THE NATIONAL JOBBANK 2006

Published by:
Adams Media, an F+W Publications Company
57 Littlefield Street, Avon MA 02322
800/872-5627

Manufactured in the United States of America.

While the publisher has made every reasonable effort to obtain accurate information and verify same, occasional errors are inevitable due to the magnitude of the database. Should you discover an error, or if a company is missing, please write the editors at the above address so that we may update future editions.

"This publication is designed to provide accurate and authoritative information with regard to the subject matter covered. It is sold with the understanding that the publisher is not engaged in rendering legal, accounting, or other professional advice. If legal advice or other expert assistance is required, the services of a competent professional person should be sought."
--From a *Declaration of Principles* jointly adopted by a Committee of the American Bar Association and a Committee of Publishers and Associations

The appearance of a listing in the book does not constitute an endorsement from the publisher.

Cover design by Peter Gouck and Chris Ciaschini.

ISBN: 1-59337-576-X
ISSN: 1051-4872

Visit us at www.adamsmedia.com

TABLE OF CONTENTS

SECTION ONE: EMPLOYER LISTINGS

SECTION TWO: CONDUCTING YOUR JOB SEARCH

SECTION THREE: EMPLOYER INDEX

EXPLANATION OF EMPLOYER LISTINGS

Employer listings are presented in alphabetical order by state.
Each listing contains some or all of the following information:

- Name of the organization or company
- Mailing address of the organization, company, or hiring department
- Phone and fax number of main office or human resources office
- Recorded jobline
- Contact person and title or department
- E-mail and World Wide Web addresses
- Detailed organization or company profile
- Company slogan
- Positions advertised
- Special programs offered
- Internship information
- Office hours
- Corporate headquarters location
- Other local, national, and international locations
- Subsidiaries
- Parent company
- Operations at this facility
- Stock exchange and symbol
- Name of President, CEO, and/or key management staff
- Annual sales/revenues
- Number of employees locally, nationally, and worldwide

ADTRAN, INC.
P.O. Box 140000, Huntsville AL 35814-4000. 256/963-8000. **Toll-free phone:** 800/9AD-TRAN. **Physical address:** 901 Explorer Boulevard, Huntsville AL 35806. **Fax:** 256/963-7040. **Contact:** Human Resources. **E-mail:** job.line@adtran.com. **World Wide Web address:** http://www.adtran.com. **Description:** ADTRAN provides digital transmission products to telephone companies and corporate end users to implement advanced digital data services over existing telephone networks. The company has three primary markets: Telco products for telephone companies; Customer Premises Equipment (CPE) for end users; and OEM products for firms who incorporate ADTRAN technology into their own products. CPE products provide end users access to Telco digital services and often include additional features for specific end user applications. Customized versions of both Telco and CPE products are supplied in OEM versions to essentially all significant suppliers of T1 multiplexers including high-volume end users, private label distributors, and other manufacturers. **Positions advertised include:** SMT Operator; Electronic Technician; Sr. Process Engineer; Test Design Engineer; Software Engineer; Bids and Proposals Administrator; Carrier Networks Technical Support Engineer. **Corporate headquarters location:** This location. **Listed on:** NASDAQ. **Stock exchange symbol:** ADTN. **Number of employees at this location:** 435.

ADVANTAGE MARKETING COMMUNICATIONS
109 20th Street North, Birmingham AL 35203. 205/328-3595. **Fax:** 205/328-9573. **Contact:** Human Resources. **World Wide Web address:** http://www.creativeguys.com. **Description:** A full-service marketing consultancy whose services include corporate recognition programs, trade show programs, product introductions, and company outings.

ALABAMA CENTRAL CREDIT UNION
3601 4th Avenue South, Birmingham AL 35222. 205/591-2228. **Fax:** 205/595-8078. **Contact:** Human Resources. **World Wide Web address:** http://www.alabamacentral.org. **Description:** A Credit Union servicing Birmingham and the surrounding communities. **Other area locations:** Creola, Decatur, Florence, Homewood, Mobile, Muscle Shoals, Russellville, Tuscaloosa.

ALABAMA CREDIT UNION
220 Paul Bryant Drive East, P.O. Box 862998, Tuscaloosa AL 35486-0027. 205/348-5944. **Fax:** 205/348-7456. **Contact:** Jon Garner. **E-mail address:** jgarner@alabamacu.com. **World Wide Web address:** http://www.alabamacu.com. **Description:** A financial institution providing its members with personal financial management services. **Positions advertised include:** Teller. **Office hours:** Monday – Thursday, 9:00 a.m. to 5:00 a.m. Friday, 9:00 a.m. to 5:30. **Corporate headquarters location:** This location. **Other area locations:** Huntsville; Vance; Indian Hill; Fayette; Huntington.

ALABAMA METAL INDUSTRIES CORPORATION (AMICO)
3245 Fayette Avenue, Birmingham AL 35208. 205/787-2611. **Toll-free phone:** 800/366-2642. **Fax:** 205/780-7838. **Contact:** Joel Maxwell, Personnel Manager. **World Wide Web address:** http://www.amico-online.com. **Description:** Manufactures steel and other metal products including studs, floor joists, and bar gratings. **Other U.S. locations:** Nationwide.

ALABAMA POWER COMPANY
600 North 18th Street, Birmingham AL 35291. 205/257-1000. **Contact:** Human Resources. **World Wide Web address:** http://www.southernco.com. **Description:** Alabama Power Company is an electric utility company serving the southern two-thirds of Alabama. The company generates, purchases, distributes, and sells electricity to 1.3 million homes, businesses, and industries. Over 82,000 miles of power lines carry electricity to customers throughout 44,500 square miles. Alabama Power Company also supplies steam service and sells electrical appliances. **NOTE:** Registration forms and job information available at: http://careers.southerncompany.com. **Positions advertised include:** Marketing Assistant; Corporate Planning Analyst; Plant Helper; Business Development Manager; Appliance Serviceman. **Corporate headquarters location:** This location. **Parent company:** Southern Company is one of the nation's largest investor-owned electric utility groups. Southern Company utilities include Georgia Power, Gulf Power, Mississippi Power, and Savannah Electric. Other subsidiaries of Southern Company include Southern Communications Services, Southern Company Services, Southern Electric International, Southern Development and Investment Group, and Southern Nuclear. **Listed on:** New York Stock Exchange. **Stock exchange symbol:** SO. **Number of employees at this location:** 6,700.

ALABAMA SHAKESPEARE FESTIVAL
One Festival Drive, Montgomery AL 36117. 334/271-5353. **Toll-free phone:** 800/841-4273. **Contact:** Human Resources. **World Wide Web address:** http://www.asf.net. **Description:** A theater dedicated to the classics and contemporary work in rotating repertory. Founded in 1972. **NOTE:** Applicants should send resumes to department of interest.

ALACAD
2687 John Hawkins Parkway, Birmingham AL 35244. 205/444-3100. **Fax:** 205/444-3111. **Contact:** Human Resources. **World Wide Web address:** http://www.alacad.com. **Description:** Resells computer hardware and software. **Corporate headquarters location:** This location. **Other area locations:** Huntsville AL; Mobile AL. **Other U.S. locations:** Jackson MS. **International Locations:** Cyprus; Singapore; Sweden; United Kingdom.

ALATAX, INC.
3001 Second Avenue South, Birmingham AL 35233. 205/324-0088. **Fax:** 205/324-1538. **Contact:** Human Resources. **World Wide Web address:** http://www.alatax.com. **Description:** Develops revenue enhancement software. **Positions advertised include:** Regional Account Manager. **Corporate headquarters location:** This location.

AMERICAN CAST IRON PIPE COMPANY (ACIPCO)
P.O. Box 2727, Birmingham AL 35202-2727. 205/325-7701. **Physical address:** 1501 31st Avenue North, Birmingham AL 35207. **Contact:** Human Resources. **World Wide Web address:** http://www.acipco.com. **Description:** Manufactures a variety of industrial products including ductile iron pipes and fittings, steel pipes, fire hydrants, and molded rubber products. **Corporate headquarters location:** This location.

AMERICAN FLAT GLASS DISTRIBUTORS, INC. (AFGD)
3350 Ball Street, Birmingham AL 35234. 205/841-6785. **Fax:** 205/841-4308. **Contact:** Human Resources. **World Wide Web address:** http://www.afgd.com. **Description:** AFGD specializes in architectural insulated glass units and custom tempering. The company manufactures a complete line of insulated glass units for commercial and residential applications. Products include clear, tint, and reflective glass; wire glass; and equipment for the handling, storage, and transportation of glass. There are 19 AFGD locations throughout the United States in metropolitan areas, with the largest facilities at Marietta, Georgia and Opelousas, Louisiana. **Positions advertised include:** Inside Sales Consultant. **Corporate headquarters location:** Atlanta GA. **Other U.S. locations:** Nationwide. **Subsidiaries include:** AFGD Canada. **Parent company:** AFG Industries, Inc. **Operations at this facility include:** Manufacturing; Sales. **Listed on:** Privately held. **Number of employees at this location:** 75. **Number of employees nationwide:** 1,000.

AMSOUTH BANCORPORATION
P.O. Box 11007, AHP7, Birmingham AL 35288. 205/326-5476. **Contact:** Human Resources. **E-mail address:** career@amsouth.com. **World Wide Web address:** http://www.amsouth.com. **Description:** One of the nation's largest banking institutions with more than 300 locations. AmSouth provides commercial, electronic, and telephone banking services. **NOTE:** Send resumes to AmSouth's Resume Processing Center Unit #168, P.O. Box 3175, Burlington MA 01803. **Positions advertised include:** Accounts Payable Manager; Assistant Branch Manager; Audit Officer; Bankruptcy Real Estate Collector; Branch Assistant; Branch Infrastructure Support Supervisor; Brokerage Hotline Representative; Business Banker V; Business Banking Assistant. **Corporate headquarters location:** This location. **Other U.S. locations:** FL; GA; LA; MS; TN. **Listed on:** New York Stock Exchange. **Stock exchange symbol:** ASO. **Number of employees at this location:** 5,000. **Number of employees nationwide:** 12,000.

ASSOCIATED GROCERS OF THE SOUTH, INC.
P.O. Box 11044, Birmingham AL 35202. 205/841-6781. **Physical address:** 3600 Vanderbilt Road, Birmingham AL 35217. **Fax:** 205/808-4896. **Contact:** Human Resources Department. **E-mail address:** jobs@agsouth.com. **World Wide Web address:** http://www.agsouth.com. **Description:** A grocery wholesaler. Founded in 1927. **Corporate headquarters location:** This location. **Number of employees at this location:** 300.

AUBURN UNIVERSITY
Langdon Hall, Auburn AL 36849. 334/844-4145. **Contact:** Human Resources. **E-mail address:** working@auburn.edu. **World Wide Web address:** http://www.auburn.edu. **Description:** A public university with approximately 22,000 students. **Positions advertised include:** Agri Technician; Broadcast Associate; Civil Engineer; Communications Specialist; Contracts & Grants Administrator; Development Officer; Financial Assistant; Research Assistant; Research Fellow;

AUTO F/X SOFTWARE
141 Village Street, Suite 2, Birmingham, AL 35242. 205/980-0056. **Fax:** 205/980-1121. **Contact:** Human Resources. **World Wide Web address:** http://www.autofx.com. **Description:** Develops automated and precreated effects and designs software for the graphic arts field.

AVOCENT
4991 Corporate Drive NW, Huntsville AL 35805. 256/430-4000. **Fax:** 256/430-4030. **Contact:** Human Resources. **World Wide Web address:** http://www.avocent.com. **Description:** A developer of switching and transmission products for computer configurations. Products include keyboard/mouse/monitor switching systems, peripheral extension and expansion products, and phone-activated power control systems for PC, Macintosh, and Sun computer platforms. Positions advertised include: Technical Writer; Sales Administrator. **Corporate headquarters location:** This location. **Other U.S. locations:** San Diego CA; Sunrise FL; Chelmsford MA; Austin TX; Redmond WA. **International locations:** Canada; Germany; Hong Kong. **Listed on:** NASDAQ. **Stock exchange symbol:** AVCT. **Number of employees worldwide:** 700.

BE&K ENGINEERING COMPANY
P.O. Box 2332, Birmingham AL 35201. 205/972-6000. **Physical address:** 2000 International Park Drive, Birmingham AL 35243. **Fax:** 205/972-6135. **Contact:** Bruce May, Human Resources Manager. **E-mail address:** bekresumes@bek.com. **World Wide Web address:** http://www.bek.com. **Description:** Provides construction, construction management, engineering, and maintenance services. **Positions advertised include:** Corporate Payroll Manager. **Other U.S. locations:** Mobile AL; Newark DE; Atlanta GA; New York NY; Raleigh NC; Trevose PA. **Parent company:** BE&K, Inc.

BAIL BONDS EXPRESS AGENCY, INC.
2301 15TH Street, Tuscaloosa AL 35401-4612. 205/759-1048. **Toll-free phone:** 800/536-8075. **Fax:** 205/759-1054. **Contact:** Human Resources. **E-mail address: World Wide Web address:** http://www.bailbondsexpress.com. **Description:** A bail bonds agency.

BANCORPSOUTH
P.O. Box 55338, Birmingham AL 35255. 205/933-8080. Fax: 205/939-0839. **Physical address:** 2211 Highland Avenue South, Birmingham AL 35205. **Recorded jobline:** 205/939-4220. **Contact:** Human Resources Department. **World Wide Web address:** http://www.bancorpsouth.com. **Description:** A bank with 240 locations in six states. **Corporate headquarters location:** Tupelo MS. **Listed on:** New York Stock Exchange. **Stock exchange symbol:** BXS.

THE BANK
17 North 20th Street, Birmingham AL 35203. 205/326-2265. **Fax:** 205/327-3865 **Contact:** Human Resources. **E-mail address:** humanresources@thebankmybank. com. **World Wide Web address:** http://www.thebankmybank.com. **Description:** A wholly-owned subsidiary of The Banc Corporation, a financial holding company. **Positions advertised include:** Platform Systems Analyst; Document Specialist. **Other area locations:** Albertville; Boaz; Decatur; Frisco City; Mt. Olive; Guntersville. **Nationwide locations:** FL. **Listed on:** NASDQ. **Symbol:** TBNC.

BAPTIST MEDICAL CENTER OF PRINCETON
701 Princeton Avenue SW, Birmingham AL 35211. 205/783-3000. **Contact:** Human Resources. **World Wide Web address:** http://www.baptistmedical.org/Princeton. **Description:** A 400-bed acute care hospital whose services include general medical and surgical procedures, heart and cancer programs, and a birthing center. **Positions advertised include:** Social Worker; Registered Nurse (Multiple Departments); Psychiatric Technician; LPN; Radiology Technologist. **NOTE:** Search and apply for positions online. **Parent company:** Baptist Health System.

BARBER DAIRIES INC.
36 Barber Court, Birmingham AL 35209. 205/942-2351. **Contact:** Human Resources. **Description:** Processes and distributes dairy products and juices. **Corporate headquarters location:** This location. **Operations at this facility include:** Administration; Divisional Headquarters; Manufacturing; Regional Headquarters; Research and Development; Sales; Service. **Annual sales/revenues:** More than $100 million. **Number of employees nationwide:** 1,000.

BARNES & NOBLE BOOKSTORES
5850A University Village, Huntsville AL 35806. 256/864-2090. **Contact:** Manager. **World Wide Web address:** http://www.barnesandnoble.com. **Description:** A bookstore chain operating nationwide. This location has a cafe in addition to its comprehensive book departments.

BIRMINGHAM POST-HERALD
THE BIRMINGHAM NEWS
2200 Fourth Avenue North, Birmingham AL 35203. 205/325-2222. **Contact:** Human Resources. **World Wide Web address:** http://www.postherald.com. **Description:** *Birmingham Post-Herald* is a daily, afternoon newspaper. *Birmingham News* (also at this location) is a daily, morning newspaper. Through a joint operating agreement, the two newspapers publish a combined Saturday morning newspaper.

THE BOEING COMPANY
P.O. Box 240002, Mail Stop JW-83, Huntsville AL 35824-6402. 256/461-2345. **Contact:** Personnel. **World Wide Web address:** http://www.boeing.com. **Description:** One of the world's largest aerospace firms. This facility performs work on a broad array of key space and defense programs including the Ground-based Midcourse Defense, International Space Station, Delta Launch Vehicles, Orbital Space Program, Avenger, Arrow and PAC-3 Missile. **NOTE:** Faxed resumes are not accepted. Search and apply for positions online. **Positions advertised include:** Engineer/Scientist; Communication Systems Design Engineer; Gmd Information Assurance Lead. **Corporate headquarters location:** St Louis MO. **Listed on:** NASDAQ. **Stock exchange symbol:** BA. Number of employees at this location: 3,300.

BOKLER SOFTWARE CORPORATION
P.O. Box 261, Huntsville AL 35804. 256/539-9901. **Fax:** 256/883-7242. **Contact:** Human Resources. **E-mail address:** info@bokler.com. **World Wide Web address:** http://www.bokler.com. **Description:** Develops cryptographic software that allows businesses to set up information security systems. **Corporate headquarters location:** This location.

BOOKS-A-MILLION, INC.
402 Industrial Lane, Birmingham AL 35211. 205/942-3737. **Contact:** Human Resources. **E-mail address:** jobs@booksamillioninc.com. **World Wide Web address:** http://www.booksamillioninc.com. **Description:** One of the nation's largest book retailers with a network of more than 200 bookstores in 18 states, primarily in the Southeast. Books-A-Million also operates a book wholesale and distribution subsidiary, American Wholesale Book Company, and an online bookstore at http://www.booksamillion.com. **Positions advertised include:** District Manager; Buyer. **Corporate headquarters location:** This location. **Subsidiaries include:** American Wholesale Book Company, Inc. **Listed on:** NASDAQ. **Stock exchange symbol:** BAMM. **President/CEO:** Clyde B. Anderson. **Annual sales/revenues:** More than $100 million.

BROOKWOOD MEDICAL CENTER
2010 Brookwood Medical Center Drive, Birmingham AL 35209. 205/877-1467. **Fax:** 205/877-2279. **Contact:** Human Resources. **World Wide Web address:** http://www.brookwood-medical.com. **Description:** A medical center. **Positions advertised include:** Surgical Support Associate; RN; LPN; OR Assistant; Insurance Associate; Respiratory Therapist.

BRUNO'S SUPERMARKETS, INC.
P.O. Box 2486, Birmingham AL 35201. 205/940-9400. **Physical address:** 800 Lakeshore Parkway, Birmingham AL 35211. **Fax:** 205/912-4628. **Contact:** Director of Employee Relations. **E-mail address:** HRRecruiting@aholdusa.com. **World Wide Web address:** http://www.brunos.com. **Description:** Operates a chain of 169 supermarkets and smaller food and liquor stores in four states. Stores include Food World, Bruno's, Food Fair, Food Max, and Food World Discount Liquors. **Corporate headquarters location:** This location. **Parent company:** AholdUSA. **Listed on:** Privately held. **Annual sales/revenues:** More than $100 million. **Number of employees nationwide:** 13,000.

BROWN INTERNATIONAL CORPORATION
2103-A West Ferry Way, Huntsville AL 35801. 256/705-1100. **Fax:** 256/705-1299. **Contact:** Human Resources. **E-mail address:** aestacio@brownintl.com. **World Wide Web address:** http://www.brownintl.com. **Description:** A defense contractor providing system designs, integration, and support for Command Control, Communications, and Computers & Intelligence (C4I) systems. **Note:** Candidates should not call to submit applications or inquire about pending applications. **Positions advertised include:** Field Service Engineer; Technician/Integrator.

CPSI (COMPUTER PROGRAMS AND SYSTEMS, INC.)
6600 Wall Street, Mobile AL 36695. 251/639-8100. **Toll-free phone:** 800/711-2774. **Fax:** 251/639-8214. **Contact:** Human Resources. **E-mail address:** employment@cpsinet.com. **World Wide Web address:** http://www.cpsinet.com. **Description:** Develops and installs business software for hospitals and other health care providers. CPSI's products assist in office management, electronic billing, and a wide range of other tasks. Founded in 1979.

CVS
2600 Morgan Road SE, Bessemer AL 35022. 205/424-3421. **Contact:** Human Resources. **World Wide Web address:** http://www.cvs.com. **Description:** CVS operates a chain of more than 4,100 stores in 34 states. Pharmacy operations make up a large portion of the company's business, offering both brand name and generic prescription drugs. CVS stores also offer a broad range of health and beauty aids, cosmetics, greeting cards, convenience foods, photo finishing services, and other general merchandise. **NOTE:** Search and apply for positions online. **Corporate headquarters location:** Woonsocket RI. **Number of employees nationwide:** 100,000.

CAREMARK RX
3000 Riverchase Galleria, Birmingham AL 35244. 205/733-8996. **Contact:** Human Resources. **World Wide Web address:** http://www.caremark.com. **Description:** A pharmaceutical company that provides pharmacy benefit management and therapeutic pharmaceutical services. Caremark Rx also offers pharmaceutical services that target chronic conditions and genetic disorders. **Corporate headquarters location:** Nashville TN. **Listed on:** New York Stock Exchange. **Stock exchange symbol:** CMX.

CAVALIER HOMES, INC.
CAVALIER HOMES OF ALABAMA, INC.
P.O. Box 300, Addison AL 35540. 256/747-1575. **Fax:** 256/747-8019. **Contact:** Sherry Jones, Personnel Director. **World Wide Web address:** http://www.cavhomesinc.com. **Description:** Cavalier Homes designs, produces, and sells prefabricated mobile homes. The company markets homes through approximately 500 independent dealers located in 32 states. Founded in 1984. **Corporate headquarters location:** This location. **Other area locations:** Hamilton AL; Winfield AL. **Other U.S. locations:** Cordele GA; Nashville NC; Robbins NC; Shippenville PA; Fort Worth TX. **Operations at this facility include:** This location houses executive offices and operates two manufacturing facilities, which function under the name Cavalier Homes of Alabama, Inc. **Listed on:** New York Stock Exchange. **Stock exchange symbol:** CAV. **Number of employees nationwide:** 1,490.

CINRAM
4905 Moores Mill Road, Huntsville AL 35811. 256/859-9042. **Fax:** 256/859-9932. **Contact:** Human Resources. **World Wide Web address:** http://www.cinram.com. **Description:** Manufactures CD-ROM drives and computer CDs on which companies can store information. **Positions advertised include:** Industrial Equipment Maintenance. **Corporate headquarters location:** Ontario, Canada. **Other U.S. locations:** Richmond IN; Commerce CA; Olyphant PA. **International locations:** Worldwide.

CITATION CORPORATION
2700 Corporate Drive, Suite 100, Birmingham AL 35242. 205/871-5731. **Fax:** 205/870-8211. **Contact:** Jim Clayton, Director of Employee Development. **World Wide Web address:** http://citation.net. **Description:** An independent U.S. manufacturer of precision ductile iron, gray iron, and steel castings for a wide variety of commercial and industrial uses. Citation operates facilities in Alabama, Illinois, Indiana, Texas, North Carolina, Michigan, and Wisconsin. **Positions advertised include:** Corporate Financial Analyst. **Corporate headquarters location:** This location. **Number of employees nationwide:** 5,000.

CLARAGE
245 Center Street North, Birmingham AL 35204. 205/581-3267. **Fax:** 205/251-6258. **Contact:** Human Resources. **E-mail address:** hr@clarage.com. **World Wide Web address:** http://www.clarage.com. **Description:** Designs, engineers and builds centrifugal fans and blowers for use in industry. **Positions advertised include:** Sales Engineer. **Note:** Resumes can be either sent to the address listed above or the corporate human resources department located at: 5959 Trenton Lane North, Minneapolis, MN 55442. Fax: 763/551-9371; e-mail: hr@tcf.com. **Parent company:** Twin City Fan Companies, Ltd.

COLONIAL BANCGROUP, INC.
P.O. Box 1108, Montgomery AL 36101-1108. 334/833-3128. **Physical address:** 32 Commerce Street, Montgomery AL. **Contact:** Human Resources. **World Wide Web address:** http://www.colonialbank.com. **Description:** A multibank holding company. Subsidiaries perform commercial banking operations and other related financial services. **Other U.S. locations:** FL; GA; NV; TN; TX. **Listed on:** New York Stock Exchange. **Stock exchange symbol:** CNB. **Number of employees nationwide:** 1,335.

COMMAND ALKON, INC.
1800 International Park Drive, Suite 400, Birmingham AL 35243. 205/879-3282. **Fax:** 205/870-1405. **Contact:** Human Resources. **E-mail:** mwhitaker@commandalkon.com. **World Wide Web address:** http://www.commandalkon.com. **Description:** Designs business software for the construction materials industry. **Positions advertised include:** Bi-Lingual Account Service Representative; Application Consultant; Engineering Manager; QA Analyst. **Corporate headquarters location:** This location.

COMMUNITY BANCSHARES, INC.
P.O. Box 1000, Blountsville AL 35031. 205/429-1000. **Contact:** Ms. Ounita Wilkes, Personnel Director. **Description:** A bank holding company. Subsidiaries perform commercial banking operations and other related financial activities. **Number of employees at this location:** 170.

COMPASS BANK
P.O. Box 10566, Birmingham AL 35296. 205/297-4900. **Physical address:** 15 South 20th Street, Birmingham AL 35233. **Fax:** 205/297-7363. **Contact:** Human Resources. **E-mail address:** jobs@compassbank.com. **World Wide Web address:** http://www.compassweb.com. **Description:** A bank holding company. Compass Bank conducts general commercial banking and trust business from 376 locations in Alabama, Arizona, Colorado, Florida, New Mexico, and Texas. **Positions advertised include:** Sales Representative; Audit Team Leader; TMS Sales Officer; Lead IT Project Manager; Financial Sales Representative; Marketing Analyst; Senior Accounting Audience; Account Administrator; Marketing Communication Manager; Insurance Administrator. **Other area locations:** Huntsville AL; Mobile AL; Montgomery AL. **Parent company:** Compass Bancshares, Inc. **Listed on:** NASDAQ. **Stock exchange symbol:** CBSS. **Number of employees nationwide:** 4,100.

COMPUTER SCIENCES CORPORATION (CSC)
4090 South Memorial Parkway, Huntsville AL 35802. 256/883-1140. **Fax:** 256/880-0367. **Contact:** Human Resources. **World Wide Web address:** http://www.csc.com. **Description:** Provides information technology solutions and technical services for the Department of Defense and intelligence agencies, federal civilian agencies and state government clients, health care organizations, and other commercial customers. Founded in 1976. **NOTE:** Entry-level positions are offered. **Positions advertised include:** Systems Analyst; Technology Architect; Help Desk/Customer Support Representative; System Engineer; Security Administrator; Application Developer; Financial Analyst; Network Engineer; Business Prospect Architect; Client Services Specialist. **Corporate headquarters location:** El Segundo CA. **Listed on:** New York Stock Exchange. **Stock exchange symbol:** CSC. **Number of employees at this location:** 1,000. **Number of employees worldwide:** 91,000.

COMSYS IT PARTNERS, INC.
5330 Stadium Trace Parkway, Suite 335, Birmingham AL 35244. 205/987-8878. **Toll-free phone:** 800/987-8878. **Fax:** 205/987-1014. **Contact:** Human Resources. **World Wide Web address:** http://www.comsys.com. **Description:** A full-service computer consulting firm. **NOTE:** Entry-level positions are offered. **Special programs:** Training. **Office hours:** Monday - Friday, 8:00 a.m. - 5:00 p.m. **Corporate headquarters location:** Houston TX. **Other U.S. locations:** Nationwide. **International locations:** Worldwide. **Annual sales/revenues:** More than $600 million. **Number of employees at this location:** 500. **Number of employees nationwide:** 5,000.

CONTINENTAL EAGLE CORPORATION
201 Gin Shop Hill Road, P.O. Box 1000, Prattville AL 36067. 334/365-8811. **Fax:** 334/361-7627. **Contact:** Human Resources Director. **E-mail address:** personnel@coneagle.com. **World Wide Web address:** http://www.coneagle.com. **Description:** A designer, manufacturer, and marketer of cotton processing and handling equipment. **NOTE:** Entry-level positions are offered. **Special programs:** Internships. **Corporate headquarters location:** This location. **Other U.S. locations:** Phoenix AZ; Visalia CA; Rayville LA; Fayetteville NC; Memphis TN; Lubbock TX. **International locations:** Australia; Brazil; West Africa. **Listed on:** Privately held. **Annual sales/revenues:** $21 - $50 million. **Number of employees at this location:** 320. **Number of employees nationwide:** 395.

CUTLER-HAMMER, INC.
104 Inverness Center Place, Birmingham AL 35242. 205/995-4510. **Contact:** Human Resources. **World Wide Web address:** http://www.eatonelectrical.com. **Description:** Produces industrial and commercial controls (electromechanical and electronic controls; motor starters, contractors, overloads, and electric drives; programmable controllers, counters, man/machine interface panels, and pushbuttons; photoelectric, proximity, temperature, and pressure sensors; circuit breakers; load centers; safety switches; panelboards; switchboards; dry type transformers; busway; meter centers; portable tool switches; commercial switches; relays; illuminated panels; annunciator panels; and electrically actuated valves and actuators); automotive and appliance controls (electromechanical and electronic controls; convenience, stalk, and concealed switches; knock sensors; climate control components; speed controls; timers; pressure switches; water valves; range controls; thermostats; gas valves; infinite switches; and temperature and humidity sensors); and specialty controls (automated material handling systems, automated guided vehicles, stacker cranes, ion implanters, engineered fasteners, golf grips, and industrial clutches and brakes). These products are sold, either directly by the company or indirectly through distributors and manufacturers' representatives, to industrial, commercial, automotive, appliance, aerospace, and government customers. **Corporate headquarters location:** Pittsburgh PA. **Parent company:** Eaton Corporation has operations in vehicle components (truck components, passenger car components, and off-highway vehicle components, which are usually sold directly from the company's plants to original equipment manufacturers of trucks, passenger cars, and off-highway vehicles) and defense systems (strategic countermeasures, tactical jamming systems, electronic intelligence, and electronic support measures for the federal government). **Number of employees nationwide:** 51,000.

DP ASSOCIATES
4900 Century Street NW, Huntsville AL 35816. 256/837-8300. **Fax:** 256/837-8454. **Contact:** Tommie Batts, Executive Vice President. **E-mail address:** info@dpa-hsv.com. **World Wide Web address:** http://www.dpa-hsv.com. **Description:** Provides contract, technical computer support services for the U.S. government and business.

DRS TEST & ENERGY MANAGEMENT, INC.
110 Wynn Drive, Huntsville AL 35805. 256/895-2006. **Fax:** 256/895-2064. **Contact:** Human Resources. **E-mail address:** humanresources@drs-tem.com. **World Wide Web address:** http://www.pei-idt.com. **Description:** Designs, develops, and produces military hardware and software.

DEATON INC.
P.O. Box 938, Birmingham AL 35201. 205/798-5555. **Contact:** Jerry Crews, President. **World Wide Web address:** http://www.deatoninc.com. **Description:** Operates a fleet of 350 trucks and 650 flatbed trailers. Founded in 1929. **Parent company:** Old Dominion Freight Lines.

DILLARD'S DEPARTMENT STORES, INC.
3300 Bel Air, Mobile AL 36606. 251/471-1551. **Contact:** Human Resources. **World Wide Web address:** http://www.dillards.com. **Description:** Operates a retail chain offering a full line of fashion brand apparel and home furnishings. Most Dillard's stores are located in suburban shopping centers of the Southwest and Midwest. **Parent company:** Mercantile Stores Company (Cincinnati OH).

DYNETICS INC.
P.O. Box 5500, Huntsville AL 35814-5500. 256/922-9230. **Physical address:** 1000 Explorer Boulevard, Huntsville AL 35806. **Fax:** 256/922-9260. **Contact:** Human Resources. **E-mail address:** Human.Resources@dynetics.com. **World Wide Web address:** http://www.dynetics.com. **Description:** A research and development firm for the defense, aerospace, and automotive industries. Products and services include software, computer imaging, systems analysis, simulation, computer modeling, and test evaluation. **Positions advertised include:** Engineer; Document Control Specialist; RF Signature Analyst; Senior Contracts Administrator; Web Application Engineering Developer; Information Systems Security Manager; Software Quality Engineer. **Corporate headquarters location:** This location. **Other U.S. locations:** Colorado Springs CO; Washington DC; Fort Walton Beach FL; Dayton OH; El Paso TX; San Antonio TX. **Subsidiaries include:** Auburn Engineering (Rochester Hills MI); Aviation and Missile Solutions (AMS) (Huntsville AL); iMs (Integrated Management Solutions) (Huntsville AL); Information Engineering (Huntsville AL). **Operations at this facility include:** Research and Development. **Number of employees at this location:** 400. **Number of employees nationwide:** 800.

EBSCO INDUSTRIES INC.
P.O. Box 1943, Birmingham AL 35201-1943. 205/991-6600. **Physical address:** 5724 Highway 280 East, Birmingham AL 35242. **Fax:** 205/995-1518. **Recorded jobline:** 205/991-1477. **Contact:** John Thompson, Human Resources Director. **E-mail address:** jobs@ebsco.com. **World Wide Web address:** http://www.ebscoind.com. **Description:** A diverse company whose principal operations include a magazine subscription service. EBSCO Industries' primary customers are academic libraries. **NOTE:** This company offers entry-level positions. **Positions advertised include:** Cancellations Clerk; Corporate Tax Accountant; Customer Service Representative; Inside Sales Representative. **Corporate headquarters location:** This location. **Other U.S. locations:** Nationwide. **Operations at this facility include:** Administration; Service. **Listed on:** Privately held. **Annual sales/revenues:** More than $100 million. **Number of employees at this location:** 700. **Number of employees nationwide:** 3,500. **Number of employees worldwide:** 4,500.

ELASTIC CORPORATION OF AMERICA
455 Highway 70 West, Columbiana AL 35051. 205/669-3101. **Fax:** 205/669-8651. **World Wide Web address:** http://www.elasticcorp.com. **Contact:** Human Resources. **Description:** A manufacturer of elastic narrow fabrics. **Corporate headquarters location:** Chestnut Hill MA. **Other U.S. locations:** Cumberland RI; Hemingway SC; Woolwine VA. **Parent company:** NFA Corporation. **Operations at this facility include:** Divisional Headquarters. **Listed on:** Privately held. **Number of employees at this location:** 430. **Number of employees nationwide:** 550.

EMERGING SYSTEMS, INC.
4620 Commercial Drive, Huntsville AL 35816. 256/721-1976. **Toll-free phone:** 800/659-4440. **Fax:** 256/721-0242. **Contact:** Human Resources. **Description:** Manufactures data storage peripherals. Products include SCSI TowerDrives and the LANRedi network appliance family.

ENERGEN CORPORATION
605 Richard Arrington Jr. Boulevard North, Birmingham AL 35203. 205/326-2700. **Contact:** Human Resources. **World Wide Web address:** http://www.energen.com. **Description:** A diversified energy holding company. **Positions advertised include:** Controlling Accountant. **Corporate headquarters location:** This location. **Subsidiaries include:** Alagasco is involved in natural gas distribution, serving approximately 445,000 homes, businesses, and industries throughout central and northern Alabama. Energen Resources Corporation acquires oil and gas properties. **Listed on:** New York Stock Exchange. **Stock exchange symbol:** EGN. **Number of employees nationwide:** 1,565.

ENOVATION GRAPHIC SYSTEMS, INC.
100 Centerview Drive, Suite 100, Birmingham AL 35216. 205/824-7699. **World Wide Web address:** http://www.enovationgraphics.com. **Contact:** Human Resources. **Description:** A worldwide distributor of plastic surgery instruments and equipment. **Parent Company:** Fuji Film.

EXPODISPLAYS
3401 Mary Taylor Road, Birmingham AL 35235. 205/439-8234. **Fax:** 205/439-8201. **Contact:** Human Resources. **E-mail address:** hr@expodisplays.com. **World Wide Web address:** http://www.expodisplays.com. **Description:** A manufacturer and designer of custom displays and exhibits. **Positions advertised include:** Sales Representative.

FEDERAL CORRECTIONAL INSTITUTION AT TALLADEGA
565 East Renfroe Road, Talladega AL 35160. 256/315-4100. **Contact:** Alan Byrd, Human Resources Manager. **Description:** A federal prison. **Special programs:** Internships. **Other U.S. locations:** Nationwide. **Parent company:** Department of Justice. **Number of employees at this location:** 365.

FIRST CITIZENS BANK, N.A.
P.O. Box 976, Talladega AL 35161. 256/362-2157. **Fax:** 256/761-2153. **Contact:** Human Resources. E-mail address: firstcitizensbank@access-bank.com. **World Wide Web address:** http://www.first-citizens-bank.com. **Description:** A bank. **Corporate headquarters location:** This location. **Operations at this facility include:** Administration. **Number of employees at this location:** 20.

FRAZIER & DEETER LLC
2000 Morris Avenue, Suite 1710, Birmingham AL 35203. 205/226-2104. **Contact:** Corporate Human Resources. **E-mail address:** hr@frazierdeeter.com. **World Wide Web address:** http://www.frazier-deeter.com. **Description:** Provides a wide-range of tax, auditing, accounting, and advisory services. **Note:** Please send resumes to the corporate office at 600 Peachtree Street, NE, Atlanta GA. **Positions advertised include:** Experienced Audit Professionals, Entry-level Audit Professionals, Entry-level Tax Professionals.

GE FANUC EMBEDDED SYSTEMS
12090 South Memorial Parkway, Huntsville AL 35803. 256/880-0444. **Fax:** 256/882-0859. **Contact:** Human Resources. **E-mail address:** human.resources@vmic.com. **World Wide Web address:** http://www.geindustrial.com/cwc/gefanuc/embedded. **Description:** Provides embedded computing products for government and commercial businesses. **Corporate headquarters location:** This location. **Other U.S. locations:** Ventura CA.

GADSDEN REGIONAL MEDICAL CENTER
1007 Goodyear Avenue, Gadsden AL 35903. 256/494-4000. **Fax:** 256/494-4579. **Recorded jobline:** 256/494-4087. **Contact:** Gale Sanders, Director of Human Resources. **Word Wide Web address:** http://www.gadsdenregional.com. **Description:** A full-service medical center. **Positions advertised include:** Licensed Physical Therapist; Occupational Therapist; Registered Nurse; Ultrasound Tech; Respiratory Therapist; Radiology Technologist. **NOTE:** Entry-level positions and second and third shifts are offered.

GOLDEN ENTERPRISES INC.
1 Golden Flake Drive, Birmingham AL 35205. 205/323-6161. **Contact:** Human Resources. **E-mail address:** human_resources@goldenflake.com. **World Wide Web address:** http://www.goldenflake.com. **Description:** A food holding company. **Subsidiaries include:** Golden Flake Snack Foods, Inc. manufactures and distributes a full line of salted snack items including potato chips, pork skins, crackers, and popcorn. **Number of employees at this location:** 1,390.

GULF STATES PAPER CORPORATION
P.O. Box 48999, 1400 Jack Warner Parkway NE, Tuscaloosa AL 35404-8999. 205/553-5000. **Contact:** Human Resources. **World Wide Web address:** http://www.gulf-states.com. **Description:** A manufacturer of paper products including pulp and paperboard, composite materials, and related products. **Positions advertised include:** Internal Audit Manager. **Corporate headquarters location:** This location. **Other area locations:** Columbiana AL; Demopolis AL; Gordo AL; Ralph AL; Cuba AL; Moundville AL. Other U.S. locations: CA; GA; PA; KY; MO; NC; TX. **Number of employees at this location:** 446.

HARBERT MANAGEMENT CORPORATION
One River Chase Parkway South, Birmingham AL 35244. 205/987-5500. **Contact:** Cathy Sinclair, Human Resources. **Description:** Provides financial management services. **Other U.S. locations:** New York NY; Richmond VA; Nashville TN. **International locations:** London UK.

HEALTHSOUTH CORPORATION
One HealthSouth Parkway, Birmingham AL 35243. 205/967-7116. **Contact:** Human Resources. **World Wide Web address:** http://www.healthsouth.com. **Description:** Provides rehabilitative health care services through approximately 250 outpatient and 40 inpatient rehabilitation facilities, and several medical centers. Services offered include rehabilitation, occupational therapy, physical therapy, head injury therapy, respiratory therapy, speech-language pathology, surgery, laser treatment of tumors, and rehabilitation nursing. **Positions advertised include:** Internal Auditor-IT; Senior Compliance Auditor; Systems Engineer; Data Warehouse Engineer; Financial Analyst. **Corporate headquarters location:** This location. **Other U.S. locations:** Nationwide. **International locations:** Australia; Puerto Rico; United Kingdom. **Listed on:** New York Stock Exchange. **Stock exchange symbol:** HRC. **Number of employees nationwide:** 42,000.

HONDA MANUFACTURING OF ALABAMA
1800 Honda Drive, Lincoln AL 35096. 205/355-5000. **Fax:** 205/355-5020. **Contact:** Human Resources. **World Wide Web address:** http://www.world.honda.com. **Description:** Manufactures Odyssey minivans and engines. Number of employees at this location: 4,300.

HONEYWELL
1327 Erie Street, Birmingham AL 35224. 205/783-9771. **Contact:** Mike Hightower, Plant Manager. **World Wide Web address:** http://www.honeywell.com. **Description:** Honeywell is engaged in the research, development, manufacture, and sale of advanced technology products and services in the fields of chemicals, electronics, automation, and controls. The company's major businesses are home and building automation and control, performance polymers and chemicals, industrial automation and control, space

and aviation systems, and defense and marine systems. **Corporate headquarters location:** Morristown NJ. **Operations at this facility include:** This location is a producer of coal tar pitch, creosote and coal tar solutions, and refined tars. **Listed on:** New York Stock Exchange. **Stock exchange symbol:** HON.

HOWARD INSTRUMENTS
4749 Appletree Street, Tuscaloosa AL 205/553-4453. **Fax:** 205/569-9267. **Contact:** Human Resources. **E-mail address:** howard@howardinstruments.com. **World Wide Web address:** http://www.howardinstruments.com. **Description:** A wholesaler of ophthalmic equipment and supplies. Howard Instruments also offers repair services.

HYUNDAI MOTOR MANUFACTURING ALABAMA
700 Hyundai Boulevard, Montgomery AL 36105. 334/387-8000. **Contact:** Human Resources. **World Wide Web address:** http://www.hyundaiusa.com. **Description:** Builds Sonata and Santa Fe model Hyundai vehicles. **Number of employees at this location:** 2,000.

INTERCONNECT SYSTEMS CORPORATION
2950 Drake Avenue, Huntsville AL 35805. 256/882-1305. **Toll-free phone:** 888/438-1305. **Contact:** Human Resources. **World Wide Web address:** http://www.interconnectsys.net. **Description:** Provides telecommunication services.

INTERGRAPH CORPORATION
288 Dunlop Boulevard, P.O. Box 240000, Huntsville AL 35824. 256/730-2000. **Fax:** 256/730-7250. **Contact:** Human Resources. **E-mail address:** jbcobb@ingr.com. **World Wide Web address:** http://www.intergraph.com. **Description:** Intergraph develops, manufactures, markets, and maintains interactive computer graphics systems that support the creation, analysis, display, output, and maintenance of virtually every type of design, drawing, map, or other graphic representation. The company's hardware products include workstations, servers, and peripherals. Software products include operating systems, database management applications, and over 1,200 graphics software programs for the CAD/CAM, engineering, design, and manufacturing industries. Clients include companies in the utilities, transportation, building, process, vehicle design, electronics, manufacturing, and publishing industries. **Positions advertised include:** Director, Corporate Communications; Internet Marketing Programs Manager. **Corporate headquarters location:** This location. **Other U.S. locations:** Nationwide. **International locations:** Worldwide. **Listed on:** NASDAQ. **Stock exchange symbol:** INGR. **Number of employees worldwide:** 3,700.

JVC DISC AMERICA INC.
One JVC Road, Tuscaloosa AL 35405. 205/556-7111. **Contact:** Victor Hamner, HR Manager. **E-mail address:** vhamner@jvcdiscusa.com. **World Wide Web address:** http://www.jvcdiscusa.com. **Description:** Manufactures DVD's and CD-ROM's. **Corporate headquarters location:** Japan. **Other U.S. locations:** Elk Grove CA.

JACKSON COUNTY HEALTHCARE AUTHORITY
P.O. Box 1050, Scottsboro AL 35768. 256/259-4444. **Fax:** 256/218-3228. **Contact:** Human Resources. **E-mail address:** ssivley@jcha.org. **World Wide Web address:** http://www.jacksoncountyhospital.com. **Description:** Operates Jackson County Hospital and North Jackson Hospital. **Positions advertised include:** RN, Emergency Department; Patient Accounts Rep; Paramedic; Certified Athletic Trainer; Physical Therapist; Certified Respiratory Therapist. **Corporate headquarters location:** This location. **Operations at this facility include:** Administration; Service.

JACKSONVILLE STATE UNIVERSITY
700 Pelham Road North, Jacksonville AL 36265. 256/218-3536. **Contact:** Gary Dempsey, Director of Personnel. **World Wide Web address:** http://www.jsu.edu. **Description:** A four-year state university offering bachelor's and master's (including MBA) degrees. Approximately 7,400 undergraduate and 1,000 graduate students attend Jacksonville State University. **Positions advertised include:** Nursing Clinic Coordinator; Disability Specialist; Department Head, Health, Physical Education & Recreation; Assistant Director, English Language Institute; Instructors, Various Departments.

JOHNSTON TEXTILES, INC.
300 General Colin Powell Parkway, Phenix City AL 36867. 334/298-9351. **Fax:** 334/298-7544. **Contact:** David Wilkerson, Manager of Human Resources. **Description:** A textile manufacturer. **Number of employees at this location:** 590.

KLEINERT'S, INC.
BUSTER BROWN
2251 Old Curtis Road, Elba AL 36323. 334/897-5764. **Contact:** Bud Daniels, Personnel Director. **Description:** Manufactures and sells infants' and children's sleepwear and other apparel.

KONICA MINOLTA PRINTING SOLUTIONS USA, INC.
One Magnum Pass, Mobile AL 36618. 251/633-4300. **Toll-free phone:** 800/523-2696. **Contact:** Todd St. Mary, Human Resources Manager. **E-mail address:** human.resources@minolta-qms.com. **World Wide Web address:** http://www.minolta-qms.com. **Description:** Develops, manufactures, and distributes laser printers and associated supplies and accessories for general office, electronic publishing, graphic design, advanced imaging, and home office applications. **NOTE:** Applications accepted only for open positions. **Positions advertised include:** Programmer Analyst; Account Executive; Inside Sales Manager. **Corporate headquarters location:** This location. **Other U.S. locations:** Orlando FL. **International locations:** Worldwide.

MARTIN INDUSTRIES
P.O. Box 128, Florence AL 35631-0128. 256/767-0330. **Physical address:** 301 East Tennessee Street, Florence AL 35630. **Contact:** Human Resources. **World Wide Web address:** http://www.martinindustries.com. **Description:** Manufactures wood and gas heat stoves and gas-fired incinerators. **Corporate headquarters location:** This location. **Subsidiaries include:** Atlanta Stove; Martin Fireplaces; Martin Gas.

MAXVISION CORPORATION
495 Production Avenue, Madison AL 35758. 256/772-3058. **Fax:** 256/772-3078. **Contact:** Human Resources. **E-mail address:** personnel@maxvision.com. **World Wide Web address:** http://www.maxvision.com. **Description:** A designer and manufacturer of Pentium Pro and Alpha-based Windows NT workstations for CAD/CAM/CAE uses. MaxVision is a leading 3-D technology developer. **Corporate headquarters location:** This location.

McWANE INC.
P.O. Box 43327, Birmingham AL 35243. 205/414-3100. **Fax:** 205/414-3170. **Contact:** Human Resources. **World Wide Web address:** http://www.mcwane.com. **Description:** Produces cast iron pressure pipe and fittings, coal, coke, and ductile iron castings. **Corporate headquarters location:** This location. **Number of employees nationwide:** 7,000.

MEADWESTVACO
P.O. Box 940, Phenix City AL 36868. 334/855-4711. **Contact:** Human Resources. **World Wide Web address:** http://www.meadwestvaco.com. **Description:** Manufactures coated paperboard for use in packaging and folding carton applications. **Corporate headquarters location:** Stamford CT.**Other U.S. locations:** Nationwide. **Operations at this facility include:** Manufacturing. **Listed on:** New York Stock Exchange. **Stock exchange symbol:** MWV. **Number of employees at this location:** 700. **Number of employees worldwide:** 30,000.

MEDIA NETWORKS, INC.
2100 Lakeshore Parkway, Birmingham AL 35209. **World Wide Web address:** http://www.mni.com. **Contact:** Human Resources. **Description:** A local market advertising company. Provides advertising and promotional placement into a network of 30 area magazines. **Corporate headquarters location:** Stamford CT. **Parent Company:** Time Warner, Inc.

MERCEDES-BENZ USA
1 Mercedes Drive, Tuscaloosa AL. 205/507-3300. **Contact:** Human Resources. **E-mail address:** careers@MBUSA.com. **World Wide Web address:** http://www.mbusa.com. **Description:** Builds M-Class and GST model Mercedes-Benz vehicles. **Corporate headquarters location:** Montvale NJ. **Number of employees at this location:** 3,500.

MOBILE COUNTY PUBLIC SCHOOLS
P.O. Box 1327, Mobile AL 36633. 251/221-4543. **Fax:** 251/221-4546. **Contact:** Human Resources. **E-mail address:** humanresources@mcpss.com. **World Wide Web address:** http://www.mcpss.com. **Description:** Provides public education through city and county schools. **NOTE:** Entry-level positions are offered. **Positions advertised include:** Principal; Assistant Principal; Teacher; High School Counselor; Diagnostician. **Office hours:** Monday - Friday, 8:00 a.m. - 4:30 p.m. **Corporate headquarters location:** This location. **Number of employees at this location:** 7,800.

MOORE-HANDLEY, INC.
P.O. Box 2607, Birmingham AL 35202. 205/663-8011. **Toll-free phone:** 800/633-3848. **Contact:** Bill Rush, Director of Human Resources. **World Wide Web address:** http://www.moorehandley.com. **Description:** A wholesale distributor of plumbing and electrical supplies, power and hand tools, lawn and garden equipment, and other hardware and building materials products. Customers, located mainly in the Southeast, include retail home centers, hardware stores, building materials dealers, combination stores, and some mass merchandisers. In connection with its wholesale distribution activities, Moore-Handley offers a wide range of marketing, advertising, and other support services designed to assist customers in maintaining and improving their market positions. These support services include computer-generated systems for the control of inventory, pricing, and gross margin, as well as advertising and store installation and design services. Products include electrical and plumbing supplies, home center products (lawn and garden equipment, paint and accessories, sporting goods, and appliances), building products (aluminum windows and doors, roofing products, and lumber), and general and shelf hardware (including power and hand tools, lock sets, and wire products.) **Corporate headquarters location:** This location. **Other U.S. locations:** Nationwide. **Listed on:** NASDAQ. **Stock exchange symbol:** MHCO. **Number of employees at this location:** 405.

MOTION INDUSTRIES
1605 Alton Road, P.O. Box 1477, Birmingham AL 35201. 205/951-1122. **Fax:** 205/951-1172. **Contact:** Human Resources. **E-mail address:** jobs@motion-ind.com. **World Wide Web address:** http://www.motionindustries.com. **Description:** Manufactures bearings, power transmission parts, and fluid replacement parts. Founded in 1946. **Other U.S. locations:** Nationwide. **International locations:** Canada; Mexico.

NEPTUNE TECHNOLOGY GROUP
1600 Alabama Highway 229, Tallassee AL 36078. 334/283-6555. **Fax:** 334/283-7287. **Contact:** Human Resources. **E-mail address:** careers@neptunetg.com. **World Wide Web address:** http:www.neptunetg.com. **Description:** A manufacturer of water meters and hand-held reading systems. **NOTE:** Entry-level positions and second and third shifts are offered. **Positions advertised include:** manufacturing Test Engineer; RF Project Engineer; RF Design Engineer; Software Design Engineer; Web Applications Specialist. **Special programs:** Internships; Training. **Operations at this facility include:** Administration; Divisional Headquarters; Manufacturing; Research and Development; Sales; Service.

NEW HORIZONS CREDIT UNION
P.O. Box 2966, Mobile AL 36652. 251/316-3240. **Physical Address:** 6320 Airport Boulevard, Mobile AL 36608. **Fax:** 251/316-3270. **Contact:** Human Resources. **World Wide Web address:** http://www.scu-mobile.org. **Description:** Scott Credit Union is a financial institution providing loans, savings, certificates of deposit, IRA (Individual Retirement Accounts), ATM and Voice Response, and credit card services to its members. **Other area locations:** Daphne AL; Theodore AL; Satsuma AL.

NEW MILLENIUM TECHNOLOGIES
P.O. Box 899, Huntsville AL 35804. 256/704-2324. **Physical address:** 120 Holmes Avenue, Suite 301, Huntsville AL 35801. **Fax:** 256/704-2327. **Contact:** Human Resources. **E-mail address:** resumes@nm-tech.com. **World Wide Web address:** www.nm-tech.com. **Description:** Provides IT implementation and management solutions. **CEO:** Larry K. Stoltz.

NUCOR STEEL BRIMINGHAM, INC.
2301 Shuttlesworth Drive, Birmingham AL 35234. 205/250-7400. **Fax:** 205/250-7465. **Contact:** Human Resources. **World Wide Web address:** http://www.nucor.com. **Description:** Nucor Steel operates mini-mills in the United States that produce steel and steel products. Primary products include steel reinforced bar (rebar) used in the construction industry and rounds, squares, flats, angles, channels, and strips (merchant products), which are sold to fabricators and other merchants. **Corporate headquarters location:** Charlotte NC. **Other U.S. locations:** Nationwide. **Listed on:** New York Stock Exchange. **Stock exchange symbol:** NUE.

O2 IDEAS INC.
2160 Highland Avenue South, Birmingham AL 35205. 205/949-9494. **Fax:** 205/949-9449. **World Wide Web address:** http://www.O2ideas.com. **Contact:** Human Resources. **Description:** A multi-cultural marketing communications firm specializing in advertising, brand planning, public relations, event planning.

PARISIAN, INC.
750 Lakeshore Parkway, Birmingham AL 35211. 205/968-4200. **Contact:** Human Resources. **World Wide Web address:** http://www.parisian.com. **Description:** A chain of fashion specialty stores offering cosmetics, clothing, shoes, and accessories for men, women, and children. Parisian operates 43 department stores throughout the Southeast and Midwest. **Other U.S. locations:** Nationwide. **Parent company:** Saks Incorporated is a department store holding company that operates approximately 360

stores in 36 states. The company's stores include Saks Fifth Avenue, Parisian, Proffit's, Younker's, Herberger's, Carson Pirie Scott, Boston Store, Bergner's, and Off 5th, the company's outlet store. Saks Incorporated also operates two retail catalogs and several retail Internet sites. **Operations at this facility include:** Administration. **Listed on:** New York Stock Exchange. **Stock exchange symbol:** SKS. **Number of employees at this location:** 850. **Number of employees nationwide:** 7,000.

PEMCO AEROPLEX, INC.
1943 50th Street North, Birmingham AL 35212. 205/592-0011. **Contact:** Department of Human Resources. **E-mail address:** jobs@pemcoair.com. **World Wide Web address:** http://www.pemcoaviationgroup.com. **Description:** Engaged in the maintenance, modification, overhaul, and repair of military and commercial multi-engine aircraft and components. **NOTE:** Resumes accepted only for open positions. **Positions advertised include:** Senior Buyer; Quality Engineer; Subcontract Administrator. **Special programs:** Internships. **Corporate headquarters location:** This location. **Subsidiaries include:** Pemco Engineers (Corona CA); Pemco World Air Services, Inc. (Dothan AL); Space Vector Corporation (Chatsworth CA). **Parent company:** Pemco Aviation Group. **Operations at this facility include:** Administration; Manufacturing; Research and Development; Sales; Service. **Listed on:** NASDAQ. **Stock exchange symbol:** PAGI.

PREMIER PROFESSIONAL SYSTEMS
7047 Old Madison Pike, Suite 350, Huntsville AL 35806-2197. 256/971-2001. **Fax:** 256/971-2008. **Contact:** Human Resources. **E-mail address:** hr@premier-inc.com. **World Wide Web address:** http://www.premier-inc.com. **Description:** Provides software development and implementation. Founded in 1990. **Positions advertised include:** Heavy Equipment Mechanics; Diesel Engine Mechanics. **President:** Jannifer J. Henderson.

PROTECTIVE LIFE CORPORATION
2801 Highway 280 South, Birmingham AL 35223. 205/268-1000. **Contact:** Human Resources. **World Wide Web address:** http://www.protective.com. **Description:** A provider of life and health insurance and investment products. **Positions advertised include:** Financial Analyst; Mortgage Loan Clerk; New Accounts Analyst; Document Fulfillment Specialist; LAD Competition Consultant; Internal Auditor. **Corporate headquarters location:** This location. **Listed on:** New York Stock Exchange. **Stock exchange symbol:** PL. **Number of employees nationwide:** 1,170.

QUANTEGY
P.O. Box 190, Opelika AL 36803-0190. 334/745-7643. **Physical address:** 2230 Marvyn Parkway, Opelika AL 36804. **Contact:** Ellis Story, Human Resources Manager. **World Wide Web address:** http://www.quantegy.com. **Description:** Manufactures audio-video systems and recording tapes. The company also manufactures computer peripherals and instrumentation technology.

QUANTUM RESEARCH INTERNATIONAL
991 Discovery Drive, Huntsville AL 35806. 256/971-1800. **Fax:** 256/971-1802. **Contact:** Human Resources. **E-mail address:** personnel@quantum-intl.com. **World Wide Web address:** http://www.quantum-intl.com. **Description:** Researches and analyzes strategic missile defense data. **Positions advertised include:** Computer Programmer; Program Analyst; Senior Staff Member; Principal Systems Engineer. **Other U.S. locations:** Bel Air MD; El Paso TX; Arlington VA. **Subsidiaries include:** Quantum Technologies, Inc.

REGIONS FINANCIAL CORPORATION
417 North 20th Street, Birmingham AL 35203. 205/944-1300. **Contact:** Human Resources. **World Wide Web address:** http://www.regions.com. **Description:** A multibank holding company with 1,400 offices in 15 states. **NOTE:** Entry-level positions, part-time jobs, and second and third shifts are offered. **Positions advertised include:** Business Analysis Manager; Senior Accountant; Loan Assistant; Commercial Loan Officer; Supervisor; Credit Administration Officer; Leasing Sales Manager. **Special programs:** Training; Summer Jobs. **Corporate headquarters location:** This location. **Operations at this facility include:** Administration; Sales; Service. **Listed on:** New York Stock Exchange. **Stock exchange symbol:** RF. **President/CEO:** Carl Jones. **Information Systems Manager:** William S. Ringler. **Annual sales/revenues:** More than $100 million. **Number of employees at this location:** 2,000. **Number of employees nationwide:** 15,000.

RUST CONSTRUCTORS, INC.
500 Corporate Parkway, Birmingham AL 35242-2928. 205/995-7171. **Fax:** 205/995-6691. **Contact:** Charlotte Lewis, Human Resources. **E-mail address:** charlotte.lewis @wgint.com. **World Wide Web address:** http://www.rustconstructors.com. **Description:** Provides construction and maintenance services to industrial customers. **Other U.S. locations:** CO; SC.

SAKS INCORPORATED
750 Lakeshore Parkway, Birmingham AL 35211. 205/940-4000. **Contact:** Human Resources. **World Wide Web address:** http://www.saksincorporated.com. **Description:** Parisian operates 43 department stores throughout the Southeast and Midwest. Saks Incorporated is a department store holding company that operates a total of approximately 360 stores in 36 states. The company's stores include Saks Fifth Avenue, Parisian, Proffit's, Younker's, Herberger's, Carson Pirie Scott, Boston Store, Bergner's, and Off 5th, the company's outlet store. Saks Incorporated also operates two retail catalogs and several retail Internet sites. **Positions advertised include:** Assistant Store Manager; Buyer; VP Product Development; Staffing Systems Coordinator; Human Resources Database Coordinator. **Corporate headquarters location:** This location. **Operations at this facility include:** This location is the corporate headquarters for Saks Incorporated, a specialty department store holding company, and Parisian, a chain of fashion specialty stores offering cosmetics, clothing, shoes, and accessories for men, women, and children. **Listed on:** New York Stock Exchange. **Stock exchange symbol:** SKS.

SANMINA-SCI CORPORATION
13000 South Memorial Parkway, Huntsville AL 35803. 256/882-4800. **Fax:** 256/882-4871. **Contact:** Human Resources. **World Wide Web address:** http://www.sci.com. **Description:** Designs, develops, manufactures, markets, distributes, and services electronic products for the computer, aerospace, defense, telecommunications, medical, and consumer industries, as well as the U.S. government. Sanmina-SCI is one of the world's largest electronics contract manufacturers and operates one of the largest surface mount technology (SMT) production facilities in the merchant market. Operations are conducted through a Commercial Division and a Government Division. The Commercial Division operates in six geographically-organized business units: Eastern, Central, and Western Regions of North America; and European and Asian Regions. Each unit operates multiple plants that manufacture components, subassemblies, and finished products for original equipment manufacturers. Design, engineering, purchasing, manufacturing, distribution, and support services are also offered. The Government Division provides data management, instrumentation, and communications services and computer subsystems to the U.S. government and its prime contractors as well as to several foreign governments. **NOTE:** Search and apply for positions online. **Positions advertised include:** Contracts Administrator; QA Engineer; Program Manager; Software Quality Assurance Engineer; Process Development Engineer. **Corporate headquarters location:** San Jose CA. **Other area locations:** Guntersville AL. **Other U.S. locations:** Nationwide. **International locations:** Worldwide. **Operations at this facility include:** Administration; Manufacturing; Research and Development. **Listed on:** NASDAQ. **Stock exchange symbol:** SANM. **Number of employees nationwide:** 22,320.

SCHNEIDER NATIONAL CARRIERS
P.O. Box Drawer 500, Evergreen AL 36401. 251/578-2836. **Contact:** Human Resources. **Description:** Provides truckload transportation services through independent contractors and commissioned sales agents.

SEARCY HOSPITAL
P.O. Box 1090, Mount Vernon AL 36560. 251/829-9411. **Fax:** 251/829-9075. **Contact:** Human Resources. **Description:** A psychiatric hospital within the state of Alabama's Department of Mental Health/Mental Retardation. The hospital provides inpatient services to individuals with serious mental illnesses while promoting the individual's quality of life, human worth, and dignity. **Positions advertised include:** RN. **Corporate headquarters location:** Montgomery AL. **Operations at this facility include:** Administration; Service. **Number of employees at this location:** 750.

SHERATON BIRMINGHAM
2101 Richard Arrington Junior Boulevard North, Birmingham AL 35203. 205/324-5000. **Fax:** 205/307-3079. **Contact:** Jean Pruiet, Employment Manager. **World Wide Web address:** http://www.sheraton.com/birmingham. **Description:** A hotel and convention center. **Other U.S. locations:** Nationwide. **International locations:** Worldwide. **Operations at this facility include:** Administration; Sales; Service. **Annual sales/revenues:** $11 - $20 million. **Number of employees at this location:** 400. **Number of employees nationwide:** 60,000. **Number of employees worldwide:** 100,000.

SHOOK & FLETCHER INSULATION COMPANY
P.O. Box 380501, Birmingham AL 35238. 205/991-7606. **Physical address:** 4625 Valleydale Road, Birmingham AL 35242. **Contact:** David Jackson, Executive Vice President. **World Wide Web address:** http://www.shookandfletcher.com. **Description:** A distributor and contractor of industrial and marine insulation. Founded in 1949. **Other area locations include:** Mobile AL. **Other U.S. locations:** Knoxville TN; Atlanta GA; Gallatin TN.

SIRSI CORPORATION
101 Washington Street SE, Huntsville AL 35801. 256/704-7000. **Fax:** 256/704-7007. **Contact:** Human Resources. **World Wide Web address:** http://www.sirsi.com. **Description:** Develops software for turnkey library systems. **Positions advertised include:** Client Care Center Representative; Systems Specialist; Web Developer. **Corporate headquarters location:** This location. **Other U.S. locations:** Monterey CA; St. Louis MO. **International locations:** Australia; Canada; France; Singapore.

SOUTHERN BANK OF COMMERCE
P.O. Box Drawer 1269, Eufaula AL 36072-1269. 334/687-3581. **Contact:** Human Resources. **Description:** A bank holding company. **Corporate headquarters location:** This location. **Number of employees at this location:** 50.

SOUTHERN NATURAL GAS COMPANY
P.O. Box 2563, Birmingham AL 35202. 205/325-3800. **Contact:** Human Resources Manager. **World Wide Web address:** http://www.premier.sonetpremier.com/sonetpremier. **Description:** An integrated oil and natural gas company. The company's two major businesses are the exploration, exploitation, and production of oil and natural gas and natural gas transmission and marketing. The company also has significant investments in the oil field services industry. **Corporate headquarters location:** This location. **Subsidiaries include:** Florida Gas Transmission Company, the principal pipeline for Florida; Sonat Energy Services Company, which manages Sonat's nonregulated natural gas businesses, principally natural gas marketing; Sonat Exploration Company, which provides exploration and production services primarily in Alabama, Arkansas, Louisiana, Oklahoma, and Texas; and Southern Natural Gas Company (also at this location), the major pipeline serving the Southeast. **Number of employees nationwide:** 1,890.

SOUTHERN NUCLEAR OPERATING COMPANY
P.O. Box 1295, Birmingham AL 35201-1295. 205/992-5316. **Physical address:** 40 Inverness Center Parkway, Birmingham AL 35242. **Toll-free phone:** 800/457-2981. **Contact:** Yancey Trucks, Human Resources Manager. **World Wide Web address:** http://www.southerncompany.com/southernnuclear. **Description:** Provides technical and administrative support to The Southern Company-owned nuclear power generating facilities. **Positions advertised include:** Accounting Assistant; Supply Chain Engineer. **Parent company:** The Southern Company.

SOUTHERN PRIDE CATFISH COMPANY LLC
P.O. Box 436, Greensboro AL 36744. 334/624-4021. **Fax:** 334/624-4444. **Contact:** Renee Barnette, Human Resources Manager. **World Wide Web address:** http://www.southernpride.net. **Description:** A processor and distributor of processed catfish products. **Corporate headquarters location:** This location. **Parent company:** American Seafoods Group, LLC. **Number of employees at this location:** 700.

SOUTHERN RESEARCH INSTITUTE
2000 Ninth Avenue South P.O. Box 55305, Birmingham AL 35255-5305. 205/581-2000. **Toll-free phone:** 800/967-6774. **Recorded jobline:** 205/581-2609. **Contact:** Human Resources. **E-mail address:** jobs@sri.org. **World Wide Web address:** http://www.sri.org. **Description:** A network of collaborative centers for scientific discovery and technology development for public and private sector clients in the pharmaceutical sciences, homeland security, automotive and engineering industries. **NOTE:** Job applicants must apply online. **Positions advertised include:** Advanced Intellectual Property Specialist; Animal Care Technician; Bacteriologist; Engineer; Materials Engineer; Project Leader; Quality Assurance Manager; Research Assistant; Research Chemist; Senior Scientist. **Corporate headquarters location:** This location. **Other area locations:** Anniston AL; Wilsonville AL. **Other U.S. locations:** Frederick MD; Fort Leonard Wood MO; Research Triangle Park NC. **Operations at this facility include:** Research and Development.

SOUTHTRUST CORPORATION
P.O. Box 2554, Birmingham AL 35290. 205/254-5000. **Contact:** Chuck Whitfield, Human Resources Manager. **World Wide Web address:** http://www.southtrust.com. **Description:** A bank holding company. Merger with Wachovia will be completed in 2005. **Positions advertised include:** Retail Trainee; Teller; Mortgage Account Representative; Finance Center Manager; Administrative Assistant. **Corporate**

headquarters location: This location. **Other U.S. locations:** FL; GA; MS; NC; SC; TN; TX. **Subsidiaries include:** SouthTrust Bank, N.A., is a regional bank operating through more than 600 offices and more than 700 ATMs in the Southeastern region; SouthTrust Securities Inc.; SouthTrust Mortgage Corporation; SouthTrust Data Services. **Corporate headquarters location:** This location. **Listed on:** NASDAQ. **Stock exchange symbol:** SOTR. **Annual sales/revenues:** $51 - $100 million.

L.V. STABLER MEMORIAL HOSPITAL
29 L.V. Stabler Drive, Greenville AL 36037. 334/383-2245. **Contact:** Human Resources. **World Wide Web address:** http://www.lvstabler.com. **Description:** A 72-bed hospital. **Positions advertised include:** CCU Registered Nurse; LPN; Medical Technologist; Registered Nurse (Multiple Positions). **Listed on:** Privately held. **Annual sales/revenues:** Less than $5 million. **Number of employees at this location:** 225.

STEELCASE INC.
214 Durham Drive, Athens AL 35611. 256/233-6716. **Fax:** 256/230-6500. **Contact:** Human Resources Manager. **World Wide Web address:** http://www.steelcase.com. **Description:** Manufactures office furniture. **Corporate headquarters location:** Grand Rapids MI. **Other U.S. locations:** Nationwide. **International locations:** Worldwide. **Operations at this facility include:** Administration; Manufacturing; Service. **Listed on:** New York Stock Exchange. **Stock exchange symbol:** SCS. **Number of employees at this location:** 750. **Number of employees worldwide:** 20,000.

SULLIVAN COMMUNICATIONS
202 Business Center Drive, Birmingham AL 35244. 205/988-5522. **Fax:** 205/988-3125. **Contact:** Joe Sullivan. **E-mail address:** joe@sullivancomm.com. **World Wide Web address:** http://www.sullivancomm.com. **Description:** A communications services and products company. **Positions advertised include:** Outside Sales Representative; Two-way Radio Technician; Part-time Clerk.

TFE TECHNOLOGY
6767 Old Madison Pike NW, Suite 300, Huntsville AL 35806. 256/922-8000. **Contact:** Maria Heflin, Human Resources. **Description:** Offers ADP/IT equipment maintenance and IT professional services to the federal government and commercial firms. **Corporate headquarters location:** Bountiful UT. **Other U.S. locations:** Nationwide. **Listed on:** Privately held.

TEC-MASTERS, INC.
1500 Perimeter Parkway, Suite 215, Huntsville AL 35806. 256/721-6616. **Contact:** Linda Case, Human Resources. **E-mail address:** lcase@tecmasters.com. **World Wide Web address:** http://www.tecmasters.com. **Description:** An engineering firm engaged in government defense projects such as weapons and logistics systems and material acquisition support. **Corporate headquarters location:** This location. **Other area locations:** Montgomery AL. **Other U.S. locations:** DC; GA; FL; KY; OK; MI. **Listed on:** Privately held. **Annual sales/revenues:** $21 - $50 million.

TELEDYNE BROWN ENGINEERING
300 Sparkman Drive, P.O. Box 070007, Huntsville AL 35807-7007. 256/726-1000. **Fax:** 256.726-3434. **Contact:** John Logan, Personnel Director. **E-mail address:** info@tbe.com. **World Wide Web address:** http://www.tbe.com. **Description:** Engaged in space and defense systems analysis, design, and development. **Other U.S. locations:** Nationwide. **Parent company:** Teledyne Technologies Incorporated. **Listed on:** New York Stock Exchange. **Stock exchange symbol:** TDY.

TELEDYNE TUNGSTEN PRODUCTS
1297 County Line Road, Madison AL 35756. 256/464-7500. **Fax:** 256/464-7550. **Contact:** Human Resources. **World Wide Web address:** http://www.tungstenprod.com. **Description:** Manufactures machinable tungsten alloys and tungsten products. **Parent company:** Teledyne, Inc.

THREE SPRINGS, INC.
1131 Eagletree Lane, Huntsville AL 35801. 256/880-3339. **Toll-free phone:** 888/758-4356. **Fax:** 256/880-3082. **Contact:** Recruitment Officer. **E-mail:** employment@threespings.com. **World Wide Web address:** http://www.threesprings.com. **Description:** Provides mental health counseling geared toward troubled teens and their families. **Positions advertised include:** Counselor. **Other U.S. locations include:** FL, GA, NC, TN, MD. **President:** Thomas M. Watson.

TORCHMARK CORPORATION
P.O. Box 2612, Birmingham AL 35202. 205/325-4200. **Fax:** 205/325-2908. **Contact:** Human Resources. **World Wide Web address:** http://www.torchmarkcorp.com. **Description:** A financial services organization and provider of supplemental insurance. **Corporate headquarters location:** This location. **Subsidiaries include:** American Income Life Insurance Company; First United American Life Insurance Company; Globe Life and Accident Insurance Company; Liberty National Life Insurance Company; United American Insurance Company; United Investors Life Insurance Company. **Listed on:** New York Stock Exchange. **Stock exchange symbol:** TMK. **Number of employees nationwide:** 6,050.

UNISYS CORPORATION
2741 Gunter Park Drive West, Montgomery AL 36109. 334/244-2800. **Contact:** Human Resources. **World Wide Web address:** http://www.unisys.com. **Description:** Unisys specializes in developing critical business solutions based on open information networks. The company's Enabling Software Team creates a variety of software projects that facilitate the building of user applications and the management of distributed systems. The Platforms Group is responsible for UNIX Operating Systems running across a wide range of multiple-processor server platforms including all peripheral and communication drivers. The Unisys Commercial Parallel Processing Team develops microkernel-based operating systems, I/O device drivers, ATM hardware, diagnostics, and system architectures. The System Management Group is in charge of the overall management of development programs for UNIX desktop and entry-server products. **Positions advertised include:** Systems Analyst; IT Storage Solutions Specialist. **Corporate headquarters location:** Blue Bell PA. **Other area locations:** Birmingham AL. **Other U.S. locations:** Nationwide. **International locations:** Worldwide.

UNIVERSITY FIELDING PRINTERS
2512 Paul W. Bryant Drive, Tuscaloosa AL 35401. 205/752-6184. **Contact:** Ray Woodbright, Owner. **Description:** A printing and publishing firm. **Corporate headquarters location:** This location.

UNIVERSITY OF ALABAMA
P.O. Box 870126, Tuscaloosa AL 35487-0126. 205/348-6690. **Recorded jobline:** 205/348-7780. **Contact:** Human Resources. **E-mail address:** uaemploy@bama.ua.edu. **World Wide Web address:** http://www.ua.edu. **Description:** A university offering bachelor's, master's, and doctoral degrees. **NOTE:** See website for application information. **Positions advertised include:** Admissions Counselor; Assistant Director Business Administration Facilities; Assistant Director for Conference Services; Associate Vice President for Administration; Benefits Specialist; Communications Specialist; Associate/Full Professor; Assistant Professor; Instructor. **Corporate headquarters location:** This location. **Number of employees at this location:** 3,700.

UNIVERSITY OF ALABAMA AT BIRMINGHAM
1530 Third Avenue South, Birmingham AL 35294. 205/934-5248. **Contact:** Patricia Robinson, Director of Employment. **World Wide Web address:** http://www.uab.edu. **Description:** A branch of the university with approximately 2,000 students. This location also operates a medical center. **NOTE:** Search for available positions online.

UNIVERSITY OF ALABAMA AT HUNTSVILLE
Madison Hall, Room 135, Huntsville AL 35899. 256/824-6545. **Contact:** Laurel Long, Director of Human Resources. **World Wide Web address:** http://www.uah.edu. **Description:** A branch of the university with approximately 6,000 students. **NOTE:** Search for available positions online.

UNIVERSITY FEDERAL CREDIT UNION
1400 south 20th Street, P.O. Box 55377, Birmingham AL 35255-5377. 205/933-9933. **Fax:** 205/930-5039. **Contact:** Human Resources. **World Wide Web address:** http://www.ufcu.com. **Description:** A financial services organization.

UNIVERSITY OF MONTEVALLO
Station 6055, Montevallo AL 35115. 205/665-6055. **Recorded jobline:** 205/665-8050. **Contact:** Human Resources. **World Wide Web address:** http://www.montevallo.edu. **Description:** A four-year, public university with an undergraduate enrollment of approximately 3,200 students and a graduate enrollment of approximately 360. Areas of study include biology, communications, English, foreign languages, international studies, math and physics, behavioral and social sciences, business, fine arts, counseling, and education. **NOTE:** See website for application information. **Positions advertised include:** Assistant Professor; Professor.

UNIVERSITY OF SOUTH ALABAMA
Administration Building, Room 286, Mobile AL 36688. 251/460-6133. **Contact:** Human Resources. **World Wide Web address:** http://www.southalabama.edu. **Description:** A university enrolling more than 13,000 students in its extensive allied health, nursing, arts and sciences, business, computer, and engineering disciplines. **NOTE:** Search for positions and application information online. **Number of employees at this location:** 5,800.

VT MILTOPE CORPORATION
3800 Richardson Road South, Hope Hull AL 36043. 334/284-8665. **Fax:** 334/613-6591.**Contact:** Vice President, Administration, Human Resource Department. **E-mail address:** hr@miltope.com. **World Wide Web address:** http://www.miltope.com. **Description:** VT Miltope Corporation manufactures microcomputers and computer peripheral equipment for military and other applications that require reliable operation in severe land, sea, and airborne environments. **Positions advertised include:** Electrical Design Engineer; Mechanical CAD Designer; Mechanical Engineer; Senior Electronic Technician. **Corporate headquarters location:** This location. **Other U.S. locations:** Boulder CO. **Parent company:** Vision Technologies Systems. **Subsidiaries include:** Miltope Business Products, Inc. produces commercial computer printer and document products.

VALSPAR PACKAGING COATINGS
90 Carson Road, Birmingham AL 35215. 205/854-5454. **Fax:** 205/856-0469. **Contact:** Human Resources. **World Wide Web address:** http://www.valspar.com. **Description:** Manufactures and distributes paint through its consumer coatings, industrial coatings, and special products divisions.

VANITY FAIR MILLS
P.O. Box 3000, Monroeville AL 36462. 251/575-2688. **Contact:** Lisa Black, Director of Human Resources. **World Wide Web address:** http://www.vfc.com. **Description:** A manufacturer of intimate apparel. **Corporate headquarters location:** Greensboro NC. **Parent company:** VF Corporation. **Listed on:** New York Stock Exchange. **Stock exchange symbol:** VFC.

VULCAN MATERIALS COMPANY
1200 Urban Center Drive P.O. Box 385014, Birmingham AL 35242-5014. 205/298-3000. **Fax:** 205/298-2960. **Contact:** Human Resources. **World Wide Web address:** http://www.vulcanmaterials.com. **Description:** A producer of construction aggregates and a manufacturer of chemicals. The company operates 129 permanent crushed stone plants, 13 sand and gravel plants, five slag plants, and four plants that produce other aggregates. Vulcan Materials' construction products are used primarily in the construction and maintenance of highways, roads, and other public works. The remainder of the company's products are used in the construction of housing and nonresidential, commercial, and industrial facilities, as well as railroad ballasts, and in nonconstruction uses such as agriculture and various industrial applications. Vulcan Chemicals Division's principal products are the coproducts chlorine and caustic soda. Primary markets for the chemicals include pulp and paper, energy, food, pharmaceuticals, chemicals processing, and fluorocarbons industries. **Positions advertised include:** Senior/Lead Programmer Analyst; Mining Engineer; Auditor; Manager, Financial Research and Reporting; Safety and Health Specialist. **Corporate headquarters location:** This location. **Other U.S. locations:** Nationwide. **Operations at this facility include:** Administration; Research and Development. **Listed on:** New York Stock Exchange. **Stock exchange symbol:** VMC. **Number of employees nationwide:** 7,000.

THE WACKENHUT CORPORATION
6610 Old Madison Pike, Suite 105B, Huntsville AL 35806. 256/837-0126. **Fax:** 256/837-9732. **Contact:** Human Resources. **E-mail address:** recruitment@wackenhut.com. **World Wide Web address:** http://www.wackenhut.com. **Description:** Provides contract security services to corporations, government agencies, and industrial and commercial customers. **Positions advertised include:** Custom Protection Officer. **Corporate headquarters location:** Palm Beach Gardens FL. **Other area locations:** Birmingham AL; Montgomery AL. **Other U.S. locations:** Nationwide. **International locations:** Worldwide. **Parent company:** Group 4 Securicor. **Number of employees worldwide:** 40,000.

WALL STREET DELI SYSTEMS, INC.
2001 Park Place, Birmingham AL 35203. 205/252-7258. **Contact:** Human Resources. **E-mail address:** jobs@wallstreetdeli.com. **World Wide Web Address:** http://www.wallstreetdeli.com. **Description:** One location of a chain of delicatessen-style restaurants operating in office buildings, business centers, and high-volume retail

districts. Through an agreement with Host Marriott, the company also franchises in airports, shopping malls, and roadside service areas. **Corporate headquarters location:** Lake Success NY. **Other U.S. locations:** Nationwide.

JIM WALTER RESOURCES, INC.
P.O. Box 133, Brookwood AL 35444. 205/554-6150. **Fax:** 205/554-6161. **Contact:** Rodger Armbrester, Personnel Manager. **E-mail address:** personnel@jimwalterresources.com. **World Wide Web address:** http://www.jimwalterresources.com. **Description:** An underground coal mining company. **Corporate headquarters location:** Tampa FL. **Parent company:** Walter Industries, Inc. **Listed on:** New York Stock Exchange. **Stock exchange symbol:** WLT.

WEST CORPORATION
5000 Bradford Drive, Huntsville AL 35805. 256/864-9600. **Toll-free phone:** 800/815-5146. **Fax:** 256/864-9703. **Contact:** Human Resources. **E-mail address:** hsvjobs@west.com. **Description:** A provider of outsourced communication solutions to many of the world's largest companies, specializing in customer acquisition, customer care, and interactive voice response services. **Positions advertised include:** Customer Service Agent. **Corporate headquarters location:** Omaha NE.

WINSTON FURNITURE COMPANY, INC.
160 Village Street, Birmingham AL 35242. 205/980-4333. **Contact:** Human Resources. **World Wide Web address:** http://www.winstonfurniture.com. **Description:** A manufacturer of outdoor patio and lawn furniture. Founded in 1975. **Corporate headquarters location:** This location. **Parent Company:** Brown Jordan International. **Number of employees nationwide:** 500.

WOLVERINE TUBE, INC.
200 Clinton Avenue West, Suite 1000, Huntsville AL 35801. 256/890-0460. **Fax:** 256/890-0470. **Contact:** Jim Neill, Corporate Human Resources Manager. **World Wide Web address:** http://www.wlv.com. **Description:** Manufactures metal tubing. **Corporate headquarters location:** This location. **Number of employees nationwide:** 2,300.

WYLE LABORATORIES
7800 Highway 20 West, Huntsville AL 35806. 256/837-4411. **Fax:** 256/830-2109. **Contact:** Human Resources. **E-mail address:** career@hnt.wylelabs.com. **World Wide Web address:** http://www.wylelabs.com. **Description:** Provides engineering and testing services to the aerospace, defense, transportation, energy, and electric utility industries. **Positions advertised include:** Senior Calibration Technician; Project Engineer; Senior Staff Electrical Engineer; Project Manager. **Corporate headquarters location:** El Segundo CA. **Other U.S. locations:** Nationwide.

XANTE CORPORATION
2800 Dauphin Street, Suite 100, Mobile AL 36606. 251/473-6502. **Fax:** 251/473-6503. **Contact:** Kathleen Parker, Human Resources Manager. **E-mail address:** employment@xante.com. **World Wide Web address:** http://www.xante.com. **Description:** Develops and manufactures laser printers and peripheral equipment. **Positions advertised include:** U.S. Sales Representative; Software Engineer; Technical Support Representative; Windows Programmer. **Corporate headquarters location:** This location. **International location:** The Netherlands. **Listed on:** Privately held. **Number of employees at this location:** 190.

XEROX CONNECT, INC.
1000 Urban Center Drive, Suite 600, Birmingham AL 35242. 205/970-4600. **Contact:** Human Resources. **World Wide Web address:** http://www.xeroxconnect.com. **Description:** Offers systems integration services. The company operates in three service groups: Consulting and Design Services, Systems Integration, and Operations and Support Services. **Positions advertised include:** Production Color Sales Executive. **Parent company:** Xerox Corporation.

A.P.I. (ALASKA PSYCHIATRIC INSTITUTE)
2900 Providence Drive, Anchorage AK 99508. 907/269-7100. **Contact:** Cynthia Keyes, Personnel Officer. **World Wide Web address:** http://www.hss.state.ak.us/dbh/api. **Description:** A comprehensive, public, mental health treatment facility that is one of the only state-run institutions of its kind in Alaska. API provides treatment to more than 1,000 patients each year through the following units: the Youth Treatment Program for children and adolescents; the Security Treatment Program for forensic patients and short-term admissions for adults in crisis; the Third Floor Unit and Denali Treatment Unit for longer term adult patients; and the Intermediate Care Program for geriatric patients and patients who are developmentally disabled or suffer long-term medical problems with accompanying psychiatric difficulties. Founded in 1962. **NOTE:** Interested jobseekers should request an application through the Department of Administration, Division of Personnel, P.O. Box 110201, Juneau AK 99811-0201. Some positions are available only to state residents; this information is available on the state Website (http://www.state.ak.us). **Positions advertised include:** Nurse I/Nurse II (Psychiatric)

ALASKA COMMERCIAL COMPANY
550 West 64th Avenue, Suite 200, Anchorage AK 99518-1720. 907/273-4600. **Fax:** 907/273-4800. **Contact:** John Stott, Director of Human Resources. **World Wide Web address:** http://www.alaskacommercial.com. **Description:** Operates a retail chain of general merchandise stores. **NOTE:** Employment application available online. **Positions advertised include:** Branch Manager; Assistant Branch Manager; Department Supervisor; Assistant Department Supervisor; Management Associate; Store Team Leader. **Corporate headquarters location:** This location. **Parent company:** The North West Company. **Annual sales/revenues:** $51 - $100 million. **Number of employees at this location:** 100. **Number of employees nationwide:** 750.

ALASKA RAILROAD CORPORATION
P.O. Box 107500, Anchorage AK 99510. 907/265-2437. **Fax:** 907/265-2542. **Contact:** Susan Lindemuth, Human Resources Manager. **E-mail address:** arjobinfo@akrr.com. **World Wide Web address:** http://www.akrr.com. **Description:** A railroad company. **Positions advertised include:** Administrative Assistant; Budget Officer; Project Manager, Capital Programs.

ALASKA REGIONAL HOSPITAL
P.O. Box 143889, Anchorage AK 99514-3889. 907/276-1131. **Physical address:** 2801 Debarr Road, Anchorage AK 99508. **Fax:** 907/264-1143. **Contact:** Human Resources. **World Wide Web address:** http://www.akreg.com. **Description:** A 238-bed, acute care hospital. The hospital has critical care units, emergency services, rehabilitation services, a maternity center, and a diagnostic imaging department. The hospital offers specialized neurosurgery, spinal surgery, and orthopedic surgery. As one of the only acute care hospitals in the state with direct airplane access, Alaska Regional Hospital serves as a medical referral center for the state. The hospital also has a referral center for cancer treatment. **Positions advertised include:** Clinical Exercise Physiologist; RN's; Occupational Therapist; Pharmacist; Physical Therapist. **Parent company:** Columbia/HCA Health Care Corporation is one of the largest health care services providers in the world, with more than 190 acute care and specialty hospitals in 26 states and two foreign countries.

ALASKA USA TRUST COMPANY
P/O Box 196613, Anchorage AK 99519-6613. 907/562-6544. **Toll-free phone:** 888/628-4567. **Fax:** 907/786-2546. **Physical address:** 4000 Credit Union Drive, Suite 605, Anchorage AK 99503. **Contact:** Human Resources. **E-mail address:** employment@alaskausa.org. **World Wide Web address:** http://www.alaskausatrust.com. **Description:** Provides a wide range of financial services. **NOTE:** Employment application available online. **Positions advertised include:** Area Manager; Assistant Sales Manager; CLA Operations Supervisor; Control Officer; Database Administrator; Enforcement Specialist; Loan Center Specialist; Network Control Specialist; Recovery Officer; Trust Systems Administrator.

ANCHORAGE DAILY NEWS
1001 Northway Drive, Anchorage AK 99508. 907/257-4275. **Recorded jobline:** 907/257-4402. **Fax:** 907/257-4472. **Contact:** Human Resources. **E-mail address:** jobs@adn.com. **World Wide Web address:** http://www.adn.com. **Description:** A newspaper with a weekday circulation of 71,700 and a Sunday circulation of 93,800. **Positions advertised include:** Administrative Assistant; Advertising Account Executive; District Manager; Home Delivery Runner; Kenai Reporter; Packaging Center Inserter; Sales Associate; Telemarketer. **Parent company:** McClatchy Newspapers is a communications company that publishes 12 daily newspapers and eight community newspapers in California, Washington, Alaska, and South Carolina.

ARCTIC SLOPE REGIONAL CORPORATION
P.O. Box 129, Barrow AK 99723. 907/852-8633. **Fax:** 907/852-5733. **Contact:** Charlotte Brower, Personnel Manager. **World Wide Web address:** http://www.asrc.com. **Description:** Arctic Slope Regional Corporation and its subsidiaries are involved in automotive merchandise sales, busing, commercial construction, communications and television operations, consulting, engineering, environmental remediation, hotel operations, manufacturing, oil field support, petroleum refining and products sales, resource exploration and development, and tourism. The company also participates in various partnerships, joint ventures, and other business activities. **Other area locations:** Anchorage AK.

BP EXPLORATION ALASKA INC.
P.O. Box 196612, Anchorage AK 99519-6612. 907/561-5111. **Contact:** Human Resources. **World Wide Web address:** http://www.bp.com/alaska. **Description:** Responsible for oil and gas exploration and development in Alaska, as well as oversight of the Trans-Alaska Pipeline System and the Kuparuk, Milne Point, and Endicott pipelines. **Positions advertised include:** Exploration and Production Attorney; Power Plant Operator; **Parent company:** BP America is one of the largest of the BP international group of companies, which operates in more than 70 countries. BP is one of the largest oil companies in the world, based on net assets, and represents about 10 percent of all domestic U.S. oil production. BP Pipelines is one of the largest oil producers in Alaska, accounting for about half of the state's total.

BARNES & NOBLE BOOKSTORES
200 East Northern Lights Boulevard, Anchorage AK 99503. 907/279-7323. **Contact:** Manager. **World Wide Web address:** http://www.bn.com. **Description:** A national bookstore chain operating nationwide. This location also has a cafe and music department.

CTG (COMPUTER TASK GROUP, INC.)
4701 Business Park Boulevard, Building J, Anchorage AK 99503. 907/261-6500. **Fax:** 907/261-6520. **Contact:** Human Resources. **World Wide Web address:** http://www.ctg.com. **Description:** Provides information technology staffing and solutions and application management outsourcing. **Corporate headquarters location:** Buffalo NY. **Other U.S. locations:** Nationwide. **International locations:** Worldwide. **Listed on:** New York Stock Exchange. **Stock exchange symbol:** CTG.

CHUGACH ALASKA CORPORATION (CAC)
560 E. 34th Avenue, Anchorage AK 99503. 907/563-8866. **Fax:** 907/563-8402. **Contact:** Human Resources. **E-mail address:** resumes@chugach-ak.com. **World Wide Web address:** http://www.chugach-ak.com. **Description:** The Chugach family consists of seven subsidiaries and several joint ventures with over 5,000 employees worldwide. CAC currently targets the following areas of business interests - base operating services, educational services, construction services, environmental services, information technology, telecommunications, and full-service employment services. **Positions advertised include:** Accountant; Senior Financial Analyst; Billing Technician.

CHUGACH ELECTRIC ASSOCIATION, INC.
P.O. Box 196300, Anchorage AK 99519-6300. 907/762-4428. **Contact:** Human Resources Department. **E-mail address:** recruitment@chugachelectric.com. **World Wide Web address:** http://www.chugachelectric.com. **Description:** Chugach is the largest electric utility in Alaska, serving more than 69,000 locations in a service territory which extends from Anchorage to the northern Kenai Peninsula. **Positions advertised include:** Record Drawing Technician; Recruitment HRIS Specialist; Safety Specialist; Substation Technician.

COMPUCOM ALASKA LEARNING CENTER
3000 C Street, Suite 102, Anchorage AK 99503. 907/562-4488. **Fax:** 907/762-9160. **Contact:** D. Renee Rasmussen, District Service Manager. **E-mail address:** rrasmuss@compucom.com. **World Wide Web address:** http://www.compucomalaska.com. **Description:** Provides computer hardware and software training for companies and business professionals. Founded in 1981. **Other U.S. locations:** Nationwide. **Parent Company:** Compucom.

CONOCOPHILLIPS ALASKA
700 G Street, Anchorage AK 99501. 907/276-1215. **Contact:** Human Resources. **World Wide Web address:** http://www.conocophillips.com. **Description:** Engaged in the exploration and production of oil, natural gas, and natural gas liquids. ConocoPhillips also markets refined products in the United States and manufactures plastics and petrochemical products. **Corporate headquarters location:** Houston TX. **Listed on:** New York Stock Exchange. **Stock exchange symbol:** COP.

CRESCENT ELECTRIC SUPPLY COMPANY
5333 Fairbank Street, Anchorage AK 99518. 907/562-2800. **Fax:** 907/564-0181. **Contact:** Human Resources. **World Wide Web address:** http://www.cesco.com. **Description:** A wholesaler of electrical supplies. **Corporate headquarters location:** East Dubuque IL. **Number of employees nationwide:** 100.

CUMMINS NORTHWEST ALASKA
2618 Commercial Drive, Anchorage AK 99501. 907/279-7594. **Fax:** 907/276-6340. **Contact:** Human Resources. **World Wide Web address:** http://www.cumminsnorthwest.com. **Description:** Manufactures and distributes heavy-duty truck, industrial, and machine parts. **Other U.S. locations:** MT; OR; WA.

DATAFLOW/ALASKA, INC.
800 East Dimond Boulevard, Suite 3-450, Anchorage AK 99515. 907/365-2700. **Fax:** 907/365-2790. **Contact:** Human Resources. **E-mail address:** resumes@dataflowalaska.com. **World Wide Web address:** http://www.dataflowalaska.com. **Description:** Provides systems analysis, programming services, technical support, and training to federal and state agencies. Founded in 1994. **Positions advertised include:** Health Systems Manager; Payroll Accountant; Cold Fusion Programmer/Analyst. **Corporate headquarters location:** This location. **Other area locations:** Juneau AK.

DENALI NATIONAL PARK AND PRESERVE
P.O. Box 9, Denali Park AK 99755. 907/683-2294. **Fax:** 907/683-9617. **Contact:** Susanne Brown, Human Resources. **World Wide Web address:** http://www.nps.gov/dena. **Description:** A 6-million-acre park. **Positions advertised include:** Park Ranger. **Special programs:** Internships. **Number of employees at this location:** 100.

ERA AVIATION, INC.
6160 Carl Brady Drive, Anchorage AK 99502. 907/248-4422. **Fax:** 907/266-8401. **Contact:** Karla Grumman, Personnel Director. **World Wide Web address:** http://www.era-aviation.com. **Description:** An air transportation company. **Positions advertised include:** Aircraft Maintenance Technician; Fleet Service Agent; Ramp Agent/Line Service Technician; Ground Maintenance Mechanic. **Corporate headquarters location:** This location. **Other U.S. locations:** Reno NV; Lake Charles LA. **Number of employees at this location:** 750. **Number of employees nationwide:** 900.

ENSR CORPORATION
1835 South Bragaw Street, Suite 490, Anchorage AK 99508. 907/561-5700. **Fax:** 907/273-4555. **Contact:** Human Resources. **World Wide Web address:** http://www.ensr.com. **Description:** Engaged in arctic engineering, soil engineering, petroleum engineering, geology, geophysics, seismology, surface and groundwater hydrology, meteorology, oceanography, environmental impact assessment, air and water quality, and biological sciences. ENSR Corporation has 70 offices in 17 countries. **Positions advertised include:** Sr. Project Manager. **Corporate headquarters location:** Westford MA. **Other area locations:** Fairbanks AK. **Other U.S. locations:** Nationwide. **International locations:** Worldwide.

FLOWLINE ALASKA, INC.
1881 Livengood Way, Fairbanks AK 99701. 907/456-4911. **Fax:** 907/456-1194. **Contact:** Human Resources. **World Wide Web address:** http://www.flowlinealaska.com. **Description:** Provides welding, fabrication, and insulation services to companies developing and managing pipelines in Alaska. Founded in 1981.

GENERAL COMMUNICATION, INC. (GCI)
2550 Denali Street, Suite 1604, Anchorage AK 99503. 907/265-5600. **Fax:** 907/868-5490. **Contact:** Human Resources. **E-mail address:** careers@gci.com. **World Wide Web address:** http://www.gci.com. **Description:** Supplies long-distance and other telecommunications products and services to residential, commercial, and government users. GCI operates in two industry segments: the message and data transmission services industry segment offers message toll, private line, and private network services; and the system sales and the service industry segment offers data communication equipment sales and technical services. **Positions advertised include:** Project Controls Analyst; LSDD Specialist; IT Testing Manager; IT Business Analyst;

Distribution Cost Specialist; Accountant. **Corporate headquarters location:** This location. **Subsidiaries include:** GCI Communication Services, Inc. provides private network, point-to-point data, and voice transmission services between Alaska, Hawaii, and the western contiguous United States. GCI Leasing Company, Inc. owns and leases undersea fiberoptic cable for switched message and private line long-distance services between Alaska and the continental United States. **Listed on:** NASDAQ. **Stock exchange symbol:** GNCMA.

HOPE COMMUNITY RESOURCES, INC.
540 West International Airport Road, Anchorage AK 99518. 907/561-5335. **Toll-free phone:** 800/478-0078. **Fax:** 907/564-7429. **Recorded jobline:** 907/562-6226. **Contact:** Eva Jo Henning, Hiring Specialist. **E-mail address:** jobs@hopealaska.com. **World Wide Web address:** http://www.hopealaska.org. **Description:** A private, nonprofit organization providing support to people with developmental disabilities. Services focus on adults and children, community building, mental health, family support, consumer rights, employment, and cultural relevance. This location also hires seasonally. Founded in 1968. **Positions advertised include:** Behavioral Health Services Clinician; Care Coordinator; Home Alliance Coordinator; Individual Support Specialist; Mental Health Associate; IT Programmer. **Special programs:** Internships; Training; Summer Jobs. **Internship information:** Summer practicums are offered for students from New York, Oregon, and Ireland. **Office hours:** Monday - Friday, 8:00 a.m. - 5:00 p.m. **Corporate headquarters location:** This location. **Other area locations:** Barrow AK; Dillingham AK; Juneau AK; Kodiak AK; Seward AK; Wasilla AK. **Listed on:** Privately held. **Executive Director:** Stephen Lesko. **Annual sales/revenues:** $11 - $20 million.

THE HOTEL CAPTAIN COOK
4th and K Street, Anchorage AK 99501. 907/276-6000. **Toll-free phone:** 800/843-1950. **Fax:** 907/343-2441. **Contact:** Raquel Edelen, Human Resources Director. **World Wide Web address:** http://www.captaincook.com. **Description:** A 565-room, luxury hotel. Founded in 1966. **NOTE:** Resumes should be sent to: 939 West Fifth Avenue, Anchorage AK 99501. **Special programs:** Summer Jobs. **Corporate headquarters location:** This location. **Listed on:** Privately held. **President:** Walter Hickel, Jr. **Number of employees at this location:** 450.

KANAKANAK HOSPITAL
BRISTOL BAY AREA HEALTH CORPORATION
P.O. Box 130, Dillingham AK 99576. 907/842-5201. **Contact:** Victor Sifof, Personnel Director. **World Wide Web address:** http://www.his.gov. **Description:** A regional hospital providing a wide range of health services including radiology, a pharmacy, outpatient services, a mental health program, maternal/child health services, a clinical laboratory, and an alcohol and drug abuse recovery program. The staff travels to over 20 villages two months out of the year. Bristol Bay Area Health Corporation (BBAHC) in 1980 became one of the first tribal organizations in the nation to assume control of a Native American hospital/service unit under the Indian Self-Determination and Education Assistance Act. Kanakanak Hospital became the centerpiece of BBAHC's range of acute, preventive, and educational services for the rest of the Bristol Bay Region. **Number of employees at this location:** 300.

KENAI FJORDS NATIONAL PARK
P.O. Box 1727, Seward AK 99664. 907/224-3175. **Physical address:** 1212 Fourth Avenue, Seward AK 99664. **Fax:** 907/224-2144. **Contact:** Human Resources. **World Wide Web address:** http://www.kenai.fjords.national-park.com. **Description:** A 580,000-acre national park established to protect the area's habitat and landscape. The national park supports unaltered natural environments and ecosystems, an ice field wilderness, unnamed waterfalls in unnamed canyons, and glaciers. Authorized commercial guides provide hiking, fishing, and kayaking services. Air charters, boat tours, and charters are also available. **Positions advertised include:** Park Ranger; Park Guide; Visitor Use Assistant; Biological Technician. **Special programs:** Internships.

KEYBANK N.A.
100 Cushman Street, Fairbanks AK 99701. 907/459-3300. **Contact:** Branch Manager. **World Wide Web address:** http://www.keybank.com. **Description:** A bank. **Corporate headquarters location:** Cleveland OH. **Other U.S. locations:** Nationwide. **Parent company:** KeyCorp is one of the nation's largest financial services holding companies. The company offers full-service commercial banking and related financial services through more than 900 offices in 12 states. Services offered by the company's financial subsidiaries include mortgage banking, investment management and trust services, insurance, and brokerage companies that operate in each of the company's banking states and other selected markets. Services handled by local offices include branch management, account management, product pricing, and lending. Services that support customer service, including information technology and operations, product development, and training, are managed by KeyCorp. **Listed on:** New York Stock Exchange. **Stock exchange symbol:** KEY.

KODIAK AREA NATIVE ASSOCIATION
3449 East Rezanof Drive, Kodiak AK 99615. 907/486-9800. **Fax:** 907/486-9898. **Contact:** Norma Peterson, Director of Human Resources. **World Wide Web address:** http://www.kanaweb.org. **Description:** A private, nonprofit organization providing health care and social services to Alaskan Native and Native American individuals. **Positions advertised include:** Community Health Aid. **Note:** The Kodiak Area Native Association is an equal opportunity employer, however, in accordance with P.L. 93-638, preference in filling vacancies is given Alaska Natives/Native American Indian candidates.

MARSH
1031 West 4th Avenue, Suite 400, Anchorage AK 99501. 907/276-5617. **Fax:** 907/257-6292. **Contact:** Human Resources. **World Wide Web address:** http://www.marsh.com. **Description:** An insurance brokerage and risk management firm. Founded in 1994.

MATANUSKA TELEPHONE ASSOCIATION, INC. (MTA)
480 Commercial Drive, Palmer AK 99645. 907/745-3211. **Fax:** 907/761-1929. **Contact:** Human Resources. **E-mail address:** careers@mta-telco.com. **World Wide Web address:** http://www.mtasolutions.com. **Description:** A cooperative telecommunications service center that provides 24-hour trouble-reporting, line assignment, central office maintenance and testing, cable maintenance, and installation and repair. Founded in 1955. **Positions advertised include:** Contract Administrator; Outside Plant construction Supervisor. **Other area locations:** Eagle River AK; Wasilla AK. **Subsidiaries include:** Cellular Connection (Wasilla AK) is a cellular telephone service company; NorthCom provides professional sales and technical support for nonregulated business telecommunications needs.

NANA DEVELOPMENT CORPORATION
1001 East Benson Boulevard, Anchorage AK 99508. 907/265-4100. **Toll-free phone:** 800/478-2000. **Fax:** 907/275-2475. **Recorded jobline:** 888/816-6262. **Contact:** Human Resources. **E-mail address:** careercenter@nana.com. **World Wide Web address:** http://www.nana.com. **Description:** NANA Development Corporation serves as the center of operations for businesses NANA oversees. **Positions advertised include:** Hospital Manager EVS; Hospital Housekeeper; Security Officer; Assistant Benefits Administrator; Cook; Civil/ Structural Designer; Civil/Structural Engineers; Electrical/Instrument Designers; Electrical Engineers; Instrumentation Engineers; Materials Coordinator; Mechanical Engineers; Mechanical/Piping Designers; Process Engineers; Project Engineers; Civil Engineer; Transportation Engineers; Transportation Planners; Geotechnical Engineer; Environmental Analyst; Entry Level Geotechnical Engineer. **Corporate headquarters location:** Kotzebue AK. **Parent company:** NANA Regional Corporation owns and manages more than 2.3 million acres of land in northwestern Alaska, which includes the mining and subsurface rights. The area is commonly mined for its abundant zinc, lead, copper, gold, coal, and jade resources. NANA Regional Corporation is engaged in engineering, government contracting, hospitality and tourism, corporate services, oilfield services, and mining activities.

NORTHERN AIR CARGO
3900 West International Airport Road, Anchorage AK 99502. 907/249-5137. **Recorded Jobline:** 907/249-5187. **Contact:** Human Resources. **World Wide Web address:** http://www.northernaircargo.com. **Description:** A transportation services company servicing Alaska and the World. Founded in 1956. **Note:** Applications are accepted in-person Monday through Friday from 8:00 a.m. to 6:00 p.m. **Positions advertised include:** Ramp Agent; Quality Assurance Auditor; GSE Mechanic; Warehouse Agent.

PROVIDENCE ALASKA MEDICAL CENTER
3200 Providence Drive, Anchorage AK 99508. 907/562-2211. **Contact:** Human Resources. **World Wide Web address:** http://www.providence.org/alaska. **Description:** An acute care hospital with 341 beds. **NOTE:** For more information about employment opportunities, contact the Providence Human Resources Service Center, 701 East Tudor Road, Suite 135, Anchorage AK 99503, 907/565-6400 or 800/478-9940. **Positions advertised include:** Analyst-Database Reporting; Assistant Clinical Manager; Certified Nurse Assistant; Dietitian; Registered Nurse; Pharmacy Intern; LPN; Medical Technologist; Occupational Therapist; Phlebotomist.

PROVIDENCE EXTENDED CARE CENTER
4900 Eagle Street, Anchorage AK 99503-7490. 907/562-2281. **Contact:** Human Resources. **World Wide Web address:** http://www.providence.org/alaska. **Description:** A 224-bed, long-term care facility for children, adolescents, adults, and the elderly. Services are for people with mental and physical disabilities due to accidents, paralysis, advanced age, Alzheimer's disease, or any other condition that has made self-care difficult. **Positions advertised include:** Accountant; Analyst-Health Information; Assistant Physical Therapist. **NOTE:** For more information about employment opportunities, contact the Providence Human Resources Service Center, 701 East Tudor Road, Suite 135, Anchorage AK 99503, 907/565-6400 or 800/478-9940.

SHANNON & WILSON
2355 Hill Road, Fairbanks AK 99709-5326. 907/479-0600. **Fax:** 907/479-5691. **Contact:** Human Resources. **E-mail address:** jobs@shanwil.com. **World Wide Web address:** http://www.shannonwilson.com. **Description:** Engaged in a variety of geotechnical, environmental, and construction materials engineering activities, including permafrost engineering, foundation engineering, engineering geology, hydrology, hydrogeology, and the design of environmental remediation projects. **Positions advertised include:** Geotechnical Engineer (Multiple positions). **Corporate headquarters location:** Seattle WA. **Other area locations:** Anchorage AK. **Other U.S. locations:** CO; IL; MA; MI; OR; WA. **Subsidiaries include:** S&W Construction Services, Inc.; Shannon & Wilson International, Inc. **Number of employees at this location:** 170.

SINBAD NETWORK COMMUNICATIONS
3101 Penland Parkway, Suite K26, Anchorage AK 99508. 907/274-6223. **Contact:** Human Resources. **World Wide Web address:** http://www.sinbad.suddenspecials.com. **Description:** Provides online services to subscribers including a Web browser, chat rooms, e-mail, personal Web pages, live news, investment tools, computer training, and bulletin boards.

TESORO CORPORATION
54741 Tesoro Road, Kenai AK 99611. 907/776-8191. **Physical address:** 2700 Gambell Street, Suite 500, Anchorage AK 99503. **Contact:** Human Resources. **World Wide Web address:** http://www.tesoropetroleum.com. **Description:** Refines petroleum products and manufactures premium unleaded gasoline. There are over 100 Tesoro stations across Alaska, including 39 7-Eleven locations. The Kenai Refinery is the company's main Alaskan producer of petroleum. The company has an exploration and production segment in south Texas, which opened in 1990. Tesoro also has operations in southern Bolivia that include significant natural gas reserves. **Positions advertised include:** Training Coordinator. **Corporate headquarters location:** San Antonio TX. Other U.S. locations: CA; HI; ND; WA. **Listed on:** New York Stock Exchange. **Stock exchange symbol:** TSO.

TOUCH N' GO SYSTEMS, INC.
406 G Street, Suite 210, Anchorage AK 99501. 907/274-6333. **Fax:** 907/274-9493. **Contact:** Human Resources. **E-mail address:** touchngo@touchngo.com. **World Wide Web address:** http://www.touchngo.com. **Description:** Develops network software and provides Website design and management services. Touch N' Go also offers computer network consulting services. **Corporate headquarters location:** This location.

U.S. BUREAU OF LAND MANAGEMENT
222 West 7th Avenue, #13, Anchorage AK 99709. 907/271-5960. **Contact:** Human Resources. **World Wide Web address:** http://www.ak.blm.gov. **Description:** Office of the federal agency that manages public lands and resources.

UNITECH OF ALASKA, INC.
P.O. Box 240167, Anchorage AK 99524-0167. 907/349-5142. **Physical address:** 2401 Cinnabar Loop, Anchorage AK 99507. **Fax:** 907/349-2733. **Contact:** Human Resources. **E-mail address:** unitech@alaska.net. **Description:** Offers environmental services, products, and equipment to the Alaskan marketplace. Founded in 1985. **Other U.S. locations:** Portland OR; Seattle WA. **Number of employees at this location:** 20.

UNITED UTILITIES, INC. (UNICOM)
5450 A Street, Anchorage AK 99518. 907/561-1674. **Toll-free phone:** 800/478-2020. **Fax:** 907/563-3185. **Contact:** Office Manager. **World Wide Web address:** http://www.unicom-alaska.com. **Description:** Provides telecommunication services to rural Alaska. **Positions advertised include:** Customer Care Representative. **Other area locations:** Bethel AK.

UNIVERSITY OF ALASKA ANCHORAGE
Human Resources Services, 3211 Providence Drive, Anchorage AK 99508. 907/786-4608. **Fax:** 907/786-4727. **Contact:** Human Resources. **World Wide Web address:** http://www.uaa.alaska.edu. **Description:** A university with over 17,000 students. Positions advertised include: Head Coach, Women's Volleyball; IS Consultant; Research Professional; Senior HRS Consultant; Assistant Professor; Various Departments. **Office hours:** Monday - Friday, 8:00 a.m. - 5:00 p.m.

UNIVERSITY OF ALASKA SOUTHEAST
11120 Glacier Highway, Juneau AK 99801. 907/465-6263. **Toll-free phone:** 877/465-4827. **Fax:** 907/465-6365. **Contact:** Human Resources. **World Wide Web address:** http://www.jun.alaska.edu. **Description:** A regional unit of the University of Alaska statewide system of higher education. The university was established in 1987 with the restructuring of the former University of Alaska Juneau, Ketchikan Community College, and Islands Community College. General education in liberal arts forms the core of the university's educational programs. The university offers certificate programs and associate's degrees in vocational/technical and business-related areas; Associate of Arts degrees; bachelor's degrees in liberal arts, sciences, education, business, and public administration; and master's degrees in education and public administration. In the University of Alaska Statewide System, this institution shares responsibility for programs in public administration, public school administration, early childhood education, and education technology. **Other area locations:** Ketchikan AK; Sitka AK.

VALLEY HOSPITAL
P.O. Box 1687, Palmer AK 99645-1687. 907/352-4850. **Recorded jobline:** 907/746-8684. **Contact:** Human Resources. **E-mail address:** skenyon@valley-hosp.com. **World Wide Web address:** http://www.valley-hosp.com. **Description:** A 36-bed acute care hospital that provides general medical and surgical services. Valley Hospital also has a retail pharmacy, birthing center, extended-hours clinic (outpatient, nontraumatic care), and home care services. **Positions advertised include:** Registered Nurse; Occupational Therapist; Physical Therapist; Director, Performance Improvement; Director, Clinical Pharmacy.

VECO CORPORATION
3601 C Street, Suite 1000, Anchorage AK 99503. 907/264-8100. **Fax:** 907/264-8130. **Contact:** Human Resources. **World Wide Web address:** http://www.veco.com. **Description:** Provides project management, engineering, procurement, construction operations and maintenance services to the energy, resource, and process industries and to the public sector. **Positions advertised include:** Structural Designer; HR Technician; Quality Assurance Engineer; Pipe Designer; Project Controls Specialist; Process Engineer; Mechanical Engineer. **Corporate headquarters location:** This location. **Other U.S. locations:** Centennial CO; Bellingham WA. **Listed on:** Privately held. **Number of employees nationwide:** 3,000.

WELLS FARGO BANK ALASKA
301 West Northern Lights, Anchorage AK 99510. 907/265-2190. **Recorded jobline:** 907/265-2197. **Contact:** Human Resources. **World Wide Web address:** http://www.wellsfargo.com. **Description:** A diversified financial institution with over $234 billion in assets. Wells Fargo serves over 23 million customers through more than 6,000 independent locations worldwide. The company also maintains several stand-alone ATMs and branches within other retail outlets. Services include community banking, credit and debit cards, home equity and mortgage loans, online banking, student loans, and insurance. Wells Fargo also offers a complete line of commercial and institutional financial services. Founded in 1852. **NOTE:** Search and apply for positions online. **Positions advertised include:** PCS Financial Consultant; Mortgage Consultant; WFF Loan Processor. **Corporate headquarters location:** San Francisco CA.

1ST NATIONAL BANK OF ARIZONA
P.O. Box 60095, Phoenix AZ 85082. 888/419-5574. **Fax:** 602/426-0280. **E-mail address:** hrd@fnbaonline.com. **World Wide Web address:** http://www.fnbaonline.com. **Contact:** Human Resources. **Description:** A full service bank providing services to both businesses and individuals. **Positions advertised include:** Project Manager; Business Applications Engineer; Treasury Management Customer Service Specialists; Treasury Management Operations Manager. **Other area locations include:** Avondale; Chandler; Charlotte; Bullhead City; Mesa; Scottsdale.

APS
P.O. Box 53999, M.S. 8012, Phoenix AZ 85072-3999. 602/250-1000. **Contact:** Human Resources. **E-mail address:** staffing@pinnaclewest.com. **World Wide Web address:** http://www.aps.com. **Description:** An electric utility serving more than 900,000 residential and commercial customers. **Positions advertised include:** Administrative Coordinator; Civil Designer; Crew Foreman. **Parent company:** Pinnacle West Capital Corporation (Phoenix AZ.) **Listed on:** New York Stock Exchange. **Stock exchange symbol:** PNW. **Number of employees nationwide:** 8,300.

APS ENERGY SERVICES
Arizona Center, 400 East Van Buren Street, Suite 750, Phoenix AZ 85004. 602/744-5000. **Toll-free phone:** 800/723-9566. **Contact:** Human Resources. **World Wide Web address:** http://www.apses.com. **Description:** An electric utility company providing service to homes and businesses in western Arizona. **Positions advertised include:** Competitive Analyst. **Other U.S. locations:** Flagstaff AZ; Tucson AZ; Long Beach CA. **Parent company:** Pinnacle West Capital Corporation. **Listed on:** New York Stock Exchange. **Stock exchange symbol:** PNW.

ASML
8555 South River Parkway, Tempe AZ 85284. 480/383-4422. **Fax:** 480/383-3986. **Contact:** Human Resources. **E-mail address:** careers@asml.com. **World Wide Web address:** http://www.asml.com. **Description:** ASML designs, develops, integrates, markets and services advanced systems used by semiconductor manufacturers to create integrated circuits that power a wide array of electronic, communications and information technology products. **Positions advertised include:** Marketing Communications Specialist; Project Manager, Installations.

AT SYSTEMS SECURITY
3001 West Indian School Road, Suite 218, Phoenix AZ 85017. 602/264-4193. **Recorded jobline:** 800/315-8442. **Contact:** Human Resources. **E-mail address:** newcareers@atsystemsinc.com. **World Wide Web address:** http://www.atsystemsinc.com. **Description:** Provides security guard services to a variety of clients.

AXA ADVISORS
1850 North Central Avenue, Suite 640, Phoenix AZ 85004. 602/241-0035. **Contact:** Human Resources. **World Wide Web address:** http://www.equitable.com. **Description:** A major life insurance company offering a variety of life insurance and annuity products and services through 8,200 career agents.

ABATIX CORPORATION
3011 East Broadway, Suite 300, Phoenix AZ 85040. 602/323-1941. **Toll-free phone:** 800/889-5186. **Fax:** 602/323-1942. **Contact:** Human Resources. **E-mail address:** hr@abatix.com. **World Wide Web address:** http://www.abatix.com. **Description:** A distributor of safety supplies, construction tools, clean-up equipment, and general safety products such as protective clothing and eyewear. The company supplies products to the asbestos and lead abatement, hazardous material remediation, and construction markets. Abatix Environmental Corporation has seven distribution centers in Texas, California, Arizona, Nevada, and Washington. **NOTE:** Please send resumes to 2801 Eastpoint Drive, Suite 500, Dallas TX 75227. **Corporate headquarters location:** Dallas TX. **Listed on:** NASDAQ. **Stock exchange symbol:** ABIX.

ACCENTURE
4742 North 24th Street, Suite 400, Phoenix AZ 85016. 602/337-4000. **Fax:** 602/337-4444. **Contact:** Personnel. **World Wide Web address:** http://www.accenture.com. **Description:** A management and technology consulting firm offering a wide range of services including business re-engineering, customer service system consulting, data system design and implementation, Internet sales systems research and design, and strategic planning. **Positions advertised include:** Oracle Application Programmer; Business Systems Analyst; Application Architect; Consultant. **Corporate headquarters location:** Chicago IL. **Other U.S. locations:** Nationwide. **International locations:** Worldwide.

ACTION PERFORMANCE COMPANIES INC.
1480 South Hohokam, Tempe AZ 85281. 602/337-3700. **Fax:** 602/337-3910. **Contact:** Terry Temple, Human Resources. **E-mail address:** ttemple@action-performance.com. **World Wide Web address:** http://www.action-performance.com. **Description:** Designs, markets, and distributes a line of licensed motor sports collectibles and consumer merchandise. **Positions advertised include:** 3D Modeling/Tooling; Attorney. **Corporate headquarters location:** This location. **Other U.S. locations:** Atlanta GA; Charlotte NC. **Listed on:** New York Stock Exchange. **Stock exchange symbol:** ATN. **Number of employees nationwide:** 600.

ACTIVE RECOGNITION TECHNOLOGIES
234 South Extension, Suite 103, Mesa AZ 85210. 480/586-3400. **Fax:** 480/586-3401. **Contact:** Human Resources. **Description:** A developer of vehicle and license plate recognition software. **Positions advertised include:** Windows Developer; Junior QA Tester.

ADAPTO, INC.
122 South Litchfield Road, Goodyear AZ 85338. 623/935-2681. **Fax:** 623/932-0939. **Contact:** Human Resources. **E-mail address:** adapto@syspac.com. **Description:** Adapto manufactures automotive parts. Founded in 1947. **NOTE:** Entry-level positions and second and third shifts are offered. **Special programs:** Training. **Corporate headquarters location:** This location. **Other U.S. locations:** South Bend IN. **Operations at this facility:** This location manufactures metal components for airbag systems. **Parent company:** SOCOR. **Listed on:** Privately held. **President:** Tom Schoaf. **Facilities Manager:** Robert Gordon. **Annual sales/revenues:** $5 - $10 million. **Number of employees at this location:** 185. **Number of employees nationwide:** 320.

ADOBEAIR, INC.
500 South 15th Street, Phoenix AZ 85034. 602/257-0060. **Fax:** 602/257-1349. **Contact:** Human Resources. **World Wide Web address:** http://www.adobeair.com. **Description:** Manufactures portable electric heaters and evaporative coolers. **Corporate headquarters location:** This location. **Parent company:** Castle Harlan. **Operations at this facility include:** Manufacturing. **Number of employees at this location:** 500.

ADVANCED SEMICONDUCTOR MATERIALS, INC.
3440 East University Drive, Phoenix AZ 85034. 602/437-1405. **Contact:** Human Resources. **Description:** Develops, manufactures, and markets a wide range of semiconductor wafer-processing equipment.

ADVANTAGE BOATS
1000 North Lake Havasu Avenue, Lake Havasu City AZ 86403. 928/680-BOAT. **Fax:** 928/680-1150. **Contact:** Human Resources Department. **World Wide Web address:** http://www.advantageboats.com. **Description:** Manufactures racing and recreational boats. **Corporate headquarters location:** This location. **President:** Harry Christensen.

ADVO, INC.
2235 South Central Avenue, Phoenix AZ 85004. 602/252-2518. **Contact:** Human Resources. **World Wide Web address:** http://www.advo.com. **Description:** A direct mail advertising company. Positions advertised include: Desktop Artist; PHX-Quality Control Artist; Print Manager; **Corporate headquarters location:** Windsor CT. **Other U.S. locations:** Nationwide.

AJILON SERVICES INC.
4647 North 32nd Street, Suite B280, Phoenix AZ 85018. 602/230-1008. **Toll-free phone:** 800/938-2342. **Fax:** 602/279-0505. **Contact:** Personnel. **E-mail address:** recruit.phoenix@ajilon.com. **World Wide Web address:** http://www.ajilon.com. **Description:** Offers computer consulting services, project support, and end user services. **Positions advertised include:** Business Analyst. **Other area locations:** Scottsdale AZ; Chandler AZ. **Other U.S. locations:** Nationwide.

ALBERTSON'S
400 South 99th Avenue, Suite 200, Tolleson AZ 85353. 602/382-5300. **Contact:** Human Resources. **E-mail address:** employment@albertsons.com. **World Wide Web address:** http://www.albertsons.com. **Description:** A full-service supermarket. Founded in 1939. **NOTE:** Search and apply for positions online. **Corporate headquarters location:** Boise ID. **Listed on:** New York Stock Exchange. **Stock exchange symbol:** ABS. **Number of employees nationwide:** 200,000.

ALLIED-BARTON SECURITY SERVICES.
702 East Osborne Street, Suite 160, Phoenix AZ 85014. 602/381-1795. **Fax:** 602/381-0265. **Contact:** Personnel. **World Wide Web address:** http://www.alliedsecurity.com. **Description:** Provides detective, guard, and armored car services.

ALLIED WASTE INDUSTRIES, INC.
15880 North Greenway-Hayden Loop, Suite 100, Scottsdale AZ 85260. 480/627-2700. **Contact:** Human Resources. **World Wide Web address:** http://www.awin.com. **Description:** One of the world's largest waste services company. Allied Waste provides collection, disposal, and recycling services to residential, commercial, and industrial customers. **Corporate headquarters location:** This location. **Listed on:** New York Stock Exchange. **Stock exchange symbol:** AW.

AMEC
2001 West Camelback Road, Suite 300, Phoenix AZ 85015. 602/343-2400. **Fax:** 602/343-2499. **Contact:** Human Resources. **E-mail address:** careers.ee.krk@amec.com. **World Wide Web address:** http://www.amec.com. **Description:** One of North America's largest full-service, environmental engineering consulting firms. There are over 250 AMEC offices worldwide. **Positions advertised include:** Senior Water Resources Project Manager; Senior Materials Engineer; Hydrology and Hydraulics Engineer. **Corporate headquarters location:** London, England. **Number of employees nationwide:** 1,300.

AMERICAN BUILDING MAINTENANCE INDUSTRIES
2632 West Medtronic Way, Tempe AZ 85281. 480/968-8300. **Fax:** 480/921-8734. **Contact:** Branch Manager. **World Wide Web address:** http://www.abm.com. **Description:** Provides janitorial and maintenance services for clients who own or manage commercial buildings of 50,000 square feet or more. **Special programs:** Internships. **Corporate headquarters location:** San Francisco CA. **Parent company:** ABM Industries Inc. **Listed on:** New York Stock Exchange. **Stock exchange symbol:** ABM.

AMERICAN CYBERNETICS, INC.
1830 West University Drive, Suite 112, Tempe AZ 85281. 480/966-9245. **Fax:** 480/966-1654. **Contact:** Human Resources Department. **Description:** A publisher of programmer editing software, including Multi-Edit for Windows and Windows NT, and Evolve, an XBase programming add-on.

AMERICAN EXPRESS TRAVEL RELATED SERVICES
20022 North 31st Avenue, Phoenix AZ 85027. 602/537-8500. **Contact:** Human Resources. **World Wide Web address:** http://www.americanexpress.com. **Description:** A diversified travel and financial services company operating in 160 countries around the world. American Express Travel Related Services offers consumers the Personal, Gold, and Platinum cards, as well as revolving credit products such as Optima Cards, which allow customers to extend payments. Other products include the American Express Corporate Card, which helps businesses manage their travel and entertainment expenditures, and the Corporate Purchasing Card, which helps businesses manage their expenditures on supplies, equipment, and services. Travel Related Services also offers American Express Traveler's Cheques and travel services, including trip planning, reservations, ticketing, and management information. Founded in 1850. **Corporate headquarters location:** New York NY. **Other U.S locations:** Fort Lauderdale FL; Jacksonville FL; Greensboro NC. **Parent company:** American Express Company. **Listed on:** New York Stock Exchange. **Stock exchange symbol:** AXP.

AMERICAN RED CROSS
P.O. Box 1129, Yuma AZ 85366. 928/782-0660. **Physical address:** 1265 South Fifth Avenue, Yuma AZ 85364. **Contact:** Human Resources. **World Wide Web address:** http://www.redcross.org. **Description:** A humanitarian organization that aids disaster victims, gathers blood for crisis distribution, trains individuals to respond to emergencies, educates individuals on various diseases, and raises funds for other charitable establishments. **Corporate headquarters location:** Washington DC. **Other U.S. locations:** Nationwide.

AMERIGAS
5140 West Bethany Home Road, Glendale AZ 85301. 623/937-9227. **Contact:** Human Resources. **World Wide Web address:** http://www.amerigas.com. **Description:** Distributes propane. **Other area locations:** Buckeye AZ; Casa Grande AZ; Holbrook AZ; Lake Havasu City AZ; Parker AZ; Sedona AZ; Show Low AZ; Sierra Vista AZ; Tucson AZ; Wickenburg AZ; Yuma AZ. **Other U.S. locations:** Nationwide. **Listed on:** New York Stock Exchange. **Stock exchange symbol:** APU.

AMKOR TECHNOLOGY
1900 South Price Road, Chandler AZ USA 85248-1604. 480/821-5000. **Fax:** 480/821-6950. **Contact:** Human Resources. **World Wide Web address:** http://www.amkor.com. **Description:** A strategic contract manufacturing resource for many of the world's leading semiconductor companies. **Positions advertised include:** Billing and Collection Coordinator; Computer Operator; Director, Financial Planning and Analysis; Network Engineer; Sr. Accounting Analyst; Sr. Technical Program Manager; Supply Chain Relationship Manager. **NOTE:** Search and apply for positions online. **Corporate headquarters location:** West Chester PA.

AMTECH SYSTEMS, INC.
131 South Clark Drive, Tempe AZ 85281. 480/967-5146. **Fax:** 480/968-3763. **Contact:** Human Resources Department. **E-mail address:** human_resources@amtechsystems.com. **World Wide Web address:** http://www.amtechsystems.com. **Description**: Amtech Systems designs, manufactures and sells products used in the fabrication of semiconductor devices and wafer manufacturing. Products include diffusion furnaces, furnace automation and wafer polishing consumables. Founded in 1981. **Listed on:** NASDAQ. **Stock exchange symbol:** ASYS.

ANALYSTS INTERNATIONAL
10851 North Black Canyon Highway, Suite 510, Phoenix AZ 85029. 602/789-7200. **Fax:** 602/789-6077. **Contact:** Human Resources. **World Wide Web address:** http://www.analysts.com. **Description:** AiC is an international computer consulting firm. The company assists clients in developing systems in a variety of industries using different programming languages and software. This involves systems analysis, design, and development. **Corporate headquarters location:** Minneapolis MN. **Listed on:** NASDAQ. **Stock exchange symbol:** ANLY.

ANIXTER
9035 South Kyrene Road, Suite 101, Tempe AZ 85284. 480/893-1166. **Toll-free phone:** 800/538-5431. **Contact:** Personnel. **E-mail address:** jobs@anixter.com. **World Wide Web address:** http://www.anixter.com. **Description:** A value-added provider of industrial wire and cabling solutions that support voice and data applications. Solutions include customized pre- and post-sale services and products. Founded in 1957. **Corporate headquarters location:** Skokie IL. **Listed on:** New York Stock Exchange. **Stock exchange symbol:** AXE.

ANTIGUA GROUP
16651 North 84th Avenue, Peoria AZ 85382-4772. 623/523-6000. **Fax:** 623/523-6016. **Contact:** Director of Human Resources. **E-mail address:** careers@antigua.com. **World Wide Web address:** http://www.antigua.com. **Description:** Specializes in the manufacture and embroidering of sporting goods and sportswear. **Positions advertised include:** Customer Service Assistant; Director of Marketing; Event Services Order Coordinator; Event Services Representative; Quality Assurance Assistant.

APACHE NITROGEN PRODUCTS, INC.
P.O. Box 700, Benson AZ 85602. 520/720-2217. **Fax:** 520/720-4158. **Contact:** Lyndon Denton, Director of Human Resources. **E-mail address:** apache@sisna.com. **World Wide Web address:** http://www.apachenitro.com. **Description:** Manufactures nitric acid and industrial and agricultural ammonium nitrate. Apache Nitrogen Products, Inc. also distributes detonating cord and blasting products.

APPLE COMPUTER, INC.
2425 East Camelback Road, Suite 550, Phoenix AZ 85016-4210. 602/957-7144. **Contact:** Human Resources. **E-mail address:** applejobs@apple.com. **World Wide Web address:** http://www.apple.com. **Description:** Apple Computer, Inc. manufactures personal computers and computer-related products for home, business, scientific, industrial, professional, and educational uses. **Positions advertised include:** Account Executive, Education Sales. **Corporate headquarters location:** Cupertino CA. **Listed on:** NASDAQ. **Stock exchange symbol:** AAPL.

ARAMARK/LAKE POWELL RESORTS AND MARINAS
P.O. Box 1597, Page AZ 86040. 928/645-1081. 928/645-2433. **Fax:** 928/645-1031. **Contact:** Human Resources. **E-mail address:** lprm-hr@aramark.com. **World Wide Web address:** http://www.aramark.com. **Description:** Operates five marinas on Lake Powell and owns resorts located throughout the Glen Canyon recreation area. **Special programs:** Internships. **Corporate headquarters location:** Philadelphia PA. **Other U.S. locations:** Nationwide. **Parent company:** ARAMARK is one of the world's leading providers of managed services. The company operates in all 50 states and 10 foreign countries, offering a broad range of services to businesses of all sizes, including most *Fortune* 500 companies and thousands of universities; hospitals; and municipal, state, and federal government facilities. ARAMARK's businesses include Food, Leisure, and Support Services including Campus Dining Services, School Nutrition Services, Business Dining Services, International Services, Health Care Support Services, Conference Center Management, and Refreshment Services; Facility Services; Correctional Services; Industrial Services; Uniform Services, which include Uniform Services and Wearguard, a direct marketer of work clothing; Health and Education Services, including Spectrum Healthcare Services and Children's World Learning Centers; and Book and Magazine Services. **Listed on:** New York Stock Exchange. **Stock exchange symbol:** RMK. **Number of employees at this location:** 1,200.

ARIZONA ATTORNEY GENERAL
1275 West Washington Street, Phoenix AZ 85007-2926. 602/542-5025. **Contact:** Human Resources. **E-mail address:** hr.recruiter@azag.gov. **World Wide Web address:** http://www.ag.state.az.us. **Description:** Administrative office of the Attorney General that handles child support issues; business complaints; housing, employment, and disability discrimination cases; and amusement or gambling registration. **NOTE:** Please send all resumes to the attention of Human Resources. **Office hours:** Monday - Friday, 8:00 a.m. - 5:00 p.m.

ARIZONA BILTMORE RESORT & SPA
2400 East Missouri Avenue, Phoenix AZ 85016. 602/955-6600. **Fax:** 602/954-2571. **Recorded jobline:** 602/954-2547. **Contact:** Director of Human Resources. **E-mail address:** resume@arizonabiltmore.com. **World Wide Web address:** http://www.arizonabiltmore.com. **Description:** A resort offering extensive lodging and dining facilities. Founded in 1929. **NOTE:** Entry-level positions and second and third shifts are offered. **Positions advertised include**: On-Call Banquet Servers; Concierge; Laundry Manager; Pool Attendant; Purchasing Storeroom Clerk; Director of Engineering; Banquet Manager. **Special programs:** Internships. **Listed on:** Privately held. **Number of employees at this location:** 900.

ARIZONA CARDINALS
P.O. Box 888, Phoenix AZ 85001. 602/379-0101. **Contact:** Human Resources. **World Wide Web address:** http://www.azcardinals.com. **Description:** Administrative offices for the NFL team.

ARIZONA CENTRAL CREDIT UNION
2020 North Central Avenue, Suite 100, Phoenix AZ 85004. 602/264-6421. **Fax:** **Contact:** Human Resources. **E-mail:** hr@azcentralcu.com. **World Wide Web address:** http://www.azcentralcu.org. **Description:** A non-profit credit cooperative providing financial services throughout the state. **Positions advertised include:** Call Center Representative; Collector; Business Development Coordinator; Accounting Representative; Accounting Supervisor. **Other area locations include:** Tempe; Chandler; Glendale; Flagstaff.

ARIZONA DEPARTMENT OF TRANSPORTATION
206 South 17th Avenue, 171A, Phoenix AZ 85007-3233. 602/712-8188. **Fax:** 602/712-3093. **Recorded jobline:** 602/712-8185. **Contact:** Human Resources. **E-mail address:** hrinfo@dot.state.az.us. **World Wide Web address:** http://www.dot.state.az.us. **Description:** Provides state-funded transportation services. **Corporate headquarters location:** This location. **Operations at this facility include:** Administration. **Number of employees at this location:** 4,800.

ARIZONA DIAMONDBACKS
P.O. Box 2095, Phoenix AZ 85001. 602/462-6500. **Recorded jobline:** 602/379-2088. **Contact:** Personnel. **World Wide Web address:** http://www.azdiamondbacks.com. **Description:** Administrative offices for the professional baseball team.

ARIZONA ELECTRIC POWER COOPERATIVE, INC.
P.O. Box 670, Benson AZ 85602. 520/586-3631. **Fax:** 520/586-5249. **Contact:** Human Resources. **World Wide Web address:** http://www.aepco.org. **Description:** An electric utility. Founded in 1961. **NOTE:** Information and application form available at: http://www.sierrasouthwest.com. Applications accepted only for open positions. **Special programs:** Internships. **Corporate headquarters location:** This location. **Number of employees at this location:** 300.

ARIZONA ENGINEERING COMPANY
419 North San Francisco Street, Flagstaff AZ 86001. 928/774-7179. **Fax:** 928/779-1041. **Contact:** Human Resources. **E-mail address:** aec@arizonaengineering.com. **World Wide Web address:** http://www.arizonaengineering.com. **Description:** A consulting firm specializing in engineering and land surveying. Caters to public agencies, institutional and industrial clients, and regulated utilities. **Other area locations:** Phoenix AZ.

ARIZONA HIGHWAYS MAGAZINE
2039 West Lewis Avenue, Phoenix AZ 85009. 602/712-2200. **Fax:** 602/254-4505. **Recorded jobline:** 602/542-4966. **Contact:** Human Resources. **Description:** A division of the Arizona Department of Transportation that publishes a magazine, books, calendars, and other products. **NOTE:** Submit resumes to: Department of Administration, Human Resources Division, 100 North 15th Avenue, Phoenix AZ 85007.

THE ARIZONA REPUBLIC
200 East Van Buren, Phoenix AZ 85004. 602/444-8000. **Contact:** Human Resources. **World Wide Web address:** http://www.azcentral.com. **Description:** A daily newspaper. Arizona Central is the online segment of the *Arizona Republic*. **Number of employees at this location:** 2,600.

ARIZONA STATE UNIVERSITY (ASU)
1551 South Rural Road, P.O. Box 875612, Tempe AZ 85287-5612. 480/965-2701. **Fax:** 480/965-0554. **Recorded jobline:** 480/965-5627. **Contact:** Human Resources. **E-mail address:** resumes@asu.edu. **World Wide Web address:** http://www.asu.edu/hr/jobs. **Description:** A four-year state university offering bachelor's, master's (including MBAs), and doctoral degrees. Approximately 30,000 undergraduate and 10,500 graduate students attend ASU. **NOTE:** Interested jobseekers are asked to call the jobline before sending a resume. Please only respond to advertised openings. **Positions advertised include:** Accountant; Administrative Assistant; Associate Director of Development; Business Manager; Computer Database Specialist; Development Officer; Event Attendant; Events Coordinator; Instructional Specialist; Office Supervisor; Program Coordinator; Research Technician; Sales Assistant; Security Officer; Technology Support Analyst.

ARIZONA STATE UNIVERSITY/WEST (ASU)
P.O. Box 37100, Phoenix AZ 85069-7100. 602/543-8400. **Physical address:** 4701 West Thunderbird Road, Glendale AZ 85306. **Fax:** 602/543-8412. **Contact:** Human Resources. **World Wide Web address:** http://www.west.asu.edu. **Description:** A four-year state university with an enrollment of more than 7,100, offering bachelor's, master's, and doctoral degrees. **Positions advertised include:** Assistant Director, Human Resources; Database and Systems Administrator; Senior Stationary Engineer; Office Specialist; Student Support Specialist.

ARIZONA VETERANS MEMORIAL COLISEUM & EXPOSITION CENTER
P.O. Box 6728, Phoenix AZ 85005. 602/252-6771. **Physical address:** 1826 West McDowell Road, Phoenix AZ 85007. **Contact:** Pamela Stocksdale, Director of Personnel. **Description:** A convention center and arena that hosts a variety of events including the Arizona Exposition & State Fair.

ARIZONA WESTERN COLLEGE
P.O. Box 929, Yuma AZ 85366-0929. 928/317-6000. **Physical address:** 9500 South Avenue 8E, Yuma AZ 85365-8834. **Toll-free phone:** 888/293-0392. **Fax:** 928/317-6001. **Contact:** Department of Human Resources. **E-mail address:** human.resources@azwestern.edu. **World Wide Web address:** http://www.awc.cc.az.us. **Description:** Arizona Western College is a two-year community college offering associate of arts and associate of applied sciences degrees. The college provides occupational programs in technical, vocational, and paraprofessional fields. Certificate programs are also available. **Positions advertised include:** Associate Dean for Distance Education; System and Network Manager; Radiology Clinical Coordinator; Head Soccer Coach; Professor, Various Departments.

THE ASSOCIATED PRESS
500 North Third Street, Suite 120, Phoenix AZ 85004. 602/258-8934. **Contact:** Steve Elliott, Bureau Chief. **E-mail address:** apjobs@ap.org. **World Wide Web address:** http://www.ap.org. **Description:** Area office of one of the largest independent news gathering organizations in the world. **Corporate headquarters location:** New York NY. **Other U.S. locations:** Nationwide. **International locations:** Worldwide.

AUTOMATIC DATA PROCESSING (ADP)
7474 West Chandler Boulevard, Chandler AZ 85226. 480/961-4553. **Contact:** Human Resources. **World Wide Web address:** http://www.adp.com. **Description:** A *Fortune* 500 company providing a variety of data processing services. ADP's Employer Services, the largest division, provides payroll processing, tax, and personnel reporting. Other services include brokerage, dealer, financial, and collision estimating services. **Corporate headquarters location:** Roseland NJ. **Operations at this facility include:**

Accounting/Auditing; Production; Regional Headquarters; Sales; Service. **Listed on:** New York Stock Exchange. **Stock exchange symbol:** ADP.

AVESIS INC.
3724 North Third Street, Suite 300, Phoenix AZ 85012. 602/241-3400. **Contact:** Shannon Barnett, Controller. **World Wide Web address:** http://www.avesis.com. **Description:** Avesis is a third-party administrator and preferred provider organization that markets and administers vision, hearing, and dental benefit plans. **Corporate headquarters location:** This location. **Number of employees at this location:** 40.

AVNET, INC.
60 South McKemy Avenue, Chandler AZ 85226. 480/643-6400. **Contact:** Human Resources. **E-mail address:** avnet.staffing@avnet.com. **World Wide Web address:** http://www.avnet.com. **Description:** Avnet, Inc. operates throughout North America and Europe as one of the largest distributors of electronic components and computer products for industrial and military customers. The company also produces and distributes other electronic, electrical, and video communications products. **Positions advertised include:** Distribution Center Rep; Maintenance Specialist; Sr. Systems Administrator. **Corporate headquarters location:** Phoenix AZ. **Other area locations:** Tempe AZ. **Operations at this facility include:** This location manufactures and distributes computers and computer-related products. **Listed on:** New York Stock Exchange. **Stock exchange symbol:** AVT.

AVNET, INC.
2211 South 47th Street, Phoenix AZ 85034. 480/643-2000. **Contact:** Human Resources. **E-mail address:** avnet.staffing@avnet.com. **World Wide Web address:** http://www.avnet.com. **Description:** Distributes electronic components and computer products for industrial and military customers. The company also produces and distributes other electronic, electrical, and video communications products. **Positions advertised include:** Computer Technician; Operations Administrator; Product Specialist; Program Manager; Systems Engineer. **Corporate headquarters location:** This location. **Listed on:** New York Stock Exchange. **Stock exchange symbol:** AVT.

AZTAR CORPORATION
2390 East Camelback Road, Suite 400, Phoenix AZ 85016. 602/381-4100. **Contact:** Human Resources. **World Wide Web address:** http://www.aztar.com. **Description:** Operates casino hotel facilities including Tropicana Casino and Resort (Atlantic City NJ), Tropicana Resort and Casino (Las Vegas NV), Ramada Express Hotel and Casino (Laughlin NV), Casino Aztar (Evansville IN), and Casino Aztar (Caruthersville MO). **Listed on:** New York Stock Exchange. **Stock exchange symbol:** AZR.

BABBITT BROTHERS TRADING COMPANY
P.O. Box 1328, Flagstaff AZ 86002. 928/774-8711. **Physical address:** 1515 East Cedar Road, Flagstaff AZ 86001. **Contact:** Human Resources. **Description:** A holding company involved in a variety of activities including commercial real estate rentals, the operation of hotels and restaurants, and concession services for the Grand Canyon. **Office hours:** Monday - Friday, 8:00 a.m. - 5:00 p.m. **Corporate headquarters location:** This location.

BANK OF AMERICA
3030 North Central Avenue, Phoenix AZ 85012. 602/248-7481. **Toll-free phone:** 800/944-0404. **Contact:** Human Resources. **World Wide Web address:** http://www.bankofamerica.com. **Description:** A full-service bank offering a complete range of services to commercial, institutional, and private customers. **Positions advertised include:** Research and Adjustments Rep; Residential Appraiser; Collector; Customer Service Team Manager; Treasury Management Sales Analyst; Operations Manager. **Corporate headquarters location:** Charlotte NC. **Other area locations:** Flagstaff AZ; Glendale AZ; Lake Havasu AZ; Mesa AZ; Prescott AZ; Scottsdale AZ; Sun City AZ; Tucson AZ; Yuma AZ. **Listed on:** New York Stock Exchange. **Stock exchange symbol:** BAC.

BANNER BEHAVIORAL HEALTH CENTER
7575 East Earll Drive, Scottsdale AZ 85251. 602/254-4357. **Fax:** 480/941-8494. **Contact:** Kathleen McFarland, Human Resources. **World Wide Web address:** http://www.bannerhealthaz.com. **Description:** A nonprofit, residential facility for the treatment of psychiatric and addiction disorders in adolescents and adults. **NOTE:** Entry-level positions and second and third shifts are offered. Search and apply for positions online. **Positions advertised include:** Clinical Care Manager Clinical Nurse; Counselor. **Special programs:** Internships. **Corporate headquarters location:** Phoenix AZ. **Operations at this facility include:** Service. **Number of employees at this location:** 225. **Number of employees nationwide:** 11,000.

BANNER HEALTH
BANNER DESERT MEDICAL CENTER
1400 South Dobson Road, Mesa AZ 85202. 480/512-3246. **Fax:** 480/512-8734. **Recorded jobline:** 480/512-3180. **Contact:** Human Resources. **World Wide Web address:** http://www.bannerhealthaz.com. **Description:** Desert Samaritan Medical Center is a 600-bed, full-service community hospital. The hospital has clinical specialties in cardiac care, emergency medicine, dialysis, labor and delivery, lithotripsy, special care nursery, pediatrics, oncology, orthopedics, pulmonary medicine, neurology, rehabilitation, and surgery. Labor and delivery services has four surgical suites; 16 private labor, delivery, and recovery rooms; and a 78-bed nursery. The hospital houses the valley's only unit dedicated to high-risk pregnancy. Annually, the cardiology department performs approximately 300 open-heart surgeries and 1,700 noninvasive cardiac procedures in its operating rooms and cardiac catheterization labs. The Center for Health Enhancement has a three-stage cardiac program for patients with heart disease. The hospital has 64 critical care and intermediate beds dedicated to intensive nursing care. The Center for Cancer Care provides diagnosis and treatment and emotional and educational support for patients and their families. **Positions advertised include:** Biomedical Technician; Certified Occupational Therapy Assistant; Child Life Specialist; Clinical Care Manager; Clinical Nurse Specialist; Coordinator Respiratory Therapist; Director of Nursing; Licensed Practical Nurse; Medical Claim Approver; Medical Sonographer; MRI Technologist. **Parent company:** Banner Health System.

BANNER HEALTH
BANNER GOOD SAMARITAN MEDICAL CENTER
1111 East McDowell Road, Phoenix AZ 85006. 602/239-2350. **Fax:** 602/239-5160. **Recorded jobline:** 602/239-3200. **Contact:** Human Resources. **World Wide Web address:** http://www.bannerhealthaz.com. **Description:** Owns and operates twelve primary care facilities, nine acute care hospitals, five behavioral health centers, an adolescent residential treatment center, three nursing care centers, and an air medical transport program. Banner Health also provides home health nursing, therapy, and supply services. Banner Health promotes wellness and prevention via community education programs, quarterly health-information television specials, health services to business and industry, and free or low-cost health screening for the community. Good Samaritan Regional Medical Center (also at this location) is one of Arizona's largest hospitals with 642 licensed beds. Good Samaritan's medical staff numbers 1,550 physicians, representing 45 specialties. The hospital's services include an emergency and trauma center, Samaritan Regional Poison Center, women and infant services, cardiology, critical care, Samaritan Rehabilitation Institute, surgery, radiology/oncology, and neurology services. Founded in 1911. **Positions advertised include:** Health Information Clerk; Charging Clerk; Diet Technician; Film Librarian; LPN; Medical Transcriptionist; MRI Technologist; Nurse Extern.

BANNER HEALTH
BANNER MESA MEDICAL CENTER
1010 North Country Club Drive, Mesa AZ 85201. 480/461-2562. **Fax:** 480/461-2939. **Recorded jobline:** 480/461-2562. **Contact:** Human Resources. **World Wide Web address:** http://www.bannerhealthaz.com/jobs. **Description:** A 320-bed full-service community medical center. Positions advertised include: Care Coordinator; Clinical Lab Assistant;

BANNER THUNDERBIRD MEDICAL CENTER
5555 West Thunderbird Road, Glendale AZ 85306. 602/865-5555. **Contact:** Human Resources. **World Wide Web address:** http://www.bannerhealthaz.com. **Description:** A 352-bed, not-for-profit, general medical and surgical hospital. **Positions advertised include:** Assistant Director, NICU; Clinical Case Manager; Clinical Dietitian; Director of Nursing; MRI Technologist; Physical Therapist; RN, Various Departments; Ultrasound Technologist. **Number of employees at this location:** 2,000.

BARKLEY AG ENTERPRISES, LLP
P.O. Box 5402, Yuma AZ 85366. 928/783-5103. **Fax:** 928/782-6392. **Contact:** Robert Barkley, President. **E-mail address:** info@barkleycompany.com. **World Wide Web address:** http://www.barkleyag.com. **Description:** Develops and merchandises cereal grain. **Corporate headquarters location:** This location.

BAR-S FOODS COMPANY
P.O. Box 29049, Phoenix AZ 85038. 602/285-5233. **Fax:** 602/285-2347. **Contact:** Karen Reo, Human Resources Manager. **E-mail address:** kreo@bar-s.com. **World Wide Web address:** http://www.bar-s.com. **Description:** Engaged primarily in the production and distribution of cheese and smoked meat products including ham, bacon, franks, sausage, and luncheon meat. **Positions advertised include:** Credit/Collections Manager. **Corporate headquarters location:** This location. **Operations at this facility include:** Administration; Sales. **Listed on:** Privately held. **Annual sales/revenues:** More than $100 million. **Number of employees at this location:** 60. **Number of employees nationwide:** 1,500.

BARNES & NOBLE BOOKSTORES
10235 North Metro Parkway East, Phoenix AZ 85051. 602/678-0088. **Contact:** Manager. **World Wide Web address:** http://www.bn.com. **Description:** A discount bookstore chain operating nationwide. This location has a cafe in addition to its comprehensive book departments. **Corporate headquarters location:** New York NY. **Listed on:** New York Stock Exchange. **Stock exchange symbol:** BKS.

BASHAS'
P.O. Box 488, Chandler AZ 85244. 480/895-9350. **Fax:** 480/895-5232. **Physical address:** 22402 South Basha Road, Chandler AZ 85248. **Contact:** Human Resources. **World Wide Web address:** http://www.bashas.com. **Description:** Operates a chain of retail grocery stores. Founded in 1932. **Corporate headquarters location:** This location. **Number of employees nationwide:** 3,400.

R.W. BECK & ASSOCIATES
14635 North Kierland Boulevard, Suite 130, Scottsdale AZ 85254. 480/998-8050. **Fax:** 480/998-1618. **Contact:** Human Resources. **E-mail address:** phoenix@rwbeck.com. **World Wide Web address:** http://www.rwbeck.com. **Description:** R.W. Beck is a diversified professional, technical, and management consulting firm. The company provides construction, environmental, technical, energy, solid waste, and water/wastewater services nationwide. **Corporate headquarters location:** Seattle WA. **Other U.S. locations:** Nationwide. **Operations at this facility include:** This location is primarily engaged in utility engineering.

BEST WESTERN COTTONWOOD INN
993 South Main Street, Cottonwood AZ 86326. 928/634-5575. **Contact:** Personnel. **World Wide Web address:** http://www.cottonwoodinn-az.com. **Description:** A full-service hotel and resort. **Other U.S. locations:** Nationwide.

BEST WESTERN INTERNATIONAL, INC.
6201 North 24th Parkway, Phoenix AZ 85016. 602/957-4200. **Contact:** Human Resources. **World Wide Web address:** http://www.bestwestern.com. **Description:** The world's largest hotel chain with over 4,000 hotels in 80 countries including over 1,000 in Europe. Best Western has over 1,900 meeting facilities worldwide including 900 in the United States. **Positions advertised include:** VP, Worldwide Sales; Sr. Accounting Analyst. **Corporate headquarters location:** This location.

BIG BROTHERS BIG SISTERS OF AMERICA
202 South First Avenue, Suite 101, Yuma AZ 85364. 928/782-7422. **Contact:** Human Resources. **World Wide Web address:** http://www.bbbsa.org. **Description:** Provides volunteer and professional services to assist children and youth in achieving their highest potential as they grow to become responsible men and women, through over 505 Big Brothers Big Sisters agencies nationwide. Across the country, more than 75,000 children are matched with adult volunteers. The agencies also provide an array of counseling, referral, and family support services to parents and children in over 110,000 families each year. Additional programs focus on children with special needs including those with physical disabilities or learning disabilities, as well as those who are abused, neglected, or have dropped out of school. Special prevention and intervention programs at many agencies address the problems of drug abuse, teen pregnancy, foster care, and juvenile delinquency. **Corporate headquarters location:** Philadelphia PA.

BILL JOHNSON'S RESTAURANTS INC.
2906 West Fairmount Avenue, Phoenix AZ 85017. 602/264-5565. **Contact:** Diane Perkins, Personnel Director. **World Wide Web address:** http://www.billjohnsons.com. **Description:** Operates the Bill Johnson's chain of family-style BBQ restaurants. **Corporate headquarters location:** This location.

BLOOD SYSTEMS
P.O. Box 1867, Scottsdale AZ 85252-1867. 480/946-4201. **Physical address:** 6210 East Oak Street, Scottsdale AZ 85257. **Fax:** 480/675-5780. **Recorded jobline:** 888/892-7598. **Contact:** Human Resources. **E-mail address:** jobs@bloodsystems.org. **World Wide Web address:** http://www.bloodsystems.org. **Description:** One of the nation's largest nonprofit blood service providers. The company collects 800,000 blood donations annually. Founded in 1943. **NOTE:** Entry-level positions and second and third shifts are offered. **Corporate headquarters location:** This location. **Other area**

locations: Tempe AZ. **Other U.S. locations:** Fort Smith AR; Ventura CA; Chicago IL; Lafayette LA; Meridian MS; Tupelo MS; Billings MT; Bismarck ND; Fargo ND; Albuquerque NM; Las Vegas NV; Reno NV; Rapid City SD; El Paso TX; Lubbock TX; McAllen TX; San Angelo TX; Cheyenne WY. **Annual sales/revenues:** $11 - $20 million.

BLOOD SYSTEMS LABORATORIES
2424 West Erie Drive, Tempe AZ 85282. 602/343-7000. **Fax:** 480/675-7025. **Recorded jobline:** 888/892-7598. **Contact:** Human Resources. **E-mail address:** jobs@bloodsystems.org. **World Wide Web address:** http://www.bloodsystems.org. **Description:** Blood Systems is one of the nation's largest nonprofit blood service providers. The company collects 800,000 blood donations annually. Founded in 1943. **NOTE:** Entry-level positions and second and third shifts are offered. **Parent company:** Blood Systems. **Other U.S. locations:** Bedford TX. **Operations at this facility include:** Administration; Research. **Annual sales/revenues:** $11 - $20 million. **Number of employees at this location:** 175.

BLUE CROSS BLUE SHIELD OF ARIZONA
2444 West Las Palmaritas Drive, Phoenix AZ 85021. 602/864-5691. **Fax:** 602/864-5685. **Recorded jobline:** 602/864-4339. **Contact:** Human Resources. **E-mail address:** resumes@phx1.bcbsaz.com. **World Wide Web address:** http://www.bcbsaz.com. **Description:** A nonprofit health care insurance organization providing managed health care plans to both individuals and groups. Blue Cross Blue Shield offers Point-of-Service, individual health, indemnity, PPO, and HMO plans, as well as vision insurance. **Positions advertised include:** Medical Policy Research and Development Specialist. **Other area locations:** Flagstaff AZ; Sun City AZ; Tempe AZ; Tucson AZ.

THE BOEING COMPANY
5000 East McDowell Road, Mesa AZ 85215. 480/891-3000. **Recorded jobline:** 800/451-1822. **Contact:** Personnel. **E-mail address:** employment@boeing.com. **World Wide Web address:** http://www.boeing.com. **Description:** Designs, develops, and produces attack and fighter aircraft; military and commercial helicopters; transport aircraft; and spare parts. The company develops and produces tactical and strategic missiles, satellite launching vehicles, lasers and laser communication systems, and defense systems, as well as defense electronic components and systems. The Boeing Company also provides financial services including commercial and private aircraft financing, as well as financing for commercial, industrial, and medical equipment. The company also offers real estate consulting services, operates a travel agency, and operates a technical services company. **Positions advertised include:** Property Management Specialist; Engineer/Scientist; Procurement Agent; Program Management Specialist; Embedded Software Engineer; Export Administrator. **NOTE:** Search and apply for positions online. **Listed on:** New York Stock Exchange. **Stock exchange symbol:** BA.

THE BOULDERS RESORT
34631 North Tom Darlington Drive, P.O. Box 2090, Carefree AZ 85377. 480/488-9009. **Recorded jobline:** 480/488-0992. **Contact:** Human Resources. **World Wide Web address:** http://www.wyndham.com. **Description:** A 160-casita, luxury resort and spa that offers a variety of activities including 36 holes of golf and six tennis courts. **NOTE:** Entry-level positions, second and third shifts, and part-time jobs are offered. Positions advertised include: Catering Manager; Senior Sales Manager; Outlet Manager; Director of Engineering. **Special programs:** Internships; Apprenticeships; Training. **Corporate headquarters location:** Dallas TX. **Parent company:** Wyndham International, Inc. **Listed on:** New York Stock Exchange. **Stock exchange symbol:** WYN. **Number of employees at this location:** 650.

BOWNE
1500 North Central Avenue, Phoenix AZ 85004. 602/223-4455. **Fax:** 602/223-4456. **Contact:** Human Resources. **World Wide Web address:** http://www.bowne.com. **Description:** A printing services firm that provides nationwide information management compliance documentation services through principal business segments. Printing activities are divided into three categories: financial, corporate, and commercial and legal printing. Services in these segments include the typesetting and printing of compliance documentation relating to corporate and municipal financing, mergers, and acquisitions; the dissemination of information by companies through annual and interim reports and proxy material; the printing of materials unrelated to compliance such as business forms and reports, newsletters, promotion aids, market letters and sales literature; and the printing of legal products such as records and briefs. Clients include architects, engineers, attorneys, and governmental agencies. **Corporate headquarters location:** New York NY. **Other U.S. locations:** Nationwide. **International locations:** Worldwide. **Listed on:** New York Stock Exchange. **Stock exchange symbol:** BNE.

BROWN & BAIN
2901 North Central Avenue, Suite 2000, Phoenix AZ 85012. 602/351-8000. **Fax:** 602/648-7074. **Contact:** Human Resources. **E-mail address:** hiringattysphoenix@brownbain.com. **World Wide Web address:** http://www.brownbain.com. **Description:** A law firm specializing in a variety of legal disciplines including banking, corporate, intellectual property, nonprofit, and tax law. **Other area locations:** Tucson AZ.

BRUSH CERAMIC PRODUCTS, INC.
6100 South Tucson Boulevard, Tucson AZ 85706. 520/746-0251. **Contact:** Human Resources. **World Wide Web address:** http://www.brushwellman.com. **Description:** Manufactures ceramic electronic components. **Corporate headquarters location:** Cleveland OH. **Parent company:** Brush Wellman. **Listed on:** New York Stock Exchange. **Stock exchange symbol:** BW.

BURGESS & NIPLE, INC.
5025 East Washington Street, Suite 212, Phoenix AZ 85034. 602/244-8100. **Contact:** Human Resources. **E-mail address:** hr@burnip.com. **World Wide Web address:** http://www.burgessniple.com. **Description:** An engineering and architecture firm engaged in study, analysis, and design services. The company specializes in waterworks, wastewater, industrial services, hydropower, energy conservation, transportation, systems analysis, HVAC, and geotechnical. Founded in 1912. **Positions advertised include:** Travel Demand Forecaster. **Corporate headquarters location:** Columbus OH.

CH2M HILL, INC.
2625 South Plaza Drive, Suite 300, Phoenix AZ 85282-3397. 480/966-8188. **Fax:** 480/966-9450. **Contact:** Human Resources. **World Wide Web address:** http://www.ch2m.com. **Description:** CH2M Hill is a group of employee-owned companies operating under the names CH2M Hill, Inc., Industrial Design Corporation, Operations Management International, CH2M Hill International, and CH2M Hill Engineering. The company provides planning, engineering design, and operation and construction management services to help clients apply technology, safeguard the environment, and develop infrastructures. The professional staff includes specialists in environmental engineering and waste management, water management, transportation, industrial facilities, and a broad spectrum of infrastructure systems. Founded in 1946. **Positions advertised include:** Water Staff Engineer; Client Service Manager; Senior Project Manager. **Corporate headquarters location:** Greenwood Village CO.

CRC INFORMATION SYSTEMS, INC.
16100 North Greenway-Hayden Loop, Scottsdale AZ 85260. 480/443-9494. **Fax:** 480/443-3656. **Contact:** Human Resources. **World Wide Web address:** http://www.crcinfosys.com. **Description:** Designs and manufactures computer software for printing and labeling companies. Founded in 1978. **Corporate headquarters location:** This location. **President/CEO:** Henry S. Hebing.

CALIFORNIA MICRO DEVICES
2000 West 14th Street, Tempe AZ 85281. 480/921-6000. **Fax:** 480/921-6598. **Contact:** Human Resources. **E-mail address:** hr@calmicro.com. **World Wide Web address:** http://www.calmicro.com. **Description:** Designs, manufactures, and markets high-performance mixed analog/digital products using state-of-the-art CMOS/BICMOS technologies for emerging communication and mixed signal markets. **Special programs:** Internships. **Corporate headquarters location:** Milpitas CA. **Operations at this facility include:** Administration; Manufacturing; Regional Headquarters; Sales; Service. **Listed on:** NASDAQ. **Stock exchange symbol:** CAMD. **Number of employees at this location:** 120.

CAREMARK
9501 East Shea Boulevard, Scottsdale AZ 85260. 480/391-4683. **Contact:** Human Resources. **World Wide Web address:** http://www.caremark.com. **Description:** Manages prescription drug benefit programs. **Positions advertised include:** PRC Technician; Director of Finance; Manager IT Audit; Sr. Pricing Analyst; Manager of Rebate Reporting; Senior Financial Analyst; Database Administrator; Project Leader. **Corporate headquarters location:** Nashville TN. **Other area locations:** Phoenix AZ. **Operations at this facility include:** Administration; Service. **Listed on:** New York Stock Exchange. **Stock exchange symbol:** CMX. **Number of employees at this location:** 1,100.

CARONDELET HOLY CROSS HOSPITAL
1171 West Target Range Road, Nogales AZ 85621-2497. 520/285-3000. **Toll-free phone:** 800/669-4979. **Contact:** Employment Office. **E-mail address:** chncareers@carondelet.org. **World Wide Web address:** http://www.carondelet.org. **Description:** An 80-bed facility, Holy Cross Hospital is part of the Carondelet Health Network, the largest and oldest not-for-profit health care provider in southern Arizona. **NOTE:** Entry-level positions and second and third shifts are offered. **Positions advertised include:** Certified Nursing Assistant; Imaging Specialist; Medical Technologist; Nuclear Medical Technologist; Nurse Assistant; Occupational Therapist; Patient Care Technician; Pharmacist; Physical Therapist; Registered Nurse; Sonographer. **Special programs:** Internships; Training.

CARONDELET MEDICAL MALL OF GREEN VALLEY
1055 North La Cañada Drive, Green Valley AZ 85614. 520/625-6469. **Toll-free phone:** 800/669-4979. **Contact:** Employment Office. **E-mail address:** chncareers@carondelet.org. **World Wide Web address:** http://www.carondelet.org. **Description:** Carondelet Medical Mall, a part of the Carondelet Health Network, provides primary, specialty and preventive care services. **NOTE:** Entry-level positions and second and third shifts are offered. **Special programs:** Internships; Training. **Positions advertised include:** Certified Nursing Assistant; Imaging Specialist; Medical Technologist; Nuclear Medical Technologist; Nurse Assistant; Occupational Therapist; Patient Care Technician; Pharmacist; Physical Therapist Registered Nurse; Sonographer. **Special programs:** Internships; Training.

CARONDELET ST. JOSEPH'S HOSPITAL
Wilmot Road, Tucson AZ 85711. 520/873-3000. **Toll-free phone:** 800/669-4979. **Contact:** Employment Office. **E-mail address:** chncareers@carondelet.org. **World Wide Web address:** http://www.carondelet.org. **Description:** A 301-bed facility, St. Joseph's Hospital is part of the Carondelet Health Network, the largest and oldest not-for-profit health care provider in southern Arizona. **NOTE:** Entry-level positions and second and third shifts are offered. **Positions advertised include:** Certified Nursing Assistant; Imaging Specialist; Medical Technologist; Nuclear Medical Technologist; Nurse Assistant; Occupational Therapist; Patient Care Technician; Pharmacist; Physical Therapist; Registered Nurse; Sonographer. **Special programs:** Internships; Training.

CASA GRANDE REGIONAL MEDICAL CENTER
1800 East Florence Boulevard, Casa Grande AZ 85222. 520/381-6300. **Fax:** 520/381-6615. **Contact:** Human Resources. **E-mail address:** recruiter@cgrmc.org. **World Wide Web address:** http://www.casagrandehospital.com. **Description:** Casa Grande Regional Medical Center is served by a 24-hour, physician-staffed emergency room. Services available at Casa Grande include maternity and newborn care, day surgery, nutritional counseling, laboratory service, pediatric care, intensive care, medical and surgical care, pharmacy services, physical therapy, respiratory therapy, radiology (CAT scans, MRIs, and mammograms), and nuclear medicine. Founded in 1984. **Positions advertised include:** Registered Nurse Contract; Unit Secretary; Nurse Technician; Nuclear Medicine Technologist; Stores Clerk; Certified Respiratory Therapist; Patient Care Coordinator.

THE CAVANAGH LAW FIRM
1850 North Central Avenue, Suite 2400, Phoenix AZ 85004. 602/322-4000. **Toll-free phone:** 888/824-3476. **Fax:** 602/322-4100. **Contact:** Human Resources. **World Wide Web address:** http://www.cavanaghlaw.com. **Description:** A law firm specializing in estate planning and administration. **Other area locations:** Sun City AZ.

CAVCO INDUSTRIES
1001 North Central Avenue, 8th Floor, Phoenix AZ 85004. 602/256-6263. **Fax:** 602/256-6189. **Contact:** Human Resources Department. **World Wide Web address:** http://www.cavco.com. **Description:** Develops, manufactures, and markets prefabricated homes. **Corporate headquarters location:** This location. **Parent company:** Centex Corporation. **Operations at this facility include:** Administration. **Number of employees at this location:** 420.

CENTRAL ARIZONA COLLEGE
8470 North Overfield Road, Coolidge AZ 85228. 520/723-4141. **Fax:** 520/876-1908. **Contact:** Office of Human Resources. **E-mail address:** human_resources@python.cac.cc.az.us. **World Wide Web address:** http://www.cac.cc.az.us. **Description:** A public, two-year community college offering a variety of programs. **Positions advertised include:** Accountant; Director of Learning Resource Center; Professor of Speech Communication; Professor of Civil Surveying; Professor of English; Assistant Director of Financial Aid. **Special programs:** Internships. **Corporate headquarters location:** This location. **Other area locations:** Apache Jct AZ; Winkelman AZ.

CENTURY 21 ANDERSON GROUP
13771 North Fountain Hills Boulevard, Suite 117, Fountain Hills AZ 85268. 480/837-1331. **Toll-free phone:** 888/678-7901. **Fax:** 480/837-7069. **Contact:** Personnel. **World Wide Web address:** http://www.andersongroup.com. **Description:** A real estate agency. Founded in 1981. **Other area locations:** Lake Havasu City AZ. **Number of employees at this location:** 60.

CENVEO
221 North 48th Avenue, Phoenix AZ 85043. 602/272-2691. **Contact:** Human Resources. **World Wide Web address:** http://www.cenveo.com. **Description:** Produces business envelopes and mail-in order forms. **Corporate headquarters location:** Englewood CO. **Other U.S. locations:** Nationwide. **Operations at this facility include:** Manufacturing. **Listed on:** New York Stock Exchange. **Stock exchange symbol:** CVO. **Number of employees at this location:** 260.

CHAMBERS BELT COMPANY
2800 East Broadway Road, Suite A200, Phoenix AZ 85040. 602/276-0016. **Contact:** Human Resources. **World Wide Web address:** http://www.chambersbelt.com. **Description:** Produces leather belts and related leather products. **NOTE:** Resumes should be sent to: 5455 Jillson Street, Commerce CA 90040. **Corporate headquarters location:** This location. **Operations at this facility include:** Manufacturing; Research and Development; Sales; Service.

CHANDLER REGIONAL HOSPITAL
475 South Dobson Road, Chandler AZ 85224. 480/821-3112. **Contact:** Human Resources. **World Wide Web address:** http://www.chandlerregional.com. **Description:** A 210-bed, nonprofit hospital. Facilities include the Family Birth Center including state-of-the-art fetal monitoring equipment, seven labor and delivery rooms, eighteen postpartum rooms, a surgery suite for Cesarean deliveries, and two nurseries; an emergency and Level II trauma center providing around-the-clock physician- and nurse-staffed emergency care; a diagnostic imaging services department providing comprehensive, state-of-the-art X-ray and diagnostic imaging services; a 12-bed intensive care unit and a 20-bed telemetry unit; inpatient and outpatient surgery; a 10-bed pediatric unit; physical rehabilitation including physical and occupational therapy, and speech pathology; cardiology services; and outpatient services. **Positions advertised include:** Anesthesia Technician; Business Office Supervisor; Charge RN; Collection Specialist; CT Technologist; EEG Technician; Financial Counselor; Housekeeper; LPN; Phlebotomist; Registrar; Site Manager. **Corporate headquarters location:** San Francisco CA. **Parent company:** Catholic Healthcare West.

CHAPMAN CHEVROLET ISUZU
1717 East Baseline Road, Tempe AZ 85283. 480/838-1234. **Contact:** Human Resources. **World Wide Web address:** http://www.chapmanauto.com. **Description:** An automotive dealership that is also engaged in automotive upholstery repair. Chapman also has an automotive paint shop.

CLEAR CHANNEL OUTDOOR
2850 East Camelback Road, Suite 300, Phoenix AZ 85016. 602/957-8116. **Fax:** 602/381-5753. **Contact:** Human Resources Department. **World Wide Web address:** http://www.clearchanneloutdoor.com. **Description:** Provides outdoor billboard advertising services. **U.S. locations:** Nationwide. **Parent company:** Clear Channel Communications, Inc.

COCONINO COMMUNITY COLLEGE
2800 South Lonetree Road, Flagstaff AZ 86001. 928/527-1222. **Toll-free phone:** 800/350-7122. **Fax:** 928/226-4114. **Contact:** Human Resources. **World Wide Web address:** http://www.coco.cc.az.us. **Description:** A community college offering 14 associate degrees and 22 certificate programs. Approximately 3,000 students are enrolled at the college. Founded in 1991. **NOTE:** The Human Resources Department only accepts completed application packets. Packets should contain a resume, a cover letter, and a completed CCC application form. Please contact the Human Resources Department at 928/226-4268 if you require additional information. **Other U.S. locations:** Fredonia AZ; Grand Canyon AZ; Page AZ; Williams AZ.

COCONINO, COUNTY OF
219 East Cherry Avenue, Flagstaff AZ 86001. 928/779-6702. **Contact:** Human Resources. **World Wide Web address:** http://co.coconino.az.us. **Description:** Houses all Coconino County administrative offices including the Department of Health Services, Parks and Recreation Department, and the Department of Public Works. **NOTE:** Applicants must fill out a county application in order to be considered for employment. Please contact Human Resources for more information. Part-time positions are offered. **Positions advertised include:** Budget Analyst; Career Coach; Community Aide; Deputy Sheriff; Detention Officer; Mechanic; Medical Examiner.

COMPREHENSIVE BUSINESS SERVICES
4431 East Broadway Boulevard, Tucson AZ 85711. 520/881-7514. **Contact:** Human Resources. **Description:** Provides a wide range of accounting services to small business owners nationwide. Services include accounting and record keeping, payroll administration, budget and business planning, and consulting.

COMPUTER ASSOCIATES INTERNATIONAL, INC.
9201 East Mountain View Road, Suite 200, Scottsdale AZ 85258. 480/657-4000. **Contact:** Recruiting. **E-mail address:** joinca@ca.com. **World Wide Web address:** http://www.ca.com. **Description:** Computer Associates International, Inc. is one of the world's leading developers of client/server and distributed computing software. The company develops, markets, and supports enterprise management, database and applications development, business applications, and consumer software products for a broad range of mainframe, midrange, and desktop computers. Computer Associates serves major business, government, research, and educational organizations. Founded in 1976. **NOTE:** Interested jobseekers should apply online or send resumes to: Computer Associates International, Inc., Human Resources Recruitment, One Computer Associates Plaza, Islandia NY 11749. **Positions advertised include:** Alliance Director; Field Partner Manager; Sales Executive, Storage; Senior Consultant; Senior Software Engineer; Software Engineer. **Special programs:** Internships; Co-ops. **Corporate headquarters location:** Islandia NY. **Other U.S. locations:** Nationwide. **Operations at this facility include:** This location is a sales and support office. **Listed on:** New York Stock Exchange. **Stock exchange symbol:** CA. **Annual sales/revenues:** More than $100 million. **Number of employees at this location:** 15. **Number of employees nationwide:** 4,000. **Number of employees worldwide:** 9,000.

COMPUWARE CORPORATION
4127 East Van Buren, Suite 100, Phoenix AZ 85008. 602/567-6300. **Contact:** Human Resources. **World Wide Web address:** http://www.compuware.com. **Description:** Offers computer consulting services specializing in the food and beverage industries. **Corporate headquarters location:** Detroit MI. **Listed on:** NASDAQ. **Stock exchange symbol:** CPWR.

CONSECO FINANCE
1580 North Fiesta Boulevard, Suite 103, Gilbert AZ 85233. 480/632-1403. **Contact:** Human Resources. **World Wide Web address:** http://www.conseco.com. **Description:** Aggregates and secures conventional manufactured home and home improvement loans and sells securities through public offerings and private placements.

CONTINENTAL PROMOTION GROUP, INC.
7405 East Monte Cristo Avenue, Scottsdale AZ 85260. 480/606-9300. **Toll-free phone:** 800/554-9838. **Fax:** 480/606-4329. **Contact:** Human Resources. **E-mail address:** hrmcpg@cpginc.com. **World Wide Web address:** http://www.cpginc.com. **Description:** Provides promotional services including rebate offers, sweepstakes, and premium fulfillment. Founded in 1989. **Positions advertised include:** Promotion Coordinator; Promotion Manager; Sales Development Manager; National Sales Manager. **Corporate headquarters location:** This location. **International locations:** Canada; Ireland; United Kingdom.

CONVERGING TECHNOLOGIES, INC.
One South Church Avenue, Suite 2200, Tucson AZ 85701. 520/670-7100. **Fax:** 520/670-7101. **Contact:** Yolanda Bay, Human Resources. **E-mail address:** ybay@spartacom.com. **World Wide Web address:** http://www.spartacom.com. **Description:** A provider of business software for networking, modem pooling and sharing, and remote control solutions. **Corporate headquarters location:** This location. **President/CEO:** Scott Moule.

JOE CONWAY TRUCKING COMPANY
6509 West Orangewood Avenue, Glendale AZ 85301. 623/937-1684. **Contact:** Gene Cooper, President. **Description:** A trucking company. **Positions advertised include:** Truck Driver. **Corporate headquarters location:** This location. **Number of employees at this location:** 50.

CORNING GILBERT, INC.
5310 West Camelback Road, Glendale AZ 85301-7597. 623/245-1050. **Fax:** 623/463-7496. **Contact:** Human Resources. **E-mail address:** hr-gilbert@corning.com. **World Wide Web address:** http://www.corning.com/corninggilbert. **Description:** A manufacturer of broadcasting equipment including coaxial cables and microwave connectors. **Corporate headquarters location:** This location. **Parent company:** Corning, Inc. (Corning NY.) **Listed on:** New York Stock Exchange. **Stock exchange symbol:** GLW. **Number of employees at this location:** 500.

CORPORATE JETS INC.
14600 North Airport Drive, Scottsdale AZ 85260. 480/948-2400. **Fax:** 480/948-3874. **Contact:** Human Resources. **E-mail address:** jobs@cjisdl.com. **World Wide Web address:** http://www.cjisdl.com. **Description:** A full-service, fixed-base corporate jet operator. The company performs a variety of services for corporate jets including refueling and aircraft charter services. **Positions advertised include:** A&P Technician. **Corporate headquarters location:** Pittsburgh PA. **Other U.S. locations:** Dallas TX. **Listed on:** Privately held. **Number of employees at this location:** 80. **Number of employees nationwide:** 700.

COURTESY CHEVROLET
1233 East Camelback Road, Phoenix AZ 85014. 602/279-3232. **Contact:** Human Resources. **World Wide Web address:** http://www.courtesychev.com. **Description:** Provides automobile sales and service. **Corporate headquarters location:** This location. **Listed on:** Privately held. **Number of employees at this location:** 260.

COX COMMUNICATIONS
20401 North 29th Avenue, Phoenix AZ 85027. 602/866-0072. **Contact:** Human Resources. **World Wide Web address:** http://www.cox.com. **Description:** One of the nation's largest broadband communications companies. **Positions advertised include:** Manager, Payroll Benefits; Account Executive; Product Manager, Interactive Media; Director Finance; Sr. Financial Analyst. **Corporate headquarters location:** Atlanta GA. **Listed on:** New York Stock Exchange. **Stock exchange symbol:** COX.

CRAZY HORSE CAMPGROUNDS
1534 Beachcomber Boulevard, Lake Havasu City AZ 86403. 928/855-4033. **Contact:** Manager. **World Wide Web address:** http://www.crazyhorsecampgrounds.com. **Description:** A year-round recreational vehicle park and campground that also houses a market and clubhouse.

CROWNE PLAZA
2532 West Peoria Avenue, Phoenix AZ 85029. 602/943-2341. **Recorded jobline:** 480/545-3668. **Contact:** Human Resources. **World Wide Web address:** http://www.ichotelsgroup.com. **Description:** A full-service hotel. **NOTE:** Interested jobseekers may apply in person Monday - Friday, 9:00 a.m. - 4:00 p.m. **Corporate headquarters location:** London, England. **Parent company:** InterContinental hotels Group. **Number of employees at this location:** 250.

CUMMINS-ALLISON CORPORATION
8146 North 23rd Avenue, Suite I, Phoenix AZ 85021. 602/995-1492. **Contact:** Human Resources. **World Wide Web address:** http://www.cumminsallison.com. **Description:** Manufactures office machines including paper shredders, perforators, and coin and currency sorters. **Positions advertised include:** Sales Representative. **Operations at this facility include:** Sales.

CUSHMAN & WAKEFIELD OF ARIZONA
2525 East Camelback Road, Suite 1000, Phoenix AZ 85016. 602/253-7900. **Contact:** Human Resources. **World Wide Web address:** http://www.cushmanwakefield.com. **Description:** A commercial and industrial real estate firm, engaged in the management and leasing of commercial office space, appraisals, project development, and related services. **Corporate headquarters location:** New York NY.

CYMA SYSTEMS, INC.
2330 West University Drive, Suite 7, Tempe AZ 85281. 480/303-2962. **Toll-free phone:** 800/292-2962. **Contact:** Human Resources. **World Wide Web address:** http://www.cyma.com. **Description:** Develops and distributes microcomputer-based software focusing on accounting, medical practice management, point-of-sale, and related vertical applications. Founded in 1980. **Corporate headquarters location:** This location. **Operations at this facility include:** Administration; Manufacturing; Research and Development; Sales; Service. **Number of employees at this location:** 60.

CYTEC ENGINEERED MATERIALS
2085 East Technology Circle, Suite 300, Tempe AZ 85284. 480/730-2000. **Fax:** 480/730-2088. **Contact:** Human Resources. **World Wide Web address:** http://www.cytec.com. **Description:** Manufactures advanced composite and adhesives for aerospace, industrial, recreational, and other applications. **Corporate headquarters**

location: West Paterson NJ. **Parent company:** Cytec Industries, Inc. **Listed on:** New York Stock Exchange. **Stock exchange symbol:** CYT.

D&Z MICROELECTRONICS
4000 North Central, Phoenix AZ 85012. 602/235-9500. **Fax:** 602/337-3213. **Contact:** Human Resources. **E-mail address:** corporate.humanresources@dayzim.com. **World Wide Web address:** http://www.dayzim.com. **Description:** Engaged in the engineering and design of clean rooms for semiconductor development. **Positions advertised include:** Semiconductor CVD Start-up Technician; Equipment Support Technician. **Corporate headquarters location:** Philadelphia PA. **Other U.S. locations:** Nationwide. **Parent company:** Day & Zimmerman International, Inc. **Listed on:** Privately held. **Annual sales/revenues:** $5 - $10 million. **Number of employees at this location:** 60. **Number of employees worldwide:** 20,000.

DAVID'S BRIDAL
Ahwatukee Foothills Towne Center, 5043 East Ray Road, Phoenix AZ 85044. 480/785-7300. **Contact:** Human Resources. **E-mail address:** staffing@davidsbridal.net. **World Wide Web address:** http://www.davidsbridal.com. **Description:** One of the nation's largest bridal retailers. The company operates more than 80 David's Bridal stores nationwide. Founded in 1950. **Corporate headquarters location:** Conshohocken PA. **Number of employees nationwide:** 1,500.

ED DEBEVIC'S RESTAURANT
2102 East Highland Avenue, Phoenix AZ 85016. 602/956-2760. **Contact:** Human Resources. **World Wide Web address:** http://www.eddebevics.com. **Description:** One location of the casual dining restaurant chain. Ed Debevic's serves American cuisine and operates a gift shop. **Corporate headquarters location:** Chicago IL. **Parent company:** Ed Debevic's Restaurant Corp.

DELOITTE & TOUCHE
2901 North Central Avenue, Suite 1200, Phoenix AZ 85012-2799. 602/234-5100. **Fax:** 602/234-5186. **Contact:** Human Resources Department. **World Wide Web address:** http://www.us.deloitte.com. **Description:** An international firm of certified public accountants providing professional accounting, auditing, tax, and management consulting services to widely diversified clients. The company has a specialized program consisting of national industry groups and functional groups that cross industry lines. Groups are involved in various disciplines including accounting, auditing, taxation management advisory services, small and growing businesses, mergers and acquisitions, and computer applications. **Positions advertised include:** ERS Consultant; Multistate Tax Manager; Federal Corporate Tax Manager; Audit Manager; International Tax Senior. **Parent company:** Deloitte Touche Tohmatsu. **Number of employees at this location:** 200.

DELUXE CHECK PRINTERS, INC.
3050 South 35th Street, Suite B, Phoenix AZ 85034. 602/431-2500. **Contact:** Human Resources. **World Wide Web address:** http://www.deluxe.com. **Description:** Engaged in printing and selling a variety of checks, deposit tickets, and related forms to banks and other financial institutions. The company also manufactures documents imprinted using magnetic ink. Printing operations are carried out at more than 50 plants throughout the United States. Founded in 1915. **Corporate headquarters location:** Shoreview MN. **Other U.S. locations:** Nationwide. **International locations:** Canada; United Kingdom. **Parent company:** Deluxe Corporation is a *Fortune* 500 company that provides check printing, electronic funds transfer processing services, and related services to the financial industry; check authorization and collection services to retailers; and electronic benefit transfer services to state governments. Deluxe Corporation also produces forms, specialty papers, and other products for small businesses, professional practices, and medical/dental offices and provides tax forms and electronic tax filing services to tax preparers. Through the direct mail channel, Deluxe Corporation sells greeting cards, gift-wrapping, and related products to households. The company entered the lithographic ink market in 1994 as a result of developing a water-washable ink. **Listed on:** New York Stock Exchange. **Stock exchange symbol:** DLX. **Number of employees at this location:** 60. **Number of employees worldwide:** 9,000.

DEX MEDIA
8900 North 22nd Avenue, Phoenix AZ 85021. 602/678-9300. **Contact:** Human Resources. **World Wide Web address:** http://www.dexmedia.com. **Description:** Provides directory publishing and Internet Yellow Pages services. **Positions advertised include:** Staff Advocate; Community Focus Accounts Representative; Account Executive. **Corporate headquarters location:** Englewood CO. **Number of employees nationwide:** 3,000.

DILLARD'S DEPARTMENT STORES, INC.
4700 North Highway 89, Flagstaff AZ 86004. 928/526-5541. **Contact:** Human Resources. **World Wide Web address:** http://www.dillards.com. **Description:** A store location of a major department store chain. The company operates 228 stores in 20 states. Dillard's offers a full line of brand-name fashion apparel and home furnishings. Founded in 1938. **International locations:** Mexico City, Mexico. **Corporate headquarters location:** Little Rock AR. **Listed on:** New York Stock Exchange. **Stock exchange symbol:** DDS.

DOLPHIN INC.
P.O. Box 6514, Phoenix AZ 85005. 602/272-6747. **Contact:** Human Resources. **Description:** An investment casting foundry that manufactures golf club heads for Ping, a brand name of golf clubs.

DOUBLETREE GUEST SUITES HOTEL
320 North 44th Street, Phoenix AZ 85008. 602/225-0500. **Fax:** 602/231-0561. **Recorded jobline:** 602/225-0328. **Contact:** Human Resources. **World Wide Web address:** http://www.doubletree.com. **Description:** An independent franchise, this location of Doubletree Guest Suites Hotel has 242 rooms and conference center facilities. **NOTE:** Entry-level positions and second and third shifts are offered. **Special programs:** Internships; Training. **Corporate headquarters location:** Beverly Hills CA. **Other U.S. locations:** Nationwide. **Parent company:** Hilton Hotels Corporation. **Listed on:** New York Stock Exchange. **Stock exchange symbol:** HLT. **Annual sales/revenues:** $5 - $10 million. **Number of employees at this location:** 200.

DYNAMIC EDUCATIONAL SYSTEMS, INC. (DESI)
8433 North Black Canyon Highway, Suite 188, Phoenix AZ 85021. **Fax:** 602-995-4091 **Contact:** HR Director. **E-mail address:** corphr@exodyne.com. **Description:** Provides career training and job placement. **Positions advertised include:** Independent Living Advisor; Finance and Administration Manager. **Parent company:** Exodyne, Inc.

DYNAMIC SCIENCE, INC. (DSI)
8433 North Black Canyon Highway, Suite 200, Phoenix AZ 85021. 602/995-3700. **Fax:** 602/995-4091. **Contact:** Human Resources. **E-mail address:** dsi@exodyne.com. **World Wide Web address:** http://www.exodyne.com. **Description:** Services cover the spectrum of developmental and operational test support and evaluation; operation and maintenance of integrated test ranges; communications system operations and maintenance; facility operation and maintenance; transportation systems research and development; aircraft and vehicle operation and maintenance; and data collection, processing, and management. DSI provides services to a broad customer base including U.S. government defense and civilian agencies, state and local governments, academic institutions, and domestic and international private industry. DSI operates through three divisions: The Defense Technical Services Division, The Exodyne Services Division, and The Research, Science, and Technology Division. Founded in 1942. **Positions advertised include:** General Manager; Air Traffic Controller; Division General Manager. **Parent company:** Exodyne, Inc.

ECT (EVERETT CHARLES TECHNOLOGIES)
3020 South Park Drive, Tempe AZ 85282. 602/438-1112. **Fax:** 602/426-9217. **Contact:** Hiring Supervisor. **World Wide Web address:** http://www.ectinfo.com. **Description:** Engaged in the design and manufacture of printed circuit boards. **Positions advertised include:** Drill Operator; Dry Film Operator; Plating Operator. **Corporate headquarters location:** Pomona CA. **Other U.S. locations:** NY; NH; IL; FL; MN; RI.

EDS (ELECTRONIC DATA SYSTEMS)
2222 West Dunlop Avenue, Suite 300, Phoenix AZ 85021. 602/997-7391. **Contact:** Human Resources. **World Wide Web address:** http://www.eds.com. **Description:** Provides consulting, systems development, systems integration, and systems management services for large-scale and industry-specific applications. Founded in 1962. **Corporate headquarters location:** Plano TX. **Listed on:** New York Stock Exchange. **Stock exchange symbol:** EDS. **Number of employees nationwide:** 54,000. **Number of employees worldwide:** 120,000.

EAGLE MILLING COMPANY
14721 West Main Avenue, Casa Grande AZ 85222. 520/836-2131. **Fax:** 520/836-2419. **Contact:** Jim Hyer, Vice President of Sales. **World Wide Web address:** http://www.eaglemilling.com. **Description:** Produces a complete range of animal feed products for dealers and commercial customers. Eagle Milling Company markets animal health products statewide. **Corporate headquarters location:** This location.

EARNHARDT FORD
P.O. Box 26878, Tempe AZ 85285-6878. 480/838-6000. **Contact:** Human Resources. **E-mail address:** jobs@earnhardt.com. **World Wide Web address:** http://www.earnhardt.com. **Description:** A retailer of new and used automobiles.

EASTER SEALS ARIZONA
2075 South Cottonwood Drive, Tempe AZ 85282. 602/252-6061. **Toll-free phone:** 800/626-6061. **Fax:** 602/252-6065. **Contact:** Human Resources. **E-mail address:** hr@azseals.org. **World Wide Web address:** http://www.easterseals arizona.org. **Description:** Provides treatment and support services for disabled individuals. **Positions advertised include:** Site Coordinator; Respite & Recreation Counselor; Camp Director; Camp Cook; Camp Nurse; Occupational Therapist.

ECLIPSYS CORPORATION
444 North 44th Street, Suite 100, Phoenix AZ 85008. 602/389-8000. **Fax:** 602/389-8111. **Contact:** Human Resources. **World Wide Web address:** http://www.eclipsnet.com. **Description:** Provides a variety of computer-related solutions to members of the health care industry. The company's businesses include software development, systems implementation, systems administration, and systems engineering. **NOTE:** Search and apply for positions online. **Company slogan:** The Outcomes Company. **Positions advertised include:** Physician Billing Coordinator; Admissions Manager; Denial Management RN. **Corporate headquarters location:** Boca Raton FL. **Listed on:** NASDAQ. **Stock exchange symbol:** ECLP.

ECONO LODGE UNIVERSITY
914 South Milton Road, Flagstaff AZ 86001-6386. 928/774-7326. **Contact:** Human Resources. **World Wide Web address:** http://www.comfortinn.com. **Description:** A 67-room economy hotel. **Corporate headquarters location:** Silver Spring MD. **Other U.S. locations:** Nationwide. **International locations:** Worldwide. **Parent company:** Choice Hotels International. **Listed on:** New York Stock Exchange. **Stock exchange symbol:** CHH.

EEGEE'S
3360 East Ajo Way, Tucson AZ 85713-5228. 520/294-3333. **Contact:** Human Resources. **World Wide Web address:** http://www.eegees.com. **Description:** Operates 21 fast-food restaurants in Tucson. The company has its own bakery on the premises and makes rolls and cookies on a daily basis.

EMBASSY SUITES AIRPORT WEST
2333 East Thomas Road, Phoenix AZ 85016. 602/957-1910. **Fax:** 602/955-2861. **Contact:** Personnel. **World Wide Web address:** http://www.embassysuites.com. **Description:** An all-suites hotel and conference facility. **Office hours:** Monday through Friday, 8:00 a.m. - 5:00 p.m. **Corporate headquarters location:** Beverly Hills CA. **Parent company:** Hilton Hotels Corporation. **Listed on:** New York Stock Exchange. **Stock exchange symbol:** HLT.

EMBASSY SUITES FLAGSTAFF
706 South Milton Road, Flagstaff AZ 86001. 928/774-4333. **Contact:** Personnel. **World Wide Web address:** http://www.embassyflagstaff.com. **Description:** An all-suites hotel. **Corporate headquarters location:** Beverly Hills CA. **Parent company:** Hilton Hotels Corporation. **Listed on:** New York Stock Exchange. **Stock exchange symbol:** HLT.

EMBRY-RIDDLE AERONAUTICAL UNIVERSITY
3200 Willow Creek Road, Prescott AZ 86301. 928/777-3728. **Toll-free phone:** 800/888-3728. **Contact:** Department of Human Resources. **World Wide Web address:** http://www.erau.edu/pr. **Description:** A private, four-year, coeducational, undergraduate institution committed to studies in aviation, aerospace, and engineering. The university's engineering program has been recognized by *U.S. News and World Report* as one of the 10 best engineering programs in the nation and has been approved by the Accreditation Board of Engineering and Technology. The university has approximately 1,500 students enrolled. **Positions advertised include:** Flight Instructor; Customer Support Technician; Eagle Card System Manager; Senior Assistant Director of Admissions; Assistant/Associate Professor of Aeronautical Science; Assistant/Associate Professor in Business Administration or Management.

EMPIRE SOUTHWEST COMPANY
1725 South Country Club Drive, Mesa AZ 85210. 480/633-4000. **Contact:** Employment Manager. **World Wide Web address:** http://www.empire-cat.com. **E-mail address:** careers@empire-cat.com. **Description:** A retailer and servicer of Caterpillar equipment. **Corporate headquarters location:** This location. **Other U.S.**

locations: Phoenix AZ; Glendale AZ; Kingman AZ; Tucson AZ; Deer Valley AZ; Yuma AZ; Imperial CA. **Subsidiaries include:** Empire Hydraulic Service; Empire Machinery; Empire Transport. **Operations at this facility include:** Administration; Sales; Service.

ERNST & YOUNG LLP
One Renaissance Square, Two North Central Avenue, Suite 2300, Phoenix AZ 85004. 602/322-3000. **Fax:** 602/322-3023. **Contact:** Human Resources. **World Wide Web address:** http://www.ey.com. **Description:** A certified public accounting firm that also provides management consulting services. Services include data processing, financial modeling, financial feasibility studies, production planning and inventory management, management sciences, health care planning, human resources, cost accounting, and budgeting systems. **Positions advertised include:** Business Risk Services Senior; Assurance Senior; Tax Manager; Technology and Security Risk Services Senior. **Corporate headquarters location:** New York NY. **Other area locations:** Tucson AZ.

ESSCENTUAL BRANDS
4835 East Cactus Road, Suite 245, Scottsdale AZ 85254. 602/889-4800. **Fax:** 602/889-4837. **Contact:** Human Resources. **E-mail address:** info@esscentualbrands.com. **World Wide Web address:** http://www.esscentualbrands.com. **Description:** Manufactures and markets fragrances, toiletries, and health care products.

ETHERTON LAW GROUP
5555 East Van Buren Street, Suite 100, Phoenix AZ 85008. 602/681-3331. **Fax:** 602/681-3339. **Contact:** Human Resources. **E-mail address:** careers@ethertonlaw.com. **World Wide Web address:** http://www.ethertonlaw.com. **Description:** A full service law firm providing a wide range of legal services including patent, tax, and securities issues. **Positions advertised include:** Intellectual Property Attorney.

EVERGREEN AIR CENTER, INC.
Pinal Air Park Road, Marana AZ 85653-9501. 520/682-4181. **Fax:** 520/682-4209. **Contact:** Recruiting. **E-mail address:** recruiting@evergreenaviation.com. **World Wide Web address:** http://www.evergreenac.com. **Description:** Evergreen Air Center is classified as an FAA Unlimited Aircraft Maintenance Repair Station. Services include Heavy C and D Check aircraft maintenance (typically performed on the Boeing 707, 727, 747, Douglas DC 8, 9, 10, and AirBus 300 aircraft); Component Overhaul and Bench Avionics; Interior Fabric and Upholstery Repair; Survival and Emergency Equipment Repair; and Composite Repair and Structural Modifications. **Positions advertised include:** Avionics Technician; Airframe & Powerplant Technician; VP Sales and Marketing. **Corporate headquarters location:** McMinnville OR. **Parent company:** Evergreen International Aviation. **Operations at this facility include:** Administration; Sales; Service. **Listed on:** Privately held. **Number of employees at this location:** 450.

EXODYNE PROPERTIES, INC. (EPI)
8433 North Black Canyon Highway, Suite 100, Phoenix AZ 85021. 602/995-0919. Fax: 602/995-8469. **Contact:** HR Director. **E-mail address:** corphr@exodyne.com. **Description:** EPI manages Exodyne's real estate holdings, including commercial office and industrial income-producing properties. EPI provides office and manufacturing facilities for approximately 30 businesses. **Parent company:** Exodyne, Inc.

EXPONENT, INC.
23445 North 19th Avenue, Phoenix AZ 85027. 623/582-6949. **Fax:** 623/581-8814. **Contact:** Human Resources. **E-mail address:** hr@exponent.com. **World Wide Web address:** http://www.exponent.com. **Description:** Performs scientific analysis of various cases in areas such as accident reconstruction, biomechanics, construction/structural engineering, aviation and marine investigations, environmental assessment, materials and product testing, warnings and labeling issues, accident statistic data analysis, and risk prevention/mitigation. Founded in 1967. **Positions advertised include:** Managing Engineer; Thermal Engineer; Systems Engineer; Senior Engineer, Vehicle Engineering. **Corporate headquarters location:** Menlo Park CA. **Listed on:** NASDAQ. **Stock exchange symbol:** EXPO.

FAIRFIELD FLAGSTAFF RESORT
1900 North Country Club Drive, Flagstaff AZ 86004. 928/526-3232. **Contact:** Human Resources. **World Wide Web address:** http://www.efairfield.com. **Description:** A golf resort and country club. **Parent company:** Cendant Corporation.

FARMERS INSURANCE GROUP OF COMPANIES
18444 North 25th Avenue, Phoenix AZ 85023. 602/588-3443. **Fax:** 602/588-3454. **Contact:** Personnel. **World Wide Web address:** http://www.farmersinsurance.com. **Description:** An insurance company with offices in 41 states. **Positions advertised include:** Claims Service Center Manger; Personal Lines Account Underwriter. **Corporate headquarters location:** Los Angeles CA. **Operations at this facility include:** Regional Headquarters. **Number of employees at this location:** 850. **Number of employees nationwide:** 18,000.

FEDERATED INSURANCE
P.O. Box 35910, Phoenix AZ 85069. 602/944-5566. **Fax:** 602/395-0664. **Contact:** Human Resources. **World Wide Web address:** http://www.federatedinsurance.com. **Description:** A multiline insurance company specializing in providing insurance to commercial businesses. Founded in 1904. **NOTE:** Entry-level positions are offered. **Positions advertised include:** Underwriter; Sales/Marketing Representative; Field Services Risk Consultant. **Special programs:** Training. **Corporate headquarters location:** Owatonna MN. **Other U.S. locations:** Atlanta GA. **Operations at this facility include:** Regional Headquarters. **Annual sales/revenues:** More than $100 million. **Number of employees at this location:** 140. **Number of employees nationwide:** 2,700.

FENDER MUSICAL INSTRUMENTS CORPORATION
8860 East Chaparral Road, Suite 100, Scottsdale AZ 85250. 480/596-9690. **Fax:** 480/596-1384. **Contact:** Human Resources. **World Wide Web address:** http://www.fender.com. **Description:** Manufactures and distributes electric and acoustic guitars, strings, accessories, amplifiers, and professional sound equipment under such brand names as Fender, Guild, Squier, and Sunn. **Corporate headquarters location:** This location. **Other U.S. locations:** CA; TN; NY; RI. **Operations at this facility include:** Administration; Research and Development; Sales; Service.

FERRELLGAS
5600 North U.S. Highway 89, Flagstaff AZ 86004. 928/526-0466. **Contact:** Human Resources. **World Wide Web address:** http://www.ferrellgas.com. **Description:** One of the nation's largest propane suppliers. **Corporate headquarters location:** Liberty MO. **Listed on:** New York Stock Exchange. **Stock exchange symbol:** FGP.

FIRST CREDIT UNION
P.O. Box 22030, Tempe AZ 85285. 480/831-2645. **Physical address:** 1232 East Baseline Road, Tempe AZ 85283. **Toll-free phone:** 800/732-6986. **Fax:** 480/756-4677. **Contact:** Human Resources. **World Wide Web address:** http://www.firstcu.net. **Description:** A nonprofit credit union serving more than 50,000 members. **Corporate headquarters location:** This location. **Other area locations:** Chandler AZ; Glendale AZ; Phoenix AZ; Tucson AZ.

FIRST CREDIT UNION
5770 West Thunderbird Road, Glendale AZ 85306. 480/831-2769. **Toll-free phone:** 800/732-6986. **Fax:** 480/756-4677. **Contact:** Human Resources. **World Wide Web address:** http://www.firstcu.net. **Description:** A nonprofit credit union serving more than 50,000 members. **NOTE:** Download application form from website. **Corporate headquarters location:** Tempe AZ. **Other area locations:** Chandler AZ; Phoenix AZ; Tucson AZ.

FIRST INVESTORS CORPORATION
1990 West Camelback Road, Suite 211, Phoenix AZ 85015-3463. 602/841-2627. **Fax:** 602/841-2565. **Contact:** Personnel. **World Wide Web address:** http://www.firstinvestors.com. **Description:** Specializes in the distribution and management of investment programs for individuals and corporations including retirement plans. **Corporate headquarters location:** New York NY. **Operations at this facility include:** Sales; Service. **Number of employees at this location:** 20. **Number of employees nationwide:** 2,000.

FLAGSTAFF, CITY OF
211 West Aspen Avenue, Flagstaff AZ 86001. 928/774-5281. **Contact:** Human Resources. **World Wide Web address:** http://www.flagstaff.az.gov. **Description:** Administrative and municipal offices for the city of Flagstaff. **Positions advertised include:** Engineering Project Manager; Urban Designer; Emergency Communications Specialist; Police Officer; Brownfield Specialist; Plant Supervisor.

FLAGSTAFF MEDICAL CENTER
1200 North Beaver Street, P.O. Box 1268, Flagstaff AZ 86001. 928/779-3366. **Toll-free phone:** 800/446-2324. **Fax:** 928/773-2579. **Recorded jobline:** 928/773-2067. **Contact:** Human Resources. **World Wide Web address:** http://www.nahealth.com. **Description:** A 238-bed acute care facility. Services include cardiology, critical care, endoscopy, imaging, pediatrics, pharmacy, cancer research and care, and cardiology. Founded in 1936. **Positions advertised include:** Neonatal Nurse Practitioner; Registered Nurse; LPN; Clinical Coordinator; Certified Nursing Assistant; Allied Health Professional; Mental Health Technician; Pharmacy Operations Manager; Echo Technician; Housekeeper. **Corporate headquarters location:** This location. **Parent company:** Northern Arizona Health Care. **Operations at this facility include:** Administration. **Number of employees at this location:** 1,800.

FLOW TECHNOLOGY, INC.
4250 East Broadway Road, Phoenix AZ 85040. 602/437-1315. **Toll-free phone:** 800/528-4225. **Fax:** 602/437-4459. **Contact:** Human Resources. **World Wide Web address:** http://www.ftimeters.com. **Description:** Manufactures solid-state image sensors for electronics applications. **Positions advertised include:** Technical Support Engineer. **Parent company:** Roper Industries.

FOAM FABRICATORS INC.
8722 East San Alberto Drive, Suite 200, Scottsdale AZ 85258-4353. 480/607-7330. **Fax:** 480/607-7333. **Contact:** Department of Human Resources. **World Wide Web address:** http://www.foamfabricatorsinc.com. **Description:** A foam fabricating company. **Operations at this facility include:** Accounting/Auditing; Administration.

FOREVER LIVING PRODUCTS
7501 East McCormick Parkway, Scottsdale AZ 85258. 480/998-8888. **Contact:** Human Resources. **World Wide Web address:** http://www.foreverliving.com. **Description:** A manufacturer of nutritional and skin care products.

FRONTIER ADJUSTERS OF AMERICA, INC.
P.O. Box 7610, Phoenix AZ 85011. 602/264-1061. **Contact:** Human Resources. **World Wide Web address:** http://www.frontieradjusters.com. **Description:** An insurance adjustment company.

FUJITSU CONSULTING
2201 East Camelback Road, Suite 310B, Phoenix AZ 85016. 602/955-0770. **Contact:** Human Resources. **World Wide Web address:** http://www.fujitsu.com. **Description:** Fujitsu designs, manufactures, develops, markets, and services large-scale, high-performance, general purpose computer systems (both hardware and software.) Customers are primarily large corporations, government agencies, and universities with high-volume data processing requirements. The company markets more than 470 different systems. **NOTE:** Search and apply for positions online. **Corporate headquarters location:** Sunnyvale CA. **Other U.S. locations:** Nationwide. **International locations:** Worldwide. **Operations at this facility include:** This location is a customer service and sales office.

FUTURE ELECTRONICS
4801 East Washington Street, Suite 225, Phoenix AZ 85034. 602/629-3013. **Toll-free phone:** 800/950-7140. **Contact:** Human Resources. **World Wide Web address:** http://www.futureelectronics.com. **Description:** Distributes electronic components.

GAB ROBINS
1661 East Camelback Road, Suite 220, Phoenix AZ 85016. 602/248-4100. **Fax:** 602/248-4129. **Contact:** Human Resources. **World Wide Web address:** http://www.gabrobinsna.com. **Description:** A nationwide firm that provides adjustment, inspection, appraisal, and management claim services to 15,000 insurance industry customers, employing 3,800 professionals in over 680 branch offices. Specific services include the settlement of claims following major disasters, appraisal, investigation, and the adjustment of auto insurance claims. **Corporate headquarters location:** Parsippany NJ.

GENERAL DYNAMICS C4 SYSTEMS
8201 E. McDowell Road, Scottsdale AZ 85257. 480/441-3033. **Fax:** 480/726-2971. **Contact:** Human Resources. **World Wide Web address:** http://www.gdds.com. **Description:** leading systems integrator of secure communication and information systems and technology in five key business areas: tactical networks, information assurance, command and control, space products and systems, and military radios. **Positions advertised include:** Communications System Engineer; Senior Software Development Engineer; Principle Systems Engineer; Digital Design Engineer; Program Control Analyst. **Corporate headquarters location:** Falls Church VA. **Other U.S. locations:** Huntsville AL; Needham MA; Columbia MD; Taunton MA. **Number of employees nationwide:** 6,500.

GTCO CALCOMP
14555 North 82nd Street, Scottsdale AZ 85260. 480/948-6540. **Fax:** 480/948-5508. **E-mail address:** az.hr@gtcocalcomp.com. **Contact:** Human Resources. **World Wide Web address:** http://www.gtcocalcomp.com. **Description:** Manufactures computer peripheral equipment including desktop graphics tablets, wide-format scanners, and large-format digitizers. Products are used in engineering, construction, and graphics applications. **Corporate headquarters location:** Columbia MD.

GIANT INDUSTRIES, INC.
23733 North Scottsdale Road, Scottsdale AZ 85255. 480/585-8888. **Fax:** 480/585-8885. **Recorded jobline:** 480/585-8844. **Contact:** Human Resources. **E-mail address:** jobs@giant.com. **World Wide Web address:** http://www.giant.com. **Description:** A refiner and marketer of petroleum products. Giant Industries owns and operates two oil refineries, Ciniza and Bloomfield, both located in New Mexico; a fleet of crude oil and finished product truck transports; and a chain of retail service stations and convenience stores in Arizona, New Mexico, and Colorado. **NOTE:** Entry-level positions and part-time jobs are offered. **Company slogan:** Unmatched service in all we do. **Office hours:** Monday - Friday, 8:00 a.m. - 5:00 p.m. **Corporate headquarters location:** This location. **Other U.S. locations:** CO; NM; UT. **Listed on:** New York Stock Exchange. **Stock exchange symbol:** GI. **Annual sales/revenues:** More than $100 million. **Number of employees at this location:** 200. **Number of employees nationwide:** 2,850.

CHARLES E. GILLMAN COMPANY
907 East Frontage Road, Rio Rico AZ 85648. 520/281-1141. **Fax:** 520/281-1372. **Contact:** Ms. Reyna Armenta, Human Resources. **World Wide Web address:** http://www.gillman.com. **Description:** Manufactures wiring harnesses and cable assemblies for sale to electronics OEMs. **Corporate headquarters location:** This location.

GLENDALE, CITY OF
5850 West Glendale Avenue, Glendale AZ 85301. 623/930-2270. **Fax:** 623/435-5347. **Recorded jobline:** 623/930-3699. **Contact:** Human Resources. **World Wide Web address:** http://www.ci.glendale.az.us. **Description:** Offices for the city of Glendale. **Positions advertised include:** Deputy City Manager; Deputy Finance Director; EMS Coordinator; Judge Pro Tempore; Laboratory Technician; Library Technology Supervisor; Marketing and Communications Manager; Materials Technician; Parks and Recreation Director.

GLENDALE COMMUNITY COLLEGE
6000 West Olive Avenue, Glendale AZ 85302. 623/845-3000. **Contact:** Human Resources. **World Wide Web address:** http://www.gc.maricopa.edu. **Description:** With 18,000 students, the college is one of the largest schools in the Maricopa County Community College District. The district serves over 2.2 million residents in Maricopa County and has one of the nation's largest community college systems. Three degrees are offered: associate of arts, associate of applied sciences, and associate of general studies. Twenty-eight career programs range from administration of justice to video production technology. Twenty-eight occupational certificates are also available in areas such as automotive, business, and child and family studies. Founded in 1965. **Positions advertised include:** College President; Faculty, Various Departments. **Office hours:** Monday - Friday, 7:30 a.m. - 4:30 p.m.

GOETTL AIR CONDITIONING INC.
1845 West 1st Street, Tempe AZ 85281. 602/275-1515. **Fax:** 602/470-4275. **Contact:** Human Resources. **World Wide Web address:** http://www.goettl.com. **Description:** Manufactures a broad range of air conditioning, heating, and air distribution products including air conditioning systems and components, heat pumps, and evaporative coolers. **Positions advertised include:** A/C Installers. **Corporate headquarters location:** This location.

GOLD'S GYM
2156 East Baseline Road, Mesa AZ 85204. 480/497-8686. **Contact:** Manager. **World Wide Web address:** http://www.goldsgym.com. **Description:** A full-service health and fitness club complete with weights and cardiovascular equipment, fitness and aerobic instruction, tanning, personal training, and child-care facilities. Overall, Gold's Gym is one of the world's largest health club chains, with over 550 locations. Founded in 1965. **NOTE:** Part-time jobs are offered.

GOLD'S GYM
1046 South Country Club Drive, Mesa AZ 85210. 480/833-0099. **Contact:** Manager. **World Wide Web address:** http://www.goldsgym.com. **Description:** A full-service health and fitness club. Each club is complete with weights and cardiovascular equipment, fitness and aerobic instruction, tanning, personal training, and child-care facilities. Overall, Gold's Gym is one of the world's largest health club chains, with over 550 locations. Founded in 1965. **NOTE:** Part-time jobs are offered.

GOLDEN WEST & ASSOCIATES
4711 East Falcon Drive, Suite 222, Mesa AZ 85215. 480/396-4653. **Contact:** Human Resources. **Description:** A real estate firm. **Corporate headquarters location:** This location.

GOODWILL INDUSTRIES OF CENTRAL ARIZONA
417 North 16th Street, Phoenix AZ 85006. 602/254-2222. **Fax:** 602/258-7047. **Contact:** Human Resources. **E-mail address:** hr@goodwillaz.org. **World Wide Web address:** http://www.goodwillcentralaz.org. **Description:** Besides operating over 1,400 thrift stores nationwide, Goodwill is a nonprofit provider of employment training for the disabled and the poor. **Positions advertised include:** Store Manager; Youth Services Program Coordinator; Youth Services Case Manager; Career Center Educator; Case Manager; Event Coordinator; Community Based Instructor. **Special programs:** Internships. **Corporate headquarters location:** Bethesda MD. **Other U.S. locations:** Nationwide. **Parent company:** Goodwill Industries International. **Number of employees at this location:** 225.

GOODRICH CORPORATION
3414 South Fifth Street, Phoenix AZ 85040. 602/243-2200. **Fax:** 602/243-2300. **Contact:** Human Resources. **World Wide Web address:** http://www.goodrich.com. **Description:** Goodrich Corporation provides aircraft systems and components, and services and manufactures a wide range of specialty chemicals. The other business units comprising the aerospace division consist of Landing Systems; Sensors and Integrated Systems; Safety Systems; and Maintenance, Repair, and Overhaul. Specialty chemical business units include Specialty Plastics, Specialty Additives, Sealants, Coatings and Adhesives, and Water Systems and Services. **Positions advertised include:** Temporary Design Engineer; Hardware Control Specialist; Operations Analyst; Manufacturing Engineer; Senior Contracts Manager; Marketing Analyst. **Corporate headquarters location:** Charlotte NC. **Listed on:** New York Stock Exchange. **Stock exchange symbol:** GR.

W.L. GORE & ASSOCIATES, INC.
1500 North Fourth Street, Flagstaff AZ 86004. 928/526-3030. **Contact:** Human Resources. **World Wide Web address:** http://www.gore.com. **Description:** W.L. Gore & Associates is a research-based organization that manufactures high-technology electronic, industrial, and medical products, as well as specialty fabric products including GORE-TEX fabric. **Positions advertised include:** MPD Plant Technical Leader; Industrial Engineer; Automation and Controls Engineer; Quality Engineer; Project Manager; Packaging Engineer; Process Engineer; Regulatory Affairs Associate; Design Engineer; Material Scientist. **Operations at this facility include:** This location manufactures a variety of medical devices used in vascular, cardiology, and facial procedures.

W.W. GRAINGER
3231 West Virginia Avenue, Phoenix AZ 85009. 602/269-3115. **Contact:** Human Resources. **World Wide Web address:** http://www.grainger.com. **Description:** Distributes a variety of equipment and components to the industrial, commercial, contracting, and institutional markets nationwide. Products include equipment and components for motors, air tools, hydraulic products, refrigeration items, power and hand tools, office equipment, computer supplies, storage equipment, replacement parts, industrial products, safety items, and sanitary supplies. **Positions advertised include:** District Sales Manager. **Corporate headquarters location:** Lake Forest IL. **Other U.S. locations:** Nationwide. **Listed on:** New York Stock Exchange. **Stock exchange symbol:** GWW.

GRAND CANYON NATIONAL PARK
P.O. Box 129, Grand Canyon AZ 86023. 928/638-7888. **Contact:** Human Resources. **World Wide Web address:** http://www.nps.gov/grca. **Description:** A national park. **NOTE:** Faxed or e-mailed job applications not accepted. **Positions advertised include:** Park Ranger; Maintenance Worker; Forestry Technician; Biological Technician; Archeological Technician. **Office hours:** Monday - Friday, 8:00 a.m. - 5:00 p.m. **Corporate headquarters location:** This location. **Operations at this facility include:** This location houses business offices for the park and is responsible for the hiring of all park personnel.

GROUPSYSTEMS
1430 East Fort Lowell Road, Suite 301, Tucson AZ 85719. 520/325-8228. **Toll-free phone:** 800/368-6338. **Contact:** Human Resources. **E-mail address:** careers@Groupsystems.com. **World Wide Web address:** http://www.groupsystems.com. **Description:** Develops group decision support software. **Corporate headquarters location:** Broomfield CO.

GRUBB & ELLIS COMMERCIAL REAL ESTATE SERVICES
2375 East Camelback Road, Suite 300, Phoenix AZ 85016. 602/954-9000. **Contact:** Bryon Carney, Sales Manager. **World Wide Web address:** http://www.grubb-ellis.com. **Description:** Office of the commercial and industrial real estate brokerage. Grubb & Ellis also specializes in property management, and institutional and individual investment. **Corporate headquarters location:** Northbrook IL. **Listed on:** New York Stock Exchange. **Stock exchange symbol:** GBE. **Number of employees at this location:** 90.

LOU GRUBB CHEVROLET
P.O. Box 11409, Phoenix AZ 85061. 602/242-5555. **Physical address:** 2646 West Camelback Road, Phoenix AZ 85017. **Contact:** Human Resources. **World Wide Web address:** http://www.lougrubbchevy.com. **Description:** An automotive dealer.

GUIDANCE INVESTORS, INC.
dba AMERICAN GRADE SCHOOLS/AMERICAN CHILD CARE CENTERS
4040 East McDowell Road, Suite 501, Phoenix AZ 85008. 602/993-6070. **Contact:** Human Resources. **Description:** Operates 25 child-care centers in Arizona, Oklahoma, and California that provide daycare and preschool services. **Special programs:** Internships. **Office hours:** Monday - Friday, 7:30 a.m. - 4:30 p.m. **Corporate headquarters location:** This location. **Operations at this facility include:** Administration. **Listed on:** Privately held.

HAMILTON SUNDSTRAND
18008 North Black Canyon Highway, Suite B, Phoenix AZ 85053. 602/439-6400. **Contact:** Ms. Chris Berry, Human Resources. **World Wide Web address:** http://www.hamiltonsundstrand.com. **Description:** Designs and develops high-technology components for aerospace, aviation, power transmission, and fluid and heat transfer. **Positions advertised include:** Associate Contract Specialist; Senior Analyst. **Parent company:** United Technologies Corporation.

HAVASU REGIONAL MEDICAL CENTER
101 Civic Center Lane, Lake Havasu City AZ 86403. 928/855-8185. **Fax:** 928/453-0810. **Contact:** Human Resources Department. **E-mail address:** humanresources@havasuregional.com. **World Wide Web address:** http://www.havasuregional.com. **Description:** A 138-bed, acute care facility providing comprehensive medical services. **Positions advertised include:** ACU Registered Nurse; Certified Nursing Assistant; Clinical Nurse; LPN; MRI Tech; Pharmacist; Ultrasound Technologist.

HEAD/PENN RACQUET SPORTS, INC.
306 South 45th Avenue, Phoenix AZ 85043. 602/269-1492. **Fax:** 602/484-7580. **Contact:** Vicky Moore, Human Resources Manager. **E-mail address:** vmoore@pennracquet.com. **World Wide Web address:** http://www.pennracquet.com. **Description:** Manufactures tennis and racquet balls for domestic and international markets. Founded in 1922. **NOTE:** Entry-level positions and second and third shifts are offered. **Office hours:** Monday - Friday, 8:00 a.m. - 4:00 p.m. **Corporate headquarters location:** This location. **International locations:** Mullingar, Ireland. **Parent company:** HEAD, USA. **Listed on:** New York Stock Exchange. **Stock exchange symbol:** HED. **Annual sales/revenues:** More than $100 million. **Number of employees at this location:** 400.

HEALTH FACTORS INTERNATIONAL
429 South Siesta Lane, Tempe AZ 85281. 480/921-1991. **Fax:** 480/921-2084. **Contact:** Human Resources. **World Wide Web address:** http://www.hfi-phx.com. **Description:** Manufactures a wide variety of vitamins and related products.

HEALTH NET OF ARIZONA
930 North Finance Center Drive, Tucson AZ 85710. 520/258-4444. **Contact:** Human Resources. **World Wide Web address:** http://www.az.health.net. **Description:** One of Arizona's leading managed health care companies. Health Net also offers third-party administrator services to self-funded employers and others; provides multi-option benefit plans, including PPO, point-of-service, and indemnity options; and provides coverage for Medicare and Medicaid recipients. **Positions advertised include:** Account Service Representative. **Corporate headquarters location:** Woodland Hills

CA. **Other area locations:** Mesa AZ; Phoenix AZ; Tempe AZ; Yuma AZ. **Parent company:** Health Net Inc. **Listed on:** New York Stock Exchange. **Stock exchange symbol:** HNT. **Number of employees nationwide:** 9,800.

HEARD MUSEUM
2301 North Central Avenue, Phoenix AZ 85004. 602/252-8840. **Contact:** Human Resources. **World Wide Web address:** http://www.heard.org. **Description:** A museum that showcases Native American art and cultural artifacts.

HEWLETT-PACKARD COMPANY
1711 West Green Tree Drive, Suite 111, Tempe AZ 85284. 480/753-4317. **Contact:** Human Resources. **World Wide Web address:** http://www.hp.com. **Description:** Hewlett-Packard is engaged in the design and manufacture of measurement and computation products and systems used in business, engineering, science, health care, and education. Principal products include integrated instrument and computer systems (including hardware and software); computer systems and peripheral products; and medical electronic equipment systems. **Positions advertised include:** Financial Analyst; Marketing Communications Consulting Manager; MS Sales Specialist; Pre-Sales Consultant; HP Educations Sales Specialist; Handheld Sales Specialist. **Corporate headquarters location:** Palo Alto CA. **Operations at this facility include:** This location is a sales office. **Listed on:** New York Stock Exchange. **Stock exchange symbol:** HWP.

HEXCEL CORPORATION
P.O. Box 15006, Casa Grande AZ 85230. 520/836-8761. **Physical address:** 1214 West Highway 84, Casa Grande AZ 85222. **Contact:** Human Resources. **World Wide Web address:** http://www.hexcel.com. **Description:** A manufacturing firm engaged in two primary business segments: structural materials and specialty chemicals and resins. Products in the structural materials segment include aerospace products, nonaerospace honeycomb, resin-impregnated industrial fabrics, and nonimpregnated fabrics. Specialty chemicals include bulk pharmaceuticals, custom and special-purpose chemicals, specialty resins, and industrial maintenance chemicals. **Positions advertised include:** Quality Assurance Engineer; Area Facilitator, Quality Assurance. **Corporate headquarters location:** Stamford CT. **Other U.S. locations:** Nationwide. **Operations at this facility include:** Administration; Manufacturing; Research and Development. **Listed on:** New York Stock Exchange. **Stock exchange symbol:** HXL. **Number of employees at this location:** 500. **Number of employees nationwide:** 2,000.

HIDDEN PALMS ALL SUITE INN
2100 Swanson Avenue, Lake Havasu City AZ 86403. 928/855-7144. **Toll-free phone:** 800/254-5611. **Fax:** 928/855-2620. **Contact:** Human Resources. **World Wide Web address:** http://www.hiddenpalms.com. **Description:** A full-service hotel offering guest suites that include kitchens and dining areas. **Office hours:** Monday - Friday, 8:00 a.m. - 8:00 p.m.

HILTON GARDEN INN FLAGSTAFF
350 West Forest Meadows Street, Flagstaff AZ 86001. 928/226-8888. **Contact:** Human Resources. **World Wide Web address:** http://www.hilton.com. **Description:** A 90-room, full-service hotel for business and leisure travelers. **Parent company:** Hilton Hotels Corporation. **Listed on:** New York Stock Exchange. **Stock exchange symbol:** HLT.

HILTON PHOENIX EAST/MESA
1011 West Holmes Avenue, Mesa AZ 85210. 480/833-5555. **Fax:** 480/649-1886. **Recorded jobline:** 480/844-6044. **Contact:** Human Resources. **World Wide Web address:** http://www.hilton.com. **Description:** A 263-room hotel. **NOTE:** Entry-level positions and second and third shifts are offered. **Positions advertised include:** Line Cook; Desk Clerk; Engineer; Room Attendant; Business Center Attendant. **Special programs:** Internships. **Corporate headquarters location:** Beverly Hills CA. **Parent company:** Hilton Hotels Corporation. **Listed on:** New York Stock Exchange. **Stock exchange symbol:** HLT. **Number of employees at this location:** 200. **Number of employees nationwide:** 800.

BERNARD HODES GROUP
2231 East Camelback Road, Suite 370, Phoenix AZ 85016. 602/956-8989. **Fax:** 602/956-9142. **Contact:** Branch Manager. **World Wide Web address:** http://www.hodes.com. **Description:** An advertising agency specializing in recruitment and employee communications. **Positions advertised include:** Account Executive. **Corporate headquarters location:** New York NY. **Other U.S. locations:** Chicago IL; Cambridge MA; Dallas TX. **Parent company:** Omnicom.

HOLSUM BAKERY INC.
2322 West Lincoln Street, Phoenix AZ 85009. 602/252-2351. **Fax:** 602/452-4109. **E-mail address:** carkeekb@holsumaz.com. **Contact:** Human Resources. **World Wide Web address:** http://www.holsumaz.com. **Description:** Produces and distributes bread and other baked goods, primarily on a wholesale basis. **Positions advertised include:** Accounts Receivable Manager; Maintenance Mechanic.

HONEYWELL
5353 West Bell Road, Glendale AZ 85308-3900. 602/436-8000. **Contact:** Human Resources. **World Wide Web address:** http://www.honeywell.com. **Description:** Manufactures completely integrated electronic cockpits. The Business and Commuter Aviation Systems group is part of Honeywell's Space and Aviation Systems business. Overall, Honeywell is engaged in the research, development, manufacture, and sale of advanced technology products and services in the fields of chemicals, electronics, automation, and controls. The company's major businesses are home and building automation and control, performance polymers and chemicals, industrial automation and control, space and aviation systems, and defense and marine systems. **NOTE:** Please see the Website to apply for a position. **Positions advertised include:** Avionics Engineer. **Corporate headquarters location:** Morristown NJ. **Listed on:** New York Stock Exchange. **Stock exchange symbol:** HON. **Annual sales/revenues:** More than $100 million. **Number of employees at this location:** 1,700.

HONEYWELL
19019 North 59th Avenue, Glendale AZ 85308. 602/822-3000. **Contact:** Human Resources. **World Wide Web address:** http://www.honeywell.com. **Description:** Honeywell is engaged in the research, development, manufacture, and sale of advanced technology products and services in the fields of chemicals, electronics, automation, and controls. The company's major businesses are home and building automation and control, performance polymers and chemicals, industrial automation and control, space and aviation systems, and defense and marine systems. **Positions advertised include:** Financial Analyst; FMS Systems Engineer; Executive Assistant; IES Software Engineer; Contracts Manager. **NOTE:** Please see the Website to apply for a position. **Corporate headquarters location:** Morristown NJ. **Operations at this facility include:** This location is engaged in the research and development, manufacture, and sale of advanced technology products and services for satellite technology. **Listed on:** New York Stock Exchange. **Stock exchange symbol:** HON. **Annual sales/revenues:** More than $100 million.

HOOLEON CORPORATION
417 South Sixth Street, Suite A, Cottonwood AZ 86326. 928/634-7515. **Contact:** Human Resources. **World Wide Web address:** http://www.hooleon.com. **Description:** Customizes computer keyboards. **President/CEO:** Joan Crozier.

HOPE PHARMACEUTICALS
8260 East Gelding Drive, Scottsdale AZ 85260. 480/607-1970. **Fax:** 480/607-1971. **Contact:** Human Resources. **World Wide Web address:** http://www.hopepharm.com. **Description:** Develops a variety of pharmaceuticals including medicines for motion sickness and acne treatments.

HYATT REGENCY PHOENIX
122 North Second Street, Phoenix AZ 85004. 602/252-1234. **Toll-free phone:** 800/223-1234. **Fax:** 602/440-3124. **Recorded jobline:** 602/440-3154. **Contact:** Valerie Saito, Director of Human Resources. **World Wide Web address:** http://www.hyatt.com. **Description:** A full-service hotel with 712 guest rooms including 45 suites. The Hyatt Regency Phoenix also features 42,000 square feet of meeting space as well as several restaurants and lounges. This location also hires seasonally. **NOTE:** Entry-level positions, part-time jobs, and second and third shifts are offered. **Positions advertised include:** Assistant Engineering Director; Assistant Restaurant Manager; Banquet Captain. **Corporate headquarters location:** Chicago IL. **Other U.S. locations:** Nationwide. **International locations:** Worldwide. **Number of employees at this location:** 500. **Number of employees worldwide:** 45,000.

HYDRO ALUMINUM NORTH AMERICA
249 South 51st Avenue, P.O. Box 6726, Phoenix AZ 85005. 602/269-2488. **Contact:** Human Resources. **World Wide Web address:** http://www.hydrona.com. **Description:** Produces aluminum. **Corporate headquarters location:** Linthicum MD. **Parent company:** Hydro (Oslo Norway). **Listed on:** New York Stock Exchange. **Stock exchange symbol:** NHY. **Number of employees at this location:** 400.

IBM CORPORATION
9000 South Rita Road, Tucson AZ 85744. 520/799-1000. **Contact:** Human Resources. **World Wide Web address:** http://www.ibm.com. **Description:** IBM is a developer, manufacturer, and marketer of advanced information processing products including computers and microelectronic technology, software, and networking systems. The company also offers information technology services. **Corporate headquarters location:** Armonk NY. **Operations at this facility include:** This facility is engaged in the development of data access and storage devices. **Subsidiaries include:** IBM Credit Corporation; IBM Instruments, Inc.; IBM World Trade Corporation. **Listed on:** New York Stock Exchange. **Stock exchange symbol:** IBM.

IKON OFFICE SOLUTIONS
P.O. Box 12369, Scottsdale AZ 85267. 602/468-4500. **Contact:** Human Resources. **World Wide Web address:** http://www.ikon.com. **Description:** A wholesaler and distributor of copy machines, fax machines, and related office supplies. **Corporate headquarters location:** Malvern PA. **Listed on:** New York Stock Exchange. **Stock exchange symbol:** IKN.

IMAGISTICS/OFFICE SOLUTIONS
4908 East McDowell Road, Suite 100, Phoenix AZ 85008. 602/371-8126. **Contact:** Human Resources. **World Wide Web address:** http://www.imagistics.com. **Description:** A direct sales, service and marketing organization offering document imaging solutions. **Corporate headquarters location:** Trumbull CT. **Parent company:** Imagistics International Inc. **Listed on:** New York Stock Exchange. **Stock exchange symbol:** IGI.

INDATA CORPORATION
1325 North Fiesta Boulevard, Suite 4, Gilbert AZ 85233. 480/497-8595. **Fax:** 480/497-1833. **Contact:** Personnel. **World Wide Web address:** http://www.indatacorp.com. **Description:** Provides a variety of imaging, video production, software development, and consulting services to trial lawyers. **Positions advertised include:** Scan/Code/Edit Personnel; Software Developer; Trial Consultant/Trainer. **Other U.S. locations:** Washington D.C.

INDOTRONIX INTERNATIONAL CORPORATION
7373 East Doubletree Ranch Road, Suite 200, Scottsdale AZ 85258. 480/998-2112. **Fax:** 480/998-2202. **Contact:** Human Resources. **World Wide Web address:** http://www.iic.com. **Description:** Develops software. **Positions advertised include:** Systems Administrator. **Corporate headquarters location:** Poughkeepsie NY. **Other U.S. locations:** Sunnyvale CA; Tampa FL; Atlanta GA; Naperville IL; Austin TX; Irving TX: Morrisville NC; Plainsboro NJ.

INFILTRATOR SYSTEMS INC.
14809 North 73rd Street, Suite 200, Scottsdale AZ 85260. 480/443-3724. **Contact:** Human Resources. **E-mail address:** jobs@infiltratorsystems.com. **World Wide Web address:** http://www.infiltratorsystems.com. **Description:** Manufactures plastic drainage chambers for septic tanks and storm water systems. **Corporate headquarters location:** Old Saybrook CT.

INSIGHT ENTERPRISES, INC.
6820 South Harl Avenue, Tempe AZ 85283. 480/902-1000. **Fax:** 480/902-1157. **Contact:** Human Resources. **E-mail address:** jobs@insight.com. **World Wide Web address:** http://www.insight.com. **Description:** A direct marketer of name brand computers, computer hardware, and software. Customers include educational institutions, businesses, and both local and national governments worldwide. **Positions advertised include:** Tax Director; Senior Project Manager; Database Administrator; Manager Marketing Strategy; Sales Manager. **Special programs:** Internships. **Corporate headquarters location:** This location. **Listed on:** NASDAQ. **Stock exchange symbol:** NSIT. **Annual sales/revenues:** More than $100 million. **Number of employees at this location:** 430.

INTEL CORPORATION
5000 West Chandler Boulevard, Chandler AZ 85226-3699. 480/554-8080. **Contact:** Human Resources. **World Wide Web address:** http://www.intel.com. **Description:** One of the largest semiconductor manufacturers in the world. Other operations of Intel Corporation include supercomputers; embedded control chips and flash memories; video technology software; multimedia hardware; and personal computer enhancement products. Intel Corporation is also engaged in the design, manufacture, and marketing of microcomputer components, modules, and systems. Intel sells its products to original equipment manufacturers and other companies that incorporate them into their own products. **Positions advertised include:** Packaging Engineer; Shift Supervisor; display Processing Architect; Business Alliance Manager; Software Engineer; Test Engineer; Sr. Mfg. Modeling Engineer; System Validation Engineer. **NOTE:** Interested

jobseekers should apply online. **Corporate headquarters location:** Santa Clara CA. **Listed on:** NASDAQ. **Stock exchange symbol:** INTC.

INTELLIGENT INSTRUMENTATION INC.
3000 East Valencia Road, Suite 100, Tucson AZ 85706. 520/573-0887. **Fax:** 520/573-9671. **Contact:** Personnel. **World Wide Web address:** http://www.instrument.com. **Description:** Manufactures networking hardware and Ethernet data collection systems. **Corporate headquarters location:** Dallas TX. **Parent company:** Texas Instruments. **Listed on:** New York Stock Exchange. **Stock exchange symbol:** TXN.

INTER-TEL INC.
1615 South 52nd Street, Suite 200, Tempe AZ 85281. 480/449-8900. **Fax:** 480/449-8929. **Contact:** Human Resources. **E-mail address:** opportunities@inter-tel.com. **World Wide Web address:** http://www.inter-tel.com. **Description:** Provides business communications systems, voice mail systems and networking applications. Inter-Tel markets and sells voice processing and unified messaging software, call accounting software, Internet Protocol (IP) telephony software, computer-telephone integration applications, long distance calling services, and other communications services. **Positions advertised include:** Senior Internal Auditor; Senior Business Analyst; Technical Analyst. **Corporate headquarters location:** This location. **Other area locations:** Chandler AZ; Phoenix AZ; Tucson AZ. **Other U.S. locations:** Orlando FL; Reno NV; Dallas TX.

IRONWOOD LITHOGRAPHERS, INC.
455 South 52nd Street, Tempe AZ 85281. 480/829-7700. **Contact:** Human Resources. **World Wide Web address:** http://www.ironwoodlitho.com. **Description:** Offers complete business communications services including electronic prepress, quality offset printing, Docutech on-demand printing, direct mail facilities, diskette duplication and packaging, and a full-service fulfillment department. **Corporate headquarters location:** This location. **Number of employees at this location:** 100. **Number of employees nationwide:** 250.

JDA SOFTWARE GROUP, INC.
14400 North 87th Street, Scottsdale AZ 85260-3649. 480/308-3000. **Fax:** 480/308-3001. **Contact:** Human Resources. **World Wide Web address:** http://www.jda.com. **Description:** Develops software for the retail industry. **Positions advertised include:** Senior Staff Accountant; Senior Business Consultant; Instructional Designer. **Listed on:** NASDAQ. **Stock exchange symbol:** JDAS.

JMC MECHANICAL
6616 West State Avenue, Glendale AZ 85301. 623/934-3206. **Contact:** Mack Crawley, President. **Description:** A utilities contractor specializing in the installation of air conditioning and plumbing systems.

JACOBS SVERDRUP
875 West Elliot Road, Suite 201, Tempe AZ 85284. 480/763-8600. **Fax:** 714/763-8601. **Contact:** Human Resources. **World Wide Web address:** http://www.jacobs.com. **Description:** An environmental engineering, architectural, and construction firm that offers consulting services, design services, and operations management to a diverse clientele. **NOTE:** Entry-level positions are offered. **Positions advertised include:** Civil Engineer; Environmental Planner; Messaging Administrator; Non-Project Assistant. **Special programs:** Internships. **Corporate headquarters location:** Pasadena CA. **Parent company:** Jacobs Engineering Group, Inc. **Operations at this facility include:** Administration; Service. **Listed on:** New York Stock Exchange. **Stock exchange symbol:** JEC. **Annual sales/revenues:** More than $100 million. **Number of employees at this location:** 100. **Number of employees worldwide:** 5,000.

JENNINGS, STROUSS, AND SALMON
The Collier Center, 11th Floor, 201 East Washington Street, Phoenix AZ 85004. 602/262-5911. **Fax:** 602/253-3255. **Contact:** Janice K. Baker, Director of Attorney Recruitment. **E-mail address:** jbaker@jsslaw.com. **World Wide Web address:** http://www.jsslaw.com. **Description:** A law firm practicing in over 35 legal disciplines including antitrust, corporate, environmental, franchising, government, and tax. **Other area locations:** Scottsdale AZ; Peoria AZ.

JOHNSON CONTROLS, INC.
2032 West Fourth Street, Tempe AZ 85281. 480/894-9193. **Contact:** Human Resources. **World Wide Web address:** http://www.johnsoncontrols.com. **Description:** Johnson Controls, Inc. provides air conditioning services, air filters, automatic temperature control, chiller services, coil cleaning, lighting services, energy management, facilities management systems, fire alarm systems, heating service, maintenance contracts, refrigeration service, and security systems. **Corporate headquarters location:** Milwaukee WI. **Operations at this facility include:** This location sells, services, and installs fire alarm controls and air conditioning systems. **Listed on:** New York Stock Exchange. **Stock exchange symbol:** JCI. **Number of employees at this location:** 65. **Number of employees worldwide:** 123,000.

JPMORGAN CHASE
170 West 16th Street, Yuma AZ 85364. 928/343-4233. **Contact:** Human Resources. **World Wide Web address:** http://www.bankone.com. **Description:** A full-service bank and financial institution. **Positions advertised include:** Accounting Supervisor; Administrative Consultant; Application Development Analyst; Arizona Middle Market Trader; Client Risk Analyst; Client Advisor. **Corporate headquarters location:** New York NY. **Listed on:** New York Stock Exchange. **Stock exchange symbol:** JPM.

JPMORGAN CHASE
3932 East Fry Boulevard, Sierra Vista AZ 85635. 520/459-1235. **Contact:** Human Resources. **World Wide Web address:** http://www.bankone.com. **Description:** A full-service bank and financial institution. **Corporate headquarters location:** New York NY. **Listed on:** New York Stock Exchange. **Stock exchange symbol:** JPM.

KFC
4515 South McClintock Drive, Suite 206, Tempe AZ 85282-7382. 480/491-5511. **Contact:** Human Resources. **World Wide Web address:** http://www.kfc.com. **Description:** KFC is a fast-food restaurant chain specializing in chicken dinners. **Corporate headquarters location:** Louisville KY. **Operations at this facility include:** This location houses administrative offices. **Parent company:** Tricon Global Restaurants, Inc. **Listed on:** New York Stock Exchange. **Stock exchange symbol:** YUM. **Number of employees at this location:** 8,500.

KISS-FM
645 East Missouri Avenue, Suite 360, Phoenix AZ 85012. 602/279-5577. **Contact:** Human Resources. **World Wide Web address:** http://www.1047kissfm.com. **Description:** A radio station that plays top 40 hits. **Positions advertised include:** Events Manager. **Corporate headquarters location:** San Antonio TX. **Parent company:** Clear Channel Communications. **Listed on:** New York Stock Exchange. **Stock exchange symbol:** CCU.

KKLT-FM
5300 North Central Avenue, Phoenix AZ 85012. 602/274-6200. **Contact:** Human Resources. **World Wide Web address:** http://www.kkltfm.com. **Description:** A radio station that plays adult contemporary light rock.

KNIX-FM
600 East Gilbert Drive, Tempe AZ 85281. 480/966-6236. **Contact:** Human Resources. **World Wide Web address:** http://www.knixcountry.com. **Description:** A country music radio station. **Positions advertised include:** Assistant Program Director; Music Director; On-Air Talent; Board Operator; Director of Promotion; Part-time Remote Technician; Research Administrator; Traffic Manager/Continuity. **Corporate headquarters location:** San Antonio TX. **Parent company:** Clear Channel Communications. **Listed on:** New York Stock Exchange. **Stock exchange symbol:** CCU. **Number of employees at this location:** 100.

KPHO-TV5
4016 North Black Canyon Highway, Phoenix AZ 85017. 602/264-1000. **Fax:** 602/274-1596. **Recorded jobline:** 602/650-5562. **Contact:** Human Resources. **World Wide Web address:** http://www.kpho.com. **Description:** A CBS-affiliated television station. Founded in 1949. **Positions advertised include:** Local Facilities Coordinator; Reporter; Morning Executive Producer; Investigative Producer; Producer; Helicopter Pilot; Credit Manager. **NOTE:** Part-time jobs are offered. **Corporate headquarters location:** Des Moines IA. **Parent company:** Meredith Corporation. **Listed on:** New York Stock Exchange. **Stock exchange symbol:** MDP. **Number of employees at this location:** 170.

KPMG
400 East Van Buren Street, Suite 1100, Phoenix AZ 85004. 602/253-2000. **Contact:** Human Resources. **World Wide Web address:** http://www.kpmg.com. **Description:** KPMG delivers a wide range of value-added assurance, tax, and consulting services. **Positions advertised include:** Associate; Senior Associate. **Corporate headquarters location:** Montvale NJ. **Parent company:** KPMG International has more than 85,000 employees worldwide, including 6,500 partners and 60,000 professional staff, serving clients in 155 countries. KPMG International is a leader among professional services firms engaged in capturing, managing, assessing, and delivering information to create knowledge that will help its clients maximize shareholder value.

KPNX-TV 12
1101 North Central Avenue, P.O. Box 711, Phoenix AZ 85004. 602/257-1212. **Contact:** Human Resources. **World Wide Web address:** http://www.12news.com. **Description:** An NBC-affiliated television broadcasting station. **Positions advertised include:** Photojournalist; News Producer; Meteorologist; Editor; Broadcast Operator.

KTAR-AM 620
5300 North Central Avenue, Phoenix AZ 85012. 602/274-6200. **Contact:** Station Manager. **World Wide Web address:** http://www.ktar.com. **Description:** A news, talk, and sports format radio station affiliated with NBC. **Positions advertised include:** VP Human Resources; HR Generalist; Promotion/Marketing Director; Account Executive.

KTVK-TV/CHANNEL 3
5555 North Seventh Avenue, Phoenix AZ 85013. 602/207-3333. **Recorded jobline:** 602/207-3530. **Contact:** Human Resources. **World Wide Web address:** http://www.azfamily.com. **Description:** A television station. **Positions advertised include:** Assignment Editor. **Corporate headquarters location:** Dallas TX. **Parent company:** Belo Corporation owns and operates newspapers and network-affiliated television stations in seven U.S. metropolitan areas. **Listed on:** New York Stock Exchange. **Stock exchange symbol:** BLC.

KAMAN AEROSPACE CORPORATION
3480 Britannia Drive, Tucson AZ 85706. 520/889-7000. **Contact:** Human Resources. **World Wide Web address:** http://www.kamanaero.com. **Description:** Kaman Aerospace is a highly diversified International 500 company operating within two segments. The Diversified Technology segment develops value-added products that solve crucial problems in niche markets for military and industrial customers. Products include artificial intelligence systems, advanced technology systems, components for commercial airliners, military subcontract programs, and laser optics systems. The Distribution Segment distributes 800,000 repair and replacement products and services to nearly every sector of heavy and light industry and sells over 13,000 musical products and instruments. **Positions advertised include:** Electro-optical Engineer; Systems Analyst. **Corporate headquarters location:** Bloomfield CT. **Operations at this facility include:** This location develops electro-optics for aircraft. **Listed on:** NASDAQ. **Stock exchange symbol:** KAMNA. **Number of employees at this location:** 50. **Number of employees nationwide:** 3,000.

KEMPER INSURANCE COMPANY
11201 North Tatum Boulevard, Suite 220, Phoenix AZ 85028. 602/765-8425. **Contact:** Human Resources. **World Wide Web address:** http://www.kemperinsurance.com. **Description:** A holding company operating in six segments including automotive insurance; property insurance; casualty insurance; reinsurance; life insurance; and diversified operations composed principally of insurance, service, and financial companies. The company's main function is to oversee these operations and to provide subsidiaries with administrative services. Kemper Insurance oversees eight wholly owned insurance company subsidiaries.

KHIMETRICS
4343 North Scottsdale Road, Suite 345, Scottsdale AZ 85251. 480/609-2833. **Contact:** Human Resources Director. **E-mail address:** hr@khimetrics.com. **World Wide Web address:** http://www.khimetrics.com. **Description:** Provides revenue management services to retailers. **Positions advertised include:** Sales Representative; Research Manager; Project Consultant; Technical Consultant; Research Analyst; Business Analyst. **President/CEO:** Brent W. Lippman.

KINDRED HOSPITAL/PHOENIX
40 East Indianola Avenue, Phoenix AZ 85012. 602/280-7000. **Fax:** 602/280-7299. **Contact:** Personnel. **World Wide Web address:** http://www.kindredhealthcare.com. **Description:** Kindred Hospital/Phoenix is a 58-bed acute care hospital. Approximately 80 percent of the hospital's patients are transferred from the intensive care units of short-term, acute care hospitals. Services provided at Kindred include some surgical procedures and full-service renal dialysis on both the general floor and the intensive care unit. Technology services include a full-service laboratory, radiology department, and pharmacy. The hospital employs approximately 200 physicians in all medical specialties. **Positions advertised include:** Licensed Practical Nurse; Registered Nurse.

Corporate headquarters location: Louisville KY. **Parent company:** Kindred Healthcare, Inc. **Listed on:** NASDAQ. **Stock exchange symbol:** KIND.

KINETICS SYSTEMS
2825 West Thomas Road, Phoenix AZ 85017. 602/685-2000. **Fax:** 602/685-2299. **Contact:** Human Resources. **World Wide Web address:** http://www.kineticsgroup.com. **Description:** One of the largest mechanical contracting firms in Arizona, and one of the top 100 in the country. Kinetics Systems provides a wide array of commercial and industrial services including process piping, heating, ventilating, air conditioning, control systems, ultra-high-purity process piping, plumbing, special projects services, energy audits and retrofits, performance contracting, air and water balance, and backflow prevention. **Positions advertised include:** Manager, Plumbing Service; Accounts Payable Clerk. **Special programs:** Training. **Corporate headquarters location:** Santa Clara CA. **Parent company:** Kinetics Group, Inc. **Operations at this facility include:** Administration; Service. **Annual sales/revenues:** $51 - $100 million. **Number of employees at this location:** 135. **Number of employees nationwide:** 600.

KINGMAN REGIONAL MEDICAL CENTER
3269 Stockton Hill Road, Kingman AZ 86401. 928/757-2101. **Contact:** Human Resources. **World Wide Web address:** http://www.azkrmc.com. **Description:** A non-profit, 213-bed medical center. The surgery department offers preoperative, intraoperative, and postoperative care for adults and children. The telemetry unit, with 15 beds, is for patients requiring continuous cardiac monitoring but not requiring the intensive care unit's total patient care. The intensive care unit, staffed by special nurses under the direction of board-certified cardiologists, cares for critically ill patients, ranging from cardiac to pediatric patients. The medical center also offers physical and occupational therapy, educational and community programs, a pharmacy, nutritional services, emergency services, labor and delivery rooms, an outpatient clinic, and a diagnostic imaging center. Kingman Regional Medical Center is accredited by the Joint Commission on Accreditation of Healthcare Organizations and is certified as a participating hospital in the Medicare program. Founded in 1992. **Positions advertised include:** Certified Nursing Assistant; Pharmacist; Pharmacy Clinical Coordinator; Recruiter; Respiratory Therapist; Registered Nurse, Various Departments; Staffing Coordinator; Unit Coordinator.

KITCHELL CORPORATION
1707 East Highland Avenue, Suite 100, Phoenix AZ 85016. 602/264-4411. **Contact:** Kay Ellis, Director of Human Resources. **World Wide Web address:** http://www.kitchell.com. **Description:** A residential and commercial construction and construction management firm. **Positions advertised include:** Assistant Director/Director of Communications; Assistant Equipment Planner; Bio-Medical Professional; Construction Project Manager; Project Director; Project Manager; Project Superintendent.

KMART
12025 North 32nd Street, Phoenix AZ 85028. 602/996-4950. **Contact:** Manager. **E-mail address:** hireme@kmart.com. **World Wide Web address:** http://www.kmartcorp.com. **Description:** The company operates 1,500 Kmart discount stores in 49 states, Puerto Rico, and the Virgin Islands. It will complete a merger with Sears, Roebuck and Co. in 2005. **Corporate headquarters location:** Troy MI. **Listed on:** New York Stock Exchange. **Stock exchange symbol:** KM.

KNOLL PHOENIX GROUP
2901 North Central Avenue, Suite 160, Phoenix AZ 85012-2702. 602/265-2231. **Contact:** Regional Manager. **World Wide Web address:** http://www.knoll.com. **Description:** A manufacturer of furniture for executive, general office, institutional, and residential space. **Other U.S. locations:** Nationwide. **Operations at this facility include:** This location is a showroom.

KNOZALL SOFTWARE, INC.
9386 North Linnet Road, Casa Grande AZ 85222. 520/876-5357. **Contact:** Human Resources. **World Wide Web address:** http://www.knozall.com. **Description:** Manufactures networking utilities for local and wide area networks. Founded in 1990. **Corporate headquarters location:** This location.

KYOCERA AMERICA INC.
7812 East Acoma Drive, Scottsdale AZ 85260. 480/831-0711. **Fax:** 480/831-2599. **Contact:** Human Resources. **World Wide Web address:** http://www.kyocera.com. **Description:** Manufactures ceramic semiconductor packages. **Corporate headquarters location:** Kyoto, Japan. **Parent company:** Kyocera Corporation. **Listed on:** New York Stock Exchange. **Stock exchange symbol:** KYO.

LA FRONTERA CENTER, INC.
502 West 29th Street, Tucson AZ 85713. 520/838-3945. **Contact:** Human Resources. **World Wide Web address:** http://www.lafrontera.org. **Description:** A nonprofit, community-based, behavioral health center that provides mental health and chemical dependency services to residents of Pima County. The center operates 30 programs in 23 different facilities throughout Pima County. La Frontera Center provides services for infants born to addicted mothers, children with developmental disabilities, chemically dependent adults, and homeless adults with mental illnesses. The center also provides outreach, rehabilitation, and substance abuse recovery programs. Founded in 1968. **Company slogan:** We give people a chance. **Positions advertised include:** Behavioral Health Technician; Case Manager; Case Manager Aide; Clinical Supervisor; Clinician; Family Team Facilitator; LPN; RN. **Office hours:** Monday - Friday, 8:00 a.m. - 5:00 p.m.

LA QUINTA INN AND SUITES FLAGSTAFF
2015 South Beulah Boulevard, Flagstaff AZ 86001. 928/556-8666. **Contact:** Human Resources. **World Wide Web address:** http://www.laquinta.com. **Description:** A full-service hotel. **Corporate headquarters location:** Irving TX. **Parent company:** La Quinta Inns operates a nationwide chain of lodging inns. The company has more than 280 locations in 28 states. **Listed on:** New York Stock Exchange. **Stock exchange symbol:** LQI.

LABORATORY CORPORATION OF AMERICA (LABCORP)
3930 East Watkins Street, Suite 301, Phoenix AZ 85034. 602/454-8000. **Contact:** Human Resources. **World Wide Web address:** http://www.labcorp.com. **Description:** One of the nation's leading clinical laboratory companies, providing services primarily to physicians, hospitals, clinics, nursing homes, and other clinical labs nationwide. LabCorp performs tests on blood, urine, and other bodily fluids and tissue, aiding the diagnosis of disease. **Positions advertised include:** Phlebotomist. **Corporate headquarters location:** Burlington NC. **Listed on:** New York Stock Exchange. **Stock exchange symbol:** LH.

E.B. LANE & ASSOCIATES, INC.
733 West McDowell Road, Phoenix AZ 85007. 602/258-5263. **Contact:** Sharon Thompson, Director of Administration. **E-mail address:** sthompson@eblane.com. **World Wide Web address:** http://www.eblane.com. **Description:** A full-service advertising agency specializing in media buying, print media, public relations, radio producing, and television producing. **Corporate headquarters location:** This location.

LANSDALE SEMICONDUCTOR INC.
2412 West Huntington Drive, Tempe AZ 85282. 602/438-0123. **Fax:** 602/438-0138. **Contact:** Cheryl Warianka, Human Resources Manager. **E-mail address:** lansdale@lansdale.com. **World Wide Web address:** http://www.lansdale.com. **Description:** Manufactures semiconductors discontinued by such major manufacturers as Intel, Motorola, National/Fairchild, and Harris, and supports spare parts requirements by purchasing lines from the original manufacturer. **Corporate headquarters location:** This location.

LARSEN SUPPLY COMPANY
7045 West Galveston Street, Chandler AZ 85226. 602/961-0971. **Contact:** Human Resources. **World Wide Web address:** http://www.lasco.net. **Description:** Manufactures and distributes a wide range of plumbing fixtures and supplies.

ANDREW LAUREN INTERIORS
1311 West 21st Street, Tempe AZ 85282. 480/829-0054. **Contact:** Human Resources. **Description:** Engaged in commercial and residential interior decorating and design. **Corporate headquarters location:** This location.

SAMUEL LAWRENCE FURNITURE
1635 South 43rd Avenue, Phoenix AZ 85009. 602/352-3980. **Contact:** Human Resources. **Description:** Manufactures bedroom furniture. **Number of employees at this location:** 850.

LEGACY PARTNERS
5333 North Seventh Street, Suite C225, Phoenix AZ 85014. 602/248-0112. **Contact:** Human Resources. **World Wide Web address:** http://www.legacyptr.com. **Description:** A property management and development company. **Corporate headquarters location:** Foster City CA.

LIBERTY MUTUAL INSURANCE GROUP
2510 West Dunlap Avenue, Phoenix AZ 85021. 602/997-4700. **Contact:** Frank W. Evans, Sales Manager. **World Wide Web address:** http://www.libertymutual.com. **Description:** One of the largest multiline insurance organizations, with over $18 billion in assets and 450 offices in the United States and Canada. Liberty Mutual Insurance Group provides all lines of property, casualty, and life insurance. The company is also one of the largest private writers of workers' compensation insurance in the United States. **Positions advertised include:** Insurance Sales Counselor; Quality Assurance Associate; Customer Claims Rep; Consultant; Regional Medical Director. **Corporate headquarters location:** Boston MA. **Number of employees at this location:** 100. **Number of employees nationwide:** 20,000.

JOHN C. LINCOLN HOSPITAL DEER VALLEY
19829 North 27th Avenue, Phoenix AZ 85027. 623/879-6100. **Contact:** Human Resources. **World Wide Web address:** http://www.jcl.com/deervalley. **Description:** A 149-bed, not-for-profit community hospital. **Positions advertised include:** Charge RN; Clinical Dietician; CVOR Tech; Medical Technologist; Radiology Supervisor; RN, Various Departments. **Number of employees at this location:** 800.

JOHN C. LINCOLN HOSPITAL NORTH MOUNTAIN
250 East Dunlap Road, Phoenix AZ 85020. 602/943-2381. **Contact:** Human Resources. **World Wide Web address:** http://www.jcl/northmountain.com. **Description:** A 262-bed, not-for-profit community hospital. **Positions advertised include:** Audit Coordinator; Charge RN; Clinical Nurse Specialist; CAN; Lab Assistant; OR Tech; Nuclear Medicine Tech. **Number of employees at this location:** 2,500.

LITTLE AMERICA HOTEL
2515 East Butler Avenue, Flagstaff AZ 86004. 928/779-2741. **Fax:** 928/779-7983. **Contact:** Human Resources. **World Wide Web address:** http://www.littleamerica.com/flagstaff. **Description:** A full-service hotel and convention center.

LOCKHEED MARTIN CORPORATION
1300 South Litchfield Road, Goodyear AZ 85338. 623/925-7000. **Contact:** Human Resources. **E-mail address:** jobs.lmc@lmco.com. **World Wide Web address:** http://www.lockheedmartin.com. **Description:** Lockheed Martin produces ground-based sensor support equipment; command, control, communications, and intelligence (C3I) systems; and computer-based training systems. **Positions advertised include:** Business Development Analyst; Computer System Design Engineer; Embedded Software Engineer; Project Engineer; Research Engineer. **Corporate headquarters location:** Bethesda MD. **Other U.S. locations:** Nationwide. **Operations at this facility include:** This location produces Synthetic-Aperture Radar (SAR) and is expanding this technology into weapon delivery applications. **Listed on:** New York Stock Exchange. **Stock exchange symbol:** LMT. **Number of employees at this location:** 480. **Number of employees worldwide:** 130,000.

LONDON BRIDGE RESORT
1477 Queens Bay Road, Lake Havasu City AZ 86403. 928/855-0880. **Fax:** 928/505-4065. **Contact:** Manager. **World Wide Web address:** http://www.londonbridgeresort.com. **Description:** A full-service hotel and resort featuring 120 studios and suites, a restaurant, a dance club, an off-track betting facility, and a nine-hole executive golf course. **Positions advertised include:** Sales Manager; Assistant Manager. **Parent company:** Epic Resorts.

LONG REALTY
900 East River Road, Suite 100, Tucson AZ 85718. 520/888-8844. **Contact:** Human Resources. **World Wide Web address:** http://www.longrealty.com. **Description:** A real estate sales and management firm. **Special programs:** Internships. **Corporate headquarters location:** This location. **Number of employees at this location:** 250.

LOOMIS, FARGO & COMPANY
1800 West Broadway, Suite 3, Tempe AZ 85282. 480/829-3552. **Fax:** 480/829-3932. **Contact:** Human Resources. **World Wide Web address:** http://www.loomisfargo.com. **Description:** Provides armored transportation, cash vault services, and ATM services. **Corporate headquarters location:** Houston TX. **Other U.S. locations:** Nationwide. **Listed on:** Privately held.

MACHINE SOLUTIONS, INC.
2951 West Shamrell Boulevard, Flagstaff AZ 86001. 928/556-3109. **Fax:** 928/556-3084. **Contact:** Human Resources. **E-mail address:** careers@ machinesolutions.org. **World Wide Web address:** http://www.machinesolutions.org. **Description:** Provides proprietary mechanical solutions to a variety of complex process and device design challenges. MSI has been instrumental in automating or semi-automating several manual processes within catheter manufacturing organizations. Founded in 1999. **Positions advertised include:** CNC Machinist; Grinder; Assembler; Software Engineer; Mechanical Engineer; Business Development Manager; Sales and Marketing Coordinator. **Corporate headquarters location:** This location.

THE MAHONEY GROUP
719 East Cottonwood Lane, Casa Grande AZ 85222. 520/836-7483. **Fax:** 520/836-6681. **Contact:** Dawn Zimbelman. **E-mail address:** dzimbelman@mahoneygroup.com. **World Wide Web address:** http://www.mahoneygroup.com. **Description:** An independent insurance agency. **Other area locations include:** Kingman; Prescott; Phoenix; Mesa; Pintetop; Globe; Tucson. **President/CEO:** Doug Fyfe.

M&I MARSHALL & ILSLEY BANK
1990 West Chandler Boulevard, Chandler AZ 85224. 480/792-6300. **Contact:** Human Resources. **World Wide Web address:** http://www.mibank.com. **Description:** Provides banking, trust, and investment services to corporate, institutional, and individual clients nationwide. Marshall & Ilsley Corporation is a diversified interstate bank holding company. Other subsidiaries of the parent company include M&I Brokerage Services, Inc. (a brokerage company providing a full range of investment products including stocks, bonds, and mutual funds for individual investors and small businesses); M&I Capital Markets Group, Inc. (invests in small and medium-sized companies to help establish new businesses or recapitalize existing companies); M&I Data Services, Inc. (supplies data processing services and software for financial institutions throughout the United States and in foreign countries); M&I First National Leasing Corp. (leases equipment and machinery to businesses throughout the United States, primarily to middle-market corporations); M&I Insurance Services, Inc. (acts as an independent insurance agency providing a full range of insurance products including a variety of high-quality annuities); M&I Investment Management Corp. (manages investment portfolios for corporations, not-for-profit organizations, and individuals throughout the United States and also acts as investment advisor to a growing family of mutual funds, the Marshall Funds); M&I Mortgage Corp. (originates and services a wide variety of home mortgages for M&I banks and other financial institutions); M&I Trust Company of Arizona (provides trust and custodial services to clients in the Southwest); Marshall & Ilsley Trust Company (provides trust and custodial services to corporate, institutional, and individual clients nationwide); Marshall & Ilsley Trust Company of Florida (provides trust and custodial services to southeastern clients); and Richter-Schroeder Company, Inc. (provides construction loans and arranges permanent financing on income properties.) **Corporate headquarters location:** Milwaukee WI. **Listed on:** New York Stock Exchange. **Stock exchange symbol:** MI.

ME GLOBAL INC.
5857 Kyrene Road, Tempe AZ 85283-1731. 480/730-7500. **Fax:** 480/730-0649. **Contact:** Human Resources. **World Wide Web address:** http://www.meglobal.com. **Description:** Manufactures steel castings used specifically in the mining industry. **Number of employees at this location:** 120.

MTD SOUTHWEST INC.
550 North 54th Street, Chandler AZ 85226. 480/961-1002. **Contact:** Human Resources. **E-mail address:** careers@mtdproducts.com. **World Wide Web address:** http://www.mtdproducts.com. **Description:** Manufactures lawn and garden products such as weed trimmers, leaf blowers, and edge trimmers. **Positions advertised include:** Product Marketing Manager; Design Engineer.

MAIN STREET RESTAURANT GROUP, INC.
5050 North 40th Street, Suite 200, Phoenix AZ 85018. 602/852-9000. **Fax:** 602/852-9086. **Contact:** Personnel. **World Wide Web address:** http://www.mainandmain.com. **Description:** A casual dining and family entertainment company that operates four restaurant brands including TGI Friday's. **NOTE:** Entry-level positions are offered. **Positions advertised include:** Store Manager; Server; Busser; Door Person; Line Cook; Dishwasher; Prep Cook. **Corporate headquarters location:** This location. **Operations at this facility include:** Sales; Service. **Listed on:** NASDAQ. **Stock exchange symbol:** MAIN. **Annual sales/revenues:** $51 - $100 million. **Number of employees nationwide:** 4,500.

MARICOPA COUNTY COMMUNITY COLLEGE DISTRICT
2411 West 14th Street, Tempe AZ 85281. 480/731-8000. **Contact:** Human Resources. **World Wide Web address:** http://www.maricopa.edu. **Description:** A college district that consists of ten colleges and two skill centers. Founded in 1962.

MARICOPA, COUNTY OF
301 West Jefferson Street, Room 200, Phoenix AZ 85003. 602/506-3755. **Fax:** 602/506-7903. **Recorded jobline:** 602/506-3329. **Contact:** Human Resources. **World Wide Web address:** http://www.maricopa.gov. **Description:** Administrative offices for Maricopa County. **Positions advertised include:** Air Quality Inspector; Appraiser; Capital Facilities Manager; Career Guidance Specialist; Contracts Manager; Counselor; Deputy Constable; Director of Research; Engineering Plan Reviewer.

MARISCAL, WEEKS, McINTYRE, AND FRIEDLANDER
2901 North Central Avenue, Suite 200, Phoenix AZ 85012. 602/285-5000. **Contact:** Human Resources. **Description:** A law firm specializing in a variety of disciplines including corporate, personal injury, commercial, bankruptcy, intellectual property, and entertainment law.

MARRIOTT CAMELBACK INN
5402 East Lincoln Drive, Scottsdale AZ 85253. 480/948-1700. **Contact:** Manager of Human Resources. **World Wide Web address:** http://www.marriott.com. **Description:** A full-service, 453-room hotel and resort facility. **Corporate headquarters location:** Bethesda MD. **Parent company:** Marriott International Inc. **Listed on:** New York Stock Exchange. **Stock exchange symbol:** MAR.

MARYVALE HOSPITAL MEDICAL CENTER
5102 West Campbell Avenue, Phoenix AZ 85031. 623/848-5050. **Toll-free phone:** 800/581-9393. **Fax:** 623/848-5959. **Recorded jobline:** 623/848-5675. **Contact:** Human Resources. **World Wide Web address:** http://www.maryvalehospital.com. **Description:** Maryvale Hospital Medical Center is a 239-bed medical facility staffed by over 400 physicians. The medical facility's services include an emergency department; women and children's services, which offer each patient a private labor, delivery, recovery, and postpartum room; special and intermediate care units; surgery; cardiology services including EKGs, echocardiograms, cardiac dopplers, and treadmill tests; magnetic resonance imaging; oncology, radiation therapy, and other types of treatments and consultations; and rehabilitation services including physical therapy, occupational therapy, and speech-language pathology. **NOTE:** Entry-level positions, part-time jobs, and second and third shifts are offered. **Positions advertised include:** Cardiac Cath Lab Tech; Certified Nurse Assistant; Director, Education; Radiology Tech; RN, Various Departments. **Special programs:** Internships; Training; Co-ops; Summer Jobs. **Corporate headquarters location:** Nashville TN. **Parent company:** Vanguard Health. **Listed on:** Privately held. **Annual sales/revenues:** $51 - $100 million. **Number of employees at this location:** 1,100.

MAYO CLINIC HOSPITAL
5777 East Mayo Boulevard, Phoenix AZ 85054. 480/515-6296. **Contact:** Human Resources. **World Wide Web address:** http://www.mayoclinic.org. **Description:** Mayo Clinic Hospital has 202 licensed beds including 166 medical/surgical beds, 20 intensive/critical care beds, 7 rehabilitation beds and 9 skilled nursing beds. The hospital provides inpatient care to support the 65 medical and surgical specialties and programs of Mayo Clinic Scottsdale. Full emergency room services and urgent care are also provided at the hospital. **NOTE:** Search and apply for positions online. **Positions advertised include:** Clinical Nurse Specialist; Coder; Contract Resource Administrator; Critical Care Therapist; HR Manager; Occupational Therapist; Perfusionist.

MAYO CLINIC SCOTTSDALE
13400 East Shea Boulevard, Scottsdale AZ 85259. 480/301-8000. **Recorded jobline:** 480/301-7678. **Contact:** Human Resources. **World Wide Web address:** http://www.mayoclinic.org/scottsdale. **Description:** Operates an outpatient, multispecialty, group practice providing clinical care, laboratory and diagnostic radiological services, graduate medical education, and basic medical research. **Positions advertised include:** Cardiac Sonographer; CME Specialist; Coordinator, Research; Financial Counselor; IT Project Analyst; LPN; Physical Therapist; Revenue Analyst; RN. **Corporate headquarters location:** Rochester MN. **Other U.S. locations:** Jacksonville FL. **Number of employees nationwide:** 18,000.

McCARTHY BUILDING COMPANIES, INC.
80 East Rio Salado Parkway, Suite 310, Tempe AZ 85281. 480/449-4700. **Fax:** 480/449-4747. **Contact:** Human Resources. **E-mail address:** phx@mccarthy.com. **World Wide Web address:** http://www.mccarthy.com. **Description:** A privately owned construction firm that also operates a separate division for work on bridges. The company currently provides a wide range of construction-related services under construction management, general contract, and design/build contractual arrangements. **NOTE:** Search and apply for positions online. **Corporate headquarters location:** St. Louis MO. **Other U.S. locations:** Irvine CA; Sacramento CA; Seattle WA.

McDUFFY'S SPORTS BAR & OFF-TRACK BETTING
P.O. Box 1570, Tempe AZ 85281. 480/966-5600. **Physical address:** 230 West Fifth Street, Tempe AZ 85281. **Fax:** 480/966-6582. **Contact:** Hiring Manager. **World Wide Web address:** http://www.mcduffys.com. **Description:** Operates a full-service restaurant and bar and offers pool tables, games, and live entertainment. McDuffy's also houses off-track betting facilities. **Other area locations:** Peoria AZ.

McKESSON CORPORATION
3200 North Central Avenue, Suite 1700, Phoenix AZ 85012. 602/230-7575. **Fax:** 602/604-1464. **Contact:** Personnel. **E-mail address:** phxhumanresources@mckesson.com. **World Wide Web address:** http://www.mckesson.com. **Description:** Produces and sells software applications catering to the specific needs of medical facilities. Some of the programs include materials management, financial accounting, patient scheduling for operating rooms, and inventory control for health clinics. **Positions advertised include:** Customer Service Representative; Implementation Specialist; Project Manager; Six Sigma Balckbelt. **Corporate headquarters location:** San Francisco CA.

MEADWESTVACO
2415 East Camelback Road, Suite 700, Phoenix AZ 85016. 602/264-0326. **Contact:** Human Resources. **World Wide Web address:** http://www.meadwestvaco.com. **Description:** Overall, MeadWestvaco manufactures envelopes, paper cups, printed films, and transparent bags. Worldwide, the company operates 50 major facilities, which include paper and paperboard mills, converting plants, chemical plants, lumber mills, research and development laboratories, and real estate operations. **Corporate headquarters location:** Stamford CT. **Operations at this facility include:** This location manufactures and prints envelopes for area schools and government offices. **Listed on:** New York Stock Exchange. **Stock exchange symbol:** MWV.

MEDICIS PHARMACEUTICAL CORPORATION
8125 North Hayden Road, Scottsdale AZ 85258. 602/808-8800. **Fax:** 602/808-0822. **Contact:** Human Resources. **E-mail address:** employment@medicis.com. **World Wide Web address:** http://www.medicis.com. **Description:** Engaged in the sale and marketing of dermatological pharmaceuticals. **Positions advertised include:** Sr. Sales Analyst; Office Services Coordinator; Field Compliance Analyst; Sr. Product Manager; Stability Program Coordinator. **Corporate headquarters location:** This location. **Listed on:** New York Stock Exchange. **Stock exchange symbol:** MRX. **Annual sales/revenues:** $11 - $20 million.

MECHTRONICS
1601 East Broadway, Phoenix AZ 85040. 602/243-3000. **Contact:** Human Resources. **World Wide Web address:** http://www.ductech.com. **Description:** Manufactures electro-mechanical assemblies and enclosures for the defense and aerospace industries. **Corporate headquarters location:** Long Beach CA. **Other U.S. locations:** Phoenix AZ. **Parent company:** Ducommun Inc. **Operations at this facility include:** Administration; Manufacturing. **Listed on:** New York Stock Exchange. **Stock exchange symbol:** DCO. **Number of employees at this location:** 300.

MEDTRONIC MICROELECTRONICS CENTER
2343 West Medtronic Way, Tempe AZ 85281. 480/968-6411. **Fax:** 480/929-5430. **Contact:** Human Resources. **World Wide Web address:** http://www.medtronic.com. **Description:** An electronics manufacturer specializing in custom, high-reliability ICs and hybrid circuits for original equipment manufacturers and the health care market. **Positions advertised include:** Manufacturing Engineer; Product Engineer; Design Engineer; Test Engineer; QA Engineer; Reliability Engineer. **Corporate headquarters location:** Minneapolis MN. **Parent company:** Medtronic, Inc. **Listed on:** New York Stock Exchange. **Stock exchange symbol:** MDT.

MERIDIAN BANK
845 North Gilbert Road, Gilbert AZ 85234. 480/539-8900. **Contact:** Human Resources. **World Wide Web address:** http://www.meridianbank.com. **Description:** A bank. **Other area locations:** Avondale AZ; Fountain Hills AZ; Glendale AZ; Kierland AZ; Peoria AZ; Phoenix AZ; Scottsdale AZ; Wickenburg AZ. **Parent company:** Marquette Financial Companies.

MERITAGE CORPORATION
MONTEREY HOMES
6613 North Scottsdale Road, Suite 200, Scottsdale AZ 85250. 480/998-8700. **Contact:** Human Resources. **World Wide Web address:** http://www.meritagecorp.com. **Description:** Designs, builds, and sells mid-priced single-family homes in Arizona, Northern California, and Texas. **Office hours:** Monday - Friday, 8:00 a.m. - 5:00 p.m. **Corporate headquarters location:** This location. **Other U.S. locations:** San Francisco CA; Plano TX. **Listed on:** New York Stock Exchange. **Stock exchange symbol:** MTH. **Annual sales/revenues:** More than $100 million.

MERRILL LYNCH
2555 East Camelback Road, Suite 900, Phoenix AZ 85016. 602/954-5000. **Fax:** 602/954-5089. **Contact:** Personnel. **World Wide Web address:** http://www.ml.com. **Description:** A diversified financial service organization. Merrill Lynch is a major broker in securities, option contracts, commodities and financial futures contracts, and insurance. The company also deals with corporate and municipal securities and investment banking. **Positions advertised include:** Finance Manager; Senior Underwriter. **Corporate headquarters location:** New York NY.

MESA COMMUNITY COLLEGE
1833 West Southern Avenue, Mesa AZ 85202. 480/461-7000. **Contact:** Human Resources. **World Wide Web address:** http://www.mc.maricopa.edu. **Description:** A comprehensive community college that operates as a member of the Maricopa County Community College District. Three degrees are offered: associate of arts, associate of applied sciences, and associate of general studies. Twenty-eight career programs range from administration of justice to video production technology. Twenty-eight occupational certificates are also available in areas such as automotive, business, and child and family studies.

MESA GENERAL HOSPITAL MEDICAL CENTER
515 North Mesa Drive, Mesa AZ 85201. 480/969-9111. **Contact:** Human Resources. **World Wide Web address:** http://www.mesageneralhospital.com. **Description:** A medical center staffed by over 200 physicians. Mesa General Hospital's medical services include cardiac catheterization and angiography; critical care/intensive care units; a telemetry unit; an emergency department; a maternity unit offering a birthing room, labor, delivery, and recovery rooms, childbirth education classes, and a specially trained obstetrical nursing staff; a pediatrics/youth care unit; and a pharmacy. Mesa General Hospital offers inpatient and outpatient diagnostic services. The hospital also participates in several health maintenance organizations and preferred provider organizations. **Positions advertised include:** RN; Director Nursing Education; Nurse Auditor; Occupational Therapy Assistant; Respiratory Therapist. **Parent company:** IASIS Healthcare.

METALTRADE INC.
3515 South Winchester Road, Apache Junction AZ 85219-8564. 480/670-4700. **Contact:** Human Resources. **Description:** Engaged in the fabrication of structural steel and platework for industrial use.

METROPOLITAN LIFE INSURANCE COMPANY
7720 North 16th Street, Suite 380, Phoenix AZ 85020. 602/995-4140. **Contact:** Martin Battock, Agency Manager. **World Wide Web address:** http://www.metlife.com. **Description:** Part of the national insurance firm offering life, health, home, auto, and retirement policies. **Positions advertised include:** Reg Training Implementation Spec; Agency Sales Director. **Special programs:** Internships. **Corporate headquarters location:** New York NY. **Other U.S. locations:** Nationwide. **Operations at this facility include:** Sales; Service. **Listed on:** New York Stock Exchange. **Stock exchange symbol:** MET. **Number of employees nationwide:** 13,500.

MICROAGE
1330 West Southern Avenue, Tempe AZ 85282. 480/366-2200. **Fax:** 480/366-2224. **Contact:** Human Resources. **E-mail address:** employment@microage.com. **World Wide Web address:** http://www.microage.com. **Description:** Provides information technology products and services to institutions and governmental agencies throughout the country and corporations worldwide. **Positions advertised include:** Account Executive; Independent Sales Consultant; Sales Operational Specialist. **Corporate headquarters location:** This location. **Subsidiaries include:** MicroAge Channel Services provides purchasing and marketing services for resellers and vendors. MicroAge Infosystems Services coordinates and services large-account marketing efforts in conjunction with franchised resellers. MicroAge Product Services provides distribution, logistics, technical, and outsourcing services. MicroAge Technologies markets to value-added resellers. **Number of employees nationwide:** 6,100.

MICROCHIP TECHNOLOGY INC.
2355 West Chandler Boulevard, Chandler AZ 85224. 480/792-7200. **Fax:** 480/792-7790. **Recorded jobline:** 480/792-7777. **Contact:** Human Resources. **E-mail address:** resumes@microchip.com. **World Wide Web address:** http://www.microchip.com. **Description:** A semiconductor manufacturer. Microchip Technology specializes in 8-bit microcontrollers, eeproms, and other nonvolatile memory products. **Positions advertised include:** Manager, Software Development Languages; Divisional Marketing Manager; Principal Test Engineer; Sr. Product Engineer; Sr. Design Engineer. **Special programs:** Internships. **Corporate headquarters location:** This location. **Other U.S. locations:** Mountain View CA; Gresham OR. **Operations at this facility include:** Administration; Manufacturing; Research and Development; Sales. **Listed on:** NASDAQ. **Stock exchange symbol:** MCHP.

MICROHELIX, INC.
4581 South Butterfield Drive, Tucson AZ 85714. 520/512-8000. **Fax:** 520/512-8800. **Contact:** Human Resources. **World Wide Web address:** http://www.microhelix.com. **Description:** Designs and manufactures probe cables for ultrasound devices. **Corporate headquarters:** Portland OR. **International locations:** Nogales, Mexico. **Listed on:** NASDAQ. **Stock exchange symbol:** MHLX.

MICROSEMI CORPORATION
8700 East Thomas Road, Scottsdale AZ 85251. 480/941-6300. **Fax:** 480/941-6361. **Contact:** Human Resources. **World Wide Web address:** http://www.microsemi.com. **Description:** Microsemi Corporation manufactures and markets semiconductors and other products and provides related services for the military, aerospace, medical, computer, and telecommunications markets. Major products include high-reliability and silicon rectifiers and zener diodes; low-leakage and high-voltage diodes; temperature-compensated zener diodes; and a family of subminiature high-power transient suppressor diodes. **Positions advertised include:** Test Engineer; Sales Representative. **Corporate headquarters location:** Irvine CA. **Other U.S. locations:** CO; MA. **Operations at this facility include:** Wafer fabrication. **Listed on:** NASDAQ. **Stock exchange symbol:** MSCC.

MICROTEST, INC.
4747 North 22nd Street, Phoenix AZ 85016-4708. 602/952-6400. **Contact:** Human Resources. **World Wide Web address:** http://www.microtest.com. **Description:** Manufactures network connectivity products including Enterprise CD/DVD-sharing products and servers. Founded in 1984. **Parent company:** Fluke Networks.

MIDWAY AUTO TEAM
2201 West Bell Road, Phoenix AZ 85023. 602/866-6662. **Fax:** 602/866-6664. **Contact:** Human Resources. **World Wide Web address:** http://www.midwayautoteam.com. **Description:** An automotive dealership. **Corporate headquarters location:** This location. **Number of employees at this location:** 225.

MOHAVE COMMUNITY COLLEGE (MCC)
1971 Jagerson Avenue, Kingman AZ 86401. 928/757-0835. **Fax:** 928/757-0875. **Contact:** Human Resources. **World Wide Web address:** http://www.mohave.edu. **Description:** Mohave Community College (MCC) uses a microwave communications system to link the three campus sites in Bullhead, Kingman, and Lake Havasu City. MCC offers three associate's degrees and more than 45 certificates, including an associate of arts degree for students planning to transfer to a four-year institution; an associate of applied science degree designed to prepare students for employment; and an associate of science degree for students pursuing a career in the life sciences, nursing, and paramedic fields. Founded in 1971. **NOTE:** Part-time jobs are offered. **Corporate headquarters location:** This location. **Operations at this facility include:** Regional Headquarters. **Number of employees at this location:** 575.

MOHAVE COMMUNITY COLLEGE (MCC)
1977 West Acoma Boulevard West, Lake Havasu City AZ 86403. 928/855-7812. **Contact:** Human Resources. **World Wide Web address:** http://www.mohave.edu. **Description:** One location of the multicampus community college. Mohave Community College (MCC) uses a microwave communications system to link the three campus sites in Bullhead, Kingman, and Lake Havasu City. MCC offers three associates degrees and more than 45 certificates, including an associate of arts degree for students planning to transfer to a four-year institution; an associate of applied science degree designed to prepare students for employment; and an associate of science degree for students pursuing a career in the life sciences, nursing, and paramedic fields. Founded in 1971. **Corporate headquarters location:** Kingman AZ. **Other U.S. locations:** Bullhead City AZ; Colorado City AZ.

MORGAN STANLEY DEAN WITTER & COMPANY
2375 East Camelback Road, Suite 600, Phoenix AZ 85016-3493. 602/957-6777. **Contact:** Human Resources. **World Wide Web address:** http://www.msdw.com. **Description:** Offers diversified financial services including equities, fixed income securities, commodities, money market instruments, and investment banking services. **Positions advertised include:** Financial Advisor Trainee; Sales Assistant. **Corporate headquarters location:** New York NY. **Operations at this facility include:** Sales. **Number of employees at this location:** 85. **Number of employees nationwide:** 5,000.

MOTION INDUSTRIES INC.
2611 South Roosevelt, Suite 102, Tempe AZ 85282. 480/921-9800. **Contact:** Human Resources. **E-mail address:** jobs@motion-ind.com. **World Wide Web address:** http://www.motionindustries.com. **Description:** Distributes power transmission equipment. **Corporate headquarters location:** Birmingham AL. **Parent company:** Genuine Parts Company. **Listed on:** New York Stock Exchange. **Stock exchange symbol:** GPC.

MOTOROLA COMPUTER GROUP
2900 South Diablo Way, Tempe AZ 85282. 602/438-5720. **Contact:** Human Resources. **World Wide Web address:** http://www.motorola.com. **Description:** Motorola Computer Group supplies embedded computer technology. The Embedded Technologies group manufactures embedded board lines. The Technical Systems group manufactures electronic products used in industrial automation, electronic imaging, and communications applications. The New Ventures group researches emerging technologies. Positions advertised include: RFPA Senior Designer; RFIC Test Engineer; Nanoenergy Engineer; Senior Financial Analyst; Product Reliability and Quality Engineer. **Corporate headquarters location:** This location. **Operations at this facility include:** This location manufactures computer hardware. **Parent company:** Motorola Inc. **Listed on:** New York Stock Exchange. **Stock exchange symbol:** MOT.

MUSEUM OF NORTHERN ARIZONA
3101 North Fort Valley Road, Flagstaff AZ 86001. 928/774-5213. **Fax:** 928/779-1527. **Contact:** Human Resources. **World Wide Web address:** http://www.musnaz.org. **Description:** Offers exhibits and programs on the art, culture, and natural science of the Grand Canyon Region and the Colorado Plateau. Founded in 1928. **Positions advertised include:** Visitor Services Staff. **Special programs:** Internships. **Internship information:** Candidates for internships must complete an application. The museum also requires copies of college or university transcripts, and a typewritten statement. For more information, please visit the museum's Website. **Office hours:** Monday - Friday, 9:00 a.m. - 5:00 p.m.

MUTUAL INSURANCE COMPANY OF ARIZONA, INC. (MICA)
2602 East Thomas Road, Phoenix AZ 85016. 602/956-5276. **Contact:** Human Resources. **World Wide Web address:** http://www.mica-az.com. **Description:** A mutual insurance provider for medical malpractice and related casualty insurance to Arizona health care providers. MICA provides professional liability coverage to physicians, their groups and facilities, hospitals, and various types of managed care entities. Founded in 1975. **Positions advertised include:** Claim Representative.

NCR CORPORATION
525 West Alameda Drive, Tempe AZ 85282. 714/529-0231. **Contact:** Human Resources. **World Wide Web address:** http://www.ncr.com. **Description:** NCR Corporation is a worldwide provider of computer products and services. The company provides computer solutions to the retail, financial, and communications industries through several business units. NCR Computer Systems Group develops, manufactures, and markets computer systems; NCR Financial Systems Group is an industry leader in three target areas: financial delivery systems, relationship banking data warehousing solutions, and payments systems/item processing; NCR Retail Systems Group is a world leader in end-to-end retail solutions serving the food, general merchandise, and hospitality industries; NCR Worldwide Services provides data warehousing services solutions and end-to-end networking services, and designs, implements, and supports complex open systems environments; NCR Systemedia Group develops, produces, and markets a complete line of information products to satisfy customers' information technology needs including transaction processing media, auto identification media, business form communication products, managing documents and media, and a full line

of integrated equipment solutions. **Corporate headquarters location:** Dayton OH. **Other U.S. locations:** Nationwide. **Operations at this facility include:** This location is a manufacturing facility and sales office. **Listed on:** New York Stock Exchange. **Stock exchange symbol:** NCR. **Annual sales/revenues:** More than $100 million. **Number of employees nationwide:** 19,000. **Number of employees worldwide:** 38,000.

NACKARD BEVERAGE
4900 East Railhead Avenue, Flagstaff AZ 86004. 928/526-2229. **Contact:** Human Resources. **Description:** A wholesale distributor of beverages including bottled water, tea, beer, and wine coolers. **Parent company:** Nackard Companies, Inc. (Flagstaff AZ.)

NATIONAL OPTICAL ASTRONOMY OBSERVATORIES
950 North Cherry Avenue, P.O. Box 26732, Tucson AZ 85726. 520/318-8386. **Fax:** 520/318-8560. **Contact:** Sandra Abbey, Human Resources Manager. **E-mail address:** hrnoao@noao.edu. **World Wide Web address:** http://www.noao.edu. **Description:** Responsible for the development and continuing operation of the Kitt Peak National Observatory, which provides observational frontier research in optical astronomy. **Positions advertised include:** Engineering Project Manager; NGSC Assistant Astronomer/Scientist; WIYN Project Scientist; Scientific Programmer. **Corporate headquarters location:** Washington DC. **Other U.S. locations:** Hilo HI; Baltimore MD; Sunspot NM. **International locations:** Chile. **Parent company:** AURA. **Number of employees at this location:** 330. **Number of employees worldwide:** 500.

NAUTICAL INN RESORT & CONFERENCE CENTER
1000 McCulloch Boulevard, Lake Havasu City AZ 86403. 928/855-2141. **Toll-free phone:** 800/892-2141. **Fax:** 928/453-5808. **Contact:** Human Resources. **E-mail address:** careers@nauticalinn.com. **World Wide Web address:** http://www.nauticalinn.com. **Description:** A hotel with 150 beachfront room and condos. The resort features a private beach and waterfront restaurants. **Positions advertised include:** Assistant to Executive Housekeeper; Steward.

NAVAJO AREA INDIAN HEALTH SERVICE
P.O. Box 9020, Window Rock AZ 86515-9020. 928/871-5880. **Contact:** Recruiting. **World Wide Web address:** http://www.navajohealthjobs.ihs.gov. **Description:** Provides direct clinical care to 230,000 Native Americans at six hospitals and seven 24-hour health centers in the Four Corners area. **NOTE:** Clerkships and residency rotations for medical students and engineers are offered. **Positions advertised include:** Environmental Health Specialist; Civil Engineering Technician. **Special programs:** Internships. **Corporate headquarters location:** This location. **Parent company:** U.S. Public Health Service. **Operations at this facility include:** Administration. **Annual sales/revenues:** More than $100 million. **Number of employees at this location:** 250. **Number of employees nationwide:** 12,000.

NAVIGANT CONSULTING
Collier Center, 201 East Washington Street, Suite 1700, Phoenix AZ 85004. 602/257-0075. **Fax:** 602/254-6163. **Contact:** Human Resources. **World Wide Web address:** http://www.navigantconsulting.com. **Description:** Provides accounting, financial, economic, engineering, and consulting services related to business disputes. **Positions advertised include:** Managing Consultant; Director/MD-Transmission Business Enterprise. **Special programs:** Internships. **Corporate headquarters location:** Chicago IL. **Other U.S. locations:** Nationwide. **Operations at this facility include:** Administration. **Listed on:** New York Stock Exchange. **Stock exchange symbol:** NCI.

NESTLE PURINA PET CARE COMPANY
4700 East Nestle Purina Avenue, Flagstaff AZ 86004. 928/526-3645. **Contact:** Human Resources. **World Wide Web address:** http://www.purina.com. **Description:** Ralston Purina is one of the world's largest producers of dog and cat foods, commercial livestock feeds, cereals, canned goods including tuna and mushrooms, soybean meal, and soybean oil. Founded in 1894. **Corporate headquarters location:** St. Louis MO. **Other U.S. locations:** Nationwide. **Operations at this facility include:** This location produces a nationally advertised line of pet foods for dogs, cats, and other domestic animals.

NETPRO COMPUTING, INC.
4747 North 22nd Street, Suite 400, Phoenix AZ 85016. 602/346-3613. **Fax:** 602/346-3610. **Contact:** Human Resources. **E-mail address:** hr@netpro.com. **World Wide Web address:** http://www.netpro.com. **Description:** Designs and sells directory services management software. Founded in 1991. **Company slogan:** The directory experts. **Positions advertised include:** Senior Regional Account Manager. **Special programs:** Internships; Summer Jobs. **Corporate headquarters location:** This location. **Listed on:** Privately held. **Annual sales/revenues:** $11 - $20 million. **Number of employees at this location:** 85. **Number of employees nationwide:** 95.

NEW ENGLAND BUSINESS SERVICE INC. (NEBS)
2000 South Thompson Street, Flagstaff AZ 86001. 520/774-5184. **Fax:** 520/779-5732. **Contact:** Barbara Morrison, Personnel. **E-mail address:** bjmorrison@nebs.com. **World Wide Web address:** http://www.nebs.com. **Description:** New England Business Service's product line consists of over 1,000 standardized imprinted manual and computer business forms including billing forms, work orders, job proposals, and purchase orders; stationery including letterheads, envelopes, and business cards; checks and check-writing systems; and marketing products including advertising labels, pricing tags and labels, signage, and seasonal greeting cards. The company also offers a line of NEBS software, which includes check-writing, billing, and mailing applications, as well as a variety of simpler form-filling software; and One-Write Plus, a line of accounting software that integrates accounting and payroll functions with basic word processing, mail merge capabilities, a spreadsheet link, a backup utility, and a menu organizer. The computer forms are compatible with over 3,500 personal computer software packages developed by third parties and used by small businesses. **Positions advertised include:** Administrative Training Specialist. **Corporate headquarters location:** Groton MA. **Operations at this facility include:** This location is a telemarketing center. **Listed on:** New York Stock Exchange. **Stock exchange symbol:** NEB.

NEW YORK & COMPANY
455 North 3rd Street, Suite 170, Phoenix AZ 85004. 602/252-1250. **Contact:** Manager. **World Wide Web address:** http://www.newyorkandcompany.com. **Description:** A retail location of the national chain of women's moderately priced fashion apparel stores. **Corporate headquarters location:** New York NY.

NEW YORK LIFE INSURANCE COMPANY
4343 North Scottsdale Road, Suite 220, Scottsdale AZ 85251. 480/840-2000. **Contact:** General Manager. **World Wide Web address:** http://www.newyorklife.com. **Description:** An insurance and financial services firm. Present activities are in the areas of life, health, and disability insurance; annuities; and a wide range of products and services combining investment and term life insurance protection into one package. Services are provided to individuals, families, and businesses. **Corporate headquarters location:** New York NY.

NEWS AMERICA MARKETING
5020 South Ash Avenue, Suite 107, Tempe AZ 85282. 480/756-2226. **Contact:** Human Resources. **World Wide Web address:** http://www.newsamerica.com. **Description:** An in-store marketing company offering demonstrations, coupon advertising, instant coupon systems, and placard advertising on shopping carts. **Positions advertised include:** Market Manager; Unit Manager; Supervisor; In-Store Representative.

NEXPAK
6270 South Country Club Road, Tucson AZ 85706. 520/294-7646. **Contact:** Human Resources. **E-mail address:** jobs@nexpak.com. **World Wide Web address:** http://www.nexpak.com. **Description:** Manufactures plastic media storage containers and security containers for videocassettes and related items. **Corporate headquarters location:** North Canton OH. **Other U.S. locations:** Camarillo CA; El Dorado Hills CA; Duluth GA; Rockaway NJ; South Hackensack NJ; East Canton OH. **International locations:** The Netherlands.

NICOLI ENTERPRISES
1702 East Highland Avenue, Suite 312, Phoenix AZ 85016. 602/266-0001. **Contact:** Human Resources Department. **Description:** A holding company with subsidiaries engaged in operating resorts, grocery stores, gas stations, motels, and trailer parks.

NORTHERN ARIZONA UNIVERSITY
P.O. Box 4113, South San Francisco Street, Flagstaff AZ 86011-4113. 928/523-2222. **Fax:** 928/523-2220. **Contact:** Human Resources. **E-mail address:** human.resources@nau.edu. **World Wide Web address:** http://www.nau.edu. **Description:** A state university with an enrollment of 13,000 undergraduate and 5,800 graduate students. **NOTE:** Application form and instructions available online. **Positions advertised include:** Curator of Visual Materials; Academic Advisor; Assistant Clinical Professor, Various Departments; Assistant Professor, Various Departments; Development Officer; Director of Annual Giving; Instructor; Library Specialist. **Number of employees at this location:** 3,650.

NORTHLAND PIONEER COLLEGE
P.O. Box 610, Holbrook AZ 86025. 928/524-7670. **Fax:** 928/524-7612. **Contact:** Human Resources. **World Wide Web address:** http://www.northland.cc.az.us. **Description:** Northland Pioneer College is a comprehensive, multicampus community college. Northland Pioneer College has four campuses in Navajo County: the Painted Desert Campus at this location, the Little Colorado Campus in Winslow, the Silver Creek Campus in Snowflake/Taylor, and the White Mountain Campus in Show Low.

NORTHLAND PUBLISHING
2900 North Fort Valley Road, P.O. Box 1389, Flagstaff AZ 86001. 928/774-5251. **Toll-free phone:** 800/346-3257. **Fax:** 928/774-0592. **Contact:** Human Resources. **World Wide Web address:** http://www.northlandpub.com. **Description:** Publishes books on a wide range of topics including natural history, cooking, Western art and history, and Native American culture. Northland Publishing also publishes a number of children's books through Rising Moon (also at this location.) Founded in 1958. **Corporate headquarters location:** This location.

NORTHROP GRUMMAN ELECTRO-OPTICAL SYSTEMS
1215 South 52nd Street, Tempe AZ 85281. 480/968-4471. **Fax:** 480/967-5655. **Contact:** Anne Townsend, Human Resources Manager. **World Wide Web address:** http://www.northropgrumman.com. **Description:** Northrop Grumman manufactures military aircraft, commercial aircraft parts, and electronic systems. Northrop Grumman has developed the B-2 Stealth Bomber, parts for the F/A-18 and the 747, and radar equipment. Other operations include computer systems development for management and scientific applications. **Positions advertised include:** Electronics Engineer; Mechanical Engineer; Business Development Engineer; Manufacturing Engineer; Quality Engineering Manager. **Corporate headquarters location:** Los Angeles CA. **Operations at this facility include:** This location designs and manufactures image intensifiers, night vision devices, and infrared detectors. Products are used in the electronic counter-measure and night vision markets for both military and commercial applications. **Listed on:** New York Stock Exchange. **Stock exchange symbol:** NOC. **Number of employees at this location:** 450.

NORTHROP GRUMMAN MISSION SYSTEMS
400 West Fry Boulevard, Sierra Vista AZ 85635. 520/458-2858. **Contact:** Human Resources. **World Wide Web address:** http://www.northropgrumman.com. **Description:** Northrop Grumman manufactures military aircraft, commercial aircraft parts, and electronic systems. **Positions advertised include:** Senior Material Expediter; TEIS Business Operations Manager; C3ISR Analyst; Quality Assurance Engineer; Software Engineer.

NORTHWEST MEDICAL CENTER
6200 North La Cholla Boulevard, Tucson AZ 85741. 520/742-9000. **Contact:** Human Resources. **World Wide Web address:** http://www.northwestmedicalcenter.com. **Description:** Offers cardiopulmonary services including a cardiac catheterization lab, nuclear imaging, and a complete open heart program. The hospital also offers an emergency department; obstetrics/neonatology care; a cancer treatment center; around-the-clock ask-a-nurse, physician referral, and medical information; and a pediatric urgent care center. The hospital, serving as a medical base for several rural areas, operates clinics in Kearney and Catalina, and is a base station for several of the ambulance companies that operate in northwest Tucson. Founded in 1983. **Positions advertised include:** Registered Nurse, Various Departments; Physical Therapist; Collection Specialist; Vascular Technologist; Licensed Practical Nurse; Pharmacy Clinical Coordinator; Radiologic Technologist; Case Manager.

THE OKONITE COMPANY
401 West Baseline, Suite 201, Tempe AZ 85283. 480/838-8596. **Contact:** Human Resources. **World Wide Web address:** http://www.okonite.com. **Description:** Manufactures power cable for large-scale users. **NOTE:** Please send resumes to Personnel Department, The Okonite Company, P.O. Box 340, Ramsey NJ 07446. **Corporate headquarters location:** Ramsey NJ.

OLYMPIAN WORLDWIDE MOVING & STORAGE
2225 South 43rd Avenue, Suite 2, Phoenix AZ 85009. 602/269-2225. **Fax:** 602/233-9810. **Contact:** Personnel Department. **E-mail address:** ddavis@moveolympian.com. **World Wide Web address:** http://www.moveolympian.com. **Description:** Part of a nationwide company engaged in moving, storing, and distributing products. **Positions advertised include:** CDL Driver; Mover; Helper; Packer; Warehouse Staff. **Special programs:** Internships. **Corporate headquarters location:** Hillside IL. **Other U.S.**

locations: Nationwide. **Parent company:** The Bekins Company. **Listed on:** Privately held. **Number of employees at this location:** 20. **Number of employees nationwide:** 900.

ORBITAL SCIENCES CORPORATION
3380 South Price Road, Chandler AZ 85248. 480/899-6000. **Contact:** Human Resources. **World Wide Web address:** http://www.orbital.com. **Description:** Designs, manufactures, operates, and markets a broad range of space products. Products include space transportation systems including space and suborbital launch vehicles and orbit transfer vehicles; spacecraft systems and payloads including space sensors and instruments; satellite-based data communications services; and environmental and remote sensing services. Founded in 1982. **Positions advertised include:** Associate Mechanical Engineer; Project Manager; Senior Designer; Senior Mechanical Design Engineer; Principal Subcontracts Administrator; Project Analyst. **Corporate headquarters location:** Dulles VA. **Operations at this facility include:** Launch Systems Group. **Listed on:** New York Stock Exchange. **Stock exchange symbol:** ORB. **Number of employees nationwide:** 1,165.

ORTHOLOGIC
1275 West Washington Street, Tempe AZ 85281-1210. 602/286-5520. **Contact:** Human Resources. **E-mail address:** recruiter@olgc.com. **World Wide Web address:** http://www.orthologic.com. **Description:** A orthobiologics drug-development company focused on commercializing several potential therapeutics. **Positions advertised include:** Clinical Operations Manager; Research Scientist; Regulatory Affairs Specialist; Toxicology Pharmacology Manager. **Corporate headquarters location:** This location. **Listed on:** NASDAQ. **Stock exchange symbol:** OLGC.

OTIS ELEVATOR COMPANY
4405 East Baseline Road, Suite 123, Phoenix AZ 85042. 602/431-1181. **Fax:** 602/431-9023. **Contact:** Human Resources. **World Wide Web address:** http://www.nao.otis.com. **Description:** A manufacturer of elevators and escalators. **Corporate headquarters location:** Hartford CT. **Parent company:** United Technologies Corp. **Listed on:** New York Stock Exchange. **Stock exchange symbol:** UTX.

OTTAWA UNIVERSITY
10020 North 25th Avenue, Phoenix AZ 85021. 602/371-1188. **Contact:** Human Resources. **World Wide Web address:** http://www.ottawa.edu. **Description:** A university offering programs in business administration, education, psychology, human services, human resources, and public administration. The university also offers a special transfer program for Maricopa Community College students and degree programs for adult learners. Graduate programs include human resources management, human resources and organizational development, and counseling. Ottawa University is accredited by the North Central Association of Colleges and Schools. Founded in 1865. **Positions advertised include:** Registration Coordinator; Business Manager; Director of Graduate Education; Adjunct Instructors. **Corporate headquarters location:** Ottawa KS. **Other area locations:** Scottsdale AZ; Mesa AZ.

PPG INDUSTRIES, INC.
4535 East Elwood Street, Suite 110, Phoenix AZ 85040. 602/276-2995. **Contact:** Al Hendrickson, Branch Manager. **World Wide Web address:** http://www.ppg.com. **Description:** PPG Industries is a supplier of products for manufacturing, building, automotive, processing, and numerous other world industries. Products include decorative and protective coatings, flat glass and fabricated glass products, continuous-strand fiberglass, and industrial and specialty chemicals. Founded in 1883. **Corporate headquarters location:** Pittsburgh PA. **International locations:** Canada; China; France; Germany; Ireland; Italy; Mexico; Portugal; Spain; Taiwan; The Netherlands; United Kingdom. **Operations at this facility include: Listed on:** New York Stock Exchange. **Stock exchange symbol:** PPG.

PACIFIC SCIENTIFIC ENERGETIC MATERIALS COMPANY
7073 West Willis Drive, Chandler AZ 85226. 480/763-3000. **Fax:** 520/796-2023. **Contact:** Human Resources. **E-mail address:** HR@psemc.com. **World Wide Web address:** http://www.psemc.com. **Description:** Manufactures a wide range of pyrotechnic devices in support of fire suppression systems on commercial and military aircraft. **Corporate headquarters location:** This location. **Other U.S. locations:** Valencia CA; Hollister CA; San Carlos CA. **Parent company:** Danaher Corporation.

PALM HARBOR HOMES INC.
309 South Perry Lane, Tempe AZ 85281. 480/967-7877. **Toll-free phone:** 800/467-7877. **Contact:** Human Resources. **World Wide Web address:** http://www.palmharbor.com. **Description:** Manufactures, sells, and finances prefabricated homes. **Corporate headquarters location:** Addison TX. **Listed on:** NASDAQ. **Stock exchange symbol:** PHHM.

PARADISE VALLEY HOSPITAL
3929 East Bell Road, Phoenix AZ 85032. 602/923-5000. **Contact:** Human Resources. **World Wide Web address:** http://www.paradisevalleyhospital.com. **Description:** A 140-bed facility. The hospital's services include the Northeast Valley's only hospital-based, 24-hour, emergency department; the Women's Center, designed for obstetrical and gynecological patients; the nursing unit; a diagnostic imaging department; and inpatient and outpatient rehabilitation services including physical, speech, and occupational therapy. The hospital also provides comprehensive mental health services to assist adults ages 55 and older suffering from emotional difficulties. **Positions advertised include:** Admitting Specialist; Case Manager; Chief Nursing Officer; ER Tech; RN, Various Departments.

PARENTS ANONYMOUS, INC.
202 South First Avenue, Suite 103, Yuma AZ 85364. 928/329-7372. **Contact:** Human Resources. **World Wide Web address:** http://www.parentsanonymous.org. **Description:** Operates the nation's largest and oldest child abuse prevention, education, and treatment programs.

PEGASUS SOLUTIONS, INC.
14000 North Pima Road, Suite 100, Scottsdale AZ 85260. 480/624-6000. **Fax:** 480/624-6687. **Contact:** Personnel. **E-mail address:** jobs@pegs.com. **World Wide Web address:** http://www.pegs.com. **Description:** A leading provider of software and other technology solutions for the travel/tourism industry. **Positions advertised include:** Reservations Agent; Business Analyst; Director, Testing: Data Services Trainer; Supervisor, Database; Database Agent; Implementations Coordinator. **Corporate headquarters:** Dallas TX. **Listed on:** NASDAQ. **Stock exchange symbol:** PEGS.

PENSKE TRUCK LEASING
3519 East 34th Street, Tucson AZ 85713. 520/327-5987. **Contact:** Larry Zitzman, Branch Manager. **World Wide Web address:** http://www.penske.com. **Description:** Offices of the automotive and bulk materials transporting company.

PEP BOYS
400 South Arizona Avenue, Chandler AZ 85225. 480/899-0822. **Contact:** Store Manager. **World Wide Web address:** http://www.pepboys.com. **Description:** Regional offices for a chain of auto parts supply and service centers. Pep Boys primarily engages in the retail sale of a wide range of automotive parts and accessories, and the installation of automobile components and merchandise through over 400 stores in 24 states. **Corporate headquarters location:** Philadelphia PA. **Listed on:** New York Stock Exchange. **Stock exchange symbol:** PBY.

PERINI BUILDING COMPANY
360 East Coronado Road, Phoenix AZ 85004. 602/256-6777. **Contact:** Human Resources. **World Wide Web address:** http://www.periniwest.com. **Description:** Provides general contracting and construction management services. **Corporate headquarters location:** Framingham MA. **Parent company:** Perini Corporation. **Operations at this facility include:** Administration. **Listed on:** American Stock Exchange. **Stock exchange symbol:** PCR.

PETER PIPER PIZZA, INC.
14635 North Kierland Boulevard, Suite 160, Scottsdale AZ 85254. 480/609-6400. **Toll-free phone:** 800/899-3425. **Fax:** 480/609-6520. **Contact:** Kenny Holmes, Director of Human Resources. **E-mail address:** recruiting@peterpiperpizza.com. **World Wide Web address:** http://www.peterpiperpizza.com. **Description:** Operates a chain of family-style pizza restaurants with 120 locations. Founded in 1973. **NOTE:** Entry-level positions and second and third shifts are offered. **Company slogan:** The pizza people pick. **Special programs:** Training; Summer Jobs. **Corporate headquarters location:** This location. **Other U.S. locations:** CA; NV; TX; UT. **Operations at this facility include:** Administration. **Annual sales/revenues:** $51 - $100 million. **Number of employees at this location:** 65. **Number of employees nationwide:** 1,600.

PETSMART, INC.
19601 North 27th Avenue, Phoenix AZ 85027. 623/580-6100. **Fax:** 623/580-6506. **Contact:** Human Resources. **World Wide Web address:** http://www.petsmart.com. **Description:** A national retail chain that sells pet supplies and animals. PETsMART also offers veterinary services, animal adoption centers, grooming services, and obedience classes. **Positions advertised include:** Payroll Specialist; Presentation Support Specialist; Industrial Engineer; Director of Engineering and Facilities; Inventory Coordinator; Financial Analyst; Senior Application Developer; Manager, Database Administration. **Corporate headquarters location:** This location. **Other U.S. locations:** Nationwide. **Listed on:** NASDAQ. **Stock exchange symbol:** PETM.

PHELPS DODGE CORP.
One North Central Avenue, Phoenix AZ 85004-4415. 602.366-8100. **Contact:** Human Resources. **World Wide Web address:** http://www.phelpsdodge.com. **Description:** The world's second-largest producer of copper and the world's largest publicly traded copper producer. The company is a world leader in the production of molybdenum, the largest producer of molybdenum-based chemicals and continuous-cast copper rod, and among the leading producers of magnet wire and carbon black. **Positions advertised include:** HR Systems Coordinator; Environmental Engineer; Sr. Accounting Analyst; Manager, Remediation Projects; Peoplesoft Systems Administrator. **Corporate headquarters location:** This location. **Listed on:** New York Stock Exchange. **Stock exchange symbol:** PD. **Number of employees worldwide:** 14,000.

PHILIPS SEMICONDUCTORS
8375 South River Parkway, Tempe AZ 85284. 480/752-8574. **Contact:** Human Resources. **World Wide Web address:** http://www.semiconductors.philips.com. **Description:** Manufactures and distributes integrated circuits for semiconductors. **Positions advertised include:** Test Engineering Manager; Design Engineer. **Corporate headquarters location:** Amsterdam, The Netherlands. **Parent company:** Koninklijke Philips Electronics NV. **Listed on:** New York Stock Exchange. **Stock exchange symbol:** PHG. **Number of employees nationwide:** 2,500.

THE PHOENICIAN
6000 East Camelback Road, Scottsdale AZ 85251. 480/423-2595. **Fax:** 480/423-2543. **Recorded jobline:** 480/423-2555. **Contact:** Alison Rodriguez, Human Resources Employment Manager. **E-mail address:** alison.rodriguez@luxurycollection.com. **World Wide Web address:** http://www.thephoenician.com. **Description:** Operates a chain of hotels and resorts. **NOTE:** Entry-level positions, part-time jobs, and second and third shifts are offered. Applications can be obtained and submitted Monday through Friday from 8:00 a.m. until 5:00 p.m. **Positions advertised include:** Human Resources Manager; Banquet Assistant Manager; Chief Engineer; Resort Manager; Spa Director; . **Special programs:** Internships. **Parent company:** Starwood Hotels & Resorts Worldwide, Inc. **Listed on:** New York Stock Exchange. **Stock exchange symbol:** HOT. **Number of employees at this location:** 1,700.

PHOENIX ART MUSEUM
1625 North Central Avenue, Phoenix AZ 85004-1685. 602/257-1880. **Fax:** 602/253-8662. **Contact:** Human Resources Manager. **E-mail address:** hr@phxart.org. **World Wide Web address:** http://www.phxart.org. **Description:** A nonprofit visual arts museum with collections including Asian art, European art, Latin American art, decorative arts, and fashion design. This location also hires seasonally. Founded in 1949. **NOTE:** Entry-level positions, part-time jobs, and second and third shifts are offered. Also, when sending resume, please list the position that you are applying for and send it to the attention of the Human Resources Manager. **Positions advertised include:** Security Shift Captain; Curatorial Assistant. **Special programs:** Internships. **Office hours:** Tuesday - Sunday, 10:00 a.m. - 5:00 p.m. **Corporate headquarters location:** This location. **Listed on:** Privately held. **Number of employees at this location:** 110.

PHOENIX COCA-COLA BOTTLING COMPANY
P.O. Box 20008, Phoenix AZ 85036. 480/345-3000. **Contact:** Human Resources. **World Wide Web address:** http://www.coca-cola.com. **Description:** Bottles, warehouses, and distributes Coca-Cola products. **Parent company:** Coca-Cola Enterprises Inc. is one of the world's largest marketers, distributors, and producers of bottle and can products of the Coca-Cola Company, which are among the most popular beverage brands in the world. The company also serves as a significant bottler of several other national and regional beverage brands such as Barq's and Dr. Pepper. Coca-Cola Enterprises is in the liquid nonalcoholic refreshment business, which extends the company's product line beyond traditional carbonated soft drink categories to beverages such as still and sparkling waters, juices, isotonics, and teas. The company operates in 38 states, the District of Columbia, the U.S. Virgin Islands, the Islands of Tortola and Grand Cayman, and the Netherlands. Including recent acquisitions, Coca-Cola Enterprises franchise territories encompass a population of over 154 million people, representing 54 percent of the population of the United States and all of the Netherlands. Coca-Cola Enterprises employs approximately 30,000 individuals who operate the 268 facilities, approximately 24,000 vehicles, and over 860,000 vending machines, beverage dispensers, and coolers used to market, distribute, and produce the company's products. **Corporate headquarters location:** Charlotte NC. **Listed on:**

NASDAQ. **Stock exchange symbol:** COKE. **Number of employees worldwide:** 30,000.

PHOENIX COLLEGE
1202 West Thomas Road, Phoenix AZ 85013. 602/264-2492. **Contact:** Human Resources. **World Wide Web address:** http://www.pc.maricopa.edu. **Description:** A two-year community college enrolling over 14,000 students. Degrees include an associate of arts, an associate of general studies, and an associate of applied science. Phoenix College also offers 45 occupational programs, several of which are the only ones of their type in the country or state, and also offers 175 computer courses for both the novice and the professional. Founded in 1920. **Positions advertised include:** Instructor, Various Departments; Dean of Instruction; Facilities Manager; Senior Associate Dean.

PHOENIX GREYHOUND PARK
P.O. Box 20300, Phoenix AZ 85036-0300. 602/273-7181. **Contact:** Human Resources. **World Wide Web address:** http://www.phoenixgreyhoundpark.com. **Description:** Operates a greyhound racing track. **Parent company:** Delaware North Companies. **Number of employees at this location:** 500.

PHOENIX MEMORIAL HEALTH SYSTEM
1201 South Seventh Avenue, Phoenix AZ 85007. 602/258-5111. **Fax:** 602/824-3420. **Contact:** Human Resources Department. **World Wide Web address:** http://www.phxmemorialhospital.com. **Description:** A general acute care hospital and health services network. Phoenix Memorial's specialties include total joint replacement and cardiovascular services. **Positions advertised include:** Charge Nurse; RN, Various Departments; Physical Therapist. **Corporate headquarters location:** This location. **Operations at this facility include:** Administration. **Number of employees at this location:** 1,100.

PHOENIX SUNS
201 East Jefferson Street, Phoenix AZ 85004. 602/379-7900. **Fax:** 602/379-7990. **Recorded jobline:** 602/379-2088. **Contact:** Human Resources. **World Wide Web address:** http://www.nba.com/suns. **Description:** Houses administrative offices for the NBA team. **Corporate headquarters location:** This location.

PIMALCO
6833 West Willis Road, Box 5050, Chandler AZ 85226. 520/796-1098. **Contact:** Human Resources. **Description:** An aluminum extrusion plant. Pimalco manufactures unfinished aluminum products including components for airplane frames and baseball bats. **Parent company:** Alcoa Inc.

PING, INC.
2201 West Desert Cove, Phoenix AZ 85029. 602/870-5000. **Fax:** 602/687-4487. **Recorded jobline:** 602/687-5779. **Contact:** Human Resources. **World Wide Web address:** http://www.pinggolf.com. **Description:** Manufactures and distributes a line of high-quality golf clubs and equipment including balls, irons, woods, and putters. **NOTE:** Please call the jobline for a listing of available positions. **Operations at this facility include:** Administration; Manufacturing; Research and Development; Service.

SECURITAS
1607 South Pantano Road, Suite 401, Tucson AZ 85710. 520/296-3833. **Fax:** 520/296-2464. **Contact:** Human Resources. **World Wide Web address:** http://www.pinkertons.com. **Description:** One of the oldest and largest nongovernmental security service organizations in the world. The company's principal business is providing high-quality security, investigative, and consulting services to commercial, industrial, institutional, governmental, and residential clients. Pinkerton Security operates through more than 125 offices in the United States, Canada, and Great Britain. Major services include industrial and nuclear plant security, institutional security, commercial and residential building security, retail security, construction security, patrol and inspection services, community security, sports and special events services, K-9 patrol services, courier services, inventory services, investigation services, security consultation, and equipment evaluation. **Parent company:** Securitas AB (Stockholm, Sweden.)

PINNACLE WEST CAPITAL CORPORATION
P.O. Box 53999, Phoenix AZ 85072-3999. 602/250-1000. **Fax:** 602/379-2545. **Contact:** Human Resources. **E-mail address:** staffing@pinnaclewest.com. **World Wide Web address:** http://www.pinnaclewest.com. **Description:** A diversified holding company with interests in electricity, banking, real estate, and mining. **Positions advertised include:** Energy Consultant; Sr. Research Analyst; Sr. FERC Regulatory Attorney. **Office hours:** Monday - Friday, 8:30 a.m. - 5:30 p.m. **Corporate headquarters location:** This location. **Subsidiaries include:** Arizona Public Service (APS) is the largest electric utility in the state, servicing over 600,000 customers in all or part of 11 of Arizona's 15 counties. SunCor Development Company develops commercial, industrial, and residential properties. Another subsidiary, El Dorado, is a venture capital investment company with diverse interests. **Listed on:** New York Stock Exchange. **Stock exchange symbol:** PNW. **Number of employees at this location:** 40.

THE POINTE HILTON AT SQUAW PEAK
7677 North 16th Street, Phoenix AZ 85020. 602/906-3880. **Fax:** 602/906-3885. **Contact:** Human Resources. **E-mail address:** pointe_sp@hilton.com. **World Wide Web address:** http://www.pointehilton.com. **Description:** A resort offering guest accommodations, five dining establishments, and recreational activities including an eight-acre water park. **Positions advertised include:** Chef de Cuisine. **Corporate headquarters location:** Beverly Hills CA. **Parent company:** Hilton Hotels Corporation is a hospitality, gaming, and lodging company. With its Hilton and Conrad brands, the company develops, owns, manages, and franchises hotel-casinos, resorts, vacation ownership, and hotel properties throughout the world. Other subsidiaries of Hilton Hotels Corporation include Conrad International, Hilton Equipment Corporation, Hilton Grand Vacation Company, and Hilton Inns, Inc. **Operations at this facility include:** Administration; Sales. **Listed on:** New York Stock Exchange. **Stock exchange symbol:** HLT. **Number of employees at this location:** 700.

THE POINTE HILTON AT TAPATIO CLIFFS
11111 North Seventh Street, Phoenix AZ 85020. 602/866-7500. **Fax:** 602/375-4660. **Contact:** Human Resources. **E-mail address:** PHXTC-Tapatio_Jobs@hilton.com. **World Wide Web address:** http://www. pointehilton.com. **Description:** A resort offering several dining establishments and recreational activities including a PGA 18-hole championship golf course. **NOTE:** Entry-level positions and second and third shifts are offered. **Positions advertised include:** Auditor; Executive Chef; Engineer. **Corporate headquarters location:** Beverly Hills CA. **Parent company:** Hilton Hotels Corporation is a hospitality, gaming, and lodging company. With its Hilton and Conrad brands, the company develops, owns, manages, and franchises hotel-casinos, resorts, vacation ownership, and hotel properties throughout the world. Other subsidiaries of Hilton Hotels Corporation include Conrad International, Hilton Equipment Corporation, Hilton Grand Vacation Company, and Hilton Inns, Inc. **Listed on:** New York Stock Exchange. **Stock exchange symbol:** HLT.

POINTE SOUTH MOUNTAIN RESORT
7777 South Pointe Parkway, Phoenix AZ 85044. 602/438-9000. **Contact:** Human Resources. **World Wide Web address:** http://www.pointesouthmtn.com. **Description:** A resort offering guest accommodations, five dining establishments, and recreational activities, including an 18-hole championship golf course. **Positions advertised include:** Food & Beverage Director; Director Group Sales; National Sales Manager. **Parent company:** Destination Hotels & Resorts.

PRESCOTT YMCA OF YAVAPI COUNTY, INC.
750 Whipple Street, Prescott AZ 86301. 928/445-7221. **Fax:** 928/445-5135. **Contact:** Human Resources. **World Wide Web address:** http://www.prescottymca.org. **Description:** A community-based, service organization dedicated to building the spirit, mind, and body of each individual with programs unique to each community. With programs emphasizing education, health, and recreation, the YMCA serves men, women, and children of all ages, religions, races, and abilities, with a focus on youth. **Corporate headquarters location:** Chicago IL.

PRICEWATERHOUSECOOPERS
1850 North Central Avenue, Suite 700, Phoenix AZ 85004-4563. 602/364-8000. **Contact:** Human Resources. **World Wide Web address:** http://www.pwcglobal.com. **Description:** One of the largest certified public accounting firms in the world. PricewaterhouseCoopers provides public accounting, business advisory, management consulting, and taxation services. Positions advertised include: Assurance Senior Associate; Systems Assurance Senior/Assoc.; Manager; Assurance Manager; ISG Senior Manager. **Corporate headquarters location:** New York NY. **Other U.S. locations:** Nationwide.

PROCTER & GAMBLE
2050 South 35th Avenue, Phoenix AZ 85009. 602/269-2171. **Contact:** Human Resources Manager. **World Wide Web address:** http://www.pg.com. **Description:** Procter & Gamble manufactures over 300 laundry, cleaning, paper, beauty, health care, food, and beverage products in more than 140 countries. Brand name products include Cover Girl, Max Factor, Vidal Sassoon, Clearasil, and Noxzema health and beauty products; Pepto-Bismol, Vicks, and NyQuil health care products; Bounce, Downy, Tide, Comet, and Mr. Clean cleaning products; Luvs, Pampers, Always, Tampax, Bounty, Charmin, and Puffs paper products; and Crisco, Folgers, Millstone, Sunny Delight, and Pringles food and beverage products. **Positions advertised include:** Manufacturing Engineer; Plant Technician. **Corporate headquarters location:** Cincinnati OH. **Operations at this facility include:** This location manufactures Metamucil. **Listed on:** New York Stock Exchange. **Stock exchange symbol:** PG.

PRODUCT DEVELOPMENT CORPORATION
402 North 37th Drive, Suite 102, Phoenix AZ 85009. 602/233-9111. **Fax:** 602/233-9223. **Contact:** Shirley Agy, Human Resources. **Description:** A nonprofit company that distributes telephone directories. **NOTE:** Entry-level positions are offered. **Office hours:** Monday - Friday, 8:00 a.m. - 4:30 p.m. **Corporate headquarters location:** Monterey CA. **Other U.S. locations:**

PRUDENTIAL SECURITIES
2415 East Camelback Road, Suite 1000, Phoenix AZ 85016-4201. 602/952-2243. **Contact:** Human Resources. **World Wide Web address:** http://www.prudential.com. **Description:** An international securities brokerage and investment firm. The company offers clients more than 70 different investment products including stocks, options, bonds, commodities, tax-favored investments, and insurance, as well as several specialized financial services. Prudential currently operates more than 240 offices in 17 countries. **Corporate headquarters location:** New York NY. **Parent company:** Prudential Insurance Company.

PULTE HOMES, INC.
15333 North Pima Road, Suite 300, Scottsdale AZ 85260. 480/598-2100. **Contact:** Human Resources. **World Wide Web address:** http://www.pulte.com. **Description:** One of the largest independent, publicly-owned home-building companies in the United States. Pulte Home Corporation's principal business is the construction and sale of moderately priced, single-family homes. **Positions advertised include:** Cost Accountant; Staff Accountant. **Corporate headquarters location:** Bloomfield Hills MI. **Listed on:** New York Stock Exchange. **Stock exchange symbol:** PHM. **Number of employees at this location:** 130. **Number of employees nationwide:** 5,000.

QUALITY HOTEL & RESORT
3600 North Second Avenue, Phoenix AZ 85013. 602/248-0222. **Contact:** Human Resources. **Description:** A 280-room hotel.

QUALITY SUITES
3101 North 32nd Street, Phoenix AZ 85018. 602/956-4900. **Contact:** Sonal Shah, General Manager. **Description:** A hotel with 76 suites. **Special programs:** Internships. **Corporate headquarters location:** El Cajon CA. **Operations at this facility include:** Service. **Listed on:** Privately held. **Number of employees at this location:** 40.

R&K BUILDING SUPPLIES
25 West Baseline Road, Gilbert AZ 85233. 480/892-0025. **Contact:** Human Resources. **World Wide Web address:** http://www.randkbuildingsupplies.com. **Description:** A wholesaler of lumber and related products. **Other area locations:** Scottsdale AZ.

R&R PRODUCTS, INC.
3334 East Milber Street, Tucson AZ 85714. 520/889-3593. **Contact:** Human Resources. **World Wide Web address:** http://www.rrproducts.com. **Description:** Manufactures replacement parts for equipment used on golf courses.

RBC DAIN RAUSCHER
16150 North Arrowhead Fountains Center Drive, Suite 300, Peoria AZ 85382. 623/334-9033. **Fax:** 623/334-2633. **Contact:** Personnel. **World Wide Web address:** http://www.rbcdain.com. **Description:** Offers investment banking and brokerage services including mutual funds, money market funds, options, commodities, tax shelters, financial futures, municipal bonds, life insurance deferred annuities, and IRA and Keogh plans. Founded in 1909. **Corporate headquarters location:** Minneapolis MN. **Other area locations:** Phoenix AZ; Scottsdale AZ; Tucson AZ. **Parent company:** Royal Bank of Canada.

THE RABB PENNY LAW FIRM
3320 North Campbell Avenue, Suite 150, Tucson AZ 85719. 520/888-6740. **World Wide Web address:** http://www.rabbpenny.com. **Contact:** Human Resources. **Description:** A law firm specializing in personal injury. **Other area locations include:** Tempe AZ; Flagstaff AZ.

RADISSON RESORT SCOTTSDALE
7171 North Scottsdale Road, Scottsdale AZ 85253. 480/991-3800. **Contact:** Human Resources. **World Wide Web address:** http://www.radisson.com. **Description:** A full-service hotel. **NOTE:** Job applicants should contact the Human Resources Department or General Manager at the property. **Corporate headquarters location:** Minneapolis MN.

RADISSON WOODLANDS HOTEL
1175 West Route 66, Flagstaff AZ 86001. 928/773-8888. **Contact:** Human Resources. **World Wide Web address:** http://www.radisson.com. **Description:** A 183-room, full-service hotel operating as part of the national chain. **NOTE:** Job applicants should contact the Human Resources Department or General Manager at the property.

RAYTHEON MISSILE SYSTEMS
P.O. Box 11337, Tucson AZ 85734. 520/794-3000. **Physical address:** 1151 East Herman Road, Tucson AZ 85706. **Contact:** Human Resources. **World Wide Web address:** http://www.raytheon.com. **Description:** Manufactures missile systems. **Positions advertised include:** Economic Analyst; Economic Engineer; Aerodynamicist; Architectural Engineer; Electrical Engineer; Financial Analyst; Sr. Logistics Specialist; Program Manager. **Corporate headquarters location:** Lexington MA. **Parent company:** Raytheon Company is a diversified firm dealing in high-technology electronic systems for space exploration; radar and electro-optics; missiles; and avionics. **Listed on:** New York Stock Exchange. **Stock exchange symbol:** RTN. **Number of employees nationwide:** 81,000.

RE/MAX EXCALIBUR
15160 North Hayden Road, Suite 100, Scottsdale AZ 85260. 480/483-3333. **Fax:** 480/483-6438. **Contact:** Stephen Proski. **World Wide Web address:** http://www.az-homes4u.com. **Description:** A real estate agency.

REMUDA RANCH CENTER
One East Apache Street, Suite A, Wickenburg AZ 85390. 928/684-3913. **Fax:** 928/684-4247. **Recorded jobline:** 800/315-3883. **Contact:** Human Resources. **E-mail address:** jobs@remudaranch.com. **World Wide Web address:** http://www.remuda-ranch.com. **Description:** A treatment center for women and adolescent girls suffering from anorexia, bulimia, and related disorders.

RENTAL SERVICE CORPORATION
6929 East Greenway Parkway, Suite 200, Scottsdale AZ 85254. 480/905-3300. **Contact:** Personnel. **World Wide Web address:** http://www.rentalservice.com. **Description:** Rents a broad line of general equipment to industrial and construction companies, government agencies, municipalities, and homeowners. Some of the company's equipment includes heavy industrial machinery such as backhoes and forklifts, and personal rentals such as lawnmowers. **Positions advertised include:** Sales Coordinator. **Other U.S. locations:** AZ; CA; FL; LA; TX. **Subsidiaries include:** Acme Dixie Inc.; Acme Duval Inc.; Acme Rents, Inc.

RESIDENCE INN FLAGSTAFF
3440 North Country Club Drive, Flagstaff AZ 86004. 928/526-5555. **Fax:** 928/527-0328. **Contact:** Human Resources. **World Wide Web address:** http://www.marriott.com/residenceinn. **Description:** An extended-stay hotel with meeting facilities. **Corporate headquarters location:** Bethesda MD. **Other U.S. locations:** Nationwide. **Parent company:** Marriott International, Inc. **Listed on:** New York Stock Exchange. **Stock exchange symbol:** MAR.

RINKER MATERIALS
701 North 44th Street, Phoenix AZ 85008. 602/220-5000. **Contact:** Human Resources. **World Wide Web address:** http://www.metromat.com. **Description:** Engaged in the sale and production of construction materials including ready-mix concrete, asphalt, sand, and gravel. **Positions advertised include:** Ready-Mix Driver; Driver Trainee. **Corporate headquarters location:** This location. **Other U.S. locations:** Flagstaff AZ; Tucson AZ. **Parent company:** CSR Limited (Australia). **Operations at this facility include:** Divisional Headquarters.

RIO SALADO COLLEGE
2323 West 14th Street, Tempe AZ 85281-6950. 480/517-8560. **Contact:** Human Resources. **World Wide Web address:** http://www.rio.maricopa.edu. **Description:** A comprehensive community college, with an enrollment of 20,000. Rio Salado is an innovative network of over 250 locations serving Maricopa County. The college does not have a traditional campus, but instead offers classes in schools, churches, businesses, and shopping malls throughout Maricopa County at locations convenient to working students. Founded in 1978. **Positions advertised include:** Adjunct Faculty.

ROAD MACHINERY COMPANY
P.O. Box 4425, Phoenix AZ 85030-4425. 602/252-7121. **Physical address:** 716 South Seventh Street, Phoenix AZ 85034-3228. **Contact:** Department of Human Resources. **E-mail address:** job-info@roadmachinery.com. **World Wide Web address:** http://www.roadmachinery.com. **Description:** Engaged in the sales and servicing of off-highway trucks and loaders. **Positions advertised include:** Account Manager; Inventory control Clerk; Field Mechanic; Vice President of Sales and Marketing.

CHAS ROBERTS AIR CONDITIONING
9828 North 19th Avenue, Phoenix AZ 85021. 602/331-2678. **Contact:** Dave Patenaude, Human Resources Director. **E-mail address:** hr@chasroberts.com. **World Wide Web address:** http://www.chasroberts.com. **Description:** Sells, installs, and services heating and air conditioning systems. **Positions advertised include:** Service Technician; Installer; Commercial/Custom Home Installer.

ROCKFORD CORPORATION
600 South Rockford Drive, Tempe AZ 85281. 480/967-3565. **Fax:** 480/967-8132. **Contact:** Human Resources. **World Wide Web address:** http://www.rockfordcorp.com. **Description:** Manufactures and markets car and home audio products. Founded in 1980. **Positions advertised include:** Corporate Controller; Senior Design Engineer; Design Engineer. **Corporate headquarters location:** This location. **Listed on:** NASDAQ. **Stock exchange symbol:** ROFO. **Number of employees at this location:** 550.

ROGERS CORPORATION
100 South Roosevelt Avenue, Chandler AZ 85226. 480/961-1382. **Fax:** 480/940-9210. **Contact:** Human Resources. **E-mail address:** employment@rogers-corp.com. **World Wide Web address:** http://www.rogers-corp.com. **Description:** Develops and manufactures specialty polymer and electronic materials for applications in communication and computer markets. **NOTE:** Resumes accepted for open positions only. **Positions advertised include:** Marketing Manager; Manufacturing Manager; Market Development Manager; Senior Process Engineer. **Special programs:** Internships. **Corporate headquarters location:** Rogers CT. **Operations at this facility include:** Administration; Manufacturing; Sales. **Listed on:** New York Stock Exchange. **Stock exchange symbol:** ROG. **Number of employees at this location:** 120. **Number of employees nationwide:** 1,200.

RURAL/METRO CORPORATION
8401 East Indian School Road, Scottsdale AZ 85251. 480/994-3886. **Fax:** 480/606-3268. **Contact:** Human Resources. **E-mail address:** recruiting@rmetro.com. **Description:** Provides emergency and non-emergency medical transportation services, fire protection, and other safety-related services. **World Wide Web address:** http://www.ruralmetro.com. **Positions advertised include:** Accounts Payable Specialist; Collector; Financial Analyst. **Special programs:** Internships. **Corporate headquarters location:** This location. **Other U.S. locations:** Nationwide. **Operations at this facility include:** Administration; Sales. **Listed on:** NASDAQ. **Stock exchange symbol:** RURL. **Number of employees at this location:** 200. **Number of employees nationwide:** 4,400.

RYLEY, CARLOCK, AND APPLEWHITE
One North Central Avenue, Suite 1200, Phoenix AZ 85004-4417. 602/258-7701. **Fax:** 602/257-9582. **Contact:** Shannon Bryant, Human Resources Director. **E-mail address:** sbryant@rcalaw.com. **World Wide Web address:** http://www.rcalaw.com. **Description:** A law firm specializing in antitrust, corporate, estate, and environmental law. Founded in 1948.

SAFEWAY, INC.
2750 South Priest Drive, Tempe AZ 85282. 480/894-4100. **Recorded jobline:** 480/894-4138. **Contact:** Personnel. **World Wide Web address:** http://www.safeway.com. **Description:** One of the world's largest food retailers. Safeway operates approximately 1,800 stores in the Western, Rocky Mountain, Southwestern, and Mid-Atlantic regions of the United States and in western Canada. Safeway also holds a 35 percent interest in The Vons Companies, Inc., one of the largest supermarket chains in Southern California, and a 49 percent interest in Casa Ley, S.A. de C.V., which operates food/variety, clothing, and wholesale outlet stores in western Mexico. **Positions advertised include:** Project Traffic Clerk. **Special programs:** Training. **Corporate headquarters location:** Pleasanton CA. **Subsidiaries include:** Dominick's Supermarkets, Inc. is a Chicago-area chain with 112 stores. **Listed on:** New York Stock Exchange. **Stock exchange symbol:** SWY.

ST. JOSEPH'S HOSPITAL & MEDICAL CENTER
350 West Thomas Road, Phoenix AZ 85013. 602/406-3000. **Contact:** Human Resources Department. **World Wide Web address:** http://www.ichosestjoes.com. **Description:** A 517-bed, not-for-profit hospital and medical center. **Positions advertised include:** Certified Nurse Assistant; Clerk; Community Outreach Program Coordinator; Customer Service Representative; Dietary Aide; Faculty Physician; Nursing Services Manager; Monitor Technician; Occupational Therapist; Physical Therapist; Plumber; Registrar; Research Assistant; Speech Pathologist; Staff Nurse; Clinical Supervisor. **Office hours:** Monday - Friday, 7:00 a.m. - 5:00 p.m. **Parent company:** Catholic Healthcare West.

ST. MARY'S HOSPITAL
1601 West St. Mary's Road, Tucson AZ 85745. 520/872-3000. **Toll-free phone:** 800/669-4979. **Contact:** Personnel. **E-mail address:** chncareers@carondelet.org. **World Wide Web address:** http://www.carondelet.org. **Description:** A 393-bed hospital, St. Mary's is part of the Carondelet Health Network, the largest and oldest not-for-profit health care provider in Southern Arizona. **NOTE:** Entry-level positions and second and third shifts are offered. **Positions advertised include:** Certified Nursing Assistant; Mammographer; Nuclear Medical Technologist; Occupational Therapist; Pharmacist; Physical Therapist; RN. **Special programs:** Internships; Training.

SAKS FIFTH AVENUE
2446 East Camelback Road, Phoenix AZ 85016. 602/955-8000. **Contact:** Personnel. **World Wide Web address:** http://www.saksincorporated.com. **Description:** Saks Fifth Avenue is a 62-store chain emphasizing soft-goods products, primarily apparel for men, women, and children. **Corporate headquarters location:** Birmingham AL. **Parent company:** Saks Incorporated is a department store holding company that operates approximately 360 stores in 36 states. The company's stores include Saks Fifth Avenue, Parisian, Proffit's, Younker's, Herberger's, Carson Pirie Scott, Boston Store, Bergner's, and Off 5th, the company's outlet store. Saks Incorporated also operates two retail catalogs and several retail Internet sites. **Operations at this facility include:** This location houses administrative offices. **Listed on:** New York Stock Exchange. **Stock exchange symbol:** SKS.

SALT RIVER VALLEY WATER USERS ASSOCIATION
P.O. Box 52025, Mail Stop PAB265, Phoenix AZ 85072-2025. 602/236-5005. **Contact:** Human Resources. **E-mail address:** staffing@srpnet.com. **World Wide Web address:** http://www.srpnet.com. **Description:** Delivers water to a 240,000-acre area in central Arizona. The association is one of two organizations under the Salt River Project. The Salt River Project's 131-mile main canal system brings domestic and irrigation water to the Valley. The four lakes on the Salt River and the two on the Verde are formed by reclamation dams operated by the Salt River Project. The pump storage electric units in Mormon Flat and Horse Mesa dams create clean, inexpensive power. **Positions advertised include:** Computer Analyst; Cost Schedule and Power Production Analyst; Power Systems Computer Analyst/Engineer; Planning Analyst; Transactional and Regulatory Attorney. **Parent company:** SRP.

THE SALVATION ARMY
P.O. Box 52177, Phoenix AZ 85072. 602/267-4100. **Physical address:** 2707 East Van Buren Street, Phoenix AZ 85008. **Contact:** Ms. Robin Harvey, Personnel Director. **World Wide Web address:** http://www.tsasw.org. **Description:** A nonprofit organization providing several service programs including day-care centers, programs for people with disabilities, substance abuse programs and tutoring for at-risk students. The Salvation Army targets its programs to assist alcoholics, battered women, drug addicts, the elderly, the homeless, people with AIDS, prison inmates, teenagers, and the unemployed. **Other U.S. locations:** Nationwide.

SANDERSON FORD, INC.
6400 North 51st Avenue, Glendale AZ 85301. 480/922-9395. **Contact:** Human Resources. **World Wide Web address:** http://www.sandersonford.com. **Description:** An automotive dealership.

SANMINA-SCI PHOENIX
5020 South 36th Street, Phoenix AZ 85040. 602/824-8300. **Contact:** Human Resources. **Description:** A leading electronics contract manufacturer serving the fastest-growing segments of the global electronics manufacturing services (EMS) market. Sanmina-SCI provides end-to-end manufacturing solutions, delivering quality and support to OEMs primarily in the communications, defense and aerospace, industrial and medical instrumentation, computer technology, and multimedia sectors. **Corporate headquarters location:** San Jose CA.

SARGENT CONTROLS & AEROSPACE
5675 West Burlingame Road, Tucson AZ 85743. 520/744-1000. **Fax:** 520/744-9290. **Contact:** Human Resources. **E-mail address:** employment@sargentcontrols.com. **World Wide Web address:** http://www.sargentcontrols.com. **Description:** Provides precision hydraulic control components and specialty and self-lubricated lined bearings for many commercial and military aircraft as well as all US Naval nuclear class submarines. **Positions advertised include:** Buyer/Planner; Electrical Project Engineer; Human Resource Generalist; Project Engineer. **Parent company:** Dover Corporation.

SCHUFF STEEL COMPANY
420 South 19th Avenue, Phoenix AZ 85009. 602/252-7787. **Contact:** Will Trujillo, Human Resources Manager. **World Wide Web address:** http://www.schuff.com. **Description:** A steel fabricating and erecting company. **Positions advertised include:** Estimator; Fitter/Welder; Project Scheduler; Structural Engineer. **Corporate headquarters location:** This location. **Parent company:** Schuff International, Inc. **Listed on:** American Stock Exchange. **Stock exchange symbol:** SHF.

SCOTTSDALE, CITY OF
7575 East Main Street, Scottsdale AZ 85251. 480/312-2491. **Fax:** 480/312-7960. **Recorded jobline:** 480/312-2395. **Contact:** Human Resources. **E-mail address:** hr@scottsdaleaz.gov. **World Wide Web address:** http://www.ci.scottsdale.az.us. **Description:** Administrative offices for the city of Scottsdale. This location also hires seasonally. **NOTE:** Entry-level positions and part-time jobs are offered. **Positions advertised include:** Public Affairs Manager; Recreation Specialist; Deputy Fire Marshal; EMS Captain; Firefighter; Plan Review Manager; Police Communications Dispatcher. **Special programs:** Summer Jobs. **Corporate headquarters location:** This location. **Number of employees at this location:** 2,000.

SCOTTSDALE COMMUNITY COLLEGE
9000 East Chaparral Road, Scottsdale AZ 85256-2626. 480/423-6000. **Contact:** Human Resources. **World Wide Web address:** http://www.sc.maricopa.edu. **Description:** A comprehensive community college that operates as a member of the Maricopa County Community College District. Three degrees are offered: associate of arts, associate of applied sciences, and associate of general studies. Twenty-eight career programs range from administration of justice to video production technology. Twenty-eight occupational certificates are also available in areas such as automotive, business, and child and family studies. **Positions advertised include:** Testing Technician.

SCOTTSDALE CONFERENCE CENTER & RESORT
7700 East McCormick Parkway, Scottsdale AZ 85258. 480/991-9000. **Contact:** Human Resources. **World Wide Web address:** http://www.benchmark.hospitalityonline.com. **Description:** A 326-room hotel with conference facilities. **Positions advertised include:** Ware Washer; House Attendant; Bus Person; Night Auditor; Dining Room Server; Business Service Center Representative; Dining Room Server; Dining Room Captain; Beverage Server; Bell Person. **Parent company:** Benchmark Hospitality.

SCOTTSDALE HEALTHCARE CORPORATION
5111 North Scottsdale Road, Suite 143, Scottsdale AZ 85250. 480/882-6950. **Contact:** Human Resources. **World Wide Web address:** http://www.shc.org. **Description:** A nonprofit health care organization that operates hospitals, home health care centers, outpatient centers, a primary health care network, and community outreach programs. **Positions advertised include:** Phlebotomist; Pharmacy Tech; Respiratory Therapist; RN; Clinical Lab Tech; Nuclear Medicine Tech; Telemetry Tech; Director, Patient Services; Physical Therapist. **Corporate headquarters location:** This location.

SCOTTSDALE HEALTHCARE OSBORN
7400 East Osborn, Scottsdale AZ 85251. 480/882-4000. **Contact:** Employment. **World Wide Web address:** http://www.shc.org. **Description:** A 305-bed, full-service hospital. **NOTE:** Search and apply for positions online. **Positions advertised include:** RN; Respiratory Therapist; Clinical Lab Tech. **Parent company:** Scottsdale Healthcare Corporation. **Number of employees at this location:** 1,900.

SCOTTSDALE HILTON RESORT & VILLAS
6333 North Scottsdale Road, Scottsdale AZ 85250. 480/948-7750. **Contact:** Human Resources. **World Wide Web address:** http://www.merv.com. **Description:** A 233-room hotel. **Parent company:** The Griffin Group. **Number of employees at this location:** 230.

SENTRY INSURANCE COMPANY
P.O. Box 9400, Phoenix AZ 85038. 480/860-7000. **Physical address:** 9060 East Via Linda, Scottsdale AZ 85258. **Contact:** Human Resources. **World Wide Web address:** http://www.sentry.com. **Description:** An insurance company specializing in property, casualty, life, and health policies. **Positions advertised include:** Claims Processor; Claims Representative; Consumer Products Specialist. **Corporate headquarters location:** Stevens Point WI. **Operations at this facility include:** Regional Claims Center; Sales.

SHAMROCK FOODS COMPANY
2540 North 29th Avenue, Phoenix AZ 85009. 602/233-6401. **Contact:** Human Resources. **E-mail address:** jobs@shamrockfoods.com. **World Wide Web address:** http://www.shamrockfoods.com. **Description:** Processes and distributes dairy and ice cream products. **Positions advertised include:** Human Resources Support. **Other U.S. locations:** San Diego CA; Commerce City CO. **Operations at this facility include:** Administration; Divisional Headquarters; Manufacturing; Regional Headquarters; Research and Development; Sales; Service. **Listed on:** Privately held. **Number of employees at this location:** 1,100. **Number of employees nationwide:** 2,400.

SCHALLER ANDERSON
4645 East Cotton Center Boulevard, Phoenix AZ 85040. 602/659-1100. **Contact:** Human Resources Generalist. **E-mail:** hr@schalleranderson.com. **World Wide Web address:** http://www.schalleranderson.com. **Description:** Manages privately funded health benefit plans for employers. Founded in 1984. **Positions advertised include:** Accounting Specialist; Sr. Actuarial Financial Analyst; Business Analyst; Claims Analyst; Quality Review Analyst; Claims Supervisor; Research and Adjustment Analyst; HR Recruiter.

SIGNAL TECHNOLOGY CORPORATION/ARIZONA OPERATION
340 North Roosevelt Avenue, Chandler AZ 85226. 480/940-1655. **Fax:** 480/961-6297. **Contact:** Polly Murray, Human Resources. **World Wide Web address:** http://www.sigtech.com. **Description:** Manufactures electronic products including oscillators, power supplies, frequency synthesizers, and related products. **Positions advertised include:** Director, Operations; Assembler; Technician; Sales Executive. **Corporate headquarters location:** Danvers MA. **Parent company:** Crane Co. **Listed on:** New York Stock Exchange. **Stock exchange symbol:** CR.

SIMULA INC.
7822 South 46th Street, Phoenix AZ 85044. 602/634-7233. **Contact:** Human Resources. **World Wide Web address:** http://www.simula.com. **Description:** Researches, develops, and manufactures crash-worthy aircraft components and related structural products for the U.S. military and prime defense contractors. Founded in 1975. **Company slogan:** Protecting people in motion. **Parent company:** Armor Holdings, Inc. **Listed on:** New York Stock Exchange. **Stock exchange symbol:** AH.

SMITH BARNEY
6710 North Scottsdale Road, Suite 250, Scottsdale AZ 85253. 480/368-6500. **Contact:** Human Resources. **World Wide Web address:** http://www.smithbarney.com. **Description:** An international investment banking firm. Salomon Smith Barney offers a wide range of financial services through more than 100 locations worldwide. **Corporate headquarters location:** New York NY. **Parent company:** Citigroup, Inc. **Listed on:** New York Stock Exchange. **Stock exchange symbol:** C.

SMURFIT-STONE CONTAINER CORPORATION
6902 West Northern Avenue, Glendale AZ 85303. 602/264-4655. **Toll-free phone:** 877/772-2932. **Contact:** Human Resources. **World Wide Web address:** http://www.smurfit-stone.com. **Description:** Smurfit-Stone Container Corporation is the world's leading paper-based packaging company. The company's main products include corrugated containers, folding cartons, and multiwall industrial bags. The company is also the world's largest collector and processor of recycled products that are then sold to a worldwide customer base. Smurfit-Stone Container Corporation also operates several paper tube, market pulp, and newsprint production facilities. **Corporate headquarters location:** Chicago IL. **Other area locations:** Snowflake AZ. **Other U.S. locations:** Nationwide. **Operations at this facility include:** This location manufactures corrugated containers. **Listed on:** NASDAQ. **Stock exchange symbol:** SSCC.

SONORA QUEST LABORATORIES
1255 West Washington Street, Tempe AZ 85281-1210. 602/685-5000. **Recorded jobline:** 602/685-5555. **Contact:** Human Resources. **World Wide Web address:** http://www.sonoraquest.com. **Description:** Provides diagnostic testing services. **Positions advertised include:** Medical Lab Technician; Medical Technologist; Phlebotomist; Spec Prep Technician.

SOUTHERN ARIZONA VA HEALTH CARE SYSTEM
3601 South Sixth Avenue, Tucson AZ 85723. 520/792-1450. **Contact:** Human Resources. **World Wide Web address:** http://www.va.gov/678savahcs. **Description:** A 325-bed medical center with accredited general medical, surgical, and psychiatric facilities. The Tucson VA Medical Center provides a full-range of medical and surgical services, including open heart and kidney transplantation. Due to its strong and active affiliation with the University of Arizona Colleges of Medicine, Nursing, and Pharmacy, a great deal of emphasis has been on education and research. Residency programs in medicine, surgery, anesthesiology, psychiatry, radiology, nuclear medicine, neurology, and pathology promote the delivery of clinical care. **Positions advertised include:** RN; Psychiatrist; Chief, Research Service; Chief, Surgical Care; Vascular Surgeon; Pharmacy Technician; Diagnostic Radiologic Technologist. **Parent company:** U.S. Department of Veterans Affairs (Washington DC.)

SOUTHWEST AMBULANCE SERVICE
222 East Main Street, Mesa AZ 85021. 480/655-7234. **Toll-free phone:** 800/341-7454. **Fax:** 480/649-7752. **Contact:** Human Resources. **E-mail address:** humanresources@swambulance.com. **World Wide Web address:** http://www.swambulance.com. **Description:** An ambulance service provider. **Positions advertised include:** Administrative Assistant; Supply Technician. **Other area locations:** Tucson AZ.

SQUARE D COMPANY
410 North 44th Street, Suite 270, Phoenix AZ 85008. 602/231-8694. **Contact:** Human Resources. **World Wide Web address:** http://www.squared.com. **Description:** An electronics firm operating in two major business segments: Electrical Equipment and Electronics Products. The Electrical Equipment segment designs, manufactures, and sells a broad range of products used in the distribution and control of electricity. Products include circuit breakers, safety switches, panel boards, switchboards, switchgear, busways, transformers, wiring devices, motor-starters, relays, limit switches, pressure switches, and vacuum switches. The Electronics Products segment includes the manufacture and sale of electrodeposited copper foil through subsidiary Yates Electronics. **Positions advertised include:** Sales Support Representative. **Corporate headquarters location:** Palatine IL. **Other U.S. locations:** Nationwide. **Subsidiaries include:** General Semiconductor Industries. **Parent company:** Groupe Schneider possesses global expertise in electrical contracting, industrial engineering, and construction. Its five major operating companies -- Jeumont-Schneider Industrie, Merlin Gerin, Spie Batignolles, Square D, and Telemecanique -- are organized in two operational sectors: Schneider Industrie designs, manufactures, and markets electrical products and systems for the distribution and control of electricity. Through Spie Batignolles, Schneider Entreprise serves as a general contractor for large-scale industrial and government construction projects around the world.

STANDARD REGISTER COMPANY
4110 North Scottsdale Road, Suite 335, Scottsdale AZ 85251. 480/423-4072. **Contact:** Human Resources. **E-mail address:** hrcorp@standardregister.com. **World Wide Web address:** http://www.standardregister.com. **Description:** Manufactures business forms, pressure sensitive products, and data systems forms for a variety of industries including business and health care. The company also offers distribution, automation, management, and software products and services. **Positions advertised include:** Production Supervisor. **Corporate headquarters location:** Dayton OH. **Listed on:** New York Stock Exchange. **Stock exchange symbol:** SR.

STANTEC CONSULTING
201 North Bonita Avenue, Tucson AZ 85745-2999. 520/750-7474. **Fax:** 520/750-7470. **Contact:** Human Resources. **E-mail address:** hr@stantec.com. **World Wide Web address:** http://www.stantec.com. **Description:** An engineering services firm. **Positions advertised include:** Engineer; Field Technician; Survey CAD Technician; Survey Crew Chief; Survey Instrument Person. **Other area locations include:** Phoenix AZ. **Other U.S. locations include:** Nationwide. **International locations:** Barbados.

STERILITE CORPORATION
2201 College Drive, Lake Havasu City AZ 86403. 928/453-5060. **Contact:** Human Resources. **E-mail address:** employment@sterilite.com. **World Wide Web address:** http://www.sterilite.com. **Description:** Manufactures plastic storage containers for food and household items. Products include trash barrels, laundry baskets, and storage drawers. Founded in 1939. **Corporate headquarters location:** Townsend MA. **Other U.S. locations:** Birmingham AL; Massillon OH; Clinton SC; Ennis TX. **International locations:** Canada.

STERIS LABORATORIES
620 North 51st Avenue, Phoenix AZ 85043. 602/278-1400. **Fax:** 602/447-3385. **Contact:** Personnel. **World Wide Web address:** http://www.watsonpharm.com. **Description:** Manufactures sterile, injectable, generic pharmaceuticals. **Positions advertised include:** Chemist; Process Operator; Warehouse Operator; Manager, Regulatory Affairs. **Corporate headquarters location:** Corona CA. **Parent company:** Watson Pharmaceuticals, Inc. **Listed on:** New York Stock Exchange. **Stock exchange symbol:** WPI.

STRATUS TECHNOLOGIES
4455 East Camelback Road, Suite 115A, Phoenix AZ 85018. 602/852-3000. **Contact:** Human Resources. **World Wide Web address:** http://www.stratus.com. **Description:** Stratus offers a broad range of computer systems, application solutions, middleware, and professional services for critical online operations. **NOTE:** Mail resumes to Stratus Technologies, 111 Powdermill Road, Maynard MA 01754. **Corporate headquarters location:** Maynard MA. **Subsidiaries include:** Shared Systems Corporation provides software and professional services to the financial services, retail, and health care industries. SoftCom Systems, Inc. provides data communications middleware and related professional services that bridge the gap between open distributed systems and legacy mainframe and midrange systems used for online applications. Isis Distributed Systems, Inc. develops advanced messaging middleware products that enable businesses to develop reliable, high-performance distributed computing applications involving networked desktop computers and shared systems. **Operations at this facility include:** This location houses engineering, customer service, and sales personnel.

SUN HEALTH
WALTER O. BOSWELL MEMORIAL HOSPITAL
10401 West Thunderbird Boulevard, Sun City AZ 85351. 623/977-7211. **Contact:** Human Resources. **World Wide Web address:** http://www.sunhealth.org. **Description:** A nonprofit health organization that operates Walter O. Boswell Memorial Hospital (also at this location), an acute care, 325-bed facility. **Positions advertised include:** Application Analyst; CNA; Manager Building Construction; MRI Technologist; CT/Radiologic Technologist; Pharmacist; Community Relations Assistant; Material Technician; RN; Radiology Technologist; Physical Therapist; Occupational Therapist.

SUNAMERICA SECURITIES
2800 North Central Avenue, Suite 2100, Phoenix AZ 85004. 619/471-3700. **Contact:** Human Resources. **World Wide Web address:** http://www.sunamericasecurities.com. **Description:** A financial services company specializing in retirement planning. **Positions advertised include:** Operations Specialist; Business Analyst; Investment Advisory Specialist; Fixed Income Trader; Advertising Compliance Analyst; Regional Management Trade Specialist. **Corporate headquarters location:** This location. **Parent company:** American International Group, Inc.

SUNCOR DEVELOPMENT COMPANY
80 East Rio Salado Parkway, Suite 410, Tempe AZ 85281. 480/317-6800. **Fax:** 480/317-6934. **Contact:** Human Resources. **World Wide Web address:** http://www.suncoraz.com. **Description:** Develops commercial, industrial, and residential properties primarily in Arizona. **Parent company:** Pinnacle West Corporation (Phoenix AZ.) **Listed on:** New York Stock Exchange. **Stock exchange symbol:** PNW.

THE SUNDT COMPANIES, INC.
1501 West Fountainhead Parkway, Suite 600, Tempe AZ 85282. 480/293-3000. **Fax:** 480/293-3079. **Contact:** Human Resources. **World Wide Web address:** http://www.sundt.com. **Description:** A general contractor providing construction management services. **Positions advertised include:** Project Administrator. **Other area locations:** Phoenix AZ; Tucson AZ. **Other U.S. locations:** Novato CA; Sacramento CA; San Diego CA; Dallas TX.

SUNDT CONSTRUCTION, INC.
2630 South 20th Place, Phoenix AZ 85034. 602/252-5881. **Contact:** Human Resources. **World Wide Web address:** http://www.sundt.com. **Description:** A general contractor providing construction management services. **Parent company:** The Sundt Companies, Inc.

SUNTRON
2401 West Grandview Road, Phoenix AZ 85023. 602/789-6600. **Toll-free phone:** 888/520-3382. **Contact:** Human Resources. **Description:** A leading provider of integrated electronics manufacturing services and solutions for the medical, defense and aerospace, semiconductor capital equipment, industrial controls and instrumentation industries. Suntron's capabilities include complete system level integration as well as printed circuit card assembly, cable and harness production, sheet metal fabrication and plastic injection molding. **NOTE:** Search and apply for positions online. **Positions advertised include:** Mechanical Commodity Manager; Product Engineer; Operations Specialist; Process Engineer; Senior Quality Engineer. **Corporate headquarters location:** This location. **Other U.S. locations:** CA; IA; KS; MA; NH; OR; TX; WA. **Listed on:** NASDAQ. **Stock exchange symbol:** SUNN.

SUNVEK
7681 East Gray, Scottsdale AZ 85260. 480/951-3223. **Fax:** 480/951-8046. **Contact:** Human Resources. **World Wide Web address:** http://www.sunvek.com. **Description:** Provides a variety of home improvement services including roofing, siding, heating/air conditioning, and plumbing.

SUPERCRITICAL SYSTEMS, INC.
2120 West Guadalupe Road, Gilbert AZ 85233-2805. 480/507-8100. **Fax:** 480/507-3103. **Contact:** Human Resources. **World Wide Web address:** http://www.telusa.com. **Description:** R&D and manufacturing of high pressure, supercritical CO2 wafer cleaning equipment. **Positions advertised include:** Applications Engineer. **Other area locations:** Phoenix AZ. **Other U.S. locations:** TX; MA. **Parent company:** Tokyo Electron Limited.

SUPERLITE BLOCK
4150 West Turney Avenue, Phoenix AZ 85063. 602/352-3813. **Contact:** Human Resources. **World Wide Web address:** http://www.superliteblock.com. **Description:** Manufactures and sells concrete masonry units and related products for masonry construction. Superlite Block's primary customers include mason contractors and dealers. **Corporate headquarters location:** This location. **Operations at this facility include:** Administration; Manufacturing; Sales.

SWENGEL-ROBBINS, INC.
837 East Southern Avenue, Phoenix AZ 85040-3144. 602/268-1724. **Contact:** Human Resources. **Description:** A construction management firm specializing in engineering and heavy construction including highways and pipelines.

SWIFT TRANSPORTATION COMPANY, INC.
P.O. Box 29243, Phoenix AZ 85038-9243. 602/269-9700. **Physical address:** 2200 South 75th Avenue, Phoenix AZ 85043. **Contact:** Human Resources. **World Wide Web address:** http://www.swifttrans.com. **Description:** One of the largest truckload motor carriers in the United States. Swift Transportation Company offers a wide variety of trailers, with more than 5,600 on the road every day. Swift Transportation has more than 2,400 power units to pull the widest variety of vans, flatbeds, and specialty trailers available to the industry. The company also provides full-service equipment leasing, dedicated fleet programs, and third-party logistics services for several major customers. **Positions advertised include:** Owner Operator; Trainer; Driver. **Corporate headquarters location:** This location. **Listed on:** NASDAQ. **Stock exchange symbol:** SWFT. **President/CEO:** Jerry C. Moyes. **Annual sales/revenues:** More than $100 million.

SYNTELLECT INC.
16610 North Black Canyon Highway, Suite 100, Phoenix AZ 85053. 602/789-2800. **Fax:** 602/789-2899. **Contact:** Human Resources. **E-mail address:** hr@syntellect.com. **World Wide Web address:** http://www.syntellect.com. **Description:** Syntellect designs software for businesses that allows customers to access automated voice systems. **Positions advertised include:** Project Manager; Systems Test Engineer; Inside Sales Representative; Manager, Product Development; Sr. Software Engineer. **Corporate headquarters location:** This location. **Listed on:** NASDAQ. **Stock exchange symbol:** SYNL.

SYSTEMS SOLUTIONS INC.
2108 East Thomas Road, Suite 103, Phoenix AZ 85016. 602/955-5566. **Fax:** 602/955-7795. **Contact:** Human Resources. **E-mail address:** jobs@syspac.com. **World Wide Web address:** http://www.syspac.com. **Description:** Provides Internet services and offers technical services and solutions for Website design, Website hosting, database programming, local- and wide-area networks, computer telephony, and software development. Systems Solutions also offers SYSPAC, a comprehensive library of distribution, inventory control, and accounting software modules. **NOTE:** Entry-level positions are offered. **Company slogan:** Full Service Computer Group Since 1982. **Special programs:** Training; Summer Jobs. **Office hours:** Monday - Friday, 8:00 a.m. - 5:00 p.m. **Corporate headquarters location:** This location. **Listed on:** Privately held. **Annual sales/revenues:** Less than $5 million. **Number of employees at this location:** 30.

TALLEY DEFENSE SYSTEMS
P.O. Box 34299, Mesa AZ 85277-4299. 480/898-2200. **Contact:** Human Resources. **World Wide Web address:** http://www.talleyds.com. **Description:** An international development and manufacturing facility using forms of solid propellant material used in automotive airbag and defense systems and subsystems for the U.S. government. The company offers a broad product line built around innovative applications of propellant technology including automotive airbag inflators; gas generators; artillery range extension devices; rocket motors; ballistic devices; stores ejector racks; dispersion and inflation systems; and direct fire weapon systems. **Positions advertised include:** Manufacturing Engineer; R & D Machinist. **Operations at this facility include:** Manufacturing; Research and Development. **Listed on:** New York Stock Exchange. **Annual sales/revenues:** $21 - $50 million. **Number of employees at this location:** 280.

TEMPE, CITY OF
20 East Sixth Street, First Floor, Tempe AZ 85281. 480/350-8278. **Recorded jobline:** 480/350-8217. **Contact:** Human Resources, Recruitment Division. **World Wide Web address:** http://www.tempe.gov. **Description:** Administrative offices for the city of Tempe. **Positions advertised include:** Deputy Development Services Manager; Detention Officer; Police Communications Dispatcher; Retail Recruiter; Sr. Civil Engineer. **NOTE:** Interested jobseekers must fill out an application to be considered for employment. Applications can be downloaded from the office's Website. E-mailed or faxed applications will not be accepted.

TETRA CORPORATION
4415 North Buckboard Trail, Suite C, Scottsdale AZ 85251. 480/949-0135. **Contact:** Personnel. **World Wide Web address:** http://www.tetracorp.com. **Description:** Provides employment counseling, training, and placement services to people with disabilities. **Positions advertised include:** Employment Interviewer; Social Worker. **Corporate headquarters location:** This location.

TEXAS INSTRUMENTS
6730 South Tucson Boulevard, Tucson AZ 85706. 520/746-1111. **Fax:** 520/746-7211. **Contact:** Human Resources. **E-mail address:** tiarizona@ti.list.com. **World Wide Web address:** http://www.ti.com. **Description:** Manufactures high-precision, high-reliability micro-electronic devices and microcomputer systems for use in data acquisition, signal conditioning, and industrial control. Texas Instruments (TI) is one of the world's largest suppliers of semiconductor products. TI's defense electronics business is a leading supplier of avionics, infrared, and weapons guidance systems to the U.S. Department of Defense and U.S. allies. The company is also a technology leader in high-performance notebook computers and model-based software development tools. TI sensors monitor and regulate pressure and temperature in products ranging from automobiles to air conditioning systems. **NOTE:** Search and apply for positions online. **Positions advertised include:** Product Engineer; Technical Marketing Engineer; Electrical Design Engineer; Test Engineer. **Corporate headquarters location:** Dallas TX. **Other U.S. locations:** Nationwide. **International locations:** Worldwide. **Operations at this facility include:** Manufacturing; Research and Development. **Listed on:** New York Stock Exchange. **Stock exchange symbol:** TXN.

THREE-FIVE SYSTEMS, INC.
1600 North Desert Drive, Tempe AZ 85281. 602/389-8884. **Fax:** 602/389-8989. **Contact:** Human Resources. **World Wide Web address:** http://www.threefive.com. **Description:** Designs and manufactures a wide range of user interface devices for operational control and informational display functions. Custom displays featuring liquid crystal displays (LCD) and light emitting diode (LED) components and technology account for a majority of revenues. Products are used in cellular telephones and other wireless communication devices, mail processing equipment, optical scanners, automotive equipment, bar code readers, home security systems, and industrial and military control products. Founded in 1985. **Corporate headquarters location:** This location. **Listed on:** New York Stock Exchange. **Stock exchange symbol:** TFS.

THUNDERBIRD
THE GARVIN SCHOOL OF INTERNATIONAL MANAGEMENT
15249 North 59th Avenue, Glendale AZ 85306-6000. 602/978-7101. **Fax:** 602/978-8305. **Contact:** Human Resources. **E-mail address:** HRResumes@t-bird.edu. **World Wide Web address:** http://www.t-bird.edu. **Description:** A graduate school of

business management with approximately 1,450 students enrolled. Founded in 1946. **Positions advertised include:** Dean of Faculty; Dean of Programs; Director, Public Relations and Rankings; Coordinator, Special Initiatives; Major Gifts Officer.

TOOH DINEH INDUSTRIES, INC.
HC 61, Box E, Winslow AZ 86047. 928/686-6477. **Fax:** 928/686-6516. **Contact:** Mary R. Begay, Human Resources. **World Wide Web address:** http://www.toohdineh.com. **Description:** A contract electronics manufacturer for the communication, transportation, and computer industries. Founded in 1983. **NOTE:** Entry-level positions and second and third shifts are offered. **Positions advertised include:** Production Operations Manager; Accounting Manager; Engineering Manager; Materials Manager; Production Supervisor. **Special programs:** Training. **Office hours:** Monday - Friday, 7:00 a.m. - 3:30 p.m. **Corporate headquarters location:** Chinle AZ. **Parent company:** Dineh Cooperatives Inc. **Operations at this facility include:** Administration; Manufacturing. **Annual sales/revenues:** $11 - $20 million. **Number of employees at this location:** 100.

TRANSPRO, INC.
2517 West McDowell Road, Suite 107, Phoenix AZ 85009. 602/484-0596. **Fax:** 602/352-1912. **Contact:** Human Resources. **World Wide Web address:** http://www.transpro.com. **Description:** A firm that manufactures and distributes replacement radiators, radiator cores, and heat products for automobiles, trucks, and industrial vehicles. **Corporate headquarters location:** New Haven CT. **Listed on:** New York Stock Exchange. **Stock exchange symbol:** TPR.

TREON, STRICK, LUCIA, AND AGUIRRE
2700 North Central Avenue, Suite 1400, Phoenix AZ 85004. 602/285-4407. **Contact:** Human Resources. **Description:** A law firm specializing in personal injury, medical malpractice, and workers' compensation.

TRI-CAD/CAM SYSTEMS, INC.
3740 East La Salle, Phoenix AZ 85040. 602/333-1600. **Fax:** 602/333-1602. **Contact:** Human Resources. **E-mail address:** HR@TriCadCam.com. **World Wide Web address:** http://www.tristar.com. **Description:** Manufactures Windows NT graphics workstations and servers. **Positions advertised include:** Solutions Architect; Associate Webmaster; Inside Sale Representative.

TRIBUNE NEWSPAPERS
120 West First Avenue, Mesa AZ 85210. 480/898-6500. **Fax:** 480/898-6401. **Recorded jobline:** 480/898-5600. **Contact:** Human Resources. **E-mail address:** tribjobs@aztrib.com. **World Wide Web address:** http://www.eastvalleytribune.com. **Description:** Publishers of the *East Valley Tribune* newspaper. **Positions advertised include:** Web Developer/Programmer. **Corporate headquarters location:** Irvine CA. **Parent company:** Freedom Communications, Inc. **Listed on:** Privately held. **Number of employees at this location:** 560.

TRIUMPH CORPORATION
2130 South Industrial Park Avenue, Tempe AZ 85282. 480/967-3337. **Fax:** 480/921-0446. **Contact:** Human Resources. **E-mail address:** personnel@triumphcorp.com. **World Wide Web address:** http://www.triumphcorp.com. **Description:** Manufactures automotive parts including distributors and valves. **Positions advertised include:** Swiss Screw Machine Operator.

TRIWEST HEALTHCARE ALLIANCE
15451 North 28th Avenue, Phoenix AZ 85053. 602/564-2000. **Contact:** Human Resources. **World Wide Web address:** http://www.triwest.com. **Description:** TriWest partners with the Department of Defense to provide access to health care for active and retired uniformed services members and their families in a 21-state area. **Positions advertised include:** Master Clinical Trainer; Administrative Trainer; Instructional Designer.

TUBA CITY INDIAN MEDICAL CENTER
167 North Main Street & East Elm Avenue, P.O. Box 600, Tuba City AZ 86045-0600. 928/283-2501. **Contact:** Human Resources. **World Wide Web address:** http://www.navajohealthjobs.ihs.gov. **Description:** A medical center serving the area's Native American population. **Positions advertised include:** Chief Executive Officer; Administrative Officer; Medical Officer Vice President of Human Resources; Health Information Management Director. **NOTE:** Search and apply for positions online. **Parent company:** Indian Health Service (IHS) agency of the U.S. Department of Health and Human Services in the Phoenix area operates eight hospitals, six health centers, one school health center, and seven health stations. In the Tucson area, Indian Health Services operates one hospital, two health centers, and one health station. Overall, IHS provides a health service delivery system to approximately 1.3 million people and acts as the principal federal health advocate for Native American population.

TUCSON CITIZEN
P.O. Box 26767, Tucson AZ 85726. 520/573-4561. **Fax:** 520/573-4569. **Contact:** Michael Chihak, Editor and Publisher. **World Wide Web address:** http://www.tucsoncitizen.com. **Description:** Publishes an evening daily newspaper with a circulation of more than 50,000. Advertising, circulation, and composing functions are operated in a partnership with the *Arizona Daily Star,* through Tucson Newspapers. **Parent company:** Gannett Company. **Operations at this facility include:** Sales; Service. **Listed on:** New York Stock Exchange. **Stock exchange symbol:** GCI.

TUCSON ELECTRIC POWER COMPANY
P.O. Box 711, Tucson AZ 85702. 520/884-3724. **Recorded jobline:** 520/884-3618. **Contact:** Personnel. **World Wide Web address:** http://www.tucsonelectric.com. **Description:** Supplies electrical service to the city of Tucson and the surrounding communities. **Positions advertised include:** Civil Engineer; Energy Settlement Analyst; Lead Plant Accountant; Substation Engineer; Web Developer; Voice Communications Administrator; Programmer/Analyst Oracle E-Business Suite; Senior Java Architect. **Corporate headquarters location:** This location. **Other area locations:** Springerville AZ. **Parent company:** UniSource Energy Corporation. **Operations at this facility include:** Administration; Service. **Number of employees at this location:** 1,200. **Number of employees nationwide:** 1,400.

TUCSON POLICE DEPARTMENT
270 South Stone Avenue, Tucson AZ 85701-1917. 520/791-4244. **Contact:** Human Resources. **World Wide Web address:** http://www.ci.tucson.az.us/police. **Description:** A local law enforcement agency providing services to the citizens of Tucson, which has a population of 463,000. **Positions advertised include:** Records Specialist; Safety Dispatcher; Service Operator. **Corporate headquarters location:** This location. **Number of employees at this location:** 1,000.

TUCSON SHOPPER
1861 West Grant Road, Tucson AZ 85745. 520/622-0101. **Fax:** 520/620-9651. **Contact:** Human Resources. **World Wide Web address:** http://www.tucson-shopper.com. **Description:** Publishers of a weekly advertising publication that is mailed to over 310,000 households weekly. The company also publishes *Conexion Hispana,* one of the nation's largest Spanish language advertising publications. **Positions advertised include:** Telemarketing Sales Representative. **Parent company:** Marks-Ferber Communications.

TURF PARADISE INC.
1501 West Bell Road, Phoenix AZ 85023. 602/942-1101. **Contact:** Human Resources. **World Wide Web address:** http://www.turfparadise.com. **Description:** Conducts an annual thoroughbred race at its 220-acre facility in Phoenix. Turf Paradise also operates a 14-acre mobile home park. **Corporate headquarters location:** This location.

TUSONIX, INC.
P.O. Box 37144, Tucson AZ 85740-7144. 520/744-0400. **Physical address:** 7741 North Business Park Drive, Tucson AZ 85743. **Contact:** Personnel. **E-mail address:** hr@tucsonix.com. **World Wide Web address:** http://www.tusonix.com. **Description:** Develops, manufactures, and markets electronic ceramic capacitors and EMI/RFI filters. The company also operates a manufacturing plant in Nogales, Mexico. **Positions advertised include:** Electronic Component Sales Representative. **Corporate headquarters location:** This location. **Operations at this facility include:** Administration; Manufacturing; Research and Development; Sales. **Listed on:** Privately held. **Number of employees at this location:** 120. **Number of employees nationwide:** 700.

U-HAUL INTERNATIONAL, INC.
2727 North Central Avenue, Phoenix AZ 85004. 602/263-6011. **Contact:** Henry Kelly, Human Resources Director. **World Wide Web address:** http://www.uhaul.com. **Description:** One of the largest consumer truck rental operations in the world, with a fleet of over 158,000 trucks and trailers. The company operates in all 50 states and all Canadian provinces, with over 12,000 dealers and 1,100 U-Haul centers. The company is one of the largest operators of self-storage units in the United States with over 700 storage locations. U-Haul has a computerized, nationwide storage reservation system. U-Haul is one of the world's largest installers of permanent trailer hitches, and is one of the largest retailers of propane fuel. Founded in 1945. **Positions advertised include:** Accountant; Adjuster; Analyst-Yellow Pages; Assistant General Counsel; Facilities Project Manager; Facility Imaging Designer; Staff Architect. **Corporate headquarters location:** This location. **Number of employees nationwide:** 15,500.

U-HAUL TECHNICAL CENTER
11298 South Priest Drive, Tempe AZ 85284. 480/940-0274. **Contact:** Human Resources. **World Wide Web address:** http://www.uhaul.com. **Description:** U-Haul Technical Center provides design, engineering and technical service for U-Haul equipment and products. Maintenance and repair assistance, purchasing supply support and product research and development are some of the functions provided by U-Haul Technical Center. **NOTE:** Search and apply for positions online. **Positions advertised include:** Buyer; Maintenance Mechanic; Repair Dispatch Specialist. **Corporate headquarters location:** Phoenix AZ.

UBS FINANCIAL SERVICES INC.
2555 East Camelback Road, Suite 600, Phoenix AZ 85016. 602/957-5100. **Contact:** James Van Steenhuyse, Division Vice President & Branch Manager. **World Wide Web address:** http://www.ubspainewebber.com. **Description:** A full-service securities firm with over 300 offices nationwide. Services include investment banking, asset management, merger and acquisition consulting, municipal securities underwriting, estate planning, retirement programs, and transaction management. UBS PaineWebber offers its services to corporations, governments, institutions, and individuals. **Corporate headquarters location:** New York NY. **Other U.S. locations:** Nationwide. **Annual sales/revenues:** More than $100 million.

UBS FINANCIAL SERVICES INC.
8501 North Scottsdale Road, Suite 100, Scottsdale AZ 85253. 480/443-5400. **Contact:** Human Resources. **World Wide Web address:** http://www.ubspainewebber.com. **Description:** A full-service securities firm with over 300 offices nationwide. Services include investment banking, asset management, merger and acquisition consulting, municipal securities underwriting, estate planning, retirement programs, and transaction management. Clients include corporations, governments, institutions, and individuals. Founded in 1879. **Corporate headquarters location:** New York NY. **Other U.S. locations:** Nationwide. **Annual sales/revenues:** More than $100 million.

UPH HOSPITAL AT KINO
2800 East Ajo Way, Tucson AZ 85713. 520/573-2815. **Fax:** 520/407-2817. **Recorded jobline:** 520/874-3603. **Contact:** Human Resources. **E-mail address:** kinojobs@upiaz.org. **World Wide Web address:** http://www.uphkino.org. **Description:** A 200-bed, full-service hospital serving southern Tucson. **Positions advertised include:** Registration Coordinator; Registered Nurse; Senior Clinical Dietician; Director, Health Information Systems; EKG Technician; Certified Nursing Assistant; Educator ICU; Radiologic Technologist; Pharmacist; Clinical Manager; Staffing Coordinator. **Parent company:** University Physicians Healthcare.

URS
7720 North 16th Street, Suite 100, Phoenix AZ 85020. 602/371-1100. **Fax:** 602/371-1615. **Contact:** Human Resources. **World Wide Web address:** http://www.urscorp.com. **Description:** An architectural, engineering, and environmental consulting firm that specializes in air transportation, environmental solutions, surface transportation, and industrial environmental and engineering concerns. **Positions advertised include:** Archaeologist; Biologist; CADD Technician; Civil Highway Engineer; Department Head; GIS Specialist. **Corporate headquarters location:** San Francisco CA. **Other area locations:** Tucson AZ. **Parent company:** URS Corporation. **Listed on:** New York Stock Exchange. **Stock exchange symbol:** URS.

U.S. BUREAU OF LAND MANAGEMENT
222 North Central Avenue, Phoenix AZ 85004. 602/417-9200. **Contact:** Human Resources. **World Wide Web address:** http://www.blm.gov. **Description:** Office of the federal agency that manages public lands and resources. **Positions advertised include:** Surveying Technician.

U.S BUREAU OF RECLAMATION
PO Box 81169, Phoenix AZ 85069-1169. 602/216-3999. **Fax:** 602/216-4000. **Contact:** Human Resources. **World Wide Web address:** http://www.usbr.gov. **Description:** Engaged in water resources development and management. The bureau's primary emphasis is on engineering.

U.S. BUREAU OF THE CENSUS
6363 South Country Club Road, Suite 151, Tucson AZ 85706-5906. 520/806-9796. **Contact:** Human Resources. **World Wide Web address:** http://www.census.gov. **Description:**. U.S. Bureau of the Census monitors social and economic development by conducting censuses and surveys. **Operations at this facility include:** This location is a telephone center.

U.S. DEPARTMENT OF AGRICULTURE
2197 South Fourth Avenue, Suite 104, Yuma AZ 85364. 928/782-0860. **Fax:** 928/782-0930. **Contact:** Human Resources. **World Wide Web address:** http://www.usda.gov. **Description:** Supports agricultural production and ensures the quality of products. The USDA provides economic and educational support to farmers and those in rural areas.

U.S. DEPARTMENT OF VETERANS AFFAIRS
CARL T. HAYDEN VA MEDICAL CENTER
650 East Indian School Road, Phoenix AZ 85012. 602/277-5551. **Recorded jobline:** 602/222-2703. **Contact:** Human Resources. **World Wide Web address:** http://www.va.gov. **Description:** A 590-bed hospital. The medical center's teaching programs include residencies in internal medicine, family practice, ophthalmology, dermatology, and general surgery; and fellowships in gastroenterology, cardiology and pulmonology. All programs are run through affiliations with accredited programs. The outpatient program includes a mental hygiene clinic, day hospital, and treatment center. Founded in 1951.

U.S. FOODSERVICE
4650 West Buckeye Road, Phoenix AZ 85043. 602/269-7241. **Contact:** Human Resources. **World Wide Web address:** http://www.usfoodservice.com. **Description:** Distributes food products, fresh meats, dairy products, and cleaning supplies to restaurants and other institutional food service establishments. **Positions advertised include:** Credit Coordinator; SIS Coordinator; Payroll Accounting Coordinator; Category Data Analyst; Internal Senior Auditor. **Corporate headquarters location:** Columbia MD. **Other U.S. locations:** Nationwide. **Number of employees nationwide:** 12,000.

U.S. GENERAL SERVICES ADMINISTRATION (GSA)
9 North Grand Avenue, Nogales AZ 85621. 520/287-4275. **Contact:** Human Resources. **World Wide Web address:** http://www.gsa.gov. **Description:** One of three of the federal government's central management agencies. The GSA seeks to ensure that government agencies are provided the best space, services, supplies, and products at the best prices. **Corporate headquarters location:** Washington DC.

U.S. POSTAL SERVICE
2400 North Postal Boulevard, Flagstaff AZ 86004-9998. 928/714-9302. **Contact:** Human Resources. **World Wide Web address:** http://www.usps.com. **Description:** The main post office for the Flagstaff area.

UNICON, INC.
3140 North Arizona Avenue, Suite 113, Chandler AZ 85225. 480/926-2368. **Fax:** 480/558-2320. **Contact:** Human Resources. **E-mail address:** hr@unicon.net. **World Wide Web address:** http://www.unicon.net. **Description:** Provides services and systems that allow clients to measure training, learning, knowledge and change management initiatives. Founded in 1993. **Positions advertised include:** Software Developer; System Administrator; uPortal Consultant. **Corporate headquarters location:** This location. **Other U.S. locations:** El Segundo CA. **Listed on:** Privately held. **President/CEO:** Ray Barker.

UNIFORMS MANUFACTURING, INC.
P.O. Box 12716, Scottsdale AZ 85267-2716. 800/222-1474. **Fax:** 480/368-8556. **E-mail address:** jobs@unifmfg.com. **Contact:** Human Resources. **World Wide Web address:** http://www.unifmfg.com. **Description:** Manufactures apparel for the hospital, recreational, institutional, and detention industries. **Positions advertised include:** Customer Service Representative.

UNISYS CORPORATION
2525 East Camelback Road, Suite 1100, Phoenix AZ 85016. 602/224-4200. **Fax:** 602/224-4258. **Contact:** Human Resources. **World Wide Web address:** http://www.unisys.com. **Description:** Unisys Corporation develops and provides information services, technology, and software. Unisys specializes in developing critical business solutions based on open information networks. The company's Enabling Software Team creates a variety of software projects that facilitate the building of user applications and the management of distributed systems. The company's Platforms Group is responsible for UNIX Operating Systems running across a wide range of multiple-processor server platforms including all peripheral and communication drivers. The Unisys Commercial Parallel Processing Team develops microkernel-based operating systems, I/O device drivers, ATM hardware, diagnostics, and system architectures. The System Management Group is in charge of the overall management of development programs for UNIX desktop and entry-server products. **Positions advertised include:** Quality Assurance Analyst; Portfolio Sales Executive. **Corporate headquarters location:** Blue Bell PA. **Other U.S. locations:** Nationwide. **Operations at this facility include:** This location houses a sales and engineering facility. **Listed on:** New York Stock Exchange. **Stock exchange symbol:** UIS. **Number of employees worldwide:** 49,000.

UNIVERSITY MEDICAL CENTER (UMC)
ARIZONA HEALTH SCIENCES CENTER
1501 North Campbell Avenue, Tucson AZ 85724. 520/694-0111. **Fax:** 520/694-2531. **Recorded jobline:** 520/694-7227. **Contact:** Human Resources. **World Wide Web address:** http://www.azumc.com. **Description:** A 312-bed, tertiary care, teaching facility. UMC serves as the teaching hospital for the University of Arizona's Colleges of Nursing and Pharmacy and the School of Health Professions, providing a training opportunity for nurses, pharmacists, medical technologists, and allied health professionals. **Positions advertised include:** Cardiac Cath Tech; Cardiologist; Clinical Social Worker; Clinical Systems Analyst; Echo Tech; Financial Analyst; Info Technology Specialist; ISS Director; Medical Lab Tech; Occupational Therapist; RN, Various Departments.

UNIVERSITY OF ARIZONA
888 North Euclid Avenue, Suite 114, P.O. Box 210158, Tucson AZ 85721-1058. 520/621-3662. **Contact:** Human Resources Department. **E-mail address:** HRInfo@email.arizona.edu. **World Wide Web address:** http://www.arizona.edu. **Description:** A four-year state university offering bachelor's, master's (including MBAs), first professional, and doctoral degrees. Approximately 34,000 students attend the University of Arizona. **Positions advertised include:** Senior Accountant; Adjunct Assistant Professor, Various Departments; Adjunct Instructor, Various Departments; Applications Systems Analyst; Assistant Vice President for Admissions and Financial Aid; Professor, Various Departments.

UNIVERSITY OF PHOENIX
4635 East Elwood Street, Phoenix AZ 85040. 480/966-7400. **Contact:** Human Resources Department. **World Wide Web address:** http://www.phoenix.edu. **Description:** A private university with 163 campuses in 33 states, Puerto Rico, and Canada enrolling over 230,000 students, including 133,000 attending via the Internet. Founded in 1976.

VF FACTORY OUTLET
2050 South Roslyn Place, Mesa AZ 85208. 480/984-0697. **Contact:** Jose Vega Bon, Store Manager. **World Wide Web address:** http://www.vffo.com. **Description:** A retailer of jeans wear, sportswear, active wear, intimate apparel, and occupational apparel with 50 stores in 27 states. **Positions advertised include:** Management Trainee; Customer Service Representative. **Other area locations:** Tucson AZ.

VAN TRAN OF TUCSON
3401 East Ajo Way, Tucson AZ 85713-5234. 520/798-1000. **Contact:** Human Resources. **World Wide Web address:** http://www.vantran.org. **Description:** A city-operated transportation service that provides van transportation to handicapped and elderly citizens of Tucson. **NOTE:** Jobseekers must apply in person.

VARIAN ELECTRONICS MANUFACTURING
615 South River Drive, Tempe AZ 85281. 480/968-6790. **Fax:** 480/829-4000. **Contact:** Human Resources. **World Wide Web address:** http://www.varianinc.com. **Description:** Varian, Inc. is a major supplier of scientific instruments, vacuum technologies, and specialized contract electronics manufacturing services for a broad range of life science and industrial customers worldwide. **Positions advertised include:** Component Engineer; Production Control Analyst; Product Assurance Engineer; SMT Operator; Manufacturing Engineer. **Corporate headquarters location:** Palo Alto CA. **Operations at this facility include:** This location manufactures printed wiring assemblies (PWAs) in low to medium volumes from a broad mixture of active component and design technologies for various internal and external customers around the country. **Listed on:** NASDAQ. **Stock exchange symbol:** VARI.

VIACOM OUTDOOR
3150 South 48th Street, Suite 200, Phoenix AZ 85040. 602/246-9569. **Fax:** 480/829-9389. **Contact:** Human Resources. **World Wide Web address:** http://www.viacomoutdoor.com. **Description:** An outdoor-advertising agency specializing in the design of billboards and posters.

VISIONQUEST
600 North Swan Road, P.O. Box 12906, Tucson AZ 85732. 520/881-3950. **Fax:** 520/881-3269. **Contact:** Human Resources. **E-mail address:** jobs@vq.com. **World Wide Web address:** http://www.vq.com. **Description:** A social service organization providing troubled kids and teens with recreational alternatives. VisionQuest allows participants to engage in such outdoor activities as camping and sailing. **NOTE:** Entry-level positions are offered. **Positions advertised include:** Cook; Family Treatment Advocate. **Corporate headquarters location:** This location. **Other U.S. locations:** PA; TX. **Subsidiaries include:** Lodgemakers. **Operations at this facility include:** Administration. **Listed on:** Privately held. **Number of employees at this location:** 60. **Number of employees nationwide:** 1,050.

VODAVI COMMUNICATIONS, INC.
4717 East Hilton Avenue, Suite 400, Phoenix AZ 85034. 480/443-6000. **Fax:** 480/443-6150. **Contact:** Human Resources. **E-mail address:** bseabolt@vodavi.com. **World Wide Web address:** http://www.vodavi.com. **Description:** Vodavi Communications manufactures and distributes telephone systems. **Positions advertised include:** Product Specialist; Product Manager; Regional Sales Engineer; Technical Support Representative. **Operations at this facility include:** This location is a sales office. **Listed on:** NASDAQ. **Stock exchange symbol:** VTEK.

VOICETRAK INC.
6420 East Tanque Verde Road, Tucson AZ 85715. 520/886-4545. **Contact:** Human Resources. **World Wide Web address:** http://www.voicetrak.com. **Description:** A national media research firm. **Corporate headquarters location:** New York NY. **Parent company:** VMS.

VULCAN MATERIALS COMPANY
1801 East University Drive, Phoenix AZ 85034. 602/254-8465. **Fax:** 602/258-8948. **Contact:** Human Resources. **World Wide Web address:** http://www.vulcanmaterials.com. **Description:** Engaged in extracting, processing, and selling of rock, sand, and gravel, either in aggregate form, or after mixture with cement. **Positions advertised include:** Dispatcher; Sales Representative. **Corporate headquarters location:** Birmingham AL. **Other area locations:** Flagstaff AZ; Tucson AZ. **Other U.S. locations:** Nationwide. **Listed on:** New York Stock Exchange. **Stock exchange symbol:** VMC.

THE WACKENHUT CORPORATION
3220 East Harbour Drive, Suite 200, Phoenix AZ 85034. 602/431-0020. **Fax:** 602/454-0870. **Contact:** Human Resources. **World Wide Web address:** http:/www.wackenhut.com. **Description:** A diversified provider of services to government, industrial, commercial, and professional organizations and agencies worldwide. The corporation has offices throughout the United States and in 49 other countries on six continents. The Wackenhut Corporation specializes in security-related services including physical security, investigations, the management of correctional and detention facilities, rehabilitative programs, and information security. The company also provides educational services and training; facility management; food service to jails and prisons; design, financial services, and construction management for correctional facilities; and fire prevention and emergency services. The Wackenhut Corporation is a leader in the privatization of public services to municipal, state, and federal governments worldwide. Founded in 1954. **Special programs:** Summer Jobs. **Corporate headquarters location:** Palm Beach Gardens FL. **Other area locations:** Tucson AZ. **Parent company:** Group 4 Securicor (London). **Listed on:** New York Stock Exchange. **Stock exchange symbol:** WAK.

WALGREEN COMPANY
2222 West Northern Avenue, Suite A101, Phoenix AZ 85021. 602/864-7517. **Fax:** 602/864-0288. **Contact:** Roy Grauer, District Manager. **World Wide Web address:** http://www.walgreens.com. **Description:** Walgreen Company operates one of the largest retail drug store chains in the United States, which sells prescription and nonprescription drugs, cosmetics, toiletries, liquor and beverages, tobacco, and general merchandise. Founded in 1901. **Positions advertised include:** PBM Account Coordinator; Rehabilitation Technology Specialist. **Corporate headquarters location:** Deerfield IL. **Operations at this facility include:** This location is a district office. **Listed on:** New York Stock Exchange. **Stock exchange symbol:** WAG. **Number of employees nationwide:** 80,000.

WASTE MANAGEMENT, INC.
7025 North Scottsdale Road, Suite 200, Scottsdale AZ 85253. 480/624-8400. **Fax:** 480/951-5280. **Contact:** Human Resources. **World Wide Web address:** http://www.wm.com. **Description:** An international provider of comprehensive waste management services, as well as engineering, construction, industrial, and related services. Waste Management has operations in 19 countries. **Positions advertised include:** Human Resource Coordinator. **Corporate headquarters location:** Houston TX. **Listed on:** New York Stock Exchange. **Stock exchange symbol:** WMI.

DEL WEBB CORPORATION
P.O. Box 29040, Phoenix AZ 85038. 602/808-8000. **Physical address:** 6001 North 24th Street, Phoenix AZ 85016. **Recorded jobline:** 602/808-7970. **Contact:** Human Resources. **World Wide Web address:** http://www.delwebb.com. **Description:** A real estate company involved in the master planning, development, and construction of active adult communities in the Sun Belt. **Number of employees at this location:** 900.

WELLS FARGO BANK
1276 East Florence Boulevard, Casa Grande AZ 85222. 520/836-8234. **Contact:** Human Resources. **World Wide Web address:** http://www.wellsfargo.com. **Description:** Wells Fargo serves over 17 million customers through 5,300 independent locations worldwide. The company also maintains several stand-alone ATMs and branches within other retail outlets. Services include community banking, credit and debit cards, home equity and mortgage loans, online banking, student loans, and insurance. Wells Fargo also offers a complete line of commercial and institutional financial services. Founded in 1852. **Positions advertised include:** Business Banking Specialist; Personal Banker; Customer Sales Service Rep. **Corporate headquarters location:** San Francisco CA. **Other U.S. locations:** Nationwide. **Listed on:** New York Stock Exchange. **Stock exchange symbol:** WFC. **Annual sales/revenues:** More than $100 million. **Number of employees worldwide:** 104,000.

WELLS FARGO BANK
1625 East Camelback Road, Phoenix AZ 85016. 602/200-9166. **Contact:** Human Resources. **World Wide Web address:** http://www.wellsfargo.com. **Description:** Wells Fargo serves over 17 million customers through 5,300 independent locations worldwide. The company also maintains several stand-alone ATMs and branches within other retail outlets. Services include community banking, credit and debit cards, home equity and mortgage loans, online banking, student loans, and insurance. Wells Fargo also offers a complete line of commercial and institutional financial services. Founded in 1852. **Positions advertised include:** Business Relationship Manager; Mortgage Consultant; Project Manager; Finance Manager; Operations Analyst. **Corporate headquarters location:** San Francisco CA. **Other U.S. locations:** Nationwide. **Listed on:** New York Stock Exchange. **Stock exchange symbol:** WFC. **Annual sales/revenues:** More than $100 million. **Number of employees worldwide:** 104,000.

WESTCHESTER CARE CENTER - VOA
6100 South Rural Road, Tempe AZ 85283. 480/831-8660. **Fax:** 480/820-7663. **Contact:** Jan Hamsen, Director of Personnel. **Description:** A nonprofit center that provides long-term care, assisted living, and independent living/retirement services. **Other U.S. locations:** Nationwide. **Parent company:** Volunteers of America. **Number of employees at this location:** 145.

WESTERN AREA POWER ADMINISTRATION
U.S. DEPARTMENT OF ENERGY
P.O. Box 6457, Phoenix AZ 85005-6457. 602/352-2770. **Contact:** Human Resources. **World Wide Web address:** http://www.wapa.gov. **Description:** A federally operated transmission system that sells and distributes electric power. **Positions advertised include:** Public Utilities Specialist.

WESTERN TECHNOLOGIES, INC.
3737 East Broadway Road, Phoenix AZ 85040. 602/437-3737. **Fax:** 602/470-1341. **Contact:** Human Resources. **World Wide Web address:** http://www.wt-us.com. **Description:** Provides engineering, consulting, and testing of environmental, geotechnical, and construction materials. Environmental services include site assessments, investigations, feasibility studies, problem solving, and remedial services. Geotechnical services are provided with use of a wide variety of exploration equipment including highly mobile drilling rigs. Materials Engineering and Testing provides analysis and quality assurance of materials and methods for clients. Materials Research develops methods of improving the strength and durability of conventional construction materials through research into the feasibility of using waste and less expensive or more available materials. Construction Quality Control provides interpretation of geotechnical reports, observation and testing of reinforced steel and concrete, visual and nondestructive evaluation of bolted and welded structural steel components, preparing concrete and asphalt mix designs, as well as sampling and testing many other architectural and structural components. Founded in 1955. **Positions advertised include:** Senior Geotechnical Engineer; Geotechnical Engineer; Environmental Scientist; Geologist; Industrial Hygienist; Senior Engineering Technician. **Company slogan:** The quality people. **Corporate headquarters location:** This location. **Listed on:** Privately held. **Annual sales/revenues:** $21 - $50 million. **Number of employees at this location:** 285.

WESTERN TECHNOLOGIES, INC.
4126 La Linda Way, Suite D, Sierra Vista AZ 85635. 520/458-0364. **Contact:** Human Resources. **World Wide Web address:** http://www.wt-us.com. **Description:** Provides engineering, consulting, and testing of environmental, geotechnical, and construction materials. Environmental services include site assessments, investigations, feasibility studies, problem solving, and remedial services. Geotechnical services are provided with the use of a wide variety of exploration equipment including highly mobile drilling rigs. Materials Engineering and Testing provides analysis and quality assurance of materials and methods for clients. Materials Research develops methods of improving the strength and durability of conventional construction materials through research into the feasibility of using waste and less expensive or more available materials. Construction Quality Control provides interpretation of geotechnical reports, observation and testing of reinforced steel and concrete, visual and nondestructive evaluation of bolted and welded structural steel components, preparing concrete and asphalt mix designs, as well as sampling and testing many other architectural and structural components. **Positions advertised include:** Senior Geotechnical Engineer; Geotechnical Engineer; Environmental Scientist; Geologist; Industrial Hygienist; Senior Engineering Technician. **Corporate headquarters location:** Phoenix AZ.

WESTERN TECHNOLOGIES, INC.
3480 South Dodge Boulevard, Tucson AZ 85713-5435. 520/748-2262. **Fax:** 520/748-0435. **Contact:** Human Resources. **World Wide Web address:** http://www.wt-us.com. **Description:** Provides engineering, consulting, and testing of environmental, geotechnical, and construction materials. Environmental services include site assessments, investigations, feasibility studies, problem solving, and remedial services. Geotechnical services are provided with the use of a wide variety of exploration equipment including highly mobile drilling rigs. Materials Engineering and Testing provides analysis and quality assurance of materials and methods for clients. Materials Research develops methods of improving the strength and durability of conventional construction materials through research into the feasibility of using waste and less expensive or more available materials. Construction Quality Control provides interpretation of geotechnical reports, observation and testing of reinforced steel and concrete, visual and nondestructive evaluation of bolted and welded structural steel components, preparing concrete and asphalt mix designs, as well as sampling and testing many other architectural and structural components. **Positions advertised include:** Senior Geotechnical Engineer; Geotechnical Engineer; Environmental Scientist; Geologist; Industrial Hygienist; Senior Engineering Technician. **Corporate headquarters location:** Phoenix AZ.

WESTEX MANUFACTURING CORPORATION
P.O. Box 6185, Nogales AZ 85628. 520/761-3064. **Physical address:** 17 West Avenida Acaponeta Drive, Rio Rico AZ 85648. **Fax:** 520/821-1467. **Contact:** Human Resources. **E-mail address:** westex@theriver.com. **World Wide Web address:** http://www.theriver.com/westex. **Description:** Manufactures aprons, napkins, and tablecloths for the hospitality industry. Founded in 1984.

WHATABURGER
4610 South 48th Street, Phoenix AZ 85040. 602/454-6453. **Contact:** Human Resources. **World Wide Web address:** http://www.whataburger.com. **Description:** A franchise location of Whataburger, a fast-food restaurant chain. Founded in 1950. **NOTE:** Entry-level positions, second and third shifts, and part-time jobs are offered. **Positions advertised include:** Assistant Manager. **Special programs:** Training; Summer Jobs. **Corporate headquarters location:** Corpus Christi TX. **Other area locations:** Statewide.

WHITE ELECTRONIC DESIGNS CORPORATION
3601 East University Drive, Phoenix AZ 85034. 602/437-1520. **Fax:** 602/437-3417. **Contact:** Human Resources. **E-mail address:** HR_DMD@wedc.com. **World Wide Web address:** http://www.wedc.com. **Description:** Designs and manufactures standard and custom high-reliability components and system products, from thick film substrates to advanced multichip modules and hybrids. Designed to meet military, industrial, and hostile environments, White Electronic Designs' components are used in airborne, missile, satellite, radar, electronic countermeasure, down hole, and ordnance applications. The company's military products are complemented by a variety of products developed for commercial, telecommunications, and data processing markets. The company provides digital design support including microprocessor-based products, and standard and custom memory modules. **Positions advertised include:** Design Engineer; Senior Buyer. **Corporate headquarters location:** This location. **Listed on:** NASDAQ. **Stock exchange symbol:** WEDC.

WIGWAM RESORT
300 Wigwam Boulevard, Litchfield Park AZ 85340. 623/935-3811. **Contact:** Human Resources. **World Wide Web address:** http://www.wigwamresort.com. **Description:** A resort and country club.

WINCUP
7980 West Buckeye Road, Phoenix AZ 85043. 623/936-1791. **Contact:** John McKelvy, Vice President of Personnel. **World Wide Web address:** http://www.wincup.com. **Description:** Produces polystyrene foam cups, containers, lids, and glasses. **Corporate headquarters location:** This location. **Parent company:** Dart & Kraft Inc. (Glenview IL) is an international food products and food packaging firm.

XEROX CORPORATION
2700 North Central Avenue, Suite 500, Phoenix AZ 85004. 602/264-4971. **Contact:** Human Resources. **E-mail address:** xerox@isearch.com. **World Wide Web address:** http://www.xerox.com. **Description:** Xerox is a global company in the document processing market. The company's activities in this area encompass the designing, developing, manufacturing, marketing, and servicing of a complete range of document processing products and systems. Xerox copiers, duplicators, electronic scanners, facsimile machines, networks, multifunction publishing machines, and related software and supplies are marketed in more than 130 countries. Founded in 1906. **Corporate headquarters location:** Stamford CT. **Operations at this facility include:** This location sells, leases, and services business machine products. **Listed on:** New York Stock Exchange. **Stock exchange symbol:** XRX.

YELLOW TRANSPORTATION INC.
2425 South 43rd Avenue, Phoenix AZ 85009. 602/269-5141. **Contact:** Human Resources. **World Wide Web address:** http://www.myyellow.com. **Description:** A national, long-haul truckload carrier, with over 585 terminal locations in 50 states, Puerto Rico, and Canada. **Corporate headquarters location:** Overland Park KS. **Parent company:** Yellow Corporation. **Listed on:** NASDAQ. **Stock exchange symbol:** YELL. **Number of employees nationwide:** 28,000.

YOH COMPANY
4000 North Central Avenue, Suite 1450, Phoenix AZ 85012. 602/235-9739. **Toll-free phone:** 888/825-9295. **Fax:** 602/280-1022. **Contact:** Human Resources. **E-mail address:** Phoenix@yoh.com. **World Wide Web address:** http://www.yoh.com. **Description:** Delivers long- and short-term temporary and direct placement of technology and professional personnel for the information technology community in the Phoenix Valley and surrounding areas. **Parent company:** Day & Zimmerman.

YUMA DAILY SUN
SUN PRINTING COMPANY
P.O. Box 271, Yuma AZ 85366 928/783-3333. **Physical address:** 2055 South Arizona Avenue, Yuma AZ 85364. **Contact:** Human Resources. **World Wide Web address:** http://www.yumasun.com. **Description:** Publishers of *Yuma Daily Sun*. **Positions advertised include:** Circulation Assistant. **Special programs:** Internships.

ZILA PHARMACEUTICALS
5227 North Seventh Street, Phoenix AZ 85014-2800. 602/266-6700. **Contact:** Marlin Steele, Human Resources. **World Wide Web address:** http://www.zila.com. **Description:** Manufactures treatments for cold sores and fever blisters. **Corporate headquarters location:** This location. **Parent company:** Zila Inc. **Operations at this facility include:** Administration; Research and Development; Sales; Service. **Listed on:** NASDAQ. **Stock exchange symbol:** ZILA. **Number of employees at this location:** 20.

AETN
350 South Donaghey Avenue, Conway AR 72034. 501/682-2386. **Fax:** 501/682-4122. **Contact:** Human Resources Supervisor. **E-mail:** applications@aetn.org. **World Wide Web address:** http://www.aetn.org. **Description:** A public education television network. **Note:** Candidates are directed to view jobs and fill out a state applications online at http://www.arstatejobs.com. **Positions advertised include:** Photographer; Television Promotion Supervisor. **Special programs:** Internships. **Corporate headquarters location:** This location. **Number of employees at this location:** 100.

ACXIOM CORPORATION
1 Information Way, Little Rock AR 72202. 501/342-1000. **Contact:** Human Resources. **World Wide Web address:** http://www.acxiom.com. **Description:** An information retrieval services company. Founded 1969. **NOTE:** Search and apply for positions online. **Positions advertised include:** Administrative Assistant; Client Delivery Analyst; Client Representative; Consultant; Data Acquisitions Manager; Data Administrator; Database Administrator; Database Developer; Decision Support Analyst; Financial Analyst; Industry Solutions Architect; Product Manager; Sales Account Manager; Software Developer; Solutions Developer. **Corporate headquarters location:** This location. **Listed on:** NASDAQ. **Stock exchange symbol:** ACXM.

AFFILIATED FOODS SOUTHWEST
8109 Interstate 30, Little Rock AR 72209. 501/570-0007. **Fax:** 501/562-0792. **Contact:** Human Resources. **E-mail address:** jroystuart@afslr.com **World Wide Web address:** http://www.harvestfoods.com. **Description:** Operates a chain of supermarkets called Harvest Foods. **Corporate headquarters location:** This location. **Listed on:** Privately held. **Number of employees at this location:** 3,200.

ALLIANCE RUBBER COMPANY
P.O. Box 20950, Hot Springs, AR 71903-0950. 501/262-2700. **Fax:** 501/262-3948. **Contact:** Human Resources. **World Wide Web address:** http://www.rubberband.com. **Description:** A manufacturer of rubber bands, mailing and shipping products, and stationery products. **Positions advertised include:** Printing Technician.

ALLTEL CORPORATION
11101 Anderson Drive, Little Rock AR 72212. 501/220-7620. **Physical address:** One Allied Drive, Little Rock AR 72202. **Contact:** Human Resources. **World Wide Web address:** http://www.alltel.com. **Description:** ALLTEL Corporation is a leading telecommunications and information services company. ALLTEL subsidiaries provide local telephone service, cellular telephone service, information services, and communications products. ALLTEL's business segments include Telephone Operations; Cellular Operations; Information Services; and Product Distribution. In addition to its four core businesses, ALLTEL operates or has investments in companies that provide wide-area paging, directory publishing, long-distance service, and cable television service. ALLTEL's local telephone operations serve 13 million customers in 26 states. **Positions advertised include:** Financial Analyst; Order Processing Specialist; Business Analyst; Sr. Operating Systems Programmer; Staff Attorney; Enterprise Network Supervisor; Engineer; Network Analyst. **NOTE:** Search and apply for positions online. **Corporate headquarters location:** This location. **Other U.S. locations:** Nationwide. **Subsidiaries include:** ALLTEL Communications Products; ALLTEL Publishing Corporation. **Listed on:** New York Stock Exchange. **Stock exchange symbol:** AT. **Number of employees nationwide:** 21,500.

ARISTOTLE INTERNET ACCESS
401 West Capitol, Suite 700, Little Rock AR 72201. 501/374-4638. **Contact:** Human Resources. **E-mail address:** info@aristotle.net. **World Wide Web address:** http://www.aristotle.net. **Description:** Provides Internet access to central Arkansas. The company also offers Website design, Internet applications training, and HTML programming. **Corporate headquarters location:** This location.

ARKANSAS BEST CORPORATION
P.O. Box 10048, Fort Smith AR 72917-0048. 479/785-6000. **Physical address:** 3801 Old Greenwood Road, Fort Smith AR 72903. **Contact:** Human Resources. **World Wide Web address:** http://www.arkbest.com. **Description:** Provides trucking and shipping services nationwide. **Corporate headquarters location:** This location. **Other U.S. locations:** Nationwide. **Subsidiaries include:** ABF Freight System, Inc.; Clipper Group; Data-Tronics Corp.; FleetNet America, LLC; Wingfoot, LLC. **Operations at this facility include:** Administration. **Listed on:** NASDAQ. **Stock exchange symbol:** ABFS. **Number of employees at this location:** 300. **Number of employees nationwide:** 15,000.

ARKANSAS CHILDREN'S HOSPITAL
800 Marshall Street, Slot 602, Little Rock AR 72202-3591. 501/364-4120. **Toll-free phone:** 800/844-1891. **Fax:** 501/364-3499. **Contact:** Employment Office. **E-mail address:** employment@archildrens.org. **World Wide Web address:** http://www.archildrens.org. **Description:** One of the largest pediatric medical centers in the United States. The private, non-profit hospital also supports the Arkansas Children's Hospital Research Institute, a nutrition research center. Through a partnership with the University of Arkansas for Medical Sciences, the hospital is the site of pediatric training for medical and nursing students, post-doctoral residents, and paramedical professionals. Service areas include emergency care including a Level I Trauma Center, the Cecil and Alice Peason Emergency Department, and Angel One, a state-of-the-art intensive care transport system; acute care including intensive care, dialysis, and treatment of pediatric cancer; life care including asthma care, an epilepsy clinic, and a lung center; and community care including the KIDS FIRST program and the Home Instruction for Preschool Youngsters program. **Positions advertised include:** Account Analyst; Anesthesia Technician; Biochemist; Control Programmer/Analyst; Clinical Nurse Specialist; Director Radiology; Housekeeper; HRIS Analyst; Radiology Technician; RN, Various Departments; Sr. VP, Medical Services; Staff Pharmacist. **Number of employees at this location:** 2,800.

ARKANSAS DEPARTMENT OF FINANCE AND ADMINISTRATION
P.O. Box 2485, Little Rock AR 72203. 501/324-9063. **Fax:** 501/683-2174. **Contact:** DFA Personnel Manager. **World Wide Web address:** http://www.state.ar.us/dfa. **Description:** Provides a variety of services for the government of Arkansas. **NOTE:** Candidates are directed to fill out a state application online at http://www.arstatejobs.com. **Positions advertised include:** Delinquent Tax Collector; Insurance Specialist; HR System Analyst; Child support Technician; Attorney; ABC Enforcement Officer. **Corporate headquarters location:** This location. **Operations at this facility include:** Administration. **Number of employees at this location:** 1,700.

ARKANSAS FARM BUREAU, INC.
P.O. Box 31, Little Rock AR 72203-0031. 501/224-4400. **Fax:** 501/228-1506. **Contact:** Kathy Heinley, Human Resources. **World Wide Web address:** http://www.arfb.com. **Description:** A fire, marine, and casualty insurance company. **Note:** Do not accept applications via e-mail. **Special programs:** Internships. **Number of employees at this location:** 250.

ARKANSAS STATE UNIVERSITY
P.O. Box 1500, State University AR 72467. 870/972-3454. **Fax:** 870/910-8041. **Contact:** Human Resources. **E-mail address:** HR@astate.edu. **World Wide Web address:** http://www.astate.edu. **Description:** A state university. **Positions advertised include:** Assistant/Associate Professor, Various Departments; College Dean; Instructor; Assistant/Associate Registrar; Computer Technician.

BALDOR ELECTRIC COMPANY
P.O. Box 2400, Fort Smith AR 72901. 501/646-4711. **Contact:** Charles Cramer, Vice President-Personnel. **World Wide Web address:** http://www.baldor.com. **Description:** Manufactures industrial electrical components such as grinders and motors. **Corporate headquarters location:** This location. **Other U.S. locations:** Nationwide. **Listed on:** New York Stock Exchange. **Stock exchange symbol:** BEZ.

BARNES & NOBLE BOOKSTORES
11500 Financial Center Parkway, Little Rock AR 72211. 501/954-7646. **Contact:** Manager. **World Wide Web address:** http://www.bn.com. **Description:** A bookstore chain operating nationwide. This location has a cafe and music department in addition to its comprehensive book departments.

E.C. BARTON & COMPANY
P.O. Box 4040, Jonesboro AR 72403. 870/932-6673. **Contact:** Wanda Lamkin, Director of Personnel. **E-mail address:** wandal@ecbarton.com. **World Wide Web Address:** http://www.ecbarton.com. **Description:** Owners and operators of retail, wholesale, and discount building material stores in eight states. **Corporate headquarters location:** This location. **Operations at this facility include:** Administration; Sales; Service. **Number of employees at this location:** 30. **Number of employees nationwide:** Over 450.

BEVERLY ENTERPRISES, INC.
1000 Beverly Way, Fort Smith AR 72919. 479/201-2000. **Contact:** Human Resources. **E-mail address:** recruit@beverlycorp.com. **World Wide Web address:** http://www.beverlycorp.com. **Description:** Operates acute care hospitals, assisted living centers, hospices, home health centers, institutional and mail services pharmacies, and nursing and rehabilitation facilities in 25 states and the District of Columbia. Founded in 1963. **Positions advertised include:** Billing Analyst; HR Director; Regional Business Development Director; Regional Sales Manager. **Corporate headquarters location:** This location. **Other U.S. locations:** Nationwide. **Operations at this facility include:** Administration. **Listed on:** New York Stock Exchange. **Stock exchange symbol:** BEV. **Number of employees nationwide:** 35,000.

CJRW
303 West Capitol Avenue, Little Rock AR 72201. 501/975-6251. **Toll-free phone:** 888/383-2579. **Fax:** 501/975-4241. **Contact:** Fran Fields, Vice President of Human Resources. **E-mail address:** fran.fields@cjrw.com. **World Wide Web address:** http://www.cjrw.com. **Description:** A full-service advertising agency. Services include strategic planning, brand development, market research, advertising development, promotions, creative development, direct marketing, media relations, public relations, public policy, public affairs, executive development, and publication services. **Number of employees at this location:** 90. **Number of employees nationwide:** 140.

CJRW NW
P.O. Box 1968, Fayetteville AR 72702-1968. 501/442-9803. **Physical address:** 3 East Colt Square, Fayetteville AR 72702. **Toll-free phone:** 800/599-9803. **Fax:** 501/975-4241. **Contact:** Human Resources. **Description:** A full-service advertising and promotions agency. The company's primary focus is on print production including package design, FSIs, and coupons for the retail food business. Founded in 1977. **Special programs:** Internships. **Office hours:** Monday - Friday, 8:00 a.m. - 5:00 p.m. **Corporate headquarters location:** Little Rock AR. **President:** Mark Blackwood. **Number of employees at this location:** 29.

COGNITIVEDATA CORPORATION
201 South Victory Street, Little Rock AR 866/243-7883. 501/975-7580. **Fax:** 866/243-7817. **Contact:** Human Resources. **World Wide Web address:** http://www.cognitivedata.com. **E-mail address:** talent@congitivedata.com. **Description:** Develops, markets and supports data quality solutions for the direct marketing industry. **Positions advertised include:** Direct Mail Database Analyst; Client Account Coordinator; Senior Database Developer; Senior Sales Executive.

COOK AND LOVE SHOES
11121 Rodney Parham Road, Little Rock AR 72212. 501/221-1833. **Fax:** 501/221-0850. **Contact:** Human Resources. **E-mail address:** info@cookandlove.com. **World Wide Web address:** http://www.cookandloveshoes.com. **Description:** A retail shoe store. **Company slogan:** Where the Sizes Are! **Positions advertised include:** Store Manager; Sales Associate. **Corporate headquarters location:** Memphis TN. **Other U.S. locations:** Nashville TN; Memphis TN; Jackson MS.

DASSAULT FALCON JET CORPORATION
P.O. Box 967, Little Rock AR 72203. 501/210-0454. **Physical address:** 3801 East Tenth Street, Adams Field, Little Rock AZ 72202. **Toll-free phone:** 800/643-9511. **Fax:** 501/210-0469. **Recorded jobline:** 501/210-0454. **Contact:** Personnel Administrator. **E-mail address:** resumes@falconjet.com. **World Wide Web address:** http://www.falconjet.com. **Description:** Manufactures and sells a line of two- and three-engine business aircraft. Also operates international jet aircraft service and maintenance centers (Falcon Jet Service Centers), engaged in a wide range of jet aircraft engine, airframe, avionics, instruments, and accessories service, repair, and maintenance. **Positions advertised include:** A & P Mechanic; Engineer; Associate Engineer; Engineering Programs Manager; Receptionist; Service Engineer; Senior Engineer. **Corporate headquarters location:** South Hackensack NJ. **Parent company:** Dassault Aviation (France). **Operations at this company include:** This location is a completion and service center for Falcon Jet Aircraft. **Number of employees at this location:** 1,300. **Number of employees nationwide:** 1,550.

DATAFIX
1203 Nettleton Circle, Jonesboro AR 72401. 870/972-5330. **Contact:** Human Resources. **World Wide Web address:** http://www.data-fix.com. **Description:** Provides repair services for most types of computers and printers. **Other area locations:** Springdale AR; Little Rock AR.

DILLARD'S DEPARTMENT STORES, INC.
1600 Cantrell Road, Little Rock AR 72201. 501/376-5200. **Contact:** Kim Kingsella, Director of Personnel. **World Wide Web address:** http://www.dillards.com. **Description:** Operates a retail chain. Dillard's offers a full line of fashion brand apparel and home furnishings. Dillard's stores are located primarily in the Southwest and Midwest including Texas, Florida, Louisiana, Oklahoma, Missouri, and Arizona. **NOTE:** Search and apply for corporate or store positions online. **Corporate**

headquarters location: This location. **International locations:** Mexico City, Mexico. **Annual sales/revenues:** More than $100 million. **Number of employees nationwide:** 44,600.

EINSTEIN SYSTEMS, INC.
201 South Victory Street, Little Rock AR 72201. 501/975-7580. **Contact:** Personnel. **World Wide Web address:** http://www.einsteinsystems.com;. **Description:** Specializes in producing commercial web pages.

ELECTRIC COOPERATIVES OF ARKANSAS
One Cooperative Way, P.O. Box 194208, Little Rock AR 72219-4208. 501/570-2200. **Contact:** Human Resources. **E-mail address:** employment@aecc.com. **World Wide Web address:** http://www.aecc.com. **Description:** Provides electricity services to 440,000 customers. Founded in 1938.

EURONET
17300 Chenal Parkway, Suite 200, Little Rock AR 72223. 501/218-7300. **Fax:** 501/218-7302. **Contact:** Human Resources. **E-mail address:** hr@euronetworldwide.com. **World Wide Web address:** http://swww.euronetworldwide.com. **Description:** Develops payment processing software for the banking industry. Founded in 1975. **Corporate headquarters location:** Leawood KS. **International locations:** Worldwide. **Listed on:** NASDAQ. **Stock exchange symbol:** EEFT. **Annual sales/revenues:** $5 - $10 million. **Number of employees at this location:** 140.

FED-EX FREIGHT EAST
2200 Forward Drive, Harrison AR 72601. 870/741-9000. **Fax:** 870/741-7325. **Contact:** Human Resources. **E-mail address:** hr@euronetworldwide.com. **World Wide Web address:** http://www.fedexfreight.fedex.com. **Description:** A trucking company providing scheduled, all-points, regional small shipment carrier service. The truckers ship a wide range of general commodities. The company uses its own drivers, equipment, and documentation process. **Positions advertised include:** Customer Service Representative; Maintenance Administration Systems Support; Programmer Analyst; Staff Accountant; Reliability Analyst; Manager, Quality Assurance; Project Manager. **Corporate headquarters location:** Chantilly VA. **Other U.S. locations:** Nationwide. **Parent company:** Federal Express. **Operations at this facility include:** Administration. **Listed on:** NASDAQ. **Stock exchange symbol:** FDX. **Annual sales/revenues:** More than $18 billion. **Number of employees worldwide:** 142,000.

GREAT LAKES CHEMICAL CORPORATION
2226 Haynesville Highway, P.O. Box 7020, El Dorado AR 71731. 870/862-5141. **Toll-free phone:** 800/428-7947. **Fax:** 870/864-1647. **Contact:** Human Resources. **World Wide Web address:** http://www.greatlakeschem.com. **Description:** A chemical compound developing company that produces synthetics of natural materials such as polymer additives and pool and spa water treatment products. **NOTE:** Search and apply for positions online. **Corporate headquarters location:** West Lafayette IN. **Other area locations:** Magnolia AR. **Other U.S. locations:** Nationwide. **International locations:** Halebank, United Kingdom; Frauenfeld, Switzerland. **Listed on:** New York Stock Exchange. **Stock exchange symbol:** GLK.

GREEN DENTAL LABORATORIES INC.
1099 Wilburn Road, Heber Springs AR 72543. 501/362-3132. **Fax:** 501/362-7934. **Contact:** Human Resources. **Description:** A dental laboratory that manufactures crowns, bridges, dentures, and other dental products.

HAJOCA CORPORATION
923 South Fillmore, Little Rock AR 72202. 501/664-4183. **Fax:** 501/664-6542. **Contact:** Human Resources. **E-mail address:** csfoster@tpwmail.com. **World Wide Web address:** http://www.hajoca.com. **Description:** A wholesale plumbing, heating, and industrial supplies distributor. Founded in 1884. **Positions advertised include:** Inside Counter Sales, Plumbing Parts Representative; Outside Sales Representative; Buyer; Truck Driver; Warehouse Staff; Profit Center Manager. **Other U.S. locations:** Nationwide.

HARMON AUTOGLASS
1200 John Barrow Road, Suite 308, Little Rock AR 72205-6529. 501/224-3331. **Contact:** Human Resources. **E-mail address:** harmonrecruiting@apogeeidd.com. **World Wide Web address:** http://www.harmonautoglass.com. **Description:** Repairs, replaces and installs windshields. **Positions advertised include:** Account Manager. **Other area locations:** Fayetteville AR; Pine Bluff AR; Springdale AR. **Other U.S. locations:** Nationwide. **Listed on:** NASDAQ. **Stock exchange symbol:** APOG.

HEALTHSOUTH
1201 Fleming Avenue, Jonesboro AR 72401. 870/932-0440. **Contact:** Human Resources. **World Wide Web address:** http://www.healthsouth.com. **Description:** Provides rehabilitative health care services through approximately 250 outpatient and 40 inpatient rehabilitation facilities, as well as through several medical centers. Services offered include rehabilitation, occupational therapy, physical therapy, head injury therapy, respiratory therapy, speech-language pathology, surgery, laser treatment of tumors, and rehabilitation nursing. **Positions advertised include:** Staff Occupational Therapist. **Operations at this facility include:** This location of HealthSouth is an acute care, inpatient, rehabilitation hospital with 60 beds. **Listed on:** New York Stock Exchange. **Stock exchange symbol:** HRC.

HEALTHSOUTH REHABILITATION CENTER
1000 East Matthews, Suite E, Jonesboro AR 72401. 870/931-4045. **Contact:** Human Resources. **World Wide Web address:** http://www.healthsouth.com. **Description:** Provides rehabilitative health care services through approximately 250 outpatient and 40 inpatient rehabilitation facilities, as well as through several medical centers. Services offered include rehabilitation, occupational therapy, physical therapy, head injury therapy, respiratory therapy, speech-language pathology, surgery, laser treatment of tumors, and rehabilitation nursing. **NOTE:** Search and apply for positions online. **Operations at this facility include:** This location of HealthSouth is a rehabilitation facility operating on an outpatient basis only. **Listed on:** New York Stock Exchange. **Stock exchange symbol:** HRC.

HEALTHSOUTH REHABILITATION CENTER
153 Country Club Road, Pocahontas AR 72455. 870/892-7072. **Contact:** Human Resources. **World Wide Web address:** http://www.healthsouth.com. **Description:** Provides rehabilitative health care services through approximately 250 outpatient and 40 inpatient rehabilitation facilities, as well as through several medical centers. Services offered include rehabilitation, occupational therapy, physical therapy, head injury therapy, respiratory therapy, speech-language pathology, surgery, laser treatment of tumors, and rehabilitation nursing. **NOTE:** Search and apply for positions online. **Operations at this facility include:** This location of HealthSouth is a rehabilitation facility operating on an outpatient basis only. **Listed on:** New York Stock Exchange. **Stock exchange symbol:** HRC.

HEALTHSOUTH REHABILITATION CENTER
4 Market Place, Paragould AR 72450. 870/236-3361. **Contact:** Human Resources. **World Wide Web address:** http://www.healthsouth.com. **Description:** Provides rehabilitative health care services through approximately 250 outpatient and 40 inpatient rehabilitation facilities, as well as through several medical centers. Services offered include rehabilitation, occupational therapy, physical therapy, head injury therapy, respiratory therapy, speech-language pathology, surgery, laser treatment of tumors, and rehabilitation nursing. **NOTE:** Search and apply for positions online. **Operations at this facility include:** This location of HealthSouth is a rehabilitation facility operating on an outpatient basis only. **Listed on:** New York Stock Exchange. **Stock exchange symbol:** HRC.

HEALTHSOUTH REHABILITATION CENTER
3906 Kelley Street, Springdale AR 72762. 479/927-4921. **Contact:** Human Resources. **World Wide Web address:** http://www.healthsouth.com. **Description:** Provides rehabilitative health care services through approximately 250 outpatient and 40 inpatient rehabilitation facilities, as well as through several medical centers. Services offered include rehabilitation, occupational therapy, physical therapy, head injury therapy, respiratory therapy, speech-language pathology, surgery, laser treatment of tumors, and rehabilitation nursing. **NOTE:** Search and apply for positions online. **Operations at this facility include:** This location of HealthSouth offers inpatient and outpatient rehabilitation services. **Listed on:** New York Stock Exchange. **Stock exchange symbol:** HRC.

IKON NORTH AMERICA
10825 Financial Centre Parkway, Little Rock AR 72211. 501/663-4044. **Fax:** 501/663-0842. **Contact:** Human Resources. **E-mail address:** resumes@ ikon.com. **World Wide Web address:** http://www.ikon.com. **Description:** Business communication and supply company. **Note:** Entry level positions available. **Corporate headquarters location:** Malvern PA. **Other area locations:** Fort Smith AR; Jonesboro AR; Pine Bluff AR; Rogers AR. **Other U.S. locations:** Nationwide. **International locations:** Worldwide. **Listed on:** New York Stock Exchange. **Stock exchange symbol:** IKN.

KEMLITE COMPANY
8500 C.W. Post Road, Jonesboro AR 72402. 870/932-9864. **Contact:** Human Resources. **World Wide Web address:** http://www.kemlite.com. **Description:** Kemlite Company is currently the world's largest manufacturer of fiberglass reinforced plastic (frp) panels. Founded in 1954. **Corporate headquarters location:** Joliet IL. **Parent company:** Crane Company.

J.B. HUNT TRANSPORT SERVICES, INC.
P.O. Box 130, 615 J.B. Hunt Corporate Drive, Lowell AR 72745. 479/820-0000. **Toll-free number:** 800-643-3622 **Contact:** Human Resources. **World Wide Web address:** http://www.jbhunt.com. **Description:** Operates one of the largest U.S. truckload carriers of general freight, serving the 48 contiguous states, British Columbia, Ontario, Quebec, and points in Mexico through arrangement with several Mexican carriers. **Positions advertised include:** PeopleSoft Programmer. **Corporate headquarters location:** This location. **Listed on:** NASDAQ. **Stock exchange symbol:** JBHT. **Number of employees nationwide:** 10,450.

LENNOX INDUSTRIES
512 West Lennox Road, P.O. Box 1170, Stuttgart AR 72160. 870/673-1531. **Fax:** 870/672-8182. **Contact:** Human Resources. **E-mail address:** employment.services@lennoxind.com. **World Wide Web address:** http://www.lennox.com. **Description:** Producer and distributor of furnaces, air conditioners, rooftop equipment and accessories, along with other products to improve heating and cooling quality of the home. Founded in 1895. **Company slogan:** A better place. **Positions advertised include:** Engineering Services Specialist. **Corporate headquarters location:** Richardson TX. **Other U.S. locations:** Nationwide. **International locations:** Worldwide. **Number of employees at this location:** 983. **Number of employees nationwide:** 4,000.

LOISLAW
105 North 28th Street, Van Buren AR 72956. 479/471-5581. **Contact:** Human Resources. **E-mail address:** info@loislaw.com; jobs@loislaw.com. **World Wide Web address:** http://www.pita.com. **Description:** An online, full-text database service providing access to state and federal law libraries. The service enables lawyers, business professionals, and government agencies to electronically research thousands of resources from their own computers. The company also publishes the information in CD-ROM format. **Parent company:** WoltersKluwer. **Corporate headquarters location:** This location.

MANGAN HOLCOMB RAINWATER CULPEPPER
2300 Cottondale Lane, Suite 300, Little Rock AR 72201. 501/376-0321. **Fax:** 501/376-6127. **Contact:** Human Resources. **E-mail address:** sharon@people-energy-ideas.com. **World Wide Web address:** http://www.people-energy-ideas.com. **Description:** An advertising agency.

MATTRESS FIRM, INC.
301 South Bowman, Suite 200, Little Rock AR 72211. 501/217-0230. **Fax:** 501/217-0225. **Contact:** Candace Stamm, Human Resources. **E-mail address:** candaces@mattfirm.com. **World Wide Web address:** http://www.mattressfirm.com. **Description:** A bedding retailer, focusing on Sealy Mattress, Inc. products. Founded in 1986. **Corporate headquarters location:** This location. **Other U.S. locations:** Nationwide.

MILLBROOK DISTRIBUTION SERVICES, INC.
P.O. Box 790, Harrison AR 72602. 870/741-3425. **Recorded jobline:** 800/375-6455, ext. 90001. **Contact:** Human Resources. **World Wide Web address:** http://www.millbrookds.com. **Description:** Arranges displays of nonfood items and specialty food items in grocery stores. **Corporate headquarters location:** Leicester MA.

MURPHY OIL CORPORATION
P.O. Box 7000, El Dorado AR 71731-7000. 870/862-6411. **Physical address:** 200 Peach Street, El Dorado AR 71730. **Fax:** 870/864-6511. **Contact:** Matt Angellette, Human Resources. **E-mail address:** matt_angellette@murphyoilcorp.com. **World Wide Web address:** http://www.murphyoilcorp.com. **Description:** A fully integrated petroleum company that operates through wholly owned subsidiaries in the United States and internationally. Founded in 1950. **Note:** Applications are provided online to submit electronically. **Corporate headquarters location:** This location. **Other U.S. locations:** Nationwide. **International locations:** Calgary, Canada; London, England. **Subsidiaries include:** Murphy Eastern Oil Company; Murphy Exploration and Production Co.; Murphy Oil Company Ltd.; Murphy Oil USA, Inc. **Listed on:** New York Stock Exchange. **Stock exchange symbol:** MUR. **Annual sales/revenues:** More than $100 million. **Number of employees nationwide:** 1,000.

PETERSON FARMS
250 South Main, Decatur AR 72722. 479/752-5296. **Fax:** 479/752-5678. **Contact:** Phillip Goff, Human Resource Manager. **World Wide Web address:** http://www.petersonfarms.com. **Description:** Engaged in poultry research and development and poultry processing. Peterson Farms also operates a cattle feedlot. **NOTE:** Entry-level positions are offered. **Positions advertised include:** Production Worker; parts/Supply Clerk; Service Technician Supervisor. **Special programs:** Internships; Training. **Corporate headquarters location:** This location. **Other U.S. locations:** Cullman AL; Trion GA; Luane MO; Olten TX. **Subsidiaries include:** Crystal Lake Foods; Decatur General Store; L&L Farms; Peterson LP Gas. **Operations at this facility include:** Administration; Research and Development; Sales. **Listed on:** Privately held. **Number of employees worldwide:** 2,000.

PILGRIM'S PRIDE CORPORATION
P.O. Box 389, De Queen AR 71832. 870/584-5000. **Fax:** 870/642-6607. **Contact:** Human Resources. **World Wide Web address:** http://www.pilgrimspride.com. **Description:** Pilgrim's Pride Corporation is a producer of chicken products and eggs for the restaurant, institutional, food service, grocery, and wholesale markets. The company's operations include breeding, hatching, growing, processing, packaging, and preparing poultry. Pilgrim's Pride Corporation also produces animal feeds and ingredients. The company is one of the largest producers of chicken products in the United States and Mexico. The company's primary domestic distribution is handled through restaurants and retailers in central, southwestern, and western United States, and through the food service industry throughout the country. **Corporate headquarters location:** Dallas TX. **Other U.S. locations:** AZ; OK; TX. **Operation:** This location is a poultry processing plant. **Listed on:** New York Stock Exchange. **Stock exchange symbol:** CHX.

PLATO LEARNING, INC.
111 Center Street, Suite 1130, Little Rock AR 72201. 800/574-3950. **Contact:** Human Resources. **E-mail address:** platojobs@plato.com. **World Wide Web address:** http://www.plato.com. **Description:** An online learning instruction system. **Positions advertised include:** Regional Curriculum and Instruction Consultant. **Corporate headquarters location:** Bloomington MN. **Other U.S. locations:** Nationwide. **International locations:** Worldwide. **Listed on:** NASDAQ-NMS. **Stock exchange symbol:** TUTR.

POTLATCH CORPORATION
P.O. Box 390, Warren AR 71671. 870/226-2611. **Fax:** 870/226-1125. **Contact:** Human Resources Department. **E-mail address:** wood@potlatch.com. **World Wide Web address:** http://www.potlatchcorp.com. **Description:** Potlatch Corporation is a diversified forest products company with 1.5 million acres of timberland in Arkansas, Idaho, and Minnesota. The corporation's facilities convert wood fiber into two main product lines: bleached fiber products and wood products, which include flooring, molding, and doorjambs. The company also operates an extensive forest regeneration program. Founded in 1903. **Corporate headquarters location:** Spokane WA. **Other area locations:** Cypress Bend AR; Prescott AR. **Other U.S. locations:** ID; MN; NV; OR. **Number of employees worldwide:** 6,300.

POTLATCH CORPORATION
P.O. Box 727, McGehee AR 71654. 870/877-2662. **Contact:** Marguerite Abowitz, Employee Relations Manager. **E-mail address:** arkansas@potlatch.com. **World Wide Web address:** http://www.potlatchcorp.com. **Description:** Potlatch Corporation is a diversified forest products company with 1.5 million acres of timberland in Arkansas, Idaho, and Minnesota. The corporation's facilities convert wood fiber into two main product lines: bleached fiber products and wood products, which include flooring, molding, and doorjambs. The company also operates an extensive forest regeneration program. Founded in 1903. **Special programs:** Internships. **Corporate headquarters location:** Spokane WA. **Other U.S. locations:** ID; MN; NV; OR. **Operations at this facility include:** Using wood chips and sawmill residue, this location produces coated and uncoated bleached paperboard for the folding carton and cup-stock markets. **Number of employees at this location:** 400. **Number of employees nationwide:** 6,300.

POTLATCH CORPORATION
10113 US Highway 371 West, Prescott AR 71857. 870/887-2605. **Contact:** Human Resources. **E-mail address:** arkansas@potlatch.com. **World Wide Web address:** http://www.potlatchcorp.com. **Description:** A diversified forest products company with 1.5 million acres of timberland in Arkansas, Idaho, and Minnesota. The corporation's facilities convert wood fiber into two main product lines: bleached fiber products and wood products, which include flooring, molding, and doorjambs. The company also operates an extensive forest regeneration program. Founded in 1903. **Corporate headquarters location:** Spokane WA. **Other U.S. locations:** ID; MN; NV; OR. **Operations at this facility include:** This location is a sawmill. **Number of employees worldwide:** 6,300.

PRODUCERS RICE MILL, INC.
P.O. Box 1248, Stuttgart AR 72160. 870/673-4444. **Fax:** 870/672-4494. **Contact:** Human Resources Director. **E-mail address:** hrdir@producersrice.com. **World Wide Web address:** http://www.producersrice.com. **Description:** Producers and distributors of rice in the South. Founded in 1943. **Corporate headquarters location:** This location. **Other area locations:** Statewide. **President/CEO:** Keith Glover.

PROFESSIONAL DENTAL TECHNOLOGIES, INC.
P.O. Box 4129, Batesville AR 72503. 870/698-2300. **Fax:** 870/698-2390. **Physical address:** 267 East Main Street, Batesville AR 72501. **Contact:** Michelle Ireland, Human Resources. **E-mail address:** mireland@prodentec.com. **World Wide Web address:** http://www.prodentec.com. **Description:** Designs and manufactures products that assist dental professionals in diagnosing, treating, and preventing periodontal and other dental diseases. Products include the Rota-dent plaque removal instrument, the Prism intra-oral camera, the Periocheck in-office enzyme test, and the PerfectByte Practice Management Software System. **Positions advertised include:** Staff Accountant; Professional Sales Representative. **Corporate headquarters location:** This location.

RITTERNET
P.O. Box 19053, Jonesboro AR 72401. 870/974-9100. **Physical address:** 3300 One Place, Jonesboro AR 72401. **Toll-free phone:** 888/659-6009. **Contact:** Human Resources. **E-mail address:** employment@callritter.com. **World Wide Web address:** http://www.ritternet.com. **Description:** An Internet access service for northeast Arkansas. **Positions advertised include:** Sales Engineer; Telecom Technician.

ROGERS TOOL WORKS
1602 East Central, Bentonville AR 72712. 479/273-2407. **Contact:** Human Resources. **World Wide Web address:** http://www.kennametal.com. **Description:** Produces carbide-tipped and solid carbide drills, reamers, end mills, and milling cutters. **Parent company:** Kennametal. **Listed on:** New York Stock Exchange. **Stock exchange symbol:** KMT.

ST. JOSEPH'S MERCY HEALTH CENTER
300 Werner Street, P.O. Box 29001, Hot Springs AR 71903. 501/622-1000. **Fax:** 501/622-2047. **Recorded jobline:** 501/622-4606. **Contact:** Lori Wozniak, Employment Supervisor. **E-mail address:** hr@saintjoesphs.com **World Wide Web address:** http://www.saintjosephs.com. **Description:** A full-service, nonprofit medical center. **NOTE:** Entry-level positions and second and third shifts are offered. **Positions advertised include:** Cardiologist; Charge RN; Dosimetrist; Family Medicine Physician; General Surgeon; Internal Medicine Physician; Licensed Practical Nurse; Neurologist; OB/GYN; Staff RN; Financial Analyst. **Special programs:** Internships; Apprenticeships; Training; Summer Jobs. **Corporate headquarters location:** St. Louis MO. **CEO:** Randy Fale. **Facilities Manager:** Randy Fortner. **Annual sales/revenues:** $5 - $10 million. **Number of employees at this location:** 1,500.

SANYO MANUFACTURING CORPORATION
P.O. Box 2000, Forest City AR 72336. 870/633-5030. **Physical address:** 3333 Sanyo Road, Forest City AR 72335. **Fax:** 870/633-0650. **Contact:** Human Resources. **World Wide Web address:** http://www.sanyo.com. **Description:** Manufactures a variety of well-known consumer home entertainment products as well as microwave ovens. **Operations at this facility include:** Manufacturing of SANYO and FISHER color televisions.

SIMMONS FOODS
P.O. Box 430, Siloam Springs AR 72761. 479/524-8151. **Contact:** Linda Ross, Vice President of Human Resources. **E-mail address:** resume@simfoods.com. **World Wide Web address:** http://www.simmonsfoods.com. **Description:** A poultry processing company and producer of pet food. The company's service base includes fast food restaurants, retailers, school programs, and other food processing companies. **Positions advertised include:** Refrigeration Supervisor; Employment Interviewer; Production Accountant; Quality Assurance Manager. **Special programs:** Internships. **Corporate headquarters location:** This location. **Other U.S. locations:** MO; OK. **Operations at this facility include:** Administration. **Number of employees nationwide:** 4,300.

SOUTHWEST TIMES RECORD
P.O. Box 1359, Fort Smith AR 72902. 479/785-7700. **Physical address:** 3600 Wheeler Avenue, Fort Smith AR 72901. **Fax:** 479/784-0476. **Contact:** Human Resources. **World Wide Web address:** http://www.stephensmedia.com. **Description:** A newspaper. **Positions advertised include:** Web Offset Press Person; Customer Service Representative. **Parent company:** Stephens Media Group.

SPACE PHOTONICS INC.
700 Research Center Boulevard, Fayetteville AR 72701. 479/575-5221. **Fax:** 479/575-7446. **Contact:** Human Resources. **E-mail address:** contact@spacephotonics.com. **World Wide Web address:** http://www.spacephotonics.com. **Description:** Develops, markets, and sells optical networking systems and components designed to address the reliability and bandwidth limitations of military and commercial aircraft and spacecraft. The company's products enable aerospace designers to embed high-capacity, optical networking capabilities into their systems. Founded in 1999.

STEPHENS, INC.
P.O. Box 3507, Little Rock AR 72203-3507. 501/377-2000. **Physical address:** 111 Center Street, Little Rock AR 72201. **Toll-free phone:** 800/643-9691. **Fax:** 501/377-2111. **Contact:** Ellen Gray, Human Resources. **E-mail address:** hr@stephens.com. **World Wide Web address:** http://www.stephens.com. **Description:** An investment banking firm. Founded in 1933. **Positions advertised include:** Financial Consultants. **Corporate headquarters location:** This location. **Operations at this facility include:** Administration; Research and Development; Sales. **Listed on:** NYSE. **Stock exchange symbol:** SIPC. **Number of employees at this location:** 650.

STONE COUNTY IRONWORKS
408 Ironworks Drive, P.O. Box 957, Mountain View AR 72560. 870/269-8108. **Contact:** Human Resources. **World Wide Web address:** http://www.stoneiron.com. **Description:** Provides hand-forged, custom blacksmith products for household use including fireplace accessories; kitchen, home, and bath products and tools; furniture and lighting; plant accessories; and handmade pottery. **Number of employees at this location:** 100.

TRACTOR SUPPLY COMPANY
5802 Warden Road, Sherwood AR 72120. 501/835-6170. **Contact:** Human Resources. **E-mail address:** careerbox1@tractorsupply.com. **World Wide Web address:** http://www.mytscstore.com. **Description:** Farm and ranch store chain with 500 retail stores in 31 states. Founded in 1938. **Positions advertised include:** Retail Store Manager; Assistant Manager; District Manager. **NOTE:** Apply for positions online. **Corporate headquarters location:** Nashville TN. **Other area locations:** Fayetteville AR; Harrison AR; Jonesboro AR; Searcy AR; Bentonville AR. **Other U.S. locations:** Nationwide. **Listed on:** NASDAQ. **Stock exchange symbol:** TSCO.

TYSON FOODS, INC.
P.O. Box 2020, Springdale AR 72765-2020. 479/290-4000. **Physical address:** 2210 West Oaklawn Drive, Springdale AR 72762. **Contact:** Personnel. **World Wide Web address:** http://www.tyson.com. **Description:** The world's largest processor and marketer of chicken, beef, and pork with more than 300 facilities in 27 states and 21 countries. **Positions advertised include:** Accountant; EEO Specialist; Exec Recruiter; Financial Analyst; Manager Income Tax; Product Manager; Production Controller. **Corporate headquarters location:** This location. **Listed on:** NASDAQ. **Stock exchange symbol:** TSN. **Number of employees worldwide:** 114,000.

USA TRUCK, INC.
P.O. Box 449, Van Buren AR 72957. 479/471-2510. **Physical address:** 3200 Industrial Park Drive, Van Buren AR 72956. **Fax:** 479/471-3877. **Contact:** Jerry Seiter, Director of Administration. **World Wide Web address:** http://www.usa-truck.com. **Description:** A trucking company that provides services for retail companies. **Positions advertised include:** Transportation/Traffic Specialist; Driver. **Corporate headquarters location:** This location. **Operations at this facility include:** Administration; Sales. **Listed on:** NASDAQ. **Stock exchange symbol:** USAK.

UNIVERSITY OF ARKANSAS FOR MEDICAL SCIENCES
4301 West Markham Street, Little Rock AR 72205. 501/686-5650. **Fax:** 501/296-1825. **Recorded jobline:** 501/686-5009. **Contact:** Betty Coller, Employment Manager. **World Wide Web address:** http://www.uams.edu. **Description:** An academic medical center providing patient care, health care education, and biomedical research. **Positions advertised include:** Account Follow-up Specialist; Administrative Assistant; Administrative Secretary; Ambulatory Technician; Cashier; Chart Technician; Hospital Operator; Medical Diagnostic Analyst; Medical/Legal Secretary; Shipping and

Receiving Clerk; Fire Safety Systems Supervisor; Journeymen Electrician; Skilled Trades Helper; Fiscal Manager; Mental health Professional; Occupational Therapist. **Operations at this facility include:** Administration; Research and Development.

VIRCO MANUFACTURING CORPORATION
Highway 65 South, Conway AR 72032 501/329-2901. **Fax:** 501/450-1140. **Contact:** Human Resources. **World Wide Web address:** http://www.virco.com. **Description:** Engaged in the manufacturing and selling of furniture products. The company's Educational Group sells furniture including school desks, tables, chairs, and cabinets to 40 of the nation's 50 largest school districts including Los Angeles, New York City, Washington DC, Philadelphia, and Dade County FL. The company's Commercial Group sells folding chairs and tables, stacking chairs, hotel and restaurant seating, office furniture, and convention and arena furniture. The company's Special Markets Group consists of all federal government and international sales. **Corporate headquarters location:** Torrance CA.

WAL-MART STORES, INC.
702 SW Eighth Street, Bentonville AR 72716. 479/273-4000. **Contact:** Recruiting. **E-mail address:** resumix@wal-mart.com. **World Wide Web address:** http://www.walmart.com. **Description:** The world's largest retailer with more than 3,600 facilities in the U.S. and more than 1,570 units in Mexico, Puerto Rico, Canada, Argentina, Brazil, China, Korea, Germany and the UK. Founded in 1962. **Positions advertised include:** Director, Global Procurement; Manager, EEO and Employment Practices; Regional Training Manager; Marketing Manager, Regional Sales; Project Coordinator, Financial Services; Programmer/Analyst; Benefits Manager; Quality Control Manager; Alarm Technician; Staff Auditor. **Special programs:** Internships. **Corporate headquarters location:** This location. **Other U.S. locations:** Nationwide. **Operations at this facility include:** Administration; Sales; Service. **Listed on:** New York Stock Exchange. **Stock exchange symbol:** WMT. **Annual sales/revenue:** $256 billion. **Number of employees worldwide:** 1.6 million.

WATERLOO INDUSTRIES
P.O. Box 1048, Pocahontas AR 72455. 870/892-4586. **Contact:** Human Resources. **E-mail address:** info@waterlooindustries.com. **World Wide Web address:** http://www.waterlooindustries.com. **Description:** Produces tool cabinets and related products, including metal saw stands. **Corporate headquarters location:** Waterloo IA. **Parent company:** Fortune Brands, Inc. **Number of employees nationwide:** 1,000.

WELLS FARGO MORTGAGE BRANCH
5525 John F. Kennedy Boulevard, Little Rock AR 72116. 501/812-4207. **Fax:** 501/812-0450. **Contact:** Human Resources. **World Wide Web address:** http://www.wellsfargo.com. **Description:** A diversified financial institution with over $234 billion in assets. Wells Fargo serves over 17 million customers through 5,300 independent locations worldwide. The company also maintains several stand-alone ATMs and branches within other retail outlets. Services include community banking, credit and debit cards, home equity and mortgage loans, on-line banking, student loans, and insurance. Wells Fargo also offers a complete line of commercial and institutional financial services. Founded in 1852. **Positions advertised include:** Consumer Loan Underwriter. **Corporate headquarters location:** San Francisco CA. **Other U.S. locations:** Nationwide. **International locations:** Worldwide. **Listed on:** New York Stock Exchange. **Stock exchange symbol:** WFC. **Annual sales/revenues:** More than $100 million. **Number of employees worldwide:** 120,000.

WHIRLPOOL CORPORATION
P.O. Box 17001, Fort Smith AR 72917-7001. 479/648-2000. **Contact:** Human Resources. **E-mail address:** careers@email.whirlpool.com. **World Wide Web address:** http://www.whirlpoolcorp.com. **Description:** Whirlpool Corporation manufactures and markets home appliances. Whirlpool also manufactures and supplies major home appliances to Sears, Roebuck and Company under the Kenmore brand name. **Positions advertised include:** Industrial Engineer; Supplier Quality Engineer; Materials Manager; Process Engineer; Product Engineer; Controls Engineer; Chemical Process Engineer. **Special programs:** Internships. **NOTE:** Search and apply for positions online. **Corporate headquarters location:** Benton Harbor MI. **Other U.S. locations:** Nationwide. **International locations:** Worldwide. **Operations at this facility include:** This location manufactures refrigerators, trash compactors, and icemakers. **Listed on:** New York Stock Exchange. **Stock exchange symbol:** WHR. **Number of employees worldwide:** 39,600.

A&R PARTNERS
201 Baldwin Avenue, San Mateo CA 94401-3914. 650/762-2800. **Fax:** 650/762-2801. **Contact:** Human Resources. **E-mail address:** hr@arpartners.com. **World Wide Web address:** http://www.arpartners.com. **Description:** A public relations firm. **NOTE:** Entry-level positions are offered. **Positions advertised include:** Director; Senior Account Execuitve; Account Executive; Account Associate. **Special programs:** Internships; Apprenticeships; Training. **Corporate headquarters location:** This location. **Other U.S. locations:** New York NY; Denver CO; Portland OR; Louisville KY; Research Triangle Park NC. **President:** Robert Angus. **Annual sales/revenues:** $5 - $10 million. **Number of employees nationwide:** Over 80.

A-MARK PRECIOUS METALS INC.
100 Wilshire Boulevard, 3rd Floor, Santa Monica CA 90401. 310/319-0200. **Fax:** 310/319-0279. **Contact:** Human Resources. **E-mail address:** hr@amark.com. **World Wide Web address:** http://www.amark.com. **Description:** A precious metals wholesaler that buys and sells gold, silver, and platinum coins. Clients include banks, brokerage houses, refiners, jewelers, investment advisors, coin dealers, and government mint officials. **Positions advertised include:** Senior Accountant; Shipping and Receiving Specialist. **Number of employees at this location:** 25.

AB&I FOUNDRY
7825 San Leandro Street, Oakland CA 94621. 510/632-3467. **Toll-free phone:** 800/GOT-IRON. **Fax:** 510/633-5292. **Contact:** Michael Lowe, Human Resources Manager. **World Wide Web address:** http://www.abifoundry.com. **Description:** A manufacturer of cast iron soil pipe, fittings, and custom castings. Founded in 1906. **Positions advertised include:** Industrial Electrician; Mechanic. **Corporate headquarters location:** This location. **Annual sales/revenues:** $21 - $50 million. **Number of employees at this location:** 180.

ABC FAMILY
10960 Wilshire Boulevard, Los Angeles CA 90024. 818/560-1000. **Contact:** Personnel. **World Wide Web address:** http://www.abcfamily.go.com. **Description:** Produces, exhibits, and distributes entertainment and informational programming as well as related products targeted at families worldwide. **NOTE:** Job listings for ABC Family are posted on the parent company's website: http://disney.go.com. **Parent company:** Disney Corporation. **Other U.S. locations:** Nationwide.

ABC, INC.
4151 Prospect Avenue, Los Angeles, CA 90067. 310/557-7777. **Contact:** Human Resources Representative. **World Wide Web address:** http://www.abc.com. **Description:** A diversified communications organization. The company is engaged in television and radio broadcasting, provides cable television service to subscribers, and publishes newspapers and other specialized publications. Broadcasting operations include ABC Television Network Group, the Broadcast Group, the Cable and International Broadcast Group, and the Multimedia Group. In addition to its network operations, the broadcasting segment consists of 8 network-affiliated television stations, 10 radio stations, cable television systems providing service to subscribers in 16 states, and the developing multimedia video-by-wire business. Publishing operations consist of 8 daily newspapers, 78 weekly newspapers, 63 shopping guides, and several other business and specialized publications. **Positions advertised include:** Director, Training; Director, Communications; Manager of Diversity; Recruitment Manager. **Parent company:** Disney Corporation.

ABC7/KGO-TV
900 Front Street, San Francisco CA 94111. 415/954-7958. **Recorded jobline:** 415/954-7958. **Contact:** Human Resources. **E-mail address:** kgo-tv.hr@abc.com. **World Wide Web address:** http://www.abclocal.go.com/kgo. **Description:** An ABC-affiliated television station. **Positions advertised include:** Web Producer; General Aswsignment News Reporter; Internet Sales Account Executive; Producer; Promotion Writer; Broadcast Systems Engineer; Broadcast Maintenance Engineer. **Special programs:** Internships. **Internship information:** Internships are offered to college juniors, seniors, and graduate students. Interns are paid minimum wage and receive college credit for their work. Approximately 16 interns are selected each semester. **Corporate headquarters location:** New York NY. **Other U.S. locations:** New York NY; Seattle WA. **Parent company:** Disney Corporation.

ABM INDUSTRIES INCORPORATED
160 Pacific Avenue, Suite 222, San Francisco CA 94111. 415/733-4000. **Fax:** 415/733-7333. **Contact:** Human Resources. **World Wide Web address:** http://www.abm.com. **Description:** A national contract maintenance firm providing janitorial, maintenance, and building management products and services in more than 60 metropolitan areas throughout the United States and Canada. **Positions advertised include:** Compensation Manager; Data Center Operator; Data Security Analyst; Documentation specialist; Project manager; Senior Internal Auditor. **Corporate headquarters location:** This location. **Listed on:** New York Stock Exchange. **Stock exchange symbol:** ABM. **Number of employees nationwide:** 70,000.

ABS CONSULTING
300 Commerce Drive, Suite 200, Irvine CA 92602. 714/734-4242. **Fax:** 714/734-4262. **Contact:** Human Resources. **E-mail address:** absgrpemp@eagle.org. **World Wide Web address:** http://www.absconsulting.com. **Description:** Offers engineering consulting for system safety and reliability and provides probable risk assessment to the energy, defense, petrochemical, and manufacturing industries. **NOTE:** Unsolicited resumes or applications not accepted. **Positions advertised include:** Program Manager; Construction Manager; Resident Engineer; Structural Engineer. **Corporate headquarters location:** Houston TX.

ACCO ENGINEERED SYSTEMS
6265 San Fernando Road, Glendale CA 91201. 818/244-6571. **Toll-free phone:** 800/998-2226. **Fax:** 818/549-0120. **Contact:** Roberta Kessler, Human Resources Director. **E-mail address:** hrglendale@accoes.com. **World Wide Web address:** http://www.accoair.com. **Description:** A mechanical contracting firm that specializes in the design and construction of HVAC systems. **Corporate headquarters location:** This location. **Other area locations:** San Leandro CA; Sacramento CA; San Diego CA; Tustin CA. **Other U.S. locations:** Orlando FL; Tampa FL; Kent WA. **Operations at this facility include:** Administration; Engineering and Design; Sales; Service. **Listed on:** Privately held. **Annual sales/revenues:** More than $100 million. **Number of employees at this location:** 300. **Number of employees nationwide:** 1,200.

ACS (AFFILIATED COMPUTER SERVICES)
One World Trade Center, Suite 2200, Long Beach CA 90831-2200. 310/513-2700. **Contact:** Human Resources. **World Wide Web address:** http://www.acs-education.com. **Description:** Administers, bills, and processes student loans acquired by individuals attending higher education institutions. **Corporate headquarters:** Dallas TX. **Parent Company:** FleetBoston Financial.

ADC TELECOMMUNICATIONS, INC.
WIRELINE SYSTEMS DIVISON
14402 Franklin Avenue, Tustin CA 92780-7013. 714/832-9922. **Toll-free phone:** 800/366-3891. **Fax:** 714/832-9924. **Contact:** Human Resources. **World Wide Web address:** http://www.adc.com. **Description:** Provides global network infrastructure products and services that enable the delivery of high-speed Internet, data, video, and voice services to consumers and businesses worldwide. Founded in 1935. **NOTE:** Jobseekers can search and apply for positions online. **Corporate headquarters location:** Minneapolis MN. **Other U.S. locations:** Nationwide. **International locations:** Worldwide. **Listed on** NASDAQ. **Stock exchange symbol:** ADCT.

ADI SYSTEMS, INC.
6851 Mowry Avenue, Newark CA 94560. 510/795-6200. **Contact:** Shelly Venegan, Human Resources Manager. **E-mail address:** personnel@adiusa.com. **World Wide Web address:** http://www.adiusa.com. **Description:** Manufactures color CRT monitors and LCD displays. **Corporate headquarters location:** This location. **Parent company:** ADI Corporation.

ADT SECURITY SERVICES
3551 Arden Road, Hayward CA 94545-3922. 650/345-6948. **Toll-free phone:** 800/228-0530. **Contact:** Human Resources Department. **World Wide Web address:** http://www.adtsecurityservices.com. **Description:** Designs, programs, markets, and installs protective systems to safeguard life and property from hazards such as burglary, hold-up, and fire. ADT Security Services has over 180,000 customers in the United States, Canada, and Western Europe. **Corporate headquarters location:** Boca Raton FL. **Parent Company:** Tyco.

ADT SECURITY SERVICES
5400 West Rosecrans Avenue, Hawthorne CA 90250. 310/725-2978. **Fax:** 310/725-2973. **Contact:** Human Resources Representative. **World Wide Web address:** http://www.adtsecurityservices.com. **Description:** Designs, programs, markets, and installs protective systems to safeguard life and property from hazards such as burglary, hold-up, and fire. ADT Security Services has over 180,000 customers in the United States, Canada, and Western Europe. **Corporate headquarters location:** Boca Raton FL. **Parent company:** Tyco. **Operations at this facility include:** Administration; Sales; Service.

AECOM TECHNOLOGY CORPORATION
555 South Flower Street, Suite 3700, Los Angeles CA 90071. 213/593-8000. **Contact:** Human Resources. **E-mail address:** aecomcareers@aecom.com. **World Wide Web address:** http://www.aecom.com. **Description:** A leading global engineering and design firm. **Corporate headquarters location:** This location. **Number of employees worldwide:** 18,000.

AFG INDUSTRIES, INC.
17300 Silica Drive, Victorville CA 92392. 760/241-2237. **Fax:** 760/241-6072. **Contact:** Human Resources. **World Wide Web address:** http://www.afg.com. **Description:** Manufactures, distributes, and packages flat glass. **Corporate headquarters location:** Kingsport TN. **Other U.S. locations:** Nationwide. **International locations:** Canada; Mexico.

ANG NEWSPAPERS
P.O. Box 28884, Oakland CA 94604. 510/208-6300. **Physical address:** 401 13th Street, Oakland CA 94612. **Fax:** 510/293-2725. **Contact:** Human Resources Department. **E-mail address:** hr@angnewspapers.com. **World Wide Web address:** http://www.insidebayarea.com. **Description:** Publishes six daily newspapers with a combined daily circulation of more than 232,000. **Positions advertised include:** Classified Call Center Supervisor; Classified Sales Executive; Classified Sales Manager; Direct Mail Sales Specialist; Sales Assistant; Copy Editor/Designer. **Parent company:** Garden State Newspapers. **Operations at this facility include:** Administration; Manufacturing; Regional Headquarters; Sales; Service. **Number of employees nationwide:** 1,000.

A.P. PHARMA
123 Saginaw Drive, Redwood City CA 94063. 650/366-2626. **Fax:** 650/365-6490. **Contact:** Sandra Squires, Human Resources. **E-mail address:** jobs@appharma.com. **World Wide Web address:** http://www.appharma.com. **Description:** A developer and marketer of polymer-based delivery systems and related technologies for use in pharmaceuticals, over-the-counter drugs, toiletries, and specialty applications. **Corporate headquarters location:** This location. **Listed on:** NASDAQ. **Stock exchange symbol:** APPA.

ASML
101 East Metro Drive, Suite 400, San Jose CA 95110. 408/452-2600. **Fax:** 408/452-2690. **Contact:** Professional Staffing. **E-mail address:** careers@asml.com. **World Wide Web address:** http://www.asml.com. **Description:** Designs and manufactures diffusion systems, oxidation systems, atmospheric pressure systems, and other equipment used to manufacture semiconductors. **Corporate headquarters location:** Veldhoven, the Netherlands. **Listed on:** NASDAQ. **Stock exchange symbol:** ASML. **President/CEO:** Doug Dunn.

ATC ASSOCIATES
50 East Foothil Boulevard, Arcadia CA 91006. 626/447-5216. **Fax:** 626/447-7593. **Contact:** Human Resources Manager. **E-mail address:** atcjobs@atc-enviro.com. **World Wide Web address:** http://www.atc-enviro.com. **Description:** Performs comprehensive environmental consulting, engineering, and on-site remediation services throughout the United States for a variety of clients including federal, state, and local government agencies. **Positions advertised include:** IH Technician; Project Manager; Staff Scientist. **Corporate headquarters location:** Woburn MA. **Other area locations:** Statewide. **Other U.S. locations:** Nationwide.

ATC ASSOCIATES
1117 Lone Palm Avenue, Suite B, Modesto CA 95351. 209/579-2221. **Fax:** 209/579-2225. **Contact:** Human Resources Manager. **E-mail address:** atcjobs@atc-enviro.com. **World Wide Web address:** http://www.atc-enviro.com. **Description:** Performs comprehensive environmental consulting, engineering, and on-site remediation services throughout the United States for a variety of clients including federal, state, and local government agencies. **Positions advertised include:** Senior Project Manager. **Corporate headquarters location:** Woburn MA. **Other area locations:** Statewide. **Other U.S. locations:** Nationwide.

AT&T GOVERNMENT SOLUTIONS
5383 Hollister Avenue, Suite 200, Santa Barbara CA 93111. 805/964-7724. **Contact:** Karen Cashman, Recruiting Manager. **World Wide Web address:** http://www.grci.com. **Description:** AT&T Government Solutions creates large-scale, decision-support systems and software engineering environments; applies operations

research and mathematical modeling to business and management systems; and implements advanced database technology. **Special programs:** Internships. **Corporate headquarters location:** Vienna VA. **Other U.S. locations:** Nationwide. **Parent company:** AT&T Corporation. **Operations at this facility include:** This location is a research and development facility. **Listed on:** New York Stock Exchange. **Stock exchange symbol:** T. **Number of employees at this location:** 120. **Number of employees worldwide:** 1,300.

AAMES FINANCIAL CORPORATION
350 South Grand Avenue, 43rd Floor, Los Angeles CA 90071. 323/210-5300. **Toll-free phone:** 800/829-2929 ext. 5300. **Fax:** 323/210-5541. **Contact:** Human Resources. **E-mail address:** info@aamesjobline.com. **World Wide Web address:** http://www.aamesfinancial.com. **Description:** Offers mortgage loans to homeowners. Aames Financial Corporation also functions as an insurance agent and mortgage trustee through some of its subsidiaries. Services include originating (brokering and funding), purchasing, selling, and servicing first and junior trust deed loans primarily for single-family residences in the western United States. **Positions advertised include:** Business Systems Analyst; Collections Officer. **Corporate headquarters location:** This location. **Other U.S. locations:** Nationwide.

ABATIX ENVIRONMENTAL CORPORATION
14068 Catalina Street, San Leandro CA 94577. 510/614-2340. **Toll-free phone:** 800/365-5795. **Fax:** 510/614-2350. **Contact:** Andrea Staub, Director of Human Resources. **E-mail address:** hr@abatix.com. **World Wide Web address:** http://www.abatix.com. **Description:** A full-line distributor of durable and nondurable supplies to the following industry segments: asbestos and lead abatement, hazardous material remediation, and construction. Products include industrial safety supplies, construction tools, general safety products such as protective clothing and eyewear, and clean-up equipment. Abatix Environmental Corporation has seven distribution centers serving customers throughout the Southwest, the Midwest, and the Pacific Coast. **NOTE:** Resumes may be sent via e-mail, mail or fax. Address resumes to: Abatix Corporation, Attention: Human Resources, 8201 Eastpoint Drive, Suite 500, Dallas TX 75227. Fax: 214/381-9513. **Corporate headquarters location:** Dallas TX. **Other U.S. locations:** Phoenix AZ; Las Vegas NV; Houston TX; Seattle WA. **Listed on:** NASDAQ. **Stock exchange symbol:** ABIX.

ABATIX ENVIRONMENTAL CORPORATION
10051 Painter Avenue, Santa Fe Springs CA 90670. 562/944-3445. **Toll-free phone:** 800/952-2284. **Fax:** 562/946-1855. **Contact:** Human Resources. **E-mail address:** hr@abatix.com. **World Wide Web address:** http://www.abatix.com. **Description:** A full-line supplier of durable and nondurable supplies to various industry segments including asbestos and lead abatement, hazardous material remediation, and construction. Products include industrial safety supplies; construction tools; general safety products such as protective clothing and eyewear; and clean-up equipment. Abatix Environmental Corporation has seven distribution centers serving customers throughout the Southwest, Midwest, and the Pacific Coast. **NOTE:** Resumes may be sent via e-mail, mail or fax. Address resumes to: Abatix Corporation, Attention: Human Resources, 8201 Eastpoint Drive, Suite 500, Dallas TX 75227. Fax: 214/381-9513. **Corporate headquarters location:** Dallas TX. **Other U.S. locations:** Phoenix AZ; Las Vegas NV; Houston TX; Seattle WA. **Listed on:** NASDAQ. **Stock exchange symbol:** ABIX.

ABAXIS, INC.
3240 Whipple Road, Union City CA 94587. 510/675-6500. **Fax:** 510/441-6151. **Contact:** Human Resources. **E-mail address:** jobs@abaxis.com. **World Wide Web address:** http://www.abaxis.com. **Description:** A research and development firm. Abaxis, Inc. is focused on the commercialization of the Piccolo System, which consists of a small, whole-blood analyzer and blood chemistry reagent rotors. The company developed Primary Health Profile, a nine-test reagent rotor marketed to veterinarians. Founded in 1989. **Positions advertised include:** Embedded Software Engineer. **Corporate headquarters location:** This location.

ABBOTT LABORATORIES
820 Mission Street, South Pasadena CA 91030. 818/410-8000. **Contact:** Human Resources. **World Wide Web address:** http://www.abbott.com. **Description:** A health care company that develops pharmaceuticals and medical devices for such conditions as AIDS, diabetes, and cancer.

ABGENIX INC.
6701 Kaiser Drive, Fremont CA 94555. 510/608-6500. **Fax:** 510/608-6511. **Contact:** Human Resources. **World Wide Web address:** http://www.abgenix.com. **Description:** A leading health technology company that develops and manufactures therapeutic antibodies. **Advertised positions:** Statistical Programming, Clinical Operations; Senior Research Associate; Compliance Specialist.

ACAPULCO RESTAURANTS
4001 Via Oro Avenue, Suite 200, Long Beach CA 90810. 310/513-7500. **Toll-free phone:** 800/735-3501. **Fax:** 310/835-3156. **Contact:** Human Resources. **World Wide Web address:** http://www.acapulcorestaurants.com. **Description:** Operates a chain of over 40 Mexican restaurants, primarily in Southern California. **Corporate headquarters location:** This location. **Other area locations:** Statewide. **Parent company:** Restaurant Associates.

ACCENTURE
2101 Rosecrans Avenue, Suite 3300, El Segundo CA 90245. 310/726-2700. **Fax:** 310/726-2950. **Contact:** Human Resources Manager. **World Wide Web address:** http://www.accenture.com. **Description:** A management and technology consulting firm. Accenture offers a wide range of services including business re-engineering, customer service system consulting, data system design and implementation, Internet sales systems research and design, and strategic planning. **NOTE:** Search and apply for positions online. **Corporate headquarters location:** Chicago IL. **Other U.S. locations:** Nationwide. **International locations:** Worldwide. **Listed on:** New York Stock Exchange. **Stock exchange symbol:** ASN.

ACCENTURE
1215 K Street, 16th Floor, Sacramento CA 95814. 916/650-2000. **Fax:** 916/650-2399. **Contact:** Personnel. **World Wide Web address:** http://www.accenture.com. **Description:** A management and technology consulting firm. Accenture offers a wide range of services including business re-engineering, customer service system consulting, data system design and implementation, Internet sales systems research and design, and strategic planning. **NOTE:** Search and apply for positions online. **Positions advertised include:** Java Programmer. **Corporate headquarters location:** Chicago IL. **Other area locations:** Los Angeles CA; Palo Alto CA; Sacramento CA; San Francisco CA; Walnut Creek CA. **Other U.S. locations:** Nationwide. **Listed on:** New York Stock Exchange. **Stock exchange symbol:** ASN.

ACCESS COMMUNICATIONS
101 Howard Street, 2nd Floor, San Francisco CA 94105-1629. 415/904-7070. **Fax:** 415/904-7055. **Contact:** Human Resources. **E-mail address:** jobs@accesspr.com. **World Wide Web address:** http://www.accesspr.com. **Description:** A public relations firm whose clients include software and other high-tech corporations. Positions advertised include: Assistant Account Executive; Senior Account Executive; Account Supervisor. **Corporate headquarters location:** This location. **Other U.S. locations:** New York NY.

ACCOM, INC.
1490 O'Brien Drive, Menlo Park CA 94025. 650/328-3818. **Fax:** 650/327-2511. **Contact:** Human Resources. **E-mail address:** personnel@accom.com. **World Wide Web address:** http://www.accom.com. **Description:** Designs, manufactures, and sells digital video production, recording, and editing equipment for the television, broadcasting, computer, and video industries. **Corporate headquarters location:** This location. **CEO:** Junaid Sheikh.

ACCURIDE INTERNATIONAL INC.
12311 Shoemaker Avenue, Santa Fe Springs CA 90670. 562/903-0200. **Fax:** 562/903-0208. **Contact:** Human Resources. **E-mail address:** careeropportunities@accuride.com. **World Wide Web address:** http://www.accuride.com. **Description:** A metals manufacturing company. Products include ball bearing slides for office furniture, copiers, computers, and tool chests. Founded in 1966. **Positions advertised include:** Market/Product Manager. **Corporate headquarters location:** This location. **Other U.S. locations:** South Bend IN; Charlotte NC. **International locations:** China; Germany; Japan; Switzerland, United Kingdom. **Listed on:** Privately held. **Number of employees at this location:** 400. **Number of employees nationwide:** 700.

ACCUTECH
2641 La Mirada Drive, Vista CA 92083. 760/599-6555. **Contact:** Human Resources. **E-mail address:** info@accutech-llc.com. **World Wide Web address:** http://www.accutech-llc.com. **Description:** Develops, manufactures, and markets disposable diagnostic tests. **Corporate headquarters location:** This location.

ACER AMERICA CORPORATION
2641 Orchard Parkway, San Jose CA 95134. 408/432-6200. **Toll-free phone:** 800/733-2237. **Fax:** 408/922-2918. **Contact:** Human Resources. **E-mail address:** careers@acer.com. **World Wide Web address:** http://www.acer.com. **Description:** One of the largest microcomputer manufacturers and OEM suppliers. The company also manufactures a variety of computer peripherals and components including monitors, keyboards, expansion cards, and CD-ROM drives. **NOTE:** Resumes may be sent via e-mail, mail, or fax. **Positions advertised include:** Business Manager, Inside Sales; Business Manager, Retail Sales. **Parent company:** Acer Inc. (Taiwan) **Number of employees at this location:** 700. **Number of employees nationwide:** 1,200. **Number of employees worldwide:** 25,000.

ACMA COMPUTERS
1505 Reliance Way, Fremont CA 94539. 510/623-1212. **Toll-free phone:** 800/786-6888. **Fax:** 510/623-0818. **Contact:** Human Resources. **World Wide Web address:** http://www.acma.com. **Description:** Manufactures custom-engineered computers and servers. **Positions advertised include:** Account Manager; Marketing Communications Specialist; In-House Sales Assistant; Technical Support Engineer; Office Assistant. **Office hours:** Monday - Friday, 8:30 a.m. - 5:30 p.m. **Corporate headquarters location:** This location.

ACOM SOLUTIONS INC.
2850 East 29th Street, Long Beach CA 90806-2313. 562/424-7899. **Fax:** 562/424-8662. **Contact:** Human Resources. **World Wide Web address:** http://www.acom.com. **Description:** Develops and markets advanced modular software systems for e-document management, e-payment management, B2B e-commerce management and e-purchasing management. **Positions advertised include:** Regional Sales Manager. **Other U.S. locations:** Los Angeles CA; Duluth GA; St. Paul MN.

ACTEL CORPORATION
6540 Lusk Boulevard, San Diego CA 92121. 858/824-0077. **Contact:** Human Resources. **World Wide Web address:** http://www.actel.com. **Description:** Designs, manufactures, and markets programmable integrated circuits used in computers, peripherals, telecommunications devices, and consumer electronics. GateField Corporation also develops the software used for its products. **Corporate headquarters location:** Mountain View CA. **Other U.S. locations:** Nationwide. **International locations:** Worldwide.

ACTEL CORPORATION
2061 Stierlin Court, Mountain View CA 94043. 650/318-4200. **Contact:** Barbara McArthur, Vice President of Human Resources. **E-mail address:** talent@actel.com. **World Wide Web address:** http://www.actel.com. **Description:** Manufactures field programmable gate arrays and develops the software to program them. **Positions advertised include:** Hardware Architect; Sr. Analog Architect; Product Marketing Manager; Military/Aerospace Business Development Manager; Sr. Staff software Engineer. **Corporate headquarters location:** This location. **Other U.S. locations:** Nationwide. **International locations:** Canada; France; Germany; Italy; Japan; Korea; United Kingdom. **Number of employees at this location:** 200.

ACTION EMBROIDERY
1315 West Brooks Street, Ontario CA 91762. 909/983-1359. **Toll-free phone:** 800/638-7223. **Fax:** 909/983-2755. **Contact:** Human Resources. **World Wide Web address:** http://www.actionemb.com. **Description:** Manufactures military emblems.

ACTIVANT SOLUTIONS INC.
7683 Southfront Road, Livermore CA 94551. 925/449-0606. **Toll-free phone:** 800/678-7423. **Fax:** 925/449-1037. **Contact:** Human Resources. **E-mail address:** info@activant.com. **World Wide Web address:** http://www.activant.com. **Description:** Develops business management software and solutions primarily for the automotive aftermarket, retail agribusiness, hardware, paint, and hardlines and lumber industries nationwide. **NOTE:** Search and apply for positions online. **Positions advertised include:** Desktop Support Analyst; Information Acquisition Specialist; Sr. Systems Analyst; Sr. Engineer; Staff Development Engineer. **Corporate headquarters location:** Austin TX. **Other U.S. locations:** Florence AL; Denver CO; Raleigh NC; Newton NJ; San Antonio TX. **International locations:** Canada; France; Ireland, United Kingdom.

ACUSHNET COMPANY
1812 Aston Avenue, Carlsbad CA 92008. 760/929-0377. **Toll-free phone:** 800/225-8500. **Contact:** Personnel. **E-mail address:** humanres@acushnetgolf.com. **World Wide Web address:** http://www.cobragolf.com. **Description:** Designs, manufactures, and markets golf clubs. The company also offers a line of men's and women's golf and

resort clothing, imported from Italy under the name Como Sport. **Corporate headquarters location:** Fairhaven MA. **Other U.S. locations:** Nationwide. **International locations:** Hamburg, Germany. **Parent company:** Fortune Brands, Inc.

ADAMS & BROOKS INC.
P.O. Box 7303, Los Angeles CA 90007. 213/749-3226. **Physical address:** 1915 South Hoover Street, Los Angeles CA 90007. **Fax:** 213/746-7614. **Contact:** Mrs. Tempe Brooks, Personnel Director. **E-mail address:** info@adams-brooks.com. **World Wide Web address:** http://www.adams-brooks.com. **Description:** Manufactures candy including P-Nuttles toffee coated peanuts, Coffee Rio caramel candy, Cup-O-Gold chocolate cups, specialty lollipops, and Fairtime Taffy. Founded in 1932. **Corporate headquarters location:** This location. **Listed on:** Privately held.

ADAPTEC, INC.
691 South Milpitas Boulevard, Milpitas CA 95035. 408/945-8600. **Fax:** 408/22-2533. **Contact:** Human Resources. **World Wide Web address:** http://www.adaptec.com. **Description:** Adaptec provides software and hardware solutions for storage connectivity and data protection, storage networking and networked storage subsystems to leading OEM and distribution channel partners. Adaptec solutions are in use by enterprises, ISPs, medium and small businesses and consumers worldwide. **NOTE:** Search and apply for positions online. **Positions advertised include:** Sr. Staff Engineer; SAP Security Administrator; Business Systems Analyst; Sr. Product Manager; OEM Sales Manager. **Corporate headquarters location:** This location. **Listed on:** NASDAQ. **Stock exchange symbol:** ADPT. **Number of employees worldwide:** 1,560.

ADOBE ANIMAL HOSPITAL
396 First Street, Los Altos CA 94022. 650/948-9661. **Fax:** 650/948-1465. **Contact:** Human Resources. **E-mail address:** srbryce10@sbcglobal.net. **World Wide Web address:** http://www.adobe-animal.com. **Description:** A fully equipped animal hospital that provides surgical, pharmaceutical, intensive care, laboratory, and radiology services. The hospital also provides regular checkups and puppy training classes. **Positions advertised include:** Registered Animal Health Technician.

ADOBE SYSTEMS, INC.
345 Park Avenue, San Jose CA 95110-2704. 408/536-6000. **Fax:** 408/537-6000. **Contact:** Human Resources. **World Wide Web address:** http://www.adobe.com. **Description:** Develops, markets, and supports computer software products and technologies that enable users to create, display, and print electronic documents for Macintosh, Windows, and OS/2 compatibles. The company distributes its products through a network of original equipment manufacturers, distributors and dealers, value-added resellers, and systems integrators. **NOTE:** Search and apply for positions online. **Positions advertised include:** Business Systems Analyst; Computer Scientist; Dabase Operations Manager; Direct Marketing Program Manager; Director, Channel & Licensing Operations. **Corporate headquarters location:** This location. **Other U.S. locations:** Seattle WA. **International locations:** Australia; Canada; Denmark; France; Germany; Ireland; Japan; the Netherlands; Norway; Spain; Sweden; UK. **Listed on:** NASDAQ. **Stock exchange symbol:** ADBE. **Number of employees worldwide:** 3,700.

ADVANCE PAPER BOX COMPANY
6100 South Gramercy Place, Los Angeles CA 90047. 323/750-2550. **Fax:** 323/752-8133. **Contact:** Bernie Konig, Personnel Manager. **World Wide Web address:** http://www.advancepaperbox.com. **Description:** Manufactures folding cartons, set-up boxes, record jackets, and other packaging products. **Office hours:** Monday – Friday, 8:00 a.m. – 5:00 p.m.

ADVANCED COMPUTER SOLUTIONS
12675 Danielson Court, Suite 407, Poway CA 92064. 858/748-6800. **Contact:** Human Resources. **E-mail address:** swardacsolutions.com. **Description:** Designs and manufactures hardware including flat-panel display systems, embedded systems, and motherboards for various industries.

ADVANCED FOAM
1745 West 134th Street, Gardena CA 90249. 310/515-0617. **Fax:** 323/515-3548. **Contact:** Human Resources. **World Wide Web address:** http://www.redicoat.com. **Description:** Manufactures specialty sheets of foam for the construction of buildings.

ADVANCED MARKETING SERVICES, INC. (AMS)
5880 Oberlin Drive, Suite 400, San Diego CA 92121-9653. 858/457-2500. **Fax:** 858/450-3593. **Contact:** Human Resources Representative. **E-mail address:** ams.jobs@advmkt.com. **World Wide Web address:** http://www.admsweb.com. **Description:** A leading distributor of general interest, computer, and business books to membership warehouse clubs and specialty retailers. Advanced Marketing Services works with leading publishers and focuses on a limited number of titles. **NOTE:** Entry-level positions are offered. **Positions advertised include:** Publisher Accounts Payable Reconciliation Analyst; Product Manager; Payroll Manager; Production Services Lead Analyst. **Corporate headquarters location:** This location. **Listed on:** New York Stock Exchange. **Stock exchange symbol:** MKT. **Annual sales/revenues:** $911 million. **Number of employees nationwide:** 1,500.

ADVANCED MICRO DEVICES, INC. (AMD)
One AMD Place, P.O. Box 3453, Sunnyvale CA 94088-3453. 408/749-4000. **Fax:** 408/774-7024. **Contact:** AMD Staffing. **E-mail address:** jobs@amd.com. **World Wide Web address:** http://www.amd.com. **Description:** Advanced Micro Devices, Inc. designs, develops, manufactures, and markets complex, monolithic integrated circuits for use by electronic equipment and systems manufacturers in instrument applications and products involved in computation and communications. **Positions advertised include:** Analog Circuit Designer; CAD Designer; Design Engineer; Device Technology Engineer; Financial Analyst; Industrial Engineer; MTS Design Engineer; Product Engineer; Wafer Fab Engineer. **Corporate headquarters location:** This location. **Other area locations:** Los Angeles CA; Pleasanton CA; Sacramento CA; San Diego CA; San Jose CA. **Other U.S. locations:** Boxborough MA; East Fishkill NY; Austin TX; Redmond WA. **International locations:** Worldwide. **Listed on:** New York Stock Exchange. **Stock exchange symbol:** AMD. **President/CEO:** Hector de Jesus Ruiz, Ph.D. **Number of employees worldwide:** 14,300.

ADVANCED PHOTONIX, INC.
1240 Avenida Acaso, Camarillo CA 93012. 805/987-0146. **Fax:** 805/484-9935. **Contact:** Human Resources Manager. **E-mail address:** hr@adavancedphotonix.com. **World Wide Web address:** http://www.advancedphotonix.com. **Description:** Advanced Photonix, Inc., with its subsidiary, Silicon Detector Corporation, develops, markets, and manufactures proprietary, advanced, solid-state silicon photodetection devices that utilize Avalanche Photodetection (APD) technology. These devices are designed to detect and amplify signals from light and radiant energy sources and convert them into electrical impulses or signals. Products are used for measurement, control, monitoring, and other functions in industrial, medical, military, scientific, and other commercial applications. Such applications include medical diagnostic imaging, airport security detection, fiber-optic communications, and nuclear radiation monitoring and detection systems. **Corporate headquarters location:** This location. **Listed on:** American Stock Exchange. **Stock exchange symbol:** API. **Number of employees at this location:** 95.

ADVANCED STERILIZATION PRODUCTS
33 Technology Drive, Irvine CA 92618. 949/581-5799. **Fax:** 949/450-6889. **Contact:** Human Resources. **E-mail address:** resumes@aspus.jnj.com. **World Wide Web address:** http://www.sterrad.com. **Description:** Manufactures sterilization equipment that is used on surgical instruments in hospitals. **Parent company:** Johnson & Johnson (New Brunswick NJ). **International locations:** Worldwide.

ADVANCED TECHNOLOGIES APPLICATIONS GROUP
3394 Carmel Mountain Road, San Diego CA 92121. 858/720-4000. **Fax:** 858/720-4137. **Contact:** Phyllis Stuart, Human Resources Administrator. **E-mail address:** jobs@jaycor.com. **World Wide Web address:** http://www.jaycor.com. **Description:** Provides scientific, high-tech research and development for public and private companies as well as the U.S. Department of Defense. The company specializes in civil engineering, communications, and biological defense systems. **Positions advertised include:** Applications Programmer; Assembler; Associate Engineer; Billing Supervisor; Chief Scientist; Communication Systems Engineer; Depot Manager; Electronic Technician; Field Engineer. **Special programs:** Internships. **Corporate headquarters location:** This location. **Other U.S. locations:** Nationwide. **Parent company:** Titan Corporation. **Operations at this facility include:** Administration; Research and Development. **Listed on:** New York Stock Exchange. **Stock exchange symbol:** TTN. **Number of employees at this location:** 120. **Number of employees nationwide:** 500.

ADVENT SOFTWARE, INC.
301 Brannan Street, 6th Floor, San Francisco CA 94107. 415/543-7696. **Toll-free phone:** 800/685-7688. **Fax:** 415/543-5070. **Contact:** Human Resources. **E-mail address:** jobs@advent.com. **World Wide Web address:** http://www.advent.com. **Description:** Develops financial planning and investment applications for investment managers, financial planners, and brokerage houses. **Positions advertised include:** Applications Engineer; Associate System Administrator; Business Analyst; Data Conversion Analyst; Interface Manager; Product Manager; Professional Services Consultant; Senior Software Engineer. **Corporate headquarters location:** This location. **Other U.S. locations:** Cambridge MA; New York NY. **International locations:** Australia; Europe. **Subsidiaries include:** MicroEdge; Second Street Securities; Advent Market Data. **Listed on:** NASDAQ. **Stock exchange symbol:** ADVS. **CEO:** Stepanie DiMarco. **Annual sales/revenues:** More than $100 million.

AEROJET
P.O. Box 13222, Sacramento CA 95813-6000. 916/355-4000. **Fax:** 916/351-8667. **Contact:** Human Resources. **E-mail address:** careers.sac@aerojet.com. **World Wide Web address:** http://www.aerojet.com. **Description:** Engaged in the research, development, testing, and production of liquid propellant rocket engines, solid rocket motors, sounding rockets, defense and aerospace systems, and waterjet propulsion systems. **NOTE:** Search and apply for positions online. **Positions advertised include:** Experimental Metalsmith; Sr. Engineer; Sr. Integrated Logistics Support Engineer; Engineering Manager; Sr. Contract Administrator; Program Manager; Inspector; Sr. Plastic Mechanic; Sr. Manufacturing Engineer. **Corporate headquarters location:** This location. **Other area locations:** Rancho Cordova CA; Vernon CA. **Other U.S. locations:** Huntsville AL; Camden AR; Washington DC; Arlington NJ; Socorro NM; Jonesboro TN; Clearfield UT; Gainesville VA; Redmond WA. **Parent company:** GenCorp, through its subsidiaries, manufactures products for the aerospace, pharmaceutical, fine chemical, and automotive industries. **Listed on:** New York Stock Exchange. **Stock Exchange Symbol:** GY.

THE AEROSPACE CORPORATION
2350 East El Segundo Boulevard, El Segundo CA 90245-4691. 310/336-5000. **Fax:** 310/336-7933. **Contact:** Professional Placement. **E-mail address:** jobs@aero.org. **World Wide Web address:** http://www.aero.org. **Description:** A nonprofit corporation engaged in space systems architecture, engineering, planning, analysis, and research, predominantly for programs managed by the Space and Missile Systems Center (SMC) of the Air Force Material Command. **NOTE:** Candidates may submit a resume via online form, e-mail, fax, or mail. Address resumes to: The Aerospace Corporation, Professional Placement, P.O. Box 92957, MS: M1/029, Los Angeles CA 90009-2957. E-mail: resume@aero.org. **Positions advertised include:** Contracts Specialist; Employee communication Director; Sr. Accountant; Sr. Research Assistant; Experimental Scientist; Info System Security Engineer. **Corporate headquarters location:** This location. **Other U.S. locations:** Colorado Springs CO; Kennedy Space Center FL; Columbia MD; Albuquerque NM; Houston TX; Crystal City VA; Chantilly VA. **Operations at this facility include:** Research and Development. **Listed on:** Privately held. **Number of employees at this location:** 3,000.

AGFA CORPORATION
1050 Rancho Conejo Boulevard, Thousand Oaks CA 91320. 805/277-6700. **Contact:** Human Resources. **World Wide Web address:** http://www.agfaus.com. **Description:** Develops, assembles, and markets computer-based systems that automate the functions of prepress production for the publishing and printing industries. Products can be separated into three categories: Automated Workflow Solutions includes servers, plateroom management tracking systems, and output file managers; Document Distribution Systems provides electronic document distribution and other communication services; and Integrated Products includes drum and flatbed scanners, and drum and computer-to-plate imagers. **NOTE:** Search and apply for open positions online. **Corporate headquarters location:** Ridgefield Park NJ. **Other U.S. locations:** Nationwide. **International locations:** Worldwide. **Parent company:** Agfa Gevaert (Belgium).

AGILENT TECHNOLOGIES
395 Page Mill Road, P.O. Box 10395, Palo Alto CA 94303. 650/752-5000. **Toll-free phone:** 877/424-4536. **Contact:** Human Resources. **World Wide Web address:** http://www.agilent.com. **Description:** Produces test, measurement, and monitoring devices; semi-conductor products; and chemical analysis. Agilent Technologies' primary clients are communications equipment manufacturers, Internet service providers, and biopharmaceutical companies. **Positions advertised include:** Legal Coordinator; R&D Engineer; Mixed-Signal RFIC Engineer; IT Consultant; Project Manager R&D Scientist. **Corporate headquarters location:** This location. **Listed on:** New York Stock Exchange. **Stock exchange symbol:** A. **Number of employees nationwide:** 11,500. **Number of employees worldwide:** 28,000.

AGILENT TECHNOLOGIES
350-370 West Trimble Road, San Jose CA 95131. 408/435-7400. **Contact:** Human Resources. **World Wide Web address:** http://www.agilent.com. **Description:** Produces test, measurement, and monitoring devices; semiconductor products; and

chemical analysis. Agilent Technologies' primary clients are communications equipment manufacturers, Internet service providers, and biopharmaceutical companies. **Positions advertised include:** R&D Engineer; Worldwide Channel Marketing Manager; Worldwide Marcom Manager; Product marketing Integrating Manager. **Corporate headquarters location:** Palo Alto CA. **Listed on:** New York Stock Exchange. **Stock exchange symbol:** A. **Number of employees nationwide:** 11,500. **Number of employees worldwide:** 28,000.

AGILENT TECHNOLOGIES
1400 Fountain Grove Parkway, Santa Rosa CA 95403. 707/577-1400. **Contact:** Human Resources. **World Wide Web address:** http://www.agilent.com. **Description:** Produces test, measurement, and monitoring devices; semi-conductor products; and chemical analysis. Agilent Technologies' primary clients are communications equipment manufacturers, Internet service providers, and biopharmaceutical companies. **Positions advertised include:** Manufacturing Electrical Engineer; RF/Microwave Hardware Engineer; R&D Software Development Engineer; Financial Analyst. **Corporate headquarters location:** Palo Alto CA. **Listed on:** New York Stock Exchange. **Stock exchange symbol:** A. **Number of employees nationwide:** 11,500. **Number of employees worldwide:** 28,000.

AGILENT TECHNOLOGIES
5301 Steven's Creek Boulevard, Santa Clara CA 95051. 408/246-4300. **Contact:** Human Resources. **World Wide Web address:** http://www.agilent.com. **Description:** Produces test, measurement, and monitoring devices; semi-conductor products; and chemical analysis. Agilent Technologies' primary clients are communications equipment manufacturers, Internet service providers, and biopharmaceutical companies. **Positions advertised include:** Web Marketing Associate; Business Development Specialist; Product Marketing Integrating Manager; Informatics Software Development Engineer. **Special programs:** Internships. **Corporate headquarters location:** Palo Alto CA. **Operations at this facility include:** Administration; Manufacturing; Research and Development; Sales; Service. **Listed on:** New York Stock Exchange. **Stock exchange symbol:** A. **Number of employees nationwide:** 11,500. **Number of employees worldwide:** 28,000.

AIMS MULTIMEDIA
20765 Superior Street, Chatsworth CA 91311. 818/773-4300. **Toll-free phone:** 800/367-2467. **Fax:** 818/341-6700. **Contact:** Adele Brant, Human Resources. **E-mail address:** info@aimsmultimedia.com. **World Wide Web address:** http://www.aimsmultimedia.com. **Description:** Engaged in educational video production and distribution. **Corporate headquarters location:** This location. **Parent company:** Discovery Education.

AIR LIQUIDE AMERICA CORPORATION
700 Decoto Road, Union City CA 94587. 510/429-4200. **Contact:** Human Resources. **E-mail address:** recruiting@airliquide.com. **World Wide Web address:** http://www.us.airliquide.com. **Description:** Air Liquide America Corporation is a diversified manufacturer engaged primarily in the recovery and sale of atmospheric industrial gases, the manufacture and sale of oil field equipment and supplies, and the distribution of welding and industrial equipment and supplies. The company operates several business segments. The Gas Group produces and sells oxygen, nitrogen, and argon in liquid and gaseous forms at approximately 20 locations in Texas, Louisiana, Florida, California, and Hawaii, operating more than 2,200 miles of pipeline. The Energy Group operates under two names (Bowen Tools and Dia-Log Companies) and manufactures and sells equipment to petroleum and natural gas companies. The Welding Group distributes electric arc welding equipment and supplies in Texas, Louisiana, California, and Hawaii for Lincoln Electric Company. **NOTE:** Search for positions online. **Corporate headquarters location:** Houston TX. **International locations:** Worldwide. **Parent company:** Air Liquide (Paris). **Operations at this facility include:** This location houses administrative offices. **Number of employees nationwide:** 2,300. **Number of employees worldwide:** 31,900.

AIRGUARD INDUSTRIES, INC.
1295 East Ontario Avenue, Unit 102, Corona CA 92881. 909/272-0708. **Fax:** 909/270-1450. **Contact:** Maria Monteon, Personnel. **E-mail address:** maverill@airguard.com. **World Wide Web address:** http://www.airguard.com. **Description:** Manufactures commercial and industrial air filtration equipment. **Corporate headquarters location:** Louisville KY. **Other U.S. locations:** Nationwide. **Parent company:** Clarcor. **Operations at this facility include:** Administration; Divisional Headquarters; Manufacturing; Regional Headquarters; Sales. **Listed on:** New York Stock Exchange. **Number of employees at this location:** 120. **Number of employees nationwide:** 1000.

AJILON SERVICES INC.
1960 East Grand Avenue, Suite 1080, El Segundo CA 90245. 310/335-4800. **Toll-free phone:** 800/811-4274. **Fax:** 310/335-4820. **Contact:** Human Resources. **E-mail address:** recruit.la@ajilon.com. **World Wide Web address:** http://www.ajilon.com. **Description:** Offers computer consulting services, project support, and end user services. **Positions advertised include:** Hyperion Brio Developer. **Corporate headquarters location:** Towson MD. **Other area locations:** Simi Valley CA; Burbank CA; Glendale CA. **Other U.S. locations:** Nationwide. **Parent company:** Adecco.

ALAMEDA COUNTY MEDICAL CENTER
1411 East 31st Street, Department 470, Oakland CA 94602. 510/437-4108. **Fax:** 510/437-5197. **Contact:** Human Resources. **E-mail address:** resumes@acmedctr.org. **World Wide Web address:** http://www.acmedctr.org. **Description:** A 300-bed, adult, acute care teaching hospital. **Positions advertised include:** RN, Various Departments; Electrocardiograph Tech; Clinical Lab Scientist; Chief Info Officer; Physician; HRIS Analyst; EEG Tech. **Corporate headquarters location:** Oakland CA. **Other area locations:** San Leandro CA. **Operations at this facility include:** Service.

ALBERTSON'S
1550 East 14th Street, San Leandro CA 94577. 510/483-0881. **Contact:** Human Resources. **E-mail address:** employment@albertsons.com. **World Wide Web address:** http://www.albertsons.com. **Description:** Operates a nationwide chain of 2,300 food and drug stores in 31 states. **Corporate headquarters location:** Boise ID. **Listed on:** New York Stock Exchange. **Stock exchange symbol:** ABS. **Number of employees nationwide:** 200,000.

ALBERTSON'S
6931 La Palma Avenue, Buena Park CA 90620-1158. 714/522-1054. **Fax:** 714/522-7601. **Contact:** Human Resources. **E-mail address:** employment@albertsons.com. **World Wide Web address:** http://www.albertsons.com. **Description:** Operates a nationwide chain of 2,300 food and drug stores in 31 states. **Corporate headquarters location:** Boise ID. **Listed on:** New York Stock Exchange. **Stock exchange symbol:** ABS. **Number of employees nationwide:** 200,000.

ALCATEL
701 East Middlefield Road, Mountain View CA 94043. 650/623-2500. **Contact:** Human Resources. **World Wide Web address:** http://www.usa.alcatel.com. **Description:** Provides communications solutions to telecommunication carriers, Internet service providers and enterprises for delivery of voice, data and video applications to their customers or employees. **NOTE:** Search and apply for positions online. **Positions advertised include:** Sr. Director Program Management; Hardware/Software Diagnostic Engineer; Marketing Manager. **Corporate headquarters location:** Plano TX. **Other U.S. locations:** Nogales AZ; Claremont NC; Raleigh NC; Reston VA. **International locations:** Worldwide. **Listed on:** New York Stock Exchange. **Stock exchange symbol:** ALA.

ALCOA FASTENING SYSTEMS
800 South State College Boulevard, Fullerton CA 92831. 714/871-1550. **Contact:** Personnel Manager. **World Wide Web address:** http://www.fairchildfasteners.com. **Description:** Manufactures and supplies precision fastening systems and components and latching devices for aerospace and industrial applications. **Corporate headquarters location:** Torrance CA. **Parent company:** Alcoa Inc. **Operations at this facility include:** Administration; Manufacturing; Research and Development; Sales; Service. **Listed on:** New York Stock Exchange. **Stock exchange symbol:** AA. **President/CEO:** Eric Steiner. **Number of employees at this location:** 600.

ALCOA FASTENING SYSTEMS
3000 West Lomita Boulevard, Torrance CA 90505. 310/530-2220. **Contact:** Human Resources Manager. **World Wide Web address:** http://www.fairchildfasteners.com. **Description:** Manufactures and supplies precision fastening systems and components and latching devices for aerospace and industrial applications. **Positions advertised include:** Staff Environmental Engineer. **Corporate headquarters location:** This location. **Listed on:** New York Stock Exchange. **Stock exchange symbol:** AA. **Parent company:** Alcoa Inc.

ALDILA, INC.
13450 Stowe Drive, Poway CA 92064. 858/513-1801. **Fax:** 858/513-3692. **Contact:** Human Resources. **E-mail address:** hradmin@aldila.com. **World Wide Web address:** http://www.aldila.com. **Description:** ALDILA is a leading manufacturer of graphite golf shafts. Founded in 1972. **Corporate headquarters location:** This location. **Other U.S. locations:** Evanston NY. **International locations:** China; Mexico. **Listed on:** NASDAQ. **Stock exchange symbol:** ALDA.

ALFA LEISURE INC.
13501 Fifth Street, Chino CA 91710. 909/628-5574. **Fax:** 909/591-7902. **Contact:** Human Resources. **E-mail address:** info@alfaleisure.com. **World Wide Web address:** http://www.alfaleisure.com. **Description:** Manufactures high-end, fifth wheel recreation trailers. Founded in 1973. **Office hours:** Monday - Friday, 8:00 a.m. - 5:00 p.m. **Corporate headquarters location:** This location. **Other U.S. locations:** Worldwide. **Annual sales/revenues:** $21 - $50 million. **Number of employees at this location:** 330.

ALGER MANUFACTURING COMPANY, INC.
724 south Bon View Avenue, Ontario CA 91761. **Toll-free phone:** 800/854-9833. **Fax:** 909/983-3351. **Contact:** Personnel Manager. **World Wide Web address:** http://www.alger1.com. **Description:** Manufactures screw machine products (nonproprietary metal components) produced in large quantities to customer specifications.

ALL-CARE ANIMAL REFERRAL CENTER
18440 Amistad Street, Fountain Valley CA 92708. 714/963-0909. **Toll-free phone:** 800/944-7387. **Fax:** 714/962-1905. **Contact:** Human Resources. **World Wide Web address:** http://www.acarc.com. **Description:** An animal hospital with a 24-hour critical care facility.

ALLDATA CORPORATION
9412 Big Horn Boulevard, Elk Grove CA 95758-1100. 916/684-5200. **Toll-free phone:** 800/697-2533. **Fax:** 916/684-5225. **Contact:** Human Resources. **E-mail address:** hr@alldata.com. **World Wide Web address:** http://www.alldata.com. **Description:** Provides dignostic, repair, and estimating information to the professional automotive service industry. **Corporate headquarters location:** This location. **Parent company:** AutoZone. **Number of employees at this location:** 300.

ALLERGAN, INC.
P.O. Box 19534, Irvine CA 92623-9534. 714/246-4500. **Physical address:** 2525 DuPont Drive, Irvine CA 92612. **Toll-free phone:** 800/347-4500. **Contact:** Personnel. **E-mail address:** resume@allergan.com. **World Wide Web address:** http://www.allergan.com. **Description:** Develops, manufactures, and distributes prescription and nonprescription pharmaceutical products in the specialty fields of ophthalmology and dermatology. Allergan, Inc.'s products are designed to treat eye and skin disorders, and to aid contact lens wearers. **Positions advertised include:** Director, Clinical Research; Sr. Clinical Data Analyst; Director, Biostatistics; Manager, Medical Writer; Principal Programmer; Biology Professional; Product Manager; Manager, Purification; Director QA. **Special programs:** Internships. **Corporate headquarters location:** This location. **International locations:** Worldwide. **Listed on:** New York Stock Exchange. **Stock exchange symbol:** AGN. **Operations at this facility include:** Administration; Divisional Headquarters; Manufacturing; Research and Development; Sales.

ALLIANCE IMAGING, INC.
1900 South State College Boulevard, Suite 600, Anaheim CA 92806. 714/688-7100. **Toll-free phone:** 800/544-3215. **Fax:** 714/688-3333. **Contact:** Human Resources Department. **E-mail address:** info@allianceimaging.com. **World Wide Web address:** http://www.allianceimaging.com. **Description:** Provides medical diagnostic imaging services to hospitals, physicians, and patients. Services include MRI, Open MRI, computer tomography (CT), ultrasound, and position emission tomography (PET). **Positions advertised include:** Patient Coordinator; PET Technologist. **Corporate headquarters location:** This location. **Other U.S. locations:** Nationwide. **Listed on:** NASDAQ. **Stock exchange symbol:** SCAN. **Chairman and CEO:** Rick Zehner.

ALLIANCE PHARMACEUTICAL CORPORATION
4660 La Jolla Village Drive, Suite 825, San Diego CA 92122. 858/410-5200. **Fax:** 858/410-5201. **Contact:** Human Resources. **World Wide Web address:** http://www.allp.com. **Description:** Develops, manufactures, and markets pharmaceutical products including Oxygent, a drug used to eliminate the need for blood transfusions during surgery; Liquivent, a drug used to treat acute respiratory illnesses; and Imagent, a diagnostic contrast agent used to enhance ultrasound images. **NOTE:** Alliance Pharmaceutical Corporation hires employees through Alcock & McFadden Employment Consultants, Inc., 3675 Ruffin Road, Suite 225, San Diego CA 92123. 619/505-0303. Fax: 619/505-0445. **Listed on:** NASDAQ. **Stock exchange symbol:** ALLP.

ALLIANT INTERNATIONAL UNIVERSITY
10455 Pomerado Road, San Diego CA 92131-1799. 858/635-4772. **Fax:** 858/635-4739. **Contact:** Human Resources. **E-mail address:** jobs@alliant.edu. **World Wide Web address:** http://www.alliant.edu. **Description:** Offers undergraduate and graduate degree programs in liberal arts, education, business, and behavioral and social sciences. **Positions advertised include:** Lecturer; Assistant Professor. **Corporate headquarters location:** This location. **Other area locations:** Fresno CA; Irvine CA; Los Angeles CA; Sacramento CA; San Francisco CA. **International locations:** Nairobi, Kenya; Mexico City, Mexico. **Number of employees nationwide:** 1,100.

ALLIANZ GLOBAL RISKS US INSURANCE COMPANY
2350 Empire Avenue, Burbank CA 91504. 818/260-7500. **Contact:** Human Resources Department. **E-mail address:** hr@aic-allianz.com. **World Wide Web address:** http://www.aic-allianz.com. **Description:** An insurance company specializing in commercial insurance including workers' compensation, specialty property, and casualty. **NOTE:** Search and apply for positions online. **Positions advertised include:** Account Engineer; Director and Associate Actuary. **Corporate headquarters location:** This location. **Other area locations:** Orange CA; Sacramento CA; San Francisco CA. **Other U.S. locations:** Atlanta GA; Chicago IL; New York NY. **Parent company:** Allianz (Germany). **Listed on:** Privately held. **Number of employees at this location:** 100. **Number of employees nationwide:** 325.

ALLIED TELESYN, INC.
960 Stewart Drive, Suite B, Sunnyvale CA 94085. 408/730-0950. **Contact:** Human Resources. **E-mail address:** jobs-na@alliedtelesyn.com. **World Wide Web address:** http://www.alliedtelesyn.com. **Description:** Manufactures a variety of hardware for the communications industry. **NOTE:** Search and apply for positions online. **Corporate headquarters location:** Bothell WA. **Other area locations:** San Jose CA. **Other U.S. locations:** Dallas TX; Olympian Fields IL; Raleigh NC; Safety Harbor FL.

ALLIED VAUGHN
5 Thomas Mellon Circle, Suite 128, Brisbane CA 94134. 415/656-2200. **Toll-free phone:** 888/691-3381. **Fax:** 415/656-2299. **Contact:** Human Resources. E-mail address: human.resources@alliedvaughn.com. **World Wide Web address:** http://www.alliedvaughn.com. **Description:** One of the nation's leading independent multimedia manufacturing companies, offering CD-audio and CD-ROM mastering and replication; videocassette and audiocassette duplication; laser video disc recording; off-line and online video editing; motion picture film processing; film-to-tape and tape-to-film transfers; and complete finishing, packaging, warehousing, and fulfillment services. **Other U.S. locations:** Nationwide.

ALTA DENA CERTIFIED DAIRY
17637 East Valley Boulevard, City of Industry CA 91744. 626/964-6401. **Recorded jobline:** 626/854-4269. **Fax:** 626/854-4227. **Contact:** Personnel. **World Wide Web address:** http://www.altadenadairy.com. **Description:** Specializes in the production of a full line of dairy products. **NOTE:** Resumes are accepted by mail or fax. **Corporate headquarters location:** This location. **Parent company:** Dean Foods. **Number of employees at this location:** 400.

ALTERA CORPORATION
101 Innovation Drive, San Jose CA 95134-1941. 408/544-7000. **Fax:** 408/544-8303. **Contact:** Staffing. **E-mail address:** hr@altera.com. **World Wide Web address:** http://www.altera.com. **Description:** Designs and develops high-performance, high-density programmable logic devices (PLDs) and associated computer-aided engineering (CAE) logic development tools. These products are used in a variety of areas including telecommunications, data communications, computers, and industrial applications. Founded in 1983. **Positions advertised include:** Advanced Applications Engineer; Senior Applications Engineer; Design Engineer; Senior Device Engineer; Field Applications Engineer; Field Sales Engineer; Hardware Engineer; Advanced Marketing Analyst; Programmer Analyst. **Special programs:** Internships. **Corporate headquarters location:** This location. **International locations:** Canada; Japan; Malaysia; United Kingdom. **Listed on:** NASDAQ. **Stock exchange symbol:** ALTR. **Annual sales/revenues:** $827 million. **Number of employees at this location:** 700. **Number of employees worldwide:** 2,000.

ALZA CORPORATION
1900 Charlestown Road, P.O. Box 7210, Mountain View CA 94039-7210. 650/564-5000. **Fax:** 650/564-5656. **Recorded jobline:** 650/494-5319. **Contact:** Darlene Markovitch, Human Resources Director. **E-mail address:** jobs@alza.com. **World Wide Web address:** http://www.alza.com. **Description:** Develops, manufactures, and markets therapeutic systems for both humans and animals. Products include drug delivery technologies that focus on the areas of urology and oncology and are used in the treatment of angina, hypertension, respiratory allergies, motion sickness, and nicotine withdrawal. Founded in 1968. **Positions advertised include:** Regulatory Affairs Associate; Research Scientist; Sr. Biostatistician; Program Manager; Sr. HR Business Partner; Sr. Financial Analyst. **Special programs:** Internships. **Corporate headquarters location:** This location. **Other U.S. locations:** Vacaville CA; Minneapolis MN. **International locations:** Canada. **Parent company:** Johnson & Johnson. **Operations at this facility include:** Administration; Manufacturing; Research and Development. **Listed on:** New York Stock Exchange. **Stock exchange symbol:** JNJ. **Number of employees at this location:** 1,000.

AMDOCS LIMITED
2570 Orchard Parkway, San Jose CA 95131. 408/965-7000. **Fax:** 408/965-4338. **Contact:** Human Resources. **E-mail address:** jobs.web@amdocs.com. **World Wide Web address:** http://www.amdocs.com. **Description:** Develops customer support management software. **Corporate headquarters location:** Chesterfield MO. **Other U.S. locations:** Boston MA; Champaign IL. **International locations:** Worldwide. **Listed on:** New York Stock Exchange. **Stock exchange symbol:** DOX.

AMELCO CORPORATION
19208 South Vermont Avenue, Gardena CA 90248-4414. 310/327-3070. **Fax:** 310/327-3599. **Contact:** Human Resources. **World Wide Web address:** http://www.amelco.net. **Description:** Provides specialty construction services primarily electrical and mechanical subcontracting. **Corporate headquarters location:** This location. **Other U.S. locations:** Hawaii. **Stock exchange symbol:** AMLC. **Number of employees nationwide:** 500.

AMERICAN ACADEMY OF OPHTHALMOLOGY
P.O. Box 7274, San Francisco CA 94120-7424. 415/561-8500. **Physical address:** 655 Beach Street, San Francisco CA 94109. **Fax:** 415/561-8533. **Contact:** Human Resources. **E-mail address:** jobs@aao.org. **World Wide Web address:** http://www.aao.org. **Description:** A lobbying group that focuses on all government legislation affecting the ophthalmology community. **Corporate headquarters location:** This location.

AMERICAN BANK NOTE COMPANY
3500 West Olive Avenue, Suite 300, Burbank CA 91505. 818/972-1700. **Contact:** Human Resources. **World Wide Web address:** http://www.abncompany.com. **Description:** A printer of counterfeit-resistant documents and one of the largest security printers in the world. American Bank Note Company creates secure documents for governments and corporations worldwide. Products include currencies; passports; stock and bond certificates; and bank, corporate, government, and traveler's checks; as well as food coupons, gift vouchers and certificates, driver's licenses, product authentication labels, and vital documents. **Corporate headquarters location:** Trevose PA. **Other area locations:** Long Beach CA; San Francisco CA. **Other U.S. locations:** Washington DC; Atlanta GA; Needham MA; St. Louis MO; Horsham PA; Huntington Valley PA; Philadelphia PA; Pittsburgh PA; Columbia TN; Dallas TX. **Parent company:** American Bank Note Corporation also operates two other subsidiaries: American Bank Note Holographics, Inc., one of the world's largest producers of the laser-generated, three-dimensional images that appear on credit cards and products requiring proof of authenticity; and American Bank Note Company Brazil, one of Brazil's largest private security printers and a provider of personalized checks, financial transaction cards, and prepaid telephone cards. **Operations at this facility include:** This location is a national sales office.

AMERICAN CANCER SOCIETY
1700 Webster Street, Oakland CA 94612. 510/832-7012. **Toll-free phone:** 800/ACS-2345. **Fax:** 510/893-0951. **Contact:** Malene Yip, Human Resources Assistant. **World Wide Web address:** http://www.cancer.org. **Description:** A nationwide, community-based, nonprofit, voluntary health organization dedicated to eliminating cancer as a major health problem by funding cancer research and public education. The society helps patients directly by offering services including transportation to treatment and rehabilitation services. **Positions advertised include:** VP, Corporate Relations. **Special programs:** Internships. **Corporate headquarters location:** Atlanta GA. **Other U.S. locations:** Nationwide. **CEO:** Patricia M. Felts. **Information Systems Manager:** Steve Levinson.

AMERICAN CANCER SOCIETY
1523 California Avenue, Bakersfield CA 93304. 661/327-2424. **Contact:** Human Resources. **World Wide Web address:** http://www.cancer.org. **Description:** A nationwide, community-based, nonprofit, voluntary health organization dedicated to eliminating cancer as a major health problem by funding cancer research and public education. The society helps patients directly by offering services including transportation to treatment and rehabilitation services. **Special programs:** Internships. **Corporate headquarters location:** Atlanta GA. **Other U.S. locations:** Nationwide.

AMERICAN CANCER SOCIETY
1240 Palmyrita Avenue, Suite A, Riverside CA 92507. 951/683-6415. **Contact:** Human Resources Manager. **World Wide Web address:** http://www.cancer.org. **Description:** A nationwide, community-based, nonprofit, voluntary health organization dedicated to eliminating cancer as a major health problem by funding cancer research and public education. The society helps patients directly by offering services including transportation to treatment and rehabilitation services. **Special programs:** Internships. **Corporate headquarters location:** Atlanta GA. **Other U.S. locations:** Nationwide.

AMERICAN EXPRESS COMPANY
455 Market Street, San Francisco CA 94105. 415/536-2600. **Toll-free phone:** 800/554-AMEX. **Contact:** Human Resources Department. **World Wide Web address:** http://www.americanexpress.com. **Description:** A diversified travel and financial services company operating in 160 countries around the world. American Express Travel Related Services offers consumers the Personal, Gold, and Platinum Cards, as well as revolving credit products such as Optima Cards, which allow customers to extend payments. Other products include the American Express Corporate Card and the Corporate Purchasing Card. Travel Related Services also offers American Express Traveler's Cheques and travel services including trip planning, reservations, ticketing, and management information. American Express Financial Advisors offers financial planning, annuities, mutual funds, insurance, investment certificates, institutional investment advisory trust services, tax preparation, and retail securities brokerage services. Founded in 1850. **Positions advertised include:** Tax Accountant; Financial Advisor. **Corporate headquarters location:** New York NY. **Other U.S. locations:** Nationwide. **International locations:** Worldwide. **Listed on:** New York Stock Exchange. **Stock exchange symbol:** AXP. **Annual sales/revenues:** $25.9 billion. **Number of employees worldwide:** 78,200.

AMERICAN GENERAL FINANCE
400 South Citrus Avenue, Covina CA 91723-2989. 626/966-0501. **Fax:** 626/332-5021. **Contact:** Teresa Molina, Manager. **World Wide Web address:** http://www.agfinance.com. **Description:** American General Finance offers wholesale and retail financing to business and industry, as well as direct consumer loans to individuals through 1,400 offices in 44 states. **NOTE:** Apply directly to a branch office. **Positions advertised include:** Management Trainee; Customer Account Administrator; Customer Account Specialist. **Corporate headquarters location:** Evansville IN. **Other U.S. locations:** Nationwide.

AMERICAN HONDA MOTOR COMPANY INC.
1919 Torrance Boulevard, Mailstop 100-1C-3A, Torrance CA 90501-2746. 310/783-2000. **Fax:** 310/783-2110. **Contact:** Rex Simpson, Manager of Employment Relations. **World Wide Web address:** http://www.hondacorporate.com. **Description:** Distributes Honda automotive, motorcycle, and power equipment products throughout the United States. Founded in 1959. **NOTE:** Candidates may submit a resume via mail, fax, or online. Positions advertised include: Tehcnical Analyst; Business Analyst; Corporate Communications Specialist; Customs Administrator; Inventory Planning and Control; Quality Assurance Manager; Sr. Project Leader; Research Specialist. **Special programs:** Internships; Training. **Corporate headquarters location:** This location. **Other U.S. locations:** Nationwide. **Subsidiaries include:** American Honda Finance Company. **Parent company:** Honda Motors Ltd. **Operations at this facility include:** Administration; Research and Development; Sales; Service. **Listed on:** New York Stock Exchange. **Stock exchange symbol:** HMC. **Number of employees at this location:** 1,800. **Number of employees nationwide:** 3,500.

AMERICAN INTERNATIONAL GROUP, INC. (AIG)
Two Rincon Center, 121 Spear Street, San Francisco CA 94105. 415/836-2700. **Contact:** Human Resources Manager. **World Wide Web address:** http://www.aig.com. **Description:** An international insurance firm that provides property and casualty coverage in 50 states and 130 jurisdictions. **NOTE:** Please use online form to submit resume. **Positions advertised include:** Financial Institutions Regional Manager; Sr. Premium Audit Technician; Sr. Underwriter; Sr. Premium Field Auditor; Quality Analyst. **Corporate headquarters location:** New York NY. **Other U.S. locations:** Phoenix AZ; Los Angeles CA; Chicago IL; Dallas TX; Seattle WA. **International locations:** Worldwide. **Operations at this facility include:** Administration; Sales; Service. **Listed on:** New York Stock Exchange. **Stock exchange symbol:** AIG.

AMERICAN MEDICAL RESPONSE INC.
20101 Hamilton Avenue, Suite 300, Torrance CA 90502. 310/851-7000. **Fax:** 925/454-6296. **Contact:** Employment Coordinator. **World Wide Web address:** http://www.amr-inc.com. **Description:** Operates an ambulance service. **NOTE:** Search and apply for positions online. **Corporate headquarters location:** Greenwood Village CO. **Other area locations:** Statewide. **Other U.S. locations:** Nationwide.

AMERICAN RED CROSS
3650 Fifth Avenue, San Diego CA 92103. 619/542-7400. **Fax:** 619/260-3528. **Contact:** Cindy DiPiero, Director of Personnel. **E-mail address:** redcross.careers@sdarc.org. **World Wide Web address:** http://www.redcross.org. **Description:** A humanitarian organization that aids disaster victims, gathers blood for crisis distribution, trains individuals to respond to emergencies, educates individuals on various diseases, and raises funds for other charitable establishments. **Positions advertised include:** Response Coordinator; Associate, Disaster Liaison. **Corporate headquarters location:** Washington DC. **Other U.S. locations:** Nationwide.

AMERICAN RED CROSS
2700 Wilshire Boulevard, Los Angeles CA 90057. 213/739-5200. **Contact:** Jennie Braun, Director of Personnel. **World Wide Web address:** http://www.redcross.org. **Description:** A humanitarian organization that aids disaster victims, gathers blood for crisis distribution, trains individuals to respond to emergencies, educates individuals on various diseases, and raises funds for other charitable establishments. **Positions advertised include:** Assistant Response Officer; Accounting Specialist; Controller. **Corporate headquarters location:** Washington DC. **Other U.S. locations:** Nationwide.

AMERICAN SHARED HOSPITAL SERVICES
Four Embarcadero Center, Suite 3700, San Francisco CA 94111-3823. 415/788-5300. **Toll-free phone:** 800/735-0641. **Fax:** 415/788-5660. **Contact:** Human Resources. **World Wide Web address:** http://www.ashs.com. **Description:** Provides shared diagnostic imaging services and respiratory therapy contract management to several hospitals, medical centers, and medical offices worldwide. The four diagnostic imaging services provided by the company are Magnetic Resonance Imaging (MRI), Computed Axial Tomography Scanning (CT), Ultrasound, and Nuclear Medicine. **Corporate headquarters location:** This location. **Other U.S. locations:** AR; CT; IL; MA; MS; NV; NJ; TX; WI.

AMERICAN VANGUARD CORPORATION
2110 Davie Avenue, City of Commerce CA 90040. 323/264-3910. **Toll-free phone:** 888/462-6822. **Fax:** 323/887-9221. **Contact:** Teresa Chavez, Human Resources. **E-mail address:** teresac@amvac-chemical.com. **World Wide Web address:** http://www.american-vanguard.com. **Description:** A holding company. **Positions advertised include:** Junior Buyer/Expeditor; Chemical Operators. **Corporate headquarters location:** This location. **Subsidiaries include:** AMVAC manufactures and formulates chemicals for crop, human, and animal health protection. These chemicals, which include insecticides, fungicides, plant growth regulators, and soil fumigants, are marketed in liquid, powder, and granular forms. **President/CEO:** Eric G. Wintemute. **Listed on:** American Stock Exchange. **Stock exchange symbol:** AVD.

AMERIGAS
4240 Rocklin Road, Suite 6, Rocklin CA 95677. 916/630-1588. **Fax:** 916/630-4279. **Contact:** Janelle Burns, Employee Relations Manager. **E-mail address:** burnsj@amerigas.com. **World Wide Web address:** http://www.amerigas.com. **Description:** The nation's largest supplier of propane, serving 1.3 million residential and commercial customers. **NOTE:** To reach Janelle Burn directly, call: 916/652-7494. Fax: 916/652-7947. **Corporate headquarters location:** Valley Forge PA. **Parent company:** UGI Corporation is a holding company whose additional businesses include UGI Utilities, Inc. and UGI Enterprises, Inc. **Operations at this facility include:** Regional Headquarters. **Listed on:** New York Stock Exchange. **Stock exchange symbol:** APU. **Number of employees nationwide:** 5,000.

AMERISOURCEBERGEN
4000 Metropolitan Drive, Orange CA 92868-3502. 714/385-4000. **Toll-free phone:** 800/442-3040. **Fax:** 714/385-1442. **Contact:** Human Resources Recruiting. **E-mail address:** techcareers@amerisourcebergen.com. **World Wide Web address:** http://www.amerisourcebergen.net. **Description:** Distributes pharmaceuticals and medical-surgical supplies. **Company slogan:** Our people make the difference. **Positions advertised include:** Project Manager, Systems Assurance; Technical Support Rep; Computer Operator. **Office hours:** Monday - Friday, 7:30 a.m. - 4:30 p.m. **Corporate headquarters location:** Valley Forge PA. **Other U.S. locations:** Nationwide (Distribution Centers). **Listed on:** New York Stock Exchange. **Stock exchange symbol:** ABC. **Number of employees nationwide:** 13,000.

AMERON INTERNATIONAL
245 South Los Robles Avenue, Pasadena CA 91101. 626/683-4000. **Fax:** 626/683-4060. **Contact:** Human Resources. **World Wide Web address:** http://www.ameron.com. **Description:** Manufactures and supplies goods and services to the industrial, utility, marine, and construction markets. The business is divided into four groups: The Protective Coatings Group develops, manufactures, and markets high-performance coatings and surface systems on a worldwide basis. These products are utilized for the preservation of major structures such as metallic and concrete facilities and equipment to prevent their decomposition by corrosion, abrasion, marine fouling, and other forms of chemical and physical attack; The Fiberglass Pipe Group develops, manufactures, and markets filament-wound and molded fiberglass pipe fittings; The Concrete and Steel Pipe Group offers products and services used in the construction of pipeline facilities for various utilities. Eight plants manufacture concrete cylinder pipe, prestressed concrete cylinder pipe, steel pipe, and reinforced concrete pipe for water transmission, and storm and industrial wastewater and sewage collection; The Construction & Allied Products Group includes the HC&D Division, which supplies ready-mix concrete, crushed and sized basaltic aggregates, dune sand, concrete pipe, and box culverts, primarily to the construction industry in Hawaii. **Corporate headquarters location:** This location. **Other area locations:** Brea CA; Rancho Cucamonga CA; Southgate CA; Ventura CA; Tracy CA. **Other U.S. locations:** Alpharetta GA; Honolulu HI; Houston TX. **Listed on:** New York Stock Exchange. **Stock exchange symbol:** AMN. **Chairman/President/CEO:** James S. Marlen.

AMERON INTERNATIONAL
10100 West Linne Road, Tracy CA 95377. 209/836-5050. **Contact:** Rosario Nunez, Personnel. **World Wide Web address:** http://www.ameron.com. **Description:** Ameron International manufactures and supplies goods and services to the industrial, utility, marine, and construction markets. The business of the company is divided into three other groups: The Protective Coatings Group develops, manufactures, and markets high-performance coatings and surfacer systems on a worldwide basis. These products are utilized for the preservation of major structures, such as metallic and concrete facilities and equipment, to prevent their degradation by corrosion, abrasion, marine fouling, and other forms of chemical and physical attack; The Fiberglass Pipe Group develops, manufactures, and markets filament-wound and molded fiberglass pipe fittings; The Construction & Allied Products Group includes the HC&D Division, which supplies ready-mix concrete, crushed and sized basaltic aggregates, dune sand, concrete pipe, and box culverts, primarily to the construction industry in Hawaii. **Corporate headquarters location:** Pasadena CA. **Other area locations:** South Gate CA; Ventura CA; Brea CA; Rancho Cucamonga CA. **Other U.S. locations:** Alpharetta GA; Honolulu HI; Houston TX. **Operations at this facility include:** Supplies products and services used in the construction of pipeline facilities for various utilities. Products include concrete cylinder pipe; prestressed concrete cylinder pipe; steel pipe; and reinforced concrete pipe for water transmission, storm and industrial wastewater, and sewage collection. **Listed on:** New York Stock Exchange. **Stock exchange symbol:** AMN. **Chairman/President/CEO:** James S. Marlen.

AMERON INTERNATIONAL
201 North Berry Street, P.O. Box 1629, Brea CA 92822-1629. 714/256-7755. **Toll-free phone:** 800/9-AMERON. **Fax:** 714/256-7750. **Contact:** Personnel Department. **World Wide Web address:** http://www.ameron.com. **Description:** This location develops, manufactures, and markets proprietary, high-performance protective coatings for the offshore, chemical processing, refining, rail, power, bridge, water and waste treatment, pulp and paper, and light industrial/commercial markets. Overall, Ameron International manufactures and supplies goods and services to the industrial, utility, marine, and construction markets. The business of the company is divided into three other groups. The Fiberglass Pipe Group develops, manufactures, and markets filament-wound and molded fiberglass pipe fittings. The Construction & Allied Products Group includes the HC&D Division, which supplies ready-mix concrete, crushed and sized basaltic aggregates, dune sand, concrete pipe, and box culverts, primarily to the construction industry in Hawaii. The Concrete and Steel Pipe Group supplies products and services used in the construction of pipeline facilities for various utilities. Products include concrete cylinder pipe, prestressed concrete cylinder pipe, steel pipe, and reinforced concrete pipe for water transmission, storm and industrial wastewater, and sewage collection. **Corporate headquarters location:** Pasadena CA. **Other area locations:** Southgate CA; Ventura CA; Tracy CA; Rancho Cucamonga CA. **Other U.S. locations:** Alpharetta GA; Honolulu HI; Houston TX. **Listed on:** New York Stock Exchange. **Stock exchange symbol:** AMN. **Chairman/President/CEO:** James S. Marlen.

AMETEK AEROSPACE
1644 Whittier Avenue, Costa Mesa CA 92627. 949/642-2400. **Contact:** Gabe Velez, Director of Human Resources. **E-mail address:** hr.gsp@ametek.com. **World Wide Web address:** http://www.ametek.com. **Description:** Manufactures electrical and electronic components, primarily for the defense industry. Products include pressure transducers for flight controls on F-16 aircraft and for engine instrumentation on F-18 and F-20 aircraft. Ametek also provides displacement and pressure transducers for engines used in a variety of military planes. **Positions advertised include:** Electro-Mechanical Designer; Program Manager; Senior Test Engineer. **NOTE:** Search and apply for positions online. **Corporate headquarters location:** Paoli PA. **Listed on:** New York Stock Exchange. **Stock exchange symbol:** AME. **Number of employees worldwide:** 7,600.

AMGEN INC.
One Amgen Center Drive, Thousand Oaks CA 91320-1799. 805/447-1000. **Toll-free phone:** 800/77-AMGEN. **Fax:** 805/447-1985. **Recorded jobline:** 800/446-4007. **Contact:** Human Resources. **E-mail address:** jobs@amgen.com. **World Wide Web address:** http://www.amgen.com. **Description:** Researches, develops, manufactures, and markets human therapeutics based on advanced cellular and molecular biology. Products include EPOGEN (Epoetin Alfa), which counteracts the symptoms of renal failure experienced by kidney dialysis patients; INFERGEN (Interferon alfacon-1); and NEUPOGEN (Filgrastim), which reduces the incidence of infection in cancer patients who receive chemotherapy. When used in conjunction with chemotherapy, NEUPOGEN selectively stimulates the bone marrow to produce neutrophil cells, accelerating the return of the patient's antibacterial defense system. In addition to its eight locations in the United States, Amgen also operates a manufacturing facility in Juncos Puerto Rico. **NOTE:** Search and apply for positions online. **Positions advertised include:** Associate Director, Marketing; Associate Director, Tax; Associate Director, Early Development; Associate Product Manager; Associate Director, Corporate Communications; Associate Director, Medical Affairs; Associate Scientist; Clinical Trial Specialist; Director, Clinical Research; Engineer; Global Safety Specialist. **Special programs:** Internships. **Corporate headquarters location:** This location. **Other U.S. locations:** Boulder CO; Longmont CO; Washington D.C.; Louisville KY; Cambridge MA; West Greenwich RI; Bothell WA; Seattle WA;. **International locations:** Worldwide. **Listed on:** NASDAQ. **Stock exchange symbol:** AMGN. **Annual sales/revenues:** $8.4 billion. **Number of employees at this location:** 2,280. **Number of employees worldwide:** 12,900.

AMISTAR CORPORATION
237 Via Vera Cruz, San Marcos CA 92069. 760/471-1700. **Fax:** 760/471-9065. **Contact:** Human Resources Department. **E-mail address:** joannej@amistar.com. **World Wide Web address:** http://www.amistar.com. **Description:** Amistar designs, develops, manufactures, markets, and services a broad variety of automatic and semi-automatic equipment for assembling electronic components to be placed in printed circuit boards. The company is also a contract assembler of printed circuit boards. **Corporate headquarters location:** This location. **Number of employees at this location:** 170. **Listed on:** NASDAQ. **Stock exchange symbol:** AMTA.

AMPEX CORPORATION
1228 Douglas Avenue, Redwood City CA 94063. 650/367-4111. **Fax:** 650/367-4669. **Contact:** Human Resources. **E-mail address:** info@ampex.com. **World Wide Web address:** http://www.ampex.com. **Description:** A manufacturer of video technology for the professional television, mass data storage, and instrumentation industries. Products include recorders, editors, switchers, special effects, robotic libraries, tapes, and interconnect equipment. **Subsidiaries include:** iNEXTV; Ampex Data Systems; MicroNet Technologies. **Corporate headquarters location:** This location. **Operations at this facility include:** Administration; Divisional Headquarters; Research and Development; Sales; Service. **Listed on:** American Stock Exchange. **Stock exchange symbol:** AXC.

AMPRO COMPUTERS INC.
5215 Hellyer Avenue, Suite 110, San Jose CA 95138-1007. 408/360-0200. **Toll-free phone:** 800/966-5200. **Fax:** 408/360-0222. **Contact:** Human Resources. **E-mail address:** careers@ampro.com. **World Wide Web address:** http://www.ampro.com. **Description:** A leading ISO 9001 manufacturer of board-level PC and PC/AT compatible computer modules for embedded applications and the originator of the PC/104 and PC/104-Plus standards. **Corporate headquarters location:** This location. **Other U.S. locations:** Nationwide. **International locations:** Worldwide. **Listed on:** Privately held. **Annual sales/revenues:** $21 - $50 million. **Number of employees at this location:** 60.

AMYLIN PHARMACEUTICALS, INC.
9360 Towne Centre Drive, Suite 110, San Diego CA 92121. 858/552-2200. **Fax:** 858/552-2212. **Contact:** Human Resources. **E-mail address:** jobs@amylin.com. **World Wide Web address:** http://www.amylin.com. **Description:** Researches the hormone amylin, which provides drug strategies for treating juvenile- and maturity-onset diabetes, and other metabolic diseases. **NOTE:** Search and apply for positions online. **Positions advertised include:** Director, Analystical Development; Sr. Statistician; Development Scientist; Global Safety Manager; Sr. Regulatory Affairs Manager; Director, Clinical Supplies; Sr. Director, Corporate Training and Development; Sr. Manager, Process Engineering. **Corporate headquarters location:** This location. **International locations:** Oxford England; Munster Germany. **Number of employees at this location:** 100. **Listed on:** NASDAQ. **Stock exchange symbol:** AMLN.

ANACOMP, INC.
15378 Avenue of Science, San Diego CA 92128. 858/716-3400. **Fax:** 858/716-3775. **Contact:** Human Resources. **World Wide Web address:** http://www.anacomp.com. **Description:** Provides document storage solutions; manufactures computer hardware and software; and develops customized financial software. **Positions advertised include:** Credit Services Representative. **Corporate headquarters location:** This location. **Other area locations:** Vista CA. **Other U.S. locations:** Nationwide. **International locations:** Austria; France; Germany; Italy; Netherlands; Sweden; Switzerland; United Kingdom. **Operations at this facility include:** Administration; Engineering and Design; Manufacturing; Marketing; Research and Development; Sales. **Number of employees worldwide:** 1,150.

ANACOMP, INC.
3855 North Freeway Boulevard, Suite 110, Sacramento CA 95834. 916/641-1280. **Contact:** Human Resources. **World Wide Web address:** http://www.anacomp.com. **Description:** Provides document storage solutions, manufactures computer hardware and software, and develops customized financial software. **Corporate headquarters location:** San Diego CA. **Other area locations:** Belmont CA; Hayward CA; Poway CA; San Francisco CA. **Other U.S. locations:** Nationwide. **International locations:** Austria; France; Germany; Italy; Netherlands; Sweden; Switzerland; United Kingdom. **Number of employees worldwide:** 1,600.

ANALOG DEVICES, INC.
1500 Space Park Drive, Santa Clara CA 95052. 408/727-9222. **Toll-free phone:** 800/446-6212. **Contact:** Personnel. **E-mail address:** candidates.hr@analog.com. **World Wide Web address:** http://www.analog.com. **Description:** Analog Devices is a *Fortune* 500 company that designs, manufactures, and markets a broad line of high-performance analog, mixed-signal, and digital integrated circuits (ICs) that address a wide range of real-world signal processing applications. The company's principal product is the general purpose, standard linear ICs. The company's largest communications application is the pan-European GSM (Global System for Mobile Communications) digital cellular telephone system. The company has direct sales offices in 17 countries including the United States. **NOTE:** Search and apply for positions online. **Special programs:** Internships; Co-ops. **Corporate headquarters location:** Norwood MA. **Other U.S. locations:** Nationwide. **Other area locations:** San Jose CA; Sunnyvale CA; Berkeley CA. **International locations:** Worldwide. **Operations at this facility include:** This location is a sales office. **Listed on:** New York Stock Exchange. **Stock exchange symbol:** ADI. **Number of employees worldwide:** 8,600.

ANALYSTS INTERNATIONAL CORPORATION (AIC)
1390 Willow Pass Road, Suite 200, Concord CA 94520-7900. 925/687-5522. **Toll-free phone:** 800/698-9411. **Fax:** 925/687-5552. **Contact:** Human Resources Manager. **E-mail address:** jobs@analysts.com. **World Wide Web address:** http://www.analysts.com. **Description:** An international computer consulting firm. The company uses different programming languages and software to assist clients in developing systems for a variety of industries. **NOTE:** Resumes are not accepted by mail or fax. Apply online or via e-mail. **Positions advertised include:** Application Consultant; Application Developer; Application Specialist; Business Analyst. **Corporate headquarters location:** Minneapolis MN. **Other U.S. locations:** Nationwide. **International locations:** Canada; United Kingdom. **Listed on:** NASDAQ. **Stock exchange symbol:** ANLY.

ANCRA INTERNATIONAL LLC
4880 West Rosecrans Avenue, Hawthorne CA 90250. 310/970-8612. **Toll-free phone:** 800/973-5092. **Contact:** Tammy Carson, Human Resources Administrator. **World Wide Web address:** http://www.ancra-llc.com. **Description:** Manufactures cargo restraint equipment for the trucking and aircraft industries including aircraft fittings, winches, cam buckles, o/c buckles, shoring beams, cargo systems, and track. Ancra also maintains off-road and marine divisions. **Corporate headquarters location:** This location. **Other U.S. locations:** Erlanger KY.

ANDERSON NEWS COMPANY
2970 North Ontario Street, Burbank CA 91504. 818/845-8347. **Contact:** Human Resources. **World Wide Web address:** http://www.andersonnews.com. **Description:** Distributes books and magazines to airports, bookstores, convenience stores, military installations, newsstands, and supermarkets. **Corporate headquarters location:** Knoxville TN.

ANDRONICO'S MARKET
1109 Washington Avenue, Albany CA 94706. **Fax:** 510/287-5978. **Fax:** 510/649-6753. **Recorded jobline:** 510/287-5978. **Contact:** Human Resources Department. **E-mail address:** humanresources@andronicos.com. **World Wide Web address:** http://www.andronicos.com. **Description:** Operates a chain of retail grocery stores. Founded in 1929. **NOTE:** Entry-level positions and part-time jobs are offered. **Special programs:** Training. **Corporate headquarters location:** This location. **Other area locations:** Berkeley CA; Danville CA; Emeryville CA; Los Altos CA; Palo Alto CA; San Anselmo CA; San Francisco CA. **Operations at this facility include:** Administration. **Listed on:** Privately held. **COO:** William J. Andronico. **Number of employees at this location:** 800.

ANDROS INC.
870 Harbour Way South, Richmond CA 94804. 510/837-3500. **Fax:** 510/837-3600. **Contact:** Human Resources. **E-mail address:** jobs@andros.com. **World Wide Web address:** http://www.andros.com. **Description:** A supplier of instrumentation and a leading worldwide designer and supplier to original equipment manufacturers of advanced infrared and fuel gas analyzers. These devices measure concentrations of carbon dioxide, carbon monoxide, and hydrocarbons. Andros also manufactures medical products that measure gases in human breath including carbon dioxide, halogenated hydrocarbon gases, and nitrous oxide. **Corporate headquarters location:** This location.

ANESTHESIA PLUS, INC.
9255 Survey Road, Suite 1, Elk Grove CA 95624. 916/686-4480. **Toll-free phone:** 800/887-8161. **Fax:** 916/686-4311. **Contact:** Human Resources. **World Wide Web address:** http://www.anesplus.com. **Description:** Manufactures and markets new and refurbished O.R. equipment. The company specializes in anesthesia and related products.

ANGELUS SANITARY CAN MACHINE COMPANY
4900 Pacific Boulevard, Los Angeles CA 90058. 323/583-2171. **Fax:** 323-587-5607. **Contact:** Mr. Wiley Fain, Personnel Director. **E-mail address:** admin@angelusmachine.com. **World Wide Web address:** http://www.angelusmachine.com. **Description:** A manufacturer and worldwide distributor of can-closing equipment. **Corporate headquarters location:** This location. **International locations:** Belgium; United Kingdom.

ANTELOPE VALLEY PRESS
P.O. Box 4050, Palmdale CA 93590-4050. 661/273-2700. **Physical address:** 37404 Sierra Highway, Palmdale CA 93550. **Contact:** Personnel Department. **World Wide Web address:** http://www.avpress.com. **Description:** Publishers of the *Antelope Valley Press,* a daily newspaper with a weekday circulation of 32,000. **Positions advertised include:** Assistant District Manager; Route Driver.

ANTHONY AND SYLVAN POOLS
1228 West Shelly Court, Orange CA 92868. 714/628-9600. **Toll-free phone:** 800/877-6657. **Contact:** Personnel. **World Wide Web address:** http://www.anthony-sylvan.com. **Description:** One of the largest builders of residential swimming pools in the United States. **NOTE:** Apply online. **Positions advertised include:** General Manager, Pool Divisions; Retail Store Manager; Operations Manager; Design Consultant; Sales Coordinator. **Parent company:** Anthony Industries, Inc. **Operations at this facility include:** Administration; Divisional Headquarters. **Other U.S. locations:** Nationwide. **Listed on:** NASDAQ. **Stock exchange symbol:** SWIM.

ANTHONY'S SEAFOOD GROUP
5232 Lovelock Street, San Diego CA 92110. 619/291-7254. **Fax:** 619/298-1212. **Contact:** Constance DeHaven, Director of Human Resources. **World Wide Web address:** http://www.gofishanthonys.com. **Description:** A family-owned restaurant chain specializing in seafood. Anthony's Fish Grotto also sells seafood to the public. **Corporate headquarters location:** This location. **Other area locations:** Chula Vista CA; Kearny Mesa CA; La Mesa CA; Mission Valley CA; Rancho Bernardo CA.

ANTIOCH, CITY OF
P.O. Box 5007, Antioch CA 94531-5007. 925/779-7020. **Fax:** 925/779-7002. **Recorded jobline:** 925/779-7022. **Contact:** Janet Sanchez, Personnel Technician. **World Wide Web address:** http://www.ci.antioch.ca.us. **Description:** Administrative offices for the city of Antioch. **Corporate headquarters location:** This location. **Operations at this facility include:** Administration. **Number of employees at this location:** 350.

AON CONSULTING
707 Wilshire Boulevard, Suite 5700, Los Angeles CA 90017. 213/630-2900. **Fax:** 213/627-6155. **Contact:** Human Resources. **E-mail address:** aonrecruitment@aon.com. **World Wide Web address:** http://www.aon.com. **Description:** An international human resources consulting and benefits brokerage firm providing integrated advisory and support services in retirement planning, health care management, organizational effectiveness, compensation, human resources-related communications, and information technologies. The company's organizational effectiveness services include advisory and support services in compensation, strategy development, organizational design, business process redesign, human resources development, management training and development, organizational communications, and information technology applications. Strategic health care services include advisory and support services in traditional group health and welfare programs, strategic health planning, strategic health care management, quality assurance, flexible benefits and compensation, financial management, data management, vendor oversight, and communications. Strategic retirement planning and educational services include consulting and support services in core actuarial applications, retirement health and welfare benefits, funding and investment strategy, record keeping and administration, employee sensing and communications, personalized retirement modeling, holistic lifestyle and family planning, and database information and proprietary studies. Information technologies services include human resources information systems development (information management strategies, systems, databases, software, and technology advisement) and human resources systems applications (human resources planning, record keeping, communication, and education). **Positions advertised include:** Systems Analyst; Consultant; Account Manager. **Corporate headquarters location:** Chicago IL. **Listed on:** New York Stock Exchange. **Stock exchange symbol:** AOC. **Number of employees worldwide:** 51,000.

AON CONSULTING
2540 North First Street, Suite 400, San Jose CA 95131. 408/321-2500. **Fax:** 408/321-2650. **Contact:** Human Resources. **World Wide Web address:** http://www.aon.com. **Description:** An international human resources consulting and benefits brokerage firm providing integrated advisory and support services in retirement planning, health care management, organizational effectiveness, compensation, human resources-related communications, and information technologies. The company's organizational effectiveness services include advisory and support services in compensation, strategy development, organizational design, business process redesign, human resources development, management training and development, organizational communications, and information technology applications. Strategic health care services include advisory and support services in traditional group health and welfare programs, strategic health planning, strategic health care management, quality assurance, flexible benefits and compensation, financial and data management, vendor oversight, and communications. Strategic retirement planning and educational services include consulting and support services in core actuarial applications, retirement health and welfare benefits, funding and investment strategy, record keeping and administration, employee sensing and communications, personalized retirement modeling, holistic lifestyle and family planning, and database information and proprietary studies. Information technologies services include human resources information systems development (information management strategies, systems, databases, software, and technology advisement) and human resources systems applications (human resources planning, record keeping, communication, and education). **Positions advertised include:** Associate Relationship Specialist. **Corporate headquarters location:** Chicago IL. **Other area locations:** Fresno CA; Irvine CA; Sacramento CA; San Francisco CA; Woodland Hills CA. **Listed on:** New York Stock Exchange. **Stock exchange symbol:** AOC.

AON RISK SERVICES
199 Fremont Street, 14th Floor, San Francisco CA 94105. 415/486-7500. **Fax:** 415/486-7026. **Contact:** Human Resources Department. **World Wide Web address:** http://www.aon.com. **Description:** AON Risk Services specializes in property and

casualty, marine, and public entities insurance. **Positions advertised include:** Consultant; Client Service Manager. **Operations at this facility include:** This location is a profit center for the large international insurance brokerage. **Listed on:** New York Stock Exchange. **Stock exchange symbol:** AOC.

AONIX
5040 Shoreham Place, Suite 100, San Diego CA 92122. 858/457-2700. **Toll-free phone:** 800/972-6649. **Fax:** 858/824-0212 **Contact:** Human Resources. **E-mail address:** resume@aonix.com. **World Wide Web address:** http://www.aonix.com. **Description:** Develops and markets computer-aided software engineering (CASE) products that allow a network of minicomputers to interact. **Positions advertised include:** Controller. **Corporate headquarters location:** This location. **International locations:** France; Germany; Sweden; United Kingdom.

APPERSON PRINT MANAGEMENT
6855 East Gage Avenue, Los Angeles CA 90040. 562/927-4718. **Fax:** 562/927-2169. **Contact:** Human Resources. **E-mail address:** apmshr@appersonprint.com. **World Wide Web address:** http://www.appersonprint.com. **Description:** Manufactures business forms. **Positions advertised include:** Sales Rep. **Corporate headquarters location:** This location. **Other area locations:** Fresno CA; San Francisco CA. **Other U.S. locations:** Rockville Center NY; Charlotte NC; Houston TX; Seattle WA. **Number of employees at this location:** 150. **Number of employees nationwide:** 400.

APPLE COMPUTER, INC.
One Infinite Loop, MS: 84-3CE, Cupertino CA 95014. 408/996-1010. **Fax:** 408/996-0275. **Recorded jobline:** 408/974-0529. **Contact:** Personnel. **E-mail address:** applejobs@apple.com. **World Wide Web address:** http://www.apple.com. **Description:** Develops, manufactures, and markets personal computer systems and peripherals. The company's desktop publishing and communications products are marketed internationally. Founded in 1976. **NOTE:** Search and apply for positions online. **Special programs:** Internships. **Corporate headquarters location:** This location. **Other area locations:** Elk Grove CA. **Other U.S. locations:** Phoenix AZ; Fountain CO; Austin TX. **Operations at this facility include:** Sales. **Listed on:** NASDAQ. **Stock exchange symbol:** AAPL. **CEO:** Steve Jobs. **Number of employees nationwide:** 10,900.

APPLE COMPUTER, INC.
2911 Laguna Boulevard, Elk Grove CA 95758. 916/394-2600. **Fax:** 916/394-5504. **Contact:** Personnel. **E-mail address:** applejobs@apple.com. **World Wide Web address:** http://www.apple.com/employment. **Description:** Apple Computer develops, manufactures, and markets personal computer systems and peripherals. The company's desktop publishing and communications products are marketed internationally. Founded in 1976. **Corporate headquarters location:** Cupertino CA. **Other U.S. locations:** Phoenix AZ; Fountain CO; Austin TX. **Operations at this facility include:** This location is the Sacramento Operations Center, which serves as a systems assembly and distribution site. **Listed on:** NASDAQ. **Stock exchange symbol:** AAPL. **CEO:** Steve Jobs. **Number of employees at this location:** 650. **Number of employees nationwide:** 10,900.

APPLIED AEROSPACE STRUCTURES CORP. (AASC)
P.O. Box 6189, Stockton CA 95206-0189. 209/982-0160. **Physical address:** 3437 South Airport Way, Stockton CA 95206. **Fax:** 209/983-3375. **Contact:** Human Resources Manager. **E-mail address:** hr@aascworld.com. **World Wide Web address:** http://www.aascworld.com. **Description:** Provides designing, engineering, and manufacturing services internationally to private and government clients in the aerospace industry. **NOTE:** Resumes are accepted by e-mail or fax. To contact Human Resources directly, call: 209/983-3279. Fax: 209/983-3333. **Special programs:** Internships. **Corporate headquarters location:** This location. **Listed on:** Privately held. **Number of employees nationwide:** 270.

APPLIED BIOSYSTEMS
850 Lincoln Centre Drive, Foster City CA 94404. 650/638-5800. **Toll-free phone:** 800/327-3002. **Fax:** 650/638-5884. **Contact:** Human Resources. **World Wide Web address:** http://www.appliedbiosystems.com. **Description:** Manufactures life science systems and analytical tools for use in such markets as biotechnology, pharmaceuticals, environmental testing, and chemical manufacturing. **Corporate headquarters location:** This location. **Parent company:** Applera Corporation. **Operations at this facility include:** Administration; Manufacturing; Research and Development; Sales; Service. **Listed on:** New York Stock Exchange. **Stock exchange symbol:** ABI. **Number of employees nationwide:** 900.

APPLIED IMAGING CORPORATION
120 Baytech Drive, San Jose CA 95134-2302. 408/719-6400. **Fax:** 408/719-6401. **Contact:** Administration Manager. **E-mail address:** info@aicorp.com. **World Wide Web address:** http://www.aicorp.com. **Description:** Develops software used by hospitals and universities for detecting genetic birth defects. **Corporate headquarters location:** This location. **Other U.S. locations:** League City TX. **International locations:** Newcastle England.

APPLIED MATERIALS, INC.
3050 Bowers Avenue, Mail Stop 1826, Santa Clara CA 95054-3299. 408/727-5555. **Contact:** Corporate Employment. **E-mail address:** jobs@appliedmaterials.com. **World Wide Web address:** http://www.appliedmaterials.com. **Description:** A *Fortune* 500 company that is a leading producer of wafer fabrication systems for the semiconductor industry. The company also sells related spare parts and services. Applied Materials' products include dry etch systems for the creation of circuit paths in semiconductors and implementation products for silicon wafers. **NOTE:** Address employment inquiries to: ask_employment@appliedmaterials.com. Resumes may be submitted via the e-mail address listed above. **Positions advertised include:** Account Technologist; Administrative Assistant; Business Process Development Manager; CAD Designer; Customer Engineer; Electrical Engineer; Financial Analyst; Human Resources Division Manager; System Design Engineer; Systems Project Manager; Technical Support Engineer. **Corporate headquarters location:** This location. **Other area locations:** Hayward CA; Irvine CA; Milpitas CA; Ontario CA; Roseville CA. **Other U.S. locations:** Nationwide. **International locations:** Worldwide. **Listed on:** NASDAQ. **Stock exchange symbol:** AMAT. **Number of employees nationwide:** 16,200.

APPLIED SIGNAL TECHNOLOGY
400 West California Avenue, Sunnyvale CA 94086. 408/749-1888. **Fax:** 408/774-2700. **Contact:** Human Resources Department. **E-mail address:** resume@appsig.com. **World Wide Web address:** http://www.appsig.com. **Description:** Designs, develops, manufactures, and markets signal processing equipment to collect and process telecommunications signals. The equipment is purchased by the U.S. government for foreign signal reconnaissance. Founded in 1984. **Positions advertised include:** Business Development Specialist; DSP Software Engineer; GUI SW Architect; Process Improvement Engineer; Program Manager; Senior Software Engineer; Senior Test Engineer; Senior System Engineer. **Corporate headquarters location:** This location. **Other U.S. locations:** MD; OR; UT; VA. **Listed on:** NASDAQ. **Stock exchange symbol:** APSG.

APRIA HEALTHCARE GROUP INC.
26220 Enterprise Court, Lake Forest CA 92630. **Toll-free phone:** 800/277-4288. **Fax:** 949/639-6258. **Contact:** Diane Cottrell, Human Resources. **E-mail address:** contact_us@apria.com. **World Wide Web address:** http://www.apria.com. **Description:** Provides a broad range of respiratory therapy services, home medical equipment, and infusion therapy services. Apria Healthcare Group's home health care services are provided to patients who have been discharged from hospitals, skilled nursing facilities, or convalescent homes and are being treated at home. In conjunction with medical professionals, Apria personnel deliver, install, and service medical equipment, as well as provide appropriate therapies and coordinate plans of care for their patients. Apria personnel also instruct patients and caregivers in the correct use of equipment and monitor the equipment's effectiveness. Patients and their families receive training from registered nurses and respiratory therapy professionals concerning the therapy administered including instruction in proper infusion technique and the care and use of equipment and supplies. **Positions advertised include:** Internal Auditor; Business Development Manager; Sr. Financial Analyst; National Nursing Manager; Vice President, Technology. **Corporate headquarters location:** This location. **Other U.S. locations:** Nationwide. **International locations:** United Kingdom. **Operations at this facility include:** Administration. **Listed on:** New York Stock Exchange. **Stock exchange symbol:** AHG. **Annual sales/revenues:** $1.4 billion. **Number of employees at this location:** 750. **Number of employees nationwide:** 9,000.

ARAMARK SPORTS AND ENTERTAINMENT SERVICES
3900 West Manchester Boulevard, Inglewood CA 90305. 310/674-2010. **Contact:** Human Resources. **World Wide Web address:** http://www.ps.aramark.com. **Description:** Provides food and beverage services; operates large-format films, theaters, and casinos; and offers venue management services. **Operations at this facility include:** This location is a food service provider for the Forum. **Listed on:** New York Stock Exchange. **Stock exchange symbol:** RMK.

ARAMARK UNIFORM SERVICES
P.O. Box 7891, Burbank CA 91510. 818/973-3700. **Physical address:** 115 North First Street, Burbank CA 91502. **Toll-free phone:** 800/ARAMARK. **Contact:** Human Resources. **World Wide Web address:** http://www.aramark-uniform.com. **Description:** One of America's largest uniform providers with over 400,000 customers. The company offers uniforms to reinforce corporate identities or to meet specialized demands for static control and flame resistance and provides a variety of products including walk-off mats, cleaning cloths, disposable towels, and other environmental control items. **Positions advertised include:** Customer Information Specialist; Assistant Regional Controller; Account Manager. **Corporate headquarters:** This location. **Parent company:** ARAMARK (Philadelphia PA) is one of the world's leading providers of managed services. The company operates in all 50 states and 10 foreign countries, offering a broad range of services to businesses of all sizes including most *Fortune* 500 companies and thousands of universities, hospitals, and municipal, state, and federal government facilities. The company is employee-owned. ARAMARK's businesses include Food, Leisure, and Support Services including Campus Dining Services, School Nutrition Services, Leisure Services, Business Dining Services, International Services, Healthcare Support Services, Conference Center Management, and Refreshment Services; Facility Services; Correctional Services; Industrial Services; Uniform Services, which includes Uniform Services and Wearguard, a direct marketer of work clothing; Health and Education Services including Spectrum Healthcare Services and Children's World Learning Centers; and Book and Magazine Services. **Listed on:** New York Stock Exchange. **Stock exchange symbol:** RMK. **Number of employees worldwide:** 200,000.

ARCADIS
1400 North Harbor Boulevard, Suite 700, Fullerton CA 92835-4127. 714/278-0992. **Fax:** 714/278-0051. **Contact:** Human Resources. **E-mail address:** arcadisgm@arcadis-us.com. **World Wide Web address:** http://www.arcadis-us.com. **Description:** A consulting firm that provides environmental and engineering services. The company focuses on the environmental, building, and infrastructure markets. Founded in 1888. **NOTE:** Search and apply for positions online. **Positions advertised include:** Scientist/Engineer; Scientist. **Corporate headquarters:** Highlands Ranch CO. **Other U.S. locations:** Nationwide. **International locations:** The Netherlands; United Kingdom. **Subsidiaries include:** JSA Environmental Inc. (Long Beach CA) provides environmental assessment and analysis services. **Listed on:** NASDAQ. **Stock exchange symbol:** ARCAF. **Number of employees worldwide:** 9,000.

ARDEN COMPANIES
9059 Hermosa, Suite A, Rancho Cucamongo CA 91730. 909/613-0998. **Contact:** Personnel Director. **World Wide Web address:** http://www.ardencompanies.com. **Description:** Manufactures shower curtains, tablecloths, placemats, swimming pools, inflatable toys, and air mattresses.

ARETE ASSOCIATES
P.O. Box 6024, Sherman Oaks CA 91413. 818/501-2880x432. **Physical address:** 5000 Van Nuys Boulevard, Suite 400, Sherman Oaks CA 91403. **Fax:** 818/501-2905. **Contact:** Human Resources. **E-mail address:** personnel@arete.com. **World Wide Web address:** http://www.arete.com. **Description:** Provides research and development in the area of signal processing as it applies to atmospheric, oceanographic, and related areas. The company is involved in the mathematical modeling of physical processes, signal and image processing, remote sensing and phenomenology, electro-optics, lidar, radar, and acoustics. Founded in 1976. **NOTE:** U.S. citizenship, a drug test, and a security investigation are required to meet position eligibility. Entry-level positions are offered. **Positions advertised include:** Research Analyst. **Corporate headquarters location:** This location. **Other U.S. locations:** AZ; FL; VA. **Operations at this facility include:** Administration; Research and Development. **Listed on:** Privately held. **Number of employees at this location:** 90. **Number of employees nationwide:** 170.

ARGONAUT GROUP, INC.
250 Middlefield Road, Menlo Park CA 94025. 650/326-0900. **Toll-free phone:** 800/222-7811. **Fax:** 650/858-6631. **Contact:** George A. Schmid, Human Resources Manager. **E-mail address:** gschmid@argonautgroup.com. **World Wide Web address:** http://www.argonautgroup.com. **Description:** Argonaut Group, Inc. is a holding company whose subsidiaries are mainly involved in the selling, underwriting, and servicing of workers' compensation and other lines of property and casualty insurance. **Positions advertised include:** Underwriter; Underwriting Assistant. **Office hours:** Monday - Friday, 8:00 a.m. - 5:00 p.m. **Corporate headquarters location:** This location. **Other area locations:** Fresno CA; San Francisco CA; San Jose CA. **Subsidiaries include:** Argonaut Great Central Insurance Company; Argonaut Insurance Company; Captive Advisory Services, Inc.; The Colony Insurance Group;

The Redwoods Group; The Rockwood Insurance Group; Trident Insurance Services; Inc. **Listed on:** NASDAQ. **Stock exchange symbol:** AGII.

ARGO-TECH COSTA MESA
671 West 17th Street, Costa Mesa CA 92627-3605. 949/764-2200. **Fax:** 949/574-9513. **Contact:** Human Resources. **E-mail address:** hrcm@argo-tech.com. **World Wide Web address:** http://www.argo-tech.com. **Description:** Formerly known as the J.C. Carter Company, this location now houses the Carter Cryogenic Products Division of the Argo-Tech Corporation. Argo-Tech designs and manufactures pumps, valves, and pressure regulators used in aircraft fuel systems. **Positions advertised include:** Environmental/Safety Manager. **Special programs:** Internships. **Corporate headquarters location:** Cleveland OH. **Other area locations:** Inglewood CA. **Other U.S. locations:** Tucson AZ. **International locations:** England; Japan.

ARRK PRODUCT DEVELOPMENT GROUP
8880 Rehco Road, San Diego CA 92121. 858/552-1587. **Toll-free phone:** 800/735-ARRK. **Fax:** 858/410-3711. **Contact:** Human Resources. **E-mail address:** hr@arrk.com. **World Wide Web address:** http://www.arrk.com. **Description:** Manufactures plastic prototypes for a variety of industries including health care. **Positions advertised include:** Software Engineer; Business Development Manager; Model Maker. **Corporate headquarters location:** This location. **Other area locations:** Los Angeles CA; San Francisco CA. **Other U.S. locations:** Atlanta GA; Detroit MI; Waxhaw NC; New York NY; Portland OR; Dallas TX. **International locations:** Australia; Canada; France; Hungary; Italy; Japan; Korea; Thailand; United Kingdom.

ARROW ELECTRONICS
3000 Bowers Avenue, Santa Clara CA 95051. 408/727-2500. **Fax:** 408/727-5896. **Contact:** Personnel Department. **World Wide Web address:** http://www.arrow.com. **Description:** Engaged in the distribution of selected lines of electronic supplies and components primarily to the electronics and computer industries, as well as to military and aerospace industries. Principal products include semiconductors, capacitors, resistors, and various computer products such as printers, video display terminals, and other products supplied by major computer manufacturing firms. **Positions advertised include:** Sales and Marketing Representative; Marketing Specialist; Material Planner. **Corporate headquarters location:** Melville NY. **Operations at this facility include:** Administration; Sales; Service. **Listed on:** New York Stock Exchange. **Stock exchange symbol:** ARW.

ARTESYN TECHNOLOGIES
47173 Benecia Street, Fremont CA 94538. 510/657-6700. **Contact:** Human Resources. **World Wide Web address:** http://www.artesyn.com. **Description:** Manufactures both standard and custom electronic products used in an array of applications including powering communications networks, controlling the manufacture of fiber optics, enabling voice messaging, providing multimedia power for global Internet servers, and operating traffic signals with real-time embedded computers. **Corporate headquarters location:** Boca Raton FL. **Other U.S. locations:** Eden Prairie MN; Redwood Falls MN. **International locations:** Germany. **Listed on:** NASDAQ. **Stock exchange symbol:** ATSN. **Number of employees worldwide:** 6,500.

ASANTE TECHNOLOGIES
2223 Old Oakland Road, San Jose CA 95131. 408/435-8388. **Contact:** Human Resources. **Fax:** 408/432-3042. **E-mail address:** hr@asante.com. **World Wide Web address:** http://www.asante.com. **Description:** Designs, develops, and manufactures Gigabit Ethernet and Fast Ethernet networking systems. **Positions advertised include:** Sr. Product Manager; Staff Software Engineer. **Corporate headquarters location:** This location. **International locations:** Germany; Austria; Switzerland. **Operations at this facility include:** Administration; Research and Development; Sales; Service. **Listed on:** NASDAQ. **Stock exchange symbol:** ASNT. **Annual sales/revenues:** $15.2 million.

ASCENT MEDIA
2813 West Alameda Avenue, Burbank CA 91505. 818/840-7000. **Fax:** 818/260-2131. **Contact:** Human Resources Department. **E-mail address:** recruiting@ascentmedia.com. **World Wide Web address:** http://www.4mc.com. **Description:** Offers creative and production services to the media and entertainment industries. **Positions advertised include:** Project Manager; Senior Financial Analyst. **Parent company:** Liberty Media Corporation. **Listed on:** New York Stock Exchange. **Stock exchange symbol:** L.

ASCO POWER TECHNOLOGIES
705 North Carlton Avenue, Stockton CA 95203. 209/941-4111. **Toll-free phone:** 800/937-ASCO. **Contact:** Eugene Hammerson, Human Resources Manager. **World Wide Web address:** http://www.asco.com. **Description:** Automatic Switch Company is an international manufacturer of an extensive line of electrical control equipment used for the automation of machinery, equipment, and industrial processes and the control of electric power. **Corporate headquarters location:** Florham Park NJ. **Other U.S. locations:** Nationwide. **Parent company:** Emerson Electric. **Operations at this facility include:** This location manufactures and assembles electronic switchgear, housings, contactors, and motor controls. **Listed on:** New York Stock Exchange. **Stock exchange symbol:** EMR.

ASHWORTH, INC.
2765 Loker Avenue West, Carlsbad CA 92008. 760/438-6610. **Fax:** 760/438-6657. **Contact:** Human Resources. **E-mail address:** jobs@ashworth.com. **World Wide Web address:** http://www.ashworthinc.com. **Description:** Designs, manufactures, and markets golf apparel including men's and women's cotton shirts, pullovers, vests, sweaters, shorts, pants, and jackets. **Corporate headquarters location:** This location. **Listed on:** NASDAQ. **Stock exchange symbol:** ASHW.

ASPECT COMMUNICATIONS CORPORATION
1310 Ridder Park Drive, San Jose CA 95131. 408/325-2200. **Fax:** 408/325-2260. **Contact:** Staffing Department. **E-mail address:** staffing@aspect.com. **World Wide Web address:** http://www.aspect.com. **Description:** Provides comprehensive business solutions for mission-critical call centers worldwide. Products include automatic call distributors, computer-telephony integration solutions, call center management and reporting software, automation solutions, and planning and forecasting packages. Founded in 1985. **NOTE:** Entry-level positions are offered. **Special programs:** Internships. **Corporate headquarters location:** This location. **Other U.S. locations:** Nationwide. **International locations:** Worldwide. **Listed on:** NASDAQ. **Stock exchange symbol:** ASPT. **President/CEO:** Gary E. Barnett. **Annual sales/revenues:** More than $363.8 million. **Number of employees worldwide:** 1,300.

AMS (ASSEMBLY AND MANUFACTURING SYSTEMS, INC.)
2222 Shasta Way, Simi Valley CA 93065. 805/583-8961. **Fax:** 805/583-0442. **Contact:** Human Resources. **E-mail address:** hr@1ams.com. **World Wide Web address:** http://www.1ams.com. **Description:** Manufactures factory automation equipment. **Positions advertised include:** Senior Applications Engineer; Project Manager; Senior Mechanical Engineer; Machine Designer; Controls Engineer; Toolmaker/Machine Builder. **Other U.S. locations:** Columbus OH. **Operations at this facility include:** Administration; Divisional Headquarters; Manufacturing; Sales; Service. **Number of employees at this location:** 50. **Number of employees nationwide:** 125.

ASTEC AMERICA
5810 Van Allen Way, Carlsbad CA 92008. 760/930-4600. **Toll-free phone:** 888/412-7832. **Fax:** 760/930-0698. **Contact:** Human Resources Department. **E-mail address:** hr@astec.com. **World Wide Web address:** http://www.astec.com. **Description:** Manufactures switch mode power supplies. **Parent company:** Emerson Electric. **International locations:** France; Germany; Hong Kong; Italy; Japan; The Netherlands, United Kingdom.

ATMEL CORPORATION
2325 Orchard Parkway, San Jose CA 95131. 408/441-0311. **Contact:** Human Resources. **E-mail address:** hr@atmel.com. **World Wide Web address:** http://www.atmel.com. **Description:** Manufactures semiconductors including integrated microcircuits. **Positions advertised include:** Contract Administrator; Electrical Design Engineer; Embedded Software Development Engineer; International Tax Manager; Manager, Business Processs Analysis; Tax Analyst. **Corporate headquarters location:** This location. **Other U.S. locations:** Colorado Springs CO; Irving TX. **International locations:** England; France; Germany. **Listed on:** NASDAQ. **Stock exchange symbol:** ATML.

AUTHENTIC FITNESS CORPORATION
6040 Bandini Boulevard, City of Commerce, CA 90040. 323/724-4693. **Contact:** Human Resources. **World Wide Web address:** http://www.speedo.com. **Description:** Owns, licenses, and markets activewear worldwide. The company's Speedo division manufactures swimwear and related accessories. Authentic Fitness also designs, sources, and markets a complete selection of skiwear including parkas, ski suits, shells, and ski pants. The company operates Authentic Fitness retail stores, which sell active fitness apparel. **Corporate headquarters location:** Van Nuys CA. **Other U.S. locations:** Nationwide. **International locations:** Canada.

AUTO-GRAPHICS, INC.
3201 Temple Avenue, Pomona CA 91768-3279. 909/595-7004. **Toll-free phone:** 800/776-6939. **Fax:** 909/595-3506. **Contact:** Human Resources. **E-mail address:** info@auto-graphics.com. **World Wide Web address:** http://www.auto-graphics.com. **Description:** Provides software and processing services to database and information publishers. Services include the computerized preparation and processing of customer-supplied information to be published in various formats including print, microform, CD-ROM, and/or online computer access. In addition, the company markets CD-ROM hardware and software packages for access to computer generated information. **Positions advertised include:** Inside Sales Representative. **Corporate headquarters location:** This location. **Subsidiaries include:** A-G Canada; Datacat; Dataquad; LibraryCard. **Number of employees at this location:** 115.

AUTODESK, INC.
111 McInnis Parkway, San Rafael CA 94903. 415/507-5000. **Fax:** 415/507-5100. **Contact:** Human Resources. **E-mail address:** resumes@autodesk.com. **World Wide Web address:** http://www.autodesk.com. **Description:** Designs, develops, markets, and supports a line of computer-aided design (CAD), engineering, and animation software products for desktop computers and workstations. **Positions advertised include:** Business Analyst; SQA Engineer; QA Engineer; Marketing Manager; Product Designer; Data Analyst; IT Project Manager; Oracle DBA; Data Architect; Sr. Soultions Manager. **Special programs:** Internships. **Corporate headquarters location:** This location. **International locations:** Worldwide. **Number of employees nationwide:** 1,800. **Listed on:** NASDAQ. **Stock exchange symbol:** ADSK.

AUTOMATIC DATA PROCESSING (ADP)
3300 Olcott Street, Santa Clara CA 95054. 408/970-7671. **Toll-free phone:** 800/225-5237. **Contact:** Human Resources. **World Wide Web address:** http://www.adp.com. **Description:** Automatic Data Processing is engaged in payroll processing services including unemployment claims management, and local, state, and federal tax filing. **Positions advertised include:** Implementation Specialist; Implementation Manager; Major Account Sales Rep. **Corporate headquarters location:** Roseland NJ. **Operations at this facility include:** This location is part of the major accounts division. **Listed on:** New York Stock Exchange. **Stock exchange symbol:** ADP. **Number of employees at this location:** 500. **Number of employees nationwide:** 20,000.

AUTOMATIC DATA PROCESSING (ADP)
5355 Orangethorpe Avenue, La Palma CA 90623. 714/228-4800. **Contact:** Human Resources. **World Wide Web address:** http://www.adp.com. **Description:** Engaged in payroll processing services including unemployment claims management and local, state, and federal tax filing. **Positions advertised include:** Leasing Solutions Rep; Associate PC Support Specialist; Implementation Specialist; Tax Service Rep. **Special programs:** Internships. **Corporate headquarters location:** Roseland NJ. **Listed on:** New York Stock Exchange. **Stock exchange symbol:** ADP. **Number of employees nationwide:** 20,000.

AUTOMOBILE CLUB OF SOUTHERN CALIFORNIA
3333 Fairview Road, Mail Stop A152, Costa Mesa 92626. 213/741-3111. **Fax:** 714/850-5058. **Contact:** Human Resources. **E-mail address:** personnel1@aaa-calif.com. **World Wide Web address:** http://www.aaa-calif.com. **Description:** Provides automotive and travel-related services and insurance to members. **NOTE:** Resumes should be sent to the attention of Human Resources at the address listed above.

AVERMEDIA
423 Dixon Landing Road, Milpitas CA 95035. 408/263-3828. **Fax:** 408/263-8132. **Contact:** Human Resources. **E-mail address:** jobs@aver.com. **World Wide Web address:** http://www.avermedia-usa.com. **Description:** Designs and manufactures digital multimedia products. Founded in 1990. **Positions advertised include:** Technical Support Specialist; Marketing Specialist; National Sales Manager; Junior Project Manager. **Number of employees worldwide:** 800.

AVERY DENNISON CORPORATION
150 North Orange Grove Boulevard, Pasadena CA 91103. 626/304-2000. **Contact:** Human Resources. **World Wide Web address:** http://www.averydennison.com. **Description:** A worldwide manufacturer of self-adhesive products, pressure-sensitive base materials, label components, labeling systems, and office products. The company services a broad range of industries with products that are used in applications for marking, identifying, labeling, decorating, fastening, filing, and indexing. **NOTE:** Search and apply for position online. **Positions advertised include:** Commodity

Manager, IT; Corporate Director, Pricing Strategy; Corporate Financial Advisor; It Internal Auditor; Research Chemist; Senior Reporting Analyst; Senior Product Architect. **Corporate headquarters location:** This location. **Other area locations:** Brea CA; Covina CA; Irwindale CA. **Other U.S. locations:** Framingham MA. **Listed on:** New York Stock Exchange. **Stock exchange symbol:** AVE. **Number of employees worldwide:** 20,300.

AVIGEN INC.
1301 harbor Bay Parkway, Alameda CA 94502. 510/748-7150. **Fax:** 510/748-7371. **Contact:** Human Resources. **E-mail address:** hr@avigen.com. **World Wide Web address:** http://www.avigen.com. **Description:** Dedicated to the development of gene therapy products and delivery technology for the treatment of series and chronic diseases. **Positions advertised:** Scientist, Neurobiology; Assistant Controller.

AVISO INC.
1301 Marina Village Parkway, Suite 210, Alameda CA 94501. 510/865-5100. **Fax:** 510/865-5165. **Contact:** Human Resources. **E-mail address:** personnel@avisoinc.com. **World Wide Web address:** http://www.avisoinc.com. **Description:** A marketing and communications firm that primarily serves the real estate and development industries. **Corporate headquarters location:** This location.

AVNET, INC.
2105 Lundy Avenue, San Jose CA 95131. 408/435-3500. **Contact:** Human Resources. **E-mail address:** human-resources@avnet.com. **World Wide Web address:** http://www.avnet.com. **Description:** A multiregional distributor of a wide variety of electronic products including wire and cable, connectors, and other passive and electromechanical products and interconnect assemblies used by customers in assembling and manufacturing electronic equipment. Kent Electronics Corporation also manufactures electronic interconnect assemblies that are built to customers' specifications. **NOTE:** Search and apply for positions online. **Positions advertised include:** Program Manager. **Corporate headquarters location:** Phoenix AZ. **International locations:** Worldwide. **Listed on:** New York Stock Exchange. **Stock exchange symbol:** AVT. **Number of employees worldwide:** 9,500.

AVON PRODUCTS INC.
2940 East Foothill Boulevard, Pasadena CA 91121. 626/578-8000. **Contact:** Human Resources. **E-mail address:** jobs@avon.com. **World Wide Web address:** http://www.avoncareers.com. **Description:** Avon Products Inc. is a direct seller of beauty care products, fashion jewelry, gifts, fragrances, and decorative products. Avon, a *Fortune* 500 company, markets its products through a network of 2.8 million independent sales representatives in 135 countries worldwide. **NOTE:** Salespeople are considered independent contractors or dealers and most work part-time. If you are interested in becoming a sales representative, please call 800/FOR-AVON, or visit the company's Website for more information. **Positions advertised include:** Division Sales Manager. **Corporate headquarters location:** New York NY. **Other U.S. locations:** Newark DE; Atlanta GA; Morton Grove NY; Rye NY; Suffern NY; Springdale OH. **Operations at this facility include:** This location is a distribution center for the West Coast.

AXELGAARD MANUFACTURING COMPANY, LTD.
1667 South Mission Road, Fallbrook CA 92028. 760/723-7554. **Fax:** 760/723-2356. **Contact:** Human Resources. **World Wide Web address:** http://www.axelgaard.com. **Description:** Manufactures electrodes for neurostimulation.

AXIOHM TRANSACTION SOLUTIONS, INC.
15070 Avenue of the Sciences, San Diego CA 92128. 858/451-3485. **Fax:** 858/451-3573. **Contact:** Paul Gardner, Director of Human Resources. **E-mail address:** paul.gardner@axiohm.com. **World Wide Web address:** http://www.axiohm.com. **Description:** One of the world's largest designers, manufacturers, and marketers of transaction printers. Axiohm Transaction Solutions also designs and manufactures bar code printers, magstripe and smartcard readers and writers, card printers, dot matrix impact printheads, magnetic heads, print and apply labeling systems, and consumables. Founded in 1977. **Corporate headquarters location:** This location. **Other U.S. locations:** Garden Grove CA; Golden CO; Ithaca NY; Riverton WY. **International locations:** Worldwide.

AXXCELERA BROADBAND WIRELESS
111 Castilian Drive, Santa Barbara CA 93117. 805/968-9621. **Fax:** 805/968-0791. **Contact:** Personnel. **E-mail address:** employment@axxcelera.com. **World Wide Web address:** http://www.axxcelera.com. **Description:** Provides a wireless access network for data, Internet, video, and voice applications. **NOTE:** Allpositions posted at: http://www.microwavedata.com/careers/employment. **Corporate headquarters location:** This location. **Other U.S. locations:** Rochester NY. **International locations:** Cambridge England; Beijing China.

AZTEC TENTS & EVENTS
540 Hawaii Avenue, Torrance CA 90503. 310/328-5060. **Toll-free phone:** 800/258-7368. **Contact:** Human Resources. **World Wide Web address:** http://www.aztectent.com. **Description:** Provides custom designed tents, structures and equipment for various special events and occasions. **Other U.S. locations:** Shelbyville KY.

B/E AEROSPACE
3355 East La Palma Avenue, Anaheim CA 92806. 714/630-5150. **Contact:** Debbi Nakamura, Director of Human Resources. **World Wide Web address:** http://www.beaerospace.com. **Description:** B/E Aerospace designs, manufactures, sells, and provides global support for one of the industry's broadest lines of commercial aircraft cabin interior products including seating products, passenger entertainment and service systems, galley structures, and inserts. The company is one of the world's largest suppliers of such products, serving most of the world's major airlines and airframe manufacturers. **Positions advertised include:** CAD Designer; R&D Engineering Technician. **Corporate headquarters location:** Wellington FL. **Other area locations:** Compton CA; Westminster CA. **Other U.S. locations:** Vista CA; Delray FL; Jacksonville FL; Miami FL; Winston-Salem NC; Arlington WA. **Listed on:** NASDAQ. **Stock exchange symbol:** BEAV. **Annual sales/revenues:** $624 million. **Number of employees nationwide:** 3,300.

B&H LABELING SYSTEMS
P.O. Box 247, Ceres CA 95307-0247. 209/537-5785. **Physical address:** 3461 Roeding Road, Ceres CA 95307. **Fax:** 209/537-8178. **Contact:** Bell Cull, Manager of Human Resources Department. **E-mail address:** bcull@bhlabeling.com. **World Wide Web address:** http://www.bhlabelingsystems.com. **Description:** A manufacturer of labeling machines for various industries including beverage and tobacco. **Corporate headquarters location:** This location. **International locations:** Mexico; Taiwan; United Kingdom.

BAE SYSTEMS
600 East Bonita Avenue, Pomona CA 91767. 909/624-8021. **Contact:** Human Resources. **E-mail address:** careers@baesystems.com. **World Wide Web address:** http://www.baesystems.com. **Description:** Manufactures microwave frequency generation and control devices, microwave integrated assemblies, and specialized semiconductors. **Positions advertised include:** Jr. Level Manufacturing Engineer. **Corporate headquarters:** Rockville MD. **Other area locations:** Barstow CA; San Diego CA; Ventura CA; Mojave CA; Ontario CA; Westlake Village CA; Los Angeles CA. **Other U.S. locations:** Nationwide. **International locations:** Worldwide. **Number of employees nationwide:** 22,000.

BBDO WEST
10960 Wilshire Boulevard, Los Angeles CA 90024. 310/444-4500. **Fax:** 310/444-4600. **Contact:** Tim Wright, Human Resources Director. **World Wide Web address:** http://www.bbdo.com. **Description:** One location of the worldwide network of advertising agencies with related businesses in public relations, direct marketing, sales promotion, graphic arts, and printing. **Corporate headquarters location:** New York NY. **Other area locations:** San Francisco CA. **Other U.S. locations:** Miami FL; Atlanta GA; Chicago IL; Wellesley MA; Southfield MI. **Parent company:** BBDO Worldwide operates 345 offices in 76 countries and 96 cities. The company operates 83 subsidiaries, affiliates, and associates engaged solely in advertising and related operations.

BBDO WEST
637 Commercial Street, 3rd Floor, San Francisco CA 94111. 415/274-6200. **Fax:** 415/274-6221. **Contact:** Human Resources. **World Wide Web address:** http://www.bbdo.com. **Description:** One location of the worldwide network of advertising agencies with related businesses in public relations, direct marketing, sales promotion, graphic arts, and printing. **Corporate headquarters location:** New York NY. **Other area locations:** Los Angeles CA. **Other U.S. locations:** Miami FL; Atlanta GA; Chicago IL; Wellesley MA; Southfield MI. **Parent company:** BBDO Worldwide operates 345 offices in 76 countries and 96 cities. The company operates 83 subsidiaries, affiliates, and associates engaged in advertising and related operations.

BD BIOSCIENCES
2350 Qume Drive, San Jose CA 95131-1807. 408/432-9475. **Toll-free phone:** 877/222-8995. **Fax:** 408/954-2347. **Contact:** Personnel. **World Wide Web address:** http://www.bdbiosciences.com. **Description:** BD Biosciences serves laboratories worldwide with research and clinical applications in immunology, hematology, and cell biology. The company also provides products and instruments for infectious disease diagnosis, which screen for microbial presence; grow and identify organisms; and test for antibiotic susceptibility. Products for the industrial microbiology market are used for food testing, environmental monitoring, and biopharmaceutical fermentation media. Tissue culture products help advance the understanding of diseases and potential therapies. **NOTE:** Search and apply for positions online. **Positions advertised include:** Systems Engineer; Scientist; Reagent Development Associate; System Specialist; Director, Program Management. **Corporate headquarters location:** Franklin Lakes NJ. **Other U.S. locations:** Nationwide. **International locations:** Worldwide. **Listed on:** New York Stock Exchange. **Stock exchange symbol:** BOX. **Number of employees at this location:** 500. **Number of employees worldwide:** 3,000.

BDS MARKETING
10 Holland, Irvine CA 92618. 949/472-6700. **Fax:** 949/597-2220. **Contact:** Human Resources. **E-mail address:** recruiters@bdsmarketing.com. **World Wide Web address:** http://www.bdsmarketing.com. **Description:** Offers a wide variety of marketing services. BDS Marketing provides ideas for sales promotions, product training, and field marketing. **Positions advertised include:** Account Coordinator; Account Director; Account Executive. **Corporate headquarters location:** This location. **Other U.S. locations:** Nationwide. **Number of employees at this location:** 140. **Number of employees nationwide:** 4,000.

BEI TECHNOLOGIES
13100 Telfair Avenue, Sylmar CA 91342. 818/362-7151. **Fax:** 818/362-1836. **Contact:** Personnel. **World Wide Web address:** http://www.bei-tech.com. **Description:** Manufactures sensors, motors, actuators and related products for automation. **Other area locations:** Concord CA; Goleta CA; San Marcos CA; San Francisco CA; Tustin CA. **Other U.S. locations:** Maumelle AR. **Listed on:** NASDAQ. **Stock exchange symbol:** BEIQ.

BMC SOFTWARE, INC.
1030 West Maude Avenue, Sunnyvale CA 94085-2810. 408/546-9000. **Fax:** 408/546-9001. **Contact:** Human Resources. **E-mail address:** resumes@bmc.com. **World Wide Web address:** http://www.bmc.com. **Description:** Develops, markets, and supports standard systems software products to enhance and increase the performance of large-scale (mainframe) computer database management systems and data communications software systems. **Positions advertised include:** Senior Product Developer; Technical Business Analyst; Staff Product Developer. **Corporate headquarters location:** Houston TX. **Other area locations:** San Francisco CA; Mountain View CA; Pleasanton CA; Irvine CA. **Other U.S. locations:** Nationwide. **International locations:** Worldwide. **Listed on:** New York Stock Exchange. **Stock exchange symbol:** BMC. **Number of employees worldwide:** 6,200.

BOC EDWARDS
3901 Burton Drive, Santa Clara CA 95054. 408/496-1177. **Fax:** 408/496-1188. **Contact:** Human Resources. **World Wide Web address:** http://www.bocedwards.com. **Description:** Manufactures vacuum systems and equipment for industrial applications. **Corporate headquarters location:** Murray Hill NJ. **Other area locations:** Concord, CA. **Parent company:** The BOC Group, Inc. **Listed on:** London Stock Exchange. **Listed on:** New York Stock Exchange. **Stock exchange symbol:** BOX.

BOC GASES
2389 Lincoln Avenue, Hayward CA 94545. 510/786-2611. **Contact:** Joe Clark, Regional Sales Manager. **World Wide Web address:** http://www.boc.com. **Description:** BOC Gases manufactures industrial, electronic, and medical gases; and cryogenic equipment. **Corporate headquarters location:** Murray Hill NJ. **International locations:** Hong Kong; Indonesia; Japan; Korea; Malaysia; Singapore. **Parent company:** The BOC Group, Inc. **Operations at this facility include:** This location manufactures industrial specialty gases.

BP AMOCO
1801 East Sepulveda Boulevard, Carson CA 90745. 310/549-6204. **Fax:** 866/836-7200. **Contact:** Human Resources. **World Wide Web address:** http://www.bpamoco.com. **Description:** BP is the largest producer of oil and natural gas and one of the largest gasoline retailers in the U.S. Their main activities are the exploration and production of crude oil and natural gas; refining, marketing, supply and transportation; and the manufacture and marketing of petrochemicals. **NOTE:** Search and apply for positions

online. **Other U.S. locations:** Nationwide. **International locations:** Worldwide. **Listed on:** New York Stock Exchange. **Stock exchange symbol:** BP. **Number of employees worldwide:** 100,000.

BRE PROPERTIES, INC.
44 Montgomery Street, 36th Floor, San Francisco CA 94104. 415/445-6530. **Fax:** 415/449-6505. **Contact:** Louisa Fossett, Vice President. **E-mail address:** humanresources@breproperties.com. **World Wide Web address:** http://www.breproperties.com. **Description:** A real estate investment trust. **Positions advertised include:** Development Administrative Assistant; Executive Assistant; Field Systems Support Technician. **Corporate headquarters location:** This location. **Listed on:** New York Stock Exchange. **Stock exchange symbol:** BRE.

BWC FINANCIAL CORPORATION
BANK OF WALNUT CREEK
1400 Civic Drive, Walnut Creek CA 94596. 925/932-5353. **Fax:** 925/256-9630. **Contact:** Human Resources Department. **E-mail address:** nfirby@bowc.com. **World Wide Web address:** http://www.bowc.com. **Description:** A holding company. **Corporate headquarters location:** This location. **Subsidiaries include:** Bank of Walnut Creek (also at this location); BWC Real Estate. **Listed on:** NASDAQ. **Stock exchange symbol:** BWCF. **Number of employees at this location:** 55.

BABCOCK, INC.
14930 East Alondra Boulevard, La Mirada CA 90638-5752. 714/994-6500. **Fax:** 714/994-0967. **Contact:** Human Resources Department. **E-mail address:** personnel@babcockinc.com. **World Wide Web address:** http://www.babcockinc.com. **Description:** Designs and manufactures electronic components including switch mode power supplies for satellites and military and aerospace applications, gas plasma and vacuum fluorescent displays, and electromagnetic relays for high-reliability aerospace applications. **Corporate headquarters location:** This location. **Parent company:** Electro-Module. **Listed on:** Privately held. **Annual sales/revenues:** $21 - $50 million. **Number of employees at this location:** 250.

BAIN & COMPANY
3 Embarcadero Center, San Francisco CA 94111. 415/627-1000. **Fax:** 415/627-1033. **Contact:** Stephanie Davis, Associate Consultant Recruiting Manager. **E-mail address:** stephanie.davis@bain.com. **World Wide Web address:** http://www.bain.com. **Description:** An international management consulting firm that helps major companies achieve higher levels of competitiveness and profitability. Founded in 1973. **NOTE:** For positions at the consultant level (MBA/PhD.), contact Victoria Bartels, victoria.bartels@bain.com. **Special programs:** Internships. **Corporate headquarters location:** Boston MA. **Other area locations:** Palo Alto CA; Los Angeles CA. **Other U.S. locations:** New York NY; Atlanta GA; Houston TX; Chicago IL. **International locations:** Worldwide.

BAKER & McKENZIE
Two Embarcadero Center, 24th Floor, San Francisco CA 94111-3909. 415/576-3000. **Fax:** 415/576-3099. **Contact:** Andrea Carr, Recruitment. **E-mail address:** andrea.l.carr@bakernet.com. **World Wide Web address:** http://www.bakerinfo.com. **Description:** An international law firm with more than 10 practice areas including banking and finance, e-commerce, intellectual property, labor and employment, tax, and U.S. litigation. **Corporate headquarters location:** Chicago IL. **Other area locations:** Palo Alto CA; San Diego CA. **Other U.S. locations:** DC; FL; IL; NY; TX. **International locations:** Worldwide.

BAKER COMMODITIES
4020 Bandini Boulevard, Los Angeles CA 90023. 323/268-2801. **Fax:** 323/268-5166. **Contact:** Maxine Taylor, Personnel Director. **World Wide Web address:** http://www.bakercommodities.com. **Description:** Manufactures animal oils, proteins, and prepared feeds. **President:** James Andreoli.

THE BAKERSFIELD CALIFORNIAN INC.
P.O. Box 440, Bakersfield CA 93302-0440. 661/395-7482. **Physical address:** 1707 Eye Street, Bakersfield CA 93301. **Fax:** 661/395-7484. **Contact:** Human Resources. **E-mail address:** jobs@bakersfield.com. **World Wide Web address:** http://www.bakersfield.com. **Description:** The *Bakersfield Californian* is a mid-sized, family-owned newspaper with a daily circulation of 84,000 and a Sunday circulation of 93,000. **Positions advertised include:** Outside Sales Representative; Business Data Analyst; Customer Service Representative; Circulation Sales Representative; Staff Accountant; Route Driver. **Special programs:** Internships. **Corporate headquarters location:** This location. **Number of employees at this location:** 500.

BALLY TOTAL FITNESS
12440 East Imperial Highway, Suite 300, Norwalk CA 90650. 562/484-2875. **Fax:** 562/484-2446. **Contact:** Diane Keller. **World Wide Web address:** http://www.ballyfitness.com. **Description:** One of the world's largest owners and operators of fitness centers. Bally Total Fitness is operated by Bally Health & Tennis Corporation, which, through the subsidiaries it controls, is a nationwide commercial operator of fitness centers in the United States. Bally Health & Tennis operates over 360 fitness centers located in 27 states with approximately 4 million members. The fitness centers operate under the Bally name in conjunction with various others including Holiday Health, Jack LaLanne, Holiday Spa, Chicago Health Clubs, Scandinavian, President's First Lady, Vic Tanny, Aerobics Plus, and as The Vertical Clubs. **Positions advertised include:** Financial Services Rep; Member Services Rep; Payment Processing. **Special programs:** Internships. **Corporate headquarters location:** Chicago IL. **Other U.S. locations:** Nationwide. **International locations:** Canada. **Parent company:** Bally's Entertainment. **Listed on:** New York Stock Exchange. **Stock exchange symbol:** BFT. **Operations at this facility include:** Regional Service Center.

BANK OF AMERICA
1275 Fell Street, San Francisco CA 94117. 650/615-4700. **Contact:** Human Resources Department. **World Wide Web address:** http://www.bankofamerica.com. **Description:** Bank of America is a full-service banking and financial institution. The company operates through four business segments: Global Corporate and Investment Banking, Principal Investing and Asset Management, Commercial Banking, and Consumer Banking. **Positions advertised include:** Banking Center Manager; Administrative Assistant; Personal Banker; Teller. **Corporate headquarters location:** Charlotte NC. **Other U.S. locations:** Nationwide. **International locations:** Worldwide. **Annual sales/revenues:** $49 billion. **Listed on:** New York Stock Exchange. **Stock exchange symbol:** BAC. **Number of employees worldwide:** 180,000.

BANK OF AMERICA
345 North Brand Boulevard, Glendale CA 91203. 818/507-6700. **Contact:** Human Resources. **World Wide Web address:** http://www.bankofamerica.com. **Description:** Bank of America is a full-service banking and financial institution. The company operates through four business segments: Global Corporate and Investment Banking, Principal Investing and Asset Management, Commercial Banking, and Consumer Banking. **Positions advertised include:** Teller. **Corporate headquarters location:** Charlotte NC. **Other U.S. locations:** Nationwide. **International locations:** Worldwide. **Operations at this facility include:** This location is a customer service office. **Listed on:** New York Stock Exchange. **Stock exchange symbol:** BAC.

BANK OF LODI, N.A.
FIRST FINANCIAL BANCORP
701 South Ham Lane, Lodi CA 95242. 209/367-2000. **Fax:** 209/365-1265. **Contact:** Becka Schumacher, Human Resources Department. **E-mail address:** bshumacher@bankoflodi.com. **World Wide Web address:** http://www.bankoflodi.com. **Description:** A full-service commercial bank providing depository accounts including checking, money market, and passbook savings accounts; and a full range of lending activities, with an emphasis on providing the agricultural, business, and professional communities with short-term commercial loans with interest rates tied to prevailing rates in the current money market. Bank of Lodi lends to light industrial, manufacturing, agricultural concerns, and professional organizations in the city of Lodi and the surrounding area. It also offers a full line of residential mortgage products and engages in limited consumer lending activities. **Corporate headquarters location:** This location. **Other area locations:** Artesia CA; Auburn CA; Downey CA; Elk Grove CA; Folsom CA; Galt CA; Plymouth CA; San Andreas CA; Woodbridge CA. **Parent company:** Placer Sierra Bank. **Number of employees at this location:** 75.

BANK OF THE WEST
180 Montgomery Street, San Francisco CA 94104. 925/942-8300. **Toll-free phone:** 800/488-2265. **Fax:** 925/938-9151. **Contact:** Human Resources Department. **World Wide Web address:** http://www.bankofthewest.com. **Description:** A full-service bank with 480 locations in 16 Western and Midwestern states. **Positions advertised include:** Sr. Cash Management Consultant; Pacific Rim Credit Analyst. **Corporate headquarters location:** This location. **Parent company:** BancWest.

BANK PRINTING COMPANY INC.
P.O. Box 296, Downey CA 90241-0296. 562/862-7001. **Physical address:** 9102 Firestone Boulevard, Unit J, Downey CA 90241. **Contact:** Human Resources. **Description:** Prints bank checks and a variety of other banking papers. **Corporate headquarters location:** This location. **Other area locations:** Cerritos CA.

BARCLAYS GLOBAL INVESTORS
45 Fremont Street, San Francisco CA 94105. 415/597-2000. **Fax:** 415/597-2171. **Contact:** Human Resources. **E-mail address:** staffing@barclaysglobal.com. **World Wide Web address:** http://www.barclaysglobal.com. **Description:** An investment banking company. **Positions advertised include:** Systems Developer; Research Analyst; Research Officer; Derivatives Trading Analyst; Business Analyst; Solutions Strategist; Portfolio Analyst; Portfolio Manager; Currency Trader; Investment Process Supervisor. **Corporate headquarters locations:** This location. **Other U.S. locations:** Chicago IL; Boston MA. **International locations:** China; India; Indonesia; Korea; Malaysia; Mexico; New Zealand; Philippines; Taiwan; Thailand. **Parent company:** Barclays (London).

BARCO OF CALIFORNIA
350 West Rosecrans Avenue, Gardena CA 90248. 310/323-7315. **Fax:** 310/719-2135. **Contact:** Human Resources. **Description:** Manufactures and markets uniforms for health care and fast-food companies. **Corporate headquarters location:** This location. **Number of employees at this location:** 250.

BARKER MECHANICAL SERVICES INC.
6800 Sierra Court, Suite L, Dublin CA 94568. 925/560-0280. **Contact:** Human Resources. **E-mail address:** info@barkermech.com. **World Wide Web address:** http://www.barkerms.com. **Description:** Sells and services heating and air-conditioning equipment to commercial and industrial clients.

BARNES & NOBLE BOOKSTORES
6326 East Pacific Coast Highway, Long Beach CA 90803. 562/431-2253. **Contact:** Manager. **World Wide Web address:** http://www.bn.com. **Description:** A bookstore chain operating nationwide. This location has a cafe and a music department in addition to its book departments. **Corporate headquarters location:** New York NY. **Listed on:** NASDAQ. **Stock exchange symbol:** BKS.

BARNES & NOBLE BOOKSTORES
1201 Third Street, Santa Monica CA 90401. 310/260-9110. **Contact:** Manager. **World Wide Web address:** http://www.barnesandnoble.com. **Description:** A bookstore chain operating nationwide. This location has a cafe and a music department in addition to its book departments. **Corporate headquarters location:** New York NY. **Listed on:** NASDAQ. **Stock exchange symbol:** BKS.

BARRA, INC.
2100 Milvia Street, Berkeley CA 94704. 510/548-5442. **Fax:** 510/548-4374. **Contact:** Human Resources. **E-mail address:** careers@barra.com. **World Wide Web address:** http://www.barra.com. **Description:** Develops, markets, and supports application software and information services used to analyze and manage portfolios of equity, fixed income, and other financial instruments. The company serves more than 750 clients in 30 countries including many of the world's largest portfolio managers, fund sponsors, pension and investment consultants, brokers/dealers, and master trustees. **NOTE:** Entry-level positions are offered. **Positions advertised include:** Research Consultant; Technical Project Consultant; Data Engineer; Market Data Analyst; Data Analyst; Office Clerk. **Special programs:** Internships; Training; Summer Jobs. **Corporate headquarters location:** This location. **Other U.S. locations:** Cranbury NJ; New York NY. **International locations:** Australia; Brazil; England; Germany; Hong Kong; Japan; South Africa. **Operations at this facility include:** Administration; Research and Development; Sales; Service. **Listed on:** NASDAQ. **Stock exchange symbol:** BARZ. **Annual sales/revenues:** More than $100 million. **Number of employees worldwide:** Over 500.

BASKIN-ROBBINS, INC.
1217 North Central Avenue, Glendale CA 91202. 818/240-2131. **Contact:** Director of Human Resources. **World Wide Web address:** http://www.baskinrobbins.com. **Description:** An ice cream manufacturer that also operates retail locations. **NOTE:** Please send resumes to: Human Resources Department, 14 Pacella Park Drive, Randolph MA 02368. **Corporate headquarters location:** Randolph MA. **International locations:** Worldwide. **Parent company:** Allied Domecq Quick Service Restaurants. **Number of employees nationwide:** 875.

BAY BANK OF COMMERCE
1495 East 14th Street, San Leandro CA 94577. 510/357-2265. **Contact:** Personnel. **World Wide Web address:** http://www.baybankofcommerce.com. **Description:** A

full-service bank. The bank's Construction Lending Division provides residential construction financing to individuals and builders throughout the East Bay area. **Corporate headquarters location:** This location. **Other area locations:** Hayward CA; San Ramon CA. **Parent company:** Greater Bay Bancorp. **Number of employees at this location:** 60. **Listed on:** NASDAQ. **Stock exchange symbol:** GBBK.

BAY MEADOWS COMPANY
P.O. Box 5050, San Mateo CA 94402. 650/574-7223. **Physical address:** 2600 South Delaware Street, San Mateo CA 94403. **Fax:** 650/349-5884. **Contact:** Human Resources. **World Wide Web address:** http://www.baymeadows.com. **Description:** Operates Bay Meadows Race Track on the San Francisco Peninsula, and California Jockey Club, an equity real estate investment trust whose principal asset is Bay Meadows Race Track. **Corporate headquarters location:** This location.

BAYER CORPORATION
808 Parker Street, P.O. Box 1986, Berkeley CA 94701. 510/705-5000. **Contact:** Personnel. **World Wide Web address:** http://www.bayerus.com. **Description:** Bayer is engaged in the development, manufacture, and distribution of health care products including pharmaceuticals and a wide range of hospital equipment. **NOTE:** Electronic submissions are preferred and will receive more immediate consideration. Please send to appropriate contact person for each job listing on the job page. **Corporate headquarters location:** Pittsburgh PA. **Other U.S. locations:** Nationwide. **International locations:** Worldwide. **Parent company:** Bayer Group (Germany). **Operations at this facility include:** This location is Bayer's biotechnology headquarters. **Listed on:** New York Stock Exchange. **Stock exchange symbol:** BAY. **Number of employees nationwide:** 21,000. **Number of employees worldwide:** 120,000.

BAYSHORE ANIMAL HOSPITAL
233 North Amphlett Boulevard, San Mateo CA 94401. 650/342-7022. **Contact:** Human Resources. **World Wide Web address:** http://www.bahospital.com. **Description:** A full-service animal hospital that provides several specialty services including eye and tooth care, in-hospital consultation with outside specialists, pharmacy, and x-ray. The hospital also provides boarding facilities when required.

BEACH PATROL INC.
1165 East 230th Street, Carson CA 90745. 310/522-2700. **Fax:** 310/952-8444. **Contact:** Lolly Padilla, Human Resources. **E-mail address:** lpadilla@beachpatrolinc.com. **World Wide Web address:** http://www.beachpatrolinc.com. **Description:** Designs swimwear and other apparel. **Positions advertised include:** Swimwear Patternmaker. **Corporate headquarters location:** This location. **Other U.S. locations:** Weston FL; Atlanta GA; New York NY; Huntington Valley PA. **International locations:** Australia; Canada; Mexico; New Zealand; Taiwan.

BEAR, STEARNS & COMPANY, INC.
1999 Avenue of the Stars, 32nd Floor, Los Angeles CA 90067-6100. 310/201-2600. **Fax:** 310/201-2755. **Contact:** Human Resources. **E-mail address:** hresources_internet@bear.com. **World Wide Web address:** http://www.bearstearns.com. **Description:** Bear, Stearns & Company, Inc. is a leading worldwide investment banking, securities trading, and brokerage firm. The firm's business includes corporate finance, mergers and acquisitions, public finance, institutional equities, fixed-income sales and trading, private client services, foreign exchange, future sales and trading, derivatives, and asset management. **Corporate headquarters location:** New York NY. **Other U.S. locations:** Nationwide. **International locations:** Worldwide. **Parent company:** The Bear Stearns Companies Inc. other subsidiaries include Bear, Stearns Securities Corporation, providing professional and correspondent clearing services including securities lending, and Custodial Trust Company, providing master trust, custody, and government securities services. **Listed on:** New York Stock Exchange. **Stock exchange symbol:** BSC. **Annual sales/revenues:** $789 million. **Number of employees nationwide:** 7,800.

BEAR, STEARNS & COMPANY, INC.
One Sansome Street, 41st Floor, Citicorp Center, San Francisco CA 94104. 415/772-2900. **Toll-free phone:** 800/688-2327. **Fax:** 415/772-3275. **Contact:** Personnel Manager. **E-mail address:** hresources_internet@bear.com. **World Wide Web address:** http://www.bearstearns.com. **Description:** A leading investment banking and securities trading and brokerage firm serving governments, corporations, institutions, and individuals worldwide. The company offers services in corporate finance, mergers and acquisitions, institutional equities, fixed income sales and trading, derivatives, futures sales and trading, asset management, and custody. **NOTE:** Please submit resume through the on-line application process. **Special programs:** Internships. **Internship information:** The company offers internships year-round. Applicants should mail or fax a resume to the Personnel Department. **Corporate headquarters location:** New York NY. **Other U.S. locations:** Nationwide. **International locations:** Worldwide. **Parent company:** The Bear Stearns Companies Inc. also operate Bear Stearns Securities Corporation, which provides professional and correspondent clearing services, including securities lending, and Custodial Trust Company, which provides master trust, custody, and government securities services. **Listed on:** New York Stock Exchange. **Stock exchange symbol:** BSC. **Annual sales/revenues:** More than $789 million. **Number of employees at this location:** 200. **Number of employees nationwide:** 7,800.

BEARINGPOINT, INC.
355 South Grand Avenue, Suite 2000, Los Angeles CA 90071. 213/443-4100. **Fax:** 213/626-0620. **Contact:** Human Resources. **World Wide Web address:** http://www.bearingpoint.com. **Description:** Delivers a wide range of value-added assurance, tax, and consulting services. **NOTE:** Search and apply for positions online. **Positions advertised include:** Management Analyst; PeopleSoft General Ledger consultant; SFA Requirements Analyst; Sr. Manager, Insurance. **Corporate headquarters location:** McLean VA. **Listed on:** New York Stock Exchange. **Stock exchange symbol:** BE.

BECHTEL CORPORATION
P.O. Box 193965, San Francisco CA 94119-3965. 415/768-1234. **Physical address:** 50 Beale Street, San Francisco CA 94105-1895. **Contact:** Human Resources. **E-mail address:** staffpx@bechtel.com. **World Wide Web address:** http://www.bechtel.com. **Description:** Operations focus on engineering, construction, financing operations and maintenance, electricity, nuclear fuel, metals, minerals, procurement management, transportation, and pollution control. **NOTE:** Search and apply for positions online. **Positions advertised include:** Contract Manager; Subconstract Manager. **Special programs:** Co-ops; Summer Jobs. **Corporate headquarters location:** This location. **Other area locations:** Martinez CA; Los Angeles CA; San Diego CA. **Other U.S. locations:** AZ; CO; KY; MD; NY; TN; TX; WA.

BECHTEL NEVADA
P.O. Box 2710, Livermore CA 94551. 925/960-2500. **Fax:** 925/960-2595. **Contact:** Lynette Simmons, Personnel Manager. **E-mail address:** bnresumes@nv.doe.gov. **World Wide Web address:** http://www.bechtelnevada.com. **Description:** Bechtel Nevada operates in the following areas: engineering, construction, financing operations and maintenance, electricity, nuclear fuel, metals, minerals, procurement management, transportation, and pollution control. **NOTE:** Resumes are by mail, fax, or e-mail. Address resumes to: Bechtel Nevada, Attention: Personnel, P.O. Box 98521, Las Vegas NV 89193. Fax: 702/295-2448. **Positions advertised include:** Senior Scientists; Engineer; Technical Staff. **Other U.S. locations:** DC; NM; NV. **Parent company:** Bechtel Corporation (San Francisco CA). **Operations at this facility include:** This location performs engineering research and development. **Number of employees at this location:** 85.

BECKMAN COULTER, INC.
4300 North Harbor Boulevard, P.O. Box 3100, Fullerton CA 92834. 714/871-4848. **Fax:** 714/773-8283. **Contact:** Employment. **E-mail address:** breahr@beckman.com. **World Wide Web address:** http://www.beckman.com. **Description:** Sells and services a diverse range of scientific instruments, reagents, and related equipment. Products include DNA synthesizers, robotic workstations, centrifuges, electrophoresis systems, detection and measurement equipment, data processing software, and specialty chemical and automated general chemical systems. Many of the company's products are used in research and development and diagnostic analysis. **NOTE:** Second and third shifts are offered. Search and apply for positions online. **Positions advertised include:** Sr. Documentation Control Specialist; Sr. Graphic Designer; Technical Operations Engineer; Finance Compliance Manager; Sr. Technical Writer; Manufacturing Associate. **Corporate headquarters location:** This location. **Other area locations:** Brea CA; Carlsbad CA; Palo Alto CA; Porterville CA; San Diego CA. **Other U.S. locations:** Nationwide. **International locations:** Worldwide. **Parent company:** Beckman Instruments, Inc. **Operations at this facility include:** Administration; Manufacturing; Research and Development. **Listed on:** New York Stock Exchange. **Stock exchange symbol:** BEC. **CEO:** Jack Wareham. **Annual sales/revenues:** $1.8 billion. **Number of employees worldwide:** 11,000.

BECKMAN COULTER, INC.
200 South Kraemer Boulevard, P.O. Box 8000, Brea CA 92822. 714/993-5321. **Fax:** 714/961-4165. **Contact:** Employment. **E-mail address:** breahr@beckman.com. **World Wide Web address:** http://www.beckman.com. **Description:** Sells and services a diverse range of scientific instruments, reagents, and related equipment. Products include DNA synthesizers, robotic workstations, centrifuges, electrophoresis systems, detection and measurement equipment, data processing software, and specialty chemical and automated general chemical systems. Many of the company's products are used in research and development and diagnostic analysis. **NOTE:** Second and third shifts are offered. Search and apply for positions online. **Positions advertised include:** Sr. Financial Analyst; Product Manager; Product Manager; Sr. Financial Analyst; Staff Development Scientist. **Corporate headquarters location:** Fullerton CA. **Other area locations:** Carlsbad CA; Palo Alto CA; Porterville CA; San Diego CA. **Other U.S. locations:** Nationwide. **International locations:** Worldwide. **Parent company:** Beckman Instruments, Inc. **Operations at this facility include:** Administration; Manufacturing; Research and Development. **Listed on:** New York Stock Exchange. **Stock exchange symbol:** BEC. **CEO:** Jack Wareham. **Annual sales/revenues:** $1.8 billion. **Number of employees worldwide:** 11,000.

BECKMAN COULTER, INC.
1050 Page Mill Road, Palo Alto CA 94304. 650/857-1150. **Fax:** 650/859-1526. **Contact:** Human Resources. **E-mail address:** palo_alto_jobs@beckman.com. **World Wide Web address:** http://www.beckman.com. **Description:** Sells and services a diverse range of scientific instruments, reagents, and related equipment. Products include DNA synthesizers, robotic workstations, centrifuges, electrophoresis systems, detection and measurement equipment, data processing software, and specialty chemical and automated general chemical systems. Many of the company's products are used in research, development and diagnostic analysis. **NOTE:** Second and third shifts are offered. Search and apply for positions online. **Positions advertised include:** Sr. Applications Developer; Sr. Financial Analyst. **Corporate headquarters location:** Fullerton CA. **Other area locations:** Brea CA; Carlsbad CA; Porterville CA; San Diego CA. **Other U.S. locations:** Nationwide. **International locations:** Worldwide. **Parent company:** Beckman Instruments, Inc. **Listed on:** New York Stock Exchange. **Stock exchange symbol:** BEC.

BECKMAN COULTER, INC.
2470 Faraday Avenue, Carlsbad CA 92008. 760/438-9151. **Fax:** 760/438-6390. **Contact:** Human Resources. **E-mail address:** clsbdhr@beckman.com. **World Wide Web address:** http://www.beckman.com. **Description:** Beckman Coulter sells and services a diverse range of scientific instruments, reagents, and related equipment. Products include DNA synthesizers, robotic workstations, centrifuges, electrophoresis systems, detection and measurement equipment, data processing software, and specialty chemical and automated general chemical systems. Many of the company's products are used in research and development or diagnostic analysis. **NOTE:** Second and third shifts are offered. Search and apply for positions online. **Positions advertised include:** Manufacturing Quality Scientist; Sr. Financial Analyst; Production Scientist; **Corporate headquarters location:** Fullerton CA. **Other area locations:** Brea CA; Palo Alto CA; Porterville CA; San Diego CA. **Other U.S. locations:** Nationwide. **International locations:** Worldwide. **Parent company:** Beckman Instruments, Inc. **Operations at this facility include:** This location develops monoclonal antibody technology for use in medical diagnostic products. **Listed on:** New York Stock Exchange. **Stock exchange symbol:** BEC.

BELL MICROPRODUCTS INC.
1941 Ringwood Avenue, San Jose CA 95131. 408/451-9400. **Toll-free phone:** 800/800-1513. **Fax:** 408/451-1600. **Contact:** Human Resources. **World Wide Web address:** http://www.bellmicro.com. **Description:** Markets and distributes a select group of computer products to original equipment manufacturers and value-added resellers. Products include logic microprocessors; disk, tape, and optical drives and subsystems; drive controllers; and board-level products. The company also provides a variety of manufacturing and value-added services to its customers including the supply of board-level products to customer specifications on a turnkey basis; certain types of components and subsystem testing services; systems integration and disk drive formatting and testing; and the packaging of electronic component kits to customer specifications. Founded in 1987. **NOTE:** Search and apply for positions online. **Positions advertised include:** Inside Sales Representative; Hardware Engineer; Retail Product Manager; Warehouse Manager. **Corporate headquarters location:** This location. **Other U.S. locations:** Nationwide. **International locations:** Argentina; Brazil; Canada; Chile; Italy; Mexico; the Netherlands; United Kingdom. **Listed on:** NASDAQ. **Stock exchange symbol:** BELM.

BENO'S FAMILY FASHIONS
1512 Santee Street, Los Angeles CA 90015. 213/748-2222. **Contact:** Personnel. **Description:** Operates a chain of retail stores in California and Nevada selling a wide variety of merchandise, with emphasis on apparel for men, women, and children. More than 55 stores are operated under the name of Beno's. **Corporate headquarters location:** This location. **Number of employees nationwide:** 550.

BENSON & NEFF
One Post Street, Suite 2150, San Francisco CA 94104-5225. 415/705-5615. **Fax:** 415/705-5633. **Contact:** Director of Personnel. **E-mail address:** bn@bensonneff.com. **World Wide Web address:** http://www.bensonneff.com. **Description:** A certified public accounting firm offering accounting, auditing, tax, computer, and other consulting services. **Corporate headquarters location:** This location. **Operations at this facility include:** Service.

BERINGER BLASS WINE ESTATES
610 Air Park Road, P.O. Box 4500, Napa CA 94558. 707/259-4500. **Fax:** 707/259-4542. **Contact:** Human Resources. **E-mail address:** bwehr@beringerblass.com. **World Wide Web address:** http://www.beringerwineestates.com. **Description:** A leading producer and marketer of premium wines. In addition to operating their own local vineyards, Beringer Blass Wine Estates imports and markets wine from France, Italy, and Chile. Brands include Beringer Vineyards, Chateau St. Jean, Meridian Vineyards, St. Clement, Rivefort de France, and Campanile. **Positions advertised include:** Hospitality Specialist; Public Relations Manager; Fulfillment Manager. **Corporate headquarters location:** This location. **Other area locations:** Cloverdale CA; Geyserville CA; Kenwood CA; Paso Robles CA; Santa Barbara CA; St. Helena CA. **Parent company:** Foster's Brewing Group Limited.

BERRY PETROLEUM COMPANY
5201 Truxtun Avenue, Suite 300, Bakersfield CA 93309-0640. 661/616-3900. **Fax:** 661/616-3885. **Contact:** Human Resources. **E-mail address:** ree@bry.com. **World Wide Web address:** http://www.bry.com. **Description:** Engaged in the production, development, exploration, blending, and marketing of crude oil and natural gas. Founded in 1909. **Positions advertised include:** Accountant; Facility Engineer; Senior Tax Accountant; Financial Analyst. **Corporate headquarters location:** This location. **Listed on:** New York Stock Exchange. **Stock exchange symbol:** BRY. **CEO/President:** Jerry Hoffman. **Annual sales/revenues:** $51 - $100 million. **Number of employees at this location:** 100.

BEST SOFTWARE, INC.
56 Technology Drive, Irvine CA 92618-2301. 949/753-1222. **Fax:** 949/753-0374. **Contact:** Human Resources. **World Wide Web address:** http://www.bestsoftware.com. **Description:** Develops, markets, and supports high-end microcomputer accounting software. **Positions advertised include:** Design Analyst; Sr. Customer Support Analyst; Sr. Accountant; Financial Analyst; Copy Writer; Director, Installed Base Sales. **Corporate headquarters location:** This location. **Parent company:** Sage Group plc. **CEO:** Ronald Verni. **Number of employees nationwide:** 2,100.

BIENVENIDOS CHILDREN'S CENTER
205 East Palms Street, Altadena CA 91001. 626/798-7222. **Fax:** 626/798-8444. **Contact:** Human Resources. **World Wide Web address:** http://www.bienvenidos.org. **Description:** Runs a group residential home for children who are placed by the courts and a foster family agency. Bienvenidos Children's Center also provides outpatient mental health services to children aged birth to 21 years.

BIGGS-GRIDLEY MEMORIAL HOSPITAL
P.O. Box 97, Gridley CA 95948. 530/846-5671. **Fax:** 530/846-9027. **Contact:** Personnel. **World Wide Web address:** http://www.frhg.org. **Description:** A 49-bed hospital. **NOTE:** Please send resumes to: Rideout Memorial Hospital, 726 Fourth Street, Marysville CA 95901. **Positions advertised include:** Registered Nurse; Billing Technician. **Parent company:** Fremont-Rideout Health Group. **Operations at this facility include:** Administration. **Listed on:** Privately held.

BINGHAM MCCUTCHEN LLP
355 South Grand Avenue, 44th Floor, Los Angeles CA 90071. 213/680-6400. **Fax:** 213/680-6499. **Contact:** Meyosha Spencer, Attorney Recruiting Manager. **E-mail address:** lalegalrecruit@bingham.com. **World Wide Web address:** http://www.bingham.com. **Description:** A law firm specializing in corporate law. This firm was formerly known as Riordan & McKinzie, and has joined Bingham McCutchen through a merger in July of 2003. **Corporate headquarters location:** Boston MA.

BIOCATALYTICS INC.
129 North Hill Avenue, Suite 103, Pasadena CA 91106-1955. 626/585-9797. **Fax:** 626/356-3999. **Contact:** Personnel Department. **E-mail address:** info@biocatalytics.com. **World Wide Web address:** http://www.biocatalytics.com. **Description:** A leading provider of technology and services for the application of enzymes. **NOTE:** Accepts resumes from applicants with a B.S., M.S., or P.H.D in microbiology, molecular biology, or biochemistry.

BIOGEN IDEC
5200 Research Place, San Diego CA 92122. 858/431-8506. **Fax:** 858/431-8750. **Contact:** Manager of Human Resources Department. **E-mail address:** resumes@biogenidec.com. **World Wide Web address:** http://www.idecpharm.com. **Description:** Manufactures chemotherapeutic pharmaceuticals for the treatment of lymphoma. The company is also in the clinical trial phase of drug development for diseases such as arthritis. **Positions advertised include:** Director, Medical Research; Manager, EHS; Sr. Scientist; Associate Director, Clinical Development; Manager, Human Resources; Sr. Director, Marketing. **Corporate headquarters location:** Cambridge MA. **Other area locations:** Oceanside CA. **Listed on:** NASDAQ. **Stock exchange symbol:** IDPH.

BIO-RAD LABORATORIES
1000 Alfred Nobel Drive, Hercules CA 94547. 510/724-7000. **Contact:** Human Resources. **World Wide Web address:** http://www.bio-rad.com. **Description:** Develops, manufactures, and markets diagnostic test kits, specialty chemicals, and related equipment used for separating complex mixtures. The company also produces analytical instruments used to detect and measure chemical components in minute quantities, as well as products for electron microscopy. **NOTE:** Candidates may search and apply for positions online. Resumes can be sent to the resume processing center: Bio-Rad Laboratories, P.O. Box 445, Burlington MA 01803. **Positions advertised include:** Administrative Associate; Business Systems Consultant; Chemist; Engineer; Environment Manager; HR Consultant; Manufacturing Engineering Manager; Oracle DBA; Product Manager. **Special programs:** Summer Internships. **Internship information:** Bio-Rad Laboratories offers summer internships for undergraduates. Internships are available in finance, human resources, marketing, information technology, engineering, biochemistry, microbiology, quality control and assurance, environmental health and safety, and research and development. **Corporate headquarters location:** This location. **Other U.S. locations:** Randolph MA; Philadelphia PA. **International locations:** Worldwide. **Operations at this facility include:** Administration; Manufacturing; Research and Development; Service. **Listed on:** American Stock Exchange. **Stock exchange symbol:** BIO.

BIOLASE TECHNOLOGY, INC.
981 Calle Amanecer, San Clemente CA 92673. 949/361-1200. **Toll-free phone:** 888/424-6527. **Fax:** 949/361-0207. **Contact:** Natalie McGregor. **E-mail address:** nmcgregor@biolase.com. **World Wide Web address:** http://www.biolase.com. **Description:** Manufactures and markets a full range of advanced dental and medical laser products. **Positions advertised include:** Western Regional Sales Manager. **Listed on:** NASDAQ. **Stock exchange symbol:** BLTI.

BIOSOURCE INTERNATIONAL, INC.
542 Flynn Road, Camarillo CA 93012. 805/987-0086. **Toll-free phone:** 800/242-0607. **Fax:** 805/383-5386. **Contact:** Personnel. **E-mail address:** hr.dept@biosource.com. **World Wide Web address:** http://www.biosource.com. **Description:** Licenses, develops, manufactures, markets, and distributes immunological reagents and enzyme-linked immunosorbent assay (ELISA) test kits used in biomedical research. BioSource International offers over 700 products for the study of cell biology and immunology research. The ELISA test kits are used by researchers and scientists to detect various immunological molecules in biological fluids found in humans, mice, rats, and primates. Founded in 1989. **NOTE:** Entry-level positions and part-time jobs are offered. **Company slogan:** The Art of Science. **Positions advertised include:** Assay Production Associate; Research Associate; Technical Production Planner; Antibody Production Associate. **Office hours:** Monday - Friday, 7:00 a.m. - 5:00 p.m. **Corporate headquarters location:** This location. **Other area locations:** Foster City CA. **Other U.S. locations:** Hopkinton MA; Rockville MD. **International locations:** Belgium, Germany, the Netherlands. **Listed on:** NASDAQ. **Stock exchange symbol:** BIOI. **President/CEO:** Leonard Hendrickson. **Annual sales/revenues:** $21 - $50 million. **Number of employees worldwide:** 271.

BIOTIME, INC.
935 Pardee Street, Berkeley CA 94710. 510/845-9535. **Fax:** 510/845-7914. **Contact:** contacts@biotimemail.com. **World Wide Web address:** http://www.biotimeinc.com. **Description:** Engaged in the research and development of aqueous-based synthetic solutions. Products are used as plasma expanders, organ preservation solutions, or solutions to replace blood volume. Founded in 1990. **Listed on:** American Stock Exchange. **Stock exchange symbol:** BTX.

BIRD PRODUCTS
1100 Bird Center Drive, Palm Springs CA 92262. 760/778-7200. **Toll-free phone:** 800/328-4139. **Fax:** 760/778-7274. **Contact:** Della Adams, Human Resources. **Description:** Manufactures respiratory care and infection control products. **Parent company:** Viasys Healthcare.

BLANC & OTUS
303 Second Street, Suite 900 South, San Francisco CA 94107. 415/856-5100. **Fax:** 415/856-5193. **Contact:** Barbara Melchin, Human Resources. **E-mail address:** bmelchin@blancandotus.com. **World Wide Web address:** http://www.bando.com. **Description:** A public relations firm that primarily serves the high-tech industry. **Positions advertised include:** Account Executive; Sr. Account Executive. **Corporate headquarters location:** This location. **Other U.S. locations:** Atlanta GA; Austin TX; Boston MA. **Parent company:** Hill and Knowlton.

BLUE SHIELD OF CALIFORNIA
50 Beale Street, San Francisco CA 94105. 415/229-5000. **Toll-free phone:** 800/200-3242. **Fax:** 415/229-5070. **Contact:** Human Resources. **World Wide Web address:** http://www.blueshieldca.com. **Description:** A health maintenance organization that provides a variety of group and individual health plan coverage and professional medical services from doctors, dentists, psychiatrists, and other medical professionals. **Positions advertised include:** Associate Business Analyst; Marketing Project Coordinator; Senior Financial Analyst; Internal Communications Manager; Senior Project Manager. **Corporate headquarters location:** This location.

BLUE SHIELD OF CALIFORNIA
6701 Center Drive West, Suite 800, Los Angeles CA 90045. 310/670-4040. **Toll-free phone:** 800/200-3242. **Contact:** Sharon Miller, Personnel Manager. **World Wide Web address:** http://www.blueshieldca.com. **Description:** A nonprofit corporation providing prepaid medical care and other health care benefits to subscribers through a variety of health care providers. The company is a member of the Blue Shield Association, an organization that provides national coordination on behalf of 69 local, autonomous Blue Shield Plans that together serve about 70 million people. **Positions advertised include:** PPO Network Manager; Senior Business Analyst; Project Manager; PC Analyst; Senior Health Data Analyst. **Corporate headquarters location:** San Francisco CA.

THE BOEING COMPANY
5301 Bolsa Avenue, Huntington Beach CA 92647-2099. 714/896-3311. **Contact:** Personnel Department. **E-mail address:** employmentoperations@boeing.com. **World Wide Web address:** http://www.boeing.com. **Description:** A major manufacturer of high-technology aerospace products including military and commercial aircraft. **NOTE:** Search and apply for positions online. **Positions advertised include:** Industrial Engineer; Business and Planning Analyst; Accountant; Engineer; Procurement Analyst. **Special programs:** Internships. **Corporate headquarters location:** Chicago IL. **Other area locations:** Anaheim CA; Canoga park; El Segundo CA; Irvine CA; Long Beach CA: Palmdale CA; Seal Beach CA; Sunnyvale CA. **Other U.S. locations:** Nationwide. **Listed on:** New York Stock Exchange. **Stock exchange symbol:** BA.

BORLAND SOFTWARE CORPORATION
100 Enterprise Way, Scotts Valley CA 95066. 831/431-1000. **Fax:** 831/431-4141. **Contact:** Human Resources. **E-mail address:** resume@borland.com. **World Wide Web address:** http://www.borland.com. **Description:** Develops, distributes, and manages tools that allow software developers to create enterprise applications that are known as Information Networks. Borland Software also provides consulting and technical support services. **Positions advertised include:** Integration Engineer; R&D Engineer. **Special programs:** Internships. **Corporate headquarters location:** This location. Other area locations: Cupertino CA; San Jose CA; Santa Ana CA. **Listed on:** NASDAQ. **Stock exchange symbol:** BORL.

BOSTON SCIENTIFIC EP TECHNOLOGIES
2710 Orchard Parkway, San Jose CA 95134. 408/895-3500. **Fax:** 408/895-2203. **Contact:** Human Resources. **World Wide Web address:** http://www.bostonscientific.com. **Description:** A worldwide developer, manufacturer, and marketer of medical devices used in a broad range of interventional procedures including the fields of cardiology, gastroenterology, pulmonary medicine, and vascular

surgery. **Special programs:** Internships. **Corporate headquarters location:** Natick MA. **Other area locations:** Fremont CA; Mountain View CA; Santa Clara CA; San Diego CA. **International locations:** Worldwide. **Listed on:** New York Stock Exchange. **Stock exchange symbol:** BSX.

BOSTON SCIENTIFIC TARGET
47900 Bayside Parkway, Fremont CA 94538. 510/440-7700. **Contact:** Human Resources Manager. **World Wide Web address:** http://www.bsci.com. **Description:** Manufactures specialized disposable microcatheters, guidewires, microcoils, and angioplasty products. **NOTE:** Search and apply for positions online. **Positions advertised include:** Technician; Repair Operations Supervisor. **Corporate headquarters location:** Natick MA. **Parent company:** Boston Scientific Corporation. **Listed on:** New York Stock Exchange. **Stock exchange symbol:** BSX.

BOURNS, INC.
1200 Columbia Avenue, Riverside CA 92507. 909/781-5690. **Toll-free phone:** 877/426-8767. **Contact:** Charles McBeth, Personnel Department. **E-mail address:** RecruitPeople@Comcast.net. **World Wide Web address:** http://www.bourns.com. **Description:** A manufacturer of electronic components and high-technology equipment. Products include semiconductor devices, aerial reconnaissance cameras, and potentiometers. **Positions advertised include:** Mechanical Design Engineer; Product Engineer. **Corporate headquarters location:** This location. **Other U.S. locations:** Barrington IL; Logan UT. **International locations:** China; Costa Rica; Ireland; Japan; Mexico; Switzerland; Taiwan; United Kingdom.

BOWNE OF LOS ANGELES, INC.
633 West Fifth Street, Suite 1400, Los Angeles CA 90071. 213/627-2200. **Fax:** 213/627-0451. **Contact:** Human Resources Department. **World Wide Web address:** http://www.bowne.com. **Description:** Engaged in financial and corporate printing services. **NOTE:** Search and apply for positions online. **Corporate headquarters location:** New York NY. **Other U.S. locations:** Nationwide. **International locations:** Worldwide. **Parent company:** Williams Lea. **Listed on:** New York Stock Exchange. **Stock exchange symbol:** BNE.

BOWNE OF SAN FRANCISCO, INC.
343 Sansome Street, 15th Floor, San Francisco CA 94104. 415/362-2300. **Fax:** 415/362-2424. **Contact:** Human Resources. **World Wide Web address:** http://www.bowne.com. **Description:** Provides financial and corporate printing services. **Corporate headquarters location:** New York NY. **Other U.S. locations:** Nationwide. **International locations:** Worldwide. **Parent company:** Williams Lea. **Listed on:** New York Stock Exchange. **Stock exchange symbol:** BNE.

BOY SCOUTS OF AMERICA
970 West Julian Avenue, San Jose CA 95126. 408/280-5088. **Contact:** Human Resources. **E-mail address:** leadership@sccc-scouting.org. **World Wide Web address:** http://www.sccc-scouting.org. **Description:** Western regional office of the national scouting organization for young adults. The Boy Scouts of America has 340 local councils nationwide. **Corporate headquarters location:** Irving TX.

BOYLE ENGINEERING CORPORATION
1501 Quail Street, Newport Beach CA 92660-2746. 949/476-3300. **Fax:** 724/258-5777. **Contact:** Recruiting Manager. **E-mail address:** recruitingmgr@boyleengineering.com. **World Wide Web address:** http://www.boyleengineering.com. **Description:** Provides comprehensive services ranging from project planning and feasibility studies to design and construction phases. The company specializes in the fields of water resources; water treatment and distribution; wastewater collection, treatment, and reuse; streets, highways, and bridges; light and heavy rail; drainage and flood control; and land planning. **NOTE:** Candidates may apply online or submit a resume via fax or mail. **Positions advertised include:** Associate Engineer; Assistant Pipeline Engineer. **Corporate headquarters location:** This location. **Other area locations:** Bakersfield CA; Fresno CA; Palmdale CA; Encino CA; Ontario CA; Sacramento CA; San Diego CA; San Luis Obispo CA; Ventura CA. **Other U.S. locations:** CO; FL; NV; NM; TX; UT.

B. BRAUN/McGAW INC.
2525 McGaw Avenue, Irvine CA 92614. 949/660-2000. **Fax:** 949/660-2821. **Recorded jobline:** 949/660-2272. **Contact:** Personnel. **E-mail address:** hr.irvine@bbraun.com. **World Wide Web address:** http://www.bbraunusa.com. **Description:** Manufactures intravenous systems and solutions. The company also offers IV accessories, critical care products, and epidural anesthesia and pharmaceutical devices. **Positions advertised include:** Microbiology Specialist; Metrology Technician; Instructional Designer; Director of Regional Pharmacy Operations; Lead, QC Process Control; Industrial Engineer; Regulatory Affairs Manager. **Corporate headquarters location:** Bethlehem PA. **Other U.S. locations:** Cherry Hill NJ; Allentown PA; Carrollton TX.

BRIDGESTONE/FIRESTONE, INC.
24196 Laguna Hills Mall, Laguna Hills CA 92653. 949/581-4700. **Contact:** Human Resources. **World Wide Web address:** http://www.bridgestone-firestone.com. **Description:** Bridgestone/Firestone is engaged in the development, manufacture, and sale of tires for the original equipment and replacement markets worldwide. **Corporate headquarters location:** Nashville TN. **Other U.S. locations:** AR; IA; IN; MI; NC; OH; OK; SC. **International locations:** Argentina; Brazil; Canada; Chile; Columbia; Costa Rica; Mexico; Venezuela. **Operations at this facility include:** This location sells a broad line of tires and wheels for the automotive aftermarket and services and maintains automobiles at its retail service centers. **Number of employees nationwide:** 60,000.

BRIDGFORD FOODS CORPORATION
1308 North Patt Street, P.O. Box 3773, Anaheim CA 92803. 714/526-5533. **Toll-free phone:** 800/527-2105. **Contact:** Personnel Director. **E-mail address:** info@bridgford.com. **World Wide Web address:** http://www.bridgford.com. **Description:** Manufactures and distributes refrigerated, frozen, and snack food products. The company markets its products throughout the United States and sells through retail and wholesale outlets, restaurants, institutions, and retail food stores. **Corporate headquarters location:** This location. **Other U.S. locations:** Chicago IL; Statesville NC; Dallas TX.

BRODERBUND LLC
100 Pine Street, Suite 1900, San Francisco CA 94111. 415/659-2000. **Contact:** Alan Byrne, Vice President of Personnel. **E-mail address:** resumes@riverdeep.net. **World Wide Web address:** http://www.broderbund.com. **Description:** Develops, publishes, and markets personal computer software for the home, school, and small business markets. Products include personal productivity and education software. **Positions advertised include:** Affiliate and Search Enginer Marketing Manager; Associate Producer, Personal Publishing; Technology Architect; Sr. Direct Marketing Manager; Art Director; Project Design Manager. **Corporate headquarters location:** This location. **Parent company:** Riverdeep, Inc. **Number of employees at this location:** 340.

BROOKS BROTHERS
150 Post Street, San Francisco CA 94108. 415/397-4500. **Contact:** Human Resources Department. **E-mail address:** hr@brooksbrothers.com. **World Wide Web address:** http://www.brooksbrothers.com. **Description:** One location of the specialty clothing store chain. Brooks Brothers operates 80 retail and 72 factory stores in the United States. **NOTE:** Apply in person for selling positions. For management positions send resume to: ATT: BB Employment Specialist, 2395 Riverlane Terrace, Fort Lauderdale FL 33312. **Corporate headquarters location:** New York NY. **International locations:** China; Japan; Taiwan.

BROOKS CAMERA
125 Kearney Street, San Francisco CA 94108. 415/362-4708. **Contact:** Don Boyle, Manager. **Description:** A retailer of photography equipment. **Corporate headquarters location:** This location. **Parent company:** Inventory Supply Company, Inc. **Operations at this facility include:** Administration; Sales. **Number of employees at this location:** 10.

BROWN & CALDWELL
201 North Civic Drive, Suite 115, Walnut Creek CA 94596-3864. 925/937-9010. **Toll-free phone:** 800/727-2224. **Fax:** 925/937-9026. **Contact:** Professional Staffing. **E-mail address:** resumes@brwncald.com. **World Wide Web address:** http://www.brownandcaldwell.com. **Description:** An employee-owned environmental engineering and consulting firm. Brown & Caldwell specializes in the planning, engineering, and design of waste management systems. The company is also engaged in construction management and environmental analytical testing. **NOTE:** Search and apply for positions online. **Positions advertised include:** Supervising Engineer; Health and Safety risk Manager; Sr. Electronic Media Specialist; Graphic Designer; Managing Scientist. **Corporate headquarters location:** This location. **Other U.S. locations:** Nationwide. **Number of employees nationwide:** 1,000.

BROWNING-FERRIS INDUSTRIES, INC. (BFI)
441 North Buchanan Circle, Pacheco CA 94553. 925/685-4716. **Fax:** 925/685-4145. **Contact:** Personnel. **World Wide Web address:** http://www.bfi.com. **Description:** Engaged primarily in the collection and disposal of solid waste for commercial, industrial, and residential customers. Services provided by Browning-Ferris Industries, Inc. include landfill services, waste-to-energy programs, hazardous waste removal, and liquid waste removal. The company has worldwide operations at more than 500 facilities. **Corporate headquarters location:** Houston TX. **Parent company:** Allied Waste Industries. **Listed on:** New York Stock Exchange. **Stock exchange symbol:** AW.

BROWNTROUT PUBLISHERS INC.
P.O. Box 280070, San Francisco CA 94128-0070. 310/316-4480. **Toll-free phone:** 800/777-7812. **Contact:** Human Resources. **World Wide Web address:** http://www.browntrout.com. **Description:** Publishes desk calendars and gift books on subjects including art, history, animals, sports, and travel. The company also customizes calendars for corporations and private businesses. **Corporate headquarters location:** This location. **International locations:** Australia; Canada; Mexico; United Kingdom.

BUCHALTER, NEMER, FIELDS & YOUNGER
333 Market Street, 25th Floor, San Francisco CA 94105-2102. 415/227-0900. **Fax:** 213/896-0400. **Contact:** Kristy Sessions, Recruiting Coordinator. **E-mail address:** ksessions@buchalter.com. **World Wide Web address:** http://www.buchalter.com. **Description:** A law firm specializing in the area of business. Practice areas include corporate, real estate, real estate finance, general litigations, labor, financial institution litigation, and multimedia entertainment and communications. **NOTE:** Address resumes to: Kristy Sessions, Recruiting Coordinator/Buchalter, Nemer, Fields, & Younger/601 South Figueroa Street, Suite 2400/Los Angeles CA 90017. Fax: 213/8986-0400. **Other area locations:** Los Angeles CA; Irvine CA.

BUCK KNIVES INC.
1900 Weld Boulevard, El Cajon CA 92020. 619/449-1100. **Toll-free number:** 800/215-BUCK. **Contact:** Human Resources. **World Wide Web address:** http://www.buckknives.com. **Description:** Manufactures a variety of sport, utility, and multipurpose knives. **Chairman/CEO:** Chuck Buck.

BUFFETS, INC.
2241 Kettner Boulevard, Suite 260, San Diego CA 92101. 619/615-5390. **Recorded jobline:** 877/7BUFFET. **Contact:** Human Resources. **World Wide Web address:** http://www.buffet.com. **Description:** Operates and franchises buffet restaurants. In addition to more than 400 buffet style restaurants throughout the country, Buffets, Inc. and its subsidiaries also operate Tahoe Joe's, a steakhouse restaurant chain with four locations in California. **NOTE:** Search and apply for positions online. For Human Resources, call 877/560-4084. **Corporate headquarters location:** Eagan MN.

BURBANK, CITY OF
275 East Olive Avenue, Burbank CA 91510. 818/238-5021. **Recorded jobline:** 818/238-5000. **Contact:** Human Resources. **World Wide Web address:** http://www.burbank.acityline.com. **Description:** Administrative offices for the city of Burbank. **Special programs:** Internships.

BURKE MERCER
2250 South 10th Street, San Jose CA 95112. 408/297-3500. **Fax:** 408/291-8401. **Contact:** Karen Lerma, Personnel Director. **World Wide Web address:** http://www.burkemercer.com. **Description:** Manufactures a wide variety of flooring products including carpet base, tile, transition strip accessories, stair tread, and floor adhesives. **Corporate headquarters location:** This location.

BURNHAM REAL ESTATE SERVICE
4435 East Gate Mall, Suite 200, San Diego CA 92121. 858/452-6500. **Fax:** 858/452-3206. **Contact:** Human Resources Department. **E-mail address:** jobs@burnhamrealestate.com. **World Wide Web address:** http://www.burnhamrealestate.com. **Description:** A real estate investor and syndicate. The firm serves as the general partner or investor in a number of real estate ventures including two public partnerships. **Corporate headquarters location:** This location.

BURSON-MARSTELLER
303 Second Street, 8th Floor, San Francisco CA 94107. 415/591-4000. **Fax:** 415/591-4030. **Contact:** Kay Fynmore, Director of Human Resources. **E-mail address:** kay_fynmore@nyc.bm.com. **World Wide Web address:** http://www.bm.com. **Description:** A public relations and public affairs firm. **NOTE:** Search and apply for positions, or submit resume online. **Positions advertised include:** PR Manager, Technology Practice. **Special programs:** Internships. **Corporate headquarters**

location: New York NY. **Other area locations:** Los Angeles CA; Sacramento CA; San Diego CA; San Francisco CA. **Other U.S. locations:** Miami FL; Chicago IL; Pittsburgh PA; Austin TX; Dallas TX. **International locations:** Worldwide. **Parent company:** Young and Rubicam, Inc.

BURTON MEDICAL PRODUCTS
21100 Lassen Street, Chatsworth CA 91311. 818/701-8700. **Fax:** 818/701-8725. **Contact:** Bonnie Tharp, Human Resource Manager. **World Wide Web address:** http://www.burtonmedical.com. **Description:** A wholesale distributor of surgical lights. **Corporate headquarters location:** This location. **Parent company:** LUXO ASA.

BYER CALIFORNIA
66 Potrero Avenue, San Francisco CA 94103. 415/626-7844. **Fax:** 415/626-7865. **Contact:** Personnel Department. **E-mail address:** clee@byer.com. **World Wide Web address:** http://www.byer.com. **Description:** Manufactures women's apparel. **Corporate headquarters location:** This location.

BYER CALIFORNIA
1201 Rio Vista Avenue, Los Angeles CA 90023. 323/266-4561. **Contact:** Personnel Department. **E-mail address:** clee@byer.com. **World Wide Web address:** http://www.byer.com. **Description:** Manufactures women's sportswear. **Corporate headquarters location:** San Francisco CA.

C&D AEROSPACE, INC.
5701 Bosla Avenue, Huntington Beach CA 92647. 714/934-0000. **Fax:** 714/934-0088. **Contact:** Human Resources. **E-mail address:** hbcareers@cdaero.com. **World Wide Web address:** http://www.cdaero.com. **Description:** Designs and manufactures aircraft interiors for commercial airlines and for various governments. **Special programs:** Internships. **Corporate headquarters location:** This location. **Other area locations:** Garden Grove CA; La Palma CA; Ontario CA; Santa Maria CA. **Other U.S. locations:** Marysville WA. **Listed on:** Privately held. **Number of employees at this location:** 700. **Number of employees nationwide:** 3,000.

CB RICHARD ELLIS
101 California Street, 44th Floor, San Francisco CA 94111. 415/772-0123. **Fax:** 415/772-0459. **Contact:** Human Resources. **E-mail address:** opps@cbre.com. **World Wide Web address:** http://www.cbrichardellis.com. **Description:** A fully integrated commercial real estate services company offering property sales and leasing, property and facility management, mortgage banking, and investment management services. **Positions advertised include:** Coordinator, Sr. Info Management; Director, Project Management; Load Production Officer. **Corporate headquarters location:** Los Angeles CA. **Other U.S. locations:** Nationwide. **International locations:** Worldwide. **Number of employees worldwide:** 13,500.

CBS CORPORATION
6121 West Sunset Boulevard, Los Angeles CA 90028. 323/460-3000. **Contact:** CBS Placement. **World Wide Web address:** http://www.cbsnews.com. **Description:** Houses the offices of CBS-2 News and KNX Radio News. **Special programs:** Internships. **Parent company:** Viacom Inc.

CCH INC.
21250 Hawthorne Boulevard, Torrance CA 90503. 310/543-6200. **Toll-free phone:** 800/PFX-9998. **Fax:** 310/543-6544. **Contact:** Human Resources. **World Wide Web address:** http://www.cch.com. **Description:** One of the nation's largest developers of income tax processing software. The company markets its software products to tax attorneys, tax accountants, and CPAs. **Positions advertised include:** Order Processing Analyst; Security Architect; Programmer Analyst; Web ArchitectProduct Manager. **Corporate headquarters location:** Riverwoods IL. **Other U.S. locations:** Chatsworth CA; Washington DC; Chicago IL; St. Cloud MN. **Parent company:** Wolters Kluwer. **Number of employees at this location:** 400.

CH2M HILL CALIFORNIA INC.
P.O. Box 12681, Oakland CA 94604. 510/251-2426. **Physical address:** 155 Grand Avenue, Suite 1000, Oakland CA 94612. **Fax:** 510/893-8205. **Contact:** Human Resources Department. **World Wide Web address:** http://www.ch2m.com. **Description:** A group of employee-owned companies operating under the names CH2M Hill, Inc., Industrial Design Corporation, Operations Management International, CH2M Hill International, and CH2M Hill Engineering. The company provides planning, engineering design, and operation and construction management services to help clients apply technology, safeguard the environment, and develop infrastructure. The professional staff includes specialists in environmental engineering and waste management, water management, transportation, industrial facilities, and a broad spectrum of infrastructure systems. Founded in 1946. **Positions advertised include:** Associate Designer; Transporation Planner Specialist; Sr. Human Resources Assistant; Hydrogeologist; Structural Engineer; Project Biologist. **Corporate headquarters location:** Greenwood Village CO. **International locations:** Worldwide. **Operations at this facility include:** Regional Headquarters.

CI DESIGN
4320 East Miraloma Avenue, Anaheim CA 92807. 714/646-0111. **Fax:** 714/646-0266. **Contact:** Human Resources. **E-mail address:** kj@cidesign.com. **World Wide Web address:** http://www.ci-design.com. **Description:** Designs and manufactures computer hardware and peripherals including storage and disk drive systems. **Positions advertised include:** Sales Representative. **Special programs:** Internships. **Corporate headquarters location:** This location. **Other U.S. locations:** Nationwide. **International locations:** The Netherlands; Taiwan.

CIS HOLLYWOOD
1144 North Las Palmas Avenue, Hollywood CA 90038. 323/463-8811. **Fax:** 323/962-1859. **Contact:** Recruiting. **E-mail address:** srichards@cishollywood.com. **World Wide Web address:** http://www.cishollywood.com. **Description:** Provides video post-production services. **NOTE:** Website includes guidelines for demo reels submission. **Corporate headquarters location:** This location.

CJ LASER BUSINESS SERVICES
654 14th Street, Oakland CA 94612. 510/832-2828. **Fax:** 510/832-1969. **Contact:** Human Resources. **World Wide Web address:** http://www.cjlaser.com. **Description:** Provides laser printer repair services and reconditions toner cartridges. **Office hours:** Monday – Friday, 9:00 a.m. – 4:00 p.m.

CKE RESTAURANTS, INC.
401 West Carl Karcher Way, P.O. Box 4349, Anaheim CA 92803-4349. 714/774-5796. **Fax:** 714/490-3630. **Recorded jobline:** 800/227-5757. **Contact:** Human Resources. **World Wide Web address:** http://www.ckr.com. **Description:** Operates Carl's Jr. restaurants. **Corporate headquarters location:** This location. **Listed on:** New York Stock Exchange. **Stock exchange symbol:** CKR.

CNF TRANSPORTATION CORPORATION
3240 Hillview Avenue, Palo Alto CA 94304. 650/494-2900. **Contact:** Personnel. **E-mail address:** jobs@cnf.com. **World Wide Web address:** http://www.cnf.com. **Description:** A motor freight carrier and air freight forwarder operating in all 50 states. Operations include import/export brokerage, overseas forwarding, and warehousing and distribution services. **Positions advertised include:** General Clerk. **Corporate headquarters location:** This location. **Other U.S. locations:** Portland OR. **Listed on:** New York Stock Exchange. **Stock exchange symbol:** CNF. **Number of employees nationwide:** 26,000.

CSE INSURANCE GROUP
P.O. Box 7764, San Francisco CA 94120-7764. 415/274-7800. **Physical address:** 50 California Street, Suite 2500, San Francisco CA 94111. **Toll-free phone:** 800/282-6848. **Fax:** 415/274-7882. **Contact:** Sarah Brotman, Human Resources Representative. **E-mail address:** sbrotman@cse-insurance.com. **World Wide Web address:** http://www.cse-insurance.com. **Description:** Provides public employees and professionals in related fields with personal lines of insurance including homeowners, automobile, life and disability, and property insurance. **Positions advertised include:** Actuarial Analyst. **Corporate headquarters location:** This location. **Other area locations:** Pasadena CA; Sacramento CA; Walnut Creek CA. **Other U.S. locations:** AZ; NV; UT. **Parent company:** AZUR-GMF Group.

CXR TELCOM
47971 Fremont Boulevard, Fremont CA 94538-6502. 510/657-8810. **Contact:** Human Resources. **World Wide Web address:** http://www.cxr.com. **Description:** Designs, manufactures, and markets electronic telecommunications test equipment and data communications equipment. The company's customers include interconnect carriers, independent telephone operating companies, private communications networks, banks, brokerage firms, and government agencies. **Corporate headquarters location:** This location. **International locations:** France; United Kingdom.

CABLE & COMPUTER TECHNOLOGY
1555 South Sinclair Street, Anaheim CA 92806. 714/937-1341. **Fax:** 714/937-1225. **World Wide Web address:** http://www.c2t.com. **Contact:** Human Resources. **Description:** Manufactures computer emulation hardware for the U.S. government. **Corporate headquarters location:** This location.

CADENCE DESIGN SYSTEMS, INC.
2655 Seely Avenue, San Jose CA 95134. 408/943-1234. **Toll-free phone:** 800/746-6223. **Fax:** 408/894-2207. **Contact:** Human Resources. **World Wide Web address:** http://www.cadence.com. **Description:** Manufactures electronic design automation software. **NOTE:** Search and apply for positions online. **Positions advertised include:** Product Engineer; Sr. Systems Engineer; Software Engineer; Sr. Marketing Manager; Legal Specialist; Principal Desgin Engineer. **Special programs:** Internships. **Corporate headquarters location:** This location. **Other area locations:** Irvine CA; San Diego CA; Santa Barbara CA. **Other U.S. locations:** MD; MA; MS; NJ; NC; OR; PA; TX. **International locations:** Canada; England; France; India; Ireland; Italy; Japan; Scotland; Taiwan. **Operations at this facility include:** Research and Development; Sales. **Listed on:** New York Stock Exchange. **Stock exchange symbol:** CDN. **Number of employees worldwide:** 4,800.

CAL-AIR CONDITIONING
1555 South Seventh Street, Building K, San Jose CA 95112. 408/283-2300. **Fax:** 562/464-3294. **Contact:** Human Resources. **E-mail address:** sozuna@calair.com. **World Wide Web address:** http://www.calair.com. **Description:** A mechanical contractor. Cal-Air Conditioning installs and services air conditioning and heating systems, and is also engaged in energy management and sheet metal fabrication. **NOTE:** Resumes may be submitted by e-mail or fax. Applicants may also mail resumes to: Cal-Air, Inc., 12393 Slauson Avenue, Whittier CA 90606. **Positions advertised include:** Energy Service Sales Representative; Service Technician. **Corporate headquarters location:** Whittier CA. **Other area locations:** Statewide. **Parent company:** Cal-Air, Inc. **Operations at this facility include:** Administration; Divisional Headquarters; Sales; Service. **Number of employees at this location:** 150. **Number of employees nationwide:** 400.

CALGENE, INC.
1920 Fifth Street, Davis CA 95616. 530/753-6313. **Fax:** 530/792-2453. **Contact:** Human Resources. **World Wide Web address:** http://www.monsanto.com. **Description:** Develops genetically engineered plants and plant products for the food and seed industries. The company's research and business efforts are focused in three main crop areas: fresh market tomato, edible and industrial plant oils, and cotton. **Corporate headquarters location:** St. Louis MO. **Parent company:** Monsanto Company.

CALAMP CORP.
1401 North Rice Avenue, Oxnard CA 93030. 805/987-9000. **Fax:** 805/987-2655. **E-mail address:** resume@calamp.com. **Contact:** Human Resources. **World Wide Web address:** http://www.calamp.com. **Description:** A leading provider of high volume wireless data delivery products for service providers, enterprises and technology developers. The company's markets include public safety, health care, wireless enterprise connectivity, digital multimedia delivery, retailing applications and residential broadband data delivery. **NOTE:** Resumes may be submitted via fax, e-mail, or US mail. **Corporate headquarters location:** This location. **International locations:** Paris France; San Paulo Brazil. **Number of employees at this location:** 335. **Listed on:** NASDAQ. **Stock exchange symbol:** CAMP.

CALIFORNIA BANK AND TRUST
11622 El Camino Real, Suite 200, San Diego CA 92130. 858/793-7400. **Fax:** 858/793-7438. **Contact:** Human Resources. **E-mail address:** careers@calbt.com. **World Wide Web address:** http://www.calbanktrust.com. **Description:** California Bank and Trust provides commercial and professional loan and deposit products, SBA loans, and construction financing. **NOTE:** Contact information for positions in the Los Angeles or Northern California area is available online. For positions in the San Diego area, address resumes to: Human Resources Division, California Bank & Trust, 4320 La Jolla Village Drive, Suite 270, San Diego CA 92122. Fax: 858/552-0473. E-mail: murphym@calbt.com. **Positions advertised include:** Processor; Customer Service Representative; Administrative Assistant; Commercial Banker. **Corporate headquarters location:** This location. **Other area locations:** Statewide. **Number of employees nationwide:** 2,000.

CALIFORNIA BEACH RESTAURANTS, INC.
17383 Sunset Boulevard, Suite 140, Pacific Palisades CA 90272. 310/459-9676. **Fax:** 310/459-9356. **Contact:** Human Resources. **World Wide Web address:** http://www.gladstones.com. **Description:** Owns and operates Gladstone's 4 Fish, and RJ's - The Rib Joint. **Corporate headquarters location:** This location. **CEO:** Dick Powell.

CALIFORNIA CARTAGE COMPANY
3545 Long Beach Boulevard, 5th Floor, Long Beach CA 90807. 310/537-1432. **Fax:** 562/427-6855. **Contact:** Personnel Director. **World Wide Web address:** http://www.calcartage.com. **Description:** A trucking company that provides freight handling, warehousing, and container freight station operations. **Corporate headquarters location:** This location. **Other area locations:** Carson CA; City of Industry CA; Compton CA; Fontana CA; National City CA; Oakland CA; Vernon CA; Wilmington CA. **Other U.S. locations:** Nationwide.

CALIFORNIA CASUALTY MANAGEMENT COMPANY
1900 Alameda de las Pulgas, San Mateo CA 94403. 650/574-4000. **Contact:** Human Resources. **World Wide Web address:** http://www.calcas.com. **Description:** A business and personal insurance firm. **NOTE:** Search and apply for positions online. **Positions advertised include:** Actuarial Analyst; Group Marketing Coordinator. **Corporate headquarters location:** This location. **Operations at this facility include:** Administration; Sales; Service.

CALIFORNIA FRINGE BENEFIT
2185 North California Boulevard, Suite 590, Walnut Creek CA 94596. 925/817-1628. **Contact:** Director of Recruiting. **E-mail address:** info@cfbretirement.com. **World Wide Web address:** http://www.cfbretirement.com. **Description:** Markets financial services and products to high-net-worth individuals and business owners. **Corporate headquarters location:** Bloomfield CT. **Parent company:** Lincoln Financial Group. **Operations at this facility include:** Administration; Sales; Service. **Listed on:** New York Stock Exchange. **Number of employees at this location:** 55.

CALIFORNIA CULINARY ACADEMY, INC.
625 Polk Street, San Francisco CA 94102. 415/771-3536. **Contact:** Human Resources. **World Wide Web address:** http://www.baychef.com. **Description:** One of the largest accredited schools for professional chef training in the United States. The academy offers instruction in classic and modern methods of food preparation in its core degree program, specialized baking and pastry certificate programs, and a full range of classes for cooking and wine enthusiasts. Founded in 1977. **Corporate headquarters location:** This location. **Listed on:** NASDAQ. **Stock exchange symbol:** COOK.

CALIFORNIA DENTAL ASSOCIATION
1201 K Street, Sacramento CA 95814. 916/443-3382. **Toll-free phone:** 800/736-7071. **Fax:** 916/443-2943. **Contact:** Human Resources Director. **E-mail address:** info@cda.org. **World Wide Web address:** http://www.cda.org. **Description:** A nonprofit dental association providing membership programs and services for California dentists. **Positions advertised include:** Associate. **Corporate headquarters location:** This location. **Operations at this facility include:** Administration; Sales; Service. **Number of employees at this location:** 200.

CALIFORNIA FIRST LEASING CORPORATION (CALFIRST LEASING)
18201 Von Karmen Avenue, Suite 800, Irvine CA 92612. 714/751-7551. **Toll-free phone:** 800/496-4640. **Fax:** 949/255-0501. **Contact:** David Wheeler, Human Resources Department. **E-mail address:** recruiter@cfnbc.com. **World Wide Web address:** http://www.calfirstbancorp.com. **Description:** A lessor of capital assets including high-technology equipment and systems. Founded in 1977. **Positions advertised include:** Account Executive; Account Representative. **Corporate headquarters location:** This location. **Parent company:** California First National Bancorp. **Listed on:** NASDAQ. **Stock exchange symbol:** CFNB.

CALIFORNIA HIGHWAY PATROL
1551 Benecia Road, Vallejo CA 94591. 707/551-4100. **Toll-free phone:** 888/422-4756. **Contact:** Recruitment Unit. **E-mail address:** recruiting@chp.ca.gov. **World Wide Web address:** http://www.chp.ca.gov. **Description:** Provides law enforcement services for the state of California. **NOTE:** Applications not accepted online. **Corporate headquarters location:** Sacramento CA. **Other area locations:** Statewide. **Number of employees nationwide:** 6,000.

CALIFORNIA MICRO DEVICES CORPORATION
430 North McCarthy Boulevard #100, Milpitas CA 95035. 408/263-3214. **Toll-free phone:** 800/325-4966. **Fax:** 408/934-2925. **Contact:** Personnel. **E-mail address:** hr@calmicro.com. **World Wide Web address:** http://www.calmicro.com. **Description:** Manufactures integrated thin film, silicon-based termination and filtering components. The company specializes in combining thin film, passive electronic components, and semiconductor devices into single-chip solutions for various electronic applications. **Positions advertised include:** ASIP Circuit Design Engineer; Customer Darketing Manager; Product Marketing Manager; Sr. Applications Engineer. **Corporate headquarters location:** This location. **Other U.S. locations:** Tempe AZ. **Listed on:** NASDAQ. **Stock exchange symbol:** CAMD. **President/CEO:** Robert V. Dickinson. **Annual sales/revenues:** $21 - $50 million. **Number of employees at this location:** 150. **Number of employees nationwide:** 280.

CALIFORNIA POLYTECHNIC STATE UNIVERSITY
One Grand Avenue, Administration Building, Room 110, San Luis Obispo CA 93407. 805/756-2236. **Fax:** 805/756-5483. **Recorded jobline:** 805/756-1533. **Contact:** Human Resources. **E-mail address:** humanresources@calpoly.edu (for inquiries only). **World Wide Web address:** http://www.calpoly.edu. **Description:** A university specializing in the field of engineering. **Positions advertised include:** Administrative Support Coordinator; Director of Donor Relations; Lecturer, Agribusiness; Full-time Lecturer, Aerospace Engineering; Medical Microbiologist; Project Manager; Provost and Vice President for Academic Affairs.

CALIFORNIA SCHOOL OF PODIATRIC MEDICINE AT SAMUEL MERRITT COLLEGE
370 Hawthorne Avenue, Oakland CA 94609. 510/869-6856. **Fax:** 510/869-6115. **Contact:** Human Resources. **E-mail address:** hr@samuelmerritt.edu. **World Wide Web address:** http://www.ccpm.edu. **Description:** A college/teaching hospital offering postgraduate programs in the field of podiatry. One of only seven podiatry schools in the U.S. **NOTE:** Search and apply for faculty or staff positions online. **Positions advertised include:** Academic Coordinator; Assistant Director of Admissions.

CALIFORNIA STATE UNIVERSITY, FULLERTON
P.O. Box 34080, Fullerton CA 92834-9480. 714/278-2425. **Physical address:** 800 North State College Boulevard, Fullerton CA 92831-3599. **Fax:** 714/278-4163. **Recorded jobline:** 714/278-3385. **Contact:** Employment Coordinator. **E-mail address:** csuf-hr@fullerton.edu. **World Wide Web address:** http://www.fullerton.edu. **Description:** A four-year state university with an enrollment of over 32,000 students. **NOTE:** Resumes are no longer accepted in hard copy form. Candidates should consult the university's extensive list of job postings and apply online. The Human Resources office is located at: 2600 East Nutwood Avenue, Suite 700, Fullerton CA 92834-6806. **Parent company:** California State University System. **Operations at this facility include:** Administration. **Number of employees at this location:** 3,200.

CALIFORNIA STATE UNIVERSITY, HAYWARD
25800 Carlos Bee Boulevard, Hayward CA 94542-3026. 510/885-3634. **Contact:** Human Resources. **E-mail address:** applycsh@csuhayward.com. **World Wide Web address:** http://www.csuhayward.edu. **Description:** One of 23 campuses of the California State University System. California State University, Hayward offers 37 bachelor's degree programs and 26 master's degree programs. **NOTE:** A CSU Hayward Employment Application must be submitted for each job. Faxed applications not accepted. **Positions advertised include:** Part-time Lecturer, Various Disciplines; Pharmacist; Speech Pathologist; Student Services Professional; Police Officer. **Office hours:** Monday – Friday, 8:00 a.m. – 5:00 p.m. **Other area locations:** Concord CA.

CALIFORNIA STATE UNIVERSITY, STANISLAUS
801 West Monte Vista Avenue, Turlock CA 95382. 209/667-3351. **Recorded jobline:** 209/667-3354. **Fax:** 209/664-7011. **Contact:** Mary Kobayashi Lee, Director of Human Resources. **E-mail address:** hr_department@csustan.edu. **World Wide Web address:** http://www.csustan.edu. **Description:** A four-year state university offering undergraduate and graduate programs of study. California State University, Stanislaus is one of 23 campuses of the California State University System. **Positions advertised include:** Dean, College of Education; Dean, College of Business Administration; Assistant Professor, Various Departments. **Other area locations:** Stockton CA.

CALIFORNIA TEACHERS ASSOCIATION
P.O. Box 2153, Santa Fe Springs CA 90670-0053. 562/942-7979. **Physical address:** 11745 East Telegraph Road, Santa Fe Springs CA 90670. **Fax:** 562/949-9438. **Contact:** Human Resources Department. **E-mail address:** employment@cta.org. **World Wide Web address:** http://www.cta.org. **Description:** An affiliate of the National Education Association, California Teachers Association represents over 175,000 public school teachers throughout the state of California. **Corporate headquarters location:** Burlingame CA. **Other area locations:** Citrus Heights CA; Los Angeles CA; Foster City CA; Norco CA.

CALIFORNIA WATER SERVICE COMPANY
2632 West 237th Street, Torrance CA 90505. 310/257-1400. **Contact:** Human Resources. **E-mail address:** jobs@calwater.com. **World Wide Web address:** http://www.calwater.com. **Description:** A public utility providing water service. **NOTE:** Address resumes to: California Water Service Company, 1720 North First Street, San Jose CA 95112. **Positions advertised include:** Government and Community Relations Specialist. **Corporate headquarters location:** San Jose CA. **Other area locations:** Statewide. **Subsidiaries include:** CWS Utility Services; Washington Water Service Company. **Listed on:** New York Stock Exchange. **Stock exchange symbol:** CWT.

CALIFORNIA WATER SERVICE COMPANY
1720 North First Street, San Jose CA 95112. 408/367-8200. **Contact:** Human Resources. **E-mail address:** jobs@calwater.com. **World Wide Web address:** http://www.calwater.com. **Description:** A public utility supplying water service through 20 separate water systems to 500,000 customers living in 38 California communities. **Corporate headquarters location:** This location. **Other area locations:** Statewide. **Parent company:** California Water Service Group. **Listed on:** New York Stock Exchange. **Stock exchange symbol:** CWT.

THE CALIFORNIAN
123 West Alisal Street, Salinas CA 93901. 831/424-2221. **Contact:** Teri James, Human Resources Manager. **E-mail address:** tjames@Salinas.gannett.com. **World Wide Web address:** http://www.californianonline.com **Description:** Publishes a daily newspaper with a circulation of 19,420. **Parent company:** Gannett Company, Inc. **Operations at this facility include:** Administration; Sales; Service. **Number of employees at this location:** 150.

CALLAWAY GOLF COMPANY
2180 Rutherford Road, Carlsbad CA 92008-7328. 760/931-1771. **Fax:** 760/930-5045. **Contact:** Human Resources. **E-mail address:** jobs@callawaygolf.com. **World Wide Web address:** http://www.callawaygolf.com. **Description:** Designs, develops, manufactures, and markets golf clubs. **Positions advertised include:** Sr. Database Administrator; Sr. Supply Chain Analyst; Associate Quality Auditor; Sr. Concept Designer. **Corporate headquarters location:** This location. **International locations:** Australia; Canada; France; Germany; Ireland; Italy; Japan; Korea; Spain; Sweden; United Kingdom. **Number of employees nationwide:** 2,300. **Listed on:** New York Stock Exchange. **Stock exchange symbol:** ELY.

CALPINE CONTAINERS INC.
140 Gregory Lane, Suite 180, Pleasant Hill CA 94523. 925/609-5124. **Fax:** 925/686-0152. **Contact:** Human Resources Director. **Description:** Produces wooden and corrugated paper boxes. **Corporate headquarters location:** This location. **Number of employees at this location:** 15. **Number of employees nationwide:** 300.

CALPINE CORPORATION
50 West San Fernando Street, Suite 500, San Jose CA 95113. 408/995-5115. **Fax:** 408/995-0505. **Contact:** Human Resources. **E-mail address:** jobs@calpine.com. **World Wide Web address:** http://www.calpine.com. **Description:** Sells steam and electricity to electric utilities, industrial companies, and government institutions. The company develops, owns, and operates independent power projects, including three geothermal and two natural gas-fired plants. Calpine Corporation is one of the largest producers of geothermal energy in the United States. **Positions advertised include:** Director, Federal Income Tax Accounting. **Corporate headquarters location:** This location. **Other area locations:** Dublin CA; Middletown CA; Walnut Creek CA. **Other U.S. locations:** Nationwide. **Listed on:** New York Stock Exchange. **Stock exchange symbol:** CPN. **Annual sales/revenues:** $8.9 billion.

CALPROP CORPORATION
13160 Mindanao Way, Suite 180, Marina Del Rey CA 90292-7903. 310/306-4314. **Fax:** 310/301-0435. **Contact:** Dori Baron, Personnel Manager. **E-mail address:** info@clpo.com. **World Wide Web address:** http://www.clpo.com. **Description:** Builds and sells single-family homes and condominiums in California. Founded in 1961. **Corporate headquarters location:** This location.

CAM COMMERCE SOLUTIONS
17075 Newhope Street, Suite A, Fountain Valley CA 92708. 714/241-9241. **Fax:** 714/241-9893. **Contact:** Human Resources. **World Wide Web address:** http://www.camcommerce.com. **Description:** Designs, manufactures, markets, and services inventory management, point-of-sale, order entry, and accounting software systems for small to medium-sized retailers and wholesalers. CAM provides its products and services on a direct basis only. The company also offers after-sale services including phone support, nationwide hardware and software service, database conversions, and regular program enhancements. Founded in 1983. **Positions advertised include:** Technical Support Specialist. **Corporate headquarters location:** This location. **Other U.S. locations:** Burlingame CA; Aurora CO; Altamonte Springs

FL; Hopkinton MA; St. Louis MO; Saddle River NJ; Henderson NV; Dallas TX. **Listed on:** NASDAQ. **Stock exchange symbol:** CADA. **Chairman and CEO:** Geoff Knapp. **Number of employees at this location:** 164.

CAMFIL FARR
2121 Paulhan Street, Rancho Dominguez CA 90220. 310/668-6300. **Fax:** 310/668-6339. **Contact:** Personnel. **World Wide Web address:** http://www.camfil.com. **Description:** Primarily engaged in the design, manufacture, and sale of air filtration systems for use in a wide variety of industrial applications. These include heating, ventilating, and air conditioning systems, as well as gas turbines and construction equipment. Other products include noise-abatement systems and engine protection equipment. **NOTE:** Submit resume to: Camfil Farr, Attention: Human Resources, One North Corporate Drive, Riverdale NJ 07457. **Corporate headquarters location:** Riverdale NJ. **Operations at this facility include:** Administration; Research and Development; Sales.

CAMPBELL SOUP COMPANY
6200 Franklin Boulevard, Sacramento CA 95824. 916/428-7890. **Contact:** Human Resources. **World Wide Web address:** http://www.campbellsoup.com. **Description:** Campbell Soup is a major producer of commercial soups, juices, pickles, frozen foods, canned beans and pasta products, spaghetti sauces, and baked goods. The company distributes its products worldwide. U.S. brands include Campbell's, Vlasic, V8, Chunky, Home Cookin', Prego, Pepperidge Farm, Inc., LeMenu, and Swanson. European brand names include Pleybin, Biscuits Delacre, Freshbake, Groko, Godiva, and Betis. **Corporate headquarters location:** Camden NJ. **Other U.S. locations:** Nationwide. **International locations:** Worldwide. **Operations at this facility include:** This location makes a variety of soups. **Listed on:** New York Stock Exchange. **Stock exchange symbol:** CPB.

CANCERVAX CORPORATION
2110 Rutherford Road, Carlsbad CA 92008. 760/494-4200. **Fax:** 760/494-4271. **Contact:** Human Resources. **E-mail address:** carlsbadcareers@cancervax.com. **World Wide Web address:** http://www.cancervax.com. **Description:** A biotechnology company focused on the creation of products for the treatment of cancer. **Advertised positions:** Regulatory Science manager; Senior Scientist; Research Associate. **Other locations:** Marina Del Rey CA.

THE CAPITAL GROUP COMPANIES
AMERICAN FUNDS DISTRIBUTORS
333 South Hope Street, 53rd Floor, Los Angeles CA 90071-1406. 310/996-6000. **Contact:** Recruiting Department. **World Wide Web address:** http://www.capgroup.com. **Description:** An investment management company with 15 mutual funds and 10 companies. American Funds Distributors (http://www.americanfunds.com) is also at this location. The company provides financial advisement services including 28 mutual funds, variable annuities, and retirement planning. **NOTE:** Search and apply for positions online. **Positions advertised include:** Research Associate; Economist; Investment Group Assistsant; Project Manager; Portfolio Control Assistant; Programmer Analyst; Java Technologist; Web Copy Editor. **Corporate headquarters location:** This location. **Other area locations:** Brea CA; San Francisco CA. **Other U.S. locations:** Washington DC; Atlanta GA; Chicago IL; Indianapolis IN; New York NY; Reno NV; San Antonio TX. **International locations:** Canada; England; Hong Kong; Japan; Singapore.

CAPITAL PACIFIC HOLDINGS
4100 MacArthur Boulevard, Suite 150, Newport Beach CA 92660. 949/622-8400. **Contact:** Kathy Smith, Human Resources. **E-mail address:** Kathy.smith@cph-inc.com. **World Wide Web address:** http://www.capitalpacifichomes.com. **Description:** Builds single-family homes throughout Orange County CA, Las Vegas NV, and Austin TX. **Corporate headquarters location:** This location. **Other U.S. locations:** Mesa AZ; Westminster CO; Austin TX. **Listed on:** American Stock Exchange. **Stock exchange symbol:** CPH.

CARDINAL HEALTH, ALARIS PRODUCTS
P.O. Box 85335, San Diego CA 92186-5335. 858/458-7000. **Physical address:** 10221 Wateridge Circle, San Diego CA 92121. **Toll-free phone:** 800/854-7128. **Fax:** 858/458-6196. **Contact:** Human Resources. **World Wide Web address:** http://www.alarismed.com. **Description:** Designs, manufactures, and markets instruments used to monitor patients and products for intravenous infusion therapy. **Positions advertised include:** Director, Infusion Information; Associate Product Manager; Senior Product Manager; Network Support Engineer. **Corporate headquarters location:** This location. **Other U.S. locations:** Creedmoor NC. **International locations:** Mexico; United Kingdom. **Parent company:** Cardinal Health. **President/CEO:** William J. Mercer.

CARGILL SALT COMPANY
7220 Central Avenue, Newark CA 94560. 510/797-1820. **Contact:** Ilene Fox, Human Resources Manager. **E-mail address:** employment@cargill.com (for inquiries only). **World Wide Web address:** http://www.cargill.com. **Description:** Processes and distributes table and industrial salts. **NOTE:** Entry-level positions are offered. **Positions advertised include:** Maintenance Supervisor. **Corporate headquarters location:** Minneapolis MN. **Parent company:** Cargill Inc. and its subsidiaries and affiliates are involved in nearly 50 individual lines of business. The company has over 130 years of service and international expertise in commodity trading, handling, transporting, processing, and risk management. Cargill is a major trader of grains and oilseeds, as well as a marketer of many other agricultural and nonagricultural commodities. Cargill is a leader in developing high-quality, competitively priced farm products and in supplying them to growers. The company's agricultural products include a wide variety of feed, seed, fertilizers, and other goods and services needed by producers worldwide. Cargill is also a leader in producing and marketing seed varieties and hybrids. Cargill's Financial Markets Division (FMD) supports Cargill and its subsidiaries with financial products and services that address the full spectrum of market conditions. Cargill's worldwide food processing businesses supply products ranging from basic ingredients used in food production to recognized brand names. Cargill also operates a number of industrial businesses including the steel production, industrial-grade starches, ethanol, and salt products. **Other U.S. locations:** Nationwide. **Listed on:** Privately held. **Number of employees worldwide:** 90,000.

CARLSMITH BALL LLP
444 South Flower Street, 9th Floor, Los Angeles CA 90071. 213/955-1200. **Fax:** 213/623-0032. **Contact:** Human Resources. **E-mail address:** recruiting@carlsmith.com. **World Wide Web address:** http://www.carlsmith.com. **Description:** A law firm that specializes in civil law. **Special programs:** Internships. **NOTE:** Address resumes to: Recruiting Coordinator, 1001 Bishop Street, ASB Tower, Suite 2200, Honolulu HI 96813. E-mail: execdirector@carlsmith.com. **Other U.S. locations:** Washington DC; Hilo HI; Honolulu HI; Kapolei HI; Kona HI; Maui HI. **International locations:** Guam; Saipan.

CARPENTER SPECIAL PRODUCTS CORPORATION
P.O. Box 609036, San Diego CA 92160-9036. 619/448-1000. **Fax:** 619/562-5776. **Contact:** Personnel Supervisor. **E-mail address:** employment@cartech.com. **World Wide Web address:** http://www.cartech.com. **Description:** Manufactures, fabricates, and markets a wide range of specialty metals for a variety of end use markets. The company also produces stainless steel, tool steel, high-temperature and electronic alloys, and other special purpose metals. **Corporate headquarters location:** Wyomissing PA. **Other U.S. locations:** Atlanta GA; Fryeburg ME; Orangeburg SC; Dallas TX. **Parent company:** Carpenter Technology Corporation. **Listed on:** New York Stock Exchange. **Stock exchange symbol:** CRS. **Number of employees at this location:** 130. **Number of employees nationwide:** 4,100.

CASA DE LAS CAMPANAS
18655 West Bernardo Drive, San Diego CA 92127. 858/592-1870. **Fax:** 858/592-1853. **Recorded jobline:** 858/592-1865. **Contact:** Jane Munson, Human Resources Manager. **World Wide Web address:** http://www.casadelascampanas.com. **Description:** A nonprofit, continuing care retirement facility with more than 500 residents. **NOTE:** Entry-level positions and second and third shifts are offered. **Positions advertised include:** Certified Nursing Assistant; Registered Nurse; Unit Clerk; Licensed Vocational Nurse; Housekeeper; Resident Helper; Lead Line Cook. **Special programs:** Internships. **Office hours:** Monday - Thursday, 10:00 a.m. - 12:00 p.m. and 3:00 p.m. - 4:00 p.m. **Parent company:** Life Care Services LLC. **Executive Director:** Craig Wyble. **Number of employees at this location:** 300.

A.M. CASTLE & COMPANY
1625 Tillie Lewis Drive, Stockton CA 95206. 209/944-1100. **Fax:** 562/944-1110. **Contact:** Administrative Supervisor. **E-mail address:** jobs@amcastle.com. **World Wide Web address:** http://www.amcastle.com. **Description:** Distributes a large variety of metals to industrial companies. Metals distributed include nickel alloys, brass, copper, titanium, stainless steel, and aluminum. **Corporate headquarters location:** Franklin Park IL. **Other area locations:** Paramount CA. **Other U.S. locations:** Nationwide. **International locations:** Canada. **Subsidiaries include:** Castle UK; Keystone Honing; Keystone Tube Company; Oliver Steel Plate; Total Plastics. **Listed on:** American Stock Exchange. **Stock exchange symbol:** CAS.

A.M. CASTLE & COMPANY
14001 Orange Avenue, Paramount CA 90723. 562/630-1400. **Fax:** 562/634-1421. **Contact:** Human Resources. **E-mail address:** jobs@amcastle.com. **World Wide Web address:** http://www.amcastle.com. **Description:** Distributes a large variety of metals to industrial companies. Metals distributed include nickel alloys, brass and copper, titanium, stainless steels, and aluminum. **Corporate headquarters location:** Franklin Park IL. **Other area locations:** Stockton CA. **Other U.S. locations:** Nationwide. **International locations:** Canada. **Subsidiaries include:** Castle UK; Keystone Honing; Keystone Tube Company; Oliver Steel Plate; Total Plastics. **Listed on:** American Stock Exchange. **Stock exchange symbol:** CAS.

CASTLE AND COOKE REALTY, INC.
10900 Wilshire Boulevard, Suite 1600, Los Angeles CA 90024. 310/208-3636. **Contact:** Human Resources. **E-mail address:** human-resources@castle-cooke.com. **World Wide Web address:** http://www.castlecooke.net. **Description:** A holding company for firms involved in construction and real estate. Castle and Cooke also owns country clubs, private membership clubs, and a horse farm. **Corporate headquarters location:** Mililani HI.

CASTLE ROCK ENTERTAINMENT
345 North Maple Drive, Suite 135, Beverly Hills CA 90210. 310/285-2300. **Fax:** 310/285-2345. **Contact:** Human Resources Department. **World Wide Web address:** http://www.castle-rock.com. **Description:** A motion picture and video production company. **NOTE:** Warner Brothers handles the hiring for Castle Rock. Please contact WB Human Resources at: 818/954-6000 for more information. **Parent Company:** Time Warner Inc. **Listed on:** New York Stock Exchange. **Stock exchange symbol:** AOL.

CATALINA YACHTS INC.
21200 Victory Boulevard, Woodland Hills CA 91367-2522. 818/884-7700. **Fax:** 818/884-3810. **Contact:** Human Resources Department. **World Wide Web address:** http://www.catalinayachts.com. **Description:** Manufactures yachts. **Corporate headquarters location:** This location. **Other U.S. locations:** Largo FL.

CATALYST SEMICONDUCTOR, INC.
1250 Borregas Avenue, Sunnyvale CA 94089. 408/542-1000. **Fax:** 408/542-1200. **Contact:** Human Resources. **E-mail address:** jobs@catsemi.com. **World Wide Web address:** http://www.catsemi.com. **Description:** Supplies nonvolatile semiconductors that provide design solutions for a broad range of applications including computers, wireless communications, networks, instrumentation, and automotive systems. The company's devices include FLASH, mixed signal devices, Serial and Parallel EEPROMs (electrically erasable programmable read-only memory), and NVRAMs. Founded in 1985. **Positions advertised include:** Quality Assaurance Manager. **Corporate headquarters location:** This location. **International locations:** Japan; Philippines; Singapore; Thailand. **Operations at this facility include:** Development; Engineering and Design; Marketing; Sales. **Listed on:** NASDAQ. **Stock exchange symbol:** CATS.

CATALYTICA ENERGY SYSTEMS, INC.
430 Ferguson Drive, Mountain View CA 94043. 650/960-3000. **Contact:** Regina Machado, Human Resources. **E-mail address:** hr@catalyticaenergy.com. **World Wide Web address:** http://www.catalyticaenergy.com. **Description:** Develops catalytic technologies for the prevention of pollution in combustion systems, advanced process technologies, and chemical products. The company also develops an ultraslow emission-combustion system for natural gas turbines. Catalytica provides contract research, development, and consulting services to the petroleum refining and chemical industries. Additional programs include the development of a process for manufacturing gasoline alkylate to eliminate the use of liquid acid catalysts, the conversion of methane to transportation fuels, and the application of nanotechnology for new catalysts and materials. The company also manufactures fine chemical products. **Positions advertised include:** Process Development Engineer. **Corporate headquarters location:** Gilbert AZ. **Operations at this facility include:** Research and Development. **Subsidiaries include:** Advanced Sensor Devices develops environmental monitoring devices including a continuous emissions monitor. **Listed on:** NASDAQ. **Stock exchange symbol:** CESI.

CATELLUS DEVELOPMENT CORPORATION
201 Mission Street, Second Floor, San Francisco CA 94105. 415/974-4500. **Contact:** Human Resources. **E-mail address:** human-resources@catellus.com. **World Wide Web address:** http://www.catellus.com. **Description:** Owns, develops, and manages industrial, retail, and office buildings. The company's properties, land holdings, and joint-venture interests are located in major markets in California and 11 other states.

Corporate headquarters location: This location. **Other area locations:** Los Angeles CA; Newport Beach CA; Norwalk CA; Oakland CA; San Jose CA. **Other U.S. locations:** Lakewood CO; Woodridge IL; Dallas TX; Seattle WA. **Listed on:** New York Stock Exchange. **Stock exchange symbol:** CDX.

CATHAY BANCORP, INC.
CATHAY BANK
777 North Broadway Street, Los Angeles CA 90012. 213/625-4700. **Fax:** jobs@cathaybank.com. **Contact:** Personnel. **World Wide Web address:** http://www.cathaybank.com. **Description:** A commercial bank operating through 17 locations. Founded in 1962. **NOTE:** Part-time jobs are offered. **Positions advertised include:** Chief Appraiser; Foreign Exchange Officer; Teller. **Corporate headquarters location:** This location. **Other area locations:** Alhambra CA; Cerritos CA; Monterey Park CA; San Gabriel CA; Valley-Stoneman CA; Westminster CA. **Other U.S. locations:** Flushing NY; New York NY; Houston TX. **Operations at this facility include:** Administration. **Listed on:** NASDAQ. **Stock exchange symbol:** CATY. **Number of employees nationwide:** 500.

CATHOLIC CHARITIES
P.O. Box 4900, Santa Rosa CA 95402. 707/528-8712. **Physical address:** 2325 Montgomery Drive, Santa Rosa CA 95405. **Fax:** 707/575-4910. **Contact:** Personnel. **E-mail address:** smmcarty@srcharities.org or amullan@srcharities.org. **World Wide Web address:** http://www.srcharities.org. **Description:** Provides social service programs for the needy in several counties of California. **Positions advertised include:** Office Assistant, Homeless Services; Director of Development; Bilingual Program Coordinator.

CEDARS-SINAI HEALTH SYSTEM
8723 Alden Drive, Room 110, Los Angeles CA 90048. 310/423-5521. **Recorded jobline:** 310/423-8230. **Fax:** 310/423-8400. **Contact:** Personnel. **E-mail address:** hr.web@cshs.org (for inquiries); jobs@cshs.org (for resume submission). **World Wide Web address:** http://www.csmc.edu. **Description:** A nonprofit health care delivery system that operates through Cedar-Sinai Medical Center, as well as a network of primary care physicians. Cedars-Sinai specializes in acute, subacute, and home patient care; biomedical research; community service; and continuing medical education. **Positions advertised include:** Registered Nurse; Health System Manager; Cytogenetic Technologist; Coder Specialist; Project Coordinator; Accounting Assistant; Chief Exercise Physiologist; Clinical Dietitian; Marketing Representative; Management Assistant. **Office hours:** Monday – Friday, 7:30 a.m. – 5:00 p.m. **Corporate headquarters location:** This location. **Operations at this facility include:** Administration; Research and Development; Service.

CELERA
180 Kimball Way, South San Francisco CA 94080. 650/829-1000. **Toll-free phone:** 877/CELERA1. **Contact:** Human Resources. **World Wide Web address:** http://www.celera.com. **Description:** Engaged in the discovery and development of innovative drugs, with a focus in oncology. **Positions advertised include:** Sr. Financial Analyst; Sr. Scientist, Biology; Director, Cell Biology; Principal Scientist; Facilities Planner; Attorney. **Special programs:** Internships. **Corporate headquarters location:** This location. **Other U.S. locations:** Rockville MD. **Listed on:** New York Stock Exchange. **Stock exchange symbol:** CRA. **Number of employees nationwide:** 538.

CELL GENESYS, INC.
500 Forbes Boulevard, South San Francisco CA 94080. 650/266-3000. **Fax:** 650/266-3010. **Contact:** Human Resources. **E-mail address:** hr@cellgenesys.com. **World Wide Web address:** http://www.cellgenesys.com. **Description:** Develops and commercializes gene therapies to treat major life-threatening diseases including cancer and cardiovascular disease. The company is conducting two multicenter Phase II human clinical trials for its GVAX cancer vaccine in prostate cancer and plans to initiate a multicenter Phase I/II trial of GVAX vaccine in lung cancer. Preclinical stage programs include gene therapy for cancer, cardiovascular disorders, hemophilia, and Parkinson's disease. **NOTE:** Search and apply for positions online. **Positions advertised include:** Biostatistician; Process Development Scientist; Research Associate; Senior Clinical Research Associate; Senior Scientist. **Corporate headquarters location:** This location. **Other area locations:** Hayward CA; San Diego CA. **Other U.S. locations:** Memphis TN. **Listed on:** NASDAQ. **Stock exchange symbol:** CEGE.

CENTER FOR GOVERNMENTAL STUDIES
10951 West Pico Boulevard, Suite 120, Los Angeles CA 90064. 310/470-6590. **Fax:** 310/475-3752. **Contact:** Rebecca Schwaner, Human Resources. **E-mail address:** rschwaner@cgs.org. **World Wide Web address:** http://www.cgs.org. **Description:** A non-profit organization dedicated to studying and implementing governmental reforms. **Special programs:** Internships. **Corporate headquarters location:** This location.

CENTRAL CONCRETE INC.
755 Stockton Avenue, San Jose CA 95126. 408/293-6272. **Fax:** 408/350-3745. **Contact:** Human Resources. **E-mail address:** nalbanese@us-concrete.com. **World Wide Web address:** http://www.centralconcrete.com. **Description:** A producer of ready-mixed concrete and concrete products. **NOTE:** Submit resume via e-mail or fax. **Positions advertised include:** Accounts Payable Assistant; Operations Manager. **Corporate headquarters location:** This location. **Parent company:** US Concrete. **Listed on:** NASDAQ. **Stock exchange symbol:** RMIX.

CENTRAL GARDEN & PET COMPANY
1340 Treat Boulevard, Suite 600, Walnut Creek CA 94597. 925/948-4000. **Contact:** Personnel Department. **World Wide Web address:** http://www.centralgardenandpet.com. **Description:** One of the nation's largest suppliers and merchandisers of lawn, garden, and pet products and a major distributor of pool supplies. **Corporate headquarters location:** This location. **Other U.S. locations:** Nationwide. **Listed on:** NASDAQ. **Stock exchange symbol:** CENT. **Number of employees nationwide:** 1,450.

CENTRAL TRANSPORT
550 South Alameda East, Compton CA 90221. **Toll-free phone:** 800/479-0501. **Fax:** 310/632-3880. **Description:** Operates a trucking service. **World Wide Web address:** http://www.centraltransportint.com. **Corporate headquarters location:** Warren MI.

CENTURY 21 AWARD
5640 Baltimore Drive, La Mesa CA 91942. 619/463-5000. **Toll-free phone:** 800/293-1657. **Contact:** Human Resources Representative. **E-mail address:** opportunities@century21award.com. **World Wide Web address:** http://www.century21award.com. **Description:** A real estate agency. **Special programs:** Career seminars held weekly for potential agents. **Other area locations:** Bonita CA; Carlsbad CA; Del Mar CA; El Cajon CA; Escondido CA; Fallbrook CA; San Diego CA.

CERADYNE, INC.
3169 Redhill Avenue, Costa Mesa CA 92626. 714/549-0421. **Fax:** 714/549-8573. **Contact:** Human Resources. **E-mail address:** hr@ceradyne.com. **World Wide Web address:** http://www.ceradyne.com. **Description:** A nationwide manufacturer specializing in high-tech ceramics for armor and commercial applications. **Positions advertised include:** Researcher; Engineer; Technician; Skilled Operator. **Corporate headquarters location:** This location. **Other U.S. locations:** Scottsdale GA; Lexington KY. **Operations at this facility include:** Administration; Manufacturing; Research and Development; Sales. **Listed on:** NASDAQ. **Stock exchange symbol:** CRDN. **Number of employees at this location:** 110. **Number of employees nationwide:** 230.

CERRELL ASSOCIATES, INC.
320 North Larchmont Boulevard, Los Angeles CA 90004. 323/466-3445. **Fax:** 323/466-8653. **Contact:** Acareli Kotero, Account Coordinator. **E-mail address:** araceli@cerrell.com. **World Wide Web address:** http://www.cerrell.com. **Description:** A public relations company specializing in local public affairs, issues management, and political campaigning. **Special programs:** Internships. **Corporate headquarters location:** This location. **Number of employees at this location:** 30.

CERRO METAL PRODUCTS
14900 Garfield Avenue, Paramount CA 90723. 562/602-6200. **Fax:** 562/531-6248. **Contact:** Lorraine Carter, Director of Human Resources Department. **World Wide Web address:** http://www.cerrometal.com. **Description:** A manufacturer of brass rods. **Corporate headquarters location:** Bellefonte PA. **Other U.S. locations:** Shenandoah VA; Weyers Cave VA. **Operations at this facility include:** Manufacturing; Sales.

CHAD THERAPEUTICS, INC.
21622 Plummer Street, Chatsworth CA 91311. 818/882-0883. **Contact:** Barbara Muskin, Human Resources Manager. **E-mail address:** bmuskin@chadtherapeutics.com. **World Wide Web address:** http://www.chadtherapeutics.com. **Description:** Designs, manufactures, and markets respiratory care devices. Products names include Oxylite, Oxymatic, and Oxymizer. **Corporate headquarters location:** This location. **Listed on:** American Stock Exchange. **Stock exchange symbol:** CTU.

CHALONE WINE GROUP, LTD.
621 Airpark Road, Napa CA 94558-6272. 707/254-4224. **Fax:** 707/254-4207. **Contact:** Tamara Damian, Human Resources Administrator. **E-mail address:** hr@chalonewinegroup.com. **World Wide Web address:** http://www.chalonewinegroup.com. **Description:** Chalone Wine Group, Ltd. produces, markets, and sells premium white and red varietal table wines, primarily Chardonnay, Pinot Noir, Cabernet Sauvignon, and Sauvignon Blanc. **Corporate headquarters location:** This location. **Other U.S. locations:** Washington. **International locations:** France. **Listed on:** NASDAQ. **Stock exchange symbol:** CHLN.

CHAMBERS BELT
5445 Jillson Street, City of Commerce CA 90040. 323/726-2109. **Contact:** Personnel. **World Wide Web address:** http://www.chambersbelt.com. **Description:** A manufacturer of leather belts for men and women. **Corporate headquarters location:** Phoenix AZ. **International locations:** Mexico.

CHARLES SCHWAB & CO., INC.
101 Montgomery Street, San Francisco CA 94104. 415/627-7000. **Fax:** 415/636-8018. **Recorded jobline:** 415/636-2077. **Contact:** Human Resources. **World Wide Web address:** http://www.schwab.com. **Description:** One of the largest discount brokerage companies in the United States. The firm has more than 200 branches and over 2.5 million active customer accounts. **NOTE:** Resumes may be submitted online. Positions advertised include: Director, Credit Risk Management; Finance Manager; Business Strategy Project Specialist; Technology Consultant; Compliance Analyst. **Special programs:** Internships. **Corporate headquarters location:** This location. **Other U.S. locations:** Nationwide. **International locations:** Worldwide. **Parent company:** Charles Schwab Corporation. **Operations at this facility include:** Administration; Sales; Service. **Listed on:** New York Stock Exchange. **Stock exchange symbol:** SCH. **Number of employees at this location:** 2,200.

CHARTERHOUSE SOFTWARE CORPORATION
2801 Townsgate Road, Suite 139, Westlake Village CA 91361. 805/494-5191. **Fax:** 805/494-8191. **Contact:** Human Resources. **World Wide Web address:** http://www.chsoft.com. **Description:** Manufactures and markets accounting software, sells business forms, and offers related consulting services.

THE CHEESECAKE FACTORY INC.
26950 Agoura Road, Calabasas Hills CA 91301. 818/871-3000. **Fax:** 818/871-3096. **Contact:** Recruiting Department. **E-mail address:** careers@thecheesecakefactory. **World Wide Web address:** http://www.thecheesecakefactory.com. **Description:** The Cheesecake Factory operates a group of restaurants featuring an extensive menu and moderate prices. The company also operates a production facility that manufactures over 50 varieties of its signature cheesecakes and other baked goods for sale both in its restaurants and through wholesale accounts. **Positions advertised include:** Bilingual Injury Counselor; Capital Projects Specialist; director of Interactive Sales; Director Purchasing; Senior Benefits Administrator. **Corporate headquarters location:** This location. **Other area locations:** Statewide. **Other U.S. locations:** Nationwide. **Listed on:** NASDAQ. **Stock exchange symbol:** CAKE.

CHEVRONTEXACO
6001 Bollinger Canyon Road, San Ramon CA 94583. 925/842-1000. **World Wide Web address:** http://www.chevrontexaco.com. **Description:** An international oil firm with operations in more than 90 countries. ChevronTexaco is engaged in worldwide integrated petroleum operations including the exploration and production of crude oil and natural gas reserves; the transportation of crude oil, natural gas, and petroleum products by pipeline, tanker, and motor equipment; the operation of oil-refining complexes; and the wholesale and retail marketing of petroleum products. **NOTE:** Search and apply for positions online. **Positions advertised include:** Research Petrophysicist; Senior Safety and Health Specialist; Information Technology Specialist; Carbon Markets Team Manager. **Special programs:** Internships. **Corporate headquarters location:** This location. **Other U.S. locations:** New Orleans LA; Houston TX. **Operations at this facility include:** Administration. **Listed on:** New York Stock Exchange. **Stock exchange symbol:** CVX. **Number of employees worldwide:** 51,000.

CHEVRONTEXACO
9525 Camino Media, Bakersfield CA 93311-1314. 661/654-7000. **Contact:** Human Resources. **World Wide Web address:** http://www.chevrontexaco.com. **Description:** An international oil firm with operations in more than 90 countries. ChevronTexaco is engaged in worldwide integrated petroleum operations including the exploration and production of crude oil and natural gas reserves; the transportation of crude oil, natural

gas, and petroleum products by pipeline, tanker, and motor equipment; the operation of oil-refining complexes; and the wholesale and retail marketing of petroleum products. **Special programs:** Internships. **NOTE:** Search and apply for positions online. **Positions advertised include:** Coordinator, Operations and Maintenance. **Corporate headquarters location:** San Ramon CA. **Listed on:** New York Stock Exchange. **Stock exchange symbol:** CVX.

CHICAGO TITLE INSURANCE COMPANY
388 Market Street, Suite 1300, San Francisco CA 94111. 415/788-0871. **Fax:** 415/781-4185. **Contact:** Human Resources. **World Wide Web address:** http://www.ctic.com. **Description:** Chicago Title Insurance Company writes title insurance policies and performs other title-related services such as escrow, collection, and trust activities in connection with real estate transactions. Founded in 1848. **NOTE:** To reach Human Resources call: 800/815-3969. **Corporate headquarters location:** Jacksonville FL. **Other U.S. locations:** Nationwide. **Subsidiaries include:** American Title Insurance; Fidelity National Title Insurance Company of New York; Fidelity National Title Insurance Company of Pennsylvania; Fidelity National Title Insurance Company of Texas; Security Title and Guaranty Company. **Parent company:** Fidelity National Financial, Inc. **Operations at this facility include:** This location houses administrative offices. **Listed on:** New York Stock Exchange. **Stock exchange symbol:** FNF. **Annual sales/revenues:** $51 - $100 million. **Number of employees nationwide:** 4,000.

CHIPMAN CORPORATION
1521 Buena Vista Avenue, Alameda CA 94501. 510/748-8700. **Toll-free phone:** 800/755-0661. **Fax:** 510/748-8714. **Contact:** Personnel. **E-mail address:** chipman@chipmancorp.com. **World Wide Web address:** http://www.chipmancorp.com. **Description:** Provides moving and storage services both domestically and internationally. **Corporate headquarters location:** This location. **Other area locations:** Concord CA; Long Beach CA; Sacramento CA; San Jose CA; Valejo CA. **Other U.S. locations:** Portland OR; Seattle WA.

CHIPX
2323 Owen Street, Santa Clara CA 95054. 408/988-2445. **Toll-free phone:** 800/95-CHIPX. **Fax:** 408/988-2449. **Contact:** Human Resources. **E-mail address:** hr@chipx.com. **World Wide Web address:** http://www.chipexpress.com. **Description:** Manufactures semiconductor chips. **NOTE:** Apply online. **Positions advertised include:** ASIC Physical Design Engineer. **Corporate headquarters location:** This location. **International locations:** Haifa, Israel. **Listed on:** Privately held.

CHIRON CORPORATION
4560 Horton Street, Emeryville CA 94608-2916. 510/655-8730. **Fax:** 510/655-9910. **Contact:** Human Resources. **E-mail address:** jobs@chiron.com. **World Wide Web address:** http://www.chiron.com. **Description:** A biotechnology company that operates within three global health care sectors including biopharmaceuticals, blood testing, and vaccines. The company specializes in products designed to prevent and treat cancer, cardiovascular disease, and infectious diseases. **NOTE:** Search and apply for positions online. **Positions advertised include:** Corp Bujsiness Development Director; Clinical QA Auditor; Clinical Director; Manager, Clinical Research; Associate Director, Investor Relations; Associate Director, Engineering. **Corporate headquarters location:** This location. **Other area locations:** Vacaville CA. **Other U.S. locations:** Annandale NJ; Seattle WA. **International locations:** Canada; France; Germany; Italy; Netherlands; United Kingdom. **Subsidiaries include:** IOLAB. **Listed on:** NASDAQ. **Stock exchange symbol:** CHIR. **Number of employees nationwide:** 1,900.

CHOLESTECH CORPORATION
3347 Investment Boulevard, Hayward CA 94545. 510/732-7200. **Fax:** 510/732-7229. **Contact:** Human Resources. **E-mail address:** ctec_hr@cholestech.com. **World Wide Web address:** http://www.cholestech.com. **Description:** Develops and markets diagnostics systems that measure cholesterol. **Positions advertised include:** Assistant Controller; New Products Marketing Manager; Senior Scientist; Quality Control Analyst. **Corporate headquarters location:** This location. **Listed on:** NASDAQ. **Stock exchange symbol:** CTEC.

CHRONTEL, INC.
2210 O'Toole Avenue, Suite 100, San Jose CA 95131. 408/383-9328. **Fax:** 408/383-9338. **Contact:** Human Resources. **E-mail address:** careers@chrontel.com. **World Wide Web address:** http://www.chrontel.com. **Description:** Manufactures computer microchips. **Positions advertised include:** Analog Design Engineer; Applications Engineer; Firmware and System Design Engineer; Algorithm Design Engineer. **Corporate headquarters location:** This location. **Number of employees at this location:** 100.

CHUBB GROUP OF INSURANCE COMPANIES
Two Embarcadero Center, Suite 1500, San Francisco CA 94111. 415/989-3000. **Fax:** 415/397-9575. **Contact:** Human Resources. **World Wide Web address:** http://www.chubb.com. **Description:** A multiple-line property and casualty insurance group that serves the public through independent agents and brokers. **Positions advertised include:** Environmental Underwriter. **Corporate headquarters location:** Warren NJ. **Other area locations:** Fresno CA; Los Angeles CA; Newport Beach CA; Pleasanton CA; Sacramento CA; San Diego CA. **Other U.S. locations:** Nationwide. **International locations:** Worldwide. **Operations at this facility include:** Administration; Sales; Service. **Listed on:** New York Stock Exchange. **Stock exchange symbol:** CB. **Number of employees worldwide:** 12,000.

CHUBB GROUP OF INSURANCE COMPANIES
801 South Figueroa Street, Suite 2400, Los Angeles CA 90017-5556. 213/612-0880. **Fax:** 213/612-5731. **Contact:** Trevor Gandy, Human Resources Manager. **World Wide Web address:** http://www.chubb.com. **Description:** A multiple-line property and casualty insurance group, serving the public through independent agents and brokers. **NOTE:** Entry-level positions are offered. **Positions advertised include:** Account Manager; Property Underwriter. **Special programs:** Internships; Training. **Corporate headquarters location:** Warren NJ. **Other area locations:** Fresno CA; Newport Beach CA; Pleasanton CA; Sacramento CA; San Diego CA; San Francisco CA. **Other U.S. locations:** Nationwide. **International locations:** Worldwide. **Listed on:** New York Stock Exchange. **Stock exchange symbol:** CB. **Number of employees worldwide:** 12,000.

CHULA VISTA, CITY OF
276 Fourth Avenue, Chula Vista CA 91910. 619/691-5096. **Recorded jobline:** 619/691-5095. **Fax:** 619/691-5199. **Contact:** Human Resources. **World Wide Web address:** http://www.chulavistaca.gov. **Description:** Administrative offices for the city of Chula Vista. **NOTE:** Resumes may not be submitted in lieu of a completed city application form. Please call the phone number above to obtain an application. **Positions advertised include:** Code Enforcement Manager; Deputy Ciy Attorney; Energy Services Manager; Human Resources Analyst; Veterinarian. **Special programs:** Internships. **Office hours:** Monday – Friday, 8:00 a.m. – 5:00 p.m. **Operations at this facility include:** Administration. **Number of employees at this location:** 800.

CIBER ENTERPRISE SOLUTIONS
1010 Battery Street, San Francisco CA 94111. 415/875-1800. **Fax:** 415/875-1801. **Contact:** Employment Administrator. **E-mail address:** recruitingsf@ciber.com. **World Wide Web address:** http://www.ciber.com. **Description:** A leading software-consulting firm serving clients in a variety of industries. The company is engaged in the implementation of HRMS, financial, distribution, manufacturing, and student systems. **Positions advertised include:** Implementation Consultant. **Corporate headquarters location:** Greenwood Village CO. **Other U.S. locations:** Chicago IL; Philadelphia PA; Dallas TX. **Parent company:** CIBER, Inc. **Listed on:** New York Stock Exchange. **Stock exchange symbol:** CBR. **Number of employees at this location:** 220.

CIRRUS LOGIC, INC.
46831 Lakeview Boulevard, Fremont CA 94538. 510/623-8300. **Contact:** Employment Manager. **World Wide Web address:** http://www.cirrus.com. **Description:** Develops innovative architectures for analog and digital systems functions and implements these architectures in very large scale integrated (VLSI) circuits for applications that include mass storage, user interface (graphics, audio, and video), communications, and data acquisition. **Positions advertised include:** Senior Digital IC Design Engineer. **Corporate headquarters location:** Austin TX. **Other U.S. locations:** Broomfield CO; Boulder CO; Boca Raton FL; Fort Wayne IN; Nashua NH. **International locations:** England; Hong Kong; Japan. **Operations at this facility include:** Administration; Divisional Headquarters; Manufacturing; Research and Development; Sales. **Listed on:** NASDAQ. **Stock exchange symbol:** CRUS. **Annual sales/revenues:** $196 million. **Number of employees worldwide:** 767.

CISCO SYSTEMS, INC.
P.O. Box 640730, San Jose 95164. 408/526-4000. **Physical address:** 170 West Tasman Drive, San Jose CA 95134. **Fax:** 800/818-9201. **Contact:** Human Resources. **E-mail address:** apply@cisco.com. **World Wide Web address:** http://www.cisco.com. **Description:** Develops, manufactures, markets, and supports high-performance internetworking systems that enable customers to build large-scale integrated computer networks. The company's products connect and manage communications among local and wide area networks that employ a variety of protocols, media interfaces, network topologies, and cable systems. **Positions advertised include:** Product Manager; Software Engineer; IT Analyst; Technical Leader; Commodity Manager; Network Consulting Engineer. **Special programs:** Internships; Co-ops. **Corporate headquarters location:** This location. **International locations:** Worldwide. **Listed on:** NASDAQ. **Stock exchange symbol:** CSCO. **Number of employees nationwide:** 15,000. **Number of employees worldwide:** 34,000.

CITIBANK
135 Main Street, San Francisco CA 94105. 415/904-1100. **Contact:** Human Resources. **World Wide Web address:** http://www.citibank.com. **Description:** A bank providing a full range of financial services. **Corporate headquarters location:** New York NY. **Parent company:** Citigroup. **Listed on:** New York Stock Exchange. **Stock exchange symbol:** C. **Annual sales/revenues:** $45.8 billion.

CITICORP
CITIBANK
One Sansome Street, San Francisco CA 94104-4448. 415/627-6000. **Recorded jobline:** 415/658-4562. **Contact:** Human Resources Department. **World Wide Web address:** http://www.citybank.com. **Description:** Provides investment and financial services to individuals, businesses, governments, and financial institutions in approximately 3,000 locations. **NOTE:** Candidates may apply via the company's online system. **Positions advertised include:** Regional Sales Manager; Accountant; Client Financial Analyst; Financial Associate; Systems Administrator. **Corporate headquarters location:** New York NY. **Parent company:** Citigroup. **Operations at this facility include:** Administration; Regional Headquarters; Sales; Service. **Listed on:** New York Stock Exchange. **Stock exchange symbol:** CIH-A. **Number of employees worldwide:** 85,000.

CITIGATE CUNNINGHAM
1530 Page Mill Road, Palo Alto CA 94304. 650/858-3700. **Fax:** 650/858-3702. **Contact:** Human Resources. **E-mail address:** careers@cunningham.com. **World Wide Web address:** http://www.cunningham.com. **Description:** A public relations agency specializing in the high-tech industry. **NOTE:** Interested candidates may also submit a general application online. **Position advertised include:** Manager; Senior Associate. **Corporate headquarters location:** This location. **Other area locations:** San Francisco CA. **Other U.S. locations:** Cambridge MA; Austin TX; Washington DC; Miami FL. **Parent company:** Incepta Group plc. **Operations at this facility include:** Administration; Service. **Listed on:** Privately held. **Number of employees at this location:** 55.

CITY CHEVROLET/GEO/VOLKSWAGEN
P.O. Box 85345, San Diego CA 92186. 619/276-6171. **Physical address:** 2111 Morena Boulevard, San Diego CA 92110. **Fax:** 619/276-6194. **Contact:** John Nieman, General Manager. **World Wide Web address:** http://www.city-chevrolet.com. **Description:** Sells new and used automobiles. **Corporate headquarters location:** This location.

CITY NATIONAL BANK
400 North Roxbury Drive, Beverly Hills CA 90210. 213/553-8272. **Contact:** Human Resources. **E-mail address:** careers@cnb.com. **World Wide Web address:** http://www.cnb.com. **Description:** A commercial bank with 50 offices in Northern and Southern California. **NOTE:** Interested candidates should apply online. To contact Human Resources directly call: 213/553-8272. **Positions advertised include:** Branch Manager; Client Services Manager; Client Services Representative; Commercial Lender; Financial Sales Officer; Mortgage Loan Representative. **Corporate headquarters location:** This location. **Other area locations:** Statewide. **Listed on:** New York Stock Exchange. **Stock exchange symbol:** CYN.

CITY NATIONAL BANK
11 Golden Shore, Long Beach CA 90802. 562/624-8600. **Contact:** Human Resources. **E-mail address:** careers@cnb.com. **World Wide Web address:** http://www.cnb.com. **Description:** A commercial bank with 50 offices in Northern and Southern California. **NOTE:** Interested candidates should apply online. To contact Human Resources directly call: 213/553-8272. **Corporate headquarters location:** Beverly Hills CA. **Other area locations:** Statewide. **Listed on:** New York Stock Exchange. **Stock exchange symbol:** CYN.

CITY NATIONAL BANK
2101 Webster Street, 14th Floor, Oakland CA 94612. 510/287-3140. **Contact:** Human Resources. **E-mail address:** careers@cnb.com. **World Wide Web address:** http://www.cnb.com. **Description:** A commercial bank with 50 offices in Northern and Southern California. **NOTE:** Apply online. To contact Human Resources directly call:

213/553-8272. **Corporate headquarters location:** Beverly Hills CA. **Other area locations:** Statewide. **Listed on:** New York Stock Exchange. **Stock exchange symbol:** CYN. **Number of employees at this location:** 115.

CITY OF HOPE NATIONAL MEDICAL CENTER
1500 East Duarte Road, Duarte CA 91010. 626/359-8111. **Toll-free phone:** 800/423-7119. **Fax:** 626/256-8601. **Recorded jobline:** 626/301-8200. **Contact:** Human Resources. **E-mail address:** jobs@coh.org. **World Wide Web address:** http://www.cityofhope.org. **Description:** A medical center that incorporates treatment for AIDS, cancer, and diabetes with counseling and helps pay patient expenses based on need. **NOTE:** Search and apply for positions online. **Positions advertised include:** Research Associate; Flow Cytometry Technologist; Clinical Trials Monitor; Occupational Therapist. **Corporate headquarters location:** This location. **Other area locations:** Irvine CA; Palm Desert CA; San Diego CA; San Francisco CA. **Other U.S. locations:** AZ; FL; GA; IL; MI; MN; NV; NY; PA; WA.

CLA-VAL COMPANY
P.O. Box 1325, Newport Beach CA 92659-0325. 949/722-4800. **Physical address:** 1701 Placentia Avenue, Costa Mesa CA 92627. **Toll-free phone:** 800/942-6326. **Fax:** 949/548-5441. **Contact:** Personnel Director. **E-mail address:** claval@cla-val.com. **World Wide Web address:** http://www.cla-val.com. **Description:** Manufactures automatic control valves used in fire protection systems, navy ship systems, farm irrigation equipment, and industrial fluid-handling systems. **Corporate headquarters location:** This location. **International locations:** Canada; England; France; Switzerland.

THE CLARK CONSTRUCTION GROUP, INC.
7677 Oakport Street, Suite 1040, Oakland CA 94621. 510/430-1700. **Fax:** 510/430-1705. **Contact:** Human Resources. **E-mail address:** hr@clarkconstruction.com. **World Wide Web address:** http://www.clarkus.com. **Description:** One of the nation's leading general contractors. Construction and renovation projects include sports facilities, civic centers, hotels, educational facilities, laboratories, and office buildings. **NOTE:** Resumes may be submitted via e-mail, mail, or fax. Address resumes to: Human Resources, The Clark Construction Group, Inc., P.O. Box 5937, Bethesda MD 20814. Fax: 301/272-8414. **Positions advertised include:** Project Manager; Superintendent; Field Engineer; Office Engineer. **Corporate headquarters location:** Bethesda MD. **Other area locations:** Costa Mesa CA. **Other U.S. locations:** Nationwide.

CLAYTON INDUSTRIES
4213 North Temple City Boulevard, P.O. Box 5530, El Monte CA 91734-1530. 626/443-9381. **Fax:** 626/442-1701. **Contact:** Human Resources. **World Wide Web address:** http://www.claytonindustries.com. **Description:** Manufactures a broad range of industrial and automotive equipment for a variety of commercial and government customers. Products include steam generators, dynamometers, and a number of automotive diagnostic components. **Special programs:** Internships. **Corporate headquarters location:** This location. **Other U.S. locations:** Nationwide. **International locations:** Worldwide. **Operations at this facility include:** Administration; Manufacturing; Research and Development; Sales; Service. **Listed on:** Privately held. **Number of employees at this location:** 135.

THE CLOROX COMPANY
P.O. Box 24305, Oakland CA 94623-1305. 510/271-7000. **Physical address:** 1221 Broadway, Oakland CA 94612. **Contact:** Corporate Staffing. **E-mail address:** cloroxjob@clorox.com. **World Wide Web address:** http://www.thecloroxcompany.com. **Description:** Clorox, a *Fortune* 500 company, is an international manufacturer and marketer of consumer food and cleaning products. Brand names include Clorox, 409, Hidden Valley Ranch, and KC Masterpiece. **NOTE:** Resumes may be submitted via mail or e-mail. **Positions advertised include:** Sr. Business Analyst; Business Systems Architect; Sr. Procurement Manager; Security Engineer; Metrics and Process Lead. **Corporate headquarters location:** This location. **Operations at this facility include:** This location houses the executive offices. **Listed on:** New York Stock Exchange. **Listed on:** New York Stock Exchange. **Stock exchange symbol:** CLX.

THE CLOROX TECHNICAL CENTER
P.O. Box 493, Pleasanton CA 94566. 925/425-6100. **Physical address:** 7200 Johnson Drive, Pleasanton CA 94888. **Contact:** Human Resources. **E-mail address:** cloroxjob@clorox.com. **World Wide Web address:** http://www.clorox.com. **Description:** Conducts research and development for The Clorox Company, which manufactures and markets a variety of consumer food and cleaning products including Clorox bleach, 409 cleaner, Hidden Valley Ranch salad dressings, and KC Masterpiece barbecue sauce. **NOTE:** Search and apply for positions online. **Positions advertised incude:** Sr. Scientist Materials Product Development; Mechancial Engineer; Project Manager; Research Associate; Sr. Scientist. **Office hours:** Monday - Friday, 8:00 a.m. - 4:30 p.m. **Corporate headquarters location:** Oakland CA. **Parent company:** The Clorox Company. **Listed on:** New York Stock Exchange. **Stock exchange symbol:** CLX.

CNET NETWORKS, INC.
235 Second Street, San Francisco CA 94105. 415/344-2000. **Contact:** Human Resources. **E-mail address:** careers@cnet.com. **World Wide Web address:** http://www.cnet.com. **Description:** A new media company that provides services and information related to computers and technology. Products and services include technology-related Internet sites, television shows, radio shows, and comparison shopping. **Positions advertised include:** Account Coordinator; Account Executive; Associate Data Producer; Associate Designer; Associate Editor; Director Sales Programs; Director of Global Marketing Communications; Executive Editor. **Special programs:** Internships. **Corporate headquarters location:** This location. **Listed on:** NASDAQ. **Stock exchange symbol:** CNET.

THE COAST DISTRIBUTION SYSTEM
350 Woodview Avenue, Morgan Hill CA 95037. 408/782-6686. **Contact:** Human Resources. **World Wide Web address:** http://www.coastdist.com. **Description:** One of North America's largest distributors of parts and accessories to the recreational vehicle and boating industries. Products include awnings, electrical and plumbing items, towing equipment and hitches, appliances, marine electronics and safety equipment, and various accessories and consumables. The company distributes its products to an active customer base of over 15,000 retailers through 19 distribution centers located throughout the United States and Canada. **Corporate headquarters location:** This location.

COAST FOUNDRY AND MANUFACTURING COMPANY
2707 North Garey Avenue, Pomona CA 91767. 909/596-1883. **Fax:** 909/596-2650. **Contact:** Human Resources. **Description:** A manufacturer of plumbing supplies. **Corporate headquarters location:** This location. **Number of employees at this location:** 300.

COGNEX CORPORATION
1001 Rengstorff Avenue, Mountain View CA 94043. 650/969-4812. **Contact:** Human Resources. **E-mail address:** human.resources@cognex.com. **World Wide Web address:** http://www.cognex.com. **Description:** Cognex Corporation designs, develops, manufactures, and markets machine vision systems used to automate a wide range of manufacturing processes. Machine vision systems are used in the electronics, semiconductor, pharmaceutical, health care, aerospace, automotive, packaging, and graphic arts industries to gauge, guide, inspect, and identify products in manufacturing operations. **NOTE:** Interested candidates may search and apply for positions online. **Corporate headquarters location:** Natick MA. **Other U.S. locations:** IL, MI, OR, PA, TX, WI. **International locations:** France; Germany; Japan; Singapore; United Kingdom. **Operations at this facility include:** This location is the West Coast regional technology center. **Listed on:** NASDAQ. **Stock exchange symbol:** CGNX.

COHERENT INC.
2303 Lindbergh Street, Auburn CA 95602. 530/823-9550. **Contact:** Human Resources. **World Wide Web address:** http://www.cohr.com. **Description:** the company produces laser-related instruments for a variety of applications. Founded in 1966. **NOTE:** Search and apply for positions online. **Positions advertised include:** Production Control Manager; Production Planner; Sr. Coater Tech. **Corporate headquarters location:** Santa Clara CA. **Other area locations:** Pleasanton CA. **Operations at this facility include:** This location is a supplier of optics, diodes, and laser instrumentation. **Listed on:** NASDAQ. **Stock exchange symbol:** COHR.

COHU, INC.
P.O. Box 85623, San Diego CA 92186. 858/277-6700. **Physical address:** 3912 Calle Fortunada, San Diego CA 92123-1827. **Fax:** 858/514-6297. **Contact:** Human Resources. **E-mail address:** hr@cohu.com (no attachments, please). **World Wide Web address:** http://www.cohu-cameras.com. **Description:** Supplies television camera equipment for use in such fields as area surveillance, teleconferencing, and industrial process control. **Corporate headquarters location:** This location. **Listed on:** NASDAQ. **Stock exchange symbol:** COHU.

COLDWELL BANKER
27271 Las Ramblas, Mission Viejo CA 92691. 949/367-1800. **Contact:** Human Resources. **World Wide Web address:** http://www.coldwellbanker.com. **Description:** A full-service real estate company focusing on commercial and residential real estate, as well as luxury home and resort sales. **Corporate headquarters location:** Parsippany NJ. **Other U.S. locations:** Nationwide. **International locations:** Canada. **Parent company:** Cendant Corporation. **Listed on:** New York Stock Exchange. **Stock exchange symbol:** CD.

COLDWELL BANKER
2633 Ocean Avenue, San Francisco CA 94132. 415/338-0100. **Contact:** Human Resources. **World Wide Web address:** http://www.coldwellbanker.com. **Description:** One of the largest residential real estate companies in the United States and Canada. **Corporate headquarters location:** Parsippany NJ. **Parent company:** Cendant Corporation. **Listed on:** New York Stock Exchange. **Stock exchange symbol:** CD.

COLDWELL BANKER
350 Bon Aire Center, Suite 100, Greenbrae CA 94904. 415/461-3220. **Contact:** Human Resources. **World Wide Web address:** http://www.coldwellbanker.com. **Description:** One of the largest residential real estate companies in the United States and Canada. **Corporate headquarters location:** Parsippany NJ. **Parent company:** Cendant Corporation. **Listed on:** New York Stock Exchange. **Stock exchange symbol:** CD.

COLLEGE OF THE DESERT
43500 Monterey Avenue, Palm Desert CA 92260-2412. 760/773-2529. **Fax:** 760/773-5877. **Contact:** Human Resources. **E-mail address:** humanresources@collegeofthedesert.edu. **World Wide Web address:** http://www.collegeofthedesert.edu. **Description:** A community college offering degrees in over 70 majors. **Positions advertised include:** Dean, Communications; Dean, Social Science & Arts; Instructor, Various Departments; Part-time Instructor, Various Departments.

COLOR FACTORY, INC.
11312 Penrose Street, Sun Valley CA 91352. 818/767-2889. **Fax:** 818/767-4062. **Contact:** Brian Smith, Human Resources Director. **E-mail address:** bsmith@colorfactoryla.com. **World Wide Web address:** http://www.colorfactoryla.com. **Description:** Develops, formulates, and manufactures a wide range of color cosmetics and other personal care products for customers that market the products under their own brand names. **Subsidiaries include:** Arnold Zegarelli Products, Inc. manufactures and distributes a line of hair care products. **Corporate headquarters location:** This location.

COMCAST SPOTLIGHT
120 Del Rey Gardens Drive, Del Rey Oaks CA 93940. 831/899-7100. **Fax:** 831/393-8382. **Contact:** Human Resources. **World Wide Web address:** http://www.cableistv.com. **Description:** Provides cable television advertising services. **Positions advertised include:** Account Representative.

COMERICA BANK CALIFORNIA
333 West Santa Clara Street, Mail Code 4805, San Jose CA 95113. 408/556-5000. **Toll-free phone:** 800/522-2265. **Contact:** Human Resources. **World Wide Web address:** http://www.comerica.com. **Description:** A bank with more than 30 offices across the state. **Positions advertised include:** Branch Manager; Branch Officer; Corporate Banking Officer; Credit Analyst; Group Manager. **Corporate headquarters location:** Detroit MI. **Other area locations:** Statewide. **Other U.S. locations:** FL; IL; MI; TX. **Parent company:** Comerica, Inc. (Detroit MI) is a bank holding company. The company offers a wide range of financial products and services for businesses and individuals through more than 400 offices nationwide. The five core business markets Comerica covers are corporate banking, consumer banking, private banking, institutional trust and investment management, and international finance and trade services. Including its subsidiaries, Comerica has operations in 16 states and two Canadian provinces. **Listed on:** New York Stock Exchange. **Stock exchange symbol:** CMA. **Number of employees at this location:** 1,000. **Number of employees nationwide:** 14,000.

COMERICA, INC.
9920 South La Cienega Boulevard, Suite 604, Inglewood CA 90301. 310/417-5600. **Contact:** Vice President. **World Wide Web address:** http://www.comerica.com. **Description:** A multistate financial services provider. **Corporate headquarters location:** Detroit MI. **Listed on:** New York Stock Exchange. **Stock exchange symbol:** CMA.

COMMERCE CASINO
6131 East Telegraph Road, Commerce CA 90040. 323/38-3351. **Fax:** 323/838-3475. **Recorded jobline:** 323/838-3399. **Contact:** Human Resources. **World Wide Web address:** http://www.commercecasino.com. **Description:** A casino that hosts poker tournaments and offers a variety of gaming facilities. **NOTE:** Please apply in person. **Positions advertised include:** Banquet Captain; Bartender; Cashier; Cook; Food Server; Houseperson; Lead Cook; Pan Dealer; Security Advisor; Security Officer; Steward; Station Attendant; Stock Clerk; Surveillance Clerk.

COMMONWEALTH FINANCIAL CORPORATION
524 Escondido Avenue, Vista CA 92084. 760/945-9891. **Toll-free phone:** 800/780-4560. **Fax:** 760/945-4991. **Contact:** Human Resources. **E-mail address:** info@cfchomeloan.com. **World Wide Web address:** http://www.cfchomeloan.com. **Description:** Provides a wide range of mortgages, home loans, and debt consolidation services. **Corporate headquarters location:** This location.

COMMUNICATION INTELLIGENCE CORPORATION (CIC)
275 Shoreline Drive, Suite 500, Redwood Shores CA 94065. 650/802-7888. **Fax:** 650/802-7777. **Contact:** Human Resources Department. **E-mail address:** jobs@cic.com. **World Wide Web address:** http://www.cic.com. **Description:** Develops, markets, and licenses handwriting recognition and related technologies for the emerging pen-based computer market. The company has created a natural input recognition system that allows a computer to recognize hand-printed character input. **Positions advertised include:** SW Applications Engineer. **Corporate headquarters location:** This location. **International locations:** China. **Listed on:** NASDAQ. **Stock exchange symbol:** CICI.

COMMUNICATIONS & POWER INDUSTRIES (CPI)
811 Hansen Way, Mail Stop B-150, P.O. Box 51625, Palo Alto CA 94303. 650/846-3700. **Fax:** 650/846-3391. **Contact:** Human Resources. **E-mail address:** hr@cpii.com. **World Wide Web address:** http://www.cpii.com/satcom. **Description:** CPI is engaged in the research, development, manufacture, and marketing of various products and services in the fields of communications, industrial equipment, medicine, and scientific research. **Positions advertised include:** Digital Design Engineer. **Corporate headquarters location:** This location. **Other U.S. locations:** Nationwide. **International locations:** Worldwide. **Operations at this facility include:** This location manufactures satellite communications equipment.

COMMUNITY BANK
505 East Colorado Boulevard, Pasadena CA 91101. 626/568-2265. **Toll-free phone:** 800/788-9999. **Fax:** 626/568-2217. **Contact:** Human Resources. **E-mail address:** cbjobs@cbank.com. **World Wide Web address:** http://www.communitybank-ca.com. **Description:** A commercial bank. **NOTE:** Candidates are strongly encouraged to apply online. **Positions advertised include:** International Trade Manager; RE Portfolio Banker. **Corporate headquarters location:** This location. **Other area locations:** Anaheim CA; Burbank CA; City of Industry CA; Corona CA; Fontana CA; Glendale CA; Huntington Park CA; Inland CA; Irvine CA; Redlands CA; San Bernardino CA; South Bay CA; Upland CA; Yucaipa CA. **Number of employees at this location:** 370.

COMMUNITY HOSPITAL OF SAN BERNARDINO
1805 Medical Center Drive, San Bernardino CA 92411. 909/887-6333. **Recorded jobline:** 909/806-1870. **Fax:** 909/887-6814. **Contact:** Human Resources. **E-mail address:** brehome@chw.edu. **World Wide Web address:** http://www.chsb.org. **Description:** A nonprofit, 321-bed community hospital whose facilities include a convalescent home and rehabilitation center. Founded in 1908. **Positions advertised include:** RN, Various Departments; Repiratory Therapist; Case Manager; Pharmacist. **Office hours:** Monday – Friday, 8:00 a.m. – 5:00 p.m. **Parent company:** Catholic Healthcare West. **Number of employees at this location:** 1,600.

COMMUNITY MEDICAL CENTERS
1925 East Dakota Avenue, Fresno CA 93726. 559/459-1919. **Fax:** 559/459-1594. **Contact:** Human Resources. **World Wide Web address:** http://www.communitymedical.org. **Description:** A nonprofit medical system with several acute care hospitals, long-term care facilities, and a variety of home care services. Specialties include cancer, cardiology, emergency services, rehabilitation, and family birthing centers. **NOTE:** Candidates may apply via mail, fax, or online. Submit a resume or application to: Human Resources, 1925 East Dakota Avenue, Suite 110, Fresno CA 93726. To obtain an application call: 559/459-1919. **Positions advertised include:** Anesthesia Technician; Cardiovascular Radiologic Technologist; Case Manager; Clinical Coordinator; Clinical Nurse Specialist; Cytotechnologist; Licensed Vocational Nurse; Medical Technologist; Occupational Therapist; Registered Nurse; Pharmacist; Sonographer; Respiratory Care Practitioner. **Corporate headquarters location:** This location. **Other U.S. locations:** Clovis CA. **Number of employees at this location:** 4,200.

COMPUTER ASSOCIATES INTERNATIONAL, INC.
10180 Telesis Court, San Diego CA 92121. 858/452-0170. **Contact:** Personnel. **World Wide Web address:** http://www.ca.com. **Description:** Computer Associates International is one of the world's leading developers of client/server and distributed computing software. The company develops, markets, and supports enterprise management, database and applications development, business applications, and consumer software products for a broad range of mainframe, midrange, and desktop computers. Computer Associates International serves major business, government, research, and educational organizations. Founded in 1976. **NOTE:** CAI prefers that candidates submit a resume via their online resume builder. Resumes may also be submitted to: Human Resource Recruitment, Computer Associates International, Inc., One Computer Associates Plaza, Islandia NY 11749. **Positions advertised include:** Software Engineer; Senior Technology Specialist. **Corporate headquarters location:** Islandia NY. **Other U.S. locations:** Nationwide. **International locations:** Worldwide. **Operations at this facility include:** This location develops software. **Listed on:** New York Stock Exchange. **Stock exchange symbol:** CA. **Annual sales/revenues:** $3.12 billion. **Number of employees nationwide:** 5,000. **Number of employees worldwide:** Over 15,000.

COMPUTER ASSOCIATES INTERNATIONAL, INC.
2040 Main Street, Irvine CA 92614. 949/797-2750. **Contact:** Human Resources. **World Wide Web address:** http://www.ca.com. **Description:** Computer Associates International is one of the world's leading developers of client/server and distributed computing software. The company develops, markets, and supports enterprise management, database and applications development, business applications, and consumer software products for a broad range of mainframe, midrange, and desktop computers. Computer Associates International serves major business, government, research, and educational organizations. Founded in 1976. **NOTE:** CAI prefers that candidates submit a resume via their online resume builder. Resumes may also be submitted to: Human Resource Recruitment, Computer Associates International, Inc., One Computer Associates Plaza, Islandia NY 11749. **Positions advertised include:** Senior Consultant; Services Partner Advocate; PMO Consultant; Sales Executive. **Corporate headquarters location:** Islandia NY. **Other U.S. locations:** Nationwide. **International locations:** Worldwide. **Operations at this facility include:** This location is a sales office. **Listed on:** New York Stock Exchange. **Stock exchange symbol:** CA. **Annual sales/revenues:** $3.12 billion. **Number of employees worldwide:** Over 15,000.

COMPUTER ASSOCIATES INTERNATIONAL, INC.
8511 Fallbrook Avenue, Suite 200, West Hills CA 91304. 818/593-0300. **Contact:** Human Resources. **World Wide Web address:** http://www.ca.com. **Description:** One of the world's leading developers of client/server and distributed computing software. The company develops, markets, and supports enterprise management, database and applications development, business applications, and consumer software products for a broad range of mainframe, midrange, and desktop computers. Computer Associates International serves major business, government, research, and educational organizations. **NOTE:** CAI prefers that candidates submit a resume via their online resume builder. Resumes may also be submitted to: Human Resource Recruitment, Computer Associates International, Inc., One Computer Associates Plaza, Islandia NY 11749. **Corporate headquarters location:** Islandia NY. **Other U.S. locations:** Nationwide. **International locations:** Worldwide. **Listed on:** New York Stock Exchange. **Stock exchange symbol:** CA. **Number of employees nationwide:** 5,000. **Number of employees worldwide:** Over 15,000.

COMPUTER ASSOCIATES INTERNATIONAL, INC.
550 South Winchester Boulevard, San Jose CA 95128. 408/878-7400. **Contact:** Human Resources. **World Wide Web address:** http://www.ca.com. **Description:** Computer Associates International is one of the world's leading developers of client/server and distributed computing software. The company develops, markets, and supports enterprise management, database and applications development, business applications, and consumer software products for a broad range of mainframe, midrange, and desktop computers. Computer Associates International serves major business, government, research, and educational organizations. Founded in 1976. **NOTE:** CAI prefers that candidates submit a resume via their online resume builder. Resumes may also be submitted to: Human Resource Recruitment, Computer Associates International, Inc., One Computer Associates Plaza, Islandia NY 11749. **Positions advertised include:** Senior Alliance Manager; Software Engineer; Product Management Director. **Corporate headquarters location:** Islandia NY. **Other U.S. locations:** Nationwide. **Operations at this facility include:** This location is engaged in the sale, research, and development of software. **Listed on:** New York Stock Exchange. **Stock exchange symbol:** CA. **Annual sales/revenues:** $3.12 billion. **Number of employees worldwide:** Over 15,000.

COMPUTER HORIZONS CORPORATION
1411 West 190th Street, Suite 470, Gardena CA 90248-4324. 310/771-0770. **Toll-free phone:** 800/711-2421. **Fax:** 310/771-0777. **Contact:** Human Resources. **World Wide Web address:** http://www.computerhorizons.com. **Description:** A full-service technology solutions company offering contract staffing, outsourcing, re-engineering, data migration, downsizing support, and network management. The company has a worldwide network of 43 offices. Founded in 1969. **Corporate headquarters location:** Mountain Lakes NJ. **International locations:** Canada; England. **Listed on:** NASDAQ. **Stock exchange symbol:** CHRZ.

COMPUTER HORIZONS CORPORATION
350 Sansome Street, Suite 810, San Francisco CA 94104. 415/434-2424. **Toll-free phone:** 800/475-7779. **Fax:** 415/434-2650. **Contact:** Human Resources. **World Wide Web address:** http://www.computerhorizons.com. **Description:** A full-service technology solutions company offering contract staffing, outsourcing, re-engineering, migration, downsizing support, and network management. The company has a worldwide network of 43 offices. Founded in 1969. **Corporate headquarters location:** Mountain Lakes NJ. **Other U.S. locations:** Nationwide. **International locations:** Canada; England. **Listed on:** NASDAQ. **Stock exchange symbol:** CHRZ.

COMPUTER SCIENCES CORPORATION
2100 East Grand Avenue, El Segundo CA 90245. 310/615-0311. **Fax:** 310/322-9768. **Contact:** Human Resources. **World Wide Web address:** http://www.csc.com. **Description:** Computer Sciences Corporation helps clients in industry and government use information technology to achieve strategic and operational objectives. The company tailors solutions from a broad suite of integrated service and technology offerings including e-business strategies and technologies; management and IT consulting; systems development and integration; application software; and IT and business process outsourcing. **NOTE:** Candidates are encouraged to apply online. **Positions advertised include:** Finance Manager; Communications Specialist; Network Engineer; Procurement Specialist; Logistics Manager; Compensation Manager. **Corporate headquarters location:** This location. **International locations:** Canada; Germany; Japan; The Netherlands; Saudi Arabia; South Korea; Spain; United Kingdom. **Operations at this facility include:** This location primarily serves the U.S. government. **Listed on:** New York Stock Exchange. **Stock exchange symbol:** CSC. **Number of employees nationwide:** 20,000. **Number of employees worldwide:** 90,000.

COMPUTER SCIENCES CORPORATION
4045 Hancock Street, San Diego CA 92110-5164. 619/225-8401. **Contact:** Human Resources. **World Wide Web address:** http://www.csc.com. **Description:** Computer Sciences Corporation is comprised of four sectors: the Systems Group Division designs, engineers, and integrates computer-based systems and communications systems, providing all of the hardware, software, training, and related elements necessary to operate such a system; the Consulting Division includes consulting and technical services in the development of computer and communication systems to nonfederal organizations; the Industry Services Group provides service to the health care, insurance, and financial services industries, as well as providing large-scale claim processing and other insurance-related services; CSC Health Care markets business systems and services to the managed health care industry, clinics, and physicians; CSC Enterprises provides consumer credit reports and account management services to credit grantors. **NOTE:** Candidates are encouraged to apply online. **Positions advertised include:** Service Delivery Manager; Application Developer; Business Analyst; Performance Engineer; Network Engineer. **Corporate headquarters location:** El Segundo CA. **International locations:** Canada; Germany; Japan; the Netherlands; Saudi Arabia; South Korea; Spain; United Kingdom. **Operations at this facility include:** This location is engaged in research and development for the U.S. Navy. **Listed on:** New York Stock Exchange. **Stock exchange symbol:** CSC. **Number of employees nationwide:** 20,000. **Number of employees worldwide:** 90,000.

COMPUWARE CORPORATION
1300 Clay Street, Suite 700, Oakland CA 94612. 510/251-8900. **Fax:** 510/2351-8950. **Contact:** Corporate Recruiting. **E-mail address:** compuware.recruiting@compuware.com. **World Wide Web address:** http://www.compuware.com. **Description:** Develops, markets, and supports an integrated line of systems software products that improve the productivity of

programmers and analysts in application program testing, test data preparation, error analysis, and maintenance. Compuware also provides a broad range of professional data processing services including business systems analysis, design, and programming, as well as systems planning and consulting. **NOTE:** Resumes may be submitted online, or by mail or fax. Address resumes to: Corporate Recruiting, Compuware Corporation, One Camous Martius, Detroit MI 48226. Fax: 877/873-6784. **Positions advertised include:** Software Sales Manager; Regional Products Director; Pre-Sales Support Engineer. **Corporate headquarters location:** Detroit MI. **Other area locations:** Irvine CA; Los Angeles CA; San Diego CA. **Other U.S. locations:** Denver CO; St. Louis MO; Cincinnati OH; Cleveland OH; Columbus OH; Nashville TN; McLean VA; Milwaukee WI. **International locations:** Canada; South Africa; United Kingdom. **Listed on:** NASDAQ. **Stock exchange symbol:** CPWR.

COMSYS
2020 Main Street, Suite 150, Irvine CA 94614. 949/885-0220. **Fax:** 949/885-0244. **Contact:** Human Resources. **World Wide Web address:** http://www.comsys.com. **Description:** A computer consulting and contracting firm that provides outsourcing, project support, vendor management, and other specialty services. Founded in 1969. **NOTE:** Search and apply for positions online. **Corporate headquarters location:** Houston TX. **Other area locations:** Folsom CA; San Francisco CA; Campbell CA. **Other U.S. locations:** Nationwide.

CONAGRA FOOD INGREDIENTS COMPANY
1350 Pacheco Pass Highway, Gilroy CA 95020. 408/846-3200. 800/289-5060. **Fax:** 408/846-3200. **Contact:** Toni Rivera, Personnel Manager. **E-mail address:** Toni.Rivera@ConAgraFoods.com. **World Wide Web address:** http://www.conagrafoods.com. **Description:** A dehydrator of vegetable products. Founded in 1959. **NOTE:** Second and third shifts are offered. Search and apply for positions online. **Special programs:** Internships; Summer Jobs. **Parent company:** ConAgra, Inc. **Operations at this facility include:** Divisional Headquarters. **Listed on:** New York Stock Exchange. **Stock exchange symbol:** CAG. **President:** Randy Tognazzini. **Annual sales/revenues:** More than $100 million. **Number of employees nationwide:** 2,000.

CONAGRA FOODS RETAIL PRODUCTS COMPANY
3353 Michaelson Drive, Irvine CA 92612. 949/437-1000. **Contact:** Human Resources. **World Wide Web address:** http://www.hunt-wesson.com. **Description:** Provider of consumer foods. **NOTE:** Search and apply for positions online. **Positions advertised include:** Product Development Leader; Recruiting Manager; Packaging Director. **Parent company:** ConAgra, Inc. **Operations at this facility include:** This is the corporate office of the Grocery Foods Group. **Listed on:** New York Stock Exchange. **Stock exchange symbol:** CAG.

CONEXANT SYSTEMS INC.
4000 Macarthur Boulevard, Newport Beach CA 92660. 949/483-4600. **Fax:** 949/483-4078. **Contact:** Personnel. **World Wide Web address:** http://www.conexant.com. **Description:** Conexant provides products for the printing, military, and aerospace industries through its electronics, automotive, and graphics divisions. Products include military and commercial communication equipment, guidance systems, electronics, components for automobiles, and printing presses. **Positions advertised include:** Mixed Signal Test Engineer; Administrative Assistant. **Corporate headquarters location:** This location. **Other U.S. locations:** Red Bank NJ; Palm Bay FL; Austin TX. **Operations at this facility include:** This location manufactures modem chips and semiconductors. **Listed on:** NASDAQ. **Stock exchange symbol:** CNXT.

CONEXANT SYSTEMS INC.
3600 Pruneridge Avenue, Suite 100, Santa Clara CA 95051. 408/551-0270. **Fax:** 408/249-7113. **Contact:** Personnel. **World Wide Web address:** http://www.conexant.com. **Description:** Provides products for the printing, military, automotive, and aerospace industries through its electronics, automotive, and graphics divisions. Products include military and commercial communications equipment, guidance systems, electronics, components for automobiles, and printing presses. **Corporate headquarters location:** Newport Beach CA. **Other U.S. locations:** Red Bank NJ; Palm Bay FL; Austin TX. **Listed on:** NASDAQ. **Stock exchange symbol:** CNXT.

CONEXANT SYSTEMS INC.
9868 Scranton Road, Suite 1000, San Diego CA 92121. 858/713-3200. **Fax:** 858/713-4008. **Contact:** Human Resources. **World Wide Web address:** http://www.conexant.com. **Description:** Conexant provides products for the printing, military, automotive, and aerospace industries through its electronics, automotive, and graphics divisions. Products include military and commercial communication equipment, guidance systems, electronics, components for automobiles, and printing presses. **Positions advertised include:** Mixed Signal IC Test Engineer; Product Manager; Product Engineer. **Corporate headquarters location:** Newport Beach CA. **Other U.S. locations:** Red Bank NJ; Palm Bay FL; Austin TX. **Operations at this facility include:** This location manufactures modem chips and semiconductors. **Listed on:** NASDAQ. **Stock exchange symbol:** CNXT.

CONSUMER PORTFOLIO SERVICES, INC.
13655 Laguna Canyon Road, Irvine CA 92618. 949/753-6800. **Fax:** 949/753-4846. **Contact:** Human Resources. **E-mail address:** humanr@consumerportfolio.com. **World Wide Web address:** http://www.consumerportfolio.com. **Description:** Consumer Portfolio Services, Inc. and its subsidiaries purchase, sell, and service retail automobile installment sales contracts originated by dealers located primarily in California. The company purchases contracts to resell them to institutional investors either as bulk sales or in the form of securities backed by the contracts. **NOTE:** Apply online, or submit resume via e-mail or fax. **Positions advertised include:** Underwriter; Collector; Credit Analyst; Customer Service Rep. **Corporate headquarters location:** This location. **Number of employees at this location:** 65. **Number of employees nationwide:** 692.

CONGRUENT SOFTWARE
2977 Ygnacio Valley Road, Suite 414, Walnut Creek CA 94598-3535. 925/934-9750. **Fax:** 925/934-9718. **Contact:** Human Resources. **E-mail address:** info@congruentsoft.com. **World Wide Web address:** http://www.congruentsoft.com. **Description:** A technical services and contingent staffing company. **NOTE:** Application available online. **Corporate headquarters location:** Bellevue WA. **International locations:** India.

CONTRA COSTA COMMUNITY COLLEGE DISTRICT
500 Court Street, Martinez CA 94553. 925/229-1000. **Fax:** 925/229-2490. **Recorded jobline:** 925/229-1000, ext. 1200. **Contact:** Ernie Fuentes, District Human Resources Technician. **E-mail address:** efuentes@4cd.net. **World Wide Web address:** http://www.4cd.net. **Description:** Administers to Contra Costa College (San Pablo CA); Diablo Valley College (Pleasant Hill CA); Los Medanos College (Pittsburg CA); San Ramon Valley Center (San Ramon CA); and Brentwood Center (Brentwood CA). Contra Costa Community College District is among the largest school districts in California. Founded in 1948. **NOTE:** Mail completed applications to: Attention: Dept. 1HR, CCCCD, 500 Court Street, Martinez CA 94553. Do not submit materials via e-mail or fax. See website for more specific information on application procedures. **Positions advertised include:** Part-Time Instructors, Various Disciplines; Adjunct Instructor, Biology; Senior Library Assistant; Office Assistant; Custodian. **Corporate headquarters location:** This location.

CONTRA COSTA TIMES
P.O. Box 5088, Walnut Creek CA 94596. 925/935-2525. **Physical address:** 2640 Shadelands Drive, Walnut Creek CA 94598. **Contact:** Laurie Fox, Human Resources Manager. **World Wide Web address:** http://www.contracostatimes.com. **Description:** Publishes the *Contra Costa Times,* a daily newspaper. **Positions advertised include:** Business Reporter. **Corporate headquarters location:** This location. **Parent company:** Knight Ridder, Inc. **Operations at this facility include:** Administration; Manufacturing. **Number of employees at this location:** 1,700.

CONTRA COSTA, COUNTY OF
651 Pine Street, 2nd Floor, Martinez CA 94553. 925/335-1701. **Recorded jobline:** 925/335-1700. **Contact:** Leslie T. Knight, Director of Human Resources. **World Wide Web address:** http://www.co.contra-costa.ca.us. **Description:** Administrative offices for the County of Contra Costa. Services offered include health, social, law and justice, public works, building inspection, agricultural inspection, animal control, and fire protection. **NOTE:** Consult website for an extensive list of job postings. **Office hours:** Monday – Friday, 8:00 a.m. – 5:00 p.m. **Corporate headquarters location:** This location. **Operations at this facility include:** Administration; Service.

CONVERA
1808 Aston Avenue, Suite 290, Carlsbad CA 92008. 760/438-7900. **Fax:** 703/761-1988. **Contact:** VP, HR and Corporate Services. **E-mail address:** recruit@convera.com. **World Wide Web address:** http://www.convera.com. **Description:** Designs, develops, markets, and supports computer software products used for the document imaging and multimedia information retrieval marketplaces. The company also offers consulting, training, maintenance, and systems integration services. In addition, the company performs research and development under contract and licenses proprietary software products for use in office, identification, and multimedia information retrieval systems. The company distributes its products through direct sales, distributors, select resellers, and vertical market suppliers. **Positions advertised include:** IT Security Specialist; Linux System Administrator; Crawler software Engineer; Information Retrieval Software Engineer. **Corporate headquarters location:** Vienna VA. **Listed on:** NASDAQ. **Stock exchange symbol:** CNVR.

COOPERSERV
3333 Gibson Street, Bakersfield CA 93308. 661/321-0271. **Contact:** Personnel. **World Wide Web address:** http://www.coopercameron.com. **Description:** COOPERSERV services power and compression equipment. **Corporate headquarters location:** Houston TX. **Other area locations:** Corona CA; Garden Grove CA; Rio Vista CA; Taft CA; Yuba City CA. **Other U.S. locations:** Nationwide. **International locations:** Worldwide. **Parent company:** Cooper Cameron. **Operations at this facility include:** This location is a sales and service office for industrial power plant engines. **Listed on:** New York Stock Exchange. **Stock exchange symbol:** CAM.

COPART, INC.
8780 Fruitridge Road, Sacramento CA 95826. 916/381-3999. **Contact:** Personnel. **E-mail address:** jobs@copart.com. **World Wide Web address:** http://www.copart.com. **Description:** Copart auctions salvage vehicles as a service to vehicle suppliers, principally major insurance companies. Copart services numerous vehicle suppliers including many of the largest insurance, financial, and rental car companies in the country. **Positions advertised include:** Assistant General Manager. **Corporate headquarters location:** Fairfield CA. **Other area locations:** Statewide.

CORNERSTONE PERIPHERALS TECHNOLOGY, INC.
225 Hammond Avenue, Fremont CA 94539. 510/580-8900. **Fax:** 510/580-8998. **Contact:** Human Resources. **E-mail address:** hr@cptmail.com. **Description:** Designs computer displays and graphics controller cards. Founded in 1986. **Special programs:** Internships. **Corporate headquarters location:** This location. **International locations:** Munich, Germany. **Listed on:** Privately held. **President/CEO:** John Noellert. **Number of employees at this location:** 55.

CORONET MANUFACTURING COMPANY INC.
16210 South Avalon Boulevard, P.O. Box 2065, Gardena CA 90247. 310/327-6700. **Fax:** 310/532-8092. **Contact:** Human Resources. **World Wide Web address:** http://www.coronetlighting.com. **Description:** Produces lamps and lighting fixtures. **Corporate headquarters location:** This location.

CORTEX PHARMACEUTICALS INCORPORATED
15231 Barranca Parkway, Irvine CA 92618. 949/727-3157. **Fax:** 949/727-3657. **Contact:** Human Resources. **E-mail address:** hr@cortexpharm.com. **World Wide Web address:** http://www.cortexpharm.com. **Description:** Researches and develops neuropharmaceuticals including the brand name AMPALEX which interacts with AMPA receptors and may increase certain types of memory. **Corporate headquarters location:** This location. **Listed on:** American Stock Exchange. **Stock exchange symbol:** COR.

CORVEL CORPORATION
2010 Main Street, Suite 600, Irvine CA 92614. 949/851-1473. **Toll-free phone:** 888/7-CORVEL. **Fax:** 949/851-1469. **Contact:** Cathy Casil, Human Resources Manager. **World Wide Web address:** http://www.corvel.com. **Description:** CorVel Corporation manages health care delivery and provider reimbursement. Many customers contract with CorVel as an outsource vendor, while others are served by its 165 branch offices located throughout the United States. CorVel maintains over 1,000 customers and its CorCare PPO network now includes over 70,000 providers located in 26 states. **NOTE:** Search for positions online. **Corporate headquarters location:** This location. **Other area locations:** Statewide. **Listed on:** NASDAQ. **Stock exchange symbol:** CRVL. **Number of employees nationwide:** 3,500.

COSMODYNE INC.
3010 Old Ranch Parkway, Suite 300, Seal Beach CA 90740. 562/795-5990. **Fax:** 562/795-5998. **Contact:** Personnel. **World Wide Web address:** http://www.cosmodyne.com. **Description:** Involved in cryogenics research and applications. **Corporate headquarters location:** This location. **Parent company:** Cryogenic Group. **Operations at this facility include:** Manufacturing. **Listed on:** Privately held. **Number of employees at this location:** 85.

COUNTRYWIDE CREDIT INDUSTRIES
4500 Park Granada, Calabasas CA 91302. 818/225-3000. **Recorded jobline:** 888/470-JOBS. **Contact:** Human Resources Department. **World Wide Web address:** http://www.countrywide.com. **Description:** A holding company. **Positions advertised include:** Senior Business Systems Analyst; Commercial Real Estate Analyst; Financial Analyst; Market Research Analyst; Project Manager; Risk Management Analyst; Vice President, Product Management; Tax Systems Analyst. **Special programs:** Internships. **Corporate headquarters location:** This location. **Subsidiaries include:** Countrywide Funding Corporation originates, purchases, sells, and services mortgage loans. The company's mortgage loans are principally first-lien loans secured by single-family residences. **Listed on:** New York Stock Exchange. **Stock exchange symbol:** CCR. **Number of employees nationwide:** 34,000

COUNTRYWIDE CREDIT INDUSTRIES
35 North Lake Avenue, Pasadena CA 91101. 626/304-8400. **Recorded jobline:** 888/470-JOBS. **Contact:** Human Resources Department. **World Wide Web address:** http://www.countrywide.com. **Description:** A holding company. **Positions advertised include:** Underwriter; Account Executive; Financial Analyst; Business Development Representative; Area Manager; Loan Specialist; Payroll Administrator. **Special programs:** Internships. **Corporate headquarters location:** Calabasas CA. **Other U.S. locations:** Nationwide. **Subsidiaries include:** Countrywide Funding Corporation originates, purchases, sells, and services mortgage loans. The company's mortgage loans are principally first-lien loans secured by single-family residences. **Operations at this facility include:** Administration; Divisional Headquarters; Regional Headquarters; Sales; Service. **Listed on:** New York Stock Exchange. **Stock exchange symbol:** CCR.

COVENANT HOUSE CALIFORNIA
1325 North Western Avenue, Hollywood CA 90027-5615. 323/461-3131. **Fax:** 323/957-7421. **Contact:** Human Resources. **E-mail address:** info@covca.org. **World Wide Web address:** http://www.covenanthouse.org. **Description:** An international human service agency for homeless and runaway adolescents. **Corporate headquarters location:** New York NY. **Other area locations:** Oakland.

COVINA, CITY OF
125 East College Street, Covina CA 91723. 626/858-7221. **Recorded jobline:** 626/331-4636, ext. 3001. **Contact:** Personnel. **World Wide Web address:** http://www.ci.covina.ca.us. **Description:** Administrative offices for the city of Covina. **Positions advertised include:** Account Clerk; Police Officer Lateral Entry; Public Works Superintendent; Recreation Services Coordinator. **Special programs:** Internships. **Operations at this facility include:** Administration. **Number of employees at this location:** 200.

COX COMMUNICATIONS, INC.
5159 Federal Boulevard, San Diego CA 92105. 619/263-9251. **Contact:** Human Resources. **World Wide Web address:** http://www.cox.com. **Description:** A local franchise of the nationwide cable television distributor. Cox Communications provides service to over 6 million customers. **NOTE:** Search and apply for positions online. **Positions advertised include:** Quality Assurance Rep; Resource Operations Manager; Business Analyst; Developer Programmer Telephony Compliance Coordinator. **Corporate headquarters location:** Atlanta GA. **Parent company:** Cox Enterprises, Inc. **Listed on:** New York Stock Exchange. **Stock exchange symbol:** COX.

CRAWFORD PIMENTEL & COMPANY, INC.
2150 Trade Zone Boulevard, Suite 200, San Jose CA 95131. 408/942-6888. **Fax:** 408/942-0194. **Contact:** Gene Gauthier, Human Resources. **E-mail address:** recruiting@cpconet.com. **World Wide Web address:** http://www.1040tax.com. **Description:** A public accounting firm that also offers management advisory, technology consulting, and business consulting services. **Special programs:** Training. **Corporate headquarters location:** This location. **Operations at this facility include:** Service. **Listed on:** Privately held. **Number of employees at this location:** 25.

CREATIVE ARTISTS AGENCY, INC. (CAA)
9830 Wilshire Boulevard, Beverly Hills CA 90212. 310/288-4545. **Fax:** 310/288-4800. **Contact:** Human Resources. **World Wide Web address:** http://www.caa.com. **Description:** Manages and represents actors, directors, and writers in the film and television industries. Founded in 1975. **CEO:** Rick Nicita. **Number of employees worldwide:** 400.

CREATIVE COMPUTER APPLICATIONS, INC.
26115-A Mureau Road, Calabasas CA 91302. 818/880-6700. **Toll-free phone:** 800/437-9000. **Fax:** 818/880-4398. **Contact:** Human Resources Department. **E-mail address:** jobs@ccainc.com. **World Wide Web address:** http://www.ccainc.com. **Description:** Designs and manufactures computer-based, clinical information systems and products that automate the acquisition and management of clinical data for the health care industry. The company sells its products and systems to hospitals, clinics, reference laboratories, veterinarians, other health care institutions, and original equipment manufacturers. **Corporate headquarters location:** This location.

CREATIVE LABS, INC.
1901 McCarthy Boulevard, Milpitas CA 95035. 408/428-6600. **Fax:** 408/546-6305. **Contact:** Recruiting. **World Wide Web address:** http://www.creative.com. **Description:** Creative Labs provides multimedia products and peripherals for personal computers. Products include graphics and audio cards, multimedia upgrade kits, and speakers. **Positions advertised include:** Assistant Controller; Brand Manager, Audio; Test Engineer; Financial Support Analyst; Marcom Manager; Marketing Copywriter. **Corporate headquarters location:** This location. **Other area locations:** Fremont CA; Scotts Valley CA. **Other U.S. locations:** Stillwater OK. **International locations:** Canada; Latin America. **Parent company:** Creative Technology, Ltd. **Operations at this facility include:** This location manufactures computer game software. **Listed on:** NASDAQ. **Stock exchange symbol:** CREAF.

CREDENCE SYSTEMS CORPORATION
1421 California Circle, Milpitas CA 95035. 408/635-4300. **Fax:** 408/635-4985. **Contact:** Human Resources. **E-mail address:** yourfuture@credence.com. **World Wide Web address:** http://www.credence.com. **Description:** Manufactures automatic testing equipment for digital and mixed-signal integrated circuits. **Positions advertised include:** Accounting Manager; Stock Administrator. **Corporate headquarters location:** This location. **Other U.S. locations:** CO; OR; TX. **International locations:** Worldwide. **Listed on:** NASDAQ. **Stock exchange symbol:** CMOS.

CROWLEY MARITIME CORPORATION
155 Grand Avenue, Oakland CA 94612. 510/251-7500. **Fax:** 510/251-7788. **Recorded jobline:** 904/727-4287. **Contact:** Personnel. **E-mail address:** resumes@Crowley.com. **World Wide Web address:** http://www.crowley.com. **Description:** Provides marine transportation and construction services. **NOTE:** Search and apply for positions online. **Corporate headquarters location:** This location.

CROWN CITY PLATING COMPANY
4350 Temple City Boulevard, El Monte CA 91731. 626/444-9291. **Fax:** 626/448-6915. **Contact:** Personnel Director. **E-mail address:** jobs@crown-city-plating.com. **World Wide Web address:** http://www.crown-city-plating.com. **Description:** Engaged in the metal finishing and plating for industrial customers. **Corporate headquarters location:** This location.

CRUSH CREATIVE
1919 Empire Avenue, Burbank CA 91504. 818/842-1121. **Contact:** Personnel. **Description:** A custom photographic lab also specializing in digital reproductions on film, inkjet, and other large format media.

CUBIC CORPORATION
MS 10-23, P.O. Box 85587, San Diego CA 92186-5587. 858/505-1540. **Physical address:** 9333 Balboa Avenue, San Diego CA 92123. **Fax:** 858/505-1524. **Recorded jobline:** 858/505-1540. **Contact:** Human Resources. **E-mail address:** jobs@cubic.com. **World Wide Web address:** http://www.cubic.com. **Description:** Cubic Corporation operates through two major segments: the Cubic Transportation Systems Group and the Cubic Defense Group. The Cubic Transportation Systems Group designs and manufactures automatic revenue collection systems throughout the world for public mass transit including railroads, buses, bridges, tunnels, toll roads, and parking lots. The Cubic Defense Group provides instrumented training systems for the U.S. Army, Air Force, and Navy, as well as avionics, data links, aerospace systems, and logistical product support. The Defense Group also provides battle command training, radio communication systems, and field service operation and maintenance. Founded in 1951. **NOTE:** Search and apply for positions online. **Positions advertised include:** Senior Auditor; Billing Analyst; Principal Systems Engineer; Senior Software Engineer; Mechanical Engineer; Senior Staff Scientist; Vice President of Sales and Marketing; Electrical Engineer; Contracts Administrator; Sales Manager; Software Engineering Director. **Corporate headquarters location:** This location. **Number of employees nationwide:** 4,700. **Listed on:** American Stock Exchange. **Stock exchange symbol:** CUB.

CULVER CITY, CITY OF
9770 Culver Boulevard, Culver City CA 90232. 310/253-5640. **Recorded jobline:** 310/253-5651. **Contact:** Human Resources Department. **World Wide Web address:** http://www.culvercity.org. **Description:** Administrative offices for Culver City. **NOTE:** Search for positions online. **Positions advertised include:** Redevelopment Project Manager; Maintenance Operations Manager. **Special programs:** Internships. **Corporate headquarters location:** This location. **Operations at this facility include:** Administration; Service. **Number of employees at this location:** 600.

CUMMINS WEST INC.
14775 Wicks Boulevard, San Leandro CA 94577-6779. 510/351-6101. **Contact:** Maryann Parrinello, Human Resources Manager. **E-mail address:** west@cummins.com. **World Wide Web address:** http://www.west.cummins.com. **Description:** Cummins West Inc. manufactures in-line and V-type diesel engines from 145 to 1600 horsepower, and replacement parts for these engines. The company also manufactures and markets a broad range of heavy-duty filters and reconditioned diesel engines and parts. **NOTE:** Apply online. Paper resumes are not accepted. **Positions advertised include:** Service Technician; Journeyman Mechanic. **Corporate headquarters location:** Columbus IN. **Operations at this facility include:** This facility is primarily a wholesale dealership. **Listed on:** New York Stock Exchange.

CUPERTINO NATIONAL BANK & TRUST
20230 Stevens Creek Boulevard, Cupertino CA 95014. 408/996-1144. **Toll-free phone:** 800/226-5262. **Fax:** 650/843-1287. **Contact:** Human Resources. **World Wide Web address:** http://www.gbbk.com. **Description:** A bank offering a variety of services including corporate and personal relationship banking, residential lending, SBA lending, and personal and corporate trust services. **Corporate headquarters location:** This location. **Other area locations:** Palo Alto CA; San Jose CA. **Parent company:** Greater Bay Bankcorp. **Listed on:** NASDAQ. **Stock exchange symbol:** GBBK.

CUSHMAN & WAKEFIELD
One Maritime Plaza, Suite 900, San Francisco CA 94111. 415/397-1700. **Contact:** Jill Campbell, Human Resources. **World Wide Web address:** http://www.cushwake.com. **Description:** An international commercial and industrial real estate services firm. The company is engaged in appraisals, financial services, project development, research services, and the management and leasing of commercial office space. **Positions advertised include:** Financial Accountant; Project Coordinator. **Corporate headquarters location:** New York NY. **Other U.S. locations:** Nationwide. **International locations:** Worldwide.

CUSTOM CHROME, INC.
16100 Jacqueline Court, Morgan Hill CA 95037. 408/778-0500. **Fax:** 408/782-6603. **Contact:** Personnel. **E-mail address:** jobs@globalmotorsport.com. **World Wide Web address:** http://www.customchrome.com. **Description:** A leading independent supplier of aftermarket parts and accessories for Harley-Davidson motorcycles. Custom Chrome distributes its own products under brand names including Rev Tech, Premium, Dyno Power, and C.C. Rider. The company also supplies products by manufacturers such as Dunlop, Champion, Hastings, and Accel. Founded in 1970. **Positions advertised include:** Accounting Manager; Business Analyst. **Parent company:** Global Motorsport Group Inc. **Listed on:** NASDAQ. **Stock exchange symbol:** CSTM.

CUSTOM CONTROL SENSORS, INC.
21111 Plummer Street, Chatsworth CA 91311. 818/341-4610. **Fax:** 818/709-0426. **Contact:** Marsha Beach, Human Resource Manager. **E-mail address:** mbeach@ccsdualsnap.com. **World Wide Web address:** http://www.ccsdualsnap.com. **Description:** Manufactures pressure, flow, and temperature switches for industrial and airborne applications. **Corporate headquarters location:** This location.

CYGNUS, INC.
400 Penobscot Drive, Redwood City CA 94063-4719. 650/369-4300. **Fax:** 650/599-3938. **Contact:** Human Resources. **E-mail address:** recruiting@cygn.com. **World Wide Web address:** http://www.cygn.com. **Description:** Develops and manufactures diagnostic medical devices. Founded in 1985. **Corporate headquarters location:** This location. **Listed on:** NASDAQ. **Stock exchange symbol:** CYGN.

CYPRESS SEMICONDUCTOR CORPORATION
198 Champion Court, San Jose CA 95134. 408/943-2600. **Fax:** 408/943-4730. **Contact:** Personnel. **World Wide Web address:** http://www.cypress.com. **Description:** Manufactures high-performance digital integrated circuits. **NOTE:** Search and apply for positions online. **Positions advertised include:** Sr. QA Engineer; Project Manager Specialist; Financial Analyst; Statistician Process Development Engineer; Applications Engineer. **Corporate headquarters location:** This location.

Listed on: New York Stock Exchange. **Stock exchange symbol:** CY. **Number of employees worldwide:** 4,000.

DCL
48641 Milmont Drive, Fremont CA 94538. 510/651-5100. **Fax:** 510/651-2261. **Contact:** Human Resources. **E-mail address:** careers@dclcorp.com. **World Wide Web address:** http://www.discopylabs.com. **Description:** Assembles discs for software developers. **Corporate headquarters location:** This location. **Other area locations:** Ontario CA.

D-LINK SYSTEMS, INC.
17595 Mt. Hermann, Fountain Valley CA 92708-4160. 800/326-1688. **Contact:** Human Resources. **E-mail address:** hr@dlink.com. **World Wide Web address:** http://www.dlink.com. **Description:** Manufactures networking, connectivity, and data communications products. The company's product line includes adapters, hubs, switches, routers, and print servers. **Positions advertised include:** Web Programmer; Manager, Channel Programs; Sr. Account Executive; Director, MSO Sales; Program Manager. **Corporate headquarters location:** This location.

DDB WORLDWIDE
340 Main Street, Los Angeles CA 90291-2524. 310/907-1500. **Contact:** Personnel Director. **World Wide Web address:** http://www.ddb.com. **Description:** A full-service, international advertising agency. **NOTE:** Submit resume online. **Corporate headquarters location:** New York NY. **Other U.S. locations:** San Francisco CA; Washington DC; Miami FL; Honolulu HI; Chicago IL; Dallas TX; Seattle WA. **Parent company:** Omnicom Group Inc. **Operations at this facility include:** Regional Headquarters. **Listed on:** New York Stock Exchange.

DEP, INC.
2101 East Via Arado, Rancho Dominguez CA 90220-6189. 310/604-0777. **Contact:** Human Resources. **World Wide Web address:** http://www.dep.com. **Description:** A leading developer, manufacturer, and distributor of diversified personal care products. Products include Dep Styling Gel, Lavoris, Cuticura, Porcelana, Nature's Family, L.A. Looks, Agree, Halsa, Topol, and Lilt. **NOTE:** Part-time jobs are offered. **Corporate headquarters location:** This location. **Parent company:** Henkel. **Operations at this facility include:** Administration; Manufacturing; Research and Development. **President:** Robert Berglass. **Annual sales/revenues:** $87 million. **Number of employees at this location:** 285.

DHL WORLDWIDE EXPRESS
50 California Street, San Francisco CA 94111. 415/677-6100. **Contact:** Human Resources. **E-mail address:** hr_jobs@us.dhl.com. **World Wide Web address:** http://www.dhl.com. **Description:** An air express network that, through its subsidiaries, services national and foreign markets in over 190 countries. **NOTE:** Search and apply for positions online. **Corporate headquarters location:** Plantation FL. **Subsidiaries include:** DHL Airways Inc.; DHL International Ltd.

DMJM
515 South Flower Street, Los Angeles CA 90071. 213/593-8100. **Fax:** 213/593-8175. **Contact:** Yvette Mitchell, Director, Recruitment. **E-mail address:** Yvette.mitchell@dmjm.com. **World Wide Web address:** http://www.dmjm.com. **Description:** Provides a wide range of architectural/engineering services to the public and private sectors. Operations include transportation, public works, and commercial architecture. **Positions advertised include:** Architect. **Special programs:** Internships. **Corporate headquarters location:** This location. **Other U.S. locations:** San Bernardino CA; San Francisco CA; Santa Monica CA. **Parent company:** AECOM Technology Corporation.

DMX MUSIC LLC
11400 West Olympic Boulevard, Suite 1100, Los Angeles CA 90064-1507. 310/444-1744. **Toll-free phone:** 800/700-4412. **Fax:** 310/477-0724. **Contact:** Human Resources Department. **E-mail address:** jobs@dmxmusic.com. **World Wide Web address:** http://www.dmxmusic.com. **Description:** Programs, distributes, and markets a premium digital music service, Digital Music Express, which provides continuous, commercial-free, CD-quality music programming. DMX is delivered by two methods: for a monthly, per-subscriber license fee, it is sent direct to cable operators by C-Band satellite for distribution to residential and commercial cable subscribers; for a monthly, per-subscriber fee, it is distributed by KuBand direct broadcast satellite (DBS) to small satellite dishes that connect through a specially designed DMX tuner to a commercial subscriber's stereo system. **Positions advertised include:** Multimedia Creative Specialist; System Sales Representative. **Corporate headquarters location:** This location. **Parent company:** Liberty Media, Inc.

DPAC TECHNOLOGIES
7321 Lincoln Way, Garden Grove CA 92841. 714/898-0007. **Fax:** 714/899-7558. **Contact:** Human Resources. **E-mail address:** hr@dpactech.com. **World Wide Web address:** http://www.dpactech.com. **Description:** Designs, develops, manufactures, and markets a broad line of standard and custom monolithic memories and memory/logic/analog modules and subsystems. The company's products are used in a variety of military, industrial, and commercial applications where high-density, high-performance, and high-reliability standards are required. Typical product applications are in the areas of communications, medical instrumentation, missiles, avionics, and space satellites. **Positions advertised include:** Systems Engineering Manager; Software Test Department Manager; Sales Technical Support Engineer. **Corporate headquarters location:** This location. **Listed on:** NASDAQ. **Stock exchange symbol:** DPAC.

DRS SIGNAL SOLUTIONS
17680 Butterfield Boulevard, Suite 100, Morgan Hill CA 95037. 408/778-7109. **Fax:** 301/948-5527. **Contact:** Human Resources. **E-mail address:** greatjobs@drs-ss.com. **World Wide Web address:** http://www.drs.com. **Description:** Manufactures and distributes microwave equipment and RF and signal intercept and location systems. **Positions advertised include:** Business Development Director; Program Manager. **Parent company:** DRS Technologies.

DSP GROUP, INC.
3120 Scott Boulevard, Santa Clara CA 95054. 408/986-4300. **Fax:** 408/986-4323. **Contact:** Professional Staffing. **E-mail address:** hr@dspg.com. **World Wide Web address:** http://www.dspg.com. **Description:** Develops, licenses, and markets digital signal processing software and digital signal processor technologies for use in digital speech products. DSP Group offers a wide range of products and licensed technologies to major original equipment manufacturers in the personal computer, telecommunications, and consumer electronics markets. Products include digital speech processors for telephone answering machines. **Corporate headquarters location:** This location. **International locations:** Israel; France; Japan; Korea. **Listed on:** NASDAQ. **Stock exchange symbol:** DSPG.

DTC COMPUTER SUPPLIES
P.O. Box 2834, Rancho Cucamonga CA 91729-2834. 909/466-7680. **Toll-free phone:** 800/700-7683. **Contact:** Human Resources Department. **World Wide Web address:** http://www.dtc1.com. **Description:** Distributes computer supplies. DTC also manufactures magnetic computer tape. **Corporate headquarters location:** This location.

DADE BEHRING, INC.
20400 Mariani Avenue, Cupertino CA 95014. 408/239-2000. **Contact:** Professional Employment. **World Wide Web address:** http://www.dadebehring.com. **Description:** Manufactures and distributes diagnostic instrument systems and other labware that serve clinical and research laboratories worldwide. Dade Behring also offers its customers support services. **NOTE:** Search and apply for positions online. **Corporate headquarters location:** Deerfield IL. **International locations:** Worldwide. **Number of employees worldwide:** 7,500.

DAILEY & ASSOCIATES ADVERTISING
8687 Melrose Avenue, Suite G300, West Hollywood CA 90069. 310/360-3100. **Fax:** 310/360-0470. **Contact:** Ms. Jean Anne Hutchinson, Director of Human Resources Administration. **E-mail address:** humanresources@daileyads.com. **World Wide Web address:** http://www.daileyads.com. **Description:** A full-service advertising agency. **Positions advertised include:** Account Executive; Broadcast Buyer; Media Planner; Media Biller; Broadcast Traffic Manager. **Office hours:** Monday – Friday, 8:30 a.m. – 5:30 p.m.

DAILY JOURNAL CORPORATION
P.O. Box 54026, Los Angeles CA 90054-0026. 213/229-5300. **Physical address:** 915 East First Street, Los Angeles CA 90012. **Contact:** Human Resources. **World Wide Web address:** http://www.dailyjournal.com. **Description:** Publishes the *Los Angeles Daily Journal, Daily Commerce, California Real Estate Journal,* and *Nevada Journal,* each based in Los Angeles; *San Francisco Daily Journal* in San Francisco; the *Daily Recorder* in Sacramento; the *Inter-City Express* in Oakland; *Marin County Court Reporter* in San Rafael; *Orange County Reporter* in Santa Ana; *San Jose Post-Record* in San Jose; *Sonoma County Daily Herald-Recorder* in Santa Rosa; *San Diego Commerce* in San Diego; *Business Journal* in Riverside; and *Washington Journal* in Seattle. The company also serves as a newspaper representative specializing in public notice advertising. **Corporate headquarters location:** This location. **Listed on:** NASDAQ. **Stock exchange symbol:** DJCO.

DAILY NEWS
P.O. Box 4200, Woodland Hills CA 91365-4200. 818/713-3000. **Fax:** 818/713-0048. **Contact:** Human Resources. **World Wide Web address:** http://www.dailynews.com. **Description:** A daily newspaper. **Parent company:** Los Angeles Newspaper Group.

DANONE WATERS OF NORTH AMERICA
3280 East Foothill Boulevard, Suite 400, Pasadena CA 91107. 626/585-1000. **Contact:** Human Resources. **Description:** Produces bottled water under the names Evian, Ferrarelle, and Volvic. **Corporate headquarters location:** Atlanta GA. **Special programs:** Internships.

DANTEL, INC.
P.O. Box 55013, Fresno CA 93717. 559/292-1111. **Physical address:** 2991 North Argyle Avenue, Fresno CA 93727. **Fax:** 559/292-7120. **Contact:** Human Resources. **E-mail address:** humres@dantel.com. **World Wide Web address:** http://www.dantel.com. **Description:** Dantel designs and manufactures alarm monitoring and alarm management solutions to companies with communications networks of all sizes. **Corporate headquarters location:** This location. **Operations at this facility include:** Administration; Manufacturing; Research and Development; Sales; Service. **Listed on:** Privately held. **Number of employees at this location:** 150.

DATA TECHNOLOGY CORPORATION (DTC)
1700 Space Park Drive, Santa Clara CA 95054. 408/745-9320. **Contact:** Human Resources. **Description:** Develops and manufactures computer peripherals including printers, disk drives, terminals, controllers, and supplies. Products are marketed to both original equipment manufacturers and distributors. **Corporate headquarters location:** This location.

DAVIS WIRE CORPORATION
5555 Irwindale Avenue, Irwindale CA 91706. 626/815-3217. **Fax:** 626/815-3232. **Contact:** Human Resources. **World Wide Web address:** http://www.daviswire.com. **Description:** Manufactures wire and related products. **Corporate headquarters location:** This location. **Other U.S. locations:** Hayward CA; Pueblo CO; Kent WA. **Parent company:** Heico. **Listed on:** Privately held. **Number of employees at this location:** 200. **Number of employees nationwide:** 550.

DAVIS ELEN ADVERTISING
865 South Figueroa Street, 12th Floor, Los Angeles CA 90017. 213/688-7071. **Fax:** 213/688-7106. **Contact:** Pamela McCarthy, VP/Director of Human Resources **E-mail address:** pammccarthy@daviselen.com. **World Wide Web address:** http://www.daviselen.com. **Description:** A full-service advertising agency. **NOTE:** Entry-level positions are offered. **Special programs:** Internships. **Corporate headquarters location:** This location. **Other area locations:** Solana Beach CA; San Francisco CA; Marina Del Ray CA. **Other U.S. locations:** Portland OR. **International locations:** Mexico; Japan. **Listed on:** Privately held.

DAY RUNNER, INC.
2750 West Moore Avenue, Fullerton CA 92833. 714/680-3500. **Fax:** 714/680-3165. **Contact:** Human Resources. **E-mail address:** human.resources@dayrunner.com. **World Wide Web address:** http://www.dayrunner.com. **Description:** A leading developer, manufacturer, and marketer of paper-based organizers for the retail market. The company markets multiple lines of organizers and planners and a wide variety of refills and accessories. **Number of employees at this location:** 550.

DAYTON/RICHMOND
13169 Slover Avenue, Suite B, Fontana CA 92316. 909/829-2765. **Fax:** 909/355-8649. **Contact:** Human Resources Department. **World Wide Web address:** http://www.daytonrichmond.com. **Description:** Manufactures concrete lifting systems, concrete modular forms, concrete accessories, and metal accessories for the construction industry. **Positions advertised include:** Precast Product Specialist; Product Specialist. **Corporate headquarters location:** Dayton OH. **Parent company:** Dayton Superior Company. **Listed on:** Privately held.

DEARDEN'S
700 South Main Street, Los Angeles CA 90014. 213/362-9600. **Contact:** Raquel Bensimon, President. **Description:** A retailer of furniture, appliances, televisions, and audio equipment. **Corporate headquarters location:** This location.

ED DEBEVIC'S RESTAURANT
134 North La Cienega Boulevard, Beverly Hills CA 90211. 310/659-1952. **Contact:** Human Resources. **World Wide Web address:** http://www.eddebevics.com. **Description:** One location of the casual dining restaurant chain. Ed Debevic's serves American cuisine and operates a gift shop. **NOTE:** Send or fax application and resume to: Ed Debevic's, Inc., 640 North Wells Street, Chicago IL 60610. Fax: 312/664-7444. **Positions advertised include:** Assistant General Manager. **Corporate headquarters location:** Chicago IL. **Parent company:** Debevic's Diners Ltd.

DECISIONONE
2323 Industrial Parkway West, Hayward CA 94545. 510/266-3000. **Contact:** Human Resources. **E-mail address:** laura.leaverton@decisionone.com. **World Wide Web address:** http://www.decisionone.com. **Description:** DecisionOne is an international supplier of plug-compatible computer equipment and accessories. Products include disk and tape storage devices, terminals, intelligent workstations and systems, controllers, printers, airline reservation systems, and a comprehensive range of computer supplies. The company operates in 27 countries around the world. **NOTE:** Search and apply for positions online. **Corporate headquarters location:** Frazer PA. **Operations at this facility include:** This location repairs computer monitors.

DECKERS OUTDOOR CORPORATION
495-A South Fairview Avenue, Goleta CA 93117. 805/967-7611. **Fax:** 805/967-3322. **Contact:** Human Resources. **World Wide Web address:** http://www.deckers.com. **Description:** Designs, manufactures, and markets footwear developed for high-performance outdoor, recreational, and sports activities, as well as casual wear. Deckers Outdoor's products are sold under the Teva, Simple, Sensi, and Picante brand names, and are marketed through leading outdoor retailers, athletic footwear stores, specialty retailers, and department stores throughout the United States and in select foreign markets. **Corporate headquarters location:** This location.

DEL MAR REYNOLDS MEDICAL, INC.
13 Whatney, Irvine CA 92618-2837. 949/699-3300. **Fax:** 949/699-3380. **Contact:** Trish Hichten, Personnel Manager. **World Wide Web address:** http://www.delmarreynolds.com. **Description:** Develops, manufactures, and markets a wide range of medical monitoring and testing equipment. Products include stress tests, ambulatory blood pressure monitors, ambulatory transesophagael testing devices, and the AVESP (Audiovisual Superimposed Electrocardiographic Presentation). **Corporate headquarters location:** This location. **Parent company:** Ferraris Group (London).

DEL MAR THOROUGHBRED CLUB
P.O. Box 700, Del Mar CA 92014. 858/755-1141. **Physical address:** 2260 Jimmy Durante Boulevard, Del Mar CA 92014. **Contact:** Joseph W. Harper, President. **E-mail address:** marys@dmtc.com. **World Wide Web address:** http://www.dmtc.com. **Description:** A horse racing facility. Del Mar Thoroughbred Club is a member of the Thoroughbred Racing Association of North America.

DEL MONTE FOODS
P.O. Box 193575, San Francisco CA 94119. 415/247-3000. **Physical address:** The Landmark at One Market Street, San Francisco CA 94105. **Contact:** Human Resources. **World Wide Web address:** http://www.delmonte.com. **Description:** A producer of canned fruits and vegetables, tomato sauces, condiments, and dessert products for the consumer, institutional, and military markets. The company operates over 60 plants worldwide where it processes food and makes, labels, and packs its own cans. Brand names include Del Monte and Contadina. Founded in 1892. **NOTE:** Search and apply for positions online. **Positions advertised include:** Operations Analyst; Sr. Associate Buyer; Financial Analyst. **Corporate headquarters location:** This location. **Listed on:** New York Stock Exchange. **Stock exchange symbol:** DLM.

DELOITTE & TOUCHE
50 Fremont Street, Suite 3100, San Francisco CA 94105. 415/783-4000. **Toll-free phone:** 888/APPLYDT. **Contact:** Human Resources. **E-mail address:** dtcareers@deloitte.com. **World Wide Web address:** http://www.us.deloitte.com. **Description:** An international firm of certified public accountants providing professional accounting, auditing, tax, and management consulting services to widely diversified clients. The company has a specialized program consisting of national industry groups and functional groups that cross industry lines. Groups are involved in various disciplines including accounting, auditing, taxation management advisory services, small and growing businesses, mergers and acquisitions, and computer applications. **Positions advertised include:** Audit Manager; BDC Director; Business Analyst; CDDT Framework Product Manager; Consultant, Technology Integration; Consultant, Network Security Specialist.

DELOITTE & TOUCHE
350 South Grand Avenue, Suite 200, Los Angeles CA 90071. 213/688-0800. **Toll-free phone:** 888/APPLYDT. **Contact:** Human Resources. **E-mail address:** dtcareers@deloitte.com. **World Wide Web address:** http://www.us.deloitte.com. **Description:** An international firm of certified public accountants providing professional accounting, auditing, tax, and management consulting services to widely diversified clients. The company has a specialized program consisting of national industry groups and functional groups that cross industry lines. Groups are involved in various disciplines including accounting, auditing, taxation management advisory services, small and growing businesses, mergers and acquisitions, and computer applications. **Positions advertised include:** Database Manager; Audit Manager, Healthcare; BDC Director; Chief Knowledge Management Officer. **Number of employees at this location:** 1,568.

DELTA DENTAL PLAN OF CALIFORNIA
100 First Street, San Francisco CA 94105. 415/972-8300. **Contact:** Recruitment and Selection. **World Wide Web address:** http://www.deltadentalca.org. **Description:** A prepaid, dental insurance firm. **NOTE:** Entry-level positions are offered. **Positions advertised include:** Sales Account Executive; Client Data Analyst; Communications Coordinator; Dental Consultant; QA Database Analyst. **Corporate headquarters location:** This location. **Other area locations:** Cerritos CA; Rancho Cordova CA. **Subsidiaries include:** Delta Dental Insurance Company (DDIC); Private Medical Care, Inc. (PMI). **Operations at this facility include:** Administration; Sales; Service. **Number of employees at this location:** 1,200. **Number of employees nationwide:** 2,500.

DELTA NATIONAL BANK
611 North Main Street, Manteca CA 95336. 209/824-4000. **Fax:** 209/823-0307. **Contact:** Human Resources. **World Wide Web address:** http://www.deltabank.net. **Description:** A commercial bank. **Parent company:** Delta National Bancorp.

DELUXE FINANCIAL SERVICES
1551 Dell Avenue, Campbell CA 95008. 408/370-8800. **Contact:** Personnel. **World Wide Web address:** http://www.deluxe.com. **Description:** Provides check printing, electronic funds transfer processing services, and related services to the financial industry; check authorization and collection services to retailers; and electronic benefit transfer services to state governments. Deluxe also produces forms, specialty papers, and other products for small businesses, professional practices, and medical/dental offices; and provides tax forms and electronic tax filing services to tax preparers. Through the direct mail channel, Deluxe sells greeting cards, gift wrapping, and related products to households. The company entered the lithographic ink market in 1994 as a result of developing a breakthrough water-washable ink. Deluxe is a *Fortune* 500 company with facilities located in the United States, Canada, and the United Kingdom. **Special programs:** Internships. **Corporate headquarters location:** Shoreview MN. **Other U.S. locations:** Nationwide. **Listed on:** New York Stock Exchange. **Stock exchange symbol:** DLX. **Number of employees nationwide:** 15,000.

DELUXE LABORATORIES, INC.
1377 Serrano Avenue, Hollywood CA 90027. 323/462-6171. **Fax:** 323/461-0608. **Contact:** Human Resources. **World Wide Web address:** http://www.bydeluxe.com. **Description:** A motion picture film developer. **Parent company:** The Rank Group plc.

DEUTSCH, INC.
5454 Beethoven Street, Los Angeles CA. 310/862-3000. **Fax:** 310/862-3104. **Recorded jobline:** 310/862-3104. **Contact:** Human Resources. **E-mail address:** job_opportunities@deutschinc.com. **World Wide Web address:** http://www.deutschinc.com. **Description:** An advertising agency. **Positions advertised include:** Print Production Manager; Print Traffic Manager; Mailroom Clerk. **Corporate headquarters location:** New York NY.

DEWALT CORPORATION
2512 Tripaldi Way, Hayward CA 94549. 510/783-3959. **Contact:** Human Resources Department. **E-mail address:** jobs@dewalt.com. **World Wide Web address:** http://www.dewalt.com. **Description:** A manufacturer of products used in and around the home and for commercial applications. The company is one of the world's largest manufacturers of power tools, power tool accessories, security hardware, and electric lawn and garden tools. **Corporate headquarters location:** Baltimore MD. **Other U.S. locations:** Mooresville NC; Bethlehem PA. **Parent company:** Black and Decker Corporation. **Listed on:** New York Stock Exchange. **Stock exchange symbol:** BDK.

DEWEY BALLANTINE
333 South Grand Avenue, Suite 2600, Los Angeles CA 90071-1530. 213/621-6288. **Fax:** 213/621-6100. **Contact:** Annmarie Gleeson, Human Resources. **E-mail address:** agleeson@deweybalantine.com. **World Wide Web address:** http://www.deweyballantine.com. **Description:** An international law firm specializing in corporate, litigation, tax, ERISA/pension, bankruptcy, and real estate law. **NOTE:** Search and apply for positions online. **Other area locations:** East Palo Alto CA. **Other U.S. locations:** New York NY; Washington DC; Austin TX; Houston TX. **International locations:** The Czech Republic; England; Germany; Hungary; Italy; Poland.

DIAGNOSTIC PRODUCTS CORPORATION
5210 Pacific concourse Drive, Los Angeles CA 90045-6900. 310/645-8200. **Toll-free phone:** 800/372-1782. **Fax:** 310/645-9999. **Contact:** Personnel Department. **E-mail address:** resumes@dpconline.com. **World Wide Web address:** http://www.dpcweb.com. **Description:** Manufactures medical immunodiagnostic test kits that are used to diagnose and treat a variety of medical conditions such as allergies, anemia, cancer, diabetes, infectious diseases, reproductive disorders, thyroid disorders, and veterinary applications. **Positions advertised include:** R&D Document Specialist; Manufacturing Supervisor; Clinical Research Associate; Regulatory Affairs Associate; Data Analysis Supervisor; Scientist; Optics Research Scientist. **Corporate headquarters location:** This location. **Operations at this facility include:** Administration; Manufacturing; Research and Development; Sales; Service. **Listed on:** New York Stock Exchange. **Stock exchange symbol:** DP. **Number of employees at this location:** 430.

DIAMOND ENTERTAINMENT CORPORATION
800 Tucker Lane, Walnut CA 91789. 909/839-1989. **Fax:** 909/635-0671. **Contact:** Human Resources. **World Wide Web address:** http://www.e-dmec.com. **Description:** A full-service video product duplicating, manufacturing, packaging, and distribution company. Through its Custom Duplication Division, the company duplicates and packages videocassettes on a custom-made basis. Customers for this service include companies and individuals within the multilevel marketing industry who use videocassettes for product information, business recruitment, training, or sales and marketing purposes. The Entertainment Division markets and sells a variety of videocassette titles to the budget home video market. The company's inventory of programs consists of more than 675 titles including children's cartoons, motion pictures, sports highlights, educational, and exercise programs. The feature motion pictures offered by the company include such film classics as *Life with Father* and *It's a Wonderful Life.* **Corporate headquarters location:** This location.

DICK CLARK PRODUCTIONS, INC.
3003 West Olive Avenue, Burbank CA 91505. 818/841-3003. **Fax:** 818/954-8609. **Contact:** Human Resources Department. **World Wide Web address:** http://www.dickclarkproductions.com. **Description:** One of the nation's top entertainment companies. The company primarily produces talk shows, made-for-TV movies, and awards shows such as the Golden Globe Awards. **Special programs:** Internships. **Corporate headquarters location:** This location.

DIGIDESIGN INC.
2001 Junipero Serra Boulevard, Daly City CA 94014-3886. 650/731-6300. **Contact:** Human Resources. **E-mail address:** jobs@digidesign.com. **World Wide Web address:** http://www.digidesign.com. **Description:** Manufactures digital audio production systems, providing the professional music, film, video, multimedia, and radio broadcast industries with tools for digital recording, MIDI sequencing, editing, signal processing, and surround mixing. **NOTE:** Search and apply for positions online. **Positions advertised include:** Localization Test Engineer; Program Manager; Application software Engineer; Hardware Product Manager. **Corporate headquarters location:** This location. **Parent company:** Avid Technology, Inc. **Operations at this facility include:** This location manufactures audio workstations for sound editing.

DIODES INC.
3050 East Hillcrest Drive, Westlake Village CA 91362-3154. 805/446-4800. **Fax:** 805/381-3840. **Contact:** Human Resources. **World Wide Web address:** http://www.diodes.com. **Description:** Diodes is a producer and distributor of electronic diodes primarily used in the semiconductor industry. **Positions advertised include:** Customer Service Representative. **Corporate headquarters location:** This location. **Operations at this facility include:** This location is a distribution and sales office. **Listed on:** NASDAQ. **Stock exchange symbol:** DIOD.

DIONEX CORPORATION
500 Mercury Drive, P.O. Box 3606, Sunnyvale CA 94088-3606. 408/737-0700. **Fax:** 408/730-9403. **Contact:** Human Resources. **E-mail address:** jobs@dionex.com. **World Wide Web address:** http://www.dionex.com. **Description:** Develops, manufactures, sells, and services systems and related products that isolate and identify the components of chemical mixtures. The company's products are used extensively for environmental analysis by the pharmaceutical, life science, biotechnology, chemical, petrochemical, power generation, and electronics industries. Customers include industrial companies, government agencies, research institutions, and universities. The company's research and development teams explore new technologies in order to enhance the performance of ion technology, high-performance liquid chromatography, capillary electrophoresis, and supercritical fluid extraction and chromatography technologies. **NOTE:** Search and apply for positions online. **Positions advertised include:** Product Manager; Chemist; Chemical Process Manager; Quality Auditor; Manufacturing Engineer Manager. **Corporate headquarters location:** This location. **Other U.S. locations:** Atlanta GA; Salt Lake City UT. **Operations at this facility include:** Administration; Manufacturing; Research and Development; Sales; Service. **Listed on:** NASDAQ. **Stock exchange symbol:** DNEX. **Number of employees nationwide:** 565.

DISCOVERY COMMUNICATIONS INC.
10100 Santa Monica Boulevard, Suite 1500, Los Angeles CA 90067. 310/551-1611. **Contact:** Personnel. **E-mail address:** explore_careers@discovery.com. **World Wide Web address:** http://www.discovery.com. **Description:** Produces the Discovery Channel, a cable television network dedicated to providing information about nature, science and technology, history, and world exploration. **NOTE:** Search and apply for positions online. **Positions advertised include:** Account Director. **Corporate headquarters location:** Silver Spring MD.

THE WALT DISNEY COMPANY
500 South Buena Vista Street, Burbank CA 91521-7235. 818/560-1811. **Contact:** Staffing Services. **World Wide Web address:** http://disney.go.com. **Description:** One of the nation's top film studios. **Positions advertised include:** VP Human Resources; Director, Business Planning; Accountant; Director Organizational Change and Development; Manager, Human Resources Communications; Digital Media Specialist; IT Coordinator. **Corporate headquarters location:** This location. **Listed on:** New York Stock Exchange. **Stock exchange symbol:** DIS.

DISNEYLAND
P.O. Box 3232, Anaheim CA 92803. 714/781-1600. **Fax:** 714/781-0065. **Recorded jobline:** 800/766-0888. **Contact:** Professional Staffing Department. **E-mail address:** dl.resort.resumes@Disney.com. **World Wide Web address:** http://www.disney.com. **Description:** One of the largest amusement/theme parks in the world. **NOTE:** Search and apply for positions online. **Positions advertised include: include:** Capital Planning Manager; Forecasting and Analysis Manager; Senior Catering and Conventions Services Manager; Sous Chef; Senior Accountant; Accounting Assistant; Market Research Manager; Vacation Planner; Candy Maker. **Corporate headquarters location:** Burbank CA. **Parent company:** The Walt Disney Company. **Operations at this facility include:** Resort/Support Functions.

DIXIELINE LUMBER COMPANY
3250 Sports Arena Boulevard, San Diego CA 92110. 619/224-4120. **Fax:** 619/222-2762. **Contact:** Brian Petretta, Human Resource Recruiter. **E-mail address:** ssolomon@dixieline.com. **World Wide Web address:** http://www.dixieline.com. **Description:** A lumber distributor. The company also operates 10 lumber and home center retail outlets throughout Southern California. **Positions advertised include:** Inside Sales Representative; Cashier; Stocker; Lumber Handler; Counter Sales Representative; Contractor Sales Representative; Load Builder; Millman; Receiving Manager; Department Manager; Forklift Operator. **Corporate headquarters location:** This location. **Operations at this facility include:** Administration; Divisional Headquarters; Sales; Service. **Listed on:** Privately held. **Number of employees at this location:** 100.

DO ALL BAY AREA
330 Commerce Circle, Sacramento CA 95815. 510/887-1331. **Toll-free phone:** 800/92-DOALL. **Contact:** Personnel. **E-mail address:** info@doall.com. **World Wide Web address:** http://www.doall.com. **Description:** A distributor of machine tools and other industrial supplies. **Corporate headquarters location:** Hartford CT.

DOCTORS MEDICAL CENTER
2000 Vale Road, San Pablo CA 94806. 510/970-5000. **Fax:** 510/970-5730. **Contact:** Human Resources. **World Wide Web address:** http://www.doctorsmedicalcenter.org. **Description:** A 232-bed acute care hospital serving the East Bay area of Northern California. **Positions advertised include:** Registered Nurse, Various Departments; Pharmacist; Laboratory Manager; Respiratory Tech; Speech Therapist; Mammography Tech; Clinical Nursing Manager; Registered Dietitian. **Parent company:** West Contra Costa Healthcare District. **Number of employees at this location:** 900.

DOCUMENTUM INC.
6801 Koll Center Parkway, Pleasanton CA 94566. 925/600-6800. **Fax:** 925/600-6850. **Contact:** Human Resources. **E-mail address:** jobs@documentum.com. **World Wide Web address:** http://www.documentum.com. **Description:** Develops client/server software for document management. **Positions advertised include:** Senior Financial Analyst. **Corporate headquarters location:** This location. **Other U.S. locations:** Dallas TX; Englewood CO; Bellevue WA; South Jordan UT; Cambridge MA. **Parent company:** EMC Corporation.

DOLE FOOD COMPANY, INC.
One Dole Drive, Westlake Village CA 91362-7300. 818/879-6600. **Contact:** Human Resources. **E-mail address:** dole@rpc.webhire.com. **World Wide Web address:** http://www.dole.com. **Description:** Processes canned fruits. Founded in 1851. **NOTE:** Candidates can search and apply for open positions online. Unsolicited resumes are not accepted. **Positions advertised include:** Senior Corporate Accountant; Consumer Response Specialist; Business Analyst; Business Systems Integrator; Director of Internal Audit; Inventory Systems Supervisor; Tax Analyst. **Special programs:** Internships. **Corporate headquarters location:** This location. **Listed on:** New York Stock Exchange. **Stock exchange symbol:** DOL. **Number of employees worldwide:** 36,000.

DOUGLAS FURNITURE OF CALIFORNIA INC.
4000 Redondo Beach Avenue, Redondo Beach CA 90278. 310/643-7200. **Contact:** Mr. Steve Wilk, Human Resources Director. **World Wide Web address:** http://www.douglasfurniture.com. **Description:** Manufactures a line of household cabinets for electronics and appliances. **Corporate headquarters location:** This location.

DOWNEY SAVINGS AND LOAN ASSOCIATION
3501 Jamboree Road, Newport Beach CA 92660. 949/509-4309. **Fax:** 949/854-4979. **Contact:** Employment Department. **E-mail address:** humanresources@downeysavings.com. **World Wide Web address:** http://www.downeysavings.com. **Description:** A retail banking and residential real estate loan institution. The association operates through 52 California offices. **Positions advertised include:** Account Officer; Business Analyst; Community Development and Investment Analyst; Sr. Database Administrator; Direct Banking Specialist; Loan Auditor. **Corporate headquarters location:** This location. **Listed on:** New York Stock Exchange. **Stock exchange symbol:** DSL.

DREYER'S GRAND ICE CREAM, INC.
5929 College Avenue, Oakland CA 94618. 510/652-8187. **Contact:** Human Resources. **World Wide Web address:** http://www.dreyersinc.com. **Description:** Manufactures and distributes ice cream and other dairy dessert products under the Edy's Grand Ice Cream brand name. **Positions advertised include:** Financial Analyst; Materials Analyst; Network Systems Analyst. **Corporate headquarters location:** This location. **Listed on:** NASDAQ. **Stock exchange symbol:** DRYR. **Number of employees nationwide:** 6,000.

DRIVER ALLIANT INSURANCE SERVICES
1620 Fifth Avenue, San Diego CA 92101-2797. 619/238-1828. **Fax:** 619/699-1323. **Contact:** Director of Human Resources. **E-mail address:** hr@driveralliant.com. **World Wide Web address:** http://www.driveralliant.com. **Description:** Provides commercial and personal insurance including automobile, business, and homeowners. **Positions advertised include:** Account Executive; Associate Broker. **Corporate headquarters location:** This location. Other area locations: Bakersfield CA; Carlsbad CA; Escondido CA; Fresno CA; Lodi CA; Newport Beach CA; Ontario CA; Sacramento CA. **Operations at this facility include:** Sales; Service. **Number of employees at this location:** 220.

DUN & BRADSTREET, INC.
725 South Figueroa Street, Los Angeles CA 90017. 213/430-9209. **Contact:** District Manager. **E-mail address:** hrsourcing@dnb.com. **World Wide Web address:** http://www.dnb.com. **Description:** Provides business-to-business credit, marketing, and investment management services. **NOTE:** Interested candidates can search and apply for positions online. **Positions advertised include:** Relationship Manager. **Corporate headquarters location:** Short Hills NJ. **Parent company:** The Dun & Bradstreet Corporation. **Operations at this facility include:** Sales. **Listed on:** New York Stock Exchange. **Stock exchange symbol:** DNB. **Number of employees worldwide:** 6,100.

DUNN-EDWARDS CORPORATION
4885 East 52nd Place, Los Angeles CA 90040. **Toll-free phone:** 888/337-2468. **Contact:** Human Resources Manager. **World Wide Web address:** http://www.dunnedwards.com. **Description:** The largest employee-owned paint manufacturer in the U.S. Operates 70 stores in Arizona, California, Nevada, New Mexico, and Texas. **Corporate headquarters location:** This location.

E! ENTERTAINMENT TELEVISION NETWORKS
5750 Wilshire Boulevard, Los Angeles CA 90036. 323/954-2400. **Recorded jobline:** 323/954-2666. **Contact:** Human Resources. **E-mail address:** hr@eentertainment.com. **World Wide Web address:** http://www.eentertainment.com. **Description:** Operates a cable network dedicated to the entertainment and fashion industries. **Positions advertised include:** Rights and Clearance Coordinator; Accounts Payable Clerk; Production Accountant, Coordinator, International Marketing; Director, Research. **Special programs:** Internships. **Internship information:** For more information regarding internships call: 323/954-2710. **Corporate headquarters location:** This location. **Other U.S. locations:** New York NY; Chicago IL; Windsor CT.

E*TRADE
532 Market Street, San Francisco CA 94104. 415/445-0101. **Contact:** Human Resources. **E-mail address:** jobs@etrade.com. **World Wide Web address:** http://www.etrade.com. **Description:** Operates a Website that provides online investing services. **NOTE:** Resumes may be submitted by e-mail, fax, or mail. Address resumes to: E*Trade Financial Corporation, P.O. Box 84, Nutting Lake MA 01865-0084. **Special programs:** Internships. **Corporate headquarters location:** New York NY. **International locations:** Worldwide. **Listed on:** New York Stock Exchange. **Stock exchange symbol:** ET.

E&Y KENNETH LEVENTHAL REAL ESTATE GROUP
2049 Century Park East, Suite 1800, Los Angeles CA 90067. 310/277-0880. **Contact:** Human Resources. **World Wide Web address:** http://www.ey.com. **Description:** A full-service real estate agency providing real estate, tax, and audit advice to developers, builders, lenders, owners, and users of real estate. **Positions advertised include:** Assurance Manager; Tax Consulting Manager; Corporate Finance Analyst; Business Risk Services Auditor; Senior Manager, Real Estate Advisory Services. **Parent company:** Ernst & Young.

EDS
2633 Camino Ramon, San Ramon CA 94583. 925/824-1700. **Fax:** 925/824-2900. **Contact:** Recruiter. **E-mail address:** careers@eds.com. **World Wide Web address:** http://www.eds.com. **Description:** Provides integrated hardware, software, and network solutions to *Fortune* 500 companies. **NOTE:** Search and apply for positions online. **Corporate headquarters location:** Plano TX. **Listed on:** New York Stock Exchange. **Stock exchange symbol:** EDS. **Number of employees worldwide:** 130,000.

EMD BIOSCIENCES
10394 Pacific Center Court, San Diego CA 92121. 858/450-9600. **Contact:** Ms. Mary O'Mally, Director of Human Resources. **E-mail address:** jobs@emdbiosciences.com. **World Wide Web address:** http://www.emdbiosciences.com. **Description:** Manufactures fine chemicals for the research, biochemical, and pharmaceutical industries. **NOTE:** Resumes submitted without salary requirements will not be considered. **Positions advertised include:** Business Development Associate; Chemical Buyer; CRM Marketing Coordinator; Import/Export Manager; Scientist. **Corporate headquarters location:** This location. **Parent company:** EMD Chemicals, Inc.

E.M.J.
10650 South Alameda Street, Lynwood CA 90262. 323/567-1122. **Fax:** 323/563-5500. **Contact:** Human Resources. **World Wide Web address:** http://www.emjmetals.com. **Description:** A nationwide distributor and processor of steel and aluminum products. Products include alloy, carbon, stainless, tool, and specialty steels. **Corporate headquarters location:** This location.

ENSR INTERNATIONAL
2850 South Red Hill Avenue, Suite 110, Santa Ana CA 92705. 949/756-2667. **Toll-free phone:** 800/722-2440. **Fax:** 949/756-8461. **Contact:** Human Resources. **E-mail address:** hrwest@ensr.com. **World Wide Web address:** http://www.ensr.com. **Description:** A full-service environmental consulting firm specializing in regulatory compliance management, risk assessment, and remediation. **NOTE:** Search and apply for positions online. **Positions advertised include:** Senior Program Manager; Senior Water Resources Specialist. **Corporate headquarters location:** Westford MA. **Other U.S. locations:** Nationwide.

EAGLE GLOBAL LOGISTICS
19600 Western Avenue, Torrance CA 90501. 310/972-5500. **Contact:** Manager of Human Resources. **World Wide Web address:** http://www.eaglegl.com. **Description:** Provides international air and ocean freight forwarding services. **Positions advertised include:** Managing Director; Operations Manager. **Corporate headquarters location:** Houston TX. **Other area locations:** Sacramento CA; San Diego CA; San Jose CA. **Other U.S. locations:** Nationwide. **International locations:** Worldwide. **Listed on:** NASDAQ. **Stock exchange symbol:** EGL.

EARTH TECH
2101 Webster Street, Suite 1000, Oakland CA 94612. 510/419-6000. **Fax:** 510/419-5122. **Contact:** Personnel Department. **E-mail address:** oaklandjobs@earthtech.com. **World Wide Web address:** http://www.earthtech.com. **Description:** Provides global water management, environmental, and transportation services. **NOTE:** Search and apply for positions online. **Positions advertised include:** Electrical Engineer. **Corporate headquarters location:** Long Beach CA. **Parent company:** Tyco International Ltd. **Listed on:** New York Stock Exchange. **Stock exchange symbol:** TYC.

EARTHLINK
220 Cochrane Circle, San Francisco CA 95037. 408/779-1162. **Fax:** 408/779-3106. **Contact:** Human Resources. **World Wide Web address:** http://www.earthlink.com. **Description:** Designs, develops, and markets telephone and Internet equipment such as Caller ID, voicemail, and e-mail. **Positions advertised include:** Product Manager; Sr. Web Developer; Account Manager; Director of Portal Engineering; Sr. Software Engineer. **Corporate headquarters location:** Atlanta GA. **Other area locations:** Pasadena CA; Pleasanton CA; Roseville CA; Sacramento CA; San Jose CA. **Other U.S. locations:** Phoenix AZ; Kansas City KS; Jackson MN; Harrisburg PA; Knoxville TN; Dallas TX. **Listed on:** NASDAQ. **Stock exchange symbol:** ELNK.

EAST LOS ANGELES COLLEGE
1301 Cesar Chavez Avenue, Monterey Park CA 91754. 323/265-8650. **Recorded jobline:** 213/419-5122. **Contact:** Human Resources. **World Wide Web address:** http://www.elac.cc.ca.us. **Description:** A two-year, community college. Part of the Los Angeles community College District. **Positions advertised include:** Mathematics Faculty; History Faculty; Respiratory Therapy Instructor**Corporate headquarters location:** This location. **Number of employees at this location:** 600.

EATON AEROSPACE
4660 Colorado Boulevard, Los Angeles CA 90039. 818/409-0200. **Contact:** Personnel Manager. **World Wide Web address:** http://www.eaton.com. **Description:** Manufactures and designs actuators, servomechanisms, AC/DC motors, solenoids, and gears. **Positions advertised include:** Senior Contracts Administrator; Test Engineer; Senior Manufacturing Engineer; Product Quality Engineer. **Corporate headquarters location:** Cleveland OH. **Other area locations:** Irvine CA; Costa Mesa CA; Pomona CA; Lafayette CA; Santa Fe Springs CA. **Listed on:** New York Stock Exchange. **Stock exchange symbol:** ETN.

EATON AEROSPACE
4520 Electronics Place, Los Angeles CA 90039. 818/550-4200. **Contact:** Human Resources. **World Wide Web address:** http://www.eaton.com. **Description:** Manufactures and designs actuators, servomechanisms, AC/DC motors, solenoids, and gears. **Positions advertised include:** Power Systems Engineer; Sales Engineer. **Corporate headquarters location:** Cleveland OH. **Other area locations:** Irvine CA; Costa Mesa CA; Pomona CA; Lafayette CA; Santa Fe Springs CA.**Operations at this facility include:** Manufacturing; Research and Development. **Listed on:** New York Stock Exchange. **Stock exchange symbol:** ETN.

eBAY, INC.
2145 Hamilton Avenue, San Jose CA 95125. 408/558-7400. **Contact:** Human Resources. **World Wide Web address:** http://www.ebay.com. **Description:** An online auction site that offers items such as antiques, coins, computers, stamps, and toys. **NOTE:** Sesarch and apply for positions online. **Positions advertised include:** Sr. Software Engineer; Content Manager; Sr. QA Engineer; Sr. Marketing Data Architect; Web Application Developer; Sr. Business Analyst. **Corporate headquarters location:** This location. **Listed on:** NASDAQ. **Stock exchange symbol:** EBAY.

EBERLINE SERVICES
2030 Wright Avenue, P.O. Box 4040, Richmond CA 94804-3823. 510/235-2633. **Toll-free phone:** 800/841-5487. **Fax:** 510/235-0438. **Contact:** Human Resources Administrator. **E-mail address:** hr@eberlineservices.com. **World Wide Web address:** http://www.eberlineservices.com. **Description:** Engaged in hazardous, radiological, and mixed-waste testing of soil and water. The company's work is related to regulatory compliance, and each of their laboratories is extensively licensed and qualified to accept radioactive samples. **Positions advertised include:** Radiochemistry Laboratory Manager. **Corporate headquarters location:** Albuquerque NM. **Other U.S. locations:** Los Alamos NM; Denver CO; Lionville PA; Oak Ridge TN; Richland WA.

EDELBROCK CORPORATION
2700 California Street, Torrance CA 90503. 310/781-2222. **Fax:** 310/972-2735. **Contact:** Human Resources. **E-mail address:** sherrmann@edelbrock.com. **World Wide Web address:** http://www.edelbrock.com. **Description:** Designs, manufactures, distributes, and markets a wide range of high-quality performance products including intake manifolds, carburetors, camshafts, cylinder heads, exhaust systems, and other components designed for most domestic V8 and selected V6 engines. These products are designed to enhance street, off-road, recreational, and competition vehicle performance through increased horsepower, torque, and maneuverability. The company also designs and markets chrome aluminum air cleaners, valve covers, and breathers, which enhance engine and vehicle appearance. **Corporate headquarters location:** This location. **Listed on:** NASDAQ. **Stock exchange symbol:** EDEL.

EDELMAN PUBLIC RELATIONS WORLDWIDE
221 Main Street, Suite 1300, San Francisco CA 94105. 415/222-9944. **Fax:** 415/222-9924. **Contact:** Recruiting. **E-mail address:** online.recruiting@edelman.com. **World Wide Web address:** http://www.edelman.com. **Description:** A public relations firm. **Positions advertised include:** Vice President; Sr. Account Executive. **Corporate headquarters location:** Chicago IL. **Special programs:** Internships.

EDGE DYNAMICS, INC.
1001 Marshall Street, Suite 500, Redwood City CA 94063. 650/780-7800. **Fax:** 650/780-7801. **Contact:** Human Resources. **World Wide Web address:** http://www.edgedynamics.com. **Description:** Edge Dynamics provides pharmaceutical manufacturers enterprise software for commerce optimization, solutions that optimize sales, distribution, and supply chain operations while complementing traditional transaction management and analytic systems.

EDIFY CORPORATION
2840 San Tomas Expressway, Santa Clara CA 95051. 408/982-2000. **Toll-free phone:** 800/944-0056. **Fax:** 408/982-0777. **Contact:** Human Resources. **E-mail address:** careers@edify.com. **World Wide Web address:** http://www.edify.com. **Description:** Develops software including Electronic Workforce, which provides a company's customers with corporate information through connections using the World Wide Web, telephone, and other interactive media. **Positions advertised include:** Senior Product Manager; Senior Software Engineer; Senior Accountant; Client Services Sales Manager. **Corporate headquarters location:** This location. **Listed on:** NASDAQ. **Stock exchange symbol:** EDFY.

EDISON INTERNATIONAL
2244 Walnut Grove Avenue, Rosemead CA 91770. 626/302-1212. **Contact:** Human Resources. **E-mail address:** employ@sce.com. **World Wide Web address:** http://www.edison.com. **Description:** A holding company. **NOTE:** Resumes may be submitted by e-mail or mail. Address resumes to: Edison International, Human Resources Staffing, P.O. Box 800, Rosemead CA 91770. **Corporate headquarters location:** This location. **Subsidiaries include:** Southern California Edison Company. **Listed on:** New York Stock Exchange. **Stock exchange symbol:** EIX.

EDUCATIONAL INSIGHTS, INC.
18730 South Wilmington Avenue, Suite 100, Rancho Dominguez 90220. 310/884-2000. **Contact:** Human Resources. **World Wide Web address:** http://www.edin.com. **Description:** Designs, develops, and markets educational supplemental materials and educationally oriented toys and games intended for use in both homes and schools. The company produces nearly 800 products including electronic teaching devices; interactive science kits; reading and language arts kits; math and geography games; and activity books. Particularly successful have been the GeoSafari interactive learning system and MathSafari, which teaches basic math concepts through fractions, decimals, and percentages to children preschool age and older. **Corporate headquarters location:** This location.

EDWARDS LIFESCIENCES
One Edwards Way, Irvine CA 92614. 949/250-2500. **Toll-free phone:** 800/428-3278. **Contact:** Human Resources. **E-mail address:** eweb@edwards.com. **World Wide Web address:** http://www.edwards.com. **Description:** Designs, develops, manufactures, and markets disposable medical devices used in the handling, processing, and purifying of blood during surgical and medical procedures. **NOTE:** Search and apply for positions online. **Positions advertised include:** Catheter Design Engineer; Clinical Research Associate; Compensation Analyst; Director, Clinical Marketing; Engineering Technician; International Tax Manager; Manager, Human Resources. **Corporate headquarters location:** This location. **International locations:** Worldwide. **Listed on:** New York Stock Exchange. **Stock exchange symbol:** EW. **Annual sales/revenues:** $860 million. **Number of employees at this location:** 1,400. **Number of employees worldwide:** 5,000.

ELAN PHARMACEUTICALS, INC.
800 Gateway Boulevard, South San Francisco CA 94080. 650/877-0900. **Fax:** 650/553-7138. **Contact:** Recruiter. **E-mail address:** careers@elanpharma.com. **World Wide Web address:** http://www.elan.com. **Description:** A research-based pharmaceutical company with a focus on drug delivery systems and specializing in neurology, cancer, pain management, and infectious diseases. **NOTE:** Search and apply for positions online. **Positions advertised include:** Accountant; Patent Attorney; Reimbursement Analyst; Scientist. **Corporate headquarters location:** Dublin, Ireland. **Parent company:** Elan Corporation. **Listed on:** New York Stock Exchange. **Stock exchange symbol:** ELN. **Number of employees worldwide:** 2,000.

ELAN PHARMACEUTICALS, INC.
7475 Lusk Boulevard, San Diego CA 92121. 858/457-2553. **Fax:** 858/457-4823. **Contact:** Human Resources. **World Wide Web address:** http://www.elan.com. **Description:** A research-based pharmaceutical company with a focus on drug delivery systems and specializing in neurology, cancer, pain management, and infectious diseases. **Positions advertised include:** Sr. Manager, Clinical Data Management; Sr. Manager, Medical Communications; Director Pharmacoeconomics & Health Outcomes. **Corporate headquarters location:** Dublin, Ireland. **Parent company:** Elan Corporation. **Listed on:** New York Stock Exchange. **Stock exchange symbol:** ELN.

ELECTRA-GEAR
1110 North Anaheim Boulevard, Anaheim CA 92801. 714/535-6061. **Toll-free phone:** 800/877-4327. **Fax:** 714/535-2489. **Contact:** April Price, Human Resources Administrator. **E-mail address:** humanresources@electragear.com. **World Wide Web address:** http://www.electragear.com. **Description:** Manufactures a wide variety of motors, gear boxes, and speed reducers. **Corporate headquarters location:** Beloit WI. **Parent company:** Regal-Beloit Corporation. **Listed on:** New York Stock Exchange. **Number of employees at this location:** 130.

ELECTRIC POWER RESEARCH INSTITUTE (EPRI)
3412 Hillview Avenue, Palo Alto CA 94304. 650/855-2000. **Contact:** Human Resources. **World Wide Web address:** http://www.epri.com. **Description:** A nonprofit research management firm specializing in all areas of electric power production, origin, transmission, distribution, storage, and end use. Founded in 1973. **NOTE:** Search and apply for positions online. **Positions advertised include:** Director, Information Technology; Research Project Manager; Senior Project Manager; Technical Leader. **Corporate headquarters location:** This location. **Number of employees at this location:** 500. **Number of employees nationwide:** 850.

ELECTRO RENT CORPORATION
6060 Sepulveda Boulevard, Van Nuys CA 91411-2512. 818/787-2100. **Toll-free phone:** 800/688-1111. **Fax:** 818/786-1602. **Contact:** Human Resources. **E-mail address:** maya@electrorent.com. **World Wide Web address:** http://www.electrorent.com. **Description:** Rents and leases electronic equipment including test and measurement instruments, workstations, personal computers, and data communication products. **NOTE:** E-mail is the preferred method of resume submission. **Positions advertised include:** Inside Sales Representative; Account Development Representative; Senior RF Technician. **Corporate headquarters location:** This location. **Other U.S. locations:** Nationwide. **Listed on:** NASDAQ. **Stock exchange symbol:** ELRC. **Annual sales/revenues:** More than $100 million. **Number of employees at this location:** 200. **Number of employees nationwide:** 500.

ELECTROGLAS, INC.
6024 Silver Creek Valley Road, San Jose CA 95138. 408/528-3000. **Contact:** Human Resources. **E-mail address:** staffing@electroglas.com. **World Wide Web address:** http://www.electroglas.com. **Description:** Develops, manufactures, markets, and services automatic wafer probing equipment for use in the fabrication of semiconductor devices. Founded in 1960. **Positions advertised include:** Applications Engineer; Field Service Sales and Marketing. **Corporate headquarters location:** This location. **Listed on:** NASDAQ. **Stock exchange symbol:** EGLS.

ELECTRONIC ARTS, INC.
209 Redwood Shore Parkway, Redwood City CA 94065. 650/628-1500. **Contact:** Human Resources. **World Wide Web address:** http://www.ea.com. **Description:** Creates, markets, and distributes interactive entertainment software for use primarily on independent game systems and IBM-compatible PCs. **Positions advertised include:** SW Engineer; Peoplesoft Developer/Analyst; Compensation Consultant; Product Manager; Art Director; Audio Engineer; Category Manager. **Corporate headquarters location:** This location. **Listed on:** NASDAQ. **Stock exchange symbol:** ERTS. **Number of employees worldwide:** 4,400.

ELECTRONIC CLEARING HOUSE, INC. (ECHO)
730 Paseo Camarillo, Camarillo CA 93010. 800/262-3246. **Fax:** 805/419-8683. **Contact:** Human Resources. **E-mail address:** hr@echo-inc.com. **World Wide Web address:** http://www.echo-inc.com. **Description:** A holding company. **Positions advertised include:** Salesperson. **Corporate headquarters location:** This location. **Subsidiaries include:** National Credit Card Reserve Corporation, which provides electronic credit card authorizations, fund transfers, and deposits for merchants, banks, and other customers; XpressCheX, Inc., which provides check guarantee services; ECHO Payment Services, Inc., which leases, rents, and sells point of sale terminals and related equipment; and Computer Based Controls, Inc., which designs, manufactures, and sells terminals and related equipment. **Listed on:** NASDAQ. **Stock exchange symbol:** ECHO.

ELECTRONIC DATA SYSTEMS CORPORATION (EDS)
1325 McCandless Drive, Milpitas CA 95035. 408/941-4600. **Fax:** 800/562-6241. **Contact:** Human Resources. **E-mail address:** careers@eds.com. **World Wide Web address:** http://www.eds.com. **Description:** An international supplier of mechanical and engineering software and services. **Listed on:** New York Stock Exchange. **Stock exchange symbol:** EDS. **Number of employees worldwide:** 1,200.

ELECTRONICS FOR IMAGING, INC.
303 Velocity Way, Foster City CA 94404. 650/357-3500. **Fax:** 650/357-3907. **Contact:** Human Resources. **E-mail address:** enghr@efi.com. **World Wide Web address:** http://www.efi.com. **Description:** Designs and markets products that enable high-quality color printing in short production runs. The company's Fiery Color Servers incorporate hardware and software technologies that transform digital color copiers into fast, high-quality color printers. **Positions advertised include:** Cost Accountant; Treasury Analyst; Corporate Counsel; Sr. UI Designer. **Corporate headquarters location:** This location. **Listed on:** NASDAQ. **Stock exchange symbol:** EFII.

ELGAR ELECTRONICS CORPORATION
9250 Brown Deer Road, San Diego CA 92121-2294. 858/450-0085. **Toll-free phone:** 800/733-5427. **Fax:** 858/458-0257. **Contact:** Tom Erickson, Vice President of Human Resources. **E-mail address:** admin@elgar.com. **World Wide Web address:** http://www.elgar.com. **Description:** Manufactures power electronics equipment including AC/DC programmable power supplies for test and measurement purposes and power conditioning/back-up systems for special applications such as harsh environments. **Positions advertised include:** Program Manager; Sr. Digital Design Engineer; Mechanical Engineer; Customer Service Engineer. **Corporate headquarters location:** This location. **Operations at this facility include:** Administration; Manufacturing; Research and Development; Sales; Service. **Number of employees at this location:** 400.

ELIXIR INDUSTRIES
17925 South Broadway, Gardena CA 90247. 310/767-3400. **Toll-free phone:** 800/421-1942. **Fax:** 310/767-3412. **Contact:** Human Resources. **E-mail address:** elixircorp@elixirind.com. **World Wide Web address:** http://www.elixirind.com. **Description:** Manufactures metal siding, roofing, doors, frame parts, roof vents, roof domes, and related mobile home products. **Corporate headquarters location:** This location. **Number of employees nationwide:** 1,300.

GEORGE ELKINS MORTGAGE BANKING COMPANY
3130 Wilshire Boulevard, Second Floor, Santa Monica CA 90403. 310/862-1000. **Fax:** 310/862-1050. **Contact:** Chad Eshaghoff. **E-mail address:** ceshaghoff@elkinsmanagement.com. **World Wide Web address:** http://www.elkinsmanagement.com. **Description:** Provides mortgage and loan services to individuals and commercial clients. **Corporate headquarters location:** This location. **Other area locations:** San Francisco CA. **Number of employees at this location:** 50.

ELPAC ELECTRONICS INC.
1562 Reynolds Avenue, Irvine CA 92614. 949/476-6070. **Toll-free phone:** 888/ELPAC80. **Fax:** 949/476-6080. **Contact:** Human Resources. **E-mail address:** employment@elpac.com. **World Wide Web address:** http://www.elpac.com. **Description:** Manufactures power supplies, capacitors, and filters. **Positions advertised include:** Regulatory Agency Engineer; Regional Sales Manager. **Corporate headquarters location:** This location. **Operations at this facility include:** Manufacturing.

EMBEE INC.
P.O. Box 15705, Santa Ana CA 92735-0705. 714/546-9842. **Physical address:** 2136 South Hathaway Street, Santa Ana CA 92705. **Fax:** 714/546-4037. **Contact:** Human Resources. **E-mail address:** embee@embee.com. **World Wide Web address:** http://www.embee.com. **Description:** Manufactures electromagnetic parts for aerospace applications. **Corporate headquarters location:** This location.

EMBEE TECHNOLOGIES
16592 Millikan Ave. Irvine, CA 92606. 949/266-1700. **Fax:** 949/435-1595. **Contact:** Human Resources. **World Wide Web address:** http://www.embee.com. **Description:** Provides a portfolio of business and technology solutions to enable our clients to improve their business performance. Embee's core portfolio comprises IT, wireless and structured cabling services. **Positions advertised include:** Account Executive, Network Project Manager/Consultant, Network Engineer, Project Manager Cabling & Wireless. **Parent company:** Embee Inc.

EMPLOYERS DIRECT INSURANCE COMPANY
P.O. Box 5043, Thousand Oaks CA 91359. 818/575-8515. **Fax:** 818/474-8645. **Contact:** June Duxler, V.P. Human Resources & Administration. **E-mail address:** HR@edicwc.com. **World Wide Web address:** http://www.edicwc.com. **Description:** Provides insurance. **Positions advertised include:** Managing Attorney; Sr. Claims Examiner; Claims Assistant.

EMULEX CORPORATION
3333 Susan Street, Costa Mesa CA 92626-7112. 714/662-5600. **Toll-free phone:** 800/EMULEX-1. **Fax:** 714/241-0792. **Contact:** Sadie Herrera, Director of Human Resources. **E-mail address:** hr@emulex.com. **World Wide Web address:** http://www.emulex.com. **Description:** Emulex Corporation specializes in intelligent interface technology for the computer industry. Emulex designs, manufactures, and markets data storage and network connectivity products, as well as advanced integrated circuits. **Positions advertised include:** Sr. Customer Program Manager; Sr. Product Marketing Manager; Marketing Director; Supply Chain Specialist; OEM Support Engineer Senior Engineer; VP, Marketing. **Corporate headquarters location:** This location. **Other U.S. locations:** Bolton MA; Longmont CO; Bothell WA. **Listed on:** NASDAQ. **Stock exchange symbol:** EMLX.

ENCAD, INC.
6059 Cornerstone Court West, San Diego CA 92121. 858/452-0882. **Toll-free phone:** 800/45-ENCAD. **Fax:** 858/457-5831. **Contact:** Human Resources. **E-mail address:** jobs1@encad.com. **World Wide Web address:** http://www.encad.com. **Description:** ENCAD, Inc. designs, develops, manufactures, and markets wide-format, color ink-jet printers and plotters. Typical users are in industries utilizing computer-aided design; architectural, engineering, and construction design; geographic information systems such as surveying and mapping; and graphic arts such as digital photo imaging and editing, sign-making, three-dimensional renderings, and presentation graphics. **Positions advertised include:** Product Manager. **Corporate headquarters location:** This location.

ENDEVCO CORPORATION
30700 Rancho Viejo Road, San Juan Capistrano CA 92675. 949/493-8181. **Toll-free phone:** 800/982-6732. **Fax:** 949/661-7231. **Contact:** Jack Marieta, Personnel Administrator. **E-mail address:** jobs@endevco.com. **World Wide Web address:** http://www.endevco.com. **Description:** Manufactures electronic instrumentation systems that measure vibration, shock, motion, and pressure. **Positions advertised include:** Applications Engineer; Product Manager; Health, Safety, and Environment Coordinator. **Corporate headquarters location:** This location. **Parent company:** Meggitt PLC. **Operations at this facility include:** Administration; Manufacturing; Research and Development; Sales; Service.

ENLOE MEDICAL CENTER
1531 Esplanade, Chico CA 95926. 530/332-7300. **Toll-free phone:** 800/822-8102x7352. **Fax:** 530/899-2010. **Recorded jobline:** 530/892-6711. **Contact:** Charlene Davis, Recruiting Manager. **E-mail address:** recruiter@enloe.org. **World Wide Web address:** http://www.enloe.org. **Description:** A nonprofit, 203-bed, regional, Level II trauma center. Enloe Medical Center offers a variety of services including breast cancer exams, cancer treatment, children's services, clinical laboratory services, educational programs, emergency/trauma services, gastroenterology, heart care, home care, hospice services, maternity care, neurological care, nutrition services, occupational health and risk assessment center, pharmacy, physical therapy, radiology, respiratory care, social services, stress management, surgery, and a trauma/surgical intensive care unit. Founded in 1913. **NOTE:** Entry-level positions and second and third shifts are offered. **Positions advertised include:** Registered Nurse; Licensed Vocational Nurse; Certified Nursing Assistant; Unit Secretary; Admissions Representative; Chief Radiology Technologist; Clinical Dietitian; Computer Operator; Emergency Medical Technician; Laboratory Assistant; Occupational Therapist; Patient Support Clerk; Pharmacist; Physical Therapist; Social Worker; Speech Therapist; Surgical Technologist. **Special programs:** Internships; Training. **Office hours:** Monday - Friday, 8:00 a.m. - 5:00 p.m. **CEO:** Phil Wolfe. **Number of employees at this location:** 1,800.

ENOVATION GRAPHIC SYSTEMS INC.
4425 Sheila Street, Los Angeles CA 90023. 323/268-9500. **Fax:** 323/260-4335. **Contact:** Personnel. **World Wide Web address:** http://www.enovationgraphics.com. **Description:** A wholesaler of electronic components. **Corporate headquarters location:** Valhalla NY. **Other U.S. locations:** Nationwide. **Parent company:** Fujifilm. **Operations at this facility include:** Administration; Regional Headquarters; Sales. **Annual sales/revenues:** More than $100 million. **Number of employees at this location:** 200. **Number of employees nationwide:** 1,500.

ENVIRON CORPORATION
6001 Shellmound Street, Suite 700, Emeryville CA 94608. 510/655-7400. **Fax:** 510/655-9517. **Contact:** Mary Eichler, Director of Human Resources. **E-mail address:** hremeryville@environcorp.com. **World Wide Web address:** http://www.environcorp.com. **Description:** A multidisciplinary environmental and health sciences consulting firm that provides a broad range of services relating to the presence of hazardous substances in the environment, consumer products, and the workplace. Services provided by ENVIRON are concentrated in the assessment and management of chemical risk. **Positions advertised include:** Associate, Due Diligence; Associate, Human Health Risk Assessment; Sr. Manager, Hydrogeology; Sr. Ecological Risk Assessor. **Corporate headquarters location:** Arlington VA. **Other area locations:** Irvine CA; Novato CA. **Other U.S. locations:** Princeton NJ; Houston TX. **Parent company:** Applied BioScience International Inc.

ENVIRON CORPORATION
2010 Main Street, Suite 900, Irvine CA 92614. 949/261-5151. **Fax:** 949/261-6202. **Contact:** Human Resources. **World Wide Web address:** http://www.environcorp.com. **Description:** A multidisciplinary environmental and health sciences consulting firm that provides a broad range of services relating to the presence of hazardous substances in the environment, consumer products, and the workplace. Services provided by ENVIRON are concentrated on the assessment and management of chemical risk. **Corporate headquarters location:** Arlington VA. **Other area locations:** Emeryville CA; Novato CA. **Other U.S. locations:** Princeton NJ; Houston TX. **Parent company:** Applied BioScience International Inc.

ENVIRON CORPORATION
101 Rowland Way, Suite 220, Novato CA 94945. 415/899-0700. **Fax:** 415/899-0707. **Contact:** Human Resources. **World Wide Web address:** http://www.environcorp.com. **Description:** A multidisciplinary environmental and health sciences consulting firm that provides a broad range of services relating to the presence of hazardous substances in the environment, consumer products, and the workplace. Services provided by ENVIRON are concentrated in the assessment and management of chemical risk. **Corporate headquarters location:** Arlington VA. **Other area locations:** Emeryville CA; Irvine CA. **Other U.S. locations:** Princeton NJ; Houston TX. **Parent company:** Applied BioScience International Inc.

EPICOR SOFTWARE CORPORATION
18200 Von Karman Avenue, Suite 1000, Irvine CA 92612. 949/585-4000. **Fax:** 949/585-4093. **Contact:** Human Resources. **E-mail address:** careers@epicor.com. **World Wide Web address:** http://www.epicor.com. **Description:** Develops financial and manufacturing software for use in a client/server environment. Epicor Software focuses exclusively on mid-market companies. Founded in 1984. **Positions advertised include:** Sr. Financial Analyst; Marketing Programs Manager; Sr. Applications Specialist; IS Support Administrator. **Office hours:** Monday - Friday, 8:00 a.m. - 5:00 p.m. **Corporate headquarters location:** This location. **Other area locations:** Oakland CA; Gold River CA; San Diego CA. **Other U.S. locations:** Nationwide. **International locations:** Worldwide. **Listed on:** NASDAQ. **Stock exchange symbol:** EPIC. **Annual sales/revenues:** $153 million. **Number of employees worldwide:** 950.

EPIMMUNE INC.
5820 Nancy Ridge Drive, San Diego CA 92121-2829. 858/860-2500. **Fax:** 858/860-2600. **Contact:** Human Resources. **E-mail address:** careers@epimmune.com. **World Wide Web address:** http://www.epimmune.com. **Description:** Researches and develops vaccines to prevent and treat infectious diseases and cancer. **Positions advertised include:** Senior Quality Assurance Associate. **Corporate headquarters location:** This location. **Listed on:** NASDAQ. **Stock exchange symbol:** EPMN.

EPLUS, INC.
1900 Point West Way, Suite 120, Sacramento CA 95815. 916/568-1555. **Toll-free phone:** 800/827-5711. **Fax:** 916/568-1590. **Contact:** Human Resources. **E-mail address:** hr@eplus.com. **World Wide Web address:** http://www.eplus.com. **Description:** Leases and sells computers and other IT equipment. ePlus also develops online software products that provide supply chain management solutions including electronic procurement, e-financing, and e-asset management. **Corporate headquarters location:** Herndon VA. **Other area locations:** Del Mar CA; San Diego CA; San Jose CA. **Other U.S. locations:** Nationwide. **Listed on:** NASDAQ. **Stock exchange symbol:** PLUS.

ERNST & YOUNG LLP
303 Almaden Boulevard, San Jose CA 95110. 408/947-5500. **Contact:** Director of Human Resources. **World Wide Web address:** http://www.ey.com. **Description:** A certified public accounting firm that also provides management consulting services. Services include data processing, financial modeling, financial feasibility studies, production planning and inventory management, management sciences, health care planning, human resources, cost accounting, and budgeting systems. **NOTE:** Search and apply for positions online. **Positions advertised include:** Assurance Manager; Senior Recruiter; Tax Manager; Technology Support Specialist; IT Audit Senior Manager. **Corporate headquarters location:** New York NY.

ERNST & YOUNG LLP
560 Mission Street, Suite 1300, San Francisco CA 94105. 415/894-8000. **Contact:** Director of Human Resources. **World Wide Web address:** http://www.ey.com. **Description:** A certified public accounting firm that also provides management consulting services. Services include data processing, financial modeling, financial feasibility studies, production planning and inventory management, management sciences, health care planning, human resources, cost accounting, and budgeting systems. **NOTE:** Search and apply for positions online. **Positions advertised include:** Tax Manager; Assurance Manager; Contract Recruiter; Business Risk Services Senior Auditor; Proposal Writer. **Corporate headquarters location:** New York NY.

EUPHONIX INC.
220 Portage Avenue, Palo Alto CA 94306-2242. 650/855-0400. **Fax:** 650/855-0410. **Contact:** Human Resources Manager. **E-mail address:** hr@euphonix.com. **World Wide Web address:** http://www.euphonix.com. **Description:** A manufacturer of digitally controlled mixing consoles and audio components. **Positions advertised include:** Software Engineer; Software Architect. **Corporate headquarters location:** This location.

EVEREX COMMUNICATIONS INC.
5020-A Brandin Court, Fremont CA 94538. 510/687-0075. **Fax:** 510/683-2021. **Contact:** Human Resources. **E-mail address:** jobs@everexcomm.net. **World Wide Web address:** http://www.everexcomm.net. **Description:** Focuses upon wireless Gateway and Internet appliance network solutions targeted at the small business and home environments. **Corporate headquarters location:** This location. **Operations at this facility include:** Administration; Manufacturing; Sales; Service. **Listed on:** Privately held.

EVERGREEN PULP
P.O. Box 218, Samoa CA 95564. 707/443-7511. **Contact:** Human Resources. **World Wide Web address:** http://www.sppulp.com. **Description:** Produces pulp, formerly known as Stockton Pacific Enterprises. **Parent company:** Lee & Man (Hong Kong).

EXAMINETICS, INC.
10920 Via Frontera, San Diego CA 92127-1704. 858/485-0933. **Fax:** 858/485-8133. **Contact:** Field Recruiting. **E-mail address:** recruiter@examinetics.com. **World Wide Web address:** http://www.examinetics.com. **Description:** A nationwide mobile health testing service. Continuum provides health screening for unions, major corporations, public utilities, and other public and private organizations. **NOTE:** Entry-level positions are offered. **Positions advertised include:** Clerk; Medical Screening Assistant; Licensed Practical Nurse; Licensed Vocational Nurse; Registered Nurse; Occupational Health Specialist; Driver Maintenance Technician. **Corporate headquarters location:** Overland Park KS.

EXAR CORPORATION
48720 Kato Road, Fremont CA 94538. 510/668-7000. **Contact:** Human Resources. **World Wide Web address:** http://www.exar.com. **Description:** Engaged in the design, manufacture, and marketing of analog and mixed signal integrated circuits and subsystems, primarily for use in telecommunications, data communications, microperipherals, and consumer electronics products. **Positions advertised include:** Senior Applications Engineer; Design Engineer; Senior Test Engineer; Senior Compliance Analyst. **Corporate headquarters location:** This location. **Listed on:** NASDAQ. **Stock exchange symbol:** EXAR. **Number of employees worldwide:** 265.

EXCELLON AUTOMATION
24751 Crenshaw Boulevard, Torrance CA 90505-5388. 310/534-6300. **Fax:** 310/534-6777. **Contact:** Human Resources Director. **E-mail address:** hr@excellon.com. **World Wide Web address:** http://www.excellon.com. **Description:** Manufactures machine tools including routers, laser drilling equipment, and high-precision drilling systems. **Corporate headquarters location:** Bellevue WA. **Parent company:** Esterline Technologies. **Operations at this facility include:** Manufacturing. **Listed on:** New York Stock Exchange. **Stock exchange symbol:** ESL. **Number of employees at this location:** 225.

EXCEPTIONAL CHILDREN'S FOUNDATION
8740 West Washington Boulevard, Culver City CA 90232. 310/204-3300. **Fax:** 310/845-8057. **Contact:** Human Resources. **E-mail address:** hrecf@ecf.net. **World Wide Web address:** http://www.ecf-la.org. **Description:** A nonprofit, educational service that provides schooling for children and adults with developmental disabilities. **Positions advertised include:** Developmental and External relations Coordinator; Educators; Developmental Instructor; Counselor; Registered Nurse Supervisor; Certified Nursing Assistant; Case Manager.

EXCITE INC.
555 Broadway, Redwood City CA 94063. 650/568-6000. **Fax:** 650/568-6030. **Contact:** Human Resources Department. **E-mail address:** positions@staff.excite.com. **World Wide Web address:** http://www.excite.com. **Description:** An Internet search engine that offers Web navigation services and features site reviews, editorial columns, news, and regional information. **Positions advertised include:** Marketing Manager; Sales Planner; Graphic Designer; System Operator. **Corporate headquarters location:** This location. **Parent company:** Ask Jeeves, Inc. **Listed on:** NASDAQ. **Stock exchange symbol:** XCIT.

EXECUTIVE SOFTWARE INTERNATIONAL
7590 North Glenoaks Boulevard, Burbank CA 91504. 818/771-1600. **Fax:** 818/252-5514. **Contact:** Becky Rager, Personnel Procurement Officer. **E-mail address:** ppo@executive.com. **World Wide Web address:** http://www.execsoft.com. **Description:** Develops and markets systems software and applications for the Windows NT operating system. **Positions advertised include:** Staff Accountant; Vice President of Public Relations; Axapta Programmer; GUI Designer; Senior Software Engineer. **Corporate headquarters location:** This location. **Listed on:** Privately held. **Annual sales/revenues:** $21 - $50 million. **Number of employees at this location:** 160.

EXELIXIS, INC.
170 Harbor Way, P.O. Box 511, South San Francisco CA 94083-0511. 650/837-7000. **Fax:** 650/837-7226. **Contact:** Human Resources. **E-mail address:** careers@exelixis.com. **World Wide Web address:** http://www.exelixis.com. **Description:** A genomics-based drug research and development company. **Positions advertised include:** Clinical Scientist; Director, Clinical Oncology Research; Senior Scientist; Vice President, Translational Medicine; Assistsant Research Scientist; Safety Technician; Senior Financial Analyst; Director, Operations. **Corporate headquarters location:** This location. **Other U.S. locations:** Portland OR. **Listed on:** NASDAQ. **Stock exchange symbol:** EXEL.

EXPONENT, INC.
149 Commonwealth Drive, Menlo Park CA 94025. 650/326-9400. **Fax:** 650/326-8072. **Contact:** Human Resources Department. **E-mail address:** hr@exponent.com. **World Wide Web address:** http://www.exponent.com. **Description:** A technical consulting firm dedicated to the investigation, analysis, and prevention of accidents and failures of an engineering or scientific nature. The company provides a multidisciplinary approach to analyze how failures occur. The company specializes in accident reconstruction, biomechanics, construction/structural engineering, aviation and marine investigations, environmental assessment, materials and product testing, warning and labeling issues, accident statistical data analysis, and risk prevention/mitigation. Founded in 1967. **NOTE:** Search and apply for positions online. **Positions advertised include:** Thermal Engineer; Senior Systems Engineer; Administrative Assistant; Civil Engineer; Senior Managing Engineer; Principal/Practice Director; Environmental Engineer; Research Assistant; Senior Software Engineer. **Special programs:** Internships. **Office hours:** Monday - Friday, 8:00 a.m. - 5:00 p.m. **Corporate headquarters location:** This location. **Other U.S. locations:** Nationwide. **Subsidiaries include:** Exponent Environmental Group; Exponent Failure Analysis; Exponent Health Group. **Listed on:** NASDAQ. **Stock exchange symbol:** EXPO. **CEO:** Michael Gaulke. **Annual sales/revenues:** $140 million. **Number of employees nationwide:** 675.

EXPONENT, INC.
5401 McConnell Avenue, Los Angeles CA 90066. 310/754-2700. **Fax:** 310/754-2799. **Contact:** Human Resources Department. **E-mail address:** hr@exponent.com. **World Wide Web address:** http://www.exponent.com. **Description:** Provides accident reconstruction, biomechanics, construction/structural engineering, aviation and marine investigations, environmental assessment, materials and product testing, warnings and labeling issues, accident statistic data analysis, and risk prevention/mitigation. Founded in 1967. **NOTE:** Search and apply for positions online. **Positions advertised include:** Senior Engineer/Architect; Managing Engineer/Architect; Civil Engineer; Biomechanical Engineer. **Corporate headquarters location:** Menlo Park CA. **Listed on:** NASDAQ. **Stock exchange symbol:** EXPO.

EXXONMOBIL CORPORATION
3700 West 190th Street, Torrance CA 90509. 310/212-2800. **Contact:** Human Resources. **World Wide Web address:** http://www.exxonmobil.com. **Description:** A refinery facility for the energy developer, producer, and distributor. **Corporate headquarters location:** Irving TX. **Listed on:** New York Stock Exchange. **Stock exchange symbol:** XOM. **Number of employees at this location:** 800.

FM GLOBAL
21860 Burbank Boulevard, Suite 300, Woodland Hills CA 91367. 818/704-1133. **Fax:** 818/883-0759. **Contact:** Human Resources. **E-mail address:** jobs@fmglobal.com. **World Wide Web address:** http://www.fmglobal.com. **Description:** A loss-control services organization. The company helps owner/company policyholders protect their properties and occupancies against damage from fire, wind, flood, and explosion; from boiler, pressure vessel, and machinery accidents; and from many other insured hazards. **NOTE:** Search and apply for positions online. **Corporate headquarters location:** Johnston RI. **Other U.S. locations:** Walnut Creek CA; Norwalk CT; Alpharetta GA; Park Ridge IL; Norwood MA; Novi MI; Plymouth MN; St. Louis MO; Charlotte NC; Parsippany NJ; New York NY; North Olmstead OH; Malvern PA; Plano TX; Houston TX; Reston VA; Bellevue WA. **International locations:** Worldwide. **Number of employees worldwide:** 4,000.

FS PRECISION TECH CO.
3025 East Victoria Street, Rancho Dominguez CA 90221. 310/638-0595. **Fax:** 310/631-2884. **Contact:** Anna Leonard, Human Resources Manager. **E-mail address:** careers@fs-precision.com. **World Wide Web address:** http://www.coastcast.com. **Description:** Manufactures precision castings for a number of specialty products including medical implants, golf clubs, hand tools, and automotive parts. **Corporate headquarters location:** This location.

FACEY MEDICAL FOUNDATION
15451 San Fernando Mission Boulevard, Suite 300, Mission Hills CA 91345. 818/837-5695. **Fax:** 818/365-5706. **Recorded jobline:** 818/837-5695. **Contact:** Marla Adams, Human Resources Representative. **E-mail address:** careers@facey.com. **World Wide**

Web address: http://www.facey.com. **Description:** A nonprofit, multispecialty health care clinic and medical group. Founded in 1922. **NOTE:** Entry-level positions, externships, and second and third shifts are offered. **Positions advertised include:** Administrative Director, Managed Care.

FACTORY 2-U STORES, INC.
15001 South Figueroa Street, Gardena CA 90248. **Fax:** 310/324-9334. **Contact:** Human Resources. **E-mail address:** mailus@factory2-u.com. **World Wide Web address:** http://www.factory2-u.com. **Description:** Operates over 200 Factory 2-U and Family Bargain Center stores, which primarily sell in-season family apparel and housewares at discounted prices. **NOTE:** Entry-level positions are offered. Search and apply for positions online. **Positions advertised include:** Import Assistant; Lease Administrator. **Corporate headquarters location:** This location. **Other U.S. locations:** AZ; LA; NV; NM; OK; OR; TX; WA. **Listed on:** NASDAQ. **Stock exchange symbol:** FTUS. **Chairman and CEO:** Mike Searles. **Annual sales/revenues:** More than $100 million. **Number of employees at this location:** 250. **Number of employees nationwide:** 4,000.

FAIR ISAAC CORPORATION
200 Smith Ranch Road, San Rafael CA 94903. 415/472-2211. **Toll-free phone:** 800/999-2955. **Fax:** 415/492-9381. **Contact:** Human Resources. **World Wide Web address:** http://www.fairisaac.com. **Description:** Develops and provides data management software and services for the consumer credit, personal lines insurance, and direct marketing industries. Founded in 1956. **NOTE:** Search and apply for open positions online. **Positions advertised include:** Analytic Science Lead; Analytic Science Engineer; Business Consulting Manager; Director. **Corporate headquarters location:** Minneapolis MN. **Other U.S. locations:** New Castle DE; Wilmington DE; Atlanta GA; Chicago IL. **Subsidiaries include:** Dynamark (Minneapolis MN); European Analytic Products Group (Birmingham, England). **Listed on:** New York Stock Exchange. **Stock exchange symbol:** FIC.

FAIR ISAAC CORPORATION
3661 Valley Center Drive, San Diego CA 92130. 858/369-8000. **Fax:** 858/369-8001. **Contact:** Human Resources. **World Wide Web address:** http://www.fairisaac.com. **Description:** Develops and markets advanced decision software for the financial services, retail, educational publishing, insurance information, Internet commerce, and market research industries. **NOTE:** Search and apply for positions online. **Positions advertised include:** Accountant; Analytic Science Lead; Analytic Science Manager; Client Relationship Manager; Director, Product Support; Engineer. **Office hours:** Monday - Friday, 8:00 a.m. - 5:00 p.m. **Corporate headquarters location:** Minneapolis MN. **Listed on:** New York Stock Exchange. **Stock exchange symbol:** FIC. **President/CEO:** Thomas G. Grudnowski. **Number of employees at this location:** 425. **Number of employees worldwide:** 2,400.

FAIRCHILD IMAGING
1801 McCarthy Boulevard, Milpitas CA 95035. 408/433-2500. **Fax:** 408/435-8259. **Contact:** Human Resources. **E-mail address:** hr@fcimg.com. **World Wide Web address:** http://www.fairchildimaging.com. **Description:** Produces visible and infrared CCDs and cameras for use in military, space, and commercial applications. **Positions advertised include:** Process Engineering Technician; Senior Systems Engineer; Manufacturing Engineer; Senior Camera Design Engineer. **Corporate headquarters location:** This location.

FAIRCHILD SEMICONDUCTOR CORPORATION
3001 Orchard Parkway, San Jose CA 95134. 408/822-2000. **Toll-free phone:** 800/341-0392. **Contact:** Recruitment. **E-mail address:** corporate.resume@fairchildsemi.com. **World Wide Web address:** http://www.fairchildsemi.com. **Description:** Manufactures semiconductors for use in telecommunications, personal computing, and digital video applications. **Note:** Interested candidates can search and apply for positions online. **Special programs:** Internships; Co-ops. **Corporate headquarters location:** South Portland ME. **Listed on:** New York Stock Exchange. **Stock exchange symbol:** FCS. **Number of employees at this location:** 300.

THE FAIRMONT HOTEL
650 California Street, 12th Floor, San Francisco CA 94108. 415/772-7800. **Fax:** 415/772-7805. **Contact:** Employment Manager. **E-mail address:** pathfinder@fairmont.com. **World Wide Web address:** http://www.fairmont.com. **Description:** A 591-room hotel. Founded in 1907. **NOTE:** Entry-level positions are offered. **Corporate headquarters location:** This location. **Other U.S. locations:** Los Angeles CA; San Jose CA; Chicago IL; New Orleans LA; Boston MA; Kansas City MO; New York NY; Dallas TX. **Operations at this facility include:** Regional Headquarters. **Listed on:** New York Stock Exchange. **Stock exchange symbol:** FHR. **Number of employees at this location:** 800.

FAMILY FUN CENTERS
1041 North Shepard Street, Anaheim CA 92806. 714/630-7212. **Contact:** Human Resources. **E-mail address:** employment@palaceentertainment.com. **World Wide Web address:** http://www.boomersparks.com. **Description:** An amusement park that features paddle boats, go carts, bumper boats, and a maze that is changed monthly. The park also includes a roller skating rink, arcade, and snack bar. **NOTE:** Send applications and resumes to: 4590 MacArthur Boulevard, Suite 400, Newport Beach CA 92660. Fax: 949/261-1414. **Corporate headquarters location:** Irvine CA. **Parent company:** Palace Entertainment Company.

FAR EAST NATIONAL BANK
350 South Grand Avenue, 41st Floor, Los Angeles CA 90071. 213/687-1200. **Fax:** 213/617-7838. **Contact:** Human Resources. **E-mail address:** hr@fenb-us.com. **World Wide Web address:** http://www.fareastnationalbank.com. **Description:** Offers commercial banking services. **NOTE:** Please mail a signed application (available to download on company Website) along with a resume and cover letter to the address listed above. **Positions advertised include:** Loan Portfolio Officer; ICFS Service Assistant; ICFS Operations Officer. **Corporate headquarters location:** This location. **Parent company:** Bank SinoPac.

FARMER JOHN MEATS COMPANY
3049 East Vernon Avenue, Los Angeles CA 90058. 323/583-4621. **Contact:** Anthony Clougherty, Personnel Director. **E-mail address:** farmerjohn@farmerjohn.com. **World Wide Web address:** http://www.farmerjohn.com. **Description:** Processes and packs meat products. **Positions advertised include:** Sanitation Supervisor. **Corporate headquarters location:** This location.

FARMERS AND MERCHANTS BANK
302 Pine Avenue, Long Beach CA 90803. 562/437-0011. **Fax:** 562/590-6307. **Contact:** Human Resources. **World Wide Web address:** http://www.fmb.com. **Description:** A commercial bank offering a wide range of services through 16 local offices. **Position advertised include:** Teller; Operations Manager; Loan Adminstrator; Administrative Assistant. **Corporate headquarters location:** This location. **Other area locations:** Fullerton CA; Garden Grove CA; Lake Forest CA; Lakewood CA; Orange CA; San Juan Capistrano CA; Santa Ana CA; Seal Beach CA. **Operations at this facility include:** Administration. **Number of employees at this location:** 100.

FARMERS INSURANCE GROUP
4680 Wilshire Boulevard, Los Angeles CA 90010. 323/932-3200. **Contact:** Human Resources. **E-mail address:** careers@farmersinsurance.com. **World Wide Web address:** http://www.farmersinsurance.com. **Description:** An insurance organization offering life, automobile, fire, and other forms of coverage to over 9 million property and casualty policyholders. **Positions advertised include:** Agency Development Analyst; Claims Legal Services Paralegal; Entry Level Accountant; Senior Secretary; Corporate Legal Supervisor. **Corporate headquarters location:** This location. **Other area locations:** Pleasanton CA; Simi Valley CA. **Other U.S. locations:** Phoenix AZ; Colorado Springs CO; Pocatello ID; Aurora IL; Columbus OH; Oklahoma City OK; Portland OR; Austin TX.

FARRELL'S ICE CREAM PARLOURS
10606 Camino Ruiz, Miramesa CA 92126. 858/578-9895. **Contact:** Store Supervisor. **World Wide Web address:** http://www.farrellsusa.com. **Description:** A restaurant franchise specializing in ice cream and ice cream products. The restaurants also sell novelties and candy. **Corporate headquarters location:** This location.

FEDERAL EXPRESS CORPORATION (FEDEX)
950 Tower Lane, Suite 770, Foster City CA 94404. 650/578-5100. **Fax:** 650/866-2235. **Recorded jobline:** 888/513-2294. **Contact:** Jon Phillips, Senior Recruitment Specialist. **World Wide Web address:** http://www.fedex.com. **Description:** One of the world's largest express transportation companies serving 212 countries worldwide. FedEx ships approximately 3.2 million packages daily. FedEx operates more than 45,000 drop-off locations, and has a fleet that consists of more than 640 aircraft and 44,5000 vehicles. Founded in 1973. **Corporate headquarters location:** Memphis TN. **Listed on:** New York Stock Exchange. **Stock exchange symbol:** FDX. **Number of employees at this location:** 100. **Number of employees nationwide:** 148,000.

FEDERAL HOME LOAN BANK OF SAN FRANCISCO
P.O. Box 7948, San Francisco CA 94120-7948. 415/616-1000. **Physical address:** 600 California Street, Suite 300, San Francisco CA 94018. **Fax:** 415/616/-2864. **Contact:** Human Resources Department. **E-mail address:** hr@fhlbnsf.com. **World Wide Web address:** http://www.fhlbsf.com. **Description:** The central bank and regulating agency to more than 200 savings and loan associations in California, Arizona, and Nevada. **Positions advertised include:** Senior Financial Analyst; AVP, Financial Systems; Senior Applications Analyst; Senior Internal Auditor; Derivatives Accounting Analyst.

FEDEX FREIGHT WEST
P.O. Box 649002, San Jose CA 95164. 408/268-9600. **Contact:** Human Resources Department. **World Wide Web address:** http://www.fedex.com/us/freight. **Description:** A trucking company. **Corporate headquarters location:** This location. **Parent company:** FedEx. **Listed on:** New York Stock Exchange. **Stock exchange symbol:** FDX.

FERGUSON ENTERPRISES, INC.
11552 Monarch Street, Garden Grove CA 92841. 714/893-1936. **Contact:** Human Resources. **E-mail address:** resumes@ferguson.com. **World Wide Web address:** http://www.ferguson.com. **Description:** Distributes an extensive variety of building materials throughout the western United States. Major product lines include plumbing supplies, valves and fittings, sprinkler and irrigation products, and solar energy components. Ferguson Enterprises operates over 500 locations in North America. **Corporate headquarters location:** Newport News VA. **Other U.S. locations:** Nationwide. **International locations:** Columbia; Mexico; Puerto Rico.

FIDELITY NATIONAL TITLE INSURANCE COMPANY
4050 Calle Real, Suite 100, Santa Barbara CA 93110. 805/879-9400. **Toll-free phone:** 800/815-3969. **Fax:** 805/879-9450. **Contact:** Ann Russell, Human Resources Director. **World Wide Web address:** http://www.fntic.com. **Description:** Writes title insurance policies and performs other title-related services such as escrow, collection, and trust activities in connection with real estate transactions. Founded in 1848. **NOTE:** To contact Human Resource directly, call the toll-free phone number listed above. **Corporate headquarters location:** Jacksonville FL. **Other U.S. locations:** Nationwide. **Parent company:** Fidelity National Financial, Inc. **Operations at this facility include:** Regional Headquarters. **Listed on:** New York Stock Exchange. **Stock exchange symbol:** FNF. **Annual sales/revenues:** $7.7 billion. **Number of employees at this location:** 150. **Number of employees nationwide:** 28,600.

FILEMAKER INC.
P.O. Box 58168, Santa Clara CA 95052. **Physical address:** 5201 Patrick Henry Drive, Santa Clara CA 95054. 408/987-7000. **Contact:** Human Resources. **E-mail address:** filemaker_hr@filemaker.com. **World Wide Web address:** http://www.filemaker.com. **Description:** Develops software including FileMaker Pro 5 and FileMaker Server 5, database systems that are designed for Windows and Macintosh operating systems. **Positions advertised include:** SQA Engineer; Senior Technical Support Engineer; Software Engineer Intern. **Special programs:** Internships. **Corporate headquarters location:** This location.

FILENET CORPORATION
3565 Harbor Boulevard, Costa Mesa CA 92626. 714/327-3400. **Contact:** Kenneth Ross, Employment Manager. **World Wide Web address:** http://www.filenet.com. **Description:** FileNET develops and markets electronic content management software and e-business solutions. Products and services are used to help corporations and organizations build intranets, create electronic portals to streamline information management, and to create, process, edit, organize, and store all forms of digital content for Internet applications. **Positions advertised include:** Internal Audit Manager; Benefits Analyst; Learning Technologist; Business Systems Manager; Applicatioin Systems Lead; Web System Lead; Sr. System Administrator; Principal Engineer. **Special programs:** Internships. **Corporate headquarters location:** This location. **Other U.S. locations:** Nationwide. **Listed on:** NASDAQ. **Stock exchange symbol:** FILE. **Number of employees at this location:** 800. **Number of employees worldwide:** 1,700.

FILIPINOS FOR AFFIRMATIVE ACTION
310 Eighth Street, Suite 306, Oakland CA 94607. 510/465-9876. **Fax:** 510/465-7548. **Contact:** Ms. Lillian Galedo, Executive Director of Human Resources Department. **E-mail address:** lgaledo@filipinos4action.org. **World Wide Web address:** http://www.filipinos4action.org. **Description:** A private, nonprofit, advocacy organization that provides employment and immigration assistance, information, and other services to the Filipino community. **Corporate headquarters location:** This location.

THE FINANCIAL RELATIONS BOARD INC.
434 Pacific Avenue, San Francisco CA 94133. 415/248-3402. **Contact:** Human Resources. **World Wide Web address:** http://www.frbinc.com. **Description:** A public relations firm that primarily serves the financial industry. **Corporate headquarters location:** Chicago IL. **Parent company:** Weber Shandwick Financial Communications.

FIREMAN'S FUND INSURANCE COMPANY
777 San Marin Drive, Novato CA 94998. 415/899-2000. **Fax:** 415/899-3600. **Contact:** Personnel. **World Wide Web address:** http://www.the-fund.com. **Description:** An insurance company offering a wide range of coverage and policies. Founded in 1863. **Positions advertised include:** Finance Intern; Administrative Specialist; Executive Assistant; Product Development Director; Claims Specialist; Claims Data Analyst; Senior Training Consultant; GCO Counselor. **Corporate headquarters location:** This location. **Other U.S. locations:** Nationwide. **Parent company:** Allianz A.G. (Munich, Germany). **Listed on:** New York Stock Exchange. **Stock exchange symbol:** AZ.

FIRESTONE TIRE & SERVICE CENTER
6102 Sunrise Mall Drive, Citrus Heights CA 95610. 916/726-7105. **Contact:** Human Resources. **World Wide Web address:** http://www.bfmastercare.com. **Description:** One location in a chain of tire and automotive service centers. **Positions advertised include:** Store Manager Trainee. **Parent company:** Bridgestone/Firestone, Inc. (Nashville TN).

THE FIRST AMERICAN CORPORATION
One First American Way, Santa Ana CA 92707-5913. 714/800-3000. **Toll-free phone:** 800/854-3643. **Fax:** 714/667-1696. **Contact:** Heather Smith, Personnel Director. **E-mail address:** corporate.hr@firstam.com. **World Wide Web address:** http://www.firstam.com. **Description:** Offers insurance services through a nationwide network of offices and agents. **Positions advertised include:** Banking Services Specialist. **Corporate headquarters location:** This location. **Other area locations:** Bakersfield CA; Los Angeles CA; Santa Barbara CA. **Listed on:** New York Stock Exchange. **Stock exchange symbol:** FAF. **Number of employees worldwide:** 25,000.

FIRST AMERICAN PROPERTY & CASUALTY INSURANCE COMPANY
114 East 5th Street, Santa Ana CA 92701. 714/560-7888. **Contact:** Human Resources. **World Wide Web address:** http://www.firstam.com. **Description:** Offers property and casualty insurance products. **Parent company:** First American Corporation.

FIRST AMERICAN TITLE COMPANY
520 North Central Avenue, Glendale CA 91203. 626/912-3664. **Contact:** Terry Hampton, Human Resources Manager. **World Wide Web address:** http://www.firstam.com. **Description:** Provides escrow and mortgage services for real estate transactions. **NOTE:** Address inquiries to: Human Resources, 3625 14th Street, P.O. Box 986, Riverside CA 92501. Phone: 909/787-1700. Fax: 909/275-5204. **Corporate headquarters location:** Santa Ana CA. **Listed on:** New York Stock Exchange. **Stock exchange symbol:** FAF.

FIRST BANK AND TRUST
550 Montgomery Street, San Francisco CA 94111. 415/781-7810. **World Wide Web address:** http://www.firstbanks.com. **Description:** A bank holding company. **Corporate headquarters location:** St. Louis MO. **Operations at this facility include:** Administration. **Listed on:** Privately held. **Number of employees at this location:** 40.

FIRST FEDERAL BANK OF CALIFORNIA
401 Wilshire Boulevard, Santa Monica CA 90401-1416. 310/319-5628. **Fax:** 310/319-5644. **Contact:** Personnel Supervisor. **E-mail address:** jobs@firstfedca.com. **World Wide Web address:** http://www.firstfedca.com. **Description:** First Federal Bank of California is a financial services organization comprised of 25 full-service branches and 6 real estate loan production offices located in Southern California. **NOTE:** Applications are available for download from the website. Completed applications may be submitted by fax or mail. **Positions advertised include:** Commercial Property Appraiser; Programmer Analyst; Residential Appraiser; Product Analyst; Credit Review Analyst; Database Administrator. **Special programs:** Internships. **Corporate headquarters location**: This location. **Parent company:** FirstFed Financial Corporation. **Number of employees nationwide:** 650. **Listed on:** New York Stock Exchange. **Stock exchange symbol:** FED.

FIRST MORTGAGE CORPORATION
3230 Fallow Field Drive, Diamond Bar CA 91765. 909/595-1996. **Fax:** 909/598-1574. **Contact:** Tammy Russ, Vice President of Human Resources. **World Wide Web address:** http://www.firstmortgage.com. **Description:** Originates, purchases, sells, and services first deed of trust loans (mortgage loans) for the purchase or refinance of owner-occupied one- to four-family residences. Founded in 1975. **Positions advertised include:** Mortgage Loan Processor. **Corporate headquarters location:** This location. **Other U.S. locations:** NV; OR; WA.

FIRST REPUBLIC BANCORP INC.
111 Pine Street, 5th floor, San Francisco CA 94111-5602. 415/392-1400. **Toll-free phone:** 800/392-1400. **Contact:** Human Resources. **World Wide Web address:** http://www.firstrepublic.com. **Description:** A leading banking and mortgage institution with growing operations in San Francisco, Los Angeles, San Diego, and Las Vegas. **Corporate headquarters location:** This location.

FISHER SCIENTIFIC COMPANY
2761 Walnut Avenue, Tustin CA 92780. 714/669-4600. **Contact:** Human Resources. **World Wide Web address:** http://www.fisherscientific.com. **Description:** Manufactures, distributes, and sells a wide range of products used in industrial and medical laboratories. Products include analytical and measuring instruments, apparatuses, and appliances; reagent chemicals and diagnostics; glassware and plasticware; and laboratory furniture. Manufacturing operations are carried out by six operating divisions in 11 U.S. locations. **Corporate headquarters:** Hampton NH. **Other U.S. locations:** Nationwide. **International locations:** Worldwide. **Listed on:** New York Stock Exchange. **Stock exchange symbol:** FSH. **Number of employees worldwide:** 10,000.

FISHKING PROCESSORS
1320 Newton Street, Los Angeles CA 90021. 213/746-1307. **Contact:** Personnel Director. **Description:** Processes and sells fresh and frozen fish products.

FLEETWOOD ENTERPRISES, INC.
P.O. Box 7638, Riverside CA 92513-7638. 951/351-3500. **Physical address:** 3125 Myers Street, Riverside CA 92503. **Contact:** John R. Moore, Vice President of Human Resources. **World Wide Web address:** http://www.fleetwood.com. **Description:** Manufactures recreational vehicles with operations worldwide. The company's recreational vehicles are primarily motor homes sold under brand names including American Eagle, Coronado, Bounder, Flair, and PaceArrow. Fleetwood Enterprises also manufactures a variety of trailers and campers and owns subsidiaries that offer financial services and supplies. **NOTE:** Search and apply for positions online. **Positions advertised include:** Financial Analyst; Public Relations Manager; Materials Administrator. **Corporate headquarters location:** This location. **Listed on:** New York Stock Exchange. **Stock exchange symbol:** FLE. **Number of employees at this location:** 19,000.

FLEISHMAN-HILLARD INC.
201 California Street, 7th Floor, San Francisco CA 94111. 415/318-4000. **Fax:** 415/318-4010. **Contact:** Human Resources. **World Wide Web address:** http://www.fleishman.com. **Description:** A public relations firm. **Positions advertised include:** Account Supervisor; Vice President Tech PR; Vice President Life Sciences. **Corporate headquarters location:** St. Louis MO. **Other area locations:** Sacramento CA; San Diego CA. **Other U.S. locations:** Nationwide. **International locations:** Worldwide. **Parent company:** Omnicom Group Inc.

FLEXTRONICS INTERNATIONAL
2090 Fortune Drive, San Jose CA 95131. 408/576-7000. **Fax:** 408/576-7454. **Contact:** Human Resources. **World Wide Web address:** http://www.flextronics.com. **Description:** Provides electronic design, engineering, and manufacturing services to OEMs in various industries. **Positions advertised include:** Corporate IT Manager; Senior Mechanical Engineer; Project Manager; Industrial Designer; Marketing Manager; Business Applications Manager. **Corporate headquarters location:** This location. **Listed on:** NASDAQ. **Stock exchange symbol:** FLEX.

FLINT INK
750 Gilman Street, Berkeley CA 94710. 510/525-1188. **Contact:** Human Resources. **World Wide Web address:** http://www.flintink.com. **Description:** A leading manufacturer of printing inks, inkjet inks, and toners for various printing applications. **NOTE:** Please send resumes to: Flint Ink, 4600 Arrow Head Drive, Ann Arbor MI 48105. **Corporate headquarters location:** Ann Arbor MI. **Other U.S. locations:** Nationwide. **International locations:** Worldwide. **Number of employees:** 4,600.

FLOWSERVE CORPORATION
6077 Egret Court, Benicia CA 94510. 707/745-3773. **Contact:** Human Resources. **World Wide Web address:** http://www.flowserve.com. **Description:** Manufactures and supplies pumps, valves, seals, and services to the process industries. **Corporate headquarters location:** Dallas TX. **Listed on:** New York Stock Exchange. **Stock exchange symbol:** FLS. **Number of employees worldwide:** 14,000.

FLOWSERVE CORPORATION
1909 East Cashdan Street, Rancho Dominguez CA 90220. 310/608-4500. **Fax:** 310/608-4540. **Contact:** Human Resources. **World Wide Web address:** http://www.flowserve.com. **Description:** Manufactures fluid control systems. **Corporate headquarters location:** Dallas TX. **Listed on:** New York Stock Exchange. **Stock exchange symbol:** FLS.

FLUOR CORPORATION
One Enterprise Drive, Aliso Viejo CA 92656. 949/349-2000. **Contact:** Human Resources Department. **E-mail address:** careers@fluor.com. **World Wide Web address:** http://www.fluor.com. **Description:** Operates within the fields of engineering, global services, coal production, and procurement and construction through four operating groups. Fluor Daniel provides engineering, procurement, and construction services. Fluor Global Services provides a wide range of products and related services including consulting services; equipment rental sales and service; operations; and maintenance services. Fluor Signature Services provides business support services to Fluor Corporation. A.T. Massey Coal Group produces coal for the steel industry. **Corporate headquarters location:** This location. **Listed on:** New York Stock Exchange. **Stock exchange symbol:** FLR. **Number of employees worldwide:** 30,000.

FOOTE, CONE & BELDING
600 Battery Street, San Francisco CA 94111. 415/820-8000. **Fax:** 415/820-8087. **Contact:** Eileen McCarthy, Human Resources Manager. **E-mail address:** sf-resume@fcb.com. **World Wide Web address:** http://www.fcb.com. **Description:** One of thc five largest advertising agencies in the world. Foote, Cone & Belding develops integrated marketing campaigns for a broad range of clients. The firm offers additional services such as merchandising, product research, package design, e-business marketing, direct marketing, sports marketing, and events marketing. **NOTE:** Entry-level positions are offered. **Special programs:** Internships; Training. **Corporate headquarters location:** Chicago IL. **Other U.S. locations:** Nationwide. **Parent company:** True North Communications. **Chairman and CEO:** Geoff Thompson. **Number of employees at this location:** 400.

FOOTHILL - DE ANZA COMMUNITY COLLEGE DISTRICT
12345 El Monte Road, Los Altos Hills CA 94022. 650/949-6217. **Recorded jobline:** 650/949-6218. **Contact:** Personnel. **E-mail address:** employment@fhda.edu. **World Wide Web address:** http://www.fhda.edu. **Description:** A nonprofit community college district composed of Foothill College (also at this location) and De Anza College (Cupertino CA). Foothill College offers associate in arts, associate in science, certificate, and transfer programs in over 80 areas of study. De Anza Community College offers two-year degrees and certificate programs in approximately 100 areas of study. **NOTE:** Entry-level positions and part-time jobs are offered. **Positions advertised include:** Dean, Business and Social Sciences; Math Instructor; Physics Instructor; ESL Composition Instructor; English Instructor; Music Instructor; Drama Instructor; History Instructor; Administrative Assistant; Nurse Practitioner. **Corporate headquarters location:** This location. **Number of employees at this location:** 2,500.

FOOTHILL INDEPENDENT BANK
510 South Grand Avenue, Glendora CA 91741-4207. 626/963-8551. **Contact:** Human Resources. **E-mail address:** resume@foothillbank.com. **World Wide Web address:** http://www.foothillbank.com. **Description:** A California state-chartered bank. The bank has 11 full-service offices located throughout the Inland Empire and San Gabriel Valley. Specialized departments include Small Business Administration Lending, Construction Lending, and Asset Based Lending. **NOTE:** Please submit completed application and resume to: Foothill Independent Bank, Attention: Human Resources, P.O. Box 3609, San Dimas CA 91773. Fax: 909/592-7945. **Positions advertised include:** Construction Loan Officer; Teller. **Corporate headquarters location:** This location. **Parent company:** Foothill Independent Bancorp. **Listed on:** NASDAQ. **Stock exchange symbol:** FOOT.

FORCE COMPUTERS, INC.
4211 Starboard Drive, Fremont CA 94538. 510/624-5300. **Toll-free phone:** 800/FORCE99. **Contact:** Human Resources. **E-mail address:** hr@fci.com. **World Wide Web address:** http://www.forcecomputers.com. **Description:** A manufacturer of embedded systems. The company supplies high-performance computer products to a broad range of worldwide telecommunications, industrial, and government customers. **NOTE:** The company has been acquired by Motorola Inc. and will be renamed The

Embedded Communications Computing Group. **Special programs:** Internships. **Corporate headquarters location:** This location. **International locations:** Germany. **Listed on:** Privately held. **Number of employees at this location:** 140.

FORTIFIBER CORPORATION
4489 Bandini Boulevard, Los Angeles CA 90023-4777. 323/268-6783. **Toll-free phone:** 800/332-5727. **Fax:** 323/264-8247. **Contact:** Human Resources Department. **World Wide Web address:** http://www.fortifiber.com. **Description:** Manufactures and markets single-ply, saturated kraft paper for use in the construction industry. **Corporate headquarters location:** Incline Village NV. **Other area locations:** Portland CA; Tracy CA. **Other U.S. locations:** Attleboro MA; Howard MI; Hanahan SC. **Operations at this facility include:** Administration; Manufacturing; Research and Development; Sales; Service.

FORTREND ENGINEERING COMPANY
404 Tasman Drive, Sunnyvale CA 94089. 408/734-9311. **Fax:** 408/734-4299. **Contact:** Human Resources. **E-mail address:** hr@fortrend.com. **World Wide Web address:** http://www.fortrend.com. **Description:** Designs and manufactures automated equipment for wafer and disk handling in the semiconductor industry. **Positions advertised include:** Customer Satisfaction/Support Engineer; Sales and Marketing Engineer. **Corporate headquarters location:** This location. **International locations:** Worldwide. **Listed on:** Privately held. **Annual sales/revenues:** $5 - $10 million. **Number of employees at this location:** 50.

49ER SHOPS, INC.
6049 East Seventh Street, Long Beach CA 90840. 562/985-7854. **Contact:** Nancy Green, Personnel Director. **E-mail address:** jobs@mail.bks.csulb.edu. **World Wide Web address:** http://www.csulb.edu/aux/49ershops. **Description:** Operates the bookstore, copy center, and food services on California State University's Long Beach campus. **Positions advertised include:** Accounting Cash Room Assistant; Sales Manager, Catering; Manager, University Dining Plaza; Convenience Stores Manager. **Corporate headquarters location:** This location. **Number of employees at this location:** 450.

FOUNTAINGLEN PROPERTIES LLC
4220 Von Karman Avenue, 2nd Floor, Newport Beach CA 92660-2002. 949/223-5000. **Fax:** 949/223-5043. **Contact:** Pam Laipple, Human Resources. **E-mail address:** PLaipple@Fountainglen.com. **World Wide Web address:** http://www.fountainglen.com. **Description:** A real estate agency specializing in residential and industrial properties. Pacific Gulf also owns apartment buildings. **Corporate headquarters location:** This location.

FOUNTAIN VIEW, INC.
27442 Portola Parkway, Foothill Ranch CA 92610. 818/556-5284. **Fax:** 949/282-5859. **Contact:** Melissa Sutton, Human Resources Manager. **Description:** Provides long-term care through the operation of skilled nursing centers and nursing homes. **NOTE:** To reach Human Resources directly call: 949/282-5977. **Corporate headquarters location:** This location. **Parent company:** Skilled Healthcare Group. **Number of employees nationwide:** 6,500.

FOUR SEASONS HOTEL
300 South Doheny Drive, Los Angeles CA 90048. 310/273-2222. **Contact:** Personnel. **Fax:** 310/385-4920. **E-mail address:** jobs.losangeles@fourseasons.com. **World Wide Web address:** http://www.fourseasons.com. **Description:** Four Seasons Hotels & Resorts operates approximately 50 luxury hotels and resorts in 22 countries. Founded in 1960. **Corporate headquarters location:** Toronto, Canada. **Operations at this facility include:** This location is a hotel with 285 guest rooms and two restaurants. The hotel also has a pool, whirlpool, fitness facilities, private cabanas, and approximately 10,000 square feet of meeting and function space. **Listed on:** New York Stock Exchange. **Stock exchange symbol:** FS.

4-D NEUROIMAGING
9727 Pacific Heights Boulevard, San Diego CA 92121. 858/453-6300. **Fax:** 858/453-4913. **Contact:** Human Resources. **World Wide Web address:** http://www.4dneuroimaging.com. **Description:** Manufactures specialized instruments for ultrasensitive magnetic field and low-temperature measurements. The company incorporates its core magnetic sensing technologies into its magnetic source imaging (MSI) system, an instrument designed to assist in the noninvasive diagnosis of a broad range of medical disorders. The MSI system developed by the company uses advanced superconducting technology to measure and locate the source of magnetic fields generated by the human body. The company is focusing the development of its technology on market applications such as brain surgery and the diagnosis and surgical planning for treatment of epilepsy and life-threatening cardiac arrhythmias. Founded in 1970. **Corporate headquarters location:** This location.

FOX TELEVISION
KTTV-FOX 11
1999 South Bundy Drive, Los Angeles CA 90025. 310/584-2000. **Fax:** 310/584-2288. **Recorded jobline:** 310/584-2280. **Contact:** Human Resources. **E-mail address:** jobs@foxtv.com. **World Wide Web address:** http://www.fox11.com. **Description:** A national television-broadcasting network. **Positions advertised include:** Associate Producer; News Writer; Maintenance Engineer; Programming Assistant. **Special programs:** Internships. **Internship information:** All internships are unpaid and are offered during summer, fall, and spring semesters. Internships in the newsroom, sports, publicity, and community relations are offered. The program requires a 12- to 15-hour-per-week commitment, and preference is given to juniors and seniors in college. Resumes should be addressed to the attention of the Internship Coordinator. **Corporate headquarters location:** Los Angeles CA. **Parent company:** Twentieth Century Fox. **Listed on:** New York Stock Exchange. **Stock exchange symbol:** FOX.

FRANKLIN RESOURCES, INC.
One Franklin Parkway, San Mateo CA 94403. 650/312-2000. **Fax:** 650/312-3655. **Contact:** Human Resources. **E-mail address:** careers@frk.com. **World Wide Web address:** http://www.franklin-templeton.com. **Description:** Provides mutual fund and money market services. **NOTE:** Search and apply for positions online. **Positions advertised include:** Sr. Financial Systems Analyst; IT Manager; Controller; software Asset Manager; Sr. Business Analyst; Marketing Research Analyst. **Special programs:** Internships. **Corporate headquarters location:** This location. **Subsidiaries include:** Franklin Templeton Group. **Listed on:** New York Stock Exchange. **Stock exchange symbol:** BEN.

FREDERICK'S OF HOLLYWOOD
6608 Hollywood Boulevard, Hollywood CA 90028. 323/466-5151. **Contact:** Human Resources. **E-mail address:** jobs@fredericks.com. **World Wide Web address:** http://www.fredericks.com. **Description:** A specialty retailer operating a chain of women's intimate-apparel stores throughout the United States. The company also has a national mail-order apparel business selling lingerie, bras, dresses, sportswear, leisurewear, swimwear, hosiery, specialty men's wear, and accessories. Frederick's of Hollywood purchases its merchandise from a variety of manufacturers. **Positions advertised include:** Associate Buyer; Creative Manager; **Corporate headquarters location:** This location.

FREEDOM COMMUNICATIONS INC.
P.O. Box 19549, Irvine CA 92623. 949/553-9292. **Physical address:** 17666 Fitch, Irvine CA 92614. **World Wide Web address:** http://www.freedom.com. **Contact:** Human Resources. **Description:** Owns the *Orange County Register* and 69 other news publications with a combined circulation of 1 million, as well as five television stations. **NOTE:** Search online for positions and application instructions.

CENTINELA FREEMAN REGIONAL MEDICAL CENTER
333 North Prairie Avenue, Inglewood CA 90301. 310/674-7050. **Contact:** Recruitment Coordinator. **World Wide Web address:** http://www.danielfreemanmemorialhospital.com. **Description:** A nonprofit hospital that offers a variety of services including behavioral health, heart care, women's and children's services, and rehabilitation. The hospital also offers a variety of specialty programs such as the Center for Heart and Health, complimentary medicine, and emergency services. **Positions advertised include:** Occupational Therapist; Physical Therapist; Dietitian; Respiratory Care Practitioner ; Licensed Vocational Nurse; Registered Nurse; Pharmacist; Human Resources Recruiter; Speech Therapist. **Corporate headquarters location:** This location. **Parent company:** Centinela Freeman HealthSystem.

FREMANTLE MEDIA
2700 Colorado Avenue, Suite 450, Santa Monica CA 90404. 310/255-4700. **Fax:** 310/255-4800. **Contact:** Human Resources. **E-mail address:** hr@fremantlemedia.com. **World Wide Web address:** http://www.fremantlemedia.com. **Description:** Produces, distributes, markets, and promotes television programs and recorded music both domestically and internationally. The company is a leading distributor of television programming in the first-run syndication and distributes, represents, or owns participations in more than 160 television series, over 250 motion pictures, a variety of children's programming, and live-event specials. **Corporate headquarters location:** London England. **Parent company:** RTL Group. **Number of employees at this location:** 125.

FREMONT GENERAL
2020 Santa Monica Boulevard, Suite 600, Santa Monica CA 90407. 310/315-5500. **Contact:** Human Resources. **Description:** A holding company with subsidiaries that conduct financial and insurance operations, primarily workers' compensation for California workers, malpractice insurance for the medical industry, life insurance, and various commercial and individual financial services. The Fremont Compensation operation deals with workmen's compensation. The medical malpractice unit offers professional liability insurance primarily for California physicians. Financial operations include asset-based lending/financing for commercial clients, thrift and loan services, and insurance. Insurance products include credit life insurance and disability coverage offered through automobile dealers, credit associations, and lending organizations. **Corporate headquarters location:** This location. **Listed on:** New York Stock Exchange. **Stock exchange symbol:** FMT.

FREMONT HOSPITAL
39001 Sundale Drive, Fremont CA 94538. 510/796-1100. **Fax:** 510/574-4877. **Contact:** Human Resources. **E-mail address:** fremonthr@ardenthealth.com. **World Wide Web address:** http://www.fremonthospital.com. **Description:** A psychiatric and chemical dependency treatment hospital. **Positions advertised include:** Case Manager; Mental Health Technician; Child Psychiatrist; Registered Nurse. **Special programs:** Internships. **Office hours:** Monday - Friday, 9:00 a.m. - 4:00 p.m. **Parent company:** Ardent Health Services. **Listed on:** Privately held. **CEO:** Terry Johnson.

FREMONT UNIFIED SCHOOL DISTRICT (FUSD)
4210 Technology Drive, Fremont CA 94538. 510/659-2545. **Toll-free phone:** 800/883-0180. **Fax:** 510/659-2507. **Contact:** Human Resources. **World Wide Web address:** http://www.fremont.k12.ca.us. **Description:** A school district comprised of 31 elementary schools, 6 junior high schools, and 12 high schools. **NOTE:** Open positions and application forms are posted online. **Number of employees nationwide:** 1,250.

FRESENIUS MEDICAL CARE NORTH AMERICA
2637 Shadelands Drive, Walnut Creek CA 94598. 925/295-0200. **Contact:** Human Resources Manager. **E-mail address:** resumes@fms-na.com. **World Wide Web address:** http://www.fmcna.com. **Description:** Manufactures, sells, and distributes systems and supplies for hemodialysis and peritoneal dialysis. Products include machines, dialyzers, equipment solutions in bio-compatible flexible plastic bags, and associated disposable tubing assemblies that serve the entire range of end-stage renal disease patients. **NOTE:** Entry-level positions are offered. **Special programs:** Training. **Corporate headquarters location:** Lexington MA. **Other U.S. locations:** Nationwide. **Parent company:** Fresenius Medical Care AG (Germany). **Listed on:** New York Stock Exchange. **Stock exchange symbol:** FMS. **Number of employees at this location:** 375.

FRESH CHOICE, INC.
485 Cochrane Circle, Morgan Hill CA 95037. 408/776-0799. **Fax:** 408/776-0798. **Contact:** Human Resources. **E-mail address:** employment@freshchoice.com. **World Wide Web address:** http://www.freshchoice.com. **Description:** Operates 36 casual, self-service restaurants in Northern California, Washington, Texas, and Washington DC. **Special programs:** Internships. **Corporate headquarters location:** This location. **Listed on:** NASDAQ. **Stock exchange symbol:** SALD. **Number of employees at this location:** 60. **Number of employees nationwide:** 3,000.

FRESNO, CITY OF
2600 Fresno Street, First Floor, Fresno CA 93721. 559/621-6950. **Recorded jobline:** 559/621-6999. **Fax:** 559/498-4775. **Contact:** Human Resources. **E-mail address:** Personnel@fresno.gov. **World Wide Web address:** http://www.fresno.gov. **Description:** This location houses the government administrative offices for Fresno CA. **NOTE:** See website for job listings. A completed application is required for any position. Apply online or print out the application and mail it to the Human Resources Office. **Positions advertised include:** Attorney; Solid Waste Management Supervisor; Water System Operator; Systems Security Administrator; Police Officer; Professional Engineer.

FRESNO, COUNTY OF
2220 Tulare Street, 14th Floor, Fresno CA 93721. 559/488-2690. **Recorded jobline:** 559/488-3017. **Fax:** 559/488-3325. **Contact:** Rosemary Kennedy, Personnel Services Manager. **E-mail address:** personnel-employmentservices@co.Fresno.ca.us. **World Wide Web address:** http://www.co.fresno.ca.us. **Description:** Administrative offices for Fresno County. **NOTE:** Open positions and application instructions are listed online. **Positions advertised include:** Occupational Therapist; Psychiatric Technician;

Psychiatrist; Reference Center Coordinator; Sr. Administrative Analyst; Sr. Engineer. **Special programs:** Internships. **Corporate headquarters location:** This location. **Operations at this facility include:** Administration; Service. **Number of employees at this location:** 7,100.

FRITO-LAY, INC.
9535 Archibald Avenue, Rancho Cucamonga CA 91730. 909/948-3600. **Contact:** Human Resources. **World Wide Web address:** http://www.fritolay.com. **Description:** A worldwide manufacturer and wholesaler of snack products including the brand names Fritos Corn Chips, Doritos Tortilla Chips, Lays Potato Chips, and Smartfood Popcorn. **NOTE:** Search and apply for positions online. **Positions advertised include:** Operations Resource; Business Unit Leader. **Corporate headquarters location:** Plano TX. **Parent company:** PepsiCo, Inc. (Purchase NY) consists of Frito-Lay, Inc., Pepsi-Cola Company, and Tropicana Products, Inc. **Listed on:** New York Stock Exchange. **Stock exchange symbol:** PEP. **Number of employees nationwide:** 29,000.

FUJICOLOR PROCESSING INC.
27105 Industrial Boulevard, Hayward CA 94545. 510/783-7000. **Toll-free phone:** 800/999-4686. **Fax:** 510/783-0535. **Contact:** Leah Mollat, Human Resources Manager. **World Wide Web address:** http://www.fujifilm.com. **Description:** Provides wholesale photofinishing services and related sales and service activities. **NOTE:** Entry-level positions, part-time jobs, and second and third shifts are offered. **Special programs:** Training; Summer Jobs. **Corporate headquarters location:** Elmsford NY. **Other U.S. locations:** Nationwide. **International locations:** Worldwide. **Parent company:** Fuji Film Ltd. **CEO:** Hank Hyyashi. **Number of employees at this location:** 225. **Number of employees nationwide:** 10,000.

FUJITSU COMPUTER PRODUCTS OF AMERICA INC.
2904 Orchard Parkway, San Jose CA 95134. 408/432-6333. **Fax:** 408/894-1700. **Contact:** Human Resources. **E-mail address:** hr@fcpa.fujitsu.com. **World Wide Web address:** http://www.fcpa.com. **Description:** Fujitsu Computer Products of America manufactures hard drives, magneto-optical drives, printers, scanners, and tape drives. **Positions advertised include:** ASIC Design Engineer; Senior Customer Support Engineer; Business Development Manager; Inside Sales Professional; Product Specialist. **Corporate headquarters location:** This location. **Other U.S. locations:** Hillsboro CO; Longmont CO. **Parent company:** Fujitsu, Ltd. (Japan). **Operations at this facility include:** This location houses administrative offices.

FUJITSU COMPUTER SYSTEMS
1250 East Arques Avenue, Sunnyvale CA 94085-3470. 408/746-6000. **Toll-free phone:** 800/538-8460. **Fax:** 408/746-7174. **Contact:** Human Resources. **World Wide Web address:** http://us.fujitsu.com/computers. **Description:** Designs, develops, manufactures, markets, and services large-scale, high-performance, general-purpose computer systems. Customers are primarily large corporations, government agencies, and large universities with high-volume data processing requirements. **Positions advertised include:** Plasma Display Operations Engineer; Alliances Account Executive. **Special programs:** Internships. **Corporate headquarters location:** This location. **Other U.S. locations:** Nationwide. **International locations:** Germany; Ireland; Italy; Portugal; Switzerland; United Kingdom. **Parent company:** Fujitsu, Ltd. **Operations at this facility include:** Administration; Manufacturing; Research and Development; Sales; Service. **Listed on:** NASDAQ. **Stock exchange symbol:** FJTSY. **CEO:** David Wright. **Number of employees at this location:** 3,500. **Number of employees nationwide:** 6,000. **Number of employees worldwide:** 9,500.

FUJITSU MICROELECTRONICS AMERICA, INC.
1250 East Arques Avenue, Sunnyvale CA 94088-3470. 408/737-5600. **Fax:** 408/737-5999. **Contact:** Human Resources. **E-mail address:** careers@fma.fujitsu.com. **World Wide Web address:** http://www.fujitsu.com/us/micro. **Description:** Fujitsu Microelectronics, Inc. manufactures microprocessors, Ethernet decoders and encoders, discrete chips, and memory products. **Corporate headquarters location:** This location. **Parent company:** Fujitsu, Ltd. (Japan). **Operations at this facility include:** This location houses administrative offices.

FUSIONWARE CORPORATION
3931 MacArthur Boulevard, Suite 212, Newport Beach CA 92660. 949/250-4800. **Fax:** 949/752-6772. **Contact:** Human Resources. **E-mail address:** info@fusionware.net. **World Wide Web address:** http://www.fusionware.net. **Description:** Engaged in systems and software integration services. **Corporate headquarters location:** Seattle WA.

GAB ROBINS
10989 Trade Center Drive, Suite 125, Rancho Cordova CA 95670. 916/853-8300. **Fax:** 916/853-8299. **Contact:** Frank Blaha, Branch Manager. **World Wide Web address:** http://www.gabrobins.com. **Description:** Provides adjustment, inspection, appraisal, and claims management services to 15,000 insurance industry customers through more than 550 branch offices. Specific services include the settlement of claims following major disasters; appraisal, investigation, and adjustment of auto insurance claims; casualty claims; and fire, marine, life, accident, health, and disability claims. **Corporate headquarters location:** Parsippany NJ. **Parent company:** SGS North America. **Number of employees nationwide:** 3,800.

GATX CAPITAL CORPORATION
4 Embarcadero Center, Suite 2200, San Francisco CA 94111. 415/955-3200. **Fax:** 415/403-3517. **Contact:** Human Resources. **E-mail address:** sfjobs@gatx.com. **World Wide Web address:** http://www.gatxcap.com. **Description:** GATX Capital is a diversified, international financial services company providing asset-based financing for transportation and industrial equipment. The company arranges full payout financing leases, secured loans, operating leases, and other structured financing both as an investing principal and with institutional partners. **Positions advertised include:** Sr. Internal Auditor. **Corporate headquarters location:** This location. **Other U.S. locations:** Tampa FL; Chicago IL; Buffalo NY. **Subsidiaries include:** GATX Rail acquires, leases, and sells railcars and locomotives for GATX Capital's own portfolio and for managed portfolios. **Parent company:** GATX Corporation. **Listed on:** New York Stock Exchange. **Stock exchange symbol:** GMT. **Number of employees at this location:** 190.

GCI GROUP
612 Howard Street, 4th Floor, San Francisco CA 94105. 415/974-6200. **Fax:** 415/974-6226. **Contact:** Human Resources. **E-mail address:** working@gcigroup.com **World Wide Web address:** http://www.gcigroup.com. **Description:** A high-tech public relations firm. **NOTE:** Send resumes to: Stephanie Lapham-Howley, GCI Group, 825 Third Avenue, New York NY 10022. **Corporate headquarters location:** New York NY.

GCI GROUP
6100 Wilshire Boulevard, Suite 840, Los Angeles CA 90048. 323/930-0811. **Fax:** 323/930-1241. **Contact:** Human Resources. **E-mail address:** working@gcigroup.com. **World Wide Web address:** http://www.gcigroup.com. **NOTE:** Send resumes to: Stephanie Lapham-Howley, GCI Group, 825 Third Avenue, New York NY 10022. **Positions advertised include:** Account Supervisor; Account Executive. **Description:** A high-tech public relations firm. **Corporate headquarters location:** New York NY.

GE COMMERCIAL FINANCE
4 Park Plaza, Irvine CA 92614-8560. 949/225-2000. **Contact:** Human Resources. **World Wide Web address:** http://www.gecommercialfinance.com. **Description:** GE Commercial Finance provides lending products, growth capital, revolving lines of credit, equipment leasing of every kind, cash flow programs, and asset financing for the healthcare, manufacturing, fleet management, communications, construction, energy, aviation, infrastructure and equipment industries. **NOTE:** Search and apply for positions online. **Parent company:** General Electric.

GE IMATRON
389 Oyster Point Boulevard, South San Francisco CA 94080. 650/583-9964. **Fax:** 650/827-7706. **Contact:** Human Resources. **World Wide Web address:** http://www.geimatron.com. **Description:** Designs, develops, manufactures, and markets electron beam tomography scanners. **NOTE:** Interested candidates can search and apply for positions online. **Positions advertised include:** Nuclear Sales Representative; Field Engineer. **Corporate headquarters location:** Milwaukee WI. **Listed on:** New York Stock Exchange. **Stock exchange symbol:** GE.

GE INFRASTRUCTURE SENSING
1055 Mission Court, Fremont CA 94539. 510/661-6000. **Fax:** 510/657-6420. **Contact:** Personnel. **World Wide Web address:** http://www.novasensor.com. **Description:** Manufactures pressure sensors for all types of applications. **Corporate headquarters location:** This location. **Parent company:** General Electric. **Listed on:** New York Stock Exchange. **Stock exchange symbol:** GE.

GKN AEROSPACE CHEM-TRONICS INC.
1150 West Bradley Avenue, El Cajon CA 92020. 619/258-5065. **Fax:** 619/258-5279. **Contact:** Human Resources. **E-mail address:** hr@chem-tronics.com. **World Wide Web address:** http://www.chem-tronics.com. **Description:** Engaged in aerospace component manufacture and repair for business and defense clients. **Positions advertised include:** Senior Contacts Administrator; Estimator; Technical Buyer; Security Guard; Manufacturing Engineer; Dimensional Inspectors; Processor; Engineering Specialist, Structural Analysis. **Corporate headquarters location:** This location. **Other U.S. locations:** Kent WA; Tulsa OK. **Parent company:** GKN Aerospace Services.

GALLEN.NEILLY & ASSOCIATES
1981 North Broadway, Suite 400, Walnut Creek CA 94596. 925/930-9848. **Fax:** 925/930-9903. **Contact:** Human Resources. **World Wide Web address:** http://www.gallen.com. **Description:** A public relations firm that primarily serves the commercial real estate industry. **Corporate headquarters location:** This location.

GALLO WINE COMPANY
2700 South Eastern Avenue, Commerce CA 90040. 323/869-6435. **Toll-free phone:** 800/499-1761. **Fax:** 323/869-6460. **Contact:** Manager of Recruiting. **E-mail address:** jobs@ejgallo.com. **World Wide Web address:** http://www.gallo.com. **Description:** Produces, markets, and distributes premium wines and brandy. Founded in 1933. **NOTE:** Search and apply for positions online. **Corporate headquarters location:** Modesto CA. **Other U.S. locations:** Nationwide. **International locations:** Worldwide. **Parent company:** E&J Gallo Winery. **Listed on:** Privately held. **Annual sales/revenues:** More than $100 million. **Number of employees at this location:** 450. **Number of employees nationwide:** 4,600.

GAP INC.
Two Folsom Street, San Francisco CA 94105. 650/952-4400. **Contact:** Personnel. **World Wide Web address:** http://www.gapinc.com. **Description:** A nationwide retailer of moderately priced casual apparel for men, women, and children. The company operates over 1,800 stores under the names Gap, GapKids, BabyGap, Banana Republic, and Old Navy Clothing Company. **NOTE:** Search and apply for positions online. **Positions advertised include:** Creative Director; Senior Financial Analyst; Strategy Manager; Merchandise Planning Manager; Data and Systems Analyst; Administrative Assistant; Marketing Director. **Corporate headquarters location:** This location. **Other U.S. locations:** Nationwide. **International locations:** Canada; France; Germany; Japan; United Kingdom. **Listed on:** New York Stock Exchange. **Stock exchange symbol:** GPS.

GARDCO LIGHTING
P.O. Box 2013, San Leandro CA 94577. 510/357-6900. **Physical address:** 2661 Alvarado Street, San Leandro CA 94577. **Fax:** 510/357-3088. **Contact:** Human Resources. **World Wide Web address:** http://www.sitelighting.com. **Description:** Thomas Industries provides lighting and compressor/vacuum pump products. **Special programs:** Internships. **Corporate headquarters location:** Louisville KY. **Other U.S. locations:** Nationwide. **Operations at this facility include:** This location produces and installs outdoor area lighting and flood lighting for parking lots, pathways, gardens, and garages. **Number of employees at this location:** 200. **Number of employees nationwide:** 3,000.

GARDEN GROVE, CITY OF
11222 Acacia Parkway, Garden Grove CA 92840. 714/741-5004. **Recorded jobline:** 714/741-5016. **Contact:** Personnel. **E-mail address:** martiw@ci.garden-grove.ca.us. **World Wide Web address:** http://www.ci.garden-grove.ca.us. **Description:** Administrative offices for the city of Garden Grove. **NOTE:** Openings and application available online. **Positions advertised include:** Police Officer. **Special programs:** Internships. **Corporate headquarters location:** This location.

GARFIELD MEDICAL CENTER
525 North Garfield Avenue, Monterey Park CA 91754. 626/573-2222. **Contact:** Human Resources. **World Wide Web address:** http://www.garfieldmedicalcenter.com. **Description:** A full-service hospital that provides acute care, emergency care, and a neonatal intensive care unit. **Positions advertised include:** Registered Nurse; Case Manager; Physical Therapist; Licensed Vocational Nurse; Surgical Technician; Pharmacist; Radiology Technologist. **Parent company:** Alhambra Hospital Medical Center.

GARRETT AVIATION SERVICES
6201 West Imperial Highway, Los Angeles CA 90045. 310/568-3700. **Toll-free phone:** 800/942-7738. **Fax:** 310/568-3992. **Contact:** Recruiter. **E-mail address:** GarrettJobs@garrettaviation.com. **World Wide Web address:** http://www.garrettaviation.com. **Description:** Specializes in the repair and service of corporate aircraft. **Corporate headquarters location:** Tempe AZ. **Other U.S. locations:** IL; NY; TX. **Number of employees at this location:** 140. **Number of employees nationwide:** 700.

GARTNER GROUP
251 & 281 River Oaks Parkway, San Jose CA 95134. 408/468-8000. **Contact:** Human Resources. **World Wide Web address:** http://www.gartner.com. **Description:** A market research company. **NOTE:** Search and apply for positions online. **Positions advertised include:** Director. **Corporate headquarters location:** Stamford CT. **Listed on:** New York Stock Exchange. **Stock exchange symbol:** IT.

GATEWAY, INC.
7565 Irvine Center Drive, Irvine CA 92618. 949/471-7000. **Toll-free phone:** 800/846-2000. **Fax:** 949/471-7041. **Contact:** Human Resources. **World Wide Web address:** http://www.gateway.com. **Description:** A leading provider of personal computers, digital cameras, camcorders, and systems and networking products. **Positions advertised include:** Sr. Software Engineer; Sr. Manager, Commodity Procurement; Consumer Electronics Engineer. **Corporate headquarters location:** This location. **Other U.S. locations:** Kansas City MO; Sioux City SD. **Number of employees worldwide:** 1,900. **Listed on:** New York Stock Exchange. **Stock exchange symbol:** GTW.

GEAC COMPUTER
2200 Powell Street, Suite 300, Emeryville CA 94608. 510/594-5700. **Fax:** 510/594-5705. **Contact:** Human Resources. **World Wide Web address:** http://www.geac.com. **Description:** Geac Computer develops and markets business applications software in the areas of human resources, materials, management, manufacturing, health care, and higher education. Products include the SmartStream series of financial software. **NOTE:** Search and apply for positions online. **Positions advertised include:** Application Engineer; Server Engineer. **Corporate headquarters location:** Ontario Canada. **Operations at this facility include:** This location is a customer support center.

GELSON'S
P.O. Box 1802, Encino CA 91426-1802. 818/906-5700. **Physical address:** 16400 Ventura Boulevard, Suite 240, Encino CA 91436. **Fax:** 818/788-3265. **Recorded jobline:** 800/700-0912. **Contact:** Human Resources Department, Attention: Recruitment. **E-mail address:** personnel@gelsons.com. **World Wide Web address:** http://www.gelsons.com. **Description:** General offices for Gelson's Markets, which operates 13 Gelson's and two Mayfair supermarkets in the greater Los Angeles area. **Corporate headquarters location:** This location. **Parent company:** Arden Group, Inc. **Listed on:** NASDAQ. **Stock exchange symbol:** ARDNA. **Number of employees nationwide:** 1,900.

GEMSTAR-TV GUIDE INTERNATIONAL, INC.
6922 Hollywood Boulevard, Hollywood CA 90028. 323/817-4600. **Fax:** 323/817-4892. **Contact:** Human Resources. **E-mail address:** jobs03@tvguide.com. **World Wide Web address:** http://www.gemstartvguide.com. **Description:** A leading media and technology company focused on consumer television guidance and home entertainment. The Company's businesses include: television media and publishing properties; interactive program guide services and products; and technology and intellectual property licensing. **NOTE:** Search and apply for positions online. **Positions advertised include:** Director, Information Security; Manager, Human Resources; Security Engineer; Sr. Financial Analyst; Director, Affiliate Marketing. **Corporate headquarters location:** This location. **Listed on:** NASDAQ. **Stock exchange symbol:** GMST.

GEN-PROBE INCORPORATED
10210 Genetic Center Drive, San Diego CA 92121. 858/410-8000. **Fax:** 800/288-3141. **Contact:** Human Resources. **E-mail address:** hr@gen-probe.com. **World Wide Web address:** http://www.gen-probe.com. **Description:** Develops and manufactures products for clinical blood testing.

GENELABS TECHNOLOGIES, INC.
505 Penobscot Drive, Redwood City CA 94063-4738. 650/369-9500. **Fax:** 650/368-6080. **Contact:** Employment Department. **E-mail address:** hr@genelabs.com. **World Wide Web address:** http://www.genelabs.com. **Description:** Develops, manufactures, and provides products for the treatment, prevention, and diagnosis of viral and severely debilitating or life-threatening diseases. The company operates through its biopharmaceutical and diagnostic divisions to clinical laboratories and physicians' offices worldwide. **Corporate headquarters location:** This location. **Listed on:** NASDAQ. **Stock exchange symbol:** GNLB.

GENENTECH, INC.
One DNA Way, South San Francisco CA 94080. 650/225-1000. **Fax:** 650/225-6000. **Contact:** Human Resources. **E-mail address:** genentechjobpost@webhirepc.com. **World Wide Web address:** http://www.gene.com. **Description:** A biotechnology company that develops, manufactures, and markets pharmaceuticals using human genetic information. Genentech specializes in products designed to treat growth deficiencies, breast cancer, and AMI. **NOTE:** Search and apply for positions online. **Positions advertised include:** Automation Engineer; Scientist, Immunology; Head, Adult Endocrinology; Business Process Analyst; Quality Manager; Operations Team Leader. **Corporate headquarters location:** This location. **Other area locations:** Vacaville CA. **Listed on:** New York Stock Exchange. **Stock exchange symbol:** DNA.

GENERAL ATOMICS
P.O. Box 85608, San Diego CA 92186-5608. 858/455-3000. **Fax:** 858/455-2232. **Recorded jobline:** 858/455-4545. **Contact:** Personnel. **World Wide Web address:** http://www.ga.com. **Description:** Provides a broad range of energy research and development programs including gas-cooled nuclear reactors, thermonuclear fusion, defense systems, hazardous and nuclear wastes, electronic instrumentation, control systems, and research reactors, as well as uranium mining, milling, and conversion. **NOTE:** Candidates may apply online, or submit a resume via fax or mail. **Positions advertised include:** Engineer; Program Manager; Software Developer; Mechanical Designer; Electrical Engineer; Logistics Manager; Accountant. **Corporate headquarters location:** This location. **Other U.S. locations:** Gore OK. **Operations at this facility include:** Administration; Research and Development. **Number of employees at this location:** 1,800.

GENERAL DYNAMICS ADVANCED INFORMATION SYSTEMS
P.O. Box 7188, Mountain View CA 94039. 650/966-2000. **Physical address:** 100 Ferguson Drive, Mountain View CA 94043. **Contact:** Millie A. Miller, Vice President of Human Resources. **E-mail address:** resumes@gd-es.com. **World Wide Web address:** http://www.gd-es.com. **Description:** Engaged in the advancement of information systems and command, control, communications, computer, and intelligence technology. General Dynamics Electronic Systems designs and produces customized systems for defense, government, and industry clients. **NOTE:** Search and apply for postions online. **Positions advertised include:** Senior Lead Systems Engineer; Human Resources Manager; Senior Lead Software Engineer; Technical Writing Specialist; Administrative Assistant. **Corporate headquarters location:** Arlington VA. **Parent company:** General Dynamics Corporation. **Listed on:** New York Stock Exchange. **Stock exchange symbol:** GD. **Number of employees worldwide:** 10,000.

GENERAL DYNAMICS ORDNANCE AND TACTICAL SYSTEMS
898 North Sepulveda Boulevard, El Segunda CA 90245. 310/662-3200. **Contact:** Human Resources Representative. **E-mail address:** staffing@gd-ots.com. **World Wide Web address:** http://www.gd-ots.com. **Description:** Research, design, development, and manufacture of medium-caliber ammunition for the military. **Corporate headquarters location:** St. Petersburg FL. **Parent company:** General Dynamics Corporation. **Operations at this facility include:** Administration; Manufacturing; Research and Development. **Listed on:** New York Stock Exchange. **Stock exchange symbol:** GD. **Annual sales/revenues:** More than $100 million. **Number of employees at this location:** 155.

GENERAL REINSURANCE CORPORATION
550 South Hope Street, Suite 600, Los Angeles CA 90071-2648. 213/630-1900. **Contact:** Human Resources. **E-mail address:** jfoulds@genre.com. **World Wide Web address:** http://www.genre.com. **Description:** Provides property and casualty reinsurance to primary insurers on a direct basis. Reinsurance is marketed and underwritten on both treaty and facultative bases. Treaty marketing efforts are focused on small to medium-sized regional and specialty property and casualty insurers. General Reinsurance does not underwrite businesses that involve aviation, ocean marine, and professional liability. **Corporate headquarters location:** Stamford CT.

GENERAL STEAMSHIP AGENCIES, INC.
575 Redwood Highway, Suite 200, Mill Valley CA 94941-3007. 415/389-5200. **Fax:** 415/389-9020. **Contact:** Janis Mahoney, Vice President of Human Resources. **E-mail address:** hr@gensteam.com. **World Wide Web address:** http://www.gensteam.com. **Description:** Operates a shipping agency. **Corporate headquarters location:** This location.

GENERAL VENEER MANUFACTURING COMPANY
8652 Otis Street, P.O. Box 1607, South Gate CA 90280. 323/564-2661. **Fax:** 323/564-8888. **Contact:** Doug S. DeWitt, Personnel Director. **World Wide Web address:** http://www.generalveneer.com. **Description:** Manufactures doors and plywood products for home, commercial, and industrial use. **Corporate headquarters location:** This location. **Other U.S. locations:** Compton CA.

GENSLER
Two Harrison Street, Suite 400, San Francisco CA 94105. 415/433-3700. **Fax:** 415/836-4599. **Contact:** Human Resources. **E-mail address:** sf_careers@gensler.com. **World Wide Web address:** http://www.gensler.com. **Description:** Provides architectural space planning, graphics, and interior design services nationwide. **NOTE:** Resumes may be submitted via mail, fax, or e-mail. **Positions advertised include:** AutoCAD Manager. **Special programs:** Internships. **Corporate headquarters location:** This location. **Other area locations:** Irvine CA; Los Angeles CA. **Other U.S. locations:** Denver CO; Washington DC; Atlanta GA; Boston MA; Detroit MI; New York NY; Houston TX. **Listed on:** Privately held. **Number of employees at this location:** 175. **Number of employees nationwide:** 800.

GENUS, INC.
1139 Karlstad Drive, Sunnyvale CA 94089. 408/747-7140. **Fax:** 408/752-2009. **Contact:** Human Resources. **World Wide Web address:** http://www.genus.com. **Description:** Designs, manufactures, markets, and services advanced systems for thin film deposition used in the fabrication of complex ultra-large-scale integration semiconductor devices. Genus's products are used for several critical process steps required to produce integrated circuits for the computer, aerospace, communications, data processing, medical, military, aeronautical, automotive, and consumer electronics industries. **Positions advertised include:** Customer Support Engineer; Field Process Engineer; Process Development Engineer; General Accountant. **Corporate headquarters location:** This location. **International locations:** Korea. **Listed on:** NASDAQ. **Stock exchange symbol:** GGNS.

GENZYME GENETICS
5300 McConnell Avenue, Los Angeles CA 90066. 310/482-5000. **Fax:** 212/258-3137. **Contact:** Human Resources. **World Wide Web address:** http://www.genzymegenetics.com. **Description:** A leading provider of genetic testing and counseling. **Other locations:** Nationwide. **Corporate headquarters location:** Westborough MA.

GEORGIA-PACIFIC CORPORATION
P.O. Box 2407, South San Francisco CA 94083. 650/873-7800. **Physical address:** 249 East Grand Avenue, South San Francisco CA 94080. **Contact:** Human Resources Manager. **World Wide Web address:** http://www.gp.com. **Description:** Georgia-Pacific Corporation is a manufacturer, wholesaler, and distributor of building products, industrial wood products, pulp, paper, packaging, and related chemicals. The company is one of the world's largest manufacturers of forest products, with facilities in 48 states and overseas. Georgia-Pacific owns 6 million acres of forestland in North America. **Corporate headquarters location:** Atlanta GA. **Operations at this facility include:** This location produces corrugated containers. **Listed on:** New York Stock Exchange. **Stock exchange symbol:** GP. **Number of employees at this location:** 220.

GILEAD SCIENCES
333 Lakeside Drive, Foster City CA 94404. 650/574-3000. **Toll-free phone:** 800/445-3235. **Fax:** 650/578-9264. **Contact:** Human Resources. **E-mail address:** gilead@rpc.webhire.com. **World Wide Web address:** http://www.gilead.com. **Description:** A biopharmaceutical company dedicated to the discovery, development, and commercialization of treatments for human diseases. The company's business is focused on making new therapies available to patients, physicians, and health care systems. The company has also developed treatments for diseases caused by HIV, the Hepatitis B virus, the Herpes simplex virus, human papilloma virus, and the influenza virus. **NOTE:** Entry-level positions are offered. Search and apply for positions online. **Positions advertised include:** Head, Commercial Operations; Desktop Support Specialist; Accounting Manager; Senior Research Associate; Senior Maintenance Technician. **Special programs:** Internships. **Corporate headquarters location:** This location. **Listed on:** NASDAQ. **Stock exchange symbol:** GILD. **Annual sales/revenues:** $836 million. **Number of employees at this location:** 270. **Number of employees worldwide:** 1,600.

GISH BIOMEDICAL, INC.
22942 Arroyo Vista, Rancho Santa Margarita CA 92688. 949/635-6200. **Toll-free phone:** 800/938-0531. **Fax:** 949/635-6291. **Contact:** Human Resources. **E-mail address:** gish@gishbiomedical.com. **World Wide Web address:** http://www.gishbiomedical.com. **Description:** Designs, produces, and markets innovative specialty surgical devices. Gish Biomedical specializes in blood handling and fluid delivery as well as blood management systems for cardiovascular surgery, oncology, and orthopedics. **Corporate headquarters location:** This location. **Parent**

company: CardioTech International. **Listed on:** American Stock Exchange. **Stock exchange symbol:** CTE.

GLACIER WATER SERVICES, INC.
1385 Park Center Drive, Vista CA 92081. 760/560-1111. **Fax:** 760/560-0226. **Contact:** Human Resources. **E-mail address:** jobs@glacierwater.com. **World Wide Web address:** http://www.glacierwater.com. **Description:** A leading provider of drinking water dispensed to consumers through coin-operated, self-service vending machines. **Positions advertised include:** Service Technician; District Manager. **Corporate headquarters location:** This location.

GLADDING McBEAN
601 Seventh Street, Lincoln CA 95648-1828. 800/776-1133. **Fax:** 916/645-1723. **Contact:** Human Resources Department. **E-mail address:** recruiter@paccoast.com. **World Wide Web address:** http://www.gladdingmcbean.com. **Description:** Manufactures clay pipe, tile, garden pottery, and architectural terra cotta. **Corporate headquarters location:** This location. **Parent company:** Pacific Coast Building Products. **Number of employees at this location:** 250.

GLASSHOUSE TECHNOLOGIES, INC.
4305 Hacienda Drive, Suite 350, Pleasanton CA 94588. 925/225-9130. **Fax:** 925/225-9144. **Contact:** Human Resources. **E-mail address:** careers@glasshouse.com. **World Wide Web address:** http://www.glasshousetech.com. **Description:** A consulting firm providing data storage strategies and solutions for the financial services, health care, biopharmaceutical, and technology sectors. Founded in 2001. **Positions advertised include:** IT Manager; Sr. Storage Consultant; Engagement Partner; Project Manager. **Corporate headquarters location:** Framingham MA. **Other U.S. locations:** Minneapolis MN; New York NY; Durham NC; Hartford CT; Washington DC. **Listed on:** Privately held.

GLENAIR INC.
1211 Air Way, Glendale CA 91201-2497. 818/247-6000. **Fax:** 818/500-9912. **Contact:** Personnel Director. **World Wide Web address:** http://www.glenair.com. **Description:** Manufactures electrical connector accessories and other electrical products. **NOTE:** Submit resume online. **Corporate headquarters location:** This location.

GLENDALE COMMUNITY COLLEGE
1500 North Verdugo Road, Glendale CA 91208. 818/240-1000. **Fax:** 818/551-5169. **Recorded jobline:** 818/291-6655. **Contact:** Office of Human Resources. **World Wide Web address:** http://www.glendale.cc.ca.us. **Description:** A two-year community college with an enrollment of over 20,000 students. **Office hours:** Monday – Friday, 8:00 a.m. – 4:30 p.m.

GLOBAL INFORMATION DISTRIBUTION (GID)
2635 Zanker Road, San Jose CA 95134-2107. 408/232-5500. **Fax:** 408/232-5501. **Contact:** Personnel. **World Wide Web address:** http://www.gid-it.com. **Description:** Manufactures film-based imaging printers and storage/retrieval hardware. **Parent company:** Softnet.

GOLD'S GYM
360 Hampton Drive, Venice CA 90291. 310/392-6004. **Fax:** 310/396-1065. **Contact:** Human Resources. **World Wide Web address:** http://www.goldsgym.com. **Description:** A full-service health and fitness club. Each club is complete with weights and cardiovascular equipment, fitness and aerobic classes, tanning, personal training, and childcare facilities. Gold's Gym is one of the world's largest health club chains, with over 550 locations. **NOTE:** Part-time jobs are offered. **Corporate headquarters location:** This location. **Other area locations:** Palm Springs CA; Palm Desert CA; Victorville CA; Temecula CA. **Parent company:** Neste Development. **Number of employees at this location:** 40.

GOLDEN EAGLE INSURANCE
525 B Street, San Diego CA 92101. 619/744-6000. **Contact:** Human Resources. **World Wide Web address:** http://www.goldeneagle-ins.com. **Description:** A carrier of property, casualty, and life insurance, licensed in all 50 states, with offices throughout the country. **Positions advertised include:** Medical and Disability Case Manager; Field Investigator; Commercial Lines Underwriter. **Special programs:** Internships; Co-ops. **Corporate headquarters location:** This location. **Parent company:** Liberty Mutual Group.

GOLDEN RAM
8 Whatney, Irvine CA 92618. 949/460-9000. **Toll-free phone:** 800/222-8861. **Fax:** 949/460-7600. **Contact:** Personnel. **E-mail address:** jobs@goldenram.com. **World Wide Web address:** http://www.goldenram.com. **Description:** Manufactures third-party memory modules for computers to increase RAM. **Positions advertised include:** Sales Representative. **Corporate headquarters location:** This location.

SAMUEL GOLDWYN COMPANY
9570 West Pico Boulevard, Suite 400, Los Angeles CA 90035. 310/860-3100. **Contact:** Human Resources. **Description:** Engaged primarily in the financing, production, and distribution of feature-length motion pictures. Samuel Goldwyn Company also finances and distributes television programs intended for licensing to cable and first-run syndication markets, and to U.S. and foreign television networks. **NOTE:** Resumes may be submitted by mail or fax. Address resumes to: Samuel Goldwyn Company, Attention: Human Resources, 10203 Santa Monica Boulevard, Los Angeles CA 90067. Fax: 310/284-9213. **Special programs:** Internships. **Corporate headquarters location:** This location. **Other U.S. locations:** New York NY. **Operations at this facility include:** Administration; Regional Headquarters; Research and Development; Sales. **Number of employees at this location:** 260.

GOLIN HARRIS INTERNATIONAL
430 Pacific Avenue, San Francisco CA 94133. 415/274-7900. **Fax:** 415/274-7933. **Contact:** Human Resources. **E-mail address:** careers@golinharris.com. **World Wide Web address:** http://www.golinharris.com. **Description:** A public relations firm that primarily serves high-tech industries. **Corporate headquarters location:** Chicago IL. **Other U.S. locations:** Nationwide.

THE GOOD GUYS!
1600 Harbor Bay Parkway, Suite 200, Alameda CA 94502. 510/747-6000. **Contact:** Human Resources. **E-mail address:** jobs@goodguys.com (no attachments, please). **World Wide Web address:** http://www.thegoodguys.com. **Description:** Owns a chain of retail consumer electronic products stores specializing in televisions, videos, home audio systems, telephones, home office systems, car audio systems and cellular phones, photographic equipment, and other related electronic products. **Positions advertised include:** Assistant Buyer; Payroll Specialist; PC Support Specialist. **Corporate headquarters location:** This location. **Parent company:** CompUSA. **Listed on:** NASDAQ. **Stock exchange symbol:** GGUY.

GOODRICH AEROSTRUCTURES GROUP
850 Lagoon Drive, Chula Vista CA 91910-2098. 619/691-4111. **Fax:** 619/691-4103. **Contact:** Mary Rose Escobedo, Senior Employment Representative. **E-mail address:** goodrich@rpc.webhire.com. **World Wide Web address:** http://www.aerostructures.goodrich.com. **Description:** Designs, integrates, manufactures, sells, and supports aircraft engine nacelle systems and components for large commercial and military aircraft. **NOTE:** Search and apply for positions online. **Positions advertised include:** Purchasing Agent; Finance Administrator; Stress/Design Engineer; Tool Design Engineer; Thermodynamicist; Aerodynamicist. **Corporate headquarters location:** This location. **Other U.S. locations:** Foley AL; Riverside CA; San Marcos TX. **International locations:** Toulouse France; Hamburg Germany. **Parent company:** Goodrich Company. **Listed on:** New York Stock Exchange. **Stock exchange symbol:** GR. **Number of employees at this location:** 2,300. **Number of employees nationwide:** 5,000.

GOODWILL INDUSTRIES OF SOUTHERN CALIFORNIA
342 North San Fernando Road, Los Angeles CA 90031. 323/223-1211. **Fax:** 323/539-2046. **Contact:** Human Resources. **World Wide Web address:** http://www.goodwillsocal.org. **Description:** Besides operating 1,400 thrift stores nationwide, Goodwill is a nonprofit provider of employment training for the disabled and the poor. **Positions advertised include:** Retail Store Manager; Employment Specialist; Contracts Director; Job Coach; Education Coordinator. **Corporate headquarters location:** Bethesda MD. **Other U.S. locations:** Nationwide.

GOODYEAR TIRE & RUBBER COMPANY
19200 South Main Street, Gardena CA 90248. 323/770-0456. **Contact:** Personnel Department. **World Wide Web address:** http://www.goodyear.com. **Description:** Develops, manufactures, distributes, and sells tires. Goodyear Tire & Rubber Company also manufactures and sells a broad spectrum of rubber products and rubber-related chemicals for various industrial and consumer markets and provides auto repair services. The company operates 32 plants in the United States, 42 plants in 29 other countries, and more than 1,800 retail tire and service centers and other distribution facilities around the globe. Strategic business units of Goodyear Tire & Rubber include North American Tire, Kelly-Springfield, Goodyear Europe, Goodyear Latin America, Goodyear Asia, Engineered Products, Chemicals, Celeron, and Goodyear Racing. **Corporate headquarters location:** Akron OH. **Listed on:** New York Stock Exchange. **Stock exchange symbol:** GT.

GOOGLE INC.
1600 Ampitheatre Parkway, Mountain View CA 94043. 650/623-4000. **Fax:** 650/618-1499. **Contact:** Human Resources. **E-mail address:** jobs@google.com. **World Wide Web address:** http://www.google.com. **Description:** Operates the world's largest Internet search engine. **NOTE:** Search and apply for positions online. **Positions advertised include:** Software Engineer; Web Specialist; Product Marketing Manager; Financial Analyst; Senior Accountant; Corporate Legal Assistant; Business Analyst; Executive Assistant. **Corporate headquarters location:** This location.

GOTTSCHALKS
7 River Park Place East, Fresno CA 93720. 559/434-8000. **Fax:** 559/434-4806. **Contact:** Renee Jones, Director of Recruitment. **E-mail address:** hr@gottschalks.com. **World Wide Web address:** http://www.gottschalks.com. **Description:** A full-line fashion department store. Founded in 1904. **NOTE:** Entry-level positions and part-time jobs are offered. This location also hires seasonally. Search and apply for positions online. **Positions advertised include:** Advertising Copywriter; Programmer Analyst. **Special programs:** Internships; Training. **Office hours:** Monday - Friday, 8:30 a.m. - 5:30 p.m. **Corporate headquarters location:** This location. **Other U.S. locations:** AK; ID; NV; OR; WA. **Listed on:** New York Stock Exchange. **Stock exchange symbol:** GOT. **Annual sales/revenues:** $667 million. **Number of employees at this location:** 500. **Number of employees nationwide:** 5,000.

GOULD'S PUMPS INC.
3951 South Capitol Avenue, City of Industry CA 91714. 562/949-2113. **Contact:** Karen Perez, Personnel Manager. **World Wide Web address:** http://www.gouldspumps.com. **Description:** Engineers, manufactures, and sells centrifugal pumps and component parts with related drivers and accessories. Gould's serves a broad variety of industries including petrochemical and refining, pulp and paper, mining, and marine. The company maintains manufacturing facilities in a number of states, as well as production and sales locations overseas. **Corporate headquarters location:** Seneca Falls NY. **Parent company:** ITT Industries. **Operations at this facility include:** Sales; Production. **Listed on:** New York Stock Exchange. **Stock exchange symbol:** ITT.

GRANITE CONSTRUCTION INC.
P.O. Box 50085, Watsonville CA 95077. 831/724-1011. **Physical address:** 585 West Beach Street, Watsonville CA 95076. **Fax:** 831/761-7871. **Contact:** Brian Fox, Director of Recruiting. **E-mail address:** brian.fox@gcinc.com. **World Wide Web address:** http://www.graniteconstruction.com. **Description:** A construction company. Founded in 1922. **Positions advertised include:** Legal Secretary/Executive Assistant; Senior Estimator; Senior Financial Analyst. **Special programs:** Internships. **Corporate headquarters location:** This location. **Other U.S. locations:** Nationwide. **Operations at this facility include:** Administration. **Listed on:** New York Stock Exchange. **Stock exchange symbol:** GVA. **Number of employees at this location:** 300. **Number of employees nationwide:** 3,000.

GRASS VALLEY GROUP
400 Providence Mine Road, P.O. Box 599000, Nevada City CA 95959. 530/478-3364. **Fax:** 530/478-3808. **Contact:** Carole McCammon, Human Resources Consultant. **E-mail address:** carole.mccammon@thomson.net. **World Wide Web address:** http://www.grassvalleygroup.com. **Description:** Manufactures television broadcasting line equipment, terminal equipment, and video switching systems and related products. **NOTE:** Please e-mail all resumes. **Positions advertised include:** Communications Specialist; Hardware Engineer; Quality Manager. **Corporate headquarters location:** Beaverton OR.

GRAYBAR ELECTRIC INC.
383 South Cheryl Lane, City of Industry CA 91789. 909/451-4300. **Toll-free phone:** 800/GRAYBAR. **Fax:** 909/451-4699. **Contact:** Manager of Human Resources Department. **E-mail address:** opportunities@gbe.com. **World Wide Web address:** http://www.graybar.com. **Description:** Engaged in the national wholesale distribution of electrical equipment, supplies, and appliances, primarily to electrical contractors, industrial plants, communications companies, power utilities, government agencies, and consumer products dealers. **Corporate headquarters location:** St Louis MO.

GREATER BAY BANCORP
2860 West Bayshore Road, Palo Alto CA 94303. 650/813-8200. **Fax:** 650/494-9193. **Contact:** Human Resources. **E-mail address:** careersearch@gbbk.com. **World Wide Web address:** http://www.gbbk.com. **Description:** A bank holding company. **NOTE:**

To request an application, applicants should call 650/813-8267. **Corporate headquarters location:** This location. **Listed on:** NASDAQ. **Stock exchange symbol:** GBBK. **Annual sales/revenues:** More than $100 million.

GRECO SYSTEMS
8030 Las Mesa Boulevard, La Mesa CA 91941. 619/442-0205. **Toll-free phone:** 800/234-7326. **Fax:** 619/447-8982. **Contact:** Personnel. **E-mail address:** hrweb@grecosystems.com. **World Wide Web address:** http://www.grecosystems.com. **Description:** Manufactures industrial computer software and hardware systems for communication and storage in factory automation facilities. **Corporate headquarters location:** This location. **Listed on:** Privately held. **Annual sales/revenues:** $5 - $10 million. **Number of employees at this location:** 60.

GREENBERG, GLUSKER, FIELDS, CLAMAN & MACHTINGER
1900 Avenue of the Stars, Suite 2100, Los Angeles CA 90067. 310/553-3610. **Fax:** 310/553-0687. **Contact:** Patricia Patrick, Recruitment Administrator. **E-mail address:** ppatrick@ggfirm.com. **World Wide Web address:** http://www.ggfirm.com. **Description:** A law firm practicing bankruptcy, business and tax, entertainment, labor and employment, litigation, and probate and estate planning law.

GRENEKER
3110 East 12th Street, Los Angeles CA 90023. 323/263-9000. **Fax:** 323/263-9543. **Contact:** Personnel Director. **World Wide Web address:** http://www.greneker.com. **Description:** Designs and manufactures mannequins and custom crafts utilizing a number of materials including fiberglass, concrete, wood and metal. **Corporate headquarters location:** This location. **Other U.S. locations:** NY; TX. **Operations at this facility include:** Administration; Manufacturing; Research and Development; Sales. **Number of employees at this location:** 285.

GRIFOLS
2410 Lillyvale Avenue, Los Angeles CA 90032-3514. **Toll-free phone:** 888/474-3657. **Contact:** Human Resources. **World Wide Web address:** http://www.grifolsusa.com. **Description:** Supplies plasma products, diagnostic reagents, automated analyzers, and dosing machines.

GUARDIAN INDUSTRIES CORPORATION
11535 East Mountain View Avenue, Kingsburg CA 93631. 559/896-6400. **Fax:** 559/896-6479. **Contact:** Human Resources. **World Wide Web address:** http://www.guardian.com. **Description:** Guardian Industries Corporation is an international manufacturer of tempered glass, reflective coatings, and insulated glass. **Corporate headquarters location:** Auburn Hills MI. **International locations:** Worldwide. **Operations at this facility include:** This location manufactures glass. **Number of employees at this location:** 240.

GUESS? INC.
1444 South Alameda Street, Los Angeles CA 90021. 213/765-3100. **Fax:** 213/744-7832. **Contact:** Recruiting Department. **E-mail address:** jobs@guess.com. **World Wide Web address:** http://www.guess.com. **Description:** Designs, develops, and markets jeans and other casual wear for men and women. **Corporate headquarters location:** This location. **Listed on:** New York Stock Exchange. **Stock exchange symbol:** GES.

GUIDANT ENDOVASCULAR SOLUTIONS
1525 O'Brien Drive, Menlo Park CA 94025. 650/617-5000. **Toll-free phone:** 800/633-7970. **Fax:** 650/470-6320. **Contact:** Human Resources. **World Wide Web address:** http://www.guidant.com. **Description:** Designs, develops, manufactures, and markets a broad range of products for use in cardiac rhythm management, coronary artery disease intervention, and other forms of minimally invasive surgery. Founded in 1986. **NOTE:** Entry-level positions are offered. **Positions advertised include:** Manufacturing Supervisor. **Office hours:** Monday - Friday, 8:00 a.m. - 5:00 p.m. **Corporate headquarters location:** Indianapolis IN. **International locations:** Brussels, Belgium. **Listed on:** New York Stock Exchange. **Stock exchange symbol:** GDT. **Annual sales/revenues:** $3.2 billion. **Number of employees at this location:** 350. **Number of employees worldwide:** 11,000.

GUIDANT VASCULAR INTERVENTION
DEVICES FOR VASCULAR INTERVENTION, INC.
P.O. Box 58167, Santa Clara CA 95052-8167. 408/845-3000. **Physical address:** 3200 Lakeside Drive, Santa Clara CA 95054-2807. **Toll-free phone:** 800/633-3375. **Fax:** 408/845-3333. **Contact:** Recruiting. **World Wide Web address:** http://www.guidant.com. **Description:** Develops and manufactures a broad line of specialized balloon catheters, guide wires, and accessories. Devices for Vascular Intervention, Inc. (also at this location) develops proprietary technologies that remove obstructive blockages from arteries. **Positions advertised include:** Meetings/Program Coordinator; Research Scientist; Customer Service Specialist; Accountant; Forecast Analyst; Senior Financial Analyst; Clinical Data Architect. **Parent company:** Guidant Corporation. **Corporate headquarters location:** Indianapolis IN. **Listed on:** New York Stock Exchange. **Stock exchange symbol:** GDT.

GYMBOREE
700 Airport Boulevard, Suite 200, Burlingame CA 94010. 650/579-0600. **Contact:** Human Resources. **World Wide Web address:** http://www.gymboree.com. **Description:** Operates a chain of retail stores that sell children's active wear and accessories. The company also franchises Gymboree Play and Music Programs for children and their parents. **Positions advertised include:** Designer; Technical Designer; Business Systems Manager; International Transportation Manager; Director of Leasing; Merchandise Planner; Inventory Control Analyst; Benefits Manager; Java Programmer; Payroll Assistant; Revenue Accountant; Production Artist. **Corporate headquarters location:** This location. **Listed on:** NASDAQ. **Stock exchange symbol:** GYMB. **Number of employees at this location:** 100. **Number of employees nationwide:** 3,700.

H&R BLOCK
366 West Portal Avenue, San Francisco CA 94127. 415/665-4540. **Recorded jobline:** 888/244-6860. **Contact:** Personnel. **E-mail address:** taxprepcareers@hrblock.com. **World Wide Web address:** http://www.hrblock.com. **Description:** Engaged in consumer tax preparation. H&R Block operates more than 9,500 offices nationwide and prepares more than 10 million tax returns each year. The company has offices in over 750 Sears, Roebuck & Co. stores in both the United States and Canada. The company is also engaged in a number of other tax-related activities including group tax programs, executive tax service, tax training schools, and real estate awareness seminars. **Other U.S. locations:** Nationwide. **Listed on:** New York Stock Exchange. **Stock exchange symbol:** HRB.

HBO PICTURES
2049 Century Park East, Suite 4100, Los Angeles CA 90067. 310/201-9200. **Contact:** Personnel Department. **World Wide Web address:** http://www.hbo.com/films. **Description:** Produces original, cable network films. **NOTE:** Search and apply for positions online. **Positions advertised include:** Assistant, HBO Films Development; Executive Assistant, HBO Films Post Production. **Corporate headquarters location:** New York NY. **Parent company:** Time Warner.

HRH INSURANCE
77-564 Country Club Drive, Suite B401, Palm Desert CA 92211. 760/360-4700. **Contact:** Human Resources. **E-mail address:** opportunities@hrh.com. **World Wide Web address:** http://www.hrhgroup.com. **Description:** Provides all types of personal and commercial insurance including life and health. **Office hours:** Monday – Friday, 8:00 a.m. – 4:30 p.m.

HRL LABORATORIES, LLC
3011 Malibu Canyon Road, Malibu CA 90265. 310/317-5000. **Contact:** Lynn W. Ross, Human Resources. **E-mail address:** staffing@hrl.com. **World Wide Web address:** http://www.hrl.com. **Description:** Researches and develops lasers, fiber optic devices and systems, computational electromagnetics, optoelectronics, and radar. **NOTE:** Search and apply for positions online. **Positions advertised include:** General Technician; Senior Development Engineer; Research Staff Member. **Special programs:** Summer internships. **Corporate headquarters location:** This location. **Parent company:** HRL Laboratories is jointly owned by Hughes Electronics Corporation and Raytheon Company.

HAMILTON SUNDSTRAND POWER SYSTEMS
P.O. Box 85757, San Diego CA 92186. 858/627-6000. **Fax:** 858/627-6601. **Contact:** Human Resources Department. **E-mail address:** professionalstaffing@hamiltonsunstrandcorp.com. **World Wide Web address:** http://www.hs-powersystems.com. **Description:** Manufactures aeronautical and aerospace equipment including auxiliary power systems. **NOTE:** Search and apply for positions at: http://www.hamiltonsundstrandcareers.com. **Positions advertised include:** Area Sales Manager; Staff Engineer; Technical Publications Analyst; Market Support Specialist. **Corporate headquarters location:** Windsor Locks CT. **Parent company:** United Technologies. **Listed on:** New York Stock Exchange. **Stock exchange symbol:** UTX. **Number of employees worldwide:** 17,200.

HAMILTON SUNSTRAND SENSOR SYSTEMS
2771 North Garey Avenue, Pomona CA 91767. 909/593-3581. **Contact:** Personnel Department. **E-mail address:** professionalstaffing@hamiltonsunstrandcorp.com. **World Wide Web address:** http://www.hamiltonsunstrand.com. **Description:** Produces orbiting satellites, small-launch vehicles, and navigational and positioning instruments and provides satellite-based communications systems for industry. **NOTE:** Search and apply for positions at: http://www.hamiltonsundstrandcareers.com. **Corporate headquarters location:** Windsor Locks CT. **Parent company:** United Technologies. **Listed on:** New York Stock Exchange. **Stock exchange symbol:** UTX.

HARPERCOLLINS SAN FRANCISCO
353 Sacramento Street, Suite 500, San Francisco CA 94111. 415/477-4400. **Contact:** Human Resources. **E-mail address:** jobs@harpercollins.com. **World Wide Web address:** http://www.harpercollins.com. **Description:** HarperCollins is a leading book publisher. **Positions advertised include:** Assistant Art Director; Interior Design Manager; Business Manager; Senior Production Editor; Rotational Associate; Senior Sales Director, Special Markets. **Special programs:** Internships. **Corporate headquarters location:** New York NY. **Other U.S. locations:** Glenview IL; Scranton PA. **Subsidiaries include:** Scott Foresman; Zondervan. **Parent company:** News Corporation. **Operations at this facility include:** This location publishes religious, academic, and psychology titles, as well as visual books such as cookbooks and gift books. **Listed on:** New York Stock Exchange. **Stock exchange symbol:** NWS. **Number of employees at this location:** 135. **Number of employees nationwide:** 3,000.

HARRIS AND FRANK INC.
17629 Ventura Boulevard, Encino CA 91316. 818/783-2739. **Contact:** Personnel Department. **Description:** A specialty fashion store chain of men's and women's clothing including a tuxedo rental department. Harris and Frank operates 19 store locations. **Operations at this facility include:** Regional Headquarters.

HARRIS CORPORATION
330 Twin Dolphin Drive, Redwood Shores CA 94065. 650/594-3290. **Contact:** Resources Manager. **World Wide Web address:** http://www.harris.com. **Description:** A communications equipment company that provides broadcast, network, government, and wireless support products and systems. Founded in 1895. **Positions advertised include:** Technical Writer. **Corporate headquarters location:** Melbourne FL. **Other U.S. locations:** Nationwide. **International locations:** Worldwide. **Listed on:** New York Stock Exchange. **Stock exchange symbol:** HRS. **Annual sales/revenues:** $2.1 billion. **Number of employees nationwide:** 10,500.

HASKEL INTERNATIONAL, INC.
100 East Graham Place, Burbank CA 91502. 818/843-4000. **Fax:** 818/841-4291. **Contact:** Human Resources. **World Wide Web address:** http://www.haskel.com. **Description:** Manufactures pneumatically driven, high-pressure liquid pumps and gas boosters for industrial, commercial, aerospace, and military applications. The company sells and distributes its own pneumatically driven pumps, gas boosters, air amplifiers, and high-pressure valves, as well as third-party valves, cylinders and actuators, and other hydraulic and pneumatic devices. The company's high-pressure pumps and systems are used worldwide in manufacturing processes for industrial pressure testing and controls, fluid storage and containment, and a wide variety of other applications. Haskel International also specializes in the trading of electronic components. Founded in 1946. **Corporate headquarters location:** This location.

HATHAWAY DINWIDDIE CONSTRUCTION COMPANY
275 Battery Street, Suite 300, San Francisco CA 94111. 415/986-2718. **Fax:** 415/956-5669. **Contact:** Human Resources. **E-mail address:** hr@hdcco.com. **World Wide Web address:** http://www.hdcco.com. **Description:** A full-service general contractor. Positions advertised include: Project Engineer; Estimator; Project Manager; Sujperintendent. **Corporate headquarters location:** This location. **Other area locations:** Los Angeles CA; Santa Clara CA.

HAYWARD, CITY OF
777 B Street, Third Floor, Hayward CA 94541-5007. 510/583-4500. **Recorded jobline:** 510/583-4555. **Contact:** Personnel. **World Wide Web address:** http://www.ci.hayward.ca.us. **Description:** Government offices for the City of Hayward. **Positions advertised include:** Neighborhood and Economic Development Manager. **Special programs:** Internships. **Corporate headquarters location:** This location. **Operations at this facility include:** Administration. **Number of employees at this location:** 800.

HEALTH NET
21282 Burbank Boulevard, Woodland Hills CA 91367. 818/676-6775. **Fax:** 818/676-8544. **Contact:** Human Resources. **E-mail address:** resume@healthnet.com. **World Wide Web address:** http://www.healthnet.com. **Description:** One of California's largest health maintenance organizations. Health Net also organizes wellness programs. **Positions advertised include:** Clinical Specialist; Senior Financial Analyst; Finance Project Manager; Grievance and Appeals Specialist; Senior Systems Analyst. **Corporate headquarters location:** This location. **Parent company:** Foundation Health Systems, Inc. **Listed on:** New York Stock Exchange. **Stock exchange symbol:** HNT.

HEALTH NET
3400 Data Drive, Rancho Cordova CA 95670. 916/631-5000. **Contact:** Human Resources. **E-mail address:** resume@healthnet.com. **World Wide Web address:** http://www.health.net. **Description:** Administers the delivery of managed care services to approximately 3.4 million individuals through its HMOs, government contracting, and specialty services managed care facilities. This location handles health plans for small businesses in Northern California. **Positions advertise include:** Customer Service Representative; Systems Programmer; Administrative Assistant; Database Administrator; Care Manager; Pharmacy Technician. **Corporate headquarters location:** Woodland Hills CA. **Listed on:** New York Stock Exchange. **Stock exchange symbol:** HNT. **Number of employees at this location:** 15,000.

HEALTH NET
3131 Camino Del Rio North, San Diego CA 92108. 619/521-4900. **Contact:** Human Resources. **E-mail address:** resume@healthnet.com. **World Wide Web address:** http://www.health.net. **Description:** Administers the delivery of managed care services to approximately 3.4 million individuals through its HMOs, government contracting, and specialty services managed care facilities. This location handles health plans for mid-sized companies. **Positions advertised include:** Alcohol and Drug Counselor; Case Manager; Utilization Review Nurse; Administrative Assistant; Customer Service Representative. **Corporate headquarters location:** Woodland Hills CA. **Operations at this facility include:** Regional office. **Listed on:** New York Stock Exchange. **Stock exchange symbol:** HNT.

HEINZ USA
757 East 11th Street, Tracy CA 95304. 209/832-4241. **Contact:** Human Resources. **World Wide Web address:** http://www.heinz.com. **Description:** A food producer. **Parent company:** H.J. Heinz Company is a worldwide producer of food products including ketchup, sauces, condiments, baby food, seafood, pet food, frozen potato products, frozen meats, beverages, and a wide selection of other processed consumables. These foods are marketed under brand names including Heinz, Steak-Umm, and Ore-Ida. The company also operates and sells franchise licenses for Weight Watchers International weight control classes and related programs. **Listed on:** New York Stock Exchange. **Stock exchange symbol:** HNZ.

HELLO DIRECT
5884 Eden Park Place, San Jose CA 95138. 408/972-1990. **Toll-free phone:** 800/444-3556. **Contact:** Human Resources. **E-mail address:** jobs@hellodirect.com. **World Wide Web address:** http://www.hellodirect.com. **Description:** A catalog retailer of telephone productivity items including headsets, cordless phones, line switches, digital adapters, and call recording devices. **Corporate headquarters location:** This location.

HEMACARE CORPORATION
21101 Oxnard Street, Woodland Hills CA 91367. 877/310-0717. **Fax:** 818/251-5300. **Contact:** Human Resources Department. **E-mail address:** jobs@hemacare.com. **World Wide Web address:** http://www.hemacare.com. **Description:** Provides blood management systems such as plasma exchange and bone marrow transplantation. The company also operates a donor center. **Positions advertised include:** Registered Nurse; Medical Assistant. **Corporate headquarters location:** This location. **Subsidiaries include:** HemaBiologics, Inc. conducts research on anti-HIV pharmaceuticals.

HENKEL INC.
P.O. Box 1282, City of Industry CA 91749-1282. 626/968-6511. **Fax:** 626/336-0526. **Contact:** Human Resources. **World Wide Web address:** http://www.henkel.com. **Description:** Manufactures coating powders and high-performance liquid encapsulates for use in the electronics industry. **Special programs:** Internships. **Corporate headquarters location:** Windsor Locks CT. **Other U.S. locations:** Nationwide. **Operations at this facility include:** Administration; Divisional Headquarters; Manufacturing; Research and Development; Sales.

HENKEL LOCTITE AEROSPACE
2850 Willow Pass Road, P.O. Box 312, Bay Point CA 94565. 925/458-8000. **Fax:** 925/458-8030. **Contact:** Human Resources. **World Wide Web address:** http://www.loctiteaero.com. **Description:** Develops and markets adhesives, sealants, and specialty chemicals. **Corporate headquarters location:** Rocky Hill CT. **Parent company:** Henkel Group. **Operations at this facility include:** This location produces adhesives and sealants for use in the aerospace industry.

THE HERRICK CORPORATION
7021 Koll Center Parkway, P.O. Box 9125, Pleasanton CA 94566. 925/484-2900. **Contact:** Marie Davies, Office Manager. **Description:** Engaged in steel fabrication and the provision of heavy industrial contracting services.

HEWLETT-PACKARD COMPANY
3000 Hanover Street, Palo Alto CA 94304-1185. 650/857-1501. **Fax:** 650/852-8138. **Contact:** Human Resources. **World Wide Web address:** http://www.hp.com. **Description:** Hewlett-Packard designs and manufactures measurement and computation products and systems used in business, engineering, science, health care, and education. Principal products include integrated instrument and computer systems such as hardware and software, peripheral products, and electronic medical equipment and systems. Products are sold through retail stores, warehouses, resellers, mail-order catalogs, and telemarketers. The company conducts business in more than 90 countries. **NOTE:** Search and apply for positions online. **Positions advertised include:** Software Territory Sales Representative; Research Associate; Advertising Director; Marketing Science Research Intern; Senior Experience Designer. **Special programs:** Internships. **Corporate headquarters location:** This location. **Other area locations:** Statewide. **Other U.S. locations:** Nationwide. **International locations:** Worldwide. **Listed on:** New York Stock Exchange. **Stock exchange symbol:** HPQ. **Number of employees worldwide:** 142,000.

HEWLETT-PACKARD COMPANY
19111 Pruneridge Avenue, Cupertino CA 95014. 408/725-8900. **Contact:** Human Resources. **World Wide Web address:** http://www.hp.com. **Description:** Hewlett-Packard designs and manufactures measurement and computation products and systems used in business, industry, engineering, science, health care, and education. Principal products include integrated instrument and computer systems such as hardware and software, peripheral products, and electronic medical equipment and systems. **NOTE:** Search and apply for positions online. **Positions advertised include:** Television Technologist; Networking Software Development Intern; Product Marketing Director; Software Design Engineer; Business Process Analyst. **Corporate headquarters location:** Palo Alto CA. **Other U.S. locations:** Nationwide. **Operations at this facility include:** This location manufactures business computer systems for interactive, online data processing, database management, and distributed data processing. **Listed on:** New York Stock Exchange. **Stock exchange symbol:** HPQ. **Number of employees nationwide:** 93,000.

HEWLETT-PACKARD COMPANY
8000 Foothills Boulevard, Roseville CA 95747. 916/786-8000. **Contact:** Human Resources. **World Wide Web address:** http://www.hp.com. **Description:** Hewlett-Packard designs and manufactures measurement and computation products and systems used in business, industry, engineering, science, health care, and education. Principal products include integrated instrument and computer systems such as hardware and software, peripheral products, and medical electronic equipment and systems. **NOTE:** Search and apply for positions online. **Positions advertised include:** Hardware Design Engineer; ASIC Engineer; R&D Network Systems Test Engineer; Engineering Program Manager; Product Marketing Manager. **Corporate headquarters location:** Palo Alto CA. **Other U.S. locations:** Nationwide. **Operations at this facility include:** This location manufactures business computer systems. **Listed on:** New York Stock Exchange. **Stock exchange symbol:** HPQ. **Number of employees nationwide:** 93,000.

HEWLETT-PACKARD COMPANY
16399 West Bernardo Drive, San Diego CA 92127. 858/655-4100. **Contact:** Human Resources. **World Wide Web address:** http://www.hp.com. **Description:** Hewlett-Packard is engaged in the design and manufacture of measurement and computation products and systems used in business, industry, engineering, science, health care, and education. Principal products include integrated instrument and computer systems such as hardware and software, peripheral products, and medical electronic equipment and systems. **NOTE:** Resumes should be sent to Employment Response Center, Hewlett-Packard Company, Mail Stop 20-APP, 3000 Hanover Street, Palo Alto CA 94304. **Positions advertised include:** . **Corporate headquarters location:** Palo Alto CA. **Other U.S. locations:** Nationwide. **Operations at this facility include:** This location manufactures printers. **Listed on:** New York Stock Exchange. **Stock exchange symbol:** HPQ. **Number of employees nationwide:** 93,000.

HEXCEL CORPORATION
11711 Dublin Boulevard, P.O. Box 2363, Dublin CA 94568. 925/551-4900. **Contact:** Corporate Staffing. **World Wide Web address:** http://www.hexcel.com. **Description:** A manufacturing firm engaged in two primary business segments: structural materials including aerospace products, nonaerospace honeycomb, resin-impregnated industrial fabrics, and nonimpregnated fabrics; and specialty chemicals including bulk pharmaceuticals, custom and special-purpose chemicals, specialty resins, and industrial maintenance chemicals. **Positions advertised include:** Laboratory Technician, Materials; Oracle Database Administrator. **Corporate headquarters location:** Stamford CT. **Other U.S. locations:** Nationwide. **Operations at this facility include:** Research and Technology Headquarters. **Listed on:** New York Stock Exchange. **Stock exchange symbol:** HXL. **Number of employees at this location:** 250. **Number of employees worldwide:** Over 4,000.

HI-SHEAR TECHNOLOGY CORPORATION
24225 Garnier Street, Torrance CA 90505. 310/784-2100. **Fax:** 310/784-7873. **Contact:** Manager of Human Resources. **E-mail address:** personnel@hstc.com. **World Wide Web address:** http://www.hstc.com. **Description:** Designs, manufactures, and markets a wide range of electronic and ordnance-related products and systems used by the aerospace and defense industries, primarily in space applications, tactical and strategic missile and weapon systems, and advanced fighter aircraft. The company also produces emergency rescue equipment; igniter assemblies for automotive airbag systems; and high-security, electromechanical locks. Aerospace products include microprocessor-based electronic sequencers, power cartridges, electronic and laser firing systems, and mechanical separation devices. **Corporate headquarters location:** This location. **Parent company:** GFI Industries. **Operations at this facility include:** Administration; Manufacturing; Research and Development; Sales. **Listed on:** American Stock Exchange. **Stock exchange symbol:** HSR. **Number of employees at this location:** 500.

HILL AND KNOWLTON INC.
303 Second Street, Suite 900 South, San Francisco 94107. 415/281-7120. **Contact:** Maya Komadina, Human Resources. **E-mail address:** mkomadina@hillandknowlton.com. **World Wide Web address:** http://www.hillandknowlton.com. **Description:** One of the world's largest public relations/public affairs counseling firms, serving more than 1,000 clients worldwide, Hill and Knowlton Inc. serves clients through more than 60 company offices and through associate arrangements with 50 leading regional firms worldwide. **NOTE:** Interested candidates should submit a resume via US mail to the address listed above. **Special programs:** Internships. **Corporate headquarters location:** New York NY. **Other U.S. locations:** Washington DC.

HILL PHOENIX
3601 Walnut Avenue, Chino CA 91710. 909/590-4432. **Contact:** Payroll. **World Wide Web address:** http://www.hillphoenix.com. **Description:** Manufactures refrigerated merchandisers, refrigeration systems, and electrical distribution centers for commercial and industrial companies. **Corporate headquarters location:** Conyers GA.

HILLVIEW MENTAL HEALTH CENTER, INC.
11500 Eldridge Avenue, Suite 206, Lake View Terrace CA 91342. 818/896-1161. **Contact:** Human Resources. **Description:** An outpatient and residential mental health services facility for individuals with persistent mental disabilities. Founded in 1985. **NOTE:** Entry-level positions and second and third shifts are offered. **Corporate headquarters location:** This location. **Number of employees at this location:** 80.

HILTON AT FISHERMAN'S WHARF
2620 Jones Street, San Francisco CA 94133. 415/885-4700. **Contact:** Personnel Department. **World Wide Web address:** http://www.hilton.com. **Description:** A 232-room hotel with a restaurant and lounge. **Corporate headquarters location:** Beverly Hills CA. **Parent company:** Hilton Group plc. **Listed on:** New York Stock Exchange. **Stock exchange symbol:** HLN.

HILTON SAN FRANCISCO & TOWERS
333 O'Farrell Street, San Francisco CA 94102. 415/771-1400. **Fax:** 415/673-6490. **Contact:** Human Resources. **World Wide Web address:** http://www.hilton.com. **Description:** A 2,000-room hotel. **NOTE:** Resumes may be submitted via mail or fax. **Positions advertised include:** Area Director, Purchasing; Assistant Director, Banquets;

Assistant Director, Housekeeping; Assistant Executive Steward; Meetings and Conventions Manager; Sales Manager. **Special programs:** Internships. **Corporate headquarters location:** Beverly Hills CA. **Other U.S. locations:** Nationwide. **Parent company:** Hilton Hotels Corporation. **Listed on:** New York Stock Exchange. **Stock exchange symbol:** HLT. **Number of employees at this location:** 1,200.

HIROSE ELECTRIC USA, INC.
2688 Westhills Court, Simi Valley CA 93065-6235. 805/522-7958. **Fax:** 805/522-0208. **Contact:** Human Resources. **E-mail address:** jobs@hirose.com. **World Wide Web address:** http://www.hiroseusa.com. **Description:** Manufactures and distributes electric, electronic, and optical connections. **Corporate headquarters location:** Tokyo, Japan. **Other U.S. locations:** IL; MI; NY; TX. **Operations at this facility include:** Administration; Divisional Headquarters; Manufacturing; Sales; Service. **Number of employees at this location:** 60.

HITACHI DATA SYSTEMS
750 Central Expressway, Santa Clara CA 95050. 408/970-1000. **Fax:** 408/727-8036. **Contact:** Human Resources. **World Wide Web address:** http://www.hds.com. **Description:** Hitachi Data Systems manufactures mainframe computers. **NOTE:** Search and apply for positions online. **Positions advertised include:** Database Administrator; Business Analyst; Attorney; Global Storage Manager. **Corporate headquarters location:** This location. **Parent company:** Hitachi Ltd. **Operations at this facility include:** This location serves as a sales and marketing office. **Listed on:** New York Stock Exchange. **Stock exchange symbol:** HIT.

HITACHI DIGITAL GRAPHICS INC.
2325 Paragon Drive, Suite 10, San Jose CA 95131. 408/392-9560. **Contact:** Human Resources. **World Wide Web address:** http://www.hitachidigital.com. **Description:** Manufactures graphics tablets with pressure sensitive pens for computers. **Parent company:** Hitachi Ltd. **Listed on:** New York Stock Exchange. **Stock exchange symbol:** HIT.

HOBART CORPORATION
5584 Bandini Boulevard, Bell CA 90201. 323/260-7321. **Contact:** Human Resources. **World Wide Web address:** http://www.hobartcorp.com. **Description:** Hobart Corporation manufactures restaurant equipment including mixers, slicers, cooking equipment, and refrigeration devices. **Corporate headquarters location:** Troy OH. **Parent company:** Premark International. **Operations at this facility include:** This location is a sales office.

HOLIDAY INN CIVIC CENTER
50 Eighth Street, San Francisco CA 94103. 415/626-6103. **Contact:** Director of Personnel. **World Wide Web address:** http://www.holiday-inn.com. **Description:** One location of the international hotel chain. Operations include the management of more than 1,750 company-owned and franchised hotels, gaming operations, restaurants, and a sea transportation subsidiary. **Corporate headquarters location:** Memphis TN. **Parent company:** Six Continents Hotels. **Listed on:** New York Stock Exchange. **Stock exchange symbol:** SXC.

HOLLYWOOD PARK INC.
P.O. Box 369, Inglewood CA 90306-0369. 310/419-1500. **Physical address:** 1050 South Prairie Avenue, Inglewood CA 90301. **Contact:** Human Resources Department. **E-mail address:** dannetteb@hollywoodpark.com. **World Wide Web address:** http://www.hollywoodpark.com. **Description:** Owns and operates a horseracing track. **Positions advertised include:** Security Officer. **Corporate headquarters location:** This location. **Parent company:** Churchill Downs Inc. **Listed on:** NASDAQ. **Stock exchange symbol:** CHDN.

HOLMES AND NARVER INC.
999 Town & Country Road, Orange CA 92868. 714/567-2567. **Fax:** 714/567-2656. **Contact:** Pam Cooper, Senior Employment Administrator. **Description:** A full-service architectural, engineering, design, and construction company. The company designs and manages the construction of government bases, airports and airfields, remote site camps, bridges, and research laboratories. **Other U.S. locations:** Anchorage AK; Denver CO. **Parent company:** USFilter.

HOLZ RUBBER COMPANY, INC.
1129 South Sacramento Street, Lodi CA 95240. 209/368-7171. **Toll-free phone:** 800/285-1600. **Fax:** 209/368-3246. **Contact:** Personnel. **World Wide Web address:** http://www.holzrubber.com. **Description:** Manufactures a wide range of molded, extruded, and hand-fabricated rubber products, tires, and related products. **Corporate headquarters location:** This location.

HONEYWELL
1430 Tully Road, Suite 415, San Jose CA 95122. 650/965-2414. **Contact:** Human Resources. **World Wide Web address:** http://www.honeywell.com. **Description:** Honeywell is engaged in the research, development, manufacture, and sale of advanced technology products and services in the fields of chemicals, electronics, automation, and controls. The company's major businesses are home and building automation and control, performance polymers and chemicals, industrial automation and control, space and aviation systems, and defense and marine systems. **Corporate headquarters location:** Morristown NJ. **Operations at this facility include:** This location manufactures industrial chemicals. **Listed on:** New York Stock Exchange. **Stock exchange symbol:** HON.

HONEYWELL
3201 West Lomita Boulevard, Torrance CA 90505. 310/530-1981. **Contact:** Human Resources. **World Wide Web address:** http://www.honeywell.com. **Description:** Honeywell is engaged in the research, development, manufacture, and sale of advanced technology products and services in the fields of chemicals, electronics, automation, and controls. The company's major businesses are home and building automation and control, performance polymers and chemicals, industrial automation and control, space and aviation systems, and defense and marine systems. **Positions advertised include:** Project Engineer. **Corporate headquarters location:** Morristown NJ. **Operations at this facility include:** This location manufactures turbochargers. **Listed on:** New York Stock Exchange. **Stock exchange symbol:** HON.

THE HORN GROUP INC.
612 Howard Street, Suite 100, San Francisco CA 94105. 415/905-4000. **Fax:** 415/977-0333. **Contact:** Director of Training. **World Wide Web address:** http://www.horngroup.com. **Description:** A public relations firm that primarily serves high-tech industries. Founded in 1991. **NOTE:** Entry-level positions are offered. Submit resume online. **Company slogan:** Pride, passion, results. **Special programs:** Internships; Summer Jobs. **Office hours:** Monday - Friday, 8:30 a.m. - 5:30 p.m. **Corporate headquarters location:** This location. **Other U.S. locations:** Braintree MA; New York NY. **Listed on:** Privately held. **Annual sales/revenues:** $5 - $10 million. **Number of employees at this location:** 40.

HOSPITAL SYSTEMS
750 Garcia Avenue, Pittsburg CA 94565. 925/427-7800. **Fax:** 925/427-0800. **Contact:** Human Resources. **World Wide Web address:** http://www.hospitalsystems.com. **Description:** Manufactures respiratory products that are used for a broad range of health services. Product lines include respiratory therapy equipment, emergency medical products, and medical gas equipment. **Corporate headquarters location:** This location.

HOT TOPIC
18305 East San Jose Avenue, City of Industry CA 91748. 626/839-4681. **Fax:** 626/581-9263. **Contact:** Personnel. **E-mail address:** jobs@hottopic.com. **World Wide Web address:** http://www.hottopic.com. **Description:** Operates a chain of mall-based retail outlets. Hot Topic's product line features clothing and accessories relating to various alternative music-related lifestyles. Founded in 1988. **NOTE:** Search and apply for positions online. **Positions advertised include:** Internet Customer Service Representative; Database Analyst; Business Analyst; Help Desk Associate; Loss Prevention Auditor. **Corporate headquarters location:** This location. **Other U.S. locations:** Nationwide. **Listed on:** NASDAQ. **Stock exchange symbol:** HOTT. **Annual sales/revenues:** Over $400 million.

HOTEL DEL CORONADO
1500 Orange Avenue, Coronado CA 92118. 619/435-6611. **Toll-free phone:** 800/HOTELDEL. **Fax:** 619/522-8160. **Recorded jobline:** 619/522-8158. **Contact:** Employment. **E-mail address:** deljobs@hoteldel.com. **World Wide Web address:** http://www.hoteldel.com. **Description:** A 691-room oceanside resort with seven restaurants, five lounges/bars, two swimming pools, and six tennis courts. Positions advertised include: Manager; Concessions Manager. **Special programs:** Internships. **Corporate headquarters location:** This location. **Listed on:** Privately held.

HOUGHTON MIFFLIN COMPANY
2001 Gateway Place, Suite 750, San Jose CA 95110. 408/392-3100. **Contact:** Human Resources. **E-mail address:** hrassist@hmco.com. **World Wide Web address:** http://www.hmco.com. **Description:** Houghton Mifflin Company is a publisher of school textbooks, fiction, nonfiction, reference books, educational software, and related multimedia products. **Corporate headquarters location:** Boston MA. **Operations at this facility include:** This location is a sales office for the Western Elementary School Division. **Listed on:** New York Stock Exchange. **Stock exchange symbol:** HTN. **Number of employees at this location:** 40.

HOUSEHOLD FINANCE CORPORATION
388 Market Street, Suite 850, San Francisco CA 94111. 415/362-4542. **Fax:** 415/362-4548. **Contact:** Branch Manager. **World Wide Web address:** http://www.hfc.com. **Description:** Offers real estate, home equity, and personal loans. **NOTE:** Search and apply for positions online. **Corporate headquarters location:** Prospect Heights IL. **Parent company:** Household International. **Operations at this facility include:** Sales; Service. **Listed on:** New York Stock Exchange. **Stock exchange symbol:** HI. **Number of employees nationwide:** 5,000.

HOYA CORPORATION USA
101 Metro Drive, Suite 500, San Jose CA 95110. 408/441-3300. **Contact:** Human Resources. **World Wide Web address:** http://www.hoya.co.jp/english/index.cfm. **Description:** Develops, produces, and markets glass, thin-film, rigid disks for use in hard drives for mobile computing applications. **NOTE:** Entry-level positions are offered. Resumes should be sent to: Human Resources, Hoya Corporation USA, 3400 Edison Way, Fremont CA 94538. **Corporate headquarters location:** This location. **Subsidiaries include:** Continuum; Probe Tech. **Parent company:** Hoya Corporation (Japan). **Listed on:** Privately held. **Number of employees at this location:** 185. **Number of employees worldwide:** Over 3,000.

HUNTER DOUGLAS
1818 South Oak Street, Los Angeles CA 90015. 213/749-6333x3205. **Fax:** 213/742-0981. **Contact:** Human Resources Department. **World Wide World Address:** http://www.hunterdouglas.com. **Description:** A manufacturer of custom-made windows. **Other U.S. locations:** Augusta GA; Chicago IL. **Parent company:** Hunter Douglas Group (The Netherlands). **Operations at this facility include:** Administration; Regional Headquarters; Sales; Service. **Number of employees at this location:** 350. **Number of employees nationwide:** 500.

HUNTER INDUSTRIES
1940 Diamond Street, San Marcos CA 92078. 760/744-5240. **Fax:** 760/744-7461. **Contact:** Human Resources Department. **E-mail address:** hr@hunterindustries.com. **World Wide Web address:** http://www.hunterindustries.com. **Description:** Manufactures irrigation equipment. Positions advertised include: Staff Accountant; Sr. Human Resources Representative; Purchasing Manager. **Corporate headquarters location:** This location. **Other area locations:** Fresno CA. **Other U.S. locations:** Cary NC.

HUSSMANN CORPORATION
48438 Milmont Drive, Fremont CA 94538. 510/354-2040. **Fax:** 510/354-3850. **Contact:** Human Resources. **E-mail address:** fremont@hussmann.com. **World Wide Web address:** http://www.hussmann.com. **Description:** A manufacturer of merchandising and refrigeration systems for the world's food industry. Products include refrigerated display cases, refrigeration systems, beverage coolers, walk-in coolers, and industrial refrigeration equipment. **Corporate headquarters location:** Bridgeton MO. **Other area locations:** Chino CA; Sacramento CA. **International locations:** Canada; Mexico; United Kingdom. **Parent company:** Ingersoll-Rand. **Listed on:** New York Stock Exchange. **Stock exchange symbol:** IR.

HUSSMANN CORPORATION
855 National Drive, Suite 109, Sacramento CA 95834. 916/920-4993. **Fax:** 916/920-2417. **Contact:** Human Resources. **E-mail address:** sacramento@hussmann.com. **World Wide Web address:** http://www.hussmann.com. **Description:** A manufacturer of merchandising and refrigeration systems for the world's food industry. Products include refrigerated display cases, refrigeration systems, beverage coolers, walk-in coolers, and industrial refrigeration equipment. **Corporate headquarters location:** Bridgeton MO. **Other area locations:** Fremont CA; Chino CA; Los Angeles CA; Carlsbad CA. **International locations:** Canada; Mexico; United Kingdom. **Parent company:** Ingersoll-Rand. **Listed on:** New York Stock Exchange. **Stock exchange symbol:** IR.

HUTCHINSON SEAL CORPORATION
NATIONAL O-RING DIVISION
11634 Patton Road, Downey CA 90241-5295. 562/862-8163. **Fax:** 562/862-4596. **Contact:** Personnel. **World Wide Web address:** http://www.hutchinsonrubber.com. **Description:** Engaged in various distribution and manufacturing operations. **Corporate headquarters location:** This location. **Subsidiaries include:** National O-Ring, which manufactures and distributes a full-range of standard-size, low-cost,

synthetic rubber o-ring sealing devices for use in automotive and industrial applications.

HYATT REGENCY LOS ANGELES
711 South Hope Street, Los Angeles CA 90017. 213/683-1234. **Contact:** Human Resources. **World Wide Web address:** http://www.hyatt.com. **Description:** A hotel and restaurant facility with 485 rooms. **NOTE:** Entry-level positions are offered. **Special programs:** Internships. **Corporate headquarters location:** Chicago IL. **Other U.S. locations:** Nationwide. **International locations:** Worldwide. **Listed on:** Privately held. **Number of employees at this location:** 300. **Number of employees nationwide:** 40,000.

HYATT REGENCY MONTEREY HOTEL CONFERENCE CENTER
One Old Golf Course Road, Monterey CA 93940-4908. 831/372-1234. **Contact:** Joe Krings, Director of Human Resources Department. **World Wide Web address:** http://www.hyatt.com. **Description:** One location of the nationwide chain of hotels. **Corporate headquarters location:** Chicago IL. **Parent company:** Hyatt Corporation. **Operations at this facility include:** Administration; Sales; Service. **Number of employees at this location:** 430. **Number of employees nationwide:** 40,000.

HYATT REGENCY SAN FRANCISCO
5 Embarcadero Center, San Francisco CA 94111. 415/788-1234. **Fax:** 415/291-6615. **Contact:** Human Resources. **World Wide Web address:** http://www.hyatt.com. **Description:** One location of the Hyatt chain of hotels, which operates hotel and recreational facilities throughout the world. **Corporate headquarters location:** Chicago IL.

HYATT REGENCY SAN FRANCISCO AIRPORT
1333 Bayshore Highway, Burlingame CA 94010. 650/347-1234. **Fax:** 650/348-2541. **Recorded jobline:** 650/696-2625. **Contact:** Henry Augustus, Human Resources. **World Wide Web address:** http://www.hyatt.com. **Description:** Operates a full-service, four-star hotel complex offering restaurants, banquet rooms, and recreational and convention facilities. **Special programs:** Training. **Office hours:** Monday - Friday, 8:00 a.m. - 5:00 p.m. **Corporate headquarters location:** Chicago IL. **Other U.S. locations:** Nationwide. **Parent company:** Hyatt Corporation. **Listed on:** Privately held. **Number of employees at this location:** 500. **Number of employees nationwide:** 40,000.

HYCOR BIOMEDICAL INC.
7272 Chapman Avenue, Garden Grove CA 92841. 714/895-9558. **Toll-free phone:** 800/382-2527. **Fax:** 714/933-3222. **Contact:** Human Resources Department. **World Wide Web address:** http://www.hycorbiomedical.com. **Description:** Develops, produces, and markets a broad range of diagnostic and medical products. The company's focus is on allergy diagnostics and therapy, microscopic urinalysis, specialized immunodiagnostics, and laboratory controls. **Corporate headquarters location:** This location. **Listed on:** NASDAQ. **Stock exchange symbol:** HYBD.

HYDREL LIGHTING
12881 Bradley Avenue, Sylmar CA 91342. 818/362-9465. **Toll-free phone:** 800/750-9773. **Fax:** 818/362-6548. **Contact:** Human Resources. **Description:** Manufactures commercial outdoor lighting. **Parent company:** Acuity Brands.

HYDRO CONDUIT
4150 North Brawley Avenue, Fresno CA 93722. 559/275-2241. **Contact:** Human Resources. **E-mail address:** hydro@rinker.com. **World Wide Web address:** http://www.csrhydroconduit.com. **Description:** Manufactures and sells a variety of concrete products including water transmission pipe and tubing, concrete pipe, and reinforced concrete pipe. **Other area locations:** Colton CA; Corona CA; Napa CA; Orland CA. **Parent company:** Rinker Materials Corporation.

HYDRO-AIRE, INC.
P.O. Box 7722, Burbank CA 91510. 818/526-2600. **Physical address:** 3000 Winona Avenue, Burbank CA 91504. **Contact:** Human Resources. **E-mail address:** hr@hydroaire.com. **World Wide Web address:** http://www.hydroairc.com. **Description:** Manufactures a variety of components for the commercial and military aircraft markets. Products include microcircuits, servovalves, fuel pumps, and braking control systems. **Positions advertised include:** Senior Design Engineer; Senior Mechanical Project Engineer. **Corporate headquarters location:** This location. **Parent company:** Crane Company. **Listed on:** New York Stock Exchange. **Stock exchange symbol:** CR. **Number of employees at this location:** 500.

I-FLOW CORPORATION
20202 Windrow Drive, Lake Forest CA 92630. 949/206-2700. **Toll-free phone:** 800/448-3569. **Fax:** 949/206-2664. **Contact:** Human Resources. **E-mail address:** hr@iflo.com. **World Wide Web address:** http://www.i-flowcorp.com. **Description:** Manufactures drug delivery systems. The company is also engaged in epidural, chronic, and wound site pain management. **Corporate headquarters location:** This location. **Listed on:** NASDAQ. **Stock exchange symbol:** IFLO.

IBM CORPORATION
5600 Cottle Road, San Jose CA 95193. 408/256-1600. **Toll-free phone:** 800/IBM4YOU. **Fax:** 408/256-8888. **Contact:** Personnel Department. **World Wide Web address:** http://www.ibm.com. **Description:** IBM is a developer, manufacturer, and marketer of advanced information processing products including computers and microelectronic technology, software, networking systems and information technology-related services. **Positions at this facility include:** Advisory Software Engineer; Software Engineer; Circuit Design Engineer; Instrumentation Engineer. **Corporate headquarters location:** White Plains NY. **Subsidiaries include:** IBM Credit Corporation; IBM Instruments, Inc.; IBM World Trade Corporation. **Operations at this facility include:** This location is engaged in the development of data access and storage devices. **Listed on:** New York Stock Exchange. **Stock exchange symbol:** IBM.

II-VI WEST
36570 Briggs Road, Murrieta CA 92563. 909/926-1866. **Fax:** 909/926-1984. **Contact:** Human Resources Manager. **E-mail address:** infowest@ii-vi.com. **World Wide Web address:** http://www.ii-vi.com. **Description:** A manufacturer of optics for high-power lasers. **Corporate headquarters location:** Saxonburg PA. **Operations at this facility include:** Administration; Manufacturing; Research and Development; Sales; Service. **Number of employees at this location:** 100.

DAILY SILVER IMP TECHNOLOGY, INC.
166 Baypointe Parkway, San Jose CA 95134. 408/433-3500. **Fax:** 408/434-5904. **Contact:** Human Resources. **E-mail address:** hr@impinc.com. **World Wide Web address:** http://www.impweb.com. **Description:** Develops and manufactures application-specific standard integrated circuits for mass storage and power management applications. **NOTE:** Send resume to IMP, Inc. 2830 North First Street, San Jose, CA 95134. **Positions advertised include:** Senior Staff Design Engineer; Senior Test Engineer; Test Engineer; Probe Card Technicians. **Parent company:** Daily Silver Holdings Limited (Hong Kong).

ISE LABS, INC.
46800 Bayside Parkway, Fremont CA 94538. 510/687-2500. **Fax:** 510/687-2573. **Contact:** Human Resources. **E-mail address:** careers@iselabs.com. **World Wide Web address:** http://www.iselabs.com. **Description:** Provides electrical and environmental testing services for integrated circuits. Founded in 1983. **Positions advertised include:** Failure Analysis Engineer. **Corporate headquarters location:** This location. **Other U.S. locations:** Manteca CA; Santa Clara CA. **International locations:** Hong Kong; Singapore. **Listed on:** Privately held. **Parent company:** ASE Test Ltd. **Listed on:** NASDAQ. **Stock exchange symbol:** ASTSF. **Annual sales/revenues:** $51 - $100 million. **Number of employees at this location:** 140. **Number of employees nationwide:** 415. **Number of employees worldwide:** 550.

ITT CANNON
666 East Dyer Road, Santa Ana CA 92705. 714/557-4700. **Contact:** Human Resources. **E-mail address:** cannonhr@itt.com. **World Wide Web address:** http://www.ittcannon.com. **Description:** Engaged in the development and manufacture of electrical interconnecting devices. Products are used in commercial, military/aerospace, and micro applications. The company's production functions are die casting, stamping, molding, plating, and machining. ITT Cannon is an operating unit of ITT Defense & Electronics, Inc. **Positions advertised include:** WW Switches and Sales Controller. **Corporate headquarters location:** White Plains NY. **Parent company:** ITT Corporation is a diversified, global enterprise engaged in three major business areas: Financial and Business Services, which includes ITT Hartford, ITT Financial Corporation, and ITT Communications and Information Services, Inc.; Manufactured Products, which includes ITT Automotive, ITT Defense & Electronics, Inc., and ITT Fluid Technology Corporation; and Sheraton Hotels (ITT Sheraton Corporation). **Operations at this facility include:** Divisional Headquarters; Manufacturing. **Listed on:** New York Stock Exchange. **Stock exchange symbol:** ITT.

ITT INDUSTRIES GILFILLAN DIVISION
7821 Orion Avenue, P.O. Box 7713, Van Nuys CA 91409-7713. 818/988-2600. **Contact:** Manager of Employment. **E-mail address:** hr.gilfillan@itt.com. **World Wide Web address:** http://www.gilfillan.itt.com. **Description:** Develops, manufactures, and services air traffic control (GCA/Landing) and air/coastal defense radar systems, and command/control systems for a wide variety of military and civil applications. **Positions advertised include:** Field Service Engineer; Technical Staff Member. **Corporate headquarters location:** New York NY. **Parent company:** ITT Corporation is a diversified, global enterprise engaged in three major business areas: Financial and Business Services, which includes ITT Hartford, ITT Financial Corporation, and ITT Communications and Information Services, Inc.; Manufactured Products, which includes ITT Automotive, ITT Defense & Electronics, Inc., and ITT Fluid Technology Corporation; and Sheraton Hotels (ITT Sheraton Corporation). **Listed on:** New York Stock Exchange. **Stock exchange symbol:** ITT.

ITT JABSCO
20 Icon, Foothill Ranch CA 92610. 949/609-5106. **Contact:** Human Resources. **World Wide Web address:** http://www.jabsco.com. **Description:** Manufactures pumps for marine craft, RVs, and industrial usage. ITT Jabsco is an operating unit of ITT Fluid Technology Corporation. **Corporate headquarters location:** This location. **Parent company:** ITT Corporation is a diversified, global enterprise engaged in three major business areas: Financial and Business Services, which includes ITT Hartford, ITT Financial Corporation, and ITT Communications and Information Services, Inc.; Manufactured Products, which includes ITT Automotive, ITT Defense & Electronics, Inc., and ITT Fluid Technology Corporation; and Sheraton Hotels (ITT Sheraton Corporation). **Listed on:** New York Stock Exchange. **Stock exchange symbol:** ITT.

IAMBIC SOFTWARE
1270 Oakmead Parkway, Suite 214, Sunnyvale CA 94085. 408/882-0390. **Contact:** Human Resources. **E-mail address:** jobs@iambic.com. **World Wide Web address:** http://www.iambic.com. **Description:** Develops and manufactures software applications for the handheld computing market. **Positions advertised include:** Software Engineer; Technical Support Engineer. **Corporate headquarters location:** This location.

IHOP CORPORATION
450 North Brand Boulevard, 7th Floor, Glendale CA 91203. 818/240-6055. **Contact:** Human Resources. **E-mail address:** jobs@ihopcorp.com. **World Wide Web address:** http://www.ihop.com. **Description:** Operates the International House of Pancakes restaurant chain. **Corporate headquarters location:** This location. **Listed on:** New York Stock Exchange. **Stock exchange symbol:** IHP.

IMAGE ENTERTAINMENT, INC.
20525 Nordhoff Street, Suite 200, Chatsworth CA 91311. 818/407-9100. **Contact:** Human Resources. **World Wide Web address:** http://www.image-entertainment.com. **Description:** One of the largest laser disc licensees and distributors in North America. The company distributes thousands of titles ranging from feature films and music videos to family, documentary, and special interest programming to over 2,500 retail outlets. The company releases exclusive titles from licensers such as Disney's Buena Vista Home Video, New Line Home Video, Orion Home Video, Playboy Home Video, and Turner Home Entertainment. **Corporate headquarters location:** This location. **Listed on:** NASDAQ. **Stock exchange symbol:** DISK.

IMAGE MICROSYSTEMS, INC.
6301 Chalet Drive, Commerce CA 90040. 562/776-3333. **Fax:** 562/776-3322. **Contact:** Human Resources. **World Wide Web address:** http://www.imagemicro.com. **Description:** A reseller of computer hardware and software. **Corporate headquarters location:** This location. **Other U.S. locations:** Austin TX; Nashville TN.

IMATION CORPORATION
300 South Lewis Road, Camarillo CA 93012-8485. 805/482-1911. **Contact:** Human Resources. **World Wide Web address:** http://www.imation.com. **Description:** Develops data storage products, medical imaging and photo products, printing and publishing systems, and customer support technologies and document imaging, and markets them under the trademark names Dry View laser imagers, Matchprint and Rainbow color proofing systems, Travan data cartridges, and LS-120 diskette technology. **Corporate headquarters location:** Oakdale MN. **Listed on:** New York Stock Exchange. **Stock exchange symbol:** IMN.

IMMUNE RESPONSE CORPORATION
5931 Darwin Court, Carlsbad CA 92008. 760/431-7080. **Fax:** 760/431-8636. **Contact:** Human Resources. **World Wide Web address:** http://www.imnr.com. **Description:**

Develops treatments in three distinct proprietary technologies, which are treatment for HIV-infected patients, autoimmune disease treatment, and gene therapy treatment. **Subsidiaries include:** TargeTech, Inc. **Corporate headquarters location:** This location. **Other U.S. locations:** King of Prussia, PA. **Listed on:** NASDAQ. **Stock exchange symbol:** IMNR.

IMPAC COMPANIES
1401 Dove Street, Suite 100, Newport Beach CA 92660. 714/556-0122. **Toll-free phone:** 800/597-4101. **Fax:** 949/475-3969. **Contact:** Sheralee Urano, Vice President, Human Resources. **World Wide Web address:** http://www.impaccompanies.com. **Description:** Provides mortgage banking services. **Corporate headquarters location:** This location. **Listed on:** American Stock Exchange. **Stock exchange symbol:** IMH.

INAWORD
1601 Cloverfield Boulevard, 2nd Floor, South Tower, Santa Monica CA 90404. 310/460-3200. **Toll-free phone:** 800/805-9673. **Fax:** 800/805-7994. **Contact:** Stella Fridman Hayes, Director of Language Services. **E-mail address:** stellaf@inaword.net. **World Wide Web address:** http://www.inaword.net. **Description:** Offers language translation services on documents including patents, legal documents, product labels, manuals and user guides, advertising copy, and Web material. The company also provides interpreters for meetings and training seminars and electronic publishing services. **Corporate headquarters location:** This location.

INAMED CORPORATION
5540 Ekwill Street, Suite D, Santa Barbara CA 93111. 805/683-6761. **Fax:** 805/692-5432. **Contact:** Human Resources. **World Wide Web address:** http://www.inamed.com. **Description:** INAMED Corporation is a medical products company with 23 subsidiaries across the United States and Europe. The company develops, manufactures, and markets implantable products including mammary prostheses, tissue expanders, and facial implants; develops, produces, and distributes premium products for dermatology, wound care, and burn treatment; and packages and sterilizes medical grade components for other medical device companies. **Positions advertised include:** Customer Care Supervisor; Senior Regional Alliance Manager; Field Marketing Manager. **Corporate headquarters location:** This location. **Listed on:** NASDAQ. **Stock exchange symbol:** IMDC.

INDEX INDUSTRIES, INC.
5362 Productiion Drive, Huntington Beach CA 92649. 800/282-8047. **Contact:** Personnel Director. **E-mail address:** jobs-lodi@interlake.com. **World Wide Web address:** http://www.interlake.com. **Description:** Manufactures and distributes materials handling equipment and other industrial and agricultural products. **Corporate headquarters location:** Naperville IL. **Parent company:** Interlake Material Handling, Inc.

INDUSTRIAL LIGHT + MAGIC
P.O. Box 2459, San Rafael CA 94912. 415/258-2200. **Recorded jobline:** 415/448-2100. **Fax:** 415/448-2850. **Contact:** Recruiting. **E-mail address:** hrdept@lucasdigital.com. **World Wide Web address:** http://www.ilm.com. **Description:** A digital effects company engaged in motion picture film production. The company is comprised of Industrial Light & Magic (ILM), a visual effects company; and Skywalker Sound, a state-of-the-art audio facility. **NOTE:** Resumes may be submitted online, or by mail or fax. **Positions advertised include:** CG Technical Assistant; Digital Matte Artist; Digital Resource Assistant; Database Administrator. **Corporate headquarters location:** This location.

INFINEON TECHNOLOGIES CORPORATION
1730 North First Street, San Jose CA 95112. 408/501-6337. **Fax:** 408/501-2430. **Contact:** Kathy Larson, Human Resources. **E-mail address:** kathy.larson@infineon.com. **World Wide Web address:** http://www.infineon.com. **Description:** Infineon Technologies Corporation is one of the world's largest semiconductor manufacturers. The company operates in five major business units. Automotive & Industrial develops and manufactures power semiconductors, optoelectronic components, microcontrollers, sensors, and discrete semiconductors for automotive and industrial applications. Communications & Peripherals develops and manufactures semiconductors, systems, and components for use in wire communications applications including cable television, LANs, and WANs. Wireless Products designs and manufactures semiconductors and complete wireless systems for such applications as cellular and cordless telephone networks and devices. Memory Products designs and manufactures memory components for computers and electronics. Security & Chip Card ICs develops and manufactures semiconductors and security components for use in applications requiring security, such as credit card systems, pay-per-view television, and traffic control. **NOTE:** Search for positions online. **Corporate headquarters location:** Munich, Germany. **Operations at this facility include:** This location is a research and development center. **Listed on:** New York Stock Exchange. **Stock exchange symbol:** IFX.

INFONET SERVICES CORPORATION
2160 East Grand Avenue, El Segundo CA 90245-5024. 310/335-2600. **Fax:** 310/335-2679. **Contact:** Ken Montgomery, Human Resources Department. **E-mail address:** ken_montgomery@infonet.com. **World Wide Web address:** http://www.infonet.com. **Description:** Provides networking services to international corporations. Founded in 1970. **Positions advertised include:** Marketing Communications Specialist; Financial Analyst; Customer Care Support Analyst; Senior Billing Specialist. **Corporate headquarters location:** This location. **Listed on:** New York Stock Exchange. **Stock exchange symbol:** IN.

INFORMATION BUILDERS INC.
1731 Technology Drive, Suite 750, San Jose CA 95110. 408/453-7600. **Contact:** Human Resources. **E-mail address:** employment_opportunities@ibi.com. **World Wide Web address:** http://www.ibi.com. **Description:** A software development firm. Products include WebFOCUS, FOCUS Solutions, EDA Middleware, and SmartMart Data Warehouse. Other services include software support and sales. **Positions advertised include:** Regional Technical Operations Manager. **Corporate headquarters location:** New York NY. **Other U.S. locations:** Nationwide. **Number of employees nationwide:** 1,800.

INFORMATION SYSTEMS SUPPORT
438 Camino Del Rio South, Suite 203, San Diego CA 92108. 619/295-1190. **Fax:** 619/295-2991. **Contact:** Human Resources. **World Wide Web address:** http://www.iss-md.com. **Description:** Provides computer consulting services including information technology and facility management support. **NOTE:** Search for positions online. **Corporate headquarters location:** Gaithersburg MD.

INFORMIX SOFTWARE, INC.
4100 Bohannon Drive, Menlo Park CA 94025. 650/926-6300. **Contact:** Human Resources. **World Wide Web address:** http://www.informix.com. **Description:** Provides database technology to build, deploy, run, and evolve applications. Informix products include distributed database management systems, application development tools, and graphical- and character-based productivity software. **Corporate headquarters location:** This location. **Other U.S. locations:** Englewood CO; Downers Grove IL; Lenexa KS; Portland OR. **International locations:** England; Singapore. **Parent company:** IBM. **Operations at this facility include:** Administration; Research and Development; Sales. **Listed on:** New York Stock Exchange. **Stock exchange symbol:** IBM. **Number of employees at this location:** 800. **Number of employees nationwide:** 1,300.

INGERSOLL-RAND EQUIPMENT SALES
1944 Marina Boulevard, San Leandro CA 94577. 510/357-9131. **Contact:** Human Resources. **World Wide Web address:** http://www.ingersoll-rand.com. **Description:** Manufactures compressors, pumps, and other nonelectrical industrial equipment and machinery. Products include air compression systems, antifriction systems, construction equipment, air tools, bearings, locks, tools, and pumps. The company operates more than 90 production facilities worldwide. **Corporate headquarters location:** Woodcliff Lake NJ. **International locations:** Worldwide. **Listed on:** New York Stock Exchange. **Stock exchange symbol:** IR.

INGRAM MICRO
1600 East Saint Andrew Place, P.O.Box 25125, Santa Ana CA 92799-5125. 714/566-1000. **Contact:** Human Resources Department. **World Wide Web address:** http://www.ingrammicro.com. **Description:** Distributes microcomputer products including desktop and notebook PCs, servers, CD-Rom drives, printers, and software. **NOTE:** Search and apply for positions onlne. **Positions advertised include:** Supply Chain Coordinator; Marketing Manager; Sr. Copywriter; Financial Analyst; Sr. Contract Negotiator; Business Process Improvement Manager. **Corporate headquarters location:** This location. **Listed on:** New York Stock Exchange. **Stock exchange symbol:** IM. **Number of employees worldwide:** 11,300.

INITIATIVE LOS ANGELES
5700 Wilshire Boulevard, Suite 400, Los Angeles CA 90036. 323/370-8000. **Fax:** 323/370-8974. **Contact:** Cynthia Carranza, Human Resources. **E-mail address:** jobs@us.initiative.com. **World Wide Web address:** http://www.wimc.com. **Description:** An advertising agency. **Corporate headquarters location:** This location.

INSIGHT HEALTH SERVICES CORPORATION
26250 Enterprise Court, Suite 100, Lake Forest CA 92630. 949/282-6000. **Fax:** 949/452-0203. **Contact:** Human Resources. **E-mail address:** employment@insighthealth.com. **World Wide Web address:** http://www.insighthealthcorp.com. **Description:** Engaged in the establishment and operation of outpatient diagnostic and treatment centers utilizing magnetic resonance imaging systems (MRI), computerized tomography systems (CT), multimodality radiologic imaging systems, cardiovascular diagnostic imaging systems, medical linear accelerators, and Leksell Stereotactic Gamma Units (Gamma Knife). **Positions advertised include:** Accounts Payable Representative; Collector; Director, Government Claims; Enterprise Operations Manager. **Office hours:** Monday - Friday, 8:00 a.m. - 5:00 p.m. **Corporate headquarters location:** This location. **Other U.S. locations:** Nationwide. **Listed on:** NASDAQ. **Stock exchange symbol:** IHSC. **Number of employees at this location:** 60. **Number of employees nationwide:** 800.

INSITE VISION INCORPORATED
965 Atlantic Avenue, Alameda CA 94501. 510/865-8800. **Fax:** 510/747-1374. **Contact:** Human Resources. **E-mail address:** careers@insite.com. **World Wide Web address:** http://www.insitevision.com. **Description:** Manufactures ophthalmic pharmaceuticals. InSite Vision is responsible for the development of the DuraSite eyedrop-based drug delivery system, which provides a steady drug flow to the eye over an elapsed period of time. **NOTE:** Submit resume online or to fax number above; do not submit resumes via email. **Corporate headquarters location:** This location. **Listed on:** American Stock Exchange. **Stock exchange symbol:** ISV.

INSPECTORATE AMERICA CORPORATION
3773 Pacheco Boulevard, Suite D, Martinez CA 94553-2130. 925/372-0958. **Contact:** Human Resources. **E-mail address:** personnel.initiatives@bsi-global.com. **World Wide Web address:** http://www.inspectorate.com. **Description:** An oil and gas field services company providing petroleum, petrochemical, and chemical inspections as well as tank calibration and meter proving. **Corporate headquarters location:** United Kingdom. **Parent company:** BSI Inspectorate.

INSURANCE COMPANY OF THE WEST
P.O. Box 85563, San Diego CA 92186-5563. 858/350-2400. **Physical address:** 11455 El Camino Real, San Diego CA 92130. **Fax:** 858/350-2697. **Contact:** Human Resources Representative. **E-mail address:** careers@icwgroup.com. **World Wide Web address:** http://www.icwgroup.com. **Description:** A commercial insurance carrier offering multirate property/casualty, workers' compensation, specialty auto, and surety lines of coverage. Founded in 1972. **Positions advertised include:** Surety Claims and Loss Control Consultant; Legal Secretary; Business Analyst; Surety Underwriter. **Corporate headquarters location:** This location. **Other U.S. locations:** AZ; CO; NV; NM; OR; TX; WA. **Operations at this facility include:** Service. **Number of employees at this location:** 230.

INTEGRATED COMMUNITY SERVICES
3020 Kerner Boulevard, Suite A, San Rafael CA 94901. 415/455-8481. **Fax:** 415/455-8483. **Contact:** Donna Lemmon, Executive Director. **E-mail address:** donna@connectics.org. **World Wide Web address:** http://www.connectics.org. **Description:** Provides job placement services and independent living skills training for individuals with disabilities. **Positions advertised include:** Job Coach; Independent Living Skills Trainer.

INTEGRATED SILICON SOLUTION, INC. (ISSI)
2231 Lawson Lane, Santa Clara CA 95054. 408/588-0800. **Fax:** 408/969-4703. **Contact:** Employment Department. **E-mail address:** jobs@issi.com. **World Wide Web address:** http://www.issi.com. **Description:** Designs, develops, and markets high-performance SRAM and nonvolatile memory integrated circuits used in personal computers, data communications, telecommunications, instrumentation, and consumer products. **Corporate headquarters location:** This location. **International locations:** Taiwan. **Listed on:** NASDAQ. **Stock exchange symbol:** ISSI. **Number of employees nationwide:** 220.

INTEL CORPORATION
2200 Mission College Boulevard, P.O. Box 58119, Santa Clara CA 95052-8119. 408/765-8080. **Contact:** Staffing Department. **World Wide Web address:** http://www.intel.com. **Description:** One of the largest semiconductor manufacturers in the world. Other products include supercomputers; embedded control chips and flash memories; motherboards; multimedia hardware; personal computer enhancement products; and the design and marketing of microcomputer components, modules, and systems. Intel sells its products to original equipment manufacturers and other

companies that incorporate them into their products. **Positions advertised include:** Audit Specialist; CAD Engineer; Senior Press Relations Specialist; Hardware Test Engineer; Manufacturing Engineer; Product Engineer; Patent Attorney; Device Engineer; Principal Research Scientist; Software Engineer. **Corporate headquarters location:** This location. **Subsidiaries include:** Shiva produces a line of direct-dial products and remote access servers. **Listed on:** NASDAQ. **Stock exchange symbol:** INTC.

INTEL CORPORATION
1900 Prairie City Road, Folsom CA 95630. 916/356-8080. **Contact:** Human Resources. **World Wide Web address:** http://www.intel.com. **Description:** Intel Corporation is one of the largest semiconductor manufacturers in the world. Other products include supercomputers; embedded control chips and flash memories; motherboards; multimedia hardware; personal computer enhancement products; and design and marketing of microcomputer components, modules, and systems. Intel sells its products to original equipment manufacturers and other companies that incorporate them into their products. **Positions advertised include:** Audit Specialist; CAD Engineer; Circuit Design Engineer; Communications Systems Engineer; Component Design Engineer; Senior Applications Architect; Senior Licensing Attorney; Senior Product Engineer. **Corporate headquarters location:** Santa Clara CA. **Operations at this facility include:** This location develops semiconductors that provide silicon connectivity, LAN switching, and WAN access solutions for telecommunications and network applications. **Listed on:** NASDAQ. **Stock exchange symbol:** INTC.

INTELLICORP
2900 lakeside Drive, Suite 221, Santa Clara CA 94054. 408/454-3500. **Fax:** 408/454-3529. **Contact:** Human Resources Department. **E-mail address:** jobs@intellicorp.com. **World Wide Web address:** http://www.intellicorp.com. **Description:** Designs, develops, and markets software development tools and provides related training, customer support, and consulting services. IntelliCorp provides its customers with object-oriented software tools for the design, development, and delivery of scalable client/server applications. **NOTE:** Resumes must be emailed; resumes submitted by postal mail or fax will not be accepted. **Positions advertised include:** Regional Sales Manager; Senior Marketing Executive; IPC Technical Consultant. **Corporate headquarters location:** This location. **Other U.S. locations:** Nationwide. **International locations:** Europe.

INTERLINK ELECTRONICS
546 Flynn Road, Camarillo CA 93012. 805/484-8855. **Fax:** 805/484-5560. **Contact:** Patrice Poleto, Human Resources. **E-mail address:** ppoleto@interlinkelectronics.com. **World Wide Web address:** http://www.interlinkelectronics.com. **Description:** Interlink's force-sensing technology transforms physical pressure applied to a sensor into a corresponding electronic response. Products incorporating a sensor using the company's force-sensing resistor (FSR) devices can react to pressure when applied by any means such as through human touch, a mechanical device, a fluid, or a gas. With supporting electronics, an FSR sensor can start, stop, intensify, select, direct, detect, or measure a desired response. **NOTE:** Resumes may be submitted via e-mail or fax. See individual postings for appropriate fax number. **Positions advertised include:** Quality Engineer. **Corporate headquarters location:** This location. **Listed on:** NASDAQ. **Stock exchange symbol:** LINK.

INTERNATIONAL CREATIVE MANAGEMENT, INC. (ICM)
8942 Wilshire Boulevard, Beverly Hills CA 90211-1934. 310/550-4000. **Fax:** 310/550-4440. **Contact:** Human Resources. **World Wide Web address:** http://www.icmtalent.com. **Description:** A talent agency managing film, music, publishing, television, theater, and public affairs clients. The agency also protects intellectual property rights. **Other U.S. locations:** New York NY. **International locations:** London; Paris; Rome. **CEO:** Jeff Berg. **Number of employees worldwide:** 500.

INTERNATIONAL MICROCOMPUTER SOFTWARE, INC. (IMSI)
100 Rowland Way, 3rd Floor, Novato CA 94945. 415/878-4000. **Fax:** 415/897-0043. **Contact:** Jackie Wandrey, Human Resources. **World Wide Web address:** http://www.imsisoft.com. **Description:** A leading developer of productivity software for business and home use. The company's Home Living Media division focuses on CD-ROM multimedia software for learning and education. IMSI's three primary product lines are business, consumer productivity, and multimedia learning software. **NOTE:** Submit resume online. **Corporate headquarters location:** This location.

INTERNATIONAL RECTIFIER
233 Kansas Street, El Segundo CA 90245. 310/726-8000. **Contact:** Human Resources. **World Wide Web address:** http://www.irf.com. **Description:** Designs and manufactures hybrid, DC-DC converters, and VHF and HF communication systems used in space and military products. **Positions advertised include:** Customer Service Representative; Automotive Sector Marketing Director; Engineering Technician; Manufacturing Technician; Layout Designer; Process Engineer; Product Engineering Manager; Financial Analyst. **Corporate headquarters location:** This location. **Other area locations:** Santa Clara CA; Temecula CA; Irvine CA. **Other U.S. locations:** North Kingstown RI; Leominster MA; Raleigh NC. **International locations:** Worldwide. **Listed on:** New York Stock Exchange. **Stock exchange symbol:** IRF. **Number of employees worldwide:** 5,800.

INTERNATIONAL REMOTE IMAGING SYSTEMS, INC. (IRIS)
9172 Eton Avenue, Chatsworth CA 91311. 818/709-1244. **Fax:** 818/700-9661. **Contact:** Human Resources. **E-mail address:** hr@proiris.com. **World Wide Web address:** http://www.proiris.com. **Description:** Manufactures and markets The Yellow IRIS, an automated urinalysis workstation. The workstation uses its patented slideless Automated Intelligent Microscopy (AIM) technology and other technology to automate the manipulative steps in routine urinalyses performed by hospital and reference clinical laboratories, including counting and classifying microscopic particles found in urine specimens. Other laboratory products manufactured by IRIS are used for blood collection, blood coagulation, and genetic analysis. **Corporate headquarters location:** This location. **Listed on:** American Stock Exchange. **Stock exchange symbol:** IRI. **Number of employees nationwide:** 65.

INTERSTATE ELECTRONICS CORPORATION
602 East Vermont Avenue, P.O. Box 3117, Anaheim CA 92803-3117. 714/758-0500. **Toll-free phone:** 800/854-6979. **Fax:** 714/758-3009. **Contact:** Personnel. **E-mail address:** iecresumes@L-3com.com. **World Wide Web address:** http://www.iechome.com. **Description:** Manufactures and markets advanced electronic systems for both military and industrial markets. **Positions advertised include:** Engineering Section Manager; Software Developer; Program Manager; Staff Engineer; Principal Engineer; Senior Chief Scientist; Quality Engineer. **Corporate headquarters location:** This location.

INTUIT, INC.
6220 Greenwich Drive, San Diego CA 92122. 858/525-8000. **Contact:** Human Resources. **World Wide Web address:** http://www.intuit.com. **Description:** Develops and markets personal finance and small business accounting software and also offers support services. Products include Quicken, which allows users to organize and manage personal finances. **Positions advertised include:** Administrative Assistant; Senior Software Engineer; Senior SCM Engineer; Accounts Receivable Specialist; Product Manager; System Engineer; Marketing Analyst; Web Editor/Writer; Image Designer. **Corporate headquarters location:** Mountain View CA. **Listed on:** NASDAQ. **Stock exchange symbol:** INTU. **Number of employees worldwide:** 6,700.

INTUIT, INC.
2632 Marine Way, Mountain View CA 94043. 650/944-6000. **Contact:** Human Resources. **World Wide Web address:** http://www.intuit.com. **Description:** Develops and markets personal finance and small business accounting software and also offers support services. Products include Quicken, which allows users to organize and manage personal finances. **Positions advertised include:** Senior Administrative Assistant; Engineering Manager; Senior PeopleSoft Application Developer; Marketing Operations Manager. **Corporate headquarters location:** This location. **Other U.S. locations:** AZ; MA; MI; NV; NY; TX; UT; VA. **International locations:** Canada; Japan; United Kingdom. **Listed on:** NASDAQ. **Stock exchange symbol:** INTU. **Number of employees worldwide:** 6,700.

INVENSYS CLIMATE CONTROLS
100 West Victoria Street, Long Beach CA 90805. 310/638-6111. **Contact:** Personnel. **World Wide Web address:** http://www.invensys.com. **Description:** A manufacturer of control instrumentation. Products include automatic controls used in homes, commercial buildings, and industrial applications to conserve energy and to enable machinery to work efficiently and automatically; level controls such as RF/microprocessor-based level controls and precision level controls; vibration detectors including monitor and control; recorders and controllers; accessories; diaphragm-actuated control valves; self-actuated temperature regulators; and control systems including system components. The company also produces Sylphon-formed bellows and assemblies, automobile thermostats, caps, water outlet housings, and heater control valves. **Corporate headquarters location:** This location.

INVIVO CORPORATION
42025 Osgood Avenue, Fremont CA 94539. 510/226-9600. **Contact:** Human Resources. **World Wide Web address:** http://www.invivocorp.com. **Description:** Manufactures sensor-based instrumentation such as pressure transducers and calibration sensors. **Corporate headquarters location:** Pleasanton CA. **Listed on:** NASDAQ. **Stock exchange symbol:** SAFE.

IRWIN NATURALS FOR HEALTH
NATURE'S SECRET
5310 Beethoven Street, Los Angeles CA 90066. 310/253-5305. **Toll-free phone:** 866/54IRWIN. **Contact:** Human Resources. **World Wide Web address:** http://www.irwinnaturals.com. **Description:** Develops herbal remedies and nutritional products. Nature's Secret is the brand name of the company's line of vitamins. **NOTE:** To contact Human Resources call: 310/306-3636 ext. 3804. **Parent company:** OMNI Neutraceuticals. **Annual sales/revenues:** $21 - $50 million.

ISIS PHARMACEUTICALS, INC.
2292 Faraday Avenue, Carlsbad CA 92008. 760/931-9200. **Fax:** 760/603-4650. **Recorded jobline:** 760/603-3858. **Contact:** Human Resources. **E-mail address:** resume@isisph.com. **World Wide Web address:** http://www.isispharm.com. **Description:** Develops antisense technology drugs and combinatorial drugs to combat cancer and infectious or inflammatory diseases. **Corporate headquarters location:** This location. **Listed on:** NASDAQ. **Stock exchange symbol:** ISIP.

ITEX CORPORATION
3400 Cottage Way, Sacramento CA 95825. 916/679-1111. **Contact:** Human Resources. **World Wide Web address:** http://www.itex.com. **Description:** ITEX Corporation operates one of the nation's largest barter exchanges with over 130 offices nationwide. ITEX operates an internationally accessible electronic trading and communications system known as BarterWire, which allows ITEX members coast-to-coast to market and purchase goods and services. The company publishes *alt.finance*, which focuses on the barter industry. All goods and services advertised within its pages are sold for ITEX trade dollars. The company also has the ITEX Express Card, the first debit/credit card in the barter industry. **Corporate headquarters location:** Bellevue WA.

ITOCHU INTERNATIONAL INC.
180 Montgomery Street, Suite 2360, San Francisco CA 94104. 415/399-3700. **Contact:** General Manager. **E-mail address:** recruiting@itochu.com. **World Wide Web address:** http://www.itochu.com. **Description:** An international, multibusiness trading and investment company. Itochu International specializes in developing and sponsoring profitable opportunities in international and domestic commerce, industry, and finance, both as a principal and as an agent. **Corporate headquarters location:** New York NY. **Parent company:** Itochu Corporation.

IWERKS ENTERTAINMENT, INC.
4520 West Valerio Street, Burbank CA 91505. 818/841-7766. **Fax:** 818/840-188. **Contact:** Human Resources. **World Wide Web address:** http://www.iwerks.com. **Description:** Designs, manufactures, installs, and services high-resolution, proprietary motion picture theater attractions in museums, visitor centers, casinos, and newly emerging entertainment venues. The company's attractions are built around a variety of theater systems including fixed and portable simulators, giant screen, 360-degree, and virtual reality theater systems. Business segments include Iwerks Attractions and Technologies, Iwerks Studios, Iwerks Cinetropolis, Iwerks Touring Technologies, and Omni Films International. **NOTE:** Entry-level positions are offered. **Special programs:** Internships. **Corporate headquarters location:** This location.

JBL PROFESSIONAL
8500 Balboa Boulevard, Northridge CA 91329. 818/894-8850. **Fax:** 818/830-7878. **Contact:** Darlene Murray, Human Resources. **E-mail address:** dmurray@harman.com. **World Wide Web address:** http://www.harman.com. **Description:** Designs, manufactures, and distributes audio loudspeaker systems for professional, automotive, and home entertainment use, both domestically and internationally. **Positions advertised include:** Human Resources Assistant. **Corporate headquarters location:** This location. **Parent company:** Harman International Industries Inc. **Number of employees at this location:** 2,500.

JDS UNIPHASE CORPORATION
1768 Automation Parkway, San Jose CA 95131. 408/546-5000. **Fax:** 408/546-4300. **Contact:** Human Resources. **World Wide Web address:** http://www.jdsu.com.

Description: Develops, manufactures, and distributes fiber-optic products including cable assemblies, fusion splicers, couplers, and lasers. Products are primarily sold to companies in the cable television and telecommunications fields. **NOTE:** Search and apply for positions online. **Positions advertised include:** Human Resources Manager; Business Systems Analyst; Market Research Analyst; Financial Analyst; Global Procurement Engineer; Development and Research Engineer. **Corporate headquarters location:** This location. **Listed on:** NASDAQ. **Stock exchange symbol:** JDSU.

JDS UNIPHASE CORPORATION
2789 Northpoint Parkway, Santa Rosa CA 95407-7397. 707/545-6440. **Contact:** Human Resources. **E-mail address:** resumes@ocli.com. **World Wide Web address:** http://www.ocli.com. **Description:** Manufactures thin film-coated components that are used in the manufacture of photographic products, office equipment, and computers. **NOTE:** Search and apply for positions online. **Positions advertised include:** Product Line Manager; Mechanical Engineer; Manufacturing Optical Engineer; Manufacturing Electrical Engineer; Engineering Technician; Senior Financial Analyst. **Corporate headquarters location:** San Jose CA. **Listed on:** NASDAQ. **Stock exchange symbol:** JDSU. **Number of employees at this location:** 900.

JDS UNIPHASE CORPORATION
1768 Automation Parkway, San Jose CA 95131. 408/546-5000. **Fax:** 408/546-4300. **Contact:** Human Resources. **World Wide Web address:** http://www.jdsu.com. **Description:** Develops, manufactures, and distributes fiber-optic products including cable assemblies, fusion splicers, couplers, and lasers. **NOTE:** Search and apply for positions online. **Positions advertised include:** Chip Development Manager; Optical Development & Research Engineer; Commodity Manager; Manufacturing Engineer; Global Quality Manager. **Corporate headquarters location:** This location. **Listed on:** NASDAQ. **Stock exchange symbol:** JDSU. **Annual sales/revenues:** $675 million.

JMAR TECHNOLOGIES, INC.
5800 Armada Drive, Carlsbad CA 92008. 760/602-3292. **Contact:** Human Resources. **World Wide Web address:** http://www.jmar.com. **Description:** Develops, manufactures, and sells cost-effective, high-reliability precision manufacturing and measurement systems to improve productivity in the microelectronics and biomedical industries. A substantial portion of the company's products incorporate advanced laser systems for performing a wide variety of welding, measurement, cutting, or drilling operations during the manufacture of precision electronics and/or medical products. **Positions advertised include:** Marketing Communications Specialist. **Corporate headquarters location:** This location. **Other area locations:** San Diego CA; McClellan CA. **Listed on:** NASDAQ. **Stock exchange symbol:** JMAR.

JS FOODS
4250 Executive Square, Suite 500, La Jolla CA 92037. 858/642-0071. **Contact:** Human Resources. **Description:** Manages Burger King, Tony Roma's, and Pacific Bagels franchises. **Corporate headquarters location:** This location.

JACK IN THE BOX INC.
9330 Balboa Avenue, San Diego CA 92123-1516. 858/571-2121. **Fax:** 858/694-1570. **Contact:** Human Resources. **E-mail address:** resumes@jackinthebox.com. **World Wide Web address:** http://www.jackinthebox.com. **Description:** Operates and franchises Jack in the Box restaurants, one of the nation's largest quick-serve hamburger chains. Jack in the Box restaurants are primarily located in the western and southwestern United States. International operations currently include restaurants in Hong Kong and Mexico. **Positions advertised include:** Accounting Representative; Information Systems/Budget Administrator; Regional Marketing Manager; Senior Project Manager; Financial Analyst; Restaurant Auditor. **Corporate headquarters location:** This location. **Listed on:** New York Stock Exchange. **Stock exchange symbol:** JBX.

JACOBS ENGINEERING GROUP INC.
1111 South Arroyo Parkway, P.O. Box 7084, Pasadena CA 91109-7084. 626/578-3500. **Fax:** 626/578-6916. **Contact:** Human Resources. **World Wide Web address:** http://www.jacobs.com. **Description:** An engineering firm offering a full range of services including environmental studies, feasibility studies, architectural services, engineering/design, procurement, construction, construction management, and construction maintenance. Jacobs Engineering Group is one of the largest engineering and construction companies in the United States. The company specializes in the chemicals and polymers, federal programs, pulp and paper, semiconductor, petroleum refining, facilities and transportation, food and consumer products, and pharmaceuticals and biotechnologies industries. **NOTE:** Search and apply for positions online. **Positions advertised include:** IT Manager; Project Manager; Security Engineer; Tax Accountant. **Corporate headquarters location:** This location. **Listed on:** New York Stock Exchange. **Stock exchange symbol:** JEC.

JAKKS PACIFIC, INC.
22619 Pacific Coast Highway, Suite 250, Malibu CA 90265. 310/456-7799. **Fax:** 310/317-8527. **Contact:** Human Resources Department. **World Wide Web address:** http://www.jakkspacific.com. **Description:** Develops, manufactures, and markets toys and similar children's products including action figures and activity kits. **Positions advertised include:** A/P Supervisor; Product Development/Mechanical Design Engineer; Packaging Designer. **Corporate headquarters location:** This location. **Listed on:** NASDAQ. **Stock exchange symbol:** JAKK. **Annual sales/revenues:** More than $300 million.

JAMS
1920 Main Street, Suite 300, Irvine CA 92614. 949/224-1810. **Fax:** 949/224-1818. **Contact:** Human Resources. **World Wide Web address:** http://www.jamsadr.com. **Description:** Provides alternative dispute resolution (ADR) judicial services, which is a means of scheduling and processing cases outside the public court system. **Corporate headquarters location:** This location.

JEFFER, MANGELS, BUTLER, & MARMARO LLP
1900 Avenue of the Stars, 7th Floor, Los Angeles CA 90067. 310/203-8080. **Fax:** 310/203-0567. **Contact:** Amy Frechette, Recruiting Manager. **E-mail address:** afl@jmbm.com. **World Wide Web address:** http://www.jmbm.com. **Description:** A law firm practicing litigation, corporate, entertainment, tax, bankruptcy, health, environment, and international law. **Special programs:** Summer Associate Program for law students. **Corporate headquarters location:** This location. **Other U.S. locations:** San Francisco CA.

JEFFERIES & COMPANY, INC.
11100 Santa Monica Boulevard, 11th Floor, Los Angeles CA 90025. 310/445-1199. **Fax:** 310/575-5165. **Contact:** Human Resources. **E-mail address:** Westcoastrecruiting@jefco.com. **World Wide Web address:** http://www.jefco.com. **Description:** Jefferies & Company is engaged in equity, convertible debt and taxable fixed income securities brokerage and trading, and corporate finance. Jefferies & Company is one of the leading national firms engaged in the distribution and trading of blocks of equity securities primarily in the third market. Founded in 1962. **NOTE:** For opportunities in IT, HR, Marketing, and Finance, contact Mel Locke, Director of People Services. E-mail: mlocke@jefco.com. Fax: 310/914-1066. **Corporate headquarters location:** This location. **Parent company:** Jefferies Group, Inc. is a holding company that, through Investment Technology Group, Inc., Jeffries & Company, Inc., Jefferies International Limited, and Jefferies Pacific Limited, is engaged in securities brokerage and trading, corporate finance, and other financial services. **Listed on:** New York Stock Exchange. **Stock exchange symbol:** JEF.

JEFFERIES & COMPANY, INC.
650 California Street, 30th Floor, San Francisco CA 94108. 415/229-1500. **Contact:** Human Resources. **E-mail address:** Westcoastrecruiting@jefco.com. **World Wide Web address:** http://www.jefco.com. **Description:** Jefferies & Company is engaged in equity, convertible debt and taxable fixed income securities brokerage and trading, and corporate finance. Founded in 1962. **NOTE:** For opportunities in IT, HR, Marketing, and Finance, contact Mel Locke, Director of People Services. E-mail: mlocke@jefco.com. Fax: 310/914-1066. **Corporate headquarters location:** Los Angeles CA. **Parent company:** Jefferies Group, Inc. is a holding company that, through Jefferies & Company, Inc.; Investment Technology Group, Inc.; Jefferies International Limited; and Jefferies Pacific Limited, is engaged in securities brokerage and trading, corporate finance, and other financial services. **Listed on:** New York Stock Exchange. **Stock exchange symbol:** JEF.

JENNY CRAIG INTERNATIONAL
5770 Fleet Street, Carlsbad CA 92008. 760/696-4000. **Fax:** 760/696-4608. **Contact:** Human Resources. **World Wide Web address:** http://www.jennycraig.com. **Description:** Provides a comprehensive weight-loss program. Jenny Craig International sells protein- and calorie-controlled food items to program participants throughout the United States and in four other countries. **Positions advertised include:** Registered Dietitian. **Corporate headquarters location:** This location. **Number of employees nationwide:** 5,370.

JENSEN INDUSTRIES, INC.
1946 East 46th Street, Los Angeles CA 90058. 323/235-6800. **Toll-free phone:** 800/325-8351. **Fax:** 323/235-6816. **Contact:** Human Resources. **E-mail address:** hr@jensen-ind.com. **World Wide Web address:** http://www.jensen-ind.com. **Description:** Primarily engaged in manufacturing building products for residential and commercial industries. The company's products include bath cabinets, vanities, lavtops, toplights, mailboxes, medicine cabinets, roof vents, range hoods, and monitor panels. **Number of employees at this location:** 200.

JETRO SAN FRANCISCO
235 Pine Street, Suite 1700, San Francisco CA 94104. 415/392-1333. **Fax:** 415/788-6927. **Contact:** Human Resources Department. **World Wide Web address:** http://www.jetrosf.org. **Description:** A nonprofit organization that provides assistance to area businesses regarding trade and investment opportunities in Japan. This location also has a Japanese information center that is open to the public. **Corporate headquarters location:** This location.

A.L. JOHNSON COMPANY
4671 Calle Carga, Camarillo CA 93012. 805/389-4631. **Fax:** 805/389-4632. **Contact:** Human Resources. **E-mail address:** aljcat@ix.netcom.com. **World Wide Web address:** http://www.aljcast.com. **Description:** Manufactures aluminum and zinc castings including machining and finishing operations. Founded in 1954. **Corporate headquarters location:** This location.

JOHNSON CONTROLS, INC.
1550 East Kimberly Avenue, Fullerton CA 92831. 714/871-7740. **Contact:** Human Resources Manager. **World Wide Web address:** http://www.johnsoncontrols.com. **Description:** Manufactures automotive storage batteries for sale to private labels. **NOTE:** Search and apply for positions online. **Special programs:** Co-ops; Internships. **Corporate headquarters location:** Milwaukee WI. **Other U.S. locations:** Nationwide. **Operations at this facility include:** Manufacturing. **Listed on:** New York Stock Exchange. **Stock exchange symbol:** JCI. **Number of employees at this location:** 300. **Number of employees worldwide:** 118,000.

JOHNSON LIFT/HYSTER
605 Freeway at Peck Road, City of Industry CA 91714. 562/692-9311. **Fax:** 562/699-6306. **Contact:** Personnel Director. **World Wide Web address:** http://www.johnson-lift.com. **Description:** Engaged in marketing material-handling equipment (industrial truck lifts and personnel lifts) and related parts and service. **Other area locations:** Anaheim CA; Oxnard CA; Riverside CA; San Diego CA. **Parent company:** Hyster-Yale Material Handling, Inc. **Operations at this facility include:** Administration; Sales.

JOSHUA TREE RECREATION
6171 Sunburst Street, Joshua Tree CA 92252-0838. 760/366-8415. **Contact:** Human Resources. **Description:** Operates the Joshua Tree Park as well as a community center, and offers a variety of classes and outdoor activity programs.

JOSLYN SUNBANK COMPANY, LLC
1740 Commerce Way, Paso Robles CA 93446. 805/238-2840. **Fax:** 805/238-0241. **Contact:** Licia Blackburn, Manager of Human Resources Department. **World Wide Web address:** http://www.sunbankcorp.com. **Description:** Manufactures electrical connector accessories (backshells) and flexible conduit cabling systems. **Corporate headquarters location:** This location. **Parent company:** Danaher Corporation. **Operations at this facility include:** Administration; Divisional Headquarters; Manufacturing; Research and Development; Sales; Service. **Listed on:** New York Stock Exchange. **Stock exchange symbol:** DHR. **Number of employees at this location:** 200.

KB HOME
10990 Wilshire Boulevard, 7th Floor, Los Angeles CA 90024. 310/231-4000. **Fax:** 310/231-4222. **Contact:** Gary Ray, Vice President of Human Resources. **World Wide Web address:** http://www.kbhome.com. **Description:** Kaufman & Broad builds and markets single-family homes; provides mortgage banking services; develops commercial projects and high-density residential properties; and acquires and develops land. **NOTE:** Search and apply for positions online. **Positions advertised include:** Senior Developer; Payroll Coordinator; Public Relations Coordinator; Web Content Administrator; Paralegal; Merchandise Manager. **Corporate headquarters location:** This location. **Other U.S. locations:** Nationwide. **Listed on:** New York Stock Exchange. **Stock exchange symbol:** KBH. **Number of employees nationwide:** 5,000.

K-SWISS INC.
31248 Oak Crest Drive, Westlake Village CA 91361. 818/706-5100. **Fax:** 818/706-5390. **Contact:** Personnel. **World Wide Web address:** http://www.kswiss.com.

Description: Manufactures athletic and casual footwear and apparel. Founded in 1966. **Corporate headquarters location:** This location. **Listed on:** NASDAQ. **Stock exchange symbol:** KSWS.

KCRA-TV
3 Television Circle, Sacramento CA 95814. 916/446-3333. **Contact:** Human Resources. **World Wide Web address:** http://www.thekcrachannel.com. **Description:** Operates one of the nation's largest television stations. In May 1999, KCRA-TV launched KCRA-DT, Northern California's first digital television station. Founded in 1955. **Positions advertised include:** Sr. Producer; Account Executive; Web Editor; Reporter. **Parent company:** Hearst-Argyle Television, Inc. **Listed on:** New York Stock Exchange. **Stock exchange symbol:** HTV.

KLA-TENCOR CORPORATION
160 Rio Robles, San Jose CA 95134. 408/875-3000. **Fax:** 408/875-4857. **Contact:** Human Resources. **E-mail address:** hr@kla-tencor.com. **World Wide Web address:** http://www.kla-tencor.com. **Description:** Manufactures high-speed, image-processing systems for the semiconductor industry. **Special programs:** Internships. **Corporate headquarters location:** This location. **Other area locations:** Milpitas CA. **Listed on:** NASDAQ. **Stock exchange symbol:** KLAC.

K.P. CORPORATION
12647 Alcosta Boulevard, Suite 425, San Ramon CA 94583. 925/543-5200. **Fax:** 925/543-5252. **Contact:** Human Resources. **E-mail address:** jobs@kpcorp.com. **World Wide Web address:** http://www.kpcorp.com. **Description:** A commercial lithographic printer. **Positions advertised include:** Sales Communications Coordinator; Project Specialist. **Corporate headquarters location:** This location.

KAISER ELECTRO-OPTICS, INC.
2752 Loker Avenue West, Carlsbad CA 92008. 760/438-9255. **Fax:** 760/438-6875. **Contact:** Human Resources. **World Wide Web address:** http://www.kaiserelectronics.com. **Description:** Designs, develops, and manufactures avionic display systems. NOTE: for current job openings, visit: http://www.rockwellcollins.com/careers/index.html. **Corporate headquarters location:** This location. **Parent company:** Rockwell Collins. **Listed on:** New York Stock Exchange. **Stock exchange symbol:** COL.

KAISER PERMANENTE
4867 West Sunset Boulevard, Los Angeles CA 90001. 323/783-6900. **Fax:** 888/805-7562. **Recorded jobline:** 800/331-3976. **Contact:** Personnel. **World Wide Web address:** http://www.kaiserpermanente.org. **Description:** A nonprofit, public-benefit, and charitable health care corporation that enrolls members and arranges for their medical services nationwide. **NOTE:** Search and apply for positions online. **Positions advertised include:** Admitting Clerk; Department Secretary; Medical Audit Clerk; Medical Secretary; Unit Manager; Project Analyst. **Special programs:** The Postgraduate Administrative Fellowship Program is a training program for talented recent graduates pursuing health care management careers. **Corporate headquarters location:** Oakland CA. **Other U.S. locations:** Nationwide. **Listed on:** Privately held. **Number of employees nationwide:** 34,000.

KAISER PERMANENTE
PROGRAM OFFICES
1 Kaiser Plaza, Oakland CA 94612. 916/973-6848. **Fax:** 978/901-9670. **Recorded jobline:** 510/271-6888. **Contact:** Recruitment. **World Wide Web address:** http://www.kaiserpermanente.org. **Description:** Kaiser Permanente is a nonprofit, public-benefit, and charitable health care organization that enrolls members and arranges for their medical, hospital, and related services nationwide. **Positions advertised include:** Area Financial Officer; Assistant Controller; Assistant Corporate Controller; Business Planner; Compliance Audit Investigator; Financial Analyst. **Corporate headquarters location:** This location. **Other U.S. locations:** Nationwide. **Operations at this facility include:** This location houses administrative offices.

KAWASAKI MOTORS CORPORATION U.S.A.
9950 Jeronimo Road, Irvine CA 92618-2084. 949/770-0400. **Fax:** 949/460-5625. **Contact:** Human Resources Department. **E-mail address:** Stephanie.Mylles@kmc-usa.com. **World Wide Web address:** http://www.kawasaki.com. **Description:** Imports and markets a variety of consumer-oriented transportation products and small engines. The company's primary product line is motorcycles, while other interests include gasoline, diesel, and turbine jet engines, as well as jet skis and portable generators. **NOTE**: Search for open positions online. Resumes may be submitted by mail, e-mail, or fax. **Corporate headquarters location:** This location. **Other U.S. locations:** Grand Rapids MI.

KAWNEER COMPANY INC.
P.O. Box 3148, Visalia CA 93278. 559/651-4000. **Physical address:** 7200 Doe Avenue, Visalia CA 93291. **Toll-free phone:** 877/505-3785. **Contact:** Personnel Manager. **World Wide Web address:** http://www.kawneer.com. **Description:** Kawneer Company manufactures and markets fabricated products. This includes nonresidential architectural building products such as storefronts, building entrances, facings, window framing, and curtainwall systems. **Corporate headquarters location:** Norcross GA. **Other U.S. locations:** AL; IN; KY; PA. **Parent company:** ALCOA Inc. **Operations at this facility include:** Administration; Manufacturing; Sales; Service. **Listed on:** New York Stock Exchange. **Stock exchange symbol:** AA. **Number of employees at this location:** 300. **Number of employees worldwide:** 14,000.

KAY COMPUTERS
722 Genevieve Street, Suite N, Solana Beach CA 92075. 858/481-0225. **Fax:** 858/481-4363. **Contact:** Human Resources. **World Wide Web address:** http://www.kaycomputers.com. **Description:** Manufactures personal computers. **Corporate headquarters location:** This location.

KEANE, INC.
133 Technology Drive, Suite 200, Irvine CA 92618. 949/450-4600. **Toll-free phone:** 800/315-8306. **Fax:** 949/450-4658. **Contact:** Edith Tarter, Human Resources. **E-mail address:** careers@keane.com. **World Wide Web address:** http://www.keane.com. **Description:** A software development and consulting firm providing systems and software applications to the transportation, finance, health care, and insurance industries. **NOTE:** Search and apply for positions online. **Positions advertised include:** Engagement Manager; Account Executive. **Office hours:** Monday - Friday, 8:00 a.m. - 5:00 p.m. **Corporate headquarters location:** Boston MA. **Listed on:** American Stock Exchange. **Stock exchange symbol:** KEA.

KELLOGG COMPANY
KELLOGG USA CONVENIENCE FOODS DIVISION
P.O. Box 5191, San Jose CA 95150. 408/295-8656. **Physical address:** 475 Eggo Way, San Jose CA 95116. **Contact:** Human Resources. **World Wide Web address:** http://www.kellogg.com. **Description:** Kellogg Company specializes in the manufacturing and marketing of ready-to-eat cereals, and other convenience foods. Kellogg products are manufactured in 18 countries in North America, Europe, Asia-Pacific, and Latin America, and are distributed in more than 150 countries. Founded in 1906. **Corporate headquarters location:** Battle Creek MI. **Other U.S. locations:** San Leandro CA; Atlanta GA; Omaha NE; Blue Anchor NJ; Lancaster PA; Muncy PA; Pottstown PA; Memphis TN; Rossville TN. **International locations:** Ontario, Canada. **Operations at this facility include:** This location manufactures products such as Kellogg's Pop-Tarts toaster pastries, Eggo waffles, Kellogg's Nutri-Grain bars, Kellogg's low-fat granola bars, Kellogg's Croutettes stuffing mix, and Kellogg's Corn Flake crumbs. **Listed on:** New York Stock Exchange. **Stock exchange symbol:** K.

KELLY HOME CARE SERVICES
2900 Bristol Street, Suite J102, Costa Mesa CA 92626. 714/979-7413. **Fax:** 714/979-6895. **Contact:** Human Resources Department. **World Wide Web address:** http://www.kellyhomecare.com. **Description:** Provides home health care aides for senior citizens. NOTE: Search and apply for positions online. **Corporate headquarters location:** Troy MI.

KELLY-MOORE PAINT COMPANY, INC.
987 Commercial Avenue, San Carlos CA 94070. 650/595-1654. **Contact:** Human Resources. **World Wide Web address:** http://www.kellymoore.com. **Description:** Manufactures and sells paint through four manufacturing facilities and more than 160 retail locations in 10 states. **Corporate headquarters location:** This location. **Number of employees nationwide:** 2,200.

KEMPER INSURANCE COMPANIES
2390 East Orangewood Avenue, Suite 400, Anaheim CA 92806. 714/935-5700. **Contact:** Personnel. **World Wide Web address:** http://www.kemperinsurance.com. **Description:** An international insurance company engaged in a wide range of insurance, financial, and related services. The company provides property, casualty, and life insurance, reinsurance, and a wide range of diversified financial services operations. **Office hours:** Monday - Friday, 8:15 a.m. - 4:30 p.m. **Corporate headquarters location:** Long Grove IL. **Other area locations:** Glendale CA; San Diego CA; Santa Ana CA; West Covina CA.

KEMPER INSURANCE COMPANIES
P.O. Box 7993, San Francisco CA 94120. 415/421-2400. **Physical address:** 475 Sansome Street, 6th Floor, San Francisco CA 94111. **Contact:** Human Resources Manager. **World Wide Web address:** http://www.kemperinsurance.com. **Description:** Provides property, casualty, and life insurance, reinsurance, and a wide range of diversified financial services operations. **Corporate headquarters location:** Long Grove IL. **Other area locations:** City of Industry CA; Glendale CA; San Diego CA; Santa Ana CA; West Covina CA.

KENSINGTON TECHNOLOGY GROUP
2000 Alameda de las Pulgas, Second Floor, San Mateo CA 94403. 650/572-2700. **Toll-free phone:** 800/243-2972. **Fax:** 650/572-9675. **Contact:** Human Resources. **E-mail address:** jobs@kensington.com. **World Wide Web address:** http://www.kensington.com. **Description:** Designs and markets computer accessories, peripherals, and software for the computer aftermarket. Products include mice and trackballs, joysticks, gamepads, surge suppressor systems, cable and lock security devices, and carrying cases. **NOTE:** Entry-level positions are offered. Search and apply for positions online. **Positions advertised include:** Channel Development Representative; Sales Planning Analyst; ID Product Designer; Sales Support Specialist. **Special programs:** Internships. **Office hours:** Monday - Friday, 8:00 a.m. - 5:00 p.m. **Corporate headquarters location:** This location. **Parent company:** ACCO Brands, Inc. **Listed on:** New York Stock Exchange. **Stock exchange symbol:** FO.

KIMBERLY-CLARK CORPORATION
2001 East Orangethorpe Avenue, Fullerton CA 92831-5396. 714/773-7500. **Contact:** Human Resources. **World Wide Web address:** http://www.kimberly-clark.com. **Description:** A major manufacturer and marketer of fiber-based products for consumer and industrial customers. Kimberly-Clark does business in three primary product classes: Consumer and Service, offering a broad range of paper-based goods such as facial tissue, table napkins, and disposable gowns for medical applications; Newsprint, Pulp, and Forest Products, providing a variety of goods to industrial clients; and Paper and Specialties, producing adhesive-coated paper for commercial printing customers. **Corporate headquarters location:** Neenah WI. **Listed on:** New York Stock Exchange. **Stock exchange symbol:** KMB.

KINGSTON TECHNOLOGY
17600 Newhope Street, Fountain Valley CA 92708. 714/435-2600. **Toll-free phone:** 877/546-4786. **Fax:** 714/427-3555. **Contact:** Human Resources. **E-mail address:** jobs@kingston.com. **World Wide Web address:** http://www.kingston.com. **Description:** A leading independent manufacturer of more than 2,000 memory, processor, and other peripheral products. Founded in 1987. **NOTE:** Entry-level positions are offered. **Positions advertised include:** Sales Account Manager. **Corporate headquarters location:** This location. **International locations:** France; Germany; Ireland; Taiwan; United Kingdom. **Listed on:** Privately held. **Annual sales/revenues:** More than $100 million. **Number of employees worldwide:** 1,200.

KIT MANUFACTURING COMPANY
3355 Linden Avenue, Long Beach CA 90807. 562/595-7451. **Contact:** Human Resources. **World Wide Web address:** http://www.kitmfg.com. **Description:** One of the largest manufacturers of travel trailers and RVs in the United States. **Corporate headquarters location:** Caldwell ID. **Listed on:** New York Stock Exchange. **Stock exchange symbol:** KIT.

KNIGHT-RIDDER
50 West San Fernando Street, Suite 1500, San Jose CA 95113. 408/938-7700. **Fax:** 408/938-7758. **Contact:** Human Resources. **World Wide Web address:** http://www.kri.com. **Description:** A major newspaper publishing company that owns 28 dailies in 15 states and 3 nondailies in suburban areas. The company also produces niche publications such as Myrtle Beach's *Golf*, *CubaNews* newsletter in Miami, and *Northland Outdoors* in Grand Forks. The larger papers include the *Miami Herald*, *Philadelphia Inquirer*, *Philadelphia Daily News*, *Detroit Free Press*, and *San Jose Mercury News*. **NOTE:** Interested candidates may search and apply for positions online. **Positions advertised include:** Sales Manager; Special Sections Editor; Marketing Director. **Corporate headquarters location:** This location. **Subsidiaries include:** Knight-Ridder also has interests in the information distribution market through Knight-Ridder Information, Inc.; Knight-Ridder Financial; and Technimetrics. Knight-Ridder's online information retrieval serves the business, scientific, technology, medical, and education communities in more than 100 countries. Knight-Ridder Financial provides real-time financial news and pricing information through products such as MoneyCenter, Digital Datafeed, ProfitCenter, and TradeCenter. Knight-Ridder also has interests in cable television and other businesses. TKR Cable, a 50-50 joint venture with Liberty Media Corporation, serves 344,000 basic subscribers in New

Jersey and New York and manages Kentucky systems with 277,000 subscribers. Through TKR Cable Partners, Knight-Ridder owns a 15 percent share of TCI/TKR L.P. Cable Systems with 867,000 subscribers in five states. Other interests include partial ownership of the Seattle Times Company, two paper mills, a newspaper advertising sales company, and SCI Holdings. **Listed on:** New York Stock Exchange. **Stock exchange symbol:** KRI. **Annual sales/revenues:** $2.9 billion.

KNOTT'S BERRY FARM
8039 Beach Boulevard, Buena Park CA 90620. 714/220-5200. **Fax:** 714/220-5150. **Recorded jobline:** 714/995-6688. **Contact:** Staffing Department. **World Wide Web address:** http://www.knotts.com. **Description:** This location is an amusement park. Overall, Knott's Berry Farm is engaged in the development and management of family restaurants, retail operations, and specialty food products manufacturing. **Positions advertised include:** Purchasing Assistant; Buyer; Catering Sales Manager; Entertainment Technician. **Special programs:** Internships. **Corporate headquarters location:** This location. **Other area locations:** Irvine CA; Moreno Valley CA; Placentia CA. **Other U.S. locations:** Bloomington MN. **Operations at this facility include:** Administration; Sales.

KNOWLEDGE LEARNING CORPORATION (KLC)
4340 Redwood Highway, Building B, San Rafael CA 94903-2121. 415/444-1600. **Fax:** 415/444-1664. **Contact:** Human Resources. **E-mail address:** familyservices@klcorp.com. **World Wide Web address:** http://www.knowledgelearning.com. **Description:** Operates one of the largest chains of childcare centers in the United States with more than 150 childcare centers in 15 states. KLC's community schools operate under the names Children's Discovery Centers, Magic Years, Learning Universe, and Hildebrandt Learning Centers. **Positions advertised include:** District Manager; Teacher; Assistant Teacher; Center Director; Assistant Center Director. **Corporate headquarters location:** This location. **Parent company:** Knowledge Universe.

KOLL COMPANY
4343 Von Karman Avenue, Newport Beach CA 92660. 949/833-3030. **Fax:** 949/250-4344. **Contact:** Corporate Recruiting. **E-mail address:** info@koll.com. **World Wide Web address:** http://www.koll.com. **Description:** A real estate development, acquisition, management, and construction firm. The company leases and manages property, operating regional divisions along the West Coast. **Corporate headquarters location:** This location.

KONICA MINOLTA BUSINESS SOLUTIONS U.S.A.
44 Montgomery Street, Suite 1010, San Francisco CA 94104. 415/398-4141. **Toll-free phone:** 800/926-7616. **Contact:** Human Resources. **E-mail address:** philbins@kmbs.konicaminolta.us. **World Wide Web address:** http://www.kmbs.konicaminolta.us. **Description:** Manufactures and distributes high-technology business equipment. **NOTE:** Entry-level positions are offered. **Positions advertised include:** Information Processing Specialist; Branch Applications Specialist; Technician. **Special programs:** Training. **Corporate headquarters location:** Ramsey NJ. **Other U.S. locations:** Nationwide. **International locations:** Worldwide. **Listed on:** Privately held. **Annual sales/revenues:** $1.5 billion. **Number of employees nationwide:** 5,900.

KONTRON AMERICA
6260 Sequence Drive, San Diego CA 92121. 858/294-4558. **Fax:** 858/677-0898. **Contact:** Human Resources. **World Wide Web address:** http://www.kontron.com. **Description:** A manufacturer of ruggedized PC chassis and a reseller of computer hardware. **NOTE:** Search and apply for positions online. **Positions advertised include:** Order Entry Administrator; Senior Program Manager; Material Handler; Executive Assistant. **Corporate headquarters location:** This location. **Other area locations:** Hayward CA. **Other U.S. locations:** Eden Prairie MN; Pittsburgh PA.

KORET OF CALIFORNIA, INC.
505 14th Street, Oakland CA 94612. 510/622-7000. **Contact:** Human Resources Department. **E-mail address:** jobs@koretsf.com. **World Wide Web address:** http://www.koretsf.com. **Description:** Manufactures and markets women's apparel. **Positions advertised include:** Fit Model; Freelance Artist; Merchandising Intern. **Special programs:** Internships. **Corporate headquarters location:** This location. **Other area locations:** Chico CA; Los Angeles CA; Napa CA. **Other U.S. locations:** Miami FL; New York NY; Price UT. **Subsidiaries include:** Koret Canada; Mr. Jax. **Parent company:** Kellwood Company. **Operations at this facility include:** Administration; Sales; Service. **Listed on:** New York Stock Exchange. **Stock exchange symbol:** KWD. **Number of employees nationwide:** 1,200.

GUY KORNBLUM & ASSOCIATES
1388 Sutter Street, Suite 820, San Francisco CA 94109. 415/440-7800. **Toll-free phone:** 888/249-7800. **Fax:** 415/440-7898. **Contact:** Human Resources. **World Wide Web address:** http://www.kornblumlaw.com. **Description:** A law firm specializing in personal injury, wrongful death, malpractice, and class action suits. **Corporate headquarters location:** This location. **Other area locations:** Los Angeles CA. **U.S. locations:** Denver CO; Indianapolis IN.

KRACO ENTERPRISES
505 East Euclid Avenue, Compton CA 90224. 310/639-0666. **Toll-free phone:** 800/678-1910 (for submission of new product concepts or prototypes only). **Contact:** Human Resources. **World Wide Web address:** http://www.kraco.com. **Description:** Manufactures a broad range of floor mats for cars, trucks, vans, and SUVs. **Corporate headquarters location:** This location. **Operations at this facility include:** Administration; Manufacturing; Research and Development; Sales. **Number of employees nationwide:** 450.

KRAFT FOODS, INC.
100 Halcyon Drive, San Leandro CA 94578. 510/639-5000. **Contact:** Human Resources. **World Wide Web address:** http://www.kraftfoods.com. **Description:** Overall, Kraft is one of the largest American-based packaged food companies. Other Kraft brands include DiGiorno, Maxwell House, Stove Top, and Oscar Mayer. **NOTE:** Search and apply for positions online. **Corporate headquarters location:** Northfield IL. **Parent company:** Philip Morris Companies Inc. **Operations at this facility include:** This location is engaged in the production of coffee, Jell-O, Log Cabin syrup, and Tang. **Listed on:** New York Stock Exchange. **Stock exchange symbol:** KFT.

KRAGEN AUTO PARTS
4240 International Boulevard, Oakland CA 94601. 510/532-1240. **Contact:** Regional Recruiter. **Description:** A retailer and distributor of automotive aftermarket products. **Company slogan:** Whatever it takes. **Operations at this facility include:** Sales; Service.

KULICKE AND SOFFA INDUSTRIES, INC. (K&S)
2210 Martin Avenue, Santa Clara CA 95050. 408/727-5040. **Fax:** 408/727-4829. **Contact:** Human Resources. **World Wide Web address:** http://www.kns.com. **Description:** Engaged in semiconductor assembly and services. The company designs, manufactures, markets, and supports equipment for IC and MCM/hybrid semiconductor manufacturers worldwide. Product lines include wafer and hard materials dicing, die bonding and wire bonding equipment, service and spare parts, and the Micro-Swiss line of bonding and dicing tools and production accessories. Founded in 1951. **Special programs:** Co-ops; Internships. **Corporate headquarters location:** Willow Grove PA. **Operations at this facility include:** Regional Headquarters. **Listed on:** NASDAQ. **Stock exchange symbol:** KLIC.

KYOCERA AMERICA, INC.
8611 Balboa Avenue, San Diego CA 92123. 858/576-2600. **Fax:** 858/268-3035. **Contact:** Human Resources. **E-mail address:** kai.hr@kyocera.com. **World Wide Web address:** http://www.kyocera.com/kai. **Description:** Manufactures a broad line of products for the electronics industry including integrated circuit packages, chip capacitors, industrial ceramics, and insulator parts. Other operations include the manufacturing of such consumer and office products as cameras, jewelry, copiers, and portable and personal computers. **NOTE:** Entry-level positions are offered. **Positions advertised include:** QA Engineer; Layout Designer. **Special programs:** Internships; Training. **Corporate headquarters location:** This location. **Parent company:** Kyocera International, Inc. **Operations at this facility include:** Administration; Manufacturing; Research and Development. **Listed on:** New York Stock Exchange. **Stock exchange symbol:** KYO. **Annual sales/revenues:** $1.8 billion. **Number of employees at this location:** 725.

L.A. GEAR, INC.
844 Moraga Drive, Los Angeles CA 90049. 310/889-3499. **Fax:** 310/889-3500. **Contact:** Human Resources. **World Wide Web address:** http://www.lagear.com. **Description:** Manufactures athletic/fashion footwear and apparel. **Operations at this facility include:** Administration; Divisional Headquarters; Research and Development; Service. **Parent company:** ACI International. **Number of employees at this location:** 200.

LSI LOGIC
1621 Barber Lane, Milpitas CA 95035. 408/954-3108. **Fax:** 408/433-8918. **Contact:** Human Resources. **World Wide Web address:** http://www.lsilogic.com. **Description:** Designs and markets integrated circuits that implement the compression, decompression, and transmission of digital full-motion video and still images for consumer electronics, communications, and computer applications such as video CD players, direct broadcast of television programming by satellites, and multimedia computing. Founded in 1988. **NOTE:** Search and apply for positions online. **Corporate headquarters location:** This location. **Other area locations:** Irvine CA; Los Angeles CA; San Diego CA. **U.S. locations:** Nationwide. **International locations:** China; France; Germany; Italy; the Netherlands; Sweden; United Kingdom. **Number of employees worldwide:** 600. **Listed on:** New York Stock Exchange. **Stock exchange symbol:** LSI.

L3 COMMUNICATIONS, INC.
130 Constitution Drive, Menlo Park CA 94025. 650/326-9500. **Contact:** Paula Moroney, Human Resources Representative. **E-mail address:** cooljobs@l-3com.com. **World Wide Web address:** http://www.l-3com.com. **Description:** Designs and manufactures integrated microwave antenna subassemblies and low-radar cross-section antenna designs and measurements. **Corporate headquarters location:** New York NY. **Number of employees at this location:** 235. **Listed on:** New York Stock Exchange. **Stock exchange symbol:** LLL.

L3 COMMUNICATIONS, INC.
9020 Balboa Avenue, San Diego CA 92123. 858/279-0411. **Fax:** 858/571-1259. **Contact:** Human Resources. **E-mail address:** cooljobs@l-3com.com. **World Wide Web address:** http://www.l-3com.com. **Description:** Designs and manufactures integrated microwave antenna subassemblies and low-radar, cross-section antenna designs and measurements. **Positions advertised include:** Business Development Manager; Senior Test Engineer; Senior Financial Analyst. **Corporate headquarters location:** New York NY. **Listed on:** New York Stock Exchange. **Stock exchange symbol:** LLL.

L3 COMMUNICATIONS, INC.
107 Woodmere Road, Folsom CA 95630. 916/351-4500. **Fax:** 916/351-4568. **Contact:** Personnel. **E-mail address:** cooljobs@l-3com.com. **World Wide Web address:** http://www.l-3com.com. **Description:** Manufactures filters/multiplexers, isolators, circulators, gain equalizers, oscillators (cavity and DRO), and integrated assemblies. **Corporate headquarters location:** New York NY. **Listed on:** New York Stock Exchange. **Stock exchange symbol:** LLL.

LA JOLLA PHARMACEUTICAL COMPANY (LJP)
6455 Nancy Ridge Drive, San Diego CA 92121-2249. 858/452-6600. **Fax:** 858/625-0155. **Contact:** Human Resources. **E-mail address:** jobs@ljpc.com. **World Wide Web address:** http://www.ljpc.com. **Description:** La Jolla Pharmaceutical Company (LJP) develops highly specific therapeutics to treat antibody-mediated and inflammatory diseases. The company is a leader in B-cell tolerance for treatment of antibody-mediated diseases and conducts Phase II clinical trials for the treatment of lupus. LJP also develops therapeutics for recurrent fetal loss, autoimmune stroke, Rh hemolytic disease of the newborn, myasthenia gravis, and Graves' disease. The company also develops compounds that control inflammation. **NOTE:** Resumes accepted only for posted positions. **Positions advertised include:** Associate Clinical Project Manager; Director, Medical Operations; Senior Clinical Manager. **Corporate headquarters location:** This location. **Listed on:** NASDAQ. **Stock exchange symbol:** LJPC.

LABORATORY CORPORATION OF AMERICA (LABCORP)
5601 Oberlin Drive, Suite 100, San Diego CA 92121. 858/455-1221. **Contact:** Personnel. **World Wide Web address:** http://www.labcorp.com. **Description:** One of the nation's leading clinical laboratory companies, providing services primarily to physicians, hospitals, clinics, nursing homes, and other clinical labs nationwide. LabCorp performs tests on blood, urine, and other body fluids and tissue, aiding the diagnosis of disease. **NOTE:** Search and apply for positions online. **Positions advertised include:** Client Inquiry Representative; Data Entry Operator; Senior Technologist; Cytology Clerk; Histotechnician. **Corporate headquarters location:** Burlington NC. **Other area locations:** San Leandro CA; Los Angeles CA. **Listed on:** New York Stock Exchange. **Stock exchange symbol:** LH.

LAGUNA CLAY COMPANY
14400 Lomitas Avenue, City of Industry CA 91746. 626/330-0631. **Toll-free phone:** 800/452-4862. **Fax:** 626/333-7694. **Contact:** Human Resources Department. **E-mail**

address: info@lagunaclay.com. **World Wide Web address:** http://www.lagunaclay.com. **Description:** Manufactures clay and ceramic materials. **Corporate headquarters location:** This location. **Other U.S. locations:** Byesville OH.

LAIDLAW TRANSIT, INC.
4337 Rowland Avenue, El Monte CA 91731. 626/448-9446. **Contact:** Personnel Director. **E-mail address:** careers@laidlawjobs.com. **World Wide Web address:** http://www.laidlawtransit.com. **Description:** Provides bus service for many districts of Los Angeles County and charter bus service to private customers. The company is also a school bus contractor. **Other area locations:** Culver City CA; Los Angeles CA. **Parent company:** Laidlaw, Inc. provides solid waste collection, compaction, transportation, treatment, transfer and disposal services; provides hazardous waste services; operates hazardous waste facilities and wastewater treatment plants; and operates passenger and school buses, transit system buses, and tour and charter buses. **Corporate headquarters location:** Kansas City KS. **Listed on:** American Stock Exchange. **Stock exchange symbol:** GLL.

LANDAMERICA LAWYERS TITLE
55 South Lake Avenue, Suite 600, Pasadena CA 91101. 626/304-9797. **Contact:** Human Resources. **E-mail address:** corprecruiter@landam.com. **World Wide Web address:** http://www.landam.com. **Description:** Provides title insurance and other real estate-related services on commercial and residential transactions in the United States, Canada, the Bahamas, Puerto Rico, and the U.S. Virgin Islands. Lawyers Title Insurance Corporation also provides search and examination services and closing services for a broad-based customer group that includes lenders, developers, real estate brokers, attorneys, and homebuyers. This location covers Alaska, Arizona, California, Hawaii, Nevada, Oregon, and Washington. **Corporate headquarters location:** Richmond VA. **Other U.S. locations:** Nationwide. **Listed on:** New York Stock Exchange. **Stock exchange symbol:** LFG.

LANTRONIX
15353 Barranca Parkway, Irvine CA 92618. 949/453-3990. **Fax:** 949/453-7165. **Contact:** Human Resources. **E-mail address:** webhr@lantronix.com. **World Wide Web address:** http://www.lantronix.com. **Description:** Provides network-enabling technology that allows for configuring and communicating over the Internet and shared networks. **Positions advertised include:** Cost Accountant; Senior Software Engineer; Test Engineer. **Corporate headquarters location:** This location. **Annual sales/revenues:** $21 - $50 million. **Listed on:** NASDAQ. **Stock exchange symbol:** LTRX.

LASCO BATHWARE, INC.
8101 East Kaiser Boulevard, Suite 130, Anaheim CA 92808. 714/993-1220. **Toll-free phone:** 800/877-2205. **Contact:** Elaine Velasco. **E-mail address:** Elaine.Velasco@lascobathware.com. **World Wide Web address:** http://www.lascobathware.com. **Description:** Manufactures bath fixtures. Products include acrylic and fiberglass bathtubs, whirlpools, showers, and shower tubs. LASCO Bathware also manufactures shower doors and steam generators. Founded in 1947. **Corporate headquarters location:** This location.

LASER EXCEL, INC.
3310 Coffey Lane, Santa Rosa CA 95403. 707/577-1301. **Toll-free phone:** 800/559-7965. **Contact:** Controller. **World Wide Web address:** http://www.laserexcel.com. **Description:** A manufacturer of laser-engraved wood and paper giftware including stationery and special occasion note cards. **Positions advertised include:** Marketing Coordinator. **Corporate headquarters location:** This location. **Other area locations:** Healdsburg CA. **Other U.S. locations:** Green Lake WI. **Operations at this facility include:** Administration; Manufacturing; Research and Development; Sales.

LASERPACIFIC MEDIA CORPORATION
809 North Cahuenga Boulevard, Hollywood CA 90038. 323/462-6266. **Fax:** 323/464-6005. **Contact:** Personnel. **World Wide Web address:** http://www.laserpacific.com. **Description:** A major supplier of film, videotape, digital sound postproduction, and multimedia services to prime time television shows. **Corporate headquarters location:** This location. **Listed on:** NASDAQ. **Stock exchange symbol:** LPAC. **Chairman and CEO:** James R. Parks. **Annual sales/revenues:** $21 - $50 million. **Number of employees nationwide:** 225.

LASERSCOPE
3070 Orchard Drive, San Jose CA 95134-2011. 408/943-0636. **Fax:** 408/943-9630. **Contact:** Human Resources. **E-mail address:** staffing@laserscope.com. **World Wide Web address:** http://www.laserscope.com. **Description:** Designs and markets an advanced line of medical laser systems and related energy delivery products. The company markets its products to hospitals, outpatient surgical centers, and physicians' offices worldwide. **Positions advertised include:** Accounting Manager; Regional Surgical Sales Manager. **Corporate headquarters location:** This location. **Operations at this facility include:** Administration; Manufacturing; Research and Development; Sales; Service. **Listed on:** NASDAQ. **Stock exchange symbol:** LSCP. **President/CEO:** Eric Reuter. **Annual sales/revenues:** $21 - $50 million. **Number of employees at this location:** 170. **Number of employees nationwide:** 220.

LATHAM & WATKINS LLP
600 West Broadway, Suite 1800, San Diego CA 92101-3375. 619/236-1234. **Contact:** Cindy D. Edson, Recruitment. **E-mail address:** cindy.edson@lw.com. **World Wide Web address:** http://www.lw.com. **Description:** A law firm practicing corporate, environmental, and real estate law. **NOTE:** For paralegal and staff positions, contact Diana L. Clarke, Human Resources Manager at: diana.clarke@lw.com or the above address. **Special programs:** Public interest fellowships for recent law graduates. **International locations:** Worldwide.

LATHROP CONSTRUCTION ASSOCIATES, INC.
4001 Park Road, P.O. Box 2005, Benicia CA 94510. 707/746-8000. **Fax:** 707/746-8080. **Contact:** Human Resources. **E-mail address:** info@lathropconstruction.com. **World Wide Web address:** http://www.lathropconstruction.com. **NOTE:** Resumes may be submitted via mail, fax, or e-mail. **Description:** A general contractor that offers a variety of services including construction management, budget development, document review, and cost estimation. **Positions advertised include:** Project Manager; Superintendent; Project Engineer. **Corporate headquarters location:** This location.

LAWRENCE BERKELEY NATIONAL LABORATORY
One Cyclotron Road, Mail Stop 937-600, Berkeley CA 94720. 510/486-7950. **Fax:** 510/486-5870. **Contact:** Recruitment. **E-mail address:** employment@lbl.gov. **World Wide Web address:** http://www.lbl.gov. **Description:** A multiprogram national research facility operated by the University of California for the Department of Energy. The oldest of the nine national laboratories, the company's major activities include the Advanced Light Source, Human Genome Center, California Institute for Energy Efficiency, and the Center for Advanced Materials. **NOTE:** Search and apply for positions online. **Positions advertised include:** Administrative Assistant; Executive Assistant; Human Resources Assistant; Software Developer; Systems Administrator; Physicist; Geological Scientist; Biologist; Radiation Safety Technician; Research Associate. **Special programs:** Internships. **Corporate headquarters location:** This location. **Operations at this facility include:** Administration; Research and Development. **Number of employees at this location:** 3,000.

LAWRENCE LIVERMORE NATIONAL LABORATORY
P.O. Box 5510, L-725, Livermore CA 94551-5510. 925/422-9367. **Physical address:** 7000 East Avenue, Livermore CA 94550-9234. **Contact:** Christine Kachiu, Recruiting Specialist. **World Wide Web address:** http://www.llnl.gov. **Description:** Engaged in basic and applied research. The laboratory's research centers around six major programs including weapon studies, magnetic fusion energy, laser isotope separation, laser fusion energy, energy and resources, and biomedical, environmental, and atmospheric sciences. NOTE: Apply online only to open positions. **Positions advertised include:** Chief Financial Officer; Division Office Manager; Program Coordinator; Administrative Specialist; Maintenance Mechanic; Chemist; Biomedical Scientist; Physicist; Software Developer; Computer Scientist. **Corporate headquarters location:** This location. **Operations at this facility include:** Research and Development. **Number of employees nationwide:** 8,000.

LEACH INTERNATIONAL
6900 Orangethorpe Avenue, P.O. Box 5032, Buena Park CA 90622-5032. 714/739-0770. **Fax:** 714/739-2206. **Contact:** Human Resources. **E-mail address:** jobs@leachintl.com. **World Wide Web address:** http://www.leachintl.com. **Description:** Manufactures equipment for power distribution and control. Positions advertised include: Mechanical Engineer; Senior Buyer; Inventory Control Supervisor; Purchasing Expeditor; Senior Manufacturing Engineer. **Corporate headquarters location:** This location.

RIVERDEEP, INC.
100 Pine Street, Suite 1900, San Francisco CA 94111. 415/659-2000. **Fax:** 415/659-1877. **Contact:** Human Resources. **E-mail address:** resumes@riverdeep.net. **World Wide Web address:** http://www.learningco.com. **Description:** Produces education software. **Positions advertised include:** Database Marketing Manager; Channel Marketing Manager; Technology Architect; Executive Producer, Schools; Senior Instructional Designer; Director of Technology. **Corporate headquarters location:** This location. **Other U.S. locations:** Cedar Rapids IA; Boston MA.

LEGATO SYSTEMS
6200 Village Parkway, Dublin CA 94568. 925/875-8000. **Contact:** Human Resources. **World Wide Web address:** http://www.legato.com. **Description:** A software development company that integrates products and solutions into a large UNIX environment. **NOTE:** Search and apply for positions online. **Positions advertised include:** Customer Service Engineer; Product Marketing Manager. **Corporate headquarters location:** Mountain View CA. **Other U.S. locations:** Chicago IL; Boston MA; New York NY; Dallas TX. **Parent company:** EMC.

LEGEND INFORMATION TECHNOLOGY
46401 Landing Parkway, Fremont CA 94538. 510/668-4933. **Contact:** Human Resources. **World Wide Web address:** http://www.legendgrp.com. **Description:** A manufacturer of computer components and motherboards. **Corporate headquarters location:** Beijing, China.

LEGGETT & PLATT, INC.
P.O. Box 4956, Whittier CA 90602. 562/945-2641. **Physical address:** 12352 East Whittier Boulevard, Whittier CA 90602. **Contact:** Personnel. **E-mail address:** resumes@leggett.com. **World Wide Web address:** http://www.leggett.com. **Description:** Manufactures and markets a broad line of components for the furniture and bedding industries. Company products also include select lines of commodity fibers and carpet cushioning materials. **Positions advertised include:** Controller; Industrial Engineer; Truck Driver. **Corporate headquarters location:** Carthage MO. **Other U.S. locations:** Nationwide. **Operations at this facility include:** Administration; Divisional Headquarters; Manufacturing; Sales. **Listed on:** New York Stock Exchange. **Number of employees at this location:** 250. **Number of employees nationwide:** 16,000.

LEVI STRAUSS & COMPANY
1155 Battery Street, San Francisco CA 94111. 415/501-6000. **Contact:** Human Resources. **World Wide Web address:** http://www.levistrauss.com. **Description:** Designs, manufactures, and markets a diversified line of apparel, primarily jeans and jeans-related products under the Levi's and Britannia brand names. The company also manufactures the Dockers line of clothing for U.S. markets. **Positions advertised include:** Senior Financial Analyst; Senior Finance Manager; Senior Business Analyst; Community Affairs Manager; Graphic Designer, Retail Environment; Inventory Analyst. **Corporate headquarters location:** This location.

LIBERTY MUTUAL INSURANCE COMPANY
6130 Stoneridge Mall Road, Suite 400, Pleasanton CA 94588. 925/734-9200. **Fax:** 925/734-0914. **Contact:** Personnel Department. **E-mail address:** careers@libertymutual.com. **World Wide Web address:** http://www.libertymutual.com. **Description:** A full-line insurance firm offering life, medical, and business insurance, as well as investment and retirement planning. **Positions advertised include:** Sales Associate; Technical Consultant; Service Director, Loss Prevention. **Corporate headquarters location:** Boston MA.

LIFESCAN, INC.
1000 Gibraltar Drive, Milpitas CA 95035. 408/263-9789. **Contact:** Human Resources. **World Wide Web address:** http://www.lifescan.com. **Description:** Manufactures and markets a wide variety of diabetic devices designed to improve the lifestyles of people with diabetes. **NOTE:** Search and apply for positions online. **Positions advertised include:** Quality Software Engineer; ELDP Associate Engineer. **Corporate headquarters location:** This location. **Parent company:** Johnson & Johnson (New Brunswick NJ). **Listed on:** New York Stock Exchange. **Stock exchange symbol:** JNJ.

LIGAND PHARMACEUTICALS INC.
10275 Science Center Drive, San Diego CA 92121. 858/550-7500. **Fax:** 858/550-7506. **Contact:** Human Resources. **E-mail address:** jobs@ligand.com. **World Wide Web address:** http://www.ligand.com. **Description:** A biopharmaceutical company that researches, develops, and markets small molecule pharmaceutical products that address the medical needs of patients with cancer, cardiovascular and inflammatory diseases, osteoporosis, and metabolic disorders. **NOTE:** Search and apply for positions online. **Positions advertised include:** Director, Clinical Operations; Clinical Research Associate. **Corporate headquarters location:** This location. **Listed on:** NASDAQ. **Stock exchange symbol:** LGND.

LINCOLN PROPERTY COMPANY
1700 Montgomery Street, San Francisco CA 94111. 415/788-3000. **Fax:** 415/788-3010. **Contact:** Human Resources. **E-mail address:** humanresources@lpc.com. **World Wide Web address:** http://www.lpc.com. **Description:** A property management and development company. Founded in 1965. **Corporate headquarters location:** Dallas TX.

LINEAR TECHNOLOGY CORPORATION
1630 McCarthy Boulevard, Milpitas CA 95035-7417. 408/432-1900. **Fax:** 408/434-0507. **Contact:** Human Resources. **E-mail address:** hr@linear.com. **World Wide Web address:** http://www.linear.com. **Description:** Designs and manufactures a broad line of standard high-performance linear integrated circuits. These circuits monitor, condition, amplify, or transform continuous analog signals. **NOTE:** Search and apply for positions online. **Positions advertised include:** Analog IC Design Engineer; CAD Engineer; Customer Service Clerk; Design Technician; ESD Specialist; Field Application Engineer. **Corporate headquarters location:** This location. **Listed on:** NASDAQ. **Stock exchange symbol:** LLTC. **Number of employees at this location:** 1,000.

LIONS GATE ENTERTAINMENT
2700 Colorado Avenue, Suite 200, Santa Monica CA 90404. 310/449-9200. **Fax:** 310/255-3870. **Contact:** Human Resources. **E-mail address:** resumes@lgf.com. **World Wide Web address:** http://www.lionsgatefilms.com. **Description:** Produces, markets, and distributes motion pictures. **Positions advertised include:** Sr. Accountant; Finance Coordinator; Budget Analyst. **Corporate headquarters location:** This location. **Other U.S. locations:** New York NY. **Listed on:** Privately held. **Annual sales/revenues:** $426.6 million.

LITHONIA LIGHTING
1405 East Locust Street, Ontario CA 91761. 909/395-9009. **Contact:** Sue Farrah, Personnel Director. **E-mail address:** recruiter@lithonia.com. **World Wide Web address:** http://www.lithonia.com. **Description:** Manufactures lighting and related products. **Corporate headquarters location:** Conyers GA. **Parent company:** Acuity Brands.

LOCKHEED MARTIN
1121 West Reeves Avenue, Ridgecrest CA 93555. 760/446-1700. **Contact:** Human Resources. **E-mail address:** jobslmc@lmco.com. **World Wide Web address:** http://www.lmco.com. **Description:** Lockheed Martin is an aerospace and technology company engaged in the design, manufacture, and management of systems and products in the fields of space, defense, electronics, communications, information management, energy, and materials. **Corporate headquarters location:** Bethesda MD. **Operations at this facility include:** This location develops threat simulation training equipment for various government agencies. **Listed on:** New York Stock Exchange. **Stock exchange symbol:** LMT. **Number of employees worldwide:** 130,000.

LOCKHEED MARTIN AERONAUTICS
1011 Lockheed Way, Palmdale CA 93550. 805/984-3683. **Contact:** Human Resources. **World Wide Web address:** http://www.lockheedmartin.com. **Description:** Location of advanced development programs, such as electronic warfare simulation systems, detailed system/tactical simulation systems, and C4ISR hardware and software. **NOTE:** Search and apply for positions online.

LOCKHEED MARTIN INTEGRATED SYSTEMS & SOLUTIONS
3200 Zanker Road, San Jose CA 95134. 408/473-3000. **Contact:** Human Resources. **World Wide Web address:** http://www.lockheedmartin.com. **Description:** Provides transformational solutions for intelligence, surveillance and reconnaissance; command and control; communications; and combat support to the U.S. Department of Defense and the intelligence community. **NOTE:** Search and apply for positions online.

LOCKHEED MARTIN SPACE SYSTEMS
P.O. Box 3504, RRC Building 150, Sunnyvale CA 94088-3504. 408/742-7151. **Fax:** 877/244-0989. **Contact:** Personnel. **E-mail address:** jobs.lmms@lmco.com. **World Wide Web address:** http://lmms.external.lmco.com. **Description:** Develops missile systems and high-tech space-related products. **Special programs:** Internships. **Corporate headquarters location:** Littleton CO. **Parent company:** Lockheed Martin Corporation operates in five major areas: Space Systems (develops space technology systems such as rocket systems, Space Shuttle support technology, and other products); Missile Systems (produces fleet ballistic missiles for military applications); Advanced Systems (operates as the research and development organization exploring military, commercial, and scientific needs); Information Processing (develops comprehensive database systems to process the specific needs of other company divisions); and the Austin Division (responsible for designing and producing military tactical support systems). **Operations at this facility include:** Administration; Research and Development. **Listed on:** New York Stock Exchange. **Stock exchange symbol:** LMT. **Number of employees at this location:** 12,000. **Number of employees nationwide:** 14,000.

LOCTITE CORPORATION
15051 East Don Julian Road, City of Industry CA 91746. 626/968-6511. **Contact:** Human Resources. **E-mail address:** hrclassifieds@loctite.com. **World Wide Web address:** http://www.loctite.com. **Description:** Develops and markets adhesives, sealants, and specialty chemicals. **Corporate headquarters location:** Rocky Hill CT. **Parent company:** Henkel Group.

LOCUS TECHNOLOGIES
299 Fairchild Drive, Mountain View CA 94043. 650/960-1640. **Fax:** 650/960-0739. **Contact:** Human Resources. **E-mail address:** humanresources@locustec.com. **World Wide Web address:** http://www.locustec.com. **Description:** A leading environmental consulting, engineering, and remediation services provider. **NOTE:** Candidates should send a resume with salary requirements and references. **Corporate headquarters location:** Walnut Creek CA. **Other area locations:** Middletown CA; Sacramento CA; Los Angeles CA. **Listed on:** Privately held.

LOCUS TECHNOLOGIES
1333 North California Boulevard, Suite 350, Walnut Creek CA 94596. 925/906-8100. **Fax:** 925/906-8101. **Contact:** Human Resources Department. **E-mail address:** humanresources@locustec.com. **World Wide Web address:** http://www.locustec.com. **Description:** A leading environmental consulting, engineering, and remediation services provider. **NOTE:** Candidates should send a resume with salary requirements and references. **Positions advertised include:** Project Scientist; Project Engineer. **Corporate headquarters location:** This location. **Other area locations:** Mountain View CA; Middletown CA; Sacramento CA; Los Angeles CA. **Listed on:** Privately held.

LODI MEMORIAL HOSPITAL
975 South Fairmont Avenue, P.O. Box 3004, Lodi CA 95240-1908. 209/334-3411. **Fax:** 209/339-7687. **Recorded jobline:** 209/339-7562. **Contact:** Mark Wallace, Manager of Human Resources Department. **E-mail address:** humanresources@lodihealth.org. **World Wide Web address:** http://www.lodihealth.org. **Description:** A 172-bed, nonprofit, acute-care hospital. Services include acute physical rehabilitation, subacute services, long-term care, home health care, and adult daycare. **NOTE:** Search and apply for positions online. **Positions advertised include:** Aide; Clerk; Clinical Dietician; Clinical Laboratory Scientist; Certified Nursing Assistant; Licensed Vocational Nurse; Pharmacist; Registered Nurse; Sonographer; Physical Therapist; Occupational Therapist. **Corporate headquarters location:** This location. **Number of employees at this location:** 1,000.

LOEWS CINEPLEX ENTERTAINMENT
1925 Century Park East, Suite 300, Los Angeles CA 90067. 310/553-5307. **Contact:** Personnel. **E-mail address:** jobopps@loewscpx.com. **World Wide Web address:** http://www.enjoytheshow.com. **Description:** One of the world's largest movie theater chains. Loews Cineplex Entertainment operates more than 2,176 screens in 200 locations. **Corporate headquarters location:** New York NY.

LOGAN HEIGHTS FAMILY HEALTH CENTER
1809 National Avenue, San Diego CA 92113. 619/515-2300. **Fax:** 619/232-1360. **Recorded jobline:** 619/515-2572. **Contact:** Human Resources Manager. **World Wide Web address:** http://www.fhcsd.org. **Description:** A nonprofit, community health center. Services include audiology, counseling, dental, dermatology, early intervention, family planning, health promotion, hearing, internal medicine, laboratory, language, OB/GYN, optometry, pediatric cardiology, pediatrics, pharmacy, radiology, social services, and speech. **Special programs:** Internships. **Other U.S. locations:** Mission Beach CA. **Operations at this facility include:** Administration. **Number of employees at this location:** 250.

LOGICAL MAINTENANCE SOLUTIONS
2205 South Wright Street, Santa Ana CA 92705. 714/549-2688. **Toll-free phone:** 800/240-8721. **Contact:** Human Resources. **E-mail address:** info@lmsservice.com. **Description:** Distributes computer printers, accessories, supplies, and enclosures. **Corporate headquarters location:** This location.

LOGITECH, INC.
6505 Kaiser Drive, Fremont CA 94555. 510/795-8500. **Fax:** 510/792-8901. **Contact:** Human Resources Manager. **World Wide Web address:** http://www.logitech.com. **Description:** Designs, develops, manufactures, and markets computer hardware and software products. Logitech is a leading worldwide manufacturer of computer pointing devices including mice, trackballs, and joysticks, and imaging devices such as scanners and cameras for PC, MAC, and other platforms. **Special programs:** Internships. **Corporate headquarters location:** This location. **Other U.S. locations:** Framingham MA; Dallas TX. **Parent company:** Logitech International S.A. **Operations at this facility include:** Administration; Research and Development; Sales. **Listed on:** NASDAQ. **Stock exchange symbol:** LOGI. **Number of employees at this location:** 350.

LONGS DRUG STORES
141 North Civic Drive, Walnut Creek CA 94596. 925/937-1170. **Fax:** 925/522-7202. **Contact:** Employment Manager. **E-mail address:** employment@longs.com. **World Wide Web address:** http://www.longs.com. **Description:** Longs Drug Stores owns and operates a chain of more than 400 retail drug stores that offer a broad range of pharmaceuticals and personal care products. **Positions advertised include:** Construction Contracts Coordinator; Administrative Assistant, Pharmacy; Project Manager; Store Operations Analyst. **Corporate headquarters location:** This location. **Operations at this facility include:** This location houses administrative offices. **Listed on:** New York Stock Exchange. **Stock exchange symbol:** LDG.

LONGVIEW FIBRE COMPANY
8511 Blaine Street, Oakland CA 94621. 510/569-2616. **Fax:** 510/569-8958. **Contact:** J. Jerry Dow, Human Resources Manager. **E-mail address:** info@longfibre.com. **World Wide Web address:** http://www.longviewfibre.com. **Description:** Owns and operates 530,000 acres of tree farms in Oregon and Washington and is a major pulp, wood, and paper products manufacturer. The company has 14 converting plants in 10 states, which produce shipping containers and grocery bags. **NOTE:** Recent college graduates are hired to fill entry-level positions. **Corporate headquarters location:** Longview WA. **Listed on:** New York Stock Exchange. **Stock exchange symbol:** LFB.

LONGWOOD MANOR SANITARIUM
4853 West Washington Boulevard, Los Angeles CA 90001. 323/935-1157. **Fax:** 323/935-3140. **Contact:** Personnel Department. **Description:** A skilled nursing home. Founded in 1970. **NOTE:** Entry-level positions and second and third shifts are offered. **Office hours:** Monday - Friday, 9:00 a.m. - 4:30 p.m.

LOS ANGELES ATHLETIC CLUB
431 West Seventh Street, Los Angeles CA 90014. 213/625-2211. **Fax:** 213/625-0128. **Contact:** Human Resources Department. **E-mail address:** laaco.jobs@laac.net. **World Wide Web address:** http://www.laac.com. **Description:** Operates an athletic facility with programs in virtually every sport, as well as concession, banquet, and guest hotel facilities. **Corporate headquarters location:** This location. **Other area locations:** Marina del Rey CA; Orange CA. **Operations at this facility include:** Administration; Sales; Service. **Listed on:** Privately held. **Number of employees at this location:** 240. **Number of employees nationwide:** 370.

THE LOS ANGELES COMMUNITY COLLEGES DISTRICT OFFICE
770 Wilshire Boulevard, Los Angeles CA 90017. 213/891-2000. **Fax:** 213/891-2411. **Contact:** Human Resources. **E-mail address:** jobs@laccd.cc.ca.us. **World Wide Web address:** http://www.laccd.edu. **Description:** Encompasses nine community colleges. **Positions advertised include:** English Instructor; Associate Vice Chancellor; Executive Assistant; Physical Sciences Laboratory Technician; Executive Legal Secretary; Registration Assistant.

LOS ANGELES, COUNTY OF
3333 Wilshire Boulevard, Suite 100, Los Angeles CA 90010. 213/738-2084. **Recorded jobline:** 800/970-5478. **Contact:** Human Resources. **World Wide Web address:** http://www.lacounty.info. **Description:** Administrative offices for the government of Los Angeles County. **NOTE:** See website for job listings and application procedures. Apply online or in person at the Human Resources office. **Special programs:** Internships. **Office hours:** Monday – Friday, 8:00 a.m. – 5:00 p.m.

THE LOS ANGELES COUNTY ARBORETUM & BOTANIC GARDEN
301 North Baldwin Avenue, Arcadia CA 91007. 626/821-3222. **Fax:** 626/445-1217.

Contact: Human Resources. **World Wide Web address:** http://www.arboretum.org. **Description:** The Arboretum is a 127-acre botanical garden and historical site jointly operated by the Los Angeles Arboretum Foundation and the Los Angeles County Department of Parks and Recreation. Founded in 1949. **Positions advertised include:** Development Manager.

LOS ANGELES COUNTY DEPARTMENT OF HEALTH SERVICES
5555 Ferguson Drive, Room 200-01, City of Commerce CA 90022. **Recorded jobline:** 800/970-5478. **Contact:** Human Resources. **E-mail address:** hr@adhs.org. **World Wide Web address:** http://www.ladhs.org. **Description:** An organization that encompasses all the county's health offices including those facilities in Acton, Torrance, Lancaster and Sylmar CA. **NOTE:** See website for job listings for all the county's health services facilities. A completed application is required for any position. See website for additional application submission procedures.

LOS ANGELES COUNTY MUSEUM OF ART
5905 Wilshire Boulevard, Los Angeles CA 90036. 323/857-6000. **Fax:** 323/857-4720. **Recorded jobline:** 323/857-6069. **Contact:** Adam Kaplan, Employment Administrator. **E-mail address:** jobs@lacma.org. **World Wide Web address:** http://www.lacma.org. **Description:** A premier visual arts museum. The museum's collection expresses the creativity of cultures from all over the world. Founded in 1938. **NOTE:** Entry-level positions and part-time jobs are offered. No phone calls please. **Positions advertised include:** Director of Conservation; Director of Development Head Librarian; Membership Systems Specialist; Senior Conservation Scientist; Membership Services Assistant. **Special programs:** Internships. **Office hours:** Monday - Friday, 8:00 a.m. - 5:00 p.m.

LOS ANGELES DODGERS
1000 Elysian Park Avenue, Los Angeles CA 90012. 323/224-1500. **Fax:** 323/224-2606. **Contact:** Human Resources. **World Wide Web address:** http://losangeles.dodgers.mlb.com. **Description:** The offices for the National League baseball team. **Positions advertised include:** Stadium Operations Assistant; Security Manager. **Special programs:** Internships.

LOS ANGELES MAGAZINE
5900 Wilshire Boulevard, 10th Floor, Los Angeles CA 90036. 323/801-0100. **Fax:** 323/801-0104. **Contact:** Human Resources. **World Wide Web address:** http://www.lamag.com. **Description:** A city magazine that focuses on local issues, people, trends, events, and lifestyles. *Los Angeles Magazine* also includes options and opportunities available throughout the Southern California area. Founded in 1960. **NOTE:** Entry-level positions are offered. **Special programs:** Internships. **Corporate headquarters location:** This location. **Parent company:** Emmis Communications Inc. **Listed on:** NASDAQ. **Stock exchange symbol:** EMMS. **Number of employees at this location:** 50.

LOS ANGELES TIMES
202 West First Street, Los Angeles CA 90012. 213/237-5000. **Contact:** Human Resources. **World Wide Web address:** http://www.latimes.com. **Description:** Publishes a daily newspaper with a circulation of over 1 million. **Parent company:** The Tribune Company (Chicago IL). **Listed on:** New York Stock Exchange. **Stock exchange symbol:** TRB.

LOS ANGELES ZOO
5333 Zoo Drive, Los Angeles CA 90027. 323/666-4650. **Contact:** Personnel. **World Wide Web address:** http://www.lazoo.org. **Description:** A zoo that houses a fully equipped animal hospital and animal health center, an animal food commissary, and a horticultural section. **NOTE:** For employment information, contact: Los Angeles City Personnel Department, Room 100, City Hall South, Los Angeles CA 90012. 213/847-9240, http://www.cityofla.org/PER/index.htm. **Number of employees at this location:** 180.

LOTUS DEVELOPMENT CORPORATION
425 Market Street, 25th Floor, San Francisco CA 94105. 415/545-3800. **Contact:** Human Resources. **World Wide Web address:** http://www.lotus.com/jobs. **Description:** Develops, manufactures, and markets applications software and services that meet the evolving technology and business applications requirements of individuals, work groups, and entire organizations. **Corporate headquarters location:** Cambridge MA. **Parent company:** IBM Corporation. **Listed on:** New York Stock Exchange. **Stock exchange symbol:** IBM.

LOYOLA MARYMOUNT UNIVERSITY
One LMU Drive, Suite 1900, Los Angeles CA 90045. 310/338-2723. **Fax:** 310/338-7711. **Recorded jobline:** 310/338-4488. **Contact:** Human Resources. **E-mail address:** jobs@lmu.edu. **World Wide Web address:** http://www.lmu.edu. **Description:** A private, four-year college offering certificates, bachelor's degrees, and master's degrees including a Master's in Business Administration. Approximately 3,800 undergraduate and 1,000 graduate students attend Loyola Marymount University. **Positions advertised include:** Assistant Director, Campus Recreation; Assistant Director, Judicial Affairs; Student Life Coordinator; Development Director; Financial Aid Counselor; Nurse Practitioner; Sports Medicine Assistant; Technology Coordinator; Therapist; Web Editor; Administrative Assistant; Lead Teacher; Teacher Assistant; Custodian.

LUCAS ARTS ENTERTAINMENT COMPANY
P.O. Box 10307, San Rafael CA 94912. 415/472-3400. **Fax:** 415/444-8438. **Contact:** HR Recruiting. **World Wide Web address:** http://www.lucasarts.com. **Description:** An international developer and publisher of entertainment software, some of which incorporate a Star Wars theme. **Positions advertised include:** Financial Analyst; Producer; Sr. Character Technical Director; Marketing Coordinator. **Corporate headquarters location:** This location.

LUCASFILM LTD.
P.O. Box 10228, San Rafael CA 94912. 415/662-1700. **Fax:** 415/662-7460. **Contact:** Human Resources. **World Wide Web address:** http://www.lucasfilm.com. **Description:** A leading film production company specializing in visual and sound effects. **Positions advertised include:** Production Finance Director; Trademark and Legal Assistant; Internal Audit Manager; Senior Human Resources Manager; Director of Publishing; Marketing Manager. **Special programs:** Internships. **Corporate headquarters location:** This location.

LUCE FORWARD
600 West Broadway, Suite 2600, San Diego CA 92101-3372. 619/236-1414. **Fax:** 619/232-8311. **Contact:** Kathryn Karpinksi, Human Resources. **E-mail address:** legalrecruiting@luce.com. **World Wide Web address:** http://www.luce.com. **Description:** A law firm specializing in corporate, environmental, immigration, and real estate law. **NOTE:** The above e-mail address is for attorney positions only. For inquiries regarding staff positions contact: staffrecruiting@luce.com. Candidates may also apply for positions online. Unsolicited resumes not accepted. **Positions advertised include:** Insurance Litigation Associate; Real Estate Associate. **Special programs:** Summer Associate Program. **Corporate headquarters location:** This location.

LUCENT TECHNOLOGIES INTERNETWORKING SYSTEMS
1001 Murphy Ranch Road, Milpitas CA 95035. 408/321-2000. **Contact:** Human Resources. **World Wide Web address:** http://www.lucent.com. **Description:** Develops, manufactures, markets, and supports a family of high-performance, multiservice wide area network (WAN) switches that enable public carrier providers and private network managers to provide cost-effective, high-speed, enhanced data communications services. These products direct and manage data communications across wide area networks that utilize different network architectures and services, and are designed to support, on a single platform, the major high-speed packet data communications services. These services include frame relay, switched multimegabit data service, and asynchronous transfer mode. The company markets its products to interexchange carriers, local exchange carriers, competitive access providers, other public network providers, and private network managers. **Corporate headquarters location:** Murray Hill NJ. **Listed on:** New York Stock Exchange. **Stock exchange symbol:** LU. **Number of employees worldwide:** 32,500.

LUCENT TECHNOLOGIES INTERNETWORKING SYSTEMS
1701 Harbor Bay Parkway, Alameda CA 94502. 510/769-6001. **Contact:** Human Resources. **World Wide Web address:** http://www.lucent.com. **Description:** Develops, manufactures, markets, and supports a family of high-performance, multiservice wide area network (WAN) switches that enable public carrier providers and private network managers to provide cost-effective, high-speed, enhanced data communications services. These products direct and manage data communications across wide area networks that utilize different network architectures and services, and are designed to support, on a single platform, the major high-speed packet data communications services. These services include frame relay, switched multimegabit data service, and asynchronous transfer mode. The company markets its products to public network providers, including interexchange carriers, local exchange carriers, competitive access providers, other public network providers, and private network managers. **Positions advertised include:** Senior Systems Engineer; Senior Security Consultant. **Corporate headquarters location:** Murray Hill NJ. **Listed on:** New York Stock Exchange. **Stock exchange symbol:** LU. **Number of employees at this location:** 80. **Number of employees worldwide:** 32,500.

LUFKIN INDUSTRIES INC.
30011 Ivy Glenn Drive, Suite 222, Laguna Niguel CA 92677-5017. 949/249-7850. **Contact:** Viron Barbay, Human Resources (Texas headquarters office). **E-mail address:** vbarbay@lufkin.com. **World Wide Web address:** http://www.lufkin.com. **NOTE:** Please submit resumes to: Human Resources, Lufkin Industries, P.O. Box 849, Lufkin TX 75902. Fax: 936/637-5475. **Description:** Lufkin Industries manufactures and markets products to global industrial, energy, and transportation companies through its four divisions: Oilfield, Foundry, Trailer, and Power Transmission. **Corporate headquarters location:** Lufkin TX. **Operations at this facility include:** This location manufactures gearboxes as part of the company's power transmission division. **Listed on:** NASDAQ. **Stock exchange symbol:** LUFK.

LUMENIS
2400 Condensa Street, Santa Clara CA 95051. 408/764-3000. **Toll-free phone:** 800/635-1313. **Fax:** 408/764-3948. **Contact:** Human Resources. **World Wide Web address:** http://www.lumenis.com. **Description:** Manufactures and markets a wide variety of specialty lasers for the medical, scientific, and commercial fields. **NOTE:** Search and apply for positions online. **Positions advertised include:** Senior Development Engineer; Service Contract Specialist; Administrative Assistant; Program Specialist; Area Sales Manager; Customer Relations Representative; Commissions Analyst. **Corporate headquarters location:** Yokneam Israel. **Other U.S. locations:** New York NY. **International locations:** Worldwide. **Operations at this facility include:** Administration; Research and Development; Sales; Service. **Listed on:** NASDAQ. **Stock exchange symbol:** LUME.

LUMETRA
One Sansome Street, Suite 600, San Francisco CA 94104-4448. 415/677-2000. **Fax:** 415/677-2190. **Contact:** Human Resources. **E-mail address:** humanresources@lumetra.com. **World Wide Web address:** http://www/lumetra.com. **Description:** A non-profit organization dedicated to improving the quality and safety of healthcare. **Positions advertised include:** Assistant Appeals Manager; Communications Specialist; Quality Improvement Advisor; Sr. Appeals Specialist. **Corporate headquarters location:** This location. **Other U.S. locations:** Columbia MD.

WILLIAM LYON COMPANY
4490 Von Karman Avenue, Newport Beach CA 92660. 949/833-3600. **Fax:** 949/252-2520. **Contact:** Personnel. **World Wide Web address:** http://www.lyonhomes.com. **Description:** Engaged in home building, financing, and land development. Assets include apartments and commercial real estate that the Hughes Investment Company and Koll Company assist in developing. Lyon also finances residential development through companies such as Warmington Homes, the Aikens Development Company, and the Lusk Company. **NOTE:** Contact information may vary. See job postings on website for more specific instructions on how to apply. **Corporate headquarters location:** This location. **Listed on:** New York Stock Exchange. **Stock exchange symbol:** WLS.

MAI SYSTEMS CORPORATION
HOTEL INFORMATION SYSTEMS
26110 Enterprise Way, Suite 200, Lake Forest CA 92630. 949/598-6000. **Toll-free phone:** 800/497-0532. **Fax:** 949/598-6324. **Contact:** Human Resources. **World Wide Web address:** http://www.maisystems.com. **Description:** A worldwide provider of information systems solutions software for the hospitality industry and mid-size manufacturers and distributors. **Positions advertised include:** Cognos Developer. **Corporate headquarters location:** This location. **Other U.S. locations:** San Francisco CA; Boston MA; Tampa FL; Washington DC; Whitehouse Station NJ; Dallas TX. **International locations:** China; Indonesia; Malaysia; Singapore; United Kingdom. **Operations at this facility include:** Administration; Manufacturing; Research and Development; Sales; Service. **Listed on:** American Stock Exchange. **Stock exchange symbol:** NOW.

MGM INC.
10250 Constellation Boulevard, Los Angeles CA 90067. 310/449-3000. **Recorded jobline:** 310/449-3569. **Contact:** Human Resources Department. **World Wide Web address:** http://www.mgm.com. **Description:** A fully integrated media company providing entertainment through the production and distribution of feature films, television programs, animation, music, and interactive games. **NOTE:** Search and apply for positions online. **Positions advertised include:** Data Warehouse Analyst; Unix Systems Administrator; Category Management Analyst. **Special programs:**

Internships. **Corporate headquarters location:** This location. **Listed on:** New York Stock Exchange. **Stock exchange symbol:** MGM.

MSC SOFTWARE CORPORATION
2 MacArthur Place, Santa Ana CA 92707. 714/540-8900. **Fax:** 714/784-4491. **Contact:** Human Resources, Professional Staffing. **E-mail address:** msc.jobs@mscsoftware.com. **World Wide Web address:** http://www.mscsoftware.com. **Description:** Develops, markets, and supports software for computer-aided engineering. **Positions advertised include:** Consulting Engineer; Manager of Compensation; Web Developer; Logistics Administrator. **Corporate headquarters location:** This location. **Listed on:** New York Stock Exchange. **Stock exchange symbol:** MNS.

MTI TECHNOLOGIES CORPORATION
14661 Franklin Avenue, Tustin CA 92780. 714/481-7800. **Fax:** 714/481-4137. **Contact:** Human Resources. **E-mail address:** jobs@mti.com. **World Wide Web address:** http://www.mti.com. **Description:** Designs, manufactures, markets, and services high-performance storage solutions for the DEC, IBM, and open UNIX systems computing environments. These storage solutions integrate MTI's proprietary application and embedded software with its advanced servers and industry standard storage peripherals. Products include NetBacker client/server application software, Infinity Automated Tape Library Series, and other systems and related application software. **Positions advertised include:** Open Software Implementation Engineer; Storage Solution Architect; Project Manager. **Corporate headquarters location:** This location.

MWH LABORATORIES
750 Royal Oaks Drive, Suite 100, Monrovia CA 91016. 626/386-1100. **Fax:** 626/386-1101. **Contact:** Corporate Human Resources. **E-mail address:** Damian J Guerin@mwhglobal.com. **World Wide Web address:** http://www.mwlaboratories.com. **Description:** Offers engineering consulting services for water, wastewater, and hazardous waste facilities. **Positions advertised include:** Staff Chemist; Administrative Assistant. **Special programs:** Internships. **Corporate headquarters location:** This location. **Other U.S. locations:** Nationwide. **Parent company:** MWH Americas, Inc. **Annual sales/revenues:** More than $100 million.

MACKENZIE COMMUNICATIONS, INC.
423 Washington Street, 6th Floor, San Francisco CA 94111. 415/403-0800. **Fax:** 415/403-0801. **Contact:** Human Resources. **E-mail address:** info@mackenziesf.com. **World Wide Web address:** http://www.mackenziesf.com. **Description:** A public relations firm that serves a wide range of industries including banking, law, and public service. **Corporate headquarters location:** This location.

MACROMEDIA, INC.
600 Townsend Street, San Francisco CA 94103. 415/252-2000. **Fax:** 415/626-0554. **Contact:** Personnel. **World Wide Web address:** http://www.macromedia.com. **Description:** Develops multimedia software for the Web. **NOTE:** Search and apply for positions online. **Positions advertised include:** Developer Support and Services Engineer; Director, Communications software Engineering; International Development Engineer; Principal Technical Writer; Media Director; Marketing Analyst. **Special programs:** Internships. **Corporate headquarters location:** This location. **Other U.S. locations:** San Diego, CA; Newton MA; Bethesda MD. **Listed on:** NASDAQ. **Stock exchange symbol:** MACR. **Number of employees worldwide:** 1,200.

MACY'S WEST
50 O'Farrell Street, San Francisco CA 94102. 415/954-6671. **Contact:** Human Resources. **World Wide Web address:** http://www.macys.com. **Description:** A location of the retail department store chain. **NOTE:** Search and apply for positions online. **Positions advertised include:** Business Manager; Database Administrator; Margin Analyst; Planner; Project Manager; Visual Merchandising Designer. **Corporate headquarters location:** New York NY. **Parent company:** Federated Department Stores.

MACY'S UNION SQUARE
170 O'Farrell Street, San Francisco CA 94102. 415/397-3333. **Contact:** Human Resources. **World Wide Web address:** http://www.macys.com. **Description:** One of three divisions of R.H. Macy Company (New York NY). Macy's Union Square operates 50 stores regionally as part of the full-line department store chain. **Corporate headquarters location:** New York NY. **Operations at this facility include:** Divisional Headquarters. **Parent company:** Federated Department Stores.

MADISON INDUSTRIES, INC.
1900 East 64th Street, Los Angeles CA 90001. 323/583-4061. **Fax:** 323/582-1015. **Contact:** Personnel. **World Wide Web address:** http://www.madisonind.com. **Description:** A construction company involved in maintenance, installations, manufacturing, engineering, and design. Madison's manufacturing facilities provide the various metal components needed to complete its building projects. **Corporate headquarters location:** This location. **Other U.S. locations:** Arizona; Oklahoma; Georgia.

MAIL BOXES ETC.
6060 Cornerstone Court West, San Diego CA 92121. 858/455-8800. **Fax:** 858/625-3159. **Contact:** Human Resources. **E-mail address:** jobs@mbe.com. **World Wide Web address:** http://www.mbe.com. **Description:** Operates through two wholly owned subsidiaries. Mail Boxes Etc. provides franchisees with a system of business training, site location, marketing, advertising programs, and management support designed to assist the franchisee in opening and operating MBE Centers. **Positions advertised include:** Technical Trainer Supervisor; Sr. Programmer Analyst; Product Development Specialist. **Corporate headquarters location:** This location. **Subsidiaries include:** Mail Boxes Etc. USA grants territorial franchise rights for the operation or sale of service centers specializing in postal, packaging, business, and communications services. MBE Service Corp. offers electronic tax filing services. **Parent company:** UPS. **Listed on:** New York Stock Exchange. **Stock exchange symbol:** UPS.

MANUFACTURERS BANK
P.O. Box 556000, Los Angeles CA 90055-1000. 213/489-6200. **Physical address:** 515 South Figueroa Street, 2nd Floor, Los Angeles CA 90071. **Contact:** Ted Mergenthaler, Director of Human Resources. **E-mail address:** hr@manubank.com. **World Wide Web address:** http://www.manubank.com. **Description:** A banking institution offering a wide range of services including checking and savings accounts; certificates of deposit; commercial, industrial, real estate, and installment loans; direct and leveraged leases; collections; escrow services; and letters of credit. **Corporate headquarters location:** This location. **Other area locations:** Beverly Hills CA; Newport Beach CA; Encino CA; Torrance CA; City of Industry CA; San Diego CA. **Parent company:** Mitsui Bank, Ltd. **Operations at this facility include:** Administration; Regional Headquarters. **Listed on:** NASDAQ. **Stock exchange symbol:** MITSY.

MANUGISTICS
26707 Agoura Road, Suite A, B, E, Calabasas CA 91302-2966. 818/737-7600. **Contact:** Human Resources. **E-mail address:** jobs@manu.com. **World Wide Web address:** http://www.manugistics.com. **Description:** Manugistics develops defense systems software. **NOTE:** Search and apply for positions online. **Positions advertised include:** Customer Service Account Manager. **Corporate headquarters location:** Rockville MD. **Other area locations:** Newport Beach CA; San Carlos CA. **Other U.S. locations:** Chicago IL; Atlanta GA. **Listed on:** NASDAQ. **Stock exchange symbol:** MANU.

MARIN COMMUNITY COLLEGE (COLLEGE OF MARIN)
835 College Avenue, Kentfield CA 94904. 415/485-9340. **Fax:** 415/485-0135. **Recorded jobline:** 415/485-9693. **E-mail address:** hrjobs@marin.cc.ca.us. **World Wide Web address:** http://www.marin.cc.ca.us. **Description:** A community college. **Positions advertised include:** Financial Aid Assistant; Instructor, Various Departments.

THE MARLEY COOLING TOWER COMPANY
150 North Wagner Avenue, Stockton CA 95215. 209/465-3451. **Contact:** Personnel. **Description:** Manufactures wooden cooling towers that are used in various industrial applications. **Corporate headquarters location:** Overland Park KS.

MARRIOTT SANTA CLARA
2700 Mission College Boulevard, Santa Clara CA 95054. 408/988-1500. **Fax:** 408/352-4353. **Contact:** Recruiter. **World Wide Web address:** http://www.marriott.com. **Description:** Operates a hotel with complete dining and recreational facilities. **Corporate headquarters location:** Washington DC. **Parent company:** Marriott International, Inc. **Listed on:** New York Stock Exchange. **Stock exchange symbol:** MAR.

MARSH RISK & INSURANCE SERVICES
777 South Figueroa Street, Los Angeles CA 90017-5822. 213/624-5555. **Contact:** Employment Manager. **E-mail address:** employment.jobs@marsh.com. **World Wide Web address:** http://www.marsh.com. **Description:** A professional firm that provides advice and services worldwide through an insurance brokerage and risk management firm, reinsurance intermediary facilities, and a consulting and financial services group, to clients concerned with the management of assets and risks. **NOTE:** Search and apply for positions online. **Positions advertised include:** Client/Carrier Accountant. **Corporate headquarters location:** New York NY. **Parent company:** Marsh & McLennan Companies, Inc.

MARSH RISK & INSURANCE SERVICES
One California Street, 5th Floor, San Francisco CA 94111. 415/743-8000. **Contact:** Human Resources. **E-mail address:** employment.jobs@marsh.com. **World Wide Web address:** http://www.marsh.com. **Description:** A professional firm that provides advice and services worldwide through an insurance brokerage and risk management firm, reinsurance intermediary facilities, and a consulting and financial services group to clients concerned with the management of assets and risks. Specific services include insurance and risk management services, reinsurance, consulting and financial services, consulting, merchandising, and investment management. **NOTE:** Search and apply for positions online. **Positions advertised include:** Client Representative. **Corporate headquarters location:** New York NY. **Parent company:** Marsh & McLennan Companies, Inc.

MARSHALLS OF SAN FRANCISCO
901 Market Street, San Francisco CA 94103. 415/974-5368. **Contact:** Human Resources. **World Wide Web address:** http://www.marshallsonline.com. **Description:** An off-price retail organization providing wide assortments of men's, women's, and children's apparel, footwear, accessories, and selected home furnishings at over 500 locations nationwide. **NOTE:** Search and apply for positions online. **Positions advertised include:** Cashier; Merchandise Associate; Processor. **Corporate headquarters location:** Framingham MA. **Parent company:** TJX. **Listed on:** New York Stock Exchange. **Stock exchange symbol:** TJX.

MASTERFOODS USA
P.O. Box 58853, Vernon CA 90058-0853. 323/587-2727. **Physical address:** 3250 East 44th Street, Vernon CA 90058. **Contact:** Personnel Director. **World Wide Web address:** http://www.mars.com. **Description:** Manufactures pet foods. Founded in 1936. **Positions advertised include:** Analytical Laboratory Technician; Customer Service Representative. **Corporate headquarters location:** This location. **Parent company:** Mars, Inc.

MATHESON TRI GAS
6775 Central Avenue, Newark CA 94560. 510/793-2559. **Fax:** 510/790-6241. **Contact:** Human Resources. **E-mail address:** hr-recruitment@matheson-trigas.com. **World Wide Web address:** http://www.mathesontrigas.com. **Description:** Distributes regulators, valves, and gas mixtures to gas companies. **Corporate headquarters location:** Parsippany NJ.

MATICH CORPORATION
P.O. Box 50000, San Bernardino CA 92412. 909/382-7400. **Physical address:** 1596 Harry Sheppard Boulevard, San Bernardino CA 92408. **Fax:** 909/382-0169. **Contact:** Human Resources. **World Wide Web address:** http://www.matichicm.com. **Description:** An asphalt paving and manufacturing company. Matich Corporation is also a highway contractor and construction management firm. Founded in 1918. **Corporate headquarters location:** This location. **Listed on:** Privately held. **Annual sales/revenues:** $21 - $50 million.

MATRIA HEALTHCARE
17701 Cowan Avenue, Suite 150, Irvine CA 92614. 949/794-6500. **Toll-free phone:** 800/456-4060. **Contact:** Human Resources. **E-mail address:** matriahr@matria.com. **World Wide Web address:** http://www.matria.com. **Description:** Offers medical services for pregnant women via 24-hour hotlines. Matria Healthcare is subcontracted through insurance companies. **Corporate headquarters location:** Marietta GA. **Listed on:** NASDAQ. **Stock exchange symbol:** MATR.

MATTEL INC.
333 Continental Boulevard, El Segundo CA 90245-5012. 310/252-2000. **Contact:** Corporate Staffing. **World Wide Web address:** http://www.mattel.com. **Description:** Produces and distributes toys, electronic products, games, books, hobby products, and family entertainment products. **Positions advertised include:** National Account Manager; Sr. HRIS Analyst; Applications Developer; Project Engineer. **Corporate headquarters location:** This location. **Other U.S. locations:** East Aurora NY; Chicago IL; Mount Laurel NJ; New York NY; Phoenix AZ; Madison WI. **Listed on:** New York Stock Exchange. **Stock exchange symbol:** MAT. **Number of employees at this location:** 2,000. **Number of employees worldwide:** 25,000.

MATTSON TECHNOLOGY
47131 Bayside Parkway, Fremont CA 94538. 510/657-5900. **Toll-free phone:** 800/635-2250. **Fax:** 510/492-5911. **Contact:** Human Resources. **E-mail address:** hr@matson.com. **World Wide Web address:** http://www.mattson.com. **Description:** Manufactures rapid thermal processing systems for the semiconductor industry. **Positions advertised include:** Software Engineer; Spare Parts Specialist. **Office hours:** Monday - Friday, 8:00 a.m. - 5:00 p.m. **Corporate headquarters location:** This location. **International locations:** Worldwide. **Parent company:** Mattson Technology, Inc. **Listed on:** NASDAQ. **Stock exchange symbol:** MTSN. **Annual sales/revenues:** $203.5 million. **Number of employees worldwide:** 687.

MAURY MICROWAVE CORPORATION
2900 Inland Empire Boulevard, Ontario CA 91764. 909/987-4715. **Fax:** 909/987-5855. **Contact:** Becky Replogle, Human Resources Manager. **E-mail address:** hr@maurymw.com. **World Wide Web address:** http://www.maurymw.com. **Description:** Manufactures microwave components and instruments. **Positions advertised include:** Controller; Microwave Tuner Engineer; Buyer. **Corporate headquarters location:** This location.

MAXTOR CORPORATION
500 McCarthy Boulevard, Milpitas Ca 95035. 408/894-5000. **Fax:** 408/894-6049. **Contact:** Human Resources. **E-mail address:** staffing_ca@maxtor.com. **World Wide Web address:** http://www.maxtor.com. **Description:** Manufactures hard disk drives and related electronic data storage equipment for computers, as well as related components for original equipment manufacturers. **Positions advertised include:** Assistant Treasurer; Senior Staff roduct Manager; Senior Technician; Senior Engineer Reliability. **Special programs:** Internships. **Corporate headquarters location:** This location. **International locations:** Hong Kong; Singapore. **Listed on:** New York Stock Exchange. **Stock exchange symbol:** MXO.

MAY DEPARTMENT STORES COMPANY
6160 Laurel Canyon Boulevard, North Hollywood CA 91606. 818/508-5226. **Contact:** Employment Office. **World Wide Web address:** http://www2.mayco.com. **Description:** Owns and operates a chain of 491 department stores in 46 states. **Corporate headquarters location:** St. Louis MO. **Listed on:** New York Stock Exchange. **Stock exchange symbol:** MAY.

THE McCLATCHY COMPANY
P.O. Box 15779, Sacramento CA 95852. 916/321-1846. **Physical address:** 2100 Q Street, Sacramento CA 95816. **Contact:** Human Resources. **World Wide Web address:** http://www.mcclatchy.com. **Description:** Publishes 12 daily and 18 community newspapers with a combined average circulation of 1.4 million daily and 1.9 million Sunday. **Positions advertised include:** Administrative Assistant; Benefits Analyst; Communications Manager; Internal Auditor. **Corporate headquarters location:** This location. **Listed on:** New York Stock Exchange. **Stock exchange symbol:** MNI. **Number of employees nationwide:** 9,300.

McCORMICK & COMPANY
P.O. Box 81311, Salinas CA 93912-1311. 831/758-2411. **Physical address:** 1311 Schilling Place, Salinas CA 93901. **Contact:** David Miller, Human Relations Manager. **World Wide Web address:** http://www.mccormick.com. **Description:** McCormick & Company is a diversified specialty food company engaged in manufacturing and marketing seasonings and flavoring products to the food industry. Products are sold in 84 countries and processed at more than 40 facilities throughout the world. Principal products include spices, herbs, vegetable products, seasoning blends, and seasoning mixes. **NOTE:** Search and apply for positions online. **Positions advertised include:** Cost Analyst. **Corporate headquarters location:** Baltimore MD. **Operations at this facility include:** This location is a spice processing plant. **Listed on:** New York Stock Exchange. **Stock exchange symbol:** MKC.

McELROY METAL INC.
P.O. Box 127, Adelanto CA 92301. 760/246-5545. **Physical address:** 17031 Koala Road, Adelanto CA 92301. **Contact:** Human Resources. **World Wide Web address:** http://www.mcelroymetal.com. **Description:** Manufactures metal siding and roofing. **Corporate headquarters location:** Shreveport LA. **Other U.S. locations:** Nationwide. **Annual sales/revenues:** Less than $5 million. **Number of employees at this location:** 35. **Number of employees nationwide:** 300.

McGRAW-HILL COMPANY
160 Spear Street, San Francisco CA 94105. 415/357-8000. **Contact:** Personnel. **E-mail address:** career_ops@mcgraw-hill.com. **World Wide Web address:** http://www.mcgraw-hill.com. **Description:** McGraw-Hill is a provider of information and services through books, magazines, newsletters, software, CD-ROMs, and online data, fax, and TV broadcasting services. The company operates four network-affiliated TV stations and also publishes *Business Week* magazine and books for college, medical, international, legal, and professional markets. McGraw-Hill also offers financial services including Standard & Poor's, commodity items, and international and logistics management products and services. **NOTE:** Search and apply for positions online. **Corporate headquarters location:** New York NY. **Listed on:** New York Stock Exchange. **Stock exchange symbol:** MHP.

McGRAW-HILL COMPANY
5939 Darwin Court, Suites 106-109, Carlsbad CA 92008. 866/433-6995. **Contact:** Human Resources. **E-mail address:** career_ops@mcgraw-hill.com. **World Wide Web address:** http://www.mcgraw-hill.com. **Description:** One of the nation's largest book and magazine publishers. McGraw-Hill is a provider of information and services through books, magazines, newsletters, software, CD-ROMs, and online data, fax, and TV broadcasting services. The company operates four network-affiliated TV stations and also publishes *Business Week* magazine and books for college, medical, international, legal, and professional markets. McGraw-Hill also offers financial services including Standard & Poor's, commodity items, and international and logistics management products and services. **Corporate headquarters location:** New York NY. **Listed on:** New York Stock Exchange. **Stock exchange symbol:** MHP.

MCGRAW-HILL EDUCATION
20 Ryan Ranch Road, Monterey CA 93940. 831/393-0700. **Contact:** Human Resources. **World Wide Web address:** http://www.mcgraw-hill.com. A leading publisher of standardized achievement tests for children and adults. **NOTE:** Search and apply for positions online. **Positions advertised include:** Sales Support Representative; Technology Development Manager; Test Engineer; Editing, Design and Production Director. **Corporate headquarters location:** New York NY. **Listed on:** New York Stock Exchange. **Stock exchange symbol:** MHP.

McJUNKIN CORPORATION
2064 East University Drive, Rancho Dominguez CA 90220-6419. 310/605-5392. **Fax:** 310/537-2464. **Contact:** Human Resources. **World Wide Web address:** http://www.mcjunkin.com. **Description:** A distributor of pipe, valves, fittings, power transmission products, and general industrial products. **Corporate headquarters location:** Charleston West Virginia. **Operations at this facility include:** Sales.

McKESSON
One Post Street, 31st Floor, San Francisco CA 94104. 415/983-8300. **Fax:** 415/983-8900. **Contact:** Personnel. **E-mail address:** jobs.infosolutions@mckesson.com. **World Wide Web address:** http://www.mckesson.com. **Description:** Provides information systems and technology to health care enterprises including hospitals, integrated delivery networks, and managed care organizations. McKessonHBOC's primary products are Pathways 2000, a family of client/server-based applications that allow the integration and uniting of health care providers; STAR, Series, and HealthQuest transaction systems; TRENDSTAR decision support system; and QUANTUM enterprise information system. The company also offers outsourcing services that include strategic information systems planning, data center operations, receivables management, business office administration, and major system conversions. Founded in 1833. **Positions advertised include:** EBIS Technical Architect; Marketing Manager; QA Analyst; Sr. EAI Specialist; Sr. Developer/Analyst. **Corporate headquarters location:** This location. **Other U.S. locations:** Nationwide. **Subsidiaries include:** Automated Healthcare Inc.; Healthcare Delivery Systems, Inc.; McKesson BioServices Corporation; McKesson Pharmacy Systems; Medis Health and Pharmaceutical Services, Inc.; MedPath; U.S. Healthcare; Zee Medical, Inc. **Operations at this facility include:** Administration. **Listed on:** New York Stock Exchange. **Stock exchange symbol:** MCK. **Number of employees at this location:** 700. **Number of employees nationwide:** 24,500.

McKESSON MEDICAL SURGICAL
30497 Canwood Street, Suite 201, Agoura Hills CA 91301. 818/879-0649. **Contact:** Personnel. **World Wide Web address:** http://www. mckesson.com. **Description:** Provides personal health management services to members and consumers through broadcast, telephone, and computer-based programs. Programs include health counseling and prevention services. **Corporate headquarters location:** San Francisco CA.

McMASTER-CARR SUPPLY COMPANY
P.O. Box 54960, Los Angeles CA 90054. 562/695-2449. **Physical Address:** 9630 Norwalk Boulevard, Santa Fe Springs CA 90670. **Contact:** Personnel. **E-mail address:** recruiting@mcmaster.com. **World Wide Web address:** http://www.mcmaster.com. **Description:** A distributor of industrial products and supplies including a complete line of products for maintaining a manufacturing facility. The company's broad customer base includes most major manufacturers in North America, as well as many major industrial firms in South and Central America, the Middle and Far East, and Africa. **Corporate headquarters location:** Chicago IL. **Other U.S. locations:** Atlanta GA; Dayton NJ; Cleveland OH. **Listed on:** Privately held.

MEADE INSTRUMENTS CORPORATION
6001 Oak Canyon, Irvine CA 92618. 949/451-1450. **Fax:** 949/451-1460. **Contact:** Human Resources. **World Wide Web address:** http://www.meade.com. **Description:** Manufactures telescopes, microscopes, and binoculars. Meade Instruments Corporation also manufactures a variety of accessories including photographic adapters, autoguiders, and eyepieces. Founded in 1972. **Corporate headquarters location:** This location. **Listed on:** NASDAQ. **Stock exchange symbol:** MEAD. **Annual sales/revenues:** More than $100 million.

MED-DESIGN CORPORATION
2810 Bunsen Avenue, Ventura CA 93003. 805/339-0375. **Fax:** 805/339-9751. **Contact:** Human Resources. **E-mail address:** hr@med-design.com. **World Wide Web address:** http://www.med-design.com. **Description:** Designs and develops medical safety devices intended to reduce the incidence of needle accidents that primarily occur in health care settings. Products developed by the company include the retractable needle hypodermic syringe, the retractable vacuum tube phlebotomy set, and the retractable intravenous catheter insertion device. **Corporate headquarters location:** This location. **Listed on:** NASDAQ. **Stock exchange symbol:** MEDC.

MEDLINE INDUSTRIES, INC.
14650 Meyer Canyon Road, Fontana CA 92336. 909/349-6000. **Contact:** Human Resources. **World Wide Web address:** http://www.medline.com. **Description:** Medline Industries manufactures and sells a broad line of health care products used by hospitals, laboratories, pharmaceutical companies, medical schools, dentists, and the general public. **Positions advertised include:** Warehouse Operator. **Corporate headquarters location:** Mundelein IL. **Operations at this facility include:** This location primarily manufactures disposable medical gloves for use in hospitals and laboratories.

MEDSEP CORPORATION
1630 Industrial Park Street, Covina CA 91722. 626/339-7388. **Toll-free phone:** 800/288-8377. **Fax:** 626/332-2518. **Contact:** Human Resources. **World Wide Web address:** http://www.pall.com. **Description:** Manufactures medical devices for collecting plasma and whole blood. Founded in 1946. **Company slogan:** Quality flows through our system. **Corporate headquarters location:** East Hills NY. **Other Other area locations:** San Diego CA. **U.S. locations:** FL; MA; MI. **International locations:** Asia; Canada; Europe; South America. **Parent company:** Pall Corporation. **Listed on:** New York Stock Exchange. **Stock exchange symbol:** PLL. **President:** Eric Krasnoff. **Annual sales/revenues:** $1.6 billion. **Number of employees at this location:** 420. **Number of employees nationwide:** 7,000. **Number of employees worldwide:** 11,000.

MEDTRONIC MINIMED
18000 Devonshire Street, Northridge CA 91325-1219. 818/362-5958. **Toll-free phone:** 800/MIN-IMED. **Fax:** 818/576-6232. **Contact:** Human Resources. **E-mail address:** hr@minimed.com. **World Wide Web address:** http://www.minimed.com. **Description:** Develops and manufactures insulin pumps and other products for the treatment of diabetes. Founded in 1980. **Positions advertised include:** Administrative Assistant; Clinical Research Director; Clinical Services Technician. **Corporate headquarters location:** This location. **Other U.S. locations:** Hollywood FL. **International locations:** Asia; Australia; Europe; South America. **Listed on:** New York Stock Exchange. **Stock exchange symbol:** MDT. **Annual sales/revenues:** More than $100 million.

MEGGITT PLC
1915 Voyager Avenue, Simi Valley CA 93063. 805/584-4100. **Contact:** Human Resources. **World Wide Web address:** http://www.meggitt.com. **Description:** Develops specialized electric and aerospace technologies. The aerospace unit manufactures systems that measure and process altitude, speed, and engine parameters; ducting systems; control valves; and fire detection/protection systems. The electronics unit manufactures sensors, circuits, and resistors for a variety of industries. **Corporate headquarters location:** This location.

MELISSA DATA
22382 Avenida Empressa, Rancho Santa Margarita CA 92688-2112. 949/589-5200. **Toll-free phone:** 800/635-4772. **Fax:** 949/589-5211. **Contact:** Human Resources. **E-mail address:** hr@melissadata.com. **World Wide Web address:** http://www.melissadata.com. **Description:** A catalog retailer of direct mail software. **Positions advertised include:** Sales Engineer. **Corporate headquarters location:** This location.

MEMEC INSIGHT
3721 Valley Centre Drive, San Diego CA 92130. 858/314-8500. **Fax:** 858/314-8550. **Contact:** Personnel. **World Wide Web address:** http://www.insight-electronics.com. **Description:** Distributes computers and semiconductors. NOTE: Search and apply for positions online. **Positions advertised include:** IT Project Manager; Sr. Manager, Corporate Development; Business Systems Analyst. **Corporate headquarters location:** This location. **Parent company:** Memec. **Number of employees worldwide:** 2,400.

MENTOR CORPORATION
201 Mentor Drive, Santa Barbara CA 93111. 805/681-6000. **Fax:** 805/964-2712. **Contact:** Human Resources. **World Wide Web address:** http://www.mentorcorp.com. **Description:** Develops, manufactures, and markets a broad range of products for plastic and reconstructive surgery, urology, and ophthalmology. Mentor Corporation's products include surgically implantable devices, diagnostic and surgical instruments, disposable instruments, and disposable products for hospitals and home health care. **NOTE:** Search and apply for positions online. **Positions advertised include:** Senior SEC Accountant; Tax Accountant; International Product Manager. **Corporate headquarters location:** This location. **Other U.S. locations:** Irving TX; Minneapolis MN. **Listed on:** NASDAQ. **Stock exchange symbol:** MNTR. **Number of employees nationwide:** 1,900.

MENTOR GRAPHICS CORPORATION
1001 Ridder Park Drive, San Jose 95131. 408/436-1500. **Toll-free phone:** 800/547-3000. **Fax:** 408/436-1501. **Contact:** Human Resources. **World Wide Web address:** http://www.mentor.com. **Description:** A provider of electronic design software and hardware used by companies to aid in the design and production of electronics. **NOTE:** Search and applyf for positions online. **Positions advertised include:** Marketing Director; Product Marketing Manager; Technical Marketing Engineer; Software Development Engineer; Senior Financial Analyst. **Corporate headquarters location:** Wilsonville OR. **Listed on:** NASDAQ. **Stock exchange symbol:** MENT.

MERCANTILE NATIONAL BANK
1880 Century Park East, Los Angeles CA 90067. 310/277-2265. **Fax:** 310/201-0629. **Contact:** Human Resources Department. **E-mail address:** hr@mnbla.com. **World Wide Web address:** http://www.mnbla.com. **Description:** A commercial bank. **Positions advertised include:** Personal Banking Officer. **Corporate headquarters location:** This location. **Listed on:** NASDAQ. **Stock exchange symbol:** MBLA.

MERCER HUMAN RESOUCE CONSULTING
777 South Figueroa Street, Suite 2000, Los Angeles CA 90017. 213/346-2200. **Fax:** 213/346-2680. **Contact:** Human Resources. **E-mail address:** careers.west@us.wmmercer.com. **World Wide Web address:** http://www.mercerhr.com. **Description:** One of the world's largest actuarial and human resources management consulting firms, providing advice to organizations on all aspects of employee/management relationships. Services include retirement, health and welfare; performance and rewards; communication; investment; human resources administration; risk finance and insurance; and health care provider consulting. **NOTE:** Search and apply for positions online. **Positions advertised include:** Actuarial Analyst; Consultant. **Special programs:** Internships. **Corporate headquarters location:** New York NY. **Listed on:** NASDAQ. **Stock exchange symbol:** MERCS.

MERCER HUMAN RESOUCE CONSULTING
3 Embarcadero Center, Suite 1500, San Francisco CA 94111. 415/743-8700. **Contact:** Human Resources. **World Wide Web address:** http://www.mercerhr.com. **Description:** One of the world's largest actuarial and human resources management consulting firms, providing advice to organizations on all aspects of employee/management relationships. Services include retirement, health and welfare; performance and rewards; communication; investment; human resources administration; risk finance and insurance; and health care provider consulting. **Positions advertised include:** Acturial Analyst. **Corporate headquarters location:** New York NY. **Listed on:** NASDAQ. **Stock exchange symbol:** MERCS.

MERCK RESEARCH LABORATORIES
3535 General Atomics Court, San Diego CA 92121. 858/202-5000. **Contact:** Human Resources. **World Wide Web address:** http://www.merck.com. **Description:** A biochemistry laboratory involved in neuroscience research. **Positions advertised include:** Business Manager, Acute Care; Animal Care Specialist; Pharmaceutical Sales Representative; Senior Research Biologist; Executive Assistant. **Corporate headquarters location:** Whitehouse Station NJ.

MERCURY AIR GROUP, INC.
5456 McConnell Avenue, Los Angeles CA 90066. 310/827-2737. **Fax:** 310/827-8921. **Contact:** Steve Antonoff, Director of Human Resources Department. **World Wide Web address:** http://www.mercuryairgroup.com. **Description:** Engaged primarily in ground support services for passenger and freight air carriers and also in the manufacturing of electronic components. Support services include aircraft refueling and maintenance. Electronic components and parts include resistors, fusing devices, circuit breakers, audio accessories, service accessories, and electrical modules. **Corporate headquarters location:** This location. **Listed on:** American Stock Exchange. **Stock exchange symbol:** MAX.

MERCURY INSURANCE GROUP
555 West Imperial Highway, Brea CA 92821. 714/671-7393. **Contact:** Human Resources. **World Wide Web address:** http://www.mercuryinsurance.com. **Description:** A property and casualty insurance firm. Founded in 1962. **NOTE:** Entry-level positions are offered. **Positions advertised include:** Phone Reporter; Support Specialist; Marketing Assistant; Underwriting Trainee; Senior File Clerk; Computer Operator; Help Center Coordinator. **Special programs:** Internships; Training; Summer Jobs. **Corporate headquarters location:** This location. **Other U.S. locations:** FL; GA; IL. **Listed on:** New York Stock Exchange. **Stock exchange symbol:** MCY. **Number of employees at this location:** 550. **Number of employees nationwide:** 1,800.

MERCURY INTERACTIVE CORPORATION
379 North Whisman Road, Mountain View CA 94043-3969. 650/603-5200. **Fax:** 650/603-5300. **Contact:** Personnel. **World Wide Web address:** http://www.mercury.com. **Description:** Develops automated software quality tools for enterprise applications testing. The company's products are used to isolate software and system errors prior to application deployment. **Positions advertised include:** Senior Manager of Business Development; Director, Business Transformation; Technical Enablement Manager; Application Support Engineer; Contracts Negotiator; Treasury Operations Manager. **Corporate headquarters location:** This location. **Listed on:** NASDAQ. **Stock exchange symbol:** MERQ. **Annual sales/revenues:** $506 million.

MERCY HEALTHCARE NORTH
2175 Rosaline Avenue, Redding CA 96001. 530/225-6000. **Fax:** 530/225-6858. **Contact:** Human Resources Department. **World Wide Web address:** http://www.mercy.org. **Description:** A 273-bed hospital that provides comprehensive health care, acute care, and a variety of special programs to a six-county region. **NOTE:** Search and apply for positions online. **Positions advertised include:** Air Ambulance Communication Specialist; Clinical Laboratory Scientist; Critical Care Specialist; Cardiac Nurse Practitioner; Registered Nurse. **Corporate headquarters location:** This location. **Parent company:** Catholic Healthcare West. **Number of employees at this location:** 1,600.

MERCY MEDICAL CENTER MERCED
301 East 13th Street, Merced CA 95340. 209/385-7000. **Fax:** 209/385-7042. **Contact:** Employment Coordinator. **E-mail address:** hr@mercymerced@chw.edu. **World Wide Web address:** http://www.mercymercedcares.org. **Description:** A nonprofit, acute care, 172-bed facility. The center is affiliated with the UC Davis School of Medicine Family Practice Residency Program. **NOTE:** Entry-level positions and second and third shifts are offered. Search and apply for positions online. **Positions advertised include:** Business Services Director; Emergency Services Director; Occupational Therapist; Physical Therapist; Pharmacist; Patient Registrar. **Special programs:** Internships; Training. **Office hours:** Monday - Friday, 8:00 a.m. - 5:00 p.m. **Parent company:** Catholic Healthcare West. **Operations at this facility include:** Administration; Service. **Administrator:** Brian Bently. **Number of employees at this location:** 1,100.

MERISEL, INC.
200 Continental Boulevard, El Segundo CA 90245. 310/615-3080. **Toll-free phone:** 800/637-4735. **Fax:** 310/535-8134. **Contact:** Personnel. **E-mail address:** hr@merisel.com. **World Wide Web address:** http://www.merisel.com. **Description:** A wholesaler of computer hardware and software products. Merisel distributes the products to computer resellers throughout the United States and Canada. **Positions advertised include:** Inside Sales Representative. **Office hours:** Monday - Friday, 8:30 a.m. - 5:30 p.m. **Corporate headquarters location:** This location. **Other U.S. locations:** Marlborough MA; Cary NC. **International locations:** Canada. **Listed on:** NASDAQ. **Stock exchange symbol:** MSEL. **Annual sales/revenues:** $96 million.

MERIT ABRASIVE PRODUCTS INC.
7301 Orangewood Avenue, P.O. Box 3195, Garden Grove CA 92842-3195. 310/639-4242. **Toll-free phone:** 800/421-1936. **Fax:** 800/472-3094. **Contact:** Human Resources Department. **World Wide Web address:** http://www.meritabrasives.com. **Description:** Manufactures coated abrasive tools. **Corporate headquarters location:** This location.

MERLE NORMAN COSMETICS
9130 Bellanca Avenue, Los Angeles CA 90045. 310/641-3000. **Toll-free phone:** 800/421-2060. **Fax:** 310/337-2364. **Recorded jobline:** 310/337-2412. **Contact:** Monica Daigle, Recruiter. **World Wide Web address:** http://www.merlenorman.com. **Description:** Manufactures a complete line of over 500 skin care and cosmetic products sold exclusively through independently owned studios. **NOTE:** Resumes may be submitted via mail or fax. **Positions advertised include:** Manager of Corporate Studios; Advertising Billing Coordinator. **Corporate headquarters location:** This location. **Operations at this facility include:** Administration; Manufacturing; Regional Headquarters; Research and Development. **Listed on:** Privately held. **Annual sales/revenues:** $100 million. **Number of employees at this location:** 450.

MERRILL LYNCH
101 California Street, Suite 1400, San Francisco CA 94111. 415/274-7000. **Fax:** 415/986-3196. **Contact:** Human Resources. **World Wide Web address:** http://www.ml.com. **Description:** Merrill Lynch provides financial services in the following areas: securities, extensive insurance, and real estate. One of the largest securities brokerage firms in the United States, the company also brokers commodity futures and options and corporate and municipal securities and is engaged in investment banking activities. The company operates three offices in San Francisco. **Positions advertised include:** Business Retirement Manager; Client Service Officer; Commercial Banking Professional. **Corporate headquarters location:** New York NY. **Operations at this facility include:** Sales. **Listed on:** New York Stock Exchange. **Stock exchange symbol:** MITT.

METALLURGICAL LABS INC.
1717 Solano Way, Suite 39, Concord CA 94520. 925/603-1080. **Contact:** Human Resources. **Description:** Engaged in analyzing metal and metal products, as well as performing chemical analyses. **Corporate headquarters location:** This location.

METRON TECHNOLOGY
4425 Fortran Drive, San Jose CA 95134. 408/719-4600. **Fax:** 408/719-0452. **Contact:** Human Resources. **E-mail address:** info@metrontech.com. **World Wide Web address:** http://www.metrontech.com. **Description:** A global provider of outsourced marketing, sales, service, and support solutions to semiconductor materials and equipment suppliers and semiconductor manufacturers. **Parent company:** Applied Materials.

METROPOLITAN STATE HOSPITAL
11401 South Bloomfield Avenue, Norwalk CA 90650. 562/863-7011. **Fax:** 562/929-3131. **Contact:** Human Resources. **World Wide Web address:** http://www.dmh.cahwnet.gov/statehospitals/metro/default.asp. **Description:** A psychiatric hospital that is part of the California Mental Health Department. **Positions advertised include:** Clinical Dietician; Hospital Police Officer; Registered Nurse; Rehabilitation Therapist; Psychiatric Social Worker.

MICHAEL J'S RESTAURANT
201 North Vineyard Street, Ontario CA 91764. 909/937-6860. **Contact:** Human Resources. **Description:** The management office for the chain of Michael J's restaurants.

MICREL
2180 Fortune Drive, San Jose CA 95131. 408/944-0800. **Fax:** 408/474-1000. **Contact:** Recruiting. **E-mail address:** recruit@micrel.com. **World Wide Web address:** http://www.micrel.com. **Description:** Designs and manufactures analog integrated circuits. Founded in 1978. **NOTE:** Search and apply for positions online. **Positions advertised include:** Applications Engineering Manager; Strategic Applications Engineer; CAD Engineer; Sr. Layout Designer; Sr. Product Marketing Manager.

Corporate headquarters location: This location. **Listed on:** NASDAQ. **Stock exchange symbol:** MCRL. **Annual sales/revenues:** More than $100 million.

MICRO DENTAL LABORATORIES
5601 Arnold Road, Dublin CA 94568. 925/829-3611. **Toll-free phone:** 800/229-0936. **Fax:** 925/828-0686. **Contact:** Human Resources Department. **E-mail address:** careers@microdental.com. **World Wide Web address:** http://www.microdental.com. **Description:** A dental laboratory that manufactures crowns, bridges, dentures, and other dental products. **Corporate headquarters location:** This location.

MICRO LINEAR CORPORATION
2050 Concourse Drive, San Jose CA 95131. 408/433-5200. **Fax:** 408/428-6595. **Contact:** Human Resources Recruiter. **E-mail address:** jobs@microlinear.com. **World Wide Web address:** http://www.microlinear.com. **Description:** Designs, develops, and markets high-performance analog and mixed-signal integrated circuits for a broad range of applications in the communications, computer, and industrial markets. The company's products provide highly integrated systems-level solutions for a variety of applications including local area networks, mass storage, telecommunications, power management, motor control, and data conversion. The company uses its proprietary design methodology and bipolar, CMOS, and BiCMOS manufacturing processes to produce standard and semistandard products. **Positions advertised include:** RFIC System Architect; Sr. RFIC Design Engineer. **Corporate headquarters location:** This location. **Other U.S. locations:** Draper UT. **Listed on:** NASDAQ. **Stock exchange symbol:** MLIN.

MICRO 2000, INC.
1100 East Broadway, 3rd Floor, Glendale CA 91205. 818/547-0125. **Toll-free phone:** 800/864-8008. **Contact:** Personnel Director. **World Wide Web address:** http://www.micro2000.com. **Description:** Develops and markets computer diagnostic products for troubleshooting. Founded in 1990. **Positions advertised include:** Appointment Setter; Sales Representative; QA Technician. **Corporate headquarters location:** This location. **International locations:** Australia; Germany; Holland; United Kingdom. **Listed on:** Privately held. **Annual sales/revenues:** $5 - $10 million. **Number of employees at this location:** 45.

MICROCHIP TECHNOLOGY INC.
25950 Acero Street, Suite 200, Mission Viejo CA 92691. 949/462-9523. **Fax:** 949/462-9608. **Contact:** Human Resources. **E-mail address:** resumes@microchip.com. **World Wide Web address:** http://www.microchip.com. **Description:** A semiconductor manufacturer. Microchip Technology specializes in eight-bit micro controllers, eproms, eeproms, and other nonvolatile memory products. **NOTE:** Microchip prefers that resumes be submitted via e-mail. **Corporate headquarters location:** Chandler AZ. **Listed on:** NASDAQ. **Stock exchange symbol:** MCHP.

MICRON IMAGING DESIGN CENTER
135 North Los Robles Avenue, 7th Floor, Pasadena CA 91101. 626/685-5100. **Contact:** Human Resources. **World Wide Web address:** http://www.micron.com. **Description:** Manufactures electronic imaging sensors, cameras, and systems. The company is a leader in CMOS Imaging Technology. Founded in 1995. **Corporate headquarters location:** Boise ID. **Other area locations:** San Jose CA. **Parent company:** Micron Technology Inc. **Listed on:** New York Stock Exchange. **Stock exchange symbol:** MU.

MICROSOFT CORPORATION
1065 La Avenida Street, Mountain View CA 94043. 650/693-1001. **Contact:** Human Resources Department. **E-mail address:** jobs@microsoft.com. **World Wide Web address:** http://www.microsoft.com. **Description:** Microsoft designs, sells and supports a product line of microcomputer software for business, home, and professional use. Microsoft also manufactures related books and hardware products. Software products include spreadsheets, desktop publishing, project management, graphics, word processing, and database applications, as well as operating systems and programming languages. **NOTE:** Register online to submit resume, create profile, or create job search agent. **Positions advertised include:** Database Analyst; Consultant; Hardware Design Engineer; Operations Analyst; Program Manager; Software Development Engineer; Systems Engineer; Human Resources Generalist; Marketing Manager. **Corporate headquarters location:** Redmond WA. **Other area locations:** Sacramento CA; San Francisco CA. **Operations at this facility include:** This location is a research and design office. **Listed on:** NASDAQ. **Stock exchange symbol:** MSFT.

MICROSOFT CORPORATION
3 Park Plaza, Suite 1800, Irvine CA 92614. 949/263-3000. **Contact:** Human Resources Department. **E-mail address:** jobs@microsoft.com. **World Wide Web address:** http://www.microsoft.com. **Description:** Microsoft designs, sells, and supports a product line of microcomputer software for business, home, and professional use. Microsoft also produces related books and hardware products. Software products include spreadsheets, desktop publishing, project management, graphics, word processing, and database applications, as well as operating systems and programming languages. **Positions advertised include:** Partner Account Manager; financial Analystis and Controls; Marketing Manager; Support Professional. **Corporate headquarters location:** Redmond WA. **Operations at this facility include:** This location is a district sales office. **Listed on:** NASDAQ. **Stock exchange symbol:** MSFT.

MIDWAY HOME ENTERTAINMENT INC.
P.O. Box 360839, Milpitas CA 95036-0839. 408/434-3700. **Physical address:** 675 Sycamore Drive, Milpitas CA 95035. **Contact:** Human Resources. **E-mail address:** hr@midwaygames.com. **World Wide Web address:** http://www.midway.com. **Description:** Develops video game software. **Positions advertised include:** Acquisition and Traffic Manager; Cinematic Art Director; Localizatioin Coordinator. **Corporate headquarters location:** Chicago IL. **Operations at this facility include:** This location is a research and development facility. **Listed on:** New York Stock Exchange. **Stock exchange symbol:** MWY.

MILLENNIUM BILTMORE HOTEL
506 South Grand Avenue, Los Angeles CA 90071. 213/624-1011. **Contact:** Human Resources. **World Wide Web address:** http://www1.millennium-hotel.com. **Description:** A luxury hotel. **Corporate headquarters location:** This location. **Operations at this facility include:** Administration; Sales. **Parent company:** CDL Group.

MILLER BREWING COMPANY
15801 East First Street, Irwindale CA 91706-2069. 626/969-6811. **Contact:** Personnel Department. **World Wide Web address:** http://www.millerbrewing.com. **Description:** Produces and distributes beer and other malt beverages. Principal beer brands include Miller Lite, Lite Ice, Miller Genuine Draft, Miller Genuine Draft Light, Miller High Life, Miller Reserve, Lowenbrau, Milwaukee's Best, Meister Brau, Red Dog, and Icehouse. Miller also produces Sharp's, a nonalcoholic brew. **NOTE:** Search and apply for positions online. **Positions advertised include:** Occupational Health/Workers Compensation Specialist; Quality Services Engineer; Mechanical Staff Engineer; Electrical Staff Engineer. **Corporate headquarters location:** Milwaukee WI. **Subsidiaries include:** Jacob Leinenkugel Brewing Company (Chippewa Falls WI) brews Leinenkugel's Original Premium, Leinenkugel's Light, Leinie's Ice, Leinenkugel's Limited, Leinenkugel's Red Lager, and four seasonal beers: Leinenkugel's Genuine Bock, Leinenkugel's Honey Weiss, Leinenkugel's Autumn Gold, and Leinenkugel's Winter Lager. Molson Breweries U.S.A., Inc. (Reston VA), one of the largest beer importers in the United States, imports Molson beers from Canada, as well as Foster's Lager and many other brands. **Parent company:** SABMiller. **Operations at this facility include:** A brewery. **Number of employees at this location:** 1,100. **Number of employees nationwide:** 155,000.

MILLER DIAL CORPORATION
P.O. Box 5868, El Monte CA 91731. 626/444-4555. **Physical address:** 4400 North Temple City Boulevard, El Monte CA 91731. **Fax:** 626/443-3267. **Contact:** Personnel Department. **World Wide Web address:** http://www.millerdial.com. **Description:** One of the world's largest manufacturers of nameplates and other function identification products including panels, dials, membrane switches, and labels. **Corporate headquarters location:** This location.

MILLS COLLEGE
5000 MacArthur Boulevard, Oakland CA 94613. 510/430-2282. **Fax:** 510/430-3311. **Recorded jobline:** 510/430-2012. **Contact:** Personnel Department. **E-mail address:** hire@mills.edu. **World Wide Web address:** http://www.mills.edu. **Description:** An independent liberal arts college for women offering bachelor's and master's degrees. Founded in 1852. **Positions advertised include:** Administrative Assistant; Maintenance Technician; Director of Human Resources; Food Service Worker; Art Instructor; Dance Instructor.

MIPS TECHNOLOGIES, INC.
1225 Charleston Road, Mountain View CA 94043-1353. 650/567-5000. **Fax:** 650/567-5150. **Contact:** Susan Raskin, Director of Human Resources. **E-mail address:** susan@mips.com. **World Wide Web address:** http://www.mips.com. **Description:** Designs 32- and 64-bit RISC processors for license to semiconductor suppliers. The company's products are then embedded in such items as digital cameras, handheld computing devices, and video game systems. **NOTE:** Search and apply for positions online. **Positions advertised include:** Sr. Programmer; Multi Media Market Development Manager; Design Verification Engineer; Sr. Core Engineer. **Corporate headquarters location:** This location. **Listed on:** NASDAQ. **Stock exchange symbol:** MIPS. **Annual sales/revenues:** $39 million.

MITCHELL INTERNATIONAL
9889 Willow Creek Road, San Diego CA 92131. 858/578-6550. **Toll-free phone:** 800/854-7030. **Fax:** 858/530-4636. **Contact:** Michael Dean Galvin, Staffing Manager. **E-mail address:** michael.galvin@mitchell.com. **World Wide Web address:** http://www.mitchell.com. **Description:** Provides printed information and electronic software products for the automotive industry. **Positions advertised include:** Automotive Editor; Configuration Mgmt Analyst; Corporate business Decision Analyst; Contract Technical Recruiter. **Special programs:** Internships. **Corporate headquarters location:** This location. **Other U.S. locations:** Chicago IL; Detroit MI; McLean VA; Milwaukee WI. **Subsidiaries include:** EH Boeckh (Milwaukee WI); Mitchell-Medical (VA); NAG's (Detroit MI). **Parent company:** Hellman & Friedman LLC. **Number of employees nationwide:** Over 700.

MIZUHO CORPORATE BANK OF CALIFORNIA
555 West Fifth Street, Los Angeles CA 90013. 213/612-2700. **Fax:** 213/612-2875. **Contact:** Vice President. **World Wide Web address:** http://www.mizuhobank.co.jp/english. **Description:** A full-service commercial bank. Founded in 1974. **NOTE:** Entry-level positions and part-time jobs are offered. **Special programs:** Summer Jobs. **Office hours:** Monday - Friday, 8:00 a.m. - 5:00 p.m. **Corporate headquarters location:** This location. **International locations:** Worldwide. **Parent company:** Mizuho Bank, Ltd. (Tokyo). **President/CEO:** Takuo Yoshida. **Number of employees at this location:** 90.

THE MODESTO BEE
1325 H Street, Modesto CA 95352. 209/578-2000. **Recorded jobline:** 209/578-2004. **Contact:** Human Resources. **E-mail address:** employment@modbee.com. **World Wide Web address:** http://www.modbee.com. **Description:** A daily newspaper. **Special programs:** Internships. **Corporate headquarters location:** Sacramento CA. **Parent company:** McClatchy Newspapers, Inc. **Listed on:** New York Stock Exchange. **Stock exchange symbol:** MNI. **Number of employees at this location:** 600.

MODESTO, CITY OF
RECREATION & NEIGHBORHOODS DEPARTMENT
P.O. Box 642, Modesto CA 95353. 209/577-5200. **Physical address:** 1010 Tenth Street, Modesto CA 95354. **Recorded jobline:** 209/577-5498. **Contact:** Human Resources. **World Wide Web address:** http://www.ci.modesto.ca.us/cnc. **Description:** The City of Modesto Parks and Recreation Department oversees the operation of all the city's parks and the Modesto Community Service Center, the Boy Scout Clubhouse, and the American Legion Hall. **Positions advertised include:** Assistant Risk Manager; Associate Civil Engineer; HUD Manager; Police Officer. **Operations at this facility include:** This location is an administrative office.

MONOGRAM SYSTEMS
P.O. Box 11189, Carson CA 90749-1189. 310/884-7000. **Physical address:** 1500 Glenn Curtiss Street, Carson CA 90746-4012. **Fax:** 310/900-2159. **Contact:** Human Resources. **E-mail address:** sschuetze@monogram.zodiac.com. **World Wide Web address:** http://www.monogramsystems.com. **Description:** Manufactures interior aircraft equipment including seats for passengers and crew, coffee machines, and lavatories. **NOTE:** Resumes may be submitted by mail, fax, or e-mail. **Positions advertised include:** Mechanical Engineer. **Corporate headquarters location:** This location.

MONTEREY PASTA COMPANY
1528 Moffett Street, Salinas CA 93905-3342. 831/753-6262. **Fax:** 831/753-0353. **Contact:** Human Resources. **E-mail address:** hr@montereypasta.com. **World Wide Web address:** http://www.montereypasta.com. **Description:** Manufactures and markets a premium line of fresh gourmet pasta and pasta sauces emphasizing natural ingredients. The company's pasta and pasta sauce products include snow crab ravioli, smoked salmon ravioli, gorgonzola roasted walnut ravioli, sweet red pepper fettuccini, Santa Fe linguine, sun dried tomato pesto sauce, and Monterey clam and mushroom sauce. **Positions advertised include:** Internal Auditor; Staff Accountant; Maintenance Mechanic. **Corporate headquarters location:** This location. **Listed on:** NASDAQ. **Stock exchange symbol:** PSTA.

MOORE BUSINESS FORMS
7801 Avenue 304, Visalia CA 93291. 559/651-2153. **Contact:** Human Resources. **World Wide Web address:** http://www.moore.com. **Description:** Moore Business Forms is a manufacturer of business systems, forms, and equipment. **Corporate headquarters location:** Bannockburn IL. **Parent company:** RR Donnelly. **Operations at this facility include:** This location prints business forms. **Listed on:** New York Stock Exchange. **Stock exchange symbol:** MCL.

MORGAN STANLEY
101 California Street, 3rd Floor, San Francisco CA 94111. 415/693-6000. **Contact:** Human Resources. **World Wide Web address:** http://www.morganstanley.com. **Description:** Offers diversified financial services including equities, fixed income securities, commodities, money market instruments, and investment banking services. **NOTE:** Positions within the firm are organized by four main divisions: Institutional Securities, the Individual Investor Group, Investment Management, and Discover Financial Services. Search and apply for positions online. **Corporate headquarters location:** New York NY. **Operations at this facility include:** This location is an individual/retail branch office. **Listed on:** New York Stock Exchange. **Stock exchange symbol:** MWD.

MORGAN STANLEY
555 California Street, Suite 2200, San Francisco CA 94104. 415/576-2000. **Contact:** Human Resources. **World Wide Web address:** http://www.morganstanley.com. **Description:** Offers diversified financial services including equities, fixed income securities, commodities, money market instruments, and investment banking services. **NOTE:** Positions within the firm are organized by four main divisions: Institutional Securities, the Individual Investor Group, Investment Management, and Discover Financial Services. Search and apply for positions online. **Corporate headquarters location:** New York NY. **Operations at this facility include:** This location is an institutional securities branch office. **Listed on:** New York Stock Exchange. **Stock exchange symbol:** MWD.

MORRISON & FOERSTER LLP
425 Market Street, San Francisco CA 94105-2482. 415/268-7000. **Fax:** 415/268-6804. **Contact:** Staff Recruiting Coordinator. **E-mail address:** jobs@mofo.com. **World Wide Web address:** http://www.mofo.com. **Description:** An international law firm specializing in corporate, financial, intellectual property, real estate, and tax law. **NOTE:** Candidates interested in Attorney positions should address resumes to: Mireille Butler, Attorney Recruiting Manager. Fax: 415/268-7522. E-mail: mbutler@mofo.com. **Positions advertised include:** Securities Litigation Associate; Patent Prosecution Associate; Financial Transactions Associate; Tax Associate; Corporate Associate; Real Estate Associate. **Corporate headquarters location:** This location. **Other area locations:** Los Angeles CA; Orange County CA; Palo Alto CA; Sacramento CA; Walnut Creek CA. **Other U.S. locations:** Denver CO; Washington DC; New York NY. **International locations:** Beijing; Brussels; Hong Kong; London; Singapore; Tokyo.

MOTOROLA, INC.
1150 Kifer Road, Suite 100, Sunnyvale CA 94086. 408/749-0510. **Contact:** Human Resources. **World Wide Web address:** http://www.motorola.com. **Description:** Designs and manufactures semiconductors and integrated circuits for the computing, communications, electronics, and transportation industries. **Positions advertised include:** Sales Account Manager; Technical Sales Engineer; MCG Account Executive. **Corporate headquarters location:** Austin TX. **Operations at this facility include:** Divisional Headquarters. **Listed on:** New York Stock Exchange. **Stock exchange symbol:** MEU.

MULTICHIP ASSEMBLY
535 East Brokaw Road, San Jose CA 95112. 408/451-2345. **Fax:** 408/451-2335. **Contact:** Human Resources. **E-mail address:** hr@multichipassy.com. **World Wide Web address:** http://www.multichipassy.com. **Description:** A contract manufacturer of tab devices and other assembly processes for the electronics industry. Founded in 1991. **Corporate headquarters location:** This location. **Listed on:** Privately held. **Annual sales/revenues:** Less than $5 million. **Number of employees at this location:** 45.

MUNCHKIN INC.
16689 Schoenborn Street, North Hills CA 91343. **Toll-free phone:** 800/344-2229. **Contact:** Personnel. **World Wide Web address:** http://www.munchkininc.com. **Description:** Manufactures baby care products and early childhood educational and developmental toys. **Corporate headquarters location:** This location.

MUSITEK
410 Bryant Circle, Suite K, Ojai CA 93023. 805/646-8051. **Toll-free phone:** 800/676-8055. **Fax:** 805/646-8099. **Contact:** Personnel. **World Wide Web address:** http://www.musitek.com. **Description:** Develops music software including MIDISCAN, which converts printed sheet music into multitrack MIDI files. **Corporate headquarters location:** This location.

NATIONAL GYPSUM COMPANY
1850 Pier B Street, Long Beach CA 90813. 562/435-4465. **Fax:** 562/495-3922. **Contact:** Caroline Dixon, Human Resources. **World Wide Web address:** http://www.nationalgypsum.com. **Description:** Manufactures gypsum wallboard and joint compounds. National Gypsum is an integrated, diversified manufacturer of products for building, construction, and shelter markets. **NOTE:** Entry-level positions and second and third shifts are offered. **Special programs:** Training. **Corporate headquarters location:** Charlotte NC. **Other U.S. locations:** Nationwide. **Listed on:** Privately held. **Number of employees at this location:** 100. **Number of employees nationwide:** 3,000.

NATIONAL MEMORY IMPAIRMENT INSTITUTE
646 Brea Canyon Road, Suite 110, Walnut CA 91789. 888/672-6577. **Fax:** 909/612-8417. **Contact:** Human Resources. **E-mail address:** info@nmi2.org. **World Wide Web address:** http://www.nmi2.org. **Description:** A non-profit organization dedicated to developing formal standards of care and a national certification program for individuals caring for the memory impaired. **Corporate headquarters location:** This location.

NATIONAL SEMICONDUCTOR CORPORATION
2900 Semiconductor Drive, P.O. Box 58090, Santa Clara CA 95052-8090. 408/721-5000. **Contact:** Staffing. **World Wide Web address:** http://www.nsc.com. **Description:** Designs, develops, and manufactures microprocessors, consumer products, integrated circuits, memory systems, computer products, telecommunications systems, and high-speed bipolar circuits. **NOTE:** Search and apply for positions onlne. **Positions advertised include:** Administrative Associate; Internal Auditor; Senior Tax Analyst; Applications Engineer; Physical Design Engineer; Sr. Failure Analysis Engineer. **Special programs:** Internships. **Corporate headquarters location:** This location. **International locations:** Scotland. **Operations at this facility include:** Administration; Manufacturing; Research and Development; Sales; Service. **Listed on:** New York Stock Exchange. **Stock exchange symbol:** NSM.

NEKTAR THERAPEUTICS
150 Industrial Road, San Carlos CA 94070. 650/631-3100. **Fax:** 650/631-3150. **Contact:** Human Resources. **World Wide Web address:** http://www.nektar.com. **Description:** Researches, develops, and manufactures aerosol drug delivery systems for the treatment of lung diseases. The system allows macromolecules of drug powder particles to be absorbed by alveoli in the lungs. **NOTE:** Search and apply for positions online. **Positions advertised include:** Senior Quality Engineer; Process Engineer; Patent Counsel; Director, Internal Audit; Director, IS Quality Management. **Special programs:** Internships. **Corporate headquarters location:** This location. **Other U.S. locations:** Huntsville AL. **Listed on:** NASDAQ. **Stock exchange symbol:** NKTR.

NESTLE USA, INC.
800 North Brand Boulevard, Glendale CA 91203. 818/549-6000. **Contact:** Human Resources. **World Wide Web address:** http://www.nestleusa.com. **Description:** One of the largest food and beverage companies in the nation. Brand names include Nestle Crunch, Baby Ruth, and Butterfinger candy bars; Taster's Choice and Nescafe coffee; Contadina tomato and refrigerated pastas and sauces; Friskies and Fancy Feast cat food; and Beringer wines. **NOTE:** Search and apply for positions online. **Positions advertised include:** Business Analyst; Marketing Associate; Auditor; IT Coordinator; Human Resources Generalist; Supply Planner; Demand Planner; Sales Forecasting Analyst. **Corporate headquarters location:** Vevey, Switzerland. **Parent company:** Nestle S.A.

NETIS TECHNOLOGY, INC.
511 Montague Expressway, Milpitas CA 95035. 408/263-0368. **Fax:** 408/263-4624. **Contact:** Human Resources. **E-mail address:** hr@netistech.com. **World Wide Web address:** http://www.netistech.com. **Description:** Provides systems integration and networking services. The company also manufactures personal computers and offers a network consulting service. Founded in 1989. **Corporate headquarters location:** This location. **Listed on:** Privately held. **Number of employees at this location:** 20.

NETSCAPE COMMUNICATIONS CORPORATION
P.O. Box 7050, Mountain View CA 94039-7050. 650/254-1900. **Physical address:** 466 Ellis Street, Mountain View CA 94043. **Fax:** 650/528-4124. **Contact:** Human Resources. **World Wide Web address:** http://www.netscape.com. **Description:** An Internet service provider. The company also provides developmental tools, commercial applications, and client/server software. **Positions advertised include:** Technical Support Engineer; Quality Assurance Manager; Senior Technical Project Manager; Software Engineer. **Special programs:** Internships. **Corporate headquarters location:** This location. **Other area locations:** Half Moon Bay CA; Sunnyvale CA; San Francisco CA. **Other U.S. locations:** Nationwide. **Parent company:** Time Warner. **Listed on:** New York Stock Exchange. **Stock exchange symbol:** AOL.

NETWORK APPLIANCE, INC.
495 East Java Drive, Sunnyvale CA 94089. 408/822-6000. **Fax:** 408/822-4501. **Contact:** Human Resources. **E-mail address:** ntapjobs@netapp.com. **World Wide Web address:** http://www.netapp.com. **Description:** Develops data storage equipment for corporate networks. **NOTE:** Search and apply for positions online. **Positions advertised include:** ATA Storage Development Engineer; Business Analyst; Business Systems Analyst; Database Application Engineer; Director of Legal; Disk Drive Sustaining Engineer. **Corporate headquarters location:** This location. **Other U.S. locations:** Morrisville NC; Cranberry Township PA; Waltham MA. **Listed on:** NASDAQ. **Stock exchange symbol:** NTAP. **Number of employees worldwide:** 2,345. **Annual sales/revenues:** $1.2 billion.

NETWORK ASSOCIATES, INC.
3965 Freedom Circle, Santa Clara CA 95054. 408/988-3832. **Contact:** Human Resources. **World Wide Web address:** http://www.nai.com. **Description:** Designs, manufactures, markets, and supports software-based analysis and monitoring tools primarily for managing enterprisewide computer networks. The company's product line consists of software and network interface cards used with portable PC-compatible computers to monitor and analyze individual local area network (LAN) or wide area network (WAN) segments. Products include VirusScan, an antivirus software. **Positions advertised include:** Senior Product Marketing Manager; Technical Support Engineer; Competitive Researcher; Business Development Manager; Corporate Development Analyst; Hardware Engineer; Senior Software Development Engineer. **Corporate headquarters location:** This location. **Other area locations:** Sunnyvale CA; Mission Viejo CA. **International locations:** Worldwide. **Listed on:** New York Stock Exchange. **Stock exchange symbol:** NET.

NEUTROGENA CORPORATION
5760 West 96th Street, Los Angeles CA 90045. 310/642-1150. **Fax:** 310/337-5537. **Contact:** Manager of Human Resources Department. **E-mail address:** neutrogenajobs@hiresystems.com. **World Wide Web address:** http://www.neutrogena.com. **Description:** Manufactures a variety of personal care products focusing on hair, skin, and cosmetics. **NOTE:** Search and apply for positions online. **Positions advertised include:** Sr. Research Scientist; Finance Manager; SAP Systems Analyst; Chemical Planner; Sr. QA Scientist; Team Leader. **Corporate headquarters location:** This location. **Parent company:** Johnson & Johnson. **Listed on:** New York Stock Exchange. **Stock exchange symbol:** JNJ.

NEW HORIZONS WORLDWIDE
1900 South State College Boulevard, Anaheim CA 92806. 714/940-8000. **Fax:** 714/938-6004. **Contact:** Personnel. **E-mail address:** career.corp@newhorizons.com. **World Wide Web address:** http://www.newhorizons.com. **Description:** Offers computer training classes to individuals and businesses. New Horizons Worldwide operates over 240 centers worldwide. Founded in 1982. **NOTE:** Search and apply for positions online. **Positions advertised include:** Treasury Director; Proposal Writer; E-Learning Specialist; Product Specialist; Regional Vice President. **Corporate headquarters location:** This location. **Other U.S. locations:** Nationwide. **International locations:** Worldwide. **Listed on:** NASDAQ. **Stock exchange symbol:** NEWH. **Annual sales/revenues:** $139 million.

NEW UNITED MOTOR MANUFACTURING INC.
45500 Fremont Boulevard, Fremont CA 94538. 510/498-5500. **Fax:** 510/770-4116. **Contact:** Human Resources Department. **E-mail address:** careers@nummi.com. **World Wide Web address:** http://www.nummi.com. **Description:** Through a joint venture between General Motors Corporation and Toyota Motor Corporation, New United Motor Manufacturing manufactures Chevrolet Prizms for the Chevrolet Motor Division of General Motors and Toyota Corolla sedans and Tacoma pickup trucks for Toyota. Founded in 1984. **NOTE:** Entry-level positions are offered. **Positions advertised include:** Business Analyst; Tax Analyst; Internal Auditor. **Special programs:** Co-ops. **Internship information:** The company offers a six-month

cooperative education program. **Corporate headquarters location:** This location. **Listed on:** Privately held. **Number of employees at this location:** 5,700.

NEWBASIS
2626 Kansas Avenue, Riverside CA 92057. 951/787-0600. **Toll-free phone:** 888/NEW-BASIS. **Fax:** 951/787-0632. **Contact:** Personnel Director. **World Wide Web address:** http://www.newbasis.com. **Description:** Manufactures concrete, lumber, and other related building materials. **Corporate headquarters location:** Auburn CA. **Other U.S. locations:** AR; FL; TX. **International locations:** Chile; Mexico.

NEWBASIS
156 Center Street, Auburn CA 95603. 530/885-2465. **Contact:** Human Resources. **World Wide Web address:** http://www.newbasis.com. **Description:** Manufactures concrete, polymer, fiberglass, and plastics products. **Corporate headquarters location:** This location. **Other U.S. locations:** AR; FL; TX. **International locations:** Chile; Mexico.

NEXTIRAONE
5 Hutton Centre, Suite 150, Santa Ana CA 92707. 714/428-3000. **Contact:** Human Resources. **World Wide Web address:** http://www.nextiraone.com. **Description:** Designs, manufactures, and supports voice-processing and health care communications systems including call center management, telephone systems, locator systems, videoconferencing, health care communications, and network and data services. **Positions advertised include:** Sales Engineer. **Corporate headquarters location:** Houston TX. **Parent company:** Platinum Equity. **Number of employees nationwide:** 2,400.

NEXWATCH
47142 Mission Falls Court, Fremont CA 94539-7818. 510/360-7800. **Fax:** 510/360-7827. **Contact:** Human Resources. **World Wide Web address:** http://www.nexwatch.com. **Description:** Manufactures access control systems. **Corporate headquarters location:** This location. **Parent company:** Honeywell, Inc. **Listed on:** New York Stock Exchange. **Stock exchange symbol:** HON.

NORCAL MUTUAL INSURANCE COMPANY
560 Davis Street, 2nd Floor, San Francisco CA 94111. 415/397-9700. **Toll-free phone:** 800/652-1051. **Fax:** 415/835-9817. **Contact:** Human Resources Department. **E-mail address:** hr@norcalmutual.com. **World Wide Web address:** http://www.norcalmutual.com. **Description:** Provides physicians with professional liability insurance. **Positions advertised include:** Quality Assurance Specialist; Risk Management Specialist; Claims Investigator Trainee; Telecommunications Specialist; Underwriter; Graphic Designer; Lead Programmer Analyst; Policyholder Services Representative. **Special programs:** Internships. **Corporate headquarters location:** This location. **Other U.S. locations:** Anchorage AK; Pasadena CA; Providence RI. **Operations at this facility include:** Administration; Sales. **Listed on:** Privately held. **Number of employees at this location:** 165.

NORCAL WASTE SYSTEMS INC.
160 Pacific Avenue, Suite 200, San Francisco CA 94111. 415/875-1000. **Fax:** 415/875-1134. **Contact:** Human Resources Department. **World Wide Web address:** http://www.norcalwaste.com. **Description:** Engaged in waste management and recycling services. **Corporate headquarters location:** This location. **Number of employees at this location:** 1,375.

NORDSTROM, INC.
285 Winston Drive, San Francisco CA 94132. 415/753-1344. **Toll-free phone:** 888/282-6060. **Contact:** Human Resources Department. **World Wide Web address:** http://www.nordstrom.com. **Description:** A specialty retailer that sells apparel, shoes, and accessories. Nordstrom operates more than 60 stores, with over 20 clearance, boutique, and leased shoe departments in 12 department stores in Hawaii and Guam. Founded in 1901. **Positions advertised include:** Accessories Sales Associate. **Corporate headquarters location:** Seattle WA. **Other area locations:** Statewide. **Listed on:** New York Stock Exchange. **Stock exchange symbol:** JWN.

NORDSTROM, INC.
865 Market Street, San Francisco CA 94103. 415/243-8500. **Toll-free phone:** 888/282-6060. **Contact:** Human Resources Department. **World Wide Web address:** http://www.nordstrom.com. **Description:** A specialty retailer that sells apparel, shoes, and accessories. Nordstrom operates more than 60 stores, with over 20 clearance, boutique, and leased shoe departments in 12 department stores in Hawaii and Guam. **Positions advertised include:** Sales Associate. **Corporate headquarters location:** Seattle WA. **Other area locations:** Statewide. **Listed on:** New York Stock Exchange. **Stock exchange symbol:** JWN.

NORTEL NETWORKS
2603 Camino Ramon, San Ramon CA 94583. 925/867-2000. **Contact:** Human Resources. **E-mail address:** work@nortelnetworks.com. **World Wide Web address:** http://www.nortelnetworks.com. **Description:** Designs, produces, and supports multimedia access devices for use in building corporate, public, and Internet networks. The primary focus of the company's services is the consolidation of voice, fax, video, and data and multimedia traffic into a single network link. **Company slogan:** How the world shares ideas. **Office hours:** Monday - Friday, 8:00 a.m. - 5:00 p.m. **Corporate headquarters location:** Ontario Canada. **Other U.S. locations:** Nationwide. **International locations:** Worldwide. **Parent company:** Nortel. **Listed on:** New York Stock Exchange; Toronto Stock Exchange. **Stock exchange symbol:** NT. **President/CEO:** William Owens. **Annual sales/revenues:** $9.8 billion. **Number of employees worldwide:** 37,000.

NORTEL NETWORKS
4655 Great America Parkway, Santa Clara CA 95054. 408/495-2400. **Contact:** Staffing. **World Wide Web address:** http://www.nortelnetworks.com. **Description:** Designs, produces, and supports multimedia access devices for use in building corporate, public, and Internet networks. The primary focus of the company's services is the consolidation of voice, fax, video, and data and multimedia traffic into a single network link. **Corporate headquarters location:** Ontario Canada. **Other U.S. locations:** Nationwide. **International locations:** Worldwide. **Listed on:** New York Stock Exchange; Toronto Stock Exchange. **Stock exchange symbol:** NT. **Annual sales/revenues:** $9.8 billion. **Number of employees worldwide:** 37,000.

THE NORTH FACE
2013 Farallon Drive, San Leandro CA 94577. 510/618-3500. **Fax:** 510/618-3531. **Contact:** Human Resources. **E-mail address:** tnf_hr@vfc.com. **World Wide Web address:** http://www.thenorthface.com. **Description:** A manufacturer, wholesaler, and retailer of outdoor equipment and apparel including tents, backpacks, sleeping bags, outerwear, skiwear, and sportswear. **Positions advertised include:** Coalition Analysis & Reporting Manager; Data Warehouse Analyst; Marketing Coordinator; Business Manager. **Corporate headquarters location:** This location. **Parent company:** VF Corporation. **Operations at this facility include:** Administration; Manufacturing; Research and Development; Sales; Service.

NORTHROP GRUMMAN CORPORATION
One Northrop Avenue, Hawthorne CA 90251. 310/332-1000. **Recorded jobline:** 310/335-3000. **Contact:** Human Resources Department. **World Wide Web address:** http://www.northgrum.com. **Description:** Manufactures military aircraft, commercial aircraft parts, and electronic systems. Northrop Grumman develops the B-2 Spirit Stealth Bomber, parts for the F/A-18 and the Boeing 747, and radar equipment. Other operations include computer systems development for management and scientific applications. **Positions advertised include:** Business Analyst; Purchasing Price Analyst; Security Specialist; Program Control Accountant. **Corporate headquarters location:** Los Angeles CA. **Operations at this facility include:** Manufacturing; Research and Development. **Listed on:** New York Stock Exchange. **Stock exchange symbol:** NOC.

NORTHROP GRUMMAN CORPORATION
1840 Century Park East, Los Angeles CA 90067-2199. 310/553-6262. **Contact:** Human Resources. **World Wide Web address:** http://www.northgrum.com. **Description:** Manufactures military aircraft, commercial aircraft parts, radar equipment, and electronic systems. Northrop Grumman develops the B-2 Spirit Stealth Bomber, as well as parts for the F/A-18 and the Boeing 747. Other operations include computer systems development for management and scientific applications. **Positions advertised include:** Executive Administrative Assistant; Senior Accountant Specialist; Paralegal; Senior Staff Counsel; Financial Reporting Specialist; Strategic Analysis Manager. **Corporate headquarters location:** This location. **Other U.S. locations:** Nationwide. **Listed on:** New York Stock Exchange. **Stock exchange symbol:** NOC.

NORTHROP GRUMMAN ELECTRONIC SYSTEMS
P.O. Box 7012, San Jose CA 95150-7012. 408/365-4747. **Physical address:** 5225 Hellyer Avenue, Suite 100, San Jose CA 95138. **Contact:** Professional Recruiting Department. **E-mail address:** jobs_esss@ngc.com. **World Wide Web address:** http://www.northgrum.com. **Description:** Designs and manufactures electronic defense systems used by the U.S. Department of Defense, other U.S. government agencies, and U.S. allies. Products include radar warning receiving systems, cover and deception systems, and surveillance systems. **Positions advertised include:** Principal Design Specialist; Systems Engineer; Senior Mechanical Engineer; Electronics Engineer; Contracts Representative. **Corporate headquarters location:** Linthicum MD. **Operations at this facility include:** Administration; Divisional Headquarters; Engineering and Design; Financial Offices; Manufacturing; Marketing; Research and Development; Sales; Service. **Listed on:** New York Stock Exchange. **Stock exchange symbol:** NOC. **Number of employees worldwide:** 24,000.

NORTHROP GRUMMAN INFORMATION TECHNOLOGY
222 North Sepulveda Boulevard, Suite 1310, El Segundo CA 90245. 310/640-1050. **Contact:** Human Resources. **World Wide Web address:** http://www.it.northropgrumman.com. **Description:** Develops state-of-the-art software and information technology systems for the U.S. military and government. **Positions advertised include:** Software Engineer; Senior Embedded Systems Developer. **Corporate headquarters location:** Herndon VA. **Other U.S. locations:** Greenbelt MD; Falls Church VA; Dallas TX; Chantilly VA. **Operations at this facility include:** Research and Development. **Listed on:** New York Stock Exchange. **Stock exchange symbol:** NOC. **Number of employees worldwide:** 19,000.

NORTHROP GRUMMAN INTEGRATED SYSTEMS
One Northrop Grumman Avenue, El Segundo CA 90245. 310/332-1000. **Recorded jobline:** 310/335-3000. **Contact:** Human Resources. **World Wide Web address:** http://www.northropgrumman.com. **Description:** Manufactures radar warning systems. **Positions advertised include:** Software Engineer; Accountant; Business Development Manager; Program Manager. **Corporate headquarters location:** This location. **Listed on:** New York Stock Exchange. **Stock exchange symbol:** NOC. **Number of employees worldwide:** 15,000.

NORTHROP GRUMMAN MISSION SYSTEMS
1475 East harry Shepard Boulevard, San Bernardino CA 92408. 909/382-6234. **Contact:** Human Resources. **World Wide Web address:** http://www.ms.northropgrumman.com. **Description:** The company is engaged in the fields of missle systems, command, control and intelligence, and technical and management services. **Positions advertised include:** Senior Analyst; Associate Analyst; Analyst; Software Engineer; Senior Software Engineer; Senior Network Administrator. **Corporate headquarters location:** Los Angeles CA. **Other area locations:** Statewide. **Other U.S. locations:** Nationwide. **Number of employees worldwide:** 18,000.

NORTHROP GRUMMAN SPACE TECHNOLOGY
One Space Park, Redondo Beach CA 90278. 310/812-4321. **Contact:** Human Resources Recruiter. **World Wide Web address:** http://www.northgrum.com. **Description:** Serves worldwide markets with commercial, consumer, industrial, professional, and defense-related products. A major business area for the division is advanced microwave components and subsystems for military radar, communications, and electronic countermeasure markets. Product technologies are focused in high-power vacuum tubes, microwave semiconductors, amplifiers and oscillators, night vision and optical devices, and military switching power supplies. NG Space Technology develops advanced space-based telecommunications systems. **Corporate headquarters location:** This location. **Operations at this facility include:** Administration; Divisional Headquarters; Manufacturing; Research and Development; Sales. **Listed on:** New York Stock Exchange. **Stock exchange symbol:** NOC. **Number of employees worldwide:** 9,000.

THE NORTHWESTERN MUTUAL LIFE INSURANCE COMPANY
STRATEGIC FINANCIAL GROUP
888 West Sixth Street, 2nd Floor, Los Angeles CA 90017. 213/243-7000. **Fax:** 213/243-7001. **Contact:** Human Resources Representative. **E-mail address:** resume@northwesternmutual.com. **World Wide Web address:** http://www.northwesternmutual.com. **Description:** An insurance and investment planning company. The Northwestern Mutual Life Insurance Company specializes in individual life insurance coverage. The company's product portfolio includes permanent and term insurance, CompLife, disability income insurance, and annuity plans for the personal, business, estate, and pension planning markets. Founded in 1857. **Special programs:** Internships; Training. **Internship information:** The Kerrigan Agency offers college agent internships. These internships offer professional experience and the flexibility required for full-time students. College agents receive extensive training allowing for hands-on learning. College agents are responsible for the development of a professional practice revolving around the sale of insurance products, annuities, mutual funds, and investments, as well as estate, retirement, education, and pension planning. Successful applicants will be independent, with strong ethics, and have a proven track

record for success. Backgrounds in marketing, entrepreneurship, management, business administration, economics, finance, and liberal arts are helpful, but not required. **Corporate headquarters location:** Milwaukee WI. **Other U.S. locations:** Nationwide. **Operations at this facility include:** Sales; Service. **Annual sales/revenues:** $16.5 billion. **Number of employees at this location:** 100.

NOVELL, INC.
1735 Technology Drive, Suite 790, San Jose CA 95110. 408/961-1037. **Contact:** Human Resources. **World Wide Web address:** http://www.novell.com. **Description:** Novell, Inc. develops software tools and systems, works in partnership with other companies, and provides computer network management services. **NOTE:** Search and apply for positions online. **Corporate headquarters location:** Waltham MA. **Other U.S. locations:** Nationwide. **International locations:** Worldwide. **Operations at this facility include:** This location is involved in marketing, software engineering, and administration. **Listed on:** NASDAQ. **Stock exchange symbol:** NOVL. **Number of employees nationwide:** 7,900.

NOVELLUS SYSTEMS, INC.
4000 North First Street, San Jose CA 95134. 408/943-9700. **Toll-free phone:** 888/321-4272. **Fax:** 408/943-3422. **Contact:** Human Resources Department. **E-mail address:** info@novellus.com. **World Wide Web address:** http://www.novellus.com. **Description:** Novellus Systems is a leading supplier of process systems used in the fabrication of advanced integrated circuits. The company is one of the world's largest suppliers of equipment for dry removal of photoresist and other mask layer materials applied to semiconductor wafers during fabrication. Novellus also offers systems for related phases of semiconductor manufacturing including thermal growth of oxide layers and selective cleaning applications. **NOTE:** Search and apply for positions online. **Positions advertised include:** Financial Analyst; Windchill Programmer; Materials Project Manager; Mechanical Engineer. **Corporate headquarters location:** This location. **Other U.S. locations:** Chandler AZ; Portland OR. **Listed on:** NASDAQ. **Stock exchange symbol:** NVLS. **Number of employees worldwide:** 2,900.

NUCLEAR PHARMACY SERVICES
6464 Canoga Avenue, Woodland Hills CA 91367-2407. 818/737-4000. **Toll-free phone:** 800/678-6779. **Contact:** Human Resources. **World Wide Web address:** http://www.nps.cardinal.com. **Description:** Compounds, dispenses, and distributes patient-specific intravenous drugs and solutions for use in diagnostic imaging and offers a complete range of pharmacy services. **Corporate headquarters location:** This location. **Parent company:** Cardinal Health. **Operations at this facility include:** Administration. **Listed on:** New York Stock Exchange. **Stock exchange symbol:** CAH. **Number of employees at this location:** 175.

THE OAKLAND ATHLETICS (A'S)
7000 Coliseum Way, Oakland CA 94621. 510/638-4900. **Recorded jobline:** 510/638-4900x2817. **Contact:** Human Resources. **E-mail address:** hr@oaklandathletics.com. **World Wide Web address:** http://oakland.athletics.mlb.com. **Description:** Business offices for the Major League Baseball team. **NOTE:** Entry-level positions and part-time jobs are offered. **Positions advertised include:** Stadium Events Staff; Guest Relations Staff. **Special programs:** Internships. **Office hours:** Monday - Friday, 8:00 a.m. - 5:00 p.m. **Corporate headquarters location:** This location. **Listed on:** Privately held.

OAKLAND, CITY OF
150 Frank H. Ogawa Plaza, Second Floor, Oakland CA 94612. 510/444-2489. **Recorded jobline:** 510/238-3111. **Contact:** Human Resources. **World Wide Web address:** http://www.oaklandnet.com. **Description:** Government and administrative offices for Oakland CA. **NOTE:** See website for job listings. A completed application is required for any position. The application can be obtained at the website and completed online, or it can downloaded and printed and mailed. Interested jobseekers can also call the Human Resources Office and request an application. **Positions advertised include:** Equal Opportunity Manager; Planner; Public Works Personnel Coordinator; Treasury Analyst; Program Analyst.

OAKLAND MARRIOTT CITY CENTER
1001 Broadway, Oakland CA 94607. 510/451-4000. **Fax:** 510/835-3460. **Recorded jobline:** 510/466-6440. **Contact:** Human Resources. **World Wide Web address:** http://www.marriott.com. **Description:** A full-service hotel and restaurant with over 400 rooms. Oakland Marriott City Center also has conference rooms and meeting space. This location also hires seasonally. **NOTE:** Entry-level positions and part-time jobs are offered. **Special programs:** Internships. **Office hours:** Monday - Friday, 9:00 a.m. - 5:00 p.m. **Corporate headquarters location:** San Francisco CA. **Parent company:** Park Lane Hotels International. **Listed on:** New York Stock Exchange. **Stock exchange symbol:** HMT. **Number of employees at this location:** 400.

OAKLAND RAIDERS
1220 Harbor Bay Parkway, Alameda CA 94502. 510/864-5000. **Contact:** Human Resources. **World Wide Web address:** http://www.raiders.com. **Description:** Offices for the National Football League team.

OAKLAND TRIBUNE, INC.
401 13th Street, Oakland CA 94612. 510/208-6300. **Fax:** 510/293-2725. **Contact:** Human Resources. **E-mail address:** hr@angnewspapers.com. **World Wide Web address:** http://www.insidebayarea.com. **Description:** Publishes a daily metropolitan newspaper with a circulation of approximately 155,000. **NOTE:** Resumes may be submitted by mail, fax, or e-mail. Address resumes to: ANG Newspapers, Attention: Human Resources, P.O. Box 28884, Oakland CA 94604. **Positions advertised include:** Senior Accountant; Call Center Supervisor; Classifieds Sales Representative; Sales Assistant; Plant Production Supervisor. **Corporate headquarters location:** This location. **Parent company:** ANG Newspapers.

OAKLEY, INC.
1 Icon, Foothill Ranch CA 92610. 949/951-0991. **Fax:** 949/454-1071. **Contact:** Human Resources. **World Wide Web address:** http//www.oakley.com. **Description:** A maker and retailer of high performance sunglasses and sports goggles. **Positions advertised include:** Apparel Development Manager; Brand Manager; Business Systems Analyst; Equipment Technician; Eyewear Test Engineer. **Corporate headquarters location:** This location. **Listed on:** New York Stock Exchange. **Stock exchange symbol:** OO.

OBJECTIVITY, INC.
640 West California Avenue, Suite 210, Sunnyvale CA 94086-2486. 408/992-7100. **Toll-free phone:** 800/767-6259. **Fax:** 408/992-7171. **Contact:** Human Resources. **E-mail address:** hr@objectivity.com. **World Wide Web address:** http://www.objectivity.com. **Description:** Manufactures computer database software. **NOTE:** Resumes may be submitted by mail, fax, or e-mail. **Corporate headquarters location:** This location.

OCCIDENTAL OF ELK HILLS, INC.
P.O. Box 1001 Tupman CA 93276. 661/763-6000. **Physical address:** 28590 Highway 119, Taft CA 93268. **Contact:** Human Resources. **World Wide Web address:** http://www.oxy.com. **Description:** Produces oil, gas, and natural gas for the Naval Petroleum Reserve in Elk Hills CA. **Corporate headquarters location:** Los Angeles CA. **Listed on:** New York Stock Exchange. **Stock exchange symbol:** OXY. **Number of employees at this location:** 500. **Number of employees worldwide:** 7,100.

OCCIDENTAL ENERGY MARKETING, INC.
WEST COAST DIVISION
111 West Ocean Boulevard, Suite 800, Long Beach CA 90802. 562/624-3263. **Contact:** Human Resources. **World Wide Web address:** http://www.oxywest.com. **Description:** OEMI markets Occidental Petroleum's California natural gas production.

OCCIDENTAL PETROLEUM CORPORATION
10889 Wilshire Boulevard, Los Angeles CA 90024. 310/208-8800. **Contact:** Human Resources. **E-mail address:** oogc_hr_staffing@oxy.com. **World Wide Web address:** http://www.oxy.com. **Description:** One of the world's leading oil and natural gas exploration companies. **Positions advertised include:** PeopleSoft Specialist. **Corporate headquarters location:** This location. **Listed on:** New York Stock Exchange. **Stock exchange symbol:** OXY.

OGILVY & MATHER
3530 Hayden Avenue, Culver City CA 90232. 310/280-2200. **Recorded jobline:** 212/237-5627. **Contact:** Mary Jensen, Director of Personnel. **World Wide Web address:** http://www.ogilvy.com. **Description:** An advertising agency. **Corporate headquarters location:** New York NY. **Other U.S. locations:** Nationwide. **Parent company:** WWP Group PLC.

OHLONE COLLEGE
43600 Mission Boulevard, P.O. Box 3909, Fremont CA 94539-0390. 510/659-6088. **Fax:** 510/659-6025. **Recorded jobline:** 510/656-8295. **Contact:** Human Resources. **E-mail address:** hr@ohlone.edu. **World Wide Web address:** http://www.ohlone.cc.ca.us. **Description:** A college offering both undergraduate and graduate degrees. **Positions advertised include:** Instructors, Various Disciplines; Director of Grants Development; Director of Institutional Research. **Other area locations:** Newark CA. **Number of employees at this location:** 550.

OLYMPIAN
999 Bayhill Drive, Suite 135, San Bruno CA 94066. 650/873-8200. **Toll-free phone:** 800/899-2376. **Fax:** 530/885-5851. **Contact:** Human Resources. **E-mail address:** hr@nellaoil.com. **World Wide Web address:** http://www.oly.com. **Description:** Distributes a wide variety of petroleum products. Founded in 1954. **NOTE:** Resumes may be submitted via mail, fax or e-mail. Address resumes to: Nella Oil Company, Attention: Human Resources, 2349 Rickenbacker Way, Auburn CA 95602. **Positions advertised include:** Cashier; Sales Associate; Gulf Transportation Driver. **Special programs:** Summer Jobs. **Corporate headquarters location:** This location. **Listed on:** Privately held. **Number of employees at this location:** 80.

ONCOLOGY THERAPEUTICS NETWORK
395 Oyster Point Boulevard, Suite 500, South San Francisco CA 94080. 650/952-8400. **Toll-free phone:** 800/482-6700. **Contact:** Human Resources. **World Wide Web address:** http://www.otnnet.com. **Description:** Distributes pharmaceuticals and related products for the treatment of cancer to oncology physicians. **Corporate headquarters location:** New York NY. **Parent company:** Bristol-Myers Squibb. **Listed on:** New York Stock Exchange. **Stock exchange symbol:** BMY.

ONE PICO RESTAURANT
One Pico Boulevard, Santa Monica CA 90405-1062. 310/587-1717. **Contact:** Manager. **World Wide Web address:** http://www.shuttersonthebeach.com/restaurants/pico. **Description:** A restaurant serving New American cuisine. The restaurant is located in Shutters Hotel.

ONYX PHARMACEUTICALS, INC.
2100 Powell Street, Emeryville CA 94608. 510/597-6500. **Fax:** 510/597-6604. **Contact:** Human Resources. **E-mail address:** resumes@onyx-pharm.com. **World Wide Web address:** http://www.onyx-pharm.com. **Description:** Engaged in the discovery and development of innovative therapeutics based on the genetics of human disease. The company's main focus is on the discovery of cancer treatments. **NOTE:** Search and apply for positions online. **Positions advertised include:** Director, Regulatory Affairs; Medical Science Liaison; Product Manager. **Corporate headquarters location:** This location. **Listed on:** NASDAQ. **Stock exchange symbol:** ONXX.

OPHTHALMIC IMAGING SYSTEMS
221 Lathrop Way, Suite I, Sacramento CA 95815. 916/646-2020. **Toll-free phone:** 800/338-8436. **Fax:** 916/646-0207. **Contact:** Human Resources. **World Wide Web address:** http://www.oisi.com. **Description:** Designs, manufactures, and markets ophthalmic digital imaging systems and other diagnostic imaging equipment used by eye care professionals. Ophthalmic Imaging Systems also develops image enhancement and analysis software. **Corporate headquarters location:** This location. **Parent company:** MediVision Medical Imaging Ltd. (Israel). **Number of employees at this location:** 25.

OPTIMAL SYSTEMS SERVICES
2722 South Fairview Street, Santa Ana CA 92704-5947. 714/957-8500. **Toll-free phone:** 800/253-3434. **Fax:** 714/957-8705. **Contact:** Human Resources. **World Wide Web address:** http://www.oss.opmr.com. **Description:** Provides consulting, networking, software support, and maintenance services. **Corporate headquarters location:** This location. **Parent company:** Optimal Robotics Inc.

ORACLE CORPORATION
500 Oracle Parkway, LTN-1, Redwood Shores CA 94065. 650/506-7000. **Contact:** Recruiting. **E-mail address:** resumes_us@oracle.com. **World Wide Web address:** http://www.oracle.com. **Description:** Designs and manufactures database and information management software for business, and provides consulting services. **NOTE:** Search and apply for positions online. **Positions advertised include:** Software Development Manager; Applications Developer; Product Management Director; Support Engineer. **Corporate headquarters location:** This location. **Other U.S. locations:** Nationwide. **Operations at this facility include:** Administration; Sales. **Listed on:** NASDAQ. **Stock exchange symbol:** ORCL. **Number of employees nationwide:** 41,000.

ORANGE COUNTY ASSOCIATION FOR RETARDED CITIZENS
225 West Carl Karcher Way, Anaheim CA 92801-2499. 714/744-5301. **Fax:** 714/744-5312. **Contact:** Human Resources. **E-mail address:** info@orangecountyarc.org.

World Wide Web address: http://www.orangecountyarc.org. **Description:** A supported employment program where adults with mental disabilities provide product packaging and assembly. **Corporate headquarters location:** This location.

ORCHARD SUPPLY HARDWARE
SEARS HARDWARE STORES
6450 Via Del Oro, San Jose CA 95119. 408/281-3500. **Fax:** 408/365-2690. **Contact:** Human Resources. **E-mail address:** jobsosh@sears.com. **World Wide Web address:** http://www.osh.com. **Description:** Operates more than 250 retail stores nationwide. Products are primarily geared toward home repair and maintenance projects. Founded in 1931. **NOTE:** Address resumes to: Orchard Supply Hardware, Attention: Human Resources, P.O. Box 49027, San Jose CA 95161-9027. **Company slogan:** We are committed to providing our customers with legendary customer service. **Positions advertised include:** Manager, Imports; Training Manager; Direct Loss Prevention Manager. **Special programs:** Internships; Training; Summer Jobs. **Corporate headquarters location:** This location. **Other U.S. locations:** Nationwide. **Parent company:** Sears, Roebuck and Company. **Number of employees at this location:** 300. **Number of employees nationwide:** 13,000.

ORIENT OVERSEAS CONTAINER LINE INC. (OOCL)
111 West Ocean Boulevard, Suite 1800, Long Beach CA 90802. 562/499-2600. **Fax:** 562/435-2750. **Contact:** Human Resources. **E-mail address:** hrinfo@oocl.com. **World Wide Web address:** http://www.oocl.com. **Description:** Provides a containerized cargo distribution system to shippers worldwide. **NOTE:** Entry-level positions and part-time jobs are offered. **Company slogan:** We take it personally. **Special programs:** Internships. **Corporate headquarters location:** This location. **Other U.S. locations:** Nationwide. **International locations:** Worldwide. **Parent company:** Orient Overseas Ltd. **Number of employees worldwide:** 4,000.

ORINCON INDUSTRIES
4770 Eastgate Mall, San Diego CA 92121. 858/455-5530. **Fax:** 858/795-8534. **Contact:** Doreen Bortos, Human Resources Administrator. **E-mail address:** resumes@orincon.com. **World Wide Web address:** http://www.orincon.com. **Description:** Engaged in the design, development, and evaluation of signal processing communications, navigation, artificial intelligence, and tracking systems for U.S. Department of Defense applications, as well as for the transportation, biotechnology, and financial markets. **NOTE:** Entry-level positions are offered. **Corporate headquarters location:** This location. **Parent company:** Lockheed Martin. **Number of employees at this location:** 100.

ORMCO CORPORATION
1717 West Collins Avenue, Orange CA 92867. 714/516-7400. **Fax:** 714/516-7953. **Contact:** Human Resources Manager. **E-mail address:** careers@sybrondental.com. **World Wide Web address:** http://www.ormco.com. **Description:** Manufactures and markets orthodontic appliances and supplies. **NOTE:** Search and apply for positions online. **Positions advertised include:** Account Management Center Representative. **Office hours:** Monday - Friday, 8:00 a.m. - 5:00 p.m. **Corporate headquarters location:** This location. **Parent company:** Sybron Dental Specialties. **Number of employees at this location:** 110.

OROWEAT/BIMBO BAKERIES USA
264 South Spruce Avenue, South San Francisco CA 94080. 650/875-3100. **Contact:** Human Resources. **World Wide Web address:** http://www.bimbobakeriesusa.com. **Description:** Manufactures and distributes a line of cakes, cookies, doughnuts, and similar baked products. **Corporate headquarters location:** Fort Worth TX. **Other U.S. locations:** Clinton CT; Greenwich CT; Trumbull CT; Chicago IL; Rolling Meadows IL; Edgewater NJ; Englewood Cliffs NJ; Saddle Brook NJ; New York NY; Cincinnati OH; Dallas TX. **International locations:** Worldwide. **Parent company:** Grupo Bimbo (Mexico).

OTIS ELEVATOR COMPANY
2303 Camino Ramon, Suite 180, San Ramon CA 94583. 925/824-4780. **Contact:** Personnel Director. **World Wide Web address:** http://www.otis.com. **Description:** Engaged in the manufacture, installation, and service of elevators and escalators. **Positions advertised include:** Account Representative. **Parent company:** United Technologies Corporation. **Listed on:** New York Stock Exchange. **Stock exchange symbol:** UTX.

THE OUTDOOR CHANNEL
43445 Business Park Drive, Suite 103, Temecula CA 92590. **Toll-free phone:** 800/770-5750. . **Fax:** 951/699-6313. **Contact:** Vicki Windham, Manager of Human Resources. **E-mail address:** vwindham@outdoorchannel.com. **World Wide Web address:** http://www.outdoorchannel.com. **Description:** A national television network. **NOTE:** No telephone call accepted. **Positions advertised include:** Media Research Analyst; Production Assistant; Freelance Camera Operator. **Corporate headquarters location:** This location. **Listed on:** NASDAQ. **Stock exchange symbol:** GLRS.

OVERTURE SERVICES, INC.
74 North Pasadena Avenue, Pasadena CA 91103. 626/685-5600. **Fax:** 626/685-5601. **Contact:** Human Resources. **World Wide Web address:** http://www.overture.com. **Description:** Provides marketing services to companies doing business online. **Positions advertised include:** Account Executive; Associate Marketing Manager; Business Planning Analyst; Customer Service Representative; Development Manager; Network Support Engineer; Senior Java Developer; Senior Product Manager. **Special programs:** Internships. **Corporate headquarters location:** This location. **Other area locations:** Carlsbad CA; Sunnyvale CA. **Other U.S. locations:** Chicago IL; New York NY. **Parent company:** Yahoo! Inc. **Number of employees at this location:** Over 800.

OWENS-CORNING FIBERGLAS CORPORATION
960 Central Expressway, Santa Clara CA 95050. 408/727-3535. **Toll-free phone:** 800/GET-PINK. **Contact:** Personnel. **E-mail address:** resume@owenscorning.com. **World Wide Web address:** http://www.owenscorning.com. **Description:** Manufactures and sells thermal and acoustical insulation products including insulation for appliances, glass fiber roofing shingles, and roof insulation and industrial asphalt. Other products of the company include windows, glass fiber textile yarns, wet process chopped strands and specialty mats, and polyester resins. **Corporate headquarters location:** Toledo OH. **Other U.S. locations:** Nationwide. **Subsidiaries include:** Barbcorp, Inc.; Dansk-Svensk Glasfiber AS; Eric Co.; European Owens-Corning Fiberglas SA; IPM Inc.; Kitsons Insulations Products Ltd.; Owens-Corning AS; Owens-Corning Building Products; Owens-Corning Finance; Owens-Corning FSC, Inc. Illinois, Inc. **Listed on:** New York Stock Exchange. **Stock exchange symbol:** OWC.

OWENS-ILLINOIS GLASS CONTAINERS
22302 Hathaway Avenue, Hayward CA 94541. 510/784-0881. **Fax:** 419/247-7107. **Contact:** Human Resources Department. **E-mail address:** resumes.oi@owens-ill.com (no attachments, please). **World Wide Web address:** http://www.o-i.com. **Description:** Owens-Illinois produces glass containers and also produces and sells containerboard, corrugated containers, printing plates and ink, plywood and dimension lumber, blown plastic containers, plastic beverage bottles, plastic drums, metal and plastic closures, tamper-resistant closures, plastic and glass prescription containers, pharmaceutical items, labels, and multipack plastic carriers for containers. **Corporate headquarters location:** Toledo OH. **Parent company:** Owens-Illinois, Inc. **Operations at this facility include:** This location manufactures glass. **Listed on:** New York Stock Exchange. **Stock exchange symbol:** OI.

OWENS-ILLINOIS GLASS CONTAINERS
3600 Alameda Avenue, Oakland CA 94601. 510/436-2000. **Contact:** Personnel Director. **E-mail address:** resumes.oi@owens-ill.com (no attachments, please). **World Wide Web address:** http://www.o-i.com. **Description:** Owens-Illinois produces glass containers and also produces and sells containerboard, corrugated containers, printing plates and ink, plywood and dimension lumber, blown plastic containers, plastic beverage bottles, plastic drums, metal and plastic closures, tamper-resistant closures, plastic and glass prescription containers, pharmaceutical items, labels and multipack plastic carriers for containers. **Corporate headquarters location:** Toledo OH. **Parent company:** Owens-Illinois, Inc. **Operations at this facility include:** This location is a diversified manufacturer of packaging products including glass containers. **Listed on:** New York Stock Exchange. **Stock exchange symbol:** OI.

OXNARD, CITY OF
300 West Third Street, First Floor, Oxnard CA 93030. 805/385-7590. **Fax:** 805/385-8352. **Recorded jobline:** 805/385-7580. **Contact:** Human Resources Department. **E-mail address:** personnel@ci.oxnard.ca.us. **World Wide Web address:** http://www.ci.oxnard.ca.us. **Description:** Provides government services for the City of Oxnard. **NOTE:** Open positions and application forms online. **Positions advertised include:** Database Administrator; Information System Specialist; Police Officer; Reference Librarian.

PAC FOUNDRIES
705 Industrial Avenue, Port Hueneme CA 93041. 805/488-6451. **Contact:** Maria De La Torre, Director of Human Resources Department. **World Wide Web address:** http://www.cfi-pac.com. **Description:** Manufactures steel and aluminum investment castings. **Parent company:** Consolidated-PAC Foundries. **Number of employees at this location:** 240.

PC PROFESSIONAL INC.
1615 Webster Street, Oakland CA 94612. 510/465-5700. **Fax:** 510/465-8327. **Contact:** Human Resources. **E-mail address:** resume@pcprofessional.com. **World Wide Web address:** http://www.pcprofessional.com. **Description:** A value-added reseller of various types of computer hardware to corporate and consumer customers. **Positions advertised include:** Sales Account Manager; Field Service Engineer. **Corporate headquarters location:** This location.

PCC STRUCTURALS
414 Hester Street, San Leandro CA 94577. 510/568-6400. **Fax:** 510/635-1922. **Contact:** Human Resources. **E-mail address:** lgossett@wyman.com. **World Wide Web address:** http://www.pccstructurals.com. **Description:** An aerospace investment casting foundry that manufactures high-technology ferrous and nonferrous castings. **Corporate headquarters location:** Portland OR.

PCMALL
2555 West 190th Street, Torrance CA 90504. 310/354-5600. **Toll-free phone:** 800/863-3282. **Contact:** Human Resources. **E-mail address:** salesrecruit@pcmall.com **World Wide Web address:** http://www.pcmall.com. **Description:** A leading reseller of computer products to businesses, governmental and educational institutions, and consumers. Founded in 1987. **Positions advertised include:** Manager of Data Mining and Analytics; Category Marketing Manager; Purchasing Manager; Account Executive. **Corporate headquarters location:** This location. **Listed on:** NASDAQ. **Stock exchange symbol:** MALL. **Annual sales/revenues:** $975 million.

PTI TECHNOLOGIES, INC.
501 Del Norte Boulevard, Oxnard CA 93030. 805/604-3700. **Toll-free phone:** 800/331-2701. **Fax:** 805/604-3772. **Contact:** Human Resources. **E-mail address:** hr@ptitechnologies.com. **World Wide Web address:** http://www.ptitechnologies.com. **Description:** Designs, manufactures, and markets filtration and coupling equipment that is used in most commercial, military, and general aviation aircraft. PTI Technologies also produces and markets filters for use in fluid power systems in heavy equipment, industrial machinery, and energy extraction applications. **Positions advertised include:** Electromechanical Engineer. **Special programs:** Summer Jobs. **Corporate headquarters location:** St. Louis MO. **Parent company:** ESCO Electronics Corporation is a diversified producer of defense systems and commercial products including valves and filters, mobile tactical systems, armament systems, automatic test equipment, utility load management equipment, and anechoic/shielding systems. ESCO's other operating subsidiaries include EMC Test Systems, L.P.; VACCO Industries; Comtrak Technologies, Inc.; Filtertek Inc.; Lindgren RF Enclosures; Distribution Control Systems, Inc.; Rantec Microwave & Electronics. **Listed on:** New York Stock Exchange. **Stock exchange symbol:** ESE.

PACIFIC GAS & ELECTRIC COMPANY (PG&E)
77 Beale Street, P.O. Box 770000, San Francisco CA 94177. 415/973-7000. **Fax:** 415/972-5972. **Contact:** Human Resources. **World Wide Web address:** http://www.pgecorp.com. **Description:** An investor-owned utility that supplies electric and natural gas service throughout northern and central California. **Positions advertised include:** Computer Systems Analyst; Associate Procurement Specialist; Systems Dispatcher; Senior Database Analyst. **Corporate headquarters location:** This location. **Listed on:** New York Stock Exchange. **Stock exchange symbol:** PCG. **Number of employees nationwide:** 21,000.

PACIFIC LIFE INSURANCE
P.O. Box 9000, Newport Beach CA 92658-9030. 949/640-3011. **Physical address:** 700 Newport Center Drive, Newport Beach CA 92660. **Fax:** 949/640-7614. **Contact:** Human Resources. **E-mail address:** plemploy@pacificlife.com. **World Wide Web address:** http://www.pacificlife.com. **Description:** Provides insurance services including group health, life, and pensions. Pacific Life Insurance also provides financial services including annuities, mutual funds, and investments. **Positions advertised include:** Accounting Manager; Reporting Representative; Business Systems Analyst; Business Service Specialist; Executive Administrative Specialist; Senior Database Administrator; Software Engineer; Securities Accounting Analyst; Benefits Plan Analyst; Contracting Specialist; Actuarial Intern; Marketing Intern; Risk Management Intern. **Special programs:** Internships. **Corporate headquarters location:** This location.

PACIFIC LUMBER COMPANY
P.O. Box 37, Scotia CA 95565. 707/764-2222. **Contact:** Personnel Department. **E-mail address:** jobs@palco.com. **World Wide Web address:** http://www.palco.com.

Description: Manufactures redwood and Douglas fir lumber. **Corporate headquarters location:** This location. **Number of employees nationwide:** 900.

PACIFIC PRECISION LABORATORIES, INC.
9207 Eton Avenue, Chatsworth CA 91311. 818/700-8977. **Fax:** 818/700-8984. **Contact:** Human Resources. **World Wide Web address:** http://www.jmar-psi.com. **Description:** Specializes in the manufacture and integration of measurement and material processing systems based on submicron motion control and optical measurement technology.

PACIFIC ROLLER DIE COMPANY INC.
1321 West Winton Avenue, Hayward CA 94545. 510/782-7242. **Fax:** 510/887-5639. **Contact:** Human Resources. **World Wide Web address:** http://www.prdcompany.com. **Description:** Designs, manufactures, and supports a full range of systems to produce spiral weldseam pipe, corrugated metal pipe and building panels, and duct products. **Corporate headquarters location:** This location.

PACIFIC SCIENTIFIC COMPANY
1800 Highland Avenue, Duarte CA 91010. 626/359-9317. **Fax:** 626/357-2107. **Contact:** Human Resources Department. **World Wide Web address:** http://www.pacsci.com. **Description:** Manufactures commercial aircraft equipment such as fire extinguishers, industrial gauges, and pressure gauges. **Corporate headquarters location:** Washington DC. **Other U.S. locations:** Silver Spring MD.

PACIFIC SCIENTIFIC QUANTIC
990 Commercial Road, San Carlos CA 94070. 650/590-4079. **Fax:** 650/637-3093. **Contact:** Personnel. **E-mail address:** hr@psemc.com. **World Wide Web address:** http://www.psemc.com. **Description:** Produces sophisticated aerospace equipment such as satellite guidance systems and aerospace ordnance devices. **Office hours:** Monday - Friday, 8:00 a.m. - 5:00 p.m. **Corporate headquarters location:** Chandler AZ. **Other area locations:** Valencia CA; Hollister CA.

PACIFIC STEEL CASTING COMPANY
1333 Second Street, Berkeley CA 94710. 510/525-9200. **Fax:** 510/524-4673. **Contact:** Ralph Hoover, Controller. **World Wide Web address:** http://www.pacificsteel.com. **Description:** Produces steel castings and is engaged in the heat-treating of metals. **Corporate headquarters location:** This location.

PACIFIC SUNWEAR
3450 East Miraloma Avenue, Anaheim CA 92806-2101. 714/414-4000. **Fax:** 714/701-4294. **Contact:** Human Resources. **E-mail address:** careers@pacificsunwear.com. **World Wide Web address:** http://www.pacsun.com. **Description:** A surf and skateboard style clothing retailer. **NOTE:** Search and apply for positions or submit resume online. **Positions advertised include:** Buyer; Designer; Director of Merchandise Planning; Director, Loss Prevention; Distribution Center Operations Manager; HR Generalist Coordinator; Instructional Designer; Manager, Corporate Facilities; Manager, Internal Audit. **Special programs:** Internships. **Corporate headquarters location:** This location. **Other U.S. locations:** Nationwide. **Listed on:** NASDAQ. **Stock exchange symbol:** PSUN. **Annual sales/revenues:** $1 billion.

PACIFICARE HEALTH SYSTEMS, INC.
5995 Plaza Drive Cypress CA 90630. 714/952-1121. **Contact:** Human Resources. **World Wide Web address:** http://www.pacificare.com. **Description:** A regionally focused health care company with six HMOs operating in California, Oklahoma, Oregon, Texas, Florida, and Washington. Services include PPOs, life and health insurance, Medicare risk management programs, dental care services, and pharmacy services. The company has a contract to provide health services to military personnel and their dependents in 19 states. **Positions advertised include:** Senior Internal Auditor. **Corporate headquarters location:** This location. **Subsidiaries include:** COMPREMIER, Inc. provides workers' compensation care; Execu-Fit Health Programs, Inc.; LifeLink, Inc., is a mental health services provider; Prescription Solutions. **Listed on:** NASDAQ. **Stock exchange symbol:** PHSY. **Number of employees nationwide:** 7,500.

PACIFICARE HEALTH SYSTEMS, INC.
2300 Clayton Road, Suite 1000, Concord CA 94520. 925/246-1300. **Contact:** Human Resources. **World Wide Web address:** http://www.pacificare.com. **Description:** A regionally focused health care company with six HMOs. Services include PPOs, life and health insurance, Medicare risk management programs, dental care, and pharmacy services. **Positions advertised include:** Marketing and Sales Associate; Clinical Operations Manager. **Corporate headquarters location:** Cypress CA. **Subsidiaries include:** COMPREMIER, Inc. provides workers' compensation care; Execu-Fit Health Programs, Inc.; LifeLink, Inc., is a mental health services provider; Prescription Solutions. **Listed on:** NASDAQ. **Stock exchange symbol:** PHSY.

PACIFICARE HEALTH SYSTEMS, INC.
3120 West Lake Center Drive, Santa Ana CA 92704. 714/825-5200. **Contact:** Human Resources. **World Wide Web address:** http://www.pacificare.com. **Description:** A regionally focused health care company with six HMOs operating in California, Oklahoma, Oregon, Texas, Florida, and Washington. Services include PPOs, life and health insurance, Medicare risk management programs, dental care services, and pharmacy services. The company has a contract to provide health services to military personnel and their dependents in 19 states. **Positions advertised include:** Sales Training Manager. **Corporate headquarters location:** Cypress CA. **Subsidiaries include:** COMPREMIER, Inc. provides workers' compensation care; Execu-Fit Health Programs, Inc.; LifeLink, Inc., is a mental health services provider; Prescription Solutions. **Listed on:** NASDAQ. **Stock exchange symbol:** PHSY.

PACO JOHNSTON PUMP COMPANY
3215 Producer Way, Pomona CA 91768. 909/594-9959. **Contact:** Human Resources. **E-mail address:** jphr@flow-products.com. **World Wide Web address:** http://www.johnston-pump.com. **Description:** Manufactures, markets, and services engineered centrifugal pumps to the commercial, construction, industrial, municipal, and irrigation markets. The company's product line includes end suction, double suction split case, in-lines, and booster systems, as well as sump and sewage pumps. **NOTE:** All hiring is conducted by the parent company. Please direct resumes to Paco Johnston Pump Company, Human Resources, 800 Koomey Road, Brookshire TX 77423. 281/934-6014. **Other U.S. locations:** Oakland CA; Portland OR; Dallas TX; Seattle WA. **Operations at this facility include:** Manufacturing; Sales; Service. **Number of employees at this location:** 20. **Number of employees nationwide:** 250.

PACTIV CORPORATION
14505 Proctor Avenue, City of Industry CA 91746. 626/968-3801. **Contact:** Charles Daniel, Personnel Manager. **World Wide Web address:** http://www.pactiv.com. **Description:** Manufactures proprietary products made entirely or partially of plastics. Major product lines include food packaging, apparel hangers, internally illuminated signs, recreational vehicle components, and swimming pool products. **Corporate headquarters location:** Lake Forest IL. **Listed on:** New York Stock Exchange. **Stock exchange symbol:** PTV.

PARAMOUNT PICTURES CORPORATION
5555 Melrose Avenue, Hollywood CA 90038-3197. 323/956-5000. **Fax:** 323/862-1134. **Recorded jobline:** 323/956-5216. **Contact:** Human Resources – Dept. WEB. **World Wide Web address:** http://www.paramount.com. **Description:** Paramount Pictures Corporation is involved in many aspects of the entertainment industry including motion pictures, television, and video production and distribution. Founded in 1905. **Positions advertised include:** Assistant Product Manager; Financial Analyst; International Product Manager; Business Systems Analyst; Sr. Programmer Analyst; Sr. Operations Auditor; Sr. Financial Analyst; Director of Accounting. **Special programs:** Internships. **Corporate headquarters location:** New York NY. **Parent company:** Viacom, Inc. Other subsidiaries of Viacom include MTV, Blockbuster, Showtime, Nickelodeon, and Simon & Schuster. **Listed on:** New York Stock Exchange. **Stock exchange symbol:** VIA. **Number of employees at this location:** 3,000.

PARASOFT CORPORATION
101 East Huntington Drive, Monrovia CA 91016. 626/256-3680. **Fax:** 626/256-6884. **Contact:** Human Resources. **E-mail address:** jobs@parasoft.com. **World Wide Web address:** http://www.parasoft.com. **Description:** Develops software using C and C++. **NOTE:** Submit resumes via e-mail or fax. **Positions advertised include:** Software Engineer; Sales Engineer; Technical Writer; Inside Sales Representative; Public Relations Specialist. **Corporate headquarters location:** This location.

PAREX INC.
11290 South Vallejo Court, French Camp CA 95231. 209/983-8002. **Toll-free phone:** 800/780-6953. **Fax:** 209/983-1431. **Contact:** Human Resources Department. **World Wide Web address:** http://www.parex.com. **Description:** A manufacturer of stucco and exterior finishing materials. **Corporate headquarters location:** Redan GA. **Parent company:** Lafarge Mortars.

PARSONS BRINCKERHOFF INC.
303 Second Street, Suite 700 North, San Francisco CA 94107. 415/243-4600. **Fax:** 415/243-9501. **Contact:** Betsy Hume, Human Resources Department. **World Wide Web address:** http://www.pbworld.com. **Description:** Provides total engineering and construction management services from project conception through completion. Services include the development of major bridges, tunnels, highways, marine facilities, buildings, industrial complexes, and railroads. **Positions advertised include:** Environmental Planner. **Special programs:** Internships. **Corporate headquarters location:** New York NY. **Other U.S. locations:** Nationwide. **Subsidiaries include:** Parsons Brinckerhoff Construction Services; Parsons Brinckerhoff International. **Number of employees worldwide:** 9,000.

PARSONS CORPORATION
100 West Walnut Street, Pasadena CA 91124. 626/440-2000. **Fax:** 626/440-2630. **Contact:** Staffing Department. **World Wide Web address:** http://www.parsons.com. **Description:** Parsons Corporation provides engineering, planning, design, project management, and related services for a variety of projects including rail systems, highways, bridges, hazardous waste management, aviation facilities, environmental engineering, resorts, power generation and delivery systems, natural resources development, defense systems, industrial and institutional facilities, and community planning and development. **NOTE:** Apply online. **Positions advertised include:** Senior Engineer; Business Development Manager; Project Manager; Operations Manager; Associate Engineer; Principal Process Engineer; Senior Transportation Engineer. **Corporate headquarters location:** This location. **Other U.S. locations:** Nationwide. **Number of employees nationwide:** 2,000.

PASADENA, CITY OF
117 East Colorado Boulevard, Pasadena CA 91105. 626/744-4366. **Recorded jobline:** 626/744-4600. **Contact:** Human Resources. **World Wide Web address:** http://www.ci.pasadena.ca.us. **Description:** The city's government offices are located at this location. **NOTE:** A completed application is required for any position. Apply online at the website or download the application and mail it to the Human Resources Office. **Positions advertised include:** Community Youth Advisor; Police Cadet; Police Officer; Project Manager; Public Health Division Manager.

PEARSON EDUCATION
1301 Sansome Street, San Francisco CA 94111. 415/402-2500. **Contact:** Kelly Ripplone, Personnel Manager. **E-mail address:** staffing@pearsoned.com. **World Wide Web address:** http://www.pearsoned.com. **Description:** Pearson Education is one of the world's largest publishers and distributors of educational materials for use in elementary and high schools, universities, and businesses. **Positions advertised include:** Assistant Editor; Editorial Assistant; Copywriter; Managing Editor; Project Editor. **Office hours:** Monday - Friday, 8:30 a.m. - 5:00 p.m. **Corporate headquarters location:** Upper Saddle River NJ. **Other U.S. locations:** Boston MA; Glenview IL; New York NY; White Plains NY. **Parent company:** Pearson plc. **Operations at this facility include:** This location primarily publishes higher education computer science and engineering materials. **Listed on:** New York Stock Exchange. **Stock exchange symbol:** PSO.

PENTAIR POOL PRODUCTS
10951 West Los Angeles Avenue, Moorpark CA 93021. 805/523-2400. **Fax:** 805/530-0177. **Contact:** Kim Cowles, Personnel Director. **World Wide Web address:** http://www.pentairpool.com. **Description:** Manufactures water recreation and hydrotherapy equipment. **NOTE:** Entry-level positions are offered. **Corporate headquarters location:** Sanford NC. **Other U.S. locations:** FL; NJ. **Operations at this facility include:** Administration; Manufacturing; Regional Headquarters; Research and Development; Sales; Service. **Listed on:** New York Stock Exchange. **Stock exchange symbol:** PNR. **Number of employees nationwide:** 14,000.

PEOPLESOFT, INC.
4460 Hacienda Drive, Pleasanton CA 94588. 925/225-3000. **Fax:** 925/694-2699. **Contact:** Human Resources. **E-mail address:** jobs@peoplesoft.com. **World Wide Web address:** http://www.peoplesoft.com. **Description:** Provides client/server applications and software solutions for businesses worldwide. PeopleSoft develops, markets, and supports a variety of enterprise solutions for accounting, materials management, distribution, manufacturing, and human resources. The company also offers industry-specific enterprise solutions to markets including financial services, health care, manufacturing, higher education, the public sector, and the federal government. **NOTE:** Entry-level positions are offered. **Positions advertised include:** Applications Consultant; Senior Financial Analyst; Lead Development Representative; Transaction/Fraud Auditor; Field Support Marketing Manager; Collections Analyst; Assistant Treasurer. **Special programs:** Internships. **Corporate headquarters location:** This location. **Other area locations:** Irvine CA; Santa Clara CA. **Other U.S.**

locations: Miami FL; Atlanta GA; Chicago IL; Bethesda MD; Boston MA; Dallas TX. **International locations:** Worldwide. **Parent company:** Oracle.

PEOPLESOFT, INC.
2525 Augustine Drive, Santa Clara CA 95054. 408/982-5700. **Contact:** Human Resources. **E-mail address:** jobs@peoplesoft.com. **World Wide Web address:** http://www.peoplesoft.com. **Description:** Provides client/server applications and software solutions for businesses worldwide. PeopleSoft develops, markets, and supports a variety of enterprise solutions for accounting, materials management, distribution, manufacturing, and human resources. The company also offers industry-specific enterprise solutions to markets including financial services, health care, manufacturing, higher education, the public sector, and the federal government. **Corporate headquarters location:** Pleasanton CA. **Other area locations:** Irvine CA. **Other U.S. locations:** Miami FL; Atlanta GA; Chicago IL; Boston MA; Bethesda MD; Dallas TX. **International locations:** Worldwide. **Parent company:** Oracle. **Listed on:** NASDAQ. **Stock exchange symbol:** PSFT. **Annual sales/revenues:** $2.8 billion. **Number of employees worldwide:** 12,000.

PEPSI-COLA BOTTLING COMPANY
7550 Reese Road, Sacramento CA 95828. 916/423-1000. **Fax:** 916/423-0111. **Contact:** Human Resources. **World Wide Web address:** http://www.pbg.com. **Description:** A bottling facility for the Pepsi-Cola Company. **Positions advertised include:** Sales Manager; Technical Manager; District Sales Leader. **Parent company:** PepsiCo, Inc. (Purchase NY) consists of Frito-Lay Company, Pepsi-Cola Company, and Tropicana Products, Inc. **Corporate headquarters location:** Purchase NY. **Listed on:** New York Stock Exchange. **Stock exchange symbol:** PBG.

PEREGRINE SYSTEMS INC.
3611 Valley Centre Drive, San Diego CA 92103. 858/481-5000. **Fax:** 858/481-1751. **Contact:** Human Resources. **World Wide Web address:** http://www.peregrine.com. **Description:** Designs and manufactures help-desk software. **NOTE:** Search and apply for positions online. **Positions advertised include:** Contract Technical Recruiter; Sr. Software Engineer; Financial Analyst; Sr. Revenue Accountant; Analytical Application Engineer. **Corporate headquarters location:** This location. **Listed on:** NASDAQ. **Stock exchange symbol:** PRGN.

PERFORMANCE TECHNOLOGIES
4669 Murphy Canyon Road, Suite 250, San Diego CA 92123. 858/627-1700. **Fax:** 858/627-1710. **Contact:** Human Resources. **World Wide Web address:** http://www.pt.com. **Description:** Develops systems, platforms, components, and software for the communications infrastructure.

PERKINELMER
2841 Lomita Boulevard, Torrance CA 90505. 310/530-1414. **Contact:** Human Resources. **World Wide Web address:** http://www.perkinelmer.com. **Description:** Manufactures specialty lamps and equipment for laser pump, medical, industrial, and aerospace applications. The company is a leading designer and supplier of arc lamps for optical pumping of solid waste, other lasers, and specialty equipment. **Corporate headquarters location:** Wellesley MA. **Listed on:** New York Stock Exchange. **Stock exchange symbol:** PKI. **Number of employees worldwide:** 10,000.

PERKINELMER OPTOELECTRONICS
44370 Christy Street, Fremont CA 94538-3180. 510/979-6500. **Toll-free phone:** 800/775-6786. **Contact:** Cris Wilbur, Director of Human Resources Department. **E-mail address:** cris.wilbur@perkinelmer.com. **World Wide Web address:** http://www.perkinelmer.com. **Description:** PerkinElmer designs and manufactures a variety of image sensors, multiplexors, and camera systems for use in medical, scientific, and document scanning applications. **Positions advertised include:** Mechanical Engineer; Administrative Assistant; Manufacturing Engineer; Senior Financial Analyst. **Corporate headquarters location:** This location. **Operations at this facility include:** This location manufactures solid-state image sensors for electronics applications. **Listed on:** New York Stock Exchange. **Stock exchange symbol:** PKI.

PETERSON TRACTOR COMPANY
P.O. Box 5258, San Leandro CA 94577. 510/357-6200. **Physical address:** 955 Marina Boulevard, San Leandro CA 94577. **Fax:** 510/357-0634. **Contact:** Rich Hasper, Director of Human Resources. **E-mail address:** hr@petersonholding.com. **World Wide Web address:** http://www.petersontractor.com. **Description:** A wholesaler of Caterpillar heavy construction equipment and diesel engines. Peterson also has retail locations. **NOTE:** Search and apply for positions online. **Positions advertised include:** Project Manager; Sales Representative; Technician Welder; Inventory Clerk. **Corporate headquarters location:** This location. **Operations at this facility include:** Administration; Sales; Service.

PHAOSTRON INSTRUMENT AND ELECTRONIC COMPANY
717 North Coney Avenue, Azusa CA 91702-2205. 626/969-6801. **Fax:** 626/334-8057. **Contact:** Ms. Jackie Cangialosi, Personnel Manager. **World Wide Web address:** http://www.phaostron.com. **Description:** Primarily engaged in the manufacture and sale of panel meters, avionic mechanisms, and edge-lighted plastic panels for a variety of aircraft. **Corporate headquarters location:** This location. **Operations at this facility include:** Manufacturing. **Number of employees at this location:** 50.

PHILADELPHIA GEAR CORPORATION
2600 East Imperial Highway, P.O. Box 700, Lynwood CA 90262. 310/605-2600. **Toll-free phone:** 800/605-1002. **Fax:** 310/898-3594. **Contact:** Human Resources. **E-mail address:** westernservicecenter@philagear.com. **World Wide Web address:** http://www.philagear.com. **Description:** Manufactures heavy machinery gear and cable equipment. **Corporate headquarters location:** Norristown PA.

PHILLIPS MEDICAL SYSTEMS
540 Alder Drive, Milpitas CA 95035. 408/321-9100. **Contact:** Vice President of Human Resources. **E-mail address:** recruit@medical.philips.com. **World Wide Web address:** http://www.medical.philips.com. **Description:** Produces medical diagnostic computer systems and components including state-of-the-art digital radiography image processing, nuclear medicine image processing, and radiation therapy planning systems. **NOTE:** Search and apply for positions online. **Positions advertised include:** Expediter; Material Handler; Product Marketing Specialist; Research Scientist; Software Development Manager. **Corporate headquarters location:** This location. **Other U.S. locations:** Washington DC; Philadelphia PA.

PHILIPS SEMICONDUCTORS
1151 McKay Drive, San Jose CA 95131. 408/434-3000. **Contact:** Human Resources. **World Wide Web address:** http://www.semiconductors.philips.com. **Description:** Designs and manufactures application-specific and application-standard integrated circuits for computer, telecommunications, consumer, and industrial uses. **Positions advertised include:** Applications Engineer; Business Development Manager; Controller; Product Marketing Manager. **Special programs:** Internships. **Corporate headquarters location:** Eindhoven, The Netherlands. **Other U.S. locations:** Tempe AZ; San Antonio TX. **Listed on:** New York Stock Exchange. **Stock exchange symbol:** PHG. **Number of employees at this location:** 1,500. **Number of employees worldwide:** 31,000.

PHOENIX TECHNOLOGIES LTD.
915 Murphy Ranch Road, Milpitas CA 95035. 408/570-1000. **Toll-free phone:** 800/677-7305. **Fax:** 408/570-1001. **Contact:** Human Resources. **World Wide Web address:** http://www.phoenix.com. **Description:** Phoenix Technologies designs, develops, and markets systems software and end user software products. The Peripherals Division designs, develops, and supplies printer emulation software, page distribution languages, and controller hardware designs for the printing industry. The PhoenixPage imaging software architecture enables printer manufacturers to offer products that are compatible with the PostScript language, the PCL printer language, and other imaging standards. Phoenix Technologies' PC Division works with leading vendors and standards committees to ensure that Phoenix products enable manufacturers to develop and deploy next-generation PCs quickly and cost-effectively. The company's Package Products Division is a single-source publisher of MS-DOS, Windows, and other software packages. **NOTE:** Entry-level positions are offered. **Positions advertised include:** Sr. Product Marketing Manager; Oracle Applications Developer; Director, QA and Operations; Principal Engineer. **Special programs:** Internships. **Corporate headquarters location:** This location. **Other U.S. locations:** Norwood MA; Durham NC; Beaverton OR; Austin TX; Houston TX; Brookfield WI. **International locations:** Worldwide. **Listed on:** NASDAQ. **Stock exchange symbol:** PTEC. **Annual sales/revenues:** $85 million. **Number of employees at this location:** 140. **Number of employees worldwide:** 800.

PHOTRONICS INC.
1905 Tarob Court, Milpitas CA 95035. 408/262-8800. **Contact:** Dolores Hudson, Human Resources. **E-mail address:** Dolores@brk.photronics.com. **World Wide Web address:** http://www.photronics.com. **Description:** A manufacturer of photomasks for the semiconductor industry. **Corporate headquarters location:** Brookfield CT. **Listed on:** NASDAQ. **Stock exchange symbol:** PLAB. **Number of employees worldwide:** 1,400.

PILKINGTON NORTH AMERICA
500 East Louise Avenue, Lathrop CA 95330. 209/858-5151. **Contact:** Human Resources Manager. **World Wide Web address:** http://www.pilkington.com. **Description:** Pilkington is a diversified industrial manufacturer of glass, laminated and molded plastic products, fluid power and fluid systems components, valves, gaskets, and fittings. **Corporate headquarters location:** Toledo OH. **Operations at this facility include:** This location primarily produces automobile window and windshield glass.

PILLSBURY WINTHROP
101 West Broadway, Suite 1800, San Diego CA 92101. 619/234-5000. **Contact:** Marcia Hommel, Recruiter. **E-mail address:** recruit_sd@pillsburywinthrop.com. **World Wide Web address:** http://www.pillsburywinthrop.com. **Description:** A law firm specializing in bankruptcy, corporate, employment, environmental, intellectual property, and real estate law. **Positions advertised include:** Associate Attorney; It Manager; Trainer. **Corporate headquarters location:** San Francisco CA.

PINNACLE SYSTEMS
280 North Bernardo Avenue, Mountain View CA 94043. 650/526-1600. **Fax:** 650/526-1601. **Contact:** Human Resources. **E-mail address:** resume@pinnaclesys.com. **World Wide Web address:** http://www.pinnaclesys.com. **Description:** Develops digital and video-editing tools for both professional and consumer markets. Products include DVExtreme, a digital special effects system; and Studio 400, a video-editing system for consumers. **Positions advertised include:** Marketing Manager; Manufacturing Engineering Manager; Product Manager; Program Manager; Quality Engineer. **Corporate headquarters location:** This location. **Listed on:** NASDAQ. **Stock exchange symbol:** PCLE.

PITNEY BOWES MANAGEMENT SERVICES
1149 South Broadway, Suite 100, Los Angeles CA 90015. 213/746-4855. **Contact:** Human Resources. **E-mail address:** staffing@pb.com. **World Wide Web address:** http://www.pb.com. **Description:** A facility management company specializing in reprographics, facsimiles, mailroom, supply room, file room, and other related office services. **Special programs:** Internships. **Corporate headquarters location:** Stamford CT. **Other U.S. locations:** Chicago IL; New York NY; Dallas TX. **Parent company:** Pitney Bowes Inc. **Operations at this facility include:** Administration; Divisional Headquarters; Regional Headquarters; Sales.

PIXAR ANIMATION STUDIOS
1200 Park Avenue, Emeryville CA 94608. 510/752-3000. **Fax:** 510/752-3151. **Contact:** Recruiting. **E-mail address:** hr@pixar.com. **World Wide Web address:** http://www.pixar.com. **Description:** A computer animation studio. Pixar Animation Studios produces various computer animated entertainment products in the form of feature films and computer software. **Positions advertised include:** Effects Technical Director; Layout Artist; Animator; Digital Painter; Set Dresser; Facilities Technician; Assistant Controller; Accounting Assistant; Software Engineer; Media Systems Engineer. **Corporate headquarters location:** This location. **Listed on:** NASDAQ. **Stock exchange symbol:** PIXR. **Number of employees at this location:** 430.

PLASTIC DRESS-UP COMPANY
11077 East Rush Street, South El Monte CA 91733. 626/442-7711. **Contact:** Human Resources Department. **World Wide Web address:** http://www.pdu.com. **Description:** Manufactures plastic trophy components. **Corporate headquarters location:** This location. **Number of employees at this location:** 550.

POLYCOM, INC.
4750 Willow Road, Pleasanton CA 94588-2708. 925/924-6000. **Toll-free phone:** 800/765-9266. **Fax:** 925/924-6100. **Contact:** Human Resources. **World Wide Web address:** http://www.polycom.com. **Description:** Creates, develops, and markets a variety of innovative videoconferencing devices and systems. **NOTE:** Search and apply for positions online. **Positions advertised include:** Assistant Corporate Controller; Financial Manager; Sr. Applications Integegration Engineer; Sr. Software Engineer. **Corporate headquarters location:** This location. **Listed on:** NASDAQ. **Stock exchange symbol:** PLCM. **Number of employees worldwide:** Over 1,000.

POMONA COLLEGE
550 North College Avenue, Alexander Hall, Room 129, Claremont CA 91711-6318. 909/621-8175. **Contact:** Anne Johnson, Personnel. **E-mail address:** anne.johnson@pomona.edu. **World Wide Web address:** http://www.pomona.edu. **Description:** A private, four-year, liberal arts college. **NOTE:** Search for positions and download application form online.

POMONA VALLEY HOSPITAL MEDICAL CENTER
1798 North Garey Avenue, Pomona CA 91767. 909/865-9500. **Fax:** 909/623-3253. **Recorded jobline:** 909/865-9840. **Contact:** Rolanda Bradshaw, Employment Specialist. **World Wide Web address:** http://www.pvhmc.com. **Description:** A 449-bed, nonprofit, acute care, teaching hospital. The hospital offers medical services through the Robert and Beverly Lewis Cancer Care Center; the Stead Heart Center; and the Women's Center. Founded in 1903. **Positions advertised include:** Registered Nurse; Admitting Representative; Claims Examiner; Phlebotomist; Patient Account Coordinator; Food Services Associate; Sous Chef; Occupational Therapist; Radiology Technologist; Sonographer; Respiratory Therapist; Medical Social Worker; Speech Therapist. **Office hours:** Monday – Friday. 7:30 a.m. – 5:00 p.m. **Operations at this facility include:** Administration; Service. **Number of employees at this location:** 2,700.

PORT OF OAKLAND
530 Water Street, Oakland CA 94607. 510/627-1100. **Contact:** Manager of Personnel and Employee Services. **E-mail address:** perstech@portofoakland.com. **World Wide Web address:** http://www.portofoakland.com. **Description:** Operates Oakland International Airport, maritime facilities, and commercial real estate properties. **NOTE:** The above e-mail address may be used to request an application. **Special programs:** Internships. **Corporate headquarters location:** This location. **Operations at this facility include:** Administration; Service. **Number of employees at this location:** 600.

PORT OF SAN FRANCISCO
Pier One, San Francisco CA 94111. 415/274-0400. **Fax:** 415/274-0528. **Contact:** Kathy Mallegni, Personnel Manager. **World Wide Web address:** http://www.sfport.com. **Description:** Operates port facilities as an agency of both the City and County of San Francisco. **NOTE:** The San Francisco municipal employment application is available online at: http://www.sfgov.org. **Positions advertised include:** Architect; Manager.

PORT OF STOCKTON
P.O. Box 2089, Stockton CA 95201. 209/946-0246. **Physical address:** 2201 West Washington Street, Stockton CA 95203. **Toll-free phone:** 800/344-3213. **Fax:** 209/941-0537. **Contact:** Human Resources. **E-mail address:** humanresources@stocktonport.com. **World Wide Web address:** http://www.portofstockton.com. **Description:** Provides berthing and warehousing facilities for inbound and outbound marine shipping. The port also provides domestic offices and warehouse space, and has land available for industrial development. **Corporate headquarters location:** This location. **Operations at this facility include:** Administration. **Annual sales/revenues:** $11 - $20 million. **Number of employees at this location:** 80.

PORTAL PUBLICATIONS
201 Alameda Del Prado, Novato CA 94949. 415/884-6200. **Fax:** 415/382-1082. **Contact:** Human Resources. **E-mail address:** recruiter@portalpub.com. **World Wide Web address:** http://www.portalpub.com. **Description:** One of the world's largest publishers of original artwork, posters, prints, cards, calendars, and related products. **Positions advertised include:** Payroll Specialist; Inside Sales Representative; Customer Service Representative; Senior Graphic Designer. **Corporate headquarters location:** This location. **Subsidiaries include:** Aird Imports Pty. Ltd., Australia; Regency House Pictures and Frames, Inc., Decatur GA; The Winn Devon Art Group, Ltd., Seattle WA. **Parent company:** Applied Graphics Technology. **Listed on:** American Stock Exchange. **Stock exchange symbol:** AGD.

PORTER NOVELLI
550 Third Street, San Francisco CA 94107. 415/975-2200. **Fax:** 415/975-2201. **Contact:** Kim Mesfin, Human Resources. **E-mail address:** bayareacareers@porternovelli.com. **World Wide Web address:** http://www.porternovelli.com. **Description:** A public relations firm primarily serving the high-tech and consumer electronics industries. **Positions advertised include:** Assistant Account Executive; Sr. Account Executive. **Corporate headquarters location:** New York NY. **Other U.S. locations:** Atlanta GA; Boston MA; New York NY; Chicago IL; Seattle WA; Washington DC.

PORTRAIT DISPLAYS, INC.
6663 Owens Drive, Pleasanton CA 94588. 925/227-2700. **Fax:** 925/227-2705. **Contact:** Human Resources Department. **E-mail address:** hr@portrait.com. **World Wide Web address:** http://www.portrait.com. **Description:** A manufacturer of pivoting, portrait-capable computer monitors. The company's software line allows the user to view and edit documents in either landscape, or portrait orientation, and offers an image rotation function as well. **Positions advertised include:** Sr. Sales/Application Engineer; Software Engineer; Software Development Manager. **Office hours:** Monday - Friday, 9:00 a.m. - 5:00 p.m. **Corporate headquarters location:** This location. **Listed on:** Privately held.

POWER-ONE, INC.
740 Calle Plano, Camarillo CA 93012. 805/987-8741. **Toll-free phone:** 800/678-9445. **Fax:** 805/389-8911. **Contact:** Melissa Dugan, Personnel Director. **E-mail address:** melissadugan@power-one.com. **World Wide Web address:** http://www.power-one.com. **Description:** Engaged in the manufacturing of DC power supplies. The company's product line includes linears, switchers, and hi-power to three kilowatts. Founded in 1973. **Positions advertised include:** Corporate Recruiter; Regional Sales Manager. **Corporate headquarters location:** This location. **Listed on:** NASDAQ. **Stock exchange symbol:** PWER. **Annual sales/revenues:** $256 million. **Number of employees at this location:** 250. **Number of employees worldwide:** Over 2,300.

POWER-SONIC CORPORATION
9163 Siempre Viva Road, Suite A, San Diego CA 92154. 619/661-2020. **Fax:** 619/661-3650. **Contact:** Ms. Kim Tran, Personnel Manager. **E-mail address:** jobs@power-sonic.com. **World Wide Web address:** http://www.power-sonic.com. **Description:** Manufactures rechargeable batteries for original equipment manufacturers. **Corporate headquarters location:** This location. **International locations:** Mexicali, Mexico. **Parent company:** Eldon Industries.

PRACTICEWARES DENTAL SUPPLY
11291 Sunrise Park Drive, Rancho Cordova CA 95742. 916/638-8147. **Contact:** Human Resources. **World Wide Web address:** http://www.practicewares.com. **Description:** Distributes professional and consumer dental products. Practicewares Dental Supply is also an authorized dealer for approximately 120 companies including 3M Dental Products, Eastman Kodak, and Premier. **Corporate headquarters location:** This location.

PRANDIUM, INC.
P.O. Box 19561, Irvine CA 92623-9561. 949/863-8500. **Fax:** 949/863-8855. **Contact:** Ken Gowen, Human Resources. **E-mail address:** careers@prandium.com. **World Wide Web address:** http://www.prandium.com. **Description:** Manages and operates Chi-Chi's restaurants in 13 states. **Corporate headquarters location:** This location. **Annual sales/revenues:** $257 million. **Number of employees at this location:** 200. **Number of employees nationwide:** 15,000.

PRICEWATERHOUSECOOPERS
400 Capital Mall, Suite 600, Sacramento CA 95814. 916/930-8100. **Contact:** Personnel. **E-mail address:** westpwcjobs@us.pwcglobal.com. **World Wide Web address:** http://www.pwcglobal.com. **Description:** One of the largest certified public accounting firms in the world. PricewaterhouseCoopers provides public accounting, business advisory, management consulting, and taxation services. **Positions advertised include:** Sr. Tax Associate; M&A Tax Manager; systems Assurnace Manager. **Corporate headquarters location:** New York NY. **Other U.S. locations:** Nationwide.

PRICEWATERHOUSECOOPERS
350 South Grand Avenue, Los Angeles CA 90071. 213/356-6000. **Fax:** 213/356-6363. **Contact:** Personnel. **E-mail address:** westpwcjobs@us.pwcglobal.com. **World Wide Web address:** http://www.pwcglobal.com. **Description:** One of the largest certified public accounting firms in the world. PricewaterhouseCoopers provides public accounting, business advisory, management consulting, and taxation services. **Positions advertised include:** Campus Recruiting Manager; International Tax Associate; Process Knowledge Manager; Middle Markets Tax Manager; Tax Associate; Senior Expatriate Tax Associate; Senior Associate, Oracle; Senior Associate, PeopleSoft; Internal Audit Manager. **Office hours:** Monday - Friday, 8:00 a.m. - 5:00 p.m. **Corporate headquarters location:** New York NY. **Other U.S. locations:** Nationwide.

PRICEWATERHOUSECOOPERS
333 Market Street, San Francisco CA 94105. 415/498-5000. **Contact:** Human Resources. **E-mail address:** westpwcjobs@us.pwcglobal.com. **World Wide Web address:** http://www.pwcglobal.com. **Description:** One of the largest certified public accounting firms in the world. PricewaterhouseCoopers provides public accounting, business advisory, management consulting, and taxation services. **Positions advertised include:** Health Policy Manager; Human Resources Manager; Senior Marketing Associate; Senior Real Estate Associate; Senior Insurance Associate; Executive Assistant, Tax; Assurance Manager. **Corporate headquarters location:** New York NY. **Other U.S. locations:** Nationwide.

PRICEWATERHOUSECOOPERS
199 Fremont Street, 7th Floor, San Francisco CA 94105. 415/498-5000. **Fax:** 415/498-5100. **Contact:** Human Resources. **E-mail address:** westpwcjobs@us.pwcglobal.com. **World Wide Web address:** http://www.pwcglobal.com. **Description:** One of the largest certified public accounting firms in the world. PricewaterhouseCoopers provides public accounting, business advisory, management consulting, and taxation services. **Positions advertised include:** Health Policy Manager; Human Resources Manager; Senior Marketing Associate; Senior Real Estate Associate; Senior Insurance Associate; Executive Assistant, Tax; Assurance Manager. **Special programs:** Internships. **Corporate headquarters location:** New York NY. **Other U.S. locations:** Nationwide.

PRIMEDIA
33046 Calle Aviador, San Juan Capistrano CA 92675. 949/496-5922. **Fax:** 949/496-7849. **Contact:** Human Resources. **World Wide Web address:** http://www.primedia.com. **Description:** Publishes *Skin Diver, Gravity Games, Surfer, Powder, Snowboarder,* and *Bike* magazines. The company also produces cable television and home video programs. **Corporate headquarters location:** New York NY. **Listed on:** New York Stock Exchange. **Stock exchange symbol:** PRM.

PRIME MEASUREMENT PRODUCTS, LLC
900 South Turnbull Canyon Road, City of Industry CA 91745. 626/961-2547. **Fax:** 626/937-0422. **Contact:** Bob Centeno, Human Resources. **E-mail address:** hr@prime-measurement.com. **World Wide Web address:** http://www.prime-measurement.com. **Description:** Develops and manufactures measurement information systems. Products are used for inventory management, flow measurement, and process monitoring control for the oil, gas, power, and chemical and petrochemical process industries. **Corporate headquarters location:** This location. **Other U.S. locations:** Nationwide. **International locations:** Worldwide.

PRINTRONIX INC.
14600 Myford Road, P.O. Box 19559, Irvine CA 92623. 949/863-1900. **Toll-free phone:** 800/665-6210. **Fax:** 714/368-2940. **Contact:** Human Resources. **E-mail address:** employment@printronix.com. **World Wide Web address:** http://www.printronix.com. **Description:** Designs, manufactures, and markets impact line printers and laser printers for use with minicomputers, microcomputers, and other computer systems. **Positions advertised include:** Industrial Engineer; Worldwide Product Manager; Human Resources Administrative Assistant; Warehouse Supervisor; Accounting Supervisor; Business Development Manager. **Corporate headquarters location:** This location. **Operations at this facility include:** Administration; Manufacturing; Research and Development; Sales; Service. **Listed on:** NASDAQ. **Stock exchange symbol:** PTNX.

PROCOPIO, CORY, HARGRAVES, & SAVITCH
530 B Street, 21st Floor, San Diego CA 92101. 619/238-1900. **Fax:** 619/235-0398. **Contact:** Human Resources Manager. **E-mail address:** bae@procopio.com. **World Wide Web address:** http://www.procopio.com. **Description:** A law firm specializing in real estate, bankruptcy, litigation, and corporate law. **Positions advertised include:** Corporate/Securities Associate; Intellectual Property Attorney; Real Estate Attorney. **Corporate headquarters location:** This location. **Operations at this facility include:** Administration. **Listed on:** Privately held. **Number of employees at this location:** 100.

PROGRESS SOFTWARE CORPORATION
10121 Miller Avenue, Suite 202, Cupertino CA 95014. 408/873-2010. **Fax:** 408/873-2019. **Contact:** Human Resources. **World Wide Web address:** http://www.progress.com. **Description:** A software company. **Corporate headquarters location:** Bedford MA. **Listed on:** NASDAQ. **Stock exchange symbol:** PRGS.

PROMINENT USA
777 South Figueroa Street, Suite 4500, Los Angeles CA 90017. 213/623-4001. **Contact:** Human Resources. **Description:** An international, multibusiness trading and investment company. Prominent USA specializes in developing and sponsoring profitable opportunities in international and domestic commerce, industry, and finance, either as a principal or as an agent. **Corporate headquarters location:** New York NY.

PROMISE TECHNOLOGY INC.
580 Cottonwood Drive, Milpitas CA 95035. 408/228-6300. **Fax:** 408/228-6407. **Contact:** Human Resources. **E-mail address:** humanresources@promise.com. **World Wide Web address:** http://www.promise.com. **Description:** Manufactures high-performance hard drive controller cards for use in IBM computers. **Positions**

advertised include: Technical Support Specialist; Senior Software Engineer; Hardware Engineer, Advanced Storage; Product Test Engineer; Staff Accountant. **Corporate headquarters location:** This location.

PROTEIN DESIGN LABS, INC.
34801 Campus Drive, Fremont CA 94555. 510/574-1400. **Fax:** 510/574-1500. **Contact:** Human Resources. **E-mail address:** careers@pdl.com. **World Wide Web address:** http://www.pdl.com. **Description:** A research and development company focused on the development of humanized and human monoclonal antibodies for the treatment and prevention of various diseases. **Positions advertised include:** Administrative Assistant; Clinical Research Associate; Medical Director; Stock/401K Administrator; Business Analyst; Network Analyst; Metrology Technician; Protein Chemistry Director. **Corporate headquarters location:** This location. **Other U.S. locations:** Plymouth MN; Brooklyn Park MN. **Listed on:** NASDAQ. **Stock exchange symbol:** PDH.

PROTEIN POLYMER TECHNOLOGIES, INC.
10655 Sorrento Valley Road, San Diego CA 92121. 858/558-6064. **Fax:** 858/558-6477. **Contact:** Human Resources. **World Wide Web address:** http://www.ppti.com. **Description:** Engaged in research and development of products for surgical repair procedures including tissue adhesives and sealants, adhesion barriers, and drug delivery devices. The company also markets a line of polymer-activated cell culture products. **Corporate headquarters location:** This location.

PROVIDIAN FINANCIAL
201 Mission Street, San Francisco CA 94105. 415/543-0404. **Contact:** Human Resources. **World Wide Web address:** http://www.providiancareers.com. **Description:** Provides lending, deposit, bankcard issuing, and other related financial services. **NOTE:** Search and apply for positions online. **Positions advertised include:** Accountant; Accounting Manager; Credit Analyst; Project Manager; Marketing Director; Marketing Analyst; Human Resources Compliance Officer; Online Product Manager. **Corporate headquarters location:** This location. **Listed on:** New York Stock Exchange. **Stock exchange symbol:** PVN.

PRUDENTIAL OVERALL SUPPLY
1661 Alton Parkway, Irvine CA 92606. 949/250-4855. **Toll-free phone:** 800/767-5536. **Fax:** 949/261-1947. **Contact:** Human Resources Manager. **E-mail address:** hrjobs@pos-clean.com. **World Wide Web address:** http://www.pos-clean.com. **Description:** An industrial laundry service. Founded in 1932. **NOTE:** Entry-level positions are offered. **Positions advertised include:** General Manager; Service Manager; Plant Superintendent; District Sales Manager; Corporate Sales Representative; Maintenance Mechanic. **Corporate headquarters location:** This location. **Other U.S. locations:** Phoenix AZ; Tucson AZ; Fresno CA; Los Angeles CA; San Diego CA; San Jose CA. **Operations at this facility include:** Administration; Manufacturing; Sales; Service. **Listed on:** Privately held. **Annual sales/revenues:** More than $100 million. **Number of employees at this location:** 100. **Number of employees nationwide:** 2,000.

PRUDENTIAL PREFERRED INSURANCE COMPANY
651 Gateway Boulevard, Suite 700, South San Francisco CA 94080. 650/952-1111. **Contact:** Human Resources. **World Wide Web address:** http://www.prudential.com. **Description:** One of the largest multiline financial services organizations in the world, with offices throughout the United States and Canada. Prudential Preferred Insurance provides a wide range of financial services for individuals and groups including individual insurance, personal investments, group insurance, reinsurance, institutional investments, group pension, and health care programs. **Positions advertised include:** Education and Enrollment Specialist; Policy Consulting Manager; Group Insurance Broker Representative. **Corporate headquarters location:** Newark NJ. **Other U.S. locations:** Westlake CA; Jacksonville FL; Chicago IL; Boston MA; Minneapolis MN; South Plainfield NJ; Philadelphia PA; Houston TX. **International locations:** Toronto, Canada. **Operations at this facility include:** Sales; Service. **Listed on:** New York Stock Exchange. **Stock exchange symbol:** PRU. **Number of employees at this location:** 65.

PRUDENTIAL FINANCIAL
1731 Technology Drive, Suite 600, San Jose CA 95110-1017. 916/789-4000. **Fax:** 916/780-8811. **Contact:** Personnel. **World Wide Web address:** http://www.prudential.com. **Description:** An international securities brokerage and investment firm. The company offers clients investment products including stocks, options, bonds, commodities, tax-favored investments, and insurance, as well as several specialized financial services. **Corporate headquarters location:** New York NY. **Listed on:** New York Stock Exchange. **Stock exchange symbol:** PRU.

PSYCHEMEDICS CORPORATION
5832 Uplander Way, Culver City CA 90230. 310/216-7776. **Toll-free phone:** 800/522-7424. **Contact:** Personnel. **World Wide Web address:** http://www.psychemedics.com. **Description:** A biotechnology company concentrating on diagnostics through the detection and measurement of substances in the body by using hair samples. The first commercial product, a testing service for the detection of abused substances, is provided principally to private sector companies. This drug test detects cocaine, marijuana, opiates, methamphetamine, and PCP. A test for methadone is used in the treatment industry. Psychemedics Corporation's testing methods use a patented technology for performing immunoassays on enzymatically dissolved hair samples with confirmation testing by gas chromatography/mass spectrometry. **Corporate headquarters location:** Acton MA. **Listed on:** American Stock Exchange. **Stock exchange symbol:** PMD. **Number of employees nationwide:** 95.

PUBLICIS & HAL RINEY
2001 The Embarcadero, San Francisco CA 94133. 415/293-2001. **Fax:** 415/293-2619. **Contact:** Human Resources. **World Wide Web address:** http://www.hrp.com. **Description:** An advertising agency. **Corporate headquarters location:** This location. **Parent company:** Publicis Worldwide.

PUBLIC POLICY INSTITUTE OF CALIFORNIA
500 Washington Street, Suite 800, San Francisco CA 94111. 415/291-4400. **Fax:** 415/291-4401. **Contact:** Human Resources. **E-mail address:** resumes@ppic.org. **World Wide Web address:** http://www.ppic.org. **Description:** A non-profit organization dedicated to independent, objective research on policy issues affecting Californians. **Positions advertised include:** Research Associate; Communications Analyst; Production Associate; Program Director. **Special programs:** Internships. **Corporate headquarters location:** This location.

PULSE ENGINEERING INC.
12220 World Trade Drive, San Diego CA 92128. 858/674-8100. **Fax:** 858/674-8262. **Contact:** Personnel Director. **E-mail address:** resumes@pulseeng.com. **World Wide Web address:** http://www.pulseeng.com. **Description:** Designs, manufactures, and markets a variety of electronic components and modules for original equipment manufacturers in the data processing, telecommunications networking, and power supply markets. **Positions advertised include:** Senior Product Manager; Senior Quality Engineer; Senior Procurement Analyst; Power Supply Design Engineer; Product Line Manager. **Special programs:** Internships. **Corporate headquarters location:** This location. **Other U.S. locations:** Wesson MI. **Parent company:** Technitrol. **Operations at this facility include:** Administration; Research and Development; Sales; Service. **Listed on:** New York Stock Exchange. **Stock exchange symbol:** TNL. **Number of employees at this location:** 170. **Number of employees worldwide:** 19,000.

PYRAMID SCREENING TECHNOLOGY, INC.
5994 West Las Positas Boulevard, Suite 225, Pleasanton CA 94588. 925/460-9228. **Fax:** 925/460-9230. **Contact:** Human Resources. **World Wide Web address:** http://www.pyramidst.com. **Description:** Provides applicant screening services for client companies. **Corporate headquarters location:** This location.

PYXIS PRODUCTS
3750 Torrey View Court, San Diego CA 92130. 858/480-6000. **Toll-free phone:** 800/367-9947. **Contact:** Human Resources. **E-mail address:** hr@pyxis.com. **World Wide Web address:** http://www.pyxis.com. **Description:** A manufacturer of automated point-of-use systems. Products are used in hospitals for distribution management and control of supplies and medicines. **NOTE:** Search and apply for positions online. **Positions advertised include:** Product Support Engineer; Sales Analyst; Financial Analyst; Systems Integration Engineer; Business Systems Analyst. **Corporate headquarters location:** This location. **Parent company:** Cardinal Health, Inc. **Listed on:** New York Stock Exchange. **Stock exchange symbol:** CAH. **Annual sales/revenues:** More than $100 million.

QAD INC.
6450 Via Real, Carpinteria CA 93013. 805/684-6614. **Fax:** 805/566-6091. **Contact:** Tom Adam, Corporate Recruiter. **E-mail address:** tma@qad.com. **World Wide Web address:** http://www.qad.com. **Description:** QAD develops software including MFG/PRO, a software package designed to aid in supply and distribution management for large companies. **NOTE:** Search and apply for positions online. **Positions advertised include:** Sr. International Tax Analyst; Project Manager; Corporate Financial Systems Administrator; Test Automation Engineer. **Corporate headquarters location:** This location. **Operations at this facility include:** This location houses administrative offices. **Listed on:** NASDAQ. **Stock exchange symbol:** QADI.

QLOGIC CORPORATION
26650 Aliso Viejo Parkway, Aliso Viejo CA 92656. 949/389-6000. **Toll-free phone:** 800/662-4471. **Fax:** 949/389-6110. **Contact:** Human Resources. **E-mail address:** hr@qlogic.com. **World Wide Web address:** http://www.qlogic.com. **Description:** Develops, manufactures, and markets network connectivity components. Founded in 1985. **NOTE:** Search and apply for positions online. **Positions advertised include:** Analog Circuit Design Engineers; Layout Engineer; Principal DVT Engineer; Embedded Software Engineer; Foundry Engineering Manager; Principal Software Engineer. **Corporate headquarters location:** This location. **Listed on:** NASDAQ. **Stock exchange symbol:** QLGC. **Annual sales/revenues:** More than $100 million.

QANTEL TECHNOLOGIES
3506 Breakwater Court, Hayward CA 94545-3611. 510/731-2080. **Toll-free phone:** 800/666-3686. **Fax:** 510/731-2075. **Contact:** Human Resources. **E-mail address:** jobs@qantel.com. **World Wide Web address:** http://www.qantel.com. **Description:** Manufactures coprocessor systems and related peripherals. **Positions advertised include:** Applications Software Developer; Java/Web Developer; Manufacturing Software Product Manager; Software Development Project Manager. **Corporate headquarters location:** This location.

QUADRAMED
22 Pelican Way, San Rafael CA 94901. 415/482-2100. **Fax:** 415/482-2110. **Contact:** Human Resources Department. **E-mail address:** resume@quadramed.com. **World Wide Web address:** http://www.quadramed.com. **Description:** Develops and markets specialized decision support software designed to improve the organizational and clinical effectiveness of hospitals, academic medical centers, managed care providers, large physician groups, and other health care providers. **Corporate headquarters location:** Reston VA. **Listed on:** NASDAQ. **Stock exchange symbol:** QMDC.

QUADREP
2635 North First Street, Suite 203, San Jose CA 95134. 408/432-3300. **Fax:** 408/432-3428. **Contact:** Personnel. **World Wide Web address:** http://www.quadrep.com. **Description:** Distributes connectors, cable assemblies, and other products manufactured by a variety of manufacturers. **Corporate headquarters location:** This location.

THE QUAKER OATS COMPANY
P.O. Box 2205, Oakland CA 94621. 510/261-5800. **Physical address:** 5625 International Boulevard, Oakland CA 94621. **Contact:** Human Resources Department. **E-mail address:** gorecruiting@quakeroats.com. **World Wide Web address:** http://www.quakeroats.com. **Description:** The Quaker Oats Company is a leading manufacturer of sports beverages, cereals, snack foods, and pasta products. **NOTE:** Please include job code in subject line of e-mail. **Positions advertised include:** Production Supervisor; Finance Manager. **Special programs:** Internships. **Corporate headquarters location:** Chicago IL. **Other U.S. locations:** Nationwide. **Parent company:** PepsiCo, Inc. **Operations at this facility include:** This location manufactures beverages and consumer food products. **Listed on:** New York Stock Exchange. **Stock exchange symbol:** PEP. **Operations at this facility include:** Manufacturing. **Number of employees at this location:** 200.

QUALCOMM INCORPORATED
5775 Morehouse Drive, San Diego CA 92191. 858/587-1121. **Recorded jobline:** 858/658-JOBS. **Contact:** Human Resources Department. **E-mail address:** resumes@qualcomm.com. **World Wide Web address:** http://www.qualcomm.com. **Description:** QUALCOMM Incorporated designs and manufactures CDMA (Code Division Multiple Access) wireless products. These products include digital cellular portable phones that use microprocessors, allowing good voice quality, low power requirements, and a wide coverage area. The company manufactures a wide variety of communications products from desktop phones to the OmniTRACS satellite communications system, all using CDMA technology. QUALCOMM Incorporated also designs and manufactures network planning software to help design wireless networks; and indoor or outdoor base stations for cellular and wireless local loop systems. The company also offers wireless network planning and deployment services. **NOTE:** Submit resume or search and apply for positions online. **Positions advertised include:** Senior Engineer; Systems Engineer; Engineering Technician; Product Manager; Speech Processing Engineer; Video Systems Engineer; Embedded Software Engineer; Failure Analysis Engineer; Marketing Analyst. **Company slogan:** We're building the wireless world. **Special programs:** Internships. **Corporate headquarters location:** This location. **Other U.S. locations:** Boulder CO. **International locations:** Argentina;

Brazil; Canada; China; India. **Operations at this facility include:** This location houses the corporate headquarters as well as CDMA University, the company's training facility. **Listed on:** NASDAQ. **Stock exchange symbol:** QCOM. **Annual sales/revenues:** Approximately $4 billion.

QUALITY SYSTEMS, INC.
18191 Von Karman Avenue, Suite 450, Irvine CA 92612. 949/255-2600. **Toll-free phone:** 800/888-7955. **Fax:** 949/255-2605. **Contact:** Human Resources. **E-mail address:** hr@qsii.com. **World Wide Web address:** http://www.qsii.com. **Description:** Develops and markets computerized information processing systems primarily to group dental and medical practices. The systems provide advanced computer-based automation in various aspects of group practice management including the retention of patient information, treatment planning, appointment scheduling, billing, insurance claims processing, electronic insurance claims submission, allocation of income among group professionals, managed care reporting, word processing, and accounting. Founded in 1973. **NOTE:** Entry-level positions are offered. **Positions advertised include:** Programmer Analyst; Customer Support Representative. **Special programs:** Internships. **Corporate headquarters location:** This location. **Other U.S. locations:** Horsham PA; Atlanta GA. **Listed on:** NASDAQ. **Stock exchange symbol:** QSII. **Number of employees nationwide:** 230.

QUANTUM CORPORATION
1650 Technology Drive, Suite 800, San Jose CA 95110-1382. 408/944-4000. **Fax:** 408/944-4040. **Contact:** Human Resources. **E-mail address:** jobs@quantum.com. **World Wide Web address:** http://www.quantum.com. **Description:** Designs, manufactures, and markets small hard disk drives used in desktop PCs, workstations, and notebook computers. **NOTE:** Search and apply for positions online. **Positions advertised include:** Software Engineer; Systems Management Architect; Finance Project Manager. **Corporate headquarters location:** This location. **Listed on:** New York Stock Exchange. **Stock exchange symbol:** DSS. **Annual sales/revenues:** $870 million. **Number of employees nationwide:** 2,455.

QUEST DIAGNOSTICS
8550 Balboa, Suite 195, Northridge CA 91325. **Toll-free phone:** 800/209-9816. **Contact:** Human Resources. **World Wide Web address:** http://www.questdiagnostics.com. **Description:** One of the largest clinical laboratories in North America, providing a broad range of clinical laboratory services to health care clients such as physicians, hospitals, clinics, dialysis centers, pharmaceutical companies, and corporations. The company offers and performs tests on blood, urine, and other bodily fluids and tissues to provide information for health and well-being. **Positions advertised include:** Account Executive; Account Sales Representative. **Corporate headquarters location:** Teterboro NJ. **Listed on:** New York Stock Exchange. **Stock exchange symbol:** DGX.

QUEST DIAGNOSTICS
7600 Tyrone Avenue, Van Nuys CA 91405. 818/989-2520. **Contact:** Human Resources Department. **World Wide Web address:** http://www.questdiagnostics.com. **Description:** One of the largest clinical laboratories in North America. The company provides a broad range of clinical laboratory services to health care clients such as physicians, hospitals, clinics, dialysis centers, pharmaceutical companies, and corporations. The company offers and performs tests on blood, urine, and other bodily fluids and tissues to provide information for health and well-being. **Corporate headquarters location:** Teterboro NJ. **Listed on:** New York Stock Exchange. **Stock exchange symbol:** DGX.

QUEST DIAGNOSTICS
3714 North Gate Boulevard, Sacramento CA 95834. 916/927-9900. **Fax:** 916/927-4124. **Contact:** Human Resources. **World Wide Web address:** http://www.questdiagnostics.com. **Description:** One of the largest clinical laboratories in North America, providing a broad range of clinical laboratory services to health care clients such as physicians, hospitals, clinics, dialysis centers, pharmaceutical companies, and corporations. The company offers and performs tests on blood, urine, and other bodily fluids and tissues to provide information for health and well-being. **Corporate headquarters location:** Teterboro NJ. **Listed on:** New York Stock Exchange. **Stock exchange symbol:** DGX.

QUEST DIAGNOSTICS
18408 Oxnard Street, Tarzana CA 91356-1504. 818/996-7300. **Recorded jobline:** 818/758-6680. **Contact:** Human Resources. **World Wide Web address:** http://www.questdiagnostics.com. **Description:** One of the largest clinical laboratories in North America, providing a broad range of clinical laboratory services to health care clients such as physicians, hospitals, clinics, dialysis centers, pharmaceutical companies, and corporations. The company offers and performs tests on blood, urine, and other bodily fluids and tissues to provide information for health and well-being. This location was formerly the headquarters for Unilab Corporation. Unilab's facilities are now part of Quest Diagnostics. **Corporate headquarters location:** Teterboro NJ. **Listed on:** New York Stock Exchange. **Stock exchange symbol:** DGX.

QUEST DIAGNOSTICS AT NICHOLS INSTITUTE
33608 Ortega Highway, San Juan Capistrano CA 92675. 949/728-4000. **Fax:** 949/728-4781. **Recorded jobline:** 949/728-4526. **Contact:** Human Resources. **World Wide Web address:** http://www.questdiagnostics.com. **Description:** One of the largest clinical laboratories in North America, providing a broad range of clinical laboratory services to health care clients such as physicians, hospitals, clinics, dialysis centers, pharmaceutical companies, and corporations. The company offers and performs tests on blood, urine, and other bodily fluids and tissues to provide information for health and well-being. **Positions advertised include:** Associate Scientific Director; Laboratory Supervisor; Laboratory Associate; Clinical Laboratory Scientist; Senior Implementation Analyst; Customer Service Assistant. **Corporate headquarters location:** Teterboro NJ. **Other U.S. locations:** Nationwide. **Listed on:** New York Stock Exchange. **Stock exchange symbol:** DGX.

QUEST DISCOVERY SERVICES, INC.
2025 Gateway Plaza, San Jose CA 95110. 408/441-7000. **Fax:** 408/441-7070. **Contact:** Human Resources. **E-mail address:** jobs@questds.com. **World Wide Web address:** http://www.questds.com. **Description:** Provides litigation support services such as deposition reporting, process serving, and large volume copy work. **NOTE:** Mail resumes to: Quest Discovery Services, Inc., Attention: Human Resources, P.O. Box 49051, San Jose CA 95161-9051. **Corporate headquarters location:** This location.

QUESTCOR PHARMACEUTICALS CORPORATION
3260 Whipple Road, Union City CA 94587. 510/400-0700. **Fax:** 510/400-0799. **Contact:** Human Resources. **E-mail address:** hr@questcor.com. **World Wide Web address:** http://www.questcor.com. **Description:** An integrated specialty pharmaceutical company that researches, develops, and markets a variety of pharmaceuticals to the health care industry. The company's products include Emitasol, Ethamolin, Inulin, Glofil-125, and NeoFlo. **NOTE:** Resumes may be submitted via fax at 928/244-3718. **Corporate headquarters location:** This location. **Listed on:** American Stock Exchange. **Stock exchange symbol:** QSC.

QUICK EAGLE NETWORKS
217 Humboldt Court, Sunnyvale CA 94089-1300. 408/745-6200. **Fax:** 408/745-6250. **E-mail address:** jobs@quickeagle.com. **Contact:** Human Resources. **World Wide Web address:** http://www.quickeagle.com. **Description:** Develops, manufactures, and markets high-speed digital access products for the WAN marketplace. **Positions advertised include:** Accounting Manager; Vice President, Engineering; Hardware Product Architect; Hardware Engineer; Technical Writer. **Corporate headquarters location:** This location.

QUICKLOGIC CORPORATION
1277 Orleans Drive, Sunnyvale CA 94089-1138. 408/990-4000. **Fax:** 408/990-4040. **Contact:** Human Resources. **E-mail address:** jobsusa@quicklogic.com. **World Wide Web address:** http://www.quicklogic.com. **Description:** Manufactures and distributes field programmable logic units. **Positions advertised include:** Marketing Communications Specialist; ERP Report Developer. **Corporate headquarters location:** This location. **International locations:** Toronto Canada; Bangalore India. **Listed on:** NASDAQ. **Stock exchange symbol:** QUIK.

QUIDEL CORPORATION
10165 McKellar Court, San Diego CA 92121. 858/552-1100. **Toll-free phone:** 800/874-1517. **Fax:** 858/453-2050. **Contact:** Human Resources. **E-mail address:** hr@quidel.com. **World Wide Web address:** http://www.quidel.com. **Description:** Engaged in the research, development, and manufacture of immunodiagnostic products designed to provide accurate testing for acute and chronic human illnesses. Customers include physicians, clinical laboratories, and consumers. **Positions advertised include:** Manufacturing Engineer; Regulatory compliance Specialist. **Office hours:** Monday - Friday, 8:00 a.m. - 5:00 p.m. **Corporate headquarters location:** This location. **Other area locations:** Santa Clara CA. **Subsidiaries include:** VHA Inc. **Listed on:** NASDAQ. **Stock exchange symbol:** QDEL. **President/CEO:** S. Wayne Kay.

RBC DAIN RAUCHER
345 California Street, Suite 2900, San Francisco CA 94104. 415/445-8500. **Fax:** 415/391-9586. **Contact:** Tony Schultz, Manager of Human Resources. **World Wide Web address:** http://www.rbcdain.com. **Description:** A full-service, regional investment brokerage firm. Founded in 1858. **Positions advertised include:** Regional Administrative Assistant; Research Associate; Financial Consultant. **Special programs:** Financial Consultant Program. **Corporate headquarters location:** Minneapolis MN. **Parent company:** Royal Bank of Canada. **Operations at this facility include:** Administration; Research and Development; Sales; Service. **Listed on:** New York Stock Exchange. **Stock exchange symbol:** RY. **Number of employees nationwide:** 5,000.

RFI ENTERPRISES
360 Turtle Creek Court, San Jose CA 95125. 408/298-5400. **Fax:** 408/882-4401. **Contact:** Human Resources. **E-mail address:** jobs@rfi.com. **World Wide Web address:** http://www.rfi-ent.com. **Description:** A multisystem integrator for low-voltage systems including alarm systems, public announcement systems, and closed circuit television. Founded in 1979. **NOTE:** Entry-level positions are offered. **Positions advertised include:** Fire Alarm System Designer; Dispatcher; Fire Alarm Test Technician; Senior Fire Technician; Service Technician; Sound Technician. **Special programs:** Internships; Apprenticeship. **Corporate headquarters location:** This location. **Other area locations:** Sacramento CA. **Other U.S. locations:** Reno NV; Beaverton OR; Eugene OR; Seattle WA. **Listed on:** Privately held. **Number of employees at this location:** 250.

RMC PACIFIC MATERIAL
6601 Koll Center Parkway, P.O. Box 5252, Pleasanton CA 94566. 925/426-8787. **Toll-free phone:** 800/227-5186. **Fax:** 925/426-2220. **Contact:** Human Resources. **World Wide Web address:** http://www.rmcpmi.com. **Description:** Manufactures cement, aggregates, and ready-mix concrete. Founded in 1988. **NOTE:** Application form available online. **Corporate headquarters location:** This location. **Parent company:** CEMEX. **Number of employees at this location:** 100.

RACAL INSTRUMENTS
4 Goodyear Street, Irvine CA 92618. 949/859-8999. **Toll-free phone:** 800/722-2528. **Fax:** 949/859-7328. **Contact:** Human Resources Department. **E-mail address:** resume@racalinst.com. **World Wide Web address:** http://www.racalinstruments.com. **Description:** Manufactures specialized electronic systems, instrumentation, and software for the test and measurement, recording, and electronic design automation markets. Products include high-end VXIbus instruments, digital word generators, subsystems for automatic test equipment, and signal-switching and routing systems. The company also produces professional recording equipment including telemetry, voice logging, and physical research systems. **NOTE:** Search and apply for positions online. **Positions advertised include:** Sr. Hardware Engineer; Software Engineer; Test Engineer; Product Marketing Engineer; International Applications Engineer; Government contracts Manager. **Corporate headquarters location:** This location. **Parent company:** EADS North America.

RADISSON WILSHIRE PLAZA HOTEL
3515 Wilshire Boulevard, Los Angeles CA 90010. 213/381-7411. **Toll-free phone:** 800/333-3333. **Fax:** 213/368-3015. **Contact:** Mr. Otho Boggs, Human Resources Director. **World Wide Web address:** http://www.radisson.com. **Description:** A 393-room hotel, restaurant, and entertainment facility. **NOTE:** Entry-level positions, part-time jobs, and second and third shifts are offered. **Special programs:** Internships; Training; Summer Jobs. **Internship information:** Unpaid internships are available in the fields of rooms; sales and marketing; food and beverage; accounting; and human resources. **Corporate headquarters location:** Minneapolis MN. **President:** Young Sun Kim.

RAINING DATA CORPORATION
17500 Cartwright Road, Irvine CA 92614-5846. 949/442-4400. **Fax:** 949/250-8187. **Contact:** Human Resources. **E-mail address:** hr@rainingdata.com. **World Wide Web address:** http://www.rainingdata.com. **Description:** Develops, markets, and supports software products for the development and deployment of applications for accessing multiuser databases in workgroup and enterprisewide client/server computing environments. The company's products are used by corporations, system integrators, small businesses, and independent consultants to deliver custom information management applications for a wide range of uses including financial management, decision support, executive information, sales and marketing, and multimedia authoring systems. In addition to these products, Raining Data provides consulting, technical support, and training to help plan, analyze, implement, and maintain applications software based on the company's technology. **Corporate headquarters location:** This location. **Listed on:** NASDAQ. **Stock exchange symbol:** RDTA.

RALEY'S & BEL AIR
500 West Capitol Avenue, West Sacramento CA 95605. 916/373-3333. **Contact:** Ronnie Cobb, Corporate Recruiter. **E-mail address:** jobs@raleys.com. **World Wide Web address:** http://www.raleys.com. **Description:** A large supermarket chain with more than 145 locations in Northern California and Nevada. Raley's owns and operates Bel Air Markets (also at this location) a supermarket chain in San Francisco. **NOTE:** Entry-level positions are offered. Interested candidates may apply online. **Positions advertised include:** Financial Analyst; Loss Prevention Agent. **Special programs:** Internships. **Corporate headquarters location:** This location. **Subsidiaries include:** Food Source; Nob Hill Foods. **Operations at this facility include:** Divisional Headquarters.

RALPHS GROCERY COMPANY
P.O. Box 54143, Los Angeles CA 90054. 310/884-9000. **Physical address:** 1100 West Artesia Boulevard, Compton CA 90200. **Recorded jobline:** 310/884-4642. **Contact:** Personnel. **World Wide Web address:** http://www.ralphs.com. **Description:** Operates a chain of grocery stores throughout California. **Corporate headquarters location:** This location. **Parent company:** The Kroger Company (Cincinnati OH). **Listed on:** New York Stock Exchange. **Stock exchange symbol:** KR.

RAMADA PLAZA HOTEL
1231 Market Street, San Francisco CA 94103. 415/626-8000. **Toll-free phone:** 800/272-6232. **Contact:** Personnel Manager. **World Wide Web address:** http://www.ramada.com. **Description:** Operates a 458-room hotel with a variety of facilities including meeting rooms and restaurants.

RANCHO LOS AMIGOS NATIONAL REHABILITATION CENTER
7601 East Imperial Highway, Downey CA 90242. 562/401-7511. **Recorded jobline:** 800/970-5478. **Contact:** Human Resources. **World Wide Web address:** http://www.rancho.org. **Description:** A rehabilitation center providing care to patients who suffer from strokes, spinal cord injuries, brain injuries, or other disabling illnesses. **NOTE:** Please consult website for more specific application instructions. **Positions advertised include:** Audiologist; Speech-Language Pathologist; Clinical Instructor, RN; Critical Care Nurse; Licensed Vocational Nurse; Nursing Attendant; Relief Nurse; Staff Nurse; Supervising Staff Nurse; Senior Student Worker; Unit Support Assistant; Occupational Therapist; Occupational Therapist Assistant; Physical Therapist; Physical Therapist Assistant.

RANCHO SANTIAGO COMMUNITY COLLEGE DISTRICT
2323 North Broadway, 4th Floor, Santa Ana CA 92706. 714/480-7485. **Recorded jobline:** 714/480-7499. **Fax:** 714/796-3939. **Contact:** Elouise Marasigan, Human Resources Coordinator. **World Wide Web address:** http://www.rsccd.org. **Description:** A college district consisting of Santa Ana College and Santiago Canyon College. Located in central Orange County, the community college district's service area includes Santa Ana, Orange, Villa Park, and portions of Garden Grove and Anaheim Hills. **NOTE:** Entry-level positions and second and third shifts are offered. Candidates may apply by mail or fax, in person, or online. **Positions advertised include:** Assistant Professor, Various Disciplines; Instructors, Various Disciplines; Student Services Specialist. **Office hours:** Monday - Friday, 8:00 a.m. - 5:00 p.m. **Corporate headquarters location:** This location. **Number of employees at this location:** 675.

RATIONAL SOFTWARE CORPORATION
18880 Homestead Road, Cupertino CA 95014. 408/863-9900. **Contact:** Human Resources. **World Wide Web address:** http://www.rational.com. **Description:** Develops, markets, and supports embedded software products for Web and e-commerce applications. The company's products operate on both Windows and UNIX systems. **Corporate headquarters location:** This location. **International locations:** Worldwide. **Parent company:** IBM. **Listed on:** NASDAQ. **Stock exchange symbol:** RATL.

RAY BURNER COMPANY
401 Parr Boulevard, Richmond CA 94801. 415/333-5800. **Toll-free phone:** 800/RAY-BURNER. **Contact:** Human Resources Department. **World Wide Web address:** http://www.rayburner.com. **Description:** Manufactures and distributes boilers and gas burners. Founded in 1872. **Corporate headquarters location:** This location.

RAYTHEON SPACE & AIRBORNE SYSTEMS
2000 East El Segundo Boulevard, El Segundo CA 90245. 310/647-1000. **Contact:** Human Resources. **E-mail address:** join-rayrecruiter@ls.rayjobs.com. (Use this e-mail address to request monthly news about Raytheon and upcoming recruiting events). **World Wide Web address:** http://www.raytheon.com. **Description:** Raytheon Systems Company is a leader in the design of military tactical communications, electronic combat, command and control, and antisubmarine warfare products and systems for the armed forces of the United States and allied nations. **NOTE:** Search and apply for positions online. **Parent company:** Raytheon Company. **Listed on:** New York Stock Exchange. **Stock exchange symbol:** RTN.

THE RECORD
P.O. Box 900, Stockton CA 95201-0900. 209/943-6397. **Physical address:** 530 East Market Street, Stockton CA 95202. **Fax:** 209/943-8502. **Contact:** Tina Vincelet, Human Resources. **E-mail address:** vincelet@recordnet.com. **World Wide Web address:** http://www.recordnet.com. **Description:** Publishes a daily newspaper with a circulation of more than 55,000. **Positions advertised include:** Managing Editor; Advertising Operations Assistant; Outside Account Executive; Inside Account Executive; Retail Advertising Manager. **Parent company:** Gannett Newspapers Group. **Listed on:** New York Stock Exchange. **Stock exchange symbol:** GCI.

REDDING RECORD SEARCHLIGHT
P.O. Box 492397, Redding CA 96049-2397. 530/243-2424. **Physical address:** 1101 Twin View Boulevard, Redding CA 96003. **Fax:** 530/225-8399. **Contact:** Cassandra Brown, Human Resources Director. **E-mail address:** cabrown@redding.com. **World Wide Web address:** http://www.redding.com. **Description:** Publishes a daily newspaper with a circulation of approximately 40,000. **NOTE:** To contact Cassandra Brown directly call: 530/225-8261. **Positions advertised include:** Accounts Receivable Bookkeeper; Press Operator; Forklift Operator; Packaging Center Clerk. **Special programs:** Internships. **Corporate headquarters location:** Cincinnati OH. **Other U.S. locations:** Nationwide. **Parent company:** The E.W. Scripps Company. **Operations at this facility include:** Administration; Sales; Service. **Listed on:** New York Stock Exchange. **Stock exchange symbol:** SSP. **Number of employees at this location:** 190.

REDENVELOPE, INC.
201 Spear Street, Third Floor, San Francisco CA 94105. 415/371-9100. **Fax:** 415/371-1134. **Contact:** Human Resources. **E-mail address:** jobs@redenvelope.com. **World Wide Web address:** http://www.redenvelope.com. **Description:** Sells unique gift items through its website and seasonal catalogs. **Positions advertised include:** Software Engineer; Receptionist; Assistant Merchandise Manager; Merchandise Assistant.

REDONDO BEACH, CITY OF
415 Diamond Street, P.O. Box 270, Redondo Beach CA 90277. 310/318-0659. **Recorded jobline:** 310/318-0660. **Contact:** Human Resources. **E-mail address:** hrd@redondo.org. **World Wide Web address:** http://www.redondo.org. **Description:** Administrative offices for the city of Redondo Beach. **Positions advertised include:** Assistant City Manager; Building Inspector; Police Officer; Librarian. **Office hours:** 7:30 a.m. – 5:30 p.m. **Corporate headquarters location:** This location. **Number of employees at this location:** 700.

REDWOOD OIL COMPANY
455 Yolanda Avenue, P.O. Box 428, Santa Rosa CA 95402. 707/546-0766. **Fax:** 707/570-2738. **Contact:** Human Resources Manager. **E-mail address:** tlong@redwoodoil.com. **World Wide Web address:** http://redwoodoil.com. **Description:** Distributes and carries various brand name petroleum products throughout northern California. Redwood Oil Company also sells, installs, and services a variety of petroleum storage and dispensing equipment. **Positions advertised include:** Customer Service Representative. **Corporate headquarters location:** This location.

REGENT BEVERLY WILSHIRE HOTEL
9500 Wilshire Boulevard, Beverly Hills CA 90212. 310/275-5200. **Toll-free phone:** 888/201-1806. **Fax:** 310/273-9212. **Contact:** Sharon Nixon, Director of Human Resources. **World Wide Web address:** http://www.regenthotels.com. **Description:** A hotel with over 290 rooms. **Corporate headquarters location:** Hong Kong. **Parent company:** Carlson Hotels Worldwide. **Listed on:** New York Stock Exchange. **Stock exchange symbol:** FS. **Number of employees at this location:** 650.

REGIONAL CENTER OF ORANGE COUNTY
P.O. Box 22010, Santa Ana CA 92702-2010. 714/796-5100. **Contact:** Personnel. **E-mail address:** jabernatha@rcocdd.com. **World Wide Web address:** http://www.rcocdd.com. **Description:** A nonprofit organization dedicated to helping individuals with all types of learning disabilities ranging from mental retardation to cerebral palsy. **Positions advertised include:** Service Coordinator; **Corporate headquarters location:** This location. **Operations at this facility include:** Administration; Service. **Listed on:** Privately held. **Number of employees at this location:** 200.

REHRIG PACIFIC COMPANY
4010 East 26th Street, Los Angeles CA 90023. 323/262-5145. **Fax:** 323/269-8506. **Contact:** Human Resources. **E-mail address:** info@rehigpacific.com. **World Wide Web address:** http://www.rehrigpacific.com. **Description:** Manufactures plastic shipping containers. **NOTE:** Contact information may vary according to position. See job postings on website. **Positions advertised include:** Plant Engineer; Sales Representative. **Corporate headquarters location:** This location.

RELIANCE STEEL & ALUMINUM COMPANY
350 South Grand Avenue, Suite 5100, Los Angeles CA 90071. 213/687-7700. **Contact:** Vice President of Human Resources. **World Wide Web address:** http://www.rsac.com. **Description:** One of the largest Western-based metals service center companies in the United States. Through a network of 20 metals service centers, the company distributes a full line of ferrous and nonferrous metal products including galvanized, hot-rolled and cold-finished steel, stainless steel, aluminum, brass, copper, and alloy steel. The company sells metal products from locations in nine states and to more than 30,000 customers engaged in a wide variety of industries. Some of these metals service centers provide processing services for specialty metals only. **Corporate headquarters location:** This location. **Subsidiaries include:** Valex Corporation manufactures and sells electropolished stainless steel tubing and fittings for use in the semiconductor, biotech, and pharmaceutical industries. **Listed on:** New York Stock Exchange. **Stock exchange symbol:** RS.

REMEC, INC.
9404 Chesapeake Drive, San Diego CA 92123. 858/560-1301. **Fax:** 858/567-7111. **Contact:** Stephanie Major, Human Resources. **E-mail address:** careers@remec.com. **World Wide Web address:** http://www.remec.com. **Description:** An electronics company engaged in the design, development, and manufacture of custom RF and microwave products. **NOTE:** Search and apply for positions online. **Positions advertised include:** Electrical Engineer; Master Technician; Mechanical Engineer; Systems Administrator; Financial Analyst; ATE Engineer. **Corporate headquarters location:** Del Mar CA. **Other area locations:** Folsom CA; Milpitas CA; Poway CA; Irvine CA; Escondido CA. **Subsidiaries include:** Humphrey, Inc. manufactures motion sensor devices. **Operations at this facility include:** Administration; Manufacturing; Research and Development. **Listed on:** NASDAQ. **Stock exchange symbol:** RMEC.

RESMED
14040 Danielson Street, Poway CA 92064-6857. 858/746-2400. **Toll-free phone:** 800/424-0737. **Fax:** 858/746-5820. **Contact:** Human Resources Manager. **E-mail address:** usjobs@resmed.com. **World Wide Web address:** http://www.resmed.com. **Description:** Develops, manufactures, and markets respiratory devices. ResMed specializes in respiratory products relating to sleep disordered breathing (SBD) including sleep apnea. Founded in 1989. **Positions advertised include:** HR Generalist; eBusiness Operations Analyst; Director, Occupational Health Marketing. **Corporate headquarters location:** This location. **International locations:** Worldwide. **Listed on:** New York Stock Exchange. **Stock exchange symbol:** RMD. **Annual sales/revenues:** $273 million. **Number of employees worldwide:** Over 1,400.

REULAND ELECTRIC
17969 East Railroad Street, City of Industry CA 91748-1192. 626/964-6411. **Fax:** 626/964-2431. **Contact:** Employee Relations. **E-mail address:** hr-ca@reuland.com. **World Wide Web address:** http://www.reuland.com. **Description:** Manufactures custom-designed motors, brakes, and controls for industrial clients. **Corporate headquarters location:** This location. **Other U.S. locations:** Howell MI.

REXEL, INC.
1990 North California Boulevard, Suite 1055, Walnut Creek CA 94596. 925/952-4295. **Fax:** 925/952-4296. **Contact:** Human Resources. **E-mail address:** job@rexel.com. **World Wide Web address:** http://www.rexelusa.com. **Description:** Distributes electrical supplies, wire, cable, switchboards, and light fixtures to small businesses, electrical contractors, and industrial customers. **Corporate headquarters location:** Dallas TX.

GEORGE RICE & SONS
2001 North Soto Street, Los Angeles CA 90032. 323/223-2020. **Contact:** Jan Miller, Human Resources Manager. **World Wide Web address:** http://wwww.quebecorworldinc.com. **Description:** Provides commercial lithography

and printing services. **NOTE:** Search for positions online. **Corporate headquarters location:** Greenwich CT. **Parent company:** Quebecor World Inc. **Listed on:** New York Stock Exchange. **Stock exchange symbol:** IQW.

RICOH BUSINESS SYSTEMS
5632 Bolsa Avenue, Huntington Beach CA 92649. 714/891-9397. **Fax:** 714/448-1323. **Contact:** Human Resources. **World Wide Web address:** http://www.ricoh-usa.com/rbs. **Description:** Develops, manufactures, and markets data handling and output equipment. The company's products include printers and digital communications equipment. **Parent company:** Ricoh Corporation.

RICOH DIGITAL CAMERA DIVISION
242 East Airport Drive, Suite 102, San Bernardino CA 92408. 909/890-9039. **Fax:** 909/890-9045. **Contact:** Human Resources. **World Wide Web address:** http://www.ricohzone.com. **Description:** The Digital Camera Division is a leader in the development, manufacture, distribution and OEM licensing of imaging products. **Corporate headquarters location:** West Caldwell NJ. **Parent company:** Ricoh Corporation.

RICOH ELECTRONIC DEVICES
One Ricoh Square, 1100 Valencia Avenue, Tustin CA 92780. 714/566-2500. **Contact:** Human Resources. **E-mail address:** jobs@rei.ricoh.com. **World Wide Web address:** http://www.rei.ricoh.com. **Description:** A manufacturer of advanced office automation equipment including digital copiers, peripherals, thermal media, and toner. **NOTE:** Search and apply for positions online. **Positions advertised include:** Process Training Coordinator; QA Engineer; Buyer; Manufacturing Engineer; Production Technician. **Other area locations:** Santa Ana CA; Irvine CA. **Other U.S. locations:** Lawrenceville GA.

RIMKUS CONSULTING GROUP, INC.
The City Tower, 333 City Boulevard West, Suite 1805, Orange CA 92868. 714/978-2044. **Fax:** 714/978-2088. **Contact:** Human Resources. **E-mail address:** careers@rimkus.com. **World Wide Web address:** http://ywtf.rimkus.com. **Description:** A diversified engineering consulting firm. Areas of expertise include automotive, chemical, environmental, cargo and roadway assessments. **NOTE:** See website for job listings. Send resumes and cover letters by e-mail or fax. **Positions advertised include:** General Contractor. **Corporate headquarters location:** Houston TX. **Other U.S. locations:** Nationwide. **International locations:** Zurich Switzerland; Kuwait City Kuwait; Madrid Spain.

RO-LAB AMERICAN RUBBER COMPANY INC.
8830 West Linne Road, Tracy CA 95378. 209/836-0965. **Toll-free phone:** 888/276-2993. **Fax:** 209/836-0465. **Contact:** John Dodge, Vice President of Personnel. **World Wide Web address:** http://www.rolabamerican.com. **Description:** Produces a wide range of rubber products, gaskets, and seals for mechanical and industrial uses. **Corporate headquarters location:** This location.

ROBERT TALBOTT INC.
P.O. Box 996, Carmel Valley CA 93924-0996. 831/649-6000. **Contact:** Human Resources. **E-mail address:** corporate@roberttalbott.com. **World Wide Web address:** http://www.roberttalbott.com. **Description:** Manufactures men's ties, dress shirts, formal wear, and related accessories. **Corporate headquarters location:** This location. **Number of employees at this location:** 250.

ROBERT TALBOTT VINEYARDS
53 West Carmel Valley Road, PO Box 449, Carmel Valley CA 93924. 831/659-3500. Fax: 831/659-3515. **Contact:** Human Resources. **World Wide Web address:** http://www.talbottvineyards.com. **Description:** A vineyard.

ROCKWELL AUTOMATION
5675 Gibraltar Drive, Pleasanton CA 94588. 925/227-0240. **Fax:** 925/227-0263. **Contact:** Human Resources. **World Wide Web address:** http://www.rockwellautomation.com. **Description:** Designs, manufactures, and markets electronic controls and control systems for industrial markets. The company's principal products are photoelectric controls, inductive proximity controls, sensing products, and mechanical limit switches used for the automation of industrial processes. **NOTE:** Search and apply for positions online. **Corporate headquarters location:** Milwaukee WI. **Listed on:** New York Stock Exchange. **Stock exchange symbol:** ROK.

ROCKWELL SCIENTIFIC COMPANY LLC
1049 Camino Dos Rios, Thousand Oaks CA 91360. 805/373-4545. **Fax:** 805/373-4775. **Contact:** Human Resources. **Description:** Rockwell Scientific Company conducts research on projects ranging from disruptive technologies intended to catalyze new business opportunities to technology application and transition. **NOTE:** Search and apply for positions online. **Positions advertised include:** Applied Computational Physicist; Compound Semiconductor Process Engineer; FPA Test Technician; Sensor Test Engineer; Camera Engineer; Sr. Cost Accounting Advisor. **Other area locations:** Camarillo CA.

ROEL CONSTRUCTION COMPANY
P.O. Box 80216, San Diego CA 92138-0216. 619/297-4156. **Physical address:** 3366 Kurtz Street, San Diego CA 92110. **Toll-free phone:** 800/662-7635. **Fax:** 619/297-1522. **Contact:** Personnel Director. **E-mail address:** careers@roel.com. **World Wide Web address:** http://www.roel.com. **Description:** A commercial and residential construction company. Roel Construction also provides tenant improvements, structural concrete construction, construction forensic services, and surety claim services. **Positions advertised include:** Assistant Project Manager; Project Engineer; Architect/Inspector. **Corporate headquarters location:** This location. **Other area locations:** Palm Desert CA; Irvine CA. **Other U.S. locations:** Las Vegas NV. **President/CEO:** Stephen Roel.

ROHM AND HAAS ELECTRONIC MATERIALS
27021 Puerta Real, Suite 270, Mission Viejo CA 92691. 949/347-2040. **Contact:** Human Resources Department. **World Wide Web address:** http://www.electronicmaterials.rohmhaas.com. **Description:** Provides materials and fabrication services for the global circuit board market, including metallization, imaging, embedded passives and optoelectronics. **Special programs:** Internships. **Corporate headquarters location:** Philadelphia PA. **Parent company:** Rohm and Haas Company. **Operations at this facility include:** Administration; Research and Development; Sales. **Listed on:** New York Stock Exchange. **Stock exchange symbol:** ROH.

ROLAND CORPORATION U.S.
P.O. Box 910921, Los Angeles CA 90091-0921. 323/890-3700. **Physical address:** 5100 South Eastern Avenue, Los Angeles CA 90040. **Fax:** 323/890-3701. **Contact:** Human Resources. **E-mail address:** employment@rolandus.com. **World Wide Web address:** http://www.rolandus.com. **Description:** A distributor of electronic musical equipment including keyboards, sound modules, digital samplers, and guitar synthesizers. **Positions advertised include:** Marketing Manager. **Corporate headquarters location:** This location. **Subsidiaries include:** Rodgers Instrument; Roland Audio Development. **Listed on:** Privately held. **Annual sales/revenues:** $51 - $100 million.

ROLLS ROYCE ENGINE SERVICES
7200 Earhart Road, Oakland CA 94621. 510/613-1000. **Fax:** 510/635-6911. **Recorded jobline:** 510/613-1011. **Contact:** Peter Caldwell, Human Resources Manager. **E-mail address:** rolls-roycecareers@rolls-royce.com. **World Wide Web address:** http://www.rolls-royce.com. **Description:** Engaged in the maintenance, repair, and overhaul of aviation and industrial gas turbine engines. Founded in 1960. **NOTE:** Entry-level positions and part-time jobs are offered. **Special programs:** Internships; Apprenticeships; Training; Co-ops. **Corporate headquarters location:** This location. **Parent company:** Rolls-Royce North America, Inc. **President/CEO:** Raj Sharma. **Annual sales/revenues:** More than $100 million. **Number of employees nationwide:** 500. **Listed on:** NASDAQ. **Stock exchange symbol:** FAVS.

ROPAK CORPORATION
660 South State College Boulevard, Fullerton CA 92831. 714/870-9757. **Toll-free phone:** 800/367-3779. **Fax:** 714/447-3871. **Contact:** Manager of Human Resources. **World Wide Web address:** http://www.ropakcorp.com. **Description:** Manufactures plastic containers for a wide range of uses. **Corporate headquarters location:** This location. **Parent company:** LINPAC Group.

ROSENFELD, MEYER & SUSMAN
9601 Wilshire Boulevard, Suite 700, Beverly Hills CA 90210-5288. 310/858-7700. **Fax:** 310/860-2430. **Contact:** Human Resource Director. **E-mail address:** rms@rmslaw.com. **World Wide Web address:** http://www.rmslaw.com. **Description:** A law firm specializing in litigation and entertainment law. **Corporate headquarters location:** This location.

RUIZ FOOD PRODUCTS, INC.
P.O. Box 37, Dinuba CA 93618. 559/591-5510. **Physical address:** 501 South Alto Avenue, Dinuba CA 93618. **Toll-free phone:** 800/477-6474. **Fax:** 559/591-1593. **Contact:** Mary McCarthy, Human Resources. **E-mail address:** jobs@ruizfoods.com. **World Wide Web address:** http://www.ruizfoods.com. **Description:** Produces Mexican-style frozen foods that are distributed throughout the United States, Mexico, and Canada. **Positions advertised include:** Sanitation Team Leader; General Mechanic; Director of Foodservice Marketing. **Corporate headquarters location:** This location. **Operations at this facility include:** Administration; Manufacturing; Research and Development; Sales; Service. **Listed on:** Privately held. **Number of employees at this location:** 800.

THE RYLAND GROUP, INC.
24025 Park Sorrento, Suite 400, Calabasas CA 91302. 818/223-7500. **Toll-free phone:** 800/638-1768. **Fax:** 818/223-7655. **Contact:** Human Resources. **E-mail address:** corpcareers@ryland.com. **World Wide Web address:** http://www.ryland.com. **Description:** One of the nation's largest homebuilders and a leading mortgage finance company. The company builds homes in six regions and more than 25 cities. **NOTE:** Search and apply for positions online. **Positions advertised include:** Executive Compensation Analyst; Senior Tax Accountant; Assistant Risk Manager; Senior Auditor. **Corporate headquarters location:** This location. **Other U.S. locations:** Nationwide. **Subsidiaries include:** Ryland Homes specializes in on-site construction of single-family attached and detached homes. Operating out of 34 retail and four wholesale branches, Ryland Mortgage Company works directly with Ryland Homes. **Listed on:** New York Stock Exchange. **Stock exchange symbol:** RYL. **Number of employees at this location:** 600. **Number of employees nationwide:** 3,200.

SAP AMERICA, INC.
18101 Von Karman Avenue, Suite 900, Irvine CA 94404. 949/636227-2200. **Fax:** 949/622-2201. **Contact:** Human Resources. **World Wide Web address:** http://www.sap.com. **Description:** Develops a variety of client/server computer software packages including programs for finance, human resources, and materials management applications. **NOTE:** Search and apply for positions online. **Corporate headquarters location:** Newtown Square PA. **Other U.S. locations:** Nationwide. **International locations:** Germany. **Parent company:** SAP AG. **Listed on:** New York Stock Exchange. **Stock exchange symbol:** SAP. **Number of employees nationwide:** 3,000. **Number of employees worldwide:** 30,000.

SEI INVESTMENTS COMPANY
300 Montgomery Street, Suite 930, San Francisco CA 94104. 415/627-1900. **Contact:** Human Resources. **E-mail address:** careers@seic.com. **World Wide Web address:** http://www.seic.com. **Description:** An investment services firm that operates in two business markets: trust and banking, and fund/sponsor investments. The company also provides an online investment accounting system for trust departments. **Corporate headquarters location:** Oaks PA. **Listed on:** NASDAQ. **Stock exchange symbol:** SEIC.

SI TECHNOLOGIES
14192 Franklin Avenue, Tustin CA 92780-7016. 714/731-1234. **Fax:** 714/573-3843. **Contact:** Personnel. **World Wide Web address:** http://www.sitechnologies.com. **Description:** Designs, manufactures, and markets industrial sensors, and weighing and factory automation systems. **Corporate headquarters location:** This location. **Other U.S. locations:** Chicago IL; Cumberland MD; Detroit MI; Mooresville NC; Eugene OR; Lynnwood WA; Seattle WA. **International locations:** Canada; France; Germany; the Netherlands; United Kingdom. **Listed on:** NASDAQ. **Stock exchange symbol:** SISI. **President/CEO:** Rick A. Beets. **Annual sales/revenues:** $21 - $50 million. **Number of employees worldwide:** 220.

SKC AMERICA, INC.
307 North Pastoria Avenue, Sunnyvale CA 94086. 408/739-4170. **Fax:** 408/720-9778. **Contact:** Human Resources/Administration Manager. **E-mail address:** resumes@skcam.com. **World Wide Web address:** http://www.sk.com. **Description:** Develops, manufactures, and markets various imaging products used for data storage, PCB, and graphic arts applications. Products include duplicate microfilm and polyester-based media for ink-jet printers. **NOTE:** Submit resume online. **Office hours:** Monday - Friday, 8:00 a.m. - 5:00 p.m. **Corporate headquarters location:** Covington GA. **Parent company:** SK Group. **Operations at this facility include:** Manufacturing; Sales.

SMS TECHNOLOGIES, INC.
9877 Waples Street, San Diego CA 92121. 858/587-6900. **Fax:** 858/457-2069. **Contact:** Personnel Manager. **E-mail address:** resumes@smstech.com. **World Wide Web address:** http://www.smstech.com. **Description:** Provides turnkey electronic manufacturing services to the telecommunications, medical electronics, computer, and

industrial equipment industries. **NOTE:** Second and third shift positions are offered. **Positions advertised include:** Manufacturing Engineer; RF Technicians; Program Manager. **Special programs:** Training. **Corporate headquarters location:** This location. **Operations at this facility include:** Administration; Divisional Headquarters; Manufacturing; Research and Development. **Listed on:** Privately held. **CEO:** Robert L. Blumberg. **Annual sales/revenues:** $21 - $50 million. **Number of employees at this location:** 200.

SRI INTERNATIONAL
333 Ravenswood Avenue, Menlo Park CA 94025-3493. 650/859-2000. **Contact:** Personnel. **E-mail address:** careers@sri.com. **World Wide Web address:** http://www.sri.com. **Description:** A multidisciplinary research, development, and consulting organization engaged in government and private industry research. SRI International provides solutions in a variety of areas including pharmaceutical discovery; biopharmaceutical development; education, health, and state policy; engineering sciences; and systems development. **Positions advertised include:** Information Systems Security Officer; Senior Researcher; Senior Secuirty Professional; Web and Graphic Designer. **Corporate headquarters location:** This location. **Listed on:** NASDAQ. **Stock exchange symbol:** STRC.

SS8 NETWORKS
91 East Tasman Drive, San Jose CA 95134. 408/944-0250. **Fax:** 408/428-3732. **Contact:** Human Resources. **E-mail address:** jobs@ss8.com. **World Wide Web address:** http://www.ss8.com. **Description:** Designs, manufactures, and markets communications systems that enable users to access and interact with a broad range of information in a variety of formats including voice, text, data, e-mail, and facsimile from a touch-tone telephone. The company's applications, such as voice messaging, facsimile store-and-forward, and interactive voice response, are integrated on the company's Adaptive Information Processing platform, a communication server that is based on industry-standard hardware and software. **Positions advertised include:** Field Service Engineer; Senior Product Manager; Telecom Applications Engineer. **Corporate headquarters location:** This location. **Operations at this facility include:** Administration; Divisional Headquarters; Manufacturing; Research and Development; Sales.

SAATCHI & SAATCHI ADVERTISING
3501 Sepulveda Boulevard, Torrance CA 90505. 310/214-6000. **Fax:** 310/214-6160. **Contact:** Human Resources. **E-mail address:** rcalhoun@saatchila.com. **World Wide Web address:** http://www.saatchi.com. **Description:** A full-service advertising agency. **Corporate headquarters location:** New York NY. **Other U.S. locations:** Nationwide. **Number of employees worldwide:** 7,000.

SACK, MILLER & ROSENDIN LLP
One Kaiser Plaza, Ordway Building, Suite 340, Oakland CA 94612. 510/286-2200. **Contact:** Human Resources. **World Wide Web address:** http://www.smrlaw.com. **Description:** A law firm specializing in a number of legal disciplines including personal and business injury, real estate, tax, and bankruptcy. **Office hours:** Monday - Friday, 9:00 a.m. - 5:00 p.m. **Corporate headquarters location:** This location.

SAFECO INSURANCE COMPANY OF AMERICA
400 Taylor Boulevard, Pleasant Hill CA 94523-2147. 925/969-2000. **Fax:** 925/969-2215. **Recorded jobline:** 800/753-5330. **Contact:** Personnel. **World Wide Web address:** http://www.safeco.com. **Description:** Provides property and casualty insurance, with strong subsidiaries in life insurance, surety, property development, credit, and investments/asset management. **Positions advertised include:** Claims Examiner; Commercial Surety Representative; Field Claims Examiner. **Corporate headquarters location:** Seattle WA. **Other U.S. locations:** Nationwide. **Parent company:** Safeco Corporation. **Listed on:** NASDAQ. **Stock exchange symbol:** SAFC. **Operations at this facility include:** Administration; Marketing.

SAFENET, INC.
50 Technology Drive, Irvine CA 92618. 949/450-7300. **Contact:** Human Resources. **E-mail address:** humanresources@safenet-inc.com. **World Wide Web address:** http://www.safenet-inc.com. **Description:** Develops security-related technology such as secure Web servers and Virtual Pirate Network acceleration boards, Internet software distribution solutions, data, voice, and satellite security systems, and smart card readers. **NOTE:** Resumes may be submitted via mail, fax, or e-mail. Send resumes to: Safenet, Inc., Attention: Human Resources, 4690 Millenium Drive, Belcamp MD 21017. Fax: 410/931-7524. **Corporate headquarters location:** Belcamp MD. **Listed on:** NASDAQ. **Stock exchange symbol:** SFNT.

SAFENET, INC.
2001 Gateway Place, Suite 335W, San Jose CA 95110. 408/452-7651. **Fax:** 408/452-5726. **Contact:** Human Resources. **E-mail address:** humanresources@safenet-inc.com. **World Wide Web address:** http://www.safenet-inc.com. **Description:** Develops and markets secure e-business solutions that protect information. The company's products protect information on the Internet as well as in local and wide area networks. Founded in 1983. **NOTE:** Resumes may be submitted via mail, fax, or e-mail. Address resumes to: SafeNet, Inc., Attention: Human Resources, 4690 Millenium Drive, Belcamp MD 21017. Fax: 410/931-7524. **Corporate headquarters location:** Belcamp MD. **Other U.S. locations:** Nationwide. **Listed on:** NASDAQ. **Stock exchange symbol:** SFNT.

SAFETY-KLEEN CORPORATION
10651 Hickson Street, El Monte CA 91731. 626/575-4685. **Fax:** 626/575-1927. **Contact:** Human Resources. **World Wide Web address:** http://www.safety-kleen.com. **Description:** A chemical waste recycler. **Corporate headquarters location:** Columbia SC.

SAFEWAY, INC.
5918 Stoneridge Mall Road, Pleasanton CA 94588-3229. 925/467-3000. **Contact:** Jean Hughes, Manager of Corporate Human Resources. **World Wide Web address:** http://www.safeway.com. **Description:** One of the world's largest food retailers. The company operates approximately 1,820 stores in the western, Rocky Mountain, southwestern, and mid-Atlantic regions of the United States and in western Canada. **NOTE:** Search and apply for positions online. **Positions advertised include:** Procurement Specialist; Federal Tax Manager; Strategic Pricing Analyst; Store Designer; Real Estate Manager. **Corporate headquarters location:** Phoenix AZ. **Other U.S. locations:** Nationwide. **International locations:** Canada. **Subsidiaries include:** Casa Ley, S.A. de C.V. operates food/variety, clothing, and wholesale outlet stores in western Mexico; The Vons Companies, Inc. is one of the largest supermarket chains in southern California. **Listed on:** New York Stock Exchange. **Stock exchange symbol:** SWY. **President/CEO:** Steven A. Burd. **Annual sales/revenues:** $35.5 billion. **Number of employees nationwide:** 111,000. **Number of employees worldwide:** 208,000.

SAGE PUBLICATIONS, INC.
2455 Teller Road, Thousand Oaks CA 91320. 805/499-0721. **Fax:** 805/375-1720. **Contact:** Director of Human Resources. **E-mail address:** hr.resume@sagepub.com. **World Wide Web address:** http://www.sagepub.com. **Description:** Publishes academic journals and textbooks for graduate and upper-level college courses in various disciplines including political science and psychology. **NOTE:** Entry-level positions and second and third shifts are offered. **Positions advertised include:** Acquisitions Editor, Journals; Circulations Analyst; Contracts Administrator; Copy Editor; Editorial Assistant; Production Editor; Publishing Editor. **Special programs:** Internships; Training. **Corporate headquarters location:** This location. **International locations:** London England; New Delhi India.

SAINT-GOBAIN CALMAR INC.
333 South Turnbull Canyon Road, City of Industry CA 91745. 626/330-3161. **Toll-free phone:** 800/599-2124. **Contact:** Human Resources Manager. **E-mail address:** jobs@calmar.com. **World Wide Web address:** http://www.calmar.com. **Description:** A leading producer of high-performance mechanical (nonaerosol) dispensing systems. Saint-Gobain Calmar Inc. also develops child-resistant and tamper-evident caps that are used by pharmaceutical firms. **Corporate headquarters location:** Watchung NJ. **Other area locations:** Cerritos CA; San Leandro CA; Union City CA. **Other U.S. locations:** Nationwide. **International locations:** Worldwide.

SAINT-GOBAIN CONTAINER CORPORATION
P.O. Box 5238, El Monte CA 91734. 626/448-9831. **Physical address:** 4000 North Arden Drive, El Monte CA 91731. **Contact:** Human Resources. **World Wide Web address:** http://www.saint-gobain.com/us. **Description:** Manufactures glass containers, such as bottles and jars for the beverage and food industries. **Corporate headquarters location:** Valley Forge PA. **Other U.S. locations:** Nationwide. **Parent company:** Saint-Gobain Group.

ST. JOHN'S HEALTH CENTER
1328 Twenty-Second Street, 6th Floor, Santa Monica CA 90404. 310/829-5511. **Toll-free phone:** 800/359-9003. **Recorded jobline:** 310/829-8323. **Contact:** Penny Bresky, Recruitment and Retention Manager. **World Wide Web address:** http://www.stjohns.org. **Description:** A private, nonprofit, 317-bed, acute health care facility. Founded in 1939. **NOTE:** Unsolicited resumes are not accepted. Search and apply for positions online. **Positions advertised include:** Administrative Specialist; Patient Care Associate; Medical Records Specialist; Case Manager; Licensed Clinical Psychologist; Physical Therapist: Respiratory Specialist; Registered Nurse; Clinical Nurse Educator; Surgical Technician. **Corporate headquarters location:** Leavenworth KS. **Other U.S. locations:** CO; KS; MT. **Parent company:** Sisters of Charity of Leavenworth. **Operations at this facility include:** Administration; Service. **Listed on:** Privately held. **Number of employees at this location:** 1,000.

ST. JON GROUP
1656 West 240th Street, Harbor City CA 90710. 310/326-2720. **Fax:** 310/326-8026. **Contact:** Human Resources. **Description:** Develops, manufactures, and markets health care products for pets. The line includes toothpaste, toothbrushes, sprays, and enzymatic rawhide chews. The brands focus on the specialty pet retail channel with Petromalt Hairball remedy products, Petrodex dental products, Petrelief anti-itch products, Nutrimalt nutritional supplements, and Breath-eze breath mints. Founded in 1982.

ST. JUDE MEDICAL
15900 Valley View Court, Sylmar CA 91342-3577. 818/362-6822. **Toll-free phone:** 800/423-5611. **Contact:** Human Resources. **World Wide Web address:** http://www.sjm.com. **Description:** Manufactures cardiac arrhythmia management devices including pacemakers and defibrillators. **NOTE:** Search and apply for positions online. **Positions advertised include:** Sr. Claims Administrator; Clinical Research Associate; Sr. Cost Analyst; Accounting Director; Program Management Director; Software Engineer. **Special programs:** Internships; Co-ops. **Corporate headquarters location:** St. Paul MN. **Listed on:** New York Stock Exchange. **Stock exchange symbol:** STJ.

ST. PAUL TRAVELERS
350 California Street, Suite 2020, San Francisco CA 94104. **Toll-free phone:** 800/995-5655. **Contact:** Human Resources Department. **E-mail address:** careers@travelers.com. **World Wide Web address:** http://www.stpaultravelers.com. **Description:** This company was formed through an April 2004 merger of the St. Paul Companies and Travelers Property and Casualty. Provides property and casualty insurance. **NOTE:** Part-time jobs are offered. **Corporate headquarters location:** Saint Paul MN. **Listed on:** New York Stock Exchange. **Stock exchange symbol:** STA. **Number of employees at this location:** 200.

SAKS FIFTH AVENUE
384 Post Street, San Francisco CA 94108. 415/986-4300. **Contact:** Ms. Bobi Eisenberg, Director of Human Resources Department. **World Wide Web address:** http://www.saksincorporated.com. **Description:** Saks Fifth Avenue is a 62-store chain emphasizing soft-goods products, primarily apparel for men, women, and children. **Corporate headquarters location:** New York NY. **Other area locations:** Palo Alto CA. **Parent company:** Saks Incorporated is a department store holding company that operates approximately 360 stores in 36 states. The company's stores include Saks Fifth Avenue, Parisian, Proffit's, Younker's, Herberger's, Carson Pirie Scott, Boston Store, Bergner's, and Off 5th, the company's outlet store. Saks Incorporated also operates two retail catalogs and several retail Internet sites. **Operations at this facility include:** This location is a part of the nationwide specialty department store chain. **Listed on:** New York Stock Exchange. **Stock exchange symbol:** SKS.

SALTZBURG, RAY & BERGMAN
12121 Wilshire Boulevard, Suite 600, Los Angeles CA 90025. 310/481-6700. **Fax:** 310/481-6720. **Contact:** Hiring Partner. **World Wide Web address:** http://www.srblaw.com. **Description:** A law firm specializing in bankruptcy, real estate, and corporate law. **Corporate headquarters location:** This location.

THE SALVATION ARMY
180 East Ocean Boulevard, Long Beach CA 90802. 562/436-7000. **Fax:** 562/491-8699. **Contact:** Personnel. **World Wide Web address:** http://www.salvationarmy.org. **Description:** A nonprofit organization providing several service programs including day-care centers, programs for people with disabilities, substance abuse programs and tutoring for at-risk students. The Salvation Army targets its programs to assist alcoholics, battered women, drug addicts, the elderly, the homeless, people with AIDS, prison inmates, teenagers, and the unemployed. **Corporate headquarters location:** Alexandria VA.

SAN DIEGO, CITY OF AND COUNTY
County Administration Center, 1600 Pacific Highway, Room 207, San Diego CA

92101. 619/531-5100. **Fax:** 619/557-4030. **Recorded jobline:** 619/531-5764. **Contact:** Dept. of Human Resources. **E-mail address:** hrwebmaster.fgg@sdcounty.ca.gov. **World Wide Web address:** http://www.sdcounty.ca.gov. **Description:** This location houses the city's and county's government offices. **NOTE:** See website for job listings, testing information and application procedures. Interested jobseekers may apply online or in person at this location or at the Human Resources Office located in 600 East Valley Parkway, Escondido CA 92025. **Positions advertised include:** Human Resources Analyst; Telecommunications Technician; Labor Relations Officer; Workers' Compensation Analyst.

SAN DIEGO COMMUNITY COLLEGE DISTRICT
3375 Camino Del Rio South, Suite 330, San Diego CA 92108. 619/388-6579. **Fax:** 619/388-6897. **Recorded jobline:** 619/388-6850. **Contact:** Beverly Dean, Employment Manager. **E-mail address:** jobs@sdccd.net. **World Wide Web address:** http://www.sdccd.cc.ca.us. **Description:** A community college district comprised of San Diego City College, San Diego Mesa College, and San Diego Miramar College. **Positions advertised include:** Adjunct Instructors, Various Disciplines; Assistant Professor, Biology; Assistant Professor, Chemistry; Assistant Professor, English; Assistant Professor, Mathematics. **Office hours:** Monday – Friday, 8:00 a.m. – 5:00 p.m. **Number of employees at this location:** 5,000.

SAN DIEGO GAS AND ELECTRIC COMPANY
P.O. Box 129831, San Diego CA 92123. 619/696-2000. **Physical address:** 101 Ash Street, San Diego CA 92101. **Recorded jobline:** 858/654-1600. **Contact:** Employment Office. **E-mail address:** jobs@semprautilities.com. **World Wide Web address:** http://www.sdge.com. **Description:** Provides gas and electricity to residential and commercial customers. **Positions advertised include:** Communications Engineer; Engineering Analyst; Environmental Specialist; Events Coordinator. **Corporate headquarters location:** This location. **Parent company:** Sempra Energy. **Listed on:** American Stock Exchange. **Stock exchange symbol:** SDO.

SAN DIEGO STATE UNIVERSITY
5500 Campanile Drive, San Diego CA 92182-1625. 619/594-6404. **Fax:** 619/594-1147. **Contact:** Sue Blair, Director of Personnel. **E-mail address:** employ@mail.sdsu.edu. **World Wide Web address:** http://www.sdsu.edu. **Description:** An undergraduate and graduate state university. **Positions advertised include:** Administrative Support Coordinator; Nutritionist; Developmental Counselor; Assistant Coach, Women's Basketball; Research Technician; Accountant; Physician; Part-time Lecturers, Various Disciplines.

SAN DIEGO ZOO
P.O. Box 120551, San Diego CA 92112-0551. 619/231-1515. **Fax:** 619/744-3326. **Recorded jobline:** 619/557-3968. **Contact:** Human Resources. **World Wide Web address:** http://www.sandiegozoo.org. **Description:** One of the nation's largest zoos. **NOTE:** Applications or resumes not accepted online or via e-mail, and are accepted only for current job openings. **Positions advertised include:** Animal Keeper; Human Resources Representative; Administrative Assistant.

SAN FRANCISCO CHRONICLE
901 Mission Street, San Francisco CA 94103. 415/777-6757. **Contact:** Human Resources. **E-mail address:** hr@sfchronicle.com. **World Wide Web address:** http://www.sfchron.com. **Description:** The largest newspaper in Northern California, with a daily circulation of 512,000, and a Sunday circulation of 540,000. **Positions advertised include:** Director of Photography; Editorial Systems Engineer. **Special programs:** Internships; Co-ops. **Parent company:** Hearst Communications, Inc.

SAN FRANCISCO, CITY OF AND COUNTY
44 Gough Street, San Francisco CA 94103. 415/554-6818. **Recorded jobline:** 415/557-4888. **Contact:** Human Resources. **World Wide Web address:** http://www.sfgov.org. **Description:** The administrative offices for the government of the City of San Francisco, including the fire and police departments, libraries, jails and public work facilities. **NOTE:** See website for job listings and contact information. Part-time and temporary positions offered. **Positions advertised include:** Automotive Machinist Supervisor; Museum Preparatory; Human Resources Director; Supervising Performance Auditor; Public Safety Communications Dispatcher; Juvenile Probation Counselor; Senior Community Development Specialist. **Office hours:** Monday – Friday, 8:00 a.m. – 5:00 p.m.

SAN FRANCISCO CONSERVATORY OF MUSIC
1201 Ortega Street, San Francisco CA 94122-4498. 415/759-3437. **Fax:** 415/759-3499. **Contact:** Karen Heather, Human Resources Manager. **E-mail address:** kjh@sfcm.edu. **World Wide Web address:** http://www.sfcm.edu. **Description:** A music conservatory with an enrollment of 270 students. **Positions advertised include:** Associate Dean for Student Life; Director of Communications.

SAN FRANCISCO EXAMINER
988 Market Street, San Francisco CA 94102. 413/359-2600. **Contact:** Brian Underwood, Human Resources. **E-mail address:** bunderwood@examiner.com. **World Wide Web address:** http://www.examiner.com. **Description:** Operates a daily afternoon newspaper with a circulation of more than 155,000. Through a joint agreement, *San Francisco Examiner* publishes a Sunday edition with competitor *San Francisco Chronicle*. **Parent company:** Hearst Corporation. **Listed on:** New York Stock Exchange. **Stock exchange symbol:** HTV.

SAN FRANCISCO MEDICAL EXAMINER'S OFFICE
850 Bryant Street, San Francisco CA 94103. 415/553-1694. **Fax:** 415/553-1650. **Recorded jobline:** 415/557-4888. **Contact:** Human Resources. **World Wide Web address:** http://www.sfgov.org. **Description:** The medical examiner's office for the City of San Francisco.

SAN FRANCISCO STATE UNIVERSITY
1600 Holloway Avenue, ADM 252, San Francisco CA 94132. 415/338-1871. **Contact:** Human Resources. **E-mail address:** hrwww@sfsu.edu. **World Wide Web address:** http://www.sfsu.edu. **Description:** A four-year, state university. San Francisco State University offers 115 bachelor's degree programs, 93 master's degree programs, a Ph.D. and Ed.D. in education with University of California Berkeley, a master's of science in physical therapy with University of California San Francisco, 28 credential programs, and 22 certificate programs. **Positions advertised include:** Director, Undergraduate Admissions; Administrative Analyst/Specialist; Police Officer. **NOTE:** Entry-level positions are offered. **Special programs:** Internships. **Parent company:** California State University System. **Number of employees at this location:** 3,000.

SAN JOSE INTERNATIONAL AIRPORT
801 North First Street, Room 207, San Jose CA 95110. 408/277-4205. **Recorded jobline:** 408/277-5627. **Contact:** Human Resources. **World Wide Web address:** http://www.sjc.org. **Description:** Operates and manages the city's airport facilities. The airport is a city-funded department, and all airport staff are City of San Jose employees. **NOTE:** Employment applications must be obtained from the City of San Jose's Human Resources Department.

SAN JOSE JOB CORPS CENTER
3485 East Hills Drive, San Jose CA 95127. 408/937-3207. **Fax:** 408/254-5667. **Contact:** Human Resources Department. **E-mail address:** coronav@jcdc.jobcorps.org. **Description:** Offers vocational and educational training for youths. **Positions advertised include:** Administration Director; Career Preparation Counselor; Admissions Counselor. **Corporate headquarters location:** Rochester NY. **Number of employees at this location:** 200. **Parent company:** Career Systems Development Corporation.

SAN JOSE MERCURY NEWS, INC.
750 Rider Park Drive, San Jose CA 95190. 408/920-5000. **Contact:** Employment Manager. **E-mail address:** jobs@sjmercury.com. **World Wide Web address:** http://www.mercurynews.com. **Description:** Publishes a daily newspaper with a circulation of 320,000. **Parent company:** Knight Ridder, Inc. **Listed on:** New York Stock Exchange.

SAN JOSE MUSEUM OF ART
110 South Market Street, San Jose CA 95113. 408/271-6840. **Contact:** Human Relations Department. **E-mail address:** hrdept@sjmusart.org. **World Wide Web address:** http://www.sjmusart.org. **Description:** A contemporary art museum. **Positions advertised include:** Development Manager for Individual Giving; Bilingual Studio Arts Educator; Visitor Service Reps. **Special programs:** Internships; Residencies; Volunteer Opportunities.

SAN JOSE SHARKS
525 West Santa Clara Street, San Jose CA 95113. 408/287-7070. **Fax:** 408/999-5797. **Contact:** Human Resources. **E-mail address:** hr@svse.net. **World Wide Web address:** http://www.sj-sharks.com. **Description:** A professional hockey team. **Corporate headquarters location:** This location.

SAN LUIS OBISPO COUNTY
1050 Monterey Street, San Luis Obispo CA 93408. 805/781-5959. **Recorded jobline:** 805/781-5958. **Contact:** Personnel. **E-mail address:** jobaps@co.slo.ca.us. **World Wide Web address:** http://www.co.slo.ca.us. **Description:** County government. **NOTE:** Application form available online. **Positions advertised include:** Administrative Analyst; Building Inspector; Clinical Lab Technologist; Correctional Nurse; Deputy Probation Officer; Engineer; Planner; Public Health Microbiologist.

SANDIA NATIONAL LABORATORIES
P.O. Box 969, Mail Stop 9111, Livermore CA 94551-0969. 925/294-3000. **Physical address:** 7011 East Avenue, Livermore CA 94550. **Recorded jobline:** 505/844-3441. **Contact:** Human Resources Department. **E-mail address:** resops@sandia.gov. **World Wide Web address:** http://www.sandia.gov. **Description:** Performs scientific research in the areas of space and defense. **Positions advertised include:** Radiation Detection Physicist; Network Engineer; Staffing Specialist. **Special programs:** Post Doctoral Fellowships. **Corporate headquarters location:** Albuquerque NM. **Parent company:** Lockheed Martin Corporation.

SANDISK CORPORATION
140 Caspian Court, Sunnyvale CA 94089. 408/542-0500. **Fax:** 408/542-0604. **Contact:** Human Resources. **E-mail address:** careers@sandisk.com. **World Wide Web address:** http://www.sandisk.com. **Description:** Manufactures computer components including memory cards. **Positions advertised include:** Developer; Business Systems Analyst; Design Engineer; Industrial Design Engineer; Software Engineer; Accountant. **Corporate headquarters location:** This location. **Listed on:** NASDAQ. **Stock exchange symbol:** SNDK. **Annual sales/revenues:** Over $1 billion.

SANMINA-SCI CORPORATION
2955 Airway Avenue, Costa Mesa CA 92626. 714/371-2800. **Fax:** 714/371-2835. **Contact:** Jackie Iten, Human Resources. **World Wide Web address:** http://www.sanmina.com. **Description:** Sanmina-SCI designs, develops, manufactures, markets, distributes, and services electronic products for the computer, aerospace, defense, telecommunications, medical, and banking industries, as well as for the United States government. Sanmina-SCI is one of the world's largest contract electronics manufacturers and operates one of the largest surface mount technology production capacities in the merchant market. Operations are conducted through a Commercial Division and a Government Division. The Commercial Division operates in five geographically organized business units: Eastern, Central, and Western North America; Europe; and Asia. Each unit operates multiple plants that manufacture components, subassemblies, and finished products primarily for original equipment manufacturers. Design, engineering, purchasing, manufacturing, distribution, and support services are also offered. The Governmental Division provides data management, instrumentation, communication, and computer subsystems to the U.S. government and several foreign governments. **Corporate headquarters location:** San Jose CA. **International locations:** Canada; France; Ireland; Mexico; Scotland; Singapore; Thailand. **Operations at this facility include:** This location Manufactures printed circuit boards and back panel assemblies. **Listed on:** NASDAQ. **Stock exchange symbol:** SANM.

SANMINA-SCI CORPORATION
2000 Ringwood Avenue, San Jose CA 95131. 408/943-6110. **Fax:** 408/943-6123. **Contact:** Human Resources. **World Wide Web address:** http://www.sci.com. **Description:** Sanmina-SCI designs, develops, manufactures, markets, distributes, and services electronic products for the computer, aerospace, defense, telecommunications, medical, and banking industries, as well as for the United States government. Sanmina-SCI is one of the world's largest contract electronics manufacturers and operates one of the largest surface mount technology production capacities in the merchant market. Operations are conducted through a Commercial Division and a Government Division. The Commercial Division operates in five geographically organized business units: Eastern, Central, and Western North America; Europe; and Asia. Each unit operates multiple plants that manufacture components, subassemblies, and finished products primarily for original equipment manufacturers. Design, engineering, purchasing, manufacturing, distribution, and support services are also offered. The Governmental Division provides data management, instrumentation, communication, and computer subsystems to the U.S. government and several foreign governments. **Corporate headquarters location:** San Jose CA. **International locations:** Canada; France; Ireland; Mexico; Scotland; Singapore; Thailand. **Operations at this facility include:** This location is a design center. **Listed on:** NASDAQ. **Stock exchange symbol:** SANM. **Annual sales/revenues:** $10.4 billion. **Number of employees worldwide:** 45,000.

SANMINA-SCI CORPORATION
30200 Avenida de las Banderas, Rancho Santa Margarita CA 92688. 949/643-7255. **Fax:** 949/643-7250. **Contact:** Human Resources. **World Wide Web address:** http://www.sanmina.com. **Description:** Manufactures custom-designed back panel

assemblies and subassemblies; multilayer, high-density printed circuit boards; and surface mount technology assemblies used in sophisticated electronics equipment. The company serves original equipment manufacturers in the telecommunication, data communication, industrial/medical, computer systems, and contract assembly business sectors. **Corporate headquarters location:** San Jose CA. **International locations:** Canada; France; Ireland; Mexico; Scotland; Singapore; Thailand. **Listed on:** NASDAQ. **Stock exchange symbol:** SANM. **Annual sales/revenues:** $10.4 billion.

SANMINA-SCI CORPORATION
2700 North First Street, San Jose CA 95134. 408/964-3500. **Fax:** 408/964-3799. **Contact:** Human Resources. **World Wide Web address:** http://www.sanmina.com. **Description:** Manufactures custom-designed backplane assemblies and subassemblies; multilayer, high-density printed circuit boards; testing equipment; and surface mount technology assemblies used in sophisticated electronics equipment with primary customers in the telecommunications, data communications, industrial/medical, computer systems, and contract assembly business sectors. **Corporate headquarters location:** This location. **Listed on:** NASDAQ. **Stock exchange symbol:** SANM. **Annual sales/revenues:** $10.4 billion. **Number of employees worldwide:** 45,000.

SANTA BARBARA LOCATION SERVICES REAL TALENT/KIDS
1214 Coast Village, Suite 12, Santa Barbara CA 93108. 805/565-1562. **Fax:** 805/969-9595. **Contact:** Ms. Ronnie Mellen, Owner. **World Wide Web address:** http://www.santabarbara-locations.com. **Description:** Assists the film industry by providing location/production coordination services. Real Talent/Kids (also at this location, 805/969-2222) is a casting company. Founded in 1983. **Number of employees at this location:** 5.

SANTA CLARA PET HOSPITAL
830 Kiely Boulevard, Santa Clara CA 95051. 408/296-5857. **Fax:** 408/243-5434. **Contact:** Human Resources Department. **World Wide Web address:** http://www.santaclarapethospital.com. **Description:** Provides general medical, surgical, dental, and radiological services to domestic and exotic animals. The hospital also provides cardiology services and avian intensive care. **Corporate headquarters location:** This location.

SANTA CLARA UNIVERSITY
500 El Camino Real, Santa Clara CA 95053-0850. 408/554-4392. **Fax:** 408/554-5488. **Contact:** Human Resources Department. **E-mail address:** hrservicedesk@scu.edu. **World Wide Web address:** http://www.scu.edu. **Description:** A four-year independent Jesuit university offering undergraduate programs through its schools of Arts and Sciences, Business, Engineering, and Education. The university also offers graduate programs through its schools of Law, Engineering, Business, Agricultural Business, and Counseling Psychology. **Positions advertised include:** Administrative Assistant; Associate Director, Planned Giving; Network Engineer; Senior Information Specialist; Lecturer, Various Disciplines. **Corporate headquarters location:** This location.

SANTA CLARA VALLEY TRANSPORTATION AUTHORITY
3331 North First Street, Building B, San Jose CA 95134. 408/321-5575. **Contact:** Personnel Director. **E-mail address:** personnel@vta.org. **World Wide Web address:** http://www.vta.org. **Description:** Provides transportation services to the San Jose area. **Positions advertised include:** Commercial Development Manager; Contracts Manager; Information Systems Manager.

SAPIENT CORPORATION
1601 cloverfield Boulevard, Suite 600 South, Santa Monica CA 90404. 310/264-6900. **Fax:** 310/264-6901. **Contact:** Director of Hiring. **World Wide Web address:** http://www.sapient.com. **Description:** Provides systems integration, consulting, and software integration services. Founded in 1991. **Corporate headquarters location:** Cambridge MA. **Other area locations:** Los Angeles CA. **Other U.S. locations:** Denver CO; Washington DC; Chicago IL; Portland ME; Minneapolis MN; Jersey City NJ; Austin TX; Dallas TX. **International locations:** Australia; England; Germany; India; Italy; Japan. **Listed on:** NASDAQ. **Stock exchange symbol:** SAPE. **Annual sales/revenues:** $184 million.

SARA LEE
955 Kennedy Street, Oakland CA 94606. 510/436-5350. **Contact:** Personnel Department. **E-mail address:** recruiting@saralee.com. **World Wide Web address:** http://www.saralee.com. **Description:** An international producer and marketer of food and consumer products. **Corporate headquarters location:** Chicago IL. **Listed on:** New York Stock Exchange. **Stock exchange symbol:** SLE.

SARA LEE
2411 Baumann Avenue, San Lorenzo CA 94580. 510/276-1300. **Contact:** Personnel. **World Wide Web address:** http://www.saralee.com. **Description:** An international producer and marketer of food and consumer products. **Corporate headquarters location:** Chicago IL. **Listed on:** New York Stock Exchange. **Stock exchange symbol:** SLE.

SATCOM TECHNOLOGIES
3111 Fujita Street, Torrance CA 90505. 310/539-6704. **Fax:** 310/539-7463. **Contact:** Hans Spieleder, Human Resources. **E-mail address:** hans.spieleder@tripointglobal.com. **World Wide Web address:** http://www.tripointglobal.com. **Description:** Designs, fabricates and tests passive microwave components and subsystems for the commercial, military and space markets. **Corporate headquarters location:** Newton NC. **Parent company:** General Dynamics.

SATCOM TECHNOLOGIES
2205 Fortune Drive, San Jose CA 95131. 408/955-1900. **Fax:** 408/955-1926. **Contact:** Human Resources. **E-mail address:** vertexrsi@tripointglobal.com. **World Wide Web address:** http://www.tripointglobal.com. **Description:** Provides TT&C antennas and systems, full motion antennas, radio telescope antennas, radar antennas and satellite monitoring systems. **Parent company:** General Dynamics.

SAVE MART SUPERMARKETS
P.O. Box 4278, Modesto CA 95352. 209/577-1600. **Physical address:** 1800 Standiford Avenue, Modesto CA 95350. **Contact:** Kit Serpa, Employment Supervisor. **Description:** Operates more than 120 grocery stores in Northern and Central California.

SAVIN CORPORATION
250 Executive Park Boulevard, South San Francisco CA 94134. 415/468-3460. **Contact:** Human Resources. **World Wide Web address:** http://www.savin.com. **Description:** Manufactures and markets a wide range of large- and small-scale electronic calculators, programmable calculators, electronic accounting machines, facsimiles, shredders, and copy machines. Products are used in a wide range of business, governmental, medical, and educational applications. Products are sold through company-owned branches in the United States and Canada. **Corporate headquarters location:** Stamford CT.

SAVVIS COMMUNICATIONS
17836 Gillette Avenue, Irvine CA 92614. 949/608-2739. **Contact:** Human Resources. **World Wide Web address:** http://www.savvis.net. **Description:** A global IT utility provider that delivers hosting, network, and application services to 110 cities in 45 countries. **NOTE:** Search and apply for positions online. **Positions advertised include:** Sr. Network Systems Engineer; Sr. Program Manager. **Corporate headquarters location:** St. Louis MO.

SCANTRON CORPORATION
34 Parker, Irvine CA 92618. **Toll-free phone:** 800/722-6876. **Fax:** 949/639-7716. **Contact:** Sherre McKaig, Director of Human Resources. **E-mail address:** hr@scantron.com. **World Wide Web address:** http://www.scantron.com. **Description:** Manufactures and markets optical mark reader, test scoring, and data entry equipment. **Positions advertised include:** Product Manager; Revenue Manager; Inside Sales Representative. **Corporate headquarters location:** This location. **Other U.S. locations:** Nationwide. **Parent company:** J.H. Harland. **Listed on:** New York Stock Exchange. **Stock exchange symbol:** JH. **Number of employees at this worldwide:** 600.

EARL SCHEIB, INC.
15206 Ventura Boulevard, Suite 200, Sherman Oaks CA 91403. 818/981-9992. **Toll-free phone:** 800/639-3275. **Contact:** Human Resources. **E-mail address:** kpickering@earlscheib.com. **World Wide Web address:** http://www.earlscheib.com. **Description:** Operates a chain of automobile paint centers throughout the United States that offer painting and light body and fender repair services. **Positions advertised include:** Manager. **Corporate headquarters location:** This location. **Other U.S. locations:** Tampa FL; Evergreen Park IL; Springfield MO. **Operations at this facility include:** Regional Headquarters. **Listed on:** American Stock Exchange. **Stock exchange symbol:** ESH.

SCHINDLER ELEVATOR CORPORATION
562 Whitney Street, San Leandro CA 94577. 510/382-2075. **Fax:** 510/382-2250. **Contact:** Human Resources. **World Wide Web address:** http://www.schindler.com. **Description:** Repairs, services, and renovates elevators and escalators produced by various manufacturers. **Corporate headquarters location:** Ebikon, Switzerland.

SCIENCE APPLICATIONS INTERNATIONAL CORPORATION
10260 Campus Point Drive, San Diego CA 92121. 858/826-7624. **Contact:** Human Resources. **E-mail address:** jobs@saic.com. **World Wide Web address:** http://www.saic.com. **Description:** Offers technology development, computer system integration, and technology support services. Founded in 1969. **NOTE:** Search and apply for positions online. **Positions advertised include:** Project Control Analyst; Tax Accountant; Executive Assistant; Human Resources Assistant; Programmer; Senior Software Engineer; Network Engineer; Senior Mechanical Engineer; Senior Radio Engineer. **Special programs:** Internships. **Corporate headquarters location:** This location. **Other area locations:** Statewide. **Subsidiaries include:** AMSEC; Carreker-Antinori; Danet; GSC; Global Integrity Corp.; Hicks & Assoc.; INTESA; Leadership 2000; Network Solutions, Inc.; PAI. **Annual sales/revenues:** $6.7 billion. **Number of employees worldwide:** 43,000.

SCIENTIFIC TECHNOLOGIES INC. (STI)
6550 Dumbarton Circle, Fremont CA 94555-3611. 510/608-3400. **Fax:** 510/744-1309. **Contact:** Human Resources. **E-mail address:** employment@sti.com. **World Wide Web address:** http://www.sti.com. **Description:** Designs, manufactures, and distributes electrical and electronic controls for the industrial market. **Positions advertised include:** Senior Electrical Engineer; Senior Mechanical Engineer; Senior Accountant. **Corporate headquarters location:** This location. **Listed on:** NASDAQ. **Stock exchange symbol:** STIZ. **President/CEO:** Joseph J. Lazzara.

SCIOS INC.
6500 Paseo Padre Parkway, Fremont CA 94555. 510/248-2405. **Contact:** Human Resources. **E-mail address:** jobs@sciosinc.com. **World Wide Web address:** http://www.sciosinc.com. **Description:** Researches, develops, and manufactures pharmaceuticals for the treatment of cardiovascular and neurological disorders. Founded in 1981. **Positions advertised include:** Accountant; Application Developer; Clinical Research Associate; Senior Medical Writer; Drug Safety Associate; Scientist. **Special programs:** Internships. **Office hours:** Monday - Friday, 8:00 a.m. - 5:00 p.m. **Corporate headquarters location:** This location. **Parent company:** Johnson & Johnson. **Listed on:** NASDAQ. **Stock exchange symbol:** SCIO. **Number of employees nationwide:** Over 700.

SCITECH SOFTWARE INC.
180 East Fourth Street, Chico CA 95928. 530/894-8400. **Fax:** 530/894-9069. **Contact:** Human Resources. **World Wide Web address:** http://www.scitechsoft.com. **Description:** A leading developer of operating system drivers for embedded systems.

SEAGATE TAPE
155 South Milpitas Boulevard, Milpitas CA 95035. 714/641-0279. **Contact:** Stephen Shoda, Personnel Manager. **World Wide Web address:** http://www.seagate.com. **Description:** Manufactures disc drives, magnetic discs, read-write heads, and tape drives. Seagate Tape also develops business intelligence software. **Corporate headquarters location:** Scotts Valley CA. **Parent company:** Seagate Technology.

SEAGATE TECHNOLOGY
920 Disc Drive, Scotts Valley CA 95067-0360. 831/438-6550. **Contact:** Human Resources. **World Wide Web address:** http://www.seagate.com. **Description:** Designs and manufactures data storage devices and related products including hard-disk drives, tape drives, software, and systems for a variety of computer-related applications and operating systems. **Positions advertised include:** Senior Programmer Analyst; Office Assistant; Senior Accountant; Investigator. **Corporate headquarters location:** This location. **Other U.S. locations:** OK. **Annual sales/revenues:** $6.5 billion. **Number of employees nationwide:** 87,000.

SECURE COMPUTING
4810 Harwood Road, San Jose CA 95124-5206. 408/979-6100. **Toll-free phone:** 800/692-5625. **Fax:** 408/979-6501. **Contact:** Human Resources. **World Wide Web address:** http://www.securecomputing.com. **Description:** Provides a variety of network security products, including firewalls, user identification and authorization software, and Web filtering applications. Its firewall and virtual private network (VPN) gateways enable companies to securely manage and maintain network access for employees, customers, and partners. Secure Computing also provides software that enables network administrators to restrict access to specific Web sites to streamline

system resources and improve employee productivity. **NOTE:** Search and apply for positions online. **Listed on:** NASDAQ. **Stock exchange symbol:** SCUR.

SECURITAS SECURITY SERVICES
1506 East Warner Avenue, Suite 114, Santa Ana CA 92707. 714/245-6800. **Fax:** 714/245-6809. **Contact:** Human Resources. **World Wide Web address:** http://www.securitasinc.com. **Description:** One of the world's largest suppliers of global, total security solutions. The company provides a broad array of security-related services to address the protection needs of customers through its 650 offices in the United States. Securitas U.S.A. has grown tremendously through its acquisition of companies such as Pinkerton, Wells Fargo, Burns, American Protective Services, and First Security. **Special programs:** Internships. **Corporate headquarters location:** Parsippany NJ. **Other U.S. locations:** Nationwide. **Parent company:** Securitas (Sweden).

SECURITAS SECURITY SERVICES
3333 Wilshire Boulevard, Suite 615, Los Angeles CA 90017. 213/637-5500. **Contact:** Personnel. **Description:** Offers a wide range of protective services and contract security guard programs to businesses and government. Formerly known as Burns International Security Services. **Number of employees nationwide:** 20,000.

SEE'S CANDIES
210 El Camino Real, South San Francisco CA 94080. 650/583-7307. **Contact:** Human Resources. **E-mail address:** resumes@sees.com. **World Wide Web address:** http://www.sees.com. **Description:** See's Candies manufactures candy. **Corporate headquarters location:** This location. **Parent company:** Berkshire-Hathaway. **Operations at this facility include:** This location houses administrative offices.

SEEBEYOND
800 East Royal Oaks Drive, Monrovia CA 91016-6347. 626/471-6000. **Fax:** 626/471-6100. **Contact:** Human Resources. **World Wide Web address:** http://www.seebeyond.com. **Description:** Develops data interface engines and database software for enterprisewide solutions. Products include e*Gate, an enterprise integration program. **Positions advertised include:** Business Process Architect; Engagement Manager; Senior Consultant; Software Engineer. **Corporate headquarters location:** This location. **Listed on:** NASDAQ. **Stock exchange symbol:** SBYN.

SEMICOA SEMICONDUCTORS, INC.
333 McCormick Avenue, Costa Mesa CA 92626. 714/979-1900. **Fax:** 714/557-4541. **Contact:** Gerri Gibb, Human Resources Manager. **E-mail address:** ggibb@semicoa.com. **World Wide Web address:** http://www.semicoa.com. **Description:** A custom manufacturer of small signal RF, discrete, bipolar transistors and photodiodes. Founded in 1968. **NOTE:** Entry-level positions and second and third shifts are offered. **Positions advertised include:** Field Sales Engineer; Senior Opto Process Development Engineer; Test Operator. **Special programs:** Training. **Corporate headquarters location:** This location. **Listed on:** Privately held. **Annual sales/revenues:** $5 - $10 million. **Number of employees at this location:** 90.

SEMICONDUCTOR PROCESS EQUIPMENT CORPORATION
27963 Franklin Parkway, Valencia CA 91355. 661/257-0934. **Fax:** 661/257-1083. **Contact:** Dede Long, Recruiter. **World Wide Web address:** http://www.team-spec.com. **Description:** A leading manufacturer of specialized processing equipment used by semiconductor manufacturers. Founded in 1986. **Office hours:** Monday - Friday, 8:00 a.m. - 5:00 p.m. **Corporate headquarters location:** This location. **Listed on:** Privately held. **Annual sales/revenues:** $11 - $20 million. **Number of employees at this location:** 125.

SEMPRA ENERGY
101 Ash Street, San Diego CA 92101-3017. 619/696-2000. **Toll-free phone:** 877/736-7721. **Fax:** 619/696-4463. **Contact:** Human Resources. **E-mail address:** careers@sempra.com. **World Wide Web address:** http://www.sempra.com. **Description:** Provides electric and natural gas products. **Positions advertised include:** Government Affairs Manager; Staff Accountant; Sr. Tax Advisor. **Special programs:** Internships. **Corporate headquarters location:** This location. **Other U.S. locations:** Nationwide. **International locations:** Worldwide. **Subsidiaries include:** Southern California Gas Co.; San Diego Gas and Electric; Sempra Energy Trading; Sempra Energy International; Sempra Energy Solutions; Sempra Energy Resources; Sempra Energy Utility Ventures. **Listed on:** New York Stock Exchange. **Stock exchange symbol:** SRE. **Annual sales/revenues:** $7.9 billion. **Number of employees worldwide:** 12,000.

SENECA DISTRICT HOSPITAL
130 Brentwood Drive, P.O. Box 737, Chester CA 96020. 530/258-2159. **Fax:** 530/258-3595. **Contact:** Doreen Turner, Director of Human Resources. **World Wide Web address:** http://www.senecahospital.org. **Description:** Provides a variety of medical services including family centered birthing, obstetrical clinic, outpatient laboratory and X-ray services including mammography and sonography, in-house pharmacy, hospice, anesthesia, inpatient and outpatient surgical services, stress testing, respiratory care, nutritional counseling, EKG, Lifeline, and patient education. Founded in 1952. **NOTE:** Entry-level positions are offered. **Positions advertised include:** Dietary Services Supervisor; CNA. **Corporate headquarters location:** This location. **CEO:** Raymond Marks. **Annual sales/revenues:** Less than $5 million. **Number of employees at this location:** 140.

SENIOR AEROSPACE
2980 North San Fernando Boulevard, Burbank CA 91504. 818/848-1193. **Contact:** Human Resources. **E-mail address:** hr@sfketema.com. **World Wide Web address:** http://www.senioraerospace.com. **Description:** Manufactures aircraft fuselages and related parts. **Positions advertised include:** Production Supervisor; Senior Planner; Manufacturing Engineer. **Corporate headquarters location:** Rickmansworth England.

SEQUOIA VOTING SYSTEMS
7677 Oakport Street, Suite 800, Oakland CA 94621. 510/875-1200. **Fax:** 510/875-1226. **Contact:** Director of Human Resources. **E-mail address:** careers@sequoiavote.com. **World Wide Web address:** http://www.seqouiavote.com. **Description:** Sequoia Pacific Systems Corporation is engaged in the printing of labels and election materials. **Corporate headquarters location:** This location. **Operations at this facility include:** This location is the major manufacturing facility and corporate office.

SEVERN TRENT LABORATORIES, INC.
1721 South Grand Avenue, Santa Ana CA 92705. 714/258-8610. **Fax:** 714/258-0921. **Contact:** Human Resources. **World Wide Web address:** http://www.stl-inc.com. **Description:** Provides a complete range of environmental testing services to private industry, engineering consultants, and government agencies in support of federal and state environmental regulations. The company also possesses analytical capabilities in the fields of air toxins, field analytical services, radiochemistry/mixed waste, and advanced technology. **Corporate headquarters location:** North Canton OH. **Other U.S. locations:** FL; MO; NC; OH; TN; TX; WA.

SEVERN TRENT LABORATORIES, INC.
880 Riverside Parkway, West Sacramento CA 95605. 916/373-5600. **Fax:** 916/372-1059. **Contact:** Joseph Schrairer, Human Resources Representative. **E-mail address:** jschairer@stl-inc.com. **World Wide Web address:** http://www.stl-inc.com. **Description:** Provides a complete range of environmental testing services to private industry, engineering consultants, and government agencies in support of federal and state environmental regulations. The company also possesses analytical capabilities in the fields of air toxins, field analytical services, radiochemistry/mixed waste, and advanced technology.

SHAKLEE CORPORATION
4747 Willow Road, Pleasanton CA 90623. 925/924-2000. **Fax:** 925/924-2862. **Contact:** Roseanne Jennings, Personnel Manager. **World Wide Web address:** http://www.shaklee.com. **Description:** Manufactures and markets vitamins, minerals, protein powders, and other nutritional products. **Corporate headquarters location:** This location.

SHARP HEALTHCARE
8695 Spectrum Center Boulevard, San Diego CA 92123. 858/499-4000. **Fax:** 858/499-5938. **Recorded jobline:** 858/499-5627. **Contact:** Human Resources. **E-mail address:** sharpjob@sharp.com. **World Wide Web address:** http://www.sharp.com. **Description:** A nonprofit organization consisting of six acute care hospitals, one specialty women's hospital, three medical groups, medical clinics, urgent care centers, skilled nursing facilities, and a variety of other community health education programs and related services. Founded in 1954. **NOTE:** Second and third shifts are offered. Apply by mail, fax, or in person. **Positions advertised include:** Account Analyst; Chaplain. **Office hours:** Monday - Friday, 7:00 a.m. - 7:00 p.m. **Corporate headquarters location:** This location. **Operations at this facility include:** Administration; Service. **Listed on:** Privately held. **CEO:** Michael Murphy.

SHARPER IMAGE CORPORATION
650 Davis Street, San Francisco CA 94111. 415/445-6000. **Contact:** Deborah Baker-Reyes, Human Resources. **World Wide Web address:** http://www.sharperimage.com. **Description:** A retailer of a wide variety of gifts in the following categories: automotive, outdoor and garden, travel and luggage, electronics, health and fitness, personal care, and home and safety. **Positions advertised include:** Account Manager; Human Resources Generalist; Senior Programmer/Analyst; Internet Content Specialist; Loss Prevention Specialist; Assistant Electronics Engineer. **Corporate headquarters location:** This location. **Listed on:** NASDAQ. **Stock exchange symbol:** SHRP.

SHASTA BEVERAGES INC.
BEVPAK MANUFACTURING
26901 Industrial Boulevard, Hayward CA 94545. 510/783-3200. **Contact:** Human Resources Director. **E-mail address:** humanresources@nationalbeverage.com. **World Wide Web address:** http://www.shastapop.com. **Description:** A producer of a variety of regular and diet soft drinks. Bevpak Manufacturing (also at this location) bottles beverages produced by Shasta. **Special programs:** Internships. **Corporate headquarters location:** This location. **Parent company:** National Beverage Corporation. **Listed on:** American Stock Exchange. **Stock exchange symbol:** FIZ.

SHASTA REGIONAL MEDICAL CENTER
1100 Butte Street, Redding CA 96001. 530/244-5150. **Fax:** 530/244-5172. **Contact:** Human Resources. **E-mail address:** srmc-employment@hospitalpartners.com. **World Wide Web address:** http://www.reddingmedicalcenter.com. **Description:** Shasta Regional Medical Center is a regional health care provider operating the California Heart Institute, the Center for Neuroscience, the Cancer Care Professionals oncology unit, the Joint Care Center for knee and hip replacement, and the Baby Place for child birthing. **NOTE:** Second and third shifts are offered. **Positions advertised include:** Pharmacist; Registered Nurse; Respiratory Therapist; Plant Maintenance Engineer. **Parent company:** Hospital Partners of America (Charlotte NC). **Number of employees at this location:** 1,400.

SHAW ENVIRONMENTAL & INFASTRUCTURE
2360 Bering Drive, San Jose CA 95131-1121. 408/382-5800. **Fax:** 408/433-1912. **Contact:** Human Resources. **World Wide Web address:** http://www.shawgrp.com. **Description:** Provides environmental engineering, consulting, and construction services to a variety of public and private sector clients. Shaw is a leader in the design and remediation of solid and hazardous waste, transfer, storage, and disposal facilities. Shaw's waste facility services include site selection and evaluation, facility design, development of preprocessing and operating plans, assistance in regulatory compliance and permitting, final closures, and end use planning and design. The company's services also include the development of programs dealing with environmental assessments and remediation of contaminated sites, as well as services related to applied sciences such as marine fate-and-effect studies and fuel spill and natural resource damage assessments. **NOTE:** Entry-level positions are offered. **Positions advertised include:** Program Manager. **Office hours:** Monday - Friday, 8:00 a.m. - 5:00 p.m. **Corporate headquarters location:** Baton Rouge LA. **Other U.S. locations:** Nationwide. **Parent company:** Shaw Group (England). **Listed on:** New York Stock Exchange. **Stock exchange symbol:** SGR.

SHAW ENVIRONMENTAL & INFRASTRUCTURE
3347 Michelson Drive, Suite 200, Irvine CA 92612. 949/261-6441. **Fax:** 949/474-8309. **Contact:** Human Resources. **World Wide Web address:** http://www.shawgrp.com. **Description:** Applies engineering, analytical, remediation, and pollution control expertise to meet the environmental needs of its clients from site assessment to remediation. **Corporate headquarters location:** Baton Rouge LA. **Number of employees worldwide:** 6,000.

J.F. SHEA COMPANY, INC.
655 Brea Canyon Road, Walnut CA 91789. 909/594-9500. **Contact:** Chief Estimator. **World Wide Web address:** http://www.jfshea.com. **Description:** Engaged in the construction of water resource, water, and wastewater treatment systems. **Corporate headquarters location:** This location. **Parent company:** Zurn Industries, Inc. (Erie PA) also has operations in three other industry segments. The Power Systems segment designs, constructs, and operates small to medium-sized alternate energy and combined-cycle power plants; designs steam generators and waste heat energy recovery and incineration systems; and produces equipment and fans to control emissions of solid particulate and gaseous pollutants. The Mechanical Power Transmission segment manufactures and markets clutches, couplings, and universal joints in the United States and Europe. The last segment, Lynx Golf, manufactures golf clubs in Nevada, which are finished and assembled in California, Mexico, and Scotland for distribution worldwide. **Operations at this facility include:** Administration; Divisional

Headquarters. **Listed on:** New York Stock Exchange. **Annual sales/revenues:** $51 - $100 million. **Number of employees at this location:** 250.

SHELL MARTINEZ REFINING COMPANY
P.O. Box 711, Martinez CA 94553-0071. 925/313-3000. **Physical address:** 3485 Pacheco Boulevard, Martinez CA 94553. **Fax:** 925/313-3839. **Recorded jobline:** 925/313-3552. **Contact:** Human Resources Department. **World Wide Web address:** http://www.shellmartinezrefinery.com. **Description:** Engaged in the exploration, development, production, purchase, transportation, and marketing of crude oil, natural gas, and related chemical products. **Positions advertised include:** Procurement Representative.

SHELL SOLAR
4650 Adohr Lane, Camarillo CA 93012. 805/482-6800. **Fax:** 805/388-6394. **Contact:** Lita Rigonan, Human Resources Manager. **E-mail address:** experiencedjobs@shell.com. **World Wide Web address:** http://www.shellsolar.com. **Description:** A manufacturer of solar cells. Founded in 1975. **Corporate headquarters location:** This location. **Other U.S. locations:** Vancouver WA. **Parent company:** Shell Solar B.V. (Amsterdam). **Number of employees at this location:** 230.

SHERATON FISHERMAN'S WHARF
2500 Mason Street, San Francisco CA 94133. 415/362-5500. **Fax:** 415/627-6529. **Recorded jobline:** 415/627-6567. **Contact:** Lisa Lucas-Yap, Human Resources Director. **World Wide Web address:** http://www.sheraton.com. **Description:** A 525-room hotel. Founded in 1998. **NOTE:** Part-time jobs are offered. To contact Human Resources call: 415/627-6526. **Corporate headquarters location:** Washington DC. **Parent company:** Starwood Hotels & Resorts Worldwide, Inc. **Listed on:** New York Stock Exchange. **Stock exchange symbol:** HOT. **Chairman and CEO:** Paul Whetsell. **Number of employees at this location:** 260. **Number of employees nationwide:** 27,000.

THE SHERWIN-WILLIAMS COMPANY INC.
1450 Sherwin Avenue, Emeryville CA 94608. 510/420-7232. **Contact:** Human Resources Manager. **World Wide Web address:** http://www.sherwin.com. **Description:** Sherwin-Williams Company manufactures, sells, and distributes coatings and related products. Coatings are produced for original equipment manufacturers in various industries, as well as for the automotive aftermarket, the industrial maintenance market, and the traffic paint market. Sherwin-Williams labeled architectural and industrial coatings are sold through company-owned specialty paint and wall covering stores. The Sherwin-Williams Company also manufactures paint under the Acme, Dutch Boy, Kem-Tone, Lucas, Martin-Senour, Minwax, Pratt & Lambert, Rogers, and Thompson brand names, as well as private labels, and markets its products to independent dealers, mass merchandisers, and home improvement centers. **Special programs:** Internships. **Office hours:** Monday - Friday, 6:30 a.m. - 3:00 p.m. **Corporate headquarters location:** Cleveland OH. **Other U.S. locations:** Nationwide. **Operations at this facility include:** This location is a support office for area stores and a facility for manufacturing emulsion paints. **Listed on:** New York Stock Exchange. **Stock exchange symbol:** SHW.

THE SHERWIN-WILLIAMS COMPANY INC.
4733 Geary Boulevard, San Francisco CA 94118. 415/751-9420. **Contact:** Human Resources. **World Wide Web address:** http://www.sherwin.com. **Description:** Sherwin-Williams manufactures, sells, and distributes coatings and related products. Coatings are produced for original equipment manufacturers in various industries, as well as for the automotive aftermarket, the industrial maintenance market, and the traffic paint market. Sherwin-Williams labeled architectural and industrial coatings are sold through company-owned specialty paint and wall covering stores. The Sherwin-Williams Company also manufactures paint under the Acme, Dutch Boy, Kem-Tone, Lucas, Martin-Senour, Minwax, Pratt & Lambert, Rogers, and Thompson brand names, as well as private labels, and markets its products to independent dealers, mass merchandisers, and home improvement centers. **Corporate headquarters location:** Cleveland OH. **Other area locations:** Redwood City CA; Burlingame CA. **Other U.S. locations:** Nationwide. **Operations at this facility include:** This location is a retail paint and wall covering store. **Listed on:** New York Stock Exchange. **Stock exchange symbol:** SHW.

THE SHERWIN-WILLIAMS COMPANY INC.
3301 McHenry Avenue, Modesto CA 95350. 209/521-1577. **Contact:** Human Resources. **World Wide Web address:** http://www.sherwin.com. **Description:** Sherwin-Williams manufactures, sells, and distributes coatings and related products. Coatings are produced for original equipment manufacturers in various industries, as well as for the automotive aftermarket, the industrial maintenance market, and the traffic paint market. Sherwin-Williams labeled architectural and industrial coatings are sold through company-owned specialty paint and wall covering stores. The Sherwin-Williams Company also manufactures paint under the Acme, Dutch Boy, Kem-Tone, Lucas, Martin-Senour, Minwax, Pratt & Lambert, Rogers, and Thompson brand names, as well as private labels, and markets its products to independent dealers, mass merchandisers, and home improvement centers. **Corporate headquarters location:** Cleveland OH. **Other U.S. locations:** Nationwide. **Operations at this facility include:** This location is a retail paint and wall covering store. **Listed on:** New York Stock Exchange. **Stock exchange symbol:** SHW.

THE SHERWIN-WILLIAMS COMPANY INC.
2125 Oak Grove Road, Suite 100, Walnut Creek CA 94598. 925/932-3363. **Fax:** 925/930-7118. **Contact:** Jim Pfohl, Human Resources Manager. **E-mail address:** jim.m.pfohl@sherwin.com. **World Wide Web address:** http://www.sherwin.com. **Description:** Sherwin-Williams manufactures, sells, and distributes coatings and related products. Coatings are produced for original equipment manufacturers in various industries, as well as for the automotive aftermarket, the industrial maintenance market, and the traffic paint market. Sherwin-Williams labeled architectural and industrial coatings are sold through company-owned specialty paint and wall covering stores. The Sherwin-Williams Company also manufactures paint under the Acme, Dutch Boy, Kem-Tone, Lucas, Martin-Senour, Minwax, Pratt & Lambert, Rogers, and Thompson brand names, as well as private labels, and markets its products to independent dealers, mass merchandisers, and home improvement centers. Founded in 1866. **Special programs:** Internships; Training; Summer Jobs. **Office hours:** Monday - Friday, 8:00 a.m. - 4:30 p.m. **Corporate headquarters location:** Cleveland OH. **Other U.S. locations:** Nationwide. **Operations at this facility include:** This location is a support office for area stores. **Listed on:** New York Stock Exchange. **Stock exchange symbol:** SHW.

SIEBEL SYSTEMS, INC.
800 Concar Drive, San Mateo CA 94402. 650/477-5000. **Toll-free phone:** 800/647-4300. **Contact:** Human Resources. **World Wide Web address:** http://www.siebel.com. **Description:** A leading provider of e-commerce application software. **NOTE:** Search and apply for positions online. **Positions advertised include:** Curriculum Developer; Lead Software Engineer; Senior QA Design Engineer; Senior Recruiter; Senior Financial Analyst; Senior Public Relations Manager. **Corporate headquarters location:** This location. **Listed on:** NASDAQ. **Stock exchange symbol:** SEBL. **Annual sales/revenues:** $1.35 billion. **Number of employees worldwide:** 5,000.

SIEMENS
1230 Shorebird Way, Mountain View CA 94309-7393. 650/969-9112. **Toll-free phone:** 800/4AC-USON. **Fax:** 650/943-7006. **Recorded jobline:** 800/3AC-USON. **Contact:** Dean Hammer, Employment Programs Specialist. **World Wide Web address:** http://www.medical.siemens.com. **Description:** A manufacturer, marketer, and service provider of diagnostic medical ultrasound systems and image management products for hospitals, clinics, and private practice physicians throughout the world. Founded in 1979. **NOTE:** Entry-level positions are offered. **Positions advertised include:** Administrative Assistant; Cardiology Sonographer; Marketing Communications Director; Human Resource Partner. **Special programs:** Internships; Summer Jobs. **Corporate headquarters location:** Malvern PA. **Other U.S. locations:** Nationwide. **International locations:** Worldwide. **Listed on:** New York Stock Exchange. **Stock exchange symbol:** SI.

SIEMENS BUSINESS COMMUNICATIONS
4900 Old Ironsides Drive, Santa Clara CA 95054. 408/492-2000. **Contact:** Human Resources. **World Wide Web address:** http://www.icn.siemens.com. **Description:** A leading provider of communications and communications integration technology such as OfficePoint ISDN systems, a high-speed integration product enabling transmission and reception of voice, data, image, and video over a single phone line. **Positions advertised include:** Pre Sales Engineer; Senior Account Manager. **Corporate headquarters location:** Boca Raton FL. **Parent company:** Siemens A.G. (Germany). **Listed on:** New York Stock Exchange. **Stock exchange symbol:** SI.

SIEMENS MEDICAL SOLUTIONS
4040 Nelson Avenue, Concord CA 94520. 925/246-8200. **Contact:** Employment Representative. **World Wide Web address:** http://www.siemensmedical.com. **Description:** Engaged in the design and manufacture of medical linear accelerators for use in radiation therapy. **Positions advertised include:** Director, Strategic Purchasing; Lead Test Engineer; Installation Service Engineer; Executive Assistant; Medical Physicist; Staff Technical Writer. **Corporate headquarters location:** Malvern PA. **Parent company:** Siemens A.G. (Berlin, Germany). **Operations at this facility include:** Administration; Manufacturing; Research and Development; Sales; Service. **Listed on:** New York Stock Exchange. **Stock exchange symbol:** SI.

SIEMENS MEDICAL SOLUTIONS HEALTH SERVICES
3010 Old Ranch Parkway, Suite 450, Seal Beach CA 90740. 562/340-4000. **Contact:** Recruiter. **World Wide Web address:** http://www.siemensmedical.com. **Description:** Siemens Medical Solutions is a leading provider of health care information systems and service solutions to hospitals, multi-entity health care corporations, integrated health networks, physician groups, and other health care providers in North America and Europe. Siemens Medical Solutions also provides a full complement of solutions for the newly emerging community health information networks, which includes payers and employers as well as providers. The company offers a comprehensive line of health care information systems including clinical, financial, administrative, ambulatory, and decision support systems, for both the public and private health care sectors. These systems are offered on computers operating at the customer site, at the Siemens Information Services Center, or as part of a distributed network. The company also provides a portfolio of professional services including systems installation, support, and education. In addition, the company provides specialized consulting services for the design and integration of software and networks, facilities management, information systems planning, and systems-related process reengineering. **NOTE:** Please contact the corporate Human Resources Department for employment information: 601/219-6300. **Corporate headquarters location:** Malvern PA. **Other U.S. locations:** Nationwide. **Operations at this facility include:** This location is a technical support office. **Listed on:** New York Stock Exchange. **Stock exchange symbol:** SI. **Number of employees worldwide:** 31,000.

SIEMENS POWER TRANSMISSION AND DISTRIBUTION
1650 Technology Drive, Suite 2, San Jose CA 95110. 408/467-3000. **Contact:** Human Resources. **World Wide Web address:** http://www.ptd.siemens.com. **Description:** Manufactures supervisory control and energy management equipment for the power and utility industries. **Corporate headquarters location:** Raleigh NC. **Parent company:** Siemens. **Listed on:** New York Stock Exchange. **Stock exchange symbol:** SI.

SIERRA CLUB
85 Second Street, 2nd Floor, San Francisco CA 94105. 415/977-5500. **Recorded jobline:** 415/977-5744. **Contact:** Human Resources Department. **E-mail address:** resumes@sierraclub.org. **World Wide Web address:** http://www.sierraclub.org. **Description:** A national, volunteer-based, nonprofit company chiefly concerned with the maintenance and preservation of national natural resources, wildlife, and wilderness areas. **NOTE:** Please call the jobline for a listing of available positions before sending a resume. **Positions advertised include:** Sr. Member Services Representative; Publicity Manager; Sr. Editor; Associate Editor. **Corporate headquarters location:** This location.

SIERRA COMMUNITY COLLEGE
5000 Rocklin Road, Rocklin CA 95677. 916/624-3333. **Toll-free phone:** 800/242-4004. **Recorded jobline:** 916/781-0424. **Contact:** Peter Kolster, Associate Vice President of Human Resources. **World Wide Web address:** http://www.sierracollege.edu. **Description:** A community college. **Positions advertised include:** Instructor, Various Disciplines. **Operations at this facility include:** Administration; Divisional Headquarters. **Number of employees at this location:** 450.

SIERRA INSURANCE GROUP
5627 Gibraltar Drive, Pleasanton CA 94566-9025. 925/416-8700. **Toll-free phone:** 800/416-8701. **Fax:** 925/416-0771. **Contact:** Human Resources. **E-mail address:** rculhane@sierrahealth.com. **World Wide Web address:** http://www.sierrainsurancegroup.com. **Description:** An insurance company. **Corporate headquarters location:** Las Vegas NV. **Other U.S. locations:** Burbank CA; Englewood CO; Gladstone MO; Reno NV; Dallas TX. **Parent company:** Sierra Insurance Group is a holding company primarily engaged in writing workers' compensation insurance through its wholly-owned subsidiaries. **Listed on:** New York Stock Exchange. **Stock exchange symbol:** SIE.

SIGNATURE FRUIT
2260 Tenaya Drive, Modesto CA 95354. 209/572-5900. **Toll-free phone:** 800/227-6746. **Fax:** 209/572-5982. **Contact:** Human Resources Manager. **World Wide Web address:** http://www.signaturefruit.com. **Description:** Processes and cans fruits and

vegetables. **NOTE:** Send resumes to: Signature Fruit Company, LLC, Attention: Human Resources Manager, P.O. Box 1338, Ceres CA 95307.

SILGAN CONTAINERS CORPORATION
21800 Oxnard Street, Suite 600, Woodland Hills CA 91367. 818/348-3700. **Contact:** Personnel Department. **World Wide Web address:** http://www.silgancontainers.com. **Description:** Manufactures metal food cans, aluminum food containers, and convenience ends for food cans. **Corporate headquarters location:** This location. **Other U.S. locations:** Nationwide. **Parent company:** Silgan Holdings. **Listed on:** NASDAQ. **Stock exchange symbol:** SLGN. **Number of employees nationwide:** 800.

SILGAN CONTAINERS CORPORATION
567 South Riverside Drive, Modesto CA 95354. 209/575-7100. **Contact:** Personnel Department. **World Wide Web address:** http://www.silgancontainers.com. **Description:** Manufactures metal food cans, aluminum food containers, and convenience ends for food cans. **Corporate headquarters location:** Woodland Hills CA. **Other U.S. locations:** Nationwide. **Parent company:** Silgan Holdings. **Listed on:** NASDAQ. **Stock exchange symbol:** SLGN. **Number of employees nationwide:** 800.

SILICON GRAPHICS INC. (SGI)
1500 Crittenden Lane, Mountain View CA 94043. 650/960-1980. **Contact:** Human Resources. **World Wide Web address:** http://www.sgi.com. **Description:** Manufactures a family of workstation and server systems that are used by engineers, scientists, and other creative professionals to develop, analyze, and simulate complex, three-dimensional objects. **Positions advertised include:** Public Relations Director; Internal Audit Director; Administrator. **Corporate headquarters location:** This location. **Listed on:** New York Stock Exchange. **Stock exchange symbol:** SGI. **Number of employees worldwide:** 3,100.

SIMCO ELECTRONICS
1178 Bordeaux Drive, Sunnyvale CA 94089. 408/734-9750. **Contact:** Lisa Clark, Manager of Human Resources. **E-mail address:** resumes@simco.com. **World Wide Web address:** http://www.simco.com. **Description:** Engaged in the calibration and repair of electronic test and measuring equipment; electrical and physical standards; physical, dimensional, mechanical gauges and tools; and the calibration and validation of biomedical process equipment. **Corporate headquarters location:** This location. **Other area locations:** Los Angeles CA; San Diego CA. **Other U.S. locations:** Nationwide. **Listed on:** Privately held. **CEO:** Lee McKenna. **Annual sales/revenues:** $11 - $20 million. **Number of employees at this location:** 70. **Number of employees nationwide:** 300.

SIMMONS COMPANY
20100 South Alameda Street, Compton CA 90220. 310/637-0101. **Fax:** 310/604-2585. **Contact:** Human Resources. **World Wide Web address:** http://www.simmons.com. **Description:** A mattress and box spring manufacturer. Simmons has 15 other plants in the United States. **Positions advertised include:** Account Coordinator. **Special programs:** Internships. **Corporate headquarters location:** Atlanta GA. **Operations at this facility include:** Administration; Divisional Headquarters; Manufacturing; Sales. **Listed on:** Privately held. **Number of employees at this location:** 220.

SIMPLETECH, INC.
3001 Daimler Street, Santa Ana CA 92705. 949/476-1180. **Toll-free phone:** 800/367-7330. **Fax:** 949/476-0852. **Contact:** Human Resources. **E-mail address:** jobs@simpletech.com. **World Wide Web address:** http://www.simpletech.com. **Description:** Designs and manufactures computer memory products, portable storage devices, and PC cards. Founded in 1990. **NOTE:** Second and third shifts are offered. **Positions advertised include:** Product Marketing Manager; Account Representative; Software Engineer; Director, Product Engineering. **Corporate headquarters location:** This location. **International locations:** Canada; Scotland. **Listed on:** NASDAQ. **Stock exchange symbol:** STEC. **Annual sales/revenues:** $211 million. **Number of employees at this location:** 300. **Number of employees nationwide:** 430.

SIMSMETAL AMERICA
699 Seaport Boulevard, Redwood City CA 94063-2712. 650/369-4161. **Contact:** Human Resources. **World Wide Web address:** http://www.sims-group.com. **Description:** A multifaceted company involved in metals recycling and related ventures. **Corporate headquarters location:** Richmond CA. **Parent company:** Simsmetal Limited (Australia).

SIMSMETAL AMERICA
600 South Fourth Street, Richmond CA 94804-3504. 510/412-5300. **Contact:** Human Resources. **World Wide Web address:** http://www.sims-group.com. **Description:** A multifaceted company involved in metals recycling and related ventures. **Corporate headquarters location:** This location. **Parent company:** Simsmetal Limited (Australia).

SIMSMETAL AMERICA
130 North 12th Street, Sacramento CA 95814. 916/444-3380. **Contact:** Human Resources. **World Wide Web address:** http://www.sims-group.com. **Description:** A multifaceted company involved in metals recycling and related ventures. **Corporate headquarters location:** Richmond CA. **Parent company:** Simsmetal Limited (Australia).

SIX FLAGS MAGIC MOUNTAIN
SIX FLAGS HURRICANE HARBOR
P.O. Box 5500, Valencia CA 91355. 661/255-4801. **Physical address:** 26101 Magic Mountain Parkway, Valencia CA 91355. **Recorded jobline:** 661/255-4800. **Contact:** Alex Hottya, Human Resources. **E-mail address:** ahottya@sftp.com. **World Wide Web address:** http://www.sixflags.com. **Description:** An amusement and water theme park. **Other U.S. locations:** Nationwide. **Corporate headquarters location:** New York NY. **Parent company:** Premier Parks (OK) owns and operates 35 theme parks nationwide. **Listed on:** New York Stock Exchange. **Stock exchange symbol:** PKS.

SIZZLER INTERNATIONAL INC.
15301 Ventura Boulevard, Garden Office Building B, Suite 300, Sherman Oaks CA 91403. 818/662-9900. **Contact:** Personnel. **E-mail address:** crogers@wrconcepts.com. **World Wide Web address:** http://www.sizzler.com. **Description:** One of the largest franchises of the KFC Corporation and the majority stockholder for the Sizzler restaurant chain. **NOTE:** Resumes may be sent to the above e-mail address. **Corporate headquarters location:** This location. **Listed on:** New York Stock Exchange. **Stock exchange symbol:** SZ.

SKYEPHARMA INC.
10450 Science Center Drive, San Diego CA 92121. 858/625-2424. **Fax:** 858/678-3999. **Contact:** Human Resources. **E-mail address:** jobs@skyepharma.com. **World Wide Web address:** http://www.skyepharma.com. **Description:** Develops proprietary, injectable material that can encapsulate a wide variety of drugs to provide sustained and controlled delivery. **Positions advertised include:** Process Engineer; Sr. Scientist; Systems Control Engineer. **Corporate headquarters location:** This location. **Parent company:** SkyePharma Plc (London). **Listed on:** NASDAQ. **Stock exchange symbol:** SKYE. **Number of employees at this location:** 60.

SMART & FINAL, INC.
600 Citadel Drive, Commerce CA 90040. 323/869-7500. **Fax:** 323/427-3443. **Contact:** Human Resources Department. **E-mail address:** hr@smartandfinal.com. **World Wide Web address:** http://www.smartandfinal.com. **Description:** One of the largest, nonmember, warehouse, grocery chains in the United States. Smart and Final operates 230 nonmembership stores in six western states and northern Mexico. Founded in 1871. **NOTE:** Mail resumes to: Smart & Final, Inc., Attention: Human Resources, P.O. Box 512377, Los Angeles CA 90051-0377. **Positions advertised include:** Logistics supervisor; Operations Manager; Sr. Payroll Coordinator; Warehouse Supervisor. **Corporate headquarters location:** This location. **Other U.S. locations:** AZ; CA; FL; NV. **International locations:** Mexico. **Listed on:** New York Stock Exchange. **Stock exchange symbol:** SMF. **Annual sales/revenues:** $1.7 billion. **Number of employees at this location:** 600. **Number of employees nationwide:** 5,000.

SMART MODULAR TECHNOLOGIES
4211 Starboard Drive, Fremont CA 94538. 510/623-1231. **Contact:** Human Resources Department. **E-mail address:** careers@smartm.com. **World Wide Web address:** http://www.smartm.com. **Description:** Manufactures and distributes computer components including PC cards and memory modules. **Positions advertised included:** Sr. PCB Designer; SEC Reporting Manager; Inventory Analyst. **Corporate headquarters location:** This location. **Other area locations:** Irvine CA. **Parent company:** Selectron. **Listed on:** New York Stock Exchange. **Stock exchange symbol:** SLR.

SMITHS AEROSPACE
1700 Business Center Drive, Duarte CA 91010. 626/359-9211. **Fax:** 626/357-0069. **Contact:** Human Resources. **World Wide Web address:** http://www.smithsaerospace.com. **Description:** Smith Aerospace is a diversified manufacturing firm that conducts business in four major industrial segments: Aerospace, Metals, Packaged Products, and Aviation. Aerospace consists of hydraulic and pneumatic valves used in military and commercial fixed-wing aircraft and helicopters, tanks, and the national aerospace program. Metals includes the production of flints and various extruded metals. Packaged Products consists principally of packaged fuels and flints. Aviation includes the chartering, servicing, and sales of helicopters and fixed-wing aircraft. **Positions advertised include:** Manufacturing Engineer; Project Engineer. **Corporate headquarters location:** Grand Rapids MI. **Parent company:** Smiths Group plc. (UK). **Operations at this facility include:** This location manufactures propellers and hydraulic engines. **Listed on:** New York Stock Exchange. **Stock exchange symbol:** SMGKE. **Annual sales/revenues:** $4.5 billion. **Number of employees at this location:** 295.

SMITHS AEROSPACE MECHANICAL SYSTEMS
2040 East Dyer Road, Santa Ana CA 92705-5710. 949/250-3123. **Fax:** 949/757-9771. **Contact:** Human Resources. **World Wide Web address:** http://www.smithsaerospace.com. **Description:** Smith Aerospace is a diversified manufacturing firm that conducts business in four major industrial segments: Aerospace, Metals, Packaged Products, and Aviation. **Positions advertised include:** Designer; Cost Accounting Manager; Sr. Production Planner. **Corporate headquarters location:** Grand Rapids MI. **Parent company:** Smiths Group plc. (UK). **Listed on:** New York Stock Exchange. **Stock exchange symbol:** SMGKE.

SMITH MICRO SOFTWARE, INC.
51 Columbia Street, Suite 200, Aliso Viejo CA 92656. 949/362-5800. **Fax:** 949/362-2300. **Contact:** Human Resources. **E-mail address:** jobs@smithmicro.com. **World Wide Web address:** http://www.smithmicro.com. **Description:** A computer consulting firm. **Positions advertised include:** Sales Representative; Customer Support Technician. **Corporate headquarters location:** This location. **Other U.S. locations:** Boulder CO. **Listed on:** NASDAQ. **Stock exchange symbol:** SMSI.

SMITH-EMERY COMPANY
791 East Washington Boulevard, Los Angeles CA 90021. 213/749-3411. **Contact:** Human Resources. **World Wide Webb address:** http://www.smithemery.com. **Description:** A testing and inspection laboratory for concrete, soil, and chemical samples. **Corporate headquarters location:** This location.

SMURFIT-STONE CONTAINER CORPORATION
201 South Hillview Drive, Milpitas CA 95035. 408/946-3600. **Toll-free phone:** 877/772-2999. **Contact:** Human Resources. **World Wide Web address:** http://www.smurfit-stone.com. **Description:** Smurfit-Stone Container Corporation is one of the world's leading paper-based packaging companies. The company's main products include corrugated containers, folding cartons, and multiwall industrial bags. The company is also one of the world's largest collectors and processors of recycled products that are then sold to a worldwide customer base. Smurfit-Stone Container Corporation also operates several paper tube, market pulp, and newsprint production facilities. **Corporate headquarters location:** Chicago IL. **Other area locations:** City of Industry CA; Corona CA; Fresno CA; Fullerton CA; Los Angeles CA; Salinas CA; Santa Fe Springs CA; Burbank CA; Santa Clara CA; Irvine CA; San Jose CA. **Operations advertised include:** This location manufactures corrugated containers. **Listed on:** NASDAQ. **Stock exchange symbol:** SSCC.

SMURFIT-STONE CONTAINER CORPORATION
2600 De La Cruz Boulevard, Santa Clara CA 95050. 408/496-5118. **Contact:** Human Resources. **World Wide Web address:** http://www.smurfit-stone.com. **Description:** Smurfit-Stone Container Corporation is one of the world's leading paper-based packaging companies. The company's main products include corrugated containers, folding cartons, and multiwall industrial bags. The company is also one of the world's largest collectors and processors of recycled products that are then sold to a worldwide customer base. **Corporate headquarters location:** Chicago IL. **Other area locations:** City of Industry CA; Corona CA; Fresno CA; Fullerton CA; Los Angeles CA; Salinas CA; Santa Fe Springs CA; Burbank CA; Milpitas CA; Irvine CA; San Jose CA. **Operations advertised include:** This location is a paper mill. **Listed on:** NASDAQ. **Stock exchange symbol:** SSCC.

SOLECTRON CORPORATION
777 Gibraltar Drive, Milpitas CA 95035. 408/957-8500. **Fax:** 408/957-6056. **Contact:** Human Resources. **World Wide Web address:** http://www.solectron.com. **Description:** Manufactures complex printed circuit boards using surface mount technology and pin-through-hole interconnection technology. The company also provides electronic subsystem testing and assembly services for OEMs in the electronics industry. **Positions advertised include:** Business Development Manager; Senior Accountant; Senior Financial Analyst; Executive Assistant. **Corporate headquarters location:** This location. **Listed on:** New York Stock Exchange. **Stock**

exchange symbol: SLR. **Annual sales/revenues:** $11 billion. **Number of employees worldwide:** 60,000.

SOLEM & ASSOCIATES
550 Kearny Street, Suite 1010, San Francisco CA 94108. 415/788-7788. **Fax:** 415/788-7858. **Contact:** Personnel. **World Wide Web address:** http://www.solem.com. **Description:** A public relations firm that primarily serves the health care, transportation, and government advocacy industries. **Corporate headquarters location:** This location.

SOLID OAK SOFTWARE, INC.
P.O. Box 6826, Santa Barbara CA 93160. 805/967-9853. **Fax:** 805/967-1614. **Contact:** Human Resources. **World Wide Web address:** http://www.solidoak.com. **Description:** Develops access-control software. **Corporate headquarters location:** This location.

SONY PICTURES ENTERTAINMENT
10202 West Washington Boulevard, Suite 3900, Culver City CA 90232-3195. 310/244-4000. **Contact:** Human Resources. **E-mail address:** resumes@spe.sony.com. **World Wide Web address:** http://www.sonypictures.com. **Description:** Sony Pictures is involved in motion pictures, television, theatrical exhibitions, and studio facilities and technology. The motion picture business distributes movies produced by Columbia TriStar Pictures. The television business, which encompasses Columbia TriStar Television, Columbia TriStar Television Distribution, and Columbia TriStar International Television, is involved with numerous cable channels and distributes and syndicates television programs such as *Days of Our Lives.* **NOTE:** Search and apply for positions online. **Positions advertised include:** Financial Analyst; Visual Development Artist; Manager, Business Development; Audio Coordinator; Designer. **Special programs:** Internships. **Corporate headquarters location:** This location. **Parent company:** Sony Corporation of America. **Operations at this facility include:** Administration; Sales. **Listed on:** New York Stock Exchange. **Stock exchange symbol:** SNE.

SOURCECORP
20500 Belshaw Avenue, Carson CA 90746. 310/763-7575. **Fax:** 310/763-7211. **Contact:** Human Resources. **E-mail address:** careers@srcp.com. **World Wide Web address:** http://www.srcp.com. **Description:** Provides full-service records management for businesses through data storage and imaging services. Data is stored on both disk and microfilm. **Corporate headquarters location:** Dallas TX. **Other area locations:** Burbank CA; Corona CA; Oakland CA. **Listed on:** NASDAQ. **Stock exchange symbol:** SRCP.

SOUTHDOWN CALIFORNIA CEMENT.
5050 83rd Street, Sacramento CA 95826-4745. 916/383-0526. **Contact:** Human Resources. **Description:** Engaged in the production, sale, and delivery of ready-mixed concrete and aggregates.

SOUTHERN CALIFORNIA EDISON (SCE)
2244 Walnut Grove Avenue, P.O. Box 999, Rosemead CA 91770. 626/302-1212. **World Wide Web address:** http://www.sce.com. **Description:** One of the nation's largest investor-owned regulated electric utilities, providing power for 800 communities in southern California. **NOTE:** Search and apply for positions online. **Positions advertised include:** Professional Recruiter; Senior Health Physicist; Nuclear Engineer. **Parent company:** Edison International. **Number of employees at this location:** 2,000.

SOUTHERN CALIFORNIA GAS COMPANY
555 West Fifth Street, Los Angeles CA 90013. 213/244-1200. **Contact:** Human Resources. **E-mail address:** jobs@sdge.com. **World Wide Web address:** http://www.socalgas.com. **Description:** Transports and distributes natural gas. **NOTE:** This company does not accept resumes through postal mail. Please be sure to include job code in the subject line of your e-mail. **Positions advertised include:** Forecasting Advisor; Project Specialist; Sr. Engineer. **Corporate headquarters location:** This location. **Parent company:** Sempra Energy is the result of the June 1998 merger between Pacific Enterprises and Enova Corporation. **Number of employees at this location:** 1,000. **Number of employees nationwide:** 8,400.

SPEAR TECHNOLOGIES
436 14th Street, Suite 200, Oakland CA 94612. 510/267-3333. **Fax:** 510/267-3344. **Contact:** Human Resources. **E-mail address:** jobs@speartechnologies.com. **World Wide Web address: http://www.speartechnologies.com. Description:** Develops, markets, and supports a line of maintenance management software for the transportation industry. **Positions advertised include:** Human Resources Manager; Sr. Software Engineer; Sr. Quality Engineer. **Corporate headquarters location:** This location. **Other U.S. locations:** Hartford CT. **International locations:** Netherlands. **Number of employees at this location:** 225.

SPECTRA-MAT, INC.
100 Westgate Drive, Watsonville CA 95076. 831/722-4116. **Fax:** 831/763-3792. **Contact:** Human Resources. **E-mail address:** hr@spectramat.com. **World Wide Web address:** http://www.spectramat.com. **Description:** Manufactures electronic components such as electron emitters. Spectra-Mat also produces materials and parts for use in thermal management and semiconductor equipment. Founded in 1963. **NOTE:** Entry-level positions and second and third shifts are offered. **Positions advertised include:** Customer Relations Representative. **Corporate headquarters location:** This location. **Operations at this facility include:** Administration; Manufacturing; Research and Development; Sales; Service. **Listed on:** Privately held. **President:** Jim Abendschan. **Annual sales/revenues:** $5 - $10 million. **Number of employees at this location:** 60.

SPECTRAL DYNAMICS INC.
1010 Timothy Drive, San Jose CA 95133. 408/918-2500. **Fax:** 408/918-2580. **Contact:** Personnel. **World Wide Web address:** http://www.spectraldynamics.com. **Description:** Specializes in the design and manufacture of computer-controlled test, measurement, and development systems and software for a wide variety of customers in three high-tech markets: electronic equipment manufacturers, mechanical equipment manufacturers, and semiconductor manufacturers. Products are used for design verification testing and process improvement. **Corporate headquarters location:** This location.

SPELLING ENTERTAINMENT INC.
5700 Wilshire Boulevard, Suite 575, Los Angeles CA 90036. 323/965-5700. **Contact:** Human Resources. **Description:** A leading producer and distributor of television, film, and interactive entertainment. The company comprises Spelling Television, which produces made-for-television movies, miniseries, and one-hour series including *Seventh Heaven* and *Sunset Beach*; Big Ticket Television, which produces sitcoms for the broadcast and first-run markets; Spelling Films, which produces and distributes feature films; Worldwide Vision, which syndicates the Spelling Entertainment library of more than 20,000 hours of television programming and thousands of feature films; Republic Entertainment, a distributor of home videos for the rental and sell-through markets; Virgin Interactive Entertainment, a developer and publisher of interactive games; and Hamilton products, a licensing and merchandising company that handles Spelling Properties. **Office hours:** Monday - Friday, 9:00 a.m. - 6:00 p.m. **Corporate headquarters location:** This location. **Parent company:** Viacom, Inc. **Listed on:** New York Stock Exchange. **Stock exchange symbol:** VIA. **Number of employees worldwide:** 1,000.

SPESCOM SOFTWARE
10052 Mesa Ridge Court, San Diego CA 92121. 858/625-3000. **Fax:** 858/625-3010. **Contact:** Human Resources. **E-mail address:** resumes@spescom.com. **World Wide Web address:** http://www.spescomsoftware.com. **Description:** Designs, develops, integrates, and markets electronic document management software for industrial, utility, commercial, and government applications. **Positions advertised include:** Configuration Management Consultant. **Corporate headquarters location:** This location. **International locations:** England. **Parent company:** Spescom Limited (South Africa). **Number of employees at this location:** 85.

THE SPORTS CLUB COMPANY
1835 Sepulveda Boulevard, Los Angeles CA 90025. 310/479-5200. **Fax:** 310/445-9819. **Recorded jobline:** 310/477-6824. **Contact:** Human Resources. **E-mail address:** hr@thesportsclub.com. **World Wide Web address:** http://www.thesportsclubla.com. **Description:** Owns and operates several health clubs throughout California under the names Sports Club and Spectrum Club. **Corporate headquarters location:** This location. **Listed on:** American Stock Exchange. **Stock exchange symbol:** SCY.

SPRAY, GOULD & BOWERS
15139 Woodlawn Avenue, Tustin CA 92780. 714/258-1550. **Fax:** 714/258-1555. **Contact:** Director of Finance and Administration. **E-mail address:** info@sgblaw.com. **World Wide Web address:** http://www.sgblaw.com. **Description:** A law firm specializing in insurance, defense, and entertainment law. **Office hours:** Monday - Friday, 8:30 a.m. - 5:00 p.m. **Corporate headquarters location:** This location. **Operations at this facility include:** Administration; Divisional Headquarters. **Listed on:** Privately held. **Number of employees at this location:** 75. **Number of employees nationwide:** 105.

SQUARE D COMPANY
21680 Gateway Center Drive, Suite 300, Diamond Bar CA 91765-2435. 909/612-5400. **Contact:** Human Resources. **E-mail address:** uwb@schneiderelectricjobs.com. **World Wide Web address:** http://www.squared.com. **Description:** A manufacturer of electrical distribution products for the construction industry. Products are used in commercial and residential construction, industrial facilities, and machinery and original equipment manufacturers' products. Residential building products feature circuit breakers with an exclusive quick-open mechanism that isolates potential dangers quickly; and a complete home wiring system connecting multiple telephone lines, audio signals, and VCR, cable, or closed circuit television. In office developments, hotels and restaurants, retail shops, and other businesses, Square D provides products ranging from parking lot gate controls and uninterrupted power systems for personal computers to space-saving remote-controlled lighting and custom circuit breaker panel boards. Square D also equips public buildings such as schools, stadiums, museums, hospitals, prisons, military bases, and wastewater treatment plants with electrical distribution systems. **NOTE:** For Human Resources Information call: 800/993-7638. **Corporate headquarters location:** Palatine IL. **Parent company:** Schneider Electric. **Operations at this facility include:** Regional Headquarters; Sales. **Listed on:** Privately held.

STAAR SURGICAL COMPANY
1911 Walker Avenue, Monrovia CA 91016. 626/303-7902. **Fax:** 626/358-9470. **Contact:** Human Resources. **E-mail address:** receptionist@staar.com. **World Wide Web address:** http://www.staar.com. **Description:** Develops, manufactures, and markets ophthalmic medical devices. The company's main product is a foldable lens used in the treatment of cataracts. Founded in 1982. **Corporate headquarters location:** This location. **Listed on:** NASDAQ. **Stock exchange symbol:** STAA.

STANDARD PACIFIC HOMES
15326 Alton Parkway, Irvine CA 92618. 949/789-1600. **Contact:** Human Resources Department. **E-mail address:** careers@stanpac.com. **World Wide Web address:** http://www.standardpacifichomes.com. **Description:** Designs, builds, and sells houses for residential use. **Positions advertised include:** Assistant Construction Manager. **Corporate headquarters location:** This location. **Listed on:** New York Stock Exchange. **Stock exchange symbol:** SPF. **Annual sales/revenues:** More than $100 million.

STANFORD UNIVERSITY
300 Pasteor Drive, Stanford CA 94305. 650/723-1888. **Contact:** Human Resources. **E-mail address:** empwebsite@lists.stanford.edu. **World Wide Web address:** http://www.stanford.edu. **Description:** A private university offering undergraduate programs through its schools of Humanities and Sciences, Engineering, and Earth Sciences. Stanford University also offers graduate programs through its professional schools of Law, Medicine, Business, and Education. Founded in 1885. **Positions advertised include:** Benefits Associate; Administrative Associate; Life Science Research Assistant; Development Associate.

STATE COMPENSATION INSURANCE FUND
1275 Market Street, 9th Floor, San Francisco CA 94103. 415/565-1234. **Contact:** Ms. Terese Carter, Human Resources. **World Wide Web address:** http://www.scif.com. **Description:** One of California's largest writers of workers' compensation insurance through more than 20 district offices. **NOTE:** Do not submit applications via e-mail. Mail applications to: State Compensation Insurance Fund, Attention: Human Resources, P.O. Box 420807, San Francisco CA 94142-0807. **Corporate headquarters location:** This location.

STERLING COMMUNICATIONS, INC.
750 University Avenue, Suite 250, Los Gatos CA 95032. 408/395-5500. **Fax:** 408/395-5533. **Contact:** Tiffany Bryant, Human Resources. **E-mail address:** tbryant@sterlingpr.com. **World Wide Web address:** http://www.sterlingpr.com. **Description:** A public relations firm that provides services to technology-based companies. **Positions advertised include:** Account Associate; Account Executive. **Corporate headquarters location:** This location.

STRADLING, YOCCA, CARLSON & RAUTH
660 Newport Center Drive, Suite 1600, Newport Beach CA 92660. 949/725-4000. **Fax:** 949/725-4100. **Contact:** Human Resources. **E-mail address:** recruiting@sycr.com. **World Wide Web address:** http://www.sycr.com. **Description:** A law firm specializing in corporate, business, estate planning, and labor law. **Corporate headquarters location:** This location.

STRATEX NETWORKS
170 Rose Orchard Way, San Jose CA 95134. 408/943-0777. **Fax:** 408/944-1701. **Contact:** Human Resources. **E-mail address:** careers@stratexnet.com. **World Wide Web address:** http://www.stratexnet.com. **Description:** Designs, manufactures, and markets wireless products for communications networks. **Positions advertised include:** Test Engineer; Manufacturing Process Engineer; SOX Compliance Analyst. **Corporate headquarters location:** This location. **International locations:** Asia; Europe; Latin America; Singapore; United Kingdom; New Zealand. **Listed on:** NASDAQ. **Stock exchange symbol:** STXN.

STRUCTURAL COMPOSITES INDUSTRIES
325 Enterprise Place, Pomona CA 91768. 909/594-7777. **Contact:** Human Resources. **E-mail address:** sci-hr@harsco.com. **World Wide Web address:** http://www.scicomposites.com. **Description:** Specializes in OSHA-approved powered-air and supplied-air systems and self-contained breathing apparatus (SCBA). Products include gas mask filters, industrial air and respiratory protection filters, Airstream helmets, the Powerflow full-facepiece respirator with a motor and filter, and the Delta line of disposable particulate respirators. The company also produces fully overwrapped composite pressure vessels used in firefighting. **Positions advertised include:** Accounting Director; Design Engineer. **Corporate headquarters location:** This location. **Parent company:** Harsco Corporation Gas and Fluid Control Group.

SUMMA INDUSTRIES
21250 Hawthorne Boulevard, Suite 500, Torrance CA 90503. 310/792-7024. **Contact:** Miriam Rivera, Human Resources. **E-mail address:** hr@summaindustries.com. **World Wide Web address:** http://www.summaindustries.com. **Description:** Manufactures plastic components for a variety of commercial and industrial markets. Products include optical components, conveyor belts, fittings, valves, coil forms, and tubing. **NOTE:** Resumes may be submitted via e-mail, mail, or fax. Mail resumes to: 3350 Shelby Street, Suite 200, Ontario CA 91764. Fax: 801/749-6952. **Corporate headquarters location:** This location. **Other U.S. locations:** FL; IL; MI; MS; OK; TN. **Listed on:** NASDAQ. **Stock exchange symbol:** SUMX. **Annual sales/revenues:** More than $100 million.

SUN MICROSYSTEMS, INC.
952Towne Centre Drive, San Diego CA 92121. 858/625-0500. **Fax:** 858/625-0691. **Contact:** Human Resources Department. **E-mail address:** resumes@sun.com. **World Wide Web address:** http://www.sun.com. **Description:** Produces high-performance computer systems, workstations, servers, CPUs, peripherals, and operating system software. The company developed its own microprocessor called SPARC. Most products are sold to engineering, scientific, technical,. and commercial markets worldwide. **NOTE:** Online applications preferred. **Positions advertised include:** Sr. Staff Engineer; Product Manager; Software Engineerin Manager; Engagement Manager. **Corporate headquarters location:** Santa Clara CA. **Subsidiaries include:** Forte Software Inc. manufactures enterprise application integration software. **Operations at this facility include:** This location is a design center. **Listed on:** NASDAQ. **Stock exchange symbol:** SUNW.

SUN MICROSYSTEMS, INC.
4150 Network Circle, UMIL 15-106, Santa Clara CA 95054. 650/960-1300. **Toll-free phone:** 800/555-9786. **Contact:** Human Resources. **World Wide Web address:** http://www.sun.com. **Description:** Produces high-performance computer systems, workstations, servers, CPUs, peripherals, and operating systems software. Products are sold to engineering, scientific, technical, and commercial markets worldwide. **NOTE:** Search and apply for positions online. **Corporate headquarters location:** This location. **Subsidiaries include:** Forte Software Inc. manufactures enterprise application integration software. **Listed on:** NASDAQ. **Stock exchange symbol:** SUNW. **Number of employees nationwide:** 26,300.

SUN SEEDS
P.O. Box 2078, Morgan Hill CA 95038-2078. 408/776-1111. **Physical address:** 18640 Sutter Boulevard, Morgan Hill CA 95037-2825. **Contact:** Human Resources Department. **E-mail address:** resumes@sunseeds.com. **World Wide Web address:** http://www.sunseeds.com. **Description:** A producer of seeds and related products for the agricultural industry. **Corporate headquarters location:** Parma ID. **Number of employees at this location:** 125.

SUN-MAID GROWERS OF CALIFORNIA
13525 South Bethel Avenue, Kingsburg CA 93631. 559/896-8000. **Contact:** Human Resources. **World Wide Web address:** http://www.sunmaid.com. **Description:** Produces and packages nationally distributed food products such as walnuts, prunes, dried fruit, and other fruit and nut products. **Corporate headquarters location:** This location. **Other area locations:** Pleasanton CA.

SUNAMERICA INC.
One SunAmerica Center, Los Angeles CA 90067-6022. 310/772-6000. **Contact:** Human Resources. **World Wide Web address:** http://www.sunamerica.com. **Description:** SunAmerica Inc. is a large financial services company specializing in long-term, tax-deferred, investment-oriented savings products. **NOTE:** Search and apply for positions online. **Corporate headquarters location:** This location. **Operations at this facility include:** Administration; Divisional Headquarters; Service. **Number of employees at this location:** 450. **Number of employees nationwide:** 1,000.

SUNGARD FINANCIAL SYSTEMS INC.
23975 Park Sorrento, Suite 400, Calabasas CA 91302. 818/223-2200. **Fax:** 818/223-2201. **Contact:** Human Resources. **E-mail address:** jobs@sungard.com. **World Wide Web address:** http://www.sungard.com. **Description:** Develops and sells investment portfolio software for financial institutions. **Corporate headquarters location:** Wayne PA. **Parent company:** SunGard Data Systems provides specialized computer services, mainly proprietary investment support systems for the financial services industry and disaster recovery services. The company's disaster recovery services include alternate-site backup, testing, and recovery services for IBM, DEC, Prime, Stratus, Tandem, and Unisys computer installations. The company's computer service unit provides remote-access IBM computer processing, direct marketing, and automated mailing services. **Listed on:** New York Stock Exchange. **Stock exchange symbol:** SDS.

SUNKIST GROWERS, INC.
P.O. Box 7888, Van Nuys CA 91409-7888. 818/986-4800. **Physical address:** 14130 Riverside Drive, Sherman Oaks CA 91423. **Fax:** 818/379-7405. **Contact:** John McGovern, Director of Human Resources. **World Wide Web address:** http://www.sunkist.com. **Description:** A citrus growing and processing cooperative, with additional operations in confections and soft drinks. **Corporate headquarters location:** This location. **Other area locations:** Los Angeles CA. **International locations:** Ontario, Canada. **Subsidiaries include:** Fruit Growers Supply Company (also at this location).

SUNRISE MEDICAL MOBILITY PRODUCTS
2842 Business Park Avenue, Fresno CA 93727. 559/292-2171. **Fax:** 559/294-2341. **Contact:** Human Resources Manager. **E-mail address:** resumes@sunmed.com. **World Wide Web address:** http://www.sunrisemedical.com. **Description:** Manufactures and markets assistive technology, patient care products, and rehabilitation products for people with disabilities as well as for use in home-care, hospitals, and nursing homes. **Positions advertised include:** Project Manager. **Corporate headquarters location:** Longmont CO. **Other area locations:** Carlsbad CA.

SUNRISE TELECOM
302 Enzo Drive, San Jose CA 95138. 408/363-8000. **Fax:** 408/363-8313. **Contact:** Human Resources. **World Wide Web address:** http://www.sunrisetelecom.com. **Description:** Manufacturer of telecommunication equipment used for fiber optics, cable, and Internet products and services. **NOTE:** See website for job listings. To apply, mail or fax resumes. Entry-level positions offered. **NOTE:** Search and apply for positions online. **Positions advertised include:** Purchasing Agent; Manufacturing Test Engineer; IP Hardware Engineer; Windows Application Software Engineer; Regional Sales Manager; National Sales/Marketing Engineer; Product Manager. **Corporate headquarters location:** This location. **Other U.S. locations:** GA. **International locations:** Canada; Italy; China; Germany, Japan. **Listed on:** NASDAQ. **Stock exchange symbol:** SRTI.

SUPERCONDUCTOR TECHNOLGIES INC. (STI)
460 Ward Drive, Santa Barbara CA 93111. 805/690-4500. **Fax:** 805/967-0342. **Contact:** Human Resources. **E-mail address:** jobs@suptech.com. **World Wide Web address:** http://www.suptech.com. **Description:** Develops, manufactures and markets high-performance wireless infrastructure products to commercial service providers, systems integrators, original equipment manufacturers, and government entities. **Positions advertised include:** Systems Electronics Engineer; Fab Process Engineer; Manufacturing Test Engineer. **Corporate headquarters location:** This location.

SUPERIOR INDUSTRIES INTERNATIONAL
7800 Woodley Avenue, Van Nuys CA 91406. 818/781-4973. **Fax:** 818/902-2531. **Contact:** Griselda Padilla, Human Resources. **E-mail address:** gpadilla@supind.com. **World Wide Web address:** http://www.supind.com. **Description:** Produces cast aluminum road wheels for original equipment manufacturers and a variety of automotive aftermarket products. **NOTE:** Entry-level positions are offered. To contact Griselda Padilla directly call: 818/902-2530. **Positions advertised include:** C.M.M. Programmer; Help Desk Coordinator; Maintenance Mechanic; Senior Internal Auditor; Database Administrator. **Corporate headquarters location:** This location. **Other U.S. locations:** AR; KS; TN. **International locations:** Mexico; Europe. **Operations at this facility include:** Administration; Manufacturing. **Annual sales/revenues:** $840 million. **Number of employees at this location:** 900. **Number of employees worldwide:** 6,600.

SUPERTEX INC.
1235 Bordeaux Drive, Sunnyvale CA 94089. 408/222-8888. **Fax:** 408/422-4805. **Contact:** Human Resources Department. **E-mail address:** jobopps@supertex.com. **World Wide Web address:** http://www.supertex.com. **Description:** Produces integrated silicon circuits and other microelectronic products for computer and electronics original equipment manufacturers. **Positions advertised include:** Payroll Accountant; Staff Applications Engineer; Sr. IC Design Engineer; Marcom Manager; Technical Marketing Manager. **Corporate headquarters location:** This location. **Operations at this facility include:** Administration; Manufacturing; Research and Development; Sales; Service. **Listed on:** NASDAQ. **Stock exchange symbol:** SUPX.

SUTTER ROSEVILLE MEDICAL CENTER
One Medical Plaza, Roseville CA 95661-3037. 916/781-1000. **Fax:** 916/781-1605. **Contact:** Human Resources. **E-mail address:** employment@sutterhealth.org. **World Wide Web address:** http://www.sutterhealth.org. **Description:** A 205-bed, acute care hospital that serves the health care needs of the Roseville community and its outlying areas. **NOTE:** Search and apply for positions online. **Positions advertised include:** Registered Nurse; Radiological Technologist; Pharmacist. **Corporate headquarters location:** Sacramento CA. **Other U.S. locations:** Honolulu HI. **Operations at this facility include:** Health Care; Service. **Number of employees at this location:** 1,250.

SUTTON PLACE HOTEL
4500 MacArthur Boulevard, Newport Beach CA 92660. 949/476-2001. **Contact:** Human Resources. **World Wide Web address:** http://www.suttonplace.com. **Description:** A 435-room hotel, also offering conference facilities.

SWINERTON INCORPORATED
260 Townsend Street, San Francisco CA 94107. 415/421-2980. **Fax:** 415/984-1306. **Contact:** Marina Aviles, Director of Employment and Staffing. **World Wide Web address:** http://www.swinerton.com. **Description:** A general contracting firm that specializes in consulting, value management, and conceptual design. The company's expertise lies with the assisted living, healthcare, public facilities, renovation and restoration, tenant improvement, and transportation markets. **Positions advertised include:** Contracts Manager; Building Manager; Project Assistant; Project Engineer; Project Manager. **Special programs:** Internships. **Corporate headquarters location:** This location. **Other area locations:** Los Angeles CA. **Other U.S. locations:** Tucson AZ; Denver CO; Portland OR. **Operations at this facility include:** Administration. **Listed on:** Privately held. **Number of employees at this location:** 100. **Number of employees nationwide:** 500.

SYAR INDUSTRIES INC.
2301 Napa Vallejo Highway, Napa CA 94558. 707/252-8711. **Fax:** 707/254-3007. **Contact:** Human Resources. **Description:** Produces high-quality rock products and asphaltic paving materials. Founded in 1938. **NOTE:** Entry-level positions and second and third shifts are offered. **Special programs:** Summer Jobs. **Corporate headquarters location:** This location. **Listed on:** Privately held. **Number of employees at this location:** 50. **Number of employees nationwide:** 375.

SYBASE, INC.
One Sybase Drive, Dublin CA 94568. 925/236-5000. **Contact:** Human Resources. **World Wide Web address:** http://www.sybase.com. **Description:** Develops, markets, and supports a full line of relational database management software products and services for integrated, enterprisewide information management systems. **NOTE:** Search and apply for positions online. **Positions advertised include:** Finance Director; Sr. Product Support Analyst; Sr. PR Specialist; Sr. Software Engineer; Sr. Project and Planning Manager. **Corporate headquarters location:** This location. **Listed on:** New York Stock Exchange. **Stock exchange symbol:** SY. **Number of employees worldwide:** 4,000.

SYBRA INC.
9255 Town Center Drive, Suite 600, San Diego CA 92121. 858/587-8534. **Contact:** Human Resources. **World Wide Web address:** http://www.sybra.com. **Description:**

Operates numerous locations of the restaurant chain Arby's. **Corporate headquarters location:** This location.

SYMANTEC CORPORATION
20330 Stevens Creek Boulevard, Cupertino CA 95014. 408/517-8000. **Contact:** Human Resources Staffing. **E-mail address:** jobs@symantec.com. **World Wide Web address:** http://www.symantec.com. **Description:** Symantec Corporation is a global organization that develops, manufactures, and markets software products for individuals and businesses. The company is a vendor of utility software for stand-alone and networked personal computers. In addition, the company offers a wide range of project management products, productivity applications, and development languages and tools. The company is organized into several product groups that are devoted to product marketing, engineering, technical support, quality assurance, and documentation. Founded in 1982. **Positions advertised include:** Senior Senior Accountant; Senior Administrative Specialist; Accounting Manager. **Special programs:** Internships. **Corporate headquarters location:** This location. **Operations at this facility include:** This location houses finance, sales, and marketing operations. **Listed on:** NASDAQ. **Stock exchange symbol:** SYMC. **Number of employees nationwide:** 1,200.

SYMBOL TECHNOLOGIES, INC.
6480 Via Del Oro, San Jose CA 95119. 408/528-2700. **Fax:** 408/528-2780. **Contact:** Professional Staffing. **E-mail address:** jobopps@symbol.com. **World Wide Web address:** http://www.symbol.com. **Description:** Designs, manufactures, and sells various lines of portable and nonportable computers and systems for business information and bill collection applications. Clients include retail food stores, drug stores, and hardware stores. **NOTE:** Resumes should be sent to Human Resources Department, Symbol Technologies, Inc., One Symbol Plaza, Holtsville NY 11742-1300. **Positions advertised include:** Business Development Services Specialist; Network Product Development Engineer; Mobile Solutions Software Architect; Software Development Manager. **Corporate headquarters location:** Holtsville NY. **Operations at this facility include:** Education; Repairs; Sales; Systems/Software Services. **Listed on:** New York Stock Exchange. **Stock exchange symbol:** SBL.

SYMMETRICOM
2300 Orchard Parkway, San Jose CA 95131. 408/433-0910. **Fax:** 408/428-7999. **Contact:** Staffing. **E-mail address:** jobs@symmetricom.com. **World Wide Web address:** http://www.symmetricom.com. **Description:** Designs, develops, manufactures, and markets precision frequency and timing instrumentation products. Datum's principal products are cesium and quartz crystal frequency standards that produce or stabilize frequencies. Datum's timing instrumentation products use a stable frequency standard to generate, encode, translate, and distribute precise time information. These products are used in a broad range of applications including accurate synchronization of telecommunications networks, synchronization of computers in local area networks, generation of precise time information, and control of global navigation satellite systems. **NOTE:** Search and apply for positions online. **Positions advertised include:** Business Systems Analyst; Human Resources Analyst; Financial Analyst; Accountant; Software Engineer. **Corporate headquarters location:** This location. **Other area locations:** Santa Rosa CA. **Other U.S. locations:** Beverly MA; Austin TX. **International locations:** China; Germany; United Kingdom. **Listed on:** NASDAQ. **Stock exchange symbol:** SYMM.

SYNBIOTICS CORPORATION
11011 Via Frontera, San Diego CA 92127. 858/451-3771. **Contact:** Human Resources. **World Wide Web address:** http://www.synbiotics.com. **Description:** Develops, manufactures, and markets products and services to veterinary specialty markets. Synbiotics provides canine reproduction products and services to purebred dog breeders and their veterinarians. In addition, the company markets a line of life-stage nutritional supplements; and PennHip, a new method for the early diagnosis and evaluation of canine hip dysplasia. **Corporate headquarters location:** This location.

SYNOPSYS INC.
700 East Middlefield Road, Mountain View CA 94043. 650/584-5000. **Toll-free phone:** 800/541-7737. **Contact:** Human Resources Department. **E-mail address:** employment@synopsys.com. **World Wide Web address:** http://www.synopsys.com. **Description:** Develops, markets, and supports high-level design automation software for designers of integrated circuits and electronic systems. **NOTE:** Search and apply for positions online. **Positions advertised include:** Compliance Analyst; Senior Applications Consultant; Corporate Applications Engineer; Financial Analyst; Marketing Director; Public Relations Specialist; Software Engineer; R&D Engineer. **Corporate headquarters location:** This location. **Listed on:** NASDAQ. **Stock exchange symbol:** SNPS. **Number of employees at this location:** 415. **Number of employees worldwide:** 4,000.

SYPRIS DATA SYSTEMS
160 East Via Verde, San Dimas CA 91773-5120. 909/962-9400. **Fax:** 909/962-9401. **Contact:** Personnel. **E-mail address:** hr@syprisdatasystems.com. **World Wide Web address:** http://www.syprisdatasystems.com. **Description:** Manufacturers of analog and digital tape recorders. **Corporate headquarters location:** This location. **Parent company:** Sypris Solutions, Inc. (Louisville KY). **Listed on:** NASDAQ. **Stock exchange symbol:** SYPR.

SYSCO FOOD SERVICE OF LOS ANGELES, INC.
20701 East Currier Road, Walnut CA 91789. 909/595-9595. **Fax:** 909/598-3115. **Contact:** Human Resources. **E-mail address:** barton.roxxanne.r045@sysco.com. **World Wide Web address:** http://www.syscola.com. **Description:** Markets and distributes a broad line of food products, beverages, and related supplies to restaurants, fast-food operations, schools, and hospitals. **Positions advertised include:** Commissioned Sales Representative. **Corporate headquarters location:** Houston TX. **Listed on:** New York Stock Exchange. **Stock exchange symbol:** SYY.

SYSCO FOOD SERVICES OF SAN FRANCISCO, INC.
5900 Stewart Avenue, Fremont CA 94538. 510/226-3000. **Fax:** 510/226-3395. **Contact:** Human Resources. **World Wide Web address:** http://www.syscosf.com. **Description:** Distributes a wide variety of food and grocery products to businesses, hospitals, and school districts. **NOTE:** Candidates must submit application available online. **Positions advertised include:** Accounting Associate; Marketing Associate. **Corporate headquarters location:** Houston TX. **Listed on:** New York Stock Exchange. **Stock exchange symbol:** SYY. **Number of employees at this location:** 1,100.

TBWA/CHIAT/DAY
55 Union Street, San Francisco CA 94111. 415/315-4100. **Recorded jobline:** 310/305-5385. **Contact:** Human Resources. **E-mail address:** hr-sf@tbwachiat.com. **World Wide Web address:** http://www.tbwachiat.com. **Description:** An advertising agency. **NOTE:** Resumes may be submitted via e-mail or regular mail. Mail resumes to: 5353 Grosvenor Boulevard, Los Angeles CA 90066-6913; hr-sf@tbwachiat.com. **Special programs:** Internships. **Corporate headquarters location:** Los Angeles. **Other U.S. locations:** New York NY. **International locations:** Toronto Canada.

TCI (TECHNOLOGY FOR COMMUNICATIONS INTERNATIONAL)
47300 Kato Road, Fremont CA 94538. 510/687-6100. **Fax:** 510/687-6101. **Contact:** Cheryl Glass, Human Resources. **World Wide Web address:** http://www.tcibr.com. **Description:** Manufactures television and broadcasting equipment and provides services such as DTV, radio broadcasting, communications management, and communications intelligence collection. **Positions advertised include:** Software Engineer. **Corporate headquarters location:** This location. **Parent company:** Dialectric Communications. **Operations at this facility include:** Manufacturing. **Listed on:** New York Stock Exchange. **Stock exchange symbol:** SPW. **Number of employees at this location:** 160. **Number of employees nationwide:** 3,100.

TDK ELECTRONICS CORPORATION
3190 East Miraloma Avenue, Anaheim CA 92806. 714/238-7900. **Contact:** Human Resources. **World Wide Web address:** http://www.tdk.com. **Description:** A manufacturer of audiocassettes and micro floppy disks. **Positions advertised include:** Warehouse Supervisor. **Corporate headquarters location:** Garden City NY. **Other U.S. locations:** Nationwide. **Operations at this facility include:** Administration; Manufacturing. **Listed on:** New York Stock Exchange. **Stock exchange symbol:** TDK. **Number of employees at this location:** 600.

THQ INC.
27001 Agoura Road, Suite 325, Calabasas Hills CA 91301. 818/871-5000. **Contact:** Human Resources. **E-mail address:** resume@thq.com. **World Wide Web address:** http://www.thq.com. **Description:** Develops, publishes, markets, and distributes video games for platforms that include the PlayStation, Nintendo 64, Game Boy, and PCs. **Positions advertised include:** Financial Analyst; Business Analyst; Product Marketing Manager; Creative Manager; Brand Manager; Production Artist; Game Designer; Quality Assurance Tester. **Corporate headquarters location:** This location. **Listed on:** NASDAQ. **Stock exchange symbol:** THQI. **Annual sales/revenues:** More than $640 million.

TMP WORLDWIDE
799 Market Street, 8th Floor, San Francisco CA 94103. 415/820-7800. **Fax:** 415/820-0540. **Contact:** Human Resources. **World Wide Web address:** http://www.monsterworldwide.com. **Description:** A B-to-B advertising agency in the recruitment and yellow pages advertising business. **NOTE:** Apply online. **Positions advertised include:** Online Marketing Manager; Associate Creative Director; Producer; Company Public Speaker; Marketing Coordinator. **Corporate headquarters location:** New York NY. **Other area locations:** Glendale CA; Laguna Hills CA; San Diego CA. **Other U.S. locations:** Boston MA; Atlanta GA; Chicago IL. **Parent company:** Monster Worldwide Inc. **Listed on:** NASDAQ. **Stock exchange symbol:** MNST.

TW METALS
2211 Tubeway Avenue, Los Angeles CA 90040. 323/728-9101. **Fax:** 323/728-5310. **Contact:** Sharon Gonzalez, Personnel Director. **World Wide Web address:** http://www.twmetals.com. **Description:** Stores and distributes steel and nickel alloy products. Provides a wide range of products to the aerospace, automotive, chemical processing, utilities, and machine industries. **Corporate headquarters location:** Exton PA.

TXI RIVERSIDE CEMENT COMPANY
19409 national Trails Highway, P.O. Box 158, Oro Grande CA 92368. 760/245-5321. **Contact:** Human Resources. **World Wide Web address:** http://www.txi.com/cement. **Description:** Manufactures cement. **Corporate headquarters location:** This location. **Listed on:** New York Stock Exchange. **Stock exchange symbol:** TXI.

TAB PRODUCTS COMPANY
12501 East Imperial Highway, Suite 120, Norwalk CA 90650. 562/868-1585. **Fax:** 562/868-1575. **Contact:** Human Resources. **E-mail address:** staffing@tab.com. **World Wide Web address:** http://www.tab.com. **Description:** A document management company specializing in managing paper-based through electronic documents. Products and services include lateral color-coding filing supplies, storage and mobile systems, document management software, imaging services, and professional services. **Corporate headquarters location:** Mayville WI. **Other U.S. locations:** Nationwide. **Listed on:** Privately held. **Number of employees worldwide:** 550.

TAITRON COMPONENTS INCORPORATED
28040 West Harrison Parkway, Valencia CA 91355. 661/257-6060. **Fax:** 661/294-1108. **Contact:** Human Resources. **E-mail address:** hr@taitron.net. **World Wide Web address:** http://www.taitroncomponents.com. **Description:** Distributes electronic components including discretes, optos, and passives. **Positions advertised include:** Marketing Analyst; Marketing Director. **Corporate headquarters location:** This location. **International locations:** Brazil; Mexico; Taiwan. **Listed on:** NASDAQ. **Stock exchange symbol:** TAIT.

TALBERT MEDICAL GROUP
9930 Talbert Avenue, Fountain Valley CA 92708. 714/964-6229. **Fax:** 714/436-4883. **Contact:** Human Resources. **E-mail address:** careers@talbertmedical.com. **World Wide Web address:** http://www.talbertmedical.com. **Description:** An HMO that offers a full range of health care products and services to over 900,000 people in California, Nevada, Utah, Arizona, Colorado, New Mexico, and Guam. Services include third-party administrative plans, and indemnity medical, group life, and workers' compensation insurance. **NOTE:** To contact Human Resources directly call: 714/436-4787. **Positions advertised include:** Medical Assistant; Registered Nurse Team Leader; Physician; Radiology Technician. **Corporate headquarters location:** This location. **Other area locations:** Anaheim CA; Compton CA; Downey CA; Huntington Beach CA; Long Beach CA; Santa Ana CA; Tustin CA.

TANABE RESEARCH LABORATORIES USA, INC.
4540 Towne Center Court, San Diego CA 92121. 858/622-7000. **Fax:** 858/558-0650. **Contact:** Human Resources. **E-mail address:** jobs@trlusa.com. **World Wide Web address:** http://www.trlusa.com. **Description:** Researches allergies, rheumatism, asthma, and arthritis. **Corporate headquarters location:** Osaka, Japan. **Parent company:** Tanabe Seiyaku Corporation, Ltd.

TECHNICOLOR, INC.
4050 Lankershim Boulevard, North Hollywood CA 91608. 818/769-8500. **Contact:** Human Resources. **E-mail address:** hrjobs@technicolor.com. **World Wide Web address:** http://www.technicolor.com. **Description:** Engaged in film processing services for the movie industry. **Corporate headquarters location:** Camarillo CA. **Other area locations:** Burbank CA; Glendale CA; Ontario CA.

TELASIC COMMUNICATIONS
1940 East Mariposa Avenue, Suite 100, El Segundo CA 90245. 310/955-3700. **Contact:** Human Resources. **E-mail address:** jobs@telasic.com. **World Wide Web address:** http://www.telasic.com. **Description:** TelASIC Communications develops high performance RF and analog mixed signal solutions for advanced wireless applications. In addition to offering commercially-available integrated circuits and supporting leading edge defense programs, TelASIC offers a complete range of digital, analog, and mixed signal design services. **Positions advertised include:** RF Design Engineer; Digital Design Engineer; Sr. Test Engineer; Sr. Product Engineer; Product Marketing Engineer.

TELE ATLAS NORTH AMERICA
1605 Adams Drive, Menlo Park CA 94025. 650/328-3825. **Contact:** Human Resources. **E-mail address:** jobs@teleatlas.com. **World Wide Web address:** http://www.na.teleatlas.com. **Description:** Develops digital mapping software for the automotive and transportation industries. **Positions advertised include:** Sr. Software Engineer. **Corporate headquarters location:** Lebanon NH.

TELEDYNE ELECTRONIC TECHNOLOGIES
1274 Terra Bella Avenue, Mountain View CA 94043. 650/691-9800. **Fax:** 650/967-4353. **Contact:** Human Resources. **World Wide Web address:** http://www.tet.com. **Description:** Engaged in the design and manufacture of passive and active devices, power supplies, and scientific instruments. Products include MMIC devices; amplifiers; integrated subsystems; voltage-controlled oscillators; microwave switches, filters, and ferrite devices; and mass spectrometry scientific instruments. **Positions advertised include:** Electrical Engineer; Sr. Design Engineer; Assembler; Manufacturing Manager; RF Technician. **Special programs:** Internships. **Corporate headquarters location:** Los Angeles CA. **Other area locations:** Statewide. **Parent company:** Teledyne Technologies. **Listed on:** New York Stock Exchange. **Stock exchange symbol:** TDY. **Number of employees at this location:** 250. **Number of employees nationwide:** 5,800.

TELEDYNE TECHNOLOGIES INC.
12333 West Olympic Boulevard, Los Angeles CA 90064. 310/893-1600. **Contact:** Human Resources Department. **World Wide Web address:** http://www.teledyne.com. **Description:** Manufactures avionics systems, broadband communications subsystems, and engines for the aerospace, defense, and manufacturing industries. The company also provides engineering and information technology services to corporate and government clients. **Positions advertised include:** Applications Engineer; Avionics Systems Engineer; Manufacturing Engineer; Software Quality Engineer. **Corporate headquarters location:** This location. **Listed on:** New York Stock Exchange. **Stock exchange symbol:** TDY.

TENDER LOVING CARE/STAFF BUILDERS
3841 North Freeway Boulevard, #130, Sacramento CA 95834. 916/646-4852. **Fax:** 916/648-9650. **Contact:** Human Resources. **World Wide Web address:** http://www.tlcathome.com. **Description:** A home health care agency. **Corporate headquarters location:** Lake Success NY. **Other U.S. locations:** Nationwide. **Number of employees nationwide:** 20,000.

TENDER LOVING CARE/STAFF BUILDERS
1510 Parkmoor Avenue, Suite B, San Jose CA 95128. 408/271-1600. **Fax:** 408/271-1601. **Contact:** Anita Richard, Human Resources Manager. **World Wide Web address:** http://www.tlcathome.com. **Description:** A home health care agency that provides services ranging from sitters and companions to 24-hour skilled nursing care. **Corporate headquarters location:** Lake Success NY. **Other U.S. locations:** Nationwide. **Number of employees nationwide:** 20,000.

TENET HEALTHCARE CORPORATION
3 Imperial Promenade, Suite 300, Santa Ana CA 92707. 714/428-6800. **Contact:** Human Resources Department. **World Wide Web address:** http://www.tenethealth.com. **Description:** A multibillion-dollar, multihospital corporation that, in conjunction with its subsidiaries, owns or operates approximately 130 acute care facilities nationwide. **Positions advertised include:** Paralegal. **Corporate headquarters location:** Dallas TX. **Listed on:** New York Stock Exchange. **Stock exchange symbol:** THC. **Number of employees nationwide:** 130,000.

TERADYNE, INC.
880 Fox Lane, San Jose CA 95131-1685. 408/437-9700. **Contact:** Personnel Department. **E-mail address:** resume@teradyne.com. **World Wide Web address:** http://www.teradyne.com. **Description:** Teradyne manufactures in-circuit testers, automated inspection systems (optical), and probe testers for printed circuit board manufacturers. **Corporate headquarters location:** Boston MA.

TERADYNE, INC.
5 Jenner, #130, Irvine CA 92618. 949/453-1061. **Contact:** Human Resources Manager. **E-mail address:** resume@teradyne.com. **World Wide Web address:** http://www.teradyne.com. **Description:** Teradyne manufactures in-circuit testers, automated inspection systems (optical), and probe testers for printed circuit board manufacturers. Founded in 1960. **Corporate headquarters location:** Boston MA. **Listed on:** New York Stock Exchange. **Stock exchange symbol:** TER. **Annual sales/revenues:** $1.4 billion. **Number of employees at this location:** 135. **Number of employees nationwide:** 6,100.

TERADYNE, INC.
SEMICONDUCTOR TEST DIVISION
30801 Agoura Road, Agoura Hills CA 91301. 818/991-9700. **Contact:** Human Resources. **E-mail address:** resume@teradyne.com. **World Wide Web address:** http://www.teradyne.com. **Description:** Teradyne manufactures in-circuit testers, automated inspection systems (optical), and probe testers for printed circuit board manufacturers. **Corporate headquarters location:** Boston MA. **Operations at this facility include:** This location of Teradyne manufactures semiconductor testers. **Listed on:** New York Stock Exchange. **Stock exchange symbol:** TER. **Number of employees nationwide:** 6,100.

TETRA TECH, INC.
3475 East Foothill Boulevard, Pasadena CA 91107. 626/351-4664. **Fax:** 626/470-2694. **Contact:** Human Resources Manager. **E-mail address:** jobs@tetratech.com. **World Wide Web address:** http://www.tetratech.com. **Description:** Tetra Tech is a leading provider of specialized management consulting and technical services in resource management, infrastructure, and communications. Founded in 1966. **NOTE:** Entry-level positions and part-time jobs are offered. **Positions adverties include:** Human Resource Assistant; Oracle Programmer; Financial Analyst; Construction Manager; Sr. Accountant. **Special programs:** Internships. **Office hours:** Monday - Friday, 8:00 a.m. - 5:00 p.m. **Corporate headquarters location:** This location. **Other U.S. locations:** Nationwide. **Subsidiaries include:** Environmental Management, Inc.; FLO Engineering; HSI GeoTrans; IWA Engineers; KCM Inc.; Simons, Li & Associates. **Listed on:** NASDAQ. **Stock exchange symbol:** TTEK. **President:** Dr. Li-San Hwang. **Number of employees at this location:** 95. **Number of employees nationwide:** 8,900.

H.R. TEXTRON, INC.
25200 West Rye Canyon Road, Santa Clarita CA 91355-1265. 661/294-6000. **Fax:** 661/702-5300. **Contact:** Human Resources. **E-mail address:** jbjoin@hrtextron.textron.com. **World Wide Web address:** http://www.systems.textron.com. **Description:** Designs and manufactures components and control systems for major aircraft manufacturers. The manufacturing group designs systems to improve performance and increase safety. **NOTE:** Resumes may be submitted via mail, fax, or e-mail. **Corporate headquarters location:** Wilmington MA. **Parent company:** Textron Systems, Inc. is a division of Textron In. Textron Inc. (Providence RI) is a diversified conglomerate with over 30 separate companies in three primary areas: Aerospace and Defense Technology; Financial Services; and Communications. The company also manufactures automobile parts, outdoor equipment, and specialty fasteners. **Listed on:** New York Stock Exchange. **Stock exchange symbol:** TXT.

THAI AIRWAYS INTERNATIONAL PUBLIC COMPANY LIMITED
222 North Sepulveda Boulevard, Suite 1950, El Segundo CA 90245. 310/640-0097. **Fax:** 310/322-8728. **Contact:** Janet Mazon, Personnel Coordinator. **World Wide Web address:** http://www.thaiair.com. **Description:** An international passenger and freight air carrier. **NOTE:** Flight crews are only hired through the Bangkok, Thailand location. **Corporate headquarters location:** Bangkok, Thailand. **Other U.S. locations:** Nationwide. **Operations at this facility include:** Regional Headquarters. **Number of employees at this location:** 50. **Number of employees nationwide:** 100.

THALES IN-FLIGHT SYSTEMS
17481 Red Hill Avenue, Irvine CA 92614. 949/660-7722. **Contact:** Erica Scott, Human Resources Department. **E-mail address:** thaleshr@thales-ifs.com. **World Wide Web address:** http://www.thalesgroup.com. **Description:** Manufactures passenger video entertainment systems, cabin video systems, and Passenger Control Units for noise control in airplanes. **Parent company:** Thomson-CSF.

THERMADOR
5551 McFadden Avenue, Huntington Beach CA 92649. 714/901-6600. **Toll-free phone:** 800/656-9226. **Contact:** Human Resources. **World Wide Web address:** http://www.thermador.com. **Description:** Manufactures built-in electrical and gas kitchen appliances. **Corporate headquarters location:** Munich, Germany. **Parent company:** Masco. **Operations at this facility include:** Manufacturing.

THERMA-WAVE, INC.
1250 Reliance Way, Fremont CA 94539. 510/668-2200. **Fax:** 510/656-3852. **Recorded jobline:** 510/668-2JOB. **Contact:** Julie Venierakis, Manager of Human Resources. **E-mail address:** careers@thermawave.com. **World Wide Web address:** http://www.thermawave.com. **Description:** Manufactures semiconductor testing equipment. **Positions advertised include:** General Ledger Sr. Accountant; Sr. Staff Mechanical Design Engineer; Sr. Mechanical Engineer. **Corporate headquarters location:** This location. **Other U.S. locations:** AZ; CO; FL; MA; OR; TX. **International locations:** England; France; Italy; Japan; Korea; Scotland; Taiwan. **Listed on:** NASDAQ. **Stock exchange symbol:** TWAV. **Annual sales/revenues:** $51 - $100 million. **Number of employees at this location:** 200.

THERMO ELECTRON
355 River Oaks Parkway, San Jose CA 95134. 408/965-6000. **Fax:** 408/965-6010. **Contact:** Human Resources. **World Wide Web address:** http://www.thermo.com. **Description:** Manufactures laboratory instruments and supplies for the health care industry. **NOTE:** Contact information may vary. See job postings for more specific instructions. **Positions advertised include:** Software Engineer; Export Customer Service Engineer; Instrument Specialist. **Corporate headquarters location:** Waltham MA. **Parent company:** Thermo Electron Corporation. **Listed on:** New York Stock Exchange. **Stock exchange symbol:** TMO. **Number of employees at this location:** 300.

THE THOMAS KINKADE COMPANY
900 Lightpost Way, Morgan Hill CA 95037. 408/201-5000. **Toll-free phone:** 800/366-3733. **Contact:** Human Resources. **E-mail address:** jobs@kinkade.com. **World Wide Web address:** http://www.mediaarts.com. **Description:** Designs, manufactures, markets, and distributes collectible, gift, and art products. **Positions advertised include:** Customer Care Rep; Licensing Manager. **Number of employees nationwide:** 450. **Corporate headquarters location:** This location. **Listed on:** New York Stock Exchange. **Stock exchange symbol:** MDA.

J. WALTER THOMPSON COMPANY
111 Sutter Street, San Francisco CA 94104. 415/733-0700. **Fax:** 415/733-0701. **Contact:** Roman Lesnau, Human Resources. **E-mail address:** roman.lesnau@jwt.com. **World Wide Web address:** http://www.jwtworld.com. **Description:** The largest full-service U.S. advertising agency. **NOTE:** Entry-level positions are offered. **Positions advertised include:** Art Director. **Corporate headquarters location:** New York NY. **International locations:** Worldwide. **Parent company:** WPP Group. **Listed on:** NASDAQ. **Stock exchange symbol:** WPPGY. **Number of employees at this location:** 175. **Number of employees worldwide:** 8,500.

3-D SYSTEMS INC.
26081 Avenue Hall, Valencia CA 91355. 661/295-5600. **Contact:** Human Resources. **E-mail address:** jobs@3dsystems.com. **World Wide Web address:** http://www.3dsystems.com. **Description:** Manufactures stereolithography equipment. Founded in 1986. **Positions advertised include:** Cost Analysis Manager. **Corporate headquarters location:** This location. **International locations:** China; France; Germany; Italy; United Kingdom. **Listed on:** NASDAQ. **Stock exchange symbol:** TDSC.

3COM CORPORATION
575 Anton Boulevard, Suite 300, Costa Mesa CA 92626. 310/348-8110. **Contact:** Human Resources. **World Wide Web address:** http://www.3com.com. **Description:** 3Com is a *Fortune* 500 company delivering global data networking solutions to organizations around the world. 3Com designs, manufactures, markets, and supports a broad range of ISO 9000-compliant global data networking solutions including routers, hubs, remote access servers, switches, and adapters for Ethernet, Token Ring, and high-speed networks. These products enable computers to communicate at high speeds and share resources including printers, disk drives, modems, and minicomputers. **Positions advertised include:** Account Executive. **Special programs:** Internships. **Corporate headquarters location:** Marlborough MA. **Other area locations:** Santa Clara CA; Los Angeles CA. **Operations at this facility include:** Administration; Manufacturing; Research and Development; Sales; Service. **Listed on:** NASDAQ. **Stock exchange symbol:** COMS. **Annual sales/revenues:** More than $100 million. **Number of employees nationwide:** 5,000.

3COM CORPORATION
5403 Betsy Ross Drive, Santa Clara CA 95054. 408/326-5000. **Contact:** Human Resources. **World Wide Web address:** http://www.3com.com. **Description:** 3Com is a *Fortune* 500 company delivering global data networking solutions to organizations around the world. 3Com designs, manufactures, markets, and supports a broad range of ISO 9000-compliant global data networking solutions including routers, hubs, remote access servers, switches, and adapters for Ethernet, Token Ring, and high-speed networks. These products enable computers to communicate at high speeds and share resources including printers, disk drives, modems, and minicomputers. **Positions advertised include:** Post Sales Systems Engineer; Web Developer; **Corporate headquarters location:** Marlborough MA. **Listed on:** NASDAQ. **Stock exchange symbol:** COMS.

3M
4080 North Palm Street, Unit 803, Fullerton CA 92835-1024. 866/320-7150. **Contact:** Human Resources. **World Wide Web address:** http://www.3m.com. **Description:** 3M manufactures products in three sectors: Industrial and Consumer; Information, Imaging, and Electronic; and Life Sciences. The Industrial and Consumer Sector includes a variety of products under brand names including 3M, Scotch, Post-it, Scotch-Brite, and Scotchgard. The Information, Imaging, and Electronic Sector is a leader in several high-growth global industries including telecommunications, electronics, electrical, imaging, and memory media. The Life Science Sector serves two broad market categories: health care, and traffic and personal safety. In the health care market, 3M is a leading provider of medical and surgical supplies, drug delivery systems, and dental products. In traffic and personal safety, 3M is a leader in products for transportation safety, worker protection, vehicle and sign graphics, and out-of-home advertising. **Corporate headquarters location:** St. Paul MN. **Operations at this facility include:** This location is an area sales office for adhesives and tapes. **Listed on:** New York Stock Exchange. **Stock exchange symbol:** MMM.

3M
18750 Minnesota Road, Corona CA 92881. 951/737-3441. **Contact:** Human Resources. **World Wide Web address:** http://www.3m.com. **Description:** 3M manufactures products in three sectors: Industrial and Consumer; Information, Imaging, and Electronic; and Life Sciences. The Industrial and Consumer Sector includes a variety of products under brand names including 3M, Scotch, Post-it, Scotch-Brite, and Scotchgard. The Information, Imaging, and Electronic Sector is a leader in several high-growth global industries including telecommunications, electronics, electrical, imaging, and memory media. The Life Science Sector serves two broad market categories: health care, and traffic and personal safety. In the health care market, 3M is a leading provider of medical and surgical supplies, drug delivery systems, and dental products. In traffic and personal safety, 3M is a leader in products for transportation safety, worker protection, vehicle and sign graphics, and out-of-home advertising. **Corporate headquarters location:** St. Paul MN. **Operations at this facility include:** This division of 3M produces roof granules used in the manufacture of shingles. **Listed on:** New York Stock Exchange. **Stock exchange symbol:** MMM.

THYSSENKRUPP ELEVATOR COMPANY
6048 Triangle Drive, Commerce CA 90040. 323/278-9888. **Contact:** Human Resources. **World Wide Web address:** http://www.thyssenelevator.com. **Description:** Provides elevator and escalator products, services, and technology. **Corporate headquarters location:** Dusseldorf Germany.

TIMES-HERALD, INC.
P.O. Box 3188, Vallejo CA 94590. 707/644-1141. **Physical address:** 440 Curtola Parkway, Vallejo CA 94590. **Contact:** Joan Rondoni, Personnel Secretary. **World Wide Web address:** http://www.timesheraldonline.com. **Description:** Publishes a daily newspaper with a circulation of more than 25,000. **Parent company:** MediaNews Group.

TITAN CORPORATION
3033 Science Park Road, San Diego CA 92121. 858/552-9500. **Contact:** Personnel. **World Wide Web address:** http://www.titan.com. **Description:** A leading provider of information technology and communications services and products primarily used by US government agencies such as the Department of Defense and the Department of Homeland Security. Founded in 1981. **NOTE:** Search and apply for positions online. **Positions advertised include:** Applications Programmer; Chief Scientist; Configuration Manager; Field Engineer; Financial Analyst; Junior Software Engineer. **Corporate headquarters location:** This location. **Listed on:** New York Stock Exchange. **Stock exchange symbol:** TTN. **Annual sales/revenues:** Approximately $2 billion. **Number of employees worldwide:** 12,000.

C.E. TOLAND & SON
5300 Industrial Way, Benicia CA 94510. 707/747-1000. **Fax:** 707/747-5300. **Contact:** Office Manager. **Description:** Engaged in the fabrication of metal and metal products. Products include stairs, railings, and toilet partitions. **NOTE:** Jobseekers interested in working in the shop or field must be union members. **Corporate headquarters location:** This location.

TORRANCE MEMORIAL MEDICAL CENTER
3330 Lomita Boulevard, Torrance CA 90505. 310/325-9110. **Recorded jobline:** 310/517-4790. **Contact:** Michele Alarcon, Human Resources Representative. **E-mail address:** michele.alarcon@tmmc.com. **World Wide Web address:** http://www.torrancememorial.org. **Description:** A nonprofit medical center. **Positions advertised include:** Registered Nurse; Emergency Department Technician; Certified Nurse Assistant; Nutrition Assistant; Physical Therapist; Occupational Therapist. **Special programs:** Training. **Corporate headquarters location:** This location.

TOSHIBA AMERICA INFORMATION SYSTEMS INC.
9740 Irvine Boulevard, Irvine CA 92718. 949/583-3000. **Fax:** 949/587-6436. **Contact:** Human Resources. **E-mail address:** employment@tais.com. **World Wide Web address:** http://www.toshiba.com. **Description:** Develops, markets, and supports computers, printers, fax machines, security imaging systems, industrial video products, voice processing systems, and medical and PC cameras. **NOTE:** Apply online or e-mail resume as a word attachment. **Positions advertised include:** Finance Manager; Tax Specialist; Senior Engineer; Technical Support Specialist; Sales Support Representative. **Corporate headquarters location:** New York NY. **Parent company:** Toshiba America Inc.

TRANS-PACIFIC CONSULTANTS
27431 Enterprise Circle West, Temecula CA 92590. 951/676-7000. **Fax:** 909/699-7324. **Contact:** Human Resources. **Description:** A full-service consulting company engaged in land planning, civil engineering, and surveying. **Corporate headquarters location:** This location.

TRANSAMERICA CORPORATION
1150 South Olive Street, Los Angeles CA 90015. 213/742-4141. **Contact:** Human Resources. **World Wide Web address:** http://www.transamerica.com. **Description:** Operates diversified financial services and insurance companies. **Corporate headquarters location:** This location. **Parent company:** AEGON N.V. (The Netherlands). **Operations at this facility include:** Administration. **Listed on:** New York Stock Exchange. **Stock exchange symbol:** TFD.

TRIDENT MICROSYSTEMS
1090 East Arques Avenue, Sunnyvale CA 94085-4601. 408/991-8800. **Fax:** 408/733-1087. **Contact:** Human Resources. **E-mail address:** hr@tridentmicro.com. **World Wide Web address:** http://www.tridentmicro.com. **Description:** Designs, develops, and markets integrated graphics ICs and multimedia audio/visual chips for PCs. Founded in 1988. **Positions advertised include:** Investor Relations Specialist. **Corporate headquarters location:** This location. **Other U.S. locations:** Chandler AZ. **Operations at this facility include:** Sales; Technical Support. **Listed on:** NASDAQ. **Stock exchange symbol:** TRID. **Number of employees at this location:** 300.

TRIKON TECHNOLOGIES, INC.
17835 New Hope Street, Fountain Valley CA 92708. 714/968-2594. 800/727-5585. **Contact:** Human Resources. **E-mail address:** website.mail@trikon.com. **World Wide Web address:** http://www.trikon.com. **Description:** Manufactures etch and deposition equipment using Etch, CVD, and PVD technologies that are necessary for semiconductor manufacturing. Trikon has three divisions: Etch, Deposition, and Global Sales and Field Operations. The Deposition Division (Newport, South Wales) houses all operations involving the Forcefill PVD and Flowfill CVD product lines. **Corporate headquarters location:** This location. **Listed on:** NASDAQ. **Stock exchange symbol:** TRKN.

TRIZEC PROPERTIES
725 South Figueroa Street, Suite 1850, Los Angeles CA 90017. 213/955-7170. **Contact:** Human Resources. **World Wide Web address:** http://www.trz.com. **Description:** Trizec is a real estate development/property management company focusing on office buildings and technology complexes with properties across the United States, Canada, and Europe. **Corporate headquarters location:** Chicago IL. **Listed:** New York Stock Exchange. **Stock exchange symbol:** TRZ.

21ST CENTURY INSURANCE GROUP
6301 Owensmouth Avenue, Woodland Hills CA 91367. 818/704-3700. **Fax:** 818/704-3485. **Contact:** Human Resources Representative. **World Wide Web address:** http://www.21stcenturyinsurance.com. **Description:** Provides automobile insurance. **Positions advertised include:** Customer Care Representative; Customer Care Manager; Information Security Analyst; Compliance Analyst. **Special programs:** Training. **Corporate headquarters location:** This location. **Listed on:** New York Stock Exchange. **Stock exchange symbol:** TW. **Number of employees at this location:** 1,400. **Number of employees nationwide:** 2,700.

UBS FINANCIAL SERVICES, INC.
555 California Street, Suite 3200, San Francisco CA 94104-1501. 415/398-6400. **Contact:** Mr. Shawn Macfarlan, Branch Manager. **World Wide Web address:** http://financialservices.ubs.com. **Description:** A full-service securities firm with over 300 offices nationwide. Services include investment banking, asset management, merger and acquisition consulting, municipal securities underwriting, estate planning, retirement programs, and transaction management. UBS offers its services to corporations, governments, institutions, and individuals. **Corporate headquarters location:** New York NY. **Other U.S. locations:** Nationwide.

UBS FINANCIAL SERVICES, INC.
One California Street, 20th Floor, San Francisco CA 94111. 415/954-6700. **Contact:** Loren Neumann, Branch Manager. **World Wide Web address:** http://financialservices.ubs.com. **Description:** One of the world's largest investment services firms. UBS assists corporations, governments, and individuals in meeting their long-term financial needs. UBS also has operations in equity and fixed-income securities. **Corporate headquarters location:** New York NY. **Other U.S. locations:** Nationwide.

UHP HEALTHCARE
3405 West Imperial Highway, Inglewood CA 90303. 310/412-3521. **Fax:** 310/412-7129. **Recorded jobline:** 310/680-3188. **Contact:** Vice President of Personnel Services. **Description:** A health maintenance organization. **Company slogan:** A commitment to caring. **Corporate headquarters location:** This location. **Number of employees at this location:** 600.

UPS SUPPLY CHAIN SOLUTIONS
1778 Carr Road, Calexico CA 92231. 760/357-5888. **Fax:** 760/357-5889. **Contact:** Human Resources. **World Wide Web address:** http://www.ups-scs.com. **Description:** A leader in global transportation and logistics. The company's services range from integrated logistics programs to traditional freight forwarding and customs brokerage. UPS SCS develops, implements, and delivers worldwide supply chain solutions for its clients. Founded in 1933. **NOTE:** Entry-level positions are offered. **Special programs:** Internships. **Corporate headquarters location:** This location. **Other U.S. locations:** Nationwide. **International locations:** Worldwide. **Parent company:** UPS. **Listed on:** New York Stock Exchange. **Stock exchange symbol:** UPS.

URS CORPORATION
600 Montgomery Street, 26th Floor, San Francisco CA 94111-2728. 415/774-2700. **Contact:** Personnel Department. **World Wide Web address:** http://www.urscorp.com. **Description:** An international professional services organization with substantial engineering, training, architectural planning, environmental, and construction management capabilities. **Positions advertised include:** Project Manager; Internal Auditor; Vice President. **Corporate headquarters location:** This location. **Listed on:** New York Stock Exchange. **Stock exchange symbol:** URS. **Number of employees worldwide:** 26,000.

URS CORPORATION
915 Wilshire Boulevard, Suite 700, Los Angeles CA 90017. 213/996-2200. **Fax:** 213/996-2515. **Contact:** Human Resources Department. **World Wide Web address:** http://www.urscorp.com. **Description:** An architectural, engineering, and environmental consulting firm that specializes in air transportation, environmental solutions, surface transportation, and industrial environmental and engineering concerns. **Positions advertised include:** Civil Geo-technical Engineer; Senior Urban Planner; Senior Water Resources Engineer. **Corporate headquarters location:** San Francisco CA. **Other area locations:** Statewide. **Listed on:** New York Stock Exchange. **Stock exchange symbol:** URS.

U.S. BANK
980 Ninth Street, Sacramento CA 95814. 916/552-5667. **Contact:** Employment Services. **World Wide Web address:** http://www.usbank.com. **Description:** A comprehensive bank with over 2,234 offices operating in 24 states. **Positions advertised include:** Account Service Representative; Mortgage Loan Officer; Commercial Banking Relationship Manager. **Corporate headquarters location:** Minneapolis MN. **Parent company:** U.S. Bancorp. **Listed on:** New York Stock Exchange. **Stock exchange symbol:** USB.

U.S. BANK
201 Montgomery Street, San Francisco CA 94104. 415/421-6364. **Contact:** Human Resources. **World Wide Web address:** http://www.usbank.com. **Description:** A comprehensive bank with over 2,234 offices operating in 24 states. **Positions advertised include:** Account Service Representative; In Store Banker; Mortgage Loan Officer; Personal Broker; Sales and Service Manager; Teller. **Corporate headquarters location:** Minneapolis MN. **Parent company:** U.S. Bancorp. **Listed on:** New York Stock Exchange. **Stock exchange symbol:** USB.

U.S. BANK
U.S. Bank Tower, 633 West Fifth Street, Los Angeles CA 90071. 213/615-6300. **Contact:** Human Resources. **World Wide Web address:** http://www.usbank.com. **Description:** A comprehensive bank with over 2,234 offices operating in 24 states. **Positions advertised include:** International Banking Specialist; Administrative Assistant. **Corporate headquarters location:** Minneapolis MN. **Parent company:** U.S. Bancorp. **Listed on:** New York Stock Exchange. **Stock exchange symbol:** USB.

U.S. BORAX INC.
26877 Tourney Road, Valencia CA 91355. 661/287-5400. **Fax:** 661/287-5652. **Contact:** Human Resources. **E-mail address:** jobs@borax.com. **World Wide Web address:** http://www.borax.com. **Description:** Produces borax, boric acid, and other boron compounds. **Positions advertised include:** Community and External Affairs Coordinator; Environmental and Health Scientist. **Special programs:** Training. **Corporate headquarters location:** This location. **Parent company:** Rio Tinto PLC. **Listed on:** New York Stock Exchange. **Stock exchange symbol:** RTP. **Number of employees at this location:** 175. **Number of employees nationwide:** 1,000.

U.S. DEPARTMENT OF VETERANS AFFAIRS
VETERANS ADMINISTRATION SAN DIEGO HEALTHCARE SYSTEM
3350 La Jolla Village Drive, San Diego CA 92161. 858/552-8585. **Contact:** Human Resources. **World Wide Web address:** http://www.san-diego.med.va.gov. **Description:** A medical center operated by the U.S. Department of Veterans Affairs. From 54 hospitals in 1930, the system has grown to include 171 medical centers; more than 364 outpatient, community and outreach clinics; 130 nursing home care units; and 37 domiciliary residences. The VA operates at least one medical center in each of the 48 contiguous states, Puerto Rico, and the District of Columbia. With approximately 76,000 medical center beds, the VA treats nearly 1 million patients in VA hospitals, 75,000 in nursing home care units, and 25,000 in domiciliary residences. The VA's outpatient clinics register approximately 24 million visits a year. The VA is affiliated with 104 medical schools, 48 dental schools, and more than 850 other schools across the country.

U.S. ENVIRONMENTAL PROTECTION AGENCY (EPA)
75 Hawthorne Street, San Francisco CA 94105. 415/972-3817. **Contact:** Human Resources. **E-mail address:** r9jobs@epa.gov. **World Wide Web address:** http://www.epa.gov. **Description:** The EPA is dedicated to improving and preserving the quality of the environment, both nationally and globally, and protecting human health and the productivity of natural resources. The agency is committed to ensuring that federal environmental laws are implemented and enforced effectively; U.S. policy, both foreign and domestic, encourages the integration of economic development and environmental protection so that economic growth can be sustained over the long term; and public and private decisions affecting energy, transportation, agriculture, industry, international trade, and natural resources fully integrate considerations of environmental quality. Founded in 1970. **NOTE:** Candidates must apply online. **Positions advertised include:** Community Involvement Specialist; Environmental Protection Specialist. **Special programs:** Internships; Co-ops; Summer Jobs. **Office hours:** Monday - Friday, 8:00 a.m. - 4:30 p.m. **Corporate headquarters location:** Washington DC. **Number of employees nationwide:** 19,000.

U.S. FEDERAL RESERVE BANK OF SAN FRANCISCO
101 Market Street, San Francisco CA 94105. 415/974-2000. **Fax:** 415/393-1906. **Contact:** Human Resources Department. **World Wide Web address:** http://www.frbsf.org. **Description:** One of 12 regional Federal Reserve banks that, along with the Federal Reserve Board of Governors in Washington DC and the Federal Open Market Committee (FOMC), comprise the Federal Reserve System, the nation's central bank. As the nation's central bank, Federal Reserve is charged with three major responsibilities: setting monetary policy, banking supervision and regulation, and payment processing. **NOTE:** Entry-level positions and second and third shifts are offered. To contact Human Resources directly call: 415/974-2727. **Positions advertised include:** Auditor; Bank Examiner; Database Analyst; Education Outreach Coordinator; Financial Analyst. **Corporate headquarters location:** This location. **Number of employees at this location:** 1,400.

U.S. FEDERAL RESERVE BANK OF SAN FRANCISCO
P.O. Box 512077, Los Angeles CA. 90051-0077 213/683-2300. **Physical address:** 950 South Grand Avenue, Los Angeles CA 90015.
Contact: Human Resources Department. **World Wide Web address:** http://www.frbsf.org. **Description:** One of 12 regional Federal Reserve banks that, along with the Federal Reserve Board of Governors in Washington DC and the Federal Open Market Committee (FOMC), comprise the Federal Reserve System, the nation's central bank. **Positions advertised include:** Community Relations & Education Specialist; District Cash Compliance Manager; Project Analyst/Manager; Sr. Examiner; Stationary Engineer. **Operations at this facility include:** This is a branch office.

U.S. FOOD AND DRUG ADMINISTRATION (FDA)
19701 Fairchild, Irvine CA 92612. 949/608-2900. **Toll-free phone:** 800/INFO-FDA. **Contact:** Human Resources. **World Wide Web address:** http://www.fda.gov. **Description:** The FDA monitors the manufacture, import, storage, and sale of consumer products. Responsibilities include checking wharves for imports of food, drugs, cosmetics, medical devices, and radiation emitting products. **Corporate headquarters location:** Rockville MD.

U.S. FOODSERVICE
15155 Northam Street, La Mirada CA 90638. 714/670-3500. **Fax:** 714/670-3794. **Recorded jobline:** 714/670-3500x5500. **Contact:** Human Resources Manager. **World Wide Web address:** http://www.usfoodservice.com. **Description:** The second largest food service distributor in the nation, U.S. Foodservice distributes food and related products to restaurants, hotels, healthcare facilities, cafeterias, and schools. **Positions advertised include:** Transportation Supervisor. **Office hours:** Monday - Friday, 8:00 a.m. - 5:00 p.m. **Corporate headquarters location:** Columbia MD. **Other U.S. locations:** Nationwide. **Parent company:** Ahold. **Listed on:** New York Stock Exchange. **Stock exchange symbol:** AHO. **Annual sales/revenues:** Over $19 billion. **Number of employees at this location:** 600. **Number of employees nationwide:** 34,000.

USA BIOMASS CORPORATION
1912 North Batavia Street, Unit C, Orange CA 92865. 714/921-2886. **Contact:** Human Resources. **Description:** USA Biomass provides waste removal and recycling services for green waste. The company is a vertically integrated green waste management business that services both corporate customers and municipalities. **Corporate headquarters location:** This location. **Operations at this facility include:** This location houses administrative offices. **Annual sales/revenues:** $6.3 million. **Number of employees at this location:** 10.

USC/NORRIS COMPREHENSIVE CANCER CENTER AND HOSPITAL
1441 Eastlake Avenue, Los Angeles CA 90033. 323/442-2660. **Fax:** 323/442-2442. **Contact:** Human Resources. **E-mail address:** careers@norris.hsc.usc.edu. **World Wide Web address:** http://www.uscnorris.com. **Description:** A 60-bed inpatient and outpatient tertiary care facility. USC Norris Comprehensive Cancer Center and Hospital is a teaching and research hospital located on the Health Sciences campus of the University of Southern California. **Positions advertised include:** Admitting Representative; Cancer Registry Abstractor; Cancer Registry Coordinator; Radiology Department Secretary; Registered Nurse; Mammography Technologist; Medical Transcriptionist. **Corporate headquarters location:** This location. **Operations at this facility include:** Administration; Service. **Number of employees at this location:** 400.

USFILTER
960 Ames Avenue, Milpitas CA 95035. 408/946-1520. **Contact:** Human Resources Department. **E-mail address:** corpstaff@usfilter.com. **World Wide Web address:** http://www.usfilter.com. **Description:** North America's largest water company, USFilter manufactures and services water purification and treatment equipment. Primary customers are entities with the need for highly purified water including the electronic, utility, and pharmaceutical industries. **Corporate headquarters location:** Palm Desert CA. **Parent company:** Siemens. **Operations at this facility include:** Administration; Marketing; Sales; Service. **Listed on:** New York Stock Exchange. **Stock exchange symbol:** VE.

USFILTER
75005 Country Club Drive, Palm Desert CA 92211. 760/340-0098. **Contact:** Human Resources. **E-mail address:** corpstaff@usfilter.com. **World Wide Web address:** http://www.usfilter.com. **Description:** North America's largest water company, USFilter manufactures and services water purification and treatment equipment. Primary customers are the electronic, utility, and pharmaceutical industries. **Positions advertised include:** Director of Technical Services/Maintenance. **Corporate headquarters location:** This location. **Parent company:** Siemens. **Listed on:** New York Stock Exchange. **Stock exchange symbol:** VE.

USS-POSCO INDUSTRIES
P.O. Box 471, Pittsburg CA 94565. 925/439-6000. **Physical address:** 900 Loveridge Road, Pittsburg CA 94565. **Fax:** 925/439-6179. **Contact:** Human Resources. **E-mail address:** recruiting@ussposco.com. **World Wide Web address:** http://www.uss-posco.com. **Description:** A steel finishing facility. **Corporate headquarters location:** This location. **Parent company:** USS-POSCO Industries is a joint venture between USX Corporation (Pittsburgh PA) and Pohang Iron and Steel Company (Republic of Korea).

ULTRATECH STEPPER, INC.
3050 Zanker Road, San Jose CA 95134. 408/321-8835. **Fax:** 408/577-3378. **Contact:** Human Resources. **World Wide Web address:** http://www.ultratech.com. **Description:** Develops, manufactures, and markets photolithography equipment designed to reduce the cost of ownership for manufacturers of integrated circuits and thin-film head magnetic recording devices. Founded in 1979. **Positions advertised include:** Corporate Controller; VP, Engineering. **Corporate headquarters location:** This location. **Other U.S. locations:** Woburn MA; Dallas TX. **Listed on:** NASDAQ. **Stock exchange symbol:** UTEK.

UNDERWRITERS LABORATORIES INC.
1655 Scott Boulevard, Santa Clara CA 95050. 408/985-2400. **Contact:** Human Resources Department. **E-mail address:** scjobs@ul.com. **World Wide Web address:** http://www.ul.com. **Description:** An independent, nonprofit corporation established to help reduce or prevent bodily injury, loss of life, and property damage. Underwriters Laboratories accomplishes its objectives by scientific investigation of various materials, devices, equipment, constructions, methods, and systems; and by the publication of standards, classifications, specifications, and other information. Engineering functions are divided between six departments: Electrical; Burglary Protection and Signaling; Casualty and Chemical Hazards; Fire Protection; Heating, Air-Conditioning, and Refrigeration; and Marine. The company also performs factory inspections. **Corporate headquarters location:** Northbrook IL.

UNION BANK OF CALIFORNIA
400 California Street, 10th Floor, San Francisco CA 94104. 415/765-3434. **Fax:** 877/217-3377. **Contact:** Corporate Staffing. **E-mail address:** careers01@uboc.com. **World Wide Web address:** http://www.uboc.com. **Description:** A full-service commercial bank providing a broad mix of financial services including retail and small business banking, middle market banking, personal and business trust services, real estate finance, corporate banking, trade finance (with a focus on the Pacific Rim), and financial management services through 246 branch offices. **NOTE:** Resumes may be submitted by e-mail, fax, or regular mail. Send resumes to: Union Bank of America, Attention: Corporate Staffing, P.O. Box 60691, Los Angeles CA 90060-0691. . **Positions advertised include:** Small Business Development Officer; Credit Examiner; Financial Services Officer; Trust Administrator; Cash Management Consultant; Senior Investment Specialist. **Special programs:** Management Training Programs. **Corporate headquarters location:** This location. **Subsidiaries include:** U.S. Investment Services, Inc. **Parent company:** UnionBanCal Corporation. **Listed on:** New York Stock Exchange. **Stock exchange symbol:** UB. **Number of employees at this location:** 3,500. **Number of employees nationwide:** 10,000.

UNISYS CORPORATION
10850 Via Frontera, San Diego CA 92127. 858/451-3000. **Fax:** 858/451-4656. **Contact:** Human Resources Manager. **World Wide Web address:** http://www.unisys.com. **Description:** Unisys Corporation provides information services, technology, and software. Unisys specializes in developing critical business solutions based on open information networks. The company's Enabling Software Team creates a variety of software projects that facilitate the building of user applications and the management of distributed systems. The company's Platforms

Group is responsible for UNIX Operating Systems running across a wide range of multiple processor server platforms including all peripheral and communication drivers. The Unisys Commercial Parallel Processing Team develops microkernel-based operating systems, I/O device drivers, ATM hardware, diagnostics, and system architectures. The System Management Group is in charge of the overall management of development programs for UNIX desktop and entry-server products. **Positions advertised include:** Accounting Analyst. **Corporate headquarters location:** Blue Bell PA. **Other U.S. locations:** Nationwide. **Operations at this facility include:** This location is a manufacturing facility. **Listed on:** New York Stock Exchange. **Stock exchange symbol:** UIS. **Number of employees worldwide:** 49,000.

UNISYS CORPORATION
2049 Century Park East, Suite 310, Los Angeles CA 90067. 310/208-1511. **Contact:** Human Resources. **World Wide Web address:** http://www.unisys.com. **Description:** Provides information services, technology, and software. Unisys Corporation specializes in developing critical business solutions based on open information networks. The company's Enabling Software Team creates a variety of software projects that facilitate the building of user applications and the management of distributed systems. The company's Platforms Group is responsible for UNIX Operating Systems running across a wide range of multiple processor server platforms including all peripheral and communication drivers. The Unisys Commercial Parallel Processing Team develops microkernel-based operating systems, I/O device drivers, ATM hardware, diagnostics, and system architectures. The System Management Group is in charge of the overall management of development programs for UNIX desktop and entry-server products. **Corporate headquarters location:** Blue Bell PA. **Other U.S. locations:** Nationwide. **Listed on:** New York Stock Exchange. **Stock exchange symbol:** UIS. **Number of employees worldwide:** 49,000.

UNISYS CORPORATION
1000 Marina Boulevard, Suite 500, Brisbane CA 94005. 650/875-4400. **Contact:** Human Resources. **World Wide Web address:** http://www.unisys.com. **Description:** Provides information services, technology, and software. Unisys Corporation specializes in developing critical business solutions based on open information networks.

UNITED HEALTHCARE
425 Market Street, 13th Floor, San Francisco CA 94105. 415/546-3300. **Contact:** Human Resources Director. **E-mail address:** resume@uhc.com. **World Wide Web address:** http://www.uhc.com. **Description:** Offers group medical insurance. **Corporate headquarters location:** Minneapolis MN. **Other area locations:** Statewide. **Parent company:** United Health Group is a diversified health and well-being company. **Listed on:** New York Stock Exchange. **Stock exchange symbol:** UNH.

UNITED PLASTICS GROUP
3125 East Coronado Street, Anaheim CA 92806. 714/630-6411. **Fax:** 714/630-3759. **Contact:** Human Resources. **E-mail address:** info@upgintl.com. **World Wide Web address:** http://www.unitedplasticsgroup.com. **Description:** Manufactures custom injection-molded plastic products. **Corporate headquarters location:** Westmont IL. **Other area locations:** Fremont CA. **Other U.S. locations:** Nationwide. **International locations:** Worldwide. **Number of employees worldwide:** 2,500.

UNITED PLASTICS GROUP
45581 Northport Loop West, Fremont CA 94538-6462. 510/657-5800. **Fax:** 510/657-6019. **Contact:** Human Resources. **E-mail address:** info@upgintl.com. **World Wide Web address:** http://www.unitedplasticsgroup.com. **Description:** Manufactures custom injection-molded plastic products. **Corporate headquarters location:** Westmont IL. **Other area locations:** Anaheim CA. **Other U.S. locations:** Nationwide. **International locations:** Worldwide. **Number of employees worldwide:** 2,500.

UNIVERSAL ELECTRONICS INC.
6101 Gateway Drive, Cypress CA 90630-4841. 714/820-1000. **Fax:** 714/820-1223. **Contact:** Human Resources. **E-mail address:** hr@ueic.com. **World Wide Web address:** http://www.universalelectronicsus.com. **Description:** Develops, designs, engineers, and markets preprogrammed universal remote controls for use with home video and audio entertainment equipment. Universal Electronics also produces home safety and automation equipment. **Positions advertised include:** Assistant Buyer; Business Development Manager; Customer Service Manager; Accounting Director; Product Manager; Program Manager; Senior Software Developer. **Special programs:** Internships. **Corporate headquarters location:** This location. **Office hours:** Monday - Friday, 7:00 a.m. - 5:00 p.m. **Number of employees at this location:** 90.

UNIVERSAL PROPULSION COMPANY
P.O. Box KK, Fairfield CA 94533. 707/422-1880. **Fax:** 707/422-3242. **Contact:** Human Resources. **World Wide Web address:** http://www.upco.goodrich.com. **Description:** Manufactures explosive devices and systems for the aerospace industry. **Corporate headquarters location:** Charlotte NC. **Parent company:** Goodrich Corporation. **Listed on:** New York Stock Exchange. **Stock exchange symbol:** GR.

UNIVERSAL STUDIOS, INC.
100 Universal City Plaza, Building 1220/1, Universal City CA 91608. 818/777-1000. **Physical address:** 3900 Lankershim Boulevard, Universal City CA 91604. **Recorded jobline:** 818/777-JOBS. **Contact:** Corporate Workforce Planning & Strategic Staffing. **E-mail address:** jobs@unistudios.com. **World Wide Web address:** http://www.universalstudios.com. **Description:** A diversified entertainment company and a worldwide leader in motion pictures, television, music, and home and location-based themed entertainment. The company's main operating divisions include Universal Studios, Universal Studios Recreation Group, Universal Studios Information Technology, Universal Studios Operations Group, Universal Music Group, Universal Pictures, Universal Networks & Worldwide Television Distribution, Universal Studios Consumer Products Group, Universal Studios Online, and Spencer Gifts. **NOTE:** Entry-level positions are offered. Online application recommended. **Positions advertised include:** Sr. Financial Analyst; Legal Assistant; Accounting Analyst. **Special programs:** Internships; Training; Co-ops; Summer Jobs. **Corporate headquarters location:** This location. **Other U.S. locations:** Orlando FL; New York NY; Memphis TN; Nashville TN; Dallas TX. **International locations:** Worldwide. **Parent company:** NBC Universal. **Annual sales/revenues:** $6.6 billion. **Number of employees worldwide:** 22,000.

UNIVERSITY COMMUNITY MEDICAL CENTER
5550 University Avenue, San Diego CA 92105. 619/582-3516. **Contact:** Human Resources. **Description:** An acute-care hospital. **Parent company:** Quantum Health Inc. **Number of employees at this location:** 280.

UNIVERSITY OF CALIFORNIA, BERKELEY
2200 University Avenue, #3540, Berkeley CA 94720. 510/642-6000. **Contact:** Human Resources. **E-mail address:** applyucb@uclink.berkeley.edu. **World Wide Web address:** http://www.berkeley.edu. **Description:** A university offering undergraduate and graduate programs in various liberal arts and professional fields. The university is a leader in teaching, research, and public service. Undergraduate divisions include the colleges of Chemistry, Engineering, Environmental Design, Letters and Science, and Natural Resources. Founded in 1868. **NOTE:** Apply online. To contact Human Resources call: 510/643-4443. **Positions advertised include:** Lecturer, Women's Studies; Scholarship Assistant; Programmer Analyst; Executive Assistant; Academic Affairs Coordinator; Prospect Development Director; Staff Research Associate; Human Resources Manager. **Operations at this facility include:** Administration; Research and Development.

UNIVERSITY OF CALIFORNIA, DAVIS
Employment Office, One Shields Avenue, Davis CA 95616. 530/752-0530. **Recorded jobline:** 530/752-1760. **Contact:** Personnel. **E-mail address:** apply@ucdavis.edu. **World Wide Web address:** http://www.ucdavis.edu. **Description:** A university offering various degrees through its colleges of Agricultural and Environmental Sciences, Engineering, and Letters and Science; Graduate School of Management; School of Law; School of Medicine; and School of Veterinary Medicine. **Positions advertised include:** Local Government Relations Director; Federal Government Relations Director; Director of Corporate Relations; Nursery Technician; Laboratory Assistant; Database Programmer.

UNIVERSITY OF CALIFORNIA, IRVINE
Berkeley Place, Suite 1000, Irvine CA 92697-4600. 949/824-5210. **Fax:** 949/824-4065. **Contact:** Human Resources. **E-mail address:** hrquestions@uci.edu. **World Wide Web address:** http://www.uci.edu. **Description:** A research university that is part of the University of California system. University of California, Irvine offers bachelors, masters, and doctoral degrees. **NOTE:** Part-time positions are offered. **Positions advertised include:** Custodian; Student Affairs Director; Fire Safety Program Manager; Laboratory Assistant; Counseling Psychologist. **Special programs:** Summer Jobs. **Operations at this facility include:** Administration; Research and Development; Service. **Number of employees at this location:** 5,000.

UNIVERSITY OF CALIFORNIA, LOS ANGELES
10920 Wilshire Boulevard, Suite 205, Los Angeles CA 90024-6504. 310/794-0890. **Fax:** 310/794-0895. **Recorded jobline:** 310/825-9151. **Contact:** Employment Services. **E-mail address:** mycareer@ucla.edu. **World Wide Web address:** http://www.chr.ucla.edu. **Description:** A campus of the state university system offering undergraduate and graduate degree programs. **NOTE:** Part-time positions are offered. **Company slogan:** UCLA - The University of Big Ideas. **Positions advertised include:** Database Developer; Programmer Analyst; Senior Custodian; Auditor; Police Officer; Laboratory Assistant; Student Affairs Officer. **Special programs:** Internships. **Corporate headquarters location:** This location. **Number of employees at this location:** 18,000.

UNIVERSITY OF CALIFORNIA, RIVERSIDE
1160 University Avenue, Suite C, Riverside CA 92521. 951/827-5627. **Fax:** 909/787-6493. **Contact:** Sheila Morris, Director of Academic Personnel. **E-mail address:** smorris@admin.ucr.edu. **World Wide Web address:** http://www.ucr.edu. **Description:** A campus of the state university system. **Positions advertised include:** Administrative Assistant; Graduate Assistant; Cook; Security Guard; Budget Director; Career Services Coordinator; Dental Hygienist; IT Manager; Orientation Coordinator; Security Analyst; Senior Human Resources Analyst. **Special programs:** Internships. **Operations at this facility include:** Research and Development; Service. **Number of employees at this location:** 2,500.

UNIVERSITY OF CALIFORNIA, SAN DIEGO
9500 Gilman Drive, Mail Code 0922, La Jolla CA 92093-0922. 858/534-2812. **Physical address:** 10280 North Torrey Pines Road, Suite 266, La Jolla CA 92093. **Contact:** Human Resources. **World Wide Web address:** http://www.ucsd.edu. **Description:** A campus of the state university system offering undergraduate and graduate programs. **Positions advertised include:** Cosmos Program Manager; Administrative Specialist; Laboratory Assistant; Fund Manager; Human Resources Specialist; Dean of Student Affairs.

UNIVERSITY OF CALIFORNIA, SAN FRANCISCO
3333 California Street, Suite 305, San Francisco CA 94143. 415/476-9000. **Fax:** 415/476-4672. **Contact:** Human Resources. **World Wide Web address:** http://www.ucsf.edu. **Description:** A medical teaching university and hospital offering degrees in dentistry, general medicine, nursing; pharmacology and research. **NOTE:** See website for job listings and application procedures. Interested jobseekers must apply online. **Special programs:** Internship. **Office hours:** Monday – Friday, 8:00 a.m. – 5:00 p.m.

UNIVERSITY OF CALIFORNIA, SANTA BARBARA
Human Resources Office, 3101 Student Affairs & Administrative Services Building, Santa Barbara CA 93106-3160. 805/893-7261. **Fax:** 805/893-8645. **Contact:** Employment Manager. **E-mail address:** hr.web@hr.ucsb.edu. **World Wide Web address:** http://www.ucsb.edu. **Description:** A campus of the state university system offering undergraduate and graduate degree programs. **NOTE:** Apply online. Paper applications are no longer accepted. **Positions advertised include:** Senior Cook; Information Systems Manager; Graduate Program Assistant; Computer Resource Specialist.

UNIVERSITY OF CALIFORNIA, SANTA CRUZ
1156 High Street, Santa Cruz CA 95064. 831/459-2009. **Recorded jobline:** 831/459-2011. **Contact:** Personnel Office. **World Wide Web address:** http://www.ucsc.edu. **Description:** This campus of the University of California emphasizes undergraduate education in the arts and sciences. The university has an undergraduate enrollment of approximately 11,000 and a graduate enrollment of approximately 1,000. **Positions advertised include:** Programmer Analyst; Administrative Assistant; Financial/Purchasing Assistant; Assistant Department Manager, Engineering; Academic Counselor.

UNIVERSITY OF SAN FRANCISCO
2130 Fulton Street, San Francisco CA 94117-1080. 415/422-6707. **Fax:** 415/386-1074. **Contact:** Human Resources. **E-mail address:** resumes@usfca.edu. **World Wide Web address:** http://www.usfca.edu. **Description:** Established as one of San Francisco's first universities, the University of San Francisco serves approximately 8,000 students in the schools of arts and sciences, business, education, nursing, law, and professional studies. The university is a nonprofit, private, Catholic and Jesuit institution. Founded in 1855. **Positions advertised include:** Associate Director, Research; Assistant Women's Track Coach; Assistant Registrar; Financial Analyst; First Assistant Athletic Trainer; Library Assistant. **Corporate headquarters location:** This location. **Other area locations:** Cupertino CA; Sacramento CA; San Ramon CA; Santa Rosa CA. **Operations at this facility include:** Administration. **President:** Father Stephen A. Privett, S.J. **Number of employees at this location:** 1,100.

UNIVERSITY OF SOUTHERN CALIFORNIA
3535 South Figueroa Street, Suite 100, Los Angeles CA 90089-1260. 213/740-7252. **Contact:** Employment Manager. **World Wide Web address:** http://www.usc.edu. **Description:** A private university offering bachelor's, master's, doctoral, and professional degrees to approximately 28,000 students. **NOTE:** Candidates must apply online. **Positions advertised include:** Account Representative; Administrative Assistant; Administrative Services Coordinator; Biller; Child Care Teacher; Community Service Officer; Computer Scientist; Office Assistant; Research Associate; Receptionist. **Office hours:** Monday – Friday, 9:30 a.m. – 3:00 p.m. **Corporate headquarters location:** This location. **Operations at this facility include:** Administration; Research and Development; Service.

UNIVERSITY OF THE PACIFIC
3601 Pacific Avenue, Stockton CA 95211. 209/946-2124. **Fax:** 209/946-2835. **Contact:** Human Resources. **E-mail address:** jobs@pacific.edu. **World Wide Web address:** http://www.uop.edu. **Description:** A four-year university offering undergraduate and graduate degree programs. **Positions advertised include:** Community Service Officer; Dental Assistant; Assistant Baseball Coach; University Budget Manager; Development Research Analyst; Financial Aid Technician; Archivist; Staff Psychologist; Systems Administrator; Police Officer. **Office hours:** Monday – Friday, 8:30 a.m. – 5:00 p.m.

UNOCAL
2141 Rosecrans Avenue, Suite 4000, El Segundo CA 90245. 310/726-7600. **Contact:** Annette Martin, Human Resources. **World Wide Web address:** http://www.unocal.com. **Description:** Explores, produces, refines, and markets petroleum and natural gas products; produces geothermal energy; manufactures gasoline, lubricant, asphalt, chemicals, and waxes; and mines minerals. **Corporate headquarters location:** This location. **Operations at this facility include:** Administration; Divisional Headquarters; Regional Headquarters. **Listed on:** New York Stock Exchange. **Stock exchange symbol:** UCL.

VACCO INDUSTRIES
10350 Vacco Street, South El Monte CA 91733-3399. 626/443-7121. **Fax:** 626/450-6486. **Contact:** Director of Human Resources. **E-mail address:** hr@vacco.com. **World Wide Web address:** http://www.vacco.com. **Description:** Manufactures high-technology valves and screens used on submarines. **Positions advertised include:** Director, Quality Assurance; Laser Technician. **Corporate headquarters location:** This location. **Parent company:** ESCO Electronics Corporation (St. Louis MO) is a diversified producer of defense systems and commercial products sold to a variety of customers worldwide. ESCO's products are broadly defined as electronic products, valves and filters, mobile tactical systems, armament systems, automatic test equipment, utility load management equipment, and anechoic/shielding systems. ESCO's other operating subsidiaries include Distribution Control Systems, Inc., EMC Test Systems. L.P., PTI Technologies, Inc., Rantec Microwave & Electronics, Comtrak Technologies, Inc., Filtertek Inc., and Lindgren RF Enclosures. **Listed on:** New York Stock Exchange. **Stock exchange symbol:** ESE.

VAGABOND INNS CORPORATION
5933 West Century Boulevard, Suite 200, Los Angeles CA 90045. 310/410-5700. **Fax:** 310/410-5771. **Contact:** Personnel. **E-mail address:** svalentino@vagabondinns.com. **World Wide Web address:** http://www.vagabondinns.com. **Description:** Owns and operates hotels. **Corporate headquarters location:** This location. **Operations at this facility include:** Administration; Sales; Service.

VARIAN MEDICAL SYSTEMS
3100 Hansen Way, Palo Alto CA 94304. 650/424-5700. **Fax:** 650/493-4636. **Contact:** Human Resources. **E-mail address:** corpresumes@us.varian.com. **World Wide Web address:** http://www.varian.com. **Description:** A diversified, international manufacturing company. Varian operates manufacturing facilities in seven countries and sales and service offices worldwide. The company is organized around the following core businesses: Health Care Systems, Instruments, Electronic Devices, and Semiconductor Equipment. Varian provides medical linear accelerators, treatment stimulators, and information management systems to hospitals and clinics worldwide. The company is a leading supplier of X-ray tubes for imaging systems of all types, as well as instruments that help in the treatment of diseases such as AIDS. Varian instruments also regulate the quality of a wide range of products, including petroleum, pharmaceuticals, ice cream, and champagne, and its vacuum pumps and leak detectors are used to create a vacuum environment. Varian is a worldwide leader in the manufacture of devices that generate, amplify, and define signals for radio and television broadcasting and satellite communications. They are also used in air traffic control, navigation, radar, fusion energy, and other scientific research applications. **NOTE:** Contact information may vary according to position type. See job postings for more specific information. **Positions advertised include:** Internal Audit Director; Senior Software Engineer; Electrical Engineer; Senior Programmer Analyst; Senior Systems Analyst; Thin Film Master Technician. **Special programs:** Internships. **Corporate headquarters location:** This location. **Other U.S. locations:** AZ; MA; UT. **Listed on:** New York Stock Exchange. **Stock exchange symbol:** VAR. **Number of employees worldwide:** 3,000.

VARIAN MDICAL SYSTEMS
2700 Mitchell Drive, Walnut Creek CA 94598. 925/939-2400. **Contact:** Human Resources. **World Wide Web address:** http://www.varian.com. **Description:** A diversified, international manufacturing company. Varian operates manufacturing facilities in seven countries and sales and service offices worldwide. The company is organized around the following core businesses: Health Care Systems, Instruments, Electronic Devices, and Semiconductor Equipment. Varian provides medical linear accelerators, treatment stimulators, and information management systems to hospitals and clinics worldwide. The company is a leading supplier of X-ray tubes for imaging systems of all types, as well as instruments that help in the treatment of diseases such as AIDS. Varian instruments also regulate the quality of a wide range of products, including petroleum, pharmaceuticals, ice cream, and champagne, and its vacuum pumps and leak detectors are used to create a vacuum environment. Varian is a worldwide leader in the manufacture of devices that generate, amplify, and define signals for radio and television broadcasting and satellite communications. They are also used in air traffic control, navigation, radar, fusion energy, and other scientific research applications. **NOTE:** Contact information may vary according to position type. See job postings for more specific information. **Corporate headquarters location:** Palo Alto CA. **Other U.S. locations:** AZ; MA; UT. **Listed on:** New York Stock Exchange. **Stock exchange symbol:** VAR. **Number of employees worldwide:** 3,000.

VARIETY, INC.
5700 Wilshire Boulevard, Suite 120, Los Angeles CA 90036. 323/857-6600. **Contact:** Employment. **E-mail address:** hrlosangeles@cahners.com. **World Wide Web address:** http://www.variety.com. **Description:** Publishes a magazine that focuses on the entertainment and film industries. **Corporate headquarters location:** This location. **Parent company:** Reed Elsevier Inc.

VERANCE
4435 Eastgate Mall, Suite 350, San Diego CA 92121. 858/202-2800. **Fax:** 858/202-2801. **Contact:** Human Resources Staffing. **E-mail address:** jobs@verance.com. **World Wide Web address:** http://www.verance.com. **Description:** Creates software to manage the copyright and legal distribution of computerized audio and visual files. **NOTE:** See website for job listings. E-mail resumes. **Positions advertised include:** Database Development Engineer; Electro Mechanical Assembler; Hardware Configuration Manager; Systems Administrator; Watermark Engine Software Engineer. **Corporate headquarters location:** This location. **Other area locations:** Los Angeles CA. **Other U.S. locations:** NY; IL.

VERIFONE, INC.
2099 Gateway Place, Suite 600, San Jose CA 95110. 408/232-7800. **Fax:** 916/630-2566. **Contact:** Human Resources. **E-mail address:** jobs@verifone.com. **World Wide Web address:** http://www.verifone.com. **Description:** VeriFone develops, manufactures, and services software for electronic payment systems that are used in a variety of industries including consumer, financial, and health care. **Positions advertised include:** Controller of SEC Reporting; Controller Revenue Recognition. **Corporate headquarters location:** This location. **Parent company:** GTCR Golder Rauner.

VERITAS SOFTWARE CORPORATION
350 Ellis Street, Mountain View CA 94043. 650/527-8000. **Contact:** Human Resources. **E-mail address:** jobs@veritas.com. **World Wide Web address:** http://www.veritas.com. **Description:** Designs, develops, and markets enterprise data and storage management software. The company's products are designed to improve system performance and to reduce administration costs. **Positions advertised include:** Business Development Manager; Global Marketing Campaign Manager; Revenue Director; Intellectual Property Attorney; Product Manager; Senior Buyer; Senior Finance Manager. **Corporate headquarters location:** This location. **Listed on:** NASDAQ. **Stock exchange symbol:** VRTS.

VERITY INC.
894 Ross Drive, Sunnyvale CA 94089. 408/541-1500. **Contact:** Human Resources Department. **E-mail address:** resumes@verity.com. **World Wide Web address:** http://www.verity.com. **Description:** Develops and markets software tools and applications for searching, retrieving, and filtering information on the Internet. **Positions advertised include:** Marketing Programs Specialist; Senior Consultant; Principal Software Engineer. **Corporate headquarters location:** This location. **Listed on:** NASDAQ. **Stock exchange symbol:** VRTY.

VERIZON COMMUNICATIONS
112 South Lavkeview Canyon Road, Westlake Village CA 91362-3831. 805/372-6000. **Contact:** Human Resources. **World Wide Web address:** http://www.verizon.com. **Description:** A full-service communications services provider. Verizon offers residential local and long distance telephone services and Internet access; wireless service plans, cellular phones, and data services; a full-line of business services including Internet access, data services, and telecommunications equipment and services; and government network solutions including Internet access, data services, telecommunications equipment and services, and enhanced communications services. **Positions advertised include:** Transport Network Engineer; Systems Billing Analyst; Operator. **Corporate headquarters location:** New York NY. **Other U.S. locations:** Nationwide. **Listed on:** New York Stock Exchange. **Stock exchange symbol:** VZ.

VERIZON WIRELESS
15505 Sand Canyon Avenue, Irvine CA 92618. 949/286-7000. **Toll-free phone:** 800/575-4473. **Contact:** Frances Allen, Senior Recruiter. **World Wide Web address:** http://www.verizonwireless.com. **Description:** Verizon Communications is a full-service communications services provider. Verizon offers residential local and long distance telephone services and Internet access; wireless service plans, cellular phones, and data services; a full-line of business services including Internet access, data services, and telecommunications equipment and services; and government network solutions including Internet access, data services, telecommunications equipment and services, and enhanced communications services. **Corporate headquarters location:** New York NY. **Operations at this facility include:** This location provides wireless communication services to customers nationwide. **Listed on:** New York Stock Exchange. **Stock exchange symbol:** VZ.

VICAL INC.
10390 Pacific Center Court, San Diego CA 92121. 858/646-1100. **Fax:** 858/646-1150. **Contact:** Karen Blade, Senior Human Resources Specialist. **E-mail address:** hr@vical.com. **World Wide Web address:** http://www.vical.com. **Description:** Provides research and development services for DNA, gene therapy, cancer, AIDS, and malaria. **Positions advertised include:** Contract Administrator; Manufacturing Engineer; Research Scientist; Evniornmental Health and Safety Manager. **Corporate headquarters location:** This location. **Listed on:** NASDAQ. **Stock exchange symbol:** VICL.

VIACOM OUTDOOR
1731 Workman Street, Los Angeles CA 90031. 323/222-7171. **Contact:** Human Resources Department. **E-mail address:** humanresources@tdi-usa.com. **World Wide Web address:** http://www.tdiworldwide.com. **Description:** An advertising agency specializing in the design of billboards and posters. **Other U.S. locations:** Nationwide. **Parent company:** Viacom Corporation. **Listed on:** New York Stock Exchange. **Stock exchange symbol:** VIA.

VICTORVILLE, CITY OF
14343 Civic Drive, Victorville CA 92392-2399. 760/955-5000. **Recorded jobline:** 760/261-1508. **Contact:** Human Resources. **World Wide Web address:** http://www.ci.victorville.ca.us. **Description:** Municipal offices for the city of Victorville. **Special programs:** Internships. **Operations at this facility include:** Administration; Service. **Number of employees at this location:** 600.

VIEWSONIC CORPORATION
381 Brea Canyon Road, Walnut CA 91789. 909/444-8888. **Fax:** 909/468-1252. **Contact:** Human Resources. **World Wide Web address:** http://www.viewsonic.com. **Description:** Manufactures computer monitors, flat-panel displays, and projectors for the business, education, entertainment, and professional markets. **Corporate headquarters location:** This location. **Office hours:** Monday - Friday, 7:00 a.m. - 6:00 p.m. **CEO:** James Chu. **Number of employees at this location:** 400. **Number of employees worldwide:** Over 600.

VIKING OFFICE PRODUCTS
P.O. Box 61144, Los Angeles CA 90061. 310/225-4500. **Physical address:** 950 West 190th Street, Torrance CA 90502. **Contact:** Human Resources. **World Wide Web address:** http://www.vikingop.com. **Description:** One of the largest direct marketing companies selling office products to small and medium-sized businesses. **Corporate headquarters location:** This location. **Parent company:** Office Depot. **Listed on:** New York Stock Exchange. **Stock exchange symbol:** ODP. **Number of employees nationwide:** 1,065.

VIRCO MANUFACTURING CORPORATION
2027 Harpers Way, Torrance CA 90501. 310/533-0474. **Contact:** Anjelica Gamble, Personnel Director. **World Wide Web address:** http://www.virco-mfg.com. **Description:** Manufactures school and office furniture. **Corporate headquarters location:** This location. **Listed on:** American Stock Exchange. **Stock exchange symbol:** VIR.

VISA INTERNATIONAL
900 Metro Center Boulevard, Foster City CA 94404. 650/432-3200. **Fax:** 650/432-7436. **Contact:** Human Resources. **World Wide Web address:** http://www.international.visa.com. **Description:** One of the largest credit card companies in the world. Founded in 1976. **NOTE:** See website for job listings and apply online. **Other U.S. locations:** Nationwide. **International locations:** Worldwide. **Listed on:** Privately held. **Number of employees worldwide:** 6,000.

VISHAY INTERTECHNOLOGY
4051 Greystone Drive, Ontario CA 91761. 909/923-3313. **Fax:** 909/923-6765. **Contact:** Personnel Department. **World Wide Web address:** http://www.vishay.com. **Description:** Manufactures a variety of electronic components including semiconductors and passive components. **Corporate headquarters location:** Malvern PA. **Listed on:** New York Stock Exchange. **Stock exchange symbol:** VSH.

VISHAY SILICONIX INC.
2201 Laurelwood Road, Santa Clara CA 95054. 408/988-8000. **Contact:** Human Resources. **World Wide Web address:** http://www.vishay.com/brands/siliconix. **Description:** Manufactures semiconductor products. **Corporate headquarters location:** Malvern PA. **Listed on:** New York Stock Exchange. **Stock exchange symbol:** VSH.

VISION SERVICE PLAN
P.O. Box 997100, Sacramento CA 95899-7100. 916/851-5000. **Physical address:** 3333 Quality Drive, Rancho Cordova CA 95670. **Fax:** 916/851-4858. **Recorded jobline:** 916/851-4700. **Contact:** Corporate Recruiter. **E-mail address:** hreoc@vsp.com. **World Wide Web address:** http://www.vsp.com. **Description:** Sells and administers a prepaid vision care plan as an employee benefit. **NOTE:** Search and apply for positions online. **Positions advertised include:** Reimbursement Management Analyst; Market Research Analyst; Project Manager; Sales Administrator; Test Engineer; Web Communications Specialist. **Special programs:** Internships. **Corporate headquarters location:** This location. **Other U.S. locations:** Nationwide. **Subsidiaries include:** Altair Eyewear. **Operations at this facility include:** Administration; Research and Development; Sales; Service. **Listed on:** Privately held. **Number of employees at this location:** 1,000. **Number of employees nationwide:** Over 2,000.

VISIONEER, INC.
5673 Gibraltar Drive, Suite 150, Pleasanton CA 94588. 925/251-6300. **Fax:** 925/416-8604. **Contact:** Human Resources. **E-mail address:** careers@visioneer.com. **World Wide Web address:** http://www.visioneer.com. **Description:** Develops software for flatbed and sheet-fed scanners. **Office hours:** Monday - Friday, 8:00 a.m. - 5:00 p.m. **Corporate headquarters location:** This location. **CEO:** Larry Smart. **Annual sales/revenues:** $51 - $100 million.

VISTA DEL MAR CHILD & FAMILY SERVICES
3200 Motor Avenue, Los Angeles CA 90034. 310/836-1223. **Fax:** 310/842-9529. **Contact:** Human Resources Director. **E-mail address:** jobs@vistadelmar.org. **World Wide Web address:** http://www.vistadelmar.org. **Description:** A residential treatment facility for children up to 18 years of age. Vista del Mar Child & Family Services offers a variety of programs including chemical dependency treatment, therapeutic schooling, adoption and foster care services, and counseling on both inpatient and outpatient bases. **NOTE:** Second and third shifts are offered. **Positions advertised include:** Youth Counselor; Secretary; Foster Care/Adoptions Coordinator; Data Entry Technician. **Corporate headquarters location:** This location. **Number of employees at this location:** 300.

VISUAL MATRIX CORPORATION
3320 North San Fernando Boulevard, Burbank CA 91504. 818/843-4831. **Fax:** 818/843-6544. **Contact:** Human Resources. **E-mail address:** jobs@visual-matrix.com. **World Wide Web address:** http://www.visual-matrix.com. **Description:** A developer and manufacture of video signal processing technology. **Positions advertised:** Hardware Engineer; Electronics Engineer; Project Engineer; Firmware Designer; Software Designer.

VISX, INCORPORATED
3400 Central Expressway, Santa Clara CA 95051. 408/773-7321. **Toll-free phone:** 800/246-VISX. **Fax:** 408/773-7200. **Contact:** Human Resources Department. **E-mail address:** greatcareers@visx.com. **World Wide Web address:** http://www.visx.com. **Description:** Designs, manufactures, and markets technologies and systems for laser vision correction. Founded in 1986. **Positions advertised include:** Software Quality Assurance Engineer; Staff Mechanical Engineer; Software Engineer; Optical Engineer. **Corporate headquarters location:** This location. **Listed on:** New York Stock Exchange. **Stock exchange symbol:** EYE. **Annual sales/revenues:** $144 million.

VITESSE SEMICONDUCTOR CORPORATION
741 Calle Plano, Camarillo CA 93012. 805/388-3700. **Toll-free phone:** 800/848-9773. **Contact:** Human Resources. **World Wide Web address:** http://www.vitesse.com. **Description:** Designs and manufactures software systems used in a variety of electronic industries. Founded in 1984. **NOTE:** See website for job listings. Apply online. Entry-level positions are offered. **Positions advertised include:** Process Engineering Technician; Systems Architecture; Technical Writer; Assembly Engineer; Key Accounts Manager; Systems Engineering Technician; Product Marketing Manager. **Corporate headquarters location:** This location. **Other U.S. locations:** MA; CO; TX; NJ. **Listed on:** NASDAQ. **Stock exchange symbol:** VTSS. **Number of employees worldwide:** 800.

VIVENDI UNIVERSAL GAMES
6080 Center Drive, 10th Floor, Los Angeles CA 90045. 310/431-4000. **Contact:** Corporate Recruiter. **E-mail address:** careers@vugames.com. **World Wide Web address:** http://www.vugames.com. **Description:** A publisher and distributor of multimedia educational and entertainment software for both the home and school markets. **Special programs:** Internships. **Corporate headquarters location:** This location. **Listed on:** New York Stock Exchange. **Stock exchange symbol:** VE.

VOITH PAPER AUTOMATION
162 Knowles Drive, Los Gatos CA 95032. 408/379-0910. **Fax:** 408/379-7275. **Contact:** Susan Rice, Human Resources. **E-mail address:** susan.rice@voith.com. **World Wide Web address:** http://www.voithpaper.com. **Description:** Develops, manufactures, sells, and services a wide variety of computer-based measurement and control systems to the paper industry. Impact's cross-direction (CD) measurement and control systems reduce CD variations in key variables occurring in the production of virtually all grades of paper. Founded in 1980. **Corporate headquarters location:** This location.

VOLCANO THERAPEUTICS, INC.
2870 Kilgore Road, Rancho Cordova CA 95670. 916/638-8008. **Fax:** 916/638-8239. **Contact:** Human Resources. **E-mail address:** jobs@volcanotherapeutics.com. **World Wide Web address:** http://www.volcanotherapeutics.com. **Description:** Manufactures medical devices that aid in the detection of diseases of the coronary arteries and vascular system. **Positions advertised include:** Signal Processing Engineer; R&D Engineer; Production Planner; Production Supervisor; Manager, Quality Assurance. **Special programs:** Internships. **Corporate headquarters location:** This location. **International locations:** Brussels Belgium.

THE VONS COMPANIES, INC.
P.O. Box 513338, Los Angeles CA 90051-1338. 626/821-7000. **Physical address:** 618 South Michillinda Avenue, Arcadia CA 91007. **Contact:** Human Resources. **World Wide Web address:** http://www.vons.com. **Description:** One of the largest operators of supermarkets and drugstores in Southern California. Vons's Super Combo stores offer video rental, dry cleaning, and photo development services in addition to traditional grocery store and drugstore products. Vons owns five EXPO stores that offer discount drugs and warehouse foods; operates a milk-processing plant; and manages ice cream, delicatessen, meat processing, and baking facilities. **NOTE:** Search and apply for positions online. **Corporate headquarters location:** This location. **Parent company:** Safeway, Inc. **Listed on:** New York Stock Exchange. **Stock exchange symbol:** SWY.

VULCAN MATERIALS COMPANY
P.O. Box 2950, Los Angeles CA 90051. 323/258-2777. **Physical address:** 3200 San Fernando Road, Los Angeles CA 90065. **Fax:** 323/258-1583. **Contact:** Human Resources. **E-mail address:** careers_ca@vmcmail.com. **World Wide Web address:** http://www.vulcanmaterials.com. **Description:** Engaged in the business of extracting, processing, and selling rock, sand, and gravel, either in aggregate form, as ready-mixed concrete, or as asphaltic concrete. **NOTE:** Search and apply for positions online. **Positions advertised include:** Environmental Manager. **Corporate headquarters location:** Birmingham AL. **Other area locations:** San Francisco CA; Ventura CA. **Listed on:** New York Stock Exchange. **Stock exchange symbol:** VMC. **Number of employees worldwide:** 9,000.

WD-40 COMPANY
1061 Cudahy Place, San Diego CA 92110-3929. 619/275-1400. **Toll-free phone:** 800/448-9340. **Fax:** 619/275-5823. **Contact:** Human Resources. **World Wide Web address:** http://www.wd40.com. **Description:** Manufactures and markets WD-40, a petroleum-based industrial lubricant spray. WD-40 is also a rust preventative, a penetrant, and a moisture displacer. **Corporate headquarters location:** This location. **Listed on:** NASDAQ. **Stock exchange symbol:** WDFC. **Number of employees at this location:** 140.

WFS FINANCIAL
15750 Alton Parkway, Irvine CA 92618. 949/727-1000. **Contact:** Human Resources. **E-mail address:** employment@wfsfinancial.com. **World Wide Web address:** http://www.wfb.com. **Description:** A financial services holding company that operates throughout the West Coast. **Positions advertised include:** Special Activities Associate; Compensation Coordinator; IRA Specialist; Senior Product Development Manager. **Corporate headquarters location:** This location. **Parent company:** Westcorp. **Listed on:** NASDAQ. **Stock exchange symbol:** WFSI. **Number of employees at this location:** 350. **Number of employees nationwide:** 1,200.

WALLACE TRANSPORT INC.
9290 East Highway 140, P.O. Box 67, Planada CA 95365. 209/382-0131. **Fax:** 209/382-1235. **Contact:** Dixie Allred, Director of Personnel & Safety. **World Wide Web address:** http://www.wallacetransport.com. **Description:** A common carrier trucking firm. **Corporate headquarters location:** This location. **Other area locations:** Fresno CA; Rancho Cucamonga CA.

WARNER BROS. STUDIOS (WB TELEVISION NETWORK)
4000 Warner Boulevard, Burbank CA 91522. 818/954-6000. **Recorded jobline:** 818/954-5400. **Contact:** Human Resources. **World Wide Web address:** http://www.warnerbros.com. **Description:** An entertainment/film production company. The company also operates a television network with nationwide affiliates. **NOTE:** Search and apply for positions online. **Positions advertised include:** Traffic Adiminstrator; Finance Coordinator; Manager, Graphics Production; Freelance Online Producer; Freelance Avid Editor; Freelance Writer/Producer. **Corporate headquarters location:** This location. **Parent company:** Time Warner. **Listed on:** New York Stock Exchange. **Stock exchange symbol:** TWX. **Annual sales/revenues:** $6.9 billion.

WASHINGTON HOSPITAL
2000 Mowry Avenue, Fremont CA 94538. 510/791-3409. **Toll-free phone:** 800/963-7070. **Fax:** 510/745-6470. **Contact:** Personnel Services. **E-mail address:** careers@whhs.com. **World Wide Web address:** http://www.whhs.com. **Description:** A general, acute care hospital that offers a community cancer program, health insurance information services, occupational medicine, and joint replacement services. **Positions advertised include:** Cardiac Sonographer; Clinical Laboratory Scientist; Budget Manager; Case Manager; Radiological Technologist; Physical Therapist; Registered Nurse; Licensed Vocational Nurse.

WASHINGTON MUTUAL
3701 Wilshire Boulevard, Los Angeles CA 90010-2810. 213/252-4320. **Contact:** Human Resources. **World Wide Web address:** http://www.wamuhomeloans.com. **Description:** Originates, acquires, sells, and services mortgage loans, principally first lien mortgage loans secured by single-family residences. North American Mortgage also sells servicing rights associated with a portion of such loans. The company operates through a network of 50 loan origination offices in 14 states, primarily in California and Texas. **Parent company:** Washington Mutual Bank. **Listed on:** New York Stock Exchange. **Stock exchange symbol:** WM.

WASTE MANAGEMENT, INC.
1970 East 213th Street, Long Beach CA 90249. 310/605-6000. **Contact:** Human Resources. **E-mail address:** careers@wm.com. **World Wide Web address:** http://www.wastemanagement.com. **Description:** Engaged in commercial and residential refuse removal. **NOTE:** Search and apply for positions online. **Corporate headquarters location:** Oak Brook IL. **Other U.S. locations:** Nationwide. **Listed on:** New York Stock Exchange. **Stock exchange symbol:** WMI.

WASTE MANAGEMENT, INC.
1675 Rogers Avenue, San Jose CA 95112. 408/392-3000. **Contact:** Human Resources. **E-mail address:** careers@wm.com. **World Wide Web address:** http://www.wastemanagement.com. **Description:** Engaged in commercial and residential refuse removal. **NOTE:** Search and apply for positions online. **Corporate headquarters location:** Oak Brook IL. **Listed on:** New York Stock Exchange. **Stock exchange symbol:** WMI.

WATERMAN INDUSTRIES INC.
25500 Route 204, P.O. Box 458, Exeter CA 93221. 559/562-4000. **Toll-free phone:** 800/331-0808. **Fax:** 559/562-2277. **Contact:** Personnel Department. **World Wide Web address:** http://www.watermanusa.com. **Description:** Manufactures water and flow control valves and irrigation equipment. **Corporate headquarters location:** This location.

WATSON PHARMACEUTICALS, INC.
311 Bonnie Circle, Corona CA 92880. 951/493-5300. **Fax:** 951/493-5836. **Contact:** Human Resources. **World Wide Web address:** http://www.watsonpharm.com. **Description:** Produces and distributes off-patent and proprietary pharmaceuticals such as analgesics, dermatological, primary care, antihypertensive, hormonal, generic, and central nervous system treatments. **NOTE:** Search and apply for positions online. **Positions advertised include:** Project Manager; Chemist; Senior Clinical Research Associate; Warehouse Operator; Finance Manager; Laboratory Technician; General Maintenance Mechanic. **Corporate headquarters location:** This location. **Subsidiaries include:** Circa Pharmaceuticals, Inc.; Oclassen Pharmaceuticals, Inc.; Watson Laboratories, Inc. **Listed on:** New York Stock Exchange. **Stock exchange symbol:** WPI. **CEO:** Dr. Allen Chao.

WAUSAU MORTGAGE CORPORATION
5820 Stoneridge Mall Road, Pleasanton CA 94588. 925/463-9200. **Contact:** Human Resources. **World Wide Web address:** http://www.wausau.com. **Description:** Sells casualty, property, and other commercial insurance products to medium- and large-sized companies. **Corporate headquarters location:** Wausau WI.

WEBER SHANDWICK INTERNATIONAL
440 Pacific Avenue, San Francisco CA 94133. 415/248-3400. **Contact:** Human Resources. **E-mail address:** jobssanfrancisco@webershandwick.com. **World Wide Web address:** http://www.webershandwick.com. **Description:** A global, full-service public relations and marketing communications agency. This office specializes in serving the Silicon Valley and San Francisco Bay area. **NOTE:** E-mail resume and cover letter to this location. Indicate desired employment position. **Corporate headquarters location:** New York NY.

WEDBUSH MORGAN SECURITIES
P.O. Box 30014, Los Angeles CA 90030. 213/688-8000. **Physical address:** 1000 Wilshire Boulevard, 9th Floor, Los Angeles CA 90017. **Contact:** Human Resources Department. **E-mail address:** hrd@wedbush.com. **World Wide Web address:** http://www.wedbush.com. **Description:** An investment banking securities brokerage. **NOTE:** Search and apply for positions online. **Positions advertised include:** Equity Research Analyst; Senior Associate, Financial Services; Director of Research; Institutional Equity Sales. **Special programs:** Internships. **Corporate headquarters location:** This location. **Listed on:** Privately held. **Number of employees at this location:** 270. **Number of employees nationwide:** 510.

WEIGH-TRONIX, INC.
3990 Brickway Boulevard, Santa Rosa CA 95403-1098. 707/527-5555. **Fax:** 707/579-1655. **Contact:** Human Resources Manager. **E-mail address:** employment@weigh-tronix.com. **World Wide Web address:** http://www.weigh-tronix.com. **Description:** Manufactures electronic weighing systems, thermal and impact printers, POS scales, mailing systems, and related products. **Corporate headquarters location:** Norwalk CT. **Other U.S. locations:** Nationwide. **Parent company:** Staveley. **Operations at this facility include:** Administration; Divisional Headquarters; Manufacturing; Research and Development; Sales; Service. **Listed on:** Privately held. **Number of employees at this location:** 85. **Number of employees nationwide:** 1,000.

WELLPOINT HEALTH NETWORKS INC.
5151 Camino Ruiz, #A, Camarillo CA 93012. 818/234-2345. **Contact:** Human Resources. **E-mail address:** employment@wellpoint.com. **World Wide Web address:** http://www.wellpoint.com. **Description:** Provides health and life insurance through Blue Cross of California and UNICARE. **Positions advertised include:** Clinical Operations Specialist; Sr. Network Specialist; Compliance Director; Field Operations Director; Sr. Financial Analyst. **Corporate headquarters location:** Indianapolis IN. **Listed on:** New York Stock Exchange. **Stock exchange symbol:** WLP. **Number of employees nationwide:** 20,000.

WELLS FARGO & COMPANY
420 Montgomery Street, San Francisco CA 94163. 800/869-3557. **Contact:** Recruitment Services. **World Wide Web address:** http://www.wellsfargo.com. **Description:** A diversified financial institution. Wells Fargo serves over 17 million customers through 5,300 independent locations worldwide. The company also maintains several stand-alone ATMs and branches within retail outlets. Services include community banking, credit and debit cards, home equity and mortgage loans, online banking, student loans, and insurance. Wells Fargo also offers a complete line of commercial and institutional financial services. Founded in 1852. **Special programs:** Internships; Training; Summer Jobs. **Internship information:** The company offers summer internships only. **Corporate headquarters location:** This location. **Other U.S. locations:** Nationwide. **International locations:** Worldwide. **Listed on:** New York Stock Exchange. **Stock exchange symbol:** WFC. **President/CEO:** Dick Kovacevich. **Annual sales/revenues:** $31.8 billion. **Number of employees worldwide:** 140,000.

WELLS FARGO FOOTHILL
2450 Colorado Avenue, Suite 300W, Santa Monica CA 90404. 800/535-1811. **Contact:** Human Resources. **World Wide Web address:** http://www.wffoothill.com. **Description:** One of the largest publicly owned commercial lenders in the nation. The company operates two businesses: commercial lending and money management. **NOTE:** Search and apply for positions online. **Positions advertised include:** Loan Portfolio Manager; Financial Analyst; Treasury Analyst; Communications Administrative Coordinator; Loan Closer; Senior Account Executive. **Corporate headquarters location:** This location. **Parent company:** Wells Fargo & Company.

WEMS ELECTRONICS INC.
4650 West Rosecrans Avenue, Hawthorne CA 90250. 310/644-0251. **Fax:** 310/644-5334. **Contact:** Theresa Sunbury, Personnel Manager. **World Wide Web address:** http://www.wems.com. **Description:** Specializes in box-build turnkey manufacturing. Current programs include electrical, electro-mechanical, pneumatic, hydraulic, and mechanical components as well as high-level electronics. Founded in 1960. **Office hours:** Monday - Friday, 8:00 a.m. - 5:00 p.m. **Corporate headquarters location:** This location. **Listed on:** Privately held. **President:** Carroll Whitney. **Number of employees at this location:** 120.

WENTZ GROUP
555 Twin Dolphin Drive, Suite 160, Redwood Shores CA 94065. 650/592-3950. **Fax:** 650/593-5632. **Contact:** Human Resources. **E-mail address:** elizabethb@wentzgroup.com. **World Wide Web address:** http://www.wentzgroup.com. **Description:** Provides general construction services. **Positions advertised include:** Sr. Project Manager; Project Executive; Superintendent; Estimator; Project Manager. **Corporate headquarters location:** This location. **Other area locations:** Sacramento CA; Newport Beach CA. **Listed on:** Privately held. **Number of employees at this location:** 30.

WESGO CERAMICS
2425 Whipple Road, Hayward CA 94544. 510/491-1100. **Fax:** 510/491-1175. **Contact:** Human Resources. **World Wide Web address:** http://www.wesgo.com. **Description:** Manufactures ceramic products for chemical, electrical, mechanical, and vacuum applications. **Parent company:** Morgan Crucible Company plc (Berkshire UK).

WEST COAST LIFE INSURANCE COMPANY
343 Sansome Street, San Francisco CA 94104. 415/591-8200. **Toll-free phone:** 800/366-9378. **Contact:** Personnel Manager. **E-mail address:** plc@resumescanning.com. **World Wide Web address:** http://www.westcoastlife.com. **Description:** Offers a complete range of life insurance services. Founded in 1906. **Positions advertised include:** Customer Service Associate. **Office hours:** Monday - Friday, 7:30 a.m. - 4:30 p.m. **Corporate headquarters location:** This location. **Parent company:** Protective Life Insurance. **President/CEO/Owner:** Jim Massengale. **Number of employees at this location:** 150.

WEST GROUP
50 California Street, 18th Floor, San Francisco CA 94111. 415/732-8888. **Fax:** 415/732-8840. **Contact:** Human Resources Manager. **World Wide Web address:** http://www.westgroup.com. **Description:** Publishes legal research information in CD-ROM and book formats for law practitioners and the judiciary. **NOTE:** Search and apply for positions online. **Positions advertised include:** Account Representative; Marketing Manager. **Corporate headquarters location:** Eagan MN. **Other U.S. locations:** Stamford CT. **Parent company:** Thomson Corporation. **Number of employees at this location:** 200.

WESTAMERICA BANK
1108 Fifth Avenue, San Rafael CA 94901. 415/257-8500. **Recorded jobline:** 707/863-6400. **Contact:** Human Resources. **E-mail address:** recruiting@westamerica.com. **World Wide Web address:** http://www.westamerica.com. **Description:** Offers a wide range of general commercial banking services including money market accounts, NOW accounts, checking accounts, savings accounts, and certificates of deposit. **NOTE:** Resumes may be submitted by fax, mail, or e-mail. Send resumes to: Westamerica Bancorporation, Recruiting Department (A-1S), P.O. Box 1200, Suisun City CA 94585. Fax: 707/863-6887. **Corporate headquarters location:** This location. **Listed on:** NASDAQ. **Stock exchange symbol:** WBKC.

WESTEC PLASTICS CORPORATION
6757-A Las Positas Road, Livermore CA 94550. 925/454-3400. **Fax:** 925/454-3410. **Contact:** Lucy Solorio, Human Resources. **E-mail address:** lsolorio@westecplastics.com. **World Wide Web address:** http://www.westecplastics.com. **Description:** Engaged in plastic injection molding for a variety of original equipment manufacturers.

WESTED
730 Harrison Street, San Francisco CA 94107. 415/565-3000. **Toll-free phone:** 877/493-7833. **Fax:** 415/565-3012. **Contact:** Personnel Manager. **E-mail address:** jobs@wested.org. **World Wide Web address:** http://www.wested.org. **Description:** WestEd is a nonprofit educational agency focused on improving the quality of education by helping policy makers and practitioners apply knowledge from research, development, and practice. Founded in 1966. **Positions advertised include:** Director, New Business Development; Contracts Assistant; Financial Assistant; Manager of Organizational Branding and Visibility; Program Assistant. **Corporate headquarters location:** This location. **Other U.S. locations:** Tucson AZ; Boston MA; Burlington VT; Washington DC. **Number of employees at this location:** 145. **Number of employees nationwide:** 165.

WESTERN DIGITAL CORPORATION
20511 Lake Forest Drive, Lake Forest CA 92630. 949/672-7000. **Fax:** 949/672-5466. **Contact:** Director of Compensation. **E-mail address:** resumix@ripley.wdc.com. **World Wide Web address:** http://www.westerndigital.com. **Description:** Engaged in information storage management. Western Digital is a leader in manufacturing hard disk drives for servers, workstations, and individual computers. **NOTE:** Search and apply for positions online. **Positions advertised include:** Administrative Assistant; Engineering Program Director; Principal Engineering Software Developer; Senior Test Engineer; Lead Claims Processor. **Corporate headquarters location:** This location. **Other area locations:** Fremont CA; San Jose CA. **Listed on:** New York Stock Exchange. **Stock exchange symbol:** WDC.

WESTERN GROWERS ASSOCIATION
P.O. Box 2130, Newport Beach CA 92658. 949/863-1000. **Physical address:** 17620 Fitch Street, Irvine CA 92614. **Fax:** 949/863-9028. **Contact:** Karen Timmins, Vice President of Human Resources. **World Wide Web address:** http://www.wga.com. **Description:** An agricultural trade association providing services such as medical insurance, workers' compensation insurance, legal advice, and marketing services. Founded in 1926. **Corporate headquarters location:** This location. **Annual sales/revenues:** $51 - $100 million. **Number of employees at this location:** 250.

WESTERN OILFIELDS SUPPLY COMPANY
dba RAIN FOR RENT
P.O. Box 2248, Bakersfield CA 93303. 661/399-9124. **Physical address:** 3404 State Road, Bakersfield CA 93308. **Fax:** 661/399-1086. **Contact:** Human Resources

Director. **E-mail address:** careers@rainforrent.com. **World Wide Web address:** http://www.rainforrent.com. **Description:** Engaged in the rental, sale, and installation of liquid handling systems, pumps, tanks, and irrigation systems to industrial and agricultural customers. Founded in 1934. **NOTE:** Search for positions online. **Office hours:** Monday - Friday, 8:00 a.m. - 5:00 p.m. **Corporate headquarters location:** This location. **Other area locations:** Riverside CA. **Other U.S. locations:** Nationwide. **International locations:** Mexico. **Number of employees at this location:** 150. **Number of employees nationwide:** 435.

WESTWOOD ONE INC.
8968 Washington Boulevard, Culver City CA 90232. 310/840-4000. **Contact:** Human Resources. **World Wide Web address:** http://www.westwoodone.com. **Description:** A radio-broadcasting network that produces and distributes syndicated radio shows. **Corporate headquarters location:** New York NY. **Other U.S. locations:** Chicago IL; Detroit MI; Arlington VA. **Listed on:** New York Stock Exchange. **Stock exchange symbol:** WON.

WEYERHAEUSER COMPANY
140 West Santa Barbara Street, Santa Paula CA 93060. 805/5225-6651. **Contact:** Recruiting, Staffing & Diversity. **E-mail address:** resume@Weyerhaeuser.com. **World Wide Web address:** http://www.weyerhaeuser.com. **Description:** A forest management and manufacturing company. The company recycles pulp, paper, and packaging products; manufactures wood products; manages timberland; and develops real estate. **NOTE:** Search for positions online. **Corporate headquarters location:** Federal Way WA. **Other U.S. locations:** Nationwide. **Operations at this facility include:** Manufacturing; Sales. **Listed on:** New York Stock Exchange. **Stock exchange symbol:** WY.

WHEREHOUSE ENTERTAINMENT
2230 Carson Street, Carson CA 90810. 310/516-4221. **Fax:** 310/516-9057. **Contact:** Human Resources. **World Wide Web address:** http://www.wherehousemusic.com. **Description:** A retailer of prerecorded music and videos. **Special programs:** Internships. **Corporate headquarters location:** This location. **Subsidiaries include:** Leopolos; Odyssey; Paradise Music; Record Shop; Rocky Mountain Records. **Parent company:** Trans World Entertainment. **Listed on:** Privately held. **Number of employees at this location:** 230. **Number of employees nationwide:** Over 5,000.

WHITTAKER CONTROLS, INC.
12838 Saticoy Street, North Hollywood CA 91605. 818/765-8160. **Fax:** 818/759-2189. **Contact:** Human Resources. **World Wide Web address:** http://www.whittakercontrols.com. **Description:** Whittaker Controls is a market leader in the design and manufacture of a broad range of fluid control devices and systems for both commercial and military aircraft, as well as various industrial applications. Controls has been a leading supplier of these products since its formation in 1942. **Parent company:** Meggitt PLC.

WHITTIER COLLEGE
13406 Philadelphia Street, P.O. Box 634, Whittier CA 90608. 562/907-4208. **Fax:** 562/907-4884. **Recorded jobline:** 562/907-4850. **Contact:** Human Resources. **World Wide Web address:** http://www.whittier.edu. **Description:** A four year liberal arts college. Whittier was founded in 1887 by members of the Religious Society of Friends. The college was named in honor of the Quaker poet and abolitionist, John Greenleaf Whittier. **Office hours:** Monday – Friday, 8:00 a.m. – 5:00 p.m.

WIEGMANN & ROSE
P.O. Box 4187, Oakland CA 94614. 510/632-8828. **Physical address:** 9131 San Leandro Street, Oakland CA 94603. **Fax:** 510/632-8920. **Contact:** John Gasparini, Vice President of Human Resources. **E-mail address:** jgasparini@wiegmannandrose.com. **World Wide Web address:** http://www.wiegmannandrose.com. **Description:** Manufactures fabricated heat exchangers. **Corporate headquarters location:** This location.

WILBUR-ELLIS COMPANY
CONNELL BROS. COMPANY
345 California Street, 27th Floor, San Francisco CA 94104. 415/772-4000. **Fax:** 415/772-4011. **Contact:** Human Resources. **World Wide Web address:** http://www.wilburellis.com. **Description:** International merchants and distributors involved in importing and exporting goods. Wilbur-Ellis trades agricultural feed and chemical products. **Corporate headquarters location:** This location. **Operations at this facility include:** Administration.

WILLIAM MORRIS AGENCY, INC.
One William Morris Place, Beverly Hills CA 90212. 310/859-4000. **Fax:** 310/859-4205. **Contact:** Human Resources. **World Wide Web address:** http://www.wma.com. **Description:** One of the largest talent and literary agencies in the world. **NOTE:** Entry-level positions are offered. **Corporate headquarters location:** This location.

WILLIAMS-SONOMA, INC.
3250 Van Ness Avenue, San Francisco CA 94109. 415/421-7900. **Fax:** 415/616-8462. **Contact:** Human Resources. **World Wide Web address:** http://www.williams-sonomainc.com. **Description:** A retailer of cookware, serving equipment, and other specialty items. Products are sold both through retail stores and mail order catalogs with the following brand names: Williams-Sonoma, Hold Everything, Gardener's Eden, Pottery Barn, and Chambers. **NOTE:** Search and apply for positions online. **Positions advertised include:** QA Analyst; Assistant Buyer; Internet Creative Manager; Catalog Production Manager; Compensation Analyst; Senior Internal Auditor; Senior Financial Analyst; Merchandise Coordinator; Senior Liquidation Analyst; Front Desk Receptionist. **Corporate headquarters location:** This location. **Listed on:** New York Stock Exchange. **Stock exchange symbol:** WSM. **Number of employees at this location:** 1,400.

GEORGE H. WILSON, INC.
P.O. Box 1140, Santa Cruz CA 95061-1140. 831/423-9522. **Physical address:** 250 Harvey West Boulevard, Santa Cruz CA 95660. **Contact:** Administrative Manager. **Description:** Provides plumbing, heating, air conditioning, and metal fabrication services. **Corporate headquarters location:** This location. **Operations at this facility include:** Administration; Manufacturing.

WINBOND ELECTRONICS
2727 North First Street, San Jose CA 95134. 408/943-6666. **Fax:** 408/544-1784. **Contact:** Human Resources. **E-mail address:** usresume@winbond.com. **World Wide Web address:** http://www.winbond.com. **Description:** Designs, develops, and markets integrated circuit products for voice recording and playback using the company's proprietary ChipCorder high-density storage technology and mixed signal expertise. The company's products offer voice reproduction, low-power consumption, and batteryless storage in a single-chip solution. **Positions advertised include:** Staff Design Engineer; Senior Design Engineer; Senior Product Engineer; Applications Engineer; Sales Manager. **Corporate headquarters location:** This location.

WIND RIVER SYSTEMS
500 Wind River Way, Alameda CA 94501. 510/748-4100. **Fax:** 510/749-2302. **Contact:** Staffing Department. **E-mail address:** resumes@careers-windriver.com. **World Wide Web address:** http://www.wrs.com. **Description:** A software engineering and development firm. **Positions advertised include:** Alliance Marketing Manager; Compiler Engineer; Data Administrator; Editor; Flash Guru. **Corporate headquarters location:** This location. **Other area locations:** Sunnyvale CA. **Listed on:** NASDAQ. **Stock exchange symbol:** WIND.

WONDERWARE CORPORATION
26561 Rancho Parkway South, Lake Forest CA 92630. 949/727-3200. **Fax:** 949/639-1830. **Contact:** Employment. **E-mail address:** employment@wonderware.com. **World Wide Web address:** http://www.wonderware.com. **Description:** A developer of industrial applications software. **Positions advertised include:** Senior Software Development Engineer; Human Resources Consultant; Senior Technical Support Specialist; Principal Marketing Research Analyst. **Corporate headquarters location:** This location.

WORKRITE UNIFORM COMPANY, INC.
P.O. Box 1192, Oxnard CA 93032. 805/483-0175. **Physical address:** 500 East Third Street, Oxnard CA 93030. **Fax:** 805/483-7622. **Contact:** Human Resources. **World Wide Web address:** http://www.workrite.com. **Description:** An apparel manufacturer specializing in flame-retardant garments. Founded in 1973. **NOTE:** Workrite Uniform Company primarily hires sewing machine operators. Entry-level positions are offered. **Special programs:** This location also hires seasonally. **Office hours:** Monday - Friday, 7:30 a.m. - 4:00 p.m. **Corporate headquarters location:** This location. **Parent company:** Williamson-Dickie Manufacturing Company. **Operations at this facility include:** Administration; Manufacturing; Sales; Service. **Listed on:** Privately held. **Annual sales/revenues:** $21 - $50 million.

WORLD SAVINGS & LOAN ASSOCIATION
1901 Harrison Street, Oakland CA 94612. 510/446-6000. **Contact:** Human Resources. **World Wide Web address:** http://www.worldsavings.com. **Description:** One of the largest savings and loan associations in the United States, with more than 50 locations nationwide. **Positions advertised include:** Accountant; Associate Creative Director; Business Analyst; Department Assistant; Design Manager; Loan Closing Specialist; Loan Processor; Project Manager; tax Accountant; Senior Web Programmer. **Corporate headquarters location:** This location. **Other area locations:** Sacramento CA; San Francisco CA; Walnut Creek CA. **Other U.S. locations:** Nationwide. **Parent company:** Golden West Financial (also at this location). **Operations at this facility include:** Administration; Service. **Listed on:** New York Stock Exchange. **Stock exchange symbol:** GDW.

WYNDHAM HOTEL SAN JOSE
1350 North First Street, San Jose CA 95112. 408/453-6200. **Contact:** Personnel Assistant. **World Wide Web address:** http://www.wyndham.com. **Description:** Operates a full-service hotel with a wide range of facilities including convention facilities, meeting rooms, suites, three lounges, two restaurants and an exercise room. **Corporate headquarters location:** Dallas TX. **Parent company:** Wyndham International. **Listed on:** New York Stock Exchange. **Stock exchange symbol:** WYN.

WYNN OIL COMPANY
1050 West Fifth Street, Azusa CA 91702-9510. 626/334-0231. **Toll-free phone:** 800/989-8363. **Fax:** 626/334-1465. **Contact:** Human Resources. **E-mail address:** wynns_humanre@wynnsusa.com. **World Wide Web address:** http://www.wynnsusa.com. **Description:** Manufactures oil and gas additives. **Corporate headquarters location:** This location. **Parent company:** Wynn's International. **Operations at this facility include:** Administration; Manufacturing; Sales; Service.

WYSE TECHNOLOGY
3471 North First Street, San Jose CA 95134. 408/473-1200. **Fax:** 408/473-2080. **Contact:** Human Resources. **E-mail address:** wysejobs@wyse.com. **World Wide Web address:** http://www.wyse.com. **Description:** Manufactures workstations that access information from a server rather than from a hard drive. **NOTE:** Search and apply for positions online. **Positions advertised include:** Business Analyst; Network Engineer; Oracle Database Administrator. **Corporate headquarters location:** This location. **CEO:** Douglas Chance. **Facilities Manager:** Lee Perry.

XENCOR
111 West Lemon Avenue, Monrovia CA 91016. 626/305-5400. **Fax:** 626/305-0350. **Contact:** Recruiting. **E-mail address:** recruiting@xencor.com. **World Wide Web address:** http://www.xencor.com. **Description:** A biotechnology company that develops protein drugs. **Positions advertised:** Associate Director, Marketing; Senior Scientist.

XENOGEN CORPORATION
860 Atlantic Avenue, Alameda CA 94501. 510/291-6100. **Fax:** 510/291-6146. **Contact:** Human Resources. **E-mail address:** employment@xenogen.com. **World Wide Web address:** http://www.xenogen.com. **Description:** Offers real-time in vivo imaging services. Xenogen's in vivo biophotonic imaging system assists pharmaceutical companies in drug discovery and development. **Positions advertised include:** Research Associate. **Corporate headquarters location:** This location. **Other U.S. locations:** Cranbury NJ.

XILINX, INC.
2100 Logic Drive, San Jose CA 95124-3400. 408/559-7778. **Fax:** 408/559-7114. **Contact:** Ms. Chris Taylor, Vice President of Human Resources. **E-mail address:** jobs@xilinx.com. **World Wide Web address:** http://www.xilinx.com. **Description:** A leading supplier of field programmable gate arrays and related development system software used by electronic systems manufacturers. **NOTE:** Apply online. Hard copy resumes are not accepted. **NOTE:** Search for positions and submit resume online. **Positions advertised include:** Applications Engineer; Process Development Engineer; Product Engineer; Senior Research Engineer; Business Development Analyst; IT Architecture Intern; Corporate Paralegal; Web Publishing Specialist. **Special programs:** Internships. **Corporate headquarters location:** This location. **Operations at this facility include:** Administration; Manufacturing; Research and Development; Sales; Service. **Listed on:** NASDAQ. **Stock exchange symbol:** XLNX. **Number of employees at this location:** 850. **Number of employees worldwide:** 2,770.

XPEDX
1381 North 10th Street, San Jose CA 95112. 408/288-9280. **Contact:** Human Resources. **E-mail address:** xpedx.recruiting@xpedx.com. **World Wide Web**

address: http://www.xpedx.com. **Description:** Distributes paper and paper products; office supplies and equipment; packaging supplies and equipment; and consumables. **Other area locations:** Hayward CA.

YMCA OF THE EAST BAY
2330 Broadway, Oakland CA 94612. 510/451-8039. **Fax:** 510/987-7449. **Contact:** Human Resources Director. **World Wide Web address:** http://www.ymca.com. **Description:** The YMCA provides health and fitness; social and personal development; sports and recreation; education and career development; and camps and conferences to children, youths, adults, the elderly, families, the disabled, refugees and foreign nationals, YMCA residents, and community residents, through a broad range of specific programs. Founded in 1879. **NOTE:** Entry-level positions are offered. **Special programs:** Internships; Training. **Corporate headquarters location:** Chicago IL. **Other U.S. locations:** Nationwide. **Number of employees at this location:** 650. **Number of employees nationwide:** 20,000.

YAHOO! INC.
701 First Avenue, Sunnyvale CA 94089. 408/349-3300. **Fax:** 408/349-3301. **Contact:** Nancy Larocca, Staffing Manager. **World Wide Web address:** http://www.yahoo.com. **Description:** A global Internet communications, commerce, and media company that offers a comprehensive branded network of services to millions of users each month. Founded in 1994. **NOTE:** The company does not accept phone calls regarding employment. Search and apply for positions online. **Positions advertised include:** Senior Financial Analyst; Software Engineer; Corporate Development Manager; Business Development Manager; Marketing Director; Web Development Manager; Customer Care Agent; Senior Business Intelligence Engineer. **Special programs:** Internships. **Office hours:** Monday - Friday, 8:00 a.m. - 6:00 p.m. **Corporate headquarters location:** This location. **Other U.S. locations:** Nationwide. **International locations:** Worldwide. **Listed on:** NASDAQ. **Stock exchange symbol:** YHOO. **Number of employees at this location:** 1,300. **Number of employees worldwide:** 2,000.

YAMAHA MOTOR CORPORATION U.S.A.
6555 Katella Avenue, Cypress CA 90630. 714/761-7300. **Contact:** Personnel Department. **World Wide Web address:** http://www.yamaha-motor.com. **Description:** Distributes motorized products including motorcycles, ATVs, snowmobiles, golf carts, outboards, and power products. **NOTE:** Search for positions online. **Positions advertised include:** Quality Control Engineer/Inspector. **Corporate headquarters location:** This location.

YORK INTERNATIONAL CORPORATION
7020 Koll Center Parkway, Suite 110, Pleasanton CA 94566. 925/426-1144. **Fax:** 925/426-1188. **Contact:** Human Resources. **World Wide Web address:** http://www.york.com. **Description:** Manufactures a full-line of residential, commercial, and industrial air conditioning and refrigeration equipment and systems, heating systems, and food systems. The company recruits internationally and markets its products in over 110 countries through 42 exclusive distribution facilities, 10 co-owned centers, and over 200 wholesalers. **Corporate headquarters location:** York PA. **Listed on:** New York Stock Exchange. **Stock exchange symbol:** YRK.

YOUNG & RUBICAM WEST
303 2nd Street, 8th Floor South Tower, San Francisco CA 94107. 415/882-0600. **Fax:** 415/882-0601. **Contact:** Ms. Whitney Ball, Human Resources Manager. **World Wide Web address:** http://www.yr.com. **Description:** An international advertising agency. The company operates through three divisions: Young & Rubicam International; Marsteller Inc., a worldwide leader in business-to-business and consumer advertising; and Young & Rubicam USA, with 14 consumer advertising agencies operating through four regional groups (except Young & Rubicam Detroit), and five specialized advertising and marketing agencies. **Positions advertised include:** PT Finance Assistant; Account Executive. **Corporate headquarters location:** New York NY.

YOUNG'S MARKET COMPANY, LLC
2164 North Batavia Street, Orange CA 92865. 714/283-4933. **Toll-free phone:** 800/317-6150. **Contact:** Director of Human Resources. **World Wide Web address:** http://www.youngsmarket.com. **Description:** A beer, wine, and spirits distributor. Founded in 1888. **Corporate headquarters location:** This location. **Other U.S. locations:** AZ; CT; DC; FL; HI; MD; NY; PA; SC.

ZENDEX CORPORATION
6780A Sierra Court, Dublin CA 94568. 925/828-3000. **Fax:** 925/828-1574. **Contact:** Human Resources. **World Wide Web address:** http://www.zendex.com. **Description:** Manufactures a variety of computers, computer boards, and PCs for use in industrial applications. **Corporate headquarters location:** This location.

ZENITH INSURANCE COMPANY
21255 Califa Street. Woodland Hills CA 91367. 818/713-1000. **Fax:** 818/592-0265. **Contact:** Human Resources. **World Wide Web address:** http://www.zenithnational.com. **Description:** Provides Workers' Compensation insurance and reinsurance packages. Zenith Insurance Company also operates a homebuilding operation in Las Vegas NV and provides workers' compensation insurance. **Positions advertised include:** Director, Business Process Innovation; Quality Control Assurance Auditor; VP, e-Business Development; Director, Internal Audit; Sr. Underwriting Clerk. **Corporate headquarters location:** This location. **Other U.S. locations:** IL; PA; TX; UT. **Parent company:** Zenith National Insurance Corp. **Listed on:** New York Stock Exchange. **Stock exchange symbol:** ZNT. **Number of employees at this location:** 500. **Number of employees nationwide:** 850.

ZEP MANUFACTURING COMPANY
25224 South Shulte Road, Tracy CA 95377. 209/830-5110. **Contact:** Human Resources. **World Wide Web address:** http://www.zepmfg.com. **Description:** A manufacturer of specialty chemical products such as soaps, waxes, disinfectants, detergents, and insecticides. **NOTE:** Submit resume online. **Corporate headquarters location:** Atlanta GA. **Other U.S. locations:** Nationwide. **Parent company:** National Service Industries. **Listed on:** New York Stock Exchange. **Stock exchange symbol:** NSI.

ZILOG, INC.
532 Race Street, San Jose CA 95126. 408/558-8500. **Fax:** 408/558-8380. **Contact:** Human Resources. **E-mail address:** careers@zilog.com. **World Wide Web address:** http://www.zilog.com. **Description:** Designs, develops, manufactures, and markets application-specific standard integrated circuits products (ASSPs) for the data communications, intelligent peripheral controller, consumer product controller, and memory markets. **Positions advertised include:** Software Engineering Director; Analog Design Engineer; Design Manager; Senior Mixed-Signal Verification Engineer. **Corporate headquarters location:** This location. **Other U.S. locations:** Meridian ID; Bellevue WA. **Operations at this facility include:** Administration; Research and Development; Sales. **Number of employees at this location:** 250. **Number of employees nationwide:** 1,500.

ZURN-WILKINS
1747 Commerce Way, Paso Robles CA 93446-3696. 805/238-7100. **Fax:** 805/238-5766. **Contact:** Human Resources Department. **E-mail address:** human.resources@zurn.com. **World Wide Web address:** http://www.zurn.com. **Description:** Manufactures backflow prevention devices and residential, commercial, and industrial pressure-reducing and regulating valves and equipment as part of the Water Control segment of Zurn Industries. **Parent company:** Zurn Industries operates in three other industry segments as well. The Mechanical Power Transmission segment manufactures and markets clutches, couplings, and universal joints in the United States and Europe. The last segment, Lynx Golf, manufactures golf clubs in Nevada, which are finished and assembled in California, Mexico, and Scotland for distribution worldwide. **Corporate headquarters location:** Erie PA.

ZYMAX ENVIROTECHNOLOGY INC.
71 Zaca Lane, San Luis Obispo CA 93401-7300. 805/544-4696. **Fax:** 805/544-8226. **Contact:** Human Resources. **E-mail address:** employment@zymaxusa.com. **World Wide Web address:** http://www.zymaxusa.com. **Description:** A high tech environmental testing company. **Advertised positions:** Inorganics Laboratory Technician; Volatiles Laboratory Specialist; Geochemist.

ZYXEL COMMUNICATIONS INC.
1130 North Miller Street, Anaheim CA 92806-2001. 714/632-0882. **Fax:** 714/632-0858. **Contact:** Human Resources. **E-mail address:** jobs@zyxel.com. **World Wide Web address:** http://www.us.zyxel.com. **Description:** ZyXEL is a manufacturer of computer modems, routers, and ISDN terminal adapters. **Positions advertised include:** Marketing Coordinator. **Corporate headquarters location:** Taiwan.

ACS STATE & LOCAL SOLUTIONS, INC.
1999 Broadway, Suite 2700, Denver CO 80202. 303/295-2860. **Contact:** Human Resources. **E-mail address:** recruiter@acs-inc.com. **World Wide Web address:** http://www.acs-inc.com. **Description:** An IT and business services consultancy. Founded in 1988. **Positions advertised include:** Associate General Manager; Payment Processing Supervisor. **President/CEO:** Jeffrey Rich.

ADP SECURITIES INDUSTRY SOFTWARE (ADP/SIS)
dba ADP/SIS
4725 Independence Street, Wheat Ridge CO 80033. 303/590-6000. **Contact:** Human Resources. **World Wide Web address:** http://www.bsg.adp.com. **Description:** Develops financial software for brokerage houses and related companies.

ADT SECURITY SERVICES
14200 East Exposition Avenue, Aurora CO 80012. 303/338-8200. **Contact:** Human Resources. **World Wide Web address:** http://www.adt.com. **Description:** Sells and installs security systems and provides electronic monitoring and maintenance services for homes and businesses. ADT has approximately 170,000 subscribers. Founded in 1993. **Other area locations:** Denver CO. **Other U.S. locations:** Miami FL; Atlanta GA; Shreveport LA; Dallas TX; Houston TX. **Number of employees nationwide:** 685.

AT&T GOVERNMENT SOLUTIONS
985 Space Center Drive, Suite 310, Colorado Springs CO 80915. 719/596-5395. **Contact:** Human Resources. **World Wide Web address:** http://www.att.com/gov. **Description:** AT&T Government Solutions provides knowledge-based professional services and technology-based product solutions to government and commercial customers. AT&T Government Solutions also provides studies and analysis capabilities for policy development and planning; modeling and simulation of hardware and software used in real-time testing of sensor, weapon, and battlefield management command, control, and communication systems; and testing and evaluation. **NOTE:** Please see company Website for more details on applying for a position. **Corporate headquarters location:** Santa Barbara CA. **Other U.S. locations:** Nationwide. **Operations at this facility include:** This location develops software for the U.S. government. **Parent company:** AT&T Corporation. **Listed on:** New York Stock Exchange. **Stock exchange symbol:** T. **Number of employees worldwide:** 1,300.

ACCREDO THERAPEUTICS INC
361 Inverness Drive South, Suite F, Englewood CO 80112-5816. 303/799-6550. **Fax:** 303/799-6551. **Contact:** Human Resources. **World Wide Web address:** http://www.accredohealth.net. **Description:** Accredo Therapeutics provides home health care services, pharmaceutical support, and supplemental staffing services. **Corporate headquarters location:** Memphis TN. **Operations at this facility include:** This location offers infusion therapy services.

ADAM'S MARK HOTEL
1550 Court Place, Denver CO 80202. 303/893-3333. **Contact:** Director of Human Resources. **World Wide Web address:** http://www.adamsmark.com. **Description:** A 1,225-room hotel with restaurant and meeting facilities. **Positions advertised include:** Front Office Manager; Pastry Chef; Reservations Manager; Sales Manager. **Corporate headquarters location:** Minneapolis MN. **Parent company:** Ash and Associates, Inc. **Number of employees at this location:** 375.

ADAMS STATE COLLEGE
208 Edgemont Boulevard, Alamosa CO 81102. 719/587-7990. **Fax:** 719/587-7938. **Contact:** Human Resources. **World Wide Web address:** http://www.adams.edu. **Description:** A state college with approximately 2,500 students. **Number of employees at this location:** 310.

AGGREGATE INDUSTRIES
1707 Cole Boulevard, Suite 100, Golden CO 80401. 303/777-3058. **World Wide Web address:** http://www.aggregate.com. **Contact:** Human Resources. **Description:** Manufactures ready-mix concrete and other aggregate products. **Positions advertised include:** Bulk Driver; Laborer; Scale Operator. **Corporate headquarters location:** This location.

AIR METHODS CORPORATION
7301 South Peoria Street, Englewood CO 80112. 303/792-7400. **Fax:** 303/790-0499. **Recorded jobline:** 303/792-7508. **Contact:** Human Resources. **World Wide Web address:** http://www.airmethods.com. **Description:** One of the largest providers of aeromedical emergency services and systems throughout North America. Air Methods Corporation operates a fleet of 41 aircraft, consisting of 29 helicopters and 12 airplanes. The company provides its services to 54 hospitals located in 14 states. The company designs, services, and installs proprietary medical interiors, allowing each aircraft to be operated as an airborne ICU. Founded in 1982. **NOTE:** Drug screening is a mandatory part of the hiring process. **Positions advertised include:** A&P Mechanic; Flights Records Specialist. **Number of employees at this location:** 250.

AIR PURIFICATION COMPANY
1860 West 64th Lane, Denver CO 80221. 303/428-2800. **Contact:** Bruce Wilde, President and Owner. **Description:** A wholesaler of air conditioning, heating, and ventilation equipment.

ALCOA PACKAGING MACHINERY
6949 South Potomac Street, Englewood CO 80112. 303/708-9044. **Contact:** Human Resources. **World Wide Web address:** http://www.apm.alcoa. com. **Description:** Designs, manufactures, and assembles can-making machinery. **Corporate headquarters location:** Pittsburgh PA. **Number of employees worldwide:** 82,600.

ALFRED MANUFACTURING COMPANY
4398 Elati Street, Denver CO 80216. 303/433-6385. **Contact:** Human Resources. **World Wide Web address:** http://www.alfredindutries.com. **Description:** Manufactures specialty dies and tools, die sets, jigs, fixtures, and industrial molds. Alfred Manufacturing Company is also engaged in machine shop production, metal stamping, welding, and special machinery operation.

ALLSTATE INSURANCE COMPANY
5500 South Quebec Street, Suite 250, Englewood CO 80111. 303/779-3700. **Contact:** Human Resources. **World Wide Web address:** http://www.allstate.com. **Description:** A homeowners, automotive, and life insurance firm.

ALPINE LUMBER COMPANY
5800 North Pecos, Denver CO 80221. 303/458-8733. **Contact:** General Manager. **World Wide Web address:** http://www.alpinelumber.com. **Description:** A retail lumberyard. **Corporate headquarters location:** This location. **Other area locations include:** Brighton CO; Denver CO.

ALTIA
5030 Corporate Plaza Drive, Colorado Springs CO 80919. 719/598-4299. **Fax:** 719/598-4392. **Contact:** Human Resources. **E-mail address:** info@altia.com. **World Wide Web address:** http://www.altia.com. **Description:** Manufactures feature prototyping software for engineers and marketing professionals. **Corporate headquarters location:** This location.

AMERICAN CENTURY INVESTMENTS
10350 Park Meadows Drive, Littleton CO 80124. 720/258-4400. **Toll-free phone:** 888/340-4545. **Contact:** Human Resources Manager. **World Wide Web address:** http://www.americancentury.com. **Description:** Provides mutual fund investment services. Founded in 1958. **Corporate headquarters location:** Kansas City MO. **Listed on:** Privately held. **Number of employees at this location:** 350. **Number of employees nationwide:** 2,000. **Number of employees worldwide:** 2,100.

AMERICAN EDUCATIONAL PRODUCTS INC.
P.O. Box 2121, Fort Collins CO 80522. 970/484-7445. **Physical address:** 401 West Hickory Street, Fort Collins CO 80524. **Contact:** Human Resources. **Description:** Manufactures and markets a wide variety of educational products including pattern blocks, cubes, geological oddities, puzzles, and arts and crafts supplies. The company also designs, develops, manufactures, markets, and services supplementary educational products including filmstrips and anatomical systems. **Number of employees at this location:** 135.

AMERICAN MANAGEMENT SYSTEMS INC.
14033 Denver West Parkway, Golden CO 80401. 303/215-3500. **Contact:** Director of Human Resources. **World Wide Web address:** http://www.amsinc.com. **Description:** American Management Systems Inc. assists large organizations in solving complex management problems by applying information technology and systems engineering solutions. Industries and markets served include financial service institutions, insurance companies, federal agencies, state and local governments, colleges and universities, telecommunications firms, health care providers, and energy companies. **Operations at this facility include:** This location designs and develops software for the telecommunications industry. **Listed on:** NASDAQ. **Stock exchange symbol:** AMSY.

AMERICAN MEDICAL RESPONSE
2901 Broadway, Denver CO 80216. 303/357-2000. **Fax:** 303/297-3639. **Contact:** Human Resources. **World Wide Web address:** http://www.amr-inc.com. **Description:** A medical transportation services company. **Other U.S. locations include:** Nationwide.

AMERICAN NATIONAL BANK
3033 East First Avenue, Denver CO 80206. 303/394-5100. **Contact:** Eileen Terrell, Personnel Director. **World Wide Web address:** http://www.anbbank.com. **Description:** A commercial bank with a complete range of services for private, commercial, and institutional customers. **Operations at this facility include:** Administration; Sales; Service.

AMERICAN PRIDE
P.O. Box 98, Henderson CO 80640. 303/659-3643. **Fax:** 303/659-3640. **Contact:** Office Manager. **Description:** Markets bulk and bagged fertilizer, agricultural chemicals, seeds, feed, and veterinary supplies. **Corporate headquarters location:** This location. **Operations at this facility include:** Administration; Sales.

AMERICOLD LOGISTICS, LLC
4475 East 50th Avenue, Denver CO 80216. 303/320-0333. **Recorded jobline:** 866/KOOL-JOB. **Contact:** Personnel. **E-mail address:** employment@amclog.com. **World Wide Web address:** http://www.americold.net. **Description:** Operates refrigerated warehouse facilities that store frozen and refrigerated food products for various food distributing and processing companies. **Positions advertised include:** HR Manager; HR Generalist; Hardware Technician; Sales Representative. **Corporate headquarters location:** Atlanta GA. **Other U.S. locations:** Portland OR.

AMERICOMM DIRECT MARKETING
4760 Oakland Street, Suite 175, Denver CO 80239. 303/373-5323. **Toll-free phone:** 877/737-5478. **Contact:** Human Resources Department. **World Wide Web address:** http://www.americomm.net. **Description:** A direct mail processing company.

AMGEN INC.
5550 Airport Boulevard, Boulder CO 80301. 303/401-1000. **Contact:** Human Resources. **World Wide Web address:** http://www.amgen.com. **Description:** Researches, develops, manufactures, and markets human therapeutics based on advanced cellular and molecular biology. Products include EPOGEN (Epoetin Alfa), which counteracts the symptoms of renal failure experienced by kidney dialysis patients; and NEUPOGEN (Filgrastim), which reduces the incidence of infection in cancer patients who receive chemotherapy. When used in conjunction with chemotherapy, NEUPOGEN selectively stimulates the bone marrow to produce neutrophil cells, accelerating the return of the patient's antibacterial defense system. **Corporate headquarters location:** Thousand Oaks CA. **Listed on:** NASDAQ. **Stock exchange symbol:** AMGN.

AMPLE BOUTIQUE
1402 South Parker Road, Denver CO 80231. 303/369-9388. **Fax:** 303/369-6860. **Contact:** Human Resources. **Description:** A clothing store specializing in the retail of plus-size women's wear. Founded in 1979. **Owner:** Stu King. **Number of employees at this location:** 5. **Number of employees nationwide:** 20.

ANALYSTS INTERNATIONAL CORPORATION (AIC)
5445 DTC Parkway, Suite 320 A, Englewood CO 80111. 303/721-6200. **Contact:** Manager of Human Resources. **World Wide Web address:** http://www.analysts.com. **Description:** AIC is an international, computer consulting firm. The company assists clients in developing systems using various programming languages and software. **Corporate headquarters location:** Minneapolis MN. **Listed on:** NASDAQ. **Stock exchange symbol:** ANLY.

ANASAZI HERITAGE CENTER
BUREAU OF LAND MANAGEMENT
27501 Highway 184, Dolores CO 81323-9217. 970/882-4811. **Fax:** 970/882-7035. **Contact:** Human Resources. **Description:** An archeological museum that focuses on the interpretation of the Anasazi culture. **Special programs:** Internships. **Corporate headquarters location:** Washington DC. **Parent company:** U.S. Department of the Interior.

ARTHUR ANDERSEN LLP
1225 17th Street, Suite 3100, Denver CO 80202. 303/295-1900. **Contact:** Human

Resources. **World Wide Web address:** http://www.arthurandersen.com. **Description:** One of the largest certified public accounting firms in the world. Arthur Andersen's four key practice areas include Audit and Business Advisory, Tax and Business Advisory, Business Consulting, and Economic and Financial Consulting. **NOTE:** This firm does not accept unsolicited resumes. Please check the Website for available positions. **Parent company:** Andersen Worldwide Organization is one of the leading providers of professional services in the world. With over 380 worldwide locations, the global practice of its member firms is conducted through two business units: Arthur Andersen and Andersen Consulting, which provides global management and technology consulting.

ANDERSON RANCH ARTS CENTER
P.O. Box 5598, Snowmass Village CO 81615. 970/923-3181. **Fax:** 970/923-3871. **Contact:** Employment. **World Wide Web address:** http://www.andersonranch.org. **Description:** Offers 100 summer workshops (one or two weeks long) in painting and drawing, ceramics, sculpture, woodworking, furniture design, photography, creative studies, and children's studies. In the winter, the center runs a studio residency program. The center also offers a visiting artists program for professional and emerging artists. **Special programs:** Internships.

ANHEUSER-BUSCH, INC.
2351 Busch Drive, Fort Collins CO 80524. 970/490-4500. **Toll-free phone:** 800/DIAL-BUD. **Contact:** Human Resources. **World Wide Web address:** http://www. anheuser-busch.com. **Description:** One of the world's largest beer brewers. Brand names include Budweiser, Michelob, and Busch beers. **Positions advertised include:** Maintenance Technician. **Corporate headquarters location:** St. Louis MO. **Parent company:** Anheuser-Busch Companies is engaged in the brewing, entertainment, baking, and manufacturing industries. In addition to its brewing operations, the company also has several related businesses including can manufacturing, paper printing, and barley malting. The company is also involved in real estate and is one of the largest operators of theme parks in the United States, with locations in Florida, Virginia, Texas, Ohio, and California. Through its subsidiary Campbell Taggart Inc., Anheuser-Busch, Inc. is also one of the largest commercial baking companies in the United States, producing foods under the Colonial brand name, among others. **Listed on:** New York Stock Exchange. **Stock exchange symbol:** BUD.

ANIXTER
14509 East 33rd Place, Suite A, Aurora CO 80011. 303/373-9200. **Contact:** Inside Sales Manager. **World Wide Web address:** http://www.anixter.com. **Description:** A value-added provider of industrial wire and cabling solutions that support voice and data applications. Solutions include customized pre- and postsale services and products from the world's leading manufacturers. Anixter operates delivery through a global distribution network with 160 sales/service locations. Founded in 1957. **Corporate headquarters location:** Skokie IL. **Other U.S. locations:** Nationwide. **International locations:** Worldwide. **Parent company:** Anixter International. **Listed on:** New York Stock Exchange. **Stock exchange symbol:** AXE. **Number of employees nationwide:** 4,100.

ANSCHUTZ CORPORATION
555 17th Street, Suite 2400, Denver CO 80202. 303/298-1000. **Contact:** Gail Ash, Payroll Manager. **World Wide Web address:** http://www.anschutz-exploration.com. **Description:** Engaged in mining, oil, and gas exploration, as well as investments.

ANTHEM BLUE CROSS BLUE SHIELD HMO COLORADO
700 Broadway, Denver CO 80273. 303/831-2131. **Toll-free phone:** 800/654-9338. **Contact:** Human Resources. **World Wide Web address:** http://www.anthem-inc.com. **Description:** A nonprofit health care insurance organization. Anthem Blue Cross Blue Shield provides hospitalization insurance coverage to individuals and groups. The company also provides group and individual insurance coverage performed by professional medical services from doctors, dentists, psychiatrists, and other medical professionals. **Positions advertised include:** Director, Application Development; Executive Director, Conversion and Integration; Executive Director, Customer Service; Manager, Performance Enhancement; Senior Financial Consultant. **Corporate headquarters location:** Indianapolis IN. **Other area locations:** Colorado Springs CO; Grand Junction CO; Greeley CO. **Parent company:** Anthem, Inc. **Listed on:** New York Stock Exchange. **Stock exchange symbol:** ATH. **CEO/President:** Larry C. Glasscock.

AON INNOVATIVE SOLUTIONS
13922 Denver West Parkway, Building 54, Golden CO 80401. 303/279-2900. **Contact:** Director of Human Resources. **World Wide Web address:** http://www.aon.com. **Description:** A provider of third-party administrative services including claims adjudication, customer service in-bound call handling, telemarketing, and fulfillment/order taking. **Corporate headquarters location:** Chicago IL. **Other U.S. locations:** Nationwide. **International locations:** Worldwide. **Parent company:** Aon Corporation. **Operations at this facility include:** Administration; Sales; Service. **Listed on:** New York Stock Exchange. **Stock exchange symbol:** AOC. **Number of employees at this location:** 200.

ARAMARK EDUCATIONAL RESOURCES (AER)
573 Park Point Drive, Golden CO 80401. 303/526-3400. **Fax:** 303/526-3393. **Recorded jobline:** 800/818-6819. **Contact:** Human Resources. **World Wide Web address:** http://www.aramarkeducation.com. **Description:** An educational service provider, serving more than 100,000 children in 28 states. AER is the umbrella organization for four divisions: Children's World Learning Centers (early care and education), Meritor Academy (private education), Medallion School Partnerships (before and after school educational programs), and ARAMARK Work/Life Partnerships (consulting services). This location also hires seasonally. **NOTE:** Entry-level positions and part-time jobs are offered. **Special programs:** Internships; Training; Summer Jobs. **Other U.S. locations:** Nationwide. **Parent company:** ARAMARK provides a broad range of services to businesses of all sizes. ARAMARK's major businesses include Food, Leisure & Support Services including Campus Dining Services, School Nutrition Services, Leisure Services, Business Dining Services, International Services, Healthcare Support Services, Conference Center Management, and Refreshment Services; Facility Services, Correctional Services, and Industrial Services; Uniform Services, which includes Wearguard, a direct marketer of work clothing; and Health & Education Services, which includes Spectrum Healthcare Services and Educational Resources. **Listed on:** New York Stock Exchange. **Stock exchange symbol:** RMK. **Number of employees at this location:** 250. **Number of employees nationwide:** 15,000.

ARCADIS GERAGHTY & MILLER, INC.
630 Plaza Drive, Suite 200, Highlands Ranch CO 80129. 303/294-1200. **Contact:** Corporate Technical Recruiter. **World Wide Web address:** http://www.arcadis-us.com. **Description:** A consulting firm that provides environmental and engineering services. The company focuses on the environmental, building, and infrastructure markets. Founded in 1888. **Other U.S. locations:** Nationwide. **International locations:** The Netherlands; United Kingdom. **Parent company:** Arcadis NV. **Listed on:** NASDAQ. **Stock exchange symbol:** ARCAF.

ARINC RESEARCH CORPORATION
1925 Aerotech Drive, Suite 212, Colorado Springs CO 80916-4219. 719/574-9001. **Contact:** Human Resources. **World Wide Web address:** http://www.arinc.com. **Description:** An engineering and management consulting firm providing technical studies, analysis, and evaluations of aircraft, ship systems, communications, and information systems. **Positions advertised include:** Staff Principal Analyst; Administrative Assistant; Public Affairs/Media Support; Security Engineer. **Corporate headquarters:** Annapolis MD. **Other U.S. locations:** Nationwide. **International locations:** Worldwide. **CEO:** James L. Pierce.

ARKANSAS VALLEY REGIONAL MEDICAL CENTER
1100 Carson Avenue, La Junta CO 81050. 719/384-5412. **Fax:** 719/383-6062. **Contact:** Director of Human Resources. **Description:** A nonprofit medical center. **Number of employees at this location:** 400.

ASPEN DISTRIBUTION INC.
11075 East 40th Avenue, Denver CO 80239. 303/371-2510. **Contact:** Personnel. **World Wide Web address:** http://www.aspendistribution.com. **Description:** A local trucking company and public warehouse.

ASPEN SYSTEMS, INC.
3900 Youngfield Street, Wheat Ridge CO 80033-3865. 303/431-4606. **Fax:** 303/431-7196. **Contact:** Personnel. **World Wide Web address:** http://www.aspsys.com. **Description:** A manufacturer of high-performance workstations and servers for the OEM, VAR, and retail industries. **Positions advertised include:** Bookkeeper/Controller; Computer Production Engineer; Sales, High Performance Computing; Senior Firmware Programmer; Senior Level Programmer; Senior Level Software Architect. **Corporate headquarters location:** This location. **Listed on:** Privately held.

ASPENBIO, INC.
1585 South Perry Street, Castle Rock CO 80104. 303/794-2000. **Contact:** Human Resources. **E-mail address:** info@aspenbio.com. **World Wide Web address:** http://www.aspenbioinc.com. **Description:** Develops, manufactures, and markets purified human antigens for manufacturers of immunodiagnostic test kits and distributors of immunochemicals. Pituitary hormones products include growth hormone, prolactin, LH, FSH, and TSH; tumor marker antigens produced include CEA, AFP, beta hCG, and alpha hCG.

ASSOCIATED GLOBAL SYSTEMS
16075 East 32nd Avenue, Aurora CO 80011. 720/858-0200. **Contact:** Human Resources. **E-mail address:** info@agsystems.com. **World Wide Web address:** http://www.agsystems.com. **Description:** An air transportation company offering domestic, international, and same-day services. **Corporate headquarters location:** New Hyde Park NY.

THE ASSOCIATED PRESS
1444 Wazee Street, Suite 130, Denver CO 80202. 303/825-0123. **Contact:** Human Resources. **E-mail address:** apjobs@ap.org. **World Wide Web address:** http://www.ap.org. **Description:** One of the largest independent news-gathering organizations in the world. **Corporate headquarters location:** New York NY. **International locations:** Worldwide.

AURORA PRESBYTERIAN HOSPITAL
1501 South Potomac Street, Aurora CO 80012. 303/363-7200. **Contact:** Human Resources. **Description:** A 146-bed, acute care hospital. Services include 24-hour emergency care; a minor emergency center; AirLife, one of Colorado's largest helicopter and fixed-wing medical evacuation services; a women's services unit with private rooms, labor and delivery suites, and comprehensive newborn care; the LifeLong Choices Awareness Program, focusing on the early detection of breast, cervical, colorectal, and skin cancers; and The Challenge Center, which promotes wellness through education, rehabilitation, and fitness. Aurora Presbyterian also features three specialty care centers: The Stereotactic Breast Biopsy Center, The Kidney Dialysis Center, and The Diagnostic Eye Center.

AUTO-TROL TECHNOLOGY CORPORATION
12500 North Washington Street, Denver CO 80241-2400. **Toll-free phone:** 800/233-2882. **Fax:** 303/252-2249. **Recorded jobline:** 303/252-2007. **Contact:** Human Resources. **E-mail address:** careers@auto-trol.com. **World Wide Web address:** http://www.auto-trol.com. **Description:** Develops and markets software for the CAD/CAM/CAE, technical illustration, network configuration, and technical information management industries. Auto-Trol Technology Corporation integrates computer hardware, operating systems, proprietary graphics software, and applications software into systems for process plant design, civil engineering, discrete manufacturing, facilities layout and design, mechanical design, technical publishing, and network configuration management. **NOTE:** Entry-level positions are offered. **Positions advertised include:** Test Engineer; Consultant/Project Manager; Sales Representative. **Special programs:** Internships. **Corporate headquarters location:** This location. **Other U.S. locations:** Nationwide. **Operations at this facility include:** Administration; Marketing; Research and Development; Sales. **Annual sales/revenues:** $5 - $10 million. **Number of employees at this location:** 200.

AUTOMATIC LAUNDRY COMPANY
P.O. Box 39365, Denver CO 80239. 303/371-9274. **Contact:** Human Resources. **World Wide Web address:** http://www.automacticlaundry.com. **Description:** Leases laundry room space and installs coin-operated laundry equipment in apartment complexes.

AUTOZONE
1108 Bonforte Boulevard, Pueblo CO 81001-1805. 719/542-9000. **Contact:** Human Resources. **World Wide Web address:** http://www.autozone.com. **Description:** A do-it-yourself, retail auto parts chain, specializing in foreign and domestic parts. **Corporate headquarters location:** Memphis TN. **Listed on:** New York Stock Exchange. **Stock exchange symbol:** AZO.

AVAYA INC.
1300 West 120th Avenue, Westminster CO 80234-2795. 303/538-1200. **Contact:** Human Resources. **World Wide Web address:** http://www.avaya.com. **Description:** Avaya Inc. manufactures communications products including switching, transmission, fiber-optic cable, wireless systems, and operations systems to supply the needs of telephone companies and other communications services providers. **Positions advertised include:** Material Planner; Technical Support Engineer; Transportation Logistics Engineer; Product Data Analyst; Product Manager, Speech Applications.

Corporate headquarters location: Basking Ridge NJ. **Other U.S. locations:** Nationwide. **International locations:** Worldwide. **Operations at this facility include:** This location is primarily a research and development facility. **Listed on:** New York Stock Exchange. **Stock exchange symbol:** AV.

BBC RESEARCH & CONSULTING
3773 Cherry Creek North Drive, Suite 850, Denver CO 80209-3827. 303/321-2547. **Contact:** Human Resources. **E-mail address:** bbc@bbcresearch.com. **World Wide Web address:** http://www.bbcresearch.com. **Description:** An economic research and management consulting firm. **Corporate headquarters location:** This location. **Listed on:** Privately held. **Number of employees at this location:** 30.

BI INCORPORATED
6400 Lookout Road, Boulder CO 80301. 303/218-1000. **Toll-free phone:** 800/241-2911. **Fax:** 303/218-1250. **Contact:** Human Resources. **E-mail address:** hdhr@bi.com. **World Wide Web address:** http://www.bi.com. **Description:** A provider of electronic home arrest and jail management systems to correctional agencies worldwide. The company also offers a computerized, interactive telephone and monitoring service for its electronic monitoring systems. **Positions advertised include:** Sales/Marketing Manager; Administrative/Account Executive; Part-time Client Administrator. **Office hours:** Monday - Friday, 8:00 a.m. - 5:30 p.m. **Corporate headquarters location:** This location. **Other U.S. locations:** GA; IL; IN; OH; OR; TX. **International locations:** Puerto Rico. **Operations at this facility include:** Administration; Manufacturing; Marketing; Research and Development; Sales. **Number of employees worldwide:** 800.

BMC WEST
6400 Arapahoe Avenue, Boulder CO 80303. 303/442-6382. **Contact:** General Manager. **World Wide Web address:** http://www.bmcwest.com. **Description:** A lumber and hardware retailer. **Corporate headquarters location:** Boise ID. **Parent company:** Building Materials Holding Corporation. **Listed on:** NASDAQ. **Stock exchange symbol:** BMHC.

BAKER ATLAS
1675 Broadway, Suite 1500, Denver CO 80202. 303/573-2781. **Contact:** Human Resources. **World Wide Web address:** http://www.bakeratlas.com. **Description:** Baker Atlas develops and markets proprietary computer software, provides management services for the petroleum and mining industries, and provides electronic data processing services. **Positions advertised include:** Directional Coordinator. **Corporate headquarters location:** Houston TX. **Operations at this facility include:** This location develops software for the oil and gas industries. **Parent company:** Baker Hughes. **Listed on:** New York Stock Exchange. **Stock exchange symbol:** BHI.

BALL AEROSPACE & TECHNOLOGIES CORP.
P.O. Box 1062, Boulder CO 80306. 303/939-4000. **Physical address:** 1600 Commerce Street, Boulder CO 80301. **Fax:** 303/939-6104. **Contact:** Human Resources. **E-mail address:** info@ball.com. **World Wide Web address:** http://www.ballaerospace.com. **Description:** Ball Aerospace & Technologies Corp. provides imaging, communications, and information systems, products, software, and services to government and commercial aerospace customers. Founded in 1956. **NOTE:** Search and apply for positions online. **Positions advertised include:** Sr. Engineer, Radiation Effects; Material Property Specialist; Sr. Business Analyst; Quality Control Inspector; Sr. Electrical Engineer; Manufacturing Director. **Listed on:** New York Stock Exchange. **Stock exchange symbol:** BLL. **Number of employees at this location:** 2,500.

BALL CORPORATION
10 Longs Peak Drive, P.O. Box 5000, Broomfield CO 80021-2510. 303/469-3131. **Contact:** Human Resources. **World Wide Web address:** http://www.ball.com. **Description:** Produces metal and plastic packaging products for foods and beverages, and provides aerospace and communications products and services to government and commercial customers. **Positions advertised include:** Project Engineer. **Corporate headquarters location:** This location. **Listed on:** New York Stock Exchange. **Stock exchange symbol:** BLL.

BAND-IT INC.
4799 Dahlia Street, Denver CO 80216-0307. 303/320-4555. **Contact:** Human Resources. **World Wide Web address:** http://www.band-it-idex.com. **Description:** Manufactures clamps, hose fittings, and brackets. **Corporate headquarters location:** Northbrook IL. **Parent company:** IDEX Corporation. **Listed on:** New York Stock Exchange. **Stock exchange symbol:** IEX.

BANK ONE COLORADO
9379 North Sheridan Boulevard, Westminster CO 80030. 303/44-5060. **Fax:** 303/430-5721. **Recorded jobline:** 303/429-8224. **Contact:** Employment Office. **World Wide Web address:** http://www.bankone.com. **Description:** A full-service bank. **NOTE:** Please call the jobline to obtain the position code for the job that interests you. Send resumes to 7301 North Federal Boulevard, Westminster CO 80030. **Corporate headquarters location:** Chicago IL. **Parent company:** Banc One Corporation (Columbus OH) is one of the nation's largest bank holding companies. Banc One Corporation operates an affiliate network of over 75 banks with 1,500 banking locations in Arizona, Colorado, Illinois, Indiana, Kentucky, Louisiana, Ohio, Oklahoma, Texas, Utah, West Virginia, and Wisconsin. Banc One Corporation also owns several additional corporations that engage in credit card merchant processing, consumer finance, mortgage banking, insurance, trust and investment management, brokerage, investment and merchant banking, venture capital, equipment leasing, and data processing. **Listed on:** New York Stock Exchange. **Stock exchange symbol:** ONE. **Number of employees at this location:** 1,000. **Number of employees nationwide:** 50,000.

BARNES & NOBLE BOOKSTORES
960 South Colorado Boulevard, Glendale CO 80246. 303/691-2998. **Fax:** 303/691-9193. **Contact:** Manager. **World Wide Web address:** http://www.bn.com. **Description:** Barnes & Noble Bookstores is a bookstore chain operating nationwide. **Corporate headquarters location:** New York NY. **Operations at this facility include:** This location houses the district headquarters as well as a bookstore. **Listed on:** New York Stock Exchange. **Stock exchange symbol:** BKS.

BAX GLOBAL
16075 East 32nd Avenue, Suite B, Aurora CO 8001. 720/859-6240. **Fax:** 720/859-6298. **Toll-free phone:** 800/525-3720. **Contact:** Human Resources. **World Wide Web address:** www.baxglobal.com. **Description:** Bax Global offers business-to-business freight delivery through a worldwide network of offices in 124 countries, with 155 offices in the U.S. **Other area locations:** Grand Junction CO. **Other U.S. locations:** Nationwide. **International locations:** Worldwide.

BAXTER HEMOGLOBIN THERAPEUTICS
2545 Central Avenue, Suite FD1, Boulder CO 80301-2857. 303/440-9988. **Fax:** 303/541-3260. **Recorded jobline:** 303/541-3366. **Contact:** Human Resources Department. **World Wide Web address:** http://www.baxter.com. **Description:** Develops specialty oxygen therapeutics and other pharmacological agents using its proprietary recombinant hemoglobin technology. The company's product, Optro, is designed to replace blood lost in surgery. **NOTE:** Entry-level positions are offered. **Positions advertised include:** Manufacturing Associate; Engineer II; Executive Assistant; Computer Validation Leader. **Corporate headquarters location:** Deerfield IL. **Parent company:** Baxter International, Inc. **Listed on:** New York Stock Exchange. **Stock exchange symbol:** BAX. **Number of employees at this location:** 200.

BEST WESTERN DENVER STAPLETON HOTEL
3535 Quebec Street, Denver CO 80207. 303/333-7711x604. **Fax:** 303/322-2262. **Contact:** Kevin Baptiste, Human Resources Administrator. **World Wide Web address:** http://www.bestwestern.com. **Description:** A 195-room hotel. **Corporate headquarters location:** San Francisco CA. **Listed on:** Privately held. **Number of employees at this location:** 115.

BESTOP, INC.
P.O. Box 307, Broomfield CO 80038. 303/465-1755. **Physical address:** 2100 West Midway Boulevard, Broomfield CO 80020. **Toll-free phone:** 800/845-3567. **Fax:** 303/466-3436. **Contact:** Human Resources Manager. **World Wide Web address:** http://www.bestop.com. **Description:** Designs and manufactures automotive soft tops and accessories for sport-utility vehicles. **NOTE:** Entry-level positions and second and third shifts are offered. **Office hours:** Monday - Friday, 7:30 a.m. - 5:00 p.m. **Corporate headquarters location:** This location. **Other U.S. locations:** Eastman GA. **International locations:** Ontario, Canada. **Operations at this facility include:** Administration; Manufacturing; Sales; Service. **President:** Ross MacLean. **Annual sales/revenues:** More than $100 million. **Number of employees at this location:** 500. **Number of employees nationwide:** 630.

BEVERAGE DISTRIBUTORS CORPORATION
14200 East Moncrieff Place, Suite G, Aurora CO 80011. 303/371-3421. **Contact:** Human Resources. **Description:** Provides beverage distribution services. **Number of employees at this location:** 385.

BLACK & VEATCH
30 Pikes Peak, Suite 200, Colorado Springs CO 80903. 719/667-7010. **Fax:** 719/667-7009. **Contact:** Human Resources Department. **World Wide Web address:** http://www.bv.com. **Description:** An environmental/civil engineering and construction firm serving utilities, commerce, industry, and government agencies in more than 40 countries throughout the world. Black & Veatch provides a broad range of study, design, construction management, and turnkey capabilities to clients in the water and wastewater fields. The firm is one of the leading authorities on drinking water treatment through the use of activated carbon, ozone, and other state-of-the-art processes. Black & Veatch is also engaged in wastewater treatment work including reclamation and reuse projects and the beneficial use of wastewater residuals. Other services are provided for solid waste recycling and disposal, transportation, and storm water management. In the energy field, Black & Veatch is a leader in providing engineering procurement and construction for electric power plants. The firm's areas of expertise include coal-fueled plants, simple and combined-cycle combustion turbines, waste-to-energy facilities, hydroelectric plants, and cogeneration facilities. Black & Veatch's capabilities also include nuclear power projects, advanced technology, air quality control, performance monitoring, plant life management, and facilities modification. In addition, Black & Veatch provides transmission and distribution services. Black & Veatch offers a variety of management and financial services including institutional strengthening, privatization, strategic financial planning, and information management. **Corporate headquarters location:** Kansas City MO.

BOEING SATELLITE SYSTEMS
1250 Academy Park Loop, Suite 134, Colorado Springs CO 80910. 719/638-5000. **Contact:** Human Resources. **World Wide Web address:** http://www.boeing.com. **Description:** Develops and produces state-of-the-art space and communications systems for military, commercial and scientific uses. These systems supply communications and meteorological observations for domestic and international customers and meet many of the military and scientific space system requirements of the U.S. government. **NOTE:** Search and apply for positions online. **Positions advertised include:** Engineer/Scientist; Ground Segment Assembly, Integration and Test Engineer; Access Administrator.

BOLDER BIOTECHNOLOGY, INC.
4056 Youngfield Street, Wheat Ridge CO 80033. 303/420-4420. **Fax:** 303/420-4426. **Contact:** Human Resources. **Description:** Bolder BioTechnology, Inc. uses advanced protein engineering technologies to create proprietary human protein pharmaceuticals with enhanced therapeutic properties. Products are intended for the treatment of hematological and endocrine disorders, cancer, and infectious disease. **Positions advertised include:** Scientist; Research Associate.

BOSTON MARKET, INC.
14103 Denver West Parkway, Golden CO 80401. 303/278-9500. **Contact:** Human Resources. **World Wide Web address:** http://www.boston-market.com. **Description:** Operates and franchises food service stores that specialize in fresh, convenient meals. Boston Market's menu features home-style entrees, fresh vegetables, salads, and other side dishes. **Corporate headquarters location:** This location.

THE BOULDER COUNTY BUSINESS REPORT
3180 Sterling Circle, Suite 201, Boulder CO 80301-2338. 303/440-4950. **Contact:** Jerry Lewis, Editor/Vice President. **World Wide Web address:** http://www.bcbr.com. **Description:** Publishes a monthly business newspaper for the Boulder County area. **Corporate headquarters location:** This location. **Operations at this facility include:** Publishing; Sales. **Number of employees at this location:** 5.

BOYLE ENGINEERING CORPORATION
215 Union, Suite 500, Lakewood CO 80228. 303/987-3443. **Contact:** Human Resources Department. **World Wide Web address:** http://www.boyleengineering.com. **Description:** Provides professional engineering services to create better infrastructure for public and private clients in the United States and abroad. Services range from project planning and feasibility studies to design and construction phases. The company is engaged in water treatment and distribution; wastewater collection, treatment, and reuse; streets, highways, and bridges construction; light and heavy rail; drainage and flood control; and land planning. **Positions advertised include:** Civil Engineer. **Corporate headquarters location:** Newport Beach CA.

BRANNAN SAND AND GRAVEL COMPANY
4800 Brighton Boulevard, Denver CO 80216. 303/534-1231. **World Wide Web address:** http://www.brannan1.com. **Contact:** Judy Carpenter, Employee Relations

Manager. **E-mail address:** judycarp@qwest.net. **Description:** Manufactures asphalt products used in construction, as well as other rock products. **Positions advertised include:** CDL Driver; Estimator; Project Superintendent; Laborer; Mechanic; Equipment Operator; Office Personnel. **Corporate headquarters location:** This location.

BRECKENRIDGE OUTDOOR EDUCATION CENTER
P.O. Box 697, Breckenridge CO 80424. 970/453-6422. **Fax:** 970/453-4676. **Contact:** Human Resources. **E-mail address:** boec@boec.org. **World Wide Web address:** http://www.boec.org. **Description:** A nonprofit organization offering year-round wilderness and adventure programs and adaptive skiing opportunities for people with disabilities and other special needs. Activities include downhill and cross-country skiing, ropes courses, rafting, rock climbing, camping, and fishing. Founded in 1976. **Special programs:** Internships. **Corporate headquarters location:** This location.

BREECE HILL LLC
246 South Taylor Avenue, Louisville CO 80027. 303/664-2000. **Contact:** Human Resources. **World Wide Web address:** http://www.breecehill.com. **Description:** A developer and manufacturer of Digital Linear Tape (DLT) drive systems. **Corporate headquarters location:** This location. **International locations:** England. **Number of employees at this location:** 100.

BRINK'S INC.
6703 East 47th Avenue Drive, Denver CO 80216. 303/355-2071. **Fax:** 303-355-9954. **Contact:** Human Resources. **World Wide Web address:** www.brinksinc.com. **Description:** An armored security service specializing in transporting currency. **Corporate headquarters location:** Dallas TX.

THE BROADMOOR HOTEL
7 Holly Avenue, Colorado Springs CO 80906. 719/634-7711. **Fax:** 719/577-5700. **Contact:** Human Resources. **World Wide Web address:** http://www.broadmoor.com. **Description:** A 700-room, five-star, five-diamond resort. Facilities include 3 championship golf courses, 15 retail outlets, 9 restaurants, 12 tennis courts, and conference rooms. Founded in 1918. **NOTE:** Entry-level positions, part-time jobs, and second and third shifts are offered. This location also hires seasonally. **Positions advertised include:** Payroll Coordinator; Finance Assistant; Assistant Banquet Supervisor; Front Desk Attendant; Operations Training Manager; National Sales Manager; Massage Therapist; Assistant Executive Steward. **Special programs:** Internships; Apprenticeships; Training. **Office hours:** Monday - Friday, 8:00 a.m. - 5:00 p.m. **Corporate headquarters location:** This location. **Parent company:** Oklahoma Publishing Company. **Annual sales/revenues:** $51 - $100 million. **Number of employees at this location:** 1,500.

BROWN PALACE HOTEL
321 17th Street, Denver CO 80202. 303/297-3111. **Fax:** 303/312-5940. **Contact:** Human Resources. **World Wide Web address:** http://www.brownpalace.com. **Description:** A full-service hotel. **NOTE:** All positions require experience in four- or five-star properties. **Special programs:** Internships. **Corporate headquarters location:** Dallas TX. **Parent company:** Quorum Hotels and Resorts. **Number of employees at this location:** 400.

BROWNING-FERRIS INDUSTRIES, INC. (BFI)
P.O. Box 5445, Denver CO 80217. 303/287-8043. **Contact:** Human Resources. **World Wide Web address:** http://www.bfi.com. **Description:** Engaged primarily in the collection and disposal of solid wastes for commercial, industrial, and residential customers. Services provided by BFI include landfill services, waste-to-energy programs, hazardous waste removal, and liquid waste removal. The company has worldwide operations at more than 500 facilities. **Corporate headquarters location:** Scottsdale AZ. **Other U.S. locations:** Nationwide. **Parent company:** Allied Waste Industries, Inc. **Listed on:** New York Stock Exchange. **Stock exchange symbol:** AW.

BURNS REALTY & TRUST
1625 Broadway, World Trade Center, Penthouse Suite, Denver CO 80202. 303/629-1899. **Contact:** Mark Gritz, Treasurer/Controller. **Description:** Engaged in real estate and investments, as well as owning and operating apartments and nonresidential buildings.

BURT CHEVROLET, INC.
5200 South Broadway, Englewood CO 80110. 303/761-0333. **Contact:** Human Resources. **World Wide Web address:** http://www.burt.com. **Description:** A new and used automobile dealership.

CH2M HILL
6161 South Syracuse Way, Suite 100, Greenwood Village CO 80111. 303/771-0900. **Contact:** Human Resources. **World Wide Web address:** http://www.ch2mhill.com. **Description:** Provides mechanical, structural, and environmental engineering services through its operating divisions. **NOTE:** Interested jobseekers should fax resumes to 781/663-3733. **Positions advertised include:** Contract Administrator; Superintendent; Client Service Manager; Associate Project Manager; Senior Construction/ Operations Manager. **Corporate headquarters location:** This location. **International locations:** Worldwide. **Subsidiaries include:** CH2M Hill Engineering; Industrial Design Corporation; Operating Management International.

CSC (COMPUTER SCIENCES CORPORATION)
1250 Academy Park Loop, Suite 240, Colorado Springs CO 80910. 719/596-7500. **Contact:** Human Resources. **World Wide Web address:** http://www.csc.com. **Description:** The company is comprised of four sectors: the Systems Group Division designs, engineers, and integrates computer-based systems and communications systems, providing all of the hardware, software, training, and related elements necessary to operate such a system; the Consulting Division includes consulting and technical services in the development of computer and communication systems to nonfederal organizations; the Industry Services Group provides service to the health care, insurance, and financial services industries; CSC Health Care markets business systems and services to the managed health care industry, clinics, and physicians; CSC Enterprises provides consumer credit reports and account management services. **Positions advertised include:** Programmer; Analyst; Program Manager; Technician; Systems Specialist. **NOTE:** Interested jobseekers should send resumes to 45154 Underwood Lane, Sterling VA 20166. **Corporate headquarters location:** El Segundo CA. **Other U.S. locations:** Nationwide. **International locations:** Worldwide. **Operations at this facility include:** This location primarily serves the U.S. federal government. **Listed on:** New York Stock Exchange. **Stock exchange symbol:** CSC. **Number of employees nationwide:** 20,000.

CSU VETERINARY TEACHING HOSPITAL
300 West Drake Road, Fort Collins CO 80523. 970/221-4535. **Contact:** Human Resources. **World Wide Web address:** http://www.cvmbs.colostate.edu/vth. **Description:** A full-service, referral, veterinary, teaching hospital. Departments include cardiology, oncology, ophthalmology, dermatology, neurology, and emergency.

CANYON RESOURCES CORPORATION
14142 Denver West Parkway, Suite 250, Golden CO 80401-3127. 303/278-8464. **Fax:** 303/279-3772. **Contact:** Human Resources Department. **World Wide Web address:** http://www.canyonresources.com. **Description:** Operates an open-pit gold mine in central Montana and other gold properties in mine development including the Briggs project in California and the McDonald Project in Montana. Canyon Resources Corporation operates the Kendall Mine in Montana, which produces gold and silver, and a mine/plant complex in Nevada. The company also conducts exploration and acquisition activities for valuable gold projects throughout the western United States, Latin America, and in select countries in Africa and the Western Pacific. **Corporate headquarters location:** This location. **Listed on:** American Stock Exchange. **Stock exchange symbol:** CAU. **Number of employees at this location:** 120.

CARDER CONCRETE PRODUCTS COMPANY
8311 West Carder Court, Littleton CO 80125. 303/791-1600. **Contact:** Human Resources. **World Wide Web address:** http://www.carderconcrete.com. **Description:** Produces concrete products including culverts, storm and drainage pipes, and box culverts. Founded in 1968. **Operations at this facility include:** Administration; Manufacturing; Regional Headquarters; Sales.

CAREFREE OF COLORADO
2145 West Sixth Avenue, Broomfield CO 80020. 303/469-3324. **Contact:** Human Resources. **E-mail address:** humanresources@carefreeofcolorado.com. **World Wide Web address:** http://www.carefreeofcolorado.com. **Description:** Manufactures a large line of products for recreational vehicles (RVs). Carefree of Colorado's product line includes awnings, add-a-rooms, and lawn furniture. **Corporate headquarters location:** This location. **Parent company:** Scott Fetzer Company.

CARGILL INC.
P.O. Box 459, Byers CO 80103. 719/775-2358. **Contact:** Human Resources Department. **E-mail address:** employment@cargill.com. **World Wide Web address:** http://www.cargill.com. **Description:** Cargill Inc., its subsidiaries, and its affiliates are involved in nearly 50 individual lines of business. Cargill Inc. has more than 130 years of service and expertise in commodity trading, handling, transporting, processing, and risk management. Cargill Inc. is a major trader of grains and oilseeds, as well as a marketer of many other agricultural and nonagricultural commodities. As a transporter, Cargill Inc. uses a network of rail and road systems, inland waterways, and ocean-going routes, combining its own fleet and contracted transportation services to move bulk commodities. As an agricultural supplier, Cargill Inc. is one of the leaders in developing and supplying farm products. Agricultural products include a wide variety of feed, seed, fertilizers, and other goods and services. Cargill Central Research, located at Cargill Inc. headquarters, is dedicated to developing new agricultural products to address the needs of its global customers. The company also provides financial and technical services. Cargill Inc.'s Financial Markets Division (FMD) supports Cargill Inc. and its subsidiaries with financial products including financial instrument trading, emerging markets instrument trading, value investing, and money management. Cargill Inc.'s worldwide food processing businesses supply products ranging from basic ingredients used in food production to recognized name brands. Cargill Inc. also operates a number of industrial businesses, including the production of steel, industrial-grade starches, ethanol, and salt products. **Corporate headquarters location:** Minneapolis MN. **Operations at this facility include:** This facility is an agricultural warehousing and storage location. **Number of employees worldwide:** 70,000.

CENTEX HOMES
9250 East Costilla Avenue, Suite 200, Greenwood Village CO 80112. 303/792-9810. **Contact:** Personnel. **World Wide Web address:** http://www.centexhomes.com. **Description:** Builds and sells residential homes nationwide. **Corporate headquarters location:** Dallas TX. **Parent company:** Centex Corporation provides home building, mortgage banking, contracting, and construction products and services. **Listed on:** New York Stock Exchange. **Stock exchange symbol:** CTX.

CENVEO
8310 South Valley Highway #400, Englewood CO 80112. 303/790-8023. **Fax:** 303/397-7438. **Contact:** Human Resources. **World Wide Web address:** http://www.cenveo.com. **Description:** Cenveo is a leading consolidator in the envelope and specialty printing industries. The company specializes in customized envelopes, filing products, labels, and printed materials. Cenveo operates approximately 70 printing plants and numerous sales offices throughout North America. **Positions advertised include:** Safety Manager; Safety Specialist; Corporate Attorney. **Office hours:** Monday - Friday, 7:30 a.m. - 5:00 p.m.

CENVEO
3500 Rockmont Drive, Denver CO 80202. 303/455-3505. **Contact:** Human Resources. **World Wide Web address:** http://www.mail-well.com. **Description:** Cenveo is a leading consolidator in the envelope and specialty printing industries. The company specializes in customized envelopes, filing products, labels, and printed materials. Cenveo operates approximately 70 printing plants and numerous sales offices throughout North America. **Corporate headquarters location:** Englewood CO. **Operations at this facility include:** This location manufactures and markets envelopes in a wide range of sizes and styles.

CEREFORM
P.O. Box 16366, Denver CO 80216. 303/287-3203. **Contact:** Calvin Bradford, Human Resources Manager. **Description:** Manufactures bakery mixes, jams, jellies, food, and oils. Cereform also sells wholesale bakery supplies and performs some chemical testing.

CHESS INC.
410 Raritan Way, Denver CO 80204. 303/573-5133. **Contact:** Human Resources Department. **World Wide Web address:** http://www.chessinc.com. **Description:** Engaged in the repair and sale of computer equipment and printers. **Other area locations:** Colorado Springs CO. **Positions advertised include:** Account Executive; Parts Administrator; Administrative Assistant; Accounts Receivable Clerk; Service Technician.

THE CHILDREN'S HOSPITAL
1056 East 19th Street, Denver CO 80218. 303/861-8888. **Fax:** 303/764-8080. **Contact:** Human Resources. **E-mail address:** jobposting@tchden.org. **World Wide Web address:** http://www.childrenshospitalden.org. **Description:** A hospital providing patient care, research, education, and advocacy. **Positions advertised include:** Insurance Coordinator; Medical Transcriptionist; Patient Service Coordinator; Staff Assistant; Unit Secretary; Dental Assistant; Case Manager; RN; Audiologist; Chaplain; Speech Pathologist; Catering Aide; Food Services Aide.

CHRISTY SPORTS, LLC
875 Parfet Street, Lakewood CO 80215. 303/237-6321. **Fax:** 303/274-4589. **Contact:** Human Resources. **World Wide Web address:** http://www.christysports.com. **Description:** Operates Christy Sports, SportStalker, and Powder Tools sporting goods stores. The company specializes in retail skiing, snowboarding, and sport clothing. In addition, Christy Sports offers patio furniture and several golf retail stores. **NOTE:** Entry-level positions are offered. **Special programs:** Training; Summer Jobs. **Corporate headquarters location:** This location. **Other U.S. locations:** UT. **Number of employees at this location:** 75. **Number of employees nationwide:** 500.

CIBER, INC.
5251 DTC Parkway, Suite 1400, Greenwood Village CO 80111. 303/220-0100. **Toll-free phone:** 800/242-3799. **Fax:** 303/220-7100. **Contact:** National Recruiting. **World Wide Web address:** http://www.ciber.com. **Description:** Provides consulting for client/server development, mainframe and legacy systems, industry-specific analysis, application-specific analysis, and network development. **Positions advertised include:** ABAP Programmer. **Corporate headquarters location:** This location. **International locations:** Canada; United Kingdom. **Listed on:** New York Stock Exchange. **Stock exchange symbol:** CBR.

CINGULAR WIRELESS
1001 16th Street, Suite C-1, Denver CO 80265-0003. 303/623-0691. **Contact:** Human Resources. **World Wide Web address:** http://www.cingular.com. **Description:** Cingular is a major cellular telephone company providing nationwide service.

CLIFTON GUNDERSON LLP
350 Interlocken Boulevard, Suite 350, Broomfield CO 80021. 303/466-8822. **Contact:** Personnel Director. **World Wide Web address:** http://www.cliftoncpa.com. **Description:** A certified public accounting and consulting firm. **Positions advertised include:** Regional Financial Services Manager.

COBANK ACB
5500 South Quebec Street, Greenwood Village CO 80111. 303/740-4000. **Fax:** 303/694-5898. **Contact:** Human Resources. **World Wide Web address:** http://www.cobank.com. **Description:** A full-service cooperative bank specializing in cooperative, agribusiness, rural utility, and agricultural export financing. Founded in 1916. **Positions advertised include:** Software Engineer; Administrative Assistant; Credit Officer; Senior Collateral Documentation Specialist; Project Manager; Lead Analyst; Application Developer; Associate Auditor; Portfolio Manager. **Corporate headquarters location:** This location.

COCA-COLA BOTTLING COMPANY OF DENVER
3825 York Street, Denver CO 80205. 303/292-2653. **Fax:** 303/291-9707. **Contact:** Ron Paxton, Human Resources Director. **World Wide Web address:** http://www.cokecce.com. **Description:** A bottler of soft drink brands including Barq's, Coca-Cola, and Dr. Pepper. **NOTE:** Please check the jobline for available positions before sending a resume. **Positions advertised include:** Full Service Driver; Bulk Driver; Home Market Delivery Merchandiser; Retail Space Specialist; Account Manager; Account Representative. **Corporate headquarters location:** Atlanta GA. **Other U.S. locations:** Nationwide. **Number of employees at this location:** 500.

COLDWELL BANKER MOORE & COMPANY
6430 South Fiddler's Green Circle, Suite 100, Greenwood Village CO 80111. 303/771-3311. **Fax:** 303/741-4024. **Contact:** Human Resources. **World Wide Web address:** http://www.coloradohomes.com. **Description:** A real estate sales company.

COLOMEX, INC.
dba TACO BELL
717 North Tejon, Colorado Springs CO 80903. 719/633-2500. **Fax:** 719/633-9610. **Contact:** Human Resources. **Description:** Colomex, Inc. owns the largest Taco Bell franchise in Colorado, operating over 30 restaurants. Taco Bell is a leader in the Mexican, fast-food restaurant industry. **Corporate headquarters location:** This location. **Listed on:** Privately held. **Number of employees at this location:** 1,000.

COLORADO BANKERS LIFE INSURANCE COMPANY
5990 Greenwood Plaza Boulevard, Suite 325, Englewood CO 80111. 303/220-8500. **Contact:** Human Resources. **World Wide Web address:** http://www.cbl-life.com. **Description:** A financial services institution providing life insurance annuities. **Parent company:** Preferred Financial Group.

COLORADO COUNCIL ON THE ARTS
1380 Lawrence Street, Denver CO 80204. 303/866-2723. **Fax:** 303/866-4266. **Contact:** Human Resources. **E-mail address:** coloarts@state.co.us. **World Wide Web address:** http://www.coloarts.state.co.us. **Description:** A state agency that awards grants to arts organizations and artists, and promotes the arts in Colorado. Founded in 1967. **Special programs:** Internships.

COLORADO CRYSTAL CORPORATION
2303 West Eighth Street, Loveland CO 80537. 970/667-9248. **Contact:** Personnel Director. **E-mail address:** info@coloradocrystal.com. **World Wide Web address:** http://www.coloradocrystal.com. **Description:** Manufactures quartz crystals for a variety of OEMs. **Corporate headquarters location:** This location.

COLORADO DIVISION OF PARKS AND RECREATION
GOLDEN GATE CANYON STATE PARK
92 Crawford Gulch Road, Golden CO 80403. 303/582-3707. **Contact:** Human Resources Department. **E-mail address:** golden.gate.park@state.co.us. **World Wide Web address:** http://parks.state.co.us. **Description:** An agency overseeing a 14,000-acre mountain park that includes more than 60 miles of hiking trails, 288 picnic sites, 164 campsites, a group camping facility, and a visitor center offering information and sales items related to natural resources. **Special programs:** Internships.

COLORADO HISTORICAL SOCIETY
1300 Broadway, Denver CO 80203. 303/866-3682. **Fax:** 303/866-4464. **Contact:** Alice Rodriguez, Personnel. **World Wide Web address:** http://www.coloradohistory.org. **Description:** A nonprofit organization that collects, preserves, and interprets the history and prehistory of Colorado and the West through educational programs and museum exhibits. Founded in 1879. **Special programs:** Internships; Summer Jobs. **Corporate headquarters location:** This location. **Number of employees at this location:** 95. **Number of employees nationwide:** 115.

COLORADO HOUSING & FINANCE AUTHORITY
1981 Blake Street, Denver CO 80202-1272. 303/297-2432. **Contact:** Becca Hagen, Human Resources Director. **E-mail address:** resumes@colohfa.org. **World Wide Web address:** http://www.colohfa.org. **Description:** A quasi-governmental organization that provides financing for housing (both rental and home ownership) for low- and moderate-income clients. Colorado Housing & Finance Authority also provides financing for small businesses. **Positions advertised include:** Asset Management Officer; Assistant Asset Management Officer; Human Resources Director; Housing Development Officer; Preservation Officer; IT Help Desk Specialist; IT Project Manager/Business Analyst; IT Senior Programmer Analyst.

COLORADO INTERSTATE GAS COMPANY
Western Pipelines, P.O. Box 1087, Colorado Springs CO 80944. 719/520-4227. **Physical address:** Western Pipelines, 2 North Nevada, Colorado Springs CO 80903. **Contact:** Human Resources. **World Wide Web address:** http://www.cigco.com. **Description:** Gathers, processes, and transports natural gas by pipeline in a six-state Rocky Mountain area to customer utility companies along the eastern front range of Colorado and southern Wyoming. **Corporate headquarters location:** Houston TX. **Other U.S. locations:** KS; OK; TX; UT; WY. **Parent company:** El Paso Corporation. **Listed on:** New York Stock Exchange. **Stock exchange symbol:** EP. **Number of employees nationwide:** 1,200.

COLORADO MENTAL HEALTH INSTITUTE AT FORT LOGAN
3550 West Oxford Avenue, Denver CO 80236. 303/866-7100. **Contact:** Human Resources. **World Wide Web address:** http://www.cdhs.state.co.us/ods/mif. **Description:** A 250-bed, state psychiatric hospital. The hospital operates in three divisions: Adolescent; Adult; and Geriatric/Deaf/Aftercare. Treatments include psychotherapy, group therapy, family therapy, behavior modification, occupational and recreational therapy, pastoral counseling, educational services, vocational counseling, and a work therapy program. The hospital is licensed by the Colorado Department of Health and is accredited by the Joint Commission on Accreditation of Hospitals.

COLORADO MOUNTAIN COLLEGE
P.O. Box 10001, Glenwood Springs CO 81602-5902. 970/945-8691. **Physical address:** 831 Grand Avenue, Glenwood Springs CO 81602. **Contact:** Director of Human Resources. **World Wide Web address:** http://www.coloradomtn.edu. **Description:** A two-year college. The school's Associate of Arts and Associate of Science degrees are academic programs designed for students who plan to transfer to a four-year college or university. Colorado Mountain College includes seven campuses in western Colorado. **NOTE:** Applications available online. **Positions advertised include:** Administrative Assistant; Chief Information Officer.

COLORADO MOUNTAIN COLLEGE/EAST
901 South U.S. Highway 24, Leadville CO 80461-9724. 719/486-2015. **Contact:** Human Resources. **World Wide Web address:** http://www.coloradomtn.edu. **Description:** A two-year college. The school's Associate of Arts and Associate of Science degrees are academic programs designed for students who plan to transfer to a four-year college or university. Colorado Mountain College includes seven campuses in western Colorado. **NOTE:** All hiring is done by the Glenwood campus.

COLORADO MUNICIPAL LEAGUE
1144 Sherman Street, Denver CO 80203-2207. 303/831-6411. **Contact:** Katy Priest, Office Manager. **E-mail address:** kpriest@cml.org. **World Wide Web address:** http://www.cml.org. **Description:** An organization comprised of Colorado municipalities.

COLORADO ROCKIES
2001 Blake Street, Denver CO 80205. 303/832-8326. **Fax:** 303/312-2028. **Recorded jobline:** 303/312-2490. **Contact:** Human Resources. **Description:** The Major League Baseball franchise of the Denver area.

COLORADO SERUM COMPANY
P.O. Box 16428, Denver CO 80216. 303/295-7527. **Fax:** 303/295-1923. **Contact:** Joe Huff, President. **E-mail address:** colorado-serum@colorado-serum.com. **World Wide Web address:** http://www.colorado-serum.com. **Description:** Develops and manufactures veterinary serums and biologics.

COLORADO SPRINGS BUSINESS JOURNAL
31 East Platte Avenue, Suite 300, Colorado Springs CO 80903. 719/634-5905. **Fax:** 719/634-5157. **Contact:** Publisher. **World Wide Web address:** http://www.csbj.com. **Description:** Publishes a weekly business newspaper. Founded in 1989. **Special programs:** Internships. **Corporate headquarters location:** This location. **Parent company:** Colorado Publishing Company. **Listed on:** Privately held. **Annual sales/revenues:** Less than $5 million. **Number of employees at this location:** 20.

COLORADO SPRINGS, CITY OF
P.O. Box 1575, Mail Code 1547, Colorado Springs CO 80901-1575. 719/385-5900. **Contact:** Lauren Kramer, City Manager. **World Wide Web address:** http://www.springsgov.com. **Description:** The administrative offices for the city of Colorado Springs.

COLORADO SPRINGS UTILITIES
P.O. Box 1103, Colorado Springs CO 80947. 719/448-4800. **Contact:** Human Resources. **E-mail address:** hrservicecenter@csu.org. **World Wide Web address:** http://www.csu.org. **Description:** Provides public utility services. **NOTE:** Apply online.

COLORADO STATE UNIVERSITY
Human Resource Services, Fort Collins CO 80523-6004. 970/491-1794. **Fax:** 970/491-2548. **Recorded jobline:** 970/491-3941. **Contact:** Human Resource Services. **World Wide Web address:** http://www.colostate.edu. **Description:** A state university offering undergraduate, graduate, and doctorate programs.

COLORADO STATE UNIVERSITY AT PUEBLO
2200 Bonforte Boulevard, Pueblo CO 81001-4901. 719/549-2100. **Contact:** Human Resources Department. **World Wide Web address:** http://www.colostate-pueblo.edu. **Description:** Colorado State/Pueblo has an enrollment of approximately 4,600 students. The university operates through five divisions: The College of Applied Science & Engineering, The School of Business, The College of Humanities and Social Science, The College of Science and Mathematics, and The Center for Teaching and Learning.

COLOREL BLINDS
13802 East 33rd Place, Unit B, Aurora CO 80011. 303/375-8181. **Fax:** 303/574-9182. **Contact:** Human Resources. **Description:** A leading national fabricator and retailer of custom-made window coverings for residential and commercial customers. **NOTE:** Entry-level positions are offered. **Special programs:** Training. **Corporate headquarters location:** This location. **Other U.S. locations:** TX; WA. **Parent company:** Colorel Corporation. **Listed on:** Privately held. **Number of employees nationwide:** 180.

COMMERCIAL FEDERAL BANK
2 Steel Street, Denver CO 80206. 303/331-3526. **Fax:** 303/331-3522. **Recorded jobline:** 402/514-5409. **Contact:** Human Resources. **E-mail address:** Colorado_Careers@commercialfed.com. **World Wide Web address:** http://www.comfedbank.com. **Description:** A branch location of the multistate bank. **Parent company:** Commercial Federal Corporation, a financial services holding company, operates 108 bank branch locations in Nebraska, Colorado, Kansas, Oklahoma, and Iowa. **Corporate headquarters location:** Omaha NE. **Listed on:** New York Stock Exchange. **Stock exchange symbol:** CFB.

COMMODORE ADVANCED SCIENCES, INC.
4251 Kipling Street, Suite 575, Wheat Ridge CO 80033. 303/421-1511. **Contact:** Human Resources. **World Wide Web address:** http://www.commodore.com. **Description:** A technical services consulting firm that provides waste management, environmental sciences, advanced technologies, and remediation. Founded in 1977. **NOTE:** Entry-level positions are offered. **Corporate headquarters location:** Alexandria VA. **Other U.S. locations:** Idaho Falls ID; Carlsbad NM; Los Alamos NM; Oak Ridge TN. **Parent company:** Commodore Applied Technologies, Inc. **Listed on:** American Stock Exchange. **Stock exchange symbol:** CXI.

COMPASSION INTERNATIONAL
12290 Voyager Parkway, Colorado Springs CO 80921. 719/487-7000. **Contact:** Recruitment. **World Wide Web address:** http://www.ci.org. **Description:** A Christian organization that aids poverty-stricken children throughout the world.

COMPUTER RESEARCH, INC.
999 18th Street, Suite 260, Denver CO 80202. 303/297-9200. **Contact:** Human Resources. **E-mail address:** crimail@crixnet.com. **World Wide Web address:** http://www.crix.com. **Description:** Provides data processing, accounting, and record-keeping services for approximately 60 investment securities firms and banks throughout the country. Clients use Computer Research, Inc. systems to maintain their customer accounts and firm records in compliance with financial industry and regulatory agency reporting requirements. These systems include a number of proprietary computer programs that the company maintains and operates, linking clients to its data centers in Pittsburgh and Denver (this location.) The programs provide online retrieval, reports, and records on a day-to-day basis using data supplied by the clients. **Corporate headquarters location:** Coraopolis PA. **Number of employees nationwide:** 50.

COMSTOR
295 Interlocken Boulevard, Suite 100, Broomfield CO 80021. 303/222-4747. **Toll-free phone:** 800/543-6098. **Fax:** 303/222-4875. **Contact:** Human Resources. **World Wide Web address:** http://www.comstor.com. **Description:** Distributes computers, internetworking products, and peripherals and provides related services. Founded in 1986. **NOTE:** Entry-level positions are offered. **Office hours:** Monday - Friday, 8:00 a.m. - 5:00 p.m. **Corporate headquarters location:** Chantilly VA. **Other U.S. locations:** Carrollton TX. **Number of employees at this location:** 140. **Number of employees nationwide:** 370.

CONAGRA FLOUR MILLING COMPANY
4545 East 64th Avenue, Commerce City CO 80022. 303/289-6141. **Contact:** Human Resources. **World Wide Web address:** http://www.conagra.com. **Description:** ConAgra Flour Milling Company is a leader in the U.S. flour milling industry with 27 mills in 14 states. Operations also include seven jointly-owned mills, three in the United States and four in Canada. **NOTE:** Interested jobseekers must be able to relocate approximately every 18 months to two years. **Office hours:** Monday - Friday, 7:00 a.m. - 4:00 p.m. **Corporate headquarters location:** Omaha NE. **Operations at this facility include:** This location is engaged in the production and sale of wheat flour products in bulk and bag units to commercial bakeries, wholesale distributors, and retail grocery companies. **Parent company:** ConAgra Foods. **Listed on:** New York Stock Exchange. **Stock exchange symbol:** CAG. **Annual sales/revenues:** More than $100 million. **Number of employees at this location:** 125.

CONAGRA FOODS
150 Main Street, Longmont CO 80501. 303/776-6611. **Contact:** Human Resources. **World Wide Web address:** http://www.conagra.com. **Description:** Engaged in poultry dressing operations. **Corporate headquarters location:** Omaha NE. **Listed on:** New York Stock Exchange. **Stock exchange symbol:** CAG.

CONOCO, INC.
5801 Brighton Boulevard, Commerce City CO 80022. 303/288-2651. **Contact:** Human Resources. **World Wide Web address:** http://www.conoco.com. **Description:** The distribution center of a refinery for gasoline, jet fuel, diesel, and asphalt. **Corporate headquarters location:** Houston TX. **Listed on:** New York Stock Exchange. **Stock exchange symbol:** COC.

COORS BREWING COMPANY/GLASS DIVISION
10619 West 50th Avenue, Wheat Ridge CO 80033. 303/425-7711. **Contact:** Human Resources. **World Wide Web address:** http://www.coors.com. **Description:** Coors Brewing Company is one of the largest brewers in the United States. Brands include Coors, Coors Light, Zima Clearmalt, and Killian's Irish Red. **NOTE:** Jobseekers should address inquiries to P.O. Box 4030, Golden CO 80401. **Operations at this facility include:** This location manufactures glass bottles.

COORSTEK
16000 Table Mountain Parkway, Golden CO 80403. 303/277-4000. **Contact:** Human Resources. **E-mail address:** careers@coorstek.com. **World Wide Web address:** http://www.coorstek.com. **Description:** Manufactures advanced technical ceramics, precision-machined metals, and engineered plastic products. **NOTE:** Apply online. **Positions advertised include:** Quality Assurance Engineer; Machinist; Thermal Processing Product Sales Manager. **Corporate headquarters location:** This location. **Other area locations:** Grand Junction, CO. **Listed on:** NASDAQ. **Stock exchange symbol:** CRTK.

COPPER MOUNTAIN RESORTS, INC.
P.O. Box 3548, Copper Mountain CO 80443. 970/968-2318. **Contact:** Human Resources Department. **World Wide Web address:** http://www.coppersummer.com. **Description:** Operates a resort with ski facilities and a wide range of warm-weather activities. Founded in 1972. **Office hours:** Sunday - Saturday, 8:00 a.m. - 5:00 p.m. **Corporate headquarters location:** This location. **Other area locations:** Dillon CO; Frisco CO; Leadville CO. **COO:** David Barry. **Facilities Manager:** Becky Yessak. **Information Systems Manager:** Doug Feeley. **Purchasing Manager:** Don Jones. **Sales Manager:** Carol Schmidt.

CORAM HEALTHCARE CORPORATION
1675 Broadway, Suite 900, Denver CO 80202. 303/672-8745. **Fax:** 303/298-0043. **Contact:** Faye Major, Human Resources. **World Wide Web address:** http://www.coramhc.com. **Description:** One of the largest home health infusion therapy companies in the United States. The company provides a wide range of alternate site delivery services including ambulatory and home infusion therapies, lithotripsy, and institutional pharmacy services. **Corporate headquarters location:** This location. **Other U.S. locations:** Nationwide. **Subsidiaries include:** Coraflex Health Services; HealthInfusion Inc.; Medisys Inc.; T2 Medical. **Listed on:** New York Stock Exchange. **Stock exchange symbol:** CRH. **Annual sales/revenues:** More than $100 million.

CORPORATE EXPRESS
One Environmental Way, Broomfield CO 80021. 303/664-2000. **Fax:** 303/664-3474. **Contact:** Personnel. **World Wide Web address:** http://www.corporateexpress.com. **Description:** A business-to-business supplier of office supplies. The company supplies products through a direct sales staff and direct mail catalogs. **Corporate headquarters location:** This location. **International locations:** Worldwide. **Listed on:** New York Stock Exchange. **Stock exchange symbol:** BUH.

COUNTRYWIDE FUNDING CORPORATION
8433 Church Ranch Boulevard, Suite 300, Westminster CO 80021. 303/410-9100. **Fax:** 303/410-9900. **World Wide Web address:** http://www.countrywide.com. **Contact:** Human Resources. **Description:** Originates, purchases, sells, and services mortgage loans. The company's mortgage loans are principally first-lien mortgage loans secured by single-family residences. **Other U.S. locations:** Nationwide. **Parent company:** Countrywide Credit Industries. **Listed on:** New York Stock Exchange. **Stock exchange symbol:** CCR.

CRAIG HOSPITAL
3425 South Clarkson Street, Englewood CO 80110. 303/789-8000. **Recorded jobline:** 303/789-8497. **Contact:** Human Resources. **E-mail address:** humanresources@craighospital.org. **World Wide Web address:** http://www.craighospital.org. **Description:** A hospital for the care and rehabilitation of patients with injuries to the brain or spinal cord. **NOTE:** Entry-level positions are offered. Please check the jobline for available positions before sending a resume. **Positions advertised include:** RN; Rehabilitation Technician; Respiratory Therapist; Clerical Coordinator; Operations Manager, HIM. **Special programs:** Internships. **Operations at this facility include:** Administration. **Number of employees at this location:** 500.

CREATIVE TOUCH INTERIORS
3301 Lewiston Street, Aurora CO 80011. 303/343-9000. **Contact:** Human Resources. **World Wide Web address:** http://www.ctihome.com. **Description:** Engaged in the installation and refinishing of hardwood floors. The company is also engaged in the installation of carpet, vinyl, ceramic tile, and related floor coverings. Founded in 1959. **Positions advertised include:** Scheduler; Production Assistant; Customer Service Representative; Field Supervisor; Warehouse Driver; Corian Fabricators; Flooring Trainee.

CREEDE REPERTORY THEATRE
P.O. Box 269, Creede CO 81130. 719/658-2541. **Fax:** 719/658-2343. **Contact:** Human Resources. **E-mail address:** crt@creederep.com. **World Wide Web address:** http://www.creederep.com. **Description:** A nonprofit theater producing eight plays annually. **Note:** This location also hires seasonally. Founded in 1969. **Special programs:** Internships. **CEO:** Richard Baxter. **Number of employees at this location:** 40.

CROSSROADS MEDICAL CENTER
1000 Alpine Street, Suite 280, Boulder CO 80304. 303/444-6400. **Contact:** Director of Personnel. **Description:** An ambulatory health care and family practice provider. Crossroads Medical Center also provides pharmacological, laboratory, and physical therapy services, as well as specialist physician services through their own group practice. **Operations at this facility include:** Administration; Divisional Headquarters; Sales.

CROWN RESOURCES CORPORATION
4251 Kipling Street, Suite 390, Wheat Ridge CO 80033. 303/534-1030. **Contact:** Human Resources. **World Wide Web address:** http://www.crownresources.com. **Description:** Engaged in gold exploration and mining.

CURRENT, INC.
1005 East Woodman Road, Colorado Springs CO 80920. 719/594-4100. **Contact:** Personnel. **World Wide Web address:** http://www.currentinc.com. **Description:** Prints and markets greeting cards, stationery, and checks. **Corporate headquarters location:** St. Paul MN. **Other U.S. locations:** Nationwide. **Parent company:** Deluxe Corporation. **Number of employees at this location:** 2,700.

DAILY CAMERA
P.O. Box 591, Boulder CO 80306. 303/442-1202. **Contact:** Human Resources Department. **E-mail address:** jobs@thedailycamera.com. **World Wide Web address:** http://www.thedailycamera.com. **Description:** Publishes a daily newspaper. **Special programs:** Internships. **Corporate headquarters location:** This location. **Parent company:** E.W. Scripps Company (Cincinnati OH). **Listed on:** New York Stock Exchange. **Stock exchange symbol:** SSP.

DAIMLERCHRYSLER CORPORATION
12225 East 39th Avenue, Denver CO 80239. 303/373-8840. **Contact:** Human Resources. **E-mail address:** resume@daimlerchrysler.com. **World Wide Web address:** http://www.daimlerchrysler.com. **Description:** DaimlerChrysler Corporation produces cars, trucks, minivans, and sport-utility vehicles for customers in more than 100 countries. **NOTE:** Please see company Website for instructions on how to apply. **Corporate headquarters location:** Auburn Hills MI. **Operations at this facility include:** This location is a parts depot. **Listed on:** New York Stock Exchange. **Stock exchange symbol:** DCX.

DATA RAY CORPORATION
12300 Pecos, Westminster CO 80234. 303/451-1300. **Contact:** Human Resources. **World Wide Web address:** http://www.data-ray.com. **Description:** Manufactures high-resolution CRT monitors.

DATATREND INFORMATION SYSTEMS, INC.
1200 17th Street, Suite 1250, Denver CO 80202. 303/572-6262. **Contact:** Human Resources. **World Wide Web address:** http://www.datatrendis.com. **Description:** Offers systems consulting services. **Positions advertised include:** PeopleSoft Functional Analyst; PeopleSoft Technical Analyst; Recruiter/Resource Manager. **Corporate headquarters location:** This location. **Other U.S. locations:** Chicago IL. **Number of employees at this location:** 25. **Number of employees nationwide:** 45.

DEERFIELD HILLS COMMUNITY CENTER
4290 Deerfield Hills Road, Colorado Springs CO 80916. 719/578-6807. **Contact:** Human Resources. **Description:** Offers programs for preschool-aged children to adults, provides rentals, and participates in several partnerships with groups such as the YMCA.

DELOITTE & TOUCHE LLP
555 17th Street, Suite 3600, Denver CO 80202-3942. 303/292-5400. **Contact:** Heather Cameron, Personnel Director. **World Wide Web address:** http://www.us.deloitte.com. **Description:** An international firm of certified public accountants providing professional accounting, auditing, tax, and management consulting services to widely diversified clients. The company has a specialized program consisting of national industry groups and functional groups that cross industry lines. Groups are involved in various disciplines including accounting, auditing, taxation management advisory services, small and growing businesses, mergers and acquisitions, and computer applications. **Special programs:** Internships. **Other U.S. locations:** Nationwide.

DENVER BRONCOS
13655 Broncos Parkway, Englewood CO 80112. 203/649-9000. **Contact:** Human Resources. **World Wide Web address:** www.denverbroncos.com. **Description:** The executive office of the NFL franchise and former Super Bowl champions.

DENVER BUSINESS JOURNAL
1700 Broadway, Suite 515, Denver CO 80290-9908. 303/837-3500. **Contact:** Human Resources. **E-mail address:** denver@bizjournals.com. **World Wide Web address:** http://www.denver.bizjournals.com. **Description:** Publishes a business journal.

DENVER CENTER THEATRE COMPANY
1245 Champa Street, Denver CO 80204-2104. 303/893-4000. **Recorded jobline:** 303/446-4873. **Contact:** Barbara Sellers, Production Director. **World Wide Web address:** http://www.denvercenter.org. **Description:** A professional acting troupe that performs a broad range of theatrical productions year-round. Founded in 1978. **Parent company:** Denver Center for the Performing Arts. **Number of employees at this location:** 300.

DENVER DISTRIBUTORS INC.
3301 Mariposa, P.O. Box 11368, Denver CO 80211. 303/433-7463. **Contact:** Mike Selby, President. **Description:** A wholesaler of electrical supplies and equipment to commercial, industrial, and residential contractors.

DENVER FEDERAL CREDIT UNION
1075 Acoma Street, Denver CO 80204. 303/573-1170. **Fax:** 303/626-0750. **Contact:** Human Resources. **E-mail address:** careers@dmfcu.org. **World Wide Web address:** http://www.dcfcu.coop. **Description:** A credit union. **Positions advertised include:** Teller.

DENVER MARRIOTT TECH CENTER
4900 South Syracuse Street, Denver CO 80237. 303/779-1100. **Recorded jobline:** 303/782-3214. **Contact:** Human Resources Department. **World Wide Web address:** http://www.marriott.com. **Description:** A 625-room hotel. **NOTE:** Entry-level positions, part-time jobs, and second and third shifts are offered. This location also hires seasonally. **Company slogan:** The difference is excellence. The difference is you. **Special programs:** Internships; Training; Summer Jobs. **Corporate headquarters location:** Bethesda MD. **Other U.S. locations:** Nationwide. **International locations:** Worldwide. **Parent company:** Marriot International, Inc. **Listed on:** New York Stock Exchange. **Stock exchange symbol:** MAR. **Annual sales/revenues:** More than $100 million. **Number of employees at this location:** 375. **Number of employees nationwide:** 100,000. **Number of employees worldwide:** 150,000.

THE DENVER POST
1560 Broadway, Denver CO 80202. 303/820-1010. **Contact:** Misty Miller, Vice President of Human Resources Department. **World Wide Web address:** http://www.denverpost.com. **Description:** Publishes a daily newspaper with a weekday circulation of more than 280,000 and a Sunday circulation of 450,000. **Special programs:** Internships. **Corporate headquarters location:** Houston TX. **Parent company:** Denver Newspaper Agency. **Operations at this facility include:** Divisional Headquarters.

DENVER REGIONAL COUNCIL OF GOVERNMENTS
4500 Cherry Creek Drive South, Suite 800, Denver CO 80246. 303/455-1000. **Fax:** 303/480-6790. **Contact:** Human Resources. **World Wide Web address:** http://www.drcog.org. **Description:** An association of local governments for 39 area cities and eight counties. **NOTE:** Entry-level positions are offered. **Special programs:** Internships. **Corporate headquarters location:** This location. **Operations at this facility include:** Administration. **Number of employees at this location:** 80.

THE DENVER ZOO
2300 Steele Street, Denver CO 80205-4899. 303/376-4800. **Contact:** Human Resources. **E-mail address:** zoohr@denverzoo.org. **World Wide Web address:** http://www.denverzoo.org. **Description:** A zoo featuring year-round exhibits including Bird World and Tropical Discovery. **Corporate headquarters location:** This location.

DEVELOPMENTAL DISABILITIES SERVICES
3824 West Princeton Circle, Denver CO 80236. 303/866-7450. **Fax:** 303/866-7470. **Contact:** Kerry Stern, Acting Director. **Description:** A nonprofit organization that provides services to individuals with developmental disabilities.

DEVELOPMENTAL DISABILITY RESOURCE CENTER (DDRC)
5685 Gray Street, Arvada CO 80002. 303/422-1305. **Contact:** Human Resources. **World Wide Web address:** http://www.ddrcco.com. **Description:** A nonprofit organization that provides services to individuals with developmental disabilities. **Positions advertised include:** Home Host Provider; Vocational Instructor Supervisor; Early Intervention Occupational Therapist.

DEVEREUX CLEO WALLACE CENTERS
8405 Church Ranch Boulevard, Westminster CO 80021. 303/639-1704. **Fax:** 303/639-1720. **Contact:** Gayle Collins, Human Resources Administrator. **World Wide Web address:** http://www.devereux.org. **Description:** A nonprofit, psychiatric treatment center offering both inpatient and outpatient treatments for children and adolescents. **NOTE:** Entry-level positions and second and third shifts are offered. **Positions advertised include:** Clinician. **Special programs:** Internships. **Corporate headquarters location:** This location. **Other area locations:** Colorado Springs CO; Westminster CO. **CEO:** James Cole. **Number of employees at this location:** 100. **Number of employees nationwide:** 600.

DIAMOND VOGEL PAINT
4500 East 48th Avenue, P.O. Box 16388, Denver CO 80216-0388. 303/333-3117. **Contact:** Human Resources. **E-mail address:** hrmanager@vogelpaint.com. **World Wide Web address:** http://www.diamondvogel.com. **Description:** Produces a variety of paints, stains, and resins. **Corporate headquarters location:** Orange City IA.

DOUBLETREE HOTEL DURANGO
501 Camino Del Rio, Durango CO 81301. 970/259-6580. **Fax:** 970/259-4398. **Contact:** Human Resources. **World Wide Web address:** www.durango.doubletree.com. **Description:** Luxury hotel within walking distance of downtown Durango and restaurants. **Parent Company:** Hilton.

DUKE ENERGY
1324 North Seventh Avenue, Greeley CO 80631. 970/454-3366. **Contact:** Human Resources. **World Wide Web address:** http://www.duke-energy.com. **Description:** Provides electric service to approximately 2 million customers, operates pipelines that deliver 12 percent of the natural gas consumed in the United States, and is a leading maker of electricity, natural gas, and natural gas liquids. **Corporate headquarters location:** Charlotte NC. **Listed on:** New York Stock Exchange. **Stock exchange symbol:** DUK.

DYNAMIC MATERIALS CORPORATION
5405 Spine Road, Boulder CO 80301. 303/665-5700. **Fax:** 303/604-1893. **Contact:** Human Resources. **E-mail address:** boom@dynamicmaterials.com. **World Wide Web address:** http://www.dynamicmaterials.com. **Description:** Engaged in the use of explosives to bond and form metals. **NOTE:** Entry-level positions and second and third shifts are offered. **Company slogan:** We strive to live up to our dynamic name. **Special programs:** Internships; Apprenticeships; Training. **Corporate headquarters location:** This location. **Other U.S. locations:** South Windsor CT; Uniontown PA. **Listed on:** NASDAQ. **Stock exchange symbol:** BOOM. **Annual sales/revenues:** $21 - $50 million. **Number of employees at this location:** 80. **Number of employees nationwide:** 135.

EDS (ELECTRONIC DATA SYSTEMS CORPORATION)
6950 West Jefferson Avenue, Suite 250, Lakewood CO 80235-2334. 303/763-3700. **Contact:** Human Resources. **World Wide Web address:** http://www.eds.com. **Description:** Provides consulting, systems development, systems integration, and systems management services for large-scale and industry-specific applications. Founded in 1962. **Corporate headquarters location:** Plano TX. **Other U.S. locations:** Nationwide. **Listed on:** New York Stock Exchange. **Stock exchange symbol:** EDS. **Number of employees nationwide:** 75,000.

EAGLEDIRECT.COM, INC.
5105 East 41st Avenue, Denver CO 80216. 303/320-5411. **Fax:** 303/393-6584. **Contact:** Human Resources. **E-mail address:** tdrinkwater@eagledirect.com. **World Wide Web address:** http://www.eagledirect. com. **Description:** Engaged in commercial and lithographic printing and design. Offers direct marketing, commercial lithography services, and an online business that allows companies to create and order printed documents and order custom marketing services.

EAST CENTRAL NEIGHBORHOOD LINK
2546 15th Street, Denver CO 80211. 303/830-0123. **Contact:** Ted Pinkowitz, President. **World Wide Web address:** http://www.ecentral.com. **Description:** Provides Internet access, e-mail accounts, and home pages on the Web to companies and individuals.

EAST DENVER YMCA
3540 East 31st Avenue, Denver CO 80205. 303/322-7761. **Contact:** Human Resources. **World Wide Web address:** http://www.ymca.com. **Description:** One of the nation's largest and most comprehensive nonprofit service organizations. The YMCA provides health and fitness, social and personal development, sports and recreation, education and career development, and camps and conferences to children, youths, adults, the elderly, families, disabled individuals, refugees and foreign nationals, YMCA residents, and community residents through a broad range of specific programs.

EASTMAN KODAK COMPANY
9952 Eastman Park Drive, Windsor CO 80551-1386. 970/686-7611. **Contact:** Jean Clark, Director of Personnel. **World Wide Web address:** http://www.kodak.com. **Description:** Eastman Kodak Company manufactures photographic equipment and supplies; medical products; information storage and retrieval systems; and copiers/duplicators. Consumer brand names include Kodak film, Bayer aspirin, d-Con pest control, Minwax wood finishes, and Resolve carpet cleaner. The company also produces cameras, photo CDs and players, software, printers, and batteries. **NOTE:** Please make sure that all resumes are in a scannable format. Interested jobseekers who have graduated from high school or obtained a GED within the last five years must also submit a high school transcript or a GED score report. **Positions advertised include:** Production Operator; Assembly/Warehouse Worker; Summer College Intern; Validation Engineer. **Special programs:** Internships. **Corporate headquarters location:** Rochester NY. **Operations at this facility include:** This location manufactures photographic and medical X-ray films. **Operations at this facility include:** Manufacturing. **Listed on:** New York Stock Exchange. **Stock exchange symbol:** EK. **Number of employees at this location:** 2,300.

EATON METAL PRODUCTS COMPANY
4800 York Street, Denver CO 80216-2237. 303/296-5729. **Contact:** Human Resources. **World Wide Web address:** http://www.eatonmetalsales.com. **Description:** Produces a broad range of fabricated metal products including structural metals, structural plates, and oil field equipment. **Positions advertised include:** Field Technician; Installer.

ECHO BAY MINES
6400 South Fiddler's Green Circle, Suite 540, Englewood CO 80111. 303/714-8800. **Contact:** Human Resources. **World Wide Web address:** http://www.echobay.com. **Description:** One of the largest gold mining operations in North America. **Listed on:** American Stock Exchange. **Stock exchange symbol:** ECO.

EMERSON PROCESS MANAGEMENT DIETERICH STANDARD, INC.
5601 North 71st Street, Boulder CO 80301. 303/530-9600. **Contact:** Human Resources. **World Wide Web address:** http://www.emersonprocess.com. **Description:** Produces a wide range of flow and process equipment. **Corporate headquarters location:** This location.

EMPIRE OLDSMOBILE/HONDA
P.O. Box 200336, Denver CO 80220. 303/399-1950. **Physical address:** 6160 East Colfax Avenue, Denver CO 80220. **Contact:** Judy Grinestaff, Payroll Supervisor. **Description:** An automobile dealership.

ENGINEERING MEASUREMENTS COMPANY
600 Diagonal Highway, Longmont CO 80501. 303/651-0550. **Fax:** 303/678-7152. **Contact:** Human Resources Director. **World Wide Web address:** http://www.emcoflow.com. **Description:** Manufactures flow meters. Founded in 1967. **NOTE:** Second and third shifts are offered. **Special programs:** Training. **Annual sales/revenues:** $5 - $10 million. **Number of employees at this location:** 90.

ENSCICON CORPORATION
518 17th Street, Suite 1350, Denver CO 80202. 303/832-8200. **Fax:** 303/832-6700. **Contact:** Staffing. **E-mail address:** info@enscicon.com. **World Wide Web address:** http://www.enscicon.com. **Description:** Provides computer science engineering and high-tech consulting services. Founded in 1994. **Positions advertised include:** Health/Safety Professional; Mechanical Designer; Drainage Engineer; Civil Engineer; Bridge Engineer; Designer/Drafter. **Corporate headquarters location:** This location. **Other U.S. locations:** Portland OR. **Listed on:** Privately held. **President:** William Smith.

EVERGREEN RESOURCES, INC.
1401 17th Street, Suite 1200, Denver CO 80202. 303/534-0400. **Contact:** Human Resources. **World Wide Web address:** http://www.evergreen-res.com. **Description:** An oil and gas exploration and production company with interests in 350 oil and gas wells in the continental United States. **Corporate headquarters location:** This location. **Subsidiaries include:** Evergreen Resources (UK) Ltd. holds six-year exploration licenses onshore in the development of methane gas and conventional hydrocarbons. Evergreen Operating Corporation is the designated operator for 193 oil and gas wells. **Listed on:** New York Stock Exchange. **Stock exchange symbol:** EVG. **President/CEO:** Mark S. Sexton. **Number of employees at this location:** 30.

EXABYTE CORPORATION
2108 55th Street, Boulder CO 80301. 303/442-4333. **Contact:** Human Resources. **World Wide Web address:** http://www.exabyte.com. **Description:** Designs, manufactures, and markets cartridge tape subsystems for data storage applications. The company's products are used in a broad spectrum of computer systems based on 8mm helical scan, 4mm helical scan, and quarter-inch technologies. Products are used in various computer systems ranging from personal computers to supercomputers. A large majority of its units are used with workstations, network file servers, and minicomputers. The capacity of these subsystems allows users to back up multiple disk drives, and in many cases, an entire computer system on a single tape cartridge. **Corporate headquarters location:** This location. **Listed on:** NASDAQ. **Stock exchange symbol:** EXBT.

EXECUTIVE TOWER HOTEL
1405 Curtis Street, Denver CO 80202. 303/571-0300. **Contact:** Human Resources. **World Wide Web address:** http://www.exectowerhotel.com. **Description:** A 337-room hotel.

EXEMPLA ST. JOSEPH HOSPITAL
1835 Franklin Street, Denver CO 80218. 303/837-7905. **Contact:** Human Resources. **World Wide Web address:** http://www.saintjosephdenver.org. **Description:** A community hospital providing patient care and education. Founded in 1873. **Positions advertised include:** Certified Nurse Assistant; Cardiac Surgery Registrar; Cardiovascular Technician; Clinical Manager; Clinical Research Coordinator; Distribution Technician; Exercise Physiologist; Environmental Services Aide; LPN; Medical Technologist; Pharmacist; Recruitment Manager. **Note:** Resumes can be submitted electronically online or mailed to the attention of the Human Resources Department.

FARMERS INSURANCE GROUP
P.O. Box 371078, Denver CO 80231. 303/283-6100. **Physical address:** 7535 East Hampden Avenue, Suite 310, Denver CO 80231-4842. **Contact:** Division Marketing Manager. **World Wide Web address:** http://www.farmersinsurance.com. **Description:** A multiline insurance agency that sells and services insurance policies to individuals, families, and businesses throughout the Denver metropolitan area. **Positions advertised include:** Insurance Agent/Broker. **Corporate headquarters location:** Los Angeles CA. **Other U.S. locations:** Phoenix AZ; Merced CA; Pleasanton CA; Santa Ana CA; Simi Valley CA; Pocatello ID; Aurora IL; Columbus OH; Portland OR; Austin TX; Vancouver WA. **Parent company:** Zurich. **Number of employees at this location:** 30.

FIBERLOK INC.
P.O. Box 1727, Fort Collins CO 80524. 970/221-1200. **Physical address:** 811 Stockton Avenue, Fort Collins CO 80824. **Contact:** Human Resources. **World Wide Web address:** http://www.fiberlok.com. **E-mail address:** info@fiberlok.com. **World Wide Web address:** http://stores.yahoo.com/fiberlok. **Description:** Manufactures heat seal transfers and sew on patches.

FIRST CLASS SECURITY SYSTEMS
3835 West 10th Street, Suite 100C, Greeley CO 80634-1551. 970/339-2449. **Fax:** 970/336-3119. **Contact:** Richard Newman, Office Manager. **Description:** Installs and services burglar and fire alarm, video surveillance, and access control systems. Founded in 1983. **Company slogan:** The best service in the business. **Office hours:** Monday - Friday, 8:00 a.m. - 5:00 p.m. **Corporate headquarters location:** This location. **Owner:** Bob Stewart. **Annual sales/revenues:** Less than $5 million.

FIRST DATA CORPORATION
6200 South Quebec Street, Greenwood Village CO 80111. 303/488-8000. **Contact:** Human Resources. **World Wide Web address:** http://www.firstdata.com. **Description:** A holding company. Through its subsidiaries, First Data provides credit card issuing and merchant transaction processing services, e-commerce solutions, money transfers, and other business services. **NOTE:** Apply online. **Positions advertised include:** Compliance Officer; Compliance Auditor; Financial Analyst; Business Analyst. **Corporate headquarters location:** This location. **Subsidiaries include:** First Data Resources. **Other U.S. locations:** Phoenix AZ; Palo Alto CA; Sunrise FL; Atlanta GA; Omaha NE; Nashville TN. **Listed on:** New York Stock Exchange. **Stock exchange symbol:** FDC.

FISCHER IMAGING CORPORATION
12300 Grant Street, Denver CO 80241. 303/452-6800. **Fax:** 303/450-4335. **Contact:** Human Resources. **World Wide Web address:** http://www.fischerimaging.com. **Description:** Develops, manufactures, and markets medical imaging systems. Fischer Imaging Corporation provides medical systems for the electrophysiology, fluoroscopic, mammography, and radiographic markets. **Positions advertised include:** X-Ray Image Scientist; Senior Hardware Engineer; Vice President of Service; Sales Representative; Field Service Engineer. **Corporate headquarters location:** This location. **Listed on:** NASDAQ. **Stock exchange symbol:** FIMG. **Number of employees at this location:** 350. **Number of employees nationwide:** 540.

FLINT ENERGY CONSTRUCTION COMPANY
P.O. Box 145, 1391 Denver Avenue, Fort Lupton CO 80621-0145. 303/857-2791. **Contact:** Human Resources. **Description:** Provides oil and gas pipeline construction and well servicing. **World Wide Web address:** http://www.flint-energy.com. **Corporate headquarters location:** Tulsa OK.

FORT CARSON
Civilian Personnel Advisory Center, 6151 Specker, Room 2080, Building 1550, Fort Carson CO 80913-5118. 719/526-4524. **Contact:** Personnel. **World Wide Web address:** http://www.carson.army.mil. **Description:** Organizes the armed forces to defend the nation's security. **NOTE:** All resumes should be sent to SWCPOC, 301 Marshall Avenue, Attention: B13, Fort Riley KS 66442-5004. **Parent company:** U.S. Department of the Army.

THE FOSS COMPANY
1224 Washington Avenue, Golden CO 80401. 303/279-3373. **Contact:** Mike Minter, Personnel Manager. **World Wide Web address:** http://www.fossco.com. **Description:** A general store, post office, pharmacy, and liquor store. This location is also headquarters for Ski Country Decanters, H.J. Foss Apparel, and The Golden Ram Restaurant. **Corporate headquarters location:** This location. **Operations at this facility include:** Administration; Sales; Service.

FOUNDERS ASSET MANAGEMENT, INC.
201 University Boulevard, Suite 800, Denver CO 80206. 303/394-4404. **Fax:** 303/394-7840. **Contact:** Human Resources. **E-mail address:** employment@founders.com. **World Wide Web address:** http://www.founders.com. **Description:** Offers mutual funds including small-stock, international funds and conservative bond funds. The company services approximately 125,000 account holders worldwide and manages assets of approximately $2 billion. Founded in 1938. **Corporate headquarters location:** This location. **Listed on:** Privately held.

FREDERIC PRINTING
14701 East 38th Avenue, Aurora CO 80011. 303/371-7990. **Contact:** Human Resources Department. **E-mail address:** info@fredericprinting.com. **World Wide Web address:** http://www.fredericprinting.com. **Description:** Provides a wide range of commercial printing services, from camera-ready art to binding. **Corporate headquarters location:** This location. **Parent company:** Consolidated Graphics. **Operations at this facility include:** Administration; Manufacturing; Sales. **Listed on:** New York Stock Exchange. **Stock exchange symbol:** CGX.

FRONTIER OIL REFINERY
4610 South Ulster Street, Suite 200, Denver CO 80237. 303/714-0100. **Contact:** Human Resources. **E-mail address:** hr@frontieroil-den.com. **World Wide Web address:** http://www.frontieroil.com. **Description:** Frontier Oil Corporation manufactures a full line of high-grade fuels from Wyoming crude oils. The company distributes more than one-half of the refinery's products throughout southern Wyoming and also supplies petroleum products to western Nebraska. **Corporate headquarters location:** Houston TX. **Operations at this facility include:** This location is a distributor of petroleum products to the Colorado Front Range. **Listed on:** New York Stock Exchange. **Stock exchange symbol:** FTO. **Number of employees nationwide:** 330.

FRONTRANGE SOLUTIONS
1125 Kelly Johnson Boulevard, Colorado Springs CO 80920. 719/531-5007. **Fax:** 719/536-0620. **Contact:** Human Resources Department. **World Wide Web address:** http://www.frontrange.com. **Description:** Develops software for support center markets such as help desks, customer service, and MIS/IS departments. **Positions advertised include:** Senior Consultant; Senior Software Engineer; PSO Practice Manager; Marketing Channel Products Manager; Director, Product Marketing.

FURNITURE ROW COMPANY
13333 East 37th Avenue, Denver CO 80239. 303/371-8560. **Contact:** Human Resources. **World Wide Web address:** http://www.furniturerow.com. **Description:** A retail furniture dealer. **Corporate headquarters location:** This location.

GALLERIA LIGHTING & DESIGN
239 Detroit Street, Denver CO 80206. 303/592-1223. **Toll-free phone:** 800/332-2066. **Fax:** 303/534-2566. **Contact:** Shelagh Stauffer, Owner. **Description:** Galleria Lighting & Design sells lighting fixtures in both retail and wholesale markets. **Positions advertised include:** Sales Executive. **Parent company:** QED. **Listed on:** Privately held. **Annual sales/revenues:** $51 - $100 million. **Number of employees at this location:** 30. **Number of employees nationwide:** 200.

GAMBRO HEALTH CARE
10810 West Collins Avenue, Lakewood CO 80215. **Toll-free phone:** 800/381-7063. **Contact:** Human Resources. **World Wide Web address:** http://www.gambro.com. **Description:** Provides dialysis and other health care services on an outpatient basis at independently operated facilities, and on an inpatient basis at hospitals.

GATES & SONS, INC.
90 South Fox Street, Denver CO 80229. 303/744-6185. **Contact:** Employment Manager. **E-mail address:** info@gatesconcreteforms.com. **World Wide Web address:** http://www.gatesconcreteforms.com. **Description:** Produces concrete forms for walls, seating, columns, prefabricated buildings, elevator shafts, and various other uses. **Corporate headquarters location:** This location.

THE GATES RUBBER COMPANY
990 South Broadway, Denver CO 80217-5887. 303/744-1911. **Physical address:** 990 South Broadway, Denver CO 80209. **Contact:** Human Resources Department. **World Wide Web address:** http://www.gates.com. **Description:** An international developer, manufacturer, and distributor of a broad range of rubber and plastic products. The company also operates area subsidiaries engaged in the production of automotive and heavy-duty batteries. **Positions advertised include:** Development Engineer; Stationary Engineer. **Corporate headquarters location:** This location.

THE GAZETTE
P.O. Box 1779, Colorado Springs CO 80901-1779. 719/632-5511. **Physical address:** 30 South Prospect, Colorado Springs CO 80903. **Contact:** Human Resources. **World Wide Web address:** http://www.gazette.com. **Description:** A newspaper with a circulation of approximately 100,000 daily and 125,000 on Sundays. **Parent company:** Freedom Communications, Inc.

GEOTRANS INC.
9101 Harlan Street, Suite 210, Westminster CO 80031. 303/426-7501. **Contact:** Human Resources. **World Wide Web address:** http://www.geotransinc.com. **Description:** Provides environmental consulting services. **NOTE:** Jobseekers should address inquiries to Judy Grant, Manager of Human Resources, HSI GeoTrans Inc.,

46050 Manekine Plaza, Suite 100, Sterling VA 20164. **Parent company:** Tetra-Tech. **Listed on:** NASDAQ. **Stock exchange symbol:** TTEK.

GLOBAL CROSSING CONFERENCING
1499 West 121st Avenue, Westminster CO 80234-0076. 303/633-3000. **Contact:** Director of Human Resources. **Description:** A supplier of audio teleconferencing equipment and services in North America and selected overseas markets. Global Crossing Conferencing provides operator-assisted and automatic audio teleconferencing services.

GOLD BUG INC.
4999 Oakland Street, Denver CO 80239. 303/371-2885. **Fax:** 303/373-8131. **Contact:** Human Resources. **Description:** Distributes children's apparel and accessories. Founded in 1968. **NOTE:** Entry-level positions and second and third shifts are offered. **Special programs:** Internships; Summer Jobs. **Office hours:** Monday - Friday, 6:00 a.m. - 6:00 p.m. **Corporate headquarters location:** This location. **Listed on:** Privately held. **Annual sales/revenues:** $21 - $50 million. **Number of employees at this location:** 120.

GOLDBERG BROTHERS INC.
P.O. Box 17048, 8000 East 40th Avenue, Denver CO 80217. 303/321-1099. **Fax:** 303/388-0749. **Contact:** Human Resources Department. **Description:** Manufactures aluminum and sheet metal products including aluminum castings, sheet metal stampings, and products made from these metals including film canisters, cases, and reels. **Corporate headquarters location:** This location. **Parent company:** J&R Film Co. **Listed on:** Privately held. **Number of employees at this location:** 40.

GOLDEN BELL PRESS INC.
2403 Champa Street, Denver CO 80205. 303/296-1600. **Contact:** Sherri Simpson, Office Manager. **World Wide Web address:** http://www.goldenbellpress.com. **Description:** Publishes periodicals and operates as an offset printer. Founded in 1936.

GOLDEN SOFTWARE, INC.
809 14th Street, Golden CO 80401-1866. 303/279-1021. **Toll-free phone:** 800/972-1021. **Contact:** Human Resources. **World Wide Web address:** http://www.goldensoftware.com. **Description:** Develops contouring, mapping, and graphing software for Windows and DOS operating systems. **Corporate headquarters location:** This location.

GOODRICH AEROSPACE
50 William White Boulevard, Pueblo CO 81001. 719/948-3500. **Contact:** Human Resources. **World Wide Web address:** http://www.goodrich.com. **Description:** Manufactures brakes for 747 airplanes. **Corporate headquarters location:** Charlotte NC. **Parent company:** Goodrich Corporation. **Listed on:** New York Stock Exchange. **Stock exchange symbol:** GR.

GOODWILL INDUSTRIES OF DENVER
6850 North Federal Boulevard, Denver CO 80221. 303/650-7700. **Fax:** 303/650-7749. **Contact:** Human Resources. **E-mail address:** info@goodwilldenver.org. **World Wide Web address:** http://www.goodwilldenver.org. **Description:** Operates 1,400 thrift stores nationwide and provides employment training for the disabled and the disadvantaged. **Other U.S. locations:** Nationwide. **CEO:** Thomas Welker. **Annual sales/revenues:** $5 - $10 million. **Number of employees at this location:** 290.

GORSUCH KIRGIS LLC
1515 Arapahoe Street, Tower One, Suite 1000, Denver CO 80202. 303/376-5000. **Fax:** 303/376-5001. **Contact:** Human Resources Director. **World Wide Web address:** http://www.gorsuch.com. **Description:** A law firm specializing in real estate, corporate, employment, health care, environmental, and bankruptcy law.

GRAND MESA, UNCOMPAHGRE, AND GUNNISON NATIONAL FOREST
2250 Highway 50, Delta CO 81416. 970/874-6609. **Contact:** Human Resources. **World Wide Web address:** http://www.fs.fed.us/r2/gmug/. **Description:** A division of the United States Department of Agriculture Forest Service. **Special programs:** Internships.

GRAND VALLEY TRANSIT
201 South Avenue, Grand Junction CO 81501. 970/256-7433. **Contact:** Ralph Power, Executive Director. **World Wide Web address:** http://www.grandvalleytransit.com. **Description:** Provides transportation services to people with disabilities.

GRANT THORNTON LLP
1600 Broadway, Suite 1800, Denver CO 80202. 303/861-5555. **Contact:** Managing Partner. **World Wide Web address:** http://www.grantthornton.com. **Description:** An international certified public accounting organization offering consulting and accounting services, as well as strategic and tactical planning assistance to a diverse clientele. **Positions advertised include:** Senior Tax Associate. **Corporate headquarters location:** Chicago IL. **Other U.S. locations:** Nationwide.

GREASE MONKEY INTERNATIONAL, INC.
7100 East Belleview Avenue, Suite 305, Greenwood Village CO 80111. 303/308-1660. **Fax:** 303/308-5906. **Contact:** Personnel. **World Wide Web address:** http://www.greasemonkeyintl.com. **Description:** The company is a franchiser, owner, and operator of retail quick lube centers. Grease Monkey centers provide customer service and preventive maintenance services for motor vehicles. **NOTE:** Entry-level positions are offered. **Special programs:** Internships. **Corporate headquarters location:** This location. **Other U.S. locations:** Nationwide. **International locations:** Mexico. **Operations at this facility include:** This location provides sales, management, marketing, administrative, accounting, MIS, human resource, franchise support, and real estate services to the organization. **Number of employees at this location:** 50. **Number of employees nationwide:** 350.

GREELEY, CITY OF
1000 10th Street, Greeley CO 80631. 970/350-9740. **Recorded jobline:** 970/350-9777x200. **Contact:** Human Resources Department. **World Wide Web address:** http://www.ci.greeley.co.us. **Description:** Administrative offices for the city of Greeley. **NOTE:** This employer does not accept unsolicited resumes. Please check the jobline for available positions or download the City of Greeley application through the http://www.nationjob.com Website by clicking on the City of Greeley logo.

GREELEY DAILY TRIBUNE
P.O. Box 1690, Greeley CO 80632. 970/352-0211. **Toll-free phone:** 800/275-0321. **Contact:** Brenda Haines, Human Resources. **World Wide Web address:** http://www.greeleytrib. com. **Description:** Publishes a daily newspaper with a circulation of more than 29,000. Founded in 1870. **Corporate headquarters location:** Reno NV. **Publisher:** Jim Elsberry.

GREYHOUND BUS LINES
12881 Highway 61, Sterling CO 80751. 970/522-5522. **Contact:** Human Resources. **World Wide Web address:** http://www.greyhound.com. **Description:** Greyhound is a major nationwide bus route service operator, with more than 3,000 stop facilities throughout the United States. Greyhound also offers passenger express bus service, sightseeing services, airport ground transportation, and independent charter bus services. **Corporate headquarters location:** Dallas TX. **Operations at this facility include:** This location is a local bus terminal.

EMILY GRIFFITH OPPORTUNITY SCHOOL
1250 Welton Street, Denver CO 80204. 303/575-4700. **Contact:** Human Resources. **World Wide Web address:** http://www.egos-school.com. **Description:** A trade school offering continuing education (high school diploma, G.E.D.), as well as classes in areas such as medicine, art, aviation, and automotive mechanics.

GROUP VOYAGERS, INC.
dba GLOBUS & COSMOS
5301 South Federal Circle, Littleton CO 80123. 303/703-7000. **Toll-free phone:** 800/851-0728. **Fax:** 303/795-6615. **Contact:** Jackie Boyd, Recruiter. **Description:** Provides travel packages to more than 70 countries on all seven continents. **NOTE:** Entry-level positions and part-time jobs are offered. **Special programs:** Training. **Office hours:** Monday - Friday, 7:00 a.m. - 6:00 p.m. **Corporate headquarters location:** This location. **Other U.S. locations:** Pasadena CA. **International locations:** Worldwide. **Listed on:** Privately held. **CEO/President:** Paulo Mantegazza. **Number of employees at this location:** 290.

GRUBB & ELLIS COMPANY
One Tabor Center, 1200 17th Street, Suite 2000, Denver CO 80202-5841. 303/572-7700. **Contact:** Fern Baker, Administrative Manager. **World Wide Web address:** http://www.grubb-ellis.com. **Description:** A commercial real estate brokerage firm offering a full range of services including transaction, management, and consultative services. Founded in 1973. **Special programs:** Internships. **Corporate headquarters location:** Northbrook IL. **Other U.S. locations:** Nationwide. **Listed on:** New York Stock Exchange. **Stock exchange symbol:** GBE.

HEI ADVANCED MEDICAL OPERATIONS
4801 North 63rd Street, Boulder CO 80301. 720/622-4100. **Fax:** 303/530-2866. **Contact:** Human Resources. **World Wide Web address:** http://www.heii.com. **Description:** Manufactures electro-mechanical medical devices, catheters, respiratory diagnostic instruments, MRI (Magnetic Resonance Imaging) systems, and similar medical devices. **Positions advertised include:** General Ledger Accountant/Payroll. **Corporate headquarters location:** Victoria MN.

H.R.H.
720 South Colorado Boulevard, North Tower, Galleria Penthouse, P.O. Box 469025, Denver CO 80246. 303/722-7776. **Contact:** Human Resources. **World Wide Web address:** http://www.hrh.com. **Description:** An agency specializing in surety bonds and commercial insurance.

THE HACH COMPANY
P.O. Box 389, Loveland CO 80539-0389. 970/669-3050. **Contact:** Human Resources. **World Wide Web address:** http://www.hach.com. **Description:** Manufactures and sells laboratory instruments, process analyzers, and test kits that analyze the chemical content and other properties of water and other aqueous solutions. The company also produces chemicals for use with its manufactured instruments and test kits. **Positions advertised include:** Sales Consultant; Technical Sales Engineer; Planner/Buyer; Regulatory Affairs Chemist; Production/Test Engineer; Technical Writer; Product Specialist; Program Manager; Regional Sales Manager; Product Manager; Electrical Engineer. **Corporate headquarters location:** This location. **Other U.S. locations:** Ames IA. **International locations:** Germany. **Parent company:** Danaker Corporation. **Operations at this facility include:** Administration; Manufacturing; Research and Development; Sales. **Number of employees at this location:** 580. **Number of employees nationwide:** 950. **Number of employees worldwide:** 980.

HAIN CELESTIAL GROUP
4600 Sleepytime Drive, Boulder CO 80301. 303/530-5300. **Contact:** Stephanie Thibault, Director of Human Resources. **World Wide Web address:** http:// www.hain-celestial.com. **Description:** Produces herbal teas and beverages. **Corporate headquarters location:** Melville NY. **Listed on:** NASDAQ. **Stock exchange symbol:** HAIN.

HAMILTON SUNDSTRAND
2800 Sundstrand Way, Grand Junction CO 81506. 970/242-2600. **Contact:** Human Resources. **World Wide Web address:** http://www.hamiltonsundstrandcorp.com. **Description:** A manufacturing facility specializing in precision machining of aerospace components. Overall, Hamilton Sundstrand manufactures a wide range of aircraft components, systems, and subsystems. **Parent company:** United Technologies Corporation.

JOHN H. HARLAND COMPANY
4700 South Syracuse Street, Suite 900, Denver CO 80237. 303/770-5190. **Toll-free phone:** 800/937-3799. **Contact:** Human Resources. **World Wide Web address:** http://www.harland.net. **Description:** A financial printing firm. Products include business and personal checks, as well as other forms and documents for the banking industry. **Corporate headquarters location:** Decatur GA. **Listed on:** New York Stock Exchange. **Stock exchange symbol:** JH. **Annual sales/revenues:** More than $100 million. **Number of employees at this location:** 90.

HARRIS CORPORATION
1999 Broadway Street, Suite 4000, Denver CO 80202-3050. 303/237-4000. **Contact:** Human Resources. **World Wide Web address:** http://www.encodasystems.com. **Description:** Develops software for television and radio stations.

THE HARTFORD
P.O. Box 5188, Denver CO 80217. 303/645-8500. **Physical address:** 7670 South Chester Street, Suite 300, Englewood CO 80112-3438. **Toll-free phone:** 800/525-7418. **Contact:** Human Resources. **World Wide Web address:** http://www.thehartford.com. **Description:** One of the largest insurance companies in the United States. The Hartford is a *Fortune* 500 company and offers business, farm, home, life, automobile, marine, and health insurance coverage as well as fidelity and surety bonds and reinsurance. Founded in 1810. **NOTE:** Entry-level positions and part-time jobs are offered. **Positions advertised include:** Senior Sales Consultant; Loss Control Manager; Health Care Provider Sales Executive; Retirement Plan Sales Director; Underwriter Trainee. **Corporate headquarters location:** Hartford CT. **Other U.S. locations:** Nationwide. **International locations:** Worldwide. **Listed on:** New York Stock Exchange. **Stock exchange symbol:** HIG. **Annual sales/revenues:** More

than $100 million. **Number of employees at this location:** 170. **Number of employees nationwide:** 22,000.

HAUSER, INC.
4161 Specialty Place, Longmont CO 80504. 720/652-7000. **Contact:** Director of Human Resources. **World Wide Web address:** http://www.hauser.com. **Description:** Hauser Chemical Research, Inc. extracts and purifies specialty products from natural resources using its proprietary technologies. **Positions advertised include:** Chemist; Scientist; Regulatory Affairs Technician; Process Operator. **Corporate headquarters location:** This location. **Number of employees at this location:** 250.

HENSEL PHELPS CONSTRUCTION COMPANY
420 Sixth Avenue, P.O. Box 0, Greeley CO 80632. 970/352-6565. **Fax:** 970/352-9311. **Contact:** Ron Norby, Vice President. **E-mail address:** careers@henselphelps.com. **World Wide Web address:** http://www.henselphelps.com. **Description:** A commercial construction company.

HEWLETT PACKARD
305 Rockrimmon Boulevard South, Colorado Springs CO 80919. 719/548-2000. **Contact:** Human Resources. **World Wide Web address:** http://www.hp.com. **Description:** Designs, manufactures, sells, and services computers, associated peripheral equipment, and related software and supplies. Applications and programs include scientific research, computation, communications, education, data analysis, industrial control, time sharing, commercial data processing, graphic arts, word processing, health care, instrumentation, engineering, and simulation. **NOTE:** Apply online. **Corporate headquarters location:** Palo Alto CA. **Listed on:** New York Stock Exchange. **Stock exchange symbol:** HPQ.

HEWLETT PACKARD
116 Inverness Drive East, Suite 300, Englewood CO 80112. 303/649-3000. **Contact:** Human Resources. **World Wide Web address:** http://www.hp.com. **Description:** Designs, manufactures, sells, and services computers, associated peripheral equipment, and related software and supplies. Applications and programs include scientific research, computation, communications, education, data analysis, industrial control, time sharing, commercial data processing, graphic arts, word processing, health care, instrumentation, engineering, and simulation. **NOTE:** Apply online. **Corporate headquarters location:** Palo Alto CA. **Listed on:** New York Stock Exchange. **Stock exchange symbol:** HPQ.

THE HIBBERT GROUP
2399 Blake Street, Denver CO 80205. 303/297-1601. **Fax:** 303/672-7320. **Contact:** Deena Lowe, Human Resources. **E-mail address:** HrDenver@hibbertgroup.com. **World Wide Web address:** http://www.hibbertgroup.com. **Description:** Provides commercial and offset printing services. **Positions advertised include:** Customer Service Representative. **Corporate headquarters location:** This location. **Other U.S. locations include:** Trenton NJ. **Parent company:** Hibbert Company (Trenton NJ).

HIX INSURANCE ASSOCIATES, INC.
4564 Arapahoe Avenue, Boulder CO 80303. 303/444-4666. **Toll-free phone:** 800/451-6448. **Fax:** 303/444-8481. **Contact:** Human Resources Department. **E-mail address:** hia@insurance-associates.com. **World Wide Web address:** http://www.insurance-associates.com. **Description:** Provides automobile, home, flood, life, and health insurance. Founded in 1919. **Corporate headquarters location:** Estes Park CO. **Listed on:** Privately held. **Number of employees at this location:** 5. **Number of employees nationwide:** 10.

BERNARD HODES GROUP
1660 17th Street, Denver CO 80202. 720/904-0461. **Contact:** Human Resources. **World Wide Web address:** http://www.hodes.com. **Description:** An advertising agency specializing in recruitment and employee communications. **Corporate headquarters location:** New York NY. **International locations:** Worldwide. **Parent company:** Omnicom.

HOLIDAY INN DENVER DOWNTOWN
1450 Glenarm Place, Denver CO 80202. 303/573-1450. **Contact:** Human Resources. **World Wide Web address:** http://www.holiday-inn.com. **Description:** One location of the nationwide hotel chain. **Corporate headquarters location:** Atlanta GA. **Parent company:** Six Continents Hotels, Inc. **Listed on:** New York Stock Exchange. **Stock exchange symbol:** SXC.

HOLLAND & HART LLP
555 17th Street, Suite 3200, Denver CO 80202. 303/295-8000. **Contact:** Sharon Curley, Personnel Director. **World Wide Web address:** http://www.hollandhart.com. **Description:** A law firm.

HOMESTEAD HOUSE
9410 Wordsworth Parkway, Arvada CO 80021. 303/425-6544. **Toll-free phone:** 800/275-0345. **Fax:** 303/425-0541. **Contact:** Director of Human Resources. **Description:** Operates a chain of home furnishings stores. **Office hours:** Monday - Friday, 8:00 a.m. - 5:00 p.m. **Corporate headquarters location:** This location. **President:** Richard L. Gill.

HOTEL JEROME
333 East Main Street, Aspen CO 81611. 970/920-1000. **Fax:** 970/925-3112. **Toll-free phone:** 800/331-7213. **Contact:** Human Resources. **E-mail address:** hr@hjerome.com. **World Wide Web address:** www.hoteljerome.com. **Description:** A 91-room landmark hotel located in downtown Aspen with an award winning restaurant.

HUSSMANN CORPORATION
11929 51st Avenue, Denver CO 80239. 303/371-5447. **Contact:** Plant Manager. **Wide Web address:** http://www.hussmann.com. **Description:** Produces merchandising and refrigeration systems for the food industry. Products include refrigerated display cases, refrigeration systems, beverage coolers, walk-in coolers, and industrial refrigeration equipment. **Parent company:** Ingersoll-Rand Company. **Listed on:** New York Stock Exchange. **Stock exchange symbol:** IR.

IBM CORPORATION
6300 Diagonal Highway, Boulder CO 80301. 303/443-9905. **Toll-free phone:** 800/796-9876. **Recorded jobline:** 800/964-4473. **Contact:** Human Resources. **World Wide Web address:** http://www.ibm.com. **Description:** IBM is a developer, manufacturer, and marketer of advanced information processing products including computers and microelectronic technology, software, networking systems, and information technology-related services. The company has operations in the United States, Canada, Europe, Middle East, Africa, Latin America, and Asia. **NOTE:** Jobseekers should send resumes to IBM Staffing Services, 1DPA/051, 3808 Six Forks Road, Raleigh NC 27609. **Corporate headquarters location:** Armonk NY. **Operations at this facility include:** This facility is engaged in the manufacture of magnetic discs and tapes. **Subsidiaries include:** IBM Credit Corporation; IBM Instruments, Inc.; IBM World Trade Corporation. **Listed on:** New York Stock Exchange. **Stock exchange symbol:** IBM.

ICG COMMUNICATIONS, INC.
161 Inverness Drive West, Englewood CO 80112. 303/414-5000. **Fax:** 303/414-8867. **Contact:** Human Resources. **World Wide Web address:** http://www.icgcom.com. **Description:** Provides data and voice network communication services. Founded in 1956. **Positions advertised include:** Financial Analyst; Marketing Manager; Director, Product Management; Director, Materials Management; Design Provisioner. **Other U.S. locations include:** Nationwide.

IHS ENERGY GROUP
15 Inverness Way East, MSB106, Englewood CO 80112-5776. 303/736-3000. **Contact:** Employment Coordinator. **E-mail address:** careers@ihs.com. **World Wide Web address:** http://www.ihsenergy.com. **Description:** Publishes oil activity information including reports, maps, and well data. **Parent company:** D&B Corporation. **Listed on:** New York Stock Exchange. **Stock exchange symbol:** DNB.

ITT INDUSTRIES
4410 East Fountain Boulevard, Colorado Springs CO 80916. 719/591-3600. **Contact:** Human Resources. **World Wide Web address:** http://www.ittind.com. **Description:** Serves the defense, energy, and communications markets with research and development services in weapons effects, computer systems, space systems, C3I, SDI, range testing, and instrumentation. **Corporate headquarters location:** White Plains NY. **Listed on:** New York Stock Exchange. **Stock exchange symbol:** ITT.

IKON OFFICE SOLUTIONS
7173 South Havana Street, Suite A, Englewood CO 80112. 720/875-8300. **Contact:** Lynn Hannblom, Director of Human Resources. **World Wide Web address:** http://www.ikon.com. **Description:** Engaged in the retail sale and service of Canon office equipment and supplies. **Corporate headquarters location:** Valley Forge PA. **Other U.S. locations:** Nationwide. **Operations at this facility include:** Administration; Regional Headquarters; Sales; Service. **Listed on:** New York Stock Exchange. **Stock exchange symbol:** IKN.

INFINITY BROADCASTING CORPORATION
1560 Broadway, Suite 1100, Denver CO 80202. 303/832-5665. **Fax:** 303/832-7000. **Contact:** Personnel. **World Wide Web address:** http://www.infinityradio.com. **Description:** Operates a radio station broadcasting oldies and classical music. **Positions advertised include:** Promotions Assistant; Afternoon Drive Personality. **Special programs:** Internships. **Office hours:** Monday - Friday, 8:30 a.m. - 5:30 p.m. **Corporate headquarters location:** Burbank CA. **Other U.S. locations:** Phoenix AZ; San Francisco CA; Atlanta GA; Detroit MI; Kansas City MO; Dallas TX; Houston TX; Seattle WA. **Parent company:** Shamrock Broadcasting, Inc. **Operations at this facility include:** Administration; Sales; Service. **Number of employees at this location:** 25.

INFORMATION HANDLING SERVICES
15 Inverness Way East, Englewood CO 80112. 303/790-0600. **Contact:** Director of Human Resources. **E-mail address:** info@ihs.com. **World Wide Web address:** http://www.ihs.com. **Description:** Assimilates and indexes technical, engineering, federal, and regulatory information and transfers it to microform and electronic media. **Positions advertised include:** Senior Systems Engineer; Production Clerk. **Corporate headquarters location:** This location. **Parent company:** Information Handling Services Group.

INLAND CONTAINER CORPORATION
5000 Oak Street, Wheat Ridge CO 80033-2298. 303/422-7700. **Contact:** Della Nugent, Human Resources Manager. **World Wide Web address:** http://www.iccnet. com. **Description:** A manufacturer of corrugated shipping containers and boxes. **Parent company:** Temple-Inland Inc. **Listed on:** New York Stock Exchange. **Stock exchange symbol:** TIN.

INTRADO, INC.
1601 Dry Creek Dive, Longmont CO 80503. 720/494-5800. **Fax:** 720/494-6652. **Contact:** Human Resources. **E-mail address:** HR@intrado.com. **World Wide Web address:** http://www.intrado.com. **Description:** Develops public safety computer software and systems that implement emergency communication networks with telephone service providers. **Positions advertised include:** Financial Analyst; Systems Administrator; Data Analyst; Telecommunicator; Internal Audit Manager. **Corporate headquarters location:** This location. **Listed on:** NASDAQ. **Stock exchange symbol:** TRDO.

ISEC, INC.
P.O. Box 6849, Englewood CO 80155. 303/790-1444. **Physical address:** 33 Inverness Drive East, Englewood CO 80112. **Contact:** Human Resources. **World Wide Web address:** http://www.isecinc.com. **Description:** Provides contract engineering services. **Positions advertised include:** Lab Design Engineer.

ISYS/ODYSSEY DEVELOPMENT, INC.
8775 East Orchard Road, Suite 811, Englewood CO 80111. 303/689-9998. **Contact:** Human Resources. **World Wide Web address:** http://www.isysdev.com. **Description:** Manufactures text retrieval software. Products include ISYS HindSite Internet utilities; ISYS Web, for online publishing; ISYS Image, for data capture and full-text search; ISYS Electronic Publisher, a retrieval and authoring tool; and ISYS for Adobe Acrobat, a search engine with PDF files.

JHB INTERNATIONAL INC.
1955 South Quince Street, Denver CO 80231. 303/751-8100. **Contact:** Personnel Coordinator. **World Wide Web address:** http://www.buttons.com. **Description:** Wholesales and exports buttons and thimbles.

JACOBS ENGINEERING GROUP, INC.
JACOBS FACILITIES, INC.
1527 Cole Boulevard, Suite 100, Lakewood CO 80401. 303/462-7000. **Contact:** Human Resources. **E-mail address:** info@jacobs.com. **World Wide Web address:** http://www.jacobs.com. **Description:** An engineering and construction company that provides engineering, procurement, construction, and maintenance services to clients and industries. These industries include chemicals and polymers, federal programs, pulp and paper, semiconductor, petroleum refining, facilities and transportation, food and consumer products, pharmaceuticals and biotechnologies, and basic resources. Through Jacobs College and other site-specific programs, the company trains more than 5,000 employees per year in project and money management, health and safety, and numerous other performance enhancing topics. CRSS Constructors, Inc. (also at this location and part of Jacobs Engineering Group, Inc.) is a management consulting company specializing in construction projects. **Positions advertised include:** Project

Manager; Project Controls Professional. **Corporate headquarters location:** Pasadena CA. **Listed on:** New York Stock Exchange. **Stock exchange symbol:** JEC.

JANUS CAPITAL
100 Fillmore Street, Denver CO 80206. 303/333-3863. **Contact:** Recruiting Manager. **World Wide Web address:** http://www.janus.com. **Description:** Manages mutual funds and offers a wide variety of account options and investment services. **Positions advertised include:** Investment Risk Analyst; Client Support Coordinator. **Corporate headquarters location:** This location. **Listed on:** Privately held. **Number of employees at this location:** 700.

JEPPESEN SANDERSON INC.
55 Inverness Drive East, Englewood CO 80112-5498. 303/799-9090. **Fax:** 303/328-4121. **Contact:** Human Resources. **E-mail address:** jobs@jeppesen.com. **World Wide Web address:** http://www.jeppesen.com. **Description:** Publishes and distributes flight information manuals, flight training supplies, and informational products. **NOTE:** If you are faxing your resume, please specify the position that you are interested in and specify a desired salary. **Positions advertised include:** Product Manager; Software Engineer; Process Analyst; Software Architect. **Other U.S. locations:** Los Gatos CA; Wilsonville OR. **International locations:** Australia; Germany; Russia; United Kingdom. **Operations at this facility include:** Administration; Divisional Headquarters; Manufacturing; Research and Development; Sales; Service. **Number of employees at this location:** 800. **Number of employees worldwide:** 1,100.

JOHNS MANVILLE CORPORATION
717 17th Street, Denver CO 80202. 303/978-2000. **Contact:** Human Resources. **E-mail address:** humanresources@jm.com. **World Wide Web address:** http:// www.jm.com. **Description:** A fiberglass manufacturer. The company produces and markets insulation products for buildings and equipment, high-efficiency air filtration media, and commercial roofing systems and textile glass used as reinforcements in buildings and industrial applications. **Positions advertised include:** Financial Analyst; Inside Sales Representative. **Corporate headquarters location:** This location. **Parent company:** Berkshire Hathaway. **Listed on:** New York Stock Exchange. **Stock exchange symbol:** BRK. **Number of employees nationwide:** 7,000.

JOHNSON PRINTING
1880 South 57th Court, Boulder CO 80301. 303/443-1576. **Contact:** Human Resources. **World Wide Web address:** http://www.jpcolorado.com. **Description:** Publishes approximately 120 nonfiction books in the areas of natural history, geology, and outdoor recreation. The company also offers commercial printing services (prepress, offset, binding, digital, and postproduction).

KAISER PERMANENTE
2500 South Havana Street, Aurora CO 80014-1622. 303/338-3900. **Recorded jobline:** 303/338-3949. **Contact:** Human Resources. **World Wide Web address:** http://www.kaiserpermanente.org. **Description:** One of the nation's leading and largest health maintenance organizations. **Positions advertised include:** Data Entry Clerk; Benefits Case Coordinator; Clinical Chemistry Manager; Contract Systems Technician; Histologic Technician; Diagnostic Medical Sonographer. **Corporate headquarters location:** Oakland CA. **Operations at this facility include:** Regional Headquarters. **Number of employees at this location:** 3,100. **Number of employees nationwide:** 75,000.

KELLOGG LLC
1801 Broadway, Suite 1000, Denver CO 80202. 303/298-8825. **Contact:** Office Manager. **E-mail address:** kellogg@kellogg-llc.com. **World Wide Web address:** http://www.kellogg-llc.com. **Description:** An international management services and engineering consulting firm for construction projects.

KEY BANK
100 Broadway, Denver CO 80203. 303/744-3228. **Contact:** Human Resources. **World Wide Web address:** http://www.keybank.com. **Description:** Offers a wide range of banking and other financial services.

KEYSTONE RESORT
P.O. Box 38, Keystone CO 80435. 970/496-4157. **Fax:** 970/496-3260. **Contact:** Director of Human Resources. **E-mail address:** keyjobs@vailresorts.com. **World Wide Web address:** http://www.keystoneresort.com. **Description:** A ski resort. **Positions advertised include:** Lift Mechanic; Employee Housing Operations Supervisor; Maintenance Technician; Reservations Statistics Accountant. **Parent company:** Vail Resorts Inc. **Listed on:** New York Stock Exchange. **Stock exchange symbol:** MTN.

KIEWIT WESTERN COMPANY
7926 South Platte Canyon Road, Littleton CO 80128-5978. 303/979-9330. **Contact:** Mark Campbell, District Business Manager. **World Wide Web address:** http:// www.kiewit.com. **Description:** A general contracting company. **Corporate headquarters location:** Omaha NE. **Parent company:** The Kiewit Companies. **Number of employees at this location:** 115.

KINDER MORGAN, INC.
370 Van Gordon Street, P.O. Box 281304, Lakewood CO 80228-8304. 303/989-1740. **Contact:** Dawn Putaturo, Director of Human Resources. **World Wide Web address:** http://www.kindermorgan.com. **Description:** A natural gas transmission and distribution company. **Positions advertised include:** Air Quality Engineer; Analyst; Senior Construction Coordinator; Systems Analyst. **Corporate headquarters location:** Houston TX. **Other U.S. locations:** Nationwide. **Listed on:** New York Stock Exchange. **Stock exchange symbol:** KMI.

KRAFT FOODS, INC.
OSCAR MAYER & COMPANY
315 Inverness Way South, Englewood CO 80112. 303/784-7500. **Contact:** Human Resources. **World Wide Web address:** http://www.kraft.com. **Description:** Kraft Foods, Inc. is one of the largest producers of packaged grocery products in North America. Major brands include Jell-O, Post, Kool-Aid, Crystal Light, Entenmann's, Miracle Whip, Stove Top, and Shake 'n Bake. Kraft Foods, Inc. markets a number of products under the Kraft brand including natural and processed cheeses and dry packaged dinners. The Oscar Mayer unit markets processed meats, poultry, lunch combinations, and pickles under the Oscar Mayer, Louis Rich, Lunchables, and Claussen brand names. Kraft Foods, Inc. is also one of the largest coffee companies with principal brands including Maxwell House, Sanka, Brim, and General Foods International Coffees. Kraft Foods Ingredients Corporation manufactures private-label and industrial food products for sale to other food processing companies. **Corporate headquarters location:** White Plains NY. **Operations at this facility include:** This location is a sales office of the consumer foods company. **Parent company:** Philip Morris Companies is a holding company whose principal wholly-owned subsidiaries are Philip Morris Inc. (Philip Morris U.S.A.), Philip Morris International Inc., Kraft Foods, Inc., and Philip Morris Capital Corporation. In the tobacco industry, Philip Morris U.S.A. and Philip Morris International together form one of the largest international cigarette operations in the world. U.S. brand names include Marlboro, Parliament, Virginia Slims, Benson & Hedges, and Merit. Philip Morris Capital Corporation is engaged in financial services and real estate. **Listed on:** New York Stock Exchange. **Stock exchange symbol:** KFT.

KUTAK ROCK LLP
1801 California Street, Suite 301, Denver CO 80202-2658. 303/297-2400. **Contact:** Recruitment. **World Wide Web address:** http://www.kutakrock.com. **Description:** A legal services firm specializing in corporate law, public and corporate finance, and litigation. **Other U.S. locations:** Nationwide.

LSI LOGIC
2950 East Harmony Road, Fort Collins CO 80525. 970/223-5100. **Contact:** Personnel. **World Wide Web address:** http://www.lsilogic.com. **Description:** LSI Logic develops, manufactures, markets, and supports complete business information systems for retail, financial, commercial, industrial, medical, educational, and government industries through the production of microelectronics. The company also manufactures and markets business forms and supplies. **Corporate headquarters location:** Milpitas CA. **Operations at this facility include:** This location manufactures, integrates, and tests circuits. **Listed on:** New York Stock Exchange. **Stock exchange symbol:** LSI.

LAFARGE NORTH AMERICA INC.
10170 Church Ranch Way, Westminster CO 80021. 303/426-1166. **Contact:** Human Resources. **World Wide Web address:** http://www.lafargenorthamerica.com. **Description:** Material supplier of ready-mix concrete aggregates and admixtures. Lafarge is a general contractor for the heavy construction industry. **Corporate headquarters location:** Herndon VA. **International locations:** Canada. **Operations at this facility include:** Administration; Regional Headquarters; Sales; Service. **Listed on:** New York Stock Exchange. **Stock exchange symbol:** LAF.

LAIDLAW TRANSIT SERVICES, INC.
6345 North Colorado Boulevard, Commerce City CO 80022. 303/288-1939. **Contact:** Human Resources. **World Wide Web address:** http://www.laidlawtransit.com. **Description:** Provides urban busing services. **Corporate headquarters location:** Overland Park KS. **Parent company:** Laidlaw, Inc. provides solid waste collection, compacting, transportation, treatment, transfer, and disposal services; provides hazardous waste services; operates hazardous waste facilities and wastewater treatment plants; and operates passenger and school buses, transit systems buses, and tour and charter buses.

LASER TECHNOLOGY, INC. (LTI)
7070 South Tucson Way, Centennial CO 80112. 303/649-1000. **Fax:** 303/649-9710. **Contact:** Angela Roth, Personnel Director. **E-mail address:** aroth@lasertech.com. **World Wide Web address:** http://www.lasertech.com. **Description:** Provides laser-based measurement systems to a wide variety of markets worldwide. Products include the Marksman, a laser speed detection system. Founded in 1985. **NOTE:** Part-time jobs are offered. **Positions advertised include:** Regional Sales Manager. **Special programs:** Apprenticeships. **Listed on:** American Stock Exchange. **Stock exchange symbol:** LSR. **President:** Eric Miller. **Annual sales/revenues:** $11 - $20 million. **Number of employees at this location:** 85. **Number of employees nationwide:** 95.

LEWAN & ASSOCIATES, INC.
1400 South Colorado Boulevard, P.O. Box 22855, Denver CO 80222. 303/759-5440. **Contact:** Human Resources. **World Wide Web address:** http://www.lewan.com. **Description:** A retail office products dealer. **Positions advertised include:** Copier Sales Representative; Inside Sales Representative. **Corporate headquarters location:** This location.

LEXISNEXIS
555 Middle Creek Parkway, Colorado Springs CO 80921. 719/488-3000. **Contact:** Human Resources. **World Wide Web address:** http://www.lexisnexis.com. **Description:** A full-service, multimedia publisher that develops legal information products and citations products in all forms of media including online and CD-ROM. **Number of employees at this location:** 850.

LIBERTY FUNDS SERVICES, INC.
12100 East Iliff Avenue, Suite 300, Aurora CO 80014. 303/337-6555. **Fax:** 303/743-6341. **Contact:** Personnel. **World Wide Web address:** http://www.libertyfunds.com. **Description:** Provides transfer agency services for the shareholders of funds managed by the parent company's other subsidiaries including Colonial Management Associates, Inc., Stein Roe and Farnham Inc., The Crabbe Huson Group, Inc., and Newport Fund Management. Founded in 1931. **Special programs:** Training. **Office hours:** Monday - Friday, 6:00 a.m. - 6:00 p.m. **Corporate headquarters location:** Boston MA. **Parent company:** FleetBoston Financial. **Listed on:** New York Stock Exchange. **Stock exchange symbol:** FBF. **Number of employees at this location:** 100. **Number of employees nationwide:** 1,500.

LIBERTY MEDIA CORPORATION
12300 Liberty Boulevard, Englewood CO 80112. 720/875-5400. **Contact:** Human Resources. **World Wide Web address:** http://www.libertymedia.com. **Description:** Provides cable television and cable programming-related services. **Corporate headquarters location:** This location. **Listed on:** New York Stock Exchange. **Stock exchange symbol:** L.

LIONSHEAD INN
705 West Lionshead Circle, Vail CO 81657. 970/476-2050. **Fax:** 970/476-9265. **Toll-free phone:** 800/283-8245. **Contact:** Human Resources. **World Wide Web address:** www.lionsheadinn.com. **Description:** Luxury inn located minutes from the Eagle Bay Gondola, shops, and restaurants.

LITTLETON ADVENTIST HOSPITAL
7700 South Broadway, Denver CO 80122. 303/730-8900. **Fax:** 303/738-2688. **Recorded jobline:** 888/808-8828. **Contact:** Human Resources. **World Wide Web address:** http:// www.littletonhosp.org. **Description:** A full service hospital serving Littleton and the surrounding areas. Founded 1989. **Positions advertised include:** Clinical Charge Auditor; Clinical Coordinator; Certified Nurse Assistant; Nursing Unit Secretary; OR Technician; Pharmacy Technician; Radiology Technician; Respiratory Therapist; Transcriptionist; Ultrasound Technician. **Parent company:** Centura Health.

LOCKHEED MARTIN ASTRONAUTICS
P.O. Box 179, Mail Stop DC1311, Denver CO 80201. 303/977-3000. **Fax:** 303/971-3324. **Recorded jobline:** 303/977-2720. **Contact:** Human Resources. **World Wide Web address:** http://www.lockheedmartin.com. **Description:** This location is part of the Space Group segment of Lockheed Martin Corporation. The Space Group is engaged in the design, development, engineering, and production of civil and military

space launch vehicles, satellites, spacecraft, space-based information and communications systems, and the Space Shuttle External Tank and associated electronics and instrumentation. **Corporate headquarters location:** Bethesda MD. **Parent company:** Lockheed Martin Corporation. **Listed on:** New York Stock Exchange. **Stock exchange symbol:** LMT. **Number of employees at this location:** 6,000. **Number of employees nationwide:** 93,000.

LONGMONT, CITY OF
350 Kimbark Street, Longmont CO 80501. 303/776-6050. **Recorded jobline:** 303/651-8710. **Contact:** Terry Rivas, Human Resources Director. **E-mail address:** Terry.Rivas@ci.longmont.co.us. **World Wide Web address:** http://www.ci.longmont.co.us. **Description:** Administrative offices for the city of Longmont. **Positions advertised include:** Preschool Teacher; Daytime Lifeguard; Pool Manager; Water Safety Instructor; Master Swim Coach.

LONGMONT UNITED HOSPITAL
1950 Mountain View Avenue, Longmont CO 80501. 303/485-4136. **Fax:** 303/485-4137. **Recorded jobline:** 303/651-5241. **Contact:** Human Resources. **World Wide Web address:** http://www.luhcares.org. **Description:** A 143-bed general, acute care, nonprofit, community hospital. Longmont United Hospital offers a cancer care center, a cardiac lab, cardiopulmonary services, a sports rehabilitation center, complimentary medicine, cardiovascular rehabilitation, trauma/emergency center, and behavioral health services. **NOTE:** Second and third shifts are offered. **Company slogan:** Here, caring is an art. **Special programs:** Training. **Corporate headquarters location:** This location. **Annual sales/revenues:** $51 - $100 million. **Number of employees at this location:** 930.

LOOMIS FARGO & COMPANY
600 South Cherry Street, Suite 314, Denver CO 80246. 303/825-0376. **Fax:** 303/355-6383. **Contact:** Personnel. **World Wide Web address:** http://www.loomisfargo.com. **Description:** An armored security service specializing in transporting currency. **NOTE:** Applications will not be mailed to jobseekers. They must be picked up in person. **Other U.S. locations:** Nationwide.

LOOMIS FARGO & COMPANY
607 South US Highway 24, Leadville CO 80461. 719/486-8265. **Fax:** 719/486-8266. **Contact:** Personnel. **World Wide Web address:** http://www.loomisfargo.com. **Description:** An armored security service specializing in transporting currency. **NOTE:** Applications will not be mailed to jobseekers. They must be picked up in person. **Other U.S. locations:** Nationwide.

LUZENAC AMERICA
345 Inverness Drive South, Suite 310, Centennial CO 80112. 303/643-0400. **Contact:** Human Resources. **World Wide Web address:** http://www.luzenac.com. **Description:** Luzenac America is a mining company with 15 locations nationwide. **Positions advertised include:** Training and Development Manager. **Corporate headquarters location:** This location.

MHC
8101 East Prentice Avenue, Suite 702, Greenwood Village CO 80111. 303/740-8366. **Contact:** Wendy Chamberlain, Office Manager. **Description:** A real estate development company specializing in mobile home parks.

MMS (MEETING MANAGEMENT SERVICES)
1765 South Eighth Street, Suite T-6, Colorado Springs CO 80906. 719/473-0557. **Toll-free phone:** 800/544-2432. **Fax:** 719/473-8750. **Contact:** Executive Assistant. **World Wide Web address:** http://www.meetingexperts.com. **Description:** A management consulting firm offering media, travel, and meeting planning services. **Special programs:** Internships. **Corporate headquarters location:** This location. **Parent company:** Benchmark Hospitality. **Operations at this facility include:** Sales; Service. **Listed on:** Privately held. **Number of employees at this location:** 20. **Number of employees nationwide:** 2,000.

MARCH OF DIMES BIRTH DEFECTS FOUNDATION
1325 South Colorado Boulevard, Suite B508, Denver CO 80222. 303/692-0011. **Contact:** Director. **E-mail address:** co611@modimes.org. **World Wide Web address:** http://www.modimes.org. **Description:** March of Dimes operates the Campaign for Healthier Babies that includes programs of research, community services, education, and advocacy. March of Dimes chapters across the country work with their communities to determine and meet the needs of women, babies, and families. Through specially designed programs, women are provided access to prenatal care. **Corporate headquarters location:** White Plains NY.

MARK VII EQUIPMENT, INC.
5981 Tennyson Street, Arvada CO 80003. 303/423-4910. **Fax:** 303/430-0139. **Contact:** Human Resources. **E-mail address:** markvii@mark7inc.com. **World Wide Web address:** http://www.mark7inc.com. **Description:** Develops and manufactures products for the automobile-washing industry. Products include the Accutime solid state timer and the Questor electronic coin rejector. The company markets its products through an intermediary network of distributors. Founded in 1966.

MARRIOTT'S MOUNTAIN VALLEY LODGE AT BRECKENRIDGE
655 Columbine Drive, Breckenridge CO 80424. 970/453-8500. **Fax:** 970/453-8100. **Contact:** Human Resources. **World Wide Web address:** www.marriott.com. **Description:** A location of the hotel chain. A 111-room hotel within walking distance of shops, restaurants, and golf.

MAXTOR CORPORATION
2452 Clover Basin Drive, Longmont CO 80503. 303/651-6000. **Contact:** Human Resources. **World Wide Web address:** http://www.maxtor.com. **Description:** Maxtor Corporation produces hard disk drives and related electronic data storage equipment for computers, as well as related components for original equipment manufacturers. The company has production plants in Hong Kong and Singapore, 10 U.S. sales offices, and 9 other sales offices in foreign nations. **Corporate headquarters location:** Milpitas CA. **Operations at this facility include:** This location is a research and development facility. **Listed on:** New York Stock Exchange. **Stock exchange symbol:** MXO.

MCI
707 17th Street, Denver CO 80202. 303/390-1000. **Contact:** Human Resources Director. **World Wide Web address:** http://www.mci.com. **Description:** One of the world's largest suppliers of local, long-distance, and international telecommunications services, and a global Internet service provider. WorldCom has operations in more than 65 countries. **Corporate headquarters location:** Clinton MS. **Other U.S. locations:** Nationwide. **Parent company:** MCI Communications Corporation. **Listed on:** NASDAQ. **Stock exchange symbol:** WCOM. **Annual sales/revenues:** More than $100 million.

MCI
2424 Garden of the Gods Road, Colorado Springs CO 80919. 719/528-1971. **Contact:** Human Resources. **World Wide Web address:** http://www.mci.com. **Description:** WorldCom is one of the world's largest suppliers of local, long-distance, and international telecommunications services, and a global Internet service provider. WorldCom has operations in more than 65 countries. **Corporate headquarters location:** Clinton MS. **Other U.S. locations:** Nationwide. **Operations at this facility include:** This location provides systems and engineering operations for the provider of domestic interstate, long-distance service throughout the continental United States, as well as Hawaii, Puerto Rico, the Virgin Islands, and all foreign countries. **Parent company:** MCI Communications Corporation. **Stock exchange symbol:** WCOM. **Annual sales/revenues:** More than $100 million.

MCI
6805 Corporate Drive, Suite 200, Colorado Springs CO 80919. 719/598-0808. **Contact:** Human Resources. **World Wide Web address:** http://www.mci.com. **Description:** WorldCom is one of the world's largest suppliers of local, long-distance, and international telecommunications services, and a global Internet service provider. WorldCom has operations in more than 65 countries. **Corporate headquarters location:** Clinton MS. **Other U.S. locations:** Nationwide. **Operations at this facility include:** This location operates as a full-scale telemarketing company providing a variety of services to clients including inbound and outbound sales, customer service, quality validation, lead generation and scriptwriting, surveys, and other marketing-related services. **Parent company:** MCI Communications Corporation. **Listed on:** NASDAQ. **Stock exchange symbol:** WCOM. **Annual sales/revenues:** More than $100 million.

McGEE COMPANY
1140 South Jason Street, Denver CO 80223. 303/777-2615. **Contact:** Human Resources. **Description:** Sells automotive equipment and supplies including tire machines, alignment machines, floor jacks, and tire patches. The company mainly sells its products to commercial clients. **CEO:** John Labreche.

McKESSON CORPORATION
285 Century Circle, Louisville CO 80027. 303/926-2000. **Contact:** Human Resources. **World Wide Web address:** http://www.mckesson.com. **Description:** McKesson Corp. is an information solutions company that provides information systems and technology to health care enterprises including hospitals, integrated delivery networks, and managed care organizations. McKesson's primary products are Pathways 2000, a family of client/server-based applications that allows for the integration and uniting of health care providers; STAR, Series, and HealthQuest transaction systems; TRENDSTAR decision support system; and QUANTUM enterprise information system. The company also offers outsourcing services that include strategic information systems planning, data center operations, receivables management, business office administration, and major system conversions. **Corporate headquarters location:** San Francisco CA. **Operations at this facility include:** This location designs and installs software for the medical industry. **Subsidiaries include:** HBO & Company (UK) Limited; HBO & Company Canada Ltd.

MEDIANEWS GROUP, INC.
1560 Broadway, Suite 2100, Denver CO 80202. 303/837-0886. **Contact:** Human Resources. **World Wide Web address:** http://www.medianewsgroup.com. **Description:** A newspaper holding company. Medianews Group manages newspaper companies including Affiliated Newspapers Investments, Inc. and Fairbanks Publishing Company.

MEDTRONIC PERFUSION SYSTEMS
18501 East Plaza Drive, Parker CO 80134. 303/840-4000. **Contact:** Manager of Personnel Department. **World Wide Web address:** http://www.medtronic.com. **Description:** Develops, manufactures, and markets computerized medical instruments that monitor human blood-clotting activity. Medtronic Perfusion Systems also supplies disposable cartridges of reagent chemicals for use in those systems. **Corporate headquarters location:** Minneapolis MN. **Parent company:** Medtronic Inc. **Listed on:** New York Stock Exchange. **Stock exchange symbol:** MDT.

MERRICK & COMPANY
2450 South Peoria Street, Aurora CO 80014. 303/751-0741. **Contact:** Human Resources. **E-mail address:** info@merrick.com. **World Wide Web address:** http://www.merrick.com. **Description:** A full-service engineering and architectural firm. Merrick & Company specializes in advanced technology, civil infrastructure, government, heavy industrial, and land development services. **Corporate headquarters location:** This location. **Other U.S. locations:** Phoenix AZ; Albuquerque NM; Los Alamos NM. **Listed on:** Privately held. **Number of employees at this location:** 270. **Number of employees nationwide:** 460.

MERRITT EQUIPMENT COMPANY
9339 Highway 85, Henderson CO 80640. 303/289-2286. **Contact:** Human Resources Department. **E-mail address:** merritt@merritt-equip.com. **World Wide Web address:** http://www.merritt-equip.com. **Description:** Manufactures livestock and commodity trailers and aluminum accessories for the trucking industry such as cab guards and toolboxes. **Corporate headquarters location:** This location. **Operations at this facility include:** Administration; Manufacturing; Sales; Service. **Number of employees at this location:** 250.

MESA LABORATORIES, INC.
12100 West Sixth Avenue, Lakewood CO 80228. 303/987-8000. **Contact:** Steve Peterson, Vice President of Finance. **World Wide Web address:** http://www.mesalabs.com. **Description:** Develops, manufactures, and markets computer-based, electronic measurement instruments used across a wide range of industries. Mesa's products include DATARACE patented instruments for measuring and recording temperature, humidity, and pressure; NUSONICS flow meters and sonic concentration analyzers; and Western Meters and the ECHO Dialyzer Reprocessor are two product lines used in kidney dialysis. **Corporate headquarters location:** This location. **Listed on:** NASDAQ. **Stock exchange symbol:** MLAB. **Number of employees at this location:** 50.

MESA STATE COLLEGE
1100 North Avenue, Grand Junction CO 81501. 970/248-1655. **Contact:** Jan Purin, Human Resources. **E-mail address:** jpurin@mesastate.edu. **World Wide Web address:** http://www.mesastate.edu. **Description:** Mesa State College grants the Bachelor of Business Administration, Bachelor of Science in Nursing, Bachelor of Arts, and Bachelor of Science degrees. The college awards Associate of Arts and Associate of Science degrees, as well as Associate of Applied Science degrees and certificates of proficiency in occupational (vocational-technical) areas. The three academic schools at Mesa State College are the School of Humanities and Social Sciences, the School of Natural Sciences and Mathematics, and the School of Professional Studies. Other Mesa State College service areas include the Unified

Technical Education Center and a continuing education program. Over 4,500 students are enrolled at the college. Founded in 1925.

METRO WASTEWATER RECLAMATION DISTRICT
6450 York Street, Denver CO 80229-7407. 303/286-3000. **Fax:** 303/286-3034. **Contact:** Human Resources. **E-mail address:** resume@mwrd.dst.co.us. **World Wide Web address:** http://www.metrowastewater.com. **Description:** A regional government agency that provides wastewater transmission and treatment services to local governments. **NOTE:** Application required. **Positions advertised include:** Staff Engineer.

METRON, INC.
1505 West Third Avenue, Denver CO 80223. 303/592-1903. **Fax:** 303/592-1969. **Contact:** Human Resources. **World Wide Web address:** http://www.metroninc.com. **Description:** A manufacturer of fire pump controllers and custom electrical products including switchgear and switchboard equipment. **Corporate headquarters location:** This location. **Number of employees at this location:** 85.

METROPOLITAN LIFE INSURANCE COMPANY
1125 17th Street, Suite 809, Denver CO 80202-1019. 303/295-0505. **Contact:** Human Resources. **World Wide Web address:** http://www.metlife.com. **Description:** Offers a wide range of individual and group insurance including life, annuity, disability, and mutual funds. **Corporate headquarters location:** New York NY. **Listed on:** New York Stock Exchange. **Stock exchange symbol:** MET.

MICRO MOTION, INC.
7070 Winchester Circle, Boulder CO 80301. 303/530-8400. **Fax:** 303/530-8007. **Recorded jobline:** 303/530-8000. **Contact:** Human Resources. **World Wide Web address:** http://www.micromotion.com. **Description:** Manufactures industrial flow meters. **Positions advertised include:** Director of Operations; Manager of Electronics Quality and Reliability. **Corporate headquarters location:** This location. **Parent company:** Emerson Process Management. **Number of employees at this location:** 650.

MICROSEMI CORPORATION
800 Hoyt Street, Broomfield CO 80020. 303/469-2161. **Fax:** 303/466-3775. **Contact:** Craig Mullin, Human Resources. **World Wide Web address:** http://www.microsemi.com. **Description:** Microsemi Corporation manufactures and markets semiconductors and similar products and provides related services, principally for the military, aerospace, medical, computer, and telecommunications applications. Major products include high-reliability silicon rectifiers and zener diodes; low-leakage and high-voltage diodes; temperature-compensated zener diodes; and a family of subminiature high-power transient suppresser diodes. **Corporate headquarters location:** Irvine CA. **Operations at this facility include:** This location manufactures rectifiers and diodes. **Listed on:** NASDAQ. **Stock exchange symbol:** MSCC. **Number of employees at this location:** 360. **Number of employees nationwide:** 1,200.

MILE HIGH EQUIPMENT COMPANY
dba ICE-O-MATIC
11100 East 45th Avenue, Denver CO 80239. 303/371-3737. **Fax:** 303/373-5434. **Contact:** Human Resources. **World Wide Web address:** http://www.iceomatic.com. **Description:** Manufactures automatic ice-making and dispensing equipment. **Corporate headquarters location:** Stamford CT. **Parent company:** Enodis Company. **Operations at this facility include:** Administration; Manufacturing; Research and Development; Sales; Service. **Listed on:** New York Stock Exchange. **Stock exchange symbol:** ENO. **Number of employees at this location:** 200.

MILE HIGH UNITED WAY
2505 18th Street, Denver CO 80211-3939. 303/433-8383. **Contact:** Human Resources. **World Wide Web address:** http://www.unitedwaydenver.org. **Description:** A nonprofit organization made up of volunteers and human service professionals. Mile High United Way provides disaster relief, emergency food and shelter, and rehabilitation and development services to needy individuals. Founded in 1887. **NOTE:** Entry-level positions are offered. **Office hours:** Monday - Friday, 8:00 a.m. - 5:00 p.m. **Annual sales/revenues:** $21 - $50 million. **Number of employees at this location:** 65.

MILES ADVERTISING, INC.
1936 Market Street, Denver CO 80202. 303/293-9191. **Toll-free phone:** 800/342-8978. **Contact:** Human Resources. **Description:** A full-service advertising agency specializing in residential real estate. Founded in 1986. **NOTE:** Entry-level positions are offered. **Special programs:** Internships. **Corporate headquarters location:** This location. **Listed on:** Privately held. **CEO:** David R. Miles. **Annual sales/revenues:** $11 - $20 million. **Number of employees at this location:** 20.

MILLENNIUM HARVEST HOUSE
1345 28th Street, Boulder CO 80302-6899. 303/443-3850. **Toll-free phone:** 800/545-6285. **Fax:** 303/443-1480. **Contact:** Human Resources Department. **E-mail address:** boulder@mhrmail.com. **World Wide Web address:** http://www.millennium-hotels.com. **Description:** A 270-room corporate and leisure hotel with meeting facilities. Founded in 1959. **Special programs:** Internships. **Corporate headquarters location:** Denver CO. **Other U.S. locations:** Nationwide. **International locations:** Worldwide. **Parent company:** Millennium & Copthorne Hotels plc. **Operations at this facility include:** Administration; Sales; Service. **Listed on:** Privately held. **Annual sales/revenues:** $11 - $20 million. **Number of employees at this location:** 200.

MINING TECHNOLOGIES INTERNATIONAL (MTI)
12002 West 35th Avenue, Wheat Ridge CO 80033. 303/452-4305. **Contact:** Human Resources. **E-mail address:** jobs@mti.com. **World Wide Web address:** http://www.mti.ca. **Description:** Produces specialized transportation equipment, primarily for the mining industry. Products include mining locomotives, carrier cars, and trucks used in mining. **Corporate headquarters location:** This location. **Parent company:** INCO. **Operations at this facility include:** Administration; Manufacturing; Sales; Service.

MOBILE TOOL INTERNATIONAL, INC. (MTI)
5600 West 88th Avenue, Westminster CO 80031. 303/427-3700. **Recorded jobline:** 303/657-2286. **Contact:** Director of Human Resources. **World Wide Web address:** http://www.mobiletool.com. **Description:** Manufactures products to serve the telecommunications, power utility, construction, and transportation industries. The five primary product groups are Puregas, Mopeco, Telsta, Holan, and PowerAll. Puregas is one of North America's leading brands of dry air pressurization systems. Puregas products are used in telecommunications, microwave, and industrial applications requiring moisture-free air to protect the quality of signal transmission or industrial processes. The Mopeco product line consists of a variety of heavy-duty ventilators and ventilator/heaters, which are used to ventilate and/or heat confined spaces. The Telsta line of noninsulated telescoping aerial lifts are sold by a nationwide direct sales force to telephone, CATV, and contracting companies. Holan is a leading manufacturer of insulated, articulated aerial lifts. These products are sold to power utilities through a nationwide network of independent distributors. The PowerAll Power Pak is a truck-mounted power source providing electric, pneumatic, and hydraulic power to support underground and road surface construction activities. Founded in 1954. **NOTE:** Entry-level positions and second and third shifts are offered. **Positions advertised include:** Assembler; Machinist; Sheet Metal Fabricator; Spray Painter; Welder. **Special programs:** Internships; Apprenticeships; Training. **Office hours:** Monday - Friday, 7:00 a.m. - 5:00 p.m. **Corporate headquarters location:** This location. **Other U.S. locations:** Nationwide. **Parent company:** Penn Central Corporation. **Listed on:** Privately held. **Annual sales/revenues:** $51 - $100 million. **Number of employees at this location:** 435. **Number of employees nationwide:** 535.

MOLI INTERNATIONAL
1150 West Virginia Avenue, Denver CO 80223. 303/777-0364. **Contact:** Van Larson, Owner. **World Wide Web address:** http://www.moliinternational.com. **Description:** Manufactures a variety of food service equipment including bins and carts.

MONIERLIFETILE LLC
10121 Dallas Street, Henderson CO 80640. 303/286-3856. **Contact:** Operations Manager. **World Wide Web address:** http://www.monierlifetile.com. **Description:** Manufactures concrete, clay, and synthetic roof tiles. **Other U.S. locations:** Nationwide.

MOUNT SAN RAFAEL HOSPITAL
410 Benedicta Avenue, Trinidad CO 81082. 719/846-9213. **Fax:** 719/846-2752. **Contact:** Human Resources. **Description:** A nonprofit, JCAHO-accredited, acute care hospital with 31 beds offering 24-hour physician coverage; an emergency department; a full laboratory; a pharmacy; X-ray facilities; physical, occupational, and speech therapy; diabetic education; home health care; and prenatal education. **NOTE:** Entry-level positions and second and third shifts are offered. **Special programs:** Training. **Office hours:** Monday - Friday, 8:00 a.m. - 4:30 p.m. **Executive Director:** James D'Agostino. **Annual sales/revenues:** Less than $5 million. **Number of employees at this location:** 165.

MOUNTAIN STATES MOTORS
1260 South Colorado Boulevard, Denver CO 80246. 303/757-7751. **Contact:** Frank Murray, Office Manager. **World Wide Web address:** http://www.vwdenver.com. **Description:** An automobile dealership specializing in Volkswagen sales and service.

NER DATA PRODUCTS, INC.
5125 Race Court, Denver CO 80216. 303/297-9900. **Contact:** Manager of Employee Relations. **World Wide Web address:** http://www.nerdata.com. **Description:** A manufacturer of office supplies, primarily ribbons and printing cartridges for typewriters, word processors, and computers. Founded in 1971. **Positions advertised include:** Inside Sales Representative. **Corporate headquarters location:** Glassboro NJ.

NATIONAL CATTLEMEN'S BEEF ASSOCIATION
P.O. Box 3469, Englewood CO 80155. 303/694-0305. **Physical address:** 9110 East Nichols Avenue, Suite 300, Centennial CO 80112. **Contact:** Human Resources. **World Wide Web address:** http://www.beef.org. **Description:** An association that operates to improve the economic, political, and social interests of the U.S. cattle industry.

NATIONAL FARMER'S UNION INSURANCE
11900 East Cornell Avenue, Aurora CO 80014-3194. 303/337-5500. **Contact:** Human Resources. **World Wide Web address:** http:// www.nfuic.com. **Description:** A national insurance company specializing in coverage for farmers. **Corporate headquarters location:** This location.

NATIONAL JEWISH MEDICAL & RESEARCH CENTER
1400 Jackson Street, G113, Denver CO 80206. 303/388-4461. **Fax:** 303/398-1775. **Recorded jobline:** 800/686-9512. **Contact:** Human Resources Director. **E-mail address:** hr@njc.org. **World Wide Web address:** http://www.njc.org. **Description:** A world leader in the research and treatment of respiratory and immune system diseases. National Jewish Medical & Research Center is a nonprofit, nonsectarian institution. Founded in 1899.

NATIONAL RENEWABLE ENERGY LABORATORIES
1617 Cole Boulevard, Golden CO 80401-3393. 303/275-3000. **Fax:** 303/384-7570. **Contact:** Human Resources. **E-mail address:** nrel_employment@nrel.gov. **World Wide Web address:** http://www.nrel.gov. **Description:** Engaged in the research and development of renewable energy technologies including wind, solar, and biomass electricity. **Positions advertised include:** Engineer; Senior Analyst; Senior Engineer; Communicator; Administrative Analyst; Specialist; Senior Technician.

NATIONAL SPORTS CENTER FOR THE DISABLED
P.O. Box 1290, Winter Park CO 80482. 970/726-1540. **Contact:** Human Resources. **World Wide Web address:** http://www.nscd.org. **Description:** Provides outdoor mountain recreational services to children and adults with disabilities. This is a nonprofit company. Founded in 1970. **Special programs:** Internships. **Corporate headquarters location:** This location. **Parent company:** Winter Park Recreation Association. **Annual sales/revenues:** Less than $5 million. **Number of employees at this location:** 55.

NATIONAL SYSTEMS AND RESEARCH COMPANY
5385 Mark Dabling Boulevard, Suite 200, Colorado Springs CO 80918. 719/590-8880. **Contact:** Human Resources. **World Wide Web address:** http://www.nsr.com. **Description:** Provides ADP support services including software development and testing for commercial and government clients in the aerospace industry. Founded in 1980. **Corporate headquarters location:** This location. **Other area locations:** Boulder CO; Golden CO; Loveland CO. **Other U.S. locations:** Camarillo CA; Tulsa OK; Portland OR; Vancouver WA. **Subsidiaries include:** NSR Information, Inc. **Operations at this facility include:** Administration. **Listed on:** Privately held. **Number of employees at this location:** 95. **Number of employees nationwide:** 500.

NATIVE AMERICAN RIGHTS FUND
1506 Broadway, Boulder CO 80302. 303/447-8760. **Contact:** Rose Cuny, Office Manager. **World Wide Web address:** http://www.narf.org. **Description:** A national legal defense fund for Native American tribes, villages, groups, and individuals throughout the United States. Founded in 1970. **Special programs:** Internships.

NATKIN CONTRACTING
2775 South Vallejo Street, Englewood CO 80110. 303/783-7500. **Contact:** Human Resources. **World Wide Web address:** http://www.natkin.com. **Description:** A mechanical contractor specializing in air conditioning, heating, piping, and plumbing. **Office hours:** Monday - Friday, 8:00 a.m. - 5:00 p.m. **Corporate headquarters location:** This location. **Other U.S. locations:** Nationwide. **Operations at this facility**

include: Administration. **Number of employees at this location:** 60. **Number of employees nationwide:** 100.

NATURESMART/NBTY
1500 East 128 Avenue, Thornton CO 80241. 303/474-2300. **Contact:** Personnel. **World Wide Web address:** http://www.nbty.com. **Description:** Develops, manufactures, and markets vitamins, nutrients, and herbal supplements.

NAUTILUS HEALTH AND FITNESS GROUP
1886 Prairie Way, Louisville CO 80027. 303/939-0100. **Contact:** Human Resources Department. **World Wide Web address:** http://www.nautilusgroup.com. **Description:** Manufactures and distributes health and fitness products. **Special programs:** Internships. **Corporate headquarters location:** Vancouver WA. **Parent company:** The Nautilus Group Inc. **Operations at this facility include:** Administration. **Listed on:** New York Stock Exchange. **Stock exchange symbol:** NLS.

NEOPLAN USA CORPORATION
700 Gottlob Auwaeter Drive, Lamar CO 81052. 719/336-3256. **Contact:** Human Resources Department. **World Wide Web address:** http://www.neoplanusa.com. **Description:** Manufactures and markets buses for international distribution. **Corporate headquarters location:** This location. **Other area locations:** Thornton CO. **Operations at this facility include:** Manufacturing.

NESTLE PURINA PET CARE COMPANY
4555 York Street, Denver CO 80216. 303/295-0818. **Contact:** Human Resources Department. **World Wide Web address:** http://www.purina.com. **Description:** Produces a line of dog foods, cat foods, and feed for other domestic animals. Founded in 1894. **Positions advertised include:** Territory Manager. **Office hours:** Monday - Friday, 7:30 a.m. - 4:00 p.m. **Corporate headquarters location:** St. Louis MO. **Number of employees worldwide:** 63,000.

NEWMONT MINING CORPORATION
1700 Lincoln Street, Denver CO 80203. 303/863-7414. **Contact:** Human Resources. **World Wide Web address:** http://www.newmont.com. **Description:** A gold exploration company that also operates, manages, and finances its gold properties in the United States. **Corporate headquarters location:** This location. **Subsidiaries include:** Newmont Exploration Limited; Newmont Gold Company. **Listed on:** New York Stock Exchange. **Stock exchange symbol:** NEM.

NEXUS CORPORATION
10983 Leroy Drive, Northglenn CO 80233. 303/457-9199. **Contact:** Human Resources. **World Wide Web address:** http://www.nexuscorp.com. **Description:** Manufactures prefabricated, metal greenhouses.

NICOLET VASCULAR INC.
6355 Joyce Drive, Golden CO 80403. 303/431-9400. **Toll-free phone:** 800/525-2519. **Fax:** 303/431-0429. **Contact:** Human Resources. **World Wide Web address:** http://www.nicoletvascular.com. **Description:** Manufactures diagnostic equipment including fetal heart detectors for determining fetal viability, and systems that aid in the diagnosis of cardiovascular disease. The company also manufactures electronic instrumentation for medical applications in neuro-physiological diagnosis and for monitoring the treatment of brain, muscle, nerve, and sleep disorders, and to test for hearing impairment. **Special programs:** Internships; Summer Jobs. **Corporate headquarters location:** Madison WI. **Parent company:** VIASYS Healthcare. **Listed on:** New York Stock Exchange. **Stock exchange symbol:** VAS. **Annual sales/revenues:** $11 - $20 million. **Number of employees at this location:** 75.

NICKELS ALUMINUM GOLDEN
P.O. Box 207, Fort Lupton CO 80621-0207. 303/659-9767. **Physical address:** 1405 East 14th Street, Fort Lupton CO 80621. **Contact:** Human Resources. **Description:** An industrial recycler producing coils for aluminum gutters and cans.

NOBEL/SYSCO FOOD SERVICES COMPANY
1101 West 48th Avenue, Denver CO 80221. 303/458-4000. **Fax:** 303/480-3370. **Recorded jobline:** 303/480-3475. **Contact:** Human Resources. **E-mail address:** jobs@nobelsysco.com. **World Wide Web address:** http://www.nobelsysco.com. **Description:** Markets and distributes a broad line of food products, beverages, and related supplies to restaurants, fast-food operations, schools, and hospitals. **Corporate headquarters location:** Houston TX. **Other U.S. locations:** Nationwide. **Parent company:** SYSCO Corporation. **Listed on:** New York Stock Exchange. **Stock exchange symbol:** SYY. **Number of employees at this location:** 1,000.

NORGREN
5400 South Delaware Street, Littleton CO 80120. 303/794-2611. **Fax:** 303/795-6200. **Contact:** Martha Parsley, Manager of Human Resources. **World Wide Web address:** http://www.usa.norgren.com. **Description:** Manufactures accessory and component parts for pneumatic systems. **Positions advertised include:** Graduate Engineer; District Sales Manager; Administrative Assistant. **Corporate headquarters location:** This location.

NORTH COLORADO MEDICAL CENTER (NCMC)
BANNER HEALTH COLORADO
1801 16th Street, Greeley CO 80631-5199. 970/352-4121. **Fax:** 970/350-6446. **Recorded jobline:** 970/350-6565. **Contact:** Director of Personnel. **World Wide Web address:** http://www.bannerhealth.com. **Description:** With more than 325 beds, NCMC is one of the largest medical facilities in the region. Notable services include 'Your Heart Team' Cardiovascular Services; the McArthur Rehabilitation Center for physical, occupational, and speech therapy; the Oncology Center; the Orthopedic Unit; the Monfort Family Birth Center; the Regional Burn Unit; North Colorado PsychCare; Family Recovery Center; The Progressive Care Rehabilitation Center, for extended inpatient rehabilitation; Emergency Services that delivers 24-hour care to more than 2,000 patients a month; Air Life of Greeley, an air ambulance transport system; and two home care agencies that complement and extend regular patient services. In addition, the center offers a Lifetime Wellness Center program that offers health education classes on such subjects as stress management, weight management, and smoking cessation; and a Patient Services Representative Program and Hospitality Program that place special emphasis on guest relations. Founded in 1995. **NOTE:** Apply online. Entry-level positions are offered. **Positions advertised include:** Activities Coordinator; RN; Business Associate; Care Coordinator; Certified Nurse Assistant; Clinical Analyst; Clinical Nurse Specialist; Clinical Resource Coordinator; Food Service Worker; Licensed Respiratory Therapist; Marketing Communications Coordinator; Medical Technologist; MRI Technologist; Patient Account Representative; Pharmacist; Physical Therapist; Radiology Engineer; Service Bureau Representative; Service Technician; Sonographer; Surgery Transporter; Surgical Technologist; Trauma Services Coordinator. **Corporate headquarters location:** Fargo ND. **Other area locations:** Brush CO; Loveland CO; Sterling CO. **Operations at this facility include:** Administration; Regional Headquarters; Service. **Annual sales/revenues:** $21 - $50 million. **Number of employees at this location:** 1,700. **Number of employees nationwide:** 14,000.

NORTH SUBURBAN MEDICAL CENTER (NSMC)
9191 Grant Street, Thornton CO 80229-4341. 303/451-7800. **Contact:** Human Resources. **World Wide Web address:** http://www.northsuburban.com. **Description:** A 200-bed, family-centered health care facility. North Suburban Medical Center offers a full range of services including orthopedics, ICU/CCU, 24-hour emergency coverage, medical and surgical, pediatrics, and oncology. In addition, NSMC also operates a 23-bed Transitional Care Center and a program for inpatient treatment of geriatric, psychiatric disorders. A full range of support services are available at NSMC and include an MRI unit, a breast diagnosis center, outpatient physical and occupational therapy, and a cardiac catheterization lab. **Positions advertised include:** RN; CS Technician; HIM Manager; Occupational Therapist; Pharmacy Director; Risk Manager; Speech Language Pathologist; OR Manager; Surgery Scheduler.

NORTHRUP GRUMMAN
MISSION SYSTEMS
985 Space Center Drive, Suite 350, Colorado Springs CO 80915. 719/596-0700. **Contact:** Human Resources. **World Wide Web address:** http://www.northgrum.com. **Description:** Focused on solutions that contribute to the welfare of the global community, the organization's technology spans three business areas: missile systems, command, control and intelligence, and technical and management services. **NOTE:** Search and apply for positions online. **Positions advertised include:** TT&C Systems Engineer; NORAD Planner; Software Engineer; Program Control Analyst; Communications Systems Engineer; Systems Integrator. **Corporate headquarters location:** Reston VA. **Number of employees worldwide:** 18,000.

NORTHWEST PIPE COMPANY
6030 North Washington Street, Denver CO 80216. 303/289-4080. **Contact:** Personnel Administrator. **World Wide Web address:** http://www.nwpipe.com. **Description:** Manufactures welded steel pipes for construction, agricultural, and industrial uses. The company also offers full-service fabricated metal and project engineering services. Founded in 1966. **Corporate headquarters location:** Portland OR. **Listed on:** NASDAQ. **Stock exchange symbol:** NWPX.

NXTREND TECHNOLOGY, INC.
5555 Tech Center Drive, Suite 300, Colorado Springs CO 80919-2309. 719/590-8940. **Fax:** 719/528-1465. **Contact:** Human Resources. **E-mail address:** jobs@nxtrend.com. **World Wide Web address:** http://www.nxtrend.com. **Description:** Develops, sells, and supports software applications for the wholesale distribution industry. **NOTE:** Entry-level positions are offered. **Special programs:** Training. **Office hours:** Monday - Friday, 8:00 a.m. - 5:00 p.m. **Corporate headquarters location:** This location. **Other U.S. locations:** Atlanta GA; Minneapolis MN; Dallas TX. **International locations:** Toronto, Canada. **Listed on:** Privately held. **Annual sales/revenues:** $51 - $100 million. **Number of employees at this location:** 220. **Number of employees nationwide:** 340.

OSI PHARMACEUTICALS, INC.
2860 Wilderness Place, Boulder CO 80301. 303/546-7600. **Fax:** 303/444-0672. **Contact:** Human Resources. **E-mail address:** employment@osip.com. **World Wide Web address:** http://www.osip.com. **Description:** A biopharmaceutical company dedicated to the discovery, development, and commercialization of treatments for human diseases. The company's business is focused on making new therapies available to patients, physicians, and health care systems. The company has also developed treatments for diseases caused by HIV, the Hepatitis B virus, the Herpes simplex virus, human papillomavirus, and the influenza virus. **Corporate headquarters location:** Melville NY. **International locations:** Worldwide. **Listed on:** NASDAQ. **Stock exchange symbol:** OSIP

OCTAGON SYSTEMS
6510 West 91st Avenue, Suite 110, Westminster CO 80031. 303/430-1500. **Fax:** 303/412-2050. **Contact:** Personnel. **E-mail address:** hrstaffing@octagonsystems.com. **World Wide Web address:** http://www.octagonsystems.com. **Description:** Manufactures personal computers for extreme environments. Founded in 1981. **Positions advertised include:** Director of Operations. **Corporate headquarters location:** This location. **Listed on:** Privately held. **Number of employees at this location:** 70.

1MAGE SOFTWARE INC.
6025 South Quebec Street, Suite 300, Englewood CO 80111. 303/694-9180. **Contact:** Human Resources. **E-mail address:** jobs@1mage.com. **World Wide Web address:** http://www.1mage.com. **Description:** Develops and markets image recording and storage systems to convert paper records into electronic format. 1mage Software also offers installation and support services. **Corporate headquarters location:** This location.

ORICA LIMITED
33101 East Quincy Avenue, Watkins CO 80137. 303/268-5000. **Contact:** Human Resources. **E-mail address:** jobs@orica.com. **World Wide Web address:** http://www.orica.com. **Description:** Manufactures commercial explosives, nitrogen products, paints, fertilizers, chemicals, and plastics. **Corporate headquarters location:** Australia. **International locations:** Worldwide. **Number of employees worldwide:** 9,000.

PC MAGAZINE
P.O. Box 53131, Boulder CO 80322-3131. 303/604-1465. **Contact:** Human Resources. **World Wide Web address:** http://www.pcmag.com. **Description:** A computer and business magazine that includes editorials, product reviews and evaluations, and other, computer-related information. **Parent company:** Ziff-Davis, Inc.

PAMCO STEWART & STEVENSON
10777 East 45th Avenue, Denver CO 80239. 303/371-0330. **Contact:** Human Resources. **World Wide Web address:** http://www.ssss.com. **Description:** Involved in the assembly of oil pumps, compressors, and engines. **NOTE:** Jobseekers should send resumes to Human Resources Manager, 5840 Dahlia Street, Commerce City CO 80022. **Positions advertised include:** Mechanic; Sales Representative; Parts Counter Attendant. **Corporate headquarters location:** Houston TX. **Parent company:** Stewart & Stevenson Power, Inc. **Operations at this facility include:** Administration; Manufacturing; Research and Development; Sales; Service. **Listed on:** NASDAQ. **Stock exchange symbol:** SSSS. **Number of employees at this location:** 125.

PARKPLACE RETIREMENT COMMUNITY
111 Emerson Street, Denver CO 80218. 303/744-0400. **Contact:** Human Resources. **World Wide Web address:** http://www.arclp.com. **Description:** A retirement community. Founded in 1978. **Positions advertised include:** Executive Director; Emergency LPN; Speech Language Pathologist. **Corporate headquarters location:**

Brentwood TN. **Parent company:** American Retirement Corporation. **Listed on:** New York Stock Exchange. **Stock exchange symbol:** ACR.

PENROSE-ST. FRANCIS HEALTH SERVICES
PENROSE HOSPITAL
P.O. Box 7021, Colorado Springs CO 80933. 719/776-5000. **Physical address:** 2215 North Cascade Avenue, Colorado Springs CO 80907. **Contact:** Human Resources. **World Wide Web address:** http://www.centura.org. **Description:** Operates a 300-bed hospital; a cytology laboratory; Huff and Puff, a children's asthma program; The Women's Life Center; ReadyCare clinics; The Penrose Cancer Center; The Namaste Alzheimer Center; The Heart Center at Penrose Hospital; The Center for Health and Nutrition; trauma rehabilitation and comprehensive rehabilitation; and The Clinical Pastoral Education Program. **Other area locations:** Green Mountain Falls CO; Woodland Park CO. **Parent company:** Centura Health.

PENTAX CORPORATION
35 Inverness Drive East, Englewood CO 80112. 303/799-8000. **Fax:** 303/728-0217. **Contact:** Roxanne Dennison, Human Resources Representative. **E-mail address:** rdennison@pentax.com. **World Wide Web address:** http://www.pentax.com. **Description:** Manufactures cameras, camera supplies, and related photographic products. **Corporate headquarters location:** This location.

PENTON TECHNOLOGY MEDIA
221 East 29th Street, Loveland CO 80538. 970/663-4700. **Contact:** Recruiter. **World Wide Web address:** http://www.pentontech.com. **Description:** Publishes technical information for IBM AS/400 and Windows NT users and financial analysts. The company produces numerous magazines, books, and textbooks. **Positions advertised include:** Marketing Associate; Promotions/Research Analyst. **Corporate headquarters location:** Cleveland OH. **Other area locations:** Lakewood CO. **International locations:** United Kingdom. **Parent company:** Penton Media, Inc. **Listed on:** New York Stock Exchange. **Stock exchange symbol:** PME. **Number of employees at this location:** 80.

PEPSI-COLA BOTTLING COMPANY
3801 Brighton Boulevard, Denver CO 80216. 303/292-9220. **Contact:** Human Resources. **World Wide Web address:** http://www.pepsico.com. **Description:** A division of Pepsi-Cola Company that produces Pepsi, Diet Pepsi, A&W Root Beer, Slice, Orange Slice, and Mountain Dew. **NOTE:** Office hours: Monday - Friday, 8:00 a.m. - 4:00 p.m. **Positions advertised include:** Quality Control Lab Technician; Vending Territory Manager; Merchandiser; Sales Manager; Technical Manager Designate; Zone Sales Leader. **Parent company:** PepsiCo, Inc. (Purchase NY) consists of Frito-Lay Company, Pepsi-Cola Company, Quaker Oats Company, and Tropicana Products, Inc. **Listed on:** New York Stock Exchange. **Stock exchange symbol:** PEP.

PETRO CANADA
1099 18th Street, Suite 400, Denver CO 80202. 303/297-2100. **Contact:** Nancy Hewitt, Human Resources Manager. **E-mail address:** nancy.hewitt@petro-canada.com. **World Wide Web address:** http://www.pretro-canada.com. **Description:** An oil and gas company engaged in the exploration, acquisition, development, and production of crude oil and natural gas. Also engaged in oil and gas property operations, oil field services, and natural gas marketing.

GERALD H. PHIPPS, INC.
1530 West 13th Avenue, Denver CO 80204-2400. 303/571-5377. **Fax:** 303/629-7467. **Contact:** Personnel. **World Wide Web address:** http://www.geraldhphipps.com. **Description:** A general contractor/construction manager for commercial buildings. Gerald H. Phipps, Inc. specializes in building medical complexes, high-tech buildings, universities, schools, offices that tenants finish, public facilities, biotechnology labs, and retail projects. Founded in 1952. **NOTE:** Entry-level positions are offered. **Special programs:** Apprenticeships. **Corporate headquarters location:** This location. **Other area locations:** Colorado Springs CO. **Listed on:** Privately held. **Annual sales/revenues:** More than $100 million. **Number of employees at this location:** 250.

PORTER ADVENTIST HOSPITAL
2525 South Downing Street, Denver CO 80210. 303/778-1955. **Contact:** Human Resources. **World Wide Web address:** http://www.centura.org. **Description:** A 369-bed, nonprofit, acute care hospital. Founded in 1930. **Positions advertised include:** CAT Scan Technician; Certified Nurse Aide; Dosimetrist; Instrument Technician; Radiology Technician; Respiratory Therapist; RN Practitioner; Secretary; Speech Pathologist. **Parent company:** Centura Health.

POUDRE VALLEY HOSPITAL
1024 South Lemay Avenue, Fort Collins CO 80524. 970/495-7300. **Fax:** 970/495-7629. **Recorded jobline:** 970/495-7310. **Contact:** Patti Oakes, Director of Human Resources. **World Wide Web address:** http://www.pvhs.org. **Description:** A hospital providing health care services in northern Colorado, western Nebraska, and southern Wyoming. **NOTE:** Please send resumes to Human Resources, 1224 Doctors Lane, Fort Collins CO 80524. Entry-level positions and second and third shifts are offered. **Positions advertised include:** RN; Physical Therapist; Application Specialist; Project Manager; Occupational Therapist; Pharmacist; Donor Phlebotomist; Nuclear Medicine Technician; Lab Support Processor; Lab Courier; Nursing Assistant; Food Service Technician; Medical Transcriptionist. **Special programs:** Internships. **Office hours:** Monday - Friday, 7:00 a.m. - 4:30 p.m. **Parent company:** Poudre Valley Health System. **President/CEO:** Rulon Stacey. **Number of employees at this location:** 1,800.

PRESBYTERIAN/ST. LUKE'S MEDICAL CENTER
1719 East 19th Avenue, Denver CO 80218. 303/839-6000. **Contact:** Human Resources. **World Wide Web address:** http://www.pslmc.com. **Description:** A 674-bed, acute care hospital. Presbyterian/St. Luke's Medical Center has comprehensive programs in pediatrics, obstetrics, oncology, cardiology, and orthopedics. The medical center is a leader in tertiary programs such as organ and bone marrow transplantation; high-risk obstetrical care; diabetes management; wound care; and head, neck, and skull surgery. **Positions advertised include:** Managed Care Coordinator; Physical Therapist; Rehabilitation Aide; Manager, Occupational Medicine; Staff Accountant; Patient Access Representative; Cashier; RN; CT Technologist; Dietician; Housekeeper; Certified Nurse Assistant; Pharmacist. **Parent company:** HealthONE facilities include Medical Center of Aurora, Spalding Rehabilitation Hospital, Swedish Medical Center, Rose Medical Center, and North Suburban Medical Center.

PRICEWATERHOUSECOOPERS
1670 Broadway Avenue, Suite 1000, Denver CO 80202. 720/931-7000. **Contact:** Recruiting. **World Wide Web address:** http://www.pwcglobal.com. **Description:** One of the largest certified public accounting firms in the world. PricewaterhouseCoopers provides public accounting, business advisory, management consulting, and taxation services. **Corporate headquarters location:** New York NY. **Other U.S. locations:** Nationwide. **International locations:** Worldwide.

PRIMEDIA BUSINESS
5680 Greenwood Plaza Boulevard, Suite 300, Greenwood Village CO 80111. 303/741-2901. **Contact:** Personnel. **World Wide Web address:** http://www.primedia.com. **Description:** A publisher of business-to-business magazines and newsletters that allow manufacturers and suppliers to provide professionals with statistics, explanations, technical advice, and product introductions that ultimately make businesses more successful. PRIMEDIA also produces 450 technical books and valuation guides. **Parent company:** PRIMEDIA Specialty Magazines. **Listed on:** New York Stock Exchange. **Stock exchange symbol:** PRM.

THE PRODUCT LINE, INC.
2370 South Trenton Way, Denver CO 80231. 303/671-8000. **Fax:** 303/696-7300. **Contact:** Human Resources. **Description:** Provides outbound telemarketing to clients in the PC software publishing, financial services, and tourism industries. Other services of the company include turnkey order entry, credit card processing, and package and literature fulfillment. Advanced technologies include two HP3000 mainframes, automatic call distribution, automatic voice response, T-1 circuitry, DNIS, and predictive dialing. Founded in 1982. **Corporate headquarters location:** This location. **Operations at this facility include:** Administration; Sales; Service. **Listed on:** Privately held. **Number of employees at this location:** 300.

PROGRESSIVE INSURANCE GROUP
1110 Chapel Hills Drive, Colorado Springs CO 80920. 719/262-5600. **Toll-free phone:** 888/838-7414. **Contact:** Human Resources Manager. **World Wide Web address:** http://www.progressive.com. **Description:** Progressive Insurance Group writes automobile, motorcycle, recreational vehicle, personal water craft, and commercial vehicle insurance in 48 states. Progressive also insures financial institutions. **Positions advertised include:** Direct Sales Representative; Massotherapist. **Corporate headquarters location:** Baltimore MD. **Other U.S. locations:** Nationwide. **Operations at this facility include:** This location is a customer service center.

PRUDENTIAL COLORADO REAL ESTATE
7995 East Hampden Avenue, Suite 100, Denver CO 80231. 303/750-3475. **Fax:** 303/337-1889. **Contact:** Human Resources. **Description:** Markets residential and commercial real estate throughout metropolitan Denver. **Positions advertised include:** Real Estate Agent. **Corporate headquarters location:** Denver CO.

PUBLIC SERVICE CREDIT UNION
7055 East Evans Avenue, Denver CO 80224. 303/691-2345. **Fax:** 303/691-8408. **Contact:** Human Resources. **E-mail address:** jobs@pscu.org. **World Wide Web address:** http://www.pscu.org. **Description:** A credit union. Founded in 1938. **Positions advertised include:** Member Service Representative. **Other area locations include:** Canon City CO; Centennial CO; Clifton CO; Colorado Springs CO.

THE PUEBLO CHIEFTAIN
P.O. Box 4040, Pueblo CO 81003. 719/544-3520. **Physical address:** 825 West 6th Street, Pueblo CO 81003. **Contact:** Executive Editor. **World Wide Web address:** http://www.chieftain.com. **Description:** Publishes the *Pueblo Chieftain*, a newspaper with a circulation of 51,000. **Corporate headquarters location:** This location.

QUALITY METAL PRODUCTS
11500 West 13th Avenue, Lakewood CO 80215. 303/232-4242. **Contact:** Human Resources. **World Wide Web address:** http://www.qualitymetalproducts.com. **Description:** Manufactures sheet metal and related products.

QUARK, INC.
1800 Grant Street, Denver CO 80203. 303/894-8888. **Contact:** Human Resources Department. **E-mail address:** employment@quark.com. **World Wide Web address:** http://www.quark.com. **Description:** Develops software including QuarkXPress, one of the leading products in desktop publishing. **International locations:** Worldwide.

QUEST DIAGNOSTICS INCORPORATED
695 South Broadway, Denver CO 80209. 303/899-6000. **Fax:** 303/899-6123. **Contact:** Human Resources. **World Wide Web address:** http://www.questdiagnostics.com. **Description:** One of the largest clinical laboratories in North America, providing a broad range of clinical laboratory services to health care clients, which include physicians, hospitals, clinics, dialysis centers, pharmaceutical companies, and corporations. The company offers and performs tests on blood, urine, and other bodily fluids and tissues to provide information for health and well-being. **Positions advertised include:** Phlebotomist; Account Representative; Specimen Technician; Specimen Entry Clerk. **Corporate headquarters location:** Teterboro NJ. **Other U.S. locations:** Nationwide. **Listed on:** New York Stock Exchange. **Stock exchange symbol:** DGX.

QWEST COMMUNICATIONS
1005 17th Street, Denver CO 80202. **Recorded jobline:** 303/896-7683. **Contact:** Manager of Human Resources. **World Wide Web address:** http://www.qwest.com. **Description:** A long-distance telecommunications carrier that provides a broad array of domestic and international voice, data, and Internet services to commercial and residential customers. Qwest Communications provides service to customers through its network of digital fiber-optic facilities. **Office hours:** Monday - Friday, 8:00 a.m. - 4:30 p.m. **Corporate headquarters location:** Denver CO. **Other U.S. locations:** Nationwide. **Listed on:** New York Stock Exchange. **Stock exchange symbol:** Q.

QWEST COMMUNICATIONS
1801 California Street, Denver CO 80202. 303/992-1400. **Recorded jobline:** 303/896-7683. **Contact:** Manager of Human Resources. **World Wide Web address:** http://www.qwest.com. **Description:** A long-distance telecommunications carrier that provides a broad array of domestic and international voice, data, and Internet services to commercial and residential customers. Qwest Communications provides service to customers through its network of digital fiber-optic facilities. **Corporate headquarters location:** This location. **Listed on:** New York Stock Exchange. **Stock exchange symbol:** Q.

REM SERVICES INC.
1520 East Mulberry, Suite 110, Fort Collins CO 80524. 970/224-9991. **Contact:** Director of Human Resources. **Description:** Provides rehabilitation services, home and job-finding services, and offers social activities to adults with mental disabilities.

RADISSON HOTELS
3200 South Parker Road, Aurora CO 80014. 303/695-1700. **Contact:** Human Resources. **World Wide Web address:** http://www.radisson.com. **Description:** One location of the nationwide hotel chain.

RADISSON STAPLETON PLAZA HOTEL
3333 Quebec Street, Denver CO 80207. 303/321-3500. **Contact:** Human Resources. **World Wide Web address:** http://www.radisson.com. **Description:** A 300-room hotel whose facilities include a fitness center and a restaurant. **NOTE:** Entry-level positions, part-time jobs, and second and third shifts are offered.

RAMTRON INTERNATIONAL CORPORATION
1850 Ramtron Drive, Colorado Springs CO 80921. 719/481-7000. **Contact:** Human Resources. **World Wide Web address:** http://www.ramtron.com. **Description:** Manufactures semiconductors. **Corporate headquarters location:** This location. **Listed on:** NASDAQ. **Stock exchange symbol:** RMTR.

RAYTHEON
16800 East Centretech Parkway, Aurora CO 80011. 303/344-6000. **Contact:** Human Resources. **World Wide Web address:** http://www.raytheon.com. **Description**: The company develops and deploys information and data management systems that command and control satellites, manage space-based assets and facilitate global communication. The Aurora business site's customers include NASA and other U.S. federal agencies, satellite manufacturers, and international commercial communications satellite operators. **NOTE:** Search and apply for positions online. **Positions advertised include:** Chief Systems Engineer; Computer Systems Technologist; Configuration Analyst; Facility Operations Specialist; Field Engineer; Accountant; Industrial Security Specialist. **Corporate headquarters location:** Waltham MA. **Number of employees at this location:** 2,600. **Number of employees worldwide:** 78,000.

REGAL ENTERTAINMENT GROUP
9110 East Nichols Avenue, Suite 200, Centennial CO 80112-3405. 303/792-3600. **Contact:** Personnel. **World Wide Web address:** http://www.regalcinemas.com. **Description:** Operates 300 movie theaters with 2,000 screens in 23 states. Founded in 1926. **Corporate headquarters location:** Knoxville TN. **Other U.S. locations:** Nationwide. **International locations:** Worldwide. **Listed on:** New York Stock Exchange. **Stock exchange symbol:** RGC. **Number of employees at this location:** 200. **Number of employees nationwide:** 11,000.

REGIS UNIVERSITY
3333 Regis Boulevard, Mail Code K-4, Denver CO 80221-1099. 303/458-4161. **Recorded jobline:** 303/458-4386. **Contact:** Human Resources. **E-mail address:** resumes@regis.edu. **World Wide Web address:** http://www.regis.edu. **Description:** A four-year, liberal arts/preprofessional, Jesuit university. Six academic divisions offer more than 30 programs of study. Approximately 1,400 students attend Regis University. **Special programs:** Internships. **Other U.S. locations:** WY. **Number of employees at this location:** 550.

RELIANCE METAL CENTER
3855 Silica Drive, Colorado Springs CO 80910. 719/390-4911. **Contact:** Human Resources. **World Wide Web address:** http://www.rsac.com. **Description:** One of the largest Western-based metals service center companies in the United States. Through a network of 20 locations, the company distributes a full line of ferrous and nonferrous metal products, including galvanized, hot-rolled and cold-finished steel, stainless steel, aluminum, brass, copper, and alloy steel. The company sells metal products from locations in nine states and to more than 30,000 customers engaged in a wide variety of industries. **Corporate headquarters location:** Los Angeles CA. **Parent company:** Reliance Steel and Aluminum Company. **Listed on:** New York Stock Exchange. **Stock exchange symbol:** RS.

RENTAL SERVICE CORP.
481 West 84th Avenue, Thornton CO 80260. 303/428-7466. **Contact:** Human Resources. **World Wide Web address:** http://www.rentalservice.com. **Description:** A general construction equipment rental company. **Parent company:** Atlas Copco Group.

REPLIDYNE, INC.
1450 Infinite Drive, Louisville CO 80027. 303/665-3450. **Fax:** 303/665-3455. **Contact:** Personnel Department. **E-mail address:** employment@replidyne.com. **World Wide Web address:** http://www.replidyne.com. **Description:** A specialty pharmaceutical company focused on developing and commercializing innovative anti-infective products. **Positions advertised include:** Clinical Microbiologist; Manager of Quality Assurance.

ROBINSON BRICK COMPANY
1845 West Dartmouth Avenue, Denver CO 80110-1308. 303/781-9002. **Contact:** Human Resources. **E-mail address:** hr@robinsonbrick.com. **World Wide Web address:** http://www.robinsonbrick.com. **Description:** Produces and markets a variety of brick and tile materials including paving brick and clay brick. Founded in 1880. **Positions advertised include:** Maintenance Technician. **Office hours:** Monday - Friday, 7:00 a.m. - 5:00 p.m. **Corporate headquarters location:** This location. **Operations at this facility include:** Administration; Manufacturing; Research and Development; Sales; Service.

ROBINSON DAIRY INC.
646 Bryant Street, Denver CO 80204. 303/825-2990. **Contact:** Human Resources. **World Wide Web address:** http://www.robinsondairy.com. **Description:** Produces a complete range of dairy products including milk and ice cream. Robinson Dairy also produces a variety of fruit-flavored drinks. **NOTE:** Fill out application at location. **Corporate headquarters location:** This location.

ROCHE COLORADO
2075 North 55th Street, Boulder CO 80301. 303/442-1926. **Fax:** 303/938-6413. **Contact:** Human Resources. **E-mail address:** boulder.hr@roche.com. **World Wide Web address:** http://www.rochecolorado.com. **Description:** An international drug development company focusing on oncology. **NOTE:** Interested jobseekers must reference specific job opening when applying for a position. Please see company Website for more details. **Parent company:** Hoffman-LaRoche Inc.

ROCK BOTTOM RESTAURANTS, INC.
248 Centennial Parkway, Suite 100, Louisville CO 80027. 303/664-4000. **Fax:** 303/664-4199. **Contact:** Human Resources Department. **World Wide Web address:** http://www.rockbottom.com. **Description:** Owns and operates 64 restaurants and breweries under the names Rock Bottom Brew Pub, Old Chicago Pizza, Walnut Brewery, Chop House, and Sing Sing. Restaurants range from casual to upscale dining. Founded in 1993. **NOTE:** Entry-level positions and part-time jobs are offered. **Company slogan:** To run great restaurants with great people. **Positions advertised include:** Restaurant Manager; Sous Chef. **Special programs:** Internships; Training; Summer Jobs. **Corporate headquarters location:** This location. **Other U.S. locations:** Nationwide. **Annual sales/revenues:** More than $100 million. **Number of employees at this location:** 70.

ROCKY MOUNTAIN CHOCOLATE FACTORY, INC.
265 Turner Drive, Durango CO 81303. 970/247-4943. **Fax:** 970/382-7371. **Contact:** Jamie Callies, Human Resources Manager. **World Wide Web address:** http://www.rmcf.com. **Description:** A retail distributor of candy products including chocolate covered fruit, fudge, and caramel apples. The company operates over 200 retail stores worldwide. Founded in 1981. **NOTE:** Part-time jobs and second and third shifts are offered. This location also hires seasonally. **Company slogan:** America's chocolatier. **Special programs:** Internships; Summer Jobs. **Office hours:** Monday - Friday, 8:00 a.m. - 5:00 p.m. **Corporate headquarters location:** This location. **Other U.S. locations:** Nationwide. **International locations:** Canada; Taiwan; United Arab Emirates. **Listed on:** NASDAQ. **Stock exchange symbol:** RMCF. **CEO:** Franklin Crail. **Annual sales/revenues:** $21 - $50 million. **Number of employees at this location:** 120. **Number of employees nationwide:** 400.

ROCKY MOUNTAIN NEWS
100 Gene Amole Way, Denver CO 80204. 303/892-5173. **Contact:** Human Resources. **World Wide Web address:** http://www.rockymountainnews.com. **Description:** Publishes a newspaper with a daily circulation of more than 344,000. **NOTE:** Please call the Human Resources department for instructions before sending a resume. **Special programs:** Internships. **Office hours:** Monday - Friday, 8:00 a.m. - 5:00 p.m. **Other U.S. locations:** Nationwide. **Parent company:** E.W. Scripps Company (Cincinnati OH.) **Operations at this facility include:** Administration; Sales; Service. **Listed on:** New York Stock Exchange. **Stock exchange symbol:** SSP. **Number of employees at this location:** 1,600.

ROCKY MOUNTAIN POISON AND DRUG CENTER
777 Bannock Street, Mail Code 0180, Denver CO 80204. 303/739-1100. **Contact:** Human Resources. **World Wide Web address:** http://www.rmpdc.org. **Description:** Provides rapid and accurate treatment recommendations over the telephone to consumers and health professionals, 24 hours a day. Registered nurses and physicians manage over 120,000 cases per year. Rocky Mountain Poison and Drug Center consults in all areas dealing with chemicals, drugs, and plants. The center's public education program focuses on early intervention and prevention education platforms.

ROCKY MOUNTAIN PRESTRESS
5801 Pecos, Denver CO 80221. 303/480-1111. **Fax:** 303/433-0451. **Contact:** Human Resources. **World Wide Web address:** http://www.rmpprestress.com. **Description:** Manufactures and sells prestressed structural concrete building materials, primarily used in heavy construction projects. **Corporate headquarters location:** This location. **Operations at this facility include:** Administration; Manufacturing; Research and Development; Sales; Service. **Number of employees at this location:** 300.

ROCKY MOUNTAIN STEEL CORPORATION
P.O. Box 316, Pueblo CO 81002. 719/561-6000. **Contact:** Supervisor of Personnel. **World Wide Web address:** http://www.oregonsteel.com. **Description:** Manufactures steel bar products, railroad rails, seamless oil country tubular pipes, and wire. **Corporate headquarters location:** Portland OR. **Parent company:** Oregon Steel Mills. **Listed on:** New York Stock Exchange. **Stock exchange symbol:** OS.

ROPER APPAREL AND FOOTWEAR
14707 East Second Avenue, 3rd Floor, Aurora CO 80011. 303/893-2320. **Contact:** Human Resources. **World Wide Web address:** http://www.eroper.com. **Description:** Manufactures Western apparel. **Corporate headquarters location:** This location.

ROSE MEDICAL CENTER
4567 East Ninth Avenue, Denver CO 80220. 303/320-2121. **Contact:** Human Resources. **World Wide Web address:** http://www.rosemed.com. **Description:** A 420-bed medical center that provides inpatient and outpatient services. Off-site services include 11 primary care centers, four physical therapy sites, and an outpatient surgery center. Rose Women's Center offers programs for parent education, infertility, and high-risk pregnancies. Women's services also include a mammography service and breast diagnostic center. Additionally, a program for middle-aged women addresses the concerns surrounding menopause and healthy aging. Comprehensive services for children include a pediatric emergency service; a 14-bed, inpatient unit; and a multispecialty outpatient service supported by general and specialty pediatricians. Other areas of specialized expertise include the treatment of diabetes, comprehensive surgical services, a regional cleft lip and palate reconstructive surgery clinic, and an institute for joint replacement surgery. Founded in 1949. **Positions advertised include:** Management Engineer; RN; Ultrasonographer; Physician Assistant; Food Service Worker; Orthopedic Specialty Clinician; Nuclear Medicine Technician; Pharmacist; Physical Therapist; Radiology Technologist. **Corporate headquarters location:** This location. **Parent company:** HealthONE. **Listed on:** Privately held. **Number of employees at this location:** 1,600.

ROSENBERG MANAGEMENT INC.
3400 East Bayaud Avenue, Suite 390, Denver CO 80209. 303/320-6067. **Contact:** Manager. **Description:** A real estate investment company involved in operating apartment buildings.

FREDERICK ROSS COMPANY
717 17th Street, Suite 2000, Denver CO 80202. 303/892-1111. **Contact:** Human Resources. **World Wide Web address:** http://www.frederickross.com. **Description:** A full-service commercial real estate firm. **Corporate headquarters location:** This location. **Parent company:** Oncor International. **Operations at this facility include:** Administration; Research and Development; Sales; Service. **Listed on:** Privately held. **Number of employees at this location:** 150.

ROTHGERBER JOHNSON & LYONS LLP
1200 17th Street, Suite 3000, Denver CO 80202-5855. 303/623-9000. **Fax:** 303/623-9222. **Contact:** Beth Martinez, Recruiter. **World Wide Web address:** http://www.rothgerber.com. **Description:** A law firm specializing in all aspects of corporate and government law including general representation and litigation. Founded in 1903. **Corporate headquarters location:** This location. **Other area locations:** Colorado Springs CO. **Other U.S. locations:** Cheyenne WY.

ROYAL & SUNALLIANCE USA
P.O. Box 3329, Englewood CO 80155. 303/754-8400. **Physical address:** 9800 South Meridian Boulevard, Englewood CO 80112. **Contact:** Human Resources. **World Wide Web address:** http://www.royalsunalliance-usa.com. **Description:** Provides commercial property and casualty insurance as well as personal and specialty insurance. **Corporate headquarters location:** London, England. **Parent company:** Royal & SunAlliance Insurance Group plc. **Listed on:** New York Stock Exchange. **Stock exchange symbol:** RSA.

ROYAL GOLD, INC.
1660 Wynkoop Street, Suite 1000, Denver CO 80202. 303/573-1660. **Contact:**

Controller. **E-mail address:** info@royalgold.com. **World Wide Web address:** http://www.royalgold.com. **Description:** Engaged in the acquisition, exploration, development, and sale of gold and precious metals properties. The company's exploration projects are located in Mono County CA; Eureka County NV; and Yavapai County AZ. Royal Gold also has gold properties located in Elko, White Pine, and Eureka Counties NV. **Corporate headquarters location:** This location. **Subsidiaries include:** Denver Mining Finance Company provides financial, operational, and management services to the mining industry. Environmental Strategies, Inc., a wholly-owned subsidiary of Denver Mining Finance Company, provides environmental consulting services to the mining industry. **Listed on:** NASDAQ. **Stock exchange symbol:** RGLD.

SAFETRAN TRAFFIC SYSTEMS, INC.
1485 Garden of the Gods, Colorado Springs CO 80907. 719/599-5600. **Contact:** Georgine Fries, Human Resources Manager. **World Wide Web address:** http://www.safetran-traffic.com. **Description:** Manufactures traffic control products and systems. **Corporate headquarters location:** This location. **Number of employees at this location:** 100.

ST. ANTHONY HOSPITAL CENTRAL
4231 West 16th Avenue, Denver CO 80204. 303/629-3511. **Contact:** Human Resources. **World Wide Web address:** http://www.centura.org. **Description:** A 500-bed, full-service hospital and the founding facility of the Provenant Health Partners health care network. St. Anthony Hospital Central provides 24-hour physician emergency room coverage, open heart surgery, and on-site emergency care. **Positions advertised include:** Anesthesia Technician; Case Manager; Communications Specialist; Echocardiographer Technician; Health Information Services Technician; LPN; RN; Medical Assistant; Mental Health Professional. **Parent company:** Centura Health.

ST. ANTHONY HOSPITAL NORTH
2551 West 84th Avenue, Westminster CO 80030. 303/426-2151. **Contact:** Human Resources. **World Wide Web address:** http://www.centura.org. **Description:** A 196-bed hospital. Major medical specialties include family practice, pediatrics, neonatology, cardiology, emergency medicine, obstetrics, oncology, and an adult psychiatric unit. **Positions advertised include:** Case Manager; CAT Scan Technician; Pharmacist; Respiratory Therapist; RN Team Leader; Staffing Coordinator. **Parent company:** Centura Health.

ST. MARY-CORWIN REGIONAL MEDICAL CENTER
1008 Minnequa Avenue, Pueblo CO 81004. 719/560-5137. **Contact:** Ms. Jackie Armstrong, Human Resources Services Representative. **World Wide Web address:** http://www.centura.org. **Description:** A hospital. **Positions advertised include:** Case Manager; Certified Nurse Assistant; Clinical Counselor; Health Unit Coordinator; Housekeeper; Laboratory Assistant; Pharmacy Technician; Physical Therapist; Radiation Therapist; Speech Language Therapist. **Corporate headquarters location:** Denver CO. **Parent company:** Centura Health. **Operations at this facility include:** Administration. **Number of employees at this location:** 1,300.

SALOMON SMITH BARNEY
370 17th Street, Suite 2800, Denver CO 80202-1370. 303/572-4000. **Contact:** Human Resources. **World Wide Web address:** http://www.salomonsmithbarney.com. **Description:** An investment banking and securities broker. Salomon Smith Barney also provides related financial services. **Parent company:** Citigroup, Inc. **Listed on:** New York Stock Exchange. **Stock exchange symbol:** C.

SAMSONITE CORPORATION
11200 East 45th Avenue, Denver CO 80239. 303/373-2000. **Contact:** Human Resources. **World Wide Web address:** http://www.samsonite.com. **Description:** Manufactures and markets luggage and business cases. **Corporate headquarters location:** This location. **Operations at this facility include:** Administration; Manufacturing; Research and Development; Service.

THE SANBORN MAP COMPANY
1935 Jamboree Drive, Suite 100, Colorado Springs CO 80920. 719/593-0093. **Fax:** 719/528-5093. **Contact:** Keith Kirkby. **E-mail address:** kkirkby@sanborn.com. **World Wide Web address:** http://www.sanbornmap.com. **Description:** The Sanborn Map Company produces high-quality, detailed maps. Founded in 1866. **Positons advertised include:** Pilot/Survey Technician.

GEORGE T. SANDERS COMPANY
10201 West 49th Avenue, Wheat Ridge CO 80033. 303/423-9660. **Fax:** 303/420-8737. **Contact:** Thomas C. Tooley, Vice President. **Description:** An independent wholesale distributor of plumbing and heating supplies. George T. Sanders Company operates seven locations in Colorado. **NOTE:** Entry-level positions and part-time jobs are offered. **Office hours:** Monday - Friday, 7:00 a.m. - 5:00 p.m. **Corporate headquarters location:** This location. **Listed on:** Privately held. **President:** Gary T. Sanders. **Purchasing Manager:** Kirk Anderson. **Annual sales/revenues:** $21 - $50 million.

SANDOZ INC MANUFACTURING
2555 West Midway Boulevard, Broomfield CO 80038-0446. 303/466-2400. **Contact:** Human Resources. **World Wide Web address:** http://www.sandoz.com. **Description:** Manufactures and distributes generic pharmaceutical products. **Positions advertised include:** Senior Software Engineer; Software Engineer; Change Specialist; Q&A Manager; Chemist; Scientist.

SANMINA-SCI CORPORATION
702 Bandley Drive, Fountain CO 80817. 719/382-2000. **Contact:** Human Resources. **World Wide Web address:** http://www.sanmina-sci.com. **Description:** SCI Systems, Inc. designs, develops, manufactures, markets, distributes, and services electronic products for the computer, aerospace, defense, telecommunications, medical, and consumer industries, as well as for the United States government. SCI is one of the world's largest electronics contract manufacturers and operates one of the largest surface mount technology (SMT) production facilities in the merchant market. Operations are conducted through a Commercial Division and a Government Division. The Commercial Division operates in six geographically-organized business units: Eastern, Central, and Western Regions of North America; and European and Asian Regions. Each unit operates multiple plants that manufacture components, subassemblies, and finished products for original equipment manufacturers. Design, engineering, purchasing, manufacturing, distribution, and support services are also offered. The Government Division provides data management, instrumentation, and communications services, and computer subsystems to the U.S. government and its prime contractors, as well as to several foreign governments. **Corporate headquarters location:** San Jose CA. **Other U.S. locations:** Arab AL; Lacey's Spring AL; San Jose CA; Watsonville CA; Graham NC; Hooksett NH; Rapid City SC. **International locations:** Canada; France; Ireland; Mexico; Scotland; Singapore; Thailand. **Operations at this facility include:** This location produces a wide range of assemblies for mass storage products including small tape backup devices, large multiple-disk array systems, and high-capacity optical storage units. **Listed on:** NASDAQ. **Stock exchange symbol:** SANM.

SCHLUMBERGER
6501 South Fiddlers Green Circle, #400, Greenwood Village CO 80111. 303/486-3200. **Fax:** 303/985-4111. **Contact:** Human Resources. **World Wide Web address:** http://www.slb.com. **Description:** Schlumberger develops and sells advanced scientific and engineering services, computer software, and digital mapping products to major oil companies and governments. **Positions advertised include:** Account Manager; Chemical Product Developer; Chemist; Customer Service Representative; Electrical Engineer; Geoscientist; Mechanical Engineer. **Corporate headquarters location:** New York NY. **Operations at this facility include:** This location provides consulting services to the oil and gas industry. **Listed on:** New York Stock Exchange. **Stock exchange symbol:** SLB.

SCIONA, INC.
1401 Walnut Street, Suite 203, Boulder CO 80302. 303/442-4300. **Fax:** 303/442-4301. **Contact:** Personnel Department. **E-mail address:** personnel@sciona.com. **World Wide Web address:** http://www.sciona.com. **Description:** Sciona researches and develops DNA screens for common gene variants that affect an individual's response to food, medications and the environment. Sciona's field of genetic personalization is a discipline aimed at creating products and services tailored to an individual's genetic makeup.

SCOTT'S LIQUID GOLD INC.
NEOTERIC COSMETICS
4880 Havana Street, P.O. Box 39-S, Denver CO 80239-0019. 303/373-4860. **Fax:** 303/576-6050. **Recorded jobline:** 800/447-1919 (Option 6.) **Contact:** Shelly Kennison, Director of Human Resources Department. **World Wide Web address:** http://www.scottsliquidgold.com. **Description:** Engaged in the manufacture and distribution of household chemical products as well as disposable cigarette filters. Principal products include Scott's Liquid Gold Wood Cleaner and Preservative, Scott's Liquid Gold Glass Cleaner, and Touch of Scent Air Freshener. Neoteric Cosmetics (also at this location) manufactures a skin care line of alpha-hydroxy products. **Corporate headquarters location:** This location.

SEAGATE TECHNOLOGY
389 Disc Drive, Longmont CO 80503. 720/684-1000. **Contact:** Human Resources. **World Wide Web address:** http://www.seagate.com. **Description:** Designs and manufactures data storage devices and related products including hard drives, tape drives, software, and systems for many computer-related applications and operating systems. These products include 2.5-inch and 3.5-inch drives with memory storage capacity between 150 megabytes and one gigabyte. **Positions advertised include:** Staff Engineer; Concept Team Director; Senior Engineer. **Corporate headquarters location:** Scotts Valley CA.

SENIORS! INC.
5840 East Evans Avenue, Denver CO 80222. 303/300-6900. **Fax:** 303/300-6936. **Contact:** Human Resources. **World Wide Web address:** http:// www.seniorsinc.org. **Description:** Provides programs and services for older persons that promote and enhance independent living. Founded in 1969. **Positions advertised include:** Bookkeeper; Cook; Caregiver. **Special programs:** Internships. **Corporate headquarters location:** This location. **Operations at this facility include:** Administration; Sales; Service. **Number of employees at this location:** 30.

7-ELEVEN, INC.
7167 South Alton Way, Englewood CO 80112. 303/740-9333. **Fax:** 303/220-1062. **Recorded jobline:** 800/711-5627. **Contact:** Human Resources. **World Wide Web address:** http://www.7-eleven.com. **Description:** The 7-Eleven convenience store chain is one of the largest store chains in the world. **Corporate headquarters location:** Dallas TX. **Operations at this facility include:** This location serves as the regional headquarters of 7-Eleven convenience stores in Colorado and Utah. **Listed on:** New York Stock Exchange. **Stock exchange symbol:** SE. **Number of employees at this location:** 3,500.

SEVERN TRENT LABORATORIES, INC.
4955 Yarrow Street, Arvada CO 80002. 303/736-0100. **Fax:** 303/431-7171. **Contact:** Human Resources. **World Wide Web address:** http://www.stl-inc.com. **Description:** Provides a complete range of environmental testing services to private industry, engineering consultants, and government agencies in support of federal and state environmental regulations. The company also possesses analytical capabilities in the fields of air toxins, field analytical services, radiochemistry/mixed waste, and advanced technology. **Positions advertised include:** Metals Department Manager; Lab Department Manager. **Parent company:** Severn Trent Services.

SHAMROCK DELIVERY SERVICES
6484 South Quebec Street, Englewood CO 80111. 303/220-1700. **Fax:** 303/220-0752. **Contact:** Human Resources. **World Wide Web address:** http://www.shamrockdelivery.com. **Description:** A delivery/courier service. Founded in 1989. **Positions advertised include:** Driver.

SIEMENS BUSINESS SERVICES
12100 East Iliff Avenue, Suite 200, Aurora CO 80014. 303/745-9600. **Contact:** Human Resources. **World Wide Web address:** http://www.sbs-usa.siemens.com. **Description:** Sells and services microcomputer systems and products, related peripherals, and software. Siemens Business Services provides training classes for software products, as well as technical and support services. **Corporate headquarters location:** Munich, Germany. **Parent company:** Siemens AG. **Listed on:** New York Stock Exchange. **Stock exchange symbol:** SI. **Number of employees at this location:** 205.

SILVER WEIBULL
5350 Joliet Street, Denver CO 80239. 303/373-2311. **Contact:** Employment. **Description:** Fabricators of heavy machinery for the food processing industry. **Parent company:** Ingersoll-Rand (Woodlake NJ.) **Operations at this facility include:** Manufacturing; Sales; Service. **Listed on:** New York Stock Exchange. **Stock exchange symbol:** IR.

SIMTEK CORPORATION
4250 Buckingham Drive, Colorado Springs CO 80907. 719/531-9444. **Fax:** 719/531-9481. **Contact:** Brian Stephens, Director of Quality Assurance. **E-mail address:** info@simtek.com. **World Wide Web address:** http://www.simtek.com. **Description:** Develops, produces, and markets nonvolatile semiconductor memories. Simtek's products are targeted for use in commercial electronic equipment markets such as high-density hard drives, modems, smart utility meters, home and commercial security

systems, portable telephones, instrumentation, and numerous military systems including communications, radar, sonar, and smart weapons.

SINTON DAIRY FOODS COMPANY, INC.
3801 North Sinton Road, Colorado Springs CO 80907. 719/633-3821. **Contact:** Human Resources. **World Wide Web address:** http://www.sintondairy.com. **Description:** Processes dairy products.

SIRENZA MICRODEVICES
303 South Technology Court, Broomfield CO 80021. 303/327-3030. **Fax:** 303/410-7088. **Contact:** Human Resources. **E-mail address:** employ@sirenza.com. **World Wide Web address:** http://www.sirenza.com. **Description:** Sirenza designs, manufactures, and markets a wide range of radio frequency and microwave signal processing components used in the wireless telecommunications industry. These components are used in commercial and military/aerospace applications such as cellular telephones and base stations, wireless local area networking, and satellite communications systems, as well as advanced radar, missile guidance, and navigational systems. The company markets its products primarily to original equipment manufacturers of commercial and defense products.

SIRNA THERAPEUTICS, INC.
2950 Wilderness Place, Boulder CO 80301. 303/449-6500. **Fax:** 303/449-6995. **Contact:** Human Resources. **E-mail address:** jobs@sirna.com. **Description:** Sirna Therapeutics is a biotechnology company focused on developing therapeutics based on RNA interference (RNAi) technology, a field of biology and medicine. The Company is using its proprietary nucleic acid technology and expertise to develop a new class of RNAi-based therapeutics that target human diseases and conditions. **Positions advertised include:** Scientist.

SKY RIDGE MEDICAL CENTER
8310 South Valley Parkway, Englewood CO 80112. 303/788-2550. **Fax:** 303/788-2590. **Contact:** Human Resources. **World Wide Web address:** http://www.skyridgemedcenter.com. **Description:** A health care facility whose services include emergency care, surgical services, cardiac services, and diagnostic and imaging services. **Positions advertised include:** RN; Case Manager; Quality Manager; Pharmacist; Dietician; Medical Records Clerk; Housekeeper; Nuclear Medicine Technologist.

SMURFIT-STONE CONTAINER CORPORATION
5050 East 50th Avenue, Denver CO 80216. 303/399-0494. **Contact:** Human Resources. **World Wide Web address:** http://www.smurfit-stone.com. **Description:** A leading paper-based packaging company. Smurfit-Stone Container Corporation's products include corrugated containers, folding cartons, and multiwall industrial bags. The company is one of the world's largest collectors and processors of recycled products that are then sold to a worldwide customer base. Smurfit-Stone Container Corporation also operates several paper tube, market pulp, and newsprint production facilities. **Corporate headquarters location:** Chicago IL. **Other U.S. locations:** Nationwide. **Listed on:** NASDAQ. **Stock exchange symbol:** SSCC.

SOURCE ONE MANAGEMENT, INC.
1225 17th Street, Suite 1500, Denver CO 80202. 303/832-8600. **Fax:** 303/832-1910. **Contact:** Director of Human Resources. **E-mail address:** resumes@sourceone.com. **World Wide Web address:** http://www.sourceone.com. **Description:** Provides staffing for government and private sector management and information technology contracts. **Positions advertised include:** Mail Clerk. **Corporate headquarters location:** This location. **Other U.S. locations:** DC; MT; ND; SD; WA. **Operations at this facility include:** Administration; Service. **Listed on:** Privately held. **Number of employees at this location:** 15. **Number of employees nationwide:** 200.

SPALDING REHABILITATION HOSPITAL
900 Potomac Street, Aurora CO 80011. 303/367-1166. **Contact:** Human Resources. **World Wide Web address:** http://www.spaldingrehab.com. **Description:** One of Denver's leading resources for physical rehabilitation services. In partnership with the HealthONE system, Spalding provides rehabilitation services. Spalding's treatment programs target an array of musculoskeletal problems and neurological disorders, including brain injury; head, neck, and spinal injuries; stroke; multiple sclerosis; and chronic pain. Founded in 1914. **Positions advertised include:** Certified Medical Assistant; RN Case Manager; Instrument Technician; Clinical Educator; Housekeeper; Pool Supervisor; Clinical Dietician; Food Service Worker; Lab Assistant; LPN; Pharmacist; Radiology Transporter; Surgical Technician. **Parent company:** HealthONE.

SPECIAL PRODUCTS COMPANY
15000 West 44th Avenue, Golden CO 80403. 303/279-5544. **Contact:** Human Resources. **Description:** Engaged in custom steel fabrication, the fabrication of screw machine products, the manufacture of agricultural equipment attachments (blades, hitches, tractor accessories, specialized digging equipment), and the fabrication of other metal products. **Corporate headquarters location:** This location.

SPECTRA LOGIC
1700 North 55th Street, Boulder CO 80301-2725. 303/449-6400. **Fax:** 303/939-8844. **Contact:** Human Resources. **E-mail address:** hireme@spectralogic.com. **World Wide Web address:** http://www.spectralogic.com. **Description:** Manufactures backup hardware and automated tape libraries. Founded in 1979. **NOTE:** Entry-level positions are offered. **Positions advertised include:** Hardware Support Technician; Test Development Engineer; Public Relations Intern; Technology Buyer; OEM Sales Representative. **Special programs:** Internships. **Internship information:** For detailed internship information, visit the company's Website. **Corporate headquarters location:** This location. **International locations:** London, England; Tokyo, Japan. **Listed on:** Privately held. **President:** Michael Sausa. **Annual sales/revenues:** $21 - $50 million. **Number of employees at this location:** 150.

THE SPECTRANETICS CORPORATION
96 Talamine Court, Colorado Springs CO 80907. 719/633-8333. **Toll-free phone:** 800/633-0960. **Fax:** 719/633-2248. **Contact:** Human Resources. **World Wide Web address:** http://www.spectranetics.com. **Description:** Researches, develops, manufactures, services, supports, and sells medical lasers and attendant catheters used in heart surgery. **Corporate headquarters location:** This location. **Other U.S. locations:** Nationwide. **International locations:** Worldwide. **Listed on:** NASDAQ. **Stock exchange symbol:** SPNC. **Number of employees at this location:** 75. **Number of employees nationwide:** 140.

SPECTRUM HUMAN RESOURCE SYSTEMS CORPORATION
707 Seventeenth Street, Suite 3800, Denver CO 80202-3438. 303/592-3200. **Toll-free phone:** 800/334-5660. **Fax:** 303/595-9970. **Contact:** Recruiter. **E-mail address:** info@ spectrumhr.com. **World Wide Web address:** http://www.spectrumhr.com. **Description:** Develops computer software for use in human resources management, benefits administration, and training development administration. Founded in 1984. **NOTE:** Entry-level positions are offered. **Positions advertised include:** Business Development Partner. **Corporate headquarters location:** This location. **Listed on:** Privately held. **Annual sales/revenues:** $5 - $10 million. **Number of employees at this location:** 100. **Number of employees nationwide:** 115.

SPORTS AUTHORITY
1050 West Hampden Avenue, Englewood CO 80110. 303/863-2297. **Fax:** 303/863-2243. **Contact:** Human Resources. **World Wide Web address:** http://www.sportsauthority.com. **Description:** Operates a chain of retail sporting goods stores. **Positions advertised include:** Department Manager. **Other U.S. locations:** Nationwide. **Listed on:** NASDAQ.

STAINLESS FABRICATING COMPANY
860 Navajo Street, Denver CO 80403. 303/573-1700. **Toll-free phone:** 800/525-8966. **Fax:** 303/573-3776. **Contact:** Jeff Manion, President/Owner. **Description:** Manufactures custom kitchen equipment for restaurants and school cafeterias. **Listed on:** Privately held. **Annual sales/revenues:** Less than $5 million. **Number of employees at this location:** 40.

STANLEY AVIATION CORPORATION
2501 Dallas Street, Aurora CO 80010. 303/340-5200. **Fax:** 303/340-5254. **Contact:** Human Resources. **E-mail address:** hr@stanleyaviation.com. **World Wide Web address:** http://www.stanleyaviation.com. **Description:** Manufactures structural sheet metal and metal tube fabrications for the aircraft industry, couplings used in aircraft and missiles, structural ground support equipment for airlines, and large metal containers. **Corporate headquarters location:** This location. **Parent company:** Flight Refueling Ltd. **Listed on:** Privately held. **Number of employees at this location:** 180.

STARTEK, INC.
100 Garfield Street, Suite 300, Denver CO 80206. 303/262-4500. **Contact:** Human Resources Department. **E-mail address:** jobs@startek.com. **World Wide Web address:** http://www.startek.com. **Description:** Provides process management services to *Fortune* 500 customers and other major corporations worldwide. Services include logistics management, e-commerce support, Internet support, technical support, order processing, packaging, distribution, inventory management, product assembly, manufacturing, fulfillment, and customer support. **Positions advertised include:** Benefits Manager; Customer Service Representative; Supervisor. **Corporate headquarters location:** This location. **Other U.S. locations:** Grand Junction CO; Greeley CO; Clarksville TN; Laramie WY. **International locations:** Hartlepool, England. **Listed on:** New York Stock Exchange. **Stock exchange symbol:** SRT.

STARZ ENCORE GROUP LLC
8900 Liberty Circle, Englewood CO 80112. 720/852-7700. **Contact:** Human Resources. **World Wide Web address:** http://starzencore.com. **Description:** Operates the Encore and Starz! premium cable movie channels.

STEWART & STEVENSON POWER INC.
5840 Dahlia Street, Commerce City CO 80022. 303/287-7441. **Contact:** Human Resources. **World Wide Web address:** http://www.ssss.com. **Description:** Stewart & Stevenson Power Inc. provides a broad line of products, most of which are diesel or gas turbine powered, serving a multitude of industries and markets. The company's principal divisions are Engine Operations, which engineers and builds power systems utilizing diesel or gas turbine engines for such uses as irrigation systems, oil well drilling rigs, and generators; Electric Operations, which produces a line of switchgear and control systems for numerous industries; and Other Operations, which includes the production of materials handling equipment and refrigeration equipment for the transportation industry. **Positions advertised include:** Mechanic; Sales Representative; Generator Sales Representative; Parts Counter Attendant. **Special programs:** Internships. **Corporate headquarters location:** Houston TX. **Operations at this facility include:** This location manufactures power units and power generators. **Parent company:** Stewart & Stevenson Services, Inc. **Listed on:** NASDAQ. **Stock exchange symbol:** SSSS. **Number of employees at this location:** 600. **Number of employees nationwide:** 4,000.

STIFEL NICOLAUS
1125 17th Street, Suite 1600, Denver CO 80202-2032. 303/296-2300. **Contact:** Human Resources. **Description:** A securities brokerage firm. **World Wide Web address:** http://www.stifel.com. **Corporate headquarters location:** This location.

STORAGETEK
One StorageTek Drive, Louisville CO 80028-0001. 719/536-4055. **Contact:** Human Resources. **World Wide Web address:** http://www.stortek.com. **Description:** StorageTek supplies high-performance computer information storage and retrieval systems for mainframe and mid-frame computers and networks. Products include automated cartridge systems, random access subsystems, and fault-tolerant disk arrays. The company also distributes equipment; sells new peripherals, software, and hardware; and offers support services. **Corporate headquarters location:** This location. **Operations at this facility include:** Administration; Manufacturing; Research and Development.

STRESSCON CORPORATION
P.O. Box 15129, Colorado Springs CO 80935. 719/390-5041. **Physical address:** 3210 Astrozon Boulevard, Colorado Springs CO 80910. **Contact:** Human Resources Department. **E-mail address:** careers@stresscon.com. **World Wide Web address:** http://www.stresscon.com. **Description:** Stresscon manufactures and distributes precast/prestressed structural concrete, architectural concrete, and concrete used in other large-scale construction projects. **Corporate headquarters location:** This location. **President:** H.W. Reinking.

SUN ENTERPRISES INC.
8877 North Washington Street, Thornton CO 80229. 303/287-7566. **Fax:** 303/287-7716. **Contact:** Gerald Bieker, Controller. **E-mail address:** sun@sunent.com. **World Wide Web address:** http://www.sunent.com. **Description:** A retailer of motorcycles, ATVs, watercraft, snowmobiles, power equipment, and related parts and accessories. **Office hours:** Tuesday - Saturday, 9:00 a.m. - 6:00 p.m. **Vice President:** Ronald Lang. **Annual sales/revenues:** $11 - $20 million. **Number of employees at this location:** 45.

SUN MICROSYSTEMS, INC.
9800 Mount Pyramid Court, Suite 300, Englewood CO 80112. 720/895-8410. **Contact:** Human Resources. **World Wide Web address:** http://www.sun.com. **Description:** Sun Microsystems Inc. produces high-performance computer systems, workstations, servers, CPUs, peripherals, and operating system software. The company also developed a microprocessor called SPARC. **Corporate headquarters location:** Palo Alto CA. **Operations at this facility include:** This location is a sales office. **Subsidiaries include:** Forte Software Inc. manufactures enterprise application integration software. **Listed on:** NASDAQ. **Stock exchange symbol:** SUNW.

SUNDYNE CORPORATION
14845 West 64th Avenue, Arvada CO 80007. 303/425-0800. **Fax:** 303/940-3141. **Contact:** Human Resources. **World Wide Web address:** http://www.sundyne.com. **Description:** Manufactures a wide range of pumps and compressors. **Parent company:** United Technologies Corporation.

SUNGARD INSURANCE SYSTEMS
14280 East Jewell Avenue, Suite 200, Aurora CO 80012. 303/283-5300. **Contact:** Human Resources. **World Wide Web address:** http://www.sungardinsurance.com. **Description:** Develops financial software for insurance companies. **Parent company:** SunGard Data Systems, Inc. **Listed on:** New York Stock Exchange. **Stock exchange symbol:** SDS.

SWAN INC.
5775 DTC Boulevard, Suite 300, Greenwood Village CO 80111. 303/220-2000. **Contact:** Human Resources. **World Wide Web address:** http://www.swanhost.com. **Description:** A company involved in hotel management and ownership. **Positions advertised include:** Administrative Assistant. **Special programs:** Internships; Co-ops. **Office hours:** Monday - Friday, 8:00 a.m. - 5:00 p.m. **Annual sales/revenues:** More than $100 million. **Number of employees at this location:** 50. **Number of employees nationwide:** 7,000.

SWISSLOG TRANSLOGIC
10825 East 47th Avenue, Denver CO 80239. 303/371-7770. **Contact:** Dave Lawson, Human Resources Director. **World Wide Web address:** http://www.translogic-corp.com. **Description:** Produces pneumatic-powered conveying systems. **Corporate headquarters location:** This location.

SYKES ENTERPRISES INC.
777 North Fourth Street, Sterling CO 80751. 970/522-6638. **Contact:** Human Resources. **E-mail address:** careers@sykes.com. **World Wide Web address:** http://www.sykes.com. **Description:** Provides computer outsourcing services, hardware and software technical support, systems consulting and integration, and documentation development. **Corporate headquarters location:** Tampa FL. **Other U.S. locations:** Nationwide. **International locations:** The Netherlands; Philippines. **Listed on:** NASDAQ. **Stock exchange symbol:** SYKE.

T-NETIX, INC.
7108 South Alton Drive, Centennial CO 80112. 720/488-9481. **Contact:** Human Resources Department. **E-mail address:** humanresources@t-netix.com. **World Wide Web address:** http://www.t-netix.com. **Description:** Manufactures software for fraud prevention and advanced call processing. **Corporate headquarters location:** Carrollton TX. **Subsidiaries include:** Cell-Tel, Tampa FL. **Listed on:** NASDAQ. **Stock exchange symbol:** TNTX. **Annual sales/revenues:** $21 - $50 million.

TVC
6709 East 38th Avenue, Denver CO 80207. 303/333-7144. **Contact:** Administrator. **Description:** A dental laboratory that manufactures crowns, bridges, and dentures.

TELEDYNE BROWN ENGINEERING
1330 Inverness Drive, Suite 350, Colorado Springs CO 80910. 719/574-7270. **Contact:** Human Resources. **World Wide Web address:** http://www.tbe.com. **Description:** Engaged in thermoelectric generator development and production. **Parent company:** Teledyne Technologies Inc. **Listed on:** New York Stock Exchange. **Stock exchange symbol:** TDY.

TIME WARNER TELECOM
5700 South Quebec Street, Greenwood Village CO 80124. 303/566-1000. **Fax:** 303/566-1008. **Contact:** Human Resources. **E-mail address:** twtelecom.resumes@twcable.com. **World Wide Web address:** http://www.twtelecom.com. **Description:** Provides telecommunications services and products. Time Warner Telecom is engaged in data communication integration for businesses, local telephone service, and network communication. **Positions advertised include:** Billing Analyst; Senior Contract Agent; Disputes Specialist; Marketing Analyst; Administrative Assistant; Sales Trainer; Trainee Coordinator; Technical Trainer. **Special programs:** Internships. **Corporate headquarters location:** This location. **Other U.S. locations:** Nationwide. **Parent company:** AOL Time Warner. **Listed on:** NASDAQ. **Stock exchange symbol:** AOL.

TRANE COMPANY
101 William White Boulevard, Pueblo CO 81001. 719/585-3800. **Contact:** Human Resources. **World Wide Web address:** http://www.trane.com. **Description:** Develops, manufactures, and sells air-conditioning equipment. **Corporate headquarters location:** Piscataway NJ. **Parent company:** American Standard Companies, Inc. **Listed on:** New York Stock Exchange. **Stock exchange symbol:** ASD.

TRANSIT MIX CONCRETE
P.O. Box 1030, Colorado Springs CO 80901. 719/475-0700. **Contact:** Human Resources Department. **World Wide Web address:** http://www.transitmixconcrete.com. **Description:** Provides ready-mixed concrete and concrete building supplies; hollow metal doors, frames, and hardware; and computer programs. **Positions advertised include:** Driver. **Operations at this facility include:** Administration; Manufacturing; Sales; Service. **Listed on:** New York Stock Exchange. **Stock exchange symbol:** TRN. **Number of employees at this location:** 170.

TRANSMONTAIGNE, INC.
P.O. Box 5660, Denver CO 80217. 303/626-8200. **Physical address:** 370 17th Street, Suite 2750, Denver CO 80202. **Contact:** Human Resources. **World Wide Web address:** http://www.transmontaigne.com. **Description:** A wholesale petroleum marketer. **Corporate headquarters location:** This location. **Listed on:** American Stock Exchange. **Stock exchange symbol:** TMG.

TRINIDAD/BENHAM CORPORATION
P.O. Box 378007, 3650 South Yosemite, Denver CO 80237. 303/220-1400. **Contact:** Human Resources Manager. **Description:** Engaged in the warehousing, packaging, and wholesaling of dry beans and aluminum foil. **Corporate headquarters location:** This location. **Other U.S. locations:** Chino CA; Murfreesboro TN; Mineola TX. **Operations at this facility include:** Administration; Sales; Service. **Listed on:** Privately held. **Number of employees at this location:** 50. **Number of employees nationwide:** 475.

UBS PAINEWEBBER INC.
370 17th Street, Suite 4100, Denver CO 80202. 303/436-9000. **Contact:** Clifford Hickerson, Human Resources Department. **World Wide Web address:** http://www.ubspainewebber. com. **Description:** A full-service securities firm with over 300 offices nationwide. Services include investment banking, asset management, merger and acquisition consulting, municipal securities underwriting, estate planning, retirement programs, and transaction management. Clients include corporations, governments, institutions, and individuals. Founded in 1879. **Corporate headquarters location:** New York NY. **Other U.S. locations:** Nationwide. **Annual sales/revenues:** More than $100 million.

URS CORPORATION
8181 East Tufts Avenue, Denver CO 80237. 303/694-2770. **Contact:** Human Resources. **World Wide Web address:** http://www.urscorp.com. **Description:** Provides regulatory compliance support, site investigation and remediation, air pollution controls, VOC and air toxins control, biotreatment, waste management, ambient and source monitoring, risk management, information management, project chemistry, specialty chemicals, remote sensing services, materials and machinery analysis, and electronic services. Founded in 1969. **Positions advertised include:** Project Manager; Assistant Project Manager; Senior Estimator; Chemist; Contract Administrator; Senior Civil Highway Engineer; Geologist; Transportation Engineer. **Corporate headquarters location:** San Francisco CA. **International locations:** Worldwide. **Listed on:** New York Stock Exchange. **Stock exchange symbol:** URS.

U.S. BANK
950 17th Street, Suite 800, Denver CO 80202. 303/585-5050. **Fax:** 303/585-4721. **Contact:** Human Resources. **World Wide Web address:** http://www.usbank.com. **Description:** Provides banking and mortgage credit services.

U.S. BUREAU OF LAND MANAGEMENT
P.O. Box 1009, Glenwood Springs CO 81602. 970/947-2800. **Contact:** Volunteers and Interns Coordinator. **World Wide Web address:** http://www.blm.gov. **Description:** A federal agency that is responsible for the balanced management of 270 million acres of public lands and resources including recreation, timber range, wildlife, minerals, watershed, wilderness, and natural, scientific, and cultural values. **Special programs:** Internships. **Corporate headquarters location:** Washington DC. **Parent company:** U.S. Department of the Interior.

U.S. BUREAU OF RECLAMATION
P.O. Box 25007, D4000, Denver CO 80225-9907. 303/445-2670. **Contact:** Human Resources. **World Wide Web address:** http://www.usbr.gov. **Description:** Engaged in the development and management of water resources in 17 western states. The bureau's primary emphasis is on engineering. **Parent company:** U.S. Department of the Interior.

U.S. DEPARTMENT OF HOUSING AND URBAN DEVELOPMENT
633 17th Street, Denver CO 80202. 303/672-5259. **Fax:** 303/672-5010. **Contact:** Human Resources. **World Wide Web address:** http://www.hud.gov. **Description:** Provides comprehensive assistance to help build and rebuild large and small communities; enforces the Fair Housing Act and other civil rights laws; identifies and combats discrimination; helps low- and moderate-income families rent or buy safe, affordable housing; and helps to create and maintain safe, affordable housing and supportive living environments for the families served by its programs.

U.S. DEPARTMENT OF VETERNS AFFAIRS
DENVER VETERANS ADMINISTRATION MEDICAL CENTER
1055 Clermont Street, Denver CO 80220-3808. 303/393-2815. **Contact:** Human Resources Management Service. **World Wide Web address:** http://www.va.gov. **Description:** A medical center.0 VA operates medical centers in each of the 48 contiguous states, Puerto Rico, and the District of Columbia. With approximately 76,000 medical center beds, VA treats nearly 1 million patients in VA hospitals, 75,000 in nursing home care units, and 25,000 in domiciliary residences. **Corporate headquarters location:** Washington DC. **Parent company:** U.S. Department of Veterans Affairs. **Number of employees at this location:** 1,600.

U.S. ENGINEERING COMPANY
P.O. Box 905, Loveland CO 80539. 970/669-1666. **Contact:** Human Resources Department. **World Wide Web address:** http://www.usengineering.com. **Description:** A contracting company that installs heating, air conditioning, piping, and sprinkler systems for businesses. **Corporate headquarters location:** Kansas City MO. **Listed on:** Privately held. **Annual sales/revenues:** More than $100 million. **Number of employees at this location:** 300. **Number of employees nationwide:** 600.

U.S. ENVIRONMENTAL PROTECTION AGENCY (EPA)
999 18th Street, Suite 300, Denver CO 80202-2466. 303/312-6259. **Contact:** Human Resources. **World Wide Web address:** http://www.epa.gov. **Description:** The EPA is dedicated to improving and preserving the quality of the environment, both nationally and globally, and protecting human health and the productivity of natural resources. The agency is committed to ensuring that federal environmental laws are implemented and enforced effectively; U.S. policy, both foreign and domestic, encourages the integration of economic development and environmental protection so that economic growth can be sustained over the long term; and public and private decisions affecting energy, transportation, agriculture, industry, international trade, and natural resources fully integrate considerations of environmental quality. Founded in 1970. **Corporate headquarters location:** Washington DC. **Other U.S. locations:** San Francisco CA; Atlanta GA; Chicago IL; Kansas City KS; Boston MA; New York NY; Philadelphia PA; Dallas TX; Seattle WA. **Number of employees nationwide:** 19,000.

U.S. FOODSERVICE
11955 East Peakview Avenue, Englewood CO 80111. 303/792-3663. **Fax:** 303/643-4702. **Contact:** Human Resources. **E-mail address:** recruit-den@allintfs.com. **World Wide Web address:** http://www.usfoodservice.com. **Description:** A broadline distributor of food products, equipment and supplies, cleaning chemicals, and disposables to a variety of food service locations including restaurants, nursing homes, hospitals, and institutional feeders. **Positions advertised include:** Center of the Plate Specialist.

U.S. FEDERAL RESERVE BANK OF KANSAS CITY
P.O. Box 5228, Denver CO 80217-5228. 303/572-2300. **Recorded jobline:** 303/572-2308. **Contact:** Human Resources. **World Wide Web address:** http://www.kc.frb. org. **Description:** A branch bank of the Federal Reserve System, which consists of 12 regional Federal Reserve banks that, along with the Federal Reserve Board of Governors in Washington DC and the Federal Open Market Committee, comprise the Federal Reserve System, the nation's central bank. As the nation's central bank, the Federal Reserve is charged with three major responsibilities: monetary policy, banking supervision and regulation, and processing payments.

U.S. GEOLOGICAL SURVEY
MIDCONTINENT ECOLOGICAL SCIENCE CENTER
Building 53, Denver Federal Center, Mail Stop 415, Box 25046, Lakewood CO 80225. 303/236-4882. **Contact:** Personnel. **World Wide Web address:** http://www.usgs.gov. **Description:** Conducts research and develops technologies to improve the understanding and management of biological systems (species, populations, communities, landscapes, and ecosystems) of the interior western United States. The

center also develops and implements inventory and monitoring programs for the accurate assessment of biological status and trends, and provides information, technical services, and training related to the management of biological resources. **Parent company:** U.S. Department of the Interior.

ULTIMATE ELECTRONICS, INC.
321 West 84th Avenue, Suite A, Thornton CO 80260. 303/412-2500. **Toll-free phone:** 800/260-2660. **Fax:** 303/412-2501. **Contact:** Human Resources. **World Wide Web address:** http://www.ultimateelectronics.com. **Description:** A specialty retailer of home entertainment and consumer electronics. The company operates stores under the SoundTrack, Audio King, and Ultimate Electronics names. Founded in 1968. **NOTE:** Entry-level positions and second and third shifts are offered. **Positions advertised include:** Audio/Video Switching Technician. **Special programs:** Training. **Corporate headquarters location:** This location. **Other area locations:** Arvada CO; Aurora CO; Boulder CO; Colorado Springs CO; Denver CO; Fort Collins CO; Littleton CO. **Other U.S. locations:** Albuquerque NM; Las Vegas NV; Murray UT; Orem UT; Salt Lake City UT. **Listed on:** NASDAQ. **Stock exchange symbol:** ULTE. **Annual sales/revenues:** More than $100 million. **Number of employees at this location:** 700. **Number of employees nationwide:** 1,600.

UNITED CEREBRAL PALSY OF COLORADO, INC.
2200 South Jasmine Street, Denver CO 80222. 303/691-9339. **Contact:** Human Resources. **World Wide Web address:** http://www.cpco.org. **Description:** A nonprofit organization that provides education, childcare, and employment services, as well as information and referrals. The organization is also engaged in donation pickup. **Corporate headquarters location:** This location. **Number of employees at this location:** 30.

UNITED PIPELINE SYSTEMS, INC.
135 Turner Drive, Durango CO 81303. 970/259-0354. **Contact:** Project Manager. **World Wide Web address:** http://www.insituform.com. **Description:** Engaged in the restoration of pipes. **Parent company:** Insituform Technologies, Inc. uses various trenchless technologies for restoration, new construction, and improvements of pipeline systems including sewers, gas lines, industrial waste lines, water lines and oil field, mining, and industrial process pipelines. **Listed on:** NASDAQ. **Stock exchange symbol:** INSUA.

UNITEDGLOBALCOM, INC.
4643 South Ulster Street, Suite 1300, Denver CO 80237. 303/770-4001. **Fax:** 303/770-4207. **Contact:** Human Resources. **E-mail address:** hr@unitedglobal.com. **World Wide Web address:** http://www.unitedglobal.com. **Description:** UnitedGlobalCom provides integrated broadband television, telephone, and Internet access services. **Corporate headquarters location:** This location. **International locations:** Worldwide. **Listed on:** NASDAQ. **Stock exchange symbol:** UCOMA. **Chairman and CEO:** Gene W. Schneider.

UNIVERSITY CORPORATION FOR ATMOSPHERIC RESEARCH
NATIONAL CENTER FOR ATMOSPHERIC RESEARCH
P.O. Box 3000, Boulder CO 80307-3000. 303/497-1000. **Physical address:** 1850 Table Mesa Drive, Boulder CO 80303. **Contact:** Human Resources. **World Wide Web address:** http://www.ucar.edu. **Description:** A nonprofit consortium of North American institutions that grants Ph.D. degrees in atmospheric and related sciences. The organization manages the National Center for Atmospheric Research, a research and facilities center sponsored by the National Science Foundation. UCAR also manages over a dozen other programs that enhance the conduct and applications of atmospheric research.

UNIVERSITY OF COLORADO AT BOULDER
3100 Marine Street, Campus Box 565, Boulder CO 80309. 303/492-6475. **Contact:** Human Resources. **World Wide Web address:** http://www.colorado.edu. **Description:** A four-year state university offering undergraduate and graduate degree programs.

UNIVERSITY OF COLORADO AT DENVER
P.O. Box 173364, Campus Box 130, Denver CO 80217-3364. 303/556-2868. **Contact:** Kevin Jacobs, Human Resources. **E-mail address:** hr@cudenver.edu. **World Wide Web address:** http://www.cudenver.edu. **Description:** A four-year state university offering undergraduate and graduate degree programs.

UNIVERSITY OF COLORADO HOSPITAL
UNIVERSITY OF COLORADO HEALTH SCIENCES CENTER
4200 East 9th Avenue, Campus Box A028, Denver CO 80262. 303/372-2121. **Fax:** 303/372-9650. **Contact:** Human Resources. **World Wide Web address:** http://www.uchsc.edu. **Description:** A regional, tertiary health care and academic medical center. University Hospital is the principal teaching hospital for the University of Colorado Health Sciences Center. Founded in 1921. **Positions advertised include:** Research Assistant; Assistant Professor; Instructor; Senior Instructor. **Special programs:** Internships. **Operations at this facility include:** Administration. **Number of employees at this location:** 2,200.

UNIVERSITY OF COLORADO FEDERAL CREDIT UNION
2900 Diagonal Highway, Boulder CO 80301. 303/443-4672. **Fax:** 303/595-0436. **Contact:** Human Resources. **World Wide Web address:** http://www.uofcfcu.com. **Description:** A credit union serving the entire state. **Positions advertised include:** Financial Service Officer; Teller; Consumer Loan Manager. **Other area locations include:** Boulder CO; Lafayette CO; Colorado Springs CO.

UNIVERSITY OF DENVER
2020 East Evans Avenue, Room 101, Denver CO 80208. 303/871-2398. **Contact:** Human Resources. **World Wide Web address:** http://www.du.edu. **Description:** A four-year university offering undergraduate, graduate, and continuing education programs to more than 8,500 students. **Positions advertised include:** Assistant Anthropology Professor; Director of Student-Athlete Support Services; Saferide Driver. **Special programs:** Internships. **Corporate headquarters location:** This location. **Operations at this facility include:** Administration; Research and Development; Service.

UNIVERSITY OF NORTHERN COLORADO
501 20th Street, Carter Hall, Room 2002, Greeley CO 80639. 970/351-2718. **Contact:** Debbi Rees, Human Resources. **World Wide Web address:** http://www.unco.edu. **Description:** A four-year university offering undergraduate and graduate degree programs to more than 12,000 students.

THE URBAN LEAGUE OF METROPOLITAN DENVER
5900 East 39th Avenue, Denver CO 80207. 303/388-5861. **Fax:** 303/388-3523. **Contact:** Personnel. **World Wide Web address:** http://www.denverurbanleague.org. **Description:** A nonprofit organization that sponsors a variety of social programs including employment services and career and outplacement counseling. **Corporate headquarters location:** This location.

VAIL RESORTS
P.O. Box 7, Vail CO 81658. 970/845-2460. **Fax:** 970/845-2465. **Recorded jobline:** 888/SKI-JOB1. **Contact:** Human Resources. **World Wide Web address:** http://www.vailresorts.com. **Description:** Operates the Vail, Breckenridge, Beaver Creek, and Keystone resorts. Founded in 1962. **NOTE:** Entry-level positions and second and third shifts are offered. **Special programs:** Internships; Training; Summer Jobs. **Office hours:** Monday - Friday, 8:00 a.m. - 5:00 p.m. **Corporate headquarters location:** This location. **Listed on:** New York Stock Exchange. **Stock exchange symbol:** MTN. **Number of employees at this location:** 6,000.

VALLEYLAB, INC.
5920 Longbow Drive, Boulder CO 80301-3299. 303/530-2300. **Toll-free phone:** 800/255-8522. **Fax:** 303/530-6525. **Recorded jobline:** 800/638-8367. **Contact:** Human Resources Department. **World Wide Web address:** http://www.valleylab.com. **Description:** Develops, manufactures, markets, and services medical equipment and accessories used in hospitals and other medical environments. Principal products are electrosurgical generators, ultrasonic surgical aspirators, and associated disposable products used to perform a variety of surgical and medical procedures. **Special programs:** Internships. **Corporate headquarters location:** New York NY. **Parent company:** Tyco Healthcare Group. **Operations at this facility include:** Administration; Divisional Headquarters; Manufacturing; Research and Development; Sales; Service.

VAN GILDER INSURANCE CORPORATION
700 Broadway, Suite 1000, Denver CO 80203. 303/837-8500. **Fax:** 303/831-5295. **Contact:** Human Resources. **World Wide Web address:** http://www.vgic.com. **Description:** Provides a full line of personal and commercial insurance. **Positions advertised include:** Personal Lines Producer; Personal Lines Account Manager. **Corporate headquarters location:** This location. **Other U.S. locations:** AZ; KS; TX; WY. **Parent company:** Assurex Global.

VANGUARD RESEARCH, INC.
770 Wooten Road, Colorado Springs CO 80915. 719/596-1174. **Contact:** General Manager. **E-mail address:** hr@vriffx.com. **World Wide Web address:** http://www.vriffx.com. **Description:** Provides engineering and technical support services. **Positions advertised include:** Aerospace Engineer; Communications Engineer; Computer Engineer; Computer Programmer; Computer Scientist; Database Manager; General Manager; Management Analyst/Consultant; Mathematician; Network/Systems Administrator; Operations Research Analyst; Secretary; Software Engineer; Systems Analyst; Systems Engineer; Systems Manager; Test Engineer. **Corporate headquarters location:** Fairfax VA. **Other U.S. locations:** Omaha NE. **President/CEO:** Mel Chaskin. **Facilities Manager:** Lee Morgan. **Number of employees at this location:** 30. **Number of employees nationwide:** 150.

VERIZON WIRELESS
8000 East Belleview Avenue, Greenwood Village CO 80111. 720/489-1223. **Contact:** Personnel. **World Wide Web address:** http://www.verizonwireless.com. **Description:** Verizon offers residential local and long-distance telephone services and Internet access; wireless service plans, cellular phones, and data services; a full-line of business services including Internet access, data services, and telecommunications equipment and services; and government network solutions including Internet access, data services, telecommunications equipment and services, and enhanced communications services. **Corporate headquarters location:** New York NY. **Parent company:** Verizon Communications. **Listed on:** New York Stock Exchange. **Stock exchange symbol:** VZ.

VICORP RESTAURANTS INC.
400 West 48th Avenue, Denver CO 80216. 303/295-4280. **Contact:** Human Resources. **World Wide Web address:** http://www.vicorpinc.com. **Description:** Operates Bakers Square and Village Inn restaurant chains and franchises restaurants under the Village Inn name. **Corporate headquarters location:** This location.

VITAL SIGNS - COLORADO
11039 East Lansing Circle, Englewood CO 80112. 303/790-4835. **Contact:** Human Resources. **E-mail address:** humanresources@vital-signs.com. **World Wide Web address:** http://www.vital-signs.com. **Description:** Manufactures disposable medical products such as facemasks, manual resuscitators, anesthesia kits, and related products. **Corporate headquarters location:** Totowa NJ. **Operations at this facility include:** Administration; Manufacturing. **Listed on:** NASDAQ. **Stock exchange symbol:** VITL. **Number of employees at this location:** 250.

WACHOVIA SECURITIES
1200 17th Street, Suite 2500, Denver CO 80202. 303/628-8000. **Contact:** Human Resources. **World Wide Web address:** http://www.wachoviasec.com. **Description:** An investment and securities firm specializing in real estate investing. **Corporate headquarters location:** Richmond VA.

THE WACKENHUT CORRECTIONS CORPORATION
15290 East Sixth Avenue, Suite 250, Aurora CO 80011. 303/341-4433. **Contact:** Human Resources Department. **World Wide Web address:** http://www.wackenhutcorrections.com. **Description:** The Wackenhut Corrections Corporation is a diversified provider of services to government, industrial, commercial, and professional organizations and agencies worldwide. The corporation has offices throughout the United States and in 49 other countries on six continents. The Wackenhut Corrections Corporation specializes in security-related services including physical security, investigations, the management of correctional and detention facilities, rehabilitative programs, and information security. The company also provides educational services and training; facility management; food service to jails and prisons; design, financial services, and construction management for correctional facilities; and fire prevention and emergency services. The Wackenhut Corrections Corporation is a leader in the privatization of public services to municipal, state, and federal governments worldwide. Founded in 1954. **Operations at this facility include:** This location provides jail and prison facility management. **Listed on:** New York Stock Exchange. **Stock exchange symbol:** WHC.

WAL-MART STORES, INC.
440 Wadsworth Boulevard, Lakewood CO 80226. 303/274-5211. **Contact:** Human Resources. **World Wide Web address:** http://www.walmartstores.com. **Description:** Wal-Mart Stores is a retail merchandise chain operating full-service discount department stores, combination grocery and discount stores, and warehouse stores requiring membership. Founded in 1962. **Corporate headquarters location:** Bentonville AR. **Listed on:** New York Stock Exchange. **Stock exchange symbol:** WMT.

WALKER ASSOCIATES
420 East 58th Avenue, Denver CO 80216. 303/292-5537. **Contact:** Human Resources. **Description:** A real estate agency whose dealings include electronic component distributor banks, ranches, and commercial properties.

WALKER COMPONENTS
5750 North Logan Street, Denver CO 80216. 303/292-6121. **Contact:** Director of Human Resources. **World Wide Web address:** http://www.walkercomponent.com. **Description:** A distributor of electronic goods to industrial contractors.

WASHINGTON GROUP INTERNATIONAL
7800 East Union Avenue, P.O. Box 5888, Denver CO 80217. 303/843-2000. **Contact:** Human Resources. **World Wide Web address:** http://www.wgint.com. **Description:** An engineering and construction firm operating through five major divisions: Government, Industrial/Process, Infrastructure & Mining, Petroleum & Chemicals, and Power. Washington Group International offers construction, engineering, and program-management services to the environmental, industrial, mining, nuclear-services, power, transportation, and water resources industries. **Operations at this facility include:** Divisional Headquarters; Service.

WASTE MANAGEMENT COLORADO
2400 West Union Avenue, Englewood CO 80110-5354. 303/797-1600. **Contact:** Human Resources. **World Wide Web address:** http://www.wmcolorado.com. **Description:** A waste disposal company specializing in the hauling of waste materials. **Parent company:** Waste Management, Inc. is an international provider of comprehensive waste management services, as well as engineering and construction, industrial, and related services, with operations in 19 countries. **Listed on:** New York Stock Exchange. **Stock exchange symbol:** WMI.

WASTE MANAGEMENT, INC.
6091 Brighton Boulevard, Commerce City CO 80022. 303/288-5115. **Contact:** Human Resources. **World Wide Web address:** http://www.wm.com. **Description:** A community provider of waste hauling, dumping, and recycling services. **Corporate headquarters location:** Houston TX. **Listed on:** New York Stock Exchange. **Stock exchange symbol:** WMI.

WATER PIK TECHNOLOGIES, INC.
1730 East Prospect Road, Fort Collins CO 80553-0001. 970/484-1352. **Contact:** Recruiter. **World Wide Web address:** http://www.waterpik.com. **Description:** Manufactures products for consumer and professional use including pulsating showerheads and point-of-use water filtration systems. Brand names include Water-Pik oral irrigators and tooth care products, Shower Massage showerhead units, and Instapure water filters. **Corporate headquarters location:** Newport Beach CA. **Listed on:** New York Stock Exchange. **Stock exchange symbol:** PIK.

WELLS FARGO BANK
1955 South Sheridan Boulevard, Denver CO 80227. 303/984-4352. **Contact:** Human Resources. **World Wide Web address:** http://www.wellsfargo.com. **Description:** A diversified financial institution with over $234 billion in assets. Wells Fargo serves over 17 million customers through 5,300 independent locations worldwide. The company also maintains several stand-alone ATMs and branches within retail outlets. Services include community banking, credit and debit cards, home equity and mortgage loans, online banking, student loans, and insurance. Wells Fargo also offers a complete line of commercial and institutional financial services. Founded in 1852. **NOTE:** Applicants should only apply for specified openings. **Corporate headquarters location:** San Francisco CA. **Other U.S. locations:** Nationwide. **International locations:** Worldwide. **Operations at this facility include:** Regional Headquarters; Sales; Service. **Parent company:** Wells Fargo & Company. **Listed on:** New York Stock Exchange. **Stock exchange symbol:** WFC. **Annual sales/revenues:** More than $100 million. **Number of employees worldwide:** 104,000.

WELLS FARGO BANK
1740 Broadway, Denver CO 80274. 303/861-8811. **Contact:** Human Resources. **World Wide Web address:** http://www.wellsfargo.com. **Description:** A diversified financial institution with over $234 billion in assets serving over 17 million customers through 5,300 independent locations worldwide. The company also maintains several stand-alone ATMs and branches within retail outlets. Services include community banking, credit and debit cards, home equity and mortgage loans, online banking, student loans, and insurance. Wells Fargo also offers a complete line of commercial and institutional financial services. Founded in 1852. **Corporate headquarters location:** San Francisco CA. **Other U.S. locations:** Nationwide. **International locations:** Worldwide. **Operations at this facility include:** This location is a full-service bank. **Parent company:** Wells Fargo & Company. **Listed on:** New York Stock Exchange. **Stock exchange symbol:** WFC. **Annual sales/revenues:** More than $100 million. **Number of employees worldwide:** 104,000.

WENDY'S INTERNATIONAL, INC.
6695 West Alameda Avenue, Denver CO 80214. 303/238-9721. **Contact:** Staffing Specialist. **World Wide Web address:** http://www.wendysintl.com. **Description:** One of the world's largest restaurant franchising companies. Wendy's International is comprised of Wendy's, a fast-food restaurant chain, and Tim Hortons, a coffee and baked goods restaurant chain. **Corporate headquarters location:** Dublin OH. **Other U.S. locations:** Nationwide. **Operations at this facility include:** Administration; Divisional Headquarters. **Listed on:** New York Stock Exchange. **Stock exchange symbol:** WEN.

WESCO FABRICS INC.
4001 Forest Street, P.O. Box 16604, Denver CO 80216. 303/388-4101. **Contact:** Human Resources. **World Wide Web address:** http://www.wescofabrics.com. **Description:** Wholesales drapery fabrics and distributes window coverings and bedspreads on a wholesale trade basis. Wesco Fabrics also manufactures bedspreads. Founded in 1946. **Corporate headquarters location:** This location. **Chairman:** Richard Gentry.

WESTERN GAS RESOURCES INC.
1099 18th Street, Denver CO 80202. 303/452-5603. **Fax:** 303/252-6025. **Contact:** Human Resources. **E-mail address:** careers@westerngas.com. **World Wide Web address:** http://www.westerngas.com. **Description:** Owns and operates natural gas gathering and processing facilities. The company also markets and transports natural gas and natural gas liquids. **Positions advertised include:** Project Engineer. **Corporate headquarters location:** This location. **Operations at this facility include:** Administration. **Listed on:** New York Stock Exchange. **Listed on:** New York Stock Exchange. **Stock exchange symbol:** WGR. **Number of employees at this location:** 350. **Number of employees nationwide:** 835.

WESTERNGECO
1625 Broadway, Suite 1300, Denver CO 80202. 303/629-9250. **Contact:** Human Resources Department. **World Wide Web address:** http://www.slb.com. **Description:** WesternGeco provides a full range of geophysical services for oil and gas exploration. Services include land and marine seismic surveys, geophysical programming, and data processing and interpretation. **Other U.S. locations:** AK; CA. **International locations:** Australia; Bolivia; Brazil; Canada; Colombia; Egypt; England; Guatemala; Italy; Pakistan; Saudi Arabia; Singapore; Tunisia. **Parent company:** Schlumberger Ltd. **Listed on:** New York Stock Exchange. **Stock exchange symbol:** SLB.

WEYERHAEUSER COMPANY
4565 Indiana Street, Golden CO 80403. 303/279-5511. **Contact:** Human Resources. **World Wide Web address:** http://www.wii.com. **Description:** Weyerhaeuser Company is a diversified, integrated forest products company with 90 plants and mills manufacturing containerboard, bag paper, fine paper, bleached hardwood market pulp, specialty printing papers, corrugated containers, business forms, cut sheet paper, paper bags, inks, lumber, plywood, particleboard, medium-density fiberboard, laminated beams, and value-added wood products. Founded in 1906. **Operations at this facility include:** This facility produces corrugated containers. **Corporate headquarters location:** Tacoma WA. **Listed on:** New York Stock Exchange. **Stock exchange symbol:** WY.

WILD OATS MARKETS
3375 Mitchell Lane, Boulder CO 80301. 303/440-5220. **Contact:** Human Resources. **World Wide Web address:** http://www.wildoats.com. **Description:** Owns and operates health food supermarkets under the Wild Oats, Alfalfa's, and Caper's names. **Positions advertised include:** Supply Chain Coordinator; Plan Development Technician; Fixed Asset Consultant; Purchasing Data Technician; Director of Corporate Brand Sourcing; Field Merchandiser; Manager of Quality Systems. **Corporate headquarters location:** This location. **Other U.S. locations:** Nationwide. **Listed on:** NASDAQ. **Stock exchange symbol:** OATS.

A.R. WILFLEY & SONS
7350 East Progress Place, Suite 200, Englewood CO 80111. 303/779-1777. **Contact:** Bill Wilbur, Director of Communications and Human Resources. **World Wide Web address:** http://www.wilfley.com. **Description:** Manufactures centrifugal pumps.

WILKERSON CORPORATION
1201 West Mansfield Avenue, Englewood CO 80110. 303/761-7601. **Fax:** 303/783-2323. **Contact:** Human Resources Administrator. **World Wide Web address:** http://www.wilkersoncorp.com. **Description:** Manufactures fluid power equipment including air dryers, filters, regulators, and lubricators. Founded in 1948. **NOTE:** Entry-level positions and second and third shifts are offered. **Corporate headquarters location:** This location. **International locations:** Germany. **Operations at this facility include:** Administration; Manufacturing; Research and Development; Sales; Service. **Number of employees at this location:** 330.

WILLIAMS
1515 Arapahoe Street, Tower 3, Suite 1000, Denver CO 80202. 303/572-3900. **Contact:** Human Resources. **E-mail address:** e-resumes@williams.com. **World Wide Web address:** http://www.williams.com. **Description:** Williams is a natural gas and oil exploration and production company with facilities in the Rocky Mountain region and Oklahoma. Williams also operates gas gathering systems and a gas processing plant in areas that are synergistic to the company's production. **Corporate headquarters location:** Tulsa OK.

WINTER PARK RESORT
P.O. Box 36, Winter Park CO 80482. 970/726-1536. **Fax:** 303/892-5823. **Recorded jobline:** 888/562-4525. **Contact:** Human Resources. **E-mail address:** wjob@mail.skiwinterpark.com. **World Wide Web address:** http://www.winterparkresort. com. **Description:** A mountain resort offering lodging, skiing, ice-skating, sleigh rides, and hot air balloon rides. **Note:** Applications are accepted in-person at the recruiting office in the Administration building. The office is open 7 days a week from 8:00 a.m. to 4:30 p.m. **Positions advertised include:** Accounting Supervisor; Catering Foreman; Equipment Room Specialist.

WONDERBREAD/HOSTESS CAKES
80 East 62nd Avenue, Denver CO 80216. 303/428-7431. **Contact:** Human Resources. **Description:** A wholesale bakery that produces Wonderbread and Hostess snack cakes. **Corporate headquarters location:** Kansas City MO.

WOODWARD GOVERNOR COMPANY
1000 East Drake Road, Fort Collins CO 80525. 970/482-5811. **Contact:** Human Resources. **World Wide Web address:** http://www.woodward.com. **Description:** Designs and manufactures engine control systems and components for engines and other turbomachinery devices for a wide range of industries. **Corporate headquarters location:** Rockford IL. **Listed on:** NASDAQ. **Stock exchange symbol:** WGOV.

WRIGHT & McGILL
P.O. Box 16011, Denver CO 80216-6011. 303/321-1481. **Physical address:** 4245 East 46th Avenue, Denver CO 80216. **Contact:** Human Resources. **World Wide Web address:** http://www.eagleclaw.com. **Description:** Manufactures a line of fishing rods and tackle. Founded in 1925. **Corporate headquarters location:** This location.

WRIGHT WATER ENGINEERS INC.
2490 West 26th Avenue, Suite 100A, Denver CO 80211-4208. 303/480-1700. **Contact:** Kenneth Wright, President. **World Wide Web address:** http:// www.wrightwater.com. **Description:** Specializes in the planning and developing of water resources.

XI GRAPHICS
1801 Broadway, Suite 1710, Denver CO 80202-3800. 303/298-7478. **Toll-free phone:** 800/946-7433. **Fax:** 303/298-1406. **Contact:** Human Resources. **E-mail address:** jobs@xig.com. **World Wide Web address:** http://www.xig.com. **Description:** Develops a line of products that enhance the graphics capabilities of PC hardware. Products include X Windows display servers, OpenGL development, and custom development. **Operations at this facility include:** Customer Service; Financial Offices; Sales; Technical Support. **Listed on:** Privately held.

XEROX CORPORATION
4600 South Ulster Street, Suite 1000, Denver CO 80237. 303/796-6200. **Contact:** Human Resources. **E-mail address:** xerox@isearch.com. **World Wide Web address:** http://www.xerox.com. **Description:** Manufactures, markets, services, and finances information processing products including copiers, duplicators, scanners, electronic printing systems, word processing systems, personal computers, and computer peripherals. Xerox does business in over 120 countries. Founded in 1906. **Corporate headquarters location:** Stamford CT. **Other U.S. locations:** Nationwide.

International locations: Worldwide. **Operations at this facility include:** This location is a regional sales and service office. **Listed on:** New York Stock Exchange. **Stock exchange symbol:** XRX. **Annual sales/revenues:** More than $100 million.

XPEDX
55 Madison Street, Suite 800, Denver CO 80206. 303/329-6644. **Contact:** Director of Human Resources. **World Wide Web address:** http://www.xpedx.com. **Description:** A wholesale distributor of paper and paper-related products. **Special programs:** Training. **Corporate headquarters location:** Covington KY.

YAHOO! INTERNET LIFE
P.O. Box 53380, Boulder CO 80323. 303/665-8930. **Contact:** Human Resources. **World Wide Web address:** http://www.yahoo.com. **Description:** An online and print magazine that reviews Internet Websites. **Corporate headquarters location:** Sunnyvale CA. **Parent company:** Yahoo! Inc. **Listed on:** NASDAQ. **Stock exchange symbol:** YHOO.

ZAXIS CORPORATION
5445 DTC Parkway, Suite 450, Greenwood Village CO 80111. 303/713-0200. **Fax:** 303/713-0299. **Contact:** Heidi O'Neil, Controller. **E-mail address:** jobs@zaxis.com. **World Wide Web address:** http://www.zaxis.com. **Description:** Designs visual evidence for legal cases using computer-generated animation and graphics. **Positions advertised include:** Flash/Lightwave Animator. **Corporate headquarters location:** This location. **Other U.S. locations:** San Francisco CA; Chicago IL; New York NY.

ZIMMERMAN METALS, INC.
201 East 58th Avenue, Denver CO 80216. 303/294-0180. **Toll-free phone:** 800/247-4202. **Fax:** 303/292-5013. **Contact:** Arla Zimmerman, Personnel Manager. **World Wide Web address:** http://www.zimmerman-metals.com. **Description:** Fabricates structural and miscellaneous steel and architectural metals. **Positions advertised include:** Fabrication Fitter; Welder; Supervisor. **Corporate headquarters location:** This location. **Operations at this facility include:** Administration; Manufacturing; Research and Development; Sales; Service.

ZYKRONIX INC.
357 Inverness Drive South, Suite C, Englewood CO 80112. 303/799-4944. **Fax:** 303/799-4978. **Contact:** Human Resources. **E-mail address:** hr@zykronix.com. **World Wide Web address:** http://www.zykronix.com. **Description:** Designs and manufactures PCs that are used mainly for industrial applications. Founded in 1990. **Positions advertised include:** Electronic Design Engineer; Senior Software Engineer; Electronic Technician. **President/CEO:** David M. Ghaemi. **Corporate headquarters location:** This location.

ABB INC.
P.O. Box 5308, Norwalk CT 06856-5308. 203/750-2200. **Physical address:** 501 Merritt Seven, Norwalk CT 06851. **Fax:** 203/750-2263. **Contact:** Human Resources. **World Wide Web address:** http://www.abb.com/us. **Description:** Provides engineering, construction, and sales support services as part of a worldwide engineering firm. Internationally, the company operates in five business segments: oil field equipment and services; power systems; engineering and construction; process equipment; and industrial products. **Corporate headquarters location:** This location. **Other U.S. locations:** Nationwide. **International locations:** Worldwide. **Subsidiaries include:** ABB Lumus Global Inc., Bloomfield NJ; ABB Simcon, Broomfield NJ. **Parent company:** ABB Asea Brown Boveri Ltd. (Baden, Switzerland.) **Number of employees worldwide:** 220,000.

AIT
639 Research Parkway, Suite 100, Meriden CT 06450. 203/782-2300. **Contact:** Human Resources. **World Wide Web address:** http://www.aitgroup.com. **Description:** A software development and applications company that specializes in telemarketing, marketing, sales, and customer service application software for the IBM midrange, UNIX client/server market. **Other U.S. locations:** Irvine CA; Cleveland OH. **International locations:** Australia; England; Paris.

AS MANAGEMENT
760 Summer Street, Suite 103, Stamford CT 06901. 203/967-4003. **Contact:** Human Resources. **Description:** Manages and operates four restaurants in Massachusetts and Florida under the name Victoria Station.

ACME UNITED CORPORATION
1931 Black Rock Turnpike, Fairfield CT 06432. 203/332-7330. **Fax:** 203/576-0007. **Contact:** Human Resources. **World Wide Web address:** http://www.acmeunited.com. **Description:** A holding company. **NOTE:** Send resumes to Human Resources, P.O. Box 458, Fremont NC 27830. **Corporate headquarters location:** This location. **Subsidiaries include:** Acme United Ltd. (England) manufactures medical scissors, household scissors and shears, nail files, and other manicure items. Acme United Limited (Canada) markets scissors, rulers, and yardsticks. Emil Schlemper GmbH (Germany) and Peter Altenbach and Son (Germany) both manufacture knives, scissors, shears, and manicure products. **Listed on:** American Stock Exchange. **Stock exchange symbol:** ACU. **Number of employees nationwide:** 570.

ADVANCED TECHNOLOGY MATERIALS, INC. (ATMI)
7 Commerce Drive, Danbury CT 06810. 203/794-1100. **Fax:** 203/792-8040. **Contact:** Human Resources Manager. **World Wide Web address:** http://www.atmi.com. **Description:** A developer of semiconductor materials and devices. ATMI specializes in chemical vapor deposition and thin-film technology, synthesis of organometallic reagents, wide bandgap semiconductor substrates and devices, and both absorption- and combustion-based air pollution abatement equipment. **Positions advertised include:** Inventory Analyst; Human Resources Administrator; Manufacturing Supervisor; Financial Analyst; Research Scientist. **Corporate headquarters location:** This location. **Other U.S. locations:** Phoenix AZ; San Jose CA. **Subsidiaries include:** EcoSys manufactures environmental equipment for the semiconductor industry. **Operations at this facility include:** Manufacturing; Research and Development. **Listed on:** NASDAQ. **Stock exchange symbol:** ATMI. **Annual sales/revenues:** $21 - $50 million. **Number of employees at this location:** 120. **Number of employees nationwide:** 225.

THE ADVEST GROUP, INC.
90 State House Square, Hartford CT 06103. 860/509-1000. **Fax:** 860/509-3849. **Contact:** Ralph J. Presutti, Human Resources. **World Wide Web address:** http://www.advest.com. **Description:** Provides diversified financial services including securities brokerage, trading, investment banking, commercial and consumer lending, and asset management. **Positions advertised include:** Compensation Consultant; Due Diligence Analyst; Internal Auditor; Margin Specialist; Mutual Fund Operations Consultant. **Corporate headquarters location:** This location. **Other U.S. locations:** Nationwide. **Subsidiaries include:** Advest, Inc. is a regional broker/dealer providing investment services to a primarily retail client base, with offices in 17 states and the District of Columbia. Advest Bank is a Connecticut-chartered savings bank offering lending, deposit, and trust services to individuals, businesses, and institutions. Boston Security Counselors is an investment management company that serves private clients and handles the proprietary mutual funds of The Advest Group, Inc. Billings & Company specializes in private placement offerings, primarily in real estate. Financial Institutions Group is a financial consulting firm that specializes in the banking and thrift industry. **Number of employees nationwide:** 1,525.

ADVO INC.
One Targeting Center, Windsor CT 06095. 860/285-6100. **Contact:** Human Resources. **World Wide Web address:** http://www.advo.com. **Description:** A direct mail advertising company. **Positions advertised include:** Client Services Account Representative; Client Marketing Manager; System and Process Support Manager; Vice President, Network and Planning Development; Human Resources Assistant. **Corporate headquarters location:** This location. **Other U.S. locations:** Nationwide. **Listed on:** New York Stock Exchange. **Stock exchange symbol:** AD. **Number of employees at this location:** 450. **Number of employees nationwide:** 5,500.

ADVO INC.
231 West Service Road, Hartford CT 06147. 860/520-6600. **Contact:** Human Resources. **World Wide Web address:** http://www.advo.com. **Description:** A direct mail advertising company. **Positions advertised include:** Account Specialist, Client Services; Client Services Regional Account Executive. **Corporate headquarters location:** Windsor CT. **Listed on:** New York Stock Exchange. **Stock exchange symbol:** AD. **Number of employees nationwide:** 5,500.

AETNA, INC.
151 Farmington Avenue, Hartford CT 06156. 860/273-0123. **Contact:** Human Resources. **World Wide Web address:** http://www.aetna.com. **NOTE:** Call Human Resources at 800/238-6247. **Description:** Provides health insurance and retirement benefit plans as well as financial services. **Positions advertised include:** Administrative Assistant; Executive Assistant; Business Information Consultant; Project Manager, Communications; Consultant; Manager, Investor Relations; Sales Support Manager; Senior Consultant; Senior Real Estate Analyst. **Special Programs:** Internships. **Corporate headquarters location:** This location. **Other area locations:** Middletown CT; Windsor CT. **Other U.S. locations:** Nationwide. **Operations at this facility include:** Administration; Service. **Listed on:** New York Stock Exchange. **Stock exchange symbol:** AET.

AHLSTROM
2 Elm Street, Windsor Locks CT 06096. 860/654-8300. **Fax:** 860/654-8596. **Contact:** Human Resources. **World Wide Web address:** http://www.ahlstrom.com. **Description:** Ahlstrom is a diverse manufacturing company whose primary products include chemical and medical products. The company is involved in molecular biology research items, as well as electronic, automotive, food packaging, and aerospace products. **Special programs:** Internships. **Corporate headquarters location:** Helsinki, Finland. **Operations at this facility include:** This division manufactures specialty paper and nonwoven products. **Number of employees at this location:** 500.

ALBERTUS MAGNUS COLLEGE
700 Prospect Street, New Haven CT 06511. 203/773-8550. **Contact:** Human Resources. **World Wide Web address:** http://www.albertus.edu. **Description:** A four-year, liberal arts and sciences college. Founded in 1925.

ALGONQUIN PARTS INC.
667 Connecticut Avenue, Norwalk CT 06854. 203/838-6548. **Contact:** Human Resources. **World Wide Web address:** http://www.algonquinparts.com. **Description:** Manufactures aircraft parts including frames, wing ribs, bulkheads, hinges, doors, flap tracks, and other related components. Founded in 1938

AMERICAN EXPRESS TRAVEL RELATED SERVICES
64 Pratt Street, 3rd Floor, Hartford CT 06103. 860/987-5500. **Contact:** Human Resources. **World Wide Web address:** http://www.americanexpress.com. **Description:** A diversified travel and financial services company operating in 160 countries around the world. American Express Travel Related Services offers consumers the Personal, Gold, and Platinum Cards, as well as revolving credit products such as Optima Cards, which allow customers to extend payments. Other products include the American Express Corporate Card, which helps businesses manage their travel and entertainment expenditures; and the Corporate Purchasing Card, which helps businesses manage their supplies, equipment, and services expenditures. American Express Travel Related Services also offers American Express Travelers' Cheques and travel services including trip planning, reservations, ticketing, and management information. American Express Financial Advisors provides a variety of financial products and services to help individuals, businesses, and institutions establish and achieve their financial goals. American Express Financial Advisors has a field of more than 8,000 financial advisors in the United States and offers products and services that include financial planning; annuities; mutual funds; insurance; investment certificates; and institutional investment advisory trust, tax preparation, and retail securities brokerage services. **Corporate headquarters location:** Cambridge MA. **Other U.S. locations:** Nationwide. **Listed on:** New York Stock Exchange. **Stock exchange symbol:** AXP.

AMERICAN FROZEN FOODS, INC.
155 Hill Street, Milford CT 06460. 203/882-6200. **Toll-free phone:** 800/233-5554. **Contact:** Bill Rappoport, Vice President of Sales. **World Wide Web address:** http://www.americanfoods.com. **Description:** Operates a customized shop-at-home food delivery service, delivering meats, vegetables, juices, desserts, and convenience items directly to the consumer. **Positions advertised include:** Sales Representative; Sales Manager; Independent Sales Agent. **Corporate headquarters location:** This location. **Other U.S. locations:** Nationwide. **Number of employees nationwide:** 1,200.

AMERICAN INSTITUTE FOR FOREIGN STUDY (AIFS)
River Plaza, 9 West Broad Street, Stamford CT 06902. 203/399-5000. **Toll-free phone:** 800/727-2437. **Contact:** Human Resources. **World Wide Web address:** http://www.aifs.org. **Description:** Engaged in the placement of au pairs in American homes, as well as the placement of American students in study programs abroad.

AMERICAN MANAGEMENT SYSTEMS, INC.
45 Glastonbury Boulevard, Glastonbury CT 06033. 860/368-2700. **Contact:** Human Resources. **World Wide Web address:** http://www.amsinc.com. **Description:** Creates custom-designed software training courses for specific computer applications used by business clientele. **Corporate headquarters location:** Fairfax VA. **Other U.S. locations:** Nationwide. **Listed on:** NASDAQ. **Stock exchange symbol:** AMSY.

AMERICAN MEDICAL RESPONSE (AMR)
55 Church Street, 6th Floor, New Haven CT 06510. 203/781-1092. **Fax:** 203/781-1192. **Contact:** Cyndee Knapp, Human Resources. **E-mail address:** Cyndee.Knapp@amr-ems.com. **World Wide Web address:** http://www.amr.net. **Description:** Provides emergency medical transportation. **Positions advertised include:** Administrative Assistant. **Corporate headquarters location:** Greenwood Village CO. **Other U.S. locations:** Nationwide.

AMERICAN PAYMENT SYSTEMS
15 Sterling Drive, P.O. Box 504415, Wallingford CT 06492. 203/679-4400. **Contact:** Human Resources. **E-mail address:** jobs@apsnet.com. **World Wide Web address:** http://www.apsnet.com. **Description:** Specializes in walk-in bill payments. Processes payments in person for various billers. Founded in 1990. **Positions advertised include:** Marketing Project Manager. **Corporate headquarters location:** This location.

AMERICAN SKANDIA LIFE ASSURANCE CORPORATION (ASLAC)
P.O. Box 883, Shelton CT 06484-0883. 203/926-1888. **Physical address:** One Corporate Drive, Shelton CT 06484. **Toll-free phone:** 800/628-6039. **Contact:** Human Resources. **World Wide Web address:** http://www.americanskandia.com. **Description:** Provides long-term savings products including variable, fixed, market-value adjusted, and immediate annuities, as well as mutual funds, qualified funds products, and variable life insurance. American Skandia Life Assurance Company also offers investment management and administrative services through a series trust that provides mutual fund options. **Special programs:** Internships.

AMPHENOL CORPORATION
358 Hall Avenue, Wallingford CT 06492. 203/265-8900. **Contact:** Human Resources. **World Wide Web address:** http://www.amphenolrf.com. **NOTE:** Submit resume online. **Description:** A manufacturer of electronic connectors and cables. **Corporate headquarters location:** This location. **Other area locations:** Danbury CT; Hamden CT. **Listed on:** New York Stock Exchange. **Stock exchange symbol:** APH. **Number of employees nationwide:** 3,070.

AMPHENOL CORPORATION
One Kennedy Avenue, Danbury CT 06810. 203/743-9272. **Contact:** Human Resources. **World Wide Web address:** http://www.amphenolrf.com. **NOTE:** Submit resume online. **Description:** Manufactures coaxial connectors and cable assemblies. **Corporate headquarters location:** Wallingford CT. **Other U.S. locations:** Hamden CT. **Listed on:** New York Stock Exchange. **Stock exchange symbol:** APH. **Number of employees nationwide:** 3,070.

AMPHENOL SPECTRA-STRAP
720 Sherman Avenue, Hamden CT 06514. 203/281-3200. **Contact:** Denise Masulli, Personnel Director. **World Wide Web address:** http://www.amphenol.com. **Description:** A producer of flat ribbon cable. **Corporate headquarters location:**

Wallingford CT. **Other U.S. locations:** Danbury CT. **Listed on:** New York Stock Exchange. **Stock exchange symbol:** APH. **Number of employees nationwide:** 3,070.

ANTEON CORPORATION
P.O. Box 220, Route 2, North Stonington CT 06359-0220. 860/599-3910. **Fax:** 860/599-6516. **Contact:** Jennifer Dauster-Bevacqua, Human Resources Administrator. **World Wide Web address:** http://www.anteon.com. **Description:** A leading provider of technology-based solutions in the areas of engineering, information technology, and interactive multimedia services. **Positions advertised include:** Telecommunications Analyst. **Corporate headquarters location:** Fairfax VA. **Other U.S. locations:** Nationwide. **International locations:** Germany; Italy; United Kingdom. **Listed on:** New York Stock Exchange. **Stock exchange symbol:** ANT. **Annual sales/revenues:** More than $100 million. **Number of employees nationwide:** 5,400.

ANTHEM
370 Bassett Road, North Haven CT 06473. 203/239-4911. **Contact:** Human Resources. **World Wide Web address:** http://www.anthem.com. **Description:** Health care benefits company. Provides health care plans, dental plans, visual and behavioral health plans, pharmacy benefits, and life insurance. Anthem is the Blue Cross and Blue Shield licensee in nine different states. **Positions advertised include:** Case Manager; RN-CVD, Diabetes. **Other U.S. locations:** Nationwide.

ANTON/BAUER INC.
14 Progress Drive, Shelton CT 06484. 203/929-1100. **Toll-free phone:** 800/422-3473. **Fax:** 203/929-4988. **Contact:** Human Resources. **World Wide Web address:** http://www.antonbauer.com. **Description:** Manufactures electronic products including battery packs and chargers for video cameras. **Corporate headquarters location:** This location. **International locations:** England; Scotland.

APPLERA CORPORATION
301 Merritt Seven, Norwalk CT 06856. 203/840-2000. **Toll-free phone:** 800/761-5381. **Fax:** 203/840-2410. **Contact:** Human Resources. **World Wide Web address:** http://www.applera.com. **Description:** A worldwide leader in the development, manufacture, and distribution of analytical and life science systems used in environmental technology, pharmaceuticals, biotechnology, chemicals, plastics, food, agriculture, and scientific research. Founded in 1937. **Positions advertised include:** Financial Analyst; Associate Benefits Administrator; Design Specialist; Travel Specialist. **Corporate headquarters location:** This location. **Subsidiaries include:** Applied Biosystems; Celera Genomics; Celera Diagnostics. **Listed on:** New York Stock Exchange. **Stock exchange symbol:** ABI.

APPLIED ENGINEERING PRODUCTS
P.O. Box 510, New Haven CT 06513-0510. 203/776-2813. **Physical address:** 104 John W. Murphy Drive, New Haven CT 06513. **Fax:** 203/776-8294. **Contact:** Human Resources. **E-mail address:** hr@aep.us. **World Wide Web address:** http://www.aepconnectors.com. **Description:** Manufactures SMB and SMC connectors for radio frequency markets.

APRIA HEALTHCARE GROUP INC.
40 Sebethe Drive, Cromwell CT 06416. 860/613-4600. **Fax:** 860/632-9673. **Contact:** Human Resources. **World Wide Web address:** http://www.apria.com. **Description:** Provides a broad range of respiratory therapy services, home medical equipment, and infusion therapy services. Apria Healthcare Group's home health care services are provided to patients who have been discharged from hospitals, skilled nursing facilities, or convalescent homes and are being treated at home. In conjunction with medical professionals, Apria personnel deliver, install, and service medical equipment, as well as provide appropriate therapies and coordinate plans of care for their patients. Apria personnel also instruct patients and care-givers in the correct use of equipment and monitor the equipment's effectiveness. Patients and their families receive training from registered nurses and respiratory therapy professionals concerning the therapy administered including instruction in proper infusion technique and the care and use of equipment and supplies. **Corporate headquarters location:** Lake Forest CA. **Other U.S. locations:** Nationwide. **Listed on:** New York Stock Exchange. **Stock exchange symbol:** AHG. **Number of employees nationwide:** 7,500.

AQUARIAN WATER COMPANY OF CONNECTICUT
600 Lindley Street, Bridgeport CT 06606. 203/337-5992. **Contact:** Jean Zanella Dyer, Manager of Human Resources. **Description:** One of the largest investor-owned water companies in New England, serving approximately 500,000 people. **NOTE:** Entry-level positions are offered. **Company slogan:** Quality water for life. **Corporate headquarters location:** This location. **Other U.S. locations:** NY; MA; NH. **Parent company:** Aquarion Company. **President:** Janet Hansen. **Annual sales/revenues:** $51 - $100 million.

ARCH CHEMICALS, INC.
501 Merritt 7, P.O. Box 5204, Norwalk CT 06856-5204. 203/229-2900. **Fax:** 203/229-3652. **Contact:** Human Resources. **E-mail address:** tcice@archchemicals.com. **World Wide Web address:** http://www.archchemicals.com. **Description:** A chemicals company specializing in treatment and performance products. **Listed on:** New York Stock Exchange. **Stock exchange symbol:** ARJ. **Number of employees worldwide:** 2,800.

ASHFORTH COMPANY
707 Summer Street, 4th Floor, Stamford CT 06901-1026. 203/359-8500. **Fax:** 203/327-5610. **Contact:** Human Resources. **E-mail address:** humanresources@ashforthcompany.com. **World Wide Web address:** http://www.ashforthcompany.com. **Description:** A property management and commercial real estate construction company. **Positions advertised include:** Tax Accountant.

AVALONBAY COMMUNITIES, INC.
220 Elm Street, Suite 200, New Canaan CT 06840. 203/801-3300. **Fax:** 203/762-1240. **Contact:** Human Resources. **World Wide Web address:** http://www.avalonbay.com. **Description:** A self-administered and self-managed equity real estate investment trust that specializes in the development, construction, acquisition, and management of apartment communities in the Mid-Atlantic and Northeastern United States. AvalonBay Communities' real estate consists of approximately 10,000 apartment homes in 33 communities located in six states and Washington DC. **Positions advertised include:** Assistant Superintendent; Financial Analyst. **Corporate headquarters location:** Washington DC. **Other U.S. locations:** Nationwide. **Listed on:** New York Stock Exchange. **Stock exchange symbol:** AVB.

B&J ELECTRIC MOTOR REPAIR COMPANY
30 Maple Street, Ansonia CT 06401. 203/734-1695. **Contact:** Alan Johns, President. **Description:** Services electrical equipment. B&J Electric Motor Repair also provides wiring supplies and related construction materials.

BVH INTEGRATED SERVICES, INC.
50 Griffin Road South, Bloomfield CT 06002. 860/286-9171. **Fax:** 860/242-0236. **Contact:** Human Resources. **E-mail address:** start@bvhis.com. **World Wide Web address:** http://www.bvhis.com. **Description:** Provides mechanical, electrical, structural, and civil engineering services.

BALDWIN TECHNOLOGY COMPANY, INC.
P.O. Box 901, 12 Commerce Drive, Shelton CT 06484. 203/925-1100. **Contact:** John Lawlor, Director of Personnel. **World Wide Web address:** http://www.baldwintech.com. **Description:** Manufactures material handling and control equipment for the printing industry. Products include cleaning systems and Web control systems. **Corporate headquarters location:** This location. **International locations:** Worldwide. **Listed on:** American Stock Exchange. **Stock exchange symbol:** BLD.

BANK OF AMERICA
New Fairfield Shopping Center, Route 37 & 39, New Fairfield CT 06812. 203/746-2596. **Contact:** Maureen Foley, Human Resources. **World Wide Web address:** http://www.bankofamerica.com. **Description:** A full-service banking institution. Along with general banking services, Bank of America performs services such as accounting, auditing, marketing, business development, insurance, operational, tax, investment, and personnel administration. **Corporate headquarters location:** Charlotte NC. **Parent company:** Bank of America. **Listed on:** New York Stock Exchange. **Stock exchange symbol:** BAC.

BANK OF AMERICA
777 Main Street, Hartford CT 06115. 860/727-5000. **Contact:** Human Resources. **World Wide Web address:** http://www.bankoramerica.com. **Description:** A full-service banking institution. Along with general banking services, Bank of America performs services such as accounting, auditing, marketing, business development, insurance, operational, tax, investment, and personnel administration. **NOTE:** Search and apply for positions online. **Positions advertised include:** District Manager; Sr. Administrative Assistant; Teller. **Corporate headquarters location:** Charlotte NC. **Parent company:** Bank of America. **Listed on:** New York Stock Exchange. **Stock exchange symbol:** BAC.

BANK OF AMERICA
21 West Main Street, Waterbury CT 06702. 203/574-7000. **Contact:** Human Resources. **World Wide Web address:** http://www.bankofamerica.com. **Description:** A full-service banking institution. Along with general banking services, Bank of America performs services such as accounting, auditing, marketing, business development, insurance, operational, tax, investment, and personnel administration. **Corporate headquarters location:** Charlotte NC. **Parent company:** Bank of America. **Listed on:** New York Stock Exchange. **Stock exchange symbol:** BAC.

BANK OF AMERICA BUSINESS CAPITAL
200 Glastonbury Boulevard, Glastonbury CT 06033. 860/659-3200. **Contact:** Human Resources. **World Wide Web address:** http://www.bankofamerica.com. **Description:** A credit institution that lends money in amounts of $5 million or greater to corporate clients. **Parent company:** Bank of America.

BARNES & NOBLE BOOKSTORES
1599 Southeast Road, Farmington CT 06032. 860/678-9494. **Contact:** Manager. **World Wide Web address:** http://www.barnesandnoble.com. **Description:** A bookstore chain. This location also has a cafe and music department. **Corporate headquarters location:** New York NY. **Other U.S. locations:** Nationwide.

BARNES & NOBLE BOOKSTORES
470 Universal Drive, North Haven CT 06473. 203/234-1805. **Contact:** Manager. **World Wide Web address:** http://www.barnesandnoble.com. **Description:** A bookstore chain. This location also has a cafe. **Corporate headquarters location:** New York NY. **Other U.S. locations:** Nationwide.

BARNES & NOBLE BOOKSTORES
360 Connecticut Avenue, Norwalk CT 06854. 203/866-2213. **Contact:** Manager. **World Wide Web address:** http://www.barnesandnoble.com. **Description:** A bookstore chain. This location also has a cafe. **Corporate headquarters location:** New York NY. **Other U.S. locations:** Nationwide.

BARNES & NOBLE BOOKSTORES
1076 Post Road East, Westport CT 06880. 203/221-7955. **Contact:** Manager. **World Wide Web address:** http://www.barnesandnoble.com. **Description:** A bookstore chain. This location also has a cafe and music department. **Corporate headquarters location:** New York NY. **Other U.S. locations:** Nationwide.

BARNES GROUP INC.
123 Main Street, Bristol CT 06010. 860/583-7070. **Contact:** James Pappas, Human Resources. **World Wide Web address:** http://www.barnesgroupinc.com. **Description:** Barnes Group distributes repair and replacement products such as fasteners, hardware, automotive parts, gas welding supplies, and industrial aerosols. The company also manufactures and distributes a wide variety of custom metal parts for mechanical purposes and machined and fabricated parts as well as assemblies. **Positions advertised include:** Administrative Services Assistant; Division Controller; Cost Analyst; Senior Internal Control Analyst. **Listed on:** New York Stock Exchange. **Stock exchange symbol:** B.

BAY TACT CORPORATION
THE PUBLIC REGISTER
440 Route 198, Woodstock Valley CT 06282. 860/974-2223. **Fax:** 860/974-2229. **Contact:** Human Resources. **World Wide Web address:** http://www.prars.com. **Description:** Bay Tact is engaged in the dissemination of financial information for publicly traded companies. The information dissemination includes 10Ks, annual reports, press releases, and promotional material. Bay Tact's client base consists of over 2,800 companies. Annual reports are distributed through The Public Register's Annual Report Service. In addition, Bay Tact publishes the *Security Traders Handbook*, a national financial publication, and *Hornsmatch*, a buy-sell cattle publication, and provides investment screening services through the PaceSetters database. **Corporate headquarters location:** This location.

BAYER CORPORATION
400 Morgan Lane, West Haven CT 06516. 203/813-2000. **Recorded jobline:** 203/812-5507. **Contact:** Personnel. **World Wide Web address:** http://www.bayerus.com. **Description:** This division conducts business through three major areas of the health care industry: prescription medicine, biological products, and biotechnology. **Corporate headquarters location:** Pittsburgh PA. **Parent company:** Bayer A.G. Worldwide. **Operations at this facility include:** This location is engaged in basic research and drug discovery as part of the Pharmaceutical Division.

W.R. BERKLEY CORPORATION
475 Steamboat Road, Greenwich CT 06830. 203/629-2880. **Contact:** Human Resources. **World Wide Web address:** http://www.wrbc.com. **Description:** W. R. Berkley Corporation is an insurance holding company which operates in five segments of the property casualty insurance business: specialty insurance, regional property casualty insurance, alternative markets, reinsurance and international. Founded in 1967. **Listed on:** New York Stock Exchange. **Stock exchange symbol:** BER.

BEST WESTERN SOVEREIGN HOTEL
9 Whitehall Avenue, Mystic CT 06355. 860/536-4281. **Contact:** Human Resources. **World Wide Web address:** http://www.bestwestern.com. **Description:** A hotel with 150 rooms. Best Western Sovereign Hotel is part of the national hotel chain. **Other U.S. locations:** Nationwide. **International locations:** Worldwide.

BIC CORPORATION
500 Bic Drive, Milford CT 06460. 203/783-2000. **Fax:** 203/783-2200. **Contact:** Paul Russo, Manager of Human Resources Administration. **World Wide Web address:** http://www.bicworldusa.com. **Description:** Manufactures consumer items including pens, lighters, shavers, and correction fluids. **Positions advertised include:** Associate Customer Development Manager; Senior Material/Design Engineer; Manufacturing Engineer; Financial Analyst; Legal Assistant; Administrative Assistant. **Corporate headquarters location:** This location. **Other U.S. locations:** Clearwater FL; St. Petersburg FL; Fort Madison IO; Charlotte NC; Fountain Inn SC; Gaffney SC. **Operations at this facility include:** Administration; Divisional Headquarters; Manufacturing; Research and Development; Sales. **Number of employees at this location:** 900. **Number of employees nationwide:** 3,000.

BIG BROTHERS BIG SISTERS OF SOUTHWESTERN CONNECTICUT
2470 Fairfield Avenue, Bridgeport CT 06605. 203/389-8734. **Fax:** 203/366-3766. **Contact:** Human Resources. **World Wide Web address:** http://www.bbbsa.org. **Description:** Provides volunteer and professional services to assist children in achieving their highest potential through over 505 Big Brothers/Big Sisters agencies nationwide. Across the country, more than 75,000 children are matched with adult volunteers. The agencies also provide counseling and family support services to parents and children in over 110,000 families each year. Additional programs focus on children with special needs including the handicapped, learning-disabled, and school dropouts, as well as those who are abused and neglected. Special prevention and intervention programs at many agencies address the problems of drug abuse, teen pregnancy, foster care, and juvenile delinquency. **Corporate headquarters location:** Philadelphia PA. **Other U.S. locations:** Nationwide.

BIO-MED DEVICES
1445 Boston Post Road, Guilford CT 06437. 203/458-0202. **Fax:** 203/458-0440. **Toll-free phone:** 800/224-6633. **Contact:** Human Resources. **World Wide Web address:** http:// www.biomeddevices.com. **Description:** Bio-Med Devices is a distributor of used medical equipment.

BLYTH INDUSTRIES, INC.
One East Weaver Street, Greenwich CT 06831. 203/661-1926. **Contact:** Jane Casey, Vice President of Organizational Development. **World Wide Web address:** http://www.blythindustries.com. **Description:** Designs, manufactures, markets, and distributes an extensive line of home fragrance products including scented candles, outdoor citronella candles, potpourri, and environmental fragrance products. The company also markets a broad range of candle accessories and decorative gift bags. Its products are sold under various brand names including Colonial Candle of Cape Cod, PartyLite Gifts, Carolina Designs, Ambria, Canterbury, Florasense, and FilterMate. The company is also a leading producer of portable heating fuel products sold under the brand names Sterno and Handy Fuel. **Corporate headquarters location:** This location. **Listed on:** New York Stock Exchange. **Stock exchange symbol:** BTH.

BOEHRINGER INGELHEIM PHARMACEUTICALS, INC.
900 Old Ridgebury Road, Ridgefield CT 06877. 203/798-9988. **Contact:** Director of Human Resources. **World Wide Web address:** http://www.boehringer-ingelheim.com. **Description:** Involved in the research, development, manufacture, and marketing of pharmaceutical products used to treat cardiovascular, pulmonary, viral, and immunological diseases. **Corporate headquarters location:** Ingelheim, Germany. **Number of employees nationwide:** 5,100.

BOMBARDIER AEROSPACE
One Bradley International Airport, Building 85-173, Windsor Locks CT 06096. 860/627-9491. **Contact:** Human Resources Department. **World Wide Web address:** http://www.aero.bombardier.com. **Description:** Bombardier Aerospace is one of the world's largest civil aircraft manufacturers. The company produces business, regional, and amphibious aircraft. **Operations at this facility include:** This location provides aircraft maintenance services.

BRADLEY INTERNATIONAL AIRPORT
CONNECTICUT DEPARTMENT OF TRANSPORTATION
Schoephoester Road, Windsor Locks CT 06096. 860/292-2000. **Contact:** Human Resources. **World Wide Web address:** http://www.bradleyairport.com. **Description:** New England's second largest airport. Bradley International Airport serves western New England with international and domestic flights. **NOTE:** Resumes should be addressed to Connecticut Department of Transportation, P.O. Box 317546, Newington CT 06131.

BRADLEY MEMORIAL HOSPITAL AND HEALTH CENTER
81 Meriden Avenue, Southington CT 06489. 860/276-5000. **Fax:** 860/276-5058. **Contact:** Human Resources. **World Wide Web address:** http://www.bradleymemorial.org. **Description:** An 84-bed acute care hospital and medical center. **Positions advertised include:** Lab Supervisor; Phlebotomist; Radiologic Technologist; Respiratory Care Practitioner; Senior Medical Technologist; Staff Pharmacist; Nursing Supervisor; Maintenance Worker.

BRANSON ULTRASONICS CORPORATION
41 Eagle Road, Danbury CT 06813. 203/796-0400. **Contact:** Human Resources. **World Wide Web address:** http://www.bransoncleaning.com. **Description:** A manufacturer of ultrasonic welders and cleaning equipment. **Corporate headquarters location:** This location. **Parent company:** Emerson Electric Company. **Number of employees at this location:** 500.

BRIDGEPORT HOSPITAL
267 Grant Street, P.O. Box 5000, Bridgeport CT 06610. 203/384-3000. **Contact:** Human Resources. **World Wide Web address:** http://www.bridgeporthospital.org. **Description:** A community hospital providing services through a trauma center, heart center, a women's care center, a joint reconstruction center, and the Norma F. Pfriem Cancer Center. **Positions advertised include:** Administrative Professional Psychiatric Nurse; Administrative Professional Nurse; Ambulatory Support Technician; Billing Analyst; Bloodless Medicine Coordinator; C.A.T. Scan Technician; Care Coordinator; Clinical Care Provider; Department Secretary; Director of Planning; Medical Technologist; Mental Health Consultant; Nurse Case Manager; Professional Nurse; Quality Improvement Nurse; Radiology Technician; Respiratory Therapist; Staff Pharmacist; Surgical Technician; Team Lead.

BRISTOL-MYERS SQUIBB COMPANY
5 Research Parkway, Wallingford CT 06492. 203/677-6000. **Contact:** Human Resources. **World Wide Web address:** http://www.bms.com. **Description:** Bristol-Myers Squibb is a manufacturer of pharmaceuticals, medical devices, nonprescription drugs, toiletries, and beauty aids. The company's pharmaceutical products include cardiovascular, anti-infective, and anticancer agents; AIDS therapy treatments; central nervous system drugs; and diagnostic agents. Its line of nonprescription products includes formulas, vitamins, analgesics, remedies, and skin care products sold under Bufferin, Excedrin, Nuprin, and Comtrex brand names. Beauty aids include Clairol and Ultress hair care and Nice n' Easy and Clairesse hair colorings, hair sprays, gels, and deodorants. **Corporate headquarters location:** New York NY. **Operations at this facility include:** This location is a pharmaceutical research facility. **Listed on:** New York Stock Exchange. **Stock exchange symbol:** BMY.

BROOKS LABORATORIES
9 Isaac Street, Norwalk CT 06850. 203/853-9792. **Contact:** Human Resources. **World Wide Web address:** http://www.brookslabs.com. **Description:** An environmental consulting firm and laboratory engaged in water testing, lead inspection, and air quality testing. **Positions advertised include:** Chemist.

J. BROWN/LMC GROUP
1010 Washington Boulevard, 8th Floor, Stamford CT 06901. 203/352-0600. **Contact:** Human Resources. **World Wide Web address:** http://www.jbrown.com. **Description:** An international engineering and construction firm serving the plastics, pharmaceutical, food, biotechnology, chemical, oil, and gas industries. **Other U.S. locations:** San Francisco CA; Chicago IL; Cincinnati OH. **Number of employees nationwide:** 185.

BROWNELL & COMPANY, INC.
423 East Adam, Moodus CT 06469. 860/873-8625. **Contact:** Human Resources. **World Wide Web address:** http://www.brownellco.com. **Description:** A producer of textiles. Principal products of Brownell & Company include twine and cordage, fishing nets, sport nets, air cargo restraint systems, archery bowstrings, camouflage netting, and helicopter nets. **Operations at this facility include:** Manufacturing.

BURNS INTERNATIONAL SECURITY SERVICES
1042 Main Street, East Hartford CT 06108. 860/289-6496. **Contact:** Human Resources. **World Wide Web address:** http://www.burnsintl.com. **Description:** Offers a wide range of protective services and contract security guard programs to businesses and government agencies. Burns International Security Services also provides electronic security systems and security planning consultation. **Parent company:** Burns International Services Corporation.

CDW
535 Connecticut Avenue, Norwalk CT 06854. 203/899-4000. **Fax:** 203/899-4242. **Contact:** Lisa Cristantiello, Director of Corporate Human Resources and Communication. **World Wide Web address:** http://www.warehouse.com. **Description:** Micro Warehouse is a specialty catalog and online retailer and direct marketer of brand name Macintosh and IBM-compatible personal computer software, accessories, and peripherals. Founded in 1987. **NOTE:** Entry-level positions are offered. **Special programs:** Internships. **Corporate headquarters location:** This location. **Other U.S. locations:** Gibbsboro NJ; Lakewood NJ; Wilmington OH. **International locations:** Canada; England; France; Germany; Mexico; Sweden; The Netherlands. **Operations at this facility include:** Administration; Sales. **Annual sales/revenues:** More than $100 million. **Number of employees at this location:** 600. **Number of employees nationwide:** 2,400. **Number of employees worldwide:** 3,500.

CTI ELECTRONICS CORPORATION
110 Old South Avenue, Stratford CT 06615. 203/386-9779. **Contact:** Human Resources. **World Wide Web address:** http://www.ctielectronics.com. **Description:** Manufactures computer peripherals including keyboards, trackballs, and joysticks. **Corporate headquarters location:** This location.

CARING COMMUNITY
84 Waterhole Road, Colchester CT 06415. 860/267-4463. **Contact:** Human Resources. **Description:** Operates group homes for the mentally retarded.

CARRIER CORPORATION
One Carrier Place, Farmington CT 06034-4015. 860/674-3000. **Contact:** Human Resources. **E-mail address:** great.jobs@carrier.utc.com. **World Wide Web address:** http://www.carrier.com. **Description:** Manufactures heating, refrigeration, and air conditioning equipment. **Positions advertised include:** Accountant/Auditor; Data Processor; Electrical/Electronics Engineer; Financial Analyst; Mechanical Engineer. **Corporate headquarters location:** This location.

THE WILLIAM CARTER COMPANY
1000 Bridgeport Avenue, P.O. Box 879, Shelton CT 06484. 203/926-5000. **Contact:** Human Resources. **World Wide Web address:** http://www.carters.com. **Description:** The William Carter Company manufactures and sells nationally-advertised apparel, primarily for children, under the Carter label. **Operations at this facility include:** This location houses financial offices.

CARVEL CORPORATION
175 Capital Boulevard, Suite 400, Rocky Hill CT 06067-4448. 860/257-4448. **Contact:** Human Resources. **World Wide Web address:** http://www.carvel.com. **Description:** Engaged in the manufacture of ice cream products and franchising operations for the chain of Carvel Ice Cream stores. **Corporate headquarters location:** This location.

CASCO PRODUCTS CORPORATION
One Waterview Drive, Shelton CT 06484. 203/922-3200. **Contact:** Human Resources. **World Wide Web address:** http://www.casco-schoeller.de. **Description:** Manufactures automotive cigarette lighters and related accessories.

CENTRAL CONNECTICUT STATE UNIVERSITY
1615 Stanley Street, New Britain CT 06050. 860/832-2278. **Contact:** Human Resources. **World Wide Web address:** http://www.ccsu.edu. **Description:** A four-year state university offering undergraduate and graduate degree programs. **Positions advertised include:** Associate Dean, School of Education and Professional Studies; Director of the Doctoral Program in Educational Leadership; Assistant Professor in Educational Leadership; Accountant; Sociologist.

CHUBB EXECUTIVE RISK INC.
555 Long Wharf Drive, P.O. Box 1903, New Haven CT 06511-5941. 203/782-4000. **Contact:** Human Resources. **World Wide Web address:** http://www.chubb.com. **Description:** Chubb Executive Risk is an insurance organization that markets and underwrites insurance coverage for executive and professional liability risks. **Positions advertised include:** Specialty Underwriting; Accountant; Claims Specialist; Customer Service Representative; Human Resources Representative; Loss Prevention Consultant. **Corporate headquarters location:** Warren NJ. **Listed on:** New York Stock Exchange. **Stock exchange symbol:** CB. **Number of employees worldwide:** 10,000.

CIGNA COMPANIES
900 Cottage Grove Road, Hartford CT 06152. 860/226-6000. **Contact:** Corporate Staffing. **Recorded jobline:** 860/226-3525. **World Wide Web address:** http://www.cigna.com. **Description:** Provides insurance and financial services to individuals and corporations worldwide. **Positions advertised include:** Lead Business Process Engineer; Sales Associate Trainee; Investment Advisor; Financial Analyst; Associate Investment Specialist; Senior Accountant. **Corporate headquarters location:** Philadelphia PA. **Subsidiaries include:** Connecticut General Life Insurance Corporation. **Parent company:** Cigna Corporation. **Listed on:** New York Stock Exchange. **Stock exchange symbol:** CI. **Number of employees worldwide:** 40,000.

CITIZENS BANK
237 Main Street, Middletown CT 06457. 860/639/4411. **Contact:** Human Resources. **World Wide Web address:** www.citizensbank.com. **Description:** Provides services in the areas of personal and commercial banking. **Positions advertised include:** Teller, Customer Service Representative, Loan Officer. **Corporate headquarters location:** Providence RI.

CITIZENS BANK
36 Fenn Road, Newington CT 06111. 860/666-7840. **Contact:** Human Resources. **World Wide Web address:** www.citizensbank.com. **Description:** Provides services in the areas of personal and commercial banking. **Positions advertised include:** Teller, Customer Service Representative, Loan Officer. **Corporate headquarters location:** Providence RI.

CITIZENS COMMUNICATIONS
3 High Ridge Park, Stamford CT 06905-1390. 203/614-5600. **Fax:** 203/614-4602. **Contact:** Christy O'Brien, Human Resources. **World Wide Web address:** http://www.czn.com. **Description:** A diversified public utility providing telecommunications, electric, gas, water, and wastewater treatment services nationwide. Founded in 1935. **Positions advertised include:** Manager, Revenue Accounting; Capital Budget and Recording Manager; Director, Labor Relations; Manager, Accounting; Tax Accountant; Senior Accountant; Financial Analyst; Senior Financial Analyst; Senior Accountant Capital. **Corporate headquarters location:** This location. **Listed on:** New York Stock Exchange. **Stock exchange symbol:** CZN. **Number of employees nationwide:** 2,300.

CLAIROL INC.
1 Blachley Road, Stamford CT 06922. 203/357-5000. **Contact:** Human Resources. **World Wide Web address:** http://www.clariol.com. **Description:** A worldwide marketer and manufacturer of hair care products for home and salon use. The company also manufactures beauty and personal care appliances. **Special programs:** Internships. **Corporate headquarters location:** This location. **Parent company:** Procter and Gamble.

CLEAN HARBORS ENVIRONMENTAL SERVICES
761 Middle Street, Bristol CT 06010. 860/583-8917. **Contact:** Human Resources. **World Wide Web address:** http://www.cleanharbors.com. **Description:** Clean Harbors, Inc., through its subsidiaries, provides a wide range of hazardous waste management and environmental support services to a diversified customer base. The company's services include treatment, storage, recycling, transportation, risk analysis, site assessment, laboratory analysis, site closure, and disposal of hazardous materials through environmentally sound methods including incineration. Environmental remediation services include emergency response, surface remediation, groundwater restoration, industrial maintenance, and facility decontamination. **Positions advertised include:** Field Service Foreman; Class A Driver; Field Technician. **Corporate headquarters location:** Braintree MA. **Other U.S. locations:** Nationwide. **Listed on:** NASDAQ. **Stock exchange symbol:** CLHB. **Number of employees nationwide:** 1,400.

CLINICAL LABORATORY PARTNERS
129 Patricia M. Genova Drive, Newington CT 06111. 860/696-8020. **Toll-free phone:** 800/286-9800. **Contact:** Human Resources. **World Wide Web address:** http://www.clinicallabpartners.com. **Description:** A laboratory that performs several different physician-ordered tests on blood.

CLUB HOTEL BY DOUBLETREE
789 Connecticut Avenue, Norwalk CT 06854. 203/853-3477. **Fax:** 203/855-9404. **Contact:** Human Resources. **World Wide Web address:** http://www.doubletree.com. **Description:** A 268-room business hotel operating as part of the Doubletree chain.

COE & BROWN COMPANY
P.O. Box 4215, Hamden CT 06514-0215. 203/288-9211. **Physical address:** 295 Treadwell Street, Hamden CT 06514. **Contact:** Human Resources. **Description:** A wholesale distributor of a wide range of industrial supplies.

COGNITRONICS CORPORATION
3 Corporate Drive, Danbury CT 06810. 203/830-3400. **Contact:** Janet Freund, Director of Human Resources. **World Wide Web address:** http://www.cognitronics.com. **Description:** Designs, manufactures, and markets voice processing systems. Products include passive announcers, which are used by telephone operating companies to inform callers about network conditions or procedures; intelligent announcers, which are primarily used by telephone companies to provide voice announcements in connection with custom calling features, such as selective call forwarding and caller originator trace; interactive voice response; audiotex, a UNIX-based voice processing platform; and call processing, automated attendant, and audiotex systems. **Corporate headquarters location:** This location. **Subsidiaries include:** Dacon Electronics, Private Legal Counsel. **Listed on:** American Stock Exchange. **Stock exchange symbol:** CGN. **Number of employees nationwide:** 80.

COHEN & WOLF
1115 Broad Street, Bridgeport CT 06604. 203/368-0211. **Contact:** Hiring Partner. **World Wide Web address:** http://www.cohenandwolf.com. **Description:** A law firm with 25 attorneys on staff. Cohen & Wolf offers corporate and personal legal services in a variety of disciplines. **Special programs:** Summer jobs. **Other area locations:** Danbury CT; Stamford CT; Westport CT.

COMMUNITY ACTION COMMITTEE OF DANBURY
66 North Street, Danbury CT 06810. 203/744-4700. **Contact:** Human Resources. **Description:** A nonprofit organization that provides daycare, heating assistance, Head Start programs, counseling, bill payment assistance, and rental assistance services to low-income families.

COMMUNITY RENEWAL TEAM (CRT)
555 Windsor Street, Hartford CT 06120. 860/560-5600. **Fax:** 860/560-5664. **Contact:** Human Resources. **World Wide Web address:** http://www.crtct.org. **Description:** Provides employment education and energy assistance to community residents. The agency also administers Head Start daycare at other locations throughout the community. **Positions advertised include:** Internal Auditor; Medical Advocate; Recreation Coordinator; Part-Time Counselor; Case Manager; Program Nurse.

COMPUTER ASSOCIATES INTERNATIONAL, INC.
1351 Washington Boulevard, Suite 800, Stamford CT 06902. 203/352-6800. **Toll-free phone:** 800/243-9462. **Fax:** 203/937-3015. **Contact:** Human Resources. **World Wide Web address:** http://www.ca.com. **Description:** Computer Associates International is one of the world's leading developers of client/server and distributed computing software. The company develops, markets, and supports enterprise management, database and applications development, business applications, and consumer software products for a broad range of mainframe, midrange, and desktop computers. Computer Associates International serves major business, government, research, and educational organizations. **Positions advertised include:** Sales Executive; Customer Relationship Manager. **Corporate headquarters location:** Islandia NY. **Other U.S. locations:** Nationwide. **Listed on:** New York Stock Exchange. **Stock exchange symbol:** CA. **Annual sales/revenues:** More than $100 million.

COMPUTER ASSOCIATES INTERNATIONAL, INC.
Hartfield Executive Park, 160 Bridge Street, Suite 300, East Windsor CT 06088. 860/627-8932. **Contact:** Human Resources. **World Wide Web address:** http://www.cai.com. **Description:** Computer Associates International is one of the world's leading developers of client/server and distributed computing software. The company develops, markets, and supports enterprise management, database and applications development, business applications, and consumer software products for a broad range of mainframe, midrange, and desktop computers. Computer Associates International serves major business, government, research, and educational organizations. **Corporate headquarters location:** Islandia NY. **Other U.S. locations:** Nationwide. **Listed on:** New York Stock Exchange. **Stock exchange symbol:** CA. **Annual sales/revenues:** More than $100 million.

COMPUTER HORIZONS CORPORATION
500 Winding Brook Drive, Glastonbury CT 06033. 860/633-4646. **Fax:** 860/657-9817. **Contact:** Personnel. **World Wide Web address:** http://www.computerhorizons.com. **Description:** A full-service technology solutions company offering contract staffing, outsourcing, re-engineering, migration, downsizing support, and network management. **Corporate headquarters location:** Mountain Lakes NJ. **Other U.S. locations:** Nationwide. **Listed on:** NASDAQ. **Stock exchange symbol:** CHRZ. **Number of employees nationwide:** 3,600.

CONAIR CORPORATION
One Cummings Point Road, Stamford CT 06902. 203/351-9000. **Fax:** 203/351-9134. **Contact:** Human Resources. **World Wide Web address:** http://www.conair.com. **Description:** Manufactures and distributes a wide range of personal and health care appliances. **Positions advertised include:** Regional Sales Manager; Sales Operation Administrator; Marketing Manager; Administrative Assistant; Electronics Engineer; Financial Manager. **Corporate headquarters location:** This location. **Listed on:** Privately held. **Number of employees at this location:** 270. **Number of employees nationwide:** 1,100.

CONNECTICUT COALITION AGAINST DOMESTIC VIOLENCE
90 Pitkin Street, East Hartford CT 06108. 860/282-7899. **Fax:** 860/282-7892. **Contact:** Executive Director. **World Wide Web address:** http://www.ctcadv.org. **Description:** Provides support services to battered women and their children. **Positions advertised include:** Family Violence Victim Advocate; Community Educator; Program Advocacy Specialist. **Parent company:** National Coalition Against Domestic Violence is a nonprofit public education and advocacy organization and a coalition of direct service programs. The coalition works toward the prevention of domestic violence by bringing about societal change. Activities of the coalition include public education and advocacy, technical assistance to member groups, information and technical assistance to public agencies and legislative committees, and professional training for law enforcement and human service workers. In addition, the coalition staff prepares policy statements and offers assistance and expertise in the preparation of protocols and practices for a wide variety of public and private entities.

CONNECTICUT DEPARTMENT OF SOCIAL SERVICES
401 West Thames Street, Unit 102, Norwich CT 06360. 860/823-5050. **Toll free phone:** 800/473-8909. **Contact:** Human Resources. **World Wide Web address:** http://www.dss.state.ct.us. **Description:** Assists the elderly, disabled, families, and individuals through the Rehabilitation Act, the Food Stamps Act, the Older Americans Act, the Social Security Act, and the state welfare program.

CONNECTICUT LIMO
230 Old Gate Lane, Milford CT 06460. 203/878-6800. **Fax:** 203/783-6992. **Contact:** Human Resources. **E-mail address:** employment@ctlimo.com. **World Wide Web address:** http://www.ctlimo.com. **Description:** A shuttle bus service that provides transportation to and from John F. Kennedy International Airport (New York NY); LaGuardia International Airport (New York NY); Newark International Airport (Newark NJ); and Bradley International Airport (Windsor Locks CT.) **Positions advertised include:** Reservation Agent; Mechanic. **Corporate headquarters location:** This location.

CONNECTICUT NATURAL GAS CORPORATION
77 Hartland Street, 4th Floor, East Hartford CT 06108-6201. 860/727-3000. **Contact:** Human Resources. **World Wide Web address:** http://www.cngcorp.com. **Description:** A major distributor of natural gas in Connecticut, serving over 140,000 customers in the Greater Hartford and Greenwich areas. **Corporate headquarters location:** This location. **Subsidiaries include:** CNG Realty Corporation; ENI Transmission Company; Energy Networks, Inc. **Parent company:** Energy East. **Number of employees nationwide:** 640.

CONNECTICUT ON-LINE COMPUTER CENTER, INC.
135 Darling Drive, Avon CT 06001. 860/678-0444. **Fax:** 860/677-1169. **Contact:** Sue W. Kittredge, Director of Human Resources. **World Wide Web address:** http://www.cocc.com. **Description:** A data processing service bureau for the banking industry. The company serves banks throughout New England and New York State. **NOTE:** Entry-level positions are offered. **Positions advertised include:** IT Internal

Audit Specialist; Reconcilement Clerk; Database Administrator. **Corporate headquarters location:** This location. **Listed on:** Privately held. **Annual sales/revenues:** $11 - $20 million. **Number of employees at this location:** 250.

THE CONNECTICUT POST
410 State Street, Bridgeport CT 06604. 203/333-0161. **Contact:** Human Resources. **World Wide Web address:** http://www.connpost.com. **Description:** A newspaper with a daily circulation of 77,000 and a Sunday circulation of 97,000. **Corporate headquarters location:** This location.

CONNECTICUT PUBLIC BROADCASTING
1049 Asylum Avenue, Hartford CT 06105. 860/278-5310. **Fax:** 860/278-2157. **Contact:** Carol Sisco, Human Resources. **E-mail address:** csisco@cptv.org. **World Wide Web address:** http://www.cpbi.org. **Description:** A member of PBS (Public Broadcasting Service) that carries a complete schedule of PBS programming, as well as programs purchased from other national sources. **Positions advertised include:** Vice President of Development; Special Events Assistant; Announcer/Board Operator. **Other area locations:** New Haven CT.

CONNECTICUT STEEL
35 Toelles Road, P.O. Box 928, Wallingford CT 06492. 203/265-0615. **Contact:** Tracy Guyette, Human Resources Manager. **E-mail address:** tguyette@connecticutsteel.com. **World Wide Web address:** http://www.connecticutsteel.com. **Description:** A mini-rolling mill that manufactures products such as steel rods. **Corporate headquarters location:** This location.

CONNECTICUT WATER COMPANY
93 West Main Street, Clinton CT 06413. 860/669-8636. **Fax:** 860.669-7328. **Contact:** Human Resources Department. **World Wide Web address:** http://www.ctwater.com. **Description:** Connecticut Water Company supplies water to over 60,000 residential, commercial, industrial, and municipal consumers throughout 31 towns in three regions of Connecticut: Naugatuck, Northern, and Shoreline. Connecticut Water Company is environmentally conscious, practicing source protection, land acquisition and management, and in-reservoir treatment through modern treatment facilities, distribution system maintenance, a leak detection program, conservation management, and certified staff members. **Parent company:** Connecticut Water Service, Inc. **Listed on:** NASDAQ. **Stock exchange symbol:** CTWS. **Number of employees at this location:** 165.

CORPORATE INFORMATION TECHNOLOGIES
314 Farmington Avenue, Suite 130, Farmington CT 06032. 860/676-2720. **Fax:** 860/676-8273. **Contact:** Human Resources. **World Wide Web address:** http://www.corpit.com. **Description:** Provides computer consulting services and software solutions to healthcare, insurance, and technology companies. Corporate Information technologies' services include application development and project management; desktop/LAN support; Helpdesk support; Mainframe support; Network administration and architecture; server/application hosting and administration; and Website and e-business development, programming, and hosting.

COURTYARD BY MARRIOTT
63 Grand Street, Waterbury CT 06702. 203/596-1000. **Fax:** 203/753-6276. **Contact:** Human Resources. **World Wide Web address:** http://www.courtyard.com. **Description:** One location of the hotel chain offering 200 rooms, a business center, and four restaurants. **Positions advertised include:** Banquet Chef. **Other U.S. locations:** Nationwide.

COURTYARD BY MARRIOTT
136 Marsh Hill Road, Orange CT 06477. 203/799-2200. **Fax:** 203/799-2626. **Contact:** Human Resources. **Description:** One location of the full-service hotel/conference facility chain. **Other U.S. locations:** Nationwide.

COX RADIO, INC.
444 Westport Avenue, 3rd Floor, Norwalk CT 06851. 203/845-3630. **Fax:** 203/845-3097. **Contact:** Human Resources. **World Wide Web address:** http://www.coxradio.com. **Description:** Owns and operates more than 15 radio stations. **Corporate headquarters location:** Atlanta GA. **Listed on:** New York Stock Exchange. **Stock exchange symbol:** CXR.

CRANE CO.
100 First Stamford Place, 4th Floor East, Stamford CT 06902. 203/363-7300. **Contact:** Human Resources. **E-mail address:** careers@craneco.com. **World Wide Web address:** http://www.craneco.com. **Description:** Manufactures fiberglass-reinforced panels, vending machines, water filtration and conditioning systems, pumps, valves, and coin machines for a variety of industries. **Subsidiaries include:** Hydro-Aire develops and manufactures brake systems, fuel pumps, and other products primarily for the aerospace industry; Huttig Sash & Door operates 47 branch warehouses across the United States. **Listed on:** New York Stock Exchange. **Stock exchange symbol:** CR.

CROMPTON CORPORATION
199 Benson Road, Middlebury CT 06749. 203/573-2000. **Contact:** Human Resources. **World Wide Web address:** http://www.cromptoncorp.com. **Description:** A manufacturer of specialty chemical and petroleum products. Products are used primarily as intermediates by other manufacturers in hundreds of industries such as personal care and household products, agricultural, automotive, housing and construction, packaging, food, and textiles. **Corporate headquarters location:** This location. **Other area locations:** Greenwich CT; Naugatuck CT. **Other U.S. locations:** Nationwide. **International locations:** Worldwide. **Listed on:** New York Stock Exchange. **Stock exchange symbol:** CK.

CROMPTON CORPORATION
DAVIS STANDARD CORPORATION
#1 Extrusion Drive, Pawcatuck CT 06379. 860/599-1010. **Contact:** Human Resources. **World Wide Web address:** http://www.cromptoncorp.com. **Description:** A manufacturer of specialty chemical and petroleum products. Products are used primarily as intermediates by other manufacturers in hundreds of industries such as personal care and household products, agricultural, automotive, housing and construction, packaging, food, and textiles. **Corporate headquarters location:** Middlebury CT. **Other area locations:** Naugatuck CT. **Other U.S. locations:** Nationwide. **International locations:** Worldwide. **Listed on:** New York Stock Exchange. **Stock exchange symbol:** CK. **Number of employees worldwide:** 7,300.

CRONIN & COMPANY
50 Nye Road, Glastonbury CT 06033. 860/659-0514. **Contact:** Human Resources. **E-mail address:** hr@cronin-co.com. **World Wide Web address:** http://www.cronin-co.com. **Description:** An advertising, direct marketing, and public relations firm. **Positions advertised include:** Rainmaker; Computer Production Artist. **Special programs:** Internships.

DHL
120 Tokeneke Road, Darien CT 06820. 203/655-7900. **Contact:** Human Resources. **World Wide Web address:** http://www.dhl.com. **Description:** An international freight forwarder, serving customers in over 135 countries. **NOTE:** Call 954/888-7000 for Human Resources. **Corporate headquarters location:** Plantation FL. **Other U.S. locations:** Nationwide.

DANAHER TOOL GROUP
125 Powder Forest Drive, P.O. Box 2004, Simsbury CT 06070. 860/843-7300. **Contact:** Human Resources. **World Wide Web address:** http://www.danaher.com. **Description:** Danaher is a producer of hand tools, automotive and transportation products, and process and environmental controls. The Danaher Tools segment manufactures tools, holders, and fasteners for industrial, professional, and consumer markets under brand names including Allen, Sears Craftsman, K-D, and NAPA. Danaher also builds control and detection systems, sensors, monitors, and measuring systems. **Corporate headquarters location:** Washington DC. **Subsidiaries include:** Fayette Tubular manufactures air conditioning equipment. Hennesey Industries manufactures a variety of automotive components including wheel aligners and balancers and brake parts. **Listed on:** New York Stock Exchange. **Stock exchange symbol:** DHR.

DANBURY, CITY OF
City Hall, 155 Deer Hill Avenue, Danbury CT 06810. 203/797-4500. **Contact:** Human Resources. **World Wide Web address:** http://www.ci.danbury.ct.us. **Description:** The administrative offices for the City of Danbury.

DEITSCH PLASTIC
14 Farwell Street, West Haven CT 06516. 203/934-6601. **Contact:** Human Resources. **World Wide Web address:** http://www.deitschplastic.com. **Description:** Manufactures plastic parts and components used in shoes, furniture, and handbags.

DELOITTE & TOUCHE
10 Westport Road, P.O. Box 820, Wilton CT 06897-0820. 203/761-3000. **Fax:** 203/761-3062. **Contact:** Human Resources. **World Wide Web address:** http://www.us.deloitte.com. **Description:** An international firm of certified public accountants providing professional accounting, auditing, tax, and management consulting services to widely diversified clients. The company has a specialized program consisting of national industry groups and functional groups that cross industry lines. Groups are involved in various disciplines including accounting, auditing, taxation management advisory services, small and growing businesses, mergers and acquisitions, and computer applications. **Positions advertised include:** Administrator; Administrative Compliance Auditor; Administrative Project Specialist; Administrative U.S. National. **Special programs:** Internships. **Corporate headquarters location:** This location. **Other U.S. locations:** Nationwide. **Parent company:** Deloitte Touche Tohmatsu International. **Number of employees worldwide:** 95,000.

DELOITTE & TOUCHE
185 Asylum Street, 33rd Floor, Hartford CT 06103. 860/280-3000. **Contact:** Human Resources. **World Wide Web address:** http://www.us.deloitte.com. **Description:** An international firm of certified public accountants providing professional accounting, auditing, tax, and management consulting services to widely diversified clients. The company has a specialized program consisting of national industry groups and functional groups that cross industry lines. Groups are involved in various disciplines including accounting, auditing, taxation management advisory services, small and growing businesses, mergers and acquisitions, and computer applications. **Corporate headquarters location:** Wilton CT. **Parent company:** Deloitte Touche Tohmatsu International. **Number of employees worldwide:** 95,000.

DEPARTMENT OF MENTAL HEALTH AND ADDICTION SERVICES
410 Capitol Avenue, P.O. Box 341431, Hartford CT 06134. 860/418-7000. **Toll-free phone:** 800/446-7348. **Contact:** Human Resources. **World Wide Web address:** http://www.dmhas.state.ct.us. **Description:** The Department of Mental Health is an agency dedicated to promoting and supporting the ability of all persons with mental disabilities. The department works with its constituents -- consumers, family members, and citizen advisory groups -- to operate a system of mental health care for all adults with mental disabilities who lack the financial means to secure adequate services on their own. The Department of Mental Health implements, coordinates, and supports homeless programs, rental assistance, and other supportive housing programs, rehabilitative programs, residential programs, assertive community treatment programs, case management services, clinical services, crisis programs, AIDS education and treatment programs, criminal justice liaison programs, educational programs, public education activities, and human resource development programs. **Positions advertised include:** Clinical Nurse; Nurse Clinical Specialist. **Special programs:** Internships. **Corporate headquarters location:** This location. **Number of employees at this location:** 150. **Number of employees nationwide:** 2,000.

DERINGER - NEY INC
2 Douglas Street, Ney Industrial Park, Bloomfield CT 06002. 860/242-2281. **Toll-free phone:** 888/JMNEY4U. **Fax:** 860/286-6113. **Contact:** Human Resources. **E-mail address:** hr@jmney.com. **World Wide Web address:** http://www.jmney.com. **Description:** A manufacturer of electronic components. Founded in 1812. **NOTE:** Second and third shifts are offered. **Special programs:** Apprenticeships. **Office hours:** Monday - Friday, 7:00 a.m. - 5:00 p.m. **Corporate headquarters location:** This location. **Facilities Manager:** John Donzella. **Information Systems Manager:** Bernie Cunningham. **Sales Manager:** Ken Beilstein. **Annual sales/revenues:** $21 - $50 million. **Number of employees at this location:** 165.

DIANON SYSTEMS, INC.
200 Watson Boulevard, Stratford CT 06615. 203/381-4000. **Toll-free phone:** 800/328-2666. **Contact:** Cynthia Yuhlan, Human Resources. **World Wide Web address:** http://www.dianon.com **Description:** A provider of testing services and diagnostic information to focused physician audiences in the United States and Europe. A wide range of laboratory tests are offered, with applications in the screening, diagnosis, prognosis, and monitoring of cancer and genetic disorders. Screening tests include those for congenital abnormalities; prostate, bladder, and ovarian cancer; and kidney disease. Prognostic testing is available for patients for whom a diagnosis has already been made regarding prostate cancer, bladder cancer, breast cancer, colon cancer, leukemia, and lymphoma. Monitoring tests are used to detect recurrent tumors and to estimate the response to therapy. **NOTE:** Does not accept resumes. Fill out online application. **Corporate headquarters location:** This location. **Other U.S. locations:** AZ; GA; MD; OH; TX. **International locations:** Amsterdam; France; Germany. **Listed on:** NASDAQ. **Stock exchange symbol:** DIAN. **Number of employees nationwide:** 300.

DICTAPHONE CORPORATION
3191 Broadbridge Avenue, Stratford CT 06614-2559. 203/381-7000. **Contact:** Human

Resources. **World Wide Web address:** http://www.dictaphone.com. **Description:** Dictaphone consists of three business units: the Healthcare Solutions Group, the Communications Recording Systems Group, and the Integrated Voice Systems Division. **NOTE:** Search and apply for positions online. **Positions advertised include:** Supervisor, Medical Record Transcription; Sr. Client Server Developer; Transcriptionist; Associate Human Resources Generalist; Sales Development Manager.

DIRECT MEDIA, INC.
200 Pemberwick Road, Greenwich CT 06830. 203/532-1000. **Contact:** Human Resources. **World Wide Web address:** http://www.directmedia.com. **Description:** Provides direct marketing services such as list management and brokerage. **Positions advertised include:** Copywriter; Package Insert Coordinator; Insert Media Sales Specialist; List Management Account Executive. **Corporate headquarters location:** This location. **Other U.S. locations:** Conway AR; Walnut Creek CA; Schaumburg IL; Merriam KS; Port Chester NY. **International locations:** Toronto, Ontario. **Number of employees worldwide:** 300.

DNE TECHNOLOGIES, INC.
50 Barnes Park North, Wallingford CT 06492. 203/265-7151. **Toll-free phone:** 800/370-4485. **Contact:** Ron Hanley, Director of Human Resources. **E-mail address:** rhanley@dne.com. **World Wide Web address:** http://www.dnetech.com. **Description:** Designs, manufactures, tests, and markets electronic and communication products and systems for the military, government, and commercial sectors. Products include multiplexors, cryptographic equipment, and signal-terminating units used for voice and data communications, both in tactical and secure office environments. Avionics products include electrical controllers, aerial refueling amplifiers, and various sensors that are used in military aircraft. **Parent company:** Superior Telecommunications. **Number of employees at this location:** 130.

DOW CHEMICAL COMPANY
39 Old Ridgebury Road, Danbury CT 06817. 203/794-2000. **Contact:** Human Resources. **World Wide Web address:** http://www.dow.com. **Description:** Dow Chemical Corporation is a science and technology company providing chemical, plastic, and agricultural products and services to consumer markets. **Parent Company:** The Dow Chemical Company.

DRESSER INDUSTRIES
250 East Main Street, Stratford CT 06614. 203/378-8281. **Contact:** Human Resources. **World Wide Web address:** http://www.dresserinstruments.com. **Description:** Manufactures pressure and temperature instruments and controls for a variety of customers. Dresser Industries supplies engineered products and technical services throughout the world. **Other area locations:** Shelton CT.

DURACELL, INC.
Berkshire Corporate Park, Bethel CT 06801. 203/796-4000. **Contact:** Human Resources. **World Wide Web address:** http://www.duracell.com. **Description:** Manufactures a line of batteries sold worldwide under the Duracell trademark. Battery types include alkaline, zinc, rechargeable, and lithium. The company also manufactures batteries used in hearing aids and photographic and communications equipment. A subsidiary conducts marketing operations for a line of lighting products under the Durabeam name. **Corporate headquarters location:** This location. **Other U.S. locations:** Alpharetta GA; Boston MA. **Parent company:** The Gillette Company.

EEW MANAGEMENT
P.O. Box 1548, Torrington CT 06790. 860/489-7575. **Physical address:** 715 Main Street, Torrington CT 06790. **Contact:** Human Resources. **World Wide Web address:** http://www.eewm.com. **Description:** Engaged in the removal and disposal of hazardous waste material.

ESPN INC.
935 Middle Street, Bristol CT 06010. 860/585-2000. **Contact:** Human Resources. **World Wide Web address:** http://www.espn.go.com. **Description:** Operates the ESPN, ESPN2, and ESPN Classic all-sports networks. **Corporate headquarters location:** This location.

EASTER SEALS
GOODWILL INDUSTRIES REHABILITATION CENTER
71 Orange Street, New Haven CT 06510. 203/770-2010. **Contact:** Director. **World Wide Web address:** http://www.volunteersolutions.org. **Description:** Easter Seals provides treatment and support services for disabled individuals. Goodwill Industries Rehabilitation Center (also at this location) provides employment training and operates 1,400 retail stores nationwide.

THE EASTERN COMPANY
112 Bridge Street, P.O. Box 460, Naugatuck CT 06770-0460. 203/729-2255. **Contact:** Human Resources. **World Wide Web address:** http://www.easterncompany.com. **Description:** The Eastern Company manufactures locks and security hardware engineered for use in industry, underground mining, and commercial construction. **Corporate headquarters location:** This location. **Subsidiaries include:** CCL Security Products Division (New Britain CT), The Illinois Lock Company Division (Wheeling IL), and World Lock Company Ltd. (Taipei, Taiwan) manufacture custom locks; Eberhard Manufacturing (Cleveland OH) and Eberhard Hardware Manufacturing, Ltd. (Ontario, Canada) produce transportation and industrial hardware; Frazer & Jones (Syracuse NY) manufactures mine roof fasteners and contract castings. **Listed on:** American Stock Exchange. **Stock exchange symbol:** EML. **Number of employees nationwide:** 475.

AG EDWARDS & SONS
2960 Post Road, Southport CT 06890. 203/255-6881. **Contact:** Human Resources. **World Wide Web address:** http://www.agedwards.com. **Description:** An investment firm offering bonds, money market accounts, mutual funds, IRAs, annuities, estate planning, and related services. **Corporate headquarters location:** St. Louis MO. **Other U.S. locations:** Nationwide. **Listed on:** New York Stock Exchange. **Stock exchange symbol:** AGE. **CEO:** Robert L. Bagby. **Number of employees nationwide:** 15,400.

EMCOR GROUP, INC.
301 Merritt Seven, 6th Floor, Norwalk CT 06851. 203/849-7800. **Contact:** Elissa Hall, Human Resources. **World Wide Web address:** http://www.emcorgroup.com. **Description:** Emcor is a diversified business services company engaged primarily in developing, integrating, and maintaining electrical and mechanical systems for the commercial construction industry. In addition to electrical and mechanical construction services, the company also provides complete facilities management services across a number of market sectors, including healthcare, hotels/hospitality, education, government/public, transportation, water/wastewater, pharmaceutical, and others. **Positions advertised include:** Desktop Support Specialist. **Corporate headquarters location:** This location. **Other U.S. locations:** Nationwide. **International locations:** Worldwide. **Listed on:** New York Stock Exchange. **Stock exchange symbol:** EME.

EMSAR, INC.
125 Access Road, Stratford CT 06615. 203/377-8100. **Contact:** Human Resources. **World Wide Web address:** http://www.emsargroup.com. **Description:** Manufactures pumps for products with aerosol sprays. **Other U.S. locations:** North Hollywood CA; Northfield IL. **International locations:** Worldwide. **Parent company:** AptarGroup, Inc.

ENGINEERING RESOURCES GROUP, LLC
37 Cherry Blossom Lane, Shelton CT 06484. 203/922-8198. **Contact:** Human Resources. **E-mail address:** engrgroup@aol.com. **World Wide Web address:** http://www.engrgroup.com. **Description:** A plastics industry. **Positions advertised include:** Sales Manager. **Corporate headquarters location:** This location.

ENVIROMED SERVICES
470 Murdock Avenue, Box 13, Meriden CT 06450. 203/786-5580. **Contact:** Personnel. **World Wide Web address:** http://www.enviromedservices.com. **Description:** Provides environmental consulting services.

ERNST & YOUNG LLP
Goodwin Square, 225 Asylum Street, Hartford CT 06103. 860/247-3100. **Contact:** Human Resources. **World Wide Web address:** http://www.ey.com. **Description:** A certified public accounting firm that also provides management consulting services. Services include data processing, financial modeling, financial feasibility studies, production planning and inventory management, management sciences, health care planning, human resources, cost accounting, and budgeting systems. **NOTE:** Mail resumes to 200 Clarendon Street, Boston MA 02116. **Positions advertised include:** Tax Compliance Manager; Tax Compliance Senior. **Special programs:** Internships. **Other U.S. locations:** Nationwide. **International locations:** Worldwide.

ETHAN ALLEN INC.
Ethan Allen Drive, Danbury CT 06811. 203/743-8000. **Contact:** Charles Farfaglia, Human Resources. **World Wide Web address:** http://www.ethanallen.com. **Description:** An international retailer of home furnishings operating approximately 350 retail locations. Founded in 1932. **Positions advertised include:** Retail Production Coordinator; Merchandise Manager, Soft Goods; Advertising Production Manager; Interior Design/Sales Professional; Designer, Store Planner. **Corporate headquarters location:** This location. **Listed on:** New York Stock Exchange. **Stock exchange symbol:** ETH.

EYELET DESIGN
574 East Main Street, P.O. Box 808, Waterbury CT 06702. 203/754-4141. **Contact:** Human Resources. **World Wide Web address:** http://www.eyeletdesign.com. **Description:** Eyelet Design produces glass containers, containerboard, corrugated containers, printing plates and ink, plywood and dimension lumber, blown plastic containers, plastic beverage bottles, plastic drums, metal and plastic closures, tamper-resistant closures, plastic and glass prescription containers, pharmaceutical items, labels, and multipack plastic carriers for containers. **Operations at this facility include:** This location manufactures aluminum caps and color tubes.

FAIRFIELD UNIVERSITY
1073 North Benson Road, Fairfield CT 06430. 203/254-4000. **Fax:** 203/254-4295. **Contact:** Office of Human Resources. **World Wide Web address:** http://www.fairfield.edu. **Description:** A four-year Jesuit university providing both undergraduate and graduate programs. Founded in 1942. **NOTE:** Entry-level positions, part-time jobs, and second and third shifts are offered. **Special programs:** Internships. **Corporate headquarters location:** This location. **Number of employees at this location:** 800.

FARMSTEAD TELEPHONE GROUP, INC.
22 Prestige Park Circle, East Hartford CT 06108. 860/610-6000. **Toll-free phone:** 888/610-6020. **Contact:** Human Resources. **World Wide Web address:** http://www.farmstead.com. **Description:** A secondary market reseller of used and/or refurbished AT&T business telephone parts and systems. The company is also a designer, manufacturer, and supplier of proprietary voice processing systems that provide automated call handling, voice and fax messaging, interactive voice response, automated call distribution, and message notification functionality. Farmstead Telephone also provides inventory management, leasing and rental services, disaster recovery services, in-house maintenance training, and other related value-added services to customers worldwide. These products and services are primarily sold to end users, ranging from small companies to large corporations including equipment wholesalers, dealers, distributors, and government agencies and municipalities. **Corporate headquarters location:** This location. **Other U.S. locations:** Nationwide. **Listed on:** American Stock Exchange. **Stock exchange symbol:** FTG.

FARREL CORPORATION
25 Main Street, Ansonia CT 06401. 203/736-5500. **Contact:** Human Resources. **World Wide Web address:** http://www.farrel.com. **Description:** Designs, manufactures, sells, and services machinery and associated equipment used in the processing and conversion of rubber and plastics. Along with sales of capital equipment, Farrel provides process engineering, process design, and related services for rubber and plastics installations. Aftermarket services consist of repair, refurbishment and upgrade, spare parts sales, and field services. **Corporate headquarters location:** This location. **Other U.S. locations:** Charlotte NC; Akron OH; Deer Park TX. **International locations:** Australia; England; Singapore.

FAST (FOOD AUTOMATION-SERVICE TECHNIQUES, INC.)
905 Honeyspot Road, Stratford CT 06615. 203/377-4414. **Fax:** 203/377-5515. **Contact:** Human Resources. **E-mail address:** pbalkonis@fastinc.com. **World Wide Web address:** http://www.fastinc.com. **Description:** A developer and manufacturer of electronic control systems and timers for the food service industry. **Positions advertised include:** Production Planner. **Special programs:** Co-ops. **Corporate headquarters location:** This location.

FEDERAL BUREAU OF INVESTIGATION (FBI)
600 State Street, New Haven CT 06511. 203/777-6311. **Contact:** Applicant Coordinator. **World Wide Web address:** http://www.fbi.gov. **Description:** The Federal Bureau of Investigation (FBI) is a federal law enforcement agency. Their special agents carry out the responsibilities of the FBI by enforcing more than 260 federal statutes. This involves conducting investigations in organized crime, white-collar crime, civil rights violations, bank robbery, kidnapping, terrorism, foreign counterintelligence, fugitive and drug trafficking matters, and many other violations against federal statutes. **Special programs:** Internships. **Corporate headquarters location:** Washington DC. **Other U.S. locations:** Nationwide.

FEDEX
347 State Street, North Haven CT 06473. **Toll-free phone:** 800/GoF-edEx. **Contact:** Human Resources. **World Wide Web address:** http://www.fedex.com. **Description:** One of the world's largest express transportation companies serving 212 countries worldwide. FedEx ships approximately 3 million packages daily through an operating fleet of over 600 aircraft, 39,500 vehicles, 2,000 ship sites, 33,800 drop boxes, and Internet shipping. **Corporate headquarters location:** Memphis TN. **Other U.S. locations:** Nationwide. **Listed on:** New York Stock Exchange. **Stock exchange symbol:** FDX.

FIBEROPTICS TECHNOLOGY INC.
1 Quasset Road, Pomfret CT 06258. 860/928-0443. **Toll-free phone:** 800/433-5248. **Contact:** Human Resources. **World Wide Web address:** http://www.fiberoptix.com. **Description:** Manufactures fiber optics for use in industrial and medical applications.

FILENE'S DEPARTMENT STORE
575 Union Street, Waterbury CT 06702. 203/757-1131. **Contact:** Human Resources. **World Wide Web address:** http://www.mayco.com/fi. **Description:** A fashion department store with 44 locations in the New England/New York area. **Positions advertised include:** General Sales Associate; Commission Sales Associate; Cosmetics Beauty Advisor. **Parent company:** May Department Stores Company.

FIRE-LITE ALARMS, INC./NOTIFIER
One Fire-Lite Place, Northford CT 06472. 203/484-7161. **Fax:** 203/484-1037. **Contact:** Joan Nichols, Human Resources Manager. **World Wide Web address:** http://www.firelite.com. **Description:** Manufactures fire alarm control panels and smoke system detectors. **Parent company:** Honeywell. **Number of employees at this location:** 325.

FISERV, INC.
151 National Drive, Glastonbury CT 06033. 860/633-9990. **Contact:** Human Resources. **World Wide Web address:** http://www.fiserv.com. **Description:** FiServ, Inc. provides data processing services to banks and credit institutions. The company also offers PC banking and e-commerce technology. **Positions advertised include:** Product Specialist. **Corporate headquarters location:** Brookfield WI. **Other U.S. locations:** Nationwide. **Listed on:** NASDAQ. **Stock exchange symbol:** FISV. **Number of employees nationwide:** 16,000.

FISERV, INC.
4 Fairfield Boulevard, Wallingford CT 06492. 203/265-3455. **Contact:** Human Resources. **World Wide Web address:** http://www.fiserv.com. **Description:** FiServ, Inc. provides data processing services to banks and credit institutions. The company also offers PC banking and e-commerce technology. **Corporate headquarters location:** Brookfield WI. **Other U.S. locations:** Nationwide. **Operations at this facility include:** Administration; Research and Development; Sales; Service. **Listed on:** NASDAQ. **Stock exchange symbol:** FISV. **Number of employees at this location:** 300. **Number of employees nationwide:** 16,000.

FLUIDYNE ANSONIA
One Riverside Drive, Ansonia CT 06401. 203/735-9311. **Toll-free phone:** 800/765-2676. **Fax:** 203/736-3489. **Contact:** Human Resources. **World Wide Web address:** http://www.granse.com. **Description:** Produces plumbing supplies and runs a contract screw machine business.

FOLEY LABORATORY SERVICES, INC.
655 Winding Brook Drive, Glastonbury CT 06033. 860/633-2660. **Toll-free phone:** 800/253-5506. **Fax:** 860/652-3259. **Contact:** Human Resources. **World Wide Web address:** http://www.dotdrugtest.com. **Description:** Provides alcohol and drug testing services. **Corporate headquarters location:** This location.

FOXWOODS RESORT CASINO
39 Norwich Westerly Road, Mashantucket CT 06339. 860/312-4170. **Contact:** Human Resources. **World Wide Web address:** http://www.foxwoods.com. **Description:** A casino. Foxwoods also offers concerts and entertainment, as well as lodging facilities. The casino is operated by the Mashantucket Pequot Indians. **NOTE:** Send resumes to: Human Resources-Employment and Staffing Division, Route 2, P.O. Box 3777, Mashantucket CT 06339.

FRANKEL
Greenwich Office Park, Building 5, Greenwich CT 06831. 203/862-6000. **Contact:** Human Resources. **World Wide Web address:** http://www.frankel.com. **Description:** Provides marketing services in the promotion, direct, interactive, brand communications, sports/entertainment, and consulting areas. **Corporate headquarters location:** This location. **Other U.S. locations:** Atlanta GA; Troy MI; Minnetonka MN; Parsippany NJ.

FUJI MEDICAL SYSTEMS USA
419 West Avenue, Stamford CT 06902. 203/324-2000. **Contact:** Human Resources. **World Wide Web address:** http://www.fujimed.com. **Description:** Manufactures and distributes X-ray machines, digital imaging systems, and radiography printers for medical offices and hospitals. **Parent company:** Fuji Photo Film Co., Ltd.

THE FUTURES GROUP INTERNATIONAL
80 Glastonbury Boulevard, Glastonbury CT 06033. 860/633-3501. **Contact:** Human Resources. **World Wide Web address:** http://www.tfgi.com. **Description:** A business and competitive intelligence consulting firm. **NOTE:** Send resumes to 1 Thomas Circle NW, Suite 200, Washington DC 20005. **Other area locations:** Durham CT **Other U.S. locations:** Washington DC. **International locations:** Worldwide.

GE CAPITAL CORPORATION
260 Long Ridge Road, Stamford CT 06927. 203/357-4000. **Contact:** Human Resources. **World Wide Web address:** http://www.gecapital.com. **Description:** GE Capital Corporation is one of the largest leasing companies in the United States and Canada, providing financing and related management services to corporate clients through 27 divisions. **NOTE:** Fill out online application at www.gecareers.com. **Corporate headquarters location:** This location. **Parent company:** General Electric Company operates in the following areas: aircraft engines (jet engines, replacement parts, and repair services for commercial, military, executive, and commuter aircraft); appliances; broadcasting (NBC); industrial (lighting products, electrical distribution and control equipment, transportation systems products, electric motors and related products, a broad range of electrical and electronic industrial automation products, and a network of electrical supply houses); materials (plastics, ABS resins, silicones, superabrasives, and laminates); power systems (products for the generation, transmission, and distribution of electricity); technical products and systems (medical systems and equipment, as well as a full range of computer-based information and data interchange services for both internal use and external commercial and industrial customers); and capital services (consumer services, financing, and specialty insurance.)

GAR-KENYON TECHNOLOGIES, LLC
238 Water Street, P.O. Box 559, Naugatuck CT 06770. 203/792-4900. **Fax:** 203/729-4950. **Contact:** Human Resources. **Description:** Develops, manufactures, and markets time equipment, hydraulic control valves, and electronic hardware components. Founded in 1997. **NOTE:** Entry-level positions and second and third shifts are offered. **Special programs:** Training; Summer Jobs. **Office hours:** Monday - Friday, 8:00 a.m. - 5:00 p.m. **Corporate headquarters location:** This location. **Listed on:** Privately held. **Annual sales/revenues:** $11 - $20 million.

GARTNER, INC.
56 Top Gallant Road, Stamford CT 06904. 203/964-0096. **Fax:** 203/316-6436. **Contact:** Human Resources. **World Wide Web address:** http:// www.gartner.com. **Description:** Gartner, Inc. is a market research and consulting firm providing strategic decision support. **Special programs:** Internships. **Corporate headquarters location:** This location. **Other U.S. locations:** San Jose CA. **International locations:** Australia; Japan; United Kingdom. **Operations at this facility include:** Research and Development; Sales. **Listed on:** NASDAQ. **Stock exchange symbol:** IT.

GATES CORRECTIONAL INSTITUTION
131 North Bridebrook Road, Niantic CT 06357. 860/691-4700. **Contact:** Human Resources. **Description:** A minimum security prison for men, run by the state of Connecticut.

GAYLORD HOSPITAL
P.O. Box 400, Wallingford CT 06492. 203/284-2830. **Physical address:** Gaylord Farm Road, Wallingford CT 06492. **Fax:** 203/284-2773. **Contact:** Nancy Ullamn, Manager of Human Resources. **E-mail address:** jobs@gaylord.org. **World Wide Web address:** http://www.gaylord.org. **Description:** Provides medical rehabilitation services for SCI, TBI, MS, chronic pulmonary, and alcohol or chemically dependent patients. **Positions advertised include:** Care Manager; Admissions Representative; Regional Healthcare Associate; Budget and Reimbursement Coordinator; Payroll Coordinator; Food Service Assistant; Certified Occupational Therapy Aide; Nursing Assistant; Certified Occupational Therapy Assistant; Licensed Practical Nurse; Senior Mobility Assistant; Nursing Supervisor; Registered Nurse; Benefit Verification Representative; Respiratory Care Practitioner; Secretary; Audiologist; Speech Pathologist. **Number of employees at this location:** 500.

GEM MANUFACTURING COMPANY INC.
P.O. Box 4550, Waterbury CT 06704. 203/574-1466. **Physical address:** 78 Brookside Road, Waterbury CT 06708. **Contact:** Human Resources. **World Wide Web address:** http://www.gemmfg.com. **Description:** Manufactures metal eyelets, fasteners, and stampings for a variety of uses.

GENERAL CABLE
1600 West Main Street, Willimantic CT 06226. 860/456-8000. **Contact:** Human Resources. **World Wide Web address:** http://www.generalcable.com. **Description:** Manufactures structured wiring systems and provides cabling solutions for military, commercial, data communications, and computer products. Shift Production Supervisors. **Special programs:** Internships. **Corporate headquarters location:** Highland Heights KY. **Listed on:** New York Stock Exchange. **Stock exchange symbol:** BGC.

GENERAL DATACOMM, INC.
6 Rubber Avenue, Naugatuck CT 06770. 203/729-0271. **Fax:** 203/729-5734. **Contact:** Anne Davino, Human Resources. **E-mail address:** jobs@gdc.com. **World Wide Web address:** http://www.gdc.com. **Description:** Provides business solutions for enterprise and telecommunications networks based on Asynchronous Transfer Mode (ATM) products and services. General DataComm operates in three areas: ATM products, internetworking products, and network access products. The company designs, assembles, markets, installs, and maintains products and services that enable telecommunications common carriers, corporations, and governments to build, upgrade, and manage their global telecommunications networks. General DataComm's networks transmit information via telephone lines, microwaves, satellites, fiber-optic cables, and other media between computers and terminals or information processing systems. Founded in 1969. **Corporate headquarters location:** This location. **International locations:** Canada; Columbia. **Annual sales/revenues:** More than $100 million. **Number of employees worldwide:** 150.

GENERAL ELECTRIC COMPANY
3135 Easton Turnpike, Fairfield CT 06828. 203/373-2211. **Contact:** Human Resources. **World Wide Web address:** http://www.ge.com. **Description:** Operates in the following areas: aircraft engines (jet engines, replacement parts, and repair services for commercial, military, executive, and commuter aircraft); appliances; broadcasting (NBC); industrial (lighting products, electrical distribution and control equipment, transportation systems products, electric motors and related products, a broad range of electrical and electronic industrial automation products, and a network of electrical supply houses); materials (plastics, ABS resins, silicones, superabrasives, and laminates); power systems (products for the generation, transmission, and distribution of electricity); technical products and systems (medical systems and equipment, as well as a full range of computer-based information and data interchange services for both internal use and external commercial and industrial customers); and capital services (consumer services, financing, and specialty insurance). **NOTE:** Apply online only. **Corporate headquarters location:** This location. **Listed on:** New York Stock Exchange. **Stock exchange symbol:** GE. **Number of employees worldwide:** 230,000.

GENERALCOLONGE RE CORPORATION
695 East Main Street, P.O. Box 10351, Stamford CT 06904. 203/328-5000. **Contact:** James Hamilton, Senior Vice President of Human Resources. **World Wide Web address:** http://www.gcre.com. **Description:** Provides property and casualty reinsurance to primary insurers on a direct basis. The company markets reinsurance directly to these insurers through its own sales team. Reinsurance is marketed and underwritten on both a treaty and facultative basis. Treaty marketing efforts are focused on small- to medium-sized regional and specialty property and casualty insurers. **Corporate headquarters location:** This location. **Other U.S. locations:** Nationwide. **International locations:** Worldwide. **Parent company:** Berkshire Hathaway Inc. **Number of employees worldwide:** 2,700.

GENERALCOLONGE RE CORPORATION
One Financial Plaza, 9th Floor, Hartford CT 06103-3400. 860/547-0200. **Contact:** Human Resources. **World Wide Web address:** http://www.gcre.com. **Description:** Provides property and casualty reinsurance to primary insurers on a direct basis through its own sales team. Reinsurance is marketed and underwritten on both treaty and facultative bases. Treaty marketing efforts are focused on small- to medium-sized regional and specialty property and casualty insurers. **NOTE:** Send resumes to the

Stamford CT location. **Corporate headquarters location:** Stamford CT. **Other U.S. locations:** Nationwide. **International locations:** Worldwide. **Parent company:** Berkshire Hathaway Inc. **Number of employees worldwide:** 2,700.

GENESEE & WYOMING INC.
66 Field Point Road, Greenwich CT 06830. 203/629-3722. **Fax:** 203/661-4106. **Contact:** Human Resources. **World Wide Web address:** http://www.gwrr.com. **Description:** Operates 18 railroads with 4,700 miles of track in the United States, Canada, Australia, and Mexico. Founded in 1895. **NOTE:** The Human Resources Department is in the Rochester NY location. Please fax resumes to 716/328-8622. **Subsidiaries include:** Allegheny & Eastern Railroad, Inc. (Punxsatawney PA); Buffalo & Pittsburgh Railroad, Inc. (Punxsatawney PA); Illinois & Midland Railroad, Inc. (Springfield IL); Portland & Western Railroad, Inc. (Albany OR); Rail Link, Inc., which provides switching, rail freight, coal loading and unloading, and locomotive leasing in North America; Rochester & Southern Railroad, Inc. (Rochester NY); Willamette & Pacific Railroad, Inc. (Albany OR). **Other U.S. locations:** IL; NY; OR; PA. **International locations:** Australia; Bolivia; Canada; Mexico. **Listed on:** NASDAQ. **Stock exchange symbol:** GNWR. **President/CEO:** Mortimer B. Fuller III.

GERALD METALS, INC.
6 High Ridge Park, Stamford CT 06905. 203/609-8300. **Fax:** 203/609-8529. **Contact:** Human Resources Department. **E-mail address:** hrdept@gerald.com. **Description:** A merchant of nonferrous and precious metals. **Positions advertised include:** Sr. Metals Merchant. **Corporate headquarters location:** This location.

GERBER COBURN OPTICAL, INC.
55 Gerber Road, South Windsor CT 06074. 860/648-6600. **Toll-free phone:** 800/843-1479. **Fax:** 860/648-6601. **Contact:** Joyce Reynolds Human Resources. **E-mail address:** joyce.reynolds@gerbercoburn.com. **World Wide Web address:** http://www.gerbercoburn.com. **Description:** Designs, manufactures, and markets computer-driven systems for eyeglass lens processing using multiaxis machinery technology. The company produces prescription lenses and edge lenses to fit eyeglass frames. **NOTE:** Entry-level positions are offered. **Positions advertised include:** Controller; Manufacturing Engineer; Materials Test Specialist. **Special programs:** Co-ops; Summer Jobs. **Office hours:** Monday - Friday, 8:00 a.m. - 4:30 p.m. **Corporate headquarters location:** This location. **Other U.S. locations:** San Marcos CA; Miami FL; Muskogee OK. **International locations:** Canada; England; The Netherlands; Singapore; South Australia. **Parent company:** Gerber Scientific, Inc. **Listed on:** New York Stock Exchange. **Stock exchange symbol:** GRB. **President:** Shawn Harrington. **Annual sales/revenues:** $21 - $50 million. **Number of employees at this location:** 110.

GERBER SCIENTIFIC, INC.
83 Gerber Road West, South Windsor CT 06074. 860/644-1551. **Contact:** Human Resources. **World Wide Web address:** http://www.gerberscientific.com. **Description:** Designs and manufactures high-tech imaging systems for the electronics, graphic arts, and a variety of other industries. **NOTE:** Entry-level positions are offered. **Positions advertised include:** Senior Sales Specialist. **Special programs:** Internships. **Corporate headquarters location:** This location. **Other U.S. locations:** Nationwide. **International locations:** Europe. **Listed on:** New York Stock Exchange. **Stock exchange symbol:** GRB. **President:** Shawn Harrington. **Annual sales/revenues:** $21 - $50 million.

GERBER TECHNOLOGY, INC.
24 Industrial Park Road West, Tolland CT 06084. 860/871-8082. **Contact:** Tamara Sehi, Human Resources Department. **World Wide Web address:** http://www.gerbertechnology.com. **Description:** Manufactures computerized garment cutting equipment. **Positions advertised include:** Purchasing Agent; Software Tester; Senior Electrical Engineer. **Corporate headquarters location:** South Windsor CT. **Other U.S. locations:** Nationwide. **Parent company:** Gerber Scientific Inc. **Operations at this facility include:** Divisional Headquarters; Manufacturing. **Listed on:** New York Stock Exchange. **Stock exchange symbol:** GRB. **President:** Shawn Harrington. **Annual sales/revenues:** $21 - $50 million **Number of employees at this location:** 350.

THE GLOBE PEQUOT PRESS
P.O. Box 480, Guilford CT 06437. 203/458-4500. **Physical address:** 246 Goose Lane, Guilford CT 06437. **Toll-free phone:** 888/249-7586. **Contact:** Human Resources. **World Wide Web address:** http://www.globe-pequot.com. **Description:** Publishes travel books, maps, language books, and outdoor recreation books. Overall, the company produces 250 new titles annually. Founded in 1947. **Corporate headquarters location:** This location. **Parent company:** Morris Communications Corporation.

GOODSPEED OPERA HOUSE
Box A, East Haddam CT 06423. 860/873-8664. **Fax:** 860/873-2329. **Contact:** Human Resources. **E-mail address:** employment@goodspeed.org. **World Wide Web address:** http://www.goodspeed.org. **Description:** A regional theater specializing in the revival and development of musical theater. Founded in 1963. **Positions advertised include:** Scenic Carpenter; Props Assistant; Costume Shop Staff; Wardrobe Staff; Production Assistant. **Special programs:** Internships; Apprenticeships.

GREENWALD INDUSTRIES
212 Middlesex Avenue, Chester CT 06412. 860/526-0800. **Fax:** 860/526-5382. **Contact:** Sue Miller, Human Resources. **E-mail address:** hr@greenwaldindustries.com. **World Wide Web address:** http://www.greenwaldindustries.com. **Description:** A designer and manufacturer of coin meter systems including the SmartCard. **Office hours:** Monday - Friday, 8:00 a.m. - 5:00 p.m. **Corporate headquarters location:** This location. **Parent company:** PubliCard, Inc. **Number of employees at this location:** 95.

GROS-ITE INDUSTRIES
1806 New Britain Avenue, Farmington CT 06032. 860/678-8140. **Fax:** 860/674-2718. **Contact:** Carol Foley, Human Resources. **World Wide Web address:** http://www.edactechnologies.com. **Description:** Offers design and manufacturing services in areas such as jet engine parts, special tooling, equipment and gauges, and components used in the manufacture, assembly, and inspection of jet engines. **Corporate headquarters location:** This location. **Subsidiaries include:** American Research offers environmental test chambers that duplicate hostile conditions such as high altitude, wind and dust, compression, humidity, decompression, temperature, and explosions; Gros-Ite Spindle specializes in the design, manufacture, and repair of precision spindles. **Parent company:** Edac Technologies offers design and manufacturing services for the medical instruments industry. Edac also maintains manufacturing and design facilities with computerized, numerically controlled machining centers; grinding, welding, and sheet metal fabrication; and painting and assembly capabilities. **Listed on:** NASDAQ. **Stock exchange symbol:** EDAC. **Number of employees nationwide:** 150.

GUARDSMARK, INC.
10 Columbus Boulevard, 2nd Floor, Hartford CT 06106. 860/560-7777. **Contact:** Human Resources. **World Wide Web address:** http://www.guardsmark.com. **Description:** Provides security, life safety, fire and protective, investigative, and consulting services. **Corporate headquarters location:** Memphis TN.

GUNTHER INTERNATIONAL, LTD.
One Winnenden Road, Norwich CT 06360. 860/823-1427. **Fax:** 860/823-3026. **Contact:** Human Resources. **E-mail address:** hr@guntherintl.com. **World Wide Web address:** http://www.guntherintl.com. **Description:** Gunther International, Ltd. designs, develops, assembles, markets, services, and maintains high-speed systems that automatically assemble printed documents; fold, staple, or bind the documents; insert completed documents into the appropriate envelopes for mailing or other distribution; and stamp the correct postage by weight. The systems are computer-driven, with scanning devices used to read bar codes printed on the documents. **Positions advertised include:** Business Development Associate; Mechanical Assembly Technician. **Corporate headquarters location:** This location. **Operations at this facility include:** Administration; Manufacturing; Research and Development; Sales; Service. **Annual sales/revenues:** $11 - $20 million. **Number of employees at this location:** 75.

HAMILTON SUNDSTRAND COMPANY
One Hamilton Road, Windsor Locks CT 06096. 860/654-6000. **Contact:** Personnel. **World Wide Web address:** http://www.hamiltonsundstrandcorp.com. **Description:** Manufactures aircraft engines and industrial products. **Positions advertised include:** Senior Mechanical Engineer; Mechanical Engineer; Senior Product Manager; Staff Engineer; Accounting Analyst; Accounting Specialist; Lead Designer, Drafting Services; Human Resources Manager. **Corporate headquarters location:** This location. **Other U.S. location:** Nationwide. **International locations:** Worldwide. **Number of employees worldwide:** 17,200.

THE HARTFORD FINANCIAL SERVICES GROUP, INC.
The Hartford Plaza, 690 Asylum Avenue, Hartford CT 06115. 860/547-5000. **Contact:** Randall Kiviet, Human Resources Department. **World Wide Web address:** http://www.thehartford.com. **Description:** One of the largest insurance companies in the United States. The Hartford is a *Fortune* 500 company and offers business, farm, home, life, automobile, marine, and health insurance coverage as well as fidelity and surety bonds and reinsurance. **Corporate headquarters location:** This location. **Other area locations:** Simsbury CT; Windsor CT. **Listed on:** New York Stock Exchange. **Stock exchange symbol:** HIG. **Number of employees worldwide:** 26,600.

HARTFORD, CITY OF
550 Main Street, Hartford CT 06103. 860/522-4888. **Contact:** Human Resources. **Description:** This location houses the executive offices for the city of Hartford including the mayor's office, city council, city manager, city treasurer, housing and planning boards, and licensing and inspection offices.

HARTFORD CIVIC CENTER
One Civic Center Plaza, Hartford CT 06103. 860/249-6333. **Contact:** Jane Dion, Personnel Director. **World Wide Web address:** http://www.hartfordciviccenter.com. **Description:** Business offices for the civic center, which is host to numerous concerts, sporting events, and entertainers year-round. The Hartford Civic Center is managed by Madison Square Garden. **Special programs:** Internships. **Corporate headquarters location:** This location.

THE HARTFORD COURANT
285 Broad Street, Hartford CT 06115. 860/241-6200. **Contact:** Human Resources. **World Wide Web address:** http://www.hartfordcourant.com. **Description:** Offices of the *Hartford Courant*, a daily newspaper with a circulation of 215,000 weekdays and 302,500 on Sundays.

HARTFORD HOSPITAL
80 Seymour Street, Hartford CT 06102. 860/545-5000. **Contact:** Human Resources Department. **World Wide Web address:** http://www.harthosp.org. **Description:** A hospital specializing in orthopedics and cardiac bypass surgery. **Positions advertised include:** Registered Nurse.

THE HARTFORD LIFE INSURANCE COMPANY
200 Hopmeadow Street, Simsbury CT 06089. 860/843-8594. **Fax:** 860/843-8723. **Contact:** Human Resources. **World Wide Web address:** http://www.thehartford.com. **Description:** The Hartford Life Insurance Company is one of the fastest-growing life insurance companies in the nation. **Positions advertised include:** Financial Analyst; Executive Assistant; Senior; Administrative Assistant; Call Specialist; Service Associate. **Special programs:** Internships; Co-ops; Temporary Positions. **Corporate headquarters location:** Hartford CT. **Other area locations:** Windsor CT. **Subsidiaries include:** HL Reinsurance; ICMG. **Operations at this facility include:** Administration; Divisional Headquarters; Sales; Service. **Listed on:** New York Stock Exchange. **Stock exchange symbol:** HIG. **Number of employees at this location:** 2,500.

THE HARTFORD STAGE COMPANY
50 Church Street, Hartford CT 06103. 860/525-5601. **Contact:** Human Resources Department. **World Wide Web address:** http://www.hartfordstage.org. **Description:** A professional, not-for-profit theater producing classic, contemporary, and new plays. Founded in 1964. **Number of employees at this location:** 80.

HARTFORD STEAM BOILER INSPECTION & INSURANCE COMPANY
One State Street, P.O. Box 5024, Hartford CT 06102-5024. 860/722-1866. **Contact:** Human Resources. **World Wide Web address:** http://www.hsb.com. **Description:** An insurance and inspection company specializing in the areas of property and equipment. **Corporate headquarters location:** This location. **Other U.S. locations:** Nationwide. **Parent company:** American International Group, Inc. **Listed on:** New York Stock Exchange. **Stock exchange symbol:** AIG.

HARTFORD SYMPHONY ORCHESTRA
228 Farmington Avenue, Hartford CT 06105. 860/246-8742. **Contact:** Personnel. **World Wide Web address:** http://www.hartfordsymphony.org. **Description:** Offices for the symphony orchestra. **Corporate headquarters location:** This location.

HEALTH NET
P.O. Box 904, Shelton CT 06484. **Physical address:** One Far Mill Crossing, Shelton CT 06484. **Toll-free phone:** 800/848-4747. **Contact:** Human Resources. **World Wide Web address:** http://www.phshealthplans.com. **Description:** One of the largest managed care companies in Connecticut. **Corporate headquarters location:** This location. **Listed on:** New York Stock Exchange. **Stock exchange symbol:** HNT.

HENKEL LOCTITE CORPORATION
1001 Trout Brook Crossing, Rocky Hill CT 06067. 860/571-5100. **Contact:** Human Resources. **World Wide Web address:** http:// www.loctite.com. **Description:** Loctite manufactures and markets a broad range of sealants, adhesives, and coatings. **Positions advertised include:** Application Engineer; Communications Editor; Director, AAM Marketing; Graphic Designer; Marketing Communications Specialist; Customer Service Representative; International Customer Service Administrative Assistant; Part-time Customer Service Representative. **Corporate headquarters location:** This location. **Other U.S. locations:** Louisville KY; Detroit MI; Cleveland OH; Sabana Grande PR. **International locations:** Worldwide. **CEO:** Heinrich Grun. **Number of employees worldwide:** 4,200.

HEXCEL CORPORATION
281 Tresser Boulevard, Two Stamford Plaza, 16th Floor, Stamford CT 06901-3261. 203/969-0666. **Contact:** Human Resources. **World Wide Web address:** http:// www.hexcel.com. **Description:** Hexcel Corporation is a manufacturing firm with two primary business segments: structural materials (including aerospace products, nonaerospace honeycomb, resin-impregnated industrial fabrics, nonimpregnated fabrics) and specialty chemicals (including bulk pharmaceuticals, custom and special purpose chemicals, specialty resins, and industrial maintenance chemicals). **Other U.S. locations:** Nationwide. **International locations:** Worldwide. **Operations at this facility include:** This location houses administrative offices. **Listed on:** New York Stock Exchange. **Stock exchange symbol:** HXL. **Number of employees nationwide:** 5,000.

HILTON MYSTIC
20 Coogan Boulevard, Mystic CT 06355. 860/572-0731. **Fax:** 860/572-0328. **Contact:** Human Resources. **Description:** Located across from the Mystic Aquarium, the hotel also offers a dining option.

HOLIDAY INN
1070 Main Street, Bridgeport CT 06604. 203/334-1234. **Contact:** Human Resources. **World Wide Web address:** www.ichotelsgroup.com. **Description:** A 234-room hotel located in the heart of downtown offering a restaurant and business amenities.

HOUSING AUTHORITY OF NEW HAVEN
360 Orange Street, P.O. Box 1912, New Haven CT 06509-1912. 203/498-8800. **Contact:** Director. **Description:** Responsible for the overall housing management of the greater New Haven community.

HUBBELL INC.
584 Derby Milford Road, Orange CT 06477. 203/799-4100. **Contact:** Human Resources. **World Wide Web address:** http:// www.hubbell.com. **Description:** An international manufacturer of electrical and electronic products, power systems, industrial lighting, industrial technology, telecommunications products, and wiring systems. **Corporate headquarters location:** This location. **Other U.S. locations:** Nationwide. **International locations:** Canada; Scotland; Switzerland. **Listed on:** New York Stock Exchange. **Stock exchange symbol:** HUBB.

HYPERION SOLUTIONS
900 Long Ridge Road, Stamford CT 06902. 203/703-3000. **Fax:** 203/322-3904. **Contact:** Human Resources. **World Wide Web address:** http://www.hyperion.com. **Description:** Hyperion Solutions develops, markets, and supports a family of network-based business information software products for large multidivision or multilocation companies worldwide. The product line provides executives, managers, and analysts with the capability to collect, process, access, and analyze critical business information in a timely manner, using networked personal computers. **Positions advertised include:** Compensation Manager; Financial Applications Instructor; Partner Technical Account Manager; Administrative Assistant; Performance Engineer; Software Engineer. **Special programs:** Internships. **Corporate headquarters location:** Sunnyvale CA. **Other U.S. locations:** Nationwide. **Operations at this facility include:** Administration; Divisional Headquarters; Regional Headquarters; Research and Development; Sales; Service. **Listed on:** NASDAQ. **Stock exchange symbol:** HYSL. **Number of employees worldwide:** 2,300.

ICU MEDICAL
129 Reservoir Road, Vernon CT 06066. 860/870-6112. **Contact:** Human Resources. **E-mail address:** jr@icumed.com. **World Wide Web address:** http://www.icumed.com. **Description:** Designs, develops, manufactures, and markets safety medical products for hospitals and medical organizations under the Punctur-Guard and Drop-It brand names. The first product was a patented blood collection needle with a mechanism that blunts the needle prior to its removal from the patient, greatly reducing the risk of accidental needle sticks that can spread hepatitis, HIV, and other infectious diseases. Other products include intravenous catheters and winged intravenous sets. **Number of employees nationwide:** 75.

IMS HEALTH INC.
1499 Post Road, Fairfield CT 06824. 203/319-4700. **Contact:** Human Resources. **World Wide Web address:** http://www.imshealth.com. **Description:** A leading provider of information solutions to the pharmaceutical and healthcare industries. **Positions advertised include:** Manager, Corporate Finance. **Corporate headquarters location:** This location. **Listed on:** New York Stock Exchange. **Stock exchange symbol:** RX. **Number of employees worldwide:** 6,400.

IPC INFORMATION SYSTEMS, INC.
42 Pequot Park Road, Westbrook CT 06498. 860/399-5981. **Contact:** Human Resources. **World Wide Web address:** http://www.ipc.com. **Description:** Provides network communications solutions for the financial industry. Through its Information Transport Systems (ITS) business, the company provides its customers with voice, data, and video solutions through the design, integration, implementation, and support of local and wide area networks. ITS solutions incorporate the latest technology and are supported by a team of systems engineers. **Corporate headquarters location:** New York NY. **Other U.S. locations:** Nationwide. **Listed on:** NASDAQ. **Stock exchange symbol:** IPCR. **Annual sales/revenues:** $21 - $50 million. **Number of employees at this location:** 70. **Number of employees nationwide:** 200. **Number of employees worldwide:** 250.

ITT INDUSTRIES
CANNON RF DIVISION
ARROWBELL COMPONENTS
860 North Main Street Extension, Wallingford CT 06492. 203/265-7741. **Toll-free phone:** 800/683-7666. **Fax:** 860/635-2010. **Contact:** Human Resources. **World Wide Web address:** http://www.ittcannon.com. **Description:** Engaged in the manufacturing of cable assemblies and coaxial connectors. **Corporate headquarters location:** New York NY. **Parent company:** ITT Corporation is a diversified, global enterprise engaged in three major business areas: Financial and Business Services, which includes ITT Hartford, ITT Financial Corporation, and ITT Communications and Information Services, Inc.; Manufactured Products, which includes ITT Automotive, ITT Defense and Electronics, Inc., and ITT Fluid Technology Corporation; and Sheraton Hotels (ITT Sheraton Corporation). **Other U.S. locations:** Nationwide. **International locations:** Worldwide. **Operations at this facility include:** Administration; Divisional Headquarters; Manufacturing; Sales. **Listed on:** New York Stock Exchange. **Stock exchange symbol:** ITT.

ITW HIGHLAND MANUFACTURING
P.O. Box 1858, 1240 Wolcott Street, Waterbury CT 06722. 203/574-3200. **Fax:** 203/575-7424. **Contact:** Human Resources. **E-mail address:** judym@itwhighland.com. **World Wide Web address:** http://www.itwhighland.com. **Description:** Manufactures automotive stampings and drawn metal products used for hardware and electrical components. **Parent company:** Illinois Tool Works Inc. develops, produces, and markets various engineered components, fasteners, assemblies, and packaging systems for clients in the industrial and construction markets. Units of the company include metal components, construction products and polymers, consumer packaging products and systems, industrial packaging systems, and finishing systems. Illinois Tool Works has over 250 operating facilities in 33 countries.

IMAGE GRAPHICS, INC.
917 Bridgeport Avenue, Shelton CT 06484. 203/926-0100. **Toll-free phone:** 888/464-6243. **Contact:** Personnel. **World Wide Web address:** http://www.igraph.com. **Description:** A systems integrator for imaging and cold systems. The company also manufactures high-resolution electronic data recorders. **Corporate headquarters location:** This location.

INDALEX ALUMINUM SOLUTIONS
500 Four Rod Road, Berlin CT 06037-2243. 860/828-4186. **Fax:** 860/828-2873. **Contact:** Human Resources. **World Wide Web address:** http://www.indalex.com. **Description:** Manufactures extruded aluminum and related products. **Corporate headquarters location:** Girard OH.

INSURITY
170 Huyshope Avenue, Hartford CT 06106. 860/616-7721. **Contact:** Human Resources. **E-mail address:** hr@insurity.com. **World Wide Web address:** http://www.insurity.com. **Description:** Develops insurance software to process workers' compensation claims. **Positions advertised include:** Database Programmer; Project Manager; Quality Assurance Analyst; Support Specialist; Programmer Analyst; Client Service Analyst. **Corporate headquarters location:** This location. **Other area locations:** East Hartford CT. **Other U.S. locations:** Cumming GA; Red Wing MN; Richardson TX.

INTERNATIONAL PAPER COMPANY
400 Atlantic Street, Stamford CT 06921. 203/541-8000. **Contact:** Human Resources. **World Wide Web address:** http://www.internationalpaper.com. **Description:** International Paper Company manufactures pulp and paper, packaging, wood products, and a range of specialty products. The company is organized into five business segments: Printing Papers, whose principal products include uncoated papers, coated papers, bristles, and pulp; Packaging, which includes industrial packaging, consumer packaging, and kraft and specialty papers; Distribution, including the sale of printing papers, graphic arts equipment and supplies, packaging materials, industrial supplies, and office products; Specialty Products, which includes imaging products, specialty panels, nonwovens, chemicals, and minerals; and Forest Products which includes logging and wood products. **Corporate headquarters location:** This location. **Subsidiaries include:** Champion Papel e Celulose (Brazil); Weldwood of Canada. **Listed on:** New York Stock Exchange. **Stock exchange symbol:** IP. **Number of employees worldwide:** 72,500.

INTERNATIONAL PAPER COMPANY
175 Park Road, Putnam CT 06260. 860/928-7901. **Contact:** Human Resources. **World Wide Web address:** http://www.internationalpaper.com. **Description:** The company is one of the world's largest forest products companies, with over 300 locations worldwide. International Paper is a manufacturer of pulp and paper, packaging, and wood products as well as a range of specialty products. Millions of acres of timberland are controlled by International Paper, making it one of the largest private landowners in the United States. The company is organized into five business segments including Printing Papers, in which principal products include uncoated papers, coated papers, bristles, and pulp; Packaging, which includes industrial packaging, consumer packaging, and kraft and specialty papers; Distribution, which includes sales of printing papers, graphic arts equipment and supplies, packaging materials, industrial supplies, and office products; Specialty Products, which includes imaging products, specialty panels, nonwovens, chemicals, and minerals; and Forest Products, including logs and wood products. **Corporate headquarters location:** Stamford CT. **Subsidiaries include:** Champion Papel e Celulose (Brazil); Weldwood of Canada. **Operations at this facility include:** This location produces corrugated containers. **Listed on:** New York Stock Exchange. **Stock exchange symbol:** IP. **Number of employees worldwide:** 72,500.

JEFFERIES & COMPANY, INC.
Metro Center, One Station Place, 3 North, Stamford CT 06902. 203/708-5800. **Contact:** Human Resources. **E-mail address:** Eastcoastrecruiting@jefco.com. **World Wide Web address:** http://www.jefco.com. **Description:** Jefferies & Company is engaged in equity, convertible debt and taxable fixed income securities brokerage and trading, and corporate finance. Jefferies is one of the leading national firms engaged in the distribution and trading of blocks of equity securities and conducts such activities primarily in the third market, which refers to transactions in listed equity securities taking place away from national securities exchanges. Founded in 1962. **Corporate headquarters location:** New York NY. **Other U.S. locations:** Nationwide. **International locations:** Worldwide. **Listed on:** New York Stock Exchange. **Stock exchange symbol:** JEF. **Number of employees worldwide:** 1,600.

JOHNSON MEMORIAL HOSPITAL, INC.
201 Chestnut Hill Road, Stafford Springs CT 06076. 860/684-4251. **Fax:** 860/684-8459. **Recorded jobline:** 860/684-8204. **Contact:** Sue Tanner, Human Resources. **E-mail address:** stanner@jmhosp.org. **World Wide Web address:** http://www.johnsonhealthnetwork.com. **Description:** An 89-bed, general, acute care hospital. **Positions advertised include:** Administrative Assistant; Development Secretary; Health Information Services Clerk; Per Diem Registered Dietician; Patient Care Technician; Mental Health Worker; Administrative Director of Emergency Services; Quality Managed Care Specialist; Crisis Worker; Mental Health Worker; Maintenance Mechanic; Environmental Technician. **Parent company:** Johnson Health Network is a nonprofit health service organization comprised of several subsidiaries: The Johnson Evergreen Corporation, which includes Evergreen Health Care Center, a 120-bed skilled nursing and rehabilitation facility; Johnson Health Care, Inc., encompassing the free-standing Johnson Surgery Center and Johnson Occupational Medicine Center in Enfield CT; The Enfield Visiting Nurse Association, Inc., which provides comprehensive home health care; Johnson Memorial Hospital Development

Fund, Inc.; and Wellcare, Inc., charged with managing Johnson Memorial's construction projects. **Operations at this facility include:** Administration; Service. **Number of employees at this location:** 700.

KPMG
744 Main Street, One Financial Plaza, Hartford CT 06103-4103. 860/522-3200. **Contact:** Human Resources. **World Wide Web address:** http://www.kpmg.com. **Description:** KPMG delivers a wide range of value-added assurance, tax, and consulting services. **Positions advertised include:** Senior Associates, Audit; Tax Professional. **Corporate headquarters location:** Woodcliff Lake NJ. **Other U.S. locations:** Nationwide. **International locations:** Worldwide. **Parent company:** KPMG International has more than 85,000 employees worldwide including 6,500 partners and 60,000 professional staff, serving clients in 844 cities in 155 countries. KPMG International is a leader among professional services firms engaged in capturing, managing, assessing, and delivering information to create knowledge that will help its clients maximize shareholder value.

KAMAN CORPORATION
1332 Blue Hills Avenue, P.O. Box 2, Bloomfield CT 06002. 860/243-7100. **Contact:** Human Resources. **E-mail address:** resumes-corp@kaman.com. **World Wide Web address:** http://www.kaman.com. **Description:** Kaman is a highly diversified *Fortune* International 500 company with two segments providing products and services in five functional areas. The Diversified Technology segment includes Kaman Instrumentation Corp., offering value-added products that solve problems in niche markets for military and industrial customers; Kamatics Corp. offers advanced information technologies and high-technology science and engineering products and services including artificial intelligence systems, advanced technology systems, and other technical professional services; and Kaman Aerospace Corp. offers commercial and military helicopter programs, components for commercial airliners, military subcontract programs, and laser optics systems. The Distribution Segment includes Kaman Industrial Technologies Corp., involving the distribution of nearly 800,000 repair and replacement products and services to nearly every sector of heavy and light industry; Kaman Music Corp. sells over 13,000 musical products and instruments. **Corporate headquarters location:** This location. **Subsidiaries include:** Kaman Aerospace Corporation; Kaman Music Corporation; Kaman Industrial Technologies Corporation. **Operations at this facility include:** This location manufactures helicopters. **Listed on:** NASDAQ. **Stock exchange symbol:** KAMNA. **Number of employees nationwide:** 4,200.

KEANE
39 Old Ridgebury Road, Suite 8, Danbury CT 06810-5108. 203/744-8877. **Fax:** 203/794-1176. **Contact:** Human Resources. **E-mail address:** info.ct@keane.com. **World Wide Web address:** http://www.keane.com. **Description:** Keane collaborates with Global 2000 and government agencies to produce software to help the agencies business strategies. **Positions advertised include:** Managing Director. **Corporate headquarters location:** Boston MA. **Other area locations:** Rocky Hill CT. **Other U.S. locations:** Nationwide. **International locations:** Coventry, England; London, England; New Delhi, India; Hyderabad, India. **Listen on:** American Stock Exchange. **Stock Exchange Symbol:** KEA.

KELLEY DRYE & WARREN LLP
2 Stamford Plaza, 281 Tresser Boulevard, 14th Floor, Stamford CT 06901. 203/324-1400. **Contact:** Personnel. **World Wide Web address:** http://www.kelleydrye.com. **Description:** An international law firm specializing in litigation, banking, labor and employment, employee benefits, bankruptcy, tax, real estate, and personal services. **Corporate headquarters location:** New York NY. **Other U.S. locations:** Los Angeles CA; Washington DC; Chicago IL; Parsippany NJ; Vienna VA. **International locations:** Belgium; Hong Kong; India; Indonesia; Japan, Thailand. **Number of employees worldwide:** 300.

KENNAMETAL INC.
1095 Day Hill Road, Suite 150, Windsor CT 06095. 860/285-0085. **Toll-free phone:** 800/446-7738. **Contact:** John DeLuco, Regional Operations Manager. **World Wide Web address:** http://www.kennametal.com. **Description:** Kennametal manufactures, purchases, and distributes a broad range of tools, tooling systems, supplies, and services for the metalworking, mining, and highway construction industries. Kennametal specializes in developing and manufacturing metal cutting tools and wear-resistant parts using a specialized type of powder metallurgy. The company's metal cutting tools are made of cemented carbides, ceramics, and other hard materials. Kennametal manufactures a complete line of toolholders and toolholding systems by machining and fabricating steel bars and other metal alloys. The company's mining and construction cutting tools are tipped with cemented carbide and are used for underground coal mining and highway construction, repair, and maintenance. Metallurgical products consist of powders made from ore concentrates, compounds, and secondary materials. **Other U.S. locations:** Nationwide. **International locations:** Worldwide. **Operations at this facility include:** This location houses customer service operations. **Listed on:** New York Stock Exchange. **Stock exchange symbol:** KMT. **Number of employees worldwide:** 12,000.

KIMBERLY-CLARK CORPORATION
58 Pickett District Road, New Milford CT 06776. 860/354-4481. **Contact:** Human Resources. **World Wide Web address:** http://www.kimberly-clark.com. **Description:** An international manufacturer of disposable consumer products including name brands such as Huggies disposable diapers, Kleenex tissue, Kotex feminine products, and Hi-Dri paper towels. **Corporate headquarters location:** Dallas TX. **Other U.S. locations:** Nationwide. **International locations:** Worldwide. **Listed on:** New York Stock Exchange. **Stock exchange symbol:** KMB. **Number of employees at this location:** 1,200.

KING INDUSTRIES INC.
P.O. Box 588, Norwalk CT 06852. 203/866-5551. **Toll-free phone:** 800/431-7900. **Physical address:** Science Road, Norwalk CT 06852. **Contact:** Human Resources. **World Wide Web address:** http://www.kingindustries.com. **Description:** A chemical plant that produces additives for coatings and lubricants.

KMART STORES
881 Wolcott Street, Waterbury CT 06705. 203/753-2191. **Contact:** Human Resources. **World Wide Web address:** http://www.bluelight.com. **Description:** One location in the discount store chain.

KNOX ENTERPRISES
33 Riverside Avenue, 5th Floor, Westport CT 06880. 203/226-6288. **Contact:** Human Resources. **World Wide Web address:** http://www.knoxandco.com. **Description:** A holding company. **Corporate headquarters location:** This location. **Subsidiaries include:** Jackburn Manufacturing, Inc. (PA) manufactures fabricated steel parts; Setterstix Corporation (DE) manufactures rolled paper products for the confectionery and health care industries. **Number of employees nationwide:** 145.

L-3 GOVERNMENT SOLUTIONS INC
25 Van Zant Street, Suite 11A, Norwalk CT 06855. 203/857-4222. **Contact:** Human Resources. **World Wide Web address:** http://www.imcwireless.com. **Description:** Engaged in the manufacture and repair of microwave radios. **Corporate headquarters location:** Chantilly VA. **Other U.S. locations:** Nationwide. **Listed on:** Privately held. **Number of employees at this location:** 35.

LAIDLAW TRANSIT SERVICES
80 Logan Street, Bridgeport CT 06607. 203/330-2600. **Contact:** Human Resources. **World Wide Web address:** http://www.laidlaw.com. **Description:** Laidlaw Transit Services operates over 200 transit lines. Laidlaw also provides transportation management services for municipalities, transit authorities, and organizations. **Parent company:** Laidlaw Inc. provides solid waste collection, compaction, transportation, treatment, transfer, and disposal services; provides hazardous waste services; operates hazardous waste facilities and wastewater treatment plants; and operates passenger and school buses, transit system buses, and tour and charter buses. **Operations at this facility include:** This location of Laidlaw Transit owns and operates school buses for the Bridgeport public school system.

LA WEIGHTLOSS CENTERS
Radisson Hotel, Danbury CT 06811. 203/778-2501. **Toll-free phone:** 800/331-4035. **Contact:** Human Resources. **World Wide Web address:** http://www.laweightloss.com. **Description:** A weight loss center. **Positions advertised include:** Sales Counselor; Bilingual Sales Counselor.

THE LEE COMPANY
P.O. Box 424, 2 Pettipaug Road, Westbrook CT 06498. 860/399-6281. **Contact:** Richard Broderick, Human Resources. **World Wide Web address:** http://www.theleeco.com. **Description:** Manufactures hydraulics for the medical and aerospace industries. **Other U.S. locations:** Nationwide. **International locations:** Worldwide.

LEGO SYSTEMS, INC.
P.O. Box 1600, 555 Taylor Road, Enfield CT 06082. 860/763-3211. **Fax:** 860/763-6681. **Contact:** Human Resources. **World Wide Web address:** http://www.lego.com. **Description:** Manufactures and distributes LEGO building block toys and accessories. LEGO Systems is one of the world's largest toy manufacturers. Founded in 1932. **Positions advertised include:** Demand Manager; In-store Account Manager; Retail Merchandiser; Seasonal Retail Merchandiser. **Parent company:** LEGO Group.

LIME ROCK PARK
497 Lime Lock Road, Lakeville CT 06039. 860/435-5000. **Contact:** Human Resources. **World Wide Web address:** http://www.limerock.com. **Description:** Operates an automobile road course.

LIMRA INTERNATIONAL
300 Day Hill Road, Windsor CT 06095-4761. 860/688-3358. **Contact:** Human Resources. **E-mail address:** hr@limra.com. **World Wide Web address:** http://www.limra.com. **Description:** A trade association and publishing company. Publications include *Recruit* magazine, dedicated to recruiters and selection process of new hires; *Managers Handbook,* dedicated to managers seeking to enhance the productivity of their workforce; *MarketFacts Quarterly,* Limra's flagship magazine that covers worldwide marketing effectiveness in the financial service industry, and *Vision.* **Positions advertised include:** Systems Analyst; Associate Client Manager.

LINCOLN SNACKS COMPANY
30 Buxton Farm Road, Stamford CT 06905. 203/329-4545. **Contact:** Human Resources. **World Wide Web address:** http://www.lincolnsnacks.com. **Description:** Manufactures and markets caramelized popcorn and glazed popcorn and nut mixes. Brand names include Poppycock, Fiddle Faddle, Screaming Yellow Zonkers, and Golden Gourmet Nuts. **Corporate headquarters location:** This location.

LINDAMOOD-BELL
2777 Summer Street, Stamford CT 06905. 203/355-0044. **Toll-free phone:** 800/300-1818. **Contact:** Human Resources. **World Wide Web address:** http://www.lindamoodbell.com. **Description:** A learning-enhancing organization. Runs process-based educational programs. Reaches students from those with severe learning disabilities to those who are extremely gifted. **NOTE:** Part time positions offered. **Positions advertised include:** Clinician. **Special programs:** Seasonal work. **Corporate headquarters location:** San Luis Obispo CA. **Other U.S. locations:** Nationwide. **International locations:** London, England.

LOUIS DREYFUS CORPORATION
20 Westport Road, Wilton CT 06897. 203/761-2000. **Fax:** 203-761-8380. **Contact:** Human Resources. **World Wide Web address:** http://www.louisdreyfus.com. **Description:** A financial company involved in the worldwide trade of agricultural and energy-related commodities. **Special programs:** Internships. **Office hours:** Monday - Friday, 9:00 a.m. - 5:00 p.m. **Other U.S. locations:** Nationwide. **International locations:** Worldwide. **Number of employees nationwide:** 1,200. **Number of employees worldwide:** 7,000.

LYDALL, INC.
P.O. Box 151, Manchester CT 06045-0151. 860/646-1233. **Physical address:** One Colonial Road, Manchester CT 06040. **Contact:** Rey Holmes, Human Resources. **World Wide Web address:** http://www.lydall.com. **Description:** Lydall, Inc. manufactures highly modified, noncommodity products primarily in the areas of air and liquid filtration, thermal barriers and insulation, electrical insulation, and materials handling. Both wet-laid and needle-punched processes are utilized in fiber and fiber composite manufacturing. Lydall designs and produces specialty materials for critical, high-performance applications. The company's divisions include: Axohm Division; Composite Materials Divisions; Logistics Management Divisions; Lydall & Foulds Division; Lydall International; Manning Non-wovens Division; Southern Products Divisions; Technical Papers Division; Westex Divisions. **Corporate headquarters location:** This location. **Listed on:** New York Stock Exchange. **Stock exchange symbol:** LDL. **Number of employees nationwide:** 1,300.

MBI, INC.
47 Richards Avenue, Norwalk CT 06857. 203/853-2000. **Contact:** Human Resources. **World Wide Web address:** http://www.mbi-inc.com. **Description:** MBI is a direct marketing firm for collectibles including coin and stamp sets, porcelain dolls, porcelain plates, and die-cast vehicles. **Positions advertised include:** General Manager. **Special programs:** Internships. **Corporate headquarters location:** This location. **Number of employees at this location:** 700.

MACDERMID INCORPORATED
245 Freight Street, Waterbury CT 06702. 203/575-5700. **Contact:** Human Resources. **World Wide Web address:** http://www.macdermid.com. **Description:** Manufactures

specialty chemicals for metal finishing. Founded in 1922. **Positions advertised include:** Technical Service Representative; Senior Research Fellow/Chemist. **Corporate headquarters location:** This location. **Listed on:** New York Stock Exchange. **Stock exchange symbol:** MRD. **Number of employees worldwide:** 3,500.

MAFCOTE, INC.
108 Main Street, Norwalk CT 06851. 203/847-8500. **Contact:** Human Resources. **E-mail address:** jobs@mafcote.com. **World Wide Web address:** http://www.mafcote.com. **Description:** Paper Manufacturer. **Positions advertised include:** Sales/Marketing Trainee; Financial Analyst; Operations Manager; Administrative Assistant; Customer Service Representative. **Corporate headquarters location:** This location. **Other U.S. locations:** Nationwide.

MARKET DATA RETRIEVAL
One Forest Parkway, Shelton CT 06484. 203/926-4800. **Contact:** Human Resources. **World Wide Web address:** http://www.schooldata.com. **Description:** Compiles lists of people to market to schools and other educational facilities. **Parent company:** Dun & Bradstreet Corporation.

MARKETING CORPORATION OF AMERICA
372 Danbury Road, Wilton CT 06897. 203/210-2600. **Contact:** Human Resources. **E-mail address:** careers@mcofa.com. **World Wide Web address:** http://www.mcofa.com. **Description:** A consulting firm. **Other U.S. locations:** San Francisco CA; Minneapolis MN; New York NY.

MASON & MADISON
23 Amity Road, Bethany CT 06524. 203/393-1101. **Contact:** Personnel. **World Wide Web address:** http://www.mason-madison.com. **Description:** An advertising and public relations agency. **Other U.S. locations:** Boston MA; New York NY.

McBEE
45 South Main Street, West Hartford CT 06107. 860/236-3500. **Toll-free phone:** 800/662-2331. **Contact:** Human Resources. **World Wide Web address:** http://www.mcbeeinc.com. **Description:** Supplies specialized business forms to small businesses in the United States and Canada. Founded in 1906. **Positions advertised include:** Sales Representative.

McGLADREY & PULLEN, LLP
One Church Street, 8th Floor, New Haven CT 06510. 203/773-1909. **Contact:** Human Resources. **World Wide Web address:** http://www.mcgladrey.com. **Description:** A certified public accounting firm providing audit, tax, management, data processing, and cost systems services. Founded in 1926. **Other U.S. locations:** Nationwide.

MEADWESTVACO
1 High Ridge Park, Stamford CT 06905. 203/461-7400. **Contact:** Human Resources. **World Wide Web address:** http://www.meadwestvaco.com. **Description:** A leading global producer of packaging, coated and specialty papers, consumer and office products, and specialty chemicals. The company operates in 29 countries and serves customers in nearly 100 nations. **Positions advertised include:** Manager, Integrated Communications. **Corporate headquarters location:** This location.

MERCATOR SOFTWARE
45 Danbury Road, Wilton CT 06897-0840. 203/761-0208. **Fax:** 203/762-9677. **Contact:** Human Resources. **E-mail address:** hr@mercator.com. **World Wide Web address:** http://www.mercator.com. **Description:** Develops electronic data interchange software (EDI) software that helps businesses become e-businesses. **Corporate headquarters location:** This location. **Other U.S. locations:** Boca Raton FL; Bannockburn IL; New York NY; Reston VA. **International locations:** Ontario, Canada.

MERCER HUMAN RESOURCE CONSULTING
601 Merritt 7, Norwalk CT 06856. 203/229-6000. **Contact:** Human Resources. **World Wide Web address:** http://www.mercer.com. **Description:** One of the world's largest actuarial and human resources management consulting firms, providing advice to organizations on all aspects of employee relations. Services include retirement, health and welfare, performance and rewards, communication, investment, human resources administration, risk, finance and insurance, and health care provider consulting. **Corporate headquarters location:** New York NY. **Other U.S. locations:** Nationwide. **International locations:** Worldwide.

MERRILL LYNCH
City Place II, 185 Asylum Street, Hartford CT 06103. 860/728-3511. **Contact:** Human Resources. **World Wide Web address:** http://www.ml.com. **Description:** A diversified financial services organization. Merrill Lynch is a major broker in securities, option contracts, commodities and financial futures contracts, and insurance. The company also deals with corporate and municipal securities and investment banking. **NOTE:** Call this location for specific information on where to mail a resume. **Corporate headquarters location:** New York NY. **Other U.S. locations:** Nationwide.

MIDDLESEX HOSPITAL
28 Crescent Street, Middletown CT 06457. 860/344-6380. **Fax:** 860/344-6973. **Recorded jobline:** 860/344-6055. **Contact:** Human Resources. **World Wide Web address:** http://www.midhosp.org. **Description:** A 275-bed, nonprofit, acute care hospital. Middlesex Hospital is affiliated with The University of Connecticut Health Center School of Medicine. **Positions advertised include:** Dietary Aide; Administrative Director, Cancer Center; Respiratory Therapist; Social Worker; Child Psychiatrist; Crisis Clinician; Registered Nurse. **Special programs:** Internships. **Operations at this facility include:** Administration. **Number of employees at this location:** 1,400.

MIDDLESEX MUTUAL ASSURANCE COMPANY
213 Court Street , Middletown CT 06457. 860/347-4621. **Contact:** Human Resources. **World Wide Web address:** http://www.middlesexmutual.com. **Description:** Provides automobile insurance to customers in Connecticut, Vermont, Maine, and Iowa. **Positions Advertised Include:** Antique Home Specialist; Claims Supervisor; Underwriting Assistant; Underwriting Trainee; Customer Service Representative. **Other U.S. locations:** Brunswick ME. **Number of employees at this location:** 360.

MILLENNIATHREE
290 Pratt Street, Mail Stop 13, Meriden CT 06450. 203/235-1806. **Contact:** Human Resources. **Description:** Provides Web design and hosting services as well as a variety of graphic design services.

MILLER COMPANY
275 Pratt Street, Meriden CT 06450. 203/235-4474. **Toll-free phone:** 800/243-3120. **Contact:** Human Resources. **World Wide Web address:** http://www.themillerco.com. **Description:** A metal rolling mill. Founded in 1844. **Corporate headquarters location:** This location. **Number of employees at this location:** 160.

MILLWARD BROWN
501 Kingshighway East, Fairfield CT 06825. 203/335-5222. **Fax:** 203/256-5470. **Contact** Human Resources. **World Wide Web address:** http://www.millwardbrown.com. **Description:** Provides research-based marketing consultancy to assist clients in building profitable brands and e-brands and in providing service. **President:** Eileen Campbell.

MINTZ & HOKE INC.
40 Tower Lane, Avon CT 06001. 860/678-0473. **Fax:** 860/679-9702. **Contact:** Dawn Hassan, Manager of Human Resources. **E-mail address:** jobs@mintz-hoke.com. **World Wide Web address:** http://www.mintz-hoke.com. **Description:** An advertising and public relations firm providing advertising creative development and execution; collateral materials development including brochures, packaging, and signage; direct mail/direct marketing; Internet services; market research; marketing communications planning; media planning, negotiating, and trafficking; positioning strategy development; and public relations services. Founded in 1971. **Company slogan:** The Street Smart Agency. **Special programs:** Internships. **Internship information:** Internships are offered for school credit only in the areas of public relations, graphic design, new business development, and media. **Corporate headquarters location:** This location. **President:** Chris Knopf. **Information Systems Manager:** Ron Perine. **Number of employees at this location:** 65.

MITCHELL COLLEGE
437 Pequot Avenue, New London CT 06320. 860/701-5000. **Fax:** 860/701-5090. **Contact:** Human Resources. **World Wide Web address:** http://www.mitchell.edu. **Description:** A private college offering two- and four-year programs. The college has approximately 650 students enrolled.

MOHEGAN SUN CASINO
One Mohegan Sun Boulevard, Uncasville CT 06382. 860/862-8000. **Toll-free phone:** 888/226-7711. **Contact:** Human Resources. **World Wide Web address:** http://www.mohegansun.com. **Description:** A casino and resort facility offering 2,500 slot machines, a wide variety of games, a night club, numerous restaurants, and a 1,500-room hotel. **Positions advertised include:** Surveillance Officer; Front Office Supervisor; Coat Room Attendant; Restaurant Host; Shuttle Driver; Valet Dispatcher; Hvac Mechanic; Retail Shift Manager; Stationary Engineer; Network Technician; Executive Housekeeper; Front Office Assistant Manager; VIP Recreation Supervisor; Voice Services Technician; Support Analyst; Retail Salesperson; Security Officer; Racebook/Keno Mechanic.

MOORE MEDICAL CORPORATION
P.O. Box 1500, New Britain CT 06050. 860/826-3600. **Contact:** Human Resources Manager. **World Wide Web address:** http://www.mooremedical.com. **Description:** A national distributor of pharmaceuticals and medical supplies. Primary customers include pharmacies, physicians, dentists, veterinarians, emergency medical services, municipalities, school systems, and correctional facilities. **Positions advertised include:** Customer Service Representative; Inside Sales Representative; Buyer; Field Sales Representative, Occupational Health; Senior Manager, Distribution Center; Returns Processor; Programmer Analyst. **Corporate headquarters location:** This location. **Other U.S. locations:** Hayward CA; Visalia CA; Lemont IL. **Operations at this facility include:** Administration; Sales; Service. **Listed on:** American Stock Exchange. **Stock exchange symbol:** MMD. **Number of employees nationwide:** 425.

MORGAN STANLEY DEAN WITTER & COMPANY
One Pickwick Plaza, Greenwich CT 06830. 203/625-4600. **Contact:** Human Resources. **World Wide Web address:** http://www.msdw.com. **Description:** One of the largest investment banking firms in the United States. Services include financing; financial advisory services; real estate services; corporate bond services; equity services; government and money market services; merger and acquisition services; investment research services; investment management services; and individual investor services. **Corporate headquarters location:** New York NY. **Other U.S. locations:** Nationwide.

MORGAN STANLEY DEAN WITTER & COMPANY
City Place One, 185 Asylum Street, 32nd Floor, Hartford CT 06103. 860/275-6300. **Contact:** Human Resources. **World Wide Web address:** http://www.msdw.com. **Description:** Offers diversified financial services including equities, fixed income securities, commodities, money market instruments, and investment banking services. **Corporate headquarters location:** New York NY. **Other U.S. locations:** Nationwide.

THE ROBERT E. MORRIS COMPANY
17 Talcott Notch Road, Farmington CT 06032-0487. 860/678-0200. **Contact:** Human Resources. **World Wide Web address:** http://www.robertemorris.com. **Description:** A distributor of machines and machine tooling. Founded in 1941. **Office hours:** Monday - Friday, 8:00 a.m. - 4:45 p.m. **Other U.S. locations:** Nationwide. **Listed on:** Privately held. **President/CEO/Owner:** Lee Morris. **Information Systems Manager:** Glenn Eigabroadt.

MOTT'S INC.
P.O. Box 3800, Stamford CT 06905-0800. 203/968-7500. **Physical address:** 6 High Ridge Park, Stamford CT 06905. **Contact:** Human Resources. **World Wide Web address:** http://www.motts.com. **Description:** A major producer of apple juice, applesauce, and related fruit products. **Positions advertised include:** Human Resources Manager; Trade Spend Analyst, Special Beverages; Master Data Analyst; Cash Application Supervisor; Procurement Category Manager; Procurement Coordinator. **Corporate headquarters location:** This location. **Other U.S. locations:** CT; FL; LA; NJ; NY; PA. **International locations:** Canada; Mexico. **Parent company:** Cadbury Schwepps plc (London, England.) **Listed on:** New York Stock Exchange. **Stock exchange symbol:** CSG.

MOTTS HOLDINGS INC.
701 Hebron Avenue, Glastonbury CT 06033. 860/682-1020. **Contact:** Human Resources. **Description:** A diversified holding company. **Subsidiaries include:** Merit Technologies Ltd. (Vancouver, Canada) manufactures and distributes cash register terminals for the retail industry; Motts/Eagle Energy Company; Mott's Super Markets.

MYSTIC AQUARIUM
INSTITUTE FOR EXPLORATION
55 Coogan Boulevard, Mystic CT 06355. 860/572-5955. **Fax:** 860/572-5969. **Contact:** Human Resources. **E-mail address:** humanresources@mysticaquarium.org. **World Wide Web address:** http://www.mysticaquarium.org. **Description:** A nonprofit organization that promotes awareness of the aquatic world through an integration of educational programs, marine-life exhibits, research and development, and ocean exploration. Mystic Aquarium's exhibits include a variety of fish and invertebrates,

African black-footed penguins, beluga whales, Stellar's sea lions, northern fur seals, harbor seals, and Atlantic bottlenose dolphins. The organization also offers the Education Center in Hartford, which provides live animal exhibits, classrooms, and a resource center. Founded in 1973. **NOTE:** Entry-level positions, part-time jobs, and second and third shifts are offered. **Positions advertised include:** Exhibit Educator; Instructor; Shipping and Receiving Clerk. **Special programs:** Internships. **Office hours:** Monday - Friday, 9:00 a.m. - 5:00 p.m. **Corporate headquarters location:** This location. **Parent company:** Sea Research Foundation, Inc. **Annual sales/revenues:** Less than $5 million. **Number of employees at this location:** 225.

MYSTIC SEAPORT
P.O. Box 6000, Mystic CT 06355-0990. 860/572-0711. **Physical address:** 75 Greenmanville Avenue, Mystic CT 06355-0990. **Contact:** Human Resources. **World Wide Web address:** http://www.mysticseaport.com. **Description:** A 19th-century maritime museum. **NOTE:** Seasonal positions offered.

NCT GROUP, INC.
20 Ketchum Street, Westport CT 06880. 203/226-4447. **Fax:** 203/348-4106. **Contact:** Human Resources. **World Wide Web address:** http://www.nct-active.com. **Description:** Designs and manufactures electronic products that reduce noise and vibration. **Office hours:** Monday - Friday, 9:00 a.m. - 5:00 p.m. **Corporate headquarters location:** This location. **International locations:** Cambridge, England.

NFO WORLDGROUP, INC.
2 Pickwick Plaza, 3rd Floor, Greenwich CT 06830. 203/629-8888. **Contact:** Human Resources. **World Wide Web address:** http://www.nfow.com. **Description:** Provides custom and syndicated market research services, primarily using a proprietary panel of prerecruited consumer households throughout the country. NFO also offers Internet-based custom marketing research. **NOTE:** Send resumes to 2700 Oregon Road, Northwood OH 43619. **Corporate headquarters location:** Canton OH. **International locations:** Worldwide. **Subsidiaries include:** Advanced Marketing Solutions, Inc. (CT) provides custom computer software systems used by clients to quickly access and analyze complex business and consumer information; Payment Systems, Inc. (FL) is a leading supplier of information to the financial services industry in the United States. **Parent company:** The Interpublic Group of Companies, Inc. **Listed on:** New York Stock Exchange. **Stock exchange symbol:** IPG. **Number of employees worldwide:** 15,000.

THE NASH ENGINEERING COMPANY
9 Trefoil Drive, Trumbull CT 06611. 203/459-3900. **Toll-free phone:** 800/553-NASH. **Fax:** 203/459-3880. **Contact:** Personnel. **E-mail address:** hr@nashelmo.com. **World Wide Web address:** http://www.nasheng.com. **Description:** Manufactures, distributes, and services compressed air and vacuum systems for industrial use worldwide. Founded in 1905. **Positions advertised include:** Global Materials Manager. **Corporate headquarters location:** This location. **Number of employees at this location:** 250.

NAUGATUCK GLASS COMPANY
P.O. Box 71, Naugatuck CT 06770. 203/729-5227. **Toll-free phone:** 800/533-3513. **Contact:** Personnel. **World Wide Web address:** http://www.naugatuckglass.com. **Description:** Cuts flat glass and flat mirror stock. Founded in 1927. **Subsidiaries include:** Bedford Mirror; Metavac, Inc.

NETPLEX
36 Lorraine Street, Hartford CT 06105. 860/233-1111. **Contact:** Human Resources. **E-mail address:** jobs@ntplx.net. **World Wide Web address:** http://www.ntplx.net. **Description:** One of Connecticut's leading Internet access providers.

NEUROGEN CORPORATION
35 NE Industrial Road, Branford CT 06405. 203/488-8201. **Fax:** 203/481-8683. **Contact:** Human Resources. **World Wide Web address:** http://www.neurogen.com. **Description:** Manufactures and markets neuropharmaceuticals for the treatment of psychiatric and neurological disorders through research involving molecular biology, medicinal chemistry, genetic engineering, and neurobiology. Development has also begun on new psychotherapeutic drugs to aid in treating a wide range of neuropsychiatric disorders including anxiety, psychosis, epilepsy, dementia, sleep- and stress-related disorders, and depression. **Positions advertised include:** Part-time Lab Assistant; Pain Pharmacologist; Research Associate; Senior Scientist. **Corporate headquarters location:** This location. **Listed on:** NASDAQ. **Stock exchange symbol:** NRGN. **Number of employees at this location:** 80.

NEW CANAAN VETERINARY HOSPITAL
7 Vitti Street, New Canaan CT 06840. 203/966-1627. **Contact:** Human Resources. **E-mail address:** ncvhdoc1@aol.com. **Description:** New Canaan Veterinary Hospital is an animal hospital. Services include radiology, dentistry, electrocardiography, surgery, diagnostic ultrasound, boarding, and kennel services.

NEW HAVEN MOVING EQUIPMENT CORPORATION
41 Washington Street, East Haven CT 06512. 203/469-6421. **Contact:** Manager. **World Wide Web address:** http://www.newhaven-usa.com. **Description:** A wholesaler of moving trucks and related equipment. **Other U.S. locations:** Nationwide.

NEW HAVEN REGISTER
40 Sargent Drive, New Haven CT 06511. 203/789-5200. **Contact:** Human Resources. **World Wide Web address:** http://www.newhavenregister.com. **Description:** Publishes a newspaper with a weekday circulation of 110,000 and a Sunday circulation of 121,000. **Corporate headquarters location:** This location.

NEW TECHNOLOGY SOLUTIONS, INC.
432 Washington Avenue, North Haven CT 06473. 203/239-6874. **Fax:** 203/239-7230. **Contact:** Human Resources. **World Wide Web address:** http://www.newtechusa.com. **Description:** Provides Microsoft Windows and VB developer training. The company offers seminars, on-site training programs, videos, and other related services. Founded in 1993. **Positions advertised include:** Systems Engineer; Senior Systems Engineer; Systems Architect; Practice Manager; Business Development Manager; Technical Services Director. **Corporate headquarters location:** This location. **Other U.S. locations:** Waltham MA; Providence RI.

THE NEWTOWN BEE
BEE PUBLISHING COMPANY
5 Church Hill Road, Newtown CT 06470. 203/426-3141. **Contact:** Human Resources. **World Wide Web address:** http://www.thebee.com. **Description:** Publishes a daily community newspaper covering events and news in western Connecticut. **Corporate headquarters location:** This location.

NORELCO CONSUMER PRODUCTS COMPANY
1010 Washington Boulevard, Stamford CT 06912. 203/973-0200. **Fax:** 203/967-9881. **Contact:** Jamie Guerrero, Director of Human Resources. **Description:** Markets electric razors and accessories for men and women, full-size irons, travel irons and steamers, air purifier systems and filters, and travel adapters and converters. **Parent company:** Philips Electronics North America Corporation is one of the larger industrial companies in the United States. The company concentrates its efforts primarily in the fields of consumer electronics, consumer products, electrical and electronics components, and professional equipment.

NORTHEAST UTILITIES
107 Seldon Street, Berlin CT 06037. 860/665-5000. **Contact:** Human Resources. **World Wide Web address:** http://www.nu.com. **Description:** A utility and real estate holding company. Northeast Utilities is among the 20 largest electric utility systems in the country and the largest in New England, serving approximately 1,684,000 customers in Connecticut, New Hampshire, and western Massachusetts. **Positions advertised include:** Associate Senior Engineer; Human Resources Information Systems Specialist; IT Telecommunications Specialist; Senior Staff Accountant. **Corporate headquarters location:** This location. **Subsidiaries include:** Charter Oak Energy, Inc.; The Connecticut Light and Power Company (also at this location); HEC Inc.; Holyoke Water Power Company; North Atlantic Energy Corporation; North Atlantic Energy Service Corporation; Northeast Nuclear Energy Company; Northeast Utilities Service Company; Public Service Company of New Hampshire; The Quinnehtuk Company; The Rocky River Realty Company; and Western Massachusetts Electric Company. **Listed on:** New York Stock Exchange. **Stock exchange symbol:** NU. **President/CEO:** Mike Morris.

NORTHERN MIDDLESEX YMCA
99 Union Street, Middletown CT 06457. 860/347-6907. **Contact:** Human Resources. **World Wide Web address:** http://www.middlesexymca.org. **Description:** One of the nation's largest and most comprehensive nonprofit service organizations. The YMCA provides health and fitness, social and personal development, sports and recreation, education and career development, and camps and conferences to children, youths, adults, the elderly, families, disabled individuals, refugees and foreign nationals, YMCA residents, and community residents through a broad range of specific programs.

NORTHROP GRUMMAN NORDEN SYSTEMS
P.O. Box 5300, Norwalk CT 06856. 203/852-5000. **Physical address:** 10 Norden Place, Norwalk CT 06856. **Contact:** Jane Nelson, Personnel Director. **World Wide Web address:** http://www.northgrum.com. **Description:** Northrop Grumman manufactures military aircraft, commercial aircraft parts, radar equipment, and electronic systems. Northrop Grumman has developed the B-2 Stealth Bomber, as well as parts for the F/A-18 and the 747. **Positions advertised include:** Electronics Engineer; Software Engineer. **Corporate headquarters location:** Los Angeles CA. **Operations at this facility include:** This location designs, develops, and manufactures advanced command, control, and communications systems; avionics systems; and data processing systems for military applications. **Listed on:** New York Stock Exchange. **Stock exchange symbol:** NOC.

NOVAMETRIX MEDICAL SYSTEMS INC.
5 Technology Drive, Wallingford CT 06492. 203/265-7701. **Fax:** 203/284-0753. **Contact:** Human Resources. **E-mail address:** hr@novrametrix.com. **World Wide Web address:** http://www.novametrix.com. **Description:** Novametrix Medical Systems Inc. develops, manufactures, and markets noninvasive, critical care blood gas monitors, respiratory monitors, and disposable products. Distributed worldwide, these electronic medical instruments provide continuous patient monitoring capabilities in hospital and nonhospital environments. The company's product line is comprised of capnographs; pulse oximeters; transcutaneous blood gas monitors; respiratory mechanics monitors; and reusable and disposable sensors, adapters, related accessories, and replacement parts. One branch of Novametrix Medical Systems, Cascadia Technology Division, is primarily a research and development group located in Redmond WA. **Corporate headquarters location:** This location. **NOTE:** Apply online at http://www.responics.appone.com. **Other U.S. locations:** Norwell MA; Redmond WA. **Listed on:** NASDAQ. **Stock exchange symbol:** NMTX. **Number of employees nationwide:** 230.

O&G INDUSTRIES INC.
112 Wall Street, Torrington CT 06790. 860/489-9261. **Contact:** Human Resources. **World Wide Web address:** http://www.ogindustries.com. **Description:** A construction firm providing building construction management, design services, heavy civil construction, environmental remediation, and construction materials. **Positions advertised include:** Accountant; Senior Buildings Estimator; Business Development Manager; Project Manager; Project Engineer. **Corporate headquarters location:** This location. **Other area locations:** Bridgeport CT; Southbury CT.

OMI CORPORATION
Metro Center, One Station Place, 7th Floor North, Stamford CT 06902. 203/602-6700. **Contact:** Human Resources. **World Wide Web address:** http://www.omicorp.com. **Description:** A large bulk shipping company with interests in 46 ocean-going bulk carriers, tankers, and gas carriers. OMI also provides logistics, crewing, technical, and commercial operations for international clients. The company has interests in OMI Petrolink Corporation and in Chiles Offshore Corporation, which operates 14 drilling rigs. **Corporate headquarters location:** This location. **Subsidiaries include:** OMI Marine Services, LLC. **Listed on:** New York Stock Exchange. **Stock exchange symbol:** OMM.

O'CONNELL, FLAHERTY & ATTMORE
280 Trumbull Street, Hartford CT 06103. 860/548-1300. **Contact:** Firm Administrator. **World Wide Web address:** http://www.ofalaw.com. **Description:** A law firm specializing in real estate, insurance, probate, and general litigation.

OLIN CORPORATION
501 Merritt Seven, Norwalk CT 06856. 203/750-3000. **Fax:** 203/495-8625. **Contact:** Human Resources. **World Wide Web address:** http://www.olin.com. **Description:** Produces copper alloys, ammunition, and chlorine and caustic soda. **Positions advertised include:** Lab Technician; Research Scientist/Engineer. **Corporate headquarters location:** This location. **Other U.S. locations:** Nationwide. **Listed on:** New York Stock Exchange. **Stock exchange symbol:** OLN. **Number of employees nationwide:** 6,700.

OMEGA ENGINEERING, INC.
One Omega Drive, P.O. Box 4047, Stamford CT 06907-0047. 203/359-1660. **Contact:** Human Resources. **World Wide Web address:** http://www.omega.com. **Description:** A manufacturer and worldwide distributor of process measurement and control instrumentation. Products include temperature, pressure, strain, and flow devices; pH equipment; and a large selection of instrument and control tools. OMEGA Engineering

also provides related consulting and engineering services. **Positions advertised include:** Client/Server Programmer Analyst; Electronic Design Engineer; Export Administrative Assistant; Industrial Product Manager; Manufacturing Engineer; Mechanical Design Engineer; Network Engineer; Planner; Buyer; Software/Systems Support; Sales-Quotations Engineer; Staff Accountant; Technical Customer Service; Technical Sales and Application Engineer. **Corporate headquarters location:** This location.

OTIS ELEVATOR COMPANY
One Farm Springs Road, Farmington CT 06032. 860/676-6000. **Contact:** Human Resources. **World Wide Web address:** http://www.nao.otis.com. **Description:** Produces and distributes a line of elevators and escalators for commercial and industrial use. Founded in 1853. **NOTE:** Apply online at www.otiscareers.com. **Corporate headquarters location:** This location. **Other U.S. locations:** Nationwide. **Parent company:** United Technologies Corporation.

OXFORD HEALTH PLANS
48 Monroe Turnpike, Trumbull CT 06611. **Toll-free phone:** 800/444-6222. **Contact:** Human Resources. **World Wide Web address:** http://www.oxhp.com. **Description:** A managed care company providing health benefit plans in New York, New Jersey, and Connecticut. The company's product lines include traditional health maintenance organizations, a point-of-service Freedom Plan, third-party administration of employer-funded benefit plans, Medicare and Medicaid supplemental plans, and dental plans. Oxford Health Plans markets its health plans to employers and individuals through its direct sales force, as well as through independent insurance agents and brokers. Founded in 1984. **Positions advertised include:** Health Care Economics Analyst; Senior Unix System Administrator; Broker Commission Representative; Case Manager; Premium Analyst; Network Developer; Actuarial Analyst; Senior Voice Network Engineer; Legal and Regulatory Specialist; Product Development Manager; Part-time Triage Nurse. **Corporate headquarters location:** This location. **Listed on:** New York Stock Exchange. **Stock exchange symbol:** OHP. **Number of employees at this location:** 350.

OZONE INDUSTRIES, INC.
P.O. Box 219, East Lyme CT 06333-0219. 860/739-4926. **Physical address:** 29 Industrial Park Road, East Lyme CT 06333. **Fax:** 860/691-2323. **Contact:** Human Resources. **E-mail address:** info@ozone-ind.com. **Description:** Ozone Industries Inc. designs, develops, and manufactures hydraulics for the aerospace and industrial markets. Products include landing gear; aircraft steering systems; and hydraulic power, control, and storage devices. **Office hours:** Monday - Friday, 8:00 a.m. - 5:00 p.m. **Corporate headquarters location:** This location. **Parent company:** BBA Group (England.) **Operations at this facility include:** This location houses manufacturing, engineering, quality control, marketing, and administrative offices. **Annual sales/revenues:** $11 - $20 million. **Number of employees at this location:** 130.

PALLFLEX
PALL CORPORATION
P.O. Box 929, Putnam CT 06260. 860/928-7761. **Physical address:** 125 Kennedy Drive, Putnam CT 06260. **Contact:** Human Resources. **World Wide Web address:** http://www.pall.com. **Description:** Pall Corporation is a world leader in filtration technology, specializing in fluid clarification and high-end separation. The company's overall business is organized into three segments: health care, aeropower, and fluid processing. Pall Corporation's products offer reliable solutions for customers, whether the client is involved in the beginning, middle, or end process of a project. In the fluid clarification market, Pall Corporation sells disposable cartridges that fit into filter houses it has sold to clients. In the separations market, the company sells complete systems, which include both semipermanent filters (which are replaced rarely) and systems that regularly consume disposable cartridges. **Corporate headquarters location:** East Hills NY. **Other U.S. locations:** Covina CA; Fort Myers FL; New Port Richey FL; Ann Arbor MI; Cortland NY; Hauppauge NY; Port Washington NY; Exton PA; Fajardo PR. **International locations:** Worldwide. **Operations at this facility include:** This location is engaged in fluid processing and clarification. **Listed on:** New York Stock Exchange. **Stock exchange symbol:** PLL. **Number of employees nationwide:** 6,500.

PARALLAX POWER COMPONENTS
902 Crescent Avenue, Bridgeport CT 06607. 203/336-0161. **Contact:** Human Resources. **E-mail address:** hr@parallaxpower.com. **World Wide Web address:** http://www.parallaxpower.com. **Description:** A designer, producer, and marketer of electrical, electronic, and industrial components and products. The company also offers services and repair support for its components. Parallax's principal products include ballasts and transformers for lighting; motors; and control components for motors and generators, systems, and controls. The company's service group rebuilds and repairs large motors, generators, and transformers primarily for utility companies and industrial manufacturers.

PATRIOT NATIONAL BANK
900 Bedford Street, Stamford CT 06901. 203/324-7500. **Fax:** 203/316-2983. **Contact:** Human Resources. **World Wide Web address:** http://www.pnbdirectonline.com. **Description:** A full-service banking institution offering a broad range of consumer and commercial banking services. Founded in 1994. **Corporate headquarters location:** This location. **Other area locations:** Greenwich CT; Norwalk CT; Old Greenwich CT.

PAUL, HASTINGS, JANOFSKY & WALKER LLP
1055 Washington Boulevard, Stamford CT 06901. 203/961-7400. **Contact:** Human Resources. **World Wide Web address:** http://www.paulhastings.com. **Description:** A law firm specializing in real estate, tax, litigation, and corporate law. Founded in 1951. **Corporate headquarters location:** San Francisco CA. **Other U.S. locations:** Los Angeles CA; Orange County CA; Washington DC; Atlanta GA; New York City NY. **International locations:** London, England; Tokyo, Japan.

PEOPLE'S BANK
850 Main Street, Bridgeport CT 06604. 203/338-7171. **Contact:** Human Resources. **World Wide Web address:** http://www.peoples.com. **Description:** Conducts business through more than 70 banking offices and one loan office in Fairfield, Hartford, Litchfield, New Haven, and Tolland Counties of Connecticut. People's Bank is one of the largest residential mortgage originators in Connecticut. Founded in 1842. **Positions advertised include:** Loss Prevention Representative; Manager/Vice President Asset/Liability; Middleware Administrator; Mortgage Underwriter; Primetime Tellers; Primetime Supermarket Bankers; Senior Financial Analyst, Customer Assistance; Statement Clerk; UNIX Systems Administrator. **Corporate headquarters location:** This location. **Parent company:** People's Mutual Holdings. **Listed on:** NASDAQ. **Stock exchange symbol:** PBCT.

PEPPERIDGE FARM INC.
595 Westport Avenue, Norwalk CT 06851. 203/846-7000. **Fax:** 203/846-7033. **Contact:** Dan Zimmerman, Director of Human Resources. **World Wide Web address:** http://www.cambpellsoup.com. **Description:** Manufactures and distributes a range of fresh and frozen baked goods and confections including bread, cookies, cakes, pastries, and crackers. **Special programs:** Internships. **Corporate headquarters location:** This location. **Parent company:** Campbell Soup Company (Camden NJ). **Listed on:** New York Stock Exchange. **Stock exchange symbol:** CPB. **Annual sales/revenues:** More than $100 million. **Number of employees at this location:** 280. **Number of employees nationwide:** 4,700.

PETROLEUM HEAT AND POWER CORPORATION
2187 Atlantic Street, Stamford CT 06902. 203/325-5400. **Recorded jobline:** 877/325-5400. **Contact:** Human Resources. **E-mail address:** greatjobs@petroheat.com. **World Wide Web address:** http://www.petro.com. **Description:** Petroleum Heat and Power Corporation is one of the nation's largest retail distributors of home heating oil. The company serves 26 Northeast and Mid-Atlantic markets including the metropolitan areas of Boston, New York, Baltimore, and Washington DC. In addition to the delivery of home heating oil, the company also installs, repairs, and services heating equipment. Founded in 1903. **Subsidiaries include:** Star Gas Corporation is one of the largest retail propane gas distributors in the country. **Number of employees at this location:** 2,400.

PFIZER INC.
Eastern Point Road, Groton CT 06340-5146. 860/441-4100. **Contact:** Human Resources. **World Wide Web address:** http://www.pfizer.com. **Description:** Pfizer is a leading pharmaceutical company that distributes products concerning cardiovascular health, central nervous system disorders, infectious diseases, and women's health worldwide. The company's brand-name products include Benadryl, Ben Gay, Cortizone, Desitin, Halls, Listerine, Sudafed, and Zantac 75. **Corporate headquarters location:** New York NY. **Operations at this facility include:** This location develops more than 400 different over-the-counter and prescription pharmaceutical products. **Listed on:** New York Stock Exchange. **Stock exchange symbol:** PFE.

PHELPS DODGE COPPER PRODUCTS COMPANY
P.O. Box 970, Norwich CT 06360-0970. 860/886-2661. **Physical address:** 41 Wawecus Street, Norwich CT 06360. **Contact:** Human Resources. **World Wide Web address:** http://www.phelpsdodge.com. **Description:** Phelps Dodge operates in two divisions. Phelps Dodge Mining Company is one of North America's largest producers of copper. It produces silver, gold, and molybdenum as by-products of its copper operations and fluorspar, gold, silver, lead, zinc, and copper from mines abroad. The company also explores for metals and minerals in the United States and abroad. Phelps Dodge Industries is the manufacturing and specialty chemicals division serving the transportation and electrical markets. The division is one of the largest international producers of carbon black (a basic raw material for the rubber industry and other industrial applications), is a major North American producer of magnet wire and specialty conductors, and has various interests in and manages companies that manufacture wire and cable products around the world. **Positions advertised include:** Chief Environmental Engineer. **Other U.S. locations:** Nationwide. **International locations:** Worldwide. **Listed on:** New York Stock Exchange. **Stock exchange symbol:** PD. **Number of employees worldwide:** 14,500.

PHIBRO INC.
500 Nyala Farms Road, Westport CT 06880. 203/221-5800. **Contact:** Human Resources. **World Wide Web address:** http://www.phibro.com. **Description:** A commodities trading group that deals with oil, gas, grain, wheat, and cocoa.

PHOENIX HOME LIFE MUTUAL INSURANCE COMPANY
One American Row, P.O. Box 5056, Hartford CT 06102-5056. 860/403-5000. **Contact:** Human Resources. **World Wide Web address:** http://www.phl.com. **Description:** One of the largest mutual life insurance companies in the United States. **Positions advertised include:** Senior Actuarial Analyst; Accounting Analyst. **Corporate headquarters location:** This location. **Other U.S. locations:** Boston MA; Braintree MA; Albany NY; East Greenbush NY. **Listed on:** New York Stock Exchange. **Stock exchange symbol:** PNX.

PHOENIX HOME LIFE MUTUAL INSURANCE COMPANY
100 Bright Meadow Boulevard, P.O. Box 1900, Enfield CT 06083-1900. 860/253-1000. **Contact:** Human Resources. **World Wide Web address:** http://www.phl.com. **Description:** One of the largest mutual life insurance companies in the United States. **Positions advertised include:** Distribution Administration Analyst; Distribution Administration Representative; Underwriter; Senior Operation Center Analyst; Senior Computer Operator. **Corporate headquarters location:** Hartford CT. **Other U.S. locations:** Boston MA; Braintree MA; Albany NY; East Greenbush NY. **Listed on:** New York Stock Exchange. **Stock exchange symbol:** PNX.

PHOTRONICS INC.
15 Secor Road, Brookfield CT 06804. 203/775-9000. **Contact:** Human Resources. **World Wide Web address:** http://www.photronics.com. **Description:** A leading manufacturer of photomasks used for the manufacture of semiconductors and integrated circuits. **Corporate headquarters location:** This location. **Other U.S. locations:** Phoenix AZ; Milpitas CA; Allen TX; Austin TX. **International locations:** China; Germany; Japan; Korea; Singapore; Taiwan; United Kingdom. **Listed on:** NASDAQ. **Stock exchange symbol:** PLAB.

PILLSBURY WINTHROP LLP
695 East Main Street, P.O. Box 6760, Stamford CT 06904-6760. 203/348-2300. **Contact:** Personnel. **World Wide Web address:** http://www.pillsburywinthrop.com. **Description:** A law firm specializing in estates, real estate, litigation, and corporate law. **Corporate headquarters location:** New York NY. **Other U.S. locations:** Nationwide. **International locations:** Australia; England; Hong Kong; Singapore; Tokyo.

PILOT PEN
60 Commerce Drive, Trumbull CT 06611. 203/377-8800. **Contact:** Human Resources. **E-mail address:** jobs@pilotpen.com. **World Wide Web address:** http://www.pilotpen.com. **Description:** Pilot Pen manufactures writing instruments. Founded in 1918. **Corporate headquarters location:** This location. **Operations at this facility include:** This location houses executive offices only.

PINKERTON CONSULTING & INVESIGATIONS
321 Research Parkway, Meriden CT 06450. 203/237-7778. **Contact:** Human Resources. **World Wide Web address:** www.ci-pinkerton.com. **Description:** America's first private investigation firm. Specializes in security solutions to corporate problems. **Corporate headquarters location:** Parsippany NJ. **Other U.S. locations:** Nationwide. **International locations:** Worldwide.

PITNEY BOWES, INC.
One Elmcroft Road, Stamford CT 06926-0700. 203/356-5000. **Fax:** 203/351-6293. **Contact:** Human Resources. **World Wide Web address:** http://www.pb.com.

Description: Pitney Bowes operates within two industry segments: Business Equipment and Services, and Financial Services. The Business Equipment and Services segment includes the manufacturing of postage meters; mailing, shipping, and facsimile systems; copiers and copier supplies; and mailroom reprographics. The Financial Services segment includes the worldwide financing operations of the company. This segment provides lease financing for the company's products, as well as other financial services for the commercial and industrial markets. Founded in 1920. **NOTE:** Apply online only. **Positions advertised include:** Accounting Analyst; Administrative Assistant; Benefits Administrator; Associate Engineer; Associate III, Payroll; Corporate Strategy Analyst; Customer Master SME; Customer Service Manager; Director, Corporate Accounting and Financial Reporting; Executive Secretary; Project Leader; Team Leader; Senior Financial Planner. **Corporate headquarters location:** This location. **International locations:** Worldwide. **Listed on:** New York Stock Exchange. **Stock exchange symbol:** PBI. **Number of employees worldwide:** 32,000.

PLAYTEX APPAREL, INC.
700 Fairfield Avenue, Stamford CT 06902. 203/356-8000. **Contact:** Dawn Cross, Vice President of Personnel. **World Wide Web address:** http://www.playtexnet.com. **Description:** Manufactures women's intimate apparel. **Parent company:** Sara Lee Corporation.

PRATT & WHITNEY
400 Main Street, East Hartford CT 06108. 860/565-4321. **Contact:** John Leary, Vice President of Human Resources. **World Wide Web address:** http://www.pratt-whitney.com. **Description:** Manufactures aircraft engine parts and blades for commercial and military engines. Founded in 1925. **Corporate headquarters location:** This location. **NOTE:** Mail resumes to United Technologies Resume Processing, Source Code PW Mail Pratt & Whitney, 89 Davis Road, Suite 160, Orinda CA 94563. **Other U.S. locations:** Columbus GA; North Berwick ME. **Parent company:** United Technologies Corporation designs and manufactures engines and space propulsion systems for commercial and general aviation. Products include large jet engines, temperature control systems, elevators and escalators, helicopters, and flight systems. The company markets its products under a variety of brand names including Carrier, Hamilton Standard, Otis, Pratt & Whitney, and Sikorsky. **Number of employees worldwide:** 30,000.

PRAXAIR TECHNOLOGY, INC.
39 Old Ridgebury Road, Danbury CT 06810. 203/837-2000. **Contact:** Barbara Harris, Vice President of Personnel. **World Wide Web address:** http://www.praxair.com. **Description:** Praxair produces gases and gas production equipment for customers in the aerospace, chemicals, electronics, food processing, health care, glass, metal fabrication, petroleum, primary metals, pulp, and paper industries. Praxair also coats customer-supplied parts and equipment with metallic and ceramic coatings for the textile, aircraft engine, paper, petrochemical, metals, and printing industries. **Positions advertised include:** Administrative Specialist; Inside Sales Representative. **Corporate headquarters location:** This location. **International locations:** Worldwide. **Listed on:** New York Stock Exchange. **Stock exchange symbol:** PX.

PREMCOR INC.
1700 East Putnam Avenue, Suite 400, Old Greenwich CT 06870. 203/698-7500. **Fax:** 203/698-7925. **Contact:** Christine Carnicelli, Human Resources. **E-mail address:** christine.carnicelli@premcor.com. **World Wide Web address:** http://www.premcor.com. **Description:** Premcor is one of the largest independent petroleum refiners and suppliers of unbranded transportation fuels, heating oil, petrochemical feedstocks, petroleum coke and other petroleum products in the United States. Premcor owns and operates refineries in Texas, Ohio, Tennessee and Delaware. **Positions advertised include:** Income Tax Accountant; Manager of IT; Property and Sales Tax Manager; Sr. Analyst; Sr. Auditor. **Listed on:** New York Stock Exchange. **Stock exchange symbol:** PCO.

PRICEWATERHOUSECOOPERS
100 Pearl Street, Hartford CT 06103. 860/241-7000. **Contact:** Human Resources. **World Wide Web address:** http://www.pricewaterhousecoopers.com. **Description:** One of the largest certified public accounting firms in the world. PricewaterhouseCoopers provides public accounting, business advisory, management consulting, and taxation services. **Corporate headquarters location:** New York NY. **Other U.S. locations:** Nationwide.

PRICEWATERHOUSECOOPERS
300 Atlantic Street, Stamford CT 06901. 203/539-3000. **Contact:** Sue Cohen, Human Resources. **World Wide Web address:** http://www.pricewaterhousecoopers.com. **Description:** One of the largest certified public accounting firms in the world. PricewaterhouseCoopers provides public accounting, business advisory, management consulting, and taxation services. **Corporate headquarters location:** New York NY. **Other U.S. locations:** Nationwide.

PRIMEDIA BUSINESS MAGAZINES & MEDIA
P.O. Box 4949, Stamford CT 06907. 203/358-9900. **Physical address:** 11 Riverbend Drive South, Stamford CT 06907. **Fax:** 203/358-4194. **Contact:** Human Resources. **World Wide Web address:** http://www.primediabusiness.com. **Description:** A publisher of business-to-business newsletters concerning the information technology and online industries. The company also publishes information on the World Wide Web, and in CD-ROM and Yellow Pages formats. Founded in 1886. **NOTE:** Part-time jobs are offered. **Special programs:** Internships. **International locations:** Worldwide. **Parent company:** PRIMEDIA. **Listed on:** New York Stock Exchange. **Stock exchange symbol:** PRM. **Number of employees at this location:** 300. **Number of employees nationwide:** 2,000.

PRINCETON REVIEW INC.
265A Post Road West, Westport CT 06880. 203/226-2662. **Contact:** Human Resources. **World Wide Web address:** http://www.princetonreview.com. **Description:** Offers a variety of review and test preparation courses for students taking exams such as the SAT, GRE, LMAT, LSAT, and GMAT. **Corporate headquarters location:** New York NY. **Listed on:** NASDAQ. **Stock exchange symbol:** REVU.

PRO-FITNESS HEALTHSOUTH
40 Richards Avenue, Norwalk CT 06854. 203/853-6478. **Contact:** Human Resources. **Description:** Pro-Fitness manages a chain of fitness centers. **Operations at this facility include:** This location houses administrative offices.

PURDUE PHARMA L.P.
One Stamford Forum, 201 Tresser Boulevard, Stamford CT 06901-3431. 203/588-8000. **Fax:** 203/588-8850. **Contact:** Human Resources. **World Wide Web address:** http://www.purduepharma.com. **Description:** Purdue is engaged in the research, development, production, sales, and licensing of both prescription and over-the-counter medicines and hospital products. **NOTE:** Candidates must apply online. No hard copy resumes will be considered. **Positions advertised include:** Sr. Statistical Programmer; Program Manager; Staff Accountant; Sr. Auditor; Clinical Research Scientist; Drug Safety Analyst; Library Coordinator; Asst. General Counsel.

THE PURDY CORPORATION
P.O. Box 1898, Manchester CT 06045-1898. 860/649-0000. **Physical address:** 586 Hillard Street, Manchester CT 06040. **Contact:** William Laramee, Human Resources. **World Wide Web address:** http://www.purdytransmissions.com. **Description:** Manufactures major parts for helicopters and other aircraft including gear box housings and components. Founded in 1946. **NOTE:** Employees are trained in advanced machining and are offered courses in computers, electronics, engineering, and mathematics. **Corporate headquarters location:** This location.

PUTNAM PRECISION MOLDING, INC.
11 Danco Road, Putnam CT 06260. 860/928-7911. **Toll-free phone:** 877/477-6462. **Contact:** Human Resources Department. **World Wide Web address:** http://www.putnamprecisionmolding.com. **Description:** Manufactures custom injection-molded plastics. **Corporate headquarters location:** This location. **Parent company:** Ensinger Industries. **Operations at this facility include:** Administration; Manufacturing.

QUEST DIAGNOSTICS
144 North Main Street, Branford CT 06405. 203/949-1260. **Contact:** Human Resources. **World Wide Web address:** http://www.questdiagnostics.com. **Description:** One of the largest clinical laboratories in North America, providing a broad range of clinical laboratory services to health care clients that include physicians, hospitals, clinics, dialysis centers, pharmaceutical companies, and corporations. The company offers and performs tests on blood, urine, and other bodily fluids and tissues to provide information for health and well-being. **Other U.S. locations:** Nationwide. **Listed on:** New York Stock Exchange. **Stock exchange symbol:** DGX.

QUEUE INC.
1450 Barnum Avenue, Bridgeport CT 06110. **Toll-free phone:** 800/232-2224. **Contact:** Personnel. **World Wide Web address:** http:// www.queueinc.com. **Description:** Develops educational software. Queue's products range from early education software to more advanced levels in the areas of history, art, math, literature, language arts, test preparation, and typing.

QUINNIPIAC UNIVERSITY
275 Mount Carmel Avenue, Hamden CT 06518. 203/582-8200. **Contact:** Human Resources. **World Wide Web address:** http://www.quinnipiac.edu. **Description:** A private university with an enrollment of 6,000 students. The university offers undergraduate degrees in business, health sciences, and liberal arts; and graduate degree programs in business, education, health sciences, mass communications, journalism, and law.

RCG INFORMATION TECHNOLOGY, INC.
50 Columbus Boulevard, 5th Floor, Hartford CT 06106. 860/278-1234. **Contact:** Human Resources. **World Wide Web address:** http://www.rcgit.com. **Description:** Provides computer consulting services. **Corporate headquarters location:** Edison NJ. **Other U.S. locations:** Washington DC; Orlando FL; Chicago IL; New York NY; Westchester NY; Philadelphia PA; Dallas TX; Houston TX. **International locations:** Philippines; South Africa.

WILLIAM RAVEIS HOME-LINK
7 Trap Falls Road, Shelton CT 06484. 203/926-1090. **Fax:** 203/929-6523. **Contact:** Human Resources. **World Wide Web address:** http://www.raveis.com. **Description:** A commercial real estate agency. Founded in 1974. **Corporate headquarters location:** This location.

WILLIAM RAVEIS HOME-LINK
3 Park Street, Norwalk CT 06851. 203/847-6633. **Contact:** Manager. **World Wide Web address:** http://www.raveis.com. **Description:** A real estate agency dealing with residential and commercial properties. Founded in 1974. **Corporate headquarters location:** Shelton CT.

RAYTECH CORPORATION
4 Corporate Drive, Suite 295, Shelton CT 06484. 203/925-8023. **Contact:** Human Resources. **World Wide Web address:** http://www.raytech.com. **Description:** Raytech Corporation is a multinational manufacturer and marketer of products for heat-resistant, inertia control, energy absorption, and transmission applications. Products are used in the automotive, aerospace, nucleonic, petrochemical, energy, metal working, construction, agricultural, utility, and electronics industries. **Corporate headquarters location:** This location. **International locations:** China; England; Germany. **Subsidiaries include:** Allomatic is a supplier of power train components; Raybestos Products develops, manufactures, and markets friction materials for wet clutch and brake applications for vehicle and component manufacturers worldwide; Raybestos Aftermarket Products and Allomatic Products provide aftermarket products for domestic automobiles and trucks, which include automatic transmission filters, and friction and reaction plates. **Listed on:** New York Stock Exchange. **Stock exchange symbol:** RAY. **Number of employees nationwide:** 1,300.

REED BUSINESS
1234 Summer Street, 6th Floor, Stamford CT 06905. 203/326-5161. **Contact:** Human Resources. **World Wide Web address:** http://www.reedbusiness.com. **Description:** Provider of a variety of communication mediums. **Positions advertised include:** Account Executive. **Parent Company:** Reed Elsevier Group PLC.

REMINGTON PRODUCTS COMPANY LLC
50 Commerce Drive, Trumbull CT 06611. 203/367-4400. **Contact:** Human Resources. **World Wide Web address:** http://www.remington-products.com. **Description:** A manufacturer, distributor, and retailer of personal care appliances including electric shavers, hair dryers, beard trimmers, and spa therapy products. Founded in 1937. **Positions advertised include:** Trade Marketing Representative. **Corporate headquarters location:** This location. **Other U.S. locations:** Nationwide. **International locations:** Worldwide. **Operations at this facility include:** Administration; Divisional Headquarters; Manufacturing; Research and Development; Sales; Service. **Listed on:** Privately held. **Annual sales/revenues:** More than $100 million. **Number of employees at this location:** 800. **Number of employees nationwide:** 1,100.

RESEARCH INTERNATIONAL
3 Landmark Square, Fourth Floor, Stamford CT 06901. 203/358-0900. **Fax:** 312/787-4156. **Contact:** Human Resources. **E-mail address:** greatjobs@research-int.com. **World Wide Web address:** http://www.research-int.com. **Description:** A company specializing in custom market research. Company teams up with clients and coaches them on making their own companies thrive. **Positions advertised include:** Senior

Research Manager. **Other U.S. locations:** Nationwide. **International locations:** Worldwide.

ROGERS CORPORATION
P.O. Box 188, Rogers CT 06263-0188. 860/774-9605. **Physical address:** One Technology Drive, Rogers CT 06263. **Contact:** Jack Richie, Director of Human Resources. **E-mail address:** employment@rogers-corp.com. **World Wide Web address:** http://www.rogers-corp.com. **Description:** Rogers Corporation develops and manufactures specialty polymer composite materials and components for the imaging, communications, computer and peripheral, consumer products, and transportation markets. Rogers Corporation is divided into segments according to the materials produced. The Poron Materials Unit (East Woodstock CT) manufactures urethane and silicone foam materials. The Elastomeric Components Unit (South Windham CT) manufactures foam and solid elastomeric components. The Microwave and Circuit Materials Divisions (Chandler AZ) manufacture high-frequency laminates used to make circuits for communications applications and flexible circuit materials used for interconnections in computers and peripherals. The Composite Materials Division (also at this location) manufactures dielectric material for most of these microwave laminates. The Molding Materials Division (Manchester CT) produces moldable composites using polymer engineering and filler technology. Durel Corporation (Tempe and Chandler AZ) is a joint venture between Rogers and 3M, whose business focuses on electroluminescent lamps. **NOTE:** Rogers Corporation does not accept unsolicited resumes. Check their Website for open positions. **Positions advertised include:** Market Development Specialist; Systems Analyst. **Corporate headquarters location:** This location. **Listed on:** New York Stock Exchange. **Stock exchange symbol:** ROG. **Number of employees nationwide:** 1,100.

ROSS AND ROBERTS, INC.
1299 West Broad Street, Stratford CT 06615. 203/378-9363. **Contact:** Susan Scovin, Personnel Manager. **Description:** Manufactures calendered vinyl film and vinyl-coated fabrics. **Operations at this facility include:** Manufacturing. **Number of employees at this location:** 125.

SCM MICROSYSTEMS
20 Carter Drive, Guilford CT 06437. 203/483-8348. **Contact:** Human Resources. **World Wide Web address:** http://www.scmmicro.com. **Description:** Manufactures computer memory and memory upgrades. **Corporate headquarters location:** Fremont CA. **Listed on:** NASDAQ. **Stock exchange symbol:** SCMM.

STR SPECIALIZED TECHNOLOGY RESOURCES
10 Water Street, Enfield CT 06082. 860/749-8371. **Fax:** 860/749-8234. **Contact:** Carol Dyjak, Business Administration & Human Resources Manager. **World Wide Web address:** http://www.strlab.com. **Description:** Provides testing and quality assurance services to assist in product development and safety evaluation of consumer products, industrial products, and raw materials. Services include regulatory compliance, product design evaluation and development, in-process quality control audits, factory audits, post-production quality assurance, preshipment verification, and management information reporting. **NOTE:** Entry-level positions and second and third shifts are offered. **Positions advertised include:** Technician Assistant; Per Diem Apparel/Textile Inspector; Extruder Operator. **Listed on:** Privately held. **Annual sales/revenues:** $21 - $50 million.

SACRED HEART UNIVERSITY
5151 Park Avenue, Fairfield CT 06825-1000. 203/371-7999. **Fax:** 203/365-7527. **Contact:** Human Resources. **E-mail address:** resumehr@sacredheart.edu. **World Wide Web address:** http://www.sacredheart.edu. **Description:** One of the largest Catholic universities in the New England area. Sacred Heart University offers programs through the College of Arts & Sciences, the College of Business, the College of Education & Health Professions, and the University College. Founded in 1963. **Positions advertised include:** Cleaning Supervisor; Director of Bands; Director of Major and Planned Gifts; Graduate Residence Hall Director; Programmer Analyst; Public Safety Officer.

ST. FRANCIS HOSPITAL & MEDICAL CENTER
114 Woodland Street, Hartford CT 06105. 860/714-4160. **Fax:** 860/714-8048. **Contact:** Human Resources. **World Wide Web address:** http://www.stfranciscare.org. **Description:** A 617-bed Catholic hospital specializing in cardiology, oncology, women's and children's services, behavioral health care, emergency/trauma care, and rehabilitation. **Positions advertised include:** Medical Staff Trainer; Clinical Educator; School Clinician; Crisis Clinician; Primary Therapist; Speech/Language Pathologist; Physical Therapist; Medical Radiation Dosimetrist; Medical Physicist; Audiologist; Certified Theraputic Recreation Specialist; Operations Supervisor; Pharmacist; Catering Supervisor; Chief Medical Physicist; Medical Assistant; Mental Health Worker; Nursing Assistant; Clinical Nursing Supervisor; Assistant Nurse Manager; Nurse Practitioner; Admission Nurse; Neonatal Nurse; Staff Physician; Geriatric Medicine Physician; Rheumatologist; Registered Nurse Endoscopy; Staff RN; Registered Nurse; Occupational Health Nurse; Coding Specialist; Secretary; Counter Aide; Porter; Driver; Food Service Assistant; Teacher Aide; Data Coordinator; Accessioning Clerk. **Special programs:** Internships. **Operations at this facility include:** Administration; Divisional Headquarters.

ST. MARY'S HOSPITAL
56 Franklin Street, Waterbury CT 06706. 203/574-6000. **Fax:** 203/575-7753. **Contact:** Dee Anderson, Human Resources. **E-mail address:** danderson@stmh.org. **World Wide Web address:** http://www.stmh.org. **Description:** A nonprofit, full-service hospital offering behavioral health care, a family health center, a children's health center, a women's center, a Level II trauma center, and pediatric care. **NOTE:** Part-time jobs and second and third shifts are offered. **Positions advertised include:** Registered Nurse; Patient Care Assistant; Secretary; Clerk; Security Officer; Clinical Supervisor; Human Resources Manager; Office Manager; Pharmacist. **CEO:** Sister Marguerite Waite. **Number of employees at this location:** 1,700.

ST. PAUL TRAVELERS
One Tower Square, Hartford CT 06183. 860/277-0111. **Contact:** Human Resources. **World Wide Web address:** http://www.stpaultravelers.com. **Description:** The second-largest commercial U.S. property-liability insurance company, St. Paul Travelers offers insurance to a wide variety of businesses and other organizations, as well as individuals, through independent insurance agents and brokers. The company also holds a nearly 80 percent majority interest in Nuveen Investments. **Positions advertised include:** Assistant Director, Data Management; Sr. Financial Consultant; Account Manager; CD Complex Claim Director; Manager, Product Development; Construction Account Manager; Sr. Business Analyst. **Corporate headquarters location:** Saint Paul MN. **Listed on:** New York Stock Exchange. **Stock exchange symbol:** STA.

THE SALVATION ARMY
30 Elm Street, Box 684, Bridgeport CT 06601. 203/334-0995. **Contact:** Human Resources. **World Wide Web address:** http://www.salvationarmy.org. **Description:** A nonprofit organization providing several service programs including day-care centers, programs for people with disabilities, substance abuse programs and tutoring for at-risk students. The Salvation Army targets its programs to assist alcoholics, battered women, drug addicts, the elderly, the homeless, people with AIDS, prison inmates, teenagers, and the unemployed. **Corporate headquarters location:** Alexandria VA. **Other U.S. locations:** Nationwide. **International locations:** Worldwide.

SARGENT MANUFACTURING
100 Sargent Drive, New Haven CT 06536. 203/562-2151. **Contact:** Jack Dwyer, Director of Human Resources. **World Wide Web address:** http://www.sargentlock.com. **Description:** The company manufactures architectural hardware and locks for residential use. **Number of employees at this location:** 700.

SAVE THE CHILDREN
54 Wilton Road, Westport CT 06880. 203/221-4000. **Toll-free phone:** 800/728-3843. **Contact:** Personnel. **World Wide Web address:** http://www.savethechildren.org. **Description:** A nonprofit organization that works to raise funds for disadvantaged children worldwide. **Positions advertised include:** Marketing Manager; Outbound Call Center Representative; Deputy Director of Education; Education Specialist; Program Specialist; Family Planning/Reproductive Health Advisor; AVP Planning, Monitoring and Evaluation. **Corporate headquarters location:** This location.

SAVIN CORPORATION
P.O. Box 10270, Stamford CT 06904-2270. 203/967-5000. **Physical address:** 333 Ludlow Street, Stamford CT 06904. **Contact:** Bob Manley, Human Resources Director. **World Wide Web address:** http://www.savin.com. **Description:** Distributes copiers and facsimile machines. **Corporate headquarters location:** This location.

SCAN-OPTICS, INC.
169 Progress Drive, Manchester CT 06040. 860/645-7878. **Fax:** 860/645-7995. **Contact:** Human Resources. **E-mail address:** mdarrell@scanoptics.com. **World Wide Web address:** http://www.scanoptics.com. **Description:** Scan-Optics designs and manufactures information processing systems used for imaging, data capture, document processing, and information management. Scan-Optics systems make it possible to process very large volumes of paper using features such as high-speed paper movement, optical character recognition, intelligent character recognition, high-speed image capture, image processing, and image storage and retrieval systems. Scan-Optics systems encompass hardware, software, and integration technologies for complete solutions. Typical applications for Scan-Optics systems include the processing of credit card sales drafts, mail order forms, federal and state tax forms, health care forms, automobile registrations, shareholder proxies, and payroll time cards. **Corporate headquarters location:** This location. **Other U.S. locations:** Dallas TX. **International locations:** England.

SCHOLASTIC, INC.
90 Sherman Turnpike, Danbury CT 06816. 203/797-3500. **Fax:** 203/797-3284. **Recorded jobline:** 203/797-3776. **Contact:** Human Resources **E-mail address:** danburyjobs@scholastic.com. **World Wide Web address:** http://www.scholastic.com. **Description:** Publishes a variety of books ranging from encyclopedias to children's books. Founded in 1896. **NOTE:** Entry-level positions are offered. **Corporate headquarters location:** New York NY. **International locations:** Worldwide. **Listed on:** NASDAQ. **Stock exchange symbol:** SCHL.

SCHOONER INC.
60 South Water Street, New Haven CT 06519. 203/865-1737. **Contact:** Human Resources. **World Wide Web address:** http://www.schoonersoundlearning.org. **Description:** A marine science company engaged in preserving the marine life of Long Island Sound and promoting environmental educational awareness.

THE SCIENCE CENTER OF CONNECTICUT
950 Trout Brook Drive, West Hartford CT 06119. 860/231-2824. **Contact:** Human Resources. **World Wide Web address:** http://www.sciencecenterct.org. **Description:** A science museum, open seven days per week in July and August, and six days per week during the rest of the year (closed on Mondays.) The Science Center of Connecticut has a wide variety of science exhibits, some of which feature interactive touch screens. Exhibits include a planetarium, an aquarium, special science exhibits for children, math exhibits featuring pool tables, and a walk-in kaleidoscope.

SCORE! LEARNING, INC.
Goodwives Shopping Center, 25 Old Kings Highway North, Suite 43, Darien CT 06820. 203/656-1455. **Toll-free phone:** 800/49SCORE. **Contact:** Human Resources. **E-mail address:** score@trm.brassring,com. **World Wide Web address:** http://www.escore.com. **Description:** Provides learning programs for children. Founded in 1992. **NOTE:** Apply online or send resume to SCORE! Recruiting, 343 Winter Street, Waltham MA 02451. **Positions advertised include:** Assistant Director. **Corporate headquarters location:** Oakland CA. **Other area locations:** Westport CT. **Other U.S. locations:** Nationwide. **Parent company:** Kaplan Inc., The Washington Post Company.

SEABOARD, INC.
P.O. Box 9503, New Haven CT 06534. 203/865-1191. **Contact:** Human Resources. **Description:** A full-service oil company specializing in home heating services.

SHARON HOSPITAL, INC.
P.O. Box 789, Sharon CT 06069-0789. 860/364-4080. **Physical address:** 50 Hospital Hill Road, Sharon CT 06069. **Contact:** Personnel. **E-mail:** hr@sharonhospital.org. **World Wide Web address:** http://www.sharon.org. **Description:** A full-service, 78-bed hospital. **NOTE:** Entry-level positions and second and third shifts are offered. **Company slogan:** Quality health care for our community. **Positions advertised include:** Registered Nurse; Manager; Nuclear Medicine Technologist; Radiology Technologist; Surgical Technologist; Patient Biller; Medical Staff Coordinator; Cashier Control Clerk; EVS Supervisor; Sterile Processing Technician. **Special programs:** Internships; Summer Jobs. **Office hours:** Monday - Friday, 8:00 a.m. - 4:30 p.m. **Corporate headquarters location:** This location. **President:** James E. Sok. **Facilities Manager:** Phil Hathaway, Jr. **Annual sales/revenues:** $21 - $50 million. **Number of employees at this location:** 500.

SHERATON DANBURY
18 Old Ridgebury Road, Danbury CT 06810. 203/794-0600. **Fax:** 203/830-5125. **Contact:** Human Resources. **World Wide Web address:** http://www.starwood.com/sheraton. **Description:** One location of the hotel chain, offering meeting facilities, a business center, two restaurants, and a fitness center. **Positions advertised include:** Catering Sales Manager. **Other U.S. locations:** Nationwide.

SHERATON HOTEL AT BRADLEY
One Bradley International Airport, Windsor Locks CT 06096. 860/627-5311. **Contact:** Human Resources. **World Wide Web address:** http://www.sheraton.com. **Description:** A 237-room hotel. Located near Bradley International Airport, the hotel also houses numerous conference and convention facilities.

SHIP ANALYTICS INC.
183 Providence-New London Turnpike, North Stonington CT 06359. 860/535-3092. **Contact:** Linda Gleason, Personnel Manager. **World Wide Web address:** http://www.shipanalytics.com. **Description:** Designs and manufactures computer hardware and software that are incorporated into the company's ship simulators. **Corporate headquarters location:** This location.

SHOREWOOD PACKAGING CORPORATION
155 South Leonard Street, Waterbury CT 06708. 203/753-3620. **Contact:** Human Resources. **World Wide Web address:** http://www.shorewoodpackaging.com. **Description:** Manufactures packaging and display units for a wide variety of products. **Parent company:** International Paper.

SIEMENS VDO NORTH AMERICA
150 Knotter Drive, Cheshire CT 06410. 203/271-6000. **Fax:** 203/271-6100. **Contact:** Susan Davis, Human Resources. **Description:** Manufactures electromechanical and electronic components and modules for automotive and off-road vehicle, information processing, telecommunications, power, and industrial equipment manufacturers. Products include automotive actuators and sensors, electronic modules, precision motors, magnetic circuit breakers, thermal sensors, speed sensors, tachometers, and indicators. **Corporate headquarters location:** Germany. **Other U.S. locations:** Nationwide. **Parent company:** Siemens AG.

SIKORSKY AIRCRAFT CORPORATION
6900 Main Street, P.O. Box 9729, Stratford CT 06615-9129. 203/386-4000. **Contact:** Human Resources. **World Wide Web address:** http://www.sikorsky.com. **Description:** Designs and manufactures helicopters for commercial, industrial, and military use. **Corporate headquarters location:** Hartford CT. **International locations:** Australia; Canada; Mexico. **Parent company:** United Technologies Corporation designs and manufactures engines and space propulsion systems for commercial and general aviation. Products include large jet engines, temperature control systems, elevators and escalators, helicopters, and flight systems. The company markets its products under a variety of brand names including Carrier, Hamilton Standard, Otis, Pratt & Whitney, and Sikorsky. **Operations at this facility include:** Administration; Divisional Headquarters; Manufacturing; Research and Development. **Listed on:** New York Stock Exchange. **Stock exchange symbol:** UTX.

SMURFIT-STONE CONTAINER CORPORATION
74 Pickering Street, Portland CT 06480. 877/772-2999. **Contact:** Human Resources. **World Wide Web address:** http://www.smurfit-stone.com. **Description:** Smurfit-Stone Container Corporation is one of the world's leading paper-based packaging companies. The company's main products include corrugated containers, folding cartons, and multiwall industrial bags. The company is also one of the world's largest collectors and processors of recycled products that are then sold to a worldwide customer base. Smurfit-Stone Container Corporation also operates several paper tube, market pulp, and newsprint production facilities. **Corporate headquarters location:** Chicago IL. **Other U.S. locations:** Nationwide. **International locations:** Worldwide. **Operations at this facility include:** This location produces corrugated containers. **Listed on:** NASDAQ. **Stock exchange symbol:** SSCC. **Annual sales/revenues:** More than $100 million.

SOMERS THIN STRIP BRASS
P.O. Box 270, Waterbury CT 06720-0270. 203/597-5000. **Physical address:** 215 Piedmont Street, Waterbury CT 06706. **Contact:** Human Resources. **Description:** Processes metals used in the manufacture of surgical equipment and a variety of industrial products.

SONALYSTS INC.
215 Parkway North, Waterford CT 06385. 860/442-4355. **Fax:** 860/447-8883. **Contact:** Human Resources. **E-mail address:** recruiting@sonalysts.com. **World Wide Web address:** http://www.sonalysts.com. **Description:** A diversified business offering operations research and systems analysis; acoustical system design, testing, and development; tactical development and evaluation for surface, submarine, and air platforms; training and trainer development; and technical services for nuclear, gas, and electric companies. Sonalysts also provides audio and visual production in full production facilities, film studios, and recording studios. **NOTE:** Entry-level positions are offered. **Positions advertised include:** Mechanical Engineer; Electronics Technician; Operations Research Analyst; Submarine Junior Officer; Logistics Manager; Electronic Engineer; Facility Management Services Engineer. **Special programs:** Internships; Apprenticeships; Training. **Corporate headquarters location:** This location. **Other U.S. locations:** Nationwide. **Operations at this facility include:** Administration; Divisional Headquarters; Research and Development; Sales; Service. **Listed on:** Privately held. **Number of employees at this location:** 350. **Number of employees nationwide:** 475.

SOUTHERN CONNECTICUT STATE UNIVERSITY
501 Crescent Street, New Haven CT 06515-1355. 203/392-5200. **Fax:** 203/392-5571. **Contact:** Personnel Department. **World Wide Web address:** http://www.southernct.edu. **Description:** A four-year state university offering a variety of undergraduate, graduate, and doctoral degree programs.

SOVEREIGN BANK NEW ENGLAND
90 State House Square, Hartford CT 06103. 860/524-5600. **Contact:** Human Resources Department. **World Wide Web address:** http://www.sovereignbank.com. **Description:** A full-service bank with 600 branches throughout Connecticut, Massachusetts, New Hampshire, and Rhode Island. **Positions advertised include:** Community Banking Manager; Customer Service Representative; Government Banking Sales Officer; Loss Prevention Investigator; Mortgage Development Officer; Personal Banking Representative; Relationship Manager, Commercial Lending; Senior Corporate Banker. **Corporate headquarters location:** Boston MA. **Parent company:** Sovereign Bancorp, Inc.

SOVEREIGN BANK NEW ENGLAND
123 Church Street, New Haven CT 06510. 203/784-7442. **Toll-free phone:** 877/768-2265. **Contact:** Human Resources Department. **World Wide Web address:** http://www.sovereignbank.com. **Description:** A full-service bank with 600 branches throughout Connecticut, Massachusetts, New Hampshire, and Rhode Island. **Corporate headquarters location:** Boston MA. **Parent company:** Sovereign Bancorp, Inc.

SPEAR TECHNOLOGIES
800 Maine Street South, Suite 210, 3rd Floor, Southbury CT 06488. 203/262-1161. **Contact:** Human Resources. **Description:** Develops, markets, and supports maintenance management software for the transportation industry. **Corporate headquarters location:** Oakland CA. **International locations:** England.

STANADYNE CORPORATION
92 Deerfield Road, Windsor CT 06095. 860/525-0821. **Fax:** 860 683-4584. **Contact:** Human Resource Department. **E-mail address:** HR@stanadyne.com. **Description:** Produces diesel fuel injection systems. **Parent company:** Kohlberg & Company.

THE STANLEY WORKS
1000 Stanley Drive, New Britain CT 06053. 860/225-5111. **Contact:** Human Resources. **World Wide Web address:** http://www.stanleyworks.com. **Description:** A worldwide marketer and manufacturer of quality tools and hardware for do-it-yourselfers and professionals. The company's business is comprised of three segments: Consumer Products including hand tools, fasteners, home hardware, garage door openers, and residential entry doors for the do-it-yourself market; Builders' Products, providing products to the professional construction industry, including architectural and residential hardware, pedestrian power-operated doors, insulated steel entry doors, garage doors and openers, automatic parking gates, and commercial doors; and Industrial Products including products sold to industrial and automotive customers, such as professional hand tools. **Corporate headquarters location:** This location. **Listed on:** New York Stock Exchange. **Stock exchange symbol:** SWK.

STEW LEONARD'S FARM FRESH FOODS
100 Westport Avenue, Norwalk CT 06851. 203/847-7214. **Contact:** Recruiting Manager. **World Wide Web address:** http://www.stew-leonards.com. **Description:** One of the world's largest retail dairy and food stores. Founded in 1969. **Company slogan:** Rule 1 - The customer is always right. Rule 2 - If the customer is ever wrong, reread Rule 1. **Special programs:** Internships. **Internship information:** Culinary and bakery internships are offered. **Corporate headquarters location:** This location. **Other U.S. locations:** Danbury CT; Yonkers NY. **Operations at this facility include:** Administration; Sales. **Annual sales/revenues:** $51 - $100 million. **Number of employees at this location:** 700. **Number of employees nationwide:** 1,400.

STOLT-NIELSEN TRANSPORTATION GROUP LTD.
P.O. Box 2300, Greenwich CT 06836. 203/625-9400. **Physical address:** 8 Sound Shore Drive, Greenwich CT 06836. **Contact:** Human Resources. **World Wide Web address:** http://www.stoltnielsen.com. **Description:** Operates the world's largest fleet of bulk chemical, oil, acid, and specialty liquid tankers. **Parent company:** Stolt-Nielsen S.A.

STURM, RUGER & COMPANY INC.
One Lacey Place, Southport CT 06890. 203/259-7843. **Contact:** Human Resources Department. **World Wide Web address:** http://www.ruger-firearms.com. **Description:** Designs, manufactures, and sells pistols, revolvers, rifles, and shotguns for a variety of sporting purposes. The company also manufactures and markets various models of police revolvers, pistols, rifles, and selective firearms for law enforcement agencies and military establishments. **Corporate headquarters location:** This location. **Subsidiaries include:** Pine Tree Castings (Newport NH) produces both chrome and stainless ferrous investment castings; Ruger Investment Casting (Prescott AZ) produces aluminum, ferrous, and titanium commercial investment castings as well as components for the company's firearm production; Uni-Cast (Manchester NH) produces a wide variety of complex parts primarily for defense-related products.

SUPERIOR ELECTRIC
383 Middle Street, Bristol CT 06010. 860/585-4500. **Contact:** Personnel. **World Wide Web address:** http://www.superiorelectric.com. **Description:** An international manufacturer of electronic and electrical control equipment, incremental motion devices (including voltage regulators and voltage conditioning equipment), and synchronous/stepping motors.

SUZIO CONCRETE COMPANY
975 Westfield Road, Meriden CT 06450. 203/237-8341. **Fax:** 203/238-9177. **Contact:** Hiring Manager. **Description:** Manufactures and distributes concrete for use in the construction and home improvement markets.

SWISS ARMY BRANDS, INC.
One Research Drive, P.O. Box 874, Shelton CT 06484-0874. 203/929-6391. **Contact:** Steve Rexford, Director of Human Resources. **World Wide Web address:** http://www.swissarmy.com. **Description:** An importer and marketer of Forschner cutlery and Swiss Army knives. **Corporate headquarters location:** This location. **Listed on:** NASDAQ. **Stock exchange symbol:** SABI.

TI AUTOMOTIVE
508 North Colony Road, Meriden CT 06450. 203/235-6180. **Contact:** Human Resources. **World Wide Web address:** http://www.tiautomotive.com. **Description:** Manufactures a variety of internal automotive equipment including brake fluid carrying systems; fuel storage and delivery systems; bellows for exhaust systems; and hoses for air conditioning, heating, and exhaust systems. The company also manufactures engine management products for chain saws, industrial engines, marine engines, and recreational vehicles.

TRC COMPANY
5 Waterside Crossing, Windsor CT 06095. 860/289-8631. **Fax:** 860/298-6385. **Contact:** Krystal Lechsit, Human Resources. **World Wide Web address:** http://www.trcsolutions.com. **Description:** TRC Company provides a wide range of services including environmental engineering and consulting, site and traffic engineering, weather modification, and specialized pollution control measurement instrumentation to the private sector and government markets. **Other U.S. locations:** Nationwide.

TECHNOSERVE INC.
49 Day Street, Norwalk CT 06854. 203/852-0377. **Fax:** 203/838-6717. **Contact:** Stacey Daves-Ohlin, Director of Human Resources. **World Wide Web address:** http://www.technoserve.org. **Description:** A private, nonprofit development aid organization that works with low-income people and development institutions in Africa, Latin America, and Eastern Europe to help establish or strengthen self-help enterprises. **NOTE:** See website for details on positions. All applicants should be fluent in French; only senior level applicants should apply. **Positions advertised include:** Trade Specialist; Agribusiness Specialist; Finance Specialist; Business Specialist Service Provider. **Special programs:** Internships. **Corporate headquarters location:** This location. **Other U.S. locations:** Washington DC. **Number of employees at this location:** 25. **Number of employees nationwide:** 220.

TEK INDUSTRIES, INC.
71 Utopia Road, Manchester CT 06040. 860/647-8738. **Contact:** Human Resources. **World Wide Web address:** http://www.tekind.com. **Description:** A manufacturer of industrial electronic products including touch-memory devices, smartcards, and telecommunications products.

TENDER LOVING CARE/STAFF BUILDERS
1234 Summer Street, 3rd Floor, Stamford CT 06905. 203/327-2680. **Contact:** Office Manager. **World Wide Web address:** http://www.tlcathome.com. **Description:** A home health care agency. **Corporate headquarters location:** Lake Success NY. **Other U.S. locations:** Nationwide. **Number of employees nationwide:** 20,000.

TENDER LOVING CARE/STAFF BUILDERS
345 North Main Street, West Hartford CT 06117. 860/233-5252. **Contact:** Office Manager. **World Wide Web address:** http://www.tlcathome.com. **Description:** A home health care agency. **Corporate headquarters location:** Lake Success NY. **Other U.S. locations:** Nationwide. **Number of employees nationwide:** 20,000.

TEREX CORPORATION
500 Post Road East, Suite 320, Westport CT 06880. 203/222-7170. **Contact:** Human Resources. **E-mail address:** hr@terex.com. **World Wide Web address:** http://www.terex.com. **Description:** Terex develops, manufactures, and markets a variety of vehicles and related components, primarily for the lifting and earth-moving industries. Products include loaders, haulers, scrapers, cranes, trucks, tractors, and replacement parts. **NOTE:** Apply online. **Corporate headquarters location:** This location. **Other U.S. locations:** Waverly IA; Olathe KS; Baruga MI; Southaven MI; Wilmington NC; Tulsa OK; Conway SC; Huron SD; Watertown SD; Milwaukee WI. **Operations at this facility include:** Administration. **Listed on:** New York Stock Exchange. **Stock exchange symbol:** TEX. **Number of employees at this location:** 30. **Number of employees nationwide:** 4,000.

TETLEY USA, INC.
100 Commerce Drive, P.O. Box 856, Shelton CT 06484-0856. 203/929-9200. **Contact:** Human Resources. **World Wide Web address:** http://www.tetleyusa.com. **Description:** Manufactures and distributes beverage and food products under the Tetley, Martinson, Bustelo, Savarin, and Medaglia D'Oro labels. **Corporate headquarters location:** This location.

THULE, INC.
42 Silvermine Road, Seymour CT 06483. 203/881-4929. **Contact:** Human Resources. **E-mail address:** jobs@thuleus.com. **World Wide Web address:** http://www.thuleracks.com. **Description:** Manufactures car rack systems for transporting skis, bicycles, and snowboards.

TILCON CONNECTICUT, INC.
1 Forest Road, North Branford CT 06471. 203/484-1421. **Contact:** Human Resources. **World Wide Web address:** http://www.tilconct.com. **Description:** Manufactures and sells paving equipment and supplies to contract service companies and asphalt companies. Tilcon Connecticut, Inc. also paves roads under government contracts. The company has 25 locations throughout Connecticut. **Corporate headquarters location:** New Britain CT.

TIMKEN
P.O. Box 1008, Torrington CT 06790-1008. 860/626-2000. **Physical address:** 59 Field Street, Torrington CT 06790. **Fax:** 860/496-3603. **Contact:** Human Resources. **World Wide Web address:** http://www.timken.com. **Description:** The firm designs, develops, and manufactures antifriction needle, roller, and ball bearings. IR Torrington also produces universal joints and precision metal components and assemblies. Founded in 1866. **Positions advertised include:** EMP; Designer; Engineer; Focus Factory Manager; Program Manager. **Special programs:** Internships; Co-ops. **Internship information:** Summer internships and co-op opportunities are generally available for mechanical engineering assignments including design/test and special projects, information technology responsibilities, and chemical engineering projects. Applications for summer internships need to be received by April 15 and applications for co-ops by April 15 or October 15. **Corporate headquarters location:** Canton OH. **Other U.S. locations:** Nationwide. **International locations:** Worldwide. **Subsidiaries include:** Kilian produces precision-machined bearings. **Parent company:** Ingersoll-Rand Company (Woodcliff Lake NJ). **Listed on:** New York Stock Exchange. **Stock exchange symbol:** IR. **Number of employees at this location:** 1,000. **Number of employees nationwide:** 8,000. **Number of employees worldwide:** 11,000.

THE TORRINGTON COMPANY
59 Field Street, P.O. Box 1008, Torrington CT 06790-1008. 860/626-2623. **Contact:** Human Resources. **World Wide Web address:** http://www.torrington.com. **Description:** A sewing needle manufacturer. Founded in 1866. **Positions advertised include:** Focus Factory Manager. **Other U.S. locations:** Nationwide. **International locations:** Worldwide. **Parent company:** Timken.

TOWERS PERRIN
One Financial Plaza, Hartford CT 06103-2613. 860-727-9400. **Contact:** Human Resources. **World Wide Web address:** http://www.towersperrin.com. Towers Perrin is a global professional services firm that helps organizations around the world optimize performance through effective people, risk and financial management. The firm provides innovative solutions to client issues in the areas of human resource strategy, design and management; actuarial and management consulting to the financial services industry; and reinsurance intermediary services. **NOTE:** Search and apply for positions online. **Positions advertised include:** Senior Claims Consultant; Disability Consultant; Actuarial Consultant (Property/Casualty); Analyst (non-actuary). **Subsidiaries include:** Tillinghast.

TRANS-LUX CORPORATION
110 Richards Avenue, Norwalk CT 06854. 203/853-4321. **Contact:** Human Resources. **World Wide Web address:** http://www.trans-lux.com. **Description:** Designs, produces, leases, sells, and services large-scale, multicolor, real-time electronic information displays for both indoor and outdoor use. These displays are used primarily in applications for the financial, banking, gaming, corporate, retail, health care, transportation, and sports markets. The company also owns an expanding chain of movie theaters in the western region of the United States and owns real estate in the United States and Canada. **Positions advertised include:** Controller. **Corporate headquarters location:** This location. **International locations:** Australia; Canada. **Subsidiaries include:** Trans-Lux Fair-Play; Trans-Lux Sports; Trans-Lux West. **Listed on:** American Stock Exchange. **Stock exchange symbol:** TLX.

TRANSPRO, INC.
100 Gando Drive, New Haven CT 06513. 203/562-5121. **Fax:** 203/865-0803. **Contact:** Melissa Chambrelli, Human Resources Manager. **World Wide Web address:** http://www.transpro.com. **Description:** A holding company that provides a variety of services to the automotive industry through its four divisions. The Safety Division provides breakaway systems for highway signs, breakaway support for light poles, and railroad crossing safety systems. The Distributor Division distributes permanent and temporary crash cushions, moveable barrier systems, traffic and weather monitoring systems, and variable message signs. The Materials Division manufactures a variety of polymer concrete products. The Precast Division manufactures barriers and curbside products, tunnel panels, and a variety of precast products. **Special programs:** Co-ops; Summer Jobs. **Corporate headquarters location:** This location. **Other U.S. locations:** Nationwide. **Subsidiaries include:** A/C Plus, Inc. remanufactures automotive air conditioning compressors; Crown Industries produces specialty van interiors; Evap, Inc. distributes a variety of automotive components including compressors, evaporators, and hose assemblies; G&O Manufacturing produces automotive radiators; GO/DAN Industries (also at this location) manufactures automotive heat transfer products. **Listed on:** New York Stock Exchange. **Stock exchange symbol:** TPR. **President/CEO:** Charles E. Johnson. **Annual sales/revenues:** More than $100 million. **Number of employees at this location:** 150. **Number of employees nationwide:** 1,650.

TRANSWITCH CORPORATION
3 Enterprise Drive, Shelton CT 06484. 203/929-8810. **Fax:** 203/926-2071. **Contact:** Paula Brunell, Human Resources. **World Wide Web address:** http://www.transwitch.com. **Description:** Designs high-speed semiconductor solutions for broadband network telecommunications and data communications applications. Products include very large scale integration (VLSI) devices for original equipment manufacturers in four markets: telephone networks, local area networks (LANs), wide area networks (WANs), and cable TV (CATV) systems. **Corporate headquarters location:** This location. **Listed on:** NASDAQ. **Stock exchange symbol:** TXCC.

TRENWICK GROUP INC.
One Canterbury Green, Stamford CT 06901. 203/353-5500. **Contact:** Human Resources. **World Wide Web address:** http://www.trenwick.com. **Description:** A holding company. **Corporate headquarters location:** Bermuda. **Subsidiaries include:** Trenwick America Reinsurance Corporation reinsures property and casualty risks primarily written by U.S. insurance companies. Virtually all of Trenwick America's business is produced by reinsurance brokers. Trenwick America divides its business into three distinct categories: facultative, treaty, and special programs. The company is authorized to write reinsurance nationwide. **Listed on:** New York Stock Exchange. **Stock exchange symbol:** TWK. **Number of employees at this location:** 70.

TRILEGIANT
100 Connecticut Avenue, Norwalk CT 06850. 203/956-1000. **Contact:** Human Resources. **E-mail address:** jobs@trilegiant.com. **World Wide Web address:** http://www.trilegiant.com. **Description:** Provider of travel, shopping, dental, health, entertainment, and consumer protection services. Company is member based. Founded in 1973. **Positions advertised include:** Director, New Product Development; Statistical Analyst, Segmentation Strategy; Financial Analyst; Senior Manager, General Accounting; Marketing Manager; Copywriter; Graphic Designer; Traffic Coordinator; Senior Art Director; IBM Mainframe Application Programmer; Interactive Coordinator. **Corporate headquarters location:** This location.

TRUELOVE & MACLEAN INC.
P.O. Box 4700, Waterbury CT 06704. 203/574-2240. **Physical address:** 984 Waterville Street, Waterbury CT 06704. **Contact:** Bruce Baker, Vice President of Human Resources. **World Wide Web address:** http://www.bouffardmetals.com. **Description:** A manufacturer of deep-drawn and progressive metal stampings. **NOTE:** Second and third shifts are offered. **Special programs:** Apprenticeships. **Operations at this facility include:** Divisional Headquarters. **Listed on:** Privately held. **Annual sales/revenues:** $51 - $100 million. **Number of employees at this location:** 190.

TURBOTEC PRODUCTS, INC.
651 Day Hill Road, Windsor CT 06095. 860/683-2005. **Toll-free phone:** 800/394-1633. **Fax:** 860/683-2133. **Contact:** Human Resources. **World Wide Web address:** http://www.turbotecproducts.com. **Description:** Turbotec designs, manufactures, and sells enhanced surface metal tubing that displays improved heat transfer characteristics, flexibility, coiling, and bendability. The tubes are used in such applications as blood oxygenators, ice-making machines, air conditioning and heating units, laser coolers, and beverage dispensers. **Corporate headquarters location:** This location.

U.S. FOODSERVICE
625 Nutmeg Road North, South Windsor CT 06074. 860/282-0101. **Toll-free phone:** 800/842-8302. **Fax:** 860/291-9763. **Contact:** Human Resources. **World Wide Web address:** http://www.usfoodservice.com. **Description:** Distributes food products, fresh meats, dairy products, and cleaning supplies to restaurants and other institutional food service establishments. **NOTE:** Send resume to Yantic location. **Corporate headquarters location:** Columbia MD. **Other U.S. locations:** Nationwide.

U.S. FOODSERVICE
P.O. Box 103, Yantic CT 06389. 860/425-3000. **Physical address:** 237 Otrobando Avenue, Yantic CT 06389. **Toll-free phone:** 800/233-5378. **Fax:** 860/885-3359. **Contact:** Human Resources Department. **World Wide Web address:** http://www.usfoodservice.com. **Description:** Distributes food products, fresh meats, dairy products, and cleaning supplies to restaurants and other institutional food service establishments. **Corporate headquarters location:** Columbia MD. **Other U.S. locations:** Nationwide.

U.S. POSTAL SERVICE
16 Washington Street, Norwalk CT 06856. 203/854-4747. **Contact:** Human Resources. **World Wide Web address:** http://www.usps.com. **Description:** Main post office for the city of Norwalk. **NOTE:** Jobseekers must apply in person.

U.S. SURGICAL
150 Glover Avenue, Norwalk CT 06856. 203/845-1000. **Contact:** Human Resources Department. **World Wide Web address:** http://www.ussurg.com. **Description:** A manufacturer of surgical instruments. **Parent company:** Tyco Healthcare Group LP.

USA HAULING & RECYCLING, INC
184 Municipal Road, Waterbury CT 06708. 203/757-3659. **Contact:** Human Resources. **Description:** Provides residential and commercial waste disposal services.

UST INC.
100 West Putnam Avenue, Greenwich CT 06830. 203/661-1100. **Fax:** 203/622-3493. **Contact:** Human Resources. **World Wide Web address:** http://www.ustinc.com. **Description:** A holding company whose subsidiaries produce and market moist, smokeless tobacco products. **Positions advertised include:** Auditor; Senior Auditor; Senior Buyer; Brand Manager; Manager, Consumer Research; Sales Representative; Senior Brand Manager. **Special programs:** Internships. **Corporate headquarters location:** This location. **Subsidiaries include:** International Wine & Spirits Ltd.; U.S.

Smokeless Tobacco Company. **Operations at this facility include:** Administration; Divisional Headquarters. **Listed on:** New York Stock Exchange. **Stock exchange symbol:** UST. **Number of employees at this location:** 500.

UTC FUEL CELLS
195 Governor's Highway, South Windsor CT 06074. 860/727-2200. **Fax:** 860/727-2319. **Contact:** Richard Knight, Personnel. **World Wide Web address:** http://www.internationalfuelcells.com. **Description:** This location is engaged in the research, design, marketing, and manufacturing of energy conversion systems. **Positions advertised include:** Manager, Materials; Assembly Chief; Senior Analyst; Commodity Manager; National Account Sales Manager; Regional Sales Manager. **Subsidiaries include:** The Onsi Corporation. **Parent company:** United Technologies Corporation provides high-technology products and support services to customers in the aerospace, building, military, and automotive industries worldwide. Products include large jet engines, temperature control systems, elevators and escalators, helicopters, and flight systems. The company markets its products under a variety of brand names including Carrier, Hamilton Standard, Otis, Pratt & Whitney, and Sikorsky. Production facilities are located in the United States, Latin America, Mexico, Canada, Australia, Europe, and Asia. **Operations at this facility include:** Administration; Divisional Headquarters; Manufacturing; Research and Development; Sales; Service. **Listed on:** New York Stock Exchange. **Stock exchange symbol:** UTX. **Number of employees at this location:** 300.

UNILEVER HOME & PERSONAL CARE USA
33 Benedict Place, Greenwich CT 06830. 203/661-2000. **Contact:** Human Resources. **World Wide Web address:** http://www.unilever.com. **Description:** Manufactures personal products and health and beauty aids including Vaseline Intensive Care Lotion and Pond's Cold Cream. **Listed on:** New York Stock Exchange. **Stock exchange symbol:** UN.

UNITED DISTILLERS & VINTNERS NORTH AMERICA, INC.
6 Landmark Square, 6th Floor, Stamford CT 06901. 203/323-3311. **Contact:** Human Resources. **Description:** A manufacturer and distributor of alcoholic beverages including Johnnie Walker, Smirnoff, Tanqueray, Jose Cuervo, Malibu, and Bailey's.

UNITED ILLUMINATING COMPANY
P.O. Box 1564, New Haven CT 06506. **Physical address:** 157 Church Street, New Haven CT 06510. **Toll-free phone:** 800/722-5584. **Fax:** 203/499-3664. **Contact:** Human Resources. **World Wide Web address:** http://www.uinet.com. **Description:** An investor-owned electric utility system in southwestern Connecticut. **Positions advertised include:** Junior Drafter; Line Worker; Senior Platform Support Specialist; Senior Business Systems Analyst; Part-time Bilingual Customer Service Representative; Process Leader, Manager of Project Managers; Analyst; Transition and Substation Group Leader; IT Internal Auditor; Compensation Analyst; Senior Internal Auditor. **Corporate headquarters location:** This location. **Operations at this facility include:** Administration; Sales. **Listed on:** New York Stock Exchange. **Stock exchange symbol:** UIL. **Number of employees at this location:** 540. **Number of employees nationwide:** 1,400.

UNITED NATURAL FOODS
260 Lake Road, P.O. Box 999, Dayville CT 06241. 860/779-2800. **Contact:** Human Resources. **World Wide Web address:** http://www.unfi.com. **Description:** a leading independent national distributor of natural foods and related products including nutritional supplements, personal care items and organic produce, in the United States.

UNITED TECHNOLOGIES CORPORATION
One Financial Plaza, Hartford CT 06103. 860/728-7000. **Contact:** Human Resources. **World Wide Web address:** http://www.utc.com. **Description:** A *Fortune* 500 company that provides high-tech products and support services to customers in the aerospace, building, military, and automotive industries worldwide. Products include large jet engines, temperature control systems, elevators and escalators, helicopters, and flight systems. The company markets its products under a variety of brand names including Carrier, Hamilton Standard, Otis, Pratt & Whitney, and Sikorsky. **Corporate headquarters location:** This location. **International locations:** Australia; Canada; Mexico. **Subsidiaries include:** Carrier; Hamilton Sundstrand; Otis; Pratt & Whitney; United Technologies Corporation Research Center; Sikorsky; UTC Fuel Cells. **Listed on:** New York Stock Exchange. **Stock exchange symbol:** UTX.

UNITED TECHNOLOGIES CORPORATION RESEARCH CENTER
411 Silver Lane, East Hartford CT 06108. 860/610-7000. **Contact:** Human Resources. **World Wide Web address:** http://www.utrc.utc.com. **Description:** United Technologies Corporation provides high-technology products and support services to customers in the aerospace, building, military, and automotive industries worldwide. Products include large jet engines, temperature control systems, elevators and escalators, helicopters, and flight systems. The company markets its products under a variety of brand names including Carrier, Hamilton Sunstrand, Otis, Pratt & Whitney, and Sikorsky. **International locations:** Australia; Canada; Mexico. **Operations at this facility include:** This location provides research in the areas of gas turbine technology, electro-optics, high energy, solid state electronics, microelectronics, microwave physics, manufacturing technology, robotics, optics, computer sciences, computer programming, materials technology, fluid mechanics, and instrument research. **Listed on:** New York Stock Exchange. **Stock exchange symbol:** UTX.

UNITED WAY OF CONNECTICUT
30 Laurel Street, Hartford CT 06106. 860/493-6800. **Contact:** Human Resources. **World Wide Web address:** http://www.unitedway.org. **Description:** A nonprofit organization that operates referral and crisis intervention services for pregnant women and parents. **Other U.S. locations:** Nationwide.

UNITED WAY OF STAMFORD
62 Palmers Hill Road, Stamford CT 06902. 203/348-7711. **Contact:** Human Resources. **World Wide Web address:** http://www.unitedway.org. **Description:** A nonprofit organization that offers referral and crisis intervention services for pregnant women and parents. **Other U.S. locations:** Nationwide.

UNIVERSITY OF BRIDGEPORT
126 Park Avenue, Bridgeport CT 06604. 203/576-4000. **Fax:** 203/576-4601. **Contact:** Human Resources. **World Wide Web address:** http://www.bridgeport.edu. **Description:** A four-year, liberal arts university offering over 30 undergraduate and 14 graduate degree programs. **Corporate headquarters location:** This location.

UNIVERSITY OF CONNECTICUT
Brown Building, Mansfield Depot Campus, 9 Walters Avenue, Unit 5075, Storrs CT 06269-5075. 860/486-3034. **Toll-free phone:** 860/486-2000. **Fax:** 860/486-0378. **Contact:** Human Resources. **World Wide Web address:** http://www.hr.uconn.edu. **Description:** This location is the main campus. University of Connecticut is a four-year, state university offering several undergraduate, graduate, and doctoral degrees. **Other area locations:** Hartford CT; Stamford CT; Waterbury CT.

UNIVERSITY OF NEW HAVEN
300 Boston Post Road, West Haven CT 06516. 203/932-7240. **Contact:** Human Resources. **World Wide Web address:** http://www.newhaven.edu. **Description:** An independent, four-year university. Founded in 1920. **NOTE:** Resumes sent via fax or e-mail will not be accepted. **Corporate headquarters location:** This location.

VECTRON INTERNATIONAL
P.O. Box 5160, Norwalk CT 06856. 203/853-4433. **Physical address:** 166 Glover Avenue, Norwalk CT 06856. **Fax:** 203/849-1423. **Contact:** Human Resources. **World Wide Web address:** http://www.vectron.com. **Description:** An electrical engineering firm. **Positions advertised include:** Board Designer; Circuit Design Engineer; Manager of Military Sales. **Special programs:** Internships. **Other U.S. locations:** Olathe KS; Hudson NH. **International locations:** Germany. **Parent company:** Dover Corporation. **Listed on:** New York Stock Exchange. **Stock exchange symbol:** DOV. **Number of employees at this location:** 250.

VION PHARMACEUTICALS
4 Science Park, New Haven CT 06511. 203/498-4210. **Fax:** 203/498-4211. **Contact:** Dan Chapman, Human Resources. **World Wide Web address:** http://www.vionpharm.com. **Description:** Engaged in research to find treatments and therapies for cancer. **Listed on:** NASDAQ. **Stock exchange symbol:** VION.

VOLTARC TECHNOLOGIES INC.
400 Captain Neville Drive, Waterbury CT 06705. 203/578-4600. **Contact:** Human Resources. **World Wide Web address:** http://www.voltarc.com. **Description:** Manufactures fluorescent tubular lighting systems used for signs, tanning beds, medical equipment, and aquariums.

WACHOVIA
60 North Main Street, Waterbury CT 06702. 203/346-6942. **Contact:** Human Resources. **World Wide Web address:** http://www.wachovia.com. **Description:** A commercial bank. **NOTE:** Please send resumes to or apply in person at Human Resources, One Jefferson Square, Waterbury CT 06702. **Positions advertised include:** Loan Review Team Leader; Management Reporting Specialist; Management Loan Review Team Leader; Teller; Resource Management Consultant; Compliance Specialist; Senior Relationship Manager. **Corporate headquarters location:** Charlotte NC. **Operations at this facility include:** Administration.

THE WACKENHUT CORPORATION
1010 Wethersfield Avenue, Suite 201, Hartford CT 06114. 860/296-4775. **Contact:** Human Resources. **World Wide Web address:** http://www.wackenhut.com. **Description:** The Wackenhut Corporation is a diversified provider of services to government, industrial, commercial, and professional organizations and agencies worldwide. The corporation has offices throughout the United States and in 49 other countries on six continents. The company also provides educational services and training, facility management, food service to jails and prisons, design, financial services and construction management for correctional facilities, and fire prevention and emergency services. The Wackenhut Corporation is a leader in the privatization of public services to municipal, state, and federal governments worldwide. Founded in 1954. **Corporate headquarters location:** Palm Beach Gardens FL. **Other U.S. locations:** Nationwide. **Operations at this facility include:** This location specializes in security-related services including physical security, investigations, the management of correctional and detention facilities, rehabilitative programs, and information security. **Listed on:** New York Stock Exchange. **Stock exchange symbol:** WAK. **Chairman/CEO:** George R. Wackenhut.

WADSWORTH ATHENEUM MUSEUM OF ART
600 Main Street, Hartford CT 06103. 860/278-2670. **Contact:** Human Resources. **World Wide Web address:** http://www.wadsworthatheneum.org. **Description:** A fine arts museum housing a collection of 19th-century American painting, Renaissance and Baroque European painting, European and American decorative arts, the Amistad Foundation collection of African-American art and artifacts, and the Nutting collection of Colonial American furniture. Founded in 1842.

THE WARNACO GROUP, INC.
470 Wheelers Farms Road, Milford CT 06460-1847. 203/301-7000. **Contact:** Human Resources. **World Wide Web address:** http://www.warnaco.com. **Description:** A large manufacturer, designer, and marketer of women's intimate apparel, men's wear, and men's accessories under brand names including Fruit of the Loom, Warner's, Olga, Chaps by Ralph Lauren, and Calvin Klein. Warnaco markets its products through a chain of 48 retail outlets, as well as department stores and mass merchandisers in North America and Europe. **Corporate headquarters location:** New York NY.

WARWICK GROUP, INC.
70 Main Street, 2nd Floor, New Canaan CT 06840. 203/966-7447. **Contact:** Human Resources. **World Wide Web address:** http://www.warwickgroup.com. **Description:** An investment bank.

WASTE MANAGEMENT, INC.
209 Pickering Street, Portland CT 06480. 860/342-0667. **Contact:** Human Resources. **E-mail address:** careers@wm.com. **World Wide Web address:** http://www.wm.com. **Description:** Provides waste removal services. **Corporate headquarters location:** Houston TX. **Other U.S. locations:** Nationwide. **Listed on:** New York Stock Exchange. **Stock exchange symbol:** WMI.

WATERBURY, CITY OF
236 Grand Street, Waterbury CT 06702. 203/574-6712. **Contact:** Human Resources. **Description:** Houses the mayor's office and other city administrative offices.

WATSON LABORATORIES, INC.
131 West Street, Danbury CT 06810. 203/744-7200. **Contact:** Human Resources. **World Wide Web address:** http://www.watsonpharm.com. **Description:** Manufactures generic prescription drugs. **Corporate headquarters location:** Corona CA. **Other U.S. locations:** Nationwide. **Parent company:** Watson Pharmaceuticals. **Listed on:** New York Stock Exchange. **Stock exchange symbol:** WPI. **Number of employees at this location:** 85.

WEBSTER BANK
2 National Place, Danbury CT 06810. 203/730-6366. **Contact:** Human Resources. **World Wide Web address:** http://www.websterbank.com. **Description:** Webster Bank is primarily involved in attracting deposits from the general public and investing these funds in mortgage loans for the purchase, construction, and refinancing of one- to four-family homes. Webster Bank also provides commercial banking services to businesses.

Corporate headquarters location: Waterbury CT. **Parent company:** Webster Financial Corporation. **Listed on:** NASDAQ. **Stock exchange symbol:** WBST.

WEBSTER BANK
145 Bank Street, Webster Plaza, Waterbury CT 06702. 203/578-2230. **Contact:** Human Resources. **World Wide Web address:** http://www.websterbank.com. **Description:** Involved in attracting deposits from the general public and investing these funds in mortgage loans for the purchase, construction, and refinancing of one- to four-family homes. Webster Bank also provides commercial banking services to businesses. Operates 145 banking offices in Connecticut, Rhode Island, Massachusetts, and New York. **Corporate headquarters location:** This location. **Parent company:** Webster Financial Corporation. **Listed on:** NASDAQ. **Stock exchange symbol:** WBST.

WESTERN CONNECTICUT STATE UNIVERSITY
181 White Street, Danbury CT 06810. 203/837-8210. **Contact:** Human Resources. **World Wide Web address:** http://www.wcsu.edu. **Description:** A four-year state university offering the Ancell School of Business, the School of Arts & Sciences, and the School of Professional Studies.

GEORGE WESTON BAKERIES, INC.
10 Hamilton Avenue, Greenwich CT 06830. 203/531-2000. **Contact:** Human Resources. **World Wide Web address:** http://www.georgewestonfoods.com.au. **Description:** An Australian-based food manufacturer.

WOODBURY TELEPHONE COMPANY
P.O. Box 5014, Woodbury CT 06798. 203/263-2121. **Physical address:** 299 Main Street South, Woodbury CT 06798. **Contact:** Vicki Deleone, Human Resources. **Description:** Provides local exchange telephone services, intrastate toll services, and access to interstate long-distance telephone services, as well as selling telephone equipment. Woodbury Telephone is the primary provider of telephone service in major portions of the towns of Woodbury, Southbury, and Bethlehem, and small portions of Oxford and Roxbury CT. **Number of employees at this location:** 75. **Parent company:** SBC

WORLD WRESTLING FEDERATION ENTERTAINMENT, INC.
1241 East Main Street, P.O. Box 3857, Stamford CT 06902. 203/352-8600. **Contact:** Human Resources. **World Wide Web address:** http://www.wwe.com. **Description:** Develops and markets television programming and pay-per-view broadcasting for the World Wrestling Federation. The company also produces and manages live wrestling events. **Positions advertised include:** Director of Internal Audit; Director of Job Notification. **Special Programs:** Internships. **Corporate headquarters location:** This location.

XL RE AMERICA, INC.
Seaview House, 70 Seaview Avenue, Stamford CT 06902. 203/964-5200. **Toll-free phone:** 800/688-1840. **Contact:** Human Resources. **World Wide Web address:** http://www.xlcapital.com. **Description:** A holding company. **Corporate headquarters location:** Bermuda. **International locations:** Worldwide. **Parent company:** XL Capital Ltd. **Number of employees worldwide:** 500.

XEROX CORPORATION
P.O. Box 1600, Stamford CT 06904. 203/968-3000. **Physical address:** 800 Long Ridge Road, Stamford CT 06904. **Contact:** Human Resources. **World Wide Web address:** http://www.xerox.com. **Description:** Develops, manufactures, markets, services, and finances information processing products including copiers, duplicators, scanners, electronic printing systems, word processing systems, personal computers, and computer peripherals. Xerox does business in over 120 countries. Founded in 1906. **Positions advertised include:** Account Executive. **Corporate headquarters location:** This location. **Other U.S. locations:** Nationwide. **Listed on:** New York Stock Exchange. **Stock exchange symbol:** XRX. **Number of employees nationwide:** 90,000.

YALE UNIVERSITY
155 Whitney Avenue, New Haven CT 06510. 203/432-2300. **Contact:** Human Resources. **World Wide Web address:** http://www.yale.edu. **Description:** One of the country's oldest universities. Yale University is a private, nonprofit institution that offers bachelor's, master's, and doctoral degrees. Founded in 1801. **Number of employees at this location:** 8,000.

YALE UNIVERSITY PRESS
P.O. Box 209040, New Haven CT 06520. 203/432-0960. **Physical address:** 302 Temple Street, New Haven CT 06511. **Contact:** Human Resources. **World Wide Web address:** http://www.yale.edu/yup. **Description:** Publishes scholarly books. **Corporate headquarters location:** This location. **Parent company:** Yale University.

YANKEE ENERGY SYSTEM, INC.
107 Selden Street, Berlin CT 06037. 203/639-4000. **Contact:** Human Resources. **World Wide Web address:** http://www.yankeegas.com. **Description:** A holding company. **Corporate headquarters location:** This location. **Subsidiaries include:** Housatonic Corporation is a single-purpose corporation holding a 10.5 percent interest in the Iroquois Gas Transmission System, a pipeline that delivers Canadian gas into the Northeast. NorConn Properties, Inc. owns the corporate office building of Yankee Energy System and another service building, both of which are leased to Yankee Gas. Yankee Energy Financial Services provides customers with equipment financing for natural gas installations. Yankee Energy Production Services funds gas-fired and other electric generation projects at selected customer sites. Yankee Gas Services Company is a natural gas distribution company regulated by the Connecticut Department of Public Utility Control. All services of the subsidiaries are provided throughout Connecticut. **Number of employees nationwide:** 670.

YORK ANALYTICAL LABORATORIES
120 Research Drive, Stratford CT 06615. 203/325-1371. **Contact:** Human Resources. **Description:** A laboratory engaged in soil, water, and air quality testing.

ZELDES NEEDLE & COOPER PC
P.O. Box 1740, Bridgeport CT 06601. 203/333-9441. **Physical address:** 1000 Lafayette Boulevard, Bridgeport CT 06604. **Contact:** Hiring Manager. **World Wide Web address:** http://www.znclaw.com. **Description:** A law firm with attorneys specializing in all areas of practice. **Number of employees at this location:** 20.

ZYGO CORPORATION
P.O. Box 448, Middlefield CT 06455-0448. 860/347-8506. **Physical address:** Laurel Brook Road, Middlefield CT 06455. **Fax:** 860/347-8136. **Contact:** Human Resources. **E-mail address:** jobs@zygo.com. **World Wide Web address:** http://www.zygo.com. **Description:** Develops and manufactures high-precision no-contact measuring instruments and precision optical components. **Positions advertised include:** Precision Systems Integration Engineer; Opto-Mechanical Systems Engineer; Optical Coating Technician; Quality Engineer; Opto-Mechanical Systems Engineer. Manufacturing; Optical Engineering Product Manager. **Corporate headquarters location:** This location. **Other U.S. locations:** Tuscon AZ; Sunnyvale CA; Delray Beach FL; Westborough MA. **International locations:** Germany; Japan; Singapore; Taiwan. **Listed on:** NASDAQ. **Stock exchange symbol:** ZIGO. **Number of employees nationwide:** 175.

ACW CORPORATION
110 South Poplar Street, Suite 102, Wilmington DE 19801. 302/427-1776. **Fax:** 302/427-1775. **Contact:** Anna Crawford, Director of Human Resources. **Description:** A franchise of Arby's restaurants. **Special programs:** Internships. **Corporate headquarters location:** This location. **Operations at this facility include:** Sales; Service. **Listed on:** Privately held. **Number of employees at this location:** 300.

AT SYSTEMS
P.O. Box 1223, Wilmington DE 19899-1223. 302/762-5444. **Physical address:** 4200 Governor Printz Boulevard, Wilmington DE 19802. **Contact:** Jerry Jackson, Recruiter. **World Wide Web address:** http://www.atsystemsinc.com. **Description:** Provides armored vehicles serving banks and other clients in need of security-intensive transportation services. **Corporate headquarters location:** This location.

AT&T WIRELESS
4120 Concord Pike, Suite 2, Wilmington DE 19803. 302/477-6969. **Contact:** Human Resources. **World Wide Web address:** http://www.attwireless.com. **Description:** A wireless communications provider. **Positions advertised include:** Communications Specialist; Lead Communications Specialist. **Other U.S. locations:** Nationwide.

THE ACCESS GROUP
1411 Foulk Rd. Wilmington DE 19803-0430. 302/477-4000. **Fax:** 302/477-4067. **Contact:** Human Resources. **E-mail address:** general@accessgroup.org. **World Wide Web address:** http://www.accessgroup.org. **Description:** A loan broker whose programs, materials, and services are designed for graduate/professional student borrowers. **Positions advertised include:** Loan Processing Associate; Loan Recovery Associate; Associate Counsel; External Account Executive.

ACE USA
One Beaver Valley Road, Wilmington DE 19850. 302/476-6000. **Contact:** Elizabeth Arment, Human Resources. **World Wide Web address:** http://www.acelimited.com. **Description:** Provides property and casualty, marine, and aerospace insurance. **Corporate headquarters location:** Philadelphia PA. **Listed on:** New York Stock Exchange. **Stock exchange symbol:** ACE.

ADVANCED NETWORKING, INC.
1316 Philadelphia Pike, Wilmington, DE 19809-1855. 302/792-9200. **Contact:** Rick Raphael, Owner. **World Wide Web address:** http://www.advnetwork.com. **Description:** Telecommunications services.

ADVO INC.
300 McIntire Drive, Newark DE 19711. 302/861-3567. **Fax:** 302/861-3552. **Contact:** Human Resources. **World Wide Web address:** http://www.advo.com. **Description:** Provides direct mail advertising services. Founded in 1929. **Positions advertised include:** Lead Operations Technician. **Corporate headquarters location:** Windsor CT. **Number of employees nationwide:** 4,700.

AMERICAN EXPRESS FINANCIAL ADVISORS
200 Bellevue Parkway, Suite 250, Wilmington DE 19809. 302/798-3199. **Contact:** Human Resources. **E-mail address:** suzan.k.cochran@aexp.com. **World Wide Web address:** http://www.americanexpress.com. **Description:** Provides a variety of financial products and services to help individuals, businesses, and institutions establish and achieve their financial goals. American Express Financial Advisors has a field of more than 8,000 financial advisors in the United States and offers financial planning, annuities, mutual funds, insurance, investment certificates. Other services include institutional investment advisory trust, tax preparation, and retail securities brokerage.

AMERICAN INTERNATIONAL GROUP, INC. (AIG)
1 Alico Plaza, 600 King Street, Wilmington DE 19801. 302/594-2000. **Fax:** 302/654-4986. **Contact:** Human Resources. **World Wide Web address:** http://www.aig.com. **Description:** An international insurance organization and an underwriter of commercial and industrial insurance in the United States for its parent company. **Corporate headquarters location:** New York NY. **Parent company:** American Life Insurance Company. **Listed on:** New York Stock Exchange. **Stock exchange symbol:** AIG.

A.H. ANGERSTEIN, INC.
315 New Road, Wilmington DE 19805. 302/996-3500. **Fax:** 302/995-1640. **Contact:** Rob Sanderson, Personnel Director. **E-mail address:** angersteins@angersteins.com. **World Wide Web address:** www.angersteins.com. **Description:** Engaged in the retail sale of building materials, glass fixtures, and kitchen and bathroom appliances.

APEX PIPING SYSTEMS INC.
302 Falco Drive, Newport DE 19804. 302/995-6136. **Fax:** 302/995-1257. **Contact:** Human Resources. **E-mail address:** resume@ apexpiping.com. **World Wide Web address:** http://www.apexpiping.com. **Description:** Fabricates pipes for petroleum and chemical companies.

ARLON
1100 Governor Lea Road, Bear DE 19701. 302/834-2100. **Fax:** 302/834-2940. **Contact:** Human Resources. **World Wide Web address:** http://www.arlonstd.com. **Description:** Manufactures silicone rubber, silicone tape, and circuit boards.

ARTESIAN WATER COMPANY, INC.
664 Churchmans Road, Newark DE 19702. 302/453-6900. **Fax:** 302/453-6904. **Contact:** Justine Joska, Human Resources. **World Wide Web address:** http://www.artesianwater.com. **Description:** Provides water utility service to over 55,000 customers in New Castle County. **Corporate headquarters location:** This location. **Parent company:** Artesian Resources Corporation's other subsidiaries include Artesian Laboratories, Inc., which provides environmental testing of water, wastewater, and solids primarily to third parties in Delaware, Maryland, Pennsylvania, and New Jersey; and Artesian Development Corporation, which operates the County Commerce Office Park.

ASHLAND NATURE CENTER
P.O. Box 700, Hockessin DE 19707. 302/239-2334. **Fax:** 302/239-2473. **Contact:** David Toman. **E-mail address:** judyp@dnsashland.org. **World Wide Web address:** http://www.delawarenaturesociety.org. **Description:** A private, nonprofit, membership organization dedicated to environmental education and the preservation of natural areas. **Positions advertised include:** Associate Director; Land Preservation Coordinator; Summer Programs Educator; Naturalists Teacher. **Special Programs:** Seasonal Programs; School Programs. **Parent company:** Delaware Nature Society operates Ashland Nature Center and Abbott's Mill, offering year-round programming for all age groups.

ASTRAZENECA PHARMACEUTICALS
P.O. Box 4520, Newark DE 19714-4520. 302/286-3500. **Physical address:** 587 Old Baltimore Pike, Newark DE. **Contact:** Human Resources. **World Wide Web address:** http://www.astrazeneca.com. **Description:** AstraZeneca Pharmaceuticals researches and develops pharmaceuticals for the treatment of cancer; infections; and disorders of the central nervous system, respiratory system, and cardiovascular system. **Operations at this facility include:** This location is a manufacturing site.

ASTRAZENECA PHARMACEUTICALS
1800 Concord Pike, P.O. Box 15437, Wilmington DE 19850-5437. 302/886-3000. **Fax:** 302/886-2972. **Contact:** Human Resources. **World Wide Web address:** http://www.astrazenecacareers.com. **Description:** Researches and develops pharmaceuticals for the treatment of cancer; infections; and disorders of the central nervous system, respiratory system, and cardiovascular system.

AVALON
65 Lukens Drive, Newark DE 19720-2718. 302/654-1633. **Fax:** 302/654-1633 **Contact:** Human Resources. **Description:** Offers services in graphic design, portable display, trade show exhibits, lobby interiors, museums, show rooms, and fulfillment programs.

AVON PRODUCTS INC.
2100 Ogletown Road, Newark DE 19712. 302/453-7700 **Fax:** 302/453-7845. **Contact:** Human Resources. **World Wide Web address:** http://www.avoncareers. com. **Description:** A direct seller of beauty care products, fashion jewelry, gifts, fragrances, and decorative products. Avon, a *Fortune* 500 company, markets its products through a network of 2.8 million independent sales representatives in 135 countries worldwide. **NOTE:** Salespeople are considered independent contractors or dealers and most work part-time. If you are interested in becoming a sales representative, please call 800/FOR-AVON, or visit the company's Website for more information. **Corporate headquarters location:** New York NY.

BALTIMORE AIRCOIL COMPANY
P.O. Box 402, Milford DE 19963. 302/422-3061. **Contact:** Human Resources. **E-mail address:** hr@baltimoreaircoil.com. **World Wide Web address:** http://www.baltaircoil.com. **Description:** A specialist in the design and manufacture of evaporative cooling equipment, cooling towers, evaporative condensers, and closed circuit cooling systems. **Other U.S. locations:** Baltimore MD; Madera CA; Paxton IL. **International Locations:** Worldwide.

BAYHEALTH MEDICAL CENTER AT MILFORD MEMORIAL HOSPITAL
21 West Clarke Avenue, P.O. Box 199, Milford DE 19963. 302/422-3311. **Fax:** 302/744-7469 **Recorded jobline:** 888/397-JOBS. **Contact:** Human Resources. **World Wide Web address:** http://www.bayhealth.org. **Description:** A medical center with facilities for 197 acute care beds, 23 rehabilitation beds, and 18 transitional care beds. **Parent company:** Bayhealth Medical Center, Inc.

BAYHEALTH MEDICAL CENTER, INC.
21 West Clarke Avenue, P.O. Box 199, Milford DE 19963. 302/422-3311. **Fax:** 302/744-7469. **Recorded jobline:** 888/397-JOBS. **Contact:** Human Resources. **World Wide Web address:** http://www.bayhealth.org. **Description:** A full-service, nonprofit, 374-bed medical center. **NOTE:** Entry-level positions and second and third shifts are offered. **Special programs:** Co-ops. **Other U.S. locations:** Milford DE. **Subsidiaries include:** Felton Laboratory; Frederica Outpatient Services Center; Harrington Outpatient Services Center; Kent General Hospital; Milford Memorial Hospital; Milton Outpatient Services Center; Smyrna Clayton Medical Services; St. Jones Center for Behavioral Health; Women's Wellness and Resources Center. **Annual sales/revenues:** $51 - $100 million. **Number of employees nationwide:** 2,000.

BEEBE MEDICAL CENTER
424 Savannah Road, Lewes DE 19958-9913. 302/645-3336. **Fax:** 302/645-0965. **Recorded jobline:** 302/856-0676. **Contact:** Human Resources. **E-mail address:** employment@bbmc.org. **World Wide Web address:** http://www.bbmc.org. **Description:** A 135-bed, acute care, community hospital with more than 35 physician specialties including cardiology, oncology, gastroenterology, internal medicine, vascular surgery, and oral surgery. Five family health centers affiliated with Beebe Medical Center have been established in Millville, Georgetown, Lewes, Rehoboth Beach, and Millsboro. Community programs include a speakers bureau, physician referral services, language bank, educational programs for health care professionals as well as the general public, a library lecture series, lending library, community sponsored events, and fund-raisers. Founded in 1916. **NOTE:** Entry-level positions and second and third shifts are offered. **Positions advertised include:** Accounts Receivable Representative; Billing Representative; Certified Occupational Therapist Assistant; Client Services Coordinator; Clinical Laboratory Assistant; Coder; Diagnostic Imaging Assistant; Director of Ambulatory Surgery Center; Risk Management Director; Echocardiographer; Floorperson; Helpdesk/Operations Coordinator; Home Health Assistant; Instructor, School of Nursing; Medical Records Assistant; Nurse Technician. **Special programs:** Summer Jobs. **Number of employees at this location:** 1,100.

BELFINT, LYONS & SCHUMAN
1011 Centre Road, Suite 310 Wilmington DE 19805. 302/225-0600. **Fax:** 302/225-0625. **Contact:** Frances Pyle, Human Resources. **E-mail address:** fpyle@belfint.com. **World Wide Web address:** http://www.belfint.com. **Description:** A certified public accounting and business consulting firm. **Positions advertised include:** Staff Accountant.

EMILY P. BISSELL HOSPITAL
3000 Newport Gap Pike, Wilmington DE 19808. 302/995-8400. **Fax:** 302/255-4437. **Contact:** Human Resources. **Description:** Long-term care facility licensed as a nursing home, with 102 beds, providing care at the skilled and intermediate levels. **Parent Company:** Delaware Health and Social Services Department.

BLUE CROSS AND BLUE SHIELD OF DELAWARE
One Brandywine Gateway, P.O. Box 1991, Wilmington DE 19899. 302/421-3000. **Fax:** 302/421-3216 **Contact:** Human Resources. **E-mail address:** humanresources@bcbsde.com **World Wide Web address:** http://www.bcbsde.com. **Description:** A nonprofit health care insurance organization providing managed health care plans to both individuals and groups. Blue Cross and Blue Shield offers Point-of-Service, individual health, PPO, and HMO plans, as well as life insurance, dental insurance, and short- and long-term disability. **Positions advertised include:** Customer Inquiry Analyst; Claims Processor; DocuTech Printer Operator. **Other U.S. locations:** Dover DE.

BOB EVANS
1650 North Dupont Highway, Dover DE 19901. 302/678-5042. **Fax:** 302/678-5192 **Contact:** Human Resources. **E-mail address:** employment@bobevans.com. **World**

Wide Web address: http://www.bobevans.com. **Description:** A family restaurant chain. Founded in 1953. **Positions advertised include:** Restaurant Manager; Restaurant Crewmember. **Corporate headquarters location:** Columbus OH. **Listed on:** NASDAQ. **Stock exchange symbol:** BOBE.

BRANDYWINE ASSET MANAGEMENT
3 Christine Centre, 201 North Walnut Street, Suite 1200, Wilmington DE 19801. 302/654-6162. **Fax:** 302/654-6530 **Contact:** Human Resources. **E-mail address:** placement@brandyami.com. **World Wide Web address:** http://www.brandywine-online.com. **Description:** An investment services company. Founded in 1982.

BROSIUS ELIASON COMPANY
508 South Street, New Castle DE 19720. 302/328-9481. **Fax:** 302/328-2761. **Contact:** Richard Armstrong, President. **E-mail address:** brosiuseliason@comcast.net. **Description:** Provides a variety of building materials including decking, doors, kitchen cabinets, lumber and plywood, molding, paint, roofing, siding, tools, and windows to the construction and retail markets.

BURRIS LOGISTICS, INC.
P.O. Box 219, Milford DE 19963-0219. 302/839-4531. **Physical address:** 501 SE 5th Street, Milford DE 19963. **Toll-free phone:** 800/805-8135. **Fax:** 302/839-5175. **Contact:** Human Resources Department. **World Wide Web address:** http://www.burrislogistics.com. **Description:** An eastern U.S. frozen food distributor and warehouser. **Corporate headquarters location:** This location. **Other U.S. locations:** Nationwide.

CHESAPEAKE UTILITIES CORPORATION
EASTERN SHORE NATURAL GAS COMPANY
909 Silver Lake Boulevard, Dover DE 19904. 302/734-6799. **Contact: Michael Adams,** Human Resources. **E-mail address:** careers@chpk.com. **World Wide Web address:** http://www.chpk.com. **Description:** A diversified utility company engaged in natural gas distribution and transmission, propane distribution, and information technology services. Chesapeake's three natural gas divisions serve approximately 32,300 residential, commercial, and industrial customers in southern Delaware, the eastern shore of Maryland, and central Florida. The company's propane segment serves approximately 22,200 customers in southern Delaware and the eastern shores of Maryland and Virginia. **Positions advertised include:** Senior Accountant; Financial Analyst. **Corporate headquarters location:** This location. **Subsidiaries include:** Eastern Shore Natural Gas Company (also at this location) operates a 271-mile interstate pipeline that transports gas from various points in Pennsylvania to the company's Delaware and Maryland distribution divisions, as well as to other utilities and industrial customers in Delaware and eastern Maryland. Capital Data Systems, Inc. and United Systems, Inc. provide software products and services to a wide variety of clients. **Listed on:** New York Stock Exchange. **Stock Exchange Symbol:** CPK.

CHICAGO BRIDGE AND IRON CO.
44 Read's Way, New Castle DE 19720. 302/325-8420. **Fax:** 302/323-0788. **Contact:** Human Resources. **World Wide Web address:** http://www.cbiepc.com. **Description:** A global engineering and construction company specializing in steel plate structures. Founded in 1889. **Listed on:** New York Stock Exchange. **Stock exchange symbol:** CBI.

CHRISTIANA CARE HEALTH SYSTEM
4755 Ogletown-Stanton Road, Newark DE 19718. 302/764-6120. **Toll-free phone:** 800/999-9169. **Contact:** Human Resources. **World Wide Web address:** http://www.christianacare.org. **Description:** An integrated health care system comprised of acute care hospitals, outpatient services, rehabilitative medicine, a primary care network, transitional/long-term care facilities, and home health care agencies. **Number of employees at this location:** 400.

CHRISTIANA CARE HEALTH SYSTEM
WILMINGTON HOSPITAL
501 West 14th Street, Wilmington DE 19801. 302/733-1000. **Toll-free phone:** 800/999-9169. **Fax:** 302/428-5770. **Contact:** Human Resources. **World Wide Web address:** http://www.christianacare.org. **Description:** Christiana Care is an integrated health care system comprised of acute care hospitals, outpatient services, rehabilitative medicine, a primary care network, transitional/long-term care facilities, and home health care agencies. **Positions advertised include:** Food and Nutrition Service Assistant; Audiologist; Registered Nurse; Patient Escort; Physical Therapist; Radiologic Technologist; Medical Technologist; Maternal Child Health Registered Nurse; Sleep Technician; Graduate Nurse; Systems Analyst; Cardiovascular Technician; Medical Technologist; Pediatric Speech Therapist; Dietician; Cook; Security Officer; Occupational Therapist; Home Health Assistant; Coding Coordinator; Pharmacist; Dental Assistant; Staff Development Specialist; Neonatal Nurse Practitioner; Office Assistant; Customer Service Manager; Nurse Extern; Staff Associate; Clinical Nurse Specialist; Mammography Technologist; Performance Improvement Coordinator; Data Collection Specialist; Systems Programmer; Licensed Practical Nurse. **Operations at this facility include:** This location is an acute care hospital. **Number of employees at this location:** 7,000.

CHURCHMAN VILLAGE
4949 Ogletown-Stanton Road, Newark, DE 19713. 302/998-6900. **Fax:** 302/998-1128. **Description:** Nursing facility providing skilled, intermediate, custodial, and respite care, including physical therapy and inhalation therapy.

CITIZENS BANK
919 North Market Street, Wilmington DE 19801. 302/421-2228. **Fax:** 302/421-2294. **Contact:** Karen Thomson, Human Resources. **E-mail address:** deljobs@citizensbank.com. **World Wide Web address:** http://www.citizensbank.com. **Description:** A savings bank. **Parent company:** Citizens Financial Group, Inc.

CITY STEEL USA
4001 Philadelphia Pike, Claymont DE 19703-2794. 302/792-5400. Recorded jobline: 320/792-5408. **Contact:** Human Resources. **Description:** A steel foundry. **Corporate headquarters location:** This location.

COKESBURY VILLAGE
726 Loveville Road, Suite 3000, Hockessin DE 19707-1536. 302/235-6800. **Fax:** 302/235-6899. **Contact:** Human Resources Department. **World Wide Web address:** http://www.pumh.org/coke_bur.htm. **Description:** A full-service facility offering assisted living care, nursing home care, and a retirement community. **Positions advertised include:** Registered Nurse; Certified Nurses Aide; Waitstaff Worker; Utility Worker.

COMPUTER AID, INC.
901 Market Street, Suite 1200, Wilmington DE 19801. 302/888-5500. **Fax:** 302/888-5799. **Contact:** Human Resources Department. **World Wide Web address:** http://www.compaid.com. **Description:** A computer consulting company. **Positions advertised include:** Document Manager; Internet Developer; Junior Programmer Analyst. **Other U.S. locations:** Nationwide. **International locations:** Worldwide.

COMPUTER SCIENCES CORPORATION (CSC)
400 Commerce Drive, Newark DE 19713. 302-391-6000. **Contact:** Human Resources. **World Wide Web address:** http://www.csc.com. **Description:** CSC provides solutions for customers worldwide by applying leading technologies and CSC's own capabilities including systems design and integration; IT and business process outsourcing; applications software development; Web and application hosting; and management consulting. Founded in 1959. **Positions advertised include:** Application Developer; Computer Scientist; Application Developer; Information Security Specialist; Performance Engineer; Financial Analyst. **Corporate headquarters location:** El Segundo CA. **Number of employees worldwide:** 79,000.

CONCENTRA MEDICAL CENTER
4110 Stanton-Ogletown Road, Newark DE 19713. 302/738-0103. **Fax:** 302/738-6612. **Contact:** Human Resources. **World Wide Web address:** http://www.concentra.com. **Description:** Provider of occupational medicine, Workers Compensation and other occupational healthcare services. **NOTE:** All applications must be submitted online. **Positions advertised include:** Administrative, Health Professional, Legal.

CONECTIV POWER DELIVERY
800 North King Street, Wilmington DE 19805. **Toll-free phone:** 800/266-3284. **Contact:** Human Resources. **World Wide Web address:** http://www.conectiv.com. **Description:** Provides electricity, gas, telecommunications, heating, and cooling services. **Corporate headquarters location:** This location. **Listed on:** New York Stock Exchange. **Stock exchange symbol:** CIV.

THE CROWELL CORPORATION
One Crowell P.O. Box 3227, Newport DE 19804-0227. 302/998-0557. **Contact:** Joan Addleman, Chief Operating Officer. **World Wide Web address:** http://www.crowellcorp.com. **Description:** Manufactures sealing tape, box tapes, paper tape, and packaging materials. Founded in 1906.

DADE BEHRING INC.
500 Gbc Drive, Newark DE 19702. 302/631-6000. **Contact:** Human Resources. **World Wide Web address:** http://www.dadebehring.com. **Description:** Dade Behring is a leader in the diagnostics industry, serving more than 24,000 laboratories worldwide with products to assist clinicians in diagnosing medical conditions and in identifying treatment options. **Positions advertised include:** Supervisor, Pricing-Sales Operations. **Number of employees worldwide:** 6,000.

DASSAULT FALCON JET CORPORATION
P.O. Box 10367, Wilmington DE 19805. 302/322-7000. **Physical address:** 191 North Dupont Highway, New Castle DE 19720. **Fax:** 302/322-7275. **Contact:** Human Resources. **World Wide Web address:** http://www.dassaultfalconjet.com. **Description:** Provides a variety of flight and aircraft services including chartered flights, aircraft maintenance, avionics work, flight support, and aircraft refurbishment. **Other U.S. locations:** Chicago IL; Teterboro NJ; Philadelphia PA; Houston TX.

M. DAVIS & SONS INC.
200 Hadco Road, Wilmington DE 19804-1000. 302/998-3385. **Toll-free phone:** 800/91-DAVIS. **Fax:** 302/655-0245. **Contact:** Human Resources. **World Wide Web address:** http://www.mdavisinc.com. **Description:** One of the area's leading industrial and commercial contractors. The company offers a variety of services including architectural and computer-aided design, electrical services, mechanical construction, and building maintenance and services. Founded in 1870. **Corporate headquarters location:** This location.

DEACON INDUSTRIAL SUPPLY COMPANY INCORPORATED
P.O. Box 765, 7 East Commons Boulevard, New Castle DE 19720. 302/322-5411. **Fax:** 610/265-6470. **Contact:** Sharon, Lawson, Human Resources. **E-mail address:** humanresources@deaconind.com. **World Wide Web address:** http://www.deaconind.com. **Description:** Distributes valves, gaskets, piping, and commercial plumbing supplies. **Note:** Mail Resumes to 165 Boro Line Road, P.O. Box 62485, King of Prussia PA 19406. **Corporate headquarters location:** This location. **Parent company:** Vail Enterprises, Inc. **Operations at this facility include:** Administration; Sales.

DELAWARE DEPARTMENT OF NATURAL RESOURCES & ENVIRONMENTAL CONTROL
89 Kings Highway, Dover DE 19901. 302/739-5823. **Contact:** Human Resources. **World Wide Web address:** http://www.dnrec.state.de.us. **Description:** Provides help with obtaining environmental permits and also provides environmental information regarding pollution, outdoor activities, waste, land and water, and whole basin management. **Positions advertised include:** Environmental Engineer; Environmental Program Manager.

DELAWARE ELECTRIC COOPERATIVE
P.O. Box 600, Greenwood DE 19950. 302/398-9090. **Toll-free phone:** 800/282-8595. **Recorded jobline:** 302/349-4575. **Fax:** 302/349-3139. **Contact:** Human Resources **World Wide Web address:** http://www.delelect.com. **Description:** An electric company. Founded in 1938.

DELAWARE GUIDANCE SERVICES
1213 Delaware Avenue, Wilmington DE 19806. 302/652-8297. **Fax:** 302/652-8297. **E-mail address:** jtaylor@delawareguidance.org. **World Wide Web address:** http://www.delawareguidance.org. **Contact:** Human Resources. **Description:** Operates mental health treatment centers for children aged 6 to 13. **Positions advertised include:** Mental Health Outpatient Therapist; Mental Health Aide; Nurse Practitioner. **Special programs:** Internships. **Corporate headquarters location:** This location. **Operations at this facility include:** Administration; Service. **Number of employees at this location:** 10. **Number of employees nationwide:** 60.

DELAWARE HEALTH AND SOCIAL SERVICES (DHSS)
1901 North DuPont Highway, Main Building, New Castle DE 19720-1100. 302/577-4580. **Recorded jobline:** 302/255-9100. **Contact:** Human Resources. **World Wide Web address:** http://www.state.de.us/dhss. **Description:** Promotes the health and well-being of Delaware's citizens. DHSS is the fifth largest employer in the state. **Number of employees nationwide:** 4,800.

DELAWARE PARK RACING ASSOCIATION
777 Delaware Park Boulevard, Wilmington DE 19804. 302/994-2521. **Contact:** Micki Nardo, Director of Human Resources. **World Wide Web address:** http://www.delpark.com. **Description:** Operates a horse racing track and off-track betting facility.

DELAWARE RIVER AND BAY AUTHORITY
P.O. Box 71 New Castle DE 19720. 302/571-6474. **Fax:** 302/571-6420. **World Wide Web address:** http://www.drba.net. **Description:** Provides vital transportation links between Delaware and New Jersey, as well as economic development in Delaware and the four southern counties of New Jersey.

DELAWARE STATE UNIVERSITY
1200 North DuPont Highway, Dover DE 19901. 302/857-6060. **Contact:** Mark Farley, Personnel Director. **World Wide Web address:** http://www.dsc.edu. **Description:** A four-year state university offering bachelor's and master's degrees.

DELAWARE TECHNICAL AND COMMUNITY COLLEGE
Terry Campus, 100 Campus Drive, Dover DE 19904-1383. 302/857-1000. **Fax:** 302/857-1297. **Contact:** Human Resources. **World Wide Web address:** http://www.dtcc.edu. **Description:** A statewide institution of higher education, providing academic, technical, continuing education, and industrial training at four campuses. Several degree programs are offered, and the Associate in Applied Science degree is granted upon successful completion of specific curriculum requirements. In addition, diploma and certificate programs are offered in a variety of technical areas at each campus. The college and its campuses are fully-accredited by the Commission on Higher Education, and Middle States Association of Colleges and Schools. In addition, several curricula have earned program-based accreditation by various professional organizations. **Other area locations:** Georgetown DE; Newark DE; Wilmington DE.

DELAWARE TECHNICAL AND COMMUNITY COLLEGE
400 Stanton Christiana Road, Newark DE 19713. 302/454-3900. **Fax:** 302/453-3028. **Contact:** Human Resources. **World Wide Web address:** http://www.dtcc.edu. **Description:** A statewide institution of higher education, providing academic, technical, continuing education, and industrial training at four campuses. Several degree programs are offered and the Associate in Applied Science degree is granted upon successful completion of specific curriculum requirements. In addition, diploma and certificate programs are offered in a variety of technical areas at each campus. The college and its campuses are fully-accredited by the Commission on Higher Education, and Middle States Association of Colleges and Schools. In addition, several curricula have earned program-based accreditation by various professional organizations.

DELPHI FINANCIAL GROUP, INC.
1105 North Market Street, Suite 1230, Wilmington DE 19899. 302/478-5142. **Contact:** Human Resources. **World Wide Web address:** http://www.delphifin.com. **Description:** An insurance holding company that, through its subsidiaries, offers a diverse portfolio of life, long-term disability, and personal accident insurance products principally to the group employee benefits market nationwide. Delphi Financial Group also offers asset accumulation products to individuals and groups. **Corporate headquarters location:** This location. **Subsidiaries include:** Reliance Standard Life Insurance Company; Safety National Casualty Corporation. **Listed on:** New York Stock Exchange. **Stock exchange symbol:** DFG.

DENTSPLY INTERNATIONAL INC.
L.D. CAULK DIVISION
38 West Clarke Avenue, P.O. Box 359, Milford DE 19963. 302/422-4511. **Fax:** 302/424-4385. **Contact:** Human Resources. **World Wide Web address:** http://www.caulk.com. **Description:** Manufactures a wide variety of dental supplies including cements for orthodontic procedures and materials for making fillings and impressions. **Corporate headquarters location:** York PA. **Other U.S. locations:** Carlsbad CA; Encino CA; Los Angeles CA; Lakewood CO; Des Plaines IL; Elgin IL; Burlington NJ; Maumee OH; Tulsa OK; Johnson City TN. **International locations:** Worldwide. **Listed on:** NASDAQ. **Stock exchange symbol:** XRAY.

DEPARTMENT OF SERVICES FOR CHILDREN, YOUTH & THEIR FAMILIES
1825 Faulkland Road, Wilmington DE 19805. 302/633-2500. **Fax:** 302/633-2684. **Contact:** Human Resources. **World Wide Web address:** http://www.state.de.us/kids. **Description:** This department's main objective is to foster positive change in the behavior of children and their families. Services include crisis help, child abuse intervention, substance abuse services, and services for delinquent youth.

EDWARD J. DESETA CO., INC.
322 A Street, Suite 200, Wilmington DE 19801-5355. 302/691-2040. **Fax:** 302/691-2041. **Contact:** Human Resources. **World Wide Web address:** http://www.ejdeseta.com. **Description:** Industrial HVAC contractors and engineers.

DODD DENTAL LABORATORIES, INC.
24 Lukens Drive, P.O. Box 1005, New Castle DE 19720-7005. 302/661-6000. **Fax:** 302/661-6016. **Contact:** Human Resources. **World Wide Web address:** http://www.doddlab.com. **Description:** A dental laboratory providing dental prosthetic devices. **Parent company:** National Dentex Corporation is one of the largest operators of dental laboratories in the United States. These dental laboratories provide a full range of custom-made dental prosthetic appliances divided into three main groups: restorative products (crowns and bridges); reconstructive products (partial and full dentures); and cosmetic products (porcelain veneers and ceramic crowns). Each lab is operated as a stand-alone facility under the direction of a local manager. All sales and marketing is done through each lab's own direct sales force.

DOVER DOWNS ENTERTAINMENT
P.O. Box 1412, Dover DE 19903-0843. 302/674-4600. **Physical address:** 1131 North DuPont Highway, Dover DE 19901. **Fax:** 302/857-3253. **E-mail address:** recruiter@doverdowns.com. **Contact:** Human Resources. **World Wide Web address:** http://www.doverdowns.com. **Description:** Operates a 5/8-mile track that provides NASCAR, PepBoys IRL, and harness racing. Dover Downs Entertainment also offers dining, concerts, and slot machines.

E.I. DUPONT DE NEMOURS AND COMPANY
1007 Market Street, Wilmington DE 19898. 302/774-1000. **Contact:** Human Resources. **World Wide Web address:** http://www.dupont.com. **Description:** Involved in the manufacture of biomedical, industrial, and consumer products (such as photographic, data-recording, and video devices); the production of manmade fiber products; polymer products (such as plastic resins, elastomers, and films); and agricultural and industrial chemicals (such as herbicides and insecticides, pigments, fluorochemicals, petroleum additives, and mineral acids); the exploration and production of crude oil and natural gas; the refining, marketing, and downstream transportation of petroleum; and the mining and distribution of steam and metallurgical coals. The company supplies products to the aerospace, agriculture, apparel, transportation, health care, and printing and publishing industries. **Corporate headquarters location:** This location. **Listed on:** New York Stock Exchange. **Stock exchange symbol:** DD. **Chairman and CEO:** Charles O. Holliday, Jr. **Annual sales/revenues:** More than $100 million. **Number of employees worldwide:** 94,000.

A. I. DUPONT HOSPITAL FOR CHILDREN & NEMOURS CHILDREN'S CLINIC
P.O. Box 269, Wilmington DE 19899. 302/651-4000. **Physical Address:** 1600 Rockland Road, Wilmington DE 19803. **Fax:** 302/651-6119. **Recorded jobline:** 800/545-0056. **Contact:** Human Resources. **World Wide Web address:** http://www.nemours.org. **Description:** Pediatric specialty hospital and clinic. **NOTE:** All applicants must adhere to specific guidelines, which can be found by calling the recorded jobline. **Positions advertised include:** Billing Liaison; Clinical Data Abstractor-Neurology; Certified Ophthalmic Technician; Administrative Secretary; Medical Secretary; Advanced Practice Nurse Cardiac; Advanced Nurse Practitioner; Registered Nurse. **Corporate headquarters location:** Jacksonville FL.

EDS (ELECTRONIC DATA SYSTEMS CORPORATION)
Bristol Building 248 Chapman Road, Suite 100, Newark DE 19702. 302/454-7622. **Contact:** Human Resources. **World Wide Web address:** http://www.eds.com. **Description:** Provides information technology services including system interaction development, management, and consulting.

FAIR, ISAAC AND CO., INC.
10 Corporate Circle, Suite 330, New Castle DE 19720. 302/324-8015. **Contact:** Human Resources. **World Wide Web address:** http://www.fairisaac.com. **Description:** Fair, Isaac and Co., Inc. develops and provides data management software and services for the consumer credit, personal lines insurance, and direct marketing industries. Founded in 1956. **Positions advertised include:** Marketing Strategy Consultant; Account Executive. **Operations at this facility include:** This location is a sales office. **Listed on:** New York Stock Exchange. **Stock exchange symbol:** FIC. **Number of employees nationwide:** 700.

FLEET CREDIT CARD SERVICES
300 North Wakefield Drive, Newark DE 19702. 302/266-5600. **Fax:** 302/266-5468. **Recorded jobline:** 302/266-JOBS. **Contact:** Human Resources. **World Wide Web address:** http://www.fleet.com. **Description:** Provides consumer credit card services. **Company slogan:** Ready when you are. **Corporate headquarters location:** Horsham PA. **Other U.S. locations:** Colorado Springs CO. **Parent company:** FleetBoston Financial. **CEO:** Joe Saunders. **Annual sales/revenues:** $11 - $20 million. **Number of employees at this location:** 700. **Number of employees nationwide:** 3,500.

FORWOOD MANOR
1912 Marsh Road, Wilmington DE 19810. 302/529-1600. **Fax:** 302/529-1689. **Contact:** Human Resources. **World Wide Web address:** http://www.sunriseseniorliving.com. **Description:** A full-service retirement community consisting of 140 apartments, 37 assisted-living suites, and 66 nursing beds. Forwood Manor's services include assisted living, daily meals, exercise facilities, housekeeping, independent living, nursing care, on-site banking, physical therapy, respite care, social activities, and transportation. **Parent company:** Marriott Corporation.

FOXFIRE PRINTING & PACKAGING, INC.
750 Dawson Drive, Newark DE 19713. 302/368-9466. **Fax:** 302/283-1825. **Contact:** Human Resources. **E-mail address:** hr@foxfireprinting.com. **World Wide Web address:** http://www.foxfireprinting.com. **Description:** A full service marketing solutions company that offers market data analysis, photography, design, digital and offset printing, web-enabled fulfillment, project-development, data management, value-added reporting, trial programs, warehousing, point-of-purchase advertising and marketing cost-benefit analysis. **Positions advertised include:** Account Executive, Digital Color Banner Operator, Digital Color Press Operator, Sales Specialist, Warehouse-Shipping Assistant, Xerox Document Management Specialist.

GENERAL CHEMICAL CORPORATION
6300 Philadelphia Pike, South Gate DE 19703. 302/792-8500. **Contact:** Human Resources. **World Wide Web address:** http://www.genchem.com. **Description:** Manufactures and distributes soda ash and calcium chloride. **Special programs:** Internships. **Corporate headquarters location:** Hampton NH. **Other U.S. locations:** Nationwide. **Listed on:** OTC BB. **Stock exchange symbol:** GNMP.OB. **Number of employees at this location:** 300. **Number of employees nationwide:** 2,000.

GENERAL MOTORS CORPORATION
Boxwood Road, P.O. Box 1512, Wilmington DE 19899. 302/428-7000. **Contact:** Human Resources. **World Wide Web address:** http://www.gm.com. **Description:** General Motors Corporation is one of the world's largest full-line vehicle manufacturers and has substantial interests in information technology, electronics, and finance. GM conducts business through the following sectors: North American Automotive Operations includes Sales/Service Groups (Buick, Cadillac, Chevrolet, GMC Truck, Oldsmobile, Pontiac, and Saturn) and Vehicle Development Groups (Powertrain, Truck Group, Small Car Group, and Midsize/Luxury Car Group); International Operations include GM Europe, Asia Pacific Operations, and Latin America, Africa, Middle East Operations; GMAC, which provides financing and insurance to GM customers and dealers, consists of North American Operations, International Operations, Motors Insurance Corporation, and GMAC Mortgage Group; EDS applies information technologies to more than 8,000 customers globally in the communications, energy/chemical, insurance, public sector, travel and transportation, financial services, manufacturing, and retail industries; GM Hughes Electronics Corporation is involved in automotive electronics, telecommunications and space electronics, and defense electronics. Founded in 1908. **Corporate headquarters location:** Detroit MI. **Operations at this facility include:** Administration; Manufacturing. This location is an automotive assembly plant for the Chevrolet Malibu. **Listed on:** New York Stock Exchange. **Stock exchange symbol:** GMA. **Annual sales/revenues:** More than $100 million. **Number of employees at this location:** 2,400.

J.R. GETTIER & ASSOCIATES INCORPORATED
2 Centerville Road, Wilmington DE 19808. 302/652-2700. **Fax:** 302/652-8699. **Contact:** Heather Shupe, Human Resources. **E-mail address:** hs@gettier.com. **World Wide Web address:** http://www.gettier.com. **Description:** Provides protective, investigative, and security services in Delaware, Maryland, New Jersey, and Pennsylvania.

GOLDEY-BEACOM COLLEGE
4701 Limestone Road, Wilmington DE 19808. 302/998-8814. **Contact:** Director of Human Resources. **E-mail address:** hr@gbc.edu. **World Wide Web address:** http://www.gbc.edu. **Description:** An independent, multilevel college of business, Goldey-Beacom offers undergraduate academic programs and a Master of Business Administration.

W.L. GORE & ASSOCIATES, INC.
P.O. Box 9206, Newark DE 19714-9206. 302/738-4880. **Physical address:** 551 Paper Mill Road, Newark DE 19711. **Contact:** Human Resources, Recruiter. **World Wide Web address:** http://www.gore.com. **Description:** Manufactures dental floss, guitar

strings, vacuum filters, and water/stain repellent. The company also produces electronic products including copper and optical signal transmission products, digital and analog cable assemblies; chemical products including a chemical polymer used to repair diseased arteries and also as an industrial sealant; and GORE-TEX fabric. **Positions advertised include:** e-Business Champion. **Corporate headquarters location:** This location. **Operations at this facility include:** Manufacturing; Research and Development; Sales; Service. **Annual sales/revenues:** More than $1.23 billion. **Number of employees nationwide:** 6,000.

GUNNIP & CO.
Little Falls Centre II, 2751 Centerville Road, Suite 300, Wilmington DE 19808. 302/225-5000. **Contact:** Human Resources. **World Wide Web address:** http://www.gunnip. com. **Description:** Provides accounting, auditing, tax, and management services to local, national, and international clients. Founded in 1947.

HAGLEY MUSEUM AND LIBRARY
P.O. Box 3630, Wilmington DE 19807-0630. 302/658-2400. **Contact:** Robert Hill, Human Resources. **World Wide Web address:** http://www.hagley.org. **Description:** A nonprofit educational institution dedicated to American business and technological history. The museum examines the development of the du Pont Company's first product, black powder.

HAPPY HARRY'S INC.
124 East Main Street, Newark DE 19711. 302/738-6333. **Contact:** Dennis Gossert, Director of Personnel. **World Wide Web address:** http://www.happy.com. **Description:** A drug store chain with locations throughout the Delaware Valley.

HOMSEY ARCHITECTURE INC.
2003 North Scott Street, Wilmington DE 19806. 302/656-4491. **Contact:** Charles Ryan, Human Resources. **E-mail address:** cryan@homsey.com. **World Wide Web address:** http://www.homsey.com. **Description:** A full-service architecture firm specializing in architecture, landscaping, and interior architectural design. Founded in 1935.

HOTEL DUPONT
11th and Market Streets, Wilmington DE 19801. 302/594-3100. **Toll-free number:** 800/941-9019. **Contact:** Human Resources. **World Wide Web address:** http://www.dupont.com/hotel. **Description:** A hotel. **NOTE:** Must apply online. **Parent company:** E.I. DuPont de Nemours & Company.

ILC DOVER, INC.
One Moonwalker Road, Frederica DE 19946. 302/335-3911. **Fax:** 302/335-0762. **Contact:** Frank J. Mossman, Director of Human Resources. **World Wide Web address:** http://www.ilcdover.com. **Description:** Develops and fabricates NASA space suits, high-tech inflatables and LTA lift systems, specialized composites, polymer-coated engineered fabrics, hardgoods/softgoods interface, human protective systems (chemical, biological masks, shelters, and suits), and environmental protective systems. **Corporate headquarters location:** Bohemia NY. **Other U.S. locations:** Houston TX. **Parent company:** ILC Industries, Inc. **Operations at this facility include:** Administration; Divisional Headquarters; Manufacturing; Research and Development; Sales; Service.

INFOQUEST SYSTEMS, INC.
15 Innovation Way, Suite 120, Newark DE 19711. 302/456-3392. **Toll-free phone:** 800/414-9899. **Fax:** 302/368-7544. **Contact:** Human Resources. **E-mail address:** jobs@iqsi.com. **World Wide Web address:** http://www.iqsi.com. **Description:** Develops software for the health care industry that assists with billing patients and scheduling appointments; attaches dictation to patients' files; and sends appointment reminders. **Corporate headquarters location:** This location.

J.P. MORGAN CHASE & COMPANY
500 Stanton Christiana Road, Newark DE 19713-2107. 302/634-1000. **Fax:** 302/634-4090. **Contact:** Human Resources. **World Wide Web address:** http://www. jpmorganchase.com. **Description:** Specializes in global financial services and retail banking. J.P. Morgan Chase and Company's services include asset management, card-member services, community development, commercial banking for middle market companies, diversified consumer lending, global markets, home finance, investment banking, private banking, private equity, regional consumer and small business banking, and treasury and securities services. **Positions advertised include:** Operations Accountant; Operations Specialist, High Yield Loan Trading Operations; Research Specialist, Merchant Disputes; Trust Officer/AVP; Credit ACD Analyst; IM Fee Billing Specialist; Private Banking Operations Accountant; Private Banking International Income Collections Specialist. **Special programs:** Internships. **Number of employees at this location:** 1,000.

JOHNSON CONTROLS INC.
700 North Broad Street, Middletown DE 19709. 302/378-9885. **Contact:** Human Resources. **World Wide Web address:** http://www.jci.com. **Description:** Johnson Controls is a global market leader in automotive seating, facility services and control systems, plastic packaging, and automotive batteries. These industries make up the four business units of the company: Automotive, Controls, Plastics, and Battery. The automotive business produces complete seat systems, seating components, and interior trim systems for cars, light trucks, and vans. The controls segment is involved in the installation and service of facility management and control systems, retrofit and service of mechanical equipment and lighting systems in nonresidential buildings, and on-site management of facility operations and maintenance. The plastics unit manufactures plastic containers for beverages, food, personal care, and household items, as well as manufacturing, installing, and servicing plastics blowmolding machinery systems. The battery segment manufactures automotive batteries for the replacement and original equipment markets and specialty batteries for telecommunications and uninterrupted power supply applications. **Corporate headquarters location:** Milwaukee WI. **Listed on:** New York Stock Exchange. **Stock exchange symbol:** JCI. **Annual sales/revenues:** More than $20 billion.

KEEN COMPRESSED GAS COMPANY
P.O. Box 15146, Wilmington DE 19850. 302/594-4545. **Physical address:** 4063 New Castle Avenue, New Castle DE 19720. **Toll-free number:** 800/533-6427. **Contact:** Human Resources. **World Wide Web address:** http://www.keengas.com. **Description:** Manufactures welding supplies, power tools, industrial gases, and medical gases. Founded in 1919.

KILLENS POND STATE PARK
5025 Killenspond Road, Felton DE 19943. 302/284-4526. **Fax:** 302/284-4694. **Contact:** Human Resources. **World Wide Web address:** http://www.destateparks.com. **Description:** A state park that offers fishing, boating, swimming, camping, hiking, and other athletic activities. Founded in 1965. **Special programs:** Seasonal opportunities; Volunteer opportunities.

KRAFT FOODS, INC.
1250 West North Street, Dover DE 19904-7756. 302/734-6100. **Contact:** Human Resources. **World Wide Web address:** http://www.kraftfoods.com. **Description:** Kraft is one of the largest producers of packaged food in North America. Major brands include Jell-O, Post, Kool-Aid, Crystal Light, Entenmann's, Miracle Whip, Stove Top, and Shake 'n Bake. Kraft Foods markets a number of products under the Kraft brand name including natural and processed cheeses and dry packaged dinners. The Oscar Mayer unit markets processed meats, poultry, lunch combinations, and pickles under the Oscar Mayer, Louis Rich, Lunchables, and Claussen brand names. Kraft is also one of the largest coffee companies, with principal brands including Maxwell House, Sanka, Brim, and General Foods International Coffees. **Corporate headquarters location:** Northfield IL. **Operations at this facility include:** This location produces rice, coconut, Kool-Aid, and Tang. **Listed on:** New York Stock Exchange. **Stock exchange symbol:** KFT.

LABORATORY CORPORATION OF AMERICA (LABCORP)
105 Faulk Road, Suite 102, Wilmington DE 19803. 302/571-8876. **Contact:** Human Resources. **World Wide Web address:** http://www.labcorp.com. **Description:** One of the nation's leading clinical laboratory companies, providing services primarily to physicians, hospitals, clinics, nursing homes, and other clinical labs nationwide. LabCorp performs tests on blood, urine, and other body fluids and tissue, aiding the diagnosis of disease. **Corporate headquarters location:** Burlington NC. **Listed on:** New York Stock Exchange. **Stock exchange symbol:** LH.

LAFARGE GYPSUM
1105 North Market Street, P.O. Box 895, Wilmington DE 19899. 302/427-9542. **Contact:** Human Resources. **World Wide Web address:** http://www.lafargenorthamerica. com. **Description:** Manufactures and sells wallboard. **Corporate headquarters location:** Herndon VA. **Parent company:** Lafarge Corporation. **Operations at this facility include:** Manufacturing; Sales. **Listed on:** New York Stock Exchange. **Stock exchange symbol:** LAF. **Number of employees at this location:** 130. **Number of employees nationwide:** 3,000. **Number of employees worldwide:** 37,000.

MBNA AMERICA
1100 North King Street, Wilmington DE 19884-0248. **Toll-free phone:** 800/441-7048. **Contact:** Human Resources. **World Wide Web address:** http://www.mbna.com. **Description:** MBNA America is a leader in issuing MasterCard Gold cards and Affinity credit cards. The company also offers home equity and personal loans. **Corporate headquarters location:** This location. **Other area locations:** Newark DE; Greenville DE; Dover DE. **Subsidiaries include:** MBNA America Bank, N.A. **Operations at this facility include:** This location oversees satellite telesales centers in Dover DE, State College PA, and Towson MD **Listed on:** New York Stock Exchange. **Stock exchange symbol:** KRB.

MOUNTAIRE OF DELMARVA INC.
P.O. Box 710, Selbyville DE 19975. 302/436-8241. **Contact:** Human Resources. **Description:** A poultry processing plant. **Corporate headquarters location:** This location.

NVF COMPANY INC.
1166 Yorklyn Road, P.O. Box 68, Yorklyn DE 19736. 302/239-5281. **Toll-free phone:** 800/388-6831. **Fax:** 302/239-4406. **Contact:** Human Resources. **World Wide Web address:** http://www.nvf.com. **Description:** Produces vulcanized fiber paper and industrial laminates. **Corporate headquarters location:** This location. **Other U.S. locations:** Newark NJ.

NATIONWIDE PROVIDENT
300 Continental Drive, Newark DE 19713. 302/452-4000. **Fax:** 302/452-7004. **Contact:** Personnel. **E-mail address:** jocros@nationwideprovident.com. **World Wide Web address:** http://www.nationwideprovident.com. **Description:** Sells various life insurance products. Provident Mutual Life Insurance Company is licensed in all 50 states and in the District of Columbia. **NOTE:** Address resumes Attn: Human Resources. **Corporate headquarters locations:** Berwyn PA.

NEWARK, CITY OF
P.O. Box 390, Newark DE 19715-1194. 302/366-7026. **Physical address:** 220 Elkton Road, Newark DE 19715. **Contact:** Human Resources. **E-mail address:** personnel@newark.de.us. **World Wide Web address:** http://newark.de.us. **Description:** The government offices for the city of Newark.

THE NEWS JOURNAL
P.O. Box 15505, Wilmington DE 19850. 302/324-2566. **Physical address:** 950 West Basin Road, New Castle DE. **Fax:** 302/324-2578. **Recorded jobline:** 302/324-2464. **Contact:** Timothy Regan, Vice President of Human Resources. **E-mail address:** jobs@delawareonline.com. **World Wide Web address:** http://www.delawareonline. com. **Description:** Publishes a daily newspaper with a weekday circulation exceeding 125,000. **Positions advertised include:** Advertising Production Supervisor; Delivery Distributor; Telemarketing Sales Representative; Construction Worker; Janitor. **Special programs:** Internships. **Parent company:** Gannett Company (Arlington VA.) **Number of employees at this location:** 625.

O.A. NEWTON & SON COMPANY
P.O. Box 397, Bridgeville DE 19933. 302/337-8211. **Contact:** Robert Rider, Jr., President. **World Wide Web address:** http://www.oanewtonirrigation.com. **Description:** A retailer of irrigation products and services.

NISOURCE INC.
300 Delaware Avenue, Suite 555, Wilmington DE 19801. 302/427-7869. **Contact:** Human Resources. **World Wide Web address:** http://www.nisource.com. **Description:** A holding company for several subsidiaries involved in the production, transmission, and distribution of natural gas. The company's five gas distribution units serve nearly 2 million customers in the residential, commercial, and industrial sectors of Pennsylvania, Ohio, Maryland, Virginia, and Kentucky. Columbia's transmission subsidiaries operate over 23,700 miles of pipeline throughout 15 states and Washington D.C. Other interests of the company include the operation of underground storage facilities; gas marketing; supply and fuel management services; propane selling; and cogeneration ventures. **Subsidiaries include:** Columbia Gas Transmission Corporation.

NIXON UNIFORM SERVICE, INC.
2925 Northeast Boulevard, Wilmington DE 19802. 302/764-7550. **Fax:** 302/351-1621. **Toll-free phone:** 888/649-6687. **Contact:** Human Resources. **E-mail address:** jobs@uniformservice.com. **World Wide Web address:** http://www.uniformservice.com. **Description:** Rents and sells casual wear, linens,

medical garments, and uniforms. **Positions advertised include:** Route Delivery Representative. **Special programs:** Internships. **Corporate headquarters location:** This location. **Other U.S. locations:** Washington DC; Baltimore MD; Newark NJ; Lancaster PA. **Number of employees at this location:** 300.

OLIVE GARDEN RESTAURANT
305 Rocky Run Parkway, Tallyville DE 19803. 302/477-0870. **Contact:** Human Resources. **World Wide Web address:** http://www.darden.com. **Description:** One location in a chain of family-style Italian restaurants. **Positions advertised include:** Host; Server; Line Cook; Preparation Cook; Alley Coordinator; Server Assistant/ Busser; Utility/Dish Machine Operator. **Parent company:** Darden Corporation. **Listed on:** New York Stock Exchange. **Stock exchange symbol:** DRI.

ONESOURCE
P.O. Box 1300, Wilmington DE 19899. 302/498-5199. **Contact:** Human Resources. **Description:** Provides janitorial, landscaping, and pest control services to public institutions, retail stores, schools, industrial facilities, and commercial buildings. **Corporate headquarters location:** Atlanta GA.

ORKIN
101 Johnson Way, New Castle DE 19720. 302/325-4410. **Contact:** Human Resources. **World Wide Web address:** http://www.orkin.com. **Description:** Pest control company.

PERDUE FARMS, INC.
255 North Rehoboth Boulevard, Milford DE 19963. 302/422-6681. **Fax:** 302/855-5555. **Contact:** Human Resources. **World Wide Web address:** http://www.perdue.com. **Description:** Perdue Farms is one of the largest suppliers of fresh poultry products in the United States. The company's products are sold in supermarkets, small grocery stores, and butcher shops from Maine to Georgia and as far west as Chicago. Perdue's operation is fully-integrated, from breeding and hatching to delivering packaged goods to market. **Positions advertised include:** Exact Weight Manager. **Special programs:** Internships. **Corporate headquarters location:** Salisbury MD. **Operations at this facility include:** This location processes poultry. **Number of employees at this location:** 1,100.

PERDUE FARMS, INC.
200 Savannah Road, Georgetown DE 19947. 302/855-5555. **Fax:** 302/855-5555. **Contact:** Human Resources. **Description:** Perdue Farms is one of the largest suppliers of fresh poultry products in the United States. The company's products are sold in supermarkets, small grocery stores, and butcher shops from Maine to Georgia and as far west as Chicago. Perdue's operation is fully-integrated, from breeding and hatching to delivering packaged goods to market. **Corporate headquarters location:** Salisbury MD. **Operations at this facility include:** This location processes chickens. **Number of employees nationwide:** 18,000.

PHILLIPS & COHEN ASSOCIATES, LTD.
258 Chapman Road, Suite 205, Newark DE 19702. 302/355-3500. **Contact:** Human Resources. **E-mail address:** info@phillips-cohen.com. **World Wide Web address:** http://www.phillips-cohen.com. **Description:** A collection agency. Founded in 1997. **Positions advertised include:** Collection Specialist.

PLAYTEX PRODUCTS, INC.
50 North DuPont Highway, P.O. Box 7016, Dover DE 19903-1516. 302/678-6000. **Fax:** 302/678-6738. **Contact:** Donna M. Griffith, Director of Human Resources. **World Wide Web address:** http://www.playtexnet.com. **Description:** Manufactures intimate apparel. **Special programs:** Internships. **Corporate headquarters location:** Westport CT. **Other U.S. locations:** Paramus NJ; Watervliet NY. **Operations at this facility include:** Administration; Distribution; Manufacturing; Research and Development; Service. **Listed on:** New York Stock Exchange. **Stock exchange symbol:** PYX. **Number of employees nationwide:** 1,500.

POTTER ANDERSON & CORROON LLP
Hercules Plaza, 1313 North Market Street, Wilmington DE 19801. 302/984-6000. **Fax:** 302/658-1192. **Contact:** Jennifer Gimler Brady, Esq., Hiring Partner. **World Wide Web address:** http://www.pacdelaware.com. **Description:** A law firm comprised of three practice groups: Corporate, Business, and Litigation.

PRICKETT, JONES & ELLIOTT
P.O. Box 1328, Wilmington DE 19899. 302/888-6500. **Physical address:** 1310 King Street, Wilmington DE 19801. **Fax:** 302/658-8111. **Contact:** Joanne Hamill, Personnel Manager. **E-mail address:** jchamill@prickett.com. **World Wide Web address:** http://www.prickett.com. **Description:** A legal services firm specializing in insurance law and corporate law. **Other area locations:** Dover DE. **Other U.S. locations:** Kennett Square PA.

PRINTPACK, INC.
River Road & Grantham Lane, P.O. Box 110, New Castle DE 19720. 302/323-4000. **Contact:** Human Resources. **E-mail address:** careers@printpack.com. **World Wide Web address:** http://www.printpack.com. **Description:** Produces facial tissues, paper towels, napkins, and paper cups; provides retail packaging for food and other consumer products; and produces boxes and cartons for packaging, groundwood papers, printing papers, and other paper products. **Corporate headquarters location:** Atlanta GA.

QUEST PHARMACEUTICAL SERVICES
Delaware Technology Park, 3 Innovation Way, Suite 240, Newark DE 19711. 302/369-5601. **Fax:** 302/369-5602. **Contact:** Human Resources. **E-mail address:** Jobs@QuestPharm.com. **World Wide Web address:** http://www.questpharm.com. **Description:** A pharmaceutical company that runs a GLP-compliant DMPK laboratory that supports drug discovery and development. **Positions advertised include:** Business Development Director, Research Scientist/Senior Research Scientist-Discovery Bioanalytical, Staff Scientist/Associate Scientist-Discovery Bioanalytical.

RICHARDS, LAYTON & FINGER, P.A.
One Rodney Square, P.O. Box 551, Wilmington DE 19899. 302/658-6541. **Contact:** Joni L. Peet, Human Resources. **World Wide Web address:** http://www.rlf.com. **Description:** A large law firm specializing in corporate law.

CAESAR RODNEY SCHOOL DISTRICT
219 Old North Road, P.O. Box 188, Camden DE 19934. 302/697-2173. **Fax:** 302/697-3406. **Contact:** Human Resources. **World Wide Web address:** http://www.crsd-k12.com. **Description:** A school district comprised of eight elementary schools, one junior high school, one high school, and one special education school. **Positions advertised include:** Custodian; General Worker; Middle School Science Teacher; Paraprofessional; School Psychologist; Speech and Hearing Pathologist.

ST. FRANCIS HOSPITAL
7th & Clayton Streets, Wilmington DE 19805-0500. 302/575-8260. **Fax:** 302/421-4265. **Contact:** Human Resources. **E-mail address:** jobs@stfrancishealthcare.org. **World Wide Web address:** http://www.stfrancishealthcare.org. **Description:** A community-based hospital consisting of more than 1,650 employees and affiliated physicians, with specialty physician practices in pediatrics and obstetrics/gynecology. **Positions advertised include:** Cardiovascular Technician; C.A.T. Scan Technician; Chief Surgical Physician Assistant; Courier; Desktop Analyst; Housekeeper; Vice President, Human Resources; HVAC Mechanic; Nurse; Nursing Senior Team Leader; RN; LPN; Patient Care Assistant; Physical Therapist; Radiographic Technologist; Respiratory Therapist; Secretary; Surgical Physician Assistant; Ultrasound Technician; Unit Clerk.

SCHMITTINGER & RODRIGUEZ, P.A.
414 South State Street, Dover DE 19903-0497. 302/674-0140. **Fax:** 302/674-0140. **Contact:** Bill Thomas, Personnel Manager. **World Wide Web address:** http://www.schmittrod.com. **Description:** A law firm.

SCHMITTINGER & RODRIGUEZ, P.A.
4602 Highway One, Corestates Building, Rehoboth Beach DE 19971. 302/227-1400. **Fax:** 302/674-1830. **Contact:** Bill Thomas, Personnel Manager. **World Wide Web address:** http:/ /www.schmittrod.com. **Description:** A law firm.

THE SCHWAN FOOD COMPANY
30083 Discount Land Road, Laurel DE 19956. 302/877-0580. **Fax:** 302/875-0667. **Contact:** Human Resources. **World Wide Web address:** http://www.schwansinc.com. **Description:** Delivers high-quality frozen foods and dairy products. **Positions advertised include:** Account Supervisor, Customer Service Specialist, Material Handler, Recruiter, Route Manager, Sales Supervisor. **Corporate headquarters location:** Marshall MN.

SEA WATCH INTERNATIONAL LTD.
242 South Rehoboth Boulevard, Milford DE 19963. 302/422-3400. **Contact:** Human Resources. **World Wide Web address:** http://www.seaclam.com. **Description:** Processes seafood including clam strips, clams, and crab cakes, and distributes its products to grocery stores and restaurants.

SECURITAS
6 Denny Road, Suite 300, Wilmington DE 19809. 302/764-1070. **Fax:** 302/764-9602. **Contact:** Human Resources. **World Wide Web address:** http://www.pinkertons.com. **Description:** Provides professional detective and security services to both commercial and private customers. Founded in 1909. **Positions advertised include:** Business Development Manager. **Other U.S. locations:** Nationwide.

J.F. SOBIESKI MECHANICAL CONTRACTORS, INC.
14 Hadco Road, Wilmington DE 19804. 302/993-0104. **Toll-free phone:** 800/665-0002. **Fax:** 302/993.0119. **Contact:** Human Resources. **E-mail address:** hr@sobieskiinc.com. **World Wide Web address:** http://www.sobieskiinc.com. **Description:** A multi-trade industrial, institutional, commercial and residential contractor specializing in process piping, heating, ventilation, air conditioning, plumbing and fire protection. **Positions advertised include:** Plumber Mechanic. **Number of employees at this location:** Over 200.

SPEAKMAN COMPANY
P.O. Box 191, Wilmington DE 19899. 302/764-7100. **Toll-free phone:** 800/537-2107. **Fax:** 800/977-2747. **Contact:** Arlene Lunbeck, Personnel Director. **World Wide Web address:** http://www.speakmancompany.com. **Description:** A manufacturer of plumbing, heating, and emergency equipment.

SNYDER, CROMPTON & ASSOCIATES, INC.
3411 Silverside Road, Hagley Building, Suite 202, Wilmington DE 19810. 302/478-6030. **Fax:** 302/478-3775. **Contact:** Jeni Albany, Human Resources Manager. **E-mail address:** jalbany@scaconstructs.com. **World Wide Web address:** http://www.scaconstructs.com. **Description:** Provides construction management and general contracting services. **Positions advertised include:** Carpenters, Construction Foreman/Site Superintendents.

STARBUCKS
1901 Concord Pike, Wilmington DE 19803. 302/654-1803. **Contact:** Human Resources. **World Wide Web address:** http://www.starbucks.com. **Description:** A chain of gourmet coffee shops. **Positions advertised include:** Store Manager. **Corporate headquarters location:** Seattle WA. **Other U.S. locations:** Nationwide. **International locations:** Worldwide.

STRATEGIC DIAGNOSTICS, INC.
111 Pencader Drive, Newark DE 19702. 302/456-6789. **Toll-free phone:** 800/544-8881. **Fax:** 302/456-6770. **Contact:** Martha Reider, Vice President of Human Resources. **World Wide Web address:** http://www.sdix.com. **Description:** Develops, manufactures, and markets immunoassay-based test kits for rapid and cost-effective detection of a wide variety of substances in three primary market categories: agricultural, water quality, and industrial. Strategic Diagnostics is a leader in the field of immunoassay research, development, and manufacturing. The company develops products in markets where the attributes of immunoassay technology (speed, ease-of-use, low cost-per-test, quantitation, and flexibility) meet specific customer needs. The substances detected by the company's test kits include chemicals used to treat drinking water, proprietary chemicals used in industrial processes, environmental contaminants, pesticides, genetically engineered traits in plants, and diseases in commercial crops. Founded in 1990. **Corporate headquarters location:** This location. **Other U.S. locations:** Ramona CA; Windham ME. **International locations:** England. **Subsidiaries include:** Strategic BioSolutions. **Listed on:** NASDAQ. **Stock exchange symbol:** SDIX. **Annual sales/revenues:** $21 - $50 million. **Number of employees at this location:** 95. **Number of employees nationwide:** 180.

STRAWBRIDGE'S
4747 Concord Pike, Wilmington DE 19803. 302/478-1860. **Contact:** Human Resources. **World Wide Web address:** http://www.mayco.com. **Description:** One location of the department store chain that operates in Delaware, Pennsylvania, and New Jersey. **Positions advertised include:** General Sales Associate; Commission Sales Associate; Cosmetics Beauty Advisor. **Corporate headquarters location:** Philadelphia PA. **Parent company:** The May Department Stores Company. **Number of employees nationwide:** 12,000.

STRAWBRIDGE'S
100 Christiana Mall, Newark DE 19702-3202. 302/366-7399. **Contact:** Human Resources. **World Wide Web address:** http://www.mayco.com. **Description:** One location of the department store chain that operates in Delaware, Pennsylvania, and

New Jersey. **NOTE:** Entry-level positions and part-time jobs are offered. **Positions advertised include:** General Sales Associate; Commission Sales Associate; Cosmetics Beauty Advisor. **Corporate headquarters location:** Philadelphia PA. **Parent company:** The May Department Stores Company. **Number of employees nationwide:** 12,000.

SUNROC CORPORATION
60 Starlifter Avenue, Kent County Aero Park, Dover DE 19901-9254. 302/678-7800. **Fax:** 302/678-7810. **Contact:** Shannon Warren, Personnel Manager. **E-mail address:** humanres@sunroc.com. **World Wide Web address:** http://www.sunroc.com. **Description:** Manufactures water coolers and drinking fountains. **NOTE:** Entry-level positions are offered. Applications are accepted Monday - Friday, 8:30 a.m. - 4:30 p.m. **Special programs:** Summer Jobs. **Corporate headquarters location:** This location. **Listed on:** Privately held. **Number of employees at this location:** 300.

THINGS REMEMBERED
3054 Dover Mall, Dover DE 19901. 302/734-8704. **Contact:** Human Resources. **E-mail address:** jobs@thingsremembered.com. **World Wide Web address:** http://www.thingsremembered.com. **Description:** A company and retail chain specializing in personalized gifts. Founded in 1966. **Positions advertised include:** Store Manager; Assistant Store Manager; Store Sales Associate. **Corporate headquarters location:** Cleveland OH.

TILCON DELAWARE INC.
P.O. Box 858, Dover DE 19903. 302/734-8632. **Physical address:** 3700 Bay Road, Dover DE 19901. **Contact:** Human Resources. **World Wide Web address:** http://www.tilconde.com. **Description:** A paving contractor that also provides asphalt, gravel, sand, and stone to the construction industry.

TRANSUNION
5300 Brandywine Parkway, Suite 100 Wilmington DE 19803. 302/433-8000. **Contact:** Human Resources. **World Wide Web address:** http://www.transunion.com. **Description:** A business intelligence service provider. Founded in 1968. **Positions advertised include:** Accounts Receivable Clerk. **Corporate headquarters location:** Chicago IL. **Other U.S. locations:** Nationwide. **International locations:** Worldwide. **Parent company:** Marmon Group. **Number of employees worldwide:** More than 3600.

U.S. DEPARTMENT OF VETERANS AFFAIRS
WILMINGTON VETERANS ADMINISTRATION MEDICAL CENTER
1601 Kirkwood Highway, Wilmington DE 19805. 302/994-2511. **Contact:** Human Resources. **World Wide Web address:** http://www.va.gov. **Description:** A medical center. From 54 hospitals in 1930, the VA health care system has grown to include more than 170 medical centers; more than 364 outpatient, community, and outreach clinics; 130 nursing home care units; and 37 domiciliaries. VA operates at least one medical center in each of the 48 contiguous states, Puerto Rico, and the District of Columbia. With approximately 76,000 medical center beds, VA treats nearly 1 million patients in VA hospitals; 75,000 in nursing home care units; and 25,000 in domiciliaries. VA's outpatient clinics register approximately 24 million visits per year.

UNION PARK
1704 Pennsylvania Avenue, Wilmington DE 19806. 866/455-4444. **Contact:** General Sales Manager. **World Wide Web address:** http://www.unionpark.com. **Description:** An automotive dealership. **Positions advertised include:** Automobile Sales Representative; Automotive Technician.

UNIVERSITY OF DELAWARE
43 Academy Street, Newark DE 19716. 302/831-2791. **Recorded jobline:** 302/831-6612. **Contact:** Human Resources. **World Wide Web address:** http://www.udel.edu. **Description:** A four-year, state university offering bachelor's, master's (including MBAs), and doctoral degrees. Approximately 15,000 undergraduate and 2,600 graduate students attend the University of Delaware. **NOTE:** Temporary positions available. **Positions advertised include:** Department of Art Chair; Assistant Professor, Instructional Technology; Assistant Professor, Department of Materials Science and Engineering; Assistant Professor, Department of Computer and Information Sciences; Associate Professor, Department of Electrical and Computer Engineering; Nursing Faculty Member; Assistant Professor, Public Financial Management; Associate Professor, Department of Plant and Social Sciences; Psychology Professor; Assistant Professor, Department of Individual and Family Studies; Assistant Professor, Inorganic or Physical Chemistry; Assistant Professor, Macromolecular Structure and Function; Assistant Professor, Wildlife Ecologist; Assistant Professor, Pedology, Plant and Social Sciences; Assistant Professor, Cellist; Assistant Professor, Orchestra Conductor; Program Coordinator, Hispanic Culture and Student Campus Programs; Web Developer, College of Agriculture and Natural Resources; Psychologist; Psychology Research Specialist; Senior Research Technician; Master Machinist; Security Officer; Senior Secretary; Library Technician; Library Coordinator; Maintenance Specialist. **Corporate headquarters location:** This location. **President:** David P. Roselle. **Number of employees at this location:** 4,500.

WILM NEWS RADIO
1215 French Street, Wilmington DE 19801. 302/656-9800. **Fax:** 302/655-1450. **Contact:** Human Resources. **World Wide Web address:** http://www.wilm.com. **Description:** An all-news AM radio station. **NOTE:** Entry-level positions are offered. **Special programs:** Internships. **Number of employees at this location:** 35.

WILMINGTON COLLEGE
320 DuPont Highway North, New Castle DE 19720. 302/328-9401. **Fax:** 302/328-7918. **Contact:** Gloria Johnson, Human Resources Director. **E-mail address:** humanresources@wilmcoll.edu **World Wide Web address:** http://www.wilmcoll.edu. **Description:** A private, career-oriented institution offering undergraduate and graduate degrees. Wilmington College is accredited by the Middle States Association of Colleges and Schools. Undergraduate enrollment is approximately 3,000. At the graduate level, the college offers a Master of Business Administration; a Master of Science with concentrations in human resources management and public administration; a Master of Education with concentrations in school leadership, instruction, elementary and secondary school counseling, and elementary studies; a Master of Science in Nursing with a concentration in family nurse practitioner studies; and a Doctor of Education in innovation and leadership.

WILMINGTON SAVINGS FUND SOCIETY, FSB
838 Market Street, Wilmington DE 19801. 302/792-6000. **Toll-free phone:** 800/WSFS-BANK. **Contact:** Human Resources. **World Wide Web address:** http://www.wsfsbank.com. **Description:** A full-service bank. **Positions advertised include:** Teller; General Applications Worker. **Corporate headquarters location:** This location. **Parent company:** WSFS Financial Corporation. **Listed on:** NASDAQ. **Stock exchange symbol:** WSFS. **Number of employees nationwide:** 430.

WILMINGTON TRUST CORPORATION
Rodney Square North, 1100 North Market Street, Wilmington DE 19890-0001. 302/651-1000. **Toll-free phone:** 800/523-2378. **Contact:** Human Resources. **World Wide Web address:** http://www.wilmingtontrust.com. **Description:** A multibank holding company. Wilmington Trust is one of the nation's leading fiduciary institutions, serving personal, institutional, and corporate clients around the world. Founded in 1903. **Positions advertised include:** Accountant/Financial Analyst; Bond Credit Analyst; Corporate Development Analyst; Credit Adjuster; Discount Clerk; Infrastructure Security Engineer.

WINNER FORD
303 East Cleveland Avenue, Newark DE 19711. 302/764-5900. **Toll-free phone:** 888/263-6032. **Contact:** Human Resources. **World Wide Web address:** http://www.winnerauto.com. **Description:** An automotive dealership. **Positions advertised include:** Parts Counter Person; Body Shop Estimator.

WINTERTHUR MUSEUM LIBRARY & GARDENS
Winterthur Museum, Winterthur DE 19735. 302/888-4600. **Toll-free phone:** 800/448-3883. **Contact:** Human Resources. **World Wide Web address:** http://www.winterthur.org. **Description:** Henry Francis du Pont's former country estate now houses his collection of American art that dates from 1640 through 1860. The estate also includes a 60-acre garden and a research library for American art studies.

XEROX CORPORATION
200 Bellevue Parkway, Suite 300, Wilmington DE 19809. 302/792-5100. **Contact:** Human Resources. **World Wide Web address:** http://www.xerox.com. **Description:** Xerox Corporation is a global company in the document processing market. The company's document processing activities encompass the designing, developing, manufacturing, marketing, and servicing of a complete range of document processing products and systems that make office work more efficient. Xerox copiers, duplicators, electronic scanners, facsimile machines, networks, multifunction publishing machines, software, and supplies are marketed in more than 130 countries. **Positions advertised include:** Account Executive. **Operations at this facility include:** This location is a sales office. **Listed on:** New York Stock Exchange. **Stock exchange symbol:** XRX. **Corporate headquarters location:** Stamford CT.

YWCA NEW CASTLE COUNTY DELAWARE
233 King Street, Wilmington DE 19801. 302/658-7161. **Contact:** Human Resources. **World Wide Web address:** http://www.ywca.org. **Description:** Provides social services for women, including childcare, housing, mortgage counseling, and career counseling.

YOUNG CONAWAY STARGATT & TAYLOR, LLP
1000 West Street, P.O. Box 391, 11th Floor Rodney Square North, Wilmington DE 19899. 302/571-6600. **Fax:** 302/576-3355. **Contact:** Polina F. Snitkovsky, Human Resources Coordinator. **E-mail address:** psnitkovsk@ycst.com. **World Wide Web address:** http://www.ycst.com. **Description:** A law firm. Founded in 1959.

ZENITH PRODUCTS CORPORATION
400 Lukens Drive, New Castle DE 19720. 302/326-8200. **Fax:** 302/326-8403. **Contact:** Human Resources. **World Wide Web address:** http://www.masco.com. **Description:** Manufactures and wholesales bathroom accessories and medicine cabinets. **Listed on:** New York Stock Exchange. **Stock exchange symbol:** MAS.

AAA MID-ATLANTIC
701 15th Street NW, Washington DC 20005. 202/331-3000. **Recorded jobline:** 877/AAA-JOB1. **Contact:** Human Resources. **World Wide Web address:** http://www.aaamidatlantic.com. **Description:** Provides insurance, travel, and a wide variety of services to motorists through a network of more than 50 branch offices. **Positions advertised include:** Branch Insurance Specialist; Senior Retail Agent; Territory Manager; Travel Agent.

ABC NEWS
1717 DeSales Street NW, Washington DC 20036. 202/222-7777. **Contact:** Ms. Francoise Drozd, Personnel Manager. **World Wide Web address:** http://www.abc.com. **Description:** The company provides cable television service to subscribers, publishes newspapers and specialized publications, and engages in television and radio broadcasting. Broadcasting operations include ABC Television Network Group, the Broadcast Group, the Cable and International Broadcast Group, and the Multimedia Group. In addition to its network operation, the broadcasting segment consists of 8 network-affiliated television stations, 10 radio stations, cable television systems providing service to subscribers in 16 states, and multimedia video-by-wire business. Publishing operations consist of 8 daily newspapers, 78 weekly newspapers, 63 shopping guides, and several other business and specialized publications. **Other U.S. locations:** Los Angeles CA; New Haven CT; Clifton NJ. **Parent company:** Walt Disney Company.

AFL-CIO ORGANIZING INSTITUTE
815 16th Street NW, Washington DC 20006. 202/637-5000. **Fax:** 202/637-5058. **Contact:** Human Resources. **E-mail address:** amarshall@aflcio.org. **World Wide Web Address:** http://www.organize.aflcio.org. **Description:** The AFLCIO Organizing Institute is a paid job training program for people who want to become involved in organizing labor. Once training is completed ninety-five percent of trainees are placed in affiliate organizations.

AEPA ARCHITECTS ENGINEERS PC
2421 Pennsylvania Avenue NW, Washington DC 20037. 202/822-8320. **Fax:** 202/457-0908. **Contact:** Director of Operations. **World Wide Web address:** http://www.aepa.com. **Description:** An architectural design firm that designs and builds biomedical research facilities. **Corporate headquarters location:** This location. **President:** Alfred H. Liu.

AEROSPACE INDUSTRIES ASSOCIATION OF AMERICA
1000 Wilson Boulevard, Suite 1700, Arlington VA 22209. 703/358-1000. **Contact:** Jane Weeden, Personnel Manager. **World Wide Web address:** http://www.aia-aerospace.org. **Description:** An organization representing companies involved in aerospace research, development, and manufacturing. The association consists of the Civil Aviation, Government, and International divisions. **Corporate headquarters location:** This location. **Number of employees at this location:** 60.

AKQA, INC.
3255 Grace Street NW, Washington DC 20007. 202/625-1111. **Fax:** 202/625-1353. **Contact:** Human Resources Manager. **World Wide Web address:** http://www.akqa.com. **Description:** Develops websites. AKQA's list of clients includes: AT&T, BMW Group, De Beers, Kit Kat, Microsoft, MTV, Nike, Sainsbury's, Smithsonian, Texas Instruments, Visa, and Xbox. **Corporate headquarters location:** This location. **Other U.S. locations:** San Francisco CA. **International locations:** London, England; Singapore.

AMERICAN ACADEMY OF OPHTHALMOLOGY
1101 Vermont Avenue NW, Suite 700, Washington DC 20005. 202/737-6662. **Fax:** 202/737-7061. **Contact:** Human Resources. **E-mail address:** jobs@aao.org. **World Wide Web address:** http://www.aao.org. **Description:** A lobbying group that tracks legislation in all areas of government that may have an effect on the ophthalmology field. **Corporate headquarters location:** San Francisco CA. **President:** Allan D. Jensen, M.D.

THE AMERICAN ASSOCIATION FOR THE ADVANCEMENT OF SCIENCE
1200 New York Avenue NW, Suite 100, Washington DC 20005. 202/326-6470. **Fax:** 202/682-1630. **Contact:** Dawn Graf, Human Resources Specialist. **World Wide Web address:** http://www.aaas.org. **Description:** A federation of scientific and engineering societies, with nearly 300 affiliate organizations. In addition, AAAS counts more than 142,000 scientists, engineers, science educators, policy makers, and interested citizens among its individual members, making it one of the largest general scientific organizations in the world. Founded in 1848. **Positions advertised include:** Editorial Assistant; Sales Coordinator; Program Associate; Program Director; Art Associate; Programmer Analyst; Project Coordinator. **Corporate headquarters location:** This location. **Number of employees at this location:** 300.

AMERICAN ASSOCIATION FOR CLINICAL CHEMISTRY
2101 L Street NW, Suite 202, Washington DC 20037-1526. 202/857-0717. **Toll-free phone:** 800/892-1400. **Fax:** 202/887-5093. **Contact:** Wanda Schwalb, Human Resources Manager. **E-mail address:** wschwalb@aacc.org. **World Wide Web address:** http://www.aacc.org. **Description:** International scientific/medical society of individuals involved in clinical chemistry and other clinical lab science-related disciplines.

AMERICAN ASSOCIATION OF UNIVERSITY WOMEN
1111 16th Street NW, Washington DC 20036. 202/785-7700. **Fax:** 202/872-1413. **Contact:** Beverly McCalop, Human Resources. **E-mail address:** aauwjobs@aauw.org. **World Wide Web address:** http://www.aauw.org. **Description:** An organization targeting the needs of women in the college community. **NOTE:** Resumes are accepted by mail, e-mail, or fax. **Positions advertised include:** Field Associate; Helpline Representative; Fellows Alumnae Network Officer; Administrative Assistant; Controller. **Internship information:** A variety of internships are offered. See website for more information regarding specific requirements and application deadlines. **Other U.S. locations:** Nationwide. **Executive Director:** Jacqueline E. Woods.

AMERICAN BUS ASSOCIATION
700 13th NW, Suite 575, Washington DC 20005-3934. 202/842-1645. **Fax:** 202/842-0850. **Contact:** Human Resources. **World Wide Web address:** http://www.buses.org. **Description:** Represents the intercity busing industry. **Corporate headquarters location:** This location.

AMERICAN CHEMICAL SOCIETY
1155 16th Street NW, Washington DC 20036. 202/872-4600. **Toll-free phone:** 800/227-5558. **Fax:** 202/872-4615. **Contact:** Human Resources. **E-mail address:** employment@acs.com. **World Wide Web address:** http://www.chemcenter.org. **Description:** Publishes directories of chemicals, journals, and student publications. **Positions advertised include:** Program Officer, Petroleum Research Fund; Administrative Associate, Publications; Controller; Senior Programmer Analyst; Lead Systems Administrator; Program Associate, Petroleum Research Fund; Library Clerk; Program Assistant, K-12 Science; Program Specialist, Executive Director's Office.

AMERICAN COUNCIL OF LIFE INSURERS
101 Constitution Avenue NW, Suite 700, Washington DC 20001-2133. 202/ 624-2361. **Contact:** Human Resources. **World Wide Web address:** http://www.acli.com. **Description:** A nonprofit trade association representing the life insurance industry. **Special programs:** Internships. **Corporate headquarters location:** This location. **Operations at this facility include:** Public Affairs. **Number of employees at this location:** 245.

AMERICAN COUNCIL OF THE BLIND (ACB)
1155 15th Street NW, Suite 1004, Washington DC 20005. 202/467-5081. **Toll-free phone:** 800/424-8666. **Fax:** 202/467-5085. **Contact:** Human Resources. **E-mail address:** info@acb.org. **World Wide Web address:** http://www.acb.org. **Description:** ACB is a national membership organization established to promote the independence, dignity, and well-being of blind and visually impaired people. ACB is one of the largest organizations of blind people in the United States with over 70 state and special interest affiliates and a national network of chapters and members. By providing numerous programs and services, ACB enables blind people to live and work independently and to advocate for their rights. Founded in 1961. **Corporate headquarters location:** This location. **Operations at this facility include:** This location houses administrative offices.

AMERICAN HEALTH CARE ASSOCIATION
1201 L Street NW, Washington DC 20005. 202/842-4444. **Fax:** 202/842-3860. **Contact:** Human Resources. **E-mail address:** hr@ahca.org. **World Wide Web address:** http://www.ahca.org. **Description:** A national association of nursing homes and related long-term care facilities. The association promotes an economic and governmental environment within which nursing homes and residential care facilities can provide quality care in safe surroundings.

AMERICAN INSTITUTE OF CERTIFIED PUBLIC ACCOUNTANTS (AICPA)
1455 Pennsylvania Avenue NW, Suite 400, Washington DC 20004-1081. 202/ 737-6600. **Fax:** 202/638-4512. **Contact:** Manager. **World Wide Web address:** http://www.aicpa.org. **Description:** A leading professional organization dedicated to serving the needs of the certified public accounting industry.

AMERICAN INSTITUTES FOR RESEARCH
1000 Thomas Jefferson Street NW, Suite 200, Washington DC 20007. 202/342-5000. **Fax:** 202/944-5454 **Contact:** Human Resources. **E-mail address:** resumes@air.org. **World Wide Web address:** http://www.air.org. **Description:** A non-profit research and analysis organization with a concentration on education, health, individual and organizational performance, and quality of life issues. Founded in 1946. **Positions advertised include:** Administrative Assistant; Education Specialist; Education Assessment Associate; English Language Arts/Reading Specialist; Health Communications Specialist; Mathematics/Reading Specialist; Social Sciences Specialist; Special Education Specialist; Field Accounting Manager; Project Assistant; Psychometrician/Statistician; Research Scientist; Research Analyst; Research Assistant; Web Developer; Word Processor. **Corporate headquarters location:** This location. **Other U.S. locations:** Palo Alto CA; Concord MA.

AMERICAN PSYCHOLOGICAL ASSOCIATION (APA)
750 First Street NE, Washington DC 20002. 202/336-5500. **Contact:** Human Resources. **E-mail address:** jobs@apa.org. **World Wide Web address:** http://www.apa.org. **Description:** Works to advance psychology as a science, a profession, and a means of promoting human welfare. The association has divisions in 49 subfields of psychology and affiliations with 57 state and Canadian provincial associations. Membership includes more than 159,000 researchers, educators, clinicians, and students. **Positions advertised include:** Accounts Receivable Specialist; Circulation Manager; Communications Manager; Senior Programmer; Federal Regulatory Affairs Specialist; Quality Assurance Manager; Operations Specialist; Production Assistant; Production Editor; Public Relations Manager; Senior Scientist; Specification Analyst; Technical Production Editor; Mail Assistant. **Corporate headquarters location:** This location. **Number of employees at this location:** 500.

AMERICAN RED CROSS
8550 Arlington Boulevard, Fairfax VA 22031. 202/728-6400. **Contact:** Director of Human Resources. **World Wide Web address:** http://www.redcross.org. **Description:** A humanitarian organization that aids disaster victims, gathers blood for crisis distribution, trains individuals to respond to emergencies, educates individuals on various diseases, and raises funds for other charitable establishments. **Positions advertised include:** Director, Major Gifts; Writer, Presidential Correspondence; Associate, International Programs; Principal Quality Auditor; Quality Design Engineer; Data Specialist; Administrative Coordinator; Security Coordinator; Law Clerk (Intern); Writer, Presidential Correspondence; Senior Associate, Nutrition; Advertising Associate; Fundraising Manager; Officer, Gift Planning. **Special programs:** Internships available. **Corporate headquarters location:** This location. **Other U.S. locations:** Nationwide.

AMERICAN SYMPHONY ORCHESTRA LEAGUE
910 17th Street NW, Suite 800, Washington DC 20006. 202/776-0215. **Fax:** 202/776-0224. **Contact:** Rachel Feinberg, Human Resources Assistant. **E-mail address:** hr@symphony.org. **World Wide Web address:** http://www. symphony.org. **Description:** A national service organization for America's professional symphony orchestras. Founded in 1942. **NOTE:** Resumes should be sent to: Rachel Feinberg, Human Resources Assistant, American Symphony Orchestra League, 33 West 60th Street, 5th Floor, New York NY 10023. Fax: 212/262-5198. Phone: 212/262-5161 ext. 245. **Special programs:** Internships. **Internship information:** Internships are available year-round. **Annual sales/revenues:** Less than $5 million. **Number of employees at this location:** 45.

AMERICAN TEXTILE MANUFACTURERS INSTITUTE
1130 Connecticut Avenue NW, Suite 1200, Washington DC 20036-3954. 202/ 862-0500. **Fax:** 202/862-0570. **Contact:** Human Resources. **World Wide Web address:** http://www.atmi.org. **Description:** A national trade association for the textile industry.

AMERICAN UNIVERSITY
4400 Massachusetts Avenue NW, Washington DC 20016-8054. 202/885-2591. **Fax:** 202/885-2558. **Contact:** Human Resources. **E-mail address:** careers@American.edu. **World Wide Web address:** http://www.american.edu. **Description:** An independent, four-year university. American University has program offerings within the School of Public Affairs, the School of Communications, the College of Arts and Sciences, the Washington College of Law, the Kogod College of Business Administration, and the School of International Services. The university also offers return-to-school programs. **NOTE:** Please check the Website for a listing of available positions. **Number of employees at this location:** 1,100.

AQUENT
1333 H Street NW, Suite 630 East, Washington DC 20005. 202/293-5700. **Contact:** Tracy Donovan. **E-mail address:** dcrecruiting@aquent.com. **World Wide Web address:** http://www.aquent.com. **Description:** A professional services firm whose specialties include marketing, information technology, and financial services. **Positions advertised include:** Senior Online Copywriter; Senior Flash Developer; Photo Archive Researcher; High End Production Artist; Senior Print Designer; Advertising Art Director; Senior Information Architect; Powerpoint Presentation Designer; Web Developer. **Corporate headquarters location:** Boston MA. **Other U.S. locations:** Nationwide. **International locations:** Worldwide.

ARENA STAGE
1101 Sixth Street SW, Washington DC 20024-2691. 202/554-9066. **Fax:** 202/488-4056. **Contact:** Administrative Director. **E-mail address:** jobs@ arenastage.org. **World Wide Web address:** http://www. arenastage.org. **Description:** A nonprofit theater company. **NOTE:** See website for individual contacts. Internships candidates should consult the website for information regarding deadlines, requirements, and types of internships offered. **Positions advertised include:** Group Sales Associate; Inbound Sales Representative; Outbound Sales Associate. **Special programs:** Internships; Apprenticeships; Fellowships. **Operations at this facility include:** Production. **Number of employees at this location:** 200.

ARMS CONTROL ASSOCIATION
1150 Connecticut Avenue NW, Suite 620, Washington DC 20036. 202/463-8270. **Fax:** 202/ 463-8273. **Contact:** Assistant to the Director. **World Wide Web address:** http://www.armscontrol.org. **Description:** An organization providing information on arms control issues. **Positions advertised include:** Research Analyst.

ARNOLD & PORTER
555 12th Street NW, Washington DC 20004. 202/942-5000. **Fax:** 202/942-5999. **Contact:** Stephanie Heeg, Recruiter. **E-mail address:** stephanie_heeg @aporter.com. **World Wide Web address:** http://www.aporter.com. **NOTE:** Candidates for Associate positions in the Washington Office should contact Diane Moore, Hiring Coordinator. Phone: 202/942-5943. E-mail address: Diane_Moore@ aporter.com. **Description:** A law firm specializing in commercial law and public policy. **Positions advertised include:** Accounts Payable Clerk; Conflicts Specialist; Director, Washington Office Operations; Legal Recruiting Manager; Legal Secretary; Litigation Support Coordinator; Marketing Coordinator; Research Analyst; Roving Desktop Support Analyst. **Special programs:** Summer Associate Program.

ASSOCIATION OF BITUMINOUS CONTRACTORS
815 Connecticut Avenue NW, Suite 620, Washington DC 20006. 202/785-4440. **Contact:** Human Resources. **Description:** A contractors' association for the construction of bituminous coal mines. Founded in 1968.

ATLANTIC VIDEO
650 Massachusetts Avenue NW, Washington DC 20001. 202/408-0900. **Fax:** 202/408-3419. **Contact:** Human Resources. **E-mail address:** hr@atlantic video.com. **World Wide Web address:** http://www.atlanticvideo.com. **NOTE:** See website for important instructions regarding applications. No phone calls please. **Description:** Provides production and postproduction services featuring studios, editing facilities, uplinking and downlinking, ancillary graphics, and audio editing facilities. **Positions advertised include:** Post Production Manager; Chief Engineer; Editor/Producer; Maintenance Engineer.

BAE SYSTEMS
1101 15th Street, Suite 603, Washington DC 20005. 703/622-1916. **Contact:** Human Resources. **World Wide Web Address:** http://www.baesystems.com. **Description:** BAE Systems is an international company engaged in the development, delivery and support of advanced defense and aerospace systems in the land, air, sea, and space. **NOTE:** Resumes may be submitted for open positions on the website.

BET SERVICES
BLACK ENTERTAINMENT TELEVISION NETWORK
1235 W Place NE, Washington DC 20018. 202/608-2000. **Fax:** 202/608-2589. **Contact:** Human Resources. **E-mail address:** resumes@bet.net. **World Wide Web address:** http://www.bet.com. **Description:** Operates the Black Entertainment Television Network (BET Network), which is an advertiser-supported basic cable television network. BET Services is also the publisher of *YSB* and *Emerge,* two magazines that are geared toward the African-American community. **Positions advertised include:** Affiliate Sales Coordinator; Senior Accountant; Receptionist. **Special programs:** Internships. **Corporate headquarters location:** This location. **Other U.S. locations:** Santa Monica CA; Chicago IL; New York NY. **Parent company:** Viacom, Inc. **Operations at this facility include:** Administration; Sales. **Listed on:** New York Stock Exchange. **Number of employees nationwide:** 475.

BANK OF AMERICA
1001 Pennsylvania Avenue NW, Washington DC 20004. 202/624-5090. **Contact:** Human Resources. **World Wide Web address:** http://www. bankofamerica.com. **Description:** This location is a bank. Overall, Bank of America is a full-service banking and financial institution. The company operates through four business segments: Global Corporate and Investment Banking, Principal Investing and Asset Management, Commercial Banking, and Consumer Banking. **Positions advertised include:** Marketing Sales Manager; Banking Center Manager; Consumer Market Manager; Teller. **Special programs:** Summer Internships. **Corporate headquarters location:** Charlotte NC. **Other area locations:** Statewide. **Other U.S. locations:** Nationwide. **Listed on:** New York Stock Exchange. **Stock exchange symbol:** BAC.

BLACKBOARD INC.
1899 L Street NW, 5th Floor, Washington DC 20036. 202/463-4860. **Toll-free phone:** 800/424-9299. **Fax:** 202/463-4863. **Contact:** Human Resources. **E-mail address:** jobs@blackboard.com. **World Wide Web address:** http://www.black board.com. **Description:** An education software provider. Founded in 1997. **Positions advertised include:** Account Manager; Developer; Administrative Assistant; Budget Analyst; Channel Sales Manager; Contracts Manager; Database Administrator; Director, Higher Education Marketing; International Developer; Software Engineer; Technical Consultant; Trademark Paralegal. **Other U.S. locations:** Phoenix AZ. **Listed on:** Privately held. **Number of employees nationwide:** 400.

B'NAI B'RITH INTERNATIONAL
2020 K Street, 7th Floor, Washington DC 20006. 202/857-6600. **Contact:** Director of Human Resources. **E-mail address:** hr@bnaibrith.org. **World Wide Web address:** http://www.bnaibrith.org. **Description:** A Jewish social services and political action organization. B'Nai B'Rith has seven district offices located across the United States. **NOTE:** Human Resources phone: 202/857-6510. **Special programs:** Internships. **Corporate headquarters location:** This location. **Operations at this facility include:** Administration; Public Affairs.

THE BROOKINGS INSTITUTION
1775 Massachusetts Avenue NW, Washington DC 20036. 202/797-6210. **Fax:** 202/797-2479. **Contact:** Human Resources. **E-mail address:** hrjobs@brookings.edu. **World Wide Web address:** http://www.brook.edu. **Description:** A private, nonprofit organization devoted to research, education, and publishing in the fields of economics, government, foreign policy, and the social sciences. Its activities are carried out through three research programs (Economic Studies, Governmental Studies, Foreign Policy Studies); the Center for Public Policy Education; Information Technology; and the Brookings Press. **Positions advertised include:** Assistant to the Vice President, Foreign Policy Studies; Staff Assistant, European Issues; Research Assistant, Russian Issues; Science and Technology Fellow; Senior External Affairs Officer. **NOTE:** This institution does not accept unsolicited resumes. Check the website for a listing of open positions. Positions are also posted on the Washington Post's website. **Special programs:** Internships; Fellowships. **President:** Strobe Talbott.

BUREAU OF ALCOHOL, FIREARMS, AND TOBACCO
607 14th Street NW, Suite 620, Washington DC 20005. 202/927-8810. **Fax:** 202/927-4024. **E-mail address:** persdiv@atf.gov. **World Wide Web address:** http://www.aft.gov. **Description:** The Bureau of Alcohol, Tobacco, Firearms and Explosives is a law enforcement agency within the Department of Justice. Its unique responsibilities include protecting the public and reducing violent crime. **NOTE:** Applications may be submitted at http://www.usajobs.opm.gov.

CBS NEWS/WASHINGTON BUREAU
2020 M Street NW, Washington DC 20036. 202/457-4321. **Contact:** Human Resources. **Description:** CBS News is one of six divisions in CBS Inc.'s Broadcast Group. **Corporate headquarters location:** New York NY.

CH2M HILL
555 11th Street NW, Suite 525, Washington DC 20004. 202/393-2426. **Fax:** 202/783-8410. **Contact:** Human Resources. **E-mail address:** hr@ch2m.com. **World Wide Web address:** http://www.ch2m.com. **Description:** An environmental engineering company specializing in water and remediation projects. **Other U.S. locations:** Nationwide. **International locations:** Worldwide.

CITY FIRST BANK OF DC
2400 14th Street NW, Suite B, Washington DC 20009. 202/332-5002. **Fax:** 202/332-8240. **E-mail address:** info@cityfirstbank.com. **World Wide Web address:** http://www.cityfirstbank.com. **Description:** City First is Washington DC's only community development bank. City First's primary mission is to spur local development.

CNN (CABLE NEWS NETWORK)
820 First Street NE, Washington DC 20002. 202/515-2916. **Recorded jobline:** 202/515-2216. **Contact:** Staffing Specialist. **World Wide Web address:** http://wwwturnerjobs.com. **Description:** A cable news network. CNN has 28 bureaus worldwide and provides 24-hour news programming worldwide. Programming includes international, domestic, and business news; sports; weather; special reports; and topical programming. Founded in 1980. **NOTE:** Entry-level positions and part-time jobs are offered. **Positions advertised include:** Associate Producer; Transportation/Facilities Specialist; Assistant Booker/Guest Greeter; News Assistant. **Special programs:** Internships. **Corporate headquarters location:** Atlanta GA. **Number of employees at this location:** 280. **Number of employees nationwide:** 3,000.

THE CAPITAL CHILDREN'S MUSEUM
800 3rd Street NE, Washington DC 20002. 202/675-4120. **Fax:** 202/675-4140. **Contact:** Human Resources. **World Wide Web address:** http://www.ccm.org. **Description:** A hands-on, interactive museum with several other divisions, which include Options School (alternative seventh grade), Community Access Computer Center, and Media Arts Center (film and animation.) Founded in 1979. **Positions advertised include:** Exhibit Educator; Vice President, Finance and Administration; Cashier/Visitor Receptionist; Reservations Assistant. **Special programs:** Internships. **Corporate headquarters location:** This location. **Operations at this facility include:** Administration; Research and Development; Service. **Number of employees at this location:** 80.

CAPITAL HILTON
1001 16th Street NW, Washington DC 20036. 202/639-5769. **Fax:** 202/942-1393. **Recorded jobline:** 202/639-5745. **Contact:** Melissa G. Storino, Employment Manager. **World Wide Web address:** http://www.hilton.com. **Description:** A full-service hotel with two restaurants. **Corporate headquarters location:** Los Angeles CA. **Parent company:** Hilton Hotels Corporation is a hospitality, gaming, and lodging company. With its Hilton and Conrad brands, the company develops, owns, manages, and franchises hotel-casinos, resorts, and hotel properties throughout the world. Other subsidiaries of Hilton Hotels Corporation include Conrad International, Hilton Equipment Corporation, Hilton Grand Vacation Company, and Hilton Inns, Inc. **Operations at this facility include:** Administration; Sales; Service. **Number of employees at this location:** 400.

CAREFIRST BLUECROSS BLUESHIELD
840 First Street NE, Washington DC 20065. 202/479-7470. **Contact:** Human Resources. **World Wide Web address:** http://www.carefirst.com. **Description:** An insurance organization administering health care coverage for private industry, government, and nongroup subscribers. **Positions advertised include:** Sales Assistant; Case Manager.

CARRAMERICA
1850 K Street NW, Suite 500, Washington DC 20006. 202/729-1700. **Fax:** 888/439-0689. **Contact:** Lynn Millar, Director of Human Resources. **E-mail address:** hr@carramerica.com. **World Wide Web address:** http://www. carramerica.com. **Description:** A real estate, architectural, and construction management firm. The company specializes in the construction and/or renovation of mixed-use developments. CarrAmerica operates in four divisions: Acquisitions, which locates, evaluates, and purchases land and buildings; Development, which defines the market, creates the initial design concept, determines economic feasibility, and arranges financing; Construction, which supervises the final design and actualizes the plan; and Operations, which markets and manages the finished product. **Corporate headquarters location:** This location. **Listed on:** New York Stock Exchange. **Stock exchange symbol:** CRE.

CASUAL CORNER
1331 Pennsylvania Avenue NW, Washington DC 20004. 202/737-9280. **Fax:** 860/741-3171 **Contact:** District Manager. **World Wide Web address:** http://www.casualcorner.com. **Description:** Area management offices for a chain of specialized retail clothing stores. **NOTE:** The personnel office can be reached at 860/741-0771. Mail Resumes to 100 Phoenix Avenue, Enfield CT 06082. **Corporate headquarters location:** Enfield CT. **Other U.S. locations:** Nationwide. **Subsidiaries**

include: August Max Woman; Petite Sophisticate. **Operations at this facility include:** Sales. **Listed on:** Privately held. **Number of employees nationwide:** 7,000.

THE CATHOLIC UNIVERSITY OF AMERICA
620 Michigan Avenue NE, Room 170, Leahy Hall, Washington DC 20064. 202/319-5050. **Fax:** 202/319-5802. **Contact:** Gigi R. Washington, Employment Manager. **E-mail address:** resumes@cua.edu. **World Wide Web address:** http://www.cua.edu. **NOTE:** See website for updated position listings. **Description:** A four-year, Catholic university offering bachelor's, master's, first professional, and doctoral degrees. Approximately 2,800 undergraduate and 3,700 graduate students attend the university. **Corporate headquarters location:** This location.

CENTER FOR INTERNATIONAL POLICY
1717 Massachusetts Avenue NW, Suite 801, Washington DC 20036. 202/232-3317. **Fax:** 202/232-3440. **E-mail address:** cip@ciponline.org. **World Wide Web Address:** http://www.ciponline.org. **Description:** Promotes a U.S foreign policy based on international demilitarization and respect for basic human rights.

CENTER FOR STRATEGIC & INTERNATIONAL STUDIES (CSIS)
1800 K Street NW, Suite 400, Washington DC 20006. 202/887-0200. **Fax:** 202/775-3199. **Contact:** Human Resources. **E-mail address:** employment@ csis.org. **World Wide Web address:** http://www.csis.org. **Description:** A nonprofit, public policy research institute. **NOTE:** Entry-level positions are offered. **Positions advertised include:** Program Coordinator, Homeland Security; Program Coordinator, International Security. **Special programs:** Internships available. **Number of employees at this location:** 240.

CHARLES P. MYRICK CPA
805 15th Street NW, Suite 805, Washington DC 20005. 202/789-8898. **Fax:** 202/789-8680. **Contact:** Human Resources. **E-mail address:** charles@myrickcpa.com. **World Wide Web address:** http://www.myrickcpa.com. **Description:** A certified public accounting firm.

CHILD WELFARE LEAGUE OF AMERICA
440 First Street NW, 3rd Floor, Washington DC 20001-2085. 202/638-2952. **Fax:** 202/638-4004. **Contact:** Human Resources. **E-mail address:** hr@cwla.org. **World Wide Web address:** http://www.cwla.org. **Description:** A national, nonprofit organization with almost 800 affiliated public and private agencies that together serve more than 2 million children and their families every year. Child Welfare League of America and its agencies offer services for the many areas of child welfare including adoption, child daycare, child protection, family foster care, chemical dependency prevention and treatment, and housing and homelessness. **President and CEO:** Shay Bilchick.

CHILDREN'S HOSPITAL
SCOTTISH RITE CENTER FOR CHILDHOOD LANGUAGE DISORDERS
1630 Columbia Road NW, Washington DC 20009. 202/939-4703. **Recorded jobline:** 202/884-2060. **Fax:** 202/939-4717. **Contact:** Human Resources. **NOTE:** Mail resumes to: Department of Human Resources, 111 Michigan Avenue NW, Washington DC 20010. The hospital only accepts resumes for open positions. **Description:** A medical center for children with language disorders. **Corporate headquarters location:** This location.

CONGRESSIONAL QUARTERLY
1255 22nd Street NW, Washington DC 20037. 202/419-8500. **Fax:** 202/419-8740. **Contact:** Human Resources. **E-mail address:** jobs@cq.com. **World Wide Web address:** http://www.cq.com. **NOTE:** The company prefers that resumes are sent by e-mail. **Description:** Publishes the *CQ Weekly* and the daily *Congressional Monitor,* as well as a wide range of government-related publications. **Positions advertised include:** Reporter; Database Editor; Department Editor; Deputy Department Editor; News/Production Editor. **Special programs:** Internships.

CORPORATE EXECUTIVE BOARD
2000 Pennsylvania Avenue NW, Suite 6000, Washington DC 20006. 202/777-5000. **Fax:** 202/777-5100. **Contact:** Human Resources. **E-mail address:** jobs@ executiveboard.com. **World Wide Web address:** http://www.executiveboard.com. **Description:** A B2B content provider whose information is geared to helping its clients improve corporate strategies, processes, and their general business framework. **Positions advertised include:** Desktop Publishing Contractor; Research Associate; Marketing Associate; Practice Manager; Strategic Research Consultant. **Special programs:** Internships available. **Listed on:** NASDAQ. **Stock exchange symbol:** EXBD.

CORPORATION FOR NATIONAL AND COMMUNITY SERVICE (CNS)
1201 New York Avenue NW, Washington DC 20525. 202/606-5000. **Fax:** 202/565-2782. **Contact:** Human Resources. **E-mail address:** jobs@cns.gov. **World Wide Web address:** http://www.cns.gov. **NOTE:** Candidates should e-mail or fax resumes. **Description:** A governmental organization geared toward matching jobseekers and volunteers with community service jobs. CNS organizes AmeriCorps, National Senior Services Corps, and Learn & Serve America. **Positions advertised include:** Assistant Inspector General; Auditor. **NOTE:** Please call or visit the Website to view available positions and application procedures. **Special programs:** Internships. **Corporate headquarters location:** This location. **Other U.S. locations:** Nationwide.

COVINGTON & BURLING
1201 Pennsylvania Avenue NW, Washington DC 20004-2401. 202/662-6000. **Fax:** 202/662-6291. **Contact:** Tiffany L. Comey, Recruitment. **E-mail address:** humanresources@cov.com. **World Wide Web address:** http://www.cov.com. **Description:** A law firm specializing in company, commercial, intellectual property, and international tax law, and food and drug regulation.

DAKA FOOD SERVICE MANAGEMENT, INC.
14th Street & Constitution Avenue NW, Washington DC 20050. 202/371-6671. **Contact:** Human Resources. **Description:** DAKA Food Service Management is a diversified restaurant company operating Fuddrucker's, DAKA Restaurants, and Champp's. Fuddrucker's owns, operates, and franchises a chain of upscale hamburger restaurants. The company operates more than 150 restaurants throughout the United States, Canada, Mexico, Argentina, Australia, and the Middle East. DAKA Restaurants is a contract food service management company that serves more than 600 corporate, educational, cultural, and health care locations, primarily in the eastern United States. **Operations at this facility include:** This location provides food services to the Smithsonian Museum of Art History.

DANAHER CORPORATION
2099 Pennsylvania Avenue NW, 12th Floor, Washington DC 20006. 202/828-0850. **Fax:** 202/828-0860. **Contact:** Human Resources. **World Wide Web address:** http://www.danaher.com. **Description:** Designs and manufactures industrial and consumer products in two divisions: Tools and Components, and Process/Environmental Controls. **Corporate headquarters location:** This location. **Listed on:** New York Stock Exchange. **Stock exchange symbol:** DHR. **Annual sales/revenues:** More than $100 million.

DELOITTE & TOUCHE
555 12th Street NW, Suite 500, Washington DC 20004-1207. 202/879-5600. **Fax:** 202/879-5309. **Contact:** Human Resources. **E-mail address:** dtcareers@deloitte.com. **World Wide Web address:** http://www.us.deloitte.com. **Description:** An international firm of certified public accountants providing professional accounting, auditing, tax, and management consulting services to widely diversified clients. The company has a specialized program consisting of national industry groups and functional groups that cross industry lines. Groups are involved in various disciplines including accounting, auditing, taxation management advisory services, small and growing businesses, mergers and acquisitions, and computer applications. **Positions advertised include:** Accounting Clerk; Administrative Assistant, National Tax Department; Tax Consultant; Director, Health Care. **Number of employees at this location:** 299.

DEMOCRATIC NATIONAL COMMITTEE
430 South Capitol Street SE, Washington DC 20003. 202/863-8000. **Contact:** Human Resources. **World Wide Web address:** http://www.democrats.org. **Description:** National headquarters for the Democratic Party. **NOTE:** The Democratic National Committee looks for individuals with campaign experience for campaigns across the country, as well as individuals with grass roots organizing, fundraising, or communications experience. **Special programs:** Internships. **Corporate headquarters location:** This location. **Annual sales/revenues:** $11 - $20 million. **Number of employees at this location:** 125.

DOGGETT ENTERPRISES, INC.
666 11th Street NW, Suite 300, Washington DC 20001. 202/638-2770. **Contact:** Human Resources. **Description:** Owns, manages, and operates parking facilities in the Washington DC area. **Corporate headquarters location:** This location.

THE DONOHOE COMPANIES, INC.
2101 Wisconsin Avenue NW, Washington DC 20007. 202/333-0880. **Fax:** 202/ 478-5104. **Contact:** Human Resources Manager. **E-mail address:** employment@ donohoe.com. **World Wide Web address:** http://www. donohoe.com. **Description:** A real estate development company. **Positions advertised include:** Assistant Facilities Manager; Senior Project Manager; HVAC Journeyman; Senior Estimator; Building Engineer. **Corporate headquarters location:** This location. **Number of employees at this location:** 300.

EDISON ELECTRIC INSTITUTE
701 Pennsylvania Avenue NW, Washington DC 20004-2696. 202/508-5000 **Fax:** 202/508-5503. **Recorded jobline:** 202/508-5492. **Contact:** Human Resources Department. **E-mail address:** hrweb@eei.org. **World Wide Web address:** http://www.eei.org. **Description:** An association of investor-owned electric utility companies in the United States. **Positions advertised include:** Manager, Federal Regulatory Affairs; Administrative Assistant, International Programs; National Accounts Administrator; Member Data Specialist. **Corporate headquarters location:** This location.

ENERGY INTELLIGENCE GROUP, INC.
1401 New York Avenue NW, Suite 500, Washington DC 20005. 202/662-0747. **Fax:** 202/662-0751. **Contact:** Human Resources. **World Wide Web address:** http://www.energyintel.com. **Description:** Publishes oil and gas industry newsletters. **Corporate headquarters location:** New York NY. **Other U.S. locations:** Houston TX. **Parent company:** EEOP. **Operations at this facility include:** Administration; Divisional Headquarters; Research and Development; Sales; Service. **President:** Edward Morse. **Number of employees at this location:** 35.

ERNST & YOUNG LLP
THE E&Y KENNETH LEVENTHAL REAL ESTATE GROUP DIVISION
1225 Connecticut Avenue NW, Washington DC 20036. 202/327-6000. **Contact:** Human Resources. **World Wide Web address:** http://www.ey.com. **Description:** A special practice unit of Ernst & Young LLP providing accounting and consulting services to the real estate and financial services industries. Overall, Ernst & Young is a certified public accounting firm that also provides management consulting services. Services include data processing, financial modeling, financial feasibility studies, production planning and inventory management, management sciences, health care planning, human resources, cost accounting, and budgeting systems. **NOTE:** Entry-level positions are offered. **Positions advertised include:** Financial Assistant; Executive Assistant; Assurance Manager; Tax Knowledge Manager. **Corporate headquarters location:** New York NY. **Other U.S. locations:** Nationwide. **Number of employees at this location:** 70.

EXPORT-IMPORT BANK OF THE UNITED STATES
811 Vermont Avenue NW, Room 771, Washington DC 20571. 202/565-3946. **Fax:** 202/565-3380. **Contact:** Human Resources. **World Wide Web address:** http://www.exim.gov. **Description:** As an agency of the federal government, the bank provides assistance to American exporters through loans, guarantees, and insurance programs. **NOTE:** This firm does not accept unsolicited resumes. Please contact this location for information about application procedures. **Special programs:** Internships. **Corporate headquarters location:** This location.

FAMILY AND CHILD SERVICES OF WASHINGTON DC
929 L Street NW, Washington DC 20001. 202/289-1510. **Fax:** 202/371-0863. **Contact:** Nolia C. Melton, Director of Human Resources. **E-mail address:** resumes@fcsdc.com. **World Wide Web address:** http://www. familyandchildservices.org. **Description:** A private, nonprofit, social services organization offering a broad range of services including counseling, adoption, family daycare, foster care, and summer and winter camping for children, as well as services for the elderly. **Positions advertised include:** Crisis Line Volunteer Coordinator; Social Worker; Program Assistant; Child Development Specialist. **Special programs:** Internships. **Corporate headquarters location:** This location. **Operations at this facility include:** Service.

FARMWORKERS JUSTICE FUND
1010 Vermont Avenue NW, Suite 915, Washington DC 20005. 202/738-2628. **Fax:** 202/783-2561. **Contact:** Ms. Baez. **E-mail address:** fjf@nclr.org. **World Wide Web address:** http://www.fwjustice.org. **Description:** Farmworkers Justice Fund helps migrant and seasonal farmworkers improve their wages and working conditions, labor and immigration policy.

FEDERAL BUREAU OF INVESTIGATION (FBI)
935 Pennsylvania Avenue NW, J. Edgar Hoover Building, Washington DC 20535-0001. 202/324-3000. **Contact:** Human Resources. **World Wide Web address:** http://www.fbi.gov. **NOTE:** Consult website for current openings and requirements.

Candidates must apply online. **Description:** Central headquarters of the national law enforcement agency.

FEDERAL DEPOSIT INSURANCE CORPORATION (FDIC)
550 17th Street NW, Washington DC 20429. 202/393-8400. **Contact:** William Roscoe, Senior Personnel Management Specialist. **E-mail address:** careers@fdic.gov. **World Wide Web address:** http://www.fdic.gov. **Description:** A federal bank regulatory agency. **Corporate headquarters location:** This location. **Number of employees nationwide:** 12,000.

FEDERAL ELECTION COMMISSION
999 E Street NW, Room 236, Washington DC 20463. 202/694-1100. **Toll-free phone:** 800/424-9530. **Contact:** Human Resources. **World Wide Web address:** http://www.fec.gov. **Description:** Regulates and monitors federal campaigning activities. Founded in 1975. **Positions advertised include:** Information Technology Specialist. **NOTE:** Faxed and/or e-mailed resumes are not accepted.

FEDERAL EMERGENCY MANAGEMENT AGENCY (FEMA)
500 C Street SW, Room 816, Washington DC 20472. 202/646-4040. **Fax:** 202/ 646-3310. **Contact:** Doug Ferher, Director of Human Resources. **World Wide Web address:** http://www.fema.gov. **Description:** Prepares for and handles disasters nationwide.

FEDERAL LABOR RELATIONS AUTHORITY
800 K Street NW, Tech World Plaza North, Washington DC 20001. 202/482-6700. **Recorded jobline:** 877/303-8945. **Contact:** Human Resources. **E-mail address:** resumes@flra.gov. **World Wide Web address:** http://www.flra.gov. **Description:** Sets guidelines and establishes policies for federal labor-management relations. Responsibilities include rectifying disputes under the Title VII Civil Service Reform Act. Founded in 1978. **Positions advertised include:** General Attorney; Attorney Advisor; Law Clerk; Legal Student Assistant; Miscellaneous Assistant; Computer Assistant. **Office hours:** Monday – Friday, 8:30 a.m. – 5:00 p.m.

FEDERAL NATIONAL MORTGAGE ASSOCIATION (FANNIE MAE)
3900 Wisconsin Avenue NW, Washington DC 20016. 202/752-7000. **Recorded jobline:** 202/752-JOBS. **Contact:** Human Resources. **World Wide Web address:** http://www.fanniemae.com. **Description:** A stockholder-owned corporation chartered by Congress for the purpose of helping to finance housing by supplementing the supply of mortgage funds. Fannie Mae purchases a variety of mortgage plans including adjustable rate mortgages, conventional fixed rate home mortgages, and second mortgages. The company also participates in pools of conventional first and second mortgages and guarantees conventional mortgage-based securities. **Positions advertised include:** Senior Developer; Credit Risk Manager; Senior Financial Engineer; Director, Finance; Senior Database Administrator; Senior Investor Relations Manager; Senior Technology Risk Specialist; Administrative Assistant; Consultant; Political Action Committee Manager; Senior Financial Analyst; Director, Human Resources. **Special programs:** Internships. **Corporate headquarters location:** This location. **Other U.S. locations:** Atlanta GA; Chicago IL; Philadelphia PA; Dallas TX. **Operations at this facility include:** Administration; Divisional Headquarters; Regional Headquarters; Sales; Service. **Listed on:** New York Stock Exchange. **Stock exchange symbol:** FNM. **Number of employees at this location:** 3,800.

THE FERTILIZER INSTITUTE
Union Center Plaza, 820 First Street NE, Suite 430, Washington DC 20002. 202/ 962-0490. **Fax:** 202/962-0577. **Contact:** Linda McAbee, Director of Conventions. **E-mail address:** lmcabee@tfi.org. **World Wide Web address:** http://www.tfi.org. **Description:** A trade association representing companies that make commercial fertilizer available to farmers worldwide. **Special programs:** Internships. **Corporate headquarters location:** This location. **Number of employees at this location:** 20.

FOUR SEASONS HOTEL
2800 Pennsylvania Avenue NW, Washington DC 20037. 202/342-0444. **Fax:** 202/944-2072. **Contact:** Human Resources. **E-mail address:** jobs.washingtondc@fourseasons.com. **World Wide Web address:** http://www.fourseasons.com. **Description:** A luxury hotel.

FRIENDS OF THE NATIONAL ZOO
3001 Connecticut Avenue NW, Washington DC 20008. 202/673-4640. **Fax:** 202/673-0289. **Contact:** Human Resources Director. **World Wide Web address:** http://www.fonz.org. **Description:** In support of the mission of the Smithsonian National Zoological Park, Friends of the National Zoo is a nonprofit company that provides biological education and environmental protection. Founded in 1958. **NOTE:** Most positions are not posted on the website. Call the number listed above for more information. See website for information regarding internships. **Special programs:** Internships; Co-ops; Summer Jobs. **Office hours:** Monday - Friday, 9:00 a.m. - 4:00 p.m. **Corporate headquarters location:** This location. **Listed on:** Privately held. **Annual sales/revenues:** $5 - $10 million. **Number of employees at this location:** 500.

GALLAUDET UNIVERSITY
800 Florida Avenue NE, Washington DC 20002. 202/651-5000. **Recorded jobline:** 202/651-5358. **Fax:** 202/651-5344. **Contact:** Human Resources Department. **World Wide Web address:** http://www.gallaudet.edu. **Description:** A liberal arts school for deaf and hearing-impaired students. Graduate programs admit both hearing and non-hearing students. Gallaudet University has an enrollment of approximately 1,500 students. **NOTE:** Please call the jobline for a listing of available positions. Unsolicited applications are not accepted. **Positions advertised include:** Director, Career Center; Database Developer; Nurse Practitioner; Development Associate; Staff Interpreter; Administrative Secretary; Assistant Professor, Social Work; Instructor, English; Instructor, American History.

GARDINER, KAMYA & ASSOCIATES PC
1717 K Street NW, Suite 601, Washington DC 20036. 202/857-1777. **Fax:** 202/857-1778. **Contact:** Human Resources Manager. **E-mail address:** gardkamy@erols.com. **World Wide Web address:** http://www.gkacpa.com. **Description:** Provides auditing and accounting, management consulting, information systems services, and taxation services. **Company slogan:** Quality, Timeliness, Responsiveness, and Value. **Corporate headquarters location:** This location. **Other U.S. locations:** Nationwide. **Subsidiaries include:** GKA Staffing Resources, LLC. **Listed on:** Privately held. **CEO:** Chris Gardiner. **Sales Manager:** John Kamya. **Number of employees at this location:** 40.

GENENTECH, INC.
808 17th Street NW, Suite 250, Washington DC 20006. 202/296-7272. **Contact:** Human Resources. **World Wide Web address:** http://www.gene.com. **Description:** A biotechnology company that develops, manufactures, and markets pharmaceuticals using human genetic information. Genentech specializes in products designed to treat growth deficiencies, breast cancer, and AMI. **Positions advertised include:** Clinical Scientist; Clinical Specialist; Medical Science Liaison. **Corporate headquarters location:** San Francisco CA. **Listed on:** New York Stock Exchange. **Stock exchange symbol:** GNE.

GEORGE WASHINGTON UNIVERSITY
2033 K Street NW, Suite 220, Washington DC 20052. 202/994-9600. **Fax:** 202/ 994-9609. **Contact:** Human Resources Department. **E-mail address:** gwujobs@gwu.edu. **World Wide Web address:** http://www.gwu.edu. **Description:** A four-year, liberal arts university offering certificates, associate's, bachelor's, master's (including MBA), and doctoral degrees. Approximately 6,000 undergraduate and 8,700 graduate students attend George Washington University. **Positions advertised include:** Library Specialist; Library Manager; Accounts Specialist; Systems Specialist; Senior Financial Analyst; Senior Events Planner; Office Manager; Executive Aide; Research Service Coordinator.

GEORGE WASHINGTON UNIVERSITY MEDICAL CENTER
2033 K Street, Suite 220 NW, Washington DC 20052. 202/994-9600. **Contact:** Manager of Personnel. **World Wide Web address:** http://www.gwumc.edu. **NOTE:** Job postings are listed on the George Washington University Human Resource Services page. **Description:** An interdisciplinary health care facility that includes the University Hospital, a top-ranked School of Medicine and Health Sciences, a comprehensive basic and clinical research program, and a health maintenance organization (George Washington University Health Plan.) Clinical services are provided through the University Hospital and Medical Faculty Associates, a group of specialists who practice and teach at George Washington. The University Hospital is a center-city facility that is also the health care provider for the president of the United States. The emergency department sees approximately 48,000 patients annually and more than 17,000 are admitted to the hospital every year. More than 1,000 physicians are affiliated with the hospital. The University Hospital is also a certified Level I trauma center.

GEORGIA-PACIFIC CORPORATION
1120 G Street NW, Suite 1050, Washington DC 20005. 202/347-4446. **Contact:** Human Resources. **World Wide Web address:** http://www.gp.com. **Description:** Manufactures, wholesales, and distributes building products, industrial wood products, pulp, paper, packaging, and related chemicals. The company is one of the world's largest manufacturers of forest products, with facilities in 48 states and overseas. **Special programs:** Internships; Co-ops.

GIANT FOOD, INC.
P.O. Box 1804, Washington DC 20013. 301/341-4100. **Contact:** Human Resources. **World Wide Web address:** http://www.giantfood.com. **Description:** Operates a retail supermarket chain of approximately 115 stores. **Corporate headquarters location:** Landover MD.

GLAXOSMITHKLINE
1500 K Street NW, Suite 650, Washington DC 20005. 202/783-1277. **Contact:** Human Resources. **World Wide Web address:** http://www.gsk.com. **Description:** A pharmaceutical preparations company whose products include AZT, an AIDS treatment drug; Zantac; and Malarone, medication for malaria. **Corporate headquarters location:** United Kingdom. **Other U.S. locations:** Nationwide. **International locations:** Worldwide. **Listed on:** New York Stock Exchange. **Stock exchange symbol:** GSK.

GNOSSOS SOFTWARE INC.
1720 I Street NW, Suite 510, Washington DC 20006. 202/463-1200. **Fax:** 202/ 785-9562. **Contact:** President. **E-mail address:** jobs@gnossos.com. **World Wide Web address:** http://www.gnossos.com. **Description:** Develops database applications software for client businesses using Paradox for Windows and Delphi. Products are marketed under the Keep In Touch brand name. Founded in 1986. **Positions advertised include:** Marketing/Sales Associate; Client Support Representative; Project Manager; Project Coordinator; Technical Writer; Software Developer; Software Tester. **Special programs:** Internships; Summer Jobs. **Corporate headquarters location:** This location. **Listed on:** Privately held. **Annual sales/revenues:** Less than $5 million. **Number of employees at this location:** 20.

GOLDBERG MARCHESANO PARTNERS, INC.
1700 Wisconsin Avenue NW, Washington DC 20007. 202/337-0700. **Fax:** 202/ 298-3477. **Contact:** Stephanie Blaine, Office Manager. **Description:** A full-service advertising agency. **Special programs:** Internships. **Corporate headquarters location:** This location. **Operations at this facility include:** Administration; Service. **Number of employees at this location:** 50.

GREATER SOUTHEAST COMMUNITY HOSPITAL
1310 Southern Avenue SE, Washington DC 20032. 202/574-6000. **Contact:** Human Resources. **Description:** A 450-bed hospital that offers comprehensive medical and surgical care, obstetrics and gynecology services, psychiatry services, pediatric care, 24-hour emergency care, rehabilitation services, and home health care. Greater Southeast Community Hospital addresses the needs of seniors through programs and services offered at the Center for the Aging, which provides long-term care for the elderly. The 183-bed Health Care Institute and the 150-bed Livingston Health Care Center offer intermediate and skilled nursing home care for residents. Founded in 1966. **Subsidiaries include:** The Fort Washington Medical Center, a 33-bed hospital in southern Prince George's County MD, provides in- and outpatient services including medical and surgical care, 24-hour emergency services, and diagnostic testing.

HILL AND KNOWLTON INC.
600 New Hampshire Avenue NW, Suite 601, Washington DC 20037. 202/333-7400. **Fax:** 202/944-1968. **Contact:** Human Resources. **World Wide Web address:** http://www.hillandknowlton.com. **Description:** One of the largest public relations/public affairs counseling firms in the world. **Corporate headquarters location:** New York NY. **Other U.S. locations:** San Francisco CA. **International locations:** Worldwide.

HOFFMANN-LA ROCHE INC.
1425 K Street NW, Suite 650, Washington DC 20005. 202/408-0090. **Contact:** Human Resources. **World Wide Web address:** http://www.rocheusa.com. **Description:** An international health care organization that develops and manufactures pharmaceuticals, diagnostics, and vitamins. **Positions advertised include:** Director of Federal Government Affairs. **Corporate headquarters location:** Nutley NJ. **Other U.S. locations:** Nationwide. **International locations:** Worldwide. **Subsidiaries include:** Roche Biomedical Laboratories; Roche Diagnostics (ethical pharmaceuticals); Roche Vitamins Inc. **Parent company:** The Roche Group. **Listed on:** Privately held. **Annual sales/revenues:** More than $100 million. **Number of employees nationwide:** 20,000. **Number of employees worldwide:** 66,000.

HORNING BROTHERS
1350 Connecticut Avenue NW, Suite 800, Washington DC 20036. 202/659-0700. **Contact:** Human Resources. **World Wide Web address:** http://www.horningbrothers.com. **Description:** A residential and commercial development, construction, and management company. **Corporate headquarters location:** This location. **Operations at this facility include:** Administration; Divisional Headquarters. **Number of employees at this location:** 15. **Number of employees nationwide:** 100.

HOTEL HARRINGTON
436 11th Street NW, Washington DC 20004-4389. 202/628-8140. **Contact:** Ann Terry, Personnel Manager. **World Wide Web address:** http://www.hotel-harrington.com. **Description:** A 300-room hotel.

HOTEL WASHINGTON
515 15th Street NW, Washington DC 20004. 202/638-5900. **Fax:** 202/638-1594. **Contact:** Human Resources. **World Wide Web address:** http://www.hotelwashington.com. **Description:** Operates a 350-room hotel with three dining rooms. **Corporate headquarters location:** Galveston TX.

HOWARD UNIVERSITY
2400 Sixth Street NW, Washington DC 20059. 202/806-7714. **Fax:** 202/806-5315. **Contact:** Human Resources. **World Wide Web address:** http://www.howard.edu. **NOTE:** Applications may be completed in person, or mailed to the following address: Howard University, Department of Employment, 400 Bryant Street NW, Washington DC 20059. **Description:** A private research university with law, dental, and medical schools. Approximately 9,500 undergraduate and 3,100 graduate students attend Howard University. **President:** H. Patrick Swygert.

HYATT REGENCY WASHINGTON DC ON CAPITOL HILL
400 New Jersey Avenue NW, Washington DC 20001. 202/737-1234. **Fax:** 202/ 942-1552. **Recorded jobline:** 202/942-1586. **Contact:** Human Resources. **World Wide Web address:** http://www.hyatt.com. **Description:** An 834-room, full-service hotel. **NOTE:** Entry-level positions, part-time jobs, and second and third shifts are offered. **Positions advertised include:** Security Officer; Cashier; Cook; Housekeeper; Server; Concierge; Bartender; Human Resources Manager; Sous Chef; Catering Administrative Assistant. **Special programs:** Internships; Training; Summer Jobs. **Corporate headquarters location:** Chicago IL. **Other U.S. locations:** Nationwide. **International locations:** Worldwide. **Parent company:** Hyatt Hotels Corporation. **Operations at this facility include:** Administration; Sales; Service. **Listed on:** Privately held. **Number of employees at this location:** 550. **Number of employees nationwide:** 40,000.

IBM CORPORATION
1301 K Street NW, Washington DC 20006. 202/515-4000. **Contact:** IBM Staffing Services. **World Wide Web address:** http://www.ibm.com. **Description:** International Business Machines (IBM) develops, manufactures, and markets advanced information processing products including computers and microelectronic technology products, software, and networking systems and provides information technology-related services. **Positions advertised include:** Procurement Specialist; Procurement Team Leader. **NOTE:** Jobseekers should send a resume to IBM Staffing Services, 1DPA/051, 3808 Six Forks Road, Raleigh NC 27609. **Corporate headquarters location:** Armonk NY. **Operations at this facility include:** This location operates as a business support center. **Subsidiaries include:** IBM Credit Corporation; IBM Instruments, Inc.; IBM World Trade Corporation. **Listed on:** New York Stock Exchange. **Stock exchange symbol:** IBM.

INSLAW INC.
1156 15th Street NW, Suite 301, Washington DC 20005-2707. 202/828-8600. **Fax:** 202/659-0755. **Contact:** Tom Nolasco. **World Wide Web address:** http://www.inslawinc.com. **Description:** Designs, manufactures, and markets case tracking management software for the legal industry.

INTELSAT
3400 International Drive NW, Washington DC 20008. 202/944-7329. **Fax:** 202/ 944-7150. **Contact:** Personnel. **E-mail address:** human. resources@ intelsat.com. **World Wide Web address:** http://www.intelsat.com. **Description:** An international telecommunications satellite organization that provides global video, data, and voice communications through 19 satellites. Founded in 1964. **NOTE:** Part-time jobs and second and third shifts are offered. **Positions advertised include:** Billing Manager; Human Resources Coordinator; Corporate Staffing Manager; Customer Service Coordinator; Government Sales Director; Principal Network Engineer; Senior Program Manager. **Special programs:** Internships; Summer Jobs. **Office hours:** Monday - Friday, 8:30 a.m. - 5:15 p.m. **Corporate headquarters location:** This location. **Number of employees at this location:** 650. **Number of employees nationwide:** 660. **Number of employees worldwide:** 670.

INTERNATIONAL MONETARY FUND
700 19th Street NW, Washington DC 20431. 202/623-7422. **Fax:** 202/623-7333. **Contact:** Human Resources. **E-mail address:** recruit@imf.org. **World Wide Web address:** http://www.imf.org. **Description:** The local office of the international lending agency primarily responsible for lending to Third World nations. **Positions advertised include:** Experienced Economist; Research Assistant; Staff Assistant; Accounts Assistant; Language Services Assistant. **Special programs:** Summer Internships; Economist Program; Research Assistants Program. **Number of employees nationwide:** 2,000.

INTERNATIONAL PAPER COMPANY
1101 Pennsylvania Avenue NW, Suite 200, Washington DC 20004. 202/628-1223. **Contact:** Human Resources. **World Wide Web address:** http://www.internationalpaper.com. **Description:** Manufactures pulp and paper, packaging, and wood products as well as a range of specialty products. Millions of acres of timberland are controlled by International Paper, making it one of the largest private landowners in the United States. The company is organized into five business segments: Printing Papers, with principal products including uncoated papers, coated papers, bristles, and pulp; Packaging, which includes industrial packaging, consumer packaging, and kraft and specialty papers; Distribution, which includes sales of printing papers, graphic arts equipment and supplies, packaging materials, industrial supplies, and office products; Specialty Products, which include imaging products, specialty panels, nonwovens, chemicals, and minerals; and Forest Products, which include logs and wood products. **Corporate headquarters location:** Stamford CT. **Listed on:** New York Stock Exchange. **Stock exchange symbol:** IP.

JOHNSTON, LEMON & COMPANY INC.
1101 Vermont Avenue NW, Suite 800, Washington DC 20005. 202/842-5500. **Toll-free phone:** 800/424-5158. **Contact:** John Clardy, Sales Manager. **E-mail address:** john_clardy@johnstonlemon.com. **World Wide Web address:** http://www.johnstonlemon.com. **Description:** Underwrites, distributes, and deals in corporate and municipal securities, revenue bonds, and mutual funds, and provides business management services.

J.A. JONES/TOMPKINS BUILDERS
1333 H Street NW, Suite 200, Washington DC 20005. 202/789-0770. **Contact:** Manager. **World Wide Web address:** http://www.turnerconstruction.com/tompkins. **Description:** A general construction contractor. **Positions advertised include:** Project Engineer; Purchasing Agent. **Parent company:** Turner Construction Company.

JONES, DAY, REAVIS & POGUE
51 Louisiana Avenue NW, Washington DC 20001-2113. 202/879-3939. **Fax:** 202/626-1700. **Contact:** Human Resources Coordinator. **World Wide Web address:** http://www.jonesday.com. **Description:** A law firm specializing in business practice law, government regulation, litigation, and tax law. **Positions advertised include:** Paralegal. **Corporate headquarters location:** Cleveland OH.

KETCHUM
2000 L Street, Suite 300, Washington DC 202/835-8800. **Fax:** 202/835-8879. **Contact:** Carol Cincotta, Director of Human Resources. **E-mail address:** dc.resume@ketchum.com. **World Wide Web address:** http://www.ketchum.com. **Description:** A public relations firm. Founded in 1923. **Positions advertised include:** Group Manager, Public Affairs; Group Manager, Healthcare; Assistant Account Executive; Senior Account Executive; Account Supervisor; Human Resources Manager. **Special programs:** Internships. **Other U.S. locations:** Nationwide. **International locations:** Worldwide. **Number of employees worldwide:** 1,200.

KPMG
2001 M Street NW, Washington DC 20036. 202/533-3000. **Contact:** Director of Human Resources. **World Wide Web address:** http://www.kpmg.com. **Description:** KPMG delivers a wide range of value-added assurance, tax, and consulting services. **NOTE:** For immediate consideration, the company encourages candidates to apply online. Resumes can also be mailed to the following address: KPMG Center, Attn: Resume Processing , 717 North Harwood Street, Suite 3100, Dallas TX 75201. Include job code in all correspondence. **Corporate headquarters location:** Montvale NJ. **Parent company:** KPMG International.

KIPLINGER WASHINGTON EDITORS INC.
1729 H Street NW, Washington DC 20006. 202/887-6400. **Fax:** 202/496-1817. **Contact:** Director of Personnel. **E-mail address:** personnel.department@kiplinger.com. **World Wide Web address:** http://www.kiplinger.com. **Description:** Publishes business newsletters, a personal finance magazine, and books. **Positions advertised include:** Associate Editor; Banking/Finance Reporter. **Special programs:** Internships available. **Corporate headquarters location:** This location.

LEVICK STRATEGIC COMMUNICATIONS
1900 M Street NW, Suite 400, Washington DC 20036. 202/973-1300. **Fax:** 202/973-1301. **E-mail address:** apery@levick.com. **World Wide Web address:** http://www.levick.com. **Description:** Communications strategist and counselor to financial institutions and corporations.

LOCKHEED MARTIN TECHNOLOGIES
400 Virginia Avenue SW, Suite 400, Washington DC 20024. 202/646-2000. **Contact:** Human Resources. **E-mail address:** jobs.lmc@lmco.com. **World Wide Web address:** http://www.lockheedmartin.com. **Description:** Lockheed Martin is an aerospace and technology company engaged in the design, manufacture, and management of systems and products for the fields of space, defense, electronics, communications, information management, energy, and materials. **NOTE:** Jobseekers should send resumes to Lockheed Martin, Director of Human Resources, 10803 Park Ridge Boulevard, Reston VA 22091. **Operations at this facility include:** This location operates under contracts with the Federal Aviation Administration. **Listed on:** New York Stock Exchange. **Stock exchange symbol:** LMT. **Number of employees worldwide:** 149,000.

LORD & TAYLOR
5255 Western Avenue NW, Washington DC 20015. 202/362-9600. **Contact:** Human Resources Manager. **World Wide Web address:** http://www. lordandtaylor.com. **Description:** A full-line department store carrying clothing, accessories, and home furnishings. Founded in 1826. **NOTE:** Part-time jobs are offered. **Positions advertised include:** General Sales Associate; Commission Sales Associate; Cosmetics Beauty Advisor. **Corporate headquarters location:** New York NY. **Parent company:** The May Department Stores Company. **Listed on:** New York Stock Exchange. **Stock exchange symbol:** MAY.

MARRIOTT AT METRO CENTER
775 12th Street NW, Washington DC 20002. 202/737-2200. **Contact:** Human Resources. **World Wide Web address:** http://www.marriott.com. **Description:** A 456-room hotel catering to business travelers. **NOTE:** See website for current listings in the DC area.

MARRIOTT WARDMAN PARK HOTEL
2660 Woodley Road NW, Washington DC 20008. 202/328-2927. **Fax:** 202/ 387-6658. **Contact:** Lombar Martinez. **E-mail address:** lombar. martinez@marriott.com. **World Wide Web address:** http://www.marriott.com. **Description:** A 1,500-room hotel with a lobby lounge, media spaces, and conference facilities. **Positions advertised include:** Stewarding Supervisor; Room Service Supervisor.

MAYA ADVERTISING AND COMMUNICATIONS
1850 M Street NW, Suite 230, Washington DC 20036. 202/530-0566. **Fax:** 202/530-0548. **Contact:** Human Resources. **E-mail address:** maya@mayadc.com. **World Wide Web address:** http://www.mayadc.com. **NOTE:** See website listings for contact information regarding specific positions. **Description:** A full service marketing and communications firm with a Latino market specialization. **Positions advertised include:** Administrative Assistant; Marketing Specialist.

McGRAW-HILL COMPANIES
1200 G Street NW, Suite 1100, Washington DC 20005-3802. 202/383-2100. **Contact:** Human Resources. **E-mail address:** career_ops@mcgraw-hill.com. **World Wide Web address:** http://www.mcgraw-hill.com. **Description:** A publishing company. McGraw-Hill is a provider of information and services through books, magazines, newsletters, software, CD-ROMs, and online data, fax, and TV broadcasting services. The company operates four network-affiliated TV stations and also publishes *Business Week* magazine and books for college, medical, international, legal, and professional markets. McGraw-Hill also offers financial services including Standard & Poor's, commodity items, and international and logistics management products and services. **Corporate headquarters location:** New York NY. **Listed on:** New York Stock Exchange. **Stock exchange symbol:** MHP.

MERCHANT'S TIRE & AUTO CENTER
1141 Bladensburg Road NE, Washington DC 20002. 202/396-3502. **Contact:** Human Resources. **World Wide Web address:** http://www.merchantstire.com. **Description:** Provides automobile parts and maintenance.

MERRILL LYNCH
1850 K Street NW, Suite 700, Washington DC 20006. 202/659-7333. **Contact:** Staff Supervisor. **World Wide Web address:** http://www.ml.com. **Description:** Provides financial services in the following areas: securities, extensive insurance, and real estate and related services. Merrill Lynch, which is one of the largest securities brokerage firms in the United States, also brokers commodity futures and options; corporate and municipal securities; and is engaged in investment banking activities. **Positions advertised include:** Consulting Relationship Manager; Senior Regional Manager; Lead Auditor; Financial Advisor. **Corporate headquarters location:** New York NY. **Operations at this facility include:** Sales. **Listed on:** New York Stock Exchange. **Stock exchange symbol:** MER.

METROPOLITAN WASHINGTON COUNCIL OF GOVERNMENTS
777 North Capitol Street NE, Suite 300, Washington DC 20002-4239. 202/962-3200. **Fax:** 202/962-3715. **Recorded jobline:** 202/962-3397. **Contact:** Office of Human Resource Management. **E-mail address:** resumes@mwcog.org. **World Wide Web address:** http://www.mwcog.org. **Description:** The only area-wide governmental organization concerned with all aspects of metropolitan development. Metropolitan Washington Council of Governments works toward solutions of regional problems such as energy, traffic congestion, inadequate housing, air and water pollution, water supply, and land use. The council also serves as the regional planning agency including transportation planning for metro Washington DC. Founded in 1957. **Positions advertised include:** Administrative Assistant; Human Services Specialist; Public Safety Project Manager. **Special programs:** Internships; Co-ops. **Office hours:** Monday - Friday, 8:30 a.m. - 5:00 p.m. **Corporate headquarters location:** This location. **Operations at this facility include:** Administration. **Executive Director:** Michael Rogers. **Number of employees at this location:** 110.

MUSCATELLOS
1331 G Street NW, Washington DC 20005. 202/393-7547. **Contact:** Human Resources. **Description:** Manufactures uniforms and other fabricated textile products. **Corporate headquarters location:** This location.

NATIONAL ACADEMY OF SCIENCES
NATIONAL RESEARCH COUNCIL (NRC)
500 5th Street NW, Washington DC 20001. 202/334-2000. **Fax:** 202/ 334-1746. **Contact:** Human Resources. **World Wide Web address:** http://www4.nationalacademies.org/nas/nashome.nsf. **Description:** A federally chartered private corporation whose primary aim is to provide an independent source of counsel to the government on matters of science and technology. Academy members are elected. The academy's research is conducted by the National Research Council (NRC.)

NATIONAL AERONAUTICS AND SPACE ADMINISTRATION (NASA)
300 E Street SW, Washington DC 20546. 202/358-0000. **Contact:** Office of Human Resources and Education. **World Wide Web address:** http://www. hq.nasa.gov. **Description:** Administers the federal space exploration program. **NOTE:** Information about current openings is available through the Career America Connection federal job hotline at 912/757-3000. **Special programs:** Internships.

NATIONAL ASSOCIATION OF MANUFACTURERS
1331 Pennsylvania Avenue NW, Suite 600, Washington DC 20004-1790. 202/ 637-3016. **Contact:** Carol Coldren. **E-mail address:** ccoldren@nam.org. **World Wide Web address:** http://www.nam.org. **Description:** An association involved in lobbying for the interests of manufacturers. **Corporate headquarters location:** This location. **Operations at this facility include:** Administration; Service.

NATIONAL CAPITAL PLANNING COMMISSION
501 Capitol Court NE, Washington DC 20002. 202/543-4110. **Fax:** 202/543-5975. **Contact:** Human Resources Office. **E-mail address:** info@ncpc.gov. **World Wide Web address:** http://www.ncpc.gov. **Description:** Coordinates all federal planning and building activities. National Capital Planning Commission strives to build upon the beauty of Washington DC and its surrounding areas, while preserving the history of the city. Founded in 1924.

NATIONAL CENTER FOR PUBLIC POLICY RESEARCH
777 North Capitol Street NE, Suite 803, Washington DC 20002. 202/371-1400. **Fax:** 202/408-7773. **Contact:** David W. Almasi, Director of Publications and Media Relations. **E-mail address:** info@nationalcenter.org. **World Wide Web address:** http://www.nationalcenter.org. **Description:** A nonprofit media and educational research foundation that publishes commentary and briefing papers and conducts special projects on policy issues from a conservative, free-market perspective. Founded in 1982. **Special programs:** Summer Jobs. **Office hours:** Monday - Friday, 9:00 a.m. - 5:30 p.m. **President:** Amy M. Ridenour.

NATIONAL DEMOCRATIC INSTITUTE FOR INTERNATIONAL AFFAIRS
2030 M Street NW, Fifth Floor, Washington DC 20036. 202/728-5500. **Fax:** 202/728-5520. **Contact:** Human Resources. **E-Mail address:** contact@ndi.org. **World Wide Web address:** http://www.ndi.org. **Description:** National Democratic Institute For International Affairs is a nonprofit organization working to expand and promote democracy worldwide. **NOTE:** Apply through website or to e-mail address: ndi@rpc.webhire.com. **Positions advertised include:** Accounting Assistant; Accounting Manager; Deputy Director of Operations; Receptionist; Operations Officer; Software Engineer.

NATIONAL EDUCATION ASSOCIATION (NEA)
1201 16th Street NW, Washington DC 20036-3290. 202/822-7600. **Fax:** 202/ 822-7619. **Recorded jobline:** 202/822-7642. **Contact:** Employment Manager. **World Wide Web address:** http://www.nea.org/jobs. **Description:** A national, nonprofit membership organization that represents teachers, the teaching profession, and education support personnel. Major programs and functions include organizing and membership, education policy, government relations, communications, publishing, research, human and civil rights, negotiations, and administration. **Corporate headquarters location:** This location. **Other U.S. locations:** Nationwide. **Number of employees at this location:** 500.

NATIONAL GALLERY OF ART
Sixth Street & Constitution Avenue NW, Washington DC 20565. 202/737-4215. **Recorded jobline:** 202/842-6298. **Fax:** 202/789-3011. **Contact:** Human Resources. **E-mail address:** staffing@nga.gov. **World Wide Web address:** http://www.nga.gov. **Description:** An art gallery hosting a variety of exhibitions and lectures in art and film. **NOTE:** If applying by mail, send resume to: National Gallery of Art, Personnel Office, 2000B South Club Drive, Landover MD 20785. **Positions advertised include:** Education Assistant; Sales Store Checker; Mason; Financial Analyst.

NATIONAL GEOGRAPHIC SOCIETY
1145 17th Street NW, Washington DC 20036. 202/857-7000. **Contact:** Human Resources. **World Wide Web address:** http://www.nationalgeographic.com. **Description:** The National Geographic Society offers various products and services. The National Geographic Education Program offers geography education programs to schools through films, computer software, videos, and other multimedia classroom materials. Since 1890, the society's Committee for Research and Exploration has supported more than 4,000 exploration and research projects in various locations. The society offers four major publications. *National Geographic* reaches over 9 million members and an estimated 40 million readers on a monthly basis. *National Geographic Traveler* provides travel information. *National Geographic World* is for children eight years old and over. *National Geographic Research and Exploration* is a scientific journal. *National Geographic* profiles geographic topics and locales from a very broad perspective. The society also offers maps and globes as well as books and games for young adults. *The National Geographic Explorer* is a two-hour cable television series with a magazine format. The society also offers various public services including an annual series of lectures and events, and the JASON Project, which provides students with access to interactive television links. **Special programs:** Apprenticeships. **Office hours:** Monday - Saturday, 9:00 a.m. - 5:00 p.m., and Sunday, 10:00 a.m. - 5:00 p.m. **Corporate headquarters location:** This location. **Other U.S. locations:** Gaithersburg MD. **Operations at this facility include:** This location houses the corporate offices as well as a museum.

NATIONAL JOURNAL
600 New Hampshire Avenue NW, Washington DC 20037. 202/739-8400. **Fax:** 202/ 833-8069. **Contact:** Human Resources Coordinator. **World Wide Web address:** http://www.nationaljournal.com. **Description:** A weekly magazine devoted to covering national politics and federal policy. Founded in 1968. **NOTE:** Candidates should apply online. **Positions advertised include:** Account Manager; Advertising Sales Coordinator; Art Director; Associate Editor; Business Development Analyst; Business Development Manager; Desktop Support Technician; Graphics Researcher; Account Executive. **Special programs:** Internships available.

NATIONAL MUSEUM OF AFRICAN ART
950 Independence Avenue SW, Washington DC 20560-0708. 202/633-4600. **Fax:** 202/357-4879. **Contact:** Human Resources. **World Wide Web address:** http://www.nmafa.si.edu. **Description:** A museum devoted exclusively to the collection, study, and exhibition of African art. An important research and reference center, the museum houses a collection of over 6,000 objects, a library, photographic archives, and a conservation laboratory. **Parent company:** Smithsonian Institution.

NATIONAL MUSEUM OF AMERICAN HISTORY
OFFICE OF INTERNSHIPS AND FELLOWSHIPS
750 9th Street NW, Victor Building, Washington DC 20560-0912. 202/633-3556. **Fax:** 202/357-3346. **Contact:** Suzanne McLaughlin, Internship/Fellowship Coordinator. **World Wide Web address:** http://americanhistory.si.edu. **Description:** A museum that investigates, interprets, collects, preserves, exhibits, and honors the heritage of America. Founded in 1846. **NOTE:** For information regarding other opportunities at the Smithsonian Institution and its various museums, call the Smithsonian's recorded jobline: 202/287-3102. **Company slogan:** The increase and diffusion of knowledge. **Special programs:** Internships. **Internship information:** The museum's internship program is open to persons enrolled in their final two years of high school and through retirement. Please contact the Office of Internships and Fellowships to receive an application packet. **Parent company:** Smithsonian Institution. **Director:** Brent D. Glass.

NATIONAL MUSEUM OF NATURAL HISTORY
750 9th Street NW, Victor Building, Washington DC 20560-0912. 202/275-1102. **Recorded jobline:** 202/287-3102. **Contact:** Human Resources. **World Wide Web address:** http://www.mnh.si.edu. **NOTE:** Interested applicants may also call the Smithonian's recorded jobline for additional information regarding openings and application procedures. **Description:** A part of the Smithsonian Institution, this museum displays natural history exhibits.

NATIONAL PUBLIC RADIO (NPR)
635 Massachusetts Avenue NW, Washington DC 20001-3753. 202/414-2000. **Fax:** 202/513-3047. **Recorded jobline:** 202/513-3030. **Contact:** Human Resources Department. **E-mail address:** employment@npr.org. **World Wide Web address:** http://www.npr.org. **Description:** Production center of the national public radio network. **NOTE:** Second and third shifts are offered. Unsolicited resumes are not accepted. No phone calls please. **Positions advertised include:** Correspondent/Reporter; Editorial Assistant; Production Assistant; Senior Web Designer; Systems Administrator; Supervising Editor; Supervising Senior Producer; Senior Accountant; Administrative Assistant; Marketing/Communications Coordinator. **Special programs:** Internships; Co-ops; Summer Jobs. **Corporate headquarters location:** This location. **Other U.S. locations:** Los Angeles CA; Chicago IL; New York NY; Boston MA. **International locations:** Worldwide. **Operations at this facility include:** Regional Headquarters. **CEO:** Kevin Klose. **Number of employees at this location:** 450. **Number of employees nationwide:** 525.

NATIONAL REHABILITATION HOSPITAL
102 Irving Street NW, Washington DC 20010-2921. 202/877-1710. **Fax:** 202/ 726-7701. **Recorded jobline:** 202/877-1700. **Contact:** Human Resources. **E-mail address:** nrhhumanresources@mhg.edu. **World Wide Web address:** http://www. nrhrehab.org. **Description:** Provides rehabilitation services through patient care, assisted technology, research, education and training, and advocacy. The hospital's patient care services include the outpatient center in Bethesda MD, providing musculoskeletal rehabilitation; the Performance Diagnostic Laboratory, offering sophisticated video and computer technology to analyze individual's movements; the Brain Injury Rehabilitation and the Stroke Recovery Program, offering day-treatment programs for those who are re-entering the community; the Department of Obstetrics and Gynecology, offering OB/GYN services for women with disabilities; and multiple sclerosis services. **Positions advertised include:** Clinical Nurse Manager; Database Developer; Occupational Therapist; Occupational Therapy Aide; Office Coordinator; Pediatric Primary Nurse; Physical Therapist; Psychologist; Rehabilitation Care Technician; Research Assistant; Speech Language Pathologist; Unit Clerk.

NATIONAL TRUST FOR HISTORIC PRESERVATION
1785 Massachusetts Avenue NW, Washington DC 20036. 202/588-6000. **Fax:** 202/588-6059. **Contact:** Human Resources Director. **E-mail address:** jobs@nthp.org. **World Wide Web address:** http://www.nthp.org. **Description:** A nonprofit organization that encourages public participation in the preservation of buildings, objects, sites, and districts that are significant to the history and culture of the nation. Founded in 1949. **Positions advertised include:** Assistant General Counsel; Executive

Assistant; Major Gifts Officer; Director of Communications; Associate Director, Preservation Programs; Database Clerk; Program Assistant.

NATIVE AMERICAN CONSULTANTS, INC.
725 Second Street NE, Washington DC 20002. 202/547-0576. **Contact:** Human Resources. **E-mail address:** nac@nativeconsultants.com. **World Wide Web address:** http://www.nativeconsultants.com. **Description:** Provides consulting services to government agencies engaged in research for Native Americans. **NOTE:** Interested applicants should send a resume to the above e-mail address. **Corporate headquarters location:** This location.

NAVAL RESEARCH LABORATORIES
4555 Overlook Avenue SW, Mail Code 1800, Washington DC 20375-5320. 202/767-3200. **Recorded jobline:** 202/767-3030. **Contact:** Human Resources Office Director. **World Wide Web address:** http://amp.nrl.navy.mil/code1800. **Description:** Provides in-house research for the physical, engineering, space, and environmental sciences; operates broadly-based exploratory and advanced development programs in response to identified and anticipated Navy needs; offers multidisciplinary support to the Naval Warfare Centers; and provides space and space systems technology development and support. **Positions advertised include:** Electronics Technician; Contract Specialist; Maintenance Mechanic; Health Physicist; Librarian; Security Specialist; Security Guard; Systems Accountant; Budget Analyst; Planner & Estimator; Telecommunications Specialist. **Special programs:** Summer Internships available. **Office hours:** Monday – Friday, 8:00 a.m. – 4:30 p.m.

OCEANA
2501 M Street NW, Suite 300, Washington DC 20037-1311. 202/833-3900. **Fax:** 202/833-2070. **Contact:** Human Resources. **E-mail address:** resumes@oceana.org. **World Wide Web address:** http://www.oceana.org. **Description:** An international, non-profit ocean protection and advocacy agency. **NOTE:** Does not accept calls regarding status of resumes or applications. **Positions advertised include:** Communications Specialist; Development Manager; Vice President for Development; Director, Major Donor Programs. **Special programs:** Seasonal Internships available. **Corporate headquarters location:** This location. **Other U.S. locations:** Los Angeles CA; Juneau AK.

OLDCASTLE MATERIALS, INC.
1055 Thomas Jefferson Street, Suite 400, Washington DC 20007. **Fax:** 202/625-2153. **Contact:** Human Resources. **E-mail address:** info@oldcastlematerials.com. **World Wide Web address:** http://www. oldcastlematerials.com. **Description:** Produces aggregate, asphalt, ready-mix concrete, and prestress concrete for road and bridge construction. **Corporate headquarters location:** This location. **Parent company:** CRH plc.

OMNI SHOREHAM HOTEL
2500 Calvert Street NW, Washington DC 20008. 202/234-0700. **Fax:** 202/756-5155. **Contact:** Human Resources. **World Wide Web address:** http://www. omnihotels.com. **Description:** A historic landmark hotel with over 700 rooms and 100,000 square feet of meeting space. **Positions advertised include:** Sales Manager; Reservation Sales Coordinator; Housekeeping Supervisor; Bartender; Beverage Porter; Room Service Supervisor; Front Desk Supervisor; Laundry Manager; Banquet Manager; Front Desk Agent; Message Therapist; Room Attendant; Catering Manager. **Special programs:** Internships. **Number of employees at this location:** 535.

OPTOELECTRONICS INDUSTRY DEVELOPMENT ASSOCIATION
1133 Connecticut Avenue NW, Suite 600, Washington DC 20036. 202/785-4426. **Fax:** 202/785-4428. **Contact:** Human Resources. **World Wide Web address:** http://www.oida.org. **Description:** A national trade association.

PALM MANAGEMENT CORPORATION
1225 19th Street NW, Washington DC 20036. 202/293-9091. **Fax:** 202/775-1468. **Contact:** Human Resources. **E-mail address:** careers@thepalm.com. **World Wide Web address:** http://www.thepalm.com. **Description:** Owns and operates Palm Restaurants.

PAN AMERICAN HEALTH ORGANIZATION
WORLD HEALTH ORGANIZATION
525 23rd Street NW, Washington DC 20037. 202/974-3396. **Fax:** 202/974-3379. **Contact:** Human Resources. **World Wide Web address:** http://www. paho.org. **Description:** An international agency responsible for assisting Latin and Caribbean governments in instituting national health programs. Services include assisting governments in the planning, development, and strengthening of laboratory networks; promoting, developing, and coordinating food protection programs; and establishing standards for the hygienic control of foods. **NOTE:** Pan American Health Organization offers the opportunity for worldwide employment. Duty stations include Martinez, Argentina; Bridgetown, Barbados; Brazzaville, Congo; Georgetown, Guyana; Port-au-Prince, Haiti; Asuncion, Paraguay; Manila, Philippines; Geneva, Switzerland. **Positions advertised include:** Administrative/Customer Support Representative; Office Assistant; Cataloger/Electronics Database Assistant. **Corporate headquarters location:** This location.

PARSONS BRINCKERHOFF INC.
1401 K Street NW, Suite 701, Washington DC 20005. 202/783-0241. **Contact:** Human Resources. **E-mail address:** careers@pbworld.com. **World Wide Web address:** http://www.pbworld.com. **Description:** An architectural engineering firm. **Special programs:** Internships available. **Corporate headquarters location:** New York NY.

THE PEACE CORPS
1111 20th Street NW, Room 2300, Washington DC 20526. 202/692-1200. **Fax:** 202/692-1201. **Contact:** Office of Human Resources. **World Wide Web address:** http://www.peacecorps.gov. **Description:** More than 150,000 people have volunteered or worked for the Peace Corps in 80 developing countries. Peace Corps members aid these countries in the areas of education, environment, health, business, and agriculture. Founded in 1961. **Positions advertised include:** Financial Management Analyst; Financial Management Specialist; Financial Management Officer; Budget Analyst.

PORTER NOVELLI INTERNATIONAL
1909 K Street NW, Suite 400, Washington DC 20006. 202/973-5800. **Contact:** Juanita Myrick, Human Resources. **World Wide Web address:** http://www. porternovelli.com. **Description:** An agency specializing in public relations, crisis management, issue advertising, and research. **Special programs:** Internships. **Corporate headquarters location:** New York NY. **Other U.S. locations:** Los Angeles CA; Chicago IL; Boston MA. **Number of employees at this location:** 65. **Number of employees nationwide:** 700.

POTOMAC ELECTRIC POWER COMPANY (PEPCO)
701 Ninth Street NW, Washington DC 20068. 202/872-2000. **Toll-free phone:** 866/23-PEPCO. **Fax:** 202/331-6850. **Contact:** Employment. **E-mail address:** employment@pepco.com. **World Wide Web address:** http://www.pepco.com. **Description:** An investor-owned electric utility serving the electricity needs of 1.9 million people in the metropolitan Washington DC area. PEPCO also sells electricity at wholesale to Southern Maryland Electric Cooperative. **Positions advertised include:** Account Investigations Representative; Accounting Analyst; Claims Clerk; Customer Service Representative; Process Manager; Senior Communications Representative; Senior Environmental Scientist. **Listed on:** New York Stock Exchange. **Stock exchange symbol:** POM.

PRICEWATERHOUSECOOPERS
1301 K Street NW, Suite 800 West, Washington DC 20005. 202/414-1000. **Contact:** Human Resources. **World Wide Web address:** http://www.pwc global.com. **Description:** One of the largest certified public accounting firms in the world. PricewaterhouseCoopers provides public accounting, business advisory, management consulting, and taxation services. **Positions advertised include:** Diversity Manager; International Tax Manager; Instructor/Trainer; Software Developer; Finance Analyst; Audit Manager; Senior Associate. **Corporate headquarters location:** New York NY. **Other U.S. locations:** Nationwide.

PROVIDENCE HOSPITAL
1150 Varnum Street NE, Washington DC 20017-2180. 202/269-7928. **Fax:** 202/ 269-7662. **Contact:** Laverne Street, Director of Human Resources. **World Wide Web address:** http://www.provhosp.org. **Description:** Offers a variety of programs, treatments, and counseling services. The Wellness Institute and Women's Center provides cancer assessments, exercise programs, and classes in nutrition, weight management, hypertension, stress management, and smoking cessation. The Senior Connection Program, Telecare, is a service that performs phone checks for seniors who, due to age, illness, or immobility, spend most of their time home alone. The Fort Lincoln Family Medicine Center provides continuous health care and serves as the outpatient training site for 21 family practice residents. Center for Life helps pregnant women in urban areas who have difficulties with language, money, and transportation. Seton Home provides inpatient and outpatient treatment, inpatient psychiatric care, and a special program for patients with both psychiatric and substance abuse problems. Umoja Treatment Service is a hospital-based alcohol and drug abuse center. **Positions advertised include:** Registered Nurse; Nurse Practitioner; Physician Assistant; Certified Nurse Midwife; Admitting/Registration Officer; Assistant Control Coordinator; Case Manager; Telephone Operator; ER Billing Coordinator. **Special programs:** Internships available.

RADIO FREE EUROPE/RADIO LIBERTY, INC.
1201 Connecticut Avenue NW, Suite 1100, Washington DC 20036. 202/457-6900. **Fax:** 202/457-6974. **Contact:** Human Resources Division. **E-mail address:** dcjobs@rferl.org. **World Wide Web address:** http://www.rferl.org. **Description:** A radio station. **Special programs:** Internships. **Internship information:** The RFE/RL journalism intern program introduces qualified graduate students to news reporting in Central Europe and the successor states of the former Soviet Union. Interns should be graduate students at schools of journalism, communications, political science, or international relations and should have some relevant on-the-job experience. Applicants are asked to submit two letters of recommendation, samples of broadcast or published material, and a resume and cover letter indicating interest and summarizing qualifications. In addition, applicants are asked to fill out an additional application form. **Corporate headquarters location:** This location.

REEDSMITH LLP
1301 K Street NW, Suite 1100, East Tower, Washington DC 20005. 202/414-9200. **Fax:** 202/414-9299. **Contact:** Cindy Schuler. **E-mail address:** dcjobs@reedsmith.com. **World Wide Web address:** http://www.reedsmith.com. **Description:** A law firm. Founded in 1877. **Positions advertised include:** Legal Secretary. **Other U.S. locations:** Harrisburg PA; Los Angeles CA; New York NY; Newark NJ; San Francisco CA; Wilmington DE. **International locations:** London.

REPUBLICAN NATIONAL COMMITTEE
310 First Street SE, Washington DC 20003. 202/863-8500. **Contact:** Personnel Director. **World Wide Web address:** http://www.rnc.org. **Description:** National headquarters for the Republican Party, engaged in a wide range of political and legislative support functions.

RESEARCH TRIANGLE INSTITUTE (RTI)
1615 M Street NW, Suite 740, Washington DC 20036. 202/728-2080. **Contact:** Human Resources. **E-mail address:** jobs@rti.org. **World Wide Web address:** http://www.rti.org. **Description:** A nonprofit, independent research organization involved in many scientific fields, under contract to business; industry; federal, state, and local governments; industrial associations; and public service agencies. The institute was created as a separately operated entity by the joint action of North Carolina State University, Duke University, and the University of North Carolina at Chapel Hill. Close ties are maintained with the universities' scientists, both through the active research community of the Research Triangle region in North Carolina and through collaborative research conducted for government and industry clients. Research Triangle Institute responds to national priorities in health, the environment, advanced technology, and social policy with contract research for the U.S. government including applications in statistics, social sciences, chemistry, life sciences, environmental sciences, engineering, and electronics. **NOTE:** Jobseekers should address all inquiries to Human Resources, P.O. Box 12194, Research Triangle Park NC 27709. **Corporate headquarters location:** Research Triangle Park NC. **Other U.S. locations:** Rockville MD; Cocoa Beach FL; Hampton VA; Atlanta GA; Chicago IL; Waltham MA; Anniston AL. **Number of employees nationwide:** 1,750.

SAUL'S LITHOGRAPH COMPANY INC.
2424 Evarts Street NE, Washington DC 20018. 202/529-9100. **Contact:** Edward Bozzella, President. **Description:** Offers a complete range of commercial printing services including offset and lithography services.

SECURITY MOVING & STORAGE
1701 Florida Avenue NW, Washington DC 20009-2697. 202/234-5600. **Fax:** 202/234-3513. **Contact:** Human Resources. **World Wide Web address:** http://www.sscw.com. **Description:** Provides general storage, cold storage, freight forwarding, moving and packing, and international trading services. **Positions advertised include:** Mover; Driver; Warehouseman. **Corporate headquarters location:** This location. **Number of employees at this location:** 160.

SEVEN WORLDWIDE
1050 Thomas Jefferson Street NW, Washington DC 20007-3871. 202/955-2518. **Contact:** Human Resources. **World Wide Web address:** http://www.agt.com.

Description: Applied Graphics Technologies (AGT) is one of the largest providers of integrated graphic communications services to advertising agencies, magazine and catalog publishers, and corporate clients in various industries throughout the world. The company's services include commercial printing, color separation and retouching, facilities management, photo CD and digital image archiving, electronic imaging services, flexo/packaging services, publication and catalog services, satellite transmission services, creative design services, technical support and training services, and black and white ad production. **NOTE:** Hiring is done through the corporate headquarters. Jobseekers should address all inquiries to: Human Resources, 450 West 33rd Street, 11th Floor, New York NY 10010. **Operations at this facility include:** This location offers publication services, four-color facsimile or digital transmittal, and a desktop service bureau.

SIBLEY MEMORIAL HOSPITAL
5255 Loughboro Road NW, Washington DC 20016. 202/537-4750. **Fax:** 202/ 363-2677. **Recorded jobline:** 202/364-8665. **Contact:** Queenie Plater, Employment Manager. **E-mail address:** qplater@sibley.org. **World Wide Web address:** http://www.sibley.org. **Description:** A 340-bed, community hospital. This is a nonprofit company. Founded in 1890. **NOTE:** Second and third shifts are offered. **Positions advertised include:** Admissions Supervisor; Admissions Representative; Admissions Manager; Gift Shop Sales Associate; Food Service Worker; Painter; Radiologic Technician; Medical Records Coder; Rehabilitation Therapist; Respiratory Therapist. **Special programs:** Summer Jobs. **Corporate headquarters location:** This location. **Number of employees at this location:** 1,200.

SMALL BUSINESS ADMINISTRATION
409 Third Street SW, Suite 4200, Washington DC 20416. 202/205-5600. **Contact:** Office of Human Resources. **World Wide Web address:** http://www. sba.gov. **Description:** Provides financial, technical, and management assistance to Americans looking to start-up and run their own small business. Founded in 1953. **Positions advertised include:** Criminal Investigator. **Corporate headquarters location:** This location. **Administrator:** Hector V. Barreto.

THE SMITH COMPANY
4455 Connecticut Avenue NW, Suite B600, Washington DC 20008. 202/895-0900. **Contact:** Human Resources. **Description:** Provides telemarketing services.

SMITHSONIAN INSTITUTION PRESS
750 Ninth Street NW, Suite 4300, Washington DC 20560-0950. 202/275-2300. **Toll-free phone:** 800/233-4830. **Fax:** 202/275-2274. **Contact:** Human Resources. **E-mail address:** info@sipress.si.edu. **World Wide Web address:** http://www.si.edu/sipress. **Description:** Publishes 60-80 books each year in general interest areas including history, popular culture, and international studies.

SO OTHERS MIGHT EAT (SOME)
71 O Street NW, Washington DC 20001-1258. 202/797-8806. **Fax:** 202/265-3849. **Contact:** Human Resources. **E-mail address:** some@some.org. **World Wide Web address:** http://www.some.org. **Description:** Provides food, clothing, and medical and dental assistance to the needy.

THOMAS SOMERVILLE COMPANY
4912 Sixth Street NE, Washington DC 20017. 301/390-9575. **Contact:** Human Resources. **World Wide Web address:** http://www.tsomerville.com. **Description:** A distributor of plumbing, heating, and air conditioning supplies. **Corporate headquarters location:** Upper Marlboro MD. **Other U.S. locations:** Annapolis MD; Hyattsville MD; Baltimore MD; Martinsburg WV; Lancaster PA; York PA; Fairfax VA; Chantilly VA.

STRAYER UNIVERSITY
1025 15th Street NW, Washington DC 20005. 202/408-2400. **Contact:** Human Resources. **World Wide Web address:** http://www.strayer.edu. **Description:** A four-year university offering business and information technology programs both on-campus and online. Its 27 campuses are located throughout Maryland, North Carolina, South Carolina, Tennessee, Virginia, and Washington DC.

TENDER LOVING CARE/STAFF BUILDERS
1212 New York Avenue, Suite 200, Washington DC 20005. 202/682-2200. **Fax:** 202/682-0822. **Contact:** Human Resources. **World Wide Web address:** http://www.tlcathome.com. **Description:** A home health care agency. **Positions advertised include:** Assistant Director of Clinical Services; Care Team Manager; Home Care Nurse; Physical Therapist; Speech Language Pathologist. **Special programs:** Apprenticeships. **Corporate headquarters location:** Lake Success NY. **Other U.S. locations:** Nationwide. **Number of employees nationwide:** 20,000.

U.S. BUREAU OF ENGRAVING AND PRINTING
14th & C Streets SW, Room 202-A, Washington DC 20228. 202/874-2633. **Contact:** Human Resources. **World Wide Web address:** http://www.bep.treas.gov. **Description:** Produces all U.S. paper currency, a majority of U.S. postage stamps, and many other security documents issued by the federal government. Research and development programs for strengthening counterfeit deterrence, improving the quality of products, and reducing manufacturing costs are integral facets of its operations. Other activities at the bureau include engraving plates and dies; manufacturing certain inks used in security products; purchasing materials, supplies, and equipment; and storing and delivering products. The bureau occupies three government-owned facilities. The main facility and annex building (Washington DC) produce Federal Reserve notes, postage stamps, and other security products. The Western Currency facility (Fort Worth TX) produces Federal Reserve notes. **Positions advertised include:** General Investigator; Currency Controller; Securities Processor; Plate Maker; Secretary; Maintenance Worker; Accounting Technician. **Parent company:** Department of Treasury.

U.S. COAST GUARD
2100 Second Street SW, Washington DC 20593-0001. 202/267-2229. **Contact:** Human Resources. **World Wide Web address:** http://www.uscg.mil. **Description:** Protects and patrols the coastal waters of the United States. **Positions advertised include:** Visual Information Specialist; General Engineer; Information Technology Specialist; Environmental Protection Specialist.

U.S. DEPARTMENT OF AGRICULTURE (USDA)
14th & Independence Avenue SW, Washington DC 20250. 202/720-2791. **Contact:** Human Resources. **World Wide Web address:** http://www.usda.gov. **Description:** Supports agricultural production and ensures the quality of products. The USDA provides economic and educational support to farmers and those in rural areas.

U.S. DEPARTMENT OF LABOR
OFFICE OF PERSONNEL MANAGEMENT SERVICES
1900 E Street NW, Washington DC 20415-0001. 202/606-1800. **Fax:** 202/606-1732. **Contact:** Human Resources. **World Wide Web address:** http://www.opm.gov. **E-mail address:** jobs4u@opm.gov. **Wide Web address:** http://www.opm.gov. **Description:** Reports on work force conditions. **Positions advertised include:** Investigator; Accountant; Financial Systems Specialist; Human Resources Specialist. **Special programs:** Internships. **Corporate headquarters location:** This location. **Operations at this facility include:** Administration; Divisional Headquarters; Service.

U.S. DEPARTMENT OF THE NAVY
Washington Navy Yard, 1014 N Street SE, Suite 1, Washington DC 20374-5050. 202/685-0077. **Fax:** 202/685-0140. **Contact:** Job Information Center. **World Wide Web address:** http://www.navy.mil. **Description:** Naval branch of the U.S. Armed Forces. **NOTE:** Entry-level positions are offered. **Special programs:** Internships; Training. **Operations at this facility include:** Administration; Divisional Headquarters; Manufacturing; Regional Headquarters; Research and Development; Sales; Service.

U.S. DEPARTMENT OF VETERANS AFFAIRS
WASHINGTON DC VETERANS AFFAIRS MEDICAL CENTER
50 Irving Street NW, Department 05-A, Washington DC 20422. 202/745-8000. **Contact:** Employment Office. **World Wide Web address:** http://www.va.gov. **Description:** A medical center operated by the U.S. Department of Veterans Affairs (VA.) From 54 hospitals in 1930, the VA health care system has grown to include 171 medical centers; more than 364 outpatient, community, and outreach clinics; 130 nursing home care units; and 37 domiciliaries. VA operates at least one medical center in each of the 48 contiguous states, Puerto Rico, and the District of Columbia. With approximately 76,000 medical center beds, VA treats nearly 1 million patients annually in VA hospitals; 75,000 in nursing home care units; and 25,000 in domiciliaries. VA's outpatient clinics register approximately 24 million visits per year.

U.S. ENVIRONMENTAL PROTECTION AGENCY (EPA)
1200 Pennsylvania Avenue NW, Washington DC 20460. 202/272-0167. **Contact:** Human Resources. **World Wide Web address:** http://www.epa.gov. **Description:** The EPA is dedicated to improving and preserving the quality of the environment, both nationally and globally, and protecting human health and the productivity of natural resources. The agency is committed to ensuring that federal environmental laws are implemented and enforced effectively; U.S. policy, both foreign and domestic, encourages the integration of economic development and environmental protection so that economic growth can be sustained over the long term; and public and private decisions affecting energy, transportation, agriculture, industry, international trade, and natural resources fully integrate considerations of environmental quality. Founded in 1970. **NOTE:** Please include the position's mail code on any application, which allows the human resources department to forward a resume to the correct department. Call the jobline for more information. **Positions advertised include:** Environmental Protection Specialist; Secretary; Management Analyst; Auditor; Technical Writer/Editor; Grant Policy Specialist. **Special programs:** Internships; Fellowships; Student Programs. **Corporate headquarters location:** This location. **Other U.S. locations:** San Francisco CA; Denver CO; Atlanta GA; Chicago IL; Kansas City KS; Boston MA; New York NY; Philadelphia PA; Dallas TX; Seattle WA. **Number of employees nationwide:** 19,000.

U.S. GENERAL SERVICES ADMINISTRATION (GSA)
1800 F Street NW, Washington DC 20405. 202/501-1805. **Contact:** Human Resources. **E-mail address:** gsajobs@gsa.gov. **World Wide Web address:** http://www.gsa.gov. **Description:** One of the federal government's three central management agencies. The GSA seeks to ensure that government agencies are provided the best space, services, supplies, and products at the best prices. There are 11 operating regional offices. **Positions advertised include:** Public Affairs Specialist; Market Program Manager; Human Capital Officer; Supervisory Realty Specialist; IT Specialist; National Accounts Manager; Program Analyst.

U.S. HOLOCAUST MEMORIAL MUSEUM
100 Raoul Wallenberg Place SW, Washington DC 20024-2126. 202/488-2674. **Fax:** 202/314-0311. **Contact:** Gerard Cataldo, Human Resources. **E-mail address:** gcataldo@ushmm.org. **World Wide Web address:** http://www.ushmm.org. **Description:** A museum dedicated to the education and remembrance of the Holocaust and genocide studies. The museum is comprised of more than 30,000 items in 18 languages.

U.S. INTERNATIONAL TRADE COMMISSION
500 E Street SW, Room 314, Washington DC 20436. 202/205-2651. **Fax:** 202/205-2008. **Contact:** Joyce Douglas, Office of Personnel. **E-mail address:** jdouglas@usitc.gov. **World Wide Web address:** http://www.usitc.gov. **Description:** Provides both the executive and legislative branches of the government with objective trade expertise. The organization analyzes the impact of trade on U.S. industries, and eliminates any unfair trade actions such as patent and copyright infringement. **Special programs:** Internships available.

U.S. NEWS & WORLD REPORT
1050 Thomas Jefferson Street NW, Washington DC 20007. 202/955-2000. **Contact:** Human Resources. **World Wide Web address:** http://www.usnews.com. **Description:** A news magazine with more than 20 million readers. **NOTE:** Hiring is done out of the New York office. Please direct resumes to Human Resources, 450 West 33rd Street, 11th Floor, New York NY 10001. 212/210-1864. **Special programs:** Internships. **Internship information:** Direct questions regarding internships to: interns@usnewscom. **Corporate headquarters location:** This location. **Other U.S. locations:** New York NY. **Operations at this facility include:** Administration.

U.S. NUCLEAR REGULATORY COMMISSION
Mail Stop 2D30, Washington DC 20555. 301/415-1534. **Recorded jobline:** 478/757-3000. **Contact:** Office of Human Resources. **World Wide Web address:** http://www.nrc.gov. **Description:** Responsible for the issuance of licenses and the regulation of companies engaged in producing and using nuclear materials and generating electricity by nuclear power. **Special programs:** Internships.

U.S. POSTAL RATE COMMISSION
1333 H Street NW, Suite 300, Washington DC 20268. 202/789-6840. **Contact:** Garry J. Sikora, Personnel Officer. **World Wide Web address:** http://www.prc.gov. **Description:** The federal government agency responsible for overseeing U.S. postal rates. **Corporate headquarters location:** This location.

U.S. POSTAL SERVICE
475 L'Enfant Plaza SW, Room 1831, Washington DC 20260-4261. 202/268-3646. **Fax:** 202/268-6195. **Contact:** Stephen A. Leavey, Manager of Corporate Personnel Management. **World Wide Web address:** http://www.usps.gov. **Description:** Field offices that provide a complete range of mail pickup and delivery services throughout the country and internationally. They also act as centers for passport acceptance, government program applications, and government registration activities. **NOTE:** Entry-level positions and second and third shifts are offered. **Company slogan:** We

deliver. **Positions advertised include:** Environmental Specialist; Accountant; Banking Relations Specialist; Operations Research Analyst; Field Liaison, Communications; Records Specialist; Business Systems Analyst; Information Systems Specialist; Labor Relations Specialist. **Special programs:** Internships; Apprenticeships; Summer Jobs. **Office hours:** Monday - Friday, 8:00 a.m. - 5:00 p.m. **Corporate headquarters location:** This location. **Other U.S. locations:** Nationwide. **Operations at this facility include:** Administration; Divisional Headquarters; Policy Development; Regional Headquarters. **Number of employees at this location:** 5,000. **Number of employees nationwide:** 800,000.

UNITED PRESS INTERNATIONAL
1510 H Street NW, Washington DC 20005. 202/898-8200. **Fax:** 202/898-8057. **Contact:** Human Resources. **E-mail address:** hr@upi.com. **World Wide Web address:** http://www.upi.com. **Description:** One of the world's largest independent news-gathering organizations with news bureaus located worldwide. **Corporate headquarters location:** This location. **Other U.S. locations:** Miami FL; Chicago IL; New York NY; Dallas TX. **Operations at this facility include:** Administration; Research and Development; Sales. **Listed on:** Privately held.

UNITED STATES SERVICE INDUSTRIES (USSI)
1424 K Street NW, 4th Floor, Washington DC 20005. 202/783-2030. **Fax:** 202/393-5541. **Contact:** Human Resources. **E-mail address:** communications@ ussiclean.com. **World Wide Web address:** http://www. ussiclean.com. **Description:** A building maintenance company offering janitorial services.

UNIVERSITY OF THE DISTRICT OF COLUMBIA
4200 Connecticut Avenue NW, Building 38, Room 301, Washington DC 20008. 202/274-5020. **Contact:** Human Resources. **World Wide Web address:** http://www.udc.edu. **Description:** Offers programs through the College of Professional Studies, which includes the School of Business and Public Administration and the School of Engineering and Applied Science; and the College of Arts and Sciences, encompassing the School of Arts and Education and the School of Science and Mathematics. Each year, 800 to 900 graduates receive one-year certificates, two-year Associate in Applied Science and Associate of Arts degrees, four-year Bachelor of Arts and Bachelor of Science degrees, and master's degrees. Founded in 1976. **Positions advertised include:** Acquisitions Librarian; Financial Aid Director; Recruitment Specialist; Police Officer.

VISITING NURSE ASSOCIATION OF WASHINGTON DC
6000 New Hampshire Avenue NE, Washington DC 20011. 202/882-6988. **Toll-free phone:** 800/634-5702. **Contact:** Human Resources Director. **Description:** Visiting Nurse Association is a home health care organization providing skilled nursing care to patients in their homes. **Operations at this facility include:** This location serves the District of Columbia, and Montgomery and Prince George's Counties in Maryland.

WJLA-TV
3007 Tilden Street NW, Washington DC 20008. **Contact:** Hiring Manager. **World Wide Web address:** http://www.wjla.com. **Description:** A television station affiliated with ABC. **NOTE:** Send resumes to: Human Resources Department, 1100 Wilson Boulevard, Arlington VA 22209. No phone calls or e-mails please. **Positions advertised include:** Designer/Animator; Executive Producer; Photographer/Editor; Research Manager; Weathercaster; Community Reporter. **Special programs:** Internships available for college Juniors and Seniors.

WRC NBC CHANNEL 4
4001 Nebraska Avenue NW, Washington DC 20016. 202/885-4000. **Fax:** 202/ 885-4913. **Contact:** Rachel Manning, Director of Employee Relations. **World Wide Web address:** http://www.nbc4.com. **Description:** An NBC-affiliated television station. **NOTE:** Resumes can be submitted by mail or fax, or on the General Electric careers website: http://www.gecareers.com. **Positions advertised include:** Producer; Station Production Manager; Account Manager. **Special programs:** Internships available.

WACHOVIA BANK
740 15th Street NW, Washington DC 20005. 202/637-7652. **Toll-free phone:** 800/398-3862. **Contact:** Personnel Department. **E-mail address:** jobs@firstunion.com. **World Wide Web address:** http://www.wachovia.com. **Description:** Formerly known as First Union National Bank of Washington DC. First Union merged with Wachovia in 2002. Bank branches are being converted on an area-by-area basis. **Parent company:** Wachovia Corporation. **Listed on:** New York Stock Exchange. **Stock exchange symbol:** WB. **Number of employees nationwide:** 32,000.

WASHINGTON HILTON AND TOWERS
1919 Connecticut Avenue NW, Washington DC 20009. 202/483-3000. **Contact:** Robin Sterrett, Director of Human Resources. **World Wide Web address:** http://www.hilton.com. **Description:** Operates a hotel with over 1,000 rooms and extensive meeting and function space. The hotel features complete dining and lounge facilities. **Corporate headquarters location:** Beverly Hills CA. **Parent company:** Hilton Hotels Corporation. **Listed on:** New York Stock Exchange. **Stock exchange symbol:** HLT. **Number of employees nationwide:** 40,000.

WASHINGTON HOSPITAL CENTER
110 Irving Street NW, Washington DC 20010-2975. 202/877-7441. **Contact:** Human Resources. **World Wide Web address:** http://www.whcenter.org. **Description:** A nonprofit hospital. Washington Heart at Washington Hospital annually performs almost 1,700 heart operations and more than 10,000 cardiac catheterization procedures. The Washington Cancer Institute provides cancer care including surgery, radiation and chemotherapy treatments, counseling, education, and community outreach. Washington Hospital Center is the home of the MedSTAR trauma unit, whose two helicopters transport more than 3,000 critically ill and injured patients each year. The center also consists of The Institute for Asthma & Allergy, a burn center, women's services, and the Washington National Eye Center. **Positions advertised include:** Anesthesiologist Assistant; Bill Audit Representative; Blood Donor Service Technician; Certified Surgical Technician; Clinical Manager; Clinical Nurse; Evening Pharmacist; Linen Supply Assistant; Material Handler; Medical Social Worker; Radiation Therapist; RN; Technical Specialist. **Parent company:** Medlantic Healthcare Group (also at this location.) **Number of employees at this location:** 5,100.

WASHINGTON PLAZA HOTEL
10 Thomas Circle NW, Massachusetts Avenue 14th Street, Washington DC 20005. 202/842-1300. **Contact:** Human Resources. **World Wide Web address:** http://www.washingtonplazahotel.com. **Description:** A 340-hotel and meeting facility catering to business travelers.

THE WASHINGTON POST COMPANY
1150 15th Street NW, Washington DC 20071. 202/334-7174. **Contact:** Cheryl Butler or Judy Havemann, Newsroom Personnel. **E-mail address:** postings@ washpost.com. **World Wide Web address:** http://www.washpostco.com. **Description:** Publishes the *Washington Post*; the *Herald* (Everett WA); *Gazette* (MD); and *Newsweek*. The company also owns cable television stations as well as television broadcasting stations in Detroit, Hartford, Houston, Jacksonville, Miami, and San Antonio. **NOTE:** For copy aide and dictationist positions, address inquiries to: Sandy Davis, Copy Aide Supervisor. **Corporate headquarters location:** This location. **Subsidiaries include:** Stanley H. Kaplan operates a regulatory computerized database. **Listed on:** New York Stock Exchange. **Stock exchange symbol:** WPO. **Number of employees nationwide:** 6,800.

THE WASHINGTON TIMES
3600 New York Avenue NE, Washington DC 20002. 202/636-3000. **Contact:** Human Resources Department. **World Wide Web address:** http://www. washtimes.com. **NOTE:** For writer, reporter, editor, and internship positions please send a resume and clips to: Ken McIntyre, Assistant Manager Editor. **Description:** A daily metropolitan newspaper. **Positions advertised include:** Telephone Sales Executive; Advertising Sales Assistant; Display Advertising Account Executive. **Special programs:** Internships. **Internship information:** The Washington Times offers an annual summer internship, primarily for college students. See the company's website for more details. **Corporate headquarters location:** This location. **Other U.S. locations:** Lanham MD. **Operations at this facility include:** Administration; Manufacturing; Regional Headquarters; Research and Development; Sales; Service. **Number of employees at this location:** 800. **Number of employees nationwide:** 900.

WASHINGTONIAN MAGAZINE
1828 L Street NW, Suite 200, Washington DC 20036. 202/296-3600. **Fax:** 202/862-3526. **Contact:** Editor. **World Wide Web address:** http://www. washingtonian.com. **Description:** A general interest magazine about Washington DC. **Special programs:** Internships available. **Internship information:** Washingtonian Magazine offers seasonal internships in the following departments: Editorial, Advertising, and Art. See website for important information on how to apply. **Annual sales/revenues:** $5 - $10 million.

WESTLAKE CONSULTING GROUP
529 14th Street NW, Suite 545, Washington DC 20045. 202/783-1100. **Toll-free phone:** 888/340-9524. **Fax:** 202/393-7727. **Contact:** Human Resources. **E-mail address:** jobs@wlcg.com. **World Wide Web address:** http://www.wlcg.com. **Description:** An Internet business and strategy consultancy.

WILEY REIN & FIELDING
1776 K Street NW, Washington DC 20006. 202/719-7000. **Fax:** 202/719-7049. **Contact:** Irena McGrath. **E-mail Address:** wrfrecruit@wrf.com. **World Wide Web Address:** http://www.wrf.com. **Description:** Wiley Rein & Fielding is a leading national law firm. **Positions Advertised Include:** Litigation Legal Assistant; Business Systems Analyst; Technical Services Analyst; Administrative Evening Manager.

WILMER CUTLER & PICKERING
2445 M Street NW, Washington DC 20037. 202/663-6000. **Fax:** 202/663-6363. **Contact:** Human Resources. **World Wide Web address:** http://www.wilmer.com. **Description:** A law firm specializing in international and corporate law. **Positions advertised include:** Bankruptcy Associate; Communications Associate; Corporate Finance Associate; Litigation Associate; Securities Associate. **Special programs:** Summer Associates Program.

XM SATELLITE RADIO
1500 Eckington Place NE, Washington DC 20002. 202/380-4000. **Fax:** 202/380-4500. **Contact:** Human Resources. **E-mail address:** jobs@xmradio.com. **World Wide Web address:** http://www.xmradio.com. **Description:** XM is one of two FCC licensees to deliver satellite radio programming. **NOTE:** Applications may be submitted at Website. **Positions advertised include:** Senior Analyst, QA; Senior Staff Accountant; Assistant Controller; Manager, OEM Marketing.

A-1 COMPONENTS, INC.
625 West 18th Street, Hialeah FL 33010. 305/885-1911. **Toll-free phone:** 800/759-2872. **Fax:** 305/884-1847. **Toll-free fax:** 800/759-9299. **Contact:** Human Resources. **E-mail address:** salessupport@a-1components.com. **World Wide Web address:** http://www.a-1components.com. **Description:** Develops, manufactures, and distributes a wide range of climate control products and related equipment. The company's products include electronics controls, timers, and start kits; mechanical valves, fittings, tubing, and driers; pressure switches and temperature control devices; cam-stat controls; chemicals; thermostat guards; capacitors; relays; transformers; and motors. **Corporate headquarters location:** This location. **Operations at this facility include:** Administration; Manufacturing; Regional Headquarters; Research and Development; Sales; Service. **Number of employees at this location:** 300.

AAA (AMERICAN AUTOMOBILE ASSOCIATION)
1000 AAA Drive, Mailstop 28, Heathrow FL 32746-5063. 407/444-7537. **Fax:** 407/444-7504. **Contact:** Human Resources. **World Wide Web address:** http://www.aaasouth.com. **Description:** A nonprofit organization that provides insurance, travel services, and related benefits to its members. **Corporate headquarters location:** This location. **Other U.S. locations:** Nationwide. **Number of employees at this location:** 1,100. **Number of employees nationwide:** 3,700.

ABC FINE WINE & SPIRITS
P.O. Box 593688, Orlando FL 32859. 407/851-0000. **Fax:** 407/857-5500. **Physical address:** 8989 South Orange Avenue, Orlando FL 32824. **Contact:** Human Resources. **E-mail address:** resumes@abcfws.com. **World Wide Web address:** http://www.abcfinewineandspirits.com. **Description:** A privately-owned retailer of cigars, fine wine, gourmet food, and liquor. ABC Fine Wine & Spirits operates over 150 stores throughout Florida. Founded in 1936. **Positions advertised include:** Sales Manager; Assistant Manager; Clerk.

ABC RESEARCH CORPORATION
3437 SW 24th Avenue, Gainesville FL 32607. 352/372-0436. **Fax:** 352/378-6483. **Contact:** Human Resources. **World Wide Web address:** http://www.abcr.com. **Description:** A laboratory specializing in food and water analysis. **Positions advertised include:** PhD Food Safety Microbiologist; Food Safety Auditor; Quality Assessment Product Manager.

ACR ELECTRONICS
5757 Ravenswood Road, Fort Lauderdale FL 33312. 954/981-3333. **Contact:** Human Resources. **World Wide Web address:** http://www.acrelectronics.com. **Description:** Manufactures survival and safety electronics equipment for the government, marine, and outdoor recreation markets.

ADAMS MARK HOTEL
225 Coast Line Drive East, Jacksonville FL 32202. 904/633-9095.**Fax:** 904/634-4566. **Contact:** Teri Borowski. **E-mail address:** tborowski@adamsmedia.com. **World Wide Web address:** http://www.adamsmark.com. **Description:** A hotel, convention, and meeting facility. **Positions advertised include:** Assistant Executive Steward; Assistant Restaurant Manager; Catering Sales Manager; Convention Services Manager; Sales Manager. **Other U.S. locations include:** Nationwide.

ADP TOTAL SOURCE
10200 Sunset Drive, Miami FL 33173. 561/615-7478. **Toll-free phone:** 800/447-3237. **Contact:** Personnel. **World Wide Web address:** http://www.adptotalsource.com. **Description:** Provides benefits, payroll, and related human resources services. **Positions advertised include:** Human Resource Manager; Client Account Representative; 401K Conversion Manager; Human Resource Consultant; Time & Attendance Implementation Manager; Administrative Assistant Executive.

AFGD, INC.
6600 Suemac Place, Jacksonville FL 32254. 904/786-6611. **Fax:** 904/781-9779. **Contact:** Stan Mesnik, Branch Manager. **World Wide Web address:** http://www.afgd.com. **Description:** Manufactures architectural insulated glass units and specializes in custom tempering. AFGD manufactures a complete line of insulated glass units for commercial and residential applications. Products include clear, tint, and reflective glass; wire glass; and equipment for the handling, storage, and transportation of glass. **Positions advertised include:** Inside Sales Representative. **Corporate headquarters location:** Atlanta GA. **Other U.S. locations:** Nationwide. **Subsidiaries include:** AFGD Canada. **Parent company:** AFG Industries, Inc. **Operations at this facility include:** Manufacturing; Sales. **Number of employees at this location:** 75. **Number of employees nationwide:** 1,000.

AJT & ASSOCIATES, INC.
8910 Astronaut Boulevard, Cape Canaveral FL 32920-4225. 321/783-7989. **Contact:** Karen Yorio, Human Resources Representative. **E-mail address:** kareny@ajt-assoc.com. **World Wide Web address:** http://www.ajt-assoc.com. **Description:** Provides environmental science and architectural engineering services.

ATC ASSOCIATES
9955 NW 116 Way, Suite 1, Miami FL 33178. 305/882-8200. **Fax:** 305/882-1200. **Contact:** Human Resources. **World Wide Web address:** http://www.atc-enviro.com. **Description:** Performs comprehensive environmental consulting, engineering, and on-site remediation services. Services include assessment of environmental regulations, investigation of contaminated sites, and the design and engineering of methods to correct or prevent the contamination. The company also performs remedial actions, and emergency response actions in cases of spills and accidental releases of hazardous waste. ATC Associates addresses hazardous and nonhazardous contaminants in municipal and industrial water supplies; in wastewater and storm water from municipal, industrial, and military installations; and in groundwater, soils, and air space. Customers include federal, state, and local government agencies. **Positions advertised include:** NDT Technician.

ATK INTEGRATED DEFENSE COMPANY
P.O. Box 4648, Clearwater FL 33758-4648. 727/572-1900. **Fax:** 727/572-2453. **Contact:** Human Resources. **E-mail address:** resume.clearwater@atk.com. **World Wide Web address:** http://www.atk.com. **Description:** An electronics testing center and manufacturing facility. **Corporate headquarters location:** Minneapolis MN. **Other U.S. locations:** Patuxent River MD; Eatontown NJ; San Antonio TX. **Parent company:** Alliant Techsystems. **Listed on:** New York Stock Exchange. **Stock exchange symbol:** ATK.

A.W. INDUSTRIES
6788 NW 17th Avenue, Fort Lauderdale FL 33309. 954/979-5696. **Fax:** 954/979-5764. **Contact:** Human Resources. **World Wide Web address:** http://www.awiconnectors.com. **Description:** Designs and manufactures electronic circuits.

ADD INC. PUBLICATIONS
1560 Kingsley Avenue, Suite 1, Orange Park FL 32073. 904/264-3200. **Fax:** 904/264-3285. **Contact:** Beth Plotner, Human Resources Department. **Description:** Publishes four local newspapers including *Jacksonville Shopping Guide* and *Clay Today*. **NOTE:** Entry-level positions are offered. **Special programs:** Internships. **Corporate headquarters location:** Waupaca WI. **Other U.S. locations:** Nationwide. **Publisher:** Joyce Lyndon. **Facilities Manager:** Tim Kult. **Annual sales/revenues:** Less than $5 million. **Number of employees at this location:** 50.

ADVANTAGE FIRE PROTECTION INC.
2750 Taylor Avenue, Orlando FL 32806. 407/855-9917. **Fax:** 407/855-9927. **Contact:** Chris Lorton. **E-mail address:** clorton@afirepro.com. **World Wide Web address:** http://www.afirepro.com. **Description:** Manufactures and installs fire protection and sprinkler systems. Founded in 1993. **Positions advertised include:** Fire Sprinkler Industry Professional. **President:** John J. Heffernan Jr.

AEROSONIC CORPORATION
1212 North Hercules Avenue, Clearwater FL 33765. 727/461-3000. **Fax:** 727/447-5926. **Contact:** Personnel. **World Wide Web address:** http://www.aerosonic.com. **Description:** Manufactures mechanical and microprocessor-based aircraft instruments. **Corporate headquarters location:** This location. **Other U.S. locations:** Wichita KS; Charlottesville VA. **Listed on:** American Stock Exchange. **Stock exchange symbol:** AIM. **Annual sales/revenues:** $5 - $10 million. **Number of employees at this location:** 140. **Number of employees nationwide:** 250.

AEROTRON-REPCO SYSTEMS, INC.
4602 Parkway Commerce Boulevard, Orlando FL 32808. 407/856-1953. **Toll-free phone:** 800/950-5633. **Fax:** 407/856-1960. **Contact:** Ted McDonald, Personnel Manager. **World Wide Web address:** http://www.aerotron-repco.com. **Description:** A manufacturer of communications equipment including wireless modems and hand-held radios. **Corporate headquarters location:** This location. **Listed on:** Privately held. **Number of employees at this location:** 55.

ALAMO RENT-A-CAR
200 South Andrews Avenue, Fort Lauderdale FL 33305. 954/320-4400. **Toll-free phone:** 800/462-5266. **Contact:** Human Resources. **World Wide Web address:** http://www.alamo.com. **Description:** One of the nation's leading car rental companies. **Corporate headquarters location:** This location. **Operations at this facility include:** Administration. **Listed on:** Privately held.

ALLEN SYSTEMS GROUP INC.
1333 Third Avenue South, Naples FL 34102. 941/263-6700. **Contact:** Human Resources. **World Wide Web address:** http://www.allensysgroup.com. **Description:** Supplies *Fortune* 1000 companies with system management, file transfer, and help desk software. **Positions advertised include:** Analyst Relations Manager; Accounts Payable Manager; Accounts Receivable Manager; Staff Accountant; Staff Attorney. **Corporate headquarters location:** This location.

ALLIANCE ENTERTAINMENT CORPORATION
4250 Coral Ridge Drive, Coral Springs FL 33065. 800/635-9082. **Fax:** 954/340-7641. **Contact:** Human Resources. **World Wide Web address:** http://www.aent.com. **Description:** Alliance Entertainment operates in two segments of the entertainment industry: the sale and distribution of prerecorded music and related products, and the acquisition and exploration of proprietary rights to recorded music, video, television, CD-ROMs, and books. **Positions advertised include:** Movie Editor; Programmer; Staff Writer. **Corporate headquarters location:** This location.

ALLIED VAUGHN
4364 35th Street, Orlando FL 32811-6502. 407/649-0008. **Toll-free phone:** 877/238-8035. **Fax:** 407/649-9005. **Contact:** Personnel. **World Wide Web address:** http://www.alliedvaughn.com. **Description:** One of the nation's leading independent multimedia manufacturing companies, offering CD-audio and CD-ROM mastering and replication; videocassette and audiocassette duplication; off-line and online video editing; motion picture film processing; film-to-tape and tape-to-film transfers; and complete finishing, packaging, warehousing, and fulfillment services. **NOTE:** When sending resumes, please specify the department to which you are applying.

ALPINE ENGINEERED PRODUCTS, INC.
P.O. Box 2225, Pompano Beach FL 33061. 954/781-3333. **Fax:** 954/784-7694. **Contact:** Human Resources. **World Wide Web address:** http://www.alpeng.com. **Description:** A manufacturer of metal connector plates for floors and roofs. Alpine Engineered Products also manufactures wood-handling equipment and saws. **Parent company:** Dorbyl Ltd. (Johannesburg, South Africa).

ALTERMAN TRANSPORT LINES
12805 NW 42nd Avenue, Opa-Locka FL 33054. 305/688-3571. **Contact:** Human Resources. **World Wide Web address:** http://www.alterman.com. **Description:** An interstate trucking company that specializes in the transport of perishable goods.

ALUMA SYSTEMS
6402 East Hanna Avenue, Tampa FL 33610. 813/626-1133. **Toll-free phone:** 800/282-9199. **Contact:** Personnel. **E-mail address:** dtweedy@aluma.com. **World Wide Web address:** http://www.aluma.com. **Description:** Supplies forming, shoring, and scaffolding products to the industrial maintenance and concrete construction industries. **Operations at this facility include:** Sales. **President/CEO:** Jim Demitrieus.

AMERICA II CORP., INC.
2600 118th Avenue North, St. Petersburg FL 33716. 727/573-0900. **Contact:** Human Resources. **E-mail address:** jobs@americaii.com. **World Wide Web address:** http://www.americaII.com. **Description:** An electronic component distributor. **Positions advertised include:** PHP Developer; Staff Accountant.

AMERICAN CANCER SOCIETY
3901 NW 79th Avenue, Suite 224, Miami FL 33166. 305/594-4363. **Contact:** Human Resources. **World Wide Web address:** http://www.cancer.org. **Description:** A nationwide, community-based, nonprofit, voluntary health organization dedicated to eliminating cancer as a major health problem by funding cancer research and public education. The society helps patients directly by offering services including transportation to treatment and rehabilitation services. **Positions advertised include:** Community Representative.

AMERICAN MEDIA, INC.
5401 NW Broken Sound Boulevard, Boca Raton FL 33487. 561/997-7733. **Contact:** Human Resources. **Description:** Publishes tabloid newspapers including the *National Enquirer, Star, Weekly World News, Country Weekly,* and *Soap Opera Magazine,* with an aggregate weekly circulation of approximately 7 million. **Corporate headquarters location:** This location. **Subsidiaries include:** Distribution Services, Inc. arranges for

the placement of its periodicals in approximately 180,000 locations in North America. **Annual sales/revenues:** More than $100 million.

AMERICAN RED CROSS
2018 Lewis Turner Boulevard, Fort Walton FL 32547. 850/314-0316. **Contact:** Manager. **World Wide Web address:** http://www.redcross.org. **Description:** A humanitarian organization that aids disaster victims, gathers blood for crisis distribution, trains individuals to respond to emergencies, educates individuals on various diseases, and raises funds for other charitable establishments. **NOTE:** http://northwestflorida.redcross.org is the Red Cross's NW Florida Chapter Web Site. **Corporate headquarters location:** Washington DC. **Other U.S. locations:** Nationwide.

AMERICAN RIBBON & TONER COMPANY
2895 West Prospect Road, Fort Lauderdale FL 33309. 954/733-4552. **Fax:** 954/733-0319. **Contact:** Personnel. **E-mail address:** info@ribbontoner.com. **World Wide Web address:** http://www.ribbontoner.com. **Description:** Manufactures ribbons and toner cartridges for printers, fax machines, and copiers.

AMERICAN WOOLEN COMPANY
P.O. Box 521399, Miami FL 33152-1399. 305/635-4000. **Physical address:** 4000 NW 30th Avenue, Miami FL 33142. **Fax:** 305/633-4997. **Contact:** Richard Marcus, President. **Description:** Manufactures blankets.

AMSOUTH BANK
70 North Baylen Street, Pensacola FL 32501. 850/444-1234. **Contact:** Sharon Hensel, Personnel. **World Wide Web address:** http://www.amsouth.com. **Description:** A commercial bank. **Positions advertised include:** Assistant Branch Manager; Branch Manager; Financial Services Associate; Head Teller; Private Banker; Registered Principal; Teller Specialist. Head Teller; Teller. **Corporate headquarters location:** Birmingham AL. **Other U.S. locations:** GA; TN.

ANALYSTS INTERNATIONAL CORPORATION (AIC)
3835 NW Boca Raton Boulevard, Suite 300C, Boca Raton FL 33431. 561/750-8588. **Contact:** Human Resources. **E-mail address:** bocajobs@analysts.com. **World Wide Web address:** http://www.analysts.com. **Description:** AIC is an international computer consulting firm. The company uses different programming languages and software to assist clients in developing systems for a variety of industries. **Corporate headquarters location:** Minneapolis MN.

ANALYSTS INTERNATIONAL CORPORATION (AIC)
550 North Reo Street, Suite 300, Tampa FL 33609. 813/261-5132. **Fax:** 813/261-5162. **Contact:** Human Resources. **E-mail address:** tampajobs@analysts.com **World Wide Web address:** http://www.analysts.com. **Description:** AIC is an international computer consulting firm. The company uses different programming languages and software to assist clients in developing systems for a variety of industries. **Corporate headquarters location:** Minneapolis MN.

ANCHOR GLASS CONTAINER CORPORATION
4343 Anchor Plaza Parkway, Tampa FL 33634. 813/884-0000. **Contact:** Human Resources. **World Wide Web address:** http://www.anchorglass.com. **Description:** Manufactures glassware, commercial and institutional chinaware, decorative and convenience hardware, glass containers, and metal and plastic closures. Operations encompass over 20 divisions and subsidiaries, with 40 plants and distribution centers worldwide. **Corporate headquarters location:** This location. **Other area locations:** Jacksonville FL.

ANCHOR GLASS CONTAINER CORPORATION
2121 Huron Street, Jacksonville FL 32254. 904/786-1010. **Contact:** Human Resources. **Description:** Manufactures glassware, commercial and institutional chinaware, decorative and convenience hardware, glass containers, and metal and plastic closures. Operations encompass over 20 divisions and subsidiaries, with 40 plants and distribution centers worldwide. **Corporate headquarters location:** Tampa FL. **Number of employees nationwide:** 6,900.

ANSWERTHINK CONSULTING GROUP
1001 Brickell Bay Drive, Suite 3000, Miami FL 33131. 305/375-8005. **Fax:** 305/379-8810. **Contact:** Human Resources. **E-mail address:** careers@answerthink.com. **World Wide Web address:** http://www.answerthink.com. **Description:** Provides computer consulting and IT services to *Fortune* 1000 companies. **Positions advertised include:** Consultant; Manager. **Corporate headquarters location:** Atlanta GA. **Other U.S. locations:** Fremont CA; Chicago IL; Burlington MA; Iselin NJ; Marlton NJ; New York NY; Hudson OH; Conshohocken PA; Dallas TX. **Listed on:** NASDAQ. **Stock exchange symbol:** ANSR.

APAC INC.
14299 Alico Road, Fort Myers FL 33913. 941/267-7767. **Contact:** Ms Elaine Paserella, Personnel Manager. **World Wide Web address:** http://www.apac.com. **Description:** APAC provides materials, services, and technology to the construction industry. **Positions advertised include:** Project Manager.

APAC INC.
4375 McCoy Drive, Pensacola FL 32503. 850/433-3001. **Contact:** Human Resources. **World Wide Web address:** http://www.apac.com. **Description:** A contractor specializing in road construction. **Positions advertised include:** Staff Accountant; Administrative Assistant.

APAC INC.
P.O. Box 2579, Sarasota FL 34230. 941/355-7178. **Contact:** Human Resources. **World Wide Web address:** http://www.apac.com. **Description:** A manufacturer of asphalt. **Positions advertised include:** Operations Manager.

APALACHICOLA TIMES
P.O. Drawer 820, Apalachicola FL 32329. 850/653-8863. **Physical address:** 82 Market Street, Apalachicola FL 32329. **Contact:** Human Resources. **World Wide Web address:** http://www.apalachtimes.com. **Description:** Oldest Area Newspaper. **Office Hours:** Monday – Friday 8:00 a.m. - 5:00 p.m.

APPLICA INCORPORATED
5980 Miami Lakes Drive East, Miami Lakes FL 33014. 305/362-2611. **Contact:** Dave Warren, Director of Human Resources. **E-mail address:** applicahr@applicamail.com. **World Wide Web address:** http://www.applicainc.com. **Description:** Manufactures small beauty appliances including hair dryers and curling irons. **Listed on:** NASDAQ. **Stock exchange symbol:** APN.

APPLIEDLOGX
1200 West Cass Street, Suite 150, Tampa FL 33606. 813/901-9728. **Fax:** 813/901-9709. **Contact:** Human Resources. **E-mail address:** info@appliedlogx.com. **World Wide Web address:** http://www.appliedlogx.com. **Description:** appliedlogx provides communication infrastructure engineering, procurement and installation services.

APRIA HEALTHCARE GROUP INC.
8509 Benjamin Road, Tampa FL 33634. 813/886-6228. **Contact:** Human Resources. **World Wide Web address:** http://www.apria.com. **Description:** One of the largest national providers of home health care products and services including a broad range of respiratory therapy services, home medical equipment, and infusion therapy services. Apria has over 400 branches throughout the United States and two respiratory therapy branches in the United Kingdom. In conjunction with medical professionals, Apria personnel deliver, install, and service medical equipment, as well as provide appropriate therapies and coordinate plans of care for their patients. Apria personnel also instruct patients and caregivers in the correct use of equipment and monitor the equipment's effectiveness. **Positions advertised include:** Collections Representative; Suspended Billing Representative; Cleaning Technician; Respiratory Therapist; Logistics Coordinator; Customer Service Representative; Delivery Technician; Patient Service Technician; Account Executive; Marketing Manager. **Corporate headquarters location:** Costa Mesa CA. **Listed on:** New York Stock Exchange. **Stock exchange symbol:** AHG.

ARAMARK CORPORATION
1301 Riverplace Boulevard, Suite C-20, Jacksonville FL 32207. 904/396-5037. **Contact:** Human Resources. **World Wide Web address:** http://www.aramark.com. **Description:** ARAMARK is one of the world's leading providers of managed services. The company operates in all 50 states and 10 foreign countries, offering a broad range of services to businesses of all sizes including many *Fortune* 500 companies and thousands of universities, hospitals, and municipal, state, and federal government facilities. ARAMARK's businesses include Food, Leisure, and Support Services including Campus Dining Services, School Nutrition Services, Leisure Services, Business Dining Services, International Services, Healthcare Support Services, Conference Center Management, and Refreshment Services; Facility Services; Correctional Services; Industrial Services; Uniform Services, which includes Wearguard, a direct marketer of work clothing; Health and Education Services including Spectrum Healthcare Services and Children's World Learning Centers; and Book and Magazine Services. **Positions advertised include:** Training Manager; District Management Trainee; Accounts Manager. **Operations at this facility include:** This location is a cafeteria. **Corporate headquarters location:** Philadelphia PA. **Number of employees nationwide:** 150,000. **Listed on:** New York Stock Exchange. **Stock exchange symbol:** RMG.

ARIZONA CHEMICAL
P.O. Box 947, 345 Kenney Mill Road, Port St. Joe FL 32456. 850/229-8271. **Contact:** Human Resources. **E-mail address:** info.arizona@paper.com. **World Wide Web address:** http://www.arizonachemical.com. **Description:** Produces chemical products by upgrading raw materials purchased from paper manufacturing companies. Arizona Chemical's products are used by other companies to manufacture glue, gum, perfume, and coatings. **NOTE:** Interested jobseekers should send resumes to ArizonaChem, Human Resources Department, P.O. Box 59447, Panama City FL 32412-0447. **Corporate headquarters location:** Jacksonville FL.

ARMOR HOLDINGS, INC.
1400 Marsh Landing Parkway #112, Jacksonville FL 32218. 904/741-5400. **Contact:** Human Resources. **World Wide Web address:** http://www.armorholdings.com. **Description:** Develops, manufactures, and markets security products including body armor to corporate and government clients worldwide. Armor Holdings, Inc. also provides security solutions such as risk analysis and electronic surveillance. **Corporate headquarters location:** This location. **Other U.S. locations:** Nationwide. **International locations:** Worldwide. **Listed on:** New York Stock Exchange. **Stock exchange symbol:** AH. **Annual sales/revenues:** More than $100 million.

ARROW AIR, INC.
P.O. Box 523726, Miami FL 33152. 305/871-3116. **Physical address:** 2000 NW 62nd Avenue, Miami FL 33122. **Toll-free phone:** 800/871-3370. **Fax:** 305/526-0933. **Contact:** Human Resources. **World Wide Web address:** http://www.arrowair.com. **Description:** An all-cargo air carrier service that serves the North and South American continents.

ARTESYN TECHNOLOGIES
7900 Glades Road, Suite 500, Boca Raton FL 33434. 561/451-1000. **Fax:** 561/451-1050. **Contact:** Personnel. **E-mail address:** jobs@artseyn.com. **World Wide Web address:** http://www.artesyn.com. **Description:** A designer and producer of electronic products and subsystems. The company manufactures both standard and custom products used in an array of applications including powering communications networks, controlling the manufacture of fiber optics, enabling voice messaging, powering multimedia applications for global Internet servers, and operating traffic signals with real-time embedded computers. The company consists of three business segments: Power Conversion supplies power systems technology to the communications industry; RTP Corporation delivers input/output products and intelligent controllers; and Heurikon Corporation designs and provides real-time computers and subsystems tailored to the markets of voice messaging, graphics, video-on-demand, machine vision, and simulation. **Positions advertised include:** Software Design Engineer. **Other U.S. locations:** Fremont CA; Pompano Beach FL; Boston MA; Madison WI. **Listed on:** NASDAQ. **Stock exchange symbol:** ATSN. **Number of employees nationwide:** 1,600.

ASHLEY ALUMINUM, LLC
dba CAMERON ASHLEY BUILDING PRODUCTS
P.O. Drawer 15398, Tampa FL 33684. 813/884-0444. **Toll-free phone:** 800/749-4067. **Contact:** Human Resources. **World Wide Web address:** http://www.cabp.com. **Description:** A manufacturer and distributor of aluminum and vinyl building products. Founded in 1967. **Office hours:** Monday - Friday, 8:00 a.m. - 5:00 p.m. **Corporate headquarters location:** This location. **Other U.S. locations:** AL; GA; KY; LA; TX. **Listed on:** New York Stock Exchange. **Stock exchange symbol:** CAB. **President:** Steve Gaffney. **Annual sales/revenues:** More than $100 million. **Number of employees at this location:** 100. **Number of employees nationwide:** 500.

ASO CORPORATION
300 Sarasota Center Boulevard, Sarasota FL 34240. 941/379-0300. **Fax:** 941/554-1434. **Contact:** Human Resources. **E-mail address:** careers@asocorp.com. **World Wide Web address:** http://www.asocorp.com. **Description:** A manufacturer and distributor of wound care products. **NOTE:** Second and third shifts are offered. **Positions advertised include:** Maintenance Mechanic. **Corporate headquarters location:** This location. **Subsidiaries include:** Aso Pharmaceutical Co., Ltd. (Kumamoto, Japan); Aso

Seiyaku Philippines, Inc. (Cebu, Philippines); Texas Aso Corporation (El Paso TX). **Parent company:** Aso International. **Listed on:** Privately held. **Number of employees at this location:** 100.

ASSURANT GROUP
11222 Quail Roost Drive, Miami FL 33157. 305/253-2244. **Contact:** Human Resources. **World Wide Web address:** http://www.assurant.com. **Description:** A holding company. Through its major subsidiaries, the company sells unemployment, accident, health, credit card, mortgage, and homeowners insurance. **Corporate headquarters location:** This location. **Number of employees at this location:** 2,100.

ATLANTIC COAST MANAGEMENT
P.O. Box 2066, Winter Park FL 32790. 407/647-4300. **Fax:** 407/647-5306. **Contact:** Joe Hayes, Vice President of Human Resources. **Description:** A restaurant management company. **Positions advertised include:** Management Trainee. **Corporate headquarters location:** This location. **Listed on:** Privately held.

ATLANTIC MARINE, INC.
ATLANTIC DRY DOCK CORPORATION
8500 Heckscher Drive, Jacksonville FL 32226. 904/251-3164. **Fax:** 904/251-1579. **Contact:** Human Resources. **World Wide Web address:** http://www.atlanticmarine.com. **E-mail address:** jaxresumes@atlanticmarine.com. **Description:** Builds, repairs, and converts ships for government, commercial, and consumer markets.

AT&T GOVERNMENT SOLUTIONS
1980 North Atlantic Avenue, Suite 1030, Cocoa Beach FL 32931. 321/784-4030. **Fax:** 321/784-2009. **Contact:** Human Resources Department. **World Wide Web address:** http://www.att.com. **Description:** This division of AT&T creates large-scale, decision-support systems and software engineering environments; applies operations research and mathematical modeling to business and management systems; and implements advanced database technology. AT&T also provides studies and analysis capabilities for policy development and planning; modeling and simulation of hardware and software used in real-time testing of sensor, weapon, and battlefield management command, control, and communication systems; and testing and evaluation. AT&T's services are offered primarily to government and commercial customers. **Other U.S. locations:** Nationwide. **Operations at this facility include:** This location provides technical services and systems engineering.

AUTONATION INC.
P.O. Box 029030, Fort Lauderdale FL 33302. 954/769-6000. **Physical address:** 110 SE Sixth Street, Fort Lauderdale FL 33301. **Contact:** Human Resources. **World Wide Web address:** http://www.autonation.com. **Description:** Sells, finances, and services new and used vehicles. The company also provides aftermarket automotive products, collision repair services, parts and accessories, and extended warranties. **Positions advertised include:** Audit Services Manager. **Corporate headquarters location:** This location. **Listed on:** New York Stock Exchange. **Stock exchange symbol:** AN.

AVATAR HOLDINGS INC.
201 Alhambra Circle, 12th Floor, Coral Gables FL 33134. 305/442-7000. **Contact:** Human Resources, Juanita Kerrigan **E-mail address:** juanita.kerrigan@avatarholdings.com. **World Wide Web address:** http://www.avatarhomes.com. **Description:** A real estate company that develops residential, resort, and recreational properties. **Listed on:** NASDAQ. **Stock exchange symbol:** AVTR.

AVINEON
15500 Light Wave Drive, Suite 200, Clearwater FL 33760. 727/539-1661. **Fax:** 727/539-0954. **Contact:** Human Resources. **World Wide Web address:** http://www.avineon.com. **Description:** Provides automated mapping, facility management, and geographic information system technologies to government and industries worldwide. **Note:** Formerly Agra Baymont. **Other U.S. locations:** Nationwide. **International locations:** Worldwide.

AVIONYX, INC.
1918 Dairy Road, West Melbourne FL 32904. 321/728-7975. **Toll-free phone:** 800/636-2833. **Fax:** 321/728-4049. **Contact:** Human Resources. **E-mail address:** jobs@avionyx.com. **World Wide Web address:** http://www.avionyx.com. **Description:** Provides full life cycle embedded software engineering services for commercial avionics systems requiring stringent development and testing standards such as DO-178B. **Positions advertised include:** Junior Software Test Engineer; IT Manager/Tech Support; Senior Software Engineer/Manager; Software/Hardware Project/Program Manager; Software Quality Engineer.

B&B CORPORATE HOLDINGS, INC.
P.O. Box 1808, Tampa FL 33601. 813/621-6411. **Contact:** Linda Toledo, Director of Human Resources. **World Wide Web address:** http://www.bnbch.com. **Description:** Operates a chain of supermarkets and convenience stores under the USave name. Founded in 1923. **Positions advertised include:** Meat Cutter; Produce Clerk; Management Trainee. **Corporate headquarters location:** This location. **Subsidiaries include:** U-Save Supermarkets. **Operations at this facility include:** Administration.

B/E AEROSPACE, INC.
1400 Corporate Center Way, Wellington FL 33414. 561/791-5000. **Fax:** 561/791-7900. **Contact:** Joseph A. Piegari, Vice President of Human Resources. **World Wide Web address:** http://www.beaerospace.com. **Description:** Designs, manufactures, sells, and supports a wide range of commercial aircraft cabin interior products including seats, passenger entertainment and service systems, lighting products, oxygen products, and galley structures and inserts. The company supplies commercial airlines and airframe manufacturers. **Positions advertised include:** Purchasing Manager; Account Manager; Cost Control Manager. **Special programs:** Internships. **Corporate headquarters location:** This location. **Other U.S. locations:** Nationwide. **International locations:** England; Singapore; Wales. **Subsidiaries include:** Aerospace Lighting Corporation; Aircraft Modular Products; Puritan-Bennett Aero Systems; SMR Aerospace; Sextant In-Flight Systems; C.F. Taylor. **Operations at this facility include:** Administration; Sales. **Listed on:** NASDAQ. **Stock exchange symbol:** BEAV. **CEO:** Robert J. Khoury. **Annual sales/revenues:** More than $100 million. **Number of employees at this location:** 30.

B/E AEROSPACE, INC.
11710 Central Parkway, Jacksonville FL 32224-7626. 904/996-3800. **Fax:** 904/996-3838. **Contact:** Julie Crosby, Human Resources Manager. **World Wide Web address:** http://www.beaerospace.com. **Description:** B/E Aerospace, Inc. designs, manufactures, sells, and supports a wide range of commercial aircraft cabin interior products including seating products, passenger entertainment and service systems, and galley structures and inserts. The company supplies major airlines and airframe manufacturers. Founded in 1965. **NOTE:** Entry-level positions and second and third shifts are offered. **Positions advertised include:** Purchasing Manager; Account Manager; Cost Control Manager. **Special programs:** Internships; Training. **Corporate headquarters location:** Wellington FL. **Other U.S. locations:** Nationwide. **International locations:** England; Singapore; Wales. **Operations at this facility include:** This location manufactures flight galleys. **Listed on:** NASDAQ. **Stock exchange symbol:** BEAV. **Annual sales/revenues:** More than $100 million. **Number of employees at this location:** 310.

B/E AEROSPACE, INC.
12807 Lake Drive, P.O. Box 130, Delray Beach FL 33447-0130. 561/276-6083. **Contact:** Personnel. **World Wide Web address:** http://www.beaerospace.com. **Description:** B/E Aerospace, Inc. designs, manufactures, sells, and provides global support for one of the industry's broadest lines of commercial aircraft cabin interior products, including seating products, passenger entertainment and service systems, and galley structures and inserts. The company supplies major airlines and airframe manufacturers. **Positions advertised include:** Purchasing Manager; Account Manager; Cost Control Manager. **Corporate headquarters location:** Wellington FL. **Other U.S. locations:** Nationwide. **International locations:** England; Singapore; Wales. **Operations at this facility include:** This location manufactures aircraft galley products. **Listed on:** NASDAQ. **Stock exchange symbol:** BEAV. **Annual sales/revenues:** More than $100 million.

BAE SYSTEMS
P.O. Box 1500, Tampa 33684. 813/885-7481. **Contact:** Personnel **E-mail address:** careers@baesystems.com. **World Wide Web address:** http://www.baesystems.com. **Description:** Designs, manufactures, and sells flight simulators, weapon systems, tactical air defense systems, small arms, and training devices for the U.S. government, as well as commercial and international customers. BAE SYSTEMS also develops simulation-based devices for the entertainment industry. The company also provides a variety of simulator-related training services at customer-owned facilities, its Tampa training center, and the British Aerospace-owned Dulles training facility. BAE SYSTEMS conducts business through its three primary operating segments: Training Devices, Training Services, and Systems Management. **Corporate headquarters location:** This location. **Subsidiaries include:** Reflectone UK Limited. **Number of employees at this location:** 400. **Number of employees nationwide:** 980.

BBDO
2 Alhambra Plaza, Suite 600, Coral Gables FL 33134. 305/446-6006. **Contact:** Human Resources. **E-mail address:** ximena.nunez@bbdo.com. **World Wide Web address:** http://www.bbdo.com. **Description:** Part of a worldwide network of advertising agencies with related businesses in public relations, direct marketing, sales promotion, graphic arts, and printing. **Corporate headquarters location:** New York NY. **Other U.S. locations:** Los Angeles CA; San Francisco CA; Atlanta GA; Chicago IL; Wellesley MA; Southfield MI. **Parent company:** BBDO Worldwide operates 83 subsidiaries, affiliates, and associates engaged solely in advertising and related operations.

BBF
10950 Belcher Road, Largo FL 33777. 727/545-8703. **Fax:** 727/548-1203. **Recorded jobline:** 727/545-8703x208. **Contact:** Eric Kemerer, Human Resources Department. **E-mail address:** hrmanager@bbfprinting.com. **World Wide Web address:** http://www.bbfprinting.com. **Description:** Supplies a full line of custom-printed forms, labels, envelopes, commercial printing, computer supplies, and promotional products. Founded in 1960. **NOTE:** Entry-level positions and second and third shifts are offered. **Positions advertised include:** Part Time Invoice Break Down Associate; Graphic Designer; Proofreader. **Special programs:** Training. **Office hours:** Monday - Friday, 8:00 a.m. - 5:00 p.m. **Corporate headquarters location:** This location. **Listed on:** Privately held. **President/CEO:** Joseph P. Baker. **Annual sales/revenues:** $51 - $100 million. **Number of employees nationwide:** 400.

BACARDI MARTINI USA, INC.
2100 Biscayne Boulevard, Miami FL 33137. 305/573-8511. **Contact:** Human Resources. **World Wide Web address:** http://www.bacardi.com. **Description:** An importer, seller, and distributor of wine and rum.

W.S. BADCOCK CORPORATION
P.O. Box 497, Mulberry FL 33860. 863/425-4921. **Physical address:** 200 Phosphate Boulevard, Mulberry FL 33860. **Contact:** Jim Vernon, Director of Personnel. **World Wide Web address:** http://www.badcock.com. **Description:** Operates a chain of retail furniture stores. **Corporate headquarters location:** This location.

BAILEY PUBLISHING & COMMUNICATIONS INC.
P.O. Box 1769, Jacksonville FL 32201. 904/356-2466. **Fax:** 904/353-2628. **Contact:** James F. Bailey, Jr., Publisher. **World Wide Web address:** http://www.baileypub.com. **Description:** Publishes several specialty newspapers including the *Financial News, Daily Record, FOCUS, GOLF News*, and the *Realty/Builder Connection*. **Positions advertised include:** Advertising Clerk; Editor; Reporter; Services Sales Representative. **Corporate headquarters location:** This location.

BAIRNCO CORPORATION
300 Primera Boulevard, Suite 432, Lake Mary FL 32746. 407/875-2222. **Contact:** Human Resources. **E-mail address:** info@bairnco.com. **World Wide Web address:** http://www.bairnco.com. **Description:** A holding company. **NOTE:** Hiring is done primarily through individual operating divisions. **Corporate headquarters location:** This location. **Subsidiaries include:** Kasco Corporation manufactures and services equipment for the supermarket industry; Arlon Inc. manufactures coated and laminated materials for industrial and commercial use. Markets include civilian and military communications, radar and computer systems, electronic testing, and other industrial, scientific, automotive, and military applications. **Listed on:** New York Stock Exchange. **Stock exchange symbol:** BZ. **Number of employees at this location:** 15. **Number of employees nationwide:** 900.

BAKER DISTRIBUTING COMPANY
7892 Baymeadows Way, Jacksonville FL 32256. 904/733-9633. **Fax:** 904/733-6722. **Contact:** Doris Spears, Payroll Manager. **E-mail address:** info@bakersdist.com. **World Wide Web address:** http://www.bakerdist.com. **Description:** A wholesaler of industrial heating and cooling equipment.

BANK OF AMERICA
50 North Laura Street, Jacksonville FL 32202. 904/791-7720. **Recorded jobline:** 800/587-5627. **Contact:** Human Resources Department. **World Wide Web address:** http://www.bankofamerica.com. **Description:** Bank of America is a full-service banking and financial institution. The company operates through four business segments: Global Corporate and Investment Banking, Principal Investing and Asset Management, Commercial Banking, and Consumer Banking. **Positions advertised include:** Applications Programming Consultant; Credit Products Officer; Application

Programming Analyst; Sales Officer; Process Design Engineer; Credit Risk Officer; Private Client Advisor. **Corporate headquarters location:** Charlotte NC. **Other U.S. locations:** Nationwide.

BANKATLANTIC
1750 East Sunrise Boulevard, Fort Lauderdale FL 33304. 954/760-5480. **Fax:** 954/760-5489. **Recorded jobline:** 954/760-5550. **Contact:** Human Resources. **World Wide Web address:** http://www.bankatlantic.com. **Description:** A federal savings and loan bank. **Positions advertised include:** Customer Service Representative; Secretary; Customer Service Specialist; Personal Banking Representative; BSA Monitoring Analyst. **Corporate headquarters location:** This location. **Parent company:** BankAtlantic Financial Corporation. **Listed on:** NASDAQ. **Stock exchange symbol:** BANCH. **Number of employees at this location:** 640.

BAPTIST MEDICAL PLAZA AT WEST KENDALL
13001 North Kendall Drive, Miami FL 33186. 786/596-3800. **Fax: Contact:** Human Resources. **E-mail address:** recruitment@baptisthealth.net. **World Wide Web address:** http://www.baptisthealth.net. **Description:** A non-profit health care facility serving south Florida. **Positions advertised include:** Corporate Analyst Manager; Corporate Director; Nurse Department Head; Manager Accreditation Readiness Person; Manager; Admitting Manager; Speech Therapist; Physical Therapist; Occupational Therapist; Pharmacist; Supervisor; Medical Technician; Clerk; Financial Representative; Office Coordinator; Coder; Executive Assistant; Billing Clerk; Research Registered Nurse; Registered Nurse; Assistant Nursing Manager; Certified Nursing Assistant; Licenses Practical Nurse; Case Manager.

BAPTIST ST. VINCENT'S HEALTH SYSTEMS
BAPTIST ST. VINCENT MEDICAL CENTER
1800 Barrs Street, Jacksonville FL 32204. 904/308-7307. **Fax:** 904/308-2951. **Contact:** Human Resources. **World Wide Web address:** http://www.jaxhealth.com. **Description:** Operates the Baptist St. Vincent Medical Center (also at this location) and the St. Catherine Laboure Manor nursing home in Jacksonville. Baptist St. Vincent Medical Center is a 711-bed hospital that provides the following services and facilities: acute care, AIDS treatment, behavioral medicine, a cancer center, cardiology, chemical dependency treatment, emergency services, geriatrics, gastroenterology, laser surgery, neonatology, neurosurgery, OB/GYN, occupational health, orthopedics, otolaryngology, otology, pediatrics, plastic surgery, psychiatric, substance abuse, and women's/children's services. Baptist St. Vincent's Health Systems is a member of the Daughters of Charity national health system, which also includes Mercy Hospital (Miami FL), Sacred Heart Hospital (Pensacola FL), and the Haven of Our Lady of Peace nursing home (Pensacola FL). **Positions advertised include:** Patient Accounting Representative; Registration Associate; Office Specialist; Medical Lab Assistant; Registration Associate; Console Operator; Registered Nurse; Licensed Practical Nurse; Nurse Manager; Unit Clerk; Behavioral Health Evaluation; Care Manager; Social Worker; Director Imaging Services; Safety Specialist; Painter. **Corporate headquarters location:** St. Louis MO. **Number of employees at this location:** 4,000.

BAPTIST ST. VINCENT'S VISITING NURSES
3563 Phillips Highway, Suite 202, Jacksonville FL 32207. 904/202-4300. **Contact:** Human Resources. **Description:** Provides home health care services as part of the greater Baptist St. Vincent's medical organization. **Positions advertised include:** Emergency Medical Technician; Paramedic; Technical Assistant; Ultrasound Technologist; CT Technologist; Medical Assistant; Senior Phlebotomist; Pharmacist; Patient Escort; RN; LPN; Certified Nurse Assistant.

BARNES & NOBLE BOOKSTORES
23654 U.S. 19 North, Clearwater FL 34625. 727/669-1688. **Contact:** Manager. **World Wide Web address:** http://www.bn.com. **Description:** A bookstore chain. This location also has a cafe and a music department. **Other area locations:** Statewide.

BAUSCH & LOMB PHARMACEUTICALS, INC.
8500 Hidden River Parkway, Tampa FL 33637. 813/975-7700. **Fax:** 813/975-7779. **Contact:** Human Resources. **World Wide Web address:** http://www.bausch.com. **Description:** Bausch & Lomb operates in selected segments of global health care and optical markets. The health care segment consists of three sectors: personal health, medical, and biomedical. The personal health sector is comprised of branded products purchased directly by consumers in health and beauty aid sections of pharmacies, food stores, and mass merchandise outlets. Products include contact lens care solutions, oral care, eye and skin care products, and nonprescription medications. The medical sector manufactures contact lenses, ophthalmic pharmaceuticals, hearing aids, dental implants, and other products sold to health care professionals or obtained by consumers through a prescription. The biomedical sector is engaged in the research and development of pharmaceuticals and the production of genetically-engineered materials. These include purpose-bred research animals, bioprocessing services, and products derived from specific pathogen-free eggs. The optics segment consists primarily of premium-priced sunglasses sold under such brand names as Ray-Ban and Revo. The company's manufacturing or marketing organizations have been established in 34 countries and the company's products are distributed in more than 70 other nations. **Positions advertised include:** Aseptic Production Operator; 3rd Shift Compounder. **Operations at this facility include:** This location manufactures contact lenses and related products, ophthalmic drugs, dental plaque removal devices, and optical items. . **Listed on:** New York Stock Exchange. **Stock exchange symbol:** BOL. **Number of employees worldwide:** 14,400.

BAXTER HEALTHCARE CORPORATION
14600 NW 60th Avenue, Miami Lakes FL 33014-2811. 305/823-5240. **Contact:** Human Resources. **World Wide Web address:** http://www.baxter.com. **Description:** An international company that manufactures and markets critical therapies for conditions involving the blood and circulatory system. The company operates within three main areas. The BioScience division manufactures products that collect, separate, and store blood. The Renal products are designed to cleanse the blood. Intravenous products are designed to help infuse drugs and other solutions into the blood stream. **Corporate headquarters location:** Deerfield IL. **Operations at this facility include:** Administration; Manufacturing; Research and Development; Sales. **Listed on:** New York Stock Exchange. **Stock exchange symbol:** BAX.

BAYFRONT MEDICAL CENTER
701 Sixth Street South, St. Petersburg FL 33701. 727/823-1234. **Contact:** Human Resources. **World Wide Web address:** http://www.bayfront.org. **Description:** A nonprofit, 502-bed hospital. **Positions advertised include:** Administrative Assistant; Assistant Operator; Certified Occupational Therapist; Histologist; Clinical Nurse Specialist; Medical Technician; Dietitian; Environmental Services Aide; Flight Nurse; Home Health Assistant. **Parent company:** Bayfront-St. Anthony's Health Care.

BAYFRONT YMCA
750 West Retta Esplanade, Punta Gorda FL 33950. 941/637-0797. **Contact:** Personnel. **Description:** The YMCA is one of the nation's largest and most comprehensive service organizations. The YMCA provides health and fitness programs; promotes social and personal development; offers sports and recreation; implements education and career development programs; and organizes camps and conferences for individuals of all ages and backgrounds. **Corporate headquarters location:** Chicago IL. **Other U.S. locations:** Nationwide. **Operations at this facility include:** Offers a variety of classes in aerobics, yoga, and tai chi and social events including dances and bridge.

BEALL'S DEPARTMENT STORES
P.O. Box 25207, Bradenton FL 34206. 941/747-2355. **Contact:** Human Resources. **World Wide Web address:** http://www.beallsinc.com. **Description:** Operates a department store chain. **Positions advertised include:** Area Sales Manager; Visual Merchandiser; Assistant Store Manager. **Corporate headquarters location:** This location.

BECKMAN COULTER, INC.
P.O. Box 169015, Miami FL 33116-9015. 305/380-3800. **Fax:** 305/380-3689. **Contact:** Human Resources. **World Wide Web address:** http://www.beckmancoulter.com. **Description:** Sells and services a diverse range of scientific instruments, reagents, and related equipment. Products include DNA synthesizers, robotic workstations, centrifuges, electrophoresis systems, detection and measurement equipment, data processing software, and specialty chemical and automated general chemical systems. Many of the company's products are used in research and development and diagnostic analysis. **Positions advertised include:** Sales Consultant. **Corporate headquarters location:** Fullerton CA.

BELL MICROPRODUCTS LATIN AMERICA
7630 NW 25th Street, Miami FL 33122. 305/477-6406. **Contact:** Human Resources. **World Wide Web address:** http://www.fti-inc.com. **Description:** Distributes a full-line of computer products to Latin America. The company also provides training, service, and technical support. **Positions advertised include:** Distributor Supervisor; Inside Sales Representative; Marketing Programs Representative; Outside Sales Representative; RMA Clerk; Warehouse Manager.

BENEFIT TECHNOLOGY INC.
2701 South Bayshore Drive, Suite 401, Miami FL 33133. 305/285-6900. **Contact:** Human Resources. **World Wide Web address:** http://www.benefittechnology.com. **Description:** Develops Visual Basic software for life insurance companies.

BENIHANA INC.
8685 NW 53rd Terrace, Suite 201, Miami FL 33166. 305/593-0770. **Fax:** 305/592-6371. **Contact:** Human Resources. **E-mail address:** contact@benihana.com. **World Wide Web address:** http://www.benihana.com. **Description:** Owns and operates more than 60 Japanese steakhouses. Additional restaurants are operated by licensees. **Corporate headquarters location:** This location. **Other U.S. locations:** Nationwide. **Subsidiaries include:** Rudy's Restaurant Group, Inc. **Listed on:** NASDAQ. **Stock exchange symbol:** BNHN. **Annual sales/revenues:** $21 - $50 million. **Number of employees nationwide:** 1,650.

BERTRAM YACHT, INC.
P.O. Box 520774 GMF, Miami FL 33152. 305/633-8011. **Fax:** 954/462-0029. **Contact:** John Marler or Manager of Human Resources. **E-mail address:** jmarler@alliedrichardbertram.com. **World Wide Web address:** http://www.alliedrichardbertram.com. **Description:** A manufacturer of yachts. **Positions advertised include:** Marine Technician Electrician; Outboard Technician; Inboard Technician. **Corporate headquarters location:** This location. **Parent company:** Bertram, Inc. **Operations at this facility include:** Manufacturing. **Number of employees at this location:** 240.

BIG CAT RESCUE
12802 Easy Street, Tampa FL 33625. 813/920-4130. **Contact:** Human Resources Department. **E-mail address:** savethecats@aol.com. **World Wide Web address:** http://www.bigcatrescue.com. **Description:** A nonprofit organization that serves as both a wildlife sanctuary for large exotic cats and a home for over 200 unwanted animals.

BLACKBEARD'S CRUISES
P.O. Box 66-1091, Miami FL 33266. 305/888-1226. **Contact:** Human Resources. **E-mail address:** jobs@blackbeard-cruises.com. **World Wide Web address:** http://www.blackbeard-cruises.com. **Description:** A cruise line that sails to the Bahamas. **Positions advertised include:** Cook; Dive Instructor; Engineer.

BLUE CROSS AND BLUE SHIELD OF FLORIDA
4800 Deerwood Campus Parkway, Building 100, Jacksonville FL 32246. 904/791-6111. **Fax:** 888/310-4797. **Contact:** Director of Human Resources. **World Wide Web address:** http://www.bcbsfl.com. **Description:** A nonprofit health care insurance organization providing managed health care plans to both individuals and groups. Blue Cross and Blue Shield offers Point-of-Service, individual health, PPO, and HMO plans, as well as life insurance, dental insurance, worker's compensation, accidental death and dismemberment, and short- and long-term disability. **Positions advertised include:** Individual Benefits Coordinator; Security Officer; FMLA Coordinator; General Counsel Associate; Computer Systems Consultant; WC Products Manager; Corporate Communications Consultant; Associate Technician; Sales Manager Trainee. **Special programs:** Internships.

BLUEGREEN CORPORATION
4960 100 Conference Way North, Suite 100, Boca Raton FL 33431. 561/912-8000. **Contact:** Human Resources. **E-mail address:** recruit@bxgcorp.com. **World Wide Web address:** http://www.bluegreen-corp.com. **Description:** A national real estate company specializing in rural land acquisitions and sales. Bluegreen Corporation also serves as a mortgage broker **Positions advertised include:** Accounting Assistant; Database Administrator; Sales Document Specialist; Clerical Assistant; Staff Accountant; Title Processor; Post Closer; Marketing Support Specialist; Junior Graphic Designer; Production Assistant; Customer Service Associate; Payment Processor. **Corporate headquarters location:** This location. **Other U.S. locations:** Nationwide. **Operations at this facility include:** Administration. **Listed on:** New York Stock Exchange. **Stock exchange symbol:** BXG. **Number of employees at this location:** 70. **Number of employees nationwide:** 400.

BOCA RATON NEWS
5801 North Congress Avenue, Boca Raton FL 33487. 561/893-6400. **Contact:** Human Resources. **World Wide Web address:** http://www.bocanews.com. **Description:** A daily newspaper.

BOCA RESEARCH
1601 Clint Moore Road, Suite 200, Boca Raton FL 33487. 561/241-8789. **Contact:** Human Resources. **World Wide Web address:** http://www.bocaresearch.com. **Description:** Manufactures computer components including network cards and video

cards. **Corporate headquarters location:** This location. **Office hours:** Monday – Friday, 8:00 a.m. – 7:30 p.m.

BODY SHOP OF AMERICA, INC.
6225 Powers Avenue, Jacksonville FL 32217-2215. 904/737-0811. **Contact:** Judy Anderson, Assistant Controller. **Description:** A retail store offering apparel for juniors.

BON SECOURS-ST. JOSEPH HOSPITAL
2500 Harbor Boulevard, Port Charlotte FL 33952. 941/766-4122. **Fax:** 941/766-4296. **Contact:** Human Resources. **World Wide Web address:** http://www.bonsecours.org. **Description:** A JCAHO-accredited, 212-bed, acute care facility with an affiliated 104-bed, long-term care facility located on the Gulf Coast of southwestern Florida. Bon Secours-St. Joseph Hospital is part of the Bon Secours Health System. **Positions advertised include:** Accounting Clerk; Certified Nurse Assistant; Chief Financial Officer; Clinical Coordinator; Employment Coordinator; Laboratory Director; Materials Technician; Chaplain; RN; Social Worker. **Special programs:** Internships. **Corporate headquarters location:** Mariottsville MD. **Other area locations:** Miami FL; St. Petersburg FL. **Other U.S. locations:** St. Clair Shores MI; Charlotte NC; Richmond VA. **Operations at this facility include:** Administration; Service. **Number of employees at this location:** 1,000.

THE BRADENTON HERALD
P.O. Box 921, Bradenton FL 34206. 941/748-0411x6801. **Physical address;** 102 Manatee Avenue, Bradenton FL 34205. **Contact:** Barbara Ferg, Human Resources Director. **E-mail address:** bferg@bradentonherald.com. **World Wide Web address:** http://www.bradenton.com. **Description:** Publisher of a daily newspaper. **Corporate headquarters location:** San Jose CA. **Parent company:** Knight-Ridder. **Number of employees at this location:** 250.

BRADENTON YMCA
3805 59th Street West, Bradenton FL 34209. 941/792-7484. **Contact:** Human Resources. **E-mail address:** manateeymca@aol.com. **World Wide Web address:** http://www.manateeymca.org. **Description:** Offers a variety of aerobics and workout classes. Bradenton YMCA's facilities include an indoor heated pool and a gym. **Positions advertised include:** Front Desk Receptionist. **Corporate headquarters location:** Chicago IL. **Other U.S. locations:** Nationwide.

BREEZE NEWSPAPERS
P.O. Box 151306, Cape Coral FL 33910. 941/574-1110. **Fax:** 941/574-1984. **Contact:** Scott Blonde, Account Manager. **World Wide Web address:** http://www.flguide.com. **Description:** Publishes over a dozen community newspapers and other publications including the *Cape Coral Daily Breeze, Fort Myers Beach Observer, Island Reporter, Sanibel-Captiva Islander, Sanibel-Captiva Chronicle, Captiva Current, Gulf Coast Woman, Lehigh Acres Citizen, Fort Myers Beach Bulletin,* and *Gasparilla Gazette.* **Corporate headquarters location:** Wheeling WV. **Operations at this facility include:** Sales. **Number of employees at this location:** 200.

BREVARD ZOO
8225 North Wickham Road, Melbourne FL 32940. 321/254-9453. **Fax:** 321/259-5966. **Contact:** Human Resources. **E-mail address:** info@brevardzoo.org. **World Wide Web address:** http://www.brevardzoo.org. **Description:** Features over 400 animals of Latin America, native Florida, and Australia in their natural habitat.

BROOKS REHABILITATION HOSPITAL
3599 University Boulevard South, Jacksonville FL 32216. 904/858-7600. **Toll-free phone:** 800/487-7342. **Fax:** **Contact:** Sandra Williamson. **E-mail address:** sandra.williamson@brookshealth.org. **World Wide Web address:** http://www.brookshealth.org. **Description:** Provides medical rehabilitation services to northeast Florida. **NOTE:** Resumes can be sent to: resume@brookshealth.org. **Positions advertised include:** Registered Nurse; Certified Nurses Aide; Physical Therapist; Referral Coordinator; Occupational Therapy Coordinator; Part Time Assistant Occupational Therapy; Rehab Aide; Speech Language Pathologist; Brooks Rehab Network President; University Center Manager. **Other area locations include:** Green Grove Springs FL; Hudson FL; Orange Park FL; Palatka FL; Palm Coast FL.

BROWN & BROWN INSURANCE
401 East Jackson Street, Suite 1700, Tampa FL 33602. 813/226-1300. **Fax:** 813/226-1313 **Contact:** Human Resources. **World Wide Web address:** http://www.brown-n-brown.com. **Description:** An independent insurance agency that provides a variety of insurance products and services to corporate, institutional, professional, and individual clients. Products and services fall into four major categories: National Programs specializes in liability and property insurance programs; Retail Operations provides property, casualty, life, and health insurance; Brokerage Operations provides property and casualty products; and Service Operations provides claims administration. **Positions advertised include:** Accountant; Accounting Manager; Benefits Manager; Internal Auditor. **Office hours:** Monday - Friday, 8:00 a.m. - 5:00 p.m. **Corporate headquarters location:** Daytona Beach FL. **Other U.S. locations:** Nationwide. **Operations at this facility include:** Administration; Sales; Service. **Listed on:** New York Stock Exchange. **Stock exchange symbol:** BRO. **Number of employees at this location:** 250. **Number of employees nationwide:** 1,000.

BROWNING-FERRIS INDUSTRIES, INC. (BFI)
1475 SW 4th Avenue, Delray Beach FL 33444. 561/278-1717. **Contact:** Human Resources. **Description:** Engaged in the collection and disposal of solid waste for commercial, industrial, and residential customers. Services provided by Browning-Ferris Industries include landfill services, waste-to-energy programs, hazardous waste removal, and liquid waste removal. The company has worldwide operations at more than 500 facilities. **Parent company:** Allied Waste Industries, Inc.

BUDGET GROUP, INC.
125 Basin Street, Suite 210, Daytona Beach FL 32114. 386/238-7035. **Contact:** Human Resources. **World Wide Web address:** http://www.bgi.com. **Description:** A holding company. **Corporate headquarters location:** This location. **Subsidiaries include:** Budget Airport Parking; Budget Car Sales, Inc.; Budget Rent A Car Corporation; Cruise America, Inc.; Premier Car Rental; Ryder TRS, Inc.; Van Pool Services, Inc.

BURDINES – MACY'S
22 East Flagler Street, 4th Floor, Miami FL 33131. 305/577-1998. **Contact:** Human Resources. **World Wide Web address:** http://www.burdinesflorida.com. **Description:** Operates a retail department store chain. **Positions advertised include:** Cosmetic Beauty Advisor; Cosmetic Counter Manager; Loss Prevention Associate; Merchandise Processor; Sales Associate; Receiving Associate; Sales Support Coordinator; Selling Supervisor; Visual Merchandiser; Associate Manager; Department Manager; Merchant Processing Manager; Merchant Team Manager; Sales Manager; Store Manager; Visual Manager. **Office hours:** Monday - Friday, 10:00 a.m. - 5:00 p.m. **Corporate headquarters location:** This location. **Parent company:** Federated Department Stores, Inc.

BURDINES – MACY'S
19503 Biscayne Boulevard, Aventura FL 33180. 305/792-6300x5. **Contact:** Employment Manager. **World Wide Web address:** http://www.burdinesflorida.com. **Description:** A retail department store. **Positions advertised include:** Cosmetic Beauty Advisor; Cosmetic Counter Manager; Loss Prevention Associate; Merchandise Processor; Sales Associate; Receiving Associate; Sales Support Coordinator; Selling Supervisor; Visual Merchandiser; Associate Manager; Department Manager; Merchant Processing Manager; Merchant Team Manager; Sales Manager; Store Manager; Visual Manager. **Special programs:** Internships. **Corporate headquarters location:** Miami FL. **Parent company:** Federated Department Stores, Inc. **Operations at this facility include:** Administration; Sales; Service.

BUSCH GARDENS TAMPA BAY
ADVENTURE ISLAND
P.O. Box 9158, Tampa FL 33674. 813/987-5400. **Physical address:** 3605 Bougainvillea Avenue, Tampa FL 33612 **Toll-free phone:** 888/800-5447. **Contact:** Human Resources. **World Wide Web address:** http://www.buschgardens.com. **Description:** A 300-acre theme park featuring shows, rides, attractions, and exotic animals. **NOTE:** All applications must be made in person at the Human Resources Office. A personal interview is required and all applicants must be a minimum of 18 years old. Please be aware that many technical and professional positions are filled by internal promotions. **Positions advertised include:** Camp Counselor.

CASA GRANDE SUITE HOTEL
834 Ocean Drive, Miami Beach FL 33139. 305/672-7003. **Fax:** 305/673-3669. **E-mail address:** info@casagrandesuitehotel.com. **Contact:** Human Resources. **World Wide Web address:** http://www.casagrandehotel.com. **Description:** A European-style luxury hotel.

CB RICHARD ELLIS
200 South Biscayne Boulevard, Suite 1150, Miami FL 33131. 305/533-1214. **Fax:** 305/533-1211. **Contact:** Human Resources. **World Wide Web address:** http://www.cbre.com. **Description:** A real estate services company offering property sales and leasing, property and facility management, mortgage banking, and investment management services. **Corporate headquarters location:** Los Angeles CA. **Other U.S. locations:** Nationwide. **Listed on:** New York Stock Exchange. **Stock exchange symbol:** CBG. **Number of employees worldwide:** 9,000.

CB RICHARD ELLIS
SUNTRUST
777 Brickell Avenue, Suite 1000, Miami FL 33131. 305/374-1000. **Fax:** 305/381-6462. **Contact:** Human Resources. **World Wide Web address:** http://www.cbre.com. **Description:** A real estate services company offering property sales and leasing, property and facility management, mortgage banking, and investment management services. **Corporate headquarters location:** Los Angeles CA. **Other U.S. locations:** Nationwide. **Listed on:** New York Stock Exchange. **Stock exchange symbol:** CBG. **Number of employees worldwide:** 9,000.

CED (CONSOLIDATED ELECTRICAL DISTRIBUTORS, INC.)
4910A Adamo Drive, Tampa FL 33605. 813/248-6699. **Contact:** Manager. **World Wide Web address:** http://www.ced.com. **E-mail address:** opps@cbre.com. **Description:** A retail store that specializes in the sale of electrical supplies. **Positions advertised include:** Maintenance Associate: Painter.

CF INDUSTRIES, INC./PLANT CITY
P.O. Drawer L, Plant City FL 33564. 813/782-1591. **Contact:** Harry Crosby, Human Resources. **World Wide Web address:** http://www.cfindustries.com. **Description:** This location manufactures phosphates for use in fertilizers.

CF INDUSTRIES, INC./TAMPA
2520 Guy Verger Boulevard, Tampa FL 33605. 813/247-5531. **Contact:** Ron Bigelow, Human Resources. **World Wide Web address:** http://www.cfindustries.com. **Description:** This location provides administrative and warehousing Human Resources. services to other locations of the company. Overall, CF Industries manufactures phosphates for use in fertilizers.

CPA SOFTWARE
125 West Romana Street, Suite 500, Pensacola FL 32502. 850/434-2685. **Toll-free phone:** 800/272-7123. **Fax:** 850/852-0470. **Contact:** Administrative Manager. **World Wide Web address:** http://www.cpasoftware.com. **Description:** Develops software for certified public accountants. **Positions advertised include:** Programmer/Analyst; Customer Service Representative; Data Conversion Specialist; Sales/Marketing Professional; Classroom Instructor. **Corporate headquarters location:** This location. **Parent company:** Fenimore Software Group, Inc. **Number of employees at this location:** 100.

CPAMERICA, INC.
2255 Glades Road, Suite 324 A, Boca Raton FL 33431. 561/988-2607. **Contact:** Human Resources. **E-mail address:** cpamerica@worldnet.att.net. **World Wide Web address:** http://www.cpamerica.com. **Description:** A consulting firm organized to market celebrities, entertainers, and concert performers to international corporations. **Corporate headquarters location:** This location. **Other U.S. locations:** Las Vegas NV. **Listed on:** Privately held. **President/CEO:** Jack Wishna. **Number of employees at this location:** 10. **Number of employees nationwide:** 20.

CSX TRANSPORTATION
500 Water Street, Jacksonville FL 32202-4423. 904/359-3100. **Contact:** Human Resources. **World Wide Web address:** http://www.csxt.com. **Description:** A railroad company that transports a variety of products for the agricultural, automotive, mining, food, and consumer markets. **Positions advertised include:** Assistant Road-master; Assistant Terminal Trainmaster; Boilermaker; Carman; Clerk; Communications Maintainer; Machinist; Police; Road Electrician; Utility Worker; Yard Worker. **Parent company:** CSX Corporation.

CTG (COMPUTER TASK GROUP, INC.)
1335 Gateway Drive, Suite 2013, Melbourne FL 32901. 321/725-1300. **Contact:** Human Resources. **World Wide Web address:** http://www.ctg.com. **Description:** A computer consulting firm that performs programming and networking services for corporate clients. **Corporate headquarters location:** Buffalo NY. **Other U.S. locations:** Nationwide. **Listed on:** New York Stock Exchange. **Stock exchange symbol:** CTG.

CAIN AND BULTMAN, INC.
2145 Dennis Street, Jacksonville FL 32204. 904/356-4812. **Contact:** Marc Kimball, Human Resources. **E-mail address:** marckimball@cain-bultman.com. **World Wide Web address:** http://www.cain-bultman.com. **Description:** A wholesale distributor of carpets and vinyl floor coverings.

CALADESI ANIMAL HOSPITAL
903 Curlew Road, Dunedin FL 34698. 813/733-9395. **Contact:** Human Resources. **E-mail address:** caladesivet@caladesi.com. **World Wide Web address:** http://www.caladesi.com. **Description:** Caladesi Animal Hospital offers general surgical and medical care, acupuncture, orthopedic surgery, boarding services, a pet taxi, and travel services.

CAPE PUBLICATIONS, INC.
P.O. Box 419000, Melbourne FL 32941-9000. 321/242-3753. **Fax:** 321/253-3801. **Physical address:** One Gannet Plaza, Melbourne FL 32940. **Contact:** Julie Lusk, Human Resources. **E-mail address:** joblink@flatoday.com. **World Wide Web address:** http://www.floridatoday.com. **Description:** Publishes *Florida Today,* a daily newspaper that serves Brevard County. Cape Publications also publishes five weekly and four monthly community newspapers. Founded in 1966. **Special programs:** Internships. **Corporate headquarters location:** Arlington VA. **Parent company:** Gannett Company, Inc. **Operations at this facility include:** Divisional Headquarters; Manufacturing; Sales. **Listed on:** New York Stock Exchange. **Stock exchange symbol:** GSI. **Number of employees at this location:** 600.

CARE MEDICAL EQUIPMENT
102 Drennen Road, Suite B-1, Orlando FL 32806. 407/856-2273. **Toll-free phone:** 800/741-2282. **Contact:** Human Resources. **E-mail address:** info@caremedicalequipment.com. **World Wide Web address:** http://www.caremedicalequipment.com. **Description:** Engaged in the short-term rental of wheelchairs, scooters, shower chairs, lifts, hospital beds, and IV stands to hotels, condos, and homes.

CARECENTRIC
1180 SW 36th Avenue, Pompano Beach FL 33069. 954/974-0707. **Toll-free phone:** 800/441-2331. **Fax:** 770/801-0789. **Contact:** Human Resources. **World Wide Web address:** http://www.carecentric.com. **Description:** Develops and publishes software for the home health care industry. **NOTE:** Jobseekers should send a resume to CareCentric, 6600 Powers Ferry Road, Atlanta GA 30339. **Positions advertised include:** Software Demo & Support Specialist. **Corporate headquarters location:** Atlanta GA. **Annual sales/revenues:** $11 - $20 million. **Number of employees at this location:** 100. **Number of employees nationwide:** 300.

CARGILL FERTILIZER
8813 U.S. Highway 41 South, Riverview FL 33569-4866. 813/677-9111. **Contact:** Human Resources Department. **World Wide Web address:** http://www.cargill.com/aghorizons/products/fert. **Description:** A chemical company that specializes in the production of phosphates for use in fertilizer.

CARIBBEAN GARDENS
1590 Goodlette-Frank Road, Naples FL 34102-5260. 239/262-5409. **Contact:** Human Resources. **E-mail address:** info@caribbeangardens.com. **World Wide Web address:** http://www.caribbeangardens.com. **Description:** A 52-acre botanical and zoological preserve featuring exhibits of endangered plant and animal species. Founded in 1919.

CARLTON FIELDS
P.O. Box 3239, Tampa FL 33601. 813/223-7000. **Contact:** Catherine Witherspoon, Human Resources. **E-mail address:** cwitherspoon@carltonfields.com. **World Wide Web address:** http://www.carltonfields.com. **Description:** A law firm specializing in real estate and construction. **Positions advertised include:** Practicing Attorney; Judicial Clerks; Legal Administration Assistant; Paralegal; Messenger; File Clerk. **Corporate headquarters location:** This location. **Operations at this facility include:** Administration; Service. **Number of employees at this location:** 420.

CARNIVAL CORPORATION
CARNIVAL CRUISE LINES
Carnival Place, 3655 NW 87th Avenue, Miami FL 33178-2428. **Toll-free phone:** 888/CARNIVAL (22764825). **Contact:** Human Resources. **World Wide Web address:** http://www.carnival.com. **Description:** A travel holding company. **NOTE:** This firm does not accept unsolicited resumes. Please only respond to advertised openings. **Positions advertised include:** International Sales; Information Systems; Hotel Operations; Guest Relations; Executive Sales; Embarkation People; Technical Operations; Ship Board Personnel; Revenue Management Accounting; Reservations; Operations Accounting; Office Sales; Marketing; Management Advisory Services; Loss Prevention; Corporate Environmental Compliance; Consumer Research. **Subsidiaries include:** Carnival Cruise Lines (also at this location) operates nine cruise ships serving the Caribbean and Mexican Riviera; Holland America Line operates seven cruise ships serving primarily the Caribbean and Alaska through the Panama Canal; Windstar Cruises operates three sail-powered vessels that call on locations inaccessible to larger ships; Holland America Westours markets sightseeing tours both separately and as a part of Holland America Line cruise/tour packages.

CAROLINA CASUALTY INSURANCE COMPANY
P.O. Box 2575, Jacksonville FL 32203. 904/363-0900. **Fax:** 904/363-8098. **Toll-free phone:** 800/874-8053. **Contact:** Human Resources Manager. **E-mail address:** info@carolinacas.com. **World Wide Web address:** http://www.carolinacas.com. **Description:** A primary insurance company. **Positions advertised include:** Underwriting Manager.

CATALINA MARKETING CORPORATION
200 Carillon Parkway, St. Petersburg FL 33716. 727/579-5000. **Toll-free phone:** 888/322-3814. **Contact:** Human Resources. **E-mail address:** resume@catalinamarketing.com. **World Wide Web address:** http://www.catmktg.com. **Description:** Provides marketing services for consumer product manufacturers and supermarket retailers. The company's point-of-scan electronic marketing network delivers checkout coupons to consumers at supermarket checkouts based on their purchases. The company also provides Internet information on retail grocery promoters. **NOTE:** Entry-level positions are offered. **Positions advertised include:** Executive Assistant; Human Resources Administrator; Customer Services Technician. **Corporate headquarters location:** This location. **Other U.S. locations:** Nationwide. **International locations:** Europe; Japan. **Subsidiaries include:** Catalina Electronic Clearing Services; Health Resource Publishing Company. **Operations at this facility include:** Administration; Divisional Headquarters. **Listed on:** New York Stock Exchange. **Stock exchange symbol:** POS. **Annual sales/revenues:** $51 - $100 million. **Number of employees at this location:** 170. **Number of employees nationwide:** 500. **Number of employees worldwide:** 1,650.

CATALINA YACHTS
7200 Bryan Dairy Road, Largo FL 33777. 727/544-6681. **Fax:** 727/546-7303. **Contact:** Georgia B. Law, Human Resources Manager. **E-mail address:** georgiacatalinayachts.com. **World Wide Web address:** http://www.catalinayachts.com. **Description:** A yacht manufacturer. Founded in 1970. **Positions advertised include:** Assembler. **Corporate headquarters location:** Woodland Hills CA. **Number of employees at this location:** 170.

CATHEDRAL RESIDENCES
601 North Newnan Street, Jacksonville FL 32202. 904/798-5360. **Contact:** Human Resources. **World Wide Web address:** http://www.cathedralresidences.org. **Description:** A nonprofit organization that focuses on the needs of elderly citizens. Cathedral Foundation operates independent living apartments and a nursing home, and provides various community services.

CAUSEWAY LUMBER COMPANY
2601 South Andrews Avenue, Fort Lauderdale FL 33316. 954/763-1224. **Contact:** Human Resources. **World Wide Web address:** http://www.causewaylumber.com. **Description:** A lumber company that offers commercial hardware, doors, lumber and plywood, roof and floor trusses, and home improvement products and accessories. **Positions advertised include:** Truss Technician; Table Leader; Assembler; Truck Driver; Outside Sales Representative; Bender.

CELEBRITY CRUISES
1050 Caribbean Way, Miami FL 33132. 305/262-6677. **Contact:** Human Resources. **E-mail address:** celebritycruises@celebrity.com. **World Wide Web address:** http://www.celebrity-cruises.com. **Description:** Operates an ocean cruise line that sails to Alaska, Bermuda, the Caribbean Islands, Europe, Hawaii, and South America. **Corporate headquarters location:** This location.

CENTEX ROONEY
7901 SW 6th Court, Plantation FL 33324. 954/585-4000. **Contact:** Human Resources. **World Wide Web address:** http://www.centex.com. **Description:** A construction and general contracting company. **Positions advertised include:** Architectural Manager; Strategic Marketing Manager; Operational Marketing Manager; Division Sales Manager; Draftsperson; Field Manager; Customer Service Manager. **Listed on:** New York Stock Exchange. **Stock exchange symbol:** CTX.

CENTRAL FLORIDA PRESS, L.C.
4560 L.B. McLeod Road, Orlando FL 32811. 407/843-5811. **Contact:** Human Resources. **Description:** Engaged in promotional printing services. **Parent company:** Cadmus Communications Corporation (Richmond VA) is a graphic communications company offering specialized products and services in three broad areas: printing, marketing, and publishing. Cadmus is one of the largest graphic communications companies in North America. Product lines include annual reports, catalogs, direct marketing financial printing, point-of-sale marketing, promotional printing, publishing, research journals, specialty magazines, and specialty packaging. Subsidiaries of Cadmus Communications include Cadmus Color Center, Inc. (Sandston VA); Cadmus Consumer Publishing (Richmond VA); Cadmus Custom Publishing (Boston MA); Cadmus Direct Marketing, Inc. (Charlotte NC); Cadmus Interactive (Tucker GA); Cadmus Journal Services (Linthicum MD; Easton MD; Richmond VA); Cadmus Marketing Services (Atlanta GA); Expert Brown (Sandston VA); Graftech Corporation (Charlotte NC); 3Score, Inc. (Tucker GA); Washburn Graphics, Inc. (Charlotte NC); and The William Byrd Press (Richmond VA).

CERTEGY
11601 North Roosevelt Boulevard, St. Petersburg FL 33716. 727/556-9000. **Fax:** 727/227-5005. **Contact:** Manager of Employment. **E-mail address:** recruit3@certegy.com. **World Wide Web address:** http://www.certegy.com. **Description:** Offers payment authorization services for financial institutions and retail establishments via national online computer systems that enable authorization of check and credit card transactions. **NOTE:** Equifax lists all job opportunities through Norrell Services. Call any local Norrell office for further information. **Positions advertised include:** Accountant; Business Analyst; AVP Risk Operations; Business Consultant; Client Relations Coordinator; Collections Account Manager; Database Analyst; Data Entry Operator; Programmer Analyst; Quality Control Specialist; Collections Supervisor. **Corporate headquarters location:** Atlanta GA. **Operations at this facility include:** Administration; Divisional Headquarters; Regional Headquarters; Research and Development; Sales Service. **Listed on:** New York Stock Exchange. **Stock exchange symbol:** EFX.

CHAMPS SPORTS
303 US 301 Boulevard, Bradenton FL 34205. 941/748-5392. **Fax:** 941/741-7170. **Contact:** Sue Campbell, Vice President of Human Resources. **World Wide Web address:** http://www.champssports.com. **Description:** A specialty sporting goods retailer located in the Desoto Square Mall. Products include hard goods, apparel, footwear, and accessories. **Special programs:** Internships. **Corporate headquarters location:** This location. **Other U.S. locations:** Nationwide. **Parent company:** Foot Locker Inc. **Listed on:** New York Stock Exchange. **Stock exchange symbol:** Z. **Number of employees at this location:** 115.

CHARLOTTE COUNTY RECORDING DEPARTMENT
P.O. Box 511687, Punta Gorda FL 33951. 941/637-2245. **Contact:** Human Resources. **Description:** Records all county records including land and court documents.

CHARLOTTE REGIONAL MEDICAL CENTER
809 East Marion Street, Punta Gorda FL 33950. 941/639-3131. **Toll-free phone:** 800/677-3132. **Fax:** 941/637-2469. **Recorded jobline:** 888/639-3166. **Contact:** Human Resources Department. **World Wide Web address:** http://www.charlotteregional.com. **Description:** A 208-bed, private, acute care hospital with specialized services including cardiac care; a sports medicine/wellness program (physical fitness, aerobics, aquatic programs, and rehabilitative services); a behavioral center (mental health and addictions treatment); sleep disorder programs; a pulmonary rehabilitation program (breathing disorder treatment); home health services; occupational medicine (offered through an outpatient clinic in North Port); an emergency department; an ambulatory care center; a critical care recovery unit (recovery from open heart surgery); a diabetes center; and a lifeline emergency response system. **Positions advertised include:** Registered Nurse; Nursing Supervisor; Case Manager; Home Health Aide; Health Information Specialist; Dietician; Cook; Medical Transcriptionist; Nutritional Services Aide; Administration Secretary Human Resources; Psych Receptionist; Unit Secretary; Respiratory Therapist; Director Material Management; Medical Social Worker; Physical Therapist; Sleep Technician. **Special programs:** Internships. **Office hours:** Monday - Friday, 8:00 a.m. - 5:00 p.m. **Corporate headquarters location:** Naples FL. **Parent company:** Health Management Associates, Inc. operates 29 hospitals in 11 states across the Southeast and Southwest, focusing on acquiring underachieving community health care facilities with solid potential. **Operations at this facility include:** Administration; Service. **Listed on:**

New York Stock Exchange. **Stock exchange symbol:** HMA. **Number of employees at this location:** 830.

CHECKERS DRIVE-IN RESTAURANTS, INC.
3300 West Cypress Street, Suite 600, Tampa FL 33607. 813/283-7000. **Contact:** Human Resources. **E-mail address:** hr@checkers.com. **World Wide Web address:** http://www.checkers.com. **Description:** Develops, owns, operates, and franchises quick-service, drive-thru restaurants under the Checkers name. **Corporate headquarters location:** This location. **Listed on:** NASDAQ. **Stock exchange symbol:** CHKR. **Number of employees at this location:** 130. **Number of employees nationwide:** 12,000.

CHICO'S FAS
11215 Metro Parkway, Fort Myers FL 33912. 239/274-4316. **Fax:** 941/277-7035. **Contact:** Human Resources. **E-mail address:** humanresources@chicos.com. **World Wide Web address:** http://www.chicos.com. **Description:** A manufacturer and retailer of women's apparel and accessories. Founded in 1983. **Corporate headquarters location:** This location. **Other U.S. locations:** Nationwide. **Listed on:** NASDAQ. **Stock exchange symbol:** CHS. **Annual sales/revenues:** More than $100 million.

CHROMALLOY FLORIDA
630 Anchors Street NW, Fort Walton Beach FL 32548. 850/244-7684. **Contact:** Human Resources. **Description:** Repairs turbine jet engine component parts. **Operations at this facility include:** Administration; Manufacturing.

CITEL AMERICA, INC.
1515 NW 167th Street, Park Center Boulevard, Suite 5 - 223, Miami FL 33169. 305/621-0022. **Contact:** Human Resources Department. **E-mail address:** citel4u@ix.Netcom.com. **World Wide Web address:** http://www.citelprotection.com. **Description:** Manufactures surge protectors for computers. **Positions advertised include:** Sales Engineer.

CITRIX SYSTEMS, INC.
851 West Cypress Creek Road, Fort Lauderdale FL 33309. 954/267-3000. **Fax:** 954/267-3018. **Contact:** Human Resources. **E-mail address:** resume@citrix.com. **World Wide Web address:** http://www.citrix.com. **Description:** Develops application server software and services. Founded in 1989. **Positions advertised include:** Customer Care Manager; Supervisor Disbursement; Test Engineer; Build Engineer; Corporate Consultant; Order Entry Representative; Marketing Operations Analyst; Product Marketing Manager; Technical Software Trainer. **Corporate headquarters location:** This location. **Listed on:** NASDAQ. **Stock exchange symbol:** CTXS. **Annual sales/revenues:** More than $100 million.

CITY NATIONAL BANK OF FLORIDA
25 West Flagler Street, Miami FL 33130-1785. 305/577-7291. **Fax:** 305/577-7689. **Recorded jobline:** 305/577-7290. **Contact:** Human Resources. **E-mail address:** employment@citynational.com. **World Wide Web address:** http://www.citynational.com. **Description:** A community bank serving Miami/Dade, Broward, and Palm Beach counties. **Positions advertised include:** Auditor; Assistant Branch Manager; Corporate Banking Officer; Commercial Real Estate Loan Officer; Information Technology Operation Specialist; Personal Service Representative. **Other area locations include:** Aventura FL; Coral Gables FL; Boca Raton FL; Ft. Lauderdale FL. **Corporate headquarters location:** This location.

CLAIRE'S ACCESSORIES
11401 NW 12th Street, Miami FL 33172. 305/436-8816. **Contact:** Manager. **World Wide Web address:** http://www.claires.com. **Description:** A specialty store offering women's accessories with over 2,200 locations in the United States and Canada. **NOTE:** For corporate positions, call human resources at 847/765-1100.

CLEVELAND CLINIC FLORIDA HOSPITAL
2950 Cleveland Clinic Boulevard, Weston FL 33331. 954/659-5000. **Fax:** 954/978-7487. **Contact:** Human Resources. **World Wide Web address:** http://www.ccf.org. **Description:** Operates an outpatient clinic and outpatient surgery center that specializes in the diagnosis and treatment of complex medical problems that have resisted previous forms of treatment. Founded in 1921. **NOTE:** Entry-level positions are offered. **Positions advertised include:** General Medicine Assistant; Practical Registered Nurse; Licensed Practical Nurse; Assistant Director Inpatient Services; Inpatient Pharmacist; Outpatient Pharmacist; Pediatric Pharmacist; Pharmacy Manager Medical Safety; Pharmacy Case Manager; Pharmacy Technician; Certified Nurse Aide; Registered Nurse; Medical Secretary. **Special programs:** Internships. **Corporate headquarters location:** Cleveland OH. **Number of employees at this location:** 500.

CLEVELAND CLINIC FLORIDA HOSPITAL
3100 Weston Road, Weston FL 33331. 954/689-5000. **Contact:** Human Resources. **World Wide Web address:** http://www.ccf.org. **Description:** A 150-bed hospital offering a wide variety of inpatient, outpatient, cardiac rehabilitation, and radiologic services. Founded in 1921. **Positions advertised include:** General Medicine Assistant; Practical Registered Nurse; Licensed Practical Nurse; Assistant Director Inpatient Services; Inpatient Pharmacist; Outpatient Pharmacist; Pediatric Pharmacist; Pharmacy Manager Medical Safety; Pharmacy Case Manager; Pharmacy Technician; Certified Nurse Aide; Registered Nurse; Medical Secretary. **Corporate headquarters location:** Cleveland OH. **Parent company:** Cleveland Clinic Foundation.

COASTAL LUMBER COMPANY
P.O. Box 1128, Havana FL 32333. 850/539-6432. **Toll-free phone:** 800/659-0521. **Contact:** Rita Taylor, Human Resources Manager. **E-mail address:** clcinfo@coastallumber.com. **World Wide Web address:** http://www.coastallumber.com. **Description:** Coastal Lumber offers lumber, lumber products, and related services. The company is also involved in environmental preservation. **Corporate headquarters location:** Weldon NC. **Operations at this facility include:** This location manufactures, treats, and markets a variety of lumber products including decking, hardwood tiles, landscape timbers, posts, and split rail fencing.

COCA-COLA BOTTLING COMPANY
3350 Pembroke Road, Hollywood FL 33021. 954/985-5000. **Contact:** Lori Welch, Director of Human Resources. **World Wide Web address:** http://www.cocacola.com. **Description:** A bottler of soft drink brands including Barq's, Dr. Pepper, and Coca-Cola. **NOTE:** Interested jobseekers should send resumes to 12333 SW 112th Avenue, Miami FL 33177. **Parent company:** Coca-Cola Enterprises, Inc. is a producer of soft drinks and nonalcoholic beverages, including spring and sparkling waters, juices, isotonics, and teas. The company operates in 38 states, the District of Columbia, the U.S. Virgin Islands, the Islands of Tortola and Grand Cayman, and the Netherlands. The company's franchises market its products to over 154 million people. Coca-Cola Enterprises operates 268 facilities; approximately 24,000 vehicles; and over 860,000 vending machines, beverage dispensers, and coolers. **Listed on:** New York Stock Exchange. **Stock exchange symbol:** KO.

COCA-COLA BOTTLING COMPANY
16569 SW 117th Avenue, Miami FL 33177. 305/378-1073. **Contact:** Human Resources. **World Wide Web address:** http://www.cocacola.com. **Description:** A bottler of soft drink brands including Barq's, Dr. Pepper, and Coca-Cola. **NOTE:** Interested jobseekers should send resumes to 12333 SW 112th Avenue, Miami FL 33177. **Parent company:** Coca-Cola Enterprises, Inc. is a producer of soft drinks and nonalcoholic beverages, including spring and sparkling waters, juices, isotonics, and teas. The company operates in 38 states, the District of Columbia, the U.S. Virgin Islands, the Islands of Tortola and Grand Cayman, and the Netherlands. The company's franchises market its products to over 154 million people. Coca-Cola Enterprises operates 268 facilities; approximately 24,000 vehicles; and over 860,000 vending machines, beverage dispensers, and coolers. **Listed on:** New York Stock Exchange. **Stock exchange symbol:** KO.

COCONUT GROVE BANK
2701 South Bayshore Drive, Miami FL 33133. 305/858-6666. **Fax:** 305/808-4001. **Contact:** David Davidoff. **E-mail address:** ddavidoff@coconutgrovebank.com. **World Wide Web address:** http://www.coconutgrovebank.com. **Description:** A community bank serving south Florida. **Positions advertised include:** Teller. **President:** Charles Umberger.

COLAMCO INC.
975 Florida Central Parkway, Suite 1100, Longwood FL 32750. 407/331-3737. **Toll-free phone:** 800/327-2722. **Contact:** Human Resources. **World Wide Web address:** http://www.colamco.com. **Description:** Sells and distributes IT products to a customer base made up of primarily small businesses.

COLDWELL BANKER
423 St. Armands Circle, Sarasota FL 34236-1483. 941/388-3966. **Contact:** Sharon Krueger, Manager of Human Resources. **World Wide Web address:** http://www.coldwellbanker.com. **Description:** One of the largest residential real estate companies in the United States and Canada. Coldwell Banker also provides relocation services to businesses worldwide. **Corporate headquarters location:** Mission Viejo CA. **Other U.S. locations:** Nationwide. **Parent company:** Cendant Corporation. **Listed on:** New York Stock Exchange. **Stock exchange symbol:** CD.

COLDWELL BANKER
5971 Cattleridge Boulevard, Suite 202, Sarasota FL 34232. 407/831-5445. **Contact:** Human Resources. **World Wide Web address:** http://www.coldwellbanker.com. **Description:** One of the largest residential real estate companies in the United States and Canada. Coldwell Banker also provides relocation services to businesses worldwide. **Corporate headquarters location:** Mission Viejo CA. **Other U.S. locations:** Nationwide. **Parent company:** Cendant Corporation. **Listed on:** New York Stock Exchange. **Stock exchange symbol:** CD.

COLUMBIA NEW PORT RICHEY HOSPITAL
5637 Marine Parkway, New Port Richey FL 34656. 727/848-1733. **Fax:** 727/845-9146. **Recorded jobline:** 727/845-4379. **Contact:** Mark Cohen, Director of Human Resources. **World Wide Web address:** http://www.communityhospitalnpr.com. **Description:** A 415-bed, JCAHO-accredited hospital. Services offered to the community include medical/surgical nursing, telemetry, psychiatry, ambulatory surgery, a catheterization lab, an in-house pool, critical care nursing, emergency rooms, and OR/RR. Columbia New Port Richey Hospital also has laboratory, radiology, nuclear medicine, pharmacy, and surgical suites. **NOTE:** Second and third shifts are offered. **Positions advertised include:** Unit Secretary; Certified Nursing Assistant; Cafeteria Aide; Nutrition Services Trayline Aide; Activity Assistant; Speech Therapist; Clinical Dietician; Administrative Assistant; Registered Nurse; Imaging Assistant; Physical Therapy Assistant; Unit Secretary General Position; Informative System General Position. **Corporate headquarters location:** Nashville TN. **CEO:** Andrew Oravec, Jr.

COMMERCIAL BANK OF FLORIDA
1550 SW 57th Avenue, Miami FL 33144-5722. 305/267-1200. **Fax:** 305/266-1323. **Contact:** Human Resources. **World Wide Web address:** http://www.commercialbankfl.com. **Description:** A Florida chartered, FDIC insured bank. **Parent Company:** Commercial Bank Shares, Inc. **Listed on:** NASDAQ. **Stock exchange symbol:** CLBK.

COMPUTER ASSOCIATES INTERNATIONAL, INC.
8014 Bayberry Road, Jacksonville FL 32256. 904/680-2674. **Contact:** Human Resources. **World Wide Web address:** http://www.cai.com. **Description:** Computer Associates International is one of the world's leading developers of client/server and distributed computing software. The company develops, markets, and supports enterprise management, database and applications development, business applications, and consumer software products for a broad range of mainframe, midrange, and desktop computers. Computer Associates International serves major business, government, research, and educational organizations. **Positions advertised include:** Associate Consultant; Call Center Program Manager; Consultant; Telesales Professional. **Corporate headquarters location:** Islandia NY. **Other U.S. locations:** Nationwide. **Annual sales/revenues:** More than $100 million. **Listed on:** New York Stock Exchange. **Stock exchange symbol:** CA. **CEO:** Sanjay Kumar.

COMSYS INC.
1800 Pembrook Drive, Suite 300, Orlando FL 32810. 407/667-3467. **Contact:** Human Resources Department. **World Wide Web address:** http://www.comsys.com. **Description:** Offers contract computer consulting services. **Positions advertised include:** Biz Talk Consultant; Data Warehouse Developer; Designer; Programmer; HP - Unix Administrator; Information Analyst; Network Engineer; Testers; UAT Lab Technologist. **Corporate headquarters location:** Houston TX. **Other U. S. locations:** Nationwide.

CONAX FLORIDA CORPORATION
2801 75th Street North, St. Petersburg FL 33710. 727/345-8000. **Fax:** 727/345-4217. **Contact:** Sandy Nitz, Personnel Administrator. **World Wide Web address:** http://www.conaxfl.com. **Description:** Manufactures temperature sensing devices, explosive actuated devices, and electrical penetrators. **Positions advertised include:** Cost Estimator; Document Engineer. **Corporate headquarters location:** This location. **Listed on:** Privately held. **Number of employees at this location:** 125.

CONCORD CAMERA CORPORATION
4000 Hollywood Boulevard, Suite 650N, Hollywood FL 33021. 954/331-4200. **Fax:** 954/981-3055. **Contact:** Human Resources. **E-mail address:** employment@concord-camera.com. **World Wide Web address:** http://www.concordcam.com. **Description:**

Designs, develops, manufactures, and markets a wide range of digital, traditional 35-mm, instant, and single-use cameras. **Corporate headquarters location:** This location. **Listed on:** NASDAQ. **Stock exchange symbol:** LENS. **Annual sales/revenues:** More than $100 million. **Number of employees worldwide:** 6,000.

CONCURRENT COMPUTER CORPORATION
2881 Gateway Drive, Pompano Beach FL 33069. 954/974-1700. **Toll-free phone:** 800/666-4544. **Fax:** 954/973-5398. **Contact:** Human Resources. **E-mail address:** resumes@ccur.com. **World Wide Web address:** http://www.ccur.com. **Description:** Provides networking systems, servers, software, technical support, and other services to companies in academic, aerospace/defense, CAD engineering, and scientific industries. **Positions advertised include:** Industry Marketing Manager. **Special programs:** Internships. **Corporate headquarters:** Duluth GA. **Listed on:** NASDAQ. **Stock exchange symbol:** CCUR. **Number of employees at this location:** 300. **Number of employees nationwide:** 425.

J.W. CONNER & SONS, INC.
P.O. Box 2522, Tampa FL 33601-2522. 813/247-4441. **Contact:** Michelle Williams, Human Resources. **Description:** A road and highway contractor.

CONSTANTINE'S WOOD CENTER OF FLORIDA
1040 East Oakland Park Boulevard, Fort Lauderdale FL 33334. 954/561-1716. **Contact:** Human Resources. **World Wide Web address:** http://www.constantine.com. **Description:** Sells tools, lumber, veneer, and related wood products.

CONSTRUCTION DATA CORPORATION
2770 Indian River Boulevard, Suite 400, Vero Beach FL 32960. 561/770-6003. **Toll-free phone:** 800/652-0008. **Fax:** 561/231-7247. **Contact:** Human Resources. **E-mail address:** jobs@cdcnew.com. **World Wide Web address:** http://www.cdcnews.com. **Description:** Publishes semiweekly construction project newspapers that include planned and upcoming projects available for bid. The company's primary subscribers are general contractors, subcontractors, and construction suppliers in the commercial, residential, industrial, and highway construction markets. **Positions advertised include:** Database Quality Control Specialist; Sales Representative; Part Time Data Entry. **Corporate headquarters location:** This location. **Other U.S. locations:** Rockland MA; Lawrenceville NJ; Austin TX. **Listed on:** Privately held. **Annual sales/revenues:** $11 - $20 million. **Number of employees at this location:** 75. **Number of employees nationwide:** 175.

CONVERGYS
285 International Parkway, Lake Mary FL 32746. 407/771-8000. **Contact:** Human Resources. **World Wide Web address:** http://www.convergys.com. **Description:** A computer software company specializing in the telecommunications industry. **Positions advertised include:** Analyst; Assistant Coordinator. **Special programs:** Internships. **Corporate headquarters location:** Cincinnati OH. **Operations at this facility include:** Regional Headquarters; Research and Development; Sales; Service. **Listed on:** New York Stock Exchange. **Stock exchange symbol:** CVG.

CORAM HEALTHCARE CORPORATION
9143 Phillips Highway, Suite 300, Jacksonville FL 32256. 904/363-3089. **Toll-free phone:** 800/365-6275. **Contact:** Human Resources. **World Wide Web address:** http://www.coram-healthcare.com. **Description:** One of the largest home health infusion therapy companies in the United States. The company provides a wide range of alternate site delivery services including ambulatory and home infusion therapies, lithotripsy, and institutional pharmacy services. Coram Healthcare Corporation has a network of more than 85 locations nationwide. **Positions advertised include:** Pharmacy Nurse Case Manager; Delivery Warehouse Technician; Pharmacy Technician; Account Manager; Nurse Manager; Clinical Pharmacist; Purchasing Representative. **NOTE:** Jobseekers should send employment inquiries to Coram Healthcare, Human Resources, 1125 17th Street, Suite 1500, Denver CO 80202. **Corporate headquarters location:** Denver CO. **Number of employees nationwide:** 4,000.

CORDIS CORPORATION
14201 NW 60th Avenue, Miami Lakes FL 33014. 305/824-2000. **Contact:** Human Resources. **World Wide Web address:** http://www.cordis.com. **Description:** Manufactures medical devices including angiographics and neurovascular products. The company also acts as a supplier for hospitals and physicians. **Positions advertised include:** Unit Manager; PQS Specialist. **Parent company:** Johnson & Johnson.

COSTA CRUISE LINES
200 South Park Road, Hollywood, FL 33021. 954/266-5600. **Contact:** Claudia Juliao, Personnel Manager. **World Wide Web address:** http://www.costacruises.com. **Description:** An ocean cruise line.

CRAWFORD & COMPANY
P.O. Box 48370, Jacksonville FL 32247-8370. 904/398-0551. **Contact:** Ronald J. Hayes, Branch Manager. **World Wide Web address:** http://www.crawford-thg.com. **Description:** A branch office of a regional insurance adjuster. **Corporate headquarters location:** Atlanta GA.

CRESTVIEW AEROSPACE CORPORATION
5486 Fairchild Road, Crestview FL 32539-8157. 850/682-2746. **Fax:** 850/682-7411. **Contact:** Jeaneane Fountain, Human Resources. **World Wide Web address:** http://www.crestview-aerospace.com. **Description:** Manufactures aircraft components and is engaged in aircraft modification. **Positions advertised include:** Resource Manager; Methods Planner; Buyer; Custom Prototype Technician. **Corporate headquarters location:** Chantilly VA. **Parent company:** Fairchild Aircraft Corporation.

CROWLEY AMERICAN TRANSPORT, INC.
P.O. Box 2110, Jacksonville FL 32203-2110. 904/727-2200. **Recorded jobline:** 904/727-4287. **Contact:** Human Resources. **World Wide Web address:** http://www.crowley.com. **Description:** An ocean freight company. **Positions advertised include:** Specialist Support Services; Security Information Administrator; Freight Service Coordinator; Inter Model Dispatcher.

CROWN CORK & SEAL COMPANY, INC.
P.O. Box 770369, Winter Garden FL 34777-0369. 407/654-0225. **Contact:** Human Resources. **World Wide Web address:** http://www.crowncork.com. **Description:** Crown Cork & Seal Company is a worldwide manufacturer and distributor of a wide range of crowns, seals, and aluminum/steel cans including aerosol and beverage cans. Crown Cork & Seal Company also manufactures bottling equipment. **Operations at this facility include:** This location manufactures two-piece aluminum soda cans and three-piece steel coffee cans. **Listed on:** New York Stock Exchange. **Stock exchange symbol:** CCK.

CUNARD LINE
6100 Blue Lagoon Drive, Suite 400, Miami FL 33126. 305/463-3000. **Toll-free phone:** 800/223-0764. **Fax:** 305/463-3035. **Contact:** Human Resources. **World Wide Web address:** http://www.cunard.com. **Description:** An ocean cruise line that calls at ports worldwide. **Positions advertised include:** Hotel Officer; Waiter; Waitress; Chef De Partie; Assistant Waiter; Assistant Waitress; Class 2, 3 Deck Officer; Ventilation Officer; Electrical Electronics Engineer; International Sales; Switchboard Operator; Regional Sales Manager; Security Operations Manager; Sales Representative; Corporate Training & Development Specialist; Business Analyst; Cruise Sales Consultant. **Corporate headquarters location:** This location. **Listed on:** New York Stock Exchange. **Stock exchange symbol:** CCL.

BILL CURRIE FORD
5815 North Dale Mabry Highway, Tampa FL 33614. 813/872-5555. **Fax:** 813/554-5354. **Contact:** Mark Jensen, Human Resources. **E-mail address:** resumes@billcurrie.com. **World Wide Web address:** http://www.billcurrie.com. **Description:** A Ford new and used car dealer. **Positions advertised include:** Customer Service Agent.

CYPRESS ELECTRONICS
10901 Malcolm McKinley Drive, Tampa FL 33612. 813/972-6000. **Fax:** 813/972-6012. **Contact:** Janice Beal, Personnel Director. **Description:** Custom designs and manufactures electronics systems, subsystems, and circuit card assemblies for the U.S. government and avionics, communications, and medical industries. **Corporate headquarters location:** This location.

CYPRESS VILLAGE
4600 Middleton Park Circle East, Jacksonville FL 32224. 904/223-6100. **Toll-free phone:** 800/228-6163. **Fax:** 904/223-6186. **Contact:** Human Resources. **World Wide Web address:** http://www.cypressvillage.com. **E-mail address:** sales@cypressvillage.com. **Description:** A nonprofit, multilevel retirement community consisting of single-family homes, townhouses, and apartments for independent living. There are also 39 assisted living units, a 120-bed skilled nursing facility, and an Alzheimer's facility with 60 beds. Founded in 1991. **NOTE:** Second and third shifts are offered. **Office hours:** Monday - Friday, 8:00 a.m. - 5:00 p.m. **Parent company:** National Benevolent Association (St. Louis MO). **Annual sales/revenues:** $11 - $20 million. **Number of employees at this location:** 300.

DANKA OFFICE IMAGING
11201 Danka Circle North, St. Petersburg FL 33716. 727/576-6003. **Contact:** Human Resources. **World Wide Web address:** http://www.danka.com. **Description:** A wholesale distributor of fax machines and photocopiers. **Positions advertised include:** Custom Support Supervisor; Customer Support Specialist; CS&S Business Support Specialist; Supply Chain Analyst; Human Resources Representative; Loyalty Process Specialist; Inbound Telesales Representative; Telephone Services Outbound Sales Representative; Information Technology Manager of System Services; Account Executive; Associate Customer Service Engineer; Staff Accountant. **Corporate headquarters location:** This location. **Listed on:** NASDAQ. **Stock exchange symbol:** DANKY.

DARDEN RESTAURANTS, INC.
P.O. Box 593330, Orlando FL 32859-3330. 407/245-4000. **Contact:** Human Resources. **World Wide Web address:** http://www.darden.com. **Description:** Operates the Red Lobster, Olive Garden, and Bahama Breeze restaurant chains. **Corporate headquarters location:** This location. **Listed on:** New York Stock Exchange. **Stock exchange symbol:** DRI. **Annual sales/revenues:** More than $100 million. **Number of employees nationwide:** 122,000.

DARTNELL CORPORATION
360 Hiatt Drive, Palm Beach Gardens FL 33410. 561/622-6520. **Toll-free phone:** 800/621-5463. **Fax:** 561/622-1375. **Contact:** Human Resources. **World Wide Web address:** http://www.dartnellcorp.com. **E-mail address:** work@lrp.com. **Description:** Dartnell publishes motivational books and newsletters that are used by companies to improve teamwork and employee morale, resolve conflicts, and increase motivation. **Positions advertised include:** Copy Editor; Editor; Legal Editor; Executive Administrative Assistant; Newsletter Sales Representative; Customer Services Representative; Marketing Assistant; Recruiter; Meeting Planner; Associated Press Cordinator.

DATACO DEREX INC.
2280 NW 33rd Court, Pompano Beach FL 33069. 954/977-6362. **Toll-free phone:** 800/825-1262. **Fax:** 913/438-1943. **Contact:** Human Resources. **World Wide Web address:** http://www.dataco.com. **Description:** Sells and services computer printers. Founded in 1979. **Corporate headquarters location:** Overland Park KS.

DAYCO PRODUCTS
3100 SE Maricamp Road, Ocala FL 34471. 352/732-6191. **Contact:** Human Resources. **World Wide Web address:** http://www.dayco.com. **E-mail address:** dayco_employment@markvauto.com. **Description:** Dayco Products is a worldwide manufacturer and distributor of a wide range of highly engineered rubber and plastic products. The company's principal markets include the agricultural, automotive, construction, energy, printing, mining, textile, and transportation industries. **Operations at this facility include:** This facility manufactures braided and woven molded rubber hose.

DAYTON-GRANGER, INC.
3299 SW 9th Avenue, Fort Lauderdale FL 33315. 954/463-0222. **Fax:** 954/761-3172. **Contact:** Personnel. **World Wide Web address:** http://www.daytongranger.com. **Description:** A manufacturer of aviation communications products. **NOTE:** Entry-level positions are offered. **Corporate headquarters location:** This location. **Operations at this facility include:** Administration; Manufacturing; Research and Development; Sales; Service. **Listed on:** Privately held. **Number of employees at this location:** 220.

DECORATOR INDUSTRIES, INC.
10011 Pines Boulevard, Suite 201, Pembroke Pines FL 33024. 954/436-8909. **Contact:** Human Resources. **World Wide Web address:** http://www.decoratorindustries.com. **E-mail address:** sales@daytongrange.com. **Description:** Manufactures draperies, bedspreads, and accessory products.

DELMONTE FRESH PRODUCE
241 Sevilla Avenue, Coral Gables FL 33134-6622. 305/520-8400. **Fax:** 305/444-0160. **Contact:** Human Resources. **World Wide Web address:** http://www.freshdelmonte.com. **Description:** Produces, distributes, and markets fresh produce. **Positions advertised include:** Line Design Engineer; Food Technologist; Quality Information Systems Assurance Manager. **International locations:** Worldwide. **Listed on:** New York Stock Exchange. **Stock exchange symbol:** FDP.

DELOITTE & TOUCHE
One Independent Drive, Suite 2801, Jacksonville FL 32202-5034. 904/356-0011. **Contact:** Human Resources. **E-mail address:** dtcareers@deloitte.com. **World Wide Web address:** http://www.us.deloitte.com. **Description:** An international firm of certified public accountants providing professional accounting, auditing, tax, and management consulting services to widely diversified clients. The company has a specialized program consisting of national industry groups and functional groups that cross industry lines. Groups are involved in various disciplines including accounting, auditing, taxation management advisory services, small and growing businesses, mergers and acquisitions, and computer applications. **International locations:** Worldwide.

DELOITTE & TOUCHE
201 East Kennedy Boulevard, Suite 1200, Tampa FL 33602-5821. 813/273-8300. **Contact:** Human Resources. **E-mail address:** dtcareers@deloitte.com. **World Wide Web address:** http://www. us.deloitte.com. **Description:** An international firm of certified public accountants providing professional accounting, auditing, tax, and management consulting services to widely diversified clients. The company has a specialized program consisting of national industry groups and functional groups that cross industry lines. Groups are involved in various disciplines including accounting, auditing, taxation management advisory services, small and growing businesses, mergers and acquisitions, and computer applications. **International locations:** Worldwide.

DELRAY MEDICAL CENTER
5352 Linton Boulevard, Suite 210, Delray Beach FL 33484. 561/498-4440. **Toll-free phone:** 800/926-8282. **Fax:** 561/637-5357. **Recorded jobline:** 561/495-3459. **Contact:** Human Resources. **World Wide Web address:** http://www. delraymedicalctr.com. **Description:** A 343-bed hospital offering a variety of specialized services including rehabilitation and psychiatric services. Founded in 1982. **Positions advertised include:** Registered Nurse; CT Scan Technician; Case Management Supervisor; Assistant Nurse Manager; Nurse Practitioner; Clinical Pharmacist; Purchasing Warehouse Assistant; Emergency Room Director; Lab Supervisor.

DELTA ENERGY SYSTEMS
One Pine Lakes Parkway North, Palm Coast FL 32137-3608. 386/445-0311. **Fax:** 386/445-0322. **Contact:** Louann Hamacher, Human Resources. **World Wide Web address:** http://www.deltaenergysystems.com. **Description:** Manufactures power packs for the computer and telecommunications industries. **Special programs:** Internships; Training; Co-ops. **Number of employees at this location:** 160.

DELTONA CORPORATION
999 Brickell Avenue, Suite 700, Miami FL 33131. 305/579-0999. **Toll-free phone:** 800/9935-6378. **Fax:** 305/358-0999. **Contact:** Human Resources. **E-mail address:** corporate@deltona.com. **World Wide Web address:** http://www.deltona.com. **Description:** Develops community housing. Founded in 1962.

DEVCON INTERNATIONAL CORPORATION
1350 East Newport Center Drive, Suite 201, Deerfield Beach FL 33442. 954/429-1500. **Contact:** Human Resources. **World Wide Web address:** http://www.devc.com. **Description:** Provides heavy construction services focusing on industrial projects in the Caribbean. **Number of employees at this location:** 640.

DICTAPHONE CORPORATION
3984 Pepsi Cola Drive, Melbourne FL 32924. **Toll-free phone:** 888/483-6266. **Contact:** Human Resources. **World Wide Web address:** http://www. dictaphone.com. **Description:** A manufacturer of voice recording equipment. Founded in 1923. **NOTE:** Jobseekers should send resumes to: Dictaphone Corporation, 3191 Broadbridge Avenue, Stratford CT 06614-2559. **Positions advertised include:** Technical Engineer; Product Specialist. **Corporate headquarters location:** Stratford CT. **Other U.S. locations:** Nationwide. **International locations:** Germany; South America; Switzerland; United Kingdom. **Annual sales/revenues:** More than $100 million.

DILLARD'S DEPARTMENT STORES, INC.
6990 Tyrone Square, St. Petersburg FL 33710. 727/341-6000. **Contact:** Human Resources. **World Wide Web address:** http://www.dillards.com. **Description:** This location is the Florida divisional headquarters. Overall, Dillard's Department Stores operates over 220 stores in 20 states. Dillard's offers a full line of fashion apparel and home furnishings. Founded in 1938. **Corporate headquarters location:** Little Rock AR. **Operations at this facility include:** Sales. **Listed on:** New York Stock Exchange. **Stock exchange symbol:** DDS. **Annual sales/revenues:** More than $100 million.

DISCOUNT AUTO PARTS, INC.
4900 South Frontage Road, Lakeland FL 33815. 863/687-9226. **Contact:** Personnel. **World Wide Web address:** http://www.discountautoparts.net. **Description:** A specialty retailer of automotive replacement parts, maintenance items, and accessories for do-it-yourself customers. Founded in 1971. **Special programs:** Training. **Corporate headquarters location:** This location. **Other U.S. locations:** AL; GA; SC. **Listed on:** New York Stock Exchange. **Stock exchange symbol:** AAP. **Number of employees nationwide:** 3,000.

EDWARD DON & COMPANY
2200 SW 45th Street, Fort Lauderdale FL 33312. 954/983-3000. **Contact:** Human Resources. **Description:** Distributes furniture and equipment to restaurants, hotels, and schools. **World Wide Web address:** http://www.don.com. **Positions advertised include:** Operations Supervisor; Transportation Manager; Sales Representative; International Sales Representative; Driver. **Operations at this facility include:** Administration; Divisional Headquarters; Sales. **Listed on:** Privately held. **Number of employees at this location:** 270. **Number of employees nationwide:** 1,200.

DONER
6200 Courtney Campbell Causeway, Suite 1050, Tampa FL 33607. 813/289-6909. **Contact:** Human Resources. **Description:** A full-service advertising agency that provides strategic planning, sales promotion, direct marketing, and public relations. **Corporate headquarters location:** Detroit MI. **Other U.S. locations:** Baltimore MD; Boston MA; Cleveland OH; Dallas TX. **International locations:** Australia; Belgium; Canada; England. **Annual sales/revenues:** More than $100 million. **Number of employees worldwide:** 600.

DURA AUTOMOTIVE SYSTEMS, INC.
9444 Florida Mining Boulevard, Jacksonville FL 32257-1178. 904/268-8300. **Fax:** 904/268-8350.**Contact:** Human Resources. **World Wide Web address:** http://www.duraauto.com. **Description:** Dura Automotive Systems designs and manufactures driver control systems, engineered components, and cable-related products for the automotive industry worldwide. **Operations at this facility include:** This location manufactures automobile windows. **Listed on:** NASDAQ. **Stock exchange symbol:** DRRA. **President/CEO:** Karl Storrie. **Annual sales/revenues:** More than $100 million.

DYCOM INDUSTRIES, INC.
First Union Center, Suite 500, 4440 PGA Boulevard, Palm Beach Gardens FL 33410. 561/627-7171. **Fax:** 561/627-7709. **Contact:** Human Resources. **E-mail address:** info@dycomind.com. **World Wide Web address:** http://www.dycomind.com. **Description:** A holding company for subsidiaries that manufacture mobile phones and provide communication services. Founded in 1969. **Corporate headquarters location:** This location. **Other U.S. locations:** Nationwide. **Listed on:** New York Stock Exchange. **Stock exchange symbol:** DY. **Annual sales/revenues:** More than $100 million. **President/CEO:** Steven E. Nielsen. **Number of employees nationwide:** 6,000.

DYNALCO CONTROLS
3690 NW 53rd Street, Fort Lauderdale FL 33309. 954/739-4300. **Contact:** Craig Woetzel, Human Resources Manager. **E-mail address:** careers@dynalco.com. **World Wide Web address:** http://www.dynalco.com. **Description:** Manufactures electronic monitors, controls, sensors, and displays, primarily for stationary engines. **Positions advertised include:** Condition – Based Maintenance Technical Supervisor. **Corporate headquarters location:** Skokie IL. **Other U.S. locations:** Long Beach CA; Billerica MA; Tulsa OK. **Parent company:** Crane Company. **Operations at this facility include:** Administration; Manufacturing; Research and Development; Sales; Service. **Number of employees at this location:** 80.

ECC INTERNATIONAL CORPORATION
2001 West Oak Ridge Road, Orlando FL 32809. 407/859-7410. **Toll-free phone:** 800/327-1020. **Fax:** 407/855-4840. **Contact:** Human Resources. **E-mail address:** marketing@eccic.com. **World Wide Web address:** http://www.eccic.com. **Description:** ECC International Corporation has two major business segments: military training and simulation, and vending machine design and manufacture. ECC provides training systems and services to the United States Department of Defense and to armed forces in over 25 countries. ECC systems are used for familiarization and maintenance training, weapons systems operation, and gunnery training. ECC's Instructional Systems Design Group also designs computer-based training systems for nonmilitary markets. **Positions advertised include:** Project Engineer. **Operations at this facility include:** This location manufactures training simulators for the government. **Subsidiaries include:** ECC Simulation Limited. **Number of employees at this location:** 780.

ECI TELECOM
1201 West Cypress Creek Road, Fort Lauderdale FL 33309. 954/772-3070. **Fax:** 954/351-4404. **Contact:** Human Resources. **World Wide Web address:** http://www.ecitele.com. **Description:** Provides wide-area network systems for voice and data systems. **Corporate headquarters location:** This location. **Other U.S. locations:** Calabasas CA; Clearwater FL; Orlando FL; Herndon VA. **International locations:** Worldwide. **Operations at this facility include:** Administration; Manufacturing; Research and Development. **Listed on:** NASDAQ. **Stock exchange symbol:** ECIL. **Number of employees at this location:** 220.

EDX ELECTRONICS, INC.
1040 Willa Springs Drive, Winter Springs FL 32708. 800/505-4100. **Fax:** 407/831-5631. **Contact:** Human Resources. **E-mail address:** hrdept@edxelectronics.com. **World Wide Web address:** http://www.edxelectronics.com. **Description:** A worldwide electronics component distributor. **Positions advertised include:** Electronic Assembly & Purchasing Specialist; Programmer.

EATON CORPORATION
2250 Whitfield Avenue, Sarasota FL 34243. 941/758-7726. **Contact:** Human Resources. **World Wide Web address:** http://www.eaton.com. **Description:** A manufacturer of airplane switches. **Positions advertised include:** ITAR Compliance Manager; Systems Development Engineer; Cost Accountant; Product Support Engineer; Electronics Mechanical Design Engineer; Electrical Design Engineer; Account Manager; Supply Chain Manager. **Listed on:** New York Stock Exchange. **Stock exchange symbol:** ETN. **Annual Revenue:** More than $100 million. **Number of employees worldwide:** 49,000.

ECKERD CORPORATION
8201 Chancellor Drive, Orlando FL 32809. 407/239-1442. **Contact:** Human Resources. **World Wide Web address:** http://www.eckerd.com. **Description:** Eckerd is one of the largest drug store chains in the United States, with over 1,715 stores in 13 states. The stores feature general merchandise, prescription and over-the-counter drugs, and photo development services. Nonpharmacy merchandise at Eckerd stores includes health and beauty aids, greeting cards, and other convenience products. The Eckerd Vision Group operates 47 optical superstores and 30 optical centers with one-hour service. Insta-Care Pharmacy Service centers provide prescription drugs and offer patient record and consulting services to health care institutions. **Positions advertised include:** Pharmacist; Pharmacy Technician; Store Management; Photo Lab Management. **Office hours:** Monday - Friday, 8:00 a.m. - 4:30 p.m. **Corporate headquarters location:** Clearwater FL. **Operations at this facility include:** This location is a distribution center. **Parent company:** JC Penney. **Listed on:** New York Stock Exchange. **Stock exchange symbol:** JCP. **Annual Revenue:** More than $100 million. **Number of employees nationwide:** 75,000.

ECKERD CORPORATION
P.O. Box 4689, Clearwater FL 33758. 727/395-6000. **Physical address:** 8333 Bryan Dairy Road, Largo FL 33777. **Recorded jobline:** 727/395-6443. **Contact:** Human Resources. **World Wide Web address:** http://www.eckerd.com. **Description:** One of the largest drug store chains in the United States, with over 1,715 stores in 13 states. The stores feature general merchandise, prescription and over-the-counter drugs, and photo development services. Nonpharmacy merchandise at Eckerd stores includes health and beauty aids, greeting cards, and other convenience products. The Eckerd Vision Group operates 47 optical superstores and 30 optical centers with one-hour service. Insta-Care Pharmacy Service centers provide prescription drugs and offer patient record and consulting services to health care institutions. **Positions advertised include:** Pharmacist; Pharmacy Technician; Store Management; Photo Lab Management. **Special programs:** Internships. **Corporate headquarters location:** This location. **Parent company:** JC Penney. **Operations at this facility include:** Administration; Research and Development. **Listed on:** New York Stock Exchange. **Stock exchange symbol:** JCP. **Number of employees at this location:** 1,000. **Number of employees nationwide:** 75,000.

EDISON COMMUNITY COLLEGE
P.O. Box 60210, Fort Myers FL 33906-6210. 239/489-9300. **Fax:** 941/489-9041. **Recorded jobline:** 941/489-9120. **Contact:** Leslie Rider, Human Resources Specialist. **World Wide Web address:** http://www.edison.edu. **Description:** A two-year college offering associate's degrees, certification programs, and noncredit continuing education

courses. **NOTE:** Part-time jobs are offered. **Positions advertised include:** Spanish Professor; Mathematics Professor; Humanities Professor; Nursing Professor; Campus Dean; Business & Technology Coordinator; Faculty Planner; Construction Manager; Student Services Specialist; Clerk Specialist; Adjunct Services Coordinator. **Office hours:** Monday - Friday, 8:30 a.m. - 4:30 p.m. **Corporate headquarters location:** This location. **Other area locations:** Naples FL; Port Charlotte FL. **Operations at this facility include:** Administration. **President:** Kenneth P. Walker. **Facilities Manager:** Ronald White. **Purchasing Manager:** Jay Collier. **Number of employees at this location:** 300.

ELIZABETH ARDEN, INC.
14100 NW 60th Avenue, Miami Lakes FL 33014. 305/818-8000. **Toll-free phone:** 800/227-2445. **Fax:** 305/818-8024. **E-mail address:** careers_miami@elizabetharden.com. **Contact:** Human Resources. **World Wide Web address:** http://www.elizabetharden.com. **Description:** A leading global marketer and manufacturer of prestige beauty products. **Positions advertised include:** Administrative Assistant; Legal Secretary. **Corporate headquarters location:** This location. **Listed on:** NASDAQ. **Stock exchange symbol:** RDEN. **Number of employees at this location:** 150.

ELTEC INSTRUMENTS INC.
P.O. Box 9610, Daytona Beach FL 32120. 386/252-0411. **Contact:** Samuel D. Mollenkof, Director of Personnel. **Description:** Develops, manufactures, and markets infrared sensors, industrial control systems, and ohm resistors. Primary customers include alarm manufacturers; building automation systems, heating, air conditioning, and lighting control marketers; and process control systems developers. **Corporate headquarters location:** This location. **Operations at this facility include:** Administration; Manufacturing; Research and Development; Sales; Service.

EMBRY-RIDDLE AERONAUTICAL UNIVERSITY
600 South Clyde Morris Boulevard, Daytona Beach FL 32114-3900. 386/226-6145. **Contact:** Human Resources. **World Wide Web address:** http://www.db.erau.edu. **Description:** A private, four-year, coeducational, undergraduate university offering studies in aviation, aerospace, and engineering. **Positions advertised include:** Department Chair Mathematics; Dean of the College of Career Education; Assistant Provost; Office Associate; Assistant Professor of Mathematics; Interactive Designer; Assistant Director Sports and Marketing and Promotions; Accounting Clerk; Assistant Center Director; Mailroom Clerk; Resident Director; Administrative Assistant; Shift Safety Officer; Serials Librarian; Data Entry Operator; Vice President Chief Financial Officer. **Special programs:** Internships. **Other U.S. locations:** Prescott AZ. **Number of employees nationwide:** 1,200.

EMERGENCY ONE INC.
P.O. Box 2710, Ocala FL 34478-2710. 352/237-1122. **Physical address:** 1601 SW 37th Street, Ocala FL 34474. **Fax:** 352/237-1151. **Contact:** Human Resources. **World Wide Web address:** http://www.e-one.com. **Description:** Manufactures fire rescue vehicles and equipment including aircraft rescue fire fighting vehicles, commercial pumpers, industrial tankers, rescue transport/ambulances, and aerial ladders and platforms. **Positions advertised include:** Product Safety Design Engineer; Environmental Manager; Chassis Design Engineer; Mechanical Designer. **Corporate headquarters location:** This location. **Parent company:** Federal Signal Corporation. **Operations at this facility include:** Administration; Manufacturing; Research and Development; Sales; Service. **Listed on:** New York Stock Exchange. **Stock exchange symbol:** FSS. **Number of employees nationwide:** 1,800.

ENCORE REAL TIME COMPUTING, INC.
1700 NW 66th Avenue, Suite 103, Fort Lauderdale FL 33313. 954/377-1100. **Fax:** 954/377-1145. **Contact:** Human Resources Department. **E-mail address:** info@encore.com. **World Wide Web address:** http://www.encore.com. **Description:** Encore specializes in the manufacture of minicomputers for aerospace, defense, simulation, energy, and information systems. **Special programs:** Internships. **Positions advertised include:** Hardware Engineer. **Corporate headquarters location:** This location. **Operations at this facility include:** Administration; Research and Development; Service.

ERNST & YOUNG LLP
390 North Orange Avenue, Suite 1700, Orlando FL 32801. 407/872-6600. **Contact:** Human Resources. **World Wide Web address:** http://www.ey.com. **Description:** A certified public accounting firm that also provides management consulting services. Services include data processing, financial modeling, financial feasibility studies, production planning and inventory management, management sciences, health care planning, human resources, cost accounting, and budgeting systems. **Other U.S. locations:** Nationwide. **International locations:** Worldwide.

ERNST & YOUNG LLP
100 North Tampa Street, Suite 2200, Tampa FL 33602. 813/225-4800. **Contact:** Human Resources. **World Wide Web address:** http://www.ey.com. **Description:** A certified public accounting firm that also provides management consulting services. Services include data processing, financial modeling, financial feasibility studies, production planning and inventory management, management sciences, health care planning, human resources, cost accounting, and budgeting systems. **Other U.S. locations:** Nationwide. **International locations:** Worldwide.

ESSILOR OF AMERICA
4900 Park Street North, St. Petersburg FL 33709. 727/541-5733. **Contact:** Clair Amrhein, Personnel Director. **World Wide Web address:** http://www.essilor.com. **Description:** A manufacturer of optical lenses for eyeglasses.

EVA-TONE
P.O. Box 7020, Clearwater FL 33758. 727/572-7000. **Toll-free phone:** 800/EVA-TONE (382-8663). **Fax:** 727/540-0088. **Contact:** Nancy Lewis, Human Resources. **E-mail address:** nancy.lewis@eva-tone.com. **World Wide Web address:** http://www.evatone.com. **Description:** Produces audio materials, CDs, CD-ROMs, and cassettes for business and marketing applications. The company also provides commercial printing, mailing, and packaging services. **Corporate headquarters location:** This location. **Operations at this facility include:** Administration; Manufacturing; Research and Development; Sales. **Listed on:** Privately held. **Number of employees at this location:** 400.

EVANS ENVIRONMENTAL CORPORATION
14505 Commerce Way, Suite 400, Miami Lakes FL 33016. 305/374-8300. **Contact:** Human Resources. **Description:** Engaged in environmental testing and consulting, and in the manufacture and distribution of remote control cable television units. **Subsidiaries include:** ABC Cable Products, Inc.; Enviropact Consultants, Inc.; Evans Environmental & Geological Sciences & Management, Inc.; Evans Management Co.; Geos Inc.

EVERGLADES BOATS
544 Air Park Road, Edgewater FL 32132. 386/409-2202. **Contact:** Brandon Von Grabe, Director of Human Resources. **E-mail address:** brandon@evergladesboats.com. **World Wide Web address:** http://www.evergladesboats.com. **Description:** Manufacturer of versatile family fishing boats. **Positions advertised include:** Manufacturing Supervisor.

EVERGLADES UNIVERSITY
1500 North West 48th Street, Fort Lauderdale FL 33309. 954/772-2655. **Toll-free phone:** 888/772-6077. **Fax:** 954/772-2695. **World Wide Web address:** http://www.evergladesuniversity.edu. **Description:** A private four-year university with graduate and undergraduate students. **Positions advertised include:** Admission Coordinator; Dean; Administrative Assistant; Financial Aide Officer; Aviation Adjunct Faculty.

EVERHOME MORTGAGE COMPANY
8100 Nations Way, Jacksonville FL 32256. 904/281-2400. **Fax:** 904/281-6165. **Contact:** Human Resources. **World Wide Web address:** http://www.everhomemortgage.com. **Description:** Engaged in the origination, purchase, sale, and servicing of residential first mortgages. Founded in 1962. **Positions advertised include:** Report & Business Analyst; Accounts Payable Supervisor; Customer Service Lead; Reconciliation Coordinator; Marketing Analyst; Loan Office Assistant; Closer; Sales Team Manager; Loss Mitigation Processor; Internet Processor; Telemarketer. **Corporate headquarters location:** This location. **Operations at this facility include:** Administration; Production; Service. **Listed on:** Privately held. **Number of employees at this location:** 250. **Number of employees nationwide:** 350

EXECUSTAY, INC.
3630 Park Central Boulevard North, Pompano Beach FL 33064. 954/975-0900. **Fax:** 954/975-0411. **Contact:** Human Resources Department. **World Wide Web address:** http://www.execustay.com. **Description:** Specializes in providing corporations and executives with interim housing throughout south Florida. **Corporate headquarters location:** This location. **Parent company:** Marriott International, Inc.

EXECUTRAIN OF FLORIDA
One Urban Center, 4830 West Kennedy Boulevard, Suite 700, Tampa FL 33609. 813/288-2000. **Contact:** Human Resources. **E-mail address:** info@executrain.com. **World Wide Web address:** http://www.executrain.com/tampa. **Description:** Trains businesses and employees in the use of computer software and offers IT certification programs. **Other U.S. locations:** Nationwide. **International locations:** Worldwide.

EXPONENT, INC.
4101 SW 71st Avenue, Miami FL 33155. 305/661-7726. **Toll-free phone:** 888/656-3976. **Contact:** Human Resources. **E-mail address:** hr@exponent.com. **World Wide Web address:** http://www.exponent.com. **Description:** Engaged in accident reconstruction, biomechanics, construction/structural engineering, aviation and marine investigations, environmental assessment, materials and product testing, warnings and labeling issues, accident statistic data analysis, and risk prevention/mitigation. Founded in 1967. **NOTE:** All hiring is conducted through the main offices of Exponent, Inc. Please send resumes to: Human Resources, 149 Commonwealth Drive, Menlo Park CA 94025. **Positions advertised include:** Civil Engineering. **Corporate headquarters location:** Menlo Park CA. **Listed on:** NASDAQ. **Stock exchange symbol:** EXPO. **Number of employees nationwide:** 675.

FDN COMMUNICATIONS
2301 Lucien Way, Suite 200, Maitland FL 32751. 407/835-0300. **Fax:** 407/835-1437. **Contact:** Human Resources. **E-mail address:** fdn-hr@mail.fdn.com. **World Wide Web address:** http://www.fdn.com. **Description:** Provides business class communication services and solutions throughout the Southeastern United States. FDN serves more than 70,000 customers with over a quarter million telephone and Internet lines. **Positions advertised include:** Account Consultant; Account Managers; Business Analyst; Corporate Sales Professional; Customer Care Representative; Inbound Corporate Sales Executive; Field Technician; Major Accounts Manager; Marketing Communications Manager; Sales Representative. **Corporate headquarters location:** This location. **Other area locations:** Atlanta FL; Fort Lauderdale FL; Jacksonville FL; Miami FL; Orlando FL; Tampa FL; West Palm Beach FL.

FDP CORPORATION
2000 South Dixie Highway, Miami FL 33133. 305/858-8200. **Fax:** 305/858-0295. **Contact:** Human Resources. **E-mail address:** jobs@insurance.sunguard.com. **World Wide Web address:** http://www.fdpcorp.com. **Description:** Develops financial software for insurance agencies. **Positions advertised include:** Sales Executive.

FMC CORPORATION
400 Fairway Avenue, Lakeland FL 33801. 863/683-5411. **Contact:** Mary Lou Polin, Human Resources. **World Wide Web address:** http://www.fmc.com. **Description:** FMC Corporation is one of the world's leading producers of chemicals and machinery for the performance chemicals, industrial chemicals, machinery and equipment, defense systems, and precious metals markets. **Corporate headquarters location:** Chicago IL. **Operations at this facility include:** This location manufactures citrus fruit processing machinery. **Listed on:** New York Stock Exchange. **Stock exchange symbol:** FMC. **Number of employees worldwide:** 6,000.

FMS MANAGEMENT SYSTEMS, INC.
dba INTERNATIONAL HOUSE OF PANCAKES
2655 NE 189th Street, North Miami Beach FL 33180. 305/931-5454. **Fax:** 305/933-3300. **Contact:** Carol Boettcher, Director of Human Resources. **World Wide Web address:** http://www.ihop.com. **Description:** Operates International House of Pancakes (IHOP) restaurants. **Positions advertised include:** General Manager. **Other U.S. locations:** Nationwide. **International locations:** Canada. **Listed on:** New York Stock Exchange. **Stock exchange symbol:** IHP.

FPL GROUP
700 Universe Boulevard, Juno Beach FL 33408. 561/694-4000. **Fax:** 305/552-3641. **Contact:** Human Resources. **World Wide Web address:** http://www.fplgroup.com. **Description:** One of the nation's largest providers of electricity-related services. **NOTE:** You may call the Recruiting Center at 800/892-2711. Job seekers should apply via the Internet or by fax. Resumes will not be accepted at address listed. **Positions advertised include:** Outage Supervisor; Meter Reader; Rad Prot Technician; Critical Maintenance Manager; Health Physics Supervisor; Lab Technician; Engineer; Warehousing Technician. **Corporate headquarters location:** This location. **Subsidiaries include:** Florida Power and Light Company serves more than 7 million people along the eastern and southern coast of Florida; FPL Energy owns and operates power plants throughout the United States and abroad; FPL FiberNet, LLC sells fiber optic network capacity wholesale to telecommunications companies in Florida. **Listed on:** New York Stock Exchange. **Stock exchange symbol:** FPL. **Annual sales/revenues:** More than $100 million.

FAMOUS AMOS RESTAURANTS, INC.
2765 Clydo Road, Jacksonville FL 32207. 904/731-3396. **Contact:** Human Resources. **Description:** Operates a chain of 10 area restaurants. **Corporate headquarters location:** This location.

FARM STORES
5800 NW 74th Avenue, Miami FL 33166. 305/471-5141. **Contact:** Human Resources. **World Wide Web address:** http://www.farmstores.com. **E-mail address:** info@farmstores.com. **Description:** Operates a regional chain of convenience stores. **Corporate headquarters location:** This location.

FARO TECHNOLOGIES, INC.
125 Technology Park, Lake Mary FL 32746. 407/333-9911. **Toll-free phone:** 800/736-0234. **Contact:** Human Resources. **World Wide Web address:** http://www.faro.com. **Description:** FARO Technologies Inc. and its international subsidiaries design, develop and market CAM2 systems and services for manufacturers of Automotive, Aerospace, Industrial and Consumer products worldwide. **Positions advertised include:** Calibration Certification Technician; Customer Service Repair Technician; Customer Service Specialist; Inside Sales Specialist. **Corporate headquarters location:** This location. **Other U.S. locations:** Chicago IL; Charlotte NC; Columbus OH; Dallas TX; Detroit MI; Kennet Square PA; Los Angeles CA; Seattle WA. **International locations:** Barcelona, Spain; Coventry, UK; Nagoya, Japan; Paris, France; Rivioli, Italy; Stuttgart, Germany.

FIDELITY FEDERAL BANK & TRUST
205 Datura Street, West Palm Beach FL 33401. 561/803/9900. Toll-free phone: 800/422-3675. **Fax:** 561/805-9992. **Contact:** Personnel. **World Wide Web address:** http://www.fidelityfederal.com. **Description:** A savings bank. Founded in 1952. **NOTE:** Entry-level positions and part-time jobs are offered. **Company slogan:** Count on us! **Position advertised include:** Senior Financial Consultant; Loan Collection Specialist; FSR/Consumer Loan Specialist; Insurance Agent; Teller; Commercial Loan Specialist; Residential/Construction Loan Officer. **Corporate headquarters location:** This location. **Annual sales/revenues:** More than $100 million. **Number of employees at this location:** 410.

FIRST AMERICAN REAL ESTATE SOLUTIONS
1800 NW 66th Avenue, Fort Lauderdale FL 33313. 954/792-2000. **Contact:** Human Resources. **World Wide Web address:** http://www.firstamres.com. **Description:** Maintains credit reports and provides information services for the real estate industry. **Positions advertised include:** Account Executive; Development Territory Manager. **NOTE:** Please send resumes to: Human Resources, 5601 East La Palma Avenue, Anaheim CA 92802. **Operations at this facility include:** Administration; Manufacturing; Regional Headquarters; Research and Development; Sales; Service. **Number of employees at this location:** 320. **Number of employees nationwide:** 1,200.

FISCHER INTERNATIONAL SYSTEMS CORPORATION
3584 Mercantile Avenue, Naples FL 34104. 239/643-1500. **Fax:** 239/643-3772. **Contact:** Human Resources. **World Wide Web address:** http://www.fisc.com. **Description:** Develops and sells software for electronic mailings, directories, and security.

FISERV INC.
1250 Grumman Place, Suite A, Titusville FL 32780. 321/268-2622. **Contact:** Human Resources. **World Wide Web address:** http://www.fiserv.com. **Description:** Conducts online data processing for credit unions. **Positions advertised include:** Internet Network Architect. **Listed on:** NASDAQ. **Stock exchange symbol:** FISV.

FISKARS POTTERY AND OUTDOOR LEISURE PRODUCTS
3000 West Orange Avenue, Apopka FL 32703. 407/889-5533. **Toll-free phone:** 800/621-4253. **Contact:** Human Resources. **World Wide Web address:** http://www.fiskars.com. **Description:** A manufacturer of plastic lawn and garden items. The company specializes in plastic flowerpots and shade structures. **Positions advertised include:** Planner; Category Manager; Assistant Product Manager; Design Engineer; Marketing Manager; Credit Collections Assistant. **Parent company:** Fiskars Consumer Products, Inc. **Number of employees at this location:** 400.

FLORIDA ATLANTIC UNIVERSITY
777 Glades Road, P.O. Box 3091, Boca Raton FL 33431. 561/297-3000. **Recorded jobline:** 561/297-3506. **Contact:** Human Resources. **World Wide Web address:** http://www.fau.edu. **Description:** A four-year liberal arts university offering bachelor's, master's (including MBA), and doctoral degrees. Approximately 11,500 undergraduate and 3,000 graduate students attend Florida Atlantic University. **Positions advertised include:** Assistant Director Student Affairs; Medical Curriculum Coordinator; Admissions Coordinator; Media Coordinator; Communications Supervisor; Facility Planning Coordinator; Athletic Academic Advisor; Student Affairs Coordinator; Chief of Police; Director Student Affairs; Program Assistant; Secretary College of Business; Registration Clerk; Secretary Women's Studies; Ocean Engineering Clerk; Office Support Specialist Admissions; Police Service Technician; Medical Research Assistant.

FLORIDA INTERNATIONAL UNIVERSITY
University Park, 11200 South West 8th Street PC 224, Miami FL 33199-0001. 305/348-2111. **Contact:** Human Resources. **World Wide Web address:** http://www.fiu.edu. **E-mail address:** hr@fiu.edu. **Description:** A multi-campus, accredited university. **Positions advertised include:** Production Manager; University Controller; Admissions Coordinator; Account Manager; PR Writer; Word Processing Operator; Inventory Clerk; Office Assistant; Engineer; Technical Writer; Librarian Technical Assistant.

FLORIDA COMMUNITY COLLEGE AT JACKSONVILLE
501 West State Street, Jacksonville FL 32202. 904/632-3210. **Recorded jobline:** 904/632-3161. **Contact:** Employment Manager, Human Resources Department. **World Wide Web address:** http://www.fccj.org. **Description:** An accredited institution offering associate's degrees, corporate and technical training, and special and continuing education programs. Total enrollment is approximately 28,000. Founded in 1966. **Positions advertised include:** Administrative Assistant; Administrative Specialist; Plant Service Manager; Plant Service Worker; Security Officer; Student Offices Advisor; Student Learning Specialist; Business Development Officer; Database Administrator; Dean of Virtual College; Network System Specialist; System Programmer; Counseling Coordinator; Administrative Specialist; Audio Visual Specialist; Security Officer. **NOTE:** Entry-level positions and part-time jobs are offered. **President:** Dr. Steven Wallace. **Number of employees at this location:** 2,700.

FLORIDA CRUSHED STONE COMPANY
P.O. Box 490180, Leesburg FL 34749-0300. 352/787-0608. **Contact:** Human Resources. **World Wide Web address:** http://www.fcsco.com. **Description:** Manufactures construction materials including cement, aggregates, and pavement components.

FLORIDA DEPARTMENT OF TRANSPORTATION
605 Suwannee Street, Mail Stop #50, Tallahassee FL 32399-0450. 850/414-5300. **Contact:** Walter R. Mitchell, Human Resources. **World Wide Web address:** http://dot.state.fl.us. **Description:** A state agency responsible for developing and maintaining Florida's transportation systems. **Positions advertised include:** Chief Executive; Account; Auditor; Office & Administrative Worker; Installation/Maintenance/Repair Worker; Business Operations Specialist; Engineer; Physical Scientist; Office Clerk; Management Analyst. **Corporate headquarters location:** This location. **Operations at this facility include:** Administration. **Number of employees at this location:** 2,000. **Number of employees nationwide:** 10,000.

FLORIDA EAST COAST RAILWAY COMPANY
P.O. Box 1048, St. Augustine FL 32085-1048. 904/826-2320. **Contact:** Gloria S. Taylor, Director of Human Resources. **Description:** A railway transportation company. **Corporate headquarters location:** This location. **Operations at this facility include:** Administration. **Number of employees at this location:** 200. **Number of employees nationwide:** 1,000.

FLORIDA ENGINEERED CONSTRUCTION PRODUCTS
P.O. Box 24567, Tampa FL 33623. 813/621-4641. **Fax:** 813/630-5476. **Contact:** Larry Toll, Human Resources. **Description:** Manufactures building materials including precast lintels and sills, prestressed concrete beams and joints, roof trusses, and architectural precast slabs. **Corporate headquarters location:** This location. **Other area locations:** Kissimmee FL; Odessa FL; Sarasota FL; West Palm Beach FL; Winter Springs FL. **Operations at this facility include:** Administration; Divisional Headquarters; Manufacturing; Regional Headquarters; Sales; Service. **Listed on:** Privately held. **Number of employees at this location:** 250. **Number of employees nationwide:** 350.

FLORIDA FURNITURE INDUSTRIES, INC.
P.O. Box 610, Palatka FL 32178. 386/328-3444. **Contact:** Human Resources. **World Wide Web address:** http://www.floridafurniture.com. **Description:** Manufactures wooden bedroom furniture.

FLORIDA GLOBAL CITRUS LIMITED
P.O. Box 37, Auburndale FL 33823. 863/967-4431. **Fax:** 863/965-2480. **Contact:** Human Resources. **Description:** Processes citrus fruits and citrus fruit by-products for bulk concentrate sales. The company is also engaged in warehousing. **Corporate headquarters location:** This location. **Operations at this facility include:** Administration; Manufacturing; Sales. **Number of employees at this location:** 200.

FLORIDA INFUSION SERVICES
1053 Progress Court, Palm Harbor FL 34683. 727/942-1829. **Fax:** 727/942-6165. **Contact:** Personnel. **World Wide Web address:** http://www.floridainfusion.com. **Description:** A distributor of pharmaceutical and medical supplies. Florida Infusion Services also provides a variety of pharmacy services.

FLORIDA KEYS ELECTRIC COOPERATIVE
P.O. Box 377, Tavernier FL 33070. 305/852-2431. **Toll-free phone:** 800/858-8845. **Fax:** 305/852-4794. **Contact:** Donna Bosold, Human Resources Manager. **E-mail address:** mail@fkec.com. **World Wide Web address:** http://www.fkec.com. **Description:** A nonprofit, electric utility company. Founded in 1940. **Positions advertised include:** Protection Specialist; Control Specialist; Journeyman; Lineman. **NOTE:** Entry-level positions are offered. **Special programs:** Apprenticeships. **Other area locations:** Marathon FL.

FLORIDA MEMORIAL COLLEGE
15800 NW 42nd Avenue, Miami FL 33054. 305/626-3622. **Fax:** 305/626-3109. **Contact:** Human Resources. **World Wide Web address:** http://www.fmc.edu. **Description:** A private, four-year, liberal arts college with an enrollment of approximately 1,500 students. **Positions advertised include:** Assistant Professor Biology; Assistant Professor Broadcasting; Assistant Professor Criminology; Assistant Professor Elementary Education; Assistant Professor Environmental Science; Assistant Professor Finance; Assistant Professor Physical Education; Assistant Professor Psychology. **Special programs:** Internships. **Operations at this facility include:** Administration. **Listed on:** Privately held. **Number of employees at this location:** 220.

FLORIDA PLYWOODS, INC.
P.O. Box 458, Greenville FL 32331. 850/948-2211. **Contact:** Arthur Maultsby, Personnel Manager. **World Wide Web address:** http://www.flply.com. **Description:** Manufactures particleboard for drawer sides, kitchen cabinets, laminated shelves, and hardwood plywood. **Operations at this facility include:** Manufacturing; Sales.

FLORIDA PROGRESS ENERGY
P.O. Box 14042, St. Petersburg FL 33733. 727/824-6400. **Physical address:** One Progress Plaza, St. Petersburg FL 33701. **Contact:** Human Resources. **World Wide Web address:** http://www.progress-energy.com. **Description:** A diversified utility holding company. **Positions advertised include:** Chemistry Program Manager; Communications Specialist; Corporate Communications & Research Assistant; Electrician; Lighting Technician; Lineman; Meter Reader; Field Coordinator. **Corporate headquarters location:** This location. **Other U.S. locations:** Raleigh NC. **Listed on:** NASDAQ. **Stock exchange symbol:** PGN.

FLORIDA ROCK INDUSTRIES
P.O. Box 4667, Jacksonville FL 32201. 904/355-1781. **Physical address:** 155 East 21st Street, Jacksonville FL 32201. **Contact:** Bob Banks, Director of Human Resources. **Description:** Manufactures concrete aggregates. Florida Rock & Tank Lines (also at this location) transports oil and gasoline. Sunbelt Transport (also at this location) is a flatbed transportation company. **Corporate headquarters location:** This location. **Operations at this facility include:** Administration. **Listed on:** New York Stock Exchange. **Stock exchange symbol:** FRK.

FLORIDA SENTINEL BULLETIN
2207 East 21st Avenue, Tampa FL 33605. 813/248-1921. **Contact:** Gwen Hayes, Editor or Human Resources. **E-mail address:** ghayes@flsentinal.com. **World Wide Web address:** http://www.flsentinel.com. **Description:** A newspaper.

THE FLORIDA STAR
P.O. Box 40629, Jacksonville FL 32203. 904/766-8834. **Fax:** 904/766-1673. **Contact:** Human Resources. **World Wide Web address:** http://www.thefloridastar.com. **Description:** A newspaper.

FLORIDA STATE HOSPITAL
P.O. Box 1000, Chattahoochee FL 32324-1000. 850/663-7258. **Contact:** Tom Carpenter, Recruitment Coordinator. **Description:** Florida State Hospital is a rehabilitative mental health institution for persons with mental/addictive illnesses.

Special programs: Internships. **Corporate headquarters location:** Tallahassee FL. **Operations at this facility include:** Administration. **Number of employees at this location:** 3,000.

FLORIDA STATE UNIVERSITY
6200-A University Center, Tallahassee FL 32306-2410. 850/644-6035. **Contact:** Phaedra Harris, Coordinator of Human Resources. **World Wide Web address:** http://www.fsu.edu. **Description:** A four-year state university offering certificates, bachelor's, master's (including MBA), and doctoral degrees. Approximately 21,500 undergraduate and 5,500 graduate students attend Florida State University. **Positions advertised include:** Assistant Director; Multi Purpose Faculty; Assistant Director University Housing; Assistant in Accounting; Assistant in Communication; Assistant Professor; Office Assistant; Office Manager; Professor & Dean; Program Assistant; Psychologist; Broadcast Specialist; Fiscal Assistant; Telecom Technician; University School Instructor. **Operations at this facility include:** Administration; Research and Development. **Number of employees at this location:** 2,500.

THE FLORIDA TIMES-UNION
FLORIDA PUBLISHING COMPANY
P.O. Box 1949, Jacksonville FL 32231. 904/359-4600. **Physical address:** One Riverside Avenue, Jacksonville FL 32202. **Fax:** 904/359-4695. **Recorded jobline:** 904/359-4588. **Contact:** Sherwin Pulmano, Human Resources Manager. **World Wide Web address:** http://www.jacksonville.com. **Description:** Florida Publishing Company publishes the *Florida Times-Union,* a daily newspaper in Jacksonville, and provides other products and services in northeastern Florida and southeastern Georgia. **Positions advertised include:** Credit Control Clerk; Staff Accountant; Accounting Executive; Contract Sales; Distributor Press; Inserters; Business Reporter; Copy Editor; Features Editor; Sports Copy Editor; Training Manager; Multimedia Real Estate Consultant; Truck Drivers. **Special programs:** Internships. **Corporate headquarters location:** Augusta GA. **Parent company:** Morris Communications Corporation. **Operations at this facility include:** Administration; Manufacturing; Research and Development; Sales; Service. **Listed on:** Privately held. **Number of employees at this location:** 1,200.

FLORIDA'S NATURAL GROWERS
P.O. Box 1111, Lake Wales FL 33859-1111. 863/676-1411. **Physical address:** 650 Highway 27 North, Lake Wales FL 33859. **Recorded jobline:** 877/842-9891. **Contact:** Human Resources. **World Wide Web address:** http://www.floridasnatural.com. **Description:** Processes and packages citrus juice. Brand names include Florida's Natural, Donald Duck, Bluebird, Texsun, and Vintage. **Positions advertised include:** General Laborer; Lab Technician; Team Resource Person; Industrial Hygiene Technician. **Corporate headquarters location:** This location. **Listed on:** Privately held. **Annual sales/revenues:** More than $100 million. **Number of employees at this location:** 900. **Number of employees nationwide:** 1,000.

FOLEY & LARDNER
One Independent Drive, Suite 1300, Jacksonville FL 32202. 904/359-2000. **Contact:** Human Resources. **World Wide Web address:** http://www.foley.com. **Description:** A law firm specializing in real estate, tax, corporate, securities, and individual planning. Founded in 1842.

FORT LAUDERDALE JET CENTER
1100 Lee Wagner Boulevard, Fort Lauderdale FL 33315. 954/359-3200. **Contact:** Personnel. **World Wide Web address:** http://www.fll-jetcenter.com. **Description:** A private airport for corporate aircraft. Fort Lauderdale Jet Center is a fixed-base operator.

FORT MYERS COCA-COLA BOTTLING COMPANY
10051 Alico Road, Fort Myers FL 33913. 941/590-2653. **Contact:** Human Resources. **Description:** A bottler of soft drink brands including Barq's, Dr. Pepper, and Coca-Cola. **Parent company:** Coca-Cola Enterprises, Inc. is a producer of soft drinks and nonalcoholic beverages including spring and sparkling waters, juices, isotonics, and teas. The company operates in 38 states, the District of Columbia, the U.S. Virgin Islands, the Islands of Tortola and Grand Cayman, and the Netherlands. The company's franchises market its products to over 154 million people. Coca-Cola Enterprises operates 268 facilities; approximately 24,000 vehicles; and over 860,000 vending machines, beverage dispensers, and coolers.

FORT PIERCE TRIBUNE
600 Edwards Road, Fort Pierce FL 34982. 561/461-2050. **Contact:** Human Resources. **World Wide Web address:** http://www.tcpalm.com. **Description:** A daily newspaper. Founded in 1920. **Positions advertised include:** Design Associate; Driver CDL Class B; Maintenance Clerk; Shipping Clerk; Receiving Clerk; Packager; Press Operator; Helper. **Parent company:** E.W. Scripps Company.

FOWLER WHITE BOGGS BANKER
P.O. Box 1438, Tampa FL 33601. **Physical address:** 501 East Kennedy Boulevard, Suite 1700, Tampa FL 33602. 813/228-7411. **Contact:** Human Resources. **World Wide Web address:** http://www.fowlerwhite.com. **Description:** A law firm specializing in corporate, business, and real estate law. **Positions advertised include:** Estate Planning Lawyer; Bankruptcy Creditor; Rights Litigator; Commercial Real Estate Transactions Coverage Litigation Associate; Estate Planning Associate; Products Liability Litigator; Securities Litigation Associate.

FRANKLIN TEMPLETON INVESTMENTS
500 East Broward Boulevard, Suite 2100, Ft. Lauderdale FL 33394. 954/527-7500. **Contact:** Human Resources. **World Wide Web address:** http://www.franklintempleton.com. **Description:** A global investment management company. **Positions advertised include:** Proposal Specialist; Research Librarian; Settlements Assistant; Trading Settlements Analyst; Performance Consultant Trainer; Mail Room Clerk; Investment Operations Manager; Financial Accounting Auditor; Administrative Assistant; Investment Operations Supervisor; Futures Program; Information Technology Manager. **Corporate headquarters location:** San Mateo CA.

FREEDOM SQUARE RETIREMENT CENTER
10801 Johnson Boulevard, Seminole FL 33772. 727/398-0379. **Contact:** Human Resources. **World Wide Web address:** http://www.arclp.com. **Description:** A retirement community providing all levels of nursing care to its clients. **Positions advertised include:** Physical Therapist; LPN; Certified Nurse Assistant. **Listed on:** New York Stock Exchange. **Stock exchange symbol:** ACR.

FREEDOM VILLAGE
6501 17th Avenue West, Bradenton FL 34209. 941/798-8200. **Employment hotline:** 941/798-8143. **Contact:** Sharon Peters, Human Resources Director. **World Wide Web address:** http://www.freedomvillage.com. **Description:** A continuing care retirement center offering skilled nursing, assisted living, and independent living options. **Positions advertised include:** Server; Utility Aide; Security Guard. **Office hours:** Monday - Friday, 8:30 a.m. - 5:00 p.m. **Corporate headquarters location:** This location. **Number of employees at this location:** 550.

G&K SERVICES, INC.
14720 NW 24th Court, Opa Locka FL 33054. **Fax:** 305/688-1179. **Contact:** Human Resources. **World Wide Web address:** http://www.gkservices.com. **Description:** Provides uniform services to more than 85,000 businesses including those in the automotive, high-tech, maintenance/repair, and manufacturing industries. G&K's services include designing uniform programs that fit customers' needs; helping customers select a company logo, garment style, and colors; and introducing the uniform program to customers' employees. Products include executive wear, industrial wear, flame-resistant garments, clean room uniforms, treated dust mops, linens, and wiping towels. G&K also provides delivery of clean garments on a weekly basis. **Positions advertised include:** Territory Sales Representative; Route Manager; District Sales Manager; Route Sales Manager; Account Manager. **Other U.S. locations:** Nationwide. **International locations:** Canada. **Listed on:** NASDAQ. **Stock exchange symbol:** GKSRA. **Number of employees nationwide:** 8,000.

G&T CONVEYOR
476 Southridge Industrial Drive, Tavares FL 32778-9118. 352/343-1500. **Fax:** 352/343-5077. **Contact:** Human Resources. **E-mail address:** careers@gtconveyor.com **World Wide Web address:** http://www.gtconveyor.com. **Description:** Manufacturer of baggage handling systems, such as those seen in airports. **Positions advertised include:** Assembly Department Supervisor; Craters/Packers; Fabrication Machine Operators; Mechanical CAD Drafters; Mechanical Designers; Mechanical Project Engineers; Parts Inventory Clerk 2nd Shift; Production Assembly; Production Painters; Production Welders.

GE AUTOMATION SERVICES
P.O. Box 7126, Pensacola FL 32534. 850/968-2191. **Contact:** Human Resources. **World Wide Web address:** http://www.geindustrial.com. **Description:** A manufacturer of industrial control instruments. **Listed on:** New York Stock Exchange. **Stock exchange symbol:** GE.

GEAC AEC BUSINESS SOLUTIONS
3938 Premier North Drive, Tampa FL 33624. 813/269-7900. **Contact:** Human Resources. **World Wide Web address:** http://www.geac.com. **Description:** Develops accounts receivable and accounts payable software.

GABLES ENGINEERING, INC.
247 Greco Avenue, Coral Gables FL 33146. 305/774-4400. **Fax:** 305/774-4465. **Contact:** Cary Reyes, Human Resources Manager. **World Wide Web address:** http://www.gableseng.com. **Description:** Designs, configures, and manufactures aircraft communication and navigation control systems. **Corporate headquarters location:** This location. **Operations at this facility include:** Manufacturing; Research and Development. **Number of employees at this location:** 220.

THE GAINESVILLE SUN
P.O. Box 147147, Gainesville FL 32614-7147. 352/374-5000. **Recorded jobline:** 352/335-3500. **Contact:** Eva Del Rio, Human Resources Manager. **E-mail address:** humanresources@gvillesun.com. **World Wide Web address:** http://www.gainesvillesun.com. **Description:** A newspaper with a daily circulation of approximately 52,550, and a Sunday circulation of 60,600.

GATORLAND
14501 South Orange Blossom Trail, Orlando FL 32837. 407/855-5496. **Toll-free phone:** 800/393-JAWS. **Contact:** Personnel. **E-mail address:** info@gatorland.com. **World Wide Web address:** http://www.gatorland.com. **Description:** An attraction featuring a cypress swamp walk, a children's water park, a children's petting zoo, and the 10-acre Alligator Breeding Marsh.

GENCOR INDUSTRIES INC.
5201 North Orange Blossom Trail, Orlando FL 32810. 407/290-6000. **Fax:** 407/578-0577. **Contact:** Personnel. **World Wide Web address:** http://www.gencor.com. **Description:** Manufactures combustion systems and related electronic heat process controls.

GENERAL DYNAMICS INC. (ADVANCED INFORMATION SYSTEMS)
960 John Sims Parkway West, Niceville FL 32578-1823. 850/678-2126. **Fax:** 850/678-3977. **Contact:** Human Resources. **World Wide Web address:** http://www.veridian.com. **Description:** General Dynamics provides engineering systems integration and technical services to government agencies. **Positions advertised include:** Defense Analysis Specialist; Systems Engineer. **Other U.S. locations:** Nationwide. **Operations at this facility include:** This location offers computer support to nearby Air Force bases. **Number of employees nationwide:** Over 5,000.

GENTIVA HEALTH SERVICES
417-B NW Race Track Road, Suite C, Fort Walton Beach FL 32547. 850/862-3240. **Contact:** Personnel. **World Wide Web address:** http://www.gentiva.com. **Description:** Gentiva Health Services provides home health care services, pharmaceutical support, and supplemental staffing services. **Positions advertised include:** Mastered Social Worker; Speech Therapist; Registered Nurse; Physical Therapist. **Operation at this facility include:** This location is a home health care agency.

GENTIVA HEALTH SERVICES
4500 North State Road 7, Building I, Suite 105, Fort Lauderdale FL 33319. 954/485-5500. **Contact:** Personnel. **World Wide Web address:** http://www.gentiva.com. **Description:** Gentiva Health Services provides home health care services, pharmaceutical support, and supplemental staffing services. **Positions advertised include:** Account Executive; Physical Therapist; Registered Nurse. **Operations at this facility include:** This location is a home health care agency.

GEORGIA-PACIFIC CORPORATION
P.O. Box 919, Palatka FL 32178. 386/325-2001. **Contact:** Michael Eichorn, Human Resources Manager. **World Wide Web address:** http://www.gp.com. **Description:** Manufactures pulp, paper, building materials, and related chemicals. **Positions advertised include:** Accountant; Accounting Supervisor. **Other U.S. locations:** Nationwide. **Listed on:** New York Stock Exchange. **Stock exchange symbol:** GP. **CEO:** Pete Correll.

GIVAUDAN FLAVORS
4705 U.S. Highway 92 East, Lakeland FL 33801. 941/665-1040. **Fax:** 773/913-0363. **Contact:** Human Resources. **E-mail address:** lakeland.hr@givaudan.com. **World Wide Web address:** http://www.givaudan.com. **Description:** Manufactures flavors and fragrances for wide variety of customers and applications. **Positions advertised**

include: Quality Control Technologist; Operations Manager. **Other U.S. locations:** Nationwide. **International locations:** Worldwide.

GOLD KIST POULTRY
P.O. Box 1000, Live Oak FL 32064. 386/362-2544. **Contact:** David Mullis, Division Human Resources Manager. **World Wide Web address:** http://www.goldkist.com. **Description:** A poultry grow-out and processing complex. **Positions advertised include:** HACCP Coordinator; Quality Assurance Specialist. **Corporate headquarters location:** Atlanta GA. **Operations at this facility include:** Divisional Headquarters. **Number of employees at this location:** 1,200. **Number of employees nationwide:** 18,000.

GOLDEN BEAR GOLF INC.
11780 U.S. Highway 1, Suite 400, North Palm Beach FL 33408. 561/626-3900. **Contact:** Linda Clark, Personnel Administrator. **World Wide Web address:** http://www.nicklaus.com. **Description:** Franchises golf practice and instruction facilities, operates golf schools, constructs golf courses through Weitz Golf International (also at this location), and sells consumer golf products and apparel. **Corporate headquarters location:** This location. **Operations at this facility include:** Service. **Listed on:** NASDAQ. **Stock exchange symbol:** JACK.

GRAPHLINE COMPANY
9409 West Commercial Boulevard, Tamarac FL 33351-4321. 954/722-3000. **Toll-free phone:** 800/998-3200. **Contact:** Director of Human Resources. **E-mail address:** humanresources@graphline.com. **World Wide Web address:** http://www.graphline.com. **Description:** Distributes graphic arts equipment, and provides service repairs to graphic arts equipment. **Corporate headquarters location:** This location. **Operations at this facility include:** Administration; Sales; Service. **Number of employees at this location:** 85. **Number of employees nationwide:** 125.

GREENBERG TRAURIG
1221 Brickell Avenue, 21st Floor, Miami FL 33131. 305/579-0500. **Fax:** 305/579-0717. **Contact:** Rosalyn Friedman, Human Resources Director. **World Wide Web address:** http://www.gtlaw.com. **Description:** A business law firm specializing in corporate and securities, entertainment, information technology, litigation, real estate, and telecommunications. **Positions advertised include:** Litigation Associate; Health Business Associate; Litigation Associate; Real Estate Associate; Reorganization Bankruptcy & Restructuring Associate; Trust & Real Estate Associate.

GULF BREEZE ZOO
5701 Gulf Breeze Parkway, Gulf Breeze FL 32561. 850/932-2229. **Fax:** 850/932-8575. **Contact:** Personnel. **E-mail address:** information@the-zoo.com. **World Wide Web address:** http://www.the-zoo.com. **Description:** An attraction that offers botanical Japanese gardens, a Safari Line train that drives through 30 acres of cageless animals, and a zoo that features more than 700 animals.

GULF COAST CENTER
5820 Buckingham Road, Fort Myers FL 33905. 239/694-2151. **Contact:** Human Resources. **Description:** A state-run residential facility for people with mental disabilities.

GULF POWER COMPANY
One Energy Place, Pensacola FL 32520-0714. **Toll-free phone:** 800/225-5797. **Recorded jobline:** 800/457-2981. **Contact:** Human Resources. **World Wide Web address:** http://www.southernco.com. **Description:** A public utility company. **NOTE:** Entry-level positions are offered. The company only accepts resumes for open positions. Please call the jobline for more information. **Positions advertised include:** Safety Specialist. **Corporate headquarters location:** Atlanta GA. **Other area locations:** Fort Walton Beach FL; Panama City FL. **Parent company:** Southern Company Services. **Operations at this facility include:** Administration; Sales; Service. **Listed on:** New York Stock Exchange. **Stock exchange symbol:** SO. **Number of employees at this location:** 1,500.

GULF STREAM LUMBER COMPANY
1415 South Federal Highway, Boynton Beach FL 33435. 561/732-9763. **Fax:** 561/732-1643. **Contact:** Human Resources. **World Wide Web address:** http://www.gulfstreamlumber.com. **Description:** Manufactures lumber, trusses, and doors **Positions advertised include:** Account Executive Window Sales; Account Executive Millwork Sales.

H.I. DEVELOPMENT, INC.
111 West Fortune Street, Tampa FL 33602. 813/229-6686. **Fax:** 813/223-9734. **Contact:** David Callen, President. **E-mail address:** mailbox@hidevelopment.com. **World Wide Web address:** http://www.hidevelopment.com. **Description:** A hotel management and consulting firm. **Corporate headquarters location:** This location. **Operations at this facility include:** Regional Headquarters.

HTE INC.
1000 Business Center Drive, Lake Mary FL 32746. 407/304-3235. **Contact:** Human Resources. **World Wide Web address:** http://www.hteinc.com. **Description:** Develops software for the government, education, law enforcement, and public safety markets. **Positions advertised include:** Applications Specialist; Customer Account Executive; Installation Specialist; Software Engineer; Support Analyst. **Listed on:** NASDAQ. **Stock exchange symbol:** HTEI. **Annual revenues:** $51 - $100 million. **Number of employees at this location:** 500.

HARDRIVES, INC.
2350 South Congress Avenue, Delray Beach FL 33445. 561/278-0456. **Contact:** Personnel Director. **World Wide Web address:** http://www.hardrivespaving.com. **Description:** Manufactures paving rouxes and related materials. **Positions advertised include:** Estimator; Heavy Equipment Operator; Field Mechanic; Truck Mechanic; Diesel Engine Re-builder; Oiler; Tandem Driver; PAN Operator. **Number of employees at this location:** 400.

HARRIS CORPORATION
1025 West NASA Boulevard, Mail Stop 19, Melbourne FL 32919. 321/727-9207. **Toll-free phone:** 800/4HA-RRIS. **Contact:** Human Resources. **World Wide Web address:** http://www.harris.com. **Description:** A communications equipment company that provides broadcast, network, government, and wireless support products and systems. **NOTE:** Send resumes to: Harris Corporation, Resume Processing, P.O. Box 549238, Suite 107, Waltham MA 02454. **Positions advertised include:** Engineering Administration; Program Manager Support Assistant; Word Processor Proposal Center; Corporate Legal Administrator; Lead Senior Auditor; Contracts Manager; Engineering Specialist; Information Systems Security Supervisor. **Corporate headquarters location:** This location. **International locations:** Worldwide. **Operations at this facility include:** Administration; Manufacturing; Research and Development; Sales; Service. **Listed on:** New York Stock Exchange. **Stock exchange symbol:** HRS. **President/CEO:** Phillip W. Farmer. **Number of employees worldwide:** 10,000.

HARRIS TECHNICAL SERVICES CORPORATION
1225 Evans Road, Melbourne FL 32904. 321/952-7550. **Toll-free phone:** 888/952-9468. **Fax:** 321/733-7570. **Contact:** Human Resources. **World Wide Web address:** http://www.harris.com. **Description:** Develops software solutions for commercial and government applications. **NOTE:** Entry-level positions are offered. Send resumes to: Harris Corporation, Resume Processing, P.O. Box 549238, Suite 107, Waltham MA 02454. **Positions advertised include:** Software Engineer; Quality Control Manager; Process Systems Engineer; Information Security Engineer; Communications Infrastructure Systems Engineer; Information and Transportation Systems Engineer; Business Development Manager; Quality Engineer. **Office hours:** Monday - Friday, 8:00 a.m. - 5:00 p.m. **International locations:** Worldwide. **Parent company:** Harris Corporation. **Listed on:** New York Stock Exchange. **Stock exchange symbol:** HRS. **President/CEO:** Phillip W. Farmer. **Number of employees worldwide:** 10,000.

THE HASKELL COMPANY
111 Riverside Avenue, Jacksonville FL 32202. 904/791-4500. **Contact:** Human Resources. **E-mail address:** recruiter@thehaskellco.com. **World Wide Web address:** http://www.thehaskellco.com. **Description:** Provides architectural, construction, engineering, and real estate services. **Positions advertised include:** Assistant Project Manager; Director of Infrastructure; Director of Software & Integration Systems; Director of Career Development; Project Manager; Project Estimator. **Corporate headquarters location:** This location. **Operations at this facility include:** Regional Headquarters.

HEALTH FIRST/HOLMES REGIONAL MEDICAL CENTER
PALM BAY COMMUNITY HOSPITAL
1350 South Hickory Street, Melbourne FL 32901. 321/434-7110. **Fax:** 321/434-8587. **Contact:** Dennis Voglas, Director of Employment. **World Wide Web address:** http://www.health-first.org. **Description:** A medical center. **Positions advertised include:** Registered Nurse; Advanced Therapist; Clinical Change Nurse; Education Technologist; Health Unit Coordinator; Medical Technologist; Practical Care Technologist; Radiological Technician; Support Technician; Winter Team Registered Nurse. **Operations at this facility include:** Service. **Number of employees at this location:** 2,800.

HEALTH MANAGEMENT ASSOCIATES, INC.
5811 Pelican Bay Boulevard, Suite 500, Naples FL 34108. 239/598-3131. **Contact:** Human Resources. **World Wide Web address:** http://www.hma-corp.com. **Description:** Provides a broad range of general, acute care health services to rural communities through its ownership of several hospitals and medical centers. **Positions advertised include:** Network Systems Engineer; Legal Secretary; Accounts Payable Clerk; Tax Manager; Reimbursement Consultant. **Listed on:** New York Stock Exchange. **Stock exchange symbol:** HMA. **Number of employees nationwide:** 5,300.

HEALTH PLAN SERVICES
3501 East Frontage Road, Tampa FL 33607. 813/289-1000. **Contact:** Human Resources. **E-mail address:** support@zywave.com. **World Wide Web address:** http://www.healthplan.com. **Description:** A third-party administrator and marketer of small group life and health insurance.

HEALTHSOUTH DOCTORS HOSPITAL
5000 University Drive, Coral Gables FL 33146. 305/666-2111. **Contact:** Director of Human Resources. **World Wide Web address:** http://www.healthsouth.com. **Description:** A 218-bed hospital offering a variety of specialized services including orthopedics, radiological imaging, neuroscience, and sports medicine. **Listed on:** New York Stock Exchange. **Stock exchange symbol:** HRC.

HEARTLAND REHABILITATION CENTER
4101 Sawyer Road, Sarasota FL 34233. 941/925-3427. **Contact:** Human Resources. **Description:** A physical therapy facility offering both inpatient and outpatient services.

HEICO AEROSPACE CORPORATION
3000 Taft Street, Hollywood FL 33021. 954/987-6101. **Fax:** 954/987-8228. **Contact:** Human Resources. **World Wide Web address:** http://www.heico.com. **Description:** Manufactures and distributes jet aircraft engine parts and repairs and overhauls engine components. **Positions advertised include:** Aviation Engineer; Aviation Sales Representative. **Parent company:** HEICO Corporation. **Listed on:** New York Stock Exchange. **Stock exchange symbol:** HEI.

HERCULES, INC.
7510 Baymeadows Way, Jacksonville FL 32256. 904/733-7110. **Contact:** Human Resources. **E-mail address:** mlevitskie@herc.com. **World Wide Web address:** http://www.herc.com. **Description:** Develops, sells, and services specialty process chemicals for the pulp and paper industry. **Special programs:** Internships. **Operations at this facility include:** Administration; Divisional Headquarters; Research and Development; Sales; Service. **Listed on:** New York Stock Exchange. **Stock exchange symbol:** HPC.

HI*TECH ELECTRONIC DISPLAYS
13900 U.S. Highway 19 North, Clearwater FL 33764. 727/531-4800. **Toll-free phone:** 800/723-9402. **Fax:** 727/524-6655. **Contact:** Laurie Danielson, Personnel. **E-mail address:** lauried@hitechled.com. **World Wide Web address:** http://www.hitechled.com. **Description:** Manufactures LED displays. Products and services include indoor and outdoor LED signs; customized graphics, logos, and animations; and software and computer accessories to run the company's LED displays. **Positions advertised include:** Customer Service Representative; Technical Support; Quality Control Inspector; Final Assembler; Cable Assembler. **NOTE:** Entry-level positions are offered. **Corporate headquarters location:** This location. **Parent company:** Paonessa Holding Company. **Annual sales/revenues:** $21 - $50 million. **Number of employees at this location:** 95.

HI-RISE RECYCLING SYSTEMS, INC.
8505 NW 74th Street, Miami FL 33166. 305/597-0243. **Fax:** 305/594-4228. **Contact:** Human Resources. **E-mail address:** info@wilkinsonhirise.com. **World Wide Web address:** http://www.hiri.com. **Description:** Sells, installs, and services the patented Hi-Rise Recycling System for use in residential and industrial buildings. Founded in 1990. **Corporate headquarters location:** This location. **Subsidiaries include:** Wilkinson Company Inc. (Stow OH) manufactures recycling, trash, and linen chutes for high-rise apartment buildings, condominiums, and hotels. **Listed on:** NASDAQ. **Stock exchange symbol:** HIRI.

HI-STAT MANUFACTURING COMPANY, INC.
7290 26th Court East, Sarasota FL 34243. 941/355-9761. **Fax:** 941/351-8342. **Contact:** Human Resources. **E-mail address:** sales@histat.com. **World Wide Web address:**

http://www.histat.com. **Description:** Manufactures and distributes automotive sensors. The company's product line includes speed, temperature, ABS, and pressure sensors. **NOTE:** Entry-level positions and second and third shifts are offered. **Corporate headquarters location:** This location. **Other U.S. locations:** Lexington OH. **Listed on:** Privately held. **Number of employees at this location:** 650. **Number of employees nationwide:** 1,500.

HILLSBOROUGH COMMUNITY COLLEGE
P.O. Box 31127, Tampa FL 33631-3127. 813/253-7000. **Physical address:** 4001 Tampa Bay Boulevard, Tampa FL 33614. **Fax:** 813/253-7034. **Recorded jobline:** 813/253-7185. **Contact:** Human Resources Department. **E-mail address:** employ@hccfl.com. **World Wide Web address:** http://www.hcc.cc.fl.us. **Description:** Hillsborough Community College is a multicampus, state-run community college accredited by the Southern Association of Colleges and Schools. **Positions advertised include:** Staff Assistant; Accountant; Aqua Culture Instructor; Dean of Health & Wellness & Sports Technician; Cashier Clerk; Lab Assistant; Shipping & Receiving Specialist; Learning Resources Technician; Nursing Instructor; Trade Worker; Child Development Associate; HVAC Station Operator. **Corporate headquarters location:** This location. **Operations at this facility include:** This location offers programs specializing in computer programming, business management, fire science, and criminal justice training. **Number of employees at this location:** 1,500.

HILLSBOROUGH, COUNTY OF
P.O. Box 1110, Tampa FL 33601. 813/272-6400. **Physical address:** 601 East Kennedy Boulevard, Tampa FL 33601. **Contact:** Human Resources. **World Wide Web address:** http://www.hillsborough.org. **Description:** The administrative offices for the Hillsborough county government. **Positions advertised include:** Appraiser; Automated Devices Mechanic; Center Coordinator; Data Clerk; Community Planner; Community Services Officer; Custodian Detention Deputy; Electrician; General Manager; Geographical Information Systems Analyst; Head Start Teacher; Plant Manager; Helicopter Pilot; Water Plant Operator; Storekeeper.

HOLLANDER HOME FASHIONS CORPORATION
6560 West Rogers Circle, Suite 19, Boca Raton FL 33487. 561/997-6900. **Fax:** 561/997-8738. **Contact:** Human Resources. **World Wide Web address:** http://www.hollander.com. **Description:** Manufactures bed pillows, comforters, mattress pads, comforter sets, and specialty bedding products. **Corporate headquarters location:** This location. **Other U.S. locations:** Nationwide. **Operations at this facility include:** Administration; Manufacturing; Research and Development; Sales. **Listed on:** Privately held. **Number of employees at this location:** 40. **Number of employees nationwide:** 1,200.

HOME SHOPPING NETWORK, INC.
One HSN Drive, St. Petersburg FL 33729. 727/872-1000. **Contact:** Human Resources. **World Wide Web address:** http://www.homeshoppingnetwork.com. **Description:** A holding company that owns and operates Home Shopping Club, Inc. (HSC), which offers jewelry, hard goods, soft goods, cosmetics, and other items via live television presentations; the Internet Shopping Network, which delivers online shopping; and HSN Direct division, which produces and airs infomercials and distributes infomercial products. **Corporate headquarters location:** This location. **Parent company:** USA Networks Inc. **Listed on:** NASDAQ. **Stock exchange symbol:** USAi. **Number of employees nationwide:** 4,500.

HONEYWELL
1401 W Cypress Creek Road, Fort Lauderdale FL 33309. 954/928-2100. **Fax:** 954/928-2619. **Contact:** Personnel. **World Wide Web address:** http://www.honeywell.com. **Description:** Honeywell is engaged in the research, development, manufacture, and sale of advanced technology products and services in the fields of chemicals, electronics, automation, and controls. The company's major businesses are home and building automation and control, performance polymers and chemicals, industrial automation and control, space and aviation systems, and defense and marine systems. **Positions advertised include:** Systems Engineer; Software Engineer; Human Resources Administration Assistant; Production Technician; Electrical Engineer. **Other U.S. locations:** Nationwide. **Operations at this facility include:** This location designs and manufactures airborne electronic equipment for the commercial airlines and military markets. **Listed on:** New York Stock Exchange. **Stock exchange symbol:** HON.

HOOVER INDUSTRIES INC.
7260 NW 68th Street, Miami FL 33166-2014. 305/888-9791. **Fax:** 305/887-4632. **Contact:** Personnel. **World Wide Web address:** http://www.hooverindustries.com. **Description:** Manufactures seat covers, cushions, and inflatable survival equipment for the aerospace industry. Founded in 1955. **Positions advertised include:** Corporate Controller; Customer Service Manager; Outside Sales; Mechanical Engineer; Aeronautical Engineer; Purchasing Traffic; Bookkeeper. **Corporate headquarters location:** This location. **Listed on:** Privately held. **Number of employees at this location:** 200.

HOSPICE BY THE SEA, INC.
1531 West Palmetto Park Road, Boca Raton FL 33486. 561/395-5031. **Fax:** 561/395-9897. **Contact:** Human Resources Department. **World Wide Web address:** http://www.hospicebytheseafl.org. **Description:** Provides nonprofit health care services to terminally ill patients and offers bereavement counseling and other services for the families of the patients. **NOTE:** Second and third shifts are offered. **Positions advertised include:** Administration Receptionist; Bilingual Team Certified Nurses Aide; Bilingual Team Physician; Donations Database Specialist; Accounting Assistant; Registered Nurse; Licensed Practical Nurse; Runner; Certified Nurses Aide; Auditor; Data Entry Medical Records; Social Worker; Volunteer Specialist. **Special programs:** Internships; Summer Jobs. **Office hours:** Monday - Friday, 8:30 a.m. - 5:00 p.m. **CEO:** Trudi Webb. **Annual sales/revenues:** $11 - $20 million. **Number of employees at this location:** 350.

HOSPICE OF NORTHEAST FLORIDA
4266 Sunbeam Road, Jacksonville FL 32257. 904/268-5200. **Contact:** Human Resources. **World Wide Web address:** http://www.hospicene.org. **Description:** Provides health care services for terminally ill patients in their homes or in nursing facilities. **Positions advertised include:** Chef; Patient Care Coordinator; Registered Nurse; Systems Specialist; Help Desk Technician; Social Service Specialist; Medical Director; Chaplain; Clinical Nurse RN; Mail Clerk.

HUBBARD CONSTRUCTION COMPANY
P.O. Box 547217, Orlando FL 32854-7217. 407/645-5500. **Contact:** Margaret Collins, Director of Personnel. **World Wide Web address:** http://www.hubbard.com. **Description:** A general construction contractor that specializes in paving, bridge-building, and highway construction. **Positions advertised include:** Asphalt Operator; Asphalt Trade; Back Hoe Operator; Trade Carpenter; Clerical Staff; Concrete Trade; Dozer Operator; Salary Estimator; Foremen; Laborer; Mechanic; Pile Driver; Quality Control; Roller Operator; Supervisor Truck Driver. **Corporate headquarters location:** This location. **Operations at this facility include:** Administration. **Number of employees at this location:** 750. **Number of employees nationwide:** 1,000.

HUGHES SUPPLY INC.
P.O. Box 2273, Orlando FL 32802-2273. 407/841-4755. **Physical address:** 20 North Orange Avenue, Suite 200, Orlando FL 32801. **Contact:** Human Resources Director. **World Wide Web address:** http://www.hughessupply.com. **Description:** A wholesale distributor of electrical, plumbing, building, and pool supplies. **Positions advertised include:** Outside Sales. **Corporate headquarters location:** This location. **Listed on:** New York Stock Exchange. **Stock exchange symbol:** HUG.

HUMANA
6101 Blue Lagoon Drive, Miami FL 33126. 305/267-6633. **Contact:** Human Resources. **World Wide Web address:** http://www.humana.com. **Description:** A managed health care company that provides comprehensive services through its health maintenance organizations, and administrative services through its workers' compensation third-party administration. **Positions advertised include:** Personal Nurse Navigator; Providing Contracting Network Relations; Smart Suite Consultant. **Listed on:** New York Stock Exchange. **Stock exchange symbol:** HUM.

HUMMINGBIRD, INC.
124 Marriott Drive, Tallahassee FL 32301. 850/942-3627. **Contact:** Cyndi Utt, Human Resources. **World Wide Web address:** http://www.hummingbird.com. **Description:** Develops document management software. Hummingbird also provides education, consulting, and support services for its products. **Positions advertised include:** Quality Assurance Analyst; Clarity System Analyst. **Listed on:** NASDAQ. **Stock exchange symbol:** HUMC.

HUSK JENNINGS GALLOWAY & ROBINSON
6 East Bay Street, Suite 600, Jacksonville FL 32202. 904/354-2600. **Fax:** 904/354-7226. **Contact:** Personnel. **World Wide Web address:** http://www.huskjennings.com. **Description:** An advertising, marketing, and public relations agency. **Positions advertised include:** Administrative Manager; Public Relations Specialist. **Corporate headquarters location:** This location. **Number of employees at this location:** 15.

HYATT REGENCY ORLANDO INTERNATIONAL AIRPORT
9300 Airport Boulevard, Orlando FL 32827. 407/825-1310. **Fax:** 407/825-1341. **Contact:** Human Resources. **World Wide Web address:** http://www.hyatt.com. **Description:** A full-service hotel that offers two restaurants, recreational facilities, air line tickets, car rental services, and meeting and banquet facilities. **Positions advertised include:** Front Desk Clerk; Housekeeper; Custodian; Security Officer. **Corporate headquarters location:** Chicago IL. **Other U.S. locations:** Nationwide. **International locations:** Worldwide. **Parent company:** Hyatt Hotel Corporation. **Operations at this facility include:** Service. **Listed on:** Privately held. **Number of employees at this location:** 400. **Number of employees nationwide:** 40,000.

HYATT REGENCY PIER SIXTY-SIX
2301 SE 17th Street Causeway, Fort Lauderdale FL 33316. 954/728-3580. **Fax:** 954/728-3509. **Contact:** Human Resources. **World Wide Web address:** http://www.hyatt.com. **Description:** A full-service hotel that offers six restaurants, multiple recreational facilities, and extensive meeting and banquet facilities. **Special programs:** Internships. **Operations at this facility include:** Administration; Divisional Headquarters; Sales. **Listed on:** Privately held. **Number of employees at this location:** 500.

HYPERION SOLUTIONS
401 East Las Olas Boulevard, Ft. Lauderdale FL 33394. 954/332-2410. **Fax:** 954/332-2411. **Contact:** Human Resources. **World Wide Web address:** http://www.hyperion.com. **Description:** Provides proprietary software to help businesses manage their operations. **Positions advertised include:** Staff Accountant. **International locations:** Worldwide. **Average annual revenue:** 490 million. **Listed on:** NASDAQ. **Exchange symbol:** HYSL.

IBM CORPORATION
3109 West Dr. Martin Luther King Junior Boulevard, Tampa FL 33607. 813/872-2277. **Toll-free phone:** 800/426-4968. **Contact:** Human Resources. **World Wide Web address:** http://www.ibm.com. **Description:** This location operates as a regional sales office. Overall, IBM is the developer, manufacturer, and marketer of advanced information processing products including computers and microelectronic technology, software, networking systems, and information technology-related services. **NOTE:** Jobseekers should send a resume to IBM Staffing Services, 1DPA/051, 3808 Six Forks Road, Raleigh NC 27609. **Corporate headquarters location:** Armonk NY. **Subsidiaries include:** IBM Credit Corporation; IBM Instruments, Inc.; IBM World Trade Corporation.

IMC PHOSPHATES
P.O. Box 2000, Mulberry FL 33860. 863/428-2500. **Contact:** Human Resources. **World Wide Web address:** http://www.imcglobal.com. **Description:** Engaged in the production of phosphate rock and related surface mining activities. **Special programs:** Apprenticeships. **Parent company:** IMC Fertilizer Group, Inc. (Mundelein IL) produces oil; natural gas; sulfur deposits; and uranium oxide, a chemical which is used in nuclear power plant fuel.

IBIS LLC
999 NW 51st Street, Suite 100, Boca Raton FL 33431. 561/489-7400. **Fax:** 561/237-2851. **Contact:** Human Resources. **E-mail address:** contact@ibisit.com. **World Wide Web address:** http://www.ibisit.com. **Description:** A technology & service company working to develop internet solutions. **Positions advertised include:** Chief Financial Advisor; Corporate Counsel; Publisher Account Manager; Publisher Account Representative; Client Services Associate; Commercial Legal Assistant; Director of Business Development; Internet Business Development Manager; Internet Marketing Specialist; Technical Support; Help Desk Representative.

IKON OFFICE SOLUTIONS TECHNOLOGY SERVICES
5445 West Cypress Street, Suite 100, Tampa FL 33607. 813/261-2000. **Fax:** 813/267-2500. **Contact:** Kim McDaniels, Human Resources. **World Wide Web address:** http://www.ikon.com. **Description:** Provides client/server and workflow consulting, network integration, product fulfillment, and technical training. Founded in 1988. **Positions advertised include:** 3rd Shift Copy Machine Operator; Account Executive Outside Sales. **Other area locations:** Fort Lauderdale FL; Jacksonville FL; Orlando FL; Tallahassee FL. **Other U.S. locations:** Pittsburgh PA. **Operations at this facility include:** Sales. **Listed on:** New York Stock Exchange. **Stock exchange symbol:** IKN. **Annual sales/revenues:** $51 - $100 million. **Number of employees at this location:** 100. **Number of employees nationwide:** 210.

INDIAN RIVER MEMORIAL HOSPITAL
1000 36th Street, Vero Beach FL 32960-6592. 772/567-4311. **Contact:** Human Resources. **World Wide Web address:** http://www.irmh.com. **Description:** A 335-bed community hospital. Founded in 1932. **Positions advertised include:** Coder; Financial Counselor; Patient Care Technician; Nursing Assistant; Accounting Clerk; Mental Health Technician;; Emergency Department Technician; Medical Assistant; Radiation Therapist; Social Worker; Clinical Dietician; Radiation Therapist; Medical Technician; Technical Support; EMT; Registered Nurse; Case Manager; Utility Worker; Environmental Services Aide.

INFINIUM LABS INC
2033 Main Street #309, Sarasota FL 34237. 941/556-8000. **Contact:** Human Resources. **E-mail address:** jobs@infiniumlabs.com. **World Wide Web address:** http://www.infiniumlabs.com. **Description:** A global entertainment and interactive game company. **Positions advertised include:** Legal Assistant.

INJECTION FOOTWEAR CORPORATION
8730 NW 36th Avenue, Miami FL 33147. 305/696-4611. **Contact:** Human Resources. **Description:** Manufactures shoes. **Corporate headquarters location:** This location. **Operations at this facility include:** Manufacturing; Sales.

INTELLECT TECHNICAL SOLUTIONS
Bay Vista Complex, 15950 Bay Vista Drive #130, Clearwater FL 33760. 727/533-9797. **Toll-free phone:** 800/599-8781. **Fax:** 727/533-0685. **Contact:** Chris Chiappetta, Human Resources. **E-mail address:** chrisc@intellectcorp.com **World Wide Web address:** http://www.intellectcorp.com. **Description:** A full service provider of technology consultants. **Positions advertised include:** Marketing Consultant; Sales Consultant.

INTERIM HEALTHCARE INC.
32644 Blossom Lane, Leesburg FL 34788. 352/326-0400. **Contact:** Human Resources. **World Wide Web address:** http://www.interimhealthcare.com. **Description:** A home health care agency.

INTERNATIONAL FLAVORS & FRAGRANCES (IFF)
2051 North Lane Avenue, Jacksonville FL 32254. 904/783-2180. **Contact:** Human Resources. **World Wide Web address:** http://www.iff.com. **Description:** A manufacturer and distributor of flavors, fragrances, and aroma chemicals. **Positions advertised include:** Associate Research Fellow; Distribution Operations Manager; Research Scientist; R&D Scientist. **Corporate headquarters location:** New York NY. **Operations at this facility include:** Administration; Manufacturing; Research and Development; Sales. **Listed on:** New York Stock Exchange. **Stock exchange symbol:** IFF.

INTERNATIONAL SPEEDWAY CORPORATION
P.O. Box 2801, Daytona Beach FL 32120-2801. 386/254-2700. **Physical address:** 1801 West International Speedway Boulevard, Daytona Beach FL 32114. **Contact:** Director of Personnel. **World Wide Web address:** http://www.daytonausa.com. **Description:** Organizes stock car, sports car, motorcycle, and go-cart racing events for spectators at six locations, including two in Daytona Beach. Among the major events conducted by the company are late-model stock car races sanctioned by the National Association for Stock Car Auto Racing, Inc. (NASCAR). The company also produces and syndicates race and race-related radio broadcasts through MRN Radio. **Other U.S. locations:** AL; AZ; NY; SC. **Subsidiaries include:** Amercrown Service Corporation conducts food, beverage, and souvenir operations. **Number of employees nationwide:** 4,620.

INVENSYS METERING SYSTEMS
9495 Delegates Drive, Orlando FL 32837. 407/851-4470. **Contact:** Human Resources. **World Wide Web address:** http://www.invensys.com. **Description:** This division manufactures water meters. Overall, Invensys manufactures temperature control products, energy management systems, and mechanical services for the commercial marketplace. **Operations at this facility include:** Administration; Manufacturing; Research and Development; Sales; Service.

ISYS/BIOVATION
6925 Lake Ellenor Drive, Suite 135, Orlando FL 32809. 407/859-2881. **Contact:** Human Resources. **World Wide Web address:** http://www.isysbiov.com. **Description:** Designs computer hardware and software to help manage laboratory information for hospitals, universities, and doctors' offices.

IVAX CORPORATION
4400 Biscayne Boulevard, Miami FL 33137. 305/575-6000. **Contact:** Human Resources. **World Wide Web address:** http://www.ivax.com. **Description:** IVAX Corporation is a holding company with subsidiaries involved in specialty chemicals, pharmaceuticals, personal care products, and medical diagnostics. The company's principal business is the research, development, manufacture, marketing, and distribution of health care products. Brand name products, marketed under the Baker Norton trade name, include the urological medications Bicitra, Polycitra, Polycitra-K, Polycitra-LC, Neutra-Phos, Neutra-Phos-K, Prohim, Urotrol, Lubraseptic Jelly, and Pro-Banthine; and cardiovascular medicines Cordilox, Triam-Co, Amil-Co, Spiro-Co, and Fru-Co. Other drugs include Proglycem, used to treat hyperinsulinism; Serenance, a neuroleptic used for psychiatric disorders; the respiratory medications Cromogen, Salamol, and Beclazone metered dose inhalers; the Steri-Nebs line of nebulization products; and Eye-Crom and Glaucol. IVAX also markets generic drugs. Through DVM Pharmaceuticals, Inc., IVAX formulates, packages, and distributes veterinary products including DermCaps, a daily dietary supplement; a line of topical therapeutics including ChlorhexiDerm Flush and shampoo, OxyDex shampoo and gel, HyLyt shampoo and rinse, and Relief shampoo, rinse, and spray; two groups of optic products known as Clear and OtiCalm; the DuraKyl and SynerKyl line of ectoparasiticidals; and the wound dressing BioDres. **Positions advertised include:** Administrative Assistant; Inside Sales Call Center Manager; Ivax Legal Secretary; People Soft Application Developer; Research Scientist; Buyer; Cost Accountant: Validation Specialist; Formulation Scientist; System Administrator; Web Producer. **Corporate headquarters location:** This location. **Listed on:** American Stock Exchange. **Stock exchange symbol:** IVX. **Number of employees nationwide:** 2,500.

IVAX PHARMACEUTICALS
4400 Biscayne Boulevard, Miami FL 33137. 305/575-6000. **Toll-free phone:** 800/327-4114. **Contact:** Human Resources Department. **World Wide Web address:** http://www.ivaxpharmaceuticals.com. **Description:** IVAX Pharmaceuticals manufactures generic pharmaceuticals. **Positions advertised include:** Senior Accountant; Regulatory Affairs Manager; Plant Engineer; Director of Systems Development; Validation Manager; Business Analyst; Windows Administrator; Health Information Technician; Senior Production Coordinator. **Parent company:** IVAX Corporation. **Listed on:** American Stock Exchange. **Stock exchange symbol:** IVX.

JACKSON MEMORIAL HOSPITAL
1611 NW 12th Avenue, Park Plaza West L-301, Miami FL 33136. 305/585-1111. **Fax:** 305/326-9470. **Recorded jobline:** 305/585-7886. **Contact:** Ruth Francis, Employment Manager. **World Wide Web address:** http://www.um-jmh.org. **Description:** A 1,567-bed, tertiary, teaching hospital offering specialized services in neurology, pediatrics, dermatology, radiology, pathology, and obstetrics and gynecology. Founded in 1952. **Positions advertised include:** Radiological Technician; Nuclear Medical Technologist; Respiratory Therapy Technologist; Physical Therapist; Hospital Billing Clerk; Health Patient Finance Associate; Nurse Educator; Social Worker; Clinical Social Worker; Practice Pharmacist; Pharmacy Technician; Research Analyst; Clinical Staff Nurse; Associate Nurse Manager; Administrative Support Specialist; Clerk; Support Associate; Health Services Associate; Operating Room Technician; Practical Nurse; Nurse Anesthetist; Patient Care Technologist; Nurse Practitioner; Dietician; Environmental Worker; Electrician Attending Physician; Executive Associate. **Operations at this facility include:** Administration.

JACKSONVILLE BUSINESS JOURNAL
1200 Riverplace Boulevard, Suite 201, Jacksonville FL 32207. 904/396-3502. **Fax:** 904/396-5706. **Contact:** Susan Warrenburg, Operations Director. **E-mail address:** Jacksonville@bizjournal.com. **World Wide Web address:** http://www.bizjournals.com/jacksonville. **Description:** Publishes a business newspaper.

JACKSONVILLE, CITY OF
117 West Duval Street, Suite 100, Jacksonville FL 32202. 904/630-1111. **Fax:** 904/630-1108. **Contact:** Human Resources. **E-mail address:** recruit@coj.net. **World Wide Web address:** http://www.coj.net. **Description:** This location houses the human resources division and is responsible for the hiring of all municipal employees for the city of Jacksonville.

JACKSONVILLE PORT AUTHORITY
2831 Talleyrand Avenue, Jacksonville FL 32206. 904/630-3080. **Fax:** 904/630-3076. **Contact:** Karen Hebert, Manager of Human Resources. **E-mail address:** recruit@coj.net. **World Wide Web address:** http://www.jaxport.com. **Description:** Oversees the daily activities of the port of Jacksonville including the operation of the Blount Island and Talleyrand Docks Marine Terminals, as well as the Jacksonville International Airport and two general aviation airports. **Corporate headquarters location:** This location. **Operations at this facility include:** Administration; Sales; Service. **Number of employees at this location:** 350.

JACKSONVILLE UNIVERSITY
2800 University Boulevard North, Jacksonville FL 32211. 904/256-8000. **Fax:** 904/256-7553. **Contact:** Career Services. **E-mail address:** careerservices@ju.edu. **World Wide Web address:** http://www.ju.edu. **Description:** A private four year liberal arts college on 260 acres in North Western Florida offering undergraduate and graduate programs. **Positions advertised include:** Assistant Professor of Art Ceramics; Assistant Professor of Biology Marine Science; Office Coordinator; Public Safety Officer; Accounting Associate.

RAYMOND JAMES AND ASSOCIATES
P.O. Box 12749, St. Petersburg FL 33733-2749. 727/573-3800. **Physical address:** 880 Carillon Parkway, St. Petersburg FL 33716. **Fax:** 727/573-8420. **Recorded jobline:** 727/573-8490. **Contact:** Human Resources. **E-mail address:** employment@hr.rjf.com. **World Wide Web address:** http://www.rjf.com. **Description:** An investment brokerage firm. Founded in 1962. **Positions advertised include:** Account Maintenance Associate; Acquisitions Analyst; Administrative Assistant; Agency Trader; Assessment Specialist. **Parent company:** Raymond James Financial, Inc. **Operations at this facility include:** Administration; Divisional Headquarters; Regional Headquarters; Research and Development; Sales; Service. **Listed on:** New York Stock Exchange. **Stock exchange symbol:** RJF.

JENKINS AND CHARLAND, INC.
3590 NW 56th Street, Fort Lauderdale FL 33309. 954/484-7777. **Toll-free phone:** 800/486-8986. **Fax:** 954/484-7834. **Contact:** Human Resources. **E-mail address:** ftl@jcengineers.com. **World Wide Web address:** http://www.jcengineers.com. **Description:** Jenkins and Charland is a construction-engineering firm. **Positions advertised include:** Structural Drafter/Designer; Senior Structural Engineer/ Engineering Manager; Structural Engineer. **Other area locations:** Fort Myers FL; Fort Pierce FL; Jacksonville FL; Sarasota FL; Tampa FL.

JOHN KNOX VILLAGE OF CENTRAL FLORIDA
101 Northlake Drive, Orange City FL 32763. 386/775-3840. **Toll-free phone:** 800/978-5669. **Contact:** Human Resources. **E-mail address:** johnknoxvillage@jkvfl.com. **World Wide Web address:** http://www.johnknoxvillage.com. **Description:** A continuing care retirement community offering skilled nursing, assisted living, and independent living.

JOHN KNOX VILLAGE OF FLORIDA
651 SW 6th Street, Pompano Beach FL 33060. 954/783-4000. **Toll-free phone:** 800/978-5669. **Contact:** Human Resources. **E-mail address:** johnknoxvillage@kvfl.com. **World Wide Web address:** http://www.johnknoxvillage.com. **Description:** A continuing care retirement community offering skilled nursing, assisted living, and independent living.

JOHN KNOX VILLAGE OF TAMPA BAY
4100 East Fletcher Avenue, Tampa FL 33613. 813/971-7038. **Toll-free phone:** 800/978-5669. **Contact:** Human Resources. **E-mail address:** johnknoxvillage@kvfl.com. **World Wide Web address:** http://www.johnknoxvillage.com. **Description:** A continuing care retirement community offering skilled nursing, assisted living, and independent living.

EDWARD JONES
1736 Thomasville Road, Tallahassee FL 32303. 850/224-1736. **Contact:** Don McClelland. **World Wide Web address:** http://www.edwardjones.com. **Description:** An investment trading company. **Positions advertised include:** Investment Representative.

JUICE BOWL PRODUCTS
P.O. Box 1048, Lakeland FL 33802-1048. 863/665-5515. **Fax:** 863/667-7137. **Contact:** Samantha Hayes, Director of Human Resources. **E-mail address:** info@juicebowl.com. **World Wide Web address:** http://www.juicebowl.com. **Description:** Cans and processes fruit. **Operations at this facility include:** Administration; Manufacturing; Research and Development; Sales; Service. **Listed on:** Privately held. **Number of employees at this location:** 175.

KPMG
One Biscayne Tower, 2 South Biscayne Boulevard, Suite 2800, Miami FL 33131-1802. 305/358-2300. **Contact:** Human Resources Department. **World Wide Web address:** http://www.kpmg.com. **Description:** KPMG delivers a wide range of value-added assurance, tax, and consulting services. **Positions advertised include:** Investigative & Integrity Advisor; International Tax Manager; Investigative Advisor; Corporate Recovery Associate. **Corporate headquarters location:** Montvale NJ. **International locations:** Worldwide. **Parent company:** KPMG International has more than 85,000 employees worldwide including 6,500 partners and 60,000 professional staff, serving clients in 844 cities in 155 countries. KPMG International is a leader among professional services firms engaged in capturing, managing, assessing, and delivering information to create knowledge that will help its clients maximize shareholder value.

KPMG
450 East Las Olas Boulevard, Suite 750, Fort Lauderdale FL 33301-3503. 954/524-6000. **Contact:** Human Resources Department. **World Wide Web address:** http://www.kpmg.com. **Description:** KPMG delivers a wide range of value-added assurance, tax, and consulting services. **Corporate headquarters location:** Montvale NJ. **Other U.S. locations:** Nationwide. **Parent company:** KPMG International has more than 85,000 employees worldwide including 6,500 partners and 60,000 professional staff, serving clients in 844 cities in 155 countries. KPMG International is a leader among professional services firms engaged in capturing, managing, assessing, and delivering information to create knowledge that will help its clients maximize shareholder value.

KANE FURNITURE
5700 70th Avenue North, Pinellas Park FL 33781. 727/545-9555. **Fax:** 727/548-0552. **Contact:** Human Resources Department. **World Wide Web address:** http://www.kanesfurniture.com. **E-mail address:** humanresources@kanesfurniture.com. **Description:** A furniture retailer. **Positions advertised include:** Sales Consultant; Store Office Customer Service; Visual Merchandiser; In Store Warehouse Personnel; Delivery Driver; Helpers; Warehouse Assistants; Furniture Repair Technician. **Corporate headquarters location:** This location. **Operations at this facility include:** Administration. **Listed on:** Privately held. **Number of employees at this location:** 250. **Number of employees nationwide:** 750.

KASH 'N KARRY FOOD STORES
6401A Harney Road, Tampa FL 33610. 813/620-1139. **Contact:** Human Resources. **World Wide Web address:** http://www.kashnkarry.com. **Description:** An operator of retail food and liquor stores. **Positions advertised include:** Cashier; Meat Cutter; Deli Clerk; Produce Clerk; Bookkeeper; Pharmacist; Truck Driver;; Front End Clerk; Stocker; Bakery Clerk; Cake Decorator; Store Manager; Department Manager; Warehouse Selector. **Corporate headquarters location:** This location. **Number of employees nationwide:** 8,400.

KELLY ASSISTED LIVING SERVICES
300 31st Street, Suite 330, St. Petersburg FL 33713. 727/327-5961. **Contact:** Human Resources. **World Wide Web address:** http://www.kellyservices.com. **Description:** Provides home health care services.

KENDALL MEDICAL CENTER
11750 SW 40th Street, Miami FL 33175. 305/223-3000. **Contact:** Human Resources. **World Wide Web address:** http://www.kendallmed.com. **Description:** A full-service hospital that features LDRP Maternity Suites, advanced diagnostic services, and a 24-hour emergency department. **Positions advertised include:** Marketing Specialist; Unit Leader; Clinical Nurse; Clinical Officer; Registered Nurse; Night Shift Staff Pharmacist; Risk Management Coordinator.

KERZNER INTERNATIONAL
1000 South Pine Island Road, Suite 800, Fort Lauderdale FL 33304. 954/713-2500. **Fax:** 954/809-2331. **Contact:** Human Resources. **E-mail address:** kerznerjobs@kerzner.com. **World Wide Web address:** http://www.kerzner.com. **Description:** Owns and operates casinos, resorts, and hotel facilities. **Listed on:** New York Stock Exchange. **Exchange symbol:** KZL.

KEY SAFETY SYSTEMS, INC.
P.O. Box 33050, Lakeland FL 33807. 863/668-6000. **Physical address:** 5300 Allen K. Breed Highway, Lakeland FL 33811. **Contact:** Human Resources. **World Wide Web address:** http://www.keysafetyinc.com. **Description:** Key Safety Systems designs and manufactures airbags, seatbelts, steering wheels and fully integrated safety systems. Its products are used in more than 300 vehicle models across 60 vehicle makes throughout North America, Europe and Asia. **Positions advertised include:** Designer; Engineer; Supervisor; Systems Administrator; Accountant; Financial Analyst; HR Clerk; HR Coordinator; Customer Service Representative; Receptionist; Material Handler; Molding Operator; Process Operator. **Corporate headquarters location:** This location. **Other U.S. locations:** St. Clair Shores MI; Sterling Heights MI; Boonton NJ; Dayton OH; Brownsville TX. **CEO:** John M. Reiss. **Number of employees at this location:** 600.

KEY WEST CITIZEN
P.O. Box 1800, Key West FL 33041. 305/294-6641. **Fax:** 305/294-0768. **Contact:** Human Resources. **World Wide Web address:** http://www.keysnews.com. **Description:** A daily newspaper. **Parent company:** Thomson Florida Keys Media Group. **Positions advertised include:** Web Designer; Designer; Internet Sales Manager; Packaging & Distributing Associate; Editor.

KHAMELEON SOFTWARE
13830 58th Street North, Suite 401, Clearwater FL 33760. 727/539-1077. **Toll-free phone:** 800/655-6598. **Fax:** 727/539-1070. **Contact:** Human Resources. **E-mail address:** hr@khameleonsoftware.com. **World Wide Web address:** http://www.khameleonsoftware.com. **Description:** Provides software design, consulting, and related services to e-focused, software, and system-integration businesses. **Special programs:** Internships. **Corporate headquarters location:** This location. **Other U.S. locations:** San Francisco CA; Atlanta GA; New York NY.

KINDRED HEALTHCARE
1859 Van Buren Street, Hollywood FL 33020. 954/920-9000. **Contact:** Human Resources. **World Wide Web address:** http://www.kindredhealthcare.com. **Description:** A hospital that specializes in the long-term critical care of patients suffering from acute-level chronic diseases. Founded in 1985. **Positions advertised include:** RN. **Corporate headquarters:** Louisville, KY. **Other U.S. locations:** Nationwide. **President/CEO:** Paul J. Diaz. **Number of employees nationwide:** 53,000.

KING PROVISION CORPORATION
P.O. Drawer U, Jacksonville FL 32203. 904/725-4122. **Contact:** Human Resources. **World Wide Web address:** http://www.kingprovision.com. **Description:** A distributor that provides food and supplies to Burger King Restaurants. **Positions advertised include:** General Manager; Management Trainee; Restaurant/Food Service Manager. **Corporate headquarters location:** This location.

J.I. KISLAK MORTGAGE CORPORATION
7900 Miami Lakes Drive West, Miami Lakes FL 33016. 305/364-4116. **Contact:** Human Resources. **Description:** A mortgage banking and real estate firm. **Positions advertised include:** Production. **Office Hours:** Monday – Friday, 8:30 a.m. – 5:00 p.m. **Corporate headquarters location:** This location.

KISSIMMEE GOOD SAMARITAN VILLAGE
1550 Aldersgate Drive, Kissimmee FL 34746. 407/933-1999. **Contact:** Human Resources. **World Wide Web address:** http://www.goodsamkiss.com. **Description:** A nursing home licensed for 166 beds. **Positions advertised include:** Staff Coordinator. **Other U.S. locations:** Nationwide.

KNIGHT-RIDDER
One Herald Plaza, Miami FL 33132. 305/376-3800. **Contact:** Human Resources. **World Wide Web address:** http://www.kri.com. **Description:** A newspaper publisher that owns 32 dailies and operates the Real Cities network of 58 Regional Websites. **Positions advertised include:** Team Member; Account Executive; Creative Services Manager; Electronic Technician. **Corporate headquarters location:** San Jose CA. **Subsidiaries include:** Knight-Ridder also has interests in the information distribution market through Knight-Ridder Information, Inc.; Knight-Ridder Financial; and Technimetrics. Knight-Ridder's online information retrieval serves the business, scientific, technology, medical, and education communities in more than 100 countries. Knight-Ridder Financial provides real-time financial news and pricing information through primary products MoneyCenter, Digital Datafeed, ProfitCenter, and TradeCenter. Knight-Ridder also has interests in cable television and other businesses. TKR Cable, a 50-50 joint venture with Liberty Media Corporation, serves 344,000 basic subscribers in New Jersey and New York and manages Kentucky systems with 277,000 subscribers. Through TKR Cable Partners, Knight-Ridder owns a 15 percent share of TCI/TKR L.P. Cable Systems with 867,000 subscribers in five states. Other interests include partial ownership of the Seattle Times Company, two paper mills, a newspaper advertising sales company, and SCI Holdings.

LBS CAPITAL MANAGEMENT, INC.
311 Park Place Boulevard, Suite 330, Clearwater FL 33759. 727/726-5656. **Toll-free phone:** 800/477-1296. **Fax:** 727/725-9173. **Contact:** Human Resources. **World Wide Web address:** http://www.lbs.com. **Description:** A financial consulting firm.

LA AMISTAD BEHAVIORAL HEALTH SERVICES
1650 Park Avenue North, Maitland FL 32751. 407/647-0660. **Fax:** 407/629-0552. **Contact:** Human Resources. **E-mail address:** laamistadhr@aol.com. **World Wide Web address:** http://www.lamistad.com. **Description:** Operates a 50-bed inpatient facility. La Amistad offers the following: Deaf and Hearing Impaired Program, Child Psychiatric Program, Adolescent Psychiatric Program, Conversion Treatment Programs, a Dual Diagnosis Psychiatric Treatment Program, an Adult Psychiatric Program, and Academic Programs. **Positions advertised include:** RN; Case Manager; Marketing Representative. **Other U.S. locations:** Winter Park FL. **Parent company:** Universal Health Services.

LA CRUISE CASINO
4738 Ocean Street, Jacksonville FL 32233. 904/241-7200. **Contact:** Human Resources. **World Wide Web address:** http://www.lacruise.com. **Description:** A 24-hour casino cruise ship. La Cruise Dockside (also at this location) is a family-style restaurant.

LAKE CITY REPORTER
P.O. Box 17109, Lake City FL 32056. 386/752-1293. **Fax:** 386/752-9400. **Contact:** Human Resources. **World Wide Web address:** http://www.lakecityreporter.com. **Description:** A newspaper published Monday through Friday. **Parent company:** The New York Times Company.

LAMBDA NOVATRONICS INC.
2855 West McNab Road, Pompano Beach FL 33069. 954/984-7000. **Toll-free phone:** 800/952-6909. **Fax:** 954/984-2479. **Contact:** Pauline Akonskey, Human Resources Department. **World Wide Web address:** http://www.lambdanovatronics.com. **Description:** Designs and manufactures power supplies, avionics, and precision equipment for the defense and electronics industries. **Positions advertised include:** Electrical Engineer; Mechanical Designer; Electrical Design Engineer. **Corporate headquarters location:** Melville NY. **Number of employees at this location:** 240.

LAND SPAN, INC.
P.O. Box 95007, Lakeland FL 33804. 863/688-1102. **Contact:** Human Resources. **World Wide Web address:** http://www.landspan.com. **Description:** An interstate trucking company that transports dry and refrigerated freight. **Positions advertised include:** Driver. **Other U.S. locations:** Norcross GA; Chicago IL; Hagerstown MD; Charlotte NC; El Paso TX; Fort Worth TX. **Parent company:** Watkins Associated Industries, Inc. **Number of employees at this location:** 300.

LANDERS AND PARTNERS, INC.
2857 Executive Drive, Suite 210, Clearwater FL 33762. 727/572-5228. **Fax:** 727/572-5910. **Contact:** Cliff Jones, President. **World Wide Web address:** http://www.landersandpartners.com. **Description:** An advertising agency. **Office hours:** Monday – Friday, 9:00 a.m. – 5:30 p.m.

LANDSTAR LIGON, INC.
P.O. Box 19137, Jacksonville FL 32245-9939. **Toll-free phone:** 800/235-4466. **Contact:** Susan Ramsey, Human Resources Director. **World Wide Web address:** http://www.landstar.com. **Description:** Landstar Ligon provides truckload transportation services through independent contractors and commissioned sales agents. **Positions advertised include:** Staff Accountant; Permit Representative; Director of Facility Operations; Credit Analyst; Trailer Utilization Coordinator; Log Compliance Representative; Contract Research Representative; Trip Envelope Processor; Per Diem Representative. **Parent company:** Landstar System, Inc. is divided into specialized freight transportation segments. Landstar is one of the only publicly traded trucking companies relying on independent owner-operators rather than salaried company drivers, with the company owning just 10 percent of the trucks in its fleet. Subsidiaries of Landstar System, Inc. include Landstar Expedited, Inc.; Landstar Express America, Inc.; Landstar Gemini, Inc.; Landstar Inway, Inc.; Landstar ITCO, Inc.; Landstar Poole, Inc.; Landstar Ranger, Inc.; Landstar T.L.C., Inc.; Landstar Transportation Service, Inc. **Listed on:** NASDAQ. **Stock exchange symbol:** LSTR.

LANDSTAR SYSTEM, INC.
13410 Sutton Park Drive, Jacksonville FL 32224. 904/398-9232. **Toll-free phone:** 800/862-9232. **Contact:** Human Resources. **World Wide Web address:** http://www.landstar.com. **Description:** Provides truckload transportation services through independent contractors and commissioned sales agents. **Positions advertised include:** Staff Accountant; Permit Representative; Director of Facility Operations; Credit Analyst; Trailer Utilization Coordinator; Log Compliance Representative; Contract Research Representative; Trip Envelope Processor; Per Diem Representative. **Corporate headquarters location:** This location. **Listed on:** NASDAQ. **Stock exchange symbol:** LSTR.

LANTANA, TOWN OF
500 Greynolds Circle, Lantana FL 33462. 561/540-5000. **Contact:** Human Resources. **World Wide Web address:** http://www.lantana.org. **Description:** Municipal offices for the town of Lantana. **Office Hours:** Monday – Friday, 8:30 a.m.- 4:30 p.m.

THE LEDGER
P.O. Box 408, Lakeland FL 33802. 863/802-7051. **Physical address:** 300 West Lime Street, Lakeland Fl 33802. **Contact:** Cindy Moates, Human Resources. **E-mail address:** cindy.moates@theledger.com. **World Wide Web address:** http://www.theledger.com. **Description:** A local Newspaper.

LEE MEMORIAL HEALTH SYSTEM
P.O. Box 2218, Fort Myers FL 33902. 239/334-5333. **Physical address:** 2776 Cleveland Avenue, Fort Myers FL 33901. **Toll-free phone:** 800/642-5267. **Fax:** 941/332-4199. **Contact:** Human Resources. **World Wide Web address:** http://www.leememorial.org. **Description:** A leading provider of health care in southwest Florida. The nonprofit hospital is comprised of three acute care hospitals, a skilled nursing facility, home health services, and physician offices. Founded in 1916. **Positions advertised include:** Certified Nursing Assistant; Nursing Director; Licensed Practical Nurse; Physical Therapist; Case Manager; Child Care Assistant; Cook; Food Service Assistant; Marketing Service Line Representative; Medical Records Representative; Monitor Technician; Registered Nurse. **NOTE:** Entry-level positions and second and third shifts are offered. **Corporate headquarters location:** This location. **Operations at this facility include:** Administration; Service. **Number of employees at this location:** 5,200.

LENNAR CORPORATION
700 NW 107th Avenue, Miami FL 33172. 305/559-4000. **Contact:** Carol Burgin, Personnel Manager. **World Wide Web address:** http://www.lennar.com. **Description:** Builds and sells homes, develops and manages commercial and residential properties, and provides real estate-related financial services. The Homebuilding Division constructs and sells single-family attached and detached multifamily homes. These activities also include the purchase, development, and sale of residential land. The company is one of the nation's largest homebuilders with operations in Florida, Arizona, and Texas. The Investment Division is involved in the development, management, leasing, acquisition, and sale of commercial and residential properties. **Positions advertised include:** Corporate Accountant; Joint Venture Assistant Controller; Staff Accountant. **Corporate headquarters location:** This location. **Subsidiaries include:** Lennar Financial Services, Inc. invests in rated portions of commercial real estate mortgage-backed securities for which Lennar's investment division is the servicer, and an investor in the unrated portion of those securities. **Operations at this facility include:** Service. **Listed on:** New York Stock Exchange. **Stock exchange symbol:** LEN. **Number of employees nationwide:** 1,300.

LEON, COUNTY OF
BOARD OF COUNTY COMMISSIONERS
301 South Monroe Street, Suite 201, Tallahassee FL 32301. 850/487-2220. **Fax:** 850/488-6293. **Contact:** Human Resources. **E-mail address:** boatwright@mail.co.leon.fl.us. **World Wide Web address:** http://www.co.leon.fl.us. **Description:** Government and administrative offices of Leon County. **Positions advertised include:** Equipment Mechanic; Fleet Mechanic; Library Services Coordinator; Paramedic; Emergency Medical Technician. **Special programs:** Internships. **Operations at this facility include:** Administration. **Number of employees at this location:** 600.

LIFE CARE SERVICES
800 NW 17th Avenue, Delray Beach FL 33445. 561/272-7779. **Contact:** Human Resources. **Description:** Provides home health care services and manages nursing staffs at various facilities.

LIGHTING COMPONENTS & DESIGN, INC.
692 South Military Trail, Deerfield Beach FL 33442. 954/425-0123. **Contact:** Human Resources. **World Wide Web address:** http://www.lightingcomponents.com. **Description:** A manufacturer of prewired electrical devices, indicator lights, and lamp holders. **Positions advertised include:** Accounting Clerk; Billing Associate; Credit Clerk; Collections & Accounts Payable Associate; Advertising Associate; Promotions Associate; Marketing Associate; Engineer; Human Resources Associate; Information Systems Associate; Machinist; Assembler; Manager; Purchasing Associate; Warehouse Associate; Logistics Associate; Quality Assurance Associate; Customer Support Representative. **Corporate headquarters location:** This location.

LIGHTPATH TECHNOLOGIES, INC.
2603 Challenger Tech Center, Suite 100, Orlando FL 32826. 407/382.4003. **Fax:** 407-382-4007. **Contact:** Human Resources. **E-mail address:** hr_mfg@lightpath.com. **World Wide Web address:** http://www.lightpath.com. **Description:** LightPath designs, develops, manufactures, and distributes optical components and assemblies, utilizing the latest optical processes and advanced manufacturing technologies. **Positions advertised include:** Machinist; Quality Control; Shipping. **Corporate headquarters location:** This location.

LINDER INDUSTRIAL MACHINERY COMPANY
P.O. Box 4589, Plant City FL 33564. 813/754-2727. **Fax:** 815/754-0772. **Physical address:** 1601 South Frontage Road, Plant City FL 33563-2014. **Contact:** Roxanne Taylor, Human Resources Coordinator. **World Wide Web address:** http://www.linderco.com. **Description:** A distributor of construction and mining equipment. **Number of employees at this location:** 200.

LINVATEC CORPORATION
11311 Concept Boulevard, Largo FL 33773. 727/392-6464. **Toll-free phone:** 800/237-0169. **Fax:** 727/399-9900. **Contact:** Human Resources. **E-mail address:** cust_serv@linvatec.com. **World Wide Web address:** http://www.linvatec.com. **Description:** Manufactures and markets medical instruments used in orthoscopy and endoscopy for minimally invasive surgery. **Positions advertised include:** Associate Product Manager; Coach / Team Facilitator; Electronic Assembler; CNC Setup Engineer; Production Machine Operator; Manufacturing Engineer; Tooling Engineer. **Corporate headquarters location:** New York NY. **Parent company:** Bristol-Myers Squibb.

LION COUNTRY SAFARI
2003 Lion Country Safari Road, Loxahatchee FL 33470-3976. 561/793-1084. **Fax:** 561/793-9603. **Contact:** Ron Cameron, Human Resources. **E-mail address:** rcameron@lioncountrysafari.com. **World Wide Web address:** http://www.lioncountrysafari.com. **NOTE:** Positions available in all departments for those who wish to work with animals. **Description:** Features two parks including the Lion Country park, a 500-acre drive-through, cageless zoo; and Safari World, an amusement park with boat cruises, rides, and animals. Founded in 1967.

LOCKHEED MARTIN ELECTRONICS & MISSILES
498 Oak Road, Ocala FL 34472-3099. 352/687-2163. **Contact:** Human Resources. **World Wide Web address:** http://www.lockheedmartin.com. **Description:** Develops, manufactures, and supports advanced combat systems, electro-optics, and air defense technology. **Corporate headquarters location:** Bethesda MD. **Listed on:** New York Stock Exchange. **Stock exchange symbol:** LMT.

LOCKHEED MARTIN MISSILES AND FIRE CONTROL
5600 Sand Lake Road, Mail Point 9, Orlando FL 32819. 407/356-5215. **Fax:** 407/356-3639. **Contact:** Bruce Czarniak, Manager of Staffing. **World Wide Web address:** http://www.lockheedmartin.com. **Description:** Develops, manufactures, and supports advanced combat systems, electro-optics, and air defense technologies. **Positions advertised include:** Human Resources Manager. **Corporate headquarters location:** Bethesda MD. **Operations at this facility include:** Administration; Manufacturing; Research and Development; Sales. **Listed on:** New York Stock Exchange. **Stock exchange symbol:** LMT. **Annual sales/revenues:** More than $100 million. **Number of employees at this location:** 3,750.

LOCKHEED MARTIN TACTICAL DEFENSE SYSTEMS
P.O. Box 6000, Clearwater FL 33758. 813/855-5711. **Fax:** 813/854-7225. **Contact:** Human Resources. **World Wide Web address:** http://www.lockheedmartin.com. **Description:** This location is a computer hardware manufacturing facility. Overall, Lockheed Martin Tactical Defense Systems designs and builds 16-bit and 32-bit technical computing systems used in mil-spec environments. Applications include electronic warfare, signal intelligence, radar, sonar, and imaging where digital signal processing or general purpose computing is required. The company is also involved in systems engineering, software development tools, computer systems, and integrated workstations of commercial architectures for proof-of-concept program phases. **NOTE:** Entry-level positions and second shifts are offered. **Positions advertised include:** Accountant; Software Engineer; Technician. **Special programs:** Training. **Corporate headquarters location:** Bethesda MD. **Other U.S. locations:** Nationwide. **International locations:** Worldwide. **Parent company:** Lockheed Martin Corporation. **Listed on:** New York Stock Exchange. **Stock exchange symbol:** LMT. **Number of employees at this location:** 500.

LOREN INDUSTRIES, INC.
2801 Greene Street, Hollywood FL 33020. 800/772-8085. **Contact:** Human Resources. **World Wide Web address:** http://www.loren.com. **Description:** A manufacturer of jewelry. **Number of employees at this location:** 185.

LOWRY PARK ZOO
1101 West Sligh Avenue, Tampa FL 33604. 813/935-8552. **Fax:** 813/935-9486. **Contact:** Human Resources. **E-mail address:** information@lowryparkzoo.com. **World Wide Web address:** http://www.lowryparkzoo.com. **Description:** A zoo hosting approximately 600,000 visitors per year. The zoo features 1,500 animals and offers a wide variety of shows and exhibits. **Positions advertised include:** Visitor Services Representative; Custodial Services Representative; Food Services Representative; Camel & Horse Ride Operator; Security Guard; Wild Australia Carriage Driver; Eco Tour Train Driver; Occasional Spanish Interpreter; Instructor / Keeper Outreach; Nite Site Instructor.

LUHRS CORPORATION
255 Diesel Road, St. Augustine FL 32084. 904/829-0500. **Toll-free phone:** 800/882-4342. **Fax:** 904/829-0683. **Contact:** Erica Stegerwald, Personnel Manager. **E-mail address:** customerservice@luhrs.com. **World Wide Web address:** http://www.luhrs.com. **Description:** Manufactures fiberglass boats. **Corporate headquarters location:** This location. **Operations at this facility include:** Administration; Manufacturing; Sales; Service. **Number of employees at this location:** 375.

LYNN UNIVERSITY
3601 North Military Trail, Boca Raton FL 33431-5598. 561/237-7853. **Fax:** 561/237-7926. **Contact:** Angela Juiliano, Human Resources. **E-mail address:** resumes@lynn.edu. **World Wide Web address:** http://www.lynn.edu. **Description:** An accredited, private university offering 38 associate's, bachelor's, master's, and doctoral degree programs. Program areas include Arts and Sciences, Business, and Education. Founded in 1962.

M.E. PRODUCTIONS
2000 SW 30th Avenue, Pembroke Park FL 33009. 954/458-4000. **Toll-free phone:** 800/544-0033. **Fax:** 954/458-4003. **Contact:** Hal Etkin, President. **World Wide Web address:** http://www.meproductions.com. **Description:** A production corporation providing sets, lighting, staging, floral arrangements, decor, audio/visual, entertainment, and music services. **Special programs:** Internships. **Corporate headquarters location:** This location. **Operations at this facility include:** Administration; Manufacturing; Sales. **Number of employees at this location:** 60.

MAC PAPERS INC.
P.O. Box 5369, Jacksonville FL 32247. 904/348-3300. **Fax:** 904/348-3340. **Physical address:** 3300 Philips Highway, Jacksonville FL 32247. **Contact:** Ms. Darnell Babbit, Human Resources Director/Corporate Office. **World Wide Web address:** http://www.macpapers.com. **Description:** Distributes envelops, graphic supplies, and printing paper to commercial printers, reproduction departments, commercial businesses, and graphic artists and designers.

MACACADEMY/WINDOWS ACADEMY
FLORIDA MARKETING INTERNATIONAL, INC.
102 East Granada Boulevard, Ormond Beach FL 32176-1712. 386/677-1918. **Toll-free phone:** 800/527-1914. **Fax:** 386/677-6717. **Contact:** Human Resources. **World Wide Web address:** http://www.macacademy.com. **Description:** Offers CD-ROM and video training for several PC and MacIntosh computer applications. The company also offers live seminars and on-site training in the United States, the United Kingdom, Australia, and Japan.

MACHO PRODUCTS INC.
10045 102nd Terrace, Sebastian FL 32958. 561/388-9892. **Toll-free phone:** 800/327-6812. **Contact:** Human Resources. **World Wide Web address:** http://www.macho.com. **Description:** Manufactures protective foam gear and padding for use in martial arts instruction. **Number of employees at this location:** 155.

MAGNUM DIGITAL SERVICES
6601 Lyons Road, Suite D-2, Coconut Creek FL 33073. 954/570-7877. **Fax:** 954/428-5349. **Contact:** Human Resources. **Description:** A printer of digital graphic images for banners, billboards, and bus displays. The company is also a Scotchprint manufacturer. **Corporate headquarters location:** This location. **Number of employees at this location:** 10.

MANATEE MEMORIAL HOSPITAL
206 Second Street East, Bradenton FL 34208. 941/746-5111. **Fax:** 941/745-6862. **Contact:** Personnel. **World Wide Web address:** http://www.manateememorial.com. **Description:** A 512-bed, acute care hospital whose departments include emergency, telemetry, ICU, CVSICU, CCU, and surgery. **Positions advertised include:** Accounting Clerk; Administrative Assistant; Emergency Room Admissions Director; Clinical Manager; Customer Service Representative; Echo Technologist; Admissions Registrar; Lab Assistant; Licensed Practical Nurse; Safety Manager; Physical Therapist; Registered Nurse; Security Officer; Unit Assistant. **Parent company:** Universal Health Services. **CEO:** Brian Flynn.

MANHATTAN TRANSFER MIAMI
1111 Lincoln Road, Suite 700, Miami Beach FL 33139. 305/674-0700. **Contact:** Human Resources. **World Wide Web address:** http://www.mtmiami.com. **Description:** Provides access to the Latin American and Spanish television markets. The company provides numerous production, post-production, and broadcast services to MTV Latino and The Discovery Channel Latin America/Iberia. Services include creative editing, film-to-tape transfer, electronic video editing, computer generated graphics, duplication, and audio services, as well as production and network facilities operations.

MARITRANS INC.
302 Knights Run Avenue, Suite 1200, Tampa FL 33602. 813/209-0600. **Fax:** 813/221-3179. **Contact:** Human Resources. **E-mail address:** hr@maritrans.com. **World Wide Web address:** http://www.maritrans.com. **Description:** Maritrans provides marine transportation for petroleum and oil storage terminals. The company also offers a full package of oil distribution services including product exchanges, marine transportation, scheduling, terminal storage, and automated truck rack delivery systems. **Positions advertised include:** Major Projects Associate; Project Engineer; Lighting Coordinator; VCE Associate; Tug Rebuilding Associate; Executive Assistant. **Corporate headquarters location:** This location. **Listed on:** New York Stock Exchange. **Stock exchange symbol:** TUG.

MARKS, GRAY, CONROY & GIBBS
P.O. Box 447, Jacksonville FL 32201. 904/398-0900. **Contact:** Office Administrator. **Description:** A law firm. **Corporate headquarters location:** This location. **Number of employees at this location:** 60.

MARSHALL & ILSLEY TRUST COMPANY OF FLORIDA
800 Laurel Oak Drive, Suite 101, Naples FL 34108. 941/597-2933. **Contact:** William Wade, President. **World Wide Web address:** http://www.mitrust.com. **Description:** Provides trust and custodial services for corporate, institutional, and individual clients in the Southeast. **Parent company:** Marshall & Ilsley Corporation (Milwaukee WI) is a diversified, interstate bank holding company. Other subsidiaries of Marshall & Ilsley include M&I Data Services, Inc. (supplies data processing services and software for financial institutions throughout the United States and in foreign countries); M&I Investment Management Corp. (manages investment portfolios for corporations, nonprofit organizations, and individuals throughout the United States and acts as an investment advisor to the Marshall Funds); M&I Marshall & Ilsley Trust Company of Arizona (provides trust and custodial services to clients in the Southwest); M&I First National Leasing Corp. (leases equipment and machinery to businesses throughout the United States, primarily to middle-market corporations); M&I Capital Markets Group, Inc. (invests in small and medium-sized companies to help establish new businesses or recapitalize existing companies); M&I Brokerage Services, Inc. (a brokerage company providing a full range of investment products including stocks, bonds, and mutual funds for individual investors and small businesses); M&I Mortgage Corp. (originates and services a wide variety of home mortgages for M&I banks and other financial institutions); Richter-Schroeder Company, Inc. (provides construction loans and arranges permanent financing on income properties); and M&I Insurance Services, Inc. (acts as an independent insurance agency providing a full range of insurance products including annuities).

MARTIN ELECTRONICS, INC.
10625 Puckett Road, Perry FL 32348. 850/584-7579. **Fax:** 850/584-2044. **Contact:** Human Resources. **World Wide Web address:** http://www.martin-electronics.com. **Description:** Manufactures pyrotechnic and explosive devices for ordnance applications. **Corporate headquarters location:** This location. **Parent company:** MEI Holdings, Inc. **Operations at this facility include:** Manufacturing. **Listed on:** Privately held. **Number of employees at this location:** 250.

MARTIN MEMORIAL HEALTH SYSTEMS, INC.
P.O. Box 9010, Stuart FL 34995. 772/287-5200. **Physical address:** 300 Hospital Avenue, Stuart FL 34994. **Contact:** Jennifer T. Slaugh, Employment Coordinator. **World Wide Web address:** http://www.mmhs.com. **Description:** A nonprofit, 336-bed, multifacility health care organization. Martin Memorial Health Systems is comprised of Martin Memorial Medical Center and Martin Memorial Hospital South, both accredited facilities. The medical center is a 236-bed, acute care facility providing a range of inpatient and outpatient services including cancer and cardiac care, a 24-hour emergency department, maternity and pediatrics, and a wide variety of laser surgeries. Martin Memorial Hospital South is a 100-bed community hospital providing inpatient and outpatient services with 92 private rooms, an 8-bed intensive care unit, and a 24-hour emergency department. **Positions advertised include:** Access Services Coordinator; Bariatric Surgery; Book Keeper; Cardiovascular Technician; Data Processing Specialist; Department Secretary; Emergency Medical Technician; Data Processing Specialist; Environmental Services Aide; Exercise Leader; Health Unit Coordinator; Imaging Services Representative; Instrument Technician; Licensed Practical Nurse; Medical Assistant; Message Therapist; Materials Data Analyst; Office Coordinator; Patient Care Technician; Pharmacist; Physician; Radiological Technician; Registered Nurse; Systems Analyst. **Corporate headquarters location:** This location. **Annual sales/revenues:** More than $100 million. **Number of employees at this location:** 2,000.

MARTINE'S CORPORATION
120 East Main Street, Suite A, Pensacola FL 32501. 850/429-8640. **Contact:** Human Resources. **Description:** Operates fast-food establishments, liquor stores, and shopping centers.

MASTEC
800 Douglas Road, Penthouse, Coral Gables FL 33134. 305/599-1800. **Fax:** 305/406-1900. **Contact:** Human Resources. **E-mail address:** opportunities@mastec.com. **World Wide Web address:** http://www.mastec.com. **Description:** A water, sewer, and power service. **Positions advertised include:** Class A Lineman; Class B Lineman; High Voltage Cable Splicer; Superintendent. **Listed on:** New York Stock Exchange. **Stock exchange symbol:** MTZ.

MAYO CLINIC
4500 San Pueblo Road, Jacksonville FL 32224. 904/953-2000. **Toll-free phone:** 800/336-2838. **Fax:** 904/296-4668. **Recorded jobline:** 904/296-5588. **Contact:** Human Resources. **E-mail address:** mcjhr@mayo.edu. **World Wide Web address:** http://www.mayo.edu. **Description:** An outpatient medical and surgical clinic offering a wide variety of specialty care services. Founded in 1986. **Positions advertised include:** Respiratory Care Practitioner; Anesthesia Technologist; Animal Care Technician; Clinical Dietician; Clinical Nurse; Educator; Controls Technologist; Medical Secretary; Medical Assistant; Medical Technician; Patient Care Technician; Phlebotomist; Regional Occupational Therapist; Registered Nurse; Surgical Technician; Telephone Operator; Unit Supervisor. **President/CEO:** Robert M. Walters. **Facilities Manager:** Gary Pezall. **Information Systems Manager:** Barbara Cummings. **Purchasing Manager:** David Johnson.

MAYORS JEWELERS
14051 NW 14th Street, Sunrise FL 33323. 954/846-8000. **Fax:** 954/846-2787. **Recorded jobline:** 800/223-6964x5408. **Contact:** Human Resources. **E-mail address:** clientservices@mayors.com. **World Wide Web address:** http://www.mayors.com. **Description:** A retailer, merchandiser, and distributor of jewelry, watches, sunglasses, fragrances, and collectibles. **Corporate headquarters location:** This location. **Other U.S. locations:** Nationwide. **Operations at this facility include:** Administration; Distribution. **Number of employees at this location:** 500.

McARTHUR DAIRY
2451 NW 7th Avenue, Miami FL 33127. 305/576-2880. **Contact:** Human Resources. **World Wide Web address:** http://www.mcarthurdairy.com. **Description:** Produces dairy products. **NOTE:** Interested jobseekers should address inquiries to: Human Resources, 500 Sawgrass Corporate Parkway, Sunrise FL 33325.

McGUIREWOODS
50 North Laura Street, Suite 3300, Jacksonville FL 32202. 904/798-3200. **Fax:** 904/798-3207. **Contact:** Human Resources. **World Wide Web address:** http://www.mcguirewoods.com. **Description:** A law firm specializing in environmental, estate trust, and labor law.

McKENZIE TANK LINES, INC.
122 Appleyard Drive, Tallahassee FL 32304. 850/576-1221. **Contact:** Paulette McElroy, Human Resources Director. **World Wide Web address:** http://www.mckenzietank.com. **Description:** An interstate trucking company.

McKESSONHBOC
1025 Greenwood Boulevard, Suite 500, Lake Mary FL 32746. 407/804-5000. **Fax:** 407/804-5005. **Contact:** Human Resources. **World Wide Web address:** http://www.hboc.com. **Description:** Provides information systems and technology to health care enterprises including hospitals, integrated delivery networks, and managed care organizations. McKessonHBOC's primary products are Pathways 2000, a family of client/server-based applications that allow the integration and uniting of health care providers; STAR, Series, and HealthQuest transaction systems; TRENDSTAR decision support system; and QUANTUM enterprise information system. The company also offers outsourcing services that include strategic information systems planning, data center operations, receivables management, business office administration, and major system conversions. **Positions advertised include:** New Business Enterprise Vice President; Network Communications Analyst. **Corporate headquarters location:** San Francisco CA. **Other U.S. locations:** San Diego CA; Chicago IL; Minneapolis MN; Bedminster NJ; Dallas TX. **Subsidiaries include:** HBO & Company (UK) Limited; HBO & Company Canada Ltd. **Number of employees nationwide:** 470.

McNEEL INTERNATIONAL CORPORATION
5401 West Kennedy Boulevard, Tampa FL 33609. 813/286-8680. **Contact:** Human Resources. **Description:** Manufactures rubber and plastic products. **Corporate headquarters location:** This location. **International locations:** Worldwide.

MEDICAL TECHNOLOGY SYSTEMS
12920 Automobile Boulevard, Clearwater FL 33762. 727/576-6311. **Fax:** 727/579-8067. **Contact:** Peter Benjamin, Vice President of Human Resources. **Description:** Manufactures and markets blister cards for drug packaging and pharmaceutical dispensing systems for use in nursing homes and hospitals. **Listed on:** NASDAQ. **Stock exchange symbol:** MSYS.

MEDTRONIC XOMED SURGICAL PRODUCTS, INC.
6743 Southpoint Drive North, Jacksonville FL 32216. 904/296-9600. **Toll-free phone:** 800/874-5797. **Contact:** Human Resources. **E-mail address:** employment@Medtronic.com. **World Wide Web address:** http://www.xomed.com. **Description:** Manufactures medical devices and products for ear, nose, and throat surgery. **Positions advertised include:** Customer Service Representative; Manufacturing Engineer; Principal Medical Design Engineer; Product Manager; Quality Assurance Technician; Financial Analyst; Quality Assurance Engineer; Regulatory Specialist; Xomed ATM Distributor; Xomed ATM Ophthalmic Disposable Representative. **Corporate headquarters location:** This location. **Operations at this facility include:** Divisional Headquarters; Manufacturing; Research and Development.

MEMORIAL HOSPITAL OF TAMPA
2901 Swann Avenue, Tampa FL 33609. 813/873-6400. **Fax:** 813/873-6494. **Contact:** Cathy Massessa, Director of Human Resources. **World Wide Web address:** http://www.memorialhospitaltampa.com. **Description:** A hospital that provides inpatient and outpatient services. **Positions advertised include:** Registered Nurse; Licensed Practical Nurse; Physical Therapist; Medical Director; Physical Therapist; Home Health Aide; House Keeping; Unit Secretary; Outpatient Coder; Case Manager; Histology Technician; Registered Dietician; Chief Nursing Officer; Medical Technologist; Quality Manager. **Corporate headquarters location:** Dallas TX. **Parent company:** AMI. **Operations at this facility include:** Service. **Number of employees at this location:** 600.

MERCY HOSPITAL
3663 South Miami Avenue, Miami FL 33133. 305/285-2929. **Recorded jobline:** 305/285-2727. **Fax:** 305/285-5015. **Contact:** Human Resources. **E-mail address:** hr@mercymiami.com. **World Wide Web address:** http://www.mercymiami.com. **Description:** A 500 bed hospital serving Miami and south Florida. **Positions advertised include:** Certified Nurse Assistant; Clinical Services Manager; Director of Surgical Services; Home Health Aide; Field RN; Respiratory Therapist; Mammography Technician; Medical Technician; Monitor Technician; Nuclear Medicine Technologist; Financial Services Coordinator; Director of Corporate Integrity; Director of Managed Care; Billing Representative; Clerk/Receptionist; Communications Operator. **Note:** Applications are accepted in person 7:30 a.m. – 4:30 p.m., Monday – Friday. **President/CEO:** John E. Matuska.

MERRILL LYNCH
50 P.O. Box 1918, Jacksonville FL 32201. 904/634-6000. **Physical address:** 50 North Laura Street, Suite 3700, Jacksonville FL 32202. **Contact:** Human Resources. **World Wide Web address:** http://www.ml.com. **Description:** A diversified financial service organization. Merrill Lynch is a major broker in securities, option contracts, commodities and financial futures contracts, and insurance. The company also deals with corporate and municipal securities and investment banking. **Positions advertised include:** Conversion Administrator; Commercial Banking Professional; Annuity Product Specialist; Controller; Correspondent Account Executive; Mortgage Underwriter; Regional Manager; Clearing Specialist; Financial Advisor. **NOTE:** Call for specific information on where to mail a resume. **Corporate headquarters location:** New York NY. **Listed on:** New York Stock Exchange. **Stock exchange symbol:** MER.

MERRILL LYNCH
1401 Manatee Avenue West, 7th Floor, Bradenton FL 34205. 941/746-1123. **Contact:** Conni Gallagher, Administrative Secretary. **World Wide Web address:** http://www.ml.com. **Description:** A diversified financial service organization. Merrill Lynch is a major broker in securities, option contracts, commodities and financial futures contracts, and insurance. The company also deals with corporate and municipal securities and investment banking. **NOTE:** Call for specific information on where to mail a resume. **Positions advertised include:** Financial Consultant. **Corporate headquarters location:** New York NY. **Listed on:** New York Stock Exchange. **Stock exchange symbol:** MER. **Number of employees at this location:** 30.

MERRILL LYNCH
601 Cleveland Street, Suite 900, Clearwater FL 33755. 727/462-2300. **Contact:** Human Resources. **World Wide Web address:** http://www.ml.com. **Description:** A diversified financial service organization. Merrill Lynch is a major broker in securities, option contracts, commodities and financial futures contracts, and insurance. The company also deals with corporate and municipal securities and investment banking. **NOTE:** Call for specific information on where to mail a resume. **Corporate headquarters location:** New York NY. **Listed on:** New York Stock Exchange. **Stock exchange symbol:** MER.

METRIC SYSTEMS CORPORATION
645 Anchors Street, Fort Walton Beach FL 32548. 850/302-3000. **Fax:** 850/302-3371. **Contact:** Martha Stevens, Human Resources Manager. **World Wide Web address:** http://www.metricsys.com. **E-mail address:** hrdept@metric-idt.com. **Description:** Designs, develops, and manufactures aerospace defense products. **Positions advertised include:** Contract Administrator; Sheet Metal Mechanic; Welder; Computer Graphics Technician; Industrial Manufacturing Engineer; Associate Computer Engineer; Program Manager; Process Engineer; Pricing Coordinator; Software Engineer. **Operations at this facility include:** Administration; Manufacturing; Research and Development; Sales; Service. **Listed on:** New York Stock Exchange. **Stock exchange symbol:** TSY. **President/CEO:** Edward R. Epstein. **Purchasing Manager:** Victor Martire. **Annual sales/revenues:** $51 - $100 million. **Number of employees at this location:** 560.

METROPOLITAN LIFE INSURANCE COMPANY
4100 Boy Scout Boulevard, Tampa FL 33607. 813/870-8000. **Contact:** Human Resources. **World Wide Web address:** http://www.metlife.com. **Description:** Metropolitan Life Insurance is an international insurance and financial services company. **Positions advertised include:** Accounting Consultant; Associate Accountant; RSC Analyst; Remittance Service Manager; Financial Services Representative; Contract Analyst; Shared Services Manager; Supervisor; Research Analyst; Claims Adjuster; Systems Analyst. **NOTE:** Positions are offered in the Metropolitan Executive Training Program for professionals with MBAs and JDs. **Operations at this facility include:** This location is the Southeast regional headquarters.

THE MIAMI CHILDREN'S HOSPITAL
3100 SW 62nd Avenue, Miami FL 33155-3009. 305/668-5567. **Toll-free phone:** 800/955-6511. **Recorded jobline:** 305/662-8295. **Contact:** Human Resources. **World Wide Web address:** http://www.mch.com. **Description:** A pediatric medical care facility. **Positions advertised include:** Practical Coordinator; Lead Office Assistant; Data Entry Clerk; Ward Secretary; Billing Analyst; Customer Greeter; Collections Physician Office Registrar; Secretary; Medical Records Clerk; Communications Specialist; Physical Therapist; Speech Pathologist; Pediatric Social Worker; Physician Assistant; Business Operations Manager; Pharmacist; Chaplain; Project Manager; Registered Dietician; Registered Nurse; Care Assistant; Licensed Practical Nurse. **CEO/President:** Thomas M. Rozek.

THE MIAMI HERALD PUBLISHING COMPANY
EL NUEVO HERALD
One Herald Plaza, Miami FL 33132. **Toll-free phone:** 800/437-2535. **Fax:** 305/995-8021. **Recorded jobline:** 305/376-2880. **Contact:** Human Resources. **Description:** Publishes a regional daily newspaper in both English and Spanish. **NOTE:** Entry-level positions and second and third shifts are offered. **Positions advertised include:** Outside Sales Representative; Data Marketing Sales Representative; Territory Inside Sales; Sales Manager; Print Manager; Industrial Electrical Technician; Call Center Representative; Telemarketing Representative; Accounting Clerk; Sales Assistant; Creative Director. **Special programs:** Internships. **Corporate headquarters location:** This location. **Parent company:** Knight-Ridder. **Operations at this facility include:** Administration; Sales. **Number of employees at this location:** 2,200.

MIAMI JEWISH HOME & HOSPITAL
5200 NE 2nd Avenue, Miami FL 33137. 305/751-8626. **Contact:** Larry McDonald, Director of Human Resources. **World Wide Web address:** http://www.douglasgardens.com. **Description:** A hospital that also operates a nursing home for senior citizens. **Positions advertised include:** Driver; Therapeutic Recreation Manager; Transporter; Food Service Supervisor; C-bord Systems Coordinator; Sous Chef; Wait Staff; Secretary; Technician Help Desk; Therapist; Nurse Supervisor; Physical Therapy Assistant; Registered Nurse; Licensed Practical Nurse.

MIAMI METROZOO
12400 SW 152nd Street, Miami FL 33177. 305/251-0400. **Contact:** Human Resources. **World Wide Web address:** http://www.miamimetrozoo.com. **Description:** Features Asian River Life, the African Plains Exhibit, and more than 700 cageless, wild animals. **Positions advertised include:** Welder; Zookeeper; Elephant Zookeeper. **NOTE:** Visit http://www.miamidade.gov/jobs for current job postings in the Miami park and recreation area.

MIAMI TIMES
900 NW 54th Street, Miami FL 33127. 305/757-1147. **Contact:** Human Resources. **Description:** Publishes a weekly newspaper. **Special programs:** Internships. **Corporate headquarters location:** This location. **Number of employees at this location:** 20.

MIAMI TODAY
P.O. Box 1368, Miami FL 33131. 305/358-2663. **Physical address:** 710 Brickell Avenue, Miami FL 33131. **Contact:** Human Resources. **World Wide Web address:** http://www.miamitodaynews.com. **Description:** Publishes a weekly newspaper that focuses on the business community. Founded in 1983. **NOTE:** Entry-level positions are offered. **Positions advertised include:** Advertising Executive; Advertising Manager; Department Manager; Management Trainee; Marketing Specialist; Reporter. **Special programs:** Internships. **Office hours:** Monday - Friday, 8:30 a.m. - 5:30 p.m. **Corporate headquarters location:** This location. **Operations at this facility include:** Administration; Production; Sales. **Sales Manager:** Kristine Cartwright. **Number of employees at this location:** 30.

MIAMI-DADE COMMUNITY COLLEGE
KENDALL CAMPUS
11011 SW 104th Street, Miami FL 33176. 305/237-2051. **Toll-free phone:** 800/955-8771. **Fax:** 305/237-0961. **Recorded jobline:** 305/237-2050. **Contact:** Human Resources. **World Wide Web address:** http://www.mdcc.edu. **Description:** A two-year state college offering an Associate in Science degree, Associate in Arts degree, and Vocational Credit Certificates. **NOTE:** Entry-level positions and second and third shifts are offered. **Positions advertised include:** Mathematics Faculty; Foreign Language Faculty; Physician Assistant Program Faculty; Emergency Medical Services Faculty; Veteran Technology Faculty; Department Chair; School of Nursing Director; Department Chair Person; Provost for Education; Director of Publications; Instructional Development Coordinator. **Corporate headquarters location:** This location. **Operations at this facility include:** Administration. **Number of employees at this location:** 2,300.

MIAMI-DADE COMMUNITY COLLEGE
MEDICAL CENTER CAMPUS
950 NW 20th Street, Miami FL 33127. 305/237-4247. **Contact:** Human Resources. **World Wide Web address:** http://www.mdcc.edu. **Description:** A two-year state college offering programs through the School of Allied Health, School of Nursing, Physical Assistant Program, and Continuing Education. **Positions advertised include:** Mathematics Faculty; Foreign Language Faculty; Physician Assistant Program Faculty; Emergency Medical Services Faculty; Veteran Technology Faculty; Department Chair; School of Nursing Director; Department Chair Person; Provost for Education; Director of Publications; Instructional Development Coordinator

MIAMI-DADE COMMUNITY COLLEGE
MITCHELL WOLFSON CAMPUS
300 NE Second Avenue, Miami FL 33132. 305/237-3000. **Contact:** Human Resources. **World Wide Web address:** http://www.mdcc.edu. **Description:** A two-year state college offering programs through the School of Allied Health, School of Nursing, Physical Assistant Program, and Continuing Education. **Positions advertised include:** Mathematics Faculty; Foreign Language Faculty; Physician Assistant Program Faculty; Emergency Medical Services Faculty; Veteran Technology Faculty; Department Chair; School of Nursing Director; Department Chair Person; Provost for Education; Director of Publications; Instructional Development Coordinator.

MIAMI-DADE COMMUNITY COLLEGE
NORTH CAMPUS
11380 NW 27th Avenue, Miami FL 33167. 305/237-1000. **Contact:** Human Resources. **World Wide Web address:** http://www.mdcc.edu. **Description:** A two-year state college offering programs through the School of Allied Health, School of Nursing, Physical Assistant Program, and Continuing Education. **Positions advertised include:** Mathematics Faculty; Foreign Language Faculty; Physician Assistant Program Faculty; Emergency Medical Services Faculty; Veteran Technology Faculty; Department Chair; School of Nursing Director; Department Chair Person; Provost for Education; Director of Publications; Instructional Development Coordinator.

MICRO SYSTEMS, INC.
35 Hill Avenue, Fort Walton Beach FL 32548. 850/244-2332. **Fax:** 850/243-1378. **Contact:** Tami L. Manard, Director of Human Resources. **World Wide Web address:** http://www.gomicrosystems.com. **Description:** Designs and manufactures real-time, microprocessor-based control systems that create interfaces between targets and their controlling ground stations. The company's equipment is built under contract for the U.S. Department of Defense. **NOTE:** Entry-level positions are offered. **Positions advertised include:** Software Engineer; Management Information Systems; Assembler; Machine Shop Estimator; CNC Programmer; Produce Service Administrator; Final Inspector; Production Training Specialist; Machinist; Accounts Payable Specialist; Incoming Inspector; Business Developing Manager; Material Buyer; Configuration Manager; Data Configuration Assistant; Executive Assistant; Human Resources Assistant; Shipping Receiving Clerk; Payroll Specialist; Drafter; Designer. **Special programs:** Internships. **Corporate headquarters location:** This location. **Listed on:** Privately held. **Annual sales/revenues:** $5 - $10 million. **Number of employees at this location:** 100.

MISENER MARINE CONSTRUCTION INC.
5600 West Commerce Street, Tampa FL 33616. 813/839-8441. **Contact:** Cindy Pierce, Human Resources. **E-mail address:** lbosworth@orionmarinegroup.com. **World Wide Web address:** http://www.misenermarine.com. **Description:** Engaged in the heavy marine construction of bridges, docks, piers, underwater pipeline and cable, and foundation piling. **Positions advertised include:** Project Manager; Project Engineer. **Corporate headquarters location:** This location.

MODCOMP INC.
1650 West McNab Road, Fort Lauderdale FL 33309. 954/974-1380. **Contact:** Julie Slovin, Human Resources Manager. **World Wide Web address:** http://www.modcomp.com. **Description:** Manufactures computers designed for industrial automation, energy transportation, and communication applications. Founded in 1970.

MODIS
One Independent Drive, Jacksonville FL 32202. 904/360-2900. **Toll-free phone:** 877/MOD-ISIT. **Fax:** 904/360-2110. **Contact:** Human Resources. **World Wide Web address:** http://www.modisit.com. **Description:** Provides a wide range of computer consulting services. **Positions advertised include:** MSI Consultant; Seibel Systems Business Analyst; Net Developer; Quality Assurance Technical Writer. **Corporate headquarters location:** This location. **Other U.S. locations:** Nationwide. **International locations:** Canada; United Kingdom; Western Europe.

MODUS OPERANDI
122 4th Avenue, Indialantic FL 32903. 321/984-3370. **Contact:** Human Resources. **E-mail address:** hr_jobs@modusoperandi.com. **World Wide Web address:** http://www.modusoperandi.com. **Description:** Designs high-tech software for the U.S. government.

MOLTECH POWER SYSTEMS, INC.
12801 US Highway 441 North, Alachua FL 32615. **Contact:** Ms. Gerry Bryant, Human Resources Department. **World Wide Web address:** http://www.moltechpower.com. **Description:** A manufacturer of rechargeable batteries. **Positions advertised include:** Drafter/Designer; Human Resources Generalist. **Special programs:** Internships. **Corporate headquarters location:** This location. **Operations at this facility include:** Administration; Manufacturing; Research and Development. **Number of employees at this location:** 1,300.

MONIERLIFETILE, INC.
135 NW 20th Street, Boca Raton FL 33431. 561/338-8200. **Toll-free phone:** 800/585-8453. **Fax:** 866/200-6872. **Contact:** Ferndo Padron, Human Resources. **World Wide Web address:** http://www.monierlifetile.com. **Description:** A manufacturer of concrete roof tile.

THE MONTICELLO COMPANY
1604 Stockton Street, Jacksonville FL 32204. 904/384-3666. **Contact:** Human Resources. **World Wide Web address:** http://www.monticellocompanies.com. **Description:** The Monticello Company manufactures and sells over-the-counter pharmaceuticals produced at the company's plant in Mexico. **Corporate headquarters location:** This location. **Operations at this facility include:** This location provides administrative services. **Parent company:** Monticello Companies.

MOORINGS PARK
111 Moorings Park Drive, Naples FL 34105. 239/261-1616. **Fax:** 239/262-7040. **Contact:** Human Resources. **E-mail address:** jwallace@mooringspark.com. **World Wide Web address:** http://www.mooringspark.com. **Description:** A continuing care retirement community offering skilled nursing, assisted living, and independent living. **Positions advertised include:** Certified Nursing Assistant; Registered Nurse; Licensed Practical Nurse; Physical Therapist; Occupational Therapist; Staff Development; Coordinator Secretary; Servers; Direct Aides; Janitor; Housekeeping. **Office hours:** Monday – Friday, 8:30 a.m. – 4:00 p.m.

MORTON PLANT HOSPITAL
300 Pinelles Street, Clearwater FL 33756. 727/462-7000. **Contact:** Human Resources. **Description:** A 687-bed community hospital offering a full range of medical/surgical services.

MORTON PLANT MEASE HEALTH CARE
601 Main Street, Dunedin FL 34698. 727/734-6435. **Fax:** 727/734-6119. **Recorded jobline:** 727/734-6937. **Contact:** Human Resources. **World Wide Web address:** http://www.mpmhealth.com. **Description:** A nonprofit, full-service hospital. Specialties include cancer treatment, cardiovascular medicine, neurosciences, orthopedics, rehabilitation, and surgery services. **Positions advertised include:** Medical Records Technician; Patient Account Services Representative; Customer Communications Specialist; Executive Assistant; Medical Records Coder; Patient Access Services Representative; Data Entry Clerk; Administrative Associate; Financial Representative; Services Representative; Certified Nursing Aide; Licensed Practical Nurse; Care Technician; Food Service Coordinator; Lab Medical Assistant; Massage Therapist; Registered Dietician; Radiology Therapist; Speech Therapist. **Corporate headquarters location:** This location. **Number of employees at this location:** 6,000.

MOTOROLA, INC.
3301 Quantum Boulevard, Boynton Beach FL 33426. 561/739-2000. **Contact:** Human Resources. **World Wide Web address:** http://www.mot.com. **Description:** Motorola provides applied research, development, manufacturing, and marketing of high-tech electronic systems and components for industry and government in the fields of communications, automotive, controls, semiconductor, information systems, and office information. Motorola manufactures communications equipment and electronic products including car radios, cellular phones, semiconductors, computer systems, cellular infrastructure equipment, pagers, cordless phones, and LANs. **Corporate headquarters location:** Schaumburg IL. **Other U.S. locations:** Nationwide. **International locations:** Worldwide. **Operations at this facility include:** This location develops and manufactures pagers. **Listed on:** New York Stock Exchange. **Stock exchange symbol:** MOT.

MOTOROLA, INC.
8000 West Sunrise Boulevard, Plantation FL 33322. 954/723-5700. **Fax:** 954/723-4490. **Contact:** Staffing Manager. **World Wide Web address:** http://www.mot.com. **Description:** Motorola provides applied research, development, manufacturing, and marketing of high-tech electronic systems and components for industry and government markets in the fields of communications, automotive, controls, semiconductor, information systems, and office information. Motorola manufactures communications equipment and electronic products including car radios, cellular phones, semiconductors, computer systems, cellular infrastructure equipment, pagers, cordless phones, and LANs. **Positions advertised include:** Electrical Engineer; Senior RF Engineer; Mechanical Design Engineer; Software Engineer; Marketing Product Planner; Senior Paralegal. **Corporate headquarters location:** Schaumburg IL. **Other U.S. locations:** Nationwide. **International locations:** Worldwide. **Operations at this facility include:** This location manufactures two-way radios. **Listed on:** New York Stock Exchange. **Stock exchange symbol:** MOT.

MP TOTAL CARE PHARMACY
615 South Ware Boulevard, Tampa FL 33619. 813/621-4800. **Toll-free phone:** 800/424-0920. **Fax:** 831/621-1610. **Contact:** Human Resources. **E-mail address:** humanresources@mptotalcare.com. **World Wide Web address:** http://www.mptotalcare.com. **Description:** Distributor of pharmacy and medical supplies. Founded in 1990. **Positions advertised include:** Patient Account Representatives; Intake Coordinator; Pharmacist; Pharmacy Technician; Customer Service Representative; Compliance Associate; Program Representatives. **Parent Company:** Charterhouse Group International, Inc. **CEO/President:** Kevin Pawlowski.

MUNTERS CORPORATION
P.O. Box 6428, Fort Myers FL 33911. 239/936-1555. **Fax:** 239/936-8858. **Physical address:** 108 Sixth Street, Fort Myers Fl 33911. **Contact:** Human Resources. **World Wide Web address:** http://www.munters-fl.com. **Description:** An environmental technology and pollution control company. **Positions advertised include:** District Manager; Industrial Account Manager; Regional Water Damage Sales Manager; Water Damage Recovery Account. **Operations at this facility include:** Administration; Manufacturing; Research and Development; Sales. **Number of employees at this location:** 120. **Number of employees nationwide:** 420.

NBC 6 / WTVJ
316 North Miami Avenue, Miami FL 33128. 305/379-6666. **Contact:** Human Resources. **Recorded jobline:** 954/622-6840. **E-mail address:** nbc6.jobs@nbc.com. **World Wide Web address:** http://www.wtvj.com. **Description:** A television station owned and operated by NBC. WTVJ serves the Miami and Ft. Lauderdale areas. **Positions advertised include:** Traffic Associate; Assistant News Director; Account Manager; Assignment Manager. **Parent company:** General Electric.

NABI BIOPHARMACEUTICALS
5800 Park of Commerce Boulevard NW, Boca Raton FL 33487. 561/989-5800x5511. **Fax:** 561/989-5874. **Contact:** Human Resources. **World Wide Web address:** http://www.nabi.com. **Description:** Provides plasma and plasma-based products that aid in the prevention and treatment of diseases and disorders. **Corporate headquarters location:** This location. **Other U.S. locations:** Rockville MD. **Listed on:** NASDAQ. **Stock exchange symbol:** NBIO.

THE NAPLES DAILY NEWS
P.O. Box 7009, Naples FL 34101. 239/262-3161. **Contact:** Human Resources. **World Wide Web address:** http://www.naplesnews.com. **Description:** Publishes a daily newspaper.

NAPLES MEDICAL CENTER
400 8th Street North, Naples FL 34102. 239/261-5511. **Fax:** 941/649-3301. **Recorded jobline:** 239/213-2275. **Contact:** Kathleen Phelps, Human Resources Director. **World Wide Web address:** http://www.naplesmedicalcenter.com. **Description:** A multispecialty medical center with diagnostic and administrative departments. Founded in 1958. **NOTE:** Entry-level positions are offered. **Positions advertised include:** Licensed Practical Nurse; Medical Records File Clerk; Medical Secretary; Medical Technician; Patient Account Collector; Representative; Phlebotomist; Radiological Therapist. **Parent company:** ProMedCo Management Corporation. **Listed on:** Privately held. **Number of employees at this location:** 230.

NATIONAL BEVERAGE CORPORATION
One North University Drive, Building A, 4th Floor, Plantation FL 33324. 954/581-0922. **Toll-free phone:** 888/462-2349. **Contact:** Human Resources. **E-mail address:** humanresources@nationalbeverage.com. **World Wide Web address:** http://www.nbcfiz.com. **Description:** National Beverage Corporation is an integrated producer and distributor of multiflavored soft drink products. Brand names include Shasta, Faygo, Big Shot, Everfresh, VooDoo Rain, and LaCroix. **Other U.S. locations:** Nationwide. **Listed on:** American Stock Exchange. **Stock exchange symbol:** FIZ.

NATIONWIDE ADVERTISING SERVICE INC.
3510 Bay to Bay Boulevard, Tampa FL 33629. 813/831-1085. **Fax:** 813/831-5086. **Contact:** Office Manager. **World Wide Web address:** http://www.hrads.com. **Description:** With offices in 36 major U.S. and Canadian cities, Nationwide Advertising Service is one of the largest and oldest independent, full-service advertising agencies exclusively specializing in human resources communications, promotions, and advertising. The company offers consultation, campaign planning, ad placement, research, and creative production. **Positions advertised include:** Regional Manager; Account Executive. **Corporate headquarters location:** Cleveland OH. **Other U.S. locations:** Detroit MI; St. Louis MO; Houston TX.

NAVAL SURFACE WARFARE CENTER
Human Resources PC, Code XPP, 6703 West Highway 98, Panama City FL 32407-7001. 850/235-5554. **Contact:** Human Resources. **Description:** The U.S. Navy's principal research and development laboratory.

NETWORK INFOSERVE, INC.
8370 West Hillsborough Avenue, Suite 201, Tampa FL 33615. 813/888-9208. **Fax:** 813/888-9481. **Contact:** Human Resources. **E-mail address:** jobs@niicorp.com. **World Wide Web address:** http://www.niicorp.com. **Description:** Engaged in systems integration.

THE NEW PIPER AIRCRAFT, INC.
2926 Piper Drive, Vero Beach FL 32960. 772/567-4361. **Fax:** 772/978-6589. **Contact:** Rosalie Webster, Vice President of Human Resources. **E-mail address:** jobs@newpiper.com. **World Wide Web address:** http://www.newpiper.com. **Description:** Manufactures personal and business aircraft including the Saratoga II TC, Warrior III, Arrow, Seminole, Saratoga II HP, Archer III, Malibu Mirage, Malibu Meridian, and Seneca V. **Positions advertised include:** Engineering Service Manager; Airframe Design Engineer; Avionics Electrical Engineer; Materials Engineer; Structural Engineer; Power Plant Mechanical Systems Engineer; Maintenance Support Worker; Lead DOA Certification Engineer; Engineering Liaison. **Corporate headquarters location:** This location. **Subsidiaries include:** Piper Financial Services, Inc. provides aircraft financing and leasing services.

NEWS HERALD
P.O. Box 1940, Panama City FL 32402-1940. 850/747-5000. **Contact:** Lorraine Grimes, Human Resources Manager. **World Wide Web address:** http://www.newsherald.com. **Description:** A daily newspaper. **Parent company:** Freedom Communications **Executive Editor:** Phil Lucas, plucas@pcnh.com

NEWSMAX MEDIA, INC.
560 Village Boulevard, Suite 270, West Palm Beach FL 33409. 561/686-1165. **Fax:** 561/686-3350. **Contact:** Human Resources. **E-mail address:** jobs@newsmax.com. **World Wide Web address:** http://www.newsmax.com. **Description:** Publisher of the magazine NewsMax.com and its corresponding Website, as well as newsletters, books, and audiotapes. **Positions advertised include:** Reporter; Sales Representative; Customer Service Representative; Telemarketer. **Corporate headquarters location:** This location. **CEO/Editor:** Christopher Ruddy.

NEWS PRESS
2442 Dr. Martin Luther King Jr. Boulevard, Fort Myers FL 33901. 239/335-0200. **Fax:** 941/335-0297. **Contact:** Human Resources. **World Wide Web address:** http://www.news-press.com. **Description:** A newspaper with a daily circulation of 89,950 and a Sunday circulation of 104,000. **Positions advertised include:** New Business Classified Sales Representative; Advertising Sales Executive; Advertising

Billing/Matrix Supervisor. **Special programs:** Internships. **Corporate headquarters location:** Arlington VA. **Parent company:** Gannett Company, Inc. **Listed on:** Privately held. **Number of employees at this location:** 650. **Number of employees nationwide:** 38,000.

NEWS-JOURNAL CORPORATION
P.O. Box 2831, Daytona Beach FL 32120-2831. 386/252-1511. **Physical address:** 901 Sixth Street, Daytona Beach FL 32117. **Contact:** Human Resources. **World Wide Web address:** http://www.news-journalonline.com. **Description:** Publishes a daily newspaper, the *News-Journal,* with a circulation of over 100,000.

NEXTIRAONE
1619 North Harrison Parkway, Building D, Sunrise FL 33323. 954/846-1601. **Fax:** 954/846-5025. **Contact:** Human Resources. **World Wide Web address:** http://www.nextiraone.com. **Description:** Manufactures data communications equipment including WANs, LANs, and access products. The company also offers related services including project management, installation, consultation, network integration, maintenance, disaster recovery, and training. **Other U.S. locations:** Irvine CA; Acton MA; Hackensack NJ; Dallas TX.

NEXTEL COMMUNICATIONS
6700 North Andrews Avenue, Suite 700, Fort Lauderdale FL 33309. 954/202-7500. **Contact:** Human Resources. **World Wide Web address:** http://www.nextel.com. **Description:** Nextel Communications is engaged in the specialized mobile radio (SMR) wireless communications business. These services permit the company's customers to dispatch fleets of vehicles and place calls using their two-way mobile radios to or from any telephone in North America through interconnection with the public switched telephone network. Nextel Communications also sells and rents two-way mobile radio equipment and provides related installation, repair, and maintenance services. **Positions advertised include:** Wireless Consultant; Store Manager; Lead Technical Support Representative; Manager In Translation.

NOBILITY HOMES, INC.
P. O. Box 1659, Ocala FL 34478. 352/732-5157. **Contact:** Human Resources. **E-mail address:** info@mobilityhomes.com. **World Wide Web address:** http://www.nobilityhomes.com. **Description:** Designs and manufactures factory-constructed homes. The company also operates real estate sales centers. **Corporate headquarters location:** This location.

NORTH LAUDERDALE, CITY OF
701 SW 71st Avenue, North Lauderdale FL 33068. 954/724-7067. **Fax:** 954/720-2064. **Recorded jobline:** 954/724-7067. **Contact:** Human Resources. **World Wide Web address:** http://www.nlauderdale.org. **Description:** Municipal offices for the city of North Lauderdale. **Positions advertised include:** Lifeguards; Counselor; Recreation Attendant.

NORTHROP GRUMMAN CORPORATION
P.O. Drawer 3447, St. Augustine FL 32085. 904/825-3300. **Contact:** Human Resources. **World Wide Web address:** http://www.northgrum.com. **Description:** Northrop Grumman manufactures military aircraft, commercial aircraft parts, and electronic systems. Northrop Grumman has developed the B-2 Stealth Bomber, parts for the F/A-18 and the 747, and radar equipment. Other operations include computer systems development for management and scientific applications. **Positions advertised include:** ISP Project Manager. **Corporate headquarters location:** Los Angeles CA. **Operations at this facility include:** This location is an aircraft overhaul and modification facility. **Listed on:** New York Stock Exchange. **Stock exchange symbol:** NOC.

NORTHROP GRUMMAN
P.O. Box 547300, Orlando, FL 32854. 407/295-4010. **Contact:** Human Resources. **World Wide Web address:** http://www.northropgrumman.com. **Description:** Designs, develops, and manufactures military and commercial laser systems. **Positions advertised include:** Assembler; Tooling Inspector; Material Coordinator; Final Assembler; Painter; Toolmaker; Program Cost Scheduler & Controller; Cost Estimator; Electrical Installer. **Corporate headquarters location:** Los Angeles CA. **Operations at this facility include:** Administration; Divisional Headquarters; Manufacturing; Research and Development. **Listed on:** New York Stock Exchange. **Stock exchange symbol:** NOC. **Number of employees at this location:** 400.

NORTHROP GRUMMAN
950 North Orlando Avenue, Suite 200, Winter Park FL 32789. 407/629-6010. **Contact:** Human Resources. **World Wide Web address:** http://northropgrumman.com. **Description:** Develops software and information technology systems for the U.S. military and government. **Positions advertised include:** Chief Engineer; Military Trainer; Subject Matter Expert. **Corporate headquarters location:** Los Angeles CA. **Listed on:** New York Stock Exchange. **Stock exchange symbol:** NOC.

THE NORTHWEST FLORIDA DAILY NEWS
P.O. Box 2949, Fort Walton Beach FL 32549. 850/863-1111. **Contact:** Human Resources. **World Wide Web address:** http://www.nfwdailynews.com. **Description:** A newspaper publisher. **Corporate headquarters location:** Atlanta GA. **Parent company:** The New York Times Company.

NORWEGIAN CRUISE LINES
7665 NW 19th Street, Miami FL 33126. 305/436-4000. **Contact:** Human Resources. **World Wide Web address:** http://www.ncl.com. **Description:** An ocean cruise line. **Positions advertised include:** Accounting Clerk; Business Analyst; Business Project Manager; Corporate & Crew Supervisor; CRS Administrator; Credit Clerk; Office Administrator; Land Agent; Production Show Supervisor; Revenue Specialist; Yield Management Supervisor.

NOVA SOUTHEASTERN UNIVERSITY
3301 College Avenue, Fort Lauderdale FL 33314. 954/262-7870. **Contact:** Human Resources. **World Wide Web address:** http://www.nova.edu. **Description:** A university offering undergraduate and graduate programs to approximately 18,000 students. **Positions advertised include:** Reference Librarian; Acquisitions Librarian; Reference Instructor Librarian; Medical Assistant; Customer Service Representative; Library Network Specialist; Buyer; Mail / Sort Clerk; Mail Researcher; Executive Assistant.

NOVEN PHARMACEUTICALS, INC.
11960 SW 144th Street, Miami FL 33186. 305/253-5099. **Fax:** 305/251-1887. **Contact:** Sandra Miller, Human Resources Administrator. **E-mail address:** hrjobs@noven.com. **World Wide Web address:** http://www.noven.com. **Description:** Develops and manufactures transdermal and transmucosal drug delivery systems. **Positions advertised include:** Analytical Chemist; Product Release Supervisor; Controlled Substance Manager. **Listed on:** NASDAQ. **Stock exchange symbol:** NOVN.

OSI COLLECTION SERVICES
5022 Gate Parkway North, Suite 204, Jacksonville FL 32256. 904/380-2600. **Contact:** Human Resources. **Description:** A collection agency. **Corporate headquarters location:** This location.

OCALA STAR-BANNER
P.O. Box 490, Ocala FL 34478. 352/867-4010. **Fax:** 352/867-4018. **Contact:** Ernestine Johnson, Human Resources Director. **Description:** A daily newspaper with a circulation of 50,000.

OCE PRINTING SYSTEMS USA
5600 Broken Sound Boulevard NW, Boca Raton FL 33487. 561/997-3100. **Contact:** Human Resources. **World Wide Web address:** http://www.oceusa.com. **Description:** Services computer printers and copiers. **Positions advertised include:** Trainer; Field Service Engineer; Buyer.

OFFICE DEPOT
2200 Old Germantown Road, Delray Beach FL 33445. 561/278-4800. **Contact:** Human Resources. **World Wide Web address:** http://www.officedepot.com. **Description:** Operates a chain of large-volume office-products warehouse stores that sell brand name office merchandise primarily to small and medium-sized businesses. The retail locations also serve the growing home office market. Major merchandise categories include general office supplies, office furniture, computer hardware and software, copiers, telephones and fax machines, paper, writing instruments, briefcases, accounting supplies, and back-to-school supplies. **Corporate headquarters location:** This location. **Other U.S. locations:** Nationwide. **International locations:** Canada. **Listed on:** New York Stock Exchange. **Stock exchange symbol:** ODP. **Number of employees nationwide:** 33,000.

OKEELANTA CORPORATION
P.O. Box 86, South Bay FL 33493. 561/996-9072. **Fax:** 561/992-7326. **Contact:** Human Resources. **Description:** Mills, refines, packages, and distributes sugar. **Listed on:** Privately held. **Number of employees at this location:** 1,250.

ORIOLE HOMES CORPORATION
1690 South Congress Avenue, Suite 200, Delray Beach FL 33445. 561/274-2000. **Contact:** Steve Mahon, Director of Human Resources. **World Wide Web address:** http://www.oriolehomes.com. **Description:** Builds and sells houses and condominiums.

ORLANDO BUSINESS JOURNAL
315 East Robinson Street, Suite 250, Orlando FL 32801-4323. 407/649-8470. **Fax:** 407/420-1625. **Contact:** Pat Beall, Editor. **E-mail address:** Orlando@bizjournals.com. **World Wide Web address:** http://www.bizjournals.com/orlando. **Description:** A weekly business newspaper. **Corporate headquarters location:** This location. **Parent company:** American City Business Journals. **Operations at this facility include:** Administration; Sales; Service.

ORLANDO REGIONAL HEALTHCARE
1414 South Kuhl Avenue, Orlando FL 32806-2008. 321/841-5111. **Fax:** 407/237-6374. **Contact:** Nancy Dinon, Vice-President. **World Wide Web address:** http://www.orhs.org. **Description:** A comprehensive medical system that operates several health care facilities throughout central Florida. **NOTE:** Entry-level positions, part-time jobs, and second and third shifts are offered. **Positions advertised include:** Orlando Regional Healthcare; Financial Manager. **Special programs:** Internships; Summer Jobs. **Number of employees nationwide:** 9,000.

ORLANDO REGIONAL LUCERNE HOSPITAL
818 Main Lane, Orlando FL 32806. 407/649-6111. **Contact:** Human Resources. **World Wide Web address:** http://www.orlandoregional.org. **Description:** A medical center serving Orlando and its surrounding cities. **Positions advertised include:** Clinical Technician; Discharge Planner; Guest Services Assistant; Medical Technician; Neurotechnologist; Occupational Therapist; Physical Therapist; Pool Physical Therapist; Registered Nurse; Security; Social Worker.

ORLANDO SENTINEL COMMUNICATIONS COMPANY
633 North Orange Avenue, Orlando FL 32801. 407/420-6253. **Fax:** 407/420-5766. **Recorded jobline:** 407/872-7200x9121. **Contact:** Human Resources. **World Wide Web address:** http://www.orlandosentinel.com. **Description:** Publishes the *Orlando Sentinel* newspaper and various niche publications. Other company divisions include interactive, direct mail, signage, and teleservices. The company is also involved in a joint venture with Time Warner Communications to produce a local 24-hour cable news channel. **Special programs:** Internships; Co-ops. **Corporate headquarters location:** Chicago IL. **Other U.S. locations:** Nationwide. **Parent company:** Tribune Company. **Number of employees at this location:** 1,500.

THE ORLANDO TIMES
4403 Vineland Road, Suite B5, Orlando FL 32811. 407/841-3710. **Fax:** 407/849-0434. **Contact:** Human Resources. **E-mail address:** news@orlando-times.com. **World Wide Web address:** http://www.orlando-times.com. **Description:** Publishes a weekly newspaper.

ORLANDO UTILITIES COMMISSION
500 South Orange Avenue, Orlando FL 32801. 407/423-9100. **Recorded jobline:** 407/423-9191. **Contact:** Human Resources. **World Wide Web address:** http://www.ouc.com. **Description:** Offers utility services to the Central Florida area. **Positions advertised include:** Electrical Engineer; Accounting Manager; Human Resources Assistant; Plant Engineer; Technician; Buyer; Customer Service Representative.

OSCEOLA REGIONAL MEDICAL CENTER
700 West Oak Street, Kissimmee FL 34741. 407/846-2266. **Contact:** Silvia Loillis, Director of Personnel. **World Wide Web address:** http://www.osceolaregional.com. **Description:** A 171-bed hospital offering a full range of services including diagnostic testing, cardiac care, and rehabilitation. **Positions advertised include:** Administrative Support Associate; Registered Nurse; Certified Pharmaceutical Technician; Certified Surgical Technician; Clinical Dietician; Lab Assistant; Nurse Specialist; Licensed Practical Nurse; Monitor Tech; Nurse Manager; Patient Care Technologist; Personal Computer Technician; Registered Nurse; Radiological Technician; Staff Pharmacist; Transcriptionist; Unit Secretary.

O'SULLIVAN CREEL, LLP
P. O. Box 12646, Pensacola FL 32574. 850/435-7400. **Fax:** 850/435-2888. **Contact:** Kathy Anthony, Firm Administrator. **World Wide Web address:** http://www.osullivancreel.com. **Description:** A full-service accounting and business

consulting firm. Founded in 1981. **Positions advertised include:** Tax Manager; Book Keeper; 401K Pension Administrator. **Special programs:** Co-ops. **Corporate headquarters location:** This location. **Listed on:** Privately held. **Annual sales/revenues:** $5 - $10 million.

OUTBACK STEAKHOUSE, INC.
2202 North West Shore Boulevard, 5th Floor, Tampa FL 33607. 813/282-1225. **Fax:** 813/282-1209. **Contact:** Trudy Cooper, Vice President of Training and Development. **World Wide Web address:** http://www.outbacksteakhouse.com. **Description:** The company operates Outback Steakhouse Restaurants. Outback Steakhouses, Inc. also owns and operates several Carraba's Italian Grill and Fleming's Prime Steakhouse and Wine Bar restaurants. **Listed on:** New York Stock Exchange. **Stock exchange symbol:** OSI. **Number of employees nationwide:** 8,800.

THE PALATKA DAILY NEWS
P.O. Box 777, Palatka FL 32178. 386/312-5200. **Fax:** 386/312-5209. **Contact:** Human Resources. **World Wide Web address:** http://www.palatkadailynews.com. **Description:** A newspaper publisher. **Positions advertised include:** Advertising Sales Representative; Editor; Reporter. **Corporate headquarters location:** Atlanta GA. **Parent company:** The New York Times Company. **Operations at this facility include:** Administration; Sales. **Number of employees at this location:** 50.

PALL AEROPOWER
5775 Rio Vista Drive, Clearwater FL 33760. 727/539-8448. **Contact:** Laurel Dinan, Personnel Director. **World Wide Web address:** http://www.pall.com. **Description:** Manufactures high-technology filtration components for hydraulic systems, fuel systems, and lubrication systems. **Corporate headquarters location:** East Hills NY. **Parent company:** Pall Corporation is a world leader in filtration end separation. The company's business is organized into three segments: Health Care, Aeropower, and Fluid Processing. In the fluid clarification market, Pall sells disposable cartridges that fit into filter houses they have sold to clients. In the separations market, the company sells complete systems, which include both semipermanent filters that are replaced rarely and systems that regularly consume disposable cartridges. **Listed on:** New York Stock Exchange. **Stock exchange symbol:** PLL.

PALL AEROPOWER
10540 Ridge Road, New Port Richey FL 34654. 727/849-9999. **Fax:** 727/848-5719. **Contact:** Human Resources. **World Wide Web address:** http://www.pall.com. **Description:** Manufactures high-technology filtration components for hydraulic systems, fuel systems, and lubrication systems. **Corporate headquarters location:** East Hills NY. **Other U.S. locations:** NJ. **Parent company:** Pall Corporation is a world leader in filtration end separation. The company's business is organized into three segments: Health Care, Aeropower, and Fluid Processing. In the fluid clarification market, Pall sells disposable cartridges that fit into filter houses they have sold to clients. In the separations market, the company sells complete systems, which include both semipermanent filters that are replaced rarely and systems that regularly consume disposable cartridges. **Operations at this facility include:** Manufacturing. **Listed on:** New York Stock Exchange. **Stock exchange symbol:** PLL.

PALM BEACH COMMUNITY COLLEGE
4200 Congress Avenue, Lake Worth FL 33461. 561/868-3114. **Fax:** 561/439-8202. **Contact:** Human Resources. **World Wide Web address:** http://www.pbcc.cc.fl.us. **Description:** A community college offering associate's degrees in the arts and sciences. **Positions advertised include:** Early Learning Coach; Learning Specialist; Program Coordinator; Program Specialist; Business Analyst; Student Services Specialist; Accounting Associate; Groundskeeper; Media Assistant; Office Assistant; Security Guard; Student Ambassador; Teacher Assistant; Nursing Tutor.

PALM BEACH NEWSPAPERS, INC.
P.O. Box 24700, West Palm Beach FL 33416-4700. 561/820-4190. **Fax:** 561/820-4192. **Recorded jobline:** 561/820-4511x1090. **Contact:** Linda Murphy, Vice President of Human Resources. **World Wide Web address:** http://www.gopbi.com. **Description:** A newspaper and shopper publisher of such titles as the *Palm Beach Post, Palm Beach Daily News,* and *Florida Pennysaver*. **Special programs:** Internships. **Corporate headquarters location:** Atlanta GA. **Parent company:** Cox Enterprises, Inc. **Operations at this facility include:** Administration; Manufacturing; Sales. **Listed on:** Privately held. **Number of employees at this location:** 1,300. **Number of employees nationwide:** 22,000.

PALM BEACH ATLANTIC UNIVERSITY
P.O Box 24708, West Palm Beach FL 33401. 561/803-2000. **Physical address:** 901 South Flagler Drive, West Palm Beach FL 33401 **Contact;** Cindi Lewis, faculty or Mona Hicks, staff. **E-mail address;** cindy_lewis@pba.edu; mona_hicks@pba.edu. **World Wide Web address:** http://www.pba.edu. **Description:** A four year private college in West Palm Beach with undergraduate and graduate programs with approximately 3000 students. **Positions advertised include:** Secretary; Academic Advisor; Administrative Assistant; Help Desk Specialist; Network Administrator; Assistant Professor; Reference Librarian.

PALM COAST DATA LTD.
11 Commerce Boulevard, Palm Coast FL 32164. 386/445-4662. **Contact:** Lynn Lawson, Director of Human Resources. **World Wide Web address:** http://www.palmcoastd.com. **Description:** Manages subscription lists for publishing companies. Founded in 1984. **Positions advertised include:** Proof Print Operator; Data Entry Assistant Supervisor; Imaging Verifier; Agency Customer Service Clerk; Mail Sorter; Building Custodian; Machine Maintenance Worker; PC Programmer; Mailing Services Director; Customer Service Manager; Business Analyst; Customer Service Manager; Customer Service Representative; Data Entry Home Keyer. **Parent company:** DIMAC Direct.

PALMER ELECTRIC COMPANY
SHOWCASE LIGHTING
875 Jackson Avenue, Winter Park FL 32789. 407/646-8700. **Contact:** Human Resources. **World Wide Web address:** http://www.palmer-electric.com. **Description:** Provides electrical services to commercial and residential customers.

PALM HARBOR HOMES
605 South Frontage Road, Plant City FL 33563. 813/719-3335. **Fax:** 813/707-1337. **Contact:** Human Resources. **E-mail address:** mvitko@palmharbor.com. **World Wide Web address:** http://www.palmharbor.com. **Description:** A home manufacturer and seller. **Positions advertised include:** Retail Sales Associate.

THE PANTRY, INC.
P.O. Box 23180, Jacksonville FL 32241. 904/464-7200. **Contact:** Manager. **World Wide Web address:** http://www.thepantry.com. **Description:** A chain of retail grocery and convenience stores. Stores operate under the names Depot, ETNA, Express Stop, Food Chief, Handy-Way, Kangaroo, Lil' Champ, Quick Stop, Smokers Express, Sprint, The Pantry, Wicker Mart, and Zip Mart. **Corporate headquarters location:** This location. **Listed on:** NASDAQ. **Stock exchange symbol:** PTRY.

PARADYNE CORPORATION
8545 126th Avenue North, Largo FL 33773. 727/530-2000. **Fax:** 727/530-8216. **Contact:** Human Resources. **World Wide Web address:** http://www.paradyne.com. **Description:** Manufactures and distributes WAN solutions including DSL, T1, and service-level management products. **Positions advertised include:** Mechanical Engineer; R&D Technician; Facilities Technician; Hardware Engineer; Support Engineer; EMS Development Engineer, **Special programs:** Internships. **Listed on:** NASDAQ. **Stock exchange symbol:** PDYN. **Number of employees at this location:** 2,150.

PARAVANT COMPUTER SYSTEMS INC.
3520 U.S. Highway 1, Palm Bay FL 32905. 321/727-3672. **Fax:** 321/725-0496. **Contact:** Human Resources. **World Wide Web address:** http://www.paravant.com. **Description:** Manufactures rugged hand-held computer systems and software for the military. **Positions advertised include:** Production Manager; Electrical Engineer; Optical Engineer; Optical Worker; Quality Engineer; Electrician Technician; Mechanical Engineer; Test Manager; Controller; Program Manager; Quality Engineer; Analog Design Electrical Engineer. **Listed on:** NASDAQ. **Stock exchange symbol:** PVAT.

PARKSON CORPORATION
2727 NW 62nd Street, Fort Lauderdale FL 33309. 954/974-6610. **Contact:** Oti Wooster, Human Resources Manager. **E-mail address:** jobs@parkson.com. **World Wide Web address:** http://www.parkson.com. **Description:** A water and wastewater treatment equipment manufacturer. Founded in 1971. **Positions advertised include:** Director of Materials; Aftermarket Sales Representative.

PARLUX FRAGRANCES, INC.
3725 SW 30th Avenue, Fort Lauderdale FL 33312. 954/316-9008x103. **Fax:** 954/316-8155. **Contact:** Tania Espinosa, Personnel Administrator. **E-mail address:** info@parlux.com. **World Wide Web address:** http://www.parlux.com. **Description:** A manufacturer and international distributor of fragrances and cosmetics. The company's product line includes Perry Ellis Cosmetics, Fred Hayman Beverly Hills, Animale Parfums, and Phantom of the Opera. **Corporate headquarters location:** This location. **International locations:** Paris, France. **Listed on:** NASDAQ. **Stock exchange symbol:** PARL.

PARROT JUNGLE AND GARDENS
11111 Parrot Jungle Trail, Miami FL 33132. 305/666-7834. **Fax:** 305/400-7293. **Contact:** Human Resources. **E-mail address:** parrots@parrotjungle.com. **World Wide Web address:** http://www.parrotjungle.com. **Description:** An attraction dedicated to parrots and the Caribbean. It features a garden with more than 1200 varieties of exotic plants, a primate exhibit, and both free-flying and trained parrot exhibits.

PAXSON COMMUNICATIONS CORPORATION
601 Clearwater Park Road, West Palm Beach FL 33401. 561/659-4122. **Contact:** Human Resources. **World Wide Web address:** http://www.paxtv.com. **Description:** Operates the PAX-TV network, with affiliates throughout the country. **Positions advertised include:** Coordinator Long Form Studies; Merchandise Manager; Accounts Services Administrator; Accounts Payable Clerk; Paralegal.

PAYFORMANCE CORPORATION
10550 Deerwood Park Boulevard, Suite 300, Jacksonville FL 32256. 904/997-6777. **Fax:** 904/997-8017. **Contact:** Human Resources. **World Wide Web address:** http://www.payformance.com. **Description:** Develops computer hardware and software designed for payment automation systems. Payformance Corporation provides services to over 3,000 corporate customers worldwide. **Positions advertised include:** Customer Service Representative; Product Manager. **Corporate headquarters location:** This location.

PAYSYS INTERNATIONAL
900 Winderley Place, Suite 140, Maitland FL 32751. 407/660-0343. **Contact:** Human Resources. **World Wide Web address:** http://www.paysys.com. **Description:** Develops credit card processing software.

PENSACOLA NEWS JOURNAL
P.O. Box 12710, Pensacola FL 32574. 850/435-8500. **Recorded jobline:** 850/470-4401. **Fax:** 850/470-4430. **Contact:** Kimberly Wheeler, Employment Manager. **World Wide Web address:** http://www.pensacolanewsjournal.com. **Description:** Publishes *Pensacola News Journal,* a newspaper with a daily circulation of 66,000, a Saturday circulation of 82,000, and a Sunday circulation of 92,000. **Positions advertised include:** Clerks; Assistants; Editor; Inside Sales: Outside Sales; Sales Supervisor; Accounts Manager; Accountant; Reporter; Copy Editor; Artist; District Manager.

PEPSI-COLA BOTTLING COMPANY
1700 Directors Row, Orlando FL 32809. 407/826-5900. **Fax:** 407/826-5999. **Recorded jobline:** 407/826-5900x330. **Contact:** Human Resources. **World Wide Web address:** http://www.pepsico.com. **Description:** A regional bottling plant. **Positions advertised include:** Warehouse Maintenance Technician; Warehouse Associate; Quality Control Manager; Production Manager; Product Availability Manager; Maintenance Manager. **Special programs:** Internships. **Parent company:** PepsiCo, Inc. (Purchase NY) consists of Frito-Lay Company, Pepsi-Cola Company, Quaker Oats Company, and Tropicana Products Inc. **Operations at this facility include:** Manufacturing; Regional Headquarters; Sales; Service. **Listed on:** New York Stock Exchange. **Stock exchange symbol:** PEP. **Annual revenues:** More than $100 million. **Number of employees at this location:** 400. **Number of employees nationwide:** 26,000.

PEPSI-COLA COMPANY
7777 NW 41st Street, Miami FL 33166. 305/592-1980. **Contact:** Human Resources. **World Wide Web address:** http://www.pepsico.com. **Description:** Manufactures, sells, and distributes Pepsi-Cola products including 7-Up and Sunkist. **Positions advertised include:** Quality Control Manager; Production Manager; Product Availability Manager; Maintenance Manager; Warehouse Associate. Lead Warehouse Associate. **Special programs:** Internships. **Parent company:** PepsiCo, Inc. (Purchase NY) consists of Frito-Lay Company, Pepsi-Cola Company, Quaker Oats Company, and Tropicana Products Inc. **Listed on:** New York Stock Exchange. **Stock exchange symbol:** PEP. **Annual revenues:** More than $100 million. **Number of employees nationwide:** 26,000.

PEPSI-COLA COMPANY
3625 Dr. Martin Luther King Jr. Boulevard, Fort Myers FL 33916. 239/337-2011. **Contact:** Human Resources. **World Wide Web address:** http://www.pepsico.com. **Description:** Distributes various beverages including the brand names Pepsi-Cola, Mountain Dew, Mug Root Beer, and Slice. **Positions advertised include:** Food Service

Sales Representative; Quality Control Manager; Production Manager; Product Availability Manager; Maintenance Manager; Territory Sales Manager; Warehouse Associate. **Parent company:** PepsiCo, Inc. (Purchase NY) consists of Frito-Lay Company, Pepsi-Cola Company, Quaker Oats Company, and Tropicana Products Inc. **Listed on:** New York Stock Exchange. **Stock exchange symbol:** PEP. **Annual revenues:** More than $100 million. **Number of employees nationwide:** 26,000.

PHARMERICA
PHARMACY MANAGEMENT SERVICES, INC. (PMSI)
175 Kelsey Lane, Tampa FL 33619. 813/626-7788. **Toll-free phone:** 800/237-7676. **Contact:** Human Resources. **World Wide Web address:** http://www.pharmerica.com. **Description:** A supplier of pharmaceuticals and related products to long-term care facilities, hospitals, and assisted living communities. PharMerica also provides nurse consultant services, infusion therapy and training, medical records consulting, and educational programs. PMSI (also at this location) offers medical equipment and supplies through mail-order delivery. **Positions advertised include:** Account Executive; Account Manager; Billing Analyst; Business Process Analyst; Cash Application Associate; Cash Associate; Clerical Assistant; Collection Associate; Computer Operator; Web Developer; Shipping, Receiving Clerk; Tax Accountant. **Corporate headquarters location:** This location. **Listed on:** New York Stock Exchange. **Stock exchange symbol:** ABC.

PIEZO TECHNOLOGY, INC. (PTI)
2525 Shader Road, Orlando FL 32804. 407/298-2000. **Fax:** 407/298-6138. **Contact:** Human Resources Department. **E-mail address:** resume@piezotech.com. **World Wide Web address:** http://www.piezotech.com. **Description:** Manufactures frequency control systems for defense industry communications systems. **Positions advertised include:** RF Oscillator Design Engineer; RF Filter Design Engineer; Crystal Processing Engineer; RF Test Measurement Engineer; Engineering Technician.

PLANTATION GENERAL HOSPITAL
401 NW 42nd Avenue, Plantation FL 33317. 954/587-5010. **Fax:** 954/587-7869. **Recorded jobline:** 954/321-4068. **Contact:** Human Resources. **World Wide Web address:** http://www.plantationgeneral.com. **Description:** A hospital offering a full range of inpatient and outpatient services. **Positions advertised include:** Registered Nurse; Unit Secretary; Women's Services Radiology; Ultra Sound Technology; CT Technologist; Physical Therapist; Case Manager; Environmental Services Aide; Housekeeping; Coding Compliance Manager. **Special programs:** Internships. **CEO:** Anthony M. Degina, Jr.

POPEYE'S
906 Lee Road, Orlando FL 32810. 407/628-0393. **Fax:** 407/628-8311. **Contact:** Human Resources. **World Wide Web address:** http://www.popeyes.com. **Description:** One location of national restaurant franchise. **Positions advertised include:** Assistant Restaurant Manager. **Corporate headquarters location:** Macon GA. **Listed on:** Privately held. **Number of employees nationwide:** 2,500.

POST, BUCKLEY, SCHUH AND JERNIGAN, INC.
2001 NW 107th Avenue, Miami FL 33172-2507. 305/592-7275. **Fax:** 305/594-9478. **Contact:** Human Resources. **World Wide Web address:** http://www.pbsj.com. **Description:** Offers architectural, engineering, and planning/design consulting services. **Positions advertised include:** Senior Project Manager; Senior Field Representative; Senior Information Solutions Developer; Office Engineer; Senior Estimator; Marketing Assistant; Finance Analyst. **Operations at this facility include:** Administration; Regional Headquarters; Sales; Service. **Number of employees nationwide:** 2,700.

POTAMKIN SOUTH
21111 South Dixie Highway, Miami FL 33189. 305/238-0000. **Contact:** General Manager. **World Wide Web address:** http://www.potamkinsouth.com. **Description:** An automobile dealership. **Special programs:** Internships. **Other U.S. locations:** Nationwide. **Listed on:** Privately held. **Number of employees at this location:** 115.

PRATT & WHITNEY
P.O. Box 109600, West Palm Beach FL 33410-9600. 561/796-2000. **Contact:** Human Resources. **World Wide Web address:** http://www.pratt-whitney.com. **Description:** Designs, manufactures, and services engines for commercial, military, and general aircraft, as well as space propulsion and power systems. **Positions advertised include:** Translator; Quality Engineer. **Corporate headquarters location:** East Hartford CT. **Operations at this facility include:** This location is the headquarters for the division of large military engines and space propulsion systems. Primary operations at the facility include the design and testing of turbine and liquid rocket engines and the production of liquid hydrogen-fuel rocket engines. **Parent company:** United Technologies Corporation designs and manufactures engines and space propulsion systems for commercial and general aviation. **Number of employees at this location:** 5,000.

PREMIO COMPUTER
1616 NW 84th Avenue, Miami FL 33126. 305/471-0199. **Contact:** Human Resources. **World Wide Web address:** http://www.premiopc.com. **Description:** A reseller of computers.

PRICEWATERHOUSECOOPERS
3111 West Dr. Martin Luther King Jr. Boulevard, Tampa FL 33607. 813/351-2300. **Fax:** 813/348-8502. **Contact:** Human Resources Department. **World Wide Web address:** http://www.pwc.com. **Description:** One of the largest certified public accounting firms in the world. PricewaterhouseCoopers provides public accounting, business advisory, management consulting, and taxation services. **Corporate headquarters location:** New York NY. **Other U.S. locations:** Nationwide.

PRICEWATERHOUSECOOPERS
First Union Financial Center, 200 South Biscayne Boulevard, Suite 1900, Miami FL 33131. 305/375-7400. **Contact:** Tammy Kline, Director of Human Resources. **World Wide Web address:** http://www.pricewaterhousecoopers.com. **Description:** One of the largest certified public accounting firms in the world. PricewaterhouseCoopers provides public accounting, business advisory, management consulting, and taxation services. **Corporate headquarters location:** New York NY. **Other U.S. locations:** Nationwide.

PRIME CARE HEALTH AGENCY INC.
8405 NW 53rd Street, Building 106, Miami FL 33166. 305/591-7774. **Toll-free phone:** 800/591-7747. **Fax:** 305/594-8951. **Recorded jobline:** 305/591-7774x815. **World Wide Web address:** http://www.primecarehealthagency.com. **E-mail address:** info@primecarehealth.com. **Contact:** Josie Melero, Human Resources Director. **Description:** Provides in-home nursing services. Founded in 1985. **Positions advertised include:** High Tech Registered Nurse; Registered Nurse; Licensed Practical Nurse; Certified Home Health Aide; Companion; Babysitter; Escort; Medical Social Worker. **Office hours:** Monday - Friday, 8:00 a.m. - 5:00 p.m. **President:** Barry G. Shoor. **Number of employees at this location:** 250. **Number of employees nationwide:** 300.

PRINTING HOUSE LTD.
1066 Strong Road, Quincy FL 32351. 850/875-1500. **Fax:** 850/627-1193. **Contact:** Human Resources. **World Wide Web address:** http://www.theprintinghouse.com. **E-mail address:** recruiter@theprintinghouse.com. **Description:** The fourth largest printing company in Florida. **Positions advertised include:** Entry level Manufacturing. **Number of employees at this location:** 250.

PROTEL, INC.
4150 Kidron Road, Lakeland FL 33811. 863/644-5558. **Toll-free phone:** 800/928-8882. **Fax:** 863/646-5855. **Contact:** Human Resources. **World Wide Web address:** http://www.protelinc.com. **Description:** Manufactures and distributes pay telephones.

PRUDENTIAL SECURITIES, INC.
P.O. Box 45049, Jacksonville FL 32232-5049. 904/391-3400. **Physical address:** 701 San Marcos Boulevard, 19th Floor, Jacksonville FL 32207. **Contact:** Branch Manager. **World Wide Web address:** http://www.prufn.com. **Description:** An international securities brokerage and investment firm. The company offers clients more than 70 investment products including stocks, options, bonds, commodities, tax-favored investments, and insurance. Prudential Securities also offers specialized financial services. **Corporate headquarters location:** New York NY.

PUBLIX SUPER MARKETS, INC.
9786 West Beaver Street, Jacksonville FL 32220. 904/781-8600. **Recorded jobline:** 904/693-6172. **Contact:** Human Resources Department. **World Wide Web address:** http://www.publix.com. **Description:** Part of a regional chain of retail supermarkets with 691 stores in Alabama, Florida, Georgia, and South Carolina. The company also produces dairy, delicatessen, and bakery items through four plants and conducts distribution operations through more than eight facilities in Florida and Georgia. **Company slogan:** Where shopping is a pleasure. **Corporate headquarters location:** Lakeland FL. **Listed on:** Privately held. **Annual sales/revenues:** More than $100 million. **Number of employees nationwide:** 122,000.

PUBLIX SUPER MARKETS, INC.
P.O. Box 407, Lakeland FL 33802-0407. 863/688-1188. **Physical address:** 1936 George Jenkins Boulevard, Lakeland FL 33815. **Recorded jobline:** 863/680-5265. **Contact:** Human Resources Department. **World Wide Web address:** http://www.publix.com. **Description:** Operates a chain of retail supermarkets with 691 stores in Alabama, Florida, Georgia, and South Carolina. The company also produces dairy, delicatessen, and bakery items through four plants and conducts distribution operations through more than eight facilities in Florida and Georgia. Founded in 1930. **Company slogan:** Where shopping is a pleasure. **Special programs:** Summer Jobs. **Corporate headquarters location:** This location. **Other U.S. locations:** AL; FL; GA; SC. **Listed on:** Privately held. **CEO:** Howard Jenkins. **Annual sales/revenues:** More than $100 million. **Number of employees at this location:** 5,000. **Number of employees nationwide:** 122,000.

PYGMY COMPUTER SYSTEMS INC.
12651 South Dixie Highway, Suite 402, Miami FL 33156. 305/253-1212. **Toll-free phone:** 800/447-7469. **E-mail address:** support@pygmy.com. **Fax:** 305/255-1876. **Contact:** Personnel. **World Wide Web address:** http://www.pygmy.com. **Description:** Resells pocket computers and associated software.

QUEST DIAGNOSTICS INCORPORATED
4225 East Fowler Avenue, Tampa FL 33617. 813/972-7100. **Toll-free phone:** 800/282-6613. **Fax:** 813/972-3986. **Contact:** Human Resources. **World Wide Web address:** http://www.questdiagnostics.com. **Description:** One of the largest clinical laboratories in North America, providing a broad range of clinical laboratory services to health care clients that include physicians, hospitals, clinics, dialysis centers, pharmaceutical companies, and corporations. The company offers and performs tests on blood, urine, and other bodily fluids and tissues to provide information for health and well-being. Founded in 1969. **Positions advertised include:** Histology; Phlebotomy; Technical Laboratory Services; Lab Management; Accounts Receivable Billing Clerk. **Other U.S. locations:** Nationwide. **Listed on:** New York Stock Exchange. **Stock exchange symbol:** DGX. **Annual revenues:** More than $100 million.

QUEST DIAGNOSTICS INCORPORATED
1605 East Plaza Drive, Tallahassee FL 32308. 850/877-5171. **Contact:** Human Resources. **World Wide Web address:** http://www.questdiagnostics.com. **Description:** Quest Diagnostics is one of the largest clinical laboratories in North America, providing a broad range of clinical laboratory services to health care clients that include physicians, hospitals, clinics, dialysis centers, pharmaceutical companies, and corporations. The company offers and performs tests on blood, urine, and other bodily fluids and tissues to provide information for health and well-being. **Other U.S. locations:** Nationwide. **Operations at this facility include:** This location is a patient service center. **Listed on:** New York Stock Exchange. **Stock exchange symbol:** DGX. **Annual revenues:** More than $100 million.

QUICK AND REILLY, INC.
420 Royal Palm Way, Palm Beach FL 33480. 561/655-8000. **Contact:** Human Resources. **World Wide Web address:** http://www.quick-reilly.com. **Description:** Quick and Reilly is a holding company that, through its subsidiaries, provides discount brokerage services primarily to retail customers throughout the United States. The company also clears securities transactions for its own customers and for other brokerage firms and banks and acts as a specialist on the floor of the New York Stock Exchange. **Number of employees nationwide:** 850.

RMC-EWELL INDUSTRIES, INC.
P.O. Box 3858, Lakeland FL 33802. 863/688-5787. **Fax:** 863/6864085. **Contact:** Human Resources. **World Wide Web address:** http://www.rmcewell.com. **Description:** Produces concrete products including ready-mix concrete and concrete piping. **Parent company:** RMC Industries Corporation. **Operations at this facility include:** Administration; Manufacturing; Sales; Service.

RWA, INC.
3050 North Horseshoe Drive, Suite 270, Naples FL 34104. 239/649-1509. **Fax:** 239/649-7056. **Contact:** Human Resources. **E-mail address:** careers@consult-rwa.com. **World Wide Web address:** http://www.consult-rwa.com. **Description:** RWA is a land development and civil engineering design firm offering solutions to both private and public sector clients. **Positions advertised include:** Director of Engineering; Engineering CAD Technician; GIS CAD Technician; Project Manager/Professional Engineer; Survey Instrument Person; Survey Party Chief. **Corporate headquarters location:** This location. **Other area locations:** Fort Myers FL.

RADISSON RIVERWALK HOTEL
1515 Prudential Drive, Jacksonville FL 32207. 904/396-5100. **Fax:** 904/398-7154. **Contact:** Human Resources. **E-mail address:** sales@radjax.com. **World Wide Web address:** http://www.radjax.com. **Description:** A hotel and conference center. **Positions advertised include:** General Maintenance Worker; Restaurant Server; Restaurant Busser; Lobby Attendant; Floor Technician; Cashier; Bartender.

RAMSAY YOUTH SERVICES, INC.
Columbus Center, One Alhambra Plaza, Suite 750, Coral Gables FL 33134. 305/569-6993. **Fax:** 305/569-4647. **Contact:** Human Resources. **World Wide Web address:** http://www.ramsay.com. **Description:** Ramsay Youth Services, Inc. is a provider and manager of juvenile justice and behavioral healthcare treatment programs and services. The programs and services are provided primarily to at-risk and troubled youth in residential and nonresidential settings. **Positions advertised include:** Administrative Assistant. **Other U.S. locations:** Nationwide. **Operations at this facility include:** Administration. **Listed on:** NASDAQ. **Stock exchange symbol:** RYOU.

RAYONIER INC.
50 North Laura Street, Jacksonville FL 32202. 904/357-9100. **Contact:** Human Resources. **World Wide Web address:** http://www.rayonier.com. **Description:** A leading international forest products company primarily engaged in the trading, merchandising, and manufacturing of logs, timber, and wood products and in the production and sale of specialty pulps. Rayonier owns, buys, and harvests timber stumpage and purchases delivered logs, primarily in North America and New Zealand, for subsequent sale into export markets (primarily to Japan, Korea, and China), as well as to domestic lumber and pulp mills. Rayonier also produces dimension and specialty products for residential construction and industrial uses. **Positions advertised include:** Auditor; Geographical Information Systems Specialist; Controller. **Corporate headquarters location:** This location. **Listed on:** New York Stock Exchange. **Stock exchange symbol:** RYN. **Number of employees worldwide:** 2,300.

RECOTON CORPORATION
2950 Lake Emma Road, Lake Mary FL 32746. 407/333-0900. **Contact:** Human Resources. **World Wide Web address:** http://www.recoton.com. **Description:** Designs, manufactures, and markets consumer electronics, car stereo speakers, and loudspeakers. **Listed on:** NASDAQ. **Stock exchange symbol:** RCOT.

REGAL MARINE INDUSTRIES, INC.
2300 Jetport Drive, Orlando FL 32809. 407/851-4360. **Fax:** 407/857-1256. **Contact:** Kim Evans, Director of Human Resources. **E-mail address:** regal@regalboats.com. **World Wide Web address:** http://www.regalboats.com. **Description:** Manufactures pleasure boats.

REGIONS BANK
P.O. Drawer 608, Milton FL 32572-0608. 850/623-3846. **Contact:** Human Resources. **World Wide Web address:** http://www.regionsbank.com. **Description:** A savings and loan bank. **Parent company:** Great Western Holding Company. **Listed on:** NASDAQ. **Stock exchange symbol:** RGBK.

REICHHOLD CHEMICALS, INC.
P.O. Box 1433, Pensacola FL 32596-1433. 850/433-7621. **Contact:** Human Resources. **E-mail address:** human.resources@reichold.com. **World Wide Web address:** http://www.reichhold.com. **Description:** A chemical plant that manufactures coating resins, epoxy, epoxy hardeners, acrylic, and copolymer resins. **Corporate headquarters location:** Durham NC. **Operations at this facility include:** Manufacturing. **Listed on:** Privately held. **Number of employees at this location:** 85.

RENAISSANCE MIAMI BISCAYNE BAY HOTEL
1601 Biscayne Boulevard, Miami FL 33132. 305/374-0000. **Fax:** 305/374-8065. **Contact:** Human Resources. **World Wide Web address:** http://www.marriott.com. **Description:** A 528-room hotel that is located atop a shopping mall. **Positions advertised include:** Sales Administrative Assistant; Assistant Restaurant Manager; Catering Sales Manager; Cook.

RESEARCH TRIANGLE INSTITUTE (RTI)
3000 North Atlantic Avenue, Suite 108, Cocoa Beach FL 32931. 321/799-1607. **Contact:** Human Resources. **E-mail address:** jobs@rti.org. **World Wide Web address:** http://www.rti.org. **Description:** A nonprofit, independent research organization involved in many scientific fields. Clients include federal, state, and local governments, industrial associations, and public service agencies. The institute was created as a separately operated entity by the joint action of North Carolina State University, Duke University, and the University of North Carolina at Chapel Hill. RTI responds to national priorities in health, the environment, advanced technology, and social policy with contract research for the U.S. government including applications in statistics, social sciences, chemistry, life sciences, environmental sciences, engineering, and electronics. The institute operates a 180-acre campus in the center of Research Triangle Park NC, which includes laboratory and office facilities for all technical programs. **Corporate headquarters location:** Research Triangle Park NC. **Other U.S. locations:** Nationwide. **International locations:** England; Indonesia; South Africa. **Number of employees nationwide:** 1,950.

RESTAURANT ADMINISTRATION SERVICES
2699 Lee Road, Suite 200, Winter Park FL 32789. 407/645-4811. **Fax:** 407/629-0641. **Contact:** Dale Lucas, Director of Personnel and Training. **Description:** Operates quick-service restaurants. **Corporate headquarters location:** This location. **Listed on:** Privately held. **Number of employees at this location:** 1,200.

REVLON
P.O. Box 37557, Jacksonville FL 32236. 904/693-1200. **Fax:** 904/693-1259. **Contact:** Human Resources. **World Wide Web address:** http://www.revlon.com. **Description:** This location manufactures hair care products. Overall, Revlon manufactures a wide variety of cosmetics and personal care products. **Corporate headquarters location:** New York NY. **Operations at this facility include:** Administration; Manufacturing; Research and Development. **Listed on:** New York Stock Exchange. **Stock exchange symbol:** REV. **Number of employees at this location:** 550.

REXALL SHOWCASE INTERNATIONAL
6111 Broken Sound Parkway NW, Boca Raton FL 33487. 561/994-2090. **Contact:** Human Resources. **World Wide Web address:** http://www.rexallshowcase.com. **Description:** Manufactures and distributes vitamins in both retail and wholesale markets. **Parent Company:** Unicity Network.

REYNOLDS, SMITH AND HILLS, INC.
P.O. Box 4850, Jacksonville FL 32201-4850. 904/256-2500. **Physical address:** 10748 Deerwood Park Boulevard, Jacksonville FL 32256. **Contact:** Jack Higson, Human Resources Director. **World Wide Web address:** http://www.rsandh.com. **Description:** Offers architectural, engineering, and planning/design consulting services. **Positions advertised include:** Senior Civil Site Design Engineer; Landscape Architect; Intern Architect; Structural Engineer. **Other area locations:** Fort Meyers; Merritt Island; Orlando; Plantation; Tampa. **Other U.S. locations:** Chicago IL; Flint MI; Duluth MN; Austin TX; Houston TX. **Number of employees nationwide:** 375.

RINKER MATERIALS CORPORATION
1501 Belvedere Road, West Palm Beach FL 33406. 561/833-5555. **Toll-free phone:** 800/226-5521. **Contact:** Tim Dugan, Personnel Manager. **World Wide Web address:** http://www.rinker.com. **Description:** Manufactures and supplies assorted concrete, cement, and aggregate products. **Corporate headquarters location:** This location. **Parent company:** CSR America. **Operations at this facility include:** Administration.

RITZ CARLTON GRANDE LAKES
4012 Central Florida Parkway, Orlando FL 32837. 407/200/2400. **Fax:** 407/206-2401. **Contact:** Human Resources, Employment Specialist. **E-mail address:** hrorlando@ritzcarlton.com. **World Wide Web address:** http://www.ritzcarlton.com. **Description:** A five star hotel located in Orlando. **Positions advertised include:** Audio Visual Technician; Houseperson Banquets.

ROBB & STUCKY
13170 South Cleveland Avenue, Fort Myers FL 33907. 239/936-8541. **Fax:** 239/437-6286. **Contact:** Sharon Dill, Director of Human Resources. **E-mail address:** personnel@robbstuckey.net. **World Wide Web address:** http://www.robbstucky.com. **Description:** A chain of furniture stores that also offers interior design services.

ROBBINS MANUFACTURING COMPANY
P.O. Box 17939, Tampa FL 33682. 813/971-3030. **Fax:** 813/972-3980. **Contact:** Human Resources. **World Wide Web address:** http://www.robbinslumber.com. **Description:** A lumber mill. **Corporate headquarters location:** This location. **Other U.S. locations:** CA; NC; TX; WA. **Listed on:** Privately held. **Number of employees at this location:** 250. **Number of employees nationwide:** 400.

ROCKWELL COLLINS
P.O. Box 1060, Melbourne FL 32902-1060. 321/725-0800. **Physical address:** 1100 West Hibiscus Boulevard, Melbourne FL 32902. **Contact:** Human Resources. **World Wide Web address:** http://www.rockwell.com. **Description:** Manufactures aircraft radio transmitters. **Corporate headquarters location:** Milwaukee WI. **Parent company:** Rockwell International Corporation provides products for the printing, military, automotive, and aerospace industries through its electronics, automotive, and graphics divisions. Products include military and commercial communication equipment, guidance systems, electronics, components for automobiles, and printing presses. Rockwell provides the government with parts and services for bombers, as well as power systems for the space station and is a major contractor for the Space Shuttle Orbiter program. **Listed on:** New York Stock Exchange. **Stock exchange symbol:** ROK. **CEO:** Don H. Davis, Jr. **Annual sales:** More than $100 million. **Number of employees worldwide:** 23,000.

ROLLINS COLLEGE
1000 Holt Avenue, Campus Box 2718, Winter Park FL 32789. 407/646-2320. **Contact:** Personnel. **World Wide Web address:** http://www.rollins.edu/hr/jobindex.htm. **Description:** A private, liberal arts college offering bachelor's and master's degrees to approximately 1,400 students. **NOTE:** Jobseekers may apply in person at the Warren Administration Building, Monday - Thursday, 9:00 a.m. - 4:00 p.m. **Positions advertised include:** Athletic Training Assistant; Director of Career Services; Assistant Professor of Acting; Assistant Professor of Elementary Secondary Education; Dispatcher; Head Provost Advisor; Integrated Past Management Technology; Marketing Assistant; Math Teacher; Project Custodian; Resident Advisor; Safety Officer; Summer Day Camp Counselor; Summer Day Camp Instructor; Facilities Management; Visiting Assistant; Professor of Economics. **Operations at this facility include:** Administration. **Listed on:** Privately held. **President:** Rita Bornstein. **Number of employees at this location:** 530.

ROSE PRINTING COMPANY, INC.
2503 Jackson Bluff Road, Tallahassee FL 32304. 850/576-4151. **Toll-free phone:** 800/227-3725. **Fax:** 850/576-4153. **Contact:** Human Resources. **World Wide Web address:** http://www.roseprinting.com. **Description:** A complete in-house book manufacturer. **Positions advertised include:** Web Press Operator; Folder Operator; Saddle Switch Operator; Bindery Worker.

ROTECH MEDICAL CORPORATION
2600 Technology Drive Suite 300, Orlando FL 32804. 407/822-4600. **Contact:** Human Resources. **E-mail address:** corporate@rotech.com. **World Wide Web address:** http://www.rotech.com. **Description:** RoTech Medical Corporation markets, provides, and delivers outpatient health care products and services to patients in physician offices and at their home. Services and products involve respiratory therapy equipment, convalescent medical equipment, prelabeled and prepackaged pharmaceuticals, and home infusion therapy products. **Other U.S. locations:** Nationwide. **Listed on:** NASDAQ. **Stock exchange symbol:** ROTC. **Number of employees at this location:** 350.

ROYAL CARIBBEAN
1050 Caribbean Way, Miami FL 33132. 305/379-2601. **Contact:** Human Resources. **World Wide Web address:** http://www.rccl.com. **Description:** An ocean cruise line that operates 22 ships sailing to the Caribbean, the Bahamas, Bermuda, Mexico, Alaska, the Mediterranean, Europe, the Greek Isles, Panama Canal, Hawaii, Scandinavia/Russia, and the Far East. **NOTE:** Job seekers are encouraged to submit their resume on-line, so that they may be considered for job opportunities as they become available. **Positions advertised include:** Accounting Clerk; Clerical Administrative Representative; Call Center Representative; Corporate Communication Representative; Culinary Associate; Customer Service Representative; General Manager; Guest Satisfaction Representative; Bar Manager; Hotel Director; Human Resources Manager; Unix System Administrator; Logistics Coordinator; Technical Superintendent; Hotel Purchasing Manager; Safety & Environmental Auditor; Guest Vacation Sales; Marketing Research Manager; Information Analyst; Vacation Sales Specialist; Quality Assurance Manager. **Corporate headquarters location:** This location. **Listed on:** New York Stock Exchange. **Stock exchange symbol:** RCL. **CEO:** Richard D. Fain. **Number of employees nationwide:** 15,000.

RYDER SYSTEM, INC.
3600 NW 82nd Avenue, Miami FL 33166. 305/500-3726. **Contact:** Human Resources. **World Wide Web address:** http://www.ryder.com. **Description:** Leases trucks, hauls automobiles, provides contract carriage and logistics services, and provides school bus transportation. Truck leasing operations are conducted in the United States, Puerto Rico, United Kingdom, Germany, and Poland with over 78,000 vehicles. The company provides maintenance, leasing, and related supplies, and also maintains over 27,000 non-leased trucks. **Positions advertised include:** Administrative Assistant; Benefit Analyst; Branch Rental Manager; Coordinator; Asset Utilization Director; Market

Research & Support Sales Director; Account Executive; Management Trainee; International Finance Manager; Market Research & Sales Support; Supply Management Manager; Supply Chain Marketing Consultant; Finance Manager; Service Manager; Service Support Leader; Staff Accountant; Tax Specialist; Customer Logistics Coordinator; Business Financial Analyst. **Corporate headquarters location:** This location. **Other U.S. locations:** Nationwide. **International locations:** Canada; Continental Europe; England; Mexico; Singapore; South America. **Listed on:** NASDAQ. **Stock exchange symbol:** R. **Number of employees worldwide:** 30,000.

S.H. MEDICAL CORPORATION
3061 NW 82nd Avenue, Miami FL 33122. 305/406-2222. **Fax:** 305/406-2113. **Contact:** Hiring Manager. **E-mail address:** shmedical@shmedical.com. **World Wide Web address:** http://www.shmedical.com. **Description:** A medical equipment distribution and export company that sells new, refurbished, and preowned medical equipment. The company specializes in diagnostic equipment, endoscopy equipment and instruments, fetal monitors, parts, pulse oximeters, surgical instruments, and ultrasounds. **Corporate headquarters location:** This location.

SACRED HEART HEALTH SYSTEMS
5151 North Ninth Avenue, Pensacola FL 32513. 850/416-7175. **Fax:** 850/416-6740. **Contact:** Sue Byrd, Director of Human Resources. **E-mail address:** shmedical@shmedical.com. **World Wide Web address:** http://www.sacred-heart.org. **Description:** A member of the Daughters of Charity national health system. Sacred Heart Health Systems is a 431-bed acute care facility. The hospital offers services in the following areas: cardiology, cardiovascular surgery, emergency, gastroenterology, laser surgery, neonatology, neurology, OB/GYN, oncology, orthopedics, otolaryngology, otology, pediatrics, and plastic surgery. Sacred Heart Health Systems also operates a skilled nursing facility, medical residence programs, and a wellness/health education center. **NOTE:** Job seekers may apply in person at the employment office from 8:00 a.m. to 3:00 p.m. The employment office is located at 5110 Bayou Boulevard, Pensacola FL 32513. **Positions advertised include:** Chief Sonnographer; Ultrasound Technician; Registered Nurse; Licensed Practical Nurse; Medical Office Secretary. **Corporate headquarters location:** St. Louis MO. **Number of employees at this location:** 2,500. **CEO:** Patrick J. Madden.

ST. AUGUSTINE FAMILY YMCA
500 Pope Road, St. Augustine FL 32084. 904/471-9622. **Contact:** Michelle Cooligan, Program Director. **World Wide Web address:** http://www.ymcaffc.org. **Description:** One of the nation's largest and most comprehensive service organizations. The YMCA provides health and fitness, social and personal development, sports and recreation, education and career development, and camps and conferences to children, youths, adults, the elderly, families, the disabled, refugees and foreign nationals, YMCA residents, and community residents through a broad range of specific programs. **Positions advertised include:** Wellness Coach; Yoga Instructor; Courtesy Counter Front Desk Clerk; Child Watch Associate. **Corporate headquarters location:** Chicago IL. **Other U.S. locations:** Nationwide.

ST. AUGUSTINE RECORD
P.O. Box 1630, St. Augustine FL 32085. 904/829-6562. **Fax:** 904/819-3558. **Physical address:** One News Place, St. Augustine FL 32086. **Contact:** Human Resources. **World Wide Web address:** http://www.staugustine.com. **Description:** A newspaper. **NOTE:** Please indicate department of interest when applying. **Parent company:** Morris Communications Corporation.

ST. IVES INC.
2025 McKinley Street, Hollywood FL 33020. 954/920-7300. **Fax:** 954/929-4324. **Contact:** Human Resources. **E-mail address:** david.neumann@st-ives.com. **World Wide Web address:** http://www.st-ives-hwd.com. **Description:** Performs a variety of prepress and printing services. **Other U.S. locations:** Cleveland OH. **Parent Company:** St. Ives plc. **President/CEO:** Wayne Angstrom. **Number of employees at this location:** Over 350.

THE ST. JOE COMPANY
245 Riverside Avenue Suite 500, Jacksonville FL 32202. 904/301-4200. **Fax:** 904/301-4201. **Contact:** Human Resources. **World Wide Web address:** http://www.joe.com. **Description:** A full-service real estate company engaged in the development, building, operation, and sale of commercial and residential real estate. The company also offers real estate financial services including brokerage, financial management, and representation. **Positions advertised include:** Sales Representative; Marketing Manager; Vice President of Land Sales & Development. **Corporate headquarters location:** This location. **Listed on:** New York Stock Exchange. **Stock exchange symbol:** JOE.

ST. PETERSBURG JUNIOR COLLEGE
P.O. Box 13489, St. Petersburg FL 33711. 727/341-3600. **Contact:** Human Resources. **World Wide Web address:** http://www.spjc.cc.fl.us. **Description:** A junior college serving Pinellas County. The school offers associate's degrees in the arts and sciences and prepares students for transferring to other institutions. **NOTE:** To apply for a position you must complete the on-line application. **Positions advertised include:** Programming Analyst; Assistant Director of Center for Teaching and Transportation Principals Program; Assistant Vice President of Financial Aide & Management; Development Coordinator Fundraising; Project Coordinator; Industrial Development Coordinator; Instructional Development Coordinator; Curriculum Designer; Curriculum Development Specialist; Orthotics & Prosthetics; Educational Technologist; Program Director; Project Technologist; Allstate Campus Provost; Scholarships & Student Financial Assistant Officer; Student Financial Assistant Officer. **Operations at this facility include:** Administration; Service. **Number of employees at this location:** 940.

ST. PETERSBURG YMCA
70 35th Street South Petersburg, FL 33711. 727/895-9622. **Contact:** Human Resources. **Description:** One of the nation's largest and most comprehensive service organizations. The YMCA provides health and fitness, social and personal development, sports and recreation, education and career development, and camps and conferences to children, youths, adults, the elderly, families, the disabled, refugees and foreign nationals, YMCA residents, and community residents through a broad range of specific programs. **Corporate headquarters location:** Chicago IL. **Other U.S. locations:** Nationwide.

SALOMON SMITH BARNEY
1301 Riverplace Boulevard, Suite 600, Jacksonville FL 32207. 904/858-2350. **Contact:** Human Resources. **World Wide Web address:** http://www.smithbarney.com. **Description:** An international investment banking, market making, and research firm serving corporations, governments, and other financial institutions. **Positions advertised include:** Project Manager; Lead Analyst; Analyst; Information Security Analyst; Manager; Technology Specialist; Program Manager. **Note:** Applicants can search and apply for current positions online. **Corporate headquarters location:** New York NY. **Parent company:** Citigroup. **Operations at this facility include:** Sales. **Listed on:** New York Stock Exchange. **Stock exchange symbol:** C.

SANFORD HERALD
P.O. Box 1667, Sanford FL 32772-1667. 407/322-2611. **Physical address:** 300 North French Avenue, Sanford FL 32771. **Fax:** 407/323-9408. **Contact:** Human Resources. **World Wide Web address:** http://www.seminoleherald.com. **Description:** A newspaper publisher. **NOTE:** Please indicate department of interest when applying.

SCHERING-PLOUGH
13900 NW 57th Court, Miami FL 33014. 305/698-4600. **Contact:** Human Resources. **World Wide Web address:** http://www.schering-plough.com. **Description:** Schering-Plough Corporation is engaged in the discovery, development, manufacture, marketing, and testing of pharmaceutical and consumer products. Pharmaceutical products include prescription drugs, over-the-counter medicines, eye care products, and animal health products promoted to the medical and allied health professions. The consumer products group consists of proprietary medicines, toiletries, cosmetics, foot care, and sun care products marketed directly to the public. Products include Coricidin cough and cold medicines and Maybelline beauty products. **Positions advertised include:** Maintenance Supervisor; Production Support Manager; Project Manager; Senior Technical Systems Analyst; Senior Validation Specialist; Production Supervisor. **Listed on:** New York Stock Exchange. **Stock exchange symbol:** SGP.

SCIENTIFIC INSTRUMENTS, INC.
4400 West Tiffany Drive, West Palm Beach FL 33407. 561/881-8500. **Contact:** Leigh Ann Capers, Human Resources Department. **E-mail address:** info@scientificinstruments.com **World Wide Web address:** http://www.scientificinstruments.com. **Description:** Manufactures temperature-sensing and controlling instruments as well as other laboratory instruments.

SCOTT TRADE
1425 West Granada Boulevard, Ormond Beach FL 32174-5900. 386/671-9303. **Toll-free phone:** 877/602-1980. **Contact:** Human Resources. **E-mail address:** support@scottrade.com. **World Wide Web address:** http://www.scottrade.com. **Description:** A stock trading investment company allowing individuals to trade online. **Positions advertised include:** Customer Service; Office Assistant.

SCOTTY'S, INC.
5300 North Recker Highway, Winter Haven FL 33880. 386/672-3343. **Contact:** Human Resources. **World Wide Web address:** http://www.scottysinc.com. **Description:** A wholesale construction supply company. **Corporate headquarters location:** This location.

SEA WORLD OF FLORIDA
7007 Sea World Drive, Orlando FL 32821. 407/351-3600. **Contact:** Professional Staffing Department. **World Wide Web address:** http://www.seaworld.com. **Description:** A marine-life park offering a variety of shows and exhibits. **Positions advertised include:** Admissions Attendants; Assistant Lead; Beer School Instructor; Cook; Education Admissions Assistant; Filtration Technician; Food Service; Game Host; Maintenance Help; Registered Nurse; Licensed Practical Nurse; Sales Clerk; Sign Maker; Walk Around Character; Warehouse Worker. **U.S. locations:** CA; TX.

SEARS, ROEBUCK & CO.
9501 Arlington Expressway, Jacksonville FL 32225. 904/727-3255. **Contact:** Human Resources. **World Wide Web address:** http://www.sears.com. **Description:** One location of the nationwide department store chain. **Positions advertised include:** District Sales Manager. **Corporate headquarters location:** Chicago IL. **Listed on:** New York Stock Exchange. **Stock exchange symbol:** S.

SECURITY PLASTICS INC.
14427 NW 60th Avenue, Miami Lakes FL 33014. 305/823-5440. **Contact:** Human Resources. **E-mail address:** hrmiami@securityplastics.com. **World Wide Web address:** http://www.securityplastics.com. **Description:** Manufactures plastic components for original equipment manufacturers. **Positions advertised include:** Sales; Engineering; Tooling. **Corporate headquarters location:** This location. **Other area locations:** St. Petersburg FL. **Other U.S. locations:** McAllen TX. **International locations:** Malaysia; Mexico. **Operations at this facility include:** Manufacturing.

SEMINOLE ELECTRIC COOPERATIVE INC.
P.O. Box 272000, Tampa FL 33688-2000. 813/963-0994. **Toll-free phone:** 800/321-6274. **Fax:** 813/264-7906. **Contact:** Faye Rampolla, Human Resources Analyst. **E-mail address:** frampolla@seminole-electric.com. **World Wide Web address:** http://www.seminole-electric.com. **Description:** A nonprofit company that owns power plants that provide electricity to utility companies. **Positions advertised include:** Associate System Coordinator. **Special programs:** Co-ops. **Corporate headquarters location:** This location. **Other area locations:** Palatka FL. **Operations at this facility include:** Divisional Headquarters. **Executive Vice-President:** Richard J. Midulla. **Annual sales/revenues:** More than $100 million.

SEMPER CARE HOSPITAL
615 North Bonita Avenue, Panama City FL 32401. 850/767-3180. **Fax:** 850/767-3190. **Contact:** Human Resources: **Description:** A hospital with 902 beds. **Positions advertised include:** Registered Nurse. **President:** Steve Johnson.

SENSORMATIC ELECTRONICS CORPORATION
6600 Congress Avenue, Boca Raton FL 33487. 561/912-6000. **Contact:** Human Resources. **World Wide Web address:** http://www.sensormatic.com. **Description:** Manufactures and services electronic security systems to retail and commercial businesses worldwide. The company's products include AC500 Access Control System, which integrates hands-free access control with video imaging; SpeedDome programmable dome camera; Alligator antishoplifting tags; AisleKeeper, SekurPost, and SuperTag antishoplifting systems; Electronic Asset Protection systems; and SekurNed systems, which monitor and track hospital patients. **Positions advertised include:** Sonitrol Branch Manager; Sales Representative; Alarm Service Technician; Business Development Manager; Operations Manager; Field Service Technician; Project Specialist; Pharmacy Regional Manager; Nuclear Pharmacist; Administrative Assistant; Production Manager; Fire Sprinkler Designer; Communications Specialist; Receptionist. **Operations at this facility include:** Administration; Manufacturing; Research and Development. **Listed on:** New York Stock Exchange. **Stock exchange symbol:** SRM. **Number of employees nationwide:** 5,500.

SEVERN TRENT LABORATORIES, INC.
3355 Meclemore Drive, Pensacola FL 32514. 850/474-1001. **Fax:** 850/478-2671. **Contact:** Human Resources. **World Wide Web address:** http://www.stl-inc.com. **Description:** Provides a complete range of environmental testing services to private industry, engineering consultants, and government agencies in support of federal and

state environmental regulations. The company also possesses analytical capabilities in the fields of air toxins, field analytical services, radiochemistry/mixed waste, and advanced technology. **Positions advertised include:** Operations Manager; Field Service Technician. **Other area locations:** Tampa FL. **Other U.S. locations:** Nationwide. **Parent Company:** Severn Trent plc. **Number of employees nationwide:** Over 2,000.

SEVERN TRENT LABORATORIES, INC.
6712 Benjamin Road Suite 100, Tampa FL 33634. 813/885-7427. **Fax:** 813/885-7049. **Contact:** Human Resources. **World Wide Web address:** http://www.stl-inc.com. **Description:** Provides a complete range of environmental testing services to private industry, engineering consultants, and government agencies in support of federal and state environmental regulations. The company also possesses analytical capabilities in the fields of air toxins, field analytical services, radiochemistry/mixed waste, and advanced technology. **Positions advertised include:** Laboratory Director; HPLC Analyst; Laboratory Technician. **Other area locations:** Pensacola FL. **Other U.S. locations:** Nationwide. **Parent Company:** Severn Trent plc. **Number of employees nationwide:** Over 2,000.

SHAKER ADVERTISING AGENCY
4920 West Cypress Street, Suite 104, Tampa FL 33607. 813/289-1100. **Contact:** Lee Ann Foster, Office Manager. **E-mail address:** hr@shaker.com. **World Wide Web address:** http://www.shaker.com. **Description:** An advertising agency. **Positions advertised include:** Human Resources Generalist. **Corporate headquarters location:** Oak Park IL. **Other area locations:** Miami/Ft. Lauderdale FL. **Other U.S. locations:** Oak Park IL; Bloomington IN; Boston MA; East Brunswick NJ; Pittsburgh PA; Milwaukee WI. **Number of employees nationwide:** 243.

SIEMENS BUSINESS COMMUNICATION SYSTEMS, INC.
900 Broken Sound Parkway, Boca Raton FL 33487. 561/923-5000. **Contact:** Human Resources. **World Wide Web address:** http://www.siemens.com. **Description:** A leading provider of communications and communications integration technology, including OfficePoint ISDN systems, a high-speed integration product enabling transmission and reception of voice, data, image, and video over a single phone line. **Positions advertised include:** 2G Project Manager; Financial Analyst Associate; Business Application Analyst; Business Development Manager; Engineer CS; Business Administrator Manager; Project Manager; System Engineer. **Corporate headquarters location:** Santa Clara CA. **Parent company:** Siemens AG (Berlin, Germany). **Listed on:** New York Stock Exchange. **Stock exchange symbol:** SI. **President/CEO:** Dr. Heinrich Pierer. **Number of employees worldwide:** 60,000.

SIEMENS STROMBERG-CARLSON
400 Rinehart Road, Lake Mary FL 32746. 407/942-5000. **Contact:** Garth Shoemaker, Human Resources. **World Wide Web address:** http://www.siemens.com. **Description:** Manufactures telecommunications equipment including broadband switching and digital central office switching equipment, Internet telephony products, and data/voice network products. **Parent company:** Siemens AG (Berlin, Germany). **Listed on:** New York Stock Exchange. **Stock exchange symbol:** SI. **President/CEO:** Dr. Heinrich Pierer. **Number of employees worldwide:** 60,000.

SIEMENS WESTINGHOUSE POWER CORPORATION
261 Lyman Road, Casselberry FL 32707. 407/736-5900. **Recorded jobline:** 407/736-2500. **Contact:** Human Resources Department. **World Wide Web address:** http://www.siemenswestinghouse.com. **Description:** Manufactures steam turbine generators. **Parent company:** Siemens AG (Berlin, Germany). **Number of employees worldwide:** 26,500.

SIGNAL TECHNOLOGY CORPORATION
84 Hill Avenue, Fort Walton Beach FL 32548. 850/244-0043. **Fax:** 850/664-5479. **Contact:** Human Resources. **E-mail address:** headricks@keltec.sigtech.com. **World Wide Web address:** http://www.sigtech.com. **Description:** Designs and manufactures power conversion equipment. **Positions advertised include:** Engineer; Manufacturer. **Other U.S. locations:** AZ; CA; MA; TX. **Listed on:** NASDAQ. **Stock exchange symbol:** STCO.

SIGNATURE FLIGHT SUPPORT
4050 SW 11th Terrace, Fort Lauderdale FL 33315. 954/359-0000. **Fax:** 954//359-2765. **Contact:** Brenda Knighton, Human Resources Department. **E-mail address:** brendaknighton@signatureflight.com. **World Wide Web address:** http://www.signatureflight.com. **Description:** A supplier and distributor of machine parts for corporate jets. The company is also involved in refueling and offers maintenance and inspections of corporate jets. **Corporate headquarters location:** Orlando FL. **Other U.S. locations:** Nationwide. **Parent company:** BBA Aviation. **Operations at this facility include:** Administration; Service. **Number of employees nationwide:** 4,500.

SIKORSKY AIRCRAFT CORPORATION
P.O. Box 109610, West Palm Beach, FL 33410-9600. 561/775-5200. **Contact:** Human Resources. **E-mail address:** sikorskywes@sikorsky.com. **World Wide Web address:** http://www.sikorsky.com. **Description:** Manufactures helicopters for commercial, industrial, and military applications. **Corporate headquarters location:** Stratford CT. **Other U.S. locations:** AL; CT. **Parent company:** United Technologies Corporation designs and manufactures engines and space propulsion systems for commercial and general aviation. **President:** Dean Borgman. **Annual revenues:** More than $100 million.

SIMPLEXGRINNELL
10550 Commerce Parkway, Miramar FL 33025. 954/431-3700. **Fax:** 954/435-6650. **Contact:** Wilma Beckman. **World Wide Web address:** http://www.simplexgrinnell.com. **Description:** Produces fire and life safety products including sprinklers, emergency lighting systems, sound alarms and communications systems, and time and workforce management systems. **Positions advertised include:** Ship Fire Protection Inspection/Maintenance Technician; Fire Suppression Sales Representative; Alarm and Detection Manager; Sprinkler Fitter. **Parent Company:** Tyco International. **Number of employees worldwide:** 200,000.

SKYWAY ANIMAL HOSPITAL
3258 Fifth Avenue South, St. Petersburg FL 33712. 727/327-5141. **Fax:** 727/327-3405. **Contact:** Human Resources. **World Wide Web address:** http://www.skywayah.com. **Description:** Provides general medical, surgical, dental, and radiological services to small animals.

SMITH DENTAL LABS
2131 Art Museum Drive, Jacksonville FL 32207. 904/398-6844. **Toll-free phone:** 800/828-9976. **Contact:** Human Resources. **World Wide Web address:** http://www.smithdentallab.com. **Description:** Provides a full range of custom-made dental prosthetic appliances, divided into three main groups: restorative products (crowns and bridges); reconstructive products (partial and full dentures); and cosmetic products (porcelain veneers and ceramic crowns.) **Positions advertised include:** Dental Lab Trainee; Skilled Technician; Department Supervisor. **Corporate headquarters location:** Wayland MA. **Parent company:** National Dentex Corporation is one of the largest operators of dental laboratories in the United States. Each lab is operated as a stand-alone facility under the direction of a local manager. All sales and marketing is done through each lab's own direct sales force. **Other U.S. locations:** Nationwide. **Listed on:** NASDAQ. **Stock exchange symbol:** NADX. **Annual sales/revenues:** Less than $5 million.

SMURFIT-STONE CONTAINER CORPORATION
P.O. Box 2000, Fernandina Beach FL 32035. 904/261-5551. **Contact:** Human Resources. **World Wide Web address:** http://www.smurfit-stone.com. **Description:** Smurfit-Stone Container Corporation is one of the world's leading paper-based packaging companies. The company's main products include corrugated containers, folding cartons, and multiwall industrial bags. The company is also one of the world's largest collectors and processors of recycled products that are then sold to a worldwide customer base. Smurfit-Stone Container Corporation also operates several paper tube, market pulp, and newsprint production facilities. **Corporate headquarters location:** Chicago IL. **Other area locations:** Jacksonville FL. **Other U.S. locations:** Nationwide. **Operations at this facility include:** This location manufactures kraft paper and corrugated shipping containers. **International locations:** Worldwide. **Listed on:** NASDAQ. **Stock exchange symbol:** SSCC.

SMURFIT-STONE CONTAINER CORPORATION
9469 Eastport Road, P.O. Box 26998, Jacksonville FL 32218. 877-772-2999. **Contact:** Human Resources. **World Wide Web address:** http://www.smurfit-stone.com. **Description:** Smurfit-Stone Container Corporation is one of the world's leading paper-based packaging companies. The company's main products include corrugated containers, folding cartons, and multiwall industrial bags. The company is also one of the world's largest collectors and processors of recycled products that are then sold to a worldwide customer base. Smurfit-Stone Container Corporation also operates several paper tube, market pulp, and newsprint production facilities. **Other area locations:** Fernandina Beach FL. **Corporate headquarters location:** Chicago IL. **Other U.S. locations:** Nationwide. **International locations:** Worldwide. **Operations at this facility include:** This location is an industrial packing plant. **Listed on:** NASDAQ. **Stock exchange symbol:** SSCC.

SOLITRON DEVICES, INC.
3301 Electronics Way, West Palm Beach FL 33407. 561/848-4311. **Fax:** 561/881-5652. **Contact:** Human Resources Department. **World Wide Web address:** http://www.solitrondevices.com. **Description:** Designs and manufactures high-density power components and circuitry. The company's semiconductor and hybrid circuit products are sold to national and international aerospace and defense programs. **Corporate headquarters location:** This location. **Other U.S. locations:** Nationwide. **Listed on:** NASDAQ. **Stock exchange symbol:** SODI. **Number of employees at this location:** 100.

SOLUTION 6 HOLDINGS LIMITED
101 North Monroe Street, Suite 800, Tallahassee FL 32301. 850/224-2200. **Contact:** Human Resources. **World Wide Web address:** http://www.solution6.com. **Description:** Develops financial software. Established in 1981. **NOTE:** Entry-level positions and part-time jobs are offered. **Special programs:** Training; Co-ops; Summer Jobs. **Corporate headquarters location:** Sydney, Australia. **Other U.S. locations:** Nationwide. **International locations:** Worldwide. **CEO:** Neil H. Gamble. **Number of employees worldwide:** 1,600.

SONOCO PRODUCTS
1854 Central Florida Parkway, Orlando FL 32837. 407/851-5800. **Contact:** Human Resources. **World Wide Web address:** http://www.sonoco.com. **Description:** Manufactures a variety of packaging materials for industrial and consumer markets. **Corporate headquarters location:** Hartsville SC. **Other U.S. locations:** Nationwide. **International locations:** Worldwide. **Listed on:** New York Stock Exchange. **Stock exchange symbol:** SON. **President/CEO:** Harris E. DeLoach, Jr. **Annual sales/revenues:** More than $100 million. **Number of employees worldwide:** 18,000.

SOUND ADVICE, INC.
301 East Las Olas Boulevard, Suite 300, Ft. Lauderdale FL 33301. 954/922-4434. **Contact:** Human Resources. **E-mail address:** hr@soundadvice-fl.com. **World Wide Web address:** http://www.wegivesoundadvice.com. **Description:** Operates retail stores that sell and service audio and video equipment for the home and automobile markets. **Corporate headquarters location:** This location.

SOUTH FLORIDA BUSINESS JOURNAL
1000 East Hillsboro Boulevard, Suite 103, Deerfield Beach FL 33441. 954/949-7600. **Contact:** Human Resources Department. **World Wide Web address:** http://www.bizjournals.com/southflorida. **Description:** A publisher of a weekly business journal. **Corporate headquarters location:** Charlotte NC. **Operations at this facility include:** Administration; Production; Sales.

SOUTHTRUST BANK
P.O. Box 7219, Jacksonville FL 32238-0219. 904/798-6300. **Contact:** Human Resources. **E-mail address:** info@southtrust.com. **World Wide Web address:** http://www.southtrust.com. **Description:** SouthTrust Bank operates through 700 offices in the Southeast. **Positions advertised include:** Private Banker; Financial Center Operations Coordinator; Financial Services Representative; Financial Center Representative; Teller; Business Banking Relationship Manager; Private Banking Team Leader; Associate Sales Representative; Commercial Relationship Manager; Peak Time Teller. **Corporate headquarters location:** Birmingham AL. **Other U.S. locations:** AL; GA; MS; NC; SC; TN; TX; VA. **Operations at this facility include:** This location is the main branch for the Jacksonville area. **Subsidiaries include:** South Trust Securities, Inc; SouthTrust Mortgage Corporation; SouthTrust Insurance, Inc. **Parent company:** SouthTrust Corporation. **Listed on:** NASDAQ. **Stock exchange symbol:** SOTR. **Annual sales/revenues:** More than $100 million. **Number of employees nationwide:** 13,000.

SPARTON ELECTRONICS
P.O. Box 788, DeLeon Springs FL 32130. 386/985-4631. **Physical address:** 5612 Johnson Lake Road, DeLeon Springs FL 32130. **Fax:** 386/985-5984. **Contact:** Human Resources. **E-mail address:** rstephens@sparten.com. **World Wide Web address:** http://www.sparton.com. **Description:** Offers electronics engineering and manufacturing services including design engineering, development engineering, manufacturing, and test engineering. Capabilities include DFMA, box build, board layout, rapid prototyping, mechanical design, system integration, full environmentals, design from concept, board-level assembly, software development, and concurrent engineering. Sparton technical design skills include electronics (analog, digital, solid-state devices, hybrid circuits, VHF transmitters, UHF receivers, custom integrated

circuits, and signal processing); mechanics (die casting, injection molding, stamping, extrusions, blow molding, and flotation systems); sensors (hydrophones, transducers, magnetics, acoustics, ultrasonics, and pressure); computers (programming, modeling, automatic test, design analysis, statistical analysis, finite element analysis, and algorithms); chemistry (electrochemistry, batteries, polymers, adhesives, and encapsulants); and environmental (hi-g shock, random vibration, humidity, temperature, altitude, high pressure, and shelf life.) **Positions advertised include:** Mechanical Engineer; Software Reliability Engineer; Test Engineer; Electrical Engineer; Project Engineer; Business Development Manager; Planner; Industrial Engineer; Quality Assurance Engineer. **Corporate headquarters location:** Jackson MI. **Other area locations:** Brooksville FL. **Other U.S. locations:** NM; NC. **International locations:** Canada. **Listed on:** New York Stock Exchange. **Stock exchange symbol:** SPA.

SPARTON ELECTRONICS
30167 Power Line Road, Brooksville FL 34602. 352/799-6520. **Fax:** 352/799-4759. **Contact:** Human Resources. **World Wide Web address:** http://www.sparton.com. **Description:** Offers electronics engineering and manufacturing services including design engineering, development engineering, manufacturing, and test engineering. Capabilities include DFMA, box build, board layout, rapid prototyping, mechanical design, system integration, full environmentals, design from concept, board-level assembly, software development, and concurrent engineering. Sparton technical design skills include electronics (analog, digital, solid-state devices, hybrid circuits, VHF transmitters, UHF receivers, custom integrated circuits, and signal processing); mechanics (die casting, injection molding, stamping, extrusions, blow molding, and flotation systems); sensors (hydrophones, transducers, magnetics, acoustics, ultrasonics, and pressure); computers (programming, modeling, automatic test, design analysis, statistical analysis, finite element analysis, and algorithms); chemistry (electrochemistry, batteries, polymers, adhesives, and encapsulants); and environmental (hi-g shock, random vibration, humidity, temperature, altitude, high pressure, and shelf life.) **Positions advertised include:** Materials Manager; Cell Manager; Customer Benefits Manager. **Corporate headquarters location:** Jackson MI. **Other area locations:** De Leon Springs FL. **Other U.S. locations:** NC; NM. **International locations:** Canada. **Listed on:** New York Stock Exchange. **Stock exchange symbol:** SPA

SPHERION
2050 Spectrum Boulevard, Fort Lauderdale FL 33309. 954/938-7600. **Contact:** Human Resources. **World Wide Web address:** http://www.spherion.com. **Description:** Spherion is an executive search firm that offers professional recruiting, testing, and assessment services. **Positions advertised include:** PeopleSoft Production Support Analyst; Staffing Branch Coordinator; Real Estate Financial Analyst; Business Analyst Process Base; Novell Engineer; Internal Auditor; Project Accountant; Controller; Outside Sales Representative; User Interface Design; Staffing Coordinator; Entry Level Staff Accountant; Online Marketing Manager; Sales Representative; Internal Auditor; Build Engineer. **Corporate headquarters location:** This location. **Other U.S. locations:** Nationwide. **International locations:** Worldwide. **Operations at this facility include:** This location houses administrative offices only. **Listed on:** New York Stock Exchange. **Stock exchange symbol:** SFN. **Number of employees worldwide:** 500,000.

STAINLESS INC.
One Stainless Plaza, Deerfield Beach FL 33441. 954/421-4290x224. **Toll-free phone:** 800/877-5177. **Fax:** 954/421-4464. **Contact:** Elizabeth Mountcastle, Manager of Human Resources. **World Wide Web address:** http://www.stainless.com. **Description:** Manufactures and distributes dining room, kitchen, and playground equipment and accessories. **Corporate headquarters location:** This location. **CEO:** Rob Kassab.

STAR MULTICARE SERVICES INC.
2221 North University Drive, Pembroke Pines FL 33024. 954/962-0926. **Contact:** Human Resources. **World Wide Web address:** http://www.starmulticare.com. **Description:** A home health care agency that also provides temporary personnel to health care facilities. **Positions advertised include:** Licensed Practical Nurse; Registered Nurse; Nurses Aide; Home Health Aide. **Corporate headquarters location:** Huntington Station NY. **Other U.S. locations:** NJ; NY; OH; PA. **Listed on:** NASDAQ. **Stock exchange symbol:** SMCS.

THE STUART NEWS
P.O. Box 9009, Stuart FL 34995. 772-464-4160. **Recorded jobline:** 877/690-6397. **Physical address:** 1939 South Federal Highway, Stuart FL 34994. **Contact:** Human Resources. **World Wide Web address:** http://www.tcpalm.com/stuart. **Description:** A community newspaper. **Positions advertised include:** Design Associate; Driver CDL Class B; Packager. **Parent company:** E.W. Scripps Company.

SUN MICROSYSTEMS, INC.
3501 Quadrangle Boulevard, Suite 150, Orlando FL 32817. 407/380-0058. **Contact:** Human Resources. **World Wide Web address:** http://www.sun.com. **Description:** Sun Microsystems produces high-performance computer systems, workstations, servers, CPUs, peripherals, and operating system software. Products include a microprocessor called SPARC. Products are sold to engineering, scientific, technical, and commercial markets worldwide. **Positions advertised include:** Finance Accounting; Project Operations Support; Mission Critical Technical Support; Sales; Sales Management; Global Account Development; Account Management; Pre Sales Technical Support; Customer Service Program Sales; Technical Consultant; Project Manager; Systems Engineer; General Controller; Sales Representative. **Corporate headquarters location:** Palo Alto CA. **Other U.S. locations:** Nationwide. **International locations:** Worldwide. **Operations at this facility include:** This location manufactures mainframe computers. **Subsidiaries include:** Forte Software Inc. manufactures enterprise application integration software. **Listed on:** NASDAQ. **Stock exchange symbol:** SUNW. **CEO:** Scott McNealy. **Annual sales/revenues:** More than $100 million. **Number of employees worldwide:** 40,000.

THE SUN-SENTINEL
200 East Las Olas Boulevard, Fort Lauderdale FL 33301-2293. 954/356-4000. **Contact:** Human Resources. **World Wide Web address:** http://www.sun-sentinel.com. **Description:** A south Florida newspaper with a daily circulation of 274,000 and a Sunday circulation of 392,000. **NOTE:** Please send resumes to: Human Resources, 333 SW 12th Avenue, Deerfield Beach FL 33442. **Parent company:** The Tribune Company.

SUNBEAM CORPORATION
2381 Executive Center Drive, Boca Raton FL 33431. 561/912-4100. **Contact:** Human Resources. **World Wide Web address:** http://www.sunbeam.com. **Description:** A designer, manufacturer, and marketer of consumer products. The company is divided into several business groups. Outdoor Products includes propane, natural gas, electric, and charcoal barbecue grills; aluminum lawn and patio furniture and related accessories; and wrought iron and wood furniture. Household Products includes electric and conventional blankets, comforters, heated throws, heating pads, bath scales, health monitoring systems, vaporizers, humidifiers, irons, steamers, and dental and hair care products. Small Kitchen Appliances includes hand mixers, blenders, food processors, juice extractors, toasters, can openers, waffle makers, and other culinary accessories. Sunbeam also produces barber and beauty products, personal care products, and animal products, as well as clocks, timers, thermometers, and weather instruments. **Positions advertised include:** Computer Operator; Commodity Manager; Director Warranty & Customer Service; Graphic Designer; Field Sales Manager; Master Black Belt. **Corporate headquarters location:** This location. **International locations:** Worldwide.

SUNRISE COMMUNITY, INC.
22300 SW 162nd Avenue, Miami FL 33170. 305/245-6150. **Contact:** Human Resources. **E-mail address:** info@sunrisegroup.com. **World Wide Web address:** http://www.sunrisegroup.org. **Description:** A residential treatment facility for individuals with developmental disabilities. **Positions advertised include:** Assistant Residential Program Director; Residential Program Director; Secretary; Training Instructor. **Other area locations:** Cape Coral FL; Clewiston FL; Lakeland FL; Naples FL; Panama City FL; St. Petersburg FL; Tallahassee FL. **Other U.S. locations:** AL; CT; GA; TN; VA. **President/CEO:** Les Leech, Jr. **Number of employees nationwide:** 4,000.

SUNRISE COMMUNITY, INC.
9040 Sunset Drive, Suite A, Miami FL 33173. 305/596-9040. **Contact:** Human Resources. **E-mail address:** info@sunrisegroup.com. **World Wide Web address:** http://www.sunrisegroup.com. **Description:** A residential treatment center for individuals with developmental disabilities. **Positions advertised include:** Assistant Residential Program Director; Residential Program Director; Secretary; Training Instructor. **Other area locations:** Cape Coral FL; Clewiston FL; Lakeland FL; Naples FL; Panama City FL; St. Petersburg FL; Tallahassee FL. **Other U.S. locations:** AL; CT; GA; TN; VA. **President/CEO:** Les Leech, Jr. **Number of employees nationwide:** 4,000.

SUNTRUST BANK, GULF COAST, N.A.
P.O. Box 2138, Sarasota FL 34230. 941/951-3307. **Contact:** Human Resources. **World Wide Web address:** http://www.suntrust.com. **Description:** A full-service commercial bank. **Positions advertised include:** Branch Manager; Business Banker; Credit Analyst; Financial Planner; Financial Services Representative; Mortgage Originator; Retail Sales Assistant; Wealth Strategist. **Corporate headquarters location:** Atlanta GA. **Other area locations:** Orlando FL; Miami FL; Tampa FL. **Other U.S. locations:** AL; DC; GA; MD; TN; VA. **Parent company:** SunTrust Banks, Inc. is a financial services company with three principal subsidiaries: SunTrust Banks of Florida, Inc.; SunTrust Banks of Georgia, Inc.; and SunTrust Banks of Tennessee, Inc. Together, these subsidiaries operate more than 1,100 full-service banking offices. The company's primary businesses include traditional deposit and credit services as well as trust and investment services. Additionally, SunTrust Banks, Inc. provides corporate finance, mortgage banking, factoring, credit card, discount brokerage, credit-related insurance, data processing, and information services. **Listed on:** New York Stock Exchange. **Stock exchange symbol:** STI. **President/CEO:** L. Phillip Humann.

SUNTRUST BANK, MIAMI, N.A.
777 Brickell Avenue, Miami FL 33131. 305/577-5244. **Fax:** 305/579-7217. **Contact:** Human Resources. **World Wide Web address:** http://www.suntrust.com. **Description:** A full-service commercial bank. **Positions advertised include:** Administrative Assistant; Financial Advisor; Branch Manager; Financial Services Representative; Mortgage Originator; Operations Specialist; Personal Trust Account Specialist; Retail Investment Consultant; Sales Representative; Service Representative. **Corporate headquarters location:** Atlanta GA. **Other area locations:** Orlando FL; Sarasota FL; Tampa FL. **Other U.S. locations:** AL; DC; GA; MD; TN; VA. **Parent company:** SunTrust Banks, Inc. is a financial services company with three principal subsidiaries: SunTrust Banks of Florida, Inc.; SunTrust Banks of Georgia, Inc.; and SunTrust Banks of Tennessee, Inc. Together, these subsidiaries operate more than 1,100 full-service banking offices. The company's primary businesses include traditional deposit and credit services as well as trust and investment services. Additionally, SunTrust Banks, Inc. provides corporate finance, mortgage banking, factoring, credit card, discount brokerage, credit-related insurance, data processing, and information services. **Listed on:** New York Stock Exchange. **Stock exchange symbol:** STI. **President/CEO:** L. Phillip Humann.

SUNTRUST BANK, TAMPA BAY, N.A.
401 East Jackson Street, 10th Floor, Tampa FL 33602. 813/224-2121. **Contact:** Human Resources. **World Wide Web address:** http://www.suntrust.com. **Description:** A full-service commercial bank. **Positions advertised include:** Administrative Assistant; Branch Manager; Business Banking Representative; Commercial Real Estate Consultant; Financial Services Representative; Human Resources Specialist; Mortgage Originator; Retail Investment Representative; Teller Coordinator. **Corporate headquarters location:** Atlanta GA. **Other area locations:** Orlando FL; Miami FL; Orlando FL; Sarasota FL. **Other U.S. locations:** AL; DC; GA; MD; TN; VA. **Parent company:** SunTrust Banks, Inc. is a financial services company with three principal subsidiaries: SunTrust Banks of Florida, Inc., SunTrust Banks of Georgia, Inc., and SunTrust Banks of Tennessee, Inc. Together, these subsidiaries operate more than 1,100 full-service banking offices. The company's primary businesses include traditional deposit and credit services as well as trust and investment services. Additionally, SunTrust Banks, Inc. provides corporate finance, mortgage banking, factoring, credit card, discount brokerage, credit-related insurance, data processing, and information services. **Listed on:** New York Stock Exchange. **Stock exchange symbol:** STI. **President/CEO:** L. Phillip Humann.

SUNTRUST BANK, CENTRAL FLORIDA, N.A.
P.O. Box 3833, Orlando FL 32802. 407/237-4153. **Contact:** Peggy Jackson, Human Resources Representative. **World Wide Web address:** http://www.suntrust.com. **Description:** A bank holding company. **Positions advertised include:** Administrative Assistant; Application Programmer; Business Banking Portfolio Specialist; Portfolio Specialist; Consumer Loan Operations Specialist; Database Analyst; Financial Analyst; Equipment Operator; Financial Planner; Personal Trust Administrator; Space Planner; Sales Representative. **Corporate headquarters location:** Atlanta GA. **Other area locations:** Orlando FL; Miami FL; Sarasota FL; Tampa FL. **Other U.S. locations:** AL; DC; GA; MD; TN; VA. **Parent company:** SunTrust Banks, Inc. is a financial services company with three principal subsidiaries: SunTrust Banks of Florida, Inc.; SunTrust Banks of Georgia, Inc.; and SunTrust Banks of Tennessee, Inc. Together, these subsidiaries operate more than 1,100 full-service banking offices. The company's primary businesses include traditional deposit and credit services as well as trust and investment services. Additionally, SunTrust Banks, Inc. provides corporate finance, mortgage banking, factoring, credit card, discount brokerage, credit-related insurance, data processing, and information services **Listed on:** New York Stock Exchange. **Stock exchange symbol:** STI. **President/CEO:** L. Phillip Humann.

SUPERIOR UNIFORM GROUP
10055 Seminole Boulevard, Seminole FL 33772. 727/397-9611. **Fax:** 727/803-2658. **Contact:** Jennifer Schmidt, Corporate Manager of Human Resources. **World Wide Web address:** http://www.superiorsurgicalmfg.com. **E-mail address:** info@superiorsurgicalmfg.com. **Description:** A manufacturer and wholesale distributor of uniforms, career apparel, and accessories for the hospital and health care fields, hotels and restaurants, and the public safety, industrial, transportation, and commercial markets. Fashion Seal Uniforms is the company's largest division and a prime supplier to the health care market. Other divisions include Worklon, Martin's Uniforms, Appel Uniforms, Universal Laundry Bags, Lamar Caribbean Sales. **Positions advertised include:** Inside Sales Account Representative; Master Data Clerks; Customer Services Representative; Costing Specialist. **Corporate headquarters location:** This location. **Listed on:** American Stock Exchange. **Stock exchange symbol:** SGC. **President:** Cliff McAlexander.

SWISHER INTERNATIONAL
P.O. Box 2230, Jacksonville FL 32203. 904/353-4311. **Contact:** Rick Dyer, Human Resources. **E-mail address;** rdyer@swisher.com. **World Wide Web address:** http://www.swisher.com. **Description:** One of the world's largest manufacturers of cigars and smokeless tobacco. Brand names include King Edward, Bering, Redwood, and Silver Creek. **Positions advertised include:** Territory Manager.

SYMETRICS INDUSTRIES
1615 West NASA Boulevard, Melbourne FL 32901. 321/254-1500. **Fax**: 321/259-4122. **Contact:** Human Resources. **E-mail address:** sberry@symetrics.com. **World Wide Web address:** http://www.symetrics.com. **Description:** Manufactures voicemail and telecommunications systems. **Positions advertised include:** Quality Engineer; Quality Inspector; Mechanical Assembler; Manufacturing Planner. **Corporate headquarters location:** This location. **Annual sales/revenues:** More than $100 million.

TI GROUP AUTOMOTIVE SYSTEMS
2660 Jewett Lane, Sanford FL 32771. 407/323-2780. **Contact:** Human Resources. **World Wide Web address:** http://www.tiauto.com. **Description:** Supplies fluid delivery and storage systems for brake, fuel, and powertrain applications to the automotive industry. **Parent company:** TI Group. **Other U.S. locations:** Nationwide. **International locations:** Worldwide. **CEO:** William J. Laule. **Number of employees worldwide:** 20,000.

TNT LOGISTICS
P.O. Box 40083, Jacksonville, FL 32203. **Toll-free phone:** 888/LOG-ISTX. **Fax:** 904/928-1547. **Contact:** Human Resources. **World Wide Web address:** http://www.tnt-logistics.com. **Description:** A third party logistics provider. Founded in 1980. **NOTE:** Entry-level positions and second and third shifts are offered. **Positions advertised include:** Business Development Manager; Internal Auditor; Logistics Engineer; Logistics Project Manager; Supervisor; Systems Engineer; Transportation Administrator; Transportation Technician. **Special programs:** Internships; Training. **Office hours:** Monday - Friday, 8:00 a.m. - 5:00 p.m. **Corporate headquarters location:** This location. **International locations:** Argentina; Brazil; Canada; Mexico; United Kingdom. **Listed on:** New York Stock Exchange. **Stock exchange symbol:** TP. **Annual sales/revenues:** More than $100 million. **Number of employees worldwide:** 116,000.

TALLAHASSEE COMMUNITY HOSPITAL
2626 Capital Medical Boulevard, Tallahassee FL 32308. 850/325-5000. **Fax:** 850/325-5198. **Contact:** Human Resources. **World Wide Web address:** http://www.tallahasseehospital.com. **World Wide Web address:** http://www.ctch.com. **Description:** A 180-bed, acute-care hospital. Founded in 1979. **Positions advertised include:** Accountant; Radiological Technologist; Registered Cardiovascular Invasive Specialist; Registered Nurse; Medical Records Processor; Environmental Services Support; Environmental Services Tech; Medical Technologist; Administrative Supervisor; Transporter; Pharmacist; Ultrasonography Technician; Respirator.

THE TALLAHASSEE DEMOCRAT
P.O. Box 900, Tallahassee FL 32302. 850/599-2128. **Physical address:** 277 North Magnolia Drive, Tallahassee FL 32301. 850/599-2128. **Contact:** Karen Sheffield, Employment Services Administrator. **E-mail address:** resumes@knightridder.com. **World Wide Web address:** http://www.tallahassee.com. **Description:** A daily newspaper. **Corporate headquarters location:** Miami FL. **Parent company:** Knight Ridder. **Operations at this facility include:** Manufacturing.

TALLAHASSEE MUSEUM OF HISTORY & NATURAL SCIENCE
3945 Museum Drive, Tallahassee FL 32310-6325. 850/575-8684. **Fax:** 850/574-8243. **Contact:** Personnel. **World Wide Web address:** http://www.tallahasseemuseum.org. **Description:** A museum and zoo featuring historical buildings, an environmental science center, and wild animals.

TAMPA ELECTRIC
P.O. Box 111, Tampa FL 33601. 813/228-4111. **Recorded jobline:** 813/228-4635. **Contact:** Human Resources. **World Wide Web address:** http://www.tampaelectric.com. **Description:** Provides electricity to residents of Tampa and outlying areas. **Positions advertised include:** Supply Diversity Manager; Financial Reporting Account Analyst. **Listed on:** New York Stock Exchange. **Stock exchange symbol:** TE. **CEO:** Robert D. Fagan.

TAMPA GENERAL HOSPITAL
P.O. Box 1289, Tampa FL 33601. 813/844-7551. **Fax:** 813/844-4345. **Recorded jobline:** 813/844-4100. **Contact:** Human Resources. **World Wide Web address:** http://www.tgh.org. **Description:** A medical facility providing hospital and ambulatory services. **Positions advertised include:** Aeromed; Anesthesia Care Technician; Cardiac Monitor Technician; Care Coordinator; Clinical Nurse; Clinical Admission Supervisor; Clinician; Epiderm Clinician; Lactation Consultant; Licensed Practical Nurse; Medical Assistant Technician; Registered Nurse; Support Services Aide; Surgical Technician; Unit Coordinator. **Special programs:** Internships. **CEO:** Ron Hytoff. **Operations at this facility include:** Administration. **Number of employees at this location:** 3,000.

TAMPA TRIBUNE
P.O. Box 191, Tampa FL 33601. 813/259-7711. **Contact:** Human Resources. **World Wide Web address:** http://www.tampatrib.com. **Description:** A daily newspaper.

TEAM STAFF RX
1901 Ulmerton Road, Suite 450, Clearwater FL 33762. 727/461-9642. **Toll-free phone:** 800/345-9642. **Fax:** 727/299-9065. **Contact:** Human Resources. **World Wide Web address:** http://www.teamstaffrx.com. **Description:** Team Staff Rx offers a full line of employer services including payroll processing, permanent and temporary placement of personnel, in-house hardware and software systems, outsourcing, facility management, employee leasing, and insurance services. **Positions advertised include:** CT Technologist; Special Procedures Technologist; Clinical Pharmacist; Staff Pharmacist; Radiological Pharmacist; Radiological Technologist; Pharmacy Director; MRI Technologist; Pharmacist. **Listed on:** NASDAQ. **Stock exchange symbol:** TSTF. **Number of employees nationwide:** 20,000.

TECH DATA CORPORATION
5350 Tech Data Drive, Clearwater FL 33760. 727/539-7429. **Contact:** Human Resources. **E-mail address:** jobs@techdata.com. **World Wide Web address:** http://www.techdata.com. **Description:** Distributes microcomputer-related hardware and software products to value-added resellers and computer retailers throughout the United States, Canada, Europe, Latin America, and the Caribbean. Tech Data Corporation purchases its products in large quantities directly from manufacturers and publishers, maintains an inventory of more than 25,000 products, and sells to an active base of over 50,000 customers. Tech Data Corporation provides its customers with products in networking, mass storage, peripherals, software, and systems from more than 600 manufacturers and publishers. Founded in 1974. **NOTE:** Entry-level positions and second and third shifts are offered. **Positions advertised include:** Compliance Coordinator; Communications Analyst; Applications Developer; Systems Application Manager; Systems Programmer; Accountant; Assistant Accountant; Credit Analyst; Credit Processor; Financial Analyst; Majors Vendor Reconciliation Specialist; Financial Analyst; Associate Counsel; Vendor Associate Manager. **Corporate headquarters location:** This location. **Other U.S. locations:** CA; GA; IN; NJ; TX. **International locations:** Canada; The Caribbean; Europe; Latin America; Middle East. **Subsidiaries include:** Computer 2000 AG (Germany); Tech Data Canada Inc. (Ontario, Canada); Tech Data Education, Inc. (Clearwater FL); Tech Data Finance, Inc. (Walnut Creek CA); Tech Data France, SNC (Bobigny, France); Tech Data Latin America (Miami FL); Tech Data Pacific, Inc. (Clearwater FL); Tech Data Product Management, Inc. (Clearwater FL). **Operations at this facility include:** Administration; Divisional Headquarters; Regional Headquarters; Sales; Service. **Listed on:** NASDAQ. **Stock exchange symbol:** TECD. **CEO:** Steven A. Raymund. **Annual sales/revenues:** More than $100 million.

TENDER LOVING CARE/STAFF BUILDERS
3225 West Commercial Boulevard, #125,, Fort Lauderdale FL 33309. 954/486-5506. **Fax:** 954/739-5129. **Contact:** Human Resources. **World Wide Web address:** http://www.tlcathome.com. **Description:** A home health care agency. **Positions advertised include:** Home Care Nurse; Licensed Practical Nurse; Physical Therapist. **Corporate headquarters location:** Lake Success NY. **Other U.S. locations:** Nationwide. **CEO:** Stephen Savitsky. **Number of employees nationwide:** 20,000.

TENDER LOVING CARE/STAFF BUILDERS
9342 South U.S. Highway 1, Village Green Plaza, Port St. Lucie FL 34952. 772-335-3255. **Fax:** 772-335-5697. **Contact:** Human Resources Department. **World Wide Web address:** http://www.tlcathome.com. **Description:** A home health care agency. **Positions advertised include:** Licensed Practical Nurse; Physical Therapist. **Corporate headquarters location:** Lake Success NY. **Other U.S. locations:** Nationwide. **CEO:** Stephen Savitsky. **Number of employees nationwide:** 20,000.

3I (IMPLANT INNOVATIONS, INC.)
4555 Riverside Drive, Palm Beach Gardens FL 33410. 561/776-6700. **Fax:** 561/776-6825. **Contact:** Human Resources. **E-mail address:** mfischer@3implant.com. **World Wide Web address:** http://www.3Ionline.com. **Description:** A manufacturer and distributor of dental implants. **Positions advertised include:** New Product Development Coordinator; Clinical Research Manager; CNVC Machinist; Customer Service Technical Representative; Product Marketing Director; Document Control Coordinator; Patient Specific Manager; Product Manager; Regulatory Services Technology Representative; Territory Sales Manager.

TIGERDIRECT, INC.
7795 West Flagler Street, Suite 35, 2nd Floor, Miami FL 33144. 305/415-2200. **Contact:** William Montes, Human Resources Manager. **E-mail address:** william.montes@tigerdirect.com. **World Wide Web address:** http://www.tigerdirect.com. **Description:** A reseller of computer hardware and software. **Positions advertised include:** Inbound Customer Service Representative; Inbound Sales Consultant. **Listed on:** New York Stock Exchange. **Stock exchange symbol:** SYX. **President:** Carl Fiorentino. **Number of employees at this location:** 435.

TIMES PUBLISHING COMPANY, INC.
P.O. Box 1121, St. Petersburg FL 33731. 727/893-8404. **Fax:** 727/892-2990. **Contact:** Human Resources. **E-mail address:** resumes@sptimes.com. **World Wide Web address:** http://www.sptimes.com. **Description:** Publishes the *St. Petersburg Times* newspaper. **Positions advertised include:** Sales Assistant; Account Representative; Administrative Assistant; Inside Classified Account Representative; Customer Sales & Service Representative; Internet Advertising Account Representative; Inside Sales Divisional Manager; Circulation Home Delivery Manager; Direct Sales Manager; Retail Marketing Administration; Retail Marketing District Manager; Telemarketing Sales; Contract Financial Services Coordinator; Direct Marketing Manager; Home Delivery District Manager; General Secretary; Human Resources Manager; Programmer; Investigative Reporter; State Educational Writer; News Reporter. **Corporate headquarters location:** This location. **Operations at this facility include:** Administration; Divisional Headquarters; Manufacturing; Sales; Service. **CEO:** Andy Barnes. **Number of employees nationwide:** 3,600.

TINGLEY SYSTEMS
31722 State Road 52, P.O. Box 700, San Antonio FL 33576. 352/588-2250. **Fax:** 352/588-4533. **Contact:** Human Resources. **E-mail address:** tsi@tingsley.net. **World Wide Web address:** http://www.tingleysystems.com. **Description:** Develops software for the health care industry.

TITAN CORPORATION
P.O. Box 550, Melbourne FL 32902-0550. 321/728-0481. **Physical address:** 1800 Penn Street, Suite 4B, Melbourne FL, 32901. **Contact:** Linda Rauscher, Director of Human Resources. **World Wide Web address:** http://www.titan.com. **Description:** Develops and manufactures advanced analytical software for use in remote sensing and orbital mechanics and electronics systems for video tracking and precision film scanning digitizer applications. The company also develops specialized electronic systems for the U.S. Defense Department. **Positions advertised include:** Electrical Engineer; Enterprise Architect; Geographical Information Systems Imagery Analyst; Mechanical Engineer; Engineer. **Corporate headquarters location:** San Diego CA. **Other U.S. locations:** Nationwide. **International locations:** Worldwide. **Listed on:** New York Stock Exchange. **Stock exchange symbol:** TTN. **Number of employees at this location:** 130. **Number of employees worldwide:** 10,000.

TITAN SYSTEMS CORPORATION
7104 Laird Street, Panama City Beach FL 32408-7666. 850/234-3940. **Fax:** 850/234-1168. **Contact:** Human Resources Department. **World Wide Web address:** http://www.titansystemscorp.com. **Description:** Provides information technology services and electronics systems to government and commercial customers worldwide. The company works principally in the following areas: Antisubmarine/Undersea Warfare, Surface Warfare, Torpedo/Electronics Countermeasures, Amphibious Warfare, War Gaming, Tactical Air Warfare, Unmanned Aerial Vehicles, and Littoral Warfare. In addition to supporting the military in system design and development, Titan Systems designs and builds its own high-tech products. These product areas include test equipment and simulation systems for the Global Positioning System markets, navigation systems for shipboard application, and air data systems for helicopters and other vertical-take-off-and-landing aircraft. **Positions advertised include:** Curriculum Developer; Reach Program Manager; Logistics Analyst; Technical Analyst; Systems Engineer; System Test Evaluation Manager; Technical Editor. **Corporate headquarters location:** San Diego CA. **Listed on:** NYSE. **Stock exchange symbol:** TTN. **Number of employees worldwide:** 10,000.

TOWNLEY MANUFACTURING
P.O. Box 221, Candler FL 32111. 352/687-3001. **Contact:** Human Resources. **World Wide Web address:** http://www.townley.net. **Description:** Manufactures heavy machinery and equipment for the mining industry as well as smaller components such as pumps, valves, and rubber hoses used in the company's products. **Positions advertised include:** Area Sales Manager; General Sales Manager; Circulation Manager; National Director Sales & Marketing; Product Line Launch Manager. **Other U.S. locations:** AZ; IL; TX; VA.

TRADER PUBLISHING COMPANY
P.O. Box 9003, Clearwater FL 33758. 727/530-5656. **Physical address:** 14549 62nd Street North, Clearwater FL 33760. **Fax:** 727/531-1748. **Recorded jobline:** 727/535-3077. **Contact:** Personnel. **World Wide Web address:** http://www.traderonline.com. **Description:** One of the nation's largest publishers devoted to classified and photo guide advertising. **Positions advertised include:** Staff Associate; Sales Representative; Sales Manager; Technical Support Analyst; Information Technology Analyst; Virtual Tour Specialist; South Florida Account Representative; Quality Control & Customer Service Representative. **Corporate headquarters location:** Norfolk VA. **Other U.S. locations:** Nationwide. **Number of employees at this location:** 300. **Number of employees nationwide:** 4,000.

TRAK MICROWAVE CORPORATION
4726 Eisenhower Boulevard, Tampa FL 33634. 813/901-7200. **Fax:** 813/901-7497. **Contact:** Linda Reynolds, Manager of Human Resources. **World Wide Web address:** http://www.trak.com. **Description:** A supplier of active and passive electronic microwave components, microwave subsystems, ferrite products, and precision timing equipment for use in communication systems and radar products. The microwave components include energy sources (oscillators and amplifiers), frequency multipliers, filters, ferrite isolators and circulators, and a broad range of passive components for modulation and control of microwave energy. The microwave subsystems consist of synthesizers, frequency converters, and microwave receiver assemblies. TRAK's microwave components and subsystems can be found in defense products such as electronic warfare equipment, defense radars, communications equipment, and missile guidance systems. Space applications include components for communication, television broadcast, meteorological, earth resource, and intelligence gathering satellites. Commercial applications include Transponder Collision Avoidance Systems, Microwave Landing Systems, radar altimeters, distance measuring equipment, and airborne weather radar. TRAK also builds timing systems for use by government and commercial organizations. Timing products are used to provide signals to time or initiate events by extracting time information from the NAVSTAR satellites of the Global Positioning System (operated by the U.S. government), and in the synchronizing of communication carrier signals between sites. **Other U.S. locations:** MD. **International locations:** Scotland. **Operations at this facility include:** Administration; Manufacturing; Sales. **Listed on:** Privately held.

TRANSITIONS OPTICAL INC.
9251 Belcher Road, Pinellas Park FL 33782. 727/545-0400. **Contact:** Human Resources. **World Wide Web address:** http://www.transitions.com. **Description:** Manufactures plastic photochromatic ophthalmic lenses. Founded in 1990. **Listed on:** Privately held. **Annual sales/revenues:** More than $100 million.

TRAVELPRO LUGGAGE
700 Banyan Trail, Boca Raton FL 33431. 561/998-2824. **Contact:** Human Resources. **World Wide Web address:** http://www.travelpro.com. **Description:** Manufactures and distributes luggage.

TREADWAY INDUSTRIES, LLC
111 Weber Avenue, Leesburg FL 34748. 352/326-3313. **Toll-free phone:** 866/TRYTWAY. **Fax:** 352/787-2888. **Contact:** Human Resources. **E-mail address:** info@treadwayindustries.com. **World Wide Web address:** http://www.treadwayindustries.com. **Description:** Treadway Industries assists customers needing architectural and decorative elements within the U.S. and overseas. The markets Treadway services include Commercial Building, Single and Multi-family Residential, Visual Merchandising, Movie and Television Set, Themeing and Props, Landscape and Hardscape, and Signage and Entryways. **Positions advertised include:** Project Coordinator.

TREND OFFSET PRINTING
10301 Busch Drive North, Jacksonville FL 32218. 904/696-8675. **Fax:** 904/696-7992. **Contact:** hr@trendoffset.com. **World Wide Web address:** http://www.trendoffset.com. **Description:** A full service, commercial and publication printing company. **Positions advertised include:** Creo Operator; Maintenance Electrician for Press/Bindery Departments; Press Operator; Rollman; Saddle Stitch Operator; Second Press Operator; Stitcher and Perfect Binder Operator. **Corporate headquarters location:** Los Alamitos CA. **Other U.S. locations:** Carrollton TX.

TRI-CITY ELECTRICAL CONTRACTORS
430 West Drive, Altamonte Springs FL 32714. 407/788-3500. **Contact:** Dori Silberman, Director of Human Resources. **Description:** Performs electrical contracting work for both commercial and residential clients.

TROPICAL SPORTSWEAR INTERNATIONAL
4902 West Waters Avenue, Tampa FL 33634. 813/249-4900. **Contact:** Human Resources. **World Wide Web address:** http://www.tsionline.com. **Description:** Manufactures men's and women's denim, twill, and corduroy casual clothing. Brand names include Savane and Bill Blass. Founded in 1927. **NOTE:** Entry-level positions and second and third shifts are offered. **Positions advertised include:** Customs Compliance Manager; Payroll Specialist; Key Account Sales Representative. **Special programs:** Internships. **Corporate headquarters location:** This location. **Other U.S. locations:** NY. **International locations:** Dominican Republic; Mexico. **Listed on:** NASDAQ. **Stock exchange symbol:** TSIC. **Annual sales/revenues:** More than $100 million. **Number of employees at this location:** 640. **Number of employees worldwide:** 1,600.

TROPICANA NORTH AMERICA
P.O. Box 338, Bradenton FL 34206. 941/747-4461. **Contact:** Human Resources. **World Wide Web address:** http://www.tropicana.com. **Description:** A leading producer and marketer of orange juice. **Corporate headquarters location:** This location. **Parent company:** PepsiCo, Inc. (Purchase NY) consists of Frito-Lay Company, Quaker Oats, Pepsi-Cola Company, and Tropicana Products, Inc. **Operations at this facility include:** Administration; Manufacturing; Research and Development; Sales; Service.

TULLY-MENARD, INC.
611 Druid Road East, Suite 407, Clearwater FL 33756. 727/298-8301. **Fax:** 727/298-8408. **Contact:** Mr. Joe Tully, President. **World Wide Web address:** http://www.tullymenard.com. **Description:** An advertising agency. **NOTE:** Part-time jobs are offered. **Office hours:** Monday - Friday, 8:30 a.m. - 5:00 p.m. **Corporate headquarters location:** This location. **Listed on:** Privately held. **Annual sales/revenues:** Less than $5 million.

TUPPERWARE CORPORATION
P.O. Box 2353, Orlando FL 32802-2353. 407/826-5050. **Fax:** 407/826-4453. **Recorded jobline:** 407/826-4496. **Contact:** Human Resources Department. **E-mail address:** resume@tupperware.com. **World Wide Web address:** http://www.tupperware.com. **Description:** Manufactures plastic food storage and service containers. **Positions advertised include:** Administration Latin America; Administrative Assistant. **Corporate headquarters location:** This location. **Other U.S. locations:** Nationwide. **International locations:** Worldwide. **Operations at this facility include:** Administration; Divisional Headquarters; Research and Development. **Listed on:** New York Stock Exchange. **Stock exchange symbol:** TUP. **CEO:** E. Goings. **Number of employees nationwide:** 7,000.

TYBRIN CORPORATION
1030 Titan Court, Fort Walton Beach FL 32547. 850/337-2500. **Toll-free phone:** 800/989-2746. **Contact:** Human Resources. **E-mail address:** support@b2secure.com. **World Wide Web address:** http://www.tybrin.com. **Description:** Tybrin Corporation provides engineering and computer support services to government and commercial customers. Founded in 1972. **Positions advertised include:** Access Analyst; Access Engineer; Lead Linux Administrative Program; Project Cost Analyst; Project Scheduler; Recruiter; Systems Test Engineer; Travel Accounting Clerk. **Corporate headquarters location:** This location. **Other U.S. locations:** Nationwide. **Listed on:** Privately held. **Number of employees nationwide:** 825.

TYCO HEALTHCARE/KENDALL
P.O. Box 62078, DeLand FL 32721-2078. 386/734-3685. **Contact:** J. Ralph Mills, Human Resources Manager. **World Wide Web address:** http://www.kendallhq.com. **Description:** Manufactures disposable hypodermic needles and syringes. Founded in 1903. **NOTE:** Second and third shifts are offered. **Positions advertised include:** Principal Electrical Engineer; Process Engineer; Project Engineer; Tooling Engineer; Supervising Maintenance. **Corporate headquarters location:** Mansfield MA. **Other U.S. locations:** Nationwide. **International locations:** Worldwide. **Parent company:** Tyco International. **Operations at this facility include:** Manufacturing. **Listed on:** New York Stock Exchange. **Stock exchange symbol:** TYC. **President/CEO:** Rich Meelia. **Annual sales/revenues:** More than $100 million.

UBS FINANCIAL INC.
One Independent Drive, 2nd Floor, Jacksonville FL 32202. 904/354-6000. **Contact:** Human Resources. **World Wide Web address:** http://www.ubspainewebber.com. **Description:** A full-service securities firm with over 300 offices nationwide. Services include investment banking, asset management, merger and acquisition consulting, municipal securities underwriting, estate planning, retirement programs, and transaction management. UBS Financial offers its services to corporations, governments, institutions, and individuals. Founded in 1879. **Special programs:** Internships. **Corporate headquarters location:** New York NY. **Other U.S. locations:** Nationwide. **Operations at this facility include:** Sales; Service. **Listed on:** New York Stock Exchange. **Stock exchange symbol:** UBS. **Annual sales/revenues:** More than $100 million.

USNR
P.O. Box 40666, Jacksonville FL 32203. 904/354-2301. **Contact:** Lynn Adams, Human Resources. **Description:** Manufactures wood-drying kilns. **World Wide Web address:** http://www.usnr.com. **Positions advertised include:** Mechanical Engineer; Electrical Engineer; Software Engineer; Capital Machinery Sales Representative; Parts Sales Representative; Welder; Fabricator; Machinist; CNC Operator; Field Service Representative; Network Administration & Support Specialist; Accounting Representative; Office Support Clerk; Purchasing Representative; Marketing Representative. **Operations at this facility include:** Divisional Headquarters.

U.S. AGRI-CHEMICALS CORPORATION
3225 State Road 630 West, Fort Meade FL 33841. 863/285-8121x231. **Fax:** 863/285-9654. **Contact:** Irene Dobson, Director of Human Resources. **Description:** Manufacturer and supplier of phosphate fertilizers for domestic and international wholesale markets. **Corporate headquarters location:** This location. **Parent company:** Sinochem. **Operations at this facility include:** Administration; Manufacturing; Regional Headquarters; Sales.

U.S. DEPARTMENT OF VETERANS AFFAIRS
BAY PINES VA MEDICAL CENTER
P.O. Box 5005, 10000 Bay Pines Boulevard, Bay Pines FL 33744. 727/398-6661. **Contact:** Human Resources. **World Wide Web address:** http://www.va.gov. **Description:** A medical center operated by the U.S. Department of Veterans Affairs. The VA health care system includes 171 medical centers; more than 364 outpatient, community, and outreach clinics; 130 nursing home care units; and 37 domiciliaries. **Positions advertised include:** Nursing Assistant; Licensed Practical Nurse. **NOTE:** Applicants must call 800/369-6008 to request application materials, applicants must refer to specific job title and location. Once received applications can be mailed to: Department of Veterans Affairs, Delegated Examining Unit, 1201 Broad Rock Boulevard #507, Richmond VA 23249. **Corporate headquarters location:** Washington DC. **Other U.S. locations:** Nationwide.

U.S. DEPARTMENT OF VETERANS AFFAIRS
MIAMI VA MEDICAL CENTER
1201 NW 16th Street, Miami FL 33125. 305/575-4455. **Fax:** 305/575-3374. **Recorded jobline:** 305/324-4455. **Contact:** Human Resources. **World Wide Web address:** http://www.va.gov/546miami. **Description:** A medical center operated by the U.S.

Department of Veterans Affairs. From 54 hospitals in 1930, the VA health care system has grown to include 171 medical centers; more than 364 outpatient, community, and outreach clinics; 130 nursing home care units; and 37 domiciliaries. VA operates at least one medical center in each of the 48 contiguous states, Puerto Rico, and the District of Columbia. With approximately 76,000 medical center beds, VA treats nearly 1 million patients in VA hospitals; 75,000 in nursing home care units; and 25,000 in domiciliaries. VA's outpatient clinics register approximately 24 million visits per year. **Positions advertised include:** Certified Respiratory Therapy Technician; Nurse Practitioner; Nurse Researcher; Advanced Registered Nurse Researcher; Dialysis Nurse; Staff Nurse; Optometrist; Physician; Physician Assistant; Podiatrist; Registered Respiratory Therapist. **Corporate headquarters location:** Washington DC. **Other U.S. locations:** Nationwide. **Operations at this facility include:** Administration; Research and Development; Service. **Number of employees at this location:** 2,700.

U.S. FEDERAL RESERVE BANK OF FLORIDA
P.O. Box 520847, Miami FL 33152. 305/597-4585. **Physical address:** 9100 NW 36th Street, Miami FL 33178. **Contact:** Amy Ginsberg, Human Resources. **World Wide Web address:** http://www.frbatlanta.org. **Description:** One of 12 regional Federal Reserve banks that, along with the Federal Reserve Board of Governors (Washington DC) and the Federal Open Market Committee (FOMC), form the Federal Reserve System, the central bank of the U.S. federal government. As the nation's central bank, the Federal Reserve is charged with three major responsibilities: monetary policy, banking supervision and regulation, and processing payments.

U.S. FOODSERVICE
P.O. Box 2246, Daytona Beach FL 32145. 386/677-2240. **Fax:** 386/672-5476. **Contact:** Personnel. **World Wide Web address:** http://www.usfoodservice.com. **Description:** An institutional food production and distribution company serving clients in the restaurant and health care industries. **Corporate headquarters location:** Columbia MD. **Other U.S. locations:** Nationwide. **Parent company:** Royal Ahold. **Listed on:** American Stock Exchange. **Stock exchange symbol:** AHLN. **Annual revenues:** Over $100 million. **Number of employees nationwide:** 34,000.

U.S. POSTAL SERVICE
5201 West Spruce Street, Tampa FL 33630-5000. **Toll-free phone:** 800/275-8777. **Contact:** Human Resources. **World Wide Web address:** http://www.usps.com. **Description:** A 24-hour airmail postal facility. **Other U.S. locations:** Nationwide.

USA TODAY
3375 Commerce Parkway, Miramar FL 33025. 954/432-6229. **Fax:** 703/854-2027. **Contact:** Human Resources. **E-mail address:** jobs@usatoday.com. **World Wide Web address:** http://www.usatoday.com. **Description:** Regional office of the national newspaper. **NOTE:** Mail your resume to: USA Today Human Resources, 7950 Jones Branch Drive, 7th Floor, McLean VA 22108. Always include the title of the position that you are applying for. **Parent company:** Gannett Co. Inc. **Listed on:** New York Stock Exchange. **Stock exchange symbol:** GCI. **President:** Tom Curley.

UNISA AMERICA INC.
10814 NW 33 Street, Suite 100, Miami FL 33172. 305/591-9397. **Fax:** 305/591-1634. **Contact:** Cindy Oliver. **E-mail address:** coliver@unisa.com. **World Wide Web address:** http://www.unisa.com. **Description:** Designer of woman's handbags and apparel. **Positions advertised include:** Store Manager; Assistant Store Manager; Key Holder; Sales Associate. **Other area locations include:** Boca Raton FL; Coconut Grove FL; The Falls FL; Naples FL; Orlando FL; Palm Beach FL. **Corporate headquarters location:** This location.

UNISON INDUSTRIES
7575 Baymeadows Way, Jacksonville FL 32256-8514. 904/739-4000. **Contact:** Bob Owens, Human Resources. **E-mail address:** jobs@unisonindustries.com. **World Wide Web address:** http://www.unisonindustries.com **Description:** Manufactures turbine aircraft ignition systems and piston products. **Corporate headquarters location:** This location. **Other U.S. locations:** IL; NY; TX. **International locations:** Mexico. **President/CEO:** Frederick Sontag. **Number of employees worldwide:** 1,400.

UNISYS CORPORATION
7000 West Palmetto Park Road, Suite 201, Boca Raton FL 33433. 561/750-5800. **Contact:** Human Resources. **World Wide Web address:** http://www.unisys.com. **Description:** Unisys Corporation provides information services, technology, and software. Unisys specializes in developing critical business solutions based on open information networks. The company's Enabling Software Team creates a variety of software projects that facilitate the building of user applications and the management of distributed systems. The company's Platforms Group is responsible for UNIX Operating Systems running across a wide range of multiple processor server platforms including all peripheral and communication drivers. The Unisys Commercial Parallel Processing Team develops microkernel-based operating systems, I/O device drivers, ATM hardware, diagnostics, and system architectures. The System Management Group is in charge of the overall management of development programs for UNIX desktop and entry-server products. **Positions advertised include:** Human Resources Business Partner; Microsoft Technology Consultant; Project Manager; Software Developer. **Corporate headquarters location:** Blue Bell PA. **Other U.S. locations:** Nationwide. **International locations:** Worldwide. **Operations at this facility include:** This location is a regional headquarters office. **Listed on:** New York Stock Exchange. **Stock exchange symbol:** UIS. **Number of employees worldwide:** 39,000.

UNITED SPACE ALLIANCE (USA)
8550 Astronaut Boulevard, Cape Canaveral FL 32920. 321/799-6800. **Contact:** Human Resources. **World Wide Web address:** http://www.unitedspacealliance.com. **Description:** A primary contractor for the NASA space shuttle operations. The company is responsible for ground operations and flight support of the Space Shuttle. **Corporate headquarters location:** Houston TX. **President/CEO:** Russell D. Turner. **Number of employees nationwide:** 10,000.

UNITED STATES GYPSUM COMPANY
P.O. Box 9579, Jacksonville FL 32208. 904/768-2501. **Contact:** Gary Jones, Human Resources Manager. **World Wide Web address:** http://www.usg.com. **Description:** Manufactures gypsum wallboard, plasters, and agricultural gypsum. **Corporate headquarters location:** Chicago IL. **Other U.S. locations:** Nationwide. **International locations:** Worldwide. **Listed on:** New York Stock Exchange. **Stock exchange symbol:** USG. **President/CEO:** William C. Foote. **Number of employees worldwide:** 14,000.

UNITED STATES SUGAR CORPORATION
111 Ponce de Leon Avenue, P.O. Box Drawer 1207, Clewiston FL 33440. 863/983-8121. **Fax:** 863/983-9827. **Contact:** Human Resources. **E-mail address:** mmaturana@ussugar.com. **World Wide Web address:** http://www.ussugar.com. **Description:** One of the nation's largest agricultural cooperatives, with primary interests in sugar and citrus. Founded in 1931. **Positions advertised include;** Cook, Waitress. **NOTE:** Be sure to include the job vacancy number on your application. **Corporate headquarters location:** This location. **Operations at this facility include:** Administration; Manufacturing; Research and Development; Sales; Service. **Number of employees at this location:** More than 3,000.

UNIVERSAL STUDIOS FLORIDA
1000 Universal Studios Plaza, Orlando FL 32819. 407/363-8000. **Fax:** 407/363-8006. **Recorded jobline:** 407/363-8080. **Contact:** Human Resources. **World Wide Web address:** http://www.universalstudios.com. **Description:** A diversified entertainment company and a worldwide leader in motion pictures, television, music, and home and location-based themed entertainment. The company's main operating divisions include Universal Studios, Universal Studios Recreation Group, Universal Studios Information Technology, Universal Studios Operations Group, Universal Music Group, Universal Pictures, Universal Networks & Worldwide Television Distribution, Universal Studios Consumer Products Group, Universal Studios Online, and Spencer Gifts. **Positions advertised include:** Oracle Program Analyst; Assistant Manager of Wardrobe; Attractions Supervisor; Executive Assistant; Park Services Supervisor; Front Teller; VIP Tours Supervisor; Brand Marketing Internet Representative; HVAC Technician; Groundskeeper; Gardener; Attractions Spiel Attendant; Certified Dive Technician; Maintenance Technician; Corporate Attorney; Sous Chef; Accounts Payable Manager; Engineer; E-commerce & Wholesale Sales Manager; Assistant Store Manager; Merchandiser; Second Cook; Legal Secretary; Ride Supervisor; Marketing Research Director; Landscape Architect; Cultural Trainer; Contracts Administrator; Animation Control Technician. **NOTE:** Entry-level positions are offered. **Company slogan:** It's a big universe. Where do you fit in? **Special programs:** Co-ops; Summer Jobs. **Corporate headquarters location:** Universal City CA. **Other U.S. locations:** Nationwide. **International locations:** Worldwide. **Parent company:** The Seagram Co. Ltd. **Listed on:** New York Stock Exchange. **Stock exchange symbol:** VOX. **Number of employees at this location:** 12,000.

UNIVERSITY COMMUNITY HOSPITAL
3100 East Fletcher Avenue, Tampa FL 33613. 813/615-7290. **Recorded jobline:** 813/615-7830. **Contact:** Bernadette Stypula, Human Resources Manager. **World Wide Web address:** http://www.uch.org. **Description:** A 431-bed, full-service, acute care hospital. **Positions advertised include:** Occupational Health Services; CT Technologist; Staff Pharmacist; Ultrasound Technologist; Physical Therapist; General Accounting Systems Manager; Ultrasound Supervisor; Speech Therapist; Public Relations Manager; Registered Nurse; Home Health Registered Nurse; Billing Representative; Press Release Manager; Respirator Therapist; Medical Coder; Surgical Technologist. **Office hours:** Monday - Friday, 8:00 a.m. - 5:00 p.m. **Operations at this facility include:** Administration; Service. **President:** Norm Stein. **Number of employees at this location:** 2,500.

UNIVERSITY HOSPITAL & MEDICAL CENTER
7710 NW, 71st Court, Suite 10, Tamarac FL 33321. 954/721-2200. **Physical address:** 7201 North University Drive, Tamarac FL 33321. **Fax:** 954/724-6666. **Recorded jobline:** 954/724-6114. **Contact:** Human Resources. **World Wide Web address:** http://www.uhmchealth.com. **Description:** A 317-bed hospital offering a full range of inpatient and outpatient health care services. Founded in 1974. **Positions advertised include:** Nurse Auditor; Registered Nurse; Nuclear Medicine Technologist; Wound Care Clinical Supervisor. **Number of employees at this location:** 1,550.

UNIVERSITY OF CENTRAL FLORIDA
12565 Research Parkway, Suite 360, Orlando FL 32826-2912. 407/823-2771. **Contact:** Mark Roberts, Human Resources Director. **World Wide Web address:** http://www.ucf.edu. **Description:** A university offering bachelor's, master's, and doctoral degrees to approximately 31,000 students. **Positions advertised include:** Assistant Vice President; Coordinator of Information Public Services; Assistant Director; Academic Support Services; Associate Director; Administrative Services Coordinator; Human Resources Coordinator; High School Coordinator; Human Resources Coordinator; Intercollegiate Athletics Coordinator; Student Affairs Coordinator; University Counseling Services Director; Academic Support Services Director; Associate Professor – School of Nursing; Student Affairs Director; Custodial Worker.

UNIVERSITY OF FLORIDA
4th Floor Stadium, P.O. Box 115002, Gainesville FL 32611. 352/392-4621. **Fax:** 352/392-7094. **Contact:** Human Resources. **World Wide Web address:** http://www.hr.ufl.edu. **Description:** A state university offering graduate, undergraduate, and professional programs to approximately 43,000 students. **NOTE:** Entry-level positions are offered. **Positions advertised include:** Registered Nurse; Laboratory Technician; Clerk; Dental Assistant; Office Manager; Library Technical Assistant; Motor Vehicle Operator; Locksmith; Custodial Worker; Clerical Aide; Accountant; Vet Care Technician; Vet Hospital Technician; Administrative Assistant; Assistant Carpenter; Secretary; Law Enforcement Officer; Program Assistant; Fiscal Assistant. **Number of employees at this location:** 11,500.

UNIVERSITY OF MIAMI
1507 Levante Avenue, Coral Gables FL 33124. 305/284-2211. **Contact:** Human Resources. **World Wide Web address:** http://www.miami.edu. **Description:** A university offering bachelor's, master's, doctoral, and professional degrees. **Positions advertised include:** Research Associate; Senior Research Associate; Postdoctoral Associate; Nurse Specialist; Pathology Program Specialist; Audiologist; Hospital Division Manager; Executive Assistant; Associate Professor of Clinical Obstetrics; Associate Professor of Clinical Surgery. **NOTE:** Jobseekers are advised to obtain a copy of the university's job bulletin through the Website for information about employment opportunities. **Number of employees at this location:** More than 9,000.

UNIVERSITY OF NORTH FLORIDA
4567 St. John's Bluff Road South, Jacksonville FL 32224. 904/620-2903. **Contact:** Human Resources. **World Wide Web address:** http://www.unf.edu. **Description:** A university offering graduate and undergraduate programs to approximately 12,000 students. **Positions advertised include:** Maintenance Mechanic; Accountant; Custodial Worker; Office Assistant; Data Entry Clerk; OPS Receptionist; Administrative Assistant; Coordinator Computer Applications; Intercollegiate Athletics Coordinator; Research Program Coordinator; Special Events Coordinator; Associate General Counsel; Research Coordinator. **President:** Annie H. Hopkins.

UNIVERSITY OF SOUTH FLORIDA (USF)
4202 East Fowler Avenue, SVC 2172, Tampa FL 33620-6980. 813/974-2974. **Contact:** Human Resources. **World Wide Web address:** http://www.usf.edu. **Description:** A state university serving approximately 37,000 undergraduate, graduate, and doctoral students. **Positions advertised include:** Advancement Coordinator; Broadcasting Coordinator; Human Services Coordinator; Student Affairs Coordinator; University Housing Coordinator.

UNIVERSITY OF WEST FLORIDA
11000 University Parkway, Pensacola FL 32514-5750. 850/474-2694. **Recorded jobline:** 850/474-2842. **Contact:** Human Resources. **World Wide Web address:** http://www.uwf.edu. **Description:** A university offering associate's, bachelor's, master's, and doctoral degrees to approximately 8,000 students. **Positions advertised include:** HVAC Operator; Police Communications Operator; Senior Fiscal Assistant; Maintenance Superintendent; Clerk Typist; Vocational Counselor/Teacher; Rehabilitative Technician; Camp Counselor; Coordinator, Educational/Trainee Programs; Coordinator, Facilities Planning; Assistant Professor; Lecturer. **President:** Dr. Morris L. Marx.

UNIWELD PRODUCTS, INC.
2850 Ravenswood Road, Fort Lauderdale FL 33312. 954/584-2000. **Contact:** Erin Mumford, Human Resources. **World Wide Web address:** http://www.uniweld.com. **Description:** Manufactures gas welding, cutting, and pressure gauge equipment and accessories. **Corporate headquarters location:** This location. **Operations at this facility include:** Administration; Manufacturing; Research and Development; Sales; Service. **Other U.S. locations:** NV; TX. **International locations:** Canada; Ecuador; Lebanon; Singapore.

VAL-PAK DIRECT MARKETING
8605 Largo Lakes Drive, Largo FL 33773. 727/399-3189. **Toll-free phone:** 800/237-2871. **Fax:** 727/399-3085. **Recorded jobline:** 727/399-3012. **Contact:** LaToy Black, Recruiting Specialist. **E-mail address:** latoy_black@valpak.com. **World Wide Web address:** http://www.valpak.com. **Description:** An international direct mail advertising company that designs, prints, and mails more than 15 billion coupons annually. **NOTE:** Entry-level positions and second and third shifts are offered. **Special programs:** Internships. **Office hours:** Monday - Friday, 8:00 a.m. - 5:00 p.m. **Corporate headquarters location:** This location. **Parent company:** Cox Enterprises, Inc. is one of the nation's largest privately held media companies with major holdings in the newspaper, television, radio, and cable industries. **Listed on:** Privately held. **President:** Joseph Bourdow. **Annual sales/revenues:** More than $100 million. **Number of employees at this location:** 1,100. **Number of employees nationwide:** 1,500.

VANN DATA SERVICES, INC.
1801 Dunn Avenue, Daytona Beach FL 32114. 386/238-1200. **Fax:** 386/238-1454. **Contact:** Human Resources. **E-mail address:** jobs@vanndata.com. **World Wide Web address:** http://www.vanndata.com. **Description:** Computer service, sales and solutions company. **CEO:** George Van Arnam.

VERITAS SOFTWARE
400 International Parkway, Heathrow FL 32746. 407/531-7500. **Contact:** Human Resources. **World Wide Web address:** http://www.veritas.com. **E-mail address:** jobs@veritas.com. **Description:** Develops and markets backup software. **Positions advertised include:** Latin America Sales Director. **Corporate headquarters:** Mountain View CA. **Other U.S. locations:** Nationwide. **International locations:** Worldwide. **Listed on:** NASDAQ. **Stock exchange symbol:** VRTS. **Number of employees worldwide:** Over 5,000.

VICORP.COM
3845 Gateway Center Boulevard, Suite 300, Pinelllas Park FL 33782. 727/572-9300. **Contact:** Human Resources. **E-mail address:** careers@vicorp.com. **World Wide Web address:** http://www.vicorp.com. **Description:** Develops software for voice enhancement services and voice dialing. Founded in 1981. **Corporate headquarters location:** This location. **International locations:** The Netherlands; Singapore; United Kingdom. **Number of employees worldwide:** 70.

VISITING NURSE ASSOCIATION
2400 SE Monterey Road, Suite 300, Stuart FL 34996. 772/286-1844. **Fax:** 772/286-8753. **Contact:** Human Resources. **E-mail address:** resumes@vnaflorida.org. **World Wide Web address:** http://www.visitingnurses.com. **Description:** A nonprofit home health agency that also offers rehabilitation and mental health services, home IV therapies, pre-op visits, private duty nurses, HIV/AIDS care, case management, and oncology care. **Other area locations include:** Bradenton FL; Clearwater FL; Lake Wales FL; Okeechobee FL; Port Richey FL; Sarasota FL; Spring Hill FL; Tampa FL.

VISITING NURSE ASSOCIATION & HOSPICE
1111 36th Street, Vero Beach FL 32960. 772/567-5551. **Contact:** Human Resources. **World Wide Web address:** http://www.vnatc.com. **Description:** A nonprofit home health agency that also offers rehabilitation and mental health services, home IV therapies, pre-op visits, private duty nurses, HIV/AIDS care, case management, and oncology care. **Positions advertised include:** Occupational Therapist; Registered Nurse; Director of Quality Education; Clinical Specialist/Educator.

WCTV
P.O. Box 3048, Tallahassee FL 32315. 850/893-6666. **Contact:** Human Resources. **Description:** A television station affiliated with CBS.

WACHOVIA
1000 Tyrone Boulevard, Saint Petersburg FL 33710. 727/892-7441. **Contact:** Human Resources. **World Wide Web address:** http://www.wachovia.com. **Description:** Wachovia Securities is one of the nation's largest bank holding companies with subsidiaries operating over 1,330 full-service bank branches in the south Atlantic states. These subsidiaries provide retail banking, retail investment, and commercial banking services. Wachovia Securities provides other financial services including mortgage banking, home equity lending, leasing, insurance, and securities brokerage services from more than 220 branch locations. The company also operates one of the nation's largest ATM networks. **Listed on:** New York Stock Exchange. **Stock exchange symbol:** WB. **Number of employees nationwide:** 32,000.

WACHOVIA BANK
450 South Australian Avenue, West Palm Beach FL 33401. 561/833-7063. **Recorded jobline:** 800/732-4754. **Contact:** Human Resources. **World Wide Web address:** http://www.wachovia.com. **Description:** A savings and mortgage bank. **Listed on:** NASDAQ. **Stock exchange symbol:** WB. **Annual sales/revenues:** More than $100 million.

WACHOVIA SECURITIES
203 Avenue A NW, Winter Haven FL 33881. 863/291-6630. **Contact:** Human Resources. **World Wide Web address:** http://www.wachovia.com. **Description:** Wachovia Security is one of the nation's largest bank holding companies with subsidiaries operating over 1,330 full-service bank branches in the south Atlantic states. These subsidiaries provide retail banking, retail investment, and commercial banking services. First Union Corporation provides other financial services including mortgage banking, home equity lending, leasing, insurance, and securities brokerage services from more than 220 branch locations. The company also operates one of the nation's largest ATM networks. **Listed on:** New York Stock Exchange. **Stock exchange symbol:** WB. **Number of employees at this location:** 400. **Number of employees nationwide:** 32,000.

WACHOVIA SECURITIES
225 Water Street, Jacksonville FL 32202. 904/361-2140. **Contact:** Human Resources. **World Wide Web address:** http://www.wachovia.com. **Description:** A full-service commercial bank that operates over 500 offices. Wachovia Securities is one of the nation's largest bank holding companies with subsidiaries operating over 1,330 full-service bank branches in the south Atlantic states. These subsidiaries provide retail banking, retail investment, and commercial banking services. First Union Corporation provides other financial services including mortgage banking, home equity lending, leasing, insurance, and securities brokerage services from more than 220 branch locations. The company also operates one of the nation's largest ATM networks. **Listed on:** New York Stock Exchange. **Stock exchange symbol:** WB. **Number of employees nationwide:** 32,000.

WACHOVIA SECURITIES
980 North Federal Highway, Boca Raton FL 33432. 561/338-2600. **Toll-free phone:** 800/325-0450. **Fax:** 561/416-1014. **Contact:** Human Resources. **World Wide Web address:** http://www.wachovia.com. **Description:** Provides a wide range of financial services including equity research, investment banking and advisory, trading, insurance annuities, and mutual funds. **Corporate headquarters location:** Richmond VA.

THE WACKENHUT CORPORATION
3974 Woodcock Drive, Suite 100, Jacksonville FL 32207. 904/398-1640. **Toll-free phone:** 800/254-4411. **Fax:** 904/396-6716. **Contact:** Human Resources. **World Wide Web address:** http://www.wackenhut.com. **Description:** Provides physical security services, correction services, and related products to businesses, governments, and individuals from more than 150 domestic and foreign offices. Specific services include security guard services; corrections staffing; private investigative services; the assembly and sale of electronic security equipment and systems; the training of security guards and fire and crash rescue personnel; providing fire protection and emergency ambulance service to municipalities; security consulting; planning, designing, and implementing integrated security systems; and providing specialized services to the nuclear power industry. Wackenhut has 90 offices located in most major United States cities. **Office hours:** Monday - Friday, 8:30 a.m. - 5:00 p.m. **Corporate headquarters location:** Palm Beach Gardens FL. **International locations:** Worldwide. **Subsidiaries include:** Wackenhut Corrections, Inc.; Wackenhut International. **Listed on:** New York Stock Exchange. **Stock exchange symbol:** WAK. **Number of employees nationwide:** 40,000.

THE WACKENHUT CORPORATION
4200 Wackenhut Drive, Building 100, Palm Beach Gardens FL 33410. 561/622-5656. **Contact:** Human Resources. **World Wide Web address:** http://www. wackenhut.com. **Description:** Provides physical security services, correction services, and related products to businesses, governments, and individuals from more than 150 domestic and foreign offices. Specific services include security guard services; corrections staffing; private investigative services; the assembly and sale of electronic security equipment and systems; the training of security guards and fire and crash rescue personnel; providing fire protection and emergency ambulance service to municipalities; security consulting; planning, designing, and implementing integrated security systems; and providing specialized services to the nuclear power industry. Wackenhut has 90 offices located in major cities throughout the United States. **Positions advertised include:** Communications Specialist; Verification Specialist; Public Records Researcher; Background Verification Specialist. **Corporate headquarters location:** This location. **Other U.S. locations:** Nationwide. **Subsidiaries include:** Wackenhut Corrections, Inc.; Wackenhut International. **Operations at this facility include:** Administration; Service. **Listed on:** New York Stock Exchange. **Stock exchange symbol:** WAK. **Number of employees at this location:** 275. **Number of employees nationwide:** 40,000.

WALT DISNEY IMAGINEERING
P.O. Box 10321, Lake Buena Vista FL 32830. 407/566-1900. **Physical address:** 200 Celebration Place, Celebration FL 34747. 407/566-1900. **Fax:** 407/566-4220. **Contact:** Human Resources. **World Wide Web address:** http://www.disney.com. **Description:** Responsible for the design, development, and construction of The Walt Disney Company's premiere attractions, resorts, and entertainment venues. **Positions advertised include:** Software Engineer; Staff Assistant; Principal Software Engineer; Assistant Technical Director. **NOTE:** Entry-level positions are offered. **Company slogan:** We make the magic! **Special programs:** Internships. **Corporate headquarters location:** Glendale CA. **Other U.S. locations:** Orlando FL. **Parent company:** The Walt Disney Company. **Operations at this facility include:** Regional Headquarters. **Listed on:** New York Stock Exchange. **Stock exchange symbol:** DIS. **Number of employees at this location:** 400. **Number of employees nationwide:** 50,000. **Number of employees worldwide:** 60,000.

WALTER INDUSTRIES
P.O. Box 31601, Tampa FL 33631. 813/871-4811. **Recorded jobline:** 813/871-4100. **Contact:** Employment Manager. **World Wide Web address:** http://www.walterind.com. **Description:** One of the nation's largest industrial companies, with leading interests in home building and financing, natural resources, and industrial manufacturing. **Positions advertised include:** Administrative Assistant; Bill of Material Management Coordinator; Executive Assistant. **Listed on:** New York Stock Exchange. **Stock exchange symbol:** WLT.

WARD NORTH AMERICA, INC.
1211 Semoran Boulevard, Suite 127, Casselberry FL 32707. 407/660-2222. **Contact:** Human Resources. **World Wide Web address:** http://www.wardnorthamerica.com. **Description:** An insurance adjuster. **Positions advertised include:** Adjuster; Claims Adjuster; Account Manager. **Other U.S. locations:** Nationwide. **International locations:** Canada.

WARNER BROTHERS PUBLICATIONS
15800 NW 48th Avenue, Miami FL 33014. 305/620-1500. **Contact:** Maria Cruz, Director of Human Resources Department. **World Wide Web address:** http://www.warnerbrospublications.com. **Description:** A printer and publisher of sheet music. **Special programs:** Internships. **Corporate headquarters location:** This location. **Parent company:** AOL Time Warner. **Listed on:** New York Stock Exchange. **Stock exchange symbol:** AOL.

WATER BONNET MANUFACTURING INC.
P.O. Box 180427, Casselberry FL 32718. 407/831-2122. **Contact:** Human Resources. **Description:** Manufactures windshields for boats and Caterpillar tractors, as well as canvas tops for boats. **Positions advertised include:** Branch Manager; Community Specialist; Design Studio Director; Server; Pantry Cook; Line Cook; Greeter; Hostess; Host; Dishwasher; Beverage Cart Attendant; Bartender; Equipment Operator; Loan Officer.

WATERMARK COMMUNITIES, INC. (WCI)
P.O. Box 5698, Sun City Center FL 33571. 813/634-3311. **Contact:** Sharon May, Director of Human Resources Department. **World Wide Web address:** http://www.wcicommunities.com. **Description:** Develops, builds, and manages resort communities. **Positions advertised include:** Community Representative; Processor; Community Specialist; Senior Project Manager; Administrative Assistant; Senior Construction Manager; Weekend Receptionist; Landscape Architect; Senior Designer; Golf Course Superintendent. **Corporate headquarters location:** This location. **Operations at this facility include:** Resort/Support Functions. **Number of employees at this location:** 3,600.

WELLCARE HEALTH PLANS, INC.
P.O. Box 26022, Tampa FL 33623. 813/290-6200. **Fax:** 813/290-6236. **Contact:** Stacy Arnold, Human Resources. **World Wide Web address:** http://www.wellcare.com. **Description:** A health insurance provider dedicated to government-sponsored health plans such as Medicare, Medicaid, State Children's Health Insurance Programs and others. **Positions advertised include:** Behavioral Health Business Analyst; Manager, Behavioral Health Community Relations; Benefits Operations & Research Analyst; Director/Manager Performance Management; Enrollment Specialist; Intake Coordinator; Human Resources Analyst; Manager, Regulatory Affairs; Medicare Product Manager; Outreach Coordinator; QI Analyst; Senior Network & Systems Engineer; Senior Process Improvement Analyst; Service Leader. **Corporate headquarters location:** This location.

WELLCRAFT MARINE
1651 Whitfield Avenue, Sarasota FL 34243. 941/753-7811. **Fax:** 941/751-7876. **Contact:** Noemi S. Vento, 941/753-7811 ext 553. Human Resources. **E-mail address:** venton@wellcraft.com. **World Wide Web address:** http://www.wellcraft.com. **Description:** Manufactures a variety of boats including cruisers, fishing boats, sport boats, and high-performance speed boats. **Corporate headquarters location:** Minneapolis MN.

WESTCHESTER GENERAL HOSPITAL, INC.
2500 SW 75th Avenue, Miami FL 33155. 305/264-5252. **Fax:** 305/264-5958. **Recorded jobline:** 305/558-9700x600. **Contact:** Human Resources. **World Wide Web address:** http://www.westchestergeneral.com. **Description:** A general acute care hospital with 192 beds.

THE WESTIN INNISBROOK RESORT
36750 U.S. Highway 19 North, Palm Harbor FL 34684. 727/942-2000. **Fax:** 727/942-5268. **Contact:** Human Resources. **World Wide Web address:** http://www.westin-innisbrook.com. **Description:** A 221-room hotel and resort that offers four golf courses, six restaurants, full-service recreational facilities, and three convention centers. **NOTE:** Entry-level positions and second and third shifts are offered. **Company slogan:** People make the difference. **Special programs:** Internships; Training; Summer Jobs. **Corporate headquarters location:** Seattle WA. **Other U.S. locations:** Nationwide. **International locations:** Worldwide. **Listed on:** Privately held. **Number of employees at this location:** 1,600. **Number of employees worldwide:** 22,000.

GEORGE WESTON BAKERIES INC.
3325 NW 62nd Street, Miami FL 33147. 305/836-4900. **Fax:** 305/835-1349. **Contact:** Human Resources. **World Wide Web address:** http://www.gwbakeries.com. **Description:** George Weston Bakeries Inc. bakes cakes, cookies, pies, and doughnuts. **Corporate headquarters location:** Bayshore NY. **Operations at this facility include:** This location is the headquarters for the Southeast Region.

WESTPOINT STEVENS
P.O. Box 625, Chipley FL 32428. 850/638-4956. **Contact:** Valerie Pettis, Personnel Director. **E-mail address:** wphumanresources@wpstv.com. **World Wide Web address:** http://www.westpointstevens.com. **Description:** Manufactures and markets bedroom and bathroom products sold in retail outlets nationwide. **Corporate headquarters location:** NY. **Other U.S. locations:** Nationwide. **International locations:** Canada; England. **Listed on:** New York Stock Exchange. **Stock exchange symbol:** WYS. **Number of employees nationwide:** 15,000.

WESTWAYNE, INC.
401 East Jackson Street, Suite 3600, Tampa FL 33602. 813/202-1200. **Fax:** 813/202-1261. **Contact:** Human Resources. **World Wide Web address:** http://www.westwayne.com. **Description:** An advertising and marketing agency. **Positions advertised include:** Account Executive; Media Buyer.

WET 'N WILD
6200 International Drive, Orlando FL 32819. 407/351-1800. **Toll-free phone:** 800/992-WILD. **Contact:** Human Resources. **E-mail address:** info@wetnwild.com. **World Wide Web address:** http://www.wetnwild.com. **Description:** A water park offering a variety of activities for all ages. **Positions advertised include:** Lifeguard; Front Gate; Surf Sky; Park Services; Food Service; Security Guard; Receptionist; Ride Operator.

WHEELED COACH INDUSTRIES, INC.
2737 North Forsyth Road, Winter Park FL 32792. 407/677-7777. **Toll-free phone:** 800/342-0720x272. **Fax:** 407/677-8984. **Contact:** Paul Holzapfel, Human Resources. **E-mail address:** paul.holzapfel@wheeledcoach.com. **World Wide Web address:** http://www.wheeledcoach.com. **Description:** One of the world's largest manufacturers of ambulances, buses, and other specialty vehicles. **Positions advertised include:** Welder; Cabinet Maker; Automotive Painter; Auto Electrician; Interior Installer. **Corporate headquarters location:** Hutchinson KS. **Other U.S. locations:** TX. **Parent company:** Collins Industries. **Operations at this facility include:** Administration; Divisional Headquarters; Manufacturing; Sales; Service.

WHITEHALL BOCA NURSING HOME
7300 Del Prado Circle South, Boca Raton FL 33433. 561/392-3000. **Contact:** Human Resources. **Fax:** 561/392-6031. **World Wide Web address:** http://www.whitehallboca.com. **Description:** A skilled nursing home that also offers some assisted living services.

WILSON MILLER
3200 Bailey Lane, Suite 200, Naples FL 34105. 239/649-4040. **Toll-free phone:** 800/649-4336. **Fax:** 239/643-5716. **Contact:** Human Resources. **E-mail address:** naples@wilsonmiller.com. **World Wide Web address:** http://www.wilsonmiller.com. **Description:** A planning, design and engineering company. **NOTE:** Search for open positions at the company website. **Positions advertised include:** Business Communications Manager; CADD Tech; Civil Designer; Crew Chief; GIS Analyst; Landscape Architect; Senior Engineer, Project Manager; Senior Project Engineer; Transportation Engineer; Water/Wastewater CADD Designer. **Other area locations:** Destin FL; Fort Myers FL; Tallahassee FL; Tampa FL; Panama City Beach FL; Port Charlotte FL; Sarasota FL.

WILSON MILLER
6900 Professional Parkway East #110, Sarasota FL 34240. 941/907-6900. **Fax:** 941/907-6910. **Contact:** Human Resources. **E-mail address:** jobs@wilsonmiller.com. **World Wide Web address:** http://www.wilsonmiller.com. **Description:** A company specializing in Engineering, Landscaping, Planning and Surveying. **Positions advertised include:** Project Engineer.

WINDJAMMER BAREFOOT CRUISES
P.O. Box 190120, Miami Beach FL 33119. 305/672-6453. **Toll-free:** 800-327-2601. **Contact:** John Horn, Personnel Director. **E-mail address:** info@windjammer.com. **World Wide Web address:** http://www.windjammer.com. **Description:** A cruise line that operates six ships sailing to the Caribbean.

WINDMOOR HEALTH CARE
11300 U.S. 19 North, Clearwater FL 33764. 727/541-2646. **Recorded jobline:** 727/541-2646. **Contact:** Human Resources. **E-mail address:** clearwaterhr@windmoor-healthcare.com. **World Wide Web address:** http://www.windmoorhealthcare.com. **Description:** A full-service hospital specializing in psychiatric treatment and chemical dependency therapy. The hospital provides both inpatient and outpatient services. **Positions advertised include:** Intake Specialist; Staff Psychologist; Case Manager; Therapist; Pool Case Manager.

WINN-DIXIE STORES, INC.
P.O. Box 585200, Orlando FL 32858. 407/578-4000. **Physical address:** 3015 Coastline Drive, Orlando FL 32808. **Fax:** 407/294-4225. **Contact:** Human Resources. **E-mail address:** hr@winn-dixie.com. **World Wide Web address:** http://www.winn-dixie.com. **Description:** Winn-Dixie is one of the largest supermarket operators in the 14 Sunbelt states. Winn-Dixie stores operate under the names Winn-Dixie, Marketplace, and Buddies. Winn-Dixie also operates 20 warehousing and distribution centers and a host of manufacturing and processing facilities. A subsidiary of the company operates 12 stores in the Bahamas. **Positions advertised include:** Corporate Finance; Marketing Associate; Corporate Accounting Associate; Human Resources Associate; Information Technology Department; Logistics Associate; Manufacturing Associate; Sales Manager. **Corporate headquarters location:** Jacksonville FL. **Operations at this facility include:** This location is the headquarters of the Orlando division of a chain of supermarkets. **Listed on:** New York Stock Exchange. **Stock exchange symbol:** WIN. **President/CEO:** Al Rowland. **Number of employees nationwide:** 120,000.

WINN-DIXIE STORES, INC.
P.O. Box B, Jacksonville FL 32203-0297. 904/783-5000. **Physical address:** 5050 Edgewood Court, Jacksonville FL 32254. **Fax:** 904/783-5235. **Contact:** Human Resources. **E-mail address:** hr@winn-dixie.com. **World Wide Web address:** http://www.winn-dixie.com. **Description:** Winn-Dixie operates supermarkets and stores in the 14 Sunbelt states under the names Winn-Dixie, Marketplace, and Buddies. Winn-Dixie also operates 20 warehousing and distribution centers and a host of manufacturing and processing facilities. A subsidiary of the company operates 12 stores in the Bahamas. **Positions advertised include:** Corporate Finance; Marketing Associate; Corporate Accounting Associate; Human Resources Associate; Information Technology Department; Logistics Associate; Manufacturing Associate; Sales Manager. **Corporate headquarters location:** This location. **Listed on:** New York Stock Exchange. **Stock exchange symbol:** WIN. **President/CEO:** Al Rowland. **Number of employees nationwide:** 120,000.

WINTER PARK MEMORIAL HOSPITAL
200 North Lakemont Avenue, Winter Park FL 32789. 407/646-7000. **Fax:** 407/646-7639. **Contact:** Human Resources Department. **E-mail address:** administrative@winterparkhospital.com. **World Wide Web address:** http://www.winterparkhospital.com. **Description:** A 334-bed medical/surgical hospital offering neonatal intensive care and oncology services. **Parent company:** Adventist Health System.

WINTER PARK TOWERS
1111 South Lakemont Avenue, Winter Park FL 32789. 407/647-4083. **Contact:** Human Resources. **World Wide Web address:** http://www.westminsterretirement.com/ccrc_wpt.html. **Description:** A retirement community offering skilled nursing, assisted living, and independent living.

WORLD FUEL SERVICES, INC.
700 South Royal Poinciana Boulevard, Suite 800, Miami Springs FL 33166. 305/884-2001. **Contact:** Ileana Garcia, Director of Human Resources. **E-mail address:** jobs@wfscorp.com. **World Wide Web address:** http://www.wfscorp.com. **Description:** Engaged in aviation fuel services for air carriers and provides used oil recycling services in the southeastern United States. **Corporate headquarters location:** This location. **Operations at this facility include:** Administration; Sales. **Listed on:** New York Stock Exchange. **Stock exchange symbol:** INT. **Annual revenues:** More than $100 million.

WYNDHAM ORLANDO RESORT
8001 International Drive, Orlando FL 32819. 407/351-2420. **Fax:** 407/352-7054. **Contact:** Human Resources Department. **World Wide Web address:** http://www.wyndham.com/hotels/MCOWD/main.wnt. **Description:** A full-service hotel that offers five restaurants, recreational facilities, and business and meeting accommodations. **Positions advertised include:** Catering Manager; Sales Manager; Housekeeping Manager; Restaurant Manager; Convention Services Manager; Director of Human Resources. **Corporate headquarters location:** Washington DC. **Parent company:** Wyndham International. **Operations at this facility include:** Administration; Sales. **Listed on:** New York Stock Exchange. **Stock exchange symbol:** WYN.

SAWICH, PEPPERDINE AND BROWN
423 South Keller, Suite 100, Orlando FL 32810. 407/875-1111. **Contact:** Julie Gochnour, Director of Human Resources. **World Wide Web address:** http://www.ypb.com. **Description:** An advertising agency. **Positions advertised include:** Vice President; Account Supervisor. **Corporate headquarters location:** This location.

ZODIAC POOL CARE, INC
2028 NW 25th Avenue, Pompano Beach FL 33069, 800/416-7665. **Toll-free phone:** 800/937-7873. **Contact:** Human Resources. **E-mail address:** info@zodiacpoolcare.com. **World Wide Web address:** http://www.zodiacpoolcare.com. **Description:** A manufacturer of automatic swimming pool vacuums and purification systems under the name of Baracuda.

AAR CORP.
5125 Blalock Ind. Boulevard, College Park GA 30349. 404/765-1885. **Fax:** 404-765-1847. **Contact:** Human Resources. **E-mail address:** hr@aarcorp.com. **World Wide Web address:** http://www.aarcorp.com. AAR is a provider of products and value-added services to the worldwide aerospace and aviation industries. Products and services include proprietary inventory management and logistic support services, encompassing supply, repair, and manufacture of spare parts and systems. Founded in 1951. **Positions advertised include:** Sr. Project Engineer. **Corporate headquarters location:** Wood Dale IL. **Number of employees nationwide:** 2,400.

ADT SECURITY SERVICES
2821 Harley Court, Columbus GA 31909-2769. 706/653-1388. **Contact:** Human Resources. **World Wide Web address:** http://www.adtsecurityservices.com. **Description:** Designs, programs, markets, and installs protective systems to safeguard life and property from hazards such as burglary, hold-up, and fire. **NOTE:** Please visit website or visit monster.com to search for jobs, and to apply online. **Office hours:** Monday – Friday, 8:00 a.m. – 5:00 p.m. **Corporate headquarters location:** Boca Raton FL. **Other area locations:** Statewide. **Other U.S. locations:** Nationwide. **International locations:** Worldwide. **Parent company:** Tyco International LTD. **Listed on:** New York Stock Exchange. **Stock exchange symbol:** TYC. **Annual revenues:** More than $100 million. **Number of employees worldwide:** 15,000.

AFC ENTERPRISES, INC.
6 Concourse Parkway, Suite 1700, Atlanta GA 30328-5352. 770/391-9500. **Fax:** 770/353-3058. **Contact:** Recruiting. **E-mail address:** afcrecruiting@afce.com. **World Wide Web address:** http://www.afce.com. **Description:** A national and international franchiser whose brand names include Church's Chicken; Cinnabon; Popeye's Chicken; and Seattle's Best Coffee. **Positions advertised include:** Supply Chain Management. **Corporate headquarters:** This location. **Listed on:** OTC. **Stock exchange symbol:** AFCE. **CEO:** Frank J. Belatti.

AGL RESOURCES INC.
P.O. Box 4569, Atlanta GA 30302-4569. 404/584-4000. 256. **Contact:** Human Resources. **E-mail address:** Jobs@aglresources.com. **World Wide Web address:** http://www.aglr.com. **Description:** Engaged in a wide variety of energy-related businesses including natural gas distribution, natural gas and power marketing, wholesale and retail propane sales, energy management services, and energy-related consumer products. **Positions advertised include:** Project Manager; State Regulatory Affairs Assistant Representative; Manager – Risk Management; Consumer Regulatory Analyst; **Corporate headquarters location:** This location. **Subsidiaries include:** Atlanta Gas Light Company; Chattanooga Gas Company; Georgia Natural Gas Services; Sequent Energy Management; Virginia Natural Gas Company. **Operations at this facility include:** Administration; Sales; Service. **Listed on:** New York Stock Exchange. **Stock exchange symbol:** ATG. **President/CEO:** Paula G. Rosput. **Number of employees at this location:** 2,100.

APCO (AUTOMOBILE PROTECTION CORPORATION)
P.O. Box 88230, Atlanta GA 30356 770/394-7070. **Physical address:** 6010 Atlantic Boulevard, Norcross GA 30071. **Toll-free phone:** 888/EASY-400. **Fax:** 770/246-2453. **Contact:** Human Resources. **E-mail Address:** jobs@easycare.com **World Wide Web address:** http://www.easycare.com. **Description:** Provides products and services to automobile dealers to enhance customer satisfaction. Services include the EasyCare Certified Pre-Owned Vehicle Program, an extended service contract for dealers and their customers. APCO promotes the vehicle service contracts, engages in customer service for the service contracts, and also arranges for insurance carriers that cover the dealer's cost of making repairs during the contract. Founded in 1984. **Positions advertised include:** Claims Adjuster; Customer Service Representative. **Corporate headquarters location:** This location. **Other U.S. locations:** Nationwide. **Subsidiaries include:** The Aegis Group, Inc. **Parent company:** Ford Motor Company. **President/CEO:** Larry I. Dorfman.

AARON RENTS, INC.
309 East Paces Ferry Road NE, Atlanta GA 30305. 404/231-0011. **Contact:** Human Resources. **World Wide Web address:** http://www.aaronrents.com. **Description:** Rents and sells residential and office furniture and business equipment from 574 stores in 42 states. Founded 1955. **Positions advertised include:** Customer Service Representative; Bilingual Manager in Training; Manager in Training; Consumer Electronics Repair Technician; Operational Auditor. **Corporate headquarters location:** This location. **Other U.S. Locations:** Nationwide. **International locations:** Ontario Canada. **Operations at this facility include:** Administration. **Listed on:** New York Stock Exchange. **Stock exchange symbol:** RNT. **Number of employees nationwide:** 3,900. **CEO:** R. Charles Loudermilk, Sr.

ABCO BUILDERS INC.
2680 Abco Court, Lithonia GA 30058. 770/981-0350. **Fax:** 770/981-5776. **Contact:** Mr. Lynn Bledsoe, Vice President. **World Wide Web address:** http://www.abcobuilders.com. **Description:** A commercial construction firm. Founded 1949. **Corporate headquarters location:** This location. **Number of employees at this location:** 350.

ACCENTURE
100 Peachtree Street NE, Suite 1300, Atlanta GA 30303. 404/880-9100. **Contact:** Personnel. **World Wide Web address:** http://www.accenture.com. **Description:** A management and technology consulting firm. Accenture offers a wide range of services including business re-engineering; customer service system consulting; data system design and implementation; Internet sales systems research and design; and strategic planning. **NOTE:** Search and apply for jobs online. **Other U.S. locations:** Nationwide. **International locations:** Worldwide. **Listed on:** New York Stock Exchange. **Stock exchange symbol:** ACN. **CEO:** Joe W. Forehand. **Number of employees worldwide:** 86,000.

ACE MARKETING SERVICES, INC.
1961 South Cobb Industrial Boulevard, Smyrna GA 30082. 770/431-2500. **Toll-free phone:** 800/962-4514. **Fax:** 770/431-2517. **Contact:** Human Resources. **E-mail address:** frontdesk@ace-marketing.com. **World Wide Web address:** http://www.acemarketingservices.com. **Description:** Offers a variety of mailing services including total project planning, package design, computer processing, production management, lettershop operation, warehousing and fulfillment, and list brokerage. **Positions advertised include:** Second Shift Lettershop Mechanic; Machine Operator; Procurement Coordinator; In-Process Auditor; Warehouseman. **Parent company:** World Marketing. **Operations at this facility include:** Administration; Manufacturing; Sales. **Listed on:** Privately held.

ADVANCED CONTROL SYSTEMS, INC.
P.O. Box 922548, Norcross GA 30010-2548. 770/446-8854. **Physical address:** 2755 Northwoods Parkway, Norcross GA 30071. **Fax:** 770/446-3502. **Contact:** Elaine Meggs, Human Resources. **E-mail address:** humanresources@acsatlanta.com. **World Wide Web address:** http://www.acsatlanta.com. **Description:** Manufactures distribution and energy management software and related hardware components. Founded 1975. **NOTE:** No phone calls regarding employment. **Positions advertised include:** Programmer. **Other U.S. locations:** CA; TX. **CEO:** John Muench.

ADVO INC.
7924 Troon Circle, Austell GA 30168. 678/945-4303. **Contact:** Human Resources. **World Wide Web address:** http://www.advo.com. **Description:** Provides direct mail advertising services. **Corporate headquarters location:** Windsor CT. **Other U.S. locations:** Nationwide. **Listed on:** New York Stock Exchange. **Stock exchange symbol:** AD. **CEO:** Gary Mulloy. **Number of employees nationwide:** 3,600.

AERUS LLC
4178 First Avenue, Tucker GA 30084. 770/939-9127. **Contact:** Human Resources Manager. **World Wide Web address:** http://www.aerusonline.com. **Description:** Manufactures and retails vacuums. Formerly Electrolux Corporation. **Corporate headquarters location:** Bristol VA. **Other U.S. locations:** Nationwide. **International locations:** Canada. **CEO:** Joseph P. Urso. **Number of employees nationwide:** 2,500.

AGCO
4205 River Green Parkway, Duluth GA 30096-2568. 770/813-9200. **Contact:** Human Resources. **E-mail address:** jobs.agco-duluth@agcocorp.com. **World Wide Web address:** http://www.agcocorp.com. **Description:** Manufactures agricultural equipment including tractors, combines, planters, and replacement parts. **Corporate headquarters location:** This location. **International locations:** Worldwide. **Listed on:** New York Stock Exchange. **Stock exchange symbol:** AG. **President/CEO:** Robert J. Ratliff. **Annual sales/revenues:** More than $100 million. **Number of employees worldwide:** 9,800.

AGNES SCOTT COLLEGE
141 East College Avenue, Decatur GA 30030-3797. 404/471-6384. **Toll-free phone:** 800/868-8602 Ext. 6384. **Fax:** 404/471-6682. **Recorded jobline:** 404/471-6383. **Contact:** Karen Gilbert, Human Resources Director. **E-mail address:** hrjobs@agnesscott.edu; kgilbert@agnesscott.edu. **World Wide Web address:** http://www.agnesscott.edu. **Description:** A four-year private college offering bachelor's and master's degrees. **Positions advertised include:** Assistant Professor of English; Visiting Assistant Professor; Director of Assessment; Director of the Science Center; Director of the Dalton Gallery; Laboratory Specialist.

AGRIBUSINESS INTERNATIONAL, INC.
P.O. Box 909, Villa Rica GA 30180. 770/459-4401. **Fax:** 770/459-6877. **Contact:** Philip Saunders, President. **E-mail address:** abigausa@worldnet.att.net. **Description:** Manufactures and supplies irrigation equipment. Founded 1955.

AIRGAS, INC.
6340 Sugarloaf Parkway, Suite 300, Duluth GA 30097. 770/717-2200. **Fax:** 770/717-2222. **Contact:** Human Resources. **World Wide Web address:** http://www.airgas.com. **Description:** Manufactures liquid carbon dioxide and related handling equipment. **NOTE:** Please visit website to search for jobs and apply online. **Corporate headquarters location:** Radnor PA. **Other area locations:** Statewide. **Other U.S. locations:** Nationwide. **Parent company:** Airgas. **Operations at this facility include:** Regional headquarters. **Listed on:** New York Stock Exchange. **Stock exchange symbol:** ARG. **CEO:** Peter McClausland. **Number of employees nationwide:** 7,600.

ALBANY ELECTRIC COMPANY
P.O. Box 5228, Albany GA 31706. 229/432-7345. **Physical address:** 800 21st Avenue, Albany GA. **Fax:** 229/436-3869. **Contact:** Human Resources. **E-mail address:** info@metropower.com. **World Wide Web address:** http://www.metropower.com. **Description:** Provides a wide range of electrical contract work including construction, maintenance, service, and design for industrial, commercial, institutional, and residential applications. **Other area locations:** Atlanta GA; Columbus GA; Macon GA; Hazelhurst GA; Norcross GA. **Other U.S. locations:** Greer SC; Andalusia AL; Beloit WI. **Parent company:** MetroPower, Inc.

ALBANY HERALD
P.O. Box 48, Albany GA 31702-0048. 229/888-9300. **Contact:** Human Resources. **World Wide Web address:** http://www.albanyherald.com. **Description:** A newspaper with a daily circulation of approximately 37,000 and 42,000 on Sundays. **Parent company:** Gray Communications Systems, Inc.

ALCON ASSOCIATES INC.
201 Baldwin Drive, Albany GA 31707. 229/432-7411. **Fax:** 229/434-1492. **Contact:** Roger Haggerty, Personnel Director. **E-mail address:** swashburn@alconassociates.com. **World Wide Web address:** http://www.alconassociates.com. **Description:** Engaged in heavy construction and operates as a general contractor. **NOTE:** Resumes are reviewed for matches with job openings, and are kept on file for one year. **Other area locations:** Columbus GA; Kennesaw GA. **President/CEO:** L.D. Bryan III, P.E.

IVAN ALLEN OFFICE FURNITURE
730 Peachtree Street NE, Suite 200, Atlanta GA 30308. 404/760-8700. **Fax:** 404/760-8670. **Contact:** Human Resources Manager. **E-mail address:** hr@ivanallen.com. **World Wide Web address:** http://www.ivanallen.com. **Description:** Engaged in the retail sale of office furniture. **Positions advertised include:** Project Designer; Inside Sales Administrator; Sales – Account Executive; Bid Representative; Small Business Development Representative. **Corporate headquarters location:** Atlanta GA. **Other area locations:** Albany GA; Augusta GA; Athens GA. **Other U.S. locations:** Chattanooga TN; Knoxville TN; Huntsville AL. **Operations at this facility include:** Administration; Sales. **CEO:** H. Inman Allen.

ALLIANCE DATA SYSTEMS
3200 Windy Hill Road Southeast, Atlanta GA 30339. 770/933-5600. **Contact:** Human Resources. **World Wide Web address:** http://www.alliancedatasystems.com. **Description:** Alliance Data Systems provides transaction, credit and marketing services to large consumer based businesses within the retail, petroleum, financial services, utility and hospitality markets. **Positions advertised include:** Project Manager; Sr. Systems Programmer Analyst; Sr. Business System Analyst; Manager, Applications Development. **Corporate headquarters location:** Dallas TX. **Listed on:** New York Stock Exchange. **Stock exchange symbol:** ADS.

ALLIANCE THEATRE COMPANY
1280 Peachtree Street NE, Atlanta GA 30309. 404/733-4650. **Contact:** Human Resources. **World Wide Web address:** http://www.alliancetheatre.org. **Description:** A theater company offering a diverse 10-performance season of contemporary plays, musical theater, world and regional premieres, and classics. **Office hours:** Monday - Friday, 9:00 a.m. - 5:00 p.m. **NOTE:** For acting positions, please contact the Casting Director. For open call information, call the Alliance Audition Information Phone Line at 404/733-4622, or the ACPA Hotline at 770/521-8338. For volunteer positions, call

the Volunteer Hotline at 404/733-4619. For Usher positions, call the Usher Hotline at 404/733-4761. **Parent company:** The Robert W. Woodruff Arts Center.

ALLIED DIAGNOSTIC IMAGING RESOURCES, INC.
5440 Oakbrook Parkway, Suite A, Norcross GA 30093. 770/448-0250. **Toll-free phone:** 800/262-9333. **Fax:** 770/448-0257. **Contact:** Human Resources. **World Wide Web address:** http://www.alliedautex.com. **Description:** Produces processing chemicals for medical, dental, graphic arts, microfilm, and industrial applications. **Parent company:** CPAC, Imaging (Leicester NY).

ALLIED SECURITY INC.
1957 Lakeside Parkway, Suite 502, Tucker GA 30339-4166. 770/492-1997. **Fax:** 770/492-1984. **Contact:** Human Resources. **World Wide Web address:** http://www.alliedsecurity.com. **Description:** One of the largest national contract security officer companies in the nation. Allied Security provides loss prevention services to private businesses and governmental agencies. **NOTE:** Please visit website for online application form. **Corporate headquarters location:** King of Prussia PA. **Other U.S. locations:** Nationwide. **Number of employees nationwide:** 20,000.

ALLISON-SMITH COMPANY
P.O. Box 20215, Atlanta GA 30325. 404/351-6430. **Physical address:** 2284 Marietta Boulevard, Atlanta GA 30318. **Fax:** 404/350-1065. **Contact:** Human Resources. **World Wide Web address:** http://www.allison-smith.com. Founded 1943. **Description:** Provides electrical contracting and engineering services. **President:** Lanny Thomas.

ALLSTATE INSURANCE COMPANY
2244 Henderson Mill Road Northeast, Atlanta GA 30345. 770/492-0194. **Toll-free phone:** 800/877-2512. **Contact:** Human Resources Manager. **E-mail address:** careers@allstate.com. **World Wide Web address:** http://www.allstatecareers.com. **Description:** As one of the nation's largest insurance companies, Allstate provides a full line of property, liability, life, reinsurance, and commercial insurance. **NOTE:** Please visit website to search for jobs and apply online. **Company slogan:** You're in good hands. **Positions advertised include:** Exclusive Agent/Independent Contractor; Exclusive Financial Specialist. **Corporate headquarters location:** Northbrook IL. **Other area locations:** Statewide. **Other U.S. locations:** Nationwide. **Listed on:** New York Stock Exchange. **Stock exchange symbol:** ALL. **President/ CEO:** Edward Liddy. **Number of employees nationwide:** 41,500.

ALOETTE COSMETICS INC.
4900 Highland Parkway, Smyrna GA 30082. 678/444-2563. **Contact:** Human Resources. **World Wide Web address:** http://www.aloette.com. **Description:** Manufactures and distributes skin care products, cosmetics, and other personal care products. The company sells approximately 130 aloe vera-based skin care products, makeup, fragrance, and cosmetic products marketed exclusively under the trade name Aloette. The company's Aloette skin care items are grouped according to individual skin type and are designed to be used in a daily regimen. Aloette's glamour products include liquid foundations, pressed powders, powder blushes, powder eye shadows, eye pencils, mascara, lipsticks, lip glosses, hair care items, and tanning products. Among the fragrance items are a bath set and men's and women's colognes. The company also sells promotional and support items to its franchises including business supplies, product samples, and sales and recruiting aids. **Corporate headquarters location:** This location.

AMEDISYS HOME HEALTH
440 Martin Luther King Jr. Boulevard, Suite 300, Macon GA 31201. 478/738-0807. **Toll-free phone:** 800/675-1073. **Fax:** 478/738-0923. **Contact:** Human Resources. **World Wide Web address:** http://www.healthfield.com. **Description:** Provides home health care nursing services. **NOTE:** Please visit website to search for jobs and apply online. **Positions advertised include:** Speech Language Pathologist; Nurse Liaison; Medical Social Worker; Clinical Manager; LPN; RN. **Other area locations:** Statewide. **Other U.S. locations:** Southern U.S. **Listed on:** NASDAQ. **Stock exchange symbol:** AMED.

AMERICAN AIRLINES, INC.
Hartsfield International Airport, Atlanta GA 30331. **Toll-free phone:** 800/433-7300. **Contact:** Human Resources. **World Wide Web address:** http://www.aa.com. **Description:** Provides scheduled jet service to more than 170 destinations primarily throughout North America, the Caribbean, Latin America, Europe, and the Pacific. **NOTE:** Please visit website to fill out an employment interest form. **Corporate headquarters location:** Fort Worth TX. **Parent company:** AMR Corporation. **Listed on:** New York Stock Exchange. **Stock exchange symbol:** AMR. **President/CEO:** Gerard J. Arpey. **Number of employees nationwide:** 100,000.

AMERICAN CANCER SOCIETY
1599 Clifton Road NE, Atlanta GA 30329. 404/320-3333. **Fax:** 404/982-3677. **Contact:** Human Resources. **E-mail address:** acs.jobs1@cancer.org. **World Wide Web address:** http://www.cancer.org. **Description:** A nationwide, community-based, nonprofit, voluntary health organization dedicated to eliminating cancer as a major health problem by funding cancer research and public education. The society helps patients directly by offering services including transportation to treatment and rehabilitation services. Founded in 1913. **Positions advertised include:** Director – Fundraising Communications; Director – National Media Relations; Online Fundraising Project Manager; HRMS Analyst; Manager – Evaluation Services; Administrative Specialist; Coordinator – CRM Projects; Network Security Engineer; Server Administrator; Assistant Controller; Associate Medical Editor; Director – Sampling and Statistics; Manager – Planned Giving Promotions; Director – Estate & Asset Services; Web Services Administrator; HelpDesk Support Analyst. **Special programs:** Internships. **Corporate headquarters location:** This location. **Other U.S. locations:** Nationwide. **Operations at this facility include:** Administration; Service.

AMERICAN FAMILY LIFE ASSURANCE COMPANY OF COLUMBUS
AFLAC Worldwide Headquarters, 1932 Wynnton Road, Columbus GA 31999. 706/323-3431. **Toll-free phone:** 800/992-3522. **Contact:** Human Resources. **World Wide Web address:** http://www.aflac.com. **Description:** American Family Life Assurance Company of Columbus (AFLAC) provides guaranteed-renewable supplemental insurance and is a *Fortune* 500 company. **NOTE:** Please visit website to register, search for jobs, and apply online. For Agent Recruiting, please fill out the interest form online. **Positions advertised include:** Accounting Specialist; Mail Specialist; Application Developer Analyst; Public Relations Representative; Manager – Systems Consulting; Senior Application Developer; Technical Support Specialist; Senior Systems Administrator; Supervisor – Software Testing; Senior Communications Specialist; Investment Consultant; Secretary. **Corporate headquarters location:** This location. **Other U.S. locations:** Nationwide. **International locations:** Japan. **Operations at this facility include:** This location houses administrative offices. **Listed on:** New York Stock Exchange. **Stock exchange symbol:** AFL. **CEO:** Dan Amos. **Number of employees worldwide:** 5,000.

AMERICAN FLAT GLASS DISTRIBUTORS, INC. (AFGD)
1600 Parkwood Circle SE, Suite 300, Atlanta GA 30339. 770/951-2343. **Toll-free phone:** 800/766-2343. **Fax:** 770/951-0001. **Contact:** Human Resources. **World Wide Web address:** http://www.afgd.com. **Description:** Manufactures a complete line of insulated glass units for commercial and residential applications. Products include clear, tint, and reflective glass; wire glass; and equipment for the handling, storage, and transportation of glass. **NOTE:** Entry-level positions are offered. **Positions advertised include:** Inside Sales Consultant. **Corporate headquarters location:** This location. **Other U.S. locations:** Nationwide. **International locations:** Canada. **Subsidiaries include:** AFGD Canada. **Parent company:** AFG Industries Inc. **Listed on:** Privately held. **Annual sales/revenues:** More than $100 million. **President:** John Stilwell.

AMERICAN FLAT GLASS DISTRIBUTORS, INC. (AFGD)
3200 Austell Road, Marietta GA 30060. 770/434-2041. **Toll-free phone:** 800/727-2343. **Fax:** 770/436-2654. **Contact:** Human Resources. **World Wide Web address:** http://www.afgd.com. **Description:** Manufactures a complete line of insulated glass units for commercial and residential applications. Products include clear, tint, and reflective glass; wire glass; and equipment for the handling, storage, and transportation of glass. **NOTE:** Please send resumes to corporate address at 1600 Parkwood Circle South East, Suite 300, Atlanta GA 30339. **Positions advertised include:** Inside Sales Consultant. **Corporate headquarters location:** Atlanta GA. **Other U.S. locations:** Nationwide. **International locations:** Canada. **Subsidiaries include:** AFGD Canada. **Parent company:** AFG Industries Inc. **Operations at this facility include:** Manufacturing; Sales. **Listed on:** Privately held. **Annual sales/revenues:** More than $100 million. **President:** John Stilwell.

AMERICAN GENERAL FINANCE
945 North Hairston Road, Suite 2, Stone Mountain GA 30083-2880. 770/498-9839. **Fax:** 770/498-9192. **Contact:** Human Resources. **World Wide Web address:** http://www.agfinance.com. **Description:** One of the largest public insurance companies in the United States. The company also provides financial services such as mortgage loans, real estate investment and development, investment counseling, and management and distribution of mutual funds. **NOTE:** Please contact your local office to learn of immediate local opportunities. **Positions advertised include:** Management Trainee; Customer Account Administrator; Customer Account Specialist. **Corporate headquarters location:** Evansville IN. **Other U.S. locations:** Nationwide.

AMERICAN INSURANCE MANAGERS
3101 Tower Creek Parkway, Suite 700, Atlanta GA 30339. 770/980-0591. **Toll-free phone:** 800/888-2464. **Fax:** 770/980-3290. **Contact:** Human Resources. **Description:** Offers insurance and related brokerage services including automobile, medical, and property and casualty insurance.

THE AMERICAN INTERCONTINENTAL UNIVERSITY
3330 Peachtree Road NE, Atlanta GA 30326. 888/999-4248. **Fax:** 404/965-5701. **Contact:** Human Resources. **World Wide Web address:** http://www.houseofedu.com/aiuat/index.jsp. **Description:** A college offering associate's and bachelor's degrees in international business, interior and fashion design, information technology, and multimedia communication. **Corporate headquarters location:** This location. **Other area locations:** Dunwoody GA. **Other U.S. locations:** Los Angeles CA; Fort Lauderdale FL; Houston TX. **International locations:** London England.

AMERICAN MEGATRENDS, INC.
6145-F Northbelt Parkway, Norcross GA 30071-2976. 770/246-8600. **Fax:** 770/246-8790. **Contact:** Human Resources. **World Wide Web address:** http://www.ami.com. **Description:** Provider of BIOS technology, motherboards, utilities, and storage solutions. **Corporate headquarters location:** This location. **International locations:** China; Germany; India; Japan; Korea; Taiwan.

AMERICAN RED CROSS
1955 Monroe Drive NE, Atlanta GA 30324-4888. 404/876-3302. **Fax:** 404/575-3086. **Contact:** Human Resources. **E-mail address:** cbattle@arcatl.org. **World Wide Web address:** http://www.redcrossatlanta.org. **Description:** A humanitarian organization that aids disaster victims, gathers blood for crisis distribution, trains individuals to respond to emergencies, educates individuals on various diseases, and raises funds for other charitable establishments. **NOTE:** Volunteer positions are also available. **Positions advertised include:** Youth Program Specialist; Media Relations Specialist; Data Entry Associate; Health Specialist. **Special programs:** Internships. **Corporate headquarters location:** Washington DC. **Other area locations:** Decatur GA; Lawrenceville GA; Marietta GA; Morrow GA. **Other U.S. locations:** Nationwide. **CEO:** Tim English. **Number of employees at this location:** 125.

AMERICAN SOFTWARE, INC.
470 East Paces Ferry Road, Atlanta GA 30305. 404/261-4381. **Toll-free phone:** 800/726-2946. **Fax:** 404/261-5206. 238-8499. **Contact:** Human Resources. **Description:** Develops, markets, and supports integrated supply-chain management and financial-control systems software. The company's multiplatform enterprise software applications are primarily used for forecasting and inventory management, purchasing and materials control, and order processing and receivables control. The company also provides consulting and outsourcing services. **Corporate headquarters location:** This location. **Operations at this facility include:** Administration; Research and Development; Sales; Service. **Listed on:** NASDAQ. **Stock exchange symbol:** AMSWA. **CEO:** James Edenfield. **Annual sales/revenues:** $51 - $100 million. **Number of employees nationwide:** 440.

AMERICAN WOODMARK CORPORATION
1017 Highway 42 South, Jackson GA 30233. 770/775-6013. **Fax:** 770/775-0383. **Contact:** Human Resources Director. **World Wide Web address:** http://www.americanwoodmark.com. **Description:** Manufactures and distributes kitchen cabinets and vanities for the remodeling and new home construction markets. The company offers almost 100 cabinet lines in a wide variety of designs, materials, and finishes. **Corporate headquarters location:** Winchester VA. **Other U.S. locations:** Nationwide. **Listed on:** NASDAQ. **Stock exchange symbol:** AMWD. **President/CEO:** James Gosa. **Number of employees nationwide:** 3,800.

AMERICA'S BEST COMPUTER DISTRIBUTORS INC. (ABCD)
108 Old Montgomeryville Road, Milledgeville GA 31061. 478/454-2299. **Toll-free phone:** 800/733-3988. **Fax:** 478/452-0737. **Contact:** Human Resources. **World Wide Web address:** http://www.abcd4less.com. **Description:** Distributes computer hardware and accessories. The company also provides on-site repairs and technical support services.

AMERICASMART
240 Peachtree Street NW, Suite 2200, Atlanta GA 30303. 404/220-3000. **Toll-free phone:** 800/285-6278. **Fax:** 678/686-5181. **Contact:** Personnel. **E-mail address:** hrdepartment@americasmart.com. **World Wide Web address:** http://www.americasmart.com. **Description:** Houses a campus of wholesale buying

facilities for gift, home furnishings, apparel, and area rug buyers. **NOTE:** Entry-level positions are offered. No phone calls regarding employment. **Positions advertised include:** Showroom Manager; Property Manager; Copier Services Technician. **Office hours:** Monday - Friday, 8:30 a.m. - 5:30 p.m. **Corporate headquarters location:** This location. **Parent company:** AMC, Inc. (also at this location) is an international trade show organizer for the wholesale and retail industries. **CEO:** John Portman. **Annual sales/revenues:** $51 - $100 million.

ANALYSTS INTERNATIONAL CORPORATION (AIC)
3169 Holcomb Bridge Road, Suite 210, Norcross GA 30071. 770/446-6971. **Toll-free phone:** 800/597-5995. **Fax:** 770/446-3028. **Contact:** Human Resources. **E-mail address:** atlantajobs@analysts.com. **World Wide Web address:** http://www.analysts.com. **Description:** AiC is an information systems consulting firm. AiC provides analytical and programming services including consulting, systems analysis, design, programming, instruction, and technical writing. **NOTE:** Please visit website to register, search for jobs, and apply online. **Corporate headquarters location:** Minneapolis MN. **Other U.S. locations:** Nationwide. **International locations:** Canada; United Kingdom. **Operations at this facility include:** Regional Headquarters. **Listed on:** NASDAQ. **Stock exchange symbol:** ANLY. **Annual sales/revenues:** More than $100 million. **President/CEO:** Mike LaVelle. **Number of employees worldwide:** 4,500.

ANCHOR GLASS CONTAINER CORPORATION
1044 Booth Road, Warner Robins GA 31088. 478/922-4271. **Contact:** Personnel Director. **Description:** Manufactures glassware, commercial and institutional chinaware, decorative and convenience hardware, glass containers, and metal and plastic closures. Operations encompass over 20 divisions and subsidiaries with 40 plants and distribution centers located in the United States and abroad. **Corporate headquarters location:** Tampa FL. **Listed on:** NASDAQ. **Stock exchange symbol:** AGCC. **President/CEO:** Richard M. Deneau.

ANCHOR HOSPITAL
5454 Yorktown Drive, Atlanta GA 30349. 770/991-6044. **Toll-free phone:** 866/667-8797. **Fax:** 770/991-3843. **Contact:** Human Resources. **World Wide Web address:** http://www.magellanhealth.com. **Description:** A specialty treatment hospital, helping teens and adults with chemical dependency or behavioral health problems. **NOTE:** Contact Human Resources at 678/251-3339. Please visit website to download employment application. **Special programs:** Internships.

ANSWERTHINK CONSULTING GROUP
1117 Perimeter Center, Suite 500, Atlanta GA 30338. 404/682-2500. **Fax:** 707/225-3650. **Contact:** Personnel. **World Wide Web address:** http://www.answerthink.com. **Description:** Provides computer consulting and IT services to *Fortune* 1000 companies. Founded 1997. **NOTE:** Please visit website to search for jobs and apply online. **Positions advertised include:** SAP Professional. **Corporate headquarters location:** This location. **Other U.S. locations:** Burlington MA; Chicago IL; Hudson OH; Miami FL; New York NY; Conshohocken PA. **International locations:** Eschborn Germany; London England. **Listed on:** NASDAQ. **Stock exchange symbol:** ANSR. **Number of employees worldwide:** 1,600.

AON CONSULTING
3565 Piedmont Road NE, Building 1, Suite 600, Atlanta GA 30305. 404/264-3141. **Fax:** 404/240-6160. **Contact:** Human Resources. **World Wide Web address:** http://www.aon.com. **Description:** An international human resources consulting and benefits brokerage firm providing integrated advisory and support services in retirement planning, health care management, organizational effectiveness, compensation, human resources-related communications, and information technologies. The company's organizational effectiveness services include advisory and support services in compensation, strategy development, organizational design, business process redesign, human resources development, management training and development, organizational communications, and information technology applications. Strategic health care services include advisory and support services in traditional group health and welfare programs, strategic health planning, strategic health care management, quality assurance, flexible benefits and compensation, financial management, data management, vendor oversight, and communications. Strategic retirement planning and educational services include consulting and support services in core actuarial applications, retirement health and welfare benefits, funding and investment strategy, record keeping and administration, employee sensing and communications, personalized retirement modeling, holistic lifestyle and family planning, and database information and proprietary studies. Information technologies services include human resources information systems development (information management strategies, systems, databases, software, and technology advisement) and human resources systems applications (human resources planning, record keeping, communication, and education). **NOTE:** Please visit website to search for jobs. For most positions, mail resumes to Aon Consulting Worldwide, P.O. Box 66, Winston-Salem NC 27102, or fax to 336/896-8359 – please see job descriptions for exact contact details. No phone calls regarding employment. **Positions advertised include:** Business Producer; Relationship Specialist; Regional Director of Commercial Market Syndication; Senior Syndicator; Benefit Specialist; Manager Trainee; Worker's Compensation Claims Adjuster; WC Medical Only Claims Adjuster; Manager of Sales Support. **Corporate headquarters location:** Chicago IL. **Other U.S. locations:** Nationwide. **International locations:** Worldwide. **Listed on:** New York Stock Exchange. **Stock exchange symbol:** AOC. **CEO:** Patrick Ryan. **Number of employees worldwide:** 51,000.

APAC, INC.
4005 Windward Plaza Drive, Suite 300, Alpharetta GA 30005. 770/664-5550. **Fax:** 770/664-5410. **Contact:** Human Resources. **E-mail address:** apac@ashland.com. **World Wide Web address:** http://www.apac.com. **Description:** Provides a variety of construction services including asphalt and concrete paving and the excavation and construction of bridges and other structures. **NOTE:** Please visit http://www.ashland.com to search for jobs and apply online. **Positions advertised include: Programmer** Analyst; Senior Sourcing Analyst; Secretary; Purchasing Agent; Payroll Processing Supervisor; Regional Plant Support Specialist; Estimator; Cash Applications Processor; Environmental Health and Safety Manager; Project Manager; Foreman; Credit Analyst; Superintendent. **Corporate headquarters location:** This location. **Other U.S. locations:** Southern and Southeastern States. **Parent company:** Ashland Inc. **Listed on:** New York Stock Exchange. **Stock exchange symbol:** ASH.

APPLIED FINANCIAL GROUP
1108 Hope Road, Atlanta GA 30350-2979. 770/992-0955. **Toll-free phone:** 800/298-9904. **Fax:** 770/594-9631. **World Wide Web address:** http://www.afg-online.com. **Description:** Provides financial planning and investment management services. **Corporate headquarters location:** This location.

ARAMARK HEALTHCARE SUPPORT SERVICES
5775 Peachtree Dunwoody Road, Building C, Suite 500, Atlanta GA 30342. 404/851-1805. **Fax:** 404/851-1911. **Contact:** Human Resources. **World Wide Web address:** http://www.aramark.com. **Description:** Serves 115 million meals annually for health care customers nationwide and offers food service, clinical nutrition management, facility services, and engineering support to health care administrators. ARAMARK Healthcare Support also provides added-value services related to resource management, revenue generation, and business planning, using an integrated program of Total Quality Management. **NOTE:** Please visit website to search for jobs and apply online. **Positions advertised include:** Assistant Director of Patient Services. **Special programs:** Internship. **Parent company:** ARAMARK (Philadelphia PA) is one of the world's leading providers of managed services. The company operates in all 50 states and 10 foreign countries, offering a broad range of services to businesses of all sizes including many *Fortune* 500 companies and thousands of universities, hospitals, and municipal, state, and federal government facilities. The company is among the market leaders in all of its businesses. ARAMARK's businesses include Food, Leisure and Support Services, which includes Campus Dining Services, School Nutrition Services, Leisure Services, Business Dining Services, International Services, Healthcare Support Services, Conference Center Management, and Refreshment Services; Facility Services; Correctional Services; Industrial Services; Uniform Services, which includes Uniform Services and Wearguard, a direct marketer of work clothing; Health and Education Services, which includes Spectrum Healthcare Services and Children's World Learning Centers; and Book and Magazine Services. **Corporate headquarters location:** Philadelphia PA. **Other U.S. locations:** Nationwide. **Operations at this facility include:** Regional Headquarters. **Listed on:** New York Stock Exchange. **Stock exchange symbol:** RMK. **President/CEO:** Joseph Neubauer. **Number of employees nationwide:** 124,000.

JOHN D. ARCHBOLD MEMORIAL HOSPITAL
P.O. Box 1018, Thomasville GA 31799-1018. 229/228-2000. **Physical address:** 915 Gordon Avenue, Thomasville GA 31792. **Fax:** 229/228-8583. **Contact:** Employment Manager. **World Wide Web address:** http://www.archbold.org. **Description:** A regional trauma center serving the southwest region of Georgia. The hospital also provides some outpatient services. **NOTE:** Human Resources phone is 229/228-2744. Please visit website to search for jobs, and to download employment application. **Positions advertised include:** Administrative Assistant; Secretary – Nursing Administration; Transcriptionist; Unit Secretary Coordinator; Cardiovascular Technician; Director of Quality Improvement; MRI Technician; Pharmacist; Pharmacy Technician; Phlebotomy Technician; Respiratory Therapist; Social Worker – Wound Management; Special Procedures Technician; Speech Language Pathologist; Computer Operator; House Supervisor; Patient Care Technician; RN – Various Departments; Transporter; Cafeteria Aide; Cook; Environmental Services Aide; Floor Technician; Nutrition Services Technician. **Corporate headquarters location:** This location. **Subsidiaries include:** Brooks County Hospital; Grady General Hospital; Mitchell County Hospital. **Operations at this facility include:** Administration; Research and Development. **Listed on:** Privately held.

ARISTA INFORMATION TECHNOLOGY
2150 Boggs Road, Building 400, Suite 430, Duluth GA 30096. 678/473-1885. **Fax:** 678/473-1051. **Contact:** Human Resources. **World Wide Web address:** http://www.aristainfo.com. **Description:** A full service laser printing and mailing company. **NOTE:** Please visit website for online application form. **Corporate headquarters location:** This location. **Other U.S. locations:** NC.

ARMSTRONG WORLD INDUSTRIES, INC.
P.O. Box 4288, 4520 Broadway, Macon GA 31213. 478/788-4811. **Fax:** 478/781-9930. **Contact:** Human Resources. **World Wide Web address:** http://www.armstrong.com. **Description:** Armstrong World Industries, Inc. manufactures flooring, ceiling systems, furniture, and industrial specialty products. Founded 1860. **Positions advertised include:** Maintenance Systems Team Manager; Process Engineer; Area Maintenance Team Manager; Sales Executive; Builder Channel Sales Manager. **Corporate headquarters location:** Lancaster PA. **Other area locations:** Atlanta. **Other U.S. locations:** Nationwide. **International locations:** Worldwide. **Listed on:** OTC. **Stock exchange symbol:** ACKHQ. **Number of employees worldwide:** 16,500.

ARRIS CORPORATION
3871 Lakefield Drive, Suite 700, Suwanee GA 30024. 770/622-8400. **Toll-free phone:** 800/469-6569. **Fax:** 770/622-8770. **Contact:** Human Resources Manager. **World Wide Web address:** http://www.arrisi.com. **Description:** Designs and manufactures telecommunications network interface systems and connection apparatus. The majority of sales are made directly to the seven regional Bell operating companies. ARRIS also manufactures various interconnect and transmission devices used in fiber-optic networks, concentrating on products for standard telephone lines installed for voice transmission. **Positions advertised include:** Internal Auditor; Technical Support Engineer. **Corporate headquarters location:** This location. **Other area locations:** Suwanee GA. **Other U.S. locations:** CO; PA; IL; CA. **International locations:** Cessnalaan Netherlands; Barcelona Spain; Cork Ireland; Tokyo Japan; Sydney Australia; Los Condes Chile. **Operations at this facility include:** Administration; Manufacturing; Research and Development; Sales; Testing. **Listed on:** NASDAQ. **Stock exchange symbol:** ARRS. **Number of employees worldwide:** 2,500.

THE ART INSTITUTE OF ATLANTA
6600 Peachtree Dunwoody Road, 100 Embassy Row, Atlanta GA 30328-1649. 770/394-8300. **Toll-free phone:** 800/275-4242. **Fax:** 770/394-9949. **Contact:** Joselyn Cassidy, Director of Human Resources. **E-mail address:** cassidyj@aii.edu. **World Wide Web address:** http://www.aia.artinstitutes.edu. **Description:** A two- and four-year art college specializing in visual communications, culinary arts, interior design, photographic imaging, video production, computer animation, multimedia, and fashion marketing. **NOTE:** Entry-level positions are offered. Direct contact phone is 770/689-4813. **Positions advertised include:** Department Chair – Media Arts and Animation. **Corporate headquarters location:** Pittsburgh PA. **Other U.S. locations:** Nationwide. **Operations at this facility include:** Administration; Sales. **Listed on:** Privately held. **Number of employees at this location:** 225. **Number of employees nationwide:** 5,000.

ARTHRITIS FOUNDATION
P.O. Box 7669, Atlanta GA 30357-0669. 404/872-7100. **Physical address:** 1330 West Peachtree Street, Atlanta GA 30309. **Fax:** 404/872-0457. **Contact:** Human Resources. **E-mail address:** resume@arthritis.org. **World Wide Web address:** http://www.arthritis.org. **Description:** Engaged in research to find a cure for arthritis. Also provides information to educate those who have the disease. **Corporate headquarters location:** This location. **Positions advertised include:** Vice President – Strategic Marketing Alliances; Manager – Year Round Program; Maintenance Technician; Group Vice President – Major Donor Relations; Regional Director – Charitable Estate Planning. **President/CEO:** John H. Klippel.

ASHLAND DISTRIBUTION
4550 NE Expressway, Doraville GA 30340. 770/448-7010. **Toll-free phone:** 800/282-8910. **Contact:** Human Resources. **World Wide Web address:** http://www.ashchem.com/adc/chemicals/. **Description:** Manufactures, markets, and distributes a wide variety of chemical products. Through its Industrial Chemical

Division, the company manufactures and markets products for water management and fuel treatment, as well as specialized chemicals for major industries. **NOTE:** Please visit http://www.ashland.com to search for jobs. **Positions advertised include:** Material Handler; Inventory Control Coordinator; Sales Specialist. **Office hours:** Monday – Friday, 8:00 a.m. – 5:00 p.m. **Corporate headquarters location:** Covington KY. **Other U.S. locations:** Nationwide. **International locations:** Worldwide. **Listed on:** New York Stock Exchange. **Stock exchange symbol:** ASH. **Number of employees worldwide:** 25,000.

ASHLEY MANUFACTURING INC.
P.O. Box 1357, Jesup GA 31598. 912/427-8734. **Physical address:** 2100 Sunset Boulevard, Jesup GA 31545. **Fax:** 912/427-0321. **Contact:** Art Stone, President. **Description:** Manufactures Halloween costumes, as well as tap, jazz, and ballet clothing. **Special programs:** Internships. **Corporate headquarters location:** This location. **Operations at this facility include:** Administration; Divisional Headquarters; Manufacturing. **Number of employees at this location:** 200.

ASSURANT PRENEED
10 Glenlake Parkway NE, Suite 500, Atlanta GA 30328. 770/206-6400. **Toll-free phone:** 800/801-0800; 800/PRENEED. **Fax:** 770/206-6389. **Contact:** Human Resources. **E-mail address:** hr@fortisfamily.com. **World Wide Web address:** http://www.fortisfamily.com. **Description:** Offers preneed funeral insurance coverage. **NOTE:** Please visit website to fill out employment information form. **Corporate headquarters location:** New York NY. **Other U.S. locations:** Rapid City SD.

ATHENS PACKAGING – KELLOGGS SNACKS
1965 Statham Drive, Statham GA 30666. 770/725-0181. **Contact:** Human Resources. **Description:** Packages cookies, crackers, and other snack foods. **Parent company:** Keebler Company (Elmhurst IL). **Number of employees at this location:** 260.

ATKINSON COUNTY SCHOOLS
506 East Roberts Avenue, Pearson GA 3642. 912/422-7373. **Fax:** 912/422-7369. **World Wide Web address:** http://www.atkinson.k12.ga.us. **Description:** Office of the Superintendent of Atkinson County Schools.

ATLANTA BOTANICAL GARDEN
1345 Piedmont Avenue NE, Atlanta GA 30309-3366. 404/876-5859. **Fax:** 404/876-7472. **Contact:** Human Resources Department. **E-mail address:** jobs@atlantabotanicalgarden.org. **World Wide Web address:** http://www.atlantabotanicalgarden.org. **Description:** Offers family entertainment featuring the Fuqua Conservatory, which contains exotic and endangered plants from around the world. The organization also maintains a lake, baseball fields, a tennis center, and bicycle trails. **NOTE:** Volunteer positions are also available. **Positions advertised include:** Security Officer; Administrative Assistant – Part-time; Summer Cam Teacher. **Special programs:** Internships. **Office hours:** Monday - Friday, 8:30 a.m. - 5:00 p.m.

ATLANTA BUSINESS JOURNAL
4405 Mall Boulevard, Suite 521, Union City GA 30291. 770/969-7711. **Fax:** 770/969-7811. **Contact:** Human Resources. **Description:** A publisher of both a quarterly magazine and a weekly newspaper.

ATLANTA CHRISTIAN COLLEGE
2605 Ben Hill Road, East Point GA 30344. 404/761-8861. **Contact:** Human Resources. **World Wide Web address:** http://www.acc.edu. **Description:** A four-year college specializing in business, humanities, and theology. **President:** Dr. R. Edwin Grover.

ATLANTA CYCLORAMA
800-C Cherokee Avenue SE, Atlanta GA 30315. 404/658-7625. **Contact:** Director. **World Wide Web address:** http://www.bcaatlanta.com. **Description:** Offers dramatic taped narrations of a day during the Civil War Battle of Atlanta. This domed, 1920s structure features a large, circular painting, viewed from a revolving stage.

ATLANTA DAILY WORLD
145 Auburn Avenue, Atlanta GA 30303-2501. 404/659-1110. **Fax:** 404/659-4988. **World Wide Web address:** http://www.atlantadailyworld.com. **Description:** One of Atlanta's oldest black newspapers. Founded 1928.

ATLANTA FIRE DEPARTMENT
675 Ponce De Leon Avenue, Suite 2001, Atlanta GA 30308. 404/853-7004. **Fax:** 404/853-7245. **Description:** The city of Atlanta's fire department. **NOTE:** You may pick up employment application at this location. **Number of employees at this location:** 960.

ATLANTA POLICE DEPARTMENT
675 Ponce de Leon Avenue NE, Atlanta GA 30308. 404/853-7650. **Fax:** 404/853-7156. **Contact:** Recruitment Unit. **World Wide Web address:** http://atlantapd.org. **Description:** Atlanta Police Department provides law enforcement services to the city of Atlanta. **NOTE:** When applying for a Police Officer position, provide a complete address – an application package will be sent to you within a week. If inquiring about civilian positions, call the City of Atlanta Personnel Section at 404/330-6377.

THE ATLANTA JOURNAL-CONSTITUTION
P.O. Box 4689, Atlanta GA 30302. 404/526-5151. **Toll-free phone:** 800/846-6672. **Recorded jobline:** 404/526-7224. **Contact:** Human Resources **Special programs:** Internships. Department. E-mail address: ejobs8@ajc.com. **World Wide Web address:** http://www.ajc.com. **Description:** Publishes a daily newspaper with a weekday circulation of 450,000. **Positions advertised include:** Collections Supervisor; Advertising Sales Manager; Account Executive; Online Coordinator; Circulation Development Manager; Systems Analyst/Software Engineer; Telephone Sales Representative; Java Server/Side Programmer Analyst; Deliver Driver; Sales Representative. **Corporate headquarters location:** This location.

ATLANTA LIFE INSURANCE COMPANY
100 Auburn Avenue NE, Atlanta GA 30303. 404/654-8894. **Toll-free phone:** 800/235-5422. **Fax:** 404/654-8808. **Contact:** Marvelyen Thomas, Human Resources Manager. **World Wide Web address:** http://www.atlantalife.com. **Description:** A life insurance company. **Note:** This location also hires seasonally. Please visit website for online application form. **Positions advertised include:** Managing Sales Agent. **Special programs:** Internships; Summer Jobs. **Office hours:** Monday - Friday, 9:00 a.m. - 5:00 p.m. **Corporate headquarters location:** This location. **Other area locations:** Augusta GA; Savannah GA; Waycross GA. **Other U.S. locations:** Nationwide. **Operations at this facility include:** Administration; Sales; Service. **President:** Charles Cornelius.

ATLANTA MARRIOTT MARQUIS
265 Peachtree Center Avenue, Atlanta GA 30303. 404/521-0000. **Toll-free phone:** 800/228-9290. **Fax:** 404/586-6299. **Contact:** Ericka Qualls, Director of Personnel. **World Wide Web address:** http://www.marriott.com. **Description:** A 1,675-room hotel with 69 suites, 48 meeting rooms, four restaurants, indoor and outdoor swimming pools, a solarium, a health club, a whirlpool, a sauna, and three golf courses. **Positions advertised include:** Director of Group Sales; Director of Loss Prevention; Executive Sous Chef. **Parent company:** Marriott International has nearly 2,300 units, with operations and franchises in 50 states and 63 countries. The company operates lodging facilities and franchises four separate brand names, each serving a different part of the lodging market: Marriott Hotels, Resorts, and Suites (full-service); Courtyard Hotels (moderate price); Residence Inn (extended stay); and Fairfield Inn (economy). The company also develops and operates Marriott Ownership Resorts (vacation time-sharing). **Corporate headquarters location:** Washington D.C. **Other U.S. locations:** Nationwide. **International locations:** Worldwide. **Listed on:** New York Stock Exchange. **Stock exchange symbol:** MAR. **CEO:** J.W. Marriott, Jr. **Number of employees worldwide:** 154,000.

ATLANTA METROPOLITAN COLLEGE
1630 Metropolitan Parkway SW, Atlanta GA 30310-4498. 404/756-4000. **Fax:** 404/756-4777. **Contact:** Regina Ray Simmons, Human Resources. **E-mail address:** hr@amcmail.atlm.peachnet.edu. **World Wide Web address:** http://www.atlm.edu. **Description:** A two-year college with an enrollment of approximately 2,000. **Positions advertised include:** Reference Librarian; Financial Aid Counselor. **Offices hours:** Monday – Friday, 8:30 a.m. – 5:15 p.m.

ATLANTA MOTOR SPEEDWAY
P.O. Box 500, Hampton GA 30228. 770/946-3931. **Physical address:** 1500 North Highway 41, Atlanta GA 30303. **Contact:** Human Resources. **World Wide Web address:** http://www.atlantamotorspeedway.com. **Description:** One of the NASCAR circuit's fastest tracks. The track hosts two annual Winston Cup championship events and is home to the Wings and Wheels Motor Fair, as well as the Busch Grand National Race. **Office hours:** Monday – Friday, 8:30 a.m. – 5:00 p.m.; Saturday, 9:00 a.m. – 5:00 p.m.; Sunday, 1:00 p.m. – 5:00 p.m. **Listed on:** New York Stock Exchange. **Stock exchange symbol:** TRK. **CEO:** O. Burton Smith.

ATLANTA TECHNICAL COLLEGE
1560 Metropolitan Parkway SW, Atlanta GA 30310. 404/756-3700. **Contact:** Human Resources. **World Wide Web address:** http://www.atlantatech.org. **Description:** A technical college whose programs of study include business and media technology, human services, health occupations, and information technology. **President:** Dr. Brenda Watts Jones.

ATLANTA UNION MISSION
P.O. Box 1807, Atlanta GA 30301. 404/367-2244. **Physical address:** 2353 Bolton Road NW, Suite 300, Atlanta GA 30318. **Contact:** T.J. Elison, Human Resources Manager. **E-mail address:** tj.elion@myaum.org. **World Wide Web address:** http://www.aumcares.org. **Description:** One of the largest homeless shelter service groups in the Southeast. Founded 1938. **NOTE:** Contact Human Resources directly at 404/526-4321. Volunteer positions are also available. **President/CEO:** David Coleman.

ATLANTA URBAN LEAGUE INC.
100 Edgewood Avenue NE, Suite 600, Atlanta GA 30303. 404/659-1150. **Fax:** 404/659-5326. **Contact:** Employment Programs. **World Wide Web address:** http://www.nul.org. **Description:** Provides a variety of services including job search assistance and training, housing counseling, summer youth programs, and mortgage counseling. Founded in 1920. **Corporate headquarters location:** New York NY. **Parent company:** National Urban League.

ATLANTA WEB PRINTERS, INC.
1585 Roadhaven Drive, Stone Mountain GA 30083-1315. 770/621-8888. **Fax:** 770/621-8866. **Contact:** Human Resources. **E-mail address:** info@atlantawebprinters.com. **World Wide Web address:** http://www.atlantawebprinters.com. **Description:** Provides commercial printing services. **President:** Rick Sauers.

ATLANTIC AMERICAN CORPORATION
P.O. Box 105480, Atlanta GA 30348. 404/266-5500. **Physical address:** 4370 Peachtree Road NE, Atlanta GA 30319. **Toll-free phone:** 800/241-1439. **Fax:** 404/266-5702. **Contact:** Human Resources. **World Wide Web address:** http://www.atlam.com. **Description:** A holding company. **Corporate headquarters location:** This location. **Subsidiaries include:** Bankers Fidelity Life Insurance Company (also at this location) provides life, accident, and health insurance; Georgia Casualty and Surety Company (also at this location) provides workers' compensation insurance. **Operations at this facility include:** Administration; Divisional Headquarters. **Listed on:** NASDAQ. **Stock exchange symbol:** AAME. **Annual sales/revenues:** $21 - $50 million. **Number of employees nationwide:** 265.

ATLANTIC SOUTHEAST AIRLINES (ASA)
100 Hartsfield Centre Parkway, Suite 800, Atlanta GA 30354-1356. 404/766-1400. **Fax:** 404/209-0162. **Contact:** Employment Department. **World Wide Web address:** http://www.flyasa.com. **Description:** One of Atlanta's largest regional airlines and a Delta connection carrier. Founded in 1979. **NOTE:** Jobseekers can request an application by sending a self-addressed, stamped envelope to this location. **Corporate headquarters location:** This location. **Other U.S. locations:** Nationwide. **Parent company:** Delta Air Lines. **Listed on:** New York Stock Exchange. **Stock exchange symbol:** DAL. **President:** W.E. Barnette. **Number of employees nationwide:** 5,500.

AUGUSTA SPORTSWEAR
P.O. Box 14939, Augusta GA 30919-0939. 706/860-4633. **Physical address:** 425 Park West Drive, Grovetown GA 30813. **Toll-free phone:** 800/237-6695. **Contact:** Human Resources. **World Wide Web address:** http://www.augustasportswear.com. **Description:** Manufactures a variety of clothing types including slacks, suits, shorts, and jogging suits. The company's products are sold to the public through its two outlet stores, and through companies that purchase and distribute the clothing to retailers.

AUSTIN KELLEY ADVERTISING, INC.
5901 Peachtree, Dunwoody Road, NE, Suite 200C, Atlanta GA 30328. 770/396-6666. **Fax:** 770/396-0301. **Contact:** Maria Beasley. **E-mail address:** maria.beasley@austinkelley.com. **World Wide Web address:** http://www.austinkelley.com. **Description:** A full-service advertising firm. **Office hours:** Monday – Friday, 9:00 a.m. – 5:00 p.m. **Corporate headquarters location:** This location. **President/CEO:** Jay Shields.

AUTOMATED SYSTEMS DESIGN (ASD)
645 Hembree Parkway, Suite D, Roswell GA 30076. 770/740-2300. **Toll-free phone:** 800/CABLING. **Fax:** 603/590-0079. **Contact:** Human Resources. **World Wide Web address:** http://www.asd-usa.com. **Description:** Installs cabling for computer networks. **President:** Bob Eskew. **Number of employees at this location:** 30.

AVON PRODUCTS INC.
425 Horizon Drive, Suwannee GA 30024. 770/271-6100. **Contact:** Human Resources. **World Wide Web address:** http://www.avoncareers.com. **Description:** A direct seller of beauty care products, fashion jewelry, gifts, fragrances, and decorative products. Avon, a *Fortune* 500 company, markets its products through a network of 2.8 million independent sales representatives in 135 countries worldwide. **NOTE:** Salespeople are considered independent contractors or dealers and most work part-time. If you are interested in becoming a sales representative, please call 800/FOR-AVON, or visit the company's Website for more information. Please visit website to search for jobs and apply online. **Positions advertised include:** Customer Service Specialist; Bilingual Customer Service Specialist; Quality Assurance Supervisor. **Special program:** Internships. **Corporate headquarters location:** New York NY. **Other area locations:** Statewide. **Other U.S. locations:** Nationwide. **International locations:** Worldwide. **Listed on:** New York Stock Exchange. **Stock exchange symbol:** AVP. **CEO:** Andrea Jung.

BBDO
3500 Lenox Road NE, Suite 1900, Atlanta GA 30326. 404/231-1700. **Contact:** Debbie Lindner, Director of Personnel. **World Wide Web address:** http://www.bbdo.com. **Description:** Part of a worldwide network of advertising agencies with related businesses in public relations, direct marketing, sales promotion, graphic arts, and printing. **NOTE:** Please visit website to take the Career Questionnaire. **Corporate headquarters location:** New York NY. **Other U.S. locations:** Los Angeles CA; San Francisco CA; Chicago IL; Miami FL; Detroit MI; Minneapolis MN. **International locations:** Worldwide. **Parent company:** BBDO Worldwide operates 156 offices in 42 countries. The company has 83 subsidiaries, affiliates, and associates engaged solely in advertising and related operations. **Number of employees nationwide:** 3,400.

B & E JACKSON
229 Peachtree Street, NE, Suite 300, Atlanta GA 30303. 404/577-4914. **Fax:** 404/577-4419. **Contact:** Edith Jackson, Director of Administration. **E-mail address:** ejackson@bejackson.com. **World Wide Web address:** http://www.bejackson.com. **Description:** A civil engineering firm whose areas of specialty include road design, hydrology studies, civil site design, GIS data manipulation, and urban planning. Founded 1988. **NOTE:** Please send resumes to 34 Peachtree Street NW, Suite 2100, Atlanta GA 30303. **Corporate headquarters location:** This location. **President:** Birdel F. Jackson.

BFI WASTE SYSTEMS
3045 Bankhead Highway NW, Atlanta GA 30318-4405. 404/792-2660. **Contact:** Human Resources. **World Wide Web address:** http://www.alliedwaste.com. **Description:** BFI is engaged primarily in the collection and disposal of solid wastes for commercial, industrial, and residential customers, landfill services, waste-to-energy programs, hazardous waste removal, and liquid waste removal. The company has worldwide operations at more than 500 facilities. **Corporate headquarters location:** Scottsdale AZ. **Parent company:** Allied Waste Industries, Inc. **Operations at this facility include:** This location hauls waste and provides waste services such as portable toilets for commercial and residential markets. **Listed on:** New York Stock Exchange. **Stock exchanges symbol:** AW. **CEO:** Thomas H. Van Weelden.

BHA GROUP, INC.
Route 2, Box 1840, Folkston GA 31537. 912/496-2583. **Physical address:** Highway 121 South, Folkston GA. **Contact:** Human Resources. **E-mail address:** hr@bha.com. **World Wide Web address:** http://www.bhagroup.com. **Description:** Designs, manufactures, and sells replacement parts and accessories for electrostatic precipitators and baghouses, and provides rehabilitation and conversion services for the types of industrial air pollution control equipment it produces. As a fully-integrated company, BHA Group manufactures mechanical and electrical products and has a full range of engineering and service capabilities. **NOTE:** Please send resumes to BHA Group Holdings Inc, 8800 East 63rd Street, Kansas City MO 64133, or fax to 816/358-8091. If you plan to e-mail your resume, please do not include it as an attachment – place it in the text of your e-mail. **Positions advertised include:** Product Engineer. **Corporate headquarters location:** Kansas City MO. **Other U.S. locations:** Nationwide. **International locations:** Worldwide. **Listed on:** NASDAQ. **Stock exchange symbol:** BHAG. **President/CEO:** James E. Lund.

BJC MEDICAL CENTER
70 Medical Center Drive, Commerce GA 30529. 706/335-1000. **Fax:** 706/335-7701. **Recorded jobline:** 706/335-1114. **Contact:** Human Resources. **E-mail address:** manglin@bjcmc.org. **World Wide Web address:** http://www.bjcmc.org. **Description:** A full-service medical center. BJC Medical Center comprises a 109-bed hospital facility and a 90-bed nursing facility. **NOTE:** Human Resources phone is 706/335-1108. **Positions advertised include:** RN – Various Departments; LPN; Certified Nursing Assistant; ARRT Registered Technician – Radiology; Controller; Housekeeping Technician; Floor Technician; Dietary Aide; Purchaser/Buyer – Materials Management. **Office hours:** Monday – Friday, 8:00 a.m. – 4:30 p.m. **Corporate headquarters location:** This location.

BP FABRICS AND FIBERS COMPANY
260 The Bluff, Austell GA 30168. 770/941-1711. **Fax:** 770/944-4745. **Contact:** Human Resources. **E-mail address:** fabrics.info@usa.com. **World Wide Web address:** http://www.fabricsandfibers.com. **Description:** BP Fabrics and Fibers Company manufactures carpet backing and other nonwoven fabrics. **Corporate headquarters location:** This location. **Other area locations:** Bainbridge GA; Dalton GA; Hazelhurst GA; Nashville GA. **Other U.S. locations:** Roanoke AL; Santa Fe Springs CA; Seneca SC. **International locations:** Brazil; Canada; Germany; Hungary; Mexico. **Parent company:** BP. **Operations at this facility include:** This location houses the executive offices. **Listed on:** New York Stock Exchange. **Stock exchange symbol:** BP. **Number of employees worldwide:** 3,500.

BALLY TOTAL FITNESS
6780 Roswell Road NW, Atlanta GA 30328. 770/392-1861. **Toll-free phone:** 800/FITNESS. **Fax:** 770/392-0229. **Contact:** Jason Rediger. **E-mail address:** jrediger@ballyfitness.com. **World Wide Web address:** http://www.ballyfitness.com. **Description:** One of the world's largest owners and operators of recreational health clubs. **Positions advertised include:** Membership Consultant; Personal Trainer; Child Care Attendant; Group Exercise Instructor; Receptionist; Maintenance Mechanic; Locker Room Attendant; Retail Sales Associate. **Corporate headquarters location:** Chicago IL. **Other area locations:** Roswell GA; Morrow GA; Norcross GA; Tucker GA. **Other U.S. locations:** Nationwide. **Listed on:** New York Stock Exchange. **Stock exchange symbol:** BFT.

BALLY TOTAL FITNESS
3101 Cobb Parkway, Atlanta GA 30339. 770/955-3845. **Toll-free phone:** 800/FITNESS. **Contact:** Human Resources. **World Wide Web address:** http://www.ballyfitness.com. **Description:** One of the world's largest owners and operators of recreational health clubs. **Positions advertised include:** Membership Consultant; Personal Trainer; Child Care Attendant; Group Exercise Instructor; Receptionist; Maintenance Mechanic; Locker Room Attendant; Retail Sales Associate. **Corporate headquarters location:** Chicago IL. **Other area locations:** Roswell GA; Morrow GA; Norcross GA; Tucker GA. **Other U.S. locations:** Nationwide. **Listed on:** New York Stock Exchange. **Stock exchange symbol:** BFT.

BANK OF AMERICA
600 Peachtree Street NE, Atlanta GA 30308. 404/607-4850. **Contact:** Human Resources. **E-mail address:** bankofamericacareers@exult.net. **World Wide Web address:** http://www.bankofamerica.com. **Description:** Bank of America is a full-service banking and financial institution. The company operates through four business segments: Global Corporate and Investment Banking, Principal Investing and Asset Management, Commercial Banking, and Consumer Banking. **NOTE:** Please visit website for online application form. Resumes are kept on file for two years. You may resubmit any time that your resume changes. **Positions advertised include:** Relationship Manager; Trust Research Specialist; Administrative Assistant; Insurance Consultant; Teller; Associate Premier Client Manager; Client Services Manager; Senior Operations Analyst; Consumer Market Executive; Operations Manager; Banking Center Service Manager; GLP Specialist; Merchant Services Field Sales Representative; Portfolio Management Assistant; Private Bank Sales Manager; Premier Client Manager. **Special programs:** Internships. **Office hours:** Monday – Thursday, 9:00 a.m. – 4:00 p.m.; Friday, 9:00 a.m. – 6:00 p.m. **Corporate headquarters location:** Charlotte NC. **Other area locations:** Statewide. **Other U.S. locations:** Nationwide. **International locations:** Worldwide. **Operations at this facility include:** This location is a bank. **Listed on:** New York Stock Exchange. **Stock exchange symbol:** BAC. **Number of employees worldwide:** 143,000.

BANKHEAD ENTERPRISES, INC.
1080 Donald L. Hollowell Parkway NW, Atlanta GA 30318. 404/894-7900. **Contact:** Personnel. **World Wide Web address:** http://www.bankheadcompanies.com. **Description:** A manufacturer and national distributor of auto-carrier trailers, as well as a fabricator of other metal products including hydraulic cylinders. The company also produces asphalt and provides machine job-shopping and paving services. **Other area locations:** Douglasville GA. **Operations at this facility include:** Administration; Divisional Headquarters; Manufacturing.

BARCO PROJECTION SYSTEMS LLC
3240 Town Point Drive, Suite 100, Kennesaw GA 30144. 770/218-3200. **Fax:** 770/218-3250. **Contact:** Human Resources. **World Wide Web address:** http://www.barco.com. **Description:** Barco Projection Systems manufactures overhead projectors and various types of monitors and displays. **NOTE:** Please visit website to search for jobs and apply online. **Positions advertised include:** Sales Assistant; Communications Manager. **Corporate headquarters location:** Belgium. **Other area locations:** Duluth GA; Lawrenceville GA. **Other U.S. locations:** Rancho Cordova CA; Logan UT; Smithville NJ; Beaverton OR; Charlotte NC; Xenia OH. **Number of employees worldwide:** 4,095.

BARD MEDICAL DIVISION
8195 Industrial Boulevard, Covington GA 30014. 770/784-6100. **Toll-free phone:** 800/526-4455. **Fax:** 800/852-1339. **Contact:** Human Resources. **World Wide Web address:** http://www.bardmedical.com. **Description:** A leader in urology medical products, and committed to diagnosing and treating urinary tract infections. **Corporate headquarters location:** Murray Hill NJ. **Parent company:** C.R. Bard. **Listed on:** New York Stock Exchange. **Stock exchange symbol:** BCR.

BARNES & NOBLE BOOKSTORES
7660 North Point Parkway, Suite 200, Alpharetta GA 30022. 770/993-8340. **Contact:** Manager. **World Wide Web address:** http://www.bn.com. **Description:** A bookstore chain operating nationwide. This location also has a cafe and music department. **Office hours:** Monday – Thursday, 9:00 a.m. – 10:00 p.m.; Friday – Saturday, 9:00 a.m. – 11:00 p.m.; Sunday 9:00 a.m. – 9:00 p.m. **Other area locations:** Statewide. **Other U.S. locations:** Nationwide.

BARRY MANUFACTURING
2303 John Glenn Drive, Chamblee GA 30341. 770/451-5476. **Fax:** 770/451-8095. **Contact:** Human Resources. **E-mail address:** employee@bettermenswear.com. **World Wide Web address:** http://www.bettermenswear.com. **Description:** Manufactures and sells suits in 38 retail stores throughout the Southeast. Founded in 1898. **Corporate headquarters location:** This location. **Other U.S. locations:** Southeastern, Southern, and Middle America. **Listed on:** Privately held.

BASSETT FURNITURE INDUSTRIES, INC.
7501 Airport Drive, Macon GA 31297. 478/788-7173. **Contact:** Personnel. **E-mail address:** bassett@bassettfurniture.com. **World Wide Web address:** http://www.bassettfurniture.com. **Description:** Manufactures and sells a full line of furniture for the home. Products include bedroom and dining suites, accent pieces, occasional tables, wall and entertainment units, upholstered sofas, chairs and love seats, recliners, and mattresses and box springs. **Special programs:** Internships. **Corporate headquarters location:** Bassett VA. **Listed on:** NASDAQ. **Stock exchange symbol:** BSET. **President/CEO:** Robert Spilman.

BAUDER COLLEGE
384 Northyards Boulevard NW, Suite 190 and 400, Atlanta GA 30313. 404/237-7573. **Toll-free phone:** 800/241-3797. **Contact:** Human Resources. **World Wide Web address:** http://www.bauder.edu. **Description:** A two-year college offering associate's degrees in business administration, fashion design, merchandising, and interior design.

BEAR, STEARNS & COMPANY, INC.
3424 Peachtree Road NE, Suite 1700, Atlanta GA 30326. 404/842-4000. **Fax:** 404/842-4523. **Toll-free phone:** 800/444-2327. **Contact:** Human Resources. **World Wide Web address:** http://www.bearstearns.com. **Description:** A leading investment banking, securities trading, and brokerage firm. Bear, Stearns & Company, Inc. serves corporations, governments, institutions, and private investors worldwide. The firm's business includes corporate finance, mergers and acquisitions, public finance, institutional equities, fixed income sales and trading, private client services, foreign exchange, future sales and trading, derivatives, and asset management. **NOTE:** Not accepting hard copy resumes for the foreseeable future. Please visit website to search for employment opportunities. **Corporate headquarters location:** New York NY. **Other U.S. locations:** Boston MA; Chicago IL; Dallas TX; Denver CO; Los Angeles CA; San Francisco CA. **International locations:** Worldwide. **Parent company:** The Bear Stearns Companies Inc. also operates Bear, Stearns Securities Corporation, providing professional and correspondent clearing services including securities lending; and Custodial Trust Company, providing master trust, custody, and government securities services. **Listed on:** New York Stock Exchange. **Stock exchange symbol:** BSC. **Annual sales/revenues:** More than $100 million. **Number of employees nationwide:** 10,500.

BEAZER HOMES USA, INC.
5775 Peachtree Dunwoody Road, Suite B-200, Atlanta GA 30342. 404/250-3420. **Fax:** 404/252-1694. **Contact:** Benefits Manager. **World Wide Web address:** http://www.beazer.com. **Description:** One of the nation's largest homebuilders. **NOTE:** Please visit website to search for jobs, apply online, and for more specific contact information. **Positions advertised include:** Internal Auditor; Office Manager; Senior Design Associate; CAD Associate; Senior CAD Associate; Design Associate. **Corporate headquarters location:** This location. **Other U.S. locations:** Nationwide. **Listed on:** New York Stock Exchange. **Stock exchange symbol:** BZH.

BEKAERT STEEL WIRE CORPORATION
301 Darlington Drive, Rome GA 30161. 706/235-4481. **Fax:** 706/235-2160. **Contact:** Human Resources. **E-mail address:** steelcord.rome@bekaert.com. **World Wide Web address:** http://www.bekaert.com. **Description:** Engaged in the manufacture of wire for tirecord, beadwire, and hose reinforcement wire. **Parent Company:** Bekaert. **Other area locations:** Kennesaw GA; Marietta GA. **Corporate headquarters location:** Belgium. **Other U.S. locations:** OH; NC; FL; TN; CA; AR; KY; MI. **International locations:** Worldwide. **Number of employees worldwide:** 17,500.

BELCO ELECTRIC
3118 Marjan Drive, Atlanta GA 30340. 770/455-4556. **Fax:** 770/458-9938. **Contact:** Human Resources. **E-mail address:** joy@belcoinc.com. **World Wide Web address:** http://www.belcoinc.com. **Description:** Electrical contractors and engineers for residential, commercial, and industrial customers. **Positions advertised include:** Electrician; Service Technician; Project Manager Trainee; Administrative Staff. **Corporate headquarters location:** This location.

BELLSOUTH CORPORATION
1155 Peachtree Street NE, Atlanta GA 30309-3610. 404/249-2000. **Recorded jobline:** 800/992-8840. **Contact:** Human Resources. **World Wide Web address:** http://www.bellsouth.com. **Description:** A communications company offering telecommunications, wireless communications, entertainment, e-commerce, and directory advertising services. **NOTE:** Please visit website to search for jobs and apply online. You must apply online to be eligible for employment. Mailed and faxed resumes are not accepted. **Positions advertised include:** Administrative Assistant; Associate Accountant Executive; Customer Operations Business Analyst; Manager – Product Marketing; Network Sales Engineer; Senior Data Entry Operator; Web Designer; Windows Architect/Programmer; Communications Specialist. **Corporate headquarters location:** This location. **Listed on:** New York Stock Exchange. **Stock exchange symbol:** BLS.

BEST MANUFACTURING COMPANY
P.O. Box 8, Menlo GA 30731-0008. 706/862-2302. **Physical address:** 579 Edison Street, Menlo GA 30731. **Contact:** Human Resources. **World Wide Web address:** http://www.bestglove.com. **Description:** Manufactures protective gloves for medical and industrial use. **Corporate headquarters location:** This location. **Other area locations:** Rome GA. **Other U.S. locations:** Moss Point AL; Fayette AL; Johnson City TN; Fall River MA; Guatemala CA. **International locations:** Canada; Belgium. Number of employees worldwide: 2,000.

BEULAH HEIGHTS BIBLE COLLEGE
892 Berne Street SE, Atlanta GA 30316. 404/627-2681. **Toll-free phone:** 888/777-2422. **Fax:** 404/627-0702. **Contact:** Human Resources. **E-mail address:** humanresources@beulah.org. **World Wide Web address:** http://www.beulah.org. **Description:** A Bible college offering two- and four-year undergraduate degrees as well as graduate degrees. The college has approximately 450 students enrolled. Founded 1918. **NOTE:** Human Resources is Extension 250. **President:** Dr. Benson M. Karanja.

BIO-LAB WATER ADDITIVES
P.O. Box 30002, Lawrenceville GA 30049-1002. 678/502-4000. **Physical address:** 1735 North Brown Road, Lawrenceville GA 30042. **Toll-free phone:** 800/600-4523. **Fax:** 678/502-4708. **Fax:** 404/371-0373. **Contact:** Human Resources. **World Wide Web address:** http://www.wateradditives.com. **Description:** Produces alkalis and chlorine. **NOTE:** Search and apply for jobs online. **Corporate headquarters location:** This location. **Other area locations:** Conyers GA; Decatur GA. **Other U.S. locations:** Lake Charles LA; Adrian MI. **International locations:** Worldwide. **Parent company:** Great Lakes Chemical. **Annual sales/revenues:** More than $100 million. **Listed on:** New York Stock Exchange. **Stock exchange symbol:** GLK. **Number of employees at this location:** 170.

BIO-LAB INC.
1700 Old Covington Highway SW, Conyers GA 30012-3996. 770/483- 2600. **Fax:** 770/922-0719. **Contact:** Human Resources. **World Wide Web address:** www.wateradditives.com. **Description:** Produces alkalis and chlorine. **NOTE:** Search and apply for jobs online. **Corporate headquarters location:** Decatur GA. **Other U.S. locations:** Lake Charles LA; Adrian MI. **Operations at this facility include:** This location is the company's principal manufacturing facility. **Parent company:** Great Lakes Chemical. **Annual sales/revenues:** More than $100 million. **Listed on:** New York Stock Exchange. **Stock exchange symbol:** GLK.

BLUE BIRD CORPORATION
P.O. Box 937, Fort Valley GA 31030. 478/825-2021. **Physical address:** 402 Blue Bird Boulevard, Fort Valley GA. **Toll-free phone:** 800/486-7122. **Fax:** 478/822-2457. **Contact:** Human Resources. **E-mail address:** hr@blue-bird.com. **World Wide Web address:** http://www.blue-bird.com. **Description:** Manufactures school and commercial buses and recreational vehicles. The company also provides financial services in the form of leasing agreements to its customers. **NOTE:** For information on employment, please visit the Georgia Department of Labor website, at http://www.dol.state.ga.us. **Parent company:** Henlys Group plc. **Number of employees worldwide:** 3,000.

BLUE CROSS AND BLUE SHIELD OF GEORGIA
3350 Peachtree Road NE, Atlanta GA 30326. 404/842-8000. **Contact:** Human Resources. **World Wide Web address:** http://www.bcbsga.com. **Description:** Offers healthcare to thousands of individuals in Georgia. **Positions advertised include:** Senior HR Associate; Business Operations Analysis Specialist; Business Data Architecture Manager; Disability Case Manager; Associate Medical Director; Director of Disease Management. **Parent company:** WellPoint owns and operates several healthcare companies, including Blue Cross of California, Blue Cross and Blue Shield of Missouri, Blue Cross and Blue Shield of Wisconsin, HealthLink, Unicare, Golden West Dental & Vision, PrecisionRx, WellPoint Behavioral Health, WellPoint Dental Services, WellPoint Pharmacy Management, and WellPoint Workers' Compensation Managed Care Services. **Corporate headquarters location:** This location. **Other area locations:** Columbus GA. **Listed on:** New York Stock Exchange. **Stock exchange symbol:** WLP.

BOB'S CANDIES
P.O. Box 3170, Albany GA 31706. 229/430-8300. **Physical address:** 1315 West Oakridge Drive, Albany GA 31707. **Fax:** 229/430-8331. **Contact:** Human Resources. **World Wide Web address:** http://www.bobscandies.com. **Description:** Manufactures candy canes and other peppermint candies.

WILLIAM L. BONNELL COMPANY, INC.
P.O. Box 428, Newnan GA 30263. 770/253-2020. **Physical address:** 25 Bonnell Street, Newnan GA 30263. **Fax:** 770/254-7708. **Contact:** Human Resources. **E-mail address:** HRUSA@bonlalum.com. **World Wide Web address:** http://www.bonlalum.com. **Description:** Manufactures and distributes a wide range of extruded aluminum shapes. **Other U.S. locations:** IN;TN. **International locations:** Canada. **Parent company:** Tredegar Industries (Richmond VA). **Operations at this facility include:** Administration; Divisional Headquarters; Manufacturing; Sales. **Listed on:** New York Stock Exchange. **Stock exchange symbol:** TG.

BOOZ ALLEN HAMILTON, INC.
230 Peachtree Street, Suite 2100, Atlanta GA 30303. 404/658-8000. **Fax:** 404/577-5709. **Contact:** Human Resources. **World Wide Web address:** http://www.bah.com. **Description:** A diversified, international management consulting organization offering services in both the commercial and public sectors. Areas of expertise include technology, strategy, and planning, as well as social research and many other technical fields. Specific services include corporate strategy and long-range planning, organization design, human resources management, financial management and control, acquisitions and divestiture, information systems and automation, manufacturing, inventory and distribution control, qualitative and quantitative market research, attitudinal and demographic trend research, marketing strategy and positioning, venture management, transportation and environmental systems, technology research, new products and process development, government programs, and regulatory compliance. **NOTE:** Please visit website to register, search for jobs, and apply online. Online application is the preferred method of applying. **Corporate headquarters location:** McLean VA. **Other area locations:** Augusta GA. **Other U.S. locations:** Nationwide. **International locations:** Worldwide. **Number of employees worldwide:** 14,000.

BORAL BRICKS INC.
123 Davis Road, Augusta GA 30906. 706/722-6831. **Toll-free phone:** 800/288-6871. **Contact:** Human Resources Director. **World Wide Web address:** http://www.boralbricks.com. **Description:** A distributor of structural clay bricks.

ROBERT BOSCH CORPORATION
855 Camp Creek Parkway, Atlanta GA 30336. 404-346-6900. **Contact:** Human Resources. **World Wide Web address:** http://www.boschusa.com. **Description:** Robert Bosch Corporation operates in three groups: Automotive-Original Equipment, Industrial Group, and Sales-Automotive Aftermarket. The largest segment of the company's business is the Automotive Group, which includes products such as antilock braking systems (ABS), airbag electronics, fuel injectors, and oxygen sensors. The Industrial Group consists of the Packaging Machinery Division (selling high-technology packaging equipment, primarily to the food processing and pharmaceutical industries); the Surftran Division (offering a range of deburring services, as well as manufacturing, selling, and servicing cleaning equipment); and Weldun International, Inc. (manufactures flexible assembly systems and automation products and assembles machinery for the Packaging Machinery Division). The Sales Group handles automotive aftermarket, mobile communications, and household goods. **NOTE:** Please visit website to submit resume online. The company regularly uses staffing agencies. Call HQ for name and contact information for specific agencies. **Corporate headquarters location:** Broadview IL. **Other U.S. locations:** Nationwide. **Operations at this facility include:** This location is a manufacturer of starters and alternators for automotive use. **Subsidiaries include:** Robert Bosch Fluid Power Corporation designs, produces, and markets hydraulic pumps, valves, and power units, and sells a full line of pneumatic products. **Number of employees worldwide:** 21,750.

BOWNE OF ATLANTA, INC.
1570 Northside Drive NW, Atlanta GA 30318. 404/350-2000. **Fax:** 404/350-2001. **Contact:** Human Resources. **World Wide Web address:** http://www.bowne.com. **Description:** A financial and corporate printer. **NOTE:** Please visit website to search for jobs and apply online. **Corporate headquarters location:** New York NY. **Other U.S. locations:** Nationwide. **Listed on:** New York Stock Exchange. **Stock exchange symbol:** BNE. **President/CEO:** Robert M. Johnson.

BOY SCOUTS OF AMERICA
P.O. Box 440728, Kennesaw GA 30160. 770/421-1601. **Contact:** Personnel. **World Wide Web address:** http://www.scouting.org. **Description:** The national scouting organization for young adults. **Corporate headquarters location:** Irving TX. **Other U.S. locations:** Nationwide. **Operations at this facility include:** Regional Headquarters. **Number of employees nationwide:** 3,950.

BOY SCOUTS OF AMERICA – ATLANTA AREA COUNCIL
1800 Circle 75 Parkway SE, Atlanta GA 30339. 770.989-8820. **Fax:** 770/989-8820. **Contact:** Makeda Moring. **World Wide Web address:** http://www.atlantabsa.org. **Description:** The local Atlanta Council for the Boy Scouts of America.

BOYS & GIRLS CLUBS OF AMERICA
1230 West Peachtree Street NW, Atlanta GA 30309. 404/487-5700. **Toll-free phone:** 800/854-CLUB. **Contact:** Human Resources Department. **E-mail address:** info@bgca.org. **World Wide Web address:** http://www.bgca.org. **Description:** A private, nonprofit organization providing developmental programs for disadvantaged young people. **NOTE:** Please visit website to search for jobs and apply online. Volunteer positions are also available. **Positions advertised include:** Federal Grants Compliance Auditor; Director – Teen Services; Senior Director – Delinquency Prevention; Supply Services Assistant; Warehouse Assistant; Program Assistant – Urban Services; Regional Service Director; Marketing Manager; Health PE Director; Director of Operations. **Corporate headquarters location:** This location. **Other U.S. locations:** Nationwide. **President:** Roxanne Spillet.

BRIGHT HOUSE
8 Puritan Mill, 916 Lowery Boulevard, Atlanta GA 30318. 404/240/2500. **Fax:** 404/240-2501. **Contact:** Human Resources. **E-mail address:** careers@brighthouse.com. **World Wide Web address:** http://www.brighthouse.com. **Description:** An ideation firm specializing in strategic thinking, trend analysis, repositioning, forecasting, new product development, and experiential marketing for business.

BROWN INDUSTRIES
P.O. Box 1103, Dalton GA 30722. **Physical address:** 205 West Industrial Boulevard, Dalton GA 30720. 706/277-1977. **Toll-free phone:** 800/241-4698. **Fax:** 706/277-3379. **Contact:** Human Resources. **World Wide Web address:** http://www.brownind.com. **Description:** Provides printing services on a variety of fabrics including paper, board, and iron-on labels. Creates merchandising systems and marketing solutions to many

industries, specializing in the floorcovering industry. Founded 1958. **Corporate headquarters location:** This location. **Subsidiaries include:** Brown Printing; Gregory Graphics; Foremost Forms & Labels; Brown Display & Fixture; Dalton Display & Wire; General Sample; Tufted Sample; Nationwide Sample; Southern Blinders; Brown Industries Distribution Services. **Number of employees nationwide:** 600.

BUCKHEAD AMERICA CORPORATION
Northpark Town Center, Building 500, 1100 Abernathy Road NE, Suite 1210, Atlanta GA 30328. 770/393-2662. **Toll-free phone:** 800/432-7992. **Contact:** Human Resources. **E-mail address:** celbers@buckheadamerica.com. **World Wide Web address:** http://www.buckheadamerica.com. **Description:** Engaged in hotel franchising, hotel management, settlement, and mortgage services. **Corporate headquarters location:** This location. **Subsidiaries include:** Country Hearth Inn is a mid-sized hotel chain.

BWAY CORPORATION
8607 Roberts Drive, Suite 250, Atlanta GA 30350. 770/645-4800. **Fax:** 770/645-4810. **Contact:** Human Resources. **E-mail address:** hr@bwaycorp.com. **World Wide Web address:** http://www.bwaycorp.com. **Description:** Manufactures container products such as cans, pails, and drums for paints and thinners, chemicals, turpentine, adhesives, insecticides, edible oils, and food products. Brockway Standard, Inc. also produces a variety of stamped metal products including metal boxes sold primarily to the Department of Defense for uses such as ammunition boxes. **Corporate headquarters location:** This location. **Other area locations:** Homerville GA. **Other U.S. locations:** Chicago IL; Cincinnati OH; Dallas TX; Fontana CA; Memphis TN; Picayune MS; Trenton NJ; York PA. **CEO:** Jean-Pierre Ergas. **Number of employees at this location:** 500. **Number of employees nationwide:** 2,000.

BYERS ENGINEERING COMPANY
6285 Barefield Road, NE, Atlanta GA 30328. 404/843-1000. **Fax:** 404/843-2278. **Contact:** Human Resources. **E-mail address:** careers-engineering@byers.com. **World Wide Web address:** http://www.byers.com. **Description:** A technical services firm serving the telecommunications and utilities industries. Founded in 1971. **NOTE:** Please visit website to download employment application. **Positions advertised include:** ROW/BICS; Software Data Service Provider. **Corporate headquarters location:** This location. **Founder & CEO:** Kenneth G. Byers, Jr. **Number of employees nationwide:** 300.

CB RICHARD ELLIS
3340 Peachtree Road, Suite 1050, Atlanta GA 30326. 404/923-1200. **Fax:** 404/923-1550. **Contact:** Human Resources. **E-mail address:** cbrejobs@cbre.com. **World Wide Web address:** http://www.cbrichardellis.com. **Description:** A real estate services company offering property sales and leasing; property and facility management; mortgage banking; and investment management services. **NOTE:** The company has three other Atlanta offices. Please visit website to register, search for jobs, and apply online. **Positions advertised include:** Senior Real Estate Analyst; Administrative Assistant; Marketing Assistant; Research Assistant; Transaction Coordinator; Building Engineer; Transaction Manager; Sales Professional. **Corporate headquarters location:** Los Angeles CA. **Other U.S. locations:** Nationwide. **Listed on:** New York Stock Exchange. **Stock exchange symbol:** CBG. **CEO:** Raymond Wirta. **Number of employees worldwide:** 13,500.

CKS PACKAGING
P.O. Box 44386, Atlanta GA 30336-4386. 404/691-8900. **Physical address:** 445 Great Southwest Parkway, Atlanta GA 30336. **Fax:** 404/691-0086. **Contact:** Human Resources. **World Wide Web address:** http://www.ckspackaging.com. **Description:** A plastic bottle manufacturer. Founded in 1985. **Other U.S. locations:** TX; KS; FL; SC; NC.

CNN (CABLE NEWS NETWORK)
One CNN Center, Atlanta GA 30303. 404/827-1700. **Contact:** Human Resources. **World Wide Web address:** http://www.cnn.com/jobs. **Description:** A cable news network. CNN has 28 bureaus worldwide and provides 24-hour news programming worldwide. Programming includes international, domestic, and business news; sports; weather; special reports; and topical programming. **NOTE:** Please visit http://www.turner.com/jobs to register, search for jobs, and apply online. **Positions advertised include:** Regional Coordinator; Supervising Producer; Executive Administrative Assistant; Producer; Production Assistant; Video Journalist; Content Sales/Business Development; Advanced Software Developer; Senior Project Manager; Advanced Quality Assurance; Technical Writer; Manager – Newsroom Operations; Vendor Relations Administrator; Associate Production Support Specialist; Local Ad Sales Promotions Manager; Receptionist; Client Systems Engineer; Editor; Staff Accountant; Recruiter; Database Administrator; VP – Business Operations. **Corporate headquarters location:** This location. **Parent Company:** AOL Time Warner. **Operations at this facility include:** Administration; Divisional Headquarters; Sales. **Listed on:** New York Stock Exchange. **Stock exchange symbol:** AOL.

CSC CONSULTING
2 Ravinia Drive, Suite 1150, Atlanta GA 30346. 770/677-3200. **Contact:** Human Resources. **World Wide Web address:** http://www.csc.com. **Description:** An independent provider of information technology consulting, systems integration, and outsourcing to industry and government. The company's services include management consulting as well as education and research programs in the strategic use of information resources and the design, engineering, development, integration, installation, and operation of computer-based systems and communications systems. CSC also provides consumer credit-related services, automated systems for health care organizations, financial insurance services, and data processing services. The company's principal markets are the U.S. federal government, U.S. commercial markets, and various international markets. Founded in 1959. **Positions advertised include:** Application Development Manager; Programmer Analyst; Strategic Management Specialist; Business Developer; System Administrator; Technician; Application Developer; Application Designer. **Corporate headquarters location:** El Segundo CA. **Listed on:** New York Stock Exchange. **Stock exchange symbol:** CSC. **Number of employees worldwide:** 90,000.

CAGLE'S INC.
2000 Hills Avenue NW, Atlanta GA 30318. 404/355-2820. **Fax:** 404/352-7353. **Contact:** Lavon Waite, Human Resources. **World Wide Web address:** http://www.cagles.net. **Description:** Produces, markets, and distributes a variety of fresh and frozen poultry products. Its operations consist of the breeding, hatching, and raising of chickens, feed milling, processing, and marketing. **Corporate headquarters location:** This location. **Other area locations:** Dalton GA; Rockmart GA; Pine Mountain Valley GA. **Other U.S. locations:** AL; KY. **Subsidiaries include:** Cagle's Farms, Inc. **CEO:** J. Douglas Cagle. **Number of employees nationwide:** 4,100.

CAGLE'S INC.
14075 Pine Mountain, Highway 116, Pine Mountain Valley GA 31213. 706/628-4251. **Contact:** O'Neal Shaw, Human Resources. **World Wide Web address:** http://www.cagles.net. **Description:** This location processes poultry. Cagle's produces, markets, and distributes a variety of fresh and frozen poultry products. Its operations consist of the breeding, hatching, and raising of chickens, feed milling, processing, and marketing. **Corporate headquarters location:** Atlanta GA. **Other area locations:** Dalton GA; Rockmart GA. **Other U.S. locations** AL; KY. **CEO:** J. Douglas Cagle. **Number of employees nationwide:** 4,100.

CALDWELL TANKS ALLIANCE, INC.
P.O. Box 608, Newnan GA 30264. 770/253-3232. **Physical address:** 57 East Broad Street, Newnan GA 30263. **Contact:** Human Resources. **Description:** Produces large-scale steel products including steel oil storage tanks, primarily for the process industries and utilities. **NOTE:** Unsolicited resumes not accepted.

CANDLER HOSPITAL
ST. JOSEPH'S/CANDLER HEALTH SYSTEM
5353 Reynolds Street,, Savannah GA 31419. 912/819-6000. **Toll-free phone:** 800/569-5463. **Fax:** 912/692-6662. **Contact:** Human Resources. **World Wide Web address:** http://www.stjosephs-candler.org. **Description:** A hospital. **NOTE:** Entry-level positions and second and third shifts are offered. Resumes should be mailed to 11700 Middleground Road, Savannah GA 31419. **Positions advertised include:** Department Secretary; Legal Secretary; Scheduling Specialist; Insurance Representative; Pharmacy Technician; Imaging Transcriptionist; Clinical Manager; Operations Manager; Nurse Manager; Program Director; Health Information Manager; Loss Prevention Manager; House Supervisor; LPN – Various Departments; RN – Various Departments. . **Annual sales/revenues:** $51 - $100 million. **President/CEO:** Paul P. Hinchey.

CARAUSTAR
P.O. Box 115, Austell GA 30168. 770/948-3100. **Physical address:** 3200 Joe Jenkins Boulevard, Austell GA 30106-3227. **Contact:** Human Resources. **E-mail address:** info@caraustar.com. **World Wide Web address:** http://www.caraustar.com. **Description:** A regional manufacturer and distributor of boxboard, paper box, and tubing products. **NOTE:** Applications are accepted in-person at this location Monday – Friday, 8:00 a.m. – 3:00 p.m. **Positions advertised include:** Export Worker. **Corporate headquarters location:** This location. **Other U.S. locations:** Nationwide. **International locations:** Mexico; Canada; United Kingdom. **Listed on:** NASDAQ. **Stock exchange symbol:** CSAR.

CARE USA
151 Ellis Street NE, Atlanta GA 30303. 404/681-2552. **Fax:** 404/589-2651. **Contact:** Human Resources. **World Wide Web address:** http://www.careusa.org. **Description:** An independent, nonprofit, cooperative organization. CARE USA is a member of CARE International, an umbrella organization that coordinates the program activities of the member organizations. CARE's purpose is to help the developing world's poor in their efforts to achieve social and economic well-being. CARE offers disaster relief, technical assistance, training, food, and other material resources and management in combinations appropriate to local needs and priorities. CARE also advocates public policies and programs that support these services. Founded in 1945. **NOTE:** Volunteer programs are also available. Please visit website to register, search for jobs, and apply online. **Positions advertised include:** Sexual and Reproductive Health Team Leader; Senior Advisor – Inter-Agency CG. **Office hours:** Monday - Friday, 8:30 a.m. - 5:00 p.m. **Corporate headquarters location:** This location. **Other U.S. locations:** Nationwide. **International locations:** Worldwide.

CARLISLE
P.O. Box 309, Bowdon GA 30108. 770/258-5551. **Fax:** 770/258-3901. **Contact:** Irene Abernathy, Personnel Manager. **E-mail address:** irenea@carlisletire.com. **World Wide Web address:** http://www.carlisletire.com. **Description:** Manufactures and distributes a wide range of molded rubber and plastic products, such as tires and wheels for the lawn and garden industries. **Corporate headquarters location:** This location. **Operations at this facility include:** Administration; Manufacturing; Research and Development; Sales; Service.

CARMIKE CINEMAS
P.O. Box 391, Columbus GA 31902-0391. 706/576-3400. **Physical address:** 1301 1st Avenue, Columbus GA 31901. **Fax:** 706/576-3441. **Contact:** Human Resources. **World Wide Web address:** http://www.carmike.com. **Description:** An operator of motion picture theaters in the United States. **Corporate headquarters location:** This location. **Listed on:** NASDAQ. **Stock exchange symbol:** CKEC. **Other U.S. locations:** Nationwide.

CARTER & ASSOCIATES INC.
1275 Peachtree Street NE, Atlanta GA 30309. 404/888-3000. **Fax:** 404/888-3006. **Contact:** Barbara Jones. **E-mail address:** bjones@carterusa.com. **World Wide Web address:** http://www.carterusa.com. **Description:** Engaged in the development, management, and sale of commercial real estate. **NOTE:** For employment information, call 404/888-3158. **Corporate headquarters location:** This location. **Other U.S. locations:** AL; FL: NC; TN. **CEO:** Bob Peterson.

CARVER BIBLE INSTITUTE & COLLEGE
P.O. Box 4335, Atlanta GA 30302. 404/527-4520. **Physical address:** 437 Nelson Street, Atlanta GA 30313. **Fax:** 404/527-4526. **Contact:** Robert Crummie, President. **World Wide Web address:** http://www.carverbiblecollege.edu. **Description:** A two- and four-year college with more than 100 undergraduates enrolled. **Listed on:** Privately held.

CDM
2030 Powers Ferry Road, Suite 325, Atlanta GA 30339. 770/952-8643. **Fax:** 770/952-9893. **Contact:** Human Resources. **World Wide Web address:** http://www.cdm.com. **Description:** A consulting, engineering, construction and operations firm aiding its clients in improving the environment in numerous ways. Founded 1947. **NOTE:** Please visit website to search for jobs and apply online. **Positions advertised include:** Environmental Engineer. **Corporate headquarters location:** Cambridge MA. **Other U.S. locations:** Nationwide. **International locations:** Worldwide. **Number of employees worldwide:** 3,600.

CENTER BROTHERS INCORPORATED
45 Ross Road, Savannah GA 31405. 912/232-6491. **Contact:** Human Resources. **Description:** Engaged in commercial, interior drywall installation as well as acoustical ceiling construction.

CERTAINTEED CORPORATION
425 Athena Drive, Athens GA 30601. 706/546-9005. **Contact:** Human Resources. **World Wide Web address:** http://www.certainteed.com. **Description:** Operates in three business segments: Building Materials, including roofing products, vinyl siding, and door and sash products; Fiberglass Products, including thermal and acoustical insulation, and a wide range of other fiberglass products; and Piping Products, which produces pipes used in industrial, irrigation, sewer, mining, construction, and manufacturing applications. A second major area facility in Savannah produces asphalt

building and roofing materials. **Office hours:** Monday – Friday, 7:30 a.m. - 6:30 p.m. **Corporate headquarters location:** Valley Forge PA. **Other U.S. locations:** Nationwide. **Parent company:** Saint-Gobain. **Operations at this facility include:** Produces fiberglass insulation products and bonded matting products for use in construction. **Parent company:** Saint-Gobain. **Number of employees nationwide:** 7,200.

CESSNA AIRCRAFT COMPANY
4800 Cargo Drive, Columbus GA 31907. 706/569-2100. **Recorded jobline:** 316/517-6155. **Contact:** Human Resources. **E-mail address:** cessnajobs@cessna.textron.com. **World Wide Web address:** http://www.cessna.com. **Description:** Cessna Aircraft Company is engaged in the engineering, fabrication, assembly, and marketing of commercial and business aircraft. **NOTE:** Please submit resumes to corporate office, at P.O. Box 7704 D837 MP, Wichita KS 67277-7704, or fax to 316/517-1432. **Corporate headquarters location:** Wichita KS. **Operations at this facility include:** This location manufactures aircraft wings and related parts through sheet metal fabrication.

CHAPARRAL BOATS INC.
P.O. Box 928, Nashville GA 31639. 229/686-7481. **Physical address:** 300 Industrial Park Boulevard, Nashville GA. **Fax:** 229/686-3660. **Contact:** Human Resources. **World Wide Web address:** http://www.chaparralboats.com. **Description:** Manufactures over 25 fiberglass boats ranging from runabouts to luxury cruisers.

CHECKFREE CORPORATION
4411 East Jones Bridge Road, Norcross GA 30092. 678/375-3387. **Contact:** Human Resources. **World Wide Web address:** http://www.checkfreecorp.com. **Description:** Provides a wide range of services and products that enable consumers, businesses, and financial institutions to conduct business over the Internet. CheckFree operates in three divisions: Electronic Commerce, Investment Services, and Software. Founded in 1981. **NOTE:** Please visit website to search for jobs and apply online. No phone calls regarding employment. **Positions advertised include:** Applications Specialist; Senior Business Process Consultant; Director Database Engineer; Revenue Accounting Manager; Insurance Sales Specialist; VP of Marketing, Strategy, and Business Development; Event Manager; Staff Project Manager; Senior Network Engineer; Software Engineer; Senior Database Administrator; Regional Sales Manager; Facilities Engineer; Manager of Operations; Project Manager; Six Sigma Black Belt; Corporate Business Continuity Program Manager. **Corporate headquarters location:** This location. **Other U.S. locations:** Nationwide. **International locations:** Canada, United Kingdom. **Listed on:** NASDAQ. **Stock exchange symbol:** CKFR. **Number of employees worldwide:** 3,300.

CHEVRON PRODUCTS U.S.A.
2300 Windy Ridge Parkway, Suite 800, Atlanta GA 30339. 770/984-3000. **Contact:** Human Resources. **World Wide Web address:** http://www.chevrontexaco.com. **Description:** An international oil firm with operations in more than 90 countries. Chevron is engaged in worldwide integrated petroleum operations including the exploration and production of crude oil and natural gas reserves; the transportation of crude oil, natural gas, and petroleum products by pipeline, tanker, and motor equipment; the operation of oil-refining complexes; and the wholesale and retail marketing of hundreds of petroleum products. **NOTE:** Please visit website to register, search for jobs, and apply online. **Corporate headquarters location:** San Francisco CA. **Other U.S. locations:** Nationwide. **Parent company:** Chevron Texaco. **Listed on:** New York Stock Exchange. **Stock exchange symbol:** CVX. **Number of employees worldwide:** 53,000.

CHILDREN'S HEALTHCARE OF ATLANTA
1600 Tullie Circle, Atlanta GA 30329. 404/325-6000. **Fax:** 404/929-8615. **Recorded jobline:** 404/929-8640. **Contact:** Human Resources. **E-mail address:** jobapplicants@choa.org. **World Wide Web address:** http://www.choa.org. **Description:** A children's hospital. **NOTE:** Volunteer positions are also available. Please visit website to register, search for jobs, and apply online. **Positions advertised include:** Lead Patients Access Specialist; Diet Clerk/Typist; Patient Care Technician; Bill Editor; Public Relations Coordinator; Writer/Editor; Director of Logistics; Unit Secretary; Customer Service Ambassador. . **Operations at this facility include:** Administration; Service. **Listed on:** Privately held. **Number of employees nationwide:** 5,250.

CHRISTIAN CITY
7290 Lester Road, Union City GA 30291-2317. 770/964-3301. **Fax:** 770/964-7041. **Recorded jobline:** 770/964-3301, Ext. 773. **Contact:** Human Resources Department. **E-mail address:** milliec@christian-city.org. **World Wide Web address:** http://www.christiancity.org. **Description:** A nonprofit company operating a home for children, retirement homes, a convalescent center, and an Alzheimer's care center. Founded in 1964. **NOTE:** Volunteer positions, entry-level positions and second and third shifts are offered. **Company slogan:** Multiple ministries. One mission. **Positions advertised include:** Activity Aids; Administrative Support; Chaplain; Courtesy Officers; Dietary Staff; Foster Parents; Housekeeping; Laundry Worker; Maintenance Worker; LPN; RN; CNA; Social Worker. **Special programs:** Summer Jobs. **Corporate headquarters location:** This location. **Listed on:** Privately held. **President/CEO:** Robert L. Crutchfield. **Number of employees at this location:** 400.

CHUBB GROUP INSURANCE
Two Live Oak Center, Suite 900, 3445 Peachtree Road NE, Suite 900, Atlanta GA 30326-1276. 404/266-4000. **Fax:** 404/264-6862. **Contact:** Angela Alper, Human Resources Manager. **World Wide Web address:** http://www.chubb.com. **Description:** A property and casualty insurance provider. The company's main business is underwriting property, casualty, marine, personal, and financial services insurance worldwide. **NOTE:** Please visit website to search for jobs, and to find more specific contact information. **Positions advertised include:** Casualty Litigation Examiner; Claims Assistant; Professional Lines Specialist; Worker's Compensation Lost Time Adjuster. **Corporate headquarters location:** Warren NJ. **Other U.S. locations:** Nationwide. **International locations:** Worldwide. **Listed on:** New York Stock Exchange. **Stock exchange symbol:** CB. **CEO:** John D. Finnegan. **Number of employees worldwide:** 12,000.

CIBA VISION CORPORATION
11460 Johns Creek Parkway, Duluth GA 30097. 678/415-3937. **Contact:** Staffing Specialist. **World Wide Web address:** http://www.cibavision.com. **Description:** Engaged in the research, development, manufacture, and sale of soft contact lenses and contact lens care products. **NOTE:** Please visit website to search for jobs and apply online. **Positions advertised include:** Business Planning Analyst; Category Manager; Channel Marketing Manager; Consumer Marketing Manager; Document Management Representative; Global Marketing Director; Manager – North American Credit; Manager – Academic Development; Payroll Administrator; Senior Administrative Assistant; Process Engineer; Patent Attorney. **Corporate headquarters location:** This location. **Other U.S. locations:** IL. **International locations:** Worldwide. **Parent company:** Novartis. **Operations at this facility include:** Administration; Manufacturing; Research and Development; Sales; Service. **Listed on:** New York Stock Exchange. **Stock exchange symbol:** NVS.

CITIFINANCIAL
8420 Abercom Street, Savannah GA 31406. 912/927-4295. **Contact:** Human Resources. **E-mail address:** jobs@citifinancial.com. **World Wide Web address:** http://www.citifinancial.com. **Description:** CitiFinancial offers loans including: bill consolidation, home equity, home improvement, and student. Citifinancial has more than 21,000 offices in the United States and Canada. Founded in 1912. **NOTE:** Please visit website to register, search for jobs, and apply online. **Positions advertised include:** Customer Service Representative. **Parent company:** Citigroup. **Other area locations:** Statewide. **Other U.S locations:** Nationwide. **International locations:** Canada. **Listed on:** New York Stock Exchange. **Stock exchange symbol:** C. **Number of employees worldwide:** 13,000.

CITIFINANCIAL
1345 South Park Street, Carrollton GA 30117. 770/834-7768. **Contact:** Human Resources. **E-mail address:** jobs@citifinancial.com. **World Wide Web address:** http://www.citifinancial.com. **Description:** CitiFinancial offers loans including: bill consolidation, home equity, home improvement, and student. Citifinancial has more than 21,000 offices in the United States and Canada. Founded in 1912. **NOTE:** Please visit website to register, search for jobs, and apply online. **Positions advertised include:** Branch Manager Trainee. **Parent company:** Citigroup. **Other area locations:** Statewide. **Other U.S locations:** Nationwide. **International locations:** Canada. **Listed on:** New York Stock Exchange. **Stock exchange symbol:** C. **Number of employees worldwide:** 13,000.

CITIZENS TRUST BANK
75 Piedmont Avenue, Suite 268, Atlanta GA 30303. 404/653-2818. **Fax:** 404/653-2851. **Contact:** Human Resources. **E-mail address:** jobs@ctbatl.com. **World Wide Web address:** http://www.ctbatl.com. **Description:** A full-service banking and financial institution offering checking, savings, and investment accounts, as well as loans, asset management, and credit card products to consumer and commercial clients. **Positions advertised include:** Mortgage Loan Officers; Investment Representatives; Junior Underwriter; Administrative Assistant; ATM Coordinator; Banking Specialist Associates; Teller. **Office hours:** Monday – Friday, 9:00 a.m. – 4:00 p.m. **Corporate headquarters location:** This location. **Other area locations:** Decatur GA; Lithonia GA; Atlanta GA; Columbus GA; East Point GA; Stone Mountain GA. **Other U.S. locations:** AL.

CLAYTON COLLEGE & STATE UNIVERSITY
5900 North Lee Street, Morrow GA 30260. 770/961-3400. **Contact:** Human Resources. **World Wide Web address:** http://www.clayton.edu. **Description:** A four-year state university enrolling nearly 6,000 students. **NOTE:** Human Resources phone is 770/961-3540. Please visit website to see job listings and to download application form. A separate application must be submitted for each position applied for. **Positions advertised include:** Head Women's Basketball Coach; Head Men's Soccer Coach; Instructor – Various Departments; Faculty – Various Departments.

CLEVELAND ELECTRIC COMPANY
1281 Fulton Industrial Boulevard NW, Atlanta GA 30336. 404/696-4550. **Toll-free phone:** 800/282-7150. **Fax:** 404/696-2849. **Contact:** Human Resources. **E-mail address:** jeffv@clevelandgroup.com. **World Wide Web address:** http://www.clevelectric.com. **Description:** Performs electric motor repair and services; and electrical, mechanical, and civil contracting. **NOTE:** There are two Atlanta office locations. Applicants are asked to fax a cover letter and resume for consideration. **Corporate headquarters location:** This location. **Other area locations:** Macon GA. **Number of employees at this location:** 2,150.

CLUB CAR, INC.
P.O. Box 204658, Augusta GA 30917-4658. 706/863-3000. **Toll-free phone:** 800/258-2227. **Fax:** 706/863-5805. **Recorded jobline:** 706/868-3890. **Contact:** Staffing Coordinator. **World Wide Web address:** http://www.clubcar.com. **Description:** Club Car, Inc. manufactures and markets four-wheel gasoline- and electric-powered golf carts and utility vehicles. **NOTE:** Entry-level positions and second and third shifts are offered. Please visit http://www.irco.com/careers/index.html to search for jobs. **Positions advertised include:** Accountant; Administrative Coordinator; Human Resources Generalist; Leasing Administration Coordinator; Logistics Planner; Manager – Design Engineer; Material Planner; Product Program Manager; Sales Order Coordinator. **Corporate headquarters location:** This location. **Parent company:** Ingersoll-Rand. **Operations at this facility include:** This location serves as the divisional headquarters. **Listed on:** NASDAQ. **Stock exchange symbol:** IR. **Annual sales/revenues:** More than $100 million. **Number of employees at this location:** 850. **Number of employees nationwide:** 1,000.

COASTAL COMMUNICATIONS
P.O. Box 1909, Hinesville GA 31310. 912/368-3300. **Physical address:** 115 Patriots Trail Hinesville GA. **Contact:** Human Resources. **World Wide Web address:** http://www.coastalnow.com. **Description:** Provides telephone service to customers throughout the area. **Corporate headquarters location:** This location. **Parent company:** Madison River Communications.

THE COCA-COLA COMPANY
P.O. Box 1734, Atlanta GA 30301. 404/676-2121. **Physical address:** One Coca-Cola Plaza NW, Atlanta GA 30310. **Contact:** Human Resources. **World Wide Web address:** http://www.coca-cola.com. **Description:** The Coca-Cola Company manufactures concentrates and syrups that are sold to bottlers and wholesalers. Brand names include Coca-Cola, Diet Coke, Coca-Cola light (international), Sprite, Diet Sprite, Mr. PiBB, Mello Yello, Fanta, TAB, Fresca, Fruitopia, Powerade, and Minute Maid. The Coca-Cola Company owns 100 supporting brands around the world including PowerAde, Aquarius, Hi-C, Georgia (canned coffee, sold in Japan), Thums Up & Limca (India), Sparletta Brands (South Africa), Nestea (distributed by Coca-Cola Enterprises Inc.)., and Seiryusabo (Japan). **NOTE:** Internships and part-time work is regularly available. Please visit website to search for jobs and apply online. **Positions advertised include:** Senior Auditor; Senior Research Manager; Senior Accountant; Security Officer; Legal Secretary; Senior Administrative Specialist; Project Chemist; Corporate Strategic Analyst; Cold Drink Technical Manager; Global Innovation Pipeline Analyst; Senior Innovation Manager; Area Service Coordinator; Customer Service Representative. **Corporate headquarters location:** This location. **Subsidiaries include:** Coca-Cola Enterprises Inc. is one of the world's largest sellers of juice and juice-related products under brands such as FiveAlive, Hi-C, Bright & Early, Bacardi, and Coca-Cola Foods. **Listed on:** New York Stock Exchange. **Stock exchange symbol:** KO.

COCA-COLA ENTERPRISES INC.
P.O. Box 723040, Atlanta GA 31139-0040. 770/989-3000. **Physical address:** 2500 Windy Ridge Parkway, Atlanta GA 30339. **Contact:** Human Resources. **World Wide**

Web address: http://www.cokecce.com. Description: Markets, distributes, and produces bottled and canned, nonalcoholic beverages. The company operates approximately 400 facilities, over 40,000 vehicles and more than 1.5 million vending machines, beverage dispensers, and coolers. The product line includes traditional carbonated soft drinks, still and sparkling waters, juices, isotonics, and teas. Positions advertised include: Warehouse Lead; Senior Executive Secretary; Senior Administrative Assistant; Delivery Driver Trainee; Senior Auditor; Organizational Development Specialist; Property Damage Claims Supervisor; Internal Audit Manager; Project Manager. Corporate headquarters location: This location. Other U.S. locations: Nationwide. Listed on: New York Stock Exchange. Stock exchange symbol: CCE. Number of employees nationwide: 72,000.

COLLIERS, CAUBLE & COMPANY
1349 West Peachtree Street, NE, Two Midtown Plaza, Suite 1110, Atlanta GA 30309. 404/888-9000. Fax: 404/870-2845. Contact: Human Resources. World Wide Web address: http://www.colliers.com. Description: Provides services and consultation to users and owners of commercial real estate. Maintains more than 250 offices in 51 countries. Founded in 1967. Corporate headquarters location: Boston MA. Other U.S. locations: Nationwide. International locations: Worldwide. Parent company: Colliers International.

COLLINS & AIKMAN CORPORATION
100 Brady Road, Americus GA 31709. 229/924-6111. Fax: 912/924-6237. Contact: Human Resources. World Wide Web address: http://www.colaik.com. Description: Manufactures RIM and RRIM fascia and injection-molded parts for Chrysler and other members of the automotive industry. Founded in 1977. NOTE: Please send resume to corporate office at 250 Stephenson Highway, Troy MI 48083, or call 248/824-1613. Special programs: Internships. Office hours: Monday – Friday, 8:00 a.m. – 5:00 p.m. Corporate headquarters location: Troy MI. Listed on: New York Stock Exchange. Stock exchange symbol: CKC. Number of employees worldwide: 23,000.

COLONIAL BANK
1041 Windy Hill Road, Smyrna GA 30080. 770/431-0500. 770/436-2421. Contact: Human Resources. World Wide Web address: http://www.colonialbank.com. Description: A full-service savings and loan bank. Positions advertised include: Regional Utility Worker; Credit Analyst; Senior Commercial Lending Officer. Corporate headquarters location: Montgomery AL. Other area locations: Statewide. Other U.S. locations: AL; FL; NV; TN; TX. Listed on: New York Stock Exchange. Stock exchange symbol: CNB.

COLONIAL GROUP
P.O. Box 576, Savannah GA 31402-0576. 912/236-1331. Physical address: 101 North Latrop Avenue, Savannah GA 31415. Toll-free phone: 800/944-3835. Fax: 912/235-3868. Contact: Human Resources. E-mail address: info@colonialgroupinc.com. World Wide Web address: http://www.colonialgroupinc.com. Description: Supplies petroleum through a pipeline to companies in New Jersey. Office hours: Monday – Friday, 8:00 a.m. – 5:00 p.m. Subsidiaries include: Colonial Oil Industries; Colonial Terminals; Georgia Kaolin Terminals; Enmark Stations; Chatham Towing Company; Colonial Energy; Colonial Chemical Solutions; Colonial Marine Industries; Compliance Systems.

COLONIAL PIPELINE COMPANY
P.O. Box 1624, Alpharetta GA 30009-9934. 678/762-2200. Physical address: 1185 Sanctuary Parkway, Suite 100, Alpharetta GA 30004-4738. Toll-free phone: 800/275-3004. Contact: Personnel. E-mail address: careers@colpipe.com. World Wide Web address: http://www.colpipe.com. Description: Supplies petroleum through a pipeline to companies in New Jersey. NOTE: Please visit website to search for open positions. Positions advertised include: Utility B Operator; Electrical Engineer; Mechanical Engineer; Computer Programmer; Associate Controller; Accountant; Administrative Support Specialist. Corporate headquarters location: This location. President/CEO: Dave Lemmon.

COLORGRAPHIC COMMUNICATIONS CORPORATION
P.O. Box 80448, Atlanta GA 30366. 770/455-3921. Physical address: 5980 Peachtree Road, Atlanta GA 30341. Toll-free phone: 877/943-3843. Contact: Human Resources. World Wide Web address: http://www.colorgraphic.net. Description: Manufactures graphic adapter boards that allow split screens on computers. Office hours: Monday – Friday, 9:00 a.m. – 5:30 p.m.

COLUMBIA THEOLOGICAL SEMINARY
P.O. Box 520, Decatur GA 30031-0520. 404/378-8821. Physical address: 701 Columbia Drive, Decatur GA 30030. Fax: 404/377-9696. Contact: Ms. Jeannie Brady, Human Resources Administrator. E-mail address: bradyj@ctsnet.edu. World Wide Web address: http://www.ctsnet.edu. Description: A theological seminary. President: Laura S. Mendenhall. NOTE: Contact Human Resources directly at 404/678-4654.

COLUMBIAN CHEMICALS COMPANY
1800 West Oak Commons Court, Marietta GA 30062. 770/792-9400. Toll-free phone: 800/235-4003. Contact: Human Resources. E-mail address: achapple@phelpsd.com. World Wide Web address: http://www.columbianchemicals.com. Description: One of the world's top producers of furnace carbon black and iron oxides. Parent company: Phelps Dodge Corporation.

COMMUNICATIONS 21
834 Inman Village Parkway, Suite 150, Atlanta GA 30307. 404/814-1330. Fax: 404/814-1332. E-mail address: jobs@c21pr.com. Contact: Human Resources. World Wide Web address: http://www.c21pr.com. Description: A full service marketing and public relations firm, specializing in media relations, marketing campaigns and brand development. Positions advertised include: Full-time and part-time PR professionals. Special programs: Internships. Corporate headquarters location: This location.

COMPREHENSIVE COMPUTER CONSULTING (CCC)
7000 Central Parkway, Suite 1000, Atlanta GA 30328. 770/512-0100. Toll-free phone: 888/451-1136. Fax: 770/512-0101. Contact: Human Resources Department. World Wide Web address: http://www.cccupclose.com. Description: Provides businesses with long-term, contract computer consultants. Founded 1978. NOTE: CCC uses the following Websites to post job listings: Computerjobs.com; and Dice.com. You may also submit your resume at their website by completing the online form. Positions advertised include: NET Developer; AutoLisp/AutoCad Developer; Capacity Planner; Digital System Installation & Operations Expert; Enterprise IT Architect; Functional Peoplesoft Consultant; Help Desk Personnel; Infrastructure/Network/SAN Analyst; Java/WebSphere Developer; Network Architect; Oracle Programmer. Corporate headquarters location: This location. Other U.S. locations: AL; NC; TX.

COMPUTER & CONTROL SOLUTIONS, INC. (CCSI)
2050 Mount Industrial Boulevard, Tucker GA 30084. 770/491-1131. Toll-free phone: 800/959-3525. Fax: 770/493-7033. Contact: Human Resources. E-mail address: hr@rackmountequipment.com. World Wide Web address: http://www.ccsisystems.com. Description: Provides systems integration services. Positions advertised include: Sales Personnel; Assembly Technician; Repair Technician.

COMPUTER ASSOCIATES INTERNATIONAL, INC.
2300 Windy Ridge Parkway, Suite 575, Atlanta GA 30339. 770/953-9276. Contact: Human Resources. World Wide Web address: http://www.ca.com. Description: Computer Associates International is one of the world's leading developers of client/server and distributed computing software. The company develops, markets, and supports enterprise management, database and applications development, business applications, and consumer software products for a broad range of mainframe, midrange, and desktop computers. The company serves major business, government, research, and educational organizations. Founded in 1976. NOTE: Please visit website to search for jobs, and to find more specific contact information. Positions advertised include: Consultant; Principal Consultant; Senior Consultant; Vice President – Finance and Administration; Account Director. Corporate headquarters location: Islandia NY. Other U.S. locations: Nationwide. International locations: Worldwide. Operations at this facility include: This location sells software and provides technical support. Listed on: New York Stock Exchange. Stock exchange symbol: CA. President/CEO: Sanjay Kumar. Number of employees nationwide: 17,000.

COMPUTER HORIZONS CORPORATION
3340 Peachtree Road NE, Suite 160, Atlanta GA 30326. 404/814-3777. Toll-free phone: 800/662-3971. Fax: 404/814-3788. Contact: Human Resources. World Wide Web address: http://www.computerhorizons.com. Description: A full-service technology solutions company offering contract staffing, outsourcing, re-engineering, migration, downsizing support, and network management services. Founded 1969. Office hours: Monday - Friday, 9:00 a.m. - 5:00 p.m. Corporate headquarters location: Mountain Lakes NJ. Other U.S. locations: Nationwide. International locations: Canada; India. Listed on: NASDAQ. Stock exchange symbol: CHRZ. President/CEO: William J. Murphy. Number of employees worldwide: 3,000.

COMPUTER INTELLIGENCE2, INC.
220 Galleria Parkway, Suite 200, Atlanta GA 30339. 770/425-2267. Toll-free phone: 888-657-3278. Fax: 770/425-1338. Contact: Human Resources. World Wide Web address: http://www.ci2.com. Description: Provides computer based technologies and services. Corporate headquarters location: This location. Other U.S. locations: Washington, D.C. CEO & President: W. Andrella Baylis.

COOPER LIGHTING
P.O. Box 1207, Americus GA 31709. 229/924-8000. Physical address: 1101 Southerfield Road, Americus GA 31719. Contact: Personnel. E-mail address: americus.recruit@lighting.com. World Wide Web address: http://www.cooperlighting.com. Description: Manufactures industrial lighting products, fixtures, and related products. Positions advertised include: Advanced Electronics Project Manager; Mechanical Project Engineer; Graphic Artist. Parent company: Cooper Industries. Corporate headquarter location: Peachtree City GA. Other area locations: Ellaville GA; Norcross GA; Preston GA. Other U.S. locations: Nationwide. International locations: Worldwide. President: David Feldman. Number of employees worldwide: 28,000.

COOPERATIVE BAPTIST FELLOWSHIP
P.O. Box 4343, Macon GA 31208-4343. 478/742-1191. Fax: 478/742-6150. Contact: Human Resources. E-mail address: contact@cbfga.org. World Wide Web address: http://www.cbfga.org. Description: A foundation dedicated to providing support to Baptist churches around the world and to providing missionaries. Corporate headquarters location: This location. Other area locations: Statewide.

CORAM HEALTHCARE CORPORATION
2140 Newmarket Parkway, Suite 106, Marietta GA 30067. 770/952-3021. Fax: 770/952-6840. Contact: Human Resources. World Wide Web address: http://www.coram-healthcare.com. Description: One of the nation's largest home health infusion therapy companies. The company provides a wide range of services including ambulatory and home infusion therapies, nutrition services, lithotripsy, hemophilia management, transplant services, and prescription services. NOTE: Please send resumes to corporate office at 1675 Broadway, Suite 900, Denver CO 80202, or fax to 303/672-8733. Be sure to mention what job you are applying for. Positions advertised include: Clinical Pharmacist; Purchasing Representative. Corporate headquarters location: Denver CO. Other U.S. locations: Nationwide. International locations: Canada. President/CEO: Daniel Crowley. Number of employees worldwide: 4,000.

CORPORATE RESOURCE DEVELOPMENT
400 Galleria Parkway, Suite 1500, Atlanta GA 30339. 770/772-4273. Fax: 770/754-7828. Contact: Human Resources. E-mail address: outcomes@crdatlanta.com. World Wide Web address: http://www.crdatlanta.com. Description: Provides marketing consulting services for management, sales, and marketing industries. The company also develops differentiation strategies for companies selling and marketing products identical to those of their competition.

COTT BEVERAGES
1000 10th Avenue, Columbus GA 31901. 706/660-9223. Fax: 706/571-9189. Contact: Human Resources. E-mail address: cottcolumbusresumes@cott.com. World Wide Web address: http://www.cott.com. Description: Produces and distributes a variety of beverages including soft drinks and water. NOTE: Please visit website to apply online. Positions advertised include: Accounts Payable Coordinator Compounding; Manager; Maintenance Mechanic. Corporate headquarters location: Ontario, Canada. Other U.S. locations: Nationwide. International locations: Canada; United Kingdom; Mexico. Listed on: New York Stock Exchange. Stock exchange symbol: COT. Number of employees nationwide: 1,400.

COTTON STATES INSURANCE GROUP
P.O. Box 105303, Atlanta GA 30348-5303. 770/391-8600. Physical address: 244 Perimeter Center Parkway NE, Atlanta GA 30346. Toll-free phone: 800/-282-6536. Contact: Human Resources Department. World Wide Web address: http://www.cottonstatesinsurance.com. Description: A group of insurance providers whose main services are individual life products. Members of the group include Cotton States Life Insurance Company, Cotton States Mutual Insurance Company, Shield Insurance Company, and Cotton States Investment Company. NOTE: Please visit website to apply online. Corporate headquarters location: This location. Other area locations: Statewide. Other U.S. locations: AL; FL; KY; TN. Subsidiaries include: CS Marketing Resources Inc.; CSI Brokerage Services, Inc. Listed on: NASDAQ. Stock exchange symbol: CSLI. President/CEO: J. Ridley Howard. Number of employees nationwide: 250.

COTTRELL INC.
2125 Candler Road, Gainesville GA 30507. 770/532-7251. Toll-free phone: 866/299-2690. Fax: 770/535-2831. Contact: Sean Blair, Human Resources. E-mail address:

sblair@cottrelltrailers.com. **World Wide Web address:** http://www.cottrelltrailers.com. **Description:** The world's largest manufacturer of car hauling equipment. Founded 1975. **Corporate headquarters location:** This location.

COX COMMUNICATIONS
P.O. Box 105357, Atlanta GA 30348. 404/843-5000. **Physical address:** 1400 Lake Hearn Drive NE, Atlanta GA 30319. **Contact:** Human Resources. **World Wide Web address:** http://www.cox.com. **Description:** A decentralized communications company specializing in mass media communication such as radio and television broadcasting, cable television, and print media. **NOTE:** Please visit website to search for jobs and apply online. Electronically submitted resumes are preferred. **Corporate headquarters location:** This location. **Other U.S. locations:** Nationwide. **Listed on:** New York Stock Exchange. **Stock exchange symbol:** COX. **Number of employees nationwide:** 22,000.

CRAWFORD & COMPANY
P.O. Box 5047, Atlanta GA 30302. 404/256-0830. **Physical address:** 5620 Glenridge Drive, Atlanta GA 30342. **Toll-free phone:** 800/241-2541. **Fax:** 404/847-4028. **Contact:** Human Resources. **E-mail address:** employment@us.crawco.com. **World Wide Web address:** http://www.crawfordandcompany.com. **Description:** A diversified services firm providing claims, risk management, health care management, and risk control services to insurance companies, self-insured corporations, and governmental entities. Founded in 1941. **NOTE:** Human Resources phone is 404/847-4080. All hiring for adjusters is done at the local branch office level. Staffing for home office support personnel is done at the above address. Please visit website to search for jobs, and to apply online. **Positions advertised include:** SAN/Storage Administrator; Unix Administrator; Database Administrator; Web Site Technical Developer. **Corporate headquarters location:** This location. **Other U.S. locations:** Nationwide. **International locations:** Worldwide. **Listed on:** New York Stock Exchange. **Stock exchange symbol:** CRDA; CRDB. **CEO:** Grover L. Davis. **Number of employees worldwide:** 10,000.

CRIDER'S POULTRY
P.O. Box 1218, Metter GA 30439. 912/562-4435. **Physical address:** 24 Rountree, Suite 5, Metter GA. **Toll-free phone:** 800/348-8449. **Fax:** 912/562-9286. **Contact:** Human Resources. **E-mail address:** info@cridercorp.com. **World Wide Web address:** http://www.cridercorp.com. **Description:** Engaged in poultry dressing operations. **Corporate headquarters location:** This location. **Other area locations:** Metter GA; Stillmore GA. **Operations at this facility include:** Manufacturing. **Number of employees nationwide:** 575.

CROWNE PLAZA HOTEL
1325 Virginia Avenue, Atlanta GA 30344. 404/768-6660. **Fax:** 404/766-6121. **Contact:** Judith Kruzich, Director of Human Resources. **World Wide Web address:** http://www.crowneplaza.com. **Description:** A 379-room hotel with several conference and meeting facilities. **NOTE:** Please visit http://www.ichotelsgroup.new-jobs.com to search for jobs and apply online. **Positions advertised include:** Corporate Group Sales Manager; Loss Prevention Manager; Controller; Assistant Banquet Manager; Director of Catering/Senior Catering Sales Manager. **Parent company:** InterContinental Hotels Group. **Listed on:** New York Stock Exchange. **Stock exchange symbol:** IHG. **Number of employees at this location:** 200.

CROWNTEX
P.O. Box 47, Wrightsville GA 31096. 478/864-2704. **Physical address:** Industrial Parkway, Wrightsville GA. **Fax:** 478/864-3076. **Contact:** Human Resources. **Description:** Manufactures men's and women's pants and slacks. Crowntex works on a contract-only basis for several companies nationwide. **Corporate headquarters location:** This location. **Number of employees at this location:** 250.

CRYOLIFE
1655 Roberts Boulevard NW, Kennesaw GA 30144. 770/419-3355. **Toll-free phone:** 800/438-8285. **Fax:** 770/426-0031. **Contact:** Human Resources Manager. **World Wide Web address:** http://www.cryolife.com. **Description:** A biomedical laboratory specializing in cryopreserved transplantable human tissues as well as the development and production of bio-adhesives. Founded in 1984. **Corporate headquarters location:** This location. **Subsidiaries include:** CryoLife International; CryoLife Europa Ltd. **Listed on:** New York Stock Exchange. **Stock exchange symbol:** CRY. **President/CEO:** Stephen G. Anderson. **Annual sales/revenues:** $51 - $100 million. **Number of employees worldwide:** 400.

CRYSTAL FARMS, INC.
CRYSTAL FARM MILLS, INC.
P.O. Box 7101, Chestnut Mountain GA 30502. 770/967-6152. **Fax:** 770/967-7248. **Contact:** Human Resources. **E-mail address:** info@crystalfarmsga.com. **World Wide Web address:** http://www.crystalfarmsga.com. **Description:** One of the largest egg producers in the state of Georgia, operating a layer complex, a hatchery, two feed mills, and two processing plants. **NOTE:** Please visit the corporate website, http://www.michaelfoods.com, for information on employment opportunities **Corporate headquarters location:** Minneapolis MN. **Parent company:** Michael Foods, Inc.

CRYSTAL SPRINGS PRINT WORKS
P.O. Box 750, Chickamauga GA 30707-0750. 706/375-2125. **Physical address:** 100 Longstreet Avenue, Chickamauga GA. **Contact:** Human Resources. **E-mail address:** textiles@cspwi.com. **World Wide Web address:** http://www.cspwi.com. **Description:** Provides fabrics printing on a contract basis. The company's products include T-shirts, sweatshirts, and jackets.

CSX TRANSPORTATION
1590 Marietta Boulevard, NW, Atlanta GA 30318. 404/350-5383. **Recorded jobline:** 800/521-1658. **E-mail address:** jobs@csxt.com. **Contact:** Human Resources Department. **World Wide Web address:** http://www.csx.com. **Description:** Provides national and international rail service. **Special programs:** Internships; Co-ops. **Corporate headquarters location:** Jacksonville FL. **Parent Company:** CSX Corporation.

DSI
7270 McGinnis Ferry Road, Suwannee GA 30024. 770/449-6300. **Fax:** 770/449-6845. **Contact:** Human Resources. **E-mail address:** info@datasuppliesinc.com. **World Wide Web address:** http://www.datasuppliesinc.com. **Description:** Provides customers with printing services and products including custom forms, notebooks, and memo pads. Founded 1966. **Corporate headquarters location:** Duluth GA. **Other area locations:** Columbus GA; Byron GA; Valdosta GA. **Other U.S. locations:** AL; FL; SC; TN.

DSI
11300 Lakefield Drive, Technology Park, Johns Creek, Duluth GA 30097-1508. 770/476-4455. **Fax:** 770/497-9431. **Contact:** Human Resources. **E-mail address:** info@datasuppliesinc.com. **World Wide Web address:** http://www.datasuppliesinc.com. **Description:** Provides customers with printing services and products including custom forms, notebooks, and memo pads. Founded 1966. **Corporate headquarters location:** This location. **Other area locations:** Suwanee GA; Columbus GA; Byron GA; Valdosta GA. **Other U.S. locations:** AL; FL; SC; TN.

THE FRANK M. DARBY COMPANY
3384 Peachtree Road, Suite 400, Atlanta GA 30326. 404/812-5900. **Fax:** 404/812-5901. **Contact:** Human Resources. **E-mail address:** amontgomery@fmdarby.com. **World Wide Web address:** http://www.fmdarby.com. **Description:** Specializes in the management and leasing of office, industrial, and investment properties in Atlanta. Founded in 1982. **Company slogan:** Signature service. **Corporate headquarters location:** This location. **Listed on:** Privately held. **President:** Frank M. Darby. **Number of employees at this location:** 30.

DATAMATX, INC.
3146 Northeast Expressway NE, Atlanta GA 30341-5345. 770/936-5600. **Toll-free phone:** 800/943-5240. **Fax:** 770/936-5614. **Contact:** Jennifer Hall, Director of Human Resources. **E-mail address:** hr@datamatx.com. **World Wide Web address:** http://www.datamatx.com. **Description:** Provides data processing services, laser printing, and mail services. Founded in 1976. **NOTE:** Entry-level positions are offered. **Other U.S. locations:** Phoenix AZ; Richmond VA. **Operations at this facility include:** Administration; Research and Development; Sales; Service. **Listed on:** Privately held. **Number of employees nationwide:** 170.

DAVOX CORPORATION
CONCERTO SOFTWARE
4450 Rivergreen Parkway, Duluth GA 30096. 770/239-4000. **Fax:** 770/239-4444. **Contact:** Human Resources Manager. **World Wide Web address:** http://www.davox.com. **Description:** Davox Corporation develops, markets, implements, supports, and services outbound and inbound/outbound management systems software for call center operations. Founded 1981. **NOTE:** Please visit website to search for jobs and apply online. **Corporate headquarters location:** Westford MA. **Other U.S. locations:** Irvine CA; Miami FL; Oak Brook IL; Fort Washington PA; Richardson TX. **International locations:** Worldwide. **Operations at this facility include:** This location is a sales office. **President/CEO:** James D. Foy.

DEKALB, COUNTY OF
1300 Commerce Drive, Suite 100, Decatur GA 30030. 404/371-2881. **Contact:** Human Resources. **World Wide Web address:** http://www.co.dekalb.ga.us. **Description:** Government offices of DeKalb County. **NOTE:** Please visit website to search for jobs, and to download an application form or apply online. You can also visit the Maloof Center in Decatur, or visit 755 Camp Drive, or call 404/371-2332 to attain an application. Resumes will not be accepted without an application. **Positions advertised include:** Animal Control Officer, Automotive Body Repair Worker, Commercial Front End Loader/Operator/Trainee; Engineer Principal; Fire and Rescue Program Manager; Fire Protection Engineer; Heavy Equipment Truck Mechanic; HVAC Mechanic Senior; Instrumentation and Controls Specialist; Internal Audit Manager; Landfill Equipment Operator; Landscape Designer; Librarian Senior; Paramedic/Firefighter; Police Officer; Property Appraiser; Quality Investigator Senior; Sanitation Driver Crew Leader and Trainee; Water Maintenance Mechanic Assistant; Water Maintenance Mechanic Senior.

DEKALB OFFICE ENVIRONMENTS
1320 Ridgeland Parkway, Alpharetta GA 30004. 770/360-0200. **Fax:** 770/360-0305. **Contact:** Human Resources Manager. **E-mail address:** humanresources@dekalboffice.com. **World Wide Web address:** http://www.dekalboffice.com. **Description:** Sells office furniture and provides facilities management services including reconfiguration, design, warehousing, project management, installation, and refinishing. **Positions advertised include:** Account Executive. **Corporate headquarters location:** This location. **Operations at this facility include:** Administration; Sales; Service. **President:** John H. Rasper. **Number of employees at this location:** 140.

DEKALB TECHNICAL COLLEGE
1085 Montreal Road Center, Clarkston GA 30021-1360. 404/297-9522. **Fax:** 404/298-3601. **Contact:** Personnel Services. **E-mail address:** employment@dekalbtech.org. **World Wide Web address:** http://www.dekalb.tec.ga.us. **Description:** A technical college offering associate's degrees in a broad range of studies. **NOTE:** Please visit website to search for jobs, find more specific contact information, and to download employment application. **Positions advertised include:** Adjunct Instructor of English; Adjunct Instructor of Psychology; Adjunct Instructor of Speech. **Office hours:** Monday – Friday, 8:00 a.m. – 5:00 p.m. **Other area locations:** Covington GA. **President:** Dr. Paul M. Starnes.

DELOITTE & TOUCHE
191 Peachtree Street, Suite 1500, Atlanta GA 30303. 404/220-1500. **Fax:** 404/220-1583; 888/APPLYDT. **Contact:** Personnel. **E-mail address:** dtcareers@deloitte.com. **World Wide Web address:** http://www.us.deloitte.com. **Description:** An international firm of certified public accountants providing professional accounting, auditing, tax, and management consulting services to widely diversified clients. The company has a specialized program consisting of national industry groups and functional groups that cross industry lines. Groups are involved in various disciplines including accounting, auditing, taxation management advisory services, small and growing businesses, mergers and acquisitions, and computer applications. **NOTE:** There are three Atlanta office locations. Pleas visit website to search for jobs and apply online. **Positions advertised include:** Manager; Administrative Assistant; Operations Manager; Senior Consultant; Energy Knowledge Manager; HR Operations and Technology Consultant; Control Assurance Consultant; Data Quality and Integrity Senior Consultant; Security Web Development Programming Consultant. **Corporate headquarters location:** New York NY. **Other U.S. locations:** Nationwide. **International locations:** Worldwide. **Parent company:** Deloitte. **Number of employees nationwide:** 30,000. **Number of employees worldwide:** 120,000.

DELTA AIR LINES
P.O. Box 20530, Atlanta GA 30320-2530. 404/715-2600. **Recorded jobline:** 800/659-2580. **Contact:** Personnel. **E-mail address:** delta.careers@delta.com. **World Wide Web address:** http://www.delta.com. **Description:** One of the largest airlines in the United States. The company provides scheduled air transportation for passengers, freight, and mail on an extensive route that covers most of the country and extends to 58 foreign nations. The route covers 218 domestic cities in 48 states, the District of Columbia, Puerto Rico, the U.S. Virgin Islands, and 131 cities abroad. Major domestic hubs include the Atlanta, Dallas/Fort Worth, Salt Lake City, and Cincinnati ports, with minor hubs located in Los Angeles and Orlando. Founded in 1929. **NOTE:** Please visit website to search for jobs. E-mailed resumes are preferred. Entry-level positions are offered. **Positions advertised include:** Accountant; Income Tax Analyst; Corporate Communications Manager; Employee and Workplace Safety Manager; International

Logistics Manager; Program Specialist – Market Planning and Intelligence; Project Leader – Finance; Senior Analyst – Financial Planning and Analysis; Senior Change Consultant; Senior Project Manager – Facilities; Senior Propulsion Engineer; Accounting Supervisor; Boarding Gate/Ticket Counter; Ramp Operator; Air Logistic Worker. **Special programs:** Internships; Co-ops. **Corporate headquarters location:** This location. **Subsidiaries include:** Comair Inc.; Southeast Airlines, Inc. **Listed on:** New York Stock Exchange. **Stock exchange symbol:** DAL. **CEO:** Gerald Grinstein. **Number of employees nationwide:** 81,000.

DELTA LIFE INSURANCE COMPANY
4370 Peachtree Road NE, Atlanta GA 30319. 404/231-2111. **Contact:** Human Resources. **World Wide Web address:** http://www.delta-life.com. **Description:** A life, accident, and health insurance company. **Corporate headquarters location:** This location. **Operations at this facility include:** Administration. **Number of employees nationwide:** 1,300.

DENON DIGITAL INDUSTRIES INC.
1380 Monticello Road, Madison GA 30650. 706/342-3425. **Contact:** Foss Hodges, Personnel Manager. **World Wide Web address:** http://www.denon.com. **Description:** Manufactures prerecorded compact discs. Founded in 1910. **Corporate headquarters location:** Pinebrook NJ. **Other U.S. locations:** CA. **International locations:** Worldwide.

THE DEVEREUX GEORGIA TREATMENT NETWORK
1291 Stanley Road NW, Kennesaw GA 30152. 770/427-0147. **Toll-free phone:** 800/342-3357. **Contact:** Michele Washington, Human Resources. **E-mail address:** mwashin2@devereux.org. **World Wide Web address:** http://www.devereux.org. **Description:** Operates a 125-bed, nonprofit, residential facility. The center provides counseling, vocational training, family counseling, and educational services for adolescents between 11 and 17 years of age who exhibit behavior disorders or delinquent behavior. **NOTE:** Please visit website to search for jobs and apply online. **Positions advertised include:** Clinical Therapist; Cook; Direct Care Professional; Head Nurse; Human Resources Assistant; LPN/LVN; RN; Special Education Teacher; Therapeutic Staff Support. **Corporate headquarters location:** Villanova PA. **Other U.S. locations:** Nationwide. **CEO:** Ronald Burd. **Number of employees nationwide:** 4,500.

DIEBOLD, INC.
1890 A West Oak Parkway, Marietta GA 30062. 678/594-5600. **Contact:** Human Resources. **World Wide Web address:** http://www.diebold.com. **Description:** Diebold, Inc. is engaged in the sale, manufacture, installation, and service of automated teller machines, physical and electronic security systems, and software for the financial and commercial industries. Other products include vaults, vault doors, lockers, safes, alarms, video surveillance systems, and data line security systems. Founded in 1859. **Positions advertised include:** Associate Customer Solutions Engineer; Implementation Coordinator. **Corporate headquarters location:** North Canton OH. **International locations:** Worldwide. **Operations at this facility include:** This location is a sales and customer service office. **Listed on:** New York Stock Exchange. **Stock exchange symbol:** DBD. **President/CEO:** Walden O'Dell. **Number of employees worldwide:** 13,000.

DIVERSITECH CORPORATION
2530 Lantrac Court, Decatur GA 30035. 770/593-0900. **Toll-free phone:** 800/397-4823. **Fax:** 770/593-8518. **Contact:** Human Resources. **World Wide Web address:** http://www.diversitech.com. **Description:** Manufactures and distributes concrete pads. **Corporate headquarters location:** This location. **Other area locations:** Conyers GA. **Other U.S. locations:** Columbus TX; Quincy FL; Adelanto CA.

DOGWOOD VETERINARY HOSPITAL
COWETA VETERINARY ASSOCIATES, P.C.
24 Hospital Road, Newnan GA 30263. 770/253-3416. **Fax:** 770/683-3416. **Contact:** Donna Robinson, Office Manager. **E-mail address:** dogwoodvet@mail.newnanutilities.org. **World Wide Web address:** http://www.dogwoodvet.com. **Description:** Offers veterinary care for small and large animals. The small animal services include general medicine, surgery, boarding, and in-house clinical and pathological testing. The large animal services include house and farm calls, pathology testing, surgery, reproductive health, and regulatory testing. **Positions advertised include:** Veterinary Technician; Veterinary Office Staff – Full-time; Office Staff – Part-time; Groomer; Kennel Staff. **Office hours:** Monday – Friday, 8:00 a.m. – 6:00 .m.; Saturday, 8::00 a.m. – 12:00 p.m.

DOLCO PACKAGING CORPORATION
252 Hosea Road, Lawrenceville GA 30245. 770/963-6191. **Fax:** 770/995-7982. **Contact:** Carleen Moscarelli, Personnel Director. **E-mail address:** info@dolco.net. **World Wide Web address:** http://tekni-plex.com/companies/dolco.html. **Description:** Dolco Packaging is a nationwide manufacturer of a wide variety of packaging and packaging materials used by the food and other industries. **Corporate headquarters location:** Somerville NJ. **Other U.S. locations:** IN; TX; WA; OH; CA; TN. **International locations:** Belgium; Argentina; Singapore. **Parent company:** Tekni-Plex Company. **Operations at this facility include:** This facility produces foam packaging trays, egg cartons, and other packaging materials.

RR DONNELLEY
WALLACE COMPUTER SERVICES
100 Wallace Street, Metter GA 30439. 912/685-6878. **Fax:** 912/685-4559. **Contact:** Human Resources Manager. **World Wide Web address:** http://www.rrdonnelley.com. **Description:** The company's products and services include custom business forms that are delivered as continuous tractor-fed forms, cut sheets, and in rolls; paper handling systems for high-speed, nonimpact printing; label products, such as prime labels (product packaging), blank and preprinted pressure-sensitive labels (fanfold, cut-sheet, and roll), thermal labels, labeling machinery and supplies, and label design and printing software; direct mail and promotional printing, personalization/customization, bindery, and mailing; commercial printing of catalogs, price sheets, and directories, as well as electronic catalogs on CD-ROMs and diskettes; direct mail catalogs offering computer and office products, accessories, and supplies under the name Visible Computer Supply; printer ribbons and paper rolls for ATM and POS systems, office machines, and computer printers; TOPS brand office supplies such as legal pads, flipcharts, steno books, phone message pads, and stock forms, sold at retail; electronic forms software; and design and implementation services. The majority of the products, services, and solutions are sold to corporate customers by the company's direct sales force. TOPS products are sold through retail office products outlets, and Visible products are marketed through direct mail catalogs. Founded in 1864. **NOTE:** Please visit website to search for jobs. Entry-level positions and second and third shifts are offered. **Corporate headquarters location:** Chicago IL. **Operations at this facility include:** This location is engaged in the printing of business forms. **Other U.S. locations:** Nationwide. **Listed on:** New York Stock Exchange. **Stock exchange symbol:** RRD. **CEO:** Mark A. Angelson. **Annual sales/revenues:** More than $100 million. **Number of employees nationwide:** 50,000.

DORNIER MEDTECH
1155 Roberts Boulevard, Kennesaw GA 30144. 770/426-1315. **Toll-free phone:** 800/367-6437. **Fax:** 770/426-6115. **Contact:** Human Resources. **E-mail address:** info@dornier.com. **World Wide Web address:** http://www.dornier.com. **Description:** Engaged in the service, sale, and installation of lithotomic, ultrasound, and laser equipment for hospitals and medical facilities. **Corporate headquarters location:** Munich, Germany. **International locations:** Worldwide.

THE DOW CHEMICAL COMPANY
2864 North Dug Gap Road, Dalton GA 30720. 706/277-1133. **Fax:** 706/277-8100. **Contact:** Human Resources. **World Wide Web address:** http://www.dow.com. **Description:** A multinational manufacturer of chemical products used in a wide variety of industries. **NOTE:** Please visit website to search for jobs and apply online. **Corporate headquarters location:** Midland MI. **Other area locations:** Atlanta GA; Marietta GA; Tucker GA. **Other U.S. locations:** Nationwide. **International locations:** Worldwide. **Operations at this facility include:** This location is engaged in producing polyurethane and latex chemicals used for the manufacturing of carpet backing. **Listed on:** New York Stock Exchange. **Stock exchange symbol:** DOW. **CEO:** William S. Stravopoulos. **Number of employees worldwide:** 46,000.

DRAFFIN & TUCKER
2617 Gillionville Road, Albany GA. 229/883-7878. **Contact:** Jeff Wright, Human Resources. **E-mail:** jwright@draffin-tucker.com. **World Wide Web address:** http://www.draffin-tucker.com. **Description:** An accounting firm that serves clients in several southern states, including Georgia, Florida, Alabama, South Carolina, and Texas. Founded 1948.

DUKE-WEEKS REALTY CORPORATION
3950 Shackleford Road, Suite 300, Duluth GA 30096-8268. 770/717-3200. **Fax:** 707/717-3310. **Contact:** Human Resources. **E-mail address:** hr@dukerealty.com. **World Wide Web address:** http://www.dukereit.com. **Description:** A developer and owner of industrial buildings and parks. The company also provides a full range of leasing, management, and construction services for its properties and industrial real estate owned by other parties. **NOTE:** Mail resumes to corporate office, at 600 East 96th Street, Suite 100, Indianapolis IN 46240, or fax to 317/808-6791. **Positions advertised include:** Lease Analyst. **Corporate headquarters location:** Indianapolis IN. **Other U.S. locations:** Eastern U.S. **Listed on:** New York Stock Exchange. **Stock exchange symbol:** DRE. **CEO:** Thomas L. Hefner. **Number of employees worldwide:** 1,050.

DUNLAP SUNBRAND INTERNATIONAL
4405 International Boulevard, Suite B-102, Norcross GA 30093. 678/924-6300. **Toll-free phone:** 800/241-6800. **Fax:** 678/924-6350. **Toll-free fax:** 800/228-7550. **Contact:** Personnel Director. **World Wide Web address:** http://www.dsinternational.com. **Description:** Engaged in the manufacture and distribution of sewing machine parts, a wide range of other related products including pressing and cutting equipment and other supplies and equipment purchased by the apparel and related industries. **Other U.S. locations:** FL; MA; TX; KY; TN; VA. **International locations:** Dominican Republic; Mexico; El Salvador; Honduras; United Kingdom; Canada. **Parent company:** Willcox & Gibb (New York NY) manufactures and markets apparel and textile supplies and equipment. **President:** Bruce McInnis.

DURACELL U.S.A.
1567 Lukken Industrial Drive West, LaGrange GA 30240. 706/884-6171. **Fax:** 706/883-1899. **Contact:** Human Resources. **World Wide Web address:** http://www.duracell.com/home.asp. **Description:** Duracell U.S.A. produces a line of batteries sold worldwide under the Duracell trademark. Battery types include alkaline, zinc, rechargeable, and lithium. The company also manufactures batteries used in hearing aids and photographic and communications equipment. **Corporate headquarters location:** Bethel CT. **Other area locations:** Alpharetta GA. **Other U.S. locations:** Nationwide. **Parent company:** The Gillette Company. **Operations at this facility include:** Nine-volt battery manufacturing. **Listed on:** New York Stock Exchange. **Stock exchange symbol:** G.

DURANGO-GEORGIA PAPER COMPANY
P.O. Box 878, St. Marys GA 31558. 912/882-0100. **Physical address:** 1000 Osborne Street, St. Mary's GA. **Toll-free phone:** 800/624-9657. **Fax:** 912/882-0423. **Contact:** Personnel Department. **World Wide Web address:** http://www.durangopaper.com/eng. **Description:** One of the nation's largest fully-integrated paper products firms. **Other area locations:** Cordele GA; Alpharetta GA. **Other U.S. locations:** TX; NJ. **Parent company:** Corparacion Durango.

EMC CORPORATION
2850 Premiere Parkway, Duluth GA 30097. 770/814-3600. **Fax:** 678/457-0003. **Contact:** Human Resources. **World Wide Web address:** http://www.emc.com. **Description:** EMC Corporation designs, manufactures, markets, and supports high-performance data storage products. The company also provides related services for selected mainframe and mid-range computer systems primarily manufactured by IBM and Unisys. **NOTE:** Please visit website to search for jobs and apply online. You may also mail resumes to corporate office at P.O. Box 65, Nutting Lake MA 01865, or fax to 508/435-8829. **Positions advertised include:** Account Manager; Channel Sales Representative; Senior Account Manager; Software Account Manager; Business Continuity Systems Integrator; Client Solutions Lead; Practice Manager; Managed Services Storage Architect. **Corporate headquarters location:** Hopkinton MA. **Other U.S. locations:** Nationwide. **International locations:** Worldwide. **Operations at this facility:** This is a sales office. **Listed on:** New York Stock Exchange. **Stock exchange symbol:** EMC. **Number of employees nationwide:** 13,100. **Number of employees worldwide:** 23,600.

EMD CHEMICALS
P.O. Box 1206, Savannah GA 31402. 912/964-9050. **Physical address:** 110 EMD Boulevard, Savannah GA 31407. **Fax:** 912/966-1891. **Contact:** Human Resources. **E-mail address:** hr@emdchemicals.com. **World Wide Web address:** http://www.emdchemicals.com. **Description:** Produces paint pigments and other specialty chemical products. **Corporate headquarters location:** Gibbstown NJ. **Other U.S. locations:** NY; OH. **Parent company:** Merck KgaA. **Number of employees worldwide:** 600.

EMAG 3495 Piedmont Road, Building 11, Suite 500, Atlanta GA 30305. 404/995-6060. **Toll-free phone:** 800/364-9838. **Fax:** 404/872-8247. **Toll-free fax:** 800/334-8273. **Contact:** Human Resources. **World Wide Web address:** http://www.emaglink.com. **Description:** EMEG provides document storage solutions, manufactures computer hardware and software, and develops customized financial software. **Corporate headquarters location:** This location. **Other U.S. locations:** NY; CA; TX. **International locations:** United Kingdom. **Operations at this facility include:** This location provides optical disk storage for IBM computers. Optical disks, also called laser disks, store data in the form of text, music, or pictures and are read by a laser that scans the surface. **Office hours:** Monday - Friday, 8:00 a.m. - 6:00 p.m. **Number of employees worldwide:** 200.

ERB INDUSTRIES
P.O. Box 1237, Woodstock GA 30188. 770/926-7944x301. **Physical address:** 1 Safety Way, Woodstock GA 30188. **Contact:** Human Resources. **World Wide Web address:** http://www.erbind.com. **Description:** Engaged in custom plastic molding and mold building, cutting and sewing, and safety equipment. **Corporate headquarters location:** This location. **Other area locations:** Jasper GA. **Operations at this facility include:** Administration; Manufacturing; Sales.

EARTHLINK, INC.
1375 Peachtree Street, Level A, Atlanta GA 30309. 404/815-0770. **Contact:** Human Resources. **World Wide Web address:** http://www.earthlink.net. **Description:** Provides Internet access and Web hosting services to individuals and small businesses. Founded in 1994. **NOTE:** Please visit website to search for jobs and apply online. **Positions advertised include:** Software Engineer; Manager – Broadband Provisioning Applications Development; Solutions Center Tier 2 Analyst; Senior Cost Analyst; Account Manager; Senior Manager – Partner Performance; Client Support Analyst; Technical Writer; Data Analyst; Project Analyst; Manager – Special Projects; Web Developer; Director – Procurement; Training Coordinator; Network Abuse Engineer; Security Analyst; Interface Design Director. **Corporate headquarters location:** This location. **Other U.S. locations:** San Francisco CA; Pasadena CA. **Listed on:** NASDAQ. **Stock exchange symbol:** ELNK.

EASTER SEALS SOCIETY
P.O. Box 847, Dublin GA 31040. 478/275-8850. **Physical address:** 602 Kellam Road, Dublin GA 31021. **Contact:** Human Resources. **World Wide Web address:** http://www.easter-seals.org. **Description:** Provides treatment and support services for disabled individuals. **NOTE:** Please visit website or contact your local office to lean about employment opportunities. **Corporate headquarters location:** Chicago IL. **Other area locations:** Albany GA; Atlanta GA; Augusta GA; Columbus GA; Roswell GA.

EASTMAN KODAK COMPANY
3003 Summit Boulevard, Suite 1100, Atlanta GA 30319. 770/668-0500. **Contact:** Staffing. **World Wide Web address:** http://www.kodak.com. **Description:** A manufacturer and distributor of photography equipment and supplies including film, paper, plates, chemicals, and other products. **NOTE:** Please send resumes to Staffing, 343 State Street, Rochester NY 14650. **Corporate headquarters location:** Rochester NY. **Other U.S. locations:** Nationwide. **Operations at this facility include:** Regional Headquarters. At this location, Eastman Kodak Company also provides related processing services and is engaged in the manufacture and distribution of office copier chemicals. **Listed on:** New York Stock Exchange. **Stock exchange symbol:** EK. **CEO:** Daniel Carp. **Number of employees nationwide:** 39,000. **Number of employees worldwide:** 70,000.

EATON CORPORATION
P.O. Box 819, Toccoa GA 30577. 706/779-3351. **Physical address:** Route 2, Box 361, Meadowbrook Road, Eastanollee GA 30538. **Contact:** Human Resources. **World Wide Web address:** http://www.eaton.com. **Description:** Manufactures aircraft parts including fittings, clamps, couplings, and other fluid-conveying products through sheet metal fabrication. **NOTE:** Please visit website to search for jobs and apply online. **Positions advertised include:** Lead Engineer. **Corporate headquarters location:** Cleveland OH. **Other area locations:** Athens GA; Austell GA; Atlanta GA; Fitzgerald GA; Lithia Springs GA. **Other U.S. locations:** Nationwide. **International locations:** Worldwide. **Listed on:** New York Stock Exchange. **Stock exchange symbol:** ETN. **CEO:** Alexander M. Cutler. **Number of employees worldwide:** 51,000.

EDWARDS BAKING COMPANY
One Lemon Lane NE, Atlanta GA 30307. 404/377-0511. **Toll-free phone:** 800/241-0559. **Contact:** Human Resources. **E-mail address:** hrdept@edwardsbaking.com. **World Wide Web address:** http://www.edwardsbaking.com. **Description:** Produces frozen bakery items. **NOTE:** Jobseekers should send resumes to Human Resources, 6875 Jimmy Carter Boulevard, Suite 3200, Norcross GA 30071. **Corporate headquarters location:** Norcross GA. **Parent company:** Edwards Fine Foods. **Number of employees at this location:** 350.

ELIXIR INDUSTRIES
1300 Pope Drive, Douglas GA 31533. 912/384-2078. **Fax:** 912/384-6480. **Contact:** Human Resources. **E-mail address:** elixirdiv24@elixirind.com. **World Wide Web address:** http://www.elixirind.com. **Description:** Manufactures metal siding, roofing, doors, frame parts, roof vents, and roof domes. Founded 1948. **NOTE:** There are two Douglas offices. **Corporate headquarters location:** Gardena CA. **Other area locations:** Fitzgerald GA 31750. **Other U.S. locations:** Nationwide. **Operations at this facility include:** The Extrusion division (this location) provides service to national and international customer with extrusion product needs, including anodizing, cutting, bending, shearing, machining, heat treating, light assembling, testing, and company-owned trucks. **President:** Christopher A. Sahm. **Number of employees nationwide:** 1,300.

ELESYS NORTH AMERICA, INC.
70 Crestridge Drive, Suite 150, Suwanee GA 30024. 770/904-3400. **Contact:** Human Resources. **E-mail address:** jobs@elesys-na.com. **World Wide Web address:** http://www.elesys-na.com. **Description:** Develops electronic automotive safety systems for automobile manufacturers. **NOTE:** Please visit website to search for jobs and apply online. **Positions advertised include:** Senior Manager, Human Resources. **Office hours:** Monday – Friday, 8:00 a.m. – 4:30 p.m. **Corporate headquarters location:** This location. **Other U.S. locations:** Plymouth MI. **International locations:** Japan. **Operations at this facility include:** Administration; Market Development. **President:** Akio Kobayashi. **Number of employees at this location:** 42. **Number of employees worldwide:** 325.

EMANUEL COUNTY SCHOOLS
P.O. Box 130, 201 North Main, Swainsboro GA 30401. 478/237-6674. **Fax:** 478/237-3404. **World Wide Web address:** http://www.emanuel.k12.ga.us. **Description:** Runs the schools in Emanuel County. **NOTE:** Please visit website to see job listings.

EMERGENCE, INC.
5150 North Royal Atlanta Drive, Atlanta GA 30084. 770/908-5650. **Fax:** 770/908-5673. **Contact:** Human Resources. **World Wide Web address:** http://www.emergencelabs.com. **Description:** Provides turnkey design and creative services to catalog producers. These services include design, layout, copywriting, studio and location photography, and coordinating services. Founded in 2000. **Corporate headquarters location:** Richmond VA. **Other U.S. locations:** Asheville NC. **CEO:** Kelly O'Keefe.

EMORY UNIVERSITY
OXFORD COLLEGE OF EMORY UNIVERSITY
1762 Clifton Road, 2nd Floor, Atlanta GA 30322. 404/727-7611. **Contact:** Employment Division, Human Resources. **World Wide Web address:** http://www.emory.edu. **Description:** An independent, four-year university offering bachelor's, master's, and doctoral degrees in a variety of disciplines. Oxford College was established as an alternative schooling option for freshmen entering Emory University. Oxford College allows students the opportunity to experience life in a small-school atmosphere. All Oxford College students matriculate into Emory University after one year. **NOTE:** Please visit http://emory.hr.emory.edu/careers.nsf to register, search for jobs, and apply online. **Positions advertised include:** Senior Accountant; Administrative Assistant; Admission Advisor; Animal Care Trainee; Applications Developer; Associate Professor – Various Departments; Assistant Professor – Various Departments; Assistant Director of Student Life; Clinical Administrator; Custodian; Cytogen Technologist; Director – Business and Finance; Genetics Counselor; Laboratory Assistant; Landscaper; Librarian; Nurse Practitioner; Post-Doctorate Fellow; Research Specialist- Various Departments; Tumor Registrar. **Office hours:** Monday – Thursday, 9:00 a.m. – 4:00 p.m.; Friday, 9:00 a.m. – 1:00 p.m.

ENGELHARD CORPORATION
P.O. Box 220, Englehard Road, Attapulgus GA 39815. 229/465-3341. **Fax:** 229/465-2258. **Contact:** Personnel Director. **World Wide Web address:** http://www.engelhard.com. **Description:** A diversified firm that manufactures catalysts, paper coatings and fillers, precious metal components and mill products, products for the electronics industry, products for dental and medical requirements, sorbents, suspension agents, lime and industrial extenders, precious metals supply/management/refining, research and development process technology, and new metallurgical specialties. The company operates 25 plants and eight principal mines in the United States and has other facilities located worldwide. **Special programs:** Internships. **Corporate headquarters location:** Iselin NJ. **Other area locations:** Gordon GA; Hartwell GA; McIntyre GA; Savannah GA. **Other U.S. locations:** Nationwide. **International locations:** Worldwide. **Operations at this facility include:** Production of catalysts used by the petroleum industry and clays used by metals-producing industries. **Listed on:** New York Stock Exchange. **Stock exchange symbol:** EC. **CEO:** Barry W. Perry.

ENPLAS U.S.A., INC.
1901 West Oak Circle, Marietta GA 30062. 770/795-1100. **Fax:** 770/795-1190. **Contact:** Human Resources. **World Wide Web address:** http://www.enplasusa.com. **Description:** Manufactures high-precision engineered plastic parts. **Corporate headquarters location:** This location. **Other U.S. locations:** Sunnyvale CA; Chicago IL. **Parent company:** Enplas Corporation.

ENTERTAINMENT PUBLICATIONS
5885 Glenridge Drive, Suite 110, Atlanta GA 30328. 888/231-7283. **Contact:** Human Resources. **World Wide Web address:** http://www.entertainment.com. **Description:** Secures agreements with restaurants, theaters, sports teams, concert venues, hotels, and retail merchandisers to provide subscribers with valuable savings, while creating a forum to stimulate consumer traffic and spending. The *Atlanta Entertainment Guide* is sold by community organizations for fundraising purposes and the Gold C Books are sold by elementary schools for fundraising as well. Entertainment Publications develops and markets discount programs and promotions. Founded in 1962. **NOTE:** Please visit website to search for jobs and apply online. **Positions advertised include:** Regional Key Account Specialist; Account Specialist; Promotions Sales Specialist; Division Business Manager; Customer Service Representative – Temporary. **Corporate headquarters location:** Troy MI. **Other U.S. locations:** Nationwide. **International locations:** Canada. **Operations at this facility include:** Publishes the Atlanta Entertainment Guide and the Gold C Books. **President/CEO:** Alan Bittker. **Number of employees nationwide:** 1,000.

EQUIFAX, INC.
P.O. Box 4081, Atlanta GA 30302. 404/885-8000. **Physical address:** 1550 Peachtree Street NE, Atlanta GA 30309. **Contact:** Human Resources. **World Wide Web address:** http://www.equifax.com. **Description:** Provides a range of financial and information management services, enabling global commerce between buyers and sellers. Equifax operates through Equifax Europe, Equifax Latin America, Knowledge Engineering, North American Information Services, and Payment Services. Operations include consumer credit reporting, collection services, credit card authorization, insurance underwriting, and hospital bill audits. Founded in 1899. **NOTE:** Please visit website to search for jobs and to apply online. **Positions advertised include:** Customer Service Consultant; Telephone Sales Representative; Vice President – Solution Shaping and Pricing; Director of Budget and Financial Analysis; Financial Analyst Senior; Director of Product Innovation; Director of Marketing; Systems Analyst; Associate Consultant; Senior Project Manager; Econometrician. **Corporate headquarters location:** This location. **Other U.S. locations:** Nationwide. **Operations at this facility include:** Administration. **Listed on:** New York Stock Exchange. **Stock exchange symbol:** EFX. **CEO:** Thomas F. Chapman. **Number of employees worldwide:** 4,800.

ERNST & YOUNG LLP
600 Peachtree Street NE, Suite 2800, Atlanta GA 30308-2215. 404/874-8300. **Contact:** Human Resources. **World Wide Web address:** http://www.ey.com. **Description:** A certified public accounting firm that also provides management consulting services. Services include data processing, financial modeling, financial feasibility studies, production planning and inventory management, management sciences, health care planning, human resources, cost accounting, and budgeting systems. **NOTE:** Entry-level positions are also available. Please visit website to search for jobs and apply online. **Positions advertised include:** Risk Management Services Manager; Transaction Tax M&A Senior; Real Estate Advisory Services Manager; Technology Support Specialist; Corporate Finance Analyst; Assurance Manager; Health Sciences Advisory Services Staff; Assistant Director of Software Development. **Corporate headquarters location:** New York NY. **Other U.S. locations:** Nationwide. **International locations:** Worldwide. **Operations at this facility include:** Regional Headquarters. **Number of employees nationwide:** 23,000. **Number of employees worldwide:** 103,000.

ETHICON, INC.
P.O. Box 70, Cornelia GA 30531. 706/778-2281. **Physical address:** 655 Ethicon Circle, Cornelia GA 30531. **Contact:** Human Resources. **World Wide Web address:** http://www.ethiconinc.com. **Description:** Manufactures products for precise wound closure including sutures, ligatures, mechanical wound closure instruments, and related products. The company makes its own surgical needles and provides thousands of needle-suture combinations to surgeons. **Office hours:** Monday – Friday, 8:00 a.m. – 6:00 p.m. **Corporate headquarters location:** Somerville NJ. **Other U.S. locations:** MA; NJ; TX. **International locations:** Mexico; Argentina. **Parent company:** Johnson & Johnson. **Listed on:** New York Stock Exchange. **Stock exchange symbol:** JNJ. **President:** Cliff Holland. **Number of employees worldwide:** 11,000.

GENE EVANS FORD, INC.
4355 Jonesboro Road, Union City GA 30291. 770/964-9801. **Toll-free phone:** 800/992-9801. **Fax:** 770/306-6715. **Contact:** Hiring Coordinator. **World Wide Web address:** http://www.geneevansford.com. **Description:** An automobile dealer. **NOTE:** Please visit website for online application form. **Corporate headquarters location:** This location. **Operations at this facility include:** Sales; Service.

FM GLOBAL
3460 Preston Ridge Road, Suite 400, Building #3, Alpharetta GA 30005. 770/777-3600. **Toll-free phone:** 888/216-9323. **Fax:** 770/777-0414. **Toll-free fax:** 888/216-9327. **Contact:** Human Resources. **World Wide Web address:** http://www.fmglobal.com. **Description:** A loss control service organization, which helps policyholders protect their properties and occupancies from damage caused by fire, wind, flood, and explosion; boiler, pressure vessel, and machinery accidents; and many other insured hazards. **NOTE:** Please visit website to search for jobs and apply online. **Corporate headquarters location:** Johnston RI. **Other U.S. locations:** Nationwide. **International locations:** Worldwide. **President/CEO:** Shivan S. Subramaniam. **Number of employees worldwide:** 5,000.

FAIR, ISAAC AND CO., INC.
3550 Engineering Drive, Suite 160, Norcross GA 30092. 770/810-8000. **Contact:** Dawn Ridz, Human Resources Recruiter. **E-mail address:** dawnridz@fairisaac.com. **World Wide Web address:** http://www.fairisaac.com. **Description:** Develops and provides data management software and services for the consumer credit, personal lines insurance, and direct marketing industries. Founded in 1956. **NOTE:** Contact is located at corporate office. Fax is 858/202-2056. Please visit website to search for jobs and apply online. **Corporate headquarters location:** San Rafael CA. **Other U.S. locations:** Nationwide. **International locations:** Worldwide. **Subsidiaries include:** CRMA Consulting; DynaMark, Inc.; Risk Management Technologies. **Listed on:** New York Stock Exchange. **Stock exchange symbol:** FIC. **President:** Thomas Grudnowski. **Number of employees nationwide:** 2,000.

LEON FARMER & COMPANY
P.O. Box 1352, Athens GA 30603. 706/353-1166. **Physical address:** 100 Rail Ridge Road, Athens GA 30607. **Fax:** 706/369-8922. **Contact:** Tim Mackey, General Manager. **Description:** A wholesale beverage distributor. **Corporate headquarters location:** This location. **Operations at this facility include:** Administration; Sales; Service.

FAYETTEVILLE POLICE DEPARTMENT
105 Johnson Avenue, Fayetteville GA 30214. 770/461-4441. **Contact:** Chief Johnny Roberts, Recruiting. **E-mail address:** jroberts@fayetteville-ga-us.org. **World Wide Web address:** http://www.fayetteville-ga-us.org/Police/Main_Page/police_index.htm. **Description:** Fayetteville's police department. **NOTE:** On weekends and after regular business hours, you may call 770/461-4357. Please visit http://www.fayetteville-ga-us.org/Personnel/Person_index.htm to search for all Fayettville town jobs, and to download an employment application.

THE WARREN FEATHERBONE COMPANY
P.O. Box 383, Gainesville GA 30503. 770/535-3000. **Physical address:** 999 Chestnut Street, Gainesville GA. **Toll-free phone:** 800/253-9476. **Contact:** Director of Human Resources. **Description:** Manufactures and markets infant clothing and related infant care products under the brand name Alexis. **Corporate headquarters location:** This location.

FEDERAL DEPOSIT INSURANCE CORPORATION (FDIC)
10 Tenth Street, NE, Suite 800, Atlanta GA 30309-3906. 678/916-2200. **Toll-free phone:** 800/765-3342. **Contact:** Human Resources Director. **E-mail address:** careersatlanta@fdic.gov. **World Wide Web address:** http://www.fdic.gov. **Description:** One location of the federal bank regulatory agency. Founded 1933. **NOTE:** Please visit website to search for jobs. **Special programs:** Internships; Summer program. **Corporate headquarters location:** Washington DC. **Operations at this facility include:** Regional Headquarters. **Other U.S. locations:** Boston MA; Chicago IL; Dallas TX; Kansas City MO; Memphis TN; New York NY; San Francisco CA. **Number of employees nationwide:** 5,200.

FEDERAL HOME LOAN BANK OF ATLANTA
P.O. Box 105565, Atlanta GA 30348-5565. 404/888-8000. **Physical address:** 1475 Peachtree Street NE, Atlanta GA 30309. **Toll-free phone:** 800/536-9650. **Fax:** 404/888-5645. **Contact:** Human Resources. **E-mail address:** staffing@fhlbatl.com. **World Wide Web address:** http://www.fhlbatl.com. **Description:** A reserve credit bank providing low-cost financing and other banking services to over 900 member financial institutions. The company offers housing financial services to consumers in Alabama, Florida, Georgia, Maryland, North Carolina, South Carolina, Virginia, and the District of Columbia. The bank is one of 12 in the national Federal Home Loan Bank system. **NOTE:** Please visit website to search for jobs and apply online. **Positions advertised include:** SEC and Financial Reporting Accountant; Senior Auditor; Senior Financial Risk Auditor; Credit and Collateral Systems Analyst; Unsecured Credit Risk Analyst; Customer and Cash Management Analyst; Mortgage Purchase Program Production Specialist; Senior Financial Risk Management Analyst; Senior Industry Relations Manager; Business Requirements Analyst; Information Security Administrator; Internet Help Desk Specialist.

FEDERATED MUTUAL INSURANCE COMPANY
P.O. Box 467500, Atlanta GA 31146. 404/497-8840. **Physical address:** 302 Perimeter Centre North, Atlanta GA 30346. **Toll-free phone:** 800/241-4945. **Fax:** 770/390-3911. **Contact:** Human Resources. **E-mail address:** iemployment@fedins.com. **World Wide Web address:** http://www.federatedinsurance.com. **Description:** A multiline insurance company concentrating primarily in the commercial lines industry. **NOTE:** Please mail resume and cover letter to corporate office at P.O. Box 328, Owatonna MN 55060-0328. **Positions advertised include:** Underwriter; Sales/Marketing Representative; Field Services Risk Consultant/Premium Auditor. **Corporate headquarters location:** Owatonna MN. **Other U.S. locations:** Nationwide. **Number of employees nationwide:** 3,100.

FERNBANK MUSEUM OF NATURAL HISTORY
767 Clifton Road NE, Atlanta GA 30307. 404/929-6300. **Fax:** 404/378-8140. **Contact:** Human Resources. **E-mail address:** human.resources@fernbank.edu. **World Wide Web address:** http://www.fernbank.edu/museum. **Description:** This facility is one of the city's largest and newest museums and one of the first major U.S. natural history museums built since the early 1900s. The Fernbank Museum offers "A Walk in Time Through Georgia" as its permanent exhibit, as well as a four-story IMAX screen. **NOTE:** Volunteer positions are also available. **Positions advertised include:** On-site Sales Representative; Member Services Volunteer Representative – Part-time; Exhibit Designer; Busser – Part-time; Dishwasher – Part-time. **Special programs:** Internships.

FIBERVISIONS, INC.
7101 Alcovy Road NE, Covington GA 30014. 770/786-7011. **Fax:** 770/784-7137. **Contact:** Human Resources. **World Wide Web address:** http://www.fibervisions.dk. **Description:** The world's largest manufacturer of polypropylene fabrics used in diapers, sanitary napkins, and adult incontinence products. **NOTE:** Entry-level positions and part-time jobs are offered. **Special programs:** Co-ops; Summer Jobs. **Office hours:** Monday - Friday, 8:00 a.m. - 4:30 p.m. **Corporate headquarters location:** This location. **International locations:** China; Denmark. **Parent company:** Hercules Inc. **Listed on:** New York Stock Exchange. **Stock exchange symbol:** HPC.

FIELDALE FARMS CORPORATION
P.O. Box 558, Baldwin GA 30511. 706/778-5100. **Contact:** Human Resources. **World Wide Web address:** http://www.fieldale.com. **Description:** Engaged in poultry processing and marketing nationwide. **Office hours:** Monday – Friday, 8:00 a.m. – 5:00 p.m. **Corporate headquarters location:** This location. **Other area locations:** Cornelia GA; Gainesville GA; Murraysville GA; Dahlonega GA; Eastanollee GA; South Clarksville GA.

FIRST DATA CORPORATION
5660 New Northside Drive, Suite 1400, Atlanta GA 30328. 770/857-0001. **Contact:** Human Resources. **World Wide Web address:** http://www.firstdatacorp.com. **Description:** A holding company. **NOTE:** Please visit website to search for jobs and apply online. **Positions advertised include:** In-House Sales Executive; MER/Account Executive; Human Resources Assistant; PB Manager; Administrative Assistant; Data Entry Operator; PB Lead; PB Coordinator; Warehouse Clerk; Mail Insert Machine Operator. **Corporate headquarters location:** Greenwood Village CO. **Subsidiaries include:** First Data Resources; First Data POS. **Listed on:** New York Stock Exchange. **Stock exchange symbol:** FDC. **CEO:** Charlie Fote. **Number of employees worldwide:** 30,000.

FIRST INSURANCE NETWORK
2889 Elmwood Drive, Smyrna GA 30080. 770/436-7575. **Toll-free phone:** 800/282-4151. **Fax:** 770/438-7228. **Contact:** Human Resources. **E-mail address:** jkimble@finusa.com. **World Wide Web address:** http://www.finusa.com. **Description:** An insurance brokerage firm involved in automobile, property, and casualty insurance. Founded in 1980. **Corporate headquarters location:** This location. **Other U.S. locations:** AZ; FL; TN.

FIRSTWAVE TECHNOLOGIES, INC.
2859 Paces Ferry Road, Overlook 3, Suite 1000, Atlanta GA 30339. 770/431-1200. **Toll-free phone:** 800/540-6061. **Fax:** 770/431-1201. **E-mail address:** careers@firstwave.net. **Contact:** Human Resources. **World Wide Web address:** http://www.firstwave.com. **Description:** Develops, markets, and supports software systems that automate the integrated sales, marketing, and customer service functions of business organizations in a wide range of industries. These sales performance solutions provide end users with closed-loop business solutions. Founded in 1984. **Corporate headquarters location:** This location. **International locations:** United Kingdom. **Operations at this facility include:** Administration; Research and Development; Sales; Service. **Listed on:** NASDAQ. **Stock exchange symbol:** FSTW. **CEO:** Richard Brock. **Annual sales/revenues:** $21 - $50 million.

FITZGERALD & COMPANY
3060 Peachtree Road, NW, Suite 500, One Buckhead Plaza, Atlanta GA 30305-2239. 404/504-6900. **Contact:** Human Resources. **E-mail Address:** hr@fitzco.com. **World Wide Web address:** http://www.fitzco.com. **Description:** A marketing and communications company comprised of three firms: The Bostford Group, which provides promotion marketing services; Weber Public Relations, which provided public relations services; and MRM providing relationship management services.

FLOWERS FOODS
1919 Flowers Circle, Thomasville GA 31757. 229/226-9110. **Contact:** Human Resources. **World Wide Web address:** http://www.flowersfoods.com. **Description:** Serves regional and national markets with a variety of branded food products including fresh and frozen baked goods and frozen specialty vegetables, fruits, and desserts. Name brands include Beebo, Blue-Bird, Broad Street Bakery, Cobblestone Mill, Dan-Co, Danish Kitchens, European Bakers, Jubilee, Nature's Own, Our Special Touch, and Pies, Inc. The company operates 34 food production facilities and conducts distribution operations through 2,300 agents to grocery, food service, restaurant, and fast food markets. Flowers Industries also owns outlet stores where surplus merchandise is sold. Founded in 1919. **NOTE:** Please visit website for online application form. **Corporate headquarters location:** This location. **Listed on:** New York Stock Exchange. **Stock exchange symbol:** FLO. **CEO:** Amos R. McMullian. **Number of employees nationwide:** 8,000.

FLOYD COLLEGE
P.O. Box 1864, Rome GA 30162-1864. 706/802-5000. **Physical address:** 3175 Cedartown Highway SE, Roma GA 30161. **Toll-free phone:** 800/332-2406. **Fax:** 706/295-6610. **Contact:** Human Resources. **E-mail address:** hr@floyd.edu. **World Wide Web address:** http://www.floyd.edu. **Description:** A two-year state college with an enrollment of approximately 3,000 students. Founded in 1970. **NOTE:** Human Resources phone is 706/802-5136. Please visit website to search for jobs and apply online. **Positions advertised include:** Director of College Relations; Enrollment Management Registrar; Assistant Professor – Accounting; Assistant Professor – Dental Hygiene; Instructor – Physical Education – Part-time; Student Financial Aid Counselor. **President:** J. Randy Pierce.

FLOYD COLLEGE
NORTH METRO CAMPUS
5198 Ross Road, Acworth GA 30102. 770/975-4088. **Fax:** 770/975-4119. **Contact:** Human Resources. **E-mail address:** hr@floyd.edu. **World Wide Web address:** http://www.floyd.edu. **Description:** A two-year state college. Founded in 1970. **NOTE:** Please send resumes to the main campus: Human Resources, P.O. Box 1864, Rome GA 30162-1864. **Positions advertised include:** Director of College Relations; Enrollment Management Registrar; Assistant Professor – Accounting; Assistant Professor – Dental Hygiene; Instructor – Physical Education – Part-time; Student Financial Aid Counselor. **President:** J. Randy Pierce.

FOCUS DEVELOPMENT, INC.
3423 Piedmont Road, Suite 325, Atlanta GA 30305. 404/816-6300. **Fax:** 404/816-6622. **Contact:** Human Resources. **World Wide Web address:** http://www.apartmentsbyfocus.com. **Description:** Develops, constructs, and manages residential real estate properties. **Corporate headquarters location:** This location. **President:** Michael Blonder.

FORD MOTOR COMPANY
340 Henry Ford II Avenue, Hapeville GA 30354. 404/669-1547. **Contact:** Wednesday Furman, Human Resources. **World Wide Web address:** http://www.ford.com.

Description: Ford Motor Company is engaged in the design, development, manufacture, and sale of cars, trucks, tractors, and related components and accessories. Ford is also one of the largest providers of financial services in the United States. Ford's two core businesses are the Automotive Group and the Financial Services Group (Ford Credit, The Associates, USL Capital, and First Nationwide). Ford is also engaged in a number of other businesses, including electronics, glass, electrical and fuel-handling products, plastics, climate-control systems, automotive service and replacement parts, vehicle leasing and rental, and land development. **Positions advertised include:** Marketing Sales and Service – Field Operations. **Corporate headquarters location:** Dearborn MI. **International locations:** Canada. **Operations at this facility include:** Manufacturing of motor vehicle bodies and serves as a regional office. **Listed on:** New York Stock Exchange. **Stock exchange symbol:** F. **CEO:** William Clay Ford, Jr. **Number of employees worldwide:** 327,531.

FOX APPLIANCE PARTS OF ATLANTA
P.O. Box 16217, Atlanta GA 30321. 404/363-3313. **Physical address:** 5375 North Parkway, Lake City GA 30260. **Contact:** Robert Taylor, Office Manager. **World Wide Web address:** http://www.foxparts.com. **Description:** A wholesale distributor of parts for major appliances and heating and air conditioning products. Founded in 1948. **NOTE:** Please visit website for online application form. **Corporate headquarters location:** This location. **Other area locations:** Statewide. **Operations at this facility include:** Administration; Sales.

FREEMAN, MATHIS, & GARY, LLP
100 Galleria Parkway, Suite 1600, Atlanta GA 30339-5948. 770/818-8000. **Fax:** 770/937-9960. **Contact:** Human Resources. **E-mail address:** pcovington@fmglaw.com. **World Wide Web address:** http://www.fmglaw.com. **Description:** A law firm servicing national corporate and government agencies. Founded in 1997. **Positions advertised include:** Litigation Associate.

FREUDENBERG-NOK
One Nok Drive, Cleveland GA 30528. 706/865-1665. **Contact:** Human Resources. **World Wide Web address:** http://www.freudenberg-nok.com. **Description:** Freudenberg-Nok manufactures sealing products, vibration control devices, and custom-molded shapes for a variety of industries. **Positions advertised include:** Process Engineer. **Office hours:** Monday – Friday, 8:00 a.m. – 5:00- p.m. **Corporate headquarters location:** Plymouth MI. **Other area locations:** LaGrange GA. **Other U.S. locations:** Nationwide. **International locations:** Worldwide. **Operations at this facility include:** Manufacturing of molded rubber parts for automobiles.

FRIGIDAIRE HOME PRODUCTS
250 Bobby Jones Expressway, Augusta GA 30907. 706/651-1751. **Contact:** Human Resources. **World Wide Web address:** http://www.frigidaire.com. **Description:** Manufactures household appliances including laundry machines, ranges, dishwashers, refrigerators, freezers, air conditioners, and garbage disposals. Founded 1918. **Special programs:** Internships. **Corporate headquarters location:** This location. **Other U.S. locations:** Eastern U.S. **Parent company:** AB Electrolux has four business areas. Household Appliances consists mainly of white goods, which account for 70 percent of sales. Other operations include floor care products, absorption refrigerators for caravans and hotel rooms, room air conditioners, sewing machines, and kitchen and bathroom cabinets. The main operations in Commercial Appliances are food service equipment for restaurants and institutions, and equipment for apartment-house laundry rooms and commercial laundries. Other operations include refrigeration equipment and freezers for shops and supermarkets, as well as vacuum cleaners and wet/dry cleaners for commercial use. Outdoor Products include garden equipment, chain saws, and other equipment for forestry operations. Garden equipment refers to portable products such as lawn trimmers and leaf blowers, as well as lawn mowers and garden tractors. Industrial Products comprise the group's second-largest business area. Over 40 percent of sales consist of profiles and other half-finished goods in aluminum, manufactured by Granges. Other main operations include car safety belts and related products for personal safety in cars, as well as materials-handling equipment. **Operations at this facility include:** Administration; Sales; Service. **Listed on:** NASDAQ. **Stock exchange symbol:** ELUX. **Number of employees worldwide:** 18,200.

FRITO-LAY, INC.
3295 River Exchange Drive, Suite 210, Norcross GA 30092. 770/734-2300. **Contact:** Human Resources. **World Wide Web address:** http://www.fritolay.com. **Description:** A worldwide manufacturer and wholesaler of snack products. Brand names include Fritos Corn Chips, Doritos Tortilla Chips, Lays Potato Chips, and Smartfood Popcorn. **NOTE:** Please visit http://www.fritolayjobs.com to register, search for jobs, and apply online. **Corporate headquarters location:** Plano TX. **Other area locations:** Statewide. **Other U.S. locations:** Nationwide. **Parent company:** PepsiCo, Inc. (Purchase NY) consists of Frito-Lay, Inc., Pepsi-Cola Company, and Tropicana Products, Inc. **Operations at this facility include:** Distribution; Manufacturing; Sales. **Listed on:** New York Stock Exchange. **Stock exchange symbol:** PEP.

FULTON SUPPLY COMPANY
342 Nelson Street SW, Atlanta GA 30313. 404/688-3400. **Fax:** 404/522-0249. **Contact:** Human Resources. **E-mail address:** cwilliams@fultonsupply.com. **World Wide Web address:** http://www.fultonsupply.com. **Description:** A wholesaler of industrial tools. Founded in 1914. **Corporate headquarters location:** This location. **Other U.S. locations:** AL; FL; SC.

GE POWER SYSTEMS
2100 Boggs Road, Duluth GA 30096. 678/844-3600. **Contact:** Human Resources. **World Wide Web address:** http://www.gepower.com/geoilandgas. **Description:** Manufactures aircraft components including tubes and propeller blades. **Corporate headquarters location:** Houston TX. **International locations:** Worldwide.

GEAC COMPUTER
66 Perimeter Center East, Atlanta GA 30346-1805. 404/239-2000. **Fax:** 404/239-2404. **Contact:** Human Resources. **World Wide Web address:** http://www.americas.geac.com. **Description:** Develops and markets business applications software in the areas of human resources, materials management, manufacturing, health care, and higher education. Products include the SmartStream series of financial software. **NOTE:** Please visit website to search for jobs and apply online. **Positions advertised include:** Accounts Receivable Administrator; Billing Analyst; Hosted Operations Systems Administrator; Senior Accountant; Senior Business Systems Analyst; Senior Financial Analyst. **Corporate headquarters location:** Ontario Canada. **Other U.S. locations:** Nationwide. **International locations:** Worldwide. **President/CEO:** Charles S. Jones. **Number of employees worldwide:** 2,400.

GEIGER BRICKEL
P.O. Box 43068, Atlanta GA 30336-0068. 404/344-1100. **Physical address:** 6095 Fulton industrial Boulevard SW, Atlanta GA. **Toll-free phone:** 800/444-8812. **Fax:** 404/346-5202. **E-mail address:** jobs@hmgeiger.com. **Contact:** Human Resources. **World Wide Web address:** http://www.hmgeiger.com. **Description:** Manufactures office furniture and case goods. **Number of employees worldwide:** 8,000.

GENERAL MOTORS CORPORATION
3900 Motors Industrial Way, Doraville GA 30360. 770/455-5255. **Contact:** Human Resources. **World Wide Web address:** http://www.gm.com. **Description:** General Motors Corporation is one of the world's largest full-line vehicle manufacturers, and also has substantial interests in information technology, electronics, and finance. GM conducts business through the following sectors: North American Automotive Operations, International Operations, General Motors Acceptance Corporation (GMAC), and GM Hughes Electronics Corporation. North American Automotive Operations includes Sales/Service Groups (Buick, Cadillac, Chevrolet, GMC Truck, Oldsmobile, Pontiac, and Saturn) and Vehicle Development Groups (Powertrain, Truck Group, Small Car Group, and Midsize/Luxury Car Group). International Operations include GM Europe; Asia Pacific Operations; and Latin America, Africa, Middle East Operations. GMAC, which provides financing and insurance to GM customers and dealers, consists of North American Operations, International Operations, Motors Insurance Corporation, and GMAC Mortgage Group. GM Hughes Electronics Corporation is involved in automotive electronics, telecommunications and space electronics, and defense electronics. Founded in 1908. **NOTE:** Please visit website to search for jobs and apply online. **Special programs:** Co-ops. **Corporate headquarters location:** Detroit MI. **Operations at this facility include:** Motor vehicle assembly. **Listed on:** New York Stock Exchange. **Stock exchange symbol:** GM. **CEO:** G. Richard Wagoner, Jr. **Number of employees worldwide:** 325,000.

GENERAL REINSURANCE CORPORATION
Seven Piedmont Center, 3525 Piedmont Road NE, Suite 7-700, Atlanta GA 30305-1533. 404/237-2555. **Fax:** 404/365-6861. **Contact:** Human Resources. **World Wide Web address:** http://www.gcr.com. **Description:** Provides property and casualty reinsurance to primary insurers on a direct basis. **Corporate headquarters location:** Stamford CT. **Other U.S. locations:** Nationwide. **International locations:** Worldwide. **Parent company:** GeneralCologne Re. **CEO:** Joseph P. Brandon. **Number of employees worldwide:** 2,700.

GENERAL SHALE PRODUCTS CORPORATION
P.O. Box 813250, Smyrna GA 30081. 404/799-8541. **Physical address:** 3195 Brick Plant Road, Atlanta GA 30318. **Fax:** 404/799-8892. **Contact:** Human Resources. **World Wide Web address:** http://www.generalshale.com. **Description:** Produces brick for construction uses. **Corporate headquarters location:** Johnson City TN. **President/CEO:** Richard Green. **Number of employees nationwide:** 2,000.

GENESIS HOME CARE
2501 Plant Avenue, Waycross GA 31501. 912/285-5200. **Fax:** 912/285-9378. **Contact:** Human Resources. **E-mail address:** genesisdma@accessate.net. **Description:** Offers home health care and medical equipment and supplies.

GENUINE PARTS COMPANY
2999 Circle 75 Parkway, Atlanta GA 30339. 770/953-1700. **Fax:** 770/956-2211. **Contact:** Human Resources. **World Wide Web address:** http://www.genpt.com. **Description:** A service organization engaged in the distribution of automotive replacement parts, industrial replacement parts, and office products. The company serves customers through more than 1,800 operations and is a member of the National Automotive Parts Association (NAPA). The company operates in three major divisions. The Automotive Parts Group, the largest division of the company, distributes automotive replacement parts and accessory items. The Industrial Parts Group distributes industrial replacement parts and related supplies through Motion Industries, Berry Bearing Company, and Oliver Industrial Supply. The Office Products Group distributes a broad line of office products ranging from furniture to computer supplies, through S.P. Richards Company. Brand name products include Sparco office supplies and Nature Saver recycled and recyclable products. Founded in 1928. **Special programs:** Internships. **Corporate headquarters location:** This location. **Other area locations:** Kennesaw GA; Norcross GA. **Other U.S. locations:** Nationwide. **International locations:** Canada; Mexico. **Operations at this facility include:** Administration. **Listed on:** New York Stock Exchange. **Stock exchange symbol:** GPC. **CEO:** Larry Prince. **Number of employees worldwide:** 31,000.

GENUINE PARTS COMPANY
120 Interstate Parkway North, Atlanta GA 30303. 770/850-2350. **Contact:** Human Resources. **World Wide Web address:** http://www.genpt.com. **Description:** Genuine Parts Company is a service organization engaged in the distribution of automotive replacement parts, industrial replacement parts, and office products. The company serves customers from more than 1,200 operations and is a member of the National Automotive Parts Association (NAPA). The company operates in three major divisions. The Automotive Parts Group, the largest division of the company, distributes automotive replacement parts and accessory items. This group operates 64 NAPA Distribution Centers and serves approximately 5,800 NAPA Auto Parts stores throughout the United States. This group also has six plants that rebuild automotive parts. The Industrial Parts Group distributes industrial replacement parts and related supplies through Motion Industries, Berry Bearing Company, and Oliver Industrial Supply. The Industrial Group distributes from more than 330 operations in 38 states. This group serves customers located in the United States, Canada, and Mexico. The Office Products Group distributes a broad line of office products ranging from furniture to computer supplies, through S.P. Richards Company. Brand name products include Sparco office supplies and Nature Saver recycled and recyclable products. This group operates 41 distribution centers in 28 states. Founded in 1928. **Corporate headquarters location:** Atlanta GA. **Other area locations:** Kennesaw GA; Norcross GA. **Other U.S. locations:** Nationwide. **International locations:** Canada; Mexico. **Operations at this facility include:** Employee Service Center. **Listed on:** New York Stock Exchange. **Stock exchange symbol:** GPC. **CEO:** Larry Prince. **Number of employees worldwide:** 31,000.

GEORGIA BUILDING AUTHORITY
7 Martin Luther King, Jr. Drive, Room 352, Atlanta GA 30334. 404/656-3869. **Contact:** Michael Carlton, Human Resources. **E-mail address:** michael.carlton@gw.gba.state.ga.us. **World Wide Web address:** http://www.state.ga.us/gba. **Description:** Serves state-owned buildings including the state capitol. **NOTE:** Please visit website to search for jobs and apply online. **Positions advertised include:** CAD Operator; Property Resources Officer; Parking Shift Supervisor; Video/Alarm Response Center Officer. **Office hours:** Monday – Friday, 8:00 a.m. – 4:00 p.m. **Corporate headquarters location:** This location. **Operations at this facility include:** Administration; Service.

GEORGIA BUREAU OF INVESTIGATION
P.O. Box 370808, Decatur GA 30037-0808. 404/244-2508. **Physical address:** 3121 Panthersville Road, Decatur GA. **Contact:** Personnel. **World Wide Web address:** http://www.ganet.org/gbi. **Description:** Supports and aides the state's criminal justice system in areas including criminal investigations and forensic lab services. **NOTE:**

Please visit website to search for jobs. **Positions advertised include:** Special Agent; Narcotics Agent; Crime Lab Specialist; Secretary. **Special programs:** Internships.

GEORGIA DEPARTMENT OF AGRICULTURE
Room 300, Agriculture Building, 19 Martin Luther King Jr. Drive SW, Atlanta Georgia 30334. 404/656-3685. **Fax:** 404/651-7957. **Contact:** Debbie Bell, Personnel. **World Wide Web address:** http://www.agr.state.ga.us. **Description:** Protects and provides support for Georgia's agriculture industry. **NOTE:** You must complete a State of Georgia employment Application. Please visit website to download an application, and to search for jobs. Personnel phone is 404/656-3615. **Positions advertised include:** Meat Inspector Trainee.

GEORGIA DUCK & CORDAGE MILL
21 Laredo Drive, Scottsdale GA 30079-0865. 404/297-3170. **Fax:** 404/296-5165. **Contact:** Michael Smith, Personnel Manager. **World Wide Web address:** http://www.gaduck.com. **Description:** Manufactures PVC, rubber, and polyurethane conveyer belting; industrial fabrics; and cordage. **Corporate headquarters location:** This location. **Parent company:** Worldwide Fenner Group. **Listed on:** Privately held.

GEORGIA FORESTRY COMMISSION
P.O. Box 819, Macon GA 31202-0819. 478/751-3500. **Physical address:** 5456 Riggins Mill Road, Dry Branch GA 31020. **Toll-free phone:** 800/GATREES. **Fax:** 478/751-3465. **Contact:** Human Resources Department. **E-mail address:** gfchrpersonnel@gfc.state.ga.us. **World Wide Web address:** http://www.gfc.state.ga.us. **Description:** Protects Georgia's forests resources, and provides education in the protection and management of those resources. **NOTE:** Mail resumes to Human Resources at 6835 James B. Rivers/Memorial Drive, Stone Mountain GA 30083. Phone is 678/476-6220, fax is 678/476-6230. **Positions advertised include:** Ranger; Forester. **Other area locations:** Statewide.

GEORGIA GULF CORPORATION
P.O. Box 105197, Atlanta GA 30348. 770/395-4500. **Physical address:** 400 Perimeter Center Terrace, Suite 595, Atlanta GA 30346. **Fax:** 770/395-4529. **Contact:** Human Resources. **E-mail address:** careers@ggc.com. **World Wide Web address:** http://www.ggc.com. **Description:** A manufacturer and worldwide marketer of several highly-integrated lines of commodity chemicals and polymers including aromatic natural gas, and electrochemical products. The company's chemical products have a number of consumer and industrial uses such as water purification, paper production, and production of high-performance plastics, pharmaceuticals, and construction materials. **Corporate headquarters location:** This location. **Other U.S. locations:** Southern U.S. **Listed on:** New York Stock Exchange. **Stock exchange symbol:** GGC. **CEO:** Edward Schmitt. **Number of employees nationwide:** 1,216.

GEORGIA INSTITUTE OF TECHNOLOGY
GEORGIA TECH RESEARCH INSTITUTE
955 Fowler Street NW, Atlanta GA 30332-0435. 404/894-9765. **Fax:** 404/894-1235. **Contact:** Human Resources. **World Wide Web address:** http://www.gatech.edu. **Description:** A public technical institute with approximately 12,000 students enrolled in its undergraduate, graduate, and doctoral programs. Georgia Tech Research Institute is a nonprofit, client-oriented, applied research and development organization. The majority of the institute's research is sponsored by the U.S. Department of Defense. The institute has a variety of research programs that focus on many areas including aerospace, information technology, occupational health and safety, and telecommunications. Founded in 1885. **NOTE:** Please visit website to search for jobs and apply online. **Positions advertised include:** Security Guard; Air Conditioning Mechanic; Grounds Keeper; Contracting Officer; Accounting Personnel; Research Technician; Administrative Assistant; Director of the Language Institute; Public Safety Officer; Maintenance Worker; Custodial Supervisor; Retail Manager; Driver; Electrical Engineer. **Number of employees at this location:** 4,000.

GEORGIA MANAGEMENT SERVICES
202 North Westover Boulevard, Albany GA 31707. 229/436-7204. **Contact:** Human Resources. **Description:** Provides bookkeeping, payroll, accounts receivable, accounts payable, and other financial management services to nursing homes.

GEORGIA PERIMETER COLLEGE
3251 Panthersville Road, Decatur GA 30034-3897. 404/244-5090. **Fax:** 404/244-5774. **Recorded jobline:** 404/244-2376. **Contact:** Human Resources. **E-mail address:** gpchrapp@gpc.edu. **World Wide Web address:** http://www.gpc.peachnet.edu. **Description:** A community college offering a variety of classes in business, fire science, foreign languages, health care, humanities, physical education, and the social sciences. Founded in 1972. **Positions advertised include:** Electronics Technician; Skills Lab Coordinator; Coordinator of Instructional Support Services; Dean of Student Services; Director of Student Life; Photographic Supervisor; Student Accounts Manager; Nursing Coordinator; Custodian; Groundskeeper; Public Safety Officer; Instructor – Various Departments – Part-time; Secretary – Part-time; Administrative Secretary – Part-time. **Other area locations:** Clarkston GA; Dunwoody GA; Alpharetta GA; Conyers GA; Lawrenceville GA. **President:** Jacquelyn M. Belcher, J.D.

GEORGIA PUBLIC BROADCASTING
260 14th Street NW, Atlanta GA 30318. 404/685-2400. **Toll-free phone:** 800/222-6006. **Contact:** Human Resources Office. **E-mail address:** jobs@gpb.org. **World Wide Web address:** http://www.gpb.org. **Description:** Operates television, radio, and educational services. Delivers PBS television programming and Georgia High School sports programming to Georgia counties. Also airs National Public Radio locally. **NOTE:** Please visit website to search for jobs. **Positions advertised include:** Senior Education Project Coordinator; Television Program Manager.

GEORGIA SOUTHERN UNIVERSITY
P.O. Box 8104, Statesboro GA 30460-8104. 912/681-5468. **Fax:** 912/681-0325. **Recorded jobline:** 912/681-0629. **Contact:** Personnel Director. **World Wide Web address:** http://www.gasou.edu. **Description:** A regional state university. Georgia Southern enrolls over 11,000 students in its undergraduate and graduate degree programs. Founded in 1906. **NOTE:** Applications are accepted Monday – Friday, 8:00 to 3:00 p.m. Please visit website to search for jobs. For faculty positions, please contact your department of interest. **Positions advertised include:** Assistant director for Health Education and Promotion; Counseling Psychologist; Director of Major Gifts; Assistant Athletics Media Relations Director; Instructional Services Coordinator; Hall Director; Academic Advisor Assistant Director of Design Services; Research Associate; Custodial Foreman; Vice President for Business and Finance; Educational Program Specialist; Conference Facilitator; Public Safety Officer; Accounting Assistant; AC Mechanic; Delivery Worker; Trades Helper. **Special programs:** Internships. **Parent company:** Board of Regents, University System of Georgia.

GEORGIA STATE DEPARTMENT OF EDUCATION
PUBLIC SCHOOL RECRUITMENT SERVICES
2 Peachtree Street, Suite 6000, Atlanta GA 30303. 404/232-2603. **Contact:** Human Resources. **World Wide Web address:** http://www.teachgeorgia.org. **Description:** Assists 180 Georgia public school systems in locating qualified teachers, administrators, and related service personnel. **Office hours:** Monday - Friday, 8:00 a.m. - 4:30 p.m.

GEORGIA STATE DEPARTMENT OF EDUCATION
2052 Twin Towers East, Atlanta GA 30334. 404/656-2510. **Fax:** 404/657-7840. **World Wide Web address:** http://www.doe.k12.ga.us. **Description:** Serves as the office for the Superintendent of Schools. Organizes educational programs and methods in the state of Georgia. **NOTE:** please visit website to search for jobs and download application form. **Positions advertised include:** Education Program Specialist; Legal Secretary; School Director; Education Facilities; Accountant; Program Associate; Education Program Specialist; Custodian; Residential Advisor; Teacher; School Social Worker; School Clinic Nurse; Speech Language Pathologist; Vocational Teacher; Teacher – Blind/Deaf; Assistant Director for Administrative Operations.

GEORGIA STATE DEPARTMENT OF TRANSPORTATION
No. 2 Capitol Square SW, Atlanta GA 30334. 404/656-5267. **Fax:** 404/463-6336. **Contact:** Human Resources. **E-mail address:** recruitment@dot.state.ga.us. **World Wide Web address:** http://www.dot.state.ga.us. **Description:** Engaged in planning, design, construction management, and maintenance of the state's transportation system. **NOTE:** Contact the Engineer Recruiter at 404/656-5260. Please visit website to search for jobs. You can find more positions listed on http://thejobsite.org. **Positions advertised include:** Civil Engineer Technologist; Transportation Engineer Associate.

GEORGIA STATE GOVERNMENT
GEORGIA MERIT SYSTEM
P.O. Box 347100, Atlanta GA 30334. 404/656-2725. **Physical address:** Floyd Veterans Memorial Building, Twin Towers West, 2 Martin Luther King Jr. Drive SE, Room 418, Atlanta GA 30334-5100. **Fax:** 404/657-4958. **Recorded jobline:** 404/656-2724. **Contact:** Job Information and Recruitment Section. **E-mail address:** staffing-info@gms.state.ga.us. **World Wide Web address:** http://www.gms.state.ga.us. **Description:** Central recruitment and applicant screening agency for many departments in the Georgia state government. The agency provides job information, applications, and advisement to jobseekers; and offers recruitment, applicant evaluation, and compensation analysis services to over 60 state agencies and authorities. **NOTE:** Please visit http://thejobsite.org to search for positions. **Company slogan:** People. Partnerships. Performance. **Office hours:** Monday - Friday, 8:00 a.m. - 5:00 p.m. **Other area locations:** Decatur GA.

GEORGIA-PACIFIC CORPORATION
133 Peachtree Street NE, Atlanta GA 30303. 404/652-4000. **Contact:** Corporate Staffing. **World Wide Web address:** http://www.gp.com. **Description:** Manufactures, wholesales, and distributes building products, industrial wood products, pulp, paper, packaging materials, and related chemicals. The company is one of the world's largest manufacturers of forest products. **NOTE:** Please visit website to search for jobs and to apply online. **Positions advertised include:** Manager; Associate Brand Manager – Brawny; Sale Representative; Sales Trainee; Senior Business Analyst; Senior Manager – Analysis; Senior Systems Analyst; Core Systems – Champion User; Account Specialist; Director of Marketing; Communications Manager; Inventory Service/Account Manager; Manager – Research; Senior Manager – Trade Marketing; Inside Account Team Leader; Industrial Sales Manager; Logistics Analyst; Regional Account Representative. **Corporate headquarters location:** This location. **Other area locations:** Statewide. **Other U.S. locations:** Nationwide. **International locations:** Canada; Europe. **Listed on:** New York Stock Exchange. **Stock exchange symbol:** GP. **CEO:** A.D. Correll. **Number of employees worldwide:** 61,000.

GEORGIA-PACIFIC CORPORATION
P.O. Box 44, Cedar Springs GA 31732. 229/372-5541. **Physical address:** Georgia Highway 273 West, Cedar Springs GA 31732. **Contact:** Bill Mayers, Human Resources Manager. **World Wide Web address:** http://www.gp.com. **Description:** Georgia-Pacific Corporation manufactures, wholesales, and distributes building products, industrial wood products, pulp, paper, packaging materials, and related chemicals. The company is one of the world's largest manufacturers of forest products. **NOTE:** Please visit website to search for jobs and to apply online. **Corporate headquarters location:** Atlanta GA. **Other area locations:** Statewide. **Other U.S. locations:** Nationwide. **International locations:** Canada; Europe. **Operations at this facility include:** Manufacturing of containerboard. **Listed on:** New York Stock Exchange. **Stock exchange symbol:** GP. **CEO:** A.D. Correll. **Number of employees worldwide:** 61,000.

GEORGIA-PACIFIC CORPORATION
405 Maxwell Drive, Albany GA 31701. 229/435-3431. **Fax:** 229/430-5353. **Contact:** Human Resources. **World Wide Web address:** http://www.gp.com. **Description:** Georgia-Pacific Corporation manufactures, wholesales, and distributes building products, industrial wood products, pulp, paper, packaging materials, and related chemicals. The company is one of the world's largest manufacturers of forest products. **NOTE:** Please visit website to search for jobs and to apply online. **Corporate headquarters location:** Atlanta GA. **Other area locations:** Statewide. **Other U.S. locations:** Nationwide. **International locations:** Canada; Europe. **Operations at this facility include:** Manufacturing of corrugated containers. **Listed on:** New York Stock Exchange. **Stock exchange symbol:** GP. **CEO:** A.D. Correll. **Number of employees worldwide:** 61,000.

GEORGIA-PACIFIC CORPORATION
P.O. Box 367, Savannah GA 31498. 912/964-2230. **Fax:** 912/963-2456. **Contact:** Human Resources. **World Wide Web address:** http://www.gp.com. **Description:** Georgia-Pacific Corporation is a manufacturer, wholesaler, and distributor of building products, industrial wood products, pulp, paper, packaging materials, and related chemicals. The company is one of the world's largest manufacturers of forest products. **NOTE:** Please visit website to search for jobs and to apply online. **Positions advertised include:** Maintenance Leader – Controls, Electrical, Mechanics. **Corporate headquarters location:** Atlanta GA. **Other area locations:** Statewide. **Other U.S. locations:** Nationwide. **International locations:** Canada; Europe. **Operations at this facility include:** Manufacturing of plywood paneling. **Listed on:** New York Stock Exchange. **Stock exchange symbol:** GP. **CEO:** A.D. Correll. **Number of employees worldwide:** 61,000.

GLENAYRE
11360 Lakefield Drive, Duluth GA 30097. 770/283-1000. **Fax:** 770/283-3993. **Contact:** Human Resources. **E-mail address:** gtti@glenayre.com. **World Wide Web address:** http://www.glenayre.com. **Description:** Develops communication network administration software. **Corporate headquarters location:** This location. **Other U.S.**

locations: TX; IL. **International locations:** Worldwide. **Listed on:** NASDAQ. **Stock exchange symbol:** GEMS. **CEO:** Clarke H. Bailey.

GLENN RAVEN CUSTOM FABRICS
P.O. Box 6107, Elberton GA 30635. 706/283-3721. **Physical address:** 120 Seaboard Street, Elberton GA. **Toll-free phone:** 800/433-1748. **Fax:** 706/283-7833. **Contact:** Human Resources. **World Wide Web address:** http://www.glenraven.com. **Description:** Produces industrial fabrics including furniture upholstery fabrics, outdoor canvasses for umbrellas, casual patio furniture, and marine applications. **Office hours:** Monday – Friday, 8:00 a.m. – 5:00 p.m. **Corporate headquarters location:** Glen Raven NC. **Other U.S. locations:** SC; NC; TX; FL. **International locations:** Worldwide. **President:** Allen Gant Jr.

GOLD KIST, INC.
P.O. Box 2210, Atlanta GA 30301. 770/393-5000. **Fax:** 770/393-5262. **Contact:** Human Resources. **E-mail address:** jobs@goldkist.com. **World Wide Web address:** http://www.goldkist.com. **Description:** A diversified agricultural cooperative with approximately 25,000 active member farms located primarily in Georgia, Alabama, Florida, North Carolina, and South Carolina. Gold Kist is one of the largest poultry processors in the country. The company also operates pork production facilities, and aquaculture research and peanut genetics research facilities. Retail poultry products are marketed under the Gold Kist Farms label or under customer's private labels. Founded in 1933. **NOTE:** Please visit website to search for jobs. **Positions advertised include:** Internal Consulting Auditor; Sales Manager; Business Application Developer; Sales Representative; Director – Public Relations. **Special programs:** Internships. **Office hours:** Monday - Friday, 8:00 a.m. - 5:00 p.m. **Corporate headquarters location:** This location. **Other U.S. locations:** AL; FL; OH; NC; SC. **Annual sales/revenues:** More than $100 million. **Number of employees nationwide:** 16,000.

GOLDEN PEANUT COMPANY
100 North Point Center East, Suite 400, Alpharetta GA 30022. 770/752-8160. **Contact:** Human Resources. **World Wide Web address:** http://www. goldenpeanut.com. **Description:** Handles and shells raw peanuts. Golden Peanut Company is one of the largest peanut procurement, processing, and marketing companies in the United States. **Corporate headquarters location:** This location. **Other area locations:** Ashburn GA; Dawson GA; Camilla GA; Bainbridge GA; Cordele GA; Blakely GA. **Other U.S. locations:** Headland AL; DeLeon TX; Seagraves TX; Ulander NC; Wakefield VA; Durant OK. **International locations:** Argentina. **Operations at this facility include:** Administration. **President/CEO:** Jimmy Dorsett.

GOODWILL INDUSTRIES OF ATLANTA, INC.
2201 Glenwood Avenue SE, Atlanta GA 30316. 404/486-8400. **Fax:** 404/371-9041. **Contact:** Human Resources. **E-mail address:** humanresources@ging.org. **World Wide Web address:** http://www.ging.org. **Description:** Operates 1,400 thrift stores nationwide. Goodwill is also a nonprofit provider of employment training for the disabled and the disadvantaged. **NOTE:** Entry-level positions are offered. **Positions advertised include:** Assistant Store Manager; Production Associate; Floor Associate; Trailer Attendant; Floor Supervisor; Director of Skills Development. Truck Driver. **Special programs:** Training. **Corporate headquarters location:** Rockville MD. **Other area locations:** Statewide. **Other U.S. locations:** Nationwide. **International locations:** Worldwide. **Parent company:** GII. **Listed on:** Privately held. **President/CEO:** George W. Kessinger. **Number of employees worldwide:** 72,000.

GOODY PRODUCTS INC.
400 Galleria Parkway, Suite 1100, Atlanta GA 30339. 770/615-4700. **Toll-free phone:** 800/631-8832. **Fax:** 770/615-4740. **Contact:** Tracy Millette, Director of Human Resources. **World Wide Web address:** http://www.goody.com. **Description:** A manufacturer of hair accessories including combs, brushes, curlers, and other products. **Positions advertised include:** Vice President of Marketing; Assistant Production Supervisor. **Corporate headquarters location:** This location. **Other area locations:** Columbus GA; Manchester GA. **Other U.S. locations:** Bentonville AR. **Parent company:** Newell Rubbermaid. **Listed on:** New York Stock Exchange. **Stock exchange symbol:** NWL. **President:** Howard C. Heckers.

GRADY MEMORIAL HOSPITAL
80 Jesse Hill Jr. Drive, Atlanta GA 30303-3050. 404/616-4307. **E-mail address:** gbedford@gmh.edu. **Contact:** Human Resources. **World Wide Web address:** http://www.gradyhealthsystem.org. **Description:** A 1,024-bed, primary care hospital. The hospital is a teaching facility for Emory University and Morehouse College. **NOTE:** Please visit website to search for jobs and apply online. Be sure to include the listed job code when applying. **Positions advertised include:** Pharmacist; Pharmacy Technician; Director of Customer Service; Director of Quality Improvement and Staff Development; Executive Director of Trauma Services; Vice President of Government Relations; Vice President of Patient Care; RN – Various Departments; Advice Nurse; Bionic Nurse; Charge Nurse; Clinical Manager; Clinical Nurse Specialist; LPN; Nurse Case Manager; Nurse Coordinator; Nurse Practitioner; Senior Staff Nurse; Surgical Technician; Coder; Coding Supervisor; Financial Counselor; Medical Transcriptionist; Quality Control Representative. **Parent company:** Grady Health System.

GRAPHIC PACKAGING CORPORATION
814 Livingston Court, Marietta GA 30067. 770/644-3000. **Contact:** Human Resources. **E-mail address:** pat.szall@graphicpkg.com. **World Wide Web address:** http://www.graphicpkg.com. **Description:** Produces coated, unbleached kraft board and packaging products including beverage and folding cartons, packaging machinery, containerboard, corrugated boxes, lumber, and plywood. **NOTE:** Please visit website to search for jobs. **Corporate headquarters location:** This location. **Other U.S. locations:** Nationwide. **International locations:** Worldwide. **Listed on:** New York Stock Exchange. **Stock exchange symbol:** GPK. **President/CEO:** Stephen M. Humphrey. **Number of employees nationwide:** 8,000.

GREAT DANE TRAILERS, INC.
P.O. Box 67, Savannah GA 31402-0067. 912/644-2100. **Physical address:** 602 East Lathrup Avenue, Savannah GA 31415. **Fax:** 912/644-2624. **E-mail Address:** hr@greatdanetrailers.com. **Contact:** Human Resources. **World Wide Web address:** http://www.greatdanetrailers.com. **Description:** Manufactures and markets flatbed and refrigerated trailers. The company also manufactures and distributes truck van bodies. **Corporate headquarters location:** This location. **Other U.S. locations:** Nationwide. **International locations:** Canada; Mexico; Colombia; Chile; Venezuela; Argentina. **Parent company:** Great Dane Limited Partnership. **Operations at this facility include:** Administration; Manufacturing; Research and Development; Sales. **President:** Kit Hammond. **Number of employees worldwide:** 4,000.

GREENHORNE & O'MARA, INC.
2211 New Market Parkway, Suite 104, Marietta GA 30067. 770/988-9555. **Toll-free phone:** 866/322-8905. **Fax:** 770/952-0653. **Contact:** Personnel. **World Wide Web address:** http://www.g-and-o.com. **Description:** Provides civil/site, environmental, transportation, and geosciences engineering services. Founded in 1950. **NOTE:** Please visit website to search for jobs and apply online. **Corporate headquarters location:** Greenbelt MD. **Other area locations:** Liburn GA. **Other U.S. locations:** FL; NC; PA; VA; WV. **Listed on:** Privately held.

GUARDIAN
1560 Lukken Industrial Drive West, LaGrange GA 30240. 706/882-2901. **Fax:** 706/882-4386. **Contact:** Scott Selby, Human Resources Manager. **World Wide Web address:** http://guardian.com. **Description:** One of the world's largest glass manufacturers. Guardian also manufactures supply products for exterior automotive purposes. **NOTE:** Please visit website to search for jobs and apply online. **Other U.S. locations:** Nationwide. **International locations:** Worldwide. **Number of employees at this location:** 325.

GULFSTREAM AEROSPACE CORPORATION
500 Gulfstream Road, Savannah GA 31408. 912/965-3000. **Contact:** Personnel. **World Wide Web address:** http://www.gulfstream.com. **Description:** Gulfstream Aerospace Corporation manufactures corporate and private executive aircraft. **NOTE:** Please visit website to search for jobs and apply online. **Positions advertised include:** Senior Certification Project Specialist; Production Trainee; Mechanical Lead; Material Control Analyst; Technical Writer; Sales Assistant; Administrative Associate; Electronics Technician; Senior Plumber; Structural Mechanic; Cabinetmaker. **Corporate headquarters location:** This location. **Other area locations:** Brunswick GA. **Other U.S. locations:** Appleton WI; Dallas TX; Mexicali Baja CA. **International locations:** London England. **Operations at this facility include:** Airplane production. **Parent company:** General Dynamics. **Listed on:** New York Stock Exchange. **Stock exchange symbol:** GD. **President:** Bryan Moss.

H&R BLOCK
2800 Old Dawson Road, Albany GA 31707. 229/883-5353. **Contact:** Human Resources Department. **World Wide Web address:** http://www.hrblock.com. **Description:** H&R Block is primarily engaged in consumer tax preparation, operating more than 10,000 U.S. offices and preparing more than 10 million tax returns each year. The company also operates more than 800 offices in Canada. H&R Block has offices in over 750 Sears stores in both the United States and Canada. Many offices operate as franchises, and some operate on a seasonal basis. H&R Block is also engaged in a number of other tax-related activities including Group Tax Programs, Premium Tax Service, Tax Training Schools, and Real Estate Tax Awareness seminars. **NOTE:** Please visit website to search for jobs and apply online. **Corporate headquarters location:** Kansas City MO. **Other area locations:** Statewide. **Other U.S. locations:** Nationwide. **International locations:** Australia; Canada; United Kingdom. **Listed on:** New York Stock Exchange. **Stock exchange symbol:** HRB. **President/CEO:** Mark A. Ernst. **Number of employees worldwide:** 24,000.

HABITAT FOR HUMANITY INTERNATIONAL
121 Habitat Street, Americus GA 31709-3498. 229/924-6935. **Toll-free phone:** 800/422-4828. **Contact:** Human Resources. **E-mail address:** hrstaffing@habitat.org. **World Wide Web address:** http://www.habitat.org. **Description:** A nonprofit, ecumenical, Christian housing ministry whose mission is to build housing for the poor around the world. **NOTE:** Please visit website to search for jobs. Volunteer positions are also available. **Positions advertised include:** Global Village Registration Coordinator; Video Producer; Media Specialist; Director of Collaborative Development; Web Communications Manager; Traffic Coordinator; User Interface Specialist; Senior Financial Analyst; Mail Processing Center Assistant; Application Support Analyst – Financial Systems; Controller; Cashier; Compensation Manager. **Corporate headquarters location:** This location. **Other U.S. locations:** Nationwide.

HAMILTON MEDICAL CENTER
P.O. Box 1168, Dalton GA 30722-1168. 706/272-6145. **Physical address:** 1200 Memorial Drive, Dalton GA 30720. **Recorded jobline:** 706/217-2020. **Fax:** 706/272-6285. **E-mail address:** employment@hhcs.org. **Contact:** Employment Services. **World Wide Web address:** http://www.hamiltonhealth.com. **Description:** A 282-bed, acute care medical center. Hamilton Medical Center provides a variety of services including cancer care, diabetes treatment, substance abuse, and psychiatric care. **Positions advertised include:** RN – Various Departments; LPN – Various Departments; Staff Pharmacist; Planning Analyst; Director of Information Services; Director of Surgery; RN Supervisor; Radiologic Technician; Staff Respiratory Therapist; Ultrasound Technologist; Reimbursement Analyst; Transcriptionist – Medical Records; Registration Clerk; CNA. **Office hours:** Monday – Thursday, 8:00 a.m. – 4:00 p.m.; Friday – 7:00 a.m. – 4:00 p.m.

HANSON PLC
100 Crescent Center Parkway, Suite 1240, Tucker GA 30084. 770/491-2777. **Contact:** Human Resources. **World Wide Web address:** http://www.hansonplc.com. **Description:** Operates an open excavation site used for obtaining building stone, slate, and limestone. **NOTE:** Send resumes to 2300 Gateway Center Boulevard, Morrisville NC 27560. **Corporate headquarters location:** London England. **Other area locations:** Statewide. **Other U.S. locations:** Nationwide. **International locations:** Worldwide. **Parent company:** Hanson PLC. **Listed on:** New York Stock Exchange. **Stock exchange symbol:** HAN. **CEO:** Christopher Collins. **Number of employees worldwide:** 28,000.

JOHN H. HARLAND COMPANY
2939 Miller Road, Decatur GA 30035. 770/981-9460. **Fax:** 770/593-5619. **Contact:** Human Resources. **World Wide Web address:** http://www.harland.net. **Description:** A financial printing firm. Products include business and personal checks, as well as other forms and documents for the banking industry. **Positions advertised include:** Configuration Specialist. **Corporate headquarters location:** This location. **Subsidiaries include:** Scanton Corporation. **Listed on:** New York Stock Exchange. **Stock exchange symbol:** JH. **CEO:** Timothy Tuff. **Number of employees nationwide:** 5,200.

HARRIS CALORIFIC
2345 Murphy Boulevard, Gainesville GA 30504-6000. 770/536-8801. **Toll-free phone:** 800/241-0804. **Fax:** 770/535-0544. **Contact:** Human Resources Department. **World Wide Web address:** http://www.harriscal.com. **Description:** Manufactures electronic welding equipment. One of the largest gas apparatus equipment creators in the world. **Corporate headquarters location:** This location. **Other U.S. locations:** CA; WI; IN; OH; NJ. **International locations:** Ireland; Italy. **Parent company:** Lincoln Electric. **President/CEO:** Dave Nangle.

THE HARTFORD
50 Glenlake Parkway NE, Suite 200 Atlanta GA 30328. 770/730-3331. **Toll-free phone:** 800/282-5855. **Fax:** 877/905-2773. **World Wide Web address:** http://www.thehartford.com. **Description:** Provider of investment, financial, and insurance products and services including life insurance, group and employee benefits, and automobile and homeowners insurance. Founded in 1810. **NOTE:** Please visit website to register, search for jobs, and apply online. **Positions advertised include:** Senior Accountant; Litigation Representative; PL Auto Claim Processor; SIU Investigator; Senior Loss Control Consultant; Assistant Manager – Service; Sales

Manager; Commercial Marine Underwriter; Construction Underwriter. **Corporate headquarters:** Hartford CT. **Other U.S. locations:** Nationwide. **International locations:** Canada. **Listed on:** New York Stock Exchange. **Stock exchange symbol:** HIG. **Number of employees nationwide:** 27,000. **Number of employees worldwide:** 29,000.

HARTRAMPF, INC.
7000 Central Parkway, Suite 1475, Atlanta GA 30328. 678/320-1888. **Fax:** 770/522-8115. **Contact:** Carol Lathem, Office Manager. **E-mail address:** hr@hartrampf.com. **World Wide Web address:** http://www.hartrampf.com. **Description:** A full-service engineering and architectural firm. Services provided include architectural, structural, mechanical, electrical, civil, environmental, and municipal engineering; surveying and energy conservation; and economic and technical feasibility studies and reports. **NOTE:** Please mail resumes to 180 Allen Road, Suite 217-N, Atlanta GA 30328-4862. Fax to 404/847-0846. **Special programs:** Internships. **Corporate headquarters location:** This location. **Operations at this facility include:** Service. **Number of employees at this location:** 28.

HAVERTY FURNITURE COMPANIES, INC.
P.O. Box 420099, Atlanta GA 30342-0099. **Physical address:** 780 Johnson Ferry Road, Suite 800, Atlanta GA 30342. 404/443-2900. **Fax:** 404/443-4170. **Contact:** Vice President of Human Resources. **E-mail address:** hr@havertys.com. **World Wide Web address:** http://www.havertys.com. **Description:** A full-service home furnishings retailer with more than 100 showrooms in 14 states. The company distributes and sells furniture lines under the Thomasville, Drexel Heritage, and Broyhill names. Founded in 1885. **Company slogan:** Making it home. **Positions advertised include:** Sales Associate; Visual Coordinator. **Special programs:** Training. **Office hours:** Monday - Friday, 8:30 a.m. - 5:00 p.m. **Corporate headquarters location:** This location. **Other U.S. locations:** Nationwide. **Listed on:** New York Stock Exchange. **Stock exchange symbol:** HVT. **CEO/President:** Clarence H. Smith. **Annual sales/revenues:** More than $100 million. **Number of employees nationwide:** 4,180.

HAWKINS & PARNELL
303 Peachtree Street NE, Suite 4000, Suntrust Plaza, Atlanta GA 30308-3243. 404/614-7400. **Fax:** 404/614-7500. **Contact:** Human Resources. **World Wide Web address:** http://www.hawkinsparnell.com. **Description:** A 54-attorney law firm specializing in civil and appellate litigation. Founded in 1963. **Corporate headquarters location:** This location. **Other U.S. locations:** Charleston WV; Dallas TX. **Number of employees at this location:** 60.

HAY GROUP
303 Peachtree Street NE, Atlanta GA 30328. 404/575-8700. **Fax:** 404/575-8711. **Contact:** Personnel. **World Wide Web address:** http://www.haygroup.com. **Description:** An international human resources and management consulting firm that provides services such as total compensation planning, strategic management, business culture, employee surveys, and outplacement. Founded 1943. **NOTE:** Please visit website to register, search for jobs, and apply online. **Positions advertised include:** Consultant. **Corporate headquarters location:** Philadelphia PA. **Other U.S. locations:** Nationwide. **International locations:** Worldwide. **Number of employees worldwide:** 2,200.

HAYSLETT SORREL
50 Glenlake Parkway, NE, Suite 430, Atlanta 30328. 770/522-8855. **Fax:** 770/522-8898. **Contact:** Human Resources. **World Wide Web address:** http://www.hayslettsorrel.com. **Description:** One of the largest and most successful public relations firms in the Atlanta area. **CEO:** Charlie Hayslett.

HEAD START PROGRAM
4332 Rosemont Drive, Columbus GA 31904. 706/327-2682. **Contact:** Human Resources. **World Wide Web address:** http://www2.acf.dhhs.gov/programs/hsb. **Description:** A state- and federally funded program for low-income families with young children. Founded in 1965. **NOTE:** Please visit website to search for jobs. **Other area locations:** Statewide. **Other U.S. locations:** Nationwide.

HEALTHFIELD INC.
6666 Powers Ferry Road, Suite 328, Atlanta GA 30339. 770/953-9510. **Fax:** 770/541-3747. **Contact:** Personnel. **World Wide Web address:** http://www.healthfield.com. **Description:** Provides home health care services throughout Georgia and Alabama. **Positions advertised include:** RN; LPN; Physical Therapist; Speech Therapist; Occupational Therapist; Case Manager; Order Manager; Pharmacist; Respiratory Therapist; Service Technician; Care Coordinator; Biller/Collector. **Parent company:** Four Seasons Healthcare Inc.

HEATCRAFT INC.
2175 West Park Place Boulevard, Stone Mountain GA 30087. 770/465-5600. **Fax:** 770/465-5990. **Contact:** Human Resources. **E-mail address:** hrpd.feedback@heatcraftrpd.com. **World Wide Web address:** http://www.heatcraftrpd.com. **Description:** Manufactures commercial refrigeration products. **NOTE:** Entry-level positions are offered. **Special programs:** Co-ops. **Corporate headquarters location:** This location. **Parent company:** Lennox International. **Operations at this facility include:** Administration; Manufacturing; Research and Development; Sales; Service. **Listed on:** New York Stock Exchange. **Stock exchange symbol:** LII.

HEBCO INC.
7980 Industrial Highway, Suite B, Macon GA 31216. 478/788-9340. **Fax:** 478/784-9087. **Contact:** Randy Williams. **E-mail address:** hebco@hebco.com. **World Wide Web address:** http://www.hebco.com. **Description:** Provides computer engineering and technical services. **Corporate headquarters location:** Oklahoma City OK. **Other U.S. locations:** AR; PA.

HERAEUS TENEVO
100 Heraeus Boulevard, Buford GA 30518. 770/945-2275. **Fax:** 770/945-4741. **Contact:** Human Resources. **World Wide Web address:** http://www.heraeus-tenevo.com. **Description:** Manufactures silica glass and quartz electronic components. **Office hours:** Monday – Friday, 8:00 a.m. – 5:00 p.m. **Corporate headquarters location:** Hanau Germany. **Other U.S. locations:** Nationwide. **Parent company:** Heraeus Group. **CEO:** Gunter Bachmann. **Number of employees worldwide:** 500.

HERTZ CORPORATION
4751 Best Road, Suite 400, Atlanta GA 30337. 404/530-2990. Fax: 404/530-2962. **Contact:** John Kreitner, Employee Relations. **E-mail address:** jkreitner@hertz.com. **World Wide Web address:** http://www.hertz.com. **Description:** Area offices for the national transportation services organization. Hertz Corporation operates nationally through three divisions: the Rent-A-Car Division, the Car Leasing Division, and the Equipment Rental and Leasing Division. **Positions advertised include:** Heavy Equipment Mechanic; Branch Manager; Management Trainee; Suburban Sales Representative; Financial Analyst. **Corporate headquarters location:** Park Ridge NJ. **Other U.S. locations:** Nationwide. **International locations:** Worldwide. **Parent company:** Ford Motor Company. **President/CEO:** Craig R. Koch. **Number of employees worldwide:** 28,900.

HERZING COLLEGE OF BUSINESS AND TECHNOLOGY
3355 Lenox Road, Suite 100, Atlanta GA 30326. 404/816-4533. **Fax:** 404/816-5576. **Contact:** Director. **World Wide Web address:** http://www.herzing.edu/atlanta. **Description:** A business and technical college offering Associate's and Bachelor's degrees. **NOTE:** Please visit website for online application form. **Corporate headquarters location:** Milwaukee WI. **Other U.S. locations:** Birmingham AL; Madison WI; Minneapolis MN; New Orleans LA; Orlando FL. **International locations:** Canada. **Parent company:** Herzing Institutes. **Operations at this facility include:** Administration; Sales; Service. **Listed on:** Privately held.

HEWITT ASSOCIATES
3350 Riverwood Parkway, Suite 80, Atlanta GA 30339-3370. 770/956-7777. **Fax:** 770/956-8780. **Contact:** Human Resources. **World Wide Web address:** http://www.hewitt.com. **Description:** Hewitt Associates is an international firm of consultants and actuaries specializing in the design, finance, communication, and administration of employee benefit and compensation programs. **NOTE:** There are two Atlanta office locations. Please visit website to search for jobs and apply online. **Positions advertised include:** Client Financial Analyst; Experienced Consultant; Market Learning Consultant; Health Management Design Consultant; Technical Programmer Analyst; Local Market Recruiter; HW Quality Assurance Analyst; Pension Administration Analyst; Business Systems Analyst; HM Project Manager; Communication Consultant; Sales Analyst; Talent Design Consultant. **Corporate headquarters location:** Lincolnshire IL. **Other U.S. locations:** Nationwide. **International locations:** Worldwide. **Operations at this facility include:** Benefits consulting. **Listed on:** New York Stock Exchange. **Stock exchange symbol:** HEW. **CEO:** Dale L. Gifford. **Number of employees worldwide:** 13,000.

HIGH MUSEUM OF ART
1280 Peachtree Street NE, Atlanta GA 30309. 404/733-4400. **Fax:** 404/733-4502. **Contact:** Personnel. **World Wide Web address:** http://www.high.org. **Description:** A contemporary art museum. Holdings include 19th- and 20th-century American furniture, 19th-century American landscape paintings, European paintings and sculptures from the 14th through the 19th centuries, African masks and ceremonial figures, folk art, and photography. The museum also offers an education gallery where performances, workshops, and classes are held, and children of all ages can participate in hands-on art activities. Founded in 1905. **Special programs:** Internships; Volunteer Opportunities. **Parent company:** The Robert W. Woodruff Arts Center. **Number of employees at this location:** 150.

HILL PHOENIX
2050 East Park Drive, Conyers GA 30013. 770/285-3100. **Fax:** 770/285-3224. **Contact:** Human Resources. **E-mail address:** hr_conyers@hillphoenix.com. **World Wide Web address:** http://www.hillphoenix.com. **Description:** Manufactures refrigeration equipment for supermarkets and convenience stores. **NOTE:** No phone calls regarding employment. **Corporate headquarters location:** This location. **Other area locations:** Covington GA. **Other U.S. locations:** CA; VA. **Parent company:** Dover Corporation. **Operations at this facility include:** Manufacturing. **Listed on:** New York Stock Exchange. **Stock exchange symbol:** DOV.

HITACHI TELECOM USA
3617 Parkway Lane, Norcross GA 30092. 770/446-8820. **Fax:** 770/242-1414. **Contact:** Personnel. **World Wide Web address:** http://www.hitel.com. **Description:** A telecommunications company engaged in the assembly and sale of telephone systems. Founded 1910. **NOTE:** For more information on the Hitachi corporation, visit http://www.hitachi.com, or http://www.hitachi.us **Corporate headquarters location:** This location. **Parent company:** Hitachi Ltd. **Listed on:** New York Stock Exchange. **Stock exchange symbol:** HIT. **President/CEO:** Etsuhiko Shoyama. **Number of employees worldwide:** 339,572.

HOLLAND & KNIGHT LLP
1201 West Peachtree Street NE, One Atlantic Center, Suite 2000, Atlanta GA 30309-3400. 404/817-8500. **Fax:** 404/881-0470. **Contact:** Human Resources. **E-mail address:** atl.careers@hklaw.com. **World Wide Web address:** http://www.hklaw.com. **Description:** An international law firm. **NOTE:** Please visit website to search for jobs. **Positions advertised include:** Paralegal. **Special programs:** Summer Associate Program.

THE HOME DEPOT
2455 Paces Ferry Road, Atlanta GA 30339-4024. 770/433-8211. **Contact:** Human Resources. **World Wide Web address:** http://www.homedepot.com. **Description:** Operates retail warehouse stores that sell a wide assortment of building materials and home improvement products, primarily to the do-it-yourself and home remodeling markets. The company operates 1,232 full-service, warehouse-style stores. The stores stock over 40,000 different kinds of building materials, home improvement supplies, and lawn and garden products. Founded in 1978. **NOTE:** Please visit website to search for jobs and apply online. **Positions advertised include:** Senior Systems Specialist; Merchandising Leadership Personnel; Inventory Supervisor; Administrative Assistant; Manager of Finance; Loss Prevention Business Specialist. **Special programs:** Internships. **Corporate headquarters location:** This location. **Other U.S. locations:** Nationwide. **International locations:** Canada; Mexico. **Listed on:** New York Stock Exchange. **Operations at this facility include:** Atlanta Store Support. **Stock exchange symbol:** HD. **CEO:** Bob Nardelli. **Annual sales/revenues:** More than $100 million. **Number of employees nationwide:** 300,000.

THE HOME DEPOT SUPPLY
3300 Breckinridge Boulevard, Suite 100, Duluth GA 30096. 770/449-7000. **Toll-free phone:** 800/395-2739. **Fax:** 770/263-4834. 441-8674. **Contact:** Human Resources. **World Wide Web address:** http://www.apexsupply.com. **Description:** A wholesale distributor of plumbing, heating, air conditioning, industrial piping products, cabinetry, appliances, and tools. The company's three major businesses are plumbing, heating and air conditioning, and building specialty products. The company distributes a variety of products including major brand names such as Kohler, Price-Pfister, Jacuzzi, Delta, and State; Trane, Honeywell, and Reznor; Jamesbury, Sarco, Nibco, Asahi, Weldbend, and US Pipe; Timberlake, Millbrook, and Plato; GE, Magic-Chef, Kitchen Aid, and Sub Zero; and Makita and Ridgid. **NOTE:** Entry-level positions are offered. Please visit website to search for jobs and apply online. **Positions advertised include:** Warehouse Operator; Outside Sales Associate. **Special programs:** Internships; Co-ops. **Corporate headquarters location:** Atlanta GA. **Other area locations:** Statewide. **Other U.S. locations:** SC; TN; FL. **Parent company:** The Home Depot. **Operations at this facility include:** Administration; Sales; Service. **Listed on:** New York Stock Exchange. **Stock exchange symbol:** HD. **Annual sales/revenues:** More than $100 million.

HOMEBANC MORTGAGE CORPORATION
5555 Glenridge Connector NE, Suite 800, Atlanta GA 30342. 404/303-4113. **Fax:** 404/303-4116. **Contact:** Human Resources. **E-mail address:** careers@homebanc.com. **World Wide Web address:** http://www.homebanc.com. **Description:** A full-service mortgage lender. **Office hours:** Monday – Friday, 8:00 a.m. – 5:00 p.m. **Corporate headquarters location:** This location. **Operations at this facility include:** Administration; Sales; Service. **CEO:** Patrick Flood.

HOMESTEAD VILLAGE INC.
2239 Powers Ferry Road, Marietta GA 30067. 770/303-0043. **Toll-free phone:** 888/782-9473. **Fax:** 770/303-0063. **Contact:** Human Resources. **World Wide Web address:** http://www.homesteadvillage.com. **Description:** An extended-stay hotel chain. Guests are typically business travelers who are on extended-stay assignments, attending seminars, or in the process of relocating to a new city. The company owns and operates 112 properties. Founded in 1992. **NOTE:** Please visit website to search for jobs and apply online. **Corporate headquarters location:** This location. **Other U.S. locations:** Nationwide. **Listed on:** American Stock Exchange. **Stock exchange symbol:** HSD. **President/CEO:** Gary A. DeLapp. **Annual sales/revenues:** $51 - $100 million. **Number of employees nationwide:** 1,800.

HONEYWELL
1190 West Druid Hills Drive NE, Suite 160, Atlanta GA 30329. 404/248-2300. 2430. **Contact:** Human Resources. **World Wide Web address:** http://www.honeywell.com. **Description:** Honeywell is engaged in the research, development, manufacture, and sale of advanced technology products and services in the fields of chemicals, electronics, automation, and controls. The company's major businesses are home and building automation and control, performance polymers and chemicals, industrial automation and control, space and aviation systems, and defense and marine systems. **NOTE:** Please visit website to search for jobs and apply online. Jobs are available for college students, both graduate and undergraduate. **Positions advertised include:** Operations Manager. **Corporate headquarters location:** Morris Township NJ. **Other area locations:** Norcross GA; Dalton GA; Duluth GA; Alpharetta GA; Elberton GA; Hapeville GA; Perry GA; Savannah GA. **Other U.S. locations:** Nationwide. **International locations:** Worldwide. **CEO:** David M. Cote. **Listed on:** New York Stock Exchange. **Stock exchange symbol:** HON. **Number of employees worldwide:** 100,000.

HOOD FLEXIBLE PACKAGING
5383 Truman Drive, Decatur GA 30035. 770/981-5400. **Fax:** 770-987-3100. **Contact:** Erica Haley. **E-mail address:** ehaley@hoodpackaging.com. **World Wide Web address:** http://www.hoodpackaging.com. **Description:** Hood Flexible Packaging offers a wide variety of product options to meet packaging needs. They specialize in producing custom made bags to meet the needs of their clients. **Positions advertised include:** Press Operator. **Corporate headquarters locations:** Madison WI. **Other U.S. locations:** Arden Hills MN, Grand Forks ND, Hamlet NC, Pine Bluff AR, Tyler TX, Valdosta GA, Wilmington OH. **Operations at this facility include:** Manufacturing; Administrative.

HOSHIZAKI AMERICA, INC.
618 Highway 74 South, Peachtree City GA 30269. 770/487-2331. **Toll-free phone:** 800/438-6087. **Fax:** 770/487-1325. **Contact:** Human Resources. **E-mail address:** hr@hoshizaki.com. **World Wide Web address:** http://www.hoshizaki.com. **Description:** Manufactures commercial ice machines, storage bins, dispensers, and refrigerators. **Positions advertised include:** National Accounts Manager; FMS Operator; Press Brake Operator; NCT Operator; Material Handler; Account Manager. **Corporate headquarters location:** This location. **Other area locations:** Griffin GA. **International locations:** Japan, England. **Parent company:** Hoshizaki Electric, Ltd. **Listed on:** Privately held. **Number of employees worldwide:** 7,000.

HOWARD SYSTEMS INTERNATIONAL
6 Concourse Parkway, Suite 2140, Atlanta GA 30328. 770/394-5700. **Toll-free phone:** 800/775-1828. **Fax:** 770/730-8470. **Contact:** Human Resources. **E-mail address:** jobopportunities@howardsystems.com; raleigh@howardsystems.com. **World Wide Web address:** http://www.howardsystems.com. **Descriptions:** An IT staffing and business solutions company. **NOTE:** Please visit website to search for jobs or to fill out the online application form. **Corporate headquarters:** Stamford CT. **Other U.S. locations:** NJ; TX; OH; CO; NY; NC. **President:** Howard Persky.

HUBER ENGINEERED MATERIALS
1000 Parkwood Circle, Suite 1000, Atlanta GA 30339. 678/247-7300. **Toll-free phone:** 800/313-6888. **Fax:** 678/247-2797. **Contact:** Human Resources. **E-mail address:** staffing@huber.com. **World Wide Web address:** http://www.huber.com. **Description:** Engineers a variety of products through science and chemistry. The company's products range from cosmetics to coatings for bridges and ships. **Corporate headquarters location:** This location. **Other area locations:** Fairmont GA; Kennesaw GA; Macon GA; Marble Hill GA; Sandersville GA; Wrens GA. **Other U.S. locations:** Etowah TN; Havre de Grace MD; Hawesville KY; Johnsonburg PA; Kingsport TN; Longview WA; Seattle WA; Marble Falls TX; Quincy IL. **International locations:** Worldwide. **Parent company:** J.M. Huber Corporation.

HUNTON & WILLIAMS
600 Peachtree Street NE, Suite 4100, Atlanta GA 30308-2216. 404/888-4000. **Fax:** 404/888-4190. **Contact:** Wanda W. Boyd, Human Resources Administrator. **E-mail address:** wboyd@hunton.com. **World Wide Web address:** http://www.hunton.com. **Description:** A law firm specializing in corporate law and securities, energy and environmental issues, international law, litigation, real estate law, and taxes. Founded in 1901. **NOTE:** Contact Theresa Kimble, Recruiter – phone is 404/888-4164, e-mail is tkimble@hunton.com – for potential lawyer positions, and Wanda W. Boyd, Human Resources Administrator – phone is 404/888-4101 –for potential staff positions. Please visit website to search for open positions. **Other U.S. locations:** Nationwide. **International locations:** Thailand, Belgium; China; London; Singapore.

HYATT REGENCY ATLANTA
265 Peachtree Street NE, Atlanta GA 30303. 404/577-1234. **Fax:** 404/588-4137. **Contact:** Human Resources. **World Wide Web address:** http://atlantaregency.hyatt.com. **Description:** Operates a luxury hotel with complete dining and entertainment facilities. **NOTE:** Please visit website to search for jobs and apply online. **Positions advertised include:** Associate Catering Director; Banquet Sous Chef; Bartender; Convention Services Manager; Culinary Lead Cook; Food Server; Greeter; HVAC Engineer; Intermediate Line Cook; Room Attendant/Housekeeper; Sales Manager; Security Officer – On-Call. **Special programs:** Internships. **Corporate headquarters location:** Chicago IL. **Other U.S. locations:** Nationwide. **Parent company:** Hyatt Hotels Corporation. **International locations:** Worldwide. **Operations at this facility include:** Administration; Regional Headquarters; Sales; Service.

HYDRO-CHEM, INC.
P.O. Box 869, Holly Springs GA 30142. 770/345-2222. **Physical address:** 110 Hickory Springs Industrial Drive, Canton GA 30015. **Fax:** 770/345-2778. **Contact:** Human Resources. **E-mail address:** norton@hydro-chem.com. **World Wide Web address:** http://www.proquip-corp.com. **Description:** Designs, engineers, and manufactures industrial gas (hydrogen, nitrogen, oxygen, and methanol) plants. **Corporate headquarters location:** Tulsa OK. **International locations:** Worldwide. **Parent company:** Pro-Quip Corporation. **Operations at this facility include:** Administration; Manufacturing; Sales; Service.

HYPERION SOFTWARE CORPORATION
3200 Town Point Drive, Suite 175, Kennesaw GA 30144. 678/797-6540. **Fax:** 678/797-6541. **Contact:** Human Resources. **World Wide Web address:** http://www.hysoft.com. **Description:** Hyperion Software Corporation develops financial applications for managers and analysts. **NOTE:** Please visit website to search for jobs and apply online. **Corporate headquarters location:** Sunnyvale CA. **Other U.S. locations:** Nationwide. **International locations:** Worldwide. **Operations at this facility include:** Regional sales office. **Listed on:** NASDAQ. **Stock exchange symbol:** HYSL. **Number of employees worldwide:** 2,600.

IBM CORPORATION
4111 Northside Parkway NW, Atlanta GA 30327. 404/238-7000. **Toll-free phone:** 800/426-4968. **Fax:** 800/262-2494. **Contact:** IBM Staffing Services. **World Wide Web address:** http://www.ibm.com. **Description:** IBM is a developer, manufacturer, and marketer of advanced information processing products including computers and microelectronic technology, software, networking systems, and information technology-related services. **NOTE:** Please visit website to search for jobs and apply online. **Positions advertised include:** Application Architect; Associate Service Delivery Representative; Business Operations/Program Manager; Portal/Lotus Specialist; Systems Services Representative; Technical eLearning Consultant. **Corporate headquarters location:** White Plains NY. **Other area locations:** Statewide. **Other U.S. locations:** Nationwide. **International locations:** Worldwide. **Operations at this facility include:** This location is a sales office. **Subsidiaries include:** IBM Credit Corporation; IBM Instruments, Inc.; IBM World Trade Corporation. **Listed on:** New York Stock Exchange. **Stock exchange symbol:** IBM. **CEO:** Samuel J. Palmisano.

IFF INC.
P.O. Box 45505, Atlanta GA 30320. 404/305-9433. **Physical address:** 452-A Plaza Drive, Cottage Park GA 30349. **Fax:** 404/209-6741. **E-mail address:** peter.halpaus@iffusa.com. **Contact:** Peter Halpaus. **World Wide Web address:** http://www.iffusa.com. **Description:** A forwarder of international freight. Founded in 1983. **Corporate headquarters location:** This location. **Other U.S. locations:** Charlotte NC; Greenville SC; Richmond VA. **President:** Jeff Smith.

IKON OFFICE SOLUTIONS
1738 Bass Road, Building 3, Macon GA 31210. 478/238-7200. **Toll-free phone:** 800/800/1060. **Fax:** 912/471-2369. **E-mail address:** resumes@ikon.com. **World Wide Web address:** http://www.ikon.com. **Description:** One of the world's largest providers of copier and printer technologies. IKON hopes to aid companies in their management of large workloads by providing the best technology and service. **NOTE:** Please visit website to search for jobs and apply online. **Positions advertised include:** Accounts Payable Associate; Cash Operations Associate; Logistics Assistant; Lease Collections Supervisor; Collector; Commercial Credit Analyst; IT Project Manager; Customer Service Representative; Recruiter; Named Account Representative; Bi-lingual Collector. **Corporate headquarters location:** Malvern PA. **Other area locations:** Statewide. **Other U.S. locations:** Nationwide. **International locations:** Canada; Denmark; France; Germany; Mexico; United Kingdom; Ireland. **Operations at this facility include:** This location serves as the main area office. **Listed on:** New York Stock Exchange. **Stock exchange symbol:** IKN. **Number of employees worldwide:** 7,000.

IPD PRINTING & DISTRIBUTING INC.
WALLACE COMPANY
5800 Peachtree Road, Chamblee GA 30341. 770/458-6351. **Toll-free phone:** 800/241-3776. **Contact:** Personnel. **World Wide Web address:** http://www.rrdonnelley.com. **Description:** Provides a wide range of commercial printing services including the printing of direct mail components, "scratch 'n sniff" magazine inserts, and quarterly financial statements. **NOTE:** Please visit website to search for jobs and apply online. **Parent company:** RR Donnelley. **Other U.S. locations:** Nationwide.

INGENICO
1003 Mansell Road, Atlanta GA 30076. 770/594-6000. **Fax:** 770/594-6003. **Contact:** Human Resources. **E-mail address:** hr@ingenico-us.com. **World Wide Web address:** http://www.ingenico-us.com. **Description:** Develops, manufactures, and markets point-of-sale payment automation systems and terminals including check readers, payment authorization systems, signature capture devices, and MICR analyzers. **Corporate headquarters location:** France. **Other U.S. locations:** Chattanooga TN; Pleasanton CA. **International locations:** Worldwide. **Annual sales/revenues:** $21 - $50 million. **Number of employees worldwide:** 2,000.

IMAGING TECHNOLOGIES
640 10th Street, Atlanta GA 30318. 404/873-5911. **Contact:** Human Resources. **E-mail address:** careers@itrepro.com. **World Wide Web address:** http://www.itrepro.com. **Description:** Provides several printing and imaging services including blue printing, quick copying, laminating, mounting, and binding. Founded 1919. **Corporate headquarters location:** This location. **Other U.S. locations:** AL; FL; NC; SC. **President:** Carter D. Pope.

IMMUCOR
P.O. Box 5625, Norcross GA 30091-5625. 770/441-2051. **Physical address:** 3130 Gateway Drive, Norcross GA 30071. **Toll-free phone:** 800/829-2553. **Fax:** 770/441-3807. **Contact:** Human Resources. **E-mail address:** hr@immucor.com. **World Wide Web address:** http://www.immucor.com. **Description:** An international in vitro diagnostic company that develops, manufactures, and markets products used by blood banks, hospitals, and clinical laboratories to test, detect, and identify properties of the human blood. Founded in 1982. **NOTE:** Entry-level positions are offered. Please visit website to search for jobs and apply online. **Positions advertised include:** Field Service Engineer; Customer Service Representative. **Office hours:** Monday – Friday, 8:30 a.m. – 5:30 p.m. **Corporate headquarters location:** This location. **Other U.S. locations:** Houston TX; Thomas VA. **International locations:** Worldwide. **Listed on:** NASDAQ. **Stock exchange symbol:** BLUD. **Number of employees nationwide:** 500. **President/CEO:** Edward Gallup.

IMPERIAL SUGAR
P.O. Box 710, Savannah GA 31498. 912/234-1261. **Physical Address:** 2 Oxnard Drive, Savannah GA 3407. **Contact:** Personnel. **E-mail address:** ischr@imperialsugar.com. **World Wide Web address:** http://www.imperialsugar.com. **Description:** The largest processor of sugar in the United States. The company markets the sugar brands Imperial, Dixie Crystals, Holly, and Spreckels. **Corporate headquarters location:** Sugar Land TX. **Operations at this facility include:** This

facility produces sugar, sugar-derived products, and liquid animal feeds. **Listed on:** NASDAQ. **Stock exchange symbol:** IPSU. **Number of employees nationwide:** 1,200.

INDUS INTERNATIONAL
3301 Windy Ridge Parkway, Atlanta GA 30339. 770/952-8444. **Fax:** 770/955-2977. **Contact:** Human Resources. **E-mail address:** recruiter_east@Indus.com. **World Wide Web address:** http://www.indus.com. **Description:** Develops software for client/server asset care applications used by manufacturing companies. **Corporate headquarter locations:** This location. **Other U.S. locations:** Columbia SC; Englewood Cliffs NJ; Pittsburg PA; Richland WA; San Francisco CA. **International locations:** Canada; United Kingdom; France; Australia; Japan; Dubai. **Listed on:** NASDAQ. **Stock exchange symbol:** IINT. **President/CEO:** Gregory J. Dukat. **Number of employees worldwide:** 600.

INFOR
3425-B Corporate Way, Duluth GA 30096. 770/418-2000. **Contact:** Human Resources. **E-mail address:** hr@infor.com. **World Wide Web address:** http://www.infor.com. **Description:** Develops software for select manufacturing and distribution industries. **Corporate headquarters location:** This location. **Other U.S. locations:** Chicago IL; Shrewsbury NJ. **CEO:** Jess Solomon.

INITIATIVE MEDIA NORTH AMERICA
15 Piedmont Center, Suite 500, Atlanta GA 30305. 404/814-8711. **Fax:** 404/949-3562. **Contact:** Human Resources. **World Wide Web address:** http://www.im-na.com. **Description:** Offers media management and planning services including strategic planning, research, and television optimization. **Corporate headquarters location:** New York NY. **Other U.S. locations:** Nationwide. **International locations:** Worldwide. **Parent company:** The Interpublic Group of Companies.

INSTITUTE OF NUCLEAR POWER OPERATIONS (INPO)
700 Galleria Parkway SE, Atlanta GA 30339-5957. 770/644-8000. **Contact:** Human Resources. **Description:** A nonprofit organization funded by electric utility companies that own and operate nuclear power plants. INPO provides services to aid these companies in the safe operation of their power plants. **Office hours:** Monday – Friday, 8:00 a.m. – 4:45 p.m. **Corporate headquarters location:** This location. **Number of employees nationwide:** 350.

INSTITUTE OF PAPER SCIENCE AND TECHNOLOGY
500 10th Street NW, Atlanta GA 30332-0620. 404/894-5700. **Toll-free phone:** 800/558-6611. **Fax:** 404/894-4778. **Contact:** Human Resources Manager. **World Wide Web address:** http://www.ipst.gatech.edu. **Description:** A graduate school offering master's and doctoral degrees in paper science engineering. **NOTE:** IPST recently merged with Georgia Institute of Technology. Please contact their employment office for information on open positions.

THE INSURANCE HOUSE
P.O. Box 28155, Atlanta GA 30358-0155. 770/952-0080. **Physical address:** 1904 Leland Drive, Marietta GA 30067. **Toll-free phone:** 800/282-7024. **Fax:** 770/858-0175. **Contact:** Human Resources. **E-mail address:** eatwood@insurancehouse.com. **World Wide Web address:** http://www.sgfgroup.com. **Description:** Provides commercial and private passenger automobile insurance, general and professional liability insurance, and commercial and personal property insurance. **Positions advertised include:** Bi-Lingual Customer Service Representative; DBA Manager; Data Entry Specialist; Product Manager; Claims Representative; Accountant. **Other U.S. locations:** Winston-Salem NC. **Parent company:** Southern General

INTERCONTINENTAL HOTELS GROUP
3 Ravinia Drive, Suite 2900, Atlanta GA 30346-2149. 770/604-2000. **Fax:** 770/604-2371. **Contact:** Human Resources. **World Wide Web address:** http://www.ihgplc.com. **Description:** Six Continents Hotels owns and operates over 3,200 hotels across 100 countries. **NOTE:** Please visit http://www.ichotelsgroup.new-jobs.com to search for jobs and apply online. **Positions advertised include:** Loyalty Marketing Manager; Director of Finance and Business Support; Analytics Analyst; Senior Market Research Consultant; Software Engineer; Global Alliances Manager; Project Manager – Investment Analysis; Lead Analyst – Technical Services; Specialist – Reporting; Director of Global Consumer Marketing; Revenue Manager. **Corporate headquarters location:** Berkshire England. **International locations:** Worldwide. **Operations at this facility include:** This location houses administrative offices. **Listed on:** New York Stock Exchange. **Stock exchange symbol:** IHG. **CEO:** Richard North. **Number of employees worldwide:** 69,953. Finance Group. **President/CEO:** Jill Jinks.

INTERDENOMINATIONAL THEOLOGY CENTER (ITC)
700 Martin Luther King Jr. Drive SW, Atlanta GA 30314-4143. 404/527-77000. 11. **Fax:** 404/614-6380. **Contact:** Janette King, Manager of Human Resources. **World Wide Web address:** http://www.itc.edu. **Description:** A graduate school of theology. **NOTE:** Direct contact phone number is 404/527-7711. **Corporate headquarters location:** This location. **Listed on:** Privately held. **President:** Dr. Michael A. Battle.

INTERFACE FLOORING SYSTEMS, INC.
P.O. Box 1503, LaGrange GA 30241. 706/882-1891. **Physical address:** 1503 Orchard Hill Road, LaGrange GA 30241. **Toll-free phone:** 800/336-0225. **Fax:** 706/845-7920. **Contact:** Tommy Bell, Director of Human Resources. **World Wide Web address:** http://www.interfaceinc.com. **Description:** A large manufacturer and seller of modular and broadloom carpeting to commercial, residential, and institutional markets. **Corporate headquarters location:** Atlanta GA. **Other U.S. locations:** Nationwide. **International locations:** Worldwide. **Parent company:** Interface, Inc. **Operations at this facility include:** Administration; Divisional Headquarters; Manufacturing; Research and Development; Sales; Service. **Listed on:** NASDAQ. **Stock exchange symbol:** IFSIA.

INTERFACE, INC.
2859 Paces Ferry Road, Suite 2000, Atlanta GA 30339. 770/437-6800. **Fax:** 770/319-0070. **Contact:** Human Resources. **World Wide Web address:** http://www.interfaceinc.com. **Description:** A large manufacturer and seller of modular and broadloom carpeting to commercial, residential, and institutional markets. The company also produces chemicals and designs, manufactures, and markets interior fabrics including upholstery and decorative window treatments. **Corporate headquarters location:** This location. **Other U.S. locations:** Nationwide. **International locations:** Worldwide. **Subsidiaries include:** Interface Flooring Systems, Inc. manufactures broadloom carpeting; Pandel manufactures vinyl carpet tile backing, specialty mats, and foam. **Listed on:** NASDAQ. **Stock exchange symbol:** IFSIA. **CEO:** Daniel Hendrix. **Number of employees worldwide:** 5,500.

INTERNATIONAL PAPER COMPANY
P.O. Box 570, Savannah GA 31402. 912/238-6000. **Physical address:** 1201 West Lathrop Avenue, Savannah GA. **Toll-free phone:** 800/841-2507. **Fax:** 912/238-6479. **Contact:** Human Resources. **World Wide Web address:** http://www.internationalpaper.com. **Description:** International Paper Company manufactures pulp and paper, packaging, wood products, and a range of specialty products. The company is organized into five business segments: Printing Papers, whose principal products include uncoated papers, coated papers, bristles, and pulp; Packaging, which includes industrial packaging, consumer packaging, and kraft and specialty papers; Distribution, including the sale of printing papers, graphic arts equipment and supplies, packaging materials, industrial supplies, and office products; Specialty Products, which includes imaging products, specialty panels, nonwovens, chemicals, and minerals; and Forest Products, which includes logging and wood products. **NOTE:** Please visit website to search for jobs and apply online. **Positions advertised include:** Paralegal. **Corporate headquarters location:** Stamford CT. **Other U.S. locations:** Nationwide. **International locations:** Africa; Asia; Canada; Europe. **Operations at this facility include:** Manufacturing of corrugated containers made from kraft paper, paper bags, and paper-treating chemicals. **Listed on:** New York Stock Exchange. **Stock exchange symbol:** IP. **Number of employees worldwide:** 83,000.

INTERPARK
615 Peachtree Street, Suite 1150, Atlanta GA 30308. 404/658-9053. **Fax:** 404/817-3617. **Contact:** Human Resources. **World Wide Web address:** http://www.interparkholdings.com. **Description:** Owns and manages a parking facility and offers consulting services in the design, construction, and operation of other such facilities. **Corporate headquarters location:** Chicago IL. **Other U.S. locations:** Nationwide.

IVIVITY
5555 Oakbrook Parkway, Suite 280, Norcross GA 30093-2286. 678/990-1550. **Fax:** 678/990-1551. **Contact:** Human Resources. **World Wide Web address:** http://www.ivivity.com. **Description:** A technology provider of intelligent storage infrastructure components and building blocks to storage networking and storage infrastructure OEMs. **Positions advertised include:** Operations Analyst; Product Manager; Field Application Engineer. **Corporate headquarters location:** This location. **President and CEO:** David Coombs.

JDA SOFTWARE GROUP
1090 Northchase Office Parkway, Suite 300, Marietta GA 30067-6402. 770/424-0100. **Contact:** Human Resources. **World Wide Web address:** http://www.jda.com. **Description:** Develops inventory control software. **NOTE:** Search and apply for jobs online. **Corporate headquarters location:** Scottsdale AZ. **Other U.S. locations:** Andover MA; Campbell CA; Columbus OH; Ann Arbor MI; St Louis Park MN; Naperville IL; Irving TX; Parsippany NJ. **International locations:** Worldwide. **Listed on:** NASDAQ. **Stock exchange symbol:** JDAS. **Number of employees worldwide:** 1,300.

JACKSON ELECTRIC MEMBER CORPORATION
P.O. Box 38, Jefferson GA 30549. 706/367-5281. **Physical address:** 850 Commerce Road, Jefferson GA. **Fax:** 706/367-6141. **Contact:** Bill Burns, Personnel Director. **E-mail address:** bburns@jacksonemc.com. **World Wide Web address:** http://www.jacksonemc.com. **Description:** A utility company offering electricity services. **Positions advertised include:** Customer Service Representative; Lineman Helper; Public Relations/Communications Representative; Mapping Database Analyst; Director – Job Training and Safety. **Corporate headquarters location:** This location. **Other area locations:** Gainseville GA; Lawrenceville GA; Hull GA. **President/CEO:** Randall Pugh.

JCPENNEY CATALOG FULFILLMENT CENTER
5500 Frontage Road, Forest Park GA 30297. 404/361-7700. **Contact:** Human Resources. **World Wide Web address:** http://www.jcpenney.net. **Description:** A catalog fulfillment center for the major national retail merchandise sales and services corporation. **Listed on:** New York Stock Exchange. **Stock exchange symbol:** JCP.

JEFFERIES & COMPANY, INC.
3414 Peachtree Road NE, Suite 810, Atlanta GA 30326. 404/264-5000. **Contact:** Human Resources. **World Wide Web address:** http://www.jefco.com. **Description:** Engaged in equity, convertible debt and taxable fixed income securities brokerage and trading, and corporate finance. Jefferies & Company, Inc. is one of the leading national firms engaged in the distribution and trading of blocks of equity securities and conducts such activities primarily in the third market, which refers to transactions in listed equity securities effected away from national securities exchanges. Founded in 1962. **NOTE:** Please visit website for more specific contact information. **Corporate headquarters location:** New York NY. **Other U.S. locations:** Nationwide. **International locations:** London England; Paris France; Zurich Switzerland; Tokyo Japan; Sydney Australia; Melbourne Australia. **Parent company:** Jefferies Group, Inc. is a holding company that, through Jefferies & Company and its three other primary subsidiaries, Investment Technology Group, Inc., Jefferies International Limited, and Jefferies Pacific Limited, is engaged in securities brokerage and trading, corporate finance, and other financial services. **Listed on:** New York Stock Exchange. **Stock exchange symbol:** JEF. **Number of employees worldwide:** 1,400.

JOHN DEERE LANDSCAPES
5610 McGinnis Ferry Road, Alpharetta GA 30005. 770/740-1874. **Contact:** Human Resources. **World Wide Web address:** http://www.johndeere.com. **Description:** Designs and manufactures a variety of tools and machines for construction, farming, and landscaping. Founded 1837. **NOTE:** Please visit website to search for jobs and apply online. **Positions advertised include:** Branch Manager. **Corporate headquarters location:** Moline IL. **Other area locations:** Statewide. **Other U.S. locations:** Nationwide. **International locations:** Worldwide. **Operations at this facility include:** This location offers landscaping and irrigation products and services. **Listed on:** New York Stock Exchange. **Stock exchange symbol:** DE. **Number of employees worldwide:** 43,000.

THE JONES COMPANY
P.O. Box 2149, Waycross GA 31501. 912/285-4011. **Physical address:** 102 Le Avenue, Waycross GA 31501. **Fax:** 912/285-5610. **Contact:** Employment. **World Wide Web address:** http://www.jonescoinc.com. **Description:** Owns and operates Flash Foods retail convenience stores. **Corporate headquarters location:** This location.

JONES WORLEY DESIGNS, INC.
723 Piedmont Road, NE, Atlanta GA 30365-0701. 404/876-9272. **Fax:** 404/876-9174. **Contact:** Human Resources. **E-mail address:** info@jonesworley.com. **World Wide Web address:** http://www.jonesworley.com. **Description:** A marketing and communications firm. **Corporate headquarters location:** This location.

JUDGE INC.
2500 Northwinds Parkway, Suite 300, Alpharetta GA 30004. 678/297-0800. **Fax:** 678/297-9014. **Contact:** Human Resources. **E-mail address:** atlantajobs@judge.com. **World Wide Web address:** http://www.judgeinc.com. **Description:** A technical

recruiting firm specializing in the food processing, pharmaceutical, retail, distribution, and information technology industries. Founded 1970. **Positions advertised include:** Production Supervisor; HAACP Coordinator. **Corporate headquarters location:** Conshohocken PA. **Other U.S. locations:** Arlington TX; Jacksonville FL; Laguna Hills CA; Tampa FL; Edison NJ.

JUST BRAKES
784 Bullsboro Drive, Newnan GA 30265. 770/252-4954. **Contact:** Human Resources. **E-mail address:** jobinfo@justbrakes.com. **World Wide Web address:** http://www.justbrakes.com. **Description:** An automotive store specializing in brake system safety. **NOTE:** Please visit website for online application form. **Positions advertised include:** Service Manager/Writer. **Other area locations:** Canton GA; Atlanta GA; Conyers GA; Stockbridge GA. **Other U.S. locations:** FL; NV; AZ; NM; TX; CO.

KFC
675 Mansell Road, Suite 200, Roswell GA 30076. 770/990-4000. **Fax:** 770/552-1739. **Contact:** Human Resources. **World Wide Web address:** http://www.kfc.com. **Description:** A worldwide fast-food chain specializing in chicken. Founded 1939. **Parent company:** Yum! Brands, Inc. **Office hours:** Monday – Friday, 8:00 a.m. – 5:00 p.m. **Corporate headquarters location:** Louisville KY. **Operations at this location include:** This location serves as a regional office. **Number of employees nationwide:** 84,000.

KPMG
303 Peachtree Street NE, Suite 2000, Atlanta GA 30308. 404/222-3000. **Contact:** Mr. Chris Beall, Director of Human Resources. **World Wide Web address:** http://www.us.kpmg.com. **Description:** Delivers a wide range of value-added assurance, tax, and consulting services, and is the U.S. member firm of KPMG International, the worldwide professional services firm. KPMG International is a leader among professional services firms engaged in capturing, managing, assessing, and delivering information to create knowledge that will help clients maximize shareholder value. Founded in 1897. **Positions advertised include:** Administrative Assistant; Desktop Support Senior Associate; Audit Manager; Senior Manager; Senior Associate; Manager – CFO Advisory Services; Career Assistance Program Manager; Audit Senior Associate; Senior Designer; Senior Financial Analyst; Senior Associate IRBS; Manager Sales and Transaction Tax. **Corporate headquarters location:** New York NY. **Other U.S. locations:** Nationwide. **International locations:** Worldwide. **CEO:** Eugene D. O'Kelly. **Number of employees nationwide:** 18,000. **Number of employees worldwide:** 100,000.

KAWNEER COMPANY, INC.
555 Guthridge Court, Norcross GA 30092. 770/449-5555. **Fax:** 770/734-1560. **Contact:** Human Resources. **World Wide Web address:** http://www.kawneer.com. **Description:** Manufactures and markets fabricated products including nonresidential architectural building products such as storefronts, building entrances, facings, window framing, and curtainwall systems. **Parent company:** Alcoa Company. **Corporate headquarters location:** This location. **Other US. locations:** Bristol IN; Greenwood IN; Bloomsburg PA; Harrisonburg VA; Hernando MS; Springdale AR; Visalia CA. **International locations:** Canada.

KEEBLER COMPANY
4375 Mead Road, Macon GA 31206. 478/781-4620. **Contact:** Human Resources. **World Wide Web address:** http://www.keebler.com. **Description:** A national manufacturer and marketer of cookies, crackers, snack foods, and other consumer food products. Keebler markets its products under the brand names Carr's, Cheez-It, Famous Amos, Murray, Plantation, and Ready Crust. Founded in 1853. **Office hours:** Monday – Friday, 8:00 a.m. – 4:00 p.m. **Corporate headquarters location:** Elmhurst IL. **Subsidiaries include:** Little Brownie's Baker is a licensed supplier of Girl Scout Cookies. **Parent company:** Kellogg USA.

KENDALL HEALTHCARE
11750 Hayes Industrial Drive, Marietta GA 30002. 770/422-3036. **Contact:** Human Resources. **World Wide Web address:** http://www.kendallhq.com. **Description:** Manufactures and distributes adult incontinence products for hospitals and nursing homes. **NOTE:** Please visit http://www.tycohealthcarecareers.com to search for jobs and apply online. **Corporate headquarters location:** Mansfield MA. **Other U.S. locations:** Nationwide. **International locations:** Canada; Mexico. **Parent company:** Tyco Healthcare. **President/CEO:** Rich Meelia.

KENNAMETAL INDUSTRIAL PRODUCTS GROUP
P.O. Box 2587, Augusta GA 30903. 706/863-7708. **Physical address:** 470 Old Evans Road, Evans GA 30809. **Toll-free phone:** 888/434-4311. **Fax:** 706/860-8559. **Contact:** Human Resources. **World Wide Web address:** http://www.kennametal.com. **Description:** Manufactures expendable cutting tools and related products used in four specific markets: Industrial, Electronics, Oil Field Equipment, and Consumer. The company primarily distributes its products to manufacturers, the federal government, electronic OEMs, electronic subcontractors, oil field pump manufacturers, do-it-yourself customers, and contractors. Kennametal is one of North America's leading producers of rotary cutting tools and suppliers of circuit board drills to the Far East. **NOTE:** Please visit website to fill out an online resume form. **Corporate headquarters location:** Latrobe PA. **Other U.S. locations:** Nationwide. **International locations:** Worldwide. **Parent company:** Kennametal, Inc. **Listed on:** New York Stock Exchange. **Stock exchange symbol:** KMT. **President/CEO:** Markos I. Tambakeras. **Annual sales/revenues:** More than $100 million. **Number of employees worldwide:** 13,500.

KENNESAW STATE UNIVERSITY
1000 Chastain Road, Kennesaw GA 30144-5591. 770/423-6031. **Fax:** 770/423-6570. **Contact:** Office of Personnel Services. **E-mail address:** personel@kennesaw.edu. **World Wide Web address:** http://www.kennesaw.edu. **Description:** A four-year state institution of higher education within the university system of Georgia. Kennesaw State University offers certificates, bachelor's, and master's degrees including a Master's of Business Administration. Approximately 12,000 undergraduate and 1,100 graduate students attend the university. **NOTE:** Please call listed number and dial 1 for the employment jobline. **Office hours:** Monday – Friday, 8:00 a.m. – 5:00 p.m.

KEN'S FOODS
155 King Mill Road, McDonough GA 30253. 770/898-8000. **Fax:** 770/898-0510. **Contact:** Allison Yi, Human Resources. **E-mail address:** ayi@kensfoods.com. **World Wide Web address:** http://www.kensfoods.com. **Description:** Produces and distributes various salad dressings and other condiments. Ken's Foods' products include over 250 salad dressings, as well as barbecue sauces, coleslaw dressings, mayonnaise and more. **Positions advertised include:** Maintenance Mechanic; Sanitation Foreman; Sanitation Supervisor; Production Scheduler; Packaging Lead. **Other U.S. locations:** Las Vegas NV, Marlborough MA. **Operations at this facility include:** Production.

KERR-McGEE CORPORATION
P.O. Box 368, Savannah GA 31402. 912/652-1000. **Physical address:** 1 Kerr McGee Road, Savannah GA 31404. **Fax:** 912/652-1168. **Contact:** Human Resources Manager. **World Wide Web address:** http://www.kerr-mcgee.com. **Description:** manufactures industrial pigments including titanium dioxide, as part of the chemical products segment of the diversified multinational organization. **Corporate headquarters location:** Oklahoma City OK. **Listed on:** New York Stock Exchange. **Stock exchange symbol:** KMG. **CEO:** Luke R. Corbett.

KEYLINK SYSTEMS
11545 Wills Road, Suite 100, Alpharetta GA 30004. 770/625-7500 **Toll-free phone:** 800/448-6177. **Fax:** 770/625-7525. **Contact:** Human Resources Department. **World Wide Web address:** http://www.keylink.pios.com. **Description:** A supplier of computers, peripherals, and software to the multi-user microcomputer industry. **Positions advertised include:** Senior Solution Architect. **Other U.S. locations:** Solon OH; Richardson TX. **Parent company:** Agilysis.

KING AND PRINCE SEAFOOD CORPORATION
GOLDEN SHORE SEAFOODS
P.O. Box 899, Brunswick GA 31521-0899. 912/265-5155. **Physical address:** One King and Prince Boulevard, Brunswick GA 31520-8603. **Toll-free phone:** 800/841-0205. **Fax:** 912/264-4812. **Contact:** Human Resources. **E-mail address:** human_res@kpseafood.com. **World Wide Web address:** http://www.kpseafood.com. **Description:** A seafood processor offering a wide range of frozen and prepared products. **Corporate headquarters location:** This location. **Number of employees at this location:** 530.

KING AMERICA FINISHING INCORPORATED
P.O. Box 75, Dover GA 30424. 912/863-4511. **Physical address:** Georgia Highway 17. Dover GA 30424. **Fax:** 912/863-7793. **Contact:** Donnie Saxon, Human Resources Manager. **E-mail address:** dsaxon@kamfin.com. **World Wide Web address:** http://www.kamfin.com. **Description:** Dyes and finishes broad-woven cotton fabric that is produced by other companies. King Finishing Company's products are sold to apparel and household furnishing stores. **NOTE:** Contact Human Resources directly at Ext. 316. **President:** Warren Back.

KYSOR/WARREN
5201 Transport Boulevard, Columbus GA 31907. 706/568-1514. **Toll-free phone:** 800/866-5596. **Fax:** 706/568-8990. **Contact:** Personnel. **World Wide Web address:** http://www.kysor.com. **Description:** Designs and manufactures high quality, energy-efficient, commercial refrigeration equipment and display cases for food stores. Founded 1882. **Corporate headquarters location:** This location. **Parent company:** Enodis PLC produces commercial vehicle products, builders' hardware, and commercial refrigeration products. **Listed on:** NASDAQ. **Stock exchange symbol:** ENO.

LXE INC.
EMS TECHNOLOGIES
125 Technology Parkway, Norcross GA 30092. 770/447-4224. **Fax:** 770/447-4405. **Contact:** Human Resources Manager. **World Wide Web address:** http://www.lxe.com. **Description:** Manufactures wireless radio equipment and data communications systems including scanners for warehouses and narrowband wireless systems. **NOTE:** Please visit http://hr.ems-t.com. to search for jobs and apply online. **Positions advertised include:** Project Leader – Product Development; Manufacturing Engineer; Marketing Specialist. **Corporate headquarters location:** This location. **Other U.S. locations:** Nationwide. **International locations:** Worldwide. **Parent company:** EMS Technologies, Inc. **Listed on:** New York Stock Exchange. **Stock exchange symbol:** ELMG. **Number of employees worldwide:** 2,000.

LABORATORY CORPORATION OF AMERICA (LABCORP)
1957 Lakeside Parkway, Suite 542, Tucker GA 30084. 770/939-4811. **Contact:** Human Resources. **World Wide Web address:** http://www.labcorp.com. **Description:** One of the nation's leading clinical laboratory companies, providing services primarily to physicians, hospitals, clinics, nursing homes, and other clinical laboratories nationwide. Labs perform tests on blood, urine, and other bodily fluids and tissue, aiding the prompt and accurate diagnosis of disease. **NOTE:** Please visit website to register, search for jobs, and apply online. **Positions advertised include:** Service Representative/Courier; Patient Services Technician Specialist; Service Representative. **Corporate headquarters location:** Burlington NC. **Other U.S. locations:** Nationwide. **Listed on:** New York Stock Exchange. **Stock exchange symbol:** LH. **Number of employees nationwide:** 23,000.

LABORATORY CORPORATION OF AMERICA (LABCORP)
2712 North Decatur Road, Decatur GA 30033. 404/294-7632. **Contact:** Human Resources. **World Wide Web address:** http://www.labcorp.com. **Description:** One of the nation's leading clinical laboratory companies, providing services primarily to physicians, hospitals, clinics, nursing homes, and other clinical labs nationwide. LabCorp performs tests on blood, urine, and other body fluids and tissue, aiding the diagnosis of disease. **NOTE:** Please visit website to register, search for jobs, and apply online. **Corporate headquarters location:** Burlington NC. **Other U.S. locations:** Nationwide. **Listed on:** New York Stock Exchange. **Stock exchange symbol:** LH. **Number of employees nationwide:** 23,000.

LANIER WORLDWIDE
2300 Parklake Drive NE, Atlanta GA 30345. 770/496-9500. **Contact:** Director of Human Resources. **E-mail address:** career@lanier.com. **World Wide Web address:** http://www.lanier.com. **Description:** Engaged in the sale and service of business equipment including copiers, fax machines, presentation systems, and dictation equipment. Founded 1934. **NOTE:** Job listings are available at http://www.monster.com. **Positions advertised include:** Staff Inventory Accountant; Senior Recruiter; Senior Business Analyst; Strategic Marketing Coordinator; Entry-Level Outside Sales; Systems Engineer; Accounts Receivable Coordinator. **Corporate headquarters location:** This location. **Other U.S. locations:** Nationwide. **International locations:** Worldwide. **Parent company:** Ricoh Corporation. **Operations at this facility include:** Administration; Research and Development; Service. **Listed on:** New York Stock Exchange. **Stock exchange symbol:** LR. **CEO:** Nori Goto. **Annual sales/revenues:** More than $100 million. **Number of employees nationwide:** 4,000.

LASON, INC.
450 Franklin Road, Suite 100, Marietta GA 30067. 770/250-2600. **Fax:** 678/797-3967. **Contact:** Human Resources. **E-mail address:** jobs@lason.com. **World Wide Web address:** http://www.lason.com. **Description:** An information processor handling data entry and processing, systems analysis, and clerical support. **NOTE:** Please visit website to search for jobs. E-mail applications are preferred. **Positions advertised include:** Sales Executive. **Corporate headquarters location:** Troy MI. **Other US. locations:** Nationwide. **International locations:** Canada; Mexico; India. **CEO:** Ronald D. Risher.

LATEX CONSTRUCTION COMPANY
P.O. Box 917, Conyers GA 30012. 770/760-0820. **Physical address:** 1353 Farmer Road NW, Conyers GA. **Fax:** 770/760-0852. **Contact:** Human Resources. **Description:** Engaged in hydrostatic testing and the manufacture of construction pipelines. **NOTE:** Information regarding employment is available through the phone menu.

LEATH FURNITURE
4370 Peachtree Road NE, 4th Floor, Atlanta GA 30319. 404/848-0880. **Contact:** Human Resources. **E-mail address:** hr@leathfurniture.com. **World Wide Web address:** http://www.leathfurniture.com. **Description:** Leath Furniture owns and operates twenty-six retail furniture stores and two distribution centers. **Corporate headquarters location:** This location. **Other U.S. locations:** IL; IN; IA; MI; WI. **Operations at this facility include:** Administrative offices.

LECTRA SYSTEMS, INC.
889 Franklin Road SE, Marietta GA 30067-7945. 770/422-8050. **Fax:** 770/422-1503. **Toll-free phone:** 877/453-2872. **Fax:** 800/746-8760. **Contact:** Human Resources. **World Wide Web address:** http://www.lectra.com. **Description:** Manufactures CAD/CAM systems for the textiles and leather processing industries. **NOTE:** Contact Human Resources directly at 800/746-3416. Please visit website to search for jobs and apply online. **Positions advertised include:** Strategic Account Manager; Welcome Center Representative; Communications Manager. **Corporate headquarters location:** Paris France. **Number of employees worldwide:** 1,520.

THE LEDGER ENQUIRER
P.O. Box 711, Columbus GA 31902. 706/324-5526. **Physical address:** 17 West 12th Street, Columbus GA 31901-2413. **Toll-free phone:** 800/282-7859. **Contact:** Human Resources. **E-mail address:** resumes@knightridder.com. **World Wide Web address:** http://www.ledger-enquirer.com. **Description:** A daily newspaper with a weekday circulation of more than 50,000 and a Sunday circulation of more than 60,000. **NOTE:** Please visit parent company website at http://www.knightridder.com to search for jobs and apply online. **Positions advertised include:** Marketing Director/Manager; City Editor; Reporter; Advertising Operations Manager; Account Executive; Advertising Director/Manager. **Parent company:** Knight-Ridder Inc. is a major newspaper publishing company that owns 28 dailies in 15 states and three nondailies in suburban areas. The company also produces niche publications such as Myrtle Beach's *Golf*, *CubaNews* newsletter in Miami, and *Northland Outdoors* in Grand Forks. The larger papers include the *Miami Herald, Philadelphia Inquirer, Philadelphia Daily News, Detroit Free Press,* and *San Jose Mercury News*. Other interests include partial ownership of the Seattle Times Company, two paper mills, a newspaper advertising sales company, and SCI Holdings. **Listed on:** New York Stock Exchange. **Stock exchange symbol:** KRI.

LEICA GEOSYSTEMS GIS & MAPPING
2801 Buford Highway NE, Suite 300, Atlanta GA 30329-2137. 404/248-9000. **Toll-free phone:** 877/463-7327. **Fax:** 404/248-9400. **Contact:** Human Resources. **E-mail address:** human.resources@leicaus.com. **World Wide Web address:** http://gis.leica-geosystems.com. **Description:** Designs geographic imaging software, which provides solutions for spectral analysis, digital photogrammetry, and map composition. One of the largest digital mapping companies in the world. The company provides the hardware and software used for the Geospatial Imaging Chain. **Positions advertised include:** Regional Sales Manager; Software Engineer; Airborne Sensor Support Engineer; Digital Photogrammetry Support Engineer; Marketing Communications Writer; Product Manager; Product Specialist; Remote Sensing Specialist; Software Engineer; Systems Integration Technician; Business Analyst; Controller Operations; Design Electro Mechanical Engineer; Key Account Manager; Strategic Purchaser. **Corporate headquarters location:** This location. **Other U.S. locations:** San Diego CA; Westford MA. **International locations:** Heerbrugg Switzerland.

LIBERTY FITECH SYSTEMS
3098 Piedmont Road NE, Suite 200, Atlanta GA 30305. 404/262-2298. **Toll-free phone:** 800/275-4374. **Fax:** 404/233-4815. **Contact:** Human Resources. **World Wide Web address:** http://www.libertysite.com/fitech. **Description:** Designs software for credit unions. Founded 1977. **Corporate headquarters location:** This location. **Other area locations:** Louisville GA. **Listed on:** Privately held. **Other U.S. locations:** Greensboro NC. **Parent company:** Liberty Enterprises Inc.

LIFE OF GEORGIA
P.O. Box 105006, Atlanta GA 30348-5006. 770/980-5100. **Physical address:** 5780 Powers Ferry Road NW, Atlanta GA 30327-4390. **Contact:** Human Resources. **World Wide Web address:** http://www.lifeofgeorgia.com. **Description:** Provides life and health insurance for more than a million policyholders in Southeastern U.S. Founded 1891. **NOTE:** Please visit http://www.ing-usa.com/careers for a link to the ING job board. You can search for jobs and apply online. Human Resources phone is 770/980-5710. **Positions advertised include:** Western Account Representative; Sales Representative. **Corporate headquarters location:** This location. **Operations at this facility include:** Administration; Research and Development; Service. **Parent company:** ING North American Insurance Corporation.

LIFE UNIVERSITY
1269 Barclay Circle, Marietta GA 30060. 770/426-2884. **Toll-free phone:** 800/543-3202. **Fax:** 770/426-2987. **Contact:** Human Resources. **World Wide Web address:** http://www.life.edu. **Description:** A four-year university that offers undergraduate and graduate degrees. Life University operates an outpatient clinic and a School of Chiropractics. **NOTE:** Human Resources phone is 770/426-2930. **Positions advertised include:** Vice President of Academic Affairs; Chief Financial Officer/Vice President of Financial Affairs; Director of Institutional Effectiveness, Planning and Assessment; Assistant Director of Post-Graduate Education; Administrative Assistant – Executive Office. **President:** Dr. Guy Riekman.

LITHONIA LIGHTING COMPANY
P.O. Box A, Conyers GA 30012. 770/922-9000. **Physical address:** 1 Lithonia Way, Conyers GA. **Fax:** 770/860-9403. **Contact:** Human Resources. **E-mail address:** recruiter@lithonia.com. **World Wide Web address:** http://www.lithonia.com. **Description:** One of North America's largest manufacturers of commercial and industrial lighting equipment and related wiring, controls, and emergency systems. **Positions advertised include:** Sales and Marketing Personnel; Finance Specialist; Human Resource Worker; Information and Management Service Provider; Manufacturer; Engineer. **Special programs:** Training. **Corporate headquarters location:** This location. **Other U.S. locations:** Nationwide. **International locations:** Canada; Mexico. **Parent company:** Acuity Lighting Group, Inc. **Number of employees worldwide:** 8,000.

LOCKHEED MARTIN
600 Corporate Pointe, Warner Robins GA 31088. 478/923-4266. **Contact:** Human Resources. **E-mail address:** jobs.lmc@lmco.com. **World Wide Web address:** http://www.lockheedmartin.com. **Description:** A technology company that provides services to the U.S. Department of Defense and federal government groups. Areas of focus include aeronautics, space systems, and information and technology services among others. **Positions advertised include:** Aircraft Mechanic; Aircraft Quality Control Inspector; Administrative Support; Aeronautical Engineer; Assembly Supervisor; Computer Systems Security Analyst; Database Administrator; Electronics Engineer; Graphic Artist; Industrial Engineer; Material Handling Workers; Mathematician; Production Control Clerk; Program Senior Manager; Subcontract Administrator; Systems Engineer; Technical Trainer; Technical Writer. **Corporate headquarters location:** Bethesda MD. **Other area locations:** Statewide. **Other U.S. locations:** Nationwide. **International locations:** Worldwide. **Listed on:** New York Stock Exchange. **Stock exchange symbol:** LMT. **CEO:** Vance D. Coffman. **Number of employees worldwide:** 130,000.

LOCKWOOD GREENE
303 Perimeter Center North, Suite 800, Atlanta GA 30346. 770/829-6500. **Fax:** 770/829-6601. **Recorded jobline:** 404/818-8301. **Contact:** Kathy Pileggi, Recruiting Manager. **World Wide Web address:** http://www.lg.com. **Description:** An international consulting, design, and construction firm. **Special programs:** Co-ops. **Corporate headquarters location:** Spartanburg SC. **Other area locations:** Augusta GA; Pooler GA. **Other U.S. locations:** Nationwide. **International locations:** Worldwide. **Operations at this facility include:** This location serves clients in the following industries: power and energy; telecommunications; general manufacturing; government; aerospace; chemicals; health care; and food and beverages. **Parent company:** Philipp Holzmann and J.A. Jones, Inc. **Listed on:** Privately held. **President/CEO:** Fred Brune. **Annual sales/revenues:** More than $100 million. **Number of employees worldwide:** 2,500.

LODGIAN, INC.
3445 Peachtree Road NE, Suite 700, Atlanta GA 30326. 404/364-9400. **Fax:** 404/364-0088. 800/862-5789. **Contact:** Personnel. **E-mail address:** hr@lodgian.com. **World Wide Web address:** http://www.lodgian.com. **Description:** Owns or manages 107 hotels located in North America. These hotels are primarily full service, providing food and beverage service as well as lodging and meeting facilities. Most of the company's hotels are affiliated with nationally recognized hospitality franchises including Holiday Inn, Best Western, Hilton, Doubletree Club Hotel, Radisson, Crowne Plaza, Comfort Inn, and Westin. Lodgian, Inc. was created through a merger between Servico, Inc. and Impac Hotel Group. **Positions advertised include:** Controller; Housekeeping Instructor; Director of Food and Beverage; Night Auditor. **Corporate headquarters location:** This location. **Other U.S. locations:** Nationwide. **International locations:** Canada. **President/CEO:** W. Thomas Parrington.

LOGMATIX INC.
1235 Kennestone Circle, Suite C, Marietta GA 30066-6029. 770/792-3777. **Toll-free phone:** 800/527-2498. **Fax:** 770/792-3737. **Contact:** President. **World Wide Web address:** http://www.logmatix.com. **Description:** Manufactures bar code, blank, and custom labels. Founded in 1983. **Office hours:** Monday – Friday, 8:00 a.m. – 5:00 p.m.

LUMMUS INDUSTRIES INC.
P.O. Box 4259, Savannah GA 31407-4259. 912/447-9000. **Physical Address:** Crossroads Business Center, One Lummus Drive, Savannah GA 31422. **Toll-free phone:** 800/458-6687. **Fax:** 912/447-9250. **Contact:** Human Resources. **World Wide Web address:** http://www.lummus.com. **Description:** Manufactures cotton gin machines and replacement parts. **NOTE:** No phone calls regarding employment. **Corporate headquarters location:** This location. **Other U.S. locations:** Greenville MI; Lubbock TX; Phoenix AZ; Fresno CA. **International locations:** Australia; Brazil. **Subsidiaries include:** Lummus Australia Ltd; Lummus Do Brasil Ltda; Belt-Wide Industries, Inc.

LYNCH SYSTEMS
601 Independent Street, Bainbridge GA 39817. 229/248-2345. **Contact:** Human Resources. **E-mail address:** bowling@lynchsystems.com. **World Wide Web address:** http://www.lynchsystems.com. **Description:** Produces bottling and packaging machinery for sale to the food and beverage processing industries worldwide. **Special programs:** Internships. **International locations:** Germany. **Parent company:** Lynch-Amav LLC. **President:** Arnold Bowling. **Number of employees at this location:** 75.

THE MACON TELEGRAPH
P.O. Box 4167, Macon GA 31208. 478/744-4200. **Physical address:** 120 Broadway, Macon GA 31201-3444. **Toll-free phone:** In-State only – 800/342-5845. **Contact:** Human Resources. **E-mail address:** resumes@knightridder.com. **World Wide Web address:** http://www.macon.com. **Description:** Publishes a daily newspaper with a weekday circulation of 70,000 and a Sunday circulation of 100,000. **NOTE:** Please visit parent company website at http://www.knightridder.com to search for jobs and apply online. **Parent company:** Knight-Ridder Inc. is a major newspaper publishing company that owns 28 dailies in 15 states and three nondailies in suburban areas. The company also produces niche publications such as Myrtle Beach's *Golf*, *CubaNews* newsletter in Miami, and *Northland Outdoors* in Grand Forks. The larger papers include the *Miami Herald, Philadelphia Inquirer, Philadelphia Daily News, Detroit Free Press,* and *San Jose Mercury News*. Other interests include partial ownership of the Seattle Times Company, two paper mills, a newspaper advertising sales company, and SCI Holdings. **Listed on:** New York Stock Exchange. **Stock exchange symbol:** KRI.

MACQUARIUM INTELLIGENT COMMUNICATIONS
1800 Peachtree, NW, Suite 250, Atlanta GA 30309. 404/554-4000. **Fax:** 404/554-4001. **Contact:** Human Resources Manager. **E-mail address:** hr@macquarium.com. **World Wide Web address:** http://www.macquarium.com. **Description:** A marketing communications firm focusing on eBusiness technologies. **Positions advertised include:** Director of Human Resources; Project Manager; Quality Assurance Manager; Executive Assistant; Interactive Flask Designer; Software Engineer – Technical Lead; Software Engineer – Tibco; Solution Architect. **President:** Kevin Foster.

MAGNOLIA HOME FASHIONS
506 Maple Street, Carrollton GA 30117. 770/832-3561. **Fax:** 770/832-9658. **Contact:** Human Resources. **E-mail address:** printfab@prodigy.net. **World Wide Web address:** http://www.magnoliahome.com. **Description:** Offers a variety of fabrics for wholesale and retail purposes. **Corporate headquarters location:** This location.

MANHATTAN ASSOCIATES
2300 Windy Ridge Parkway, Suite 700, Atlanta GA 30339. 770/955-7070. **Fax:** 770/955-0302. **E-mail address:** careers@manh.com. **World Wide Web address:** http://www.manh.com. **Description:** A leading supply chain execution company, providing companies with the means to ship inventory faster. **NOTE:** Please visit website to search for jobs and apply online. **Positions advertised include:** Call Center Consultant; RFID Consultant; Senior Software Consultant; WMS Labor Management Software Expert; Corporate Catering and Food Coordinator; Demand Generation Representative; Junior Business Analyst; Program Manager; Software Analyst; Senior Software Analyst; Technical Lead; Technical Support Consultant; Senior Internet

Software Engineer; Software Engineer. **Corporate headquarters location:** This location. **Other U.S. locations:** Burlington MA; Carmel IN; Mishawaka IN; Vienna VA. **International locations:** Worldwide. **Listed on:** NASDAQ. **Stock exchange symbol:** MANH. **President/CEO:** Richard Haddrill.

MANNING SELVAGE & LEE
1170 Peachtree Street NE, Suite 400, Atlanta GA 30309. 404/875-1444. **Fax:** 404/892-1274. **Contact:** Human Resources. **E-mail Address:** careers@mlsrp.com. **World Wide Web address:** http://www.mslpr.com. **Description:** Provides public relations services for the health care, real estate, business-to-business, and consumer relations industries. **NOTE:** Please visit website to search for jobs, and to download an employment application or a Self-ID form. **Positions advertised include:** Account Executive. **Special programs:** Internships. **Corporate headquarters location:** New York NY. **Other U.S. locations:** Boston MA; Chicago IL; Detroit MI; Los Angeles CA; San Francisco CA; San Antonio TX; Washington D.C. **International locations:** Worldwide. **CEO:** Lou Capozzi.

MAR-JAC INC.
P.O. Box 1017, Gainesville GA 30501. 770/531-5000. **Physical address:** 1020 Aviation Boulevard Gainesville GA 30503. **Fax:** 770/531-5049. **Contact:** Personnel. **E-mail address:** careers@marjacpoultry.com. **World Wide Web address:** http://www.marjacpoultry.com. **Description:** Engaged in poultry processing. **NOTE:** Personnel phone is 770/531-5007. **Positions advertised:** Supervisor. **Corporate headquarters location:** This location.

MARIETTA, CITY OF
205 Lawrence Street, 3rd Floor, Marietta GA 30060. 770/794-5562. **Fax:** 770/794-5565. **Recorded jobline:** 770/794-5571. **Hearing impaired phone:** 770/794-5560. **Contact:** Miriam Corbin, Personnel. **E-mail address:** mcorbin@mariettaga.gov. **World Wide Web address:** http://www.city.marietta.ga.us. **Description:** Administrative offices of the city of Marietta. **NOTE:** Please visit website to search for jobs and to download a City of Marietta/BLW Employment Application. **Positions advertised include:** Administrative Secretary; City Service Worker; Day Camp Coordinator; Electrical Director; Housing Assistant Officer; Inspector Code Enforcement Worker; Prisoner Transport Officer. **Office hours:** Monday – Friday, 8:00 a.m. – 5:00 p.m. **Corporate headquarters location:** This location. **Operations at this facility include:** Service.

MARIETTA FIRE DEPARTMENT
112 Haynes Street, Marietta GA 30060-1973. 770/794-5450. **Fax:** 770/794-5465. **Contact:** Recruitment. **E-mail address:** mcorbin@mariettaga.gov. **World Wide Web address:** http://www.city.marietta.ga.us/fire Fire/home.htm. **Description:** Fire department for the city of Marietta.

MASTER FOODS USA
P.O. Box 3289, Albany GA 31706-3289. 229/883-4000. **Physical address:** 1209 West Oakridge Drive, Albany GA 31707. **Contact:** Personnel Manager. **World Wide Web address:** http://www.masterfoods.com. **Description:** Manufactures food and snack products. Brands include M&Ms, Snickers, Starburst, and Combos. **NOTE:** Please visit http://www.mars.com to search for jobs and apply online. **Positions advertised include:** Scheduling and Outbound Logistics. **Other U.S. locations:** Nationwide. **Operations at this location:** This location is a manufacturing facility. **Parent company:** MARS Incorporated.

MASTERACK
LEGGETT & PLATT, INC.
905 Memorial Drive SE, Atlanta GA 30316. 404/525-5501. **Toll-free phone:** 800/334-4183. **Fax:** 404/739-4005. **Contact:** Parnell Bryant, Human Resources Manager. **World Wide Web address:** http://www.masterack.com. **Description:** Manufactures car and van racks, bottle racks, lighting fixtures, and bunk beds for prison cells. **Parent company:** Legget & Platt, Inc. **Operations at this facility include:** Manufacturing; Research and Development; Sales. **Listed on:** New York Stock Exchange. **Stock exchange symbol:** LEG. **CEO:** Felix Wright.

McDONALD'S CORPORATION
5901 Peachtree Dunwoody Road NE, Suite C-500, Atlanta GA 30328. 770/698-7498. **Fax:** 770/885-4100. **Contact:** Human Resources. **World Wide Web address:** http://www.mcdonalds.com. **Description:** McDonald's is one of the largest restaurant chains and food service organizations in the world, operating more than 30,000 restaurants in all 50 states and in more than 121 countries. **NOTE:** Please visit http://www.monster.com to search for jobs. **Positions advertised include:** Finance Manager. **Corporate headquarters location:** Oakbrook IL. **Other U.S. locations:** Nationwide. **International locations:** Worldwide. **Operations at this facility include:** Area administrative offices for the worldwide developer, operator, franchiser, and servicer of a system of restaurants that process, package, and sell fast foods. **Listed on:** New York Stock Exchange. **Stock exchange symbol:** MCD. **CEO:** Jim Cantalupo. **Number of employees worldwide:** 418,000.

McKESSON INFORMATION SOLUTIONS
5995 Windward Parkway, Alpharetta GA 30005. 404/338-6000. **Contact:** Human Resources. **World Wide Web address:** http://www.mckhboc.com. **Description:** Provides information systems and technology to health care enterprises including hospitals, integrated delivery networks, and managed care organizations. McKesson's primary products are Pathways 2000, a family of client/server-based applications that allows the integration and uniting of health care providers; STAR, Series, and HealthQuest transaction systems; TRENDSTAR decision support system; and QUANTUM enterprise information system. The company also offers outsourcing services that include strategic information systems planning, data center operations, receivables management, business office administration, and major system conversions. **Positions advertised include:** Senior Business Analyst; Product Support Analyst; Business Analyst R&D and Services; Manager of Financial Planning and Analysis; Senior Financial Analyst; Senior Oracle Database Administrator; Enterprise Vice President – Sales; Sales Support Product Consultant; Staff Accountant; Technology Licensing Attorney; Auditor; Project Manager – Clinical Demo Systems; Sales Associate; Network/Desktop Systems Specialist; Enterprise Sales Executive; HRIS Call Center Analyst; Security Infrastructure Engineer. **Corporate headquarters location:** San Francisco CA. **Other U.S. locations:** Carrollton TX. **Parent company:** McKesson Corporation. **Listed on:** New York Stock Exchange. **Stock exchange symbol:** MCK. **CEO:** John H. Hammergren.

MCMICHAEL'S CONSTRUCTION COMPANY, INC.
90 Almon Road, Covington GA 30014. 770/483-1080. **Fax:** 770/483-0445. **Contact:** Human Resources. **World Wide Web address:** http://www.mcmbuilds.com. **Description:** A construction company that serves the Southeast United States. **Positions advertised include:** Project Manager; Trade Professional; Laborer. **Corporate headquarters location:** This location.

MEADWESTVACO
1040 West Marietta Street, Atlanta GA 30318. 404/875-2711. **Contact:** Human Resources Manager. **World Wide Web address:** http://www.meadwestvaco.com. **Description:** Manufactures paperboard and a variety of packaging systems and equipment for the conversion of paper products. **NOTE:** Please visit http://www.monster.com to search for jobs and apply online. **Positions advertised include:** Mechanical Design Engineer; Director of Worldwide Finance. **Special programs:** Co-ops; Internships. **Office hours:** Monday – Friday, 8:00 a.m. – 5:00 p.m. **Corporate headquarters location:** Stamford CT. **Other U.S. locations:** Nationwide. **International locations:** Worldwide. **Listed on:** New York Stock Exchange. **Stock exchange symbol:** MWV. **Number of employees nationwide:** 23,000. **Number of employees worldwide:** 30,000.

MEDIA BIN, INC.
3525 Piedmont Road, Seven Piedmont Center NE, Suite 600, Atlanta GA 30305-1530. 404/264-8000. **Fax:** 404/264-8300. **Contact:** Human Resources. **E-mail address:** jobs@mediabin.com. **World Wide Web address:** http://www.mediabin.com. **Description:** Develops digital imaging technologies and software. Founded in 1987. **Corporate headquarters location:** Sunnyvale CA. **Other U.S. locations:** Newport Beach CA; Bethesda MD; Chicago IL; Waltham MA; Dallas TX; New York NY; Bellevue WA. **International locations:** Worldwide. **Listed on:** NASDAQ. **Stock exchange symbol:** IWOV. **CEO:** Martin Brauns. **Number of employees worldwide:** 700.

MEDTRONIC
3225 Cumberland Boulevard SE, Suite 500, Atlanta GA 30339. 770/955-3808. **Contact:** Human Resources. **World Wide Web address:** http://www.medtronic.com. **Description:** The world's leader in medical technology. Medtronic develops technology that treats vascular illnesses, neurological disorders, and heart disease. **NOTE:** Please visit website to search for jobs and apply online. **Positions advertised include:** District Sales Manager; Field Service Representative; Regional Health Care Economics Manager; Senior Human Resources Manager. **Corporate headquarters location:** Minneapolis MN. **Other area locations:** Albany GA; Alpharetta GA; Augusta GA; Cordele GA; Macon GA; Savannah GA; Valdosta GA. **Other U.S. locations:** Nationwide. **International locations:** Worldwide. **Listed on:** New York Stock Exchange. **Stock exchange symbol:** MDT. **Number of employees worldwide:** 29,000.

MERCER UNIVERSITY
3001 Mercer University Drive, Room 103, Atlanta GA 30341-4155. 678/547-6000. **Fax:** 678/547-6157. **Recorded jobline:** 678/547-6015. **Contact:** Human Resources. **E-mail address:** jobinfo@mercer.edu. **World Wide Web address:** http://www.mercer.edu. **Description:** The Atlanta location of the independent four-year university. Mercer University offers undergraduate and graduate degrees and enrolls approximately 1,000 students at this location. **NOTE:** Human Resources phone is 678/547-6155. If interested in a position, you must complete an online application. Please visit website to register, search for jobs, and apply online. Online applications are the only accepted format. You may submit a resume with your application. **Positions advertised include:** Assistant Professor – Various Departments; Director of Media Center; Faculty – Nursing; Maintenance Technician; Police Officer; Tenure Track Faculty – Pharmaceutical Sciences. **Office hours:** Monday, Wednesday, Friday, 7:30 a.m. – 3:30 p.m. **Other area locations:** Macon GA.

MERCK & COMPANY, INC.
3517 Radium Springs Road, Albany GA 31705. 229/420-3000. **Contact:** Human Resources. **World Wide Web address:** http://www.merck.com. **Description:** Merck discovers, develops, manufactures, and markets a broad range of pharmaceutical products to improve human and animal health. The Merck-Medco Managed Care Division manages pharmacy benefits for more than 40 million Americans, encourages the appropriate uses of medicines, and provides disease management programs. **NOTE:** Please visit website to search for jobs and apply online. **Positions advertised include:** Hospital Sales Representative; Specialty Sales Representative. **Corporate headquarters location:** Whitehouse Station NJ. **Other U.S. locations:** Rahway NJ; Wilson NC; Danville PA; Elkton VA. **International locations:** Worldwide. **Operations at this facility include:** Manufacturing of prescription drugs. **Listed on:** New York Stock Exchange. **Stock exchange symbol:** MRK. **President/CEO:** Raymond V. Gilmartin.

MERCURY INTERACTIVE CORPORATION
5 Concourse Parkway, Suite 2350, Atlanta GA 30328. 770/804-5895. **Fax:** 770/804-5894. **Toll-free phone:** 800/TEST-911. **Contact:** Human Resources Department. **World Wide Web address:** http://www.mercuryinteractive.com. **Description:** Mercury Interactive is a developer of automated software quality (ASQ) tools for enterprise applications testing. The company's products are used to isolate software and system errors prior to application deployment. **NOTE:** Please visit website to search for jobs and for more details on applying for specific positions. **Positions advertised include:** Consulting Project Manager; Expert Consultant – Technology Integration; Process Engineer; Solution Consultant; Application Delivery Testing Systems Engineer. **Corporate headquarters location:** Sunnyvale CA. **Other U.S. locations:** Nationwide. **Operations at this facility include:** This location is a sales office. **Listed on:** NASDAQ. **Stock exchange symbol:** MERQ. **CEO:** Amnon Landan. **Annual sales/revenues:** More than $100 million. **Number of employees worldwide:** 2,322.

MERIAL LTD.
3239 Satellite Boulevard NW, Duluth GA 30096. 678/638-3000. **Contact:** Human Resources. **World Wide Web address:** http://www.merial.com. **Description:** Develops veterinary vaccines and pharmaceuticals. **NOTE:** Please visit website to search for jobs and apply online. **Positions advertised include:** Financial Analyst; Associate Manager; Biostatistician; Accountant; Administrative Associate; Director – Financial Analyst; Senior Database Administrator; Senior Manager; Senior Business Analyst; Project Leader. **Corporate headquarters location:** This location. **Other area locations:** Athens GA; Gainesville GA. **Other U.S. locations:** Nationwide. **International locations:** Worldwide. **Subsidiaries include:** Hubbard ISA. **Operations at this facility include:** This location serves as the North American headquarters. **Number of employees worldwide:** 6,500.

METROPOLITAN ATLANTA RAPID TRANSIT AUTHORITY (MARTA)
2424 Piedmont Road NE, Atlanta GA 30324-3311. 404/848-5000. **Fax:** 404/848-5687. **Recorded jobline:** 404/848-5627. **Contact:** Recruiting. **World Wide Web address:** http://www.itsmarta.com. **Description:** Operates the bus and subway systems for the city of Atlanta. **NOTE:** You may also apply by contacting the Georgia Department of Labor in the metropolitan Atlanta area. **Positions advertised include:** Director – Infrastructure and System Management; Senior IT Program Manager; Planning/Research Project Coordinator; Transit Police Officer; Performance Administrator; Strategic Planner; Manager of Compensation; ITS/GIC Analyst; Technical Engineer. **Special programs:** Internships. **Corporate headquarters location:** This location. **Operations at this facility include:** Administration.

MICROMERITICS INSTRUMENT CORPORATION
One Micromeritics Drive, Norcross GA 30093-1877. 770/662-3620. 3678. **Fax:** 770/662-3696. **Contact:** Human Resources. **E-mail address:** hr@micromeritics.com. **World Wide Web address:** http://www.micromeritics.com. **Description:** Produces and distributes laboratory analysis equipment used in various health care and scientific applications including liquid chromatographs. **NOTE:** Please visit website to search for jobs and apply online. **Corporate headquarters location:** This location. **International locations:** China; Italy; Belgium; France; Germany. **Operations at this facility include:** Manufacturing; Research and Development. **Subsidiaries include:** Alcott Chromatography. **Number of employees worldwide:** 240.

MIKART
1750 Chattahoochee Avenue NW, Atlanta GA 30318. 404/351-4510. **Toll-free phone:** 888/4MIKART. **Fax:** 404/350-0432. **Contact:** Human Resources. **E-mail address:** resumes1@mikart.com. **World Wide Web address:** http://www.mikart.com. **Description:** Engaged in the formulation, manufacturing, and packaging of generic and prescription drugs. **NOTE:** No phone calls regarding employment. **Positions advertised include:** Formulation Scientist; Analytical Methods Development Chemist. **Corporate headquarters location:** This location. **Number of employees at this location:** 170.

MILLER BREWING COMPANY
405 Cordele Road, Albany GA 31705-2109. 229/420-5000. **Recorded jobline:** 229/420-5153. **Contact:** Personnel. **World Wide Web address:** http://www.millerbrewing.com. **Description:** Produces and distributes beer and other malt beverages. Principal beer brands include Miller Lite, Lite Ice, Miller Genuine Draft, Miller Genuine Draft Light, Miller High Life, Miller Reserve, Lowenbrau, Milwaukee's Best, and Meister Brau, as well as Red Dog and Icehouse, which are brewed at the Plank Road Brewery. Miller also produces Sharp's, a nonalcoholic brew. Founded 1855. **NOTE:** Please visit website to search for jobs and apply online. Resumes are kept on file for two years. **Positions advertised include:** Electrician; Maintenance Mechanic; Work Group Manager. **Corporate headquarters location:** Milwaukee WI. **Other U.S. locations:** Irwindale CA; Chippewa Falls WI; Trenton OH; Fort Worth TX; Eden NC. **Subsidiaries include:** Jacob Leinenkugel Brewing Company (Chippewa Falls WI) brews Leinenkugel's Original Premium, Leinenkugel's Light, Leinie's Ice, Leinenkugel's Limited, Leinenkugel's Red Lager, and four seasonal beers: Leinenkugel's Genuine Bock, Leinenkugel's Honey Weiss, Leinenkugel's Autumn Gold, and Leinenkugel's Winter Lager; Molson Breweries U.S.A., Inc. (Reston VA) imports Molson beers from Canada as well as Foster's Lager and many other brands. Miller is also majority owner of Celis Brewery Inc. in Austin TX. **Parent company:** SABMiller plc. **Operations at this facility include:** Manufacturing. **President/CEO:** Norman Adami. **Number of employees at this location:** 700. **Number of employees worldwide:** 6,500.

MILLER/ZELL INC.
4715 Frederick Drive SW, Atlanta GA 30336. 404/691-7400. **Fax:** 404/699-2189. **Contact:** Brenda B. Redding, Manager of Personnel Administration. **E-mail address:** recruitme@millerzell.com. **World Wide Web address:** http://www.millerzell.com. **Description:** Purchases store fixtures, furniture, displays, prefabricated building products, and interior design products; prints graphics and point-of-purchase signage and fixtures; and provides fixtures, graphics, and service to retail companies. **NOTE:** Please visit website to search or jobs and apply online. **Positions advertised include:** Corporate Training Director; Print Planner; Senior Programmer/Analyst, JD Edwards. **Corporate headquarters location:** This location. **Other U.S. locations:** New York NY; Washington D.C. Bentonville AR. **International locations:** Worldwide. **Operations at this facility include:** Administration; Manufacturing; Sales. **CEO:** Sandy Miller. **Number of employees at this location:** 350.

MISSION TO THE WORLD
1600 North Brown Road, Lawrenceville GA 30043-8141. 678/823-0004. **Fax:** 678/823-0027. **Contact:** Courtney Rogers, Personnel. **E-mail address:** crogers@mtw.org. **World Wide Web address:** http://www.mtw.org. **Description:** Provides support services including funding and advisory services to missionaries for the Presbyterian Church of America. **NOTE:** Contact Personnel directly at Ext. 278. **Special programs:** Internships. **Corporate headquarters location:** This location.

MITCHELL COUNTY BOARD OF EDUCATION
108 South Harney Street, Camilla GA 31730. 229/336-4543. **Fax:** 229/336-1615. **World Wide Web address:** http://www.mitchell.k12.ga.us. **Description:** Runs the schools in Mitchell County.

MOHAWK INDUSTRIES
P.O. Box 12069, Calhoun GA 30703. 706/629-7721. **Physical address:** 160 South Industrial Boulevard, Calhoun GA 30701. **Toll-free phone:** 800/241-4494. **Contact:** Personnel. **World Wide Web address:** http://www.mohawkind.com. **Description:** A carpet mill and a leading producer of area rugs and mats for both the residential and commercial markets. Mohawk manufactures and markets broadloom carpet, area and accent rugs, and indoor and outdoor mats, covering all significant market segments, distribution channels, and price points. Brand names include Aladdin, Alexander Smith, American Rug Craftsmen, Bigelow, Eden, Galaxy, Harbinger, Horizon, Karastan, and Mohawk. **Corporate headquarters location:** This location. **Other area locations:** Statewide. **Other U.S. locations:** Nationwide. **Listed on:** New York Stock Exchange. **Stock exchange symbol:** MHK. **President/CEO:** Jeffrey S. Lorberbaum. **Number of employees worldwide:** 33,300.

MOHAWK INDUSTRIES
200 Industrial Drive, Cartersville GA 30120. 770/382-6485. **Contact:** Personnel. **World Wide Web address:** http://www.mohawkind.com. **Description:** A carpet mill and a leading producer of area rugs and mats for both the residential and commercial markets. Mohawk manufactures and markets broadloom carpet, area and accent rugs, and indoor and outdoor mats, covering all major market segments, distribution channels, and price points. Brand names include Aladdin, Alexander Smith, American Rug Craftsmen, Bigelow, Eden, Galaxy, Harbinger, Horizon, Karastan, and Mohawk. **Corporate headquarters location:** Calhoun GA. **Other area locations:** Statewide. **Other U.S. locations:** Nationwide. **Listed on:** New York Stock Exchange. **Stock exchange symbol:** MHK. **President/CEO:** Jeffrey S. Lorberbaum. **Number of employees worldwide:** 33,300.

MOHAWK INDUSTRIES
500 Town Park Lane, Suite 400, Kennesaw GA 30144. 770/792-6300. **Contact:** Personnel Director. **World Wide Web address:** http://www.mohawkind.com. **Description:** A carpet mill and producer of area rugs and mats for both the residential and commercial markets. Mohawk manufactures and markets broadloom carpet, area and accent rugs, and indoor and outdoor mats, covering all major market segments, distribution channels, and price points. Brand names include Aladdin, Alexander Smith, American Rug Craftsmen, Bigelow, Eden, Galaxy, Harbinger, Horizon, Karastan, and Mohawk. **Corporate headquarters location:** Calhoun GA. **Other area locations:** Statewide. **Other U.S. locations:** Nationwide. **Listed on:** New York Stock Exchange. **Stock exchange symbol:** MHK. **President/CEO:** Jeffrey S. Lorberbaum. **Number of employees worldwide:** 33,300.

MOHAWK INDUSTRIES
365 Patterson Avenue, Fort Oglethorpe GA 30742. 706/866-7528. **Contact:** Personnel Director. **World Wide Web address:** http://www.mohawkind.com. **Description:** A carpet mill and a leading producer of area rugs and mats for both the residential and commercial markets. Mohawk manufactures and markets broadloom carpet, area and accent rugs, and indoor and outdoor mats, covering all significant market segments, distribution channels, and price points. Brand names include Aladdin, Alexander Smith, American Rug Craftsmen, Bigelow, Eden, Galaxy, Harbinger, Horizon, Karastan, and Mohawk. **Corporate headquarters location:** Calhoun GA. **Other area locations:** Statewide. **Other U.S. locations:** Nationwide. **Listed on:** New York Stock Exchange. **Stock exchange symbol:** MHK. **President/CEO:** Jeffrey S. Lorberbaum. **Number of employees worldwide:** 33,300.

MONTGOMERY INSURANCE COMPANY
3555 Koger Boulevard, Suite 200, Duluth GA 30096. 678/380-8734. **Toll-free phone:** 800/762-5573. **Fax:** 678/380-7675. **Contact:** Personnel. **World Wide Web address:** http://www.montgomery-ins.com. **Description:** A carrier of property, casualty, and life insurance. **NOTE:** Please visit Liberty Mutual Group's career search site to search for jobs and apply online. You can find a link to this site on the Montgomery Insurance website. **Positions advertised include:** Claims Trainee. **Corporate headquarters location:** Sandy Spring MD. **Other U.S. locations:** Charlotte NC. **Parent company:** Regional Agency Markets of Liberty Mutual. **President/CEO:** John C. Robinson.

MOREHOUSE COLLEGE
830 Westview Drive SW, Suite 207, Gloster Hall, Atlanta GA 30314. 404/681-2800. **Recorded jobline:** 404/614-6048. **Contact:** Human Resources. **World Wide Web address:** http://www.morehouse.edu. **Description:** A four-year liberal arts college. Morehouse College also offers medical studies through the Morehouse School of Medicine. For more information about the medical school please call 404/752-1500 or visit the Website. **NOTE:** Entry-level positions are offered. Interested jobseekers should place inquiries between 10:00 a.m. and 12:00 p.m. or 2:00 p.m. and 4:00 p.m., Tuesdays through Thursdays only. When applying for faculty positions, please contact the specific department. **President:** Dr. Walter E. Massey. **Annual sales/revenues:** $51 - $100 million.

MORRIS BROWN COLLEGE
643 Martin Luther King, Jr. Drive NW, Atlanta GA 30314. 404/739-1000. **Contact:** Human Resources. **World Wide Web address:** http://www.morrisbrown.edu. **Description:** A four-year college offering bachelor of arts and bachelor of science degrees. Founded 1881. **President:** Dolores E. Cross, PhD.

MORRIS NEWSPAPER CORPORATION
27 Abercorn Street, Savannah GA 31401. 912/233-1281. **Fax:** 912/238-2059. **Contact:** Human Resources Department. **E-mail address:** info@morrismultimedia.com. **World Wide Web address:** http://www.morrismultimedia.com. **Description:** A newspaper conglomerate that also operates broadcasting stations. **Corporate headquarters location:** This location. **President/CEO:** Charles H. Morris.

MORRISON HOMES
3655 Brookside Parkway, Suite 400, Alpharetta GA 30022. 770/360-8700. **World Wide Web address:** http://www.morrisonhomes.com. **Description:** Builds residential homes. Founded 1984. **NOTE:** Please visit website to search for jobs and apply online. **Positions advertised include:** IS Functional Analyst; AIX Engineer; CADD Operator. **Corporate headquarters location:** This location. **Other area locations:** Marietta GA. **Other U.S. locations:** TX; CA; CO; FL; AZ. **Parent company:** George Wimpley PLC.

MOTION INDUSTRIES
106 Hemlock Street, Valdosta GA 31601. 229/244-4548. **Fax:** 229/244-4528. **Contact:** Human Resources Department. **E-mail address:** jobs@motion-ind.com. **World Wide Web address:** http://www.motion-industries.com. **Description:** Motion Industries manufactures bearings, power transmission parts, and fluid replacement parts. **NOTE:** Please visit website to apply online. Please mail your resume to the corporate office at P.O. Box 1477, Birmingham AL 35201-1477; fax is 205/951-1172. **Corporate headquarters location:** Birmingham AL. **Other area locations:** Statewide. **Other U.S. locations:** Nationwide. **International locations:** Canada. **Operations at this facility include:** A distribution center for various transmission and replacement parts. **Parent company:** Genuine Parts Company. **Number of employees worldwide:** 6,000.

MOUNT VERNON MILLS
APPAREL FABRICS GROUP
821 South Elm Street, Commerce GA. 706/335-3171. **Contact:** Human Resources. **World Wide Web address:** http://www.mvmills.com. **Description:** Produces and distributes cotton fabrics to clothing and other textile manufacturers. **Corporate headquarters location:** Greenville SC. **Other U.S. locations:** AL; CA; MS; SC; TX. **President:** Roger W. Chastain. **Number of employees nationwide:** 5,500.

MUNICH AMERICAN REASSURANCE COMPANY
P.O. Box 3210, Atlanta GA 30302-3210. 770/350-3200. **Physical address:** 56 Perimeter Center E, Suite 500, Atlanta GA 30346-2290. **Fax:** 770/350-3300. **Contact:** Kay Yoest, Personnel Administrator. **E-mail address:** careers@marclife.com. **World Wide Web address:** http://www.marclife.com. **Description:** The U.S. offices of an international insurance carrier. Munich American Reassurance offers a wide variety of life, accident, and health reinsurance coverage. Founded 1959. **Positions advertised include:** Actuarial Assistant; General Accountant; Long Term Care Administrator. **Office hours:** Monday – Friday, 8:00 a.m. – 4:15 p.m. **Corporate headquarters location:** This location. **Other U.S. locations:** Chicago IL. **Parent company:** Munich Re Group.

NCR CORPORATION
2651 Satellite Boulevard, Duluth GA 30096. 770/623-7000. **Contact:** Human Resources. **World Wide Web address:** http://www.ncr.com. **Description:** A worldwide provider of computer products and services. The company provides computer solutions to three targeted industries: retail, financial, and communication. NCR Computer Systems Group develops, manufactures, and markets computer systems. NCR Financial Systems Group is an industry leader in financial delivery systems, relationship banking data warehousing solutions, and payments systems/item processing. NCR Retail Systems Group is a world leader in end-to-end retail solutions serving the food, general merchandise, and hospitality segments. NCR Worldwide Services provides data warehousing services solutions; end-to-end networking services; and designing, implementing, and supporting complex open systems environments. NCR Systemedia Group develops, produces, and markets a complete line of information products to satisfy customers' information technology needs including transaction processing media, auto identification media, business form communication products, managing documents and media, and a full line of integrated equipment

solutions. **NOTE:** Please visit website to search for jobs and apply online. **Positions advertised include:** Pricing Director; Financial Planning Analyst; Compris Controller; GIS IC Food; Sales Representative; Channel Marketing Manager; Industrial Design Engineer; Product Management Business Analyst; Production Planning Manager. **Corporate headquarters location:** Dayton OH. **Other U.S. locations:** El Segundo CA; San Diego CA; Columbia SC. **International locations:** Worldwide. **Listed on:** New York Stock Exchange. **Stock exchange symbol:** NCR. **Number of employees worldwide:** 29,000.

NDCHEALTH CORPORATION
4 Corporate Square NE, Atlanta GA 30329. 404/728-2000. **Toll-free phone:** 800/225-5632. **Fax:** 404/728-3904. **Contact:** Director of Staffing. **E-mail address:** careers@ndchealth.com. **World Wide Web address:** http://www.ndchealth.com. **Description:** A provider of information systems and services to the health care market. NDCHealth offers patient eligibility, claims processing, consulting, billing and other services to doctors, hospitals, pharmacies, government agencies, and managed care organizations. The company's clients include more than 55,000 pharmacies, 100,000 physicians, and more than 1,200 hospitals. Founded 1977. **NOTE:** Please visit website to search for jobs and apply online. **Positions advertised include:** Director of Finance; Training Specialist; Senior Payroll Representative; Senior Paralegal; Senior Administrative Assistant; Senior Recruiter; Lead Systems Engineer; Senior Financial Analyst; Manager – Training and Development; Maintenance Electrician; Senior Attorney; Senior Internal Auditor; Director - IHR. **Corporate headquarters location:** This location. **Other U.S. locations:** Nationwide. **International locations:** Canada; Germany; United Kingdom. **Listed on:** New York Stock Exchange. **Stock exchange symbol:** NDC. **President/CEO:** William Hoff. **Number of employees worldwide:** 1,800.

KRAFT FOODS
1400 Murphy Avenue SW, Atlanta GA 30310. 404/756-6000. **Contact:** Human Resources Manager. **World Wide Web address:** http://www.kraft.com. **Description:** Kraft Foods is one of the largest consumer foods operations in the country. The company markets a broad line of cookie and cracker products under such brand names as Oreo, Ritz, Premium, Teddy Grahams, Chips Ahoy!, and Wheat Thins. The company operates 13 cake and cookie bakeries, a flourmill, and a cheese plant. Over 150 biscuit brands reach the consumer via Nabisco's distribution network. **NOTE:** Employment opportunities are listed on the Georgia Department of Labor website. **Office hours:** Monday – Friday 8:00 a.m. – 4:00 p.m. **Corporate headquarters location:** Northfield IL. **Other U.S. locations:** Nationwide. **International locations:** Worldwide. **Operations at this facility include:** This location manufactures cookies. **Listed on:** New York Stock Exchange. **Stock exchange symbol:** KFT. **CEO:** Roger Deromedi. **Number of employees worldwide:** 109,000.

NLC HOLDINGS
25 Dart Road, Newnan GA 30265. 770/304-7660. **Toll-free phone:** 800/521-8266. **Fax:** 800/342-1276. **Contact:** Human Resources Manager. **Description:** Manufactures plastic and vinyl toilet seats. **Special programs:** Internships. **Corporate headquarters location:** This location. **Operations at this facility include:** Manufacturing. **Listed on:** Privately held. **President/CEO:** William Marsh.

NATIONAL DISTRIBUTING COMPANY INC.
P.O. Box 44127, Atlanta GA 30336. 404/696-9440. **Physical address:** One National Drive SW, Atlanta GA 30336. **Toll-free phone:** 800/282-3548. **Fax:** 404/505-1013. **Contact:** Human Resources. **World Wide Web address:** http://www.natdistco.com. **Description:** Engaged in wholesale beverage (beer, wine, and spirits) distribution and the linen supply business. **Corporate headquarters location:** This location. **Other U.S. locations:** Nationwide. **CEO:** Jay M. Davis. **Number of employees nationwide:** 2,500.

NATIONAL SERVICE INDUSTRIES INC.
NATIONAL LINEN SERVICE
1420 Peachtree Street NE, Suite 500, Atlanta GA 30309. 404/853-6000. **Toll-free phone:** 800/225-4636. **Fax:** 404/853-6002. **Contact:** Recruiter. **E-mail address:** recruiter@nationallinen.com. **World Wide Web address:** http://www.national-linen.com. **Description:** A total linen solution services company primarily for dining and food service, healthcare, lodging and country club, and facility service markets. **NOTE:** Please visit website to search for jobs and apply online. You may also fax your resume to 404/853-6200. **Positions advertised include:** Area Manager; Plant Manager; Production Supervisor; Service Manager. **Corporate headquarters location:** This location. **Other U.S. locations:** Southeastern U.S. **Parent company:** National Service Industries, Inc. operates in two segments: the textile rental segment, National Linen Service, and the envelope segment, Atlantic Envelope Company (Smyrna GA). **President:** Gerry Knotek. **Number of employees nationwide:** 5,884.

NATIONAL VISION
296 Grayson Highway, Lawrenceville GA 30045. 770/822-3600. **Fax:** 770/822-6206. **Recorded jobline:** 888/261-3937. **Contact:** Human Resources. **E-mail address:** jobs@nationalvision.com. **World Wide Web address:** http://www.nationalvision.com. **Description:** National Vision operates five separate retail divisions offering a variety of products and services for eye care and eyewear needs. **Positions advertised include:** Legal Secretary; Human Resources Generalist. **Office hours:** Monday – Friday, 8:30 a.m. – 5:00 p.m. **Corporate headquarters location:** This location. **Listed on:** American Stock Exchange. **Stock exchange symbol:** NVI. **President/CEO:** L. Reade Fahs. **Number of employees worldwide:** 2,930.

NEIMAN MARCUS
3393 Peachtree Road NE, Atlanta GA 30326. 404/266-8200. **Toll-free phone:** 800/555-5077. **Contact:** Human Resources Manager. **World Wide Web address:** http://www.neimanmarcus.com. **Description:** A retailer of men's and women's apparel, fashion accessories, precious jewelry, fine china, and moderately priced crystal and silver. Neiman Marcus has 33 stores nationwide. **NOTE:** Entry-level positions are offered. **Corporate headquarters location:** Dallas TX. **Other area locations:** Lawrenceville GA. **Other U.S. locations:** Nationwide. **Subsidiaries include:** Bergdorf Goodman Stores (NY); NM Direct, a direct marketing company. **Operations at this facility include:** Administration; Sales; Service. **Listed on:** New York Stock Exchange. **Stock exchange symbol:** NMG/A. **President/CEO:** Burton Tansky. **Number of employees nationwide:** 15,400.

NORTEL NETWORKS
5405 Windward Parkway, Alpharetta GA 30004. 770/708-4000. **Contact:** Human Resources. **World Wide Web address:** http://www.nortel.com. **Description:** Nortel Networks designs, produces, and supports multimedia access devices for use in building corporate, public, and Internet networks. The primary focus of the company's services is the consolidation of voice, fax, video, and data and multimedia traffic into a single network link. **NOTE:** Please visit website to search for jobs and apply online. **Corporate headquarters location:** Ontario, Canada. **Other U.S. locations:** Richardson TX; Santa Clara CA; Simi Valley CA; San Ramon CA; Billerica MA; Triangle Park NC; Schaumburg IL. **Operations at this facility include:** This location develops software. **Listed on:** New York Stock Exchange. **Stock exchange symbol:** NT. **President/CEO:** Frank A. Dunn.

NORTHLAKE MEDICAL CENTER
1455 Montreal Road, Tucker GA 30084. 770/270-3000. **Fax:** 770/270-3046. **Recorded jobline:** 770/270-3080. **Contact:** Kevin Trameri, Human Resources. **E-mail address:** kevin.trameri@hcahealthcare.com. **World Wide Web address:** http://www.northlakemedical..com. **Description:** A 120-bed general acute care medical center. **NOTE:** Direct contact phone number is 770/270-3118. Please visit website to search for jobs. Part-time jobs, second and third shifts, and volunteer positions are also offered. **Positions advertised include:** Mammography Technician; RN – Various Departments; Occupational Therapist; Physician Assistant; Physical Therapist; CT Technician. **Special programs:** Internships.

NOVA INFORMATION SYSTEMS, INC.
One Concourse Parkway, Suite 300, Atlanta GA 30328. 770/396-1456. **Toll-free phone:** 800/226-9332. **Contact:** Human Resources. **E-mail address:** novaresume@novainfo.com. **World Wide Web address:** http://www.novainfo.com. **Description:** Develops and markets credit and debit card processing software. **Office hours:** Monday – Friday, 8:30 a.m. – 5:30 p.m. **Corporate headquarters location:** This location. **Other U.S. locations:** Knoxville TN. **Listed on:** New York Stock Exchange. **Stock exchange symbol:** NIS. **Annual sales/revenues:** More than $100 million. **CEO:** Edward Grzedzinski. **Number of employees nationwide:** 1,500.

OCONEE REGIONAL MEDICAL CENTER
821 North Cobb Street, P.O. Box 690, Milledgeville GA 31061. 478/454-3500. **Recorded jobline:** 478/454-3545. **Contact:** Human Resources. **E-mail address:** jobs@oconeeregional.com. **World Wide Web address:** http://www.oconeeregional.com. **Description:** A medical center. **NOTE:** Human Resources phone is 478/454-3540. Please visit website to search for jobs and download employment application. Volunteer positions are also available. **Positions advertised include:** Accounting Clerk; Accounting Supervisor; Billing Specialist; Conversion Assistant; Director of Foundation and Development; Driver – Non-emergency Transportation; EMT/Paramedic; Maintenance Mechanic - Engineering; Monitor Technician – Radiology; Nuclear Medicine Technologist – Radiology; OB Nurse Manager; PBX Operator; Physical Therapy Assistant; RN; - Various Departments; Registration Representative; Respiratory Care Practitioner; Transcriptionist; Transport/Monitor Technician; Ultrasound Technologist. **Special programs:** Internships. **Operations at this facility include:** Administration. **Listed on:** Privately held. **President/CEO:** Brian Riddle.

OGLETHORPE POWER CORPORATION
P.O. Box 1349, Tucker GA 30085-1349. 770/270-7600. **Physical address:** 2100 East Exchange Place, Tucker GA. **Toll-free phone:** 800/241-5374. **Contact:** Human Resources. **World Wide Web address:** http://www.opc.com. **Description:** A nonprofit electric generation and transmission cooperative, entirely owned by its 39 retail electric distribution cooperative members, who, in turn, are entirely owned by their retail consumers. The principal business of the company is to provide wholesale electric service to the members, where each member purchases capacity and energy from the company. Oglethorpe Power Corporation is one of the largest generation and transmission cooperatives in the country in terms of operating revenues, assets, kilowatt-hour sales, and consumers served. **NOTE:** Please visit website to search for jobs and apply online. **Positions advertised include:** Analyst; Craft Supervisor. **Corporate headquarters location:** This location. **President/CEO:** Thomas A. Smith.

OGLETHORPE UNIVERSITY
4484 Peachtree Road NE, Atlanta GA 30319. 404/261-1441. **Toll-free phone:** 800/428-4484. **Contact:** Human Resources. **World Wide Web address:** http://www.oglethorpe.edu. **Description:** A four-year university offering bachelor of arts, bachelor of science, and master's degrees; total enrollment is approximately 1,200. Founded in 1835. **NOTE:** Please visit website to search for jobs, and for more details on applying for specific jobs. Human Resources phone is 404/364-8325. **Positions advertised include:** University College Administration Operations Coordinator; Assistant Professor – Management; Assistant Professor – Social Psychology; Director of Admissions. **President:** Larry D. Large.

OLAN MILLS STUDIOS
2400 Wisteria Drive SW, Suite 6, Snellville GA 30078. 770/978-2433. **Contact:** Human Resources. **World Wide Web address:** http://www.olanmills.com. **Description:** A photography studio offering portrait services and sales of photography-related products. Founded 1932. **NOTE:** Please visit website to browse career categories and job openings. Please indicate area of interest: photography, telemarketing, or scheduling appointments. **Corporate headquarters location:** Chattanooga TN. **Other area locations:** Statewide. **Other U.S. locations:** Nationwide. **International locations:** UK.

OLIN CORPORATION
P.O. Box 1234, Augusta GA 30903-1234. 706/798-1510. **Physical address:** 2402 Doug Barbard Parkway, Augusta GA 30906-2139. **Contact:** Human Resources. **World Wide Web address:** http://www.olin.com. **Description:** Olin produces copper alloys, ammunition, and chlorine and caustic soda. The company has expanding interests in electronic materials, defense, aerospace management, and water management. **NOTE:** Please visit website to search for jobs. **Corporate headquarters location:** Norwalk CT. **Other U.S. locations:** Nationwide. **Operations at this facility include:** Alkaline production. **Listed on:** New York Stock Exchange. **Stock exchange symbol:** OLN. **Number of employees nationwide:** 6,200.

OMNI HOTEL AT CNN CENTER
100 CNN Center, Atlanta GA 30303. 404/659-0000. **Fax:** 404/525-5050. **Contact:** Human Resources Manager. **World Wide Web address:** http://www.omnihotels.com. **Description:** A luxury hotel offering lodging, dining, lounge, and meeting facilities. **NOTE:** Please visit website to search for jobs and apply online. **Positions advertised include:** Senior Convention Services Manager; Business Travel Sales Manager; Omni Express Sales Manager. **Corporate headquarters location:** Irving TX. **Other U.S. locations:** Nationwide. **International locations:** Canada; Mexico. **Parent company:** Omni Hotels. **Operations at this facility include:** Sales; Service. **President:** James D. Caldwell. **Number of employees worldwide:** 10,000.

ONESOURCE
1600 Parkwood Circle, Suite 400, Atlanta GA 30339. 770/436-9900. **Contact:** Human Resources. **World Wide Web address:** http://www.2onesource.com. **Description:** Provides facility management including janitorial and landscaping services. **Corporate headquarters location:** This location. **Other area locations:** Statewide.

ONESOURCE
3120 Medlock Bridge Road NW, Norcross GA 30071. 770/368-1062. **Contact:** Human Resource Manager. **World Wide Web address:** http://www.2onesource.com. **Description:** Provides environmental services, facility management, janitorial services,

and landscaping services. **Corporate headquarters location:** Atlanta GA. **Other area locations:** Statewide.

OWENS CORNING
4795 Frederick Drive, Atlanta GA 30336. 404/691-3910. **Contact:** Human Resources. **World Wide Web address:** http://www.owenscorning.com. **Description:** Owens Corning manufactures and sells thermal and acoustical insulation products including insulation for appliances, glass fiber roofing shingles, and roof insulation and industrial asphalt. Other products of the company include windows, glass fiber textile yarns, wet process chopped strands and specialty mats, and polyester resins. **NOTE:** Please visit website to search for jobs and apply online. **Positions advertised include:** Production Supervisor. **Corporate headquarters location:** Toledo OH. **Other U.S. locations:** Nationwide. **International locations:** Worldwide. **Operation at this facility include:** This location houses the area administrative and manufacturing facilities. **Listed on:** Over-The-Counter. **Stock exchange symbol:** OWENQ. **CEO:** Dave Brown. **Number of employees worldwide:** 17,000.

OXFORD INDUSTRIES, INC.
222 Piedmont Avenue NE, Atlanta GA 30308. 404/659-2424. **Fax:** 404/653-1545. **Contact:** Human Resources. **World Wide Web address:** http://www.oxfordinc.com. **Description:** Manufactures private-label clothing including men's and boys' tailored sports jackets, slacks, and dress shirts; and women's dresses, separates, and collections. **Corporate headquarters location:** This location. **Listed on:** New York Stock Exchange. **Stock exchange symbol:** OXM. **CEO:** J. Hicks Lanier.

PCA (PACKAGING CORPORATION OF AMERICA)
P.O. Box 1048, Valdosta GA 31603-1048. 229/559-7911. **Physical address:** 5495 Lake Park, Statenville GA 31648. Fax: 229/559-0546. **Contact:** Human Resources. **World Wide Web address:** http://www.packagingcorp.com. **Description:** Manufactures containerboard, kraft linerboard, and corrugated packaging. Products are primarily used to ship manufactured goods. **NOTE:** Contact corporate office at 847/482-2111; fax is 847/482-2238. **Corporate headquarters location:** Lake Forest IL. **Listed on:** New York Stock Exchange. **Stock exchange symbol:** PKG. **CEO:** Paul T. Stecko. **Number of employees nationwide:** 7,900.

PGI – POLYMER GROUP
2100 Atlanta Highway, Gainesville GA 30504. 770/532-3161. **Contact:** Personnel Director. **E-mail address:** recruiter@pginw.com. **World Wide Web address:** http://www.polymergroupinc.com. **Description:** Manufactures a variety of fabrics sold to a broad range of industrial and commercial customers. The company also manufactures diapers for the private label market segment. **NOTE:** Send resume to corporate office at 201 North Church Street, Mooresville NC 28115. **Corporate headquarters location:** Mooresville NC. **Other U.S. locations:** Nationwide. **International locations:** Worldwide. **Listed on:** Over-The-Counter. **Stock exchange symbol:** POLGA. **Number of employees worldwide:** 3,600.

PPG INDUSTRIES, INC.
1377 Oakleigh Drive, East Point GA 30344. 404/761-7771. **Contact:** Human Resources. **World Wide Web address:** http://www.ppg.com. **Description:** PPG Industries supplies products for manufacturing, building, automotive, processing, and numerous other world industries. The company manufactures decorative and protective coatings, flat glass and fabricated glass products, continuous-strand fiberglass, and industrial and specialty chemicals. PPG operates 120 manufacturing facilities worldwide. Founded in 1883. **Office hours:** Monday – Friday, 8:00 a.m. – 4:30 p.m. **Corporate headquarters location:** Pittsburgh PA. **Other U.S. locations:** Nationwide. **International locations:** Worldwide. **Operations at this facility include:** This facility manufactures a variety of coating products for the professional and consumer house paint markets. **Listed on:** New York Stock Exchange. **Stock exchange symbol:** PPG. **CEO:** Raymond LeBoeuf. **Number of employees worldwide:** 32,900.

PRG-SCHULTZ INTERNATIONAL, INC.
600 Galleria Parkway, Suite 100, Atlanta GA 30339. 770/779-3900. **Toll-free phone:** 800/752-5894. **Fax:** 770/779-3250. **Contact:** Personnel. **E-mail address:** personnel@prgx.com. **World Wide Web address:** http://www.prgx.com. **Description:** A profit-recovery firm. Profit recovery group offers services in logistics, tax, communications, and payables. **NOTE:** Please visit website to download application form. Visit http://www.monster.com to search for jobs and apply online. **Positions advertised include:** Reports Analyst; Network Operations Analyst; Regional Human Resources Manager. **Corporate headquarters location:** This location. **Other U.S. locations:** San Juan Capistrano CA; West Valley City UT; Fort Collins CO; New York NY; Parsippany NJ. **International locations:** Worldwide. **Listed on:** NASDAQ. **Stock exchange symbol:** PRGX. **President/CEO:** John Cook. **Annual sales/revenues:** More than $100 million. **Number of employees worldwide:** 3,500.

PACTIV CORPORATION
7670 Airport Drive, Macon GA 31297. 478/788-2000. **Contact:** Human Resources. **World Wide Web address:** http://www.pactiv.com. **Description:** A worldwide manufacturer of paper, corrugated paper, paperboard, aluminum, and plastic packaging material. Products are used in the packaging of food, paper and paper products, metal products, rubber and plastics, automotive products, point-of-purchase displays, soap, detergent, and food products, as well as residential construction. **Office hours:** Monday – Friday, 8:00 a.m. – 5:00 p.m. **Corporate headquarters location:** Lake Forest IL. **Listed on:** New York Stock Exchange. **Stock exchange symbol:** PTV.

PANDUIT CORPORATION
1819 Atlanta Highway, Cumming GA 30040. 770/889-3522. **Contact:** Linda Skorb, Human Resources. **E-mail address:** ga-employment@panduit.com. **World Wide Web address:** http://www.panduit.com. **Description:** Panduit is a manufacturer of products for wiring and communications applications. Panduit's major products include network cabling systems, cable ties, wiring accessories, surface raceway and wiring duct, terminals, power connectors, installation tooling, identification products, heat shrink products, communication connectors and cable management systems. **Positions advertised include:** Technical Writer; Drafter; Construction Engineer; Business Development Manager; Corporate Quality Engineer; System Test Engineer; Wireless LAN Business Development Manager; Manufacturing Engineer; Product Design Engineer; Production Foreperson; Marketing Project Manager. **Corporate headquarters location:** Tinley Park IL. **Other U.S. locations:** Nationwide. **Number of employees worldwide:** 3,000.

PANASONIC AUTOMOTIVE SYSTEMS COMPANY
776 Highway 74 South, Peachtree City GA 30269. 770/487-3356. **Fax:** 770/487-3357. **Contact:** Human Resources. **E-mail address:** richh@panasonic-mcusa.com. **World Wide Web address:** http://www.panasonic.com. **Description:** A manufacturer of original equipment car audio parts. The company also manufactures telecommunications products including digital business systems (DBS). **NOTE:** Please visit website to search for jobs. **Positions advertised include:** Manager of Human Resources. **Corporate headquarters location:** Secaucus NJ. **Other U.S. locations:** Nationwide. **International locations:** Worldwide. **Parent company:** Matsushita.

PARKER AEROSPACE – CONTROL SYSTEMS DIVISION
2010 Waldrep Industrial Boulevard, Dublin GA 31021-2648. 478/275-4030. **Fax:** 478/277-9228. **Contact:** Human Resources. **World Wide Web address:** http://www.parker.com/ag/cce. **Description:** Designs and manufactures flight, missile, and engine controls for both commercial and military programs. The product lines consist of electronics, hydraulics, and electrohydraulic components. **NOTE:** Please visit http://www.monster.com to search for jobs and apply online. **Positions advertised include:** Aerospace Engineer; Quality Engineer; **Listed on:** New York Stock Exchange. **Stock exchange symbol:** PH.

PAUL, HASTINGS, JANOFSKY & WALKER
600 Peachtree Street NE, Suite 2400, Atlanta GA 30308. 404/815-2400. **Fax:** 404/815-2424. **Contact:** Hiring Attorney. **E-mail address:** recruitatl@paulhastings.com. **World Wide Web address:** http://www.paulhastings.com. **Description:** A law firm specializing in corporate, employment, immigration, litigation, and real estate. **NOTE:** Please visit website to see job listings. **Positions advertised include:** Immigration Administrative Case Manager. **Special programs:** Summer Associate program. **Other U.S. locations:** Costa Mesa CA; Los Angeles CA; New York NY; San Diego CA; San Francisco CA; Stamford CT; Washington D.C. **International locations:** Beijing China; Hong Kong China; London England; Shanghai China; Tokyo Japan. **Number of employees at this location:** 83. **Number of employees worldwide:** 900.

PEACHTREE PLANNING CORPORATION
5040 Roswell Road, Atlanta GA 30342. 404/260/1600. 231-0839. **Toll-free phone:** 800/366-0839. **Fax:** 404/260-1700. **Contact:** Sarah Brannon, Director of Manpower Development. **E-mail address:** sarah.brannon@glic.com. **World Wide Web address:** http://www.peachtreeplanning.com. **Description:** Specializes in estate planning (wealth creation and wealth conservation). Product lines include stocks, bonds, mutual funds, life insurance, disability insurance, and annuities. **NOTE:** Contact Director of Manpower Development at 404/260-1627 or at listed toll-free number, ext. 1627; fax is 404/260-1727. Please visit website to complete online employment form. **Corporate headquarters location:** This location. **Other area locations:** Statewide. **Number of employees at this location:** 45.

PEPSI BOTTLING GROUP
1480 Chattahoochee Avenue NW, Atlanta GA 30318. 404/355-1480. **Contact:** Human Resources Director. **World Wide Web address:** http://www.pbg.com. **Description:** Bottles and distributes the complete line of Pepsi-Cola soft drink products. This facility is independent of PepsiCo, Inc. **NOTE:** Please visit http://www.pbgjobs.com to search for jobs and apply online. **Positions advertised include:** Plant Manager; Production Manager; Quality Control Manager; Product Availability Manager; Maintenance Manager. **Corporate headquarters location:** Somers NY. **Other area locations:** Rome GA; Gainesville GA; Bogart GA; Macon GA. **Other U.S. locations:** Nationwide. **International locations:** Canada; Greece; Mexico; Russia; Spain; Turkey. **Listed on:** New York Stock Exchange. **Stock exchange symbol:** PBG. **Number of employees worldwide:** 65,000. **CEO:** John T. Cahill.

PEOPLESOFT
3353 Peachtree Road NE, Suite 600, Atlanta GA 38326. 404/439-5900. **Contact:** Human Resources. **World Wide Web address:** http://www.peoplesoft.com. **Description:** Creates a variety of software. Founded 1987. **NOTE:** Please visit website to search for jobs and apply online. **Positions advertised include:** PGS Manager; Client Executive Healthcare; Staff Proposal Specialist; Revenue Management Systems Solution Consultant; Senior Consultant. **Corporate headquarters location:** Pleasanton CA. **Other area locations:** Atlanta GA. **Other U.S. locations:** Nationwide. **International locations:** Worldwide. **Listed on:** NASDAQ. **Stock exchange symbol:** PSFT. **Number of employees worldwide:** 12,000.

PEREGRINE SYSTEMS
12600 Deerfield Parkway, First Floor, Alpharetta GA 30004. 678/566-3825. Fax: 678/566-3551. **Contact:** Human Resources. **World Wide Web address:** http://www.peregrine.com. **Description:** Develops IT asset management software for businesses. Founded 1981. **NOTE:** Entry-level positions and second and third shifts are offered. Please visit website to search for jobs and apply online. Mail resumes to corporate office at 3611 Valley Centre Drive, Floor 1, San Diego CA 92130; phone is 858/481-5000; fax is 858/720-5275. **Corporate headquarters location:** San Diego CA. **Other U.S. locations:** Nationwide. **International locations:** Worldwide. **Listed on:** NASDAQ. **Stock exchange symbol:** PRGN. **CEO:** John Mutch. **Number of employees worldwide:** 650.

PER-SE TECHNOLOGIES, INC.
1145 Sanctuary Parkway, Suite 200, Alpharetta GA 30004. 770/237-4300. **Toll-free phone:** 877/737-3773. **Contact:** Human Resources. **World Wide Web address:** http://www.per-se.com. **Description:** A provider of comprehensive business management services, financial and clinical software, and Internet solutions to physicians and other healthcare professionals. **Positions advertised include:** Senior Software Engineer; Product Director; Corporate Communications Associate; Staff Financial Analyst; Help Desk Administrator; Senior Coding Consultant; Healthcare Consulting Sales Director; Practice/Account Manager; Client Enrollment Specialist. **Corporate headquarters location:** This location. **Other U.S.** locations: Nationwide. **Listed on:** NASDAQ. **Stock exchange symbol:** PSTI. **President/CEO:** Phillip M. Pead. **Number of employees nationwide:** 5,000.

PFIZER
P.O Box 2347, Augusta GA 30903. 706/303-6000. **Physical address:** 1736 Lover's Lane, Augusta GA 30901. **Contact:** Human Resources Department. **World Wide Web address:** http://www.pfizer.com. **Description:** Develops and manufactures prescription medicines and other products for both humans and animals. Medicines include Celebrex, Diflucan, Viagra, Zoloft, and Zyrtec. Over the counter products include Benadryl, e.p.t., Listerine, Lubriderm, Rolaids, Sudafed, and Visine. **NOTE:** Please visit the Georgia Department of Labor in person or online – http://www.dol.state.ga.us – for a listing of Pfizer job opportunities. **Office hours:** Monday – Friday, 8:00 a.m. – 4:30 p.m. **Corporate headquarters location:** New York NY. **Other U.S. locations:** Nationwide. **International locations:** Worldwide. **Listed on:** New York Stock Exchange. **Stock exchange symbol:** PFE. CEO: Hank McKinnell. **Number of employees worldwide:** 122,000.

PHILIPS CONSUMER ELECTRONICS COMPANY
64 Perimeter Center East, P.O. Box 467300, Atlanta GA 31146-7300. 770/821-2400. **Fax:** 770/821-3126. **Contact:** Personnel Director. **World Wide Web address:** http://www.usa.philips.com. **Description:** Engaged in the manufacture and sale of a line of dictating machines including portable recorders, desktop dictation and transcription units, and a state-of-the-art, PC-based, digital dictation system. Units are marketed under the Philips and Norelco brand names. **NOTE:** Please visit http://www.careers.philips.com to search for jobs and apply online. **Positions advertised include:** Account Manager; Administrative Assistant; Administrative Support; Business Analyst; Director – Sales Connected Flat Displays; Multi-Vendor Service Sales Specialist; Order Processing Support; Sales Representative; Service Sales

Specialist; Surgery Demo Specialist; Team Leader – Category Management; Technical Support Engineer; Ultra-High Field MR Business Development. **Parent company:** Royal Philips Electronics of the Netherlands is a multimarket manufacturing organization with worldwide locations and various subsidiaries. The company concentrates its efforts primarily in the fields of consumer electronics, consumer products, electrical and electronics components, and professional equipment. **Listed on:** New York Stock Exchange. **Stock exchange symbol:** PHG. **Number of employees worldwide:** 164,000.

PHOTOCIRCUITS ATLANTA
350 Dividend Drive, Peachtree City GA 30269. 770/487-8888. **Fax:** 770/632-2105. **Contact:** Human Resources. **E-mail address:** ptrecruiter@photocircuits.com. **World Wide Web address:** http://www.photocircuits.com. **Description:** One of the leading manufacturers of printed circuit boards in North America. Founded 1951. **NOTE:** Please visit website to search for jobs and to fill out online employment form. **Positions advertised include:** Product Engineer; Process Engineering Technician; HVAC Mechanic. **Corporate headquarters location:** Glen Cove NY. **International locations:** Philippines; Costa Rica; Mexico. **Operations at this facility include:** Manufacturing. **Number of employees at this location:** 800. **Number of employees worldwide:** 2,500.

PILGRIM'S PRIDE
920 Queen City Parkway, Gainseville GA 30501. 770/536-3413. **Fax:** 770/287-7662. **Contact:** Rick Bailey, Divisional Personnel Manager. **E-mail address:** rick.bailey@pilgrimspride.com. **World Wide Web address:** http://www.pilgrimspride.com. **Description:** The nation's second largest poultry company. Founded 1946. **NOTE:** Please visit website to search for jobs, or to download an employment application. **Positions advertised include:** Regional CI Manager; Processing Shift Manager; Sanitation Supervisor. **Corporate headquarters location:** Pittsburg TX. **Other area locations:** Athens GA; Canton GA; Duluth GA; Elberton GA; Dalton GA; Atlanta GA. **Other U.S. locations:** Southern U.S. **International locations:** Puerto Rico; Mexico. **Number of employees worldwide:** 40,000.

PILGRIM'S PRIDE
898 Barber Street, Athens GA 30601. 706/549-2810. **Contact:** Daniel Haggard, Personnel Manager. **E-mail address:** dan.hoggard@pilgrimspride.com. **World Wide Web address:** http://www. pilgrimspride.com. **Description:** The nation's second largest poultry company. Founded 1946. **NOTE:** Please visit website to search for jobs, or to download an employment application. Direct contact phone is 706/425-7657. **Positions advertised include:** Maintenance Supervisor; Registered Nurse. **Corporate headquarters location:** Pittsburg TX. **Other area locations:** Canton GA; Duluth GA; Elberton GA; Gainesville GA; Dalton GA; Atlanta GA. **Other U.S. locations:** Southern U.S. **International locations:** Puerto Rico; Mexico. **Number of employees worldwide:** 40,000.

PILGRIM'S PRIDE
P.O. Box 519, Elberton GA 30635. 706/283-3821. **Physical address:** 1129 Old Middleton Road, Elberton GA 30635. **Contact:** Human Resources Manager. **E-mail address:** jobs@pilgrimspride.com. **World Wide Web address:** http://www.pilgrimspride.com. **Description:** The nation's second largest poultry company. Founded 1946. **NOTE:** Please visit website to search for jobs, or to download an employment application. **Positions advertised include:** Safety Manager. **Corporate headquarters location:** Pittsburg TX. **Other area locations:** Athens GA; Canton GA; Duluth GA; Gainesville GA; Dalton GA; Atlanta GA. **Other U.S. locations:** Southern U.S. **International locations:** Puerto Rico; Mexico. **Number of employees worldwide:** 40,000.

PILGRIM'S PRIDE
P.O. Box 1389, Duluth GA 30096. 770/232-4200. **Physical address:** 2475 Meadowbrook Parkway, Suite A, Duluth GA 30096. **Contact:** Human Resources. **E-mail address:** jobs@pilgrimspride.com. **World Wide Web address:** http://www.pilgrimspride.com. **Description:** The nation's second largest poultry company. Founded 1946. **NOTE:** Please visit website to search for jobs, or to download an employment application. **Positions advertised include:** Transportation Planner. **Corporate headquarters location:** Pittsburg TX. **Other area locations:** Athens GA; Canton GA; Duluth GA; Gainesville GA; Dalton GA; Atlanta GA. **Other U.S. locations:** Southern U.S. **International locations:** Puerto Rico; Mexico. **Number of employees worldwide:** 40,000.

PITTMAN DENTAL LABORATORY
2355 Centennial Circle, Gainesville GA 30504. 770/534-4457. **Fax:** 770/503-1173. **World Wide Web address:** http://www.pittmandental.com. **Contact:** Human Resources. **Description:** A dental laboratory that manufactures crowns, bridges, and dentures.

PIZZA HUT, INC.
675 Mansell Road, Suite 200, Roswell GA 30076. 770/990-2000. **Contact:** Human Resources. **World Wide Web address:** http://www.pizzahut.com. **Description:** Pizza Hut is a worldwide operator of family restaurants, with more than 12,000 locations. **NOTE:** Entry-level positions are offered. Please visit http://www.yumcareers.com to search for jobs. **Office hours: Monday – Friday,** 8:00 a.m. – 5:00 p.m. **Corporate headquarters location:** Dallas TX. **Other U.S. locations:** Nationwide. **International locations:** Worldwide. **Operations at this facility include:** Home to the administrative offices for the southern region. **Parent company:** Yum! Brands Inc.

PLANTATION PIPE LINE COMPANY
1720 Windward Concourse, Suite 325, Alpharetta GA 30005. 770/751-4000. **Fax:** 770/751-4130. **Contact:** Human Resources. **World Wide Web address:** http://www.plantation-ppl.com. **Description:** A manufacturer of refined-petroleum pipelines. Founded in 1940. **NOTE:** Please visit parent company website at http://www.kindermorgan.com to search for jobs. **Corporate headquarters location:** This location. **Other area locations:** Doraville GA. **Parent company:** Kinder Morgan, Inc.

PLASTICAN
101 Lillian Drive, Macon GA 31201. 478/746-7744. **Fax:** 478/742-7742. **Contact:** Human Resources. **World Wide Web address:** http://www.plastican.com. **Description:** Manufactures plastic pails, milk crates, and recycling bins. **NOTE:** Please send resumes to corporate office at 196 Industrial Road, Leominster MA 01453. **Corporate headquarters location:** Leominster MA. **Other U.S. locations:** Phoenix AZ; Dallas TX.

PORSCHE CARS N.A., INC.
980 Hammond Drive NE, Suite 1000, Atlanta GA 30328. 770/290-3500. **Contact:** Personnel. **E-mail address:** resumes@porschecars.com. **World Wide Web address:** http://www.us.porsche.com. **Description:** Porsche Cars N.A. is a manufacturer of sports cars. The United States is Porsche's largest export market. The Porsche Development Center (Weissach, Germany) is the site for the company's design, research, and development. Founded in 1931. **International locations:** Worldwide. **Operations at this facility include:** This location is the North American headquarters, importing and distributing cars and parts to the United States and Canada. **Listed on:** Privately held.

POST PROPERTIES, INC.
One Riverside, 4401 Northside Parkway, Suite 800, Atlanta GA 30327-3057. 404/846-5000. **Fax:** 404/504-9369. **Contact:** Human Resources. **E-mail address:** careers@postproperties.com. **World Wide Web address:** http://www.postproperties.com. **Description:** Operates a real estate investment trust. Post Properties is one of the largest owners and operators of multifamily apartment communities in the southeastern United States. Founded 1971. **NOTE:** Search and apply for jobs online. Contact Human Resources directly at 404/846-6171. **Special programs:** Internships. **Positions advertised include:** Leasing Consultant; Housekeeper; Property Monitor; Property Engineer; Assistant Property Engineer; Preventative Maintenance Engineer; Maintenance Groundsperson; Floriculture Groundsperson; Maintenance Assistant-in-Training; Seasonal Groundsperson. **Corporate headquarters location:** This location. **Listed on:** New York Stock Exchange. **Stock exchange symbol:** PPS. **President/CEO:** David Stockert.

PRATT & WHITNEY
8801 Macon Road, Columbus GA 31901. 706/568-5400. **Contact:** Human Resources. **World Wide Web address:** http://www.pratt-whitney.com. **Description:** Forges disks for commercial and military jet engines. **NOTE:** Please visit website to search for jobs and apply online. **Positions advertised include:** Quality Engineer; Production Planning and Scheduling Coordinator; Human Resources Manager. **Special programs:** Co-ops; Internships. **Corporate headquarters location:** East Hartford CT. **Other area locations:** Marietta GA. **Other U.S. locations:** Nationwide. **International locations:** Worldwide. **Parent company:** United Technologies Corporation. **President:** Louis Chehevert. **Number of employees worldwide:** 30,000.

PRECISION ROLL GRINDERS, INC.
400 Barnes Drive, GA 30117. 770/830-6323. **Fax:** 770/830-7024. **Contact:** Human Resources. **E-mail address:** gahr@precisionrollgrinders.com. **World Wide Web address:** http://www.precisionrollgrinders.com. **Description:** PRG provides high-accuracy grinding of cylindrical rolls and shafts of virtually all weights, sizes and compositions. Roll grinding and roll service is PRG's primary business. **Positions advertised include:** Mechanic; Account Manager; Manufacturing Engineer. **Corporate headquarters location:** Allentown PA. **Other U.S. locations:** Lewisport KY; Allentown PA; Texarkana AR.

PRICEWATERHOUSECOOPERS
10 Tenth Street, Suite 1400, Atlanta GA 30309. 678/419-1000. **Fax:** 678/419-1239. **Contact:** Jim Klee, Director of Human Resources. **World Wide Web address:** http://www.pricewaterhousecoopers.com. **Description:** One of the largest certified public accounting firms in the world. PricewaterhouseCoopers provides public accounting, business advisory, management consulting, and taxation services. **NOTE:** Please visit website to search for jobs and apply online. **Positions advertised include:** BCS Senior Associate; Healthcare Associate; Internal Audit Associate; CIPS Experienced Associate; Service Center Consultant; Recruiting Manager; Health and Welfare SE Practice Leader; Assurance Manager; Real Estate Senior Associate; Campus Recruiting Manager; BCS Data Specialist; Trainer; Transaction Services Manager; Manager. **Corporate headquarters location:** New York NY. **Other U.S. locations:** Nationwide. **International locations:** Worldwide. **CEO:** Samuel A. Di Piazza, Jr. **Number of employees worldwide:** 120,000.

PRIMEDIA BUSINESS MAGAZINES AND MEDIA
6151 Powers Ferry Road NW, Suite 200, Atlanta GA 30339. 770/955-2500. **Fax:** 770/618-0204. **Contact:** Office Manager. **World Wide Web address:** http://www.primediabusiness.com. **Description:** A publisher of business-to-business magazines and newsletters that allow manufacturers and suppliers to provide professionals with statistics, explanations, technical advice, and product introductions that ultimately make businesses more successful. Intertec Publishing also produces 450 technical books and valuation guides. **NOTE:** Please visit website to search for jobs and apply online. **Corporate headquarters location:** Overland Park KS. **Other U.S. locations:** Nationwide. **Parent company:** PRIMEDIA. **Listed on:** New York Stock Exchange. **Stock exchange symbol:** PRM. President/**CEO:** Kelly P. Conlin.

PRIMERICA FINANCIAL SERVICES
3120 Breckinridge Boulevard, Duluth GA 30099. 770/381-1000. **Fax:** 770/564-6110. **Contact:** Human Resources. **Wide Web address:** http://www.primerica.com. **Description:** Provides financial services including insurance and securities. **Corporate headquarters location:** This location. **Parent company:** Citigroup. **Other U.S. locations:** Nationwide. **International locations:** Asia; Europe. **Number of employees worldwide:** 100,000.

PRINTPACK INC.
P.O. Box 43687, Atlanta GA 30336. 404/691-5830. **Physical address:** 4335 Wendell Drive, Atlanta GA. **Fax:** 404/699-6116. **Contact:** Human Resources. **E-mail address:** careers@printpack.com. **World Wide Web address:** http://www.printpack.com. **Description:** Produces flexible packaging material for the snack, candy, meat, and cookie industries. **Corporate headquarters location:** This location. **Other U.S. locations:** Nationwide. **International locations:** England; Mexico. **Operations at this facility include:** Administration; Manufacturing; Regional Headquarters; Research and Development; Sales; Service. **Listed on:** Privately held. **President:** Dennis Love. **Number of employees worldwide:** 4,300.

PROCTER & GAMBLE – PAPER PRODUCTS
P.O. Box 1747, Albany GA 31702. 229/430-8260. **Physical address:** 512 Liberty Expressway SE, Albany GA 31705. **Contact:** Human Resources. **World Wide Web address:** http://www.pg.com. **Description:** Procter & Gamble manufactures over 300 laundry, cleaning, paper, beauty, health care, food, and beverage products in more than 140 countries. Brand name products include Cover Girl, Max Factor, Vidal Sassoon, Clearasil, and Noxzema health and beauty products; Pepto-Bismol, Vicks, and NyQuil health care products; Bounce, Downy, Tide, Comet, and Mr. Clean cleaning products; Luvs, Pampers, Always, Tampax, Bounty, Charmin, and Puffs paper products; and Crisco, Folgers, Millstone, Sunny Delight, and Pringles food and beverage products. **NOTE:** Please contact the Georgia Department of Labor to learn about employment opportunities. Their phone is 229/430-5010. **Corporate headquarters location:** Cincinnati OH. **International locations:** Worldwide. **Operations at this facility include:** This location manufactures consumer paper products including toilet tissue and paper towels. **Listed on:** New York Stock Exchange. **Stock exchange symbol:** PG. **Number of employees worldwide:** 98,000.

PRUDENTIAL PREFERRED FINANCIAL SERVICES
3500 Lenox Road, Suite 1200, Atlanta GA 30326. 404/262-2600. **Fax:** 404/262-1835. **Contact:** Human Resources. **World Wide Web address:** http://www.prudential.com.

Description: Markets a complete portfolio of insurance (group life and health) and financial services products to business owners, professionals, and upper-income individuals. Founded in 1875. **NOTE:** Please visit website to search for jobs and apply online. **Positions advertised include:** Annuities Wholesaler; Investment Associate Manager of Financial Services. **Special programs:** Training. **Office hours:** Monday - Friday, 8:00 a.m. - 5:00 p.m. **Corporate headquarters location:** Newark NJ. **Other area locations:** Statewide. **Other U.S. locations:** Nationwide. **International locations:** Worldwide. **Listed on:** New York Stock Exchange. **Stock exchange symbol:** PRU. **Parent company:** Prudential Insurance Company of America. **Operations at this facility include:** Administration; Sales; Service. **Annual sales/revenues:** More than $100 million. **Number of employees worldwide:** 39,400.

TRAVIS PRUITT & ASSOCIATES, P.C.
4317 Park Drive, Suite 400, Norcross GA 30093. 770/416-7511. **Toll-free phone:** 800/909-7511. **Fax:** 770/416-0659. **Contact:** Human Resources. **E-mail address:** pete@travispruitt.com. **World Wide Web address:** http://www.travispruitt.com. **Description:** A consulting firm specializing in civil engineering, land surveys, and landscape architecture. The company also offers environmental engineering services. Founded in 1972. **Positions advertised include:** CAD Technician; Civil Engineer; Survey Party Chief and Personnel; Survey Technician. **Office hours:** Monday - Friday, 8:00 a.m. - 5:00 p.m. **Corporate headquarters location:** This location. **President:** Travis Pruitt, Sr. **Number of employees at this location:** 105.

PYRAMID MASONRY CONTRACTORS INC.
2330 Mellon Court, Decatur GA 30035. 770/987-4750. **Fax:** 770/981-7142. **Contact:** Human Resources. **World Wide Web address:** http://www.pyramidmasonry.net. **Description:** A special trade contractor engaged in masonry stone setting projects. **Other U.S. locations:** FL; NC. **President:** John C. Doherty.

QUAD/GRAPHICS, INC.
100 Duplainville Road, The Rock GA 30285. 706/648-5000. **Contact:** Employee Services. **E-mail address:** quadjobs@qg.com. **World Wide Web address:** http://www.qg.com. **Description:** A printing press that offers web offset printing, imaging, finishing, and distribution for newsweekly and monthly magazines. **NOTE:** Please visit website to search for jobs and apply online. **Positions advertised include:** Digital Assembly Technician; Finishing Material Handler; Imaging Retouch Artist; Operator in Training – Finishing; Substance Abuse Counselor. **Special programs:** Internships. **Corporate headquarters location:** Pewaukee WI. **Other U.S. locations:** Nationwide. **Operations at this facility include:** Manufacturing. **Listed on:** Privately held. **International locations:** Argentina; Brazil: Poland. **Number of employees worldwide:** 12,000.

QUEBECOR WORLD DIRECT
4301 Evans To Locks Road, Evans GA 30809. 706/860-8000. **Fax:** 706/860-9046. **Contact:** Human Resources. **E-mail address:** usacareers@quebcorworld.com. **World Wide Web address:** http://www.quebecorworld.com. **Description:** Quebecor World prints timetables, directories, promotional pieces, direct mail, and other specialty items. **Corporate headquarters location:** Montreal Quebec Canada. **Other area locations:** Atlanta GA; Forest Park GA. **Other U.S. locations:** Nationwide. **International locations:** Worldwide. **Operations at this facility include:** This location publishes and prints periodicals. **Listed on:** New York Stock Exchange. **Stock exchange symbol:** IQW. **CEO:** Pierre Karl Peladeau. **Number of employees worldwide:** 37,000.

QUEBECOR WORLD DIRECT
3101 McCall Drive, Atlanta GA 30340. 770/936-7100. **Toll-free phone:** 866/936-7100. **Fax:** 770/986-7306. **Contact:** Human Resources. **World Wide Web address:** http://www.quebecorworld.com. **Description:** Quebecor World prints timetables, directories, promotional pieces, direct mail, and other specialty items. **Corporate headquarters location:** Quebec Canada. **Other area locations:** Forest Park GA; Evans GA. **Other U.S. locations:** Nationwide. **International locations:** Worldwide. **Listed on:** New York Stock Exchange. **Stock exchange symbol:** IQW. **CEO:** Pierre Karl Peladeau. **Number of employees worldwide:** 37,000.

QUEST DIAGNOSTICS INCORPORATED
3175 Presidential Drive, Atlanta GA 30340. 770/452-1590. **Contact:** Human Resources. **E-mail address:** careers@questdiagnostics.com. **World Wide Web address:** http://www.questdiagnostics.com. **Description:** Quest Diagnostics is one of the largest clinical laboratories in North America, providing a broad range of clinical laboratory services to health care clients that include physicians, hospitals, clinics, dialysis centers, pharmaceutical companies, and corporations. The company offers and performs tests on blood, urine, and other bodily fluids and tissues to provide information for health and well-being. **NOTE:** Please visit website to search for jobs. **Positions advertised include:** Phlebotomy Service Floater; Floater; Representative of Phlebotomy Services. **Corporate headquarters location:** Teterboro NJ. **Other area locations:** Statewide. **Other U.S. locations:** Nationwide. **Operations at this facility include:** This location is engaged in specimen collection. **Listed on:** New York Stock Exchange. **Stock exchange symbol:** DGX. **CEO:** Kenneth Freeman. **Number of employees worldwide:** 37,000.

QUEST DIAGNOSTICS INCORPORATED
1777 Montreal Circle, Tucker GA 30084. 770/934-9200. **Contact:** Human Resources. **E-mail address:** careers@questdiagnostics.com. **World Wide Web address:** http://www.questdiagnostics.com. **Description:** One of the largest clinical laboratories in North America, providing a broad range of clinical laboratory services to health care clients that include physicians, hospitals, clinics, dialysis centers, pharmaceutical companies, and corporations. The company offers and performs tests on blood, urine, and other bodily fluids and tissues to provide information for health and well-being. **NOTE:** Please visit website to search for jobs. **Positions advertised include:** Lab Assistant; Medical Technologist; Client Systems Analyst; Laboratory Manager; Supervisor; Transcriptionist; Data Entry Operator; Cytotechnologist; Phlebotomy Service Floater; Phlebotomy Services Representative. **Corporate headquarters location:** Teterboro NJ. **Other area locations:** Statewide. **Other U.S. locations:** Nationwide. **Operations at this facility include:** This location is the main testing laboratory. **Listed on:** New York Stock Exchange. **Stock exchange symbol:** DGX. **CEO:** Kenneth Freeman. **Number of employees worldwide:** 37,000.

QUEST DIAGNOSTICS INCORPORATED
83 Upper Riverdale Road, Riverdale GA 30274. 770/991-2030. **Contact:** Human Resources. **E-mail address:** careers@questdiagnostics.com. **World Wide Web address:** http://www.questdiagnostics.com. **Description:** Quest Diagnostics is one of the largest clinical laboratories in North America, providing a broad range of clinical laboratory services to health care clients that include physicians, hospitals, clinics, dialysis centers, pharmaceutical companies, and corporations. The company offers and performs tests on blood, urine, and other bodily fluids and tissues to provide information for health and well-being. **NOTE:** Please visit website to search for jobs. **Positions advertised include:** Phlebotomy Service Floater. **Office hours:** Monday – Friday, 7:30 a.m. – 5:00 p.m.; Saturday, 8:00 a.m. – 11:45 a.m. **Corporate headquarters location:** Teterboro NJ. **Other area locations:** Statewide. **Other U.S. locations:** Nationwide. **Operations at this facility include:** This location is engaged in specimen collection for laboratory processing. **Listed on:** New York Stock Exchange. **Stock exchange symbol:** DGX. **CEO:** Kenneth Freeman. **Number of employees worldwide:** 37,000.

QUEST DIAGNOSTICS INCORPORATED
446 Poplar Street, Suite A, Macon GA 31201. 478/745-8576. **Contact:** Human Resources. **E-mail address:** careers@questdiagnostics.com. **World Wide Web address:** http://www.questdiagnostics.com. **Description:** Quest Diagnostics is one of the largest clinical laboratories in North America, providing a broad range of clinical laboratory services to health care clients that include physicians, hospitals, clinics, dialysis centers, pharmaceutical companies, and corporations. The company offers and performs tests on blood, urine, and other bodily fluids and tissues to provide information for health and well-being. **NOTE:** Please visit website to search for jobs. **Office hours:** Monday – Friday, 8:00 a.m. – 5:00 p.m. **Corporate headquarters location:** Teterboro NJ. **Other area locations:** Statewide. **Other U.S. locations:** Nationwide. **Operations at this facility include:** This location is engaged in blood testing and specimen collection. **Listed on:** New York Stock Exchange. **Stock exchange symbol:** DGX. **CEO:** Kenneth Freeman. **Number of employees worldwide:** 37,000.

THE QUICKRETE COMPANIES
One Security Centre, 3490 Piedmont Road, Suite 1300, Atlanta GA 30305. 404/634-9100. **Contact:** Human Resources. **E-mail address:** careers@quikrete.com. **World Wide Web address:** http://www.quickrete.com. **Description:** Manufactures and distributes packaged concrete and concrete repair products. **Corporate headquarters location:** This location. **Other U.S. locations:** Nationwide. **International locations:** Canada; South America.

RBC CENTURA
2355 Main Street, Tucker GA 30084. 404/495-6400. **Contact:** Human Resources. **World Wide Web address:** http://www.justrightbank.com. **Description:** A bank offering investments, mutual finds, deposit accounts, business and personal loans, insurance, and residential and commercial mortgages. **NOTE:** Entry-level positions are offered. Please visit website to search for jobs and apply online. **Corporate headquarters location:** Rocky Mount NC. **Other area locations:** Statewide. **Other U.S. locations:** Nationwide. **Listed on:** New York Stock Exchange. **Stock exchange symbol:** RY. **CEO:** H. Kel Landis.

RBM OF ATLANTA, INC.
7640 Roswell Road, Atlanta GA 30350-4839. 770/390-0700. **Fax:** 770/395-7521. **Contact:** Office Manager. **World Wide Web address:** http://www.atlanta.mercedescenter.com. **Description:** A retail dealer and servicer of Mercedes-Benz automobiles.

RDA CORPORATION
980 Hammond Drive, Suite 350, Atlanta GA 30328. 770/668-9200. **Toll-free phone:** 877/678-9200. **Fax:** 770/668-9280. **Contact:** Human Resources Manager. **World Wide Web address:** http://www.rdacorp.com. **Description:** Provides IT integration and security services. Founded in 1988. **NOTE:** Please visit website to search for jobs and apply online. **Corporate headquarters location:** Baltimore MD. **Other U.S. locations include:** IL, PA; VA. **CEO:** Don Awalt. **Number of employees nationwide:** 206.

RTM RESTAURANT GROUP
5995 Barfield Road, Atlanta GA 30328. 404/256-4900. **Contact:** Human Resources. **World Wide Web address:** http://www.rtminc.com. **Description:** Operates and franchises national restaurant chains including Arby's, Lee's Famous Recipe Chicken, Mrs. Winner's Chicken & Biscuits, Del Taco Mexican Restaurants, Pasta Connection, Sbarro, and T.J. Cinnamons. **Positions advertised include:** Assistant Manager; General Manager; Operating Partner; Area Supervisor; Director of Operations; Region Vice President of Operations. **Corporate headquarters location:** This location. **Other U.S. locations:** Nationwide. **Operations at this facility include:** Administration; Research and Development. **CEO:** Russ Umphenour. **Number of employees nationwide:** 20,000.

RAILCAR MANAGEMENT, INC.
1819 Peachtree Road, NE, Suite 303, Atlanta GA 30309. 404/355-6734. **Fax:** 404/352-8814. **Contact:** Rachel M. Emigh, Assistant Vice President of Human Resources. **E-mail address:** hr@railcarmgt.com. **World Wide Web address:** http://www.railcarmgt.com. **Description:** Provides IT services and e-Commerce solutions to the railroad industry. Founded in 1979. **NOTE:** No phone calls regarding employment. **Corporate headquarters location:** This location.

RANDALL BROTHERS, INC.
P.O. Box 1678, Atlanta GA 30371. 404/892-6666. **Physical address:** 665 Marietta Street NW, Atlanta GA. **Toll-free phone:** 800/476-4539. **Fax:** 404/875-6102. **Contact:** Personnel. **World Wide Web address:** http://www.randallbrothers.com. **Description:** A woodworking firm that treats lumber and prepares building materials. Founded in 1885. **NOTE:** Please visit website to search for jobs and download application form.

RARE HOSPITALITY INTERNATIONAL, INC.
8215 Roswell Road, Building 600, Atlanta GA 30350. 770/399-9595. **Contact:** Director of Employment. **E-mail address:** careeropportunities@rarehospitality.com. **World Wide Web address:** http://www.rarehospitality.com. **Description:** Franchises 193 restaurants and operates 190 LongHorn Steakhouses (located in the southeastern and midwestern United States), 25 Bugaboo Creek Steak Houses, 17 Capital Grille Restaurants (nationwide), Hemenway's Seafood Grill And Oyster Bar, and The Old Grist Mill Tavern. Founded in 1981. **NOTE:** Contact Employment directly at 770/551-5464. **Corporate headquarters location:** This location. **Listed on:** NASDAQ. **Stock exchange symbol:** RARE. **President/CEO:** Philip Hickey, Jr. **Annual sales/revenues:** More than $100 million. **Number of employees nationwide:** 11,200.

RAYOVAC CORPORATION
6 Concourse Parkway, Suite 330, Atlanta GA 30328. 770/829-6200. **Contact:** Human Resources. **World Wide Web address:** http://www.rayovac.com. **Description:** One of the top three battery manufacturers in the country. **NOTE:** Please visit website to apply online. Send resume with cover letter to P.O. Box 44960, Madison WI 53744-4960. **Positions advertised include:** Administrative Assistant; Financial Analyst; Manager of Corporate Planning. **Corporate headquarters location:** Madison WI. **Other U.S. locations:** Bentonville AR; Boca Raton FL; Fennimore WI; Portage WI; Dixon IL; LaVergne TN; Fresno CA. **International locations:** Worldwide. **Listed on:** New York Stock Exchange. **Stock exchange symbol:** ROV.

REDMAX/KOMATSU ZENOAH AMERICA, INC.
4344 Shackleford Road, Suite 500, Norcross GA 30093. 770/381-5147. **Toll-free phone:** 800/291-8251. **Fax:** 770/381-5150. **Contact:** Human Resources. **World Wide web address:** http://www.redmax.com. **Description:** Imports and wholesales gas-

powered, hand-held outdoor equipment including leaf blowers and brush trimmers for commercial use. **Corporate headquarters location:** This location. **Parent company:** Komatsu Japan.

REINHARDT COLLEGE
7300 Reinhardt College Circle, Waleska GA 30183-2981. 770/720-5600. **Fax:** 770/720-9215. **Contact:** Tammy Edge, Human Resources Specialist. **E-mail address:** TJE@reinhardt.edu. **World Wide Web address:** http://www.reinhardt.edu. **Description:** An undergraduate college offering two- and four-year degrees in the liberal arts. Approximately 1,100 students are enrolled at the college. Founded 1883. **NOTE:** Please visit website for a listing of jobs. Contact Human Resources directly at 770/720-5661. **Positions advertised include:** Vice President for Academic Affairs; Dean of College; Assistant Professor – Communication; Assistant Professor – History, Western Civilization; Adjunct Instructor – Various Departments; Assistant Director of Admissions; College Chaplain; Head Softball Coach.

RELIANCE ELECTRIC COMPANY
P.O. Box 809, 195 Collins Industrial #B, Athens GA 30601. 706/549-3871. **Contact:** Human Resources. **World Wide Web address:** http://www.reliance.com. **Description:** Reliance Electric Company designs, manufactures, and distributes industrial equipment including electric motors in a wide range of horsepowers; mechanical power transmission components; control systems; telecommunications equipment; and industrial scales. Nationally, products fall into four business segments: Electrical, Weighing and Controls, Mechanical, and Telecommunications. **Office hours:** Monday – Friday, 7:30 a.m. - 4:30 p.m. **Corporate headquarters location:** Greenville SC. **Operations at this facility include:** This facility primarily produces electric motors and control systems.

REYNOLDS & REYNOLDS, INC.
3575 Koger Boulevard, Suite 400, Duluth GA 30096. 770/806-3300. **Contact:** Human Resources. **World Wide Web address:** http://www.reyrey.com. **Description:** Reynolds & Reynolds provides systems integration and analysis for the health care and automotive industries. **NOTE:** Please visit website to search for jobs and apply online. **Positions advertised include:** Dealer Relations Specialist; Product Operations Manager; Product Operations Professional. **Special programs:** Internships; Co-ops. **Corporate headquarters location:** Kettering OH. **Other U.S. locations:** Nationwide. **International locations:** Canada. **Listed on:** New York Stock Exchange. **Stock exchange symbol:** REY. **President/CEO:** Buzz Waterhouse. **Number of employees worldwide:** 4,500.

RHEEM RUUD MANUFACTURING
P.O. Box 2098, Milledgeville GA 31061. 478/453-7575. **Physical address:** 138 Roberson Mill Road, Milledgeville GA 31061. **Contact:** Human Resources. **World Wide Web address:** http://www.rheem.com. **Description:** A national manufacturer of central heating and air conditioning equipment. **Office hours:** Monday – Friday, 8:00 a.m. – 5:00 p.m. **Positions advertised include:** Manufacturing Control Manager.

RICH SEAPAK CORPORATION
127 Airport Road, P.O. Box 20670, St. Simons Island GA 31522. 912/638-5000. **Toll-free phone:** 800/654-9731. **Fax:** 912/634-3104. **Contact:** Human Resources. **E-mail address:** recruiter@rich-seapak.com. **World Wide Web address:** http://www.seapak.com. **Description:** Processes and distributes frozen seafood and vegetable products. Founded 1948. **NOTE:** Entry-level positions and part-time jobs are offered. Please visit website to search for jobs. **Positions advertised include:** Administrative Coordinator. **Corporate headquarters location:** This location. **Other area locations:** Brunswick GA; Waycross GA. **Other U.S. locations:** Brownsville TX; Vineland NJ; Gallatin TN. **Parent company:** Rich Products Corporation (Buffalo NY) is a family-owned, frozen foods manufacturer. The company operates manufacturing sites and field offices throughout North America and abroad. Rich Products also operates more than 30 production facilities involved in producing a wide spectrum of products including nondairy creamers, toppings, and icings; frozen dough; baked goods; sweet goods; pastas; and specialty meats.

RIVERSIDE MANUFACTURING COMPANY
P.O. Box 460, Moultrie GA 31776-0460. 229/985-5210. **Physical address:** 301 Riverside Drive, Moultrie GA. **Contact:** Personnel Manager. **World Wide Web address:** http://www.riversideuniforms.com. **Description:** Manufactures industrial uniforms and work clothing including shirts, aprons, and other careerwear. The company also produces a line of apparel products including men's blazers and dress pants. Founded 1911. **Corporate headquarters location:** This location. **Other area locations:** Atlanta GA. **Other U.S. locations:** Prichard WV; Reno NV. **International locations:** Dundalk Ireland.

RLG-MACY'S
223 Perimeter Center Parkway, Atlanta GA 30346. 770/913-4000. 4123. **Contact:** Human Resources. **World Wide Web address:** http://www.federated-fds.com. **Description:** Operates Rich's-Macy's, Lazarus-Macy's, and Goldsmith-Macy's in the Southeastern states. **NOTE:** Please visit http://www.retailology.com to search for jobs and apply online. **Positions advertised include:** Assistant Buyer; Beauty Advisor – Various Brands; Bedding Specialist; Hair Stylist; Loss Prevention Associate; Manager – Seasonal Planning; Regional Merchandise Manager; Sales Associate – Various Departments; Stock/Support Associate. **Corporate headquarters location:** This location. **Other U.S. locations:** Southeastern U.S. **Parent company:** Federated Department Stores, Inc. **Listed on:** New York Stock Exchange. **Stock exchange symbol:** FD. **Number of employees nationwide:** 15,500.

ROADWAY EXPRESS INC.
2701 Moreland Avenue SE, Atlanta GA 30315. 404/361-0861. **Fax:** 404/361-0988. **Contact:** Personnel Manager. **World Wide Web address:** http://www.roadway.com. **Description:** Operates a freight consolidation and distribution terminal for one of the largest common carriers in the United States, with terminals in more than 633 cities nationwide. Founded 1930. **NOTE:** Please visit website to search for jobs. **Corporate headquarters location:** Akron OH. **Other area locations:** Statewide. **Other U.S. locations:** Nationwide. **International locations:** Puerto Rico; Guam; Mexico; Canada. **Parent company:** Yellow Roadway. **Listed on:** NASDAQ. **Stock exchange symbol:** YELL. **Number of employees worldwide:** 24,800.

ROCK-TENN COMPANY
P.O. Box 4098, Norcross GA 30091. 770/448-2193. **Physical address:** 504 Thrasher Street, Norcross GA 30071. **Fax:** 678/291-7666. **Contact:** Human Resources. **World Wide Web address:** http://www.rocktenn.com. **Description:** Manufactures 100 percent recycled paperboard and paperboard products. Over two-thirds of paperboard production is done by the company's own converting plants to produce folding cartons, book and notebook covers, components for the furniture industry, and solid fiber partitions used in shipping glass and plastic containers. Founded 1936. **NOTE:** Please visit website to register, search for jobs, and apply online. **Corporate headquarters location:** This location. **Other U.S. locations:** Nationwide. **International locations:** Canada; Mexico; Chile. **Listed on:** New York Stock Exchange. **Stock exchange symbol:** RKT. **Number of employees worldwide:** 8,800.

ROCKWELL AUTOMATION
720 Industrial Boulevard, Dublin GA 31021. 478/274.2600. **Contact:** Personnel Manager. **World Wide Web address:** http://www.automation.rockwell.com. **Description:** Manufactures programmable controllers. **Parent company:** Rockwell International Corporation manufactures products for the printing, military, automotive, and aerospace industries through its electronics, automotive, and graphics division. Products include military and commercial communication equipment, guidance systems, electronics, components for automobiles, and printing presses. Rockwell provides the U.S. government with parts and services for bombers, as well as power systems for the space station. The company is also a major contractor for the Space Shuttle Orbiter program. **NOTE:** Please visit website to search for jobs and apply online. **Positions advertised include:** Safety/Environmental Analyst. **Corporate Headquarters location:** Milwaukee WI. **International locations:** Worldwide. **Listed on:** New York Stock Exchange. **Stock exchange symbol:** ROK. **President/CEO:** Keith Nosbusch. **Number of employees worldwide:** 20,000.

ROLLINS INC.
P.O. Box 647, Atlanta GA 30301. 404/888-2000. **Physical address:** 2170 Piedmont Road NE, Atlanta GA 30324. **Fax:** 404/888-2672. **Recorded jobline:** 404/888-2125. **Contact:** Human Resources. **E-mail address:** jobs@rollinscorp.com. **World Wide Web address:** http://www.rollinscorp.com. **Description:** A nationwide chain providing termite and other pest control services. **Positions advertised include:** Vice President of Training; Orkin National Accounts Receivable Representative; Commercial Sales Director; Accounts Payable Telecom Specialist; Customer Service Assistant; Corporate Controller; Collector; Senior Claims Adjuster; New Customer Specialist. **Corporate headquarters location:** This location. **Other U.S. locations:** Nationwide. **Subsidiaries include:** Orkin Pest Control. **Listed on:** New York Stock Exchange. **Stock exchange symbol:** ROL. **President/CEO:** Gary W. Rollins.

ROPER INDUSTRIES INC.
2160 Satellite Boulevard, Suite 200, Duluth GA 30097. 770/495-5100. **Fax:** 770/495-5150. **Contact:** Director of Human Resources. **World Wide Web address:** http://www.roperind.com. **Description:** Manufactures industrial control systems, valves, pumps, and related equipment. **Corporate headquarters location:** This location. **Other U.S. locations:** Nationwide. **International locations:** France; United Kingdom. **Listed on:** New York Stock Exchange. **Stock exchange symbol:** ROP. **CEO:** Brian Jellison. **Annual sales/revenues:** More than $100 million. **Number of employees worldwide:** 3,700.

ROSSER INTERNATIONAL, INC.
524 West Peachtree Street NW, Atlanta GA 30308. 404/876-3800. **Fax:** 404/888-6863. **Contact:** Human Resources. **E-mail address:** employment@rosser.com. **World Wide Web address:** http://www.rosser.com. **Description:** An architectural and engineering design firm. Projects include prisons, stadiums, hangars, commercial retail space, and other facilities. **Positions advertised include:** Design Architect; Business Development Coordinator. **Office hours:** Monday - Friday, 8:00 a.m. - 5:00 p.m. **Corporate headquarters location:** This location. **Other area locations:** Cartersville GA; Jackson GA; Savannah GA. **Listed on:** Privately held. **Number of employees nationwide:** 170.

ROYAL OAK ENTERPRISES SALES
One Royal Oak Avenue, Roswell GA 30076. 678/461-3200. **Toll-free phone:** 800/241-3955. **Fax:** 678/461-3233. **Contact:** Personnel Director. **E-mail address:** royaloak@worldnet.att.net. **Description:** A manufacturer and distributor of charcoal briquettes, industrial carbon, and related products. Founded 1986. **Number of employees at this location:** 80.

RYERSON TULL
4400 Peachtree Industrial Boulevard, P.O. Box 4725, Norcross GA 30071. 770/368-4200. **Contact:** Human Resources. **World Wide Web address:** http://www.ryersontull.com. **Description:** A wholesale distributor of a wide variety of ferrous and nonferrous metal products. **NOTE:** Please visit website to search for jobs and apply online. **Positions advertised include:** Administrative Specialist. **Corporate headquarters location:** Chicago IL. **Other U.S. locations:** Nationwide. **Parent company:** Ryerson Tull (Chicago IL) is one of the nation's largest distributors of metals and industrial plastics. **Listed on:** New York Stock Exchange. **Stock exchange symbol:** RT.

SED INTERNATIONAL
4916 North Royal Atlanta Drive, Tucker GA 30085. 770/491-8962. **Toll-free phone:** 800/444-8962. **Fax:** 770/938-1235. **Toll-free fax:** 800/329-2733. **Contact:** Human Resources Department. **E-mail address:** humanresources@sedintl.com. **World Wide Web address:** http://www.sedonline.com. **Description:** A wholesaler of computer systems and cellular phones. Founded 1980. **NOTE:** Please visit website for job listings. **Positions advertised include:** Inside Sales Representative. **Corporate headquarters location:** This location. **Other U.S. locations:** City of Industry CA; Dallas TC; Miami FL. **International locations:** Argentina; Puerto Rico; Columbia. **Listed on:** NASDAQ. **Stock exchange symbol:** SECX. **CEO:** Mark Diamond. **Number of employees worldwide:** 287.

SIU (SOUTHERN INSURANCE UNDERWRITERS)
P.O. Box 105609, Atlanta GA 30348-5609. 678/498-4500. **Physical address:** 4500 Mansell Road, Alpharetta GA 30022. **Toll-free phone:** 800/568-1700. **Fax:** 678/498-4600. **Contact:** Nanci Lamborn, Human Resources Manager. **E-mail address:** nanci.lamborn@siuins.com. **World Wide Web address:** http://www.siuins.com. **Description:** A full-service insurance company that provides personal, commercial, automobile, and property insurance to customers in the states of Georgia, South Carolina, Florida, Alabama, and Texas. Founded 1964. **NOTE:** Human Resources phone is 678/498-4517, fax is 678/498-4605. **Office hours:** Monday – Friday, 8:15 a.m. – 5:00 p.m. **Corporate headquarters location:** This location. **Other U.S. locations:** Winter Park FL.

SMI GEORGIA REBAR
P.O. Box 368, Lawrenceville GA 30046-0368. 770/963-6251. **Physical address:** 251 Hosea Road, Lawrenceville GA. **Fax:** 770/339-6623. **Contact:** Employee Relations. **World Wide Web address:** http://www.commercialmetals.com. **Description:** Produces structural and reinforcing steel used in large-scale construction. **Positions advertised include:** Civil Engineer. **Corporate headquarters location:** Irving TX. **Other U.S. locations:** Nationwide. **Parent company:** Commercial Metals Company. **Operations at this facility include:** Manufacturing. **Listed on:** New York Stock Exchange. **Stock exchange symbol:** CMC.

SAFT AMERICA INC.
711 Gil Harbin Industrial Boulevard, Valdosta GA 31601. 229/247-2331. **Contact:** Human Resources. **World Wide Web address:** http://www.saftamerica.com.

Description: Manufactures industrial aviation batteries and other storage batteries for industrial use. **Corporate headquarters location:** Bangolet France. **International locations:** Worldwide. **Number of employees worldwide:** 4,000.

SAMPO TECHNOLOGY CORPORATION
5550 Peachtree Industrial Boulevard, Suite 100, Norcross GA 30071. 770/449-6220. **Fax:** 770/447-1109. **Contact:** Personnel Manager. **World Wide Web address:** http://www.sampotech.com. **Description:** Distributes computer monitors. **Corporate headquarters location:** Taiwan. **Other U.S. locations:** Irvine CA. **International locations:** The Netherlands; China; Philippines. **Operations at this facility include:** Administration; Sales; Service. **CEO:** H.C. Ho. **Number of employees worldwide:** 1,500.

SARA LEE BAKERY GROUP
10 Darlington Drive, Rome GA 30161. 706/232-4494. **Contact:** Job Service Center. **World Wide Web address:** http://www.saraleebakery.com. **Description:** Produces and distributes cookies and similar snack products. **NOTE:** For employment information, contact the Georgia Department of Labor at 706/295-6145 (Rome GA). **Office hours:** Monday – Friday, 8:00 a.m. – 5:00 p.m. **Corporate headquarters location:** St. Louis MO. **Operations at this facility include:** Administration; Manufacturing. **Other U.S. locations:** Nationwide. **Parent company:** Sara Lee Corporation. **CEO:** Richard A. Noll. **Number of employees nationwide:** 22,300. **Number of employees worldwide:** 145,000.

SARA LEE BAKERY GROUP
273 Central Avenue, Forest Park GA 30297. 404/361-7211. **Contact:** Human Resources Manager. **World Wide Web address:** http://www.saraleebakery.com. **Description:** Produces a variety of bakery products, including refrigerated dough and toaster pastries. **Corporate headquarters location:** St. Louis MO. **Operations at this facility include:** Administration; Manufacturing. **Other U.S. locations:** Nationwide. **Parent company:** Sara Lee Corporation. **CEO:** Richard A. Noll. **Number of employees nationwide:** 22,300. **Number of employees worldwide:** 145,000.

SATILLA CARDIAC AND PULMONARY REHABILITATION CENTER
2004 Pioneer Street, Waycross GA 31501. 912/284-2410. **Contact:** Human Resources. **E-mail address:** recruiting@satilla.org. **World Wide Web address:** http://www.satilla.org. **Description:** An outpatient facility that provides rehabilitation services and instructions on lifestyle changes to patients diagnosed with heart disease. **NOTE:** Human Resources phone is 912/287-2630. Please visit website to search for jobs and apply online. **Positions advertised include:** Cash Control Officer; Cardiac Sonographer; Pharmacist; Occupational Therapist; Ultrasound Radiology Technologist; CRT-RCP; RN – Various Departments; LPN – Various Department; CNA; Dietary Manager. **Parent company:** Satilla Health Services, Inc. **CEO:** Robert M. Trimm.

SATILLA REGIONAL MEDICAL CENTER
SATILLA HEALTH SERVICES, INC.
P.O. Box 139, Waycross GA 31501. 912/283-3030. **Physical address:** 410 Darling Avenue, Waycross GA 31501. 912/283-3030. **Fax:** 912/287-2632. **Recorded jobline:** 912/338-6308.**Contact:** Human Resources. **E-mail address:** recruiting@satilla.org. **World Wide Web address:** http://www.satilla.org. **Description:** A 257-bed acute care hospital. **NOTE:** Human Resources phone is 912/287-2630. Please visit website to search for jobs and apply online, or write to request an application. Applications are accepted Tuesday, Wednesday, and Thursday, from 9:00 a.m. – 3:00 p.m. **Positions advertised include:** Cash Control Officer; Cardiac Sonographer; Pharmacist; Occupational Therapist; Ultrasound Radiology Technologist; CRT-RCP; RN – Various Departments; LPN – Various Department; CNA; Dietary Manager. **Parent company:** Satilla Health Services, Inc. (also at this location). **President/CEO:** Robert M. Trimm.

SAVANNAH DESOTO HILTON
15 East Liberty Street, Savannah GA 31401. 912/232-9000. **Fax:** 912/232-3089. **Contact:** Human Resources. **World Wide Web address:** http://www.hilton.com. **Description:** A 250-room hotel. **Special programs:** Internships. **Parent company:** Hilton Hotels Corporation is engaged in the operation and management of hotels and inns throughout the world including more than 1,800 franchised hotels operating in the United States. **Corporate headquarters location:** Beverly Hills CA. **Other U.S. locations:** Nationwide. **Listed on:** New York Stock Exchange. **Stock exchange symbol:** HLT. **President/CEO:** Stephen F. Bollenbach.

SAVANNAH ELECTRIC
600 East Bay Street, Savannah GA 31401. 912/644-7171. **Toll-free phone:** 800/437-3890. **Contact:** Human Resources. **World Wide Web address:** http://www.southerncompany.com/savannah. **Description:** A public utility company that serves the Savannah metro area. **NOTE:** Please visit corporate site - http://www.southerncompany.com – to search for jobs and apply online. **Special programs:** Internships; Co-ops. **Corporate headquarters location:** This location. **Parent company:** The Southern Company (Atlanta GA) operates a total of five electric utilities in the Southeast including Georgia Power, which serves the rest of the state. These five companies operate with jointly-owned generating facilities, interconnecting transmission lines, and the exchange of power. **Listed on:** New York Stock Exchange. **Stock exchange symbol:** SO. **President/CEO:** Anthony R. James. **Number of employees nationwide:** 25,762.

SAVANNAH MORNING NEWS
P.O. Box 1088, Savannah GA 31402-1088. 912/236-9511. **Physical address:** 111 West Bay Street, Savannah GA 31402. **Fax:** 912/652-0264. **Contact:** Human Resources. **E-mail address:** lacey.bartlett@savannahnow.com. **World Wide Web address:** http://www.savannahnow.com. **Description:** A daily newspaper with a circulation of 57,000. **NOTE:** Contact Human Resources at 912/652-0310.

SAVELL & WILLIAMS
100 Peachtree Street, Suite 1500, The Equitable Building, Atlanta GA 30303. 404/521-1282. **Fax:** 404/584-0026. **Contact:** Jennifer Chapin, Hiring Partner. **E-mail address:** jhc@savellwilliams.com. **World Wide Web address:** http://www.savellwilliams.com. **Description:** A law firm specializing in insurance, litigation, liability, adoption, and worker's compensation law.

SCIENTIFIC-ATLANTA, INC.
BROADBAND COMMUNICATIONS SYSTEMS
5030 Sugarloaf Parkway, Lawrenceville GA 30044-2869. 770/903-5000. **Toll-free phone:** 800/722-2009. **Contact:** Personnel. **World Wide Web address:** http://www.sciatl.com. **Description:** Scientific-Atlanta, Inc. is a provider of communications equipment, electronics, instrumentation products, and satellite-based network systems. Products and systems are used by cable operations in more than 100 countries, as well as in 9,000 local cable sites in the United States. Scientific-Atlanta also designs, manufactures, installs, operates, and services Earth Station systems and networks that provide audio, video, and data communication services to 135 countries. Founded in 1951. **NOTE:** Please visit website to register, search for jobs, and apply online. **Positions advertised include:** Accountant; Associate Staff – IT Systems Programmer; Associate Staff – Network Supply Engineer. **Corporate headquarters location:** This location. **Other area locations:** Atlanta GA. **Other U.S. locations:** Nationwide. **International locations:** Worldwide. **Operations at this facility include:** This location develops, manufactures, and supports a line of equipment and systems for broadband terrestrial network delivery of cable television, telephony, and electric utility services. **Listed on:** New York Stock Exchange. **Stock exchange symbol:** SFA. **President/CEO:** James F. McDonald. **Number of employees worldwide:** 6,500.

SEASONS 4 INC.
4500 Industrial Access Road, Douglasville GA 30134. 770/489-0716. **Fax:** 770/489-2938. **Contact:** Human Resources. **World Wide Web address:** http://www.seasons4.net. **Description:** Installs heating and air conditioning units in commercial buildings such as supermarkets. Founded 1971. **Corporate headquarters location:** This location.

SECURITAS SECURITY SERVICES
400 Chastain Center, Suite 410, Kennesaw GA 30144. 770/426-5262. **Fax:** 770/426-5480. **Contact:** Human Resources. **World Wide Web address:** http://www.pinkertons.com. **Description:** America's largest security provider. **Positions advertised include:** Account Executive. **Other U.S. locations:** Nationwide. **International locations:** Worldwide. **Operations at this facility include:** Regional Headquarters for the Southeast. **Number of employees worldwide:** 200,000.

SECURITAS – PINKERTON
5555 Oak Brook Parkway, Suite 300, Norcross GA 30093. 770/248-9800. **Contact:** Personnel Manager. **World Wide Web address:** http://www.securitasinc.com. **Description:** The company offers a full range of specialized protective services including premier property and high-rise services, health care and hospital services, special event services, ATM services, and patrol services. The company serves thousands of companies worldwide with investigation services, threat assessment services, and executive protection. **NOTE:** Please visit website to search for jobs. **Corporate headquarters location:** Chicago IL. **Other area locations:** Statewide. **Other U.S. locations:** Nationwide. **International locations:** Worldwide. **Operations at this facility include:** District offices. **International locations:** Worldwide. **Number of employees worldwide:** 93,000.

SELIG CHEMICAL INDUSTRIES
P.O. Box 2015, Atlanta GA 30301. 404/691-9220. **Physical address:** 4401 Northside Parkway, Suite 700, Atlanta GA 30327. **Toll-free phone:** 800/447-3544. **Fax:** 404/603-7764. **Contact:** Human Resources. **World Wide Web address:** http://www.acuitybrands.com. **Description:** Manufactures specialty cleaning, polishing, and sanitation preparations. Founded in 1896. **Corporate headquarters location:** This location. **Other U.S. locations:** CA; FL; KY; LA; NC; TX. **Parent company:** Acuity Brands, Inc. **Listed on:** New York Stock Exchange. **Stock exchange symbol:** AYI. **Annual sales/revenues:** $21 - $50 million.

SERVIDYNE SYSTEMS, INC.
1945 The Exchange, Suite 325, Atlanta GA 30339. 404/352-2050. **Toll-free phone:** 800/241-8996. **Fax:** 770/953-9922. **Contact:** Corporate Recruiter. **World Wide Web address:** http://www.servidyne.com. **Description:** Provides facilities performance management consulting. Servidyne Systems utilizes systematic engineering processes to prevent and solve building operations problems in order to enhance energy efficiency and labor productivity. **NOTE:** Entry-level positions are offered. **Corporate headquarters location:** This location. **Parent company:** Abrams Industries. **Operations at this facility include:** Administration; Manufacturing; Sales; Service. **Listed on:** NASDAQ. **Stock exchange symbol:** ABRI. **President:** Alan Abrams.

SHAW INDUSTRIES, INC.
P.O. Drawer 2128, 616 East Walnut Avenue, Dalton GA 30722-2128. 706/278-3812. **Contact:** Human Resources. **World Wide Web address:** http://www.shawinc.com. **Description:** The company manufactures tufted floor coverings and related products. The company manufactures and sells tufted carpet for both residential and commercial use. All products are marketed through retailers, distributors, and other end users and are exported to over 150 countries. Brand names include Philadelphia Carpet Company, Fashion Statements, Expressive Designs, Sutton, Shaw Commercial Carpets, ShawRugs, Stratton Commercial Carpets, and Salemcarpets. **NOTE:** Please visit website to search for jobs and apply online. Call the Employment Center at 706/275-2615. **Positions advertised include:** Bi-Lingual Specialist; Systems Engineer; Mechanic Trainee; Technician; Financial Services Trainee; Flex Nurse; Occupational Health Nurse; Assistant Brand Manager; Process Engineer; Senior Systems Analyst. **Corporate headquarters location:** This location. **Other area locations:** Statewide. **Other U.S. locations:** Nationwide. **Parent company:** Berkshire Hathaway, Inc. **CEO:** Robert E. Shaw. **Number of employees worldwide:** 30,000.

SHAW INDUSTRIES, INC.
185 South Industrial Boulevard, Calhoun GA. 706/629-9234. **Contact:** Human Resources. **World Wide Web address:** http://www.shawinc.com. **Description:** The company manufactures tufted floor coverings and related products. The company manufactures and sells tufted carpet for both residential and commercial use. All products are marketed through retailers, distributors, and other end users and are exported to over 150 countries. Brand names include Philadelphia Carpet Company, Fashion Statements, Expressive Designs, Sutton, Shaw Commercial Carpets, ShawRugs, Stratton Commercial Carpets, and Salemcarpets. **NOTE:** Please visit website to search for jobs and apply online. Call the Employment Center at 706/275-2615. **Positions advertised include:** Bi-Lingual Specialist; Systems Engineer; Mechanic Trainee; Technician; Financial Services Trainee; Flex Nurse; Occupational Health Nurse; Assistant Brand Manager; Process Engineer; Senior Systems Analyst. **Corporate headquarters location:** This location. **Other area locations:** Statewide. **Other U.S. locations:** Nationwide. **Parent company:** Berkshire Hathaway, Inc. **CEO:** Robert E. Shaw. **Number of employees worldwide:** 30,000.

SHORTER COLLEGE
Box 2119, 315 Shorter Avenue, Rome GA 30165. 706/291-2121. **Toll-free phone:** 800/868-6980. **Fax:** 706/236-1514. **Contact:** Brenda Newman, Human Resources. **E-mail address:** bnewman@shorter.edu. **World Wide Web address:** http://www.shorter.edu. **Description:** A liberal arts college. **NOTE:** Please visit website to search for jobs, download application form, and for more details about applying to specific positions. **Positions advertised include:** Adjunct Teacher – School of Professional Programs; Assistant Professor of Music. **President:** Ed L. Schrader.

SIEMENS ENERGY & AUTOMATION, INC.
2037 Weems Road, Tucker GA 30384. 770/939-7230. **Contact:** Personnel Manager. **World Wide Web address:** http://www.sea.siemens.com. **Description:** Manufactures and markets a broad range of primarily large-scale electrical products including a variety of circuit protection devices that are sold to electronics OEMs throughout the country. The company also produces circuit-breaker load centers, metering panels, and related accessories. These products are sold to electric utilities and industrial manufacturers. **NOTE:** Please visit website to search for jobs and apply online.

Positions advertised include: Quality Assurance Manager. **Corporate headquarters location:** Alpharetta GA. **Other area locations:** Statewide. **Other U.S. locations:** Nationwide. **President/CEO:** Auburt Martin. **Number of employees nationwide:** 9,460.

SIEMENS ENERGY & AUTOMATION, INC.
3333 Old Milton Parkway, Alpharetta GA 30005. 770/751-2000. **Toll-free phone:** 800/964-4114. **Contact:** Corporate Human Resources Manager. **World Wide Web address:** http://www.sea.siemens.com. **Description:** Manufactures and markets a broad range of primarily large-scale electrical products including a variety of circuit protection devices that are sold to electronics OEMs throughout the country. The company also produces circuit-breaker load centers, metering panels, and related accessories. These products are sold primarily to electric utilities and industrial manufacturers. **NOTE:** Please visit website to search for jobs and apply online. **Positions advertised include:** Administrative Assistant; Applications Analyst; Associate Engineer; Commodity Manager; Contract Administrator; Human Resources Specialist; Information Security Specialist; Logistics Administrator; Product Consultant; Quality Assurance Manager; Senior Accounting Specialist; Senior Business Analyst; Senior Designer/Drafter; Systems Engineer. **Special programs:** Co-ops; Internships. **Corporate headquarters location:** This location. **Other area locations:** Statewide. **Other U.S. locations:** Nationwide. **Parent company:** Siemens Corporation. **Operations at this facility include:** Administration; Sales; Service. **Listed on:** New York Stock Exchange. **Stock exchange symbol:** SI. **President/CEO:** Auburt Martin. **Number of employees nationwide:** 9,460.

SIMMONS COMPANY
One Concourse Parkway, Suite 800, Atlanta GA 30328-6188. 770/512-7700. **Fax:** 770/392-2560. **Contact:** Personnel. **World Wide Web address:** http://www.simmons.com. **Description:** Simmons manufactures various name brand mattresses and boxsprings. Simmons Company has been in the bedding business since 1876 and now operates 18 plants throughout the United States. **NOTE:** Please visit website to search for jobs and apply online. **Positions advertised include:** Senior Internal Auditor; Project Manager – Application Development; National Purchasing Manager; Director of Product Design and Testing; **Corporate headquarters location:** This location. **Other U.S. locations:** Nationwide. **Operations at this facility include:** Administration. **CEO:** Charles R. Eitel. **Number of employees nationwide:** 2,500.

SIMMONS COMPANY
3450 Simmons Drive, Waycross GA 31503. 912/283-3996. **Fax:** 912/338-7560. **Contact:** Human Resources. **World Wide Web address:** http://www.simmons.com. **Description:** Simmons manufactures various name brand mattresses and boxsprings. Simmons Company has been in the bedding business since 1876 and now operates 18 plants throughout the United States. **NOTE:** Please visit website to search for jobs and apply online. **Positions advertised include:** Human Resources Manager; Lab Manager; Operations Manager; Materials Manager; Production Manager; Assistant Production Manager; Production Control Clerk; Vice President of Supply Chain; Maintenance Mechanic; Electrical Engineer; Mechanical Engineer. **Corporate headquarters location:** Atlanta GA. **Other U.S. locations:** Nationwide. **Operations at this facility include:** Manufacturing. **CEO:** Charles R. Eitel. **Number of employees nationwide:** 2,500.

SIMMONS MANUFACTURING COMPANY
P.O. Box 1509, McDonough GA 30253. 770/957-3976. **Physical address:** 1608 Conyers Road, McDonough GA. **Fax:** 770/957-3979. **Contact:** Personnel. **E-mail address:** info@simmonsmfg.com. **World Wide Web address:** http://www.simmonsmfg.com. **Description:** Produces a variety of water well flow control products including valves, seals, and hydrants. Founded in 1957. **Office hours:** Monday – Friday, 8:00 a.m. – 4:30 p.m. **Corporate headquarters location:** This location.

SIMTROL
2220 Norcross Parkway, Suite 255, Norcross GA 30071.678/533-1200. **Fax:** 770/441-1823. **Toll-free phone:** 800/474-6876. **Contact:** Human Resources. **World Wide Web address:** http://www.simtrol.com. **Description:** Designs, produces, and markets tailored software for interactive group video conferencing systems. Using standard telecommunication transmissions, Simtrol products allow many people at different geographic locations to see and hear one another on live television. **Corporate headquarters location:** This location. **CEO:** Rick Egan.

SIX FLAGS OVER GEORGIA
P.O. Box 43187, Atlanta GA 30336. 770/948-9290. **Physical address:** 275 Riverside Parkway, Austell GA 30168. **Contact:** Debbie McGraw, Human Resources Manager. **E-mail address:** sgrecrut@sftp.com. **World Wide Web address:** http://www.sixflags.com/parks/overgeorgia. **Description:** A state-of-the-art theme park with more than 100 rides, shows, and attractions. Main attractions include the Looping Starship, Mindbender, and the Great American Scream Machine. **NOTE:** Please visit website to search for jobs, apply online, and to find details about applying for specific jobs. Seasonal, Part-time, and Full-time jobs are offered. **Positions advertised include:** Admission Attendant; Food Services Attendant; Host/Hostess – Games, Housekeeping, Merchandise, Park Services, Rides, Security. **Parent company:** Premier Parks (OK) owns and operates 40 theme parks nationwide. **Listed on:** New York Stock Exchange. **Stock exchange symbol:** PKS.

SKANSKA
70 Ellis Street NE, Atlanta GA 30303. 404/659-1970. **Fax:** 404/656-1665. **Contact:** Human Resources. **World Wide Web address:** http://www.skanska.com. **Description:** A construction firm primarily engaged in large-scale commercial and industrial construction projects. **Special programs:** Internships. **Corporate headquarters location:** Sweden. **Other U.S. locations:** Nationwide. **International locations:** Worldwide. **Number of employees worldwide:** 69,700.

SMALL BUSINESS SOLUTION
PEACHTREE SOFTWARE
1505 Pavilion Place, Norcross GA 30093. 770/724-4000. **Contact:** Human Resources. **E-mail address:** humanresources@bestsoftware.com. **World Wide Web address:** http://www.peachtree.com. **Description:** Develops, manufactures, and markets accounting software. **NOTE:** Please visit website to search for jobs and apply online. No phone calls regarding employment. **Positions advertised include:** Web Managing Editor; Inside Software Sales Representative; Design Analyst – Windows GUI; Associate Marketing Manager; ACT Lead Qualifying Sales Representative; Shipping and Receiving Clerk; Customer Support Manager; Vice President of Product Management; Director of Corporate Sales; Network Engineer; Senior Marketing Manager; Vice President of Direct Mail. **Corporate headquarters location:** This location. **Parent company:** Best Software.

SMITH BARNEY
3455 Peachtree Road NE, Suite 1400, The Pinnacle Building, Atlanta GA 30326. 404/266-0090. **Toll-free phone:** 800/241-4277. **Fax:** 404/842-2393. **Contact:** Human Resources. **World Wide Web address:** http://www.smithbarney.com. **Description:** An international investment banking, market making, and research firm serving corporations, state and local governments, sovereign and provincial governments and their agencies, central banks, and other financial institutions. **Office hours:** Monday – Friday, 8:00 a.m. – 5;00 p.m. **Corporate headquarters location:** New York NY. **Other U.S. locations:** Nationwide. **Parent company:** Citigroup. **Listed on:** New York Stock Exchange. **Stock exchange symbol:** C.

SMURFIT-STONE CONTAINER CORPORATION
1311 Walker Street, Augusta GA 30901. 706/722-9603. **Contact:** Human Resources. **World Wide Web address:** http://www.smurfit-stone.com. **Description:** One of the world's leading paper-based packaging companies. The company's main products include corrugated containers, folding cartons, and multiwall industrial bags. The company is also one of the world's largest collectors and processors of recycled products that are then sold to a worldwide customer base. Smurfit-Stone Container Corporation also operates several paper tube, market pulp, and newsprint production facilities. **Corporate headquarters location:** Chicago IL. **Other U.S. locations:** Nationwide. **Operations at this facility include:** Recycling. **Listed on:** NASDAQ. **Stock exchange symbol:** SSCC. **CEO:** Patrick Moore. **Number of employees nationwide:** 38,600.

SNAPPER, INC.
535 Macon Street, McDonough GA 30253. 770/957-9141. **Toll-free phone:** 800/935-2967. **Fax:** 770/957-7981. **Contact:** Emily James-Lesser, Vice President of Human Resources. **E-mail address:** info@snapper.com. **World Wide Web address:** http://www.snapper.com. **Description:** Manufactures Snapper brand power lawnmowers, lawn tractors, garden tillers, snowthrowers, and related parts and accessories. Lawnmowers include rear-engine riding mowers, front-engine riding mowers, and self-propelled and push-type mowers. Snapper also manufactures a line of commercial lawn and turf equipment. Founded in 1950. **NOTE:** Human Resources phone is 770/954-2532. **Office hours:** Monday - Friday, 8:00 a.m. - 5:00 p.m. **Corporate headquarters location:** This location. **Parent company:** Simplicity Manufacturing, Inc. **President:** James Weir.

SOLO CUP COMPANY
1455 Highway 138 NE, Conyers GA 30013. 770/483-9556. **Contact:** Human Resources. **E-mail address:** hr@sweetheart.com. **World Wide Web address:** http://www.solocup.com. **Description:** Manufactures and distributes a variety of food serviceware including plates, cups, bowls, knives, in addition to food containers and plastic lids. **Office hours:** Monday – Friday, 8:00 a.m. – 4:45 p.m. **Corporate headquarters location:** Highland Park IL. **Other U.S. locations:** Nationwide. **CEO:** Robert L. Hulseman.

SOLVAY PHARMACEUTICALS
901 Sawyer Road, Marietta GA 30062. 770/578-9000. **Fax:** 770/578-5597. **Contact:** Human Resources. **World Wide Web address:** http://www.solvay.com. **Description:** A manufacturer of prescription drugs. **Corporate headquarters location:** Brussels Belgium. **Other U.S. locations:** Nationwide. **International locations:** Worldwide. **Parent company:** Solvay S.A. **Listed on:** Over-the-Counter. **Stock exchange symbol:** SVYSY. **Number of employees worldwide:** 30,302.

SONOCO STANCAP
3150 Clinton Court, Norcross GA 30071. 770/476-9088. **Fax:** 770/476-0765. **Contact:** Human Resources. **World Wide Web address:** http://www.sonoco.com. **Description:** Prints and produces paperboard closures for hotel room-service trays. **Corporate headquarters location:** Hartsville SC. **Listed on:** New York Stock Exchange. **Stock Exchange symbol:** SON. **CEO:** Harris DeLoach, Jr. **Number of employees nationwide:** 17,400.

SONY MUSIC ENTERTAINMENT, INC.
5152 Columbia Drive, Carrollton GA 30117. 770/836-2000. **Contact:** Employment Manager. **World Wide Web address:** http://www.sonymusic.com. **Description:** Produces prerecorded discs and tapes. **Special programs:** Internships. **Corporate headquarters location:** New York NY. **CEO:** Andrew Lack. **Number of employees nationwide:** 15,000.

SOUTH FULTON MEDICAL CENTER
1170 Cleveland Avenue, East Point GA 30344. 404/466-1170. **Fax:** 404/466-1120. **Recorded jobline:** 404/466-1200, Ext. 1. **Contact:** Recruitment. **World Wide Web address:** http://www.southfultonmedicalcenter.com. **Description:** A nonprofit, 392-bed, acute care facility serving the metropolitan Atlanta area. South Fulton Medical Center is affiliated with Emory University System of Health. Founded in 1963. **NOTE:** Please visit website to search for jobs and access online application form. **Positions advertised include:** RN – Various Departments; Case Manager; Secretary; Patient Care Assistant; Emergency Room Technician; Radiology Technician; MRI/CT Scanner Technician; Unit Supervisor – Nursing/SNF Rehabilitation; HVAC Mechanic; Transport/Courier; Accountant; Pharmacy Technician. **Parent company:** Tenet Healthcare Corporation. **Listed on:** New York Stock Exchange. **Stock exchange symbol:** THC.

SOUTHEAST GEORGIA REGIONAL MEDICAL CENTER
2415 Parkwood Drive, Brunswick GA 31520. 912/466-7000. **Fax:** 912/466-3113. **Recorded jobline:** Nursing positions – 912/466-5512; Non-nursing positions – 912/466-5515. **Contact:** Human Resources. **E-mail address:** careers@sghs.org. **World Wide Web address:** http://www.sghs.org/brunswick.php. **Description:** A 316-bed hospital offering full medical service, except open heart surgery. **NOTE:** Please visit website to search for jobs. **Positions advertised include:** **Manager** – Core Laboratory; CT Technologist; CAN; LPN; RN; Physical Therapist; MRI Technologist; Team Coordinator; Unit Coordinator Applications Analyst; Medical Office Assistant; Application Analyst; Director of Development; Family Nurse Practitioner; Occupational Therapist; Operating Room Assistant; Clerical Assistant; Senior Financial analyst; Clinical Auditor; Coding Specialist; HR Generalist; Maintenance Assistant; Infection Control Practitioner. **Special programs:** Internships. **Other area location:** Camden GA. **Parent company:** Southeast Georgia Health System. **Operations at this facility include:** Administration; Service. **Number of employees at this location:** 1,500.

THE SOUTHERN COMPANY
270 Peachtree Street NW, Atlanta GA 30303. 404/506-5000. **Contact:** Staffing Center. **World Wide Web address:** http://www.southernco.com. **Description:** A holding company for one of the nation's largest investor-owned electric utility groups. The company has five utilities serving approximately 11 million customers with the generation, transmission, and distribution of electricity. **NOTE:** Please visit website to search for jobs and apply online. **Special programs:** Internships; Co-ops. **Corporate headquarters location:** This location. **Other U.S. locations:** Washington D.C. **Subsidiaries include:** Alabama Power; Georgia Power; Gulf Power; Mississippi Power; Savannah Electric; Southern Communications Services provides wireless communications services to The Southern Company subsidiaries and their customers;

Southern Company Services provides The Southern Company subsidiaries with engineering, computer planning, research, financial and accounting services, and support; Southern Development and Investment Group develops new business opportunities for the company related to energy products and services; Southern Electric International develops, builds, owns, and operates cogeneration and independent power production facilities in the United States and around the world; Southern Nuclear provides specialized services for The Southern Company's three nuclear power plants. **Listed on:** New York Stock Exchange. **Stock exchange symbol:** SO. **CEO:** Daniel P. Amos. **Number of employees nationwide:** 26,100.

SOUTHERN MILLS
P.O. Box 289, Union City GA 30291. 770/969-1000. **Physical address:** 6501 Mall Boulevard, Union City GA. **Fax:** 770/969-6846. **Contact:** Human Resources. **World Wide Web address:** http://www.somills.com. **Description:** Manufactures industrial fabrics for use by other manufacturing companies. Southern Mills also manufactures press pads and covers for dry cleaning and laundry services. **Corporate headquarters location:** This location. **President/CEO:** Philip S. Vincent. **Number of employees nationwide:** 600.

SOUTHERN POLYTECHNIC STATE UNIVERSITY
Building V, Norton Dormitory, 1100 South Marietta Parkway, Marietta GA 30060-2896. 770/528-7200. **Toll-free phone:** 800/635-3204. **Fax:** 770/528-3535. **Recorded jobline:** 770/528-5534. **E-mail address:** human_resources@spsu.edu. **World Wide Web address:** http://www.spsu.edu. **Description:** A state university specializing in technology and enrolling 4,000 students. Founded 1948. **NOTE:** Human Resources phone is 770/528-7331. Please visit website to search for jobs and download application form. **Positions advertised include:** Tenure Track Professor – Apparel/Textile; Catalog/Serials Librarian; Dean – School of Engineering, Technology, and Management; Adjunct Professor – Various Departments; Area Program Coordinator – Residential Life; Assistant Director of Budget; Loan Specialist; Public Safety Officer.

SOUTHERN STATES, LLC.
30 Georgia Avenue, Hampton GA 30228. 770/946-4562. **Fax:** 770/946-8106. **Contact:** Marlin Gilbert, Personnel Director. **E-mail address:** m.gilbert@southernstatesllc.com. **World Wide Web address:** http://www.southernstatesinc.com. **Description:** Manufactures high-voltage switchgear, cut-outs, power fuses, and protective devices for the transmission and distribution of electricity. Founded 1916. **NOTE:** Please visit website to search for jobs and apply online. **Positions advertised include:** Quality Assurance Manager. **Corporate headquarters location:** This location.

SOUTHERN TEA LLC
1267 Cobb Industrial Drive, Marietta GA 30066. 770/428-5555. **Contact:** Personnel. **Description:** Processes and packages tea and coffee products. **Office hours:** Monday - Friday, 8:00 a.m. - 5:00 p.m. **Corporate headquarters location:** This location.

SOUTHERN TRUST INSURANCE COMPANY
P.O. Box 250, Macon GA 31202-0250. 478/474-0555. **Physical address:** 5444 Riverside Drive, Macon GA. **Contact:** Human Resources Department. **World Wide Web address:** http://www.stins.com. **Description:** Operates a multiline property/casualty insurance company. Offers personal and business insurance products. Founded 1968. **Corporate headquarters location:** This location.

SOUTHTRUST BANK
600 West Peachtree Street, Suite 300, Atlanta GA 30308. 770/612-6500. **Toll-free phone:** 800/606-0634. **Contact:** Human Resources. **World Wide Web address:** http://www.southtrust.com. **Description:** A full-service bank offering trust services as well as international operations. **Positions advertised include:** Investment Sales Representative; Credit Analyst; Financial Center Support Representative; Commercial Business Sales Manager; Systems and Technology Manager; Teller/Financial Services Representative; Charitable Trust Relationship Manager; Commercial Segment Sales Manager; Private Banker; Private Banking Teamleader; Credit Administrator; Insurance Agent; Loan Review Analyst; Commercial Account Manager; Desktop Support Specialist; Project Manager; Administrative Assistant. **Office hours:** Monday – Friday. 9:00 a.m. – 4:00 p.m. **Corporate headquarters location:** Birmingham AL. **Other area locations:** Statewide. **Other U.S. locations:** Southern U.S. **Listed on:** NASDAQ. **Stock exchange symbol:** SOTR. **CEO:** Wallace D. Malone.

SOUTHWIRE COMPANY
P.O. Box 1000, Carrollton GA 30119. 770/832-4242. **Physical address:** One Southwire Drive, Carrollton GA 30119. **Contact:** Mike Wiggins, Assistant Vice President of Human Resources. **World Wide Web address:** http://www.mysouthwire.com. **Description:** The largest manufacturer of building wire and utility cable in North America. **Positions advertised include:** Accountant; Finance Specialist; Administrative Office Worker; Engineer; Machinist; Electronic Technician; Information Technology Worker; Logistics Specialist; Sales Specialist; Marketing Specialist. **Corporate headquarters location:** This location. **Other U.S. locations:** Nationwide. **President/CEO:** Stuart Thorn. **Number of employees nationwide:** 3,300.

SPELMAN COLLEGE
350 Spelman Lane SW, Box 1133, Atlanta GA 30314-4399. 404/681-3643. **Fax:** 866/289-0968. **Contact:** Human Resources. **E-mail address:** resumes@spelmancareers.net. **World Wide Web address:** http://www.spelman.edu. **Description:** A women's four-year liberal arts college offering bachelor of arts and bachelor of science degrees. **NOTE:** Human resources phone is 866/289-0968. **Positions advertised include:** Groundsperson; Police Officer/Public Safety Officer; Associate Coordinator of Student Accounts; Director of Research Resources; Vice Provost for Academic Affairs; LPN. **President:** Dr. Beverly Daniel Tatum.

SPRINGS INDUSTRIES, INC.
175 South Industrial Boulevard, Calhoun GA 30701. 706/629-4541. **Contact:** Personnel. **E-mail address:** springsjobs@springs.com. **World Wide Web address:** http://www.springs.com. **Description:** Manufactures a variety of home furnishing products including shower curtains, bath rugs, towels, sheets, comforters, and infant bedding. **NOTE:** Contact Personnel directly at 706/625-6606. **Corporate headquarters location:** Fort Mills SC. **Other U.S. locations:** Nationwide. **International locations:** Canada; Mexico. **Operations at this facility include:** Administration; Divisional Headquarters; Service. **Number of employees worldwide:** 17,000.

STATE UNIVERSITY OF WEST GEORGIA
1601 Maple Street, Carrollton GA 30118. 678/839-5000. **Recorded jobline:** 770/830-2280. **Contact:** Human Resources Department. **E-mail address:** personnel@westga.edu. **World Wide Web address:** http://www.westga.edu. **Description:** A four-year college offering associate's, bachelor's, and master's degrees including MBAs. **NOTE:** Human Resources phone is 770/836-6403; fax: 770/836-4637. Please visit website to search for jobs, for more specific details on applying for positions, and to access the online application form. . **Positions advertised include:** Public Safety Officer; Assistant to the Registrar; Assistant Director of Greek Life and Community Outreach; Assistant Director of Residence Life; Academy Residential Coordinator; Custodian; Coordinator of First Year and Academic Support Programs; Teaching Assistant; Senior Network Engineer; Residence Life and Judicial Coordinator; Vice President for University Advancement; Assistant Professor – Various Departments. **President:** Beheruz N. Sethna. **Number of employees at this location:** 900.

STEVENS GRAPHICS, INC.
713 R.D. Abernathy Boulevard SW, Atlanta GA 30310. 404/753-1121. **Fax:** 404/752-0514. **Contact:** Ricki Bryant, Staffing. **World Wide Web address:** http://www.stevensgraphicsinc.com. **Description:** A commercial printer of directories. **Corporate headquarters location:** This location. **Other U.S. locations:** Birmingham AL. **Parent company:** BellSouth. **Number of employees nationwide:** 570.

STEWART & STEVENSON
S&S TUG AIRLINE GROUND SUPPORT
815 Allgood Road, Marietta GA 30062. 770/422-7230. **Fax:** 770/428-7315. **Contact:** Director of Human Resources. **World Wide Web address:** http://www.ssss.com/sstug. **Description:** Manufactures airline and industrial material handling equipment. **NOTE:** Please visit website to search for jobs. **Positions advertised include:** Ground Support Equipment Technician; TUG Shop Inside Marketer; Human Resources Coordinator. **Corporate headquarters location:** Houston TX. **Parent company:** Stewart & Stevenson Services, Inc. **Number of employees worldwide:** 3,600.

STOCK BUILDING SUPPLY
P.O. Box 45, Tucker GA 30085. 770/934-1400. **Physical address:** 3386 Lawrenceville Highway, Tucker GA. **Fax:** 770/492-1865. **Contact:** Carol Jones. **E-mail address:** recruitment@stocksupply.com. **World Wide Web address:** http://www.stockbuildingsupply.com. **Description:** Manufactures and sells wooden building products, such as doors and frames. **NOTE:** Entry-level positions and second and third shifts are offered. Please send resumes to P.O. Box 58515, Raleigh NC 27658. **Special programs:** Apprenticeships; Training. **Corporate headquarters location:** Raleigh NC. **Other area locations:** Statewide. **Other U.S. locations:** Nationwide. **Number of employees at this location:** 85.

STOFFEL SEALS CORPORATION
P.O. Box 217, Tallapoosa GA 30176. 770/574-2382. **Physical address:** One Stoffel Drive, Tallapoosa GA. **Toll-free phone:** 800/422-8247. **Fax:** 770/574-7937. **Toll-free fax:** 800/551-8545. **Contact:** Personnel Manager. **E-mail address:** info@stoffel.com. **World Wide Web address:** http://www.stoffel.com. **Description:** Engaged in graphic and offset commercial printing. **Corporate headquarters location:** Nyack NY. **Number of employees nationwide:** 500.

STORK GAMCO
P.O. Box 1258, Gainesville GA 30503. 770/532-7041. **Fax:** 770/532-5672. **Contact:** Human Resources. **E-mail address:** h.r.dept@stork.com. **World Wide Web address:** http://www.stork-gamco.com. **Description:** Produces and markets a variety of products and equipment used in the poultry processing industry. **NOTE:** Please visit website to view job listings. **Corporate headquarters location:** This location. **Parent company:** Stork N.V. **Number of employees at this location:** 180.

SUMTER COUNTY SCHOOLS
100 Learning Lane, Americus GA 31719. 229/931-8500. **Fax:** 229/931-8555. **World Wide Web address:** http://www.sumter.k12.ga.us. **Contact:** Dr. James Drew, Assistant Superintendent. **NOTE:** Please visit http://www.teachgeorgia.org to search for jobs.

SUNGARD DATA SYSTEMS
11560 Great Oaks Way, Suite 200, Alpharetta GA 30022. 770/587-6800. **Fax:** 770/587-6808. **Contact:** Human Resources. **World Wide Web address:** http://www.sungard.com. **Description:** Develops financial software for insurance companies. **NOTE:** Please visit website to search for jobs. Visit http://www.sungard.apply2jobs.com to apply online. **Positions advertised include:** Manager of Professional Services; Consultant. **Corporate headquarters location:** Wayne PA. **International locations:** Worldwide. **Parent company:** SunGard Financial Systems. **Listed on:** New York Stock Exchange. **Stock exchange symbol:** SDS. **President/CEO:** Cristobal I. Conde. **Number of employees at worldwide:** 10,000.

SUNTRUST BANK, ATLANTA, N.A.
SUNTRUST BANKS, INC.
P.O. Box 4418, 019, Atlanta GA 30302. 404/588-7711. **Physical address:** 303 Peachtree Street NE, Atlanta GA 30308. **Toll-free phone:** 800/786-8787. **Fax:** 404/332-3875. **Contact:** Human Resources. **World Wide Web address:** http://www.suntrust.com. **Description:** A full-service bank. **NOTE:** Please visit website to search for jobs and apply online. **Positions advertised include:** Accountant; Administrative Assistant; Applications Programmer; Assistant Branch Manager; Attorney; Audit Project Manager; Branch Manager; Business Analyst; Client Services Specialist; Corporate Financier; Credit Advisor; CRM Director; Customer Service Specialist; Equity Research Associate; Financial Analyst; Healthcare Associate; Human Resources Specialist; Marketing Manager; Loan Review Administrator; Portfolio Manager; Private Financial Advisor. **Corporate headquarters location:** This location. **Other area locations:** Statewide. **Other U.S. locations:** AL; FL; MD; TN; VA. **Parent company:** SunTrust Banks, Inc. (also at this location) is a financial services company. The company's primary businesses include traditional deposit and credit services, as well as trust and investment services. Additionally, SunTrust Banks, Inc. provides corporate finance, mortgage banking, factoring, credit cards, discount brokerage, credit-related insurance, and data processing and information services. **Operations at this facility include:** Administration. **Listed on:** New York Stock Exchange. **Stock exchange symbol:** STI. **President/CEO:** L. Phillip Humann. **Number of employees nationwide:** 27,578.

SUNTRUST BANK, AUGUSTA, N.A.
P.O. Box 927, Augusta GA 30903. 706/821-2000. **Contact:** Personnel. **World Wide Web address:** http://www.suntrust.com. **Description:** A full-service commercial bank. **Positions advertised include:** Accountant; Administrative Assistant; Applications Programmer; Assistant Branch Manager; Attorney; Audit Project Manager; Branch Manager; Business Analyst; Client Services Specialist; Corporate Financier; Credit Advisor; CRM Director; Customer Service Specialist; Equity Research Associate; Financial Analyst; Healthcare Associate; Human Resources Specialist; Marketing Manager; Loan Review Administrator; Portfolio Manager; Private Financial Advisor; Retail Investment Consultant; Tax Specialist. **NOTE:** Please visit website to search for jobs and apply online. **Corporate headquarters location:** Atlanta GA. **Other U.S. locations:** AL; FL; MD; TN; VA. **Parent company:** SunTrust Banks, Inc. (Atlanta GA) is a financial services company. The company's primary businesses include traditional deposit and credit services as well as trust and investment services. Additionally, SunTrust Banks, Inc. provides corporate finance, mortgage banking,

factoring, credit cards, discount brokerage, credit-related insurance, data processing, and information services. **Listed on:** New York Stock Exchange. **Stock exchange symbol:** STI. **President/CEO:** L. Phillip Humann. **Number of employees nationwide:**27,578.

SUNTRUST BANK, MIDDLE GEORGIA, N.A.
P.O. Box 4248, Macon GA 31208. 478/741-2265. **Contact:** Human Resources. **World Wide Web address:** http://www.suntrust.com. **Description:** A full-service commercial bank. **Positions advertised include:** Accountant; Administrative Assistant; Applications Programmer; Assistant Branch Manager; Attorney; Audit Project Manager; Branch Manager; Business Analyst; Client Services Specialist; Corporate Financier; Credit Advisor; CRM Director; Customer Service Specialist; Equity Research Associate; Financial Analyst; Healthcare Associate; Human Resources Specialist; Marketing Manager; Loan Review Administrator; Portfolio Manager; Private Financial Advisor; Retail Investment Consultant; Tax Specialist. **NOTE:** Please visit website to search for jobs and apply online. **Corporate headquarters location:** Atlanta GA. **Other U.S. locations:** AL; FL; MD; TN; VA. **Parent company:** SunTrust Banks, Inc. (Atlanta GA) is a financial services company. The company's primary businesses include traditional deposit and credit services as well as trust and investment services. Additionally, SunTrust Banks, Inc. provides corporate finance, mortgage banking, factoring, credit cards, discount brokerage, credit-related insurance, data processing, and information services. **Listed on:** New York Stock Exchange. **Stock exchange symbol:** STI. **President/CEO:** L. Phillip Humann. **Number of employees nationwide:** 27,578.

SUNTRUST ROBINSON-HUMPHREY COMPANY
Atlanta Financial Center, 3333 Peachtree Road NE, Atlanta GA 30326. 404/926-5000. **Contact:** Human Resources. **World Wide Web address:** https://www.suntrustrh.com. **Description:** Provides debt capital and equity financing solutions to growing companies. **Positions advertised include:** Analyst; Associate. **Corporate headquarters location:** This location. **Other U.S. locations:** New York NY; San Francisco CA; Boston MA; Nashville TN. **Parent company:** Suntrust Capital Markets, Inc.

SURGICAL INFORMATION SYSTEMS
3650 Mansell Road, Suite 300, Alpharetta GA 30022. 770/643-5555. **Toll-free phone:** 800/866-0656. **Fax:** 770/643-5777. **Contact:** Human Resources. **E-mail address:** jobs@orsoftware.com. **World Wide Web address:** http://www.orsoftware.com. **Description:** Provides physician management services for hospitals and health care facilities. The company's divisions serve the health care industry by assisting hospitals and physicians in the organization and operation of cost-effective health care, improved productivity and low costs in operating rooms, and physician placement services. **NOTE:** Please visit website for a listing of jobs. **Positions advertised include:** Surgical Software Implementation Consultant.

SWIFT, CURIE, McGHEE & HIERS
1355 Peachtree Street NE, Suite 300, Atlanta GA 30309. 404/874-8800. **Fax:** 404/888-6199. **Contact:** Human Resources. **World Wide Web address:** http://www.scmhlaw.com. **Description:** A legal services firm specializing in worker's compensation law. **NOTE:** Please visit website to see job listings and to submit resume online. For those interested in attorney jobs, contact Patricia L. Young, Attorney Recruiting Manager at 404/888-6199. **Positions advertised include:** Paralegal. **Special programs:** Summer Associate Program. **Corporate headquarters location:** This location.

SYNOVUS FINANCIAL CORPORATION
P.O. Box 120, Columbus GA 31902. 706/649-2311. **Physical address:** 901 Front Avenue, One Arsenal Place, Columbus GA 31902. **Fax:** 706/641-6555. **Recorded jobline:** 706/649-4758. **Contact:** Human Resources. **E-mail address:** careers@sfcts.com. **World Wide Web address:** http://www.synovus.com. **Description:** A multiservice financial company. Synovus Financial owns 80 percent of Total Systems Services, Inc. (also at this location, http://www.tsys.com), one of the largest credit, debit, commercial, and private label processing companies in the world. Synovus Financial Corporation also operates 38 banks in the Southeast. Founded in 1888. **NOTE:** Please visit website to search for jobs and apply online. All applicants should contact the jobline for available positions. Entry-level positions and second and third shifts are offered. If applying for more than one position, please submit a separate resume for each position. **Positions advertised include:** Commercial Sales Trainer; Teller; Accounting Manager; Marketing Project Coordinator; Operations Associate; Operations Associate Adjustments; Receptionist; Database Administrator; Assistant Financial Reporting Manager; Balancing Clerk; Manager – Security Applications; Call Support Analyst. **Corporate headquarters location:** This location. **Other U.S. locations:** AL; FL; SC. **Special programs:** Internships; Training; Summer Jobs. **Subsidiaries include:** Synovus Securities, Inc. is a full-service brokerage firm; Synovus Trust Company is one of the Southeast's largest providers of trust services; Synovus Mortgage Corporation offers mortgage servicing throughout the Southeast; Synovus Leasing Company offers equipment leasing; Synovus Insurance Services offers insurance services. **Listed on:** New York Stock Exchange. **Stock exchange symbol:** SNV. **CEO:** James H. Blanchard. **Annual sales/revenues:** $21 - $50 million. **Number of employees nationwide:** 11,000.

T-MOBILE USA, INC.
One Concourse Parkway NE, Suite 500, Atlanta GA 30328. 770/522-3400. **Contact:** Human Resources. **World Wide Web address:** http://www.t-mobile.com. **Description:** A cellular networking communications company. **Corporate headquarters location:** Bellevue WA. **Other area locations:** Statewide. **Other U.S. locations:** Nationwide. **Parent company:** Deutsche Telekom AG. **Listed on:** New York Stock Exchange. **Stock exchange symbol:** DT. **CEO:** John Stanton. **Number of employees worldwide:** 22,000.

TDK ELECTRONICS CORPORATION
1 TDK Boulevard, Peachtree City GA 30269-2047. 770/631-0410. **Fax:** 770/631-0425. **Contact:** Human Resources. **World Wide Web address:** http://www.tdk.com. **Description:** TDK Electronics Corporation is one of the world's largest manufacturers of magnetic recording tapes, ferrite products, and CD-ROMs. **NOTE:** Please visit website to register, search for jobs, and apply online. **Corporate headquarters location:** Garden City NY. **Other U.S. locations:** Nationwide. **International locations:** Brazil. **Operations at this facility include:** This location manufactures video recording tapes. **Listed on:** New York Stock Exchange. **Stock exchange symbol:** TDK. **President:** Hajime Sawabe. **Number of employees worldwide:** 29,747.

TARA MATERIALS, INC.
P.O. Box 646, Lawrenceville GA 30046. 770/963-5256. **Physical address:** 111 Fredrix Alley, Lawrenceville GA. **Contact:** Rosemary Rose, Human Resources Director. **World Wide Web address:** http://www.taramaterials.com. **Description:** Produces and distributes canvases used by professional artists. **Corporate headquarters location:** This location. **Subsidiaries include:** Fredrix Artist Canvas; Fredrix PrintCanvas; Fredrix Floorcloths; Tara Picture Frames. **Operations at this facility include:** Administration; Manufacturing; Research and Development; Sales.

TARGET STORES
4502 Old Union Road, Tifton GA 31793. 229/387-3000. **Contact:** Human Resources Department. **World Wide Web address:** http://www.target.com. **Description:** A national chain of upscale discount retail stores. **NOTE:** Please visit http://www.targetcorp.com to search for jobs. **Positions advertised include:** Operations Senior Group Leader; Facility Operations Manager; Group Leader; Regional Transportation Supervisor; Facility Operations Group Leader. **Corporate headquarters location:** Minneapolis MN. **Other U.S. locations:** Nationwide. **Operations at this facility include:** The Southeast's distribution center for Target retail stores. **Listed on:** New York Stock Exchange. **Stock exchange symbol:** TGT. **CEO:** Bob Ulrich. **Number of employees nationwide:** 245,000.

TASQ TECHNOLOGY
2155 Barrett Park Drive, Suite 215, Kennesaw GA 30144. 770/218-5000. **Contact:** Human Resources. **World Wide Web address:** http://www.tasq.com. **Description:** Provides point-of-sale equipment and resolutions for electronic payment purposes. **Corporate headquarters location:** Rocklin CA. **Parent company:** First Data Corporation.

TELULAR CORPORATION
420 Thornton Road, Suite 109, Lithia Springs GA 30122. 678/945-7770. **Toll-free phone:** 800/229-2326. **Fax:** 678/945-7758. **Contact:** Human Resources Department. **E-mail address:** jobs@telular.com. **World Wide Web address:** http://www.telular.com. **Description:** The world's leading developer of cellular fixed wireless telecommunication products. Also designs, manufactures, and markets electronic security products, custom precision sheet metal, and printed circuit boards. **Corporate headquarters location:** Vernon Hills IL. **Other U.S. locations:** Hauppauge NY. **International locations:** United Kingdom; Singapore. **Listed on:** NASDAQ. **Stock exchange symbol:** WRLS. **President/CEO:** Kenneth E. Millard.

TENDER LOVING CARE/STAFF BUILDERS
100 Hannover Park Road, Atlanta GA 30350. 678/323-1640. **Fax:** 678/323-1641. **Contact:** Human Resources. **World Wide Web address:** http://www.tlcathome.com. **Description:** A nonprofit home health care agency. **NOTE:** There are two locations in Atlanta. Another office is located at 3401 Norman Berry Drive # 138. Entry-level positions are offered. Please visit website to register, search for jobs, and apply online. **Positions advertised include:** Home Care Nurse; Occupational Therapist; Physical Therapist. **Corporate headquarters location:** Lake Success NY. **Other U.S. locations:** Nationwide. **CEO:** James Happ. **Number of employees nationwide:** 20,000.

TEXICAN INDUSTRIAL ENERGY MARKETING
100 Glenridge Point Parkway, Suite 550, Atlanta GA 30342. 404/851-3000. **Fax:** 404/851-3001. **Contact:** Human Resources Manager. **E-mail address:** texican@texicangas.com. **World Wide Web address:** http://www.texicangas.com. **Description:** Provides energy products and services. Founded in 1985. **Corporate headquarters location:** This location. **Other U.S. locations include:** Houston TX; Mobile AL. **Listed on:** Privately held.

THIELE KAOLIN COMPANY
P.O. Box 1056, Sandersville GA 31082. 478/552-3951. **Physical address:** 520 Kaolin Road, Sandersville GA. **Contact:** Human Resources. **World Wide Web address:** http://www.thielekaolin.com. **Description:** The company primarily mines nonmetallic minerals including kaolin and clay. **Corporate headquarters location:** This location. **Operations at this facility include:** This location is a processing plant.

THERAGENICS CORPORATION
5203 Bristol Industrial Way, Buford GA 30518. 770/271-0233. **Toll-free phone:** 800/998-8479. **Fax:** 770/831-4369. **Contact:** Human Resources. **E-mail address:** pfeiferk@theragenics.com. **World Wide Web address:** http://www.theragenics.com. **Description:** Develops and manufactures implantable radiation devices for the treatment of prostate cancer. Founded in 1981. **Positions advertised include:** Advanced Process Chemical Development Engineer; Network Systems Administrator. **Corporate headquarters location:** This location. **Other U.S. locations:** Oak Ridge TN. **Listed on:** New York Stock Exchange. **Stock exchange symbol:** TGX.

THERMAL CERAMICS
P.O. Box 923, Department 101, Augusta GA 30903-0923. 706/796-4200. **Physical address:** 2102 Old Savannah Road, Augusta GA 30906. **Fax:** 706/796-4398. **Contact:** Director of Personnel. **E-mail address:** tceramics@thermalceramics.com. **World Wide Web address:** http://www.thermalceramics.com/home.html. **Description:** Manufactures a variety of high-temperature insulation products including castables and firebrick. **International locations:** Worldwide.

THERMO KING CORPORATION
1430 State Highway 24 East, Louisville GA 30434. 478/625-7241. **Fax:** 478/625-7756. **Contact:** Human Resources. **World Wide Web address:** http://www.thermoking.com. **Description:** Thermo King Corporation serves the refrigeration and air conditioning needs of buses and tractor-trailer centers. **NOTE:** Please visit website to see job listings. **Corporate headquarters location:** Minneapolis MN. **Other U.S. locations:** Lowell AR; Clayton CA; Hastings NE. **International locations:** Worldwide. **Parent company:** Ingersoll-Rand. **Operations at this facility include:** This location manufactures refrigeration units.

J. WALTER THOMPSON COMPANY
10B Glenlake Parkway NE, North Tower, Atlanta GA 30328. 404/365-7300. **Contact:** Director of Human Resources. **World Wide Web address:** http://www.jwtworld.com. **Description:** A full-service advertising agency. Founded 1864. **Corporate headquarters location:** New York NY. **Other U.S. locations:** Nationwide. **International locations:** Worldwide. **CEO:** Bob Jeffrey. **Number of employees worldwide:** 8,500.

TIP TOP POULTRY INC.
P.O. Box 6338, Marietta GA 30065-6338. 770/973-8070. **Physical address:** 327 Wallace Road, Marietta GA 30062. **Toll-free phone:** 800/241-5230. **Fax:** 770/579-4261. **Contact:** Personnel Manager. **E-mail address:** mpersonnel@tiptoppoultry.com. **World Wide Web address:** http://www.tiptoppoultry.com. **Description:** Engaged in poultry processing and distributing. **Corporate headquarters location:** This location. **Other area locations:** Rockmart GA; Atlanta GA.

TOM'S FOODS
P.O. Box 60, Columbus GA 31901. 706/323-2721. **Physical address:** 900 8th Street, Columbus GA. **Fax:** 706/256-0153. **Contact:** Human Resources. **E-mail address:** hr@tomsfoods.com. **World Wide Web address:** http://www.tomsfoods.com. **Description:** A nationwide manufacturer and distributor of snack food products

including potato chips, peanuts, candy, crackers, and bakery items. Founded 1925. **NOTE:** Please visit website to see job listings, and to apply online. **Positions advertised include:** Route Sales Representative. **Corporate headquarters location:** This location. **Other U.S. locations:** Fresno CA; Perry FL; Knoxville TN; Corsicana TX. **Operations at this facility include:** Administration; Manufacturing; Research and Development; Sales; Service. **Listed on:** Privately held.

TOTO USA
1155 Southern Road, Morrow GA 30260. 770/282-8686. **Fax:** 770/282-0001. **Contact:** Human Resources. **E-mail address:** humanres@totousa.com. **World Wide Web address:** http://www.totousa.com. **Description:** The world's largest manufacturer of toilets. **Corporate headquarters location:** Atlanta GA. **Other U.S. locations:** Orange CA; New York NY. **Parent company:** TOTO Ltd. **President:** Hiromichi Tabata.

TOTO USA
1800 Murphy Avenue SW, Atlanta GA 30310. 404/755-2834. **Contact:** Human Resources. **E-mail address:** humanres@totousa.com. **World Wide Web address:** http://www.totousa.com. **Description:** The world's largest manufacturer of toilets. **Corporate headquarters location:** This location. **Other U.S. locations:** Orange CA; New York NY. **Parent company:** TOTO Ltd. **President:** Hiromichi Tabata.

TRANSMONTAIGNE INC.
P.O. Box 103076, Roswell GA 30076. 770/518-3500. **Physical address:** 200 Mansell Court East, Suite 600, Roswell GA. **Fax:** 770/518-3567. **Contact:** Human Resources. **E-mail address:** openpositions@transmontaigne.com. **World Wide Web address:** http://www.transmontaigne.com. **Description:** A wholesale petroleum marketer. **Corporate headquarters location:** Denver CO. **Other area locations:** Statewide. **Other U.S. locations:** Eastern and Southeastern U.S. **Listed on:** American Stock Exchange. **Stock exchange symbol:** TMG. **CEO:** Donald H. Anderson.

TRIDIA CORPORATION
1000 Cobb Place Boulevard NW, Building 200, Suite 220, Kennesaw GA 30144-3684. 770/428-5000. **Toll-free phone:** 800/582-9337. **Fax:** 770/428-5009. **Contact:** Human Resources. **World Wide Web address:** http://www.tridia.com. **Description:** A provider of SCO UNIX-based solutions and a software developer and reseller. The company's product line includes DOUBLEVISION remote control software, which allows a user to connect to another user's screen. Founded 1987. **Office hours:** Monday – Friday, 8:30 a.m. – 5:00 p.m. **Corporate headquarters location:** This location. **CEO:** Vincent Frese, II.

TRONCALLI NISSAN
1625 Church Street, Decatur GA 30033. 404/292-3853; 404/292-6828. **Contact:** General Sales Manager. **World Wide Web address:** http://www.troncallinissan.com. **Description:** A franchised dealer of Nissan, Jaguar, and Chrysler-Plymouth automobiles. **NOTE:** Please visit website for online application form. **Operations at this facility include:** Administration; Sales; Service.

TUCKER DOOR & TRIM COMPANY
650 Highway 83, Monroe GA 30655. 770/267-4622. **Contact:** Marion Harris, Sales Manager. **Description:** A manufacturer of doors. The company is also engaged in wholesale millwork.

TURNER BROADCASTING SYSTEM, INC.
P.O. Box 105366, Atlanta GA 30348. 404/827-1700. **Fax:** 404/827-2437. **Physical address:** One CNN Center, 100 International Boulevard, Atlanta GA. **World Wide Web address:** http://www.turner.com. **Description:** A broadcasting company that operates television stations and websites, as well as real estate ventures and sports teams. **NOTE:** Please visit parent company's website at http://www.timewarner.com to search for jobs. **Positions advertised include:** Advanced Business System Analyst; BOC Coordinator; Legal Counsel; Staff Accountant; Administrative Assistant; Business Systems Analyst Specialist; Marketing Manager; Business Systems Analysis Specialist; Senior Project Manager; Senior Financial Analyst; Associate Producer; Receptionist. **Subsidiaries include:** CNN; TBS Superstation; TNT; Cartoon Network; Turner Classic Movies; nascar.com; pga.com. **Parent company:** Time Warner. **CEO:** Philip I. Kent. **Number of employees worldwide:** 8,000.

TY COBB HEALTHCARE SYSTEM, INC.
P.O. Box 589, Royston GA 30662. 706/245-5071. **Physical address:** 521 Franklin Springs Street, Royston GA. **Fax:** 706/245-1831. **Contact:** Personnel. **World Wide Web address:** http://www.tycobbhealthcare.org. **Description:** Operates a 71-bed hospital. Specializations include physical and speech therapy, as well as pediatric and occupational therapy. **NOTE:** Contact Personnel directly at 706/245-1846. Entry-level positions and second and third shifts are offered. Please visit website to search for jobs. **Positions advertised include:** RN; CNA; Dietician; Food Service Worker; Respiratory Therapist; Case Manager; Administrative Assistant; Patient Access Representative; Pharmacist; Custodian; RN Supervisor; Dietary Aide; Radiology Technician. **Special programs:** Training. **CEO:** Chuck Adams.

TYCO PLASTICS
KING PACKAGING
407 Sangamore Road, Bremen GA 30110. 770/537-5548. **Toll-free phone:** 800/888-5464. **Contact:** Sophia Chivers, Human Resources. **World Wide Web address:** http://www.kingpackaging.com. **Description:** One of the largest manufacturers of plastic films products in the United States, producing items such as plastic sheeting, plastic bags, shrink wrap and stretch film. **Parent company:** Tyco International Ltd. **Corporate headquarters location:** This location.

TYSON FOODS, INC.
P.O. Box 247, Cumming GA 30028. 770/887-2344. **Physical Address:** 340 West Maple Street, Cumming GA 30040. **Fax:** 770/889-3250. **Contact:** Personnel. **World Wide Web address:** http://www.tysonfoodsinc.com. **Description:** Tyson Foods, Inc. is one of the world's largest fully-integrated producers, processors, and marketers of poultry-based food products. Products include Tyson Holly Farms Fresh Chicken, Weaver, Louis Kemp Crab, Lobster Delights, Healthy Portion, Beef Stir Fry, and Crab Delights Stir Fry. **NOTE:** Please visit website to search for jobs and apply online. **Corporate headquarters location:** Springdale AR. **Other area locations:** Buena Vista GA; Dahlonega GA; Dawson GA; Fairmont GA; Gainesville GA; Lawrenceville GA; Oglethorpe GA; Vienna GA. **Other U.S. locations:** Nationwide. **Operations at this facility include:** This location processes poultry. **Listed on:** New York Stock Exchange. **Stock exchange symbol:** TSN.

TYSON FOODS, INC.
P.O. Box 415, Vienna GA 31092. 229/268-3400. **Physical address:** Pine Street, Vienna GA. **Fax:** 229/268-1276. **Contact:** Human Resources. **World Wide Web address:** http://www.tysonfoodsinc.com. **Description:** Tyson Foods, Inc. is one of the world's largest fully-integrated producers, processors, and marketers of poultry-based food products. Products include Tyson Holly Farms Fresh Chicken, Weaver, Louis Kemp Crab, Lobster Delights, Healthy Portion, Beef Stir Fry, and Crab Delights Stir Fry. **NOTE:** Please visit website to search for jobs and apply online. **Corporate headquarters location:** Springdale AR. **Other area locations:** Buena Vista GA; Dahlonega GA; Dawson GA; Fairmont GA; Gainesville GA; Lawrenceville GA; Oglethorpe GA; Summing GA. **Other U.S. locations:** Nationwide. **Operations at this facility include:** This location processes poultry. **Listed on:** New York Stock Exchange. **Stock exchange symbol:** TSN.

URS CORPORATION
400 Northpark Town Center, 1000 Abernathy Road NE, Suite 900, Atlanta GA 30328. 678/808-8800. **Fax:** 678/808-8400. **Contact:** Human Resources. **World Wide Web address:** http://www.urscorp.com. **Description:** Develops and alters transportation systems, buildings, and industrial facilities. URS Corporation is also involved in environmental reconstruction and preservation services. Founded in 1969. **Positions advertised include:** Civil Engineer; Graduate Civil Engineer; Graduate Water Resources Engineer; MIS Coordinator; Project Accountant/Accounting Manager; Project Civil Engineer; Project Environmental Scientist; Project Transportation Engineer; Senior Accountant; Senior CADD Designer; Senior Civil-Bridge Engineer; Water Resources Engineer. **Special programs:** Internships; Co-ops. **Corporate headquarters location:** San Francisco CA. **Other U.S. locations:** Nationwide. **International locations:** Worldwide. **Listed on:** New York Stock Exchange. **Stock exchange symbol:** URS. **Number of employees worldwide:** 26,000.

U.S. CENTERS FOR DISEASE CONTROL & PREVENTION
1600 Clifton Road NE, Mail Stop K05, Atlanta GA 30333. 404/639-3311. **Toll-free phone:** 800/311-3435. **Contact:** Human Resources. **World Wide Web address:** http://www.cdc.gov. **Description:** A federal agency responsible for promoting health and the quality of life by preventing, researching, and controlling disease, injury, and disability. **NOTE:** Please visit website to search for jobs. **Positions advertised include:** Administrative Officer; Budget Analyst; Communication Officer; Computer Scientist; Deputy Director for Public Health Science; Director – Various Departments; Epidemiologist; Health Communication Specialist; Lead Behavioral Scientist; Management and Operations Officer; Management and Program Analyst; Medical Officer; Microbiologist; Planning and Evaluation Officer; Program Specialist; Supervisor – Various Departments. **Corporate headquarters location:** This location. **Other U.S. locations:** Nationwide. **Number of employees at this location:** 1,600. **Number of employees nationwide:** 8,500.

U.S. ENVIRONMENTAL PROTECTION AGENCY (EPA)
61 Forsyth Street SW, Atlanta GA 30303-3104. 404/562-9900. **Toll-free phone:** 800/241-1754. **Fax:** 404/562-8174. **Contact:** Human Resources. **World Wide Web address:** http://www.epa.gov. **Description:** The EPA is dedicated to improving and preserving the quality of the environment, both nationally and globally, and protecting human health and the productivity of natural resources. The EPA is committed to ensuring that federal environmental laws are implemented and enforced effectively; that U.S. policy, both foreign and domestic, fosters the integration of economic development and environmental protection so that economic growth can be sustained over the long term; and that public and private decisions affecting the energy, transportation, agriculture, industry, international trade, and natural resources markets fully integrate considerations of environmental quality. **NOTE:** Contact Human Resources directly at 404/562-8182. Please visit website to search for jobs and apply online. Resumes and applications are only accepted via the internet. For more details, please visit the website or contact the Human Resources department. **Positions advertised include:** Environmental Protection Specialist; Biologist. **Special programs:** Internships. **Corporate headquarters location:** Washington DC. **Other U.S. locations:** Nationwide. **Operations at this facility include:** This location of the EPA serves Alabama, Florida, Georgia, Kentucky, Mississippi, North Carolina, South Carolina, and Tennessee. **Number of employees nationwide:** 18,000.

U.S. FEDERAL RESERVE BANK OF ATLANTA
1000 Peachtree Street, Atlanta GA 30309-4470. 404/498-8500. **Contact:** Employment Specialist. **World Wide Web address:** http://www.frbatlanta.org. **Description:** One of 12 regional Federal Reserve banks that, along with the Federal Reserve Board of Governors in Washington DC and the Federal Open Market Committee, comprise the Federal Reserve System, the nation's central bank charged with three major responsibilities: monetary policy, banking supervision and regulation, and processing payments. **NOTE:** Please visit website to search for jobs and apply online. **Positions advertised include:** Associate Examiner; Capital Markets Specialist; Editor and Publications Manager; Financial Analyst; Information Resources Manager; Information Security Coordinator; Senior Economic Analyst; Senior Statistics Reports Analyst. **Corporate headquarters location:** This location. **Other U.S. locations:** Birmingham AL; Jacksonville FL; Miami FL; Nashville TN; New Orleans LA.

U.S SOCIAL SECURITY ADMINISTRATION
61 Forsyth Street SW, Suite 22T64, Atlanta GA 30303-8907. 404/562-1201. **Toll-free phone:** 800/772-1213. **Contact:** Personnel Operations. **World Wide Web address:** http://www.ssa.gov. **Description:** Administers the Social Security program and provides benefits and services to recipients residing in the state of Georgia. **Positions advertised include:** Information Technology Specialist. **Special programs:** Internships. **Corporate headquarters location:** Baltimore MD. **Other area locations:** Statewide. **Other U.S. locations:** Nationwide. **Operations at this facility include:** This office serves as a regional headquarters for Alabama, Florida, Georgia, Kentucky, Mississippi, North Carolina, South Carolina, and Tennessee.

U.S. TRAFFIC CORPORATION
6301 Best Friend Road, Norcross GA 30071. 770/662-5400. **Fax:** 770/409-5064. **Contact:** Human Resources. **E-mail address:** hr@myerspowerproducts.com. **World Wide Web address:** http://www.ustraffic.net. **Description:** Manufactures a variety of electronic and electric information display equipment including scoreboards, advertising media, and transport terminal arrival/departure boards. **NOTE:** Please visit website to download application form. Send application and resume to corporate office, at 9601 John Street, Santa Fe Springs CA 90670. **Corporate headquarters location:** Santa Fe Springs CA 90670. **Other U.S. locations:** WA; OR; IL; TX; CT. **International locations:** Mexico. **Operations at this facility include:** This location serves as a regional sales office.

ULINE
2165 Northmont Parkway, Duluth GA 30096. 800/958-5463. **Fax:** 770/495-7504. **Contact:** Human Resources. **E-mail address:** ulinejobs@uline.com. **World Wide Web address:** http://www.uline.com. **Description:** Uline is a nationwide leading distributor of packaging and industrial supplies. **Positions advertised include:** Administrative Assistant; Custodian, Customer Service Representative; Operations Analyst; Warehouse Management; Warehouse Supervisor; General Warehouse; Sales Representative. **Corporate headquarters location:** Waukegan IL. **Other U.S. locations:** Breinigsville PA; Eagan MN; Duluth GA; Coppell TX. **Operations at this facility include:** Manufacturing; Administrative.

UNICOMP
3478 Putnam Ford Drive, Suite E207, Woodstock GA 30189. 770/424-3684. **Fax:** 770/424-5558. **Contact:** Human Resources. **E-mail address:** careers@unicomp.com. **World Wide Web address:** http://www.unicomp.com. **Description:** Creates interactive and automated wireless kiosks for retail operations. Retailers such as Target, Kmart, Estée Lauder, Lollytogs, and A&P use uniComp products. **Corporate headquarters location:** Fletcher NC. **CEO:** Stephen A. Hafer.

UNISOURCE
6600 Governors Lake Parkway, Norcross GA 30071. 770/447-9000. **Toll-free phone:** 800/864-7687. **Contact:** Ray Millet, Operations. **World Wide Web address:** http://www.unisourcelink.com. **Description:** Manufactures and wholesales fine papers in addition to marketing and distributing commercial printing and business imaging materials. **NOTE:** Please visit website to submit resume online. **Corporate headquarters location:** This location. **Other area locations:** Atlanta GA; Doraville GA; Riverside GA; Marietta GA; Roswell GA. **Other U.S. locations:** Nationwide. **International locations:** Canada.

UNISYS CORPORATION
5550-A Peachtree Parkway, 1st Floor, Norcross GA 30092. 770/368-6000. **Fax:** 770/368-6152. **Contact:** Human Resources. **World Wide Web address:** http://www.unisys.com. **Description:** Unisys Corporation provides information services, technology, and software. Unisys specializes in developing critical business solutions based on open information networks. The company's Enabling Software Team creates a variety of software projects that facilitate the building of user applications and the management of distributed systems. The company's Platforms Group is responsible for UNIX Operating Systems running across a wide range of multiple processor server platforms including all peripheral and communication drivers. The Unisys Commercial Parallel Processing Team develops microkernel-based operating systems, I/O device drivers, ATM hardware, diagnostics, and system architectures. The System Management Group is in charge of the overall management of development programs for UNIX desktop and entry-server products. **NOTE:** Please visit website to register, search for jobs, and apply online. **Positions advertised include:** Portfolio Sales Executive; Mail Clerk; CRM Manager; Client Focus Manager. **Corporate headquarters location:** Blue Bell PA. **Other area locations:** Savannah GA. **Other U.S. locations:** Nationwide. **International locations:** Worldwide. **Operations at this facility include:** This location provides information services and global customer support. **Listed on:** New York Stock Exchange. **Stock exchange symbol:** UIS. **Number of employees worldwide:** 37,000. **President/CEO:** Lawrence A. Wrinbach.

UNITED PARCEL SERVICE (UPS)
55 Glenlake Parkway NE, Atlanta GA 30328. 404/828-6000. **Fax:** 404/828-6440. **Recorded jobline:** 888/967-5877. **Contact:** Human Resources. **World Wide Web address:** http://www.ups.com. **Description:** United Parcel Service is a package pickup and delivery service organization, providing service to all 50 states and to more than 185 countries and territories worldwide. The company delivers approximately 12 million packages daily. **NOTE:** Please visit website to search for jobs and apply online. **Positions advertised include:** Contact Manager; CSC Industrial Engineer; Print Production Supervisor; Strategic Customer Communications Supervisor; Project Design Specialist; Treasury Specialist; Contract Administrator; Brand Identity Manager; Database Marketing Specialist; Junior Finance Specialist; Plant Engineering Designer; Associate Financial Analyst; Lead Accountant; Warehouse Associate; Paralegal; Regional Account Manager. **Special programs:** Internships. **Corporate headquarters location:** This location. **Other U.S. locations:** Nationwide. **International locations:** Worldwide. **Operations at this facility include:** This location houses the administrative offices. **Listed on:** New York Stock Exchange. **Stock exchange symbol:** UPS. **CEO:** Michael Eskew. **Number of employees nationwide:** 355,000.

UNITED WAY OF METROPOLITAN ATLANTA INC.
100 Edgewood Avenue NE, Second Floor, Atlanta GA 30303. 404/527-7200. **Contact:** Human Resources. **E-mail address:** cberube@unitedwayatlanta.org. **World Wide Web address:** http://www.unitedwayatl.org. **Description:** Through a network of volunteers and local charities, United Way organizations throughout America help meet the health and human care needs of millions of people. The United Way system includes approximately 1,900 community-based organizations. United Way volunteers raise funds that are used for human services ranging from disaster relief, emergency food and shelter, and crisis intervention to daycare, physical rehabilitation, and youth development. **NOTE:** Please visit website to search for jobs. **Positions advertised include:** Grant Accountant; Building Accountant. **Corporate headquarters location:** Alexandria VA. **Parent company:** United Way of America is the national service and training center, supporting its members with national services that include advertising, training, corporate relations, research, networks, and government relations.

UNIVERSAL SOLUTIONS INC.
2084-M Lake Industrial Court, Conyers GA 30013. 770/785-9710. **Contact:** Human Resources. **E-mail address:** recruiter@usiinc.net. **World Wide Web address:** http://www.usiinc.net. **Description:** A pharmaceutical company engaged in the disposal of outdated pills and medical products. **Positions advertised include:** Technical Specialist; Account Manager; Account Development Manager. **Corporate headquarters location:** Winston-Salem NC.

UNIVERSITY HEALTH CARE SYSTEM
UNIVERSITY HOSPITAL
1350 Walton Way, Augusta GA 30901-2629. 706/774-8982. **Toll-free phone:** 800/338-9599. **Fax:** 706/774-8782. **Recorded jobline:** 706/774-8933. **Contact:** Human Resources. **World Wide Web address:** http://www.universityhealth.org. **Description:** A nonprofit, comprehensive healthcare system. University Hospital (also at this location) is a full-service, 612-bed hospital. Founded in 1818. **NOTE:** Please visit website to search for jobs and apply online. Entry-level positions and second and third shifts are offered. Printed lists of open positions are available for pickup at the Human Resources lobby during office hours. **Special programs:** Internships. **Office hours:** Monday – Friday, 7:00 a.m. – 7:00 p.m. **Corporate headquarters location:** This location. **Operations at this facility include:** Administration; Service. **Listed on:** Privately held.

UNIVERSITY OF GEORGIA
215 South Jackson Street, Human Resources Building, Athens GA 30602-4135. 706/542-2623. **Fax:** 706/542-7321. **Contact:** Employment Department. **World Wide Web address:** http://www.uga.edu. **Description:** The University of Georgia offers a broad range of studies at the undergraduate, graduate, and doctoral levels. The university enrolls more than 30,000 students. **NOTE:** Please visit website to search for jobs and apply online. **Positions advertised include:** Accounting Assistant; Administrative Secretary; Cashier Clerk; Library Assistant; Senior Accounting Assistant; Senior Secretary; Cafeteria Manager; Chief Cook; Child Development Aide; Construction Foreman; Custodian; Equipment Operator; Food Service Worker; Housekeeper; Public Safety Officer; Security Guard; Skilled Trades Worker; Utility Worker; Computer Services Specialist; Management Information Specialist; Academic Advisor; Art Coordinator; Assistant Director of Housing; Assistant to the Dean; Program Coordinator; Laboratory Technician; Clinical Nurse; Medical Records Technician; Agricultural Specialist; Research Technician.

VCG INC.
1805 Old Alabama Road, Roswell GA 30076. 770/246-2300. **Toll-free phone:** 800/318-4983. **Fax:** 770/449-3638. **Contact:** Missy DuToit, Human Resources Manager. **E-mail address:** hr@vcgsoftware.com. **World Wide Web address:** http://www.vcgsoftware.com. **Description:** Distributes computer hardware and staffing software. Founded in 1976. **NOTE:** Please visit website to search for jobs. **Positions advertised include:** Data Migration Engineer; Regional Sales Manager; Application Support Representative; C++ Analyst; Quality Assurance Analyst; Web Design Developer. **Corporate headquarters location:** This location. **Operations at this facility include:** Accounting/Auditing; Customer Service; Marketing; Sales. **Annual sales/revenues:** $11 - $20 million.

VALDOSTA STATE UNIVERSITY
1500 North Patterson Street, Valdosta GA 31698. 229/333-5800. **Toll-free phone:** 800/618-1878. **Fax:** 229/259-5030. **Contact:** Amy Reed, Employment Manager. **World Wide Web address:** http://www.valdosta.edu. **Description:** A state university with 9,700 students enrolled. **NOTE:** Human Resources is located at 1205 North Patterson, Valdosta GA. Contact them at 229/333-5709. Please visit website to download an employment application, or pick one up at the Business and Finance offices at the University Center. **Positions advertised include:** Maintenance Worker; Trades Helper; Public Safety Officer; Nursing Supervisor; Library Assistant; Computer Service Specialist; House Director; Bus Operator.

VERIZON WIRELESS
One Verizon Place, Building 1, Alpharetta GA 30004. 678/339-4000. **Fax:** 678/339-8602. **Contact:** Personnel. **World Wide Web address:** http://www.verizon.com. **Description:** Verizon Communications is a full-service communications services provider. Verizon offers residential local and long distance telephone services and Internet access; wireless service plans, cellular phones, and data services; a full-line of business services including Internet access, data services, and telecommunications equipment and services; and government network solutions including Internet access, data services, telecommunications equipment and services, and enhanced communications services. **NOTE:** Please visit website to search for jobs and apply online. **Positions advertised include:** Inside Sales Representative. **Corporate headquarters location:** New York NY. **Listed on:** New York Stock Exchange. **Stock exchange symbol:** VZ. **CEO:** Ivan G. Seidenberg. **Number of employees worldwide:** 203,100.

VERSO TECHNOLOGIES
400 Galleria Parkway, Suite 300, Atlanta GA 30339. 678/589-3500. **Fax:** 678/589-3750. **Contact:** Julie Prye, Vice President of Human Resources. **E-mail address:** jobs@verso.com. **World Wide Web address:** http://www.verso.com. **Description:** Develops and installs wINNfinity and LANmark management systems. Founded 1984. **NOTE:** Please visit website to search for jobs. No phone calls regarding employment. **Positions advertised include:** Training and Installation Specialist; Bilingual Customer Care Agent; Customer Care Agent; Senior Software Engineer. **Corporate headquarters location:** This location. **Other U.S. locations:** Oakbrook Terrace IL. **Listed on:** NASDAQ. **Stock exchange symbol:** VRSO. **CEO:** Steve Odom. **Number of employees nationwide:** 450.

VIACOM OUTDOOR SYSTEMS ADVERTISING
3745 Atlanta Industrial Drive, Atlanta GA 30331. 404/699-1499. **Fax:** 404/505-7013. **Contact:** Human Resources. **World Wide Web address:** http://www.infoutdoor.com. **Description:** An advertising agency specializing in the design of billboards and posters. **Other U.S. locations:** Nationwide. **Parent company:** VIACOM. **CEO:** Wally Kelly.

VIDEO DISPLAY CORPORATION
1868 Tucker Industrial Road, Tucker GA 30084. 770/938-2080. **Toll-free phone:** 800/241-5005. **Fax:** 770/493-3903. **Contact:** Personnel. **E-mail address:** videodisplaycorp@aol.com. **World Wide Web address:** http://www.videodisplay.com. **Description:** One of the leading international manufacturers of new and recycled cathode ray tubes (CRTs) and component parts. Video Display Corporation is also one of the largest domestic distributors of consumer electronic parts and accessories. Founded in 1975. **Office hours:** Monday – Friday, 8:30 a.m. – 6:00 p.m. **Corporate headquarters location:** This location. **Subsidiaries include:** Aydin Displays; Chroma; Datagraphix; Infodex; Lexel Imaging Systems; Megascan, MII; Novatron; Precision; Southeast Vacuum Devices; ISY; Video Display Europe; VDC Display Systems; Wintron Technologies; XKD Corporation; Z-Axis; Data Display; Teltron. Fox International is one of the largest domestic distributors of warranty and nonwarranty consumer electronic parts and accessories.

VISITING NURSE HEALTH SYSTEM
1066 Bay Circle, Norcross GA 30071. 770/454-0900. **Toll-free phone:** 800/800-8647. **Recorded jobline:** 770/451-4044. **Contact:** Human Resources. **World Wide Web address:** http://www.vnhs.org. **Description:** A nonprofit home health care agency. Founded in 1940. **NOTE:** Second and third shifts are offered. Please mail resumes to 6610 Bay Circle Suite A Norcross GA 30071; fax to 770/936-1044. **Positions advertised include:** Health Information Specialist; Medical Collector; Medical Records Coordinator; Pharmacy Billing Clerk; Delivery Technician; Equipment Technician II; Occupational Therapist; Pharmacist; Pharmacy Operations Manager; Respiratory Therapist; Area Nursing Director; Evening Nursing Team Leader; Level II RN; LPN Floater; Weekend Admissions Nurse. **Special programs:** Internships. **Other area locations:** Buford GA.

VOUGHT AIRCRAFT INDUSTRIES
90 Highway 22 West, Milledgeville GA 31061-9699. 478/454-4200. **Contact:** Wendell Barr, Human Resources Director. **E-mail address:** vought_resume@voughtaircraft.com. **World Wide Web address:** http://www.voughtaircraft.com. **Description:** Develops, designs, and manufactures aerostructures. **NOTE:** Contact Human Resources directly at 478/454-4238. **Special programs:** Internships. **Corporate headquarters location:** Dallas TX. **Other U.S. locations:** Brea CA; Everett WA; Grand Prairie TX; Hawthorne CA; Nashville TN; Stuart FL. **Parent company:** The Carlyle Group. **Operations at this facility include:** Material fabrication; Assembly. **President/CEO:** Ronald D. Sugar. **Number of employees at this location:** 460. **Number of employees nationwide:** 6,000.

VULCAN MATERIALS COMPANY
2299 Perimeter Park Drive, Atlanta GA 30341. 770/458-4481. **Fax:** 770/454-7581. **Contact:** Director of Human Resources. **World Wide Web address:** http://www.vulcanmaterials.com. **Description:** Vulcan Materials Company has 22 plant locations throughout the Southeast. The company primarily produces crushed stone and aggregates. **Corporate headquarters location:** Birmingham AL. **Other**

area locations: Statewide. **Operations at this facility include:** This location houses administrative offices for the construction aggregates division. **Listed on:** New York Stock Exchange. **Stock exchange symbol:** VMC. **CEO:** Donald M. James. **Annual sales/revenues:** More than $100 million. **Number of employees nationwide:** 8,500.

WALB-TV
P.O. Box 3130, Albany GA 31706-3130. 229/446-1010. **Physical address:** 1709 Stuart Avenue, Albany GA 31706-3130. **Fax:** 229/446-4000. **Contact:** Human Resources. **World Wide Web address:** http://www.walb.com. **Description:** An NBC-affiliated television station. **NOTE:** Please visit website to download application form.

WTVM
P.O. Box 1848, Columbus GA 31902-1848. 706/324-6471. **Fax:** 706/322-7527. **Contact:** Jennifer Cameron, Human Resources. **E-mail address:** jennifercameron@wtvm.com. **World Wide Web address:** http://www.wtvm.com. **Description:** An ABC-affiliated television station. **NOTE:** Please visit website to search for jobs. **Positions advertised include:** Producer; New Director; Reporter/Photographer; National Sales Assistant.

WAFFLE HOUSE, INC.
P.O. Box 6450, Norcross GA 30091. 770/729-5700. **Physical address:** 5986 Financial Drive, Norcross GA 30071. **Fax:** 770/729-5834. **Contact:** Recruiting. **E-mail address:** info@wafflehouse.com. **World Wide Web address:** http://www.wafflehouse.com. **Description:** One of the largest 24-hour restaurant chains in the country, with more than 1,200 restaurants in 20 states. Founded in 1955. **NOTE:** Contact Recruiting at 770/729-5825. **Corporate headquarters location:** This location. **Listed on:** Privately held.

WALTON FABRICS, INC.
119 1st Street, Monroe GA 30655. 770/267-9411. **Contact:** Human Resources. **World Wide Web address:** http://www.avondalemills.com. **Description:** Manufactures woven textiles and other piece goods. **Parent company:** Avondale Mills, Inc. **Corporate headquarters location:** This location.

WATKINS ASSOCIATED INDUSTRIES
1958 Monroe Drive NE, Atlanta GA 30324. 404/872-3841. **Fax:** 404/872-2812. **Contact:** Human Resources. **Description:** Operates a variety of companies, including trucking company, real estate development, door and window manufacturing, and seafood processing. **Corporate headquarters location:** This location. **Other U.S. locations:** Nationwide. **International locations:** Canada; Mexico; Puerto Rico. **President/CEO:** Mike Watkins. **Number of employees nationwide:** 9,000.

WAYNE FARMS LLC
4110 Continental Drive, Oakwood GA 30566. 678/450-3100. **Toll-free phone:** 800/392-0844. **Contact:** Human Resources. **E-mail address:** jobs@waynedqh.com. **World Wide Web address:** http://www.waynefarmsllc.com. **Description:** Engaged in poultry processing. **Corporate headquarters location:** This location. **Other area locations:** Pendergrass GA; College Park GA; Douglas GA. **Other U.S. locations:** AL; NC; MS, LA; AR. **Parent company:** ContiGroup Companies.

WAYNE MEMORIAL HOSPITAL
P.O. Box 410, Jesup GA 31598. 912/427-6811. **Physical address:** 865 South First Street, Jesup GA 31545. **Fax:** 912/530-3106. **Contact:** Human Resources. **E-mail address:** sdaniel@wmhweb.com. **World Wide Web address:** http://www.wmhweb.com. **Description:** A short-term health care facility. **NOTE:** Please visit website to see listed jobs. Contact Human Resources at 912/530-3309. **Positions advertised include:** Nuclear Medical Technician; Medical Lab Technologist; Respiratory Therapist; Clinical Pharmacist; Physical Therapist; Physical Therapist Director.

THE WEATHER CHANNEL, INC.
300 Interstate North Parkway, Atlanta GA 30339. 770/226-0000. **Contact:** Human Resource Manager. **World Wide Web address:** http://www.weather.com. **Description:** A cable television network with 24-hour live weather service. Founded in 1982. **NOTE:** Please visit website to search for jobs and apply online. **Positions advertised include:** On Camera Meteorologist; Director/Master Control; Graphic Meteorologist; Marketing Research Coordinator; Account Manager; Technical Project Manager; Ad Master; Radio Broadcast Meteorologist; Directory of Financial Reporting, Planning and Analysis; Senior Project Manager; Vice President of Ad Products and Integrated Content; Web Metrics Analyst; Vice President of Desktop Applications; Database Administrator; Broadband Writer/Producer; Senior Writer/Producer. **Special programs:** Internships. **Parent company:** Landmark Communications, Inc. **Operations at this facility include:** Administration; Divisional Headquarters; Sales; Service. **Listed on:** Privately held.

WEATHERLY INC.
1100 Spring Street NW, Suite 800, Atlanta GA 30309. 404/873-5030. **Fax:** 404/873-1303. **Contact:** Ms. G.C. Bailey, Executive Assistant. **E-mail address:** info@weatherlyinc.com. **World Wide Web address:** http://www.chematur.se. **Description:** Designs, engineers, and constructs chemical process plants. **Corporate headquarters location:** This location. **Parent company:** Chematur Engineering. **Operations at this facility include:** Administration; Engineering and Design; Sales; Service.

WEB CONVERTING
2272 Park Central Boulevard, Decatur GA 30035. 770/593-2004. **Fax:** 770/593-1942. **Contact:** Human Resources. **World Wide Web address:** http://www.webconverting.com. **Description:** Web Converting is a custom contractor that works with various foils, plastics, and woven and nonwoven materials, changing them into different forms for use by other companies. **Corporate headquarters location:** Westborough MA. **Other U.S. locations:** Holliston MA; Indianapolis IN; Dallas TX; Phoenix AZ. **Operations at this facility include:** This location converts large rolls of plastic into smaller rolls. **Parent company:** Web Industries. **President:** Don Romine. **Number of employees nationwide:** 280.

WEGENER CORPORATION
11350 Technology Circle, Duluth GA 30097. 770/814-4000. **Fax:** 770/814-4061. **Contact:** Human Resources. **E-mail address:** careers@wegener.com. **World Wide Web address:** http://www.wegener.com. **Description:** Manufactures electronics including digital compression products for cable television operators, radio and television broadcasters, the music business industry, data communications, and private network systems. **Corporate headquarters location:** This location. **Listed on:** NASDAQ. **Stock exchange symbol:** WGNR. **President/CEO:** Robert A. Placek. **Number of employees nationwide:** 89.

WELDING SERVICES, INC.
2225 Skyland Court, Norcross GA 30071. 678/728-9100. **Fax:** 770/449-4684. **Contact:** Human Resources. **World Wide Web address:** http://www.weldingservices.com. **Description:** Provides repair welding at nationwide nuclear and fossil fuel power plants. **Corporate headquarters location:** This location. **International locations:** Venezuela; The Netherlands. **Operations at this facility include:** Administration; Manufacturing; Research and Development; Sales; Service.

WELLESLEY INN HOTEL
1377 Virginia Avenue, Atlanta GA 30344. 404/762-5111. **Contact:** Human Resources. **World Wide Web address:** http://www.wellesleyonline.com. **Description:** Operates a full-service hotel with complete lodging facilities.

WELLINGTON LEISURE PRODUCTS INC.
P.O. Box 244, Madison GA 30650. 706/342-1916. **Physical address:** 1140 Monticello Highway, Madison GA. **Fax:** 706/342-7911. **Contact:** Thomas Little, Director of Human Resources. **E-mail address:** jrdavis@wellingtoninc.com. **World Wide Web address:** http://www.wellingtoninc.com. **Description:** Manufactures cordage and twine that is used in water and outdoor sport equipment. **NOTE:** Please visit website to see listed positions. **Corporate headquarters location:** This location. **Number of employees nationwide:** 1,500.

WELLS FARGO FINANCIAL
975 Dawsonville Highway, Suite 18, Gainesville GA 30501. 770/536-5070. **Contact:** Human Resources. **World Wide Web address:** http://www.financial.wellsfargo.com. **Description:** Wells Fargo Financial offers real estate and automobile loans and financing solutions. They also provide credit cards to retailers through private labels and co-brands, and also directly to customers. Founded in 1897. **NOTE:** Please visit website to explore career opportunities. **Corporate headquarters location:** Des Moines IA. **Other U.S. locations:** Nationwide. **International locations:** Worldwide. **Parent company:** Wells Fargo. **Operations at this facility include:** This location provides loans to small businesses and individuals. **President:** Thomas P. Shippee. **Annual sales/revenues:** More than $100 million. **Number of employees worldwide:** 16,500.

WESLEY WOODS CENTER OF EMORY UNIVERSITY
1817 Clifton Road, Atlanta GA 30329. 404/728-6200. **Contact:** Employment Coordinator. **E-mail address:** careers@emoryhealthcare.org. **World Wide Web address:** http://www.emoryhealthcare.org/departments/WW/index.html. **Description:** A 100-bed geriatric hospital specializing in rehabilitation, psychiatry, and neurology. Wesley Woods is a residential facility providing intermediate health care. **NOTE:** Contact corporate Employment office at 404/712-4938. Please visit website to register, search for jobs, and apply online, **Positions advertised include:** Accounting Assistant; Clinical Nutritionist; Computer Tomography Technologist; Environmental Services Aide; Food Services Attendant; Infection Control Assistant; LPN; Nursing Technician; Occupational Therapist; Occupational Therapy Assistant; Physical Therapist; Receptionist; RN; Respiratory Therapist; Speech Pathologist; Supervisor – Nursing Administration. **Special programs:** Internships. **Parent company:** Emory Heathcare. **Number of employees at this location:** 868.

WEST INFORMATION CENTER
245 Peachtree Center Avenue, Suite 1000, Atlanta GA 30303. 404/881-0454. **Toll-free phone:** 800/336-5768. **Fax:** 404/881-0873. **Contact:** Human Resources. **World Wide Web address:** http://www.westlaw.com. **Description:** An online information company that provides access to public and court records for clients such as lawyers, bankers, investigators, and those involved with commercial transactions and business litigation. **Parent company:** Thompson West.

WEST WAYNE
1170 Peachtree Street, Suite 1500, Atlanta GA 30309. 404/347-8700. **Fax:** 404/347-8800. **Contact:** Cristi Axon, Director of Human Resources. **E-mail address:** wwijobs@westwayne.com. **World Wide Web address:** http://www.westwayne.com. **Description:** An advertising agency. **NOTE:** Human Resources phone is 404/347-8754; fax is 404/347-8919. Please visit website to search for jobs and apply online. **Positions advertised include:** Administrative Assistant; Senior Broadcast Traffic Manager; Part-time Technology Assistant. **Corporate headquarters location:** This location. **Other U.S. locations:** Tampa FL. **President/CEO:** Jeff Johnson.

WEYERHAEUSER COMPANY
P.O. Box 238, Oglethorpe GA 31068-0238. 478/472-2527. **Physical address:** Old Stagecoach Road, Oglethorpe GA. **Fax:** 478/472-5508. **Contact:** Human Resources. **World Wide Web address:** http://www.weyerhaeuser.com. **Description:** Weyerhaeuser Company's principal businesses include the growing and harvesting of timber; the manufacture, distribution, and sale of forest products including logs, wood chips, and building products; real estate development and construction; and financial services. Weyerhaeuser Company is one of the world's largest private owners of marketable softwood timber and also one of the largest producers of softwood lumber and pulp. The company is one of North America's largest producers of forest products and recyclers of office wastepaper, newspaper, and corrugated boxes. Weyerhaeuser Company sells electricity to utility companies generated from its 15 trash-to-energy plants and 6 small cogeneration plants. The Water Division manufactures and operates facilities and systems for water purification, water treatment, and managed by-products. The Air Division designs, manufactures, and integrates air pollution emission control and measurement systems and related equipment. **Corporate headquarters location:** Federal Way WA. **Other area locations:** Statewide. **Other U.S. locations:** Nationwide. **International locations:** Worldwide. **Operations at this facility include:** This location manufactures paper. **Listed on:** New York Stock Exchange. **Stock exchange symbol:** WY. **Number of employees worldwide:** 57,000.

WEYERHAEUSER COMPANY
5099 North Royal Atlanta Drive, Atlanta GA 30084-3034. 770/938-4077. **Contact:** Human Resources. **World Wide Web address:** http://www.weyerhaeuser.com. **Description:** Weyerhaeuser Company's principal businesses are the growing and harvesting of timber; the manufacture, distribution, and sale of forest products including logs, wood chips, and building products; real estate development and construction; and financial services. Weyerhaeuser Company is one of the world's largest private owners of marketable softwood timber and also one of the largest producers of softwood lumber and pulp. The company is one of North America's largest producers of forest products and recyclers of office wastepaper, newspaper, and corrugated boxes. Weyerhaeuser Company sells electricity to utility companies generated from its 15 trash-to-energy plants and 6 small cogeneration or recycling plants. The Water Division manufactures and operates facilities and systems for water purification, water treatment, and managed by-products. The Air Division designs, manufactures, and integrates air pollution emission control and measurement systems and related equipment. **Corporate headquarters location:** Federal Way WA. **Other area locations:** Statewide. **Other U.S. locations:** Nationwide. **International locations:** Worldwide. **Operations at this facility include:** This location is a packing facility. **Listed on:** New York Stock Exchange. **Stock exchange symbol:** WY. **Number of employees worldwide:** 57,000.

WEYERHAEUSER COMPANY
P.O. Box 8787, Columbus GA 31908-8787. 706/568-0050. **Physical address:** 4847 Cargo Drive, Columbus GA 31907-1905. **Contact:** Human Resources. **World Wide Web address:** http://www.weyerhaeuser.com. **Description:** Weyerhaeuser Company's principal businesses include the growing and harvesting of timber; the manufacture, distribution, and sale of forest products including logs, wood chips, and building products; real estate development and construction; and financial services. Weyerhaeuser Company is one of the world's largest private owners of marketable softwood timber and also one of the largest producers of softwood lumber and pulp. The company is one of North America's largest producers of forest products and recyclers of office wastepaper, newspaper, and corrugated boxes. Weyerhaeuser Company sells electricity generated from its 15 trash-to-energy plants and 6 small cogeneration plants to utility companies. The Water Division manufactures and operates facilities and systems for water purification, water treatment, and managed by-products. The Air Division designs, manufactures, and integrates air pollution emission control and measurement systems and related equipment. **Corporate headquarters location:** Federal Way WA. **Other area locations:** Statewide. **Other U.S. locations:** Nationwide. **International locations:** Worldwide. **Operations at this facility include:** This location is a packing facility. **Listed on:** New York Stock Exchange. **Stock exchange symbol:** WY. **Number of employees worldwide:** 57,000.

WEYERHAEUSER
One Bonnybridge Road, Port Wentworth GA 31407. 912/964-1271. **Contact:** Human Resources. **World Wide Web address:** http://www.weyerhaeuser.com. **Description:** Weyerhaeuser Company's principal businesses include the growing and harvesting of timber; the manufacture, distribution, and sale of forest products including logs, wood chips, and building products; real estate development and construction; and financial services. Weyerhaeuser Company is one of the world's largest private owners of marketable softwood timber and also one of the largest producers of softwood lumber and pulp. The company is one of North America's largest producers of forest products and recyclers of office wastepaper, newspaper, and corrugated boxes. Weyerhaeuser Company sells electricity generated from its 15 trash-to-energy plants and 6 small cogeneration plants to utility companies. The Water Division manufactures and operates facilities and systems for water purification, water treatment, and managed by-products. The Air Division designs, manufactures, and integrates air pollution emission control and measurement systems and related equipment. **Corporate headquarters location:** Federal Way WA. **Other area locations:** Statewide. **Other U.S. locations:** Nationwide. **International locations:** Worldwide. **Listed on:** New York Stock Exchange. **Stock exchange symbol:** WY. **CEO:** Steven R. Rogel. **Number of employees nationwide:** 57,000.

WHITE PROPERTY ACQUISITIONS
4485 Pench Road, Suite 510, Suwanee GA 30024. 770/452-8778. **Fax:** 770/613-0501. **Contact:** Human Resources. **Description:** A general contracting company that specializes in fire damage repairs. Founded in 1960. **NOTE:** Entry-level positions are offered. **Corporate headquarters location:** This location. **Listed on:** Privately held. **Annual sales/revenues:** Less than $5 million.

RALPH WHITEHEAD ASSOCIATES
3505 Koger Boulevard, Suite 205, Duluth GA 30096. 770/452-0797. **Fax:** 770/936-9171. **Contact:** Human Resources. **E-mail address:** atl@rwhitehead.com. **World Wide Web address:** http://www.rwhitehead.com. Founded 1961. **Description:** A civil engineering consulting firm. **NOTE:** Please visit website to search for jobs. **Positions advertised include:** Project Manager/Senior Engineer; Highway/Roadway Engineer; Stormwater Services Engineer; Geotechnical Engineer; Project Engineer; Designer; Project Design Engineer – Railway; Project Design/Engineer – Transportation; Engineering Technician – Construction Service. **Corporate headquarters location:** Charlotte NC. **Other U.S. locations:** Overland Park KS; Jacksonville FL; Charleston SC; Rock Hill SC; Raleigh NC; Richmond VA. **Number of employees nationwide:** 120.

JOHN WIELAND HOMES, INC.
P.O. Box 87363, Atlanta GA 30337. 770/996-6065. 1400. **Fax:** 770/907-3485. **Contact:** Human Resources. **E-mail address:** hr@jwhomes.com. **World Wide Web address:** http://www.jwhomes.com. **Description:** A real estate developer and construction company specializing in single-family homes. **NOTE:** Please visit website to search for jobs and apply online. **Positions advertised include:** Project Sales Consultant; Pricing Project Coordinator; Loan Officer Part-time Human Resources Assistant; Superintendent; Architectural Product Leader; Estimating Coordinator; Design Consultant; Accounting Coordinator; Licensed Sales Assistant; Architect; Crew Member; Director of Risk Management; Receptionist; Manager of Administration; Corporate Office Manager; Structural Engineer; Boxtruck Driver; Assembler – Windows; Piggyback Driver; Flatbed Driver. **Corporate headquarters location:** This location. **Other U.S. locations:** Mount Pleasant SC; Franklin TN; Morrisville NC; Charlotte NC.

WIGHT NURSERY
P.O. Box 390, Cairo GA 31728. 229/377-3033. **Physical address:** 1579 Highway 111 South, Cairo GA. **Toll-free phone:** 800/342-6012. **Fax:** 229/377-9394. **Contact:** Human Resources. **E-mail address:** hrcairo@monrovia.com. **World Wide Web address:** http://www.monrovia.com. **Description:** A wholesaler of shrubberies. **NOTE:** Please visit website to see jobs listings. **Corporate headquarters location:** Azusa CA. **Other U.S. locations:** Visalia CA; Dayton OR; Springfield OH; La Grange NC. **Parent company:** Monrovia.

WILEN PROFESSIONAL CLEANING PRODUCTS, INC.
3760 Southside Industrial Parkway, Atlanta GA 30354. 404/366-2111. **Toll-free phone:** 800/325-1051. **Fax:** 404/361-8832. **Toll-free fax:** 800/327-5492. **Contact:** Personnel Director. **E-mail address:** kmills@wilen.com. **World Wide Web address:** http://www.wilen.com. **Description:** Manufactures industrial cleaning tools, such as dust mops, wet mops, brooms, and brushes. Founded 1938. **Parent company:** Katy Industries.

WILLIAMS PRINTING CO.
1240 Spring Street NW, Atlanta GA 30309. 404/875-6611. **Fax:** 404/872-4025. **Contact:** Employment. **E-mail address:** williams@wpcatlanta.com. **World Wide Web address:** http://www.wpcatlanta.com. **Description:** A full-service graphic communications company offering services including corporate, commercial, and financial printing; and direct response, reprographic, and educational printing services. **NOTE:** Please visit website to search for jobs and apply online. **Operations at this facility include:** This location manufactures corrugated boxes.

WILLIAMS TILE AND MARBLE CO.
1870 South Cobb Industrial Boulevard, Smyrna GA 30082. 770/432-2201. **Fax:** 770/438-7466. **Contact:** Employment. **E-mail address:** wtile@bellsouth.net. **World Wide Web address:** http://www.williamstileandmarble.com. **Description:** A subcontractor for such products as ceramic tile, terrazzo, marble, and granite.

WINCUP
4640 Lewis Road, Stone Mountain GA 30083. 770/938-5281. **Contact:** Human Resources. **World Wide Web address:** http://www.wincup.com. **Description:** Produces polystyrene foam cups, containers, lids, and glasses. **Office hours:** Monday – Friday, 8:00 a.m. – 5:00 p.m. **Corporate headquarters location:** Phoenix AZ. **Other U.S. locations:** TX; FL; CA; LA; IL; OH; NJ. **International locations:** Finland; Germany; Poland; Scandinavia; Ireland; Russia.

WINDSOR GROUP
P.O. Box 105091, Atlanta GA 30348-5091. 678/627-8000. **Physical address:** 11700 Great Oaks Way, Alpharetta GA 30022. **Toll-free phone:** 800/852-8208. **Contact:** Human Resources. **World Wide Web address:** http://www. windsorgroup.com. **Description:** Provides automobile insurance. **Corporate headquarters location:** This location. **Other U.S. locations:** Nationwide. **Number of employees nationwide:** 15,000.

WINTER CONSTRUCTION COMPANY
1330 Spring Street NW, Atlanta GA 30309. 404/588-3300. **Fax:** 404/223-5753. **Contact:** Personnel. **World Wide Web address:** http://www.wintercompanies.com. **Description:** A general contracting and construction company that specializes in commercial construction. **NOTE:** Please visit website to search for jobs and apply online. **Positions advertised include:** Assistant Project Manager; Contract Administrator; Environmental Project Engineer; Estimator; Project Manager; Project Superintendent; Senior Estimator; Senior Project Manager; Superintendent – Institutional; Superintendent – Environmental Services. **Special programs:** Internships. **Corporate headquarters location:** This location. **Parent company:** The Winter Companies (also at this location). **Operations at this facility include:** Administration; Research and Development; Sales; Service. **President/CEO:** Brent Reid.

ROGER WOOD FOODS INC.
P.O. Box 2926, Savannah GA 31402. 912/964-6335. **Physical address:** 7 Alfred Street, Savannah GA 31408. **Toll-free phone:** 800/849-9272. **Fax:** 912/964-6367. **Contact:** Human Resources. **World Wide Web address:** http://www.rogerwoodfoods.com. **Description:** A meat processing plant producing hot dogs and a variety of smoked meats. **Corporate headquarters location:** This location.

WS PACKAGING GROUP
100 Clover Green, Peachtree City GA 30269. 770/487-7575. **Toll-free phone:** 800/232-7833. **Toll-free fax:** 800/288-4949. **Contact:** Human Resources. **World Wide Web address:** http://www.wspackaging.com. **Description:** A manufacturer of pressure-sensitive label and tag printing. **NOTE:** Please visit website to search for jobs. **Corporate headquarters location:** Algoma WI. **Other U.S. locations:** AZ; CA; NV; NH; OR; OK; OH; TX. **Operations at this facility include:** Administration; Manufacturing; Research and Development; Sales; Service.

XEROX CONNECT, INC.
100 North Point Center East, Suite 500, Alpharetta GA 30022. 770/751-0199. **Fax:** 770/751-0273. **Contact:** Human Resources. **World Wide Web address:** http://www.xeroxconnect.com. **Description:** Offers systems integration services. The company operates in three service groups: Consulting and Design Services, Systems Integration, and Operations and Support Services. **Corporate headquarters location:** Stamford CT. **International locations:** Worldwide. **Parent company:** Xerox Corporation.

YKK USA INC.
1300 Cobb Industrial Drive, Marietta GA 30066. 770/427-5521. **Fax:** 770/421-8150. **Contact:** Human Resources. **World Wide Web address:** http://www.ykkamerica.com. **Description:** Develops and manufactures a variety of slide fasteners, primarily zippers. YKK USA also manufactures other closure devices used in the manufacture of luggage. **NOTE:** To inquire about employment opportunities, please contact the Georgia Department of Labor. **Corporate headquarters location:** This locations. **Other area locations:** Macon GA. **Other U.S. locations:** Nationwide. **Parent company:** YKK. **Operations at this facility include:** Administration; Divisional Headquarters; Manufacturing; Research and Development. **Number of employees nationwide:** 3,500.

YMCA OF METRO ATLANTA
100 Edgewood Avenue NE, Suite 1100, Atlanta GA 30303. 404/588-9622. **Contact:** Human Resources. **E-mail address:** comments@ymcaatl.org. **World Wide Web address:** http://www.ymcaatlanta.org. **Description:** One of the nation's largest and most comprehensive service organizations. The YMCA provides health and fitness; social and personal development; sports and recreation; education and career development; and camps and conferences to children, youths, adults, the elderly, families, the disabled, refugees and foreign nationals, YMCA residents, and community residents, through a broad range of specific programs. **NOTE:** Volunteer positions are also available. **Other U.S. locations:** Nationwide.

YWCA OF BRUNSWICK
144 Scranton Connector, Brunswick GA 31525-0514. 912/265-4100. **Fax:** 912/265-8059. **Contact:** Katie O'Shea, Human Resources Director. **World Wide Web address:** http://www.ywcabrunswickga. **Description:** An organization that represents more than 25 million women worldwide. YWCA is committed to empowering women to overcome racism and injustice. YWCA provides shelter to women and children who are homeless or have been victims of domestic violence. Day care services include training programs for baby sitters and other child care providers. YWCA also offers employment training including GED and ESL courses, Welfare-to-Work programs, and career counseling workshops. The organization is a member of the YWCA/Nike Sports Program and the United States Olympic Committee. **NOTE:** Please visit website to see job listings, and to download application form. **Positions advertised include:** Executive Director; After School Activity Leader; Facilities Assistant; Lifeguard; Child Care Associate Teacher; After School Site Coordinator; Swim Instructor; Membership Services Assistant. **Corporate headquarters location:** New York NY. **Other area locations:** Macon GA; Marietta GA; Atlanta GA.

YAMAHA MOTOR MANUFACTURING CORPORATION
1000 Georgia Highway 34 East, Newnan GA 30265. 770/254-4000. **Contact:** Human Resource Manager. **World Wide Web address:** http://www.yamaha-motor.com. **Description:** A wholesale distributor of motorized products including motorcycles, ATV's, snowmobiles, golf carts, outboards, and power products. **NOTE:** Please visit website to search for jobs, and for more specific details on applying for positions. **Positions advertised include:** Leasing Specialist; Regional Technical Advisor; District Service Representative; Marine Sales/Technical Support Coordinator; Regional Service Representative; Business Analyst; Buyer; District Manager Inside Sales. **Corporate headquarters location:** Cypress CA. **Other area locations:** Kennesaw GA. **Operations at this facility include:** This location manufactures ATVs, Golf Cars, and Water Vehicles, in addition to housing the Yamaha Golf-Car Company.

YELLOW TRANSPORTATION
1892 Airport Industrial Park Drive SE, Marietta GA 30060. 770/952-9341. **Contact:** Human Resources Department. **World Wide Web address:** http://www.myyellow.com. **Description:** Yellow Freight Systems, Inc. is a national long-haul truckload carrier, with over 400 terminal locations. **NOTE:** Please visit website to search for jobs. **Corporate headquarters location:** Overland Park KS. **Operations at this facility include:** This location operates one of the company's 17 nationwide hub stations.

YOKOGAWA CORPORATION OF AMERICA
2 Dart Road, Newnan GA 30265. 770/253-7000. **Fax:** 770/253-8174. **Contact:** Human Resources. **E-mail address:** employment@us.yokogawa.com. **World Wide Web address:** http://us.yokogawa.com. **Description:** Engaged in the manufacture, sale, and service of metering instrumentation. **Positions advertised include:** Area Sales Manager; Field Construction Lead Technician; Market Development Sales Engineer; Field Systems Service Specialist; Project Engineer; CAD Designer; Project Coordinator; Application Engineer; Technical Support Engineer; Design Technician. **Corporate headquarters location:** This location. **Other U.S. locations:** Germantown MD; Stafford TX; Coldspring TX. **International locations:** Worldwide. **Parent company:** Yokogawa Electric Corporation.

ZEP MANUFACTURING COMPANY
P.O. Box 2015, Atlanta GA 30301. 404/352-1680. **Physical address:** 4401 Riverside Parkway, Atlanta GA 30327. **Toll-free phone:** 877/428-9937. **Fax:** 404/630-7764. **Contact:** Human Resources. **World Wide Web address:** http://www.zepmfg.com. **Description:** Manufactures and distributes industrial cleaning products. Founded 1937. **NOTE:** Entry-level positions are offered. **Positions advertised include:** Sales Representative. **Corporate headquarters location:** This location. **Other U.S. locations:** Nationwide. **Parent company:** Acuity Brands. **Listed on:** New York Stock Exchange. **Stock exchange symbol:** AYI.

ABB ALSTOM POWER
91-111 Kalaeloa Boulevard, Barbers Point HI 96862. 808/682-5344. **Contact:** Human Resources. **World Wide Web address:** http://www.power.alstom.com. **Description:** Alstom produces a large variety of power generating systems, equipment and also services products in the electrical generation industry. **Company slogan:** The full service provider, in power generation. **Positions advertised include:** Communication Specialist; Engineer; Finance Associate; General Service Associate; Human Resource Associate; Information Technology Associate; Legal Associate; Maintenance Worker; Quality Associate; Sales & Marketing Associates; & Strategy Associate. **Other U.S. locations:** Nationwide. **International locations:** Worldwide. **Number of employees worldwide:** 45,000.

AES HAWAII, INC.
91-086 Kaomi Loop, Kapolei HI 96862. 808/682-5330. **Fax:** 808/682-4915. **Contact:** Human Resources. **World Wide Web address:** http://www.aesc.com. **Description:** A cogeneration plant. **Corporate headquarters location:** Arlington VA. **Parent company:** A developer, owner, and operator of independent electric power generating facilities. The company owns or has an interest in 112 plants, totaling over 43,000 megawatts in 17 countries. Founded in 1981. **Office Hours:** Monday- Friday, 7:00 a.m. - 5:00 p.m. **Operations at this facility include:** Administration; Service. **Listed on:** New York Stock Exchange. **Stock exchange symbol:** AES. **Annual sales/revenues:** More than $100 million. **Number of employees at this location:** 60. **Number of employees worldwide:** 54,000.

ALEXANDER & BALDWIN, INC.
P.O. Box 3440, Honolulu HI 96801-3440. 808/525-6611. **Physical address:** 822 Bishop Street, Honolulu HI 96813-3924. **Contact:** John Gasher, Vice President of Human Resources. **World Wide Web address:** http://www.alexanderbaldwin.com. **Description:** Involved in ocean transportation, property development and management, trucking and storage, and sugar production and refinement. Founded in 1870. **Office hours:** Monday – Friday, 8:00 a.m. – 4:30 p.m. **Corporate headquarters location:** This location. **Other U.S. locations:** Crokett CA; San Francisco CA; Kauai HI; Maui HI. **Subsidiaries include:** Matson Navigation Company offers a shuttle service across the Pacific serving ports in the continental United States and Canada, the Marshall Islands, and Johnston Island; Matson Terminals; Matson Services; Matson Leasing is one of the world's largest leasing companies involved in marine containers with 145,000 units; Matson Intermodal System; Hawaiian Commercial & Sugar; McBryde Sugar; A&B Hawaii; Kahului Trucking & Storage; East Maui Irrigation Company; Kauai Coffee Company; Kauai Commercial Company; California & Hawaiian Sugar Company (C&H). **Listed on:** NASDAQ. **Stock exchange symbol:** ALEX.

BAE SYSTEMS NORTH AMERICA
1942 Gaffney Street, Suite 500, Pearl Harbor HI 96860. 808/473-2849. **Contact:** Human Resources. **World Wide Web address:** http://www.na.baesystems.com. **Description:** The Technology Solutions Sector of BAE Systems North America provides systems engineering, technical services, and ordnance systems. Its full life-cycle systems capabilities include system design, integration and test; software development, engineering, and maintenance; and integrated logistics support. **NOTE:** Search and apply for positions online. **Positions advertised include:** Operations Site Support Engineer; Computer Operator; Data Entry Operator; Associate Computer Operator; Associate Systems Administrator. **Operations at this facility include:** Naval Submarine Support Command.

BANK OF HAWAII
P.O. Box 2900, Honolulu HI 96846-2900. 808/537-8844. **Contact:** Human Resources. **World Wide Web address:** http://www.boh.com. **Description:** A bank holding company that provides a variety of financial services. **NOTE:** Above address is the human resources address, not the address for a branch location. **Company Slogan:** Where people make quality happen. **Positions advertised include:** Administrative Assistant; Consumer Lending Associate; Sales Manager; Mortgage Banker; Banking Officer; Service Representative. **Other Area Locations:** Island of Hawaii; Island of Kaui; Island of Lanai; Island of Maui; Island of Molokai; Island of Oahu. **International locations:** American Somoa; Saipan, Marianas Islands; Guam; Palau. **Listed on:** New York Stock Exchange. **Stock exchange symbol:** BOH.

BARNWELL INDUSTRIES, INC.
1100 Alakea Street, Suite 2900, Honolulu HI 96813. 808/531-8400. **Fax:** 808/531-7181. **Contact:** Human Resources. **World Wide Web address:** http://www.brninc.com. **Description:** Engaged in the business of exploring for, developing, producing, and selling oil and natural gas in Canada and the United States; investing in leasehold land in Hawaii; and drilling and maintaining water systems in the state of Hawaii. **Office Hours:** Monday – Friday, 7:30 a.m. – 5:30 p.m. **Corporate headquarters location:** This location. **Other area locations:** Kamuela HI. **Other U.S. locations:** New York NY. **International locations:** Calgary, Alberta, Canada. **Subsidiaries include:** Barnwell of Canada; Kaupulehu Developments; Water Resources International, Inc. **Listed on:** American Stock Exchange. **Stock exchange symbol:** BRN.

BOEING LTS
535 Lipoa Parkway, Suite 200, Kihei HI 96753. 808/875-4500. **Contact:** Cathy Oleson, Human Resources. **Toll-free phone:** 800/254-1591. **World Wide Web address:** http://www.boeing.com. **Email address:** employmentoperations@boeing.com. **Description:** Operates a U.S. Air Force Observatory that provides the government with parts and services for bombers, as well as power systems for the space station, and is a major contractor for the Space Shuttle Orbiter program. **NOTE:** Boeing accepts applications and resumes online only. Faxed resumes will not be accepted. Please visit their Website for further information (http://www.boeing.com/ employment). **Company Slogan:** You'll be making tomorrow better. **Positions advertised include:** Delivery Systems Generalist. **Office Hours:** Monday – Friday 7:00 a.m. – 4:00p.m. **Corporate headquarters location:** Chicago IL. **Other U.S. locations:** Nationwide. **Operations at this facility include:** Administration; Research and Development; Service. **Listed on:** New York Stock Exchange. **Stock exchange symbol:** BA. **Number of employees at this location:** 100.

CPB INC.
CENTRAL PACIFIC BANK
P.O. Box 3590, Honolulu HI 96811-3590. 808/544-0500. **Physical address:** 220 South King Street, Honolulu HI 96813. **Contact:** Lyris Kaneshiro, Human Resources Staffing Officer. **E-mail address:** info@centralpacificbank.com. **World Wide Web address:** http://www.cpbi.com. **Description:** A bank holding company whose subsidiary, Central Pacific Bank, is a full-service commercial bank with 26 banking offices located throughout the state of Hawaii. Central Pacific Bank is also a member of the Federal Home Loan Bank of Seattle. **Office hours:** Monday – Friday, 8:30 a.m. – 3:00 p.m. **Special programs:** Internships. **Corporate headquarters location:** This location. **Operations at this facility include:** This location houses administrative offices as well as a bank. **Listed on:** New York Stock Exchange. **Stock exchange symbol:** CPF. **Number of employees at this location:** 500.

CADES SCHUTTE FLEMING & WRIGHT
1000 Bishop Street, Suite 1200, Honolulu HI 96813. 808/544-3893. **Fax:** 808/521-9210. **Contact:** Grace Nihei Kido, Human Resources. **E-mail address:** gkido@cades.com. **World Wide Web address:** http://www.cades.com. **Description:** A law firm that specializes in corporate, probate, real estate, and taxation law. Founded in 1922. **Special programs:** Summer Associate Program. **Corporate headquarters location:** This location. **Other area locations:** Kailua-Kona HI.

CARLSMITH BALL LLP
P.O. Box 656, Honolulu HI 96813. 808/523-2500. **Fax:** 808/523-0842. **Physical address:** 1001 Bishop Street, Pacific Tower, Suite 2200, Honolulu HI 96813. **Contact:** Carlsmith Ball LLP, Recruiting Coordinator. **E-mail address:** execdirector@carlsmith.com. **World Wide Web address:** http://www.carlsmith.com. **Description:** A law firm that specializes in corporate, finance, and taxation law. **Office hours:** Monday – Friday, 7:30 a.m. – 5:00 p.m. **Special programs:** Summer Associate Program. **Other area locations:** Hilo HI; Kapolei HI; Kona HI; Maui HI. **Other U.S. locations:** Los Angeles CA; Washington DC. **International locations:** Guam; Saipan.

CASTLE MEDICAL CENTER
640 Ulukahiki Street, Kailua HI 96734-4498. 808/263-5500. **Fax:** 808/266-3617. **Recorded jobline:** 808/263-5151. **Contact:** Human Resources. **E-mail address:** meyerka@castlep.ah.org. **World Wide Web address:** http://www.castlemed.com. **Description:** A full-service, acute care hospital offering both inpatient care and outpatient programs. The 160-bed facility offers a full spectrum of services, ranging from preventative health programs and maternity care to emergency medicine and critical care. Castle Medical Center is staffed by more than 800 employees, 250 volunteers, and nearly 300 physicians representing a broad range of specialties and subspecialties. **Positions advertised include:** Nursing; Certified Nurses Aids; Registered Staff Nurses; Surgical Unit; Telemetry; Data Entry; Pharmacy Technician 1; Laboratory aid; Pharmacy Technician II. **Special programs:** Volunteer Opportunities available. Call 808/263-5252, or E-mail kongfk@ah.org. **Parent company:** Adventist Health System/West.

CHAMINADE UNIVERSITY
3140 Waialae Avenue, Honolulu HI 96816. 808/735-4730. **Toll-free phone:** 800/735-3733. **Contact:** Personnel Director. **E-mail address:** hr@chaminade.edu. **World Wide Web address:** http://www.chaminade.edu. **Office Hours:** Monday – Friday, 7:30 a.m. – 4:30 p.m. **Description:** A Catholic, Marianist university offering 25 undergraduate degrees and 6 graduate degree programs. Undergraduate majors include biology, business, communications, criminal justice, education, history, international studies, and interior design. Graduate programs include the master of science in counseling psychology, master of science in criminal science, master of Japanese business studies, master of science in teaching, master of public administration, and master of business administration. The university has approximately 800 undergraduates, 1,400 part-time undergraduates in its evening program, and 300 graduate students. Chaminade's special programs and services include an accredited early childhood education program, education courses in the evening, and an interior design program. **Positions advertised include:** Assistant Professor of education; Off Campus Program Coordinator; Records Specialist; Assistant Employee training; Lecturer's. **Company Slogan:** Inspiring Success. **Office hours:** Monday – Friday, 7:30 a.m. – 4:30 p.m.

CHEVRONTEXACO CORPORATION
91-480 Mala Kole Street, Kapolei HI 96707. 808/682-2209. **Contact:** Mary Beth Kelly, Personnel Manager. **E-mail address:** ktakekawa@chevrontexaco.com. **World Wide Web address:** http://www.chevrontexaco.com. **Description:** An international oil firm with operations in more than 90 countries. Chevron is engaged in worldwide integrated petroleum operations including the exploration and production of crude oil and natural gas reserves; the transportation of crude oil, natural gas, and petroleum products by pipeline, tanker, and motor equipment; the operation of oil-refining complexes; and the wholesale and retail marketing of hundreds of petroleum products. **Corporate headquarters location:** San Francisco CA. **Operations at this facility include:** Regional Headquarters. **Listed on:** New York Stock Exchange. **Stock exchange symbol:** CVX. **Number of employees at this location:** 80.

CHILD AND FAMILY SERVICES
91-1841 Fort Weaver Road, Ewa Beach HI 96706. 808/681-3500. **Fax:** 808/681-1486. **Recorded jobline:** 808/543-8483. **Contact:** Human Resources. **E-mail address:** cfsjobs-web@cfs-hawaii.org. **World Wide Web address:** http://www.cfs-hawaii.org. **Description:** A private human services organization. Works to strengthen families and assist the proper development of children. **Note:** Positions are available by level of education. **Positions advertised include:** Social Worker, Clinical Director; Program Services Director; Group Facility Associate; Mental Health Worker; Social Worker, Accounting Manager; Budget Manager; Case Manager; Child Development Specialist; Crisis Outreach Specialist; Information Technology; Teacher; Substitute Teacher; Residential Coordinator; Systems Analyst Associate; Case Manager- part time. **Corporate headquarters location:** This location. **Other area locations:** Maui HI; Kauai HI; Big Island HI; Molokai HI; Lanai HI.

CITY BANK
P.O. Box 3709, Honolulu HI 96813. 808/535-2500. **Physical address:** 201 Merchant Street, Honolulu HI 96813. **Fax:** 808/535-2876. **Recorded jobline:** 808/535-2885. **Contact:** Human Resources Manager. **E-mail address:** humanresources@cb-hi.net. **World Wide Web address:** http://www.citybankhawaii.com. **Description:** A full-service bank. The bank's general services include checking accounts such as regular personal and business checking accounts; personal and business interest-bearing accounts; and savings accounts such as personal and business statement savings accounts, personal and business certificates of deposits, Christmas savings accounts, and individual retirement accounts. City Bank is also part of a worldwide network of ATMs. The bank's business services include money market accounts, a wide variety of loans, international business services, business credit cards, merchant credit card services, direct payroll deposit, bank by mail, safe deposit boxes, cashier's checks and money orders, and utility payments. **Positions advertised include:** Accounting Clerk; Administrative Support; Credit Clerk, part time; Customer Sales Service Representative; Loan Processor; Loan Specialist; Bank Teller. **Office Hours:** Monday – Friday, 9:00 a.m. – 3:00 p.m. **Corporate headquarters location:** This location. **Parent company:** CB Bancshares, Inc. **Listed on:** NASDAQ. **Stock exchange symbol:** CBBI.

CHILI'S GRILL AND BAR
2350 Kuhio, Honolulu HI 96815. 808/922-9697. **Fax:** 808/922-9698. **Contact:** Human Resources. **World Wide Web address:** http://www.chilis.com. **Description:** A worldwide franchised restaurant chain. Founded in 1975. **Company Slogan:** Like No Place Else. **Positions advertised include:** Manager; Server. **Corporate headquarters location:** Dallas TX. **Other area locations:** Kapolei HI; Mililani HI; Aiea HI; Waipahu HI. **Other U.S. locations:** Nationwide. **International locations:** Worldwide. **Parent company:** Brinker, International. **Listed on:** New York Stock Exchange. **Stock

exchange symbol: EAT. **CEO:** Ronald A. McDougall. **President:** Douglas H. Brooks.

COCA-COLA BOTTLING COMPANY OF HAWAII
949 Mapunapuna Street, Honolulu HI 96819. 808/839-6719. **Contact:** Joy Takanishi, Area Human Resources Manager. **World Wide Web address:** http://www.cocacola.com. **Description:** A bottling company for Coca-Cola, Barq's, and Dr. Pepper soft drinks. **Parent company:** Coca-Cola Company is one of the world's largest marketers, distributors, and producers of bottle and can products. Coca-Cola Enterprises, part of the Coca-Cola Company, is in the liquid nonalcoholic refreshment business, which includes traditional carbonated soft drinks, still and sparkling waters, juices, isotonics, and teas. The company operates in 38 states, the District of Columbia, the U.S. Virgin Islands, the Islands of Tortola and Grand Cayman, and the Netherlands. Including recent acquisitions, Coca-Cola Enterprises' franchise territories encompass a population of over 154 million people. Coca-Cola Enterprises operates 268 facilities, approximately 24,000 vehicles, and over 860,000 vending machines, beverage dispensers, and coolers used to market, distribute, and produce the company's products. **Office Hours:** Monday – Friday, 8:00 a.m. – 5:00 p.m. **Corporate headquarters location:** Atlanta GA. **Other U.S. locations:** Nationwide. **Listed on:** New York Stock Exchange. **Stock exchange symbol:** KO. **Number of employees worldwide:** 30,000.

COMPUTER TRAINING ACADEMY
NETWORK RESOURCE CENTER
550 Paiea Street, Suite 222, Honolulu HI 96819. 808/839-2200. **Contact:** Human Resources. **E-mail address:** info@cta.net. **World Wide Web address:** http://www.cta.net. **Description:** One of the largest computer training companies in Hawaii. The center is certified as a Microsoft solution provider and a Novell-authorized education center. **Company Slogan:** Your talent and technology partner. **Positions advertised include:** Payroll Specialist; Customer Claims; Senior Information Processor; Part Time Office Assistant; Administrative Assistant; Accounting Assistant; Receptionist; Human Resources Assistant; Bilingual Service Representative; Executive Administrative Assistant. **Office Hours:** Monday – Friday. 8:00 a.m. – 5:00 p.m.

CRAZY SHIRTS
99-969 Iwaena Street, Aiea HI 96701. 808/487-9919. **Fax:** 808/486-6354. **Recorded jobline:** 808/483-2205. **Contact:** Human Resources Department. **E-mail address:** resumes@crazyshirts.com. **World Wide Web address:** http://www.crazyshirts.com. **Description:** Manufactures and sells custom-imprinted or embroidered sportswear apparel. Founded in 1964. **Positions advertised include:** Sales – Part time. **Office hours:** Monday - Friday, 8:00 a.m. - 5:00 p.m. **Corporate headquarters location:** This location. **Other U.S. locations:** CA; FL; LA; NV. **International locations:** Guam. **Listed on:** Privately held. **Annual sales/revenues:** $51 - $100 million. **Number of employees nationwide:** 1,000.

CYANOTECH CORPORATION
73-4460 Queen Kaahumanu Highway, Suite 102, Kailua-Kona HI 96740. 808/326-1353. **Fax:** 808/329-4533. **Toll-free phone:** 800/393-1353. **Contact:** Human Resources. **Email address:** info@cyanotech.com. **World Wide Web address:** http://www.cyanotech.com. **Office Hours:** Monday – Friday, 8:00 a.m. – 5:00 p.m. HST. **Description:** Develops and produces natural products from microalgae. The company manufactures products for use in nutritional supplements, immunological diagnostics, and aquaculture/pigments. Founded in 1983. **Corporate headquarters location:** This location. **Other U.S. locations:** NV. **Subsidiaries include:** Cyanotech International FSC, Inc.; Nutrex, Inc. **Listed on:** NASDAQ. **Stock exchange symbol:** CYAN. **President/CEO:** Gerald R. Cysewski. **Number of employees at this location:** 80.

DEL MONTE FRESH PRODUCE (HAWAII), INC.
P.O. Box 200, Kunia HI 96759. 808/621-1221. **Fax:** 808/621-1213. **Contact:** Human Resources. **World Wide Web address:** http://www.delmonte.com. **Description:** A producer of canned fruits and vegetables, tomato sauces, condiments, and dessert products for the consumer, institutional, and military markets. The company operates over 60 plants worldwide at which it processes food and manufactures, labels, and packs its own cans. Brand names include Del Monte, Morton Munchwich, Snack Cups, Bonanza, Ortega, Sunkist Plus, and Summer Crisp. Founded in 1892. **Corporate headquarters location:** San Francisco CA. **Other U.S. locations:** CA; TX; WA. **International locations:** Venezuela. **Operations at this facility include:** This location grows and processes pineapples. **Listed on:** New York Stock Exchange. **Stock exchange symbol:** DLM. **Number of employees worldwide:** 2,700.

DELOITTE AND TOUCHE
1132 Bishop Street, Suite 1200, Honolulu HI 96813-2870. 808/543-0700. **Fax:** 808/526-0225. **E-mail address:** dtcareers@deloitte.com. **Contact:** Human Resources. **World Wide Web address:** http://www.deloitte.com. **Description:** A professional service firm providing financial consulting. **Positions advertised include:** Senior Consultant.

DOLE FOOD COMPANY HAWAII
1116 Whitmore Avenue, Wahiawa HI 96786. 808/621-3200. **Contact:** Human Resources. **World Wide Web address:** http://www.dole.com. **Description:** Processes canned fruits. Founded in 1851. **NOTE:** You must include the job number you are applying for when submitting your resume. Please check the Website for information on current openings. Dole does not accept unsolicited resumes. **Listed on:** New York Stock Exchange. **Stock exchange symbol:** DOL. **Number of employees worldwide:** 51,000.

FIREMAN'S FUND INSURANCE COMPANY
P.O. Box 2079, Honolulu HI 96805. 808/523-6500. **Contact:** Debbie Hisatake, Personnel Department. **World Wide Web address:** http://www.the-fund.com. **Description:** An insurance company. **Corporate headquarters location:** Novato CA. **Other U.S. locations:** Nationwide.

FIRST HAWAIIAN BANK
P.O. Box 3200, Honolulu HI 96847. 808/525-7000. **Physical address:** 999 Bishop Street, 29th Floor, Honolulu HI 96813. **Fax:** 808/525-5798. **Recorded jobline:** 808/525-5627. **Contact:** Human Resources. **World Wide Web address:** http://www.fhb.com. **Description:** A bank with 59 branch locations throughout the state of Hawaii, two locations in Guam, and one location in Saipan. **Positions advertised include:** Assistant Liability Analyst; Bus Help; HR Assistant; Kitchen Help; Personal Banker; Personal Trust Assistant; Private Banking; Production Management; Real Estate Loan; Receiving Clerks; Trust Administrator; Teller. **Office Hours:** Monday – Friday, 8:00 a.m. – 4:30 p.m. **Corporate headquarters location:** This location. **Operations at this facility include:** Service. **Parent company:** BancWest Corporation (a subsidiary of BNP Paribas.) **Number of employees at this location:** 400. **Number of employees nationwide:** 2,800.

FIRST INSURANCE COMPANY OF HAWAII, LTD.
P.O. Box 2866, Honolulu HI 96803. 808/527-7777. **Physical address:** 1100 Ward Avenue, Honolulu HI 96814. **Fax:** 808/527-7451. **Contact:** Human Resources. **E-mail address:** jobs@ficoh.com. **World Wide Web address:** http://www.ficoh.com. **Description:** Provides automobile, casualty, homeowner's, and workman's compensation insurance. Established in 1911. **Positions advertised include:** Underwriting Associate; Loss Control Associate; Claims Adjuster; Actuarial. **Corporate headquarters location:** This location. **Subsidiaries include:** First Fire & Casualty Insurance of Hawaii; First Indemnity Insurance of Hawaii.

FOODLAND
3536 Harding Avenue, Honolulu HI 96816. 808/732-0791. **Contact:** Human Resources. **E-mail address:** services@foodland.com. **World Wide Web address:** http://www.foodland.com. **Description:** Operates 24 Foodland supermarkets. **Corporate headquarters location:** This location.

HAWAII PACIFIC HEALTH
KAPIOLANI HEALTH
55 Merchant Street, 23rd Floor, Honolulu HI 96813. 808/535-7555. **Contact:** Human Resources. **World Wide Web address:** http://www.kapiolani.org. **Description:** Kapiolani Health Care System operates Kapiolani Medical Center for Women and Children and Kapiolani Medical Center at Pali Momi. Kapiolani Medical Center for Women and Children is a 240-bed, 90-bassinet hospital with health services featuring obstetrics/gynecology; personalized maternity services; labor, delivery, and recovery suites; perinatal special care unit; and a fetal diagnostic center. The pediatrics unit has 24-hour emergency services, newborn normal and intermediate care nurseries, and neonatal and pediatric intensive care units. The outreach programs include a sex abuse treatment center, a child protective services team, a teen intervention program, and a neonatal intensive care follow-up team. KMC for Women and Children is a teaching hospital affiliated with the University of Hawaii John A. Burns School of Medicine. Kapiolani Medical Center at Pali Momi is a 116-bed, acute care hospital. Its services include a 24-hour physician-staffed emergency department; private rooms for all guests; a critical care unit; inpatient and same-day surgery; cardiology, neurology, and OB/GYN screening services; a cardiac catheterization lab; oncology; home health services; and rehabilitation services. **Company slogan:** Keeping you healthy for life. **Positions advertised include:** Accountant; Activity Aid; Administrative Assistant; Administrative Support Specialist; Anesthesia Assistants; Business Office Assistant Breast Center; Business Support Analysis; Cancer Patient data; Cardial Technician.

HAWAII PACIFIC UNIVERSITY
1164 Bishop Street, Honolulu HI 96813. 808/544-0200. **Toll-free phone:** 866/CALL-HPU. **Contact:** Linda Kawamura, Associate Vice President of Human Resources. **E-mail address:** hr@hpu.edu. **Office Hours:** Monday – Friday, 8:00 a.m. – 5:00 p.m. **World Wide Web address:** http://www.hpu.edu. **Description:** A nonprofit, coeducational university with approximately 6,700 undergraduate and 1,200 graduate students enrolled. Graduate degrees include master of science in business administration, master of science in information systems, and master of art in human resource management. Founded in 1965. **Special programs:** Internships; Co-ops. **Positions advertised include:** Accounting Professor; Biology Professor; Chemistry Professor; Communication Professor; Computer Science Professor; Finance Professor; Geography Professor; Management Professor; Mathematics Professor; Military Professor; Nursing Professor; Oceanography Professor; Physics Professor. Logo and Promotions Associate; Secretary; Shuttle Van Driver.

HAWAII PROTECTIVE ASSOCIATION LTD.
1290A Maunakea Street, Honolulu HI 96817. 808/537-5938. **Contact:** Personnel. **Description:** A security firm that provides uniformed guards and motorized patrols to various clients throughout the state of Hawaii. **NOTE:** Entry-level positions are offered. Applicants must come in person to fill out an application. **Corporate headquarters location:** This location. **Number of employees at this location:** 400.

HAWAII STATE FEDERAL CREDIT UNION
P.O. Box 3072, Honolulu HI 96802-3072. 808/587-2735 x872. **Physical address:** 560 Halekauwila Street, Honolulu HI 93813-5085. **Fax:** 808/587-3235. **Contact:** Human Resources. **E-mail address:** hr@hsfcu.com. **World Wide Web address:** http://www.hsfcu.com. **Description:** A credit union. **Positions advertised include:** Business Developer Specialist; Teller; Call Center Representative; Part time Teller.

HAWAIIAN AIRLINES, INC.
P.O. Box 30008, Honolulu HI 96820. 808/835-3700. **Fax:** 808/835-3649. **Recorded jobline:** 808/835-3730. **Contact:** Human Resources. **World Wide Web address:** http://www.hawaiianair.com. **Description:** A regional airline for passengers, cargo, and mail over a route consisting of six major Hawaiian islands, cities on the West Coast, and some cities in the South Pacific. **NOTE:** Address resumes Attn: People Services Group. **Positions advertised include:** Technology Buyer; Security Director; Technical Specialist Supervisor; Human Resource Administrator; Management Business; Credit Clerk; Online Advertising Tech; Computer Services; Maintenance. **Corporate headquarters location:** This location. **Other U.S. locations:** Los Angeles CA; San Francisco CA; Las Vegas NV; Portland OR; Seattle WA. **Operations at this facility include:** Administration; Research and Development; Sales. **Listed on:** American Stock Exchange. **Stock exchange symbol:** HA. **Number of employees nationwide:** 3,300.

HAWAIIAN DREDGING CONSTRUCTION COMPANY
P.O. Box 4088, Honolulu HI 96812-4088. 808/735-3211. **Fax:** 808/735-7416. **Physical address:** 614 Kapahulu Avenue, Honolulu HI 96815-3891. **Contact:** Human Resources. **E-mail address:** employmenti@hdcc.com. **World Wide Web address:** http://www.hdcc.com. **Description:** A residential and commercial construction company. **Parent company:** Dillingham Construction Corporation.

HILO HATTIE
700 North Nimitz Highway, Honolulu HI 96817. 808/524-3966. **Toll-free phone:** 800/233-8912. **Toll-free Fax:** 888/526-5696. **Contact:** Human Resources Department. **World Wide Web address:** http://www.hilohattie.com. **E-mail address:** customer.service@hilohattie.com **Office hours:** Monday – Friday, 8:00 a.m. – 5:00 p.m. HST. **Description:** Manufactures and sells Hawaiian tropical wear, covering a wide variety of styles and imprints. Hilo Hattie designs its own prints and styles, which are sold through five Hilo Hattie stores. Founded in 1963. **Positions advertised include:** Management Opportunities; Retail Positions. **Corporate headquarters location:** This location. **Other area locations:** Hilo HI; Kona HI; Kihei HI; Lahaina HI; Lihue HI. **Other U.S. locations:** Phoenix AZ; Anaheim CA; Miami FL; Nashville TN.

HILO MEDICAL CENTER
1190 Waianuenue Avenue, Hilo HI 96720. 808/974-6837. **Fax:** 808/733-4028. **Contact:** Human Resources. **E-mail address:** hmcrecruit@hhsc.org. **World Wide Web address:** http://www.hmc.hhsc.org. **Description:** A 274-bed facility providing

acute, long-term care, and psychiatric services to the island's central, eastern, and southern sectors. **NOTE:** Entry-level positions as well as second and third shifts are offered. **Company Slogan:** We Care For Our Community. **Positions advertised include:** Health Unit Clerk; Licensed Practical Nurse; Per Diem Nurse; Radiological Tech; Radiation Therapist; Certified Nurses Aid; Nurse; Director Material Management; Accountant; Admitting Clerk; Blomed Engineer; Maintenance. **Special programs:** Internships. **Office hours:** Monday - Friday, 7:30 a.m. - 4:00 p.m. **Corporate headquarters location:** Honolulu HI. **Parent company:** Hawaii Health Systems Corporation. **Operations at this facility include:** Administration; Service. **Number of employees at this location:** 850.

HILTON HAWAIIAN VILLAGE
2005 Kalia Road, Honolulu HI 96815. 808/949-4321. **Fax:** 808/947-7904. **Recorded jobline:** 808/948-7742. **Contact:** Personnel Department. **World Wide Web address:** http://www.hilton.com. **Description:** Operates hotels and restaurants. **NOTE:** Entry-level positions are offered. **Positions advertised include:** Front Service Desk Representative; Secretary; Services Manager; Bartender; Wait Help; Cafeteria Attendant; Recreational Manager; Concierge Manager; Door Attendant; Maintenance; Air Conditioning Specialist; Front Office Clerk; Linguist; Parking Valet. . **Special programs:** Internships; Apprenticeships. **Office hours:** Monday - Thursday, 8:00 a.m. - 4:00 p.m. Friday hours: 8:00 a.m. – 3:00 p.m. **Corporate headquarters location:** Beverly Hills CA. **Other U.S. locations:** Nationwide. **International locations:** Worldwide. **Listed on:** New York Stock Exchange. **Stock exchange symbol:** HLT. **Annual sales/revenues:** $51 - $100 million. **Number of employees at this location:** 1,800.

HIPOINT SOFTWARE, LLC
1314 S. King Street, Suite 864, Honolulu HI 96822. 808/597-8851. **Fax:** 808/597-8861. **Contact:** Human Resources Department. **E-mail address:** info@hipointsoftware.com. **World Wide Web address:** http://www.hipointsoftware.com. **Description:** A computer consulting firm specializing in data collection and management applications for distribution companies. **Corporate headquarters location:** This location. **Other U.S. locations:** New York NY. **President:** Brian Ho.

HON-CAD
1000 Bishop Street, Suite 500, Honolulu HI 96813. 808/440-5006. **Fax:** 808/440-5001. **Contact:** Human Resources. **World Wide Web address:** http://www.hon-cad.com. **Description:** Provides CAD training, services, and products to Hawaii's architecture, engineering, and construction market. **Positions advertised include:** CAD Applications Engineer.

HYATT REGENCY WAIKIKI
2424 Kalakaua Avenue, Honolulu HI 96815. 808/923-1234. **Contact:** Renee Kagimoto, Director of Human Resources. **World Wide Web address:** http://waikiki.hyatt.com. **Description:** A hotel/restaurant facility. **Positions advertised include:** Banquet Server; Beauty Specialist; Concierge; Convention Service Representative; Housekeeper; Massage Practitioner; Regency Club Attendant; Security Officer; Utility Steward; Wait Help. **Corporate headquarters location:** Chicago IL. **Parent company:** Hyatt Hotels Corporation. **Operations at this facility include:** Service. **Listed on:** Privately held. **Number of employees at this location:** 850. **Number of employees nationwide:** 40,000.

KAHI MOHALA BEHAVIORAL HEALTH
91-2301 Fort Weaver Road, Ewa Beach HI 96706. 808/677-2525. **Toll-free phone:** 800/999-9889. **Fax:** 808/677-2570. **Recorded jobline:** 808/948-2525. **Contact:** Christina Enoka, Director of Human Resources. **World Wide Web address:** http://www.kahimohala.org. **Description:** A JCAHO-accredited, psychiatric hospital providing mental health and chemical dependency services for children on both inpatient and outpatient bases. **Positions advertised include:** Maintenance Worker; PBS Operator; Cook; Call Center Coordinator; Unit Clerk; Registered Nurse. **Special programs:** Training. **Corporate headquarters location:** Sacramento CA. **Parent company:** Sutter Health. **Operations at this facility include:** Administration; Service. **Annual sales/revenues:** $11 - $20 million. **Number of employees at this location:** 225.

KAISER PERMANENTE
Ala Moana Building, 1441 Kapiolani Boulevard, 17th Floor, Honolulu HI 96814. 808/432-4900. **Fax:** 808/432-4989. **Contact:** Carolyn Jennings, Regional Human Resources Leader. **World Wide Web address:** http://www.kaiserpermanente.org. **Office hours:** Monday – Friday, 8:00 a.m. – 5:00p.m. **Description:** A nonprofit, public-benefit and charitable health care corporation that enrolls members and arranges for their medical, hospital, and related services nationwide. Founded in 1945. **Positions advertised include:** Assistant Director HIM; Behavioral Specialist; Cardiological Tech; Chart Clerk; Data Entry Clerk; Director Laboratory; Film Clerk; Genetic Counselor; Hospital Aid; Human Resource Assistant. **Corporate headquarters location:** Oakland CA. **Operations at this facility include:** Administration; Health Care; Regional Headquarters; Sales; Service. **Listed on:** Privately held. **Number of employees at this location:** 3,800.

KAMEHAMEHA SCHOOLS
567 South King Street, Honolulu HI 96813. 808/523-6200. **Fax:** 808/842-8405. **Contact:** Human Resources. **E-mail address:** recruit@ksbe.edu. **World Wide Web address:** http://www.ksbe.edu. **Description:** Kamehameha Schools serves more than 4,900 students in preschool through grade 12. Founded in 1887. **Note:** E-mail resume in Microsoft Word 97 format. Resumes must be received by 4:15 p.m. **Positions advertised include:** Extended Day Teacher; Security Officer; Assistant Athletic Director; Substitute Teachers; Performing Arts Teacher; General Contracting Teachers; Business and Leadership Teacher; Vice Principal; Student Activities Coordinator.

LEEWARD COMMUNITY COLLEGE
96-045 Ala Ike, Pearl City HI 96782. 808/455-0326. **Contact:** Human Resources. **E-mail address:** lcccdc@hawaii.edu. **World Wide Web address:** http://www.lcc.hawaii.edu. **Description:** One of several community colleges in the University of Hawaii System. Many of its programs and classes coordinate with those at the University of Hawaii campuses at Manoa, Hilo, and West Oahu. The college offers approximately 500 courses in four academic divisions and two vocational divisions, as well as short-term courses through the Office of Special Programs and Community Services. Degrees and certificates include an associate in arts degree, an associate of science degree, a certificate of achievement, and a certificate of completion. Over 5,000 students attend the college. Founded in 1968. **Office Hours:** Monday – Friday. 7:45 a.m.– 4:30 p.m. **Note:** Check http://workatuh.Hawaii.edu for job postings. **Positions advertised include:** Associate Dean; Associate Dean Academic Affairs; Chancellor; Dean College of Agriculture; Director Waikiki Aquarium.

MACY'S
1450 Ala Moana Boulevard, Honolulu HI 96814. 808/941-2345. **Contact:** Human Resources. **World Wide Web address:** http://www.macysjobs.com. **Description:** A department store. **Positions advertised include:** Sales, Cosmetics - Clinique; Origins; Channel; Loss Prevention; Receiving; Fine Jewelry Sales; Sales Associates; Support Associates; Woman's Shoes. **Corporate headquarters location:** Cincinnati OH. **Other U.S. locations:** Nationwide. **Parent company:** Federated Department Stores, Inc.

MAUI ELECTRIC COMPANY, LTD.
P.O. Box 398, Kahului HI 96733. 808/871-8461. **Physical Address:** 210 West Kamehameha Avenue, Kahului HI 96732. **Contact:** Ms. Merle Minami-Shima, Human Resources. **World Wide Web address:** http://www.hei.com. **Description:** An electric utility company. **Parent company:** Hawaiian Electric Industries, Inc. **Positions advertised include:** Auto Mechanic; Mechanic Helper; Project Manager; Engineer; Auto Attendant; Drafting Tech. **Office Hours:** Monday – Friday, 7:00 a.m. – 4:00 p.m.

THE MAUNA LANI BAY HOTEL & BUNGALOWS
68-1400 Mauna Lani Drive, Kohala Coast HI 96743. 808/885-6622. **Recorded Job Line:** 808/881-7973. **Contact:** Human Resources. **World Wide Web address:** http://www.maunalani.com. **Description:** A resort with hotel rooms; one, two, and three-bedroom villas; and five private bungalows. The resort offers golf, tennis, and water sports activities. **Office Hours:** Monday – Friday, 8:00 a.m. – 4:30 p.m. **Positions advertised include:** Wait Staff; Buss Staff; Hostess; Bartender; Assistant Store Manager; Food Runner; Cook; Pantry; Kitchen Utility; House Keeper; Trolly Driver; Assistant Hotel Manager; Security Manager.

MEADOW GOLD DAIRIES
P.O. Box 1880, Honolulu HI 96805-1880. 808/949-6161. **Physical address:** 925 Cedar Street, Honolulu HI 96814. **Contact:** Darrel Tajima, Human Resources Representative. **E-mail address:** hgardner@meadowgold.com. **World Wide Web address:** http://www.meadowgold.com. **Description:** Meadow Gold Dairies is a manufacturer and wholesale distributor of dairy cultured products, juices and fruit drinks, ice cream, purified drinking water, and other foodstuffs. **Positions advertised include:** Manufacturing, Sales, Administrative. **Corporate headquarters location:** Kahului HI. **Operations at this facility include:** A small dairy farm producing raw milk on the islands of Kauai and Oahu. **Listed on:** Privately held. **Annual sales/revenues:** $5 - $10 million. **Information Systems Manager:** Derek Loui. **Number of employees at this location:** 285.

MEADOW GOLD DAIRIES
55 South Wakea Avenue, Kahului HI 96732-1395. 808/877-5541. **Fax:** 808/871-6224. **Contact:** Personnel. **World Wide Web address:** http://www.meadowgold.com. **Description:** A manufacturer and wholesale distributor of dairy cultured products, juices and fruit drinks, ice cream, purified drinking water, and other foodstuffs. Founded in 1896. **NOTE:** Entry-level positions are offered. **Special programs:** Training. **Positions advertised include:** Manufacturing, Sales, Administrative. **Corporate headquarters location:** This location. **Operations at this facility include:** Regional Headquarters. **Listed on:** Privately held. **Annual sales/revenues:** $5 - $10 million. **Number of employees at this location:** 70.

NISSAN MOTOR CORPORATION IN HAWAII, LTD.
2880 Kilihau Street, Honolulu HI 96819. 808/836-0888. **Contact:** Lynn Sato, Human Resources. **World Wide Web address:** http://www.nissanhawaii.com. **Description:** Distributes cars, trucks, forklifts, and parts. **Corporate headquarters location:** Tokyo, Japan. **Parent company:** Nissan Motor Corporation, Ltd. **Operations at this facility include:** Administration; Sales; Service.

NOVASOL
23rd Floor, 1100 Alakea Street, Honolulu HI 96813. 808/441-3600. **Fax:** 808/441-3601. **Contact:** Human Resources. **E-mail address:** hr_dept@nova-sol.com. **World Wide Web address:** http://www.nova-sol.com. **Description:** Provides text-based technical support for military, industrial, medical, and environmental problems. Founded in 1998. **Positions advertised include:** Scientist, Analyst for Imaging Spectroscopy; Optical Scientist; Principal Engineer; Software Engineer D1 program; Software Engineer; Mechanical Engineer. **Corporate headquarters location:** This location. **Other area locations:** Waipahu HI. **Other U.S. locations:** San Diego CA; Orlando FL.

OCEANIC CABLE
P.O. Box 860200, Wahiawa HI 96786-0200. 808/625-2100. **Physical address:** 200 Akamainui Street, Mililani HI 96789. **Recorded jobline:** 808/625-8559. **Contact:** Marcia Taira, Director of Human Resources. **Office Hours:** Monday – Friday, 8:00 a.m. – 4:00 p.m. **World Wide Web address:** http://www.oceanic.com. **Note:** Check http://www.aoltimewarner.com/careers for positions. Oceanic Cable only accepts application for advertised positions. **Description:** Provides cable television services. **Parent company:** AOL Time Warner.

THE PARK SHORE
2586 Kalakaua Avenue, Honolulu HI 96815. 808/923-0411. **Fax:** 808/921-7645. **Contact:** Personnel. **World Wide Web address:** http://www.parkshorewaikiki.com. **Description:** A full-service hotel offering three restaurants, a shopping plaza, and a car rental service. **Parent company:** Wyndham International. **Positions advertised include:** Front Office; Night auditor; Security.

PARSONS BRINCKERHOFF INC.
American Savings Bank Tower, Suite 3000, 1001 Bishop Street, Honolulu HI 96813. 808/531-7094. **Fax:** 808/528-2368. **Contact:** Human Resources. **E-mail address:** careers@pbworld.com. **World Wide Web address:** http://www.pbworld.com. **Description:** An engineering and design firm engaged in the design of bridges, tunnels, rapid transit systems, hydroelectric facilities, water supply systems, and marine facilities. Founded in 1885. **Corporate headquarters location:** New York NY. **Other U.S. locations:** Nationwide. **International locations:** Worldwide. **Number of employees worldwide:** 9,000.

THE QUEEN'S MEDICAL CENTER
1301 Punchbowl Street, Honolulu HI 96813. 808/538-9011. **Contact:** Human Resources. **E-mail address:** employment@queens.org. **World Wide Web address:** http://www.queens.org. **Description:** A private, nonprofit, acute care medical facility. It is one of the largest private hospitals in Hawaii and the Pacific Basin, licensed to operate 530 acute care beds, 30 subacute beds, and 30 trauma/ER beds. As a leading medical referral center in Hawaii and the Pacific Basin, The Queen's Medical Center offers a comprehensive range of primary and specialized care services. The hospital's departments include oncology, orthopedics, cardiology, obstetrics, and trauma and critical care. The hospital also offers a broad spectrum of adult mental health services. **Positions advertised include:** Management Opportunities; Registered Nurse; Licensed

Practical Nurse; Psychiatric Assistant; Technical Professor. **Special Programs:** Volunteer work available. Contact Queen's Volunteer Services at 808/547-4397. **Corporate headquarters location:** This location. **Parent company:** The Queen's Health Systems. **Operations at this facility include:** Administration. **Number of employees nationwide:** 3,500.

REHABILITATION HOSPITAL OF THE PACIFIC
226 North Kuakini Street, Honolulu HI 96817. 808/544-3334. **Toll-free phone:** 800/973-4226. **Fax:** 808/544-3337. **Contact:** Human Resources. **E-mail address:** hr@rehabhospital.org. **World Wide Web address:** http://www.rehabhospital.org. **Description:** A comprehensive physical rehabilitation hospital offering both inpatient and outpatient services to individuals with physical disabilities. The hospital is licensed for 100 acute beds. The outpatient network consists of clinics located at various sites on the islands of Hawaii (Hilo and Kona), Kauai, Maui, and Oahu. **Positions advertised include:** Physical Therapist; Rehab Nurse; Speech & Language Pathologists; Occupational Therapist; Patient Care Services Clerk; Ward Clerk; Patient Registrar; Food Services Worker; Security Officer. **Corporate headquarters location:** This location. **Number of employees at this location:** 400.

SAFEWAY STORES, INC.
680 Iwilei Road, Suite 590, Honolulu HI 96817. 808/524-4554. **Contact:** Human Resources. **World Wide Web address:** http://www.safeway.com. **Description:** Operates approximately 1,080 stores in the Western, Rocky Mountain, Southwestern, and Mid-Atlantic regions of the United States and in western Canada. The company also operates a network of distribution, manufacturing, and food processing facilities. Safeway also holds a 35 percent interest in The Vons Companies, Inc. and a 49 percent interest in Casa Ley, S.A. de C.V., which operates food/variety, clothing, and wholesale outlet stores in western Mexico. **NOTE:** Applicants should fill out an application form in person. **Positions advertised include:** Food Clerk; Checker Clerk; Deli Associate; Bakery Associate; Dairy Stock Associate; Meat Associate; Produce Associate; Corporate Associate; Pharmacy Associate. **Corporate headquarters location:** Pleasanton CA. **Operations at this facility include:** This location houses the district offices for Safeway supermarkets.

ST. FRANCIS HEALTHCARE SYSTEM OF HAWAII
P.O. Box 30100, Honolulu HI 96820. 808/566-4721. **Physical address:** 2230 Liliha St. Honolulu HI 96820. **Fax:** 808/547-6352. **Contact:** Marge Mattos, Human Resources. **World Wide Web address:** http://www.sfhs-hi.org. **E-mail address:** apply@sfhs-hi.org **Note**: Applicants may only apply for positions listed currently online. **Description:** A nonprofit, acute care hospital. **NOTE:** Entry-level positions and second and third shifts are offered. **Positions advertised include:** Clinical Dietitian; Dietary Aide; Homecare Physical Therapist; Home Health Aide; Licensed Practical Nurse; Nursing Assistant; Personal Care Attendant; Physical Therapy Assistant; Registered Nurse; Speech Language Pathologist. **Special programs:** Internships; Training; Summer Jobs. **Office hours:** Monday - Friday, 7:30 a.m. - 4:30 p.m. **Subsidiaries include:** St. Francis Medical Center; St. Francis-West. **CEO:** Beatrice Tom. **Number of employees at this location:** 2,400.

SCHULER HOMES, INC.
828 Fort Street Mall, 4th Floor, Honolulu HI 96813. 808/521-5661. Toll-free phone: 888/890-4622. **Fax:** 808/538-1476. **E-mail address**: salesinfo@shlr.com. **Contact:** Office Manager. **World Wide Web address:** http://www.schulerhawaii.com. **Description:** Designs, builds, and sells single-family homes, townhouses, and condominiums. Founded in 1973. **Corporate headquarters location:** This location. **Other U.S. locations:** CA; CO; OR; WA. **President/CEO:** James K. Schuler. **Annual sales/revenues:** More than $100 million.

SHERATON WAIKIKI HOTEL
2255 Kalakaua Avenue, Honolulu HI 96815. 808/922-4422. **Fax:** 808/931-8297. **Recorded jobline:** 808/931-8294. **Contact:** Human Resources Department. **E-mail address:** resume.waikiki@sheraton.com. **World Wide Web address:** http://www.sheraton-waikiki.com. **Description:** A hotel. **Office Hours:** MWF 8:30 a.m. – 12:00 p.m. T, TH; 1:00 p.m. – 4:30 p.m. **NOTE:** Apply in person, or send resume for current advertised positions only. **Positions advertised include:** Assistant Manager; Electrician; Housekeeper; Sales Manager; Hourly Manager; Telephone Operator; Bartender; Bus Help; Food Help; Mini-bar; Weight Help; Night Auditor; Bilingual Speaker of English and Japanese.

SPIRENT COMMUNICATIONS
First Hawaiian Center, 999 Bishop Street, 17th Floor, Honolulu HI 96813. 808/734-3300. **Fax:** 808/734-7100. **Toll-free phone:** 800/348-0080. **Contact:** Recruitment Specialist. **E-mail address:** opportunities@spirentcom.com. **World Wide Web address:** http://www.spirentcom.com. **Description:** The Adtech Division of Spirent Communications offers a full range of comprehensive test solutions for today's communications technologies, including: optical networking, voice over IP (VoIP), 3G wireless, routing and online test and measurement (OLTM).

STAR MARKETS
P.O. Box 2367, Honolulu HI 96804-2367. 808/832-8400. **Contact:** Human Resources. **World Wide Web address:** http://www.shaws.com. **Note:** Shaw's owns Star Supermarkets. **Description:** Grocery Store. **Positions advertised include:** Store Manager; Department Manager; Bakery Associate; Customer Service Representative; Deli Associate; Front End Representative; Grocery Stock Clerk; Meat Stock Clerk; Produce Stock Clerk; Seafood Stock Clerk.

STRAUB CLINIC & HOSPITAL, INC.
888 South King Street, Honolulu HI 96813. 808/522-4000. **Fax:** 808/522-4060. **Contact:** Personnel. **World Wide Web address:** http://www.straubhealth.com. **Description:** A private, nonprofit hospital and clinic with approximately 150 physicians and a 159-bed hospital. The main clinic and seven satellite clinics are located on Oahu. Founded in 1921. **Positions advertised include:** Accountant; Administrative Assistant; Support & Specialist in Administration; Business Systems Analyst; Charge Entry Specialist; Clinic Customer Service Representative; Clinical Assistant. **Corporate headquarters location:** This location. **Listed on:** Privately held. **CEO:** Dr. Blake Waterhouse. **Number of employees at this location:** 2,000.

SYNCADD SYSTEMS INC.
1833 Kalakaua Avenue, Suite 608, Honolulu HI 96815. 808/941-8286. **Fax:** 808/941-7173. **Contact:** Human Resources. **World Wide Web address:** http://www.syncadd.com. **Description:** Provides consulting, application design and development, and data capture as related to facilities management and GIS.

TECHNOLOGY INTEGRATION GROUP (TIG)
1221 Kapiolani Boulevard Suite 410, Honolulu HI 96814. 808/524-6652. **Contact:** Michelle McWilliams. **E-mail address:** michelle.mcwilliams@tig.com. **World Wide Web address:** http://www.tig.com. **Description:** Provides IT solutions to small and medium organizations. Founded in 1981. **Positions advertised include:** Account Executive. **Corporate headquarters location:** San Diego CA. **Number of employees nationwide:** 320.

UNIVERSITY OF HAWAII AT HILO
200 West Kawili Street, Hilo HI 96720-4091. 808/974-7687. **Fax:** 808/974-7689. **Contact:** Human Resources. **World Wide Web address:** http://www.uhh.hawaii.edu. **Description:** A four-year university made up of the College of Arts and Sciences, the College of Agriculture, and the College of Continuing Education and Community Service. The College of Arts and Sciences has approximately 130 faculty and 3,000 students. The College of Agriculture offers a low student-faculty ratio, hands-on production techniques, basic management programs, and basic science courses. The College of Continuing Education and Community Service, formed in 1971, serves as the outreach arm of the university. The university is accredited by the Accrediting Commission for Senior Colleges and Universities of the Western Association of Schools and Colleges. Founded in 1947. **Positions advertised include:** Assistant Professor's in the following subjects: Marine Science; Japanese; Geography and Environmental History; World History; Marketing; Biology; Physical Education; Sociology.

UNIVERSITY OF HAWAII AT MANOA
2444 Dole Street, Honolulu HI 96822. 808/956-7753. **Fax:** 808/956-8294. **Contact:** Evelyn Nowaki, Director of Human Resources. **World Wide Web address:** http://www.uhm.hawaii.edu. **Description:** Offers undergraduate, graduate, professional, and postdoctoral studies. The university is accredited by the Accrediting Commission for Senior Colleges and the Universities of the Western Association of Schools and Colleges.

VERIFONE, INC.
100 Kahelu Avenue, Mililani HI 96789-3909. 808/623-2911. **Fax:** 916/630-2566. **Contact:** Human Resources. **E-mail address:** jobs@verifone.com. **World Wide Web address:** http://www.verifone.com. **Description:** VeriFone develops, manufactures, and services software for electronic payment systems that are used in a variety of industries including consumer, financial, and health care. **Corporate headquarters location:** Santa Clara CA. **Operations at this facility include:** This location houses a research and development facility for operating system software. **Positions advertised include:** Project Manager; Software Engineer; Quality Assurance Tech; Software Design; Firmware Engineer; Product Manager; Software Engineer Tools; Help Desk Customer Service Support; Software Design Engineer; Financial Analyst; West Coast Sales Representative.

VERIZON HAWAIIAN COMMUNICATIONS
P.O. Box 2200, Honolulu HI 96841. 808/546-4511. **Contact:** Personnel. **World Wide Web address:** http://www.verizon.com. **Description:** Verizon is a full-service communications services provider. Verizon offers residential local and long distance telephone services and Internet access; wireless service plans, cellular phones, and data services; a full line of business services including Internet access, data services, and telecommunications equipment and services; and government network solutions including Internet access, data services, telecommunications equipment and services, and enhanced communications services. **Positions advertised include:** Building Services Tech; Real Estate Project Manager; Inside Sales Representative; Network Engineer; Power Engineer. **Corporate headquarters location:** New York NY. **Other U.S. locations:** Nationwide. **Operations at this facility include:** This location provides telecommunication services and products in Hawaii and the Pacific Basin. **Listed on:** New York Stock Exchange. **Stock exchange symbol:** VZ.

WILCOX MEMORIAL HOSPITAL
3420 Kuhio Highway, Lihue HI 96766. 808/245-1100. **Fax:** 808/245-1211. **Contact:** Human Resources. **World Wide Web address:** http://www.wilcoxhealth.org. **Office Hours:** Monday – Friday, 7:00 a.m. – 4:30 p.m. **Description:** A 185-bed, acute and long-term care, JCAHO-accredited hospital. **Positions advertised include:** Activities Aid; Bay Health Specialist; Departmental Nurses; Registered Nurse; Licensed Practical Nurse; File Clerk; Manager; PDX Operator; Pharmacist; **Corporate headquarters location:** This location. **Number of employees at this location:** 640.

AMI SEMICONDUCTOR
2300 Buckskin Road, Pocatello ID 83201. 208/233-4690. **Toll-free phone:** 800/639-7264. **Contact:** Human Resources. **E-mail address:** us_jobs@amis.com. **World Wide Web address:** http://www.amis.com. **Description:** Specializes in digital and mixed-signal application-specific integrated circuits (ASIC) design, foundry, and manufacturing. AMI's digital ASIC Standard Library contains over 500 cells and operates from 2.5 to 5.0 volts. The library supports both gate arrays and standard cells and is process- and technology-independent, creating a path for future cost reductions through process migrations. Arrays have up to 300,000 usable gates. Megacells include RAM, ROM, dual port ROM microprocessors, and controllers. AMI's ACCESS Design Tools software optimizes digital ASIC designs at customer sites. AMI's mixed-signal offering includes Mixed Signal Design Solution (MSDS) software for automating the design, simulation, and test of mixed signal ASICs. **Positions advertised include:** Applications Engineer; Product Management Director; Process Engineer; Fab 9 Operations Director; Director of Quality; Device Reliability Technician; Line Maintenance Stores Manager; Corporate Attorney; Senior RF ASIC Designer. **Corporate headquarters location:** This location. **Other U.S. Locations:** Nationwide. **International locations:** Worldwide. **President/CEO:** Christine King. **Number of employees at this location:** 1100. **Number of employees Worldwide:** 2500.

AMS SERVICES INC.
7600 North Mineral Drive, Suite 400, Coeur d'Alene ID 83815. 208/772-8900. **Contact:** Human Resources. **World Wide Web address:** http://www.ams-services.com. **Description:** Develops and markets insurance software. **Corporate headquarters location:** Windsor CT. **Other U.S. locations:** FL; GA; IL; MA; TX; WA.

ATK (ALLIANT TECHSYSTEMS)
d.b.a CCI/Speer
2299 Snake River Avenue, P.O. Box 856, Lewiston ID 83501. 208/746-2351. **Toll-free phone:** 800/627-3640. **Contact:** Human Resources. **Email address:** CCI/SPEER@ATK.com. **World Wide Web address:** http://www.atk.com. **Description:** ATK had two operating systems: Aerospace and Defense. This location supplies defense products to the U.S. Department of Defense and other allied nations. Internships available. **Corporate headquarters location:** Edina, MN. **Other U.S. locations:** CA; FL; MI; MO; MN; MS; UT; WV. **Listed on:** New York Stock Exchange. **Stock Exchange Symbol:** ATK. **Number of employees nationwide:** Approximately 12,500.

ADAGER CORPORATION
Adager Way, P.O. Box 3000, Sun Valley ID 83353-3000. 208/726-9100. **Fax:** 208/726-8191. **Contact:** Human Resources. **E-mail address:** info@adager.com. **World Wide Web address:** http://www.adager.com. **Description:** A database utility firm. Adager's hardware is oriented to any type of HP3000 hardware, operating system, or IMAGE/SQL version.

ADVANCED INPUT DEVICES
600 West Wilbur Avenue, Coeur d'Alene ID 83815. 208/765-8000. **Toll-free phone:** 800/444-5923. **Fax:** 208/772-7807. **Contact:** Personnel. **E-mail address:** personnel @advanced-input.com. **World Wide Web address:** http://www.advanced-input.com. **Description:** A leading manufacturer of custom keyboards for electronic instruments and systems. **Special programs:** Internships. **Corporate headquarters location:** This location. **Other U.S. locations:** MI **International locations:** Hampshire, England. **Parent company:** Esterline Technologies. **Listed on:** New York Stock Exchange. **Stock exchange symbol:** ESL.

AGENCY SOFTWARE, INC.
215 West Commerce Drive, Hayden Lake ID 83835. 208/762-7188. **Toll-free phone:** 800/342-7327. **Fax:** 208/762-1265 **Contact:** Human Resources Department. **World Wide Web address:** http://www.agencysoft.com. **Description:** Develops software for the insurance industry.

ALBERTSON'S, INC.
P.O. Box 20, Boise ID 83726. 208/395-6200. **Physical address:** 250 East Parkcenter Boulevard, Boise ID 83706 **Fax:** 208/395-4880. **Contact:** Human Resources. **Email address:** employment@albertsons.com. **World Wide Web address:** http://www.albertsons.com. **Description:** One of the largest retail food-drug chains in the United States. The company operates approximately 2,300 stores in 31 states. Founded in 1939. **Positions advertised include:** Marketing Analyst; Brand Manager; Product Developer. **Internship information:** Offers full time internships. Rotated through various departments including finance and accounting to gain a variety of experience. **Office hours:** Monday - Friday, 8:00 a.m. - 5:00 p.m. **Corporate headquarters location:** This location. **Other U.S. locations:** Nationwide. **Listed on:** New York Stock Exchange. **Stock exchange symbol:** ABS. **CEO:** Lawrence R. Johnston. **Annual sales/revenues:** 37.9 billion. **Number of employees nationwide:** 220,000.

AMALGAMATED SUGAR COMPANY
138 West Karcher Road, P.O. Box 8787, Nampa ID 83653. 208/466-3541. **Contact:** Ken Baumgatner, Human Resources. **World Wide Web address:** http://www.amalgamatedsugar.com. **Description:** This location is one of the largest beet factories in the world. The factory processes over 10,000 tons of sugar beets every 24 hours during the 140-day season. Overall, the Amalgamated Sugar Company is one of the nation's largest producers of sugar, accounting for nearly 10 percent of the annual sugar production in the United States. The company's White Satin brand sugar is sold primarily to industrial users in the Pacific, Intermountain, and Midwestern states. Approximately 80 percent of the company's sugar sales are to wholesalers or retailers in consumer-sized packages. **Corporate headquarters location**: Ogden, UT **Other U.S. locations:** CO; IL; KS; OR; UT; WA.

AMALGAMATED SUGAR COMPANY
2320 Orchard East, P.O. Box 127, Twin Falls ID 83303. 208/733-4104. **Fax:** 208/735-5433. **Contact:** Carol McCoy. **World Wide Web address:** http://www.amalgamatedsugar.com. **Description:** A producer of sugar, accounting for nearly 10 percent of the annual sugar production in the United States. The company's White Satin brand sugar is sold primarily to industrial users in the Pacific, Intermountain, and Midwestern states. Approximately 80 percent of the company's sugar sales are to wholesalers or retailers in consumer-sized packages. **Other U.S. locations:** CO; IL; KS; OR; UT; WA.

AMERISTAR CASINOS, INC.
550 Blue Lakes Boulevard North, Twin Falls ID 83301. 208/733-2282. **Contact:** Human Resources. **World Wide Web address:** http://www.ameristarcasinos.com. **Description:** Owns and operates Cactus Pete's Resort Casino and The Horseshu Hotel and Casino. **NOTE:** Resumes should be sent to the corporate office, 777 West Lake Mead Drive, Henderson NV 89015. **Corporate headquarters location:** Henderson, NV. **Subsidiaries include:** Ameristar Casino Vicksburg, Inc., also owns and operates a riverboat-themed dockside casino and related land-based facilities in Vicksburg MS; Ameristar Casino Council Bluffs, Inc. was awarded one of two riverboat gaming licenses in Council Bluffs IA; Ameristar Casino Lawrenceburg, Inc. is one of seven applicants seeking a single gaming license in Lawrenceburg IA. **Listed on:** NASDAQ. **Stock exchange symbol:** ASCA. **President/CEO:** Craig H. Neilsen.

BMC WEST CORPORATION
P.O. Box 70006, Boise ID 83707. 208/331-4300. **Physical address:** 720 Park Boulevard Suite 200, Boise ID 83712. **Toll-free phone:** 888/868-2629. **Fax:** 208/331-4367. **Contact:** Neil Watterson, Director of Human Resources. **World Wide Web address:** http://www.bmcwest.com. **Description:** BMC West Corporation is a regional distributor and retailer of building materials in the western United States. Products are sold primarily to professional contractors and consumers. In addition to distributing products from other manufacturers, the company conducts value-added conversion activities that include prehanging doors, fabricating roof trusses, preassembling windows, and precutting lumber to meet customer specifications. **Positions advertised include:** Door Plant Management; Sales and Production; Truss Plant Management; Sales Design and Production; Senior, General, Administrative and Sales Management. **Special programs:** Internships. **Corporate headquarters location:** This location. **Other U.S. locations:** Nationwide. **Parent company:** Building Materials Holding Corporation. **Listed on:** NASDAQ. **Stock exchange symbol:** BMHC. **Number of employees nationwide:** More than 4,500.

BARNES & NOBLE BOOKSTORES
1315 North Milwaukee Street, Boise ID 83704. 208/375-4454. **Contact:** Manager. **World Wide Web address:** http://www.barnesandnoble.com. **Description:** A bookstore chain operating nationwide. This location has a cafe and music department in addition to its book departments. **Listed on:** NASDAQ. **Stock exchange symbol:** BNBN.

BENEWAH COMMUNITY HOSPITAL
229 South Seventh Street, Saint Maries ID 83861. 208/245-5551. **Contact:** Jacquae Moore, Human Resources Department. **World Wide Web address:** http://www.nihn.net/benewah. **Description:** Benewah Community Hospital is a 25-bed, acute care, county hospital offering a full range of services including inpatient and outpatient surgeries. **Number of employees:** 137.

BINGHAM MEMORIAL HOSPITAL
98 Poplar Street, Blackfoot ID 83221-1758. 208/785-3840. **Fax:** 208/785-3842. **Contact:** Human Resources. **E-mail address:** dkarren@binghammemorial.org. **World Wide Web address:** http://www.binghammemorial.org. **Description:** Bingham Memorial Hospital has a 40-bed acute care division, a birthing center, and a variety of rehabilitative outpatient services including physical therapy. Bingham County Extended Care Facility (also at this location) is a 100-bed long-term care facility. **Note:** Applications may be downloaded from the hospital's website, or contact human resources at 208/785-3841 to have one mailed to you. **Positions advertised include:** Registered Nurse, Critical Care; Registered Nurse, Surgery; Registered Nurse, Part Time. **Number of employees at this location:** 300.

BLUE CROSS OF IDAHO
P.O. Box 7408 Meridian ID 83707. 208/345-4550. **Fax:** 208/331-7682. **Physical address:** 3000 East Pine Avenue, Meridian ID 83642. **Recorded jobline:** 208/331-7683. **Contact:** Human Resources. **E-mail address:** hr@bcidaho.com. **World Wide Web address:** http://www.bcidaho.com. **Description:** A nonprofit health care insurance organization providing managed health care plans to both individuals and groups including Medicare Supplement, dental, PPO, and HMO plans. **NOTE:** Does not accept unsolicited applications or resumes. See website for information on how to apply. **Positions advertised include:** Care Coordination Nurse; Case Management Nurse; Dental Sales Manager; Sales District Manager. **Corporate headquarters location:** Chicago IL.

BOISE CASCADE CORPORATION
1111 West Jefferson Street, P.O. Box 50, Boise ID 83728. 208/384-6161. **Fax:** 208/384-7189. **Contact:** Human Resources. **World Wide Web address:** http://www.bc.com. **Description:** A producer and distributor of pulp and paper, a direct distributor of office products, and a manufacturer and distributor of building products. The company has more than 90 manufacturing and distribution locations in 27 states. Boise Cascade Corporation's paper is used for commercial printing and publishing, forms, envelopes, reprographics, tablets, and packaging. Boise Cascade Corporation provides direct delivery of office products including office and computer supplies and xerographic paper. The company also produces engineered wood products such as laminated veneer lumber and wood I-joists. Founded in 1957. **NOTE:** Does not accept unsolicited resumes or applications. See website for information on how to apply for specific positions. **Positions advertised include:** Accounting Specialist. **Special Programs:** Internships available. **Corporate headquarters location:** This location. **Other U.S. locations:** Nationwide. **International locations:** Australia; Brazil; New Zealand. **Listed on:** New York Stock Exchange. **Stock exchange symbol:** BCC. **CEO:** George Harad. **Number of employees worldwide:** 24,000.

BOISE STATE UNIVERSITY
Human Resources Services, Administration Building Room 218, 1910 University Drive, Boise ID 83725. 208/426-1616. **Fax:** 208/426-3100. **Contact:** Viola Boman, Employment Manager. **Email address:** vboman@boisestate.edu. **World Wide Web address:** http://www.idbsu.edu. **Description:** Boise State University has one of the largest student enrollments in Idaho with approximately 17,000 students. The university offers courses in seven colleges: Arts and Sciences, Business, Education, Health Science, Social Sciences and Public Affairs, Technology, and Graduate Studies. The university is fully accredited by the Northwest Association of Schools and Colleges and is a member of the College Entrance Examination Board and the College Scholarship Service Assembly. Founded in 1932. **NOTE:** Applicants for classified jobs must apply on the state of Idaho website: http://www.dhr.state.id.us. **Positions advertised include:** Underwriting Account Executive; Assistant Professor, Bilingual Education and English as a Second Language; University Internship Coordinator; Assistant Director, University Conference Services; Assistant Professor (Tenure Track), Department of Curriculum. **Office hours:** Monday-Friday 8 a.m.-5 p.m.; Summer hours: Monday-Thursday 8 a.m.-5 p.m., Friday 7:30 a.m.-11:30 a.m. **President:** Dr. Bob Kustra. **Number of employees at this location:** 1,500.

BON-MACY'S
918 West Idaho Street, Boise ID 83702. 208/388-7000. **Contact:** Human Resources. **World Wide Web address:** http://www.bon-macys.com. **Description:** Formally known as The Bon Marche, a regional department store. The Bon Marche and Macy's have integrated to form Bon-Macy's, a retail department store chain with 50 locations in the Pacific Northwest. **Positions advertised include:** Storeline Sales & Sales Support Associate; Storeline Management. **Corporate headquarters location:** Seattle, WA. **Other U.S. locations:** ID; MT; OR; WA; WY. **Parent company:** Federated Department Stores. **Number of employees nationwide:** 6,900. **Annual sales/revenues in 2002:** $963 million.

BUSINESS PSYCHOLOGY ASSOCIATES
300 Mallard Drive, Suite 350, Boise ID 83706. 208/343-4080. **Toll-free phone:** 800/486-4372. **Fax:** 208/344-7430. **Contact:** Sarah Woodley, Manager of Operations. **World Wide Web address:** http://www.bpahealth.com. **Description:** Business Psychology Services provides managed behavioral health and employee assistance programs on an out-patient basis. **NOTE:** Applicants for counselor positions should address inquiries to the attention of Bruce Wixson, Clinical Supervisor. Applicants for office administrative positions should address inquiries to Sarah Woodley, Manager of Operations.

COEUR D'ALENE MINES CORPORATION
505 Front Avenue, Coeur d'Alene ID 83814. 208/667-3511. **Toll-free phone:** 800/624-2824. **Fax:** 208/769-5080. **Contact:** Human Resources. **Email address:** mharper@coeur.com. **World Wide Web address:** http://www.coeur.com. **Description:** Coeur d'Alene Mines is a gold and silver producer. **Corporate headquarters location:** This location. **Other U.S. locations:** NV, AK. **International locations:** Chile, Argentina, Bolivia. **Listed on:** New York Stock Exchange. **Stock exchange symbol:** CDE. **Chairman and CEO:** Dennis E. Wheeler.

CORRECTIONAL INDUSTRIES
1299 North Orchard Suite 110, Boise ID 83706. 208/658-2163. **Toll-free Phone:** 800/334-5314. **Contact:** Human Resources. **World Wide Web address:** http://www.ci.state.id.us. **Description:** Correctional Industries, a self-supporting division of the Department of Corrections, employs inmates and civilians to provide a wide range of products and services. The company mimics private sector employment in organizational structure, production, management, and standards. Products include office and systems furniture, carpentry, upholstery and seating, metal fabrication, custom and traffic signs, decals, moving services, and printing services. **Corporate headquarters location:** This location. **Operations at this facility include:** Administration; Manufacturing; Sales.

CSHQA, ARCHITECTS/ENGINEERS/PLANNERS
C.W. Moore Plaza, 250 South Fifth Street, Boise ID 83702. 208/343-4635. **Fax:** 208/343-2017. **Contact:** Human Resources. **E-mail address:** hr@cshqa.com. **World Wide Web address:** http://www.cshqa.com. **Description:** Full service engineering and architectural firm. Founded in 1889. **Positions advertised include:** Business Development Coordinator. **Other U.S. locations:** CA; OR. **President:** Jeffrey A. Shneider, AIA.

DEDICATED DEVICES INC.
5680 east Franklin Road, Suite 250, Nampa ID 83687. 208/442-1248. **Fax:** 208/442-1281. **Contact:** Human Resources. **E-mail address:** hr@dedicateddev.com. **World Wide Web address:** http://www.dedicateddev.com. **Description:** Designs integrated digital home media technology devices.

DOUBLETREE RIVERSIDE
2900 Chinden Boulevard, Boise ID 83714. 208/343-1871. **Fax:** 208/344-1079. **Contact:** Director of Human Resources. **World Wide Web address:** http://www.doubletree.com. **Description:** A major hotel. The facilities include 14 meeting rooms, the largest accommodating up to 1,000 people, and complete catering and convention planning services. **Parent company:** Hilton Hotel.

EAST IDAHO CREDIT UNION
865 South Woodruff Avenue, P.O. Box 1865, Idaho Falls ID 83403. 208/523-9068. **Fax:** 280/523-4755. **Contact:** Cindy Mitchell, Branch Manager. **E-mail address:** cmitchell@eastidahocu.org. **World Wide Web address:** http://www.eastidahocu.org. **Description:** A member-owned financial cooperative, offering loan and other financial services. The credit union has nine offices throughout Idaho, plus a telephone-teller line. Financial services include savings services; share draft accounts; VISA debit/draft guarantee cards; ATM Access; travelers' checks; financial counseling; and an electronic federal tax filing. The credit union's loan service covers a wide range of loan programs. Founded in 1935. **Office hours:** Monday-Friday 9 a.m.-5:30 p.m.; Saturday 9 a.m.-1 p.m.

EMERGECORE NETWORKS LLC
6149 North Meeker Place, Suite 200, Boise ID 83713. 208/947-8555. **Fax:** 208/947-8556. **Contact:** Human Resources. **E-mail address:** salesmgr@emergecore.com. **World Wide Web address:** http://www.emergecore.com. **Description:** Develops integrated IT solutions for small businesses.

EXTENDED SYSTEMS, INC.
5777 North Meeker Avenue, Boise ID 83711. **Toll-free phone:** 800/235-7576. **Fax:** 208/327-5004. **Contact:** Human Resources. **E-mail address:** jobs@extendsys.com. **World Wide Web address:** http://www.extendsys.com. **Description:** Designs, manufactures, and markets computer enhancement products, primarily printer sharing products and network print servers. **Positions advertised include:** General Counsel; Staff Accountant/Analyst. **Special programs:** Internships, Student Part-time Employment; Co-op. **Corporate headquarters location:** This location. **International locations:** France; Germany; Italy; The Netherlands; Singapore; United Kingdom. **Operations at this facility include:** Administration; Manufacturing; Research and Development; Sales; Service. **Listed on:** NASDAQ. **Stock exchange symbol:** XTND.

EXTREME RVS
P.O. Box 990, Caldwell ID 83606. 208/453-2500. **Physical address:** 412 South Kit Avenue, Caldwell ID 83605. **Contact:** Human Resources. **World Wide Web address:** http://www.extremervs.com. **Description:** One of the largest manufacturers of travel trailers and fifth wheels in the United States. The company also manufactures a wide range of recreational vehicle (RV) products. Products are sold under the Road Ranger, Companion, and Sportsmaster brand names.

GEOENGINEERS
802 West Bannock Street, Suite 700, Boise ID 83702. 208/433-8098. **Fax:** 208/433-8092. **Contact:** Human Resources. **E-mail address:** employment@geoengineers.com. **World Wide Web address:** http://www.geoengineers.com. **NOTE:** Apply online. **Description:** Provides earth science, environmental, and technology consulting services focusing on the areas of transportation, energy, development, government services, and water and natural resources. **Corporate headquarters location:** Redmond WA. **location: Other locations:** Anchorage AK; Honolulu HI; Springfield MO; Portland OR.

THE GROVE HOTEL
245 South Capital Boulevard, Boise ID 83702. 208/333-8000. **Fax:** 208/333-8800. **Contact:** Rhonna Dunten. **World Wide Web address:** http://www.westcoasthotels.com/grove. **Description:** A luxury hotel with 250 rooms and suites, executive boardrooms, and a full-service athletic facility. **NOTE:** For salaried positions send resumes to: 201 West North River Drive, Spokane WA 99201 or fax 509/325-7324. **Corporate headquarters location:** Spokane Washington. **Parent company:** West Coast Hospitality Corporation. **Listed on:** New York Stock Exchange. **Stock exchange symbol:** WEH.

THE HAGADONE CORPORATION
111 South First Street, Coeur d'Alene ID 83814. 208/667-3431. **Fax:** 208/664-7206. **Contact:** Personnel. **World Wide Web address:** http://www.hagadone.com. **Description:** A newspaper publisher. Hagadone is also engaged in hotel and motel operations.

HECLA MINING COMPANY
6500 North Mineral Drive, Suite 200, Coeur d'Alene ID 83815-9408. 208/769-4100. **Fax:** 208/769-7612. **Contact:** Robert Buckham, Director of Human Resources. **E-mail address:** rcsumc@hecla-mining.com. **World Wide Web address:** http://www.hecla-mining.com. **Description:** A silver and gold mining company. A leader in the silver business for decades, Hecla controls nearly 76 million ounces of proven and probable silver reserves. Hecla is also a growing gold producer. Founded in 1896. **Subsidiaries include:** Kentucky-Tennessee Clay Company, a major supplier of ball clay, kaolin, and feldspar. **Listed on:** New York Stock Exchange. **Stock exchange symbol:** HL. **CEO:** Arthur Brown. **Number of employees at this location:** 800.

HEWLETT PACKARD
1311 Chinden Boulevard, Boise ID 83714. 208/396-6000. **Fax:** 208/396-3457. **Contact:** Human Resources. **World Wide Web address:** http://www.hp.com. **Description:** Hewlett-Packard designs and manufactures measurement and computation products and systems used in business, industry, engineering, science, health care, and education. Principal products include integrated instrument and computer systems such as hardware and software, peripheral products, and electronic medical equipment and systems. **NOTE:** Search and apply for positions online. **Corporate headquarters location:** Palo Alto CA. **Other U.S. locations:** Nationwide.

HOLLAND & HART LLP
P.O. Box 2527, Boise ID 83701. 208/342-5000. **Physical address**: U.S. Bank Plaza, 101 South Capitol Boulevard Suite 1400, Boise ID 83702. **Contact:** Hiring Partner. **World Wide Web address:** http://www.hollandhart.com. **Description:** A law firm with a wide range of practice areas. **Note:** Go to http://www.hhjobs.com_for information on how to apply. **Special Programs:** Summer Clerkship. **Other U.S. locations:** CO; DC; MO; NM; UT; WY. **Number of employees nationwide:** 250.

HOME-STYLE INDUSTRIES INC.
P.O. Box 1500, Nampa ID 83653. 208/466-8481. **Physical address:** 1324 Eleventh Avenue North Extension, Nampa ID 83651. **Fax:** 208/467-9942. **Contact:** Human Resources. **Description:** Manufactures furniture. **Corporate headquarters location:** This location.

IDAHO DEPARTMENT OF CORRECTIONS
1299 North Orchard Street, Suite 110, Boise ID 83706. 208/658-2000. **Toll-free number:** 800/260-2684. **Contact:** Human Resources Office. **E-mail address:** hr@corr.state.id.us. **World Wide Web address:** http://www.corr.state.id.us. **Description:** Provides incarceration facilities for adult felons. This location is the central office, additionally there are eight correctional institutions, five community work centers, and 24 parole offices. **Positions advertised include:** Sentencing Specialist; Deputy Administrator, Operations; Correctional Lieutenant; Correctional Industries, Driver. **Other area locations:** Orofino ID; Cottonwood ID; Pocatello ID; St. Anthony ID; Nampa ID; Twin Falls ID; Coeur d'Alene ID; Sandpoint ID; Walden ID; Lewiston ID; Grangeville ID; Caldwell ID; Moscow ID; Emmett ID; Weiser ID. **Number of employees:** 1,400.

IDAHO ELKS REHABILITATION HOSPITAL
600 North Robbins Road, P.O. Box 1100, Boise ID 83702. 208/489-4444. **Fax:** 208/489-4005. **Contact:** Jim Atkins, Director-Employee Services. **Email address:** jatkins@ierh.org. **World Wide Web address:** http://www.idahoelks.com. **Description:** A rehabilitation hospital providing in patient and outpatient services. Founded in 1941, this hospital began as a convalescent home for children recovering from Polio. A new, state-of-the-art facility was opened in 2001. **Positions advertised include:** Speech Pathologist; Audiology Clinical Secretary; Registered Nurse; Respiratory Therapist; Physical Therapist; Medical Transcriptionist.

IDAHO POWER COMPANY
P.O. Box 70, Boise ID 83707. 208/388-2965. **Physical address:** 1221 West Idaho, Boise ID 83702. **Fax:** 208/388-6695. **Recorded jobline:** 800/789-2950. **Contact:** Personnel. **E-mail address:** ipcohr@idahopower.com. **World Wide Web address:** http://www.idahopower.com. **Description:** Idaho Power Company is an independent, investor-owned utility that provides electricity to parts of southern Idaho, eastern Oregon, and northern Nevada. The company has 17 hydroelectric plants and is part owner of three coal-fired generating plants. **Positions advertised include:** Computer Operator; Building Maintenance Technician. **Parent company:** IDACORP, Inc. **Listed on:** New York Stock Exchange. **Stock exchange symbol:** IDA. **President/CEO:** Jan B. Packwood.

IDAHO STATE UNIVERSITY
Campus Box 8107, Pocatello ID 83209. 208/282-2517. **Physical address:** 741 South Seventh Avenue, Pocatello ID 83209. **Fax:** 208/282-4976. **Contact:** David Miller, Director of Personnel. **E-mail address:** hr@isu.edu **World Wide Web address:** http://www.isu.edu. **Description:** A four-year state university offering a variety of programs in the colleges of Arts and Sciences, Business, Education, Engineering, Health Professions, and Pharmacy. Family Medicine is a post-graduate medical training program for physicians seeking specialization in rural family practice. The university also has a School of Graduate Studies and Research and a School of Applied Technology. **Positions advertised include:** Assistant Professor of Health and Nutrition; Assistant Professor of English; Assistant Professor of Pharmacy Science; Assistant Professor of Neuroscience and Human Anatomy; Director of Special Education and Summer Programs; Government Documents Librarian; Teacher/Parent Involvement Coordinator.

IDAHOAN FOODS
P.O. Box 130, 529 North 3500 East, Lewisville ID 83431. 208/754-4686. **Toll-free phone:** 800/635-6100. **Fax:** 208/754-0094. **Contact:** Rodney Roberts, Chief Financial Officer. **World Wide Web address:** http://www.idahoan.com. **Description:** A producer of dehydrated potato products. **Corporate headquarters location:** This location. **Number of employees this location:** 500.

JCPENNEY COMPANY, INC.
300 North Milwaukee, Boise ID 83704. 208/376-0555. **Fax:** 208/376-0050. **Contact:** Steven Fuss, Store Manager. **World Wide Web address:** http://www.jcpenney.com. **Description:** This location is a retail store. JCPenney Company, Inc. is an international retail merchandise sales and service corporation. The company sells its merchandise through a chain of department stores as well as through its catalog. **Special programs:**

Internships. **Corporate headquarters location:** Plano TX. **Operations at this facility include:** Sales. **Listed on:** New York Stock Exchange. **Stock exchange symbol:** JCP. **CEO:** Allen Questrom. **Other U.S. locations:** Nationwide.

KEYBANK OF IDAHO
702 West Idaho, Boise ID 83702. 208/364-8510. **Recorded jobline:** 208/364-8700. **Contact:** Patricia McKinnis, Manager of Human Resources. **World Wide Web address:** http://www.keybank.com. **Description:** Provides banking services. **Positions advertised include:** Small Business Team Leader; Part-time Teller; Relationship Manager; Business Development Manager. **Corporate headquarters location:** Cleveland OH. **Parent company:** KeyCorp. **Operations at this facility include:** Divisional Headquarters. **Listed on:** New York Stock Exchange. **Stock exchange symbol:** KEY.

WALTER KNOX MEMORIAL HOSPITAL
1202 East Locust Street, Emmett ID 83617-2715. 208/365-3561. **Contact:** Michael Cornell, Human Resources Department. **Email address:** cornellm@wkmh.org. **World Wide Web address:** http://www.wkmh.org. **Description:** A 24-bed, acute care hospital that offers general medical and surgical services and also has a birthing center. **Positions advertised include:** X-Ray and Lab Technician; Registered Nurse. **CEO:** Max Long.

LAMB WESTON, INC.
P.O. Box 128, Twin Falls ID 83303-0128. 208/733-5664. **Fax:** 208/736-5607. **Contact:** Personnel. **E-mail:** resume@lambweston.com. **World Wide Web address:** http://www.lambweston.com. **Description:** A processor of a broad line of nationally distributed frozen potato products including french fries and potato wedges. **Corporate headquarters location:** Kennewick WA. **Other U.S. locations:** MN; NC; OR; WA. **International locations:** Canada; Holland. **Parent company:** ConAgra, Inc**Operations at this facility include:** Administration; Manufacturing. **Listed on:** New York Stock Exchange. **Stock exchange symbol:** CAG.

LEWIS-CLARK STATE COLLEGE
500 Eighth Avenue, Lewiston ID 83501. 208/792-2269. **Fax:** 208/792-2872. **Contact:** Lori Gaskill, Director of Human Resources. **Email:** lgaskill@lcsc.edu. **World Wide Web address:** http://www.lcsc.edu. **Description:** A public undergraduate college serving a diverse student population. Lewis-Clark State College offers programs in the liberal arts and sciences, as well in professional and applied technical fields. Founded in 1893. **Positions advertised include:** Division Chair of Nursing and Health Sciences. **Office hours:** Monday-Friday, 8:00 a.m. - 5:00 p.m. **President:** Dene Kay Thomas, Ph. D.

LOUISIANA-PACIFIC CORPORATION
P.O. Box 4000-98, Hayden Lake ID 83835. 208/772-6011. **Fax:** 208/762-2461. **Contact:** Human Resources. **World Wide Web address:** http://www.lpcorp.com. **Description:** A forest products firm that harvests timber and converts it into a wide range of wood products including lumber, panel products, doors, and other goods. Louisiana-Pacific operates more than 100 manufacturing facilities and 20 distribution centers in the United States and Canada. **Note:** Louisiana-Pacific's website lists salaried job openings only. For hourly positions, contact the Human Resources Manager at specific facilities to inquire. **Positions advertised include:** National Sales Manager, Lumber. **Corporate headquarters location:** OR. **Other U.S. locations:** Nationwide. **International locations:** Canada; Chile; Ireland. **Listed on:** New York Stock Exchange. **Stock exchange symbol:** LPX. **CEO:** Mark Suwyn.

MPC COMPUTERS
906 East Karcher Road, Nampa ID 83687. 208/893-3434. **Toll-free phone:** 800/828-0416. **Fax:** 208/893-7044. **Contact:** Human Resources. **E-mail address:** jobs@buympc.com. **World Wide Web address:** http://www.buympc.com. **Description:** Develops, manufactures, markets, and supports a line of memory intensive, high-performance notebook and desktop PCs and NetFRAME servers, along with related hardware and software products for the business, consumer, government, and education industries. Positions advertised include: Account Executive-State, Local and Educational Markets for Los Angeles; Account Executive-Federal Government/Civilian for DC; Account Executive- New York/New Jersey Area; Inside Sales Representative, Army. **NOTE:** Unsolicited resumes and applications not accepted. **Special programs:** Internships. **Office hours:** Monday - Friday, 8:00 a.m. - 5:00 p.m. **Corporate headquarters location:** This location. **Subsidiaries include:** SpecTek processes and markets various grades of DRAM products under the SpecTek brand name. **Parent company:** Gores Technology Group. **President/CEO:** Michael S. Adkins.

MAGIC VALLEY REGIONAL MEDICAL CENTER
P.O. Box 409, Twin Falls ID 83303. 208/737-2000. **Recorded jobline:** 208/737-2775. **Contact:** Human Resources. **E-mail address:** jamesg@mvrmc.com **World Wide Web address:** http://www.mvrmc.org. **Description:** A 165-bed, general acute care facility governed by a volunteer hospital board and managed by Quorum Resources, Inc. The hospital's services include the Southern Idaho Regional Cancer Center, home care services, a same-day surgery center, an intensive care unit, emergency transport services, a 24-hour physician-staffed emergency department, maternity and newborn services, physical therapy, and a pharmacy. **NOTE:** Applicants must apply online. **Positions advertised include:** Registered Nurse; Licensed Practitioner Nurse; Anesthesia Technician; Certified Surgical Technician; Chemical Dependency Counselor; Respiratory Therapist; Social Worker; Phlebotomy/Lab Assistant; Computer Systems Specialist; Physical Therapist; Pediatric Speech Pathologist; Community Connections Coordinator; Construction Worker.

MELALEUCA
3910 South Yellowstone Highway, Idaho Falls ID 83402. 208/522-0700. **Toll-free Phone:** 800/742-2444. **Fax:** 888/528-2090. **Contact:** Human Resources. **E-mail address:** info@melaleuca.com. **World Wide Web address:** http://www.melaleuca.com. **Description:** A consumer-direct marketing company. Melaleuca produces and distributes personal care, home hygiene, nutritional, and pharmaceutical products. **Corporate headquarters location:** This location. **Other U.S. locations:** Nationwide. **International locations:** Canada. **Operations at this facility include:** Administration; Manufacturing; Research and Development; Sales; Service. **President/CEO:** Frank L. VanderSloot. **Number of employees nationwide:** 1,300.

MERCY MEDICAL CENTER
1512 12th Avenue Road, Nampa ID 83686. 208/463-5800. **Recorded jobline:** 208/463-5802. **Contact:** Human Resources. **World Wide Web address:** http://www.mercymedicalnampa.com. **Description:** Mercy Medical Center is a 152-bed community-based, acute care hospital. **Positions advertised include:** Mammography Technician; Nuclear Medicine Technician; Monitor Technician; Medical Technician; Phlebotomist; Physical Therapist; Pharmacist; Radiology Technician; Speech Therapist; Ultrasound Technician; Cook; Registered Nurse. **Parent Company:** Catholic Health Initiatives (CHI.) **Number of employees at this location:** 700.

MICRON TECHNOLOGY, INC.
8000 South Federal Way, P.O. Box 6, Mail Stop 707, Boise ID 83707-0006. 208/368-4141. **Fax:** 208/363-2322. **Recorded jobline:** 800/932-4991. **Contact:** Human Resources. **E-mail address:** jobs@micron.com. **World Wide Web address:** http://www.micron.com. **Description:** Manufactures and markets 16- and 64-megabyte dynamic random access memory (DRAM) components in varying word widths (x4, x8, x16); Graphics DRAMs; Synchronous SRAMs, pipelined and nonpipelined; and Flash Memory. The company also manufactures integrated circuits and small semiconductor dies. **NOTE:** See Website for specific instructions on mailing or faxing resumes. **Positions advertised include:** Budget Analyst; CAD Engineer; Equipment Maintenance Technician; Calibration Test Engineer; Characterization Engineer; Cost Accountant; Design Engineer; Flash Process Integration Technician; Flash Process Reliability Engineer; Junior Chemist; Process Engineer; Yield Enhancement Engineer. **Special programs:** Internships; College Recruiting. **Corporate headquarters location:** This location. **Other U.S. Locations:** CA, MN, TX, UT, VA. **International Locations:** Worldwide. **Subsidiaries include:** Micron Communications; Micron Display Technology; Micron Europe Limited; Micron Quantum Devices, Inc.; Micron Semiconductor (Deutschland) GmbH; Micron Semiconductor Asia Pacific Pte. Ltd.; Micron Semiconductor Asia Pacific, Inc.; Micron Semiconductor Products, Inc.; Micron Technology Japan, K.K. **Operations at this facility include:** Administration; Manufacturing; Research and Development; Sales. **Listed on:** New York Stock Exchange. **Stock exchange symbol:** MU. **President/CEO:** Steve Appleton. **Number of employees at this location:** 7,825. **Number of employees nationwide:** 11,400. **Number of employees worldwide:** 16,900

NORTH WIND INC.
P.O. Box 51174, 1423 Hingham Street, Idaho Falls ID 83405. 208/528-8718. **Fax:** 208/528-8714. **Contact:** Human Resources. **World Wide Web address:** http://www.nwindenv.com. **Description:** An environmental restoration, engineering, program management, geosciences, waste management, and civil construction services company operating from over a dozen offices. **NOTE:** Search and apply for positions online. **Positions advertised include:** Archaeologist; Chemist; Construction Project Manager; Environmental Engineer; Industrial Hygienist. **Corporate office location:** This location. **Other area locations:** Kellogg ID; Salmon ID.

NORTHWEST NAZARENE UNIVERSITY
623 Holly Street, Nampa ID 83686. 208/467-8011. **Toll-free phone:** 800/NNU-4YOU. **Fax:** 208/467-8597. **Contact:** Human Resources. **World Wide Web address:** http://www.nnu.edu. **Description:** A liberal arts college affiliated with the Church of the Nazarene. Founded in 1913. **NOTE:** See Website for contact information regarding specific positions. **Positions advertised include:** Secretary; Professor of Social Work; Professor of Media Studies; Professor of Spanish; Security; Visit Coordinator. **President:** Dr. Richard A. Hagood.

NORTHWEST PRINTING
3430 Americana Terrace, Boise ID 83706. 208/345-4545. **Toll-free phone:** 800/325-3906. **Fax:** 208/345-4564. **Contact:** Personnel. **Email:** cdirstine@nwprinting.com. **World Wide Web address:** http://www.nwprinting.com. **Description:** Northwest Printing is one of the premier printers of the Northwest. The company's operations include an electronic prepress department, a camera department, a press department, and a bindery department.

POSITRON SYSTEMS
6151 North Discovery Way, Boise ID 83713. 208/672-1923. **Fax:** 208/672-8012. **Contact:** Human Resources. **World Wide Web address:** http://www.positronsystems.com. **Description:** Performs nondestructive testing that identifies structural integrity, fatigue, and embrittlement problems at the atomic level.

POTLATCH CORPORATION
P.O. Box 1388, Lewiston ID 83501. 208/799-0123. **Physical address:** 805 Mill Road, Lewiston ID 83501. **Contact:** Scott Dean, Employee Relations Manager. **E-mail address:** jobs@potlatchcorp.com. **World Wide Web address:** http://www.potlatchcorp.com. **Description:** Potlatch Corporation is a diversified forest products company with approximately 1.5 million acres of timberland in Arkansas, Idaho, Minnesota, Nevada, and Oklahoma. Founded in 1903. **NOTE:** Only on-line applications will be accepted. For assistance with the application process, address questions to the e-mail address listed above. **Positions advertised include:** Internal Auditor; Research Technician-Temporary/Casual; Business Planning Manager; Wildlife Technician-Temporary/Casual; Business Analyst; Sawmill Shift Supervisor. **Corporate headquarters location:** WA. **Other area locations:** St. Maries ID; Bovil ID. **Other U.S. locations:** AR; MN; NV; OR. **Operations at this facility include:** This location produces bleached kraft pulp, while the paperboard operation produces bleached paperboard. **Listed on:** New York Stock Exchange. **Stock exchange symbol:** PCH. **Number of employees worldwide:** 4,200.

PROCLARITY CORPORATION
P.O. Box 8064, Boise ID 83707. 208/344-1630. **Fax:** 208/343-6128. **Contact:** Human Resources. **E-mail address:** employment@proclarity.com. **World Wide Web address:** http://www.proclarity.com. **Description:** Develops analytical solutions for retail, healthcare, financial service and insurance organizations that allows for smarter faster decisions. **Positions advertised include:** Inside Sale Representative; Presales Engineer.

SCP GLOBAL TECHNOLOGIES INC.
8455 West Park Street, Boise ID 83704. 208/685-5000. **Fax:** 208/685-4540. **Toll-free phone:** 800/223-1691. **Contact:** Human Resources. **World Wide Web address:** http://www.scpglobal.com. **Description:** Develops and markets cleaning technology for the semiconductor industry.

SAINT LUKE'S REGIONAL MEDICAL CENTER
148 East Jefferson Street, Boise ID 83712. **Toll-free phone:** 800/722-7052. **Fax:** 208/381-4649. **Recorded jobline:** 208/381-1187. **Contact:** Human Resources. **E-mail address:** jobs@slrmc.org. **World Wide Web address:** http://www.stlukesonline.org. **Description:** Idaho's largest healthcare provider. Three full service hospitals and twenty-five outpatient treatment facilities and clinics. Serving Idaho and the six neighboring states. **Positions advertised include:** Medical Imaging Film Librarian; Health Records Specialist; Patient Business Associate; Mountain States Tumor Institute Secretary; Cardio Vascular Surgery Unit Clerk; Clinical Assistant Personnel; Nurse Apprentice; Laundry Production Operator; Purchasing Sales Clerk; Unit Service Associate; Certified Surgical Technician; Certified Engineering Technician; MRI Technologist; Pharmacy Technician; Radiology Staff Technician; Women's Unit Clinical Director; Communication Specialist; Performance Improvements/Outcomes Manager/Director; Family Financial Counselor; Occupational Therapist; Office

Manager; Desktop Support Supervisor; Registered Nurse. **Other area locations:** Meridian ID; Ketchum ID.

SALTZER MEDICAL GROUP
215 East Hawaii Avenue, Nampa ID 83686. 208/463-3000. **Contact:** Human Resources. **World Wide Web address:** http://www.saltzermedicalgroup.com. **Description:** A clinic with approximately 40 physicians. Saltzer Medical Group offers a wide variety of services including emergency care, dermatology, cardiology, and pediatrics. **Note:** See website for information on downloading and faxing applications. **Corporate Headquarters:** Granite Bay CA. **CEO:** Jim Steeb.

SCIENTECH INC.
200 South Woodruff Avenue, Idaho Falls ID 83402. 208/524-9200. **Fax:** 208/529-4721. **Contact:** Human Resources. **World Wide Web address:** http://www.scientech.com. **Description:** SCIENTECH Inc. is a nationwide scientific and technical consulting firm specializing in information systems, environmental, and engineering projects. **NOTE:** Unless otherwise stated on Website, send resumes to: Human Resources Department, 910 Clopper Road, Gaithersburg MD 20878. **Fax:** 301/258-2463. **Positions advertised include:** Electronic Design/Engineering Manager. **Other U.S. locations:** Nationwide. **Subsidiaries include:** Belfort Engineering. **Listed on:** Privately held. **President/CEO:** Paul Loch. **Number of employees nationwide:** 350.

SENICA FOODS
P.O. Box 460, Payette ID 83661. 208/642-9061. **Fax:** 208/642-6310. **Physical address:** 25 North Sixth Street, Payette ID 83661. **Contact:** Human Resources. **World Wide Web address:** http://www.senicafoods.com. **Description:** Senica is an independent, publicly–traded, food processing company. Senica is a fully integrated producer, having made significant investments in facilities and technologies to enhance manufacturing processes, increase line speeds, and guarantee premium quality. **Corporate headquarters location:** Marion NY.

SHOSHONE MEDICAL CENTER
25 Jacobs Gulch, Kellogg ID 83837. 208/784-1221. **Fax:** 208/784-0961. **Contact:** Wanda Groves, Human Resources. **E-mail address:** wgroves@shomed.org. **World Wide Web address:** http://www.shomed.org. **Description:** A nonprofit, 25-bed, acute care facility. Shoshone Medical Center has an obstetrics unit, 24-hour emergency services, a walk-in immediate care center open 365 days per year, primary and specialty care physician clinics, North Idaho Addiction Recovery Center, and Healthworks Fitness Center. Founded in 1958. **Company slogan:** Excellence in health care. **Positions advertised include:** Registered Nurse; Radiological Technologist; Operating Room Nurse. **Corporate headquarters location:** This location. **CEO:** Gary M. Moore.

J.R. SIMPLOT COMPANY/MINERAL & CHEMICAL GROUP
P.O. Box 27, Boise ID 83702. 208/672-2700. **Contact:** Human Resources. **E-mail address:** questions@simplotjobs. **World Wide Web address:** http://www.simplot.com. **Description:** Operates four fertilizer manufacturing plants. **Other U.S. locations:** CA. **International locations:** Manitoba, Canada. **Parent company:** J.R. Simplot Company, a privately held agribusiness corporation. **Annual sales/revenues:** More than $100 million.

J.R. SIMPLOT COMPANY/CALDWELL
P.O. Box 1059, Caldwell ID 83606-1059. 208/459-0071. **Fax:** 208/454-4393. **Contact:** Human Resources. **World Wide Web address:** http://www.simplot.com. **Description:** A potato-processing plant. **Corporate headquarters location:** Boise ID. **Parent company:** J.R. Simplot Company, a privately held agribusiness corporation. **Annual sales/revenues:** More than $100 million.

SIMPLOT LIVESTOCK COMPANY
1301 Highway 67 Grandview ID 83624. 208/834-2231. **Contact:** Mr. Vern Bohn, Personnel Director. **World Wide Web address:** http://www.simplot.com. **Description:** The Simplot Livestock Company raises livestock. **Corporate headquarters location:** Boise ID. **Parent company:** J.R. Simplot Company, a privately held agribusiness corporation. **Annual sales/revenues:** More than $100 million.

SOLUTIA, INC.
P.O. Box 816, Soda Springs ID 83276-0816. 208/547-4300. **Physical address:** 1853 Highway 34, Soda Springs ID 83276-5227. **Fax:** 208/547-3312. **Contact:** Mr. Mark Dooley, Human Resources Supervisor. **World Wide Web address:** http://www.solutia.com. **Description:** Produces high-purity phosphorous. Founded in 1997. **Parent company:** Monsanto Chemical Company. **Corporate headquarters location:** St. Louis MO. **Other US. locations:** Nationwide. **International locations:** Worldwide. **Listed on:** New York Stock Exchange. **Stock exchange symbol:** SOI.

STATE HOSPITAL NORTH
300 Hospital Drive, Orofino ID 83544. 208/476-4511. **Fax:** 208/476-7898. **Contact:** Quinn Galbraith or Sharon Larson, Human Resources Staff. **Description:** A 60-bed residential psychiatric hospital for adults. State Hospital North also has a chemical dependency unit.

STATE HOSPITAL SOUTH
P.O. Box 400, Blackfoot ID 83221. 208/785-1200. **Physical address:** 700 East Alice Street, Blackfoot ID 83221. **Contact:** Human Resources Director. **Description:** A 130-bed residential psychiatric hospital for adolescents (ages 12 - 18) and adults.

SUN VALLEY COMPANY
P.O. Box 10, Sun Valley ID 83353. 208/622-2078. **Toll-free phone:** 800/894/9946. **Fax:** 208/622-2082. **Contact:** Human Resources. **E-mail address:** svpersonnel@sunvalley.com **World Wide Web address:** http://www.sunvalley.com. **Description:** Operates a hotel and ski resort on 4,000 acres in the Idaho Rockies. **Positions advertised include:** Cook; Restaurant Manager; Night Baker; Journeymen Electrician; Journeymen Plumber; Diesel Mechanic; Wait Staff; Bartender; Grounds Maintenance; Flower Specialist; Laundry Attendant; Housekeeper; Airport Driver; Deli Counter Help; Lift Operator; Trail Crew; Ticket Sales; Mechanic Help; Stable Help; Golf Cashier; Bike Mechanic. **Corporate headquarters location:** This location.

TREETOP TECHNOLOGIES INC.
6148 Discovery Way, Suite 105, Boise ID 83713. 208/342-5668. **Fax:** 208/345-8808. **Contact:** Human Resources. **E-mail address:** resumes@treetoptech.com. **World Wide Web address:** http://www.treetoptech.com. **Description:** A computer consulting company that designs IT portfolios for organizations to improve cost effectiveness and efficiency. **Positions advertised include:** Source Code Management Analyst; Java Developer; Oracle Developer.

TRIBUNE PUBLISHING COMPANY
P.O. Box 957, Lewiston ID 83501. 208/743-9411. **Contact:** JoAnn Thompson, Human Resources Director. **E-mail address:** jthompson@lmtribune.com **World Wide Web address:** http://www.lmtribune.com. **Description:** Publishes the daily Lewiston Morning Tribune newspaper. **NOTE:** Jobseekers must apply to a specific department of interest. **Positions advertised include:** District Manager; Delivery Person.

TRUS JOIST MACMILLAN
200 East Mallard Drive, Boise ID 83706. 208/364-1200. **Toll-free phone:** 800/338-0515. **Fax:** 208/364-1300. **Contact:** Rob Adams, Director of Human Resources. **World Wide Web address:** http://www.trusjoist.com. **Description:** Markets industrial construction materials, concentrating on wood-and-steel composite truss. The company focuses on engineered wood, sized to fit custom needs. Products include Microllam LVL; TimberStrand LSL; Parallam PSL, and Form-I Joists. **Corporate headquarters location:** This location. **Other U.S. locations:** Nationwide. **International locations:** Canada. **Parent company:** Weyerhaeuser Company. **Listed on:** NASDAQ. **Stock exchange symbol:** TJCO. **President/CEO:** Tom Denig. **Annual sales/revenues:** More than $100 million. **Number of employees worldwide:** 4,000.

UNITED HERITAGE MUTUAL LIFE INSURANCE COMPANY
P.O. Box 7777, Meridian ID 83680-7777. 208/466-7856. **Physical address:** 707 East United Heritage Court, Meridian ID 83642. **Toll-free phone:** 800/657-6351. **Fax:** 208/475-1015. **Contact:** Marge Hopkins, Human Resources. **World Wide Web address:** http://www.unitedheritage.com. **Description:** Provides life insurance. **Corporate headquarters location:** This location. **Other U.S. locations:** Nineteen western states.

UNIVERSITY OF IDAHO
P.O. Box 444332, Moscow ID 83844-4332. 208/885-3609. **Physical address:** 415 West Sixth Street, Moscow ID 83844-4332. **Fax:** 208/885-3602. **Contact:** Human Resources. **E-mail address:** employment@ uidaho.edu. **World Wide Web address:** http://www.uidaho.edu/hrs. **Description:** A state university. **Positions advertised include:** Scientific Aide; Financial Technician; Office Specialist/Shipping Coordinator; Steam Plant Manager; HVAC Control Technician; Program Advisor; Assistant Ticket Manager; Fuel Supply Handler; Scholarship Advisor; Hazardous Materials Specialist; Technical Support Assistant; Counseling Psychologist; Visiting Assistant Professor of Voice; Dean of Agriculture and Life Sciences; Post Doctoral Fellow; Faculty Secretary; Supervisor, Food Processing Facility; Assistant Vice President for Facilities.

WASHINGTON GROUP INTERNATIONAL
P.O. Box 73, Boise ID 83729. 208/386-5000. **Fax:** 208/386-5191. **Recorded jobline:** 208/386-6966. **Contact:** Human Resources. **World Wide Web address:** http://www.wgint.com. **Description:** Provides construction, engineering, environmental, and mining services. The company works through four major divisions: Engineering & Construction Group, Environmental/Government Group, Heavy Civil Construction Group, and the Mining Group. **NOTE:** Entry-level positions are offered. **Positions advertised include:** Senior Executive Secretary. **Special programs:** Internships; Co-ops; Summer Jobs. **Corporate headquarters location:** This location. **Other U.S. locations:** Nationwide. **International locations:** Worldwide. **Parent Company:** Morrison Knudsen Corporation. **CEO:** Steve Hanks. **Number of employees worldwide:** 38,000.

WELLS FARGO BANK
3295 Elder St., Boise ID 83705. **Physical Address:** 1400 Vista Avenue, Boise ID 83705. 208/338-5500. **Contact:** Human Resources. **E-mail address:** cindy.gonzalez@wellsfargo.com. **World Wide Web address:** http://www.wellsfargo.com. **Description:** A diversified financial institution with over $234 billion in assets. Wells Fargo serves over 17 million customers through 5,300 independent locations worldwide. Services include community banking, credit and debit cards, home equity and mortgage loans, on-line banking, student loans, and insurance. Founded in 1852. **Positions advertised include:** Personal Banker; Teller. **Corporate headquarters location:** San Francisco CA. **Other U.S. locations:** Nationwide. **International locations:** Worldwide. **Operations at this facility include:** Administration; Regional Headquarters; Sales; Service. **Listed on:** New York Stock Exchange. **Stock exchange symbol:** WFC. **Annual sales/revenues:** More than $100 million. **Number of employees worldwide:** 120,000.

WESTERN AIRCRAFT
4300 South Kennedy Street, Boise ID 83705. 208/338-1800. **Toll-free phone:** 800/333-3442. **Fax:** 208/338-1830. **Contact:** Angela Robinson, Human Resources Manager. **E-mail address:** angelar@westair.com. **Description:** A service center and repair station for many top business aircraft manufacturers. **Company Slogan:** Professionals serving professionals. **Positions advertised include:** Hawker Aircraft Mechanic; Falcon Aircraft Mechanic. **CEO:** Mike Cleary.

WEST VALLEY MEDICAL CENTER
1717 Arlington Avenue, Caldwell ID 83605. 208/455-3835. **Fax:** 208/455-4057. **Recorded jobline:** 208/455-3828. **Contact:** Dona Blakley, Human Resources. **E-mail address:** donablakley@hcahealthcare.com. **World Wide Web address:** http://www.westvalleymedctr.com. **Description:** West Valley Medical Center is a 150-bed hospital serving many western Idaho communities as well as eastern Oregon. The medical center offers resident services such as oncology and laser surgery. The hospital also offers cardiac and pulmonary rehabilitation; diabetes education and outpatient services; a hospice program, providing patients and their families an alternative for terminal illness management in their home; and a birthing center. Founded in 1950. **Positions advertised include:** Payroll Clerk; Registered Nurse- Critical Care Unit/Nights; Registered Nurse- Operating Room; Impatient/Outpatient Physical Therapist; Full-Time Speech Therapist; Part-Time Speech Therapist.

ZILOG MANUFACTURING, INC.
2601 11th Avenue North Extension, Nampa ID 83687. 208/465-3413. **Contact:** Human Resources. **E-mail address:** nampajobs@zilog.com. **World Wide Web address:** http://www.zilog.com. **Description:** This location manufactures semiconductors. Zilog designs, develops, manufactures, and markets application-specific standard integrated circuits products (ASSPs) for the data communications, intelligent peripheral controller, consumer product controller, and memory markets. Zilog uses its proprietary superintegration design technology to combine cores and cells from its library of customer-familiar microprocessor, microcontroller, memory, and logic circuits to meet the design, cost, and time-to-market requirements of its customers. **Corporate headquarters location:** San Jose CA. **Other U.S. Locations:** CA, WA, TX. **International locations:** Philippines; Bangalore. **Listed on:** Privately held. **President/CEO:** Jim Thornburn. **Annual sales/revenues:** More than $100 million. **Number of employees nationwide:** 800.

AAR
One AAR Place, 1100 North Wood Dale Road, Wood Dale IL 60191. 630/227-2000. **Fax:** 630/227-2019. **Contact:** Human Resources. **World Wide Web address:** http://www.aarcorp.com. **Description:** Provides trading, overhaul, and manufacturing services, primarily to aviation-related customers including commercial airlines, the government, original equipment manufacturers, and aviation service companies. In trading, AAR buys, sells, and leases aircraft, engines, and airframe components and distributes factory-new airframe and engine hardware. The company also customizes programs for airlines seeking inventory management. Overhaul includes the maintenance of aircraft and components including instruments; hydraulic, pneumatic, and electrical systems; landing gear; and engine parts. AAR also designs and manufactures a variety of aviation products with an emphasis on air cargo transport systems and related materials. Founded in 1951. **Corporate headquarters location:** Wood Dale, IL. **Listed on:** New York Stock Exchange. **Stock exchange symbol:** AIR.

ABF FREIGHT SYSTEM, INC.
1970 Weisbrook Drive, Oswego IL 60543. 630/966-0606. **Toll-free phone:** 800/610-5544. **Fax:** 800/599-2810 **Contact:** Branch Manager. **World Wide Web address:** http://www.abfs.com. **Description:** One of the nation's largest motor carriers. **NOTE:** Apply online at website. Special programs: Management Training. **Positions advertised include:** Drivers; Office Clerk; Operations Supervisor; Quotation Analyst; Industrial Engineer. **Corporate headquarters location:** Fort Smith, AK.

ACNIELSEN
150 North Martingale Road, Schaumburg IL 60173-2076. 847/605-5000. **Fax:** 847/605-2559. **Contact:** Human Resources. **World Wide Web address:** http://www.acnielsen.com. **Description:** Provides demographic and related information such as television audience rating services and consumer polling for the consumer goods industry. **NOTE:** AC Nielsen has additional locations in Illinois. See its website for locations and job listings and apply online. **Positions advertised include:** Associate Database Specialist; Business Analyst; Operations Director; Consumer Insight Director; Order Conversion Specialist. **Corporate headquarters location:** New York NY. **Parent company:** VNU. **Operations at this facility include:** Administration; Regional Headquarters; Research and Development; Sales; Service. **Number of employees worldwide:** 21,000.

AMD INDUSTRIES, INC.
4620 West 19th Street, Cicero IL 60804. 708/863-8900. **Toll-free phone:** 800/367-9999. **Fax:** 708/863-2065. **Contact:** Human Resources Director. **World Wide Web address:** http://www.amdpop.com. **Description:** Manufactures and sells point-of-purchase (P.O.P.) displays. **Corporate headquarters location:** This location. **Other U.S. locations:** OH; WI. **Listed on:** Privately held.

A1 TRAVEL
1506 Wabash Avenue, Springfield IL 62704. 217/546-1090. **Contact:** Hiring Manager. **Description:** A travel agency. A1 Travel also offers classes for individuals who are considering becoming travel consultants. **Corporate headquarters location:** This location.

APV INVENSYS, INC.
5100 North River Road, 3rd Floor, Schiller Park IL 60176. 847/678-4300. **Contact:** Human Resources. **World Wide Web address:** http://www.apv.com. **Description:** Designs, engineers, and installs food and beverage processing equipment. APV Invensys, Inc. has four regional sales offices, each responsible for selling processing systems and parts for existing systems. Once a system has been sold, the sales force submits the engineering work to the Systems Engineering Group at this location. These engineers design dairy and food processing systems for APV's customers. After the design phase is complete, the engineers travel to job sites to supervise the installation of the processing equipment. They remain on-site until the processing systems are installed and running and the customer has been fully trained to operate the systems. **NOTE:** Apply online at this company's website. **Special programs:** Internships. **Other U.S. locations:** Cerritos CA. **Operations at this facility include:** Sales. **Number of employees worldwide:** 80,000.

ATC
419 Eisenhower Lane South, Lombard IL 60148-5706. 630/916-7272. **Fax:** 630/916-7013. **Contact:** Human Resources. **World Wide Web address:** http://www.atc-enviro.com. **Description:** Provides comprehensive environmental consulting, engineering, and on-site remediation services throughout the United States for clients including federal, state, and local government agencies. ATC's services include assessment of environmental regulations, investigation of contaminated sites, and the design and engineering of methods to correct or prevent contamination. The company addresses hazardous and non-hazardous contaminants in municipal and industrial water supplies; wastewater and storm water from municipal, industrial, and military installations; groundwater, soils, and air space surrounding these types of complexes; and contaminants in buildings and facilities such as asbestos, lead paint, and radioactive contamination. **NOTE:** Apply online. **Positions advertised include:** Project Scientist; Group Leader/Manager.

ABBOTT LABORATORIES
100 Abbott Park Road, Abbott Park IL 60064-3500. 847/937-6100. **Fax:** 847/937-1511. **Contact:** Human Resources. **World Wide Web address:** http://www.abbott.com. **Description:** Manufactures pharmaceuticals and liquid nutrition products including Similac, Pedialyte, and Ensure. The company also manufactures anesthetics, blood pressure monitors, and intravenous systems. **NOTE:** Apply online at this company's website. **Positions advertised include:** Secretary; Senior Financial Analyst; Manager of Strategy and Development; Contract Coordinator; Project Engineer; Secretary; Technical Project Leader/Architect; Project Engineer. **Corporate headquarters location:** This location. **Other U.S. locations:** AZ; CA; GA; MA; MI; NJ; OH; TX; UT; VA. **Operations at this facility include:** Administration; Manufacturing; Research and Development; Sales; Service. **Listed on:** New York Stock Exchange. **Stock exchange symbol:** ABT. **Number of employees worldwide:** 52,000.

ACCENTURE
161 North Clark Street, 44th Floor, Chicago IL 60601. 312/693-0161. **Fax:** 312/693-0507. **Contact:** Human Resources. **World Wide Web address:** http://www.accenture.com. **Description:** A management and technology consulting firm. Accenture offers a wide range of services including business re-engineering; customer service system consulting; data system design and implementation; Internet sales systems research and design; and strategic planning. **NOTE:** This company provides job listings for all its Illinois, U.S. and global offices. Apply online. **Positions advertised include:** Entry-Level Programmers; Oracle PL; Tester; Cobol. **Corporate headquarters location:** This location. **Other U.S. locations:** Nationwide. **International locations:** Worldwide. **Listed on:** New York Stock Exchange. **Stock exchange symbol:** ACN. **Number of employees worldwide:** 75,000.

ACCO USA, INC.
300 Tower Parkway, Lincolnshire IL 60069. 847/541-9500. **Toll-free phone:** 800/222-6462. **Fax:** 847/484-4492. **Contact:** Human Resources Department. **World Wide Web address:** http://www.acco.com. **Description:** Manufactures a wide variety of office supplies and equipment. **NOTE:** Apply online at this company's website. **Positions advertised include:** Market Development Manager; Recruiter; Unix/Oracle Manager; Senior System Analyst; Credit Risk Analyst. **Corporate headquarters location:** This location. **Parent company:** American Brands, Inc. (New York NY).

ACE DORAN HAULING & RIGGING COMPANY
5529 Dial Drive, Granite City IL 62040. 618/797-0047. **Contact:** Human Resources. **World Wide Web address:** http://www.acedoran.com. **Description:** Provides truck transportation of heavy and specialized commodities such as steel, aluminum, self-propelled vehicles in excess of 15,000 pounds, and construction equipment. **NOTE:** For driver positions, apply online. For all other positions, send resumes to: Ace Doran Hauling & Rigging Company, Human Resources, 1601 Blue Rock Street, Cincinnati OH 45223.

ACE HARDWARE CORPORATION
2200 Kensington Court, Oak Brook IL 60523. 630/990-6600. **Fax:** 630/990-6838. **Contact:** Director of Human Resources. **World Wide Web address:** http://www.acehardware.com. **Description:** A worldwide dealer-owned cooperative operating through 5,100 hardware retailers in 62 countries. Ace Hardware Corporation also produces a line of hand and power tools, plumbing products, lawn and garden products, cleaning supplies, and manufactures a line of paint. **NOTE:** Apply online at the company's website. **Positions advertised include:** Advertising Distribution Analyst; Financial Analyst; Senior Audit Consultant; POR Operator; Network Administrator; Assistant Buyer. **Corporate headquarters location:** This location.

ACXIOM CORPORATION
1501 Opus Place, Downers Grove IL 60515. 630/964-1501. **Contact:** Human Resources. **World Wide Web address:** http://www.acxiom.com. **Description:** Provides a variety of services including data integration services, data products, and information technology outsourcing. **NOTE:** Entry-level positions offered. Apply online for all positions. **Positions advertised include:** Client Executive; Client Representative; Decision Support Analyst. **Special programs:** Internships. **Corporate headquarters location:** Little Rock AR. **Listed on:** NASDAQ. **Stock exchange symbol:** ACXM.

ADLER PLANETARIUM & ASTRONOMY MUSEUM
1300 South Lake Shore Drive, Chicago IL 60605. 312/322-0591. **Fax:** 312/322-9909. **Contact:** Marguerite E. Dawson, Human Resources Manager. **E-mail address:** mdawson@adlernet.org. **World Wide Web address:** http://www.adlerplanetarium.org. **Description:** A planetarium and science museum focusing on astronomy. Founded in 1930. **NOTE:** Entry-level and part-time positions are offered. **Positions advertised include:** Distance Learning Educator; Museum Service Staff. **Special programs:** Internships; Training; Volunteer. **Corporate headquarters location:** This location. **Operations at this facility include:** Administration.

ADVANCE MECHANICAL SYSTEMS INC.
2080 South Carboy, Mount Prospect IL 60056-5750. 847/593-2510. **Contact:** Human Resources. **World Wide Web address:** http://www.advmech.com. **Description:** An engineering firm specializing in mechanical and HVAC contracting.

ADVANCE TRANSFORMER COMPANY
10275 West Higgins Road, Rosemont IL 60018. 847/390-5000. **Toll-free phone:** 800/322-2086. **Contact:** Human Resources. **World Wide Web address:** http://www.advancetransformer.com. **Description:** Manufactures magnetic and electronic fluorescent lamp ballasts. Advance Transformer Company also manufactures high-intensity discharge ballasts for the starting and regulating of fluorescent and high-intensity discharge lamps. The company focuses primarily in the fields of consumer electronics, consumer products, electrical and electronics components, and professional equipment.

ADVOCATE ILLINOIS MASONIC MEDICAL CENTER
836 West Wellington Avenue, Chicago IL 60657. 773/975-1600. Contact: Human Resources. **World Wide Web address:** http://www.advocatehealth.com/immc. **Description:** A hospital specializing in oncology, cardiology and emergency care. **NOTE:** Apply online.

AIR LIQUIDE AMERICA CORPORATION
5230 South East Avenue, Countryside IL 60525. 708/482-8400. **Fax:** 708/579-7702. **Contact:** Ronald J. Nowak, Manager of Administration. **World Wide Web address:** http://www.airliquide.com. **Description:** Air Liquide America Corporation is a diversified manufacturer engaged in the recovery and sale of atmospheric industrial gases, the manufacture and sale of oil field equipment and supplies, and the distribution of welding and industrial equipment and supplies. The company operates several business segments. The Gas Group produces and sells oxygen, nitrogen, and argon in liquid and gaseous forms through approximately 20 locations, operating more than 2,200 miles of pipeline; The Energy Group operates under two names, Bowen Tools and Dia-Log Companies, and manufactures and sells equipment to petroleum and natural gas companies; The Welding Group distributes electric arc welding equipment and supplies. **NOTE:** Apply online. **Special programs:** Internships. **Corporate headquarters location:** Houston TX. **Other U.S. locations:** CA; FL; HI; LA. **Operations at this facility include:** This location is a technology center involved in the engineering and research of industrial gases and related equipment. **Parent company:** L'Air Liquide. **Number of employees worldwide:** 30,000.

AKZO NOBEL CHEMICALS, INC.
525 West Van Buren Street, Chicago IL 60607. 312/544-7000. **Contact:** Human Resources. **World Wide Web address:** http://www.akzonobelusa.com. **Description:** Akzo Nobel is a diverse manufacturing company whose primary products include chemical and medical products. The company is involved in molecular biology research as well as electronic, automotive, food packaging, and aerospace products. **NOTE:** There are several Akzo Nobel divisions at this location: Akzo Nobel Functional Chemicals (Chelates and Micronutrients); Akzo Nobel Polymer Chemicals and Akzo Nobel Surface Chemistry. The website provides job listings for all divisions. Apply online. **Operations at this facility include:** This location researches, develops, and manufactures industrial coatings and finishes. **Listed on:** NASDAQ. **Stock exchange symbol:** AKZOY.

ALBANY BANK & TRUST COMPANY N.A.
3400 West Lawrence Avenue, Chicago IL 60625. 773/267-7300. **Contact:** Human Resources. **World Wide Web address:** http://www.albanybank.com. **Description:** A full-service bank with three locations throughout the Chicago metropolitan area. **Parent company:** Albank Corporation.

ALBERTO-CULVER COMPANY
2525 West Armitage Avenue, Melrose Park IL 60160. 708/450-3000. **Fax:** 708/450-3354. **Contact:** Corporate Human Resources. **World Wide Web address:** http://www.alberto.com. **Description:** Manufactures health and beauty aids and operates a chain of beauty supply stores. Products include shampoos, hair colorings, conditioners, fixatives, deodorants, antistatic sprays, and furniture polish. Brand names include Alberto VO5, Static Guard, TCB, and Kleen Guard. The company also produces consumer food items such as sweeteners, Mrs. Dash seasonings, and the Molly McButter butter substitute. **NOTE:** See website for job postings and contact information. **Positions advertised include:** Executive Secretary; Customer Business Manager; Account Executive; Corporate Auditor; Buyer. **Subsidiaries include:** Cederroth International AB is a manufacturer of bandages, antacid powder, and other consumer goods; Sally Beauty Supply is one of the world's largest chains of beauty supply stores, which operates through 2,000 units in the United States and the United Kingdom. **Listed on:** New York Stock Exchange. **Stock exchange symbol:** ACV.

ALBERTSON'S INC.
3030 Cullerton Drive, Franklin Park IL 60131. **Toll-free phone:** 800/964-1434. **Fax:** 888/541-5793. **Contact:** Director of Recruiting. **World Wide Web address:** http://www.albertsons.com. **Description:** One of the largest retail food-drug chains in the United States. The company operates approximately 2,300 stores in 33 states. **NOTE:** Entry-level positions and part-time jobs are offered. **Positions advertised include:** Programmer Analyst; Computer Programmer; Management Trainee; Pharmacist; Systems Analyst. **Corporate headquarters location:** Boise ID. **Listed on:** New York Stock Exchange. **Stock exchange symbol:** ABS.

ALCAN PACKAGING
1731 S. Mont Prospect Road, Des Plaines IL 60018. 847/298-5626. **Fax:** 773/399-3005. **Contact:** Human Resources. **World Wide Web address:** https://www.alcan.com. **Description:** Provider of aluminum and packaging solutions to companies worldwide. **Positions advertised include:** Cost Accountant; HR Assistant; Production Mechanic Technician; Quality Assurance Manager; Senior Engineer.

ALDI INC.
2080 West Main Street, Batavia IL 60510. 630/879-8100. **Contact:** Human Resources. **World Wide Web address:** http://www.aldifoods.com. **Description:** Operates a chain of discount grocery stores throughout the Midwest. **Corporate headquarters location:** This location.

ALERI
Two Prudential Plaza, 41st Floor, Chicago IL 60601. 312/540-0100. **Fax:** 312/540-0717. **Contact:** Human Resources. **E-mail address:** careers@aleri.com. **World Wide Web address:** http://www.aleri.com. **Description:** Designs and develops solutions for financial institutions including the ATLAS software product line, a series of financial transaction processing systems that allow companies to increase productivity and reduce operating costs. Founded in 1981.

ALEXIAN BROTHERS MEDICAL CENTER
800 Biesterfield Road, Elk Grove Village IL 60007. 847/437-5500. **Contact:** Human Resources. **World Wide Web address:** http://www.alexian.org. **Description:** A nonprofit, acute care hospital. Alexian Brothers Medical Center offers a wide range of health care services including oncology, radiology, mental health, and obstetrics. Founded in 1972. **NOTE:** This medical center is part of the Alexian Brothers Health System, which includes Alexian Brothers Behavioral Hospital and St. Alexius Medical Center, both in Hoffman Estates IL. Job listings for this hospital and the others can be found at http://www.alexianjobs.org. **Positions advertised include:** Registered Nurse; LPN; Education Coordinator; Critical Care Respiratory Therapist; Staff Chaplains; Administrative Director Perioperative Services, Cardiology Services Director.

ALLIANCE SHIPPERS, INC.
15515 South 70th Court, Orland Park IL 60462. 708/802-7000. **Contact:** Manager. **World Wide Web address:** http://www.alliance.com. **Description:** Transports packages for businesses and consumers throughout the world. **Corporate headquarters location:** This location. **International locations:** Worldwide.

ALLIED TUBE & CONDUIT CORPORATION
16100 South Lathrop Avenue, Harvey IL 60426. 708/339-1610. **Toll-free phone:** 800/882-5543. **Fax:** 708/339-2399. **Contact:** Human Resources. **World Wide Web address:** http://www.alliedtube.com. **Description:** Manufactures steel tubing for a variety of commercial and industrial uses. **Parent company:** Tyco International.

ALLIED VAN LINES
700 Oakmont Lane, Westmont IL 60559. 630/570-3000. **Fax:** 630/570-3606. **Contact:** Human Resources. **World Wide Web address:** http://www.alliedvan.com. **Description:** A moving company whose major markets are household goods moving and specialized transportation services. **NOTE:** To see job listings and to apply, visit the corporate website at http://www.careers.sirva.com. **Positions advertised include:** Customer Service Manager; Transportation Manager; IT Quality Assurance Analyst; Claims Adjustor. **Corporate headquarters location:** This location. **Parent company:** SIRVA. **Number of employees at this location:** 690.

ALLIED VAUGHN
1200 Thorndale Avenue, Elk Grove Village IL 60007. 847/595-2900. **Toll-free phone:** 800/759-4087. **Fax:** 847/595-8677. **Contact:** Human Resources. **World Wide Web address:** http://www.alliedvaughn.com. **Description:** One of the nation's leading independent multimedia manufacturing companies offering CD-audio and CD-ROM mastering and replication, videocassette and audiocassette duplication, off-line and online video editing, motion picture film processing, film-to-tape and tape-to-film transfers, and complete finishing, packaging, warehousing, and fulfillment services. **Positions advertised include:** Sales Executive. **Corporate headquarters location:** Minneapolis MN.

ALLSTATE CORPORATION
2775 Sanders Road, Building A1, Northbrook IL 60052. 847/402-5000. **Toll-free phone:** 800/574-3553. **Fax:** 847/402-5000. **Contact:** Employment Manager. **World Wide Web address:** http://www.allstate.com. **Description:** Provides property, liability, life, reinsurance, and commercial lines of insurance. **NOTE:** Apply online at the company's website. **Company slogan:** You're in good hands. **Special programs:** Internships. **Corporate headquarters location:** This location. **Operations at this facility include:** Administration; Service. **Listed on:** New York Stock Exchange. **Stock exchange symbol:** ALL. **Number of employees nationwide:** 37,600.

ALLSTATE INSURANCE COMPANY
South Barrington Plaza, 51 West Higgins Road, South Barrington IL 60010-9300. 847/551-2000. **Contact:** Human Resources Manager. **World Wide Web address:** http://www.allstate.com. **Description:** Provides property, liability, life, reinsurance, and commercial lines of insurance. **NOTE:** Apply online at the company's website. **Company slogan:** You're in good hands. **Corporate headquarters location:** Northbrook IL. **Listed on:** New York Stock Exchange. **Stock exchange symbol:** ALL. **Number of employees nationwide:** 37,600.

ALPHA BAKING COMPANY
4545 West Lyndale Avenue, Chicago IL 60639-3419. 773/489-5400. **Fax:** 773/489-2711. **Contact:** Human Resources. **World Wide Web address:** http://www.alphabaking.com. **Description:** Specializes in preparing and baking breads and rolls. Trucks deliver products east of the Rocky Mountains. An institutional route system delivers products locally. **Corporate headquarters location:** This location. **Operations at this facility include:** Administration; Manufacturing; Sales. **Listed on:** Privately held. **Number of employees nationwide:** 1,000.

ALRA LABORATORIES, INC.
3850 Clearview Court, Gurnee IL 60031. 847/244-9440. **Toll-free phone:** 800/248-ARLA. **Fax:** 847/244-9464. **Contact:** Human Resources. **Description:** Researches, develops, and manufactures generic pharmaceuticals. Products include eryzole, gelpirin, multivitamins, and methalgen cream. Founded in 1982. **Corporate headquarters location:** This location.

ALTON MENTAL HEALTH CENTER
4500 College Avenue, Alton IL 62002. 618/474-3200. **Contact:** Human Resources. **Description:** An inpatient medical facility specializing in the treatment of psychiatric developmental disabilities. Part of the Illinois Department of Human Services.

ALVORD, BURDICK & HOWSON
20 North Wacker Drive, Suite 1401, Chicago IL 60606. 312/236-9147. **Fax:** 312/236-0692. **Contact:** Mr. Bon G. Mui, Partner. **E-mail address:** bmui@abhengineers.com. **World Wide Web address:** http://www.abhengineers.com. **Description:** An environmental consulting and engineering firm that is also engaged in mechanical, civil, and structural engineering. **NOTE:** Mail or e-mail resumes to Mr. Mui.

AMBITECH ENGINEERING CORPORATION
1333 Butterfield Road, Suite 200, Downers Grove IL 60515. 630/963-5800. **Fax:** 630/963-8099. **Contact:** Carrie Koenig, Human Resources Manager. **E-mail address:** ckoenig@ambitech.com. **World Wide Web address:** http://www.ambitech.com. **Description:** A consulting and engineering firm engaged in the engineering and design of petroleum refineries, chemical plants, and petrochemical plants including. **NOTE:** See website for application. **Positions advertised include:** Instrumentation and Controls Programmer; Mechanical Engineer; Senior Piping Engineer; Senior Process Engineer. **Corporate headquarters location:** This location. **Listed on:** Privately held.

AMCORE BANK ROCKFORD
501 Seventh Street, P.O. Box 1537, Rockford IL 61104. 815/968-2241. **Contact:** Human Resources. **World Wide Web address:** http://www.amcore.com. **Description:** A chain of banks with more than 65 locations in Illinois, Wisconsin and Iowa. Founded in 1910. **NOTE:** This company's website includes job listings and contact information for all its locations. See website for specific contact information. **Listed on:** NASDAQ. **Stock exchange symbol:** AMFI.

AMERENCIPS
CENTRAL ILLINOIS PUBLIC SERVICE
607 East Adams Street, Springfield IL 62739. 217/523-3600. **Fax:** 877/226-3736. **Contact:** Employee Development Supervisor. **World Wide Web address:** http://www.ameren.com. **Description:** An electric and gas utility company serving central and southern Illinois. **NOTE:** This company's website provides job listings. Apply online **Parent company:** Ameren Corporation. **Listed on:** New York Stock Exchange. **Stock exchange symbol:** AEE.

AMERENIP
500 South 27th Street, Decatur IL 62521. 217/424-6600. **Toll-free phone:** 800/755-5000. **Contact:** Human Resources. **World Wide Web address:** http://www.amerenip.com. **Description:** An electric and gas utility serving 1.4 million customers in Illinois. **Listed on:** New York Stock Exchange. **Stock exchange symbol:** AEE.

AMERICAN BAR ASSOCIATION
321 North Clark Street, Chicago IL 60610. 312/988-5000. **Contact:** Human Resources. **World Wide Web address:** http://www.abanet.org. **Description:** A professional association serving the legal profession. **Corporate headquarters location:** This location.

AMERICAN COLLOID COMPANY
1500 West Shure Drive, Arlington Heights IL 60004. 847/392-4600. **Fax:** 847/506-6199. **Contact:** Human Resources. **World Wide Web address:** http://www.colloid.com. **Description:** American Colloid mines bentonite clay. The company's Volclay sodium bentonite is used in oil well drilling and foundry forming applications.

AMERICAN DENTAL ASSOCIATION
211 East Chicago Avenue, Chicago IL 60611. 312/440-2500. **Contact:** Human Resources. **E-mail address:** jobs@ada.org. **World Wide Web address:** http://www.ada.org. **Description:** A professional association serving the dental community. **Positions advertised include:** Senior Manager, Corporate Relations and Marketing; Marketing Communications Director; Operations Specialist; Editorial/Advertising Assistant; Production Associate, Client Services. **Corporate headquarters location:** This location.

AMERICAN LIBRARY ASSOCIATION
50 East Huron Street, Chicago IL 60611. 312/944-6780. **Fax:** 314/944-6763. **Contact:** Human Resources. **World Wide Web address:** http://www.ala.org. **Description:** A membership association focusing on library information science. The association works with legislators to obtain federal support for libraries; engages in public educational programs; maintains a library and research center; presents over 100 awards, scholarships, and grants including the Newbury and Caldecott Medals for children's literature; publishes journals, monographs, and reference works; and holds two conferences each year for its members. **NOTE:** See website for job listings and contact information. **Corporate headquarters location:** This location. **Other U.S. locations:** Washington DC.

AMERICAN NTN BEARING MANUFACTURING CORPORATION
1500 Holmes Road, Elgin IL 60123. 847/741-4545. **Contact:** Human Resources. **World Wide Web address:** http://www.ntnamerica.com. **Description:** Manufactures bearings. **Corporate headquarters location:** This location. **Other U.S. locations:** Schiller Park IL. **Parent company:** NTN. **Operations at this facility include:** Administration; Manufacturing.

AMERICAN OSTEOPATHIC ASSOCIATION
142 East Ontario Street, Chicago IL 60611-2864. 312/202-8000. **Toll-free phone:** 800/621-1773. **Fax:** 312/202-8200. **Contact:** Human Resources. **E-mail address:** recruiter@osteopathic.org. **World Wide Web address:** http://www.osteopathic.org. **Description:** The AOA is a member association representing more than 54,000 osteopathic physicians. The AOA serves as the primary certifying body for osteopathic physicians and is the accrediting agency for all osteopathic medical colleges and health care facilities. The AOA's mission is to advance the philosophy and practice of osteopathic medicine by promoting excellence in education, research, and the delivery of quality, cost-effective healthcare within a distinct, unified profession. **NOTE:** Search for open positions online. **Positions advertised include:** Administrative Assistant; Editorial Assistant; HR Manager; Program Educational Specialist; Research Director. **Corporate headquarters location:** This location.

AMERICAN PHARMACEUTICAL SERVICES
1717 Park Street, Naperville IL 60563. 630/305-8000. **Contact:** Human Resources. **Description:** A pharmaceutical delivery service whose primary customers are nursing homes.

AMERICAN RED CROSS OF GREATER CHICAGO
2200 W. Harrison Street, Chicago IL 60612. 312/729-6100. **Fax:** 312/729-6306. **Contact:** Human Resources. **E-mail address:** chicagohr@usa.redcross.org. **World Wide Web address:** http://www.chicagoredcross.org. **Description:** A humanitarian organization that aids disaster victims, gathers blood for crisis distribution, trains individuals to respond to emergencies, educates individuals on various diseases, and raises funds for other charitable establishments. **Positions advertised include:** Training Specialist (Per Diem). **Special programs:** Internships. **Corporate headquarters location:** Washington DC. **Other U.S. locations:** Nationwide.

AMERIDRIVES INTERNATIONAL
MARLAND CLUTCH PRODUCTS
650 East Elm Avenue, La Grange IL 60525. 708/352-3330. **Contact:** Human Resources. **World Wide Web address:** http://www.ameridrives.com. **Description:** Manufactures couplings, backstops, and RINGSPANN freewheel clutches.

AMPHENOL CORPORATION
FIBER OPTICS DIVISION
61925A Ohio Street, Lisle IL 60532. 630/960-1010. **Fax:** 630/810-5640. **Contact:** Human Resources. **World Wide Web address:** http://www.amphenol-fiberoptics.com. **Description:** Manufactures fiber optic products. **Parent company:** Amphenol (Wallingford CT).

AMSTED INDUSTRIES
205 North Michigan Avenue, 44th Floor, Chicago IL 60601. 312/645-1700. **Fax:** 312/819-8494. **Contact:** Human Resources. **E-mail address:** jobs@amsted.com. **World Wide Web address:** http://www.amsted.com. **Description:** Amsted Industries manufactures steel industrial products for the railroad and construction industries. **Corporate headquarters location:** This location. **Other U.S. locations:** Nationwide. **Operations at this facility include:** This location houses administrative offices. **Listed on:** Privately held.

ANALYSTS INTERNATIONAL CORPORATION (AIC)
1101 Perimeter Drive, Suite 837, Schaumburg IL 60173-5060. 847/619-4673. **Fax:** 847/605-9489. **Contact:** Human Resources. **World Wide Web address:** http://www.analysts.com. **Description:** AIC is an international computer consulting firm. The company assists clients in developing systems in a variety of industries using different programming languages and software. **NOTE:** Apply online. **Corporate headquarters location:** Minneapolis MN. **Listed on:** NASDAQ. **Stock exchange symbol:** ANLY.

ARTHUR ANDERSEN
33 West Monroe Street, Chicago IL 60603. 312/580-0033. **Fax:** 312/507-6748. **Contact:** Human Resources. **World Wide Web address:** http://www.arthurandersen.com. **Description:** One of the largest certified public accounting firms in the world. Andersen's four key practice areas are Audit and Business Advisory, Tax and Business Advisory, Business Consulting, and Economic and Financial Consulting. **NOTE:** This firm does not accept unsolicited resumes. Please check its website for available positions. **Corporate headquarters location:** This location.

ANDREW CORPORATION
10500 West 153rd Street, Orland Park IL 60462. 708/349-3300. **Fax:** 708/873-3640. **Contact:** Human Resources. **World Wide Web address:** http://www.andrew.com. **Description:** A manufacturer of telecommunications equipment including Earth Station Satellite, cellular, and microwave antennas, towers, shelters, cables, and associated equipment. **Positions advertised include:** Buyer; Compensation Analyst; Corporate Communications Writer; Cost Accounting Assistant; Customer Relationship Representative; Operations Supervisor; Project Manager; Senior Engineer Industrial. **Special programs:** Internships. **Corporate headquarters location:** This location. **Operations at this facility include:** Administration; Manufacturing; Research and Development; Sales; Service. **Listed on:** NASDAQ. **Stock exchange symbol:** ANDW.

ANIXTER CENTER
6610 Clark Street, Chicago IL 60626-4062. 773/973-7900. **Fax:** 773/973-2180. **Contact:** Debbie Thom, Human Resources Director. **World Wide Web address:** http://www.anixter.org. **Description:** A nonprofit job training and rehabilitation organization for people with developmental disabilities. **NOTE:** Part-time positions offered. **Positions advertised include:** Advocate; Certified Nursing Assistant; Certified Occupational Therapist; Certified Special Educators; Child Care Worker; Mental Health Professional; Occupational Therapy Consultant; Substance Abuse Counselor; Teaching Assistant/Substitute Teacher.

ANIXTER INC.
2301 Patriot Boulevard, Glenview IL 60025-8020. Toll-free phone: 800/264-9837. **Contact:** Human Resources. **World Wide Web address:** http://www.anixter.com. **Description:** A value-added provider of industrial wire and cabling solutions that support voice and data applications. Solutions include customized pre- and post-sale services and products. **Positions advertised include:** Inventory Group Accountant; Staff Accountant. **Corporate headquarters location:** This location. **Other U.S. locations:** Nationwide. **Parent company:** Anixter International. **Operations at this facility include:** Administration; Marketing; Research and Development; Service. **Listed on:** New York Stock Exchange. **Stock exchange symbol:** AXE.

ANNING-JOHNSON COMPANY
1959 Anson Drive, Melrose Park IL 60160. 708/681-1300. **Fax:** 708/681-1386. **Contact:** Human Resources. **World Wide Web address:** http://www.anningjohnson.com. **Description:** Engaged in a variety of areas including acoustical ceiling, drywall, fireproofing, metal floor decks, metal siding, roofing, and geotechnical fill. Founded in 1940. **Corporate headquarters location:** This location. **Parent company:** Anson Industries Inc.

AON CORPORATION
200 East Randolph Street, Suite 900, Chicago IL 60601. 312/381-4800. Fax: 312/381-0240. **Contact:** Human Resources. **World Wide Web address:** http://www.aon.com. **Description:** An insurance holding company. **NOTE:** This company provides job listings for all its Illinois offices. Apply online. **Positions advertised include:** Risk Analyst; Licensing Administrator; Administrative Assistant; Treaty Drafter; Senior Communications Consultant; Production Assistant; Executive Assistant; Vice President; System Administrator. **Corporate headquarters location:** This location. **Subsidiaries include:** Aon Risk Services; Aon Consulting Worldwide; Aon Services Group; Aon Re Worldwide; Aon Warranty Group; Combined Insurance Company; Virginia Surety Company. **Operations at this facility include:** Administration; Sales; Service. **Listed on:** New York Stock Exchange. **Stock exchange symbol:** AOC.

APPLIED COMPOSITES
333 North Sixth Street, St. Charles IL 60174. 877/653-9577x122. Fax: 630/584-5365. **Contact:** Human Resources. **E-mail address:** Istritzel@appliedcompositecorp.com. **World Wide Web address:** http://www.appliedcompositescorp.com. **Description:** Manufactures fiber-reinforced plastic. **Positions advertised include:** Outside Sales Engineer; Customer Relations Manager; Plant Manager; Production Supervisor; Quality Manager; Human Resources Manager. **Corporate headquarters location:** This location. **Operations at this facility include:** Administration; Manufacturing; Research and Development; Sales; Service.

APPLIED SYSTEMS, INC.
200 Applied Parkway, University Park IL 60466. 708/534-5575. **Contact:** Director of Human Resources. **World Wide Web address:** http://www.appliedsystems.com. **Description:** Provides computer systems integration and design services to the insurance industry. **Positions advertised include:** Equipment Maintenance Technician; Web Development Engineer; Web Product Engineer.

ARAMARK
1801 South Meyers Road, Suite 300, Oak Brook Terrace IL 60181. 630/568-2500. **Contact:** Human Resources. **World Wide Web address:** http://www.aramark.com. **Description:** ARAMARK Correctional Services provides food to more than 125,000 inmates at 175 prisons and jail facilities in 27 states and Puerto Rico. The company also offers facility management services. **Parent company:** ARAMARK is one of the world's leading providers of managed services. The company operates in all 50 states and 15 foreign countries, offering a broad range of services to businesses of all sizes including most *Fortune* 500 companies and thousands of universities, hospitals, and municipal, state, and federal government facilities. The company is employee-owned. With revenues over $7 billion, the company is among the market leaders in all of its businesses. ARAMARK's businesses include Food, Leisure and Support Services including Campus Dining Services, School Nutrition Services, Leisure Services, Business Dining Services, International Services, Healthcare Support Services, Conference Center Management, and Refreshment Services; Facility Services; Correctional Services; Industrial Services; Uniform Services, which includes Uniform Services and Wearguard, a direct marketer of work clothing; Health and Education Services including Spectrum Healthcare Services and Children's World Learning Centers; and Book and Magazine Services. **NOTE:** Apply online.

ARCADIS GERAGHTY & MILLER, INC.
35 East Wacker Drive, Suite 1000, Chicago IL 60601. 312/263-6703. **Fax:** 317/231-6514. **Contact:** Phil Hutton, Office Administrator. **World Wide Web address:** http://www.arcadis-us.com. **Description:** A consulting firm that provides environmental and engineering services. The company focuses on the environmental, building, and infrastructure markets. Founded in 1888. **NOTE:** Apply online at the company's website. **Positions advertised include:** Principal Scientist; Engineer. **Corporate headquarters location:** Denver CO. **International locations:** Worldwide. **Listed on:** NASDAQ. **Stock exchange symbol:** ARCAF.

ARCHER DANIELS MIDLAND COMPANY
P.O. Box 1470, Decatur IL 62525. 217/424-5230. **Physical address:** 4666 Faries Parkway, Decatur IL 62526. **Toll-free phone:** 800/637-5843. **Fax:** 217/424-4383. **Contact:** Employment. **World Wide Web address:** http://www.admworld.com. **Description:** A worldwide firm engaged in the procuring, transporting, storing, processing, and merchandising of agricultural commodities. The company processes agricultural products such as corn, soybeans, wheat, rice, cottonseed, and canola and produces a variety of products including vegetable oils, cooking oil, margarine, vitamin E, soy flour, soy isolates, soy protein, soy milk, TVP, high-fructose corn syrup, sorbitol, starch, ethanol, xanthan gum, tryptophan, vitamin C, fermentation products, pasta, and cottonseed flour products. Founded in 1902. **NOTE:** Entry-level positions are offered. Apply online for all positions. **Positions advertised include:** Assistant Building and Grounds; Business Analyst; Clerk; Client Server; Commodity Trader; Construction Superintendent; Control Systems/Automation Specialist. **Corporate headquarters location:** This location. **Other U.S. locations:** Nationwide. **International locations:** Worldwide. **Operations at this facility include:** Administration; Research and Development; Sales. **Listed on:** New York Stock Exchange. **Stock exchange symbol:** ADM. **Number of employees worldwide:** 23,000.

ARCHER DANIELS MIDLAND COMPANY
One Edmund Street, Peoria IL 61602. 309/673-7828. **Contact:** Human Resources. **World Wide Web address:** http://www.admworld.com. **Description:** Archer Daniels Midland Company is a worldwide firm engaged in the procuring, transporting, storing, processing, and merchandising of agricultural commodities. **NOTE:** Apply online at this company's website. **Corporate headquarters location:** Decatur IL. **Operations at this facility include:** This location produces alcohol.

ARGONNE NATIONAL LABORATORY
9700 South Cass Avenue, Argonne IL 60439. 630/252-2000. **Contact:** Human Resources. **World Wide Web address:** http://www.anl.gov. **Description:** One of the Department of Energy's largest research centers. Argonne National Laboratory's research falls into three broad categories: engineering research including research on meltdown-proof nuclear reactors, advanced batteries, and fuel cells; physical research including materials science, physics, chemistry, mathematics, and computer science; and energy, environmental, and biological research including research into the causes and cures of cancer, alternate energy systems, and environmental and economic impact assessments. The laboratory is operated by the University of Chicago for the U.S. Department of Energy. **NOTE:** Apply online at the laboratory's website. **Positions advertised include:** Assistant Electrical Engineer; Contract Specialist; STA Lifeguard; Senior Secretary; Supervisor of Subcontracts.

ARNSTEIN & LEHR
120 South Riverside Plaza, Suite 1200, Chicago IL 60606. 312/876-7100. **Fax:** 312/876-0288. **Contact:** Denise Simms, Manager of Human Resources. **World Wide Web address:** http://www.arnstein.com. **Description:** A law firm specializing in antitrust, corporate, environmental, insurance, real estate, and tax law. This law firm also has offices in Hoffman Estates IL. **Positions advertised include:** Word Processor; Network Administrator. **Corporate headquarters location:** This location. Other U.S. locations: WI; FL. **Operations at this facility include:** Administration. **Listed on:** Privately held.

ART INSTITUTE OF CHICAGO
111 South Michigan Avenue, Chicago IL 60603. 312/443-3600. **Fax:** 312/857-0141. **Contact:** Human Resources. **E-mail address:** aic.jobs@artic.edu. **World Wide Web address:** http://www.artic.edu. **Description:** An art museum that provides educational programs, family workshops, artist demonstrations, and lectures. Exhibits include African and Ancient American Art, Architecture, Arms and Armor, Impressionism and Post-Impressionism, Modern Art, and Textiles. **NOTE:** Part-time and temporary positions available. E-mail or fax resumes and cover letters. An application is available also online. It can be downloaded and e-mailed or faxed. **Positions advertised include:** Auxiliary Board Assistant Director; Evening Associates Assistant Director; Membership Associate Director; Coordinator; Day Security Officer; Housekeeper; Information Systems Assistant. **Special programs:** Volunteer; Internship. **Office hours:** Monday - Friday, 9:00 a.m. - 5:00 p.m.

ASPIRE
9901 Derby Lane, Westchester IL 60154. 708/547-3550x3577. **Fax:** 708/547-4067. **Contact:** Human Resources Administrator. **E-mail address:** chrishunt@aspireofillinois.org **World Wide Web address:** http://www.aspireofillinois.org. **Description:** A private, nonprofit agency serving the developmental, residential, and vocational needs of adults and children with developmental and mental disabilities. **NOTE:** Apply in person at the Human Resources Office. **Special programs:** Internships; Volunteers. **Office hours:** Monday – Friday, 9:00 a.m. – 3:00 p.m. **Corporate headquarters location:** This location. **Listed on:** Privately held.

ASTRO BUILDING SERVICES INC.
2510 North Illinois Street, Belleville IL 62226. 618/235-4006. **Contact:** Human Resources. **Description:** Provides contract floor cleaning and shining services to retail stores.

AUDIT BUREAU OF CIRCULATIONS (ABC)
900 North Meacham Road, Schaumburg IL 60173. 847/605-0909. **Toll-free phone:** 800/285-2220. **Fax:** 847/605-9771. **Contact:** Manager of Human Resources. **World Wide Web address:** http://www.accessabc.com. **Description:** A nonprofit membership organization created by advertisers and publishers to ensure that circulating facts and statistics are compliant with industry bylaws and rules. Founded in 1914. **NOTE:** Entry-level positions are offered. **Positions advertised include:** Field Auditor. **Special programs:** Training. **Office hours:** Monday - Friday, 7:30 a.m. - 5:00 p.m. **Corporate headquarters location:** This location. **Other U.S. locations:** Nationwide. **Operations at this facility include:** Administration; Regional Headquarters.

AURORA, CITY OF
44 East Downer Place, Aurora IL 60507. 630/844-3626. **Fax:** 630/892-8837. **Recorded jobline:** 630/906-7415. **Contact:** Human Resources. **World Wide Web address:** http://www.ci.aurora.il.us. **Description:** Houses administrative, municipal, and government offices for the city of Aurora. **NOTE:** Seasonal positions offered. A completed application is required for any position. Apply online. **Office hours:** Monday – Friday, 8:00 a.m. – 5:00 p.m.

AURORA PUMP
800 Airport Road, North Aurora IL 60542. 630/859-7000. **Contact:** Vicki Swaine, Human Resources. **World Wide Web address:** http://www.aurorapump.com. **Description:** Manufactures water pumps for sprinkler systems.

AURORA UNIVERSITY
347 South Gladstone Avenue, Aurora IL 60506. 630/844-5493. **Fax:** 630/844-5650. **Contact:** Human Resources. **E-mail address:** hr@aurora.edu. **World Wide Web address:** http://www.aurora.edu. **Description:** A private university with an enrollment of approximately 2,000 graduate and undergraduate students. Programs are offered through the School of Business and Professional Studies; the School of Education of George Williams College; the University College of Arts & Sciences; the New College (adult learning center); the School of Nursing; the School of Physical Education, Recreation, and Athletics of George Williams College; and the School of Social Work. **NOTE:** Resumes and cover letters may be faxed, e-mailed, or mailed. Interested jobseekers may also apply online at the university's website. **Positions advertised include:** Assistant Professor (Various); Adjunct Faculty; Assistant Dean of Campus Activities; Director of Publications; Director of Field Experiences; Program Secretary; La Aurora Program Secretary.

AUTOMATIC DATA PROCESSING, INC. (ADP)
100 Northwest Point Boulevard, Elk Grove Village IL 60007. 847/718-2000. **Contact:** Senior Employment Specialist. **World Wide Web address:** http://www.adp.com. **Description:** Automatic Data Processing (ADP) helps over 300,000 clients improve their business performance by providing computerized transaction processing, data communications, and information services. The company's services include payroll, payroll tax, and human resource information management; brokerage industry market data; back-office and proxy services; industry-specific services to auto and truck dealers; and computerized auto repair and replacement estimating for auto insurance companies and body repair shops. **Positions advertised include:** Help Desk Coordinator; Express Representative; Product Manager; Teledata Representative; Staffing Specialist; Program Manager; Billing Specialist; CVR Regional Director; Tax Data Representative. **Corporate headquarters location:** Roseland NJ. **Operations at this facility include:** Administration; Regional Headquarters; Sales; Service. **Listed on:** New York Stock Exchange. **Stock exchange symbol:** ADP.

AUTOMATION INTERNATIONAL, INC.
1020 Bahls Street, Danville IL 61832. 217/446-9500. **Fax:** 217/446-6855. **Contact:** Mr. Terry Prosser, CEO. **World Wide Web address:** http://www.automation-intl.com. **Description:** Produces custom-designed resistance and arc welding equipment. The company also remanufactures and rebuilds used equipment. Brand names include Swift-Ohio and Federal. Founded in 1991. **Corporate headquarters location:** Quincy IL. **Operations at this facility include:** Manufacturing; Sales; Service. **Number of employees at this location:** 100.

AVON PRODUCTS INC.
6901 Golf Road, Morton Grove IL 60053. 847/966-0200. **Contact:** Human Resources. **World Wide Web address:** http://www.avoncareers.com. **Description:** A direct seller of beauty care products, fashion jewelry, gifts, fragrances, and decorative products. Avon, a *Fortune* 500 company, markets its products through a network of 2.8 million independent sales representatives in 135 countries worldwide. Founded in 1886. **NOTE:** For corporate positions, see job listings on the website. Salespeople are considered independent contractors or dealers and most work part-time. If you are interested in becoming a sales representative, please call 800/FOR-AVON, or visit the company's website for more information. **Positions advertised include:** Order Fulfillment Supervisor; Order Fulfillment Supervisor; Packaging Advisor; Customer Service Specialist. **Corporate headquarters location:** New York NY. **Other U.S. locations:** Pasadena CA; Newark DE; Atlanta GA; Suffern NY; Springdale OH. **Operations at this facility include:** Manufacturing. **Listed on:** New York Stock Exchange. **Stock exchange symbol:** AVP. **CEO/President:** Andrea Jung. **Number of employees nationwide:** 40,000.

AXIS INC.
2201 West Townline Road, Peoria IL 61615. 309/691-3988. **Fax:** 309/691-4172. **Contact:** Human Resources. **E-mail address:** careers@axis-inc.com. **World Wide Web address:** http://www.axis-inc.com. **Description:** Engaged in civil and mechanical engineering, information technology, and client-site technical services. Founded in 1987. **NOTE:** See list of job openings at the company's website. **Other U.S. locations:** Indianapolis IN. **International locations:** Australia; United Kingdom. **Subsidiaries include:** Axis Software, Inc. (Indianapolis IN); Axis Computers Ltd. (New Delhi, India); Axis EU Ltd. (London, England).

BBDO CHICAGO INC.
410 North Michigan Avenue, Chicago IL 60611. 312/337-7860. **Contact:** Human Resources. **World Wide Web address:** http://www.bbdo.com. **Description:** A worldwide advertising agency with related businesses in public relations, direct marketing, sales promotion, graphic arts, and printing. **NOTE:** Apply online. **Special programs:** Internships. **Corporate headquarters location:** New York NY. **Other U.S. locations:** Los Angeles CA; San Francisco CA; Miami FL; Atlanta GA; Wellesley MA; Southfield MI. **Parent company:** BBDO Worldwide operates 156 offices in 42 countries and 96 cities. The company also operates 83 subsidiaries, affiliates, and associates engaged solely in advertising and related operations. **Operations at this facility include:** Administration; Service.

BDO SEIDMAN, LLP
130 East Randolph Drive, Suite 2800, Chicago IL 60601. 312/240-1236. **Fax:** 312/540-1750. **Contact:** Human Resources. **E-mail address:** r7@bdo.com. **World Wide Web address:** http://www.bdo.com. **Description:** A public accounting and consulting firm. **NOTE:** This company has other Illinois locations. See website for addresses. Apply online. **Positions advertised include:** Business Development Manager; Valuation Manager; Administrative Assistant. **Corporate headquarters location:** This location. **Other U.S. locations:** Boston MA.

BDO SEIDMAN, LLP
233 North Michigan Avenue, Suite 2500, Chicago IL 60601. 312/856-9100. **Fax:** 312/856-1379. **Contact:** Human Resources. **World Wide Web address:** http://www.bdo.com. **Description:** A location of the public accounting and consulting firm. **NOTE:** Apply online at the company's website. **Special programs:** Internships. **Operations at this facility include:** Sales. **Other U.S. locations:** Boston MA.

BP AMOCO
28100 Torch Parkway, Warrenville IL 60555-3938. 630/420-5111. **Contact:** Human Resources. **World Wide Web address:** http://www.bp.com. **Description:** Engaged in the energy business, principally domestic oil and natural gas. The firm is a major holder of domestic crude oil reserves and is also involved in the refining and marketing of petroleum products. **NOTE:** This company provides job listings for all its Illinois, United States and international locations. See website and apply online. **Corporate headquarters location:** This location. **Parent company:** BP (United Kingdom). **Listed on:** New York Stock Exchange. **Stock exchange symbol:** BP. **Number of employees worldwide:** 104,000.

BP CHEMICAL
28100 Torch Park Way, Warrenville IL 60555. 877/701-2726. **Contact:** Human Resources. **World Wide Web address:** http://www.bp.com/chemicals. **Description:** Manufactures industrial intermediate petrochemicals. Overall, BP is a major supplier of fuel for transportation, energy for heat and light, solar power, and petrochemicals for plastics, fabrics, and fibers. The company is also one of the world's largest marketers of aviation fuels, and a major supplier of fuels and lubricants to the global market. **Special programs:** Internships. **NOTE:** This company provides job listings for all its Illinois, United States and international locations. See website and apply online. **Corporate headquarters location:** This location. **Parent company:** BP (United Kingdom). **Operations at this facility include:** Administration.

BAGCRAFT PACKAGING LLC
3900 West 43rd Street, Chicago IL 60632. 773/254-8000. **Toll-free phone:** 800/621-8468. **Fax:** 773/254-8204. **Contact:** Human Resources. **E-mail address:** hr@bagcraft.com. **World Wide Web address:** http://www.bagcraft.com. **Description:** Manufactures flexible packaging and laminating materials. **Parent company:** Packaging Dynamics.

BAIRD & WARNER
120 South LaSalle Street, Suite 2000, Chicago IL 60603. 312/368-1855. **Toll-free phone:** 800/644-1855. **Fax:** 302/368-1490. **Contact:** Wendy Adametz, Human Resources Director. **World Wide Web address:** http://www.bairdwarner.com. **Description:** A full-service, residential real estate broker operating 30 offices in the Chicago area. **NOTE:** Part-time positions offered. See website for all job listings. **Positions advertised include:** Mortgage Underwriter; Loan Officer. **Corporate headquarters location:** This location.

BAKER & McKENZIE
One Prudential Plaza, 130 East Randolph Drive, Chicago IL 60601. 312/861-8800. **Fax:** 312/861-8823. **Contact:** Bethany Phillips, Recruiter. **World Wide Web address:** http://www.bakernet.com. **Description:** A general practice law firm. **Corporate headquarters location:** This location.

BALL HORTICULTURAL COMPANY
622 Town Road, West Chicago IL 60185-2698. 630/231-3600. **Fax:** 630/231-3605. **Contact:** Human Resources. **E-mail address:** careers@ballhort.com. **World Wide Web address:** http://www.ballhort.com. **Description:** An international horticulture producer and distributor. **Positions advertised include:** Production Research Specialist; Sales Trainee; Technical Manager. **NOTE:** Entry-level positions are

offered. **Corporate headquarters location:** This location. **Subsidiaries include:** Ball FloraPlant; Ball Seed Company; Ball Superior Ltd.; ColorLink; PanAmerican Seed Company; Vegmo Plant, BV.

BALLY TOTAL FITNESS CORPORATION
8700 West Bryn Mawr Avenue, Chicago IL 60631. 773/399-1300. **Contact:** Personnel Director. **World Wide Web address:** http://www.ballyfitness.com. **Description:** Bally Total Fitness operates 360 fitness centers located in 27 states with approximately 4.2 million members. The fitness centers operate under the Bally name in conjunction with various others including Holiday Health, Jack LaLanne, Holiday Spa, Chicago Health Clubs, Scandinavian, President's First Lady, Vic Tanny and Aerobics Plus, and The Vertical Clubs. In addition, the company operates four fitness centers in Canada. **NOTE:** Bally has offices throughout the United States. Their website provides job listings and contact information for each location. See website. **Positions advertised include:** Staff Accountant; Senior Auditor; Financial Reporting Manager. **Special programs:** Internships. **Corporate headquarters location:** This location. **Other U.S. locations:** Nationwide. **Listed on:** New York Stock Exchange. **Stock exchange symbol:** BFT.

BANCO POPULAR BANK & TRUST COMPANY
4000 West North Avenue, Chicago IL 60639. 773/772-8600. **Contact:** Human Resources. **World Wide Web address:** http://www.bancopopular.com. **Description:** A bank. **NOTE:** This bank has branches throughout Illinois. See its website for additional locations. Apply online.

BANK OF AMERICA
23 Public Square, Belleville IL 62222. 618/233-6600. **Contact:** Human Resources. **World Wide Web address:** http://www.bankofamerica.com. **Description:** Bank of America is a full-service banking and financial institution. The company operates through four business segments: Global Corporate and Investment Banking, Principal Investing and Asset Management, Commercial Banking, and Consumer Banking. **Corporate headquarters location:** Charlotte NC. **Other U.S. locations:** Nationwide. **Listed on:** New York Stock Exchange. **Stock exchange symbol:** BAC.

BANK ONE
120 North Scott Street, Joliet IL 60432. 815/727-2601. **Contact:** Human Resources. **World Wide Web address:** http://www.bankone.com. **Description:** Bank One is a bank holding company that provides a broad range of commercial and investment banking, trust services, and financial and other services on a worldwide basis to individuals, businesses, and governmental units. **Corporate headquarters location:** Chicago IL. **Operations at this facility include:** This locations is a bank. **Listed on:** New York Stock Exchange. **Stock exchange symbol:** ONE. **Number of employees nationwide:** 73,500.

BANK ONE
8001 Lincoln Avenue, Skokie IL 60077. 847/673-2500. **Contact:** Human Resources. **World Wide Web address:** http://www.bankone.com. **Description:** Bank One is a bank holding company that provides a broad range of commercial and investment banking, trust services, and financial and other services on a worldwide basis to individuals, businesses, and governmental units. **Corporate headquarters location:** Chicago IL. **Operations at this facility include:** This locations is a bank. **Listed on:** New York Stock Exchange. **Stock exchange symbol:** ONE. **Number of employees nationwide:** 73,500.

BANK ONE CORPORATION
One Bank One Plaza, Chicago IL 60670. 312/732-4000. **Contact:** Human Resources. **World Wide Web address:** http://www.bankone.com. **Description:** A bank holding company that provides a broad range of commercial and investment banking, trust services, and financial and other services on a worldwide basis to individuals, businesses, and governmental units. **Corporate headquarters location:** This location. **Listed on:** New York Stock Exchange. **Stock exchange symbol:** ONE. **Number of employees nationwide:** 73,500.

BANK ONE LA GRANGE, N.A.
14 South La Grange Road, La Grange IL 60525. 708/579-4400. **Contact:** Human Resources. **World Wide Web address:** http://www.bankone.com. **Description:** A full-service bank. **Corporate headquarters location:** Chicago IL. **Other U.S. locations:** Nationwide. **Parent company:** Bank One Corporation is one of the nation's largest bank holding companies. Bank One has an affiliate network of over 75 banks with more than 1,500 banking locations. In addition, Bank One operates corporations involved in data processing, venture capital, investment and merchant banking, trust, brokerage, investment management, leasing, mortgage banking, consumer finance, and insurance. **Listed on:** New York Stock Exchange. **Stock exchange symbol:** ONE. **Number of employees nationwide:** 73,500.

BANK ONE SPRINGFIELD, N.A.
One East Old State Capital Plaza, Springfield IL 62701. 217/525-9733. **Contact:** Human Resources. **World Wide Web address:** http://www.bankone.com. **Description:** A bank. **Parent company:** Bank One Corporation is one of the nation's largest bank holding companies. Bank One has an affiliate network of over 75 banks with more than 1,500 banking locations. In addition, Bank One operates corporations involved in data processing, venture capital, investment and merchant banking, trust, brokerage, investment management, leasing, mortgage banking, consumer finance, and insurance. **Listed on:** New York Stock Exchange. **Stock exchange symbol:** ONE. **Number of employees nationwide:** 73,500.

BANKERS LIFE AND CASUALTY COMPANY
222 Merchandise Mart Plaza, 19th Floor, Chicago IL 60654. 312/396-7170. **Fax:** 312/396-5969. **Contact:** Human Resources. **World Wide Web address:** http://www.bankerslife.com. **Description:** Offers a variety of health plans including Medicare supplements, long-term care, and managed care, as well as life, annuity, and disability product lines. **NOTE:** Entry-level positions offered. Apply online for all positions. **Positions advertised include:** Actuarial Assistant; Adjuster; Organizational Trainer and Developer; Help Desk Manager; Claims Vice President; Branch Office Sales Managers. **Corporate headquarters location:** This location. **Parent company:** The Conseco Companies. **Operations at this facility include:** Administration; Service.

BANSLEY & KIENER
8745 West Higgins Road, Suite 200, Chicago IL 60631. 312/263-2700. **Fax:** 312/263-6935. **Contact:** Human Resources. **E-mail address:** humanresources@bk-cpa.com. **World Wide Web address:** http://www.bk-cpa.com. **Description:** A certified public accounting firm. **NOTE:** Fax or e-mail resumes. **Positions advertised include:** Senior In-Charge Auditors; Staff Assistants; Payroll Compliance Auditor; Paraprofessionals. **Special programs:** Internships. **Corporate headquarters location:** This location. **Operations at this facility include:** Service.

BANTA DIRECT MARKETING GROUP
2075 Busse Road, Elk Grove Village IL 60007-5791. 847/593-1200. **Contact:** Human Resources. **E-mail address:** apply@Banta.com. **World Wide Web address:** http://www.banta.com. **Description:** Produces direct mail products including brochures, publication and package inserts, coupons, reply cards, return envelopes, and specialty booklets for national advertisers, direct marketers, publishers, and ad agencies. **NOTE:** Apply online to open positions. For general employment inquiries, e-mail the company. **Positions advertised include:** Customer Service Representative; Executive Assistant; Marketing Assistant/Database Coordinator; Sales and Marketing Assistant. **Parent company:** Banta Corporation (Menasha WI) is a technology and market leader in printing and digital imaging. The corporation serves publishers of educational and general books, special-interest magazines, consumer and business catalogs, and direct marketing materials. In addition to printing and digital imaging, Banta offers multimedia and software packages, interactive media, point-of-purchase materials, and single-use products. Banta operates through the following groups: Banta Book Group; Banta Catalog Group; Banta Digital Group; Banta Direct Marketing Group; Banta Information Services Group; Banta Publications Group; Signs, Displays, Labels & Stamps; and Single-Use Products. **Listed on:** New York Stock Exchange. **Stock exchange symbol:** BN.

BARNES & NOBLE BOOKSTORES
1550 West 75th Street, Downers Grove IL 60516. 630/663-0181. **Fax:** 630/663-0188. **Contact:** Manager. **World Wide Web address:** http://www.barnesandnobleinc.com. **Description:** One location of the nationwide bookstore chain. This location has a cafe in addition to its book departments. **NOTE:** Apply online or at the nearest retail location. **Positions advertised include:** Book Seller; Music Seller; Café Attendant; Department Manager; Community Relations Manager. **Corporate headquarters location:** New York NY. **Other U.S. locations:** Nationwide. **Listed on:** NASDAQ. **Stock exchange symbol:** BNBN.

BARNES & NOBLE BOOKSTORES
47 East Chicago Avenue, Suite 132, Naperville IL 60540. 630/579-0200. **Fax:** 630/579-6921. **Contact:** Manager. **World Wide Web address:** http://www.barnesandnobleinc.com. **Description:** One location of the nationwide bookstore chain. **NOTE:** Apply online or at the nearest retail location. **Positions advertised include:** Book Seller; Music Seller; Café Attendant; Department Manager; Community Relations Manager. **Corporate headquarters location:** New York NY. **Listed on:** NASDAQ. **Other U.S. locations:** Nationwide. **Stock exchange symbol:** BNBN.

BASLER ELECTRIC
P.O. Box 269, Route 143, Highland IL 62249. 618/654-2341. **Fax:** 618-654-2341. **Contact:** Human Resources. **E-mail address:** info@basler.com. **World Wide Web address:** http://www.basler.com. **Description:** Manufactures transformers and electronic equipment. **Other U.S. locations:** Carway AR; Corning AR; Miami FL. **Operations at this facility include:** Administration; Manufacturing; Research and Development; Sales; Service. **Number of employees nationwide:** 1,500.

BAXTER HEALTHCARE CORPORATION
Route 120 and Wilson Road, Round Lake IL 60073. 847/270-5850. **Contact:** Human Resources. **World Wide Web address:** http://www.baxter.com. **Description:** Baxter Healthcare operates four global businesses: Biotechnology develops therapies and products in transfusion medicine; Cardiovascular Medicine develops products and provides services to treat late-stage cardiovascular disease; Renal Therapy develops products and provides services to improve therapies to fight kidney disease; and Intravenous Systems/Medical Products develops technologies and systems to improve intravenous medication delivery and distributes disposable medical products. **NOTE:** Apply online at the company's website. **Corporate headquarters location:** Deerfield IL. **Operations at this facility include:** This location is a research facility. **Listed on:** New York Stock Exchange. **Stock exchange symbol:** BAX. **Number of employees worldwide:** 48,000.

BAXTER INTERNATIONAL, INC.
One Baxter Parkway, Deerfield IL 60015. 847/948-2000. **Toll-free phone:** 800/422-9827. **Fax:** 847/948-2964. **Contact:** Human Resources. **World Wide Web address:** http://www.baxter.com. **Description:** A global medical products and services company that is a leader in technologies related to blood and the circulatory system. The company operates four global businesses: Biotechnology develops therapies and products in transfusion medicine; Cardiovascular Medicine develops products and provides services to treat late-stage cardiovascular disease; Renal Therapy develops products and provides services to improve therapies to fight kidney disease; and Intravenous Systems/Medical Products develops technologies and systems to improve intravenous medication delivery and distributes disposable medical products. **NOTE:** Apply online. **Positions advertised include:** Communications Manager; Senior Paralegal; Training and eLearning. . **Special programs:** Internships. **Corporate headquarters location:** This location. **Operations at this facility include:** Administration. **Listed on:** New York Stock Exchange. **Stock exchange symbol:** BAX. **Number of employees worldwide:** 48,000.

THE BEACON NEWS
101 South River Street, Aurora IL 60506. 630/844-5811. **Contact:** Human Resources. **World Wide Web address:** http://www.suburbanchicagonews.com. **Description:** A daily newspaper serving De Kalb, DuPage, Kane, and Kendall Counties. The paper has a daily circulation of approximately 90,000. Founded in 1846. **Parent company:** The Copley Press (La Jolla CA) publishes 45 newspapers nationwide.

BEALL MANUFACTURING INC.
P.O. Box 70, East Alton IL 62024. 618/259-8154. **Contact:** Human Resources. **Description:** Manufactures heat-treated spring steel parts. Major markets served by Beall Manufacturing include the agricultural, railroad, construction, and outdoor recreation markets. **Corporate headquarters location:** This location. **Operations at this facility include:** Manufacturing. **Listed on:** Privately held.

BEAR, STEARNS & COMPANY, INC.
3 First National Plaza, Chicago IL 60602. 800/753-2327. **Contact:** Human Resources. **World Wide Web address:** http://www.bearstearns.com. **Description:** A leading investment banking and securities trading and brokerage firm serving governments, corporations, institutions, and individuals worldwide. The company offers services in corporate finance, mergers, acquisitions, institutional equities, fixed income sales and trading, derivatives, futures sales and trading, asset management, and custody. **NOTE:** This company provides job listings for all its lo locations on its website. See website and apply online. **Corporate headquarters location:** New York NY. **Other U.S. locations:** Nationwide **International locations:** Worldwide. **Parent company:** The Bear Stearns Companies Inc. **Listed on:** NASDAQ. **Stock exchange symbol:** BSC. **Number of employees nationwide:** 10,500.

BEKINS VAN LINES
330 South Mannheim Road, Hillside IL 60162. 708/547-2000. **Fax:** 708/547-3228. **Contact:** Human Resources. **World Wide Web address:** http://www.bekins.com. **Description:** A moving and storage company. **Positions advertised include:** Driver. **Corporate headquarters location:** This location. **Parent company:** The Bekins Company. **Operations at this facility include:** Service. **Listed on:** Privately held.

BELCAN CORPORATION
Woodland Courte Office Center, 3130 Finley Road, Suite 520, Downers Grove IL 60515. 630/786-9900. **Contact:** Human Resources. **World Wide Web address:** http://www.belcan.com. **Description:** An engineering and consulting firm offering long-term, client-site consulting services in the Midwest. **NOTE:** Entry-level positions are offered. This company has many locations throughout Illinois. See website for additional offices and apply online. **Positions advertised include:** Civil Project Engineer; Design Engineer; Electrical Engineer; Physical-Electrical Designer. **Corporate headquarters location:** Ann Arbor MI. **International locations:** England. **Listed on:** Privately held.

BELL AND GOSSETT DOMESTIC PUMP
ITT INDUSTRIES
8200 North Austin Avenue, Morton Grove IL 60053. 847/966-3700. **Contact:** Bill Dempsey, Employee Relations Manager. **World Wide Web address:** http://www.bgasp.ittind.com. **Description:** Produces heat exchangers, plumbing equipment, and pumps. **Corporate headquarters location:** White Plains NY. **Parent company:** ITT Industries is a diversified, global enterprise engaged in four major business areas: Electronic Components; Defense Electronics and Services; Fluid Technology; and Motion and Flow Control. **Listed on:** New York Stock Exchange. **Stock exchange symbol:** ITT.

BELL SPORTS
1924 County Road, Rantoul IL 61866. 217/893-9300. **Toll-free phone:** 800-456-2355. **Contact:** Human Resources. **World Wide Web address:** http://www.bellsports.com. **Description:** Manufactures helmets and other safety equipment. **Special programs:** Internships. **Corporate headquarters location:** Scottsdale AZ. **Other U.S. locations:** Los Gatos CA; East Providence RI. **Operations at this facility include:** Manufacturing.

BELLEVILLE SHOE MANUFACTURING COMPANY
100 Premier Drive, Belleville IL 62220. 618/233-5600. **Fax:** 618/233-5617. **Contact:** Human Resources. **World Wide Web address:** http://www.bellevilleshoe.com. **Description:** Manufactures men's and boys' shoes.

BEMIS COMPANY INC.
P.O. Box 568, Peoria IL 61651. 309/682-5406. **Physical address:** One Sloan Street, Peoria IL 61603. **Contact:** Human Resources. **World Wide Web address:** http://www.bemis.com. **Description**: Bemis Company is a diversified producer of consumer and industrial packaging materials, film products, and business products. Packaging products include tapes and paper bags for pharmaceuticals, candy, toilet paper, and detergents. The company also produces sheetprint stock, roll labels, laminates, and adhesive products. **NOTE:** Apply online at the company's website. **Corporate headquarters location:** Minneapolis MN. **Operations at this facility include: :** This location manufactures paper bags. **Listed on:** New York Stock Exchange. **Stock exchange symbol:** BMS.

BEVERLY FARM FOUNDATION INC.
6301 Humbert Road, Godfrey IL 62035. 618/466-0367. **Contact:** Peggy Price, Human Resources. **E-mail address:** pprice@beverlyfarm.org. **World Wide Web address:** http://www.beverlyfarm.org. **Description:** A nonprofit residential care facility for developmentally disabled individuals. **Positions advertised include:** Dietary Aide; Client Program Coordinator. **Office hours:** Monday – Friday, 8:00 a.m. – 4:30 p.m.

BIG RIVER ZINC CORPORATION
2401 Mississippi Avenue, Sauget IL 62201. 618/274-5000. **Toll-free phone:** 800/274-4002. **Fax:** 618/274-4444. **Contact:** Human Resources. **World Wide Web address:** http://www.bigriverzinc.com. **Description:** A foundry producing primary zinc. **NOTE:** Entry-level positions are offered. **Special programs:** Apprenticeships. **Corporate headquarters location:** This location. **International locations:** Worldwide. **Parent company:** Korea Zinc (Seoul, Korea). **Operations at this facility include:** Manufacturing; Research and Development; Sales. **Listed on:** Privately held.

BITUMINOUS INSURANCE COMPANY
320 18th Street, Rock Island IL 61201. 309/786-5401. **Toll-free phone:** 800/475-4777. **Fax:** 309/786-4716. **Contact:** Senior Vice President of Administrative Services. **E-mail address:** hr@bituminous.com. **World Wide Web address:** http://www.bituminousinsurance.com. **Description:** Offers a wide variety of individual insurance plans including property and casualty. **NOTE:** Interested jobseekers may apply by sending their resumes via fax, e-mail or mail. An online application may also be completed at the company's website.

BLISTEX, INC.
1800 Swift Drive, Oak Brook IL 60523. 630/571-2870. **Toll-free phone:** 800/837-1800. **Contact:** Human Resources. **World Wide Web address:** http://www.blistex.com. **Description:** Manufactures a line of lip care products under the Blistex and DCT brand names. **NOTE:** Resumes and cover letters must be mailed. **Corporate headquarters location:** This location.

BLOOM ENGINEERING COMPANY, INC.
18161 Morris Avenue, Homewood IL 60430. 412/760-8737. **Contact:** Human Resources. **E-mail address:** tfennell@bloomeng.com. **World Wide Web address:** http://www.bloomeng.com. **Description:** Provides innovative energy and environmental solutions to industry. **Positions advertised include:** Combustion Technician; Boiler Technician; Controls Technician. **Corporate headquarters location:** Pittsburgh PA.

BLUE CROSS AND BLUE SHIELD OF ILLINOIS
300 East Randolph Street, Chicago IL 60601-5099. 312/938-6000. Fax: 312/240-0386. **Contact:** Pat O'Connor, Human Resources. **World Wide Web address:** http://www.bcbsil.com. **Description:** A nonprofit health care insurance organization providing managed health care plans to both individuals and groups. Blue Cross and Blue Shield offers Point-of-Service, individual health, PPO, and HMO plans, as well as vision and dental insurance. **NOTE:** See website for job listings. Fax resume or apply online. **Positions advertised include:** Source Control Technician; Medical Management Program Administrator; Information Systems; Auditor; Senior Internal Auditor; Senior Information Systems Auditor; Financial Analyst; Care Coordinator I; Medical Management Results Coordinator; Senior Project Coordinator. Parent company: Health Care Service Corporation.

BODINE ELECTRIC COMPANY
2500 West Bradley Place, Chicago IL 60618. 773/478-3515. **Fax:** 773/478-3232. **Contact:** Human Resources. **E-mail address:** careers@bodine-electric.com. **World Wide Web address:** http://www.bodine-electric.com. **Description:** Manufactures fractional horsepower electric motors, gear motors, and motor controls. Founded in 1905. **NOTE:** Entry-level positions and second and third shifts are offered. **Other U.S. locations:** Peosta IA. **Operations at this facility include:** Administration; Manufacturing; Research and Development; Sales; Service. **Listed on:** Privately held.

BOHLER-UDDEHOLM CORPORATION
4902 Tollview Drive, Rolling Meadows IL 60008. 847/577-2220. **Contact:** Human Resources Manager. **World Wide Web address:** http://www.bohler-uddeholm.com. **Description:** A steel distributor. This location also hires seasonally. **NOTE:** Entry-level positions and part-time jobs are offered. **Special programs:** Internships; Summer Jobs. **Corporate headquarters location:** This location. **Other U.S. locations:** Nationwide. **International locations:** Austria; Canada; Germany; Sweden. **Operations at this facility include:** Administration. **Listed on:** Privately held. **Number of employees worldwide:** 10,000.

BOISE OFFICE SOLUTIONS
CORPORATE HEADQUARTERS
150 East Pierce Road, Itasca IL 60143. **Toll-Free phone:** 800-47BOISE. **Fax:** 800/57BOISE. **Contact:** Human Resources. **World Wide Web address:** http://www.bcop.com. **Description:** A business-to-business distributor of office and computer supplies, furniture, paper products, and promotional products. Founded in 1964. **NOTE:** Apply online. **International locations:** Australia; Canada; England; France; Germany; Spain. **Subsidiaries include:** Boise Marketing Services, Inc.; Grande Toy; JPG; Neat Ideas; Reliable. **Parent company:** Boise Cascade Corporation. **Listed on:** New York Stock Exchange. **Stock exchange symbol:** BCC.

BOISE OFFICE SOLUTIONS
CHICAGO DISTRIBUTION CENTER
800 West Bryn Mawr Avenue, Itasca IL 60143-1594. **Toll-Free phone:** 800-47BOISE. **Fax:** 800/57BOISE. **Contact:** Human Resources. **World Wide Web address:** http://www.bcop.com. **Description:** The company's main distribution office. **Parent company:** Boise Cascade Corporation. **Listed on:** New York Stock Exchange. **Stock exchange symbol:** BCC.

BOND SAFEGUARD INSURANCE COMPANY
1919 South Highland Avenue, Building A, Suite 300, Lombard IL 60148. 630/495-9380. **Toll-free phone:** 800/962-5212. **Fax:** 630/495-9272. **Contact:** Human Resources. **World Wide Web address:** http://www.bondsafeguard.com. **Description:** Offers bond insurance.

BORG-WARNER AUTOMOTIVE
700 25th Avenue, Bellwood IL 60104. 708/547-2600. **Contact:** Director of Human Resources. **World Wide Web address:** http://www.bwauto.com. **Description:** Manufactures powertrain components for original equipment manufacturers and original equipment suppliers in the automobile industry. **Corporate headquarters location:** Chicago IL. Operations at this facility include: This location is a powertrain engine manufacturing facility. **Listed on:** New York Stock Exchange. **Stock exchange symbol:** BWA.

BORG-WARNER AUTOMOTIVE
200 South Michigan Avenue, Chicago IL 60604. 312/322-8500. **Fax:** 312/322-8500. **Contact:** Director of Human Resources. **World Wide Web address:** http://www.bwauto.com. **Description:** Manufactures powertrain components for original equipment manufacturers and original equipment suppliers in the automobile industry. Operations include powertrain assembly and the manufacture of automatic transmission systems, and chain and control systems. **Corporate headquarters location:** This location. **Operations at this facility include:** Administration. **Listed on:** New York Stock Exchange. **Stock exchange symbol:** BWA.

ROBERT BOSCH CORPORATION
P.O. Box 4601, Carol Stream IL 60197. 708/865-5200. **Physical address:** 2800 South 25th Avenue, Broadview IL 60155. **Fax:** 708/865-6430. **Contact:** Human Resources. **World Wide Web address:** http://www.bosch.com. **Description:** Robert Bosch Corporation operates through three groups: Automotive Equipment, Industrial Technology, and Consumer Goods and Building Technology. The largest segment of the company's business is the Automotive Equipment group, which includes products such as antilock braking systems, airbag electronics, fuel injectors, and oxygen sensors. The Industrial Technology group consists of the Packaging Technology Division, which sells high-tech packaging equipment, primarily to the food processing and pharmaceutical industries; the Bosch Rexroth Division, which creates products that control motors and motion equipment; and Metal Technology Division, which manufactures water pipes for various industries. The Consumer Goods and Building Technology group has five divisions: Power Tools (sold in many hardware stores); Thermotechnology (residential and industrial heating systems); Household Appliances; and Broadband Networks. **NOTE:** This company provides job listings for all its locations on its website. Apply online. **Corporate headquarters location:** This location.

ROBERT BOSCH TOOL COMPANY
1800 West Central Road, Mont Prospect IL 60056. 224/232-2000. **Contact:** Human Resources. **World Wide Web address:** http://www.boschtools.com. **Description:** Manufactures hand and power tools. **Other U.S. locations:** Nationwide. **Operations at this facility include:** Administration; Research and Development.

BOWE BELL & HOWELL COMPANY
760 South Wolf Road, Wheeling IL 60090-6232. 847/675-7600. **Contact:** Human Resources. **World Wide Web address:** http://www.bellhowell.com. **Description:** Bell & Howell is a diversified corporation operating in three major areas: Specialized Business Equipment, which manufactures items including microfilm recorders, readers, and jackets, as well as micropublishing, office collation, and mailing machines; Learning Systems and Materials, which operates technical training schools in electronics and computer science, publishes textbooks, and produces a variety of instructional materials at all levels; and Instrumentation, which manufactures measuring and recording equipment, magnetic tape instrumentation, and a variety of semiconductor compounds, optics equipment, and photoplates for integrated circuits. **NOTE:** See the corporate website for job listings. **Operations at this facility include:** Administrative; Production.

THE BRADFORD GROUP
9333 North Milwaukee Avenue, Niles IL 60714. 847/966-2770. **Fax:** 847/581-8630. **Contact:** Recruiter. **E-mail address:** jobs@collectiblestoday.com. **World Wide Web address:** http://www.collectiblestoday.com. **Description:** An international direct marketing company specializing in fine arts and collectibles. **NOTE:** Entry-level

positions are offered. **Positions advertised include:** Marketing Professional; Product Manager; Product Designer; Product Development Associate. **Special programs:** Internships. **Corporate headquarters location:** This location. **Listed on:** Privately held.

BRADLEY UNIVERSITY
1501 West Bradley Avenue, Peoria IL 61625. 309/676-7611. **Fax:** 309/677-3223. **Contact:** Human Resources. **World Wide Web address:** http://www.bradley.edu. **Description:** A private, four-year university offering both undergraduate and graduate degrees. Programs are offered through the Slane College of Communications and Fine Arts; Engineering and Technology; Education and Health Sciences; Liberal Arts and Sciences; and the Foster College of Business Administration. Founded in 1897. **NOTE:** See website for job listings and contact information. **Office hours:** Monday – Friday, 8:00 a.m. – 5:00 p.m. (closed between noon and 1:00 p.m.)

BRAKE PARTS INC.
4400 Prime Parkway, McHenry IL 60050. 815/363-9000. **Fax:** 815/363-9303. **Contact:** Human Resources. **World Wide Web address:** http://www.raybestos.com. **Description:** Manufactures and distributes a variety of automotive brake products. **NOTE:** Mail resume or apply online in persona at this location's Human Resources office. **Parent company:** Dana Corporation. **Operations at this facility include:** Administration; Manufacturing; Sales; Service.

BRICKKICKER
849 North Ellsworth, Naperville IL 60563. 630/420-9900. **Toll-free phone:** 800/821-1820. **Fax:** 630/420-2270.**Contact:** Human Resources. **World Wide Web address:** http://www.brickkicker.com. **Description:** Performs home and building inspections.

BRIDGESTONE/FIRESTONE, INC.
RETAIL AND COMMERCIAL DIVISION
333 East Lake Street Bloomingdale IL 60108. 630/259-9000. **Fax:** 630/259-9158. **Contact:** Human Resources. **World Wide Web address:** http://www.mastercareusa.com. **Description:** This location is the support center and headquarters for the Bridgestone/Firestone, Inc. retail stores, MasterCare. Founded in 1900. **NOTE:** Entry-level positions and part-time jobs are offered. Apply online at the website. **Office hours:** Monday - Friday, 8:00 a.m. - 5:00 p.m. **Corporate headquarters location:** Nashville TN. **Other U.S. locations:** Nationwide. **International locations:** Worldwide. **Parent company:** Bridgestone. **Operations at this facility include:** Administration; Divisional Headquarters; Service.

BROADVIEW MEDIA
142 East Ontario, 3rd Floor, Chicago IL 60611. 312/337-6000. **Contact:** Human Resources. **World Wide Web address:** http://www.broadviewmedia.com. **Description:** A full-service film and video production company involved in production, editing, audio, consumer graphics, and distribution, servicing broadcast and cable networks, corporate advertising agencies, and business to business markets. **NOTE:** Entry-level positions are offered.

BROMENN REGIONAL MEDICAL CENTER
Franklin & Virginia Streets, Normal IL 61761. 309/268-5717. **Contact:** Human Resources. **World Wide Web address:** http://www.bromenn.org. **Description:** A 244-bed hospital offering a variety of inpatient, outpatient, rehabilitation, acute, and preventive health care services including women's and children's, emergency and trauma, neurological, cardiac, and pulmonary, and orthopedic. **NOTE:** A completed application is required for any position. Apply online. **Positions advertised include:** Cardiovascular Operating Room Technician; Coder; Cook; Help Desk Operator; Lead Nursing Technician; Physical Therapist. **Parent company:** Bromenn Healthcare. **Operations at this facility include:** Administration; Service.

BRONSON & BRATTON
220 Shore Drive, Burr Ridge IL 60527. 630/986-1815. **Fax:** 630/655-3801. **Contact:** Human Resources. **World Wide Web address:** http://www.brons.com. **Description:** Manufactures small-lot, specialty tools and dies, specializing in hard-to-machine metals and ceramics.

BROWN PRINTING
11595 McConnell Road, Woodstock IL 60098. 815/338-6750. **Contact:** Ed Davis, Human Resources Manager. **E-mail address:** ed.davis@bpc.com. **World Wide Web address:** http://www.bpc.com. **Description:** Provides color printing, binding, and related services to the publishers of trade and special-interest magazines. Services include selective binding, ink-jet technology, carrier-route sorting, and bar coding of customers' subscriber lists.

LEO BURNETT USA
35 West Wacker Drive, Chicago IL 60601. 312/220-5959. **Contact:** Human Resources. **World Wide Web address:** http://www.leoburnett.com. **Description:** One of the world's largest advertising agencies, with 200 operating units worldwide. Leo Burnett USA also provides direct marketing, promotional, interactive, and public relations services. Founded in 1935. **NOTE:** Apply online at the company's website. **Positions advertised include:** Digital Studio Artist; Creative Director; Database Analyst. **Special programs:** Internships. **Number of employees worldwide:** 8,000.

BURNSIDE CONSTRUCTION COMPANY
2400 Wisconsin Avenue, Downers Grove IL 60515-4019. 630/515-9999. **Contact:** Human Resources. **World Wide Web address:** http://www.burnsidehomes.com. **Description:** A residential construction company. Founded in 1911.

BUTTERNUT BAKERY
CHICAGO BAKING COMPANY
40 East Garfield Boulevard, Chicago IL 60615. 773/536-7700. **Contact:** Joseph Schulz, Personnel Manager. **Description:** A producer and wholesaler of bread products. **Corporate headquarters location:** Kansas City MO. **Parent company:** Interstate Brands Corporation. **Operations at this facility include:** Manufacturing.

CBS INC.
630 North McClurg Court, Chicago IL 60611. 312/202-2222. **Contact:** Human Resources. **World Wide Web address:** http://www.cbs.com. **Description:** CBS Inc. is a broad-based entertainment and communications company that operates one of the country's four major commercial television networks and two nationwide radio networks, which include 8 AM and 13 FM stations. **NOTE:** Interested jobseekers should mail their resumes and indicate in their cover letters if they are applying for TV, AM or FM radio positions. **Operations at this facility include:** This location houses regional administrative offices.

CCL CUSTOM MANUFACTURING INC.
One West Hegeler Lane, Danville IL 61832. 217/442-1400. **Contact:** Human Resources Department. **World Wide Web address:** http://www.cclind.com. **Description:** Engaged in the contract filling and packaging of aerosol and liquid containers for a variety of household and automotive purposes. **NOTE:** Apply online. **Corporate headquarters location:** Chicago IL. **Other U.S. locations:** Wixom MI; Cumberland RI; Memphis TN.

CDW COMPUTER CENTERS, INC.
200 North Milwaukee Avenue, Vernon Hills IL 60061. 847/465-6000. **Fax:** 847/465-3858. **Contact:** Human Resources. **World Wide Web address:** http://www.cdw.com. **Description:** Resells name-brand computers and peripherals to small and medium-sized businesses through catalog, phone, and online sales. **NOTE:** Apply online. **Corporate headquarters location:** This location. **Listed on:** NASDAQ. **Stock exchange symbol:** CDWC. **Annual sales/revenues:** More than $100 million.

CF INDUSTRIES, INC.
One Salem Lake Drive, Long Grove IL 60047-8402. 847/438-9500. **Fax:** 847/438-0211. **Contact:** Human Resources. **World Wide Web address:** http://www.cfindustries.com. **Description:** One of North America's largest manufacturers and distributors of fertilizer products. Founded in 1946. **NOTE:** Entry-level positions are offered. **Corporate headquarters location:** This location. **Listed on:** Privately held.

CGH MEDICAL CENTER
100 East LeFevre Road, Sterling IL 61081-1279. 815/625-0400. **Contact:** Director of Human Resources. **World Wide Web address:** http://www.cghmc.com. **Description:** An acute care trauma center housing a variety of specialty centers including home nursing, home health, sleep disorder, and speech and hearing. **NOTE:** See website for job listings. An application is required for any position. Download an application from the website and mail it or apply online. **Positions advertised include:** Patient Registration Clerk; RN.

CH2M HILL
8501 West Higgins Road, Suite 300,Chicago IL 60631-2801. 773/693-3809. **Contact:** Human Resources. **World Wide Web address:** http://www.ch2m.com. **Description:** CH2M Hill is a group of employee-owned companies operating under the names CH2M Hill, Inc., Industrial Design Corporation, Operations Management International, CH2M Hill International, and CH2M Hill Engineering. The professional staff includes specialists in environmental engineering, waste management, water management, transportation, industrial facilities, and a broad spectrum of infrastructure systems. **NOTE:** This company has offices throughout Chicago, Illinois and the United States. See website for job listings and apply online. **Operations at this facility include:** This location provides transportation and environmental engineering services.

CII TECHNOLOGIES
844 East Rockland Road, Libertyville IL 60048-3375. 847/680-7400. **Fax:** 847/680-8169. **Contact:** Human Resources. **World Wide Web address:** http://www.cor.com. **Description:** One of the world's largest suppliers of radio frequency interference (RFI) filters. Products are used to control noise pollution in a wide variety of digital electronic devices. Founded in 1955. **Corporate headquarters location:** This location. **Parent company:** Tyco Electronics. **Listed on:** New York Stock Exchange. **Stock exchange symbol:** TYC.

CNA INSURANCE COMPANIES
CNA Plaza, 333 South Wabash Avenue, 31st Floor, Chicago IL 60685. 312/822-5000. **Contact:** Human Resources. **World Wide Web address:** http://www.cna.com. **Description:** An insurance holding company. **NOTE:** Apply online at the company's website. **Corporate headquarters location:** This location. **Subsidiaries include:** American Casualty Company; Continental Assurance Company; National Fire Insurance Company. **Listed on:** New York Stock Exchange. **Stock exchange symbol:** CNA.

CPC (CERTIFIED PACKAGING CORPORATION)
3800 Hawthorne Court, Waukegan IL 60087. 888/438-1515. **Contact:** Human Resources. **World Wide Web address:** http://www.cpcpack.com. **Description:** The company is a contract packaging firm offering shrink wrapping, promotional packs, gift set assembly, and compounding/filling services. **Operations at this facility include:** This location manufactures consumer products such as candles and over-the-counter drugs for other companies.

CABOT CORPORATION
CAB-O-SIL DIVISION
700 East U.S. Highway 36, Tuscola IL 61953-9643. 217/253-3370. **Fax:** 217/253-4334. **Contact:** Human Resources. **World Wide Web address:** http://www.cabot-corp.com/cabosil. **Description:** Cabot Corporation's operations are in specialty chemicals, materials, and energy. The company produces carbon black, an essential reinforcing agent in tires and rubber products and a pigment in inks, coatings, and plastics. The company also produces fumed silica, electronic materials, and refractory metals. Cabot Corporation is a European producer of plastic concentrates and compounds. Cabot Corporation also makes eyewear, hearing protection, and industrial noise control products. **NOTE:** Apply online or mail resumes. **Corporate headquarters location:** Boston. **Listed on:** New York Stock Exchange. Stock exchange symbol: CBT.

CAMPBELL MITHUN
101 East Erie, 10th Floor, Chicago IL 60611. 312/278-6000. Fax: 312/278-6210. **Contact:** Human Resources. **E-mail address:** careers@campbell-mithun.com. **World Wide Web address:** http://www.campbellmithun.com. **Description:** A full-service advertising agency. Campbell Mithun also offers public relations services including corporate relations, marketing support, employee relations, financial relations, government affairs, and community relations.

CANON BUSINESS SOLUTIONS
425 North Martingale Road, Schaumburg IL 60173. 847/706-3480. **Fax:** 847/706-3419. **Contact:** Recruiter. **World Wide Web address:** http://www.solutions.canon.com. **Description:** Offers customized solutions for business offices. Canon Business Solutions markets the full line of Canon office equipment including copiers, laser printers, fax machines, and scanners. Founded in 1974. **NOTE:** Entry-level positions are offered. **NOTE:** Apply online at this website for open positions. **Positions advertised include:** Sales Manager; Field Service Technician. **Corporate headquarters location:** This location. **Parent company:** Canon USA. **Listed on:** New York Stock Exchange. **Stock exchange symbol:** CAJ.

CANTEEN CORPORATION
216 West Diversey Avenue, Elmhurst IL 60126. 630/833-3666. **Contact:** Human Resources. **World Wide Web address:** http://www.canteen.com. **Description:** One of the world's largest food and beverage vending companies. Canteen Corporation has over 150,000 vending machines in service. **Positions advertised include:** Branch Manager; Customer Service Manager; Supervisor; Route Driver. **Corporate**

headquarters location: This location. **Parent company:** Compass Group plc (London, England).

CAPITOL CONSTRUCTION GROUP
220 North Smith Street, Suite 210, Palatine Il 60067. 847/654-4700. Fax: 847/358-7331. **Contact:** Human Resources. **E-mail address:** info@capitol.com. **World Wide Web address:** http://www.capitolconstruction.com. **Description:** A general contractor. **NOTE:** Interested jobseekers should fax or e-mail their resumes. **Positions advertised include:** Project Manager; Construction Superintendent. **Other U.S. locations:** Phoenix AZ; Tampa FL; St. Louis MO.

CARDINAL GLASS COMPANY
1087 Research Parkway, Rockford IL 61109. 815/394-1400. **Contact:** Human Resources. **Description:** Replaces automobile glass, distributes flat glass, and performs commercial and residential glazing.

CARDINAL HEALTH
1430 Waukegan Road, McGraw Park IL 60085. 847/578-9500. **Contact:** Human Resources. **World Wide Web address:** http://www.cardinal.com. **Description:** Cardinal Health is a producer, developer, and distributor of medical products and technologies for use in hospitals and other health care settings. The company operates through two industry segments: medical specialties, and medical/laboratory products and distribution. **NOTE:** Apply online. **Corporate headquarters location:** Dublin OH. **Operations at this facility include:** This location distributes medical supplies to hospitals and government facilities. Number of employees worldwide: 55,000. **Listed on:** New York Stock Exchange. **Stock exchange symbol:** CAH.

CAREMARK INTERNATIONAL
2211 Sanders Road, Northbrook IL 60062. 847/559-4700. **Contact:** Director of Human Resources. **World Wide Web address:** http://www.caremark.com. **Description:** A leading provider of patient services through health care networks. Divisions include physician practice management and pharmaceutical services, which includes one of the country's largest independent pharmacy benefit management programs, serving approximately 29 million Americans through a mail-order and retail network of pharmacies. AdvancePCS, a mail-order prescription company, is also part of Caremark. Apply online. **International locations:** Worldwide. **Operations at this facility include:** Administration; Operations. **Listed on:** New York Stock Exchange. **Stock exchange symbol:** CMX.

CARLE FOUNDATION HOSPITAL
611 West Park Street, Urbana IL 61801. 217/383-4000. **Fax:** 217/383-3373. **Contact:** Human Resources. **E-mail address:** Foundation.HR@carle.com. **World Wide Web address:** http://www.carle.com/CFH/about. **Description:** A 295-bed, tertiary care and regional trauma center. Carle Foundation Hospital also includes a 295-bed, long-term care facility, home care agency, retail pharmacy, daycare center, and psychiatric and chemical dependency services. This hospital also provides services for the Carle Medical Clinic, (located in the same building) as well as other healthcare facilities throughout Illinois. **NOTE:** Interested jobseekers may mail or apply online for open positions. Resumes and applications are also accepted in the Human Resources office. **Positions advertised include:** Certified/Registered Coder; Inpatient Coding Coordinator; Therapy Office Coordinator; Health Care Technician; Advanced Practice Nurse; Physical Therapist; Telemedicine and Mobile Clinic Coordinator; Contract Administrator; Physician Services Director. **Office hours:** Monday – Friday, 7:00 a.m. – 5:00 p.m.

CARRY TRANSIT
7830 West 71st Street, Bridgeview IL 60455. 800/777-2288. **Fax:** 708-594-5110. **Contact:** Neil Desmond, Human Resources. **E-mail address:** ndesmond@carrytransit.com. **World Wide Web address:** http://www.carrytransit.com. **Description:** Operates one of the nation's largest fleets of stainless steel food grade tankers, serving as a liquid and dry bulk distribution partner to various food products manufacturers. **Positions advertised include:** Local Truck Driver; Truck Driver CDL; Trucking Terminal Manager. **Corporate headquarters location:** This location.

CARSON PIRIE SCOTT & COMPANY
One South State Street, Chicago IL 60603. 312/641-7000. **Fax:** 312/641-7088. **Contact:** Hiring Manager. **World Wide Web address:** http://www.carsons.com. **Description:** The department store chain's flagship store in downtown Chicago. Overall, Carson Pirie Scott & Company operates a department store chain with more than 50 Midwest locations. **Parent company:** Saks Incorporated operates a number of retail stores offering fashion apparel, accessories, cosmetics, and home furnishings. Saks Incorporated operates more than 350 stores in 38 states. Stores include: Proffitt's, McRae's, Younkers, and Saks Fifth Avenue. The company also operates two direct mail companies, Folio and Bullock & James. **NOTE:** This chain has several locations throughout the Chicago area and Illinois and the Midwest. To apply, see the corporate website for open positions; or visit the nearest store location. **Listed on:** New York Stock Exchange. **Stock exchange symbol:** SKS.

CARSON PIRIE SCOTT & COMPANY/BERGNERS DISTRIBUTION CENTER
4650 Shepherd Trail, Rockford IL 61103. 815/654-5420. **Contact:** Human Resources. **World Wide Web address:** http://www.carsons.com. **Description:** Carson Pirie Scott & Company Bergner's Company operate department store chains with more than 100 Midwest locations. **Parent company:** Saks Incorporated operates a number of retail stores offering fashion apparel, accessories, cosmetics, and home furnishings. Saks Incorporated operates more than 350 stores in 38 states. Other stores include: Proffitt's, McRae's, Younkers, and Saks Fifth Avenue. The company also operates two direct mail companies, Folio and Bullock & James. **NOTE:** Interested jobseekers must visit this facility's Human Resources Office. **Office hours:** Monday – Thursday, 7:00 a.m. – 4:30 p.m.; Friday, 8:00 a.m. to noon. **Operations at this facility include:** This location is the distribution center for Carson Pirie Scott and Bergner's. **Listed on:** New York Stock Exchange. **Stock exchange symbol:** SKS.

CATERPILLAR INC.
P.O. Box 504, Joliet IL 60434-0504. 815/729-5511. **Contact:** Human Resources. **World Wide Web address:** http://www.cat.com. **Description:** Caterpillar is one of the world's largest manufacturers of construction and mining equipment, natural gas engines, and industrial gas turbines; and a leading global supplier of diesel engines. Products range from track-type tractors to hydraulic excavators, backhoe loaders, motor graders, and off-highway trucks. They are used in the construction, road building, mining, forestry, energy, transportation, and material-handling industries. Caterpillar products and components are manufactured in more than 70 plants worldwide. **NOTE:** Apply online at the corporate website. **Corporate headquarters location:** Peoria IL. **Operations at this facility include:** This location is part of Cat Logistics, a division of Caterpillar. It manufactures hydraulic components and fabrications such as valves, pumps, motors, and cylinders.

CATERPILLAR INC.
100 North East Adams Street, Peoria IL 61629-8300. 309/675-5923. **Fax:** 309/675-6476. **Contact:** Corporate Employment Services. **World Wide Web address:** http://www.cat.com. **Description:** Caterpillar is one of the world's largest manufacturers of construction and mining equipment and machine engines. In addition, the company provides a number of business services such as logistics, automation and financial services. **NOTE:** Entry-level positions are offered. This company provides job listings for its corporate office, division offices and manufacturing facilities on its website. See website and apply online. **Special programs:** Internships. **Corporate headquarters location:** This location. **Listed on:** New York Stock Exchange. **Stock exchange symbol:** CAT. **Number of employees worldwide:** 72,000.

CATERPILLAR INC.
CATERPILLAR LOGISTICS
500 North Morton Avenue, Morton IL 61550-0474. **Toll-free phone:** 800/240-2126. **Contact:** Human Resources. **World Wide Web address:** http://www.cat.com. **Description:** Caterpillar Logistics Division provides products and services that help businesses and government agencies manage their supply chains. **NOTE:** Caterpillar Logistics has another location in Aurora IL. See website for street address. Apply online at the corporate website for all open positions in Caterpillar and Caterpillar Logistics. **Corporate headquarters location:** Peoria IL. **Operations at this facility include:** Administration. This location is the headquarters for Caterpillar Logistics. **Listed on:** New York Stock Exchange. **Stock exchange symbol:** CAT. **Number of employees worldwide:** 72,000.

CATHOLIC CHARITIES OF THE ARCHDIOCESE OF CHICAGO
126 North Desplaines Street, Chicago IL 60661. 312/655-7000. **Fax:** 312/831-1321. **Recorded jobline:** 312/655-7118. **Contact:** Employment Services. **World Wide Web address:** http://www.catholiccharities.net. **Description:** A network of private social service organizations that provides food, shelter, and clothing to more than 10 million poor and homeless people each year. **NOTE:** This organization provides a complete list of open positions and contact information on its website. See website. **Positions advertised include:** Intake/Marketing Specialist; Supervisor; Bi-Lingual Receptionist/Clerk; Social Work/Coordinator.

CENTRAL DUPAGE HOSPITAL
BEHAVIORAL HEALTH SERVICES
25 North Winfield Road, Winfield IL 60190. 630/653-4000. **Fax:** 630/933-2652. **Contact:** Human Resources. **E-mail address:** hr@cdh.org. **World Wide Web address:** http://www.cdh.org. **Description:** A mental health and chemical dependency outpatient and inpatient treatment center. **Positions advertised include:** Purchasing Assistant; Physician Peer Review Clinical Decision Support; RN (Various); Home Health Aide.

CENTRAL STEEL AND WIRE COMPANY
3000 West 51st Street, Chicago IL 60632. 773/471-3800. **Toll-free phone:** 800/232-9279. **Contact:** Matthews Professional Employment, Inc. **E-mail address:** ppaulmatthews@aol.com. **World Wide Web address:** http://www.centralsteel.com. **Description:** Distributes many types and forms of processed and non-processed, ferrous and nonferrous metals purchased from producing mills and specialty mills. **NOTE:** To apply for positions, contact Matthews Professional Employment via e-mail or fax at 847/249-1133.

CENVEO
3001 North Rockwell Street, Chicago IL 60618. 773/267-3600. **Contact:** Human Resources. **World Wide Web address:** http://www.mail-wellenvelope.com. **Description:** An envelope manufacturer. **Corporate headquarters location:** Englewood CO. **Operations at this facility include:** This is a manufacturing plant. **Other area locations:** DeKalb IL; Kankakee IL. **Other U.S. locations:** Nationwide. **Listed on:** New York Stock Exchange. **Stock exchange symbol:** CVO.

CERRO FLOW PRODUCTS, INC.
3000 Mississippi Avenue, Sauget IL 62206. 618/337-6000. **Toll-free phone:** 888/237-7611. **Fax:** 618/337-6958. **Contact:** Human Resources. **World Wide Web address:** http://www.cerrocu.com. **Description:** Manufactures and sells copper tubing. **NOTE:** Resumes should be sent to Human Resources, P.O. Box 66800, St. Louis MO 63166. Interested jobseekers may also apply online at the corporate website.

CERTIFIED GROCERS MIDWEST, INC.
One Certified Drive, Hodgkins IL 60525. 708/579-2100. Fax: 708/354-7502. **Contact:** Human Resources. **World Wide Web address:** http://www.certisaver.com. **Description:** A food wholesaler. **Corporate headquarters location:** This location.

CHAMBERLAIN GROUP
845 Larch Avenue, Elmhurst IL 60126. 630/530-6752. **Toll-free phone:** 800/528-5880. **Fax:** 630/530-6091. **Contact:** Melanie Ditore, Human Resources. **E-mail address:** mditore@chamberlian.com. **World Wide Web address:** http://www.chamberlaingroup.com. **Description:** Manufactures garage door openers, waxers, and gate openers. **NOTE:** Mail or e-mail resumes and cover letters. **Positions advertised include:** PC Support Specialist; Graphic Design Specialist; Marketing Support Representative; Financial Analyst. **Parent company:** Duchossois Industries, Inc.

CHAPMAN AND CUTLER
111 West Monroe Street, Chicago IL 60603. 312/845-3898. **Fax:** 312/701-2361. **Contact:** Human Resources. **World Wide Web address:** http://www.chapman.com. **Description:** A law firm specializing in corporate financing, litigation, and tax law. **NOTE:** To apply for attorney positions, contact Stacey Kielbasa, Legal Personnel and Recruitment Manager, at kielbasa@chapman.com. Transcripts must be submitted with cover letters and resumes. For corporate and support positions, send resumes to Kimberly Wongstrom-Torvik via fax at 312/516-1488 or e-mail at legalresumes@chapman.com. **Special programs:** Summer Associates. **Corporate headquarters location:** This location. **Operations at this facility include:** Administration; Service. **Listed on:** Privately held.

CHARTER ONE BANK
6700 West North Avenue, Chicago IL 60707. 773/622-5000. **Contact:** Human Resources. **World Wide Web address:** http://www.charteronebank.com. **Description:** A federally chartered savings and loan bank. **NOTE:** Part-time shifts offered. Apply online or at the nearest branch location for all positions. **Positions advertised include:** Assistant Sales. **Corporate headquarters location:** This location. **Operations at this facility include:** Administration; Sales; Service.

CHEF SOLUTIONS INC.
20 North Martingale Road, Suite 600, Schaumburg IL 60173. 847/762-8500. **Toll-free phone:** 800/877-1157. **Fax:** 847/762-8605. **Contact:** Human Resources. **E-mail address:** resumes@chefsolutions.com. **World Wide Web address:**

http://www.chefsolutions.com. **Description:** Markets a variety of chilled, freshly prepared foods for restaurants, wholesalers, and consumers. **NOTE:** Entry-level positions and second and third shifts are offered. **Special programs:** Internships. **Corporate headquarters location:** This location. **Other area locations:** Wheeling IL (Manufacturing); Northlake IL (Bakery); Mt. Prospect IL (Research and Development). **U.S. locations:** CA; TX; MN; CT; NY; OH; KS; NJ; GA. **International locations:** Mexico. **Parent company:** Questor Management (Southfield MI). **Listed on:** Privately held.

THE CHERRY ELECTRICAL CORPORATION
P.O. Box 581913, Pleasant Prairie IL 53158-0913. 847/662-9200. **Contact:** Human Resources. **World Wide Web address:** http://www.cherrycorp.com. **Description:** Manufactures and distributes a wide range of electrical components for the computer, automotive, consumer, and commercial markets worldwide. The principal segments are electromechanical devices including snap-action, selector, and special-use switches principally for use in automobiles, home appliances, office and industrial equipment, and vending machines; and electronic assemblies including keyboards, keyboard switches, gas discharge displays, and automotive electronics for use in data entry terminals, automobiles, industrial and commercial control devices, business machines, and amusement products. **Corporate headquarters location:** This location. **Subsidiaries include:** Cherry Automotive Division (this location); Cherry Electrical Products Division (Pleasant Prairie WI); Cherry de Mexico (Mexico).

CHICAGO ACADEMY OF SCIENCES
PEGGY NOTEBAERT NATURE MUSEUM
2340 North Cannon Drive, Chicago IL 60614. 773/755-5100. **Fax:** 773/549-5199. **Contact:** Human Resources. **World Wide Web address:** http://www.chias.org. **Description:** A natural history museum. The Nature Museum, located on the North Pier, offers hands-on exhibits and also runs week-long summer nature camps June through August each year. Founded in 1857. **NOTE:** See website for job listings and specific contact information.

CHICAGO ASSOCIATION FOR RETARDED CITIZENS (CARC)
8 South Michigan Avenue, Suite 1700, Chicago IL 60603. 312/346/6230. **Contact:** Recruiting Manager. **E-mail address:** recruiting@chgoarc.org. **Description:** Provides self-help and vocational training skills to people with physical and mental disabilities. Operates 14 education and vocational centers throughout the Chicago area. **NOTE:** See website for center locations. Send all resumes and cover letters to this address. **Positions advertised include:** Special Education Teacher; QMRP/Counselor.

CHICAGO BLOWER CORPORATION
1675 Glen Ellyn Road, Glendale Heights IL 60139. 630/858-2600. **Fax:** 630/858-7172. **Contact:** Human Resources. **E-mail address:** cbc@fan.net. **World Wide Web address:** http://www.chiblo.com. **Description:** Designs and manufactures industrial fans and blowers. **NOTE:** Interested jobseekers may also apply in person.

THE CHICAGO BOARD OF TRADE
141 West Jackson Boulevard, Suite 2080, Chicago IL 60604. 312/435-3494. **Fax:** 312/435-7150. **Contact:** Employment Office. **World Wide Web address:** http://www.cbot.com. **Description:** A commodities, futures, and options exchange. **Positions advertised include:** Trading Systems Analyst; e-CBOT Senior Systems Administrator; Program Office Administrator; Revenue Auditor; Senior Programmer Analyst; Systems Integration Specialist. **Corporate headquarters location:** This location.

THE CHICAGO BOARD OPTIONS EXCHANGE
400 South LaSalle Street, Chicago IL 60605. 312/786-7800. **Toll-free phone:** 877/THE-CODE. **Fax:** 312/786-7808. **Contact:** Human Resources. **World Wide Web address:** http://www.cboe.com. **Description:** A nonprofit financial institution engaged in options trading. **NOTE:** Entry-level positions are offered. **Positions advertised include:** Senior Business Analyst; VIP Help Desk Director; Examiner; Investigator; Engineer. **Corporate headquarters location:** This location.

CHICAGO BOTANIC GARDEN
1000 Lake Cook Road, Glencoe IL 60022. 847/835-8300. **Fax:** 847/835-4263. **Contact:** Human Resources. **E-mail address:** employment@chicagobotanic.org. **World Wide Web address:** http://www.chicago-botanic.org. **Description:** Contains horticultural displays used to promote the understanding of plants, gardening, and natural resource conservation. Founded in 1965. **NOTE:** See website for job listings and e-mail resumes and cover letters. **Positions advertised include:** College First Instructor; Curriculum Development Coordinator; Coordinator Retail Events Floor Supervisor. **Special programs:** Internships.

CHICAGO BRIDGE AND IRON COMPANY (CB&I)
14109 South Route 59, Plainfield IL 60544-8984. 815/439-6000. **Fax:** 815/439-6010. **Contact:** Human Resources. **E-mail address:** employment@CBIepc.com. **World Wide Web address:** http://www.chicago-bridge.com. **Description:** A global engineering and construction company specializing in the engineering, design, fabrication, erection, and repair of petroleum terminals, steel tanks, refinery pressure vessels, low temperature and cryogenic storage facilities, and other steel-plated structures and their associated systems. Founded in 1889. **NOTE:** E-mail resumes and cover letters. **Special programs:** Engineer Training. **Corporate headquarters location:** The Netherlands. **Operations at this facility include:** This location houses the main offices for CB&I Industrial Division and CB&I Water Group. **Listed on:** New York Stock Exchange. **Stock exchange symbol:** CBI. **Number of employees worldwide:** 7,500.

CHICAGO, CITY OF
City Hall, 121 North LaSalle Street, Chicago IL 60602. 312/742-5955. **Recorded jobline:** 312/744-1369. **Contact:** Department of Personnel Service Center. **World Wide Web address:** http://www.cityofchicago.org. **Description:** Administrative offices for the City of Chicago's government departments, agencies and services. **NOTE:** The Department of Personnel only accepts resumes and applications for open positions. Interested jobseekers may call the jobline to hear about current openings; or, they may visit the Department at City Hall in Room 100. An application can be obtained online at the City's website. **Special programs:** Internships. **Office hours:** Monday – Friday, 8:00 a.m. – 5:00 p.m.

CHICAGO CUBS
Wrigley Field, 1060 West Addison Street, Chicago IL 60613. 773/404-2827. **Contact:** Director of Human Resources. **World Wide Web address:** http://www.cubs.com. **Description:** The administrative offices for the professional baseball team. **NOTE:** See website.

CHICAGO DISPLAY MARKETING CORPORATION
1999 North Ruby Street, Melrose Park IL 60160. 708/681-4340. **Fax:** 708/681-5852. **Contact:** Human Resources. **World Wide Web address:** http://www.chicagodisplay.com. **Description:** Designs and markets advertising display materials for merchandisers and manufacturers.

CHICAGO EXTRUDED METALS COMPANY
1601 South 54th Avenue, Cicero IL 60804. 708/656-7900. **Fax:** 708/780-3479. **Contact:** Human Resources. **World Wide Web address:** http://www.cxm.com. **Description:** Manufactures screw machine products, brass wire rods, and other related products. **NOTE:** Apply online. **Corporate headquarters location:** This location.

THE CHICAGO FAUCET COMPANY
2100 South Clearwater Drive, Des Plaines IL 60018. 847/803-5000. **Fax:** 847/803-44995454. **Contact:** Human Resources. **World Wide Web address:** http://www.chicagofaucets.com. **Description:** Manufactures brass products including plumbing fittings.

THE CHICAGO GROUP, INC.
744 North Wells Street, Chicago IL 60610. 312/751-0303. **Fax:** 312/751-0470. **Contact:** Human Resources. **World Wide Web address:** http://www.thechicagogroup.com. **Description:** A management consulting firm specializing in strategic marketing for utility, telecommunications, industrial, technology, and service businesses. **Positions advertised include:** Analyst; Consultant; Director; Manager. **Corporate headquarters location:** This location. **Listed on:** Privately held.

CHICAGO MARRIOTT DOWNTOWN
540 North Michigan Avenue, Chicago IL 60611-3822. 312/836-0100. **Contact:** Human Resources. **World Wide Web address:** http://www.marriott.com. **Description:** A full-service hotel chain offering 1,172 rooms and 20 meeting facilities. **NOTE:** Apply online. **Other U.S. locations:** Nationwide. **Listed on:** New York Stock Exchange. **Stock exchange symbol:** MAR.

CHICAGO MERCANTILE EXCHANGE
20 South Wacker Drive, Chicago IL 60606. 312/930-8240. **Fax:** 312/930-2036. **Contact:** Human Resources. **World Wide Web address:** http://www.cme.com. **Description:** One of the world's largest commodities, futures, and options exchanges. **Positions advertised include:** Associate Director of Product Communication; Senior Internal Auditor; Business Analyst; Market Reporter; Assistant General Counsel. **Special programs:** Internships. **Corporate headquarters location:** This location. **Other U.S. locations:** Washington DC; New York NY. **Listed on:** American Stock Exchange. **Stock exchange symbol:** CME.

CHICAGO MICROSYSTEMS, INC.
1825 Elmdale Avenue, Glenview IL 60026-1297. 847/998-9970. **Fax:** 847/998-9975. **Contact:** Human Resources. **World Wide Web address:** http://www.chimicro.com. **Description:** A computer reseller and an Internet service provider.

CHICAGO RAWHIDE
890 North State Road, Elgin IL 60123. 847/742-7840. **Contact:** Human Resources. **World Wide Web address:** http://www.chicago-rawhide.com. **Description:** Manufactures oil seals, filters, gaskets, and other custom-molded products. **Corporate headquarters location:** This location. **Parent company:** SKF. **Operations at this facility include:** Manufacturing.

CHICAGO STATE UNIVERSITY
9501 South King Drive, Chicago IL 60628. 773/995-2000. **Contact:** Human Resources. **World Wide Web address:** http://www.csu.edu. **Description:** A four-year, state university offering undergraduate and graduate degree programs through its colleges of Arts and Sciences, Business, Education, and Health Sciences. **NOTE:** See website for job listings and contact information. **Office hours:** Monday – Friday, 8:30 a.m. – 5:00 p.m.

CHICAGO STOCK EXCHANGE INC.
440 South LaSalle Street, Chicago IL 60657. 312/663-2526. **Contact:** Human Resources. **E-mail address:** hrrecruiting@chx.com. **World Wide Web address:** http://www.chx.com. **Description:** A stock exchange offering securities trading and depository services. **NOTE:** Send resumes by fax or e-mail only. **Positions advertised include:** Surveillance Investigator; Enforcement Attorney; Senior Programmer Analyst. **Corporate headquarters location:** This location. **Other U.S. locations:** New York NY.

CHICAGO SUN-TIMES INC.
350 North Orleans, Chicago IL 60604. 312/321-3000. **Contact:** Employment Manager. **World Wide Web address:** http://www.suntimes.com. **Description:** Publishes one of the largest daily newspapers in the United States. **Special programs:** Internships. **Corporate headquarters location:** This location. **Parent company:** American Publishing Company. **Operations at this facility include:** Administration; Manufacturing; Sales; Service.

CHICAGO SYMPHONY ORCHESTRA
220 South Michigan Avenue, Chicago IL 60604. 312/294-3333. **Fax:** 312/294-3838. **Recorded jobline:** 312/294-3326. **Contact:** Human Resources. **E-mail address:** hr@cso.org. **World Wide Web address:** http://www.chicagosymphony.org. **Description:** One of the nation's most prestigious orchestras. **Positions advertised include:** Director of Research; Ticket Sales and Service Associate. **Special programs:** Internship. **Corporate headquarters location:** This location.

CHICAGO TITLE & TRUST COMPANY
171 North Clark Street, Chicago IL 60601. 312/223-2000. **Toll-free phone:** 800/815-3969. **Contact:** Human Resources. **World Wide Web address:** http://www.ctic.com. **Description:** Provides a variety of insurance related services including credit services, marketing information, flood insurance, field services, and consolidated reconveyance. **Operations at this facility include:** Administration; Sales; Service.

CHICAGO TOUR GUIDES INSTITUTE, INC.
EUROPEAN LANGUAGE CENTER INC.
60 East Chestnut, Suite 381, Chicago IL 60611. 773/276-6683. **Fax:** 773/252-3729. **Contact:** Human Resources Department. **World Wide Web address:** http://www.chicagoguide.net. **Description:** Offers tours of Chicago. The European Language Center (also at this location) hires part-time and full-time foreign language interpreters for U.S. and foreign companies. **NOTE:** Guides earn $15 to $25 per hour and need to have comprehensive knowledge of the city including local museums, architecture, art, and city history. **Positions advertised include:** Tour Guide. **Corporate headquarters location:** This location.

CHICAGO YOUTH CENTERS
104 South Michigan Avenue, 14th Floor, Chicago IL 60603-5902. 312/648-1550. **Fax:** 312/795-3520. **Contact:** Human Resources. **World Wide Web address:**

http://www.chicagoyouthcenters.org. **Description:** Provides recreational and educational opportunities for children.

CINCH CONNECTORS
1700 Finley Road, Lombard IL 60148. 630/705-6000. **Toll-free phone:** 800/323-9612. **Fax:** 630/705-6054. **Contact:** Human Resources. **E-mail address:** careers@cinch.com. **World Wide Web address:** http://www.cinch.com. **Description:** Produces connectors, interconnection systems, IC sockets, relay sockets, tube sockets, terminal strips, barrier blocks, crimp terminals, communications cross-connect systems, harness assemblies, and adapters. Major markets served include military/aerospace, telecommunications, computer and instrumentation, and automotive. **Operations at this facility include:** Administration; Divisional Headquarters; Manufacturing; Research and Development; Sales; Service.

CINTAS
5600 West 73rd Street, Chicago IL 60638. 708/563-4913. **Fax:** 708/563-4360. **Contact:** Human Resources. **World Wide Web address:** http://www.cintas.com. **Description:** Designs, manufactures, and markets specialty apparel for the hospitality, restaurant, and entertainment industries. **Corporate headquarters location:** This location. **International locations:** Canada; Mexico; Puerto Rico. **Operations at this facility include:** Administration; Regional Headquarters; Research and Development; Sales; Service. **Listed on:** NASDAQ. **Stock exchange symbol:** CTAS.

CIRCA '21 DINNER PLAYHOUSE
1828 Third Avenue, Rock Island IL 61201. 309/786-2667. **Fax:** 309/786-4119. **Contact:** Dennis Hitchcock, Producer. **E-mail address:** dlaake@circa21.com. **World Wide Web address:** http://www.circa21.com. **Description:** Produces musicals and modern comedies, as well as a series of children's plays and concerts year-round. Circa '21 Dinner Playhouse has produced numerous national tours. Founded in 1977. **NOTE:** Part-time jobs are offered. Interested jobseekers may fill out an application in person at the office or e-mail their resumes. **Positions advertised include:** Housekeeper; Cook; Dishwasher; Maintenance Worker. **Special programs:** Internships. **Listed on:** Privately held.

CITATION
7800 North Austin Avenue, Skokie IL 60077-2675. 847/966-5050. **Fax:** 847/966-9128. **Contact:** Bill Herrmann, Human Resources. **E-mail address:** billh@skokie.citation.net. **World Wide Web address:** http://www.citation.net. **Description:** Citation Corporation is a manufacturer of cast, forged and machined components for the capital and durable goods industries. This location offers four different casting production solutions under one facility. **Positions advertised include:** Casting/Pattern Engineer; Industrial Maintenance Supervisor; Network Administrator; Production Supervisor; Sharepoint Portal Application Developer; Shipping Supervisor. **Corporate headquarters location:** Birmingham AL. **Other area locations:** Lake Zurich IL. **Other U.S. locations:** Berlin WI, Browntown WI, Menomonee Falls WI, Grand Rapids MI, Butler IN, Lufkin TX, Columbiana AL, Biscoe NC.

CITGO PETROLEUM CORPORATION
3737 South Cicero Avenue, Cicero IL 60804. 708/780-5700. **Contact:** Human Resources. **World Wide Web address:** http://www.citgo.com. **Description:** Citgo Petroleum wholesales gasoline that is then sold to gas stations by a distributor. **Corporate headquarters location:** Tulsa OK. **Operations at this facility include:** This location manufactures lubricants.

CITGO PETROLEUM CORPORATION
135th Street & New Avenue, Lemont IL 60439. 630/257-7761. **Contact:** Personnel. **World Wide Web address:** http://www.citgo.com. **Description:** Citgo Petroleum wholesales gasoline that is then sold to gas stations by a distributor. **Positions advertised include:** Chemical Engineer; Electrical Engineer; Mechanical Engineer. **Corporate headquarters location:** Tulsa OK. **Operations at this facility include:** This location is a refinery.

CITIBANK
500 West Madison Street, 5th Floor, Chicago IL 60661. 312/627-5231. **Fax:** 312/627-5235. **Recorded jobline:** 312/627-5299. **Contact:** Strategic Staffing. **World Wide Web address:** http://www.citibank.com. **Description:** Citibank operates a global, full-service consumer franchise encompassing branch banking, credit and charge cards, and private banking. In branch banking, Citibank services almost 20 million accounts in 41 countries and territories. In global card products, Citibank is one of the world's largest bankcard and charge card issuers, with almost 50 million cards in force (34 million bankcards in the United States, 9 million in other countries, and almost 7 million Diners Club cards). In addition, Citibank issues and services approximately 5 million private-label cards for department stores and retail outlets. Citibank Private Bank's offices in 31 countries and territories provide a full-range of wealth management services and give clients access to the full range of Citibank's global capabilities. **NOTE:** This company lists all its open positions in its Chicago area, Illinois and United States locations. See website and apply online. **Special programs:** Internships. **Corporate headquarters location:** New York NY. **Other U.S. locations:** Nationwide. **Parent company:** Citigroup. **Operations at this facility include:** Divisional Headquarters. **Listed on:** New York Stock Exchange. **Stock exchange symbol:** C.

CLARK NATIONAL, INC.
CLARK FOODSERVICE PRODUCTS, INC.
950 Arthur Avenue, Elk Grove Village IL 60007. 847/956-1730. **Fax:** 847/956-0199. **Contact:** Human Resources. **World Wide Web address:** http://www.clarkfoodservice.com. **Description:** Distributes cleaning supplies, food service disposables, and groceries to the food service industry. **NOTE:** The parent company, Clark National Inc., is located also at this facility. **Positions advertised include:** Corporate Sales Executive. **Operations at this facility include:** Administration; Sales.

CLAUSSEN PICKLE COMPANY
1300 Claussen Drive, Woodstock IL 60098. 815/338-7000. **Contact:** Human Resources. **World Wide Web address:** http://www.kraftfoods.com/cla. **Description:** A producer and distributor of pickles. **NOTE:** Kraft's corporate website provides job listings for Claussen and its other divisions. To see job listings and to apply, visit http://www.kraftfoods.com/careers. **Parent company:** Kraft Foods. **Operations at this facility include:** Manufacturing. **Listed on:** New York Stock Exchange. **Stock exchange symbol:** KFT.

CLAYTON GROUP SERVICES, INC.
3140 Finley Road, Downers Grove IL 60515. 630/795-3200. **Fax:** 630/795-1130. **Contact:** Human Resources. **E-mail address:** hr@claytongrp.com. **World Wide Web address:** http://www.claytongrp.com. **Description:** An environmental consulting firm that also offers occupational health and safety, strategic environmental management, environmental risk management, and laboratory services. **NOTE:** Resumes may be sent to Human Resources, 45525 Grand River Avenue, Suite 200, Novi, MI 48374; or, they may be faxed to 248/344-0229. Indicate job code in cover letter.

CLEAN HARBORS, INC.
11800 South Stony Island Avenue, Chicago IL 60617. 773/646-6202. **Fax:** 773/646-6381. **Contact:** Human Resources. **World Wide Web address:** http://www.cleanharbors.com. **Description:** Clean Harbors, Inc., through its subsidiaries, provides comprehensive environmental services in 35 states in the Northeast, Midwest, Central, and Mid-Atlantic regions. Clean Harbors provides a wide range of hazardous waste management and environmental support services to a diversified customer base from over 40 locations. The company's hazardous waste management services include treatment, storage, recycling, transportation, risk analysis, site assessment, laboratory analysis, site closure, and disposal of hazardous materials through environmentally sound methods including incineration. Environmental remediation services include emergency response, surface remediation, groundwater restoration, industrial maintenance, and facility decontamination. **NOTE:** See website for job listings and contact information. **Positions advertised include:** Field Technician. **Corporate headquarters location:** Braintree MA. **Other U.S. locations:** Nationwide.

CLIFTON GUNDERSON L.L.C.
P.O. Box 1835, Peoria IL 61656-1835. 309/671-4500. **Physical address:** 301 Southwest Adams Street, Peoria IL 61656-1835. **Fax:** 309/671-4508. **Contact:** Human Resources. **World Wide Web address:** http://www.cliftoncpa.com. **Description:** A certified public accounting and consulting firm. **NOTE:** Send resumes to: Clifton Gunderson L.L.C., Human Resources, 2323 North Mayfair Road, Milwaukee WI 53226. **Positions advertised include:** Accountant; Human Resources Professional; Statistical Typist; Accounting Software Sales; Network Infrastructure Sales Consultant. **Corporate headquarters location:** This location.

CLINTON ELECTRONICS CORPORATION
6701 Clinton Road, Loves Park IL 61111. 815/633-1444. **Toll-free phone:** 800/447-3306. **Fax:** 815/633-8712. **Contact:** Employee Relations Supervisor. **World Wide Web address:** http://www.cec-displays.com. **Description:** Manufactures cathode ray tubes for use in computer screens.

COBRA ELECTRONICS CORPORATION
6500 West Cortland Street, Chicago IL 60707. 773/889-8870. **Fax:** 773/889-4453. **Contact:** Human Resources. **World Wide Web address:** http://www.cobraelec.com. **Description:** Manufactures telephones and consumer electronics products. **NOTE:** Interested jobseekers may mail or fax resumes or apply online at the company's website. **Positions advertised include:** Regional Sales Manager. **Corporate headquarters location:** This location. **Operations at this facility include:** Administration; Manufacturing; Sales; Service. **Listed on:** NASDAQ. **Stock exchange symbol:** COBR.

COGNEX CORPORATION
850 East Diehl Road, Suite 125, Naperville IL 60563. 630/505-9990. **Fax:** 630/505-9995. **Contact:** Human Resources. **World Wide Web address:** http://www.cognex.com. **Description:** Designs, develops, manufactures, and markets machine vision systems used to automate a wide range of manufacturing processes. Cognex machine vision systems are used in the electronics, semiconductor, pharmaceutical, health care, aerospace, automotive, packaging, and graphic arts industries to gauge, guide, inspect, and identify products in manufacturing operations. **NOTE:** Resumes should be sent to Human Resources, Cognex Corporation, One Vision Drive, Natick MA 01760-2059. Fax: 508/650-3340. **Corporate headquarters location:** Natick MA. **Other U.S. locations:** CA. **International locations:** France; Germany; Japan; Singapore; United Kingdom. **Operations at this facility include:** This location is the company's Midwest Regional Technology Center. **Listed on:** NASDAQ. **Stock exchange symbol:** CGNX.

COLDWELL BANKER RESIDENTIAL BROKERAGE
875 North Michigan Avenue, Suite 3500, Chicago IL 60611. 312/751-9100. **Fax:** 312/751-9293. **Contact:** Human Resources. **World Wide Web address:** http://www.coldwellbanker.com. **Description:** One of the largest residential real estate companies in the United States and Canada. **Corporate headquarters location:** Parsippany NJ.

COLE TAYLOR BANK
9550 West Higgins Road, Rosemont IL 60018. 847/653-7978.x350. East Dundee Road, Wheeling IL 60090. 847/459-6666. **Contact:** Human Resources. **World Wide Web address:** http://www.ctbnk.com. **Description:** A full-service bank with multiple locations throughout the Greater Chicago area. **Positions advertised include:** Chief Financial Officer; Consumer Loan Specialist; Systems Project Manager; Vice President of Product Development.

COLE-PARMER INSTRUMENT COMPANY
625 East Bunker Court, Vernon Hills IL 60061. 847/549-7600. **Toll-free phone:** 800/323-4340. **Fax:** 847/549-1515. **Contact:** Human Resources. **E-mail address:** hr@coleparmer.com. **World Wide Web address:** http://www.coleparmer.com. **Description:** An international exporter and distributor of scientific instruments for laboratories. **NOTE:** See website for job listings. Apply online or e-mail resumes. **Positions advertised include:** Application Specialist; Desktop Publishing Specialist; Financial Analyst.

COLLEGE OF LAKE COUNTY
19351 West Washington Street, Grayslake IL 60030. 847/543-2065. **Fax:** 847/223-0824. 223-6601. **Contact:** Human Resources. **E-mail address:** personnel@clcillinois.edu. **World Wide Web address:** http://www.clcillinois.edu. **Description:** A two-year community college. College of Lake County offers a variety of transfer and career preparation programs to over 14,000 students. The college is a nonresidential institution. **NOTE:** See website for job listings, contact information and application procedures. Positions advertised include: Dental Hygiene Instructor; Architectural Technology Instructor; Medical Imaging Instructor; Director of Nursing Education. **Office hours:** Monday – Friday, 8:00 a.m. – 4:30 p.m.

COLLINSVILLE HOLIDAY INN
1000 Eastport Plaza Drive, Collinsville IL 62234. 618/345-2800. **Fax:** 618/345-9804. **Contact:** Human Resources. **World Wide Web address:** http://www.holidayinncollinsville.com. **Description:** A nationwide hotel chain. Overall, Holiday Inn's operations include the management of more than 1,750 company-owned and franchised hotels, gaming operations, restaurants, and a sea transportation subsidiary. **Corporate headquarters location:** Atlanta GA.

COLUMBIA COLLEGE
600 South Michigan Avenue, Chicago IL 60605-1996. 312/663-1600. **Contact:** Human Resources. **World Wide Web address:** http://www.colum.edu. **Description:** A college

offering bachelor's and master's degrees and specializing in communications, media, applied and fine arts, theatrical and performing arts, and management and marketing. Columbia College's enrollment is approximately 7,300 students. At the graduate level, Columbia offers the master of arts degree in seven disciplines: arts, entertainment, and media management; teaching of writing; dance/movement therapy; interdisciplinary arts; journalism; multicultural education; and photography. The master of fine arts degree is awarded in creative writing, film and video, and photography. **NOTE:** See website for job listings, contact information and application procedures. **Positions advertised include:** Attorney; Director of L.A. Semester; Coordinator of Sports Management; Professor (Various).

COMCAST
5N301 Medinah Road, Addison IL 60101. 708/383-7280. **Contact:** Human Resources. **World Wide Web address:** http://www.comcast.com. **Description:** One of the nation's largest cable television and broadband services companies. **NOTE:** In addition to this location, Comcast has several locations in Illinois. Jobseekers are encouraged to apply via the company's website. Positions advertised include: Recruiting Assistant; Collections Representative; Supervisor of Inbound Sales/Retention. **Corporate headquarters location:** Philadelphia PA. **Listed on:** NASDAQ. **Stock exchange symbol:** CMCSA. **Number of employees worldwide:** 150,000.

COMMERCE CLEARING HOUSE, INC. (CCH, INC.)
4025 West Peterson, Chicago IL 60646. 773/583-8500. **Contact:** Human Resources. **World Wide Web address:** http://www. cch.com. **Description:** Provides business law information to the legal and accounting professions by publishing loose-leaf news reports and books primarily on tax and business law. The company also provides corporate services to lawyers and offers computer services for processing income tax returns. It also provides information to the healthcare and human resources industries. **NOTE:** See website for job listings and apply online. **Corporate headquarters location:** Riverwoods IL. **Other U.S. locations:** Quail Hill CA; Washington DC; St. Petersburg FL; Clark NJ; New York NY. **Operations at this facility include:** Administration; Manufacturing; Service.

COMMERCIAL FORGED PRODUCTS
5757 West 65th Street, Bedford Park IL 60638. 708/458-1220. **Fax:** 708/458-9346. **Contact:** Human Resources. **World Wide Web address:** http://www.commercialforged.com. **Description:** Engaged in upset forging of spindles, axles, drill bits, and tie rods. **Corporate headquarters location:** Oakbrook Terrace IL. **Listed on:** Privately held.

COMMERCIAL LIGHT COMPANY
245 Fencl Lane, Hillside IL 60162. 708/449-6900. **Fax:** 708/449-6942. **Contact:** Human Resources. **World Wide Web address:** http://www.clcats.com. **Description:** An electrical contractor. Founded in 1915.

COMPUTER ASSOCIATES INTERNATIONAL, INC.
2400 Cabot Drive, Lisle IL 60532. 630/505-6000. **Contact:** Human Resources. **World Wide Web address:** http://www.cai.com. **Description:** Computer Associates International is one of the world's leading developers of client/server and distributed computing software. The company develops, markets, and supports enterprise management, database and applications development, business applications, and consumer software products for a broad range of mainframe, midrange, and desktop computers. Computer Associates International serves major business, government, research, and educational organizations. Founded in 1976. **NOTE:** Apply online at the website or send resumes for open positions to the company's headquarters: One Computer Associates Plaza, Islandia NY 11749, Attention: Human Resources Recruitment. **Positions advertised include:** Technology Services Architect; Consultant; Customer Advocate; Sales. **Corporate headquarters location:** Islandia NY. **Other U.S. locations:** Nationwide. **Listed on:** New York Stock Exchange. **Stock exchange symbol:** CA. **Number of employees nationwide:** 16,000.

COMPUTER HORIZONS CORPORATION
RECRUITING CENTER, MIDWEST REGION
6400 Shafer Court, Suite 600, Rosemont IL 60018. 847/698-6800. **Toll-free phone:** 800/877-2421. **Fax:** 847/698-6823. **Contact:** Staffing Manager. **World Wide Web address:** http://www.computerhorizons.com. **Description:** Computer Horizons is a full-service technology solutions company offering contract staffing, outsourcing, re-engineering, migration, downsizing support, and network management. Founded in 1969. **NOTE:** Apply online at the company's website. **Corporate headquarters location:** Mountain Lakes NJ.

COMPUTER SCIENCES CORPORATION (CSC)
935 Lakeview Parkway, Suite 190, Vernon Hills IL 60061. 847/573-4400. **Contact:** Human Resources. **World Wide Web address:** http://www.csc.com. **Description:** Develops software for the many industries and governments, and provides solutions to client/server, e-business, and mainframe applications. Founded in 1959. **Listed on:** New York Stock Exchange. **Stock exchange symbol:** CSC. **Number of employees worldwide:** 90,000.

COMPUWARE CORPORATION
2 Pierce Place, Suite 1900, Itasca IL 60143. 630/285-8560. **Contact:** Human Resources. **World Wide Web address:** http://www.compuware.com. **Description:** Develops, markets, and supports an integrated line of systems software products that improve the productivity of programmers and analysts in application program testing, test data preparation, error analysis, and maintenance. Compuware also provides a broad range of professional data processing services including business systems analysis, design, and programming, as well as systems planning and consulting. **NOTE:** Apply online to open positions. **Corporate headquarters location:** Farmington Hills MI.

CONAGRA REFRIGERATED PREPARED FOODS
215 West Diehl Road, Naperville IL 60563. 630/857-1000. **Fax:** 630/857-1901. **Contact:** Human Resources. **World Wide Web address:** http://www.conagrafoods.com. **Description:** Processes meats such as bacon, ham, fresh smoked and dry sausage, and luncheon meats under the brand names Armour Star, Brown 'N Serve, Butterball, Eckrich, Healthy Choice, and Swift Premium. **NOTE:** Apply online at the parent company's Conagra's, website: http://www.conagrafoods.com. **Corporate headquarters location:** Omaha NE. **Other U.S. locations:** Nationwide. **Parent company:** ConAgra, Inc. **Operations at this facility include:** Administration; Divisional Headquarters; Regional Headquarters; Sales.

CONESTOGA ROVERS & ASSOCIATES
8615 West Bryn Mawr, Chicago IL 60631. 773/380-9933. **Contact:** Human Resources. **World Wide Web address:** http://www.craworld.com. **Description:** An environmental engineering and consulting firm. Founded in 1976. Apply online at this company's website.

CONSOER TOWNSEND ENVIRODYNE ENGINEERS, INC.
303 East Wacker Drive, Suite 600, Chicago IL 60601. 312/938-0300. **Fax:** 312/938-1109. **Contact:** Director of Human Resources. **E-mail address:** jobs@cte-eng.com. **World Wide Web address:** http://www.cte-eng.com. **Description:** Provides engineering consulting for highways, airports, and waste management projects. **NOTE:** Apply online at the company's website or e-mail resumes.

CONTINENTAL PLASTIC CONTAINERS
2727 East Higgins, Elk Grove IL 60007. 847/364-3800. **Contact:** Human Resources. **Description:** A leading developer, manufacturer, and marketer of custom extrusion, blow-molded plastic containers. Founded in 1904. **Other U.S. locations:** Nationwide. **Parent company:** Continental Can Company, Inc. is an international packaging company with several subsidiaries in Europe. **Operations at this facility include:** This location is a technical center. **Listed on:** New York Stock Exchange. **Stock exchange symbol:** CAN.

CONTRACTING & MATERIAL COMPANY
9550 West 55th Street, Suite B, McCook IL 60525. 708/588-6000. **Contact:** Human Resources. **World Wide Web address:** http://www.candmcompany.com. **Description:** Provides contract construction services for electrical, pipeline, highway, and heavy construction projects. **NOTE:** Garages are located at 5401 West Harrison Street, Chicago IL 60644-5030.

CONVERGYS
2 Pierce Place, Itasca IL 60143-3153. 630/775-1700. **Fax:** 630/775-8890. **Contact:** Human Resources. **World Wide Web address:** http://www.convergys.com. **Description:** Designs and markets information systems, and provides consulting and technical services for telecommunications companies. **NOTE:** Apply online at the website. **Positions advertised include:** Senior Manager of Professional Services; Engagement Director.

COOK COMMUNICATIONS MINISTRIES
850 North Grove Avenue, Elgin IL 60120. 847/741-2400. **Contact:** Human Resources. **World Wide Web address:** http://www.cookministries.com. **Description:** Creates, designs, produces, prints, publishes, markets, and distributes evangelical material. **Positions advertised include:** Internet Product Coordinator; Clerical Assistant; Marketing Specialist; Publicist; Senior Accountant; Sales Representative; Marketing Brand Manager. **Corporate headquarters location:** This location. **Operations at this facility include:** Administration; Manufacturing; Research and Development; Sales; Service.

COOPER B-LINE SYSTEMS INC.
509 West Monroe Street, Highland IL 62249. **Toll-free phone:** 800/851-7415. **Fax:** 800/356-1438. **Contact:** Human Resources. **World Wide Web address:** http://www.b-line.com. **Description:** Manufactures steel, aluminum, and nonmetallic products used in the support and installation of equipment in industrial, commercial, utility, customer premises, and original equipment manufacturer installations for the mechanical, electrical, and electronics industries. Metal fabrication operations include roll forming, CNC laser, CNC press, welding, assembly, painting, and finishing. Founded in 1969. **Special programs:** Internships; Training. **Internship information:** Internships are available at certain locations in sales, marketing, engineering, human resources, and other disciplines. Applicants should mail resumes including availability, to the Highland IL address for consideration. **Corporate headquarters location:** This location. **Other U.S. locations:** Modesto CA; Denver CO; Atlanta GA; Troy IL; Reno NV; Portland OR; Sherman TX. **Parent company:** Cooper Industries. **Operations at this facility include:** Administration; Manufacturing; Research and Development; Sales; Service.

COOPER INDUSTRIES, INC.
1830 Howard Street, Suite B, Elk Grove Village IL 60007. 847/228-1199. **Contact:** Human Resources. **E-mail address:** egv.recruit@cooperlighting.com. **World Wide Web address:** http://www.cooperlighting.com. **Description:** The Cooper Lighting Division of Cooper Industries produces lighting fixtures sold under the Lumark, McGraw-Edison, Sure-Lites, Iris, Optiance, Halo, and Metalux brand names. Products include indoor and outdoor lighting, recessed and track lighting, fluorescent lighting, and vandal-resistant lighting products. Overall, Cooper Industries manufactures electrical power equipment, tools and hardware, automotive products, and petroleum and industrial equipment. **NOTE:** Apply online. **Corporate headquarters location:** Peachtree City GA.

COPPERWELD
1855 East 122nd Street, Chicago IL 60633. 773/646-4500. **Toll-free phone:** 800/733-5683. **Fax:** 773/646-6128. **Contact:** Human Resources Coordinator. **World Wide Web address:** http://www.copperweld.com. **Description:** Manufactures and sells welded steel tubing. Products are used in low- and medium-rise construction; automotive, railroad and industrial equipment; farm implements and equipment; boat, car, and truck trailers; and industrial storage facilities. **Corporate headquarters location:** Pittsburgh PA. **International locations:** United Kingdom. **Number of employees worldwide:** 2,900.

CORMARK, INC.
1701 S. Winthrop Drive, Des Plaines IL 60018. 847/364-5900. **Toll-free phone:** 800/211-9646. **Contact:** Human Resources. **E-mail address:** recruit2@cormarkinc.com. **World Wide Web address:** http://www.cormarkinc.com. **Description:** A merchandising company. **Positions advertised include:** Business Unit Manager, Graphic Designer, Industrial Designer, Project Engineers, Project Manager. **Corporate headquarters location:** This location.

CORN PRODUCTS INTERNATIONAL
5 Westbrook Corporate Center, Westchester IL 60154. 708/551-2600. **Fax:** 708/551-2800. **Contact:** Human Resources. **E-mail address:** hr@cornproducts.com. **World Wide Web address:** http://www.cornproducts.com. **Description:** Supplies sweeteners and starches that come from the corn refining process. Corn Products International serves the brewing, corrugating, food, pharmaceutical, and soft drink industries. **NOTE:** Mail or e-mail resumes. **Listed on:** New York Stock Exchange. **Stock exchange symbol:** CPO.

CORPORATE DISK COMPANY
4610 Prime Parkway, McHenry IL 60050. 815/331-6000. **Toll-free phone:** 800/634-3475. **Fax:** 815/331-6030. **Contact:** Human Resources. **World Wide Web address:** http://www.disk.com. **Description:** Manufactures and develops software packages and provides related support services.

CORUS BANK, N.A.
3959 North Lincoln Avenue, Chicago IL 60613. 773/880-7900. **Fax:** 773/832-5262. **Contact:** Human Resources. **World Wide Web address:** http://www.corusbank.com. **Description:** A full-service banking institution. **NOTE:** Entry-level and part-time

positions are offered. This bank has several branches throughout the Chicago area. See website for additional locations and job listings. Apply online. **Parent company:** Corus Bankshares. **Listed on:** NASDAQ. **Stock exchange symbol:** CORS.

COUNTRY COMPANIES INSURANCE GROUP
P.O. Box 2020, Bloomington IL 61702-2020. 309/821-3000. **Toll-free phone:** 866/255-7965. **Fax:** 309/821-5160. **Physical address:** 1711 GE Road, Bloomington IL 61702. **Contact:** Human Resources. **E-mail address:** jake.dressler@countryfinancial.com. **World Wide Web address:** http://www.countryfinancial.com. **Description:** Offers a full line of insurance products including auto, home, life, health, disability income, long-term care, farm, ranch, and commercial insurance, as well as annuities, mutual funds, and financial and estate planning. Country Companies include Country Life, Country Mutual, Country Casualty Insurance Companies, and Country Investors Life Assurance Company. Founded in 1925. **NOTE:** Entry-level positions and second and third shifts are offered. Mail, fax or e-mail resumes. **Positions advertised include:** Field Claims Representative. **Special programs:** Internships; Training. **Corporate headquarters location:** This location. **Other U.S. locations:** AK; AZ; CO; KS; MO; NV; OK; OR; WA. **Operations at this facility include:** Administration; Sales; Service. **Listed on:** Privately held.

THE COURIER NEWS
P.O. Box 351, Elgin IL 60121. 847/888-7800. **Physical address:** 300 Lake Street, Elgin IL 60120. **Contact:** Human Resources. **World Wide Web address:** http://www.suburbanchicagonews.com. **Description:** A daily newspaper with a circulation of approximately 30,000.

CRABAR/GBF
200 West Railroad Avenue, Princeton IL 61356. **Toll-free phone:** 800/423-4569. **Contact:** Human Resources. **World Wide Web address:** http://www.crabargbf.com. **Description:** A full-service commercial printer specializing in customized business forms and direct mail printing. Founded in 1952. **Corporate headquarters location:** Dayton OH. **Other U.S. locations:** Nationwide. **Listed on:** Privately held.

CRAIN COMMUNICATIONS
360 North Michigan Avenue, Chicago IL 60601. 312/649-5200. **Fax:** 312/649-5331. **Contact:** Human Resources. **E-mail address:** chicago_jobs@crain.com. **World Wide Web address:** http://www.craincommunications.com. **Description:** Publishes health, trade, and business magazines and newspapers.

JOHN CRANE INC.
6400 West Oakton Street, Morton Grove IL 60053. 847/967-2400. **Fax:** 847/967-3040. **Contact:** Employee Relations Department. **E-mail address:** recruiter@johncrane.com. **World Wide Web address:** http://www.johncrane.com. **Description:** Manufactures and markets mechanical seals, packaging, and Teflon products for the industrial, automotive, and marine aftermarkets. John Crane operates over 40 branches throughout the United States including sales, service, and engineering operations. Founded in 1917. **Positions advertised include:** International Documentation Clerk; Mechanical Engineer. **Corporate headquarters location:** This location. **Parent company:** Smiths Group PLC. **Operations at this facility include:** Administration; Manufacturing; Research and Development; Sales; Service.

CREATIVE COMPUTERS INTEGRATED TECHNOLOGIES
1155 West Dundee Road, Suite 100, Arlington Heights IL 60004. 224/625-8800. **Toll-free phone:** 800/700-1000. **Contact:** Human Resources. **World Wide Web address:** http://www.cc-inc.com. **Description:** Owns and operates a chain of retail stores that sell computers and related accessories. This company also sells computers on the Internet. **NOTE:** Entry-level positions are offered. **Corporate headquarters location:** This location. **Other U.S. locations:** CO; IN; KS. **Parent company:** PC Mall (Torrance CA).

CULLIGAN INTERNATIONAL COMPANY
One Culligan Parkway, Northbrook IL 60062. 847/205-60005902. **Contact:** Manager of Human Resources. **World Wide Web address:** http://www.culligan.com. **Description:** A manufacturer of water filtration equipment and systems. **Positions advertised include:** Accountant; Human Resources Manager. **Corporate headquarters location:** This location. **Parent company:** Astrum, International.

CUSHMAN/AMBERG COMMUNICATIONS INC.
180 North Michigan Avenue, Suite 1600, Chicago IL 60601. 312/263-2500. **Contact:** Thomas Amberg. **World Wide Web address:** http://www.cushmanamberg.com. **Description:** A public relations agency. Founded in 1952. **Corporate headquarters location:** This location.

CYBORG SYSTEMS INC.
120 South Riverside Plaza, 17th Floor, Chicago IL 60606. 312/279-7000. **Contact:** Human Resources. **E-mail address:** careers@cyborg.com. **World Wide Web address:** http://www.cyborg.com. **Description:** Designs software for human resources departments. **NOTE:** Entry-level positions are offered. **International locations:** Africa; Asia; Australia; Canada; Latin America; United Kingdom. **Parent company:** Hewitt Associates.

DDB CHICAGO, INC.
200 East Randolph Drive, Chicago IL 60601. 312/552-6000. **Contact:** Human Resources. **World Wide Web address:** http://www.ddbjobs.com. **Description:** A full-service, international advertising agency. **NOTE:** Apply online. **Corporate headquarters location:** New York NY. **Other U.S. locations:** Los Angeles CA. **Parent company:** Omnicom. **Operations at this facility include:** Administration; Marketing; Research and Development; Service.

DSM DESOTECH INC.
1122 St. Charles Street, Elgin IL 60120. 847/697-0400. **Toll-free phone:** 800/223-7191. **Fax:** 847/468-7795. **Contact:** Human Resources Department. **World Wide Web address:** http://www.dsmdesotech.com. **Description:** A researcher, formulator, and manufacturer of ultraviolet and electron beam curable materials and technology. **NOTE:** Apply online to open positions. **Corporate headquarters location:** This location.

DADE BEHRING, INC.
1717 Deerfield Road, Deerfield IL 60015-0778. 847/267-5300. **Fax:** 847/267-5408. **Contact:** Human Resources. **World Wide Web address:** http://www.dadebehring.com. **Description:** Manufactures and distributes diagnostic instrument systems and other labware that serve clinical and research laboratories worldwide. Dade Behring also offers its customers support services. **Positions advertised include:** Bilingual Customer Satisfaction Representative; Office Services Clerk; Systems Analyst. **Corporate headquarters location:** This location. **International locations:** Worldwide.

DAILY HERALD
PADDOCK PUBLICATIONS, INC.
P.O. Box 280, Arlington Heights IL 60006-0280. 847/427-4300. **Fax:** 847/427-1270. **Recorded jobline:** 847/427-4398. **Contact:** Employment Recruiter. **E-mail address:** staffing@dailyherald.com. **World Wide Web address:** http://www.dailyherald.com. **Description:** Publishes a daily newspaper. Founded in 1872. **NOTE:** Entry-level positions, part-time jobs, and second and third shifts are offered. **NOTE:** See website or call the recorded job line for open positions. Fax or e-mail resumes. **Special programs:** Internships; Training; Co-ops. **Corporate headquarters location:** This location. **Listed on:** Privately held.

THE DAILY SOUTHTOWN
6901 West 159th Street, Tinley Park IL 60477. 708/633-6700. **Contact:** Human Resources. **World Wide Web address:** http://www.dailysouthtown.com. **Description:** A daily newspaper serving the Chicago metropolitan area. **Corporate headquarters location:** This location.

DANA BRAKE PARTS INC.
1600 North Industrial Drive, McHenry IL 60050. 815/385-7000. **Contact:** Employment Relations Manager. **World Wide Web address:** http://www.dana.com. **Description:** Manufactures and distributes a variety of automotive brake products. **NOTE:** Mail resume or apply online in persona at this location's Human Resources office.

DANA CORPORATION
1945 Ohio Street, Lisle IL 60532. 630/960-4200. **Contact:** Human Resources. **World Wide Web address:** http://www.dana.com. **Description:** Dana Corporation is a global leader in engineering, manufacturing, and marketing products and systems for the worldwide vehicular, industrial, and mobile off-highway original equipment markets and is a major supplier to the related aftermarkets. Dana Corporation also provides lease financing services in selected markets. The company's products include drivetrain components such as axles, driveshafts, clutches, and transmissions; engine parts such as gaskets, piston rings, seals, pistons, and filters; chassis products such as vehicular frames and cradles and heavy-duty side rails; fluid power components such as pumps, motors, and control valves; and industrial products such as electrical and mechanical brakes and clutches, drives, and motion control devices. Dana's vehicular components and parts are used on automobiles, pickup trucks, vans, minivans, sport utility vehicles, medium and heavy trucks, and off-highway vehicles. The company's industrial products include mobile off-highway and stationary equipment. **Corporate headquarters location:** Toledo OH. **Operations at this facility include:** This location manufactures gaskets for automobiles and tractors.

DANVILLE METAL STAMPING COMPANY, INC.
20 Oakwood Avenue, Danville IL 61832. 217/446-0647. **Contact:** Human Resources. **World Wide Web address:** http://www.danvillemetal.com. **Description:** Develops and produces fabricated metal components for the aerospace and gas turbine industries. Founded in 1946. This company has another facility in Danville IL at 1100 Martin Street.

DATA COMMUNICATION FOR BUSINESS INC.
2949 County Road, 1000 East, Dewey IL 61840. 217/897-6600. **Fax:** 217/897-1331. **Contact:** Human Resources. **World Wide Web address:** http://www.dcbnet.com. **Description:** Manufactures and markets data communications equipment. The company also aids in network installation by providing assistance with accessory equipment, communications lines and suppliers, site planning, and installation.

DATALOGICS INC.
101 North Wacker Drive, Suite 1800, Chicago IL 60606. 312/853-8200. **Fax:** 312/853-8282. **Contact:** Human Resources. **World Wide Web address:** http://www.datalogics.com. **Description:** Develops and markets software for publishing companies. **Positions advertised include:** Marketing Manager; Sales Engineer/Web Developer. **Corporate headquarters location:** This location.

DEAN FOODS COMPANY
3600 North River Road, Franklin Park IL 60131. 847/678-1680. **Contact:** Human Resources. **World Wide Web address:** http://www.deanfoods.com. **Description:** A producer and distributor of dairy and specialty food items. Products include milk, cheese, yogurt, sour cream, eggnog, ice cream, vegetables, pickles, salad dressings, pudding, dips, and other condiments. The company also sells and distributes canned meat products to the federal government. **Special programs:** Internships. **Corporate headquarters location:** Dallas TX. **Other U.S. locations:** Nationwide. **Listed on:** New York Stock Exchange. **Stock exchange symbol:** DF.

DEARBORN FINANCIAL PUBLISHING
30 South Wacker Drive, Suite 2500, Chicago IL 60606. 312/836-4400. **Toll-free phone:** 800/824-8742. **Contact:** Human Resources. **World Wide Web address:** http://www.dearborn.com. **Description:** A publisher of financial, educational, and trade materials.

ED DEBEVIC'S RESTAURANT
640 North Wells, Chicago IL 60610. 312/664-1707. **Fax:** 312/345-85251. **Contact:** Human Resources. **World Wide Web address:** http://www.eddebevics.com. **Description:** A casual dining restaurant chain. Ed Debevic's serves American cuisine and operates a gift shop.

DEERE & COMPANY
One John Deere Place, Moline IL 61265. 309/765-8000. **Contact:** Director of Human Resources. **World Wide Web address:** http://www.deere.com. **Description:** Manufactures, distributes, and finances the sale of heavy equipment and machinery for use in the agricultural and industrial equipment industries. The Agricultural Equipment Sector manufactures tractors, soil, seeding, and harvesting equipment. The Industrial Equipment Segment manufactures a variety of earth moving equipment, tractors, loaders, and excavators. The Consumer Products Division manufactures tractors and products for the homeowner. **NOTE:** On its website, this company provides all of its job listings for all of its locations. Apply online. **Corporate headquarters location:** This location.

DELNOR COMMUNITY HOSPITAL
300 Randall Road, Geneva IL 60134. 630/208-3000. **Contact:** Human Resources. **World Wide Web address:** http://www.delnor.com. **Description:** A 118-bed hospital offering a variety of specialized services including massage therapy, orthopedics, heart care, pediatrics, and cancer care. **NOTE:** Apply online. **Positions advertised include:** RN (Various); Nursing Coordinator; RN Patient Care Coordinator; Special Procedure Anesthetist; Cardiac Ultrasonographer.

DEPARTMENT OF TRANSPORTATION/CHICAGO
30 North LaSalle Street, Room 600, Chicago IL 60602. 312/744-3674. **Fax:** 312/747-6021. **Recorded jobline:** 312/744-1369. **Contact:** Human Resources.

http://www.ci.chi.il.us/transportation. **Description:** Maintains roads and highways and manages transportation infrastructure throughout the city of Chicago. **NOTE:** To apply for a position, visit the City of Chicago's website at http://www.ci.chi.il.us. To apply in person, apply with the City of Chicago's Department of Personnel; City Hall – Room 100, 121 North LaSalle Street, Chicago IL 60602. Office hours: Monday – Friday, 8:00 a.m. – 5:00 p.m.

DES PLAINES, CITY OF
1420 Miner Street, Des Plaines IL 60016. 847/391-5480. **Contact:** Human Resources. **World Wide Web address:** http://www.desplaines.org. **Description:** This location houses the governmental administrative offices for the City of Des Plaines IL, including its Police Department. **NOTE:** See website for job listings and application procedures. **Positions advertised include:** Police Officer; Director of Community Development.

DESOTO, INC.
P.O. Box 609, Joliet IL 60433. 815/727-4931. **Contact:** Anita Jackson, Director of Human Resources. **Description:** A diversified manufacturer of consumer paints, industrial coatings, and specialty products.

DEVLIEG-BULLARD SERVICES GROUP
10100 Forest Hills Road, Rockford IL 61115. 815/282-4100. **Toll-free phone:** 800/248-8120. **Fax:** 815/282-4949. **Contact:** Human Resources Manager. **World Wide Web address:** http://www.devliegbullard.com. **Description:** Supplies aftermarket parts and services including rebuilding services to the machine tool industry. **Corporate headquarters location:** Westport CT. **Other U.S. locations:** Cypress CA; Cromwell CT; Twinsburg OH; Abbottstown PA. **Parent company:** DeVlieg-Bullard, Inc. **Operations at this facility include:** Administration; Divisional Headquarters; Sales; Service.

DEVRY INSTITUTE OF TECHNOLOGY
3300 North Campbell Avenue, Chicago IL 60618. 773/929-8500. **Fax:** 773/348-1780. **Contact:** Peggy O'Brien, Human Resources Manager. **World Wide Web address:** http://www.chi.devry.edu. **Description:** A technical training institute that provides courses in electronics technology, computer information systems, business operations, telecommunications management, accounting, and technical management. Founded in 1931. **Corporate headquarters location:** Oakbrook Terrace IL. **International locations:** Canada. **Listed on:** New York Stock Exchange. **Stock exchange symbol:** DV.

DIAMONDCLUSTER INTERNATIONAL
875 North Michigan Avenue, Suite 3000, John Hancock Center, Chicago IL 60611. 312/255-5000. **Fax:** 312/255-6000. **Contact:** Aneeta Muradali, Human Resources. **World Wide Web address:** http://www.diamondcluster.com. **Description:** Develops e-commerce solutions for companies. Founded in 1994. **NOTE:** Apply online at this company's website. **Special programs:** Internships. **Corporate headquarters location:** This location. **Other U.S. locations:** San Francisco CA. **International locations:** London, England. **Listed on:** NASDAQ. **Stock exchange symbol:** DTPI.

DICKEY-JOHN CORPORATION
P.O. Box 10, Auburn IL 62615. 217/438-3371. **Toll-free phone:** 800/637-2952. 2243. **Fax:** 217/438-3623. **Contact:** Human Resources. **World Wide Web address:** http://www.dickey-john.com. **Description:** DICKEY-john Corporation is an electronic design and manufacturing company. Products include application control systems, grain moisture monitoring equipment, ice control systems, and hand-held analytical viscometers. The company's primary markets are the agriculture, public works, and construction industries. **NOTE:** See website for job listings and apply online. **Special programs:** Internships. **Corporate headquarters location:** This location. **Parent company:** Churchill Companies. **Operations at this facility include:** Administration; Manufacturing; Research and Development; Sales; Service.

THE DO-ALL COMPANY
254 North Laurel Avenue, Des Plaines IL 60016. 847/824-1122. **Fax:** 847/699-7524. **Contact:** Human Resources. **World Wide Web address:** http://www.doall.com. **Description:** Distributes machine tools and other supplies primarily for the metalworking and industrial markets. **NOTE:** Apply online.

DOMINICK'S FINER FOODS
711 Jorie Boulevard, Oak Brook IL 60523. 888/723-3929. **Contact:** Human Resources. **World Wide Web address:** http://www.dominicks.com. **Description:** Operates a chain of retail grocery stores. **NOTE:** Apply online at this company's website. **Corporate headquarters location:** This location.

EDWARD DON & COMPANY
2500 South Harlem Avenue, North Riverside IL 60546. 708/442-9400. **Toll-free phone:** 800/777-4366. **Fax:** 708/883-8268. **Contact:** Bill Doucette, Human Resources Manager. **World Wide Web address:** http://www.don.com. **Description:** Distributes food service equipment and supplies. **NOTE:** Apply online. **Positions advertised include:** Customer Service Representative; Credit Representative; Sales Representative. **Special programs:** Internships. **Corporate headquarters location:** This location. **Listed on:** Privately held.

R.R. DONNELLEY & SONS COMPANY
77 West Wacker Drive, Chicago IL 60601-1696. 312/326-8000. **Fax:** 312/326-8543. **Contact:** Human Resources. **World Wide Web address:** http://www.rrdonnelley.com. **Description:** A world leader in managing, reproducing, and distributing print and digital information for publishing, merchandising, and information technology customers. The company is one of the largest commercial printers in the world, producing catalogs, inserts, magazines, books, directories, computer documentation, and financial printing. R.R. Donnelley has more than 180 sales offices and production facilities. Principal services offered by the company are conventional and digital prepress operations; computerized printing and binding; sophisticated pool shipping and distribution services for printed products; information repackaging into multiple formats including print, magnetic, and optical media; database management, list rental, list enhancement, and direct mail production services; turnkey computer documentation services including outsourcing, translation, printing, binding, diskette replication, kitting, licensing, republishing, and fulfillment; reprographics and facilities management; creative design and communication services; and digital and conventional map creation and related services. Founded in 1864. **NOTE:** See website for job listings and apply online. **Corporate headquarters location:** This location. **Other U.S. locations:** Nationwide. **International locations:** Worldwide. **Listed on:** New York Stock Exchange. **Stock exchange symbol:** RRD.

DUDEK & BOCK SPRING MANUFACTURING
5100 West Roosevelt Road, Chicago IL 60644. 773/379-4100. **Contact:** Jeff Kopacz, Human Resources. **World Wide Web address:** http://www.dudek-bock.com. **Description:** Manufactures springs, wireforms, and light metal stampings.

DUKANE CORPORATION
2900 Dukane Drive, St. Charles IL 60174. 630/584-2300. **Fax:** 630/584-2370. **Contact:** Human Resources. **E-mail address:** hr@dukane.com. **World Wide Web address:** http://www.dukane.com. **Description:** An electronics firm operating through four divisions: Communications; Audio/Visual; Ultrasonics; and Sea Com, which manufactures underwater locators for aircraft.

DUO-FAST
2400 Galvin Drive, Elgin IL 60123. 847/783-5500. **Fax:** 847/783-5705. **Contact:** Human Resources. **E-mail address:** duofastjobs@paslode.com. **World Wide Web address:** http://www.duofast.com. **Description:** A manufacturer of industrial staples and nailing tools. **NOTE:** See website for Fax or e-mail resumes.

EGS ELECTRICAL GROUP
9377 West Higgins Road, Rosemont Il 60018. 847/679-7800. **Fax:** 847/763-6011. **Contact:** Human Resources. **E-mail address:** recruiter@egseg.com. **World Wide Web address:** http://www.egseg.com. **Description:** Manufactures electronic components such as conduit bodies and boxes, plugs and receptacles, industrial lighting fixtures, cord reels, and junction bodies. **NOTE:** E-mail or fax resumes. **Positions advertised include:** Customer Service Representative; Quality Engineer; **Corporate headquarters location:** This location. **Parent company:** Emerson Electric Company and SPX Corporation

EASTERN ILLINOIS UNIVERSITY
600 West Lincoln Avenue, Charleston IL 61920. 217/581-3463. **Fax:** 217/581-7266. **Contact:** Human Resources. **World Wide Web address:** http://www.eiu.edu. **Description:** A four-year, state university offering a variety of degree programs to approximately 9,200 undergraduate and 1,400 graduate students. **NOTE:** An application must be completed for any open position. Interested jobseekers must apply in person at the Human Resources office on Tuesdays and Thursdays from 8:00 a.m. – 4:30 p.m.

EBIX.COM
1900 East Golf Street, Suite 1200, Schaumburg IL 60173. 847/789-3047. **Fax:** 847/619-4773. **Contact:** Human Resources. **World Wide Web address:** http://www.ebix.com. **Description:** Develops agency management applications software for insurance companies.

ECOLAB INC.
3001 Channahon Road, Joliet IL 60436. 815/729-4900. **Fax:** 815/729-7303. **Contact:** Human Resources. **World Wide Web address:** http://www.ecolab.com. **Description:** Manufactures industrial-strength surface cleaners and disinfectants for use in hospitals, restaurants, schools, dairy farms, and other industrial facilities. **NOTE:** Apply online. **Positions advertised include:** Water Care Specialist; Route Manager; Account Sales Executive; Service Technician; Warehouse Supervisor; Corporate Account Manager.

EDELMAN WORLDWIDE
200 East Randolph Drive, Suite 6300, Chicago IL 60601. 312/240-3000. **Fax:** 312/240-2900. **Contact:** Human Resources. **World Wide Web address:** http://www.edelman.com. **Description:** A public relations firm. Founded in 1952. **NOTE:** Apply online at the company's website. **Positions advertised include:** Editorial Supervisor; Senior Account Executive; Administrative Assistant; Print Production Coordinator.

EDGE SYSTEMS, INC.
1805 High Point Drive, Suite 103, Naperville IL 60563-9359. 630/810-9669. **Fax:** 630/810-9228. **Contact:** Human Resources Director. **World Wide Web address:** http://www.edge.com. **Description:** Engaged in systems integration and information resource management solutions. **Corporate headquarters location:** This location. **Other area locations:** Chicago IL (Sales).

EDSAL MANUFACTURING
4400 South Packers Avenue, Chicago IL 60609. 773/254-0600. **Fax:** 773/254-1303. **Contact:** Barbara Kazsuk, Director of Human Resources. **World Wide Web address:** http://www.edsalmfg.com. **Description:** Manufactures and markets industrial furniture and steel equipment such as shelves, storage racks, lockers, benches, and shop desks.

EDWARD HOSPITAL
801 South Washington Street, Naperville IL 60540. 630/527-3401. **Contact:** Human Resources. **World Wide Web address:** http://www.edward.org. **Description:** A 159-bed full-service, nonprofit hospital. Edward Hospital provides a number of health services ranging from preventive education to advanced treatment technology. Its 50-acre campus supports a state-of-the-art, all-private-room inpatient facility; Edward Cardiovascular Institute; Edward Health & Fitness Center; Edward Hospital Cancer Center, affiliated with the Oncology Institute at Loyola University Medical Center; CARE Center, a diagnostic program for sexually abused children; and Linden Oaks Hospital, a private psychiatric facility. The hospital also operates Edward Healthcare Center in Bolingbrook, a satellite health care center with primary and specialty care physicians and a full range of diagnostic services. **NOTE:** Complete the online application located on the hospital's website.

EESCO, INC.
3939 South Karlov Avenue, Chicago IL 60632-3813. 773/376-8750. **Fax:** 773/376-8288. **Contact:** Paul Morris, Human Resources. **World Wide Web address:** http://www.eescodist.com. **Description:** A wholesale distributor of electrical, electronic, and communication systems products. **NOTE:** Interested jobseekers may also apply in person. **Corporate headquarters location:** This location. **Other U.S. locations:** FL; GA; IN; MI; MN; SC; WI. **Operations at this facility include:** Sales.

ELECTRO RENT CORPORATION
200 West Mark Street, Woodale IL 60191. 630/860-3991. **Contact:** Human Resources. **World Wide Web address:** http://www.electrorent.com. **Description:** Rents and leases electronic equipment including test and measurement instruments, workstations, personal computers, and data communication products. **Corporate headquarters location:** Van Nuys CA. **Other U.S. locations:** Nationwide.

ELECTRO SWITCH
60 Orland Square Drive, Suite 5, Orland Park IL 60462. 708/226-6982. **Contact:** Human Resources. **World Wide Web address:** http://www.electro-nc.com. **Description:** Designs and manufactures electromechanical switches and controls. **Corporate headquarters location:** Raleigh NC. **Operations at this facility include:** Administration; Manufacturing; Research and Development; Sales; Service.

ELECTROLUX HOME CARE PRODUCTS NA
807 North Main Street, Bloomington IL 61701. 309/828-2367. **Fax:** 309/823-5203. **Contact:** Denise Younge, Human Resources. **E-mail address:** eureka.hrdept@eureka.com. **World Wide Web address:** http://www.eureka.com.

Description: A manufacturer of vacuum cleaners. **Positions advertised include:** Controller; National Accounts Sales Director. **Corporate headquarters location:** This location. **Other U.S. locations:** El Paso TX. **Parent company:** WCI, Inc. **Operations at this facility include:** Administration; Divisional Headquarters; Manufacturing; Research and Development; Sales; Service.

ELEMENTIS PIGMENTS, INC.
2051 Lynch Avenue, East St. Louis IL 62205. 618/646-2110. **Toll-free phone:** 800/323-7796. **Fax:** 618/646-2178. **Contact:** Human Resources. **E-mail:** pigments.info@elementis-na.com. **World Wide Web address:** http://www.elementis.com. **Description:** Manufactures synthetic, natural, and magnetic iron oxides, colors, extender pigments, and barytes. **NOTE:** E-mail resumes and cover letters.

ELGIN, JOLIET & EASTERN RAILWAY COMPANY
1141 Maple Road, Joliet IL 60432. 815/740-6760. **Fax:** 815/740-6757. **Contact:** Human Resources. **World Wide Web address:** http://www.tstarinc.com. **Description:** A common carrier freight line. **NOTE:** Resumes only accepted for open positions. The company's website provides job listings. Apply online or fax or e-mail resumes. **Positions advertised include:** Motor Car Repairman; Trainman/Remote Control/Locomotive Engineer Trainee. **Other U.S. locations:** IN. **Parent company:** Transtar (Monroeville PA). **Operations at this facility include:** Service.

ELGIN MENTAL HEALTH CENTER
750 South State Street, Elgin IL 60123. 847/742-1040. **Contact:** Director of Employee Services. **Description:** An inpatient, psychiatric hospital serving the metropolitan and suburban Chicago areas. Part of the Illinois Department of Human Services. **NOTE:** Download an application at the Department of Human Service's website: http://www.dhs.state.i.us/careers.

ELGIN NATIONAL INDUSTRIES
2001 Butterfield Road, Suite 1020, Downers Grove IL 60515-1050. 630/434-7200. **Fax:** 630/434-7272. **Contact:** Harry Chase, Human Resources. **World Wide Web address:** http://www.eni.com. **Description:** A diversified company engaged in coal engineering and manufacturing. **NOTE:** See website for companies that operate under the Elgin name.

ELKAY MANUFACTURING COMPANY
2222 Camden Court, Oak Brook IL 60523. 630/574-8484. **Fax:** 630/574-5012. **Contact:** Human Resources. **World Wide Web address:** http://www.elkay.com. **Description:** Manufactures stainless steel sinks, faucets, water coolers, and kitchen cabinets. **NOTE:** Entry-level positions are offered. Apply online for all positions. **Corporate headquarters location:** This location. **Listed on:** Privately held.

ELMHURST COLLEGE
190 Prospect Avenue, Elmhurst IL 60126. 630/617-3016. **Fax:** 630/617-3746. **Recorded jobline:** 630/617-3779. **Contact:** Kathryn Patera, Human Resources Secretary. **E-mail address:** kathyp@elmhurst.edu. **World Wide Web address:** http://www.elmhurst.edu. **Description:** A four-year, private, liberal arts college affiliated with the United Church of Christ. The college has 22 academic departments and offers 48 majors. Preprofessional studies in dentistry, medicine, law, engineering, and theology are also offered. Founded in 1871. **NOTE:** Entry-level positions and second and third shifts are offered. **Special programs:** Internships; Apprenticeships; Summer Jobs. **Office hours:** Monday - Friday, 8:30 a.m. - 5:00 p.m.

EMPIRE COMFORT SYSTEMS
918 Freeburg Avenue, Belleville IL 62220. 618/233-7420. **Fax:** 618/233-7097. **Contact:** Mary Bruns, Human Resources Director. **World Wide Web address:** http://www.empirecomfort.com. **Description:** Manufactures gas-fired heating equipment. Founded in 1932.

ENCYCLOPAEDIA BRITANNICA
310 South Michigan Avenue, Chicago IL 60604. 312/347-7000. **Fax:** 312/294-2135. **Contact:** Human Resources. **E-mail address:** staffing@eb.com. **World Wide Web address:** http://www.britannica.com. **Description:** An international publisher of reference books and other educational materials. **Corporate headquarters location:** This location.

ENERFAB
1913 South Briggs Street, Joliet IL 60433. 815/727-4624. **Fax:** 815/727-0776. **Contact:** Human Resources. **World Wide Web address:** http://www.enerfab.com. **Description:** A mechanical engineering company that provides a variety of services including HVAC, power piping, fabrication, and plumbing. **Corporate headquarters location:** Cincinnati OH.

ENTHONE-OMI INC.
9809 Industrial Drive, Bridgeview IL 60455. 708/598-3210. **Fax:** 708/598-1719. **Contact:** Human Resources. **World Wide Web address:** http://www.enthone-omi.com. **Description:** A wholesale manufacturer and distributor of plating equipment and supplies.

EQUISTAR CHEMICALS LLP
8805 North Tabler Road, Morris IL 60450. 815/942-7011. **Fax:** 815/942-7331. **Contact:** Human Resources Department. **World Wide Web address:** http://www.equistarchem.com. **Description:** A leading producer of ethylene, propylene, and polyethylene. **Parent company:** Lyondell Chemical Company (Houston TX). **Listed on:** New York Stock Exchange. **Stock exchange symbol:** LYO.

EURO RSCG TATHAM
36 East Grand Avenue, Chicago IL 60611. 312/337-4400. **Contact:** Teresa Mogush, Director of Talent Development. **E-mail address:** TathamHR@eurorscg.com. **World Wide Web address:** http://www.eurorscgchicago.com. **Description:** An advertising agency. **Corporate headquarters location:** New York NY. **Operations at this facility include:** Administration; Research and Development; Sales. **Listed on:** Privately held.

EVANSTON HOSPITAL CORPORATION
2650 Ridge Avenue, Evanston IL 60201. 847/570-2600. **Fax:** 847/570-1903. **Contact:** Employment Office. **World Wide Web address:** http://www.enh.org. **Description:** Operates Evanston Hospital (also at this location), as well as Glenbrook Hospital (Glenview IL). **NOTE:** Apply online. **Positions advertised include:** RN (Various); Staff Nurse; Physical Medicine Aide; Research Scientist; Audiologist; Patient Service Representative; Nursing Assistant. **Corporate headquarters location:** This location. **Operations at this facility include:** Administration; Regional Headquarters; Service.

EXELON CORPORATION
P.O. Box 805379, Chicago IL 60680. 312/394-7398. **Contact:** Human Resources. **E-mail address:** ccresumes@exeloncorp.com. **World Wide Web address:** http://www.exeloncorp.com. **Description:** A holding company. **NOTE:** See website for job listings. E-mail resumes. **Positions advertised include:** Testing Group Supervisor; Communications Manager; Senior Planning Analyst; Corporate Crisis Management; **Corporate headquarters location:** This location. **Subsidiaries include:** Commonwealth Edison is a utility company that provides electricity to northern Illinois.

EXPERIAN
955 American Lane, Schaumburg IL 60173. 847/517-5600. **Contact:** Human Resources. **World Wide Web address:** http://www.experian.com. **Description:** Maintains credit reports and provides information services for the real estate industry. **NOTE:** Send resumes to: Experian, Human Resources Department, 475 Anton Boulevard, Building D, Costa Mesa CA 92626. Resumes may also be faxed. **Positions advertised include:** Administrative Assistant; Channel Manager; Inside Sales; Account Executive; Data Quality Analyst; Client Services Analyst. **Other U.S. locations:** Nationwide.

EXXONMOBIL CORPORATION
P.O. Box 874, Joliet IL 60410. 815/423-5571. **Contact:** Employee Relations Manager. **World Wide Web address:** http://www.exxon.mobil.com. **Description:** ExxonMobil is an integrated oil company engaged in petroleum and chemical products marketing, refining, manufacturing, exploration, production, transportation, and research and development worldwide. **NOTE:** For administrative positions, visit the nearest ExxonMobil office location. For technician positions, apply online at the corporate website. **Corporate headquarters location:** Irving TX. **Operations at this facility include:** This location is the Midwest regional office and also houses a refinery. **Listed on:** New York Stock Exchange. **Stock exchange symbol:** XON.

F&F FOODS, INC.
3501 West 48th Place, Chicago IL 60632. 773/927-3737. **Contact:** Joe Nelson, Human Resources. **World Wide Web address:** http://www.fffoods.com. **Description:** Manufactures cough drops, dietary supplements, candy, crackers, and a variety of other items under the product names Fast Dry Zinc, F&F Dietary Supplements, Daily C, Smith Brothers Cough Drops, and Foxes.

FM GLOBAL
300 South Northwest Highway, Park Ridge IL 60068. 847/430-7000. **Contact:** Human Resources. **World Wide Web address:** http://www.fmglobal.com. **Description:** Offers corporate property insurance and risk management services for commercial and industrial organizations. **NOTE:** The company only accepts resumes for current openings. See the website for job listings. **Corporate headquarters location:** Johnston RI. **Other U.S. locations:** Nationwide. **International locations:** Worldwide.

FMC TECHNOLOGIES
FMC FOODTECH
200 East Randolph Drive, Chicago IL 60601. 312/861-6000. **Contact:** Human Resources. **World Wide Web address:** http://www.fmctechnologies.com. **Description:** FMC Technologies is a diversified manufacturer of specialty, industrial, and agricultural chemicals; defense-related systems; industrial machinery. FMC, a subsidiary, creates computerized systems for the food industry. **Corporate headquarters location:** This location is the corporate office for the parent company, FMC Technologies and its subsidiary FMC Foodtech. **Subsidiaries include:** FMC Energy Systems; FMC Airport Systems; FMC Technologies A.G.

FAIRMOUNT PARK
OGDEN FAIRMOUNT INC.
9301 Collinsville Road, Collinsville IL 62234-1799. 618/345-4300. **Contact:** Human Resources. **World Wide Web address:** http://www.fairmountpark.com. **Description:** A horse racing track.

FARMERS INSURANCE GROUP
P.O. Box 948, Aurora IL 60507. 630/907-0030. **Physical address:** 2245 Sequoia Drive, Aurora IL 60506. **Fax:** 630/907-3498. **Contact:** Joy Brokaw, Human Resources Manager. **World Wide Web address:** http://www.farmersinsurance.com. **Description:** Farmers Insurance Group is one of the nation's largest property and casualty insurance groups. Founded in 1928. **Positions advertised include:** Workman's Compensation Commercial Underwriter; Trial Attorney; Human Resources Operations Specialist. **Corporate headquarters location:** Los Angeles CA. **Operations at this facility include:** This location houses the business support center and commercial operations.

FARMLAND FOODS INC.
1220 North Sixth Street Road, Monmouth IL 61462. 309/734-5353. **Contact:** Human Resources. **World Wide Web address:** http://www.farmland.com. **Description:** A pork processing facility. **Parent company:** Farmland Industries Inc. is one of the largest farmer-owned agricultural food marketing and manufacturing cooperative associations in the United States. The company is engaged in grain marketing, pork and beef processing, and manufacturing of fertilizers, livestock feeds, and petroleum products. Membership includes farmers from Iowa, Kansas, Oklahoma, South Dakota, Illinois, Nebraska, and Mexico.

FEDERAL EXPRESS CORPORATION (FEDEX)
500 Commerce Street, Aurora IL 60504. 630/820-1061. **Toll-free phone:** 800/463-3339. **Contact:** Human Resources. **World Wide Web address:** http://www.fedex.com. **Description:** One of the world's largest express transportation companies serving 212 countries worldwide. FedEx ships approximately 3.2 million packages daily. FedEx operates more than 45,000 drop-off locations, and has a fleet that consists of more than 640 aircraft and 44,5000 vehicles. **NOTE:** Apply online at the company's website. **Corporate headquarters location:** Memphis TN. **Other U.S. locations:** Nationwide. **Operations at this facility include:** This location is a World Service Center.

FEDERAL SIGNAL CORPORATION
SIGNAL DIVISION
2645 Federal Signal Drive, University Park IL 60466-3195. 708/534-4756. **Fax:** 708/534-4852. **Contact:** Peggy Szumski, Human Resources Representative. **World Wide Web address:** http://www.fedsig.com. **Description:** A manufacturer of audio and visual emergency warning equipment for vehicle and industrial applications. **NOTE:** See the corporate website, http://www.federalsignaljobs.com, for job listings and contact information. **Positions advertised include:** Customer Service Representative; Marketing Manager; Project Coordinator; Quality Manager; Regional Systems Sales Manager; Section Manager; Senior Mechanical Engineer. **Special programs:** Training. **Corporate headquarters location:** Oak Brook IL. **Operations at this facility include:** This location is manufactures signals.

FELLOWES MANUFACTURING COMPANY
1789 Norwood Avenue, Itasca IL 60143. 630/893-1600. **Contact:** Director of Human Resources. **World Wide Web address:** http://www.fellowes.com. **Description:** Manufactures corrugated boxes. Fellowes Manufacturing also manufactures, markets,

and sells a variety of office equipment and supplies. **NOTE:** Apply online for open job positions at this company's website.

THE FEMALE HEALTH COMPANY
515 North State Street, Suite 2225, Chicago IL 60610. 312/595-9123. **Fax:** 312/595-9122. **Contact:** Human Resources. **World Wide Web address:** http://www.femalehealth.com. **Description:** Markets and distributes a proprietary female barrier contraceptive product known as the Reality female condom. **Corporate headquarters location:** This location. **Parent company:** Wisconsin Pharmacal Company, Inc. (Jackson WI).

FERMI NATIONAL ACCELERATOR LABORATORY
P.O. Box 500, MS 116, Batavia IL 60510. 630/840-3324. **Fax:** 630/840-2306. **Contact:** Employment Manager. **World Wide Web address:** http://www.fnal.gov. **Description:** A federally funded, nonprofit organization dedicated to basic research in the field of high-energy physics. **NOTE:** See website for job listings and contact information. **Special programs:** Internships. **Corporate headquarters location:** Washington DC. **Parent company:** Universities Research Association. **Operations at this facility include:** Research and Development.

THE FIELD MUSEUM OF NATURAL HISTORY
1400 South Lake Shore Drive, Chicago IL 60605. 312/922-9410. **Fax:** 312/665-7272. **Contact:** Human Resource. **E-mail address:** hr@fieldmuseum.org. **World Wide Web address:** http://www.fmnh.org. **Description:** A natural history museum. The museum provides both formal and informal educational opportunities for the public and conducts its own research in the fields of anthropology, geology, zoology, and biology. Founded in 1893. **NOTE:** The museum only accepts online applications via its website. Entry-level positions are offered. **Positions advertised include:** Annual Giving Manager; Campaign Manager; Enterprise Application and Project Manager; Major Gifts Office, Prospect Research Coordinator. **Special programs:** Internships; Volunteer. **Corporate headquarters location:** This location. **Operations at this facility include:** Administration; Research and Development; Service.

FIFTH THIRD BANK
105 South York Street, Elmhurst IL 60126. 630/941-5200. **Contact:** Human Resources. **World Wide Web address:** http://www.53.com. **Description:** A single branch of a bank that provides commercial and personal banking and trust services. **NOTE:** Fifth Third Bank has locations throughout Chicago and the midwestern part of the United States. See its website for job listings at specific branch locations. **Positions advertised include:** Lockbox Extractor; Lockbox Processor; Proof Operator. **Parent company:** Fifth Third Bancorp.

FILTERTEK, INC.
11411 Price Road, Hebron IL 60034-8936. 815/648-2416. **Fax:** 815/648-1168. **Contact:** Mary Ellen Nilles, Director of Human Resources. **World Wide Web address:** http://www.filtertek.com. **Description:** This location manufactures custom-molded filters. Overall, Filtertek, Inc. manufactures filtration elements used in the automotive, health care, and various other industrial and consumer markets. The company sells its automotive filters directly to automotive manufacturers, automotive suppliers, and companies reselling filters in the automotive aftermarket. Filtertek produces filter products ranging from highly sophisticated disposable medical filters that filter contamination from blood, to a simple air filter used to protect machinery from dust contamination. **NOTE:** Apply online at the company's website. **Corporate headquarters location:** This location. **Parent company:** ESCO Electronics Corporation is a diversified producer of commercial products that are sold to a variety of customers worldwide. ESCO's products include electronic equipment, valves and filters, filtration and fluid flow components, automatic test equipment, utility load management equipment, and anechoic/shielding systems. ESCO's other operating subsidiaries include PTI Technologies, Inc.; VACCO Industries; Distribution Control Systems, Inc.; Rantec Microwave & Electronics; Lindgren RF Enclosures; Comtrak Technologies, Inc.; and EMC Test Systems, L.P. **Operations at this facility include:** Administration; Divisional Headquarters; Research and Development; Sales.

A. FINKL & SONS COMPANY
2011 North Southport Avenue, Chicago IL 60614. 773/975-2624. **Fax:** 773/975-2636. **Contact:** Human Resources. **E-mail address:** Jobs@Finkl.com. **World Wide Web address:** http://www.finkl.com. **Description:** A steel forgings manufacturer with domestic and international warehousing operations. A. Finkl & Sons manufactures custom forgings, plastic mold steel, and hot work die steel. **Corporate headquarters location:** This location. **Operations at this facility include:** Administration; Manufacturing; Sales; Service. **Listed on:** Privately held.

FIRST ALERT
BRK BRANDS, INC.
3901 Liberty Street Road, Aurora IL 60504. 630/851-7330. **Contact:** Human Resources. **World Wide Web address:** http://www.firstalert.com. **Description:** First Alert operates through its subsidiaries to manufacture smoke alarms, fire alarms, carbon monoxide detectors, fire extinguishers, fire escape ladders, rechargeable flashlights, and related home safety products. **Subsidiaries include:** BRK Brands Canada (Ontario, Canada); BRK Brands Europe, Ltd. (Berkshire, England); BRK Brands, Inc. (also at this location); BRK Brands Pty Ltd. (Parramatta, Australia); Electronica RBK de Mexico S.A. de C.V. (Chihuahua, Mexico). **Corporate headquarters location:** This location.

FIRST HEALTH
3200 Highland Avenue, Downers Grove IL 60515-1223. 630/737-7900. **Contact:** Human Resources. **World Wide Web address:** http://www.firsthealth.com. **Description:** A managed health care company that provides group health benefit programs for employers nationwide. **NOTE:** This company provides jobs listings on its website for all its locations. Apply online.

FIRST MIDWEST BANK
300 Park Boulevard, Suite 405, Itasca, IL 60143. 630/875-7450. **Fax:** 630/875-7369. **Recorded jobline:** 866/562-7362. **Contact:** Human Resources. **World Wide Web address:** http://www.firstmidwest.com. **Description:** A full-service bank with approximately 70 offices throughout northern Illinois and eastern Iowa. **NOTE:** This bank provides job listings for all its branch locations. See its website and apply online. **Listed on:** NASDAQ. **Stock exchange symbol:** FMBI.

FLEX-O-GLASS, INC.
1100 N. Cicero Avenue, Chicago IL 60651. 773/379-7878. **Contact:** Human Resources. **World Wide Web address:** http://www.flexoglass.com. **Description:** Manufacturer of Innovative plastic products. Founded over 81 years ago. Their product lines include, construction and agricultural plastic sheeting, acrylic sheet, lawn and garden products, trash bags, ribbed floor runner and shelf liners, and packaging films. **Positions advertised include:** Plastic Extrusion Setup; Production Leadman. **Other area locations:** Dixon IL.

FOLLETT CORPORATION
2233 West Street, River Grove IL 60171. 708/583-2000. **Toll-free phone:** 800/621-4345. **Fax:** 708/452-9347. **Contact:** Rene Collier, Director of Human Resources. **World Wide Web address:** http://www.follett.com. **Description:** Distributes educational textbooks, library books, and software systems for library management. Follett is also engaged in the nationwide operation of college bookstores. **NOTE:** Temporary and part-time positions offered. This company has other positions throughout the state of Illinois. See its website for additional locations and job listings. **Positions advertised include:** Plant Operator, Facility Maintenance; Marketing Specialist; Operational Auditor; Financial Analyst; Gold Planner; Inside Sales Representatives.

FOOTE CONE & BELDING
101 East Erie Street, Chicago IL 60611. 312/425-5000. **Fax:** 312/425-5010. **Contact:** Human Resources. **E-mail address:** CareersChi@fcb.com. **World Wide Web address:** http://www.fcb.com. **Description:** One of the largest advertising agencies in the world. Foote Cone & Belding analyzes the advertising needs of clients, plans and creates advertising for their products and services, and places advertising in various mass-market media. The firm offers additional services such as the design and production of merchandising and promotional programs, product research, and package design. **Corporate headquarters location:** New York NY. **Other U.S. locations:** Nationwide.

FOOTE-JONES/ILLINOIS GEAR
2102 North Natchez Avenue, Chicago IL 60707. 773/622-8000. **Fax:** 773/622-8176. **Contact:** Human Resources Manager. **World Wide Web address:** http://www.footejones.com. **Description:** Manufactures precision gears, gearboxes, and other machine parts.

FORD MOTOR COMPANY
12600 South Torrance Avenue, Chicago IL 60633. 773/646-3100. **Contact:** Human Resources. **World Wide Web address:** http://www.ford.com. **Description:** Ford Motor Company is engaged in the design, development, manufacture, and sale of cars, trucks, tractors, and related components and accessories. Ford is also one of the largest providers of financial services in the United States. Ford's two core businesses are the Automotive Group and the Financial Services Group (Ford Credit, The Associates, USL Capital, and First Nationwide). Ford is also engaged in a number of other businesses including electronics, glass, electrical and fuel-handling products, plastics, climate-control systems, automotive service and replacement parts, vehicle leasing and rental, and land development. **NOTE:** For hourly positions, contact the plant or the nearest state employment center office. For managerial positions, see the company's website for job listings and application procedures. **Corporate headquarters location:** Dearborn MI. **Operations at this facility include:** This location is an assembly plant.

FORT DEARBORN LIFE INSURANCE COMPANY
1020 West Thirty-First Street, Downers Grove IL 60515-5591. **Toll-free phone:** 800/633-3696. **Contact:** Human Resources. **World Wide Web address:** http://www.fdl-life.com. **Description:** Provides group life and disability insurance, as well as other financial services. **Corporate headquarters location:** This location.

FORTUNE BRANDS INC.
300 Tower Parkway, Lincolnshire IL 60069. 847/484-4400. **Contact:** Human Resources. **World Wide Web address:** http://www.fortunebrands.com. **Description:** A consumer products company offering home and office products, golf equipment, and spirits and wine. **Brand names include:** Jim Beam, Master Lock, Moen, El Tesoro, Acco, Dekuyper, Titlelist; Footjoy. **NOTE:** For positions with a specific Fortune Brand company, see its corporate website for links to the its subsidiaries' websites. **Corporate headquarters location:** This location. **Listed on:** New York Stock Exchange. **Stock exchange symbol:** FO.

FRAMATOME ANP DE&S
215 Shuman Boulevard, Suite 172, Naperville IL 60563. 630/778-0100. **Fax:** 630/778-4343. **Contact:** Human Resources Department. **World Wide Web address:** http://www.framatome.com. **Description:** Engaged in environmental engineering and consulting with expertise in nuclear engineering and management. **NOTE:** Entry-level positions are offered. **Special programs:** Internships; Co-ops; Summer Employment.

FRASCA INTERNATIONAL, INC.
906 East Airport Road, Urbana IL 61802-7407. 217/344-9200. **Fax:** 217/344-9207. **Contact:** Human Resources. **E-mail address:**personnel@frasca.com. **World Wide Web address:** http://www.frasca.com. **Description:** Manufactures certified full-flight simulators, flight training devices, cockpit procedures trainers, and noncertified ab-initio trainers for the airline, military, and general aviation industries. Modifications and upgrades of flight simulation and training equipment are available. Frasca also offers engineering and consulting services. Founded in 1958.

FRY, INC.
740 Pasquinelli Drive, Suite 100, Westmont IL 60559. 630/850-9144. **Toll-free phone:** 800/FRY-6858. **Fax:** 630/850-8043. **Contact:** Human Resources. **World Wide Web address:** http://www.fry.com. **Description:** Fry, Inc. designs, develops, and manages high scale ebusiness brands, applications, and systems. Fry was one of the first companies to offer ecommerce, branding sites, and extranets to its clients. **Positions advertised include:** Account Director; Director of Business Development; E-commerce Project Manager; Office Manager; Proposal Writer. **Corporate headquarters location:** Ann Arbor MI. **Other U.S. locations:** New York NY.

FUCHS LUBRICANTS COMPANY
17050 Lathrop Avenue, Harvey IL 60426. 708/333-8900. **Contact:** Human Resources. **E-mail address:** jobs@fuchs.com. **World Wide Web address:** http://www.fuchs.com. **Description:** Manufactures and markets specialty lubricants primarily for the metalworking and mining industries. Founded in 1924. **Parent company:** Fuchs Worldwide Group.

FUJISAWA HEALTHCARE, INC.
Three Parkway North, Deerfield IL 60015. 847/317-8800. **Fax:** 847/317-1245. **Contact:** Human Resources. **E-mail address:** employment@fujisawa.com. **World Wide Web address:** http://www.fujisawausa.com. **Description:** A pharmaceutical company that markets products in the area of anti-infectives, cardiovasculars, transplantation, and dermatology. **NOTE:** Apply online at the company's website for specific job openings. Resumes may also be e-mailed for specific job openings. **Positions advertised include:** Assistant/Associate Director Regulatory Affairs; Senior Corporate Records Assistant; Senior Medical Writer; Project Assistant. **Corporate headquarters location:** This location. **Parent company:** Fujisawa Company Ltd.

FUJITSU IT HOLDINGS, INC.
9399 West Higgins Road, Suite 1000, Rosemont IL 60018. 847/692-6940. **Contact:** Human Resources. **World Wide Web address:** http://www.amdahl.com. **Description:**

Designs, develops, manufactures, markets, and services more than 470 large-scale, high-performance, general purpose computer systems. Customers are primarily large corporations, government agencies, and large universities with high-volume data processing requirements. **Corporate headquarters location:** Sunnyvale CA. Other area locations: Rosemont IL (Fujitsu Computer Systems). Operations at this facility include: This is a office for Fujitsu Computer Systems. **Parent company:** Fujitsu Limited.

FUTURESOURCE
955 Parkview Boulevard, Lombard IL 60148. 630/620-8444. **Fax:** 630/792-2600. **Contact:** Human Resources. **World Wide Web address:** http://www.futuresource.com. **Description:** An online, real-time, financial news provider.

G&W ELECTRIC COMPANY
3500 West 127th Street, Blue Island IL 60406. 708/388-5010. **Contact:** Human Resources. **E-mail address:** hr@gwelec.com. **World Wide Web address:** http://www.gwelec.com. **Description:** Manufactures power cable terminals, switches, and splices. **Corporate headquarters location:** This location. **Operations at this facility include:** Administration; Manufacturing; Research and Development; Sales; Service. **Listed on:** Privately held.

GATX CORPORATION
500 West Monroe Street, 42nd Floor, Chicago IL 60661. 312/621-6200. **Fax:** 312/621-8062. **Contact:** Human Resources. **E-mail address:** jobs@gatx.com. **World Wide Web address:** http://www.gatx.com. **Description:** A holding company engaged in the lease and sale of rail cars and storage tanks for petroleum transport; equipment and capital asset financing and related services; the operation of tank storage terminals, pipelines, and related facilities; the operation of warehouses; and distribution and logistics support. Founded in 1898. **NOTE:** Entry-level positions are offered. **Positions advertised include:** Payroll Specialist; Senior Financial Analyst. **Special programs:** Internships. **Office hours:** Monday - Friday, 8:30 a.m. - 4:45 p.m. **Corporate headquarters location:** This location. **Other U.S. locations:** Nationwide. **International locations:** Worldwide. **Subsidiaries include:** American Steamship Company; GATX Capital Corporation; GATX Logistics; GATX Terminals Corporation; General American Trans. **Operations at this facility include:** Administration. **Listed on:** New York Stock Exchange. **Stock exchange symbol:** GMT.

GE CAPITAL CORPORATION
540 West Northwest Highway, Barrington IL 60010. 847/277-4000. **Contact:** Human Resources. **World Wide Web address:** http://www.gecareers.com. **Description:** GE Capital Corporation is one of the largest vehicle leasing and financing companies in the United States and Canada, providing fleet and related management services to corporate clients. **Parent company:** General Electric Company operates in the following areas: aircraft engines (jet engines, replacement parts, and repair services for commercial, military, executive, and commuter aircraft); appliances; broadcasting (NBC); industrial (lighting products, electrical distribution and control equipment, transportation systems products, electric motors and related products, a broad range of electrical and electronic industrial automation products, and a network of electrical supply houses); materials (plastics, ABS resins, silicones, superabrasives, and laminates); power systems (products for the generation, transmission, and distribution of electricity); technical products and systems (medical systems and equipment, as well as a full range of computer-based information and data interchange services for both internal use and external commercial and industrial customers); and capital services (consumer services, financing, and specialty insurance). **Operations at this facility include:** This location provides automobile leasing and financing. **Listed on:** New York Stock Exchange. **Stock exchange symbol:** GE.

GE CAPITAL CORPORATION
500 West Monroe Street, Chicago IL 60661. 312/441-7000. **Fax:** 305/476-6550. **Contact:** Human Resources. **World Wide Web address:** http://www.gecas.com. **Description:** Provides financing and leasing services to small and mid-sized businesses including equipment, real estate, and capital loans. **Parent company:** General Electric Company.

GE CAPITAL RAILCAR SERVICES
161 North Clark Street, Chicago IL 60601. 312/853-5000. **Contact:** Employment Manager. **World Wide Web address:** http://www.gecareers.com. **Description:** A major lessor of railcars in North America. The company's primary areas of business are: leasing and managing railcar equipment, financing, car repair and maintenance, and wheel services. The company's fleet includes covered hoppers, tank cars, boxcars, intermodal cars, pressure differential cars, coal cars, and other specialty cars. The company offers a full variety of lease types and equipment management services. **Special programs:** Internships. **Other U.S. locations:** El Cerrito CA; Englewood CO; Atlanta GA; Oak Brook IL; Albany NY; Bala-Cynwyd PA; Houston TX. **Parent company:** General Electric Company.

GE FINANCIAL ASSURANCE PARTNERSHIP MARKETING
200 North Martingale Road, Schaumburg IL 60173. 847/605-3000. **Contact:** Human Resources. **World Wide Web address:** http://www.gecareers.com. **Description:** One of the nation's largest telemarketing and direct mail companies. GE Financial Assurance offers retail, wholesale, enhancement, and employee assistance and benefit programs. The company also markets several of the country's largest auto, dental, and legal services plans. Founded in 1966. **Corporate headquarters location:** This location. **Other U.S. locations:** Nationwide. **Parent company:** General Electric Company. **Listed on:** New York Stock Exchange. **Stock exchange symbol:** GE.

GE HEALTH
3350 North Ridge Avenue, Arlington Heights IL 60004. 847/398-8400. **Fax:** 847/818-6629. **Contact:** Human Resources. **World Wide Web address:** http://www.gehealthcare.com. **Description:** Researches, develops, and manufactures nuclear medicine and radiopharmaceuticals. **NOTE:** For a list of job openings, visit the website. To apply, either fax or e-mail resumes and cover letters, stating desired position. **Operations at this facility include:** Manufacturing; Research and Development.

GNB TECHNOLOGIES, INC.
2475 West Station Street, Kankakee IL 60901. 815/937-6925. **Contact:** Human Resources. **World Wide Web address:** http://www.gnb.com. **Description:** Manufactures and recycles lead-acid batteries for a wide range of consumer and industrial uses. **Corporate headquarters location:** Princeton NJ.

GTI
1700 South Mount Prospect Road, Des Plaines IL 60018. 847/768-0500. **Fax:** 847/468-0501. **Contact:** Human Resources. **E-mail address:** hr@gastechnology.org. **World Wide Web address:** http://www.gastechnology.org. **Description:** A nonprofit research and development institution serving the energy field including gas companies and the Department of Energy. **NOTE:** See website for job listings. Mail, fax or e-mail resumes. Temporary positions are offered. **Positions advertised include:** Research and Development; Administrative; Non-Technical. **Special programs:** Internships.

GABRIEL ENVIRONMENTAL SERVICES
1421 North Elston Avenue, Chicago IL 60622. 773/486-2123. **Fax:** 773/486-0004. **Contact:** Human Resources. **World Wide Web address:** http://www.gabrielenvironmental.com. **Description:** Provides environmental consulting, fieldwork, and laboratory services. **Special programs:** Internships. **Corporate headquarters location:** This location.

GALENA-STRAUSS HOSPITAL & NURSING CARE FACILITY
215 Summit Street, Galena IL 61036. 815/777-1340. **Contact:** Melissa Kaiser, Human Resources Manager. **E-mail address:** mjkaiser@galenastauss.org. **World Wide Web address:** http://www.galenahealth.org. **Description:** A 25-bed, nonprofit, acute care hospital and 60-bed nursing home. Founded in 1962. **NOTE:** Entry-level positions and second and third shifts are offered. **Positions advertised include:** Exercise Specialist; Certified Nurses' Assistant; Laboratory Manager; Assistant Director of Nursing. **Office hours:** Monday - Friday, 8:00 a.m. - 4:00 p.m. **Corporate headquarters location:** This location.

GALILEO INTERNATIONAL
9700 West Higgins Road, Suite 400, Rosemont IL 60018. 847/518-4000. **Contact:** Human Resources. **World Wide Web address:** http://www.galileo.com. **Description:** Designs and installs software for the travel industry that provides access to inventory, scheduling, and pricing information. **NOTE:** Apply online at this company's website. **Corporate headquarters location:** Parsippany NJ. **Other U.S. locations:** Centennial CO. **International locations:** UK; Saudi Arabia; India. **Operations at this facility include:** This office is a corporate regional office.

ARTHUR J. GALLAGHER & CO.
2 Pierce Place, Itasca IL 60143-3141. 630/773-3800. **Fax:** 630/285-4000. **Contact:** Human Resources. **World Wide Web address:** http://www.ajg.com. **Description:** An insurance brokerage offering property, casualty, and employee benefit plans. Founded in 1927. **NOTE:** Contact this location for job openings and mail or fax resumes. **Special programs:** Internships. **Office hours:** Monday - Friday, 9:00 a.m. - 5:00 p.m. **Corporate headquarters location:** This location. **Listed on:** New York Stock Exchange. **Stock exchange symbol:** AJG.

GANNETT FLEMING
222 South Riverside Plaza, Suite 1860, Chicago IL 60606. 312/454-9494. **Fax:** 312/454-1277. **Contact:** Human Resources. **E-mail address:** employment@gfnet.com. **World Wide Web address:** http://www.gannettfleming.com. **Description:** Provides civil and structural engineering consulting services.

GARRETT AVIATION SERVICES
1200 North Airport Drive, Springfield IL 62707-8417. 217/544-3431. **Toll-free phone:** 800/731-7371. **Fax:** 217/544-8911. **Contact:** Steve Fox, Human Resources. **World Wide Web address:** http://www.garrettaviation.com. **Description:** Provides a comprehensive group of services to the general aviation industry. Garrett performs airframe, engine, and modification services at its six domestic locations. **NOTE:** Second and third shifts are offered. **Office hours:** Monday - Friday, 8:00 a.m. - 5:00 p.m. **Corporate headquarters location:** Annapolis MD. **Other U.S. locations:** Los Angeles CA; Van Nuys CA; Augusta GA; Ronkonkoma NY; Houston TX. **Parent company:** General Electric Company. **Operations at this facility include:** Administration; Sales; Service. **Listed on:** New York Stock Exchange. **Stock exchange symbol:** GE.

GENERAL BINDING CORPORATION
One GBC Plaza, Northbrook IL 60062-4195. 847/272-3700. **Contact:** Human Resources. **World Wide Web address:** http://www.generalbinding.com. **Description:** An international manufacturer and distributor of office binding and laminating systems and supplies. **NOTE:** Apply online at this company's website. **Positions advertised include:** Mechanical Engineer; Print Estimator. **Operations at this facility include:** Administration; Manufacturing; Research and Development.

GENERAL ELECTRIC COMPANY (GE)
AIRCRAFT ENGINES DIVISION
1543 South 54th Avenue, Cicero IL 60804. 708/780-2600. **Contact:** Human Resources. **World Wide Web address:** http://www.ge.com. **Description:** GE operates in the following areas: aircraft engines (jet engines, replacement parts, and repair services for commercial, military, executive, and commuter aircraft); appliances; broadcasting (NBC); industrial (lighting products, electrical distribution and control equipment, transportation systems products, electric motors and related products, a broad range of electrical and electronic industrial automation products, and a network of electrical supply houses); materials (plastics, ABS resins, silicones, superabrasives, and laminates); power systems (products for the generation, transmission, and distribution of electricity); technical products and systems (medical systems and equipment, as well as a full range of computer-based information and data interchange services for both internal use and external commercial and industrial customers); and capital services (consumer services, financing, and specialty insurance). **NOTE:** Apply online at http://www.gecareers.com. **Company slogan:** We bring good things to life. **Corporate headquarters location:** Fairfield CT. **Operations at this facility include:** This location manufactures aircraft engines and engine parts. **Listed on:** New York Stock Exchange. **Stock exchange symbol:** GE.

GENERAL ELECTRIC COMPANY (GE)
CONSUMER PRODUCTS DIVISION
709 West Wall Street, Morrison IL 61270. 815/772-2131. **Contact:** Human Resources. **World Wide Web address:** http://www.ge.com. **Description:** General Electric operates in the following areas: aircraft engines (jet engines, replacement parts, and repair services for commercial, military, executive, and commuter aircraft); appliances; broadcasting (NBC); industrial (lighting products, electrical distribution and control equipment, transportation systems products, electric motors and related products, a broad range of electrical and electronic industrial automation products, and a network of electrical supply houses); materials (plastics, ABS resins, silicones, superabrasives, and laminates); power systems (products for the generation, transmission, and distribution of electricity); technical products and systems (medical systems and equipment, as well as a full range of computer-based information and data interchange services for both internal use and external commercial and industrial customers); and capital services (consumer services, financing, and specialty insurance). **NOTE:** Apply online at http://www.gecareers.com. **Company slogan:** We bring good things to life **Corporate headquarters location:** Fairfield CT. **Operations at this facility include:** This location is engaged in quality control for General Electric appliances. **Listed on:** New York Stock Exchange. **Stock exchange symbol:** GE.

GENERAL GROWTH PROPERTIES, INC.
110 North Wacker Drive, Chicago IL 60606. 312/960-5000. **Fax:** 312/960-5475. **Contact:** Human Resources. **E-mail address:** careers@generalgrowth.com. **World Wide Web address:** http://www.generalgrowth.com. **Description:** Owns, operates, develops, and renovates shopping malls. Mail or e-mail resume and cover letters, stating interest in a specific type of position. Special programs: Internships. **Positions advertised include:** CAD Specialist; Director of Grocery Store Leasing; Director of Operations; Group Vice President of Marketing. **Corporate headquarters location:** This location. **Parent company:** Sears, Roebuck & Co. **Listed on:** New York Stock Exchange. **Stock exchange symbol:** GGP.

GENERAL LEARNING CORPORATION
CAREER WORLD
900 Skokie Boulevard, Suite 200, Northbrook IL 60062-4028. 847/205-3000. **Toll-free phone:** 800/641-3912. **Fax:** 847/564-8197. **Contact:** Human Resources. **World Wide Web address:** http://www.glcomm.com. **Description:** Publishes *Career World,* a career guidance magazine with a circulation of approximately 85,000.

GENERAL MILLS, INC.
704 West Washington Street, West Chicago IL 60185. 630/231-1140. **Fax:** 630/876-4217. **Contact:** Human Resources. **World Wide Web address:** http://www.genmills.com. **Description:** Produces and markets consumer foods including Cheerios, Wheaties, and Total cereals; Betty Crocker desserts, frostings, and baking mixes; Pop Secret microwave popcorn; Gorton's frozen seafood; Yoplait yogurt; Bisquick pancake mix; and Gold Medal flour. Founded in 1866. **NOTE:** This company provides job listings for all its offices throughout the United States. Visit its website and apply online. **Corporate headquarters location:** Minneapolis MN. **Operations at this facility include:** This location is the office for the company's Package Foods Operations Division. **Listed on:** New York Stock Exchange. **Stock exchange symbol:** GIS.

GERBER PLUMBING FIXTURES CORPORATION
4600 West Touhy Avenue, Lincolnwood IL 60712. 847/675-6570. **Fax:** 847/675-5192. **Contact:** Human Resources. **World Wide Web address:** http://www.gerberonline.com. **Description:** Manufactures a variety of bathroom and kitchen plumbing products including faucets, valves, lavatories, toilets, and vanities. **Corporate headquarters location:** This location.

GLENAYRE ELECTRONICS, INC.
One Glenayre Way, Quincy IL 62301. 217/223-3211. **Fax:** 217/221-6489. **Contact:** Ed Danielski, Human Resources Manager. **World Wide Web address:** http://www.glenayre.com. **Description:** Provides infrastructure equipment to providers of wireless communication services such as paging and voice messaging. **NOTE:** Send resumes to: Glenayre Electronics, Inc., 11360 Lakefield Drive, Duluth GA 30097. **Special programs:** Internships. **Corporate headquarters location:** Duluth GA. **Other U.S. locations:** Duluth GA. **Parent company:** Glenayre Technologies, Inc. provides paging products and systems including messaging pagers. Other services are for both mobile and fixed telecommunication systems and include voice mail, fax messaging, and debit/prepaid calling card platforms. **Operations at this facility include:** Administration; Manufacturing; Research and Development; Sales; Service. **Listed on:** NASDAQ. **Stock exchange symbol:** GEMS.

GLENBROOK HOSPITAL
2100 Pfingsten Road, Glenview IL 60026. 847/657-5800. **Contact:** Human Resources. **World Wide Web address:** http://www.enh.org. **Description:** A 136-bed hospital offering a variety of health services including coronary care, plastic surgery, cancer care, and joint replacement. **NOTE:** Apply online. **Positions advertised include:** Medical Secretary; MRI Technologist; EKG Technician; Ophthalmic Technician; Senior Secretary. **Parent company:** Evanston Northwestern Healthcare.

GLENOAKS HOSPITAL
701 Winthrop Avenue, Glendale Heights IL 60139. 630/545-7300. **Fax:** 630/545-3999. **Contact:** Human Resources. **World Wide Web address:** http://www.ahsmidwest.org. **Description:** A 186-bed, nonprofit, acute care hospital. The hospital is affiliated with the Seventh-Day Adventist Church. Founded in 1980. **NOTE:** Apply online. **Positions advertised include:** Case Manager; Certified Nurse Midwife; Charge Nurse; CT Technologist; Quality Management Director. **Special programs:** Training. **Office hours:** Monday - Friday, 7:30 a.m. - 4:30 p.m. **Corporate headquarters location:** Washington DC. **Parent company:** Adventist Health System.

GONNELLA BAKING CO.
2002 West Erie Street, Chicago IL 60612. 312/733-2020x376 or x189. **Fax:** 312/733-7670. **Contact:** Lauren Slipkowsky, Human Resources. **World Wide Web address:** http://www.gonnella.com. **Description:** Makers of bread, rolls, frozen dough, garlic bread, and other bakery products. Founded in 1886. **NOTE:** Entry-level positions, part-time jobs, and second and third shifts are offered. This location hires for its corporate offices as well as its plants. Apply online or in person at the Human Resources Office. **Positions advertised include:** Maintenance Mechanic; Route Sales Representative. **Special programs:** Internships; Apprenticeships; Training; Summer Jobs. **Office hours:** Tuesday, 2:00 p.m. – 4:00 p.m.; Thursday, 9:00 a.m. – 11:00 a.m. **Corporate headquarters location:** This location. **Listed on:** Privately held.

GONNELLA FROZEN PRODUCTS, INC.
1117 East Wiley Road, Schaumburg, IL 60173. 847/884-8829x5212. **Fax:** 847/884-9469. **Contact:** James Mazukelli, Human Resources and Safety Manager. **World Wide Web address:** http://www.gonnella.com. **Description:** The frozen food division of Gonnella Baking Company. **NOTE:** apply online or in person at the human resources office. **Positions advertised include:** Maintenance Mechanic. **Office hours:** Monday – Friday, 8:00 a.m. – 5:00 p.m.

GOOD SAMARITAN HOSPITAL
3815 Highland Avenue, Downers Grove IL 60515. 630/275-5900. **Contact:** Human Resources. **World Wide Web address:** http://www.advocatehealth.com. **Description:** A 300-bed hospital offering a wide range of health services from emergency care to pediatrics. **NOTE:** Apply online. **Positions advertised include:** Central Outpatient Scheduler; Cleaning and Process Technician; Clinical Education Specialist; RN (Various); Physician (Various).

GOODMAN THEATRE
170 North Dearborn Street, Chicago IL 60601. 312/443-3811. **Contact:** Human Resources. **World Wide Web address:** http://www.goodman-theatre.org. **Description:** A nonprofit theater producing both classic and contemporary works. Founded in 1925. **NOTE:** See the theatre's website for job listings and contact information.

GOSS GRAPHIC SYSTEMS, INC.
3 Territorial Court, Bolingbrook IL 60440-3557. 630/755-9300. **Fax:** 630/755-9301. **Contact:** Human Resources. **World Wide Web address:** http://www.gossgraphic.com. **Description:** A world leader in color offset printing, press manufacturing, and development. The company offers color printing services for newspapers and magazines. **Office hours:** Monday - Friday, 8:00 a.m. - 5:00 p.m. **Corporate headquarters location:** This location. **International locations:** Japan; United Kingdom; France; China.

GOVERNORS STATE UNIVERSITY
One University Parkway, University Park IL 60466. 708/534-5000. **Contact:** Human Resources. **World Wide Web address:** http://www.govst.edu. **Description:** A state university offering 42 degree programs to juniors, seniors, and master's candidates. **NOTE:** See website for job listings and contact and application information.

RAY GRAHAM ASSOCIATION
2801 Finley Road, Downers Grove IL 60515. 630/620-2222. **Fax:** 630/628-2351. **Contact:** Human Resources. **E-mail address:** rgajobs@yahoo.com. **World Wide Web address:** http://www.ray-graham.org. **Description:** A consumer-driven organization that responds to the needs of people with disabilities and their families. **NOTE:** An application is required for any position and must be completed in person at the Human Resources office. **Positions advertised include:** Dietary Technician; Lab Technician; Community Support Specialist; ADT/AM Aide. **Corporate headquarters location:** This location. **Operations at this facility include:** Administration.

W.W. GRAINGER
100 Grainger Parkway, Lake Forest IL 60045. 847/535-1000. **Contact:** Human Resources. **World Wide Web address:** http://www.grainger.com. **Description:** Distributes a variety of equipment and components to the industrial, commercial, contracting, and institutional markets nationwide. The company operates 337 branches in all 50 states and Puerto Rico. Products include equipment and components for motors, air tools, hydraulic products, refrigeration items, power and hand tools, office equipment, computer supplies, storage equipment, replacement parts, industrial products, safety items, cold weather clothing, and sanitary supplies. **NOTE:** This company provides job listings for this location and its other locations on its website. Apply online. **Corporate headquarters location:** This location.

GRAINGER PARTS
1657 Shermer Road, Northbrook IL 60062. 847/498-5900. **Fax:** 847/559-6192. **Contact:** Human Resources. **World Wide Web address:** http://www.grainger.com. **Description:** Distributes repair and replacement parts to industrial and commercial markets. **Corporate headquarters location:** Skokie IL. **Parent company:** W.W. Grainger, Inc. (Skokie IL). **Operations at this facility include:** Administration; Divisional Headquarters; Sales; Service.

GRANITE CITY WORKS
UNITED STATES STEEL CORPORATION
1951 State Street, Granite City IL 62040. 618/451-3456. **Contact:** Human Resources. **Description:** A manufacturer of steel.

GRAYHILL, INC.
561 Hillgrove Avenue, LaGrange IL 60525. 708/354-1040. **Fax:** 708/354-2820. **Contact:** Human Resources. **E-mail address:** resumes@grayhill.com. **World Wide Web address:** http://www.grayhill.com. **Description:** Manufactures rotary, push-button, and DIP switches, keyboards and keypads, encoders, wireless products, I/O modules, and industrial control systems. **Corporate headquarters location:** This location. **Other U.S. locations:** Carpentersville IL; Fox River Grove IL; Iola WI. **Operations at this facility include:** Administration; Manufacturing; Research and Development; Sales. **Listed on:** Privately held.

GREAT LAKES ANALYTICAL
1380 Busch Parkway, Buffalo Grove IL 60089. 847/808-7766. **Fax:** 847/808-7772. **Contact:** Human Resources. **World Wide Web address:** http://www.glalabs.com. **Description:** An analytical laboratory that provides a full spectrum of environmental analyses on soil, water, and waste samples. Founded in 1990. **NOTE:** Entry-level positions, part-time jobs, and second and third shifts are offered. **Special programs:** Co-ops; Summer Jobs. **Corporate headquarters location:** This location. **Other U.S. locations:** AZ; CA; CO; HI; NV; OR; PA; TX; WA. **Listed on:** Privately held.

GREAT LAKES MAINTENANCE & SECURITY CORPORATION
8734 South Cottage Grove, Suite 200, Chicago IL 60619-6924. 773/994-1899. **Contact:** Human Resources. **Description:** Provides maintenance, cleaning, and security guard services.

GREAT LAKES NAVAL HOSPITAL
3001A Sixth Street, Great Lakes IL 60088. 847/688-4561. **Contact:** Human Resources. **World Wide Web address:** http://www.greatlakes.med.navy.mil. **Description:** A military hospital serving active and retired military personnel and their families in the Midwest region. **NOTE:** This hospital has jobs for military personnel and civilians. Call the regional Human Resources Office at 847/688-2222 to hear job listings and how application procedures.

GREELEY AND HANSEN
100 South Wacker Drive, Suite 1400, Chicago IL 60606. 312/558-9000. **Contact:** Human Resources. **E-mail address:** careers@greeley-hansen.com. **World Wide Web address:** http://www.greeley-hansen.com. **Description:** A consulting engineering firm specializing in water and wastewater treatment. The company also provides construction management, design engineering, and operations assistance. **Positions advertised include:** Civil Engineer; Management Consultant; Administrative Support. **Listed on:** Privately held.

GREENBRIER & RUSSEL, INC.
1450 East American Lane, Suite 1700, Schaumburg IL 60173. 847/706-4000. **Toll-free phone:** 800/453-0347. **Fax:** 847/706-4020. **Contact:** Sherry Greer, Recruiter. **E-mail address:** recruiting@gr.com. **World Wide Web address:** http://www.gr.com. **Description:** A leader in providing strategic business solutions through technical services and software. The company offers technical and management consulting, information systems training, and a wide range of intranet and client/server software. The consulting division is a national practice that focuses on helping clients meet business goals through the use of technology. The company's training division offers instructor-led intranet, client/server, AS/400, and DB2 classes. **NOTE:** Entry-level positions are offered. **Positions advertised include:** Senior Business Objects Developer; Data Warehouse Architect; MS Analysis Services Consultant; Oracle Application DBA; Student Systems Functional Consultant; CRM Functional Consultant. **Corporate headquarters location:** This location. **Other U.S. locations:** Milwaukee WI; Appleton WI; Minneapolis MN; Atlanta GA; Dallas TX.

GREIF BROTHERS CORPORATION
P.O. Box 248, Oreana IL 62554. 800/468-2396. **Fax:** 217/468-2264. **Contact:** Human Resources. **World Wide Web address:** http://www.gbcdecatur.com. **Description:**

Produces and sells shipping containers and materials including fiber, steel and plastic drums, multiwall bags, and other related items. The company also produces and sells containerboard and related products including corrugated paper, and corrugated containers. **NOTE:** For career opportunities, see Greif Inc's website, http://www.greif.com/careers/. Resumes may also be mailed or faxed to the corporate Human Resources Manager at Greif Inc., 425 Winter Road, Delaware, OH 433015 or fax, 740/549-6100. **Positions advertised include:** Account Manager; Lead/Set-up Person Molding Department.

GRIFFITH LABORATORIES
One Griffith Center, Alsip IL 60803. 708/371-0900. **Contact:** Human Resources. **E-mail address:** contactjobsna@griffithlabs.com. **World Wide Web address:** http://www.griffithlabs.com. **Description:** Manufactures food seasonings, coatings, and mixes including soup, gravy, breadcrumbs, batters, sauces, and marinades.

GRUBB & ELLIS COMPANY
2215 Sanders Road, Suite 400, Northbrook IL 60062. 847/753-9010. **Contact:** Human Resources. **World Wide Web address:** http://www.grubb-ellis.com. **Description:** A commercial and residential real estate brokerage firm. **Corporate headquarters location:** This location.

GUARDIAN ELECTRIC MANUFACTURING COMPANY
1425 Lake Avenue, Woodstock IL 60098. 815/337-0050. **Fax:** 815/337-0377. **Contact:** Human Resources. **World Wide Web address:** http://www.guardian-electric.com. **Description:** Manufactures electromechanical components and relays.

T.J. GUNDLACH MACHINE COMPANY
P.O. Box 385, Belleville IL 62222-0385. 618/233-7208. **Fax:** 618/233-7208. **Physical address:** One Freedom Drive, Belleville IL. **Contact:** Human Resources. **World Wide Web address:** http://www.tjgundlach.com. **Description:** Manufactures and sells crushing and sizing machinery and equipment used in the mining industry.

KENNETH HALL REGIONAL HOSPITAL
129 North Eighth Street, East St. Louis IL 62201. 618/482-7129. **Fax:** 618/482-7015. **Contact:** Shirley Simmons, Human Resources Specialist. **Description:** A Level II trauma center offering a variety of health services. **NOTE:** Call the Human Resources for job listings and application information. **Corporate headquarters location:** Hobart IN. **Other U.S. locations:** Chicago IL; Fort Wayne IN. **Parent company:** Southern Illinois Health Foundation. **Operations at this facility include:** Regional Headquarters.

HAMILTON SUNDSTRAND CORPORATION
4747 Harrison Avenue, P.O. Box 7002, Rockford IL 61125-7002. 815/226-6000. **Contact:** Human Resources. **World Wide Web address:** http://www.hamiltonsundstrandcorp.com. **Description:** Manufactures a wide range of aircraft components, systems, and subsystems. **NOTE:** This company provides job listings for this location and its other U.S. facilities. See its website and apply online.

HANDEX OF ILLINOIS
1701 West Quincy Avenue, Naperville IL 60540. 630/527-1666. **Contact:** Human Resources. **World Wide Web address:** http://www.handex.com. **Description:** Provides environmental services including overseeing the installation and removal of underground storage tanks, as well as groundwater and soil sampling. **NOTE:** To apply for a position, contact Paula Griffin, Human Resources Director, Handex Group, Inc., 30914 Suneagle Drive, Mt. Dora FL 32757; 800/989-3753 (phone); 352/735-1904 (fax). **Corporate headquarters location:** Dora FL.

HANSON ENGINEERS
1525 South Sixth Street, Springfield IL 62703. 217/788-2450. **Fax:** 217/788-2503. **Contact:** Human Resources. **World Wide Web address:** http://www.hansonengineers.com. **Description:** A consulting firm that provides a variety of architectural, engineering, and scientific services. Founded in 1954. **Corporate headquarters location:** This location. **Other U.S. locations:** Nationwide.

HARDING ESE
8901 North Industrial Road, Peoria IL 61615. **Toll-free phone:** 800/373-1999. **Fax:** 309/692-9364. **Contact:** Human Resources. **World Wide Web address:** http://www.mactec.com. **Description:** An engineering and consulting company providing environmental and infrastructure services to commercial and municipal clients, as well as to state and federal government agencies. Founded in 1965. **NOTE:** Send resumes to: Harding ESE, Human Resources, 440 North Cumberland Avenue, Suite 250, Chicago IL 60656. **Positions advertised include:** Lead CADD Operator; Principal Engineer; Senior Bridge Engineer; Senior Civil/Transportation Engineer; Wastewater Treatment Operator. **Special programs:** Internships; Co-ops. **Office hours:** Monday - Friday, 8:00 a.m. - 5:00 p.m. **Other U.S. locations:** Nationwide. **Parent company:** MACTEC, Inc. **Listed on:** Privately held.

HAROLD WASHINGTON COLLEGE
30 East Lake Street, Chicago IL 60601. 312/553-5600. **Contact:** Steve Crosby, Director of Personnel. **World Wide Web address:** http://www.hwashingtonccc.edu. **Description:** A four-year college operating as part of the City Colleges of Chicago system. The college offers associate's degrees and certificates to approximately 9,400 students. **NOTE:** Apply online at the college's website or visit the Human Resources Office during regular business hours. **Office hours:** Monday – Friday, 9:00 a.m. – 4:30 p.m.

HARPER COLLEGE
1200 West Algonquin Road, Palatine IL 60067. 847/925-6000. **Contact:** Human Resources. **World Wide Web address:** http://www.harpercollege.edu. **Description:** A community college offering associate's degrees and certificates to approximately 23,000 students. **NOTE:** Harper College no longer will accept mailed or faxed resumes. Apply online at its website. **Positions advertised include:** Counselor; Instructors (Various); Professors (Various); Student Development Specialist; Coordinator of Accommodations; Secretary; Custodian; Career Mentor; Computer Support and Training.

HARPO INC.
110 North Carpenter Street, Chicago IL 60607. 312/633-1000. **Contact:** Human Resources. **World Wide Web address:** http://www.oprah.com. **Description:** Engaged in film and television production. **Corporate headquarters location:** This location. **President:** Oprah Winfrey.

HARRIS BANK
P.O. Box 755, Chicago IL 60690. 312/461-2121. **Physical address:** 111 West Monroe Street, Chicago IL 60603. **Contact:** Human Resources. **World Wide Web address:** http://www.harrisbank.com. **Description:** Provides a wide range of banking, trust, and investment services to individuals and small businesses. Harris Bank has 140 locations in the greater Chicago area. **NOTE:** Apply online at the company's website. **Parent company:** Bank of Montreal.

HARRIS MARCUS GROUP
3757 South Ashland Avenue, Chicago IL 60609. 773/247-7500. **Contact:** Human Resources. **World Wide Web address:** http://www.harris-marcus.com. **Description:** Engaged in the manufacture of lamps, furniture, and accessories for the home. **Corporate headquarters location:** This location. **Operations at this facility include:** Administration; Manufacturing. **Listed on:** Privately held.

HARRISBURG MEDICAL CENTER
100 Hospital Drive, P.O. Box 428, Harrisburg IL 62946. 618/253-7671x300. **Fax:** 618/252-2077. **Contact:** Human Resources. **World Wide Web address:** http://www.harrisburgmedicalcenter.com. **Description:** A hospital. **NOTE:** See the center's website for application procedures. **Office hours:** Monday – Friday, 8:00 a.m. – 11:00 a.m. or 1:00 p.m. – 4:30 p.m.

HARTMARX CORPORATION
101 North Wacker Drive, Chicago IL 60606. 312/372-6300. **Fax:** 312/444-2679. **Contact:** Susan Klawitter, Director of Human Resources Administration. **World Wide Web address:** http://www.hartmarx.com. **Description:** A manufacturer of men's tailored clothing under the labels Hart Schaffner & Marx, Austin Reed, Tommy Hilfiger, and Krizia. Hartmarx Corporation also manufactures women's clothing and sportswear under the brand names Hart Schaffner & Marx, Pierre Cardin, Austin Reed, and Hickey-Freeman. The company conducts direct marketing and catalog sales operations worldwide. **Corporate headquarters location:** This location. **Other U.S. locations:** Winchester KY; Cape Girardeau MO; New York NY. **Operations at this facility include:** Administration; Manufacturing; Sales; Service.

HEALTH MANAGEMENT SYSTEMS
820 West Jackson Boulevard, Chicago IL 60607. 312/962-6100. **Contact:** Laura Pontarelli, Human Resources Director. **World Wide Web address:** http://www.hmsy.com. **Description:** Develops software for the health insurance and health care industries. **NOTE:** Entry-level positions are offered. **Corporate headquarters location:** New York NY. **Other U.S. locations:** Nationwide. **Operations at this facility include:** Administration; Research and Development; Sales; Service. **Listed on:** Privately held.

H.J. HEINZ COMPANY
2301 Shermer Road, Northbrook IL 60062. 847/291-3900. **Contact:** Human Resources Manager. **World Wide Web address:** http://www.heinz.com **Description:** Produces bouillon, dry soup, pasta, and pasta sauces. Brand names include Catelli, Creamette, Prince, R&F, Ronco, and Wyler's. **NOTE:** Apply online. **Special programs:** Internships. **Corporate headquarters location:** Pittsburgh PA. **Listed on:** New York Stock Exchange. **Stock exchange symbol:** HNZ.

HELP AT HOME INC.
17 North State Street, Suite 1400, Chicago IL 60602. 312/762-9999. **Fax:** 312/704-0022. **Contact:** Human Resources. **World Wide Web address:** http://www.helpathome.com. **Description:** Provides homemaker and nurses aide services for the elderly. **Corporate headquarters location:** This location. **Other area locations:** Danville IL; East Alton IL; Galesburg IL; Joliet IL; Macomb IL; Mount Vernon IL; Oak Forest IL; Ottawa IL; Rock Island IL; Rockford IL; Skokie IL; Springfield IL; St. Charles IL; Waukegan IL. **Other U.S. locations:** IN; MO; MI; AL; MS; TN. **Subsidiaries include:** Oxford Health Care. **Listed on:** NASDAQ. **Stock exchange symbol:** HAHI.

HENDRICKSON INTERNATIONAL
800 South Frontage Road, Woodridge IL 60517. 630/910-2800. **Fax:** 630/910-2899. **Contact:** Beth Bretz, Human Resources. **World Wide Web address:** http://www.hendrickson-intl.com. **Description:** A worldwide supplier of engineered products for the truck and automotive industries. Hendrickson International designs, develops, and manufactures suspension systems, leaf springs, and heavy stampings primarily for heavy-duty trucks. **NOTE:** See website for contact information. **Corporate headquarters location:** This location. **Parent company:** The Boler Company. **Listed on:** Privately held.

HENRI STUDIO
1250 Henri Drive, Wauconda IL 60084. 847/526-5200. **Contact:** Diane Walters, Human Resources. **World Wide Web address:** http://www.henristudio.com. **Description:** Manufactures concrete statues, fountains, birdbaths, and planters. **Subsidiaries include:** Henri Studio Edmonton, Ltd.; Henri Studio Europe, Ltd.

HEWITT ASSOCIATES
100 Half Day Road, Lincolnshire IL 60069. 847/295-5000. **Contact:** Human Resources. **World Wide Web address:** http://www.hewitt.com. **Description:** Hewitt Associates is an international firm of consultants and actuaries specializing in the design, financing, communication, and administration of employee benefit and compensation programs. **Positions advertised include:** Programmer Analyst; WM Analyst; Compliance Specialist; Financial Consultant; Client Coordinator. **Corporate headquarters location:** This location.

HIGHLAND SUPPLY CORPORATION
1111 Sixth Street, Highland IL 62249. 618/654-2161. **Contact:** Human Resources. **World Wide Web address:** http://www.highlandsupply.com. **Description:** Manufactures foils, polypropylene film, cellophane, and printed and plain bags. **Corporate headquarters location:** This location.

HINCKLEY SPRINGS
6155 South Harlem Avenue, Chicago IL 60638. 773/586-8600. **Fax:** 773/586-6542. **Recorded jobline:** 800/329-0835. **Contact:** Judy Archer, Human Resources. **World Wide Web address:** http://www.water.com. **Description:** Hinkley Springs processes and distributes bottled water. Founded in 1888. **NOTE:** Entry-level positions and second and third shifts are offered. **Office hours:** Monday - Friday, 8:15 a.m. - 5:00 p.m. **Corporate headquarters location:** Atlanta GA. **Other U.S. locations:** Indianapolis IN; Kansas City MO. **Parent company:** Suntory Water Group. **Operations at this facility include:** Divisional Headquarters. **Listed on:** Privately held.

BERNARD HODES ADVERTISING
430 North Michigan Avenue, Suite 1101, Chicago IL 60611. 312/288-2550. **Contact:** Human Resources. **World Wide Web address:** http://www.hodes.com. **Description:** An advertising agency specializing in recruitment and employee communications. **Positions advertised include:** Client Services Account Executive. **Special programs:** Internships. **Corporate headquarters location:** New York NY. **Other U.S. locations:** Phoenix AZ; Cambridge MA; Dallas TX. **Parent company:** Omnicom.

HOFFER PLASTICS CORPORATION
500 North Collins Street, South Elgin IL 60177-1195. 847/741-5740. **Fax:** 847/741-2675. **Contact:** Human Resources. **World Wide Web address:** http://www.hofferplastics.com. **Description:** A custom injection molder of thermoplastics products. **NOTE:** Fax resumes or apply in person at the Human Resources Office. **Office hours:** Monday – Friday, 8:00 a.m. - 4:00 p.m.

HOLIDAY INN CHICAGO-CITY CENTRE
300 East Ohio Street, Chicago IL 60611. 312/787-6100. **Fax:** 312/787-3055. **Contact:** Human Resources. **World Wide Web address:** http://www.chicc.com. **Description:** A 500-room hotel. **Parent company:** TR Streeterville Hotel Corporation.

HOLIDAY INN CITY CENTRE
500 Hamilton Boulevard, Peoria IL 61602. 309/674-2500. **Fax:** 309/674-8705. **Contact:** Human Resources. **World Wide Web address:** http://www.holidayinnpeoria.com. **Description:** A 300-room hotel. The Holiday Inn City Centre also houses one of Illinois' largest convention centers. **NOTE:** To apply, visit the company's website. Positions advertised include: Bennigan's Bar Manager; Sales Manager; Catering Assistant; Sales Assistant.

HOLIDAY INN O'HARE INTERNATIONAL
5440 North River Road, Rosemont IL 60018. 847/671-6350. **Contact:** Staffing. **World Wide Web address:** http://chi-ohare.holiday-inn.com. **Description:** A 507-room location of the large hotel chain. **Parent company:** Six Continents Hotels.

HOLLYMATIC CORPORATION
600 East Plainfield Road, Countryside IL 60525. 708/579-3700. **Fax:** 708/579-1057. **Contact:** Human Resources. **World Wide Web address:** http://www.hollymatic.com. **Description:** Manufactures food processing machines and parts, and paper products. **Corporate headquarters location:** This location.

HOLLYWOOD CASINO AURORA
49 North Golino Boulevard, Aurora IL 60506. 630/801-7000. **Contact:** Human Resources. **World Wide Web address:** http://www.pngaming.com. **Description:** Operates a fixed riverboat casino featuring movie memorabilia. **NOTE:** Apply online at the website. **Positions advertised include:** Bartender; Casino Cashier; Casino Scheduler Internal Auditor. **Parent company:** Penn National Gaming.

HOLY CROSS HOSPITAL
2701 West 68th Street, Chicago IL 60629. 773/471-9050. **Fax:** 773/884-8013. **Contact:** Human Resources. **E-mail address:** hrd@holycrosshospital.org. **World Wide Web address:** http://www.holycrosshospital.org. **Description:** A 331-bed, nonprofit, community hospital offering a wide range of inpatient and outpatient health services. **NOTE:** See website for job listings. Resumes may be mailed or faxed. Interested jobseekers may also apply in person at the Human Resources Office. **Office hours:** Monday – Friday, 8:00 a.m. – 4:30 p.m.

HOME NURSERY, INC.
P.O. Box 307, Edwardsville IL 62025. 618/656-1470. **Contact:** Employment Manager. **World Wide Web address:** http://www.homenursery.com. **Description:** A nursery engaged in the wholesale and retail sale of lawn and garden supplies. **Operations at this facility include:** Administration; Accounting.

HONEYWELL
1500 West Dundee Road, Arlington Heights IL 60004. 847/797-4000. **Contact:** Human Resources. **World Wide Web address:** http://www.honeywell.com. **Description:** Honeywell is engaged in the research, development, manufacture, and sale of advanced technology products and services in the fields of chemicals, electronics, automation, and controls. The company's major businesses are home and building automation and control, performance polymers and chemicals, industrial automation and control, space and aviation systems, and defense and marine systems. **NOTE:** See job listings on Honeywell's website and apply online. **Operation at this facility include:** This location manufactures home heating and air-conditioning controls. **Listed on:** New York Stock Exchange. **Stock exchange symbol:** HON.

THE HORACE MANN COMPANIES
One Horace Mann Plaza, Springfield IL 62715. 217/788-5153. **Fax:** 217/535-7129. **Contact:** Employment Office. **World Wide Web address:** http://www.horacemann.com. **Description:** A multiline insurance company serving the education industry. **NOTE:** See website for job listings and application information. **Positions advertised include:** Programmer Analyst; Assistant Actuary; Home Office Analyst; Director of Planning; Data Input Operator. **Special programs:** Internships. **Operations at this facility include:** Administration; Sales; Service.

HOSTMARK HOSPITALITY GROUP
1111 Plaza Drive, Suite 200, Schaumburg IL 60173. 847/517-9100. **Fax:** 847/517-9797. **Contact:** Human Resources. **World Wide Web address:** http://www.hostmark.com. **Description:** HostMark Hospitality Group is a hotel property management company. **Positions advertised include:** Director of Sales.

HOTEL 71
71 East Wacker Drive, Chicago IL 60601. 312/346-7100. **Toll-free phone:** 800/621-4005. **Fax:** 312/346-1721. **Contact:** Recruitment Manager. **E-mail address:** jobs@hotel71.com. **World Wide Web address:** http://www.hotel71.com. **Description:** A 417-room full-service hotel. Founded in 1958.

HOUSEHOLD FINANCE CORPORATION
961 Weigel Drive, Elmhurst IL 60126. 630/617-7000. **Contact:** Human Resources. **World Wide Web address:** http://www.householdfinance.com. **Description:** Household Finance Corporation is one of the oldest and largest independent consumer finance companies in the United States, providing secured and unsecured loans for home improvement, education, bill consolidation, and leisure activities to 1.7 million customers through 400 branches and two regional headquarters. **NOTE:** Apply to job listings found on the company's website. **Positions advertised include:** Underwriter; Sales Assistant Beneficial; Bankruptcy Specialist; Collection Representative; Operations Systems Associate. **Special programs:** Internships. **Other U.S. locations:** San Francisco CA; Wood Dale IL. **Parent company:** Household International (Prospect Heights IL).

HUDSON RESPIRATORY CARE INC.
900 West University Drive, Arlington Heights IL 60004. 847/259-7400. **Contact:** Althea J. Schuler, Human Resources Manager. **World Wide Web address:** http://www.hudsonrci.com. **Description:** A specialized manufacturer of sterile disposable products for respiratory therapy. **NOTE:** Apply online or fax resumes for open positions. **Positions advertised include:** Territory Sales Manager; Quality Assurance Compliance Specialist. **Corporate headquarters location:** Temecula CA. **Operations at this facility include:** Administration; Manufacturing. **Listed on:** Privately held.

HUMPHREYS, INC.
2009 West Hastings Street, Chicago IL 60608. 312/997-2358. **Toll-free phone:** 800/843-8455. **Fax:** 312/997-2147. **Contact:** Marilyn Bly, Office Manager. **E-mail address:** blym@randacorp.com. **World Wide Web address:** http://www.humphreysinc.com. **Description:** Manufactures belts, wallets, and other leather accessories. **NOTE:** Fax or e-mail resumes to Ms. Bly.

HYATT REGENCY CHICAGO
151 East Wacker Drive, Chicago IL 60601. 312/565-1234. **Contact:** Human Resources. **World Wide Web address:** http://www.chicagohyatt.com. **Description:** A hotel with over 2,000 rooms. **NOTE:** Apply online at the website. **Positions advertised include:** Deli Attendant; Food Server Assistant; Front Office Supervisor; Master Accounts Coordinator; Off-Premises Catering Driver.

HYDAC TECHNOLOGY CORPORATION
445 Windy Point Drive, Glendale Heights IL 60139. 630/545-0800. **Fax:** 630/545-0033. **Contact:** Human Resources. **World Wide Web address:** http://www.hydacusa.com. **Description:** Provides fluid power solutions intended to increase the efficiency, longevity, and safety of fluid power systems. **Positions advertised include:** Computer Network Support Specialist; Product Manager; Regional Sales Manager. **Corporate headquarters location:** Bethlehem PA. **Other U.S. locations:** Nationwide.

HYDRO GEAR
1411 S. Hamilton Street Sullivan IL 61951. 217/728-7665. **Fax:** 866/207-7512. **Contact:** Christina O'Brien. **E-mail address:** careers@hydro-gear.com. **World Wide Web address:** http://hydro-gear.com. **Description:** Hydro Gear designs, manufactures, sells, and services hydrostatic drive systems for the lawn and garden industry. They produce high-performance hydrostatic transmissions, gear reduction drives, piston pumps, wheel motors, and accessories for both the consumer and commercial markets. **NOTE:** Search for open positions online. **Positions advertised include:** Buyer; Market Development Manager; Model Shop Technician; Production Supervisor. **Operations at this facility include:** Administrative; Production.

IBM CORPORATION
One IBM Plaza, Chicago IL 60611. 312/245-6383. **Contact:** IBM Staffing Services. **World Wide Web address:** http://www.ibm.com. **Description:** IBM is a developer, manufacturer, and marketer of advanced information processing products including computers and microelectronic technology, software, networking systems, and information technology-related services. **Corporate headquarters location:** Armonk NY. **International locations:** Africa; Asia; Canada; Europe; Latin America; Middle East. **Operations at this facility include:** This location is a marketing office. **Listed on:** New York Stock Exchange. **Stock exchange symbol:** IBM.

IBM CORPORATION
6250 River Road, Suite 7050, Rosemont IL 60018. 877/683-6235. **Contact:** Human Resources. **World Wide Web address:** http://www.ibm.com. **Description:** IBM is a developer, manufacturer, and marketer of advanced information processing products including computers and microelectronic technology, software, networking systems, and information technology-related services. Founded in 1983. **Corporate headquarters location:** Beaverton OR. **International locations:** Worldwide. **Operations at this facility include:** This location is a sales office. **Subsidiaries include:** IBM Credit Corporation; IBM Instruments, Inc.; IBM World Trade Corporation. **Listed on:** New York Stock Exchange. **Stock exchange symbol:** IBM.

ITW BRANDS
955 National Parkway, Suite 9500, Schaumburg IL 60173. 847/944-2260. **Contact:** Human Resources. **World Wide Web address:** http://www.itwinc.com. **Description:** A division of Illinois Tool Works, this company manufactures tools and fasteners. It also operates as a warehousing facility.

ITW INDUSTRIAL FINISHING
195 International Boulevard, Glendale Heights IL 60139. 630/237-5000. **Fax:** 630/237-5011. **Contact:** Human Resources. **Description:** A manufacturer of spray finishing and coating application equipment.

ITW SIGNODE CORPORATION
3650 West Lake Avenue, Glenview IL 60025. 800/531-1022. **Contact:** Human Resources. **World Wide Web address:** http://www.signode.com. **Description:** ITW Signode manufactures and distributes strapping systems for use in packaging and materials handling by a broad range of industries. **Parent company:** Illinois Tool Works Inc. (Glenview IL) develops, produces, and markets various highly-engineered components, fasteners, assemblies, and packaging systems for clients in the industrial and construction markets. Products of the company include metal components, construction products and polymers, consumer packaging products and systems, industrial packaging systems, and finishing systems. Illinois Tool Works has over 250 operating facilities in 33 countries.

ILLINOIS CENTRAL RAILROAD COMPANY
455 North Cityfront Plaza Drive, Chicago IL 60611-5317. 312/755-7500. **Contact:** Human Resources. **World Wide Web address:** http://www.cn.ca. **Description:** Operates one of the largest rail networks in the United States. The company's network includes 2,700 miles of main lines; 1,700 miles of passing, yard, and switching track; and 300 miles of secondary main lines. The company serves land shippers in Illinois, Louisiana, Michigan, Alabama, Kentucky, and Tennessee. Illinois Central's equipment consists of locomotives; freight cars; work equipment; and highway trailers and tractors. **NOTE:** Apply online. **Positions advertised include:** Communication Technician. **Corporate headquarters location:** This location. **Parent company:** Canadian National Railway.

ILLINOIS INSTITUTE OF TECHNOLOGY
3300 South Federal Street, Main Building, Room 302, Chicago IL 60616. 312/567-3318. **Fax:** 312/567-3450. 000. **Contact:** Human Resources. **E-mail address:** hr@iit.edu. **World Wide Web address:** http://www.iit.edu. **Description:** A four-year college offering bachelor's, master's (including MBA), and doctoral degrees. Approximately 2,500 undergraduate and 2,500 graduate students attend Illinois Institute of Technology. **NOTE:** The Human Resources Office prefers resumes to be sent via e-mail. **Positions advertised include:** Assistant to the Director; Service Coordinator; Administrative Assistant; Career Specialist; International Student Advisor; Web Programmer; Help Desk Supervisor.

ILLINOIS STATE UNIVERSITY
Campus Box 1300, Normal IL 61790. 309/438-8311. **Contact:** Human Resources. **World Wide Web address:** http://www.ilstu.edu. **Description:** A four-year, state

university offering bachelor's, master's, and doctoral degrees to approximately 20,000 students. **NOTE:** To apply for administrative and professional positions, see website for job listings and contact information. To apply for civil service positions, an application is required and can be obtained on the website or in person at the Human Resources Office in the Nelson Smith Building, Room 101 Applications may also be faxed to Human Resources at 309/438-7421. **Office hours:** Monday – Friday, 7:30 a.m. – 4:30 p.m.

ILLINOIS TOOL WORKS INC. (ITW)
3600 West Lake Avenue, Glenview IL 60025. 847/724-7500. **Contact:** Barbara Morris, Manager of Human Resources. **World Wide Web address:** http://www.itwinc.com. **Description:** Illinois Tool Works develops, produces, and markets various components, fasteners, assemblies, and packaging systems for clients in the industrial and construction markets. Products include metal components, construction products and polymers, consumer packaging products and systems, industrial packaging systems, and finishing systems. The company has over 250 operating facilities worldwide. **Corporate headquarters location:** This location. **Listed on:** New York Stock Exchange. **Stock exchange symbol:** ITW. **Number of employees worldwide:** 52,000.

INFORMATION RESOURCES, INC.
150 North Clinton Street, Chicago IL 60661. 312/726-1221. **Fax:** 312/726-5304. **Contact:** Human Resources. **World Wide Web address:** http://www.infores.com. **Description:** Develops and maintains computerized proprietary databases, decision support software, and analytical models to assist clients, primarily in the consumer packaged goods industry, in testing and evaluating their marketing plans for new products, media advertising, price, and sales promotions. **NOTE:** Apply online. **Corporate headquarters location:** This location. **Other U.S. locations:** Los Angeles CA; San Francisco CA; Darien CT; Waltham MA; Fairfield NJ; Cincinnati OH. **Operations at this facility include:** Administration.

INGENIENT TECHNOLOGIES, INC.
1701 West Golf Road, Tower 1, Suite 300, Rolling Meadows IL 60008. 847/357-1980. **Fax:** 847/357-1981. **Contact:** Human Resources. **E-mail address:** hr@ingenient.com. **World Wide Web address:** http://www.ingenient.com. **Description:** A technology company that develops multimedia product solutions based upon embedded Digital Signal Processors (DSPs) and General Purpose Processors (GPPs). **NOTE:** Search for open positions on the company website. **Positions advertised include:** Business Development Manager; Design Verification and Testing Engineer; Firmware Engineers; Hardware Engineers; Senior DSP Engineer; WindowsCE Software Engineer. **Corporate headquarters location:** This location. **Other U.S. locations:** Baltimore MD.

INGERSOLL MILLING MACHINE COMPANY
707 Fulton Avenue, Rockford IL 61103. 815/987-6000. **Fax:** 815/987-6725. **Contact:** Human Resources. **World Wide Web address:** http://www.ingersoll.com. **Description:** Manufactures industrial machinery including diemaking and various types of milling machines. **NOTE:** Call the company's Human Resources Office to hear bout employment opportunities. **Subsidiaries include:** Ingersoll Milling Machines (Rockford IL); Ingersoll Production Systems (Rockland IL); Ingersoll Rapid Response (Rockford IL); Ingersoll Contract Manufacturing Company; Ingersoll Automation (Machesney Park, IL).

INRULE SOLUTIONS
224 North Des Plaines, Suite 601, Chicago IL 60661. 312/648-1800. **Fax:** 312/873-3851. **Contact:** Rick Chomko, Chief Product Officer. **E-mail address:** resume@inrule.com. **World Wide Web address:** http://www.inrule.com. **Description:** Manufacturer of software (InRuleSuite) that helps streamline the development of program coding. Primary clients are those in the insurance, finance, manufacturing and professional markets. **NOTE:** E-mail resumes. **Listed on:** Privately held.

INSIGHT ENTERPRISES, INC.
444 Scott Drive, Bloomingdale IL 60108-3111. 630/924-6700. **Toll-free phone:** 800/723-2254. **Contact:** Human Resources. **World Wide Web address:** http://www.corp.insight.com. **Description:** Sells and distributes computer hardware, software and peripherals to *Fortune* 500 companies. Founded in 1988. **Positions advertised include:** Wireless Sales Engineer; Corporate Sales Representative; Inside Sales Representative; Procurement Specialist; Software Sales Engineer. **Office hours:** Monday - Friday, 8:00 a.m. - 5:00 p.m. **Corporate headquarters location:** This location. **Other U.S. locations:** Nationwide. **Listed on:** NASDAQ. **Stock exchange symbol:** NSIT.

INTERIM HEALTHCARE
3020 West Willow Knolls Drive, Peoria IL 61614. 309/693-7665. **Toll-free phone:** 800/373-0659. **Fax:** 309/693-7664. **Contact:** Human Resources. **World Wide Web address:** http://www.interimhealthcare.com/peoria_il. **Description:** Provides home health care services. **Positions advertised include:** RN; LPN; Physical Therapist; Occupational Therapist; Dental Hygienists; Dental Assistants.

INTERLAKE MATERIAL HANDLING, INC.
1230 East Diehl Road, Suite 400, Naperville IL 60563. 630/245-8800. **Toll-free phone:** 800/468-3752. **Fax:** 630/245-8906. **Contact:** Human Resources. **E-mail address:** career@interlake.com. **World Wide Web address:** http://www.interlake.com. **Description:** Operates through two divisions: Engineered Materials Division manufactures ferrous powders used in aircraft parts; Handling Division produces warehouse storage equipment, conveyor systems, and inventory control systems. **NOTE:** Visit the company's website to review job listings. E-mail resumes indicating desired position. **Positions advertised include:** Designer; Business Development Manager. **Corporate headquarters location:** This location.

INTERMATIC, INC.
7777 Winn Road, Intermatic Plaza, Spring Grove IL 60081. 815/675-2321. **Contact:** Human Resources. **World Wide Web address:** http://www.intermatic.com. **Description:** A manufacturer of electromechanical and electronic timers and photo controls. **NOTE:** Apply online at this company's website.

INTERNATIONAL PAPER FOOD SERVICE
500 Dacey Drive, Shelbyville IL 62565. 217/774-2176. **Contact:** Human Resources. **World Wide Web address:** http://www.ipfoodservice.com. **Description:** Manufactures cartons and containers for the food service industry. **NOTE:** Apply online at the parent company's website: http://www.internationalpaper.com. **Parent company:** International Paper Company (Purchase NY). **Listed on:** New York Stock Exchange. **Stock exchange symbol:** IP.

INTERSTATE BRANDS CORPORATION
HOSTESS BAKERY
9555 West Soreng Avenue, Schiller Park IL 60176. 847/994-9699. **Fax:** 847/678-9651. **Recorded jobline:** 847/994-9690. **Contact:** Russ Hinkle, Human Resources. **Description:** Produces Hostess snack products such as cupcakes and Twinkies. **Special programs:** Apprenticeships; Training. **Corporate headquarters location:** Kansas City MO.

INTERTECH NASHVILLE
18355 Enterprise Avenue, Nashville IL 62263. 618/327-4416. **Contact:** Human Resources. **Description:** Manufactures interior panels and seat frames for automobiles.

INVENSYS CLIMATE CONTROLS AMERICA
191 East North Avenue, Carol Stream IL 60188. 630/260-3402. **Contact:** Human Resources. **World Wide Web address:** http://www.icca.invensys.com. **Description:** Manufactures thermostats, smoke detectors, and carbon monoxide detectors. **NOTE:** See website for job listings.

IVEX PACKAGING CORPORATION
100 Tri-State International, Suite 200, Lincolnshire IL 60069. 847/945-9100. **Contact:** Human Resources. **World Wide Web address:** http://www.ivexpackaging.com. **Description:** Manufactures paper and plastic packaging products including dessert trays, containers, and toilet tissue overwraps. **Corporate headquarters location:** This location. **Operations at this facility include:** Administration.

IVEX PACKAGING CORPORATION
8100 South 77th Avenue, Bridgeview IL 60455. 708/458-8084. **Contact:** Shelly Dentzman, Human Resources. **World Wide Web address:** http://www.ivexpackaging.com. **Description:** Manufactures corrugated packaging and mailers. **Corporate headquarters location:** Lincolnshire IL.

JMB REALTY CORPORATION
J&V URBAN RETAIL PROPERTIES COMPANY
900 North Michigan Avenue, Chicago IL 60611. 312/440-4800. **Fax:** 312/915-2310. **Contact:** Human Resources. **Description:** Owns and manages shopping malls and strip malls nationwide. **Corporate headquarters location:** This location. **Other U.S. locations:** Nationwide. **Listed on:** Privately held.

JACKSON PARK HOSPITAL
7531 Stony Island Avenue, Chicago IL 60649. 773/947-7512. **Contact:** Human Resources. **World Wide Web address:** http://www.jacksonparkhospital.com. **Description:** A 326-bed hospital offering inpatient and outpatient services. **NOTE:** Apply in person at the hospital's Human Resources Office. **Office hours:** Monday – Friday: 8:00 a.m. – 4:30 p.m. **Operations at this facility include:** Administration; Service.

JAKEL, INCORPORATED
400 Broadway, Highland IL 62249. 618/654-2371. **Fax:** 618/654-5320. **Contact:** Human Resources. **E-mail address:** humanresources@jakelinc.com. **World Wide Web address:** http://www.jakelinc.com. **Description:** Manufactures subfractional horsepower electric motors for the small appliance and HVAC industry. Founded in 1946. **NOTE:** Entry-level positions are offered. **Special programs:** Internships; Co-ops. **Office hours:** Monday - Friday, 8:00 a.m. - 5:00 p.m. **Corporate headquarters location:** This location. **Other U.S. locations:** Murray KY. **International locations:** Mexico; China. **Operations at this facility include:** Administration; Manufacturing; Research and Development; Sales; Service.

JANE ADDAMS HULL HOUSE ASSOCIATION
10 South Riverside Plaza, Suite 1700, Chicago IL 60606. 312/906-8600. **Contact:** Staffing Coordinator. **World Wide Web address:** http://www.hullhouse.org. **Description:** A nonprofit, multiservice social agency dedicated to helping people build better lives for themselves and their families. Jane Addams Hull House Association has 6 community centers and 35 satellite locations throughout metropolitan Chicago. The organization serves approximately 225,000 people from geographically, culturally, and economically diverse backgrounds each year. **NOTE:** See website for job listings and contact information. **Positions advertised include:** Literacy Aide; Case Management Supervisor; Program Supervisor; Caseworker; Administrative Assistant. **Corporate headquarters location:** This location.

JC PENNEY COMPANY, INC.
3 Woodfield Mall, Schaumburg IL 60173. 847/240-5000. **Contact:** Human Resources. **World Wide Web address:** http://www.jcpenney.net. **Description:** A national retail service corporation with department stores in most major American cities. JC Penney sells apparel, home furnishings, and leisure lines in catalogs and 1,900 retail stores. Other operations include JC Penney Life Insurance Company, which sells life, health, and credit insurance; and JC Penney National Bank. **Corporate headquarters location:** Dallas TX. **Other U.S. locations:** Ford City IL; Lombard IL; North Riverside IL. **Operations at this facility include:** Regional Headquarters. **Listed on:** New York Stock Exchange. **Stock exchange symbol:** JCP.

JEFFERIES & COMPANY, INC.
DERIVATIVES DIRECT
55 West Monroe Street, Suite 3500, Chicago IL 60603. 312/750-4700. **Contact:** Human Resources. **World Wide Web address:** http://www.jefco.com. **Description:** Jefferies & Company is engaged in equity, convertible debt, and taxable fixed income securities brokerage and trading, and corporate finance. Jefferies & Company is one of the leading national firms engaged in the distribution and trading of blocks of equity securities and conducts such activities primarily in the third market. Founded in 1962. **NOTE:** To apply for investment banking positions, contact Dee Dee Bird, Recruiting Coordinator, at dbird@jefco.com or by fax at 310/575-5165. To apply for other positions, contact Mel Locke, Director of People Services at mlocke@jefco.com or via fax at 310/914-1066. **Corporate headquarters location:** Los Angeles CA. **Parent company:** Jefferies Group, Inc. is a holding company that operates several subsidiaries in the securities brokerage and trading, corporate finance, and financial services markets.

JEL SERT COMPANY
P.O. Box 261, West Chicago IL 60186. 630/231-7590. **Contact:** Human Resources. **E-mail address:** hr@jelsert.com. **World Wide Web address:** http://www.jelsert.com. **Description:** Manufactures Fla-Vor-Ice, FlavorAid, Mondo, Otter Pops, Pop Ice, and Wyler's products. **NOTE:** Apply online. **Positions advertised include:** Quality Assurance Lab Technician.

JEWEL OSCO
1955 West North Avenue, Melrose Park IL 60160. 708/531-6000. **Fax:** 708/531-6047. **Contact:** Employment Manager. **E-mail address:** JJ.JobsAtJEWELCO@ALBERTSONS.COM. **World Wide Web address:** http://www.jewelosco.com. **Description:** Operates a chain of retail food stores. **NOTE:** For store management positions, e-mail resumes. For retail positions, apply at the nearest Jewel Osco location. For pharmacy employment, send resume to Recruiting Department, 3030 Cullerton, Franklin Park, IL 60130; fax: 888/541-5793; or e-mail:

pharmacyrecruiting@Albertsons.com. When sending a resume, please indicate department of interest. Special programs: Internships; Store Management Training. **Corporate headquarters location:** This location.

JIM BEAM BRANDS COMPANY
510 Lake Cook Road, Suite 200, Deerfield IL 60015. 847/948-8888. **Contact:** Human Resources. **World Wide Web address:** http://www.jimbeam.com. **Description:** Distills bourbon. **Parent company:** Fortune Brands (Lincolnshire IL).

JOHN DEERE HISTORIC SITE
8393 South Main, Grand Detour, Dixon IL 61021. 815/652-4551. **Contact:** Human Resources. **World Wide Web address:** http://www.deere.com. **Description:** The historic site of John Deere, who founded one of the country's largest agricultural manufacturing companies. This location houses a museum and a blacksmith shop.

JOHNSON CONTROLS, INC.
300 South Glengarry Drive, Geneva IL 60134. 630/232-4270. **Contact:** Human Resources. **World Wide Web address:** http://www.jci.com. **Description:** Johnson Controls, Inc. provides air conditioning services, air filters, automatic temperature control, chiller services, coil cleaning, lighting services, energy management, facilities management systems, fire alarm systems, heating service, maintenance contracts, refrigeration service, and security systems. **NOTE:** Apply online. **Corporate headquarters location:** Milwaukee WI. **Operations at this facility include:** This location manufactures automobile batteries. **Listed on:** New York Stock Exchange. **Stock exchange symbol:** JCI.

JOHNSON PUBLISHING COMPANY, INC.
820 South Michigan Avenue, Chicago IL 60605. 312/322-9200. **Contact:** LaDoris Foster, Personnel Director. **World Wide Web address:** http://www.ebony.com. **Description:** Publishes Ebony and Jet magazines. The company also markets the Fashion Fair cosmetics line. **Corporate headquarters location:** This location.

JOLIET JUNIOR COLLEGE
1215 Houbolt Road, Joliet IL 60431-8938. 815/280-2266. **Fax:** 815/729-3331. **Contact:** Human Resources. **E-mail address:** hr@jjc.edu. **World Wide Web address:** http://www.jjc.cc.il.us. **Description:** A community college offering associate degrees and career and technical degrees and certificates. Founded in 1901. **NOTE:** An application is required. See website to download a copy or contact the Human Resources Office to have one mailed or faxed. Entry-level positions and second and third shifts are offered. **Positions advertised include:** Office Systems Instructor; Pastry and Baking Instructor; Adjunct Faculty (Various).

EARLE M. JORGENSEN COMPANY
1900 Mitchell Boulevard, Schaumburg IL 60193. 847/301-6100. **Fax:** 847/301-6114. **Contact:** Human Resources. **World Wide Web address:** http://www.emjmetals.com. **Description:** A full-line steel and aluminum distributor with approximately 40 domestic and international locations. **Corporate headquarters location:** Brea CA. **Other U.S. locations:** Nationwide. **Listed on:** Privately held.

JOSLYN MANUFACTURING COMPANY
3700 South Morgan Street, Chicago IL 60609. 773/927-1420. **Contact:** Human Resources. **World Wide Web address:** http://www.joslynmfg.com. **Description:** Manufactures a variety of products associated with power utility distribution and transmission lines and communication systems. This company has two plants in the Chicago area and one in Franklin Park, IL.

K'S MERCHANDISE
3103 North Charles Street, Decatur IL 62526. 217/875-1440. **Fax:** 217/875-6978. **Contact:** Human Resources. **World Wide Web address:** http://www.catalog.ksmerchandise.com. **Description:** A retail catalog showroom chain. **Positions advertised include:** Store Manager Trainee; Jewelry Assistant; Jewelry Manager; Jeweler Promotional Coordinator; Jeweler. **Corporate headquarters location:** This location. **Operations at this facility include:** Administration; Manufacturing; Sales; Service.

KPMG
303 East Wacker Drive, Chicago IL 60601. 312/665-1000. **Fax:** 312/665-6000. **Contact:** Human Resources. **World Wide Web address:** http://www.kpmgcareers.com. **Description:** KPMG delivers a wide range of value-added assurance, tax, and consulting services. **NOTE:** KPMG prefers job candidates to apply online at its website; however, it possible to fax a scannable resume. See website and job listings for additional information. Positions advertised include: Senior Associate; Senior Actuarial Manager; Public Sector Audit; Internal Audit Manager; Senior Writer. **Corporate headquarters location:** Montvale NJ. **Parent company:** KPMG International is a leader among professional services firms engaged in capturing, managing, assessing, and delivering information to create knowledge that will help its clients maximize shareholder value.

KAPLAN UNIVERSITY
550 West Van Buren, 7th Floor, Chicago IL 60607. 312/777-6333. **Fax:** 312-777-6704. **Contact:** Human Resources. **E-mail address:** kaplaninc@trm.brassring.com. **World Wide Web address:** http://www.kaplan.edu. **Description:** Kaplan is an online university offering Associates, Bachelors, Masters, and Certificate programs to students who wish to learn over the Internet. **NOTE:** Search and apply for positions online. **Positions advertised include:** Editorial Assistant; Faculty; Advanced Website Design Technicians. **Corporate headquarters location:** Fort Lauderdale FL.

A.T. KEARNEY PROCUREMENT SOLUTIONS
222 West Adams Street, Suite 2500, Chicago IL 60606. 312/648-0111. **Toll-free phone:** 888/327-3842. **Fax:** 312/223-7070. **Contact:** Human Resources. **E-mail services:** atkps_careers@atkearney.com. **World Wide Web address:** http://www.atkearney.com. **Description:** A general management consulting firm. **NOTE:** E-mail resumes. **Positions advertised include:** eSourcing Manager.

KEEBLER COMPANY
545 Lamont Road, Elmhurst IL 60126. 630/833-2900. **Contact:** Human Resources. **World Wide Web address:** http://www.keebler.com. **Description:** A national manufacturer and marketer of cookies, crackers, snack foods, and other consumer food products. Keebler markets its products under the brand names Carr's, Cheez-It, Famous Amos, Murray, Plantation, and Ready Crust. Founded in 1853. **NOTE:** For Keebler job listings, visit Kellogg's website: http://www.careers.kelloggs.com. Apply online. **Corporate headquarters location:** Battle Creek MI. **Other U.S. locations:** Denver CO; Macon GA; Grand Rapids MI; Cincinnati OH. **Subsidiaries include:** Little Brownie's Baker is a licensed supplier of Girl Scout Cookies. **Parent company:** Kellogg Company. **Operations at this facility include:** Administration; Research and Development.

KELLY-SPRINGFIELD TIRE COMPANY
3769 U.S. Route 20 East, Freeport IL 61032-9653. 815/235-4185. **Contact:** Human Resources. **World Wide Web address:** http://www.kelly-springfield.com. **Description:** Manufactures tires. **Corporate headquarters location:** Cumberland MD. **Other U.S. locations:** Fayetteville NC; Tyler TX. **International locations:** Worldwide. **Parent company:** Goodyear Tire & Rubber Company's principal business is the development, manufacture, distribution, marketing, and sale of tires for most applications worldwide. The company also manufactures and sells a broad spectrum of rubber products and rubber-related chemicals for various industrial and consumer markets, and provides auto repair services. Goodyear operates 32 plants in the United States, 42 plants in 29 other countries, and more than 1,800 retail tire and service centers and other distribution facilities around the globe. **Listed on:** New York Stock Exchange. **Stock exchange symbol:** GT.

KEMPER INSURANCE COMPANIES
One Kemper Drive, Long Grove IL 60049. 847/320-2000. **Fax:** 847/320-5624. **Contact:** Human Resources. **World Wide Web address:** http://www.kemperinsurance.com. **Description:** Provides property, casualty, and life insurance, reinsurance, and a wide range of diversified financial services operations. Founded in 1912. **NOTE:** Entry-level positions and second and third shifts are offered. **Positions advertised include:** Claim Specialist; Environmental Claims Handler. **Special programs:** Internships; Training; Co-ops; Summer Jobs. **Corporate headquarters location:** This location. **Subsidiaries include:** Eagle Pacific Insurance Company and Pacific Eagle Insurance Company. **Other U.S. locations:** Nationwide.

KENNY CONSTRUCTION COMPANY
250 Northgate Parkway, Wheeling IL 60090. 847/541- 8200. **Fax:** 847/541-8358. **Contact:** Human Resources. **World Wide Web address:** http://www.kennyconstruction.com. **Description:** A construction company that handles various large scale projects such as subways, tunnels, airports, stadiums, buildings, hotels, power plants, mass transit, bridges, highways and all manner of Infrastructure projects. Kenny Construction operates primarily in five operating groups: Tunnels, Transportation, Underground, Building, and Power. **Positions advertised include:** Accounts Payable Clerk, Construction Superintendent, Cost Control Engineer, Office Assistant, Project Engineer, Project Manager. **Corporate headquarters location:** This location.

KETCHUM
200 East Randolph Street, Chicago IL 60601. 312/228-6800. **Contact:** Human Resources. **World Wide Web address:** http://www.ketchum.com. **Description:** A communications agency specializing in advertising, public relations, and directory advertising. **NOTE:** Apply online for open positions. **Positions advertised include:** Office Manager/Human Resources Coordinator; Financial Analyst; Corporate Vice President. **Special programs:** Internships. **Corporate headquarters location:** New York NY. **Other U.S. locations:** Nationwide. **International locations:** United Kingdom. **Parent company:** Omnicom.

KINDRED HOSPITAL/NORTHLAKE
365 East North Avenue, Northlake IL 60164. 708/345-8100. **Contact:** Human Resources. **World Wide Web address:** http://www.kindrednorthlake.com. **Description:** A hospital specializing in wound care; pulmonary medicine; rehabilitative medicine; and vision care. **NOTE:** Apply online. **Positions advertised include:** RN; LPN; Pharmacist; Occupational Therapist; Monitor Technician; Dietary Aide. **Parent company:** Kindred Healthcare.

KINETICSYSTEMS COMPANY, LLC
900 North State Street, Lockport IL 60441. 815/838-0005. **Fax:** 815/838-0095. **Contact:** Human Resources. **World Wide Web address:** http://www.kscorp.com. **Description:** A manufacturer of high-performance data acquisition and control systems. Products include modules such as analog to digital converters; digital to analog converters; signal conditioners; timers; counters; buffer memories; computer interfaces; software packages and drivers; mainframes; and VXI slot-0 controllers. Founded in 1970.

KLEINSCHMIDT INC.
450 Lake Cook Road, Deerfield IL 60015. 847/945-1000. **Contact:** Human Resources. **World Wide Web address:** http://www.kleinschmidt.com. **Description:** Offers third-party computer networking services.

KNIGHT'S ACTION PARK & CARIBBEAN WATER ADVENTURE
1700 Recreation Drive, Springfield IL 62707. 217/546-8881. **Contact:** Human Resources. **E-mail address:** knightsap@aol.com. **World Wide Web address:** http://www.knightsactionpark.com. **Description:** An action and water park offering bumper boats, batting cages, miniature golf, a driving range, laser tag, and other activities. **NOTE:** E-mail resumes or drop by the park to fill out an application. **Positions advertised include:** Office; Cashier; Maintenance; Ride Operator; Lifeguard; Food Service; Housekeeping; Parking Attendant; Guest Greeter; Landscaping.

KNOX COUNTY COUNCIL FOR DEVELOPMENTAL DISABILITIES
2015 Windish Drive, Galesburg IL 61401. 309/344-2600. **Contact:** Deputy Executive Director. **World Wide Web address:** http://www.kccdd.com. **Description:** A nonprofit agency serving people with developmental disabilities. **Special programs:** Volunteers. **Corporate headquarters location:** This location. **Operations at this facility include:** Administration; Manufacturing; Service.

KOHL CHILDREN'S MUSEUM
165 Green Bay Road, Wilmette IL 60091. 847/256-6056. **Fax:** 847/853-9154. **Contact:** Human Resources. **World Wide Web address:** http://www.kohlchildrensmuseum.org. **Description:** A children's museum with multisensory exhibits and programs intended to enhance children's understanding of themselves and the world around them. **Positions advertised include:** Exhibit Guide. **Special programs:** Internships; Volunteers. **Corporate headquarters location:** This location.

KOMATSU AMERICA
440 North Fairway Drive, Vernon Hills IL 60061. 847/970-4100. **Fax:** 847/970-5737. **Contact:** Human Resources. **World Wide Web address:** http://www.komatsuamerica.com. **Description:** Manufactures mining trucks, excavators, and haulers. The company also offers mining equipment repair services. **NOTE:** This company's website provides job listings for all its Illinois locations. Apply online. **Corporate headquarters location:** This location. **Other area locations:** Peoria IL (Manufacturing); Downers Grove IL (Financial Facility). **Parent company:** Komatsu Global (Japan). **Operations at this facility include:** Manufacturing.

KRAFT FOODS, INC.
Three Lakes Drive, Northfield IL 60093. 847/646-2000. **Fax:** 847/646-6005. **Contact:** Corporate Staffing. **World Wide Web address:** http://www.kraft.com/careers.

Description: One of the largest producers of packaged food in North America. Major brands include Jell-O, Post, Kool-Aid, Crystal Light, Entenmann's, Miracle Whip, Stove Top, and Shake 'n Bake. Kraft Foods markets a number of products under the Kraft brand name including natural and processed cheeses and dry packaged dinners. The Oscar Mayer unit markets processed meats, poultry, lunch combinations, and pickles under the Oscar Mayer, Louis Rich, Lunchables, and Claussen brand names. Kraft is also one of the largest coffee companies with principal brands including Maxwell House, Sanka, Brim, and General Foods International Coffees. **NOTE:** On its website, Kraft provides job listings for its corporate offices and division facilities. Apply online. **Corporate headquarters location:** This location. **Parent company:** Philip Morris Companies (New York) is a holding company whose principal wholly-owned subsidiaries are Philip Morris Inc. (Philip Morris U.S.A.), Philip Morris International Inc., Kraft Foods, Inc., and Philip Morris Capital Corporation. In the tobacco industry, Philip Morris U.S.A. and Philip Morris International together form one of the largest international cigarette operations in the world. U.S. brand names include Marlboro, Parliament, Virginia Slims, Benson & Hedges, and Merit. Philip Morris Capital Corporation is engaged in financial services and real estate. **Listed on:** New York Stock Exchange. **Stock exchange symbol:** KFT.

KREIDER CENTER
P.O. Box 366, Dixon IL 61021. 815/288-6691. **Physical address:** 500 Anchor Road, Dixon IL. **Contact:** Human Resources. **World Wide Web address:** http://www.kreiderservices.org. **Description:** Provides residential and day services for adults with mental disabilities.

LA RABIDA CHILDREN'S HOSPITAL
East 65th Street at Lake Michigan, Chicago IL 60649. 773/363-6700x635. **Fax:** 773/363-7905. **Recorded jobline:** 773/363-6700x500. **Contact:** Recruiter. **E-mail address:** gchurnovic@larabida.org. **World Wide Web address:** http://www.larabida.org. **Description:** A 77-bed pediatric hospital specializing in treating children with chronic illnesses and long-term disabilities. Founded in 1896. **NOTE:** Mail, fax or e-mail resumes or visit the Human Resources Office to fill out an application. **Positions advertised include:** Nutritionist; Senior Physical Therapist; Medical Technologist; Speech Language Pathologist; Respiratory Therapist; RN; LPN; Certified Nurse Assistants.

LAIDLAW TRANSIT, INC.
SCHOOL BUS DIVISION
1240 East Diehl Road, Suite 100, Naperville IL 60563. 630/955-0003. **Fax:** 630/955-0653. **Contact:** Human Resources. **World Wide Web address:** http://www.laidlawschoolbus.com. **Description:** Provides busing services. **NOTE:** Apply online. **Positions advertised include:** School Bus Driver; Dispatcher; Mechanic; Safety Supervisor; Location Manager. **Parent company:** Laidlaw, Inc. provides solid waste collection, compaction, transportation, treatment, transfer and disposal services; provides hazardous waste services; operates hazardous waste facilities and wastewater treatment plants; and operates passenger and school buses, transit system buses, and tour and charter buses.

LAKEVIEW TECHNOLOGY
1901 South Meyers Road, Suite 600, Oak Brook Terrace IL 60181. 630/282-8100. **Toll-free phone:** 800/573-8371. **Fax:** 630/282-8500. **Contact:** Human Resources. **E-mail address:** hr@lakeviewtech.com. **World Wide Web address:** http://www.lakeviewtech.com. **Description:** Resells IBM products and services. LAS also provides training, education, and software development services.

LAKEWOOD ENGINEERING & MANUFACTURING COMPANY
501 North Sacramento Boulevard, Chicago IL 60612. 773/722-4300. **Toll-free phone:** 800/621-4277. **Fax:** 773/722-1541. **Contact:** Human Resources. **World Wide Web address:** http://www.lakewoodeng.com. **Description:** Manufactures ventilating fans, electric heaters, and other products.

LANDAMERICA
10 South LaSalle Street, Suite 2501, Chicago IL 60603. 312/558-5445. **Contact:** Human Resources. **World Wide Web address:** http://www.landam.com. **Description:** Provides title insurance and other real estate services on commercial and residential transactions in the United States, Canada, the Bahamas, Puerto Rico, and the U.S. Virgin Islands. LandAmerica also provides search and examination services, and closing services for a broad-based customer group that includes lenders, developers, real estate brokers, attorneys, and homebuyers. **Corporate headquarters location:** Richmond VA. **NOTE:** This company has locations throughout Illinois. See website for locations, job listings and contact information. **Other area locations:** Statewide. **Other U.S. locations:** Nationwide. **Operations at this facility include:** This location is a regional office. **Listed on:** New York Stock Exchange. **Stock exchange symbol:** LFG.

LANDAUER, INC.
2 Science Road, Glenwood IL 60425. 708/755-7000. **Toll-free phone:** 800/323-8830. **Fax:** 708/755-7016. **Contact:** Lana Gowen, Human Resources. **World Wide Web address:** http://www.landauerinc.com. **Description:** Provides environmental testing services that determine exposure to occupational and environmental radiation hazards. The company also provides radiation dosimetry services to a number of industries in which radiation is a threat to employees. Founded in 1954.

LANDSTAR EXPRESS AMERICA, INC.
2136 12th Street, Suite 106, Rockford IL 61104. 815/226-2170. **Contact:** Human Resources. **World Wide Web address:** http://www.landstar.com. **Description:** Performs expedited and emergency air and truck freight services. **Corporate headquarters location:** Jacksonville FL. **Parent company:** Landstar System, Inc. is divided into specialized freight transportation segments: Landstar Carrier Group and Landstar Logistics. **Listed on:** NASDAQ. **Stock exchange symbol:** LSTR.

LANDSTAR CARRIER GROUP
P.O. Box 7013, Rockford IL 61125-7013. 815/972-5000. **Physical address:** 1000 Simpson Road, Rockford IL 61102. **Contact:** Human Resources. **World Wide Web address:** http://www.landstar.com. **Description:** Provides truckload transportation services through independent contractors and commission sales agents. **Corporate headquarters location:** Jacksonville FL.

LANTER DELIVERY SYSTEMS
One Caine Drive, Madison IL 62060 618/452-5300x257. **Fax:** 618/452-5931. 305B South Lee, Bloomington IL 61701. 309/828-5383. **Contact:** Human Resources. **World Wide Web address:** http://www.lanterdeliverysystems.com. **Description:** A chain of courier companies located in the Midwest providing delivery service throughout the United States and Canada. **Corporate headquarters location:** Madison WI. **Other U.S. locations:** KS; GA; IN; KY.

LANTER DELIVERY SYSTEMS
1636 New Milford School Road, Rockford IL 61109. 815/874-0401. **Contact:** Human Resources. **Description:** One location of a chain the Lanter Delivery Systems courier company.

LASALLE BANK N.A.
5250 North Harlem Avenue, Chicago IL 60656. 773/775-6800. **Fax:** 877/619-2005. **Recorded jobline:** 312/904-5627. **Contact:** Human Resources. **World Wide Web address:** http://www.lasallebanks.com. **Description:** A full-service savings and loan bank. **NOTE:** Apply online at ABN ARMO's website: http://www.abnamro.com. **Parent company:** ABN ARMO Bank N.V. is one of the world's largest banking institutions, with more than 1,900 locations in 71 countries.

LASALLE BANK N.A.
5200 West Fullerton Avenue, Chicago IL 60639. 773/889-1000. **Fax:** 877/619-2005. **Recorded jobline:** 312/904-5627. **Contact:** Human Resources. **World Wide Web address:** http://www.lasallebanks.com. **Description:** A location of the largest savings bank in Illinois. **NOTE:** Apply online at ABN ARMO's website: http://www.abnamro.com. **Parent company:** ABN ARMO Bank N.V. is one of the world's largest banking institutions, with more than 1,900 locations in 71 countries.

LASALLE BANK N.A.
135 South LaSalle Street, Suite 3300, Chicago IL 60603. 312/904-2000. **Fax:** 877/619-2005. **Recorded jobline:** 312/904-5627. **Contact:** Human Resources. **World Wide Web address:** http://www.lasallebanks.com. **Description:** A divisional headquarters of the bank chain. **NOTE:** Apply online at ABN ARMO's website: http://www.abnamro.com. **Parent company:** ABN ARMO Bank N.V. is one of the world's largest banking institutions, with more than 1,900 locations in 71 countries.

LASALLE BANK N.A.
5501 South Kedzie Avenue, Chicago IL 60629. 773/434-3322. **Fax:** 877/619-2005. **Recorded jobline:** 312/904-5627. **Contact:** Human Resources. **World Wide Web address:** http://www.lasallebanks.com. **Description:** This is the regional headquarters for LaSalle Bank. **NOTE:** Apply online at ABN ARMO's website: http://www.abnamro.com. **Parent company:** ABN ARMO Bank N.V. is one of the world's largest banking institutions, with more than 1,900 locations in 71 countries. **Operations at this facility include:** Administration.

LASALLE BANK N.A.
4747 West Irving Park Road, Chicago IL 60641. 773/777-7700. **Fax:** 877/619-2005. **Recorded jobline:** 312/904-5627. **Contact:** Human Resources. **World Wide Web address:** http://www.lasallebanks.com. **Description:** A location of the largest savings bank in Illinois. **NOTE:** Apply online at ABN ARMO's website: http://www.abnamro.com. **Parent company:** ABN ARMO Bank N.V. is one of the world's largest banking institutions, with more than 1,900 locations in 71 countries.

LASER PRECISION
1755 Butterfield Road, Suite B, Libertyville IL 60048. 847/367-0282. **Fax:** 847/367-0236. **Contact:** Human Resources. **E-mail address:** brake@laserprecision.com. **World Wide Web address:** http://www.laserprecision.com. **Description:** Laser Precision utilizes lasers and turret punching to manufacture parts for the food, medical, transportation and agricultural industries. **Positions advertised include:** Machinist, Press Brake Set-Up, Quality Control Inspector, Sheet Metal Estimator, Welder. **Operations at this facility include:** Administration; Production.

SCOTT LAUDER ASSOCIATES
1580 South Milwaukee, Suite 207, Libertyville IL 60048. 847/549-6262. **Contact:** Sandra White, Office Manager. **E-mail address:** swhite@v2gfk.com. **World Wide Web address:** http://www.scottlauderassociates.com. **Description:** Engaged in a variety of business services including custom market research. **NOTE:** Send resumes via e-mail, fax or mail to Ms. White at V2 GfK, 587 Skippack Pike, Blue Bell PA 19422. Fax: 215/283-3201. **Parent company:** V2 GfK (Blue Bell PA).

LAWSON PRODUCTS, INC.
1666 East Touhy Avenue, Des Plaines IL 60018. 847/827-9666. **Toll-free phone:** 800/448-8985. **Fax:** 847/827-0083. **Contact:** Human Resources. **World Wide Web address:** http://www.lawsonproducts.com. **Description:** Distributes a variety of industrial parts and fasteners for machinery, automobiles, and other industrial products. **NOTE:** Apply online.

LEICA NORTH AMERICA
2345 Waukegan Road, Bannockburn IL 60015. 847/405-0123. **Contact:** Human Resources. **World Wide Web address:** http://www.leica.com. **Description:** Manufactures and sells microscopes and other scientific instruments.

LETTUCE ENTERTAIN YOU ENTERPRISES INC.
5419 North Sheridan Road, Suite 104, Chicago IL 60640. 773/878-7340. **Fax:** 773/878-0113. **Contact:** Human Resources. **E-mail address:** resumes@leye.com. **World Wide Web address:** http://www.leye.com. **Description:** A restaurant management company operating casual, moderately priced dining establishments. **NOTE:** Call the Recruiting Office at 773/878-5588 for current job listings. Fax or e-mail resumes.

CHARLES LEVY CIRCULATING COMPANY
1140 N. North Branch Street, Chicago IL 60622. 312/440-4400. **Contact:** Steve Damiani, Human Resources. **World Wide Web address:** http://www.chaslevy.com. **Description:** A wholesale distributor of magazines, books, videos, cassettes, CDs, and other consumer products. **Corporate headquarters location:** Melrose Park IL. **Other U.S. locations:** Grand Rapids MI; Philadelphia PA. **Operations at this facility include:** Sales; Service. **Listed on:** Privately held.

LEWIS & CLARK COMMUNITY COLLEGE
5800 Godfrey Road, Godfrey IL 62035. 618/466-3410 or 618/468-3920. **Fax:** 618/468-3105. **Recorded jobline:** 618/468-5627. **Contact:** Human Resources. **World Wide Web address:** http://www.lc.cc.il.us. **Description:** A two-year junior college. **NOTE:** See website for job listings. An application is required. Complete it online or download it and fax it to the Human Resources Office. Interested jobseekers may also apply in person at the Human Resources Office in Erickson Hall, Room 107.

LEXIS DOCUMENT SERVICES
801 Adlai Stevenson Drive, Springfield IL 62703. 217/529-5599. **Contact:** Human Resources. **E-mail address:** Employment.HR@lexisnexis.com. **World Wide Web address:** http://www.lexisnexis.com. **Description:** Offers searching, filing, and retrieval services for law firms and financial organizations. This facility provides document service and storage for the Midwest region. **NOTE:** Apply online.

LIBERTY MUTUAL INSURANCE GROUP
555 West Pierce Road, Suite 100, Itasca IL 60143. 630/250-7100. **Contact:** Human Resources. **World Wide Web address:** http://www.libertymutual.com. **Description:** A full-line insurance firm offering life, medical, and business insurance, as well as investment and retirement plans. **NOTE:** Apply online at the corporate website. **Corporate headquarters location:** Boston MA. **Other area locations:** Des Plaines IL; Lisle IL; Matteson IL. **Operations at this facility include:** Divisional Headquarters.

LINCOLN FINANCIAL ADVISORS
8755 West Higgins Road, Suite 550, Chicago IL 60631. 773/380-8518. **Fax:** 773/693-2531. **Contact:** Linda Proskurniak, Vice President of Professional Development. **E-mail address:** Lsproskurniak@LNC.com. **World Wide Web address:** http://www.lfachicago.com. **Description:** Lincoln Financial Advisors markets financial planning, permanent and term life insurance, annuities, disability coverage, and investment products to business owners and professionals. The company also provides complex estate planning and business planning advice. Founded in 1905. **Corporate headquarters location:** Fort Wayne IN. **Other U.S. locations:** Nationwide. **International locations:** Argentina; China; United Kingdom. **Parent company:** Lincoln Financial Group. **Operations at this facility include:** Regional Headquarters; Sales. **Listed on:** New York Stock Exchange. **Stock exchange symbol:** LNC.

LINCOLN PARK ZOO
P.O. Box 14903, 2001 North Clark Street, Chicago IL 60614. 312/742-2000. **Fax:** 312/742-2299. **Contact:** Human Resources. **World Wide Web address:** http://www.lpzoo.com. **Description:** The Greater Chicago area's zoological exhibit, including amusement rides, a train and restaurants. **NOTE:** A completed application must be submitted for any position. . See website for job listings, application and submission procedures. Part-time and seasonal positions are offered. **Positions advertised include:** Education Interpreter; Retail Greeter; Production Manager; Curator; Guest Services Attendant. **Special programs:** Volunteer.

LINDEN OAKS HOSPITAL
801 South Washington Street, Naperville IL 60540. 630/305-5500. **Contact:** Human Resources. **World Wide Web address:** http://www.edward.org. **Description:** A full-service behavioral health care system meeting the needs of persons with emotional, behavioral, and substance abuse problems, as well as eating disorders. Linden Oaks Hospital is located on 10 acres of the Edward Hospital medical campus. **NOTE:** Interested jobseekers may apply online at the hospital's website or in person at the Human Resources Office. **Positions advertised include:** File Clerk; Customer Service Specialist; ER Physician Coder; Financial Counselor; Float Unit Secretary; Case Manager; Mammography Technician. **Special programs:** Internships. **Corporate headquarters location:** Macon GA. **Other U.S. locations:** Nationwide. **Operations at this facility include:** Service. **Listed on:** Privately held.

LIONS CLUBS INTERNATIONAL
300 West 22nd Street, Oak Brook IL 60523-8842. 630/571-5466. **Contact:** Human Resources. **World Wide Web address:** http://www.lionsclubs.org. **Description:** An international service organization. This location is the headquarters for the International Activities and Program Planning Division. **NOTE:** See website for job listings.

LITTELFUSE, INC.
800 East Northwest Highway, Des Plaines IL 60016. 847/824-1188. **Fax:** 847/391-0434. **Contact:** Human Resources. **World Wide Web address:** http://www.littelfuse.com. **Description:** Manufactures a wide variety of fuses. **Special programs:** Internships. **Corporate headquarters location:** This location. **Other area locations:** Arcola IL. **Other U.S. locations:** TX. **International locations:** Worldwide. **Operations at this facility include:** Administration; Manufacturing; Research and Development; Sales; Service.

LITTLE COMPANY OF MARY HOSPITAL
2800 West 95th Street, Evergreen Park IL 60805. 708/422-6200. **Recorded jobline:** 708/229-5050. **Contact:** Human Resources. **World Wide Web address:** http://www.lcmh.org. **Description:** A nonprofit hospital offering a variety of services including oncology, orthopedics, pediatrics, mother/baby care, home care, senior services, and a full-service emergency room. **NOTE:** Jobseekers are encouraged to apply via the website. **Positions advertised include:** Ultrasound Technologist; RN (Various); Surgical Technician; Nurse Manager; Medical Assistant. **Special programs:** Internships; Summer Jobs.

LODERS CROKLAAN
24708 West Durkee Road, Channahon IL 60410. 815/730-5200. **Contact:** Human Resources. **World Wide Web address:** http://www.croklaan.com. **Description:** Loders Croklaan processes, packages, and ships cooking oils. **Operations at this facility include:** This location is a vegetable oil refinery. **Parent company:** Unilever Corporation (New York NY).

LOMBART MIDWEST INSTRUMENTS
1312 Marquette Drive, Suite G, Romeoville IL 60446. 630/759-7666. **Toll-free phone:** 800/831-1194. **Fax:** 630/759-1744. **Contact:** Human Resources. **Description:** Lombart Midwest Instruments manufactures nonsurgical, ophthalmic equipment for examinations.

LOYOLA UNIVERSITY OF CHICAGO
6525 North Sheridan Road, Chicago IL 60626. 773/274-3000. **Contact:** Human Resources. **World Wide Web address:** http://www.luc.edu. **Description:** A private university and medical center. Loyola University operates four additional campuses in the greater Chicago area including Loyola University Medical Center in Maywood, Lake Shore and Water Tower campuses in Chicago, and Mallinckrodt campus in Wilmette. **NOTE:** See website for staff and faculty job listings and application and resume submission procedures. The Human Resources Office is located at 820 North Michigan Avenue. **Corporate headquarters location:** This location.

LUNAN CORPORATION
414 North Orleans Street, Suite 402, Chicago IL 60610. 312/645-9898. **Contact:** Human Resources. **World Wide Web address:** http://www.arbysrestaurants.com. **Description:** The restaurant management company of the fast food chain Arby's. **Corporate headquarters location:** This location.

LUNAN CORPORATION
7451 Woodward Avenue, Suite 109, Woodridge IL. 630/515-9797. **Fax:** 630/515-9462. **Contact:** Human Resources. **E-mail address:** operations@lunancorparbys.com. **World Wide Web address:** http://www.arbysrestaurants.com. **Description:** This location is the corporation's Operations Headquarters. **NOTE:** Fax or e-mail resumes. **Positions advertised include:** Restaurant Managers; Assistant Managers.

LYON METAL PRODUCTS LLC
P.O. Box 671, Aurora IL 60507-0671. 630/892-8941. **Fax:** 630/264-4548. **Contact:** Carol Stathis, Human Resources Manager. **World Wide Web address:** http://www.lyonworkspace.com. **Description:** Manufactures metal storage products including lockers, cabinets, shelving, office products, and ergonomic furniture. Founded in 1901.

LYRIC OPERA OF CHICAGO
20 North Wacker Drive, Chicago IL 60606. 312/332-2244. **Fax:** 312/419-1082. **Contact:** Human Resources. **E-mail address:** jobs@lyricopera.org. **World Wide Web address:** http://www.lyricopera.org. **Description:** Engaged in the study of opera, music, and the fine arts. Lyric Opera is a nonprofit organization that sponsors, produces, and encourages opera and musical performances in Chicago and the surrounding areas. Founded in 1954. **NOTE:** Part-time, seasonal and entry-level positions are offered. See website for job listings. Fax, mail or e-mail resumes. **Special programs:** Internships. **Corporate headquarters location:** This location.

MB FINANCIAL BANK
2 South LaSalle Street, Chicago IL 60602. 312/782-6200. **Contact:** Human Resources Director. **World Wide Web address:** http://www.mbfinancial.com. **Description:** A bank. **NOTE:** See website for job listings and resume submission procedures. Part-time positions offered. **Special program:** Internships. **Listed on:** NASDAQ. **Stock exchange symbol:** MBFI.

M+W ZANDER
549 West Randolph Street, Chicago IL 60661. 312/577-3200. **Contact:** Human Resources. **World Wide Web address:** http://www.mw-zander.com. **Description:** An architectural and engineering firm. Founded in 1945.

MCI
205 North Michigan Avenue, Suite 2600, Chicago IL 60601. 312/470-2121. **Contact:** Human Resources. **World Wide Web address:** http://www.mci.com. **Description:** One of the world's largest suppliers of local, long distance, and international telecommunications services, and a global Internet service provider. Founded in 1968. MCI services more than 150 countries and places. **Corporate headquarters location:** Ashburn VA. **Other U.S. locations:** Nationwide. **Parent company:** MCI Communications Corporation. **Listed on:** NASDAQ. **Stock exchange symbol:** MCIP. Number of employees worldwide: 50,000.

MPC PRODUCTS CORPORATION
7426 North Linder Avenue, Skokie IL 60077. 847/673-8300. **Fax:** 847/673-7144. **Contact:** Human Resources. **E-mail address:** human_resources@mpcproducts.com. **World Wide Web address:** http://www.mpcproducts.com. **Description:** Engineers and manufactures electromechanical equipment including motors, gears, and electronics for the government and aerospace companies. **NOTE:** See website for job listings and apply online.

MACKIE CONSULTANTS, INC.
9575 West Higgins Road, Suite 500, Rosemont IL 60018. 847/696-1400. **Contact:** Human Resources. **Description:** An engineering consulting firm providing a variety of engineering services as well as land surveying and grading.

MACLEAN FASTENERS
MACLEAN-FOGG COMPANY
1000 Allanson Road, Mundelein IL 60060. 847/566-0010. **Toll-free phone:** 800/323-4536. **Fax:** 847/566-0026. **Contact:** Human Resources. **World Wide Web address:** http://www.maclean-fogg.com. **Description:** Manufactures fasteners including nuts and bolts. Founded in 1925. This is also the location for MacLean Vehicle Systems. **Office hours:** Monday - Friday, 8:00 a.m. - 5:00 p.m. **Corporate headquarters location:** This location. **Other area locations:** Franklin Park IL; Richmond IL. **Other U.S. locations:** Pocohantas AR; Royal Oak MI. **Listed on:** Privately held.

MANUFACTURERS' NEWS, INC.
1633 Central Street, Evanston IL 60201. 847/864-7000. **Fax:** 847/332-1100. **Contact:** Human Resources. **World Wide Web address:** http://www.mninfo.com. **Description:** Compiles and publishes directories and databases of U.S. manufacturers. Founded in 1912. **NOTE:** Part-time jobs are offered. **Office hours:** Monday – Friday, 8:30 a.m. – 4:30 p.m.

MARSH INC.
500 West Monroe Street, Suite 2100, Chicago IL 60661-3630. 312/627-6000. **Contact:** Human Resources. **World Wide Web address:** http://www.marsh.com. **Description:** Provides advice and services worldwide through an insurance brokerage and risk management firm, reinsurance intermediary facilities, and a consulting and financial services group, to clients concerned with the management of assets and risks. Specific services include insurance and risk management services, reinsurance, consulting and financial services, merchandising, and investment management. The company has subsidiaries and affiliates in 57 countries, with correspondents in 20 other countries. **Corporate headquarters location:** New York NY. **Parent company:** Marsh & McLennan Companies, Inc.

MARSHALL ASSOCIATES, INC.
680 N. Lake Shore Drive, Chicago IL 60611. 312/266-8500. **Fax:** 312/266-7925. **Contact:** Human Resources. **E-mail address:** jobs@marshassoc.com. **World Wide Web address:** http://www.marshassoc.com. **Description:** Marshall Associates is a sales and merchandising company that sells consumer products to retailers across the country. They act on behalf of specific manufacturers to serve as their direct sales force. Marshall Associates' primary product categories include lawn & garden, toys, sporting goods and furniture. **Positions advertised include:** Inside Sales Representative; In-Store Sales Merchandiser; Receptionist. **Corporate headquarters location:** This location. **Other U.S. locations:** Nationwide.

MARTIN ENGINEERING
One Martin Place, Neponset IL 61345. 309/594-2384. **Contact:** Human Resources. **World Wide Web address:** http://www.martinengineering.com. **Description:** Manufactures and markets products designed to make the handling of bulk materials safer, cleaner, and more expedient. The company serves the coal, metallic and nonmetallic mineral, pulp and paper, aggregate, and cement industries among many others. Founded in 1944. **Positions advertised include:** Customer Development Representative; International Operations Engineer; Distribution Supervisor.

THE MARTIN-BROWER COMPANY
9500 West Bryn Mawr Avenue, Suite 700, Rosemont IL 60018. 847/227-6500. **Fax:** 847/227-6550. **Contact:** Human Resources. **Description:** An international company that provides food distribution services to the restaurant industry. **Corporate headquarters location:** This location. **Parent company:** Reyes Holdings.

MARYVILLE CITY OF YOUTH
1150 North River Road, Des Plaines IL 60016. 847/824-6126. **Fax:** 847/824-7190. **Contact:** Human Resources Department. **World Wide Web address:** http://www.maryvilleacademy.org. **Description:** A residential home for orphaned and homeless children. Founded in 1882. **Positions advertised include:** Family Educator. **Special programs:** Volunteers. **Corporate headquarters location:** This location.

MASONITE
1955 Powis Road, West Chicago IL 60185. 630/584-6330. **Contact:** Human Resources Manager. **World Wide Web address:** http://www.masonite.com. **Description:** Masonite manufactures doors. **Other U.S. locations:** Nationwide. **International locations:** Worldwide. **Operations at this facility include:** Sales.

GEORGE S. MAY INTERNATIONAL COMPANY
303 South Northwest Highway, Park Ridge IL 60068. 847/825-8806. **Toll-free phone:** 800/999-3020. Fax: 847/825-2951. **Contact:** Human Resources. **World Wide Web address:** http://www.georgesmay.com. **Description:** One of the world's largest and oldest management consulting firms. George S. May International focuses on consulting for small businesses. **NOTE:** Visit the website to submit a resume or download the online application and fax it. **Positions advertised include:** Field Service Representative; Executive Analyst; Staff Executive; Marketing Assistant. **Listed on:** Privately held. **President:** Israel Kushnir.

McCORMICK PLACE
2301 South Lake Shore Drive, Chicago IL 60616. 312/791-7000. **Fax:** 312/791-6001. **Recorded jobline:** 312/791-6090. **Contact:** Human Resources Director. **World Wide Web address:** http://www.mccormickplace.com. **Description:** A convention center that features three theaters, 114 meeting rooms, a ballroom, and over 2 million square feet of exhibition space. **NOTE:** An application is required for any position. See website for application. **Positions advertised include:** Production Coordinator.

McCOY SECURITY, INC.
404 South Wells, 4th Floor, Chicago IL 60607. 312/322-4900. **Fax:** 312/322-0078. **Contact:** Personnel Manager. **E-mail address:** jobs@mccoysecurity.com. **World Wide Web address:** http://www.mccoysecurity.com. **Description:** A security firm providing primarily unarmed guards and patrolmen in the greater Chicago area. **NOTE:** Call or an appointment, e-mail resume or complete the online application.

MCDONNELL AND MILLER
ITT INDUSTRIES
3500 North Spaulding Avenue, Chicago IL 60618. 773/267-1600. **Contact:** Kathy Stone, Director of Human Resources. **World Wide Web address:** http://www.mcdonnellmiller.com. **Description:** Produces water control valves and boiler equipment for heating and air conditioning systems. **Corporate headquarters location:** White Plains NY. **Parent company:** ITT Industries is a diversified, global enterprise engaged in four major business areas: Electronic Components; Defense Electronics and Services; Fluid Technology; and Motion and Flow Control. **Listed on:** New York Stock Exchange. **Stock exchange symbol:** ITT.

McDONALD'S CORPORATION
2111 McDonald's Drive, Oak Brook IL 60523. 630/623-3000. **Contact:** Human Resources. **World Wide Web address:** http://www.mcdonalds.com. **Description:** McDonald's is one of the largest restaurant chains and food service organizations in the world, operating more than 26,000 restaurants in 119 countries. **NOTE:** For corporate positions, see the website. For restaurant jobs, see http://www.McState.com or apply in person at the nearest location. **Corporate headquarters location:** This location. **Other U.S. locations:** Nationwide. **International locations:** Worldwide. **Listed on:** New York Stock Exchange. **Stock exchange symbol:** MCD.

McDONOUGH DISTRICT HOSPITAL
525 East Grant Street, Macomb IL 61455. 309/833-4101. **Fax:** 309/836-1677. **Contact:** Human Resources. **E-mail address:** info@mdh.org. **World Wide Web address:** http://www.mdh.org. **Description:** A 120-bed, nonprofit community hospital. **NOTE:** A completed application is require for any position. See website to download an application and mail or fax it or deliver it in person to the Human Resources Office. **Positions advertised include:** Cardiac Rehabilitation Nurse; Physical Therapist; RN (Various); Staff Dietitian; Nursing Instructor. **Office hours:** Monday – Friday, 7:00 a.m. – 4:30 p.m.

McGLADREY & PULLEN, LLP
20 North Martingale Road, Schaumburg IL 60173. 847/517-7070. **Contact:** Human Resources. **E-mail address:** careers@rsmi.com. **World Wide Web address:** http://www.mcgladrey.com. **Description:** A certified public accounting firm providing audit, tax, management, data processing, and cost systems services. **NOTE:** Entry-level positions are offered. **Positions advertised include:** Audit Manager **Special programs:** Internships. **Corporate headquarters location:** Bloomington MN. **Other U.S. locations:** Nationwide. **Operations at this facility include:** Administration; Service.

MCGRAW-HILL CONTEMPORARY PUBLISHING
10 NE Prudential Plaza, Chicago IL 60601. 312/233-6500. **Fax:** 847/679-2494. **Contact:** Human Resources Manager. **World Wide Web address:** http://www.mhcontemporary.com. **Description:** A division of McGraw-Hill that publishes career, foreign language, travel, reference, business, and children's books. **NOTE:** Apply online at the parent company's website: http://www.mcgraw-hill.com/careers. **Special programs:** Internships. **Corporate headquarters location:** Columbus OH. **International locations:** Markham, Ontario.

McKENDREE COLLEGE
701 College Road, Lebanon IL 62254. 618/537-6524. **Fax:** 618/537-6960. **Contact:** Hubert Place, Human Resources Director. **E-mail address:** HumanResource@McKendree.edu. **World Wide Web address:** http://www.mckendree.edu. **Description:** A four-year college offering 28 academic majors to an enrollment of over 1,000. **NOTE:** Mail, fax or e-mail resumes to Mr. Place. Entry-level and part-time positions are offered. **Positions advertised include:** Adjunct Faculty (Various); Assistant Men and Women's Soccer Coach; Residence Hall Director; Student Services Specialist. **Corporate headquarters location:** This location. **Other U.S. locations:** Louisville KY; Radcliff KY.

McKESSON CORPORATION
1400 South Wolf Road, Wheeling IL 60090. 847/537-4800. **Toll-free phone:** 800/323-8154. **Fax:** 847/537-4866. **Contact:** Recruiter. **World Wide Web address:** http://www.mckesson.com. **Description:** Produces and sells software applications catering to the specific needs of medical facilities. Some of the programs include materials management, financial accounting, patient scheduling for operating rooms, and inventory control for health clinics. Founded in 1974. **NOTE:** See website for job listings and apply online. Entry-level positions are offered. **Positions advertised include:** VP Health Systems National Accounts; Sales Support Product Demonstrator; Staff Pharmacist; Director of National Accounts; Product Manager/Development Manager. **Special programs:** Internships. **Corporate headquarters location:** San Francisco CA. **Other U.S. locations:** Boulder CO. **Listed on:** New York Stock Exchange. **Stock exchange symbol:** MCK.

MCMASTER-CARR SUPPLY
600 County Line Road, Elmhurst IL 60126. 630/833-0300. **Fax:** 630/993-3008. **Contact:** Human Resources. **E-mail address:** rita.lally@mcmaster.com. **World Wide Web address:** http://www.mcmaster.com. **Description:** Publishes a catalog of more than 420,000 industrial supplies used in a multitude of different fields. McMaster keeps 98% of that merchandise on their own warehouse shelves and ready to ship as soon as orders are placed. **Positions advertised include:** Accountant; Customer Service; Data Entry; Marketing Research Assistant; Proofreader; Warehouse Distribution Specialist. **Other U.S. locations:** Atlanta GA, Cleveland OH, Los Angeles CA, Dayton NJ.

MEDLINE INDUSTRIES, INC.
One Medline Place, Mundelein IL 60060. 847/949-5500. **Toll-free phone:** 800/MED-LINE. **Fax:** 847/949-2109. **Contact:** Human Resources. **E-mail address:** employment@medline.com. **World Wide Web address:** http://www.medline.net. **Description:** One of the largest privately held manufacturers and distributors of health care products including beds, cots, gowns, and wheelchairs. Founded in 1910. **NOTE:** For sales positions, mail resumes to the Sales Recruiter at this location or send resumes via e-mail to salesrecruiter@medline.com. Entry-level positions and second and third shifts are offered. **Positions advertised include:** Product Manager; Quality Control Inspector; Administrative Assistant; Sales Administration Coordinator; Customer Relations Specialist. **Special programs:** Internships; Co-ops; Summer Jobs. **Office hours:** Monday - Friday, 8:00 a.m. - 5:00 p.m. **Corporate headquarters location:** This location. **Other U.S. locations:** Nationwide. **Operations at this facility include:** Administration; Manufacturing; Sales. **Listed on:** Privately held.

MELMEDICA CHILDREN'S HEALTHCARE
17600 South Pulaski Road, Country Club Hills IL 60478. 708/335-3331. **Toll-free phone:** 800/387-PEDS. **Fax:** 630/357-4696. **Contact:** Human Resources. **World Wide Web address:** http://www.melmedica.com. **Description:** Provides private, in-home nursing care primarily in pediatrics. The company also offers limited obstetric services. **NOTE:** For all RN positions, call 800/387-7337 or fax resumes to 800/434-7337.

MEMORIAL HOSPITAL
4500 Memorial Drive, Belleville IL 62226-5399. 618/257-5230. **Fax:** 618/257-6911. **Recorded jobline:** 618/257-5627. **Contact:** Recruiter. **E-mail address:** personnel@memhosp.com. **World Wide Web address:** http://www.memhosp.com. **Description:** A nonprofit, acute and long-term care hospital, housing 346 adult and pediatric beds, 32 bassinets, and a 108-bed skilled nursing facility. **NOTE:** Entry-level, second and third shifts are offered. See website for online application or e-mail resumes. **Positions advertised include:** RN; LPN; CT Scan Technologist; Phlebotomist; Occupational Therapist; Security; Admitting Supervisor; Unit Secretary. **Number of employees at this location:** 2,200.

MERCHANDISE MART PROPERTIES, INC.
200 World Trade Center, Suite 470, Chicago IL 60654. 312/527-7792. **Fax:** 312/527-7905. **Contact:** Tom Fitzpatrick, Director of Human Resources. **E-mail address:** careers@mmart.com. **World Wide Web address:** http://www.merchandisemart.com. **Description:** The management and leasing agent for prominent wholesale showroom facilities, which include the Merchandise Mart and Apparel Center (Chicago), the Decorators and Designers Building (New York), and the Washington Design Center (Washington DC). **Positions advertised include:** Concierge; Administrative Assistant. **Special programs:** Internships. **Corporate headquarters location:** This location. **Other U.S. locations:** Washington DC; High Point NC. **Parent company:** Vornado Realty Trust. **Operations at this facility include:** Administration; Research and Development; Sales; Service. **Listed on:** Privately held.

MERCURY INTERACTIVE CORPORATION
10255 West Higgins Road, Suite 620, Rosemont IL 60018. 847/803-3176. **Fax:** 847/803-5686. **Contact:** Human Resources. **World Wide Web address:** http://www.mercuryinteractive.com. **Description:** Mercury Interactive is a developer of automated software quality (ASQ) tools for enterprise applications testing. The company's products are used to isolate software and system errors prior to application deployment. **NOTE:** See website for job listings and apply online. **Corporate headquarters location:** Sunnyvale CA. **Operations at this facility include:** This location is a sales office. **Listed on:** NASDAQ. **Stock exchange symbol:** MERQ.

MERCY HOSPITAL & MEDICAL CENTER
2525 South Michigan Avenue, Chicago IL 60616. 312/567-2011. **Fax:** 312/567-5562. **Contact:** Kay Jensen, Human Resources Director. **E-mail address:** employment@mercy-chicago.org. **World Wide Web address:** http://www.mercy-chicago.org. **Description:** A mid-size teaching hospital that is part of a network of satellite clinic facilities. NOTE: An application is required for any position. See website for job listings and application. Part-time and second and third shifts are offered. **Positions advertised include:** RN (Various); LPN; Patient Care Attendant; Clinical Lab Assistant; Physical Therapist; Clinical Educator; Speech Pathologist; Coding and Data Research Manager; Laboratory Supervisor; Application Business Analyst. **Operations at this facility include:** Administration; Research and Development; Service.

MERIDIAN RAIL
1545 State Street, Chicago Heights IL 60411. 708/757-8223. **Contact:** Human Resources. **World Wide Web address:** http://www.meridianrail.com. **Description:** Manufactures and markets replacement and original equipment products for the railroad industry. Products include railroad tracks, wheels, brake shoes, and signals. **Other area locations:** Cicero IL (Manufacturing).

MERRILL LYNCH
33 West Monroe Street, Suite 2200, Chicago IL 60603. 312/269-5100. **Fax:** 312/269-5092. **Contact:** Human Resources. **World Wide Web address:** http://www.ml.com. **Description:** One of the largest securities brokerage firms in the world, Merrill Lynch provides financial services in securities, financial planning, insurance, estate planning, mortgages, and related areas. The company also brokers commodity futures and options, is a major underwriter of new securities issues, and is a dealer in corporate and municipal securities. **NOTE:** This company has other locations throughout Chicago, Illinois and the United States. See website for additional locations and job listings. Apply online. **Special programs:** Internships. **Corporate headquarters location:** New York NY. **Operations at this facility include:** Sales; Service.

MERRILL LYNCH/HOWARD JOHNSON & COMPANY
300 South Wacker Drive, Suite 2600, Chicago IL 60606. 312/697-1040. **Contact:** Human Resources. **World Wide Web address:** http://www.ml.com. **Description:** As a

subsidiary of Merrill Lynch, Howard Johnson & Co. has been specializing in employee benefits consulting on a national basis for over 30 years. **NOTE:** See website for job listings and apply online. . **Corporate headquarters location:** New York NY. **Other U.S. locations:** San Francisco CA; Seattle WA. **Operations at this facility include:** Divisional Headquarters.

MESSENGER MOUSE
7818 Forest Hills Road, Loves Park IL 61111. 815/877-2224. **Contact:** Human Resources. **Description:** Offers package delivery services to companies and individual consumers throughout Illinois and Wisconsin.

METHODIST HOSPITAL OF CHICAGO
5015 North Paulina Street, Chicago IL 60640. 773/271-9040. **Contact:** Human Resources. **World Wide Web address:** http://www.bethanymethodist.org. **Description:** A 235-bed, nonprofit, acute care facility that specializes in geriatrics. The hospital is affiliated with a nursing home, retirement community, and immediate care centers. Founded in 1887. **NOTE:** Fax resume or apply in person at the Human Resources Office. Entry-level positions and second and third shifts are offered. **Positions advertised include:** RN; LPN; Coder; Mental Health Social Worker; Phlebotomist. **Internship information:** Internships in Human Resources are coordinated through area schools. Applications for summer internships must be submitted by mid-April. **Parent company:** Bethany Methodist.

METROPOLITAN FAMILY SERVICES
14 East Jackson Boulevard, 14th Floor, Chicago IL 60604. 312/986-4000. **Fax:** 312/986-4347. **Contact:** Human Resources. **E-mail address:** resumes@metrofamily.org. **World Wide Web address:** http://www.metrofamily.org. **Description:** A nonprofit, social services agency that provides counseling and support services to low-income families and individuals. The agency operates 23 other locations in the Chicago area. Positions advertised include: Bi-lingual Social Worker; Program Supervisor; Social Worker or Counselor. **Special programs:** Internships. **Corporate headquarters location:** This location. **Operations at this facility include:** Administration; Service.

MICRO SOLUTIONS COMPUTER PRODUCTS INC.
132 West Lincoln Highway, DeKalb IL 60115. 815/756-3411. **Contact:** Human Resources. **World Wide Web address:** http://www.micro-solutions.com. **Description:** Manufactures parallel printer port computer drives.

MB FINANCIAL BANK
S La Salle Street, Chicago IL 60603. 773/645-3333. **Contact:** Human Resources. **World Wide Web address:** http://www.mbfinancial.com. **Description:** A bank. **NOTE:** See website for job listings and contact information.

MIDAMERICA BANK
55th Street & Holmes Avenue, Clarendon Hills IL 60514. 630/325-7300. **Contact:** Teresa Colson, Human Resources Manager. **World Wide Web address:** http://www.midamerica-bank.com. **Description:** A full-service bank. **NOTE:** See website for job listings and apply online. **Corporate headquarters location:** Westchester IL. **Other area locations:** Cicero IL; La Grange Park IL; Naperville IL; Riverside IL; St. Charles IL; Wheaton IL. **Parent company:** MAF Bancorp, Inc. **Listed on:** NASDAQ. **Stock exchange symbol:** MAFB.

MIDWAY GAMES INC.
2704 West Roscoe Street, Chicago IL 60618. 773/961-1000. **Contact:** Human Resources. **World Wide Web address:** http://www.midway.com. **Description:** Develops a wide variety of coin-operated arcade and home video game entertainment and software products. Midway produces games for Sony, Nintendo, and Saga platforms. **Positions advertised include:** Executive Producer; Financial Planning Analyst. **Special programs:** Internships. **Corporate headquarters location:** This location. **International locations:** Midway Games Limited, London England. **Listed on:** New York Stock Exchange. **Stock exchange symbol:** MWY.

MIDWEST DENTAL PRODUCTS CORPORATION
901 West Oakton Street, Des Plaines IL 60018. 847/640-4800. **Toll-free phone:** 800/800-2888. **Contact:** Human Resources. **World Wide Web address:** http://www.midwestdental.com. **Description:** Designs, develops, manufactures, and markets a full line of medical and dental X-ray equipment. **Parent company:** DENTSPLY International.

MIDWEST TELEVISION, INC.
WCIA-CHANNEL 3
P.O. Box 20, Champaign IL 61824-0020. 217/356-8333. **Contact:** Human Resources. **World Wide Web address:** http://www.wcia.com. **Description:** A television and radio broadcasting company. **NOTE:** See website for contact information. **Positions advertised include:** Traffic Assistant; News Photographer/Sports Reporter.

MIDWESTERN REGIONAL MEDICAL CENTER
2520 Elisha Avenue, Zion IL 60099. 847/872-4561. **Contact:** Human Resources. **World Wide Web address:** http://www.cancercenter.com. **Description:** A community hospital specializing in treating various forms of cancer. **NOTE:** Apply online at http://www.cancercenter.com/employment. **Positions advertised include:** Assistant Director of Imaging; Bone Marrow Transplant; Case Manager; Clinical Manager Assistant; Housekeeper; Medical Technologist.

MILLER FLUID POWER CORPORATION
800 North York Road, Bensenville IL 60106. 630/766-3400. **Fax:** 630/766-2013. **Contact:** Human Resources. **E-mail address:** employment@millerfp.com. **World Wide Web address:** http://www.millerfluidpower.com. **Description:** A manufacturer of pneumatic and hydraulic cylinders and components. **Corporate headquarters location:** This location. **Operations at this facility include:** Administration; Manufacturing; Research and Development; Sales; Service.

MILLIKIN UNIVERSITY
1184 West Main Street, Decatur IL 62522-2084. 217/362-6416. **Fax:** 217/424-6468. **Contact:** Human Resources. **World Wide Web address:** http://www.millikin.edu. **Description:** A liberal arts university affiliated with the Presbyterian Church. Approximately 2,000 students are enrolled at Millikin University. **NOTE:** See website for job listings and application. Interested jobseekers may apply to open positions by mailing or faxing resumes. Interested jobseekers may also apply in person at the Human Resources Office, Room 212 of Shilling Hall. **Office hours:** Monday – Friday, 8:00 a.m. – 5:00 p.m. **Positions advertised include:** Continuing Education Services Coordinator and Research/Instruction Librarian; Instructor of Nursing; Assistant Professor; Acting Department Chair; Hall Director; Database Analyst; Team Coach (Various); Executive Secretary. **Special programs:** Internships. **Corporate headquarters location:** This location. **Operations at this facility include:** Administration. **Listed on:** Privately held.

MISSISSIPPI LIME COMPANY
P.O. Box 2247, 7 Alby Street, Alton IL 62002. 618/465-7741. **Contact:** Human Resources. **World Wide Web address:** http://www.mississippilime.com. **Description:** Engaged in the production of limestone, sand, and rock. **Operations at this facility include:** This is the main wholesale office.

MITEK CORPORATION
One Mitek Plaza, Winslow IL 61089. 815/367-3000. **Contact:** Teresa Stamm, Director of Human Resources. **World Wide Web address:** http://www.mitekcorp.com. **Description:** Engaged in the developing, manufacturing, and marketing of automotive, home, and professional loudspeakers. **NOTE:** Apply online. **Corporate headquarters location:** Phoenix AZ. **Other U.S. locations:** Monroe WI. **Operations at this facility include:** Administration; Manufacturing; Research and Development; Sales; Service. **Listed on:** Privately held.

MITEL TELECOMMUNICATIONS SYSTEMS
241 South Furnace Road, Suite 37, Burr Ridge IL 60527. 630/850-2170. **Contact:** Human Resources. **World Wide Web address:** http://www.mitel.com. **Description:** Sells and services a variety of business telephone systems including voicemail. **NOTE:** Send resumes to the corporate headquarters' Human Resources Office – Mitel Networks, 350 Legget Drive, Kanata, Ontario, Canada, K2K 2W7. Or phone: 613/592-2122 for additional employment information. **Operations at this facility include:** This is a sales office.

MODERN DROP FORGE COMPANY
13810 South Western Avenue, Blue Island IL 60406. 708/388-1806. **Contact:** Human Resources. **World Wide Web address:** http://www.modernforge.com. **Description:** Operates a steel forging plant. **Corporate headquarters location:** This location.

MOHN CUSTOM INTERIORS
601 South MacArthur Boulevard, Springfield IL 62704. 217/787-6251. **Contact:** Manager. **World Wide Web address:** http://www.mohninteriors.com. **Description:** Provides professional interior design and furniture upholstering services. Founded in 1968. **Office hours:** Monday – Friday, 9:00 a.m. – 5:00 p.m.; Saturday – 10:00 a.m. – 12:00 p.m.

MOLEX INC.
2222 Wellington Court, Lisle IL 60532. 630/969-4550. **Contact:** Human Resources. **World Wide Web address:** http://www.molex.com. **Description:** Designs, manufactures, and distributes electrical and electronic devices such as terminals, connectors, switches, and related application tooling. Products are used by television, stereo, home computer, electronic game, audio, video, and other consumer manufacturing firms, as well as by the automotive and farm equipment industries. Founded in 1938. **NOTE:** Apply online for corporate positions. **Corporate headquarters location:** This location. **Other area locations:** Addison IL; Downers Grove IL; Schaumburg IL.

MONSANTO CORPORATION
3100 Sycamore Road, De Kalb IL 60115. 815/758-3461. **Fax:** 815/756-2676. **Contact:** Human Resources. **World Wide Web address:** http://www.monsanto.com. **Description:** Manufactures and markets agricultural products, performance chemicals used in consumer products, prescription pharmaceuticals, and food ingredients. **NOTE:** See website for job listings and apply online. **Corporate headquarters location:** Peapack NJ. **Other U.S. locations:** Nationwide. **Operations at this facility include:** This is the DeKalb Genetics Corporation's main office.

MOORE WALLACE
1200 South Lakeside Drive, Bannockburn IL 60015. 847/607-6000. **Contact:** Human Resources. **World Wide Web address:** http://www.rrdonnelley.com. **Description:** A manufacturer of business systems, forms, and equipment. The company has more than 280 locations in 39 countries. **NOTE:** Apply online at the corporate website for open positions. **Special programs:** Internships. **Corporate headquarters location:** This location. **Parent company:** RR Donnelley.

MORAINE VALLEY COMMUNITY COLLEGE
10900 South 88th Avenue, Palos Hills IL 60465. 708/974-4300. **Contact:** Director of Human Resources. **World Wide Web address:** http://www.moraine.cc.il.us. **Description:** A community college offering programs for students who are planning to transfer to a four-year institution. Founded in 1967.

F.E. MORAN
2265 Carlson Drive, Northbrook IL 60062. 847/498-4800. **Contact:** Human Resources. **World Wide Web address:** http://www.femoran.com. **Description:** An international mechanical contracting company specializing in fire detection, heating, air conditioning, plumbing, and ventilation systems. **NOTE:** See website for job listings and contact information. **Corporate headquarters location:** This location.

THE MOSAIC COMPANY
100 South Saunders Street, Lake Forest IL 60045. 847/739-1200. **Fax:** 847/739-1617. **Contact:** Director of Human Resources. **E-mail address:** careers@mosaicco.com. **World Wide Web address:** http://www.mosaicco.com. **Description:** Mosaic mines and manufactures crop nutrients including potash and phosphates; supplies animal feed ingredients necessary for raising livestock; and produces salt for road maintenance. **Corporate headquarters location:** Minneapolis MN. **Listed on:** New York Stock Exchange. **Stock exchange symbol:** MOS. **Number of employees worldwide:** 8,000.

MOTOROLA, INC.
1303 East Algonquin Road, Schaumburg IL 60196. 847/576-5000. **Contact:** Human Resources. **World Wide Web address:** http://www.motorola.com. **Description:** Motorola manufactures communications equipment and electronic products including car radios, cellular phones, semiconductors, computer systems, cellular infrastructure equipment, pagers, cordless phones, and LANs. **NOTE:** Apply online for open positions. **Corporate headquarters location:** This location. **Other U.S. locations:** Nationwide. **International locations:** Worldwide. **Listed on:** New York Stock Exchange. **Stock exchange symbol:** MOT.

MOUNT SINAI HOSPITAL
California Avenue at 15th Street, Chicago IL 60608. 773/542-6236. **Contact:** Human Resources. **World Wide Web address:** http://www.sinai.org. **Description:** A 432-bed, tertiary care hospital. Mount Sinai Hospital also serves as a teaching hospital for The Chicago Medical School. **NOTE:** See website for job listings and contact information. Entry-level, part-time and evening positions offered. Jobseekers interested in nursing positions should call 773/257-6566.

MUSEUM OF CONTEMPORARY ART
220 East Chicago Avenue, Chicago IL 60611. 312/280-2660. **Toll-free phone:** 800/MCA-7858. **Fax:** 312/397-4095. **Recorded jobline:** 312/397-4050. **Contact:**

Susan Kieffer, Human Resources Manager. **E-mail address:** skieffer@mcachicago.org. **World Wide Web address:** http://www.mcachicago.org. **Description:** A nonprofit, contemporary art museum offering exhibitions of international works from 1945 to the present, with a permanent collection of over 1,500 works. **NOTE:** See website for job listings. Submit resumes and cover letters by mail or fax. An application may also be completed in person at the Human Resources Office. Entry-level positions, part-time jobs, and second and third shifts are offered. **Positions advertised include:** Accounts Payable/Payroll Accountant; Coordinator of Interpretive Training; Accounting Assistant; Marketing Coordinator; Media Relations Coordinator; Box Office Associate; Free-Lance Preparators; Gallery Officers; Visitor Services Associate; Coatroom Attendants. **Special programs:** Internships; Summer Jobs. **Office hours:** Monday - Friday, 10:00 a.m. - 5:00 p.m.

MUSEUM OF SCIENCE & INDUSTRY
57th Street & Lake Shore Drive, Chicago IL 60637. 773/684-1414. **Fax:** 773/684-0019. **Contact:** Human Resources. **E-mail address:** Human.Resources@msichicago.org. **World Wide Web address:** http://www.msichicago.org. **Description:** One of the largest science museums in the world. Museum of Science & Industry offers over 800 exhibits. Founded in 1933. **NOTE:** Interested jobseekers may fax, mail or e-mail resumes. Walk-in applicants are also accepted in the Human Resources Office. Part-time and temporary positions are offered. **Positions advertised include:** Demonstrator; Public Programs; Internal Auditor; Program Interpreters; Administration Assistant; Retail Businesses and Technology Services; Director of Marketing; Maintenance Technician; Manager of Program Development. **Special programs:** Internships; Volunteers. **Office hours:** Monday, Tuesday and Wednesday – 10:00 a.m. – 3:00 p.m. **Corporate headquarters location:** This location.

NTN-BOWER
711 North Bower Road, Macomb IL 61455. 309/833-4541. **Contact:** Human Resources. **World Wide Web address:** http://www.ntnamerica.com. **Description:** Manufactures bearings and joints for the automotive, airline, and industrial fields. **NOTE:** This company also has offices in Illinois. See website for addresses.

NABISCO BRANDS, INC.
7300 South Kedzie Avenue, Chicago IL 60629. 773/925-4300. **Contact:** Human Resources. **World Wide Web address:** http://www.kraft.com. **Description:** A producer and distributor of cookies and crackers. **NOTE:** See website for job listings. Apply online. **Other U.S. locations:** Nationwide. **International locations:** Asia; Canada; Europe. **Parent company:** Kraft Foods. **Listed on:** New York Stock Exchange. **Stock exchange symbol:** KFT.

NABISCO BRANDS, INC.
7777 North Caldwell Avenue, Niles IL 60714. 847/967-6201. **Contact:** Human Resources. **World Wide Web address:** http://www.kraft.com. **Description:** A producer and distributor of cookies and crackers. **NOTE:** See website for job listings. **Parent company:** Kraft Foods. **Operations at this facility include:** This is a manufacturing plant and research and development facility.

NALCO CHEMICAL COMPANY
1601 West Diehl Road, Naperville IL 60563-1198. 877/813-3523. **Fax:** 630/305-2900. **Contact:** Human Resources. **World Wide Web address:** http://www.nalco.com. **Description:** Engaged in the manufacture and sale of highly specialized service chemicals used in water treatment, pollution control, energy conservation, oil production and refining, steel making, paper making, mining, and other industrial processes. Founded in 1928. **NOTE:** Apply online. **Positions advertised include:** Paper Industry Development Manager; Administrative Services Specialist. **Corporate headquarters location:** This location. **Operations at this facility include:** Administration; Research and Development; Sales. **Number of employees at this location:** 1,200. **Number of employees worldwide:** 6,500.

NAPERVILLE, CITY OF
Municipal Center, 400 South Eagle Street, Naperville IL 60566-7020. 630/420-6111. **Fax:** 630/305-4048. **Contact:** Human Resources. **E-mail address:** apply@naperville.il.us. **World Wide Web address:** http://www.naperville.il.us. **Description:** The administrative offices for the City of Naperville. **NOTE:** See website for job listings. Mail, fax or e-mail resumes and cover letters. Interested jobseekers may also apply in person at the Human Resources Office located in the ground floor of the Municipal Center. **Positions advertised include:** Engineering Technician; Community Relations Specialist; Ground Technician.

NATIONAL CITY BANK
120 West State Street, Rockford IL 61101. 815/987-2000. **Fax:** 815/987-2185. **Contact:** Human Resources. **World Wide Web address:** http://www.nationalcity.com. **Description:** One of the largest banks in the Midwest. National City offers a wide variety of financial services including mortgages, checking accounts, and mutual funds. **NOTE:** Apply online at the corporate website. **Special programs:** Internships. **Corporate headquarters location:** Cleveland OH. **Other U.S. locations:** AZ; FL; IN; MI; MO; NC; SC. **Listed on:** New York Stock Exchange. **Stock exchange symbol:** NCC. **Number of employees worldwide:** 32,300.

NATIONAL CITY BANK
One Old Capital Plaza North, Springfield IL 62701. 217/753-7100. **Contact:** Human Resources. **World Wide Web address:** http://www.nationalcity.com. **Description:** One of the largest banks in the Midwest. **NOTE:** Apply online at the corporate website.

NATIONAL CITY BANK
325 North Milwaukee Avenue, Libertyville IL 60048. 847/362-3000. **Fax:** 847/816-5798. **Contact:** Human Resources. **World Wide Web address:** http://www.nationalcity.com. **Description:** The regional headquarters for this chain of banks. **NOTE:** Apply online at the corporate website. **Operations at this facility include:** Administration; Sales; Service.

NATIONAL CITY BANK
301 SW Adams Street, Peoria IL 61602. 309/655-5000. **Contact:** Human Resources. **World Wide Web address:** http://www.nationalcity.com. **Description:** A branch of the largest banks in the Midwest. Founded in 1845. **NOTE:** Apply online at the corporate website. **Operations at this facility include:** Private Client Group and NatCity Investments.

NATIONAL EDUCATION TRAINING GROUP (NETG)
1751 West Diehl Road, Suite 200, Naperville IL 60563. 630/369-3000. **Toll-free phone:** 877/561-6384. **Fax:** 630/983-4877. **Contact:** Human Resources. **World Wide Web address:** http://www.netg.com. **Description:** A source of products and services for training and education in the areas of advanced technologies. **NOTE:** Apply online. **Positions advertised include:** Corporate/Financial Analyst; Senior Systems Specialist; Lead Product Development Manager; Contract Analyst; Senior Software Engineer. **Corporate headquarters location:** This location. **Parent company:** Thomson Corporation.

NATIONAL METALWARES INC.
900 North Russell Avenue, Aurora IL 60506. 630/892-9000. **Fax:** 630/892-2573. **Contact:** Marietta Ryan, Management Recruiter. **E-mail address:** info@nationalmetalwares.com. **World Wide Web address:** http://www.nationalmetalwares.com. **Description:** Manufactures fabricated steel tubing and components. **Corporate headquarters location:** This location. **Parent company:** Varlen Corporation.

NATIONAL-LOUIS UNIVERSITY
1000 Capitol Drive, Wheeling IL 60090. 847/465-0575. **Fax:** 847/465-5610. **Recorded jobline:** 847/465-5400. **Contact:** Human Resources. **World Wide Web address:** http://www.nl.edu. **Description:** A university offering undergraduate and graduate programs to approximately 1,600 students. **NOTE:** See website for job postings and contact information. Entry-level positions, part-time jobs, and second and third shifts are offered. **Positions advertised include:** Administrative Assistant; Enrollment Representative; Associate Director of Alumni Relations; Director of School-College Relations; Construction Manager. **Office hours:** Monday - Friday, 8:30 a.m. - 4:30 p.m. **Corporate headquarters location:** This location. **Other area locations:** Chicago IL; Evanston IL. **Other U.S. locations:** Washington DC; Orlando FL; Tampa FL; Atlanta GA; St. Louis MO; Milwaukee WI.

NEIGHBORCARE
1250 East Diehl Road, Suite 208, Naperville IL 60563. 630/245-4800. **Fax:** 630/505-1319. **Contact:** Human Resources. **World Wide Web address:** http://www.neighborcare.com. **Description:** An institutional pharmacy provider that offers services such as infusion therapy, drug distribution, patient management, educational services, and consulting services for managing health care costs. **Corporate headquarters location:** Baltimore MD.

NETWORK CHICAGO
5400 North St. Louis Avenue, Chicago IL 60625-4698. 773/583-5000. **Fax:** 773/583-5300. **Recorded jobline:** 773/509-5333. **Contact:** Laura Backus, Vice President, Human Resources. **E-mail address:** job@networkchicago.com. **World Wide Web address:** http://www.networkchicago.com. **Description:** Owns and operates WTTW Channel 11, The Chicago Production Center, and WFMT & The Radio Networks. **NOTE:** E-mail or fax resumes to Ms. Backus. Resumes may also be mailed to her at Window To the World Communications, Inc., 5400 North St. Louis Avenue, Chicago IL 60625. **Special programs:** Internships. **Corporate headquarters location:** This location.

NEW HOLLAND CONSTRUCTION
245 East North Avenue, Carol Stream IL 60188. 630/260-4000. **Contact:** Human Resources. **World Wide Web address:** http://www.newholland.com. **Description:** Distributes parts for industrial equipment including tractors and backhoes.

NEW YORK & COMPANY
4190-E North Harlem Avenue, Chicago IL 60634. 773/625-9684. **Contact:** Human Resources. **E-mail address:** recruiting@nyandcompany.com. **World Wide Web address:** http://www.nyandcompany.com. **Description:** New York & Company sells moderately priced women's fashions through a chain of retail stores. **NOTE:** See website for corporate job listings. To apply for retail positions, visit the nearest store location. **Operations at this facility include:** This location houses administrative offices. **Parent company:** The Limited, Inc.

NEWARK ELECTRONICS
4801 North Ravenswood Avenue, Chicago IL 60640. 773/784-5100. **Fax:** 773/907-5218. **Contact:** Human Resources. **World Wide Web address:** http://www.newark.com. **Description:** An electronics distributor with sales offices located throughout North America. **Positions advertised include:** Customer Database Specialist; Senior Financial Analyst; Director of Product Management; Government Associate Marketing Manager. **Corporate headquarters location:** Leeds, England. **Operations at this facility include:** Administration; Divisional Headquarters.

NEWARK INONE
1919 South Highland Avenue, A320, Lombard IL 60148-6119. **Toll-free phone:** 800/263-9275. **Fax:** 630/424-8048. **Contact:** Human Resources. **E-mail address:** chicago@newarkinone.com. **World Wide Web address:** http://www.newark.com. **Description:** A sales office of the electronics distributor Newark Electronics. **Positions advertised include:** Account Representative.

NEWELL RUBBERMAID
29 East Stephenson Street, Freeport IL 61032. 815/235-4171. **Contact:** Human Resources. **World Wide Web address:** http://www.newellco.com. **Description:** A manufacturer of housewares, hardware, home furnishings, office products, hair accessories, beauty organizers, picture frames, specialty glass products, and industrial plastics. **NOTE:** This company has facilities throughout Illinois and the Midwest area. See website for job listings and apply online. **Corporate headquarters location:** This location. **Operations at this facility include:** Administration. **Listed on:** New York Stock Exchange. **Stock exchange symbol:** NWL.

THE NEWS SUN
2383 North Delany Road, Waukegan, IL 60087. 847/336-7000. **Fax:** 847/249-7254. **Contact:** Chris Cashman, Managing Editor. **World Wide Web address:** http://www.suburbanchicagonews.com. **Description:** A daily newspaper that serves Waukegan and Lake counties. **Corporate headquarters location:** This location. **Other U.S. locations:** Lake Villa IL; Libertyville IL. **Parent company:** The Copley Press (La Jolla CA) publishes 45 newspapers nationwide. **Operations at this facility include:** Administration.

NICOR GAS
1844 West Ferry Road, Naperville IL 60563. 630/983-8676. **Contact:** Human Resources. **E-mail address:** nigashr@nigas.com. **World Wide Web address:** http://www.nicorinc.com. **Description:** One of the nation's largest gas distribution companies. NICOR Gas delivers natural gas to more than 1.8 million customers including transportation service, gas storage, and gas supply backup to approximately 18,000 commercial and industrial customers. **NOTE:** Apply online. Entry-level positions are offered. **Positions advertised include:** Meter Reader; General Clerk Legal Secretary; HVAC Install Helper; Accountant; Credit Analyst; Mapping Analyst; Risk Analyst; Sourcing Specialist; Staff Manager. **Special programs:** Internships. **Corporate headquarters location:** This location. **Other area locations:** Bellwood IL; Crystal Lake IL; Glen Ellyn IL; Glenview IL; Glenwood IL; Joliet IL; Rockford IL. **Parent company:** NICOR Inc. (also at this location). **Operations at this facility include:** Administration; Regional Headquarters; Research and Development; Sales. **Listed on:** New York Stock Exchange. **Stock exchange symbol:** GAS.

NISSAN FORKLIFT CORPORATION, NORTH AMERICA
240 North Prospect Street, Marengo IL 60152-3298. 815/568-0061. **Toll-free phone:** 800/871-LIFT. **Fax:** 815/568-0181. **Contact:** Human Resources Manager. **E-mail address:** careers@nfcna.com. **World Wide Web address:** http://www.nissanforklift.com. **Description:** Manufactures forklifts including electric-powered and internal combustion engines. Founded in 1988. **NOTE:** Cover letters and resumes may be mailed, faxed or e-mailed. Entry-level positions, part-time jobs, and second shifts are offered. **Positions advertised include:** Parts Marketing Manager; Product Service Specialist; Design/Product Engineer; Electrical Project Engineer. **Special programs:** Internships; Summer Jobs. **Office hours:** Monday - Friday, 8:00 a.m. - 5:00 p.m. **Corporate headquarters location:** This location. **International locations:** Japan; Spain. **Parent company:** Nissan Motor Company, Ltd. **Operations at this facility include:** Administration; Manufacturing; Research and Development; Sales; Service. **Listed on:** Privately held.

NORTH AMERICAN COMPANY FOR LIFE AND HEALTH INSURANCE
525 West Van Buren, Chicago IL 60607. 312/648-7600. **Toll-free phone:** 800/733-2524. **Fax:** 312/648-7765. **Contact:** Michael Haley, Vice President of Human Resources. **E-mail address:** mhaley@nacolah.com. **World Wide Web address:** http://www.nacolah.com. **Description:** Provides a variety of annuities and individual life insurance policies. **Positions advertised include:** Agency Services Associate/Consultant; Marketing Communications Specialist. **Corporate headquarters location:** This location. **Other U.S. locations:** Woodland Hills CA; Garden City NY. **Operations at this facility include:** Administration; Sales; Service. **Listed on:** Privately held.

NORTH CENTRAL REGIONAL EDUCATIONAL LAB INC.
1120 East Diehl Road, Suite 200, Naperville IL 60563. 630/649-6500. **Contact:** Human Resources. **E-mail address:** jobs@learningpt.org. **World Wide Web address:** http://www.ncrel.org. **Description:** A nonprofit organization that promotes education by providing information access through research-based resources to teachers, parents, students, and policymakers. Founded in 1984. **NOTE:** For job listings, visit http://www.learningpt.org/employ/. **Positions advertised include:** Applied Research and Development Director; Program Specialist; Senior Research Associate; Program Associate.

NORTHEASTERN ILLINOIS UNIVERSITY
5500 North St. Louis Avenue, Chicago IL 60625. 773/583-4050. **Contact:** Human Resources. **World Wide Web address:** http://www.neiu.edu. **Description:** A state university serving more than 10,000 commuter students with over 80 graduate and undergraduate programs. **NOTE:** See website for job listings and contact information and application requirements. **Positions advertised include:** Associate Director of Admissions; Clinical Psychologist of Counseling Office; Director of Public Safety; Professor (Various); Assistant Professor (Various); Secretary.

NORTHERN ILLINOIS UNIVERSITY
1515 West Lincoln Highway, De Kalb IL 60115. 815/753-6021. **Contact:** Human Resources. **World Wide Web address:** http://www.niu.edu. **Description:** A university comprised of seven colleges offering more than 100 graduate and undergraduate programs to approximately 23,000 students. **NOTE:** See web site for job listings, contact information and application procedures. **Positions advertised include:** Assistant Area Coordinator; Professor (Various); Assistant Professor (Various); Information Technology Associate; Route Driver; Secretary.

THE NORTHERN TRUST COMPANY
50 South LaSalle Street, Chicago IL 60675. 312/630-6000. **Contact:** Human Resources. **World Wide Web address:** http://www.ntrs.com. **Description:** A full-service bank engaged in commercial lending services, trust services, financial services, bond services, financial management, and other related services. **NOTE:** This company has branches throughout Illinois. See its website for jobs listings and location information. Apply online for open positions. **Positions advertised include:** Private Banker; Marketing Representative; Broker; Process Manager; Teller Services Team Leader. **Special programs:** Internships. **Corporate headquarters location:** This location.

NORTHFIELD LABORATORIES, INC.
1560 Sherman Avenue, Suite 1000, Evanston IL 60201-4422. 847/864-3500. **Fax:** 847/864-0353. **Contact:** Human Resources. **World Wide Web address:** http://www.northfieldlabs.com. **Description:** Develops chemically altered human hemoglobin as an alternative for blood transfusion where acute blood loss has occurred. The company markets PolyHeme, a blood substitute product that carries as much oxygen and loads and unloads oxygen in the same manner as transfused blood. **Listed on:** NASDAQ. **Stock exchange symbol:** NFLD.

NORTHROP GRUMMAN CORPORATION
600 Hicks Road, Room U-3100, Rolling Meadows IL 60008. 847/259-9600. **Contact:** Human Resources. **E-mail address:** northgrum@rpc.webhire.com. **World Wide Web address:** http://www.northropgrumman.com. **Description:** Northrop Grumman makes military aircraft, commercial aircraft parts, and electronic systems. Northrop Grumman has developed the B-2 Spirit Stealth Bomber, as well as parts for the F/A-18 and the Boeing 747. Other operations include computer systems development for management and scientific applications and radar equipment. **NOTE:** See website for job listings and to apply online. **Positions advertised include:** Rates and Budgets; Mechanical Technician; Business Planner; Electronics Engineer; Systems Engineer. **Special programs:** Internships. **Corporate headquarters location:** Los Angeles CA. **Operations at this facility include:** This location is engaged in the manufacturing of electronic countermeasures for military applications. **Listed on:** New York Stock Exchange. **Stock exchange symbol:** NOC.

NORTHSTAR AEROSPACE
WINDSOR DIVISION
6006 West 73rd Street, Bedford Park IL 60638. 708/728-2000. **Fax:** 708/728-2009. **Contact:** Human Resources. **World Wide Web address:** http://www.windsor.northstar-aerospace.com. **Description:** Manufactures parts for helicopters including transmissions, gear boxes, and flap drives.

NORTHWESTERN MEMORIAL HOSPITAL
251 East Huron Street, Chicago IL 60611. 312/908-2000. **Contact:** Human Resources. **World Wide Web address:** http://www.nmh.org. **Description:** A hospital offering a variety of specialized services ranging from preventive medicine to organ transplantation. Northwestern Memorial also serves as the teaching hospital for Northwestern University Medical School. **NOTE:** See website for job listings and contact information. **Special programs:** Internship.

NORTHWESTERN UNIVERSITY
720 University Place, Evanston IL 60208. 847/491-7507. **Contact:** Human Resources. **E-mail address:** resume@northwestern.edu. **World Wide Web address:** http://www.nwu.edu. **Description:** One of the country's largest private research universities. The university offers academic specialties in 12 colleges to its 17,700 students. **NOTE:** See website for job listings and contact information. **Positions advertised include:** Administrative Secretary; Animal Care Technician; Group Leader; Library Assistant; Research Technologist; Program Assistant.

NK SEEDS
5300 Katrine Avenue, Downers Grove IL 60515-4095. 630/969-6300. **Fax:** 630/969-6373. **Contact:** Human Resources. **World Wide Web address:** http://www.nk-us.com. **Description:** A horticulture broker. **Special programs:** Internships. **Corporate headquarters location:** The Netherlands. **Parent company:** Syngenta. **Operations at this facility include:** Administration; Manufacturing; Research and Development; Sales. **Listed on:** Privately held.

NUARC COMPANY INC.
One North 372 Main Street, Glen Ellyn IL 60137. 847/967-4400. **Toll-free phone:** 800/962-8883. **Contact:** Human Resources. **World Wide Web address:** http://www.mrprint.com/nuarc. **Description:** Manufactures graphic arts equipment such as exposure systems. **Corporate headquarters location:** This location.

NUTRASWEET COMPANY
200 World Trade Center, Merchandise Mart, Suite 900, Chicago IL 60654. 312/873-5000. **Contact:** Human Resources. **World Wide Web address:** http://www.nutrasweet.com. **Description:** Manufactures and markets agricultural products, performance chemicals used in consumer products, prescription pharmaceuticals, and food ingredients.

JOHN NUVEEN & COMPANY, INC.
333 West Wacker Drive, 34th Floor, Chicago IL 60606. 312/917-7700. **Toll-free phone:** 800/257-8787. **Fax:** 312/917-8049. **Contact:** Wendy Lindquist, Human Resources Assistant. **World Wide Web address:** http://www.nuveen.com. **Description:** An investment banking company. **Positions advertised include:** Advisor Support Manager; Internal Adviser Services Representative; Data Specialist; Sales; Administrative Assistant.

NYSTROM COMPANY
3333 Elston Avenue, Chicago IL 60618. 773/463-1144. **Toll-free phone:** 800/621-8086. **Fax:** 773/463-0515. **Contact:** Paige Johnson, Human Resources Director. **World Wide Web address:** http://www.nystromnet.com. **Description:** Manufactures and publishes charts, maps, globes, and other visual learning instruments. **Parent company:** Herff Jones, Inc. **Operations at this facility include:** This location is the main office for Herff Jones Education Division.

OAKTON COMMUNITY COLLEGE
1600 East Golf Road, Des Plaines IL 60016. 847/635-1675 **Fax:** 847/635-1764. **Contact:** Human Resources. **E-mail address:** hr@oakton.edu. **World Wide Web address:** http://www.oakton.edu. **Description:** A community college offering programs for students who are planning to transfer to a four-year institution. The college also offers training courses and career programs. **NOTE:** See website for job listings, contact information and application form. **Positions advertised include:** Director of Resource Development; Admission Specialist; Health Services Manager; Learning Center Specialist; Faculty (Various); System Director.

O'BRYAN BROTHERS
4220 West Belmont Avenue, Chicago IL 60641. 773/283-3000. **Contact:** Eva Vollrath, Human Resources Director. **Description:** Manufactures ladies' loungewear and lingerie. **Corporate headquarters location:** This location.

OCE-USA, INC.
1800 Bruning Drive West, Itasca IL 60143. 630/351-2900. **Toll-free phone:** 800/445-3526. **Contact:** Human Resources. **World Wide Web address:** http://www.oceusa.com. **Description:** The company manufactures office printers, high-speed printing systems, copy machines, and scanners. **NOTE:** Resumes should be directed to Jim Sunberg, Director of Staffing and Organizational Development, 5450 North Cumberland, Chicago IL 60656. Interested jobseekers may also apply online at the company's website. **Positions advertised include:** Staffing Specialist; Customer Delivery Coordinator Manager; Inventory Analyst; Display Graphics Sales Executive. **Corporate headquarters location:** Chicago IL. **Operations at this facility include:** This location is a sales office. **Number of employees at this location:** 3,000.

OGILVY & MATHER
111 East Wacker Drive, Chicago IL 60601. 312/856-8200.**Fax:** 312/856-8420. **Recorded jobline:** 212/237-5627. **Contact:** Human Resources. **World Wide Web address:** http://www.ogilvy.com. **Description:** An advertising agency. **Other U.S. locations:** New York NY. **Parent company:** WWP.

OLD REPUBLIC INTERNATIONAL CORPORATION
307 North Michigan Avenue, Chicago IL 60601. 312/346-8100. **Fax:** 312/726-0309. **Contact:** Human Resources Director. **World Wide Web address:** http://www.oldrepublic.com. **Description:** An insurance holding company. **Corporate headquarters location:** This location. **International locations:** Canada; Hong Kong; Puerto Rico. **Listed on:** New York Stock Exchange.

OLD SECOND NATIONAL BANK
37 South River Street, Aurora IL 60506. 630/892-0202. **Contact:** Bob Dicosola, Director of Human Resources. **World Wide Web address:** http://www.o2bancorp.com. **E-mail address:** rdicosola@o2bancorp.com. **Description:** A full-service bank whose services include savings bonds; investment services; large commercial, business, personal, student, parent PLUS, and automobile loans; and wire transfer services. **NOTE:** See website for job listings and contact information. For general resume submissions, e-mail or write to Mr. Dicosola. **Positions advertised include:** Credit Analyst.

ONEAC CORPORATION
27944 North Bradley Road, Libertyville IL 60048. 847/816-6000. **Toll-free phone:** 800/327-801. **Fax:** 847/680-5124. **Contact:** Human Resources. **E-mail address:** hr@oneac.com. **World Wide Web address:** http://www.oneac.com. **Description:** Manufactures power conditioners that protect electrical systems from lightning and other electrical surges. **NOTE:** Mail resumes and cover letters. **Positions advertised include:** Manufacturing Engineer.

W.E. O'NEIL CONSTRUCTION COMPANY
2751 North Clybourn Avenue, Chicago IL 60614. 773/755-1611. **Fax:** 773/327-4806. **Contact:** Pat McGowan, Organizational Development Director. **E-mail address:** chicago.careers@oneilind.com. **World Wide Web address:** http://www.oneilind.com. **Description:** A general construction company specializing in construction management, general contracting, design/build, and preconstruction. **NOTE:**

Jobseekers should indicate the department in which they are interested in a cover letter. **Corporate headquarters location:** This location. **Parent company:** O'Neil Industries, Inc. (also at this location).

OPW FUEL MANAGEMENT SYSTEMS
6900 Santa Fe Drive, Hodgkins IL 60525. 708/485-4200. **Contact:** Human Resources. **World Wide Web address:** http://www.petrovend.com. **Description:** Develops automated fuel systems for oil companies. **NOTE:** Apply online. **Positions advertised include:** Service Technician.

OTIS ELEVATOR COMPANY
651 West Washington Boulevard, Suite 1-N, Chicago IL 60661. 312/454-1616. **Fax:** 312/454-0217. **Contact:** Gretchen E. Simpson, Human Resources Manager. **World Wide Web address:** http://www.otis.com. **Description:** One of the world's largest manufacturers of elevators and escalators. Founded in 1853. **NOTE:** This company has offices throughout the Greater Chicago area and Illinois. See website for job listings and contact information. **Positions advertised include:** Sales Representative; Project Manager. **Corporate headquarters location:** Farmington CT. **Parent company:** United Technologies.

OTTAWA DENTAL LABORATORY
1304 Starfire Drive, P.O. Box 771, Ottawa IL 61350. **Toll-free phone:** 800/851-8239. **Fax:** 815/434-0760. **Contact:** Joanie Bretag, Human Resources. **E-mail address:** hrodl@ottawadentallab.com. **World Wide Web address:** http://www.ottawadentallab.com. **Description:** A dental lab that manufactures dentures, crowns, bridges, and other dental products. **NOTE:** Apply online.

OUR LADY OF THE RESURRECTION MEDICAL CENTER
5645 West Addison Street, Chicago IL 60634. 773/282-7000. **Recorded jobline:** 877/737-4636(option 9). **Fax:** 773/794-8467. **Contact:** Human Resources. **World Wide Web address:** http://www.reshealth.org. **Description:** A 288-bed, acute care, community hospital. **NOTE:** The hospital only accepts resumes for open positions. See website for job listings and apply online. Evening and part-time positions offered. **Positions advertised include:** Activities Assistant; Certified Nursing Assistant; Environmental Service Worker; Nurse Practitioner; Occupational Therapist.

R.S. OWENS AND COMPANY INC.
5535 North Lynch Avenue, Chicago IL 60630. 773/282-6000. **Contact:** Human Resources. **World Wide Web address:** http://www.rsowens.com. **Description:** Manufactures trophies, plaques, and awards. **Corporate headquarters location:** This location.

OWENS-ILLINOIS
315 Tolle Lane, Godfrey IL 62035. 618/466-8811. **Contact:** Human Resources. **World Wide Web address:** http://www.o-i.com. **Description:** Owens-Illinois is a diversified manufacturer of glass making equipment. **Operations at this facility include:** This location manufactures machines used to manufacture glass containers. **NOTE:** See website for job listings. Entry-level positions offered.

OXXFORD CLOTHES
1220 West Van Buren Street, Chicago IL 60607. 312/829-3600. **Toll-free phone:** 800/525-4727. **Fax:** 312/829-6075. **Contact:** Human Resources. **World Wide Web address:** http://www.oxxfordclothes.com. **Description:** A manufacturer of hand-sewn suits and coats for men. **NOTE:** Entry-level positions are offered. **Parent company:** Tom James Company. **Operations at this facility include:** Administration; Manufacturing; Sales.

OZINGA BROTHERS
2255 South Lumber Street, Chicago IL 606016. 312/432-8100. **Fax:** 312/432-8101. **Contact:** Human Resources. **World Wide Web address:** http://www.ozinga.com. **Description:** Manufactures concrete and plaster materials for use in construction. Founded in 1928. **NOTE:** See website for job listings, contact information and application forms. Fax or e-mail resumes. **Positions advertised include:** Quality Control Technician; Driver.

PC WHOLESALE
444 Scott Drive, Bloomingdale IL 60108. 630/307-1700. **Fax:** 630/307-2450. **Contact:** Human Resources. **World Wide Web address:** http://www.pcwholesale.com. **Description:** Distributes computer systems, peripherals, and supplies to an international client base. PC Wholesale also offers support services. Founded in 1989. **Corporate headquarters location:** This location. **Other U.S. locations:** MN; NJ: GA.

PACKER ENGINEERING INC.
1950 North Washington Street, Naperville IL 60563. 630/505-5722. **Toll-free phone:** 800/323-0114. **Fax:** 630/505-3010. **Contact:** Human Resources. **E-mail address:** pejobs@packereng.com. **World Wide Web address:** http://www.packereng.com. **Description:** A multidisciplinary engineering, consulting, and technical services company. The practice includes failure analysis; accident investigation and reconstruction; fire/explosion cause and origin studies; product design evaluations; process design assessments; customized and routine testing; applied research; commercial product development; and litigation support. **NOTE:** Apply online for all positions. Entry-level positions are offered. **Special programs:** Internships. **Internship information:** Paid summer internships are available through The Packer Foundation. For additional information, visit the Foundation's website at http://www.packerfoundation.com/internships. **Corporate headquarters location:** This location. **Other U.S. locations:** Nationwide. **Parent company:** The Packer Group.

PACTIV CORPORATION
1900 West Field Court, Lake Forest IL 60045. 847/482-2000. **Toll-free phone:** 888/828-2850. **Fax:** 847/482-4738. **Contact:** Human Resources. **World Wide Web address:** http://www.pactiv.com. **Description:** A worldwide manufacturer of paper, corrugated paper, paperboard, aluminum, and plastic packaging material. Products are used in the packaging of food, paper and paper products, metal products, rubber and plastics, automotive products, point-of-purchase displays, soap, detergent, and food products, as well as residential construction. Brands include Hefty paper and plastic products. **Special programs:** Internships. **Corporate headquarters location:** This location. **Listed on:** New York Stock Exchange. **Stock exchange symbol:** PTV.

PALOS COMMUNITY HOSPITAL
12251 South 80th Avenue, Palos Heights IL 60463. 708/923-4880. **Fax:** 708/923-4888. **Recorded jobline:** 708/923-8088. **Contact:** Human Resources. **World Wide Web address:** http://www.paloshospital.org. **Description:** A community hospital. For professional positions, e-mail resumes to holly_brasher@paloscommunityhospital.org. For support staff positions, e-mail resumes to diane_jorgensen@paoloscommunityhospital.org. For nursing positions, e-mail regina_sibley@paloscommunityhospital.org. Part-time jobs and second and third shifts are offered. **Special programs:** Volunteers.

J.S. PALUCH COMPANY, INC.
3708 River Road, Suite 400, Franklin Park IL 60131. 847/678-9300. **Contact:** Linda Kaup, Manager of Human Resources. **World Wide Web address:** http://www.jspaluch.com. **Description:** Publishes and prints religious material such as computer software, educational bulletins, Sunday bulletins, and worship aids.

PANASONIC
1707 North Randall Road, Elgin IL 60123. 847/468-4010. **Contact:** Human Resources. **World Wide Web address:** http://www.panasonic.com. **Description:** Manufactures and sells consumer electronic appliances such as televisions, microwave ovens, and videotape machines. **Positions advertised include:** Sales Representative.

PANDUIT CORPORATION
17301 South Ridgeland Avenue, Tinley Park IL 60477. 708/532-1800. **Toll-free phone:** 888/506-5400. **Fax:** 708/532-1811. **Contact:** Cheryl Lewis, Supervisor of Corporate Recruiting. **World Wide Web address:** http://www.panduit.com. **Description:** Manufactures electrical wiring components, electrical accessories, and communications products. **NOTE:** See website for job listings and to submit resume. Entry-level positions are offered. **Special programs:** Internships. **Corporate headquarters location:** This location. **Other U.S. locations:** Nationwide. **International locations:** Worldwide. **Listed on:** Privately held.

PARKER HANNIFIN CORPORATION
595 Schelter Road, Lincolnshire IL 60069. 847/821-1500. **Fax:** 847/821-7600. **Contact:** Human Resources. **World Wide Web address:** http://www.parker.com. **Description:** An international fluid power firm that manufactures components and replacement parts for hydraulic and pneumatic power systems that are used by the automotive, aviation, industrial, and marine industries. Parker Hannifin has also entered the biomedical market to research and help produce equipment and products for treating chronic illnesses. **Operations at this facility include:** This location manufactures truck hydraulic parts and systems.

PARKER HANNIFIN CORPORATION
500 South Wolf Road, Des Plaines IL 60016. 847/298-2400. **Contact:** Lou Ford, Human Resources Manager. **E-mail address:** cylmktg@parker.com. **World Wide Web address:** http://www.parker.com. **Description:** Parker Hannifin Corporation is an international fluid power firm that manufactures components and replacement parts for hydraulic and pneumatic power systems that are used by the automotive, aviation, industrial, and marine industries. Parker Hannifin has also entered the biomedical market to research and help produce equipment and products for treating chronic illnesses. **NOTE:** To apply, visit the company's website. **Positions advertised include:** Senior Design Engineer. **Corporate headquarters location:** Cleveland OH. **Other U.S. locations:** Nationwide. **Operations at this facility include:** This location is a sales office for the Cylinder Division.

PARKVIEW METAL PRODUCTS
4931 West Armitage Avenue, Chicago IL 60639. 773/622-8414. **Fax:** 73/622-8446. **Contact:** Human Resources. **E-mail address:** HRCHICAGO@parky.com. **World Wide Web address:** http://www.parkviewmetal.com. **Description:** A metal stampings manufacturer servicing metal trades industries nationwide. Parkview Metal Products also builds and maintains progressive dies. **Special programs:** Internships. **Corporate headquarters location:** This location. **Other U.S. locations:** San Marcos TX. **International locations:** Mexico. **Operations at this facility include:** Administration; Manufacturing; Sales.

PARSONS TRANSPORTATION GROUP
10 South Riverside, Suite 400, Chicago IL 60606. 312/930-5100. **Fax:** 312/930-0018. **Contact:** Technical Recruiter. **World Wide Web address:** http://www.parsons.com. **Description:** Designs and builds roads, bridges, highways, and other transportation infrastructure. **NOTE:** Apply online. **Positions advertised include:** Project Manager; Associate Engineer; Principal Designer. **Corporate headquarters location:** Washington DC.

PATRICK ENGINEERING
4970 Varsity Drive, Lisle IL 60532. 630/790-7200. **Fax:** 630/790-1681. **Contact:** Human Resources. **E-mail address:** hr_jobs@patrickengineering.com. **World Wide Web address:** http://www.patrickengineering.com. **Description:** Offers solid waste planning, architecture, surveying, and engineering services in the civil, transportation, environmental, geotechnical, hydraulic, water resources, structural, and electrical sectors. Founded in 1979. **Other area locations:** Chicago IL; Springfield IL. **Other U.S. locations:** MI: WI; PA.

PAYMASTER TECHNOLOGIES, INC.
900 Pratt Boulevard, Elk Grove Village IL 60007. 773/878-9200. **Toll-free phone:** 800/462-4477. **Fax:** 847/758-0123. **Contact:** Human Resources. **E-mail address:** paymaster@paymastertech.com. **World Wide Web address:** http://www.paymastertech.com. **Description:** Manufactures and sells check-writing machines and check protectors. **Corporate headquarters location:** This location.

PEKIN HOSPITAL
600 South 13th Street, Pekin IL 61554. 309/347-1151. **Fax:** 309/347-1249. **Contact:** Human Resources. **E-mail address:** hr@phs1.org. **World Wide Web address:** http://www.pekinhospital.org. **Description:** A hospital engaged in allied health services. **NOTE:** See website for job listings and online application. **Positions advertised include:** Decision Support Analyst; House Supervisor; RN(Various); Surgical Technologist. **Operations at this facility include:** Administration; Service.

PEOPLESOFT
233 South Wacker Drive, 45th Floor, Chicago IL 60606. 312/651-8000. **Contact:** Human Resources. **World Wide Web address:** http://www.peoplesoft.com. **Description:** PeopleSoft designs, markets, and supports a wide variety of business software applications. **Corporate headquarters location:** Pleasanton CA. **Other U.S. locations:** Nationwide. **International locations:** Worldwide. **Parent company:** Oracle. **Operations at this facility include:** This location serves as the Midwestern U.S. Regional Headquarters for the company. **Listed on:** NASDAQ. **Stock exchange symbol:** PSFT.

PEORIA JOURNAL STAR, INC.
One News Plaza, Peoria IL 61643. 309/686-3125. **Fax:** 309/686-3297. **Contact:** Julie O'Donnnell, Human Resources Manager. **E-mail address:** jodonnell@pjstar.com. **World Wide Web address:** http://www.pjstar.com. **Description:** Publishes a daily newspaper with a circulation of 72,000.

PEPPERIDGE FARM, INC.
230 Second Street, Downers Grove IL 60515. 630/968-4000. **Contact:** Mary Harris, Human Resources Manager. **World Wide Web address:** http://www.pepperidgefarm.com. **Description:** Manufactures and distributes a range of fresh and frozen baked goods and confections including bread, cookies, cakes, pastries, and crackers. **NOTE:** Apply online at Campbell's website: http://www.careers.campbellsoupcompany.com. **Parent company:** Campbells Soup. **Operations at this facility include:** This location is a bakery.

PEPSIAMERICAS, INC.
3501 Algonquin Road, Rolling Meadows IL 60008. 847/818-5000. **Contact:** Human Resources. **World Wide Web address:** http://www.pepsiamericas.com. **Description:** PepsiAmericas is a holding company for food and beverages. **Corporate headquarters location:** This location. **NOTE:** Apply online. **Positions advertised include:** Sales Specialist; Logistics Analyst; Warehouse Manager. **Operations at this facility include:** This location houses administrative offices.

PEPSI-COLA BOTTLING COMPANY
1881 Bilter Road, Aurora IL 60504. 630/898-1300. **Fax:** 630/898-1717. **Contact:** Human Resources. **World Wide Web address:** http://www.pepsiamericas.com. **Description:** A bottling facility and a division of Pepsi-Cola Company. **NOTE:** Apply online. **Other U.S. locations:** Nationwide. **Parent company:** PepsiCo, Inc. (Purchase NY) consists of Frito-Lay Company, Pepsi-Cola Company, Quaker Oats, and Tropicana Products, Inc. **Operations at this facility include:** This location is a bottling plant. **Listed on:** New York Stock Exchange. **Stock exchange symbol:** PEP.

PERKINELMER
2200 Warrenville Road, Downers Grove IL 60515. 630/969-6000. **Toll-free phone:** 800/323-5891. **Fax:** 630/969-6511. **Contact:** Human Resources. **World Wide Web address:** http://www.perkinelmer.com. **Description:** Manufactures biomedical instruments that test blood for disease including the scintillation gamma counter. Primary customers are hospitals and universities located worldwide. **NOTE:** Final Acceptance Testing; Electrical Engineering Manager; Technical Services Manager.

PERKINS & WILL
330 North Wabash Avenue, Suite 3600, Chicago IL 60611. 312/755-0770. **Toll-free phone:** 800/837-9455. **Fax:** 312/755-4788. **Contact:** Human Resources. **E-mail address:** hr@perkinswill.com. **World Wide Web address:** http://www.perkinswill.com. **Description:** An architectural, interior design and planning firm that serves both commercial and industrial companies. The company also provides an IDP/IDEP program for unlicensed designers. This location also hires seasonally. Founded in 1935. **NOTE:** Mail, fax or e-mail resumes. Entry-level positions and part-time jobs are offered. **Positions advertised include:** Environmental Graphics Designer; Marketing Coordinator. **Corporate headquarters location:** This location. **Other U.S. locations:** Los Angeles CA; Miami FL; Atlanta GA; Minneapolis MN; Charlotte NC; New York NY. **International locations:** Paris, France. **Subsidiaries include:** TY Lin, Inc. **Parent company:** Dar Al Handesah. **Listed on:** Privately held.

PETERSEN ALUMINUM CORPORATION
1005 Tonne Road, Elk Grove Village IL 60007. 847/228-7150. **Contact:** Human Resources. **World Wide Web address:** http://www.pac-clad.com. **Description:** Manufactures and distributes aluminum and steel. Petersen Aluminum also manufactures roofing panels.

FERRO PFANSTIEHL LABORATORIES, INC.
1219 Glen Rock Avenue, Waukegan IL 60085. 847/623-0370. **Fax:** 847/623-9173. **Contact:** Human Resources. **E-mail address:** resume@ferro.com. **World Wide Web address:** http://www.ferro.com. **Description:** A chemical laboratory specializing in the production of carbohydrates and biological chemicals. Clients are primarily pharmaceutical companies. **NOTE:** See website for job requirements and e-mail resumes. **Corporate headquarters location:** Cleveland, OH. **Listed on:** New York Stock Exchange. **Stock exchange symbol:** FOE.

PFIZER
5500 Forest Hills Road, Rockford IL 61105. 815/877-8081. **Contact:** Human Resources. **World Wide Web address:** http://www.pfizer.com. **Description:** Pfizer is a leading pharmaceutical company that distributes products concerning cardiovascular health, central nervous system disorders, infectious diseases, and women's health worldwide. The company's brand-name products include Benadryl, Ben Gay, Cortizone, Desitin, Halls, Listerine, Sudafed, and Zantac 75. **NOTE:** This company has other locations in Illinois. See website for job listings and locations. Apply online. **Positions advertised include:** Buyer/Planner; Oncology Sales Consultant. **Corporate headquarters location:** New York NY. **Operations at this facility include:** This location manufactures gum. **Listed on:** New York Stock Exchange. **Stock exchange symbol:** PFE.

PHEASANT RUN RESORT & CONVENTION CENTER
4051 East Main Street, St. Charles IL 60174-5200. 630/584-6300. **Fax:** 630/762-0509. **Contact:** Human Resources. **E-mail address:** lbabusch@pheasantrun.com. **World Wide Web address:** http://www.pheasantrun.com. **Description:** A hotel and convention center. **NOTE:** Fax or e-mail resumes. Interested jobseekers may also apply in person at the Human Resources Office. **Positions advertise include:** Administrative Assistant; Cook; Bartender; Front Desk Agent; Rooms Director; Security. **Office hours:** Monday – Friday, 8:30 a.m. – 5:00 p.m. **Corporate headquarters location:** This location. **Operations at this facility include:** Sales; Service.

PILKINGTON COMPANY
20th and Center Streets, Ottawa IL 61350. 815/433-0932. **Fax:** 815/434-8088. **Contact:** Human Resources. **World Wide Web address:** http://www.pilkington.com. **Description:** Pilkington-Libby-Owens-Ford Company is a diversified manufacturer of fluid power and fluid systems components, automotive glass, flat and tinted glass products, decorative laminates, and molded plastics. **NOTE:** See website for job listings. **Listed on:** Privately held.

PIPER MARBURY RUDNICK & WOLFE LLP
203 North LaSalle Street, Suite 1400, Chicago IL 60601. 312/368-4000. **Fax:** 312/236-7516. **Contact:** Marguerite E. Strubing, Legal Recruiting Manager. **E-mail address:** marguerite.strubing@piperrudnick.com. **World Wide Web address:** http://www.piperrudnick.com. **Description:** A law firm specializing in bankruptcy, corporate, labor, insurance, and tax law. **Special programs:** Summer employment. **Other U.S. locations:** Nationwide.

PITNEY BOWES DOCUMENT MESSAGING TECHNOLOGIES
220 Western Court, Suite 100, Lisle IL 60532. 630/435-7500. **Contact:** Human Resources. **World Wide Web address:** http://www.pbdmt.com. **Description:** Develops information management software for customer service, marketing, and systems integration applications. **Parent company:** Pitney Bowes Inc.

PIZZA HUT OF AMERICA, INC.
4575 Weaver Parkway, Suite 200, Warrenville IL 60555. 630/791-1000. **Fax:** 630/955-0577. **Contact:** Human Resources. **World Wide Web address:** http://www.pizzahut.com. **Description:** Part of the large, worldwide restaurant chain. **NOTE:** Apply in person at this location or online at http://www.yum.com. **Positions advertised include:** Assistant Manager; Management Trainee. **Special programs:** Internships. **Other U.S. locations:** Nationwide. **Parent company:** Yum Brands.

PLASTOFILM INDUSTRIES, INC.
935 West Union Avenue, Wheaton IL 60187. 630/668-2838. **Contact:** Human Resources. **Description:** Manufactures plastic packaging for cosmetics, pharmaceuticals, toys, and small tools. **Corporate headquarters location:** Lincolnshire IL.

PLAYBOY ENTERPRISES
680 North Lake Shore Drive, 15th Floor, Chicago IL 60611. 312/751-8000. **Contact:** Human Resources. **World Wide Web address:** http://www.playboy.com. **Description:** Publishes and markets products in almost 200 countries through six business groups. The Casino Gaming Group has plans to open a club in London, England. The Catalog Group markets print and online versions of Critic's Choice Video and Collector's Choice Music Catalogs. The Entertainment Group operates Playboy TV networks and home video markets. Playboy.com INC. operates the company's Website. The Product Marketing Group markets accessories and apparel. The Publishing Group publishes *Playboy* magazine and books. **NOTE:** Apply online. **Listed on:** New York Stock Exchange. **Stock exchange symbol:** PLA.

PRECISION TWIST DRILL COMPANY
One Precision Plaza, P.O. Box 9000, Crystal Lake IL 60039. 815/459-2040. **Contact:** Human Resources Director. **World Wide Web address:** http://www.precisiontwistdrill.com. **Description:** Manufactures drills and cutting tools for the aerospace, automotive, and construction industries. **Corporate headquarters location:** This location. **Subsidiaries include:** Triumph Twist Drill Company. **Operations at this facility include:** Administration; Manufacturing; Research and Development; Sales. **Listed on:** Privately held.

PREMCOR INC.
201 East Hawthorne Street, Hartford IL 62048. 618/254-7301. **Fax:** 618/254-4661. Christine Carnicelli, Human Resources. **E-mail address:** christine.carnicelli@premcor.com. **World Wide Web address:** http://www.premcorinc.com. **Description:** Manufactures petroleum products. **NOTE:** Contact Ms. Carnicelli at 1700 East Putnam, Suite 400, Old Greenwich CT 06870, or via phone at 203/698-5649. **Positions advertised include:** Senior Safety Specialist; Electrician; Process Engineer. **Operations at this facility include:** This location is a terminal facility.

PRICEWATERHOUSECOOPERS
One North Wacker Drive, Chicago IL 60606. 312/298-2000. **Contact:** Human Resources. **World Wide Web address:** http://www.pwcglobal.com. **Description:** A location of one of the largest certified public accounting firms in the world. PricewaterhouseCoopers provides public accounting, business advisory, management consulting, and taxation services. **NOTE:** Apply online. **Corporate headquarters location:** New York NY. **Other U.S. locations:** Nationwide.

PRICEWATERHOUSECOOPERS
411 Hamilton Boulevard, Suite 1110, Peoria IL 61602-1135. 309/676-8557. **Contact:** Human Resources. **World Wide Web address:** http://www.pwcglobal.com. **Description:** A location of one of the largest certified public accounting firms in the world. PricewaterhouseCoopers provides public accounting, business advisory, management consulting, and taxation services. **NOTE:** Apply online. **Corporate headquarters location:** New York NY. **Other U.S. locations:** Nationwide.

PROCTOR HOSPITAL
5409 North Knoxville Avenue, Peoria IL 61614. 309/691-1062. **Fax:** 309/689-6062. **Contact:** Human Resources. **World Wide Web address:** http://www.proctor.org. **Description:** A 200-bed general hospital with a specialty addiction recovery clinic. **NOTE:** Entry-level, second- and third- shifts are offered. See website for job listings and application procedures. For nursing opportunities, contact Sheila Johnson at 309/683-6062. **Positions advertised include:** Linen Handler; Medical Lab Technician; Phlebotomist; RN (Various); LPN (Various).

PROVENA COVENANT MEDICAL CENTER
1400 West Park Street, Urbana IL 61801-2334. 217/337-2224. **Fax:** 217/337-2619. **Contact:** Human Resources. **World Wide Web address:** http://www.provenacovenant.org. **Description:** A 280-bed, nonprofit, acute care hospital. **NOTE:** Apply online. Entry-level positions are offered. **Positions advertised include:** Assistant to the President; Charge RN: Certified Occupational Therapy Assistant; Coder; Communication/Scheduler; Food Service Worker. **Corporate headquarters location:** Mokena IL. **Parent company:** Provena Health.

PROVENA MERCY CENTER FOR HEALTH CARE
1325 North Highland Avenue, Aurora IL 60506. 630/859-2222. **Contact:** Human Resource. **World Wide Web address:** http://www.provenamercy.com. **Description:** A 356-bed hospital offering general health and behavioral services. **NOTE:** Apply online. **Positions advertised include:** Central Scheduling; Clinical Coordinator; Intake Counselor; LPN; Physical Therapist; On-Call Social Worker.

PRUDENTIAL INSURANCE
1901 Butterfield Road, Suite 250, Downers Grove IL 60515. 630/493-0585. **Contact:** Human Resources. **World Wide Web address:** http://www.prudential.com. **Description:** Provides underwriting risk analysis and selection services for 18 midwestern and northeastern states; provides claims services for policyholders in several midwestern states; and provides nonclaims services to policyholders nationwide. Overall, Prudential Property & Casualty Insurance underwrites family automobile and homeowner policies. Founded in 1969. **NOTE:** Apply online. **Parent company:** Prudential Insurance Company of America.

PUBLICATIONS INTERNATIONAL LTD.
7373 North Cicero Avenue, Lincolnwood IL 60712. 847/676-3470. **Contact:** Human Resources. **World Wide Web address:** http://www.pubint.com. **Description:** A publisher of fiction, nonfiction, and consumer guides.

QUADRAMED
440 North Wells, Suite 505, Chicago IL 60610. 312/396-0700. **Toll-free phone:**

800/634-0800. **Fax:** 312/396-0800. **Contact:** Human Resources. **E-mail address:** resume@quadramed.com. **World Wide Web address:** http://www.quadramed.com. **Description:** Develops and markets specialized decision support software designed to improve the organizational and clinical effectiveness of hospitals, academic medical centers, managed care providers, large physician groups, and other health care providers. **NOTE:** See website for job listings. Apply online or e-mail resumes. Resumes may also be faxed to the company's corporate office in Santa Ana CA at 714/371-1700. **Positions advertised include:** Nurse Consultant; Support Analyst.

THE QUAKER OATS COMPANY
555 West Monroe, Suite 16-01, Chicago IL 60604. 312/821-1000. **Contact:** Human Resources. **World Wide Web address:** http://www.quakeroats.com. **Description:** A producer of grain-based foods and sports beverages. Products include Gatorade; Golden Grain pasta and rice; and Quaker Oats hot and ready-to-eat cereals, granola bars, and rice cakes. Founded in 1877. NOTE: Apply online. **Corporate headquarters location:** This location. **Other U.S. locations:** Nationwide. **International locations:** Worldwide. **Parent company:** Pepsico. **Listed on:** New York Stock Exchange. **Stock exchange symbol:** PEP.

QUEST DIAGNOSTICS INCORPORATED
1614 W. Central Road, Arlington Heights IL 60005. 847/342-0344. **Contact:** Human Resources. **World Wide Web address:** http://www.questdiagnostics.com. **Description:** Quest Diagnostics is one of the largest clinical laboratories in North America, providing a broad range of clinical laboratory services to health care clients that include physicians, hospitals, clinics, dialysis centers, pharmaceutical companies, and corporations. The company offers and performs tests on blood, urine, and other bodily fluids and tissues to provide information for health and well-being. **NOTE:** This company has locations throughout Illinois and the United States. See website for locations and job listings. **Operations at this facility include:** This location is a testing laboratory. **Listed on:** New York Stock Exchange. **Stock exchange symbol:** DGX.

QUEST DIAGNOSTICS INCORPORATED
37B East Center Street, Alton IL 62002. 618/465-5877. **Contact:** Human Resources. **World Wide Web address:** http://www.questdiagnostics.com. **Description:** Quest Diagnostics is one of the largest clinical laboratories in North America, providing a broad range of clinical laboratory services to health care clients that include physicians, hospitals, clinics, dialysis centers, pharmaceutical companies, and corporations. The company offers and performs tests on blood, urine, and other bodily fluids and tissues to provide information for health and well-being. **NOTE:** This company has locations throughout Illinois and the United States. See website for locations and job listings. **Operations at this facility include:** This location is a satellite blood-drawing laboratory.

QUINCY COMPRESSOR
3501 Wismann Lane, Quincy IL 62301. 217/222-7700. **Contact:** Tina Engelmeyer, Human Resources. **E-mail address:** Tina.Engelmeyer@quincycompressor.com. **World Wide Web address:** http://www.quincycompressor.com. **Description:** Manufactures and sells air compressors and vacuum pumps. Their products are used around the world in manufacturing plants, hospitals, and climate control systems. **Positions advertised include:** Customer Service Manager; Manufacturing Engineer; Market Specialist; Packaging Engineer. **Corporate headquarters location:** This location. **Other U.S. locations:** Bay Minette AL.

RLI CORPORATION
9025 North Lindbergh Drive, Peoria IL 61615-1431. 309/692-1000. **Fax:** 309/692-1068. **Contact:** Human Resources. **World Wide Web address:** http://www.rlicorp.com. **Description:** Underwrites property and casualty insurance policies. **NOTE:** Apply online for all positions. Part-time positions are offered. **Positions advertised include:** Graphic Designer; Paralegal; Applications Analyst; Post Press Technician. **Listed on:** New York Stock Exchange. **Stock exchange symbol:** RLI.

RSM MCGLADREY, INC.
191 North Wacker Drive, Suite 1400, Chicago IL 60606. 312/207-2124. **Contact:** Human Resources. **World Wide Web address:** http://www.rsmmcgladrey.com. **Description:** An accounting firm. **NOTE:** Apply online. **Positions advertised include:** Consulting Actuary; Programmer Analyst; Actuarial Analyst; Audit Senior Associate; Audit Manager.

RAGNAR BENSON INC.
250 South Northwest Highway, Park Ridge IL 60068-4252. 847/698-4900. **Fax:** 847/692-9320. **Contact:** Human Resources. **World Wide Web address:** http://www.ragnarbenson.com. **Description:** An engineering and construction firm that specializes in design-build, construction management, and general contracting. Founded in 1922. **Positions advertised include:** Project Superintendent.

RADIAN CORPORATION
6718 West Plank Road, Peoria IL 61604. 309/697-4400. **Contact:** Human Resources. **E-mail address:** careers@radiancorp.com. **World Wide Web address:** http://www.radiancorp.com. **Description:** Rohn Industries manufactures cabinets for housing electrical equipment; steel and concrete fencing; prefabricated concrete units; and cattle handling equipment, stalls, and corrals. **Operations at this facility include:** This location is the primary plant for the manufacturing of tower and pole products used to mount transmitting devices.

RAMADA PLAZA HOTEL O'HARE
6600 North Mannheim Road, Rosemont IL 60018. 847/827-5131. **Contact:** Human Resources. **World Wide Web address:** http://www.ramadaplazaohare.com. **Description:** A hotel and conference facility. Ramada has locations nationwide, including Stouffers/Renaissance Hotel Properties. **NOTE:** Entry-level positions are offered. **Special programs:** Internships; Training. **Corporate headquarters location:** Solon OH. **Other U.S. locations:** Nationwide. **Parent company:** Cendant Corporation. **Operations at this facility include:** Sales; Service.

RAND McNALLY & COMPANY
8255 North Central Park Avenue, Skokie IL 60076. 847/329-8100. **Toll-free phone:** 800/333-0136. **Fax:** 847/329-6361. **Contact:** Human Resources. **World Wide Web address:** http://www.randmcnally.com. **Description:** A book, map, and road atlas publisher. **NOTE:** Apply online. **Corporate headquarters location:** This location. **Positions advertised include:** Customer Service Representative; Senior Category Manager; National Account Manager; Internet Marketing Manager.

RAPID DISPLAYS
4300 West 47th Street, Chicago IL 60632. 800/356-5775. **Fax:** 773/927-1091. **Contact:** Human Resources. **World Wide Web address:** http://www.rapiddisplays.com. **Description:** Manufactures signs and advertising displays. Founded in 1938. **NOTE:** See website for job listings. Mail or fax resumes. **Positions advertised include:** Estimator; Design Technician; Illustrator; Account Executive; Customer Service. **Operations at this facility include:** This is a sales and production office.

RAULAND-BORG CORPORATION
3450 West Oakton Street, Skokie IL 60076. 847/679-0900. **Fax:** 847/679-0793. **Contact:** Human Resources. **E-mail address:** jobs@rauland.com. **World Wide Web address:** http://www.rauland.com. **Description:** Manufactures electronic communications and sound equipment. **Positions advertised include:** Regional Manager. **Corporate headquarters location:** This location. **Operations at this facility include:** Administration; Manufacturing; Research and Development.

RAYMOND PROFESSIONAL GROUP, INC.
550 West Van Buren Street, Suite 400, Chicago IL 60607. 312/935-3200. **Fax:** 312/935-3201. **Contact:** Human Resources. **World Wide Web address:** http://www.raymondgroup.com. **Description:** A multidisciplinary engineering consulting firm. Services include electrical, mechanical, and structural engineering.

RED BUD REGIONAL HOSPITAL
325 Spring Street, Red Bud IL 62278. 618/282-3831. **Contact:** Human Resources Assistant. **World Wide Web address:** http://www.redbudhospital.org. **Description:** An acute care hospital and a long-term, rehabilitative care, skilled nursing facility. **NOTE:** See website for job listings, contact information and application procedures. Second and third shifts are offered.

RE/MAX TEAM 2000
7130 West 127th Street, Palos Heights IL 60463. 708/361-5950. **Contact:** Human Resources. **World Wide Web address:** http://www.chicago-area-homes.com. **Description:** A residential and commercial real estate agency.

REED BUSINESS INFORMATION
2000 Clearwater Drive, Oak Brook IL 60523. 847/635-8800. **Contact:** Human Resources. **World Wide Web address:** http://www.reedbusiness.com. **Description:** Publishes travel information guides. **Positions advertised include:** Sale Representative; Human Resources Manager; Data Enhancer; Senior Editor. **Operations at this facility include:** Administration; Sales.

THE REHABILITATION INSTITUTE OF CHICAGO
345 East Superior Street, Chicago IL 60611. 312/238-6290. **Toll-free phone:** 800/782-7342. **Fax:** 312/238-1263. **Recorded jobline:** 312/238-5600. **Contact:** Human Resources. **World Wide Web address:** http://www.rehabchicago.org. **Description:** A comprehensive rehabilitation facility offering inpatient, outpatient, subacute, and day treatment. The Rehabilitation Institute of Chicago also offers at home rehabilitation services. **NOTE:** Part-time, second and third shifts are offered. **Positions advertised include:** Clinical Instructor; Help Desk Specialist; Nurse Manager; Phlebotomist; Occupational Therapist; Fitness Instructor; Director of Development; Financial Clearance Coordinator. **Corporate headquarters location:** This location.

THE RELIABLE CORPORATION
1501 East Woodfield Road, Suite 300 West, Schaumburg IL 60173. 847/413-1300. **Contact:** Human Resources. **World Wide Web address:** http://www.reliable.com. **Description:** A wholesaler of a wide variety of office supplies sold primarily through a mail-order catalog. **Corporate headquarters location:** This location. **Parent company:** Boise Cascade. **Operations at this facility include:** Administration.

RESOURCE INFORMATION MANAGEMENT SYSTEMS, INC.
500 Technology Drive, Naperville IL 60563. 630/369-5300. **Contact:** Human Resources. **E-mail address:** recruiting@rims.com. **World Wide Web address:** http://www.rims.com. **Description:** Develops software programs to help medical and dental insurance agencies manage their claim systems.

REVCOR, INC.
251 Edwards Avenue, Carpentersville IL 60110. 847/428-4411. **Fax:** 847/426-0589. **Contact:** Human Resources. **World Wide Web address:** http://www.revcor.com. **Description:** Manufactures fans and blowers for computerized electronic systems. **Corporate headquarters location:** This location. **Other U.S. locations:** Fort Worth TX. **Operations at this facility include:** Administration; Manufacturing; Research and Development; Sales; Service.

REXAM BEVERAGE CAN COMPANY
8770 West Bryn Mawr Avenue, Chicago IL 60631. 773/399-3000. **Contact:** Director of Human Resources. **World Wide Web address:** http://www.rexam.com. **Description:** Manufactures a variety of container and packaging products. **Corporate headquarters location:** This location.

REXAM BEVERAGE CAN COMPANY
2250 Lively Boulevard, Elk Grove Village IL 60007. 847/734-5500. **Contact:** Human Resources. **World Wide Web address:** http://www.rexam.com. **Description:** Manufactures a variety of container and packaging products. **NOTE:** Human Resources is located at 8770 West Bryn Mawr Avenue, Chicago IL 60631. 773-399-3000. **Corporate headquarters location:** Chicago IL. **Operations at this facility include:** This location is a research and development facility.

RHC SPACEMASTER
1400 North 25th Avenue, Melrose Park IL 60160. 708/345-2500. **Contact:** Linda Atkinson, Personnel Director. **World Wide Web address:** http://www.rhcspacemaster.com. **Description:** Manufactures store fixtures, office furniture, and library equipment. **Corporate headquarters location:** This location.

RICHARDS-WILCOX, INC.
600 South Lake Street, Aurora IL 60506. 630/897-6951. **Fax:** 630/897-4011. **Contact:** Human Resources. **E-mail address:** RWHR@richrdswilcox.com. **World Wide Web address:** http://www.richards-wilcox.com. **Description:** Engaged in the manufacture and distribution of materials handling equipment and office systems products. Products include overhead chain conveyors, horizontal and vertical carousels, general hardware, Aurora shelving, Timer 2, and mobile base. **Corporate headquarters location:** This location. **Operations at this facility include:** Administration; Manufacturing; Research and Development; Sales.

RICHARDSON ELECTRONICS, LTD.
P.O. Box 393, LaFox IL 60147-0393. 630/208-2200. **Fax:** 630/208-2550. **Contact:** Human Resources. **World Wide Web address:** http://www.rell.com. **Description:** An international distributor of electronic components such as electron tubes, RF and microwave components, semiconductors, and security equipment. **NOTE:** See job listings and contact information on the website. **Positions advertised include:** EDI Programmer; Industrial Engineer; Glassblower; Mechanical Engineer. **Corporate headquarters location:** This location. **International locations:** Worldwide.

Operations at this facility include: Administration; Sales; Service. **Listed on:** NASDAQ. **Stock exchange symbol:** RELL.

ROBERTS & SCHAEFER COMPANY
120 South Riverside Plaza, Suite 400, Chicago IL 60606. 312/236-7292. **Contact:** Human Resources. **World Wide Web address:** http://www.r-s.com. **Description:** A multidisciplinary engineering firm. Founded in 1903.

ROCKFORD MEMORIAL HOSPITAL
2400 North Rockton Avenue, Rockford IL 61103. 815/968-6861. **Contact:** Human Resources. **World Wide Web address:** http://www.rhsnet.org. **Description:** A 490-bed hospital. **NOTE:** Apply online at the hospital's website. **Parent company:** Rockford Health System. **Special programs:** Internships.

ROCKFORD POWERTRAIN, INC.
1200 Windsor Road, Loves Park IL 61111. 815/633-7460. **Contact:** Human Resources. **World Wide Web address:** http://www.rockfordpowertrain.com. **Description:** Manufactures clutch and driveline equipment for off-road vehicles.

ROCKFORD PRODUCTS CORPORATION
707 Harrison Avenue, Rockford IL 61104-7197. 815/229-4349. **Contact:** Human Resources. **World Wide Web address:** http://www.rpc-usa.com. **Description:** Manufactures metal fasteners. Founded in 1926. **Special programs:** Internships; Training. **Corporate headquarters location:** This location. **Listed on:** Privately held.

ROESCH INC.
P.O. Box 328, Belleville IL 62222-0328. 618/233-2760. **Physical Address:** 100 N. 24th Street, Belleville IL 62222. **Fax:** 618/233-1186. **Contact:** Human Resources. **World Wide Web address:** http://www.roeschinc.com. **Description:** Manufactures steel stampings, porcelain enameling, and refrigerated ice merchandisers.

ROHM & HAAS COMPANY
123 North Wacker Drive, Chicago IL 60606. 312/807-2000. **Contact:** Human Resources. **World Wide Web address:** http://www.rohmhaas.com. **Description:** A diverse manufacturer of industrial and consumer items including Morton brand salt. The company is also a large producer of inflatable air bags for the automotive industry, adhesives for the packaging industry, liquid plastic coatings for automobiles, electronic products used in printed circuit boards and semiconductor wafers, and dyes used by the printing industry. **International locations:** Bahamas; Canada; Europe; Mexico. **Listed on:** New York Stock Exchange. **Stock exchange symbol:** ROH.

ROHM & HAAS COMPANY
5005 Barnard Mill Road, Ringwood IL 60072. 815/653-2411. **Contact:** Human Resources. **World Wide Web address:** http://www.rohmhaas.com. **Description:** A location of Rohm and Haas company.

ROHM & HAAS COMPANY
2701 East 170th Street, Lansing IL 60438. 708/474-7000. **Fax:** 708/868-7490. **Contact:** Human Resources. **Description:** A location of Rohm & Haas Company.

ROOSEVELT UNIVERSITY
430 South Michigan Avenue, Chicago IL 60605. 312/341-3500. **Contact:** Human Resources. **World Wide Web address:** http://www.roosevelt.edu. **Description:** A university offering graduate and undergraduate programs through its colleges of Arts and Sciences, Business, Education, and Performing Arts. **NOTE:** See website for job listings and application procedures.

ROSCOR CORPORATION
1061 Feehanville Drive, Mount Prospect IL 60056. 847/299-8080. **Fax:** 847/803-8089. **Contact:** Human Resources. **E-mail address:** opportunities@roscor.com. **World Wide Web address:** http://www.roscor.com. **Description:** Distributes industrial video equipment.

ROTADYNE
2512 West 24th Street, Chicago IL 60608. 800/621-8521. **Contact:** Human Resources. **World Wide Web address:** http://www.rotadyne.com. **Description:** Manufactures roller manufacturing equipment and rollers used in the graphic arts industry. **Corporate headquarters location:** Hinsdale IL. **Operations at this facility include:** Divisional Headquarters; Manufacturing; Research and Development; Service.

ROTARY INTERNATIONAL
One Rotary Center, 1560 Sherman Avenue, Evanston IL 60201. 847/866-3000. **Fax:** 847/866-5766. **Contact:** Human Resources. **World Wide Web address:** http://www.rotary.org. **Description:** Rotary International is one of the largest international, nonprofit, service organizations in the world. Founded in 1905. **Special programs:** Internships. **Corporate headquarters location:** This location. **Operations at this facility include:** This location provides administrative services to Rotary clubs including publicity and the administration of humanitarian and scholarship programs funded by the Rotary Foundation.

RUSH UNIVERSITY MEDICAL CENTER
1650 West Harrison, Chicago IL 60612. 312/942-5000. **Contact:** Human Resources. **World Wide Web address:** http://www.rush.edu. **Description:** A 825-bed hospital, specializing in children's medicine. It is the teaching hospital for Rush University. **NOTE:** Apply online. **Positions advertised include:** Dosimetrist; Supervisor of Billing; Applications Analyst; Assistant Professor; Staff Pharmacist; Polysomnographic Technician.

RUST-OLEUM CORPORATION
11 Hawthorne Parkway, Vernon Hills IL 60061. 847/367-7700. **Fax:** 847/816-2230. **Contact:** Human Resources. **E-mail address:** corporatejobs1@rustoleum.com. **World Wide Web address:** http://www.rustoleum.com. **Description:** Manufactures rust fighting, decorative, and roof repair paints for the commercial and industrial markets. **NOTE:** Apply online. **Corporate headquarters location:** This location. **Other U.S. locations:** Evanston IL.

RYERSON TULL
2558 West 16th Street Chicago IL 60608. 773/762-2121. **Fax:** 773/762-0437. **Contact:** Human Resources. **World Wide Web address:** http://www.ryersontull.com. **Description:** Ryerson Tull operates 70 metal service centers and supplies carbon and alloy steel, stainless steel and aluminum, nickel and copper alloys, and a wide range of industrial plastics. Joseph T. Ryerson & Son (also at this location) distributes industrial materials through three divisions: Plastics, Grinding, and Industrial Catalog. Founded in 1842. **Positions advertised include:** Marketing Representative; Corporate Internal Auditor; Inside Sales Professional; Administrative Assistant; Regional Transportation Manager. **Parent company:** Inland Steel Industries, Inc. **Listed on:** New York Stock Exchange. **Stock exchange symbol:** RT.

RYERSON TULL COILING
720 East 111th Street, Chicago IL 60628. 773/468-2121. **Contact:** Human Resources. **World Wide Web address:** http://www.ryersontull.com. **Description:** A steel works and blast furnace company. **NOTE:** Apply online. **Parent company:** Ryerson Tull. **Listed on:** New York Stock Exchange. **Stock exchange symbol:** RT.

RYERSON TULL
JOSEPH T. RYERSON & SON, INC.
P.O. Box 8000, Chicago IL 60680. 773/762-2121. **Physical address:** 2621 West Fifteenth Place, Chicago IL 60608. **Fax:** 773/788-4210. **Contact:** Human Resources. **World Wide Web address:** http://www.ryersontull.com. **Description:** Ryerson Tull operates 70 metal service centers and supplies carbon and alloy steel, stainless steel and aluminum, nickel and copper alloys, and a wide range of industrial plastics. Joseph T. Ryerson & Son (also at this location) distributes industrial materials through three divisions: Plastics, Grinding, and Industrial Catalog. Founded in 1842. **NOTE:** Entry-level positions, part-time jobs, and second and third shifts are offered. **Positions advertised include:** Procurement Specialist; Business Process Improvement Specialist; Direct Sales Representative; Administrative Assistant. **Special programs:** Internships; Training. **Office hours:** Monday - Friday, 8:00 a.m. - 5:00 p.m. **Corporate headquarters location:** This location. **Other U.S. locations:** Nationwide. **Parent company:** Inland Steel Industries, Inc. **Operations at this facility include:** Administration; Manufacturing; Sales; Service. **Listed on:** New York Stock Exchange. **Stock exchange symbol:** RT.

S&C ELECTRIC COMPANY
6601 North Ridge Boulevard, Chicago IL 60626. 773/338-1000. **Contact:** Human Resources. **World Wide Web address:** http://www.sandc.com. **Description:** Manufactures switchgear and switchboard apparatus. **NOTE:** Apply online.

S&S AUTOMOTIVE, INC.
740 North Larch Avenue, Elmhurst IL 60126. 630/279-1600. **Contact:** Human Resources. **Description:** A wholesaler of janitorial products and automotive accessories to car dealerships.

S.I. TECH, INC.
P.O. Box 609, Geneva IL 60134. 630/761-3640. **Fax:** 630/761-3644. **Contact:** Ramesh Sheth, Human Resources Manager. **World Wide Web address:** http://www.sitech-bitdriver.com. **Description:** Manufactures and markets fiber-optic products such as modems, multiplexers, F.O. hubs, LAN/WAN products, short-haul modems, and cable assemblies for data communications use. Founded in 1984. **Office hours:** Monday - Friday, 7:00 a.m. - 7:00 p.m. **Corporate headquarters location:** This location. **Listed on:** Privately held.

SPSS INC.
233 South Wacker Drive, Suite 1100, Chicago IL 60606. 312/651-3000. **Contact:** Human Resources. **World Wide Web address:** http://www.spss.com. **Description:** Develops, markets, and supports statistical software. **NOTE:** See this company's website for job listings. Apply online.

SAFECO INSURANCE COMPANIES
2800 West Higgins Road, Suite 1100, Hoffman Estates IL 60195. 847/490-2900. **Fax:** 847/490-2452. **Recorded jobline:** 800/753-5330. **Contact:** Human Resources Manager. **World Wide Web address:** http://www.safeco.com. **Description:** An insurance company offering personal, homeowner's, auto, commercial, property, casualty, life, and health insurance products and services. Founded in 1923. **NOTE:** Apply online. Entry-level positions are offered. **Positions advertised include:** Legal Secretary; Casualty Claims Examiner; Contract Surety Representative; Personal Lines Claims Specialist; Risk Control Specialist; Workers Compensation Claims Examiner. **Special programs:** Internships; Training. **Office hours:** Monday - Friday, 8:00 a.m. - 4:30 p.m. **Corporate headquarters location:** Seattle WA. **Parent company:** Safeco Insurance Corporation. **Operations at this facility include:** Regional Headquarters.

ST. ANTHONY'S HOSPITAL
P.O. Box 340, St. Anthony's Way, Alton IL 62002-0340. 618/465-2571. **Contact:** Personnel Director. **World Wide Web address:** http://www.sahc.org. **Description:** A general hospital. **NOTE:** Apply online or download the application at the hospital's website and mail it in. **Positions advertised include:** RN; Nurse Assistant; Nuclear Medicine Technologist; Intervention Specialist.

ST. JOHN'S HOSPITAL
800 East Carpenter Street, Springfield IL 62769. 217/525-5644. **Toll-free phone:** 800/419-2296. **Fax:** 217/525-5601. **Recorded jobline:** 217/525-5600. **Contact:** Human Resources. **World Wide Web address:** http://www.st-johns.org. **Description:** A 750-bed, nonprofit, tertiary care, teaching facility affiliated with Southern Illinois University School of Medicine. **Positions advertised include:** File Clerk; Unit Clerk; RN (Various). **NOTE:** Entry-level positions and second and third shifts are offered. **Corporate headquarters location:** This location. **Other U.S. locations:** WI. **Parent company:** Hospital Sisters Health System.

ST. JOSEPH'S HOSPITAL
1515 Main Street, Highland IL 62249. 618/654-7421x2396. **Contact:** Human Resources. **World Wide Web address:** http://www.stjosephs-highland.org. **Description:** A general hospital. **NOTE:** Part-time and weekend shifts offered. Call or visit the Human Resources Office for more information. **Positions advertised include:** RN (Various).

ST. JOSEPH MEDICAL CENTER
77 North Airlite Street, Elgin IL 60123. 847/931-5505. **Contact:** Human Resources. **World Wide Web address:** http://www.provenasaintjoseph.com. **Description:** A 280-bed, acute care hospital with satellite facilities in surrounding communities. **NOTE:** Apply online. **Corporate headquarters location:** Frankfort IL. **Other U.S. locations:** Avilla IN. **Parent company:** Provena Health.

THE ST. PAUL TRAVELERS COMPANIES, INC.
540 Lake Cook Road, Deerfield IL 60015. 847/374-2400. **Fax:** 847/374-1306. **Contact:** Human Resources. **World Wide Web address:** http://www.stpaultravelers.com. **Description:** Provides property liability and life insurance services. **NOTE:** Apply online. **Corporate headquarters location:** St. Paul MN.

SAFECO INSURANCE
225 West Washington Street, Suite 1400, Chicago IL 60606. **Fax:** 847/490-2452. **Contact:** Human Resources. **E-mail address:** stehas@safeco.com. **World Wide Web address:** http://www.safeco.com. **Description:** Sells a comprehensive mix of insurance through a network of independent agents, brokers, and financial advisors nationwide. Safeco products include auto, home, and business insurance, and surety bonds. **Corporate headquarters location:** Seattle WA. **Other U.S. locations:** Nationwide.

SAKS FIFTH AVENUE
700 North Michigan Avenue, Chicago IL 60611. 312/944-6500. **Contact:** Human Resources. **World Wide Web address:** http://www.saksincorporated.com. **Description:** Saks Fifth Avenue is a 62-store chain emphasizing soft-goods products, primarily apparel for men, women, and children. **NOTE:** See website for job listings and apply online. **Parent company:** Saks Incorporated is a department store holding company that operates approximately 360 stores in 36 states. The company's stores include Saks Fifth Avenue, Parisian, Proffit's, Younker's, Herberger's, Carson Pirie Scott, Boston Store, Bergner's, and Off 5th, the company's outlet store. Saks Incorporated also operates two retail catalogs and several retail Internet sites. **Operations at this facility include:** This location is a part of the nationwide specialty department store chain. **Listed on:** New York Stock Exchange. **Stock exchange symbol:** SKS.

W.H. SALISBURY & COMPANY
7520 North Long Avenue, Skokie IL 60077. 847/679-6700. **Fax:** 847/679-2401.**Contact:** Rosa Martinez, Human Resources Manager. **World Wide Web address:** http://www.whsalisbury.com. **Description:** Manufactures a variety of insulating equipment that protects workers from electrical shock. The company also manufactures temporary grounding equipment, plastic covers, and insulated bypass jumpers. **Corporate headquarters location:** This location.

SALTON, INC.
1955 West Field Court, Lake Forest IL 60045. 847/803-4600. **Fax:** 847/803-1186.**Contact:** Human Resources. **World Wide Web address:** http://www.saltoninc.com. **Description:** Designs and markets home appliances, housewares, and beauty care products. Products include the George Foreman grill and the Juiceman juicer. **Corporate headquarters location:** This location. **Listed on:** New York Stock Exchange. **Stock exchange symbol:** SFP. **Annual sales/revenues:** More than $100 million.

SANFORD CORPORATION
2707 Butterfield Road, Oak Brook IL 60523. 708/547-6650. **Fax:** 708/649-3440. **Contact:** Human Resources. **E-mail address:** recruiter.sanford@sanfordcorp.com. **World Wide Web address:** http://www.sanfordcorp.com. **Description:** Manufactures felt-tip pens and other writing implements. **NOTE:** See website for job listings. Mail or e-mail resumes and cover letters. Entry-level positions, part-time jobs, and second and third shifts are offered. **Corporate headquarters location:** This location. **Other U.S. locations:** TN. **International locations:** Worldwide. **Parent company:** Newell Inc. **Operations at this facility include:** Administration; Divisional Headquarters; Manufacturing; Research and Development; Sales; Service. **Listed on:** New York Stock Exchange. **Stock exchange symbol:** NWL.

SANGAMON, COUNTY OF
200 South Ninth Street, Springfield IL 62701. 217/753-6650. **Contact:** Human Resources. **World Wide Web address:** http://www.co.sangamon.il.us. **Description:** Houses the administrative and government offices for Sangamon County. **NOTE:** See website for job listings, contact information and application procedures. **Positions advertised include:** Assistant Administrator of Finance; Accounting Technician.

SARA LEE COFFEE AND TEA
3800 Golf Road, Rolling Meadows IL 60008. 630/860-1400. **Contact:** Human Resources. **World Wide Web address:** http://www.saraleecoffeeandtea.com. **Description:** Produces and sells coffee, tea, salad dressings, syrups, and vending products. **NOTE:** For job listings, visit the Career Section at Sara Lee's website at http://www.saralee.com. Apply online. **Corporate headquarters location:** This location. **Other area locations:** Chicago IL; Elk Grove Village IL.

SARA LEE CORPORATION
3 First National Plaza, Chicago IL 60602. 312/726-2600. **Contact:** Human Resources. **World Wide Web address:** http://www.saralee.com. **Description:** This location houses the administrative offices of the international food and consumer products company. **NOTE:** For employment opportunities, see the company's website for job listings and apply online. **Corporate headquarters location:** This location.

SARGENT & LUNDY
55 East Monroe Street, Chicago IL 60603. 312/269-2000. **Fax:** 312/269-1960. **Contact:** Kathleen A. Lynch, Human Resources. **E-mail address:** kathleen.a.lynch@sargentlundy.com. **World Wide Web address:** http://www.sargentlundy.com. **Description:** Provides a broad range of engineering services. Founded in 1891. **NOTE:** See website for job listings and contact information. Entry-level and temporary positions are offered. **Corporate headquarters location:** This location. **Other U.S. locations:** Nationwide. **International locations:** Worldwide. **Listed on:** Privately held.

SARGENT-WELCH SCIENTIFIC COMPANY
911 Commerce Court, Buffalo Grove IL 60089. 800/727-4368. **Contact:** Human Resources. **E-mail address:** sarwel@sargentwelch.com. **World Wide Web address:** http://www.sargentwelch.com. **Description:** Sargent-Welch Scientific Company is a distributor and manufacturer of a wide range of analytical instruments, scientific apparatus, lab equipment, supplies, chemicals, and furniture. **Corporate headquarters location:** West Chester PA. **Parent company:** VWR Corporation. **Operations at this facility include:** This location houses customer service offices.

SCHAFER GEAR & MACHINE, INC.
5876 Sandy Hollow Road, Rockford IL 61109. 815/874-4327. **Contact:** Human Resources. **World Wide Web address:** http://www.schafergear.com. **Description:** Manufactures gears.

SCHAWK, INC.
1695 River Road, Des Plaines IL 60018. 847/827-9494. **Fax:** 847/827-1264. **Contact:** Human Resources. **E-mail address:** recruit@schawk.com. **World Wide Web address:** http://www.schawk.com. **Description:** Schawk offers an entire range of creative and prepress capabilities for books, magazines, directories, retail and catalog advertising, and corporate communications. Services include design, copywriting, editorial development, photography, electronic composition, color separations, and data management. **NOTE:** See website for job listings. E-mail resumes and cover letters. **Corporate headquarters location:** This location. **Other U.S. locations:** GA; MI; MN; NJ; NY. **Operations at this facility include:** Administration; Service.

SCHAWK, INC.
6115 Official Road, Crystal Lake IL 60014. 815/459-8520. **Fax:** 815/459-7259. **Contact:** Human Resources. **World Wide Web address:** http://www.schawk.com. **Description:** Schawk offers an entire range of creative and prepress capabilities for books, magazines, directories, retail and catalog advertising, and corporate communications. Services include design, copywriting, editorial development, photography, electronic composition, color separations, and data management. **Corporate headquarters location:** Des Plaines IL. **Other U.S. locations:** GA; MI; MN; NJ; NY. **Operations at this facility include:** Administration; Service.

SCHOLLE CORPORATION
200 West North Avenue, Northlake IL 60164. 708/562-7290. **Contact:** Human Resources. **World Wide Web address:** http://www.scholle.com. **Description:** A manufacturer and distributor of flexible film packaging for the food and beverage industries; specialty chemical solutions for coating and related industries; and bulk and packaged acid. Scholle also manufactures filling equipment for food and beverage packages. **NOTE:** See website for job listings and contact information. **Corporate headquarters location:** This location. **Operations at this facility include:** Administration; Manufacturing; Research and Development; Sales; Service. **Listed on:** Privately held.

SCIAKY INC.
4915 West 67th Street, Bedford Park IL 60638. 708/594-3800. **Fax:** 708/496-6191. **Contact:** Comptroller. **World Wide Web address:** http://www.sciaky.com. **Description:** A manufacturer of precision-integrated welding systems. The company engineers and manufactures systems for resistance, advanced arc, electron beam, and laser welding. **NOTE:** See website for job listings. Fax resumes and cover letters to the attention of the Comptroller. **Positions advertised include:** Lathe Operator; Gear Cutter; Senior Mechanical Engineer; Proposal Engineer; Machinist; Machine Builder. **Parent company:** Phillips Service Industries. **Operations at this facility include:** Administration; Divisional Headquarters; Manufacturing; Research and Development; Sales; Service.

SCOTT FORESMAN
1900 East Lake Avenue, Glenview IL 60025. 847/729-3000. **Fax:** 847/486-3968. **Recorded jobline:** 847/657-3920. **Contact:** Human Resources. **World Wide Web address:** http://www.scottforesman.com. **Description:** One of the largest educational publishers in the United States. The company publishes teaching materials including textbooks, computer software, video, and CD-ROM products for elementary and high school students in all major disciplines. **Special programs:** Internships. **Corporate headquarters location:** This location. **Listed on:** Privately held.

SCOTTISH DEVELOPMENT INTERNATIONAL
1020 31st Street, Lower Level 20, Downers Grove IL. 60515. 630/968-6555. **Contact:** Human Resources Department. **World Wide Web address:** http://www.scottishdevelopmentinternational.com. **Description:** A nonprofit, economic development agency for the British government engaged in attracting new business to Scotland.

SCULLY-JONES CORPORATION
1901 South Rockwell Street, Chicago IL 60608. 773/247-5900. **Contact:** Gerald Walton, Human Resources. **World Wide Web address:** http://www.scullyjones.com. **Description:** A manufacturer of precision tool holders for machine tools. **Corporate headquarters location:** This location. **Operations at this facility include:** Administration; Manufacturing. **Listed on:** Privately held.

SEAQUISTPERFECT DISPENSING
1160 North Silver Lake Road, Cary IL 60013. 847/639-2124. **Contact:** Rob Revak, Human Resources. **World Wide Web address:** http://www.seaqperf.com. **Description:** Manufactures aerosol valves and spray pumps. **Special programs:** Internships. **Corporate headquarters location:** This location. **Parent company:** Aptar Group. **Operations at this facility include:** Administration; Manufacturing; Research and Development.

SEARS, ROEBUCK & CO.
3333 Beverly Road, Hoffman Estates IL 60179. 847/286-2500. **Contact:** Director of Human Resources. **World Wide Web address:** http://www.sears.com. **Description:** Operates a chain of department stores. **Corporate headquarters location:** This location. **Subsidiaries include:** Advantis, a partnership formed by Sears and IBM, is a networking technology company that provides businesses with data, voice, and multimedia services; Allstate Insurance Group is one of the nation's largest publicly held property and casualty insurance companies, with more than 20 million customers and approximately 14,600 full-time agents in the United States and Canada. Allstate offers automobile insurance, homeowners insurance, life insurance, annuity and pension products, business insurance (insurance for small and mid-size businesses, as well as reinsurance for other insurers), and mortgage guaranty insurance (through Allstate's wholly-owned subsidiary, PMI Mortgage Insurance Company); Homart is one of the country's leading developers, owners, and managers of regional shopping malls and community centers; Prodigy, a Sears/IBM partnership, is a home computer network providing a wide variety of personal Internet services including news, shopping, bulletin boards, travel ticketing, brokerage, banking, and e-mail services; and Sears Merchandise Group is a leading retailer of apparel, home, and automotive products and related services for families throughout North America. **Listed on:** New York Stock Exchange. **NOTE:** For corporate positions, apply online. For retail positions, visit the nearest retail location. **Stock exchange symbol:** S.

SERVICEMASTER COMPANY
3250 Lacey Road, Suite 600, Downers Grove IL 60515. 630/663-2000. **Fax:** 901/766-1157. **Contact:** Gina DePompei, People Services Director. **E-mail address:** careers@servicemaster.com. **World Wide Web address:** http://www.servicemaster.com. **Description:** A housekeeping, maintenance, and management company that provides services to residential, commercial, educational, industrial, and health care facilities in 50 states, Washington DC, and 15 foreign countries. Other services include lawn care (through TruGreen and ChemLawn), cleaning and restoration, pest control, radon testing, and child care. **NOTE:** E-mail or fax resumes to the attention of Corporate People Services – Careers. Resumes may also be mailed to the Corporate People Services – Careers' office at ServiceMaster Consumer Services, 860 Ridge Lake Boulevard, Suite AL-1099, Memphis TN 38120. **Corporate headquarters location:** This location. **Listed on:** New York Stock Exchange. **Stock exchange symbol:** SVM.

SEVEN WORLDWIDE, INC.
225 West Superior Street, Chicago IL 60610. 312/616-7777. **Contact:** Human Resources. **World Wide Web address:** http://www.sevenww.com. **Description:** A commercial graphic arts company providing digital imaging prepress services. Founded in 1953.

SHAY HEALTH CARE SERVICES
5730 West 159th Street, Oak Forest IL 60452. 708/535-4300. **Fax:** 708/535-7520. **Contact:** Karen Carter, Human Resources Coordinator. **Description:** A home health care agency. Founded in 1981. **NOTE:** Entry-level positions and second and third shifts are offered. **Company slogan:** Beyond business as usual. **Positions advertised include:** Certified Nurses Aide; Daycare Worker; Home Health Aide; Licensed

Practical Nurse; Registered Nurse. **Office hours:** Monday - Friday, 8:00 a.m. - 4:00 p.m. **Corporate headquarters location:** Chicago IL. **Listed on:** Privately held.

SHEDD AQUARIUM
1200 South Lake Shore Drive, Chicago IL 60605. 312/939-2426. **Contact:** Tina Ausley, Human Resources Recruiter. **E-mail address:** jobs@sheddaquarium.org. **World Wide Web address:** http://www.shedd.org. **Description:** An aquarium and oceanarium offering a wide range of exhibits, outreach programs, and educational workshops. **NOTE:** See website for job listings. Part-time positions offered. Mail or e-mail resumes for all positions. **Positions advertised include:** Admissions Associate; Aquarist; Interpretive Naturalist; Membership Associate; Audio-Visual Operator; Multimedia Manager. **Corporate headquarters location:** This location.

SHEFFIELD STEEL CORPORATION
P.O. Box 727, One Industry Avenue, Joliet IL 60434-0727. 815/723-9335. **Contact:** Human Resources. **World Wide Web address:** http://www.sheffieldsteel.com. **Description:** Operates the largest subsidiary component of Penn Dixie Industries, a multiproduct corporation primarily serving the construction industry. Sheffield Steel Corporation manufactures steel, industrial and welding wire, nails, fencing, welded wire fabric, and other products. Facilities are located in several western and midwestern states. **NOTE:** See website for contact information. **Corporate headquarters location:** Kokomo IN. **Operations at this facility include:** This location manufactures hot-rolled steel merchant bars and lightweight structural steel shapes.

THE SHERWIN-WILLIAMS COMPANY
619 Howard Street, Evanston IL 60202. 847/869-9030. **Contact:** Human Resources. **World Wide Web address:** http://www.sherwin.com. **Description:** Sherwin-Williams Company manufactures, sells, and distributes coatings and related products. Coatings are produced for original equipment manufacturers in various industries, as well as for the automotive aftermarket, the industrial maintenance market, and the traffic paint market. Sherwin-Williams labeled architectural and industrial coatings are sold through company-owned specialty paint and wallcovering stores. The Sherwin-Williams Company also manufactures paint under the Acme, Dutch Boy, Kem-Tone, Lucas, Martin-Senour, Minwax, Pratt & Lambert, Rogers, and Thompson brand names, as well as private labels, and markets its products to independent dealers, mass merchandisers, and home improvement centers. **NOTE:** Apply in person at this location. See website for corporate job listings. **Corporate headquarters location:** Cleveland OH. **Operations at this facility include:** This location is a retail and wholesale outlet.

SHURE INC.
5800 West Tilley Avenue, Niles IL 60714-4608. 847/600-2000. **Toll-free phone:** 800/2574873. **Fax:** 847/600-6303. **Contact:** Marcie Austen, Human Resources Manager. **E-mail address:** careers@shure.com. **World Wide Web address:** http://www.shure.com. **Description:** Manufactures a wide range of electronic equipment including microphones, mixers, audio processors, and wireless systems. **NOTE:** See website for job listings. Apply online or fax resume. **Corporate headquarters location:** This location. **Other U.S. locations:** Douglas AZ; El Paso TX. **Operations at this facility include:** Administration; Manufacturing; Research and Development; Sales; Service. **Listed on:** Privately held.

SIEMENS BUILDING TECHNOLOGIES, INC.
1000 Deerfield Parkway, Buffalo Grove IL 60089. 847/215-1000. **Contact:** Human Resources. **World Wide Web address:** http://www.sbt.siemens.com. **Description:** A designer, manufacturer, and installer of computer-based heating and cooling controls for nonresidential buildings. The company's integrated building systems manage energy usage, HVAC, fire safety, and security. **NOTE:** Apply online at the parent company's website – http:/www.siemens.com. **Parent company:** Siemens.

SIEMENS BUSINESS SERVICES
3041 Woodcreek Drive, Suite 100, Downers Grove IL 60515. 630/724-8000. **Fax:** 630/336-1222. **Contact:** Recruiter. **E-mail address:** careers@sbs.siemens.com. **World Wide Web address:** http://www.sbs-usa.siemens.com. **Description:** Provides systems integration services and resells software. **NOTE:** See website for job listings.

SIEMENS ENERGY & AUTOMATION, INC.
1000 McKee Street, Batavia IL 60510. 630/879-6000. **Contact:** Human Resources. **World Wide Web address:** http://www.sea.siemens.com. **Description:** Develops, manufactures, and markets an expanding line of electronic control products and systems for a wide variety of industrial applications. **NOTE:** Apply online. **Other U.S. locations:** Nationwide. **Operations at this facility include:** Administration; Manufacturing; Research and Development; Sales; Service.

SILLIKER LABORATORIES GROUP, INC.
900 Maple Road, Homewood IL 60430. 708/957-7878. **Fax:** 708/957-3798. **Contact:** Margo Neetz, Human Resources Generalist. **E-mail address:** human.resources@silliker.com. **World Wide Web address:** http://www.silliker.com. **Description:** Operates a network of food testing laboratories. The labs test for pathogens and microbes and serve to verify the accuracy of nutritional labeling. Founded in 1967. **NOTE:** See website for job listings. Apply online or e-mail or mail resumes. Entry-level positions and part-time jobs are offered. **Special programs:** Summer Jobs. **Corporate headquarters location:** This location. **International locations:** Worldwide. **Listed on:** Privately held.

SILVON SOFTWARE INC.
900 Oakmont Lane, Suite 400, Westmont IL 60559. 630/655-3313. **Contact:** Human Resources. **World Wide Web address:** http://www.silvon.com. **Description:** Develops sales tracking software. **NOTE:** See website for job listings and contact information.

SIMPSON ELECTRIC COMPANY
853 Dundee Avenue, Elgin IL 60120. 847/697-2260. **Fax:** 847/697-2272. **Contact:** Human Resources. **World Wide Web address:** http://www.simpsonelectric.com. **Description:** Manufactures instruments and panel meters.

SIX FLAGS GREAT AMERICA
P.O. Box 1776, Gurnee IL 60031. 847/249-2133. **Contact:** Human Resources. **World Wide Web address:** http://www.sixflags.com. **Description:** A theme park. **NOTE:** Apply in person at the company's Human Resources Office. **Special programs:** Internships. **Office hours:** Monday – Friday, 1:00 p.m. – 5:00 p.m.; Saturday, 11:00 a.m. – 3:00 p.m. **Other U.S. locations:** CA; GA; NJ; TX. **International locations:** Toronto, Canada. **Parent company:** Premier Parks (OK) owns and operates 35 theme parks nationwide. **Operations at this facility include:** Administration; Sales.

SLOAN VALVE COMPANY
10500 Seymour Avenue, Franklin Park IL 60131. 847/671-4300. **Contact:** Human Resources. **World Wide Web address:** http://www.sloanvalve.com. **Description:** An international manufacturer of valves for toilets, railroad cars, air brakes, and faucets. Brand names include Slimline, Flushmate, Act-O-Matic, and Optima. **Corporate headquarters location:** This location. **Other U.S. locations:** AR. **Listed on:** Privately held.

SMITH, BUCKLIN AND ASSOCIATES
401 North Michigan Avenue, Suite 2200, Chicago IL 60611. 312/644-6610. **Fax:** 312/673-6580. **Contact:** Human Resources. **E-mail address:** ChicagoHR@smithbucklin.com. **World Wide Web address:** http://www.sba.com. **Description:** Provides daily management services for nonprofit organizations worldwide and for full-service and contract clients.

SMITHFIELD CONSTRUCTION GROUP, INC.
400 W. Huron, Chicago IL 60610. 312/266-9800. **Fax:** 312/2669530. **Contact:** Adrienne Pearlman, Human Resources. **E-mail address:** apearlman@smith-field.com. **World Wide Web address:** http://www.smith-field.com. **Description:** Residential, commercial, and industrial construction company. **Positions advertised include:** Safety Director.

SMURFIT-STONE CONTAINER CORPORATION
401 Alton Street, Alton IL 62002. 618/463-6000. **Contact:** Human Resources. **World Wide Web address:** http://www.smurfit-stone.com. **Description:** Smurfit-Stone Container Corporation is one of the world's leading paper-based packaging companies. The company's main products include corrugated containers, folding cartons, and multiwall industrial bags. The company is also one of the world's largest collectors and processors of recycled products that are then sold to a worldwide customer base. Smurfit-Stone Container Corporation also operates several paper tube, market pulp, and newsprint production facilities. **Corporate headquarters location:** Chicago IL. **Other U.S. locations:** Nationwide. **International locations:** Dublin, Ireland. **Operations at this facility include:** This location manufactures corrugated shipping containers. It is also a Midwest Regional Sales office. **Listed on:** NASDAQ. **Stock exchange symbol:** SSCC.

SMURFIT-STONE CONTAINER CORPORATION
150 North Michigan Avenue, Chicago IL 60601. 312/346-6600. **Contact:** Recruiting Specialist. **World Wide Web address:** http://www.smurfit-stone.com. **Description:** One of the world's leading paper-based packaging companies. Smurfit-Stone Container Corporation's main products include corrugated containers, folding cartons, and multiwall industrial bags. The company is also one of the world's largest collectors and processors of recycled products. Smurfit-Stone Container Corporation also operates several paper tube, market pulp, and newsprint production facilities. **Corporate headquarters location:** This location. **Other U.S. locations:** Nationwide. **Listed on:** NASDAQ. **Stock exchange symbol:** SSCC.

GEORGE SOLLITT CONSTRUCTION COMPANY
790 North Central, Wood Dale IL 60191. 630/860-7333. **Fax:** 630/860-7347. **Contact:** Howard Strong, Vice President of Operations. **World Wide Web address:** http://www.sollitt.com. **Description:** A leading general contractor/construction management firm. Clients include hospitals, schools, and major corporations. Founded in 1838. **NOTE:** Entry-level positions are offered. **Special programs:** Training. **Corporate headquarters location:** This location. **Listed on:** Privately held.

SOLO CUP COMPANY
1501 East 96th Street, Chicago IL 60628. 773/721-3600. **Contact:** Director of Human Resources. **World Wide Web address:** http://www.solocup.com. **Description:** A manufacturer and distributor of paper cups, paper plates, and other disposable products. **NOTE:** See website for job listings. **Corporate headquarters location:** Champaign IL.

SOLO CUP COMPANY, INC.
7575 South Kostner Avenue, Chicago IL 60652. 773/767-3300. **Contact:** Human Resources Manager. **World Wide Web address:** http://www.solocup.com. **Description:** A manufacturer and distributor of paper cups, paper plates, and other disposable products. **NOTE:** Apply online. **Positions advertised include:** Human Resources Generalist; Quality Manager; Production Supervisor. **Corporate headquarters location:** Champaign IL.

SOLUCIENT
1007 Church Street, Suite 700, Evanston IL 60201. 800/366-PLAN. **Contact:** Human Resources. **World Wide Web address:** http://www.solucient.com. **Description:** Solucient provides healthcare business intelligence to the healthcare industry. The company maintains the nation's largest healthcare database, comprised of more than 22.6 million hospital discharges per year. Serving a client base of more than 3,300 customers, Solucient provides information resources to more than 2,000 hospitals, as well as many of the largest pharmaceutical manufacturers in the United States. **Positions advertised include:** Desktop Services Supervisor; Director of Vendor Management; Senior Systems Database Administrator. **Corporate headquarters location:** This location.

SOUTH SHORE HOSPITAL
8012 South Crandon Avenue, Chicago IL 60617. 773/768-0810. **Fax:** 773/468-0749. **Contact:** Joe Perez, Human Resources Director. **E-mail address:** jobs@southshorehospital.com. **World Wide Web address:** http://www.southshorehospital.com. **Description:** A 170-bed, acute care hospital offering a full range of inpatient and outpatient health services. **NOTE:** This company prefers that resumes be mailed or faxed; however, there is an online application form available on its website.

SOUTHERN ILLINOIS HEALTHCARE
405 West Jackson Street, Carbondale IL 62902. 618/457-5200. **Contact:** Human Resources. **World Wide Web address:** http://www.sih.net. **Description:** A nonprofit health care corporation that operates six hospitals and several rural clinics. Southern Illinois Healthcare also offers home health care and outreach programs. **NOTE:** This company has three hospitals in its network: Herrin Hospital; Memorial Hospital of Carbondale, and St. Joseph Medical Center. It also has other medical facilities. See website for job listings for all locations. An application may also be completed at the Human Resources office for each location. **Corporate headquarters location:** This location.

SOUTHERN ILLINOIS UNIVERSITY AT CARBONDALE
803 South Elizabeth Street, Carbondale IL 62901. 618/536-3369. **Recorded jobline:** 618/536-2116. **Fax:** 618/453-1353. **Contact:** Employment Manager. **World Wide Web address:** http://www.siu.edu. **Description:** A four-year public university offering both undergraduate and graduate degree programs. **NOTE:** See website for job listings and contact information.

SOUTHERN ILLINOIS UNIVERSITY AT EDWARDSVILLE
Campus Box 1040, Edwardsville IL 62026. 618/650-2190. **Fax:** 618/650-2696. **Contact:** Human Resources. **World Wide Web address:** http://www.siue.edu. **Description:** A state university offering both undergraduate and graduate programs. **NOTE:** See website for administrative, faculty, professional staff, and civil service positions and related contact and application procedure information. Interested jobseekers may also visit the Human Resources office located at Rendleman Hall, Room 3210. **Office hours:** Monday – Friday, 8:00 a.m. – 4:00 p.m.

SOUTHWESTERN ILLINOIS COLLEGE
2500 Carlyle Avenue, Belleville IL 62221. 618/235-2700. **Fax:** 618/277-7346. **Contact:** Larry Friederich, Human Resources. **E-mail address:** humanresourccs@swic.edu. **World Wide Web address:** http://www.southwestern.cc.il.us. **Description:** A public, two-year community college. **NOTE:** Mail resumes to Mr. Friederich's attention. **Positions advertised include:** Americorps Field Coordinator; Public Safety Officers; Assistant Professor (Various); Adjunct Instructors (Various); Systems Analyst-Programmer.

SPECTRULITE CONSORTIUM, INC.
P.O. Box 258, 1001 College Avenue, Madison IL 62060. 618/452-5190. **Fax:** 618/798-3190. **Contact:** Human Resources. **World Wide Web address:** http://www.spectrulite.com. **Description:** Engaged in problem solving for the design, use, and application of lightweight metal technology. Spectrulite is one of the largest producers of magnesium and aluminum wrought products in the United States. The company is also involved in the graphic arts industry, producing magnesium photo-sensitized plate and other flexographic products through its facility in Findlay OH. **Operations at this facility include:** Administration; Manufacturing; Sales; Service.

SPIEGEL, INC.
3500 Lacey Road, Downers Grove IL 60515. 630/986-8800. **Fax:** 630/769-2012. **Contact:** Human Resources. **E-mail address:** careers@spgl.com. **World Wide Web address:** http://www.spiegel.com. **Description:** A retailer of goods and services for the home, as well as current fashions for women, men, and children. **NOTE:** See website for job listings and apply online. **Positions advertised include:** Recruiter. **Corporate headquarters location:** This location. **Subsidiaries include:** Eddie Bauer, Inc.

SPRAYING SYSTEMS COMPANY
P.O. Box 7900, Wheaton IL 60189. 630/665-5000. **Fax:** 630/260-0842. **Contact:** Jim Yehling, Director of Human Resources. **World Wide Web address:** http://www.spray.com. **Description:** Manufactures spraying components for industrial use. Products include air atomizing, tank wash, air control, spray/dry, and gas conditioning nozzles; spray guns; and portable spray systems. **Corporate headquarters location:** This location.

SPRINGFIELD AIRPORT AUTHORITY
1200 Capital Airport Drive, Springfield IL 62707-8419. 217/788-1060. **Contact:** Human Resources. **World Wide Web address:** http://www.flyspi.com. **Description:** Operates the Capital Airport. Founded in 1947. **Corporate headquarters location:** This location.

SPRINGFIELD HILTON
700 East Adams Street, Springfield IL 62701-1601. 217/789-1530. **Fax:** 217/789-0709. **Contact:** Human Resources. **World Wide Web address:** http://www.hilton.com. **Description:** A 30-story hotel with 368 guest rooms. The hotel also offers long-term guest services. **Parent company:** Hilton Hotels Corporation. **Listed on:** New York Stock Exchange. **Stock exchange symbol:** HLT.

STANDARD EDUCATIONAL COMPANY
900 North Shore Drive, Suite 252, Lake Bluff IL 60044. 847/283-0301. **Contact:** Human Resources Manager. **World Wide Web address:** http://www.fergpubco.com. **Description:** Publishers of the *Careers in Focus* series and numerous other career and training-related books and CD-ROMs.

STAR PUBLICATIONS, INC.
6901 West 159th Street, Tinley Park IL 60477. 708/802-8800. **Contact:** Human Resources. **World Wide Web address:** http://www.starnewspapers.com. **Description:** Publishes biweekly community newspapers. **NOTE:** Entry-level positions are offered. **Special programs:** Internships. **Corporate headquarters location:** West Frankfort IL. **Parent company:** American Publishing Company. **Operations at this facility include:** Administration; Manufacturing; Sales; Service.

STARTSPOT MEDIAWORKS, INC.
1840 Oak Avenue, Evanston IL 60201. 847/866-1830. **Fax:** 847/866-1880. **Contact:** Human Resources. **World Wide Web address:** http://www.startspot.com. **Description:** Develops a group of informational websites that work as search engines. StartSpot's sites include: LibrarySpot is library resource site; BookSpot offers book reviews and reading lists, along with lists of authors, publishers, and the latest news on happenings in the book world; GourmetSpot offers advice and links to some of the best recipes, restaurants, culinary equipment, and wine available; EmploymentSpot provides information and related links for jobseekers.

STATE FARM INSURANCE
P.O. Box 2315, Bloomington IL 61702. 309/766-2311. **Fax:** 309/735-3422. **Contact:** Human Resources. **World Wide Web address:** http://www.statefarm.com. **Description:** Provides homeowner's, health, auto, and life insurance. **NOTE:** See website for job listings and resume submission guidelines. **Positions advertised include:** Collections Representative; Collection Supervisor; Asset/Liability Management Analyst. **Special programs:** Internships. **Corporate headquarters location:** This location. **Operations at this facility include:** Administration.

THE STATE JOURNAL-REGISTER
One Copley Plaza, Springfield IL 62701. 217/788-1330. **Contact:** Elaine Kerhlikar, Human Resources. **World Wide Web address:** http://www.sj-r.com. **Description:** Publishes a morning, daily newspaper covering 11 central Illinois counties. **NOTE:** Part-time positions offered. **Parent company:** The Copley Press (La Jolla CA) publishes 45 newspapers nationwide.

STATE LINE INSURANCE COMPANY
P.O. Box 69, Orangeville IL 61060-0069. 815/789-3366. **Contact:** Human Resources. **Description:** Offers a wide variety of insurance to individuals including property and casualty.

STEIN ROE INVESTMENT COUNSEL
One South Wacker Drive, Chicago IL 60606. 312/368-7700. **Fax:** 312/368-8129. **Contact:** Human Resources. **World Wide Web address:** http://www.sric.net. **Description:** An investment counseling firm offering professional advice and services to individuals, institutions, and other organizations. Stein Roe & Farnham also manages 20 no-load mutual funds. **NOTE:** Apply online. **Corporate headquarters location:** This location. **Other U.S. locations:** San Francisco CA; New York NY; Cleveland OH. **International locations:** San Juan, Puerto Rico.

STENOGRAPH CORPORATION
1500 Bishop Court, Mount Prospect IL 60056. **Toll-free phone:** 800/323-4247. **Contact:** Human Resources. **World Wide Web address:** http://www.stenograph.com. **Description:** Manufactures court reporting equipment.

STEPAN COMPANY
22 West Frontage Road, Northfield IL 60093. 847/446-7500. **Fax:** 847/501-2100. **Contact:** Human Resources. **World Wide Web address:** http://www.stepan.com. **Description:** Develops, manufactures, and markets a wide range of chemical intermediates sold to producers of shampoos, toothpastes, household detergents, and other personal care items. Products are also used as ingredients in industrial detergents and cleansers, agricultural fertilizers, herbicides, and petroleum-based detergents. Stepan Company is a major producer of phthalic anhydride, an essential ingredient in plastics and polyesters, and also manufactures urethane foam systems and other specialty products. **NOTE:** Apply online. **Corporate headquarters location:** This location. **Operations at this facility include:** Administration; Research and Development; Sales. **Listed on:** New York Stock Exchange. **Stock exchange symbol:** SCL.

STEPPENWOLF THEATRE COMPANY
758 West North Avenue, 4th Floor, Chicago IL 60610. 312/335-1888. **Fax:** 312/335-0808. **Contact:** Human Resources. **World Wide Web address:** http://www.steppenwolf.org. **Description:** A Tony Award-winning theater company. **NOTE:** See website for job listings and contact information. **Positions advertised include:** Technical Director; Fundraising; Theatre Sales. **Special programs:** Internships; Volunteers.

STERICYCLE, INC.
28161 North Keith Drive, Lake Forest IL 60045. **Toll-free phone:** 800/643-0240. **Fax:** 847/367-9493. **Contact:** Human Resources. **E-mail address:** careers@stericycle.com. **World Wide Web address:** http://www.stericycle.com. **Description:** Provides medical waste management services. Services include regulated medical waste collection, transportation, treatment, disposal, and reduction services. Founded in 1989. **NOTE:** See website for job listings. Entry-level, part-time and temporary positions offered. **Corporate headquarters location:** This location. **Listed on:** NASDAQ. **Stock exchange symbol:** SRCL.

STERLING PLUMBING GROUP, INC.
2900 Golf Road, Rolling Meadows IL 60008. 847/734-1777. **Contact:** Human Resources. **World Wide Web address:** http://www.sterlingplumbing.com. **Description:** Manufactures sinks, faucets, tubs, and toilets as well as other plumbing supplies for kitchens and bathrooms. **NOTE:** For job listings, visit Kohler's website at http://www.hr.kohler.com/careers. Parent company: Kohler.

STEVENS INDUSTRIES INC.
704 West Main Street, Teutopolis IL 62467. 217/857-6411. **Fax:** 217/540-3101. **Contact:** Human Resources. **E-mail address:** joant@stevensind.com. **World Wide Web address:** http://www.stevensind.com. **Description:** A manufacturer of laminated case goods, integrated component parts, and panels. **NOTE:** See website for job listings. E-mail resumes or apply in person in the Human Resources Office. Second- and third-shift positions are offered. **Positions advertised include:** Team Leader; Estimator; Inventory Clerk; Machine Operator, Supervisor. **Office hours:** Monday – Friday, 8:00 a.m. – 4:00 p.m. **Corporate headquarters location:** This location. **Operations at this facility include:** Administration; Manufacturing; Research and Development; Sales; Service. **Listed on:** Privately held.

STRATFORD HALL
6253 West 74th Street, Box 2001, Bedford Park IL 60499-2001. 800/258-4084. **Contact:** Human Resources. **World Wide Web address:** http://www.stratfordhall.com. **Description:** Engaged in the catalog sale of personalized holiday cards for businesses. **Corporate headquarters location:** This location.

STRATOS LIGHTWAVE, INC.
7444 West Wilson Avenue, Harwood Heights IL 60706. 708/867-9600. **Contact:** Human Resources. **World Wide Web address:** http://www.stratoslightwave.com. **Description:** Stratos Lightwave develops, manufactures, and sells optical subsystems and components for high data rate networking, data storage, and telecommunications applications. **NOTE:** Apply online. **Corporate headquarters location:** This location. **Other area locations:** Carthage IL; Rolling Meadows IL; Warsaw IL. **International locations:** Singapore; United Kingdom. **Listed on:** NASDAQ. **Stock exchange symbol:** STLW.

STREAMWOOD BEHAVIORAL HEALTH CENTER
1400 East Irving Park Road, Streamwood IL 60107. 630/837-9000. **Fax:** 630/540-4290. **Contact:** Mark Paladino, Director of Human Resources. **World Wide Web address:** http://www.streamwoodhospital.com. **Description:** A psychiatric hospital for children and adolescents aged 3 through 18. **NOTE:** Apply online. Entry-level positions and second and third shifts are offered. **Special programs:** Internships. **Listed on:** Privately held.

STROMBECKER CORPORATION
700 North Sacramento Boulevard, Suite 321, Chicago IL 60612. 773/638-1000. **Toll-free phone:** 800/944-8697. **Fax:** 773/638-3679. **Contact:** Robert Knorrek, Director of Human Resources. **E-mail address:** rknorrek@compuserve.com. **World Wide Web address:** http://www.tootsietoy.com. **Description:** Manufactures toys under the Tootsie Toy logo. **NOTE:** Entry-level positions are offered. **Office hours:** Monday - Friday, 8:00 a.m. - 5:00 p.m. **Other U.S. locations:** Nationwide. **International locations:** Worldwide.

SUN CHEMICAL
135 West Lake Street, Northlake IL 60164. 708/562-0550. **Fax:** 708/562-0580. **Contact:** Human Resources. **World Wide Web address:** http://www.sunchemicalink.com. **Description:** One of the world's largest producers of printing inks and organic pigments. Sun Chemical also designs and manufactures graphic arts equipment.

SUNGARD INSURANCE SYSTEMS
321 Susan Drive, Suite C, Normal IL 61761. 309/862-4300. **Fax:** 309/888-2130. **Contact:** Human Resources. **World Wide Web address:** http://www.sungardinsurance.com. **Description:** Develops computer software for the insurance industry. **NOTE:** Apply online. **Special programs:** Internships. **Corporate headquarters location:** Atlanta GA. **Other U.S. locations:** Denver CO. **Parent**

company: SunGard Corporation. **Listed on:** New York Stock Exchange. **Stock exchange symbol:** SDS.

THE SUNSTAR BUTLER COMPANY
4635 W. Foster Avenue, Chicago IL 60630. 800/265-8353. **Fax:** 773/777-9226. **Contact:** R. Varra, Human Resources. **E-mail address:** hr6@jbutler.com. **World Wide Web address:** http://www.jbutler.com. **Description:** Manufactures oral health care products. **Positions advertised include:** Lead Molding Technician. **Corporate headquarters location:** This location. **Other area locations:** Elgin IL. **International locations:** Canada, Germany, and Sweden. **Number of employees worldwide:** 600.

SWITCHCRAFT, INC.
5555 North Elston Avenue, Chicago IL 60630. 773/792-2700. **Fax:** 773/792-8529. **Contact:** Debbie Zumsteg, Human Resources Director. **E-mail address:** dzumsteg@switchcraft.com. **World Wide Web address:** http://www.switchcraft.com. **Description:** Manufactures electronic components including switches, connectors, jacks, plugs, cable assemblies, and cords. **NOTE:** See website for job listings. Fax or e-mail resumes. **Positions advertised include:** CAD Operator; Product Engineer. **Corporate headquarters location:** This location.

SYMONS CORPORATION
200 East Touhy Avenue, Des Plaines IL 60018. 847/298-3200. **Fax:** 847/635-9287. **Contact:** Human Resources. **E-mail address:** jobs@symons.com. **World Wide Web address:** http://www.symons.com. **Description:** An international manufacturer of standard, custom, and fiberglass concrete-forming equipment. The company also manufactures chemical systems including acrylic sealers, bonding agents, construction grouts, and curing compounds. **NOTE:** See website for job listings. Fax resumes or apply online. **Positions advertised include:** Customer Service Coordinator; Senior Account Manager; Senior Form Designer; Administrative Assistant; Corporate Health and Safety Specialist. **Corporate headquarters location:** This location.

SYNOVATE
222 South Riverside Plaza, Chicago IL 60606. 312/526-4000. **Contact:** Human Resources. **E-mail address:** HR.Resumes@synovate.com. **World Wide Web address:** http://www.synovate.com. **Description:** A market research firm that provides services to the government as well as to national and international companies. **NOTE:** Apply online. **Positions advertised include:** Account Director; Account Group Manager; Associate Data Director; Business Systems Analyst; Executive Assistant. . **Other U.S. locations:** Nationwide. **International locations:** Worldwide. **Parent company:** Aegis.

SYSCO FOOD SERVICES
250 Wieboldt Drive, Des Plaines IL 60016. 847/699-5400. **Fax:** 847/298-3048. **Contact:** Human Resources. **World Wide Web address:** http://www. sysco.com. **Description:** Sells and distributes food service products through more than 65 locations nationwide. **NOTE:** Mail resumes to this location. Entry-level positions and second and third shifts are offered. **Corporate headquarters location:** Houston TX. **Other U.S. locations:** Nationwide.

SYSTEM SENSOR
3825 Ohio Avenue, St. Charles IL 60174. 630/377-6580. **Toll-free phone:** 800/736-7672. **Fax:** 630/377-6593. **Contact:** Human Resources. **E-mail address:** careers@systemsensor.com. **World Wide Web address:** http://www.systemsensor.com. **Description:** Manufactures commercial smoke and heat detection devices. **NOTE:** See website for job listings. E-mail resumes or apply online. **Positions advertised include:** Regional Sales Manager; Senior Material Analyst/Planner; Associate Engineer; Electrical Engineer; Director of Marketing. **Corporate headquarters location:** This location. **Parent company:** Pittway Corporation. **Operations at this facility include:** Advertising; Manufacturing; Research and Development; Sales; Service.

SSA GLOBAL
500 West Madison, Suite 1600, Chicago IL 60661. 312/258-6000. **Fax:** 312/474-7500. **Contact:** Human Resources. **E-mail address:** careersops@ssaglobal.com. **World Wide Web address:** http://www.ssagt.com. **Description:** System Software Associates develops, markets, and supports an integrated line of business application, computer-aided software engineering (CASE), and electronic data interchange (EDI) software, primarily for IBM minicomputers and workstations. **NOTE:** See website for job listings and mail or e-mail resumes. **Corporate headquarters:** This location. **Other U.S. locations:** Nationwide. **International locations:** Worldwide.

T&D METAL PRODUCTS INC.
602 East Walnut Street, Watseka IL 60970. 815/432-4938. **Contact:** Human Resources. **World Wide Web address:** http://www.tdmetal.com. **Description:** Manufactures toolboxes, table bases, and go-carts. **Special programs:** Internships. **Corporate headquarters location:** This location. **Other U.S. locations:** Paris IL; Yorkville IL. **Listed on:** Privately held.

TCF BANK
4192 South Archer Avenue, Chicago IL 60632. 773/847-1140. **Contact:** Human Resources. **World Wide Web address:** http://www.tcfbank.com. **Description:** A full-service bank with more than 300 branch offices in five states. **NOTE:** See website for job listings and apply online. \ **Corporate headquarters location:** Minneapolis MN. **Other U.S. locations:** CO, MI, MN, WI.

TTX COMPANY
101 North Wacker Drive, Chicago IL 60606. 312/853-3223. **Contact:** Human Resources. **World Wide Web address:** http://www.ttx.com. **Description:** A rail transportation company.

TALK-A-PHONE COMPANY
5013 North Kedzie Avenue, Chicago IL 60625. 773/539-1100. **Contact:** Human Resources. **World Wide Web address:** http://www.talkaphone.com. **Description:** Manufactures emergency phones and intercom units.

TATE & LYLE
2200 East El Dorado, Decatur IL 62525. 217/423-4411. **Contact:** Human Resources. **World Wide Web address:** http://www.tateandlyle.com. **Description:** A wet mill corn refinery that produces corn products including animal feed, ethanol, starches, and sweeteners. Founded in 1898. **NOTE:** See website for job listings. **Positions advertised include:** Grain Accounting Clerk; Rate Analyst. **Corporate headquarters location:** London.

TAYLOR COMPANY
750 North Blackhawk Boulevard, Rockton IL 61072. 815/624-8333. **Contact:** Human Resources. **World Wide Web address:** http://www.taylor-company.com. **Description:** Manufactures soft-serve ice cream freezers and other food preparation equipment.

TECHNIUM, INC.
8745 West Higgins Road, Suite 350, Chicago IL 60631. 773/380-0555. **Fax:** 773/380-0568. **Contact:** Jim Archuleta, Human Resources. **E-mail address:** jarchuleta@technium.com. **World Wide Web address:** http://www.technium.com. **Description:** Technium provides computer consulting services focusing on client/server technologies. The company's client base represents a variety of industries, from consumer products and health care to financial services and software. Technium provides a full range of services to deploy client/server applications including architecture planning, application analysis, visualization, and design; graphical user interface development, using Visual C++, Visual Basic, PowerBuilder, and Delphi; object-oriented development with C, C++, and Smalltalk; relational database development in SQL Server, Microsoft Access, Oracle, and Sybase; and decision support systems development using OLAP and Data Warehousing technologies. **NOTE:** E-mail resumes. Entry-level positions are offered. **Special programs:** Training. **Corporate headquarters location:** This location. **Other U.S. locations:** Dallas TX; Milwaukee WI. **Listed on:** Privately held.

THE TELEGRAPH
P.O. Box 278, Alton IL 62002. 618/463-2500. **Contact:** Human Resources. **World Wide Web address:** http://www.thetelegraph.com. **Description:** Publishes the *Telegraph*, a large daily newspaper.

TELEPHONE AND DATA SYSTEMS, INC. (TDS)
30 North LaSalle Street, Suite 4000, Chicago IL 60602. 312/630-1900. **Fax:** 312/630-1908. **Contact:** Human Resources. **E-mail address:** careers@teldta.com. **World Wide Web address:** http://www.teldta.com. **Description:** Provides local telecommunications services including cellular, landline telephone, and paging to customers nationwide. TDS's strategic business units include United States Cellular Corporation, which manages and invests in cellular systems throughout the nation; TDS Telecommunications Corporation, which provides local telephone and access service to rural and suburban areas across the nation and acquires operating telephone companies; American Paging, Inc., which operates paging and voicemail systems; and Aerial Communications, Inc., which is one of the largest licensees of personal communications services in the United States. Founded in 1968. **NOTE:** See website for job listings. E-mail resumes. **Positions advertised include:** Accountant; Support Analyst; Distribution Clerk; Machine Operator; Senior Credit Analyst; Communications Manager. **Special programs:** Internships. **Corporate headquarters location:** This location. **Other U.S. locations:** Nationwide. **Subsidiaries include:** Suttle Press, Inc. is a commercial printing subsidiary; TDS Computing Services, Inc. is an information systems subsidiary. **Operations at this facility include:** Administration.

TELLABS
1415 West Diehl Road, Naperville IL 60563. 630/378-8800. **Fax:** 630/798-2000. **Contact:** Human Resources. **World Wide Web address:** http://www.tellabs.com. **Description:** Designs, manufactures, markets, and services voice and data transport systems and network access systems used worldwide by public telephone companies, long-distance carriers, alternate service providers, cellular and wireless service providers, cable operators, government agencies, and businesses. Founded in 1975. **NOTE:** See website for job listings and apply online. Entry-level positions are offered. **Special programs:** Internships. **Internship information:** Tellabs hires summer to work in software and hardware development and testing areas. See website for more information. **Corporate headquarters location:** This location. **Other U.S. locations:** Boston MA; Hawthorne NY; Round Rock TX; Ashburn VA. **International locations:** Helsinki, Finland; Shannon, Ireland. **Operations at this facility include:** Administration; Manufacturing; Research and Development; Sales; Service. **Listed on:** NASDAQ. **Stock exchange symbol:** TLAB.

TEMPEL STEEL COMPANY
5500 North Wolcott, Chicago IL 60640. 773/250-8000. **Fax:** 773/250-8000. **Contact:** Human Resources. **World Wide Web address:** http://www.tempel.com. **Description:** A manufacturer of steel magnetic laminations for electric motors and transformers. **Positions advertised include:** Database Administrator; Programmer Analyst. **Special programs:** Internships. **Corporate headquarters location:** Skokie IL. **Other U.S. locations:** Elk Grove Village IL; Libertyville IL. **Operations at this facility include:** Administration; Divisional Headquarters; Manufacturing. **Listed on:** Privately held.

TEMPLETON, KENLY & COMPANY, INC.
2525 Gardner Road, Broadview IL 60155. 708/865-1500. **Toll-free phone:** 800/275-5225. **Fax:** 708/865-0894. **Contact:** Human Resources. **World Wide Web address:** http://www.tksimplex.com. **Description:** Manufactures hydraulic and mechanical jacks under the brand name Simplex. **Corporate headquarters location:** This location.

TENNECO AUTOMOTIVE
500 North Field Drive, Lake Forest IL 60045. 847/482-5000. **Contact:** Human Resources. **World Wide Web address:** http://www.tenneco-automotive.com. **Description:** Develops and manufactures suspension systems and engine mounting systems providing noise, shock, and vibration control for the transportation industry. **NOTE:** Submit resume online at the company's website. **Corporate headquarters location:** This location. **Parent company:** Tenneco (Greenwich CT). **Listed on:** New York Stock Exchange. **Stock exchange symbol:** TEN.

TEST AMERICA
1090 Rock Road Lane, Suite 11, East Dundee IL 60118. 847/783-4960. **Fax:** 847/783-4969. **Contact:** Human Resources. **World Wide Web address:** http://www. testamericainc.com. **Description:** Performs testing of wastewater, hazardous waste, and food. **NOTE:** See website for job listings and contact information. **Operations at this facility include:** Service; Sales.

TETRA PAK INC.
101 Corporate Woods Parkway, Vernon Hills IL 60061. 847/955-6000. **Contact:** Human Resources. **E-mail address:** tpincjobs@tetrapak.com. **World Wide Web address:** http://www.tetrapakusa.com. **Description:** Manufactures food processing equipment. **NOTE:** See the corporate website for job listings – http://www.tetrapak.com. Apply online or e-mail resumes. **Operations at this facility:** Sales.

TEXTRON FASTENING SYSTEMS
516 18th Avenue, Rockford IL 61104-5181. 815/961-5000. **Fax:** 815/961-5399. **Contact:** Corporate Human Resources Manager. **World Wide Web address:** http://www.camcar.textron.com. **Description:** A world leader in the cold-forming of custom fasteners. **NOTE:** Submit resumes by mail to Textron Fastening Systems – Aerospace, Human Resources Department, 1224 East Warner Avenue, Santa Ana CA 92707. Resumes may also be faxed to 714/957-2142 or e-mailed to crbrown@tfs.textron.com. **Corporate headquarters location:** Troy MI. **Parent company:** Textron. **Operations at this facility include:** Administration;

Manufacturing; Research and Development; Sales; Service. **Number of employees worldwide:** Over 5,000.

R&D THIEL INC.
2340 Newburg Road, Belvidere IL 61008. 815/544-1699. **Contact:** Human Resources. **E-mail address:** HumanResources@rdthiel.com. **World Wide Web address:** http://www.rdthiel.com. **Description:** Provides a variety of construction services ranging from carpentry labor to completed residential housing. **NOTE:** See website for job listings and contact information. **Positions advertised include:** Wall Panel Designer; Truss Designers; Carpenter Helpers; Carpenters; Lead Carpenters; Jobsite Foreman. **Corporate headquarters location:** This location.

THIRD WORLD PRESS
7822 South Dobson, Chicago IL 60619. 773/651-0700. **Contact:** Human Resources. **World Wide Web address:** http://www.thirdworldpressinc.com. **Description:** A publisher of fiction, nonfiction, and children's stories by African-American authors. Third World Press also publishes titles on audio and produces some videos. **Corporate headquarters location:** This location.

THOMAS ELECTRONICS
300 South LaLonde Avenue, Addison IL 60101. 630/543-6444. **Fax:** 630/543-0287. **Contact:** Human Resources. **World Wide Web address:** http://www.thomaselectronics.com. **Description:** Manufactures deflective yokes for CRTs. **NOTE:** Resumes should be mailed to Thomas Electronics Human Resources Department, 208 Davis Parkway, Clyde NY 14433.

J. WALTER THOMPSON COMPANY
900 North Michigan Avenue, Chicago IL 60611. 312/951-4000. **Contact:** Human Resources. **World Wide Web address:** http://www.jwtworld.com. **Description:** An advertising agency. **NOTE:** Apply online. **Other U.S. locations:** Nationwide.

THOMPSON STEEL COMPANY
9470 King Street, Franklin Park IL 60131. 847/678-0400. **Contact:** Human Resources. **World Wide Web address:** http://www.thompsonsteelco.com. **Description:** Engaged in the cold-roll reduction of strip steel. **Corporate headquarters location:** This location.

THOREK HOSPITAL AND MEDICAL CENTER
850 West Irving Park Road, Chicago IL 60613. 773/525-6780. **Fax:** 773/975-6839. **Contact:** Human Resources. **E-mail address:** humanresources@thorek.org. **World Wide Web address:** http://www.thorek.org. **Description:** A medical center. Thorek also offers The Center for Male Health. **Positions advertised include:** RN; LPN.

3COM CORPORATION
3800 Golf Road, Rolling Meadows IL 60008. 847/262-5000. **Contact:** Human Resources. **World Wide Web address:** http://www.3com.com. **Description:** 3Com is a billion-dollar *Fortune* 500 company delivering global data networking solutions to organizations around the world. 3Com designs, manufactures, markets, and supports a broad range of ISO 9000-compliant global data networking solutions including routers, hubs, remote access servers, switches, and adapters for Ethernet, Token Ring, and high-speed networks. These products enable computers to communicate at high speeds and share resources including printers, disk drives, modems, and minicomputers. **NOTE:** Apply online. **Positions advertised include:** Customer Operations Representative; Program Manager; Software Engineer; Technical Voice Education Developer; Product Engineer.

3M
22614 Route 84 North Cordova, IL 61242-9779. 309/654-2291. **Contact:** Human Resources. **World Wide Web address:** http://www.3m.com. **Description:** 3M manufactures products in three sectors. The Industrial and Consumer sector includes a variety of products under brand names including 3M, Scotch, Post-it, Scotch-Brite, and Scotchgard. The Information, Imaging, and Electronic sector is a leader in several high-growth, global industries including telecommunications, electronics, electrical, imaging, and memory media. The Life Science sector serves two broad market categories: health care, and traffic and personal safety. In the health care market, 3M is a leading provider of medical and surgical supplies, drug delivery systems, and dental products; in traffic and personal safety, 3M is a leader in products for transportation safety, worker protection, vehicle and sign graphics, and out-of-home advertising. **NOTE:** Apply online. **Corporate headquarters location:** St. Paul MN. **International locations:** Worldwide. **Operations at this facility include:** Manufacturing plant.

TICOR TITLE INSURANCE
203 North LaSalle Street, Suite 1390, Chicago IL 60601. 312/621-5000. **Fax:** 312/621-5033. **Contact:** Human Resources. **World Wide Web address:** http://www.ticortitle.com. **Description:** Specializes in real estate title insurance and escrow services. **Corporate headquarters location:** Los Angeles CA. **Other area locations:** Joliet IL; Oaklawn IL; Schaumburg IL.

TIGER DIRECT
175 Ambassador Drive, Naperville IL 60540. 630/355-3000. **Contact:** Human Resources. **World Wide Web address:** http://www.tigerdirect.com. **Description:** Manufactures a wide variety of computer supplies including hardware, software, and computer office equipment. **Operations at this facility include:** This location is a distribution center.

TOOTSIE ROLL INDUSTRIES, INC.
7401 South Cicero Avenue, Chicago IL 60629. 773/838-3400. **Contact:** Human Resources. **World Wide Web address:** http://www.tootsie.com. **Description:** Manufactures and distributes candy, sold primarily under the Tootsie Roll brand name. The company also produces Cella's and Mason candies. Tootsie Roll Industries is one of the largest U.S. confectioners of lollipops sold mainly under the Charms and Blow-Pop brand names. **Corporate headquarters location:** This location.

TOPCO ASSOCIATES, INC.
7711 Gross Point Road, Skokie IL 60077. 847/676-3030. **Fax:** 847/329-3621. **Contact:** Dennis Pieper, Human Resources Manager. **E-mail address:** dpieper@topco.com. **World Wide Web address:** http://www.topco.com. **Description:** A leader in private label procurement and brand management for the supermarket and food service industries. The company specializes in procuring, packaging, and distributing corporate brands, perishables, and pharmaceutical products. **NOTE:** Fax or e-mail resumes to Mr. Pieper. **Corporate headquarters location:** This location. **Other U.S. locations:** Visalia CA; Lakeland FL. **Listed on:** Privately held.

TRADER PUBLISHING COMPANY
840 Oak Creek Drive, Lombard IL 60148. 630/620-7355. **Contact:** Human Resources. **World Wide Web address:** http://www.traderonline.com. **Description:** Publishes classified advertising magazines that feature used vehicles along with parts and accessories. **NOTE:** Submit resumes by mail indicating department of interest.

TRAILMOBILE, INC.
1101 Skokie Boulevard, Suite 350, Northbrook IL 60062. 847/504-2000. **Toll-free phone:** 800/877-4990. **Fax:** 847/480-9262. 1000 North 14th Street, Charleston IL 60921. 217/348-8181. **Contact:** Human Resources. **World Wide Web address:** http://www.trailmobile.com. **Description:** Trailmobile manufactures over-the-road semitrailers. **Operations at this facility include:** Administration; Sales; Manufacturing.

TRANSX
720 Greenleaf Avenue, Elk Grove Village IL 60007. 630/458-1310. **Contact:** Human Resources. **World Wide Web address:** http://www.transx.com. **Description:** A trucking and air freight company. **NOTE:** To apply, visit the website and complete the online application. Interested jobseekers may also contact the Recruiter by phone at 800/385-5005 or via e-mail at jnesbitt@transx.com.

TRI-COR INDUSTRIES, INC.
5 Eagle Center, Suite 8, O'Fallon IL 62269. 618/632-9804. **Fax:** 618/632-9805. **Contact:** Bill Welsch, Deputy Manager. **E-mail address:** b.welsch@tricorind.com. **World Wide Web address:** http://www.tricorind.com. **Description:** Develops software for Department of Defense applications and offers technical support. **NOTE:** Submit resumes and cover letters indicating area of interest. E-mail resumes to Mr. Welsch or download the application found on the website and fax it to his attention.

THE TRIBUNE COMPANY
435 North Michigan Avenue, Chicago IL 60611. 312/222-9100. **Contact:** Human Resources. **World Wide Web address:** http://www.tribune.com. **Description:** Publishes daily newspapers including the *Chicago Tribune, Fort Lauderdale Sun-Sentinel, Los Angeles Times, Baltimore Sun, Hartford Courant, Orlando Sentinel,* and *Daily Press.* The company also owns eight independent TV stations in Illinois, New York, Colorado, Pennsylvania, California, Massachusetts, Georgia, and Louisiana; six radio stations in Illinois, New York, Colorado, and California; and the Chicago Cubs baseball team. **NOTE:** See website for job listings and contact information. Mail resumes to this location. **Special programs:** Internships. **Corporate headquarters location:** This location. **Subsidiaries include:** Independent Network News; The Wright Group; Tribune Entertainment Company. **Listed on:** New York Stock Exchange. **Stock exchange symbol:** TRB.

TRUE VALUE COMPANY
8600 West Bryn Mawr Avenue, Chicago IL 60631-3505. 773/695-5000. **Contact:** Human Resources. **E-mail address:** jobs@truevalue.com. **World Wide Web address:** http://www.truevaluecompany.com. **Description:** A *Fortune* 500 company that operates the True Value, Home & Garden Showplace, and Taylor Rental national retail chains. **NOTE:** Apply online. **Positions advertised include:** Import Logistics Manager; Import Coordinator; Inventory Analyst; Field Marketing Manager; Retail Project Supervisor; Accounts Payable Manager; Transportation Compliance Analyst. **Corporate headquarters location:** This location.

TRUMAN COLLEGE
1145 West Wilson Avenue, Chicago IL 60640. 773/878-1700. **Contact:** Human Resources. **World Wide Web address:** http://www.trumancollege.cc. **Description:** A community college offering automotive, cosmetology, ESL, and continuing education classes. **NOTE:** See website for job listings and contact information. Positions advertised include: Faculty (Various); Nursing Laboratory Coordinator.

TRUSTMARK INSURANCE COMPANY
400 Field Drive, Lake Forest IL 60045. 847/615-1500. **Contact:** Human Resources. **World Wide Web address:** http://www.trustmarkinsurance.com. **Description:** A legal reserve life insurance company. Trustmark Insurance Company issues a wide variety of individual and group life, disability, annuity, hospital, and medical policies, as well as administrative service-only arrangements for larger groups. **Positions advertised include:** Actuarial; Direct Sales Manager; Bindery Operator; Investigative Analyst; Senior Staff Assistant; Telecommunications Manager; Underwriter. **Corporate headquarters location:** This location. **Other U.S. locations:** Nationwide. **Operations at this facility include:** Administration; Sales.

TURTLE WAX, INC.
5655 West 73rd Street, Chicago IL 60638. 708/563-3600. **Fax:** 708/563-3559. **Contact:** Sean Speilman, Human Resources. **E-mail address:** Recruiting@turtlewax.com. **World Wide Web address:** http://www.turtlewax.com. **Description:** Manufactures Turtle Wax brand polishing products. **NOTE:** See website for job listings. Mail, fax e-mail resumes. **Corporate headquarters location:** This location.

TUTHILL CORPORATION
12500 South Pulaski Road, Alsip IL 60805. 708/389-2500. **Contact:** Human Resources. **E-mail address:** jobs@tuthill.com. **World Wide Web address:** http://www.tuthill.com. **Description:** An international distributor and manufacturer of rotary pumps, positive displacement gear, test plugs, and tube connectors. **NOTE:** See website for job listings. **Corporate headquarters location:** Burr Ridge IL. **Operations at this facility include:** Manufacturing.

TYNDALE HOUSE PUBLISHERS, INC.
P.O. Box 80, Wheaton IL 60189. 630/668-8300. **Contact:** Human Resources. **World Wide Web address:** http://www.tyndalebooksellers.com. **Description:** Publishes *The Living Bible,* as well as other religious products including books, movies, calendars, audio books, and Bible reference products. Founded in 1962. **Office hours:** Monday - Friday, 8:00 a.m. - 4:30 p.m. **Corporate headquarters location:** This location. **Listed on:** Privately held.

UOP, INC.
25 East Algonquin Road, Des Plaines IL 60017. 847/391-2000. **Fax:** 847/391-2253. **Contact:** Human Resources. **World Wide Web address:** http://www.uop.com. **Description:** Provides research, development, engineering, and manufacturing services relating to process technology and products for the petroleum and petrochemical industries. **NOTE:** Apply online. Part-time positions offered. **Positions advertised include:** Project Engineer; MRO Buyer; Web Coordinator; Development Chemist; Research Technician; Field Technical Advisor. **Special programs:** Internships. **Corporate headquarters location:** This location. **Listed on:** Privately held.

UOP, INC.
P.O. Box 163, Riverside IL 60546. 708/442-7400. **Contact:** Human Resources. **World Wide Web address:** http://www.uop.com. **Description:** UOP provides research, development, engineering, and manufacturing services relating to process technology

and products for the petroleum and petrochemical industries. **NOTE:** Apply online. **Operations at this facility include:** This location is a research center.

U.S. BUREAU OF ALCOHOL, TOBACCO, AND FIREARMS
300 South Riverside Plaza, Suite 350, Chicago IL 60606. 312/353-6935. **Contact:** Human Resources Department. **World Wide Web address:** http://www.atf.treas.gov/jobs/index.htm. **Description:** A government agency responsible for enforcing alcohol, tobacco, and firearms laws. **NOTE:** See website for job listings and application procedures. **Special programs:** Internship; Volunteer. **Operations at this facility include:** This is the Midwest Regional Audit Office.

U.S. CAN COMPANY
700 East Butterfield, Suite 250, Lombard IL 60148. 630/678-8000. **Contact:** Human Resources. **E-mail address:** humanresources@uscanco.com. **World Wide Web address:** http://www.uscanco.com. **Description:** A manufacturer of metal containers for personal care, household, automotive, paint, and industrial products. In addition, the company manufactures specialty cans. **NOTE:** E-mail resumes and cover letters. **Special programs:** Internships. **Corporate headquarters location:** This location.

U.S. DEPARTMENT OF VETERANS AFFAIRS
JESSE BROWN VA MEDICAL CENTER
820 South Damen Avenue, HRMS, Chicago IL 60612. 312/569-8387. **Contact:** Human Resources. **World Wide Web address:** http://www.vagreatlakes.org. **Description:** A medical center operated by the U.S. Department of Veterans Affairs. From 54 hospitals in 1930, the system has grown to include 171 medical centers; more than 364 outpatient, community and outreach clinics; 130 nursing home care units; and 37 domiciliary residences. The VA operates at least one medical center in each of the 48 contiguous states, Puerto Rico, and the District of Columbia. With approximately 76,000 medical center beds, the VA treats nearly 1 million patients in VA hospitals, 75,000 in nursing home care units, and 25,000 in domiciliary residences. The VA is affiliated with 104 medical schools, 48 dental schools, and more than 850 other schools across the country. **NOTE:** For job listings at this facility, visit http://www.vacareers.com. Send resumes and inquiries to Edward Hines Jr. VA Hospital, Human Resources, Chicago Network, HRMS-05, Hines IL 60141. 708/343-7200. Indicate to which center or for which job you are applying. **Corporate headquarters location:** Washington DC. **Other U.S. locations:** Nationwide. **Operations at this facility include:** Administration; Service.

U.S. DEPARTMENT OF VETERANS AFFAIRS
LAKESIDE CLINIC
333 East Huron Street, Chicago IL 60611. 312/569-8387. **Contact:** Human Resources. **World Wide Web address:** http://www.vagreatlakes.org. **Description:** An outpatient center dedicating to serving veterans and their dependents. The hospital is operated by the U.S. Department of Veterans Affairs. **NOTE:** For job listings at this facility, visit http://www.vacareers.com. Send resumes and inquiries to Edward Hines Jr. VA Hospital, Human Resources, Chicago Network, HRMS-05, Hines IL 60141. 708/343-7200. Indicate to which center or for which job you are applying. **Other U.S. locations:** Nationwide.

U.S. DEPARTMENT OF VETERANS AFFAIRS
EDWARD HINES JR. VA HOSPITAL
P.O. Box 5000, Hines IL 60141. 708/202-8387. **Contact:** Human Resources. **World Wide Web address:** http://www.vagreatlakes.org. **Description:** A medical center operated by the U.S. Department of Veterans Affairs. **NOTE:** For job listings at this facility, visit http://www.vacareers.com. Mail resumes to this location and indicate to which center or for which job you are applying.

U.S. ENVIRONMENTAL PROTECTION AGENCY (EPA)
77 West Jackson Boulevard, Chicago IL 60604. 312/353-2000. **Contact:** Human Resources. **World Wide Web address:** http://www.epa.gov. **Description:** The EPA is dedicated to improving and preserving the quality of the environment, both nationally and globally, and protecting human health and the productivity of natural resources. The agency is committed to ensuring that federal environmental laws are implemented and enforced effectively; U.S. policy, both foreign and domestic, encourages the integration of economic development and environmental protection so that economic growth can be sustained over the long term; and public and private decisions affecting energy, transportation, agriculture, industry, international trade, and natural resources fully integrate considerations of environmental quality. Founded in 1970. **Special programs:** Internships. **Corporate headquarters location:** Washington DC. **Other U.S. locations:** Nationwide.

U.S. ENVIRONMENTAL PROTECTION AGENCY (EPA)
1021 North Grand Avenue East, Springfield IL 62794. 217/782-3397. **Contact:** Human Resources. **World Wide Web address:** http://www.epa.gov. **Description:** The EPA is dedicated to improving and preserving the quality of the environment, both nationally and globally, and protecting human health and the productivity of natural resources. The agency is committed to ensuring that federal environmental laws are implemented and enforced effectively; U.S. policy, both foreign and domestic, encourages the integration of economic development and environmental protection so that economic growth can be sustained over the long term; and public and private decisions affecting energy, transportation, agriculture, industry, international trade, and natural resources fully integrate considerations of environmental quality. Founded in 1970. **Corporate headquarters location:** Washington DC. **Other U.S. locations:** Nationwide.

U.S. FEDERAL RESERVE BANK OF CHICAGO
230 South LaSalle Street, Chicago IL 60604. 312/322-5490. **Fax:** 312/322-5332. **Contact:** Staffing Division. **World Wide Web address:** http://www.chicagofed.org. **Description:** One of 12 regional Federal Reserve banks that, along with the Federal Reserve Board of Governors in Washington DC and the Federal Open Market Committee, comprise the Federal Reserve System (the nation's central bank). As the nation's central bank, Federal Reserve is charged with three major responsibilities: setting monetary policy, banking supervision and regulation, and payment processing. **Office hours:** Monday - Friday, 8:15 a.m. - 5:00 p.m. **Corporate headquarters location:** Washington DC.

U.S. FOODSERVICE
800 Supreme Drive, Bensenville IL 60106. 630/595-1200. **Fax:** 630/250-4202. **Contact:** Personnel. **World Wide Web address:** http://www.usfoodservice.com. **Description:** A broad-line distributor of food products, equipment and supplies, cleaning chemicals, and disposables to a variety of food service locations such as restaurants, nursing homes, hospitals, and institutional dining facilities. **Parent company:** Royal Ahold. **Listed on:** New York Stock Exchange. **Stock exchange symbol:** AHO. **Number of employees worldwide:** 34,000.

U.S. FOODSERVICE
One Sexton Drive, Glendale Heights IL 60139. 630/980-3000. **Fax:** 630/924-2970. **Contact:** Human Resources Department. **World Wide Web address:** http://www.usfoodservice.com. **Description:** An institutional food production and distribution company with clients in the restaurant and health care industries. **Corporate headquarters location:** Columbia MD. **Other U.S. locations:** Nationwide. **Parent company:** Royal Ahold. **Listed on:** New York Stock Exchange. **Stock exchange symbol:** AHO. **Number of employees worldwide:** 34,000.

U.S. FOODSERVICE
One Quality Lane, Streator IL 61364. 815/673-3311. **Contact:** Human Resources. **World Wide Web address:** http://www.usfoodservice.com. **Description:** An institutional food production and distribution company with clients in the restaurant and health care industries. **Corporate headquarters location:** Columbia MD. **Other U.S. locations:** Nationwide. **Parent company:** Royal Ahold. **Listed on:** New York Stock Exchange. **Stock exchange symbol:** AHO. **Number of employees worldwide:** 34,000.

U.S. FREIGHTWAYS
8550 West Bryn Mawr Avenue, Suite 700, Chicago IL 60631. 773/824-1000. **Contact:** Human Resources. **World Wide Web address:** http://www.usfreightways.com. **Description:** U.S. Freightways offers assembly and distribution, domestic and international freight forwarding, and logistics. **Positions advertised include:** Director of Carrier Systems; EDI Coordinator; Senior Programmer/Analyst; Systems Engineer; Systems Support Administrator. **NOTE:** Applicants should indicate the department in which they are interested.

U.S. POSTAL SERVICE
1824 North 25th Avenue, Melrose Park IL 60160. 708/343-2150. **Contact:** Human Resources. **World Wide Web address:** http://www.usps.com. **Description:** A full-service post office serving the Melrose Park area.

U.S. PRECISION GLASS COMPANY
1900 Holmes Road, Elgin IL 60123. 847/931-1200. **Fax:** 847/931-4144. **Contact:** Lynn M. Sprangers, Human Resources Manager. **World Wide Web address:** http://www.uspg.com. **Description:** Fabricates precision glass for appliance, commercial, industrial, and technical applications. **Special programs:** Internships. **Corporate headquarters location:** This location. **Other U.S. locations:** Lewisburg OH; Jefferson TX. **Operations at this facility include:** Administration; Manufacturing; Research and Development; Sales; Service.

USFILTER/ HPD
23562 West Main Street, Plainfield IL 60544. 815/436-3013. **Contact:** Human Resources. **World Wide Web address:** http://www.usfilter.com. **Description:** USFilter is engaged in the manufacture and servicing of water purification and treatment equipment. Primary customers include the electronics industry, utilities, pharmaceutical companies, and other entities with the need for highly purified water. **Operations at this facility include:** This location is a research and development facility for pollution control products. **Parent company:** Veolia Environment.

USFILTER
55 Shuman Boulevard, Naperville IL 60563. 630/357-7330. **Contact:** Janice Slawinski, Human Resources Manager. **World Wide Web address:** http://www.usfilter.com. **Description:** USFilter is engaged in the manufacture and servicing of water purification and treatment equipment. Primary customers include the electronics industry, utilities, pharmaceutical companies, and other entities with the need for highly purified water. **Operations at this facility include:** This location is a design facility for the company's water purification and treatment technologies. **Parent company:** Veolia Environment.

USFILTER
1501 East Woodfield Road, Suite 200 West, Schaumburg IL 60173. 847/706-6900. **Contact:** Human Resources. **World Wide Web address:** http://www.usfilter.com. **Description:** USFilter is engaged in the manufacture and servicing of water purification and treatment equipment. Primary customers include the electronics industry, utilities, pharmaceutical companies, and other entities with the need for highly purified water. **Operations at this facility include:** This location engineers and manufactures air pollution control equipment. **Parent company:** Veolia Environment.

USG CORPORATION
UNITED STATES GYPSUM COMPANY
125 South Franklin Street, Chicago IL 60606. 312/606-4390. **Contact:** Greg Puchalski, Vice President of Human Resources. **World Wide Web address:** http://www.usgcorp.com. **Description:** Manufacturers a wide range of products for use in building construction, repair, and remodeling, and in many industry processes. Products include wallboard, plasters, and agricultural gypsum. The company operates more than 100 plants. **Positions advertised include:** Plant Manager; Production Engineer; Project Engineer; Services Manager; Lab Director; Senior Development Associate; Accountant; Corporate Auditor; Financial Analyst. **Corporate headquarters location:** This location. **International locations:** Canada; Europe; Mexico. **Operations at this facility include:** Administration.

UNDERWRITERS LABORATORIES INC.
333 Pfingsten Road, Northbrook IL 60062. 847/272-8800. **Fax:** 847/509-6300. **Contact:** Human Resources **E-mail address:** northbrook@us.ul.com. **World Wide Web address:** http://www.ul.com. **Description:** An independent, nonprofit corporation established to help reduce or prevent bodily injury, loss of life, and property damage. Engineering functions are divided between six departments: Electrical Department; Burglary Protection and Signaling Department; Casualty and Chemical Hazards Department; Fire Protection Department; Heating, Air Conditioning, and Refrigeration Department; and Marine Department. The company also provides factory inspection services through offices in the United States and 54 other countries. **Corporate headquarters location:** This location. **Other U.S. locations:** CA; NC; NY; WA. **Operations at this facility include:** Administration; Service.

UNILEVER HOME & PERSONAL CARE
205 North Michigan Avenue, Suite 3200, Chicago IL 60601. 312/661-0222. **Contact:** Human Resources. **World Wide Web address:** http://www.unilever.com. **Description:** Develops, manufactures, and sells personal care products including hair and skin care items and deodorants. The company also operates a unit that manufactures and markets similar products for use in beauty salons.

UNISON INDUSTRIES
530 Blackhawk Park Avenue, Rockford IL 61104. 815/965-4700. **Contact:** Human Resources. **World Wide Web address:** http://www.unisonindustries.com. **Description:** Manufactures aircraft equipment including ignition parts, digital engine control systems, sensors, and power generation equipment.

UNISYS CORPORATION
333 Butterfield Road, One Unisys Center, Lombard IL 60148. 630/810-8000. **Contact:** Human Resources. **World Wide Web address:** http://www.unisys.com. **Description:**

Unisys Corporation provides information services, technology, and software. Unisys specializes in developing critical business solutions based on open information networks. The company's Enabling Software Team creates a variety of software projects that facilitate the building of user applications and the management of distributed systems. The company's Platforms Group is responsible for UNIX Operating Systems running across a wide range of multiple processor server platforms including all peripheral and communication drivers. The Unisys Commercial Parallel Processing Team develops microkernel-based operating systems, I/O device drivers, ATM hardware, diagnostics, and system architectures. The System Management Group is in charge of the overall management of development programs for UNIX desktop and entry-server products. **Corporate headquarters location:** Blue Bell PA. **Other U.S. locations:** Nationwide. **Operations at this facility include:** This location is a sales office. **Listed on:** New York Stock Exchange. **Stock exchange symbol:** UIS.

UNITED AIRLINES, INC. (UAL)
P.O. Box 66100, Chicago IL 60666. 847/700-4000. **Physical address:** 1200 East Algonquin Road, Elk Grove Township IL 60007. **Fax:** 847/700-5287. **Contact:** Human Resources. **World Wide Web address:** http://www.ual.com. **Description:** United Airlines services 159 airports in the United States and 32 foreign countries in Europe, North and South America, and Asia. Domestic hubs are located in Chicago, Denver, San Francisco, and Washington DC. International hubs are located in Japan and England. **Special programs:** Internships. **Corporate headquarters location:** This location. **Operations at this facility include:** Administration; Sales.

THE UNITED CENTER
1901 West Madison Street, Chicago IL 60612. 312/455-4500. **Fax:** 312/455-4750. **Contact:** Human Resources. **World Wide Web address:** http://www.united-center.com. **Description:** A state-of-the-art stadium and entertainment facility. The United Center is home to the Chicago Bulls basketball team and the Chicago Blackhawks ice hockey team. **Operations at this facility include:** Administration; Sales; Service.

UNITED STATES TOBACCO MANUFACTURING COMPANY
11601 Copenhagen Court, Franklin Park IL 60131. 847/957-8200. **Contact:** Human Resources. **World Wide Web address:** http://www.ustshareholder.com. **Description:** A manufacturing plant for moist, smokeless tobacco products and a distribution warehouse. Products include Skoal, Copenhagen, and Happy Days smokeless tobaccos. **Corporate headquarters location:** Greenwich CT.

UNITED STATIONERS SUPPLY COMPANY
2200 East Golf Road, Des Plaines IL 60016. 847/699-5000. **Fax:** 847/699-8046. **Contact:** Personnel. **World Wide Web address:** http://www.unitedstationers.com. **Description:** A wholesale distributor of office supplies, furniture, and machines. **Corporate headquarters location:** This location. **Other U.S. locations:** Nationwide. **Operations at this facility include:** Administration; Sales; Service.

UNITRIN, INC.
One East Wacker Drive, Chicago IL 60601. 312/661-4600. **Toll-free phone:** 800/999-0546. **Contact:** Personnel. **World Wide Web address:** http://www.unitrin.com. **Description:** A financial services company with subsidiaries engaged in three business areas: life and health insurance, property and casualty insurance, and consumer finance. Founded in 1990. **Positions advertised include:** Actuarial Services Manager; Product Technician; Territory Sales Manager; Regional Claims Manager. **Special programs:** Internships; Summer Jobs. **Office hours:** Monday - Friday, 8:00 a.m. - 4:30 p.m. **Corporate headquarters location:** This location. **Listed on:** NASDAQ. **Stock exchange symbol:** UTR.

UNIVAR USA INC.
P.O. Box 446 Summit IL 60501-0446. 708/728-6740. **Physical address:** 8500 West 68th Street, Bedford Park IL 60501. **Contact:** Human Resources. **World Wide Web address:** http://www.univarusa.com. **Description:** Manufactures and wholesales chemical pesticides and industrial chemicals.

UNIVERSITY OF CHICAGO
956 East 58th Street, Chicago IL 60637. 773/702-8900. **Contact:** Human Resources. **World Wide Web address:** http://www.uchicago.edu. **Description:** A university with a total enrollment of over 12,000 students. Founded in 1892. **NOTE:** Apply online.

UNIVERSITY OF CHICAGO HOSPITALS & HEALTH SYSTEM
5841 South Maryland Avenue, Chicago IL 60637. 773/702-0198. **Contact:** Human Resources. **World Wide Web address:** http://www.uchospitals.edu. **Description:** A hospital. **NOTE:** Applicants should send resumes to the Employment Office, 800 East 55th Street, Chicago IL 60615. **Positions advertised include:** Certified Nurses Aide; Certified Occupational Therapy Assistant; Dietician/Nutritionist; EEG Technologist; EKG Technician; Emergency Medical Technician; Home Health Aide; Medical Records Technician; Nuclear Medicine Technologist; Occupational Therapist; Pharmacist; Physical Therapist; Physician; Radiological Technologist; Registered Nurse; Respiratory Therapist; Social Worker; Speech-Language Pathologist. **Operations at this facility include:** Administration.

UNIVERSITY OF CHICAGO PRESS
1427 East 60th Street, Chicago IL 60637. 773/702-7700. **Contact:** Human Resources. **World Wide Web address:** http://www.press.uchicago.edu. **Description:** A nonfiction book and periodical publisher. **Positions advertised include:** Advertising Clerk. **Parent company:** University of Chicago. **Operations at this facility include:** Administration.

UNIVERSITY OF ILLINOIS AT CHICAGO
715 South Wood Street, Mail Code 862, Chicago IL 60612. 312/996-0840. **Fax:** 312/413-1190. **Contact:** Associate Director of Employment. **World Wide Web address:** http://www.uic.edu. **Description:** One location of the state university offering graduate and undergraduate programs of study to approximately 25,000 students. **NOTE:** Applicants must apply online. **Operations at this facility include:** Administration; Research and Development; Service.

UNIVERSITY OF ILLINOIS AT SPRINGFIELD
P.O. Box 19243, Springfield IL 62794-9243. 217/206-6600. **Contact:** Human Resources. **World Wide Web address:** http://www.uis.edu. **Description:** One location of the state university specializing in liberal arts and professional studies. The university offers undergraduate and graduate programs of study. Founded in 1969.

UNIVERSITY OF ILLINOIS AT URBANA-CHAMPAIGN
52 East Gregory Drive, Champaign IL 61820. 217/333-2137. **Contact:** Human Resources. **World Wide Web address:** http://www.uiuc.edu. **Description:** The main campus of the state university. Graduate and undergraduate programs are offered through the colleges of Communications; Liberal Arts and Sciences; Fine and Applied Arts; Agriculture, Consumer, and Environmental Sciences; Commerce and Business Administration; Applied Life Sciences; Library and Information Science; Law; Social Work; Medicine; and Veterinary Medicine.

VALUE CITY FURNITURE
15770 S. La Grange Road, Orland Park IL 60462. 708/226-8121. **Fax:** 708/226-8177. **Contact:** John Jacobe, General Manager. **E-mail address:** John.Jacobe@vcf.com. **World Wide Web address:** http://www.vcf.com. **Description:** A furniture retailer with over 100 stores throughout the Midwestern, Eastern, and Southern United States. **Positions advertised include:** Delivery Driver; General Warehouse Worker; Sales Professional; Service Technician; Visual Merchandiser. **Other U.S. locations:** Nationwide.

VAN KAMPEN INVESTMENTS
One Parkview Plaza, P.O. Box 5555, Oakbrook Terrace IL 60181. 630/684-6000. **Contact:** Human Resources. **World Wide Web address:** http://www.vankampen.com. **Description:** An investment management firm.

VAN LEER CONTAINERS, INC.
4300 West 130th Street, Alsip IL 60803. 708/371-4777. **Fax:** 708/371-2047. **Contact:** Human Resources. **World Wide Web address:** http://www.greif.com. **Description:** Manufactures plastic and fiber containers including intermediate bulk containers and closures. The consumer packaging business includes molded fiber products, flexible packaging such as metalized paper, strength films, folding cartons, tubs, and lids. **NOTE:** Current job openings are listed on http://www.hotjobs.com. The Human Resources address is: 425 Winter Road, Delaware OH 43015, Fax: 740/549-6100. **Positions advertised include:** Physical Therapist; CNC Operator; Lead Maintenance Technician. **Corporate headquarters location:** This location. **Other U.S. locations:** Atlanta GA; Florence KY; Canton MS; Greenville OH; Warminster PA. **Parent company:** Greif Brothers. **Operations at this facility include:** Administration; Divisional Headquarters; Manufacturing; Research and Development; Sales; Service.

VAPOR BUS INTERNATIONAL
1010 Johnson Drive, Buffalo Grove IL 60089. 847/777-6429. **Fax:** 847/520-2225. **Contact:** Dennis E. Huebner, Director Human resources. **Description:** Manufactures transit, shuttle, commuter, and tour coach bus doors. **Corporate headquarters location:** This location.

VAUGHAN & BUSHNELL MANUFACTURING COMPANY
P.O. Box 208, Bushnell IL 61422. 309/772-2131. **Contact:** Human Resources. **World Wide Web address:** http://www.vaughanmfg.com. **Description:** Manufactures hand tools including hammers, saws, hatchets, axes and landscaping tools.

VEDDER, PRICE, KAUFMAN, & KAMMHOLZ
222 North LaSalle Street, Suite 2600, Chicago IL 60601. 312/609-7500. **Fax:** 312/609-5005. **Contact:** Gina Grunloh, Human Resources. **E-mail address:** ggrunloh@vedderprice.com. **World Wide Web address:** http://www.vedderprice.com. **Description:** A law firm engaged in a variety of legal services including labor, litigation, corporate, health, and pro bono law. **Other U.S. locations:** New York NY; Roseland NJ.

VERIZON COMMUNICATIONS
1312 East Empire Street, Bloomington IL 61701. 309/663-3311. **Contact:** Human Resources Director. **World Wide Web address:** http://www.verizon.com. **Description:** A full-service communications services provider. Verizon offers residential local and long distance telephone services and Internet access; wireless service plans, cellular phones, and data services; a full-line of business services including Internet access, data services, and telecommunications equipment and services; and government network solutions including Internet access, data services, telecommunications equipment and services, and enhanced communications services. **Corporate headquarters location:** New York NY. **Other U.S. locations:** Nationwide. **Operations at this facility include:** Engineering and Design; Payroll; Regional Headquarters; Sales. **Listed on:** New York Stock Exchange. **Stock exchange symbol:** VZ.

VICTORY MEMORIAL HOSPITAL
1324 North Sheridan Road, Waukegan IL 60085. 847/360-4170. **Fax:** 847/360-4230. **Contact:** Human Resources. **World Wide Web address:** http://www.vistahealth.com. **Description:** A hospital that provides inpatient, outpatient, and home health care services. **Positions advertised include:** Transcriptionist; Evening & Nights Manager; Medical Technologist; Pharmacist; Senior Environmental Services Aides; Patient Care Technician; Registered Nurse; Transporter. **Other area locations:** Lindenhurst IL. **Parent company:** Vista Health Services.

VIDEOJET TECHNOLOGIES
1500 North Mittel Boulevard, Wood Dale IL 60191-1073. 630/860-7300. **Fax:** 630/616-3678. **Contact:** Human Resources. **World Wide Web address:** http://www.videojet.com. **Description:** Provides development, manufacturing, sales, and service of nonimpact ink-jet coding and marking equipment. **Positions advertised include:** International Customer Service Representative; Buyer/Planner; Procurement Buyer; Strategic Account Manager.

VIDEOJET TECHNOLOGIES
P.O. Box 388, Belleville IL 62222. 618/234-1122. **Contact:** Human Resources. **World Wide Web address:** http://www.videojet.com. **Description:** Engaged in the manufacture of microprocessor-controlled and mechanical marking, coding, and packing equipment for industrial use. **Positions advertised include:** International Customer Service Representative; Buyer/Planner; Procurement Buyer; Strategic Account Manager. **Special programs:** Internships. **Operations at this facility include:** Administration; Manufacturing; Research and Development; Sales.

VIENNA BEEF LTD.
2501 North Damen Avenue, Chicago IL 60647. 773/278-7800. **Fax:** 773/278-4759. **Contact:** Human Resources. **E-mail address:** jobs@viennabeef.com. **World Wide Web address:** http://www.viennabeef.com. **Description:** Vienna Beef Ltd. is an international distributor and processor of meat and sausage. **Positions advertised include:** Human Resources Clerk. **Corporate headquarters location:** This location. **Operations at this facility include:** This location houses the corporate headquarters as well as a meat-cutting plant.

VISITING NURSE ASSOCIATION
1245 Corporate Boulevard, 5th Floor, Aurora IL 60504. 630/978-2532. **Contact:** Human Resources. **World Wide Web address:** http://www.vnafoxvalley.com. **Description:** Provides home health services to patients. Services include nursing, physical therapy, occupational therapy, speech pathology, nutritional therapy, mental health and enterostomal therapy, medical social services, and hospice care. **Other U.S. locations:** Nationwide.

VISITING NURSE ASSOCIATION
720 North Bond Street, Springfield IL 62702. 217/523-4113. **Contact:** Human Resources. **Description:** Provides home health services to patients. Services include nursing, physical therapy, occupational therapy, speech pathology, nutritional therapy, mental health and enterostomal therapy, medical social services, and hospice care.

VISKASE CORPORATION
625 Willowbrook Center Parkway, Willowbrook IL 60527. 630/789-4900. **Toll-free phone:** 800/323-8562. **Fax:** 630/455-2155. **Contact:** Human Resources. **World Wide Web address:** http://www.viskase.com. **Description:** Manufactures cellulose casings and flexible packaging used primarily in the food industry. **Special programs:** Internships. **Corporate headquarters location:** This location. **Parent company:** Envirodyne Industries.

VISTA INTERNATIONAL
dba THE DRAKE HOTEL
140 East Walton Place, Chicago IL 60611. 312/787-2200. **Contact:** Human Resources. **World Wide Web address:** http://www.hilton.com. **Description:** A 535-room hotel and restaurant.

WFLD FOX 32
205 North Michigan Avenue, Chicago IL 60601. 312/565-5532. **Recorded jobline:** 312/565-5555. **Contact:** Human Resources Department. **World Wide Web address:** http://www.foxchicago.com. **Description:** Owns WFLD-TV, a Fox affiliate. **Positions advertised include:** Stage Hand; Transmitter Supervisor; Local Account Executive; Engineering Manager. **Special programs:** Internships. **Corporate headquarters location:** Los Angeles CA.

WMAY
P.O. Box 460, Springfield IL 62705. 217/629-7077. **Fax:** 217/629-7952. **Contact:** Human Resources. **World Wide Web address:** http://www.wmay.com. **Description:** A talk radio station.

WMS INDUSTRIES, INC.
3401 North California Avenue, Chicago IL 60618. 773/961-1620. **Fax:** 773/961-1025. **Contact:** Human Resources. **E-mail address:** hr@wmsgaming.com. **World Wide Web address:** http://www.wmsgaming.com. **Description:** WMS Industries operates in three divisions: the gaming division designs and manufactures slot machines; the pinball and cabinets division; and the contract manufacturing division produces coin-operated video games for Midway Games. **Positions advertised include:** BOM Analyst; Electrical Lab Assistant; Lead Artist; Manufacturing Engineer; Planner; Principal Engineer; Software Engineer. **Subsidiaries include:** WMS Gaming Inc. **Listed on:** New York Stock Exchange. **Stock exchange symbol:** WMS.

WPS/MEDICARE
2108 Cimarron Drive Freeport IL 61032. 815/233-5196. **Contact:** Human Resources. **World Wide Web address:** http://www.wpsic.com. **Description:** A managed health care insurance provider for private industry, government, and non-group subscribers. **Corporate headquarters location:** Madison WI.

WACHOVIA SECURITIES, INC.
77 West Wacker Drive, 25th Floor, Chicago IL 60601. 312/574-6000. **Contact:** Human Resources Department. **World Wide Web address:** http://www.wachoviasec.com. **Description:** A full-service brokerage firm with more than 300 offices serving 1.5 million clients. **Other U.S. locations:** Nationwide. **Parent company:** Wachovia Corporation. **Listed on:** New York Stock Exchange. **Stock exchange symbol:** WB.

WALGREEN COMPANY
200 Wilmot Road, Deerfield IL 60015. 847/940-2500. **Contact:** Personnel Recruiting. **World Wide Web address:** http://www.walgreens.com. **Description:** Walgreen operates one of the largest retail drug store chains in the United States, which sells prescription and nonprescription drugs, cosmetics, toiletries, liquor and beverages, tobacco, and general merchandise. **Corporate headquarters location:** This location.

THE WALSH GROUP
929 West Adams, Chicago IL 60607. 312/563-5400. **Fax:** 312/563-5453. **Contact:** Human Resources. **E-mail address:** agonzalez@walshgroup.com. **World Wide Web address:** http://www.walshgroup.com. **Description:** A construction contracting company. **Positions advertised include:** Payroll Data Entry Clerk; Field Secretary; Project Engineer.

WAREHOUSE EQUIPMENT, INC.
2500 York Road, Elk Grove Village IL 60007. 847/595-9400. **Fax:** 847/595-2126. **Contact:** General Manager. **World Wide Web address:** http://www.weinet.com. **Description:** Manufactures and distributes material handling products, provides engineering services for product handling systems, and designs storage and retrieval equipment. Founded in 1971. **NOTE:** Jobseekers may apply for open positions online. **Corporate headquarters location:** This location.

WASHINGTON MUTUAL HOMELOANS
75 North Fairway Drive, Vernon Hills IL 60061. 847/549-6500. **Fax:** 847/549-2568. **Contact:** Human Resources. **World Wide Web address:** http://www.wamumortgage.com. **Description:** A full-service mortgage banking company that originates, acquires, and services residential mortgage loans. **Operations at this facility include:** Administration; Divisional Headquarters; Service.

WASTE MANAGEMENT, INC.
720 East Butterfield Road, Lombard IL 60148. 630/572-8800. **Contact:** Human Resources Manager. **World Wide Web address:** http://www.wm.com. **Description:** An international provider of comprehensive waste management services as well as engineering, construction, industrial, and related service. **Corporate headquarters location:** Houston TX. **International locations:** Worldwide. **Listed on:** New York Stock Exchange. **Stock exchange symbol:** WMI.

WAUBONSEE COMMUNITY COLLEGE
Route 47 at Waubonsee Drive, Building A, Sugar Grove IL 60554. 630/466-4811. **Contact:** Michele Morey, Director of Human Resources. **World Wide Web address:** http://www.wcc.cc.il.us. **Description:** A community college offering occupational programs and programs to students who are planning to transfer to a four-year institution. **Positions advertised include:** Adult Education Student Records Clerk; Bookstore Clerk; Child Care Center Aide; ESL Secretary; Public Safety Cadet; Fitness Center Technical Assistant; Site Manager.

WAUSAU INSURANCE COMPANIES
1431 Opus Place, Suite 300, Downers Grove IL 60515. 630/719-0717. **Toll-free phone:** 800/835-0060. **Contact:** Human Resources. **World Wide Web address:** http://www.wausau.com. **Description:** Offers a full line of business insurance services including casualty, property, and group insurance, through 7 divisional offices and 100 field offices across the United States. **Positions advertised include:** Account Manager; Underwriter; Claims Case Manager; Associate Business Analyst; Claims Specialist; Property Loss Contents Adjuster; Sales Associate; Law Clerk. **Corporate headquarters location:** Wausau WI. **Other U.S. locations:** Nationwide. **Operations at this facility include:** Divisional Headquarters.

WEBER MARKING SYSTEMS, INC.
711 West Algonquin Road, Arlington Heights IL 60005. 847/364-8570. **Fax:** 847/364-8572. **Contact:** Shirley Hurley, Vice President of Human Resources. **E-mail address:** hrdept@webermarketing.com. **World Wide Web address:** http://www.webermarking.com. **Description:** An international distributor of product identification addressing, labeling, industrial, and marking machines and devices. Weber Marking Systems also operates several sales locations. **Corporate headquarters location:** This location.

WELLS FARGO
225 West Wacker Drive, Suite 2550, Chicago IL 60606-2228. 312/592-5600. **Fax:** 312/782-0969. **Contact:** Human Resources. **World Wide Web address:** http://www.wellsfargo.com. **Description**: Wells Fargo is a diversified financial institution with over $234 billion in assets. Wells Fargo serves over 17 million customers through 5,300 independent locations worldwide. The company also maintains several stand-alone ATMs and branches within retail outlets. Services include community banking, credit and debit cards, home equity and mortgage loans, online banking, student loans, and insurance. Wells Fargo also offers a complete line of commercial and institutional financial services. Founded in 1852. **Corporate headquarters location:** San Francisco CA. **Other U.S. locations:** Nationwide. **International locations:** Worldwide. **Listed on:** New York Stock Exchange. **Stock exchange symbol:** WFC.

WELLS FARGO HOME MORTGAGE
4800 West Wallbash Road, Springfield IL 62711. 217/547-7500. **Contact:** Human Resources. **World Wide Web address:** http://www.wellsfargo.com. **Description**: Wells Fargo is a diversified financial institution with over $234 billion in assets. Wells Fargo serves over 17 million customers through 5,300 independent locations worldwide. The company also maintains several stand-alone ATMs and branches within retail outlets. Services include community banking, credit and debit cards, home equity and mortgage loans, online banking, student loans, and insurance. Wells Fargo also offers a complete line of commercial and institutional financial services. Founded in 1852. **Corporate headquarters location:** San Francisco CA. **Other U.S. locations:** Nationwide. **International locations:** Worldwide. **Operations at this facility include:** This location offers home equity and mortgage services. **Listed on:** New York Stock Exchange. **Stock exchange symbol:** WFC.

WELLS MANUFACTURING COMPANY
2100 West Lake Shore Drive, Woodstock IL 60098. 815/338-3900. **Contact:** Human Resources. **Description:** National distributor of electric furnace gray and alloyed iron castings, and cast iron bar stock. **Special programs:** Internships. **Corporate headquarters location:** This location.

WELLS-GARDNER ELECTRONICS CORPORATION
9500 West 55th Street, Suite A, McCook IL 60525. 708/290-2100. **Toll-free phone:** 800/336-6630. **Fax:** 708/290-2200. **Contact:** Gene Ahner, Human Resources Director. **E-mail address:** gahner@wellsgardner.com. **World Wide Web address:** http://www.wgec.com. **Description:** Designs and manufactures CRT video monitors for arcade games, and for the leisure and fitness, automotive, intranet, and video wall markets. Founded in 1925. **Corporate headquarters location:** This location. **Operations at this facility include:** Administration; Engineering and Design; Manufacturing; Research and Development.

WEN PRODUCTS, INC.
501 Davis Road, Elgin IL 60123. 847/289-0386. **Fax:** 847/289-0387. **Contact:** Controller. **World Wide Web address:** http://www.wenproducts.com. **Description:** Manufactures a complete line of power tools including electrical soldering guns, sanders, and electric saws. **Other U.S. locations:** Akron IN; Fowler IN. **Parent company:** Great Lakes Tools.

WERNER COMPANY
10800 West Belmont Avenue, Franklin Park IL 60131. 847/455-9450. **Contact:** Human Resources. **World Wide Web address:** http://www.wernerco.com. **Description:** Manufactures aluminum extrusions and ladders. **Corporate headquarters location:** Greenville PA.

WEST SUBURBAN BANK
711 South Meyers Road, Lombard IL 60148. 630/629-4200. **Contact:** Human Resources. **World Wide Web address:** http://www.westsuburbanbank.com. **Description:** A full-service bank. **Positions advertised include:** Branch Manager; Teller; Loan Servicer; Shift Leader; Personal Banker; Administrative Assistant.

WESTELL TECHNOLOGIES INC.
750 North Commons Drive, Aurora IL 60504. 630/898-2500. **Fax:** 630/375-4148. **Contact:** Human Resources Department. **E-mail address:** employment@ westell.com. **World Wide Web address:** http://www.westell.com. **Description:** Manufactures telecommunications access products. The company's DSL products enable telephone companies to provide interactive media services through existing telephone lines. These products are used to provide faster Internet access as well as telecommuting opportunities. **Positions advertised include:** Account Manager; Account Representative. **Corporate headquarters location:** This location. **Subsidiaries include:** Westell, Inc. **Listed on:** NASDAQ. **Stock exchange symbol:** WSTL.

WESTERN ILLINOIS UNIVERSITY
One University Circle, 105 Sherman Hall, Macomb IL 61455. 309/298-1971. **Fax:** 309/298-2300. **Contact:** Pam Bowman, Director Human Resources. **World Wide Web address:** http://www.wiu.edu. **Description:** A university offering over 80 graduate and undergraduate programs of study.

GEORGE WESTON BAKERIES
ENTENMANN'S
300 West North Avenue, North Lake IL 60164. 708/562-6311. **Contact:** Human Resources Manager. **World Wide Web address:** http://www.gwbakeries.com. **Description:** George Weston Bakeries operates in two distinct business segments; food processing and food distribution. **Corporate headquarters location:** Bayshore NY. **Operations at this facility include:** This location bakes cakes, cookies, and pies.

WESTWOOD ONE INC.
111 East Wacker Drive, Suite 955, Chicago IL 60601. 312/938-0222. **Fax:** 312/938-0353. **Contact:** Office Manager. **World Wide Web address:**

http://www.westwoodone.com. **Description:** A broadcasting network serving over 7,500 radio stations. **Positions advertised include:** Account Representative; Sales Representative. **Office hours:** Monday - Friday, 9:00 a.m. - 5:00 p.m. **Other U.S. locations:** Culver City CA; Detroit MI; New York NY; Arlington VA. **International locations:** London, England; Tokyo, Japan. **Subsidiaries include:** Shadow Broadcast Service. **Listed on:** New York Sock Exchange. **Stock exchange symbol:** WON.

WEYERHAEUSER COMPANY
4160 Campus Drive, Aurora IL 60504. 630/585-3400. **Contact:** Human Resources. **World Wide Web address:** http://www.weyerhaeuser.com. **Description:** A forest management and manufacturing company. Weyerhauser recycles pulp, paper, and packaging products; manufactures wood products; manages timberland; and develops real estate. **Positions advertised include:** Automation Representative; Outside Sales Representative; Customer Service Manager; Human Resources Manager. **Corporate headquarters location:** Tacoma WA. **Other U.S. locations:** Nationwide.

WHEATON COLLEGE
501 College Avenue, Wheaton IL 60187. 630/752-5060. **Contact:** Human Resources. **E-mail address:** hr@wheaton.edu. **World Wide Web address:** http://www.wheaton.edu. **Description:** A private, coeducational, Christian college with an undergraduate enrollment of 2,300.

WHITE SWAN META UNIFORM COMPANY
13975 Polo Trail, Suite 101, Lake Forest IL 60045. 847/247-0380. **Contact:** Human Resources. **Description:** White Swan Meta Uniform Company manufactures uniforms. **Operations at this facility include:** This location is the sales and service office.

WHITING CORPORATION
26000 Whiting Way, Monee IL 60449. 708/587-4000. **Fax:** 708/587-2041. **Contact:** Human Resources. **World Wide Web address:** http://www.whitingcorp.com. **Description:** A manufacturer of heavy overhead gantry cranes, metallurgical process equipment, and transportation maintenance and repair equipment. **Corporate headquarters location:** This location. **Operations at this facility include:** Manufacturing; Sales; Service.

WICKES INC.
706 Deerpath Drive, Vernon Hills IL 60061. 847/367-3400. **Fax:** 847/3673767. **Contact:** Human Resources. **E-mail address:** humanresources@wickes.com. **World Wide Web address:** http://www.wickes.com. **Description:** One of the largest suppliers of building materials in the United States. Wickes's manufacturing facilities produce prehung door units, window assemblies, roof and floor trusses, and framed wall panels. **Corporate headquarters location:** This location. **Other U.S. locations:** Denver CO; Elwood IN; Ocean Springs MS; Lomira WI. **Listed on:** NASDAQ. **Stock exchange symbol:** WIKS.

WICKS ORGAN COMPANY
1100 5th Street, Highland IL 62249. 618/654-2191. **Fax:** 618/654-3770. **Contact:** Scott Wick, Vice President. **World Wide Web address:** http://www.wicks.com. **Description:** A manufacturer of church pipe organs. **Positions advertised include:** Sales Representative. **Corporate headquarters location:** This location. **Operations at this facility include:** Manufacturing; Sales; Service.

WILDMAN, HARROLD, ALLEN & DIXON
2300 Cabot Drive, Suite 455, Lisle IL 60532. 630/955-0555. **Contact:** Human Resources. **World Wide Web address:** http://www.whad.com. **Description:** Wildman, Harrold, Allen & Dixon specialize in corporate, divorce, medical malpractice, real estate, and wills and trusts law. **NOTE:** Resumes should be directed to the corporate headquarters, located at 225 West Wacker Drive, Chicago IL 60606-1229. **Corporate headquarters location:** Chicago IL. **Operations at this facility include:** This location is a satellite office with 12 attorneys.

WILDMAN, HARROLD, ALLEN & DIXON
225 West Wacker Drive, Suite 3000, Chicago IL 60606-1229. 312/201-2000. **Contact:** Human Resources. **World Wide Web address:** http://www.whad.com. **Description:** A law firm specializing in corporate, divorce, medical malpractice, real estate, and wills and trusts law. **Special programs:** Summer Internship. **Office hours:** Monday - Friday, 8:00 a.m. - 6:00 p.m. **Corporate headquarters location:** This location.

WILSON SPORTING GOODS COMPANY
8700 West Bryn Mawr Avenue, Chicago IL 60631. 773/714-6400. **Contact:** Human Resources. **World Wide Web address:** http://www.wilsonsports.com. **Description:** Manufactures sporting goods for golf, tennis, and team sports. Wilson has been affiliated with the NFL since 1941, has produced the official baseball of the NCAA championships since 1986, and has produced the official ball of many of professional baseball's minor league teams. Wilson also manufactures and supplies uniforms to the NFL, MLB, NBA, and many colleges, universities, and high schools throughout the United States. **Corporate headquarters location:** This location. **Parent company:** Amer Group, plc (Helsinki, Finland) is engaged in the marketing of motor vehicles, paper, communications services, and tobacco. **Operations at this facility include:** Administration; Research and Development; Sales; Service.

WOLFRAM RESEARCH, INC.
100 Trade Center Drive, Champaign IL 61820. 217/398-0700. **Fax:** 217/398-0747. **Contact:** Human Resources. **E-mail address:** resumes@wolfram.com. **World Wide Web address:** http://www.wri.com. **Description:** Develops mathematical software and services including Mathematica. **Positions advertised include:** NKS Development Director; Project Assistant; Numerical Computation Developer; Analysis Developer; Symbolic Computation Developer; Software Quality Engineer; Academic Account Sales Executive; Commercial Sales Representative; Technical Product Manager.

WOODHEAD INDUSTRIES, INC.
3 Parkway North, Suite 550, Deerfield IL 60015. 847/236-9300. **Physical address:** 3411 Woodhead Drive, Northbrook IL 60062. **Fax:** 847/236-0503. **Contact:** Human Resources. **World Wide Web address:** http://www.woodhead.com. **Description:** Manufactures a wide variety of specialty electrical commercial and industrial products including portable lighting and power boxes.

THE WOODLAWN ORGANIZATION (TWO)
6040 South Harper Avenue, Chicago IL 60637. 773/288-5840. **Contact:** Human Resources. **Description:** Provides social services including a detoxification center, a child abuse treatment center, mental health facilities, two early childhood development programs, secretarial and word-processing training programs, a youth try-out employment project, and HUD real estate management services. **Corporate headquarters location:** This location. **Operations at this facility include:** Administration.

WOODS EQUIPMENT COMPANY
2606 South Illinois Route 2, P.O. Box 1000, Oregon IL 61061. 815/732-2141. **Fax:** 815/732-7580. **Contact:** Human Resources. **World Wide Web address:** http://www.woodsequipment.com. **Description:** Manufacturer of farm equipment, and lawn and garden products. **Positions advertised include:** Agriculture & Turf Sales Specialist; Construction Equipment Sales Specialist; General Manager; Operations Manager; Manufacturing Engineer. **Corporate headquarters location:** This location. **Other U.S. locations:** Nationwide.

WORLD BOOK INTERNATIONAL
233 North Michigan Avenue, Suite 2000, Chicago IL 60601. 312/729-5800. **Fax:** 312/729-5600. **Contact:** Director of Human Resources. **World Wide Web address:** http://www.worldbook.com. **Description:** An encyclopedia publisher.

WORLD KITCHENS, INC.
5500 Pearl Street, Suite 400, Rosemont IL 60018. 847/678-8600. **Fax:** 847/678-9424. **Contact:** Human Resources. **Description:** A manufacturer and wholesaler of bakeware and kitchen gadgets.

WORLD'S FINEST CHOCOLATE
4801 South Lawndale Avenue, Chicago IL 60632. 773/847-4600. **Toll-free phone:** 800/366-2462. **Fax:** 773/847-7804. **Contact:** Human Resources. **E-mail address:** humanresources@wfchocolate.com. **World Wide Web address:** http://www.wfchocolate.com. **Description:** An international manufacturer of chocolate and cocoa products. **Corporate headquarters location:** This location.

WILLIAM WRIGLEY JR. COMPANY
410 North Michigan Avenue, Chicago IL 60611. 312/644-2121. **Contact:** Human Resources. **World Wide Web address:** http://www.wrigley.com. **Description:** One of the largest producers of chewing gum in the world. Brand name gums include Wrigley's Spearmint, Juicy Fruit, Big Red, Extra, and Freedent. **Positions advertised include:** Chemist; Receptionist; Mechanic; Lab Technician; Machine Operator; Occupational Health Therapist; Sensory Development Scientist. **Corporate headquarters location:** This location. **Other U.S. locations:** GA; NJ. **International locations:** Worldwide. **Subsidiaries include:** Amurol Products Company manufactures and markets novelty chewing gum products; Northwestern Flavors, Inc. produces flavors and mint oil for Wrigley's gums and other food-related products; WRICO Packaging converts raw paper and carton stock into printed packaging materials used by the company; and L.A. Dreyfus manufactures chewing gum base. **Listed on:** New York Stock Exchange. **Stock exchange symbol:** WWY.

WUNDERMAN
233 North Michigan Avenue, Suite 1500, Chicago IL 60601-5519. 312/596-2500. **Contact:** Human Resources. **World Wide Web address:** http://www.wunderman.com. **Description:** An advertising agency.

XPEDX
3555 North Kimball Avenue, Chicago IL 60618. 773/463-0822. **Fax:** 773/463-4862. **Contact:** Human Resources. **World Wide Web address:** http://www.xpedx.com. **Description:** A retailer of paper and office products. **NOTE:** For corporate positions, send resumes and cover letters to Bill Alexander, Human Resources Manager, at this location. For retail positions, contact Tom Phillips at 773/463-6423. **Corporate headquarters location:** This location. **Parent company:** International Paper Company. **Operations at this facility include:** Administration; Sales; Service. **Listed on:** New York Stock Exchange. **Stock exchange symbol:** IP.

YMCA OF METROPOLITAN CHICAGO
801 North Dearborn, Chicago IL 60610. 312/932-1200. **Contact:** Human Resources. **World Wide Web address:** http://www.ymcachgo.org. **Description:** One of the nation's largest and most comprehensive service organizations. The YMCA provides health and fitness; social and personal development; sports and recreation; education and career development; and camps and conferences to children, youths, adults, the elderly, families, the disabled, refugees and foreign nationals, YMCA residents, and community residents, through a broad range of specific programs. **Special programs:** Internships.

YOUNG & RUBICAM, INC./CHICAGO
233 North Michigan Avenue, Suite 1600, Chicago IL 60601. 312/596-3000. **Contact:** Human Resources. **World Wide Web address:** http://www.yandr.com. **Description:** An international advertising agency. The company operates through three divisions: Young & Rubicam International; Marsteller Inc., a worldwide leader in business-to-business and consumer advertising; and Young & Rubicam USA, with 14 consumer advertising agencies operating through four regional groups, and five specialized advertising and marketing agencies. **Corporate headquarters location:** New York NY. **Other U.S. locations:** Nationwide. **International locations:** Worldwide. **Subsidiaries include:** Burson-Marsteller provides public relations services throughout the world.

ZEBRA TECHNOLOGIES CORPORATION
333 Corporate Woods Parkway, Vernon Hills IL 60061. 847/634-6700. **Fax:** 847/913-8766. **Contact:** Human Resource Director. **World Wide Web address:** http://www.zebra.com. **Description:** Designs, manufactures, sells, and supports a broad line of computerized label and ticket printing systems and related specialty supplies. The company provides barcode labeling solutions to manufacturing customers and government entities worldwide for use in automatic identification and data collection systems. **Positions advertised include:** Administrative Assistant; Billing Specialist; Corporate Reservation Agent; Data Entry Specialist; IP Counsel; Claims Coordinator; Cost Accountant; Credit Coordinator; Staff Accountant.

ZENITH ELECTRONICS CORPORATION
2000 Millbrook Drive, Lincolnshire IL 60069. 847/391-7000. **Fax:** 847/941-8200. **Contact:** Human Resources. **E-mail address:** careers@zenith.com. **World Wide Web address:** http://www.zenith.com. **Description:** Designs, manufactures, and markets consumer electronics products including televisions, videocassette recorders, and cable television and network systems. **Special programs:** Internships. **Corporate headquarters location:** This location.

ZURICH DIRECT
1400 American Lane, Schaumburg IL 60173. 847/605-6000. **Contact:** Human Resources. **World Wide Web address:** http://www.zurichdirect.com. **Description:** A life insurance company with worldwide operations. **Corporate headquarters location:** This location. **Parent company:** Zurich Kemper Life.

AET PACKAGING FILMS
P.O. Box 5038, Terre Haute IN 47805-0038. 812/466-4277. **Physical address:** U.S. Highway 41 North, Terre Haute IN 47805. **Fax:** 812/462-5100. **Contact:** Ken Baker, Human Resources Manager. **World Wide Web address:** http://www.aetfilms.com. **Description:** A leading manufacturer of plastic films for flexible packaging applications. AET's polypropylene film products are used for snack food and candy packaging, labels for bottles and cans, and other packaging, labeling, and overwrap applications. **Special programs:** Internships. **Corporate headquarters location:** Newcastle DE. **Other U.S. locations:** Covington VA; Chicago IL **International locations:** Australia; Brazil; Canada; Mexico. **Parent company:** Applied Extrusion Technologies, Inc.

AM GENERAL CORPORATION
105 North Niles Avenue, South Bend IN 46634. 574/237-6222. **Fax:** 574/284-2910. **Contact:** Human Resources Department. **World Wide Web address:** http://www.amgeneral.com. **Description:** Manufactures the Hummer, an oversized truck built primarily for the military. **Other U.S. locations:** Mishawaka IN. **President and CEO:** James A. Armour.

AP IMAGE TEAM INC.
1620-B North Ironwood Drive, South Bend IN 46635. 574/259-7112. **Fax:** 574/259-0574. **Toll-free phone:** 866/259-7112. **Contact:** Human Resources. **E-mail address:** info@APImageTM.com. **World Wide Web address:** www.apimagetm.com. **Description:** A promotional marketing company founded in 1991 that provides web/graphic design services. **Positions advertised include:** Java Programmer; Customer Service Representative.

ARC OPPORTUNITIES, INC.
0235 West 300 North, Howe IN 46746. 260/463-2653. **Fax:** 260/463-2046. **Contact:** Human Resources. **E-mail address:** info@arcopportunities.com. **World Wide Web address:** http://www.thearclink.org. **Description:** ARC Opportunities offers a skills workshop and some contract factory work opportunities for handicapped adults and helps these individuals attain jobs in the community. ARC also hosts the First Steps program, which aids infants and children with physical and learning disabilities.

ATC ASSOCIATES INC.
7988 Centerpoint Drive, Suite 100, Indianapolis IN 46256. 317/849-4990. **Fax:** 317/849-4278. **Contact:** Human Resources Department. **E-mail address:** atcjobs@atc-enviro.com. **World Wide Web address:** http://www.atc-enviro.com. **Description:** An environmental consulting services firm. **Positions advertised include:** Industrial Hygienist.

ADESA CORPORATION
310 East 96th Street, Suite 400, Indianapolis IN 46024. 317/815-4077. **Fax:** 317/249-4651. **Contact:** Human Resources. **E-mail address:** Careers@adessa.com. **World Wide Web address:** http://www.adesa.com. **Description:** Auctions used cars and other vehicles to franchised auto dealerships. Adesa also provides auto reconditioning and vehicle transport services.

ADVANCED MICROELECTRONICS, INC.
6001 East Old Highway 50, Vincennes IN 47591. 812/726-4500. **Fax:** 812/726-4551. **Contact:** Human Resources. **E-mail address:** info@ advancedmicro.com. **World Wide Web address:** http://www.advancedmicro.com. **Description:** Provides computer repair services and computer sales. **Positions advertised include:** Software Engineer; Sales Account Representative; Field Service Technician; Network Engineer.

ADVO INC.
8910 Purdue Road, Suite 650, Indianapolis IN 46268. 317/879-4710. **Contact:** Human Resources. **World Wide Web address:** http://www.advo.com. **Description:** A direct mail advertising company. Founded in 1929. **NOTE:** Send resumes to 10176 Dixie Highway, Florence KY 41042. **Corporate headquarters location:** Windsor CT. **Other U.S. locations:** Nationwide.

AETNA U.S. HEALTHCARE
3500 Coliseum Boulevard East, Fort Wayne IN 46805. 260/496-5400. **Fax:** 260/496-5401. **Contact:** Human Resources. **World Wide Web address:** http://www.aetna.com. **Description:** Provides managed health care benefits, indemnity health care benefits, dental, pharmacy, vision, and group insurance coverage. **Corporate headquarters location:** Hartford CT.

AIR ROAD EXPRESS
3150 Chief Lane, Indianapolis IN 46241. 317/390-6500. **Toll-free phone:** 800/899-3812. **Contact:** Jim Lape, Human Resources Director. **World Wide Web address:** http://www.airroad.com. **Description:** An air transportation company. **Positions advertised include:** Company Driver; Owner Operator.

AIRGUARD
2234 East Market Street, New Albany IN 47150. 812/944-6793. **Fax:** 812/949-3509. **Contact:** Sherrie Reas, Human Resources Manager. **World Wide Web address:** http://www.airguard.com. **Description:** Manufactures commercial and industrial air-filtration equipment.

ALCOA (ALUMINUM COMPANY OF AMERICA)
P.O. Box 10, Newburgh IN 47629-0010. 812/853-6111. **Fax:** 812/853-1086. **Contact:** Human Resources. **World Wide Web address:** http://www.alcoa.com. **Description:** Engaged in all aspects of the aluminum industry including mining, refining, smelting, fabricating, and recycling. ALCOA also manufactures ceramic packaging for the semiconductor industry, alumina chemicals, plastic bottle closures, vinyl siding, packaging machinery, and electrical distribution systems for automobiles. **Positions advertised include:** Controller; Director, Alcoa Business System; Product Marketing Manager.

ALLTRISTA CONSUMER PRODUCTS COMPANY
345 South High Street. Suite 201, Muncie IN 47305. 765/281-5000. **Fax:** 765/281-5403. **Contact:** Human Resources. **World Wide Web address:** http://www.alltrista.com. **Description:** Alltrista Consumer Products Company manufactures a line of home food preservation products including consumer jars, jar closures, and related food products. **Operations at this facility include:** This location houses administrative and marketing offices. **Parent company:** Jarden Corporation is a diversified manufacturer operating in a number of product and service areas such as high-barrier, multilayer, coextruded plastic products, including sheet-formed containers and retort containers; copper-plated zinc penny blanks, cans for use in zinc/carbon batteries, and other industrial zinc products; protective coating application and decorative lithography services; tin-plated steel aluminum and light-gauge rolled products; thermoformed plastic refrigerator door liners, separators, and evaporator trays; injection molded plastics products; and software and hardware for nondestructive inspection systems.

ALPINE ELECTRONICS MANUFACTURING OF AMERICA
421 North Emerson Avenue, Greenwood IN 46214. 317/881-7700. **Contact:** Gary Sexton, Senior Manager of Human Resources. **World Wide Web address:** http://www.alpine.com. **Description:** Manufactures car stereos and accessories.

AMERIANA BANK & TRUST
P.O. Box H, New Castle IN 47362. 765/529-2230. **Physical address:** 2118 Bundy Avenue, Newcastle IN 47362. **Contact:** Jane K. Moyer, Assistant Vice President of Personnel and Administrative Services. **World Wide Web address:** http://www.ameriana.com. **Description:** A savings and loan bank. **Parent company:** Ameriana Bancorp.

AMERICAN BOTTLING CO.
401 North Railroad Avenue, Northlake IN 60164. 708/492-0514. **Contact:** Human Resources. **Description:** Produces a variety of soft drink and juice products.

AMERICAN COMMERCIAL LINES HOLDINGS LLC (ACL)
P.O. Box 610, Jeffersonville IN 47130. 812/288-0100. **Fax:** 812/288-0413. **Contact:** Human Resources. **World Wide Web address:** http://www.acbl.net. **Description:** A large, diversified transportation network operating in North and South America. American Commercial Lines Holdings also operates marine construction facilities and river terminals, and provides communications and repair services. **NOTE:** Entry-level positions, part-time jobs, and second and third shifts are offered. **Special programs:** Internships. **Office hours:** Monday - Friday, 8:00 a.m. - 5:00 p.m. **Corporate headquarters location:** This location. **Other U.S. locations:** New Orleans LA; St. Louis MO. **International locations:** Argentina; Venezuela. **Subsidiaries include:** ACBL; ACT; Jeffboat; Louisiana Dock Company; Watercom. **CEO:** Stephen A, Frasher.

AMERICAN ELECTRONIC COMPONENTS
23590 Country Road 6, Elkhart IN 46514. 574/264-1116. **Fax:** 574/264-4681. **Contact:** Human Resources. **World Wide Web address:** http://www.aecsensors.com. **Description:** Manufactures and markets electronic components. **Operations at this facility include:** This location designs and manufactures specialized electronic and electrical components including highly engineered sensors.

AMERICAN ELECTRIC POWER (AEP)
P.O. Box 60, Fort Wayne IN 46801. 260/425-2111. **Fax:** 614/716-1864. **Contact:** Jeff Keifer, Human Resources Manager. **World Wide Web address:** http://www.aep.com. **Description:** An electric utility company. **NOTE:** Send resumes to: American Electric Power, Human Resources, One Riverside Plaza, Columbus OH 43215. **Corporate headquarters location:** This location. **Operations at this facility include:** Administration.

AMERICAN GENERAL FINANCE
P.O. Box 59, Evansville IN 47708. 812/468-5677. **Physical address:** 601 North West Second Street, Evansville IN 47708. **Fax:** 812/468-5119. **Recorded jobline:** 812/468-5600. **Contact:** Human Resources. **World Wide Web address:** http://www.agfinance.com. **Description:** One of the country's largest public insurance companies. American General Finance also provides financial services including mortgage loans, real estate investment and development, investment counseling, and management and distribution of mutual funds. Founded in 1920. **Positions advertised include:** Accounting Analyst; Business/Financial Analyst; Customer Service Representative; Collector; Senior Mail Clerk; Design Specialist; Quality Assurance Supervisor; Retail Credit Analyst; Specialist Programmer. **Corporate headquarters location:** This location. **Other U.S. locations:** Nationwide. **Subsidiaries include:** MorEquity. **Parent company:** American General Corporation.

AMERICAN SAVINGS BANK, FSB
8230 Hohman Avenue, Munster IN 46321. 219/836-5870. **Fax:** 219/836-5883. **Contact:** Human Resources. **World Wide Web address:** http://www.ambfinancial.com. **Description:** A full-service bank.

AMERICAN UNITED LIFE INSURANCE COMPANY
P.O. Box 368, Indianapolis IN 46206-0368. 800/249-6269. **Physical address:** One American Square, Indianapolis IN 46282. **Fax:** 317/285-1931. **Recorded jobline:** 317/285-4444. **Contact:** Employment. **E-mail address:** aul_employment@aul.com. **World Wide Web address:** http://www.aul.com. **Description:** Provides insurance, annuities, reinsurance, and investment services. **Positions advertised include:** Processor; Process Improvement Analyst; Senior Operations Audit Consultant; Transition Consultant; Policyholder Service Specialist; Corporate Development Manager; Staff Accountant; Bindery/Printing Specialist; Part-time Recruiter; Project Manager; Technical Support Specialist; Senior Programmer Analyst; Compliance Supervisor. **Special programs:** Internships. **Internship information:** A variety of internships are offered. See website for a detailed listing. **Office hours:** Monday - Friday, 8:00 a.m. - 5:00 p.m. **Corporate headquarters location:** This location. **Subsidiaries include:** State Life Insurance. **Operations at this facility include:** Administration; Sales. **Listed on:** Privately held.

ANALYSTS INTERNATIONAL CORPORATION (AIC)
5750 Castle Creek Parkway North, Suite 259, Indianapolis IN 46250. 317/ 842-1100. **Contact:** Human Resources. **World Wide Web address:** http://www.analysts.com. **Description:** An international computer consulting firm. The company assists clients in analyzing, designing, and developing systems using different programming languages and software. Founded in 1966. **Office hours:** Monday - Friday, 7:30 a.m. - 5:00 p.m. **Corporate headquarters location:** Minneapolis MN. **Other U.S. locations:** Nationwide. **Operations at this facility include:** Regional Headquarters. **Listed on:** NASDAQ. **Stock exchange symbol:** ANLY.

ANCHOR GLASS CONTAINER CORPORATION
603 East North Street, Winchester IN 47394. 765/584-6101. **Contact:** Rhonda Rust, Human Resources Manager. **E-mail address:** webhr@anchorglass.com. **World Wide Web address:** http://www.anchorglass.com. **Description:** Manufactures glass containers for food, beverage, and pharmaceutical industries, along with consumer glassware. Operations encompass over 20 divisions and subsidiaries with 40 plants and distribution centers located in the United States and abroad. **Corporate headquarters location:** Tampa FL.

ANCILLA SYSTEMS, INC.
1000 South Lake Park Avenue, Hobart IN 46342. 219/947-8500. **Contact:** Molly Lawlor. **E-mail address:** mlawlor@ancilla.org. **World Wide Web address:** http://www.ancilla.org. **Description:** A multi-institutional, nonprofit health care corporation. Ancilla Systems is sponsored by the Poor Handmaids of Jesus Christ. The company operates seven hospitals in Illinois and Indiana, a home health care affiliate, and a community hospital. Founded in 1857. **Corporate headquarters location:** This location. **Subsidiaries include:** Harbor Health Services, Inc.; Lakeshore Health Systems Incorporated; Michiana Community Hospital, Inc.; St. Elizabeth's Hospital of

Chicago, Inc.; St. Joseph Medical Center of Fort Wayne; St. Joseph Mishawaka Health Services, Inc.; St. Mary's Hospital of East St. Louis, Inc. **Listed on:** Privately held.

ANTHEM, INC.
220 Virginia Avenue, Indianapolis IN 46203. 317/488-6000. **Toll-free phone:** 800/331-1476. **Fax:** 317/488-6028. **Contact:** Human Resources. **World Wide Web address:** http://www.anthem-inc.com. **Description:** Provides health insurance. **Positions advertised include:** Account Manager; Systems Advisor; Customer Service Representative. **Corporate headquarters location:** Indianapolis IN. **President and CEO:** Larry C. Glasscock.

AREA FIVE AGENCY ON AGING AND COMMUNITY SERVICES
1801 Smith Street, Logansport IN 46947. 574/722-4451. **Fax:** 574/722-3447. **Contact:** Human Resources. **World Wide Web address:** http://www.areafive.com. **Description:** A social services organization that offers nursing home placement for the elderly, childcare services, and home weatherizing services. Area Five also hosts the local Head Start Program. **Positions advertised include:** Case Manager.

ARVIN INDUSTRIES, INC.
One Noblitt Plaza, Box 3000, Columbus IN 47202. 812/378-1500. **Contact:** Mr. Raymond P. Mack, Vice President of Human Resources Department. **World Wide Web address:** http://www.arvinmeritor.com. **Description:** Engaged in the manufacture of exhaust systems (OEM and aftermarket) and ride control products that serve the automotive, consumer, and industrial markets. **Positions advertised include:** Senior Technician; Senior Engineer; Process Engineer. **Corporate headquarters location:** This location. **Parent company:** Arvin Meritor. **Listed on:** New York Stock Exchange. **Stock exchange symbol:** ARM.

ASCOT ENTERPRISES, INC.
P.O. Box 165, Nappanee IN 46550-0165. 574/773-7751. **Physical address:** 503 South Main Street, Nappanee IN 46550. **Toll-free phone:** 877/773-7751. **Fax:** 574/773-2894. **Contact:** Human Resources. **World Wide Web address:** http://www.ascotent.com. **Description:** Engaged in the manufacture of window coverings and bedding for homes, recreational vehicles, and the hospitality industry. Founded in 1976. **Other U.S. locations:** CA; FL; GA; OH; OR; PA; TX.

ASHER AGENCY, INC.
P.O. Box 2535, Fort Wayne IN 46801-2535. 260/424-3373. **Physical address:** 535 West Wayne Street. Fort Wayne, IN 46801. **Toll-free phone:** 800/900-7031. **Contact:** Tom Borne, President. **E-mail address:** tomb@ asheragency.com. **World Wide Web address:** http://www.asheragency.com. **Description:** An advertising agency.

ASSOCIATION OF RETIRED AMERICANS
6505 East 82nd Street, Suite 130, Indianapolis IN 46250. 317/915-2500. **Fax:** 317/915-2510. **Contact:** Human Resources. **World Wide Web address:** http://www.ara-usa.org. **Description:** Provides insurance discounts, hearing and vision care discounts, and car rental discounts for members.

ATLAS VAN LINES, INC.
1212 St. George Road, Evansville IN 47711. 812/424-4326. **Fax:** 812/421-7155. **Contact:** Pam Brio. **E-mail address:** pambrio@atlasworldgroup.com. **World Wide Web address:** http://www.atlasvanlines.com. **Description:** A worldwide common carrier, principally engaged in the transportation of used household goods, general commodities, special products, and freight forwarding. **Positions advertised include:** Driver. **Corporate headquarters location:** This location.

ATWOOD CENTER
1120 North Main Street, Elkhart IN 46514. 574/264-2131. **Contact:** Human Resources. **World Wide Web address:** http://www.atwoodmobile.com. **Description:** Designs, manufactures, and supplies window and door systems to the combined automobile, light truck and van, bus, heavy truck, and recreational vehicle markets in North America. Product categories include automotive windows and doors, automotive regulators, mass transit/RV/heavy trucks, and plastic products.

AURORA CASKET COMPANY, INC.
10944 Marsh Road, Aurora IN 47001. 812/926-1111. **Fax:** 812/926-0208. **Contact:** Human Resources. **E-mail address:** kflory@auroracasket.com. **World Wide Web address:** http://www.auroracasket.com. **Description:** Manufactures and distributes caskets. **Positions advertised include:** Metal Supervisor; Sales Representative; Supervisor of Paint Operations. **Corporate headquarters location:** This location. **President:** William E. Barrott III.

AVIS INDUSTRIAL CORPORATION
P.O. Box 548, Upland IN 46989. 765/998-8100. **Physical address:** 1909 South Main Street, Upland IN 46989. **Fax:** 765/998-8111. **Contact:** Peggy Sheets, Personnel Director. **World Wide Web address:** http://www.avisindustrial.com. **Description:** Avis Industrial Corporation and its subsidiaries manufacture industrial construction equipment, steel tubing, forgings, and metal fasteners. Founded in 1959. **Corporate headquarters location:** This location. **Other U.S. locations:** Nationwide. **Operations at this facility include:** This location houses administrative offices. **Listed on:** Privately held.

BI MONITORING
P.O. Box 1336, Anderson IN 46015. 765/641-2496. **Physical address:** 800 Main Street, Anderson IN 46015. **Fax:** 765/609-3018. **Contact:** Human Resources. **E-mail address:** resumes@bi.com. **World Wide Web address:** http://www.bi.com. **Description:** A leading provider of electronic home arrest and jail management systems to corrections agencies worldwide. The company also offers computerized interactive telephone service and monitoring service for its electronic monitoring systems. BI Monitoring operates through the following divisions: Research and Development, Manufacturing, Quality Assurance, Sales, Marketing, Product Service, Account Management, Monitoring, Administration, and Management. **Corporate headquarters location:** Boulder CO. **Other U.S. locations:** GA; IL; OH; TX.

BFI
2017 North Fares Avenue, Evansville IN 47711-3967. 812/424-3345. **Contact:** Human Resources. **World Wide Web address:** http://www.bfi.com. **Description:** Specializes in residential, medical, and commercial solid waste collection, processing, and disposal. **Other U.S. locations:** Nationwide. **Parent company:** Allied Waste Industries, Inc. **Listed on:** New York Stock Exchange. **Stock exchange symbol:** AW.

BKD LLP
P.O. Box 44998, Indianapolis IN 46244. 317/383-4000. **Physical address:** 201 North Illinois Street, Suite 700, Indianapolis IN 46402. **Fax:** 317/383-4200. **Contact:** David L. Leising, Recruiter. **E-mail address:** dleising@bkd.com. **World Wide Web address:** http://www.bkd.com. **NOTE:** To reach David Leising directly dial ext. 4215. **Description:** A full-service certified public accounting and consulting firm. **Special programs:** Internships. **Office hours:** Monday - Friday, 8:00 a.m. - 5:00 p.m. **Corporate headquarters location:** This location.

BMG ENTERTAINMENT
6550 East 30th Street, Indianapolis IN 46219. 317/542-6000. **Contact:** Human Resources. **World Wide Web address:** http://www.bmg.com. **Description:** Engaged in the production of music and entertainment through 200 music labels, music publishing, direct marketing, and CD and cassette manufacturing. **Special programs:** Internships. **Corporate headquarters location:** New York NY. **Parent company:** Bertelsmann AG.

BP AMOCO PLC
2815 Indianapolis Boulevard, P.O. Box 710, Whiting IN 46394. 219/473-7700. **Contact:** Human Resources. **World Wide Web address:** http://www. bpamoco.com. **Description:** Manufactures, transports, and markets petroleum products.

BPB CELOTEX
P.O. Box 157, Lagro IN 46941-0157. 260/782-2211. **Contact:** Personnel Department. **E-mail address:** hr@bpb-na.com. **World Wide Web address:** http://www.bpb-na.com. **Description:** Manufactures molded acoustical ceiling tile and mineral wool. **Operations at this facility include:** Manufacturing.

BAKER & DANIELS
300 North Meridian Street, Suite 2700, Indianapolis IN 46204. 317/237-1299. **Fax:** 317/237-1000. **Contact:** Kristin Givens, Legal Recruiting Administrator. **E-mail address:** Kristin.givens@bakerd.com. **World Wide Web address:** http://www.bakerdaniels.com. **Description:** A legal services firm specializing in corporate, environmental, and international law. Baker & Daniels employs 20 practice teams to serve its clients. **Positions advertised include:** Legal Secretary. **Special programs:** Summer Associate Programs.

BALL MEMORIAL HOSPITAL
2401 West University Avenue, Muncie IN 47303-3499. 765/747-3007. **Fax:** 765/747-4476. **Recorded jobline:** 765/747-3636. **Contact:** Human Resources. **World Wide Web address:** http://www.ballhospital.org. **NOTE:** The jobine is updated on the 15th and 30th of every month. For current job listings and descriptions visit the parent company's website: http://www.cardinalhealthsystems.org. **Description:** A 550-bed teaching hospital and medical referral center for east central Indiana. The hospital has comprehensive rehabilitation services and a full-service laboratory. **Special programs:** Internships. **Parent company:** Cardinal Health System. **Listed on:** Privately held.

BALLET INTERNATIONALE
502 North Capitol Avenue, Suite B, Indianapolis IN 46204. 317/637-8979. **Fax:** 317/637-1637. **Contact:** Carolyn Treeby, Company Manager. **E-mail address:** ctreeby@balletinternationale.org. **World Wide Web address:** http://www.balletinternationale.org. **Description:** A professional ballet company that performs nationally. **Special programs:** Internships. **Corporate headquarters location:** This location.

BANK ONE
211 West Washington Street, South Bend IN 46601. 574/283-4100. **Contact:** Human Resources Department. **World Wide Web address:** http://www.bankone.com. **Description:** A full-service bank. **Positions advertised include:** Assistant Banking Center Manager; Banking Center Manager; Teller. **Other area locations:** Statewide. **Other U.S. locations:** Nationwide.

BANK ONE INDIANA, N.A.
111 Monument Circle, Suite 102, Indianapolis IN 46277. 317/321-7020. **Contact:** Human Resources Department. **World Wide Web address:** http://www.bankone.com. **Description:** A full-service bank. **Positions advertised include:** Asset Based Lender; Assistant Banking Center Manager; Banking Center Manager; Banker. **Special programs:** Internships. **Corporate headquarters location:** Columbus OH. **Other U.S. locations:** Nationwide. **Parent company:** Banc One Corporation (Columbus OH) is one of the nation's largest bank holding companies. Banc One operates an affiliate network of over 75 banks with more than 1,500 banking locations. In addition, Banc One operates corporations involved in data processing, venture capital, investment and merchant banking, trust, brokerage, investment management, leasing, mortgage banking, consumer finance, and insurance. **Operations at this facility include:** Regional Headquarters.

BARNES & NOBLE BOOKSTORES
3748 East 82nd Street, Indianapolis IN 46240. 317/594-7525. **Contact:** Human Resources. **World Wide Web address:** http://www.bn.com. **Description:** A discount bookstore chain. This location has a cafe and music department in addition to its comprehensive book departments. **Other U.S. locations:** Nationwide.

BARNES & NOBLE BOOKSTORES
2240 East 80th Avenue, Merrillville IN 46410. 219/735-7788. **Fax:** 219/736-0841. **Contact:** Human Resources. **World Wide Web address:** http://www.bn.com. **Description:** A discount bookstore chain. **Other U.S. locations:** Nationwide.

BARNES & THORNBURG
11 South Meridian Street, Indianapolis IN 46204. 317/236-1313. **Fax:** 317/231-7433. **Contact:** Joseph Eaton, Chair of Recruiting Committee. **World Wide Web address:** http://www.btlaw.com. **Description:** A legal firm specializing in international, trade, business, utility, taxes, and real estate law.

BATES USA
117 East Washington Street, Indianapolis IN 46204. 317/686-7800. **Contact:** Shawna Lake, Personnel Manager. **World Wide Web address:** http://www.batesusa.com. **Description:** An advertising agency. **Corporate headquarters location:** New York NY.

BATESVILLE CASKET COMPANY, INC.
One Batesville Boulevard, Batesville IN 47006. 812/934-7444. **Contact:** Human Resources. **E-mail address:** employment@batesvillecasket.net. **World Wide Web address:** http://www.batesville.com. **Description:** Manufactures funeral-related products including caskets and urns. **Corporate headquarters location:** This location. **Parent company:** Hillenbrand Industries, Inc.

BAYER CORPORATION
P.O. Box 40, Elkhart IN 46515. 574/264-8111. **Physical address:** 1884 Miles Avenue, Elkhart IN 46514. **Fax:** 574/262-7450. **Contact:** William Gross, Human Resources Director. **World Wide Web address:** http://www.bayerus.com. **Description:** Produces citric acid monitoring systems for blood and urine, over-the-counter cold remedy products, and vitamins. **NOTE:** To increase chances of consideration, applicants

should submit a resume online in reference to a specific job posting. **Special programs:** Internships; Co-ops.

BELDEN WIRE AND CABLE COMPANY
P.O. Box 1980, Richmond IN 47375-1980. 765/983-5200. **Physical address:** 2200 U.S. Highway 27 South, Richmond IN 47374. **Fax:** 765 983-5294. **Contact:** Human Resources. **E-mail address:** hr@belden.com. **World Wide Web address:** http://www.bwcecom.belden.com. **Description:** Designs and manufactures wire, cable, and cord products. Belden serves the computer market with a broad range of multiconductor, coaxial, flat, and fiber optic cables. Belden cable links various segments of broadcast and cable television including broadcast studios, post-production and sound mixing facilities, satellite transmission centers, and home cable television systems. Belden's electrical products include power supply cords, electrical motor lead wire, and Canadian building wire. The cord products division focuses on the electrical cord market. Belden also serves the industrial market by providing a broad spectrum of industrial products, ranging from general purpose control cables to highly sophisticated cables for process control. **NOTE:** No unsolicited resumes.

BELDEN WIRE AND CABLE COMPANY
P.O. Box 1327, Richmond IN 47375. 765/962-7561. **Physical address:** 350 NW N Street, Richmond IN 47374. **Contact:** Human Resources. **World Wide Web address:** http://www.belden.com. **Description:** This location is the manufacturing plant for Belden Wire and cable company. See listing above for a detailed description of the company and its products. .

BELL TECH.LOGIX
5604 Fortune Circle South, Suite G-N, Indianapolis IN 46241. 317/227-6700. **Contact:** General Manager. **World Wide Web address:** http://www.belltechlogix.com. **Description:** Bell Tech.logix is a leading distributor of computer-related electronic components, semiconductors, and microcomputer products. **Operations at this facility include:** This location is engaged in computer product development, training, and systems engineering.

BEMIS COMPANY INC.
1350 North Fruitridge Avenue, Terre Haute IN 47804. 812/466-2213. **Contact:** Recruiting Specialist. **World Wide Web address:** http://www.bemisppg.com. **Description:** A diversified producer of consumer and industrial packaging materials, film products, and business products. Packaging products include tapes, paper bags, and packaging for pharmaceuticals, candy, toilet paper, and detergents. Bemis Company also produces sheetprint stock, roll labels, laminates, and adhesive products. **Corporate headquarters location:** Minneapolis MN.

BERNE APPAREL COMPANY INC.
P.O. Box 309, Berne IN 46711-0309. 260/589-3136. **Physical address:** 104 East Main Street, Berne IN 46711. **Toll-free phone:** 800/843-7657. **Fax:** 260/589-8192. **Contact:** Human Resources. **World Wide Web address:** http://www.berneapparel.com. **Description:** Manufactures work clothing, safety clothing, and hunting apparel. Founded in 1915. **NOTE:** All hiring done through a staffing firm.

BERRY PLASTICS CORPORATION
P.O. Box 959, Evansville IN 47706. 812/424-2904. **Physical address:** 101 Oakley Street, Evansville IN 47706. **Contact:** Human Resources. **World Wide Web address:** http://www.berryplastics.com. **Description:** Manufactures and markets plastic packaging products including caps for aerosol cans and rigid open-top containers.

BEST ACCESS SYSTEMS
P.O. Box 50444, Indianapolis IN 46250-0444. 317/849-2250. **Physical address:** 6161 East 75th Street, Indianapolis IN 46250. **Fax:** 317/806-3521. **Contact:** Human Resources. **E-mail address:** employment@bestlock.com. **World Wide Web address:** http://www.bestaccess.com. **Description:** Best Access Systems manufactures and distributes access control and security systems for corporations and institutions worldwide. **Corporate headquarters location:** This location. **Other U.S. locations:** Nationwide. **Operations at this facility include:** Administration; Manufacturing; Regional Headquarters.

BIG SISTERS OF CENTRAL INDIANA
2960 North Meridian Street, Suite 150, Indianapolis IN 46206. 317/921-2201. **Fax:** 317/921-2202. **Contact:** Human Resources. **World Wide Web address:** http://www.bbbsci.org. **Description:** Provides volunteer and professional services to young girls. The agency also provides an array of counseling, referral, and family support services to parents and children. Additional programs focus on children with special needs including physical or learning disabilities, as well as those who are abused, neglected, or have dropped out of school. Special prevention and intervention programs at many agencies address the problems of drug abuse, teen pregnancy, foster care, and juvenile delinquency. **Other U.S. locations:** Nationwide.

BINDLEY WESTERN INDUSTRIES, INC.
10333 North Meridian Street, Suite 300, Indianapolis IN 46290. 317/297-9900. **Fax:** 317/297-5372. **Contact:** Human Resources. **World Wide Web address:** http://www.bindley.com. **Description:** Distributes prescription pharmaceuticals to drug stores, hospitals, clinics, and other health care providers. The company also distributes non-pharmaceutical products including health and beauty aids. **Corporate headquarters location:** This location. **Parent company:** Cardinal Health. **Listed on:** New York Stock Exchange. **Stock exchange symbol:** BDY.

BIOMET, INC.
P.O. Box 587, Warsaw IN 46581. 574/267-6639. **Physical address:** 56 East Bell Drive, Warsaw IN 46582. **Fax:** 574/267-8137. **Contact:** Human Resources. **E-mail address:** human.resources@biomet.com. **World Wide Web address:** http://www.biomet.com. **Description:** Designs, manufactures, and markets products used by orthopedic medical specialists in both surgical and non-surgical therapy. Products include reconstructive and trauma devices, electrical bone growth stimulators, orthopedic support devices, operating room supplies, powered surgical instruments, general surgical instruments, arthroscopy products, and oral-maxillofacial implants and instruments. **NOTE:** Resumes that do not adhere to the guidelines indicated on the website will not be considered. **Corporate headquarters location:** This location. **International locations:** Worldwide.

BIVONA MEDICAL TECHNOLOGIES
5700 West 23rd Avenue, Gary IN 46406. 219/989-9150. **Contact:** Human Resources. **Description:** Specializes in the manufacture of silicone catheters. **Parent company:** Smiths Group.

BLACK BEAUTY COAL COMPANY
414 South Fares Avenue, Evansville IN 47714. 812/424-9000. **Fax:** 812/924-6551. **Contact:** Judy Hipp, Human Resources. **Description:** A coal mining company that sells low-, medium-, and high-sulfur coal to power companies and industrial users. Black Beauty Coal Company operates eight mines in Indiana and three in southern Illinois.

BLOOMINGTON HOSPITAL
P.O. Box 1149, Bloomington IN 47402. 812/336-9535. **Toll-free phone:** 800/354-0561. **Fax:** 812/353-5447. **Contact:** Human Resources Department. **E-mail address:** careers@bloomhealth.org. **World Wide Web address:** http://www.bhhs.org. **Description:** A 314-bed, nonprofit, acute care hospital. **Positions advertised include:** Chief Clinical Microbiologist; Assistant Director of Nursing; Certified Nursing Assistant; Clinical Educator, Oncology; Cook; Dietary Aide; Occupational Therapist; Physical Therapist; Registered Nurse; House Orderly; Patient Services Secretary; Phlebotomist; Respiratory Technician. **Listed on:** Privately held.

BLUE & CO., LLC
12800 North Meridian Street, Suite 400, Carmel IN 46032. 317/848-8920. **Fax:** 317/573-2458. **Contact:** Human Resources. **E-mail address:** jobs@ blueandco.com. **World Wide Web address:** http://www.blueandco.com. **Description:** A public accounting and consulting firm with specialties in health care, manufacturing, construction, litigation support, and retirement planning. **Positions advertised include:** Audit Manager; Tax Accountant; Staff Accountant. **Special programs:** Internships. **Internship information:** Internships are offered January through April. **Corporate headquarters location:** This location. **Other U.S. locations:** KY. **Listed on:** Privately held.

BORG-WARNER AUTOMOTIVE
5401 Kilgore Avenue, Muncie IN 47304. 765/286-6100. **Contact:** Employment. **World Wide Web address:** http://www.bwauto.com. **Description:** Manufactures automotive equipment for engines, transmissions, and four-wheel drive systems. **Corporate headquarters location:** Chicago IL.

BOSTON SCIENTIFIC CORPORATION
780 Brookside Drive, Spencer IN 47460. 812/829-4877. **Contact:** Human Resources Director. **World Wide Web address:** http://www.bsci.com. **Description:** Boston Scientific Corporation is a worldwide developer, manufacturer, and marketer of medical devices used in a broad range of interventional medical procedures including cardiology, gastroenterology, pulmonary medicine, radiology, urology, and vascular surgery. Boston Scientific's products are used by physicians to perform less invasive procedures. **Positions advertised include:** Principal Learning and Development Specialist. **Corporate headquarters location:** Natick MA. **Other U.S. locations:** San Jose CA; Mansfield MA; Milford MA; Redmond WA. **Operations at this facility include:** This location manufactures disposable medical devices such as catheters.

BRADFORD WOODS OUTDOOR CENTER
5040 State Road 67 North, Martinsville IN 46151. 765/342-2915. **Fax:** 765/349-1086. **Contact:** Human Resources. **E-mail address:** bradwood@indiana.edu. **World Wide Web address:** http://www.bradwoods.org. **Description:** Offers environmental education and recreation programs. Bradford Woods is affiliated with Indiana University. **NOTE:** Seasonal and Part-time positions are available. **Positions advertised include:** Field Instructor; Summer Camp Counselor; Administrative Assistant; Office Services Assistant; Accounting Assistant; Account Representative. **Special programs:** Internships.

BRIGHTPOINT INC.
501 Airtech Parkway, Plainfield IN 46168. 317/707-2355. **Fax:** 317/707-2521. **Contact:** Human Resources. **E-mail address:** hr2@brightpoint.com. **World Wide Web address:** http://www.brightpoint.com. **Description:** A wholesale distributor of cellular telephones including a variety of brands of vehicle-mounted, transportable, and hand-held portable cellular telephones. Brightpoint also distributes cellular telephone accessories, such as batteries, battery eliminators and chargers, antennas, and cases. Brand-name products include Motorola, Uniden, OKI, NEC, Nokia, Pioneer, Audiovox, Mitsubishi International, and Fujitsu. The company distributes its products to over 2,000 customers including cellular carriers, agents, dealers, and retailers worldwide. **Positions advertised include:** Training Coordinator; Payroll/Benefits Coordinator; Recruitment/HR Generalist; Field Sales Representative. **CEO:** Robert J. Laikin.

BROAD RIPPLE ANIMAL CLINIC, PC
6225 North Broadway Street, Indianapolis IN 46220. 317/257-5334. **Fax:** 317/255-3371. **Contact:** Corry Lampe, Patient Services Coordinator. **E-mail address:** branimal@aol.com. **World Wide Web address:** http://www.bracpet.com. **Description:** A veterinary hospital. **Positions advertised include:** Veterinary Technician.

BRYAN STEAM CORPORATION
783 North Chili Avenue, Peru IN 46970. 765/473-6651. **Contact:** Human Resources. **World Wide Web address:** http://www.bryanboilers.com. **Description:** Manufactures and sells oil boilers, gas boilers, electrically fired boilers, commercial water heaters, and swimming pool heaters. Bryan Boilers also manufactures and sells storage tanks and other vessels for use with its boilers.

BURGESS & NIPLE, LTD.
251 North Illinois Street, Capital Center, Suite 920, Indianapolis IN 46204. 317/237-2760. **Fax:** 614/459-9433. **Contact:** Human Resources. **E-mail address:** hr@burnip.com. **World Wide Web address:** http://www.burgessniple.com. **Description:** An engineering and architecture firm engaged in study, analysis, and design services. The company specializes in waterworks, wastewater, industrial services, hydropower, energy conservation, transportation, systems analysis, HVAC, and geotechnical. **NOTE:** Applicants can e-mail or fax resumes using the information provided in this listing. Resumes sent via regular mail should be addressed as follows: Human Resources, Burgess & Niple, 5085 Reed Road, Columbus OH 43220. **Positions advertised include:** Transportation Planner; Travel Demand Forecaster. **Corporate headquarters location:** Columbus OH.

BURKHART ADVERTISING INC.
1335 Mishawaka Avenue, South Bend IN 46615. 260/233-2101. **Toll-free phone:** 800/777-8122. **Fax:** 219/236-1953. **Contact:** Human Resources. **E-mail address:** info@burkhartadv.com. **World Wide Web address:** http://www.burkhartadv.com. **Description:** An advertising agency that specializes in outdoor billboards and advertising panels for buses and commuter transit in southern Indiana.

CB RICHARD ELLIS
202 South Michigan, Suite 900, South Bend IN 46601. 574/237-6000. **Fax:** 574/237-6001. **Contact:** Personnel. **E-mail address:** cbrejobs@cbre.com. **World Wide Web address:** http://www.cbrichardellis.com. **Description:** A real estate services company offering property sales and leasing; property and facility management; mortgage banking; and investment management services. **Corporate headquarters location:**

Los Angeles CA. **Listed on:** New York Stock Exchange. **Stock exchange symbol:** CBG.

CB RICHARD ELLIS
115 West Washington Street, Suite 1170 South Tower, Indianapolis IN 46204-3421. 317/269-1000. **Fax:** 317/637-4404. **Contact:** Personnel. **E-mail address:** cbrejobs@cbre.com. **World Wide Web address:** http://www.cbrichardellis.com. **Description:** A real estate services company offering property sales and leasing; property and facility management; mortgage banking; and investment management services. **Corporate headquarters location:** Los Angeles CA. **Other U.S. locations:** Nationwide. **Listed on:** New York Stock Exchange. **Stock exchange symbol:** CBG.

CFM
VERMONT CASTINGS
1000 East Market Street, Huntington IN 46750. 260/356-8000. **Fax:** 260/358-9265. **Contact:** Personnel. **World Wide Web address:** http://www.majesticproducts.com. **Description:** Manufactures gas and wood fireplaces. **Corporate headquarters location:** This location. **Other U.S. locations:** Austin TX.

CIT GROUP
3500 DePauw Boulevard, Suite 1070, Indianapolis IN 46268. 317/872-5631. **Contact:** Human Resources Department. **World Wide Web address:** http://www.citgroup.com. **Description:** Provides financing of capital equipment for commercial customers worldwide. **Positions advertised include:** Account Executive. **Listed on:** New York Stock Exchange. **Stock exchange symbol:** CIT.

CTS CORPORATION
905 West Boulevard North, Elkhart IN 46514. 574/293-7511. **Fax:** 574/293-6146. **Contact:** Human Resources. **E-mail address:** recruiting@ctscorps.com. **World Wide Web address:** http://www.ctscorp.com. **Description:** CTS Corporation designs, manufactures, and sells electronic components. **NOTE:** The company prefers that resumes are submitted via e-mail, but also accepts submissions by fax or mail. **Positions advertised include:** Internal Auditor; Quality and Environmental Systems Coordinator; Patent Counsel; Staff Accountant. **Corporate headquarters location:** This location. **Operations at this facility include:** This location houses administrative offices.

CTS CORPORATION
406 Parr Road, Berne IN 46711. 260/589-3111. **Fax:** 260/589-3243. **Contact:** Human Resources. **World Wide Web address:** http://www.ctscorp.com. **Description:** CTS Corporation designs, manufactures, and sells electronic components. **Corporate headquarters location:** Elkhart IN. **Operations at this facility include:** This location manufactures electronic resistor networks.

CAPITOL TECHNOLOGIES
3615 West Voorde Drive, South Bend IN 46628. 574/232-3311. **Fax:** 260/233-1607. **Contact:** Human Resources. **E-mail address:** jobs-cti@capitoltech.com. **World Wide Web address:** http://www.capitoltech.com. **Description:** Produces die-cast machinery for industrial manufacturing plants. **Positions advertised include:** Sales Engineer; Project Engineer; Machine Design Engineer; Machine Designer; Control Designer; Assembler; Die Maker; Field Service Representative. **Parent company:** Hess Industries.

CARLETON INC.
P.O. Box 570, South Bend IN 46624. 574/243-6040. **Physical address:** 3975 William Richardson Drive, South Bend IN 46628. **Toll-free phone:** 800/433-0090. **Fax:** 574/243-6060. **Contact:** Human Resources. **World Wide Web address:** http://www.carletoninc.com. **Description:** Develops software for the consumer credit and credit insurance industries. Carleton also sells preprogrammed, hand-held computers.

CARPENTER COMPANY
P.O. Box 2386, Elkhart IN 46515. 574/522-2800. **Physical address:** 195 County Road 15 South, Elkhart IN 46516. **Fax:** 574/295-9714. **Contact:** Rich Trownsell. **E-mail address:** rich.trownsell@carpenter.com. **World Wide Web address:** http://www.carpenter.com. **Description:** A division of one of the world's largest producers of polyurethane foam and comfort cushioning products. Founded in 1948. **NOTE:** Entry-level positions and second and third shifts are offered. **Company slogan:** We bring comfort to your life. **Positions advertised include:** Management Development Associate. **Note:** HR contact is based out of Virginia. When contacting, indicate that you are applying for a position in Indiana. **Office hours:** Monday - Friday, 7:00 a.m. - 5:00 p.m. **Corporate headquarters location:** Richmond VA. **Listed on:** Privately held.

CASTING SERVICE
P.O. Box 488. La Porte IN 46352. 219/362-1000. **Physical address:** 300 Philadelphia Street, La Porte IN 46350. **Fax:** 219/362-4413. **Contact:** Cindy Johnson, Human Resources Manager. **E-mail address:** cjohnson@alleghenytechnologies.com. **World Wide Web address:** http://www. castingservice.com. **Description:** Manufactures gray and ductile iron castings.

CATERPILLAR, INC.
3701 State Road 26 East, Lafayette IN 47905. 765/448-5000. **Contact:** Human Resources. **World Wide Web address:** http://www.cat.com. **Description:** A global leader in the production of large diesel and natural gas engines and engine systems that satisfy a wide variety of power needs for marine, petroleum, and construction equipment. The company also offers electric power generating systems for communities, and provides emergency power to hospitals, schools, and airports. Caterpillar operates 40 manufacturing facilities nationwide. **Special programs:** Internships. **International locations:** Worldwide.

CELADON GROUP, INC.
9503 East 33rd Street, Indianapolis IN 46235. 317/972-7000. **Toll-free phone:** 800/235-2366. **Fax:** 317/890-1619. **Contact:** Personnel. **World Wide Web address:** http://www.celadontrucking.com. **Description:** An international truckload carrier specializing in freight shipments between the United States, Canada, and Mexico. **Corporate headquarters location:** This location. **Other U.S. locations:** Laredo TX. **Subsidiaries include:** Cheetah Transportation (Mooresville NC); Gerth Transportation (Ontario, Canada); Jaguar Transportation (Mexico); and Zipp Express (Indianapolis IN). **President:** Stephen Russell.

CENTRAL INDIANA COUNCIL ON THE AGING (CICOA)
4755 Kingsway Drive, Suite 200, Indianapolis IN 46205. 317/254-5465. **Fax:** 317/803-6273. **Contact:** Human Resources. **World Wide Web address:** http://www.cicoa.org. **Description:** Coordinates in-home services such as home health care and respite care for elderly individuals.

CENTRAL INDIANA REGIONAL BLOOD CENTER
3450 North Meridian Street, Indianapolis IN 46208. 317/916-5150. **Fax:** 317/916-5085. **Contact:** Human Resources. **E-mail address:** employment @cirbc.org. **World Wide Web address:** http://www.cirbc.org. **Description:** A nonprofit blood center and one of the nation's largest blood banking institutions. The Central Indiana Regional Blood Center provides blood services as well as bone and tissue products. Founded in 1952. **Positions advertised include:** Blood Collection Technician; Components Technician; Director of Testing; Field Recruiter; Laboratory Assistant; Materials Handler; Telephone Recruiter.

CERESTAR U.S.A.
1100 Indianapolis Boulevard, Hammond IN 46320. 219/659-2000. **Contact:** Human Resources. **World Wide Web address:** http://www.cerestar.com. **Description:** Cerestar is also a leading manufacturer and marketer of tobacco products. The tobacco products business manufactures and markets cigars with brand names including Swisher Sweets, King Edward, Optimo, Bering, and a variety of smokeless tobacco products including Silver Creek and Redwood moist snuff; Navy and Railroad Mills dry snuff; and Chattanooga Chew, Lancaster, and Mail Pouch chewing tobaccos. **Corporate headquarters location:** Stamford CT. **Other U.S. locations:** Decatur AL; Dimmitt TX. **Operations at this facility include:** This location processes corn into a wide variety of products including sweeteners (corn syrup and high fructose corn syrup) and food starches.

CHICAGO STEEL & TINPLATE INC.
700 Chase Street, Suite 100, Gary IN 46404. 219/949-1111. **Fax:** 219/977-4289. **Contact:** Human Resources. **World Wide Web address:** http://www. chisteel.com. **Description:** Engaged in tension leveling steel for other companies. Services also include cleaning, drying, degreasing, and recoiling.

CHILDCRAFT INDUSTRIES
P.O. Box 444, Salem IN 47167. 812/883-3111. **Physical address:** 501 East Market Street, Salem IN 47167. **Contact:** Human Resources. **World Wide Web address:** http://www.childcraftind.com. **Description:** Manufactures baby beds and related accessories.

THE CHILDREN'S MUSEUM OF INDIANAPOLIS
P.O. Box 3000, Indianapolis IN 46206. 317/334-3322. **Toll-free phone:** 800/820-6214. **Fax:** 317/920-2047. **Contact:** Manager of Recruiting Services. **E-mail address:** hrweb@childrensmuseum.org. **World Wide Web address:** http://www.childrensmuseum.org. **Description:** A nonprofit, interactive museum for children. The Children's Museum of Indianapolis is one of the largest and fourth oldest children's museum in the world. Founded in 1925. **NOTE:** Entry-level positions, part-time jobs, and second and third shifts are offered. **Positions advertised include:** Vertebrate Paleontologist; Dinosphere Interpretation Manager; Chief Development Officer; Planetarium Show Specialist; Educational Gallery Assistant; Box Office Sales Assistant; Visitor Services Assistant. **Special programs:** Internships; Training; Summer Jobs; Scholarships. **Office hours:** Monday - Friday, 9:00 a.m. - 5:00 p.m. **Corporate headquarters location:** This location. **Operations at this facility include:** Research and Development; Sales; Service. **Listed on:** Privately held.

THE CHINET COMPANY
6629 Indianapolis Boulevard, Hammond IN 46320. 219/844-8950. **Contact:** Human Resources. **World Wide Web address:** http://www.chinetco.com. **Description:** Manufactures paper and plastic plates and cutlery. **Parent company:** Huhtamaki.

CHORE-TIME BROCK
P.O. Box 2000, Milford IN 46542-2000. 574/658-4101. **Fax:** 574/658-4133. **Contact:** Human Resources. **E-mail address:** hr@ctbinc.com. **World Wide Web address:** http://www.ctbinc.com. **Description:** Manufactures farm machinery and related equipment. Chore-Time Brock's products include watering, feeding, and ventilation equipment.

CHROMCRAFT REVINGTON, INC.
P.O. Box 238, Delphi IN 46923-0238. 765/564-3500. **Fax:** 765/564-3722. **Physical address:** 1100 North Washington Street, Delphi IN 46923. **Contact:** Personnel Director. **Description:** A national designer, manufacturer, and seller of furniture sold under the Chromcraft, Peters-Revington, and Silver Furniture brand names. **Other U.S. locations:** Sentobia MS; Knoxville TN. **President and CEO:** Michael E. Thomas.

CINERGY/PSI
30 Jackson Street, New Albany IN 47150. 812/944-8471. **Fax:** 812/949-6404. **Contact:** Human Resources. **World Wide Web address:** http://www.cinergy.com. **Description:** Provides electric and gas service in the southwestern portion of Ohio and adjacent areas in Kentucky and Indiana, an area covering approximately 3,000 square miles with an estimated population of 1.7 million. **Special programs:** Internships; Co-ops. **Operations at this facility include:** This location is a generating station.

CITIZENS GAS & COKE UTILITY
2950 Prospect Street, Indianapolis IN 46203. 317/924-3311. **Fax:** 317/931-4159. **Contact:** Human Resources. **E-mail address:** employment@cgcu.com. **World Wide Web address:** http://www.citizensgas.com. **Description:** A utility company that provides gas services to its customers. **NOTE:** Mail resumes to: Employment, Citizens Gas & Coke Utility, 2020 North Meridian Street, Indianapolis IN 46202. **Positions advertised include:** Journeyman Plumber; Ammonia Destruct and Desulfurization Operator; Customer Relations Cashier; Marketing Sales Assistant.

CLARIAN HEALTH PARTNERS
550 University Boulevard, Room 1653, Indianapolis IN 46202. 317/278-2980. **Contact:** Human Resources. **World Wide Web address:** http://www.clarian.com. **Description:** In 1997, Indiana University Hospital, Methodist Hospital, and Riley Hospital joined to form Clarian Health Partners. **NOTE:** See website for information on how to contact recruiters. **Positions advertised include:** Medical Technologist; Medical Assistant; Patient Care Assistant; Respiratory Therapist; Surgical Technologist; Social Worker; Pharmacy Technician; Registered Nurse; Clinical Educator. **Special programs:** Internships; Externships; Scholarships; Educational Opportunities.

CLARK FOODSERVICE, INC.
1901 Bendix Drive, South Bend IN 46628. 574/234-5011. **Fax:** 574/232-4515. **Contact:** Personnel. **World Wide Web address:** http://www.clarkfoodservice.com. **Description:** A wholesale distributor that supplies groceries, food service disposables, and cleaning supplies to colleges, hospitals, hotels, and restaurants. Clark Foodservice also produces a private-label product line of packaged foods that are available in three grades. Founded in 1912. **Positions advertised include:** Corporate Sales Executive.

CLARK MEMORIAL HOSPITAL
1220 Missouri Avenue, Jeffersonville IN 47130. 812/282-2216. **Recorded jobline:** 812/283-2213. **Contact:** Human Resources Department. **World Wide Web address:** http://www.clarkmemorial.org. **Description:** Affiliated with Jewish Hospital HealthCare Services since 1992, the hospital provides services including the CompCare occupational medicine program, emergency care, maternal-child health, inpatient psychiatric care, pediatrics, home health, and cardiology. Founded in 1922. **NOTE:** Entry-level positions and second and third shifts are offered. **Positions advertised include:** Cardiac Rehabilitation Specialist; Occupational Therapist; Patient Care Associate; Charge Nurse; Registered Nurse. **Special programs:** Internships; Training; Co-ops; Summer Jobs.

CLARK NURSING & REHABILITATION CENTER
1964 Clark Road, Gary IN 46404. 219/949-5600. **Contact:** Human Resources. **World Wide Web address:** http://www.clarknursinghome.com. **Description:** Offers long-term and respite health care. Clark Nursing & Rehabilitation Center also arranges occupational, speech, and physical therapy.

COACHMEN INDUSTRIES, INC.
P.O. Box 3300, Elkhart IN 46515. 574/262-0123. **Fax:** 260/724-8987. **Contact:** Human Resources. **World Wide Web address:** http://www.coachmen.com. **Description:** Coachmen Industries manufactures recreational vehicles such as motor homes, travel trailers, camping trailers, truck campers, and van campers. The company also manufactures parts and supplies for all of these vehicles. **Positions advertised include:** Construction Manager. **Corporate headquarters location:** This location. **Operations at this facility include:** This location houses corporate offices. **Subsidiaries include:** Coachmen Recreational Vehicles, Inc.

COACHMEN RECREATIONAL VEHICLES, INC.
423 North Main Street, P.O. Box 30, Middlebury IN 46540. 574/825-5821. **Contact:** Human Resources. **World Wide Web address:** http://www. coachmenrv.com. **Description:** Manufactures recreational vehicles such as motor homes, travel trailers, camping trailers, truck campers, and van campers. The company also manufactures parts and supplies for all of its vehicles. **Corporate headquarters location:** Elkhart IN. **Parent company:** Coachmen Industries, Inc.

COMCAST CABLEVISION
720 Taylor Street, Fort Wayne IN 46802. 260/456-9000. **Contact:** Human Resources. **World Wide Web address:** http://www.comcast.com. **Description:** Provides residential cable television services. **Office hours:** Monday - Friday, 8:00 a.m. - 6:00 p.m.; Saturday, 8:00 a.m. - 5:00 p.m. **Corporate headquarters location:** Philadelphia PA.

COMMUNITY ACTION PROGRAM (CAP)
27 Pasco Avenue, Evansville IN 47713. 812/425-4241. **Fax:** 812/425-4255. **Contact:** Laurie Brown, Human Resources. **Description:** A community service center that offers energy assistance services, weatherizing and housing services, and other community programs. CAP also hosts the local Head Start program.

COMMUNITY ACTION PROGRAM (CAP)
P.O. Box 188, Covington IN 47932. 765/793-4881. **Physical address:** 418 Washington Street, Covington IN 47932. **Fax:** 765/793-4884. **Contact:** Human Resources. **Description:** A community service center that offers energy assistance services, weatherizing and housing services, and other community programs. CAP also hosts the local Head Start program.

COMMUNITY ACTION SOUTHERN INDIANA
1613 East Eighth Street, Jeffersonville IN 47130. 812/288-6451. **Fax:** 812/284-8314. **Contact:** Human Resources. **Description:** A community service center that offers energy assistance services, weatherizing and housing services, and other community programs. CAP also hosts the local Head Start program. Community Action Southern Indiana also sponsors several programs for youth including Four Cs (a developmental program for toddlers), Head Start, and Achieve.

COMMUNITY BANK OF SOUTHERN INDIANA
COMMUNITY BANK SHARES OF INDIANA, INC.
101 West Spring Street, New Albany IN 47150. 812/944-2224. **Fax:** 812/949-6870. **Contact:** Director of Human Resources. **E-mail address:** nharbaugh@cbinonline.com. **World Wide Web address:** http://www. cbinonline.com. **Description:** A full-service savings and loan bank. **Corporate headquarters location:** This location. **Parent company:** Community Bank Shares of Indiana, Inc. (also at this location).

COMMUNITY CENTERS OF INDIANAPOLIS
615 North Alabama Street, Suite 600, Indianapolis IN 46204. 317/638-3360x22. **Fax:** 317/638-3675. **Contact:** Human Resources. **World Wide Web address:** http://www.ccicorp.org. **Description:** A service organization that operates 14 community service centers in Indianapolis. Services include individual and family counseling, assessment, and referral, as well as emergency assistance food and clothing banks; housing revitalization; senior citizen activities, hot lunches, residential facility, and homemaker assistance; transportation for low-income seniors and disabled persons to center-related activities; summer day camp; summer youth activities; tutoring and remedial education; outpatient and residential drug and alcohol treatment programs for adolescents; recreation and social development for all ages; training for job readiness and job skills seminars; well baby clinics, health clinics, and a dental clinic; Women, Infants and Children nutrition programs (WIC); food stamp distribution; immigration and naturalization help; ESL classes; library extensions; meeting places for scout troops, community groups, and Alcoholics Anonymous; and offices for the Indiana State Employment Service.

COMMUNITY HARVEST FOOD BANK
999 East Tillman Road, Fort Wayne IN 46816. 260/447-3696. **Fax:** 260/447-4859. **Contact:** Jane Avery, Executive Director. **E-mail address:** info@ communityharvest.org. **World Wide Web address:** http://www. communityharvest.org. **Description:** Collects and distributes food donations. The food bank operates as part of a group of over 400 agencies in northeast Indiana and Allen County. Founded in 1983.

THE COMMUNITY HOSPITAL
901 MacArthur Boulevard, Munster IN 46321. 219/836-4568. **Fax:** 219/852-6434. **Contact:** Personnel. **E-mail address:** personnel@comhs.org. **World Wide Web address:** http://www.communityhospital.org. **Description:** A 305-bed hospital with a staff of over 1,900 employees, offering a wide range of medical services. The hospital operates one of the area's most advanced neonatal intensive care units, as well as an oncology center. Founded in 1973. **Positions advertised include:** Accountant; Operational Secretary; Massage Therapist; Coder; Microbiologist; Home Care Registered Nurse; Nursing Assistant; Pharmacy Technician; Physical Therapist; Speech/Language Pathologist; Exercise Instructor; Transcriptionist; Cancer Registry Technician. **Office hours:** Monday – Friday, 8:00 a.m. – 4:30 p.m.

COMPUTER HORIZONS CORPORATION
8720 Castle Creek Parkway, Suite 121, Indianapolis IN 46250. 317/574-1000. **Contact:** Human Resources. **World Wide Web address:** http://www. computerhorizons.com. **Description:** A full-service technology solutions company offering contract staffing, outsourcing, re-engineering, migration, downsizing support, and network management. **Corporate headquarters location:** Mountain Lakes NJ. **Other U.S. locations:** Nationwide. **President and CEO:** William J. Murphy.

THE CONSECO COMPANIES
11815 North Pennsylvania Street, P. O. Box 1911, Carmel IN 46032. 317/817-6100. **Fax:** 317/817-6327. **Contact:** Human Resources. **World Wide Web address:** http://www.conseco.com. **Description:** Offers life and health insurance, investment, and lending products. **Positions advertised include:** Mail Clerk; Legal Administrative Secretary; Paralegal; Project Manager; Analyst; Claims Adjuster. **Corporate headquarters location:** This location.

CONSOLIDATED FABRICATION AND CONSTRUCTORS, INC.
3851 Ellsworth Street, Gary IN 46408. 219/884-6150. **Fax:** 219/884-6652. **Contact:** Human Resources. **World Wide Web address:** http://www.consfab.com. **Description:** A mechanical contracting company for industrial applications including the repair of oil refineries and chemical plants. Consolidated Fabrication and Constructors also manufactures and repairs tanks and pressure valves.

CONTINENTAL DESIGN & ENGINEERING
2710 Enterprise Drive, Anderson IN 46013. 765/778-9999. **Toll-free phone:** 800/875-4557. **Fax:** 765/778-3078. **Contact:** Cathy Mellinger, Director of Technical Recruiting. **E-mail address:** cdcin@continental-design.com. **World Wide Web address:** http://www.continental-design.com. **Description:** Continental Design & Engineering provides computer-aided engineering and design services. **Corporate headquarters location:** This location. **Other U.S. locations:** Troy MI. **Operations at this facility include:** This location houses administrative offices as well as the engineering and design center.

CONTINENTAL ELECTRIC COMPANY
P.O. Box 2710, Gary IN 46403. 219/938-3460. **Physical address:** 9501 East Fifth Avenue, Gary IN 46403. **Fax:** 219/938-3469. **Contact:** Human Resources. **World Wide Web address:** http://www.continentalelectric.com. **Description:** Provides electrical contracting services to residential and industrial clients.

COUNTRYMARK COOPERATIVE, INC.
1200 Refinery Road, Mount Vernon IN 47620. 812/838-4341. **Contact:** Human Resources. **World Wide Web address:** http://www.countrymark.com. **Description:** Manufactures, purchases, distributes, markets, and sells agricultural inputs and products.

COURIER KENDALLVILLE, INC.
2500 Marion Drive, Kendallville IN 46755. 260/347-3044. **Fax:** 260/347-3507. **Contact:** Human Resources Director. **E-mail address:** hr@courier.com. **World Wide Web address:** http://www.courier.com. **Description:** A manufacturer of books, religious products, reference texts, software manuals, and technical documentation. The company also provides electronic prepress and fulfillment services. **Positions advertised include:** Web Press Operator; Assistant Web Press Operator; Application Specialist. **Corporate headquarters location:** Lowell MA. **Other U.S. locations:** North Chelmsford MA; Stoughton MA; Westford MA; Philadelphia PA. **Parent company:** Courier Corporation.

COVANCE LABORATORIES INC.
8211 Scicore Drive, Indianapolis IN 46214. 317/271-1200. **Contact:** Human Resources. **World Wide Web address:** http://www.covance.com. **Description:** A life sciences firm providing biological and chemical research services. Covance Laboratories is also a supplier of laboratory animals and biological products. Clients include research institutes, industrial companies, government agencies, and manufacturers of pharmaceuticals, chemicals, food, and cosmetics. **Positions advertised include:** Assistant Buyer; Technical Associate; Extraction Analyst; Pathologist Associate; Special Chemistry Technologist. **Corporate headquarters location:** Princeton NJ.

CRAWFORD INDUSTRIES
1414 Crawford Drive, P.O. Box 191, Crawfordsville IN 47933. 765/362-6733. **Contact:** Human Resources. **World Wide Web address:** http://www.crawford-industries.com. **Description:** Manufactures polyurethane office binders.

CROSSMAN COMMUNITIES, INC.
4072 Mossy Bank Road, Suite 300, Indianapolis IN 46234. 317/328-0501. **Contact:** Human Resources Department. **World Wide Web address:** http://www.croscom.com. **Description:** A holding company that operates through subsidiaries that design, develop, and build single-family detached homes. **Number of employees nationwide:** 170.

CROWN CORK & SEAL COMPANY, INC.
400 North Walnut Street, Crawfordsville IN 47933. 765/362-3200. **Fax:** 765/362-4532. **Contact:** Human Resources. **World Wide Web address:** http://www.crowncork.com. **Description:** Crown Cork & Seal manufactures cans, plastic bottles, metal and plastic closures, machinery for the packaging industry, and disposable medical devices and closures. **International locations:** Worldwide. **Operations at this facility include:** This location manufactures metal bottle caps.

CROWN INTERNATIONAL
P.O. Box 1000, Elkhart IN 46515-1000. 574/294-8000. **Physical address:** 1718 West Mishawaka Road, Elkhart IN 46517. **Fax:** 574/294-8083. **Contact:** Human Resources Department. **E-mail address:** atrim@crownintl.com. **World Wide Web address:** http://www.crownintl.com. **Description:** Manufactures a wide variety of amplification equipment for the professional audio and industrial markets. The company also manufactures microphones, amplifiers, and transmitters for the broadcast market, and amplifiers and imaging products for the medical industry. **NOTE:** Second and third shifts are offered. **Special programs:** Summer Jobs. **Corporate headquarters location:** This location. **Operations at this facility include:** Administration; Manufacturing; Research and Development; Sales; Service. **Listed on:** Privately held.

CUMMINS ENGINE COMPANY, INC.
500 Jackson Street, P.O. Box 3005, Columbus IN 47202-3005. 812/377-5000. **Contact:** Human Resources Department. **World Wide Web address:** http://www.cummins.com. **Description:** One of the world's leading producers of diesel engines for heavy-duty trucks, engine parts, and powertrain systems for the mining,

military, construction, transportation, agricultural, and industrial vehicle markets. **Positions advertised include:** College Recruiting Coordinator; Corporate Audit Manager; Custom Manufacturing Engineer; Facility Engineer; Mechanical Engineer; Editor/Production Specialist; Labor Relations Specialist; Project Manager.

CURTIS MAGAZINE GROUP
INDIANA BUSINESS MAGAZINE
1100 Waterway Boulevard, Suite 300, Indianapolis IN 46202. 317/692-1200. **Toll-free phone:** 800/473-2526. **Fax:** 317/692-4250. **Contact:** Human Resources. **World Wide Web address:** http://www.indianabusiness.com. **Description:** A monthly, statewide business publication. Curtis Magazine Group also issues a business directory of Indiana's top 2,500 firms. **Corporate headquarters location:** This location. **Operations at this facility include:** Administration; Sales; Service.

DAIMLERCHRYSLER CORPORATION
2401 South Reed Road, Kokomo IN 46902. 765/454-1000. **Contact:** Employment Office. **World Wide Web address:** http://www1.daimlerchrysler.com. **Description:** Produces cars, trucks, minivans, and sport-utility vehicles for customers in more than 100 countries.

DALTON CORPORATION
P.O. Box 1388, Warsaw IN 46581-0230. 574/267-8111. **Fax:** 219/371-5285. **Contact:** Jim Dutka, Human Resources. **World Wide Web address:** http://www.daltonfoundries.com. **Description:** A premium supplier of gray iron castings for the air conditioning and refrigeration, engine, gearbox, stationary transmission, automotive, heavy-duty truck transmission, marine, motor frame, and municipal water industries worldwide. **NOTE:** Resumes are accepted by mail or fax. **Corporate headquarters location:** This location. **Other area locations:** Kendallville IN. **Other U.S. locations:** Ashland OH. **Listed on:** Privately held.

DEFLECTO CORPORATION
7035 East 86th Street, P.O. Box 50057, Indianapolis IN 46250. 800/428-4328. **Contact:** Human Resources. **E-mail address:** jobs@deflecto.com. **World Wide Web address:** http://www.deflecto.com. **Description:** Manufacturer and distributor in the air distribution, dryer venting, office products, and literature display industries. **NOTE:** Search and apply for positions online. **Positions advertised include:** Inventory Supervisor; Process Engineer; Sales Coordinator; Shipping Clerk. **Corporate headquarters location:** This location. **Parent company:** Jordan Industries.

DEISTER MACHINE COMPANY INC.
P.O. Box 1, Fort Wayne IN 46801. 260/426-7495. **Physical address:** 1933 East Wayne Street, Fort Wayne IN 46803. **Fax:** 260/422-1523. **Contact:** Human Resources. **World Wide Web address:** http://www.deistermachine.com. **Description:** Manufactures sizing and separating mining machinery for stone quarries. Founded in 1912.

DELOITTE & TOUCHE
111 Monument Circle, Suite 2000, Indianapolis IN 46204. 317/464-8600. **Contact:** Human Resources. **World Wide Web address:** http://www. us.deloitte.com. **Description:** An international firm of certified public accountants providing professional accounting, auditing, tax, and management consulting services to widely diversified clients. The company has a specialized program consisting of national industry groups and functional groups that cross industry lines. Groups are involved in various disciplines including accounting, auditing, taxation management advisory services, small and growing businesses, mergers and acquisitions, and computer applications.

DELPHI DELCO ELECTRONIC SYSTEMS
2151 East Lincoln, P.O. Box 9005, Kokomo IN 46904-9005. 765/451-5011. **Fax:** 765/451-5426. **Contact:** Human Resources. **World Wide Web address:** http://www.delphi.com. **Description:** Produces automotive starting, generating, ignition systems, and a wide variety of related parts and systems. **Special programs:** Internships; Co-ops. **Corporate headquarters location:** Troy MI.

DEPAUW UNIVERSITY
Office of Human Resources, 313 South Locust Street, Greencastle IN 46135. 765/658-4181. **Contact:** Susan Hacker, Human Resources Specialist. **E-mail address:** susanhacker@depauw.edu. **World Wide Web address:** http://www.depauw.edu. **Description:** A selective undergraduate liberal arts college with a separate school of music. DePauw offers a variety of academic programs and educational opportunities. Special programs for students include: The Honor Scholar Program; The Management Fellows Program; The Media Fellows Program; The Science Research Fellows Program. DePauw has an enrollment of approximately 2,300 students. Founded in 1837 by the Methodist Episcopal Church. **Positions advertised include:** Professor, Latin American History; Professor, English; Choral Director. **President:** Robert G. Bottoms.

DEPUY INC.
P.O. Box 988, Warsaw IN 46581-0988. 574/267-8143. **Physical address:** 700 Orthopaedic Drive, Warsaw IN 46582. **Contact:** Human Resources. **World Wide Web address:** http://www.depuy.com. **Description:** A medical device manufacturing company specializing in orthopedic products including total joint replacement and fracture management devices. **Special programs:** Internships. **Corporate headquarters location:** This location. **Other U.S. locations:** Jackson MI; Albuquerque NM. **Parent company:** Johnson & Johnson. **Operations at this facility include:** Administration; Manufacturing; Research and Development; Service.

DIALAMERICA MARKETING INC.
2952 East Covenanter Drive, Bloomington IN 47401. 812/332-2628. **Fax:** 812/333-7238. **Contact:** Manager of Human Resources. **World Wide Web address:** http://www.dialamerica.com/bloomington. **Description:** A telemarketing agency. Founded in 1957. **Positions advertised include:** Branch Manager; Branch Office Assistant; Teleservice Representative; Sales Supervisor. **Office hours:** Monday - Friday, 8:00 a.m. - 10:00 p.m. **Corporate headquarters location:** Mahwah NJ. **Other U.S. locations:** Nationwide. **Listed on:** Privately held.

DIGITECH
8455 Castlewood Drive, Suite C, Indianapolis IN 46250. 317/863-0025. **Fax:** 317/863-0029. **Contact:** Human Resources. **E-mail address:** info@itdept4u.com. **World Wide Web address:** http://www.itdept4u.com. **Description:** An information technology services company. **Positions advertised include:** Network Technician. **NOTE:** Search and apply for positions online.

DISCOUNT LABELS, INC.
4115 Profit Court, New Albany IN 47150. 812/945-2617. **Fax:** 812/949-3578. **Contact:** Human Resources. **World Wide Web address:** http://www.discountlabels.com. **Description:** A leading provider of labels for the quick-print market and one of the largest short-run label printers in the United States. Products include self-adhesive labels, rubber stamps, and other related products such as laser labels, bumper stickers, barcode labels, and hot stamp labels. **Corporate headquarters location:** This location. **Parent company:** American Business Products. **Operations at this facility include:** Administration; Divisional Headquarters; Manufacturing; Sales.

DO IT BEST CORPORATION
6502 Nelson Road, Fort Wayne IN 46801. 260/748-5300. **Fax:** 260/748-5608. **Contact:** Human Resources. **World Wide Web address:** http://doitbest.com. **Description:** A cooperative wholesale supplier of hardware, lumber, and building materials to retailers throughout the world. **Positions advertised include:** Accounting Supervisor; Account Executive; Web Developer; Public Relations Coordinator; Communications Coordinator; Retail Store Designer; Retail Development Specialist. **Special programs:** Internships; Co-ops. **Corporate headquarters location:** This location. **Other U.S. locations:** Nationwide. **President and CEO:** Bob Taylor.

DOMETIC CORPORATION
509 South Poplar Street, Lagrange IN 46761. 260/463-2191. **Contact:** Human Resources. **World Wide Web address:** http://www.dometic.com. **Description:** Manufactures a variety of products for recreational vehicles. The company's products include air conditioning systems, antennae, awnings, heating systems, ovens and ranges, refrigerators, roof vents, icemakers, and generators.

DONALDSON COMPANY, INC.
3260 West State Road 28, Frankfort IN 46041. 765/659-4766. **Contact:** Human Resources. **World Wide Web address:** http://www.donaldson.com. **Description:** Manufactures and sells filtration systems and replacement parts worldwide. **Positions advertised include:** Manufacturing Engineer; Production Manager. **Corporate headquarters location:** Bloomington MN. **International locations:** Worldwide.

R.R. DONNELLEY & SONS COMPANY
State Road 32 West, Crawfordsville IN 47933. 765/362-1300. **Contact:** Human Resources. **E-mail address:** rrdonnelley@hiresystems.com. **World Wide Web address:** http://www.rrdonnelley.com. **Description:** R.R. Donnelley & Sons is a world leader in managing, reproducing, and distributing print and digital information for publishing, merchandising, and information technology customers. The company is one of the largest commercial printers in the world, producing catalogs, inserts, magazines, books, directories, computer documentation, and financial printing. Principal services offered by the company are conventional and digital prepress operations, computerized printing and binding, and sophisticated shipping and distribution services for printed products; information repackaging into multiple formats (print, magnetic, and optical media); database management, list rental, list enhancement, and direct mail production services; turnkey computer documentation services (outsourcing, translation, printing, binding, diskette replication, kitting, licensing, republishing, and fulfillment); reprographics and facilities management; creative design and communication services; and digital and conventional map creation and related services. Founded in 1864. **Corporate headquarters location:** Chicago IL. **Other U.S. locations:** Nationwide. **International locations:** Worldwide. **Operations at this facility include:** This location performs various manufacturing, printing, and publishing functions. **Listed on:** New York Stock Exchange. **Stock exchange symbol:** DNY.

R.R. DONNELLEY & SONS COMPANY
P.O. Box 837, Warsaw IN 46581-0837. 574/267-7101. **Contact:** Human Resources Department. **E-mail address:** rrdonnelley@hiresystems.com. **World Wide Web address:** http://www.rrdonnelley.com. **Description:** R.R. Donnelley & Sons is a world leader in managing, reproducing, and distributing print and digital information for publishing, merchandising, and information technology customers. The company is one of the largest commercial printers in the world, producing catalogs, inserts, magazines, books, directories, computer documentation, and financial printing. Principal services offered by the company are conventional and digital prepress operations, computerized printing and binding, and sophisticated shipping and distribution services for printed products; information repackaging into multiple formats (print, magnetic, and optical media); database management, list rental, list enhancement, and direct mail production services; turnkey computer documentation services (outsourcing, translation, printing, binding, diskette replication, kitting, licensing, republishing, and fulfillment); reprographics and facilities management; creative design and communication services; and digital and conventional map creation and related services. Founded in 1864. **Corporate headquarters location:** Chicago IL. **Other U.S. locations:** Nationwide. **International locations:** Worldwide. **Operations at this facility include:** This location is involved in catalog printing. **Listed on:** New York Stock Exchange. **Stock exchange symbol:** DNY.

DOW AGROSCIENCES LLC
9330 Zionsville Road, Indianapolis IN 46268. 317/337-3000. **Contact:** Human Resources Department. **World Wide Web address:** http://www.dowagro.com. **Description:** Produces a variety of agricultural products including herbicides and insecticides. Founded in 1989. **NOTE:** Entry-level positions are offered. **Company slogan:** Improving the quality of life around the world. **Positions advertised include:** Analytical/Product Chemist. **Special programs:** Internships; Training. **Office hours:** Monday - Friday, 7:30 a.m. - 4:30 p.m. **Corporate headquarters location:** This location. **Other U.S. locations:** Nationwide. **International locations:** Worldwide. **Parent company:** Dow Chemical Company. **Operations at this facility include:** Administration; Research and Development; Sales; Service.

DRESSER INDUSTRIES
900 West Mount Street, Connersville IN 47331. 765/827-9200. **Contact:** Human Resources. **World Wide Web address:** http://www.rootsblower.com. **Description:** The Roots Division supplies blowers and vacuum pumps to a variety of customers. Overall, Dresser Industries is a supplier of technology, products, and services to worldwide energy, natural resources, and industrial markets. Operations include petroleum, energy processing and conversion, mining and construction, and general industry. The company markets its products and services in more than 100 countries. **Corporate headquarters location:** Dallas TX. **Operations at this facility include:** Administration; Divisional Headquarters; Manufacturing; Research and Development; Sales; Service.

DUKE-WEEKS REALTY CORPORATION
600 East 96th Street, Suite 100, Indianapolis IN 46240. 317/846-4700. **Fax:** 317/808-6791. **Contact:** Human Resources. **E-mail address:** hr@ dukerealty.com. **World Wide Web address:** http://www.dukereit.com. **Description:** Duke-Weeks Realty Corporation is a self-administered real estate investment trust that provides leasing, management, development, construction, and other tenant-related services for its properties and for about 12 million square feet of properties owned by third parties. The company provides leasing, property and asset management, development, construction, build-to-suit, and related services for more than 1,200 tenants at properties managed and leased by Duke for third-party customers. **NOTE:** Resumes may be submitted via e-mail, fax, or mail. **Positions advertised include:** Staff Internal Auditor; Systems

Administrator; Project Manager. **Corporate headquarters location:** This location. **Operations at this facility include:** Administration; Sales.

DUPONT PHOTOMASKS, INC.
P.O. Box 4088, Kokomo IN 46904-4088. 765/854-7500. **Physical address:** 1901 East Morgan Street, Kokomo IN 46901. **Fax:** 765/854-7633. **Contact:** Human Resources. **World Wide Web address:** http://www.photomask.com. **Description:** Manufactures biomedical, industrial, and consumer products including photographic, data-recording, and video devices; man-made fiber products and polymer products including plastic resins, elastomers, and films; and agricultural and industrial chemicals including herbicides and insecticides, pigments, fluorochemicals, petroleum additives, and mineral acids. DuPont Photomasks also specializes in the exploration and production of crude oil and natural gas; the refining, marketing, and downstream transportation of petroleum; and the mining and distribution of steam and metallurgical coals. Industries served include aerospace, agriculture, apparel, transportation, health care, printing, and publishing.

EATON CORPORATION
201 Brandon Street, Auburn IN 46706. 260/925-3800. **Contact:** Human Resources. **World Wide Web address:** http://www.eaton.com. **Description:** Eaton Corporation is a worldwide manufacturer of hydraulic products, fluid connectors, electrical power distribution equipment, engine components, and truck drivetrain systems. The company serves the automotive, aerospace, industrial, and semiconductor industries. Founded in 1905. **Positions advertised include:** Product Reliability Engineer; Senior Financial Analyst; Process Engineer. **Corporate headquarters location:** Cleveland OH. **Operations at this facility include:** This location manufactures automotive clutches. **Subsidiaries include:** Aeroquip-Vickers, Inc. manufactures a wide range of engineered products and systems for the industrial, aerospace, defense, and automotive markets.

EDGEWATER SYSTEMS FOR BALANCED LIVING
1100 West Sixth Avenue, Gary IN 46402. 219/885-4264. **Fax:** 219/885-0165. **Contact:** Personnel Recruiter. **World Wide Web address:** http://www. edgewatersystems.org. **Description:** A not-for-profit outpatient facility that offers behavioral health care services, mental health services, alcoholism and addiction treatment, crisis intervention, and counseling. Edgewater Systems for Balanced Living also provides short-term residential care for children and teenagers, and offers an Employee Assistance Program. **Positions advertised include:** Therapist; Addictions Specialist; Childcare Worker; Case Manager; Client Affairs Counselor; Administrative Assistant; Driver.

EITELJORG MUSEUM
500 West Washington Street, Indianapolis IN 46204. 317/636-9378. **Fax:** 317/264-1724. **Contact:** Lezlie Laxton, Personnel Coordinator. **E-mail address:** personnel@eiteljorg.com. **Description:** A museum of Native American and Western art. **Positions advertised include:** Exhibit Specialist.

ELI LILLY AND COMPANY
Lilly Corporate Center, Indianapolis IN 46285. 317/277-7731. **Contact:** Human Resources. **World Wide Web address:** http://www.lilly.com. **Description:** Discovers, develops, manufactures, and sells a broad line of human health products and pharmaceuticals including diagnostic products; monoclonal antibody-based diagnostic tests for colon, prostate, and testicular cancer; medical devices; patient vital-signs measurement and electrocardiograph systems; implantable cardiac pacemakers and related medical systems; and anti-infectives and diabetic care products. The company also produces animal health products such as animal antibiotics and special animal feed additives. **NOTE:** Jobseekers are encouraged to apply via the Website: https://jobs.lilly.com. **Positions advertised include:** Analytical Chemist; Associate Biologist; Associate Environmental Consultant; Associate Project Manager; Behavioral Pharmacologist; Biologist, Cancer Research; Clinical Data Management Coordinator. **Corporate headquarters location:** This location. **Listed on:** New York Stock Exchange. **Stock exchange symbol:** LLY.

ELI LILLY AND COMPANY
10500 South State Road 63, P.O. Box 99, Clinton IN 47842. 765/832-4400. **Contact:** Human Resources. **World Wide Web address:** http://www.lilly.com. **Description:** Discovers, develops, manufactures, and sells a broad line of human health products and pharmaceuticals such as diagnostic products; monoclonal antibody-based diagnostic tests for colon, prostate, and testicular cancer; medical devices; patient vital-signs measurement and electrocardiograph systems; implantable cardiac pacemakers, and other related medical systems; and anti-infective and diabetic care products. The company also produces animal health products such as animal antibiotics and special animal feed additives. **NOTE:** Jobseekers are encouraged to apply via the Website: https://jobs.lilly.com. **Positions advertised include:** Manager, Quality Control Laboratory; Project Engineering Consultant. **Corporate headquarters location:** Indianapolis IN. **Listed on:** New York Stock Exchange. **Stock exchange symbol:** LLY.

EMMIS COMMUNICATIONS
40 Monument Circle, One Emmis Plaza, Suite 500, Indianapolis IN 46204. 317/266-0100. **Contact:** Personnel Director. **World Wide Web address:** http://www.emmis.com. **Description:** Owns and operates FM radio stations and publishes a monthly statistical publication for the radio industry. **Positions advertised include:** Account Executive; Assistant Promotions Director; News Reporter, Anchor; Vice President, Engineering; Receptionist. **Special programs:** Internships. **Corporate headquarters location:** This location.

ERNST & YOUNG LLP
111 Monument Circle, One Indiana Square, Suite 2600, Indianapolis IN 46204. 317/681-7000. **Contact:** Personnel. **World Wide Web address:** http://www.ey.com. **Description:** A certified public accounting firm that also provides management consulting services. Services include data processing, financial modeling, financial feasibility studies, production planning and inventory management, management sciences, health care planning, human resources, cost accounting, and budgeting systems. **International locations:** Worldwide.

ERNST & YOUNG LLP
National City Center, Suite 2300, 110 Westberry Street, Fort Wayne IN 46802. 260/424-2233. **Contact:** Personnel. **E-mail address:** erica.knuth@ey.com. **World Wide Web address:** http://www.ey.com. **Description:** A certified public accounting firm that also provides management consulting services. Services include data processing, financial modeling, financial feasibility studies, production planning and inventory management, management sciences, health care planning, human resources, cost accounting, and budgeting systems. **International locations:** Worldwide.

ESCALADE SPORTS
P.O. Box 889, Evansville IN 47706. 812/467-1200. **Physical address:** 817 Maxwell Avenue, Evansville IN 47711. **Contact:** Director of Employment Services. **E-mail address:** gallan@escaladesports.com. **World Wide Web address:** http://www.escaladesports.com. **Description:** Manufactures and sells a variety of sporting goods such as table tennis tables and accessories, archery equipment, basketball backboards, goals, and home fitness accessories. **Corporate headquarters location:** This location. **Parent company:** Escalade, Inc.

FAIRMONT HOMES, INC.
P.O. Box 27, Nappanee IN 46550. 574/773-7941. **Physical address:** 502 South Oakland, Nappanee IN 46550. **Fax:** 574/773-2185. **Contact:** Human Resources. **World Wide Web address:** http://www.fairmonthomes.com. **Description:** Manufactures and markets sectional housing, modular homes, and recreational vehicles nationwide. **Corporate headquarters location:** This location. **Other U.S. locations:** Montevideo MN. **Listed on:** Privately held.

FARBEST FOODS INC.
P.O. Box 480, Huntingburg IN 47542. 812/683-4200. **Fax:** 812/683-4226. **Contact:** Human Resources Manager. **E-mail address:** jjochem@farbestfoods.com. **World Wide Web address:** http://www.farbestfoods.com. **Description:** A turkey processing plant. **Corporate headquarters location:** This location. **Listed on:** Privately held.

FEDERAL-MOGUL CORPORATION
2845 West State Road 28, Frankfort IN 46041. 765/654-8761. **Contact:** Human Resources Department. **World Wide Web address:** http://www.federal-mogul.com. **Description:** Federal-Mogul Corporation manufactures cylindrical and tapered roller bearings, bushings, sleeve bearings, ball bearings, thrust washers, and related products for the automotive industry. The company also produces and distributes precision parts to original equipment manufacturers and replacement parts such as fuel systems, suspension parts, and lighting and electrical products to worldwide markets. Brand names of manufactured goods include Federal-Mogul, Glyco, Bruss, National, Mather, and Signal-Stat. **NOTE:** Interested candidates should send a resume or curriculum vitae to: Federal-Mogul Corporation, Attention: Human Resources Staffing, 26555 Northwestern Highway, Southfield MI 48034. **Positions advertised include:** Manufacturing Engineer; Quality Engineer; Inventory Analyst; Financial Analyst; Credit Analyst; Sales Representative. **Special programs:** Internships; Co-ops. **Corporate headquarters location:** Southfield MI. **Operations at this facility include:** This location manufactures oil seals for the automotive industry. **Listed on:** New York Stock Exchange. **Stock exchange symbol:** FMO. **Number of employees at this location:** 820.

FEDERAL-MOGUL CORPORATION
101 Industrial Boulevard, Logansport IN 46947. 574/722-6141. **Fax:** 574/722-9426. **Contact:** Human Resources Manager. **World Wide Web address:** http://www.federal-mogul.com. **Description:** Federal-Mogul Corporation manufactures cylindrical and tapered roller bearings, oil seals, bushings, sleeve bearings, ball bearings, thrust washers, and related products for the automotive industry. The company also produces and distributes precision parts to original equipment manufacturers and replacement parts such as fuel systems, suspension parts, and lighting and electrical products to worldwide markets. Brand names include Federal-Mogul, Glyco, Bruss, National, Mather, and Signal-Stat. **NOTE:** Interested candidates should send a resume or curriculum vitae to: Federal-Mogul Corporation, Attention: Human Resources Staffing, 26555 Northwestern Highway, Southfield MI 48034. **Corporate headquarters location:** Southfield MI. **Operations at this facility include:** This location manufactures electrical lighting systems for tractor-trailers, and electrical and diesel fuel pumps for the automotive industry. **Listed on:** New York Stock Exchange. **Stock exchange symbol:** FMO.

FEDERAL-MOGUL WIPER PRODUCTS
402 Royal Road, Michigan City IN 46360. 219/872-5150. **Contact:** Joyce Clark, Human Resources. **World Wide Web address:** http://www.federal-mogul.com. **Description:** An automotive parts assembly plant. **Corporate headquarters location:** Southfield MI. **Parent company:** Federal-Mogul Corporation manufactures cylindrical and tapered roller bearings, bushings, sleeve bearings, ball bearings, thrust washers, and related products for the automotive industry. The company also produces and distributes precision parts to original equipment manufacturers and replacement parts such as fuel systems, suspension parts, and lighting and electrical products to worldwide markets. Brand names of manufactured goods include Federal-Mogul, Glyco, Bruss, National, Mather, and Signal-Stat. **Operations at this facility include:** Divisional Headquarters. **Listed on:** New York Stock Exchange. **Stock exchange symbol:** FMO.

FINISH LINE INC.
3308 North Mitthoeffer Road, Indianapolis IN 46235. 888/777-3949. **Fax** 317/613-6701. **Contact:** Human Resources. **E-mail address:** hr@finishline.com. **World Wide Web address:** http://www.thefinishline.com. **Description:** Finish Line Inc. operates retail stores that offer a broad selection of current men's, women's, and children's brand name athletic and leisure footwear, active-wear, and accessories. **Positions advertised include:** Store Cash Reconciliation Associate; Controller; Human Resources Specialist; Staff Attorney; Paralegal; Loss Prevention Officer; In-Store Production Coordinator; Product Merchandiser; Senior Tax Accountant. **Corporate headquarters location:** This location.

FIRST INDIANA BANK
135 North Pennsylvania Street, Indianapolis IN 46204. 317/269-1304. **Fax:** 317/859-4723. **Contact:** Human Resources Department. **E-mail address:** jobs@firstindiana.com. **World Wide Web address:** http://wwwfirstindiana.com. **Description:** A full-service bank. **Positions advertised include:** Commercial Real Estate Loan Officer; Construction Loan Officer; Credit Analyst; Customer Service Representative; Financial Reporting Accountant; Loan Review Officer. **Corporate headquarters location:** This location. **Parent company:** First Indiana Corporation (also at this location) is a holding company whose principal subsidiary is First Indiana Bank. The corporation is engaged primarily in retail banking and lending through 29 banking centers including Mid-West Federal Savings Bank, First Federal Savings and Loan of Rushville, and Mooresville Savings Bank. In addition, the corporation operates six mortgage services offices in central Indiana. One Mortgage Corporation, a subsidiary, operates offices in Florida and North Carolina. First Indiana Corporation's other subsidiaries, One Insurance Agency, One Investment Corporation, and One Property Corporation, are engaged in insurance sales, investments, and full-service securities brokerage. **Operations at this facility include:** Administration; Divisional Headquarters; Sales.

FIRST MERCHANTS BANK N.A.
P.O. Box 792, Muncie IN 47308-0792. 765/747-1500. **Physical address:** 200 East Jackson Street, Muncie IN 47305. **Fax:** 765/747-1485. **Contact:** Human Resources. **E-mail address:** jobs@firstmerchants.com. **World Wide Web address:** http://www.firstmerchants.com. **Description:** A bank that operates one of the largest trust departments in Indiana. **NOTE:** Human Resources phone: 765/747-1537. **Positions advertised include:** Associate Loan Review Specialist; Loan Accounting Supervisor; Service Associate. **Parent company:** First Merchants Corporation provides

service through 21 offices located in Delaware, Madison, and Henry Counties in Indiana. Subsidiaries of First Merchants, including Pendleton Banking Company and First United Bank, conduct a full range of banking activities including commercial, industrial, consumer and real estate lending, deposit and investment services, and other banking services.

FISERV, INC.
3575 Moreau Court, Suite 2, South Bend IN 46628. 574/282-3300. **Contact:** Human Resources. **World Wide Web address:** http://www.fiserv.com. **Description:** Develops software for the mortgage industry. **Positions advertised include:** Executive Assistant; Project Manager. **Other U.S. locations:** Nationwide. **Listed on:** NASDAQ. **Stock exchange symbol:** FISV.

FLEETWOOD MOTOR HOMES, INC.
1031 U.S. Highway 224 East, P.O. Box 31, Decatur IN 46733. 260/728-2121. **Contact:** Personnel. **World Wide Web address:** http://www.fleetwoodhomes.com. **Description:** Produces recreational vehicles and manufactured housing with operations in the United States, Canada, and Germany. The company's recreational vehicles are primarily motor homes sold under brand names including American Eagle, Coronado, Bounder, Flair, and PaceArrow. Fleetwood also manufactures a variety of trailers and campers and owns subsidiaries that offer financial services and supplies. The company has an 80 percent interest in Niesmann & Bischoff, a motor home manufacturer in Germany. **Corporate headquarters location:** Riverside CA. **Listed on:** New York Stock Exchange. **Stock exchange symbol:** FLE.

FLOYD COUNTY AUDITOR'S OFFICE
311 West First Street, Suite 118, City County Building, New Albany IN 47150. 812/948-5433. **Contact:** Human Resources. **World Wide Web address:** www.cityofnewalbany.com. **Description:** Manages control audits, statewide financial and compliance audits, special investigations, classification compliance audits, briefing reports, legislative requests, and special issue areas.

FLOYD MEMORIAL HOSPITAL AND HEALTH SERVICES
1850 State Street, New Albany IN 47150. 812/944-7701. **Recorded jobline:** 812/949-5660. **Contact:** Personnel. **World Wide Web address:** http://www.floydmemorial.org. **Description:** An acute care hospital offering 24-hour adult and pediatric emergency care. Floyd Memorial Hospital and Health Services also has an oncology unit, a critical care cardiac unit, and a full surgery center. **Positions advertised include:** Case Manager; Certified Nursing Assistant; Director, Rehabilitation Services; Environmental Services Aide; Home Health Aide; Imaging Systems Coordinator; Medical Technologist; Nurse Practitioner; Orderly; Radiation Therapist; Receptionist; Registered Nurse.

FOAMEX INTERNATIONAL, INC.
2211 South Wayne Street, Auburn IN 46706. 260/925-1073. **Contact:** Human Resources. **E-mail address:** recruiting@foamex.com. **World Wide Web address:** http://www.foamex.com. **Description:** One of the nation's largest manufacturers of flexible polyurethane foam products. Foamex products are classified into four groups: cushion foams, carpet cushion foams, automotive foams, and technical foams. Cushion foams are used for mattresses, quilting and borders, home and office furniture, computer and electronics packaging, and padding for health care equipment. Carpet cushion foams include prime, bonded, sponge rubber, felt carpet cushion, synthetic grass turf, and a variety of textured carpeting and wall covering. Automotive foams include foams for cushioning and seating, acoustical foams, headliner foams, trim foams, and foams for door panel parts. Technical foams include those for filtration, reservoiring, sound absorption and transmission, carburetors, high-speed inkjet printers, speaker grilles, oxygenators, and EKG pads, as well as cosmetic applicators, mop heads, paint brushes, and diapers. **NOTE:** Direct resumes to: Director of Staffing and Development, Foamex International Inc., 1000 Columbia Avenue, Linwood PA 19061. **Other U.S. locations:** Nationwide. **International locations:** Canada; Mexico. **Listed on:** NASDAQ. **Stock exchange symbol:** FMXI.

FORD METER BOX COMPANY
P.O. Box 398, 775 Manchester Avenue, Wabash IN 46992-0398. 260/563-3171. **Contact:** Human Resources Department. **World Wide Web address:** http://www.fordmeterbox.com. **Description:** Manufactures brass valves and fittings for the water works industry.

FORETHOUGHT FINANCIAL SERVICES
One Forethought Center, Highway 46 East, Batesville IN 47006. 812/934-8148. **Contact:** Human Resources. **World Wide Web address:** http://www.forethought.com. **Description:** Provides financial services for the planning of funeral arrangements. **Corporate headquarters location:** This location.

FORT WAYNE CHILDREN'S ZOO
3411 Sherman Boulevard, Fort Wayne IN 46808. 260/427-6800. **Contact:** Human Resources. **World Wide Web address:** http://www.kidszoo.com. **Description:** A children's zoo featuring African, Indonesian Rain Forest, and Australian exhibits. The zoo also offers a miniature train ride and a dugout canoe ride as well as the Wild Wings Bird Show. **Positions advertised include:** Seasonal Zoo Attendant. **Special programs:** Internships; Apprenticeships.

FRANKLIN ELECTRIC COMPANY, INC.
400 East Spring Street, Bluffton IN 46714. 260/824-2900. **Contact:** Human Resources. **World Wide Web address:** http://www.fele.com. **Description:** One of the world's largest manufacturers of submersible electric motors. Franklin Electric is also a leading producer of engineered specialty electric motor products and electronic controls used by original equipment manufacturers for residential, industrial, and municipal applications. The principal application for Franklin's submersible motors is providing electrical power for water and pumping systems, oil wells, and wastewater handling systems. Franklin's engineered specialty electric motor products and electronic controls are used in a wide variety of industrial products including gasoline dispensers, paint sprayers, electric hoists, explosion-proof vapor exhaust fans, vacuum pumping systems, livestock feeding systems, and soft ice cream machines. **Positions advertised include:** Electrical Design Engineer. **Other U.S. locations:** Siloam Springs AR; Tulsa OK; Wilburton OK; McFarland WI. **International locations:** Australia; Czech Republic; Germany; Mexico; South Africa.

FRANKLIN UNITED METHODIST COMMUNITY
1070 West Jefferson Street, Franklin IN 46131. 317/736-7185. **Fax:** 317/736-1150. **Contact:** Kathi Couch, Human Resources Director. **E-mail address:** kcouch@fumeth.com. **World Wide Web address:** http://www.fumeth.com. **Description:** A continuing care retirement community. Founded in 1957. **Positions advertised include:** Activity Director; Certified Nursing Assistant; Dietary Cart Personnel; Dining Room Waitress; Staff Nurse; Unit Charge Nurse; Qualified Medication Aide; Housekeeper; Beauty Shop Operator. **Office hours:** Monday - Friday, 8:00 a.m. - 4:30 p.m.

FRITO-LAY, INC.
323 South County Road 300 West, Frankfort IN 46041. 765/659-1831. **Contact:** Human Resources. **World Wide Web address:** http://www.fritolay.com. **Description:** A worldwide manufacturer and wholesaler of snack products including the brand names Fritos Corn Chips, Doritos Tortilla Chips, Lays Potato Chips, and Smartfood Popcorn. **Corporate headquarters location:** Plano TX. **Parent company:** PepsiCo, Inc. (Purchase NY) consists of Frito-Lay Company, Pepsi-Cola Company, Quaker Oats, and Tropicana Products, Inc. **Listed on:** New York Stock Exchange. **Stock exchange symbol:** PEP.

GD LEASING COMPANY
2399 East 15th Avenue, Gary IN 46402. 219/881-0215. **Contact:** Human Resources. **World Wide Web address:** http://www.falcon.com. **Description:** A truck driving company servicing the continental United States and Canada.

GE INDUSTRIAL SYSTEMS
1635 Broadway, Fort Wayne IN 46802. 260/439-2000. **Contact:** Manager of Human Resources. **World Wide Web address:** http://www.geindustrial.com. **Description:** General Electric Company operates in the following areas: aircraft engines (jet engines, replacement parts, and repair services for commercial, military, executive, and commuter aircraft); appliances; broadcasting (NBC); industrial (lighting products, electrical distribution and control equipment, transportation systems products, electric motors and related products, a broad range of electrical and electronic industrial automation products, and a network of electrical supply houses); materials (plastics, ABS resins, silicones, superabrasives, and laminates); power systems (products for the generation, transmission, and distribution of electricity); technical products and systems (medical systems and equipment, as well as a full range of computer-based information and data interchange services for both internal use and external commercial and industrial customers); and capital services (consumer services, financing, and specialty insurance). **Positions advertised include:** Senior Underwriter; Accounting Specialist; Advanced Manufacturing Engineer; Services Associate. **Special programs:** Internships. **Operations at this facility include:** This location manufactures motors and transformers.

GE INDUSTRIAL SYSTEMS
1412 13th Street, Tell City IN 47586. 812/547-2311. **Contact:** Human Resources. **World Wide Web address:** http://www.ge.com. **Description:** General Electric Company operates in the following areas: aircraft engines (jet engines, replacement parts, and repair services for commercial, military, executive, and commuter aircraft); appliances; broadcasting (NBC); industrial (lighting products, electrical distribution and control equipment, transportation systems products, electric motors and related products, a broad range of electrical and electronic industrial automation products, and a network of electrical supply houses); materials (plastics, ABS resins, silicones, superabrasives, and laminates); power systems (products for the generation, transmission, and distribution of electricity); technical products and systems (medical systems and equipment, as well as a full range of computer-based information and data interchange services for both internal use and external commercial and industrial customers); and capital services (consumer services, financing, and specialty insurance). **Operations at this facility include:** This location manufactures motors and industrial systems.

GALLAGHER BASSETT SERVICES, INC.
5775 Nimtz Parkway, Suite 100, South Bend IN 46628. 574/234-0028. **Contact:** Human Resources. **World Wide Web address:** http://www.gallagherbassett.com. **Description:** A full-service property and casualty administrator that focuses on workmen's compensation and liability. Gallagher Bassett Services, Inc. offers risk management programs as well as loss reduction and investigative services to assess claims and appraisals for corporate clients. Founded in 1962. **Other U.S. locations:** Nationwide. **International locations:** Worldwide.

GARY PUBLIC TRANSPORTATION
P.O. Box 857, Gary IN 46402-0857. 219/885-7555. **Physical address:** 100 West Fourth Avenue, Gary IN 46402. **Contact:** Human Resources. **Description:** Gary Public Transportation Corporation operates the local bus and public transit system. **Operations at this facility include:** This location houses administrative offices.

GECOM CORPORATION
1025 Barachel Lane, Greensburg IN 47240. 812/663-2270. **Fax:** 812/663-1781. **Contact:** Human Resources. **E-mail address:** hr@gecom.com. **World Wide Web address:** http://www.gecomcorp.com. **Description:** A QS-9000 certified automotive parts supplier to Honda, Toyota, Mazda, Isuzu, and other OEMs. GECOM manufactures opener and latch assemblies. Founded in 1987. **NOTE:** Entry-level positions are offered. **Company slogan:** Opening doors to the automotive world. **Special programs:** Apprenticeships. **Corporate headquarters location:** This location. **Other U.S. locations:** Southfield MI. **International locations:** China; England; Japan; Thailand. **Subsidiaries include:** NAC, Inc. **Parent company:** Mitsui Kinzoku. **Operations at this facility include:** Administration; Manufacturing; Service. **Listed on:** Privately held.

GEMINUS CORPORATION
8400 Louisiana Street, Merrillville IN 46410. 219/757-1800. **Fax:** 219/757-1831. **Contact:** Diane Johnson, Human Resources. **E-mail address:** diane.johnson@geminus.org. **World Wide Web address:** http://www. geminus.org. **Description:** Operates Head Start programs and performs accounting, marketing, and human resource functions for Southlake Center for Mental Health, an inpatient and outpatient mental health center, and Tri-City Mental Health, an outpatient mental health center. **Positions advertised include:** Staff Accountant; Collection Specialist; Psychologist; Social Worker; Residential Assistant; Staff Nurse; Clinician; Addictions Therapist; Van Driver. **Special programs:** Internships. **Corporate headquarters location:** This location. **Operations at this facility include:** Service. **Listed on:** Privately held.

GENCORP
One General Street, P.O. Box 507, Wabash IN 46992. 260/563-1121. **Contact:** Human Resources. **World Wide Web address:** http://www.gdxautomotive.com. **Description:** An international corporation that manufactures rubber products, plastics, industrial products, wall coverings, athletic products, rocket propulsion ordnance systems, and electronic sensors. **Corporate headquarters location:** Fairlawn OH.

GENERAL ELECTRIC COMPANY
301 North Curry Pike, Bloomington IN 47404. 812/334-9500. **Contact:** Human Resources. **World Wide Web address:** http://www.ge.com. **Description:** General Electric Company operates in the following areas: aircraft engines (jet engines, replacement parts, and repair services for commercial, military, executive, and commuter aircraft); appliances; broadcasting (NBC); industrial (lighting products, electrical distribution and control equipment, transportation systems products, electric motors and related products, a broad range of electrical and electronic industrial

automation products, and a network of electrical supply houses); materials (plastics, ABS resins, silicones, superabrasives, and laminates); power systems (products for the generation, transmission, and distribution of electricity); technical products and systems (medical systems and equipment, as well as a full range of computer-based information and data interchange services for both internal use and external commercial and industrial customers); and capital services (consumer services, financing, and specialty insurance). **Operations at this facility include:** This location manufactures side-by-side refrigerators. **Listed on:** New York Stock Exchange. **Stock exchange symbol:** GE.

GENERAL MOTORS CORPORATION (GM)
P.O. Box 388, Indianapolis IN 46206. 317/269-5830. **Contact:** Human Resources. **World Wide Web address:** http://www.gm.com. **Description:** General Motors Corporation is one of the world's largest full-line vehicle manufacturers. The company also has substantial interests in information technology, electronics, and finance. GM conducts business through six different sectors. North American Automotive Operations includes Sales/Service Groups (Buick, Cadillac, Chevrolet, GMC Truck, Oldsmobile, Pontiac, and Saturn) and Vehicle Development Groups (Powertrain, Truck Group, Small Car Group, and Midsize/Luxury Car Group). International Operations include GM Europe (GME), Asia Pacific Operations (APO), and Latin America, Africa, Middle East Operations (LAAMO). General Motors Acceptance Corporation (GMAC) provides financing and insurance to GM customers and dealers, and consists of North American Operations, International Operations, Motors Insurance Corporation, and GMAC Mortgage Group. Electronic Data Systems (EDS) applies information technologies to more than 8,000 customers globally in the communications, energy/chemical, insurance, public sector, travel and transportation, financial services, manufacturing, and retail industries. GM Hughes Electronics Corporation is involved in automotive electronics, telecommunications and space electronics, and defense electronics. Founded in 1908. **Corporate headquarters location:** Detroit MI. **Operations at this facility include:** This location stamps metal for pick-up trucks. **Listed on:** New York Stock Exchange. **Stock exchange symbol:** GM.

GENERAL MOTORS CORPORATION (GM)
C-P-C GROUP
2400 West Second Street, Marion IN 46952. 765/668-2000. **Contact:** Human Resources. **World Wide Web address:** http://www.gm.com. **Description:** One of the world's largest full-line vehicle manufacturers. The company also has substantial interests in information technology, electronics, and finance. GM conducts business through six different sectors. North American Automotive Operations includes Sales/Service Groups (Buick, Cadillac, Chevrolet, GMC Truck, Oldsmobile, Pontiac, and Saturn) and Vehicle Development Groups (Powertrain, Truck Group, Small Car Group, and Midsize/Luxury Car Group). International Operations include GM Europe (GME), Asia Pacific Operations (APO), and Latin America, Africa, Middle East Operations (LAAMO). General Motors Acceptance Corporation (GMAC) provides financing and insurance to GM customers and dealers, and consists of North American Operations, International Operations, Motors Insurance Corporation, and GMAC Mortgage Group. Electronic Data Systems (EDS) applies information technologies to more than 8,000 customers globally in the communications, energy/chemical, insurance, public sector, travel and transportation, financial services, manufacturing, and retail industries. GM Hughes Electronics Corporation is involved in automotive electronics, telecommunications and space electronics, and defense electronics. Founded in 1908. **Corporate headquarters location:** Detroit MI. **Listed on:** New York Stock Exchange. **Stock exchange symbol:** GM.

GENERAL MOTORS CORPORATION (GM)
GM FORT WAYNE TRUCK AND BUS
12200 Lafayette Center Road, Roanoke IN 46783. 260/673-2000. **Contact:** Human Resources. **World Wide Web address:** http://www.gm.com. **Description:** General Motors Corporation is one of the world's largest full-line vehicle manufacturers. The company also has substantial interests in information technology, electronics, and finance. GM conducts business through six different sectors. North American Automotive Operations includes Sales/Service Groups (Buick, Cadillac, Chevrolet, GMC Truck, Oldsmobile, Pontiac, and Saturn) and Vehicle Development Groups (Powertrain, Truck Group, Small Car Group, and Midsize/Luxury Car Group). International Operations include GM Europe (GME), Asia Pacific Operations (APO), and Latin America, Africa, Middle East Operations (LAAMO). General Motors Acceptance Corporation (GMAC) provides financing and insurance to GM customers and dealers, and consists of North American Operations, International Operations, Motors Insurance Corporation, and GMAC Mortgage Group. Electronic Data Systems (EDS) applies information technologies to more than 8,000 customers globally in the communications, energy/chemical, insurance, public sector, travel and transportation, financial services, manufacturing, and retail industries. GM Hughes Electronics Corporation is involved in automotive electronics, telecommunications and space electronics, and defense electronics. Founded in 1908. **Corporate headquarters location:** Detroit MI. **Operations at this facility include:** This location manufactures trucks. **Listed on:** New York Stock Exchange. **Stock exchange symbol:** GM.

GENERAL PETROLEUM
P.O. Box 10688, Fort Wayne IN 46853. 260/489-8504. **Physical address:** 7404 Disalle Boulevard, Fort Wayne IN 46825. **Fax:** 260/489-6468. **Contact:** Human Resources. **World Wide Web address:** http://www.genpet.com. **Description:** A lubricant wholesaler and distributor. **Corporate headquarters location:** This location. **Other area locations:** Fishers IN.

GIRL SCOUTS OF LIMBERLOST
2135 Spy Run Avenue, Fort Wayne IN 46805. 260/422-3417. **Contact:** Human Resources. **World Wide Web address:** http://www.girlscouts.org. **Description:** A social service organization aimed at meeting the social and developmental needs of adolescent girls. **Corporate headquarters location:** New York NY. **Parent company:** Girl Scouts USA.

GOLDEN RULE INSURANCE COMPANY
7440 Woodland Drive, Indianapolis IN 46278. 317/297-4123. **Fax:** 317/299-7416. **Contact:** Human Resources. **E-mail address:** jobs@goldenrule.com. **World Wide Web address:** http://www.goldenrule.com. **Description:** Provides life, health, and group insurance nationwide. **Positions advertised include:** Underwriter; Data Security Analyst; Management Trainee; Marketing Coordinator; Sales Representative.

GOOD SAMARITAN HOSPITAL
GOOD SAMARITAN HEART CENTER
520 South Seventh Street, Vincennes IN 47591. 812/885-3373. **Fax:** 812/885-3961. **Recorded jobline:** 888/866-9356. **Contact:** Human Resources. **World Wide Web address:** http://www.gshvin.org. **Description:** A 262-bed, acute care facility. The hospital provides a full range of services including cardiovascular surgery; neurosurgery; a Women and Infants Center; a cancer program; physical, occupational, and speech therapy; and hemodialysis. Good Samaritan Hospital also provides mental health and home health care services to the community. Good Samaritan Heart Center (also at this location; 812/885-3243) offers prevention, diagnosis, intervention (balloon angioplasty and pacemakers), surgery, and rehabilitation for a variety of heart ailments. **Positions advertised include:** Registered Nurse; Environmental Services Assistant; Case Manager; Clinical Psychologist; Laboratory Assistant; Radiologic Technologist; Staff Nurse; Staff Pharmacist.

GRAND VICTORIA CASINO & RESORT BY HYATT
600 Grand Victoria Drive, Rising Sun IN 47040. 812/438-1234. **Toll-free phone:** 800/GRA-ND11. **Contact:** Human Resources. **World Wide Web address:** http://www.hyatt.com. **Description:** A 200-room hotel and resort featuring an 18-hole golf course, a casino, and multiple banquet facilities.

GREAT DANE TRAILERS, INC.
P.O. Box 350, Brazil IN 47834. 812/443-4711. **Contact:** Human Resources. **World Wide Web address:** http://www.greatdanetrailers.com. **Description:** Manufactures flatbed and refrigerated trailers, and truck and van bodies.

GREAT LAKES CHEMICAL CORPORATION
One Great Lakes Boulevard, West Lafayette IN 47996-2200. 765/497-6100. **Recorded jobline:** 765/497-6377. **Contact:** Human Resources Department. **World Wide Web address:** http://www.greatlakeschem.com. **Description:** A leading supplier of specialty chemical solutions to customers in the plastics, additives, and life sciences industries. The company also develops performance chemicals for use in fire protection, oil and gas drilling, and recreational water treatment. **NOTE:** Please call the jobline for application procedures and a list of available positions before sending a resume. **Office hours:** Monday – Friday, 8:00 a.m. – 5:00 p.m. **Corporate headquarters location:** This location. **Listed on:** New York Stock Exchange. **Stock exchange symbol:** GLK.

GROTE INDUSTRIES COMPANY
P.O. Box 1550, Madison IN 47250. 812/273-2121. **Toll-free phone:** 800/628-0809. **Fax:** 812/265-8440. **Physical address:** 2600 Lanier Drive, Madison IN 47250. **Contact:** Human Resources. **World Wide Web address:** http://www.grote.com. **Description:** Manufactures vehicular lighting products.

GUARDIAN INDUSTRIES CORPORATION
1900 South Center Street, Auburn IN 46706. 260/925-5656. **Contact:** Human Resources. **E-mail address:** auburnhr@guardian.com. **World Wide Web address:** http://www.guardian.com. **Description:** Guardian Industries Corporation is an international manufacturer of glass including tempered glass, reflective coatings, and insulated glass. **Positions advertised include:** Production Supervisor.

GUIDANT CORPORATION
111 Monument Circle, Suite 2900, Indianapolis IN 46204. 317/971-2000. **Fax:** 317/971-2040. **Contact:** Human Resources. **World Wide Web address:** http://www.guidant.com. **Description:** Designs, develops, manufactures, and markets a broad range of products for use in cardiac rhythm management, coronary artery disease intervention, and other forms of minimally invasive surgery. **Corporate headquarters location:** This location. **Listed on:** New York Stock Exchange. **Stock exchange symbol:** GDT.

HAGERMAN
P.O. Box 502710, Indianapolis IN 46250-7710. 317/713-0636. **Physical address:** 7930 Castleway Drive, Indianapolis IN 46250. **Contact:** Human Resources. **Fax:** 317/577-6841. **World Wide Web address:** http://www.hagermangc.com. **Description:** Engaged in construction management and general contracting services. **Positions advertised include:** Estimator. **Corporate headquarters location:** This location. **Operations at this facility include:** Administration. **Number of employees at this location:** 100.

HAMMOND GROUP, INC.
P.O. Box 6408, Hammond IN 46325. 219/931-9360. **Fax:** 219/931-2140. **Contact:** Human Resources. **E-mail address:** info@hmndgroup.com. **World Wide Web address:** http://www.hmndgroup.com. **Description:** Hammond Group manufactures lead chemicals and products under the name Hammond Lead Products including lead carbonates, silicates, and sulfates for a variety of industries. The company also manufactures a de-dusted granular litharge called 400Y. **Corporate headquarters location:** This location. **Operations at this facility include:** This location houses administrative offices.

HAMPTON INN
105 South Meridian Street, Indianapolis IN 46225. 317/261-1200. **Contact:** Human Resources. **World Wide Web address:** www.hamptoninn.com. **Description:** Located downtown within walking distance of Conseco Field House, the RCA Dome, and numerous restaurants. **Other U.S. locations:** Nationwide. **Parent Company:** Hilton.

HARRIS & HARRIS
222 North Buffalo Street, Warsaw IN 46580. 574/267-2111. **Contact:** Recruitment. **Description:** A law firm specializing in diverse areas including corporate, banking, taxation, real estate, environmental, family/domestic, bankruptcy, and estate planning law.

HARRISON STEEL CASTINGS COMPANY
P.O. Box 60, Attica IN 47918. 765/762-2481. **Physical address:** 900 Mound Street, Attica IN 47918. **Fax:** 765/762-2487. **Contact:** Geoff Curtis, Human Resources. **E-mail address:** curtisgh@hscast.com. **World Wide Web address:** http://www.hscast.com. **Description:** Operates a steel works and blast furnace.

HAYNES INTERNATIONAL, INC.
P.O. Box 9013, Kokomo IN 46904-9013. 765/456-6000. **Physical address:** 1020 West Park Avenue, Kokomo IN 46901. **Toll-free phone:** 800/428-8857. **Contact:** Employment Manager. **E-mail address:** human_relations_info@haynesintl.com. **World Wide Web address:** http://www.haynesintl.com. **Description:** One of the world's leading manufacturers of nickel- and cobalt-based, heat-resistant, and corrosion-resistant alloys. **NOTE:** Entry-level positions and second and third shifts are offered. **Special programs:** Internships; Apprenticeships; Co-ops. **Office hours:** Monday - Friday, 8:00 a.m. - 5:00 p.m. **Corporate headquarters location:** This location. **Other U.S. locations:** Anaheim CA; Windsor CT; Arcadia LA; Houston TX. **International locations:** Openshaw, England; Paris, France; Zurich, Switzerland. **Operations at this facility include:** Administration; Manufacturing; Research and Development; Sales; Service.

THE HERALD-PRESS
7 North Jefferson Street, Huntington IN 46750. 260/356-6700. **Contact:** Human Resources. **World Wide Web address:** http://www.h-ponline.com. **Description:** A community newspaper with a weekday circulation of 8,800 and a Sunday circulation of 9,200. Founded in 1848.

HILL-ROM COMPANY, INC.
1069 State Route 46 East, Batesville IN 47006. 812/934-7777. **Fax:** 812/934-8329. **Contact:** Human Resources. **E-mail address:** careers@hill-rom.com. **World Wide Web address:** http://www.hill-rom.com. **Description:** Manufactures and rents a variety of health care products including birthing beds, hospital beds, and stretchers. **Positions advertised include:** Project Test Engineer; Quality Engineer; Advanced Electrical Design Engineer; Marketing Manager; Asset Management Analyst. **Corporate headquarters location:** This location. **Parent company:** Hillenbrand Industries, Inc.

HILLENBRAND INDUSTRIES, INC.
700 State Route 46 East, Mail Code Y-20, Batesville IN 47006. 812/934-7771. **Fax:** 812/934-1998. **Contact:** Director, Administrative Services **E-mail address:** resume_admin@Hillenbrand.com. **World Wide Web address:** http://www.hillenbrand.com. **Description:** A holding company. **Corporate headquarters location:** This location. **Subsidiaries include:** Batesville Casket Company, Inc. (Batesville IN) manufactures funeral-related products including caskets and urns. Forethought Financial Services (Batesville IN) provides financial services for the purpose of planning funeral arrangements. Hill-Rom Company, Inc. (Batesville IN) manufactures and rents a variety of health care products including birthing beds, hospital beds, and stretchers.

HILLIARD-LYONS INC.
P.O. Box 98, Evansville IN 47701. 812/426-1481. **Fax:** 812/428-8697. **Contact:** Human Resources. **E-mail address:** careers@hilliard.com. **World Wide Web address:** http://www.hilliard.com. **Description:** A security broker and dealer offering stocks, bonds, mutual funds, and other financial services. **Corporate headquarters location:** Louisville KY.

HILTON FORT WAYNE
1020 South Calhoun Street, Fort Wayne IN 46802-3005. 260/420-1100. **Fax:** 260/424-7775. **Contact:** Human Resources. **World Wide Web address:** www.hilton.com. **Description:** A 246-room hotel attached to the Grand Wayne Convention Center offering downtown conveniences and business amenities.

HOLM INDUSTRIES INC.
P.O. Box 450, Scottsburg IN 47170. 812/752-2526. **Fax:** 812/752-3563. **Contact:** Human Resources. **Description:** Involved in the extrusion of plastic, rubber, and vinyl for the appliance and building trade industries. **Corporate headquarters location:** This location. **Other U.S. locations:** Hartselle AL; San Diego CA; St. Charles IL; New Ulm MN. **Operations at this facility include:** Administration; Manufacturing; Research and Development; Sales.

HOME HOSPITAL
2400 South Street, Lafayette IN 47904. 765/423-6175. **Fax:** 765/423-6475. **Contact:** Human Resources. **World Wide Web address:** http://www.glhsi.org. **Description:** A 365-bed hospital with surgery facilities, a recovery unit, Ambulatory Surgery Center, Critical Care Center, Neonatal Intensive Care Nursery, and Hook Rehabilitation Center. **Positions advertised include:** Registered Nurse; Social Worker; Nurse Technician; Home Health Aide; Educator; Certified Surgical Technologist; Bereavement Coordinator; Chaplain; Spiritual Counselor; Radiographer; Pharmacist; Speech Pathologist; Paramedic; Phlebotomist; Food Services Worker; Cook; Housekeeper. **Special programs:** Internships; Scholarships. **Office hours:** Monday – Friday, 8:00 a.m. – 5:00 p.m.

HONEYWELL
3520 Westmore Street, South Bend IN 46628. 574/223-2000. **Contact:** Human Resources. **World Wide Web address:** http://www.honeywell.com. **Description:** Honeywell is engaged in the research, development, manufacture, and sale of advanced technology products and services in the fields of chemicals, electronics, automation, and controls. The company's major businesses are home and building automation and control, performance polymers and chemicals, industrial automation and control, space and aviation systems, and defense and marine systems. **NOTE:** Jobseekers are encouraged to apply via the Website: http://www.honeywell.com/careers. **Listed on:** New York Stock Exchange. **Stock exchange symbol:** HON. **Other U.S. locations:** Nationwide. **Operations at this facility include:** This location manufactures aircraft landing systems, aircraft engine controls and subsystems, aircraft electronics, and aircraft equipment.

HOOSIER NATIONAL FOREST/BROWNSTONE DISTRICT
U.S. FOREST SERVICE
811 Constitution Avenue, Bedford IN 47421. 812/275-5987. **Contact:** Human Resources. **World Wide Web address:** http://www.fs.fed.us/r9/hoosier. **Description:** Manages approximately 100,000 acres of national forestland.

HOWARD COMMUNITY HOSPITAL
3500 South Lafountain Street, Kokomo IN 46901. 765/453-8560. **Fax:** 765/453-8380. **Recorded jobline:** 765/453-8185. **Contact:** Lee Springer, Human Resources. **E-mail address:** lspringe@hch-kokomo.org. **World Wide Web address:** http://www.howardcommunity.org. **Description:** A nonprofit, 125-bed, community-based medical facility. The hospital also operates as a regional mental health center. Founded in 1961. **Positions advertised include:** Home Health Aide; Registered Nurse; Nuclear Medicine Technologist; Respiratory Therapist; Staff Pharmacist.

HOWMET CASTINGS
1110 East Lincoln Way, La Porte IN 46350. 219/326-7400. **Fax:** 219/324-3193. **Contact:** Human Resources. **World Wide Web address:** http://www.howmet.com. **Description:** Manufactures high-temperature engines for the automotive and aerospace industries. Howmet is partly owned by Pechiney, a diversified international corporation that has operations in packaging, aluminum, turbine components, and related industrial sectors. **Corporate headquarters location:** Greenwich CT. **Parent Company:** Alcoa.

HUNT CONSTRUCTION GROUP
P.O. Box 128, Indianapolis IN 46206. 317/241-6301. **Physical address:** 2450 South Tibbs Avenue, Indianapolis IN 46241. **Fax:** 317/227-7830. **Contact:** Human Resources. **E-mail address:** incareers@huntconstructiongroup.com. **World Wide Web address:** http://www.huntconstructiongroup.com. **Description:** A general contract and construction management firm. **NOTE:** No phone calls please. Direct application materials to the attention of: Employment Opportunities. No personal names are necessary. . **Positions advertised include:** Project Engineer; Assistant Project Engineer; Superintendent. **Corporate headquarters location:** This location.

HURCO COMPANIES, INC.
One Technology Way, Indianapolis IN 46268. 317/293-5309. **Contact:** Human Resources Manager. **E-mail address:** info@hurco.com. **World Wide Web address:** http://www.hurco.com. **Description:** Designs, manufactures, and sells computer numerical control (CNC) systems and software, as well as CNC machine tools for the international machine tool industry. Hurco is among the largest U.S. manufacturers of CNC systems for stand-alone machine tools. These CNC systems and software are either integrated with machine tools sold by Hurco or sold to machine tool end users. Products are also sold to original equipment manufacturers (OEMs), who combine them with their own machine tools. The company's CNC systems include Autocon Technologies, Inc. (Delta Series) CNC Controls, Ultimax controls and software, and Autobend CNC and press brake gauging systems. Among the company's integrated machine tool products are CNC machining centers and CNC milling machines. Hurco's products are sold through the company's international network of distributors. Clients for the company's products include independent contract manufacturing operations, short-run, precision, tool, die, and mold manufacturers, and large companies that cut or form metal parts. Industries served include aerospace, computer, defense, medical equipment, farm implement, construction equipment, energy, and transportation.

ITT EDUCATIONAL SERVICES, INC. (ESI)
9511 Angola Court, Indianapolis IN 46268. 317/875-8640 **Toll-free phone:** 800/937-4488. **Fax:** 317/594-4327. **Contact:** Human Resources. **World Wide Web address:** http://www.itttech.edu. **Description:** A leading private college system providing associate's and bachelor's degrees in technology-based disciplines. ESI operates 67 ITT Technical Institutes in 27 states. **Company slogan:** We teach technology. **Corporate headquarters location:** This location. **Listed on:** New York Stock Exchange. **Stock exchange symbol:** ESI.

ITT INDUSTRIES
1919 West Cook Road, P.O. Box 3700, Fort Wayne IN 46801-3700. 260/451-6000. **Contact:** Mike E. Evans, Senior Technical Recruiter. **E-mail address:** mike.evans@itt.com. **Wide Web address:** http://www.acd.itt.com. **Description:** Maintains fully-equipped facilities for research, engineering, manufacturing, and product support in the fields of voice and data battlefield communications, aerospace navigation, and weather satellite imagine/IR sensors. **NOTE:** Jobseekers are encouraged to apply via the Website: http://www.ittind.com/careers. **Corporate headquarters location:** New York NY. **Other U.S. locations:** San Diego CA; Clifton NJ. **Parent company:** ITT Corporation is a diversified, global enterprise engaged in three major business areas: Financial and Business Services, which includes ITT Hartford, ITT Financial Corporation, and ITT Communications and Information Services, Inc.; Manufactured Products, which includes ITT Automotive, ITT Defense and Electronics, Inc., and ITT Fluid Technology Corporation; and the Sheraton Hotels (ITT Sheraton Corporation). **Listed on:** New York Stock Exchange. **Stock exchange symbol:** ITT.

ITW GEMA
ITW RANSBURG
4141 West 54th Street, Indianapolis IN 46254. 317/298-5000. **Toll-free phone:** 800/628-0601. **Fax:** 317/298-5010. **Contact:** Human Resources. **World Wide Web address:** http://www.itwgema.com. **Description:** Designs and sells powder coating equipment. ITW also manufactures and sells wheel-balancing systems.

INDIANA AMERICAN WATER COMPANY
P.O. Box 570, Greenwood IN 46142. 219/886-3770. **Contact:** Human Resources. **World Wide Web address:** http://www.indiana-american.com. **Description:** Supplies water for residential, commercial, and industrial use. **NOTE:** Indiana American Water Company accepts resumes only for positions currently listed.

INDIANA DEPARTMENT OF ENVIRONMENTAL MANAGEMENT
P.O. Box 6015, Indianapolis IN 46206-6015. 317/232-8603. **Physical address:** 100 North Senate Avenue, Indianapolis IN 46204. **Toll-free phone:** 800/451-6027. **Fax:** 317/233-6339. **Contact:** Rachel Scudder, Human Resources Director. **E-mail address:** jobs@dem.state.in.us. **World Wide Web address:** http://www.state.in.us/idem. **Description:** A state governmental agency that protects public health and the environment by regulating air, water, solid, and hazardous waste. **NOTE:** Address applications to: IDEM, Attention: Human Resources Management, Room N1322, 100 North Senate Avenue, Indianapolis IN 46206. **Positions advertised include:** Environmental Manager. **Special programs:** Internships; Summer Jobs. **Corporate headquarters location:** This location.

INDIANA DEPARTMENT OF TRANSPORTATION
100 North Senate Avenue, Room IGCN-755, Indianapolis IN 46204. 317/232-5533. **Fax:** 317/233-1481. **Contact:** Human Resources. **World Wide Web address:** http://www.state.in.us/dot. **Description:** A state agency involved in the construction and maintenance of all interstate and state highways in Indiana. **Positions advertised include:** Draftsman; Electronic Technician; Highway Engineer; Program Director. **Special programs:** Internships. **Corporate headquarters location:** This location. **Operations at this facility include:** Administration; Research and Development; Service.

INDIANA DEPARTMENT OF WORKFORCE DEVELOPMENT
10 North Senate Avenue, Indianapolis IN 46204. **Toll free:** 888/967-5663. **Contact:** Human Resources. **World Wide Web address:** http://www.state.in.us/dwd. **Description:** A state employment office that offers job placement, individual skill/needs assessment, counseling, skills training, unemployment insurance protection, and labor market information for the state of Indiana. **Corporate headquarters location:** Indianapolis IN.

INDIANA GLASS COMPANY
Route 2, P.O. Box 171, Dunkirk IN 47336. 765/768-6789. **Physical address:** 717 West E Street, Dunkirk IN 47336. **Contact:** Human Resources. **Description:** Manufactures glass housewares including glasses, mugs, and ashtrays.

INDIANA HARBOR COKE COMPANY LP
3210 Watling Street, East Chicago IN 46312. 219/397-0243. **Fax:** 219/397-4590. **Contact:** Human Resources. **Description:** Indiana Harbor Coke Company is a coal refinery that produces coke for blast furnaces.

INDIANA INSURANCE REGIONAL AGENCY MARKET
P.O. Box 1967, Indianapolis IN 46240. 317/581-6400. **Contact:** Human Resources. **Description:** Offers property and casualty, personal, and commercial lines of insurance.

INDIANA MILLS AND MANUFACTURING INC.
P.O. Box 408, Westfield IN 46074. 317/896-9531. **Physical address:** 18881 US 31 North, Westfield IN 46074. **Contact:** Human Resources. **E-mail address:** resumes@imminet.com. **World Wide Web address:** http://www.imminet.com. **Description:** Manufactures and distributes seatbelts for commercial vehicles, child and infant seats, and off-road machinery.

THE INDIANA REPERTORY THEATRE
140 West Washington Street, Indianapolis IN 46204. 317/635-5277. **Contact:** Employment. **E-mail address:** indianarep@indianarep.com. **World Wide Web address:** http://www.indianarep.com. **Description:** A nonprofit theatre operating from October to May of each year. Founded in 1971. **NOTE:** Jobseekers interested in administrative positions should contact Jane Robison, General Manager. Those interested in production positions should contact Josh Friedman, Production Manager.

INDIANA RIBBON INC.
P.O. Box 355, Wolcott IN 47995-0355. 219/279-2112. **Physical address:** 106 North Second Street, Wolcott IN 47995. **Toll-free phone:** 800/531-3100. **Fax:** 219/279-3174. **Contact:** Personnel. **World Wide Web address:** http://www.giftwrapgifts.com. **Description:** Manufactures bows, ribbons, and other gift-wrapping products. Indiana Ribbon also offers embossing, custom printing, and color tinting. Giftwrap.com is the company's online storefront. Founded in 1951.

INDIANA STATE UNIVERSITY/TERRE HAUTE
210 North Seventh Street, Rankin Hall, Terre Haute IN 47809. 812/237-4371. **Fax:** 812/237-8331. **Contact:** Human Resources. **E-mail address:** jobs@ind.state.edu. **World Wide Web address:** http://www.indstate.edu. **Description:** A four-year state university offering associate's, bachelor's, master's (including MBA), and doctoral degrees. Approximately 10,200 undergraduate and 1,500 graduate students attend Indiana State University. **NOTE:** Jobseekers must obtain an application from the university before sending a resume. Resumes without applications will be returned. Candidates for faculty positions should consult the website for departmental contacts and requirements. **Positions advertised include:** Graphic Designer; Student Services Assistant; Custodial Worker; Public Safety Officer; Director of Admissions; Assistant Professor, Creative Writing; Assistant Professor, Music Education; Assistant Professor, American Politics. **Office hours:** Monday – Friday, 8:00 a.m. – 4:30 p.m.

INDIANA UNIVERSITY BLOOMINGTON
Poplars Building, 400 East Seventh Street, Bloomington IN 47405-3085. 812/855-2172. **Recorded jobline:** 812/855-9102. **Contact:** Human Resources. **World Wide Web address:** http://www.indiana.edu. **Description:** A branch of the state university offering bachelor's, master's (including MBA), first professional, and doctoral degrees. The School of Business and the School of Public and Environmental Affairs are also at this location. **NOTE:** Application procedures vary according to the type of position. See website for specific instructions. **Office hours:** Monday – Friday, 8:00 a.m. – 5:00 p.m. **Other area locations:** Kokomo IN; Gary IN; South Bend IN; New Albany IN.

INDIANA UNIVERSITY/PURDUE UNIVERSITY AT FORT WAYNE
2101 Coliseum Boulevard East, Fort Wayne IN 46805-1499. 260/481-6840. **Contact:** Human Resources. **E-mail address:** jobs@ipfw.edu. **World Wide Web address:** http://www.ipfw.edu. **Description:** Branches of the two state universities. **Office hours:** Monday – Friday, 8:00 a.m. – 5:00 p.m.

INDIANA UNIVERSITY/PURDUE UNIVERSITY AT INDIANAPOLIS
620 Union Drive, Student Union Building, Room 340, Indianapolis IN 46202-5168. 317/274-7617. **Fax:** 317/274-5481. **Contact:** Human Resources Administration. **E-mail address:** hra@iupui.edu. **World Wide Web address:** http://www.iupui.edu. **Description:** A four-year state university with professional schools, teaching hospitals, and schools of medicine and dentistry. IUPUI offers degrees from both Indiana University and Purdue University.

INDIANAPOLIS COLTS
7001 West 56th Street, Indianapolis IN 46254. 317/297-7000. **Fax:** 317/297-7000. **Contact:** Executive Vice President of Operations. **E-mail address:** info@colts.com. **World Wide Web address:** http://www.colts.com. **Description:** Administrative offices for the National Football League team. **Special programs:** Internships. **Internship information:** Please check the Website for specific internship information. **Corporate headquarters location:** This location.

INDIANAPOLIS MUSEUM OF ART
4000 Michigan Avenue, Indianapolis IN 46208. 317/923-1331. **Fax:** 317/931-1978. **Recorded jobline:** 317/920-2670. **Contact:** Human Resources. **World Wide Web address:** http://www.ima-art.org. **Description:** One of the largest general art museums in the U.S. **NOTE:** Unsolicited resumes are not accepted. **Special programs:** Internships.

INDIANAPOLIS NEWSPAPERS, INC.
307 North Pennsylvania Street, Indianapolis IN 46204. 317/633-1240. **Contact:** Human Resources. **World Wide Web address:** http://www.starnews.com. **Description:** Publishes the *Indianapolis Star* and the *Indianapolis News*. *Indianapolis Star* is a morning newspaper with a Monday through Saturday circulation of more than 228,000 and a Sunday circulation of more than 391,000. *Indianapolis News* is an evening newspaper with a Monday through Saturday circulation of more than 41,000. **Special programs:** Internships.

INDIANAPOLIS POWER & LIGHT COMPANY
One Monument Circle, Indianapolis IN 46204. 317/261-8222. **Recorded jobline:** 800/735-8515. **Contact:** Human Resources. **World Wide Web address:** http://www.ipalco.com. **Description:** An electric company. Indianapolis Power & Light Company provides electricity to 420,000 residential, commercial, and industrial customers in the greater Indianapolis area. **NOTE:** Please call the jobline for current openings and application procedures. Unsolicited resumes are not accepted. **Parent company:** AES IPALCO Enterprises, Inc. is a multistate energy company.

INDIANAPOLIS WATER COMPANY (IWC)
1220 Waterway Boulevard, Indianapolis IN 46202. 317/639-1501. **Contact:** Michelle Howard, Human Resources. **World Wide Web address:** http://www.indianapoliswater.com. **Description:** A holding company with subsidiaries that own and operate waterworks systems that supply water for residential, commercial, and industrial use.

THE INDIANAPOLIS ZOO
1200 West Washington Street, Indianapolis IN 46222. 317/630-2041. **Fax:** 317/630-2194. **Contact:** Human Resources. **E-mail address:** jobs@indyzoo.com. **World Wide Web address:** http://www.indyzoo.com. **Description:** The Indianapolis Zoo's collection includes a hoofed animal complex, a display garden, an education center, and a library. Founded in 1944. **Positions advertised include:** Encounter Keeper; Zoo Educator; Gardener; Seasonal Butterfly Gardener. **Special programs:** Internships; Volunteer Opportunities.

INDUSTRIAL COMBUSTION ENGINEER, INC.
7000 West 21st Avenue, Gary IN 46406. 219/949-5066. **Fax:** 219/944-7683. **Contact:** Personnel. **World Wide Web address:** http://www.indcomb.com. **Description:** Designs and manufactures industrial heaters, ovens, furnaces, and electrical panels.

INLAND CONTAINER CORPORATION
4030 Vincennes Road, Indianapolis IN 46268. 317/879-9747. **Contact:** Human Resources. **World Wide Web address:** http://www.myinland.com. **Description:** Manufactures corrugated shipping containers and boxes. **Corporate headquarters location:** This location.

INTEGRA BANK
P.O. Box 1217, Vincennes IN 47591. 812/882-9310. **Physical address:** 619 Main Street Vincennes IN 47591. **Contact:** Robbie Lane, Human Resources. **World Wide Web address:** http://www.integrabank.com. **Description:** A full-service savings bank. **Other U.S. locations:** Lexington KY; Louisville KY; Akron OH; Columbus OH; Dayton OH; Toledo OH.

INTERNATIONAL STEEL GROUP
3001 Dickey Road, East Chicago IN 46312. 219/391-2000. **Contact:** Employment. **World Wide Web address:** http://www.intlsteel.com. **Description:** A large, fully integrated U.S. steel manufacturer whose principal products include hot-rolled, cold-rolled, and coated steel sheets, as well as tubular and tin mill products serving the automotive, appliance, and electrical equipment industries. LTV operates two integrated mills in Ohio and Indiana, as well as various finishing and processing facilities and tubular and tin mill plants.

INTERNATIONAL STEEL REVOLVING DOOR COMPANY
2138 North Sixth Avenue, Evansville IN 47710. 812/425-3311. **Toll-free phone:** 800/745-4726. **Fax:** 812/426-2682. **Contact:** Human Resources. **World Wide Web address:** http://www.internationalrevolvingdoors.com. **Description:** Designs and builds custom revolving doors. The company also performs metal stamping. Founded in 1963. **Special programs:** Internships; Apprenticeships. **Corporate headquarters location:** This location. **Listed on:** Privately held.

INTERNATIONAL TRUCK AND ENGINE CORPORATION
5565 Brookville Road, Indianapolis IN 46219. 317/352-4500. **Contact:** Personnel. **World Wide Web address:** http://www.nav-international.com. **Description:** Manufactures large and medium-sized heavy-duty trucks, chassis, and mid-range diesel engines. Other operations include financing for dealers and customers, service operations, and replacement parts distribution. The company operates seven production facilities in the United States and one in Canada and sells its products throughout more than 70 countries.

INTERSTATE BRANDS CORPORATION
2929 North Shadeland Avenue, Indianapolis IN 46219. 317/547-9421. **Contact:** Human Resources. **Description:** Interstate Brands Corporation manufactures and distributes a line of bread and cake products with brand names including Wonder Bread and Hostess. **Operations at this facility include:** This location operates as part of a national wholesale bakery.

INVENSYS APPLIANCE CONTROLS
703 West South Street, North Manchester IN 46962. 260/982-2161. **Contact:** Personnel. **World Wide Web address:** http://www.invensysappliance.com. **Description:** Manufactures electro-mechanical control units and small appliance motors. **Corporate headquarters location:** Richmond VA.

IRWIN MORTGAGE CORPORATION
9265 Counselor's Row, Indianapolis IN 46240. 317/844-7788. **Contact:** Human Resources. **World Wide Web address:** http://www.irwinmortgage.com. **Description:** A financial services company specializing in the refinancing of loans.

IRWIN UNION BANK
P.O. Box 929, Columbus IN 47202-0929. 812/376-1020. **Physical address:** 500 Washington Street, Columbus IN 47201. **Contact:** Human Resources. **E-mail address:** human.resources@irwinunion.com. **World Wide Web address:** http://www.irwinunion.com. **Description:** A diversified financial services company that offers commercial banking, credit card services, insurance services, mortgage banking, investment services, and other financial activities. **Positions advertised include:** Teller; Administrative Assistant; Vice President, Bank Operations.

JAMAX CORPORATION
12247 Southmill Street, Terre Haute IN 47802. 812/298-2100. **Contact:** Human Resources. **Description:** Offers commercial and residential trash removal services and roll-off containers for businesses.

JOHNS DENTAL LABORATORY INC.
P.O. Box 606, Terre Haute IN 47808-0606. 812/232-6026. **Physical address:** 423 South 13th Street, Terre Haute IN 47807. **Contact:** Human Resources. **World Wide Web address:** http://www.johnsdental.com. **Description:** A full-service dental laboratory.

JOHNSON CONTROLS, INC.
1302 East Monroe Street, Goshen IN 46528. 574/538-6100. **Contact:** Carol Senour, Personnel Director. **World Wide Web address:** http://www.johnsoncontrols.com. **Description:** Johnson Controls, Inc. conducts operations in four business units. The automotive business produces complete seat systems, seating components, and interior trim systems for cars, light trucks, and vans. The controls segment is involved in the installation and service of facility management and control systems, retrofitting and service of mechanical equipment and lighting systems in nonresidential buildings, and on-site management of facility operations and maintenance. The plastics unit manufactures plastic containers for beverages, food, personal care products, and household items, as well as manufacturing, installing, and servicing plastics molding machinery. The battery segment manufactures automotive batteries for the replacement and original equipment markets, and specialty batteries for telecommunications and uninterruptible power supply (UPS) applications. **Special programs:** Internships; Co-ops. **Corporate headquarters location:** Milwaukee WI. **Operations at this facility include:** This location manufactures refrigeration controls and flow control values.

JUHL MARKETING COMMUNICATIONS
401 East Colfax, Suite 100, South Bend IN 46617. 574/472-0472. **Fax:** 574/472-5358. **Contact:** Office Manager. **E-mail address:** jobs@juhl.com. **World Wide Web address:** http://www.juhl.com. **Description:** An advertising and public relations agency. **NOTE:** Entry-level positions are offered.

KMC CONTROLS, INC.
19476 Industrial Drive, New Paris IN 46553. 574/831-5250. **Fax:** 574/831-5252. **Contact:** Human Resources. **E-mail address:** info@kmccontrols.com. **World Wide Web address:** http://www.kmccontrols.com. **Description:** Manufacturer of HVAC and Building Automation controls. **Positions advertised include:** Sales Engineer; Software Developer; Web Systems Developer.

KPMG
2400 First Indiana Plaza, 135 North Pennsylvania Street, Indianapolis IN 46204. 317/636-5592. **Contact:** Human Resources Department. **World Wide Web address:** http://www.kpmg.com. **Description:** Delivers a range of value-added assurance, tax, and consulting services. **Corporate headquarters location:** Montvale NJ. **Other U.S. locations:** Nationwide.

KAWNEER COMPANY, INC.
P.O. Box 3, Bristol IN 46507. 574/848-7616. **Contact:** Human Resources. **World Wide Web address:** http://www.kawneer.com. **Description:** Manufactures and markets nonresidential architectural building products including storefronts, building entrances, facings, window framing, and curtain wall systems. **Parent company:** Alcoa is one of the largest aluminum producers in North America.

KELLER CRESCENT COMPANY, INC.
110 East Louisiana Street, P.O. Box 3, Evansville IN 47701. 812/464-2461. **Fax:** 812/426-7578. **Contact:** Mr. Chris Feagans, Vice President of Human Resources. **E-mail address:** cooljobs@kellercrescent.com. **World Wide Web address:** http://www.kellercrescent.com. **Description:** A marketing communications company offering advertising, media, public relations, sales promotion, audio/visual production, and marketing services, as well as printing and packaging facilities. **Other area locations:** Indianapolis IN. **Other U.S. locations:** St. Louis MO. **Operations at this facility include:** Administration; Manufacturing; Sales. **Listed on:** Privately held.

KENWAL STEEL COMPANY
307 Tech Drive, Burns Harbor IN 46304. 219/763-7500. **Contact:** Human Resources. **World Wide Web address:** http://www.kenwal.com. **Description:** A steel company that processes and sells coils that are used in the tubing and automotive industries.

KIMBALL INTERNATIONAL, INC.
Kimball Boulevard Center, Jasper IN 47549. 812/482-1600. **Fax:** 812/482-8803. **Contact:** Corporate Recruitment. **E-mail address:** recruit@kimball.com. **World Wide Web address:** http://www.kimball.com. **Description:** A leading supplier of high-quality wood furnishings for offices, hotels, resorts, and health care facilities. Products include office furniture and seating under the Kimball, National, and Harpers brand names; Kimball and Bosendorfer pianos; Kimball hospitality furniture; Kimball health care furniture; Harmony Woods home office furniture; and Kimball Victorian and French furniture reproductions. Kimball International operates as a contract/OEM manufacturer through its subsidiaries, which produce electronic assemblies, cabinetry, molded plastics, carbide cutting tools, and metal stampings, and also produce a variety of brand name products marketed in such industries as home entertainment and furnishings, consumer electronics, marine, and automotive. **Positions advertised include:** Customer Care Representative; Design Engineer; Financial Manager; General Accountant; Product Engineer; Sales Coordinator. **Corporate headquarters location:** This location.

KING SYSTEMS
15011 Herriman Boulevard, Noblesville IN 46060. 317/776-6823. **Fax:** 317/776-6827. **Contact:** Bill Stephan, Human Resources Director. **World Wide Web address:** http://www.kingsystems.com. **Description:** Manufactures plastic disposable breathing circuits used for the delivery of anesthesia in the operating room. **NOTE:** Entry-level positions and second and third shifts are offered. **Corporate headquarters location:** This location. **Listed on:** Privately held.

KING'S DAUGHTER'S HOSPITAL
One King's Daughter's Drive, Madison IN 47250. 812/265-5211. **Recorded jobline:** 812/265-0265. **Contact:** Debbie Temple, Human Resources Director. **Description:** A hospital that offers a surgery unit with outpatient capabilities; an obstetrics unit with several birthing options; specialized areas for pediatrics and geriatrics; laser surgery; emergency services; an ICU; radiology; diagnostic services; oncology; respiratory care; home health care; and physical therapy. Founded in 1915. **Office hours:** Monday – Friday, 8:00 a.m. – 4:30 p.m.

KITTLE'S FURNITURE
8600 Allisonville Road, Indianapolis IN 46250. 317/849-5300. **Fax:** 317/579-7394. **Contact:** Human Resources. **E-mail address:** mrenskers@kittles.com. **World Wide Web address:** http://www.kittles.com. **Description:** A fine furniture and appliance retailer consisting of 17 stores located throughout the Midwest. **Positions advertised include:** Information Technology Manager; Sales Manager. **Corporate headquarters location:** This location.

KNAUF FIBER GLASS
One Knauf Drive, Shelbyville IN 46176. 317/398-4434. **Fax:** 317/398-3675. **Contact:** Mike Hudson, Human Resources. **E-mail address:** mike.hudson@knaufusa.com. **World Wide Web address:** http://www. knauffiberglass.com. **Description:** Manufactures fiberglass for both commercial and residential uses.

KOCH ORIGINALS, INC.
P.O. Box 3436, Evansville IN 47733-3436. 812/421-5600. **Contact:** Human Resources Manager. **World Wide Web address:** http://www.koch-originals.com. **Description:** Manufactures brass-plated, metal furnishings for resale.

KREAMO BAKERS
1910 Lincoln Way West, South Bend IN 46628. 574/234-0188. **Contact:** Human Resources. **Description:** A baked goods company that sells bread and buns in bulk to grocery stores, hospitals, restaurants, and schools. Kreamco Bakers also sells to nursing homes and arranges regular delivery to several area homes.

KROGER'S
2864 Charlestown Road, New Albany IN 47150. 812/944-7016. **Contact:** Human Resources. **World Wide Web address:** http://www.kroger.com. **Description:** A supermarket.

KROGER'S
3400 Grant Line Road, New Albany IN 47150. 812/944-5839. **Contact:** Human Resources. **World Wide Web address:** http://www.kroger.com. **Description:** A supermarket.

KROGER'S
200 New Albany Plaza, New Albany IN 47150. 812/948-2817. **Contact:** Human Resources. **World Wide Web address:** http://www.kroger.com. **Description:** A supermarket.

LAFAYETTE SAVINGS BANK
P.O. Box 1628, Lafayette IN 47902-1628. 765/742-1064. **Physical address:** 101 Main Street, Lafayette IN 47901. **Fax:** 765/742-0354. **Contact:** Human Resources. **E-mail address:** careers@lsbank.com. **World Wide Web address:** http://www.lsbank.com. **Description:** A savings and loan bank. **Positions advertised include:** Commercial Loan Officer; Mortgage Loan Originator; Teller.

LAKE CITY BANK
P.O. Box 1387, Warsaw IN 46581-1387. 574/267-9180. **Physical address:** 202 East Center Street, Warsaw IN 46581. **Contact:** Human Resources. **World Wide Web address:** http://www.lakecitybank.com. **Description:** A bank that performs commercial banking operations, credit card services, and mortgage banking services.

LAKE ERIE PRODUCTS
3595 West State Road 28, Frankfort IN 46041. 765/654-0477. **Toll-free phone:** 800/444-3743. **Fax:** 765/659-7159. **Contact:** Betsy Broadhurst. **E-mail address:** bbroadhurst@lepinc.com. **World Wide Web address:** http://www.lepinc.com. **Description:** A manufacturing company that specializes in producing standard and custom-designed ferrous, nonferrous and special alloy fasteners and build-to-print large diameter fasteners for the agricultural and transportation equipment, construction and fabricated metal products and commercial and industrial maintenance markets. **Positions advertised include:** Financial Analyst; Logistics Manager; Planner Scheduler; Plant Cost Accountant; Staff Accountant. **Corporate headquarters location:** This location.

LAMAR ADVERTISING COMPANY
1770 West 41st Avenue, Gary IN 46408. 219/980-7046. **Fax:** 219/980-1208. **Contact:** Human Resources. **World Wide Web address:** http://www.lamar.com. **Description:** An advertising agency that specializes in outdoor and transit advertising such as billboards, postings, and bulletins. **Corporate headquarters location:** Baton Rouge LA. **Other U.S. locations:** Nationwide.

LANGSDALE RECYCLING
832 Langsdale Avenue, Indianapolis IN 46206. 317/926-5492. **Contact:** Human Resources. **World Wide Web address:** http://www.therecyclinggroup.com. **Description:** Specializes in paper recycling and processing. Langsdale Recycling purchases recyclable paper products, provides recycling containers, and offers pick-up services for businesses. Founded in 1979.

LASALLE BRISTOL
601 Country Road 17, Elkhart IN 46516. 574/295-4400. **Fax:** 574/295-5290. **Contact:** Human Resources. **World Wide Web address:** http://www.lasallebristol.com. **Description:** A wholesaler and manufacturer of furniture, lighting, flooring, and plumbing for the manufactured home and recreational vehicle industries. **Corporate headquarters location:** This location.

LEE'S INNS OF AMERICA
P.O. Box 86, North Vernon IN 47265-0086. 812/346-5072. **Physical address:** 130 North State Street, North Vernon IN 47265. **Fax:** 812/346-7521. **Contact:** Becky Hook, Human Resources. **World Wide Web address:** http://www.leesinn.com. **Description:** Owns and operates 21 limited-service hotels throughout Indiana, Illinois, Michigan, and Ohio. **NOTE:** Entry-level positions are offered. **Special programs:** Internships; Training. **Corporate headquarters location:** This location. **Listed on:** Privately held.

LEISURE DISTRIBUTORS INC.
4220 East Morgan Avenue, Evansville IN 47715. 812/473-9684. **Contact:** Human Resources. **Description:** Distributes patio and fireplace equipment including gas grills, fireplaces, and gas logs.

LIBERTY HOMES, INC.
P.O. Box 35, Goshen IN 46527-0035. 574/533-0431. **Physical address:** 1101 Eisenhower Drive N, Goshen IN 46527. **Fax:** 574/533-0438. **Contact:** Human Resources. **World Wide Web address:** http://www.libertyhomesinc.com. **Description:** Designs, manufactures, and sells single section and multi-sectional manufactured homes.

LIBERTY MUTUAL INSURANCE GROUP
100 Lincolnway West, Mishawaka IN 46544. 574/258-4400. **Contact:** Human Resources. **World Wide Web address:** http://www.libertymutual.com. **Description:** A full-line insurance firm offering life, medical, and business insurance, as well as investment and retirement plans. **Positions advertised include:** Customer Service Representative. **Subsidiaries include:** Wausau Insurance Company.

LINCOLN FINANCIAL GROUP
P.O. Box 1110, Fort Wayne IN 46801-1110. 260/455-2000. **Physical address:** 1300 South Clinton Street, Fort Wayne IN 46802. **Fax:** 260/455-4268. **Contact:** Human Resources Department. **World Wide Web address:** http://www.lfg.com. **Description:** An insurance holding company whose businesses sell insurance and investment products. **NOTE:** Apply online. **Positions advertised include:** Actuarial Consultant; Business Systems Analyst; Customer Service Representative. **Subsidiaries include:** Delaware Investments (investment management services); First Penn-Pacific Life Insurance Company (life insurance); Lincoln National Life Insurance Company (individual life, annuities, and pensions); Lincoln Re (life and health reinsurance); Vantage Investment Advisors (investment management services).

LINCOLN FOODSERVICE PRODUCTS, INC.
P.O. Box 1229, Fort Wayne IN 46804. 260/459-8200. **Physical address:** 1111 North Hadley Road, Fort Wayne IN 46804. **Fax:** 260/436-0735. **Contact:** Human Resources. **World Wide Web address:** http://www.lincolnfp.com. **Description:** Designs, manufactures, and markets commercial and institutional food service cooking equipment and kitchenware supplies.

LINDE GAS LLC
3930 Michigan Street, Hammond IN 46323. 219/989-9030. **Fax:** 219/845-4956. **Contact:** Human Resources. **World Wide Web address:** http://www.us.lindegas.com. **Description:** A manufacturer and marketer of industrial gases. Linde Gas LLC offers a variety of gas products, services and delivery capabilities in the United States. **Positions advertised include:** Bulk Driver; Delivery Driver; Liquid Tanker Drivers; Project Manager; Specialty Gas Product Engineer. **Corporate headquarters location:** Independence OH. **Other U.S. locations:** Nationwide.

LITHONIA LIGHTING
P.O. Box 72, 1615 East Elmore Street, Crawfordsville IN 47933-0072. 765/362-1837. **Contact:** Human Resources. **E-mail address:** recruiter@lithonia.com. **World Wide Web address:** http://www.lithonia.com. **Description:** A manufacturer of a wide variety of light fixtures including industrial, indoor, and outdoor fixtures. **NOTE:** To contact human resources directly, address inquiries and resumes to: Human Resources, One Lithonia Way, Conyers GA 30012. Phone: 770/922-9000. Fax: 770/860-9403. **Corporate headquarters:** Conyers GA.

LOCK JOINT TUBE INC.
515 West Ireland Road, South Bend IN 46614. 574/299-5326. **Toll-free phone:** 800/524-6233. **Fax:** 574/299-3460. **Contact:** Human Resources. **E-mail address:** info@lockjointtube.com. **World Wide Web address:** http://www.lockjointtube.com. **Description:** Manufactures steel pipes and tubes for distribution to large retailers. **Number of employees at this location:** 275.

LOGANSPORT STATE HOSPITAL
1098 South State Road 25, Logansport IN 46947. 574/722-4141. **Contact:** Human Resources. **World Wide Web address:** http://www.lshonline.org. **Description:** A district psychiatric hospital serving 24 counties in northwest and north central Indiana. **Parent company:** Indiana Family and Social Services Administration. **Administrator:** Dr. Jeffrey H. Smith. **Number of employees at this location:** 700.

LOGO ATHLETICS, INC.
8677 Logo Athletics Court, Indianapolis IN 46219. 317/895-7000. **Contact:** Human Resources Department. **Description:** A manufacturer of sports apparel featuring licensed team logos. The company licenses for most major professional and collegiate sports teams.

LOOMIS FARGO
122 North College Avenue, Indianapolis IN 46202. 317/632-3421. **Fax:** 317/955-1278. **Contact:** Human Resources. **World Wide Web address:** www.loomisfargo.com. **Description:** An armored car service specializing in transporting currency. **Other U.S. locations:** Nationwide.

LUCENT TECHNOLOGIES INC.
2855 North Franklin Road, Indianapolis IN 46219. 317/322-6530. **Contact:** Human Resources. **World Wide Web address:** http://www.lucent.com. **Description:** Manufactures communications products including switching and transmission equipment, fiber-optic cable, wireless systems, and operations systems, to supply telephone companies and other communications service providers. The Customer Information Center is responsible for the production and distribution of product manuals and literature for the company's products. **Special programs:** Internships.

LUTHERAN HOME OF NORTHWEST INDIANA
1200 East Luther Drive, Crown Point IN 46307. 219/663-3860. **Fax:** 219/662-3070. **Contact:** Human Resources. **Description:** A nursing home. The Lutheran Home of Northwest Indiana also offers assisted living and independent living programs, and arranges for home health care for clients in these programs.

MZD (MONTGOMERY ZUKERMAN DAVIS, INC.)
1800 North Meridian Street, Suite 200, Indianapolis IN 46202. 317/924-6271. **Fax:** 317/925-3854. **Contact:** Human Resources. **World Wide Web address:** http://www.mzd.com. **Description:** An advertising, strategic marketing, and public relations agency. MZD offers creative planning, Website development, market research, promotional assistance, and a variety of marketing services. MZD also owns a video and audio production company, Telematrix, and offers both video and audio production services, as well as computer graphics development. Founded in 1950. **Corporate headquarters location:** This location. **Other U.S. locations:** Chicago IL; Detroit MI.

MAGNUM SECURITY SERVICES
601 South Bend Avenue, South Bend IN 46617. 574/232-9653. **Contact:** Human Resources. **Description:** Provides security guards and other security personnel for commercial establishments.

MAILCODE
1500 Kepner Drive, P.O. Box 5625, Lafayette IN 47903-5625. 765/447-8888. **Fax:** 765/447-1828. **Contact:** Human Resources. **E-mail address:** careers@mailcode.com. **World Wide Web address:** http://www.mailcode.com. **Description:** Develops, manufactures and delivers mail processing software solutions. Their various software applications include local, remote and voice encoding, as well as OCR technologies. **Positions advertised include:** Senior Accounting Clerk; Application Engineer; Development Controls Engineer, Electrical; Director, International Sales; Process Engineering Technician; Senior Software Engineer. **Corporate headquarters location:** This location. **Parent Company:** Pitney Bowes.

MALLORY CONTROLS
2831 Waterfront Parkway, East Drive, Indianapolis IN 46214-2016. 317/328-4032. **Fax:** 317/328-4118. **World Wide Web address:** http://www. mallorycontrols.com. **Contact:** Sula Dippold, Human Resources Representative. **Description:** Manufactures electromechanical controls, automotive switches, and timers. **Special programs:** Co-ops. **Parent company:** Emerson Electric Co.

MARATHON ASHLAND PETROLEUM LLC
1304 Olin Avenue, Indianapolis IN 46222. 317/244-9551. **Contact:** Human Resources. **World Wide Web address:** http://www.mapllc.com. **Description:** A petroleum refinery and distribution company. Marathon Ashland also provides terminal transportation of petroleum to client corporations. **Special programs:** Internships; Co-ops. **Corporate headquarters location:** Findlay OH. **Other U.S. locations:** Nationwide.

MARC USA/INDIANAPOLIS
1314 North Meridian Street, Indianapolis IN 46202. 317/632-6501. **Fax:** 317/632-4438. **Contact:** Julie Muncy, Human Resources Director. **E-mail address:** jmuncy@marcusa.com. **World Wide Web address:** http://www.marc-usa.com/indianapolis. **Description:** An advertising agency that offers integrated marketing, creative development, public relations, and market research. Caldwell VanRiper/MARC also offers new media development for client companies.

MARRIOTT
123 North Joseph Street, South Bend IN 46601. 574/234-2000. **Fax:** 574/234-2252. **Contact:** Human Resources. **World Wide Web address:** www.marriott.com. **Description:** A 298 room hotel located in downtown South Bend, across from the College Football Hall of Fame. **Other area locations:** Statewide. **Other U.S. locations:** Nationwide.

MARSH SUPERMARKETS, INC.
520 North New Jersey Street, Indianapolis IN 46204. 317/615-1609. **Contact:** Human Resources. **E-mail address:** resume@marsh.net. **World Wide Web address:** http://www.marsh.net. **Description:** Through three divisions, the company operates Marsh Supermarkets, LoBill Foods, Village Pantry Convenience Stores in Indiana and Ohio, and CSDC, a convenience store distribution company. Founded in 1931. **Positions advertised include:** Chef; Meat Cutter; Floral Department Manager; Pharmacist; Sea Food Manager; Cashier; Espresso Bar Server; Cake Decorator. **Corporate headquarters location:** This location.

MASTERBRAND CABINETS, INC.,
One MasterBrand Cabinets Drive, P.O. Box 420, Jasper IN 47547-0420. 812/482-2527. **Fax:** 812/482-9872. **Contact:** Human Resources. **World Wide Web address:** http://www.masterbrand.com. **Description:** One of the world's largest cabinetry manufacturers. MasterBrand Cabinets' brands include Aristokraft, Decorá, Diamond, Kemper, NHB, and Schrock. MasterBrand Cabinets also makes bathroom vanity products. It produces Home Depot's Thomasville-brand cabinets and owns Omega Group cabinetry. Products are sold through home centers, lumber outlets, and specialty retailers. **NOTE:** Search and apply for positions online. **Positions advertised include:** Controller; Benefits Manager; Logistics Manager; Planner; Senior Buyer. **Parent company:** Fortune Brands. **Other U.S. locations:** Nationwide.

McDONALD'S CORPORATION
D&J PARTNERSHIP
3042 State Street, Columbus IN 47201. 812/376-0552. **Contact:** Human Resources. **World Wide Web address:** http://www.mcdonalds.com. **Description:** A franchisee of McDonald's Restaurants that operates 11 restaurants in Indiana. McDonald's Corporation develops, operates, franchises, and services a worldwide system of restaurants that process, package, and sell a variety of fast foods. McDonald's is one of the largest restaurant operations in the world. The company operates more than 26,000 McDonald's restaurants in all 50 states and in 119 foreign countries.

MEAD JOHNSON NUTRITIONALS
2400 West Lloyd Expressway, Evansville IN 47721. 812/429-5000. **Contact:** Employment. **World Wide Web address:** http://www.meadjohnson.com. **Description:** Engaged in the research, manufacture, and marketing of pharmaceutical and nutritional products for the consumer and pharmaceutical markets. **Corporate headquarters location:** This location. **Parent company:** Bristol-Myers Squibb Company. **Number of employees at this location:** 2,500. **Number of employees worldwide:** 5,000.

MEADWESTVACO
6302 Churchman Bypass, Indianapolis IN 46203. 317/787-3361. **Contact:** Human Resources. **World Wide Web address:** http://www.meadwestvaco.com. **Description:** Manufactures carbonless copy paper rolls. MeadWestvaco's primary customers are printers of business forms. **Parent company:** MeadWestvaco manufactures, sells, and markets pulp, paper, paperboard, shipping containers, packaging, lumber, school and office supplies, stationery products, and electronic publishing and information retrieval systems.

MEMORIAL HOSPITAL
615 North Michigan Street, South Bend IN 46601. 574/234-9041. **Contact:** Human Resources. **World Wide Web address:** http://www.qualityoflife.org. **Description:** A 525-bed, general medical and surgical hospital. **Positions advertised include:** Patient Care Manager; Market Research Analyst; Medical Assistant; Nurse Manager; Coder/Analyst; Occupational Therapist; Physical Therapist; Registered Nurse; Surgical Technologist.

MENARD'S
6050 West Ridge Road, Gary IN 46408. 219/838-6134. **Contact:** Human Resources. **World Wide Web address:** http://www.menards.com. **Description:** An electronics, hardware, and home supplies retail outlet. Menard's sells building materials; electricity and lighting equipment; doors, windows, floor supplies and carpeting; home heating equipment; plumbing tools and supplies; and electronics.

MERIDIAN AUTOMOTIVE SYSTEMS INC.
14123 Roth Road, Grabill IN 46741. 260/627-3612. **Contact:** Human Resources. **World Wide Web address:** http://www.meridianautosystems.com. **Description:** Manufactures blow moldings, injection moldings, and plastic interior items for automobiles.

MERIDIAN MUTUAL INSURANCE COMPANY
P.O. Box 1980, Indianapolis IN 46206-1980. 317/931-7173. **Fax:** 317/931-7263. **Recorded jobline:** 317/931-7180. **Contact:** Human Resources. **World Wide Web address:** http://www.stateauto.com. **Description:** A regional property and casualty insurance company. **Corporate headquarters location:** This location. **Other U.S. locations:** Louisville KY; Lansing MI. **Operations at this facility include:** Administration.

MERRILL LYNCH
130 West Main Street, Fort Wayne IN 46802. 260/424-2424. **Fax:** 219/423-3493. **Contact:** Human Resources. **World Wide Web address:** http://www. ml.com. **Description:** One of the largest securities brokerage firms in the world, Merrill Lynch provides financial services in corporate and municipal securities, financial planning, insurance, estate planning, mortgages, and related areas. The company also provides investment banking services. **Positions advertised include:** Consulting Relationship Manager; Client Associate; Financial Advisor. **Other U.S. locations:** Nationwide.

MID-AMERICA CLINICAL LABORATORIES
1500 North Ritter Avenue, Indianapolis IN 46219. 317/803-1010. **Fax:** 317/803-0097. **Contact:** Jane Lloyd, Human Resources. **E-mail address:** hr@macl1.com. **World Wide Web address:** http://www.maclonline.com. **Description:** This location houses administrative offices. Overall, Mid-America Clinical Laboratories provide lab services for Community East Hospital.

MID-AMERICA MAILERS, INC.
430 Russell Street, P.O. Box 646, Hammond IN 46325-0646. 219/933-0137. **Fax:** 219/931-3336. **Contact:** Human Resources. **World Wide Web address:** http://www.midam-mail.com. **Description:** A lettershop and data processing company engaged in direct mail advertising. Mid-America Mailers provides data processing, personalization, sorting, and mailing services for client companies.

MIDLAND ENGINEERING COMPANY
P.O. Box 1019, South Bend IN 46624. 574/272-0200. **Physical address:** 52369 Indiana State Route, South Bend IN 46637. **Fax:** 574/272-7400. **Contact:** Human Resources. **World Wide Web address:** http://www.midlandengineering.com. **Description:** A contract construction firm that focuses on residential work such as roofing, sheet metal, waterproofing, and restoration.

MILLENNIUM INDUSTRIES
P.O. Box 350, Ligonier IN 46767-0350. 260/894-3163. **Physical address:** 925 North Main Street, Ligonier IN 46767. **Contact:** Human Resources. **World Wide Web address:** http://www.mill-ind.com. **Description:** Engaged in product design, brazed assemblies, precision stamping, refrigeration products, and auto parts. **Corporate headquarters location:** Auburn Hills MI.

MILLER BUILDING SYSTEMS, INC.
58120 County Road 3 South, Elkhart IN 46517. 574/295-1214. **Fax:** 574/295-2232. **Contact:** Human Resources. **World Wide Web address:** http://www.mbsionline.com. **Description:** Designs, manufactures, and markets prefabricated buildings. **Subsidiaries include:** Miller Structures, Inc. serves both the modular and mobile office market, as well as (through its Residential Division) the modular housing market. The company's main clients are firms that sell, lease, and rent modular and mobile office structures, as well as residential housing builders and dealers. Miller Telecom Services, Inc. is responsible for telecommunication shelters and pre-cast concrete assemblies for prisons, hazardous waste, and material confinement structures. The main market for Miller Telecom is end users with specific requirements for specialized applications.

MONACO COACH CORPORATION
P.O. Box 4313, Elkhart IN 46517. 574/295-8060. **Contact:** Human Resources. **World Wide Web address:** http://www.monaco-online.com. **Description:** One of the nation's leading manufacturers of high-line motor coaches. The company has five distinct lines: the Windsor, the Dynasty, the Executive, the Crowne Royale Signature Series, and Royale Coach bus conversions. Monaco offers its customers after-sale service and support including company-sponsored rallies, membership in one of its two owners' clubs, and a subscription to Lifestyles, its owners' magazine. **Corporate headquarters location:** Coburg OR.

MOODY'S KMV
130 South Main Street, Suite 300, South Bend IN 46601. 574/472-5700. **Toll-free phone:** 800/523-2627. **Fax:** 574/245-7670. **E-mail address:** resumes@mkmv.com. **World Wide Web address:** http://www.moodyskmv.com. **Description:** Provider of quantitative credit analysis tools to lenders, investors, and corporations. **Positions advertised include:** Advisory Services Associate; Application Support Engineer; Global Client Services Associate; Quality Assurance Engineer; Senior Sales Associate; Senior Software Engineer. **Other U.S. locations:** CA; NY. **International locations:** Tokyo, Japan; London, UK; Relgate, UK.

MORGAN DRIVE AWAY, INC.
THE MORGAN GROUP, INC.
2746 Old US 20 West, Elkhart IN 46514. 574/295-2200. **Toll-free phone:** 800/289-7565. **Contact:** Personnel. **World Wide Web address:** http://www. morgrp.com. **Description:** Arranges transportation services for the movement and delivery of manufactured houses and recreational vehicles. Morgan Drive Away also arranges the movement of commercial vehicles, office trailers, automobiles, buses, and other vehicles and freight. The company operates a network of approximately 1,900 independent owner-operators and drivers, and 1,100 part-time drive-away employees in 108 offices nationwide. **Parent company:** The Morgan Group, Inc. (also at this location) manages the delivery of manufactured homes, commercialized equipment, and related equipment. The company operates through more than 100 offices nationwide. Subsidiaries of the parent company include: Interstate Indemnity; Morgan Finance, Inc. **Listed on:** American Stock Exchange. **Stock exchange symbol:** MG.

MORRISON CONSTRUCTION CO.
1834 Summer Street, Hammond IN 46320. 219/932-5036. **Fax:** 219/933-7302. **Contact:** Human Resources. **E-mail address:** info@morrisonconst.com. **World Wide Web address:** http://www.morrisonconst.com. **Description:** Manufactures and services pipe fittings for blast furnaces and boiler makers.

MOSSBERG & COMPANY INC.
P.O. Box 210, South Bend IN 46624. 574/289-9253. **Physical address:** 301 East Sample Street, South Bend IN 46601. **Toll-free phone:** 800/428-3340. **Fax:** 574/289-6622. **Contact:** Human Resources. **World Wide Web address:** http://www.mossbergco.com. **Description:** A commercial printing company that creates brochures, letterheads, graphics, labels, annual reports, and other printed material for client companies. Mossberg & Company handles both low- and high-volume printing projects.

MOTION INDUSTRIES
3620 Calumet Avenue, Hammond IN 46320. 219/931-3010. **Contact:** Personnel. **World Wide Web address:** http://www.motion-industries.com. **Description:** A distributor of industrial machinery parts including belts, pulleys, bearings, and other power transmission parts.

NTN-BCA
987 North U.S. Highway 421, Greensburg IN 47240. 812/663-3361. **Contact:** Human Resources. **Description:** Manufactures ball bearings that are used in the automotive and agriculture industries. **Number of employees at this location:** 375.

NABISCO BRANDS, INC.
151 West Ohio Street, Kendallville IN 46755. 260/347-1300. **Contact:** Human Resources. **World Wide Web address:** http://www.nabisco.com. **Description:** This location manufactures caramel candies. **Parent company:** Kraft Foods.

NASCO INDUSTRIES
P.O. Box 427, Washington IN 47501. 812/254-7393. **Physical address:** 3 North East 21st Street, Washington IN 47501. **Fax:** 812/254-6476. **Contact:** Human Resources Department. **E-mail address:** info@nasco.com. **World Wide Web address:** http://www.nascoinc.com. **Description:** Manufactures waterproof outerwear and industrial safety clothing.

NATIONAL ASSOCIATION OF THE SELF-EMPLOYED
3939 Priority Way, Indianapolis IN 46240. 317/571-0307. **Contact:** Human Resources. **World Wide Web address:** http://www.nase.org. **Description:** A professional association that offers members a wide range of services including group hospitalization insurance.

NATIONAL CITY BANK
P.O. Box 730, Kokomo IN 46903-0730. 765/457-5551. **Physical address:** 200 West Mulberry Street, Kokomo IN 46901. **Contact:** Personnel. **World Wide Web address:** http://www.national-city.com. **Description:** A full-service savings bank. **NOTE:** Jobseekers are encouraged to apply via the Website. **Corporate headquarters location:** Cleveland OH. **Other U.S. locations:** Lexington KY; Louisville KY; Dayton OH; Toledo OH; Akron OH; Columbus OH. **Operations at this facility include:** Regional Headquarters.

NATIONAL CITY BANK
110 West Berry Street, Fort Wayne IN 46802. 260/426-0555. **Contact:** Personnel. **World Wide Web address:** http://www.national-city.com. **Description:** A full-service savings bank. **NOTE:** Jobseekers are encouraged to apply via the website: http://www.nationalcity.com/ employment. **Corporate headquarters location:** Cleveland OH. **Other U.S. locations:** Lexington KY; Louisville KY; Akron OH; Columbus OH; Dayton OH; Toledo OH. **Parent company:** Fort Wayne National Corporation.

NATIONAL SERVE-ALL
P.O. Box 2234, Fort Wayne IN 46801. 260/747-4117. **Physical address:** 6231 Macbeth Road, Fort Wayne IN 46809. **Contact:** Human Resources. **Description:** A full-service waste management company that offers corporate and residential waste removal, recycling services, and waste chemical handling and disposal.

NATIONAL STARCH & CHEMICAL
1515 South Drover Street, Indianapolis IN 46221. 317/635-4455. **Contact:** Human Resources. **World Wide Web address:** http://www.nationalstarch.com. **Description:** An industrial chemical manufacturer producing adhesives, resins, starches, and specialty chemicals for the packaging, textile, paper, food, furniture, electronic materials, and automotive markets. The company operates 100 facilities worldwide. **NOTE:** The company strongly encourages candidates to apply online.

NAVAL SURFACE WARFARE CENTER
NSWC Crane Division, Code 0642-RT, 300 Highway 361, Building 5, Crane IN 47522. 812/854-4242. **Recorded jobline:** 812/854-3529. **Contact:** Human Resources. **E-mail address:** resume@crane.navy.mil. **World Wide Web address:** http://www.crane.navy.mil. **Description:** Provides engineering, technical, and material support to the Navy Fleet. **NOTE:** Entry-level positions are offered. **Corporate headquarters location:** Washington DC.

NEW ALBANY COMPONENT & TRUSS
56 Galt Street, New Albany IN 47150. 812/945-2155. **Contact:** Human Resources. **Description:** Manufactures structural wooden trusses and other construction components.

NEW HORIZONS REHABILITATION, INC.
P.O. Box 98, Batesville IN 47006. 812/934-4528. **Physical address:** 237 Six Pine Ranch Road, Batesville IN 47006. **Fax:** 812/934-2522. **Contact:** Marie Dausch, Executive Director. **World Wide Web address:** http://www.nhrehab.org. **Description:** A nonprofit job service that helps people with disabilities find jobs within the community. **Office hours:** Monday – Friday, 7:30 a.m. – 4:00 p.m.

NIAGARA LASALLE STEEL COMPANY
1412 150th Street, Hammond IN 46327. 219/853-6000. **Contact:** Human Resources. **E-mail address:** info@niagaralasalle.com. **World Wide Web address:** http://www.niagaralasalle.com. **Description:** Niagara LaSalle Steel is a national producer of cold-finished and special-purpose steel bar products. The automotive industry primarily uses the company's steel bar products for making component parts, which include shafts, gears, pins, rods, and plug shells. Surface Operations is responsible for the company's line of precision surface steel bars. The fluid power facility (Griffith IN) produces a line of induction-hardened, chrome-plated steel bars for piston rods and hydraulic cylinders. **Corporate headquarters location:** Houston TX. **Parent company:** Quanex Corporation. **Operations at this facility include:** This location's cold drawn facilities produce more than 200 standard carbon and alloy grades.

NIBCO, INC.
P.O. Box 1167, Elkhart IN 46515-1167. 574/295-3000. **Physical address:** 1516 Middlebury Street, Elkhart IN 46516. **Fax:** 574/295-3307. **Contact:** Corporate Human Resources. **E-mail address:** hr@nibco.com. **World Wide Web address:** http://www.nibco.com. **Description:** Manufactures flow control solutions, fittings, and valves. **NOTE:** Entry-level positions are offered. **Positions advertised include:** Sales Engineer; Software Engineer. **Special programs:** Internships. **Corporate headquarters location:** This location. **Other U.S. locations:** Nationwide. **Operations at this facility include:** Administration; Manufacturing. **Listed on:** Privately held.

NISOURCE INC.
801 East 86th Avenue, Merrillville IN 46410. 219/647-5990. **Contact:** Human Resources. **World Wide Web address:** http://www.nisource.com. **Description:** A holding company. Through its subsidiaries, NiSource Inc. distributes electricity, natural gas, and water throughout the Midwest and the Northeast. **Positions advertised include:** Executive Assistant; Facilities Administrator. **Corporate headquarters location:** This location.

NORTH AMERICAN PRODUCTS CORPORATION
1180 Wernsing Road, Jasper IN 47546. 812/482-2000. **Contact:** Human Resources. **World Wide Web address:** http://www.naptools.com. **Description:** Manufactures and services carbide-tipped cutting tools for the wood and metal industries. **Corporate headquarters location:** This location. **Other U.S. locations:** Nationwide. **Listed on:** Privately held.

NORTHERN INDIANA PUBLIC SERVICE COMPANY (NIPSCO)
801 East 86th Avenue, Merrillville IN 46410. 219/853-5200. **Contact:** Employment and Compensation Consultant. **E-mail address:** hrquestions@nisource.com. **World Wide Web address:** http://www.nipsco.com. **Description:** A gas and electric public utility company. NIPSCO provides energy to the northern third of Indiana. **NOTE:** Apply online. **Corporate headquarters location:** This location. **Parent company:** NiSource Inc.

NUCOR STEEL
4537 South Nucor Road, Crawfordsville IN 47933. 765/364-1323. **Contact:** Human Resources. **World Wide Web address:** http://www.ns-ind.com. **Description:** Produces bars, angles, light structural, sheet, and special steel products. **Parent company:** Nucor Corporation is a manufacturer of steel products, whose other divisions include Vulcraft, one of the nation's largest producers of steel joists and joist girders; Nucor Cold Finish, which produces cold-finished steel bars used extensively for shafting and machined precision parts; Nucor Grinding Balls, which produces steel grinding balls in Utah for the mining industry; Nucor Fastener, a facility that makes steel bolts; Nucor Bearing Products, Inc., which produces steel bearings and machined steel parts; and Nucor Building Systems, which produces metal buildings and components.

OLD NATIONAL BANCORP
One Main Street, Evansville IN 47708. 812/464-1414. **Contact:** Human Resources. **World Wide Web address:** http://www.oldnational.com. **Description:** A multibank holding company. The company provides a comprehensive range of financial services including commercial and retail banking, trust, brokerage, correspondent banking, and insurance. **Corporate headquarters location:** This location.

OLD NATIONAL BANCORP
110 East Main Street, Muncie IN 47305. 765/747-7575. **Contact:** Debbie DenHouter, Human Resources. **World Wide Web address:** http://www. oldnational.com.

Description: A bank that offers commercial banking and other related financial services.

ONTARIO SYSTEMS CORPORATION
1150 West Kilgore Avenue, Muncie IN 47305. 765/751-7000. **Fax:** 765/751-7818. **Contact:** Human Resources Specialist. **E-mail address:** careers@osntariosystems.com. **World Wide Web address:** http://www.ontariosystems.com. **Description:** Develops software for businesses that offer accounts receivable management, collection, and teleservicing services. **NOTE:** Part-time jobs are offered. **Company slogan:** People are our foundation. **Positions advertised include:** Systems Analyst; Technical Communicator. **Special programs:** Training. **Office hours:** Monday - Friday, 8:00 a.m. - 5:00 p.m. **Corporate headquarters location:** This location. **Other U.S. locations:** Berlin OH; Cle Elum WA. **Subsidiaries include:** CDS Leopold; Sherry Labs. **Parent company:** Ontario Corporation. **Listed on:** Privately held.

ORBITAL ENGINEERING
3800 179th Street, Hammond IN 46323. 219/989-3300. **Contact:** Human Resources. **E-mail address:** japhilips@orbitalengr.com. **World Wide Web address:** http://www.orbitaleng.com. **Description:** A design consulting firm providing a variety of engineering services. **Corporate headquarters location:** Pittsburgh PA.

OTIS ELEVATOR COMPANY
P.O. Box 516, Bloomington IN 47402-0516. 812/339-2281. **Physical address:** 1331 South Curry Pike, Bloomington IN 47403. **Contact:** John Korzec, Director of Human Resources. **World Wide Web address:** http://www.nao.otis.com. **Description:** Produces and distributes a line of elevators and escalators for commercial and industrial use. **Parent company:** United Technologies Corporation provides high-tech products and support services to customers in the aerospace, building, military, and automotive industries worldwide. Products include large jet engines, temperature control systems, elevators and escalators, helicopters, and flight systems. The company markets its products under a variety of brand names including Carrier, Hamilton Standard, Otis, Pratt & Whitney, and Sikorsky. Production facilities are located in the United States, Latin America, Mexico, Canada, Australia, Europe, and Asia.

OWENS-BROCKWAY GLASS INC.
P.O. Box 368, Lapel IN 46051-0368. 765/534-3121. **Contact:** Human Resources. **Description:** One of several area divisions of the diversified manufacturer of packaging products. Principal products are glass containers, although the company also produces and sells containerboard, corrugated containers, printing plates and ink, plywood and dimension lumber, blown plastic containers, plastic beverage bottles, plastic drums, metal and plastic closures, tamper-resistant closures, plastic and glass prescription containers, pharmaceutical items, labels, and multipack plastic carriers for containers. Specialized glass products made and sold by the company include Libbey Tumblers, stemware, and decorative glassware; television bulbs for picture tubes; and Kimble scientific and laboratory ware. Some overseas affiliates also manufacture flat glass and related products.

OWENS CORNING
P.O. Box 1366, Elkhart IN 46515. 574/522-8473. **Contact:** Human Resources Director. **World Wide Web address:** http://www.owenscorning.com. **Description:** Produces and supplies exterior components to the building and construction, manufactured housing, recreational vehicle, and transportation/cargo industries.

OXFORD AUTOMOTIVE
2190 Landmark Avenue, Corydon IN 47112. 812/738-5900. **Contact:** Human Resources. **World Wide Web address:** http://www.oxauto.com. **Description:** A full-service supplier of metal stampings and welded assemblies, primarily to the automotive industry. **NOTE:** Interested candidates can submit a resume online, or address a resume to: Oxford Automotive, Human Resources Department, 1250 Stephenson Highway, Troy MI 48083. **Corporate headquarters location:** Troy MI.

OXFORD GROUP LTD.
P.O. Box 80238, Indianapolis IN 46280-0238. 317/843-5678. **Fax:** 317/843-5679. **Contact:** Human Resources. **World Wide Web address:** http://www. ofac.com. **Description:** Specializes in financial and investment advising for wealthy individuals and institutions.

PPG INDUSTRIES
424 East Inglefield Road, Evansville IN 47725. 812/867-6601. **Contact:** Human Resources. **World Wide Web address:** http://www.ppg.com. **Description:** Manufactures decorative and protective coatings, flat glass and fabricated glass products, continuous-strand fiberglass, and industrial and specialty chemicals. The company supplies its products to manufacturing, building, automotive, and processing industries. Founded in 1883. **International locations:** Worldwide.

PARKER-GOSHEN
501 South Sycamore Street, Syracuse IN 46567. 574/457-3141. **Fax:** 574/457-5009. **Contact:** Brenda Foster, Human Resources Manager. **World Wide Web address:** http://www.parker.com. **Description:** Manufactures molded rubber products. **Special programs:** Internships. **Corporate headquarters location:** Goshen IN. **Other U.S. locations:** Nationwide.

PARKER HANNIFIN CORPORATION
10801 Rose Avenue, New Haven IN 46774. 260/748-6000. **Contact:** Human Resources. **World Wide Web address:** http://www.parker.com. **Description:** Parker Hannifin Corporation is a worldwide manufacturer of hydraulic products, fluid connectors, electrical power distribution equipment, engine components, and truck drivetrain systems. The company serves the automotive, aerospace, industrial, and semiconductor industries. **NOTE:** Hires through a staffing firm. **Operations at this facility include:** This location manufactures air conditioning and heating equipment.

PARKVIEW HOSPITAL
2200 Randallia Drive, Fort Wayne IN 46805. 260/373-4000. **Contact:** Human Resources. **World Wide Web address:** http://www.parkview.com. **Description:** A nonprofit health system comprised of several hospitals, a health plan, a foundation of employed physicians, and a managed services organization. The hospital offers cardiopulmonary services including endoscopy, pulmonary rehabilitation, and respiratory care; corporate health services including industrial rehabilitation and occupational medicine; a critical care center; diagnostic imaging; dietetics and food service; a laboratory; Lindenview Regional Behavioral Center; Parkside Fitness Center; a regional diabetes care center; a regional heart center; a regional neurology center including a neurology unit, occupational therapy, physical therapy, rehabilitation services, and speech pathology; a regional oncology center; a regional orthopedic center; a regional trauma center; senior health services; social services; a surgical care center; and women and children's health services including a fertility center, genetics lab, new life center, pediatric care, and women's health center. **Positions advertised include:** Registered Nurse; Occupational Therapist; Women's Health Specialist; Lab Technician; Flight Paramedic; Licensed Practical Nurse; Certified Nursing Assistant; Medical Technologist; Pharmacist. **Special programs:** Internships. **Operations at this facility include:** Administration; Divisional Headquarters; Regional Headquarters; Research and Development; Service. **Listed on:** Privately held.

PATHOLOGISTS ASSOCIATED
1200 West White River Boulevard, Muncie IN 47303. 765/284-7795. **Fax:** 765/741-5604. **Contact:** Human Resources. **World Wide Web address:** http://www.palab.com. **Description:** A clinical laboratory that provides services for Ball Memorial Hospital. **NOTE:** Interested applicants should complete the employment application available on the website. Submit applications to: Pathologists Association, Attention: Human Resources Department, 1200 West White River Boulevard, Muncie IN 47303. **Positions advertised include:** Phlebotomist; Medical Technologist; Lab Supply Coordinator; Specimen Processing Assistant.

PEARSON EDUCATION
201 West 103rd Street, Indianapolis IN 46290. 317/581-3500. **Toll-free phone:** 800/545-5914. **Fax:** 317/581-4960. **Contact:** Human Resources. **World Wide Web address:** http://www.pearsoned.com. **Description:** A leading integrated education company. Pearson Education published textbooks, develops educational software, and operates several education-related websites. **Special programs:** Internships.

PHELPS DODGE MAGNET WIRE COMPANY
One Technology Center, 2131 South Coliseum Boulevard, Fort Wayne IN 46803. 260/421-5400. **Contact:** Human Resources Department. **World Wide Web address:** http://www.phelpsdodge.com. **Description:** Manufactures magnet wire and houses the company's technology center.

PILKINGTON COMPANY
300 Northridge Drive, Shelbyville IN 46176. 317/392-7000. **Contact:** Human Resources. **World Wide Web address:** http://www.pilkington.com. **Description:** A diversified manufacturer of fluid power and fluid systems components, automotive glass, flat and tinted glass products, decorative laminates, and molded plastics.

PILLSBURY COMPANY
707 Pillsbury Lane, New Albany IN 47150. 812/944-8411. **Contact:** Human Resources. **World Wide Web address:** http://www.pillsbury.com. **Description:** Manufactures and markets food products for consumer, industrial, and international markets.

PINNACLE SYSTEMS
7340 Shadeland Station, Suite 200, Indianapolis IN 46256. 317/841-0332. **Fax:** 317/577-8779. **Contact:** Human Resources. **World Wide Web address:** http://www.pinnaclesys.com. **Description:** Develops PC digital video cards for desktop video production. **Corporate headquarters location:** Mountainview CA.

POLAROID ID SYSTEMS
4640 Executive Boulevard, Fort Wayne IN 46808. 260/484-0611. **Fax:** 781/386-3925. **Contact:** Human Resources. **E-mail address:** globalstaff1@polaroid.com. **World Wide Web address:** http://www.polaroid-id.com. **Description:** Develops, manufactures, and markets a variety of image recording products worldwide. The company manufactures instant photo cameras and films, electronic recording imaging devices, videotapes, a full range of standard films, and camera filters and lenses for a variety of industries including consumer, real estate, architecture, insurance, and education. Other products are primarily for medical and scientific use and office applications. **NOTE:** Candidates should e-mail or fax resumes with salary history using the information listed above. **Corporate headquarters location:** Waltham MA.

POLLUTION CONTROL INDUSTRIES
4343 Kennedy Avenue, East Chicago IN 46312. 219/397-3951. **Contact:** Human Resources. **E-mail address:** nsanders@pollutioncontrol.com. **World Wide Web address:** http://www.pollutioncontrol.com. **Description:** Engaged in the handling and disposal of hazardous materials. Pollution Control Industries provides assessments of waste chemicals and operates remote control units and secure containment equipment to handle and remove the material safely.

PORTER MEMORIAL HOSPITAL SYSTEM
814 La Porte Avenue, Valparaiso IN 46383. 219/465-4653. **Fax:** 219/531-7017. **Contact:** Human Resources. **World Wide Web address:** http://www.portermemorial.org. **Description:** Offers a growing number of health care services. The hospital's specialties include family practice, obstetrics, pediatrics, and cardiology. **Positions advertised include:** Patient Registrar; Registered Nurse; Certified Nursing Assistant; Special Projects Analyst; Professional Recruiter; Infection Control Coordinator; Medical Technologist; Pharmacist; Emergency Department Director; Administrative Supervisor; Security Officer; Food Service Worker; Housekeeper.

POWERWAY, INC.
6919 Hillsdale Court Indianapolis, IN 46250. 317/598-1760. **Toll-free phone:** 800/964-9004. **Fax:** 317/598-1740. **Contact:** Human Resources. **E-mail address:** info@powerwayinc.com. **World Wide Web address:** http://www.powerwayinc.com. **Description:** Powerway is a software company that delivers innovative technology solutions that help manufacturing companies accelerate time to market and improve product quality while reducing risks and costs. **Positions advertised include:** Database Designer. **International locations:** Mexico; UK.

PRAXAIR SURFACE TECHNOLOGY, INC.
1500 Polco Street, Indianapolis IN 46222. 317/240-2500. **Contact:** Marilyn Harvey, Human Resources. **World Wide Web address:** http://www.praxair.com. **Description:** Applies metallic and ceramic coatings to products manufactured by other companies. **Parent company:** Praxair, Inc. produces gases and gas production equipment in 185 plants worldwide for customers in the aerospace, chemicals, electronics, food processing, health care, glass, metal fabrication, petroleum, primary metals, pulp, and paper industries. These gases are distributed through pipelines, merchants, and packaged products. The two major pipeline networks are in Illinois and Texas. Praxair also coats customer-supplied parts and equipment with metallic and ceramic coatings for the textile, aircraft engine, paper, petrochemical, metals, and printing industries. **Corporate headquarters location:** This location.

PRINTPACK
1505 West Main Street, Greensburg IN 47240. 812/663-5091. **Contact:** Human Resources. **E-mail address:** careers@printpack.com. **World Wide Web address:** http://www.printpack.com. **Description:** Manufactures a variety of paper products, plastic tableware, and retail packaging products including cartons, bags, and wraps. Paper products include tissues, towels, business and correspondence paper, coated papers for catalogs, and premium printing papers.

PROXYMED LAB SERVICES
2633 Grant Line Road, New Albany IN 47150. 812/944-3865. **Contact:** Human Resources. **World Wide Web address:** http://www.proxymed.com. **Description:** Manufactures computer components and installs computer systems for the clinical laboratory industry.

PURDUE UNIVERSITY
Freehafer Hall of Administrative Services, 401 South Grant Street, West Lafayette IN 47907. 765/494-9687. **Fax:** 765/494-6138. **Recorded jobline:** 765/496-5627. **Contact:** Human Resources. **E-mail address:** resumes@purdue.edu. **World Wide Web address:** http://www.purdue.edu. **Description:** Purdue has an enrollment of approximately 64,000 students across five campuses with numerous teaching and research sites statewide. Degrees are offered in agriculture, consumer and family sciences, education, engineering, health sciences, liberal arts, management, nursing, pharmacy and pharmaceutical sciences, science, technology, and veterinary medicine. **Positions advertised include:** Web Development Manager; Office Manager; Career Services Consultant; Editor; Computer Systems Administrator; NMR Applications Scientist; Research Assistant; Research Associate; Laboratory Technician; Secretary; Library Assistant; Account Clerk. **Special programs:** Internships. **Office hours:** Monday – Friday, 8:00 a.m. – 5:00 p.m. **Corporate headquarters location:** This location.

PURDUE UNIVERSITY/CALUMET
2200 169th Street, Hammond IN 46323-2094. 219/989-2251. **Fax:** 219/989-2185. **Contact:** Personnel. **E-mail address:** jobs@calumet.purdue.edu. **World Wide Web address:** http://www.calumet.purdue.edu. **Description:** A regional campus of the university. **Positions advertised include:** Information Clerk; Accounting Clerk; Secretary; Coordinator, Northwest Indiana Writing Project.

QUALITY DINING, INC.
4220 Edison Lakes Parkway, Mishawaka IN 46545. 574/271-4600. **Fax:** 574/271-4612. **Contact:** Human Resources Manager. **World Wide Web address:** http://www.qdi.com. **Description:** A franchiser of restaurants. The company operates 71 quick-service Burger King Restaurants, 29 restaurants under the name Chili's Bar & Grill, five casual dining restaurants under the name Papa Vino's, three casual dining restaurants under the name Spageddie's, and 36 casual dining restaurants under the name Grady's American Grill. **Special programs:** Internships; Summer Jobs. **Corporate headquarters location:** This location. **Other U.S. locations:** Nationwide. **Listed on:** NASDAQ. **Stock exchange symbol:** QDIN.

RMG FOUNDRY
500 South Union Street, Mishawaka IN 46544. 574/256-4208. **Fax:** 219/256-4624. **Contact:** Mike Burns, Human Resources Manager. **World Wide Web address:** http://www.rmgfoundry.com. **Description:** Operates a gray and ductile iron foundry and manufactures conveyor-belt motors. **Parent company:** Rockwell Automation.

RAYBESTOS PRODUCTS COMPANY
1204 Darlington Avenue, Crawfordsville IN 47933. 765/362-3500. **Contact:** Human Resources. **World Wide Web address:** http://www.raybestosproducts.com. **Description:** Manufactures friction products including transmission plates for automobile and tractor engines.

RAY'S TRASH SERVICES
3859 East U.S. Highway 40, Clayton IN 46118. 317/539-2024. **Contact:** Human Resources. **E-mail address:** rays2026@iquest.net. **World Wide Web address:** http://www.raystrash.com. **Description:** Provides residential and commercial garbage pick-up, roll-off containers, and compactors.

RAYTHEON SYSTEMS COMPANY
1010 Production Road, Fort Wayne IN 46808-4106. 260/429-6000. **Contact:** Human Resources. **World Wide Web address:** http://www.raytheon.com. **Description:** A leader in the design of military tactical communications, electronic combat, command and control, and antisubmarine warfare products and systems for the Armed Forces of the United States and Allied Nations. **NOTE:** Entry-level positions are offered. **Company slogan:** Expect great things. **Positions advertised include:** Senior Reliability Engineer; Management Assistant. **Special programs:** Internships. **Office hours:** Monday - Friday, 7:30 a.m. - 4:30 p.m. **Corporate headquarters location:** Lexington MA. **Other U.S. locations:** Nationwide. **Parent company:** Raytheon Company. **Operations at this facility include:** Administration; Divisional Headquarters; Manufacturing; Research and Development; Sales.

RED SPOT PAINT & VARNISH COMPANY, INC.
1107 East Louisiana Street, Evansville IN 47711-0418. 800/457-3544. **Contact:** Human Resources. **E-mail address:** hrevansville@redspot.com. **World Wide Web address:** http://www.redspot.com. **Description:** Manufactures household paints and varnish, automotive plastics, and related coatings. Founded in 1903. **Positions advertised include:** Chemist. **NOTE:** Please send resumes to Human Resources, P.O. Box 418, Evansville IN 47703-0418. **Corporate headquarters location:** This location.

REHABILITATION HOSPITAL OF INDIANA
4141 Shore Drive, Indianapolis IN 46254-2607. 317/329-2233. **Contact:** Human Resources. **E-mail address:** resumes@rhin.com. **World Wide Web address:** http://www.rhin.com. **Description:** An 89-bed, nonprofit, physical rehabilitation facility. Rehabilitation Hospital of Indiana provides specialized care, through both inpatient and outpatient services, for patients who have experienced spinal cord injuries, head injuries, stroke, amputation, orthopedic problems, or neuromuscular disease. **Positions advertised include:** Registered Nurse; Admissions Nurse; House Coordinator; Licensed Practical Nurse; Unit Secretary; Nursing Rehabilitation Technician; Physical Therapist; Occupational Therapist; Fiscal Services Clerk; Radiology Technician. **Operations at this facility include:** Administration; Service.

REPUBLIC ENGINEERED PRODUCTS LLC
2800 East Dunes Highway, Gary IN 46402. 219/886-8100. **Contact:** Human Resources. **World Wide Web address:** http://www.republicengineered.com. **Description:** Produces stainless steel, alloy steel, billets, bar, rod, wire, special shapes, and nickel-based alloys.

REPUBLIC SERVICES
P.O. Box 36098, Indianapolis IN 46236. 317/823-6881. **Contact:** Human Resources. **World Wide Web address:** http://www.republicservices.com. **Description:** Specializes in residential and commercial solid waste collection, processing, and disposal as well as medical waste collection and recycling. **NOTE:** Entry-level positions are offered. **Corporate headquarters location:** Houston TX. **Other U.S. locations:** Nationwide. **Parent companies:** Allied Waste Industries.

REXAM CLOSURES
3245 Kansas Road, Evansville IN 47725. 812/867-6671x223. **Fax:** 812/867-6289. **Contact:** Scott Harrell, Manager of Employment. **E-mail address:** employment@rexamclosures.com. **World Wide Web address:** http://www.rexamclosures.com. **Description:** Designs, develops, manufactures, and markets closure systems for the packaging industry. The company's products include child-resistant closures, dispensers, screw caps, and tamper-evident systems. Customers include pharmaceutical companies; over-the-counter drug companies; food and cosmetics companies; household, industrial, and agricultural chemical companies; swimming pool chemical companies; and packagers of household cleaners, automotive aftermarket products, and beverages. Founded in 1953. **Corporate headquarters location:** This location. **Other U.S. locations:** Princeton IN. **Parent company:** Rexam. **Operations at this facility include:** Administration; Manufacturing; Research and Development; Sales.

RHODIA CHEMICAL
2000 Michigan Street, Hammond IN 46320. 219/932-7651. **Fax:** 219/932-0524. **Contact:** Human Resources. **E-mail address:** rhodia@rpc.webhire.com. **World Wide Web address:** http://www.us.rhodia.com. **Description:** Produces acid that is mainly used in the manufacturing of gasoline. **Parent company:** Rhone-Poulenc Basic Chemicals.

ROLLS ROYCE ALLISON
2355 South Tibbs Avenue, Indianapolis IN 46241. 317/487-8292. **Contact:** Human Resources. **World Wide Web address:** http://www.rolls-royce.com. **Description:** Manufactures precision bearings, locomotive parts, and gas turbine engines for automotive, marine, and aircraft applications. **Parent company:** General Motors. **Operations at this facility include:** Administration; Divisional Headquarters; Manufacturing; Research and Development; Sales; Service.

ROYALE COACH BY MONACO
21330 Wade Drive, P.O. Box 4319, Elkhart IN 46514. 574/262-9278. **Contact:** Human Resources. **World Wide Web address:** http://www.monaco-online.com. **Description:** A manufacturing and conversion facility for the Royale Coach bus line. **Corporate headquarters location:** Coburg OR. **Parent company:** Monaco Coach Corporation is one of the nation's leading manufacturers of motor coaches. The company has five distinct lines: the Windsor, the Dynasty, the Executive, the Crowne Royale Signature Series, and Royale Coach bus conversions. Monaco offers its customers after-sale service and support including company-sponsored rallies, membership in one of its two owners' clubs, and a subscription to Lifestyles, its owners' magazine.

RUTTER COMMUNICATIONS NETWORK
420 West Washington Street, Muncie IN 47305. 765/289-2113. **Fax:** 765/284-6970. **Contact:** Human Resources. **E-mail address:** hr@rutter.net. **World Wide Web address:** http://www. rutter.net. **Description:** An advertising firm that specializes in network cable advertising.

SBC XAMERITECH
4401 South Meeker Avenue, Muncie IN 47302. 765/287-8153. **Recorded jobline:** 866/967-5722. **Contact:** Human Resources Department. **World Wide Web address:** http://www.sbc.com. **Description:** Provides pay phone, long-distance telephone, and cellular telephone service. **Parent Company:** SBC Communications is one of the largest telephone holding companies in the United States. Ameritech provides local telephone service to 17.9 million customers in five midwestern states. Subsidiaries of Ameritech Corporation include: Ameritech Mobile, a wireless communications company providing services to one million clients and over 500,000 pagers. Other subsidiaries conduct advertising, publishing, research and development, messaging, financing, and leasing services. SBC Communications acquired Ameritech in 1999.

SAFECO/AMERICAN STATES INSURANCE
500 North Meridian Street, Indianapolis IN 46204. 317/262-6262. **Fax:** 317/262-6397. **Recorded jobline:** 800/753-5330. **Contact:** Dan Guio, Human Resources Manager. **World Wide Web address:** http://www.safeco.com. **Description:** Provides a range of insurance coverage including commercial, personal, and small business. **Positions advertised include:** Environmental Claims Representative; National Catastrophe Field Examiner. **Parent company:** SAFECO Corporation.

ST. ANTHONY MEDICAL CENTER
1201 South Main Street, Crown Point IN 46307. 219/663-8120. **Contact:** Personnel. **World Wide Web address:** http://www.stanthonymedicalcenter.com. **Description:** An acute care hospital. **NOTE:** Human Resources phone: 219/757-6451. **Positions advertised include:** Registered Nurse; Receptionist; Scheduling Clerk; Physical Therapist; Speech Pathologist; Receptionist; Medical Staff Coordinator; Respiratory Therapist; Food Service Aide; Environmental Service Attendant.

ST. JOSEPH HOSPITAL & HEALTH CENTER
1907 West Sycamore Street, Kokomo IN 46904. 765/456-5403. **Fax:** 765/456-5823. **Contact:** Human Resources. **World Wide Web address:** http://www.stjhhc.org. **Description:** A nonprofit, acute care medical facility that offers diagnostic and therapeutic services. **NOTE:** Entry-level positions, part-time jobs, and second and third shifts are offered. **Positions advertised include:** Physical Therapist; Respiratory Therapist; Pharmacist; Staff Nurse; Nursing Assistant. **Special programs:** Training. **Operations at this facility include:** Administration.

ST. JOSEPH HOSPITAL
700 Broadway, Fort Wayne IN 46802. 260/425-3016. **Contact:** Human Resources Manager. **World Wide Web address:** http://www.lutheranhealthnetwork.com/stjoe. **Description:** A nonprofit, medical center offering primary and secondary acute care, neighborhood clinics, preventative outreach programs, and a satellite surgery center. Founded in 1869. **NOTE:** Second and third shifts are offered. **Positions advertised include:** Registered Nurse; Home Health Care Nurse; Licensed Practical Nurse; Lead Therapist; Medical Assistant; Nursing Assistant; Medical Transcriptionist; ; Respiratory Care Clinician; Pharmacy Technician. **Corporate headquarters location:** Hobart IN. **Other U.S. locations:** Chicago IL; St. Louis MO. **Parent company:** Lutheran Health Network. **Operations at this facility include:** Administration; Divisional Headquarters; Service.

ST. MARY'S HOSPITAL
3700 Washington Avenue, Evansville IN 47750. 812/485-4000. **Fax:** 812/485-6735. **Contact:** Human Resources. **E-mail address:** llcollins@stmarys.org. **World Wide Web address:** http://www.stmarys.org. **Description:** A general hospital with over 400 beds providing a wide range of medical and surgical services. Founded in 1894. **Positions advertised include:** Speech Language Pathologist; Nuclear Medicine Technologist; Occupational Therapist; Patient Care Technician; Respiratory Therapist; Group Exercise Instructor; Pharmacist; Licensed Practical Nurse; Registered Nurse; Cook; Paramedic.

SALOMON SMITH BARNEY
8900 Keystone Crossing, Suite 900, Indianapolis IN 46240. 317/581-5200. **Contact:** Human Resources. **World Wide Web address:** http://www. salomonsmithbarney.com. **Description:** An international investment banking, market making, and research firm serving corporations, state, local, and foreign governments, central banks, and other financial institutions. **Corporate headquarters location:** New York NY. **Other U.S. locations:** Nationwide.

HOWARD W. SAMS
9850 East 30th Street, Indianapolis IN 46269. 317/396-9850. **Toll-free phone:** 800/428-SAMS. **Fax:** 800/552-3910. **Contact:** Human Resources. **World Wide Web address:** http://www.samswebsite.com. **Description:** A technical publisher. **NOTE:** Second and third shifts are offered. **Corporate headquarters location:** This location.

SCHAFER GEAR WORKS
4701 Nimtz Parkway, South Bend IN 46628. 574/234-4116. **Fax:** 574/234-4115. **Contact:** Human Resources Manager. **E-mail address:** hr@schafergear.com. **World Wide Web address:** http://www.schafergear.com. **Description:** A manufacturer of precision gears. **Corporate headquarters location:** This location. **Other area locations:** Elkhart IN; Fort Wayne IN. **Operations at this facility include:** Administration; Manufacturing; Sales.

SCHWARZ PHARMA MANUFACTURING
P.O. Box 328, Seymour IN 47274-0328. 812/523-5400. **Physical address:** 1101 C Avenue West, Seymour IN 47274. **Contact:** Rhonda Wells, Human Resources Manager. **World Wide Web address:** http://www.schwarzusa.com. **Description:** Specializes in the manufacture of prescription cardiovascular pharmaceuticals, such as treatments for high blood pressure. Schwarz Pharma Manufacturing also produces tablet and liquid cough suppressants, analgesics, cold medications, and other nonprescription drugs under the Schwarz label.

JOSEPH E. SEAGRAM & SONS INCORPORATED
7 Ridge Avenue, Lawrenceburg IN 47025. 812/537-0700. **Contact:** Human Resources. **World Wide Web address:** http://www.seagram.com. **Description:** A producer of distilled wines. **Parent company:** Pernod Ricard.

SECURITAS
4265 Counselors Road, Indianapolis IN 46240. 317/569-1149. **Contact:** Human Resources. **World Wide Web address:** http://www.securitasinc.com. **Description:** Offers a wide range of protective services and contract security guard programs to businesses and government. **Other U.S. locations:** Nationwide

SECURITAS USA
1086 Ohio Street, Terre Haute IN 47807. 812/234-3724. **Contact:** Human Resources. **World Wide Web address:** http://www.pinkertons.com. **Description:** Offers a full range of specialized protective services including premier property and high-rise services, health care and hospital services, special event services, ATM services, and patrol services. The company serves thousands of companies worldwide with investigation, threat assessment, and executive protection services. **Corporate headquarters location:** Westlake Village CA. **Other U.S. locations:** Nationwide.

SECURITAS USA
445 Crosspointe Boulevard, Suite 130, Evansville IN 47715. 812/477-8295. **Contact:** Human Resources. **World Wide Web address:** http://www.securitasusa.com. **Description:** Offers a full range of specialized protective services including premier property and high-rise services, health care and hospital services, special event services, ATM services, and patrol services. The company serves thousands of companies worldwide with investigation, threat assessment, and executive protection services. **Corporate headquarters location:** Westlake Village CA. **Other U.S. locations:** Nationwide.

THE SELMER LUDWIG COMPANY
P.O. Box 310, Elkhart IN 46515. 574/522-1675. **Contact:** Michelle Hammer, Human Resources Department. **World Wide Web address:** http://www.selmer.com. **Description:** Manufactures and distributes musical instruments and related accessories.

SENIOR EMPLOYMENT
2912 East 83rd Place, Merrillville IN 46410. 219/942-4097. **Contact:** Human Resources. **Description:** Provides employment services for senior citizens (over age 55) with limited income.

SERADYN INC.
7998 Georgetown Road, Suite 1000, Indianapolis IN 46268. 317/610-3800. **Contact:** Human Resources Department. **World Wide Web address:** http://www.seradyn.com. **Description:** Seradyn consists of three distinct divisions: Diagnostics, Particle Technology, and Photovolt. Products include industrial and diagnostic instruments, as well as a full line of medical diagnostic reagents. **Corporate headquarters location:** This location. **Operations at this facility include:** This location manufactures medical test kits. **Parent company:** Mitsubishi Chemical Corporation.

SENSIENT FLAVORS
5600 West Raymond Street, Indianapolis IN 46241. 317/243-3521. **Fax:** 317/240-1524. **Contact:** Human Resources. **E-mail address:** employment@sensient-tech.com. **World Wide Web address:** http://www.sensient-tech.com. **Description:** A manufacturer of flavors for the food and beverage industry.

SHOE CARNIVAL, INC.
4595 University Drive, Evansville IN 47712. 812/421-2260. **Contact:** Human Resources. **World Wide Web address:** http://www.shoecarnival.com. **Description:** Operates specialty shoe stores.

SIVITAR CORPORATION
300 Main Street, Suite 100, West Lafayette IN 47902. 765/449-4415. **Fax:** 765/463-1234. **Contact:** Human Resources Department. **E-mail address:** hr@mbds.com. **World Wide Web address:** http://www.sivitar.com. **Description:** Manufactures database management systems software for small computers and artificial intelligence systems. **Corporate headquarters location:** This location. **Operations at this facility include:** Administration; Computer Programming; Research and Development; Sales; Service.

SKYLINE CORPORATION
2520 By-Pass Road, Elkhart IN 46514. 574/294-6521. **Contact:** Human Resources. **E-mail address:** hresources@skylinecorp.com. **World Wide Web address:** http://www.skylinecorp.com. **Description:** Designs, produces, and distributes mobile homes and recreational vehicles such as travel trailers, park models, mini motor homes, and fifth wheels. **Positions advertised include:** Production Worker. **Corporate headquarters location:** This location.

SMITHS AEROSPACE COMPONENTS
333 South Third Street, Terre Haute IN 47807. 812/234-1591. **Contact:** Human Resources. **World Wide Web address:** http://www.triindustries.com. **Description:** Engaged in a variety of sheet metal work, primarily for the aerospace industry.

SOUTH BEND TRIBUNE
225 West Colfax Avenue, South Bend IN 46626. 260/235-6161. **Contact:** Human Resources Department. **World Wide Web address:** http://www. southbendtribune.com. **Description:** A newspaper with a daily circulation of nearly 80,000 and a Sunday circulation of more than 113,000.

SOUTHERN INDIANA GAS AND ELECTRIC COMPANY (SIGECO)
P.O. Box 209, Evansville IN 47702-0209. 812/491-4000. **Contact:** Human Resources. **World Wide Web address:** http://www.vectren.com. **Description:** Generates and distributes electricity to over 120,000 customers, and purchases, transports, and distributes natural gas to over 104,000 customers. The service area covers 10 counties in southwestern Indiana. SIGECO also sells power to municipalities and to other companies and public utilities. **Parent company:** Vectren.

SPLASH DOWN DUNES
150 East U.S. Highway 20, Porter IN 46304. 219/929-1181. **Contact:** Human Resources. **World Wide Web address:** http://www.splashdowndunes.com. **Description:** A water amusement park. Splash Down Dunes is the largest water park in Indiana and is open during the summer only (May through September).

SQUARE D COMPANY
252 North Tippecanoe Street, Peru IN 46970. 765/472-3381. **Contact:** Human Resources. **World Wide Web address:** http://www.squared.com. **Description:** A manufacturer of electrical distribution products for the construction industry. Products are used in commercial and residential construction, industrial facilities, and machinery, as well as original equipment manufacturers' products. Residential building products feature circuit breakers with an exclusive quick-open mechanism that isolates potential dangers quickly. Square D also equips public buildings such as schools, stadiums, museums, hospitals, prisons, military bases, and wastewater treatment plants with electrical distribution systems.

STANT MANUFACTURING, INC.
1620 Columbia Avenue, Connersville IN 47331. 765/825-3121. **Contact:** Human Resources. **World Wide Web address:** http://www.stant.com. **Description:** Manufactures radiator and fuel pumps, radiator valves, oil caps, and coolant systems pressure gauges. **Parent company:** Stant Corporation manufactures windshield wiper blades, closure caps, engine thermostats, grease guns, power steering components, and other automotive parts.

STARCRAFT AUTOMOTIVE GROUP, INC.
1123 Indiana Avenue, Goshen IN 46527. 574/534-7827. **Contact:** Human Resources. **World Wide Web address:** http://www.starcraftcorp.com. **Description:** Specializes in upscale, custom vehicles and is one of the largest conversion van manufacturers in the United States. In addition to converting full-size vans and minivans, the company customizes pick-up trucks and sport-utility vehicles. Starcraft Automotive Group sells its products through a network of approximately 900 authorized automotive dealers worldwide. **Corporate headquarters location:** This location.

STARCRAFT MONARCH MARINE
201 Starcraft Drive, P.O. Box 517, Topeka IN 46571. 260/593-2500. **Contact:** Human Resources Department. **World Wide Web address:** http://www.starcraftmarine.com. **Description:** Manufactures marine products including power motors and pleasure boating equipment. **Corporate headquarters location:** Goshen IN.

STEAK N SHAKE
36 South Pennsylvania Street, 500 Century Building, Indianapolis IN 46204. 317/633-4100. **Fax:** 317/633-4105. **Contact:** Human Resources Manager. **E-mail address:** careers@steaknshake.com. **World Wide Web address:** http://www.steaknshake.com. **Description:** Owns and operates a chain of casual-dining restaurants. Steak n Shake operates over 370 locations throughout the Midwest and Southeast. Founded in 1934. **NOTE:** Resumes are accepted by e-mail or regular mail. **Special programs:** Internships. **Internship information:** Corporate and Management internships are offered. **Other U.S. locations:** Nationwide. **Listed on:** New York Stock Exchange. **Stock exchange symbol:** SNS.

SUBARU OF INDIANA AUTOMOTIVE, INC.
P.O. Box 5689, Lafayette IN 47905. 765/449-1111. **Contact:** Human Resources. **World Wide Web address:** http://www.subaru-sia.com. **Description:** Indiana-based automobile manufacturer of Subaru vehicles. **Positions advertised include:** Industrial Engineer. **Operations at this facility:** Administrative; Production. **Number of employees at this location:** 2757.

SUNOCO, INC.
705 Pillsbury Lane, New Albany IN 47150. 812/945-0224. **Contact:** Human Resources. **World Wide Web address:** http://www.sunocoinc.com. **Description:** Sunoco is one of the country's largest independent petroleum refiners and marketers, with 3,800 stations operating under the Sunoco brand name in 17 states. Sunoco's lubricant and petrochemical products are marketed worldwide.

SUPERIOR CONSTRUCTION COMPANY INC.
2045 East Dunes Highway, P.O. Box 64888, Gary IN 46402. 219/886-3728. **Fax:** 219/885-4328. **Contact:** Human Resources. **World Wide Web address:** http://www.superior-construction.com. **Description:** A contract construction company that focuses on nonresidential business and highway construction.

SUPERIOR ENGINEERING LLC
2345 167th Street, Hammond IN 46323. 219/844-7030. **Fax:** 219/844-4217. **Contact:** Human Resources. **World Wide Web address:** http://www. superiorengineering.com. **Description:** Offers structural, electrical, and mechanical engineering services.

SUPERIOR ESSEX
1601 Wall Street, Fort Wayne IN 46802. 260/461-4000. **Contact:** Human Resources Manager. **E-mail address:** career_ops@superioressex.com. **World Wide Web address:** http://www.superioressex.com. **Description:** Manufactures and distributes electrical cable and insulation products including magnetic wire, building wire, and telephone cable. **Positions advertised include:** Collection Specialist. **Corporate headquarters location:** Atlanta GA.

SUPERVALU INC.
4815 Executive Boulevard, Fort Wayne IN 46808. 260/483-2146. **Contact:** Human Resources. **E-mail address:** careers@supervalu.com. **World Wide Web address:** http://www.supervalu.com. **Description:** One of the nation's largest food retailers and

distribution companies, supplying grocery, health and beauty aids, and general merchandise products to over 4,000 customers. In the corporate retail sector, SUPERVALU operates over 300 stores under the following names: Bigg's, Cub Foods, Shop 'n Save, Save-A-Lot, Scott's Foods, Laneco, and Hornbachers. **Corporate headquarters location:** Eden Prairie MN. **Subsidiaries include:** Hazelwood Farms Bakeries manufactures frozen bakery products. **Listed on:** New York Stock Exchange. **Stock exchange symbol:** SVU.

SUPREME INDUSTRIES, INC.
P.O. Box 463, Goshen IN 46526. 800/642-4889. **Physical address:** 2581 East Kercher Road, Goshen IN 46526. **Fax:** 574/642-4729. **Contact:** Human Resources. **World Wide Web address:** http://www.supremeind.com. **Description:** A manufacturer and distributor of specialized truck bodies. The company also installs the bodies and other equipment on truck chassis.

TJ MAXX
3301 Maxx Road, Evansville IN 47711. 812/424-0932. **Contact:** Human Resources. **World Wide Web address:** http://www.tjmaxx.com. **Description:** TJ Maxx operates a chain of discount stores. **Corporate headquarters location:** Framingham MA. **Other U.S. locations:** Nationwide. **Parent company:** The TJX Companies, Inc. owns both TJ Maxx and Marshall's. TJ Maxx/Marshall's is one of the largest chains in the off-price industry, with over 1,000 stores nationwide. The TJX Companies, Inc. also operates Winners Apparel Ltd. and HomeGoods stores. **Operations at this facility include:** This location is a retail distribution and loss control center.

TLC/STAFF BUILDERS
823 East Westfield Boulevard, Indianapolis IN 46220. 317/205-6010. **Contact:** Human Resources. **World Wide Web address:** http://www.tlcathome.com. **Description:** A home health care agency. **Corporate headquarters location:** Success NY. **Other U.S. locations:** Nationwide.

TMP WORLDWIDE
115 East Spring Street, Suite 100 & 600, New Albany IN 47150. 812/945-9780. **Fax:** 219/436-0307. **Contact:** Human Resources Department. **World Wide Web address:** http://www.tmpw.com. **Description:** TMP Worldwide is a Yellow Pages advertising agency that also does online and interactive advertising, recruitment advertising, offers staffing services, and operates the popular career site Monster.com. Founded in 1967. **Corporate headquarters location:** New York NY. **Other U.S. locations:** Nationwide. **International locations:** Worldwide. **Operations at this facility include:** This location focuses on graphic design.

TRW
800 Heath Street, P.O. Box 60, Lafayette IN 47902. 765/423-5377. **Contact:** Director of Human Resources. **World Wide Web address:** http://www.trw.com. **Description:** TRW is a diversified technology firm with operations in electronics and space systems; car and truck equipment for both original equipment manufacturers and the replacement market; and a wide variety of industrial and energy components including aircraft parts, welding systems, and electromechanical assemblies. **Corporate headquarters location:** Cleveland OH. **Operations at this facility include:** This location manufactures manual and power steering gears and components for trucks, farm equipment, construction and industrial equipment, low-speed high-torque hydraulic motors, and gear pumps.

TELESERVICES DIRECT
6050 Corporate Way, Indianapolis IN 46278. 317/216-2240. **Fax:** 317/216-2248. **Contact:** Human Resources. **E-mail address:** jobs@teleservicesdirect.com. **World Wide Web address:** http://www.teleservicesdirect.com. **Description:** Providers of outsourced telemarketing solutions. **NOTE:** Search and apply for positions online. **Positions advertised include**: Call Center Team Leader; Senior Account Executive. **Corporate headquarters location:** This location.

THEORIS
8888 Keystone Crossing, Suite 1550, Indianapolis IN 46240. 317/849-4444. **Fax:** 317/576-6934. **Contact:** Recruiting Coordinator. **E-mail address:** info@theoris.com. **World Wide Web address:** http://www.theoris.com. **Description:** A computer consulting firm. **NOTE:** Address all employment inquiries to the corporate office. **Corporate headquarters location:** This location.

THERMA-TRU CORPORATION
108 Mutzfeld Road, Butler IN 46721. 260/868-5811. **Contact:** Human Resources. **E-mail address:** mgray@thermatru.com. **World Wide Web address:** http://www.thermatru.com. **Description:** Manufactures fiberglass doors and steel doors. **NOTE:** Interested candidates should mail resumes to: Therma-Tru Corporation, Corporate Human Resources, P.O. Box 8780, Maumee OH 43537.

THERMWOOD CORPORATION
P.O. Box 436, Dale IN 47523. 812/937-4476. **Physical address:** 904 Buffaloville Road, Dale IN 47523. **Toll-free phone:** 800/937-2956. **Fax:** 800/533-6901. **Contact:** Human Resources Department. **World Wide Web address:** http://www.thermwood.com. **Description:** Develops, manufactures, markets, and services computer-controlled industrial systems that perform high-speed machining and routing functions.

3M
304 South 075 East, Hartford City IN 47348. 765/348-3200. **Contact:** Human Resources. **World Wide Web address:** http://www.3m.com. **Description:** 3M manufactures products in three sectors. The Industrial and Consumer sector includes a variety of products under brand names including 3M, Scotch, Post-it, Scotch-Brite, and Scotchgard. The Information, Imaging, and Electronic sector is a leader in several high-growth global industries including telecommunications, electronics, electrical, imaging, and memory media. The Life Science sector serves two broad market categories: health care, and traffic and personal safety. In the health care market, 3M provides medical and surgical supplies, drug-delivery systems, and dental products; in traffic and personal safety, 3M produces products for transportation safety, worker protection, vehicle and sign graphics, and out-of-home advertising. **Corporate headquarters location:** St. Paul MN. **International locations:** Worldwide. **Operations at this facility include:** This location manufactures label stock, microcapsule, and electrical specialties tape. **Listed on:** New York Stock Exchange. **Stock exchange symbol:** MMM.

THUNDERBIRD PRODUCTS CORPORATION
P.O. Box 1003, Decatur IN 46733-5003. 260/724-9111. **Physical address:** 2200 West Monroe Street, Decatur IN 46733. **Contact:** Human Resources. **World Wide Web address:** http://www.thunderbirdboats.com. **Description:** Engaged in boat building and repairing services.

TIPTON COUNTY MEMORIAL HOSPITAL
1000 South Main Street, Tipton IN 46072. 765/675-8500. **Contact:** Human Resources. **World Wide Web address:** http://www.tiptonhospital.org. **Description:** A nonprofit, acute-care, community hospital. **NOTE:** Entry-level positions and second and third shifts are offered. **Positions advertised include:** Registered Nurse; Licensed Practical Nurse; Office Nurse; Housekeeping Aide. **Corporate headquarters location:** This location.

TOKHEIM CORPORATION
1600 Wabash Avenue, Fort Wayne IN 46803. 260/470-4600. **Fax:** 260/470-4718. **Contact:** Human Resources. **World Wide Web address:** http://www.tokheim.com. **Description:** Designs, manufactures, and markets electronic petroleum and monitoring systems such as service station equipment, point-of-sale control systems, card-activated transaction systems, and underground tank monitoring equipment. The company also designs, manufactures, and produces process control automation systems, solid-state time delays, and time and temperature control devices. **Office hours:** Monday - Friday, 8:00 a.m. - 5:00 p.m.

TOTALEMS LLC
One Technology Way, Caller Box 7011, Logansport IN 46947. 574/739-2929. **Fax:** 574/722-1870. **Contact:** Human Resources. **World Wide Web address:** http://www.totalems.com. **Description:** Designs and manufactures electronic controls. **Positions advertised include:** Industrial Maintenance Apprentice; Electronic Technician Assistant; Material Handling Specialist; Material Planning Specialist. **Corporate headquarters location:** This location. **Operations at this facility include:** Administration; Manufacturing; Sales; Service. **Listed on:** Privately held.

THE TOWNSEND GILBERT COMPANY
101 Main Street, P.O. Box 128, Parker City IN 47368. **Toll-free phone:** 800/428-8128. **Fax:** 765/468-3131. **Contact:** Human Resources. **World Wide Web address:** http://www.townsendtree.com. **Description:** A construction contracting firm specializing in pipeline, sewer, and marine projects.

TOYOTA MOTOR CORPORATION
5555 Inwood Drive, Columbus IN 47201. 812/342-0060. **Physical address:** P.O. Box 2487, Columbus IN 47202-2487. **Contact:** Human Resources. **World Wide Web address:** http://www.toyota.com. **Description:** Toyota Motor Corporation is involved in the research, design, and manufacture of a broad line of automobiles, trucks, and SUVs. **Operations at this facility include:** This location manufactures Tundra pick-up trucks and other SUVs.

TRANS TECH ELECTRIC
4601 Cleveland Road, South Bend IN 46628. 574/272-9673. **Contact:** Human Resources. **E-mail address:** lboren@transtechelectric.com. **World Wide Web address:** http://www.tte-inc.com. **Description:** Offers ongoing commercial and traffic electrical repair and servicing.

TRANS-APPAREL GROUP
5000 South Ohio Street, Michigan City IN 46360. 219/879-7341. **Contact:** Human Resources. **World Wide Web address:** http://www.transapparel.com. **Description:** A manufacturer of men's slacks. Trans-Apparel Group has a nationwide sales force. **Corporate headquarters location:** This location. **Operations at this facility include:** Manufacturing.

TRANSPO
901 East Northside Boulevard, South Bend IN 46617. 574/232-9901. **Fax:** 219/239-2309. **Contact:** Personnel. **World Wide Web address:** http://www. transpo.com. **Description:** Provides transportation planning services and offers research on alleviating and managing traffic. Founded in 1975. **Corporate headquarters location:** Kirkland WA.

TRI-CITY COMMUNITY MENTAL HEALTH CENTER
3903 Indianapolis Boulevard, East Chicago IN 46312. 219/392-6001. **Contact:** Human Resources. **World Wide Web address:** http://www.tricitycenter.org. **Description:** A mental health care facility that primarily provides care on an outpatient basis. Other services offered by Tri-City Community Mental Health Center include a detoxification unit for adults and residential care for adolescent women. **NOTE:** Resumes for Tri-City Community Mental Health Center must be sent to Geminus Corporation, Attention Dee Dee Shoemaker, Human Resources Associate, 5281 Fountain Drive, Crown Point IN 46307. **Positions advertised include:** Therapist; Psychiatric Technician; Case Manager.

TRIBUNE-STAR PUBLISHING COMPANY
P.O. Box 149, Terre Haute IN 47808. 812/231-4200. **Physical address:** 222 South 7th Street, Terre Haute IN 47808. **Contact:** Human Resources. **World Wide Web address:** http://www.tribstar.com. **Description:** Publishes the *Terre Haute Tribune-Star* newspaper with a daily circulation of 36,000 and a Sunday circulation of 47,000.

TRILLIUM PROPERTIES
8901 East 5th Avenue, Gary IN 46403. 219/938-1600. **Contact:** Human Resources. **Description:** Manages several apartment complexes in Gary and East Chicago.

TWIGG CORPORATION
659 East York Street, Martinsville IN 46151. 765/342-7126. **Fax:** 765/342-1553. **Contact:** Human Resources. **E-mail address:** info@twiggcorp.com. **World Wide Web address:** http://www.twiggcorp.com. **Description:** Manufactures commercial and military jet engine parts.

TYSON FOODS, INC.
545 Valley Road, Corydon IN 47112. 812/738-3217. **Contact:** Human Resources Manager. **World Wide Web address:** http://www.tyson.com. **Description:** One of the world's largest producers, processors, and marketers of poultry products, as well as a marketer of other food items including meats, seafood, and pork products. Tyson is involved in all stages of poultry production including genetic research, feeding mills, and veterinary services. Products are sold primarily to hospitals, schools, airlines, retail stores, and wholesaling markets under the brand names Weaver, Tyson Holly Farms, Healthy Portion, Premium Pies, Complete Kits, Louis Kemp Crab, and Lobster Delights. **Corporate headquarters location:** Springdale AR.

UBS FINANCIAL SERVICES INC.
8888 Keystone Crossing, 10th Floor, Indianapolis IN 46240. 317/816-0800. **Contact:** Human Resources. **World Wide Web address:** http://www.ubs.com/financialservicesinc. **Description:** A full-service securities firm with over 300 offices nationwide. Services include investment banking, asset management, merger and acquisition consulting, municipal securities underwriting, estate planning, retirement programs, and transaction management. UBS PaineWebber offers its services to corporations, governments, institutions, and individuals. Founded

in 1879. **Corporate headquarters location:** New York NY. **Other U.S. locations:** Nationwide.

UNDERWRITERS LABORATORIES, INC.
110 South Hill Street, South Bend IN 46617. **Toll-free phone:** 800/332-4345. **Fax:** 574/233-8207. **Contact:** Human Resources. **E-mail address:** ehl@ehl.ul.com. **World Wide Web address:** http://www.ul.com. **Description:** A not-for-profit product-safety testing and certification organization. Underwriters Laboratories (UL) has been testing products for more than a century. **Positions advertised include:** EHL Operations Manager; Fire Protection Engineer; Inside Sales; Quality Registration Sales Position; Suppression Reviewer. **Other U.S. locations:** CA; CO; FL; GA; IL; MA; MI; MN; MO; NC; NV; NY; TX; WA.

UNILEVER HPC
1200 Calumet Avenue, Hammond IN 46320. 219/659-3200. **Contact:** Human Resources. **E-mail address:** na.recruiting@unilever.com. **World Wide Web address:** http://www.unilever.com. **Description:** Unilever is an international manufacturer and distributor of soaps and cleaning products, specialty foods, toothpastes, and detergents. **Special programs:** Internships. **Operations at this facility include:** This location produces a variety of soap and detergent products.

UNION ACCEPTANCE CORPORATION
250 North Shadeland Avenue, Indianapolis IN 46219. 317/231-6400. **Fax:** 317/231-2756. **Contact:** Human Resources. **E-mail address:** careers@uaca.com. **World wide Web address:** http://www.uaca.com. **Description:** Purchases, collects, and services motor vehicle retail installment contracts.

UNION HOSPITAL HEALTH GROUP
1606 North Seventh Street, Terre Haute IN 47804. 812/238-7000. **Recorded jobline:** 812/238-7200. **Contact:** Mary Halsted, Employment Manager. **World Wide Web address:** http://www.uhhg.org. **Description:** Owns and operates two hospitals, a physicians/surgeons clinic, and physician office sites. Union Hospital Health Group is a nonprofit, regional referral center. **NOTE:** Entry-level positions, part-time jobs, and second and third shifts are offered. **Positions advertised include:** Occupational Therapist; Respiratory Therapist; Physical Therapist; Pharmacist; Registered Nurse; Licensed Practical Nurse; Psychologist; Speech Language Pathologist; Nutrition Assistant. **Special programs:** Internships. **Office hours:** Monday - Friday, 8:00 a.m. - 4:30 p.m. **Corporate headquarters location:** This location. **Other area locations:** Clinton IN.

UNITED FIDELITY BANK, FSB
18 NW 4th Street, Evansville IN 47708. 812/424-0921. **Contact:** Human Resources. **World Wide Web address:** http://www.unitedfidelity.com. **Description:** Services include savings deposits, which the bank then invests in consumer installment loans, commercial loans for owner-occupied one- to four-family homes in Indiana, and in investment and money market securities. **Subsidiaries include:** United Fidelity Bank also owns, develops, builds, rents, and manages affordable housing projects through Village Management Corporation, Village Community Development Corporation, and Village Housing Corporation.

UNITED TECHNOLOGIES CARRIER SECURITY
7310 West Morris, Indianapolis IN 46231. 317/243-0851. **Contact:** Salaried Human Resources. **World Wide Web address:** http://www.utc.com. **Description:** A commercial manufacturer of HVAC equipment. **NOTE:** Apply online at www.carrier.com. **International locations:** Asia; Australia; Canada; Europe; Latin America; Mexico. **Parent company:** United Technologies provides high-technology products and support services to customers in the aerospace, building, military, and automotive industries worldwide. Products include large jet engines, temperature control systems, elevators and escalators, helicopters, and flight systems. The company markets its products under a variety of brand names including Carrier, Hamilton Standard, Otis, Pratt & Whitney, and Sikorsky.

UNITED TECHNOLOGIES CORPORATION
3650 West 200 North, Huntington IN 46750. 260/358-0888. **Contact:** Director of Human Resources. **World Wide Web address:** http://www.utc.com. **Description:** United Technologies Corporation provides high-technology products and support services to customers in the aerospace, building, military, and automotive industries worldwide. Products include large jet engines, temperature control systems, elevators and escalators, helicopters, and flight systems. The company markets its products under a variety of brand names including Carrier, Hamilton Standard, Otis, Pratt & Whitney, and Sikorsky. **International locations:** Asia; Australia; Canada; Europe; Latin America; Mexico. **Operations at this facility include:** This location manufactures electronic controls primarily used in heating and air conditioning equipment.

UNITED WAY OF CENTRAL INDIANA
3901 North Meridian Street, Indianapolis IN 46208. 317/923-1466. **Fax:** 317/921-1388. **Contact:** Human Resources. **World Wide Web address:** http://www.uwci.org. **Description:** An organization that raises and distributes funds for community service needs. **Special programs:** Internships; Volunteer Opportunities. **Internship information:** Paid and unpaid internships are offered in a variety of areas throughout the year. **Other U.S. locations:** Nationwide.

UNITED WAY OF HOWARD COUNTY
210 West Walnut, Room 201, Kokomo IN 46901. 765/457-6691. **Contact:** Carl Graber, President. **World Wide Web address:** http://www.unitedwayhoco.org. **Description:** An organization that raises and distributes funds for community service needs. **Special programs:** Internships. **Other U.S. locations:** Nationwide.

UNIVERSITY OF EVANSVILLE
1800 Lincoln Avenue, Evansville IN 47722. 812/479-2943. **Fax:** 812/479-2320. **Contact:** Director of Human Resources. **World Wide Web address:** http://www.evansville.edu. **Description:** A nonprofit, four-year university offering bachelor's and master's degrees. Approximately 2,600 undergraduate and 500 graduate students attend the University of Evansville. Founded in 1854. **NOTE:** Entry-level positions and second and third shifts are offered. **Positions advertised include:** Administrative Assistant; University Chaplain; Assistant Professor, Physics; Assistant Professor, Political Science; Assistant Professor, Nursing. **Corporate headquarters location:** This location. **Operations at this facility include:** Administration. **Listed on:** Privately held.

UNIVERSITY OF INDIANAPOLIS
1400 East Hanna Avenue, Indianapolis IN 46227. 317/788-3368. **Fax:** 317/788-3468. **Contact:** Human Resources. **E-mail address:** sclark@uindy.edu. **World Wide Web address:** http://www.uindy.edu. **Description:** A four-year university offering associate's, bachelor's, and master's degrees including MBAs. Enrollment is approximately 1,900 undergraduate and 460 graduate students. **Positions advertised include:** Assistant Professor, Art; Assistant Football Coach; Coaching Coordinator.

UNIVERSITY OF NOTRE DAME
Office of Human Resources, 100 Grace Hall, Notre Dame IN 46556-5612. 574/631-5900. **Fax:** 574/631-6790. **Contact:** Human Resources. **E-mail address:** hr@nd.edu. **World Wide Web address:** http://www.nd.edu. **Description:** An independent Catholic university offering undergraduate, graduate, and professional degree programs. The university's graduate school offers 44 master's degree programs, and 22 doctoral degree programs. The campus is located in Notre Dame, adjacent to the city of South Bend, Indiana. Founded in 1842. **Positions advertised include:** Operations Manager; Writer/Editor; Assistant Director, Non-Degree Programs; Banquet Server; Senior Research Technician. **President:** Rev. Edward A. Malloy, C.S.C.

UNIVERSITY OF SOUTHERN INDIANA
8600 University Boulevard, Evansville IN 47712-3596. 812/464-1844. **Recorded jobline:** 812/465-7117. **Contact:** Human Resources. **E-mail address:** humanres@usi.edu. **World Wide Web address:** http://www.usi.edu. **Description:** A public university offering both undergraduate and graduate degrees in a broad range of disciplines. Approximately 8,700 students are enrolled at the university. Founded in 1965. **Positions advertised include:** English Instructor; Assistant Professor, Chemistry; Residence Life Coordinator; Special Funds Accountant; Benefits Supervisor. **Office hours:** Monday – Friday, 8:00 a.m. – 4:30 p.m.

UNIVERSITY PLACE
850 West Michigan Street, Indianapolis IN 46202-5198. 317/269-9000. **Toll-free phone:** 800/410-MEET. **Fax:** 317/231-5050. **Contact:** Human Resources Director. **E-mail address:** iuplace@iupui.edu. **NOTE:** Fill out application or apply through www.careerbuilder.com. **World Wide Web address:** http://www.universityplace.iupui.edu. **Description:** A conference center and hotel. University Place offers 28 meeting rooms and a 340-seat auditorium.

US STEEL
GARY WORKS
One North Broadway, Gary IN 46402. 219/888-4492. **Contact:** Human Resources. **E-mail address:** HResources-GaryWorks@uss.com. **World Wide Web address:** www.ussteel.com. **Description:** Manufactures tin products for the automotive, construction, and food container industries.

UTILIMASTER CORPORATION
65288 State Road 19, P.O. Box 585, Wakarusa IN 46573. 574/862-4561. **Contact:** Human Resources. **E-mail address:** jobs@utilimaster.com. **World Wide Web address:** http://www.utilimaster.com. **Description:** A manufacturer of truck and bus bodies. **NOTE:** Resumes are accepted by mail or e-mail.

VALEO SYLVANIA
1231 A Avenue North, Seymour IN 47274. 812/523-5200. **Contact:** Human Resources. **World Wide Web address:** http://www.sylvania.com. **Description:** Manufactures vehicle lighting systems. Products include headlights and tail lamps for cars, motorcycles, and airplanes. **Corporate headquarters location:** Danvers MA. **Parent company:** OSRAM SYLVANIA.

VECTREN CORPORATION
P.O. Box 209, Evansville IN 47702. 812/491-4000. **Physical address:** 20 NW 4th Street, Evansville IN 47741. **Contact:** Human Resources. **World Wide Web address:** http://www.vectren.com. **Description:** A holding company that provides natural gas and electric power and related products. **Positions advertised include:** Warehouse Manager; Business Unit Analyst. **Corporate headquarters location:** This location. **Listed on:** New York Stock Exchange. **Stock exchange symbol:** VVC.

VERIZON COMMUNICATIONS
19845 U.S. 31 North, Westfield IN 46074. 317/896-6464. **Contact:** Human Resources. **World Wide Web address:** http://www.verizon.com. **Description:** A full-service communications services provider. Verizon offers residential local and long distance telephone services and Internet access; wireless service plans, cellular phones, and data services; a full-line of business services including Internet access, data services, and telecommunications equipment and services; and government network solutions including Internet access, data services, telecommunications equipment and services, and enhanced communications services. **Corporate headquarters location:** New York NY. **Other U.S. locations:** Nationwide. **Listed on:** New York Stock Exchange. **Stock exchange symbol:** VZ.

VIBRACOUSTIC
1497 Gerber Street, Ligonier IN 46767. 260/894-7183. **Contact:** Human Resources Manager. **World Wide Web address:** http://www.freudenberg.com. **Description:** Manufactures vibration control parts including engine mounts for automobiles.

VISKASE CORPORATION
102 East Bailie Street, Kentland IN 47951. 219/474-5101. **Contact:** Human Resources. **World Wide Web address:** http://www.viskase.com. **Description:** Manufactures cellulose casings and flexible packaging primarily used for food industry applications.

VOLT INFORMATION SCIENCES
1099 North Meridian, Suite 180, Indianapolis IN 46204. 317/630-3700. **Contact:** Human Resources. **World Wide Web address:** http://www.volt.com. **Description:** Provides prepress printing services for directory publishers. **NOTE:** Jobseekers are encouraged to submit their resumes via the Website. **Positions advertised include:** Technical Writer; Software Controls Engineer; Visual Basic Developer.

WISH-TV 8
1950 North Meridian Street, Indianapolis IN 46202. 317/923-8888. **Fax:** 317/926-1144. **Contact:** Human Resources. **E-mail address:** careers@ wishtv.com. **World Wide Web address:** http://www.wish-tv.com. **Description:** A CBS affiliate broadcasting throughout central Indiana. **Positions advertised include:** Broadcast Graphic Designer. **Number of employees at this location:** 150.

WTIU-TV
1229 East Seventh Street, Bloomington IN 47405. 812/855-5900. **Contact:** Human Resources. **World Wide Web address:** http://www.wtiu.indiana.edu. **Description:** A public television station serving south central Indiana. Founded in 1969. **NOTE:** Hiring is done through Indiana University. **Positions advertised include:** Producer/Director; Chief Videographer/Editor.

WZPL
MYSTAR COMMUNICATIONS
9245 North Meridian Street, Suite 300, Indianapolis IN 46260. 317/816-4000. **Contact:** Human Resources. **World Wide Web address:** http://www.wzpl.com. **Description:** A contemporary music radio station.

WABASH ALLOYS
4525 West Old 24, P.O. Box 466, Wabash IN 46992. 260/563-7461. **Fax:** 260/563-5997. **Contact:** Human Resources. **World Wide Web address:** http://www.wabashalloys.com. **Description:** Engaged in the smelting of secondary aluminum. **Other U.S. locations:** Nationwide. **Parent company:** Connell Limited Partnership. **Operations at this facility include:** Divisional Headquarters; Manufacturing; Sales. **Listed on:** Privately held.

WABASH NATIONAL CORPORATION
P.O. Box 6129, Lafayette IN 47903. 765/771-5300. **Contact:** Human Resources Department. **Recorded jobline:** 765/771-5451. **World Wide Web address:** http://www.wabashnational.com. **Description:** Designs, manufactures, and markets standard and customized truck trailers including dry freight vans, refrigerated trailers, and bimodal vehicles, as well as parts and related equipment. Wabash National markets its products through dealers to truckload and less-than-truckload common carriers, private fleet operators, household moving and storage companies, package carriers, and intermodal carriers including railroads. Founded in 1985. **Corporate headquarters location:** This location. **Operations at this facility include:** Administration; Manufacturing.

WABASH TECHNOLOGIES
P.O. Box 829, Huntington IN 46750-0829. 260/356-8300. **Physical address:** 1375 Swan Street, Huntington IN 46750. **Fax:** 260/355-4246. **Contact:** Human Resources. **E-mail address:** bstouder@wabashtech.com. **World Wide Web address:** http://www.wabashtech.com. **Description:** Manufactures sensors, coils, and other electronic parts and equipment for use in the automotive industry.

WALKER INFORMATION
3939 Priority Way South Drive, Indianapolis IN 46240. 317/843-3939. **Fax:** 317/843-8584. **Contact:** Human Resources. **E-mail address:** walkerhr@walkerinfo.com. **World Wide Web address:** http://www.walker info.com. **Description:** Provides marketing research and data collection for clients. Walker Information collects data from its clients' customers using the Internet, paper questionnaires, and telephone interviewing. Founded in 1939. **NOTE:** Entry-level positions are offered. **Special programs:** Internships. **Corporate headquarters location:** This location. **International locations:** Hamburg, Germany; Toronto, Canada. **Listed on:** Privately held.

WALSH & KELLY INC.
24358 State Road 23, South Bend IN 46614. 574/288-4811. **Fax:** 574/289-7174. **Contact:** Doug Kesler, Operations Manager. **World Wide Web address:** http://www.walshkelly.com. **Description:** Sells asphalt and does paving, concrete curbs and sidewalks, piping, and site preparation and grading.

WASTE MANAGEMENT, INC.
3200 West Bertha Street, Indianapolis IN 46222. 317/635-2491. **Contact:** Human Resources. **E-mail address:** careers@wm.com. **World Wide Web address:** http://www.wm.com. **Description:** Provides waste collection, removal, and disposal services to its residential, commercial, and industrial customers. **Other U.S. locations:** Nationwide.

WASTE MANAGEMENT, INC.
2000 Domby Road, Portage IN 46368. 219/763-2502. **Fax:** 219/764-1344. **Contact:** Sally Lawton, Human Resources. **E-mail address:** careers@ wm.com. **World Wide Web address:** http://www.wm.com. **Description:** Provides waste collection, removal, and disposal services to its residential, commercial, and industrial customers. **Other U.S. locations:** Nationwide.

WATERFURNACE INTERNATIONAL
9000 Conservation Way, Fort Wayne IN 46809. 260/478-5667. **Fax:** 260/479-3284. **Contact:** Human Resources. **E-mail address:** hr@waterfurnance.com. **World Wide Web address:** http://www.waterfurnace.com. **Description:** One of North America's leading manufacturers and distributors of geothermal heating and cooling systems for residential and commercial applications. WaterFurnace products are sold and serviced through commercial representatives and residential authorized dealers, and supported by independent distributors and regional direct-sales branches throughout the United States, Canada, and Australia. **Parent company:** WFI Industries, Ltd. **Operations at this facility include:** Administration; Distribution; Manufacturing; Marketing; Research and Development.

WEIL McLAIN
500 Blaine Street, Michigan City IN 46360. 219/879-6561. **Contact:** Human Resources. **World Wide Web address:** http://www.weil-mclain.com. **Description:** Manufactures heating equipment including boilers for the home construction and industrial markets. **Office hours:** Monday - Friday, 7:30 a.m. - 4:30 p.m.

WELLS FARGO BANK
111 East Wayne Street, Fort Wayne IN 46802. 260/461-6401. **Contact:** Human Resources. **World Wide Web address:** http://www.wellsfargo.com. **Description:** A diversified financial institution with over $234 billion in assets. Wells Fargo serves over 17 million customers through 5,300 independent locations worldwide. The company also maintains several stand-alone ATMs and branches within retail outlets. Services include community banking, credit and debit cards, home equity and mortgage loans, online banking, student loans, and insurance. Wells Fargo also offers a complete line of commercial and institutional financial services. Founded in 1852. **Corporate headquarters location:** San Francisco CA. **Other U.S. locations:** Nationwide. **International locations:** Worldwide. **Listed on:** New York Stock Exchange. **Stock exchange symbol:** WFC.

WHIRLPOOL CORPORATION
1900 Whirlpool Drive, LaPorte IN 46350. 765/463-0900. **Contact:** Human Resources. **World Wide Web address:** http://www.whirlpool.com. **Description:** Manufactures and markets home appliances. Whirlpool Corporation markets its products worldwide under brand names such as Whirlpool, KitchenAid, Roper, Estate, Bauknecht, Ignis, Laden, and Inglis. Whirlpool also manufactures and supplies major home appliances to Sears, Roebuck and Company under the Kenmore brand name.

WHITECO INDUSTRIES
1000 East 80th Place, Suite 700 North, Merrillville IN 46410. 219/769-6601. **Fax:** 219/757-3510. **Contact:** Personnel. **World Wide Web address:** http://www.whiteco.com. **Description:** An advertising agency specializing in the hotel and real estate industries.

WOLF PARK
Wolf Park, Battle Ground IN 47920. 765/567-2265. **Fax:** 765/567-4299. **Contact:** Manager. **World Wide Web address:** http://www.wolfpark.org. **Description:** A nonprofit research organization focusing on wolf behavior and preservation. The park offers walking tours, lectures, and seminars to the public. Founded in 1972. **Special programs:** Internships; Co-ops. **Corporate headquarters location:** This location. **Parent company:** North American Wildlife Park Foundation, Inc.

WOODS INDUSTRIES
510 Third Avenue SW, Carmel IN 46032. 317/844-7261. **Fax:** 317/814-7207. **Contact:** Human Resources. **World Wide Web address:** http://www.woods.com. **Description:** Manufactures electrical wiring products used in a wide variety of applications.

WYANDOT, INC.
125 Peacely Street, Jeffersonville IN 47130. 812/283-3528. **Contact:** Human Resources. **World Wide Web address:** http://www.wyandotsnacks.com. **Description:** Manufactures potato chips, corn chips, and other snack foods.

YMCA CAMP POTAWOTAMI
P.O. Box 38, South Milford IN 46786. 260/351-2525. **Toll-free phone:** 800/966-9622. **Fax:** 260/351-3915. **Contact:** Executive Director. **World Wide Web address:** http://www.camp-potawotami.org. **Description:** The YMCA provides health and fitness, social and personal development, sports and recreation, education and career development, and camps and conferences to children, youths, adults, the elderly, families, and the disabled. **Operations at this facility include:** This location is a resident camp offering programs to children, families, and organizations throughout the Midwest.

ZIMMER INC.
P.O. Box 708, Warsaw IN 46581. 574/267-6131. **Physical address:** 1800 West Center Street, Warsaw IN 46581. 800/613-6131. **Fax:** 574/372-4988. **Contact:** Employment Office. **World Wide Web address:** http://www.zimmer.com. **Description:** Develops, manufactures, and markets orthopedic products for human implant and patient care. Zimmer's primary customers are hospitals. **Positions advertised include:** Inventory Accountant; Process Engineer; Quality Engineer; Tax Manager; Product Manager; Brand Manager. **Corporate headquarters location:** This location. **Operations at this facility include:** Administration; Manufacturing; Research and Development. **Listed on:** New York Stock Exchange. **Stock exchange symbol:** ZMH.

ZIOLKOWSKI CONSTRUCTION INC.
1005 South Lafayette Boulevard, South Bend IN 46601. 574/287-1811. **Fax:** 574/234-0151. **Contact:** Human Resources Department. **World Wide Web address:** http://www.ziolkowskiconst.com. **Description:** A contract construction company with divisions for general construction, masonry, painting, design and architecture, and interiors.

AALFS MANUFACTURING, INC.
P.O. Box 3567, Sioux City IA 51102. 712/252-1877. **Physical address:** 1005 Fourth Street, Sioux City IA 51101. **Contact:** Melanie Nieman, Director of Personnel. **E-mail address:** hresources@aalfs.com. **World Wide Web address:** http://www.aalfs.com. **Description:** Aalfs Manufacturing, Inc. manufactures and sells men's and boys' clothing specializing in denim apparel. It contracts for such outlets as JCPenney, Tommy Hilfiger, Lands' End, GAP, Old Nave, and Harley Davidson among others. The company has sales and marketing operations in Dallas TX, a distribution center in Mena AR, and seven manufacturing partnerships in Mexico. Founded in 1914. **Corporate headquarters location:** This location. **Other area locations:** Bridgeport IA; Sheldon IA; Spencer IA; Yankton IA. **Other U.S. locations:** AR; TX. **Operations at this facility include:** Corporate administration; Manufacturing.

AG SERVICES OF AMERICA, INC.
P.O. Box 668, Cedar Falls IA 50613-0668. 319/277-0261. **Physical address:** 1309 Technology Parkway, Cedar Falls IA 50613. **Toll-free Phone:** 800-395-8505. **Fax:** 319/277-0144. **Contact:** Cindy Eckhoff, Human Resources Director. **E-mail address:** cindy.eckhoff@agservices.com. **World Wide Web address:** http://www.agservices.com. **Description:** Supplies farm inputs including seed; fertilizer; agricultural chemicals; crop insurance; and cash advances for rent, fuel, and irrigation, to farmers primarily in the central United States. Ag Services extends credit and provides farmers with the convenience of purchasing and financing a wide variety of farm inputs from a single source at competitive prices. Founded in 1985. **Positions advertised include:** Administrative Assistant. **Corporate headquarters location:** This location. **Listed on:** New York Stock Exchange. **Stock exchange symbol:** ASV. **Chairman:** Gaylen D. Miller. **Annual sales/revenues:** $387 million. **Number of employees:** 164.

AVG AUTOMATION
P.O. Box 1327, Bettendorf IA 52722. 630/668-3900. **Physical address:** 4140 Utica Ridge Road, Bettendorf IA 52722. **Fax:** 563/359-9094. **Contact:** Linda Wooten, Human Resources Manager. **World Wide Web address:** http://www.avg.net. **Description:** The AVG Group of companies, which includes former Uticor Technologies, manufactures computer hardware, monitors, message displays, motion controls, operator interface technologies, and other electronic products.

ADVANCED TECHNOLOGIES GROUP, INC.
1601 48th Street, Suite 220, West Des Moines IA 50266. 515/221-9344. **Fax:** 515/221-1266. **Contact:** Human Resources. **World Wide Web address:** http://www.a-t-g.com. **Description:** Web design and technology consulting service for corporations and state agencies and is a certified Microsoft Windows platform consulting service. Founded in 1991. **Listed on:** Privately held. **Chairman/CEO:** Atul Gupta. **Annual sales/revenues:** $6.1 million. **Number of employees:** 45.

AEGON USA, INC.
4333 Edgewood Road NE, Cedar Rapids IA 52499. 319/363-5400. **Toll-free phone:** 800/238-4309. **Fax:** 319/398-7915. **Contact:** Human Resources. **World Wide Web address:** http://www.aegonins.com. **Description:** AEGON USA operates through four groups encompassing 11 insurance divisions: Agency, Asset Accumulation, Health, and Home Services. The Individual, Western Reserve Life, and Monumental Life Divisions sell life and health insurance products, mutual funds, and annuities. The Insurance Center administers group hospital expense insurance programs that are sold exclusively to the more than 300,000 members of the National Association for the Self-Employed. The NOL Division markets traditional and interest-sensitive life insurance and disability income products. Servicing the financial planning need of high-income, high-net-worth clients, the Advanced Products Division offers estate planning, deferred compensation, capital transfer, and key-man programs. Offering plan design, participant communication programs, record-keeping services, and technical guidance, the Diversified Investment Advisors service the retirement plan markets. The Financial Markets Division provides fixed and variable annuity products through national and state banks, savings and loans, and regional brokerage firms. Monumental General has seven business units, each with district objectives, including credit, Medicare Supplement, and accidental death insurance. The Long Term Care Division markets long-term care/nursing home products including nursing home, home health, assisted living, and adult daycare services, while the Supplemental Insurance Division markets intensive care, long-term care, and accident insurance products. **NOTE:** Applicants can apply to positions by submitting resume online through the company Website. For career information: 319/398-8018. **Positions advertised include:** Accountant; Accounting Associate; Actuarial Analyst; Administrative Assistant; Advanced Marketing Analyst; AFP Service Representative; Assistant General Counsel; Audit Manager; Benefits Project Coordinator; Business Systems Analyst; Call Center Consultant; Cash Flow Analyst; Client Associate; Corporate Director of Security; Customer Service Consultant; Career Agent; Data Entry Associate; Document Processing Associate; Facilities Manager; Information Security Architect; Lead Internal Auditor; Mortgage Loan Analyst; Network Engineer; Payroll Associate; Print Operator; Research Analyst; Risk Analyst; Senior Accountant; Senior Asset Manager; Senior Programmer; Senior Tax Accountant. **Special programs:** Internships and student employment. **Corporate headquarters location:** Baltimore MD. **Other U.S. locations:** Nationwide. **International locations:** Canada. **Subsidiaries include:** Aegon USA Realty Advisers, Inc.; Life Companies; Transamerica. **Parent company:** AEGON N.V. Insurance Group. **Operations at this facility include:** Corporate administration; Investment Management, Inc.; Diversified Investment Advisers; Financial Markets Division; Individual Division. **Chairman:** Donald J. Shepard. **Annual sales/revenues:** $16 billion. **Number of employees at this location:** 2,300. **Number of employees nationwide:** 13,081.

AIN COMPANY, LLC
1223 Oakes Drive, Iowa City IA 52245. 319/621-7995. **Contact:** Human Resources. **E-mail address:** info@aincompany.com. **World Wide Web address:** http://www.aincompany.com. **Description:** Develops software for simulating neurobiology.

ALCOA (ALUMINUM COMPANY OF AMERICA)
P.O. Box 3567, Bettendorf IA 52722. 563/459-2000. **Fax:** 563/459-1697. **Recorded jobline:** 563-459-2832 **Contact:** Human Resources. **World Wide Web address:** http://www.alcoa.com. **Description:** Engaged in all aspects of the aluminum industry including mining, refining, smelting, fabricating, and recycling. ALCOA also manufactures ceramic packaging for the semiconductor industry, alumina chemicals, plastic bottle closures, vinyl siding, packaging machinery, and electrical distribution systems for automobiles. **Positions advertised include:** Maintenance; Brick Mason; Mechanic; Machinist. **Corporate headquarters location:** Pittsburgh PA. **Other U.S. locations:** Nationwide. **International Locations:** Worldwide. **Subsidiaries include:** Alcoa Fujikura Ltd.; Howmet Castings; Integris Metals, Inc.; Ivex Packaging Corp. **Operations at this facility include:** The Davenport Works in Riverdale produces fabricated aluminum products, sheeting, and plating for aerospace components and other industries; Administrative offices in Bettendorf. **Listed on:** New York Stock Exchange. **Stock exchange symbol:** AA. **Chairman/President/CEO:** Alain J. P. Belda. **Annual sales/revenues:** $20.3 billion. **Number of employees worldwide:** 129,000.

ALLEN MEMORIAL HOSPITAL
1825 Logan Avenue, Waterloo IA 50703. 319/235-3941. **Fax:** 319/235-5260. **Contact:** Ken Leibold, Director of Human Resources. **World Wide Web address:** http://www.allenhospital.org. **Description:** Part of the Iowa Health System, this 240-bed hospital's programs and services include an ambulatory medical center, an ambulatory surgery center, anesthesiology, angiography, angioplasty, audiology, a back injury program, neurology, nuclear medicine, radiology services, senior services, hospice services, home health services, infection control, intensive/coronary care, CT scan, MRI, mental health services, tele-care, trauma center, wellness center, women's health center, oncology, open heart surgery, ophthalmology, orthopedics, nursing school, International Diabetes Center/North Iowa Affiliate, speech pathology, urology, hyperbaric oxygen for extremities, maxillofacial surgery, and an emergency department. **NOTE:** For consideration applicants must submit a completed application available from the company Website. Human Resources phone: 319/235-3605. **Positions advertised include:** Family Practice Physician; Cardiologist; Emergency Medicine Physician; Obstetrics and Gynecology Physician; Nursing Assistant; Admitting Technician; Licensed Practical Nurse; Medical Transcriptionist; Registered Nurse; Physical Therapist; Patient Service Representative; Development Assistant; Diagnostic Radiographer; Respiratory Therapist; Cytotechnologist. **Other clinic locations:** Cedar Falls IA; Eldora IA; Sumner IA. **Affiliates include:** Allen College. **Parent company:** Allen Health System, Inc.

ALLIANT ENERGY
1000 Main Street, P.O. Box 769, Dubuque IA 52004-0769. 800/851-0658. **Fax:** 563/567-2282. **Contact:** Human Resources. **E-mail address:** jobsdbq@alliantenergy.com. **World Wide Web address:** http://www.alliantenergy.com. **Description:** An electric and gas utility formed in 1998 from the three-way merger of WPL Holdings, IES Industries, and Interstate Power serving 1.3 million customers in northern Iowa, southern Minnesota, northwest Illinois, and Wisconsin. **NOTE:** For clerical positions in Iowa, contact Human Resources, P.O. Box 77007, Madison WI 53707; or E-mail: jobsmsn@alliantenergy.com; or Fax: 608/458-0119. **Positions advertised include:** Maintenance Manager; Coal & Ash Operator; Gas Distribution Engineer; Payment & Corporate Credit Coordinator; IT PeopleSoft Security Analyst. **Corporate headquarters location:** Madison WI. **Other area locations:** Cedar Rapids IA. **Operations at this facility include:** Prairie Creek Generating Facility; Administration. **Listed on:** New York Stock Exchange. **Stock exchange symbol:** LNT. **Chairman/President/CEO:** Erroll B. Davis Jr. **Annual sales/revenues:** $2.6 billion. **Number of employees nationwide:** 8,585.

ALLIED GROUP, INC.
701 Fifth Avenue, Des Moines IA 50391. 515/280-4211. **Toll-free phone:** 800/532-1436. **Fax:** 515/280-4904. **Contact:** Senior Employment Representative. **World Wide Web address:** http://www.alliedinsurance.com. **Description:** With its regional unit, Allied Property and Casualty Insurance, offers various property, casualty, auto, farm, homeowners, and life insurance policies for individual and commercial customers. **Positions advertised include:** Actuarial Assistant; Commercial Underwriting Manager; Claims Manager; Claims Service Representative; Compliance Analyst; General Counsel; Direct Sales Agent; Loss Control Representative; Damage Claims Appraiser; Multiline Master Claims Representative; Output Operator; PBX Operator; Product Underwriting Consultant; Programmer Analyst; Service Center Representative; Software Specialist; Senior Applications Database Analyst; Senior Compliance Analyst; Program Project Leader; System Manager; Web Communications Designer. **NOTE:** Post resumes and apply online at the company Website. **Corporate headquarters location:** This location. **Other U.S. locations:** Nationwide. **Subsidiaries/Affiliates include:** AMCO Insurance; Depositors Insurance; Allied Property; Casualty Insurance. **Parent company:** Nationwide Insurance. **Operations at this facility include:** Administration; Sales; Service. **President/CEO:** Douglas L. Andersen. **Number of employees at this location:** 1,600. **Number of employees nationwide:** 4,100.

AMANA APPLIANCES
2800 220th Trail, Amana IA 52204. 319/622-2208. **Fax:** 319/622-8286. **Contact:** Human Resources. **World Wide Web address:** http://www.amana.com. **Description:** Since becoming a part of the Maytag family of brands in a 2001 acquisition from the Goodman Manufacturing Company, the Amana Appliance Division designs, develops, manufactures, and sells major consumer appliances including dishwashers, refrigerators, and microwaves as well as commercial microwave ovens. Founded in 1934. **NOTE:** Resumes and applications are accepted through the parent company Website: http://www.careers.maytag.com. **Positions advertised include:** Commercial Products Manager. **Corporate headquarters location:** This location. **Parent company:** Maytag Corporation. **Operations at this facility include:** Administration; Manufacturing; Research and Development; Sales; Service.

AMERICA MEDIA
421 121st Street, Urbandale IA 50323. 515/224-0919. **Toll-free phone:** 888/776-8268. **Fax:** 515/224-0256. **Contact:** Human Resources. **World Wide Web address:** http://www.amedia.com. **Description:** A leading producer of corporate training products and services. The company offers audio, interactive multimedia, and video products. **Positions advertised include:** Account Manager; Multimedia Designer. **Listed on:** NASDAQ.

AMERICAN IDENTITY
1520 Albany Place SE, Orange City IA 51041. 712/737-4925. **Recorded jobline:** 866/313-5154. **Contact:** Deborah Anderson, Employment Coordinator. **E-mail address:** jobs@americanid.com. **World Wide Web address:** http://www.americanid.com. **Description:** A full-line, promotional products supplier offering wearables, caps, and specialty products for men, women, and children. This location also hires seasonally. **NOTE:** Second and third shifts are offered. **Office hours:** Monday - Friday 7:30 a.m. - 4:30 p.m. **Corporate headquarters location:** Kansas City MO. **Other U.S. locations:** Bonner Springs KS; Maumee OH; Shawnee KS; Tigard OR. **Operations at this facility include:** Distribution; Sales. **Number of employees nationwide:** 1,375.

AMERUS GROUP CO.
dba AMERUS LIFE INSURANCE
699 Walnut Street Des Moines 50309-3948. 515/362-3600. **Fax:** 515/557-2635. **Contact:** Human Resources. **World Wide Web address:** http://www.amerusgroup.com. **Description:** Through its subsidiaries, the company underwrites and sells individual whole life, universal life, and term life insurance policies offering fixed annuities. **NOTE:** Entry-level positions are offered. Post resumes and apply for specific positions via the company's Website. **Positions advertised include:** Director of Advanced Markets; Marketing Specialist; Part-Time Project Coordinator; Administrative Assistant; Supply Clerk; Account Executive. **Corporate headquarters location:** This location. **Other area locations:** Statewide.

Subsidiaries include: AmerUS Life Insurance; AmerUS Home Lending; AmerUS Annuity Group; Bankers Life Insurance Company of New York; Indianapolis Life Insurance Company. **Operations at this facility include:** Corporate Administration; Services. **Listed on:** New York Stock Exchange. **Stock exchange symbol;** AMH. **Chairman/President/CEO:** Roger K. Brooks. **Annual sales/revenues:** $1.4 billion. **Number of employees at this location:** 300. **Number of employees nationwide:** 1,133.

AMES LABORATORY
105 Technical and Administrative Services Facility, Iowa State University, Ames IA 50011-3020. 515/294-2680. **Fax:** 525/294-5741. **Contact:** Human Resources. **World Wide Web address:** http://www.ameslab.gov. **Description:** A U.S. Department of Energy laboratory operated by Iowa State University. The lab performs basic and applied energy research. **NOTE:** Applicants must apply online at http://www.iastatejobs.com. **Positions advertised include:** Administrator; Scientist; Engineer; Chemist; Physicist. **Operations at this facility include:** Research and Development.

ARCHER DANIELS MIDLAND COMPANY CORN PROCESSING DIVISION
1251 Beaver Channel Parkway, Clinton IA 52732. 563/242-1121. **Contact:** Jim Woll, Plant Manager. **World Wide Web address:** http://www.admworld.com. **Description:** Archer Daniels Midland processes corn and other agricultural products such as soybeans, dry-milled grains (wheat, rice, and masa), cottonseed, and canola. The company also produces a variety of products including vegetable oils (lecithin, cooking oil, and margarine), vitamin E, protein (soy flour, soy solates, soy protein, soy milk, and TVP), high fructose corn syrup, sorbitol, starch, ethanol, xanthan gum, tryptophan, vitamin C, fermentation products (lysine, threonine, lactic acid, citric acid, and MSG), pasta, and cottonseed flour products. **NOTE:** Post resumes and apply for positions through the company Website: http://careers.admworld.com. **Company slogan:** Supermarket to the World. **Positions advertised include:** Plant Engineer. **Special programs:** Internships; Coops. **Corporate headquarters location:** Decatur IL. **Other area locations:** Atlantic IA; Burlington IA; Cedar Rapids IA; Des Moines IA; Keokuk IA. **Other U.S. locations:** Nationwide. **International locations:** Worldwide. **Subsidiaries include:** ADM Alliance Nutrition, Inc. **Operations at this facility include:** Corn processing plant; Soybean Production and Merchandising Division. The ADM Milling Co. is in Des Moines IA. **Listed on:** New York Stock Exchange. **Stock exchange symbol:** ADM. **Chairman/CEO:** G. Allen Andreas. **Annual sales/revenues:** $25 billion. **Number of employees:** 25,000.

ART'S-WAY MANUFACTURING COMPANY INC.
P.O. Box 288, Armstrong IA 50514. 712/864-3131. **Physical address:** Highway 9 West, Armstrong IA 50514. **Fax:** 712/864-3154. **Contact:** Brenda Evans, Personnel Manager. **World Wide Web address:** http://www.artsway-mfg.com. **Description:** A manufacturer and distributor of animal feed processing products, sugar beet harvesting equipment, minimum/no-till seed bed preparation equipment, and other agricultural products. Founded in 1956. **Company slogan:** Building on a Tradition of Quality. **Positions advertised include:** Engineer; Operations/Production Manager. **Listed on:** NASDAQ. **Stock Exchange Symbol:** ARTW. **Chairman:** James L. Koley. **Annual sales/revenues:** $10 million. **Number of employees at this location:** 100.

BANDAG, INC.
2905 North Highway 61, Muscatine IA 52761-5886. 563/262-1400. **Fax:** 563/262-1069. **Contact:** Employee Services. **E-mail address:** recruiter@badag.com. **World Wide Web address:** http://www.bandag.com. **Description:** The company's Traditional Business division manufactures and sells procured tread rubber and retreading equipment and supplies producing over 500 varieties of tire tread. Through its Tire Distribution Systems subsidiary the company operates 40 franchise and manufacturing locations, and over 100 commercial and industrial outlets in 16 states. **Corporate headquarters location:** This location. **Other U.S. locations:** Abilene TX; Griffin GA; Long Beach CA; Muncie IN; Oxford NC. **International locations:** Worldwide. **Subsidiaries include:** Tire Distribution Systems, Inc.; Tire Management Solutions. **Operations at this facility include:** Corporate administration; Research and Development; Retreading at the Bandag Equipment Plant. **Listed on:** NASDAQ; New York Stock Exchange. **Stock Exchange Symbol:** BDG. **Chairman/President/CEO:** Martin G. Carver. **Annual sales/revenues:** $912 million. **Number of employees:** 4,000.

BANK OF AMERICA
6200 Aurora Avenue, Des Moines IA 50322. 515/235-2910. **Contact:** Personnel. **E-mail address:** bankofamerica@efunds.com. **World Wide Web address:** http://www.bankofamerica.com. **Description:** A full-service banking and financial institution. The company operates through four business segments: Global Corporate and Investment Banking, Principal Investing and Asset Management, Commercial Banking, and Consumer Banking. **NOTE:** Applications and resumes can be submitted via the company Website. **Positions advertised include:** Teller; Personal Banker; Associate Teller; Banking Center Manager; Marketing Retail Lending Account Executive; Executive Teller. **Corporate headquarters location:** Charlotte NC. **Other U.S. locations:** Nationwide. **Listed on:** New York Stock Exchange. **Stock exchange symbol:** BAC. **Chairman/President/CEO:** Kenneth D. Lewis. **Annual sales/revenues:** $53 billion. **Number of employees worldwide:** 143,000.

BARNES & NOBLE BOOKSTORES
4550 University Avenue, West Des Moines IA 50266-1025. 515/221-9171. **Fax:** 515/226-0930. **Contact:** Store Manager. **World Wide Web address:** http://www.barnesandnobleinc.com. **Description:** A bookstore chain operating 900 stores nationwide. This location has a cafe and music department in addition to its book comprehensive departments. **NOTE:** Applications should be submitted via the company Website: http://www.barnesandnobleinc.com/jobs/index.html. **Corporate headquarters location:** New York NY. **Other area locations:** Cedar Rapids IA; Coralville IA; Waterloo IA. **Other U.S. locations:** Nationwide. **Listed on:** New York Stock Exchange. **Stock exchange symbol:** BKS. **Chairman:** Leonard S. Riggio. **Annual sales/revenues:** $5.2 billion. **Number of employees worldwide:** 37,000.

BARNSTEAD-THERMOLYNE CORPORATION
P.O. Box 797, Dubuque IA 52204-0797. 563/556-2241. **Physical address:** 2555 Kerper Boulevard, Dubuque IA 52001. **Fax:** 563/589-0516. **Contact:** Human Resources. **World Wide Web address:** http://www.barnsteadthermolyne.com. **Description:** Develops, manufactures, and markets precision heating, stirring, and temperature control apparatuses; water purification systems; liquid handling equipment; and replacement parts for such products. Heating, stirring, and temperature control apparatuses include hot plates, stirrers, heating tapes, muffle furnaces, incubators, dribaths, and cryogenic storage apparatus. Barnstead-Thermolyne offers a full range of systems to produce ultra pure water, which incorporate distillation, deionization, reverse osmosis, ultraviolet oxidation, and absorption or filtration technologies. Barnstead-Thermolyne products are marketed primarily to industrial, clinical, academic, governmental, and biotechnological laboratories in the United States and abroad through independent distributors. **Corporate headquarters location:** This location. **Other locations:** Boston MA. **Parent company:** Apogent Technologies Inc., formerly Sybron International Corporation, has four operating subsidiaries that hold leadership product positions in laboratory and professional orthodontic and dental markets in the United States and abroad.

BIOFORCE NANOSCIENCES
1615 Golden Aspen Drive, Suite 101, Ames IA 50010. 515/233-8333. **Fax:** 515/233-8337. **Contact:** Human Relations. **E-mail address:** hr@bioforcenano.com. **World Wide Web address:** http://www.bioforcenano.com. **Description:** A rapidly expanding developer of ultra-miniaturized array technologies for biomolecular analysis. **Positions advertised include:** Molecular/Cell Biology Research Associate.

BLACKHAWK ENGINEERING
118 Blackhawk Lane, Cedar Falls IA 50613. 319/266-2681. **Contact:** Gayla Hoppenworth, Human Resources. **E-mail address:** ghoppenworth@newcor.com. **Description:** Manufacturer of high-quality tool and die products specializing in contract production work. The company operates this Production Division, a machining facility, and the Engineering and Tooling Division in Waterloo IA. It designs and builds tooling and fixturing and other special machines with complete Computer-Aided Design based proposal and engineering departments with complete machine shop capability and assembly bay areas. Founded in 1971. **Positions advertised include:** Wiring Harness Pro-E Engineer; Electronics Technician; Electromagnetic Compatibility Test Technician; Senior Electromagnetic Compatibility Engineer; Environmental Test Technician; Maintenance Mechanic. **Other area locations:** Waterloo IA. **Parent company:** Newcor, Inc. (Bloom Hills, MI).

BROADLAWNS MEDICAL CENTER
1801 Hickman Road, Des Moines IA 50314. 515/282-2200. **Fax:** 515-282-2526. **Contact:** Human Resources. **World Wide Web address:** http://www.broadlawns.org. **Description:** A 200-bed general medical and psychiatric hospital serving the residents of Polk County. Both inpatient and outpatient services are performed at Broadlawns with a wide range of diagnostic procedures and support departments to ensure complete continuity of patient care. Departments include emergency, pharmacy, laboratory, physical therapy, respiratory therapy, radiology, diagnostic services, specialty clinics, social service, outreach project, and chaplaincy services. Broadlawns's Mental Health Service offers an extensive program of inpatient and outpatient mental health services including a crisis intervention program and day treatment programs for adults and adolescents. The Family Health Center provides patients with continuity of care through a personal physician, and offers the following programs: the Family Practice Residency Program, dental clinic, WIC, and family planning. The Primary Care Center is a federal community health center whose purpose is to provide patients without a family physician the opportunity to acquire their own personal health care provider. Patients receive a full range of primary health care and are offered a continuity of care from their own provider. Additional programs include Polk County Jail Health Services, providing on-site medical, dental, and psychological health care to Polk County Jail inmates, and a Speakers Bureau, offering the community free speakers on various topics. Founded in 1925. **NOTE:** Applications filled out on the company Website: http://www.broadlawns.org/application.htm. Human Resources phone: 515/282-2210. **Positions advertised include:** Director of Development; Program Specialist Supervisor; Coder; Medical Lab Technician; Radiology Technician; Residential Treatment Worker; Health Service Technician; Emergency Department Technician; Licensed Practical Nurse; Certified Medical Assistant; Transcriptionist; Communications Clerk; Patient Access Representative; Pre-Registration Clerk; Intensive Care Nurse; Medical/Surgical Nurse; Adult Psychologist.

BRODERBUND AND THE LEARNING COMPANY
222 Third Avenue SE, Cedar Rapids IA 52401. 319/395-9626. **Fax:** 319/395-0217. **Contact:** Human Resources. **E-mail address:** resumes@riverdeep.net. **World Wide Web address:** http://www.broderbund.com. **Description:** Develops more than 80 software programs for a wide range of business applications and provides technical support services. **Corporate headquarters location:** Novato CA. **Other U.S. locations:** CA; MA; WA. **International locations:** Ireland; Israel. **Parent company:** Riverdeep Group, PLC (Dublin, Ireland).

CARGILL CORPORATION
300 Ninth Street, Onawa IA 51040. 712/423-1521. **Toll-free phone:** 800/247-2017. **Contact:** Human Resources. **E-mail address:** For career information (no resumes): employment@cargill.com. **World Wide Web address:** http://www.cargill.com. **Description:** Cargill Corporation, its subsidiaries, and its affiliates are involved in nearly 50 individual lines of business. The company is engaged in commodity trading, handling, transporting, processing, and risk management. Cargill is a major trader of grains and oilseeds, as well as a marketer of many other agricultural and nonagricultural commodities. Agricultural products include a wide variety of feed, seed, fertilizers, and other goods and services needed by producers worldwide. Cargill is also a leader in producing and marketing seed varieties and hybrids. Cargill Central Research is engaged in developing new agricultural products. The company also provides financial and technical services. Cargill's Financial Markets Division (FMD) supports Cargill and its subsidiaries with financial products and services that address market conditions including financial instrument trading, emerging markets instrument trading, value investing, and money management. Cargill's worldwide food processing businesses supply products ranging from basic ingredients used in food production to recognized name brands. Cargill also operates a number of industrial businesses including the production of steel, industrial-grade starches, ethanol, and salt products. **NOTE:** Scannable resumes should be sent to: Cargill Incorporated, Selection Department #10, P.O. Box 5697, Minneapolis MN 55440-5697, or posted to the Cargill Resume Builder Website: http://www.cargill.com/jobs/index.htm. **Positions advertised include:** HFT Project Manager; Project Engineer; Plant Manager; Engineer; Production Supervisor; Chemist. **Corporate headquarters location:** Minneapolis MN. **Other area locations include:** Ankeny IA; Belmond IA; Buffalo IA; Cedar Rapids IA; Des Moines IA; Eddyville IA; Greeley IA; Hamburg IA; Sioux City IA; Woodward IA. **Other U.S. locations:** Nationwide. **International locations:** Worldwide. **Subsidiaries include:** Cargill Dow LLC; Cargill Steel; North Star Steel Incorporated. **Operations in Iowa include:** Production; Research and Development; Refineries; Soy Laboratories; Corn Mills. **Listed on:** Privately held. **Chairman/CEO:** Warren R. Staley. **Annual sales/revenues:** $50.1 billion. **Number of employees worldwide:** 97,000.

CENTRAL IOWA HEALTH SYSTEM
1313 High Street, Suite 111, Des Moines IA 50309. 515/241-6313. **Toll-free phone:** 800/843-4522. **Fax:** 515/241-8515. **E-mail address:** careers@ihs.org. **Contact:** Personnel. **World Wide Web address:** http://www.iowahealth.org. **Description:** Iowa Methodist Medical Center, Iowa Lutheran Hospital, and St. Luke's are affiliated hospitals under the Central Iowa Health System. They form one of Iowa's largest nonprofit medical facilities with a combined total of 1,175 beds. Iowa Methodist is central Iowa's only designated trauma center and is also a teaching, regional referral center. Iowa Lutheran is a community hospital that focuses on family medicine and behavioral health sciences. St. Luke's is a general hospital located in Cedar Rapids.

Positions advertised include: Care Manager; CDTR Community Services; Certified Occupational Therapy Assistant; Chemical Depression Counselor; Clinical Lab Technician; Clinical Education Specialist; Clinical Nurse Specialist; Certified Medical Assistant; Coder/Abstractor; Facilities Manager; Financial Counselor; Housekeeper; Licensed Practical Nurse; Medical Lab Technician; Medical Records Technician; Medical Technologist; Nursing Manager; Health Information Manager; Nuclear Medicine Technologist; Occupational Therapist. **NOTE:** Post resumes on the company Website. **Corporate headquarters location:** This location. **Other area locations:** Knoxville IA. **Subsidiaries include:** Blank Children's Hospital; Iowa Lutheran Hospital; Iowa Methodist Medical Center. **Parent company:** Iowa Health Systems. **Number of employees at this location:** 5,200. **Number of employees statewide:** 7,000.

CLOW VALVE COMPANY
902 South Second Street, Oskaloosa IA 52577. 641/673-8611. **Fax:** 641/673-1934. **Contact:** Human Resources Director. **World Wide Web address:** http://www.clowvalve.com. **Description:** Produces valves and hydrants used for water and wastewater treatment, water distribution, and fire line projects. Founded in 1878. **Positions advertised include:** Nurse Administrator. **Corporate headquarters location:** This location. **Other locations:** Corona CA; Piedmont SC. **Parent company:** McWane, Inc. **Operations at this facility include:** Iron and brass foundries; Corporate administration; Manufacturing; Distribution.

CONAGRA FOODS
RETAIL PRODUCTS COMPANY
1023 South Fourth Street, Council Bluffs IA 51503. 712/322-0203. **Fax:** 712/325-5239. **Contact:** Human Resources. **E-mail address:** careers@conagrafoods.com. **World Wide Web address:** http://www.conagrafoods.com. **Description:** The Retail Products division, part of the ConAgra Packaged Foods Segment, produces and markets a variety of leading brands to retailers in North America with business in Mexico, the Caribbean and Canada. The Frozen Foods division manufactures potpies and other frozen and microwaveable foods. **NOTE:** Human Resources phone: 712/322-0203. **Positions advertised include:** Shipping and Warehouse Supervisor; Processing Supervisor. **Corporate headquarters location:** Omaha NE. **Other area locations:** Snack Foods Group in Hamburg IA. **Parent company:** ConAgra Foods, Inc. **Operations at this facility include:** Frozen Foods Group. **Listed on:** New York Stock Exchange. **Stock exchange symbol:** CAG. **Chairman/President/CEO:** Bruce C. Rhode. **Annual sales/revenues:** $27.6 billion. **Number of employees:** 80,000.

CUNA MUTUAL LIFE INSURANCE COMPANY
2000 Heritage Way, Waverly IA 50677. 319/352-1000. **Fax:** 319/352-1272. **Contact:** Manager of Human Resources. **World Wide Web address:** http://www.cunamutual.com. **Description:** The company, part of the Cuna Mutual Group, designs markets and administers individual investments, life insurance plans, long term care insurance and annuity products. Founded in 1935. **NOTE:** Applicants are requested to register and apply for positions through the company's Online Response Form. **Positions advertised include:** Mail Clerk; Imaging & Retrieval Specialist; HVAC Mechanic; Service Representative; Financial Services Sales Assistant. **Corporate headquarters location:** Madison WI. **Other are locations:** Dubuque IA. **Parent company:** Cuna Mutual Group. **Chairman:** James L. Bryan. **Annual sales/revenues:** $2 billion. **Number of employees nationwide:** 5,000.

CURRIES COMPANY
1502 12th Street NW, Mason City IA 50401-2542. 641/423-1334. **Fax:** 641/422-2650. **Contact:** Mark Evers, Director of Human Resources. **E-mail address:** mark.evers@doorgroup.com. **World Wide Web address:** http://www.curries.com. **Description:** Part of the ESSEX Total Openings Group, Curries Company manufactures doors and frames for the construction market. The company's custom and pre-engineered products are created with the building designer in mind including doors and frames in a variety of construction systems, styles, fire ratings, and steel types. Founded in 1958. **Affiliates include:** ESSEX Total Openings Group. **Parent company:** ASSA ABLOY Inc. **President:** Jerry Currie.

CUSTOM-PAK INC.
86 16th Avenue North, Clinton IA 52732. **Contact:** Vice President of Human Resources. **World Wide Web address:** http://www.custom-pak.com. **Description:** Manufactures molded plastic products.

DECO PRODUCTS COMPANY
506 Sanford Street, Decorah IA 52101. 563/382-4264. **Fax:** 319/382-9845. **Contact:** Human Resources. **World Wide Web address:** http://www.decoprod.com. **Description:** Designs, produces, and delivers zinc die cast parts for manufacturers and suppliers nationwide. The company also offers complete finishing and secondary operations including complete assembly capabilities (drilling and stamping); contract manufacturing; flash-free, trim, and breakoff capabilities; plating, powder coating, and other finishes; and engraved casting, such as a company logo, part or patent number, textured designs, or instructions. Deco's products include large castings; medium castings; small, precision castings; castings with exterior threads cast in; castings with inserts (other metal components molded directly into the casting); castings with complex configurations (4-slide technology); CNC machined castings; powder-coated castings; custom powder coatings on customers' metal components; assembly technology; assemblies of all types; industrial hose clamps; and clamp application tools. Founded in 1960. **Positions advertised include:** Accountant; Metals Engineer; Manufacturing Engineer. **Annual sales/revenues:** $21 - $50 million. **Number of employees at this location:** 400.

DELONG SPORTSWEAR, INC.
821 Fifth Avenue, P.O. Box 189, Grinnell IA 50112-0189. 641/236-3106. **Fax:** 641/236-5183. **Contact:** Human Resources. **World Wide Web address:** http://www.delong-sportswear.com. **Description:** Manufacturer and designer of school and college athletic sportswear specializing in uniforms, sports outerwear, team headwear, award jackets, and other leisure apparel. **Positions advertised include:** Accountant; Engineer; Manufacturer's/Wholesaler's Sales Rep; Marketing Specialist. **Operations at this facility include:** Administration; Customer Service; Manufacturing; Marketing; Sales. A retail outlet and the Material Distribution Center are also in Grinnell IA.

DES MOINES AREA COMMUNITY COLLEGE
2006 South Ankeny Boulevard, Ankeny IA 50021. 515/964-6200. **Fax:** 515/965-7316. **Contact:** Human Resources. **E-mail address:** jobs@dmacc.org. **World Wide Web address:** http://www.dmacc.cc.ia.us. **Description:** A publicly supported, two-year institution serving the Des Moines metropolitan area and surrounding counties. DMACC offers the Associate in Arts degree, which is primarily a general education degree intended for transfer; Associate in Science degree, a college transfer degree designed especially for students desiring additional career specialization during their first two years of college; Associate in Applied Science degree, which is awarded for the satisfactory completion of an approved two-year preparatory vocational and technical program; the Associate in General Studies Degree, designed for individuals who wish to choose a vocational and technical course of study suited to their unique needs; the diploma, awarded to those individuals who complete an approved program of at least 30 semester hours of credit; the certificate of specialization, awarded for the satisfactory completion of a curriculum in selected areas of study; and the certificate of completion, normally issued at the completion of a specific short-term course of study. **NOTE:** Applications available on the company website. Human Resources phone: 515/964-6301. **Positions advertised include:** Student Activities and Housing Coordinator; Volleyball Coach; Industrial Outreach Specialist; Training Consultant; Counselor; Math Instructor. **President:** David C. England.

DES MOINES REGISTER & TRIBUNE CO.
P.O. Box 957, Des Moines IA 50304. 515/284-8000. **Physical address:** 715 Locust Street, Des Moines IA 50309. **Fax:** 515/286-2526. **Recorded jobline:** 515/284-8437. **Contact:** Sue Decker, Recruiter/Program Manager. **E-mail address:** sdecker@dmreg.com. **World Wide Web address:** http://www.dmregister.com. **Description:** One of the largest regional newspapers in the Midwest publishing three daily editions covering the entire state of Iowa. Founded in 1849. **NOTE:** Apply online through the company Website. **Positions advertised include:** Sales Executive; Inside Account Executive; Outside Account Executive; Advertising Operations Coordinator Supervisor; Circulation Assistant; Route Driver; Financial Analyst; Computer Specialist; Market Research Analyst; Copy Editor; Sports Page Designer; Truck Loader. **Special programs:** Internships. **Other locations:** Statewide. **Parent company:** Gannett Co., Inc.

R.K. DIXON COMPANY
5700 Utica Ridge Road, Davenport IA 52807. 563/344-9100. **Contact:** Human Resources. **E-mail address:** employment@rkdixon.com. **World Wide Web address:** http://www.rkdixon.com. **Description:** Sells and services copiers, fax machines, and filing systems, and installs computer networks for offices. Authorized Canon dealer at some locations. Founded in 1983. **Other area locations:** Dubuque IA. **Other U.S. locations:** Bloomington IL; Peoria IL; Rockford IL; Springfield IL. **Subsidiaries include:** Copy Products Corporation; Network Integration Services. **President:** Bryan Dixon. **Number of employees:** 150.

EMC INSURANCE GROUP, INC.
dba EMC INSURANCE COMPANIES
P.O. Box 712, Des Moines IA 50303. 515/280-2604. **Physical address:** 717 Mulberry Street, Des Moines IA 50309-3872. **Fax:** 515/280-2961. **Recorded jobline:** 515/237-2151. **Contact:** Human Resources. **E-mail addresses:** humanresources@emcins.com. **World Wide Web address:** http://www.emcins.com. **Description:** Provides complete property, casualty, and life insurance mainly in the Midwest with a worldwide reinsurance business marketing and underwriting through several property and casualty subsidiaries and affiliates. Founded in 1911. **Positions advertised include:** Medical Case Manager; Risk Improvement Consultant; Marketing Consultant; Claims Rep Comp.; Underwriter/Assistant Underwriter. **Corporate headquarters location:** This location. **Other U.S. locations:** Nationwide. **Subsidiaries include:** EMCASCO Insurance; Illinois EMCASCO; Dakota Fire Insurance; Farm and City Insurance; EMC Underwriters; EMC Reinsurance; Union Insurance Company of Providence; EMC Property and Casualty; Hamilton Mutual Insurance Company; Employers Modern Life; EMC Risk Service, Inc. **Parent company:** Employers Mutual Casualty. **Operations at this facility include:** Administration; Service. **Listed on:** NASDAQ. **Stock exchange symbol:** EMCI. **Chairman:** George W. Kochheiser. **Number of employees at this location:** 900. **Number of employees nationwide:** 2,000.

EAGLE POINT SOFTWARE CORPORATION
4131 Westmark Drive, Dubuque IA 52002-2627. 563/556-8392. **Toll-free phone:** 800/678-6565. **Fax:** 563/556-5321. **Contact:** Human Resources. **E-mail address:** hr@eaglepoint.com. **World Wide Web address:** http://www.eaglepoint.com. **Description:** Develops integrated software for the architectural, landscaping, civil engineering, and structural marketplaces. Founded in 1983. **Positions advertised include:** Field Business Consultant; Administrative Assistant; Architect; Civil Engineer; Landscape Architect. **Office hours:** Monday - Friday, 8:00 a.m. - 5:00 p.m. **Corporate headquarters location:** This location. **Other U.S. locations:** Church Hill TN. **Subsidiaries include:** Land Development Today Magazine. **Listed on:** Privately held. **President/CEO:** John F. Biver. **Annual sales/revenues:** $17 million. **Number of employees:** 130.

ING US FINANCIAL SERVICES
dba ING EQUITABLE LIFE OF IOWA
909 Locust Street, Des Moines IA 50309. 515/698-7000. **Toll-free phone:** 800/555-1899. **Fax:** 515/698-2005. **Contact:** Human Resources. **E-mail address:** fsius_hr_services@ing-dm.com. **World Wide Web address:** http://www.ing-usa.com. **Description:** Formerly Equitable of Iowa Companies, it is engaged primarily in the sale of individual life insurance policies and annuities. Founded in 1977. **Positions advertised include:** Commissions Coordinator; Financial Communications Specialist; Associate Business Analyst; Policy Services Coordinator; Training Specialist; Licensing Coordinator; Call Center Team Leader; Work Flow Coordinator; Commissions Coordinator; Contact Center Communications Specialist; Commissions Manager; New Business Manager. **Corporate headquarters location:** Atlanta GA. **Parent company:** ING Groep N.V. (Amsterdam, Netherlands). **Subsidiaries include:** Equitable Life Insurance Company of Iowa. **CEO:** Thomas J. McInerney. **Number of employees nationwide:** 10,000.

EXOPACK
1400 Chase Boulevard #2, Box 278, Sibley IA 51249. 712/754-3613. **Fax:** 712/754-4109. **Contact:** Human Resources. **World Wide Web address:** http://www.exopack.com. **Description:** Exopack, formerly International Paper operates in the areas of forest-based products, minerals, land development, chemicals, retail building supplies, and cartons and containers. **Corporate headquarters location:** Spartanburg SC. **Other locations:** AR; GA; PA; WI. **Operations at this location include:** The Chase Bag Plant manufacturing paper bags.

FARM BUREAU FINANCIAL SERVICES
5400 University Avenue, West Des Moines IA 50266. 515/225-5400. **Fax:** 515/226-6053. **Recorded jobline:** 515/225-5627. **Contact:** Human Resources Department. **World Wide Web address:** http://www.fbfs.com. **Description:** Provides life, disability, and property/casualty insurance; annuities; and mutual funds. **Positions advertised include:** Agency Services Manager; Office Assistant; Administrative Assistant; District Claims Manager; Coder; Senior Purchasing Assistant; Claims Clerk; Senior Writer; Bills Claims Representative; Quality Assurance Associate; Director of Communications; Underwriter; Programmer; Claim Representative. **NOTE:** Applicants are requested to complete application online. **Corporate headquarters location:** This location. **Operations at this facility include:** Administration. **Listed on:** New York Stock Exchange. **Stock exchange symbol:** FFG. **Number of employees at this location:** 850. **Number of employees nationwide:** 1,600.

FARMLAND MUTUAL INSURANCE COMPANY
1100 Locust Street, Des Moines IA 50391. 515/245-8800. **Toll-free phone:** 877/256-0382. **Fax:** 515/245-4055. **Recorded jobline:** 515/245-8817. **Contact:** Human Resources. **World Wide Web address:** http://www.farmlandins.com. **Description:** Offers agribusiness, property, and casualty commercial insurance as well as specialty coverage for greenhouse and nursery operations. **Positions advertised include:** Claims Service Representative; Commercial Underwriter; General Utility Clerk; Senior Commercial Underwriter; Underwriter/Assistant Underwriter. **Corporate headquarters location:** This location. **Affiliates include:** Nationwide Agribusiness Insurance Company. **Parent company:** Nationwide Insurance. **Operations at this facility include:** Administration; Sales. **President/COO:** Steve S. Rasmussen.

FEDERAL MOGUL IGNITION PRODUCTS
dba CHAMPION SPARK PLUG COMPANY
3009 Sylvania Drive, Burlington IA 52601. 319/753-5401. **Fax:** 319/753-0682. **Contact:** Human Resources. **World Wide Web address:** http://federal-mogul.com. **Description:** Manufactures spark plugs for automotive OEMs and aftermarket, heavy equipment, and industrial applications. Founded in 1899. **NOTE:** Resumes should be sent to the parent company's corporate address: Corporate Human Resources Staffing, Federal-Mogul Corporation, 26555 Northwestern Highway, Southfield MI 48034. **Positions advertised include:** Manufacturing Engineer; Quality Assurance Representative; Quality Engineer; Inventory Analyst; Purchasing/Materials Analyst; Expediter; **Special programs:** Internships; Coops. **Parent company:** Federal-Mogul Corporation. **Operations at this facility include:** Manufacturing and Distribution of Champion Spark Plugs. **Plant Manager:** Greg Scott.

THE FINLEY HOSPITAL
350 North Grandview Avenue, Dubuque IA 52001. 563/589-2457. **Toll-free phone:** 800/582-1891. **Fax:** 563/557-2846. **Recorded jobline:** 563/557-2841. **Contact:** Kelly Wagner, Employment Coordinator. **E-mail address:** kelli.wagner@finleyhospital.org. **World Wide Web address:** http://www.finleyhospital.org. **Description:** A 158-bed, non-profit, locally owned and controlled, regional hospital serving the tri-state area offering comprehensive health care services. **Positions advertised include:** Certified Nurse Assistant; Mental Health Technician; Nurse Practitioner; Occupational Therapist; Operating Room Technician; Licensed Practical Nurse; Radiographer; Registered Nurse; Speech Language Pathologist; Unit Technician. **Other area locations:** Elkader IA. **Affiliates include:** Cascade Medical Center; Galena Health Clinic; Hazel Green Health Clinic; Home Healthcare; Business Health. **Parent company:** Iowa Health Systems. **President/CEO:** Kevin Rogols. **Number of employees:** 800.

FLEXSTEEL INDUSTRIES, INC.
P.O. Box 877, Dubuque IA 52004-0877. 563/556-7730. **Physical address:** 3400 Jackson Street, Dubuque IA 52001. **Fax:** 563/556-8345. **Contact:** Human Resources. **World Wide Web address:** http://www.flexsteel.com. **Description:** Manufactures and markets upholstered furniture for the retail furniture market and the recreational vehicle field. Products of Flexsteel Industries include a variety of wood and upholstered chairs, rockers, sofas, sofa beds, loveseats, buckets seats, and convertible bedding units for use in offices, homes, vans, and recreational vehicles. **Company slogan:** Furniture to Last a Lifetime. **Positions advertised include:** Accountant; Administrative Assistant; Applications Engineer; AS400 Programmer Analyst; Auditor; Buyer; Chief Financial Officer; Computer Operator; Computer Programmer; Controller; Cost Estimator; Credit Manager; Customer Service Representative; Design Engineer; Draftsperson; General Manager; Human Resources Manager; Industrial Engineer; Manufacturing Engineer; Marketing Manager; Mechanical Engineer; MIS Specialist; Operations Manager; Production Manager; Purchasing Agent/Manager; Quality Control Supervisor; Registered Nurse; Sales Manager; Sales Representative; Secretary. **Corporate headquarters location:** This location. **Other U.S. locations:** Harrison AR; Riverside CA; Dublin GA; Elkhart IN; New Paris IN; Starkville MS; Lancaster PA. **Listed on:** NASDAQ. **Stock exchange symbol:** FLXS. **Chairman:** L. Bruce Boylen. **Annual sales/revenues:** $280 million. **Number of employees at this location:** 800. **Number of employees nationwide:** 2,300.

FORT DODGE ANIMAL HEALTH
800 Fifth Street NW, Fort Dodge IA 50501. 515/955-4600. **Contact:** Staffing Manager. **World Wide Web address:** http://www.wyeth.com. **Description:** Formerly part of the American Home Products Corporation, this division manufactures and distributes prescription and over-the-counter animal health care products distributing to over 100 countries and specializing in veterinary biological vaccines. Founded in 1912. **NOTE:** Inquiries and resumes should be sent to the company headquarters: Staffing Manager, 9401 Indian Creek Parkway, Suite 1500, Overland Park KS 66210, or fax: 913/664-7195. **Corporate headquarters location:** Overland Park KS. **Affiliates include:** Wyeth Pharmaceuticals; Wyeth Research; Wyeth Consumer Healthcare. **Parent company:** Wyeth (Collegeville PA). **Operations at this facility include:** Manufacturing of pharmaceuticals and biological vaccines. **Number of employees at this location:** 450. **Number of employees nationwide:** 1,700. **Number of employees worldwide:** 4,000.

FRIENDSHIP HAVEN, INC.
420 Kenyon Road, Fort Dodge, IA 50501. 515/573-2121. **Toll-free phone:** 800/593-2121. **Fax:** 515/573-6013. **Contact:** Amy Porter, Human Resources Director. **World Wide Web address:** http://www.friendshiphaven.org. **Description:** A nonprofit retirement community offering continuing care ranging from independent living to 24-hour nursing care. Founded in 1950. **NOTE:** Entry-level positions and second and third shifts are offered. Human Resources phone: 515/573-6006. **Company slogan:** A tradition of caring. **Positions advertised include:** Staff Accountant; Certified Nurses Aide; Licensed Practical Nurse; Registered Nurse. **Office hours:** Monday - Friday, 8:00 a.m. - 4:30 p.m. **CEO/President:** Craig Johnsen. **Annual sales/revenues:** Less than $5 million. **Number of employees at this location:** 385.

GAZETTE COMMUNICATIONS, INC.
P.O. Box 511, Cedar Rapids IA 52406. 319/398-8211. **Contact:** Trish Thoms, Employment Manager. **E-mail address:** gazcohr@fyiowa.com. **World Wide Web address:** http://www.gazettecommunications.com. **Description:** A multimedia company with several publications, broadcast outlets, and a software company. *The Gazette* and *The Iowa City Gazette* have daily circulations of 65,500 and 80,000 on Sundays serving eastern Iowa. Publications include *The Penny Saver, The Community News Advertiser, Iowa Farmer Today, Midwest Marketer,* and *Iowa Equipment Today.* The company's new media division operates several Internet Websites, audiotex services and direct marketing services. Affiliates KCRG TV-9 and KCRG SportsRadio broadcast local news. Software development firms Decisionmark and Gazette Technologies provide media-related software products. Founded in 1883. **Positions advertised include:** Reporter; Advertising Business Manager; Classified Outbound/Inbound Media Consultant; Director of Sales; Copywriter; Customer Service Representative. **Corporate headquarters location:** This location. **Parent company:** The Gazette Company. **Number of employees:** 800.

HAPPY JOE'S PIZZA AND ICE CREAM
2705 Happy Joe Drive, Bettendorf IA 52722. 563/332-8811. **Fax:** 563/332-5822. **Contact:** Stacy Drezek, Human Resources. **E-mail address:** staceed@happyjoes.com. **World Wide Web address:** http://www.happyjoes.com. **Description:** A restaurant chain that serves pizza, pasta, and ice cream. **Positions advertised include:** General Manager; Restaurant Worker Positions. **Operations at this facility include:** Administration; Divisional Headquarters; Research and Development. **Number of employees at this location:** 30.

HBOC
700 Locust Street, Suite 500, Dubuque IA 52001. 563/556-3131. **Fax:** 563/557-3951. **Contact:** Human Resources. **World Wide Web address:** http://www.mckesson.com. **Description:** A leading provider of management information systems, related support services, and electronic data interchange services for medical group practices, faculty practice plans, and medical enterprises. **Parent company:** McKesson Information Solutions. **Operations at this facility include:** Administration; Research and Development; Service.

HEARTLAND EXPRESS, INC.
2777 Heartland Drive, Coralville IA 52241. 319/545-2728. **Fax:** 319/545-1349. **Contact:** Human Resources. **E-mail address:** careers@heartlandexpress.com. **World Wide Web address:** http://www.heartlandexpress.com. **Description:** An irregular-route carrier that is authorized to transport general commodities in interstate commerce throughout the 48 contiguous states. **NOTE:** Entry-level positions are offered. Human Resources phone: 800/654-1175. **Positions advertised include:** Professional Driver; Owner Operator; Recruiting Verification Clerk; Safety Data Entry Clerk; MIS Desktop Support; Road Breakdown Coordinator. **Corporate headquarters location:** This location. **Other U.S. locations:** Nationwide. **Operations at this facility include:** Administration; Divisional Headquarters; Regional Headquarters; Sales; Service. **Listed on:** NASDAQ. **Stock exchange symbol:** HTLD. **Chairman/ President/CEO/ Secretary:** Russell A. Gerdin. **Annual sales/revenues:** $341 million. **Number of employees nationwide:** 2,000.

THE HON COMPANY
200 Oak Street, P.O. Box 1109, Muscatine IA 52761. 563/264-7100. **Toll-free phone:** 800/624-9212. **Contact:** Human Resources. **World Wide Web address:** http://www.hon.com. **Description:** A manufacturer of office furniture and related equipment. Founded in 1944. **Positions advertised include:** Industrial Engineer; Mechanical Engineer; Production Manager; Sales Representative; Secretary; Systems Analyst. **Corporate headquarters location:** This location. **Other U.S. locations:** Nationwide. **Parent company:** Hon Industries, Inc. is a diversified manufacturer and marketer of office furniture, work space accessories, and home building products, and is comprised of nine operating companies with offices, showrooms, distribution centers, and manufacturing plants nationwide. Five other operating companies, marketing under various brand names (Gunlocke Company, BPI, and Holga) participate in the office furniture industry. Heatilator, Inc. manufactures and markets factory-built fireplaces, fireplace inserts, heating stoves, and accessories. HON Export Limited markets the corporation's products worldwide. **Operations at this facility include:** Administration. **Number of employees at this location:** 200.

INTEGRATED DNA TECHNOLOGIES, INC.
1710 Commercial Park, Coralville IA 52241. 319/626-8400. **Toll-free phone:** 800/328-2661. **Fax:** 319/626-8444. **Contact:** Heidi Skow, Human Resources Assistant. **E-mail address:** hskow@idtdna.com. **World Wide Web address:** http://www.idtdna.com. **Description:** Integrated DNA Technologies, Inc. researches and supplies oligonucleotide synthesis to biotechnology firms. Since 1987. **NOTE:** For sales positions contact executive offices: IDT, 8930 Gross Point Road, Suite 700, Skokie IL 60077. **Positions advertised include:** Customer Service Representative; Senior Enterprise Applications Specialist; Senior Database Administrator; Senior Technical Writer; Order Administrator; Entry-Level Enterprise Applications Specialist; Patent Technical Assistant; Programmer/Business Analyst. **Corporate headquarters location:** This location. **Operations at this facility include:** Administration; Research and Development.

INTERMEC TECHNOLOGIES CORPORATION
550 Second Street SE, Cedar Rapids IA 52401. 319/369-3100. **Fax:** 319/369-3453. **Contact:** Human Resources. **World Wide Web address:** http://www.intermec.com. **Description:** Manufactures and markets portable, computerized data collection systems and hand-held radio frequency terminals used in a wide range of applications including route accounting, inventory management, and warehouse data management. These systems are used by companies to improve accountability, productivity, and management control. The company's testing laboratories are in Fairfax IA with Sales and Service at this facility. **Positions advertised include:** Logistics Industry Marketing Director; Technical Trainer; Developer; Senior Developer; Software Engineer; Applications Programmer; Administrative Manager; Research Analyst; Engineer. **Corporate headquarters location:** Everett WA. **Parent company:** UNOVA. **Operations at this facility include:** Administration; Manufacturing; Research and Development; Sales; Service. **President/CEO:** Larry Brady. **Annual sales/revenues:** $655 million. **Number of employees nationwide:** 2,700.

INTERSTATE BRANDS CORPORATION
P.O. Box 3989, Davenport IA 52808. 563/323-3647. **Physical address:** 1034 East River Drive, Davenport IA 52803. **Fax:** 563/323-6309. **Contact:** Human Resources. **World Wide Web address:** http://wonderbread.com. **Description:** A wholesale bakery that produces Wonder Bread and Hostess snack cakes. The bakery in Waterloo IA produces Wonder Bread. **Corporate headquarters location:** Kansas City MO. **Other area locations:** Waterloo IA. **Other U.S. locations:** Nationwide. **Listed on:** New York Stock Exchange. **Stock exchange symbol:** IBC. **Chairman:** Charles A. Sullivan. **Annual sales/revenues:** $3.5 billion. **Number of employees nationwide:** 34,000.

IOWA FOUNDATION FOR MEDICAL CARE INFORMATION SYSTEMS
6000 Westown Parkway, Suite 350E, West Des Moines IA 50266-7771. 515/223-2900. **Fax:** 515/453-8118. **Contact:** Ronna Pochter, Vice President. **E-mail address:** rpochter@ifmc.org. **World Wide Web address:** http://www.ifmc.org. **Description:** IFMC seeks to optimize the quality of medical care and health through collaborative relationships, education, and health information management. IFMC employs more than 500 people in seven offices throughout the United States. **Positions advertised include:** Coordinator, Review; Coordinator, Review Medical Support; Coordinator, Review Disease Management; Coordinator, Review Enhanced Primary Care Case Management; Manager, Government; Assistant, Review II.

IOWA, STATE OF
IOWA DEPARTMENT OF PERSONNEL
Grimes State Office Building, 400 East 14th Street, Des Moines IA 50319-0150. 515/281-3087. **Fax:** 515/281-7970. **Contact:** Human Resources. **World Wide Web address:** http://www.state.ia.us/government/idop. **Description:** The Iowa Department of Personnel serves as a Central Personnel Department for the Executive Branch of the

state government, consisting of 35 departments or divisions of departments. **Positions advertised include:** Clerk Specialist; Receptionist; Word Processor; Senior Correctional Officer; Correctional Supervisor; Correctional Counselor; Workforce Associate; Executive Officer; Management Analyst; Registered Nurse; Social Worker; Income Maintenance Worker; Child Support Recovery Officer; Motor Vehicles Officer; Soil Conservation Technician; Environmental Engineer; Natural Resources Biologist; Power Plant Engineer; Plant Operations Manager; Military Aircraft Crew Chief; Information Technology Specialist; Equipment Operator; Design Technician Associate. **Special programs:** Internships. **Office hours:** Monday - Friday, 8:00 a.m. - 4:30 p.m. **Number of employees at this location:** 18,750.

IOWA STATE UNIVERSITY
Recruitment and Employment Office, 3810 Beardshear Hall, Ames IA 50011-2033. 515/294-2936. **Contact:** Human Resources Services. **World Wide Web address:** http://www.iastate.edu/jobs. **Description:** A four-year university offering bachelor's, master's (including MBA), and doctoral degrees. Approximately 24,000 students attend Iowa State University. **NOTE:** Applicants must apply online at http://www.iastatejobs.com. **Positions advertised include:** Education Lecturer; Sociology Lecturer; Veterinary Microbiology Assistant Professor; Zoology & Microbiology Lecturer; Administrative Specialist; Program Coordinator; Biomedical Research Associate; Kitchen Helper; Athletic Equipment Manager; Post-Doctoral Botany Researcher. **President:** Gregory L. Geoffroy. **Annual revenues:** $743 million. **Number of employees:** 6,157.

JOHN DEERE POWER SYSTEMS & ENGINE WORKS
3801 West Ridgeway Avenue, Waterloo IA 50704-5100. 319/292-5643. **Fax:** 319/292-5075. **Contact:** Human Resources. **World Wide Web address:** http://www.deere.com. **Description:** Manufactures farm and construction equipment, as well as industrial, forestry, and lawn-care equipment specializing in tractors, tillers, harvesting machinery, soil-preparation machinery, backhoes, and excavators. Deere also produces diesel engines, drivetrain parts, chain saws, leaf and snow blowers. Founded in 1837. **NOTE:** The company prefers resumes to be submitted online through their Website. **Company slogan:** Nothing Runs Like a Deere. **Positions advertised include:** Test Engineer; Electrical Systems Engineer; Senior Engineer; Engineer; Software Engineer; Design Engineer; Supervisor; Advanced Engineering Analyst; Industrial Maintenance Engineer. **Special programs:** Internships. **Corporate headquarters location:** Moline IL. **Other area locations:** Cedar Falls IA; Davenport IA; Des Moines IA; Dubuque IA; Johnston IA; Ottumwa IA. **Other U.S. locations:** Nationwide. **International locations:** Worldwide. **Parent company:** Deere & Company. **Listed on:** New York Stock Exchange. **Stock exchange symbol:** DE. **Chairman/President/CEO:** Robert W. Lane. **Annual sales/revenues:** $13.9 billion. **Number of employees worldwide:** 43,000.

KEANE, INC.
383 Collins Road NE, Cedar Rapids IA 52402. 319/393-3343. **Fax:** 319/378-1342. **Contact:** Human Resources. **World Wide Web address:** http://www.keane.com. **Description:** Keane offers businesses a variety of computer consulting services and also assists in project management. Founded in 1965. **Corporate headquarters location:** Boston MA. **Other U.S. locations:** Nationwide. **Operations at this facility include:** Design, development, and managing of software for corporations and health care facilities. **Listed on:** American Stock Exchange. **Stock exchange symbol:** KEA. **Chairman:** John F. Keane, Sr. **Annual sales/revenues:** $873 million. **Number of employees nationwide:** 7,800.

KEMIN INDUSTRIES
2100 Maury Street, Des Moines IA 50317-1110. 515/559-5100. **Fax:** 515/559-5232. **Toll-free phone:** 800/777-8307. **Contact:** Human Resources. **E-mail address:** jobs@kemin.com. **World Wide Web address:** http://www.kemin.com. **NOTE:** Fill out online application. **Description:** A nutritional ingredient manufacturer. **Corporate headquarters location:** This location. **International locations:** Worldwide.

LEE ENTERPRISES
201 North Harrison Street, Suite 600, Davenport IA 52801-1924. 563/383-2100. **Fax:** 563/328-4331. **Contact:** Vytenis P. Kuraitis, Vice President, Human Resources. **E-mail address:** jobs@lee.net. **World Wide Web address:** http://www.lee.net. **Description:** A media publishing company with interests in 45 daily newspapers and over 175 weekly, shoppers, and specialty publications concentrated in Midwestern and Northwestern markets. This location houses administrative offices and the *Quad-City Times* is also published in Davenport IA. Founded in 1890. **NOTE:** Entry-level positions are offered. **Positions advertised include:** Benefits Manager; Executive Assistant; Financial Analyst; Human Resources Coordinator; Managing Editor; Outbound Sales Manager; Retail Advertising Sales Representative; Sports Reporter; Reporter. **Corporate headquarters location:** This location. **Other area locations:** Mason City IA; Muscatine IA; Sioux City IA; Waterloo/Cedar Falls IA. **Other U.S. locations:** Nationwide. **Subsidiaries/Affiliates include:** La Cross Tribune Online; *Lincoln Journal Star;* Madison Newspapers; *Mason City Globe Gazette; Racine Journal Times; The Bismarck Tribune.* **Listed on:** New York Stock Exchange. **Stock exchange symbol:** LEE. **Annual sales/revenues:** $460 million. **Number of employees nationwide:** 6,700.

LENNOX INDUSTRIES INC.
P.O. Box 250, Marshalltown IA 50158-0250. 641/754-4011. **Fax:** 515/754-4214. **Contact:** Human Resources. **E-mail address:** employment. services@lennoxind.com. **World Wide Web address:** http://www.lennox.com. **Description:** Lennox Industries, manufacturer of heating, ventilation, air conditioning, and refrigeration, is a subsidiary of Lennox International Inc., which has operations in over 70 countries. **Positions advertised include:** Department Manager; Draftsperson; Electrician; Heating/AC/Refrigeration Technician; Machinist; Mechanical Engineer; Precision Assembler; Quality Control Supervisor; Secretary; Tool and Die Maker; Welder. **Corporate headquarters location:** This location. **Parent company:** Lennox International Inc. **Operations at this facility include:** Manufacturing. **Number of employees at this location:** 1,050.

MCI
102 Sergeant Square Drive, Sergeant Bluff IA 51054. 712/943-1000. **Contact:** Human Resources. **World Wide Web address:** http://www.mci.com. **Description:** One of the world's largest suppliers of local, long distance, and international telecommunications services, and a global Internet service provider. **NOTE:** Search and apply for positions online. **Corporate headquarters location:** Ashburn VA. **Other area locations:** Cedar Rapids IA. **Other U.S. locations:** Nationwide. **Subsidiaries/Affiliates include:** SkyTel Communications, Inc. **Parent company:** MCI, Inc. **Listed on:** NASDAQ. **Stock exchange symbol:** MCIP.

MARSHALL ENGINEERED PRODUCTS CO. LLC
dba MEPCO
811 East Main Street, Marshalltown IA 50158. 641/752-4291. **Toll-free phone:** 888/853-7350. **Fax:** 641/753-0496. **Contact:** Dick White, Human Resources. **World Wide Web address:** http://www.mepcollc.com. **Description:** A manufacturer of commercial steam and hot water heating system components and centrifugal pumps. Founded in 1903. **Positions advertised include:** Engineer; Draftsperson; Electrical/Electronics Engineer; Industrial Engineer; Manufacturing Engineer; Mechanical Engineer; Operations/Production Manager; Project Manager; Quality Control Supervisor. **Corporate headquarters location:** This location. **Other U.S. locations:** Nationwide. **International locations:** Worldwide. **Operations at this facility include:** Manufacturing; Sales; Service. **Listed on:** Privately held. **Number of employees at this location:** 105.

MARSHALLTOWN MEDICAL & SURGICAL CENTER
3 South Fourth Avenue, Marshalltown IA 50158. 641/754-5113. **Fax:** 641/753-2570. **Recorded jobline:** 641/754-5339. **Contact:** Human Resources. **World Wide Web address**: http://www.everydaychampions.org. **Description:** A 176-bed, acute care medical center with a rehabilitation and sports medicine facility. **Positions advertised include:** Emergency Department Assistant; Interpreter; Phlebotomist; Medical Registered Nurse; Surgical Registered Nurse; Pediatric Registered Nurse; Respiratory Therapist; Staff Radiographer; Operating Room Surgical Technologist; Physician Assistant. **Number of employees:** 700.

MAYTAG CORPORATION
403 West Fourth Street North, P.O. Box 39, Newton IA 50208. 641/792-8000. **Fax:** 641/787-6209. **Contact:** Mark W. Krivoruchka, Human Resources. **World Wide Web address:** http://www.maytagcorp.com. **Description:** Global manufacturer of home appliances: washers, dryers, dishwashers, refrigerators, and cooking appliances. Name brands include: Maytag, Jenn-Air, Magic Chef, Admiral, Hoover vacuums, and soda machines for Coca Cola and Pepsi. Operates network of retailers, dealers, and distributors. **NOTE:** Online application available on the company Website. **Positions advertised include:** Product Manager; Senior Supply Team Leader-Metals Commodity; Income Tax Manager; Indirect Materials and Services Sourcing Manager; Accountant; Design Engineer; Mechanical Engineer; Sales Representative. **Corporate headquarters location:** This location. **Subsidiaries include:** Dixie-Narco, Inc.; G.S. Blodgett Corp.; Maytag Appliances; Maytag International; The Hoover Company; Dysastyn Range; Jenn-Air; Amana. **Listed on:** New York Stock Exchange. **Stock exchange symbol:** MYG. **Annual sales/revenues:** $4.7 billion. **Chairman/CEO:** Ralph F. Hake. **Number of employees at this location:** 3,000. **Number of employees nationwide:** 21,000.

A.Y. McDONALD MANUFACTURING COMPANY
P.O. Box 508, Dubuque IA 52004-0508. 563/583-7311. **Physical address:** 4800 Chavenelle Road, Dubuque IA 52002. **Fax:** 888/840-2438. **Contact:** Chad A Huntington, Human Resource Director. **E-mail address:** hr@aymcdonald.com. **World Wide Web address:** http://www.aymcdonald.com. **Description:** Manufactures water service valves and fittings, gas valves, pumps, water systems for domestic and commercial applications, plumbing and industrial valves, and petroleum equipment. Products are made of brass, cast iron, aluminum, stainless steel, and plastic. The company sells and distributes its five major product lines nationally and internationally. Founded in 1856. **Positions advertised include:** Electrician; Manufacturer's/ Wholesaler's Sales Representative; Operations/ Production Manager. **Corporate headquarters location:** This location. **Other area locations:** Albia IA. **Other U.S. locations:** Elizabethton TN; Sparks NV. **Subsidiaries include:** A.Y.M. Inc. **Operations at this facility include:** Corporate administration; Brass Foundry; Main Manufacturing Plant. **Listed on:** Privately held. **Number of employees at this location:** 270. **Number of employees nationwide:** 350.

McGRAW-HILL COMPANY
2460 Kerper Boulevard, Dubuque IA 52001. 563/588-1451. **Contact:** Human Resources. **World Wide Web address:** http://www.mcgraw-hill.com. **Description:** McGraw-Hill is a provider of information and services through books, magazines, newsletters, software, CD-ROMs, and online data, fax, and TV broadcasting services. The company operates four network-affiliated TV stations and also publishes *Business Week* magazine and books for the college, medical, international, legal, and professional markets. McGraw-Hill also offers financial services including Standard & Poor's, commodity items, and international and logistics management products and services. Founded in 1888. **NOTE:** Post resumes and complete applications online or send to: The McGraw-Hill Companies, Human Resources Service Center, Resume Scanning Center, 148 Princeton-Heightstown Road, Hightstown, NJ 08520-1450. **Positions advertised include:** Design Manager; Software Tester. **Corporate headquarters location:** New York NY. **Other area locations:** West Des Moines IA. **Operations at this facility include:** Administration; Divisional Headquarters; Manufacturing; Sales. **Listed on:** New York Stock Exchange. **Stock exchange symbol:** MHP. **Chairman/President/CEO:** Harold W. (Terry) McGraw III. **Annual sales/revenues:** $4.8 billion. **Number of employees nationwide:** 16,500.

MEDICAL INDUSTRIES AMERICA INC.
2636 289th Place, Adel IA 50003-8021. 515/993-5001. **Fax:** 515/993-4172. **Contact:** Human Resources. **World Wide Web address:** http://www.medindustries.com. **Description:** Manufactures and distributes a line of home respiratory care equipment.

MERCY HOSPITAL MEDICAL CENTER
11116 Sixth Avenue, Des Moines IA 50314. 515/247-3121. **Fax:** 515/643-8831. **Contact:** Human Resources. **World Wide Web address:** http://www.mercydesmoines.org. **Description:** A 917-bed hospital. **Positions advertised include:** Obstetrician; Allied Health Administrator; Pharmacist; Interpreter/Translator; Clinic Supervisor; Medical Records Supervisor; Physical Therapist; Primary Counselor; Nuclear Medicine Technician; Cytotechnologist; Radiology Technologist; Respiratory Therapist; Surgical Technician; Coder; Certified Medical Assistant. **Corporate headquarters location:** Omaha NE. **Parent company:** Catholic Health Corporation. **Listed on:** Privately held.

MERCY MEDICAL CENTER
801 Fifth Street, Sioux City IA 51102. 712/279-2010. **Fax:** 712/279-5624. **Contact:** Patricia Rodriguez, Recruiter. **E-mail address:** mercysiouxcity@mercyhealth.com. **World Wide Web address:** http://www.mercysiouxcity.com. **Description:** A nonprofit, regional medical center. Mercy Medical Center serves as the state-designated trauma center for the region and provides a vital lifesaving link to rural areas via the hospital's helicopter ambulance service. Mercy Medical also provides a full range of comprehensive medical services including balloon angioplasty, atherectomy, full diagnostic capabilities, and open-heart surgery. **Positions advertised include:** Central Processing Technician; Certified Surgical Technologist; Certified Nursing Assistant; Customer Service Technician; Maintenance Worker; Medical Assistant; Medical Records Clerk; Medical Technologist; Medical Transcriptionist; Pharmacy Intern; Physical Therapist; Physical Therapy Assistant; Registered Nurse; Licensed Practical Nurse; Speech Pathologist; Staff Pharmacist. **NOTE:** Human Resources phone: 712/279-5921.

MEREDITH CORPORATION
1716 Locust Street, Des Moines IA 50309. 515/284-3000. **Fax:** 515/284-2958. **Contact:** Kandis Bock, Employment Opportunities Manager. **Recorded jobline:** 888/424-2562. **World Wide Web address:** http://www.meredith.com. **Description:** Meredith publishes books and magazines, operates cable TV systems, owns television stations, and has real estate interests. The company produces 15 magazines including *Better Homes & Gardens, Country Home, WOOD, Golf for Women,* and *Ladies' Home Journal;* publishes 47 special interest publications on topics including home improvement, crafts, decorating, food, garden care, and family affairs; and produces 175 home and family service books. Meredith also owns five TV stations in Nevada, Missouri, Arizona, Michigan, and Florida, and two cable systems. The company also operates national real estate marketing services. **Positions advertised include:** Application Developer; Art Director; Associate Art Director; Associate Design Director; Billing Specialist; Business Manager; Business Office Assistant; Category Management Analyst; Consumer Products Marketing Director; Corporate Auditor; Interior Design Head; Food & Entertaining Editor; Garden Editor; Senior Garden Editor; Graphic Designer; Senior Account Manager; Senior Corporate Auditor; Paint Decoration Senior Editor; Building & Remodeling Senior Editor; Decorating Senior Editor; Senior Graphic Designer; Senior Designer; Senior System Administrator; Senior Business Manager. **NOTE:** Human Resources phone: 515/284-2211. **Other U.S. locations:** New York NY; Chicago IL. **Listed on:** New York Stock Exchange. **Stock exchange symbol:** MDP. **Chairman/CEO:** William T. Kerr. **Annual sales/revenues:** $989 million. **Number of employees nationwide:** 2,570.

METROPOLITAN MEDICAL CENTER
603 East 12th Street, Des Moines IA 50309. 515/263-5200. **Contact:** Human Resources. **World Wide Web address:** http://www.metmedical.com. **Description:** A nonprofit hospital offering a complete range of health care services including inpatient and outpatient surgical services, rehabilitation services, Gateway (centers for both inpatient and outpatient treatment of addictions), Connections (mental health care for adults 55 and older), obstetrical services, One Call Information Services, Des Moines General Family Practice Clinics, skilled nursing services, home health services, neurological services, inpatient and outpatient cardiac diagnostic and rehabilitation services, diagnostic imaging services, critical care services, and emergency services. **NOTE:** Human Resources phone: 515/263-4845.

MICROFRONTIER, INC.
P.O. Box 269, Winterset, IA 50237. 515/462-5930. **Contact:** Human Resources. **World Wide Web address:** http://www.microfrontier.com. **Description:** Develops graphic arts software. Founded in 1987. **NOTE:** Entry-level positions are offered. **Positions advertised include:** Computer Programmer; Marketing Specialist; Sales Representative; Software Engineer. **Number of employees at this location:** 15.

MIDAMERICAN ENERGY HOLDINGS COMPANY
666 Grand Avenue, P.O. Box 657, Des Moines IA 50303. 515/281-4300. **Fax:** 515/281-2389. **Recorded jobline:** 888/257-1369. **Contact:** Human Resources. **E-mail address:** employment@midamerican.com. **World Wide Web address:** http://www.midamerican.com. **Description:** One of Iowa's largest energy companies. MidAmerican provides electric and natural gas service in a 10,600 square-mile area with a population of 1.7 million. The service area includes much of Iowa and portions of Illinois, Nebraska, and South Dakota. MidAmerican provides service to 648,000 electric customers and 619,000 natural gas customers. **Positions advertised include:** Business Systems Analyst; Environmental Compliance Manager; Senior Customer Office Analyst; Senior Environmental Coordinator; Service Supervisor; Administrative Specialist; Journeyman; Garage Mechanic. **Special programs:** Internships. **Internship information:** The company offers some 20 summer engineering internships. **Corporate headquarters location:** This location. **Other area locations:** Statewide. **Other U.S. locations:** Omaha NE; Salt Lake City UT; Edina MN. **International locations:** Newcastle on Tyne, England. **Subsidiaries include:** HomeServices of America, Inc.; Northern Natural Gas Company; Northern and Yorkshire Electric; CalEnergy; Kern River Gas Transmission Company. **Operations at this facility include:** Administration. **Listed on:** Privately held. **Chairman/CEO:** David L. Sokol. **Annual sales/revenues:** $5.3 billion. **Number of employees:** 9,780.

JOHN MORRELL & COMPANY
1200 Bluff Road, Sioux City IA 51107. 712/279-7398. **Fax:** 712/279-7342. **Contact:** Steve Joyce, Human Resources. **World Wide Web address:** http://www.johnmorrell.com. **Description:** Fresh pork producer and meat processor producing and distributing through its four subsidiaries under 13 regional brands which include: Dinner Bell; Rath; John Morrell; Preyton's; Hunter; Kretschmar; E-Z-Cut; Rodeo; Shenson; Tobin's First Prize; Farmers Hickory Brand; and Iowa Quality. Founded in 1827. **NOTE:** Contact address for the company's Human Resources office is: Aggie Carlson, 1400 North Weber Avenue, Sioux Falls SD 57103. **Corporate headquarters location:** Cincinnati OH. **Other area locations:** Clive IA; Des Moines IA. **Other U.S. locations:** Nationwide. **Subsidiaries include:** Curly's Foods; Mohawk Packaging; Saratoga Specialties; Iowa Quality Meats. **Parent company:** Smithfield Foods, Inc. (Smithfield VA). **Operations at this facility include:** Both the Sioux City and Des Moines slaughterhouses produce Cooked Meats and Foodservice Specialty Items.

MOUNT ARBOR NURSERIES
201 East Ferguson, P.O. Box 129, Shenandoah IA 51601. 712/246-4250. **Fax:** 712/246-1841. **Contact:** Human Resources. **Description:** A grower and wholesaler of nursery stock. **Positions advertised include:** Supervisor; Customer Service Representative.

PAUL MUELLER COMPANY
P.O. Box 320, Osceola IA 50213. 641/342-6531. **Physical address:** 1000 Tieken Drive, Osceola IA. **Fax:** 417/575-9669. **Contact:** Human Resources. **E-mail address:** personnel@muel.com. **World Wide Web address:** http://www.paulmueller.com. **Description:** Paul Mueller Company specializes in the manufacture of stainless steel tanks and industrial processing equipment. Products include dairy farm equipment; food, dairy, meat and poultry processing equipment; beer, wine and beverage equipment; chemical and pharmaceutical equipment; industrial heat transfer equipment; thermal energy storage equipment; and water distilling/pure steam equipment. Founded in 1940. **Positions advertised include:** Project Manager; Craftsman; Fabricator; Sales Manager; Heat Transfer Engineer; Process Engineer. **Corporate headquarters location:** Springfield MO. **Subsidiaries include:** Mueller International Sales Corporation. **Listed on:** NASDAQ. **Stock exchange symbol:** MUEL. **Chairman:** Paul Mueller. **Annual sales/revenues:** $114 million. **Number of employees at this location:** 100. **Number of employees nationwide:** 1,000.

NCMIC GROUP INC.
14001 University Avenue, Clive IA 50325. 515/222-1736. **Toll-free phone:** 800/769-2000. **Fax:** 515/313-4479. **Contact:** Liz Patfield. Human Resources. **World Wide Web address:** http://www.nfcfinance.com/nfc. **Description:** A direct writer of chiropractic malpractice insurance. **Positions advertised include:** Adjuster; Claim Representative; Customer Service Representative; Underwriter/Assistant Underwriter.

NEWLINK GENETICS CORPORATION
2901 South Loop Drive, Suite 3900, Ames IA 50010. 515/296-5555. **Fax:** 515/296-5557. **Contact:** Shelley Kinnear. **E-mail address:** skinnear@linkp.com. **World Wide Web address:** http://www.newlinkgenetics.com. **Description:** A biopharmaceutical company that works to produce diagnostic and therapeutic agents to improve the lives of cancer patients.

NORPLEX
665 Lybrand Street, Postville IA 52162-0977. 563/864-7321. **Fax:** 563/864-4231. **Contact:** Human Resources. **World Wide Web address:** http://www.ilnorplex.com. **Description:** Manufactures copper clad and unclad plastic laminates that are used in a broad range of industries including automotive, electrical, electronic, and structural. **Corporate headquarters location:** Morristown NJ.

NOVARTIS ANIMAL HEALTH US INC.
1447 140th Street, Larchwood IA 51241. 712/477-2811. **Contact:** Human Resources. **World Wide Web address:** http://www.livestock.novartis.com. **Description:** A division of Novartis that focuses on the research and development of vaccines for livestock.

PAXTON & VIERLING STEEL COMPANY
501 Avenue H, Carter Lake IA 51510. 712/347-5500. **Contact:** Human Resources. **E-mail address:** hrpvx@pvsteel.com. **World Wide Web address:** http://www.pvsteel.com. **Description:** Engaged in in-plant steel fabrication for buildings, bridges, and industry and the sale of steel products to manufacturers, contractors, and other steel users. Paxton & Vierling is also engaged in tool steel sales. Founded in 1885. **NOTE:** Resumes should be sent to Human Resources, P.O. Box 1085, Omaha NE 68101. **Positions advertised include:** Laborer; Welder; Draftsperson. **Corporate headquarters location:** Omaha NE. **Parent company:** Owen Industries, Inc.

PELLA CORPORATION
102 Main Street, Pella IA 50219. 641/621-6040. **Fax:** 641/621-6976. **Contact:** Human Resources. **World Wide Web address:** http://www.pella.com. **Description:** A leading manufacturer of windows and doors. **Corporate headquarters location:** This location.

PHARMACOM CORPORATION
100 Oakdale Campus, Iowa City IA 52242. 319/335-4771. **Fax:** 319/335-4482. **Contact:** Human Resources. **E-mail address:** hr@pharmacom.us. **World Wide Web address:** http://www.pharmacom.us. **Description:** Develops lab-on-a-chip technology. **NOTE:** Apply online. **Positions advertised include:** Research Scientist; Nanotechnologists; Software Developers; Bioinformatics Scientists; Lab Technicians.

PHYTODYNE INC.
2711 South Loop Drive, Building 4, Suite 4400, Ames IA 50010. 515/296-5513. **Fax:** 515/296-5583. **Contact:** Human Resources. **E-mail address:** leafstedt@phytodyne-inc.com. **World Wide Web address:** http://www.phytodyne-inc.com. **Description:** A leader in the development and commercialization of advanced biotech crop improvement through genome modification.

PIONEER HI-BRED INTERNATIONAL, INC.
400 Locust Street, Suite 800, Des Moines IA 50309. 515/248-4800. **Toll-free phone:** 800/247-6803 ext.4000. **Fax:** 515/248-4999. **Recorded jobline:** 515/270-4000, or 800/247-6803x4000. **Contact:** Pat Sabine, Human Resources. **E-mail address:** apply@pioneer.com. **World Wide Web address:** http://www.pioneer.com. **Description:** A biotechnology company and the largest soybean seed and corn producer, the company genetically engineers high-yield hybrid seeds for farmers growing animal feeds. The company manufactures seeds for alfalfa, canola, sorghum, sunflowers, wheat, silage and hay inoculants. Founded in 1926. **NOTE:** Entry-level positions and part-time jobs are offered. E-mail address for employment inquiries: jobs@pioneer.com. E-mail address for sending resumes: apply@pioneer.com. **Positions advertised include:** Administrative Assistant; Postdoctoral Researcher; Human Resource Director; Human Resource Manager; Laboratory Technician; Market Research Analyst; Production Technician; Public Relations Coordinator; Purchasing Operations Manager; Research Associate; Research Coordinator; Research Scientist; Security Officer; Senior Application Developer. **Special programs:** Internships. **Corporate headquarters location:** This location. **International locations:** Worldwide. **Parent company:** Dupont. **President:** Richard L. (Rick) McConnell. **Annual sales/revenues:** $2 billion. **Number of employees:** 5,000.

PRINCIPAL FINANCIAL GROUP, INC.
711 High Street, Des Moines IA 50392-0001. 515/247-5111. **Toll-free phone:** 800/986-3343. **Fax:** 515/246-5475. **Contact:** Human Resources. **World Wide Web address:** http://www.principal.com. **Description:** Provides financial services including annuities, home mortgages, mutual funds, and retirement plans. The Principal Financial Group also offers dental, disability, health, life, and vision insurance policies. **Positions advertised include:** Retirement Resource Consultant; Underwriting Director; Coordinator; International Human Resources Associate; New Business Case Specialist; Marketing Consultant; Customer Service Assistant; Investment Accountant; Product Development Manager; Asset Management Representative; Human Resource Officer; Financial Accountant; Associate Technician Consultant; Senior Product Manager; Sales Support Leader; Underwriter; Communications Specialist. **NOTE:** Human Resources phone: 515/248-3476. **Corporate headquarters location:** This location. **Subsidiaries include:** Principal Bank; Principal Capital; Principal Life Insurance Company; Principal Residential Mortgage, Inc. **Listed on:** New York Stock Exchange. **Stock exchange symbol:** PFG. **Chairman/President/CEO:** J. Barry Griswell. **Annual sales/revenues:** $9.2 billion. **Number of employees:** 17,600.

QUAD-CITY TIMES
P.O. Box 3828, Davenport IA 52808. 563/383-2200. **Physical address:** 500 East Third Street, Davenport IA 52804. **Contact:** Jill DeKaiser, Human Resources. **World Wide Web address:** http://www.qctimes.com. **Description:** Publishes a daily newspaper with a circulation of 56,000 daily and more than 87,000 on Sunday. Founded in 1878. **Positions advertised include:** Advertising Clerk; Commercial Artist; Editor; Reporter. **Corporate headquarters location:** Davenport IA. **Other U.S. locations:** AZ; IL; MT; NM; OR; WI. **Parent company:** Lee Enterprises, Inc. **Operations at this facility include:** Divisional Headquarters. **Number of employees at this location:** 400.

QUAKER FOODS & BEVERAGES
418 Second Street NE, P.O. Box 1848, Cedar Rapids IA 52406-5668. 319/362-3121. **Fax:** 319/298-1728. **Contact:** Human Resources. **World Wide Web address:** http://www.quakeroats.com. **Description:** Manufacturer and marketer of premium consumer grocery products specializing in cereal and grain products. **NOTE:** Information on current open positions is posted on the parent company's Website, the

PepsiCo Career Center: http://www.pepsicojobs.com. **Positions advertised include:** Ready to Eat Cereals Supervisor; Senior Project Engineer; Quality Control Specialist. **Corporate headquarters location:** Chicago IL. **Parent company:** PepsiCo, Inc. **Operations at this facility include:** Cedar Rapids cereal milling plant.

RSM McGLADREY, INC.
212 North Brady Street, 2nd Floor, Davenport IA 52801. 563/324-0447. **Fax:** 563/324-0211. **Contact:** Human Resources. **E-mail address:** careers@rsmi.com. **World Wide Web address:** http://www.rsmmcgladrey.com. **Description:** One of the largest accounting and consulting firms in the United States with 70 offices from coast to coast. Clients range from large, publicly held corporations to small organizations and individuals. Services rendered include auditing services, tax consulting services, and managerial and operational consulting. **NOTE:** Apply for positions online. Though they are separate companies, RSM McGladrey, Inc. and McGladrey & Pullen, LLP are affiliated through an alternative practice structure. Audit positions are with McGladrey & Pullen, however, RSM McGladrey performs recruiting services for McGladrey & Pullen through a service agreement. **Positions advertised include:** Accountant; Financial Institution Consultant; Global Systems Administrator; Network Consultant; Network Senior Consultant; Payroll Administrator; Public Accountant; Quality Assurance Analyst; SALT Consulting Analyst; Senior Tax Accountant; Supervisor; Tax Manager. **Parent company:** H&R Block. **Corporate headquarters location:** Bloomington MN. **Other area locations:** Burlington IA; Cedar Rapids IA; Des Moines IA; Dubuque IA; Iowa City IA; Waterloo IA. **Other U.S. locations:** Nationwide. **International locations:** Worldwide. **President/CEO:** Tom Rotherham. **Number of employees:** 4,400

RADISYS CORPORATION
1240 Office Plaza Drive, W. Des Moines IA 50266. 515/223-8000. **Fax:** 515/327-2484. **Contact:** Human Resources. **World Wide Web address:** http://www.radisys.com. **Description:** Develops embedded systems software for a wide range of applications including development of the OS-9 real-time operating system, Intel IXP 1200 Network Processor solutions, the Microcode Solutions Library, and consulting services projects. **Corporate headquarters location:** Hillsboro OR. **Other U.S. locations:** Boca Raton FL; Charlotte NC; Cheshire CT; Cranbury and Mount Laurel NJ; Flower Mound TX; Marlboro MA; San Diego CA. **International locations:** Worldwide. **Operations at this facility include:** This site serves as the headquarters for RadiSys' Microwave Software, part of the Communications Software Division. **Listed on:** NASDAQ. **Stock exchange symbol:** RSYS. **Chairman:** C. Scott Gibson. **Annual sales/revenues:** $200 million. **Number of employees:** 818.

RACING CHAMPIONS ERTL, CORP.
P.O. Box 500, Highways 136 and 20, Dyersville IA 52040-0500. 563/875-2000. **Fax:** 563/875-5658. **Contact:** Human Resources. **World Wide Web address:** http://www.ertltoys.com. **Description:** An international toy manufacturer. **Positions advertised include:** Ceramics Engineer; Computer Programmer; Customer Service Representative; Designer; Draftsperson; Industrial Engineer; Mechanical Engineer; Operations/Production Manager; Software Engineer; Systems Analyst. **Corporate headquarters location:** Glen Ellyn IL. **Subsidiaries include:** Die Cast Express. **Operations at this facility include:** Manufacturing; Research and Development; Sales; Service. **Listed on:** NASDAQ. **Stock exchange symbol:** RACN. **Chairman:** Robert E. (Bob) Dods. **Annual sales/revenues:** $214 million. **Number of employees at this location:** 1,100. **Number of employees worldwide:** 2,500.

ROCKWELL COLLINS, INC.
400 Collins Road NE, Cedar Rapids IA 52498. 319/295-1000. **Fax:** 319/295-5429. **Contact:** Human Resources. **World Wide Web address:** http://www.rockwellcollins.com. **Description:** Operates two divisions, Collins Air Transport Division and Collins General Aviation Division, which provide aviation electronics products, systems, and services to commercial, business, and general aviation aircraft markets worldwide. Overall, Rockwell Collins is an international company providing aviation electronics for global aircraft manufacturers and over 400 airline companies and militaries. **NOTE:** Applicants are requested to post resumes and apply on the company Website. **Positions advertised include:** Satellite Computer Operator; Lead Information Systems Auditor; Media Relations Manager; Mechanical Engineer; Principal Electrical Engineer; Principal Engineering Manager; Principal Marketing Manager; Principal Systems Engineer; Programmer Analyst; Senior Business Integration Analyst; Senior Electrical Engineer; Senior Product Integrity Engineer; Senior Software Engineer; Senior Subcontract Administrator; Senior Systems Engineer; Senior Writer. **Corporate headquarters location:** This location. **Parent company:** Rockwell Automation. **Operations at this facility include:** Administration; Manufacturing; Research and Development; Sales; Service. **Listed on:** New York Stock Exchange. **Stock exchange symbol:** COL. **Chairman/President/CEO:** Clayton M. (Clay) Jones. **Annual sales/revenues:** $2.5 billion. **Number of employees:** 14,500.

ROQUETTE AMERICA
1417 Exchange Street, P.O. Box 6647, Keokuk IA 52632. 319/524-5757. **Fax:** 319/526-2542. **Contact:** Human Resources Department. **E-mail address:** drhrecrut@roquette.com. **World Wide Web address:** http://www.roquette.com. **Description:** Produces cornstarch and syrup. **NOTE:** Applications and resumes should be sent to: Roquette Frères, Service du personnel, 62136 Lestrem, France. **Other U.S. locations:** Gurnee IL; Stockport IA.

RYKO MANUFACTURING COMPANY
11600 NW 54th Avenue, Grimes IA 50111. 515/986-3700. **Contact:** Human Resources. **World Wide Web address:** http://www.ryko.com. **Description:** The largest manufacturer of car wash equipment and accessories in North America. Offers a full line of touch-free and self-service car wash systems.

ST. ANTHONY REGIONAL HOSPITAL
311 South Clark Street, P.O. Box 628, Carroll IA 51401. 712/792-3581. **Fax:** 712/792-2124. **Contact:** Gina Ramaekers, Human Resources Representative. **World Wide Web address:** http://www.stanthonyhospital.org. **Description:** A 99-bed nonprofit, full-service community hospital with a 79-bed nursing home. **NOTE:** Entry-level positions and second and third shifts are offered. **Company slogan:** People Caring for People. **Positions advertised include:** Certified Registered Anesthesia Nurse; Dietary Aide; Licensed Practical Medical Nurse; Advanced Cardiac Life Support Nurse; Licensed Practical Surgical Nurse; Certified Nursing Assistant; Licensed Practical Pediatric Nurse; Registered Nurse; Registered Mental Health Nurse; Licensed Practical Nursery Nurse; Director of Surgical Services; Surgery Technician; Certified Occupational Therapy Assistant; Certified Nursing Home Assistant; Intensive Care Registered Nurse; Housekeeper; Pharmacy Technician. **President/CEO:** Gary Riedmann. **Number of employees at this location:** 420.

ST. LUKE'S HEALTH CARE SYSTEM
2720 Stone Park Boulevard, Sioux City IA 51104. 712/279-3634. **Fax:** 712/279-3368. **Contact:** Laura Hill, Human Resources. **E-mail address:** hilll@stlukes.org. **World Wide Web address:** http://www.stlukes.org. **Description:** A regional health care system that operates over 20 facilities including outpatient rehabilitation centers, physician clinics, a senior living community, and a charitable foundation. St. Luke's Health Care System is also affiliated with several area hospitals. Founded in 1884. **NOTE:** Human Resources phone: 712/279-3160. Applicants must apply online. **Positions advertised include:** Computer-aided Tomography Technician; Dietitian; Emergency Room Technician; Respiratory Care Instructor; Clinical Coordinator; Licensed Practical Nurse; Medical Laboratory Technician; Medical Records Clerk; MRI Technologist; Nursing Assistant; Registered Nurse Manager; Surgical Technician; Pharmacist; Pharmacy Technician; Burn Unit Registered Nurse; Respiratory Therapist; Women/Children's Services Director; Staff Histologist. **Other area locations:** Sergeant Bluffs IA. **Number of employees at this location:** 1,450.

SAUER-DANFOSS INC.
2800 East 13th Street, Ames IA 50010. 515/239-6000. **Fax:** 515/239-6318. **Contact:** Human Resources. **World Wide Web address:** http://www.sauer-danfoss.com. **Description:** Sauer-Danfoss provides controlled hydraulic power systems and components to manufacturers of off-highway vehicles throughout the world. Products include hydrostatic transmissions, piston pumps and motors, gear pumps and motors, mechanical gearboxes, and electronic and electrohydraulic controls. **NOTE:** The company lists current job openings through the Iowa Smart Career Move Website: http://www.smartcareermove.com. **Positions advertised include:** Mechanical Engineer; Agricultural Engineer; Electrical Engineer; Software Engineer; Industrial/Manufacturing Engineer; Quality Control Engineer; Information Technology Specialist; Maintenance Technician; Electrical/Electronic Technician; Production Machinist; Hydraulic Technician. **Special programs:** Engineering Internships; Engineering Coops. **Corporate headquarters location:** This location. **Other area locations:** West Branch IA. **Other U.S. locations:** IL; KS; MN; OR; SC; WI. **International locations:** China; Denmark; England; Germany; Slovakia; Sweden. **Operations at this facility include:** Administration; Research and Development; Sales; Service. The manufacturing plant focuses on piston pumps and motors for hydrostatic transmissions and system integration for all Sauer-Danfoss products. The plant in West Branch IA focuses on aluminum style, and cast iron construction style gear pumps specializing in open circuit pumps. **Listed on:** New York Stock Exchange. **Stock exchange symbol:** SHS. **Chairman:** Klaus H. Murmann. **Annual sales/revenues:** $252 million. **Number of employees at this location:** 600. **Number of employees nationwide:** 1,700. **Number of employees worldwide:** 6,900.

SHEAFFER PEN
301 Avenue H, Fort Madison IA 52627. 319/372-3300. **Fax:** 319/372-7539. **Contact:** Human Resources. **World Wide Web address:** http://www.sheaffer.com. **Description:** Manufactures ballpoint pens, pencils, and other desk accessories. Founded in 1907. **Positions advertised include:** Clerical Supervisor; Customer Service Representative; Design Engineer; Industrial Engineer; Mechanical Engineer; Quality Control Supervisor. **Other U.S. locations:** Milford CT. **Parent company:** Bic USA Inc. **Operations at this facility include:** Administration; Divisional Headquarters; Manufacturing; Research and Development; Service. **Listed on:** Privately held. **Number of employees at this location:** 500. **Number of employees worldwide:** 700.

SHENANDOAH MEMORIAL HOSPITAL
300 Pershing Avenue, Shenandoah IA 51601. 712/246-1230. **Fax:** 712/246-7357. **Contact:** Linda Braden, Human Resources Director. **E-mail address:** lbraden@shenandoahmedcenter.com. **World Wide Web address:** http://www.shenandoahmedcenter.com. **Description:** A nonprofit hospital offering acute care, outpatient services, skilled nursing, long-term care, and home health services. **NOTE:** Entry-level positions and second and third shifts are offered. Human Resources phone: 712/246-7102. **Positions advertised include:** Nurse Manager; Program Director; Physical Therapist; Physical Therapy Assistant; Home Health Aide; Housekeeper; Registered Nurse. **Office hours:** Monday - Friday, 8:00 a.m. - 4:30 p.m. **Corporate headquarters location:** This location. **CEO:** Chuck Millburg. **Annual sales/revenues:** $5 - $10 million. **Number of employees at this location:** 200.

SPENCER MUNICIPAL HOSPITAL
1200 First Avenue East, Spencer IA 51301. 712/264-6198. **Fax:** 712/264-6466. **Contact:** Michael Schauer, Human Resources. **E-mail address:** mschauer@spencerhospital.org. **World Wide Web address:** http://www.spencerhospital.org. **Description:** A 99-bed, nonprofit hospital. **NOTE:** Entry-level positions and second and third shifts are offered. Applicants are requested to send resumes by e-mail noting the position applying for and will receive an automatic reply by e-mail with an attached job application to be completed. Send resumes to: hr@spencerhospital.org. Human Resources phone: 712/264-6205. **Positions advertised include:** Registered Nurse; Mental Health Nurse; Medical/Surgical Nurse; Diagnostic Imaging Director; Clinical Nurse Coordinator; Respiratory Therapist; Radiation Therapist; Mental Health Department Manager; Certified Nurse Aide; Certified Occupational Therapy Assistant; Physical Therapist; Radiologic Technologist; Dietitian; Coder; Social Worker; Central Supply Clerk. **Office hours:** Monday - Friday, 8:00 a.m. - 4:30 p.m. **President/CEO:** John W. Allen. **Number of employees:** 500.

SWISS VALLEY FARMS COMPANY, INC.
P.O. Box 4493, Davenport IA 52808. 563/391-3341. **Fax:** 563/391-7479. **Contact:** Deb Sullivan, Director of Personnel. **World Wide Web address:** http://www.swissvalley.com. **Description:** A producer of cheese, milk, and ice cream. **Other area locations:** Luana IA; St. Olaf IA.

TERRA INDUSTRIES INC.
600 Fourth Street, P.O. Box 6000, Sioux City IA 51101. 712/277-1340. **Physical address:** 600 Fourth Street, Sioux City IA 51102. **Fax:** 712/277-7364. **Contact:** Rebecca Boyd, Human Resources. **World Wide Web address:** http://www.terraindustries.com. **Description:** Markets and produces nitrogen fertilizers and crop protection products such as herbicides, insecticides, plant growth regulators, and fungicides. Terra Industries also provides seeds and crop protection services to farmers. **Positions advertised include:** Programmer; Public Relations Specialist. **Corporate headquarters location:** This location. **Listed on:** New York Stock Exchange. **Stock exchange symbol:** TRA. **Chairman:** Harry R. Slack. **Annual sales/revenues:** $1 billion. **Number of employees:** 1,250.

3M
3406 East Pleasant Street, Knoxville IA 50138. 641/828-7000. **Contact:** Human Resources. **World Wide Web address:** http://www.mmm.com. **Description:** The company manufactures products in three sectors: Industrial and Consumer; Information, Imaging, and Electronic; and Life Sciences. The Industrial and Consumer Sector includes a variety of products under brand names including 3M, Scotch, Post-it, Scotch-Brite, and Scotchgard. The Information, Imaging, and Electronic Sector is a leader in several high-growth global industries, including telecommunications, electronics, electrical, imaging, and memory media. The Life Science Sector serves two broad market categories: health care, and traffic and personal safety. In the health care market, 3M is a leading provider of medical and surgical supplies, drug-delivery

systems, and dental products; in traffic and personal safety, 3M is a leader in products for transportation safety, worker protection, vehicle and sign graphics, and out-of-home advertising. **Corporate headquarters location:** St. Paul MN. **Operations at this facility include:** Manufacturing of tape products. **Listed on:** New York Stock Exchange. **Stock exchange symbol:** MMM. **Chairman/CEO:** W. James McNerney, Jr. **Annual sales/revenues:** $16.3 million. **Number of employees:** 71,700.

TRUCK COUNTRY
4300 NE 14th Street, Des Moines IA 50313. 515/265-7361. **Toll-free phone:** 888/201-6222. **Fax:** 515/265-6443. **Contact:** Erik Thoms. **E-mail address:** erikthoms@truckcountry.com. **World Wide Web address:** http://www.truckcountry.com. **Description:** Truck Country is one of the largest Freightliner dealers in the U.S. They serve their customers in 11 locations throughout the mid-west offering a large selection of new and used trucks. In addition, they provide 24-hour parts and service, 7 days a week, to support truckers after the sale. **Positions advertised include:** Diesel Technician, Lot Assistant/Detailer, Office Manager, Outside Parts Sales, Parts Counter Salesperson, Shipping & Receiving, Service Manager, Assistant Service Manager, Service Advisor, Inventory Control Clerk, Truck Transfer Driver, Business Analyst, Custodian.

TURBINE FUEL TECHNOLOGIES
811 Fourth Street, P.O. Box 65100, West Des Moines IA 50265. 515/274-1561. **Fax:** 515/271-7243. **Contact:** Human Resources. **World Wide Web address:** http://www.tft.goodrich.com. **Description:** Manufactures turbine engines for aircraft. Founded in 1938. **NOTE:** Second and third shifts are offered. **Positions advertised include:** Administrative Assistant; Design Engineer; Draftsperson; Management Trainee; Manufacturing Engineer; Mechanical Engineer; Sales Representative. **Office hours:** Monday - Friday, 7:30 a.m. - 4:00 p.m. **Corporate headquarters location:** Charlotte NC. **Other U.S. locations:** Carroll IA. **Parent company:** Goodrich Corporation. **Operations at this facility include:** Divisional Headquarters. **Listed on:** New York Stock Exchange. **Stock exchange symbol:** GR. **President:** James Baker. **Number of employees at this location:** 400.

TUR-PAK FOODS, INC.
6201 MacArthur Street, P.O. Box 116, Sioux City IA 51102. 712/277-8484. **Fax:** 712/277-3760. **Contact:** Human Resources. **Description:** A custom meat processing company specializing in portion controlled and vacuum packaged pork according to customer specifications. **Positions advertised include:** Electrician; Food Scientist/Technologist; Manager; Mechanical Engineer; Operations/Production Manager; Quality Control Supervisor. **Corporate headquarters location:** This location. **Parent company:** Kustom Pak Foods, Ltd. **Operations at this facility include:** Administration; Manufacturing; Sales. **Listed on:** Privately held. **President:** Stanley A. Sherman. **Number of employees at this location:** 300.

U. S. DEPARTMENT OF VETERAN AFFAIRS
VETERANS ADMINISTRATION CENTRAL IOWA HEALTH CARE SYSTEM
1515 West Pleasant, Knoxville IA 50138. 641/842-3101. **Contact:** Human Resources. **Description:** Provides a variety of inpatient and outpatient services including acute, long-term, and community-based psychiatric, rehabilitative, and medical care. The center has more than 600 beds. **Positions advertised include:** Licensed Practical Nurse; Pharmacist; Physical Therapist; Physician; Registered Nurse; Respiratory Therapist. **Corporate headquarters location:** Washington DC. **Other U.S. locations:** Nationwide. **Parent company:** U.S. Department of Veterans Affairs. **Operations at this facility include:** Administration; Health Care. **Number of employees at this location:** 830.

UNIVERSITY OF IOWA
120 USB, Iowa City IA 52242-1411. 319/335-3500. **Fax:** 319/335-0202. **Recorded jobline:** 319/335-2682. **Contact:** Employment Services. **World Wide Web address:** http://www.uiowa.edu. **Description:** A university with 27,900 students enrolled in over 150 areas of study. **NOTE:** Entry-level positions, part-time jobs, and second and third shifts are offered. Contact info: Employment Services, 102 University Services Building, Suite 21, Iowa City IA 52242-1911. 319/335-2656. **Positions advertised include:** Clerk; Library Assistant; Nursing Unit Clerk; Patient Account Representative; Pharmacy Technician; Secretary; Custodian; Nursing Assistant; Psychiatric Nursing Assistant; Dental Assistant; Radiographer; Steamfitter; Surgical Technologist. **Number of employees at this location:** 15,000.

UNIVERSITY OF IOWA HOSPITALS AND CLINICS
200 Hawkins Drive, Iowa City IA 52242. 319/356-2120. **Toll-free phone:** 800/777-4692. **Contact:** Human Resources. **World Wide Web address:** http://www.uihealthcare.com. **Description:** A university-affiliated tertiary health care center with 800 beds and a 22-suite perioperative nursing division. **NOTE:** Second and third shifts are offered. **Positions advertised include:** Research Assistant; Postdoctoral Research Scholar; Postdoctoral Scholar; Assistant Anatomy Professor; Anesthesiologist; Ophthalmology Professor; Clinical Lab Scientist; Social Worker; Stem Cell Biologist; Bone Marrow Transplant Physician; Staff Nurse.

VIDEO KING GAMING SYSTEMS
3211 Nebraska Avenue, Council Bluffs IA 51501. 712/323-1488. **Fax:** 712/890-3936. **Contact:** Human Resources. **E-mail address:** jryan@vkge.com. **World Wide Web address:** http://www.bingoking.com. **Description:** Manufactures and distributes a line of bingo cards, break-open tickets, ink markers, electronic equipment, supplies, and accessories. VKGS's products are sold primarily to distributors, who resell them to fraternal, charitable, religious, and social organizations; lodges; hospitals; nursing homes; PTA groups; military clubs; and other similar organizations that use products to raise money and provide entertainment. The company's products are also sold to charitable and commercial bingo halls and to government lottery agencies through company-owned retail stores in Canada, mail-order catalogs, and promotional flyers. Through its Colorado-based subsidiary, the company also makes and distributes electronic gaming equipment. **Corporate headquarters location:** St. Catharines, Ontario, Canada. **International locations:** Canada; Mexico. **Subsidiaries include:** Bazaar & Novelty, Canada; Video King, Littleton CO. **Listed on:** NASDAQ. **Stock exchange symbol:** STUA. **CEO:** Al Barber.

VIKING PUMP, INC.
P.O. Box 8, Cedar Falls IA 50613. 319/266-1741. **Physical address:** 406 State Street, Cedar Falls IA 50613-0008. **Fax:** 803/216-7008. **Contact:** Human Resources. **E-mail address:** careers.viking@idexcorp.com. **World Wide Web address:** http://www.vikingpump.com. **Description:** Manufactures positive displacement pumps and ferrous and nonferrous castings. Founded in 1911. **Positions advertised include:** Project Engineer; Safety and Environmental Compliance Engineer. **Parent company:** IDEX Corporation. **Number of employees nationwide:** 475.

VON MAUR, INC.
6565 Brady Street, Davenport IA 52806. 563/388-2200. **Fax:** 563/388-2242. **Contact:** Human Resources. **World Wide Web address:** http://www.vonmaur.com. **Description:** A department store carrying a full line of clothing, shoes, and accessories for men, women, and children. **Positions advertised include:** Buyer; Department Manager; Management Trainee; Retail Manager. **Corporate headquarters location:** This location. **Other U.S. locations:** Nationwide. **Operations at this facility include:** Administration; Distribution. **Listed on:** Privately held. **Number of employees at this location:** 300. **Number of employees nationwide:** 2,800.

VONHOFFMANN GRAPHICS, INC.
400 South 14th Avenue, Eldridge IA 52748. 563/285-4800. **Fax:** 563/285-8240. **Contact:** Personnel. **World Wide Web address:** http://www.vonhoffmann.com. **Description:** A commercial printing company offering a variety of services including complete test printing capabilities, typesetting, keylining, negatives, proofs, plates, printing, die-cutting, collating, stitching, trimming, consecutive numbering, sealing, wrapping, packaging, and distribution. Founded in 1908. **Corporate headquarters location:** Darien IL. **Operations at this facility include:** Binding Production; Distribution; Administration; Customer Service. **Listed on:** Privately held.

THE WALDINGER CORPORATION
2601 Bell Avenue, Des Moines IA 50321-1189. 515/284-1911. **Fax:** 515/247-9644. **Contact:** Human Resources. **World Wide Web address:** http://www.waldinger.com. **Description:** Engaged in mechanical and sheet metal construction. The company also designs, manufactures, installs, and maintains heating, air conditioning, ventilation, piping, and plumbing systems. Founded in 1906. **Positions advertised include:** Accountant; Engineer; Industrial Engineer; Project Manager; Service Manager; Service Sales Representative; Service Technician; Computer Programmer; Draftsperson; Mechanical Engineer. **Office hours:** Monday - Friday, 8:00 a.m. - 5:00 p.m. **Corporate headquarters location:** This location. **Annual sales/revenues:** Over $100 million. **Number of employees:** 1,000.

WASHINGTON COUNTY HOSPITAL
400 East Polk Street, Washington IA 52353. 319/653-5481x246. **Fax:** 319/653-4271. **Contact:** Director of Human Resources. **E-mail address:** jobs@wchc.org. **World Wide Web address:** http://www.wchc.org. **Description:** A nonprofit, rural health care facility including a 48-bed hospital and 43-bed nursing home with 24-hour emergency care, a family birthing center, medical/surgical care, an intensive care unit, skilled care, home health services, and broad diagnostic capabilities providing inpatient, outpatient, long-term care and emergency services for the Washington County area. Founded in 1912. **NOTE:** Entry-level positions, part-time jobs, and second and third shifts are offered. Human Resources phone: 319/863-3909. **Company slogan:** We Treat You Like Family. **Positions advertised include:** Medical/Surgery Registered Nurse; Obstetric Registered Nurse; Operating Room Nurse; Certified Nurses Aide; Radiology Technologist; clinical Dietician; Coder; Lab Technician; Licensed Practical Nurse. **Number of employees at this location:** 230.

WELLS FARGO
13621 University Avenue, Des Moines, IA 50325. 515/237-5882. **Contact:** Human Resources **World Wide Web address:** http://www.wellsfargo.com. **Description:** A diversified financial institution with over $234 billion in assets. Wells Fargo serves over 17 million customers through 5,300 independent locations worldwide. The company also maintains several stand-alone ATMs and branches within other retail outlets. Services include community banking, credit and debit cards, home equity and mortgage loans, online banking, student loans, and insurance. Wells Fargo also offers a complete line of commercial and institutional financial services. Founded in 1852. **Positions advertised include:** Accounting Clerk; Administrative Assistant; Systems Engineer; Business Systems Consultant; Client Service Consultant; Customer Service Representative; Database Analyst; Financial Consultant. **Corporate headquarters location:** San Francisco CA. **Subsidiaries include:** Acordia, Inc.; H.D. Vest, Inc.; Ragen MacKenzie Group Incorporated; Wells Capital Management. **Operations at this facility include:** Administration; Sales; Service. **Listed on:** New York Stock Exchange. **Stock exchange symbol:** WFC.

WINNEBAGO INDUSTRIES, INC.
605 West Crystal Lake Road, P.O. Box 152, Forest City IA 50436. 641/585-3535. **Fax:** 641/585-6966. **Contact:** Human Resources. **E-mail address:** hr@winnebagoind.com. **World Wide Web address:** http://www.winnebagoind.com. **Description:** A manufacturer and distributor of recreational and camping vehicles. **Positions advertised include:** Accountant; Computer Specialist; Electrical Engineer; Industrial Engineer; Information Technologist; Manufacturing Engineer; Marketing Representative; Mechanical Engineer; Inspector; Production Assembler; Quality Control Technician; Painter; Vehicle Technician; Welder. **Corporate headquarters location:** This location. **Operations at this facility include:** Administration; Manufacturing; Research and Development; Sales; Service. **Listed on:** New York Stock Exchange. **Stock exchange symbol:** WGO. **Chairman/CEO/President:** Bruce D. Hertzke. **Annual sales/revenues:** $328 million. **Number of employees:** 3,685.

WOODWARD COMMUNICATIONS, INC.
P.O. Box 688, Dubuque IA 52004-0688. 563/588-5687. **Fax:** 563/588-4539. **Contact:** Human Resources. **World Wide Web address:** http://www.wcinet.com. **Description:** Operates a daily newspaper, radio stations, weekly publications, specialty publications, and offers Internet services. **Positions advertised include:** Customer Service Representative; Editor; General Manager; Operations/Production Manager; Radio/TV Announcer/Broadcaster; Reporter. **Corporate headquarters location:** This location. **Other area locations:** Cascade IA; Dyersville IA. **Other U.S. locations:** IL; WI. **Operations at this facility include:** Administration; Sales; Service. **Listed on:** Privately held. **Number of employees:** 600.

WORKSTREAM
505 North Fourth Street, Fairfield IA 52556. 641/472/7720. **Toll-free phone:** 800/247-0077. **Fax:** 641/472-7105. **Contact:** Human Resources. **World Wide Web address:** http://www.workstreaminc.com. **Description:** Develops and provides human resource-related business software and services. Founded in 1996. **NOTE:** Search and apply for positions online. **Corporate headquarters location:** Ottawa Canada. **Other U.S. locations:** FL; CA. **Listed on:** NASDAQ. **Stock exchange symbol:** WSTM.

ACTUATE CORPORATION
12980 Metcalf Avenue, Suite 300, Overland Park KS 66213. 913/851-2200. **Contact:** Human Resources. **World Wide Web address:** http://www.actuate.com. **Description:** A provider of information delivery software products and services. The company offers a platform for retrieving business information from corporate databases as well as designing spreadsheet technology for Web-based computing. Founded in 1993. **Corporate headquarters location:** South San Francisco CA. **Other U.S. locations:** Nationwide. **International locations:** Worldwide. **Operations at this location:** Actuate's F-1 Division. **Listed on:** NASDAQ. **Stock exchange symbol:** ACTU. **Chairman:** Nicholas Nierenberg. **Annual sales/revenues:** $109 billion. **Number of employees worldwide:** 575.

AEROCOMM
11160 Thompson Avenue, Lenexa KS 66219. 913/492-2320. **Toll-free phone:** 800/492-2320. **Fax:** 913/492-1243. **Contact:** Human Resources Department. **E-mail address:** wireless@aerocomm.com. **World Wide Web address:** http://www.aerocomm.com. **Description:** Designs, manufactures, and markets Instant Wireless data communications for equipment manufacturers and spread spectrum data radios for OEM integration or commercial plug-and-play. **Positions advertised include:** Inside Sales Representative; OEM Sales Representative; RF Technician. **Corporate headquarters location:** This location. **Other U.S. locations:** Salt Lake City UT. **Listed on:** Privately Held.

AIR MIDWEST, INC.
dba US AIRWAYS EXPRESS
2203 Air Cargo Road, Wichita KS 67209. 316/944-2563. **Fax:** 316/945-0947. **Contact:** Personnel. **World Wide Web address:** http://www.mesa-air.com. **E-mail address:** mesarecruiting@mesa-air.com. **Description:** A regional subsidiary of Mesa Air Group providing scheduled passenger and airfreight service in the lower Midwest region of the U.S. The company operates turboprop aircraft as US Airways Express under agreement at US Airways' hub operations in Pittsburgh, Philadelphia, Kansas City MO, and Tampa, as well as code-sharing with Midwest Express and US Airways. Air Midwest also operates as Mesa Airlines in Albuquerque NM. **Note:** Resumes sent by e-mail should be in Microsoft Word or Adobe Acrobat Reader format. **Positions advertised include:** Crew Tracker; Dispatcher; Flight Simulator Instructor; Flight Attendant; Maintenance Worker. **Corporate headquarters location:** Phoenix AZ. **Other area locations:** Dodge City KS; Great Bend KS; Manhattan KS; Shawnee Mission; Topeka KS. **Parent company:** Mesa Airlines, Inc. (Farmington NM). **Operations at this facility include:** Administration; Sales; Service. **Listed on:** NASDAQ. **Stock exchange symbol:** MESA. **President:** Greg Stephens. **Annual sales/revenues:** $497 million. **Number of employees at this location:** 100. **Number of employees nationwide:** 3,100.

AMERICAN RED CROSS
707 North Main Street, Wichita KS 67203 316/268-0800. **Fax:** 316/268-0888. **World Wide Web address:** http://www.midwaykansas.redcross.org. **Description:** A humanitarian organization that aids disaster victims, gathers blood for crisis distribution, trains individuals to respond to emergencies, educates individuals on various diseases, and raises funds for other charitable establishments. **Other area locations:** Throughout Kansas. **Other U.S. locations:** Nationwide.

AMERICAN RESTAURANT PARTNERS
RESTAURANT MANAGEMENT COMPANY
3020 North Cypress Road, Suite 100, Wichita KS 67226. 316/634-1190. **Fax:** 316/634-1662. **Contact:** Human Resources. **World Wide Web address:** http://www.restaurantmanagement.hcareers.com. **Description:** A limited partnership operating more than 120 restaurants and delivery/carry-out facilities (including Kentucky Fried Chicken, Pizza Hut, and Long John Silvers) located primarily in Texas, Montana, Oklahoma, Georgia, Louisiana, and Wyoming. **NOTE:** Entry-level positions are offered. **Positions advertised include:** Assistant Manager; Manager Trainee; Restaurant General Manager; Shift Manager; Food Service Manager. **Special programs:** Training. **Corporate headquarters location:** This location. **Other area locations:** Dodge City KS; El Dorado KS; Newton KS; Park City KS. **Operations at this facility include:** Administration. **Chairman/CEO:** Hal W. McCoy. **Annual sales/revenues:** $64 million. **Number of employees nationwide:** 3,000.

AEROFLEX, INC.
10200 West York Street, Wichita KS 67215. 316/522-4981. **Toll-free phone:** 800/855-2352. **Fax:** 316/524-2623. **E-mail address:** info-test@aeroflex.com. **Contact:** Human Resources Manager. **World Wide Web address:** http://www.ifrsys.com. **Note:** Formerly IFR Systems Inc. **Description:** Designs and manufactures electronic test equipment for analyzing frequency transmission ability and power levels of communications systems including signal generators, spectrum analyzers, attenuators, power supplies, counters, and ground station and satellite simulators. The company produces radio test systems used in defense communications as well as automatic test and optical inspection equipment for the manufacture of electronic components. Founded in 1968. **Positions advertised include:** Software Engineer; Area Sales Manager; PXI Sales Specialist; Senior Software Engineer. **Corporate headquarters location:** This location. **International locations:** United Kingdom. **Parent company:** Aeroflex, Inc. **Operations at this facility include:** Administration; Engineering and Design; Manufacturing; Sales; Service. **President/CEO:** Jeffrey A. Bloomer. **Annual sales/revenues:** $118 billion. **Number of employees at this location:** 550. **Number of employees worldwide:** 1,200.

ASH GROVE CEMENT COMPANY
11011 Cody Street, Overland Park KS 66210. 913/451-8900. **Toll-free phone:** 800/545-1882. **Fax:** 913/345-4263. **Contact:** Employment & Compensation Manager. **World Wide Web address:** http://www.ashgrove.com. **E-mail address:** info@ashgrove.com. **Description:** The company operates cement and lime plants in nine states across the country with an annual production capacity of more 7.8 million tons of cement. In addition to manufacturing port cement, masonry, and ready-mix cements, the company operates rock quarries in Texas; a lime plant in Oregon; and a quarry in British Columbia. Incorporated in 1882. **Company slogan:** Best on earth. **Positions advertised include:** Plant Manager; Production Manager; Maintenance Manager; Process Engineer; Plant Engineer; Chief Chemist; Environmental and Safety Manager; Quarry Superintendent; Human Resource Manager. **Corporate headquarters location:** This location. **Other area locations:** Chanute KS; Kansas City KS. **Other U.S. locations:** Portland OR. **Subsidiaries include:** Ash Grove Aggregates; Ash Grove Materials Corporation; Ash Grove Packaging Group; Cedar Creek Properties, Inc.; Century Concrete, Inc.; Fordyce Concrete Co.; Materials Packaging Corp.; Precision Packaging, Inc.; Permanent Paving, Inc.; Quikrete Materials, Inc.; and others. **Operations at this facility include:** Operations, Marketing, and Midwest Division Office. **Listed on:** Privately held. **Chairman:** Charles T. Sunderland. **Annual sales/revenues:** $900 million. **Number of employees at this location:** 100. **Number of employees nationwide:** 1,800.

ASSOCIATED WHOLESALE GROCERS, INC.
P.O. Box 2932, Kansas City KS 66110-2932. 913/288-1510. **Physical address:** 5000 Kansas Avenue, Kansas City KS 66106. **Fax:** 913/288-1547. **Contact:** Human Resources Manager. **E-mail address:** hr.kc@awginc.com. **World Wide Web address:** http://www.awginc.com. **Description:** A wholesale grocery cooperative with distribution centers supplying products to 850 stores in 10 states, as well as supermarket chains in Kansas, Missouri, and Oklahoma. Founded in 1926. **NOTE:** Entry-level positions, as well as second and third shifts are offered. **Positions advertised include:** Category Managers; Design and Décor Source Group Clerk; Education and Training Associate; Human Resources Representative; Information Technology Associate; In Store Marketing Representative; Legal Associate; Merchandising Associate; Payroll Clerk; Print shop Specialist; Purchasing & Facilities Clerk; Retail Associate; Shelving Associate; Traffic Associate; Grocery Associate; Produce Associate; Meat Clerk; Bakery Clerk; Bakery Clerk; Deli Help. **Special programs:** Training. **Corporate headquarters location:** This location. **Other area locations:** Fort Scott KS; Shawnee Mission KS. **Other U.S. locations:** Springfield MO; Oklahoma City OK. **Subsidiaries include:** Associated Retail Grocers; Falley's; Food 4 Less; Homeland Stores, Inc. **Listed on:** Privately held. **Chairman:** J. Fred Ball. **Annual sales/revenues:** $3.1 billion. **Number of employees at this location:** 1,200. **Number of employees nationwide:** 2,700.

BANK OF AMERICA
100 North Broadway, Wichita KS 67202. 316/261-4251. **Contact:** Personnel. **E-mail address:** bankofamerica@efunds.com. **World Wide Web address:** http://www.bankofamerica.com. **Description:** A full-service banking and financial institution. The company operates through four business segments: Global Corporate and Investment Banking, Principal Investing and Asset Management, Commercial Banking, and Consumer Banking. **NOTE:** Applications and resumes can be submitted via the company Website. **Positions advertised include:** Banking Center Manager; Business Manager; Operations Representative; Home Services Specialist; Loan Specialist; Credit Officer; Fiduciary Specialist; Consumer Market Executive; Teller. **Corporate** Office Hours: Monday – Thursday, 9:00 a.m. – 3:00 p.m. Friday, 9:00 a.m. – 5:00 p.m. **Headquarters location:** Charlotte NC. **Other U.S. locations:** Nationwide. **Listed on:** New York Stock Exchange. **Stock exchange symbol:** BAC. **Chairman/President/CEO:** Kenneth D. Lewis. **Annual sales/revenues:** $53 billion. **Number of employees worldwide:** 143,000.

BARNES & NOBLE BOOKSTORES
6130 SW 17th Street, Topeka KS 66615. 785/273-9600. **Contact:** Manager. **World Wide Web address:** http://www.barnesandnobleinc.com. **Description:** A bookstore chain operating 900 stores nationwide. This location has a cafe and music department in addition to its book departments. **Note:** Applications may be submitted online at web address. **Positions advertised include:** Book Seller; Café Seller; Music Seller; Receiver; Lead Position; Head Cashier; Community Relations Manager; Assistant Store Manager; Store Manager; District Manager. **Office hours:** Monday – Friday, 9:00 a.m. – 11:00 p.m. **Corporate headquarters location:** New York NY. **Other area locations:** Leawood KS; Wichita KS. **Other U.S. locations:** Nationwide. **Listed on:** New York Stock Exchange. **Stock exchange symbol:** BKS. **Chairman:** Leonard S. Riggio. **Annual sales/revenues:** $5.2 billion. **Number of employees worldwide:** 37,000.

BOARD OF PUBLIC UTILITIES, KANSAS CITY
540 Minnesota Avenue, Kansas City KS 66101. 913/573-9000. **Fax:** 913/573-9990. **Recorded jobline:** 913/573-6900. **Contact:** Don Woodson, Human Resources. **E-mail address:** jobs@bpu.com. **World Wide Web address:** http://www.bpu.com. **Description:** Provides electricity, water, and water pollution treatment to the Kansas City KS area. Founded in 1929. **NOTE:** Entry-level positions and second and third shifts are offered. **Positions advertised include:** Carpenter; Benefits Coordinator. **Office hours:** Monday, 8:00 a.m. – 12:00 p.m. Wednesday, 1:00 p.m. – 4:00 p.m. **Corporate headquarters location:** This location. **Number of employees at this location:** 680.

THE BOEING COMPANY
3801 South Oliver Street, Wichita KS 67210. 316/526-2121. **Recorded jobline:** 316/526-1065. **Contact:** Employment Services. **E-mail address:** employmentoperations@boeing.com. **World Wide Web address:** http://www.boeing.com. **Description:** A manufacturer of commercial airplanes, the company also develops air traffic control systems as well as products and services for defense, intelligence, communications, and space. **Note:** Provides applications on Website. **Positions advertised include:** Engineer; 767 System Safety; Production Support; Business & Planning Analyst. **Special programs:** Internships. **Corporate headquarters location:** Chicago IL. **Other U.S. locations:** Nationwide. **Subsidiaries include:** Boeing Commercial Airplanes; Boeing Integrated Defense Systems; United Space Alliance. **Operations at this facility include:** Airplane Services; Commercial Airplanes; Integrated Defense Systems; Shared Service Group; Administration; Research and Development. **Listed on:** New York Stock Exchange. **Stock exchange symbol:** BA. **Chairman/CEO:** Philip M. Condit. **Annual sales/revenues:** $54 billion. **Number of employees at this location:** 17,000. **Number of employees nationwide:** 169,000.

BOMBARDIER AEROSPACE
dba LEARJET INC.
P.O. Box 7707 MS 15, Wichita KS 67277-7707. 316/946-2200. **Physical address:** One Learjet Way, Wichita KS 67209. **Fax:** 316/946-2861. **Contact:** Human Resources. **World Wide Web address:** http://www.aero.bombardier.com. **Description:** Bombardier Aerospace manufactures business and civil aircraft at its Wichita KS location under the brands Challenger and Learjet. Learjet Inc., is a wholly-owned subsidiary producing high-performance business jets at the Wichita plant. Learjet interiors are assembled at the Tucson AZ Completion Center and wings are assembled in Canada. The company also manufactures other aerospace products. **NOTE:** Applicants are encouraged to submit resumes via the company website. **Positions advertised include:** Project Engineer; Airframe Designer; Regional Sales Manager; Senior Business Administration Analyst; Structures Designer; Safety and Reliability Engineer; Aerospace Engineer; Aircraft Mechanic/Engine Specialist; Structural Engineer. **Special programs:** Internships. **Internship information:** Internships are only offered for local students. **Corporate headquarters location:** Quebec, Canada. **Other U.S. locations:** Tucson AZ. **Subsidiaries include:** Learjet Inc. **Operations at this facility include:** Learjet Corporate Headquarters; Learjet Services; Challenger 300; Flight Test Center; Administration; Manufacturing; Research and Development; Sales; Service. **Listed on:** Toronto Stock Exchange. **Stock exchange symbol:** BBD.B. **Annual sales/revenues:** $13.6 billion. **Number of employees at this location:** 2,800. **Number of employees nationwide:** 5,000. **Number of employees worldwide:** 79,000.

BUSHNELL CORPORATION
dba BUSHNELL SPORTS OPTICS
9200 Cody Street, Overland Park KS 66214. 913/752-3400. **Fax:** 913/752-3568. **Contact:** Human Resources. **World Wide Web address:** http://www.bushnell.com.

Office Hours: Monday – Friday, 8:00 a.m. – 4:00 p.m. **Description:** Designs, markets, and distributes a wide range of optical products including binoculars, night vision, speed guns, laser rangefinders, digital compasses, telescopes, spotting scopes, riflescopes, premium sunglasses, sport shields, and ski goggles through retail outlets. Founded in 1947. **Corporate headquarters location:** This location. **International locations:** Australia; Canada; France; Hong Kong.

CENTRAL KANSAS MEDICAL CENTER
ST. ROSE HOSPITAL CAMPUS
3515 Broadway, Great Bend KS 67530. 620/786—6186. **Fax:** 620/792-1605. **Contact:** Human Resources. **E-mail address:** deniseschreiber@catholichealth.net. **World Wide Web address:** http://www.ckmc.org. **Description:** A two-campus, 121-bed regional medical center with the main, St. Rose campus in Great Bend and a second, St. Joseph Hospital in Larned. Founded by the Dominican Sisters in 1902. **Positions advertised include:** Registered Nurse; Licensed Practical Nurse; Medical Record File Clerk; Respiratory Therapist; Cook; Plant Mechanic Coder; Nurse Manager; Physician. **Other area locations:** Larned KS (St. Joseph Memorial Hospital). **Operations at this facility include:** St. Rose Hospital; Golden Belt Home Health & Hospice. **Number of employees at this location:** 630.

CERTAINTEED CORPORATION
P.O. Box 15080, Kansas City KS 66115. 913/342-6624. **Physical address:** 103 Funston Road, Kansas City KS 66115. **Contact:** Human Resources Development. **E-mail address:** ctrecruitment@saint-gobain.com. **World Wide Web address:** http://www.certainteed.com. **Description:** Manufacturer of building materials including roofing, siding, insulation, windows, doors, ventilation, fence, decking, foundations and piping. Located in Valley Forge, Pennsylvania, the company operates more than 45 facilities in the U.S. (Parent company Saint-Gobain has 173,000 employees in over 45 countries, and in the U.S. operates some 200 manufacturing locations with 28,000 employees.) The CertainTeed subsidiary operates in three sectors—building materials; fiberglass products; and pipes—producing abrasives, roofing products, vinyl and sash products, containers, flat glass, industrial ceramics, thermal and acoustical insulation, reinforcements, and piping. **Positions advertised include:** Sales. **Corporate headquarters location:** 750 East Swedesford Road, Valley Forge PA 19482. **Other area locations:** McPherson KS. **Other U.S. locations:** CA; GA; PA. **Parent company:** Compagnie de Saint Gobain (Paris, France) operates through four branches: Abrasives, Construction Materials, Industrial Ceramics, and Insulation and Reinforcements. The Saint-Gobain companies based in North America are organized under the umbrella of the Saint-Gobain Corporation, which include CertainTeed Corporation, Norton Company, and all of their subsidiaries. **Chairman/President/CEO:** Jean-Francois Phelizon. **Annual sales/revenues:** $2.6 billion. **Number of employees nationwide:** 7,800.

CESSNA AIRCRAFT COMPANY
P.O. Box 1996, Independence KS 67301. 620/332-0111. **Physical address:** Two Cessna Boulevard, Wichita KS 67215. **Fax:** 620/332-0144. **Recorded jobline:** 316/517-6155. **Contact:** Director of Employment. **E-mail address:** jobs@cessna.textron.com. **World Wide Web address:** http://www.cessna.com. **Description:** Engaged in the engineering, fabrication, assembly, and marketing of business jets including seven variations of its signature Citation jet; the utility turboprop Caravan for freight, bush, amphibious and commercial use; and small single-engine aircraft used for personal and small-business purposes; as well as offering shared ownership of business jets. **Office hours:** Monday – Friday. 8:00 a.m. – 4:30 p.m. **NOTE:** Check the company's website (http://www.cessnajobs.com) for current employment information; resumes can be submitted online. **Positions advertised include:** Technical Support Mechanic; Avionics Technician; A&B Mechanic; Technical Support Services; Instrumentation Technician; Electrical/Electronics Engineer; Mechanical Engineer. **Corporate headquarters location:** This location. **Parent company:** Textron Inc. **Operations at this facility include:** Administration; Manufacturing; Research and Development; Sales; Service. **CEO:** Russ Meyer. **Annual sales/revenues:** $3 billion.

COBALT BOATS
1715 North 8th Street, Neodesha KS 66757. 620/325-2653 ext. 710. **Fax:** 620/325-2361. **Contact:** Human Resources. **World Wide Web address:** http://www.cobaltboats.com. **Description:** Manufacturer of luxury boats ranging in length from 20 to 36 feet. Founded in 1968. **Positions advertised include:** Product Engineer.

COCA-COLA BOTTLING COMPANY OF MID-AMERICA/COCA-COLA ENTERPRISES, INC.
9000 Marshall Drive, Shawnee Mission KA 66215. 913/492-8100. **Fax:** 913/599-9288. **Recorded jobline:** 913/599-9360. **Contact:** Human Resources. **E-mail address:** marecruiting@na.cokecce.com. **World Wide Web addresses:** http://www.cokecce.com/careers or http://www.ccecareers.com. **Description:** Coca-Cola Enterprises (CCE), a 38-percent-owned subsidiary of The Coca-Cola Company (TCCC) bottles and distributes the soft drinks. With 463 facilities, CCE is the top bottler in the world accounting for 80 percent of all North American sales of Coca-Cola products. The company also bottles and distributes Canada Dry, Dr Pepper, Barq's, Nestea, bottled water and juices distributing to 46 states, Canada, and Europe. **NOTE:** Provides job opening information and applications online. **Positions advertised include:** Side Load Driver; Maintenance Mechanic; Fleet Mechanic; Bulk Merchandiser. **Special programs:** Internships. **Corporate headquarters location:** Atlanta GA. **Other area locations:** Concordia KS; Fort Scott KS; Lenexa KS; Victoria KS; Wichita KS. **Parent company:** The Coca-Cola Company. **Operations at this facility include:** Administration; Divisional Headquarters; Manufacturing; Sales. **Listed on:** NASDAQ. **Stock exchange symbol:** CCE. **Chairman/CEO:** Lowry F. Kline. **Annual sales/revenues:** $16.9 billion. **Number of employees at this location:** 1,550. **Number of employees worldwide:** 72,000.

COFFEYVILLE REGIONAL MEDICAL CENTER
1400 West Fourth Street, Coffeyville KS 67337. 620/252-1500. **Toll-free phone:** 800/540-2762. **Fax:** 620/252-1562. **Recorded jobline:** 800/914-8732. **Contact:** Human Resources Director. **E-mail address:** humanresources@crmcinc.com. **World Wide Web address:** http://www.crmcinc.com. **Description:** A 110-bed, not-for-profit, community hospital providing acute care and skilled care services, as well as outpatient health care services to Southeast Kansas and Northeast Oklahoma. **Note:** Applicants may apply for positions online. **Positions advertised include:** Registered Nurse; Certified Nurses Aid; Health Information Clerk; Health Information Scanner; Maintenance Worker; Housekeeping Clerk. **Operations at this facility include:** Administration; Service. **Number of employees at this location:** 450.

THE COLEMAN COMPANY, INC.
Dept 531 P.O. Box 2931, Wichita KS 67201-2931. 316/832-2692. **Physical address:** 3600 North Hydraulic, Wichita KS 67219. **Fax:** 316/832-3060. **Recorded jobline:** 316/832-8777. **Contact:** Human Resources. **E-mail address:** careers@coleman.com. **World Wide Web address:** http://www.colemancareers.com. **Description:** The Coleman Company manufactures, markets, and distributes outdoor recreation gear such as sleeping bags, lanterns, flashlights, coolers, backpacks, camp stoves, canoes and fishing boats, water ski boats, sleeping bags, fuel, and hot tubs. Nationally, the company manufactures the following brands: Coleman, Campingaz, Peak 1, Outing Sports Products; Hobie Cat and O'Brien Marine Products; Coleman Camping Trailers; Home Heating and Air Conditioning Products; and Recreational Vehicle Products. Its Coleman Powermate division produces portable generators, fuel cell generators, and compressors. The company operates internationally through Coleman Canadian Sales and Coleman Foreign Sales. **NOTE:** Resumes accepted through the company website. **Positions advertised include:** Accounting Assistant; Black Belt-Appliances; Category Manager; Graphic Design Associate; Administrative Associate; Advertising Associate; Business Intelligence & Shelf Space Management Analyst; Sales Manager; Manufacturing Engineer; Security Guard; Shipping Supervisor- 3rd Shift; Sourcing Manager; Textile Engineer; Warehouse Control Coordinator. **Corporate headquarters location:** This location. **Other area locations:** Shawnee Mission KS; Maize KS. **Other U.S. locations:** AR; FL; OK; SC; TX. **International locations:** Worldwide. **Subsidiaries include:** Coleman Powermate, Inc. **Parent company:** American Household (formerly Sunbeam). **Operations at this facility include:** Unitary Products/Evcon division; Administration; Manufacturing of home heating, air conditioning, and heat pump products. **Chairman:** Jerry W. Levin. **Annual sales/revenues:** $1 billion. **Number of employees at this location:** 1,300. **Number of employees nationwide:** 2,000.

COLLINS INDUSTRIES, INC.
P.O. Box 2946, Hutchinson KS 67504-2946. 620/663-5551. **Physical address:** 15 Compound Drive, Hutchinson KS 67502. **Toll-free phone:** 866/669-1842. **Fax:** 620/663-1630. **Contact:** Human Resources. **World Wide Web address:** http://www.collinsind.com. **Description:** Designs, manufactures, and sells ambulances, specialty vehicles, and products which include school buses, shuttle buses, commercial bus chassis, road construction equipment, wheelchair lifts, medical support vans, and terminal trucks used to move trailers and containers in warehouses. All products are marketed under its subsidiary brand names. Founded in 1971. **NOTE:** Application materials can be sent to parent company headquarters or directly to the subsidiary. **Positions advertised include:** Master Painter; Chassis Painter; Customer Service Representative; Engineer; Production Manager; Sales Representative. **Corporate headquarters location:** This location. **Other area locations:** South Hutchinson KS. **Other U.S. locations:** FL; TX. **Subsidiaries include:** Capacity of Texas, Inc. (terminal trucks); Collins Bus Corporation; Lay-Mor (road construction); Mid Bus Corporation (small school buses); Waldon Equipment; Wheeled Coach Industries (ambulances); World Trans, Inc. (commercial buses). **Listed on:** NASDAQ. **Stock exchange symbol:** COLL. **Chairman:** Don L. Collins. **Annual sales/revenues:** $200 million. **Number of employees nationwide:** 1000.

COMMERCE BANK
150 North Main Street, Wichita KS 67202. 316/261-4924. **Contact:** Personnel Manager. **E-mail address:** webhr@commercebank.com. **World Wide Web address:** http://www.commercebank.com. **Description:** Commerce Bank, N.A. (Kansas) is one of the subsidiaries of the holding company Commerce Bancshares, Inc. that operates over 300 branches in Missouri, Illinois, and Kansas, with a credit card division in Nebraska. Founded in 1865, the bank makes business and consumer loans as well as writing mortgages and construction loans, most of which are made in the St. Louis and Kansas City MO markets. Commerce Bank, N.A. (Kansas) is a full-service bank operating branches throughout Kansas. **Positions advertised include:** Portfolio Manager; Credit Analyst; Teller; Teller Supervisor. **Other U.S. locations:** IL; MO. **Parent company:** Commerce Bancshares, Inc. 1000 Walnut, P.O. Box 13686, Kansas City MO 64199. **Listed on:** NASDAQ. **Stock exchange symbol:** CBSH. **Chairman/President/CEO:** David W. Kemper. **Annual sales/revenues:** $652 million. **Number of employees nationwide:** 5,400.

CONTROL SYSTEMS INTERNATIONAL INC.
8040 Nieman Road, Lenexa KS 66214. 913/599-5010. **Fax:** 913/599-5013. **Contact:** Human Resources. **E-mail address:** resume@csiks.com. **World Wide Web address:** http://www.csiks.com. **Description:** Manufactures networking systems that aid in fuel distribution management. Founded in 1968. **NOTE:** Entry-level positions are offered. **Positions advertised include:** Electrical/Electronics Engineer; Software Engineer. **Corporate headquarters location:** This location. **Other U.S. locations:** Irvine CA. **International locations:** London, England. **Listed on:** Privately held. **Annual sales/revenues:** $21 - $50 million. **Number of employees worldwide:** 160.

COVANSYS CORPORATION
dba PDA SOFTWARE SERVICES, INC.
7701 College Boulevard, Overland Park KS 66210. 913/469-8700. **Fax:** 913/469-5814. **Contact:** Shari Maple, Recruiting Manager. **E-mail address:** Smaple@covansys.com. **World Wide Web address:** http://www.pdainc.com. **Description:** As of June 2002 Covansys Corp. acquired PDA, which had been a wholly owned subsidiary of Selective Insurance Group, Inc. Founded in 1975 PDA develops and maintains information systems for states that are required to meet federal tracking mandates of the WIC Program (Women, Infants & Children) and offers the Web-based product, FloodConnect for private insurers managing flood insurance through the National Flood Insurance Program. The company provides software consulting, application development and processing services, which include Web development, and data exchange for federal and state agencies as well as for insurance, agrochemical, and pharmaceutical industries. **Positions advertised include:** IIPAA Privacy Consultant; Director/Senior Director. **Corporate headquarters location:** Farmington Hills MI. **Listed on:** NASDAQ. **Stock exchange symbol:** CVNS. **Co-Chairmen:** Ned Lautenbach and Rajendra Vattikuti. **Annual sales/revenues:** CVNS: $383 million; PDA: $18 million. **Number of employees at this location:** 190. **Number of employees worldwide:** 4,500

COX COMMUNICATIONS, INC.
701 East Douglas, Wichita KS 67202. 316/262-0661. **Contact:** Human Resources. **World Wide Web address:** http://www.cox.com. **Description:** A full-service telecom and cable company offering advanced digital video services as Cox Digital Cable to 6.3 million customers and telephone service as Cox Digital Telephone. Cox High Speed Internet provides Internet access and Cox Business Services specialize in commercial voice and data services with a fiber-optic network. Founded in 1962. **NOTE:** Applicants can register resumes and apply via the company's Cox SpotLighter online resume website: http://www.cox.com/coxcareer/spotlighter.asp. **Positions advertised include:** Field Maintenance Worker; Customer Care Associate; Marketing Associate; Information Technology Associate; Sales Associate; Human Resources Representative; Vice President Customer Care. **Corporate headquarters location:** Atlanta GA. **Other area locations:** Coffeyville KS; Dodge City KS; Junction City KS; Pittsburg KS; Topeka KS. **Other U.S. locations:** Nationwide. **Parent company:** Cox Enterprises. **Listed on:** New York Stock Exchange. **Stock exchange symbol:** COX. **Chairman:** James Cox Kennedy. **Annual sales/revenues:** $ 8 billion. **Number of employees:** 21,000.

DEARBORN MID-WEST CONVEYOR CO.
2601 Mid-West Drive, Kansas City KS 66111. 913/261-2403. **Fax:** 913/441-8348. **Contact:** Tom Joslin, Personnel Manager. **E-mail address:** tomj@dmwcc.com. **World Wide Web address:** http://www.dmwcc.com. **Description:** Manufacturer of postal and bulk conveyors as well as skid and floor conveyors. It also provides integrated material handling systems for automotive and industrial assembly operations, postal facilities, and bulk handling. Founded in 1947. **Positions advertised include:** Buyer; Design Engineer; Designer; Draftsperson; Electrician; Mechanical Engineer; Project Manager; Structural Engineer. **Corporate headquarters location:** Taylor MI. **Other U.S. locations:** DE; MI; MO; WI. **Parent company:** Tomkins Industries, Inc. **Operations at this facility include:** Administration; Manufacturing; Research and Development; Sales. **President/CEO:** Wes Paisley. **Annual sales/revenues:** $200 million. **Number of employees at this location:** 210. **Number of employees nationwide:** 320.

DELUXE CORPORATION
16505 West 113th Street, Lenexa KS 66219. 913/541-7952. **Contact:** Human Resources. **World Wide Web address:** http://www.deluxe.com. **Description:** Provides check printing, electronic funds transfer processing services, and related services to the financial industry; check authorization and collection services to retailers; and electronic benefit transfer services to state governments. Deluxe also produces forms, specialty papers, and other products for small businesses, professional practices, and medical/dental offices; and provides tax forms and electronic tax filing services to tax preparers. Through the direct mail channel, Deluxe sells greeting cards, gift-wrap, and related products to households. The company also produces a water-washable ink. Founded in 1915. **NOTE:** The company strongly discourages paper, e-mail and faxed resumes. The preferred method of submitting a resume is via the company website: http://www.deluxe.com/dlxab/deluxe-jobs-main.jsp. **Positions advertised include:** ONE Phone Trainer; Technology Solutions Manager; Customer Service Representative; Production Worker. **Special programs:** Internships; Training; Summer Jobs. **Corporate headquarters location:** Shoreview MN. **Other U.S. locations:** Nationwide. **Listed on:** New York Stock Exchange. **Stock exchange symbol:** DLX. **Chairman/CEO:** Lawrence J. Mosner. **Annual sales/revenues:** $1.3 billion. **Number of employees nationwide:** 6,700.

DUCKWALL-ALCO STORES, INC.
401 Cottage Avenue, Abilene KS 67410. 785/263-3350. **Fax:** 785/263-1789. **Contact:** Dan Curoe, Vice President of Training & Recruiting. **E-mail address:** dcuroe@duckwall.com. **World Wide Web address:** http://www.duckwall.com. **Description:** A regional retailer operating 170 ALCO discount stores and over 90 Duckwell variety stores in small towns in 21 Midwest states. It distributes a full-line of 35,000 sundry discount items. Founded in 1901. **Positions advertised include:** Management Trainee; Assistant Manager; Store Manager; Store Associate. **Special programs:** Management Training Program; full-time and part-time positions. **Office hours:** Monday - Friday, 8:00 a.m. - 5:00 p.m. **Corporate headquarters location:** This location. **Listed on:** NASDAQ. **Stock exchange symbol:** DUCK. **Chairman/President/CEO:** Glen L. Shank. **Annual sales/revenues:** $4.5 million. **Number of employees at this location:** 200. **Number of employees nationwide:** 5,200.

MARTIN K. EBY CONSTRUCTION CO., INC.
P.O. Box 1679, Wichita KS 67201-1679. 316/268-3500. **Physical address:** 610 North Main Street, Wichita KS 67203. **Fax:** 316/268-3616. **Contact:** Larry Cheatham, Vice President of Corporate Services. **E-mail address:** cheatham@ebycorp.com. **World Wide Web address:** http://www.ebycorp.com. **Description:** A general contractor for commercial buildings, treatment plants, pipelines, heavy highways, locks, dams, and power plants. Founded in 1937. **NOTE:** Entry-level positions are offered. **Positions advertised include:** Project Engineer; Superintendent; Project Manager; Estimator; Civil Engineer; Foreman; Carpenter; Bricklayer; Ironworker; Cement Finisher; Laborer. **Special programs:** Internships; Co-ops. **Corporate headquarters location:** This location. **Other U.S. locations:** Maitland FL; Austin TX; Bedford TX. **Parent company:** Eby Corporation. **Listed on:** Privately held. **President:** Rich Bean. **Annual sales/revenues:** More than $170 million. **Number of employees nationwide:** 800.

ELECTRO DYNAMICS CRYSTAL CORPORATION (EDC)
9075 Cody Street, Overland Park KS 66214. 913/888-1750. **Toll-free phone:** 800/332-9825. **Fax:** 913/888-1260. **Contact:** Jane Madsen, Personnel Director. **E-mail address:** janem@electrodynamics.com. **World Wide Web address:** http://www.electrodynamics.com. **Description:** Manufactures a variety of components used in consumer entertainment products and the defense electronics industry specializing in top quality crystals, filters, and oscillators. Founded in 1963. **Parent company:** SFE Technologies. **President:** Tim Abbott.

GE GLOBAL INSURANCE HOLDING CORP.
dba EMPLOYERS REINSURANCE CORPORATION
P.O. Box 2991, Shawnee Mission KS 66201. 913/676-5200. **Toll-free phone:** 800/255-6931. **Physical address:** 5200 Metcalf Avenue, Overland Park KS 66202. **Fax:** 913/676-5221. **Contact:** Human Resources. **World Wide Web address:** http://www.geinsurancesolutions.com. **Description:** The GE Global Insurance Holding Corporation is a family of ten insurance companies with Employers Reinsurance Corporation the flagship company providing property, casualty, life, and health reinsurance. **NOTE:** Resumes can be submitted online via the company website or by sending to: GE Suite #26, P.O. Box 549231, Waltham MA 02454-9231. **Positions advertised include:** Commercial Compliance Leader; Commercial Insurance Communicator; Underwriting Associate; Audit leader; Actuarial Associate; Project Manager; Information Technology Security; Claims Specialist; Accounting; Administrative Assistant; Training & Change Management; P & C Global Compliance Leader; Insurance Auditor; Call Center Associate; Health Care Actuary Representative. **Parent company:** General Electric. **Chairman/President/CEO:** Ron Pressman. **Annual sales/revenues:** $8.8 billion. **Number of employees:** 3,200.

EXCEL CORPORATION
151 North Main, Wichita KS 67202. 316/291-2500. **Recorded jobline:** 877/292-6570. **Contact:** Corporate Recruiter. **E-mail address:** excelmeats@hiresystems.com. **World Wide Web address:** http://www.excelmeats.com. **Description:** A wholly owned subsidiary of Cargill Incorporated providing innovative red meat solutions by offering an extensive line of premium quality beef and pork products and programs to recognized retail and commercial foodservice markets worldwide. It is the second largest beef and pork packing company in the U.S. Founded in 1936. **NOTE:** Resumes must be submitted online via the company website or by sending to: Excel Corporation Resume Processing, Box 540247, Waltham MA 02454. **Positions advertised include:** Plant Systems Associate; Customer Service Representative; Financial Analyst. **Special programs:** Training program, internships, and entry-level positions are offered. **Corporate headquarters location:** This location. **Other area locations:** Dodge City KS. **Other U.S. locations:** Nationwide. **International locations:** Australia; China; Honduras; Japan; Korea; Taiwan. **Parent company:** Cargill, Inc. **Listed on:** Privately held. **President:** Bill Buckner. **Annual sales/revenues:** More than $100 million. **Number of employees at this location:** 600. **Number of employees nationwide:** 21,000.

FUNK MANUFACTURING COMPANY
P.O. Box 577, Coffeyville KS 67337. 620/251-3400. **Physical address:** Industrial Park Highway 169 North, Coffeyville KS 67337. **Fax:** 620/252-3252. **Contact:** Human Resources. **World Wide Web address:** http://www.deere.com/jdpower. **Description:** Engaged in the design and manufacture of power transmissions. Primary applications include heavy-duty, off-road equipment, serving customers in the construction, mining, railway maintenance, forestry, and agricultural markets. Founded in 1941. **NOTE:** The company does not accept faxed, paper, or hand delivered resumes. Applicants must apply online at http://www.johndeere.com and select "John Deere Careers", click "Job Search", Select "Kansas", and search. **Positions advertised include:** Accountant/Auditor; Computer Programmer; Draftsperson; Industrial Engineer; Manufacturer's/Wholesaler's Sales Representative; Marketing Specialist; Mechanical Engineer; Quality Control Supervisor; Systems Analyst. **Corporate headquarters location:** This location. **Other area locations:** Lenexa KS. **Other U.S. locations:** Nationwide. **Parent company:** Deere Power Systems. **Operations at this facility include:** Administration; Manufacturing; Research and Development; Sales.

GENERAL MOTORS CORPORATION, NORTH AMERICA
3201 Fairfax Traffic Way, Kansas City KS 66115. 913/573-7000. **Contact:** Human Resources. **World Wide Web address:** http://www.gm.com. **Description:** General Motors is the world's number one car and truck maker with operations in 30 countries and interests in communications, locomotives, finance, and insurance. GM North America, one of GM's four regional automobile divisions, designs, manufactures, and markets vehicles under the brands: Chevrolet, Pontiac, GMC, Buick, Cadillac, Saturn, and Hummer. The Fairfax II Assembly Plant at this location manufactures the Pontiac Grand Prix and is being retooled to produce the new Malibu. Founded in 1908. **NOTE:** Resumes may be submitted online for open positions. **Positions advertised include:** Senior Plant Engineer; Production Supervisor. **Corporate headquarters location:** Detroit MI. **Other area locations:** Olathe KS; Shawnee Mission KS; Topeka KS. **Listed on:** New York Stock Exchange. **Stock exchange symbol:** GM. **President:** (of GMNA) Gary L. Cowgar. **Annual sales/revenues:** $187 billion. **Number of employees at this location:** 3,000. **Number of employees worldwide:** 340,000.

GOODRICH CORPORATION
400 New Century Parkway, New Century KS 66031. 913/764-2452. **Contact:** Human Resources. **World Wide Web address:** http://www.goodrich.com. **Description:** The Goodrich Corporation, formerly the BF Goodrich tire maker, is now focused on its aerospace business: Airframe Systems, Electronic Systems, and Engine Systems. The company also services Boeing and Airbus with aircraft maintenance and repair operating 133 facilities in 20 countries. **Office Hours:** Monday – Friday, 8:00 a.m. – 5:00 p.m. **NOTE:** The company receives resumes via their Online Resume Tool. **Positions advertised include:** Electronic Assembler. **Corporate headquarters location:** Charlotte NC. **Other area locations:** New Century KS. **Other U.S. locations:** Nationwide. **International locations:** Worldwide. **Operations at this facility include:** Goodrich Aerospace Aircraft Wheel & Brake Overhaul facility; JcAIR Avionics Equipment Testing Systems in New Century KS. **Listed on:** New York Stock Exchange. **Stock exchange symbol:** GR. **Chairman/CEO:** Marshall O. Larsen. **Annual sales/revenues:** $4 billion. **Number of employees worldwide:** 19,200.

GOODYEAR TIRE & RUBBER COMPANY
P.O. Box 1069, Topeka KS 66601. 785/295-7111. **Physical address:** 2000 Northwest Highway 24, Topeka KS 66618. **Recorded jobline:** 800/782-4473. **Contact:** Human Resources. **World Wide Web address:** http://www.goodyear.com. **Description:** This location manufactures tires. Overall, Goodyear Tire & Rubber Company's principal business is the development, manufacture, distribution, and sale of tires for most applications worldwide. Goodyear also manufactures and sells a broad spectrum of rubber products and rubber-related chemicals for various industrial and consumer markets, and provides auto repair services at over 2,000 service center outlets. **NOTE:** Applications accepted via the company's Website. For this location check http://www.keystaffing.com for current employment opportunities. **Positions advertised include:** Auto Tech; General Maintenance; Sales Associate; Store Management Trainee. **Office Hours:** Monday – Friday. 7:30 a.m. – 4:30 p.m. **Special programs:** Store Management Training. **Corporate headquarters location:** Akron OH. **Other area locations:** Independence KS; Ottowa KS; Shawnee Mission KS. **Other U.S. locations:** Nationwide. **International locations:** Worldwide. **Subsidiaries include:** Celeron; Goodyear Asia; Goodyear Europe; Goodyear Latin America; Goodyear Racing; Kelly-Springfield; North American Tire. **Operations at this location:** In addition to several retail service centers in the state, the company operates the Topeka tire plant. **Listed on:** New York Stock Exchange. **Stock exchange symbol:** GT. **Chairman:** Samir G. Gibara. **Annual sales/revenues:** $14.1 billion. **Number of employees at the Topeka Tire Plant:** 1,700. **Number of employees worldwide:** 96,000.

HALLMARK CARDS INC.
P.O. Box 99, Lawrence KS 66044. 785/843-9050. **Physical address:** 101 Mcdonald Drive, Lawrence KS 66044. **Fax:** 785/841-4508. **Contact:** Human Resources. **World Wide Web address:** http://www.hallmark.com. **Description:** Produces a variety of gift cards for many occasions and sells under brand names Hallmark, Shoebox, and Ambassador in more than 42,000 retail stores nationwide. **NOTE:** This location hires only through local job service agencies. **Corporate headquarters location:** Kansas City MO. **Other area locations:** Topeka (factory) KS; Leavenworth (factory) KS. **Subsidiaries include:** Binney & Smith, Inc.; Crown Center Redevelopment Corp.; Crown Media Holdings, Inc.; Day Spring Cards, Inc.; Gift Certificate Center; Hallmark Entertainment, Inc.; Halls Merchandising, Inc.; Image Arts; InterArt; Irresistible Ink, Inc.; Litho-Krane Co.; The Picture People; William Arthur. **Operations at this facility include:** Manufacturing activities at all three Kansas factories. **Chairman:** Donald J. Hall. **Number of employees at this location:** over 500. **Number of employees worldwide:** 21,700.

HILLS PET NUTRITION, INC.
P.O. Box 148, Topeka KS 66601. 785/354-8523. **Physical address:** 400 Southwest 8th Avenue. **Toll-free phone:** 800/255-0449. **Fax:** 785/368-5915. **Contact:** Human Resources. **World Wide Web address:** http://www.hillspet.com. **Description:** Manufacturer and distributor of premium pet food lines including: Science Diet, Pet Nutrition, and over 30 Prescription Diet products only available through veterinarians. The company specializes in producing products for pets' dietary requirements, medical conditions and ages, and are sold in more than 85 countries. Founded in 1943. **NOTE:** Resumes can be submitted online through the company website. **Office Hours:** Monday – Friday, 9:00 a.m. – 4:00 p.m. **Positions advertised include:** Scientific Spokesperson. **Corporate headquarters location:** This location. **Other area locations:** Meriden KS; Lawrence KS; Seneca KS. **Other U.S. locations:** AZ; CA; KY; MO; OR; TX. **Parent company:** Colgate-Palmolive Company. **Operations at this facility include:** Science & Technology Center; Manufacturing Plant;

Administrative Offices. **Chairman/CEO:** Robert C. Wheeler. **Annual sales/revenues:** $1.2 billion.

HONEYWELL AEROSPACE
dba BENDIX/KING AVIONICS
One Technology Center, 23500 West 105th Street, Olathe KS 66061. 913/712-0400. **Toll-free phone:** 800/247-0230. **Fax:** 913/712-3145. **Contact:** Human Resources. **World Wide Web address:** http://www.honeywellaerospace.com. **Description:** Honeywell Aerospace, a division of Honeywell International, produces aircraft engines and systems, aerospace electronics, and landing gear components, as well as hydraulic systems and pneumatic products. Honeywell now manufactures products under the Bendix/King brand name products, which include communication and navigation avionics, weather radar, flight controls, flight information services, Integrated Hazard Avoidance Systems, and multi-function displays, as well as landing gear brakes and wheels for aircraft manufacturers, airlines, business and general aviation, military, space, and airport operations. **NOTE:** Applications and resumes can be submitted via the company website: http://www.honeywell.com/careers. **Positions advertised include:** Financial Accounting Representative. **Special programs:** Internships. **Corporate headquarters location:** Phoenix AZ. **Other are locations:** Independence KS; Lawrence KS; Ottowa KS; Shawnee Mission KS; Wichita KS. **Other U.S. locations:** AZ; FL; IN; MD; MN; NM; OH. **Parent company:** Honeywell International, Inc. **Operations at this facility include:** Bendix/King productions; Wingman Services; Sales & Marketing; Administration. **Listed on:** New York Stock Exchange; London Stock Exchange; Chicago Stock Exchange; Pacific Stock Exchange. **Stock exchange symbol:** HON. **President/CEO:** Robert D. Johnson. **Annual sales/revenues:** $10 billion. **Number of employees:** 120,000.

HUHTAMAKI
9201 Packaging Drive, De Soto KS 66018. 913/583-3025. **Fax:** 913/583-8756 **Contact:** Human Resources. **World Wide Web address:** http://www.huhtamaki.com. **Description:** Consumer packaging company operating facilities in 36 countries. It manufactures plastic packaging, disposable tableware, and paper cups as well as packaging for dairy products, frozen meals, fresh produce, and deli items under such brand names as Sealright and Chinet. Founded in 1920. **Corporate headquarters location:** Espoo, Finland. **Other U.S. locations:** AL; AZ; CA; IN; ME; MI; NY; PA; OH. **International locations:** Worldwide. **Operations at this facility include:** Huhtamaki North America Division Headquarters; Foodservice Business Unit Headquarters; Consumer Packaging Business Unit Headquarters; Paperboard production; Administration; Manufacturing. **Listed on:** Helsinki Stock Exchange. **Stock exchange symbol:** HUH. **Chairman:** Veli Sunback. **NA Division President:** Larry Mason. **Annual sales/revenues:** $2.1 billion. **Number of employees worldwide:** 16,000.

IBM
16011 College Boulevard, Lenexa KS 66219. 913/599-7112. **Contact:** Helen Porter-Ferguson, Human Resources. **World Wide Web address:** http://www.ibm.com. **Description:** Provides database technology to build, deploy, run, and evolve applications. Products include powerful distributed database management systems, application development tools, and graphic- and character-based productivity software for delivering information to every significant desktop platform. **NOTE:** Resumes may be submitted via IBM's Global Employment website: http://www.ibm.com/employment. **Positions advertised include:** Senior Software Engineer; Services Support Representative; Customer Engineer; Computer Programmer. **Special programs:** Internships. **Corporate headquarters location:** White Plains NY. **Other area locations:** Overland Park KS; Shawnee Mission KS; Topeka KS; Wichita KS. **U.S. locations:** Nationwide. **International locations:** Worldwide. **Subsidiaries include:** Hitachi Global Storage Technologies; IBM Canada Ltd; IBM-Microelectronics; IBM-Hardware; IBM-Services; IBM-Software; Lotus Development Corporation; Tivoli Software. **Listed on:** New York Stock Exchange. **Stock exchange symbol:** IBM. **President/Chairman/CEO:** Samuel J. Palmisano. **Annual sales/revenues:** $81 billion. **Number of employees worldwide:** 320,000

IBP FRESH MEATS GROUP
2101 West Sixth Avenue, Emporia KS 66801. 620/343-3640. **Contact:** Processing Personnel. **E-mail address:** ibpstaff@ibpinc.com. **World Wide Web address:** http://www.ibpinc.com. **Description:** Fresh meat processor which slaughters and sells boxed beef, fresh pork, and value-added meats with 20 processing sites in North America and sales offices worldwide, and also operates swine research and breeding facilities. Formerly Iowa Beef Processors, under Tyson the company was reorganized to focus only on its 350 fresh meats products including the Thomas E. Wilson brand with processed and frozen foods operations moved to other Tyson units. Founded in 1960. **NOTE:** Resumes and cover letters should be sent directly to: Corporate Recruiter, Tyson's IBP Fresh Meats Headquarters, 800 Stevens Port Drive, Suite 818, Dakota Dunes SD 570490; or fax to: 605/235-2025. **Corporate headquarters location:** Dakota Dunes SD. **Other area locations:** Finney County KS; Hutchinson KS; Olathe KS; South Hutchinson KS. **Other U.S. locations:** Nationwide. **International locations:** England; Japan; Taiwan; China; Korea; Russia; Mexico. **Parent company:** Tyson Foods. **Operations at this facility include:** Beef processing plant; Cold storage warehouse. **Vice President:** Eugene D. Leman. **Annual sales/revenues:** $13 billion. **Number of employees worldwide:** 41,000.

IBT INC.
9400 West 55th Street, Merriam KS 66203. 913/677-3151. **Toll-free phone:** 800/332-2114. **Fax:** 913/362-1413. **E-mail address:** ibtinfo@ibtinc.com. **Contact:** Human Resources Manager. **World Wide Web address:** http://www.ibtinc.com. **Description:** Manufacturer and distributor of belts, bearings, transmission products and other industrial products with 48 service centers in 11 Midwest states. In addition to industrial supplies, the company distributes rubber hoses, belting products, electrical supplies, and material-handling equipment, as well as providing engineering and media production services. Founded in 1949. **Corporate headquarters location:** This location. **Other area locations:** Statewide. **Operations at this facility include:** Administration; Central Distribution Center. **President/CEO:** Stephen R. Cloud. **Number of employees:** 120.

KANSAS DEPARTMENT OF TRANSPORTATION (KDOT)
Docking State Office Building, 915 SW Harrison Street, 7th Floor, Topeka KS 66612. 785/296-3566. **Fax:** 785/296-0287. **E-mail address:** recruit@ksdot.org. **Contact:** Ruth Marstall. **World Wide Web address:** http://wwwksdot.org. **Description:** Engaged in the construction and maintenance of Kansas's state and interstate highways. **Positions advertised include:** Engineering Associate-Bridge Sector; Engineering Associate-Road Sector; Engineering Associate-Traffic Sector; Civil Engineer; Programmer; Inspector; Surveyor. **Special programs:** Internships. **Corporate headquarters location:** This location. **Number of employees at this location:** 3,200.

KANSAS DEPARTMENT OF WILDLIFE AND PARKS
512 SE 25th Avenue, Pratt KS 67124. 785/296-2281. **Contact:** Human Resources. **World Wide Web address:** http://www.kdwp.state.ks.us. **Description:** State Park agency and nature conservation organization maintaining the state's open spaces and public lands as well as preserving the state's natural heritage, wildlife, and habitat. **Positions advertised include:** Public Service Executive II; Environmental Scientist II; Natural Resource Officer; Environmental Scientist I. **Special programs:** Seasonal positions include Creel Clerk; Fishing Clinic Instructor; Fisheries Aide. **Other area locations:** Statewide.

KANSAS WESLEYAN UNIVERSITY
100 East Claflin Avenue, Salina KS 67401-6196. 785/827-5541. **Contact:** Human Resources. **World Wide Web address:** http://www.kwu.edu. **Description:** A university affiliated with the United Methodist Church with an enrollment of 800 students. Founded in 1886. **Positions advertised include:** Controller; Communications Faculty; Sociology Faculty; Resident Director.

KOCH-GLITSCH, LP
4111 East 37th Street North, Wichita KS 67220. 316/828-5110. **Fax:** 316/828-5263. **Contact:** Human Resources. **E-mail address:** kgjob@kochind.com. **World Wide Web address:** http://www.koch-glitsch.com. **Description:** Koch-Glitsch (pronounced 'coke') is a refinery equipment manufacturer fabricating metal plates, sheet metal, and petroleum processing equipment, pollution control equipment, and mesh products for the automotive industry, and a leading producer of mass transfer, mist elimination, and motionless mixer technology. **NOTE:** Send resumes to: Applicant Center, P.O. Box 8127, Wichita KS 67208. **Positions advertised include:** Accounting Clerk; NCPP Operator; Shear Operator. **Other U.S. locations:** Nationwide. **International locations:** Italy; Japan. **Parent company:** Koch Chemical Technology Group, LLC.

KOCH INDUSTRIES, INC.
P.O. Box 2972, Wichita KS 67201. 316/828-5500. **Physical address:** 4111 East 37th Street North, Wichita KS 67220. **Fax:** 316/828-5739. **Recorded jobline:** 316/828-5627. **Contact:** Human Resources Manager. **E-mail address:** jobs@kochind.com. **World Wide Web address:** http://www.kochind.com. **Description:** A fully integrated energy company with holdings in oil, gas, chemicals, minerals, ranching, and securities including two refineries. It operates pipeline networks, processes natural gas liquids, and operates gas gathering systems and has interests in commodity trading, asphalt marketing, and chemical manufacture equipment. Controlled by the Koch brothers. **NOTE:** Resumes are requested to be posted to the company website: http://www.kochcareers.com. **Positions advertised include:** Accountant; Analyst; Controller; EH & S Compliance Systems Manager; Groundskeeper; Help Desk Specialist; Information Technologist Administrator; Payroll; Risk Analyst; Shear Operator; Tax Analyst; Work Station Technologist. **Corporate headquarters location:** This location. **Other area locations:** Dodge City KS; El Dorado KS; Eureka KS; Hutchinson KS; Kansas City KS; McPherson KS; Salina KS. **Other U.S. locations:** Nationwide. **International locations:** Worldwide. **Listed on:** Privately held. **Chairman/CEO:** Charles G. Koch. **Annual sales/revenues:** $40 billion. **Number of employees at this location:** 2,000. **Number of employees worldwide:** 11,000.

KRAUSE CORPORATION
P.O. Box 2707, Hutchinson KS 67504-2707. 620/663-6161. **Physical address:** 305 South Monroe, Hutchinson KS 67501. **Toll-free phone:** 800/957-2873. **Contact:** Personnel Manager. **World Wide Web address:** http://www.krauseco.com. **Description:** A family-owned corporation that manufactures and markets plows, tilling systems, farm machinery, and waste management equipment. The company is also engaged in truck-mounted hoists, compactors, captive-foundry forging and ductile iron forging. Founded in 1920. **Positions advertised include:** Engineer; Manager. **Corporate headquarters location:** This location. **Operations at this facility include:** Administration; Manufacturing; Research and Development; Sales; Service. **Listed on:** Privately held. **Chairman:** Norman L. Krause.

LSI LOGIC
3718 North Rock Road, Wichita KS 67226. 316/636-8000. **Contact:** Human Resources. **World Wide Web address:** http://www.lsilogic.com. **Description:** Manufactures and designs communications systems and storage semiconductors that access, interconnect, and store data, voice, and video. The company produces standard and custom integrated circuits specializing in broadband and wireless communications, consumer electronics, and data networking. In addition to its system-on-a-chip devices the company supplies servers, storage network solutions, and software for storage area networks. Founded in 1981. **Positions advertised include:** Human Resources Administrative Assistant; Failure Analysis Technician; Director of Manufacturing Engineering; Material Handler; Production Planning and Control; Manufacturing Manager; Storage Assembly Specialist; Buyer; Test Engineering Technician; Design Engineer; Applications Engineer. **Corporate headquarters location:** Milpitas CA. **Other U.S. locations:** Nationwide. **International locations:** Worldwide. **Listed on:** New York Stock Exchange. **Stock exchange symbol:** LSI. **Chairman/CEO:** Wilfred J. Corrigan. **Annual sales/revenues:** $1.8 billion. **Number of employees worldwide:** 6,000.

LA PETITE ACADEMY, INC.
8717 West 110th Street, Suite 300, Overland Park KS 66210. 913/345-1250. **Toll-free phone:** 888/568-5115. **Contact:** Human Resources. **E-mail address:** careers@lpacorp.com. **World Wide Web address:** http://www.lapetite.com. **Description:** Operator of a system of proprietary childcare facilities and preschool education centers with over 700 centers in 36 states with some 75,000 children from six-weeks to 12-years of age. La Petite Academy and Montessori Unlimited provide full- and part-time childcare, early learning, educational and developmental programs, and workplace childcare. Founded in 1970, J.P. Morgan Partners owns a controlling interest in the company. **NOTE:** See website for current employment opportunities. **Positions advertised include:** AIM. **Corporate Headquarters location:** Chicago IL. **Other area locations:** Lawrence KS; Olathe KS; Overland Park KS; Shawnee Mission KS; Topeka KS; Wichita KS. **Other U.S. locations:** Nationwide. **Operations at this facility include:** Regional headquarters; Administration. **Listed on:** Privately held. **President/CEO:** Judith A. Rogala. **Annual sales/revenues:** $385 million. **Number of employees nationwide:** 12,800.

LABONE INC.
10101 Renner Boulevard, Lenexa KS 66219. 913/888-1770. **Recorded jobline:** 913/577-1249. **Contact:** Human Resources. **E-mail address:** jobs@labone.com. **World Wide Web address:** http://www.labone.com. **Description:** Provides medical and drug testing for the insurance industry as well as for employees to detect the existence of infection, cardiovascular disease, HIV, and tobacco use. The company's tests are specifically designed to provide a standardized format to assist insurance companies in objectively evaluating the mortality or morbidity risk posed by policy applicants. Formerly Home Office Reference Laboratory, the company is a centralized laboratory in the Kansas City area that provides testing and information services including risk assessment information, healthcare services, and drug testing to determine eligibility and premium payment levels. Testing uses individual specimens as well as telephone inspections and motor vehicle reports. The company also performs substance abuse testing, urinalysis, and Pap smears. Founded in 1972, the company has

two divisions: Risk Assessment and Clinical. **Positions advertised include:** Marketing Representative; Buyer Position; Currier Supervisor Positions; Associate C Engineer Position; Medical Lab Tech; Setup Associate; Technical Account Manager; Account Marketing Associate. **Corporate headquarters location:** This location. **Other area locations:** Olathe KS; Shawnee Mission KS; Topeka KS. **Other U.S. locations:** MO. **International locations:** Canada. **Subsidiaries include:** Osborn Group, Inc.; LabOne Canada, Inc.; Systematic Business Services Inc.; ExamOne World Wide, Inc.; Intellisys. **Listed on:** NASDAQ. **Stock exchange symbol:** LABS. **Chairman/President/CEO:** W. Thomas Grant III. **Annual sales/revenues:** $234 million. **Number of employees:** 1,625.

LANDOLL CORPORATION
1900 North Street, Marysville KS 66508. 785/562-4705. **Fax:** 785/562-4851. **Contact:** Ramona Wienck, Human Resource Manager. **E-mail address:** Ramona_wienck@landoll.com. **World Wide Web address:** http://www.landoll.com. **Description:** Designs, manufactures, and markets products and services for agriculture, transportation, material handling, OEM, and government. **Positions advertised include:** Drafter; Mechanical Engineer; Industrial Engineer.

LAWRENCE, CITY OF
P.O. Box 708, Lawrence KS 66044-0708. 785/832-3203. **Physical address:** 6 East Sixth Street, Lawrence KS 66044. **Fax:** 785/832-3305. **Recorded jobline:** 785/832-3333. **Contact:** Personnel Manager. **E-mail address:** personnel@ci.lawrence.ks.us. **World Wide Web address:** http://www.ci.lawrence.ks.us. **Description:** The city of Lawrence's administrative offices provide city services for the community. This location also hires seasonally. **NOTE:** Part-time jobs are offered. A listing of job titles is available to the public at this location and online. Applications are accepted by the city of Lawrence for posted positions only. Clerical positions require a minimum typing score of 40 wpm, and the typing test must be taken at the State Job Service Center (833 Ohio Street, Lawrence KS) before an application can be obtained. **Positions advertised include:** Engineering Intern; Life Guard; Pool Cashier; Utility Billing Clerk; Golf Shop Attendent. **Special programs:** Internships. **Office hours:** Monday - Friday, 8:00 a.m. - 5:00 p.m. **Operations at this facility include:** Administration. **Number of employees at this location:** 650.

LAWRENCE MEMORIAL HOSPITAL
325 Maine Street, Lawrence KS 66044. 785/749-6100. **Fax:** 785/840-3006. **Contact:** Deborah Thompson, Vice President of Human Resources. **E-mail address:** lmhcares@lmh.org **Note:** Applicants may apply online for current positions. **World Wide Web address:** http://www.lmh.org. **Description:** A 177-bed, nonprofit community hospital with a third surgical unit, a 12-bed intensive care unit, a 10-bed rehabilitation unit, an 8-bed pediatric department, a 16-bed mental health unit, and a 13-bed maternity care unit. **NOTE:** Entry-level positions as well as second and third shifts are offered. **Positions advertised include:** Clinical Associate; Registered Nurse; Licensed Practical Nurse; Systems Engineer; Testing Coordinator; Lab Assistant; Clerk III. **Number of employees at this location:** 850.

LEE COMPANY, INC.
P.O. Box 2940, Shawnee Mission KS 66201-1340. 913/789-0679. **Physical address:** One Lee Drive, Merriam KS 66202. **Contact:** Human Resources. **World Wide Web address:** http://www.leejeans.com. **Description:** The Lee Apparel Company is a division of the VF Corporation (NYSE: VF) that manufactures, markets, and distributes brand name jeans, denim and other apparel including casual pants, shirts, fleece, and knit apparel. Founded in 1889. **NOTE:** Jobs posted on parent company website: http://jobsearch.vfc.newjobs.com. **Corporate headquarters location:** This location. **Parent company:** VF Corporation (Greensboro NC). **Number of employees nationwide:** 400.

LONE STAR STEAKHOUSE & SALOON, INC.
P.O. Box 12726, Wichita KS 67277-2726. 316/264-8899. **Physical address:** 224 East Douglas, Suite 700, Wichita KS 67202. **Fax:** 888/384-8326. **Contact:** Human Resources. **E-mail address:** team@thesteakcompany.com. **World Wide Web address:** http://www.lonestarsteakhouse.com. **Description:** Owner/Operator of chain of 250 U.S. restaurants offering mid-priced, full-service, casual dining as well as 20 restaurants worldwide. Specializing in mesquite-grilled steaks, ribs, chicken, and fish with Texas paraphernalia, neon bear signs, and country music. It also operates 15 upscale Sullivan's Steakhouses and five Del Frisco's Double Eagle Steak Houses. **Positions advertised include:** General Manager; Regional Manager; Management Trainee; Restaurant/Food Service Manager Assistant Manager. **Special programs:** Internships. **Corporate headquarters location:** This location. **Other area locations:** Garden City KS; Shawnee Mission KS. **Other U.S. locations:** Nationwide. **Operations at this facility include:** Sales; Service. **Listed on:** NASDAQ. **Stock exchange symbol:** STAR. **CEO:** Jamie B. Coulter. **Annual sales/revenues:** $598 million. **Number of employees nationwide:** 18,425.

MGP INGREDIENTS, INC.
P.O. Box 130, Atchison KS 66002-0130. 913/367-1480. **Physical address:** 1300 Main Street, Atchison KS 66002. **Toll-free phone:** 800/255-0302. **Fax:** 913/367-0192. **Contact:** David E. Rindom, Corporate Director of Human Resources. **E-mail address:** daver@mgpingrediants.com. **World Wide Web address:** http://www.midwestgrain.com. **Description:** Formerly Midwest Grain Products, the company buys wheat locally and produces food additives, alcohol, and flour used in food and beverage processing. By-products are used as additives in alcohol products as well as in animal feed. The Cray family owns a controlling interest in the company. **Company slogan:** Supporting your innovations. **Positions advertised include:** Quality Assurance Chemist. **Special programs:** Internships. **Corporate headquarters location:** This location. **Other area locations:** Kansas City KS. **Other U.S. locations:** Pekin IL **Operations at this facility include:** Administration; Assembly; Distillery; Flour mill; Manufacturing; Research and Development; Sales; Service; Wheat gluten and specialty wheat protein recovery facility; Wheat starch recovery facility. **Listed on:** NASDAQ. **Stock exchange symbol:** MGPI. **Chairman:** Cloud L. (Bud) Cray Jr. **Annual sales/revenues:** $215 million. **Number of employees at this location:** 320. **Number of employees nationwide:** 436.

MEDICALODGES, INC.
P.O. Box 509, Coffeyville KS 67337-0509. 620/251-6700. **Physical address:** 201 West Eighth, Coffeyville KS 67337. **Fax:** 620/251-6427. **Contact:** Director of Training and Resources. **Email address:** mwcarey-ranes@medicalodges.com. **World Wide Web address:** http://www.medicalodges.com. **Description:** An employee-owned health care company operating 23 skilled nursing facilities, 11 assisted living centers, five residential care units, two resident care facilities for the developmentally disabled, a skilled facility for the mentally handicapped, two geriatric psychiatry units, and several specialized units. Most facilities are in rural areas with centers in the Kansas City and Wichita areas. Founded in 1961. **Company slogan:** Quality Care with Dignity **Positions advertised include:** Information Systems Specialist; Nurse Consultant; Regional Business Specialist; Activities Director; Administrative In Training; Certified Medication Aide; Certified Nursing Assistant; Charge Nurse; Directory Service; Housekeeping; Maintenance Plant Supervisor; Marketing Director; Medical Records Clerk; Nurses Aid. **Special programs:** Internships. **Corporate headquarters location:** This location. **Other area locations:** Statewide. **Other U.S. locations:** AR; MO; OK. **Operations at this facility include:** Administration; Service. **Number of employees nationwide:** 2,600.

MEDIWARE INFORMATION SYSTEMS, INC.
11711 West 79th Street, Lenexa KS 66214. 913/307-1000. **Fax:** 913/307-1111. **Contact:** Human Resources. **E-mail address:** hr@mediware.com. **World Wide Web address:** http://www.mediware.com. **Description:** Develops software and data management systems for pharmacies, hospitals, surgical centers, and blood banks specializing in clinical information systems to manage health care facilities. Provides pharmacy stock control systems through its British subsidiary, JAC. Founded in 1980. **Positions advertised include:** Clinical Project Manager; Implementation Consultant; Clinical Sales Consultant; Implementation Specialist; National Sales Director. **Other U.S. locations:** Scotts Valley CA; Melville NY; Lake Oswego OR; Dallas TX. **International locations:** United Kingdom. **Listed on:** NASDAQ. **Stock exchange symbol:** MEDW. **Chairman/Secretary:** Lawrence Auriana. **Annual sales/revenues:** $31 million.

MICROTECH COMPUTERS, INC.
4921 Legends Drive, Lawrence KS 66049. 785/841-9513. **Fax:** 785/841-1809. **Contact:** Personnel. **World Wide Web address:** http://www.microtechcomp.com. **Description:** Develops, manufactures, markets, installs, and services personal computers and related equipment. Primary customers are end users, retailers, corporations, and government agencies. Founded in 1986. **Company slogan:** Your key business partner. **Corporate headquarters location:** This location. **Other area locations:** Shawnee Mission KS; Topeka KS. **Subsidiaries include:** A-Plus Open; MicroOpen; Atipa Technologies. **Operations at this facility include:** Accounting; Administration; Distribution; Manufacturing; Research and Development; Sales; Support Service; Warehouse. **Listed on:** Privately held. **President:** Mike Zheng. **Annual sales/revenues:** $5 million. **Number of employees:** 80.

MODINE MANUFACTURING COMPANY
1401 Industrial Road, Emporia KS 66801. 620/343-1120. **Fax:** 620/343-7480. **Contact:** Human Resources Manager. **World Wide Web address:** http://www.modine.com. **Description:** The world leader in heat-transfer and heat-storage technology for the automotive and building industries with more than 50 locations in 13 countries. Manufactures and markets heat exchanges and technology used in heating, ventilation, and air-conditioning of original equipment manufacturers and for replacement parts such as radiators, oil coolers, air conditioning condensers, building/HVAC products, and radiator cores. Founded in 1916. **Positions advertised include:** Manufacturing Engineer; Production Supervisor. **Note:** Positions are listed on Career Builder http://www.careerbuilder.com **Corporate headquarters location:** Racine WI. **Other U.S. locations:** Nationwide. **International locations:** Worldwide. **Subsidiaries include:** Langerer & Reich (L&R); Austria Warmetauscher GmbH (AWG). **Operations at this facility include:** Manufacturing. **Listed on:** NASDAQ. **Stock exchange symbol:** MODI. **Chairman:** Donald R. Johnson. **Annual sales/revenues:** $1 billion. **Number of employees worldwide:** 7,700.

MT. CARMEL REGIONAL MEDICAL CENTER, INC.
1102 East Centennial, Pittsburg KS 66762. 620/232-0170. **Fax:** 620/232-3586. **Recorded jobline:** 620/235-3535. **Contact:** Human Resources. **E-mail address for nursing:** jhenderson@via-christi.org. **E-mail address for allied health/clerical:** cpuckett@via-christi.org. **World Wide Web address:** http://www.mtcarmel.org. **Description:** A nonprofit medical center with 188 beds offering home health services, inpatient care, emergency care, and a community cancer therapy program. Programs include First Steps, prenatal care for low-income women; Lifetime, a day respite program for those with Alzheimer's disease; CareVan, free transportation to and from medical appointments; Kids Care, a daycare program for sick children; Care Calls, a daily check-in service for those who live alone; and CareLink, an emergency home response system. MCRMC is: a member of Via Christi Health System of Wichita; sponsored by the Sisters of St. Joseph of Wichita and the Sisters of the Sorrowful Mother; and accredited by JCAHO. Founded in 1903. **NOTE:** Applicants accepted for employment must pass an alcohol and drug test as well as a health assessment; an investigative background check of criminal records; past employer information; review of educational institutions and the public or private agencies that issued certification or license; a Medical sanction review; and orientation. Resumes can be submitted through the company's website and applications can be filled out online. **Positions advertised include:** Staff Nurses; Nursing Assistants; CT/MRI Tester; Technologist Nuclear Medicine; Administrative Secretary; Physician Coder; Developmental Coordinator. **Office Hours:** Monday – Friday, 8:00 a.m. – 4:30 p.m. **Special programs:** Nursing Scholarships; Internships. **Subsidiaries include:** Mt. Carmel Medical Center; Mt. Carmel Cancer Center; Mt. Carmel Durable Medical Equipment; Crossroads Counseling Center. **Operations at this facility include:** Administration; Manufacturing; Service. **Annual sales/revenues:** $141 million. **Number of employees at this location:** 1,000.

NCRA (NATIONAL COOPERATIVE REFINERY ASSOCIATION)
P.O. Box 1404, McPherson KS 67460-1404. 620/241-2340. **Physical address:** 1391 Iron Horse Road, McPherson KS 67460. **Fax:** 620/241-5531. **Contact:** Dennis McMurray, Manager of Employee Relations. **E-mail address:** jobs@ncrarefinery.com. **World Wide Web address:** http://www.ncrarefinery.com. **Description:** Operates an oil refinery producing 72,000 barrels per day as well as a products pipeline network throughout the Midwest. Along with corporate headquarters at McPherson the cooperative operates an underground petroleum storage installation at Conway and crude oil trucking and pipeline operations. NCRA has ownership in several subsidiaries; Founded in 1943. **Positions advertised include:** Process Engineer; Truck Driver Gauger; Chemical Engineer. **Corporate headquarters location:** This location. **Other area locations:** Conway KS; Council Bluffs IA; Great Bend KS; Plainville KS; Wichita KS. **Other U.S. locations:** Denver CO; Tulsa OK; Dallas TX. **Subsidiaries include:** Jayhawk Pipline, LLC; Osage Pipe Line Co.; Kaw Pipe Line Co.; Globe Oil Refinery & Pipeline; Clear Creek; AnSon Transportation Company; Refined Products; Crude Purchasing. **Parent company:** CENEX (majority owner at 74.2 percent). **Operations at this facility include:** Refinery; Corporate Administration; Truck Terminal. **Annual sales/revenues:** $700 million. **Number of employees at this location:** 420. **Number of employees nationwide:** 560.

NPC INTERNATIONAL
720 West 20th Street, Pittsburg KS 66762. 620/231-3390. **Fax:** 620/231-3746. **Contact:** Corporate Recruitment Department. **World Wide Web address:** http://www.npcinternational.com. **Description:** NPC, formerly National Pizza Company, owns and operates 840 Pizza Hut restaurants in 27 states. The company recapitalized its controlling majority of the Tony Roma's Restaurant chain in 1998 and retains a minority interest. In August 2001 founder and chairman Gene Bicknell purchased the 35 percent he did not own in a stockholder-approved merger through which the company went private. Founded in 1962. **NOTE:** The above address is for

the Restaurant Service Office; The Chairman/CEO's office is located at 100 North Pine, Pittsburg KS 66762; and NPC's Executive Board is located at 14400 College Boulevard, Suite 201, Lenexa KS 66215. For restaurant positions, see manager. For management positions, send E-mail to: phillips@npcinternational.com. **Positions advertised include:** Dough Master; Cook; Waiter/Waitress; Customer Service Representative; Delivery Driver; Restaurant Shift Manager; Assistant Restaurant Manager; Restaurant Manager; Area Manager. **Special programs:** Internships. **Corporate headquarters location:** This location. **Restaurant locations:** Chanute KS; Emporia KS; Fort Scott KS; Frontenac KS; Girard KS; Parsons KS; Pittsburg KS; Topeka KS. **Listed on:** Privately held. **President/CEO:** O. Gene Bicknell. **Annual sales/revenues:** $536 million. **Number of employees nationwide:** 18,000.

OGDEN PUBLICATIONS, INC.
1503 SW 42nd Street, Topeka KS 66609. 785/274-4300. **Fax:** 785/274-4305. **Contact:** Human Resources. **World Wide Web address:** http://www.ogdenpubs.com. **Description:** Publisher of magazines and books on sustainability, rural lifestyles, and farm memorabilia as well as offering insurance, subscription and financial services. **NOTE:** See parent company Website for employment information: http://www.oweb.com. **Positions advertised include:** Promotions Assistant; Art Director; Associate Editor; Editorial Assistant; Graphic Designer. **Corporate headquarters location:** Wheeling WV. **Subsidiaries/magazines include:** *Capper's; Mother Earth News; Grit; Farm Collector; John Deere Tradition; Iron-Men Album; Gas Engine*. **Parent company:** Ogden Newspapers, Inc. **Number of employees at this location:** 100.

OLATHE HEALTH SYSTEMS, INC.
dba OLATHE MEDICAL CENTER, INC.
20333 West 151st Street, Suite 356, Olathe KS 66061. 913/791-4243. **Fax:** 913/791-4240. **Recorded jobline:** 913/791-4246. **Contact:** Human Resources. **E-mail address:** resumes@ohsi.com. **World Wide Web address:** http://www.ohsi.com. **Description:** Since beginning as the Olathe Health Foundation, this regional hospital has a reputation for its rehabilitation services; hospice and home health; cardiology, emergency services, obstetrics, oncology and women's health. The Olathe Health System operates several subsidiary corporations including the main Medical Center campus at I-35 and 151st Street which is one of the largest in the country. Founded in 1948. **Positions advertised include:** Film Librarian Clerk; Radiology Registered Nurse; Registered Nurse; Unit Secretary; Clinical Resource Nurse; Security Officer; Accounts Payable Coder; Medical Records Transcriber; Patient Registration Clerk; Housekeeping Associate; Cashier. **Special programs:** Internships. **Subsidiaries include:** Olathe Medical Center, Inc.; Miami County Medical Center; Olathe Medical Services; Olathe Medical Center Charitable Fund; Olathe Health Development Corporation; Health Access; Cedar Lake Village, Inc. **Operations at this facility include:** Administration. **President/CEO:** Frank H. Devocelle. **Number of employees at this location:** 965.

PARSONS BRINCKERHOFF INC.
dba PARSONS BRINCKERHOFF QUADE & DOUGLAS, INC.
225 North Market Street, Suite 350, Wichita KS 67202. 316/263-6121. **Fax:** 316/263-8989. **Contact:** Human Resources. **World Wide Web address:** http://www.pbworld.com. **E-mail address:** careers@pbworld.com. **Description:** Provides complete engineering and construction management services, including the development of major bridges, tunnels, highways, marine facilities, buildings, industrial complexes, and railroads for transportation, power buildings, and telecommunications projects with more than 250 worldwide offices. Founded in 1885. **Special programs:** Internships. **Corporate headquarters location:** New York NY. **Other area locations:** Lenexa KS. **Other U.S. locations:** Nationwide. **International locations:** Worldwide. **Operations at this facility include:** The Wichita office is part of the U.S. infrastructure arm of PB. **Chairman:** Robert (Bob) Prieto. **Annual sales/revenues:** $1.4 billion. **Number of employees worldwide:** 9,300.

PITTSBURG STATE UNIVERSITY
1701 South Broadway, Pittsburg KS 66762. 620/235-4191. **Contact:** Budget & Human Resource Services Staff. **E-mail address:** hrs@pittstate.edu. **World Wide Web address:** http://www.pittstate.edu. **Description:** A state university with four colleges offering over 50 degree programs. Fall 2002 enrollment was 6,751 in the four colleges: College of Arts and Sciences; The Kelce College of Business; College of Education; College of Technology. **Positions advertised include:** Staff Attorney; Applications Programmer; Analyst III; Corrections Manager; Office Assistant; Plumber. **President:** Tom W. Bryant. **Number of employees at this location:** 675.

PRAIRIE VIEW INC.
P.O. Box 467, Newton KS 67114. 316/284-6311. **Physical address:** 1901 East First Street, Newton KS 67114. **Human Resources address:** 7570 West 21st Street North, Wichita KS 67205. **Fax:** 316/284-6491. **Contact:** Joy Robb, Personnel. **E-mail address:** robbjh@pvi.org. **World Wide Web address:** http://www.prairieview.com. **Description:** Established by the Mennonite churches, Prairie View is a private, nonprofit regional behavioral and mental health system with eight locations including the 70-acre headquarters in Newton. Prairie View provides a complete range of psychiatric services including individual, marriage and family therapy, aging services, pastoral counseling, treatment for severe and persistent mental illness, depression, anxiety, stress, anger, eating disorders, dementia, sexually related issues, grief, cognitive disorders, chemical dependency, and alcoholism, offering child and adolescent services, trauma treatment, sex offender treatment, psychiatric hospitalization, an adventure course, an accredited day school, and employee assistance programs. A 60-bed psychiatric hospital and partial hospitalization program are also available as well as outpatient services. **Positions advertised include:** Administrative Assistant; Registered Nurse; Licensed Practical Nurse; Mental Health Worker; Psychiatrist; Community Case Manager. **Corporate headquarters location:** This location. **Other area locations:** Hutchinson KS; Marion KS; McPherson KS; Newton KS; Salina KS; Wichita KS. **Operations at this facility include:** Administration; Services. **Number of employees at this location:** 250. **Number of employees nationwide:** 375.

PRIMEDIA BUSINESS MAGAZINES & MEDIA
PO Box 19201, Overland Park KS 666282. 913/341-1300. **Fax:** 913/967-1898. **Physical Address:** 9800 Metcalf Avenue, Overland Park KS 66212. **Contact:** Personnel. **World Wide Web address:** http://www.primediabusiness.com. **Description:** A publisher of 300 business-to-business publications, special interest and trade magazines, newsletters, business directories, databases, and guides. The magazines allow manufacturers and suppliers to provide professionals with statistics, explanations, technical advice, and product introductions. It also operates over 1,000 Websites. **NOTE:** Resumes can be submitted via the company Website and there is a Response Profile available online. **Positions advertised include:** Industry Information Manager; Payroll; Human Resources Administrator. **Corporate headquarters location:** This location. **Parent company:** Primedia, Inc. **Operations at this facility include:** Corporate Administration; Offices of over two dozen specialty publications. **Listed on:** New York Stock Exchange. **Stock exchange symbol:** PRM. **Chairman/CEO:** Thomas Rogers. **Annual sales/revenues:** $1.7 billion. **Number of employees nationwide:** 6,550.

PROCTER & GAMBLE
P.O. Box 2906, Kansas City KS 66110. 913/573-0200. **Physical address:** 1900 Kansas Avenue, Kansas City KS 66105. **Contact:** Human Resources. **World Wide Web address:** http://www.pg.com. **Description:** P&G manufactures 300 consumer products in four categories—Baby, Feminine and Family Care; Fabric and Home Care; Beauty Care; Health and food and beverage—and markets them worldwide. The P&G Plant in Kansas City is the company's second oldest and produces both dishwashing detergents (i.e. Dawn, Ivory Liquid, and Joy) and specialty chemicals. The company has over two dozen divisions, affiliates, and subsidiaries. Established in 1837. **NOTE:** Applications may be submitted online. **Positions advertised include:** Administrative Assistant; Engineer; Manufacturing Intern. **Special programs:** Internships; Online courses. **Corporate headquarters location:** Cincinnati OH. **Other area locations:** Shawnee Mission KS. **Other U.S. locations:** Nationwide. **International locations:** Worldwide. **Subsidiaries include:** The Iams Company; Refect.com, LLC; Clairol; Millstone Coffee. **Operations at this facility include:** The Kansas City Soap Plant, built in 1904, produces light duty liquids and specialty chemicals. **Listed on:** New York Stock Exchange. **Stock exchange symbol:** PG. **Chairman/President/CEO:** Alan G. (A.G.) Lafley. **Annual sales/revenues:** $41 billion. **Number of employees worldwide:** 106,000.

FRED PRYOR SEMINARS
A DIVISION OF PRYOR RESOURCES, INC.
9757 Metcalf Avenue, Overland Park KS 66212. 913/967-8599. **Fax:** 913/967-8580. **Contact:** Human Resources. **E-mail address:** careeropportunities@pryor.com. **World Wide Web address:** http://www.pryor.com. **Description:** Fred Pryor Seminars and CareerTrack Seminars provide motivational and professional training for individuals and corporations. **Positions advertised include:** On-Site Training Consultant; Inside Sales Representative; Contract Trainer.

RAYTHEON AIRCRAFT COMPANY
P.O. Box 85, Wichita KS 67201-0085. 316/676-7111. **Physical address:** 9709 East Central Avenue, Wichita KS 67206. **Fax:** 316/676-6618. **Contact:** Employment. **World Wide Web address:** http://www.raytheonaircraft.com. **Description:** Wichita-based subsidiary of Raytheon Company, the Raytheon Aircraft division provides aircraft products, services, and support for government, military, corporate, and commercial customers specializing in the design, manufacture, and marketing of the Hawker and Beechjet line of jets, King Air turboprops, the Baron and Bonanza piston-powered aircraft, and Executive airliners. The company also sells used aircraft as well as offering charter, management, and maintenance services. **NOTE:** Human Resources phone: 316/676-8435. Resumes and applications may be submitted via the company's My Rayjobs Website: http://www.rayjobs.com. **Positions advertised include:** Aircraft Engineer; Finance Accountant. **Special programs:** Internships. **Corporate headquarters location:** This location. **Other area locations:** Andover KS; Salina KS; Little Rock AR. **Affiliates include:** Raytheon Aircraft Charter and Management Company; Raytheon Aircraft Services, Inc.; United Beechcraft, Inc.; Travelers Air Insurance. **Parent company:** Raytheon Company, a diversified, international, technology-based company with over 100 facilities in 28 states and overseas facilities and representative offices in 26 countries, principally in Europe, the Middle East, and the Pacific Rim. The company has four business segments: Electronics; Major Appliances; Aircraft Products; and Energy and Environmental. **Operations at this facility include:** Raytheon Aircraft Company corporate administration; Manufacturing division—business jets, turboprops, piston-powered craft, and airliners; Sales; Service. **Chairman/CEO:** James E. Schuster. **Annual sales/revenues:** $3 billion. **Number of employees:** 11,800.

REECE & NICHOLS REALTORS
11500 Granada, Leawood KS 66211. 913/491-1001. **Fax:** 913/491-0930. **Contact:** Sam Hartman, Director of Human Resources. **E-mail address:** samh@reeceandnichols.com. **World Wide Web address:** http://www.reeceandnichols.com. **Description:** Engaged in residential real estate, new home developments, resale, property management, and corporate relocation. **NOTE:** In addition to the company's Director of Human Resources, the company also uses an outside employment agency; check the careers page of the company Website. **Positions advertised include:** Home Mortgage Consultant; Home Mortgage Associate. **Other area locations:** Twenty branches in the greater Kansas City area. **Number of employees:** 1,400.

RIMPULL CORPORATION
P.O. Box 748, Olathe KS 66051-0748. 913/782-4000. **Physical address:** 157 and 169 Highway, Olathe KS 66161. **Toll-free phone:** 800/7467855. **E-mail address:** global@rimpull.com. **Contact:** Personnel Manager. **World Wide Web address:** http://www.rimpull.com. **Description:** Manufactures off-highway vehicles for the coal mining industry and heavy earthmoving trucks. Founded in 1971. **Corporate headquarters location:** This location. **Other locations:** IN; NM; TX; WV; WY. **Special programs:** Internships. **Internship information:** Paid summer internship open to sophomore or junior engineering students familiar with computers and CAD with opportunity for full-time employment after graduation. Resumes should be sent to John Byrne, P.O. Box 748, Olathe KS 66051.

SEABOARD CORPORATION
P.O. Box 2972, Shawnee Mission KS 66202-2972. 913/676-8800. **Physical address:** 9000 West 67th Street, Shawnee Mission KS 66202. **Fax:** 913/676-8862. **Contact:** Personnel Manager. **E-mail address:** hr@seaboardcorp.com. **World Wide Web address:** http://www.seaboardcorp.com. **Description:** A diversified international food processing and transportation company specializing in pork products and overseas shipping and milling as well as power generation. Food operations include poultry and pork processing, primarily in the eastern United States, with hog farrowing plants in Colorado and Oklahoma; flour milling and baked goods production in Puerto Rico; and fruit, vegetables, shrimp, flour, pen-raised salmon, and animal feed processing and production. Seaboard Corporation operates an ocean-liner service for cargo, with routes running between Florida and Latin America; and operates bulk carriers in the Atlantic Basin. The company also trades bulk grain and oil seed commodities. **NOTE:** For international management positions contact: opportunities@seaboardcorp.com. **Positions advertised include:** Senior Program Analyst. **Corporate headquarters location:** This location. **Other area locations:** Feed mills in Leoti and Rolla KS. **Other U.S. locations:** Marine Division in Miami FL. **Operations at this location include:** Corporate Headquarters for Seaboard Corp.; Seaboard Farms, Inc.; and Commodity, Trading & Milling Division. **Listed on:** American Stock Exchange. **Stock exchange symbol:** SEB. **Chairman/President/CEO:** H. Harry Bresky. **Annual sales/revenues:** $1.8 billion. **Number of employees nationwide:** 5,000. **Number of employees worldwide:** 9,500.

SHEPLER'S
6501 West Kellogg, Wichita KS 67209. 316/946-3600. **Fax:** 316/946-3652. **Contact:** Human Resources. **E-mail address:** khunt@sheplers.com. **World Wide Web address:** http://www.sheplers.com. **Description:** Engaged in retail, catalog, and Internet sales of Western-style apparel operating 19 stores in 9 central and western states. **Positions**

advertised include: Internet Graphic Artist; Bi-lingual Customer Service Representative; Department Supervisor. **Special programs:** Internships. **Corporate headquarters location:** This location. **Operations at this facility include:** Corporate Administration and Catalog Warehouse. **Listed on:** Privately held. **Number of employees at this location:** 350. **Number of employees nationwide:** 1,500.

SKILLPATH SEMINARS
P.O. Box 2768, Shawnee Mission KS 66201-2768. 913/362-3900. **Physical address:** 6900 Squibb Road, Shawnee Mission KS 66202. **Fax:** 913/362-4241. **Toll-free phone:** 800/873-7545. **Contact:** Personnel Department. **E-mail address:** opportunities@skillpath.net. **World Wide Web address:** http://www.skillpath.com. **Description:** A training company that conducts educational seminars targeted to professionals from a variety of businesses and organizations. **NOTE:** Contact Human Resources at extension 129. For contract trainer positions contact Christy Gaddis: cgaddis@skillpath.net. **Positions advertised include:** Contract Trainer; (Canada-based) Business and Management Skills Trainer. **Parent company:** The Graceland College Center for Professional Development and Lifelong Learning, Inc.

SNYDER MEMORIAL RESEARCH FOUNDATION
1407 Wheat Road, Winfield KS 67156. 620/221-4080. **Fax:** 620/221-2684. **Contact:** Human Resources. **E-mail address:** tsmith@snydermri.org. **World Wide Web address:** http://www.snydermri.org. **Description:** A foundation focusing on biomedical and cancer research. **Positions advertised include:** Biological Scientist. **Operations at this facility include:** Research and Development. **President:** Jim Barnthouse. **Number of employees at this location:** 10.

SPECIALTY HOSPITAL OF MID AMERICA
6509 West 103rd Street, Overland Park KS 66212. 913/649-3701. **Fax:** 913/649-2408. **Contact:** Human Resources. **Description:** Provides health care services including nursing care, rehabilitation, and other therapies; institutional pharmacy services; specialty care to Alzheimer's patients; and subacute care. The hospital's specialty and subacute care units provide a range of specialized services including post-acute medical care; rehabilitative ventilator care; infusion therapy; stroke, pain, and wound management; and physical rehabilitation.

SPRINT CORPORATION
2330 Shawnee Mission Parkway, Westwood KS 66205. 913/624-3000. **Fax:** 913/624-3281. **Contact:** Human Resources Manager. **World Wide Web address:** http://www.sprint.com. **Description:** A diversified telecommunications company with a nationwide, all-digital, fiber-optic network. Sprint's divisions provide global long-distance, voice, data, and video products and services; local telephone services in 19 states; and cellular operations that serve 42 metropolitan markets and more than 50 rural service areas. **NOTE:** Resumes should be submitted directly through the company website: http://www.careers.sprint.com. **Positions advertised include:** Account Executive; Accountant; Attorney; Billing Analyst; Billing Revenue Consultant; Client Solutions Representative; Customer Service Representative; Data Analyst; Employee Relations Specialist; Human Resources Manager; Business Market Planning Manager; Partner Development Manager; Indirect Account Executive Partner; Process Analyst/Engineer; Program Manager; Security Engineer; Senior Process Analyst; Site Development Analyst; Small Business Sales Specialist; Software Engineer; Marketing Vice President. **Special programs:** Internships. **Corporate headquarters location:** This location. **Other area locations:** Kansas City KS; Lawrence KS; Topeka KS; Wichita KS. **Other U.S. locations:** Nationwide. **Subsidiaries/Affiliates/Divisions include:** Sprint PCS; Local Telecommunications Division; Business Services Division; Customer Services Group; Sprint North Supply; Sprint Publishing and Advertising. **Listed on:** New York Stock Exchange. **Stock exchange symbol:** FON. **Chairman/CEO:** William T. Esrey. **Annual sales/revenues:** $26 billion. **Number of employees nationwide:** 83,700.

TELECOMMMUNICATIONS RESEARCH ASSOCIATES (TRA)
P.O. Box A, St. Marys KS 66536-0016. 785/437-2000. **Physical address:** 505 West Bertrand Avenue, St. Marys KS 66536. **Toll-free phone:** 800/872-4736. **Fax:** 785/437-2600. **Contact:** Human Resources. **E-mail address:** humanresources@tra.com. **World Wide Web address:** http://www.tra.com. **Description:** A technology training vendor for the communications industry. TRA also offers on-site training and some material on CD-Rom.

TERRACON COMPANIES, INC.
16000 College Boulevard, Lenexa KS 66219. 913/599-6886. **Toll-free phone:** 800/593-7777. **Fax:** 913/599-0574. **Contact:** Human Resources Director. **E-mail address:** careers@terracon.com. **World Wide Web address:** http://www.terracon.com. **Description:** An employee-owned engineering and consulting company providing geotechnical, environmental, construction, and facilities management services with 55 offices in 23 states. Founded in 1965. **NOTE:** Please submit resumes at website. **Positions advertised include:** Environmental Scientist; Industrial Hygiene Professional; Asbestos Air Quality Control Technician; Microsoft Applications Programmer; Construction Services Assistant; Secretary; Environmental Project Engineer; Constructions Materials Technician; Geotechnical Engineer. **Corporate headquarters location:** This location. **Other area locations:** Garden City KS; Kansas City KS; Topeka KS; Wichita KS; **Other U.S. locations:** Nationwide. **Subsidiaries include:** HBC/Terracon; Titan Atlantic Group, Inc.; Infrastructure Management Services, Inc.; The Terra Group of Chicago, Inc. **President/CEO:** David Gaboury. **Number of employees nationwide:** 1,400.

THALES ATM, INC.
23501 West 84th Street, Shawnee Mission KS 66227. 913/422-2600. **Fax:** 913/422-2989. **Contact:** Sherry Parnell, Manager of Personnel. **World Wide Web address:** http://www.thalesatm.com. **Description:** Manufactures instrument landing systems and distance measuring equipment, and provides turnkey installation and training for airports. Airsys ATM also supports MSSR radar production, formerly managed by Cardion Inc. **Corporate headquarters location:** Bagneux Cedex, France. **International locations:** Australia; Germany; Italy; United Kingdom.

THE TOPEKA CAPITAL-JOURNAL
616 SE Jefferson Street, Topeka KS 66607. 785/295-1218. **Fax:** 785/295-5637. **Contact:** Heather Johannins, Human Resources Manager. **E-mail address:** heather.johannins@cjonline.com. **World Wide Web address:** http://www.cjonline.com. **Description:** Publishes a daily newspaper with a circulation of approximately 60,000 daily, and 67,000 on Sundays. **NOTE:** Contact the Human Resources Director at: 785/295-1218. **Positions advertised include:** New Media Assistant; Content Editor; News Designer; Copy Editor; Graphic Artist; Sports Editor; District Circulation Manager; Inside (Circulation) Sales; Accounts Receivables Assistant; Classified Adviser. **Special programs:** Internships. **Corporate headquarters location:** Augusta GA. **Parent company:** Morris Communications Corporation, Inc. **Operations at this facility include:** Administration; Sales; Service. **Number of employees at this location:** 350.

TYSON PREPARED FOODS
P.O. Box 1570, Hutchinson KS 67504. 620/663-6141. **Physical address:** 9 North Washington Street, South Hutchinson KS 67505. **Contact:** Richard Gary, Human Resources. **World Wide Web address:** http://www.tyson.com. **Description:** Tyson Prepared Foods produces precooked meats and sausages. **Corporate headquarters location:** Springdale AR. **Listed on:** New York Stock Exchange. **Stock exchange symbol:** TSN. **Number of employees worldwide:** 52,000.

U.S. DEPARTMENT OF VETERANS AFFAIRS MEDICAL AND REGIONAL OFFICE CENTER
5500 East Kellogg, Wichita KS 67218. 316/651-3625. **Contact:** Human Resources. **World Wide Web address:** http://www.vets.org. **Description:** This location is a medical and regional office of the U.S. Department of Veterans Affairs. From 54 hospitals in 1930, the VA health care system has grown to include 171 medical centers; more than 364 outpatient, community, and outreach clinics; 130 nursing home care units; and 37 domiciliary residences. VA operates at least one medical center in each of the 48 contiguous states, Puerto Rico, and the District of Columbia. With approximately 76,000 medical center beds, VA treats nearly 1 million patients in VA hospitals; 75,000 in nursing home care units; and 25,000 in domiciliary residences. VA's outpatient clinics register approximately 24 million visits per year. **Special programs:** Internships. **Corporate headquarters location:** Washington DC. **Operations at this facility include:** Administration; Regional Headquarters; Research and Development. **Number of employees at this location:** 890.

U.S. ENVIRONMENTAL PROTECTION AGENCY (EPA)
901 North Fifth Street, Kansas City KS 66101. 913/551-7000. **Recorded jobline:** 913/551-7068. **Contact:** Personnel. **World Wide Web address:** http://www.epa.gov. **Note:** Applicants must apply online, no paper applications accepted. **Description:** The EPA is dedicated to improving and preserving the quality of the environment, both nationally and globally, and protecting human health and the productivity of natural resources with 10 regional offices and 17 laboratories. **Positions advertised include:** Criminal Investigator; Supervisory Environmental Protection Specialist; Environmental Engineer. **NOTE:** Applicants are encouraged to use the EPA's Web-based ezhire@EPA system to register and apply to EPA jobs; Paper applications are not accepted. Human Resources phone: 913/551-7041. **Special programs:** Fellowships; Internships; Student employment. **Corporate headquarters location:** Washington DC. **Other U.S. locations:** Nationwide. **Number of employees nationwide:** 18,000.

UNIVERSITY OF KANSAS
1246 West Campus Road, Room 103, Lawrence KS 66045-7505. 785/864-3686. **Fax:** 785/864-3689. **Contact:** Human Resources. **E-mail address:** equalop@ku.edu. **World Wide Web address:** http://www.ukans.edu. **Description:** A four-year university serving as a comprehensive research and teaching institution. Founded in 1864. **NOTE:** Human Resources phone: 785/864-4946. **Positions advertised include:** Accounting Specialist; Administration Assistant; Assistant Professor; Associate Dean; Design Chair Person; Director of Laboratory; Financial Analyst; Information Technology Manager; Instructor Education / Chemistry; Lecturer; Network Manager; Research Aide; University Police Officer; Vice Provost for Research.

UNIVERSITY OF KANSAS MEDICAL CENTER
3901 Rainbow Boulevard, Kansas City KS 66160. 913/588-5080. **Fax:** 913/588-5042. **Contact:** Director of Human Resources. **E-mail address:** kumchr@kumc.edu. **World Wide Web address:** http://www.kumc.edu. **Description:** A medical center providing a full range of health care services and offering health education. **NOTE:** Offers applications on website. **Positions advertised include:** Administrative Specialist; Administrative Assistant; Division Director of Nephrology; Research Associate; Medical Billing; Student Financial Aid Advisor; Nurse Manager; Assistant Professor; Post Doctoral Fellow; Senior Coordinator. **Other area locations:** Wichita KS.

WADDELL & REED INC.
P.O. Box 29217, Shawnee Mission KS 66201-9217. 913/236-2000. **Physical address:** 6301 Glennwood Avenue, Shawnee Mission KS 66201. **Toll-free phone:** 800/532-2757. **Fax:** 913/236-1909. **Contact:** Human Resources. **E-mail address:** jobs@waddell.com. **World Wide Web address:** http://www.waddell.com. The company and its affiliates administer over 45 mutual funds and manage accounts for institutional investors and individual clients, as well as selling annuities and insurance. Founded in 1937. **Positions advertised include:** Administrative Assistant; IT Administration Specialist; Fund Pricing Manager; Investor Departmental Operations; Siebel Business Analyst; Siebel Configuration; IT Administrative Support; Senior Systems Administrator. **Office hours:** Monday - Friday, 8:00 a.m. - 4:30 p.m. **Corporate headquarters location:** This location. **Other area locations:** Statewide. **Other U.S. locations:** Nationwide. **Parent company:** Waddell & Reed Financial, Inc. **Listed on:** New York Stock Exchange. **Stock exchange symbol:** WDR. **Chairman/CEO:** Keith A Tucker. **Annual sales/revenues:** $435 million. **Number of employees at this location:** 400. **Number of employees worldwide:** 1,430.

WALLACE, SAUNDERS, AUSTIN, BROWN & ENOCHS
10111 West 87th Street, Overland Park KS 66282. 913/888-1000. **Fax:** 913/888-1065. **Contact:** Julie Cramm, Human Resources Director. **World Wide Web address:** http://www.wsabe.com. **Description:** A law firm of 60 attorneys handling a variety of cases involving insurance claims, child custody, divorce, and automobile accidents. Founded in 1963. **Other locations:** Kansas City MO; Wichita KS; Springfield MO.

WASHBURN UNIVERSITY
1700 SW College Avenue, Topeka KS 66621. 785/231-1010. **Contact:** Personnel Office. **World Wide Web address:** http://www.washburn.edu. **Description:** A public, four-year university offering undergraduate and graduate degrees in Arts & Sciences, Business, and Law with a Nursing School and a continuing education program. **NOTE:** Contact Human Resources at extension 1538.

WESTAR ENERGY
P.O. Box 889, Topeka KS 66601-889. 785/575-6300. **Physical address:** 818 South Kansas Avenue, Topeka KS 66612. **Fax:** 785/575-6523. **Contact:** Human Resources. **E-mail address:** wrjobs@wr.com. **World Wide Web address:** http://www.wstnres.com. **Description:** Formerly Western Resources, the company supplies electricity, natural gas, and security monitoring services specializing in electric utility operations. Affiliates generate 6,000 MW serving 640,000 customers in Kansas. **NOTE:** Applications must be submitted online. **Positions advertised include:** Associate Financial Assistant; Intern; Systems Analyst; Technical Specialist IT. **Other area locations:** Wichita KS. **Affiliates include:** KPL Utility; KGE Utility. **Corporate headquarters location:** This location. **Listed on:** New York Stock Exchange. **Stock exchange symbol:** WR. **Chairman:** James S. Haines Jr. **Annual sales/revenues:** $2 billion. **Number of employees:** 5,600.

WICHITA AREA TECHNICAL COLLEGE
201 North Water, Wichita KS 67202. 316/677-9282. **Contact:** Personnel Services. **World Wide Web address:** http://www.wichitatech.com. **Description:** A nonprofit

technical college. **NOTE:** Entry-level positions are offered. Personnel Services phone: 316/973-4710. **Positions advertised include:** CATIA Instructor; Geriatric Aide.

THE WICHITA EAGLE
P.O. Box 820, Wichita KS 67201-0820. 316/268-6000. **Contact:** Human Resources. **E-mail address:** circserv@wichitaeagle.com. **World Wide Web address:** http://www.wichitaeagle.com. **Description:** Publishes an independent daily newspaper. Weekday circulation exceeds 120,000; Sunday circulation exceeds 195,000.

WICHITA SPECIALTY HOSPITAL
8080 East Pawnee, Wichita KS 67207. 316/682-0004. **Fax:** 316/682-5790. **Contact:** Human Resources. **Description:** Wichita Specialty Hospital is a long-term, acute care hospital.

WICHITA STATE UNIVERSITY
1845 Fairmount Street, Box 15, Wichita KS 67260-0015. 316/978-3065. **Fax:** 316/978-3201. **Recorded jobline:** 316/978-3344. **Contact:** Office of Human Resources. **E-mail address:** career.services@Wichita.edu. **World Wide Web address:** http://www.wichita.edu. **Description:** A state university with an enrollment of approximately 13,000 part-time students who are predominantly beyond the traditional college age. The university offers undergraduate, graduate, and continuing education courses. **NOTE:** Entry-level positions as well as second and third shifts are offered. To apply for the state positions applicants must register with the State of Kansas. **Positions advertised include:** Custodial Specialist; Seasonal Grounds Worker; Administrative Assistant; Equipment Operator Trainee- Greenhouse; Assistant Director Financial Aid; Registered Nurse; Administrative Representative. **Number of employees:** 3,000.

WOLF CREEK NUCLEAR OPERATING CORPORATION
P.O. Box 411, Burlington KS 66839-0411. 620/364-4141. **Fax:** 620/364-4155. **Physical address:** 1550 Oxen Lane Northeast, Burlington KS 66839. **Contact:** David O. Reynolds. **E-mail address:** doreyno@ucnoc.com. **World Wide Web address:** http://www.wcnoc.com. **Description:** A commercial nuclear electric power generating station. **Special programs:** Internships. **Parent company:** Westar Energy. **Number of employees at this location:** 1,000.

YELLOW ROADWAY CORPORATION
P.O. Box 7950, Overland Park KS 66207. 913/696-6100. **Physical address:** 10990 Roe Avenue, Overland Park KS 66211. **Fax:** 913/234-9142. **Contact:** Human Resources. **E-mail address:** yfs.hr@yellowcorp.com. **World Wide Web address:** http://www.myyellow.com. **Description:** The company's main subsidiary, Yellow Roadway Corporation formerly know as Yellow Transportation, is a national, long-haul truckload carrier, with over 585 terminal locations in North America operating a fleet of 8,000 tractors and 35,000 trailers. Founded 1924. **Positions advertised include:** Account Executive; Administrative Clerk Assistant; Control Dispatcher; Payroll Analyst; Revenue Management Specialist. **Corporate headquarters location:** This location. **Other area locations:** Abilene KS; Baxter Springs KS; Great Bend KS; Topeka KS; Wichita KS.

ACNIELSEN BASES
50 West Rivercenter Boulevard, Suite 600, Covington KY 41011. 859/905-4000. **Fax:** 859/905-5000. **Contact:** Jamie Kennedy, Human Resources. **E-mail address:** hr@bases.com. **World Wide Web address:** http://www.acnielsenbases.com. **Description:** An operating unit of ACNielsen Corporation, this is a marketing research firm that specializes in forecasting sales of new consumer packaged goods and products through the use of simulated test markets and market models. **Positions advertised include:** Associate Business Analyst; Tabulation Analyst/Manager. **Special programs:** Training. **Corporate headquarters location:** This location. **Other U.S. locations:** Westport CT; Chicago IL; Parsippany NJ. **International locations:** Argentina; Mexico; Brazil; Belgium; Canada; China; France; United Kingdom; Australia. **Parent company:** VNU. **President:** John Willke.

ACS
1084 South Laurel Road, London KY 40744. 606/878-7900. **Contact:** Human Resources. **World Wide Web address:** http://www.acs-inc.com. **Description:** Affiliated Computer Services, Incorporated provides business and information technology solutions to a wide range of clients. **Positions advertised include:** Microsystems Analyst. **Special programs:** Internships; Training; Career Development Program. **Corporate headquarters location:** Dallas TX. **Other area locations:** Lexington KY; Richmond KY. **Other U.S. locations:** Nationwide. **International locations:** Worldwide. **CEO:** Jeff Rich. **Sales/revenues:** Approximately $4 billion. **Number of employees worldwide:** Over 40,000.

ACCURIDE CORPORATION
2315 Adams Lane, Henderson KY 42420. 270/826-5000. **Fax:** 270/827-7656. **Contact:** Human Resources. **E-mail address:** employment@accuridecorp.com. **Contact:** Jackie Askins. **World Wide Web address:** http://www.accuridecorp.com. **Description:** Manufactures rims and wheels for cars and semitrailers. **NOTE:** Resumes may be submitted online. **Positions advertised include:** Team Leader; Administrative Associate; Maintenance Associate. **Special programs:** Internships. **Corporate headquarters location:** Evansville IN. **Other U.S. locations:** Cuyahoga Falls OH; Springfield OH; Northville MI; Taylor MI; Erie PA; Columbia TN. **International locations:** Canada; Mexico. **Parent Company:** Kohlberg Kravis and Roberts (KKR). **Operations at this facility include:** Administration; Manufacturing; Research and Development. **Number of employees at this location:** 650.

AEGON COMPANIES
P.O. Box 32830, Louisville KY 40232. 502/560-2000. **Physical address:** 400 West Market Street, Louisville KY 40202. **Fax:** 502/560-2957. **Contact:** Human Resources. **World Wide Web address:** http://www.aegonins.com. **Description:** Engaged in a wide variety of insurance, financial services, and related activities. AEGON offers health, automobile, homeowner's, life, and property and casualty insurance. The company also offers money market accounts and certificates of deposit. Founded in 1969. **Note:** Applicants may submit resume online. **Positions advertised include:** Junior/Intermediate Underwriter; Institutional Marketing Lead Analyst; Senior Administrative Assistant; Senior Financial Analyst; Financial Analysis Director; Senior Marketing Analyst; Senior Account Manager; Spread Contract Evaluation Analyst. **Corporate headquarters location:** Baltimore MD. **Other U.S. locations:** Nationwide. **International locations:** Asia; Hungary; The Netherlands; Spain; United Kingdom; Belgium; Italy. **Listed on:** New York Stock Exchange; also, stock exchanges in Frankfurt, London, Tokyo, and Zurich. **Stock exchange symbol:** AEG US. **CEO:** Don Shepard. **Number of employees worldwide:** Over 25,000.

AG EDWARDS
130 Thompson Poynter Road, First Floor, P.O. Box 2368, London KY 40743. 606/864-8400. **World Wide Web address:** http://www.agedwards.com. **Description:** A financial consulting company with over 700 offices nationwide. Ag Edwards offers informative investment information for planning for the future. **Company slogan:** Fully invested in our clients. **Positions advertised include:** Sales, Financial Consultant. **Number of employees worldwide:** Over 7,000 in the US and in Europe.

AJILON CONSULTING
6060 Dutchmans Lane, Suite 430, Louisville KY 40205. 502/454-5840. **Toll-free phone:** 800/364-9078. **Fax:** 502/454-9742. **Contact:** Rebecca Tinley, Human Resources. **E-mail address:** recruit.louisville@ajilon.com. **World Wide Web address:** http://www.ajilonconsulting.com. **Description:** Offers computer consulting services, project support, and end user services with specializations in the areas of information technology, communications, finance and accounting, and legal and office. **NOTE:** Job seekers may apply online for consideration. **Positions advertised include:** P/A Oracle Programmer; IT Security Consultant; TSM Administrator; Java Web Architect. **Special programs:** Tuition Reimbursement Program. **Corporate headquarters location:** Baltimore MD. **Other U.S. locations:** Nationwide. **Subsidiaries include:** Software Quality Partners; Computer People, Incorporated. **Parent company:** Adecco. **President:** Mark E. Fusco.

AKZO NOBEL CHEMICALS
4730 Crittenden Drive, Louisville KY 40233. 502/375-5322. **Fax:** 502/375-2755. **Contact:** Paula Burke, Human Resources. **E-mail address:** paula.burke@akzonobel.com. **World Wide Web address:** http://www.akzonobel.com. **Description:** An industrial organization with companies in more than 50 countries. Akzo Nobel's product range includes salt and chemicals, coatings, health care products, and fibers. Business activities are conducted in four units: Chemicals, Coatings, Pharma, and Fibers. The Chemicals Group produces polymer chemicals, catalysts, detergents, surfactants, functional chemicals, salt, chlor-alkali, and industrial chemicals. The Coatings Group produces decorative coatings, car refinishes, industrial coatings, industrial wood finishes, aerospace finishes, automotive finishes, and resins. The Pharma Group includes ethical drugs, hospital supplies, nonprescription products, raw materials for the pharmaceuticals industry, generics, and veterinary products. The Fibers Group produces textile, industrial, and high-performance fibers; industrial nonwovens; and membranes for medical, technical, and industrial uses. Extensive research and development takes place in all units. **Positions advertised include:** Chemist. **Special programs:** Internships. **Corporate headquarters location:** Chicago IL. **Other U.S. locations:** Nationwide. **International locations:** Worldwide. **Operations at this facility include:** This location produces resins and coatings. **Listed on:** NASDAQ; Amsterdam Euronext; Belgium Euronext; Paris Euronext. **Stock exchange symbol:** NASDAQ (AKZOY); Euronext (AKZ). **Sales/revenues:** $13 billion. **Number of employees worldwide:** 68,000.

AMERICAN GREETINGS CORPORATION
800 American Drive, Bardstown KY 40004. 502/348-1000. **Fax:** 502/348-7348. **Contact:** Roger Bias, Human Resources. **World Wide Web address:** http://www.americangreetings.com. **Description:** One of the world's largest publicly-owned manufacturers and distributors of greeting cards and related social expression products which are printed in 16 languages at 31 plants and facilities throughout the United States, Canada, the United Kingdom, France, and Mexico, and distributed through a global network of about 97,000 retail outlets in 68 countries. Founded in 1906. **Note:** Applications can be submitted online for posted jobs, This location does not accept applications at the plant. **Corporate headquarters location:** Cleveland OH. **International locations:** Canada; United Kingdom; Mexico; Australia; New Zealand. **Subsidiaries include:** Acme Frame Products, a manufacturer of quality picture frames under the brand names Acme and Royal Gallery of Frames; A.G. Industries, a designer and manufacturer of custom permanent display fixtures and merchandising systems for American Greetings, its subsidiaries, consumer product companies, and retailers; CreataCard, a marketer of interactive, multimedia kiosks that allow consumers to write, personalize, and print greetings cards; Magnivision, a manufacturer and distributor of nonprescription, over-the-counter reading glasses produced primarily for mass retail distribution; Plus Mark, a manufacturer and distributor of promotional Christmas gift-wrap, boxed cards, and accessories under the brand names Plus Mark and Greeneville Press; Those Characters From Cleveland, a developer and marketer of licensed characters; and Wilhold, a manufacturer and distributor of hair accessories designed for mass retail distribution. **Listed on:** New York Stock Exchange. **Stock exchange symbol:** AM. **President/COO:** James C. Spira. **Sales/revenues:** $2,355 million. **Number of employees worldwide:** Over 20,000.

AMERICAN PRINTING HOUSE FOR THE BLIND, INC.
P.O. Box 6085, Louisville KY 40206-0085. 502/895-2405x238. **Physical address:** 1839 Frankfort Avenue, Louisville KY 40206. **Toll-free phone:** 800/223-1839. **Fax:** 502/899-2274. **Contact:** Jane Thompson, Human Resources. **E-mail address:** info@aph.org. **World Wide Web address:** http://www.aph.org. **Description:** A nonprofit company that creates educational, workplace, and lifestyle products and services to support the independence of visually impaired people. Products include books and magazines in Braille, large type, recorded, and computer disk form and instructional aids, tools, and supplies. Other services are offered through the APH-CARL textbook reference database and a center for ongoing research. Founded in 1858. **Positions advertised include:** Early Childhood Project Leader; Accessible Media Editor; Research Assistant. **Operations at this facility include:** Production; Sales; Research and development.

ANALYSTS INTERNATIONAL CORPORATION (AIC)
2365 Harrodsburg Road, Suite B-450, Lexington KY 40504-3342. 859/223-0001. **Toll-free phone:** 800/279-8433. **Fax:** 859/224-4389. **Contact:** Corporate Recruiter. **E-mail address:** jobs@analysts.com. **World Wide Web address:** http://www.analysts.com. **Description:** An international computer consulting firm. The company assists clients in developing systems in a variety of industries using different programming languages and software. **NOTE:** Job seekers may apply online for specific positions or general consideration. **Positions advertised include:** Firmware Developer; Hardware Engineer; Senior Lotus Notes Administrator. **Corporate headquarters location:** Minneapolis MN. **Other area locations:** Bowling Green KY; Louisville KY; Paducah KY. **Other U.S. locations:** Nationwide. **International locations:** Canada; United Kingdom. **Subsidiaries include:** Sequoia Services Group; Managed Services Group; IT Supplemental Resources. **Listed on:** NASDAQ. **Stock exchange symbol:** ANLY. **Sales/revenues:** Over $550 million. **Number of employees worldwide:** Over 3,800.

APPALACHIAN REGIONAL HEALTHCARE (ARH)
100 Medical Center Drive, Hazard KY 41701. 606/439-1331. **Contact:** Human Resources. **E-mail address:** humanresources@arh.org. **World Wide Web address:** http://www.arh.org. **Description:** A nonprofit health care system with hospitals, clinics, home health agencies, and other health services in the central Appalachian region of Kentucky, West Virginia, and Virginia. Products and services offered by ARH include hospital care, home health, durable medical equipment, psychiatric care, ambulatory clinics, laboratory, and EEG/EKG/Holter monitoring. **NOTE:** Resumes should be mailed to Marilyn Hamblin, ARH System Professional Recruiter, at P.O. Box 8086, Lexington KY 40533, or faxed to 859/226-2586. **Positions advertised include:** Certified Registered Nurse. **Special programs:** Internships. **Other area locations:** Harlan KY; McDowell KY; Middlesboro KY; South Williamson KY; West Liberty KY; Whitesburg KY. **Other U.S. locations:** Wise VA; Beckley WV; Hinton WV; Man WV. **President/CEO:** Stephen C. Hanson. **Number of employees nationwide:** 5,000.

ARCO ALUMINUM, INC.
9960 Corporate Campus Drive, Suite 3000, Louisville KY 40223-4032. 502/566-5700. **Toll-free phone:** 800/662-2726. **Fax:** 502/566-5741. **Contact:** Human Resources. **Description:** Produces aluminum products. Founded in 1950. **Corporate headquarters location:** This location. **Parent Company:** Atlantic Richfield Company. **President:** Patrick Franc.

ASHLAND INC.
P.O. Box 391, 50 East River Center Boulevard, Covington KY 41012-0191. 859/815-3333. **Fax:** 859/357-3344. **Contact:** Joe Lake, Human Resources Consultant. **World Wide Web address:** http://www.ashland.com. **Description:** A diversified company with operations in distribution, specialty chemicals, motor oil and car care products, and highway construction. Ashland also has equity interests in petroleum refining and marketing and coal. Founded in 1924. **NOTE:** Jobseekers must call the Employment Department for current openings. Entry-level positions are offered. **Special programs:** Internships. **Office hours:** Monday - Friday, 8:00 a.m. - 5:00 p.m. **Corporate headquarters location:** This location. **Other U.S. locations:** Nationwide. **International locations:** Worldwide. **Subsidiaries include:** Ashland Chemical; Ashland Petroleum Company (also at this location); SuperAmerica; Valvoline. **Listed on:** New York Stock Exchange. **Stock exchange symbol:** ASH. **CEO/Chairman:** James J. O'Brien. **Sales/revenues:** $6.7 billion. **Number of employees at this location:** 70. **Number of employees worldwide:** 24,000.

AUTOMATIC DATA PROCESSING, INC. (ADP)
13425 Eastpoint Center Drive, Suite 124, Louisville KY 40223. 859/971-9696. **Contact:** Sales Manager. **World Wide Web address:** http://www.adp.com. **Description:** Provides computerized transaction processing, data communications, and information services through its four primary businesses. The company's Employer Services Division provides payroll processing, payroll tax filing, job costing, labor distribution, automated bill payment, management reports, unemployment compensation management, human resource information, and benefits administration support to over 300,000 businesses. Other divisions include Claims, Dealer, and Brokerage Services. **NOTE:** Entry-level and part-time positions are offered. **Positions advertised include:** District Manager. **Special programs:** Tuition Reimbursement Program; Scholarship Program; Internships. **Corporate headquarters location:** Roseland NJ. **Other U.S. locations:** Nationwide. **Listed on:** New York Stock Exchange. **Stock exchange symbol:** ADP. **CEO/Chairman:** Arthur F. Weinbach. **Sales/revenues:** $6.6 billion. **Number of employees nationwide:** 25,000. **Number of employees worldwide:** Over 40,000.

BANDY, CARROLL & HELLIGE ADVERTISING
307 West Muhammad Ali Boulevard, Louisville KY 40202. 502/589-7711. **Fax:** 502/589-0390. **Contact:** Human Resources. **E-mail address:** employment@bch.com. **World Wide Web address:** http://www.bch.com. **Description:** An advertising agency. **Other U.S. locations:** Indianapolis IN; South Bend IN.

BAPTIST HEALTHCARE SYSTEM INC.
4007 Kresge Way, Louisville KY 40207. 502/896-5000. **Fax:** 502/896-5097. **Contact:** David Rhodes, Vice President of Human Resources. **E-mail address:** recruiter@bhsi.com. **World Wide Web address:** http://www.bhsi.com. **Note:** Applicants can submit job interest form online. **Description:** A nonprofit health care system with acute care hospitals in Louisville, Paducah, Lexington, Corbin, and La Grange, Kentucky. The system has over 1,500 licensed beds and is comprised of Baptist Hospital East, Western Baptist Hospital, Central Baptist Hospital, Baptist Regional Medical Center, and Tri-County Baptist Hospital. **NOTE:** Online applications are available. To contact the Human Resources Department directly, call 502/896-5032. **Positions advertised include:** Data Base Administrative Analyst; IS Support Systems; Network Control Technician; Business Systems Analyst. **Corporate headquarters location:** This location. **Number of employees nationwide:** 6,700.

BELDEN WIRE AND CABLE COMPANY
1211 Columbia Avenue, Monticello KY 42633. 606/348-8433. **Fax:** 606/348-3499. **Contact:** Larry P. Bates, Human Resources Manager. **World Wide Web address:** http://www.belden.com. **Description:** Designs and manufactures wire, cable, and cord products. Belden serves the computer, audio/video, industrial, and electrical markets worldwide, as well as the computer market with a broad range of multi-conductor, coaxial, flat, and fiber-optic cables. Belden cable links segments of broadcast and cable television including broadcast studios, postproduction and sound mixing facilities, satellite transmission centers, and home cable television systems. Belden's electrical products include power supply cords, electrical motor lead wire, and Canadian building wire. Belden also serves the industrial market by providing a broad spectrum of industrial products, ranging from general-purpose control cables to highly sophisticated cables for process control. **Corporate headquarters location:** St. Louis MO. **Other U.S. locations:** Phoenix AZ; Richmond IN. **International locations:** Canada; Australia; Germany; Hungary; the Netherlands; Singapore. **Listed on:** New York Stock Exchange. **Stock exchange symbol:** BWC. **President/CEO/Chairman:** C. Baker Cunningham. **Number of employees at this location:** 350. **Number of employees nationwide:** 2,500. **Number of employees worldwide:** 5,000.

BELLARMINE UNIVERSITY
2001 Newburg Road, Louisville KY 40205. 502/452-8435. **Toll-free phone:** 800/274-4723. **Fax:** 502/452-8293. **Contact:** Human Resources. **E-mail address:** hr@bellarmine.edu. **World Wide Web address:** http://www.bellarmine.edu. **Description:** A Catholic liberal arts university that supplies undergraduate and graduate degree programs through its central college, the Rubel School of Business, the Lansing School of Nursing and Health Sciences, and the Thornton School of Education. **NOTE:** For faculty positions, contact the appropriate department chair or search committee member. **Positions advertised include:** Help Desk Technician; Secretary; Assistant Facilities Director; Athletic Director; Part-time Volley Ball Coach; Assistant Professor of Theology; Assistant Professor of Mathematics. **President:** Joseph J. McGowan.

BOSCH REXROTH CORPORATION
1953 Mercer Road, Lexington KY 40514. 859/254-8031. **Fax:** 859/281-3477. **Contact:** Erma Emerson, Human Resources Department. **World Wide Web address:** http://www.boschrexroth.com. **Description:** Manufactures and markets valves, cylinders, and other control and motion products for machine tool and factory automation applications. **Corporate headquarters location:** Hoffman Estates IL. **Other U.S. locations:** Nationwide. **International locations:** Worldwide. **Parent Company:** Robert Bosch GmbH. **Operations at this facility include:** This location is the home of the company's Pneumatics division. **President/CEO:** Robert L. Rickert. **Sales/revenues:** $567 million. **Number of employees at this location:** 290. **Number of employees nationwide:** 2,200. **Number of employees worldwide:** 26,000.

BROWN-FORMAN CORPORATION
P.O. Box 1080, Louisville KY 40201-1080. 502/585-1100. **Physical address:** 850 Dixie Highway, Louisville KY 40210. **Contact:** Human Resources. **E-mail address:** brown-foreman@b-f.com. **World Wide Web address:** http://www.brown-forman.com. **Note:** Can search for positions and submit resumes online. **Description:** A distiller, marketer, and importer of alcoholic beverages such as hard liquors, wines, and champagnes. Brands include Jack Daniels, Southern Comfort, Korbel, Bolla, and Canadian Mist. The company also produces durable goods such as china, crystal, and giftware, which are sold through retail stores and company-affiliated outlets. Other businesses include an aquaculture operation. **Positions advertised include:** Senior Business Analyst; Legal Assistant; Security Administrator Consultant; Audit Consultant. **Corporate headquarters location:** This location. **Listed on:** New York Stock Exchange. **Stock exchange symbol:** BFB. **CEO:** Owsley Brown II. **Sales/revenues:** $2.2 billion. **Number of employees worldwide:** 7,000.

BURGESS & NIPLE, LTD.
220 Lexington Green Circle, Suite 110, Lexington KY 40503. 859/273-0557. **Fax:** 859/273-3332. **Contact:** Mark Willis, District Director. **E-mail address:** hr@burnip.com. **World Wide Web address:** http://www.burgessniple.com. **Note:** Applicants can search and submit applications for advertised positions online. **Description:** An engineering and architecture firm engaged in study, analysis, and design services. The company specializes in waterworks, wastewater, industrial services, hydropower, energy conservation, transportation, systems analysis, HVAC, and geotechnical services. **Positions advertised include:** Travel Demand Forecaster; CAD Designer. **Corporate headquarters location:** Columbus OH. **Other U.S. locations:** AZ; IN; OH; VA; WV; PA. **Sales/revenues:** $75 million. **Number of employees nationwide:** Approximately 700.

CABBAGE PATCH SETTLEMENT HOUSE
1413 South Sixth Street, Louisville KY 40208. 502/634-0811. **Fax:** 502/637-9943. **Contact:** Julie Meiman, Human Resources. **E-mail address:** cabbagepatch@cabbagepatch.org. **World Wide Web address:** http://www.cabbagepatch.org. **Description:** An independently funded, nonprofit, Christian charity that assists underprivileged, inner-city individuals through daycare, family services, and recreational/educational programs. Services include an Educational Opportunities Program, counseling, financial assistance for struggling families, childcare, and youth recreation and development programs. Founded in 1910. **Office hours:** Monday – Friday, 9:00 a.m. – 5:00 p.m. **Corporate headquarters location:** This location. **Number of employees at this location:** 30.

CARETENDERS HEALTH CORPORATION
9510 Ornsby Station Road, Suite 300, Louisville KY 40223. 502/899-5355. **Toll-free phone:** 800/845-6987. **Fax:** 502/891-8073. **Contact:** Elaine Styles, Human Resources. **E-mail address:** info@afam-inc.com. **World Wide Web Address:** http://www.almost-family.com. **Description:** Caretenders Health Corporation is a visiting nurse service that provides a full array of home health care and adult day care options. **Positions advertised include:** Payroll Clerk; Home Health Aide. **Other U.S. locations:** FL; AL; IN; OH; MD; CT; MA. **Parent Company:** Almost Family. **Listed on:** NASDAQ. **Stock exchange symbol:** CTND. **CEO:** William B. Yarmuth.

CENTRAL BAPTIST HOSPITAL
1740 Nicholasville Road, Lexington KY 40503. 859/275-6100. **Fax:** 859/260-6069. **Contact:** Human Resources. **World Wide Web address:** http://www.centralbap.com. **Description:** A 373-bed hospital. In addition to its WomanCare Plaza, Central Baptist Hospital also provides cardiology, outpatient services, oncology, and home health care services. Other programs and services include medical and surgical nursing; women's and children's services; ambulatory care; critical care; surgical services (inpatient, outpatient, and recovery); biomed; laboratory; pharmacy; education department; discharge planning/social services; utilization review/medical records; child development center; respiratory care; radiology; and rehabilitation services. Founded in 1954. **Positions advertised include:** Care Management Specialist; Secretary II; Patient Accounts Representative; HR Assistant; Receptionist; Transporter; Respiratory Therapist; Registered Nurse; Licensed Practical Nurse; Housekeeper. **Special programs:** Tuition Reimbursement Program. **Parent company:** Baptist Healthcare System. **Number of employees at this location:** 1,680.

CHI-CHI'S INC.
10200 Linn Station Road, Louisville KY 40223. 502/426-3900. **Toll-free phone:** 888/374-3746. **Contact:** Human Resources. **E-mail address:** careers@prandium.com. **World Wide Web address:** http://www.chi-chis.com. **Description:** A Mexican restaurant chain that operates from 130 locations throughout the mid-western and eastern U.S. **Positions advertised include:** General Manager; Assistant Manager; Shift Leader. **Corporate headquarters location:** This location. **Other U.S. locations:** Nationwide. **Parent company:** Prandium, Incorporated. **Listed on:** Privately held. **Number of employees nationwide:** 8,900.

CHRISTIAN CARE CENTER
308 West Maple Avenue, Lancaster KY 40444. 859/792-6844. **Fax:** 859/792-6844. **Contact:** Human Resources. **Description:** A nonprofit, acute care hospital and long-term care facility offering a variety of services on both inpatient and outpatient bases. Founded in 1950. **NOTE:** Entry-level positions and second and third shifts are offered. **Company slogan:** Close to your heart, close to your home. **Special programs:** Training; Co-ops. **Office hours:** Monday - Friday, 9:00 a.m. - 5:00 p.m. **Number of employees at this location:** 199.

CHURCHILL DOWNS, INC.
700 Central Avenue, Louisville KY 40208. 502/636-4400. **Toll-free phone:** 800/28DERBY. **Fax:** 502/635-0742. **Contact:** Human Resources Manager. **World Wide Web address:** http://www.churchilldowns.com. **Description:** A horse racetrack and home to the Kentucky Derby. The grounds also include the Eclipse Dining Room and Terrace; Silks Restaurant; the Jockey Club and Balcony; the Skye Terrace; the Clubhouse Gardens; the paddock, where the horses are saddled for the races; the Kentucky Derby Museum, one of the world's largest museums dedicated to thoroughbred racing; and the Churchill Downs Sports Spectrum, where wagering is available on live, televised racing from Keeneland, Turfway Park, Ellis Park, and top racetracks around the country. Founded in 1874. **Positions advertised include:** IT Help Desk Support; CDSN Administrative Assistant; Website Production Manager. **Listed on:** NASDAQ. **Stock exchange symbol:** CHDN. **President/CEO:** Thomas Meeker. **Sales/revenues:** $329 million. **Number of employees at this location:** 1,500.

CLARK MATERIAL HANDLING COMPANY
700 Enterprise Drive, Lexington KY 40517. 859/422-6537. **Fax:** 859/422-7400. **Contact:** Sherry Myers, Human Resources. **E-mail address:** sherrymyers@clarkmhc.com. **World Wide Web address:** http://www.clarkmhc.com. **Description:** An industrial equipment manufacturer whose products include lift trucks, gasoline, LPG, dual and diesel fuels, narrow-aisle stackers, and electric riders. **Positions advertised include:** Accounting Clerk; Graphic Designer; Sales & Marketing Coordinator; Part Time Accounting Clerk. **Special programs:** Tuition Reimbursement Program. **International locations:** Korea; Germany; Brazil. **CEO:** Kevin Reardon. **Number of employees at this location:** 1,600.

CLEAR CHANNEL
50 East Rivercenter Boulevard, 12th Floor, Covington KY 41011. 859/655-2267. **Contact:** Personnel. **World Wide Web address:** http://www.clearchannel.com. **Description:** Clear Channel is one of the world's largest media outlets, it owns 1,225 radio stations and 66 television stations in 66 countries. **NOTE:** Jobseekers can inquire about openings through the San Antonio HR office: 210/822-2828. **Corporate headquarters location:** San Antonio TX. **Other U.S. locations:** Phoenix AZ; Los Angeles CA; Sherman Oaks CA; New York NY. **International locations:** London, England. **Subsidiaries include:** SFX Entertainment, Incorporated; Dauphin; AMFM, Incorporated; Jacor Communications; Eller Media Company; More Group, plc. **Listed on:** New York Stock Exchange. **Stock exchange symbol:** CCU. **CEO/Chairman:** Lowry Mays.

COMMONWEALTH ALUMINUM
P.O. Box 480, 1372 State Road 1957, Lewisport KY 42351. 270/295-3451. **Contact:** Human Resources. **World Wide Web address:** http://www.cacky.com. **Description:** Engaged in the manufacture of aluminum sheet for the beverage, building, and aerospace industries. **Special programs:** Internships. **Corporate headquarters location:** Louisville KY. **Other U.S. locations:** Battleboro NC; Kings Mountain NC; Torrance CA; Rancho Dominguez CA; Long Beach CA; Bedford OH; Uhrichville OH. **Parent company:** Commonwealth Industries, Incorporated. **Operations at this facility include:** Administration; Manufacturing; Service. **Listed on:** NASDAQ. **Stock exchange symbol:** CMIN. **President/CEO:** Mark V. Kaminski. **Number of employees at this location:** 1,000. **Number of employees nationwide:** Over 2,000.

COMMONWEALTH CREDIT UNION
P.O. Box 978, Frankfort KY 40602-0978. 502/564-4775. **Physical address:** 417 High Street, Frankfort KY. **Toll-free phone:** 800/228/6420. **Contact:** Human Resources. **E-mail address:** hrinfo@cwcu.com. **World Wide Web address:** http://www.ccuk.org. **Description:** A not-for-profit financial institution offering banking and loan services. **Positions advertised include:** Compliance Officer; Marketing Assistant; Teller. **Other area locations:** Lexington KY; Louisville KY.

COMPUTER ANALYTICAL SYSTEMS
1418 South Third Street, Louisville KY 40208. 502/635-2019. **Toll-free phone:** 800/977-3475. **Fax:** 502/636-9157. **Contact:** Human Resources. **E-mail address:** info@c-a-s-i.com. **World Wide Web address:** http://www.c-a-s-i.com. **Description:** A technical consulting firm offering a variety of services including database development and maintenance, custom programming, hardware/software sales solutions, networking, and systems integration and management. Founded in 1988. **Office hours:** Monday – Friday, 8:00 a.m. – 5:00 p.m.

CONCORD CUSTOM CLEANERS
P.O. Box 55910, Lexington KY 40555-5910. 859/422-4800. **Physical address:** 1850 Bryant Road, Suite 400, Lexington KY 40509. **Fax:** 859/422-4801. **Contact:** Human Resources. **E-mail address:** info@concordcustomcleaners.com. **World Wide Web**

address: http://www.concordcustomcleaners.com. **Description:** A retail chain of dry cleaning stores that operates from 140 locations across the U.S. Founded in 1957. **Corporate headquarters location:** This location. **Other U.S. locations:** AL; FL; IL; IN; IA; MI; MO; OH; TN; VA.

COURIER-JOURNAL AND LOUISVILLE TIMES COMPANY
P.O. Box 740031, Louisville KY 40201-7431. 502/582-4561. **Physical address:** 525 West Broadway, Louisville KY 40202. **Fax:** 502/582-4001. **Recorded jobline:** 502/582-7000. **Contact:** Human Resources. **E-mail address:** jobs@courier-journal.com. **World Wide Web address:** http://www.courier-journal.com. **Description:** Publishes an independent daily newspaper. Weekday circulation exceeds 244,000, with a Sunday circulation of more than 330,000. **NOTE:** Applicants must apply in person. This firm does not accept unsolicited resumes. **Positions advertised include:** Telemarketing Sales Associate; Sales Specialist; Customer Sales Specialist; Outside Real Estate Account Executive; Corporate Sales; Distribution Associate. **Special programs:** Internships. **Office hours:** Monday – Friday, 9:00 a.m. – 5:00 p.m.

COX INTERIOR, INC.
1751 Old Columbia Road, Campbellsville KY 42718. 270/789-3129. **Toll-free phone:** 800/733-1751. **Fax:** 270/465-7977. **Contact:** Cathy Priddy, Human Resources Department. **E-mail address:** contact@coxinterior.com. **World Wide Web address:** http://www.coxinterior.com. **Description:** Manufactures stair parts, doors, mantels, and other hardwood trim products. Primary materials are poplar, oak, and cherry woods. **Corporate headquarters location:** This location. **Number of employees at this location:** 480. **Number of employees nationwide:** Over 800.

CUMBERLAND COLLEGE
7000 College Station Drive, Williamsburg KY 40769. 606/549-2200. **Physical address:** 816 Walnut Street, Williamsburg KY 40769. **Fax:** 606/549-2828. **Contact:** Human Resources. **World Wide Web address:** http://www.cumber.edu. **Description:** A four-year college offering a traditional liberal arts program. Degrees offered include bachelors of arts, science, general studies, and music and master of arts in education. Preprofessional degrees include medical technology, ministry and religious vocations, pre-engineering, premedicine, pre-veterinary science, predentistry, prepharmacy, and prenursing. Founded in 1889. **President:** Jim Taylor.

DMI FURNITURE
One Oxmoor Place, 101 Bullitt Lane, Suite 205, Louisville KY 40222. 502/429-6285. **Fax:** 800/755-2878. **Contact:** K. Lyn Sale, Human Resources Manager. **E-mail address:** lsale@dmifurniture.com. **World Wide Web address:** http://www.dmifurniture.com. **Description:** Manufactures, imports, and markets office furniture, residential desks, and bedroom furniture. **Corporate headquarters location:** This location. **Other U.S. locations:** IN. **International locations:** China; Thailand. **Listed on:** NASDAQ. **Stock exchange symbol:** DMIF. **President/CEO/Chairman:** Donald D. Dreher.

D.R.E., INC.
1800 Williamson Court, Louisville KY 40223-4114. 502/244-4444. **Toll-free phone:** 800/499-9220. **Fax:** 502/244-0369. **Contact:** Human Resources. **E-mail address:** info@dremedical.com. **World Wide Web address:** http://www.dremedical.com. **Description:** A distributor of new and used medical equipment. The Domestic Medical Equipment Division sells anesthesia equipment, surgical equipment, and operating room tables. The company also has a Veterinary Medical Equipment Division. **Corporate headquarters location:** This location. **President:** Mike Dirr. **Number of employees at this location:** 30.

DOE-ANDERSON ADVERTISING
620 West Main Street, Louisville KY 40202. 502/589-1700. **Fax:** 502/587-8349. **Contact:** Crystal Peterson, Personnel. **E-mail address:** cpeterson@doeanderson.com. **World Wide Web address:** http://www.doeanderson.com. **Description:** A full-service advertising and public relations agency. Founded in 1915. **NOTE:** Entry-level positions are offered. Job seekers may apply online for advertised openings. **Positions advertised include:** Broadcast Coordinator; Senior Account Manager. **Special programs:** Internships. **Corporate headquarters location:** This location. **Listed on:** Privately held. **CEO:** Dave Wilkins. **Sales/revenues:** $51 - $100 million. **Number of employees at this location:** 135.

R.R. DONNELLEY & SONS COMPANY
3201 Lebanon Road, Danville KY 40422. 859/238-7910. **Contact:** Keith Lile, Human Resources Department. **E-mail address:** rrdonnelley@hiresystems.com. **World Wide Web address:** http://www.rrdonnelley.com. **Description:** R.R. Donnelley & Sons manages, reproduces, and distributes print and digital information for publishing, merchandising, and information technology customers. Among the company's products are catalogs, inserts, magazines, books, directories, computer documentation, and financial printing. R.R. Donnelley has more than 180 strategically located sales offices and production facilities. Principal services offered by the company are conventional and digital prepress operations, computerized printing and binding, and sophisticated pool shipping and distribution services for printed products; information repackaging into multiple formats (print, magnetic, and optical media); database management, list rental, list enhancement, and direct mail production services; turnkey computer documentation services (outsourcing, translation, printing, binding, diskette replication, kitting, licensing, republishing, and fulfillment); reprographics and facilities management; creative design and communication services; and digital and conventional map creation and related services. Founded in 1864. **NOTE:** Entry-level positions are offered. Submit resumes by e-mail to rrdonnelley@hiresystems.com. **Positions advertised include:** Regional Sourcing Leader; Desktop Support Technician; Process Manager. **Special programs:** Training. **Corporate headquarters location:** Chicago IL. **Other U.S. locations:** Nationwide. **International locations:** Worldwide. **Operations at this facility include:** Administration; Manufacturing. **Listed on:** New York Stock Exchange. **Stock exchange symbol:** DNY. **President/CEO/Chairman:** William L. Davis. **Sales/revenues:** $5.3 billion. **Number of employees at this location:** 1,100. **Number of employees nationwide:** 30,000. **Number of employees worldwide:** 35,000.

R.R. DONNELLEY & SONS COMPANY
Glasgow Division, 120 Donnelley Drive, Glasgow KY 42141. 270/678-2121. **Contact:** Human Resources. **E-mail address:** rrdonnelley@hiresystems.com. **World Wide Web address:** http://www.rrdonnelley.com. **Description:** Also known as The Lakeside Press, R.R. Donnelley & Sons manages, reproduces, and distributes print and digital information for publishing, merchandising, and information technology customers. Among the company's products are catalogs, inserts, magazines, books, directories, computer documentation, and financial printing. R.R. Donnelley has more than 180 strategically located sales offices and production facilities. R.R. Principal services offered by the company are conventional and digital prepress operations, computerized printing and binding, and sophisticated pool shipping and distribution services for printed products; information repackaging into multiple formats (print, magnetic, and optical media); database management, list rental, list enhancement, and direct mail production services; turnkey computer documentation services (outsourcing, translation, printing, binding, diskette replication, kitting, licensing, republishing, and fulfillment); reprographics and facilities management; creative design and communication services; and digital and conventional map creation and related services. Founded in 1864. **NOTE:** Entry-level positions are offered. Submit resumes by e-mail to rrdonnelley@hiresystems.com. **Positions advertised include:** Pressroom Supervisor; Plant Finance Manager. **Special Programs:** Training. **Corporate headquarters location:** Chicago IL. **Other U.S. locations:** Nationwide. **International locations:** Worldwide. **Operations at this facility include:** This location prints magazines. **Listed on:** New York Stock Exchange. **Stock exchange symbol:** DNY. **President/CEO/Chairman:** William L. Davis. **Sales/revenues:** $5.3 billion. **Number of employees nationwide:** 30,000. **Number of employees worldwide:** 35,000.

DOW CORNING CORPORATION
P.O. Box 310, 4770 Highway 42 East, Carrollton KY 41008. 502/732-2000. **Contact:** Rick Heinke, Human Resources. **E-mail address:** resume@downcorning.com. **World Wide Web address:** http://www.dowcorning.com. **Description:** Develops, manufactures, and markets silicones, related specialty chemical materials, polycrystalline silicone, and specialty health care products. Dow Corning serves the following industries: automotive; chemicals and petrochemicals; construction; consumer products; electrical and electronics; food processing; medical products; paints and coatings; personal, household, and automotive care; pharmaceuticals; plastics; pressure-sensitive adhesives; and textiles and leather. The company operates 40 manufacturing and service locations worldwide. Founded in 1943. **Positions advertised include:** Human Resources Generalist; Senior Process Specialist; Meteorology Specialist. **Special programs:** Co-ops; Summer Internships. **Corporate headquarters location:** Midland MI. **Other U.S. locations:** MI; IN; NC; CA; OH. **International locations:** Worldwide. **Operations at this facility include:** This location produces silicon-based products for a variety of industries. **Listed on:** Privately held. **President/COO:** Stephanie A. Burns. **Number of employees worldwide:** 8,200.

DOW CORNING CORPORATION
760 Hodgenville Road, Elizabethtown KY 42701. 270/737-6466. **Fax:** 270/737-6798. **Contact:** Dave Soldan, Human Resources. **E-mail address:** resume@dowcorning.com. **Wide Web address:** http://www.dowcorning.com. **Description:** Develops, manufactures, and markets silicones, related specialty chemical materials, polycrystalline silicone, and specialty health care products. Dow Corning serves the following industries: automotive; chemicals and petrochemicals; construction; consumer products; electrical and electronics; food processing; medical products; paints and coatings; personal, household, and automotive care; pharmaceuticals; plastics; pressure-sensitive adhesives; and textiles and leather. The company operates 40 manufacturing and service locations worldwide. Founded in 1943. **Positions advertised include:** Senior Process Specialist; Meteorology Specialist. **Special programs:** Co-ops; Summer Internships. **Corporate headquarters location:** Midland MI. **Other U.S. locations:** MI; IN; NC; CA; OH. **International locations:** Worldwide. **Operations at this facility include:** This location produces silicon-based products for a variety of industries. **Listed on:** Privately held. **President/COO:** Stephanie A. Burns. **Number of employees worldwide:** 8,200.

E.I. DUPONT DE NEMOURS & COMPANY
4200 Camp Ground Road, Louisville KY 40216. 502/775-3115. **Contact:** Human Resources. **World Wide Web address:** http://www.dupont-dow.com. **Description:** E.I. DuPont de Nemours & Company's activities include the manufacturing of biomedical, industrial, and consumer products such as photographic, data-recording, and video devices; the production of man-made fiber products with applications in a variety of consumer and commercial industries; polymer products such as plastic resins, elastomers, and films; agricultural and industrial chemicals such as herbicides and insecticides, pigments, fluorochemicals, petroleum additives, and mineral acids; the exploration and production of crude oil and natural gas; the refining, marketing, and downstream transportation of petroleum; and the mining and distribution of steam and metallurgical coals. The company has clients in the aerospace, agriculture, apparel, transportation, health care, and printing and publishing industries. **Corporate headquarters location:** Wilmington DE. **International locations:** Worldwide. **Operations at this facility include:** This location manufactures latex and acids. **Listed on:** New York Stock Exchange. **Stock exchange symbol:** DD. **CEO/Chairman:** Charles Holliday, Junior. **Sales/revenues:** Approximately $25 billion. **Number of employees worldwide:** 1,500.

DURO BAG MANUFACTURING COMPANY
7600 Empire Drive, Florence KY 41042. 859/371-2150 **Toll-free phone:** 800/829-3876. **Contact:** Jason Wiehe, Human Resources. **E-mail address:** jwiehe@durobag.com. **World Wide Web address:** http://www.durobag.com. **Description:** An integrated manufacturer of paper and plastic bags, sold primarily to the retail industry and other users of specialty bags. Founded in 1953. **NOTE:** Entry-level positions are offered. **Corporate headquarters location:** Ludlow KY. **Other area locations:** Covington KY; Walton KY. **Other U.S. locations:** Tampa FL; Brownsville TX; Richmond VA; Hudson WI; Tolleson AZ; Elizabeth NJ; Alsip IL. **International locations:** Rio Bravo, Mexico. **Subsidiaries include:** S&G Packaging. **Operations at this facility include:** This location is a manufacturing facility whose products include fast food, grocery, and lawn and leaf bags. **Listed on:** Privately held. **President/CEO:** Charles Shor. **Sales/revenues:** Over $100 million. **Number of employees at this location:** 100. **Number of employees nationwide:** 1,400. **Number of employees worldwide:** 2,300.

DURO BAG MANUFACTURING COMPANY
Corporate Headquarters, P.O. Box 16250, Davies & Oak Street, Ludlow KY 41016. 859/581-8200. **Toll-free phone:** 800/829-3876. **Fax:** 859/581-8327. **Contact:** Jackie Isaacs or David Schlageter, Human Resources. **E-mail address:** jisaacs@durobag.com or dschlageter@durobag.com. **World Wide Web address:** http://www.durobag.com. **Description:** An integrated manufacturer of paper and plastic bags, sold primarily to the retail industry and other users of specialty bags. Founded in 1953. **NOTE:** Entry-level positions and second and third shifts are offered. **Corporate headquarters location:** This location. **Other area locations:** Covington KY; Walton KY; Florence KY. **Other U.S. locations:** Tampa FL; Brownsville TX; Richmond VA; Hudson WI; Tolleson AZ; Elizabeth NJ; Alsip IL. **International locations:** Rio Bravo, Mexico. **Subsidiaries include:** S&G Packaging. **Operations at this facility include:** Administration. **Listed on:** Privately held. **President/ CEO:** Charles Shor. **Sales/revenues:** Over $100 million. **Number of employees at this location:** 100. **Number of employees nationwide:** 1,400. **Number of employees worldwide:** 2,300.

EXECUTIVE INN RIVERMONT
One Executive Boulevard, Owensboro KY 42301. 270/926-8000. **Toll-free phone:** 800/626-1936. **Fax:** 270/926-9047. **Contact:** Human Resources. **E-mail address:** exeinnrivermont@cs.com. **World Wide Web Address:** http://www.executiveinnrivermont.com. **Description:** A hotel/convention center featuring 650 guest rooms and suites, 22 meeting rooms, and an exposition center.

FIELD PACKING COMPANY INC.
P.O. Box 20003, Owensboro KY 42304. 270/926-2324. **Physical address:** 6 Dublin Lane, Owensboro KY 42301. **Fax:** 270/926-4067. **Contact:** Human Resources. **World Wide Web address:** http://www.kentuckiangold.com. **Description:** Field Packing Company Inc. is engaged in the processing of fresh and cured pork products and is most noted for its Kentuckian Gold Premium deli line. Products include ham, bacon, bologna, and hot dogs. **Corporate headquarters location:** This location. **Parent company:** Soparind Corporation.

FOAM DESIGN, INC.
P.O. Box 12178, Lexington KY 40581. 859/231-7006. **Physical address:** 444 Transport Court, Lexington KY 40511. **Toll-free phone:** 800/238-8574. **Fax:** 859/231-7731. **Contact:** Marianne McCartt, Human Resources. **E-mail address:** lex@foamdesign.com. **World Wide Web address:** http://www. foamdesign.com. **Description:** Manufactures foam, foam products, and cushioning products made of polyethylene, polyurethane, and polystyrene foams for the protection of typewriters, printed circuit boards, medical instruments, electronic components, and related merchandise. Cushioning products are used to package consumer goods, for the transport of aerospace and military missile components and related hardware, for the handling and shipping of automotive parts, and in the packaging of electronics components and assemblies. Foam Design also manufactures consumer products such as camping pads, bodyboards, and archery targets. **Corporate headquarters location:** This location. **Other U.S. locations:** Research Triangle NC; Sioux Falls SD; Memphis TN. **Operations at this facility include:** Administration; Manufacturing. **CEO:** Walter Gradek.

FORD MOTOR COMPANY
P.O. Box 32310, Louisville KY 40232. 502/429-2000. **Physical address:** 3001 Chamberlain Lane, Louisville KY 40241. **Toll-free phone:** 800/248-4444. **Contact:** Director of Personnel. **World Wide Web address:** http://www.ford.com. **Description:** Engaged in the design, development, manufacture, and sale of cars, trucks, tractors, and related components and accessories. The company's two core businesses are the Automotive Group and the Financial Services Group (Ford Credit, The Associates, USL Capital, and First Nationwide). Ford is also engaged in a number of other businesses, including electronics, glass, electrical and fuel-handling products, plastics, climate-control systems, automotive service and replacement parts, vehicle leasing and rental, and land development. **Corporate headquarters location:** Dearborn MI. **Other U.S. locations:** Nationwide. **International locations:** Worldwide. **Subsidiaries include:** Ford Motor Company of Canada, Limited; Ford Motor Credit Company. **Operations at this facility include:** This location manufactures trucks. **Listed on:** New York Stock Exchange. **Stock exchange symbol:** F. **CEO/Chairman:** William Clay Ford, Junior. **Sales/revenues:** Approximately $163 million. **Number of employees worldwide:** Over 350,000.

FRUIT OF THE LOOM, INC.
One Fruit of the Loom Drive, P.O. Box 90015, Bowling Green KY 42102-9015. 270/781-6400. **Contact:** Vicki Gibson, Human Resources. **E-mail address:** jobs@fruit.com. **World Wide Web address:** http://www.fruit.com. **Description:** An international marketer and manufacturer of basic family apparel. The casualwear, sportswear, and activewear categories account for more than 60 percent of Fruit of the Loom's total business. Fruit of the Loom also manufactures and markets a complete line of athletic sportswear featuring the Wilson Sporting Goods brand. Activewear includes the production of blank T-shirts, shorts, knit shirts, and fleecewear, primarily for garment imprinters and decorators. Fruit of the Loom maintains a large share of the men's and boys' underwear market and also produces women's, girls', infants', and toddlers' underwear. **Corporate headquarters location:** This location. **Other area locations:** Franklin KY; Greensburg KY; Jamestown KY. **International locations:** Canada, the Republic of Ireland; Northern Ireland; Morocco. **Subsidiaries include:** Salem Sportswear Corporation, a designer and marketer of sports apparel under licenses granted by major professional sports leagues, players' associations, and colleges and universities; and Josten Sportswear, a manufacturer and wholesaler of decorated sportswear, which also licenses cartoon characters including those from Disney, Peanuts, and Looney Tunes. **Parent company:** Berkshire Hathaway, Incorporated. **Number of employees worldwide:** Approximately 23,000.

FRUIT OF THE LOOM, INC.
P.O. Box 170, Jamestown KY 42629. 270/343-2501. **Physical address:** South Highway 127, Jamestown KY 42629. **Fax:** 270/343-3598. **Contact:** Trish Popplewell, Personnel Manager. **World Wide Web address:** http://www.fruit.com. **Description:** An international marketer and manufacturer of basic family apparel. The casualwear, sportswear, and activewear categories account for more than 60 percent of Fruit of the Loom's total business. Fruit of the Loom also manufactures and markets a complete line of athletic sportswear featuring the Wilson Sporting Goods brand. Activewear business includes the production of blank T-shirts, shorts, knit shirts, and fleecewear, primarily for garment imprinters and decorators. Fruit of the Loom maintains a large share of men's and boys' underwear market and also produces women's, girls', infants', and toddlers' underwear. **Corporate headquarters location:** Bowling Green KY. **Other area locations:** Bowling Green KY; Franklin KY; Greensburg KY. **International locations:** Canada; the Republic of Ireland; Northern Ireland; Morocco. **Operations at this facility include:** This location manufactures T-shirts, sweatshirts, shorts, and men's and boys' briefs. **Subsidiaries include:** Salem Sportswear Corporation, a designer and marketer of sports apparel under licenses granted by major professional sports leagues, players' associations, and colleges and universities; and Josten Sportswear, a manufacturer and wholesaler of decorated sportswear, which also licenses cartoon characters including those from Disney, Peanuts, and Looney Tunes. **Parent company:** Berkshire Hathaway, Incorporated. **Number of employees worldwide:** Approximately 23,000.

GE APPLIANCES
GE Appliance Park, Building 3, Room 175, Louisville KY 40225. 502/452-4311. **Physical address:** 9500 Williamsburg Office Plaza, Louisville Kentucky 40222. **Toll-free phone:** 800/626-2000. **Fax:** 502/452-0217. **Contact:** Patty Blair, Professional Relations. **World Wide Web address:** http://www.gecareers.com. **Description:** General Electric is a diversified services, technology, and manufacturing company with operations in the following areas: aircraft engines (jet engines, replacement parts, and repair services for commercial, military, executive, and commuter aircraft); appliances; broadcasting (NBC); industrial and power systems (lighting products, electrical distribution and control equipment, transportation systems products, electric motors and related products, a broad range of electrical and electronic industrial automation products, and a network of electrical supply houses); materials (plastics, ABS resins, silicones, superabrasives, and laminates); power systems (products for the generation, transmission, and distribution of electricity); technical products and systems (medical systems and equipment, as well as a full range of computer-based information and data interchange services for both internal use and external commercial and industrial customers); and capital services (consumer services, financing, and specialty insurance). **Positions advertised include:** Field-service Engineer. **Special programs:** Internships; Training; Co-ops. **Corporate headquarters location:** Fairfield CT. **Other U.S. locations:** Nationwide. **International locations:** Worldwide. **Parent company:** General Electric Company. **Operations at this facility include:** This is the headquarters location for GE Appliances, which is part of the GE Consumer Products division. GE Appliances markets its products under such brand names as Monogram, GE Profile, GE, and Hotpoint. **Listed on:** New York Stock Exchange. **Stock exchange symbol:** GE. **President/CEO:** James P. Campbell. **Number of employees worldwide:** Approximately 45,000 in the Consumer Products division.

GE CAPITAL IT SOLUTIONS
One Riverfront Place, Suite 500, Newport KY 41071. 859/815-7000. **Fax:** 859/815-7027. **Contact:** Recruiting Department. **World Wide Web address:** http://www.gecareers.com. **Description:** Resells computer products to commercial, governmental, and educational users. The company's products and services include value-added systems, systems integration, networking services, support, maintenance, facilities management, outsourcing, software and business consulting services, and rental services. **NOTE:** Entry-level positions are offered. **Special programs:** Internships; Co-ops. **Corporate headquarters location:** This location. **Other U.S. locations:** Nationwide. **International locations:** Worldwide. **Parent Company:** General Electric Company. **Listed on:** New York Stock Exchange. **Stock exchange symbol:** GE. **Number of employees nationwide:** 2,100.

GE MOTORS
3301 Old Hartford Road, Owensboro KY 42303. 270/926-8500. **Fax:** 270/686-1226. **Contact:** Cathie Pace, Human Resources Director. **World Wide Web address:** http://www.ge.com. **Description:** General Electric is a diversified services, technology, and manufacturing company with operations in the following areas: aircraft engines (jet engines, replacement parts, and repair services for commercial, military, executive, and commuter aircraft); appliances; capital services (consumer services, financing, and specialty insurance); industrial (lighting products, electrical distribution and control equipment, transportation systems products, electric motors and related products, and a broad range of electrical and electronic industrial automation products); technical products and services (medical systems and equipment sold worldwide to hospitals and medical facilities as well as a full range of computer-based information and data interchange services for both internal use and external commercial and industrial customers); broadcasting (NBC); materials (plastics, ABS resins, silicones, and superabrasives); power systems (products for the generation, transmission, and distribution of electricity); technical products and systems (medical systems and equipment, as well as a full range of computer-based information and data interchange services for both internal use and external commercial and industrial customers); and capital services (consumer services, financing, and specialty insurance). **Positions advertised include:** EHS Manager. **Corporate headquarters location:** Plainville CT. **Operations at this facility include:** This location manufactures industrial air-conditioning and is part of the GE Industrial Services division. GE Industrial Services supplies industrial, electrical, and security equipment, systems, and services. **President/CEO:** Lloyd G. Trotter. **Sales/revenues:** $6 billion. **Number of employees at this location:** 500. **Number of employees worldwide:** Approximately 40,000 in the Industrial Services division.

GALL'S INC.
2680 Palumbo Drive, Lexington KY 40509. 859/266-7227. **Fax:** 859/269-3492. **Recorded jobline:** 859/266-7227 x5627. **Contact:** Human Resources. **E-mail address:** resume@galls.com. **World Wide Web address:** http://www.gallsinc.com. **Description:** A retailer of public safety equipment. Products include vehicle equipment (radar, lightbars, and security screens); bags and organizers; public safety accessories (scanners, cameras, surveillance systems); flashlights and spotlights; traffic safety products (lock picks, barrier tape, traffic warning supplies); law enforcement products (ear protection, weapon storage units, gun cleaning and lubrication systems, handcuffs, bullet proof vests, and breath tests); fire rescue products (helmets, hoods, and clothing); medical supplies; badges and identification; apparel and uniforms; and footwear. **NOTE:** Online applications are available. To send by e-mail, resumes and cover letters must be attached in Microsoft Word format. **Positions advertised include:** Sales Manager; Account Manager; Customer Service Representative. **Office hours:** Monday – Friday, 8:00 a.m. – 5:00 p.m. **Corporate headquarters location:** This location. **Subsidiaries include:** DynaMed. **Listed on:** Privately held. **President:** Thomas Vozzo. **Number of employees at this location:** 275.

GENERAL CABLE
4 Tesseneer Drive, Highland Heights KY 41076. 859/572-8000. **Fax:** 859/572-8919. **Contact:** Human Resources. **E-mail address:** resumes-hr@generalcable.com. **World Wide Web address:** http://www.generalcable.com. **Description:** A manufacturer of cable wire. The company's business units include the Electrical Group, the Telecommunications and Electronics Group, the Consumer Products Group, and the Manufacturing Group. The Electrical Group operates under the business units General Cable/Guardian, which manufactures and distributes a full line of copper building wire, tray cable, power cable, and other cable products; Carol Cable Electrical, which manufactures industrial, power, and mining cable, control cable, THHN building wire, entertainment cable, rubber portable cord, and cordsets insulated with plastic and thermosetting compounds; and Capital Wire and Cable, which manufactures insulated wire and cable using both aluminum and copper conductors. The Telecommunications and Electronics Group operates under the business units Outside Products, which markets wire and cable designed for use in the outside plant network; Premise Products, which manufactures wire products that support the central office and commercial premise markets; and Electronics, which manufactures computer and control cables, IBM cabling products, ethernet, coaxial, twin axial, and fire alarm cables. The Consumer Products Group operates under the business units Carol Cable, which manufactures extension cords, portable lights, and home office power supplies; General/Capital Wire Retail, which sells building wire to the retail market; and the OEM Engineered Cordsets Division, which manufactures cord and cordsets for data processing equipment, tools, floor care products, and other appliances. The Manufacturing Group provides specialized support and expertise in the areas of purchasing, transportation, engineering, labor relations, manufacturing, and environmental and safety support. **NOTE:** Resumes and applications may be submitted online. **Positions advertised include:** Compliance Controls Auditor; Inside Accounts Representative. **Corporate headquarters location:** This location. **International locations:** New Zealand; Spain; United Kingdom; Mexico; Canada. **Listed on:** New York Stock Exchange. **Stock exchange symbol:** BGC. **President/CEO/Director:** Gregory Kenny. **Sales/revenues:** $1.5 billion. **Number of employees worldwide:** 6,400.

GENERAL ELECTRIC COMPANY
1801 Edison Drive, Lexington KY 40503. 859/277-1161. **Fax:** 859/276-7969. **Contact:** Tony Colluci, Human Resources. **World Wide Web address:** http://www.gecareers.com. **Description:** General Electric is a diversified services, technology, and manufacturing company with operations in the following areas: aircraft engines (jet engines, replacement parts, and repair services for commercial, military, executive, and commuter aircraft); appliances; broadcasting (NBC); industrial and power systems (lighting products, electrical distribution and control equipment,

transportation systems products, electric motors and related products, a broad range of electrical and electronic industrial automation products, and a network of electrical supply houses); materials (plastics, ABS resins, silicones, superabrasives, and laminates); power systems (products for the generation, transmission, and distribution of electricity); technical products and systems (medical systems and equipment, as well as a full range of computer-based information and data interchange services for both internal use and external commercial and industrial customers); and capital services (consumer services, financing, and specialty insurance). **Corporate headquarters location:** Louisville KY. **Other U.S. locations:** Nationwide. **International locations:** Worldwide. **Operations at this facility include:** This location manufactures headlamps for automobiles for GE Lighting, which is part of the Consumer Products division. **President/CEO:** James P. Campbell. **Number of employees at this location:** 470. **Number of employees worldwide:** Approximately 45,000 in the Consumer Products division.

GEORGETOWN COLLEGE
400 East College Street, Georgetown KY 40324. 502/863-8149. **Fax:** 502/868-7737. **Contact:** Human Resources. **E-mail address:** humanresources@georgetowncollege.edu. **World Wide Web address:** http://www.georgetowncollege.edu. **Description:** A private, four-year, Christian liberal arts college, which also offers several pre-professional academic programs. The student body is made up of approximately 1,200 undergraduates. **NOTE:** Those applying for faculty positions must contact the Vice President of Academic Affairs. **Positions advertised include:** Controller; Student Life Person; Art History Assistant Professor; Computer Science Assistant Professor; Psychology Assistant Professor; Exercise Science Assistant Professor; Physics Assistant Professor; Media Assistant Professor; Religion Assistant Professor; Spanish Assistant Professor; Technical Theatre Assistant Professor; Voice Assistant Professor; Wait Staff Caters. **President:** William H. Crouch.

JAMES N. GRAY COMPANY
10 Quality Street, Lexington KY 40507-1450. 859/281-5000. **Fax:** 859/281-9313. **Contact:** Jeri Tackett, Human Resources Director. **E-mail address:** humanresources@jngray.com. **World Wide Web address:** http://www.jngray.com. **Description:** Specializes in commercial construction. Founded in 1960. **Positions advertised include:** Project Manager; Senior Project Manager; Design Manger; CADD Operator. **Note:** E-mail resume to human resources for consideration of these and other potential positions. **Special programs:** Educational Assistance Program. **Other area locations:** Glasgow KY; Hopkinsville KY; Louisville KY. **Other U.S. locations:** Birmingham AL; Anaheim CA; Floral Park NY; Richmond VA. **Sales/revenues:** $330 million. **Number of employees at this location:** 282.

HK SYSTEMS INC.
2100 Litton Lane, Hebron KY 41048. 859/334-3400. **Fax:** 859/334-2329. **Contact:** Betty Baker, Human Resources. **World Wide Web address:** http://www.hksystems.com. **Description:** Provides business solutions and services for material handling systems. HK Systems also manufactures automated guided vehicles, automated storage and retrieval machines, conveyors, palletizers, and sortation equipment. **Positions advertised include:** Account Executive; Pharmaceutical Industry Account Representative; Maintenance Technician; Sales Director; Proposal Manager. **Corporate headquarters location:** New Berlin WI. **Other U.S. locations:** Bountiful UT; Salt Lake City UT; Montgomery AL; Charlotte NC; Duluth GA; Gainsville GA; Grapevine TX; Novi MI; St. Louis MO. **International locations:** Mississauga, Ontario, Canada. **Subsidiaries include:** Irista. **President/CEO:** John W. Splude. **Sales/revenues:** $250 million. **Number of employees worldwide:** 1,200.

HARLAN APPALACHIAN REGIONAL HEALTHCARE
81 Ball Park Road, Harlan KY 40831. 606/573-8100. **Fax:** 606/573-8200. **Contact:** Ms. Sabra Howard, Director of Personnel. **E-mail address:** mhamblin@arh.org. **World Wide Web address:** http://www.arh.org. **Description:** A 150-bed acute care hospital that provides a full range of primary and secondary health care services. **Positions advertised include:** Community Chief Financial Officer; Pharmacy Director. **Special programs:** Internships. **Parent company:** Appalachian Regional Healthcare is a nonprofit health care system with hospitals, clinics, home health agencies, and other health services in the central Appalachian region of Kentucky, West Virginia, and Virginia. Products and services offered by ARH include hospital care, home health, durable medical equipment, psychiatric care, ambulatory clinics, sterile laundry, laboratory, and EEG/EKG/Holter monitoring. **NOTE:** Send resumes to Marilyn Hamblin, ARH Systems Professional Recruiter, Appalachian Regional Healthcare, P.O. Box 8086, Lexington KY 40533, or fax to 859/226-2586. **President/CEO:** Stephen C. Hanson. **Number of employees at this location:** 450.

HORSE CAVE THEATRE
P.O. Box 215, Horse Cave KY 42749. 270/786-1200. **Physical address:** 101 East Main Street, Horse Cave KY 42749. **Fax:** 270/786-5298. **Contact:** Robert Brock, Executive Director. **World Wide Web address:** http://www.horsecavetheatre.org. **Description:** A nonprofit repertory theater promoting professional and educational theater programs. **Special programs:** Internships. **Corporate headquarters location:** This location. **Number of employees at this location:** 10.

HOST COMMUNICATIONS, INC.
546 East Main Street, Lexington KY 40508. 859/226-4678. **Fax:** 859/226-4221. **Contact:** Human Resources. **World Wide Web address:** http://www.hostcommunications.com. **Description:** Provides media and marketing services to universities, athletic conferences, and the National Collegiate Athletic Association (NCAA). These services primarily include the production, sales, and syndication of Internet, radio, and television broadcasts of football and basketball games; the publishing and printing of athletic and championship programs and magazines; and the management of NCAA Corporate Partner Program. The company's sports services include five national radio broadcasts, one national NCAA magazine, nationally televised NCAA football and basketball shows, and numerous Internet sites. Host Communications, Inc. also manages the NCAA Corporate Partner Program, which features blue chip companies. Included in its products is the Historically Black Collegiate Coalition (HBCC), a collection of more than 20 historically black institutions. The company's Main Street Productions Division operates recording studios that provide live broadcast productions and soundtracks for radio, video, and multirange presentations. The company's publishing division produces 400 annual publications and NCAA basketball championship programs. The printing division of the company offers services including graphic design, computerized typesetting and image assembly, and printing and binding. **Positions advertised include:** Event Coordinator; Administrative Associate; Executive Director; Database & Dues Coordinator. **Corporate headquarters location:** This location. **Parent company:** Bull Run Corporation (Atlanta GA) is a diversified holding company with other subsidiaries including Gray Communications Systems, Incorporated (Albany GA) and Datasouth Computer Corporation (Charlotte NC). **Listed on:** NASDAQ. **Stock exchange symbol:** BULL. **President/COO:** Gordon Whitener. **Number of employees nationwide:** Approximately 350.

HUMANA, INC.
500 West Main Street, Louisville KY 40202. 502/580-1000. **Contact:** Vivian Tate, Human Resources. **World Wide Web address:** http://www.humana.com. **Description:** A managed care company operating in 17 markets in 11 states throughout the Southeast and Midwest. The company's health plans serve over 1.6 million people through three product lines: commercial, Medicare risk, and Medicare supplement plans. Commercial health care products are delivered through health maintenance organizations (HMOs) and preferred provider organizations (PPOs), which share the financial risks of delivering cost-effective services. The Medicare risk product is an HMO for Medicare recipients, and the Medicare supplement program covers medical costs for which the Medicare beneficiary is usually responsible. **NOTE:** Resumes must be submitted online. **Positions advertised include:** Beneficiary Services Representative; Learning Specialist; Web Design Developer; Contract Systems Coordinator; Administrative Services Coordinator; HR Customer Service Specialist; Frontline Leader Billing & Enrollment Associate; Senior Auditor; Education Consultant; Clinical Advisor Analyst; HR Director; Policy Consultant; Marketing Consultant; Technology Project Manager; Research Scientist; Computer Scientist; Data Analyst. **Special programs:** Co-ops; Internships; Tuition Reimbursement Program; Scholarship Program. **Corporate headquarters location:** This location. **Listed on:** New York Stock Exchange. **Stock exchange symbol:** HUM. **President/CEO:** Mike McCallister. **Sales/revenues:** $10.2 billion.

IBM CORPORATION
230 Lexington Green Circle, Suite 500, Lexington KY 40503. **Toll-free phone:** 800/796-9876. **Contact:** IBM Staffing Services. **World Wide Web address:** http://www.ibm.com. **Description:** Formerly Databeam Corporation. IBM is an advanced information technologies company that manufactures and markets a wide range of products, including computer systems, software, networking systems, microelectronics, and storage devices. **Special programs:** Training. **Corporate headquarters location:** Armonk NY. **Other U.S. locations:** Nationwide. **International locations:** Worldwide. **Subsidiaries include:** Hitachi Global Storage Technologies; IBM Canada Limited; IBM Global Services; IBM Software; Lotus Development Corporation; Tivoli Software. **Operations at this facility include:** This location develops document conferencing software applications for end users. **Listed on:** New York Stock Exchange. **Stock exchange symbol:** IBM. **President/CEO/Chairman:** Samuel J. Palmisano. **Sales/revenues:** $81,186 million. **Number of employees worldwide:** 319,876.

ICHIKOH MANUFACTURING INC.
6601 Midland Industrial Drive, Shelbyville KY 40065. 502/633-4936. **Fax:** 502/633-6251. **Contact:** Bob Hart, Human Resources Manager. **World Wide Web address:** http://www.ichikoh.com. **Description:** A manufacturer of rearview and sideview mirrors for vehicles. Founded in 1987. **Parent company:** Ichikoh, Japan. **Listed on:** Tokyo Stock Exchange. **President:** Yukio Ichikawa. **Sales/revenues:** $83.5 billion. **Number of employees at this location:** 400. **Number of employees worldwide:** 2,130.

JOHNSON CONTROLS, INC.
P.O. Box 503-A, Cadiz KY 42211. 270/522-3221. **Physical address:** 340 Hopkinsville Road, Cadiz KY 42211. **Fax:** 270/522-3881. **Contact:** Terry Birdsong, Personnel Manager. **World Wide Web address:** http://www.jci.com. **Description: Operations at this facility include:** A manufacturer and marketer of automotive seating, facility services and control systems, plastic packaging, and automotive batteries. The company is composed of four business units: Automotive, Controls, Plastics, and Battery. The automotive business produces complete seat systems, seating components, and interior trim systems for cars, light trucks, and vans. The controls segment is involved in the installation and service of facility management and control systems, retrofit and service of mechanical equipment and lighting systems in nonresidential buildings, and on-site management of facility operations and maintenance. The plastics unit manufactures plastic containers for beverages, food, personal care, and household items, as well as manufacturing, installing, and servicing plastics blowmolding machinery systems. The battery segment manufactures automotive batteries for the replacement and original equipment markets and specialty batteries for telecommunications and uninterrupted power supply applications. Founded in 1885. **Special programs:** Internships; Co-ops. **Corporate headquarters location:** Milwaukee WI. **Other area locations:** Florence KY; Georgetown KY. **Other U.S. locations:** Nationwide. **International locations:** Worldwide. **Operations at this facility include:** This location manufactures automotive seat frames. **Listed on:** New York Stock Exchange. **Stock exchange symbol:** JCI. **President/CEO:** John M. Barth. **Sales/revenues:** $20 billion. **Number of employees worldwide:** 113,000.

JOHNSON CONTROLS, INC.
8040 Bluegrass Drive, Florence KY 41042. 859/371-6030. **Contact:** Personnel. **World Wide Web address:** http://www.johnsoncontrols.com. **Description:** A manufacturer and marketer of automotive seating, facility services and control systems, plastic packaging, and automotive batteries. The company is composed of four business units: Automotive, Controls, Plastics, and Battery. The automotive business produces complete seat systems, seating components, and interior trim systems for cars, light trucks, and vans. The controls segment is involved in the installation and service of facility management and control systems, retrofit and service of mechanical equipment and lighting systems in nonresidential buildings, and on-site management of facility operations and maintenance. The plastics unit manufactures plastic containers for beverages, food, personal care, and household items, as well as manufacturing, installing, and servicing plastics blowmolding machinery systems. The battery segment manufactures automotive batteries for the replacement and original equipment markets and specialty batteries for telecommunications and uninterrupted power supply applications. **Special programs:** Internships; Co-ops. **Corporate headquarters location:** Milwaukee WI. **Other area locations:** Cadiz KY; Georgetown KY. **Other U.S. locations:** Nationwide. **International locations:** Worldwide. **Operations at this facility include:** This location manufactures plastic cases for batteries. **Listed on:** New York Stock Exchange. **Stock exchange symbol:** JCI. **President/CEO:** John M. Barth. **Sales/revenues:** $20 billion. **Number of employees worldwide:** 113,000.

JOHNSON CONTROLS, INC.
824 Lemons Mill Road, Georgetown KY 40324. 502/863-0400. **Contact:** Personnel. **World Wide Web address:** http://www.johnsoncontrols.com. **Description:** A manufacturer and marketer of automotive seating, facility services and control systems, plastic packaging, and automotive batteries. The company is composed of four business units: Automotive, Controls, Plastics, and Battery. The automotive business produces complete seat systems, seating components, and interior trim systems for cars, light trucks, and vans. The controls segment is involved in the installation and service of facility management and control systems, retrofit and service of mechanical equipment and lighting systems in nonresidential buildings, and on-site management of facility operations and maintenance. The plastics unit manufactures plastic containers for beverages, food, personal care, and household items, as well as manufacturing, installing, and servicing plastics blowmolding machinery systems. The battery segment manufactures automotive batteries for the replacement and original equipment markets

and specialty batteries for telecommunications and uninterrupted power supply applications. Founded in 1885. **Special programs:** Internships; Co-ops. **Corporate headquarters location:** Milwaukee WI. **Other area locations:** Cadiz KY; Florence KY. **Other U.S. locations:** Nationwide. **International locations:** Worldwide. **Operations at this facility include:** This location manufactures metal frames for automobile seats, primarily for Toyota/Camry. **Listed on:** New York Stock Exchange. **Stock exchange symbol:** JCI. **President/CEO:** John M. Barth. **Sales/revenues:** $20 billion. **Number of employees worldwide:** 113,000.

KEANE, INC.
9300 Shelbyville Road, Suite 205, Louisville KY 40222. 502/423-9958. **Contact:** Human Resources. **E-mail address:** careers@keane.com. **World Wide Web address:** http://www.keane.com. **Description:** Offers businesses a variety of computer consulting services. Keane also develops, markets, and manages software for its clients and assists in project management. **Positions advertised include:** Project Manager; Help Desk Administrator; Database Administrator. **Special programs:** Tuition Assistance Program; Training. **Corporate headquarters location:** Boston MA. **Other U.S. locations:** Nationwide. **International locations:** London, UK; Coventry, UK; Halifax, Nova Scotia; Noida, India; Hyderabad, India. **Subsidiaries include:** Metro Information Services. **Listed on:** American Stock Exchange. **Stock exchange symbol:** KEA. **CEO:** Brian T. Keane. **Sales/revenues:** $212.5 million.

KENTUCKY FARM BUREAU INSURANCE
9201 Bunsen Parkway, Louisville KY 40220. 502/495-5000. **Fax:** 502/495-7779. **Contact:** Human Resources. **E-mail address:** info_humanresources@kyfins.com. **World Wide Web address:** http://www.kyfbins.com. **Description:** A property and casualty insurance company that serves all 120 Kentucky counties. A wide range of personal and commercial insurance lines are offered, principally auto, homeowner, farmowner, general liability, and worker's compensation. The company also writes life and health insurance and individual retirement accounts. Founded in 1944. **NOTE:** To contact Human Resources directly, call 502/495-7780. **Positions advertised include:** Java Programmer; Programmer Analyst. **Corporate headquarters location:** This location. **Operations at this facility include:** Administration; Sales; Service.

THE KENTUCKY NETWORK
KENTUCKY EDUCATIONAL TELEVISION
600 Cooper Drive, Lexington KY 40502. 859/258-7231. **Fax:** 859/258-7766. **Contact:** Human Resources. **E-mail address:** jobsl@ket.org. **World Wide Web address:** http://www.ket.org. **Description:** A broadcasting network with a viewership of approximately 640,000 Kentuckians. **NOTE:** To contact Human Resources directly, call 859/258-7030. **Positions advertised include:** Publication Director; Latin Teacher Assistant. **Special programs:** Internships. **Corporate headquarters location:** This location. **Operations at this facility include:** Administration. **Number of employees at this location:** 260.

THE KENTUCKY POST
P.O. Box 2678, Covington KY 41012-2678. 859/292-2600. **Fax:** 859/291-2525. **E-mail address:** mphilipps@cincypost.com. **Physical address:** 421 Madison Avenue, Covington KY 41001. **Contact:** Mike Phillips, Editor. **World Wide Web address:** http://www.kypost.com. **NOTE:** Mail resumes to 125 East Court Street, Cincinnati OH 45202. **Description:** The *Kentucky Post* has a circulation of 45,000 and became a member of the Associated Press in 1984. The company also publishes the *Post Extra*, a total-market-coverage weekly edition. **Corporate headquarters location:** Cincinnati OH.

KENTUCKY STATE UNIVERSITY
400 East Main Street, Frankfort KY 40601. 502/597-6000. **Contact:** Office of Personnel. **E-mail address:** jobs@gwmail.kysu.edu. **World Wide Web address:** http://www.kysu.edu. **Description:** A liberal arts university that offers undergraduate degrees through its College of Arts, Social Sciences, and Interdisciplanry Studies, College of Mathematics, Sciences, Technology and Health, and the College of Professional Studies. **Positions advertised include:** Assistant Bursar; Counselor/Advisor; Administrative Assistant; Security Officer. **President:** Mary Evans Sias.

KENTUCKY TEXTILES
One 20th Street, Paris KY 40361. 859/987-5228. **Fax:** 859/987-1871. **Contact:** Human Resources. **World Wide Web address:** http://www.kentuckytextiles.com. **Description:** An apparel manufacturer and catalog retailer of a line of women's casual wear under the name SloppyJoe's casual wear. The company's products include printed and nonprinted T-shirts, sweatshirts, shorts, leggings, casual dresses, and tote bags. **Office hours:** Monday – Friday, 7:30 a.m. – 4:30 p.m.

KINDRED HEALTHCARE
680 South Fourth Avenue, Louisville KY 40202. 502/596-7300. **Fax:** 502/596-4052. **Contact:** Brenda Kadel, Human Resources. **World Wide Web address:** http://www.kindredhealthcare.com. **Description:** A healthcare network that operates 61 hospitals and pulmonary units, 315 nursing centers, and contract rehabilitation services in 43 states. **Note:** Job seekers may apply for openings online. Part-time positions are offered. Positions are listed on http://www.monster.com as well as Kindred Health Care's website. **Positions advertised include:** Director of Business Development; Rehabilitation Recruiting Manager; Reimbursement Analyst; Programming Analyst; Internal Auditing; Regional Quality Education; Human Resource Payroll Benefits Analyst. **Special programs:** Tuition Reimbursement Program. **Corporate headquarters location:** This location. **Listed on:** New York Stock Exchange. **Stock exchange symbol:** KIND. **Number of employees nationwide:** 53,000.

KOSAIR CHILDREN'S HOSPITAL
231 East Chestnut Street, Louisville KY 40202. 502/629-6000. **Contact:** Human Resources. **World Wide Web address:** http://www.nortonhealthcare.com. **Description:** A full-service, tertiary care, 235-bed children's hospital. Kosair Children's Hospital offers a full range of services including Pediatric Intensive Care, one of the nation's largest neonatal intensive care nurseries, a pediatric trauma center, and a poison center. The hospital operates a self-contained pediatric burn unit; infant/pediatric heart, kidney, and bone marrow transplant programs; and special units for oncology, orthopedics, diabetes, psychiatry, and pediatric surgery. Kosair Children's Hospital was one of the first hospitals in the country to perform an infant heart transplant and is one of the only facilities in the region to offer extra corporeal membrane oxygenation, a miniature heart-lung bypass procedure that gives lungs of premature infants the chance to heal and mature. **Positions advertised include:** Patient Care Associate; Neonatal Nurse; Registered Nurse; Supervising Nurse; Certified Respiratory Care Practitioner. **NOTE:** All hiring is conducted through the parent company. Resumes should be directed to Human Resources, Norton Healthcare, 200 East Chestnut Street, Louisville KY 40202. To contact the Human Resources Department directly, call 502/629-5950. **Parent company:** Norton Healthcare.

KROGER
810 Indian Mound Drive, Mount Sterling KY 40305. 859/497-4314. **Contact:** Human Resources Manager. **World Wide Web address:** http://www.Kroger.com. **Description:** A Grocery food chain. **Positions advertised include:** Management Trainee; Engineer; Cashier; Deli Clerk; Stock Associate. **Corporate Headquarters location:** Cincinnati Ohio. **Listed on:** New York Stock Exchange. **Stock exchange symbol:** KR.

KUHLMAN ELECTRIC CORPORATION
101 Kuhlman Boulevard, Versailles KY 40383. 859/879-2999. **Toll-free phone:** 800/395-6932. **Fax:** 859/873-8032. **Contact:** Human Resources Manager. **World Wide Web address:** http://www.keco.com. **Description:** Designs, manufactures, and markets electrical transformers. **Corporate headquarters location:** This location. **Other U.S. locations:** Nationwide. **Parent Company:** The Carlyle Group, an equity investment firm. **Operations at this facility include:** Administration; Manufacturing.

LG&E ENERGY
P.O. Box 32010, 220 West Main Street, Louisville KY 40232. 502/627-2000. **Toll-free phone:** 800/331-7370. **Fax:** 502/627-4660. **Contact:** Human Resources. **World Wide Web address:** http://www.lgeenergy.com. **Description:** An energy-services holding company operating power generation, retail gas, and electric utility services businesses. **NOTE:** Part-time positions are offered. **Positions advertised include:** Call Center Outage Representative. **Office hours:** Monday – Friday, 8:00 a.m. – 5:00 p.m. **Corporate headquarters location:** This location. **Subsidiaries include:** Louisville Gas & Electric; Kentucky Utilities; Western Kentucky Energy; Old Dominion Power. **Parent company:** Powergen plc. **Sales/revenues:** More than $100 million.

LANDSTAR SYSTEM, INC.
dba RISK MANAGEMENT CLAIM SERVICES, INC.
P.O. Box 70, Madisonville KY 42431. 270/821-0400. **Physical address:** 1850 Lantaff Boulevard, Suite 107, Madisonville KY 42431. **Contact:** Human Resources. **World Wide Web address:** http://www.landstar.com. **Description:** Landstar System, Incorporated is a North American multimodal transportation services company, which is divided into specialized freight transportation segments. Landstar is one of the only publicly traded trucking companies relying on independent owner-operators rather than salaried company drivers, with the company owning just 10 percent of the trucks in its fleet. **Corporate headquarters location:** Jacksonville FL. **Other U.S. locations:** Jacksonville FL; Romulus MI; Springfield VA. **Subsidiaries include:** Landstar Expedited, Incorporated; Landstar Express America, Incorporated; Landstar Gemini, Incorporated; Landstar Inway, Incorporated; Landstar ITCO, Incorporated; Landstar Ligon, Incorporated; Landstar Poole, Incorporated; Landstar Ranger, Incorporated; Landstar T.L.C., Incorporated; Landstar Transportation Service, Incorporated. **Listed on:** NASDAQ. **Stock exchange symbol:** LSTR. **Chairman/CEO:** Jeffrey C. Crowe. **Number of employees nationwide:** 2,500.

LANTECH, INC.
11000 Bluegrass Parkway, Louisville KY 40299. 502/267-4200. **Toll-free phone:** 800/866-0322. **Fax:** 502/267-5637. **Contact:** Human Resources. **E-mail address:** hr@lantech.com. **World Wide Web address:** http://www.lantech.com. **Description:** Researches, develops, and manufactures industrial packaging equipment that uses stretch wrapping to palletize or wrap product loads. **Positions advertised include:** Engineer; Field Service Technician; Welder; Production Associate; Micro Application Engineer. **Corporate headquarters location:** This location. **Operations at this facility include:** Administration; Manufacturing; Research and Development; Sales; Service. **President:** Jim Lancaster.

LEGGETT & PLATT, INC.
P.O. Box 367, Simpsonville KY 40067. 502/722-8811. **Physical address:** 211 Main Street, Simpsonville KY 40067. **Fax:** 502/722-8007. **Contact:** Human Resources Manager. **World Wide Web address:** http://www.leggett.com. **Description:** Specializes in the manufacture and marketing of a broad line of components for the furniture and bedding industries. Products include a select line of commodity fibers and carpet cushioning materials. A variety of diversified products are produced and sold in different markets. **Corporate headquarters location:** Carthage MO. **Other area locations:** Winchester KY. **Other U.S. locations:** Villa Rica GA; Pineville NC; Cincinnati OH; Nashville TN; Mexica TX. **Operations at this location include:** This location manufactures motion furniture products for recliner chairs, swivel chairs, rockers, and sleeper sofas. **Listed on:** New York Stock Exchange. **Stock exchange symbol:** LEG. **Sales/revenues:** $4.3 billion. **Number of employees worldwide:** 35,000.

LEGGETT & PLATT, INC.
P.O. Box 4037, Winchester KY 40391. 859/744-4626x100. **Physical address:** 101 New Street, Winchester KY 40392. **Fax:** 859/744-0957. **Contact:** Bill Bowman, Human Resources. **World Wide Web address:** http://www.leggett.com. **Description:** Leggett & Platt specializes in the manufacturing and marketing of a broad line of components for the furniture and bedding industries. Products include a select line of commodity fibers and carpet cushioning materials. The Textile Products Division is an operating division of Leggett & Platt, Inc., with a number of manufacturing locations across the nation. Operating locations manufacture products made from recycled fiber materials. Products include bedding and furniture fiber components, textile commodities, industrial wiping cloths, and synthetic fiber carpet cushions. **Corporate headquarters location:** Carthage MO. **Other area locations:** Simpsonville KY. **Other U.S. locations:** Villa Rica GA; Pineville NC; Cincinnati OH; Nashville TN; Mexica TX. **Operations at this facility include:** This location manufactures bed components, such as boxsprings, inner springs, and bed railings. **Listed on:** New York Stock Exchange. **Stock exchange symbol:** LEG. **Sales/revenues:** $4.3 billion. **Number of employees worldwide:** 35,000.

LEXMARK INTERNATIONAL, INC.
740 New Circle Road, Lexington KY 40511. 859/232-2379. **Contact:** Recruiting Office. **E-mail address:** recruiting@lexmark.com. **World Wide Web address:** http://www.lexmark.com. **Note:** All applications can be submitted online. **Description:** Develops, manufactures, and markets printers, typewriters, computer keyboards, and related supplies. **Positions advertised include:** Human Resources Professional; IT Business Professional; Research Engineering Associate; Inside Retail Sales Representative; Hardware Engineer; Research Engineer; Development Engineering Associate; External Communications Representative; General Accounting Associate; Finance Representative; Facilities Engineering Associate; Drafter Designer Associate. **Special programs:** Internships; Co-ops. **Corporate headquarters location:** This location. **Other U.S. locations:** Boulder CO. **International locations:** Worldwide. **Operations at this facility include:** Manufacturing; Research and Development; Sales. **Listed on:** New York Stock Exchange. **Stock exchange symbol:** LXK. **CEO/Chairman:** Paul J. Curlander. **Sales/revenues:** $4.4 billion. **Number of employees at this location:** 4,000.

LEXNET, INC.
268 Southland Drive, Suite 120, Lexington KY 40503. 859/266-1141. **Fax:** 859/268-6196. **Contact:** Craig or Debbie Rouse, Human Resources. **E-mail address:** Jobs@lexnetinc.com. **World Wide Web address:** http://www.lexnetinc.com. **Description:** Provides computer network consulting and training. **NOTE:** Online applications are available. **Positions advertised include:** Sales Consultant; Hardware Technician; System Engineer; AccPac Accounting Support; Application Specialist; Citrix Engineer; Printer Engineer.

LINK-BELT CONSTRUCTION EQUIPMENT COMPANY
P.O. Box 13600, 2651 Palumbo Drive, Lexington KY 40509. 859/263-5200. **Fax:** 859/264-6214. **Contact:** Marsha Brock, Employee Relations Manager. **World Wide Web address:** http://www.linkbelt.com. **Description:** Produces construction machinery and equipment including cranes and excavators. **Special programs:** Scholarship Program; Educational Assistance Program. **Corporate headquarters location:** This location. **Parent company:** Sumitomo Heavy Industries. **Operations at this facility include:** Administration; Manufacturing. **President:** Chuck Martz. **Number of employees at this location:** 800. **Number of employees nationwide:** 850.

LOUISVILLE BEDDING COMPANY
10400 Bunsen Way, Louisville KY 40299. 502/491-3370. **Toll-free phone:** 800/626-2594. **Fax:** 502/493-7706. **Contact:** Human Resources. **E-mail address:** hr@loubed.com. **World Wide Web address:** http://www.loubed.com. **Description:** A manufacturer of bed pillows, mattress pads, and chair pads. **Corporate headquarters location:** This location. **Other area locations:** Munfordville KY. **Other U.S. locations:** Ontario CA. **Subsidiaries include:** Aerated Home Fashions.

MARRIOTT RESORT
1800 Newtown Pike, Lexington KY 40511. 859/231-5100. **Toll-free phone:** 800/228-9290. **Fax:** 859/255-9944. **Contact:** Angela Brown, Director of Human Resources. **World Wide Web address:** http://www.marriott.com. **Description:** A full-service hotel that also includes a swimming pool, a gift shop, convention and banquet facilities, restaurant and lounge, tennis courts, and a golf course. **Corporate headquarters location:** Washington DC. **Other U.S. locations:** Nationwide. **Parent company:** Marriott International was launched as a public company following the division of the former Marriott Corporation. The company has operations and franchises in 50 states and 25 countries and operates lodging facilities franchised under four separate brand names: Marriott Hotels, Resorts, and Suites (full-service), Courtyard Hotels (moderate price), Residence Inn (extended stay), and Fairfield Inn (economy). The company also develops and operates Marriott Ownership Resorts (vacation timesharing). The full-service Marriott hotel system includes 251 Marriott Hotels, Resorts, and Suites located in 39 states and 18 foreign countries with over 100,000 guest rooms. **Listed on:** New York Stock Exchange. **Stock exchange symbol:** MAR. **Sales/revenues:** $20 billion. **Number of employees at this location:** 600. **Number of employees nationwide:** 145,000.

MEDIAPLEX SYSTEMS
5111 Commerce Crossing, Suite 200, Louisville KY 40229-2100. 502/810-5000. **Fax:** 502/810-5179. **Contact:** Personnel. **World Wide Web address:** http://www.adware.com. **Description:** Develops and manufactures software for advertising agencies. **Other U.S. locations:** Los Angeles CA; Indianapolis IN; New York NY. **International locations:** Toronto, Canada. **Parent company:** Valueclick.

MESSENGER – ENQUIRER
P.O. Box 1480, Owensburo KY 42302. 270/926-0123. **Physical address:** 1401 Federica Street, Owensburo KY 42302. **Contact:** Human Resources Manager. **Positions advertised include:** Advertising Sales Representative. **Description:** A leading local newspaper. **Number of employees at this location:** 155.

METTLER TOLEDO INC.
2549 Richmond Road, Suite 400, Lexington KY 40509. 859/266-3000. **Contact:** Human Resources. **World Wide Web address:** http://www.mt.com. **Description:** Develops automation software for rock and cement company manufacturing plants. Mettler Toledo, Incorporated is comprised of five business units: Laboratory, Industrial, Process Analytics, Packaging Industry, and Retail. **NOTE:** Job seekers may apply for advertised positions online. **Corporate headquarters location:** Columbus OH. **Other U.S. locations:** Nationwide. **International locations:** Worldwide. **Listed on:** New York Stock Exchange. **Stock exchange symbol:** MTD. **President/CEO:** Robert F. Spoerry. **Sales/revenues:** Over $1 billion. **Number of employees nationwide:** 3,000. **Number of employees worldwide:** Over 8,000.

MID-SOUTH ELECTRONICS, INC.
P.O. Box 400, Annville KY 40402. 606/364-5142. **Fax:** 606/364-8350. **Contact:** Frank Elkins, Human Resources. **E-mail address:** hr-ky@msi-mfg.com. **World Wide Web address:** http://www.msi-mfg.com. **Description:** Through its four subsidiaries and additional affiliates, MidSouth Industries manufactures various commercial products for customers in the transportation, large appliance, office products, and communications industries. **Positions advertised include:** Manufacturing Engineer; Quality Assurance Engineer; Program Development Manager. **Operations at this facility include:** This location manufactures printed circuit boards and plastic injection molding and provides electro-mechanical assembly. **Other area locations:** London KY. **Other U.S. locations:** Dayton OH; Gadsden AL; Raleigh NC. **International locations:** Germany; Mexico. **Parent company:** MidSouth Industries. **Sales/revenues:** Over $390 million. **Number of employees at this location:** 900. **Number of employees nationwide:** Over 2,000.

MOREHEAD STATE UNIVERSITY
101 Howell-McDowell Administration Building, Morehead KY 40351. 606/783-2097. **Physical address:** 150 University Boulevard, Morehead KY 40351. **Fax:** 606/783-5028. **Contact:** Office of Human Resources. **E-mail address:** humanresources@moreheadstate.edu. **World Wide Web address:** http://www.morehead-st.edu. **Description:** A state university with approximately 8,200 undergraduate and graduate students enrolled. **Positions advertised include:** Assistant Professor of Nursing; Electrical Engineer; Student Personnel Coordinator; Police Officer; Athletics Director Assistant. **Corporate headquarters location:** This location. **President:** Robert G. Eaglin. **Number of employees at this location:** 920.

MURRAY STATE UNIVERSITY
Murray State University, 404 Sparks Hall, Murray KY 42071-0009. 270/762-2146. **Toll-free phone:** 800/272-4MSU. **Fax:** 270/762-3464. **Contact:** Rita Culver, Human Resources. **E-mail address:** human.resources@murraystate.edu. **World Wide Web address:** http://www.mursuky.edu. **Description:** A state university comprised of five academic colleges: Business and Public Affairs, Humanities and Fine Arts, Health Sciences and Human Resources, Engineering and Technology, and a School of Agriculture. **NOTE:** Contact Human Resources directly at 270/762-3509. For faculty positions, contact appropriate department or search committee member. Entry-level positions are offered. **Positions advertised include:** Assistant Professor; Readmissions Clerk; Bookkeeper; Evening Weekend Supervisor; Administrative Secretary; Assistant Football Coach; Program Coordinator. **President:** F. King Alexander.

NS GROUP INC.
P.O. Box 1670, Newport KY 41072. 859/292-6809. **Physical Address:** 530 West Ninth Street, Newport KY 41071. **Fax:** 859/292-0593. **Contact:** Susan Vaughn, Human Resources. **World Wide Web address:** http://www.newportsteel.com. **Description:** Manufactures tubular goods and line pipe for oil and natural gas drilling and production, construction, and water transmission applications. **Positions advertised include:** Staff Accountant; Cashier Specialist; Melt Shop General Specialist. **Corporate headquarters location:** This location. **Subsidiaries include:** Newport Steel Corporation; Koppel Steel. **Listed on:** New York Stock Exchange. **Stock exchange symbol:** NSS. **President/CEO:** Rene J. Robichaud. **Number of employees at this location:** 725.

NATIONAL CITY BANK
P.O. Box 36000, Louisville KY 40233. 502/581-4200. **Physical address:** 101 South Fifth Street, Louisville KY 40202. **Contact:** Human Resources. **World Wide Web address:** http://www.nationalcity.com. **Description:** A bank. **Positions advertised include:** Auditor; Branch Assistant Manager; Sales / Service Consultant; Credit Analyst; Human Resources Recruiter. **Parent company:** National City Corporation is a major bank holding company with assets of $29.9 billion and subsidiaries engaging in full-service banking, trust, mortgage banking, merchant banking, insurance, and item processing products and services. The company operates 32 commercial banks that have over 600 branches in Ohio, Kentucky, and Indiana. **NOTE:** Entry-level positions are offered. **Corporate headquarters location:** Cleveland OH. **Subsidiaries include:** National Processing, Incorporated. **Listed on:** New York Stock Exchange. **Stock exchange symbol:** NCC. **CEO/Chairman:** David A. Daberko. **Number of employees nationwide:** Over 9,000.

THE NEWS – ENTERPRISE
408 West Drive Avenue, Elizabethtown KY 42701. 270/ 769-1200x358. **Fax:** 270/ 765-7318. **Contact:** Lisa D'Alessio, Human Resources. **E-mail address:** lisad@mail-the-ne.com. **World Wide Web address:** http://www.newsenterpriseonline.com. **Description:** The Hardin County newspaper. **Office Hours:** Monday – Friday, 8:00 a.m. – 5:00 p.m. **Parent Company:** Landmark Publications. **Number of employees at this location:** 110.

NORTHERN KENTUCKY UNIVERSITY (NKU)
708 Lucas Administrative Center, Highland Heights KY 41099-8125. 859/572-5200. **Physical address:** Nunn Drive, Highland Heights KY 41099. **Toll-free phone:** 800/637-9948. **Fax:** 859/572-6998. **Contact:** Denny Allen, Employment Manager. **E-mail address:** hr@nku.edu or allend@nku.edu. **World Wide Web address:** http://www.nku.edu. **Description:** NKU is a diverse, metropolitan university offering 19 associate's degree programs, 51 bachelor's degree programs, five graduate degree programs, and a joint JD/MBA program. **NOTE:** Jobseekers must indicate on their cover letter the position of interest. For faculty positions, contact the proper department chairperson or search committee member. Person's looking for employment information may check http://jobs.nku.edu for latest listings and apply online. **Positions advertised include:** Budget Analyst; Campus Nurse; Custodian; Extended Campus Initiative Director; Head Men's Basketball Coach. **Number of employees at this location:** 1,200.

NORTON HEALTHCARE
P.O. Box 35070, Louisville KY 40232. 502/629-8025. **Physical address:** 200 East Chestnut Street, Louisville KY 40202. **Toll-free phone:** 800/852-4456. **Contact:** Human Resources. **World Wide Web address:** http://www.nortonhealthcare.com. **Description:** A healthcare system that operates seven hospitals including Norton Hospital and Kosair Children's Hospital and provides services throughout Kentucky and southern Indiana. **NOTE:** Hiring for all of Norton Healthcare's hospitals takes place at this location. Entry-level positions are offered. Applicants may check http://careers.nortonhealthcare.com/seajob.asp. The number for Human Resources is 502/629-8400. **Positions advertised include:** Registered Nurse; Radiology Vice President. **Special programs:** Norton Scholar Program; Internships. **Corporate headquarters location:** This location (Norton Hospital). **President/CEO:** Stephen A. Williams. **Number of employees at this location:** 1,913.

OMNICARE, INC.
100 East Rivercenter Boulevard, Suite 1600, Covington KY 41011-1558. 859/392-3300. **Fax:** 859/392-3330. **Contact:** Patty Kingdom, Human Resources. **E-mail address:** human.resources@omnicare.com. **World Wide Web address:** http://www.omnicare.com. **Description:** Provides pharmaceutical services to long-term care facilities including nursing homes and rehabilitation centers. **NOTE:** Resumes may be submitted via e-mail. **Corporate headquarters location:** This location. **Other U.S. locations:** Nationwide. **Listed on:** New York Stock Exchange. **Stock exchange symbol:** OCR. **President/CEO:** Joel F. Gemunder.

OWENSBORO MERCY HEALTH SYSTEM
P.O. Box 20007, Owensboro KY 42304. 270/688-2780. **Physical address:** 811 East Parrish Avenue, Owensboro KY 42303. **Fax:** 270/688-1610. **Recorded jobline:** 270/688-2790. **Contact:** Personnel Department. **World Wide Web address:** http://www.omhs.org. **Description:** A comprehensive health system that operates hospitals and other medical facilities in Kentucky and Indiana. **Positions advertised include:** Physical Therapy Associate; Physical Therapist; Vascular Lab Tech; Certified Surgical Technician; Registered Nurse; Licensed Practical Nurse; Nurses Aide; Financial Counselor. **Office hours:** Monday – Friday, 7:00 a.m. – 4:30 p.m. **Number of employees at this location:** 2,400.

PEPSI-COLA BOTTLING COMPANY
554 South Forbes Road, Lexington KY 40504. 859/255-3375. **Fax:** 859/253-0154. **Recorded jobline:** 859/226-5881 **Contact:** Human Resources Manager. **World Wide Web address:** http://www.pepsico.com. **Description:** An independently-owned bottler of PepsiCo, Incorporated brand beverages including Pepsi, Diet Pepsi, 7-Up, Mountain Dew, Mug Root Beer, and Slice. **Listed on:** New York Stock Exchange. **Stock exchange symbol:** PEP. **CEO/Chairman:** Steve Reinemund. **Number of employees at this location:** 250. **Number of employees worldwide:** Over 135,000.

POMEROY COMPUTER RESOURCES
1020 Petersburg Road, Hebron KY 41048-9605. 859/586-0600. **Toll-free phone:** 800/846-8727. **Fax:** 859/586-4414. **Contact:** Corporate Recruiting Manager. **World Wide Web address:** http://www.pomeroy.com. **Description:** A full-service systems integration company that sells, installs, and services microcomputers and microcomputer equipment primarily for business, professional, educational, and government customers. The company also offers customer support services including network analysis and design, systems configuration, custom installation, training, maintenance, and repair. Founded in 1992. **NOTE:** Online applications are available. **Positions advertised include:** SOL ASP Java Web Developer; Solutions & RFF

Proposal Coordinator. **Corporate headquarters location:** This location. **Other area locations:** Lexington KY; Louisville KY. **Other U.S. locations:** Cincinnati OH; Louisville OH; Kingsport TN; Knoxville TN; Nashville TN. **Subsidiaries include:** Xenas Multimedia. **Listed on:** NASDAQ. **Stock exchange symbol:** PMRY. **CEO/Chairman:** David B. Pomeroy II. **Sales/revenues:** $702 million. **Number of employees at this location:** 120. **Number of employees nationwide:** 1,765.

PRICEWEBER MARKETING COMMUNICATIONS, INC.
2101 Production Drive, Louisville KY 40299. 502/499-9220. **Fax:** 502/491-5593. **Contact:** Susan Hovekanp, Human Resources Director. **World Wide Web address:** http://www.priceweber.com. **Description:** An advertising agency. **Positions advertised include:** Senior-level Writer; Art Director; Account Manager; Advertising Specialist; Web Developer/Software Designer; Writer; Buyer; Photographer. **President:** Shanna Columbus.

PUBLISHERS PRESS, INC.
100 Frank E. Simon Avenue, Shepherdsville KY 40165. 502/543-2251. **Fax:** 502/543-2830. **Contact:** Personnel Manager. **World Wide Web address:** http://www.pubpress.com. **Description:** Offers a complete line of printing and production services such as complete composition, image assembly, prepress, press, bindery, and mailing services. This also includes typesetting, desktop film output, digitized or conventional separations, Opticopy imposition, ink jetting, and mail list conversion. Publishers Press has two facilities with ten full webs, five half webs, seven saddle stitchers, and four adhesive binders. Company departments include Composition, which now incorporates desktop publishing as well as traditional typesetting and paste-up services; Reprographics, which also utilizes desktop and conventional methods; Image Assembly; the Prepress department; and Bindery and Shipping, where the final publications are assembled and processed for distribution. Publishers Press prints *Sports Car International, Ocean Realm, Scuba Times, Climbing World, Art World,* and *Birder's World* magazines. Founded in 1866. **Special programs:** Training. **Number of employees nationwide:** Over 160.

QUEBECOR WORLD
100 U.S. 60 Bypass, Versailles KY 40384. 859/873-3181. **Fax:** 859/879-0067. **Contact:** Jim Thompson, Personnel Department. **E-mail address:** usa.careers@quebecorworld.com. **World Wide Web address:** http://www.quebecorworld.com. **Description:** Quebecor World is engaged in bookbinding and loose-leaf packaging. Binding styles include Smyth sewn, side sewn, center sewn, Wire-O, plastic comb, and spiral. The loose-leaf operations handle a wide variety of styles and materials including square, round, or brass corners; turned edge, vinyl heatseal, custom index tabs; and covers from polyethylene to cow-hide leather. **Positions advertised include:** Financial Accountant II. **Special programs:** Education Reimbursement Program; Quebecor World Scholarship Program. **Corporate headquarters location:** Greenwich CT. **Other area locations:** Franklin KY; Lexington KY. **Other U.S. locations:** Nationwide. **International locations:** Canada; Belgium; France; United Kingdom; Spain; Switzerland; Austria; Sweden; Finland; Brazil; Chile; Argentina; Peru; Colombia; Mexico; India. **Operations at this facility include:** Production; Sales. **Listed on:** New York Stock Exchange. **Stock exchange symbol:** IQW. **Number of employees at this location:** 975. **Number of employees worldwide:** Approximately 40,000.

QUEST DIAGNOSTICS
2277 Charleston Drive, Lexington KY 40505. 859/299-3866. **Toll-free phone:** 800/366-7522. **Fax:** 859/293-7409. **Contact:** Mickey Dobson, Human Resources. **World Wide Web Address:** http://www.questdiagnostics.com. **Description:** Provides a broad range of clinical laboratory services to health care clients that include physicians, hospitals, clinics, dialysis centers, pharmaceutical companies, and corporations. The company performs tests on blood, urine, and other bodily fluids and tissues to provide information for health and well-being. **NOTE:** Online applications are available. **Positions advertised include:** Route Service Representative; Phlebotomy Services Representative; Genomics & Esoteric Test Specialist; Specimen I Technician. **Office hours:** Monday – Friday, 8:00 a.m. – 5:00 p.m. **Corporate headquarters location:** Teterboro NJ. **Other area locations:** Bowling Green KY; Frankfort KY; Louisville KY. **Other U.S. locations:** Nationwide. **International locations:** Mexico; United Kingdom; Germany; France; Belgium; Brazil. **Listed on:** New York Stock Exchange. **Stock exchange symbol:** DGX. **CEO/Chairman:** Kenneth W. Freeman.

RED7E
637 West Main Street, Louisville KY 40202. 502/585-3403. **Fax:** 502/582-2043. **Contact:** Human Resources. **E-mail address:** info@red7e.com. **World Wide Web address:** http://www.red7e.com. **Description:** Red7e provides a broad range of planning, creative, direct marketing, public relations, sales promotion, production, and media services to customers in the construction, health care, restaurant, business, financial, and manufacturing industries. Founded in 1974. **Special programs:** Internships. **Corporate headquarters location:** This location. **Number of employees at this location:** 40.

REPUBLIC BANK & TRUST COMPANY
601 West Market Street, Louisville KY 40202. 502/584-3600. **Recorded jobline:** 888/584-3600x8630. **Contact:** Human Resources. **E-mail address:** rwhite@republicbank.com. **World Wide Web address:** http://www.republicbank.com. **NOTE:** Send resumes to 9600 Brownsboro Road, Louisville KY 40241-1122. **Description:** Provides personal and commercial banking services throughout North Central and Central Kentucky. **Other area locations:** Bowling Green KY; Elizabethtown KY; Frankfort KY; Georgetown KY; Lexington KY; Louisville KY; Owensboro KY; Shelbyville KY. **Parent Company:** Republic Bancorp Inc.

REPUBLIC SERVICES
2343 Alexandria Drive, Suite 400, Lexington KY 40504. 859/885-5138. **Contact:** Human Resources. **World Wide Web address:** http://www.republicservices.com. **Description:** Provides environmental services such as waste collection, recycling, and disposal, as well as mining. **NOTE:** All employment inquiries should be directed to the Fort Lauderdale office: 110 Southeast 6th Street, Suite 2100, Fort Lauderdale FL 33301. **Office hours:** Monday – Friday, 8:00 a.m. – 5:00 p.m. **Corporate headquarters location:** Fort Lauderdale FL. **Operations at this facility include:** Administration; Sales. **Other U.S. locations:** Nationwide. **Listed on:** New York Stock Exchange. **Stock exchange symbol:** RSG. **CEO/Chairman:** James E. O'Conner. **Number of employees at this location:** 50. **Number of employees nationwide:** 12,700.

RES-CARE INCORPORATED
10140 Linn Station Road, Louisville KY 40223. 502/394-2100. **Fax:** 502/394-2235. **Contact:** Leigh Brady, Human Resources. **E-mail address:** lbrady@rescare.com. **World Wide Web address:** http://www.rescare.com. **Description:** Provides support and training service for people with mental disabilities or other developmental disabilities. **NOTE:** To contact Human Resources directly, call 502/394-2168. **Positions advertised include:** A/R Analyst; Revenue & Cash A/R Manager; Chief Compliance Officer; Computer Hardware Specialist; Labor Relations Director; Financial Analyst; Human Resource Information Specialist Analyst; Payroll Assistant. **Other U.S. locations:** Nationwide. **International locations:** Canada; Puerto Rico. **Listed on:** NASDAQ. **Stock exchange symbol:** RSCR. **Number of employees worldwide:** Approximately 29,000.

RJ REYNOLDS
401 South Fourth Street, Louisville KY 40202. 502/568-7000. **Toll-free phone:** 800/341-5211. **Fax:** 502/568-7120. **Contact:** Manager Recruitment. **World Wide Web address:** http://www.rjrt.com. **Description:** RJ Reynolds researches, develops, manufactures, and markets tobacco products including cigarettes. **Special programs:** Tuition Reimbursement Program; Management Development Program; Internships. **Corporate headquarters location:** Winston Salem NC. **Other U.S. locations:** Nationwide. **Operations at this facility include:** Administration.

RICHMOND REGISTER
P.O. Box 99, Richmond KY 40475. 859/ 623-1669. **Physical address:** 380 Big Hill Avenue, Richmond KY 40475. **Fax:** 859/623-2337. **Contact:** Human Resources. **E-mail address:** publisher@richmondregister.com. **World Wide Web address:** http://www.richmondregister.com. **Description:** A local newspaper service Richmond Kentucky. **Positions advertised include:** Press Room Manager. **Company Slogan:** Homemade Everyday Just For You.

ROOD & RIDDLE EQUINE HOSPITAL
P.O. Box 12070, 2150 Georgetown Road, Lexington KY 40580. 859/233-0371. **Fax:** 859/255-5367. **Physical address:** 2150 Georgetown Road, Lexington KY 40511. **Contact:** Personnel. **E-mail address:** rreh@roodandriddle.com. **World Wide Web address:** http://www.roodandriddle.com. **Positions advertised include:** Surgery Technician; Nursing Staff. **Description:** A full-service equine hospital. This full service equine hospital specializes in horse care practicing medical, surgical, functions as well as internal medicine. In cases of emergency the hospital will even provide ambulatory services. Founded in 1986. **Special programs:** Internships; Training. **Hospital Director:** William A. Rood, D.M.V.

SAFETRAN SYSTEMS CORPORATION
2400 Nelson Miller Parkway, Louisville KY 40223. 502/244-7400. **Toll-free phone:** 800/626-2710. **Fax:** 502/253-3764. **Contact:** Manager of Human Resources. **E-mail address:** resumes.engineering@invensys.com. **World Wide Web address:** http://www.safetran.com. **Description:** Manufactures railroad accessories and safety devices including electrical control systems, electro-mechanical signal devices, and communication systems. **Positions advertised include:** (Embedded Real Time Software) Design Engineer. **Other U.S. locations:** Rancho Cucamonga CA; Louisville KY. **Parent company:** BTR, plc. **Operations at this facility include:** Administration; Divisional Headquarters; Manufacturing; Research and Development; Sales; Service. **President:** George L. Kline. **Number of employees at this location:** 250. **Number of employees nationwide:** 700.

ST. JOSEPH HOSPITAL
One Saint Joseph Drive, Lexington KY 40504. 859/313-1000. **Fax:** 859/313-3100. **Contact:** Director of Human Resources. **E-mail address:** hrinfo@sjhlex.org. **World Wide Web address:** http://www.sjhlex.org. **Description:** A private, nonprofit hospital that is one of eight divisions of the Sisters of Charity of Nazareth Health Corporation. The hospital offers a broad spectrum of specialized services. St. Joseph Heart Institute employs cardiologists and cardiovascular surgeons and has more than 100 patient rooms, with more than 3,000 patients undergoing cardiac catheterizations and angioplasty procedures every year. The St. Joseph Cancer Center provides care for patients and their families with 32 private rooms, as well as a solarium and self-contained kitchen. Diagnostic options include CT scanning, nuclear medicine studies, X-rays, magnetic resonance imaging, and complex blood and tissue tests. St. Joseph Hospital also offers outpatient services, surgical services, medical/surgical and intensive care services, orthopedics and neurosciences, a sleep disorders center, mental health services, a chemical recovery center, emergency services, and aeromedical services. **Positions advertised include:** Medical Records Specialist; Health Data Analyst; Business Office Registrar; Unit Secretary; Radiology Dispatch; Radiology Secretary; Transcriptionist Supervisor; Technician; Case Manager; Echo Vascular Tech; Endoscopy Tech; Anesthesia Technician; Registered Nurse; Lab Support Specialist; Licenses Practical Nurse; Nurses Aide. .

SARGENT & GREENLEAF, INC.
P.O. Box 930, Nicholasville KY 40340. 859/885-9411. **Physical address:** One Security Drive, Nicholasville KY 40356. **Toll-free phone:** 800/826-7652. **Fax:** 859/885-3063. **Contact:** Shirlean Herron, Industrial Relations Manager. **World Wide Web address:** http://www.sglocks.com. **Description:** Produces high-security locks and access controls and devices. Founded in 1857. **Corporate headquarters location:** This location.

SQUARE D SCHNEIDER ELECTRIC
1601 Mercer Road, Lexington KY 40511. 859/243-8000. **Fax:** 859/243-8000. **Contact:** Human Resources Supervisor. **E-mail address:** UWB@SchneiderElectricJobs.com. **World Wide Web address:** http://www.squared.com. **Description:** A manufacturer of electrical distribution and industrial control and automation products for the construction industry. Products are used in commercial and residential construction, industrial facilities, and machinery, as well as OEM's products. Residential building products feature circuit breakers with an exclusive quick-open mechanism that isolates potential dangers quickly. Square D also equips public buildings such as schools, stadiums, museums, hospitals, prisons, military bases, and wastewater treatment plants with electrical distribution systems. **Positions advertised include:** Marketing Manager. **Special programs:** Training. **Corporate headquarters location:** Palatine IL. **Other U.S. locations:** Nationwide. **International locations:** Worldwide. **Parent company:** Schneider Electric, which is based in Paris, France. **Listed on:** Euronext Paris. **Stock exchange symbol:** SU. **CEO/Chairman:** Henri Lachmann. **Sales/revenues:** Approximately $8.8 billion. **Number of employees worldwide:** Over 66,000.

STAGE ONE
501 West Main Street, Louisville KY 40202-2957. 502/589-5946. **Fax:** 502/588-5910. **Contact:** Human Resources. **E-mail address:** stageone@stageone.org. **World Wide Web address:** http://www.stageone.org. **Description:** A professional theater company that targets youth audiences, their families and the education community. **Artistic Director:** J. Daniel Herring.

STEEL TECHNOLOGIES, INC.
15415 Shelbyville Road, Louisville KY 40245. 502/245-2110. **Fax:** 502/254-9413. **Contact:** Vicki Taylor, Director of Personnel. **World Wide Web address:** http://www.steeltechnologies.com. **Description:** Processes precision flat-rolled steel for customers in a variety of industries including automotive, appliance, electrical, communications, machinery, and office equipment. **Corporate headquarters location:**

This location. **Other area locations:** Ghent KY; Eminence KY. **Other U.S. locations:** Wayne MI; Canton MI; Cleveland OH; Murfreesboro TN; Greensburg IN; Portage IN; Clinton NC; Berkley SC; San Diego CA. **International locations:** Mexico. **Operations at this location include:** This location manufactures value-added strip steel for the automotive and appliance markets. **Listed on:** NASDAQ. **Stock exchange symbol:** STTX. **Number of employees worldwide:** Over 1,200.

JENNIE STUART MEDICAL CENTER
P.O. Box 2400, 320 West 18th Street, Hopkinsville KY 42240-2400. 270/887-0100. **Fax:** 270/887-0178. **Recorded jobline:** 270/887-0654. **Contact:** Austin Moss, Human Resources Director. **World Wide Web address:** http://www.jsmc.org. **Description:** A 195-bed, acute care hospital offering a full range of services. **NOTE:** Online applications are available. To contact Human Resources directly, call 270/887-0177. **Positions advertised include:** Physician; Radiology Technician; Operating Room Registered Nurse; Medical Technician; Microbiologist; Medical Surgeon Registered Nurse; Licensed Practical Nurse; Ambulatory Services Licensed Practical Nurse. **CEO:** Terry Peeples. **Number of employees at this location:** 600.

THOMAS INDUSTRIES, INC.
P.O. Box 35120, 4360 Brownsboro Road, Suite 300, Louisville KY 40232-5120. 502/893-4600. **Fax:** 502/895-6618. **Contact:** Human Resources. **E-mail address:** thomasmail@thomasind.com. **World Wide Web address:** http://www.thomasind.com. **Description:** Manufactures compressors and vacuum pumps for original equipment manufacturers. The primary products include piston, diaphragm, and rotary air compressors and vacuum pumps; vibrating-diaphragm and linear air compressors and pumps; peristaltic liquid pumps; air motors; and air-powered vacuum pumps, which serve the medical, mobile, instrumentation, business, packaging, vapor recovery, and vending equipment markets. **Positions advertised include:** Sales Engineer; Internal Technical Support. **Corporate headquarters location:** This location. **Other U.S. locations:** Monroe LA; Los Angeles CA; San Leandro CA; Tupelo MS; Sheboygan WI. **International locations:** Canada; Taiwan; Australia; Japan; Germany. **Subsidiaries include:** Werner Rietschle GmbH & Company. **Listed on:** New York Stock Exchange. **Stock exchange symbol:** TII. **President/CEO/Chairman:** Timothy C. Brown.

UNIVERSITY OF LOUISVILLE
1900 Arthur Street, Louisville KY 40208-2776. 502/852-6258. **Toll-free phone:** 800/334-8635. **Fax:** 502/852-5665. **Contact:** Human Resources. **E-mail address:** employ@Louisville.edu. **World Wide Web address:** http://www.louisville.edu. **Description:** The University of Louisville is run by the state of Kentucky and is in the largest metropolitan area in the state. It has three campuses. It enrolls 27K students and offers many different courses including undergraduate and graduate school programs. **Company Slogan:** Dare to be great. **Positions advertised include:** Accounting Clerk; Administrative Assistant; Human Resources Assistant; Nurse Practitioner; Research Technologist.

U.S. DEPARTMENT OF VETERANS AFFAIRS
VETERANS ADMINISTRATION MEDICAL CENTER
1101 Veteran's Drive, Lexington KY 40502-2236. 859/233-4511. **Contact:** Personnel Director. **Description:** A medical center operated by the U.S. Department of Veterans Affairs that provides acute and extended care services. From 54 hospitals in 1930, the VA health care system has grown to include 171 medical centers; more than 364 outpatient, community, and outreach clinics; 130 nursing home care units; and 37 domiciles. VA operates at least one medical center in each of the 48 contiguous states, Puerto Rico, and the District of Columbia. With approximately 76,000 medical center beds, VA treats nearly 1 million patients in VA hospitals; 75,000 in nursing home care units; and 25,000 in domiciles. VA's outpatient clinics register approximately 24 million visits per year. **Number of employees at this location:** 2,000.

U.S. FOREST SERVICE
LAND BETWEEN THE LAKES NATIONAL RECREATION AREA
100 Van Morgan Drive, Golden Pond KY 42211. 270/924-2089. **Fax:** 270/924-2060. **E-mail address:** rweakly@fs.fed.us. **Contact:** Human Resources Manager. **World Wide Web address:** http://www2.lbl.org/lbl. **Description:** A designated national recreation area under the management of the USDA Forest Service that additionally features environmental education opportunities. The park's facilities include a living history farm, a nature center, a planetarium and observatory, a horseback riding campground and public horse stable, and an elk and bison prairie interpretive site. **Special programs:** Internships; Apprenticeships.

UNITED L-N GLASS, INC.
102 Kuhlman Drive, Versailles KY 40383. 859/873-2800. **Contact:** Jessica Salmon, Human Resources. **World Wide Web address:** http://www.nsgamerica.com. **Description:** Processes solid sheets of glass into automotive windshields and windows. **Positions advertised:** Equipment Engineer. **Parent company:** Nippon Sheet Glass Company, Limited, a glass manufacturing and materials supplier headquartered in Osaka, Japan.

UNIVERSITY OF KENTUCKY
112 Scovell Hall, Lexington KY 40506. 859/257-9555. **Fax:** 859/257-1736. **Contact:** Human Resources. **E-mail address:** ukjobs@email.uky.edu. **World Wide Web address:** http://www.uky.edu. **Description:** A state university with an enrollment of over 24,000, which is composed of a graduate school and 16 academic colleges. UK Hospital, a 473-bed facility at this location, cares for more than 21,000 inpatients yearly and is ranked as one of the top 100 hospitals by Modern Healthcare magazine. The university is designated a Research University of the First Class by the Carnegie Foundation, one of 59 public universities in the country to have earned this distinction. Founded in 1865. **NOTE:** Part-time and temporary positions are offered. **Positions advertised include:** Accounting Manager; Administrative Staff Officer; Administrative Support; Administrative Coordinator; Cardiac Catheter Technician; Obstetrician Case Manager; Clinical Research Executive; Data Center Analyst; Dental Assistant; Registered Dietitian; Psychiatric Director; Image Management Specialist; Lab Animal Technician; Laboratory Technician; Multimedia Specialist; Nursing Care Worker; Research Analyst; Scientist. **President:** Lee Todd. **Number of employees at this location:** 7,500. **Number of employees nationwide:** 11,500.

VAC MAGNETICS
101 Magnet Drive, Elizabethtown KY 42701. 270/769-1333. **Fax:** 270/765-3118. **Contact:** Human Resources. **World Wide Web address:** http://www.vaccorp.com. **Description:** Manufacturer of permanent magnets (ceramic, cast, and rare earth) for automotive, computer, and various other applications. **Corporate headquarters location:** Terrace Park OH. **Other U.S. locations:** Nationwide. **International locations:** Worldwide. **Parent company:** VAC GmbH & Company, the Magnetics Division of The Morgan Crucible Company, plc. **Listed on:** Privately held. **Number of employees at this location:** 500. **Number of employees worldwide:** Over 3,000.

THE VALVOLINE COMPANY
P.O. Box 14000, Lexington KY 40512. 859/357-7181. **Physical address:** 3499 Blazer Parkway, Lexington KY 40509. **Toll-free phone:** 800/782-4669. **Contact:** Human Resources. **World Wide Web address:** http://www.valvoline.com. **Description:** Manufactures, markets, and sells motor oils, lubricants, and automotive chemicals. **NOTE:** See parent company Website (www.ashland.com) for Valvoline job opportunities. Unsolicited resumes are not accepted. **Positions advertised include:** Retail Marketing Manager; Account Support Representative; Administrative Assistant; Product Specialist; Expense & Project Control Manager. **Corporate headquarters location:** This location. **Other U.S. locations:** Nationwide. **Parent company:** Ashland, Incorporated. **Operations at this facility include:** Administration; Sales; Service. **Listed on:** New York Stock Exchange. **Stock exchange symbol:** ASH. **Number of employees nationwide:** 3,100.

VAN METER INSURANCE
P.O. Box 785, Owensboro KY 42302. 270/685-5581x2116. **Physical address:** 2009 Frederica Street, Owensboro KY 42302. **Fax:** 270/685-3342. **Contact:** Molly Humphreys, Personnel. **E-mail address:** info@vanmeterins.com. **World Wide Web address:** http://www.vanmeterins.com. **Description:** An insurance company specializing in commercial insurance, loss control service, bonds, contractors advantage program, personal lines insurance, life/health insurance, and employee benefits. **Corporate headquarters:** Bowling Green KY. **Other area locations:** Lexington KY. **Other U.S. locations:** Franklin TN. **Parent company:** Synaxis Group. **President:** Jerry Heming.

VETERINARY ASSOCIATES STONEFIELD
203 Moser Road, Louisville KY 40223. 502/245-7863. **Fax:** 502/245-2869. **Contact:** Ginger Lanham, Human Resources Department. **E-mail address:** aviansam@aol.com. **World Wide Web address:** http://www.vetcity.com. **Description:** Offers general medical and surgical care to domestic and exotic animals. **Office hours:** Monday – Thursday, 7:30 a.m. – 8:00 p.m., Friday, 7:30 a.m. – 5:30 p.m., Saturday, 8:00 a.m. – 2:00 p.m.

WLRS-FM
520 South Fourth Street, Louisville KY 40202. 502/625-1220. **Fax:** 502/825-1225. **Contact:** Human Resources. **World Wide Web address:** http;//www.wlrs.com. **Description:** An alternative rock radio station. **Note:** Internship in promotional sales available. **Company slogan:** I am the Walrus. **Parent Company:** Radio-One Communications.

WHAS-TV
P.O. Box 1100, Louisville KY 40202. 502/582-7840. **Physical address:** 520 West Chestnut Street, Louisville KY 40202. **Fax:** 502/582-7279. **Contact:** Terrence Spence, Director of Human Resources. **World Wide Web address:** http://www.whas11.com. **Description:** An ABC-affiliated television station. **Positions advertised include:** Office Manager; Receptionist; Marketing Research Director; Photographer; Reporter; Producer. **Special programs:** Internships. **Parent company:** Providence Journal Company. **Number of employees at this location:** 145.

WELLS FARGO BANK
171 West Lowry Lane, Lexington KY 40503. 859/276-5322. **Contact:** Human Resources. **World Wide Web address:** http://www.wellsfargo.com. **Description:** A diversified financial institution with over $234 billion in assets. Wells Fargo serves over 17 million customers through 5,300 independent locations worldwide. The company also maintains several stand-alone ATMs and branches within other retail outlets. Services include community banking, credit and debit cards, home equity and mortgage loans, on-line banking, student loans, and insurance. Wells Fargo also offers a complete line of commercial and institutional financial services. Founded in 1852. **Corporate headquarters location:** San Francisco CA. **Other U.S. locations:** Nationwide. **International locations:** Worldwide. **Listed on:** New York Stock Exchange. **Stock exchange symbol:** WFC. **Annual sales/revenues:** More than $100 million. **Number of employees worldwide:** 120,000.

WESTERN KENTUCKY UNIVERSITY
One Big Red Way, Weatherby Administrative Building 42, Bowling Green KY 42101. 270/745-2071. **Fax:** 270/745-5882. **Contact:** Tony Glisson, Human Resources. **World Wide Web address:** http://www.wku.edu. **Description:** A liberal arts university that offers 88 academic majors and variety of professional and pre-professional programs. **NOTE:** Part-time positions are offered. Job seekers may submit applications online. **Positions advertised include** Accounting Associate; Office Associate; Lab Technician; Teachers; Assistant Farm Manager; Building Services Attendant. **Special programs:** Tuition Scholarship Program; Wellness Program. **President:** Gary A. Ransdell.

WILLIAMS GAS PIPELINE - TEXAS GAS
P.O. Box 20008, 3800 Frederica Street, Owensboro KY 42301. 270/926-8686. **Fax:** 270/688-5870. **Contact:** Human Resources. **World Wide Web address:** http://www.txgt.com. **Description:** Engaged in the transportation of natural gas. **Special programs:** Training; Internships. **Corporate headquarters location:** Houston TX. **Other U.S. locations:** Salt Lake City UT; Tulsa OK. **Parent company:** Williams provides a full range of energy and communications services. **President/CEO/Chairman:** Steven J. Malcolm. **Listed on:** New York Stock Exchange. **Stock exchange symbol:** WMB. **Number of employees nationwide:** 830.

YUM! BRANDS, INC.
P.O. Box 32220, Louisville KY 40212. 502/874-8300. **Physical address:** 1441 Gardiner Lane, Louisville KY 40213. **Fax:** 502/874-2452. **Contact:** Human Resources. **World Wide Web address:** http://www.yum.com. **Description:** Operates and franchises fast food restaurants including KFC, Pizza Hut, Long John Silver's, A&W All-American Food, Yum! Restaurants International, and Taco Bell. **Positions advertised include:** General Manager; Shift Supervisor; Assistant Manager. **Corporate headquarters location:** This location. **Listed on:** New York Stock Exchange. **Stock exchange symbol:** YUM.

AEP SOUTHWESTERN ELECTRIC POWER COMPANY
P.O. Box 21106, Shreveport LA 71156. 318/222-2141. **Physical address:** 428 Travis Street, Shreveport LA 71101. **Recorded jobline:** 800/300-1858. **Contact:** Personnel Director. **World Wide Web address:** http://www.aep.com. **Description:** As a division of AEP North American Energy Delivery, Southwestern Electric Power Company generates, purchases, transmits, and sells electric energy in portions of northeastern Texas, northwestern Louisiana, and western Arkansas. **NOTE:** Search current job openings and apply online, either for specific positions or general consideration. Resumes can also be mailed to the Human Resources Department at 1 Riverside Plaza, Columbus OH 43215, or faxed to 614/716-1864. **Positions advertised include:** Engineer. **Special programs:** Internships; Co-ops. **Corporate headquarters location:** Columbus OH. **Other U.S. locations:** AR; IN; KY; LA; MI; OH; OK; TN; TX; VA; WV. **International locations:** Australia; Brazil; China; Mexico; Norway; Sweden; United Kingdom; continental Europe. **Parent company:** Central and South West Corporation (CSW) is a diversified electric utility holding company that provides electric power through subsidiaries including Central Power & Light, Public Service of Oklahoma, Southwestern Electric Power, and West Texas Utilities. Other operations include interstate natural gas gathering, transmission, processing, storage, and marketing, as well as communications and accounting services. **Listed on:** New York Stock Exchange. **Stock exchange symbol:** AEP. **President/CEO/Chairman:** E. Linn Draper, Junior. **Sales/Revenues:** $61.3 billion. **Number of employees nationwide:** 21,000.

THE ADVOCATE
525 Lafayette Street, Baton Rouge LA 70821. 225/383-1111. **Recorded jobline:** 225/388-0171. **Contact:** Human Resources. **World Wide Web address:** http://www.theadvocate.com. **Description:** Publishes *The Advocate*, a local newspaper. **Positions advertised include:** Packaging Department Operator. **Special programs:** Internships. **Corporate headquarters location:** This location. **Operations at this facility include:** Administration; Manufacturing; Research and Development; Sales; Service. **Number of employees at this location:** 560.

ALBEMARLE CORPORATION ADMINISTRATIVE HEADQUARTERS
451 Florida Street, Baton Rouge LA 70801-1765. 225/388-7402. **Toll-free phone:** 800/535-3030. **Fax:** 225/388-7848. **Contact:** Human Resources. **World Wide Web address:** http://www.albemarle.com. **NOTE:** Please do not e-mail resumes and employee inquiries. **Description:** A global supplier of specialty and performance chemicals such as polymers, alpha olefins, bromine chemicals and ibuprofen, whose operations are divided into two segments: Polymer Chemicals and Fine Chemicals. The company serves markets for petroleum and agricultural chemicals, detergents, polymers, electronics, and pharmaceuticals. **Positions advertised include:** Entry level Corporate Tax Accountant; Intellectual Property Attorney; Polymer Chemist. **Special programs:** Education Assistance Program. **Corporate headquarters location:** Richmond VA. **Other U.S. locations:** Magnolia AR; Dayton OH; Tyrone PA; Orangeburg SC; Houston TX; Richmond VA. **International locations:** Worldwide. **Subsidiaries include:** Albemarle Holdings Company Limited; Martinswerk GmbH; Albermale Cytec Industries, Incorporated; Asano Corporation. **Operations at this facility include:** This location is the company's administrative headquarters. **Listed on:** New York Stock Exchange. **Stock exchange symbol:** ALB. **President/CEO/Director:** Mark Rohr. **Sales/revenues:** $980.2 million. **Number of employees worldwide:** 3,000.

ALBEMARLE CORPORATION
P.O. Box 341, Baton Rouge LA 70821-0341. 225/768-5600. **Toll-free phone:** 800/535-3030. **Contact:** Personnel. **World Wide Web address:** http://www.albemarle.com. **NOTE:** Please do not e-mail resumes and employee inquiries. **Description:** A global supplier of specialty and performance chemicals such as polymers, alpha olefins, bromine chemicals and ibuprofen, whose operations are divided into two segments: Polymer Chemicals and Fine Chemicals. The company serves markets for petroleum and agricultural chemicals, detergents, polymers, electronics, and pharmaceuticals. **Corporate headquarters location:** Richmond VA. **Other U.S. locations:** Magnolia AR; Dayton OH; Tyrone PA; Orangeburg SC; Houston TX; Richmond VA. **International locations:** Worldwide. **Subsidiaries include:** Albermarle Holdings Company Limited; Martinswerk GmbH; Albermarle Cytec Industries, Incorporated; Asano Corporation. **Operations at this facility include:** This location is the company's research and development center. **Listed on:** New York Stock Exchange. **Stock exchange symbol:** ALB. **President/CEO/Director:** Mark Rohr. **Sales/revenues:** $980.2 million. **Number of employees worldwide:** 3,000.

ALCOA (ALUMINUM COMPANY OF AMERICA)
3502 South Riverview Drive, Port Allen LA 70767. 225/389-9945. **Fax:** 225/389-9957. **Contact:** Human Resources. **World Wide Web address:** http://www.alcoa.com. **Description:** Engaged in all aspects of the aluminum industry including mining, refining, smelting, fabricating, and recycling. ALCOA also manufactures ceramic packaging for the semiconductor industry, alumina chemicals, plastic bottle closures, vinyl siding, packaging machinery, and electrical distribution systems for automobiles. **NOTE:** Job openings are posted online. **Special programs:** Tuition Assistance Program. **Corporate headquarters location:** Pittsburgh PA. **Other area locations:** Vidalia; Lake Charles; Lake Charles; Shreveport; West Monroe. **Other U.S. locations:** Nationwide. **International locations:** Worldwide. **Operations at this facility include:** This location produces Alumina chemicals. **Listed on:** New York Stock Exchange; the Electronical Swiss Stock Exchange; Australian Stock Exchange; stock exchanges in Brussels, Frankfurt, and London. **Stock exchange symbol:** AA. **CEO:** Alan J.P. Belda. **Sales/revenues:** $20.3 billion. **Number of employees worldwide:** 127,000.

AMBAR LONESTAR
P.O. Box 51271, Lafayette LA 70508-3283. 337/237-5300. **Physical address:** 221 Rue de Jean, Suite 301, Lafayette LA 70508. **Toll-free phone:** 800/642-6227. **Fax:** 337/232-9696. **Contact:** Human Resources. **E-mail address:** info@amstarfluids.com. **World Wide Web address:** http://www.ambarlonestar.com. **Description:** Designs, blends, and markets fluids and chemicals, and provides environmental services primarily to oil and gas operators in Louisiana and Texas, as well as to other locations along the Gulf Coast. The company divides its products and service lines into two industry segments: Oil Field products and services and Environmental products and services. AMBAR Lonestar provides total fluids management with a comprehensive range of products and services primarily used in the drilling, completion, and workover (repair and maintenance) of oil and gas wells. The company markets high-density brines (HDBs) primarily to operators of offshore oil and gas wells for use in completion and workover operations performed on such wells. **Corporate headquarters location:** This location. **Operations at this facility include:** Administration; Divisional Headquarters; Research and Development; Sales. **Number of employees at this location:** 90.

AMCOL HEALTH AND BEAUTY SOLUTIONS
301 Laser Lane, Lafayette LA 70507. 337/232-6838. **Toll-free phone:** 866/657-0743. **Fax:** 337/235-8118. **Contact:** Human Resources. **World Wide Web address:** http://www.healthbeautysolutions.com. **Description:** AMCOL Health & Beauty Solutions, Inc. uses technology and a staff of chemists and engineers to provide Personal Care, Cosmetics, Pharmaceutical, and Nutraceutical products. **Corporate headquarters location:** Arlington Heights IL. **Parent company:** AMCOL International Corporation.

AMERICA FIRST
P.O. Box 1300, Ruston LA 71273-1300. 318/255-2622. **Toll-free phone:** 800/372-4823. **Fax:** 318/254-4522. **Contact:** Human Resources Department. **World Wide Web address:** http://www.americafirst-ins.com. **Description:** A carrier of property, casualty, and life insurance. America First is a member of the Regional Agency Markets (RAM) unit of Liberty Mutual. **NOTE:** For a list of job openings, see Liberty Mutual Group's career search site at www.jobs.brassring.com. **Positions advertised include:** Service Manager; Sales Associate; Law Clerk; Paralegal; Subrogation Counsel; Adjuster – Workman's Comp. **Corporate headquarters location:** Dallas TX. **Other U.S. locations:** AR; TX; OK. **Operations at this facility include:** This location is a regional claims office. **Parent company:** Liberty Mutual Group. **President/CEO:** Phil Broughton.

AMERICAN FLAT GLASS DISTRIBUTORS, INC. (AFGD)
710 West Landry, Opelousas LA 70570. 337/942-6539. **Toll-free phone:** 800/489-3386. **Fax:** 800/639-6754. **Contact:** Human Resources. **World Wide Web address:** http://www.afgd.com. **Description:** Specializes in architectural insulated units and custom tempering. The firm manufactures a complete line of insulated units for commercial and residential applications. The product line includes clear, tint, and reflective float glass; laminated, low-emissivity, tempered, acrylic, mirror, obscure, insulated, and polished wire glass; and a complete line of glass handling, storage, and transportation equipment. **NOTE:** Entry-level positions are offered. Please visit website to submit a resume online. **Corporate headquarters location:** Atlanta GA. **Other U.S. locations:** Nationwide. **International locations:** Canada. **Subsidiaries include:** AFGD Canada. **Parent company:** AFG Industries, Incorporated. **Operations at this facility include:** Manufacturing; Sales. **Listed on:** Privately held. **President:** John Stilwell. **Number of employees at this location:** 200. **Number of employees nationwide:** 1,000.

AMERICAN PRESS
P.O. Box 2893, Lake Charles LA 70602-2893. 337/433-3000. **Physical address:** 4900 Highway 90 East, Lake Charles LA 70615. **Fax:** 337/494-4059. **Contact:** Anita Tinsley, Business Manager. **World Wide Web address:** http://www.americanpress.com. **Description:** A daily newspaper distributed in southwestern Louisiana. Founded in 1895. **NOTE:** Part-time positions are offered. **Special programs:** Internships. **Office hours:** Monday – Friday, 8:00 a.m. – 5:00 p.m. **Corporate headquarters location:** This location. **Parent company:** Spearman Corporation. **Other U.S. locations:** Trinidad CO; Hobbes NM. **Sales/revenues:** $11 - $20 million.

ANCO INDUSTRIES
15981 Airline Highway, Baton Rouge LA 70817. 225/752-4333. **Toll-free phone:** 800/766-7677. **Fax:** 225/756-7666. **Contact:** Human Resources. **World Wide Web address:** http://www.basicindustries.com. **Description:** A diversified company with business segments in refining, petrochemicals, power and utilities, paper and pulp, and maintenance or new construction. The company offers services such as industrial insulating, scaffolding, fireproofing, and asbestos abatement. **NOTE:** Contact Human Resources to learn about employment opportunities. **Special programs:** Apprenticeships; Training. **Corporate headquarters location:** This location. **Other U.S. locations:** NC; TX; Washington D.C. **Subsidiaries include:** Basic Industries. **Listed on:** Privately held. **President:** Dean Bordelon. **Sales/revenues:** $158 million.

APPRO SYSTEMS INC.
7173 Florida Boulevard, Suite 100, Baton Rouge LA 70806. 225/490-2400. **Toll-free phone:** 866/277-7612. **Fax:** 225/490-2700. **Contact:** Human Resources. **E-mail address:** hr@approsystems.com. **World Wide Web address:** http://www.approsystems.com. **NOTE:** Please visit website for information on how to apply for available positions. **Description:** Designs, develops, and markets financial risk assessment software for consumer, small business, and retail banking use. The company's core product is LoanCenter. Founded in 1979. **Positions advertised include:** ASP.NET and C# Programmer; Crystal Reports Trainer; Desktop Support; First Level Support Manager; Internal Developer; Product Specialist. **Listed on:** Privately held. **CEO/Chairman:** Steve Uffman. **Number of employees nationwide:** Over 200.

BASF CORPORATION
8800 Line Avenue, Shreveport LA 71106. 318/861-8200. **Fax:** 318/861-8297. **Contact:** Human Resources Department. **E-mail address:** recruiting@basf.com. **World Wide Web address:** http://www.basf.com. **Description:** A chemical company whose diverse product line includes plastics, colorants and pigments, dispersions, fine chemicals, automotive and industrial coatings, crop-protection agents, and oil and gas. **NOTE:** Entry-level positions are offered. Job seekers may submit applications online. **Company slogan:** We don't make a lot of the products you buy. We make a lot of the products you buy better. **Positions advertised include:** EHS Team Member. **Special programs:** Internships; Professional Development Program; Tuition Reimbursement Program; Employee Stock Purchase Program. **Corporate headquarters location:** Mount Olive NJ. **Other area locations:** Geismar LA. **Other U.S. locations:** Nationwide. **International locations:** Worldwide. **Subsidiaries include:** BASF Aktiengesllschaft; BASF Canada; BASF Mexicana. **Parent company:** BASF AG. **Operations at this facility include:** Production. **Listed on:** New York Stock Exchange; major European stock exchanges in Frankfurt, London, Paris, and Zurich. **Stock exchange symbol:** New York (BF); Frankfurt (BAS); London (BFA); Paris (BA); Zurich (BAS). **CEO/Chairman:** Klaus Peter Lobbe. **Sales/revenues:** $29 billion. **Number of employees at this location:** Over 100. **Number of employees nationwide:** 12,000. **Number of employees worldwide:** Over 93,000.

BANK OF LOUISIANA
3340 Severn Avenue, Metairie LA 70002. 504/889-9376. **Toll-free phone:** 800/288-9811. **Fax:** 504/889-9444. **Contact:** Human Resources. **World Wide Web address:** http://www.bankoflouisiana.com. **Positions advertised include:** Loans Clerk. **Description:** A bank holding company with subsidiaries that perform commercial banking operations and other related financial activities. **Office hours:** Monday – Thursday, 9:00 a.m. – 3:00 p.m., Friday, 9:00 a.m. – 6:00 p.m., Saturday, 9:00 a.m. – 12:00 p.m. **Corporate headquarters location:** New Orleans LA. **Operations at this location include:** This location is the company's Operations Center.

BATON ROUGE GENERAL MEDICAL CENTER
P.O. Box 2511, Baton Rouge LA 70806. 225/387-7000. **Physical address:** Baton Rouge General Medical Center, 3600 Florida Boulevard, Baton Rouge LA 70806. **Fax:** 225/381-6825. **Recorded jobline:** 866/800-1126. **Contact:** Human Resources. **E-mail:** human.resources@brgeneral.org. **World Wide Web address:**

http://www.generalhealth.org. **Description:** A non-profit, full-service hospital that is considered the flagship entity of General Health System. General Health System is a unified health care delivery system consisting of 27 health care companies. Services provided by General Health include radiology; cardiology; regional cancer care; regional burn center; obstetrics; physical therapy; laser surgery; pathology; diabetes education and treatment; chemical dependency treatment; graduate medical education; intergenerational daycare; home health care; respiratory care; health screenings; managed care services; continuing medical education; occupational therapy; long-term care; industrial rehabilitation; imaging and diagnostics; cardiac rehabilitation; gynecology; mental health care; infusion therapy; speech therapy; mammography; sleep disorders; geriatric assessment; wellness and health promotion; neurological services; laboratory testing; emergency care; assisted living centers; nutritional counseling; pediatrics; and inpatient and outpatient surgeries. **Positions advertised include:** Accessioning Tech; Accounts Payable Assistant; Administrative Secretary; Cashier; Charge Posting Clerk; Cook; Crew Member; ER Tech; HIM Specialist; Health Information Management Manager; Hospitality Associate; Hospitality Hostess; LPN; Medical Lab Technician; Mental Health Technician; Patient Access Representative; Patient Care Associate; Pharmacy Incentives; Pharmacy Tech; Phlebotomist; Physical Therapist; RN; RN – Various Departments. **Office hours:** Monday – Friday, 8:00 a.m. – 4:30 p.m. **President/CEO:** William R. Holman. **Number of employees at this location:** 2,000.

BAYOU STEEL CORPORATION
P.O. Box 5000, La Place LA 70069-1156. 985/652-4900. **Physical address:** 138 Highway 3217, La Place LA 70069. **Fax:** 985/652-0339. **Contact:** Steve Turner, Human Resources Department. **E-mail address:** hr@bayousteel.com. **World Wide Web address:** http://www.bayousteel.com. **Description:** Owns and operates a steel minimill located on the Mississippi River. The company's principal raw material, scrap metal, is melted in electric arc furnaces and continuously cast into billets, then rolled on its rolling mill into a variety of steel structural shapes. The company rolls angles, channels, flats, standard beams, and wide-flange beams. These products are sold principally to steel service centers that supply various end users in manufacturing and construction. The company ships billets and steel structural shapes and receives scrap steel using barge transportation. **Other U.S. locations:** Harriman TN; Tulsa OK; Pittsburgh PA; Chicago IL. **Operations at this facility include:** Administration; Manufacturing; Sales; Service. **Listed on:** American Stock Exchange. **Stock exchange symbol:** BYX. **CEO/Chairman:** Howard Meyers. **Sales/revenues:** $142.1 million. **Number of employees at this location:** 400.

BLUE CROSS BLUE SHIELD OF LOUISIANA
P.O. Box 98029, Baton Rouge LA 70898-9029. 225/295-3307. **Physical address:** 5525 Reitz Avenue, Baton Rouge LA 70809. **Fax:** 225/295-2082. **Contact:** Human Resources. **E-mail address:** job.posting@bcbsla.com. **World Wide Web address:** http://www.bcbsla.com. **Description:** A nonprofit health care insurance organization that provides managed health care plans to both individuals and groups. Blue Cross and Blue Shield offers Point-of-Service, PPO, and HMO plans, as well as life insurance. **NOTE:** When e-mailing your resume, include the job number for which you are applying. No phone calls please. **Positions advertised include:** Advisory Systems Programmer; Associate Medical Director; Case Management RN; Senior Systems Engineer; SNL Programmer Analyst; TPA Correspondence Clerk; TPA System Audit Specialist. **Office hours:** Monday – Friday, 8:00 a.m. – 4:20 p.m. **Other area locations include:** Shreveport; Monroe; Alexandria; Lake Charles; Lafayette; Houma; New Orleans. **Subsidiaries include:** HMO Louisiana, Incorporated; Southern National Life Insurance, Incorporated; The Louisiana Child Caring Foundation. **Operations at this facility include:** Administration; Sales; Service. **President/CEO:** Kathryn Sullivan. **Number of employees nationwide:** 1,500.

BOOMTOWN WESTBANK
4132 Peters Road, Harvey LA 70058-1805. 504/366-7711. **Toll-free phone:** 800/366-7711. **Fax:** 504/364-8796. **Contact:** Human Resources. **World Wide Web address:** http://www.boomtownneworleans.com. **Description:** A 50-acre complex whose primary operations include the Boomtown Belle Casino, a replica of a paddle-wheel riverboat. It accommodates 1,400 passengers and a crew of 200. The Boomtown Belle Casino cruises the Inter-Coastal Waterway when not anchored beside Boomtown Westbank's site on the Harvey Canal. The complex's dockside facility offers such amenities as the 200-seat Boomer's Cabaret entertainment lounge, the Mossy Horn Cafe, and a family entertainment center. A second floor of the center features additional food service facilities and entertainment. **NOTE:** Online applications are available. Please visit website to download application. **Special programs:** Tuition Reimbursement Program; G.E.D. Program; Computer Classes. **Other U.S. locations:** Biloxi MS; Reno NV. **Parent company:** Boomtown, Incorporated, a subsidiary of Pinnacle Entertainment.

BRENT HOUSE HOTEL
1512 Jefferson Highway, New Orleans LA 70112. 504/842-4140. **Toll-free phone:** 800/535-3986. **Fax:** 504/842-4160. **Contact:** Shelly Williams, Human Resources Coordinator. **World Wide Web address:** http://www.brenthouse.com. **Description:** The 150-room Brent House Hotel is immediately adjacent to the patient care facilities at Ochsner Clinic and Ochsner Foundation Hospital in New Orleans. This hotel provides lodging for ambulatory and convalescent patients and their families.

CENTRAL LOUISIANA ELECTRIC COMPANY INC. (CLECO)
P.O. Box 5000, Pineville LA 71361-5000. 318/484-7628. **Physical address:** 2030 Donahue Ferry Road, Pineville LA 71361-5000. **Toll-free phone:** 800/622-6537. **Fax:** 318/484-7488. **Contact:** Human Resources. **World Wide Web address:** http://www.cleco.com. **NOTE:** Please visit website for online application form. **Description:** An electric company that serves approximately 218,000 customers in a 14,000-square-mile region of Louisiana that includes mainly small communities and rural areas. Generating units are fueled by coal, Louisiana lignite, and natural gas. **Special programs:** Summer Employment; School-to-Work Program; Tuition Reimbursement Program; Home Computer Finance Program; Adoption Assistance Program. **Corporate headquarters location:** This location. **Subsidiaries include:** Cleco Power; Cleco Midstream Resources; Cleco Energy; Cleco Generation Services; Cleco Marketing and Trading. **Operations at this facility include:** Administration. **Listed on:** New York Stock Exchange; Pacific Stock Exchange. **Stock exchange symbol:** CNL. **President/CEO/Director:** David Eppler. **Sales/revenues:** $721.2 million. **Number of employees at this location:** 300. **Number of employees nationwide:** Over 1,300.

CENTURYTEL
100 CenturyTel Drive, Monroe LA 71203. 318/388-9500. **Fax:** 318/340-5393. **Contact:** Human Resources Manager. **E-mail address:** staffing@centurytel.com. **World Wide Web address:** http://www.centurytel.com. **NOTE:** Please visit website to create a profile and apply for positions online. **Description:** Provides local exchange telephone service and mobile communications services. The company's telephone subsidiaries serve portions of 15 states. Through Century Cellunet, the company also provides cellular mobile telephone service and nationwide radio paging services. **Positions advertised include:** Communications Technician; Supervisor Collections; Security Representative; Analyst; Customer Service Representative; Senior Systems Programmer; PC/LAN Specialist; Manager – Billing; Manage – Customer Retention; Systems Administrator; Supervisor – Internet Network Operations; Senior Network Analyst. **Special programs:** Tuition Assistance Program; Training. **Other U.S. locations:** Nationwide. **Subsidiaries include:** Central Telephone Company; Interactive Communications, Incorporated; Delta Security Alarm Company, Incorporated; Pacific Telecom, Incorporated; Century Protection Systems; CSW Net, Incorporated. **Listed on:** New York Stock Exchange. **Stock exchange symbol:** CTL. **CEO/Chairman:** Glen F. Post III. **Number of employees nationwide:** 3,000.

CHRISTUS ST. PATRICK HOSPITAL
P.O. Box 3401, Lake Charles LA 70602-3401. 337/436-2511. **Physical address:** 524 South Ryan Street, Lake Charles LA 70601. **Toll-free phone:** 888/72B-WELL. **Fax:** 337/491-7157. **Recorded jobline:** 337/491-7519. **Contact:** Recruiting Department. **World Wide Web address:** http://www.stpatrickhospital.org. **NOTE:** Please visit website to create a profile and apply for positions online. Applications will be kept on file for six months. **Description:** A nonprofit hospital that offers a variety of services including cardiovascular care, inpatient and outpatient services, cancer treatment, rehabilitation, physical therapy, and behavioral health services. Founded in 1908. **NOTE:** Entry-level positions are offered. Job seekers may submit resumes online. **Positions advertised include:** Controller; Director Business Development; Director of Materials Management; LPN; Manager GI Lab; Manager Home Health/Jennings; Pharmacy Tech; Physical Therapist; Registered Nurse; Respiratory Therapist; RN – Diabetes Educator; RN Service Director; Speech Pathologist; Staff Pharmacist; Vice President – Medical Affairs. **Special programs:** Tuition Reimbursement Program; Continuing Education Program; Internships. **Other U.S. locations:** AR; TX; OK; UT. **Parent company:** Christus Health. **CEO:** Ellen Jones. **Number of employees at this location:** 1,500. **Number of employees nationwide:** 20,000.

COMPUTER SOURCE
3814 Williams Boulevard, Kenner LA 70065. 504/443-4100. **Toll-free phone:** 800/524-9696. **Fax:** 504/443-6275. **Contact:** Human Resources. **E-mail address:** lwallace@compsource.com. **World Wide Web address:** http://www.compsource.com. **Description:** A computer reseller that also provides technical support, networking, and business solutions to its customers. **NOTE:** Contract, fee-paid direct, and internal jobs are posted on the company Website. Resumes may be submitted via e-mail. **Positions advertised include:** Marketing Intern; Hardware Service Technician; Desktop Support Specialist; Network Support Specialist; Account Manager; Executive Sales Assistant; Civil/Structural Designer; Scanning Technician; CAD Instructor; Document Specialist; Civil Engineer; Civil Engineering Draftsman; Structural Consulting Engineer; Senior Consultant; Civil-Environmental Engineer. **Special programs:** Internships. **Corporate headquarters location:** This location.

CONAGRA POULTRY COMPANY
6648 Highway Fifteen North, Farmerville LA 71241-0726. 318/368-4258. **Contact:** Human Resources. **E-mail address:** careers@conagra.com. **World Wide Web address:** http://www.conagra.com. **NOTE:** Please visit website to post resume and search for job listings. **Description:** The poultry division of ConAgra Foods, Incorporated. ConAgra Foods is a diversified international food company. Products range from prepared foods to farming supplies. ConAgra has major businesses in branded grocery products including shelf-stable and frozen foods, processed meats, chicken and turkey products, and cheeses, as well as major businesses in potato products, private label grocery products, beef, pork, seafood, grain and pulse (edible beans) merchandising, grain processing, specialty trailing, crop protection chemicals, fertilizers, and animal feed. ConAgra is a family of independent operating companies in three industry segments: prepared foods, trading and processing, and agri-products. **Special programs:** Tuition Reimbursement Program; Scholarship Assistance Program; Employee Discount Program. **Corporate headquarters location:** Omaha NE. **Other U.S. locations:** Nationwide. **Operations at this facility include:** Production of frozen and cooked chickens. **Corporate headquarters location:** Omaha NE. **Parent Company:** ConAgra Foods, Incorporated. **Listed on:** New York Stock Exchange. **Stock exchange symbol:** CAG. **Sales/revenues:** $27 billion.

CONAGRA POULTRY COMPANY
P.O. Box 1008, Natchitoches LA 71458-1008. 318/352-9600. **Physical address:** 7088 Highway One Bypass, Natchitoches LA 71457. **Fax:** 318/352-8210. **Contact:** Human Resources. **E-mail address:** careers@conagra.com. **Wide Web address:** http://www.conagra.com. **NOTE:** Please visit website to post resume and search for job listings. **Description:** The poultry division of ConAgra Foods, Incorporated. ConAgra Foods is a diversified international food company. Products range from prepared foods to farming supplies. ConAgra has major businesses in branded grocery products including shelf-stable and frozen foods, processed meats, chicken and turkey products, and cheeses, as well as major businesses in potato products, private label grocery products, beef, pork, seafood, grain and pulse (edible beans) merchandising, grain processing, specialty trailing, crop protection chemicals, fertilizers, and animal feed. ConAgra is a family of independent operating companies in three industry segments: prepared foods, trading and processing, and agri-products. **Special programs:** Tuition Reimbursement Program; Scholarship Assistance Program; Employee Discount Program. **Corporate headquarters location:** Omaha NE. **Other U.S. locations:** Nationwide. **Parent company:** ConAgra Foods, Incorporated. **Operations at this facility include:** This location processes chickens. **Corporate headquarters location:** Omaha NE. **Listed on:** New York Stock Exchange. **Stock exchange symbol:** CAG. **CEO/Chairman:** Bruce Rohde. **Sales/revenues:** $27 billion.

CONESTOGA-ROVERS & ASSOCIATES
4915 South Sherwood Forest Boulevard, Baton Rouge LA 70816. 225/292-9007. **Fax:** 225/291-1022. **Contact:** Human Resources. **E-mail address:** hr@craworld.com. **World Wide Web address:** http://www.rovers.com. **Description:** Provides engineering, environmental, construction, and information technology services. Founded in 1976. **NOTE:** Entry-level positions and part-time jobs are offered. Job seekers may apply for advertised positions online. **Special programs include:** Fitness Reimbursement; Training; Professional Development Program. **Positions advertised include:** Scientist; Chemist; Environmental Scientist; Environmental Compliance Engineer; Regional Safety Manager; Engineer/Geologist. **Office hours:** Monday - Friday, 7:30 a.m. - 5:00 p.m. **Corporate headquarters location:** Niagara Falls NY. **Other area locations:** Shreveport LA. **Other U.S. locations:** Nationwide. **International locations:** Canada; Mexico; United Kingdom. **Subsidiaries include:** CRA Contractors, Limited; CRA Developments, Limited; CNA Services; Inspec-Sol, Incorporated; Soil Enrichment Systems. **Operations at this facility include:** Divisional Headquarters. **Listed on:** Privately held. **Sales/revenues:** $21 - $50 million. **Number of employees at this location:** 75. **Number of employees nationwide:** 250. **Number of employees worldwide:** 1,600.

AL COPELAND INVESTMENTS
1405 Airline Drive, Metairie LA 70001. 504/830-1000. **Fax:** 504/832-8918. **Contact:** Human Resources. **World Wide Web address:** http://www.alcopeland.com.

Description: Owns and operates several franchises, including Popeye's Famous Fried Chicken restaurants, Copeland's of New Orleans restaurants, and Copeland's Cheesecake Bistro. The company also owns a Diversified Food and Seasonings manufacturing company, an improv comedy club, a hotel and a Cajun diner. **Positions advertised include:** Manager; Hourly help. **Corporate headquarters location:** This location.

DATEC INC.
401 Whitney Avenue, Suite 406, Gretna LA 70056. 504/368-2097. **Fax:** 504/368-2989. **Contact:** Human Resources. **World Wide Web address:** http://www.datecinc.com. **Description:** Sells computer hardware and software including the Integraph brand. The company also provides computer aided design (CAD) and technical document management (TDM) services, as well as computer training classes. Founded in 1978. **Other area locations:** Baton Rouge LA. **Other U.S. locations:** Mobile AL. **Listed on:** Privately held. **President:** Bill Regan.

DELTA QUEEN STEAMBOAT COMPANY
Robin Street Wharf, 1380 Port of New Orleans Place, New Orleans LA 70130-1890. 504/586-0631. **Toll-free phone:** 800/543-1949. **Fax:** 504/585-0630. **Contact:** Human Resources Manager. **World Wide Web address:** http://www.deltaqueen.com. **Description:** Owns and operates three steamboat cruise lines: the *Delta Queen*, the *Mississippi Queen*, and the *American Queen*. Founded in 1890. **NOTE:** Online applications are available. **Office hours:** Monday – Friday 8:00 a.m. – 8:00 p.m., Saturday & Sunday 9:00 a.m. – 5:00 p.m. **Parent company:** Delaware North Companies, Incorporated. **Number of employees nationwide:** Over 400.

DOMINION E&P
CNG Tower, 1450 Poydras Street, New Orleans LA 70112-6000. 504/593-7000. **Contact:** Human Resources. **E-mail address:** human_resources@dom.com. **World Wide Web address:** http://www.dom.com. **Description:** As the oil and gas exploration and production unit of Dominion, this company operates on and offshore in the Gulf of Mexico and the Gulf Coast, the Appalachian region, the Southwest, the Rockies, and northeast British Columbia. **NOTE:** Job openings are posted online at www.dom.com/jobs, where applicants may also submit resumes. **Positions advertised include:** Accountant; Administrative Assistant; Associate Safety Specialist; Business Systems Analyst; Document Imaging Processor; Planning and Budgeting Analyst. **Special programs:** Dominion Scholarship Program; Dominion Power Start Program; Professional Development Program; Tuition Reimbursement Program; Co-ops; Internships. **Corporate headquarters location:** Richmond VA. **Other U.S. locations:** Nationwide. **International locations:** Canada. **Subsidiaries include:** Louis Dreyfuss Natural Gas; CNG Retail Services Corporation. **Parent company:** Dominion Resources provides electricity, natural gas, and related services to customers in the U.S. **Listed on:** New York Stock Exchange. **Stock exchange symbol:** D. **President/CEO/Chairman:** Thos. E. Capps. **Sales/revenues:** $10.6 billion.

ELMWOOD FITNESS CENTER
1200 South Clearview Parkway, Suite 1200, Harahan LA 70123. 504/733-1600. **Fax:** 504/799-1684. **Contact:** Lorilea Craft, Human Resources. **E-mail address:** lcraft@ochsner.com. **World Wide Web address:** http://www.elmwoodfitness.com. **NOTE:** Please visit website to search positions and apply online. **Description:** A full-service fitness center offering programs for the entire family. Recreational activities include indoor and outdoor pools; racquetball, volleyball, and basketball courts; weight training; and aquatics. The center includes two aerobic studios; the Cardiovascular Health Center; and Kidsports, a facility for children's activities. **Positions advertised include:** Club Instructor; Clerk – Accounting; Environmental Services; Club Staff; Staff Supervisor; Maintenance Person – Mechanical. **Other area locations:** Metairie. **Operations at this facility include:** This location is the main health club. **Parent company:** Ochsner Clinic Foundation, a health-care facility.

ENTERGY CORPORATION
639 Loyola Avenue, New Orleans LA 70113. 504/529-5262. **Contact:** Personnel. **E-mail address:** career@entergy.com (for experienced applicants); college@entergy.com (for recent college graduates). **World Wide Web address:** http://www.entergy.com. **Description:** An investor-owned, diversified energy company that produces and distributes power through its domestic and international power plants. Entergy serves more than 2.4 million retail customers through its operating companies in Arkansas, Louisiana, Mississippi, and Texas. Through its subsidiary, Entergy-Koch, L.P., it also operates natural gas pipeline and storage facilities, and provides wholesale energy trading services. **NOTE:** See posted jobs and submit resumes online at http://watss.entergy.com/jobsearch.asp. **Positions advertised include:** Administrative Associate; Security Specialist; Communications Specialist; Senior Secretary; Management Aide. **Special programs:** Co-ops; Internships; Educational Reimbursement Program; Career Development Program. **Corporate headquarters location:** This location. **Subsidiaries include:** Arkansas Power & Light; Louisiana Power & Light; Mississippi Power & Light; New Orleans Public Service, which provides electricity to more than 1.7 million commercial, private, and industrial consumers; System Energy Resources, which has a 90 percent interest in Grand Gulf 1, a nuclear power plant; and Gulf States Utilities, which services parts of Texas and Louisiana and owns 70 percent of the River Bend nuclear power plant. **Listed on:** New York Stock Exchange. **Stock exchange symbol:** ETR. **President/CEO:** E. Renae Conley. **Sales/revenues:** Over $8 billion. **Number of employees at this location:** 2,200. **Number of employees nationwide:** 14,000.

EXXONMOBIL CHEMICAL AMERICAS
P.O. Box 241, Baton Rouge LA 70821. 225/977-7011. **Contact:** Director of Personnel. **World Wide Web address:** http://www.exxon.mobil.com. **NOTE:** Apply online at http://www.prod.exxonmobil.com/careers/usa. **Description:** ExxonMobil is an integrated oil company engaged in petroleum and chemical products marketing, refining, manufacturing, exploration, production, transportation, and research and development worldwide. Other products include fabricated plastics, films, food bags, housewares, garbage bags, and building materials. The company also has subsidiaries involved in real estate development and mining operations. **Special programs:** Summer Internships; Co-ops. **Office hours:** Monday – Friday, 7:45 a.m. – 4:15 p.m. **Corporate headquarters location:** Irving TX. **Other U.S. locations:** Nationwide. **International locations:** Worldwide. **Operations at this facility include:** This location produces industrial organic chemicals and synthetic rubber. **Listed on:** New York Stock Exchange. **Stock exchange symbol:** XOM. **CEO/Chairman:** Lee R. Raymond. **Sales/revenues:** $204.5 billion.

EXXONMOBIL CORPORATION
500 West St. Bernard's Highway 500, Chalmette LA 70043. 504/279-9481. **Contact:** Human Resources. **World Wide Web address:** http://www.exxon.mobil.com. **Description:** ExxonMobil is an integrated oil company engaged in petroleum and chemical products marketing, refining, manufacturing, exploration, production, transportation, and research and development worldwide. Other products include fabricated plastics, films, food bags, housewares, garbage bags, and building materials. The company also has subsidiaries involved in real estate development and mining operations. **NOTE:** Apply online at http://www.prod.exxonmobil.com/careers/usa. **Special programs:** Summer Internships; Co-ops. **Corporate headquarters location:** Irving TX. **Other U.S. locations:** Nationwide. **International locations:** Worldwide. **Operations at this facility include:** This location is a petroleum refining facility. **Listed on:** New York Stock Exchange. **Stock exchange symbol:** XOM. **CEO/Chairman:** Lee R. Raymond. **Sales/revenues:** $204.5 billion.

FIBREBOND CORPORATION
1300 Davenport Drive, Minden LA 71055. 318/377-1030. **Toll-free phone:** 800/824-2614. **Fax:** 318/377-5756. **Contact:** Human Resources. **World Wide Web address:** http://www.fibrebond.com. **Description:** Manufactures prefabricated buildings and structures. The company also provides cellular and PCS installation services. **Corporate headquarters location:** This location. **Other U.S. locations:** Fairfield CA. **CEO/Chairman:** Claud B. Walker.

GLOBAL INDUSTRIES, LTD.
P.O. Box 442, Sulphur LA 70064-0442. 337/583-5000. **Physical address:** 8000 Global Drive, Carlyss LA 70665. **Fax:** 337/583-5100. **Contact:** Human Resources. **World Wide Web address:** http://www.globalind.com. **Description:** Provides construction and diving services to the offshore oil and gas industry. Global's operations include Global Pipeline PLUS, Incorporated; Global Movable Offshore; Global Divers and Contractors; Pelican Transportation; and The Red Adair Company. PLUS's barges have various combinations of pipelay, pipebury, and derrick capabilities, which offer a wide range of services including deepwater installation, pipelay by the reel method, and pipeline maintenance and repair. Global Movable Offshore's three derrick barges provide offshore lifting services including installation and removal of platforms and associated components, drilling and workover rigs, and other equipment. Global Divers' dive support vessels (DSV) provide diving services for offshore oil and gas development and production. Global Divers is a leader in deepwater diving, underwater welding technology, subsea completions, and nuclear power plant diving services. A full-service trucking company, Pelican transports general commodities as well as oil field equipment, pipe, and supplies. The Red Adair Company is a worldwide leader in wild well control. In addition to fire fighting, the company offers contingency planning and training, engineering, well plug, and abandonment and rig inspection services. **Corporate headquarters location:** This location. **Other area locations:** New Iberia LA; New Orleans LA. **Other U.S. locations:** Houston TX. **International locations:** Worldwide. **Listed on:** NASDAQ. **Stock exchange symbol:** GLBL. **CEO/Chairman:** William Dore. **Sales/revenues:** Approximately $400 million. **Number of employees worldwide:** Over 2,100.

GREEN CLINIC L.L.C.
1200 South Farmerville Street, Ruston LA 71270. 318/255-3690. **Fax:** 318/255-4360. **Contact:** Human Resources. **World Wide Web address:** http://www.green-clinic.com. **Description:** A health clinic consisting of an in-house physical therapy department and an outpatient ambulatory surgical center. Founded in 1948. **Positions advertised include:** Licensed Practical Nurse. **Office hours:** Monday – Friday, 8:00 a.m. – 5:00 p.m. **Number of employees at this location:** 225.

HIBERNIA NATIONAL BANK
P.O. Box 3402, Lake Charles LA 70602. 337/494-3380. **Physical address:** One Lakeshore Drive, 3rd Floor, Lake Charles LA 70629. **Recorded jobline:** 877/446-2562. **Contact:** Human Resources. **World Wide Web address:** http://www.hiberniabank.com. **Description:** A commercial bank that offers personal, Internet, small business, and mortgage options, as well as investment, insurance, and trust services. **NOTE:** Resumes may be submitted online. Please visit website to learn about Applicant Walk-in Days at a location near you. At this location, Applicant Walk-in hours are Tuesdays 9:00 a.m. – 11:00 a.m. **Positions advertised include:** Corporate Relationship Manager; Personal Banker; Teller. **Corporate headquarters location:** This location. **Other U.S. locations:** AR; TX; MS. **Parent company:** Hibernia Corporation offers consumer banking, commercial middle market and small business lending, and trust services in Louisiana. **Listed on:** New York Stock Exchange. **Stock exchange symbol:** HIB.

HONEYWELL INTERNATIONAL
P.O. Box 2830, Baton Rouge LA 70821-2830. 225/383-5222. **Physical address:** 2966 Lupine Avenue, Baton Rouge LA 70801. **Fax:** 225/346-3627. **Recorded jobline:** 225/346-3685. **Contact:** Human Resources Department. **World Wide Web address:** http://www.honeywell.com. **Description:** Honeywell is engaged in the research, development, manufacture, and sale of advanced technology products and services in the fields of chemicals, electronics, automation, and controls. The company's major businesses are home and building automation and control, performance polymers and chemicals, industrial automation and control, space and aviation systems, and defense and marine systems. **Positions advertised include:** Account Executive. **Special programs:** Internships; Training; Co-ops; Summer Jobs. **NOTE:** Please see website to register and search for jobs internships and other college jobs. **Office hours:** Monday - Friday, 8:00 a.m. - 5:00 p.m. **Corporate headquarters location:** Morristown NJ. **Other U.S. locations:** Nationwide. **International locations:** Worldwide. **Subsidiaries include:** ADEMCO Group; Honeywell Aerospace; Honeywell International Specialty Materials; UOP L.L.C.; Sensotec, Incorporated. **Operations at this facility include:** This location manufactures environmentally safe refrigerants. **Listed on:** New York Stock Exchange; also, the London, Chicago, and Pacific Stock Exchanges. **Stock exchange symbol:** HON. **President/CEO:** David M. Cote. **Sales/revenues:** $22 million. **Number of employees at this location:** 250. **Number of employees worldwide:** 125,000.

INTERNATIONAL SHIPHOLDING CORP.
P.O. Box 53425, New Orleans LA 70153. 504/529-1300. **Physical address:** 1700 Poydras Center, 650 Poydras Street, New Orleans LA 70153-3425. **Toll-free phone:** 888/354-5274. **Fax:** 504/593-6401. **Contact:** Human Resources. **E-mail address:** fli-seafarers-employmt@intship.com. **World Wide Web address:** http://www.forest-lines.com. **Description:** Operates a diversified fleet of U.S. and foreign flag vessels that transport various shipments including forest products, automobiles, military cargo, petroleum products, and dry bulk cargo. **Corporate headquarters location:** This location. **Other U.S. locations:** New York NY; Washington D.C.; Houston TX; Chicago IL. **International locations:** Singapore **Subsidiaries include:** Central Gulf Lines; Lash Marine Services; Waterman Steamship Corporation. **Operations at this facility include:** Administration. **Listed on:** New York Stock Exchange. **Stock exchange symbol:** ISH. **CEO/Chairman:** Niels W. Johnson. **Sales/revenues:** $227.4 million. **Number of employees at this location:** 225. **Number of employees nationwide:** 800.

JACOBS ENGINEERING GROUP, INC.
4949 Essen Lane, Baton Rouge LA 70809. 225/769-7700. **Fax:** 225/768-5087. **World Wide Web address:** http://www.jacobs.com. **NOTE:** Please visit website to search for jobs and apply online. **Description:** Provides professional technical services, including scientific consulting, construction, and engineering, to companies worldwide. Specialties include aerospace, oil and gas, biotechnology, pulp and paper, buildings,

and pharmaceuticals. **Positions advertised include:** CAE Technical Specialist; Civil/Structural Designer; Civil/Structural Engineer; Clerical/Office Worker; Control Systems Designer; Control Systems Engineer; Control Systems/Electrical Drafter; Document Control; Engineering Project Manager; Mechanical Designer; Pipe Design Drafter; Piping Drafter; Planner/Scheduler; Principal Engineer; Project Engineer; Runner; Senior Civil/Structural Designer; Senior Instrument Lead Designer; Senior Piping Designer/Checker. **Corporate headquarters location:** Pasadena CA. **Other area locations:** Lake Charles; Port Allen. **Other U.S locations:** Nationwide. **International locations:** Worldwide. **Listed on:** New York Stock Exchange. **Stock exchange symbol:** JEC.

JEFFERIES & COMPANY, INC.
650 Poydras Street, Suite 2215, New Orleans LA 70130. 504/681-5700. **Contact:** Human Resources. **World Wide Web address:** http://www.jefco.com. **Description:** Engaged in equity, convertible debt, and taxable fixed income securities brokerage, and trading and corporate finance. The company is a national firm that distributes and trades blocks of equity securities primarily in the third market. Founded in 1962. **Corporate headquarters location:** New York NY. **Other U.S. locations:** Nationwide. **International locations:** England; France; Switzerland; Japan; Australia. **Parent company:** Jefferies Group, Incorporated is a holding company that, through Jefferies & Company and its three other primary subsidiaries, Investment Technology Group, Incorporated, Jefferies International Limited, and Jefferies Pacific Limited, is engaged in securities brokerage and trading, corporate finance, and other financial services. **Listed on:** New York Stock Exchange. **Stock exchange symbol:** JEF. **Number of employees worldwide:** 1,400.

LEWIS COMPUTER SERVICES, INC.
8549 United Plaza Boulevard, Suite 310, Baton Rouge LA 70809. 225/709-2000. **Fax:** 225/709-2010. **Contact:** Human Resources. **E-mail address:** jobs@lewis.com. **World Wide Web address:** http://www.lewis.com. **NOTE:** Please visit website for online application form. **Description:** Develops software for home health agencies. The company's products include Prompt IPS, PROMPT-LINK, and PROMPT-LITE. **Positions advertised include:** Account Executive; Clinical Software Trainer; Crystal Report Developer; C++ Developer; Development Manager; Director of Sales; Manager of Client Training; Research Analyst; Software Developer; Software Implementation Specialist; SQL Server Developer; Support Technician; XML Developer. **Corporate headquarters location:** This location. **Other U.S. locations:** Chicago IL. **President:** Jeffrey Lewis. **Number of employees at this location:** Over 100.

LIFECARE HOSPITALS, INC.
9320 Linwood Avenue, Shreveport LA 71106. 318/688-8504. **Toll-free phone:** 800/280-5433. **Fax:** 318/683-4545. **Contact:** Human Resources. **E-mail address:** ShreveportHR@lifecare-hospitals.com. **World Wide Web address:** http://www.lifecare-hospitals.com/Default.htm. **Description:** A long-term, acute care hospital with 130 beds that specializes in individualized, therapy-driven treatment. LifeCare services include respiratory, physical, occupational, speech, and recreational therapy. **NOTE:** Entry-level positions and second and third shifts are offered. **Positions advertised include:** RN; LPN; Physical Therapist; Charge Nurse. **Office hours:** Monday - Friday, 8:00 a.m. - 5:00 p.m. **Corporate headquarters location:** This location. **Other area locations:** New Orleans LA. **Other U.S. locations:** NV; TX; OH; PA; MI; NC; CO. **Listed on:** Privately held. **CEO:** Robert A. Loepp. **Number of employees at this location:** 160.

LOUISIANA TECH UNIVERSITY
P.O. Box 3178, Ruston LA 71272. 318/257-2235. **Toll-free phone:** 800/LATECH-1. **Fax:** 318/257-2482. **Contact:** Personnel. **World Wide Web address:** http://www.latech.edu. **NOTE:** Please visit website for details on applying to particular positions. **Description:** A technical university that offers a broad range of fully-accredited undergraduate degrees, master's degrees in a variety of areas, and doctoral programs in business administration and engineering. Approximately 10,000 students are enrolled. Founded in 1894. **Positions advertised include:** Carpenter; Laborer; Instructor on Continuing Appointment; Director of Retention and Advertising; Office Coordinator; Word Processor Operator Specialist; Secretary; Custodian; Administrative Secretary; Library Specialist Supervisor; Head Women's Soccer Coach; Head Bowling Coach; Assistant Football Coach; Clerk; Assistant Professor – Various Departments; Dean; Faculty Positions – Various Departments, Tenure-track and Non-Tenure-track; Spatial Data Laboratory Supervisor; Rehabilitation Technology Specialist. **Office hours:** Monday - Friday, 8:00 a.m. - 5:00 p.m. **President:** Dr. Daniel D. Reneau.

LOYOLA UNIVERSITY NEW ORLEANS
Box 16, 6363 St. Charles Avenue, New Orleans LA 70118. 504/864-7757. **Fax:** 504/864-7100. **Recorded jobline:** 504/864-7700. **Contact:** Sue Metzner, Director Human Resources. **E-mail address:** resumes@loyno.edu. **World Wide Web address:** http://www.loyno.edu. **Description:** A large Catholic University that offers graduate and undergraduate programs and is composed of a College of Arts and Sciences, Business Administration, and Music, as well as a School of Law, the Loyola Institute for Ministry, and the Loyola Intensive English Program. The school has a total enrollment of 5,500 students, including 3,500 undergraduates. It was founded by a group of Jesuits in 1912. **NOTE:** Job seekers may apply in person at 2020 Calhoun Street, Mercy Hall, Room 102. **Positions advertised include:** Law Faculty Secretary; Web Designer; Engineer; Police Officer; Substitute – Children's Center; Temporary Preschool Teacher; Temporary Processing/Binding Assistant; Assistant Professor – Various Departments; Outreach Librarian; Catalog Librarian; **Special programs:** Training; Tuition Remission Program. **Office hours:** Monday – Friday, 8:30 a.m. – 4:45 p.m. **President:** Reverend William J. Byron, S.J.

LUDWIG BUILDING SYSTEMS
P.O. Box 23134, Harahan LA 70183. 504/733-6260. **Physical address:** 521 Timesaver Avenue, Harahan LA 70123. **Fax:** 504/733-7458. **Contact:** Human Resources. **Description:** Engaged in the manufacture and construction of commercial, retail, and industrial steel buildings. **Corporate headquarters location:** This location. **Operations at this facility include:** Administration; Manufacturing; Sales.

McDERMOTT INTERNATIONAL INC.
P.O. Box 60035, Mail Station 2228, New Orleans LA 70160. 504/587-4411. **Fax:** 504/587-6153. **Physical address:** 1450 Poydras Street, New Orleans LA 70112. **Contact:** Recruiting Manager. **E-mail address:** jobopps@mcdermott.com. **World Wide Web address:** http://www.mcdermott.com. **Description:** Designs, constructs, and installs specialized offshore fixed platforms and marine pipelines for the oil and gas industry; operates a shipyard; performs ship maintenance; and engineers and constructs oil, gas, and petrochemical processing plants. Babcock & Wilcox (also at this location) is a supplier of steam generating systems and associated equipment such as boiler cleaning systems. **Positions advertised include:** Director – Global Procurement and Contract Administration. **Corporate headquarters location:** This location. **Other area locations:** Morgan City LA. **Other U.S. locations:** Rocky Flats CO; Boise ID; Houston TX; West Point MS; Lynchburg VA; Alliance OH; Barberton OH; Lancaster OH; Miamisburg OH. **International locations:** Worldwide. **Subsidiaries include:** J. Ray McDermott, S.A.; The Babcock & Wilcox Company; McDermott Technology, Incorporated; BWX Technologies, Incorporated. **Listed on:** New York Stock Exchange. **Stock exchange symbol:** MDR. **CEO/Chairman:** Bruce W. Wilkinson. **Number of employees worldwide:** 25,000.

McILHENNY COMPANY
Highway 329, Avery Island LA 70513. 337/365-8173. **Contact:** Human Resources. **World Wide Web address:** http://www.tabasco.com. **Description:** Manufactures Tabasco brand pepper sauces. **Corporate headquarters location:** This location. **Other area locations:** New Orleans; Breaux Bridge; New Iberia. **Other U.S. locations:** Nationwide. **International locations:** Brokers/distributors exist worldwide. **Operations at this facility include:** Production; Tours. **President/CEO:** Paul C.P. McIlhenny. **Sales/revenues:** Approximately $150 million.

MIDSOUTH BANCORP, INC.
P.O. Box 3745, Lafayette LA 70502. 337/237-8343. **Physical address:** 102 Versailles Boulevard, Lafayette LA 70501. **Toll-free phone:** 800/213-BANK. **Fax:** 337/291-4989. **Recorded jobline:** 337/267-4310. **Contact:** Personnel. **E-mail address:** jobs@midsouthbank.com. **World Wide Web address:** http://www.midsouthbank.com. **Description:** A one-bank holding company with assets of $97.7 million. The company offers complete banking services to commercial and retail customers through its wholly-owned subsidiary, MidSouth National Bank. The bank has nineteen offices spanning the state. Founded in 1985. **Positions advertised include:** Retail Store Manager; Retail Operations Manager; Part-time Counter; Full-time Counter; File Clerk; Team Leader; Full-time; Executive Administrative Assistant; Electronic Banking Associate; Commercial Loan Assistant; Mortgage Originator. **Office hours:** Monday – Thursday, 9:00 a.m. – 4:00 p.m., Friday, 9:00 a.m. – 6:00 p.m. **Listed on:** American Stock Exchange. **Stock exchange symbol:** MSL. **President:** C.R. Rusty Cloutier. **Sales/revenues:** Approximately $1 million.

MURPHY EXPLORATION AND PRODUCTION COMPANY
131 South Robertson Street, New Orleans LA 70112. 504/561-2811. **Contact:** Personnel. **World Wide Web address:** http://www.murphyoilcorp.com. **Description:** Engaged in crude oil and natural gas exploration and production. **NOTE:** Online applications are available. **Positions advertised include:** Store Manager. **Special Programs:** Training. **Corporate headquarters location:** This location. **Parent Company:** Murphy Oil Corporation. **Listed on:** New York Stock Exchange. **Stock exchange symbol:** MUR. **President:** Claiborne P. Deming. **Number of employees worldwide:** Over 4,000.

NEW ORLEANS COLD STORAGE & WAREHOUSE COMPANY
P.O. Box 26308, New Orleans LA 70186. 504/944-4400. **Physical address:** 3401 Alvar Street, New Orleans LA 70126. **Toll-free phone:** 800/782-2653. **Fax:** 504/944-8539. **Contact:** Human Resources. **E-mail address:** info@nocs.com. **World Wide Web address:** http://www.nocs.com. **Description:** Through its Warehousing Division, the company offers refrigerated storage and distribution, and through its Transport Division, conveys a wide variety of temperature-sensitive products to destinations throughout the U.S. **Corporate headquarters location:** This location. **Other U.S. locations:** Charleston SC; Houston TX. **Operations at this facility include:** Administration; Service.

OAKDALE COMMUNITY HOSPITAL
P.O. Box 629, Oakdale LA 71463-0629. 318/335-3700. **Physical address:** 130 North Hospital Drive, Oakdale LA 71463. **Fax:** 318/215-3024. **Contact:** Human Resources Department. **World Wide Web address:** http://www.oakdalecommunityhospital.com. **Description:** A community hospital that provides a wide array of both inpatient and outpatient services. **NOTE:** Entry-level positions and second and third shifts are offered. Contact the Human Resources Department at 318/215-3256. For physician opportunities, contact CEO Kevin Fowler at 318/335-3700. **Positions advertised include:** Medical Technologist; LPN; Patient Care Assistant; RN – Various Departments. **Special programs:** Summer Jobs. **Office hours:** Monday - Friday, 8:00 a.m. - 5:00 p.m. **CEO:** Kevin Fowler. **Number of employees at this location:** 200.

OCHSNER CLINIC
9001 Summa Avenue, Baton Rouge LA 70809. 225/761-5200. **Toll-free phone:** 800/874-8984. **Contact:** Human Resources. **World Wide Web address:** http://www.ochsner.org. **Description:** An integrated health care system that is a regional affiliate of Ochsner Clinic Foundation in New Orleans and provides outpatient services. A medical staff of 70 practices in over 25 specialties at the main location and at one neighborhood clinic. **NOTE:** Online applications are available. For physician positions, call 800/488-2240, fax 225/761-5441, or e-mail kwascom@ochsner.org. **Positions advertised include:** File Clerk – Radiology; Appointment Coordinator; Audit Entry Specialist; Patient Registration Associate; Medical Assistant – Various Departments; EEG Tech; RN Clinical Lead; RN – Practitioner; Physician Assistant. **Operations at this facility include:** Health care; Research; Education. **Number of employees at this location:** Over 430.

OCHSNER CLINIC
1514 Jefferson Highway, New Orleans LA 70121. 504/842-4000. **Toll-free phone:** 800/874-8984. **Contact:** Human Resources. **World Wide Web address:** http://www.ochsner.org. **Description:** Operates satellite clinics throughout Louisiana. Each clinic provides family medical services and offers laboratory and X-ray services for routine care. Founded in 1942. **NOTE:** Online applications are available. For physician positions, call 800/488-2240, fax 225/761-5441, or e-mail kwascom@ochsner.org. **Positions advertised include:** Unit Secretary; Administrative Secretary; Patient Services Associate; HR Assistant; Guest Services Representative; Cancer Registrar; Receiving Clerk; Patient Services Float Associate – Outpatient Patient Registration; Cashier; Assistant Buyer; Department Secretary; OR Assistant; Physical Therapist; Radiology Tech; Surgical Technician; Laboratory Supervisor; Area Support Associate; Sonographer; Special Imaging Tech; LPM – Various Departments; RN – Various Departments. **Corporate headquarters location:** This location. **Number of employees nationwide:** 1,675.

ALTON OCHSNER MEDICAL FOUNDATION
1516 Jefferson Highway, Jefferson LA 70121. 504/842-3000. **Fax:** 504/842-5856. **Contact:** Human Resources. **World Wide Web address:** http://www.ochsner.org. **Description:** A nonprofit organization offering patient care, medical education, and clinical research activities. The foundation conducts a postgraduate medical education program, with approximately 250 residents and fellows in 24 training programs. It offers 10 professional education programs in its School of Allied Health Sciences. The foundation's patient care activities are delivered in the 532-bed Ochsner Foundation Hospital, which admits 18,000 patients annually. The research activities of the foundation are carried out in the Richard W. Freeman Research Institute. Founded in 1944. **Operations at this facility include:** Administration; Research and Development. **Listed on:** Privately held. **Number of employees at this location:** 6,000.

OFFSHORE LOGISTICS, INC.
4605 Industrial Drive, New Iberia LA 70563. 337/365-6771. **Fax:** 337/365-6039. **Contact:** Human Resources. **E-mail address:** intlhr@olog.com. **World Wide Web address:** http://www.olog.com. **Description:** Through its subsidiaries, Offshore Logistics, Incorporated is one of the leading suppliers of helicopter transportation services to oil and gas production companies. **Positions advertised include:** Accountant; Distribution Manager; Technical Help Desk Support; Administrative Assistant; Helicopter Pilot; Technical Services Representative. **Corporate headquarters location:** This location. **Other U.S. locations:** AK. **International locations:** England. **Subsidiaries include:** Air Logistics, Air Logistics of Alaska, and Air Logistics International make up one of the world's largest helicopter operators providing customers with a complete aviation infrastructure in both the Gulf of Mexico and Alaska. From the company's operating bases along the Gulf Coast and in Alaska, the company transports personnel and high-priority equipment needed to find, produce, and transport oil and gas. Internationally, Offshore Logistics works through joint ventures and affiliations to supply aircraft and technical expertise in many of the oil and gas producing areas of the world. Grasso Production Management (GPM) provides personnel, contract production and engineering services, transportation, and medical services to oil and gas customers both onshore and offshore. Cathodic Protection Services (CPS) sells, designs, constructs, installs, and monitors corrosion protection systems for the domestic and international oil and gas industry, oil and gas pipelines, and municipalities. **Listed on:** New York Stock Exchange. **Stock exchange symbol:** OLG. **President/CEO:** George M. Small. **Sales/revenues:** $420 million. **Number of employees worldwide:** 3,267.

OUR LADY OF THE LAKE REGIONAL MEDICAL CENTER
5000 Hennessy Boulevard, Baton Rouge LA 70808. 225/765-6565. **Recorded jobline:** 225/765-1004. **Contact:** Human Resources. **World Wide Web address:** http://www.ololrmc.com. **Description:** Established by the Franciscan Missionaries of Our Lady, Our Lady of the Lake is a major medical center located on a 100-acre campus. The hospital has 852 beds and a medical staff with 700 physicians. Services range from emergency room to home health and outpatient programs, and include intermediate care such as skilled nursing. Founded in 1923. **NOTE:** To contact the Human Resources Department directly, call 225/765-8803, or send resume to 5311 Dijon, Baton Rouge LA 70808. **Positions advertised include:** Assistant Physician Practice Manager; Blood Donor Tech; Child Life Specialist; Director Pastoral Care; Food Service Worker; LPN – Various Departments; Medical Technologist – Various Departments; Nurse Supervisor – Various Departments; Nurse Assistant – Various Departments; Physical Therapist; Registered Nurse – Various Departments; Staff Pharmacist. **Office hours:** Monday – Friday, 8:00 a.m. – 5:00 p.m. **CEO:** Robert C. Davidge. **Number of employees at this location:** 3,500.

PELLERIN MILNOR CORPORATION
P.O. Box 400, Kenner LA 70063-0400. 504/467-9591. **Physical address:** 700 Jackson Street, Kenner LA 70062. **Contact:** Human Resources Director. **NOTE:** Human Resources phone is 504/712-7702. **World Wide Web address:** http://www.milnor.com. **Description:** An international manufacturer of industrial and commercial laundry machinery including washers, dryers, and presses. Founded in 1947. **Special programs:** Internships. **Corporate headquarters location:** This location. **Operations at this facility include:** Administration; Manufacturing; Research and Development; Sales; Service.

PETROLEUM HELICOPTERS, INC.
P.O. Box 90808, Lafayette LA 70509. 337/235-2452. **Physical address:** 2001 SE Evangeline Thruway, Lafayette LA 70508. **Fax:** 337/232-6537. **Contact:** Richard Rovinelli, Director of Human Resources. **E-mail address:** rrovinelli@phihelico.com. **World Wide Web address:** http://www.phihelico.com. **Description:** Provides a full range of services to businesses engaged in the domestic oil and gas industry, aeronautical services, and in the international marketplace. The company is primarily engaged in providing helicopter transportation and related services. The predominant portion of its revenue is derived from transporting offshore oil and gas production and drilling workers on a worldwide basis. The company also performs helicopter transportation services for a variety of hospital and medical programs and provides aircraft maintenance to outside parties. PHI's helicopter fleet consists of 266 aircraft, which operate from 34 domestic and six foreign bases. Founded in 1949. **NOTE:** Applicants may e-mail resumes to resumes@phihelico.com. **Positions advertised include:** Maintenance Technician; Pilot. **Special programs:** Training. **Corporate headquarters location:** This location. **Operations at this facility include:** Overhaul; Maintenance. **Listed on:** NASDAQ. **Stock exchange symbol:** PHELK. **President/CEO:** Lance F. Bospflug. **Sales/revenues:** Approximately $300 million. **Number of employees nationwide:** 1,778.

PICCADILLY CAFETERIAS, INC.
P.O. Box 2467, Baton Rouge LA 70821-2467. 225/293-9440. **Physical address:** 3232 Sherwood Forest Boulevard, Baton Rouge LA 70816. **Toll-free phone:** 800/552-7422. **Contact:** Director of Management Training. **World Wide Web address:** http://www.piccadilly.com. **Description:** Operates over 150 restaurants located in 14 Sunbelt states from coast to coast. Founded in 1944. **NOTE:** Please visit website for online application form. **Special programs:** Training. **Corporate headquarters location:** This location. **Other U.S. locations:** Nationwide. **Office hours:** Monday - Friday, 8:00 a.m. – 4:30 p.m. **Number of employees nationwide:** Over 6,000.

PRE-ENGINEERING SOFTWARE CORPORATION
5800 One Perkins Place Drive, Suite 10-D, Baton Rouge LA 70808. 225/769-3728. **Fax:** 225/769-3661. **Contact:** Human Resources. **E-mail address:** mail@pre-engineering.com. **World Wide Web address:** http://www.pre-engineering.com. **Description:** Develops and publishes software programs and other teaching tools used to reinforce students' math and science skills while encouraging an interest in the engineering field.

QUEST DIAGNOSTICS
4648 South Interstate 10 Service Road West, Metairie LA 70001. 504/889-2307. **Fax:** 504/889-2678. **Contact:** Kara E. Hoerner, Human Resources. **E-mail address:** kara.e.hoerner@questdiagnostics.com. **World Wide Web address:** http://www.questdiagnostics.com. **NOTE:** Please visit website to register, search for jobs, and apply online. **Description:** Provides a broad range of clinical laboratory services to health care clients such as physicians, hospitals, clinics, dialysis centers, pharmaceutical companies, and corporations. The company offers and performs tests on blood, urine, and other bodily fluids and tissues to provide information for health and well-being. **NOTE:** Online applications are available. **Positions advertised include:** Account Manager; Account Sales Representative; Cytotechnologist; Phlebotomy Services Representative; Specimen Processor; Physician Client Service Provider; Distributor. **Corporate headquarters location:** Teterboro NJ. **Other U.S. locations:** Nationwide. **Listed on:** New York Stock Exchange. **Stock exchange symbol:** DGX. **CEO/Chairman:** Kenneth Freeman. **Sales/revenues:** $4.11 billion. **Number of employees nationwide:** 27,000.

RANDA CORPORATION
WEMCO
200 James Drive East, Saint Rose LA 70087. 504/712-7100. **Toll-free phone:** 800/827-8437. **Fax:** 504/712-7101. **Contact:** William T. Rogers, Vice President of Human Resources. **E-mail address:** rogerst@randacorp.com. **World Wide Web address:** http://www.randacorp.com. **Description:** A manufacturer and distributor of neckwear for men and boys. Founded in 1935. **Other U.S. locations:** New York NY; Chicago IL; Chalfont PA. **International locations:** Shanghai, China; Glenrothes, Scotland; Como, Italy; London, U.K.; Mississauga, Ontario, Canada; Australia. **Subsidiaries include:** WEMCO, Incorporated; Humphreys Accessories, L.L.C.; MCG Retail; Countess Mara; Randa Canada, Limited; Randa International, s.p.a.; Woodstock Neckwear, Limited; Randa Shanghai, Limited. **Operations at this facility include:** This location is the company's main production and distribution center for the U.S. and South America. **President/CEO:** Jeffrey Spiegel. **Number of employees worldwide:** Over 1,000.

REGIONS BANK
P.O. Box 11240, New Iberia LA 70562-1240. 337/365-6761. **Physical address:** 800 South Lewis Street, New Iberia LA. **Contact:** Human Resources. **World Wide Web address:** http://www.regions.com. **Description:** A full-service bank that operates from over 680 offices throughout the southern U.S. **Positions advertised include:** Commercial Loan Officer; Residential Area Manager; Teller; Corporate Trust Officer. **Special programs:** Training; Tuition Reimbursement Program; Professional Development Program. **Corporate headquarters location:** This location. **Other U.S. locations:** AL; AR; FL; GA; KY; NC; SC; TN; TX. **Parent company:** Regions Financial Corporation. **Listed on:** New York Stock Exchange. **Stock exchange symbol:** RF. **President/CEO:** Carl E. Jones, Junior. **Sales/revenues:** $47.9 billion. **Number of employees nationwide:** Approximately 16,000.

RICHLAND PARISH HOSPITAL
407 Cincinnati Street, Delhi LA 71232. 318/878-5171. **Contact:** Personnel Director. **Description:** A nonprofit hospital with affiliated home care, cardiac rehabilitation programs, KidMed children's services, and outpatient psychiatric care for the elderly. **NOTE:** To contact Personnel directly, call 318/878-6327. **Special programs:** Internships. **Administrator:** Michael Carroll. **Number of employees at this location:** 200.

SCP POOL CORPORATION
109 Northpark Boulevard, 4th Floor, Covington LA 70433. 985/892-5521. **Contact:** Human Resources. **E-mail address:** jobs@scppool.com. **World Wide Web address:** http://www.scppool.com. **Description:** Operates over 100 retail locations in the United States and Europe that offer pool equipment and pool maintenance supplies. Founded in 1980. **Positions advertised include:** Accounts Receivable Manager; Branch Manager; CDL Driver; Counter Sales Person; Customer Service Representative; Office Manager; Operations Manager; Outside Sales; Purchaser; Receptionist; Warehouse Workers; Warehouse Manager; Corporate Office Workers. **Special programs:** Educational Reimbursement Program. **Corporate headquarters location:** This location. **Other U.S. locations:** Nationwide. **Listed on:** NASDAQ. **Stock exchange symbol:** POOL. **President/CEO:** Manual J. Perez de la Mesa. **Sales/revenues:** More than $100 million. **Number of employees nationwide:** Over 2,300.

ST. FRANCIS COMMUNITY HEALTH CENTER
920 Oliver Road, Monroe LA 71201. 318/327-6200. **Contact:** Human Resources. **World Wide Web address:** http://www.stfran.com. **Description:** A community-based health center that is part of the St. Francis network of healthcare providers. St. Francis Community Health Center offers a variety of services and programs, including the Shots for Tots immunization program; women's health; OccuMed, an industrial medicine program; outpatient rehabilitation; preoperative strengthening, mobility adaptations, and other services; cardiac rehabilitation; pulmonary rehabilitation; laboratory services; radiology and mammography; pharmacy; pharmacy home services; diagnostic testing; community health education; counseling; speech therapy; and enterostomal therapy. **NOTE:** Human Resources phone is 318/327-4148. Please visit website to search for jobs by location and to apply online. **Positions advertised include:** Administrative Technician; Blood Bank Supervisor; Certified Nursing Assistant – Various Departments; Coding Coordinator; Director – Health Information; ER Technician; Housekeeper; Information Clerk; LPN – Various Departments; Pharmacist; Physical Therapy Assistant – Various Departments; Radiologic Technologist; Registered Nurse – Various Departments; Security Officer; Special Officer; Surgical Tech. **Special programs:** Tuition Reimbursement Program; Continuing Education Program.

ST. FRANCIS MEDICAL CENTER
309 Jackson Street, Monroe LA 71201. 318/327-40004826. **Fax:** 318/327-4870. **Recorded jobline:** 318/327-4562. **Contact:** Human Resources. **World Wide Web address:** http://www.stfran.com. **Description:** A modern, 450-bed, private hospital sponsored by the Franciscan Missionaries of Our Lady. St. Francis offers a full range of medical and surgical specialties including cardiology; neuroscience; oncology; physical medicine; critical care for infants, children, and adults; obstetrics; surgery; general medicine; skilled care; rehabilitation; and outpatient care. St. Francis's medical staff is composed of family practitioners and specialists. The medical center is fully accredited by the Joint Commission on Accreditation of Healthcare Organizations. Founded in 1913. **NOTE:** Human Resources phone is 318/327-4148. Please visit website to search for jobs by location and to apply online. **Positions advertised include:** Administrative Technician; Blood Bank Supervisor; Certified Nursing Assistant – Various Departments; Coding Coordinator; Director – Health Information; ER Technician; Housekeeper; Information Clerk; LPN – Various Departments; Pharmacist; Physical Therapy Assistant – Various Departments; Radiologic Technologist; Registered Nurse – Various Departments; Security Officer; Special Officer; Surgical Tech. **Number of employees at this location:** 1,700.

SEACOR MARINE INC.
P.O. Box 2291, Morgan City LA 70381. 985/385-3475. **Physical address:** 5005 Railroad Avenue, Morgan City LA 70380. **Fax:** 985/385-1130. **Contact:** Personnel. **E-mail address:** domestic@seacormarine.com. **World Wide Web address:** http://www.seacormarine.com. **Description:** Operates a diversified fleet of marine vessels primarily dedicated to supporting offshore oil and gas exploration and development in the Gulf of Mexico, the North Sea, and offshore West Africa. The company's vessels provide services for exploration, development, and production activities, such as towing and anchor handling of mobile rigs, delivery of cargo and supplies to offshore rigs and platforms, transportation for offshore construction and maintenance work, and standby safety support. SEACOR Marine also furnishes vessels for special projects, such as seismic mapping, well stimulation, freight hauling, and environmental clean-up and emergency response. **Positions advertised include:** Captain; Mate; Licensed Engineer; Able Seaman; QMED/Oiler; Ordinary Seaman; Wiper; First Captain; Second Captain; Unlicensed Engineer; Deckhand. **Corporate headquarters location:** Houston TX. **Other U.S. locations:** New York NY. **International locations:** Worldwide. **Listed on:** New York Stock Exchange. **Stock**

exchange symbol: CKH. **President/CEO:** Charles Fabrikant. **Number of employees worldwide:** 3,100.

SHAW ENVIRONMENTAL & INFRASTRUCTURE, INC.
4171 Essen Lane, Baton Rouge LA 70809. 225/932-2500. **Fax:** 225/932-2661. **Contact:** Human Resources. **E-mail address:** jobssouth@shawgrp.com. **World Wide Web address:** http://www.theitgroup.com. **Description:** Delivers a full range of environmental management services through an integrated approach for total turnkey solutions. The company applies engineering, analytical, remediation, and pollution control expertise to meet the environmental needs of its clients, from site assessment to remediation. **NOTE:** Resumes may be submitted online as specified on the company Website, or via mail. **Positions advertised include:** Engineering Technician; Project Manager; Senior Assistant Engineer; Draftsperson; Engineer; Field Technician; Senior Consultant; Computer Technician. **Other U.S. locations:** Nationwide. **Subsidiaries:** The IT Group; Stone & Webster, Incorporated. **Parent company:** The Shaw Group Incorporated. **Listed on:** New York Stock Exchange. **Stock exchange symbol:** SGR. **President/CEO:** J.M. Bernard, Junior. **Number of employees worldwide:** 6,000.

SHELL OFFSHORE, INC.
P.O. Box 61933, New Orleans LA 70161-1933. 504/728-6161. **Physical address:** 701 Poydras Street, New Orleans LA 70139. **Contact:** Human Resources. **E-mail address:** recruitment@shell.com. **World Wide Web address:** http://www.shellus.com. **Description:** An oil and gas exploration and production company operating principally in the Gulf of Mexico, Michigan, and South Texas. **Special programs:** Internships. **Corporate headquarters location:** Houston TX. **Subsidiaries include:** Aera Energy, L.L.C. **Parent company:** Shell Oil Company. **Operations at this facility include:** Divisional Headquarters. **President/CEO:** Raoul Restucci. **Number of employees worldwide:** 2,000.

SIZELER PROPERTY INVESTORS, INC.
2542 Williams Boulevard, Kenner LA 70062. 504/471-6200. **Fax:** 504/471-6291. **Contact:** Human Resources. **World Wide Web address:** http://www.sizeler.net. **Description:** A self-administered equity real estate investment trust that invests in shopping center and apartment properties in the southern United States. The company's investment portfolio includes interests in three enclosed regional shopping malls, two shopping centers, 11 community shopping centers, and 12 apartment complexes. Fifteen of the company's properties are located in Louisiana, eight in Florida, four in Alabama, and one in Texas. **Listed on:** New York Stock Exchange. **Stock exchange symbol:** SIZ. **CEO:** Sidney W. Lassen. **Sales/revenues:** $52.8 million.

SOUTHEAST FOODS
P.O. Box 2230, Monroe LA 71207. 318/388-1884. **Physical address:** 1001 North 11th Street, Monroe LA 71207-2230. **Fax:** 318/322-0110. **Contact:** Austin White, Controller. Human Resources. **Description:** Owns and operates a franchised food store chain. **Corporate headquarters location:** This location. **Operations at this facility include:** This location houses the administrative offices for the grocery store chain located in Louisiana, Arkansas, and Mississippi. **CEO:** Jim Creel. **Number of employees at this location:** 30. **Number of employees nationwide:** 750.

SOUTHEASTERN LOUISIANA UNIVERSITY
SLU 10799, Hammond LA 70402. 985/549-2001. **Recorded jobline:** 985/549-5065. **Contact:** Jessie R. Roberts, Human Resources Director. **E-mail address:** jroberts@selu.edu. **World Wide Web address:** http://www.selu.edu. **Description:** A state university offering a variety of academic programs. Founded in 1925. **Positions advertised include:** University Police Department Secretary; Police Radio Dispatcher; Associate Professor; Community Music School Director; Visual Arts Gallery Director; Director of Athletic Training Program; Dean; College of Arts and Sciences Department Head; Department of Foreign Language and Literature Department Head; Technical Director. **NOTE:** For faculty positions, do not e-mail or send resumes to the Human Resources Office. Contact the appropriate search committee. **Positions advertised include:** Parking Lot Attendant; Police Officer; Secretary – Various Departments; Word Processor Operator; Assistant/Associate Professor – Various Departments; Department Head – Various Departments; Executive Assistant; Production Specialist; Research Associate; Student Advisor. **Office hours:** Monday – Friday, 7:45 a.m. – 4:30 p.m. **Corporate headquarters location:** This location. **Operations at this facility include:** Administration; Service. **President:** Randy Moffat. **Number of employees at this location:** 1,500.

STEWART ENTERPRISES, INC.
110 Veterans Memorial Boulevard, Metairie LA 70005. 504/837-5880. **Toll-free phone:** 800/535-6017. **Contact:** Human Resources. **E-mail address:** hrinfo@stei.com. **World Wide Web address:** http://www.stewartenterprises.com. **Description:** A funeral service provider. Through its subsidiaries, the company operates 134 funeral homes and 95 cemeteries in 16 states, as well as abroad. **Positions advertised include:** Funeral Director; Assistant Funeral Director; Funeral Home Administrator; Embalmer; Housekeeper; Florist; Driver; Attendant; Receptionist; Sales Representative; Manager; Cemetery Administrator; Landscaper; Groundskeeper; Mechanic; Accounts Payable; Treasurer. **NOTE:** Please contact facility to learn of open positions. **Special programs:** Educational Assistance Program; Internships. **Corporate headquarters location:** This location. **Other U.S. locations:** Nationwide. **International locations:** Puerto Rico; Australia; New Zealand; Canada; Spain; Belgium; the Netherlands; Argentina; France. **Operations at this facility include:** Administration; Sales; Marketing. **Listed on:** NASDAQ. **Stock exchange symbol:** STEI. **President/CEO:** William E. Rowe. **Sales/revenues:** $76 million. **Number of employees worldwide:** 6,500.

TENMAST SOFTWARE
1503 Goodwin Road, Suite 100, Ruston LA 71270. 318/251-2392. **Fax:** 318/251-2205. **Contact:** Human Resources. **World Wide Web address:** http://www.tenmast.com. **Description:** Develops PC-HAP housing management software and provides network services for its clients. **NOTE:** Entry-level positions are offered. **Corporate headquarters location:** Lexington KY. **Listed on:** Privately held. **President:** James C. Mauch. **Sales/revenues:** Approximately $5 million.

THE TIMES-PICAYUNE
3800 Howard Avenue, New Orleans LA 70125-1429. 504/826-3270. **Recorded jobline:** 504/826-3270. **Contact:** Personnel. **World Wide Web address:** http://www.timespicayune.com. **Description:** Publishes a daily newspaper with circulation exceeding 275,000. **NOTE:** Jobs are posted in lobby of building at 3800 Howard Avenue, and are advertised in the Times-Picayune paper. Applications kept on file for three months. You may write to have an application sent to you if you live more than 100 miles from New Orleans. **Office hours:** Monday – Friday, 7:30 a.m. – 5:00 p.m. **Other area locations:** Covington LA; Metairie LA; La Place LA; Slidell LA; Chalmette LA; Gretna LA. **Parent company:** Newhouse Newspaper Group.

TOURO INFIRMARY
1401 Foucher Street, New Orleans LA 70115. 504/897-7011. **Fax:** 504/897-8719. **Recorded jobline:** 504/897-8222. **Contact:** Lynne Jones, Human Resources Recruiter. **E-mail address:** resumes@touro.com. **World Wide Web address:** http://www.touro.com. **Description:** A nonprofit 350-bed hospital composed of centers for physical medicine and rehabilitation, obstetrics and gynecology, mental health services, and cancer care and treatment. Founded in 1852. **NOTE:** Second and third shifts are offered. **Company slogan:** We treat everyone like family. **Positions advertised include:** Registered Nurse – Various Departments; LPN – Various Departments; MRI/CT Tech; Patient Care Supervisor; Reimbursement Log Clerk; Home Health Speech Therapist; Exercise Leader; General Mechanic; Temporary Courier; Pathology Clerk; Manager of Reimbursement; Emergency Department Tech; Neuro Trauma Unit Certified Nursing Assistant; Food Service Worker; Evening Housekeeper; Application Analyst; Trayline Supervisor; Health Record Analyst. **Special programs:** Internships. **Office hours:** Monday – Friday, 8:30 a.m. – 4:00 p.m. **President/CEO:** Gary M. Stein. **Number of employees at this location:** 1,400.

TUCKER AND ASSOCIATES INC.
616 Girod Street, Suite 300, New Orleans LA 70130-3738. 504/522-4627. **Contact:** Human Resources. **Description:** Provides technical support for companies that are changing their computer networks or setting up a new network. The firm also provides management consulting services.

TULANE UNIVERSITY
Uptown Square, 200 Broadway, Suite 120, New Orleans LA 70118-5680. 504/865-5280. **Fax:** 504/865-6727. **Recorded jobline:** 504/865-5627. **Contact:** Human Resources – Judy Payne or Cassandra Manning. **E-mail address:** jpayne@tulane.edu or cmanning@tulane.edu. **World Wide Web address:** http://www2.tulane.edu. **Description:** A university comprised of several academic schools including a business school. **Positions advertised include:** Account Analyst; Administrative Assistant; Administrative Secretary – Various Departments; Lab Assistant; Collector; Project Assistant; Carpenter; Custodian; Grounds Worker; Painter; Plumber, Licensed; Police Officer; Teacher – Child Care Center; Animal Care Tech; Clinical Protocol Technician; Lab Assistant – Various Departments; Laboratory Research Technician – Various Departments; Licensed Practical Nurse; Medical Research Specialist – Various Departments; Veterinary Technician; Legal Secretary; Project Assistant; Library Clerk; Senior Computer Operator; Senior Accountant. **NOTE:** Unsolicited resumes are not accepted. For further information about job openings, contact Cassandra Manning at 865-5280 for positions at the Uptown Campus or Judy Payne at 588-5425 for the Health Sciences Center. **Office hours:** Monday – Friday, 8:30 a.m. – 4:00 p.m. **President:** Scott S. Cowen. **Number of employees at this location:** Over 5,000.

TULANE UNIVERSITY SCHOOL OF MEDICINE
1430 Tulane Avenue, EP-13, New Orleans LA 70112. 504/582-7800. **Recorded jobline:** 504/865-5627. **Contact:** Barbara Brauner, Personnel Director. **World Wide Web address:** http://www.mcl.tulane.edu. **Description:** Medical school for the New Orleans university. **Positions advertised include:** Animal Care Tech; Clinical Protocol Technician; Lab Assistant – Various Departments; Laboratory Research Technician – Various Departments; Licensed Practical Nurse; Medical Research Specialist – Various Departments; Veterinary Technician. **NOTE:** Mail resumes to 127 Elk Place, 4th Floor, New Orleans LA 70112 or fax to 504/865-5627. Human Resources can be contacted directly by calling 504/588-5425. **Number of employees at this location:** Approximately 2,000.

TURNER INDUSTRIES
P.O. Box 2750, Baton Rouge LA 70821. 225/922-5050. **Physical address:** 8687 United Plaza Boulevard, Baton Rouge LA 70809. **Toll-free phone:** 800/288-6503. **Fax:** 225/922-5055. **Contact:** Personnel. **World Wide Web address:** http://www.turner-industries.com. **NOTE:** Please visit website to fill out profile data form. **Description:** An industrial services provider that offers industrial construction, contract maintenance, and outsourcing to customers in the oil refinement, petrochemical, power generation, and pulp and paper industries. Turner Industries also provides staffing services and maintenance and materials management. **Corporate headquarters location:** This location. **Subsidiaries include:** Harmony, L.L.C.; International Maintenance Company, L.L.C.; International Piping Systems, L.L.C.; Nichols Construction Company, L.L.C.; Scafco, L.L.C; Specialized Welding Services; Turner Industrial Technical, L.L.C.; Turner International Piping Systems, Incorporated; Turner Staffing, Limited. **President:** Thomas H. Turner. **Sales/revenues:** $800 million. **Number of employees nationwide:** 12,000. **Number of employees worldwide:** Over 25,000.

URS CORPORATION
600 Carondelet Street, New Orleans LA 70130-3587. 504/586-8111. **Fax:** 504/522-0554. **Contact:** Human Resources. **E-mail address:** recruiter@urscorp.com. **World Wide Web address:** http://www.urscorp.com. **Description:** A fully-integrated engineering and architectural organization that specializes in the project management, design, and construction management of industrial, private, and government facilities. URS Corporation also provides process and environmental engineering, architectural design, and total support services. **NOTE:** Please visit website to apply online; this is the preferred method of application and resume submission. **Positions advertised include:** CADD Supervisor; Electrical Engineer; Field Technician Supervisor; Mechanical Designer; Principal Civil/Chemical Engineer; Project Manager; Project Mechanical Engineer; Records Clerk; Senior Chemical Engineer; Senior Civil Engineer; Senior Cost/Schedule Specialist; Senior Electrical Engineer. **Special programs:** Tuition Reimbursement Program; Professional Development Program; Internships. **Corporate headquarters location:** San Francisco CA. **Other area locations:** Baton Rouge LA; Lake Charles LA; Metairie LA; Shreveport LA. **Other U.S. locations:** Nationwide. **International locations:** Worldwide. **Number of employees at this location:** 400. **Listed on:** New York Stock Exchange. **Stock exchange symbol:** URS. **President/CEO/Chairman:** Martin M. Koffel. **Sales/revenues:** $2.43 billion. **Number of employees nationwide:** 600. **Number of employees worldwide:** 25,000.

UNIVERSITY OF LOUISIANA
P.O. Box 40196, Lafayette LA 70504. 337/482-6242. **Physical address:** 104 University Circle, Lafayette LA 70504. **Contact:** Office of Personnel Services. **E-mail address:** gbj3997@louisiana.edu. **World Wide Web address:** http://www.louisiana.edu. **Description:** A university that offers 108 majors in 11 colleges and schools and provides both undergraduate and graduate programs of study. **Positions advertised include:** Assistant Professor – Various Departments; Associate Professor – Various Departments; Art/Design Materials Curator; Endowed Chair; Coordinator; Instructor; Polymer Lab Technician; Research Assistant; Field Agent; Clinical Veterinarian; Software Engineer; Staff Physician; Program Advisor; Research Scientist. **NOTE:** For faculty positions, contact appropriate search committee member. **President:** Dr. Ray Authement. **Number of employees at this location:** 1,200.

UNIVERSITY OF NEW ORLEANS
2000 Lakeshore Drive, New Orleans LA 70148. 504/280-6259. **Toll-free phone:** 888/514-4275. **Fax:** 504/280-6390. **Contact:** Human Resources. **World Wide Web address:** http://www.uno.edu. **Description:** A university with an enrollment of approximately 16,000 students, that offers both graduate and undergraduate programs of study. **Special programs:** Training and Development Program. **Other area locations:** Slidell LA. **Chancellor:** Greg O'Brien.

VALENTINE PAPER COMPANY
139 Joe Brown Road, Lockport LA 70374. 985/532-3313. **Fax:** 985/5322969. **World Wide Web address:** http://www.valentinepaper.com. **Contact:** Personnel. **Description:** A paper mill. The company's products include writing paper, offset paper, and envelopes. **Corporate headquarters location:** This location.

WELLS FARGO BANK
1701 Old Minden Road, Suite 21, Bossier City LA 71111. 318/742-0141. **Contact:** Human Resources. **World Wide Web address:** http://www.wellsfargo.com. **NOTE:** Please visit website to search for jobs and apply online. **Description:** A diversified financial institution with over $234 billion in assets. Wells Fargo serves over 17 million customers through 5,300 independent locations worldwide. The company also maintains several stand-alone ATMs and branches within other retail outlets. Services include community banking, credit and debit cards, home equity and mortgage loans, on-line banking, student loans, and insurance. Wells Fargo also offers a complete line of commercial and institutional financial services. Founded in 1852. **Corporate headquarters location:** San Francisco CA. **Other U.S. locations:** Nationwide. **International locations:** Worldwide. **Listed on:** New York Stock Exchange and the Chicago Stock Exchange. **Stock exchange symbol:** WFC. **Annual sales/revenues:** More than $100 million. **Number of employees worldwide:** 139,000.

WEYERHAEUSER COMPANY
P.O. Box 377, Campti LA 71411-0377. 318/476-3392. **Physical address:** 4537 Highway 480, Red River Mill, Campti LA 71411. **Fax:** 318/476-2525. **Contact:** Human Resources. **World Wide Web address:** http://www.weyerhaeuser.com. **Description:** Engaged in the growing and harvesting of timber; the manufacture, distribution, and sale of forest products including logs, wood chips, and building products; real estate development and construction; and financial services. Weyerhaeuser is one of the world's largest private owners of marketable softwood timber and one of the largest producers of softwood lumber and pulp. The company is also one of North America's largest producers of forest products and recyclers of office wastepaper, newspaper, and corrugated boxes. Weyerhaeuser Company also sells electricity to utility companies generated from its 15 trash-to-energy plants and 6 small cogeneration and recycling plants. Founded in 1900. **Special programs:** Tuition Reimbursement Program; Training; Mentorship. **Corporate headquarters location:** Federal Way WA. **Other U.S. locations:** Nationwide. **International locations:** Worldwide. **Operations at this facility include:** This location manufactures paper, pulp, and linerboard. **Listed on:** New York Stock Exchange. **Stock exchange symbol:** WY. **President/CEO/Chairman:** Steven Rogel. **Sales/revenues:** $19.9 billion. **Number of employees worldwide:** 57,000.

WEYERHAEUSER COMPANY
P.O. Box 1100, Ruston LA 71273-1100. 318/255-6258. **Physical address:** 603 Reynolds Drive, Ruston LA 71270. **Contact:** Manager of Human Resources. **World Wide Web address:** http://www.weyerhaeuser.com. **Description:** Engaged principally in the growing and harvesting of timber; the manufacture, distribution, and sale of forest products including logs, wood chips, and building products; real estate development and construction; and financial services. Founded in 1900. **Special programs:** Tuition Reimbursement Program; Training; Mentorship. **Corporate headquarters location:** Federal Way WA. **Other U.S. locations:** Nationwide. **International locations:** Worldwide. **Operations at this facility include:** This location produces plywood. **Listed on:** New York Stock Exchange. **Stock exchange symbol:** WY. **President/CEO/Chairman:** Steven Rogel. **Sales/revenues:** $19.9 billion. **Number of employees worldwide:** 57,000.

WOMEN'S HOSPITAL
P.O. Box 95009, Baton Rouge LA 70895-9009. 225/927-1300. **Physical address:** 9050 Airline Highway, Baton Rouge LA 70815. **Fax:** 225/928-8850. **Contact:** Human Resources. **World Wide Web address:** http://www.womans.com. **Description:** A 225-bed, non-profit women's specialty hospital composed of a Breast Center, Osteoporosis Center, Cosmetic Surgery Center, Urinary Incontinence Center, Genetics Clinic, Woman's Center for Fertility and Advanced Reproductive Medicine, and a Women's Fitness Center. Other services include prenatal and women's health education; gynecologic and prenatal surgery and care; physical, speech, respiratory, and occupational therapy; as well as pediatric subspecialty clinics. Founded in 1968. **NOTE:** To contact Human Resources directly, call 225/924-8655. **Positions advertised include:** Volunteer positions; Aesthetician; Licensed Nail Technician; Maintenance Tech; Clinical Applications Consultant; Nursing Applications Coordinator; Patient Information Coordinator; Graphic Designer; Physician Marketing Representative; Occupational Therapist; Physical Therapist Assistant; RN – Various Departments; Secretary; Neonatal Care Technician; Nurse Tech; Nursing Assistant; Health Information Management Auditor; Phlebotomy Technician; Imaging Assistant; Child Care Aide; Massage Therapist; Gift Shop Assistant; Guest Relations. **Special Programs:** Tuition Reimbursement Program; Staff Development Program. **Office hours:** Monday – Friday, 7:30 a.m. – 4:00 p.m. **President/CEO:** Teri G. Fontenot. **Number of employees at this location:** 1,500.

ACADIA INSURANCE COMPANY
One Acadia Commons, P.O. Box 9010, Westbrook ME 04098-5010. 207/772-4300. **Toll-free phone:** 800/773-4300. **Contact:** Human Resources. **World Wide Web address:** http://www.acadiainsurance.com. **Description:** Offers personal and commercial lines of property and casualty insurance. Acadia Insurance Company handles claim, audit, loss control, automation, and underwriting services. **Positions advertised include:** Imaging Specialist; Inland Marine Associate Underwriter; Manager – Home Office Marketing; Marketing Specialist; Rating Technician; Staff Attorney. **Other U.S. locations:** Marlborough MA; Manchester NH; Bedford NH; Syracuse NY; South Burlington VT; Farmington CT. **Parent company:** W.R. Berkley Corporation. **Listed on:** New York Stock Exchange. **Stock exchange symbol:** BER.

ANDOVER COLLEGE
901 Washington Avenue, Portland ME 04103. 207/774-6126. **Toll-free phone:** 800/639-3110. **Fax:** 207/774-1715. **Contact:** Human resources. **World Wide Web address:** http://www.andovercollege.com. **Description:** A two-year college offering associate's degrees and certificate programs in the fields of accounting, business administration, computer technology, criminal justice, legal studies, medical assisting, office administration, travel and tourism, and childhood education. Founded in 1966. **NOTE:** Entry-level positions and part-time jobs are offered. No phone calls regarding employment please. **Company slogan:** Skills for success in a changing work place. **Positions advertised include:** Adjunct Instructor – Various Departments; Adjunct Instructor – Early Childhood Education Program; Certified Nurse's Assistant Instructor. **Special programs:** Internships; Co-ops. **Office hours:** Monday - Friday, 7:30 a.m. - 6:00 p.m. **Corporate headquarters location:** This location. **Listed on:** Privately held. **CEO/President:** Stephen K. Ingram. **Annual sales/revenues:** Less than $5 million. **Number of employees at this location:** 60.

ANTHEM BLUE CROSS AND BLUE SHIELD
2 Gannett Drive, South Portland ME 04106-6911. 207/822-7000. **Contact:** Human Resources. **World Wide Web address:** http://www.anthem.com. **Description:** A health insurance provider and managed care company. Anthem Blue Cross and Blue Shield offers individual insurance, Medigap supplemental insurance for persons over 65, group coverage for small businesses, and group dental coverage for businesses with 50 or more employees. **NOTE:** Please visit website to register and apply online. **Positions advertised include:** Senior Systems Analyst. **Corporate headquarters location:** Indianapolis IN. **Other area location:** Augusta; Bangor; Portland; Presque Isle; Westbrook. **Other U.S. locations:** Denver CO; North Haven CT; Indianapolis IN; Louisville KY; Manchester NH; South Reno NV; Mason OH; Richmond VA. **Listed on:** New York Stock Exchange. **Stock exchange symbol:** ATH. **Parent company:** Anthem Insurance Companies Inc. **Number of employees nationwide:** 6,000.

THE AROOSTOOK MEDICAL CENTER
P.O. Box 151, 140 Academy Street, Presque Isle ME 04769. 207/768-4000. **Fax:** 207/768-4045. **Contact:** Human Resources. **World Wide Web address:** http://www.tamc.org. **Description:** A 212-bed, tri-campus facility located in northern Maine. The center is a nonprofit organization and offers a wide range of services. Founded in 1912. **NOTE:** Entry-level positions, part-time jobs, and second and third shifts are offered. Human Resources phone is 207/768-4026. **Positions advertised include:** CPT – Physical Therapist; Food Service Attendant; Medical Assistant; LPN/Office Nurse; Billing Technician; Central Registration Representative; Clinical Coordinator; Clinical Social Worker; CAN; EMT; Nuclear Medical Technician; Nursing Home Administrator; Radiology Technician; Receptionist; RN – OR; Secretary/Receptionist; Transcriptionist; Ultrasound Technician; VP of Nursing Services; Warehouse Receiving Clerk; RN – Labor and Delivery. **Corporate headquarters location:** This location. **Number of employees at this location:** 650.

AUGUSTA SCHOOL DEPARTMENT
40 Pierce Drive, Suite 3, Augusta ME 04330. 207/626-2468. **Fax:** 207/626-2444. **Contact:** Lisa Boucher, Director of Human Resources. **E-mail address:** lboucher@catc.augusta.k12.me.us. **World Wide Web address:** http://www.cony-hs.augusta.k12.me.us. **Description:** Manages and staffs all public schools in Augusta, including one high, two middle, four elementary, and one secondary technical school.

THE BAKER COMPANY
P.O. Drawer E, 161 Gatehouse Road, Sanford ME 04073. 207/324-8773. **Toll-free phone:** 800/992-2537. **Fax:** 207/324-3869. **E-mail address:** bakerco@bakerco.com. **World Wide Web address:** http://www.bakerco.com. **Description:** Designs and manufactures air containment and clean air products for life science, pharmaceutical, industrial, and medical applications. **Corporate headquarters location:** This location. **Other U.S. locations:** Nationwide. **Number of employees at this location:** 180.

BAKER NEWMAN & NOYES
280 Fore Street, Portland ME 04112. 207/879-2100. **Fax:** 207/774-1793. **Contact:** Human Resources. **World Wide Web address:** http://bnncpa.com. **Description:** A certified public accounting firm that provides a variety of services including audits and tax planning. **NOTE:** Human Resources fax is 207/791-7160. **Positions advertised include:** Staff Accountant; Audit Manager; Audit Senior; Audit Senior Manager; Tax Intern; Tax Accountant; Tax Senior; Tax Manager; Tax Senior Manager; Staff Consultant; Senior Staff Consultant; Manager; Senior Manager; Marketing Staff Consultant. **Other U.S. locations:** Manchester NH; Portsmouth NH.

BANGOR HYDRO-ELECTRIC COMPANY
P.O. Box 932, Bangor ME 04402-0932. 207/945-5621. **Physical address:** 33 State Street, Bangor ME 04401. **Toll-free phone:** 800/499-6600. **Fax:** 207/990-6990. **Contact:** Personnel. **E-mail address:** jobs@bhe.com. **World Wide Web address:** http://www.bhe.com. **Description:** One of the largest electric utilities in Maine. The company serves a population of about 195,000 in eastern Maine. The company is a member of the New England Power Pool and is interconnected with other New England utilities to the south and with New Brunswick Power Corporation to the north. Founded in 1924. **NOTE:** You may pick up an application in person at 33 State Street, or at 45 Oak Street. **Corporate headquarters location:** This location. **Subsidiaries include:** Bangor Var; Penobscot Hydro Company, Inc. **Parent company:** Emera. **Listed on:** New York Stock Exchange. **Number of employees at this location:** 200. **Number of employees nationwide:** 275.

BANGOR SAVINGS BANK
P.O. Box 930, Bangor ME 04402-0930. 207/942-5211. **Physical address:** 203 Maine Avenue, Bangor ME 04401. **Toll-free phone:** 877/Bangor1. **Contact:** Human Resources. **Email address:** careers@bangor.com. **World Wide Web address:** http://www.bangor.com. **Description:** A mutual savings institution with 14 branch locations throughout the state of Maine. The bank holds accounts for Maine residents only. Founded in 1852. **NOTE:** Please visit website for online application form. Positions advertised include: Application Developer; Assistant Branch Manager; Commercial Lending Officer; Director of Insurance Sales; Financial Consultant; Payroll Application Administrator; Retail Banking Assistant; Secretary; Teller (Part-time). **Corporate headquarters location:** This location.

BANGOR SCHOOL DEPARTMENT
73 Harlow Street, Bangor ME 04401. 207/945-4400. **Contact:** Human Resources. **World Wide Web address:** http://www.bangorschools.net. **Description:** Responsible for the management and staffing of 10 local schools including Bangor High School, two middle schools (grades 6-7), two intermediate level schools (grades 4-5), and five elementary level schools (K-3). **NOTE:** Please visit website for online application form. **Positions advertised include:** Custodian; Educational Technician; Secretary; Substitute Teacher – Various Positions; Tutor – Various Grades/Positions.

BANK OF AMERICA
1176 Union Street, Bangor ME 04401. 207/947-0362. **Toll-free phone:** 866/ 826-8989. **Contact:** Human Resources. **World Wide Web address:** http://www.bankofamerica.com. **Description:** Provides full-service personal, corporate, and small business banking services statewide. **Corporate headquarters location:** Charlotte NC. **Other area locations:** Statewide. **Other U.S. locations:** Nationwide.

BANK OF AMERICA
One City Center, Portland ME 04101. 207/874-5574. **Toll-free phone:** 866/ 826-8989. **Fax:** 207/874-5569. **Contact:** Human Resources. **World Wide Web address:** http://www.bankofamerica.com. **Description:** Provides full-service personal, corporate, and small business banking services statewide. **Positions advertised include:** Branch Ops Supervisor; Teller; Training Specialist. **Office hours:** Monday – Friday, 9:00 a.m. – 4:00 p.m. **Corporate headquarters location:** Charlotte NC. **Other area locations:** Statewide. **Other U.S. locations:** Nationwide.

BAR HARBOR BANKING & TRUST COMPANY
82 Main Street, P.O. Box 400, Bar Harbor ME 04609-0400. 207/288-3314. **Toll-free phone:** In state – 800/924-7787; Out of state – 800/237-9601. **Fax:** 207/288-2811. **Contact:** Sonya Hubbard, Human Resources Manager. **E-mail address:** shubbard@bhbt.com. **World Wide Web address:** http://www.bhbt.com. **Description:** A commercial bank with 10 branch locations in eastern Maine. Founded in 1887. **Positions advertised include:** Seasonal Teller. **Corporate headquarters location:** This location. **Other area locations:** Statewide.

BARNES & NOBLE BOOKSTORES
9 Market Place Drive, Augusta ME 04330. 207/621-0038. **Contact:** Manager. **World Wide Web address:** http://www.bn.com. **Description:** A bookstore chain. This location also has a cafe and a music department. **NOTE:** For employment information, contact Human Resources in Westbury NY at 516/338-8000. **Other U.S. locations:** Nationwide. **Listed on:** NASDAQ. **Stock exchange symbol:** BNBN.

G.H. BASS & COMPANY
100 Clarks Pond Parkway, South Portland ME 04106. 207/761-7059. **Toll-free phone:** 800/950-2277 **Fax:** 207/791-4909. **Contact:** Human Resources. **E-mail address:** bassresumes@pvh.com. **World Wide Web address:** http://www.bassstore.net. **Description:** G.H. Bass & Company operates over 200 factory outlet stores. **Corporate headquarters location:** New York NY. **Parent company:** Phillips-Van Heusen Corporation. **Listed on:** New York Stock Exchange.

BATES COLLEGE
215 College Street, Lewiston ME 04240. 207/786-6140. **Contact:** Human Resources. **Fax:** 207/786-6170. **E-mail address:** hrdept@bates.edu. **World Wide Web address:** http://www.bates.edu. **Description:** A four-year, liberal arts college offering 32 bachelor's degree programs. Approximately 1,600 students attend Bates College. Founded in 1855. **Positions advertised include:** Lecturer – Various Departments; Assistant Professor – Various Departments; Behavioral/Cognitive Neuroscientist; Tenure-track Position – Various Departments; Dean of Students; Life Model; Leadership Gifts Officer; Operations Coordinator for Planned Giving; Sanitation – Dining Room; On-Call Caterer; Director – Archives; On-Call Security Dispatcher.

BATH IRON WORKS CORPORATION
700 Washington Street, Bath ME 04530. 207/443-3311. **Fax:** 207/442-1567. **Contact:** Nancy Fortin. **E-mail address:** employment@gdbiw.com. **World Wide Web address:** http://www.gdbiw.com. **Description:** Engineers and builds ships including navy frigates and destroyers. The company also sells shipbuilding and repair technology worldwide. **Other U.S. locations:** Nationwide. **Parent company:** General Dynamics (Falls Church VA). **Listed on:** Privately held.

BINAX INC.
217 Read Road, Portland ME 04103. 207/772-3988. **Fax:** 207/871-5751. **Toll-free phone:** 800/323-3199. **Contact:** Human Resources. **E-mail address:** ddende@binax.com. **World Wide Web address:** http://www.binax.com. **Description:** A biotechnology company focused on developing technology for rapid diagnostic testing.

BIODESIGN INTERNATIONAL
60 Industrial Park Road, Saco ME 04072. 207/283-6500. **Toll-free phone:** 888/530-0140. **Fax:** 207/283-4800. **Contact:**General Manager. **E-mail address:** LDiou@biodesign.com. **World Wide Web address:** http://www.biodesign.com. **Description:** Manufactures and markets polyclonal and monoclonal antibodies, purified antigens, and assay development reagents. BIODESIGN International also offers custom services for research and industrial clients. Custom services include antibody production, analysis, conjugation, and other laboratory processes. Founded in 1987. **Positions advertised include:** Marketing/Product Manager. **Corporate headquarters location:** This location.

BLUE MARBLE GEOGRAPHICS
345 Water Street, Gardiner ME 04345. 207/582-6747. **Toll-free phone:** 800/ 616-2725. **Fax:** 207/582-7001. **Contact:** Human Resources Department. **E-mail address:** hr@bluemarblegeo.com. **World Wide Web address:** http://www.bluemarblegeo.com. **Description:** Develops and markets mapping software. Products include coordinate and data translator programs, tracking and GPS programs, and a wide array of mapping software development and application tools. Founded in 1993. **NOTE:** E-mail is preferred when responding to job openings. **Positions advertised include:** Software Developer; Entry Level Software Salesperson. **Corporate headquarters location:** This location.

BLUE ROCK INDUSTRIES
58 Main Street, Westbrook ME 04092. 207/854-2561. **Toll-free phone:** 877/439-2561. **Contact:** Human Resources. **E-mail address:** info@bluerockmaine.com. **World Wide Web address:** http://www.bluerockmaine.com. **Description:** Manufactures and supplies aggregates, sands, gravel, ready-mix concrete, and hot and cold bituminous pavement to the construction industry and private consumers. Blue Rock Industries is also a paving contractor serving commercial and residential markets. The company also maintains its own heavy equipment maintenance facilities for its own fleet and offers repair services to commercial clients. The company's Blue Rock Stone Center sells and offers custom fabrication of marble and granite countertops, wallstones, flagstones, and

decorative stone items. Founded in 1920. **NOTE:** There are both seasonal positions and year-round positions offered. **Office hours:** Monday – Friday, 8:00 a.m. – 4:30 p.m. **Corporate headquarters location:** This location. **Other area locations:** Cumberland ME; Leeds ME; Sidney ME. **President:** Mark Humphrey.

BOWDOIN COLLEGE
3501 College Station, Brunswick ME 04011-8426. 207/725-3837. **Fax:** 207/725-3976. **Recorded jobline:** 207/725-3923. **Contact:** Kimberly Bonsey, Manager of Employment. **E-mail address:** kbonsey@bowdoin.edu; hr@bowdoin.edu. **World Wide Web address:** http://www.bowdoin.edu. **Description:** A private, four-year, liberal arts college with approximately 1,500 students. **NOTE:** Please call the jobline for a listing of available positions before applying. Human Resources address is McLellan Building, 85 Union Street, Brunswick. Please visit the Human Resources website at http://www.bowdoin.edu/hr. **Positions advertised include:** Tenure-track positions – Various Departments; Visiting Fellow in Education; Groundskeeper; Coordinator of Multicultural Student Programs; Academic Department Coordinator; Administrative Coordinator; Associate Director of Academic Communications; Housekeeper; Assistant Director of Residential Life; Capital Gifts Officer; Mail Clerk; Secretary; Substitute Teacher; Communication Officer. **Special programs:** Internships; Summer Jobs. **Number of employees at this location:** 1,000.

N.H. BRAGG & SONS
92 Perry Road, P.O. Box 927, Bangor ME 04402-0927. 207/947-8615. **Toll-free phone:** 877/NHBRAGG. **Fax:** 800/281-6752. **Contact:** Personnel. **E-mail address:** nhbragg@nhbragg.com. **World Wide Web address:** http://www.nhbragg.com. **Description:** A wholesaler and distributor of a variety of industrial welding supplies and automotive products. N.H. Bragg & Sons also operates auto parts retail outlets and distribution centers throughout Maine. Founded in 1854. **Corporate headquarters location:** This location. **Other area locations:** Statewide.

BREWER SCHOOL DEPARTMENT
49 Capri Street, Brewer ME 04412. 207/989-3160. **Fax:** 207/989-8622. **Contact:** Betsy Webb, Superintendent. **E-mail address:** bwebb@breweredu.org. **World Wide Web address:** http://www.breweredu.org. **Description:** Responsible for the management and staffing of the area's schools. Brewer School Department consists of Brewer High School, Brewer Middle School, and four elementary schools.

BURGESS ADVERTISING & ASSOCIATES, INC.
1290 Congress Street, Portland ME 04102-2150. 207/775-5227. **Fax:** 207/775-3157. **Contact:** Human Resources. **E-mail address:** adburg@burgessadv.com. **World Wide Web address:** http://www. burgessadv.com. **Description:** A full-service marketing, public relations, and advertising firm. Burgess Advertising & Associates also offers market research, new media, and collateral services. Founded in 1986. **Company slogan:** Advertising that works. **Corporate headquarters location:** This location.

BURGESS COMPUTER INC.
101 Centre Street, Bath ME 04530. 207/443-9554. **Fax:** 207/443-3856. **Toll-free phone:** 800/498-8642. **Contact:** Human Resources. **E-mail address:** craig@burgessinc.com. **World Wide Web address:** http://www.burgessinc.com. **Description:** Provides technology consulting and implementation services.

CANTEEN SERVICES COMPANY
P.O. Box 895, Bangor ME 04402-0895. 207/945-5688. **Physical address:** 244 Perry Road, Bangor ME 04401. **Toll-free phone:** 800/432-7919. **Fax:** 207/947-3430. **Contact:** Human Resources Department. **E-mail address:** food@canteenmaine.com; bangor@canteenmaine.com. **World Wide Web address:** http://www.canteenmaine.com. **Description:** Sells, rents, and services vending machines. Canteen Services Company also offers catering and office coffee services. **Other area locations:** Saco ME; Lewiston ME.

CASCO DEVELOPMENT INC.
2 Portland Fish Pier, Portland ME 04101. 207/773-0944. **Fax:** 207/773-0524. **Contact:** Hiring Manager. **E-mail address:** jobs@cascodev.com. **World Wide Web address:** http://www.cascodev.com. **Description:** A developer and provider of labor related data collection and reporting software.

CENTRAL MAINE MEDICAL CENTER
300 Main Street, Lewiston ME 04240-0305. 207/795-2390. **Fax:** 207/753-7250. **Contact:** Human Resources. **E-mail address:** recruitment@cmhc.org. **World Wide Web address:** http://www.cmmc.org. **Description:** A 250-bed medical center offering a full-range of medical services including cardiac care, emergency services, rehabilitation services, cancer care, and LifeFlight of Maine, a medical helicopter service. **NOTE:** Please visit website to apply online. **Positions advertised include:** Aerobic Instructor; Biomedical Equipment Technician; Budget Analyst; Cat Scan Technologist; Clinical Assistant; LPN; Clinical Dietician; Clinical Lab Scientist; Cytotechnologist; Environmental Services Aide; ER Office Manager; Groundskeeper; Insurance Follow-up Representative; Medical Technologist; Nursing Supervisor; Outpatient Licensed Clinical Social Worker; Pediatric Nurse Practitioner; Phlebotomist; Respiratory Therapist; RN – Various Departments; Security Officer; Staff Therapist – Occupational Therapy and Physical Therapy. **Parent company:** Central Maine Health Care. **Number of employees at this location:** 1,100.

CENTRAL MAINE NEWSPAPERS
31 Front Street, Waterville ME 04901. 207/621-5740. **Toll-free phone:** 800/ 537-5508. **Fax:** 207/621-5610. **Contact:** Karen O'Connor, Human Resources Director. **E-mail address:** kconnor@centralmaine.com. **World Wide Web address:** http://www.centralmaine.com. **Description:** Publishes two daily morning newspapers: the *Central Maine Morning Sentinel* and the *Kennebec Journal*.

CENTRAL MAINE POWER COMPANY
83 Edison Drive, Augusta ME 04336. 207/623-3521. **Fax:** 207/621-5851. **Toll-free phone:** 800/565-0121. **Contact:** Human Resources. **E-mail address:** hr@cmpco.com. **World Wide Web address:** http://www.cmpco.com. **Description:** Provides electric service to more than 450,000 customers in an 11,000 square-mile area in southern and central Maine. The company owns or has an interest in hydroelectric, nuclear, and oil generating stations. It also meets its customer's needs through energy management programs and purchases from independent power producers from New England and Canadian utilities. Central Maine Power is a member of the New England Power Pool and is interconnected with both southern New England and New Brunswick, Canada. **Positions advertised include:** Regulatory Service Analyst; Real Estate Analyst; Risk Management Lead Analyst. **Office hours:** Monday – Friday, 7:30 a.m. – 4:00 p.m. **Parent company:** Energy East. **Listed on:** New York Stock Exchange. **Stock exchange symbol:** EAS. **Number of employees nationwide:** 1,500.

CIANBRO CORPORATION
P.O. Box 1000, One Hunnewell Square, Pittsfield ME 04967. 207/487-3311. **Fax:** 207/487-3861. **Contact:** Amy Chute, Assistant Human Resources Manager. **E-mail address:** jobscorp@cianbro.com. **World Wide Web address:** http://www.cianbro.com. **Description:** An employee-owned, civil and industrial construction company. Cianbro Corporation is primarily involved in facilities construction and renovation in the eastern United States. Founded in 1949. **Positions advertised include:** Pipewelder; Pipefitter; Structural Welder; First Class Linesman. **Corporate headquarters location:** This location. **Other area locations:** Portland ME. **Other U.S. locations:** Bloomfield CT; Baltimore MD. **Listed on:** Privately held. **Number of employees at this location:** 150. **Number of employees nationwide:** 1,200.

CINGULAR WIRELESS
75 John Roberts Road, Suite 2A, South Portland ME 04106. 207/772-9805. **Contact:** Owen Smith, Human Resources. **Toll-free phone:** 800/888-7600. **World Wide Web address:** http://www.cingular.com. **Description:** Provides wireless services to 10.1 million customers. AT&T Wireless Services also offers wireless data communications services to corporate clients. **Positions advertised include:** Lead Communication Specialist. **Corporate headquarters location:** Anaheim Hills CA. **Other U.S. locations:** Nationwide. **Listed on:** New York Stock Exchange. **Stock exchange symbol:** AWE. **Number of employees nationwide:** 30,000.

CITIGROUP GLOBAL TRANSACTION SERVICES
3 Canal Plaza, Portland ME 04101. 207/879-1900. **Fax:** 207/874-2159. **Contact:** Human Resources Department. **E-mail address:** recruiting@citigroupfundservices.com. **World Wide Web address:** http://www.funds.transactionservices.citigroup.com. **Description:** A financial services firm. **Positions advertised include:** Cash Management Analyst; Shareholder Services Representative.

CLEAN HARBORS ENVIRONMENTAL SERVICES
17 Main Street, South Portland ME 04106. 207/799-8111; 800/526-9191. **Toll-free phone:** 800/OIL-TANK. **Fax:** 207/779-0349. **Contact:** Human Resources. **World Wide Web address:** http://www.cleanharbors.com. **Description:** Clean Harbors, Inc., through its subsidiaries, provides comprehensive environmental services in 35 states in the Northeast, Midwest, Central, and Mid-Atlantic regions. Clean Harbors provides a wide range of hazardous waste management and environmental support services to a diversified customer base from over 40 locations. The company's hazardous waste management services include treatment, storage, recycling, transportation, risk analysis, site assessment, laboratory analysis, site closure, and disposal of hazardous materials through environmentally sound methods including incineration. Environmental remediation services include emergency response, surface remediation, groundwater restoration, industrial maintenance, and facility decontamination. Customers include nearly 300 of the *Fortune* 500 companies; regional utilities; oil, pharmaceutical, and chemical companies; small businesses; and the high-tech and biotech industries. **Positions advertised include:** Field Service Foreman; Class A Driver; Field Technician. **Corporate headquarters location:** Braintree MA. **Other area locations:** Newburgh ME. **Other U.S. locations:** Nationwide. **Number of employees nationwide:** 1,400.

COASTAL ENTERPRISES, INC.
P.O. Box 268, Wiscasset ME 04578. 207/882-7552. **Physical address:** 36 Water Street, Wiscasset ME 04578. **Fax:** 207/882-7308. **Contact:** Personnel Department. **E-mail address:** cei@ceimaine.org. **World Wide Web address:** http://www.ceimaine.org. **Description:** A non-profit social and economic development organization. **Other area locations:** Portland; Lewiston; Augusta; Sanford; Fairfield; Farmington; Unity; Bangor.

COCA-COLA ENTERPRISES INC.
91 Dowd Road, Bangor ME 04401. 207/942-5546. **Contact:** Human Resources. **World Wide Web address:** http://www.cokecce.com. **Description:** An independent company that markets, produces, and distributes Coca-Cola beverage products. The company also distributes Dr Pepper and other beverage products. **Corporate headquarters location:** Atlanta GA. **Other area locations:** South Portland ME. **Other U.S. locations:** Nationwide. **International locations:** Canada, Belgium, France, Great Britain, Luxembourg, Monaco, the Netherlands. **Parent company:** The Coca-Cola Company owns 100 supporting brands around the world including Powerade, Aquarius, Hi-C, Georgia (canned coffee, sold in Japan), Thums Up & Limca (India), Sparletta Brands (South Africa), Nestea (distributed by Coca-Cola Enterprises Inc)., and Seiryusabo (Japan). The Coca-Cola Company has owning interest in many bottlers including 44 percent of Coca-Cola Enterprises Inc., as well as Coca-Cola Foods, the world's largest seller of juice and juice-related products under brands such as FiveAlive, Hi-C, Bright & Early, and Bacardi. **Listed on:** New York Stock Exchange. **Stock exchange symbol:** CCE.

COLBY COLLEGE
4000 Mayflower Hill Drive, Waterville ME 04901. 207/872-3000. **Contact:** Office of Personnel. **World Wide Web address:** http://www.colby.edu. **Description:** A small, four-year, liberal arts college serving approximately 1,800 undergraduate students, most of whom live on the campus. Colby College offers a variety of bachelor's degree programs and gives students the option to establish their own unique degree program. The college has a January semester between its regular spring and fall semesters. Colby College offers a variety of facilities for students including the Olin Science Center and the Colby Museum of Art. **NOTE:** Please visit website for information on applying for specific positions. **Positions advertised include:** Visiting Assistant Professor – Various Departments; Faculty Fellow – Various Departments; Tenure-track Assistant Professor – Various Departments; Chair – Psychology; Interim Assistant Coach of Football; Dean of Students; Director of Donor Relations; Director of Outdoor Safety and Education; RN. **Listed on:** Privately held.

COLDWELL BANKER
THOMAS AGENCY
75 Main Street, Winthrop ME 04364. 207/377-2121. **Fax:** 207/377-8015. **Contact:** Human Resources. **World Wide Web address:** http://www.coldwellbanker.com. **Description:** A real estate agency specializing in residential waterfront properties. **NOTE:** Please visit website to search for jobs, and to fill out the Career Information Request form. **Corporate headquarters location:** Parsippany NJ. **Other area locations:** Statewide. **Other U.S. locations:** Nationwide. **Listed on:** New York Stock Exchange. **Stock exchange symbol:** CD. **President/CEO:** Alex Perriello.

COMMON CENSUS
90 Bridge Street, 1st Floor, Westbrook ME 04092. 207/854-5454. **Fax:** 207/854-3154. **Contact:** Human Resources. **E-mail address:** hr@commoncensus.com. **World Wide Web address:** http://www.commoncensus.com. **Description:** Produces an operating system that allows businesses to manage employee benefits.

COOPER WIRING DEVICES
One Cressey Road, Brunswick ME 04011-1539. 207/729-6734. **Contact:** Personnel. **E-mail address:** jobs@cooperwiringdevices.com. **World Wide Web address:**

http://www.cooperwiringdevices.com. **Description:** Cooper Industries has major business segments that include Electrical Products, Electrical Power Equipment, Tools and Hardware, Automotive, and Petroleum and Industrial Equipment. **Corporate headquarters location:** Houston TX. **Other U.S. locations:** Nationwide. **International locations:** Worldwide. **Operations at this facility include:** This location manufactures electrical switches and receptacles.

CORNING INCORPORATED
2 Alfred Road, Kennebunk ME 04043. 207/985-3111. **Fax:** 207/985-5203. **Contact:** Human Resources. **World Wide Web address:** http://www.corning.com. **Description:** Engaged in the design, development, manufacture, and sale of disposable plastic research labware, sold under the Corning Costar name. **Positions advertised include:** Senior Process Engineer; Molding Supervisor; Development Platform Manager; Cell Structure Assay Analyst. **Special programs:** Internships. **Corporate headquarters location:** Corning NY. **Other U.S. locations:** Nationwide. **International locations:** Worldwide. **Parent company:** Corning Inc. **Listed on:** New York Stock Exchange. **Stock exchange symbol:** GLW. **Number of employees at this location:** 350. **Number of employees nationwide:** 800.

COYNE TEXTILE SERVICES
95 Spring Street, Lewiston ME 04240-7520. 207/786-8772. **Contact:** Human Resources. **World Wide Web address:** http://www.coynetextileservices.com. **Description:** Offers commercial laundry services to hospitals, industrial facilities, and institutions. Coyne Textile Services also sells and rents work garments, protective clothing, floor mats, and towels. **NOTE:** Please visit website for a list of current jobs, and to apply online. Mail resumes to 20 Howard Avenue, New Bedford MA 02745. **Corporate headquarters location:** Syracuse NY. **Other U.S. locations:** Nationwide.

CRITICAL INSIGHTS
120 Exchange Street, Portland ME 04101. 207/772-4011. **Fax:** 207/772-7027. **Contact:** Nancy Harman. **E-mail address:** insights@criticalinsights.com. **World Wide Web address:** http://www.criticalinsights.com. **Description:** A strategic market and public opinion research firm. **NOTE:** Reach listed contact at 207/780-8096. **Positions advertised include:** Day/Evening Interviewer.

CUMBERLAND COUNTY YMCA
70 Forest Avenue, P.O. Box 1078, Portland ME 04101. 207/874-1111. **Fax:** 207/874-1114. **Contact:** Human Resources. **World Wide Web address:** http://www.cascobayymca.org. **Description:** Provides a wide range of social and educational services including health and lodging. Founded 1853. **NOTE:** For childcare positions, resumes should be directed to Pam Washington, Director of Childcare. For positions in finance, resumes should be directed to Ludmila Tutunaru, Director of Finance. You may search for and apply to jobs through http://jobsinme.com. Volunteer positions are also available. **Positions advertised include:** Youth Program Assistant; Teen Program Assistant; Substitute Childcare Provider. **Special programs:** Internships, including health and lodging. **Other area locations:** Freeport ME; New Gloucester ME; Standish ME.

CYRO INDUSTRIES
P.O. Box 591, Sanford ME 04073. 207/324-6000. **Physical address:** 1796 Maine Street, Sanford ME 04073. **Contact:** Human Resources. **E-mail address:** human_resources@cyro.com. **World Wide Web address:** http://www.cyro.com. **Description:** CYRO Industries manufactures, sells, and distributes plastics. **NOTE:** Please send resume and cover letter to Corporate Headquarters at – Human Resources Supervisor, 100 Enterprise Drive, Rockaway NJ 07866. **Corporate headquarters location:** Rockaway NJ. **Operations at this facility include:** This location manufactures acrylic sheets. **Number of employees at this location:** 400.

DARLING'S INC.
P.O. Box 277, Brewer ME 04412. 207/941-1240. **Physical address:** 153 Perry Road, Bangor ME 04401. **Contact:** Personnel. **World Wide Web address:** http://www.darlings.com. **Description:** This location houses the corporate and accounting offices for the four Darling's automobile dealerships. **Corporate headquarters location:** This location. **Other area locations:** Augusta ME; Lewiston ME, Waterville ME.

DEAD RIVER COMPANY
55 Broadway, Bangor ME 04402-1427. 207/947-8641. **Contact:** Human Resources. **E-mail address:** hr@deadriver.com. **World Wide Web address:** http://www.deadriver.com. **Description:** Distributes petroleum products to residential and commercial customers in northern New England. The company also offers maintenance services and equipment installations, as well as convenience stores that feature fast food and deli services. Founded 1907. **Positions advertised include:** Service Technician Trainer; Controller/Tax Manager; Oil Delivery Driver – Seasonal/Full-time; Licensed Propane or Oil Burner Service Technician. **Office hours:** Monday – Friday, 8:00 a.m. – 5:00 p.m. **Corporate headquarters location:** This location. **Other area locations:** Statewide. **Other U.S. locations:** NH; VT.

DELORME MAPPING
Two DeLorme Drive, Yarmouth ME 04096. 207/846-7000.**Fax:** 207/846-7071. **Contact:** Human Resources. **E-mail address:** jobs@delorme.com. **World Wide Web address:** http://www.delorme.com. **Description:** Publishes atlases, maps, mapping software, and online mapping applications. Founded in 1976. **Positions advertised include:** Mechanical Design Engineer; Applications Marketing Engineer. **Corporate headquarters location:** This location.

DEXTER SHOE COMPANY
71 Railroad Avenue, Dexter ME 04930. 207/924-7341. **Contact:** Human Resources. **World Wide Web address:** http://www.dextershoe.com. **Description:** A shoe manufacturer and distributor. Dexter Shoe Company produces general street shoes, golf shoes, and bowling shoes. **Office hours:** Monday – Friday, 8:00 a.m. – 4:30 p.m.

DIELECTRIC COMMUNICATIONS
22 Tower Road, Raymond ME 04071. 207/655-4555. **Toll-free phone:** 800/341-9678. **Fax:** 207/655-7120. **Recorded jobline:** 207/655-2662. **Contact:** Human Resources. **World Wide Web address:** http://www.dielectric.com. **Description:** Manufactures and supplies broadcasting equipment and pressurization products for commercial, military, and industrial applications. Founded in 1942. **Corporate headquarters location:** This location. **Subsidiaries include:** TCI; Central Towers; Flash Technology; Brookstone Telecom. **Operations at this facility include:** Administration; Manufacturing; Sales. **President:** John Capasso.

DIVERSIFIED COMMUNICATIONS
P.O. Box 7437, Portland ME 04112-7437. 207/842-5500. **Physical address:** 121 Free Street, Portland ME 04101. **Fax:** 207/842-5503. **Contact:** Jan Crosby, Human Resources. **E-mail address:** jcrosby@divcom.com. **World Wide Web address:** http://www.divbusiness.com. **Description:** A communications organization. Diversified Communications has a broadcast division with four television stations and a cable division, in addition to a publishing division that produces publications related to the seafood and fishing industry. Another division organizes trade shows for the seafood and fishing industry. **Corporate headquarters location:** This location. **Other U.S. locations:** Seattle WA; Mondeville LA. **International locations:** Victoria Australia; Markham Ontario; West Sussex United Kingdom. **Subsidiaries include:** Diversified Business Communications. **Number of employees at this location:** 100. **Number of employees nationwide:** 450.

DOMTAR
144 Main Street, Baileyville ME 04694-9656. 207/427-3311. **Fax:** 207/427-4013. **Contact:** Human Resources. **E-mail address:** careers@ dotmar.com. **World Wide Web address:** http://www.domtar.com. **Description:** A manufacturer, wholesaler, and distributor of building products, industrial wood products, pulp, paper, packaging, and related chemicals. The company is one of the world's largest manufacturers of forest products, with facilities in 48 states and overseas. Domtar owns 4.7 million acres of forestland in North America. **NOTE:** Please visit website for online application form. **Special programs:** Internships. **Corporate headquarters location:** Quebec, Canada. **Other U.S. locations:** WI; MI; AR; GA. **International locations:** Canada. **Number of employees at this location:** 555.

DRAGON PRODUCTS CORPORATION
P.O. Box 1521, Portland ME 04104-1521. 207/774-6355. **Physical address:** 38 Preble Street, Portland ME 04101. **Toll-free phone:** Maine – 800/427-6368; National – 800/828-8352. **Fax:** 207/761-5694. **Contact:** Human Resources. **E-mail address:** info@dragonproducts.com. **World Wide Web address:** http://www.dragonproducts.com. **Description:** Manufactures, markets, and distributes ready-mix cement. Dragon Products Corporation also manufactures and sells crushed aggregate, sand, and concrete blocks. **Corporate headquarters location:** This location. **Other area locations:** Statewide. **Other U.S. locations:** Newington NH; Boston MA.

DRESSER & ASSOCIATES
243 Route 1, Scarborough ME 04074. 207/885-0809. **Toll-free phone:** 866/885-7212. **Fax:** 207/885-0816. **Contact:** Human Resources. **E-mail address:** mfdresser@dresserassociates.com. **World Wide Web address:** http://www.dresserassociates.com. **Description:** An operational management and performance consultancy. **Positions advertised include:** Inside Sales Representative; Account Executive; Software Implementation Consultant.

DURATHERM WINDOW CORPORATION
YORK SPIRAL STAIR
720 Main Street, North Vassalboro ME 04962. 207/872-5558. **Toll-free phone:** 800/996-5558. **Fax:** 207/872-6731. **Contact:** Personnel. **E-mail address:** info@durathermwindow.com. **World Wide Web address:** http://www.durathermwindow.com. **Description:** Manufactures standard and custom wooden window systems, doors, and spiral stairs. Customers include architects, contractors, private residences, retail stores, and companies.

EASTLAND PARK HOTEL
157 High Street, Portland ME 04101. 207/775-5411. **Toll-free phone:** 888/671-8008. **Fax:** 207/775-2872. **Contact:** Personnel. **E-mail address:** info@eastlandparkhotel.com. **World Wide Web address:** http://www.eastlandparkhotel.com. **Description:** A 200-room hotel. Founded in 1927.

EMERY-WATERHOUSE COMPANY, INC.
P.O. Box 659, Portland ME 04104. 207/283-0236 **Fax:** 207/775-5206. **Physical address:** 7 Rand Road, Portland ME 04104. **Toll-free phone:** 800/283-0236. **Contact:** Human Resources Department. **E-mail address:** info@emeryonline.com. **World Wide Web address:** http://www.emery-waterhouse.com. **Description:** A hardware wholesaler. Emery-Waterhouse sells hardware and various seasonal items to retail businesses. Founded in 1842. **Corporate headquarters location:** This locatio

ENVIROLOGIX
500 Riverside Industrial Parkway, Portland ME 04103-1486. 207/797-0300. **Fax:** 207/797-7533. **Toll-free phone:** 866/408-4597. **Contact:** Human Resources. **E-mail address:** hr-web@envirologix.com. **World Wide Web address:** http://www.envirologix.com. **Description:** Develops and produces rapid test kits for identifying molds, fungi, and natural toxins. **NOTE:** Employment application available online.

FACE MAGAZINE
P.O. Box 336, Bar Harbor ME 04609-0336. 207/288-4500. Physical address: 93 Cotton Street, Bar Harbor ME 04609. **Fax:** 207/288-0220. **World Wide Web address:** http://www.facemag.com. **E-mail address:** mail@facemag.com. **Description:** A weekly newspaper offering features on local and regional musicians; reviews on major, independent, and local recorded music and performances; and comprehensive club listings.

FAIRCHILD SEMICONDUCTOR CORPORATION
82 Running Hill Road, South Portland ME 04106. 207/775-8100. **Toll-free phone:** In-state – 800/832-5505; Out-of-state – 800/341-0392. **Contact:** Human Resources Department. **World Wide Web address:** http://www.fairchildsemi.com. **Description:** Manufactures semiconductors for use in telecommunications, personal computing, and digital video applications. **NOTE:** Please visit website for online application form. **Special programs:** Co-ops; Internships. **Corporate headquarters:** This location. **Other U.S. locations:** Nationwide. **International locations:** Worldwide.

FEDERAL DISTRIBUTORS
P.O. Box 2007, Lewiston ME 04240-2007. 207/783-1777. **Physical address:** 2075 Lisbon Road, Lewiston ME 04240. **Fax:** 207/783-1176. **Contact:** Rita St. Amand, Vice President of Human Resources. **E-mail address:** rstamand@federaldistributors.com **World Wide Web address:** http://www.federaldistributors.com. **Description:** A regional distributor of Anheuser-Busch products

FIRST NATIONAL BANK OF DAMARISCOTTA
223 Main Street, P.O. Box 940, Damariscotta ME 04543-0940. 207/563-3195. **Toll-free phone:** 800/564-3195. **Fax:** 207/563-6853. **Contact:** Human Resources. **E-mail address:** hr@the1st.com. **World Wide Web address:** http://www.the1st.com. **Description:** A bank providing a full range of banking services to individual and corporate customers in Maine. **Positions advertised include:** Securities Operations Associate; Item Processing Supervisor. **Corporate headquarters location:** This location. **Other area locations:** Statewide.

FIRST TECHNOLOGY
228 Northeast Road, Standish ME 04084-6919. 207/642-4535. **Fax:** 207/642-0198. **Toll-free phone:** 800/392-3908. **Contact:** Human Resources. **E-mail address:**

info@1firsttech.com. **World Wide Web address:** http://www.1firsttech.com. **Description:** A manufacturer of control devices such as ceramic sensors for automobiles. **Corporate headquarters location:** This location. **Other U.S. locations:** Caribou ME; Southfield MI; Grand Blanc MI. **International locations:** Dominican Republic, France; Japan; Korea; The Netherlands; United Kingdom.

FIRST TEK TECHNOLOGIES INC.
482 Congress Street, Suite 203, Portland ME 04101. 207/699-2885. **Fax:** 207/221-1005. **Contact:** Human Resources. **E-mail address:** erma@first-tek.com. **World Wide Web address:** http://www.first-tek.com. **Description:** An IT and e-commerce solution provider that performs services as well as delivers products. **Positions advertised include:** Program Analyst; Software Engineer; Systems Analyst; Business Analyst. **Other U.S. locations:** North Brunswick NJ; Chicago IL; Sioux Falls SD; Omaha NE; Newark DE; Des Moines IA.

FISHER ENGINEERING
50 Gordon Drive, P.O. Box 529, Rockland ME 04841. 207/701-4200. **Fax:** 207/701-4313. **Contact:** Human Resources Department. **World Wide Web address:** http://www.fisherplows.com. **Description:** Designs and manufactures snow plows and other ice management products. Founded in 1948. **Corporate headquarters:** This location. **Other U.S. locations:** Milwaukee WI; Johnson City TN. **Parent company:** Douglas Dynamics LLC. **Number of employees at this location:** 200.

FRANKLIN MEMORIAL HOSPITAL
111 Franklin Health Commons, Farmington ME 04938. 207/778-6031. **Toll-free phone:** 800/398-6031. **Fax:** 207/779-2606. **Contact:** Human Resources. **E-mail address:** humanresources@fchn.org. **World Wide Web address:** http://www.fchn.org/fmh. **Description:** A 70-bed, acute care, community hospital serving west central Maine. This is a nonprofit company. **NOTE:** Human Resources phone is 207/779-2363. Please visit website to download an application. **Positions advertised include:** Clinician Counselor; Radiologic Technologist; Evening Radiologic Technologist; Ultrasound Sonographer; OR Staff Nurse; ICU RN. **Parent company:** Franklin Community Health Network. **Operations at this facility include:** Administration; Service. **Number of employees at this location:** 465.

FRASER PAPERS LTD.
82 Bridge Avenue, Madawaska ME 04756. 207/728-3321. **Fax:** 207/728-8701. **Contact:** Human Resources. **World Wide Web address:** http://www.fraserpapers.com. **Description:** A specialty paper company. Fraser Papers produces glossy paper for products such as magazines and catalogs. **Corporate headquarters location:** Stamford CT. **Other area locations:** Ashland ME. **Other U.S. locations:** CT; NH; IL; WI. **International locations:** Canada. **Parent company:** Nexfor Inc. **Number of employees worldwide:** 3,700.

GZA GEOENVIRONMENTAL SERVICES
4 Free Street, Portland ME 04101-3926. 207/879-9190. **Fax:** 207/879-0099. **Contact:** Tom Lawless, Office Manager. **World Wide Web address:** http://www.gza.net. **Description:** Provides consulting and remediation services, as well as geotechnical services, principally in the Northeast and the Midwest. The company also maintains its own drilling, laboratory, and instrumentation facilities to support environmental and geotechnical activities. Environmental services range from initial assessment and evaluation of contaminated sites to design, construction, and operation of remediation systems for treating, controlling, or removing contamination. **Corporate headquarters location:** Norwood MA. **Other U.S. locations:** MA; NY; MI; CT; NH; NJ; WI; RI; PA. . **Subsidiaries include:** GZA Drilling, Inc.; Soil and Rock Instrumental Division. **Number of employees nationwide:** 500.

GEARY BREWING
38 Evergreen Drive, Portland ME 04103. 207/878-2337. **Contact:** Personnel. **E-mail address:** info@gearybrewing.com. **World Wide Web address:** http://www.gearybrewing.com. **Description:** A beer brewing facility. **Corporate headquarters location:** This location.

GEEKTEAM.COM
197 Sullivan Road, Greene ME 04236. 207/946-2455. **Fax:** 603/372-4538. **Toll-free phone:** 888/517-7816. **Contact:** Bill Clarke. **E-mail address:** employment@geekteam.com. **World Wide Web address:** http://www.geekteam.com. **Description:** Designs and builds custom web applications. Also develops web-based software products. **Positions advertised include:** Application/Information Architect; Application Programmer.

GEIGER
P.O. Box 1609, 70 Mount Hope Avenue, Lewiston ME 04240. 207/755-2000. **Fax:** 207/755-2431. **Contact:** Human Resources. **E-mail address:** jobs@geiger.com. **World Wide Web address:** http://www.geiger.com. **Description:** Sells over 50,000 promotional products ranging from coffee mugs to lollipops. Geiger also offers sales consulting and merchandising services to support its promotional products business. The company also distributes the *Farmers' Almanac* and manufactures calendars and personal organizers. **NOTE:** Please visit website for online application form. **Positions advertised include:** Sales Partner; Customer Relations Specialist; Freight Administrator; Horhauf Covermaking Machine Operator; Krathern Daily Date Machine Operator; OEM Account Executive; Sales Service Coordinator; Senior Financial Analyst. **Corporate headquarters location:** This location. **Other area locations:** Auburn ME. **Other U.S. locations:** Nationwide.

GENERAL ELECTRIC COMPANY
534 Griffin Road, Bangor ME 04401-3086. 207/941-2500. **Contact:** Personnel. **World Wide Web address:** http://www.ge.com. **Description:** General Electric operates in the following areas: aircraft engines (jet engines, replacement parts, and repair services for commercial, military, executive, and commuter aircraft); appliances; broadcasting (NBC); industrial (lighting products, electrical distribution and control equipment, transportation systems products, electric motors and related products, a broad range of electrical and electronic industrial automation products, and a network of electrical supply houses); materials (plastics, ABS resins, silicones, superabrasives, and laminates); power systems (products for the generation, transmission, and distribution of electricity); technical products and systems (medical systems and equipment, as well as a full range of computer-based information and data interchange services for both internal use and external commercial and industrial customers); and capital services (consumer services, financing, and specialty insurance). **Operations at this facility include:** This facility produces components for steam turbines. **Listed on:** New York Stock Exchange. **Stock exchange symbol:** GE. **Number of employees worldwide:** 315,000.

GEORGIA-PACIFIC CORPORATION
One Portland Street, Old Town ME 04468. 207/827-7711. **Fax:** 207/827-0669. **Contact:** Human Resources. **World Wide Web address:** http://www.gp.com. **Description:** Produces sanitary paper products such as facial tissues, paper towels, and napkins; produces food service products such as paper cups; provides retail packaging for food and other consumer products; produces boxes and cartons for packaging; and produces groundwood papers, printing papers, and other paper products. **Corporate headquarters location:** Atlanta GA. **Other area locations:** Portland ME; Milo ME; Milford ME; Baileyville ME. **Other U.S. locations:** Nationwide. **International locations:** Worldwide. **Listed on:** New York Stock Exchange. **Stock exchange symbol:** GP. **Stock exchange symbol:** GP-CUSIP. **Number of employees worldwide:** 61,000.

GORHAM SAVINGS BANK
10 Wentworth Drive, Gorham ME 04038. 207/839-4450. **Physical address:** 64 Maine Street, Gorham ME 04038. **Fax:** 207/839-4790. **Contact:** Human Resources. **World Wide Web address:** http://www.gorhamsavingsbank.com. **Description:** A community bank serving Gorham and the surrounding areas. **NOTE:** Human Resources phone is 207/839-5209 Ext. 3354. Fax is 207/839-3994. **Positions advertised include:** Customer Service Representative; Teller. **Other area locations include:** Scarborough ME; Windham ME; Standish ME; Waterboro ME; West Falmouth ME; South Portland ME.

GRITTY McDUFF'S
396 Fore Street, Portland ME 04101. 207/772-2739. **Fax:** 207/772-6204. **Contact:** Manager. **E-mail address:** grittys@grittys.com. **World Wide Web address:** http://www.grittys.com. **Description:** A brew pub in the Old Port section of Portland. **Other area locations:** Freeport ME.

H.O.M.E., INC.
P.O. Box 10, 90 School House Road, Orland ME 04472. 207/469-7961. **Fax:** 207/469-1023. **Contact:** Father Randy Eldridge, Internship Coordinator. **E-mail address:** info@homecoop.net. **World Wide Web address:** http://www.homecoop.net/index.html. **Description:** Provides self-sufficiency instruction to individuals. In addition, this nonprofit company provides education, an outlet for people to sell their crafts, and health care for low-income individuals. H.O.M.E., Inc. also gives job training workshops and provides housing. Founded in 1970. **Special programs:** Internships. **Internship information:** Interns receive training, room and board, and a small stipend. **Corporate headquarters location:** This location. **Number of employees at this location:** 55.

HANCOCK LUMBER COMPANY
P.O. Box 299, Casco ME 04015. 207/627-7631. **Physical address:** 4 Edes Falls Road, Casco ME. **Contact:** Personnel. **E-mail address:** info@hancocklumber.com. **World Wide Web address:** http://www.hancocklumber.com. **Description:** A lumber company. Founded 1848. **NOTE:** Please visit website for online application form. Positions advertised include: Window and Door Specialist; Assistant Designer; Truck Driver – Class B or C; Custom Cabinet Maker; Delivery Dispatch Assistant; Draftsman; Driver-Support Service Associate; Estimator; Maintenance Worker; Moulder; General Warehouse Laborer; Home Planning Center Coordinator; Inside Sales Support; Insulation Installer; Kitchen Designer; Bath Designer; Manager Trainee; Receiver; Counter Person. **Corporate headquarters location:** This location. **Other area locations:** Statewide. **Other U.S. locations:** Hookset NH.

HANNAFORD BROS. COMPANY
P.O. Box 1000, Portland ME 04104. 207/883-2911. **Physical address:** 145 Pleasant Hill Road, Scarborough ME 04074. **Contact:** Human Resources. **E-mail address:** working@hannaford.com. **World Wide Web address:** http://www.hannaford.com. **Description:** A multiregional food retailer located throughout Maine and in parts of New Hampshire, Vermont, upstate New York, Massachusetts, North Carolina, and South Carolina. Supermarkets operate primarily under the names Shop 'n Save, Wilson's, and Sun Foods. **NOTE:** Please see website for specific email contact for your desired profession. **Positions advertised include:** Retail System Specialist; Department Manager Trainee; Store Loss Prevention Coordinator; Meat Manager; Warehouse Order Selector; Pharmacy Opportunities. **Corporate headquarters location:** This location. **Other U.S. locations:** MA; NH; NY; VT.

HARRASEEKET INN
162 Main Street, Freeport ME 04032. 207/865-9377. **Toll-free phone:** 800/342-6423. **Fax:** 207/865-1684. **Contact:** John Jacobs, Business Office. **World Wide Web address:** http://www.harraseeketinn.com. **Description:** An 84-room inn featuring two restaurants and an indoor pool. **Positions advertised include:** Banquet Server.

HEALTHREACH NETWORK
8 Highwood Street, P.O. Box 829, Waterville ME 04903-0829. 207/861-3400. **Toll-free phone:** 800/427-1127. **Contact:** Human Resources. **World Wide Web address:** http://www.mainegeneral.org/locations/healthreach/default.asp. **Description:** Provides a variety of health care services ranging from counseling to home health nursing. **Positions advertised include:** Medical Care Review Coordinator; Medical Physicist; Occupational Therapist; Pharmacist; Physical Therapist; Physical Therapy Assistant; Speech-Language Pathologist Float; Mental Health/Substance Abuse Clinician; Substance Abuse Counselor; RN – various Departments; Float RN – Various Departments; Dialysis Technician; Nursing Unit Assistant; Phlebotomist; Rehab Technician; Health Information Clerk; Registration Representative; Team Leader. **Other area locations:** Statewide. Parent company: **Parent company:** MaineGeneral. **Number of employees nationwide:** 376.

HUHTAMAKI FOODSERVICE, INC.
242 College Avenue, P.O. Box 1716, Waterville ME 04903-1016. 207/873-3351. **Toll-free phone:** 800/244-6382. **Fax:** 207/877-6254. **Contact:** Human Resources. **E-mail address:** foodservice@huhtamaki.com. **World Wide Web address:** http://www.us.huhtamaki.com. **Description:** Manufactures paper and plastic food service products including plates, cups, utensils, and food storage products. The Chinet Company also manufactures trays designed for ovens such as frozen food trays. **NOTE:** Please visit website for online application form. **Corporate headquarters location:**De Soto KS. **Other U.S. locations:** Nationwide. **International locations:** Worldwide.

HUMPTY DUMPTY
75 Westminster Street, Lewiston ME 04240. 207/782-7215. **Toll-free phone:** 800/274-2447. **Fax:** 207/885-0773. **Physical address:** 86 Pleasant Hill Road, Scarborough ME 04074. **Fax:** 207/885-0773. **Contact:** Personnel. **World Wide Web address:** http://www.humptydumpty.com. **Description:** Manufactures potato chips. **NOTE:** Entry-level positions are offered. **Company slogan:** A taste worth falling for. **Office hours:** Monday - Friday, 8:30 a.m. - 5:00 p.m. **Corporate headquarters location:** Brampton Ontario. **CEO:** Gerald P. Schmalz. **Annual sales/revenues:** $170 million. **Number of employees worldwide:** 1000.

HUSSON COLLEGE
One College Circle, Bangor ME 04401-2999. 207/941-7162. **Fax:** 207/941-7935. **Contact:** Human Resources. **World Wide Web address:** http://www.husson.edu.

Description: A four-year college with certificate, associate, bachelor, and graduate degree programs. Approximately 1,800 students attend Husson College.

I-MANY, INC.
537 Congress Street, Suite 500, Portland ME 04101. 207/774-3244. **Contact:** Human Resources. **World Wide Web address:** http://www.imanyinc.com. **Description:** Develops and manufactures contract management software, and provides Internet-based solutions for the medical, surgical, and pharmaceutical fields. **NOTE:** Please visit website for online application form. **Listed on:** NASDAQ. **Stock exchange symbol:** IMNY.

IDEXX LABORATORIES, INC.
One IDEXX Drive, Westbrook ME 04092. 207/856-0300. **Toll-free phone:** 800/548-6733. **Fax:** 207/856-0346. **Contact:** Donalee Santoro, Director of Human Resources. **World Wide Web address:** http://www.idexx.com. **Description:** Develops and commercializes advanced biotechnology-based and chemistry-based detection systems for veterinary, food, and environmental testing applications. IDEXX markets more than 90 products to customers in over 50 countries. The veterinary products are used to detect and monitor diseases, physiologic disorders, immune status, hormone and enzyme levels, blood chemistry and electrolyte levels, blood counts, and other substances or conditions in animals. The food and environmental products are used to detect various microbiological and chemical contaminants in food products and water, and the biomedical products are used in clinical research, pharmaceutical development, and other life applications. **Other area locations:** Portland ME. **Other U.S. locations:** Nationwide. **International locations:** Worldwide. **Number of employees worldwide:** 500.

IMMUCELL CORPORATION
56 Evergreen Drive, Portland ME 04103. 207/878-2770. **Toll-free phone:** 800/466-8235. **Fax:** 207/878-2117. **Contact:** Human Resources. **E-mail address:** info@immucell.com. **World Wide Web address:** http://www.immucell.com. **Description:** Develops, manufactures, and markets milk-derived, passive, antibody products to prevent gastrointestinal diseases in both humans and animals. The company's business is to utilize its core technology (the production of commercial quantities of pathogen-specific antibodies from cow's milk) in two business areas that share research, development, and manufacturing technologies and resources: human disease treatment and prevention products, and dairy and beef animal health products. **Listed on:** NASDAQ. **Stock exchange symbol:** ICCC.

INLAND HOSPITAL
200 Kennedy Memorial Drive, Waterville ME 04901. 207/861-3028. **Fax:** 207/861-3053. **Contact:** Human Resources. **World Wide Web address:** http://www.inlandhospital.org. **Description:** A 78-bed, nonprofit, acute care hospital that uses both osteopathic and allopathic physicians. **NOTE:** Please visit website for online application form. **Positions advertised include:** File Clerk – Radiology; Occupational Therapist; Occupational Therapy Assistant; Physical Therapist; Physical Therapy Assistant; Radiology Technician; RN – Various Departments; Home Health Aide; Anesthesia Technician; Phlebotomist; Housekeeping Aide; Medical Assistant. **Corporate headquarters location:** This location. **Parent company:** Eastern Maine Healthcare. **Number of employees at this location:** 315.

INTELLICARE
500 Southborough Drive, South Portland ME 04106. 207/775-2600. **Fax:** 207/775-0250. **Toll-free phone:** 800/524-1484. **Contact:** Human Resources. **E-mail address:** jobs@intellicare.com. **World Wide Web address:** http://www.intellicare.com. **Description:** Operates the largest network of medical call centers in the U.S., with over 225 organizations using the company's technology to provide more efficient and effective care. **Positions advertised include:** Clinical Service Provider Nurse Consultant; Customer Service Representative; Helpline Screener. **Other U.S. locations:** Williamsville NY; Columbia MD; Dallas TX; Knoxville TN; Earth City MO.

INTERIM HEALTHCARE
Wonderbrook Center, 57 Portland Road, Kennebunk ME 04043. 207/985-8586. **Fax:** 207/985-4581. **Contact:** Human Resources. **World Wide Web address:** http://www.interimhealthcare.com. **Description:** A home health care agency. **NOTE:** Please visit website to register, search for jobs, and apply online. **Corporate headquarters location:** Sunrise FL. **Other area locations:** Brunswick ME; Lewiston ME; South Portland ME. **Other U.S. locations:** Nationwide.

INTERNATIONAL PAPER COMPANY
P.O. Box O, Livermore Falls ME 04254-1215. 207/897-1936. **Physical address:** 22 Church Street, Livermore Falls ME 04254. **Contact:** Manager. **World Wide Web address:** http://www.internationalpaper.com. **Description:** International Paper Company manufactures pulp and paper, packaging, wood products, and a range of specialty products. The company is organized into five business segments: Printing Papers, whose principal products include uncoated papers, coated papers, bristles, and pulp; Packaging, which includes industrial packaging, consumer packaging, and kraft and specialty papers; Distribution, including the sale of printing papers, graphic arts equipment and supplies, packaging materials, industrial supplies, and office products; Specialty Products, which includes imaging products, specialty panels, nonwovens, chemicals, and minerals; and Forest Products, which includes logging and wood products. **Special programs:** Summer Jobs. **Corporate headquarters location:** Stamford CT. **Other area locations:** Bucksport ME; Costigan ME; Carmel ME; Jay ME; Roxbury ME. **Other U.S. locations:** Nationwide. **International locations:** Worldwide. **Operations at this facility include:** This location purchases wood chips and distributes them to the company's mills. **CEO:** John V. Faraci. **Number of employees worldwide:** 90,000.

INTERNATIONAL PAPER COMPANY
P.O. Box 20, Jay ME 04239-0020. 207/897-3431. Physical Address: Riley Road, Jay ME 04239. **Contact:** Human Resources. **World Wide Web address:** http://www.internationalpaper.com. **Description:** International Paper Company, one of the world's largest forest products companies with over 300 locations worldwide, manufactures pulp and paper, packaging, and wood products, as well as a range of specialty products. Millions of acres of timberland are controlled by International Paper, making it one of the largest private landowners in the United States. The company is organized into five business segments including Printing Papers, in which principal products include uncoated papers, coated papers, bristles, and pulp; Packaging, which includes industrial packaging, consumer packaging, and kraft and specialty papers; Distribution, which includes sales of printing papers, graphic arts equipment and supplies, packaging materials, industrial supplies, and office products; Specialty Products, which include imaging products, specialty panels, nonwovens, chemicals, and minerals; and Forest Products, including Logs and Wood Products. **Corporate headquarters location:** Stamford CT. **Other area locations:** Bucksport ME; Costigan ME; Carmel ME; Jay ME; Roxbury ME. **Other U.S. locations:** Nationwide. **International locations:** Worldwide. **Operations at this facility include:** This location is a paper mill. **Number of employees worldwide:**90,000.

THE JACKSON LABORATORY
600 Main Street, Bar Harbor ME 04609. 207/288-6000. **Fax:** 207/288-6106. **Contact:** Human Resources. **E-mail address:** jobs@jax.com. **World Wide Web address:** http://www.jax.org. **Description:** The Jackson Laboratory is an independent, nonprofit institution. A staff of more than 30 scientists conducts research directed toward two general goals: the development of new knowledge of mammalian genetics through the use of inbred and mutant mice, and the investigation of basic biological processes and their relationships to human diseases by combining genetic knowledge with that of other disciplines. In addition to research, the laboratory distributes nearly 2 million mice annually and offers research training programs for high school, undergraduate, graduate, and postdoctoral level students. **NOTE:** You may mail resumes to 610 Main Street, Bar Harbor ME; e-mail is preferred. **Positions advertised include:** Grants Coordinator; Senior Product Coordinator; Human Resourcse Information Systems Assistant; Production Technician Trainee; Technical Information Services Specialist; Data Architect; Security Guard; Environmental Monitoring Technician; Research Assistant; Laboratory Technician; Director of Directed Research; Biomedical Technologist; Database User Support Specialist; Manager – Biostatistician; Scientific Curator – Various Departments; Senior Veterinarian. **Corporate headquarters location:** This location. **Number of employees at this location:** 650.

JARDEN PLASTIC SOLUTIONS
JARDEN HOME BRANDS
P.O. Box 657, Wilton ME 04294. 207/645-2574. **Physical address:** 5 Mill, Wilton ME 04294. **Contact:** Human Resources. **World Wide Web address:** http://www.unimarkplastics.com. **Description:** Manufactures and distributes wood and plastic household products including toothpicks, match boxes and books, and plastic cutlery. **Corporate headquarters location:** Greenville SC. **Other area locations:** Dryden ME; Strong ME. **Subsidiaries include:** Ball; Bernardin; Diamond, Forster; Kerr; Lady Dianne. **Parent company:** Jarden Corporation. **Listed on:** New York Stock Exchange. **Stock exchange symbol:** JAH

KATAHDIN PAPER
One Katahdin Avenue, Millinocket ME 04462. 207/723-5131. **Contact:** Human Resources. **Description:** Operates two pulp and paper mills, a lumber mill, and a woodlands division. **Other U.S. locations:** Catawba SC; Calhoun TN.

KEYBANK N.A.
One Monument Square, Portland ME 04101. 207/776-7720. **Contact:** Human Resources. **World Wide Web address:** http://www.keybank.com. **Description:** Provides customers with all types of personal and business financial services. There are over 100 branch locations in the state of Maine. **Office hours:** Monday – Friday, 9:00 a.m. – 4:00 p.m. **Corporate headquarters location:** Cleveland OH. **Other area locations:** Statewide. **Other U.S. locations:** Nationwide. **Parent company:** KeyCorp. **Listed on:** American Stock Exchange. **Stock exchange symbol:** KEY. **Number of employees nationwide:** 1,500.

KITTERY TRADING POST
P.O. Box 904, Route 1, Kittery ME 03904-0904. 207/439-2700. **Toll-free phone:** 888/587-6246. **Contact:** Human Resources. **World Wide Web address:** http://www.kitterytradingpost.com. **Description:** A large retail store that sells a wide variety of sporting goods including clothing, footwear, camping gear, shooting and archery equipment, cross country skis, kayaks, and fishing gear. **NOTE:** Please visit website for online application form.

L.L. BEAN, INC.
One Casco Street, Freeport ME 04033. 207/865-4761. **Toll-free phone:** 800/441-5713. **Fax:** 207/552-3080. **Contact:** Human Resources. **E-mail address:** recruit@llbean.com. **World Wide Web address:** http://www.llbean.com. **Description:** A mail order sporting goods and clothing retailer. All types of outdoor clothing and gear are available both at the Freeport retail location (open 24 hours) and through regular seasonal catalogs. **Positions advertised include:** Apparel Designers – Men's and Women's. **Number of employees nationwide:** 4,000.

LABREE'S BAKERY, INC.
169 Gillman Falls Avenue, P.O. Box 555, Old Town ME 04468. 207/827-6121. **Fax:** 207/827-2525. **Contact:** Personnel. **E-mail address:** info@labrees.com; labrees@labrees.com. **World Wide Web address:** http://www.labrees.com. **Description:** A wholesaler and baker of a variety of baked goods including donuts and cakes. LaBree's Bakery, Inc. also runs a retail thrift shop at this location. **Number of employees nationwide:** 150.

LANE CONSTRUCTION CORPORATION
P.O. Box 103, Bangor ME 04402. 207/945-0850. **Physical address:** 1067 Odlin Road, Hermon ME 04401. **Contact:** Human Resources. **World Wide Web address:** http://www.laneconstruct.com. **Description:** A construction company specializing in paving. **Corporate headquarters location:** Meridan CT. **Other U.S. locations:** Nationwide.

LAPOINTE LUMBER COMPANY
2385 North Belfast Avenue, Augusta ME 04330. 207/622-5025. **Toll-free phone:** 800/287-5025. **Fax:** 207/623-3594. **Contact:** Peggy Lord, President of Personnel. **E-mail address:** plord@lapointelumber.com. **World Wide Web address:** http://www.lapointelumber.com. **Description:** Produces and sells lumber and other related products. **Office hours:** Monday – Friday, 7:00 a.m. – 5:00 p.m.; Saturday, 7:00 a.m. – 12:00 p.m. **Corporate headquarters location:** This location.

LIBERTY MUTUAL INSURANCE GROUP
1775 Lisbon Road, Lewiston ME 04240. 207/784-4011. **Toll-free phone:** 800/346-0052. **Fax:** 207/783-8011. **Contact:** Human Resources. **World Wide Web address:** http://www.libertymutual.com. **Description:** A $20 billion insurance and financial services company. **NOTE:** Please visit website to register, search for jobs, and apply online. **Positions advertised include:** Office Assistant; Managing Attorney; Legal Secretary; Legal Office Manager; Senior Underwriting Technician. **Special programs:** Internships. **Corporate headquarters location:** Boston MA. **Other area locations:** Bangor ME; South Portland ME; Kennebunk ME. **Other U.S. locations:** Nationwide. **International locations:** Worldwide. **Number of employees nationwide:** 37,000.

MACDONALD PAGE SCHATZ FLETCHER & CO., LLC
227 Water Street, Augusta ME 04332-1071. 207/774-5701. **Fax:** 207/774-7835. **Contact:** Dan Alley, Human Resources Manager. **E-mail address:** dsa@macpage.com; cpa@macpage.com. **World Wide Web address:** http://www.macpage.com. **Description:** Engaged in all types of accounting for both individual clients and corporations. **Special programs:** Internships. **Other area locations:** South Portland ME; Camden ME. **Number of employees nationwide:** 80.

MADISON PAPER INDUSTRIES
P.O. Box 129, Madison ME 04950. 207/696-3307. **Contact:** Human Resources. **World Wide Web address:** http://www.madisonpaper.com. **Description:** Madison Paper is a mill that produces super-glossy calendar paper for printing catalog-quality material. The company does work for magazines such as *Rolling Stone*. **NOTE:** For salaried employment, please mail resume. For hourly employment, contact the Maine Career Center in Waterville. **Corporate headquarters location:** Norwalk CT. **Parent company:** Myllykoski Corporation. **Listed on:** New York Stock Exchange. **Stock exchange symbol:** NYT. **Number of employees nationwide:** 3,700.

MAINE BIOTECHNOLOGY SERVICES, INC.
1037-R Forest Avenue, Portland ME 04103. 207/797-5454. **Toll-free phone:** 800/925-9476. **Fax:** 207/797-5595. **Contact:** Human Resources. **E-mail address:** msullivan@mainebiotechnology.com. **World Wide Web address:** http://www.mainebiotechnology.com. **Description:** A contracting firm that produces monoclonal and polyclonal antibodies for biotechnology companies.

MAINE DEPARTMENT OF ENVIRONMENTAL PROTECTION
17 Statehouse Station, Augusta ME 04333-0017. 207/287-7688. **Toll-free phone:** 800/452-1942. **Contact:** Alan Lane, Personnel. **E-mail address:** alan.m.lane@state.me.us. **World Wide Web address:** http://www.state.me.us/dep. **Description:** An agency responsible for environmental protection and regulation in the state of Maine. The Maine DEP issues various permits and licenses and enforces state and federal laws, rules, and regulations. **NOTE:** Please visit website to download State of Maine application form. **Positions advertised include:** Conservation Aide. **Other area locations:** Bangor ME; Portland ME; Presque Isle ME.

MAINE DEPARTMENT OF FISHERIES AND WILDLIFE
284 State Street, 41 State House Station, Augusta ME 04333-0041. 207/287-8000. **Toll-free phone:** 800/482-0777. **Contact:** Personnel. **World Wide Web address:** http://www.state.me.us/ifw. **Description:** Regulates and studies Maine's fisheries and wildlife areas. **NOTE:** Please visit website to download State of Maine application form. **Positions advertised include:** Conservation Aide; Biologist; Reservation Clerk; Fish Culturist; AmeriCorps Position. **Other area locations:** Statewide.

MAINE GENERAL MEDICAL CENTER
149 North Street, Waterville ME 04901. 207/872-1000. **Contact:** Human Resources. **World Wide Web address:** http://www.mainegeneral.org. **Description:** A hospital serving central Maine. **NOTE:** Human Resources phone is 207/872-4660. Please visit website to download application form. Applications are kept on record for one year. **Positions advertised include:** Medical Care Review Coordinator; Medical Physicist; Occupational Therapist; Pharmacist; Physical Therapist; Speech-Language Pathologist Float; Mental Health/Substance Abuse Clinician; Substance Abuse Counselor; RN – Various Departments; Dialysis Technician; Nursing Unit Assistant; Phlebotomist; Rehab Technician; Central Scheduler; Health Information Clerk; Registration Representative; Team Leader. **Other area locations:** Augusta ME; Gardiner ME; Manchester ME; Jackman ME; Skowhegan; Winthrop ME. **Number of employees at this location:** 1,738.

MAINE MARITIME ACADEMY
Co-op Administration, Pleasant Street, Castine ME 04421. 207/326-2206. **Toll-free phone:** In-state – 800/464-6565; Out-of-state – 800/277-8465. **Contact:** Human Resources. **World Wide Web address:** http://www.mainemaritime.edu; http://www.mma.edu. **Description:** A four-year college with associate, bachelor's, and master's degree programs in engineering, science, and management. **Positions advertised include:** Master, Small Craft Waterfront; Assistant/Associate Professor – Various Departments; Foundation Officer; STCW Auditor; Summer Sea Session Residential Counselor; Adjunct Instructor – Various Departments; Assistant Men's Basketball Coach; Head Men's Lacrosse Coach; Instructor – Continuing Education; Technical Reader. **Special programs:** Internships. **NOTE:** Human Resources phone is 207/326-2360.

MAINE MEDICAL CENTER
22 Bramhall Street, Portland ME 04102-3175. 207/871-2974. **Recorded jobline:** 877/JOBSMMC. **Fax:** 207/871-4999. **Contact:** Human Resources. **E-mail address:** resumes@mmc.org. **World Wide Web address:** http://www.mmc.org. **Description:** A 598-bed teaching and referral hospital serving northern New England. NOTE: Please visit website for online application form. **Positions advertised include:** Administrative Secretary; Admitting Representative; Billing Representative; Care Coordinator; Certified Nursing Assistant – Various Departments; Chief Nuclear Medical Tech; Clinical Medical Physicist; Clinical Nurse – Various Departments; Clinical Pharmacist; Diagnostic Medical Sonographer; Employee Relations Manager; Executive Director; Financial Planning Specialist; HR Receptionist; Medical Office Assistant; Medical Transcriptionist; Nurse Manager; Nursing Unit Secretary; Pediatric Clinical Nurse Specialist; Physical Therapist; Research Fellow; Secretary – Various Departments.

MAINE PUBLIC SERVICE COMPANY
P.O. Box 1209, Presque Isle ME 04769-1209. 207/760-2435. **Toll-free phone:** 877/655-4448. **Fax:** 207/264-6586. **Contact:** Sherri Jordan, Human Resources. **World Wide Web address:** http://www.mainepublicservice.com. **Description:** A large, investor-owned electric utility located in northern Maine providing energy to more than 34,500 retail customers in a 3,600-square-mile area. Maine Public Service Company has a mixture of generation sources made up of power produced by hydroelectric, nuclear, and oil-fueled facilities, as well as an independent wood-burning cogenerator. **Positions advertised include:** Manager – Financial Planning and Analysis; Corporate Accountant. **Number of employees at this location:** 140.

MAINE STATE MUSIC THEATRE INC.
22 Elm Street, Brunswick ME 04011. 207/725-8760. **Fax:** 207/725-1199. **Contact:** Kathy Kacinski, Company Manager. **E-mail address:** jobs@msmt.org. **World Wide Web address:** http://www.msmt.org. **Description:** A nonprofit music theater company that produces five shows per summer. Maine State Music Theatre also trains theater professionals. **Special programs:** Internships. **Office hours:** Monday - Saturday, 9:00 a.m. - 5:00 p.m. **Corporate headquarters location:** This location.

MAINE WILD BLUEBERRY COMPANY, INC.
P.O. Box 128, Cherryfield ME 04622. 207/255-8364. **Physical address:** Elm, Machias ME 04654. **Contact:** Nancy Merritt, Personnel Manager. **Description:** Producers of wild blueberries and frozen and canned fruits and other products. **Parent company:** Oxford Frozen Foods.

MARRIOTT HOTEL
200 Sable Oaks Drive, South Portland ME 04106-3212. 207/871-8000. **Fax:** 207/871-7971. **Contact:** Human Resources. **World Wide Web address:** http://marriotthotels.com/pwmap. **Description:** A 227-room hotel offering both lodging and restaurant services. **Special programs:** Internships. **Corporate headquarters location:** Washington D.C. **Other area locations:** Statewide. **Other U.S. locations:** Nationwide. **Listed on:** New York Stock Exchange. **Stock exchange symbol:** MAR. **Number of employees at this location:** 150. **Number of employees worldwide:** 128,000.

MCBEE
1321 Washington Avenue, Portland ME 04103. 207/797-5908. **Fax:** 207/797-0312. **Contact:** Human Resources. **E-mail address:** jobs@ mcbeeinc.com. **World Wide Web address:** http://www.mcbeeinc.com. **Description:** Produces specialized business forms including check and payroll forms. Founded 1908. **Positions advertised include:** Sales Representative. **Corporate headquarters location:** Thorofare NJ.

MEADWESTVACO
35 Hartford Street, Rumford ME 04276. 207/364-4521. **Contact:** Human Resources. **World Wide Web address:** http://www.meadwestvaco.com. **Description:** Produces and distributes pulp and paper, directly distributes office products, and manufactures and distributes building products. **Corporate headquarters location:** Stamford CT. **Other area locations:** Augusta ME. **Other U.S. locations:** Nationwide. **International locations:** Worldwide. **Listed on:** New York Stock Exchange. **Stock exchange symbol:** MWV.

MERCY HOSPITAL
144 State Street, Portland ME 04101. 207/879-3000. **Toll-free phone:** 800/293-6583. **Recorded jobline:** 207/879-3674. **Contact:** Human Resources Department. **E-mail address:** resumes@careers-mercy hospital.org. **World Wide Web address:** http://www.mercyhospital.org. **Description:** A hospital providing service to Portland ME and the surrounding communities. **NOTE:** Please visit website for online application form. Human Resources phone is 207/879-3464. **Positions advertised include:** Accountant; Cafeteria Service Assistant; Certified Surgical Technologist; Clinical Dietitian; Clinical Nurse Educator; Clinical Nurse – Various Departments; CRNA; Environmental Service Assistant; Food Service Assistant; Lab Assistant; Nuclear Medicine Technologist; Out-Patient Counselor; Physical Therapist; Radiology Client Service Coordinator; Security Officer; Switchboard Operator; Therapist; Ultrasound Technician.

MORGAN BAYSIDE
MORGAN REAL ESTATE INC.
711 Bayside Road, Ellsworth ME 04605. 207/667-3845. **Toll-free phone:** 800/660-3845. **Fax:** 207/667-7383. **Contact:** Human Resources. **E-mail address:** sold@mbre.net. **World Wide Web address:** http://www.mbre.net. **Description:** Engaged in residential and commercial property sales and rental.

MOUNT DESERT ISLAND HOSPITAL
10 Wayman Lane, Bar Harbor ME 04609. 207/288-5081. **Fax:** 207/288-5874. **Contact:** Human Resources. **E-mail address:** hr@mdihospital.org. **World Wide Web address:** http://www.mdihospital.org. **Description:** A nonprofit hospital with physician practices. Founded in 1897. **NOTE:** Human Resources is Extension 410. Entry-level positions and second and third shifts are offered. Please visit website, call, or email to request an application form. You may also print an application form from the website. **Positions advertised include:** Health Care Systems Trainer; Health Center Clinical Operations Educator; Medical Assistant; Health Center Receptionist; CNA; Environmental Services Aide; RN – OR; X-ray Technician; Ultrasonographer; Radiologic Technologist. **Number of employees at this location:** 310.

NAVIGATOR PUBLISHING
P.O. Box 569, Portland ME 04112. 207/772-2466. **Physical address:** 58 Fore Street, Portland ME 04101. **Fax:** 207/772-2879. **Contact:** Human Resources. **World Wide Web address:** http://www.navigatorpublishing.com. **Description:** A magazine publishing company. Titles include two bimonthly publications, *Ocean Navigator* and *Professional Mariner*.

NEW BALANCE ATHLETIC SHOE INC.
13 Walnut Street, Skowhegan ME 04976-1514. 207/474-6231. **Contact:** Personnel Department. **World Wide Web address:** http://www.newbalance.com. **Description:** New Balance Athletic Shoes manufactures and distributes running and other athletic shoes. **Corporate headquarters location:** Boston MA. **Other area locations:** Norway ME; Norridgewock ME. **Other U.S. locations:** Lawrence MA. **International locations:** Worldwide. **Operations at this facility include:** This location is a manufacturing facility. **Number of employees worldwide:** 2,500

NEW ENGLAND HOME HEALTH CARE
P.O. Box 722, Bangor ME 04402-0722. 207/945-3374. **Physical address:** 412 State Street, Bangor ME 04402. **Toll-free phone:** 800/287-0338. **Fax:** 207/942-1022. **Contact:** Jen Ashmore, Human Resources Manager. **E-mail address:** jen@nehhc.com. **World Wide Web address:** http://www.nehhc.com. **Description:** Provides home care services in Penobscot, Piscataquis, and Hancock Counties of Maine. The company also provides temporary staffing services to hospitals, boarding homes, assisted living centers, nursing homes, and other home care agencies. Founded in 1984. **NOTE:** Please visit website for online application form. Second and third shifts are offered. New England Home Health Care also offers a personal care attendant training program three times a year. **Company slogan:** Helping you meet the challenges of today and tomorrow. **Positions advertised include:** CAN – Various Departments. **Special programs:** Summer Jobs. **Listed on:** Privately held. **Other area locations:** Statewide. **President:** Margaret Michaud-Cain. **Number of employees at this location:** 200.

NICHOLS PORTLAND
2400 Congress Street, Portland ME 04102. 207/774-6121. **Fax:** 207/774-3601. **Contact:** Human Resources Department. **World Wide Web address:** http://www.parker.com/nichport. **Description:** Manufactures motion control products including fluid power systems, electromechanical controls, and related components. Products are sold through direct sales employees and more than 4,900 distributors. Repair and replacement components account for about half of the total sales. The product lines of the industrial sector cover most of the components of control systems. The Motion and Control Group makes hydraulic pumps, power units, control valves, accumulators, cylinders, actuators, and automation devices to remove contaminants from air, fuel, oil, water, and other fluids. The Fluid Connectors Group makes connectors, tube and hose fittings, hoses, and couplers that transmit fluid. The Seal Group makes sealing devices, gaskets, and packing that ensure leak-proof connections. The Automotive and Refrigeration Groups make components for use in industrial and automotive air conditioning and refrigeration systems. Principal products of the aerospace segment are hydraulic, pneumatic, and fuel systems and components. **Positions advertised include:** Manufacturing Personnel; Maintenance Electrician. **Office hours:** Monday – Friday, 8:00 a.m. – 4:30 p.m. **Parent company:** Parker Hannifin Corporation. **Number of employees at this location:** 500.

NORDX LABORATORIES
102 Campus Drive, Scarborough ME 04074. 207/885-7877. **Fax:** 207/885-7880. **Contact:** Human Resources. **E-mail address:** hr@nordx.org. **World Wide Web**

address: http://www.nordx.org. **Description:** Provides comprehensive laboratory services for the Northeast medical community.

NORTHEAST MECHANICAL CORPORATION
139 Cash Street, P.O. Box 2829, South Portland ME 04116. 207/799-8533. **Toll-free phone:** 800/883-7661. **Fax:** 207/799-5642. **Contact:** Human Resources. **E-mail address:** info@nemech.com. **World Wide Web address:** http://www.nemech.com. **Description:** Provides energy solutions to Maine and New Hampshire. Founded 1963. **Positions advertised include:** Burner Service Technician. **Corporate headquarters location:** This location. **Other area locations:** Brewer ME. **Other U.S. locations:** Manchester NH.

NORWAY SAVINGS BANK
P.O. Box 347, Norway ME 04268. 207/743-7986. **Physical address:** 261 Main Street, Norway ME 04268. **Toll-free phone:** 888/725-2207. **Fax:** 207/743-5378. **Contact:** Human Resources Department. **E-mail address:** info@norwaysavingsbank.com. **World Wide Web address:** http://www.norwaysavingsbank.com. **Description:** Offers a full range of business and individual banking products and services. **NOTE:** Please visit website to download application form. **Positions advertised include:** Customer Relations Representative; Customer Service Representative; Full-time Teller; Part-time Teller. **Office hours:** Monday – Thursday, 9:00 a.m. – 3:00 p.m.; Friday, 9:00 a.m. – 5:00 p.m. **Corporate headquarters location:** This location. **Other area locations:** Statewide. **Number of employees nationwide:** 250.

OLIVE GARDEN ITALIAN RESTAURANT
741 Hogan Road, Bangor ME 04401-3625. 207/942-6209. **Fax:** 207/947-6575. **Contact:** Mr. Chris Fowler, General Manager. **World Wide Web address:** http://www.olivegarden.com. **Description:** One location of the nationwide restaurant chain. **NOTE:** Applications must be filled out at the restaurant. **Office hours:** Sunday – Thursday, 11:00 a.m. – 10:00 p.m.; Friday – Saturday, 11:00 a.m. – 11:00 p.m.

OSRAM-SYLVANIA, INC.
405 Friendship Street, Waldoboro ME 04572. 207/832-5313. **Contact:** Human Resources Manager. **World Wide Web address:** http://www.sylvania.com. **Description:** A producer of lighting filaments. OSRAM-SYLVANIA, Inc. operates in the following divisions: Coated Coil Operation, which involves the production of tungsten filaments coated with high-performance insulator aluminum oxide used in television electron guns; Special Refractory Products, which manufactures products made from refractory metals that are used as furnace hardware; the Ceramics Department, which produces various types of steatite ceramic electrical insulators used in bases of light bulbs; and the Quartz Department, which produces and finishes quartz crucibles for use by the semiconductor industry. **Corporate headquarters location:** Danvers MA. **Other U.S. locations:** Nationwide. **Parent company:** OSRAM GmbH of Munich, Germany. **Operations at this facility include:** This location manufactures precision materials and components. **Number of employees at this location:** 250. **Number of employees worldwide:** 35,000.

PEOPLE'S HERITAGE BANK
One Portland Square, P.O. Box 9540, Portland ME 04112-9540. 207/761-8500. **Fax:** 207/828-7578. **Contact:** Human Resources. **E-mail address:** hrme@banknorth.com. **World Wide Web address:** http://www.peoplesheritage.com. **Description:** A bank that is a holding company. People's Heritage conducts residential and commercial real estate operations; originates construction, commercial, and consumer loans; invests in government securities; and operates equipment leasing and financial planning services. **Positions advertised include:** Consumer Credit Representative; Teller; In-store Service Associate; Compliance Specialist; Asset Liability Analyst; IT Auditor. **Listed on:** New York Stock Exchange. **Stock exchange symbol:** BNK. **Parent company:** Banknorth, N.A. **President:** Michael W. McNamara.

PEPSI BOTTLING GROUP
19 Penobscot Meadow Drive, Hampden ME 04444. 207/973-2200. **Contact:** Personnel. **World Wide Web address:** http://www.pepsico.com. **Description:** Distributes beverages bottled under the Pepsi-Cola name. **NOTE:** Jobs are posted at the Career Center, located at 45 Oak Street in Bangor. Their phone is 207/561-4050. **Office hours:** Monday – Friday, 8:00 a.m. – 5:00 p.m. **Parent company:** PepsiCo, Inc. (Purchase NY) consists of Frito-Lay Company, Pepsi-Cola Company, Quaker, Gatorade, and Tropicana Products, Inc. **Listed on:** New York Stock Exchange. **Stock exchange symbol:** PEP.

PHILIPS ELMET
1560 Lisbon Street, Lewiston ME 04240. 207/784-3591. **Toll-free phone:** 800/343-8008. **Fax:** 207/786-8924. **Contact:** Human Resources. **World Wide Web address:** http://www.lighting.philips.com/elmet. **Description:** A refractory metals division of the company, which manufactures molybdenum and tungsten products including rods and studs. Philips Elmet also has a division that produces fine wire for lightbulb coils. Founded 1929. **Corporate headquarters location:** This location. **Number of employees at this location:** 350.

PHOENIX FOOTWEAR
P.O. Box 545, Old Town ME 04468-1417. 207/827-4431. **Physical address:** 107 Main Street, Old Town ME 04468. **Contact:** Personnel Manager. **World Wide Web address:** http://www.phoenixfootwear.com. **Description:** Designs, manufactures, imports, and sells women's casual, sport, and leisure footwear, including fashion boots and sandals. Founded 1882. **Corporate headquarters location:** Carlsbad CA. **Listed on:** American Stock Exchange. **Stock exchange symbol:** PXG.

PINE STATE TRADING COMPANY
8 Ellis Avenue, Augusta ME 04330. 207/622-3741. **Toll-free phone:** In-state – 800/452-4633; Out-of-state – 800/451-5500. **Contact:** Personnel. **World Wide Web address:** http://www.pinestatetrading.com. **Description:** A wholesaler of a wide variety of foods and other products for retail stores. **Corporate headquarters location:** This location. **Other area locations:** Bangor. **Other U.S. locations:** Manchester NH; East Montpelier VT; Millbury MA. **CEO:** Charles F. Canning.

PIONITE DECORATIVE SURFACES
P.O. Box 1014, Auburn ME 04211-1014. 207/784-9111. **Physical address:** One Pionite Road, Auburn ME 04210. **Toll-free phone:** 800/746-6483. **Fax:** 207/784-0392. **Contact:** Human Resources. **World Wide Web address:** http://www.pionite.com/pionite/index.html. **Description:** A manufacturer of high-pressure decorative laminates, treated papers, and specialty resins. **Corporate headquarters location:** Shelton CT. **Parent company:** Panolam Industries International/ **Number of employees at this location:** 700.

PORTLAND MAGAZINE
722 Congress Street, Portland ME 04102. 207/775-4339. **Contact:** Colin Sargent, Publisher. **E-mail address:** editor@portlandmonthly.com. **World Wide Web address:** http://www.portlandmonthly.com. **Description:** Publishes a monthly periodical. **Special programs:** Internships. **Corporate headquarters location:** This location. **Parent company:** Sargent Publishing. **Operations at this facility include:** Administration; Sales. **Listed on:** Privately held.

PORTLAND PIRATES
531 Congress Street, Portland ME 04101. 207/828-4665. **Fax:** 207/773-3278. **Contact:** Human Resources. **E-mail address:** info@portlandpirates. com. **World Wide Web address:** http://www.portlandpirates.com. **Description:** A minor league professional hockey franchise. The Portland Pirates play in the AHL (American Hockey League) and are an affiliate of the Washington Capitals. The team plays in the Cumberland County Civic Center. The team's offices include the following departments: a ticket office, souvenir sales, media relations, team services, and community relations. **Office hours:** Monday - Thursday, 9:00 a.m. - 3:00 p.m.; Friday, 9:00 a.m. - 1:00 p.m.

PORTLAND SEA DOGS
P.O. Box 626, Portland ME 04102. 207/874-9300. **Physical address:** 271 Park Avenue, Portland ME 04102. **Toll-free phone:** 800/936-3647. **Contact:** Personnel. **World Wide Web address:** http://www.portlandseadogs.com. **Description:** A minor league baseball franchise. The Portland Sea Dogs are the AA affiliate of the Florida Marlins Major League Baseball franchise. **Corporate headquarters location:** This location.

PORTLAND STAGE COMPANY
P.O. Box 1458, Portland ME 04104. 207/774-1043. **Physical address:** 25 Forest Avenue, Portland ME 04104. **Fax:** 207/774-0576. **E-mail address:** info@portlandstage.com. **World Wide Web address:** http://www.portlandstage.com. **Description:** A nonprofit professional theater. Founded 1974. **Special programs:** Internships. **Corporate headquarters location:** This location. **Number of employees at this location:** 30.

PRATT & WHITNEY
113 Wells Street, North Berwick ME 03906. 207/676-4100. **Fax:** 207/676-4123. **Contact:** Human Resources. **World Wide Web address:** http://www.pratt-whitney.com. **Description:** Manufactures blades, vanes, and bearing compartments for commercial and military engines. **Special programs:** Internships; Co-ops. **Corporate headquarters location:** East Hartford CT. **Other U.S. locations:** Nationwide. **International locations:** Worldwide. **Parent company:** United Technologies Corporation. **Listed on:** New York Stock Exchange. **Stock exchange symbol:** UTX. **Number of employees at this location:** 1,500.

PRECAST CONCRETE PRODUCTS OF MAINE
P.O. Box 307, Topsham ME 04086. 207/729-1628. **Physical address:** Route 201 Augusta Road, Topsham ME. **Fax:** 207/729-8710. **Contact:** Ben Gray, Personnel. **E-mail address:** bgray@suscom-maine.net. **World Wide Web address:** http://www.gwi.net/precast. **Description:** Manufactures a wide range of precast concrete products including concrete blocks and septic tanks. **Positions advertised include:** Mixer Truck Driver. **Office hours:** Monday – Friday, 7:00 a.m. – 5:00 p.m. **Corporate headquarters location:** This location.

PROCTER & GAMBLE
2879 Hotel Road, Auburn ME 04210. 207/753-4000. **Contact:** Human Resource. **World Wide Web address:** http://www.pg.com. **Description:** P&G is a manufacturer and marketer of consumer healthcare and sanitary products.

REDINGTON-FAIRVIEW GENERAL HOSPITAL
P.O. Box 468, Skowhegan ME 04976. 207/474-5121. **Physical address:** 46 Fariview Avenue, Skowhegan ME. **Fax:** 207/474-7004. **Contact:** Debbie Buckingham, Human Resources Director. **E-mail address:** wbrooks@rfgh.net. **World Wide Web address:** http://www.rfgh.net. **Description:** A nonprofit, acute care hospital. Founded in 1969. **NOTE:** Entry-level positions, part-time jobs, and second and third shifts are offered. Volunteer positions are also available. Human Resources Extensions are 301, 304, and 425. Please visit website to download application form. **Positions advertised include:** Clinic/CAN; Endoscopy Aide; General Maintenance Worker/Plumber; Infection Control Practitioner; MT/MLT; Occupational Therapist; Phlebotomist; Physical Therapist; RN – Various Departments. **President/CEO:** Richard Willett. **Number of employees at this location:** 540.

S.A.S. PITTSFIELD INC. (SAN ANTONIO SHOE)
P.O. Box 250, Pittsfield ME 04967-0250. 207/487-3252. **Physical address:** Northeast Drive, Pittsfield ME. **Contact:** Personnel. **Description:** S.A.S. Pittsfield Inc. is a shoe manufacturer. **Number of employees at this location:** 250.

SACO RIVER TECHNOLOGIES
70 Shadagee Road, Saco ME 04072. 207/727-5795. **Fax:** 207/727-5793. **Contact:** Hiring Manager. **World Wide Web address:** http://www.sacorivertech.com. **Description:** Provides a variety of computer services including consulting, programming, and Web design to help clients understand their technology options. Founded in 1991. **Office hours:** Monday - Friday, 9:00 a.m. - 5:00 p.m. **Corporate headquarters location:** This location.

ST. ANDREWS HOSPITAL & HEALTHCARE CENTER
P.O. Box 417, 6 Saint Andrew's Lane, Boothbay Harbor ME 04538. 207/633-2121. **Fax:** 207/633-4209. **Contact:** Human Resources. **World Wide Web address:** http://www.standrewshealthcare.org. **Description:** A nonprofit hospital that offers acute care, long-term care, a family medical practice, home health care, emergency services, and a retirement community center. Founded in 1908. **NOTE:** Second and third shifts are offered. **Company slogan:** A tradition of caring. **Office hours:** Monday - Friday, 8:00 a.m. - 5:00 p.m. **Listed on:** Privately held. **President:** Peggy Pinkham. **Annual sales/revenues:** $5 - $10 million. **Number of employees at this location:** 185.

SAINT-GOBAIN BTI, INC.
43 Bibber Parkway, Brunswick ME 04011. 207/729-7792. **Toll-free phone:** 888/284-2667. **Fax:** 207/729-7877. **Contact:** Human Resources. **World Wide Web address:** http://www.brunswicktech.com. **Description:** Develops and manufactures engineered reinforcements for the composites industry. Products are constructed with glass, carbon and Kevlar™ in a variety of widths, weights, and fiber orientations. **Corporate headquarters location:** This location. **Other U.S. locations:** Seguin TX. **International locations:** Andover, England. **Number of employees worldwide:** 195.

ST. JOSEPH'S COLLEGE
278 Whites Bridge Road, Standish ME 04084-5263. 207/892-6766. **Contact:** Jane LaFlamme, Director of Human Resources. **E-mail address:** jlaflemme@sjcme.edu. **World Wide Web address:** http://www.sjcme.edu. **Description:** A four-year college with associate and bachelor's degree programs, as well as master's degrees in health care administration. **NOTE:** Please visit website for online application form. Human Resources phone is 207/893-7755. **Positions advertised include:** Assistant Professor of Nursing; Assistant Professor Elementary Education; Adjunct Professor – Various

Departments; Library Assistant; Area Coordinator; Campus Services Assistant; Volleyball Coach; Field Hockey Coach; Van/Mini Bus Driver; HVAC Technician; Peer Reviewer for Master in Health Administrative Program; Security Officer.

ST. MARY'S REGIONAL MEDICAL CENTER
Campus Avenue, Lewiston ME 04243. 207/777-8100. **Fax:** 207/777-8783. **Contact:** Nicole Moran-Scribner, Employee Relations Director. **World Wide Web address:** http://www.stmarysmaine.com. **Description:** A hospital that operates as part of the Sisters of Charity Health System. **NOTE:** Please visit website for online application form. Human Resources phone is 207/777-8779. **Positions advertised include:** Certified Nurse Assistant; Office Secretary; Account Representative; Behavioral Services Technician; Director – Imaging Services; Nurse Practitioner; Respiratory Care Practitioner; RN – Various Departments; Washperson – Personal Laundry; Medical Assistant; Cytotechnologist; Phlebotomist; Behavioral Services Technician; Laboratory Technical Assistant; Dental Assistant; Dental Hygenist; Resident Technician; Office Clinical Assistant; Occupational Therapist; Social Worker; Call Center Associate; LPN; Polysomnography – Registered. **Operations at this facility include:** Administration. **Number of employees at this location:** 1,400.

SALT MAGAZINE
P.O. Box 7800, Portland ME 04112-7800. 207/761-0660. **Physical address:** 110 Exchange Street, Portland ME. **Fax:** 207/761-2913. **Contact:** Human Resources. **E-mail address:** info@salt.edu. **World Wide Web address:** http://www.salt.edu. **Description:** Publishes a magazine focused on contemporary Maine, displaying the writing and black and white photography of Salt Institute for Documentary Studies students. **Office hours:** Monday – Friday, 9:00 a.m. – 4:00 p.m.

H.E. SARGENT, INC.
P.O. Box 435, 101 Bennoch Road, Stillwater ME 04489. 207/827-4435. **Fax:** 207/827-6150. **Contact:** Personnel. **World Wide Web address:** http://www.hesargent.com. **Description:** A general and heavy construction firm engaging in earth and civil work.

SCOTIA PRINCE CRUISES
468 Commercial Street, Portland ME 04101. 207/775-5611. **Toll-free phone:** 800/845-4073. **E-mail address:** info@scotiaprince.com. **World Wide Web address:** http://www.scotiaprince.com. **Description:** An ocean cruise line.

SHAPE INC.
RNV INDUSTRIES
90 Community Drive, Sanford ME 04073. 207/324-5200. **Fax:** 207/324-0875. **Contact:** Human Resources. **E-mail address:** careers@shapeglobal.com. **World Wide Web address:** http://www.shapenet.com. **Description:** A manufacturing company specializing in audio- and videocassettes and other magnetic media. **Positions advertised include:** Senior Toolmaker. **Corporate headquarters location:** This location. **Subsidiaries include:** Shape Audio Product Division, an independent manufacturer of audiocassettes; Shape Video Products, which provides a complete range of manufacturing services from the production of VHS cassettes to the loading, packaging, and distribution of private-label cassettes; Shape Segoma, which manufactures high-quality computer printer ribbons for OEM manufacturers and storage media; and Shape South, Inc., which designs and manufactures precision products for the computer, video, and other magnetic media industries. **Operations at this facility include:** Administration; Sales.

SHAW'S SUPERMARKETS
P.O. Box 3566, Portland ME 04104. 207/773-0211. **Physical address:** 190 Riverside Street, Portland ME. **Contact:** Human Resources. **World Wide Web address:** http://www.shaws.com. **Description:** This is the northern regional office location of the Shaw's Supermarkets chain of grocery stores, serving as the hub for the retail locations throughout the state of Maine. Founded 1860. **NOTE:** Please visit website for online application form. **Corporate headquarters location:** East Bridgewater MA. **Other area locations:** Statewide. **Other U.S. locations:** CT; MA; NH; RI; VT. **Parent company:** J. Sainsbury plc. **Operations at this facility include:** Regional Headquarters. **Number of employees nationwide:** 30,000.

SHAW'S SUPERMARKETS
46 Springer Drive, Bangor ME 04401. 207/942-1608. **Contact:** Manager. **E-mail address:** resume@shaws.com. **World Wide Web address:** http://www.shaws.com. **Description:** A supermarket. **NOTE:** Please visit website for online application form. **Corporate headquarters location:** East Bridgewater MA. **Other U.S. locations:** CT; MA; NH; RI; VT. **Parent company:** J. Sainsbury plc. **Number of employees nationwide:** 30,000.

SHERIDAN CORPORATION
P.O. Box 359, Fairfield ME 04937. 207/453-9311. **Physical address:** 33 Sheridan Road, Fairfield ME 04937. **Fax:** 207/453-2820. **Contact:** Personnel. **E-mail address:** jobs@sheridancorp.com. **World Wide Web address:** http://www.sheridancorp.com. **Description:** A general contractor specializing in residential and commercial construction. **Positions advertised include:** Laborer; Steel Erector; Metal Roof Installer; Form Carpenter; Welder; Metal Siding Installer; Project Supervisor; Rough Carpenter; Steel Fabricator; Crane Operator; Sales Consultant; Administrative Worker; Proposal Coordinator; Project Manager; Health and Safety Personnel; Engineer; CAD Operator. **Office hours:** Monday – Friday, 8:00 a.m. – 5:00 p.m. **Other area locations:** Portland ME.

SOMIX TECHNOLOGIES INC.
1293 Main Street, Sanford ME 04073. 207/324-8805. **Fax:** 207/324-8683. **Contact:** Human Resources. **E-mail address:** jobs@somix.com. **World Wide Web address:** http://www.somix.com. **Description:** Develops web-based IT and system management applications.

SOUTHWORTH PRODUCTS
P.O. Box 1380, Portland ME 04104. 207/878-0700. **Physical address:** 11 Gray Road, Falmouth ME 04105. **Toll-free phone:** 800/743-1000. **Fax:** 207/ 797-4734. **Contact:** John Lemire, Director of Human Resources. **World Wide Web address:** http://www.southworthproducts.com. **Description:** Manufactures hydraulic lift tables, packaging equipment, conveyors, and material handling systems. **Corporate headquarters location:** This location. **Other area locations:** Falmouth ME. **Operations at this facility include:** Administration; Sales.

SPRING HARBOR HOSPITAL
123 Andover Road, Westbrook ME 04092. 207/761-2200. **Toll-free phone:** 888/524-0080. **Fax:** 207/761-2388. **Contact:** Wendy Worcester, Employment Specialist. **E-mail address:** recruitment@springharbor.org. **World Wide Web address:** http://www.springharbor.org. **Description:** A psychiatric hospital that offers inpatient treatment and outpatient counseling services to people of all ages. **NOTE:** Entry-level positions and second and third shifts are offered. Please visit website for online application form. **Positions advertised include:** Payroll Specialist; Psychiatric NP; Psych Tech; RN; Behavioral Ph]sychologist; Discharge Planner; Clinical Nurse Manager; Dietary Aide. **Special programs:** Internships. **Office hours:** Monday - Friday, 8:00 a.m. - 4:30 p.m. **Number of employees at this location:** 500.

STEPHENS MEMORIAL HOSPITAL
181 Main Street, Norway ME 04268-1297. 207/743-5933. **Contact:** Human Resources. **E-mail address:** benochl@wmhcc.org. **World Wide Web address:** http://www.wmhcc.com. **Description:** A hospital offering a special care unit, pace paramedic service, and educational programs on health issues. **NOTE:** Please visit website for online application form. **Positions advertised include:** CNA – Various Departments; LPN – Various Departments; RN – Various Departments; CT Technologist; PT or PTA; Ultrasonographer. **Parent company:** Western Maine Health. **CEO:** Timothy A. Churchill. **Number of employees at this location:** 400

STINSON SEAFOOD
65 Bowery Street, Bath ME 04530 P.O. Box 69, Route 186, Prospect Harbor ME 04669. 207/963-7331. **Toll-free phone:** 800/334-3696. **Fax:** 207/963-5590. 8235. **Contact:** Human Resources Manager. **World Description:** Catches, processes, cans, packages, and ships sardines and sardine products. Plants also manufacture the aluminum cans used in packaging. The company's plants are located in Bath (not this location), Belfast, and Prospect Harbor. **NOTE:** Employment information is available at this location. **Other area locations:** Bath ME.

SUGARLOAF/USA
Box 5092, Carrabasset Valley ME 04947. 207/237-6922. **Fax:** 207/237-6778. **Contact:** Marilyn Curry, Human Resources Director. **World Wide Web address:** http://www.sugarloaf.com. **Description:** An operator of a ski mountain and resort. Races and other events are held year-round. Features at Sugarloaf include a number of cross-country trails, an Olympic-size ice-skating rink, and an 18-hole golf course. **NOTE:** Contact Human Resources Director at 207/237-6932. Please visit website to download application form. **Positions advertised include:** Certified Massage Therapist; Costume Character; Hotel Housekeeper; Lift Dispatcher; Lift Operator; Marketing Services and Interactive Manager; Nordic Pro/Shop Sales; Owner Services Secretary; Race and Event Crew; Security Dispatcher; Security Officer; Snow Shoveler; Sugarloaf Food Service Provider; Water Utilities Technician. **Special programs:** Internships. **Corporate headquarters location:** This location. **Parent company:** American Skiing Company. **Operations at this facility include:** Administration; Sales; Service. **Number of employees at this location:** 750.

SUNDAY RIVER SKI AREA
P.O. Box 450, Bethel ME 04217. 207/824-3000. **Toll-free phone:** 877/4-SNOW_JOB. **Fax:** 207/824-5110. **Contact:** Human Resources Department. **E-mail address:** jobs@sundayriver.com. **World Wide Web address:** http://www.sundayriver.com. **Description:** Operates more than 120 ski trails on eight mountains. **NOTE:** Minimum employment age is 16 years old. Contact Human Resources directly at 207/824-5160. Please visit website for online application form. **Positions advertised include:** Lift Operator; Electrician; Hotel Administrative Assistant; Hotel Line Cook; Housekeeper; Rental Technician; Event Staff Member; Snowboard Professional.

SYSCO FOOD SERVICES OF NORTHERN NEW ENGLAND
P.O. Box 4657, Portland ME 04112-4657. 207/871-0700. **Physical address:** 36 Thomas Drive, Westbrook ME. **Toll-free phone:** 800/632-4446. **Fax:** 207/253-7233. **Contact:** Richard Euler, Director of Human Resources. **E-mail address:** employment@sysconne.com. **World Wide Web address:** http://www.sysconne.com. **Description:** Sysco is one of the largest foodservice distributors in the United States. They distribute fresh and frozen meats, canned products, dairy products, as well as disposable items and medical equipment. **Positions advertised include:** Marketing Associate; Cycle Counter; Warehouse Selector; Delivery Driver; Shuttle Driver. **Parent company:** Sysco Corporation. **Listed on:** New York Stock Exchange. **Stock exchange symbol:** SYY.

THE THEATER AT MONMOUTH
P.O. Box 385, Monmouth ME 04259-0385. 207/933-2952. **Contact:** David Greenham, Producing Director. **E-mail address:** tamoffice@theateratmonmouth.org. **World Wide Web address:** http://www.theateratmonmouth.org. **Description:** A small, professional, summer theater in central Maine, performing in a national historic landmark Victorian opera house. **NOTE:** The theater offers seasonal employment for professionals in the technical, costume, administrative, and performance departments. **Special programs:** Internships. **Office hours:** Monday - Friday, 9:00 a.m. - 5:00 p.m. **Corporate headquarters location:** This location. **Operations at this facility include:** Administration; Sales. **Number of employees at this location:** 40.

THOMAS COLLEGE
180 West River Road, Waterville ME 04901. 207/859-1111. **Fax:** 207/859-1114. **Contact:** Human Resources. **E-mail address:** its@thomas.edu. **World Wide Web address:** http://www.thomas.edu. **Description:** A four-year college with associate, bachelor's, and master's degree programs. NOTE: Thomas College accepts letters of interest for adjunct faculty positions. **Positions advertised include:** Adjunct Faculty – Various Departments; Security Officer; Student Financial Services Counselor; Custodian.

THORNDIKE PRESS
P.O. Box 159, Thorndike ME 04986. 207/859-1000. **Physical address:** 295 Kennedy Memorial Drive, Waterville ME 04901. **Contact:** Human Resources. **World Wide Web address:** http://www.galegroup.com. **Description:** Purchases the rights to books that have already been published and publishes them in large-print. **Parent Company:** Gale Group.

TIME WARNER CABLE
118 Johnson Road, Portland ME 04102-1911. 207/775-2381. **Contact:** Human Resources. **World Wide Web address:** http://www.twmaine.com. **Description:** A cable television company serving local Maine communities. **Other area locations:** Presque Isle ME; Saco ME. **Parent company:** AOL Time Warner.

TOM'S OF MAINE
302 Lafayette Center, P.O. Box 710, Kennebunk ME 04043. 207/985-2944. **Toll-free phone:** 800/775-2388. **Contact:** Human Resources. **World Wide Web address:** http://www.toms-of-maine.com. **Description:** Manufactures oral and body care products using only natural ingredients. Products include fluoride and nonfluoride toothpaste; children's toothpaste (made with fruit extracts); flossing ribbon made with vegetable waxes; alcohol-free mouthwash; moisturizing, deodorant, and mild children's soaps; shampoo; deodorant and antiperspirant; and shaving cream. **Corporate headquarters location:** This location.

TOWER PUBLISHING COMPANY
588 Saco Road, Standish ME 04084. 207/642-5400. **Toll-free phone:** 800/969-8693. **Fax:** 207/642-5463. **Contact:** Michael Lyons, Publisher. **E-mail address:**

info@towerpub.com. **World Wide Web address:** http://www.towerpublishingcompany.com. **Description:** A publishing company specializing in business and legal directories for northern New England. Founded in 1820. **Annual sales/revenues:** Less than $5 million.

U.S. OCCUPATIONAL SAFETY AND HEALTH ADMINISTRATION
100 Middle Street, Suite 410 West, Portland ME 04101. 207/780-3178. **Contact:** Human Resources. **World Wide Web address:** http://www.osha.gov. **Description:** Conducts unannounced inspections of businesses to ensure government standards are being met. **Parent company:** U.S. Department of Labor.

UNITED PUBLICATIONS INC.
106 Lafayette Street, Yarmouth ME 04096. 207/846-0600. **Fax:** 207/846-0657. **Contact:** Human Resources. **World Wide Web address:** http://www.ccnews.com. **Description:** A newspaper publishing company that produces six specialty trade publications.

UNIVERSITY OF MAINE AT FARMINGTON
224 Main Street, Farmington ME 04938. 207/778-7246. **Fax:** 207/778-7247. **Contact:** Director of Personnel. **E-mail address:** lgardner@maine.edu. **World Wide Web address:** http://www.umf.maine.edu. **Description:** One location of the state university. University of Maine is a four-year, undergraduate, public university with an emphasis on education and liberal arts. **Positions advertised include:** Assistant English Professor; Assistant/Associate Professor of Computer Science; Assistant Director of Facilities Management; Administrative Assistant; Plumber. **Operations at this facility include:** Administration; Service. **Number of employees at this location:** 330.

UNIVERSITY OF MAINE AT MACHIAS
9 O'Brien Avenue, Machias ME 04654. 207/255-1200. **Contact:** Personnel. **E-mail address:** ummjobs@maine.edu. **World Wide Web address:** http://www.umm.maine.edu. **Description:** One location of the state university. The University of Maine is a four-year, undergraduate, public university with an emphasis on education and liberal arts. **Positions advertised include:** Part-time teaching positions for the following disciplines: Mathematics, Psychology, History, Humanities, and Art.

UNIVERSITY OF MAINE AT ORONO
124 Corbett Hall, Orono ME 04469-5717. 207/581-2362. **Contact:** Allan Boggs. **E-mail address:** aboggs@maine.edu. **World Wide Web address:** http://www.umaine.edu. **Description:** One location of the state university. The University of Maine is a four-year, undergraduate, public university with an emphasis on education and liberal arts.

UNIVERSITY OF MAINE AT PRESQUE ISLE
181 Main Street, Presque Isle ME 04769-2888. 207/768-9400. **Contact:** Personnel. **World Wide Web address:** http://www.umpi.maine.edu. **Description:** One location of the state university. The University of Maine is a four-year, undergraduate, public university with an emphasis on education and liberal arts. **Positions advertised include:** Faculty tenure positions for the following disciplines: Educational Computing; Pedagogy/Adapted Physical Education; Recreation and Leisure Services; Director of Instructional Technology and Support Services; Administrative Assistant.

UNIVERSITY OF MAINE COOPERATIVE EXTENSION
133 Western Avenue, Auburn ME 04210. 207/786-0376. **Contact:** Human Resources. **World Wide Web address:** http://www.umext.maine.edu. **Description:** Loosely affiliated with University of Maine at Orono, University of Maine Cooperative Extension provides community-based, noncredit workshops in four main areas: agriculture; backyard landscape for wildlife; family matters (nutrition, parenting, and other programs); and kids at risk.

UNIVERSITY OF NEW ENGLAND
11 Hills Beach Road, Biddeford ME 04005. 207/797-7261. **Contact:** Human Resources. **World Wide Web address:** http://www.une.edu. **Description:** A four-year college offering associate's, bachelor's, and master's degree programs, with a total student enrollment of 2,800. Founded in 1831. **NOTE:** Entry-level positions and part-time jobs are offered. **Positions advertised include:** Visiting Biology Instructor; Associate Education Professor; Assistant Professor of Political Science; Computer Purchasing and Support Specialist; Veterinarian; Staff Physician; Director of Marine Science Center; Payroll Manager. **Number of employees at this location:** 525.

UNIVERSITY OF SOUTHERN MAINE (USM)
96 Falmouth Street, P.O. Box 9300, Portland ME 04104-9300. 207/780-4141. **Toll-free phone:** 800/800-4USM. **Contact:** Employment Manager. **World Wide Web address:** http://www.usm.maine.edu. **Description:** University of Southern Maine has an enrollment of approximately 10,500. The university is a comprehensive public institution comprised of eight academic units including applied science, arts and sciences, business, education and human development, law, Lewiston-Auburn College, Muskie School of Public Service, and nursing and health professions. **NOTE:** Part-time jobs and second and third shifts are offered. **Positions advertised include:** Administrative Assistant; Plumber Coordinator; Police Officer; Refrigeration Mechanic; Teacher Assistant; Truck Driver; Database Applications Developer; Project Assistant; Project Specialist; Research Associate; Senior Policy Analyst; Woman's Volleyball Coach. **Number of employees at this location:** 1,200.

UNUMPROVIDENT CORPORATION
2211 Congress Street, Portland ME 04122. 207/262-0018. **Contact:** Human Resources. **World Wide Web address:** http://www.unumprovident.com. **Description:** An insurance company providing income protection to small and medium-sized employers through a broad range of life, health, disability, and retirement products. **Corporate headquarters location:** This location. **Other U.S. locations:** Nationwide. **International locations:** Argentina, Canada, France, Japan, Netherlands, Great Britain. **Listed on:** New York Stock Exchange. **Stock exchange symbol:** UNM.

VERRILL AND DANA
P.O. Box 586, Portland ME 04112-0586. 207/774-4000. **Physical address:** One Portland Square, Portland ME. **Contact:** David Bois, Director of Administration. **E-mail address:** hiring@verrilldana.com. **World Wide Web address:** http://www.verdan.com. **Description:** A law firm with a wide variety of specialties. **Positions advertised include:** Legal Secretary; Summer Associate. **Other area locations:** Portland ME; Kennebunk ME; Augusta ME. **Other U.S. locations:** Kansas City KA; Washington DC.

VISHAY SPRAGUE INC.
P.O. Box 1754, Sanford ME 04073. 207/324-4140. **Physical address:** 678 Main Street, Route 109, Sanford ME. **Contact:** Sandy Gold, Human Resources. **World Wide Web address:** http://www.vishay.com. **Description:** Manufactures tantalum capacitors used in a wide range of products including airplanes, automobiles, telephones, and computers. Founded in 1962. **International locations:** Worldwide. **Parent company:** Vishay Intertechnology designs, manufactures, and sells precision stress analysis systems and services, as well as high-precision resistive systems. The company owns several subsidiaries. **Listed on:** New York Stock Exchange. **Stock exchange symbol:** VSH. **Number of employees at this location:** 1,360.

WGME-TV CHANNEL 13
1335 Washington Avenue, Portland ME. 207/797-1313. **Contact:** Human Resources. **World Wide Web address:** http://www.wgme.com. **Description:** A television broadcasting station.

WAHLCOMETROFLEX
29 Lexington Street, Lewiston ME 04240. 207/784-2338. **Toll-free phone:** 800/272-6652. **Contact:** Human Resources. **E-mail address:** wmx@wahlcometroflex.com. **World Wide Web address:** http://www.wahlcometroflex.com **Description:** Manufactures metal fabricators, diverters, and conversion belts. **Number of employees at this location:** 100.

WAL-MART STORES, INC.
458 Kennedy Memorial Drive, Waterville ME 04901. 207/877-8774. **Contact:** Manager. **World Wide Web address:** http://www.walmart.com. **Description:** Wal-Mart Stores is one of the largest retail merchandise chains in the country, operating full-service discount department stores, combination grocery and discount stores, and warehouse stores requiring membership. Founded in 1962. **Corporate headquarters location:** Bentonville AR. **Other area locations:** Sanford ME. **Listed on:** New York Stock Exchange. **Stock exchange symbol:** WMT.

J. WESTON WALCH PUBLISHER
P.O. Box 658, Portland ME 04104-0658. 207/772-2846. **Physical address:** 321 Valley Street, Portland ME 04102. **Contact:** Melanie Arsenault, Human Resources Director. **World Wide Web address:** http://www.walch.com. **Description:** A book publishing company specializing in supplementary educational materials for middle schools, high schools, and adult learning schools.

WASHBURN & DOUGHTY ASSOCIATES, INC.
P.O. Box 296, East Boothbay ME 04544. 207/633-6517. **Physical address:** 7 Enterprise Street, East Boothbay ME 04544. **Fax:** 207/633-7007. **Contact:** Human Resources. **E-mail address:** info@washburndoughty.com. **World Wide Web address:** http://www.washburndoughty.com. **Description:** Washburn & Doughty runs a shipyard where the company manufactures steel and aluminum vessels and barges. **Corporate headquarters location:** This location.

WEBBER ENERGY FUELS
P.O. Box 929, Bangor ME 04402-0929. 207/942-5501. **Physical address:** 700 Main Street, Bangor ME 04401. **Toll-free phone:** 800/238-5505. **Contact:** Human Resources. **World Wide Web address:** http://www.wenergy.com. **Description:** An oil company.

WISE BUSINESS FORMS INC.
2301 Congress Street, Portland ME 04102. 207/774-6560. **Toll-free phone:** 800/866-6560. **Fax:** 207/775-4728. **Contact:** Tina Miller, Human Resources. **World Wide Web address:** http://www.epx-group.com. **Description:** A commercial printer offering business forms, digital printing, and variable imaging. EPX Group also provides mailing, warehouse, and distribution services. Founded in 1941. **NOTE:** Entry-level positions, part-time jobs, and second and third shifts are offered. **Corporate headquarters location:** Alpharetta GA. **Other U.S. locations:** Fort Wayne IN; Butler PA; Piedmont SC. **President/CEO:** William D. Prettyman. **Number of employees nationwide:** 600.

WONDER BREAD
NISSEN BAKERY
One Bakers Way, Biddeford ME 04005. 207/286-1200. **Contact:** Human Resources Manager. **World Wide Web address:** http://www. wonderbread.com. **Description:** Wonder Bread is part of Interstate Bakeries Corporation, one of the largest bakery groups in the United States. J.J. Nissen is a brand produced by Wonder and IBC. **Corporate headquarters location:** Kansas City MO. **Other area locations:** Statewide. **Other U.S. locations:** Nationwide. **Parent company:** Interstate Bakeries Corporation. **Listed on:** New York Stock Exchange. **Stock exchange symbol:** IBC. **Number of employees nationwide:** 34,000.

WRIGHT-PIERCE ENGINEERS
99 Main Street, Topsham ME 04086. 207/725-8721. **Fax:** 947/762-7002. **Contact:** Human Resources. **E-mail address:** hr@wright-pierce.com. **World Wide Web address:** http://www.wright-pierce.com. **Description:** A full-service civil and environmental engineering firm. The company specializes in civil and transportation engineering; structural engineering; environmental laboratory services; and water, wastewater, and solid waste treatment. **Corporate headquarters location:** This location. **Other area locations:** Portland ME. **Other U.S. locations:** Middletown CT; Portsmouth NH. **Number of employees at this location:** 95.

ZF LEMFORDER CORPORATION
55 Baker Boulevard, Brewer ME 04412-2200. 207/989-1310. **Contact:** Human Resources. **World Wide Web address:** http://www.zf-group.com. **Description:** Manufactures steering and suspension components for automobiles.

ZURICH COMMERCIAL INSURANCE
P.O. Box 455, Portland ME 04112. 207/874-9451. **Physical address:** 2 Monument Square, Portland ME 04112. **Toll-free phone:** 800/382-2150. **Fax:** 847/762-7002. **Contact:** Personnel. **E-mail address:** careers@zurichna.com. **World Wide Web address:** http://www.zurichna.com. **Description:** Provides commercial insurance.

AAI CORPORATION
P.O. Box 126, Hunt Valley MD 21030-0126. 410/666-1400. **Toll-free number:** 800/655-2616. **Physical address:** 124 Industry Lane, Hunt Valley MD 21030-0126. **Fax:** 410/628-8746. **Contact:** Linda Napoli, Human Resources. **E-mail address:** careercenter@aaicorp.com. **World Wide Web address:** http://www.aaicorp.com. **Description:** Manufactures electronic warfare simulation systems, automatic test systems, combat vehicle ordnance, remotely piloted vehicles (RPVs), and materials handling equipment. The company is divided into four business units: Defense Systems, Unmanned Air Vehicle Systems; Fluid Test Systems, Transportation Systems, and Engineering and Maintenance Services. **Positions advertised include:** Administrative Clerk; Secretary; Custodian; Engineering Aide; Financial Analyst; Security Staff Assistant; Associate Engineer; Publications Specialist; Business Area Manager; Program Manager; Assembly Mechanic; Composite Lab Technician; Journeyman Electrician; Utility Person. **Corporate headquarters location:** This location. **Other U.S. locations:** Summerville SC; Brea CA. **Parent company:** United Industrial Corporation. **Listed on:** New York Stock Exchange. **Stock exchange symbol:** UIC. **President:** Frederick M. Strader. **Sales/revenues:** Over $170 million. **Number of employees nationwide:** 1,400.

ABS CONSULTING
4 Research Place, 200-A, Rockville MD 20850. 301/907-9100. **Contact:** Human Resources. **Fax:** 301/921-0373. **E-mail address:** ABSGRPEMP@eagle.org. **World Wide Web address:** http://www.absconsulting.com. **Description:** Provides consulting services to clients in the education, industrial, government, transportation, healthcare, and finance industries. **Positions advertised include:** Product Manager. **Special programs:** Tuition Reimbursement Program. **Corporate headquarters location:** Houston TX. **Other U.S. locations:** Nationwide. **International locations:** Worldwide. **Subsidiaries include:** ABS Group, Incorporated; EQE International, Incorporated. **President:** Christopher J. Wiernicki. **Sales/revenues:** Over $130 million. **Number of employees worldwide:** Over 1,100.

ACS GOVERNMENT SOLUTIONS GROUP, INC.
One Curie Court, Rockville MD 20850. 301/921-7000. **Contact:** Human Resources. **World Wide Web address:** http://www.acs-nih.com. **Description:** Provides contract computer services to the government including data processing and systems integration. **NOTE:** Online applications are available. **Positions advertised include:** Subcontracting Manager; Network Engineer; Scanner Operator; Portfolio Reporting Analyst; Senior Business Analyst; Quality Assurance Manager; Street Business Unit Manager; Test Engineer; Operations Analyst; Windows Systems Engineer. **Special programs:** Internships. **Corporate headquarters location:** Dallas TX. **Other U.S. locations:** Nationwide. **Subsidiaries include:** Analytical Systems Engineering Corporation; Betac Corporation. **Parent company:** Computer Services, Incorporated. **Listed on:** New York Stock Exchange. **Stock exchange symbol:** ACS. **President/CEO:** William Woodard. **Number of employees nationwide:** 4,100.

ADP INTEGRATED MEDICAL SOLUTIONS
401 North Washington Street, Rockville MD 20850. 301/296-7000. **Toll-free phone:** 800/205-8881. **Fax:** 301/296-7017. **Contact:** Human Resources. **World Wide Web address:** http://www.adpims.com. **Description:** As part of Automatic Data Processing (ADP), a worldwide independent computing services firm, ADP Integrated Medical Solutions audits medical bills for insurance companies. **NOTE:** Apply online. **Positions advertised include:** Software Engineer; Director Development; SBS Outside Sales; Major Account Recruiter; Installation Special Assistant; Technical Editor Associate; Administrative Assistant. **Corporate headquarters location:** This location. **Other U.S. locations:** Lake Mary FL; Honolulu HI; Westmont IL; Norristown PA. **Listed on:** New York Stock Exchange. **Stock exchange symbol:** ADP. **Sales/revenues:** Over $6 billion.

ARINC INCORPORATED
2551 Riva Road, Annapolis MD 21401-7465. 410/266-4000. **Fax:** 410/266-3201. **Contact:** Staffing. **World Wide Web address:** http://www.arinc.com. **Description:** An engineering and management consulting firm that provides technical studies, analyses, and evaluations of aircraft and ship communication and information systems. Customers of ARINC include the Department of Defense, the Department of Energy, the Department of Transportation, and the Federal Aviation Administration. **Positions advertised include** Market Research Analyst; GPS Engineer; GPS Software Engineer; Antenna Electromagnetic Engineer; Analyst; Operation Analyst; Interoperability Test Analyst; Network Test Engineer; Systems Analyst; Pricing Intern; Junior Java Developer; Marketing Communications Writer; Mechanical Design Engineer; Principal Engineer. **Special programs:** Internships. **Corporate headquarters location:** This location. **Other area locations:** Rockville MD; Patuxent River MD; Millersville MD; Baltimore MD. **Other U.S. locations:** Nationwide. **International locations:** Canada; United Kingdom; France; Spain; Germany; China; Japan; Taiwan; Thailand. **Operations at this facility include:** Administration; Research and Development; Sales. **Listed on:** Privately held. **President/CEO:** John M. Belcher. **Number of employees at this location:** 2,600. **Number of employees worldwide:** Over 3,000.

ATC ASSOCIATES INC.
8989 Herrmann Drive, Suite 300, Columbia MD 21045. 410/381-0232. **Fax:** 410/381-0247. **Contact:** Wilma Smith, Human Resources. **E-mail address:** AFCJobs@atc-enviro.com. **World Wide Web address:** http://www.atc-enviro.com. **Description:** Provides geotechnical engineering and consulting services to customers in the environmental field. Founded in 1982. **Positions advertised include:** Project Manager. **Corporate headquarters location:** Woburn MA. **Other U.S. locations:** Nationwide. **Number of employees nationwide:** 1,800.

ATK THIOKOL PROPULSION COMPANY
P.O. Box 241, Elkton MD 21922. 410/392-1000. **Fax:** 410/392-1013. **Contact:** Staffing Representative. **E-mail address:** resume_elkton@atk.com. **World Wide Web address:** http://www.atk.com/aerospace. **Description:** A developer and producer of solid rocket motors for aerospace, defense, and commercial launch applications, and a manufacturer of precision fastening systems for aerospace and industrial markets worldwide. ATK Thiokol produces solid rocket motors for most of the nation's satellite systems, solid rocket motors for the Space Shuttle, and the Castor 120 motor for commercial launch vehicles. For the defense market, the company produces components of the first and second stages of the Navy's Trident II missile system, and propulsion systems for tactical missiles. **NOTE:** Online applications are available. **Positions advertised include:** Ballistician; Quality Assurance Engineer; Material Distribution; Product Planning Associate; Programmer Analyst; Project Engineer; Trooling Engineer; Regional Sales Manager; Contract Specialist; Electrical Engineer. **Special programs:** Internships. **Corporate headquarters location:** Edina MN. **Parent company:** Alliant Techsystems (ATK). **Listed on:** New York Stock Exchange. **Stock exchange symbol:** ATK. **Number of employees nationwide:** Approximately 5,700.

ABERDEEN PROVING GROUND (APG)
Commander, USAGAPG, 2201 Aberdeen Boulevard, Attention: AMSSB-GCP, Aberdeen Proving Ground MD 21005-5001. 410/278-5201. **Recorded jobline:** 410/306-2722. **Contact:** Civilian Personnel Advisory Center. **World Wide Web address:** http://www.apg.army.mil. **Description:** APG is a military installation that employs civilians in the research, development, testing, and evaluation of military materials for use by soldiers on the battlefield. Founded in 1917. **Positions advertised include:** Chemical Engineer; Dental Assistant; Electronics Engineer; Operations Engineer; Physical Scientist; Mechanical Engineer; Proto-call officer; Industrial Specialist; Research Biologist; Geographical Forester. **Special programs:** Training. **Office hours:** Monday – Friday, 7:30 a.m. – 4:30 p.m. **Number of employees at this location:** Over 7,500.

ACE*COMM
704 Quince Orchard Road, Suite 100, Gaithersburg MD 20878. 301/721-3000. **Fax:** 301/721-3001. **Contact:** Human Resources. **E-mail address:** hr@acecomm.com. **World Wide Web address:** http://www.acecomm.com. **Description:** Develops networking systems for the telecommunications industry. **NOTE:** If submitting resume via e-mail, all attachments must either be MS Word 97 or ASCII text files. **Positions advertised include:** Accounts Payable Clerk; Director of Strategic Accounts; Field Service Engineer; Purchasing & Materials Manager; Software Test Engineer; Senior Manager; Technical Support Engineer; Vice President of Sales. **Corporate headquarters location:** This location. **Other U.S. locations:** Flemington NJ. **International locations:** Canada; China; Philippines; New Zealand. **Listed on:** NASDAQ. **Stock exchange symbol:** ACEC.

ACTERNA CORPORATION
12410 Milestone Center Drive, Germantown MD 20876-4023. 301/353-1550. **Toll-free phone:** 800/638-2049. **Fax:** 301/404-2298. **Contact:** Personnel. **World Wide Web address:** http://www.acterna.com. **Description:** Provides equipment and services that support and build worldwide information infrastructures. **Positions advertised include:** Client Services Specialist; Application Engineer; Corporate Manager; Buyer; Financial Analyst; Administrative Assistant; Collection Specialist. **Special programs:** Co-ops; Internships. **Corporate headquarters location:** This location. **Other U.S. locations:** Nationwide. **International locations:** Worldwide. **Operations at this facility include:** This location manufactures portable and digital test equipment for the communications industry. **Listed on:** NASDAQ. **Stock exchange symbol:** ACTR. **Number of employees at this location:** 900.

ADVANCED MARKETING SERVICES, INC. (AMS)
1020 Airport 100 Way, Hanover MD 21076. 410/993-0066. **Fax:** 410/859-0551. **Contact:** Human Resources. **World Wide Web address:** http://www.admsweb.com. **Description:** A leading distributor of general interest, computer, and business books to membership warehouse clubs and office product superstores. AMS provides product selection advice, specialized merchandising, and product development programs and services to its customers. **Positions advertised include:** Human Resources Manager. **Corporate headquarters location:** San Diego CA. **International locations:** Australia; Canada; England; Mexico; Singapore. **Listed on:** New York Stock Exchange. **Stock exchange symbol:** MKT.

AEGON USA, INC.
MONUMENTAL LIFE INSURANCE COMPANY
1111 North Charles Street, Baltimore MD 21201-5574. 410/576-4571. **Contact:** Human Resources. **World Wide Web address:** http://www.aegon.com. **Description:** AEGON USA operates through four groups encompassing 11 insurance divisions. The four groups are Agency, Asset Accumulation, Health, and Home Services. The Individual Division, Western Reserve Life, and Monumental Life Insurance Company (also at this location) sell life and health insurance products, mutual funds, and annuities. The Insurance Center administers group hospital expense insurance programs that are sold exclusively to the more than 300,000 members of the National Association for the Self-Employed. The NOL Division markets traditional and interest-sensitive life insurance and disability income products. Servicing the financial planning needs of high-income, high-net-worth clients, the Advanced Products Division offers estate planning, deferred compensation, capital transfer, and key-man programs. Offering plan design, participant communication programs, record-keeping services, and technical guidance, the Diversified Investment Advisors services the retirement plan markets. The Financial Markets Division provides fixed and variable annuity products through national and state banks, savings and loans, and regional brokerage firms. Monumental General has seven business units, each with district objectives including credit, Medicare supplement, and accidental death insurance. The Long Term Care Division markets long-term care/nursing home products including nursing home, home health, assisted living, and adult daycare services, while the Supplemental Insurance Division markets intensive care, long-term care, and accident insurance products. **Corporate headquarters location:** This location. **Other U.S. locations:** Cedar Rapids IA. **International locations:** Worldwide. **Parent company:** AEGON Insurance Group. **Listed on:** New York Stock Exchange; also, stock exchanges in Amsterdam, Frankfurt, London, Tokyo, and Zurich. **Stock exchange symbol:** AEG.

AFRO-AMERICAN NEWSPAPERS INC.
2519 North Charles Street, Baltimore MD 21218. 410/554-8221. **Contact:** Ms. Verdell Elliott, Director of Human Resources. **World Wide Web address:** http://www.afro.com. **Description:** Publishes the *Baltimore Afro-American,* a newspaper marketed to the African-American community. Founded in 1892. **Special programs:** Internships. **Corporate headquarters location:** This location. **Other U.S. locations:** Nationwide. **Listed on:** Privately held. **Number of employees at this location:** 55. **Number of employees nationwide:** 90.

AGORA, INC.
P.O. Box 1936, Baltimore MD 21203. 410/783-8499. **Physical address:** 14 West Mt. Vernon Place, Baltimore MD 21201. **Fax:** 410/783-8455. **Contact:** Elizabeth Masing, Personnel Manager. **E-mail address:** personnel@agora-inc.com. **World Wide Web address:** http://www.agora-inc.com. **Description:** A publisher of health, travel, financial, and entrepreneurial books and newsletters. Founded in 1979. **NOTE:** Entry-level positions and part-time jobs are offered. **Positions advertised include:** Editorial Associate; Marketing Assistant; Fulfillment Assistant; Customer Service Representative. **Special programs:** Internships; Summer Jobs. **Office hours:** Monday - Friday, 8:30 a.m. - 5:30 p.m. **Corporate headquarters location:** This location. **International locations:** Ireland. **Listed on:** Privately held. **President/Founder:** William Bonner. **Number of employees at this location:** Over 200.

AIRGAS
2900 52nd Avenue, Hyattsville MD 20781. 301/981-3702. **Fax:** 301/864-4875. **Contact:** Jamie Weatherford. **E-mail address:** james.weatherford@airgas.com. **World Wide Web address:** http://www.airgas.com. **Description:** Distributor of industrial, medical, and specialty gases and related equipment, safety supplies and MRO products and services to industrial and commercial customers. **Positions advertised include:** Filler (First Shift). **Corporate headquarters location:** Radnor PA. **Other U.S. locations:** Nationwide. **Listed on:** New York Stock Exchange. **Stock exchange symbol:** ARG. **Chairman and CEO:** Peter McCausland.

AIRPAX CORPORATION
POWER PROTECTION PRODUCTS
P.O. Box 520, 807 Woods Road, Cambridge MD 21613-0520. 410/228-4600. **Fax:** 410/221-9568. **Contact:** Human Resources. **E-mail address:** ppphr@airpax.net. **World Wide Web address:** http://www.airpax.net. **Description:** Designs, manufactures, and markets various electronic components for applications in the industrial, power conditioning, telecommunications, medical and information processing, marine, and military fields. **Other area locations:** Frederick MD. **International locations:** Matamoros, Mexico. **Subsidiaries include:** Power Protection Products; Thermal Sensing Products. **Operations at this facility include:** This location manufactures circuit breakers, thermostats, and microcircuits.

AJILON SERVICES INC.
210 West Pennsylvania Avenue, Suite 500, Towson MD 21204. 410/821-0435. **Fax:** 410/828-7389. **Contact:** Janet Metzger, Human Resources. **World Wide Web address:** http://www.ajilon.com. **Description:** Offers computer consulting services, project support, and end user services. **Positions advertised include:** Accounts Payable Supervisor; Payroll Accountant. **Special programs:** Tuition Reimbursement Program. **Other U.S. locations:** Nationwide. **International locations:** Canada. **President/COO:** Mark E. Fusco.

ALBAN TRACTOR COMPANY, INC.
8531 Pulaski Highway, Baltimore MD 21237-3092. 410/686-7777. **Toll-free phone:** 800/492-6994. **Fax:** 410/780-3481. **Contact:** Human Resources. **World Wide Web address:** http://www.albancat.com. **Description:** Involved in the resale and service of Caterpillar equipment. Founded in 1927. **Positions advertised include:** Construction Equipment Attachment Manager; Parts Counter Help. **Corporate headquarters location:** This location. **Other area locations:** Statewide. **Other U.S. locations:** DE; VA. **Listed on:** Privately held.

ALION SCIENCE AND TECHNOLOGY
185 Admiral Cochrane Drive, Annapolis MD 21401. 410/573-7223. **Fax:** 410/573-7033. **Contact:** Human Resources. **World Wide Web address:** http://www.alionscience.com. **Description:** A research and development company whose primary customer is the U.S. government. **Positions advertised include:** Assistant Programming Analyst; Assistant Engineer; Research Communications Analyst. **Note:** Applicants can search and submit for specific jobs listed currently online. **Corporate headquarters location:** McLean VA. **Other area locations:** Lanham MD. **Other U.S. locations:** IL; NY; FL; PA; AL; IN; MI; VA; WA. **Operations at this facility include:** Administration; Research and Development. **CEO/Chairman:** Bahman Atefi. **Number of employees at this location:** 500. **Number of employees nationwide:** 1,700.

ALLIED VAUGHN
819 Brightseat Road, Landover MD 20785. 301/808-6100. **Toll-free phone:** 800/379-9412. **Fax:** 301/808-9585. **Contact:** Human Resources. **World Wide Web address:** http://www.alliedvaughn. **Description:** An independent multimedia manufacturing company that offers CD-audio and CD-ROM mastering and replication, videocassette and audiocassette duplication, off-line and online video editing, motion picture film processing, film-to-tape and tape-to-film transfers, and complete finishing, packaging, warehousing, and fulfillment services. **Corporate headquarters location:** Minneapolis MN. **Other U.S. locations:** Nationwide. **Subsidiaries include:** TangibleData, Incorporated. **CEO:** Dave Willette.

ALPHARMA USPD
7205 Windsor Boulevard, Baltimore MD 21244. 410/298-1000. **Toll-free phone:** 800/638-9096. **Fax:** 410/298-8187. **Contact:** Human Resources. **World Wide Web address:** http://www.alpharma.com. **Description:** Alpha, Incorporated is an international pharmaceutical company that develops, manufactures, and markets specialty generic and proprietary human pharmaceuticals and animal health products. Business segments include The Animal Health Division, which manufactures and markets antibiotics and other feed additives to the poultry and swine industries; The Aquatic Animal Health Division, which serves the aquaculture industry and is a manufacturer and marketer of vaccines for farmed fish; and The Fine Chemicals Division, which is a basic producer of specialty bulk antibiotics. **NOTE:** Online applications are available. **Positions advertised include:** Validation Engineer; Training Specialist; Microbiologist; Quality Control Analytical Lab Supervision; Technical Service Metrology Supervisor. **Corporate headquarters location:** Fort Lee NJ. **Other area locations:** Columbia MD; Owing Mills MD. **Other U.S. locations:** Elizabeth NJ; Lincolnton NC. **International locations:** Oslo, Norway. **Operations at this facility include:** This location is part of Alpha, Incorporated's U.S. Pharmaceuticals Division and manufactures liquid pharmaceuticals, creams, and ointments. **Listed on:** New York Stock Exchange. **Stock exchange symbol:** ALO. **Annual sales/revenues:** More than $100 million. **Number of employees at this location:** 600. **Number of employees nationwide:** 1,200.

AMERICA'S BODY COMPANY
INDEPENDENCE DIVISION
6401 Aaron Lane, Clinton MD 20735. 301/868-0540. **Toll-free phone:** 800/872-4831. **Contact:** Human Resources. **E-mail address:** abcemploy@abctruck.com. **World Wide Web address:** http://www.abctruck.com. **Description:** Manufactures and wholesales truck bodies and related parts and equipment. **Positions advertised include:** National Account Sales; Telemarketer. **Corporate headquarters location:** Oakwood Village OH. **Other U.S. locations:** Louisville KY; Kansas City MO; Detroit MI; Nanticoke PA; Philadelphia PA; Portland OR; Cleveland OH; Columbus OH; Tampa FL. **Number of employees nationwide:** 875.

AMERICAN PORT SERVICES
dba HOBELMAN PORT SERVICES, INC.
401 East Pratt Street, World Trade Suite 1344, Baltimore MD 21202. 410/625-1370. **Fax:** 410/354-8812. **Contact:** Human Resources. **E-mail address:** info@amports.com. **World Wide Web address:** http://www.amerport.com. **Description:** A global transportation provider that owns and operates marine and airport terminals worldwide. **Other U.S. locations:** Benicia CA; Jacksonville FL; Brunswick GA. **Office hours:** Monday – Friday, 8:00 a.m –5:00 p.m. **International locations:** Zeebrugge, Belgium. **Parent company:** Associated British Ports. **Operations at this facility include:** This location operates as part of the Sea Port Division and processes import and export automobiles in the United States.

AMERICAN POWER CONVERSION CORPORATION (APC)
128 Cockeysville Road, Hunt Valley MD 21030. 410/584-2700. **Contact:** Human Resources. **World Wide Web address:** http://www.apcc.com. **Description:** Manufactures power protection and management solutions for computer, communications, and electronic applications. **Corporate headquarters location:** West Kingston RI. **Other U.S. locations:** West Warwick RI; East Providence RI; North Billerica MA; St. Louis MO; Dallas TX; Miami FL. **International locations:** Worldwide. **Subsidiaries include:** Silicon™. **Operations at this facility include:** This location is part of the APC Cables division. **Listed on:** NASDAQ. **Stock exchange symbol:** ADCC. **President/CEO/Chairman:** Rodger Dowdell. **Sales/revenues:** Approximately $1.4 billion.

THE AMERITAS/ACACIA COMPANY
7315 Wisconsin Avenue, Bethesda MD 20814. 301/280-1000. **Toll-free phone:** 800/444-1889. **Fax:** 301/280-1261. **Contact:** Human Resources. **E-mail address:** hr@acaciagroup.com. **World Wide Web address:** http://www.acaciagroup.com. **Description:** Provides diversified financial and insurance services through its operating companies. **NOTE:** Resumes for advertised positions may be submitted online. **Positions advertised include:** Executive Assistant; Telecommunications Analyst; Compliance Director; Administrative Assistant; Investor Relations Representative. **Corporate headquarters location:** This location. **Other U.S. locations:** Nationwide. **Subsidiaries include:** Acacia Life and Acacia National Life offer life insurance policies. The Advisors Group provides investment management services. The Calvert Group, Limited offers mutual fund management services. Acacia Federal Savings Bank provides traditional savings and loan services. **Parent company:** Ameritas Acacia Mutual Holding Company. **Operations at this facility include:** Administration; Service. **Number of employees at this location:** 300. **Number of employees nationwide:** 1,000.

AMTOTE INTERNATIONAL, INC.
11200 Pepper Road, Hunt Valley MD 21031-1324. 410/771-8700. **Fax:** 410/785-5239. **Contact:** Human Resources. **E-mail address:** jobs@amtote.com. **World Wide Web address:** http://www.amtote.com. **Description:** Manufactures Totalisator machines for the pari-mutuel wagering industry. **Corporate headquarters location:** This location.

ANDREWS FEDERAL CREDIT UNION
5711 Allentown Road, Suite 418, Suitland MD 20746. 301/702-5500. **Fax:** 301/702-5336. **Contact:** Employment Manager. **E-mail address:** employmentdc@andrewsfcu.org. **World Wide Web address:** http://www.andrewsfcu.org. **Description:** Provides financial services to members of the military and their families. **Positions advertised include:** Auditor; Loan Specialist; Consumer Loan Officer; Teller; Member Services Representative; Telecommunications Engineering; Delivery Team Operations Supervisor; Promotions Specialist; Telephone Sales Representative. **Special programs:** Tuition Assistance Program. **Office hours:** Monday – Friday, 9:30 a.m. – 4:30 p.m. **Corporate headquarters location:** This location. **Other area locations:** Rockville MD; Andrews AFB MD. **Other U.S. locations:** Burlington NJ; Wrightstown NJ; Maguire AFB NJ; Falls Church VA; Rockville VA; Springfield VA. **International locations:** Belgium; Germany; the Netherlands. **Operations at this facility include:** This location houses the administrative offices and a credit union.

ANTEX BIOLOGICS INC.
300 Professional Drive, Suite 100, Gaithersburg MD 20879. 301/590-0129. **Fax:** 301/590-1251. **Contact:** Human Resources. **E-mail address:** hr@antexbiologics.com. **World Wide Web address:** http://www.antexbio.com. **Description:** Develops pharmaceuticals to treat, detect, and prevent infectious diseases. Antex operates under three business units: AntexBiologics, AntexPharma, and AntexProteomics. **Positions advertised include:** Director of Formulation Development; Director of Process and Analytical Development; Manager of Analytical Methods; Quality Assurance/Regulatory Manager. **Corporate headquarters location:** This location. **Listed on:** American Stock Exchange. **Stock exchange symbol:** ANX.

AON CONSULTING
10451 Mill Run Circle, Owings Mills MD 21117. 410/363-5500. **Fax:** 410/363-5697. **Contact:** Sue Elligson, Human Resources Director. **World Wide Web address:** http://www.aon.com. **Description:** Aon is an international human resources consulting and benefits brokerage firm providing integrated advisory and support services in retirement planning, health care management, organizational effectiveness, compensation, human resources-related communications, and information technologies. **Positions advertised include:** Plant Manager. **Corporate headquarters location:** Chicago IL. **Other area locations:** Baltimore MD. **Other U.S. locations:** Nationwide. **International locations:** Worldwide. **Listed on:** New York Stock Exchange. **Stock exchange symbol:** AOC. **CEO/Chairman:** Patrick G. Ryan. **Sales/revenues:** Over $8 billion. **Number of employees worldwide:** Over 53,000.

ARONSON & COMPANY
700 King Farm Boulevard, Suite 300, Rockville MD 20850. 301/231-6200. **Fax:** 301/231-7630. **Contact:** Angel Rutch, Human Resources. **E-mail address:** info@aronsoncompany.com. **World Wide Web address:** http://www.aronsoncompany.com. **Description:** A certified public accounting and consulting firm whose services include audit and assurance, technology/accounting systems, tax, investment banking, litigation support, and valuation. **NOTE:** Resumes may be submitted online. **Positions advertised include:** Accountant; Administrative Assistant; Audit & Accounting Controller; Financial Accounting Consultant; Human Resource Director; Public Accountant; Technical Consultant; Timberline Consultant. **Number of employees at this location:** 100. **Number of employees nationwide:** Over 200.

ANNE ARUNDEL MEDICAL CENTER
Wayson Pavilion, Suite 350, 2001 Medical Parkway, Annapolis MD 21401. 443/481-1950. **Toll-free phone:** 800/242-2262. **Fax:** 443/481-1951. **Contact:** Human Resources. **World Wide Web address:** http://www.aahs.org. **Description:** A 290-bed, nonprofit, acute care hospital serving more than 64,000 people annually. The medical center's family practice and internal medicine physicians provide comprehensive care for family members including diagnosis, treatment, and prevention of illnesses. Other affiliates of the medical center include Anne Arundel Diagnostics, a complete outpatient radiology service that offers general and specialized radiology services; Anne Arundel Magnetic Resonance Imaging, which diagnoses disorders; and Pathways, a 40-bed treatment facility for adolescents and young adults aged 12 to 25 who suffer from substance abuse or chemical dependency. Founded in 1902. **NOTE:** Entry-level positions are offered. Job seekers may view current openings and apply online. To contact Nursing Recruitment, call 443/481-1958, fax 443/481-1321, or e-mail nursingrecruitment@aahs.org. **Special programs:** Tuition Assistance Program. **Positions advertised include:** Certified Orthopedic Technologist; Clinical Escort; Clinical Nurse; Clinical Specialist; Coding Technician; Compliance Auditor; Database Administrator; Nursing Director; Insurance Validation Unit Team Leader; Intake Counselor; Paralegal; Programming Analyst; Social Worker; Staff Pharmacist.

ASPEN SYSTEMS CORPORATION
2277 Research Boulevard, Rockville MD 20850. 301/519-5000. **Fax:** 301/519-5445. **Contact:** Human Resources. **World Wide Web address:** http://www.aspensys.com. **Description:** Provides a broad range of analytical, technical, and information support services in the energy, environment, health, housing, education, justice, and legal services fields. These support services reach both the private and public sectors at the national, regional, state, and local levels. Founded in 1970. **Special programs:**

Training; Tuition Reimbursement Program; Scholarship Opportunities. **Corporate headquarters location:** This location. **Subsidiaries include:** Hunter Medical, Incorporated; StaffXpress. **President:** Al Lampert. **Number of employees nationwide:** Over 1,600.

ATLANTIC BEVERAGE COMPANY
8106 Stayton Drive, Jessup MD 20794. 410/792-7055. **Fax:** 301/604-0205. **Contact:** Human Resources. **E-mail address:** info@aspensys.com. **World Wide Web address:** http://www.atlanticbeverage.net. **Description:** An independent, wholesale distributor of specialty nonalcoholic beverages for retail trade in the greater Baltimore and metropolitan Washington DC area. Products include teas, natural sodas, sparkling waters with juice, fruit juices, and juice drinks. Atlantic Beverage Company distributes its specialty beverage products to independent grocery stores, delicatessens, restaurants, and convenience store chains. **Corporate headquarters location:** This location. **Number of employees nationwide:** 320.

ATLANTIC GENERAL HOSPITAL
9733 Health Way Drive, Berlin MD 21811. 410/641-9612. **Fax:** 410/641-9715. **Toll-free phone:** 877/641-1100. **Contact:** Trish Tanski, Human Resources. **E-mail address:** ttanski@atlanticgeneral.org. **World Wide Web address:** http://www.atlanticgeneral.org. **Description:** 62 Bed Facility with 163 Physician that opened in 1993. **Positions advertised include:** Medical Technician; Medical Licensed Technician; Certified Nursing Assistant; Nurse Technician; Outpatient Services Technician; Respiratory Therapist; Registered Nurse.

ATLIS SYSTEMS INC.
8455 Colesville Road, Suite 1050, Silver Spring MD 20910. 301/578-4200. **Fax:** 301/650-2043. **Contact:** President. **E-mail address:** info@atlis.com. **World Wide Web address:** http://www.atlis.com. **Description:** Provides various computer-related services including document coding, systems integration, information processing, and electronic publishing. **NOTE:** Part-time, temporary, and entry-level positions are offered. **Positions advertised include:** TeX Application Programmer. **Corporate headquarters location:** This location. **Other U.S. locations:** Camp Hill PA.

AUTOMATED GRAPHIC SYSTEMS, INC.
4590 Graphics Drive, White Plains MD 20695. 301/843-7185. **Toll-free phone:** 800/678-8760. **Fax:** 301/843-6339. **Contact:** Dottie Moats, Director of Human Resources. **E-mail address:** mdjobs@ags.com. **World Wide Web address:** http://www.ags.com. **Description:** Provides printing and graphic communication services including design, desktop publishing, prepress services, on-demand printing, binding, fulfillment, mailing, and storage as well as CD-ROM production and disk replication. **Positions advertised include:** Digital Color Press Operator. **Corporate headquarters location:** This location. **Other U.S. locations:** Washington DC; Macedonia OH.

AVEMCO INSURANCE COMPANY
411 Aviation Way, Frederick MD 21701. 301/694-5700. **Toll-free phone:** 888/241-7891. **Fax:** 301/694-4376. **Contact:** Human Resources. **E-mail address:** avemco@ave.com. **World Wide Web address:** http://www.avemco.com. **Description:** An aviation insurance company. Founded in 1961. **Office hours:** Monday – Friday, 8:00 a.m. – 7:30 p.m. **International locations:** Canada. **Parent company:** HCC Insurance Holdings, Incorporated.

AXCELIS TECHNOLOGIES, INC.
7600 Standish Place, Rockville MD 20855-2798. 301/284-5900. **Contact:** Human Resources. **World Wide Web address:** http://www.axcelis.com. **Description:** Axcelis supplies ultraviolet curing equipment and photostabilizers and ashers to the semiconductor industry. **NOTE:** Resumes may be submitted online. **Positions advertised include** Software Application Engineer. **Special programs:** Internships; Co-ops. **Corporate headquarters location:** Beverly MA. **Other U.S. locations:** Nationwide. **International locations:** Worldwide. **Operations at this facility include:** Administrative Divisional Headquarters Research and Development; Sales; Service. **Listed on:** NASDAQ. **Stock exchange symbol:** ACLS. **President/CEO:** Mary G. Puma. **Sales/revenue:** $941 million. **Number of employees worldwide:** Approximately 2,000.

BAE SYSTEMS
23481 Cottonwood Parkway, California MD 20619. 301/862-9300. **Fax:** 301/863-0715. **Contact:** Human Resources. **World Wide Web address:** http://www.baesystems.com. **Description:** Provides a full spectrum of systems engineering and technical services in the areas of systems development, operation, and maintenance for commercial and government clientele. Technical services include system design, integration, and testing; software development, engineering, and maintenance; and integrated logistics support, including safety, reliability, and quality assurance engineering. **NOTE:** All applications must be done online. Entry-level positions are offered. **Positions advertised include:** Editor; Technical Manager; Systems Engineer; IS Program Manager; Unix System Administrator; Database Management Specialist; Training Specialist; RDECOM Site Manager. **Corporate headquarters location:** Rockville MD. **International locations:** Worldwide. **Operations at this facility include:** This location is part of the company's Technical Services sector, and is engaged in the testing and evaluation of U.S. Navy electronics, communications, radar, sonar, and combat systems; as well as surface ship and submarine maintenance. **President/CEO:** Mark Ronald. **Sales/revenue:** Approximately $4 billion. **Number of employees nationwide:** 22,000. **Number of employees worldwide:** Over 100,000.

BAE SYSTEMS
139000 Connecticut Avenue, Silver Spring MD 20906. 301/231-3400. **Contact:** Human Resources. **World Wide Web address:** http://www.baesystems.com. **Description:** Provides a full spectrum of systems engineering and technical services in the areas of systems development, operation, and maintenance for commercial and government clientele. Information Systems manufactures network-based computing archives and dissemination systems, and automated support systems. **NOTE:** All applications should be done online. **Positions advertised include:** Unix Systems Administrator; Hardware Configuration Manager; Windows 2000 System Administrator. **Corporate headquarters location:** Rockville MD. **International locations:** Worldwide. **Operations at this facility include:** This location is part of the company's Information Systems sector. **President/CEO:** Mark Ronald. **Sales/revenue:** Approximately $4 billion. **Number of employees at this location:** 500. **Number of employees nationwide:** 22,000. **Number of employees worldwide:** Over 100,000.

BAE SYSTEMS
1601 Research Boulevard, Rockville MD 20850. 301/838-6000. **Toll-free phone:** 800/638-8512. **Fax:** 301/838-6925. **Contact:** Kenneth Aubrey, Employment Manager. **World Wide Web address:** http://www.baesystems.com. **Description:** Provides a full spectrum of systems engineering and technical services in the areas of systems development, operation, and maintenance for commercial and government clientele. Technical services include system design, integration, and testing; software development, engineering, and maintenance; and integrated logistics support including safety, reliability, and quality assurance engineering. **NOTE:** All applications should be done online. **Positions advertised include:** System Analyst; Rapid Prototyping Mechanical Engineer; Contract Administrator; Administrative Assistant; Financial Manager; Financial Analyst; Mechanical Systems Associate; E-commerce Manager; Technical Advisor Program Manager; Vice President Business Development. **Special programs:** Internships; Co-ops. **Corporate headquarters location:** This location. **Other U.S. locations:** Nationwide. **International locations:** Worldwide. **President/CEO:** Mark Ronald. **Sales/revenue:** Approximately $4 billion. **Number of employees nationwide:** 22,000. **Number of employees worldwide:** Over 100,000.

BB&T (BRANCH BANKING & TRUST COMPANY)
3505 Hamilton Street, Hyattsville MD 20782. 301/985-1120. **Contact:** Human Resources. **World Wide Web address:** http://www.bbandt.com. **Description:** A full-service bank. **Special programs:** Internships. **Corporate headquarters location:** Winston-Salem NC. **Subsidiaries include:** BB&T Insurance Services, Incorporated; BB&T Investment Services; BB&T Leasing Corporation; BB&T Factors Association. **Parent company:** BB&T Corporation is a financial holding company whose subsidiaries include more than 55 community banks, over 70 insurance companies, and 21 non-bank financial services businesses. **Listed on:** NASDAQ. **Stock exchange symbol:** BB&T. **President:** Kelly King.

BD BIOSCIENCES
P.O. Box 999, 7 Loveton Circle, Sparks MD 21152. 410/316-4000. **Fax:** 410/316-4156. **Contact:** Human Resources. **World Wide Web address:** http://www.bdbiosciences.com. **Description:** Through its four business units: Clontech, Discovery Labware, Immunocyotmetry Systems, and Pharmingen, BD Biosciences manufactures health care products, medical instrumentation, a line of diagnostic products, and industrial safety equipment. Medical equipment includes hypodermics, intravenous equipment, operating room products, thermometers, gloves, and specialty needles. The company also offers contract packaging services. **Special programs:** Training; Educational Assistance Program. **Corporate headquarters location:** Franklin Lakes NJ. **International locations:** Worldwide. **Parent company:** Becton, Dickinson & Company. **Operations at this facility include:** Divisional Headquarters; Manufacturing; Research and Development; Sales; Service. The Diagnostics and Industrial Products division manufactures and sells a broad range of medical supplies, devices, and diagnostic systems for use by health care professionals, medical research institutions, and the general public. **Listed on:** New York Stock Exchange. **Stock exchange symbol:** BDX. **President:** Deborah J. Neff. **Number of employees worldwide:** Over 3,000.

BP AMOCO
One West Pennsylvania Avenue, Suite 400, Towson MD 21204. 410/825-4122. **Fax:** 410/494-3755. **Contact:** Human Resources Department. **World Wide Web address:** http://www.bpamoco.com. **Description:** A major supplier of fuel for transportation, energy for heat and light, solar power, and petrochemicals for plastics, fabrics, and fibers. The company also markets of aviation fuels, and supplies fuels and lubricants to the global market. **Special programs:** Internships; Co-ops. **Office hours:** Monday - Friday, 8:30 a.m. - 5:00 p.m. **Corporate headquarters location:** London, England. **Other U.S. locations:** Atlanta GA; Chicago IL; Cleveland OH. **International locations:** Worldwide. **Operations at this facility include:** Regional Headquarters. **Listed on:** New York Stock Exchange. **Stock exchange symbol:** BP. **Annual sales/revenues:** More than $100 million. **Number of employees at this location:** 200.

BP SOLAR
630 Solarex Court, Frederick MD 21703. 301/698-4200. **Fax:** 301/698-4336. **Contact:** Human Resources. **World Wide Web address:** http://www.bpsolar.com. **Description:** BP Solar is engaged in the research, development, and manufacturing of solar electric systems, primarily photovoltaic cells and panels. **Positions advertised include:** Systems Engineer; Product Engineer; Product Delivery Manager. **Corporate headquarters location:** Linthicum MD. **International locations:** Worldwide. **Parent company:** BP, plc. **Listed on:** New York Stock Exchange; London Stock Exchange. **Stock exchange symbol:** BPA. **Number of employees worldwide:** Approximately 2,200.

BALLY TOTAL FITNESS
300 East Joppa Road, Towson MD 21286. 410/296-8800. **Fax:** 410/853-4923. **Contact:** Human Resources. **World Wide Web address:** http://www.ballyfitness.com. **Description:** Through its subsidiaries, Bally's Total Fitness, operates over 330 fitness centers located in 27 states with approximately 4.2 million members. The fitness centers operate under the Bally's name in conjunction with various others including Holiday Health, Jack LaLanne, Holiday Spa, Chicago Health Clubs, Scandinavian, President's First Lady, Vic Tanny and Aerobics Plus, and the Vertical Clubs. **Positions advertised include:** Management Trainee; Service Manager; Program Instructor; Group Fitness Instructor; Personal Trainer; Lifeguard; Receptionist; Childcare Attendant; Housekeeper. **Special programs:** Internships. **Corporate headquarters location:** Chicago IL. **Other U.S. locations:** Phoenix AZ; Los Angeles CA; Denver CO; Washington DC; Miami FL; Atlanta GA; Chicago IL; Detroit MI; Minneapolis MN; New York NY; Cleveland OH; Philadelphia PA; Dallas TX; Houston TX; Seattle WA. **Listed on:** New York Stock Exchange. **Stock exchange symbol:** BFT.

BALTIMORE AIRCOIL COMPANY
P.O. Box 7322, Baltimore MD 21227. 410/799-6200. **Physical address:** 7595 Montevideo Road, Jessup MD 20794. **Fax:** 410/799-6564. **Contact:** Marian Thompson, Manager of Human Resources. **E-mail address:** hr@baltimoreaircoil.com. **World Wide Web address:** http://www.baltaircoil.com. **Description:** Designs and manufactures evaporative cooling equipment, cooling towers, evaporative condensers, and closed circuit cooling systems at 10 manufacturing plants worldwide.

BALTIMORE BAYHAWKS
2219 York Road, Suite 201, Timonium MD 21093. 866/994-2957. **Contact:** Tucker Parnell, or Kellen Williams, Personnel. **E-mail address:** tparnell@baltimorebayhawks.com, or kwilliams@baltimorebayhawks.com. **World Wide Web address:** http://www.baltimorebayhawks.com. **Description:** Baltimore's Major League Lacrosse franchise, and the 2002 MLL champions. **Positions advertised include:** Internships.

BALTIMORE DREDGES, LLC
1425 Wicomico Street, Baltimore MD 21230. 410/625-0808. **Fax:** 410/545-0200. **Contact:** Human Resources. **E-mail address:** jobs@dredge.com. **World Wide Web address:** http://www.dredge.com. **Description:** Produces dredges, dredging machinery, and related equipment. **Positions advertised include:** Manufacturing Estimator; Field Service Engineer. **Corporate headquarters location:** This location. **Operations at this facility include:** Administration; Manufacturing.

THE BALTIMORE LIFE INSURANCE COMPANY
10075 Red Run Boulevard, Owings Mills MD 21117. 410/581-6629. **Fax:** 410/581-6604. **Contact:** Rosalind McElrath, Assistant Vice President of Human Resources. **World Wide Web address:** http://www.baltimorelife.com. **Description:** A mutual life insurance company, Baltimore Life Insurance Company provides individual life insurance products and annuities. Founded in 1882. **Positions advertised include:** Unlicensed Agency Services Associate; Office Manager; Agent. **Special programs:** Internships. **Corporate headquarters location:** This location. **President/CEO/Chairman:** L. John Pearson. **Sales/revenue:** Approximately $4.7 million. **Number of employees at this location:** 200.

BALTIMORE ORIOLES
333 West Camden Street, Baltimore MD 21201-2435. 410/685-9800. **Fax:** 410/547-6273. **Contact:** Personnel. **World Wide Web address:** http://www.orioles.mlb.com. **Description:** Administrative offices for the major league baseball team. **Corporate headquarters location:** This location.

BALTIMORE PUBLIC WORKS BUREAU
600 Abel Wolman Municipal Building, Room 200, Baltimore MD 21202. 410/396-3330. **Contact:** Personnel Department. **World Wide Web address:** http://www.ci.Baltimore.nd.us/government/dpw/index.html. **Description:** Operates in four divisions: general services, which cleans and maintains public buildings; solid waste, which provides trash pick-up; transportation, which is responsible for the upkeep of city highways and street lights; and water/wastewater, which operates filtration plants to purify city water going into the Chesapeake Bay.

BALTIMORE RAVENS
1 Winning Drive, Training Facility, Owings Mills MD 21117. 410/407-4000. **Contact:** Personnel. **E-mail address:** inquiries@baltimoreravens.com. **World Wide Web address:** http://www.baltimoreravens.com. **Description:** Baltimore's NFL franchise and Super Bowl XXXV champions. **NOTE:** Offers internships.

THE BALTIMORE SUN
P.O. Box 1377, 501 North Calvert Street, Baltimore MD 21278. 410/332-6000. **Toll-free phone:** 800/829-8000. **Fax:** 410/783-2548. **Contact:** Human Resources. **E-mail address:** tribune@hiresystems.com. **World Wide Web address:** http://www.sunspot.net. **Description:** Publishes a newspaper with a daily circulation of 430,000 and a Sunday circulation of 540,000. **Positions advertised include:** Free Lance Business Writer. **Note:** Applicants can e-mail theamon@batimoresun.com for freelance position. **Special programs**: Internships. **Office hours:** Monday – Friday, 6:00 a.m. – 5:00 p.m., Saturday, Sunday, 8:00 a.m. – 12:00 p.m. **Corporate headquarters location:** Chicago IL. **Parent company:** Tribune Company. **Operations at this facility include:** Administration; Manufacturing; Sales; Service. **Listed on:** New York Stock Exchange. **Stock exchange symbol:** TRB. **CEO/Publisher:** Denise E. Palmer. **Number of employees at this location:** 2,300.

BANK OF AMERICA
100 South Charles Street, Baltimore MD 21201-2725. 410/547-4403. **Contact:** Human Resources Department. **World Wide Web address:** http://www.bankofamerica.com. **Description:** A full-service banking and financial institution. The company operates through four business segments: Global, Corporate, and Investment Banking; Principal Investing and Asset Management; Commercial Banking; and Consumer Banking. **Positions advertised include:** Associate Operations Representative; Full Time Teller. **Office hours:** Monday – Friday, 9:00 a.m. – 3:00 p.m. **Corporate headquarters location:** Charlotte NC. **Other area locations:** Statewide. **Other U.S. locations:** Nationwide. **Operations at this facility include:** This location is a bank. **Listed on:** New York Stock Exchange. **Stock exchange symbol:** BAC.

BANK OF AMERICA
7316 Wisconsin Avenue, Bethesda MD 20814. 301/951-8220. **Contact:** Human Resources. **World Wide Web address:** http://www.bankofamerica.com. **Description:** A full-service banking and financial institution. The company operates through four business segments: Global, Corporate, and Investment Banking; Principal Investing and Asset Management; Commercial Banking; and Consumer Banking. **Positions advertised include:** Customer Service Representative, Full Time Teller. **Corporate headquarters location:** Charlotte NC. **Other area locations:** Statewide. **Other U.S. locations:** Nationwide.

BANNER LIFE INSURANCE COMPANY
1701 Research Boulevard, Rockville MD 20850. 301/279-4128. **Toll-free phone:** 800/638-8428. **Fax:** 301/294-6961. **Contact:** Human Resources. **World Wide Web address:** http://www.lgamerica.com. **Description:** An insurance company that specializes in individual life insurance products and annuities. **Corporate headquarters location:** This location. **Other U.S. locations:** Nationwide. **International locations:** District of Columbia. **Subsidiaries include:** William Penn Life Insurance Company. **Parent company:** The Legal and General America Companies. **Operations at this facility include:** Administration; Service. **Number of employees at this location:** 150.

BARNES & NOBLE BOOKSTORES
620A Marketplace Drive, Bel Air MD 21014. 410/638-7023. **Fax:** 410/6387029. **Contact:** Lori Stark. **World Wide Web address:** http://www.bn.com. **Description:** A bookstore chain. This location also features a cafe and music department. **Corporate headquarters location:** New York NY. **Other U.S. locations:** Nationwide. **Listed on:** New York Stock Exchange. **Stock exchange symbol:** BKS.

BARTON-COTTON INC.
1405 Parker Road, Baltimore MD 21227. 410/247-4800. **Toll-free phone:** 800/638-4652. **Fax:** 410/204-7599. **E-mail address:** customer.service@bartoncotton.com. **Contact:** Melissa Scheidt, Human Resources. **World Wide Web address:** http://www.bartoncotton.com. **Description:** Prints and publishes religious greeting cards and stationary. **Office hours:** Monday – Friday, 8:30 a.m. – 6:00 p.m.

BAXTER
9000 Virginia Manner Road, Beltsville MD 20705. 847/948-2000. **Contact:** Human Resources. **World Wide Web address:** http://www.baxter.com. **Description:** A global health-care company that, through its subsidiaries, applies expertise in medical devices, pharmaceuticals, and biotechnology to assist health-care professionals and their patients with treatment of complex medical conditions. **Positions advertised include:** IT Project Manager; Marketing Group Manager; Medical Supervisor; Quality Associate. **Corporate headquarters location:** Deerfield IL. **International locations:** Worldwide. **Listed on:** New York Stock Exchange. **Stock exchange symbol:** BAX. **Number of employees worldwide:** 51,000.

BEATTY SATCHELL BUSINESS SERVICES, INC.
P.O. Box 1187, Easton MD 21601. 410/822-6950. **Physical address:** 125 Bay Street, Easton MD 21601. **Fax:** 410/820-9042. **Contact:** Human Resources. **Description:** An accounting and business services firm that specializes in taxes, pension administration, and estate planning. **Corporate headquarters location:** This location. **Other area locations:** Denton MD. **Number of employees at this location:** 10. **Number of employees nationwide:** 60.

BERLYN, INC.
P.O. Box 1229, Seabrook MD 20703. 301/306-9500. **Physical address:** 9458 Lanham-Severn Road, Suite 203, Seabrook MD 20703. **Fax:** 301/306-0134. **Contact:** Human Resources. **World Wide Web address:** http://www.thesentinel.com. **Description:** Publishes two weekly newspapers, the *Prince George Sentinel* and the *Montgomery Sentinel,* with a combined circulation of more than 100,000. **NOTE:** Entry-level positions and part-time jobs are offered. **Company slogan:** Watch us grow. **Special programs:** Internships; Summer Jobs. **Office hours:** Monday - Friday, 8:30 a.m. - 5:00 p.m. **Corporate headquarters location:** This location. **Operations at this facility include:** Sales; Service. **CEO:** Lynn G. Kapiloff. **Annual sales/revenues:** Less than $5 million. **Number of employees at this location:** 30.

BETHESDA MARRIOTT HOTEL
5151 Pooks Hill Road, Bethesda MD 20814. 301/897-9400. **Fax:** 301/897-0192. **Contact:** Human Resources. **World Wide Web address:** http://www.marriott.com. **Description:** A 407-room hotel with three restaurants, 23 meeting rooms, and a business center. **Corporate headquarters location:** Washington, D.C. **Other U.S. locations:** Nationwide. **International locations:** Worldwide. **Parent company:** Marriott International, Incorporated. **Listed on:** New York Stock Exchange. **Stock exchange symbol:** MAR. **Sales/revenue:** Over $20 billion. **Number of employees worldwide:** Approximately 145,000.

BIORELIANCE
14920 Broschart Road, Rockville MD 20850-3349. 301/738-1000. **Fax:** 301/738-1033. **Contact:** Human Resources. **E-mail address:** info@bioreliance.com. **World Wide Web address:** http://www.bioreliance.com. **Description:** A contract service organization that provides development and nonclinical services to biotechnology and pharmaceutical companies. BioReliance provides development, testing, and manufacturing services that cover the product from preclinical development through licensed production. **Positions advertised include:** Account Management; Business Analyst; Chemical Repository Coordinator; Desktop Supply Specialist; Laboratory Assistant; Laboratory Directory; Maintenance Technician; QA Auditor; Receptionist; Financial Analyst; Study Director; Test Article Reception. **Corporate headquarters location:** This location. **Other U.S. locations:** Bethesda MD. **International locations:** Heidelberg, Germany; Tokyo, Japan; Stirling, Scotland. **Listed on:** NASDAQ. **Stock exchange symbol:** BREL. **CEO:** Capers McDonald. **Number of employees worldwide:** Approximately 600.

BLACK & DECKER CORPORATION
701 East Joppa Road, Towson MD 21286. 410/716-3900. **Fax:** 410/716-7867. **Contact:** Human Resources. **World Wide Web address:** http://www.blackanddecker.com. **Description:** A global marketer and manufacturer of products used in and around the home and for commercial applications. The company is also a major supplier of information technology and services to government and commercial clients worldwide. The company's products include power tools, power tool accessories, security hardware, and electric lawn and garden tools. **NOTE:** Resumes may be submitted online. **Positions advertised include:** Reliability Engineer. **Special programs:** Training; Internships. **Corporate headquarters location:** This location. **Other U.S. locations:** Nationwide. **International locations:** Worldwide. **Operations at this facility include:** This location houses administrative offices. **Listed on:** New York Stock Exchange. **Stock exchange symbol:** BDK. **President/CEO:** Nolan Archibald. **Sales/revenue:** $4.4 billion. **Number of employees worldwide:** 22,300.

BLACK & DECKER CORPORATION
626 Hanover Pike, Hampstead MD 21074. 410/239-5000. **Contact:** Human Resources. **World Wide Web address:** http://www.blackanddecker.com. **Description:** A global marketer and manufacturer of products used in and around the home and for commercial applications. The company is also a major supplier of information technology and services to government and commercial clients worldwide. The company's products include power tools, power tool accessories, security hardware, and electric lawn and garden tools. **NOTE:** Resumes may be submitted online. **Special programs:** Training; Internships. **Office hours:** Monday – Friday, 8:00 a.m. – 5:00 p.m. **Corporate headquarters location:** Towson MD. **Other U.S. locations:** Nationwide. **International locations:** Worldwide. **Operations at this facility include:** This location is a distribution center. **Listed on:** New York Stock Exchange. **Stock exchange symbol:** BDK. **President/CEO:** Nolan Archibald. **Sales/revenue:** $4.4 billion. **Number of employees worldwide:** 22,300.

BLUMENTHAL-KAHN ELECTRIC L.P.
10233 South Dolfield Road, Owings Mills MD 21117. 410/363-1200. **Fax:** 410/363-1215. **Contact:** Human Resources. **E-mail address:** info@kelp.com. **World Wide Web address:** http://www.bkelp.com. **Description:** Engaged in heavy industrial and commercial electrical construction projects. **CEO:** Todd Bowlings.

BON SECOURS HOSPITAL
2000 West Baltimore Street, Baltimore MD 21223. 410/362-3000. **Fax:** 410/947-3210. **Recorded jobline:** 410/362-3414. **Contact:** Human Resources. **World Wide Web address:** http://www.bshsi.com. **Description:** An acute care hospital. **Positions advertised include:** Accounts Payable Assistant; Dance Movement Instructor; Addict Counselor; Project Specialist; Administrative Secretary; Registered Nurse; Clinical Nurse; Physical Therapist; Social Worker; Unit Secretary; Communication Support Specialist; Imaging Services Technician; Special Programming Associate; CT Technician; Environmental Services Associate; Licensed Practical Nurse; Medical Technician; Mental Health Assistant; Network Auditor. **Corporate headquarters location:** Marriottsville MD. **Other U.S. locations:** MI; NY; NJ; PA; VA; FL; KY; SC. **Parent company:** Bon Secours Health System, Incorporated.

BOOKS-A-MILLION, INC.
7000 Arundel Mills Circle, Space B3, Hanover MD 21076. 443/755-0210. **Contact:** Human Resources. **E-mail address:** jobs@booksamillioninc.com. **World Wide Web address:** http://www.booksamillioninc.com. **Description:** One of the nation's largest book retailers with a network of 182 bookstores in 17 states, primarily in the Southeast. Books-A-Million also operates an online bookstore at http://www.booksamillion.com. **Positions advertised include:** Bookseller; Café Barista; Café Manager; Co-Manager; General Manager; Customer Services Representative; District Manager; Investigator; Business to Business Representative. **Corporate headquarters location:** Birmingham AL. **Subsidiaries include:** American Wholesale Book Company, Incorporated. **Listed on:** NASDAQ. **Stock exchange symbol:** BAMM. **President/CEO:** Clyde B. Anderson. **Sales/revenues:** $443 million. **Number of employees nationwide:** 5,100.

BOWIE STATE UNIVERSITY
14000 Jericho Park Road, Bowie MD 20715. 301/860-3450. **Fax:** 301/860-3454. **Recorded jobline:** 301/860-3449. **Contact:** Human Resources. **E-mail address:** hr@bowiestate.edu. **World Wide Web address:** http://www.bowiestate.edu. **Description:** A four-year, state university offering bachelor's and master's degrees. Approximately 3,200 undergraduate and 1,600 graduate students attend Bowie State. **Positions advertised include:** University Police Officer; Assistant Men's Basketball Coach; Application Software Developer; Software Systems Analyst; Administrative Assistant; Professor of Sociology/Criminal Justice; Nursing Department Chair; Mass Communications/Public Relations Professor; English Lecturer; Theatre/Dance Teacher.

CACI SECURITY GROUP
6835 Deerpath Road, Elkridge MD 21075. 410/796-7200. **Contact:** Human Resources. **E-mail address:** jobs@caci.com. **World Wide Web address:** http://www.caci.com. **Description:** Manufactures access control systems and security systems. The company also provides software support for the U.S. Navy. **NOTE:** Resumes should be sent to: 14151 Park Meadow Drive, Attn: Recruiters, Chantilly VA 20151, or faxed to 703/679-4510. Resumes may also be submitted online. **Positions advertised include:** OPELINT Analyst; All Source Analyst; Team Leader; Security Manager; Program Manager; Project Manager; Operation Research Analyst. **Corporate headquarters location:** Arlington VA. **Other U.S. locations:** Nationwide. **International locations:** England; Scotland. **Parent company:** CACI International, Incorporated. **Listed on:** NASDAQ. **Stock exchange symbol:** CACI.

CADMUS PROFESSIONAL COMMUNICATIONS
940 Elkridge Landing Road, Linthicum MD 21090-2908. 410/691-6229. **Contact:** Michelle Anders, Human Resources Manager. **E-mail address:** andersm@cadmus.com. **World Wide Web address:** http://www.cadmus.com. **Description:** A division of Cadmus Communications Corporation, Cadmus Professional Communications produces research journals. The company's product line serves four distinct markets: medical and biomedical; technical and scientific; scholarly; and mathematics. **NOTE:** Online applications are available. **Positions advertised include:** Proofreader; Team Leader; General Application Specialist. **Special programs:** Internships; Tuition Reimbursement Program. **Corporate headquarters location:** Richmond VA. **Other area locations:** Easton MD. **Other U.S. locations:** Richmond VA; Ephrata PA. **Parent company:** Cadmus Communications Corporation is a graphic communications company offering specialized products and services in three broad areas: printing, marketing, and publishing. Product lines include annual reports, catalogs, direct marketing, financial printing, point-of-sale marketing, promotional printing, publishing, research journals, specialty magazines, and specialty packaging. Subsidiaries of Cadmus Communications include Cadmus Consumer Publishing (Richmond VA); Cadmus Custom Publishing (Boston MA); Cadmus Direct Marketing, Incorporated (Charlotte NC); Cadmus Interactive (Tucker GA); Cadmus Marketing Services (Atlanta GA); Central Florida Press, L.C. (Orlando FL); Expert Brown (Sandston VA); Graftech Corporation (Charlotte NC); 3Score, Incorporated (Tucker GA); Washburn Graphics, Incorporated (Charlotte NC); and The William Byrd Press (Richmond VA). **Listed on:** NASDAQ. **Stock exchange symbol:** CDMS. **Number of employees nationwide:** 2,500.

CALL FOR ACTION, INC.
5272 River Road, Suite 300, Bethesda MD 20816-1405. 301/657-8260. **Contact:** Human Resources. **World Wide Web address:** http://www.callforaction.org. **Description:** A nonprofit consumer group engaged in mediation between manufacturers and dissatisfied consumers through a network of consumer hotlines. **Office hours:** Tuesday – Friday, 11:00 a.m. – 1:00 p.m. **Corporate headquarters location:** This location. **Other U.S. locations:** Nationwide. **International locations:** Buenos Aires, Argentina.

THE CALVERT GROUP, LTD.
4550 Montgomery Avenue, Suite 1000 N, Bethesda MD 20814. 301/951-4800. **Toll-free phone:** 800/369-2748. **Fax:** 301/657-7000. **Contact:** Personnel. **E-mail address:** calvertjobs@calvert.com. **World Wide Web address:** http://www.calvertgroup.com. **Description:** Offers mutual fund management services. Founded in 1976. **Note:** Apply via email. **Positions advertised include:** Performance Analytics Supervisor; Senior Technical Support Specialist; Institutional Coordinator. **Special programs:** Education Program; Tuition Reimbursement Program. **Subsidiaries include:** Calvert Asset Management Company, Incorporated; Calvert Shareholder Services, Incorporated; Calvert Administrative Services Company, Incorporated; Calvert Distributors, Incorporated. **Parent company:** The Acacia Group (Bethesda MD). **CEO:** Barbara Krumsiek.

CAMBREX BIOSCIENCE WALKERSVILLE, INC.
8330 Biggs Ford Road, Walkersville MD 21793. 301/898-7025. **Fax:** 301/845-7774. **Contact:** Human Resources. **E-mail address:** human.resources@cambrex.com. **World Wide Web address:** http://www.cambrex.com. **Description:** Manufactures cell culture products used to develop drugs and vaccines. Cell culture products include living cell cultures; chemically defined nutrient medics necessary for growing the cell cultures; and sera used to supplement the media. BioWhittaker, Incorporated also manufactures endotoxin detection products, which aid pharmaceutical and medical device manufacturers in determining whether their products are safe for humans. **NOTE:** Entry-level positions are offered. **Positions advertised include:** Controllership Financial Representative; Staff Accountant; Accounting Manager; Tax Research & Plan Manager; Treasurer; Facilities Technician; Maintenance Technician; Human Resources Director; Manufacturing Manager; Fermentation Support; Quality Assurance Technician; Material Handler; Operations Technician; Quality Assurance Analyst. **Special programs:** Internships; Training; Summer Jobs; Tuition Reimbursement Program; Scholarship Program. **Office hours:** Monday - Friday, 8:00 a.m. - 5:00 p.m. **Corporate headquarters location:** East Rutherford NJ. **Parent company:** Cambrex Corporation. **Listed on:** New York Stock Exchange. **Stock exchange symbol:** CBM. **CEO:** James A. Mack. **Sales/revenues:** Approximately $530 million. **Number of employees worldwide:** Over 2,000.

CANAM STEEL CORPORATION
P.O. Box 285, 4010 Clay Street, Point of Rocks MD 21777-0285. 301/874-5141. **Toll-free phone:** 800/370-7833. **Fax:** 301/874-5626. **Contact:** Human Resources. **World Wide Web address:** http://www.canammanac.com. **Description:** Manufactures steel and other fabricated metal alloys. **Other U.S. locations:** Washington MO; Columbus OH; Woodridge IL; Easton MA. **International locations:** Canada. **Parent company:** Canam Manac Group (Saint-Georges, Quebec, Canada). **President/General Manager:** Pierre Arcand.

CANTEEN VENDING SERVICE
4501 Auth Place, Suitland MD 20746. 301/702-1267. **Toll-free phone:** 800/357-0012. **Fax:** 301/702-1984. **E-mail address:** randy.morris@each.compass-usa.com. **Contact:** Carlson Knight, Human Resources. **World Wide Web address:** http://www.canteen-usa.com. **Description:** Operates a food and vending service, as well as several cafeterias. **Positions advertised include:** Branch Manager; Customer Service Manager; Supervisor; Route Driver. **Parent company:** Compass Group (also at this location) is a national contract food service management firm, serving 10,000 clients across the United States and in Canada. The three principal operating divisions of Service America are Dining Services, which concentrates on Corporate America; Vending Services, one of the largest vending machine operators in the country with over 60,000 units; and Recreation Services, which provides food for convention centers, sports arenas, and performing arts centers.

CAPITAL-GAZETTE COMMUNICATIONS, INC.
P.O. Box 911, Annapolis MD 21404. 410/268-5000. **Physical address:** 2000 Capital Drive, Annapolis MD 21401. **Fax:** 410/268-4643. **Contact:** Loretta Haring, Managing Editor. **World Wide Web address:** http://www.hometownannapolis.com. **Description:** Publishes the *Annapolis Evening Capital,* a newspaper with a daily circulation of 50,000. **Corporate headquarters location:** This location. **Subsidiaries include:** Capital-Gazette Newspapers. **Publisher:** Eleanor Merrill. **Number of employees at this location:** 500.

CARAUSTAR
P.O. Box 987, Hunt Valley MD 21031. 410/785-2233. **Physical address:** 11000 Gilroy Road, Hunt Valley MD 21031. **Fax:** 410/785-4815. **Contact:** Human Resources. **World Wide Web address:** http://www.caraustar.com. **Description:** Produces folding and corrugated boxes, recycled paperboard, custom packaging, plastics, and adhesives. The company is divided into four business units: the Mill Group, the Custom Packaging Group, the Industrial and Consumer Products Group, and the Recovered Fiber Group. **Corporate headquarters location:** Austell GA. **Other U.S. locations:** Nationwide. **International locations:** Mexico; England; Canada. **Operations at this facility include:** This location manufactures folding cartons. **Listed on:** NASDAQ. **Stock exchange symbol:** CSAR.

CARDINAL HEALTH
8851 McGaw Road, Columbia MD 21045. 410/290-8500. **Fax:** 410/290-7906. **Contact:** Personnel. **World Wide Web address:** http://www.cardinal.com. **Description:** A producer, developer, and distributor of medical products and technologies for use in hospitals and other health care settings. The company also provides consulting services. **NOTE:** Entry-level positions are offered. **Positions advertised include:** Nuclear Medical Technician. **Special programs:** Internships. **Corporate headquarters location:** Dublin OH. **Other U.S. locations:** Nationwide. **International locations:** Worldwide **Operations at this location include:** This location distributes medical supplies to hospitals. **President/CEO:** George L. Fotiades. **Sales/revenues:** $40 billion. **Number of employees worldwide:** Over 49,000.

CAREFIRST BLUECROSS BLUESHIELD
10455 Mill Run Circle, Owings Mills MD 21117. 410/581-3000. **Fax:** 410/998-5313. **Contact:** Personnel. **World Wide Web address:** http://www.carefirst.com. **Description:** An insurance organization administering health care coverage for private industry, government, and nongroup subscribers. **NOTE:** Resumes may be submitted online. **Positions advertised include:** Medical Assistant; Case Manager; Financial Auditor; Support Clerk; Oncology Case Manager; Utilization Review Specialist; Office Assistant. **Corporate headquarters location:** This location. **Other U.S. locations:** Delaware; Washington, D.C. **Subsidiaries include:** CareFirst of Maryland, Incorporated; Group Hospitalization and Medical Services, Incorporated; BCBSD, Incorporated. **Number of employees nationwide:** 6,400.

CARR-LOWREY GLASS COMPANY
2201 Kloman Street, Baltimore MD 21230. 410/347-8800. **Fax:** 410/727-3019. **Contact:** Human Resources. **E-mail address:** glassworks@carrlowry.com. **World Wide Web address:** http://www.carrlowrey.com. **Description:** Produces glass bottles, jars, and labels and decorates glass products. Founded in 1889. **Corporate headquarters location:** This location. **International locations:** Paris, France. **Listed on:** Privately held. **Sales/revenues:** $21 - $50 million. **Number of employees at this location:** 550.

CARROLL COUNTY GENERAL HOSPITAL
200 Memorial Avenue, Westminster MD 21157. 410/871-6833. **Fax:** 410/871-6989. **Recorded jobline:** 410/871-7147. **Contact:** Human Resources. **E-mail address:** hr@ccgh.com. **World Wide Web address:** http://www.ccgh.com. **Description:** A private, nonprofit, 158-bed hospital governed by a community-based board which offers comprehensive laboratory and radiology services, an ambulatory surgery center, a cardiac catheterization lab and angiography service, and an inpatient psychiatric unit. **Positions advertised include:** Clinical Social Worker; Director; Clinical Representative; Registered Nurse; Licensed Practical Nurse; Applications Coordinator; Team Leader; Clinical Education Coordinator; Unit Secretary; Emergency Room Registrar; Attendant; Nuclear Medical Technician; Environmental Services Associate; Phlebotomist; Representative Therapist. **Special programs:** Internships; Tuition Reimbursement Program. **Office hours:** Monday – Friday, 7:30 a.m. – 3:00 p.m.

CARROLL INDEPENDENT FUEL COMPANY
2700 Loch Raven Road, Baltimore MD 21218. 410/261-5461. **Toll-free phone:** 800/834-8590. **Contact:** Human Resources. **E-mail address:** hr@carrollfuel.com. **World Wide Web address:** http://www.carrollfuel.com. **Description:** An oil company that provides delivery and service to its customers. **NOTE:** Online applications are available. To contact Human Resources directly, call 410/261-5461. **Positions advertised include:** Customer Service Representative; HVAC Service Technician; Driver. **Operations at this facility include:** This location houses administrative offices.

CARROLLTON BANK
P.O. Box 24129, Baltimore MD. 410/536-4600. **Contact:** Allison Cwiek, Human Resources Department. **World Wide Web address:** http://www.carrolltonbank.com. **Description:** Operates a full-service commercial bank. **Corporate headquarters location:** This location.

CASTROL HEAVY DUTY LUBRICANTS
9300 Pulaski Highway, Baltimore MD 21220. 410/574-5000. **Toll-free phone:** 800/777-1466. **Fax:** 410/682-9486. **Contact:** Human Resources. **Description:** A manufacturer of oils and greases. **Corporate headquarters location:** This location. **Office hours:** Monday – Friday, 7:00 a.m. – 6:30 p.m. **Operations at this facility include:** Administration; Manufacturing; Research and Development; Sales; Service.

CAT HOSPITAL AT TOWSON
6701 York Road, Baltimore MD 21212. 410/377-7900. **Contact:** Human Resources. **E-mail address:** catdoc@catdoc.com. **World Wide Web address:** http://www.catdoc.com. **Description:** Provides general medical and surgical services as well as chemotherapy, electrocardiograms, and dental care for cats. **Office hours:** Monday – Thursday, 8:00 a.m. – 8:00 p.m., Friday, 8:00 a.m. – 6:00 p.m., Saturday, 8:00 a.m. – 4:00 p.m.

CENTURY ENGINEERING, INC.
32 West Road, Towson MD 21204. 410/823-8070. **Fax:** 410/823-2184. **Contact:** Ken Stratemeyer, Human Resources. **E-mail address:** kstratemeyer@centuryeng.com. **World Wide Web address:** http://www.centuryeng.com. **Description:** Provides electrical, mechanical, civil, structural, and geotechnical engineering services to private firms and government agencies in the U.S. **NOTE:** Entry-level positions are offered. **Positions advertised include:** Instrument Operations; Environmental Structures Engineer; Hydraulics Engineer; Structural Engineer; Traffic Engineer; Transportation Planner; Electrical Engineer. **Corporate headquarters location:** This location. **Other area locations:** Oakland MD. **Other U.S. locations:** Dover DE; Elkins WV. **CEO:** Francis X. Smyth. **Number of employees at this location:** 100. **Number of employees nationwide:** Approximately 170.

CENTURY TECHNOLOGIES, INC. (CENTECH)
8403 Colesville Road, Suite 920, Silver Spring MD 20910. 301/585-4800. **Fax:** 301/588-1619. **Contact:** Human Resources. **E-mail address:** resumes@centech.com. **World Wide Web address:** http://www.centech.com. **Description:** A systems integrator that provides telecommunications and networking services to clientele in the public and private sectors. Founded in 1977. **Positions advertised include:** Microsoft Certified Consultant. **Corporate headquarters location:** This location. **Other U.S. locations:** Beavercreek OH; Del City OK. **Number of employees nationwide:** 300.

CENVEO
1820 Portal Street, Baltimore MD 21224. 410/633-4200. **Contact:** Human Resources. **World Wide Web address:** http://www.cenveo.com. **Description:** Involved in all aspects of printing and book-making including composition and binding services, typesetting, and lithography. Founded in 1830. **Note:** Employment phone number: 410/633-1284. **Corporate headquarters location:** This location. **Operations at this facility include:** Administration; Manufacturing; Sales; Service. **President:** Barry Heyman. **Number of employees at this location:** 200.

CERTAINTEED CORPORATION
P.O. Box 290, Williamsport MD 21795. 301/223-7900. **Physical address:** 10131 Governor Lane Boulevard, Williamsport MD 21795. **Fax:** 301/582-5510. **Contact:** Human Resources. **World Wide Web address:** http://www.certainteed.com. **Description:** Manufactures and distributes building materials, fiberglass products, and piping products. Principal products are used in residential, commercial, and industrial construction; repair and remodeling; fiberglass reinforcement applications; water and sewer systems; and other underground utility systems. Other products include roofing, acoustical insulation, fiberglass thermal insulation, air handling products, glass fiber, vinyl siding, and PVC piping. **Corporate headquarters location:** Valley Forge PA. **Other area locations:** Hagerstown MD. **Other U.S. locations:** Nationwide. **Parent company:** Saint-Gobain Corporation. **Operations at this facility include:** This location is a vinyl siding and windows manufacturing plant. **Sales/revenues:** Over $2.5 billion. **Number of employees nationwide:** Approximately 7,000.

CHESAPEAKE AND OHIO CANAL NATIONAL HISTORICAL PARK
1850 Dual Highway, Suite 100, Hagerstown MD 21740-6620. 301/739-4200. **Fax:** 301/432-5897. **Contact:** Human Resources. **E-mail address:** choh_superintendent@nps.gov. **World Wide Web address:** http://www.nps.gov/choh. **Description:** Preserves the cultural and national history of the Chesapeake and Ohio Canal, which operated as a transportation route from 1828 to 1924. The canal runs for 184.5 miles along the Potomac River from Washington DC to Cumberland MD. **Special programs:** Internships.

CHESAPEAKE BIOLOGICAL LABORATORIES, INC.
1111 South Paca Street, Baltimore MD 21230-2591. 410/843-5000. **Toll-free phone:** 800/441-4225. **Fax:** 410/843-4414. **Contact:** Human Resources. **E-mail address:** info@cblinc.com. **World Wide Web address:** http://www.cblinc.com. **Description:** A pharmaceuticals manufacturing company that provides sterile finish processing and specializes in single-dose vials and syringes. **Special programs:** Training and Development Program.

CHESAPEAKE PUBLISHING CORPORATION
P.O. Box 600, 29088 Airpark Drive, Easton MD 21601-0600. 410/822-1500. **Fax:** 410/770-4012. **Contact:** Human Resources. **World Wide Web address:** http://www.chespub.com. **Description:** Chesapeake Publishing publishes 50 newspapers including *Enterprise* (circulation: 14,000); *Maryland Independent* (circulation: 12,500); *South County Current* (circulation: 33,000); *Calvert County Recorder* (circulation: 5,500); and *Flightline* (circulation: 9,000). The company also provides commercial printing services. **Corporate headquarters location:** This location. **Other area locations:** Elkton MD; Beltsville MD. **Operations at this facility include:** This location publishes the *Star Democratic*. **Number of employees nationwide:** Approximately 500.

CHESAPEAKE PUBLISHING CORPORATION
601 North Bridge Street, Elkton MD 21922-0429. 410/398-3311. **Fax:** 410/398-4044. **Contact:** Human Resources. **World Wide Web address:** http://www.chespub.com. **Description:** Chesapeake Publishing publishes 50 newspapers including: *Enterprise* (circulation: 14,000); *Maryland Independent* (circulation: 12,500); *South County Current* (circulation: 33,000); *Calvert County Recorder* (circulation: 5,500); and *Flightline* (circulation: 9,000). The company also provides commercial printing services. **Corporate headquarters location:** Easton MD. **Other area locations:** Beltsville MD. **Operations at this facility include:** This location publishes the *Cecil Whig*. **Number of employees nationwide:** Approximately 500.

CHEVY CHASE BANK
7501 Wisconsin Avenue, Bethesda MD 20814. 240/497-7700. **Fax:** 240/497-4688. **Contact:** Human Resources. **World Wide Web address:** http://www.chevychasebank.com. **Description:** Commercial lending headquarters of the largest bank in the DC metro area, with over 220 branches and 850 ATMs. **Other area locations:** Baltimore MD, Chevy Chase MD, Laurel MD.

CHEVY CHASE BANK
6151 Chevy Chase Drive, Laurel MD 20707. 301/287-7300. **Fax:** 301/369-3023. **Contact:** Human Resources. **Description:** Financial institution with branches throughout MD, DC, Northern VA, and DE. **Other area locations:** Baltimore MD, Bethesda MD.

THE CHIMES, INC.
4814 Seton Drive, Baltimore MD 21215. 410/358-6400. **Toll-free phone:** 800/CHI-MES1. **Fax:** 410/358-6165. **Recorded jobline:** 410/358-6006. **Contact:** Human Resources. **E-mail address:** hrmail@chimes.org. **World Wide Web address:** http://www.chimes.org. **Description:** A nonsectarian, nonprofit agency that offers a broad range of vocational, rehabilitative, residential, educational, and support services for thousands of individuals in central Maryland, northern Virginia, and Washington DC. The Chimes helps children, adults, and senior citizens with mental and related disabilities to lead more independent lives. Founded in 1947. **Positions advertised include:** Single and Multi Site Job Coach; Food Service Manager; House Manager; Research Proven Technician; Program Coordinator; Instructor; Executive Assistant; Accounts Payable Manager; Environmental Services. **Office hours:** Monday – Thursday, 9:00 a.m. – 3:00 p.m. **Corporate headquarters location:** This location. **Other U.S. locations:** CA; DE; DC; IA; VA. **International locations:** Israel. **President/CEO:** Terry Allen Perl. **Number of employees nationwide:** 600.

CHOICE HOTELS INTERNATIONAL
10750 Columbia Pike, Silver Spring MD 20901. 301/592-5000. **Contact:** Human Resources. **E-mail address:** choicehotels@hiresystems.com. **World Wide Web address:** http://www.choicehotels.com. **Description:** An internationally franchised hotel company. **NOTE:** Resumes may be submitted online for advertised positions. **Positions advertised include:** Database Administrator; Strategic Planner; Coordinating Marketer; Director FRAN – Operations Mexico; Marketing Analyst; Marketing Communications Specialist; Administrative Assistant; Database Marketing Specialist; Revenue Coordinator; People Soft Financial Programmer. **Corporate headquarters location:** This location. **Other U.S. locations:** Nationwide. **International locations:** Worldwide. **Subsidiaries include:** Clarion Hotels; Comfort Inns; Econo Lodge; Main Stay Suites; Quality Inns; Rodeway; Sleep Inns. **Operations at this facility include:** Sales. **Listed on:** New York Stock Exchange. **Stock exchange symbol:** CHH. **President/CEO:** Charles A. Ledsinger, Junior. **Sales/revenue:** $365 million. **Number of employees worldwide:** Approximately 2,000.

CINGULAR WIRELESS
7855 Walker Drive, Suite 100, Greenbelt MD 20770. 301/220-3787. **Contact:** Personnel. **World Wide Web address:** http://www.cingular.com. **Description:** Manufactures and sells mobile phone systems. **NOTE:** Online applications are available. **Positions advertised include:** Business Account Executive; Federal Government Key Account Executive; Key Account Executive; Federal Government Operations; Floating Assistant Store Manager. **Special programs:** Tuition Reimbursement Program. **Office hours:** Monday – Friday, 8:00 a.m. – 5:00 p.m. **Corporate headquarters location:** Atlanta GA. **Other U.S. locations:** Nationwide. **Parent company:** Joint venture of BellSouth and SBC. **Listed on:** New York Stock Exchange. **Stock exchange symbol:** BLS; SBC. **Sales/revenue:** $4.7 billion. **Number of employees nationwide:** 35,000.

CISCO SYSTEMS
8865 Stanford Boulevard Suite 201, Columbia MD 21045. 410/309-4800. **Fax:** 410/309-4899. **Contact:** Human Resources. **World Wide Web address:** http://www.cisco.com **Description:** Cisco Systems is the leader for networking and the Internet. **Note:** Applications may be submitted online. **Positions advertised include:** Finance Business Specialist; Safety Manager. **Corporate Headquarters location:** San Jose, CA. **Other U.S. locations:** Nation wide. **International locations:** World Wide. **Listed on:** NASDAQ. **Stock exchange symbol:** CSCO.

CITIFINANCIAL
300 St. Paul Place, Baltimore MD 21202. 410/332-3000. **Contact:** Human Resources. **World Wide Web address:** http://www.citifinancial.com. **Description:** Provides bill consolidation, debt refinancing, home improvement, home equity, and other small personal loans. **Positions advertised include:** Program Manager; Project Manager; Business Systems Analyst; Administrative Technician; Dealer Developer Representative; Dispatch Analyst; Field Investigator; Accountant; Financial Analyst; Staff Accountant; Supervisor Fields Representative; Money Desk Manager; Processor; Executive Secretary; Information Technology Reporting Analyst; Account Manager; Operations Manager; Director Operations Assistant; Quality Control Team Leader. **Corporate headquarters location:** This location. **Other U.S. locations:** Nationwide. **International locations:** Canada. **Parent company:** Citigroup, Incorporated. **Operations at this facility include:** Administration. **Listed on:** New York Stock Exchange. **Stock exchange symbol:** C. **President/CEO:** Michael S. Knapp. **Number of employees at this location:** 450. **Number of employees nationwide:** 4,000. **Number of employees worldwide:** Over 13,000.

CITIFINANCIAL
841 Russell Avenue, Gaithersburg MD 20879. 240/632-5640. **Contact:** Human Resources. **World Wide Web address:** http://www.citifinancial.com. **Description:** Provides bill consolidation, debt refinancing, home improvement, home equity, and other small personal loans. **Corporate headquarters location:** Baltimore MD. **Other U.S. locations:** Nationwide. **International locations:** Canada. **Parent company:** Citigroup, Incorporated. **Listed on:** New York Stock Exchange. **Stock exchange symbol:** C. **President/CEO:** Michael S. Knapp. **Number of employees nationwide:** 4,000. **Number of employees worldwide:** Over 13,000.

CIVISTA MEDICAL CENTER
P.O. Box 1070, 701 East Charles Street, La Plata MD 20646. 301/609-4444. **Fax:** 301/609-4417. **Recorded jobline:** 301/638-1805. **Contact:** Human Resources. **E-mail address:** hr@civista.org. **World Wide Web address:** http://www.civista.org. **Description:** A 131-bed, full-service community hospital. Founded in 1939. **Positions advertised include:** Business Associate; Clerical Imaging Technician; CT Technician; Exercise Physiologist; Medical Technician; Practical Registered Nurse; Nuclear Medical Technologist; Patient Account Representative; Pharmacist. **Special programs:** Internships. **Office hours:** Monday - Tuesday, Thursday – Friday, 8:30 a.m. – 4:00 p.m., Wednesday, 8:00 a.m. – 4:00 p.m. **Corporate headquarters location:** Waldorf MD. **Parent company:** Civista Health is a non-profit organization that delivers health care services to southern Maryland. **Operations at this facility include:** Administration; Divisional Headquarters; Regional Headquarters; Service. **Number of employees at this location:** 750.

THE CLARK CONSTRUCTION GROUP, INC.
7500 Old Georgetown Road, Bethesda MD 20814. 301/272-8100. **Fax:** 301/272-8414. **Contact:** Personnel. **E-mail address:** hr@clarkconstruction.com. **World Wide Web address:** http://www.clarkconstruction.com. **Description:** Provides general contract construction. Founded in 1906. **NOTE:** Resumes submitted via e-mail must be in Microsoft Word, WordPerfect, or text file format. **Positions advertised include:** Estimator; Field Engineer; Office Engineer; Project Manager; Safety Representative; Superintendent. **Special programs:** Internships; Co-ops. **Corporate headquarters location:** This location. **Other U.S. locations:** Costa Mesa CA; Oakland CA; Tampa FL; Chicago IL; Boston MA. **Sales/revenue:** $2 billion.

CLEAN HARBORS ENVIRONMENTAL SERVICES, INC.
3527 Whisky Bottom Road, Laurel MD 20724. 301/939-6000. **Fax:** 301/939-6066. **Contact:** Human Resources. **World Wide Web address:** http://www.cleanharbors.com. **Description:** Provides comprehensive environmental services in 35 states in the northeast, midwest, central, and mid-Atlantic regions through its subsidiaries. Clean Harbors provides a wide range of hazardous waste management and environmental support services to a diversified customer base from over 40 locations. The company's hazardous waste management services include

treatment, storage, recycling, transportation, risk analysis, site assessment, laboratory analysis, site closure, and disposal of hazardous materials through environmentally sound methods including incineration. Environmental remediation services include emergency response, surface remediation, groundwater restoration, industrial maintenance, and facility decontamination. Customers include nearly 300 of the *Fortune* 500 companies, regional utilities, oil, pharmaceutical, and chemical companies, small businesses, and the high-tech and biotech industries. **Positions advertised include:** Field Technician; Class A Driver; Field Service Technician. **Corporate headquarters location:** Braintree MA. **Other U.S. locations:** Nationwide. **International locations:** Canada; Mexico; Puerto Rico. **Listed on:** NASDAQ. **Stock exchange symbol:** CLHB. **CEO:** Alan S. McKim. **Number of employees nationwide:** 1,400.

CLENDENIN BROTHERS, INC.
4309 Erdman Avenue, Baltimore MD 21213. 410/327-4500. **Fax:** 410/327-0241. **Contact:** Human Resources. **Description:** Manufactures brass, copper, aluminum, and stainless steel products.

CLIFTON GUNDERSON LLP
9515 Deereco Road, Suite 500, Timonium MD 21093. 410/453-0900. **Fax:** 410/453-0914. **Contact:** Human Resources. **World Wide Web address:** http://www.cliftoncpa.com. **Description:** A certified public accounting and consulting firm that provides services to customers in the agribusiness, contracting, financial, government, health care, and manufacturing industries. **Positions advertised include:** Assurance Manager; Assurance Associate. **Special programs:** Internships; Tuition Assistance Program; Relocation Program. **Corporate headquarters location:** Peoria IL. **Other area locations:** Calverton MD; Forest Hill MD. **Other U.S. locations:** Nationwide. **Subsidiaries include:** R.S. Wells L.L.C.; CG Financial Services. **CEO:** Carl R. George. **Number of employees nationwide:** Over 1,400.

CLIFTON GUNDERSON
4041 Powder Mill Road, Beltsville MD 20705. 301/931-2050. **Contact:** Human Resources. **World Wide Web address:** http://www.cliftoncpa.com. **Description:** Provides accounting, auditing, tax, and consulting services. Founded in 1921. **NOTE:** Online applications are available. **Positions advertised include:** Tax Specialist; Accountant. **Special programs:** Internships.

CLOVERLAND GREEN SPRING DAIRY
2701 Loch Raven Road, Baltimore MD 21218. 410/235-4477. **Fax:** 410/889-3690. **Contact:** Human Resources. **E-mail address:** personnel@cloverlanddairy.com. **World Wide Web address:** http://www.cloverlanddairy.com. **Description:** Produces and distributes milk, ice cream, bakery products, and citrus juices. Founded in 1919. **Positions advertised include:** Truck Driver/Route Salesperson; Cooler/Warehouse Worker; Blow Molder Operator. **Corporate headquarters location:** This location. **Number of employees at this location:** Approximately 300.

COASTAL SUNBELT PRODUCE
8704 Bollman place, Savage MD 20763. 410/694-4040. **Fax:** 410/694-4052. **E-mail address:** chunt@coastalsunbelt.com. **Contact:** Human Resources Manager. **World Wide Web address:** http://www.coastalsunbelt.com. **Description:** A produce company specializing in servicing restaurants from Bertucci's to Outback Steakhouse and Ruby Tuesday's. **Positions advertised include:** Operations Clerk. **Company Slogan:** Keeping Promises is how we do business. **Number of employees:** 150.

COMMUNITY COLLEGE OF BALTIMORE COUNTY
800 South Rolling Road, Baltimore MD 21228. 410/869-7137. **Fax:** 410/869-7149. **Contact:** Gary S. Slowe, Employment and Recruitment Administrator. **E-mail address:** gslowe2@ccbcmd.edu. **World Wide Web address:** http://www.ccbc.cc.md.us. **Description:** One location of the community college that offers more than 60 degree and certificate programs. **NOTE:** Online applications are available. **Positions advertised include:** Assistant Director; Director Public Safety; Evening Receptionist; Grants Revenue Coordinator; Information Assistant Instructor; Registration Information Specialist; Switchboard Operator; Video Production Assistant. **President:** Dr. Andrew C. Jones.

COMPRO SYSTEMS, INC.
8560 Laureldale Drive, Laurel MD 20724. 301/497-7650. **Fax:** 301/497-7653. **Contact:** Human Resources. **World Wide Web address:** http://www.compro.com. **Description:** Fulfills the automation needs of clients through systems integration, LANs, networking, the Internet, customized application software development, database management, document image processing, and business modeling. ComPro's customers include both government and commercial clients. Founded in 1982. **Positions advertised include:** Queue Coordinator; Help Desk Administrator; Cross Functional Queue Manager; Tools Applicant Support; Network Systems Administrator; Network Storage Area Associate; Sonet Engineer; Service Writer; Configuration Manager; Desktop Support Systems Administrator; UNIX Infrastructure Administrator; Web Architect; Windows NT2000 Server Administrator; Fiber Optics Technician. **Corporate headquarters location:** This location. **International locations:** India. **Listed on:** Privately held. **Sales/revenues:** $11 - $20 million. **Number of employees at this location:** 15. **Number of employees nationwide:** 225.

COMPUTER SCIENCES CORPORATION
15245 Shady Grove Road, Suite 200, Rockville MD 20850. 301/921-3000. **Contact:** Human Resources. **World Wide Web address:** http://www.csc.com. **Description:** A diversified company comprised of four sectors: the Systems Group Division designs, engineers, and integrates computer-based systems and communications systems, providing all the hardware, software, training, and related elements necessary to operate such a system; the Consulting Division provides consulting and technical services in the development of computer and communication systems to nonfederal organizations; the Industry Services Group serves the health care, insurance, and financial services industries, and provides large-scale claim processing and other insurance-related services; CSC Health Care and CSC Enterprises make up the CSC Divisions. CSC Health Care markets business systems and services to the managed health care industry, clinics, and physicians. CSC Enterprises provides consumer credit reports and account management services to credit grantors. **Positions advertised include:** Systems Analyst; Applications Developer; Contract Specialist. **Corporate headquarters location:** El Segundo CA. **Other U.S. locations:** Nationwide. **International locations:** Worldwide. **Subsidiaries include:** DynaCorp. **Operations at this facility include:** This location is the Systems Sciences division headquarters, and primarily serves the U.S. government. **Listed on:** New York Stock Exchange. **Stock exchange symbol:** CSC. **President/COO:** Edward P. Boykin. **Sales/revenue:** $11.3 billion. **Number of employees nationwide:** 20,000. **Number of employees worldwide:** 90,000.

COMSO, INC.
6303 Ivy Lane, Suite 300, Greenbelt MD 20770. 301/345-0046. **Fax:** 301/345-0047. **Contact:** Recruiting. **E-mail address:** recruit@comso.com. **World Wide Web address:** http://www.comso.com. **Description:** A computer systems integration firm. Founded in 1988. **Positions advertised include:** Director of Business; Development Sales. **Other area locations:** Silver Spring MD; Landover MD; Fort Meade MD. **Other U.S. locations:** Arlington VA; McClean VA; Reston VA; Washington D.C.

COMSYS
9737 Washingtonian Boulevard, Gaithersburg MD 20878. 301/921-3600. **Toll-free phone:** 800/926-6797. **Fax:** 301/921-3660. **Contact:** Human Resources. **World Wide Web address:** http://www.comsys.com. **Description:** Provides contract programming and computer and software consulting services. **Positions advertised include:** Contract Administrator; Database Technician; Expert Approval Import Processing; HTML Programmer; Logistic Support Engineer; Mechanical Engineer; Performance Test Coordinator; Resident Source Inspector; Service Level Management; Subcontract Administrator; UNIX Administrator. **Corporate headquarters location:** Houston TX. **Other area locations:** Baltimore MD. **Other U.S. locations:** Nationwide. **President/CEO:** Michael T. Willis.

CONESTOGA WOOD SPECIALTIES, INC.
3502 Hughes Road, Darlington MD 21034. 410/457-5123. **Contact:** Human Resources. **World Wide Web address:** http://www.conestoga.com. **Description:** Produces millwork, primarily wooden kitchen and bathroom cabinet doors. Founded in 1964. **Office hours:** Monday – Friday, 8:00 a.m. – 4:00 p.m. **Corporate headquarters location:** East Earl PA. **Other U.S. locations:** Jacksonville AR; Mountain View AR; Kenly NC; Hamilton OH; Beavertown PA. **Number of employees nationwide:** Approximately 2,000.

COOPERATIVE HOUSING FOUNDATION
8601 Georgia Avenue, Suite 800, Silver Spring MD 20910. 301/587-4700. **Fax:** 301/587-7315. **Contact:** Human Resources. **E-mail address:** hrrec@chfhq.org. **World Wide Web address:** http://www.chfhq.org. **Description:** A foundation providing housing, economic, infrastructure, and health assistance. **NOTE:** When submitting via e-mail, attach resume and cover letter as separate documents. **Positions advertised include:** Communications Assistant; Security Offices; Short Term Consultant; A/R Accountant; Credit Manager; Credit Analyst; Operations Support Officer; Municipal Financial Specialist; Program Officer; Program Manager. **Corporate headquarters location:** This location. **Operations at this facility include:** Regional Headquarters. **President/CEO:** Michael Doyle.

COPPIN STATE COLLEGE
2500 West North Avenue, Baltimore MD 21216. 410/951-3666. **Fax:** 410/951-3667. **Contact:** Human Resources. **E-mail address:** careers@coppin.edu. **World Wide Web address:** http://www.coppin.edu. **Description:** A four-year, liberal arts college offering both bachelor's and master's degrees. Approximately 2,500 undergraduate and 275 graduate students attend the college. **Positions advertised include:** Counselor; Assistant Professor; Assistant Director. **NOTE:** Applications are available online. **Special programs:** Internships; Training. **Office hours:** Monday – Friday, 8:00 a.m. – 5:30 p.m. **Corporate headquarters location:** This location. **President:** Dr. Stanley F. Battle. **Number of employees at this location:** 530.

COUNTY DEPARTMENT OF AGING
520 North Market Street, Frederick MD 21701. 301/694-1605. **Contact:** Human Resources. **World Wide Web address:** http://www.co.frederick.md.us/COA/. **Description:** A department that studies and advocates the rights of the elderly. **Office hours:** Monday – Friday, 8:30 a.m. – 4:00 p.m.

CRAFTSMAN PRESS, INC.
2300 Craftsman Circle, Cheverly MD 20781-1133. 301/773-9400. **Toll-free phone:** 877/773-9400. **Fax:** 301/341-7667. **Contact:** Human Resources. **World Wide Web address:** http://www.craftsman-press.com. **Description:** Provides a wide range of commercial printing services. **Other U.S. locations:** Holmdel NJ.

CROWN CENTRAL PETROLEUM CORPORATION
P.O. Box 1168, Baltimore MD 21203. 410/539-7400. **Physical address:** One North Charles Street, Baltimore MD 21201. **Fax:** 410/659-4875. **Contact:** Jim Weaver, Human Resources Department. **E-mail address:** recruiter@crowncentral.com. **World Wide Web address:** http://www.crowncentral.com. **Description:** Crown Central Petroleum refines and markets petroleum products and petrochemicals and has subsidiaries in the convenience store market. The company owns two refineries in Texas and operates 17 terminals across the Southeastern and Midwestern United States. Petroleum products are marketed through 18 states and Washington DC. The company also operates approximately 350 convenience stores and gas outlets under the Fast Fare and Zippy Mart names in Alabama, North and South Carolina, and Georgia. Founded in 1917. **NOTE:** Entry-level positions are offered. **Special programs:** Internships; Summer Jobs. **Corporate headquarters location:** This location. **Other U.S. locations:** PA; VA; NC; SC; TX; GA; AL. **Number of employees at this location:** 250. **Number of employees nationwide:** 3,300.

CYTEC ENGINEERED MATERIALS
1300 Revolution Street, Havre de Grace MD 21078. 410/939-1910. **Contact:** Human Resources. **World Wide Web address:** http://www.cytec.com. **Description:** Manufactures advanced composite and adhesives for aerospace, industrial, recreational, and other applications. **Corporate headquarters:** West Paterson NJ. **Other U.S. locations:** Nationwide. **International locations:** Worldwide. **Parent company:** Cytec Industries Incorporated. **Operations at this facility include:** This location is part of the Engineered Materials division and produces sealants, film adhesives, primers, syntactic foams, and potting compounds, in addition to conducting research. **Listed on:** New York Stock Exchange. **Stock exchange symbol:** CYT. **President/CEO/Chairman:** David Lilley.

DAP INC.
2400 Boston Street, Suite 200, Baltimore MD 21224. 410/675-2100. **Toll-free phone:** 800/543-3840. **Fax:** 410/558-1084. **Contact:** Linda Bennet, Human Resources. **E-mail address:** hresources@dap.com. **World Wide Web address:** http://www.dap.com. **Description:** Manufactures and markets sealant and adhesive products for customers for home repair and construction applications. **Positions advertised include:** Territory Manager; Channel Manager; Human Resources Safety Manager; Channel Manager. **Corporate headquarters location:** This location. **Number of employees at this location:** Over 130. **Number of employees worldwide:** 700.

DRS ELECTRONIC SYSTEMS, INC.
200 Professional Drive, Gaithersburg MD 20879. 301/921-8100. **Contact:** Human Resources. **E-mail address:** resume@drs-esg.com. **World Wide Web address:** http://www.drs.com. **Description:** Manufactures and sells a diverse range of electronic products for communication, technological, transportation, and defense applications. **Positions advertised include:** Electrical Engineer; Radar Systems Engineer; Software Engineer; Software Configuration Management Support; Technical Display Software Systems Engineer; UNIX Administration. **Corporate headquarters location:** Parsippany NJ. **Other U.S. locations:** Nationwide. **International locations:** Canada;

England. **Parent company:** DRS Technologies, Incorporated is a defense electronic systems supplier that serves customers in both government and commercial sectors. **Listed on:** American Stock Exchange. **Stock exchange symbol:** DRS. **President/Chairman/CEO:** Mark S. Newman.

DRS SIGNAL RECORDING TECHNOLOGIES
9790 Patuxent Woods Drive, Suite H, Columbia MD 21046. 410/290-7711. **Contact:** Human Resources. **E-mail address:** employment@drs-srt.com. **World Wide Web address:** http://www.drs-srt.com. **Description:** Manufactures hardware for supercomputers. **NOTE:** Resumes may be submitted online. **Positions advertised include:** Analog Design Engineer; Hardware Engineer; Software Engineer. **Operations at this facility include:** Sales.

DALE CARNEGIE TRAINING
11140 Rockville Pike, Suite 650, Rockville MD 20852. 301/770-2444. **Fax:** 301/984-3118. **Contact:** Personnel. **E-mail address:** Carla_lee@dalecarnegie.com. **World Wide Web address:** http://www.washingtondc.dalecarnegie.com. **Description:** A professional services institute offering training for sales people in the areas of motivation, time management, and leadership. Founded in 1912. **Corporate headquarters location:** New York NY.

DALY COMPUTERS
22521 Gateway Center Drive, Clarksburg MD 20871. 301/670-0381. **Toll-free phone:** 800/955-DALY. **Fax:** 301/515-9366. **Contact:** Human Resources. **E-mail address:** hr@daly.com. **World Wide Web address:** http://www.daly.com. **Description:** An information technologies service provider geared primarily toward the public sector. **Positions advertised include:** Inside Sales Person; Outside Sales Person; Computer Engineer. **Corporate headquarters location:** This location. **Other U.S. locations:** Miami FL; Chicago IL; Harrisburg PA; Richmond VA; Roanoke VA.

C.R. DANIELS, INC.
3451 Ellicott Center Drive, Ellicott City MD 21042. 410/461-2100. **Fax:** 410/461-2987. **Contact:** Human Resources. **E-mail address:** info@crdaniels.com. **World Wide Web address:** http://www.crdaniels.com. **Description:** Produces a wide range of aviation products including seats, nets, and cushions; material handling containers; industrial and other premium fabric products; canvas and synthetic tarpaulins; and conveyor belts. Founded in 1918. **Corporate headquarters location:** This location. **Other U.S. locations:** Rutledge TN. **Number of employees at this location:** 170.

DAVENPORT INSULATION INC.
P.O. Box 57, 15445 Depot Lane, Upper Marlboro MD 20772. 301/627-1800. **Fax:** 301/627-6999. **Contact:** Human Resources. **Description:** A contracting and retail operation specializing in the installation and servicing of insulation and related products.

DAVID-EDWARD LTD.
1407 Parker Road, Baltimore MD 21227. 410/242-2222. **Contact:** Human Resources. **World Wide Web address:** http://www.davidedward.com. **Description:** Manufactures custom-made upholstered chairs and sofas. **Corporate headquarters location:** This location. **Number of employees at this location:** 300.

DECRANE AIRCRAFT SYSTEMS INTEGRATION GROUP (DASIG)
9570 Berger Road, Columbia MD 21046. 410/381-5533x183. **Fax:** 410/290-6960. **Contact:** Ellen Leache, Human Resources. **E-mail address:** leache@patsinc.com. **World Wide Web address:** http://www.patsinc.com. **Description:** Manufactures long-range fuel tanks, APUs, and air stairs and provides personal service for VIP and Head-of-State aircraft. **Corporate headquarters location:** El Segundo CA. **Other U.S. locations:** Georgetown DE. **Parent company:** DeCrane Aircraft Holdings, Incorporated.

DEUTSCHE BANC ALEX. BROWN
One South Street, Baltimore MD 21202. 410/727-1700. **Toll-free phone:** 800/ 638-2596. **Fax:** 410/895-3450. **Recorded jobline:** 410/895-5350. **Contact:** Human Resources. **World Wide Web address:** http://www.alexbrown.db.com. **Description:** A financial services, investment advisory, and investment banking firm. Founded in 1800. **Corporate headquarters location:** This location. **Other U.S. locations:** Atlanta GA; Boston MA; Winston-Salem NC; Chicago IL; Greenwich CT; Los Angeles CA; San Francisco CA; Philadelphia PA; Houston TX; Dallas TX; New York NY. **Parent Company:** Deutsche Bank Securities, Incorporated. **Listed on:** New York Stock Exchange. **Stock exchange symbol:** DB. **CEO:** Tom Hughes.

DIGICON CORPORATION
1355 Piccard Drive, Suite 200, Rockville MD 20850. 301/721-6300. **Contact:** Maryanne Kozorous, Recruiter. **E-mail address:** careers@digicon.com. **World Wide Web address:** http://www.digicon.com. **Description:** A systems integration firm that provides telecommunications, networking, information technology, and enterprise systems management services. **NOTE:** Resumes submitted online must be in Word format. **Positions advertised include:** Service Center Engineer; Contract Manager; HQ Capture Manager; Oracle Developer; Project Manager; N/H-IT Acquisition Specialist; HQ Network Engineer; Software Engineer Manager; Staff Accountant. **Subsidiaries include:** DTx Incorporated; Digicon Technologies. **Sales/revenue:** Approximately $55 million. **Number of employees nationwide:** Over 300.

DISTRICT PHOTO, INC.
10501 Rhode Island Avenue, Beltsville MD 20705. 301/937-5300. **Contact:** Human Resources. **Description:** Engaged in the retail sale of photographic equipment and supplies. District Photo also provides amateur photofinishing services.

DOCUCORP INTERNATIONAL
8455 Colesville Road, Suite 820, Silver Spring MD 20910. 301/589-6300. **Contact:** Human Resources. **E-mail address:** recruiter@docucorp.com. **World Wide Web address:** http://www.docucorp.com. **Description:** Develops business solution software for document management and automation purposes. The company's services include insurance policy production, financial fulfillment, electronic bill presentment and payment, and customer statements and billings. **NOTE:** Resumes should be sent to: Docucorp, Attn: Recruiter, 5910 North Central Expressway, Suite 800, Dallas TX 75206. Fax to: 214/987-8187 **Positions advertised include:** Lead Writer. **Corporate headquarters location:** Dallas TX. **Other U.S. locations:** Atlanta GA; Portland ME; Bedford NH; Dallas TX. **International locations:** London, England. **Listed on:** NASDAQ. **Stock exchange symbol:** DOCC. **President/CEO:** Michael D. Andereck. **Sales/revenue:** $72 billion. **Number of employees nationwide:** 400.

DOMINO SUGAR CORPORATION
1100 Key Highway East, Baltimore MD 21230. 410/752-6150. **Contact:** Human Resources. **World Wide Web address:** http://www.dominosugar.com. **Description:** Refines primarily cane sugar for retail and industrial customers. Domino Sugar Corporation is one of the leading domestic brands of sugar in the United States. **Operations at this facility include:** This location is a raw sugar refinery.

R.R. DONNELLEY FINANCIAL
2 North Charles Street, Suite 920, Baltimore MD 21201. 410/752-3100. **Fax:** 410/752-6970. **Contact:** Human Resources. **E-mail address:** rrdonnelley@hiresystems.com. **World Wide Web address:** http://www.rrdfin.com. **Description:** Prints financial materials for the capital markets, health care, and mutual funds markets. **NOTE:** If sending resume via e-mail, include the code DNY/ in the subject or body of the message and format the document as either Microsoft Word or ASCII text. **Office hours:** Monday – Friday, 8:00 a.m. – 8:00 p.m. **Other U.S. locations:** Nationwide. **International locations:** Worldwide. **Parent company:** R.R. Donnelley & Sons (Chicago IL) is a world leader in managing, reproducing, and distributing print and digital information for publishing, merchandising, and information technology customers. The company is one of the largest commercial printers in the world, producing catalogs, inserts, magazines, books, directories, computer documentation, and financial materials. R.R. Donnelley has more than 180 sales offices and production facilities. Principal services offered by the company are conventional and digital prepress operations; computerized printing and binding; sophisticated pool shipping and distribution services for printed products; information repackaging into multiple formats (print, magnetic, and optical media); database management, list rental, list enhancement, and direct mail production services; turnkey computer documentation services (outsourcing, translation, printing, binding, diskette replication, kitting, licensing, republishing, and fulfillment); reprographics and facilities management; creative design and communication services; and digital and conventional map creation and related services. **Listed on:** New York Stock Exchange; Pacific Stock Exchange; Midwest Stock Exchange. **Stock exchange symbol:** DNY. **President:** Terry Trayvick. **Sales revenue:** Approximately $4 million. **Number of employees worldwide:** Over 30,000.

DOW JONES & COMPANY, INC.
11501 Columbia Pike, Silver Spring MD 20904. 301/680-2900. **Contact:** Human Resources. **E-mail address:** djcareers@dowjones.com. **World Wide Web address:** http://www.dowjones.com. **Description:** Prints the *Wall Street Journal*. Dow Jones is a national financial news service and publishing company with operating units in print publishing, electronic publishing and community newspapers. **Special programs:** Internships; Educational Assistance Plan; Educational Loan Program; Scholarship Program. **Corporate headquarters location:** New York NY. **Other U.S. locations:** Nationwide. **Listed on:** New York Stock Exchange. **Stock exchange symbol:** DJ. **CEO/Chairman:** Peter R. Kann. **Sales/revenue:** Approximately $1.8 billion. **Number of employees worldwide:** 8,000.

DURATEK, INC.
10100 Old Columbia Road, Columbia MD 21046. 410/312-5100. **Contact:** Human Resources. **E-mail address:** corprec@duratekinc.com. **World Wide Web address:** http://www.duratekinc.com. **Description:** An environmental and technology services company specializing in the process of solidifying nuclear waste into glass (vitrification). The Department of Energy and other companies employ Duratek to vitrify and dispose of their radioactive and nuclear wastes. **Positions advertised include:** Environmental Health Associate; Safety Director. **Corporate headquarters location:** This location. **Other U.S. locations:** Oak Ridge TN; Memphis TN; Kingston TN; Lakewood CO; Barnwell SC; Richland WA; Los Alamos NM. **Subsidiaries include:** Waste Management Nuclear Services. **Listed on:** NASDAQ. **Stock exchange symbol:** DRTK. **Sales/revenue:** $300 million.

DURON PAINTS & WALL COVERINGS
10406 Tucker Street, Beltsville MD 20705-2297. 301/937-4600. **Toll-free phone:** 800/723-8766. **Fax:** 301/595-0435. **Contact:** Human Resources. **E-mail address:** employment@duron.com. **World Wide Web address:** http://www.duron.com. **Description:** A manufacturer and wholesaler of paint and related products. **Positions advertised include:** Collector Adjuster; Computer Technician; Inside Sales Counter Representative; Machine Operator; Maintenance Technician; Material Handler Associate; Paint Maker Associate; Technician. **Corporate headquarters location:** This location. **Other U.S. locations:** Nationwide. **Operations at this facility include:** Administration; Manufacturing; Regional Headquarters; Research and Development; Sales; Service. **Listed on:** Privately held. **Number of employees at this location:** 375. **Number of employees nationwide:** 1,500.

DYNAMAC CORPORATION
2275 Research Boulevard, Suite 300, Rockville MD 20850-3218. 301/417-9800. **Fax:** 301/417-6125. **Contact:** Michael Ray, Human Resources. **E-mail address:** hr@dynamac.com. **World Wide Web address:** http://www.dynamac.com. **Description:** Develops environmental software geared toward database applications. **Positions advertised include:** Litigation Support Specialist; Records Specialist; NEPA Specialist; Webmaster; Administration Assistant. **NOTE:** Resumes submitted via e-mail must be in Microsoft Word or ASCII text format. **Corporate headquarters location:** This location. **Other area locations:** Germantown MD; Aberdeen Proving Ground MD. **Other U.S. locations:** OR; ID; OK; KS; TX; SC; NC; FL; PA. **CEO/Chairman:** Diana MacArthur.

E&G CLASSICS, INC.
8910 McGaw Court, Columbia MD 21045. 410/381-4900. **Contact:** Human Resources. **World Wide Web address:** http://www.egclassic.com. **Description:** Manufactures automotive restyling products including convertible tops, gold and silver grilles, classic spares, sunroofs, leather interiors, smoothie bumpers, and roll pans. **Corporate headquarters location:** This location. **Other U.S. locations:** Gardena CA; Oakland Park FL; Wood Dale IL.

EA ENGINEERING, SCIENCE, AND TECHNOLOGY, INC.
11019 McCormick Road, Hunt Valley MD 21031. 410/584-7000. **Fax:** 410/771-1780. **Contact:** Human Resources. **E-mail address:** careers@eaest.com. **World Wide Web address:** http://www.eaest.com. **Description:** An engineering firm that operates ecological and environmental testing laboratories. Founded in 1973. **NOTE:** Online applications are available. **Positions advertised include:** Administrative Assistant; Engineer; Geologist; Technician; Scientist; Natural Resource Management. **Special programs:** Internships; Tuition Reimbursement Program. **Other area locations:** Baltimore MD; Sparks MD. **Other U.S. locations:** Nationwide.

EARLE PALMER BROWN
6400 Goldsboro Road, Suite 500, Bethesda MD 20817. 301/263-2200. **Contact:** Human Resources. **Description:** An agency offering advertising, public relations, marketing research, direct marketing, and sales promotion services. Founded in 1952. **Special programs:** Internships. **Corporate headquarters location:** New York NY. **Other U.S. locations:** Richmond VA; St. Petersburg FL; Philadelphia PA. **Operations at this facility include:** Administration. **Listed on:** Privately held.

EDITORS PRESS, INC.
1701 Cabin Branch Drive, Cheverly MD 20785. 301/853-4900. **Toll-free phone:** 800/242-2484. **Fax:** 301/853-4933. **Contact:** Michelle Cirrincione, Personnel. **E-mail address:** synergy@edpress.com. **World Wide Web address:** http://www.edpress.com. **Description:** Provides a variety of commercial printing and direct mail services including the printing of advertising literature, brochures, folders, booklets, pamphlets, maps, catalogs, and periodicals. **Positions advertised include:** Sales Executive; Sales Trainee. **Corporate headquarters location:** This location.

EISNER PETROU AND ASSOCIATES
509 South Exeter Street, Baltimore MD 21202. 410/843-3100. **Fax:** 410/685-4771. **Contact:** Sue Friedman, Hiring Manager. **E-mail address:** info@eisnerpetrou.com. **World Wide Web address:** http://www.eisnerpetrou.com. **Description:** An advertising and public relations agency. **Special programs:** Internships. **Corporate headquarters location:** This location. **Other U.S. locations:** Washington DC. **Operations at this facility include:** Administration. **Listed on:** Privately held. **President/CEO:** David M. Petrou. **Number of employees at this location:** 65.

ENTERPRISE LEASING COMPANY
2 Research Place, Suite 300, Rockville MD 20850. 301/670-8649. **Fax:** 301/840-1758. **Contact:** Megan Trimm, Human Resources. **World Wide Web address:** http://www.enterprise.com. **Description:** A nationwide automotive leasing and rent-a-car company with over 2,000 offices coast-to-coast. **Special programs:** Internships; Management Training Program. **Corporate headquarters location:** St. Louis MO. **Other U.S. locations:** Nationwide. **International locations:** Canada; Germany; Ireland; United Kingdom. **Listed on:** Privately held. **CEO/Chairman:** Andrew C. Taylor. **Sales/revenue:** $6 billion. **Number of employees at this location:** 250. **Number of employees nationwide:** 12,000. **Number of employees worldwide:** Over 50,000.

ENVIRONMENTAL ELEMENTS CORPORATION
3700 Koppers Street, Baltimore MD 21227. 410/368-7000. **Toll-free phone:** 800/333-4331. **Fax:** 410/368-7344. **Contact:** Human Resources. **E-mail address:** hr@eec1.com. **World Wide Web address:** http://www.eec1.com. **Description:** Designs and engineers air pollution control systems and equipment, and offers related services. Founded in 1946. **NOTE:** Entry-level positions and part-time jobs are offered. Resumes submitted via e-mail must be formatted in Microsoft or ASCII text. **Positions advertised include:** Regional Sales Manager; Service Engineer/Manager. **Company slogan:** A breath of fresh air. **Special programs:** Internships; Co-ops; Summer Jobs. **Office hours:** Monday - Friday, 8:00 a.m. - 5:00 p.m. **Corporate headquarters location:** This location. **Listed on:** American Stock Exchange. **Stock exchange symbol:** EEC. **President/CEO:** John L. Sams. **Sales/revenues:** Approximately $70 million. **Number of employees at this location:** 130. **Number of employees nationwide:** 160.

EPISCOPAL MINISTRIES TO THE AGING
576 Johnsville Road, Eldersburg MD 21784. 410/970-2000. **Contact:** Human Resources. **World Wide Web address:** http://www.emaseniorcare.org. **Description:** A nonprofit company that provides a variety of programs and services to the elderly. EMA operates two residential and outpatient facilities, a continuing care retirement community, a research and development institute devoted to the care of the aging, and various other retirement and nursing facilities in the Baltimore area. **NOTE:** Entry-level positions and second and third shifts are offered. See Website for further information on Human Resource contacts for the Copper Ridge, Fairhaven, and Buckingham's Choice facilities. **Positions advertised include:** Director of Budget and Cost; Maintenance Technician; LPN; Registered Nurse; Unit Clerk; Laundry Assistant; Sous Chef; Certified Medicine Aide; Wait Staff; Server/Cashier; Beautician; Housekeeping Assistant; Assistant Director of Activities. **Special programs:** Training; Tuition Reimbursement Program; Scholarship Program. **Office hours:** Monday - Friday, 9:00 a.m. - 5:00 p.m. **Corporate headquarters location:** This location. **Subsidiaries include:** Fairhaven Incorporated is a continuing care retirement community with 420 residents in independent living, assisted living, and comprehensive care units. Copper Ridge, Incorporated is a nursing facility specializing in care for the memory-impaired, with accommodations for 126 residents in its assisted living and comprehensive care units. Buckingham's Choice is a continuing care retirement community. **Number of employees nationwide:** Over 1,000.

ERACHEM COMILOG, INC.
610 Pittman Road, Baltimore MD 21226-1788. 410/789-8800. **Fax:** 410/636-7134. **Contact:** Melissa O'Connor, Administrative Assistant of Human Resources. **World Wide Web address:** http://www.erachem-comilog.com. **Description:** A producer of manganese chemicals and related products. **Special programs:** Internships. **Office hours:** Monday – Friday, 8:00 a.m. – 5:00 p.m. **Corporate headquarters location:** This location. **Other U.S. locations:** TN. **Parent company:** Eramet Comilog is an integrated mining and metallurgy group. **Operations at this facility include:** Administration; Manufacturing; Research and Development; Sales; Service. **Listed on:** Privately held. **Number of employees at this location:** 160. **Number of employees nationwide:** 275.

ERNST & YOUNG LLP
One North Charles Street, Baltimore MD 21201. 410/539-7940. **Contact:** Director of Administration. **World Wide Web address:** http://www.ey.com. **Description:** A certified public accounting firm that also provides management consulting services. The company offers assurance and advisory business services, comprehensive support for emerging growth companies, corporate finance solutions, and a wide range of tax services. **NOTE:** Applications are available online. **Positions advertised include:** Technology and Security Risk Services Assurance Associate; Production Assistant; Business Risk Group Manager; Business Risk Auditor. **Special programs:** Internships. **Corporate headquarters location:** New York NY. **Other U.S. locations:** Nationwide. **International locations:** Worldwide. **CEO/Chairman:** James S. Turley. **Sales/revenue:** $10.1 billion. **Number of employees worldwide:** 110,000.

EULER AMERICAN CREDIT INDEMNITY
100 East Pratt Street, 5th Floor, Baltimore MD 21202. 410/837-2031. **Toll-free phone:** 888/909-3224. **Fax:** 410/554-0606. **Contact:** Human Resources. **E-mail address:** jobs.eaci@eulergroup.com. **World Wide Web address:** http://www.eulergroup.com/aci. **Description:** One of North America's largest providers of business credit insurance. **Positions advertised include:** Sales Agent; Business Development Specialist. **Special Programs:** Tuition Reimbursement Program. **Corporate headquarters location:** This location. **Other U.S. locations:** Nationwide. **International locations:** Worldwide. **Operations at this facility include:** Administration. **President/CEO:** Paul Overeem. **Sales/revenue:** $130 million. **Number of employees at this location:** 165. **Number of employees nationwide:** 300.

EVAPCO, INC.
5151 Allendale Lane, Taneytown MD 21787. 410/756-2600. **Fax:** 410/756-6450. **Contact:** Human Resources. **World Wide Web address:** http://www.evapco.com. **Description:** Manufactures evaporative condensers and closed-circuit coolers. **Positions advertised include:** Manufacturing Associate; Marketing Associate; Engineering Associate; CAD Operating Associate; Mechanics Associate; Welding Associate. **Corporate headquarters location:** This location. **Other U.S. locations:** TX; CA; IA; IL. **International locations:** China; Italy; Egypt; Belgium; Germany; United Kingdom; South Africa; Australia. **Operations at this facility include:** Administration; Research and Development.

FMC CORPORATION
1701 East Patapsco Avenue, Baltimore MD 21226. 410/355-6400. **Fax:** 410/354-5019. **Contact:** Human Resources. **World Wide Web address:** http://www.fmc.com. **Description:** A diversified chemicals company that participates on a worldwide basis in selected segments of five markets: industrial chemicals, agricultural chemicals, machinery and equipment, defense systems, and precious metals. **Special programs:** Internships. **Corporate headquarters location:** Philadelphia PA. **Other U.S. locations:** Nationwide. **Operations at this facility include:** This location is part of the Agricultural Chemicals Group, which produces crop protection and pest control chemicals for markets worldwide. **Listed on:** New York Stock Exchange. **Stock exchange symbol:** FMC. **Number of employees at this location:** 310. **Number of employees worldwide:** Approximately 5,700.

FAIR, ISAAC AND CO., INC.
8010 Corporate Drive, Suite G, Baltimore MD 21236. 410/931-7800. **Fax:** 410/931-7801. **Contact:** Human Resources. **E-mail address:** info@fairisaac.com. **World Wide Web address:** http://www.fairisaac.com. **Description:** Provides consulting services to financial institutions, service organizations, and government support institutions. Services include statistical analysis, database development and reporting, and actuarial management of customer portfolios through software decision support systems. **Positions advertised include:** Business Risk Consulting Director; Business Risk Consulting Manager. **Special programs:** Tuition Reimbursement Program. **Corporate headquarters location:** San Rafael CA. **Other U.S. locations:** Nationwide. **International locations:** Worldwide. **Subsidiaries include:** Nykamp Consulting Group, Incorporated; Prevision; Risk Management Technologies; Credit and Risk Management Associates. **Listed on:** New York Stock Exchange. **Stock exchange symbol:** FIC. **CEO:** Thomas G. Grudnowski.

FARMERS AND MECHANICS NATIONAL BANK
P.O. Box 518, Frederick MD 21705. 301/694-4186. **Physical address:** 110 Thomas Johnson Drive, Frederick MD 21702. **Toll-free phone:** 800/445-3626. **Fax:** 301/698-4626. **Contact:** Human Resources. **World Wide Web address:** http://www.fmbancorp.com. **Description:** A bank offering retail, commercial, trust, and investment management services. **Positions advertised include:** Mortgage Loan Originator; Wealth Advisor. **Office hours:** Monday – Thursday, 9:00 a.m. – 5:00 p.m., Friday, 9:00 a.m. – 6:00 p.m. **Parent company:** F&M Bancorp. **Listed on:** NASDAQ. **Stock exchange symbol:** FMBN. **President/CEO:** Faye E. Cannon.

FAWN INDUSTRIES, INC.
1920 Greenspring Drive, Suite 140, Timonium MD 21093. 410/308-9200. **Contact:** Human Resources. **World Wide Web address:** http://www.fawn-ind.com. **Description:** Manufactures electronic subassemblies and related injection-molded plastic parts used by the automotive, medical instrumentation, office/business, industrial electronics, and personal computer industries. Company operations are divided into two segments: Plastics and Electronics. Founded in 1953. **Corporate headquarters location:** This location. **Other U.S. locations:** MI; NC; TN. **International locations:** Mexico.

FEDERAL REALTY INVESTMENT TRUST
1626 East Jefferson Street, Rockville MD 20852-4041. 301/998-8100. **Toll-free phone:** 800/658-8980. **Contact:** Human Resources. **World Wide Web address:** http://www.federalrealty.com. **Description:** An equity real estate investment firm that acquires and develops prime retail properties. **Positions advertised include:** Accounting Manager; Administrative Assistant; Executive Assistant; Human Resource Training Coordinator; Lease Administration Associate; Network Administration Associate; Programmer; Director of Acquisition. **Special programs:** Training. **Corporate headquarters location:** This location. **Operations at this facility include:** Administration; Sales; Service. **Listed on:** New York Stock Exchange. **Stock exchange symbol:** FRT. **President/CEO:** Donald C. Wood.

FILETEK, INC.
9400 Key West Avenue, Rockville MD 20850. 301/251-0600. **Fax:** 301/251-1990. **Contact:** Debbie Mobley, Manager of Human Resources. **E-mail address:** employment@filetek.com. **World Wide Web address:** http://www.filetek.com. **Description:** Uses hierarchical relational database technology to design, develop, and deliver mass data storage software systems for large corporations. Founded in 1984. **NOTE:** To contact Human Resources directly, call 301/517-1840. **Special programs:** Tuition Reimbursement Program. **Corporate headquarters location:** This location. **Other U.S. locations:** Nationwide. **International locations:** Belgium; Germany; United Kingdom. **Listed on:** Privately held. **President/CEO:** William C. Thompson. **Number of employees at this location:** 100.

FRANKLIN SQUARE HOSPITAL CENTER
9000 Franklin Square Drive, Baltimore MD 21237-3998. 443/777-7000. **Fax:** 443/777-7910. **Contact:** Frank Heine, Human Resources Generalist. **E-mail address:** frank.heine@medstar.net. **World Wide Web address:** http://www.franklinsquare.org. **Description:** A 405-bed acute care community hospital in Baltimore County. Franklin Square specializes as a teaching hospital and offers emergency medicine, oncology, cardiology, labor and delivery, and general medicine. Other major programs include family health, neonatology, psychiatry, and pediatrics. **NOTE:** Online applications are available. To contact Human Resources directly, call 443/777-7233. **Positions advertised include:** Care Associate; Case Manager; Clinical Administrator; Clinical Aide; Administrative Coordinator; Diagnostic Technician; Environmental Support Associate; Generalist; Infection Control Practitioner; Lactating Consultant; Linen Handler; Mammographer; Materials Handler; Mechanic; Medical Assistant; Medical Technician; OD Specialist; Patient Care Associate; Plumber; Program Manager; Registered Nurse; Respiratory Therapist; Site Coordinator; Speech Therapist; Materials Management; Sterile Processing Technician; Ultrasound Technician. **Parent company:** MedStar Health is a diversified health care system comprised of over 30 businesses, including seven hospitals in the Baltimore/Washington area. **President:** Charles J. Schindelar.

FROSTBURG STATE UNIVERSITY
101 Braddock Road, 3rd Floor, Hitchins Building, Frostburg MD 21532-1099. 301/687-4105. **Fax:** 301/687-4118. **Contact:** Beth Clark, Human Resources. **E-mail address:** bclark@frostburg.edu, or humanresources@frostburg.edu. **World Wide Web address:** http://www.frostburg.edu. **Description:** A four year state university focusing in liberal arts, business and education with graduate and undergraduate student body. **Positions advertised include:** Consulting Psychologist; University Police Officer.

FUTRON CORPORATION
7315 Wisconsin Avenue, Suite 900W, Bethesda MD 20814-3202. 301/913-9372. **Fax:** 301/913-9475. **Contact:** Robin Andrusko, Human Resources Director. **E-mail address:** resume@futron.com. **World Wide Web address:** http://www.futron.com. **Description:** Provides management consulting to the aerospace industry. Services focus on information technology and management; space market forecasting; risk-based decision support; education and outreach; and aerospace safety, reliability management, and quality assurance. **NOTE:** Entry-level positions and part-time jobs are offered. Resumes submitted via e-mail must be in either Microsoft Word or text format. **Positions advertised include:** Engineer; Program Manager. **Special programs:** Internships; Training. **Office hours:** Monday - Friday, 8:30 a.m. - 5:00 p.m. **Corporate headquarters location:** This location. **Other U.S. locations:** Houston TX. **Listed on:** Privately held. **President:** Joseph Fuller, Junior. **Number of employees at this location:** 35. **Number of employees nationwide:** 85.

GAF MATERIALS CORPORATION
1500 South Ponca Street, Baltimore MD 21224. 410/633-7200. **Contact:** Matt Sterrett, Human Resources Manager. **E-mail address:** employment@gaf.com. **World Wide Web address:** http://www.gaf.com. **Description:** Produces prepared roofing, roll roofing, built-up roofing systems, single-ply roofing, and insulation products. Founded in 1886. **Corporate headquarters location:** Wayne NJ. **Other U.S. locations:** Nationwide. **International locations:** Worldwide. **Sales/revenue:** $1.2 billion.

GE GLOBAL EXCHANGE SERVICES
100 Edison Park Drive, Gaithersburg MD 20878. 301/947-9627. **Contact:** Human Resources. **E-mail address:** opportunities@gxs.ge.com. **World Wide Web address:** http://www.gxs.com. **Description:** Provides business productivity solutions through management consulting. **Positions advertised include:** Channel Manager; Business Operations Director. **Special programs:** Internships; Co-ops. **Corporate headquarters location:** This location. **Other U.S. locations:** Nationwide. **International locations:** Worldwide. **Parent company:** General Electric Company (Fairfield CT) operates in the following areas: aircraft engines (jet engines, replacement parts, and repair services for commercial, military, executive, and commuter aircraft); appliances; broadcasting (NBC); industrial (lighting products, electrical distribution and control equipment, transportation systems products, electric motors and related products, a broad range of electrical and electronic industrial automation products, and a network of electrical supply houses); materials (plastics, ABS resins, silicones, superabrasives, and laminates); power systems (products for the generation, transmission, and distribution of electricity); technical products and systems (medical systems and equipment, as well as a full range of computer-based information and data interchange services for both internal use and external commercial and industrial customers); and capital services (consumer services, financing, and specialty insurance). **Listed on:** New York Stock Exchange. **Stock exchange symbol:** GE. **CEO:** Harvey Seegers. **Number of employees worldwide:** 230,000.

GSE SYSTEMS
9189 Red Branch Road, Columbia MD 21045-2013. 410/772-3500. **Fax:** 410/772-3616. **Contact:** Human Resources. **E-mail address:** employ@gses.com. **World Wide Web address:** http://www.gses.com. **Description:** Creates power simulation, nuclear simulation, and process controls programs. **Corporate headquarters location:** This location. **Other area locations:** Columbia MD. **Other U.S. locations:** Aiken SC; Shelby NC; Pittsburgh PA; Houston TX; Baton Rouge LA; St. Mary's GA. **International locations:** Japan; Sweden. **Listed on:** American Stock Exchange. **Stock exchange symbol:** GVP. **President/COO:** Chin-Our Jerry Jen. **Sales/revenue:** Over $50 million. **Number of employees worldwide:** Approximately 250.

GTCO CALCOMP, INC.
7125 Riverwood Drive, Columbia MD 21046. 410/381-6688. **Toll-free phone:** 800/344-4723. **Fax:** 410/290-9065. **Contact:** Human Resources. **E-mail address:** md.hr@gtcocalcomp.com. **World Wide Web address:** http://www.gtcocalcomp.com. **Description:** Manufactures input peripherals. Founded in 1975. **Positions advertised include:** Sales Representative. **Special programs:** Tuition Reimbursement Program. **Corporate headquarters location:** This location. **Other U.S. locations:** Scottsdale AZ. **International locations:** Vienna, Austria; Munich, Germany. **President:** Eric Timmons. **Number of employees at this location:** 60.

GST AUTO LEATHER
15717 Clear Spring Road, Williamsport MD 21795-1010. 301/223-7500. **Fax:** 240/313-4942. **Contact:** Human Resources. **E-mail address:** hr@gstautoleather.com. **World Wide Web address:** http://www.gstautoleather.com. **Description:** Produces leather for use in the manufacture of automobile upholstery. Founded in 1933. **Positions advertised include:** Production Control Supervisor. **NOTE:** Entry-level positions and second and third shifts are offered. **Special programs:** Internships. **Corporate headquarters location:** Hagerstown MD. **Other U.S. locations:** Adrian MI; Fleetwood PA; Reading PA. **International locations:** Mexico; China; Argentina.

GARRETT COUNTY MEMORIAL HOSPITAL
251 North Fourth Street, Oakland MD 21550. 301/533-4000. **Fax:** 301/533-4328. **Contact:** Human Resources. **World Wide Web address:** http://www.gcmh.com. **Description:** A county hospital offering comprehensive health care services. **NOTE:** To contact Human Resources directly, call 301/533-4325. **Positions advertised include:** Registered Nurse; Staff Registered Nurse; Certified Nursing Aide; Radiographer; Phlebotomist; Admissions Clerk. **Office hours:** Monday – Friday, 9:00 a.m. – 3:00 p.m. **President/CEO:** Donald P. Battista. **Number of employees at this location:** 350.

GENERAL DYNAMICS ADVANCED INFORMATION SYSTEMS
22309 Exploration Drive, Lexington Park MD 20653. 301/863-4200. **Fax:** 301/863-2530. **Contact:** Human Resources. **World Wide Web address:** http://www.veridian.com. **Description:** Assists various military branches with software engineering, systems integration, and project development. **NOTE:** Online applications are available. **Positions advertised include:** Principal Engineering Systems; Technical Writing Specialist; Principal Engineer; Lead Engineer; Administrative Assistant; Technical Support Engineer; Information Technology Engineer; Finance Specialist; Software Quality Assurance Engineer. **Corporate headquarters location:** Arlington VA. **Other area locations:** California MD; Aberdeen MD. **Other U.S. locations:** Nationwide. **Operations at this facility include:** This location offers computer support to the Naval Air Warfare Center. **President/CEO:** David H. Langstaff. **Number of employees nationwide:** Over 7,000.

GENERAL MOTORS TRUCK GROUP
2122 Broening Highway, Baltimore MD 21224. 410/631-2501. **Contact:** Human Resources. **World Wide Web address:** http://www.gm.com. **Description:** General Motors Corporation (GM) is one of the world's largest full-line vehicle manufacturers, and also has substantial interests in electronics and finance. GM conducts business through the following sectors: North American Automotive Operations, International Operations, General Motors Acceptance Corporation (GMAC), and GM Hughes Electronics Corporation. North American Automotive Operations includes Sales/Service Groups (Buick, Cadillac, Chevrolet, GMC Truck, Oldsmobile, Pontiac, and Saturn) and Vehicle Development Groups (Powertrain, Truck Group, Small Car Group, and Midsize/Luxury Car Group). International Operations include GM Europe; Asia Pacific Operations; and Latin America, Africa, Middle East Operations. GMAC, which provides financing and insurance to GM customers and dealers, consists of North American Operations, International Operations, Motors Insurance Corporation, and GMAC Mortgage Group. GM Hughes Electronics Corporation is involved in automotive, telecommunications, space, and defense electronics. Founded in 1908. **Positions advertised include:** Staff Assistant. **Corporate headquarters location:** Detroit MI. **Other U.S. locations:** Nationwide. **International locations:** Worldwide. **Operations at this facility include:** This location manufactures bus and truck bodies. **Listed on:** New York Stock Exchange. **Stock exchange symbol:** GM. **President/CEO:** G. Richard Wagoner, Junior. **Number of employees worldwide:** Approximately 355,000.

GENERAL PHYSICS CORPORATION
6095 Marshalee Drive, Elkridge MD 21075. 410/379-3600. **Toll-free phone:** 800/727-6677. **Fax:** 410/540-5312. **Contact:** Human Resources. **E-mail address:** hr@gpworldwide.com. **World Wide Web address:** http://www.gpworldwide.com. **Description:** A performance improvement firm that provides training, engineering, and technical services to clients in the aerospace, automotive, defense, government, manufacturing, utility, independent power, pharmaceutical, and process industries. Founded in 1966. **NOTE:** Entry-level positions are offered. **Company slogan:** Leading the world to better performance. **Positions advertised include:** Program Manager Technician; Unix Administrator. **Special programs:** Internships; Training. **Office hours:** Monday - Friday, 8:30 a.m. - 5:00 p.m. **Corporate headquarters location:** This location. **Other area locations:** Aberdeen Proving Ground MD; Edgewood MD. **Other U.S. locations:** Nationwide. **International locations:** Brazil; Canada; Malaysia; Mexico; England. **Parent company:** GP Strategies Corporation. **Operations at this facility include:** Administration. **Listed on:** New York Stock Exchange. **Stock exchange symbol:** GPX. **Sales/revenue:** Approximately $180 million. **Number of employees at this location:** 200. **Number of employees nationwide:** 1,400. **Number of employees worldwide:** 2,200.

GENERAL SCIENCES CORPORATION
10218 Southward Drive, Beltsville MD 20705. 301/931-2900. **Contact:** Personnel Manager. **World Wide Web address:** http://www.saic-gsc.com. **Description:** Develops software for a variety of scientific applications. **Positions advertised include:** Software Engineer; Support Scientist. **Special programs:** Training; Educational Assistance Program. **Parent company:** Science Applications International Corporation (SAIC).

GENETIC THERAPY INC.
9 West Watkins Mill Road, Gaithersburg MD 20878. 301/258-4600. **Contact:** Human Resources. **E-mail address:** gtijobs@pharma.novartis.com. **World Wide Web address:** http://www.novartis.com. **Description:** Researches and develops gene therapy products for the treatment of various diseases. **Special programs:** Internships. **Corporate headquarters location:** Basel, Switzerland. **International locations:** Worldwide. **Parent company:** Novartis. **Listed on:** New York Stock Exchange. **Stock exchange symbol:** NVS. **CEO:** Paulo Costa. **Number of employees at this location:** 140.

GOLDWELL COSMETICS USA
981 Corporate Boulevard, Linthicum Heights MD 21090. 410/850-7555. **Fax:** 410/592-2478. **Contact:** Personnel. **E-mail:** rwilson@goldwell.com. **World Wide Web address:** http://www.goldwellusa.com. **Description:** Manufactures a full line of hair care products sold exclusively to salons. **President/COO:** Andrew D. Biazis.

GOODELL, DEVRIES, LEECH & DANN, LLP
One South Street, 20th Floor, Baltimore MD 21202. 410/783-4000. **Fax:** 410/783-4040. **Contact:** Human Resources. **E-mail address:** info@gdldlaw.com. **World Wide Web address:** http://www.gdldlaw.com. **Description:** A law firm specializing in litigation. Founded in 1988. **NOTE:** Entry-level positions are offered. **Positions advertised include:** Entry level Associates; Lateral Entry Attorney.

W.L. GORE & ASSOCIATES
105 Vieve's Way, Elkton MD 21921. 410/392-3600. **Contact:** Human Resources. **E-mail address:** info@wlgore.com. **World Wide Web address:** http://www.gore.com. **Description:** A company that specializes in fluoropolymer products, primarily manufacturing windproof and waterproof clothing for outdoor sports including fishing, golf, hiking, hunting, sailing, and snow sports. Other non-apparel products include sealants, insulated wires and cables, guitar strings, dental floss, space suits, and medical membranes and sutures. **NOTE:** Interested jobseekers should direct resumes to: W.L. Gore & Associates, Incorporated, Resume Processing Center, P.O. Box 549259, Suite 247, Waltham MA 02454-9259. **Positions advertised include:** Environmental Health & Safety Associate; Cardiac Marketing Leader. **Corporate headquarters location:** Newark DE. **International locations:** Worldwide. **President/CEO:** Robert W. Gore. **Sales/revenue:** $1.23 billion. **Number of employees worldwide:** Approximately 6,000.

W.R. GRACE & COMPANY
7500 Grace Drive, Columbia MD 21044. 410/531-4000. **Fax:** 410/531-4367. **Contact:** Human Resources. **E-mail address:** careers@grace.com. **World Wide Web address:** http://www.grace.com. **Description:** A specialty chemicals and flexible packaging supplier. W.R. Grace operates through four major divisions. Grace Packaging specializes in flexible packaging systems for meat, poultry, cheese, and other perishable food products, as well as shrink packaging materials for consumer and industrial products. Grace Davison catalysts crack crude oil into fuel and related by-products. Davison polyolefin catalysts are involved in polyethylene production, and its silica and zeolite adsorbents are ingredients in industrial and consumer applications. Grace Construction products include concrete and cement additives, fireproofing, and waterproofing systems that strengthen concrete, fight corrosion, stop water damage, and protect structural steel from fire damage. Grace Container includes container sealant systems that keep food and beverages protected from bacteria and other contaminants, extend shelf life, and preserve flavor. **Corporate headquarters location:** This location. **International locations:** Worldwide. **Operations at this facility include:** Administration. **Listed on:** New York Stock Exchange. **Stock exchange symbol:** GRA. **President/CEO/Chairman:** Paul J. Norris. **Number of employees nationwide:** 17,000.

GRANT THORNTON LLP
2 Hopkins Plaza, Suite 700, Baltimore MD 21201-2998. 410/685-4000. **Contact:** Recruiting Coordinator. **World Wide Web address:** http://www.granthornton.com. **Description:** An international, certified public accounting organization offering a comprehensive scope of consulting and accounting services as well as strategic and tactical planning assistance to a diverse clientele. **Corporate headquarters location:**

Chicago IL. **Other U.S. locations:** Nationwide. **International locations:** Worldwide. **Sales/revenue:** $1.7 billion. **Number of employees nationwide:** Over 3,000. **Number of employees worldwide:** 21,500.

GREATER BALTIMORE ALLIANCE
111 South Calvert Street, Suite 2220, Baltimore MD 21202-6180. 410/468-0100. **Toll-free phone:** 888/298-4322. **Fax:** 410/468-3383. **Contact:** Director. **E-mail address:** info@greaterbaltimore.org. **World Wide Web address:** http://www.greaterbaltimore.org. **Description:** A nonprofit, regional, economic development corporation. The organization provides services to employers moving to the greater Baltimore area and works to improve existing regional businesses. **Corporate headquarters location:** This location. **President/CEO:** Ioanna T. Morfeissis.

GRIFFITH ENERGY SERVICES, INC.
2510 Schuster Drive, Cheverly MD 20781. 301/322-3111. **Contact:** Personnel. **E-mail address:** info@griffithoil.com. **World Wide Web address:** http://www.griffithoil.com. **Description:** A full-service, independent, retail distributor of petroleum products, primarily heating oil and gasoline. Griffith Consumers Company also sells diesel fuel, heavy oils, kerosene, and products and services related to its energy business. Founded in 1898. **Corporate headquarters location:** This location. **Other area locations:** Hagerstown MD; Baltimore MD; Frederick MD. **Other U.S. locations:** DE; VA; WV. **Operations at this facility include:** Administration; Research and Development; Sales; Service.

GROUP 1 SOFTWARE, INC.
4200 Parliament Place, Suite 600, Lanham MD 20706-1844. 301/731-2300. **Toll-free phone:** 888/413-6763. **Contact:** Rachel Holstein, Human Resources. **E-mail address:** rachel_holstein@g1.com. **World Wide Web address:** http://www.g1.com. **Description:** Develops, acquires, and markets specialized, integrated list management, mail management, and marketing support software systems. Group 1 Software also publishes list and mail management software products. Founded in 1982. **Positions advertised include:** Sales Executive; Sales Manager; Development Manager; Principal Engineer; Software Engineer; Technical Support Representative; Staff Attorney. **Special programs:** Training. **Corporate headquarters location:** This location. **Other U.S. locations:** CA; GA; IL; MN; NV; NJ; TX; VA; FL. **International locations:** Worldwide. **Operations at this facility include:** Administration; Research and Development; Sales. **Listed on:** NASDAQ. **Stock exchange symbol:** GSOF. **CEO:** Robert S. Bowen. **Sales/revenues:** $21 - $50 million. **Number of employees at this location:** 250. **Number of employees nationwide:** 325. **Number of employees worldwide:** 365.

HANGER PROSTHETICS AND ORTHOPEDICS
SOUTHERN MARYLAND BRACE AND LIMB
P.O. Box 588, Hughesville MD 20637. 301/274-4548. **Contact:** Human Resources. **E-mail address:** sking@hanger.com. **World Wide Web address:** http://www.hanger.com. **Description:** Manufactures braces and prosthetic limbs for hospitals and retail stores. **NOTE:** Interested applicants should send resumes to: Hanger Orthopedic Group, Incorporated, 2 Bethesda Metro Center, Suite 1200, Bethesda MD 20814. **Positions advertised include:** Prosthetist; Orthotist. **Corporate headquarters location:** Bethesda MD. **Other U.S. locations:** Nationwide. **Parent company:** Hanger Orthopedic Group, Incorporated, which is comprised of Hanger Prosthetics and Orthopedics, Incorporated, OPNET, Incorporated, and Southern Prosthetic Supply, Incorporated. **Listed on:** New York Stock Exchange. **Stock exchange symbol:** HGR. **CEO/Chairman:** Ivan R. Sabel. **Number of employees nationwide:** Over 1,000.

HARFORD MUTUAL INSURANCE COMPANIES
200 North Main Street, Bel Air MD 21014-3544. 410/838-4000. **Contact:** Ellen Truant, Human Resources Manager. **E-mail address:** hr@harfordmutual.com. **World Wide Web address:** http://www.harfordmutual.com. **Description:** A fire and casualty insurance company. Founded in 1842. **President:** Phillip Raub. **Number of employees nationwide:** 115.

HARITON, MANCUSO & JONES, P.C.
11140 Rockville Pike, Suite 340, North Bethesda MD 20852. 301/984-6400. **Fax:** 301/984-0028. **Contact:** Personnel Director. **Description:** An accounting firm. **Listed on:** Privately held. **Number of employees at this location:** 30.

HARTE-HANKS, INC.
4545 Annapolis Road, Baltimore MD 21227. **Fax:** 410/789-0159. **Contact:** Jeff Romans. **E-mail address:** jeff_romans@harte-hanks.com. **World Wide Web address:** http://www.harte-hanks.com. **Description:** Worldwide, direct and targeted marketing company that provides direct marketing services and shopper advertising opportunities to a wide range of local, regional, national and international consumer and business-to-business marketers. **Positions advertised include:** Account Manager; Programmer. **Corporate headquarters location:** San Antonio, Texas. **Other U.S. locations:** Nationwide. **International locations:** Worldwide.

HARTZ & COMPANY, INC.
1341 Hughes Ford Road, Frederick MD 21701. 301/662-7500. **Fax:** 301/662-0461. **Contact:** Human Resources. **World Wide Web address:** http://www.hartzco.com. **Description:** A manufacturer of men's clothing. Founded in 1893. **Corporate headquarters location:** This location. **Other U.S. locations:** New York NY; Broadway VA. **Operations at this facility include:** Administration; Manufacturing; Research and Development. **Listed on:** Privately held. **CEO:** Robert M. Watson. **Number of employees at this location:** 350. **Number of employees nationwide:** 850.

HARVARD CUSTOM MANUFACTURING
600 Glen Avenue, Salisbury MD 21804. 410/548-7800. **Toll-free phone:** 800/ 228-0064. **Fax:** 410/548-7839. **Contact:** Steve Robertson, Corporate Director of Human Resources. **E-mail address:** srobertson@harvardgrp.com. **World Wide Web address:** http://www.harvardgrp.com. **Description:** Provides electronic assembly cables and harnesses for the military and commercial telecommunications industries. **NOTE:** Completed application is required. **Corporate headquarters location:** This location. **Other U.S. locations:** NY; MA; IL; TX. **Listed on:** Privately held. **Number of employees at this location:** 220.

HEDWIN CORPORATION
1600 Roland Heights Avenue, Baltimore MD 21211. 410/467-8209. **Toll-free phone:** 800/638-1012. **Contact:** Director of Human Resources. **World Wide Web address:** http://www.hedwin.com. **Description:** Manufactures plastic containers for industrial applications. The company offers three product lines: Cubitainer Combination Package, Blow Molded Products, and the Hedwin Liner Group. **Corporate headquarters location:** This location. **Other U.S. locations:** La Porte IN. **Parent company:** Solvay America. **Operations at this facility include:** Administration; Manufacturing; Research and Development; Sales; Service.

HEWLETT PACKARD
6406 Ivy Lane, Greenbelt MD 20770. 301/459-7900. **Toll-free phone:** 800/544-9944. **Contact:** Human Resources. **World Wide Web address:** http://www.hp.com. **Description:** Designs, manufactures, sells, and services computers, peripheral equipment, and related software and supplies. Applications and programs include scientific research, computation, communications, education, data analysis, industrial control, time sharing, commercial data processing, graphic arts, word processing, health care, instrumentation, engineering, and simulation. **NOTE:** Previously Compaq Computer Corporation. The two companies merged in May 2002. **Positions advertised include:** Business Process Transition Manager; Director of Consulting; Global Deployment Manager; Global Solutions Manager; ITO Operations Consultant; HP Service Tax Manager; Financial Analyst; Program Manager; Project Manager. **Corporate headquarters location:** Palo Alto CA. **Other U.S. locations:** Nationwide. **International locations:** Worldwide. **Operations at this facility include:** This location is a sales office. **Listed on:** New York Stock Exchange. **Stock exchange symbol:** HP. **Sales/revenue:** $72 billion. **Number of employees worldwide:** 140,000.

HOLY CROSS HOSPITAL
1500 Forest Glen Road, Silver Spring MD 20910. 301/754-7050. **Fax:** 301/754-7031. **Recorded jobline:** 301/754-7044. **Contact:** Human Resources. **World Wide Web address:** http://www.holycrosshealth.org. **Description:** A nonprofit, 442-bed, community teaching hospital that provides primary and secondary health care in both Montgomery and Prince George's Counties, serving almost 200,000 patients each year. Holy Cross Hospital has teaching affiliations with George Washington University School of Medicine in obstetrics and gynecology, general medicine, and surgery, and with Children's National Medical Center in pediatrics. Holy Cross Hospital also offers Healthy Side, a program providing health seminars, classes, support groups, and special events. **NOTE:** Entry-level positions and second and third shifts are offered. **Positions advertised include:** Home Health Services Registered Nurse; Nurse Practitioner; Administrative Coordinator; Depart Patient Care Services; Clinical Nurse. **Special programs:** Internships. **Parent company:** Trinity Health (Novi MI).

HOMECALL, INC.
92 Thomas Johnson Drive, Suite 140, Frederick MD 21702-4383. 301/664-3086. **Toll-free phone:** 800/695-7820. **Contact:** Human Resources. **World Wide Web address:** http://www.homecallinc.com. **Description:** HomeCall provides nursing care to patients who are confined to their homes. **Positions advertised include:** Registered Nurse; LPN; Private Duty Case Nursing Assistant; Home Health Aide; Physical Therapist; Occupational Therapist; Speech Therapist; Medical Social Worker; Medical Records Clerk; Nursing Supervisor; MIS Senior Programmer. **Special programs:** Educational Assistance Program; Mileage Reimbursement Program. **Corporate headquarters location:** This location. **Other area locations:** Statewide. **Subsidiaries include:** FirstCall, Incorporated. **Parent company:** Mid-Atlantic Medical Services, Incorporated (MAMSI), a holding company whose subsidiaries also include HomeCall Pharmaceutical Services and HomeCall Hospice Services. Mid-Atlantic is one of the largest managed care companies in its market, which currently includes Maryland, Virginia, Washington DC, and West Virginia.

HOOD COLLEGE
401 Rosemont Avenue, Frederick MD 21701-8575. 301/696-3592. **Fax:** 301/696-3880. **Contact:** Human Resources. **E-mail address:** humanresources@hood.edu. **World Wide Web address:** http://www.hood.edu. **Description:** A liberal arts college that specializes in science programs. The school offers both undergraduate and graduate programs with residential housing available for undergraduate and graduate women; male students are day students only. Hood College has approximately 1,100 undergraduate students and 900 graduate students. **NOTE:** Part-time positions are offered. **Positions advertised include:** Assistant Biology Professor; Building Services Manager; Set-up and Delivery Technician; Library Technician; Floor-Care Specialist; Director of Graduate School Marketing and Recruitment; Accounting Clerk. **Special programs:** Tuition Exchange Program. **President:** Ronald J. Volpe.

HOUSING AUTHORITY OF BALTIMORE CITY
417 East Fayette Street, Suite 1339, Baltimore MD 21202. 410/396-3237. **Contact:** Penny Milson, Human Resources. **E-mail address:** penny.milson@habc.org. **World Wide Web address:** http://www.baltimorehousing.org. **Description:** Responsible for the overall housing management of the greater Baltimore area. **NOTE:** Unsolicited resumes will not be accepted. Please see the Website for more information. **Positions advertised include:** Project Coordinator; Weatherization Inspector; Accounting Associate; Equipment Operator; Project Manager; Carpenter.

HOWARD COUNTY GENERAL HOSPITAL
5755 Cedar Lane, Columbia MD 21044. 410/740-7815. **Fax:** 410/740-7532. **Recorded jobline:** 410/884-4567. **Contact:** Personnel. **E-mail address:** careers@hcgh.org. **World Wide Web address:** http://www.hcgh.org. **Description:** A full-service hospital. **Positions advertised include:** Department of Diagnostic Imaging Administrator; Admitting Counselor; Biomedical Engineering Technician; Cardiographic Technician; Cardiovascular Radiologic Technologist; Chaplain Associate; Cross-Sectional Imaging Supervisor; Dietary Assistant; Director of Plant Operations; Environmental Services Technician; Health Information Clerk; Hostess; LPN; MRI Technician; Medical Social Work Associate; Newborn Hearing Screening Technician; Nuclear Medicine Technologist; Occupational Therapist; Operating Room Technician; Patient Care Technician; Physician Assistant; Registered Nurse Case Manager; Psychiatric Assistant. **Special programs:** Internships; Tuition Assistance Program. **Parent company:** Johns Hopkins Medicine. **Operations at this facility include:** Administration. **Listed on:** Privately held. **Number of employees at this location:** 1,600.

J.M. HUBER CORPORATION
P.O. Box 310, 907 Revolution Street, Havre de Grace MD 21078. 410/939-3500. **Contact:** Human Resources. **World Wide Web address:** http://www.huber.com. **Description:** An internationally diversified company producing oil and natural gas, carbon black, kaolin (china) clay, synthetic inorganic pigments, printing inks, and equipment for the petroleum and pipeline industries. J.M. Huber Corporation provides ingredients for products sold to oil refineries and related facilities as well as to many other industries including rubber, paper, printing, paint, adhesives, plastics, insecticides, ceramics, animal feed, packaging, and home construction. Founded in 1883. **Corporate headquarters location:** Edison NJ. **Other U.S. locations:** Nationwide. **International locations:** Worldwide. **Operations at this facility include:** This location is part of the Engineered Materials division and manufactures inorganic chemicals. **Listed on:** Privately held. **President/CEO/Chairman:** Peter T. Francis. **Sales/revenues:** Approximately $1 billion. **Number of employees at this location:** 150. **Number of employees nationwide:** Over 3,000.

HUGHES NETWORK SYSTEMS
11717 Exploration Lane, Germantown MD 20876. 301/428-5500. **Contact:** Human Resources. **World Wide Web address:** http://www.hns.com. **Description:** The company operates through four divisions. In the Defense Division, there are four

product groups including radar and communication systems, electro-optical systems, weapons systems, and information systems. Products in the defense division include airborne, land- and ship-based radar, laser rangefinders, cruise and tactical-guided missiles, and command and control systems. The Telemarketing and Space Division produces satellites and satellite-based telecommunication systems and services. The corporation's Automotive Electronics Division develops, manufactures, and markets electronics for vehicles worldwide including airbag electronics, antilock brake modules, remote keyless entry, engine and transmission controls, and pressure sensors. The Commercial Technologies Division utilizes core defense and space technologies for commercial and nondefense government applications. Major products include large-scale database management systems, air traffic control systems, and large-screen projector systems. **NOTE:** Online applications are available. **Positions advertised include:** Senior Department Specialist; Program Manager; Engineer; Spaceway NOCC Software Systems Associate; Accounting Payload Controller; Shift Supervisor; Network Controller; Network Administrator; Systems Analyst; Sattelite Payload Engineer. **Special programs:** Training. **International locations:** United Kingdom; Germany; Italy; Czech Republic; Brazil; China; Japan; Indonesia; United Arab Emirates; South Africa; Mexico. **Operations at this facility include:** This location markets and services high-technology electronic systems and products for global defense, telecommunications, and space and automotive industries. **CEO/Chairman:** Pradman P. Kaul. **Number of employees at this location:** 340. **Number of employees nationwide:** 1,050.

HUMAN GENOME SCIENCES, INC.
14200 Shady Grove Road, Rockville MD 20850-3338. 301/309-8504. **Fax:** 301/309-1845. **Contact:** Human Resources. **E-mail address:** resume@hgsi.com. **World Wide Web address:** http://www.hgsi.com. **Description:** A biotechnology research firm employing cell biology, molecular biology, genomic research, and other sciences in order to discover ways to prevent and cure diseases by using the body's own proteins to make pharmaceuticals. The company is also involved in the isolation and characterization of human genes. **Positions advertised include:** Associate Director; Bio Processing Associate; Engineering Scientist; Cleaning & Analytical Validation Manager; Clinical Applications Systems Administration; Clinical Systems Administration Custodian. **Special programs:** Educational Assistance Program. **Corporate headquarters location:** This location. **Listed on:** NASDAQ. **Stock exchange symbol:** HGSI. **CEO/Chairman:** William A. Haseltine.

HYDRO ALUMINUM NORTH AMERICA
801 International Drive, Suite 200, Linthicum MD 21090. 410/487-4500. **Fax:** 410/487-8053. **Contact:** Human Resources. **E-mail address:** halnacareers@hydrona.com. **World Wide Web address:** http://www.hydroaluminuma.com. **Description:** An extruder, finisher, and manufacturer of aluminum products. The company operates through four business units: Extruded Products, Components and Assemblies, Metal Products, and Trading, Recycling, and Commercial Services. **Positions advertised include:** Senior Accountant; Staff Accountant; Logistics Manager; Sales Support Administrator; Sourcing Support Administrator; IS/IT Director; Contract Hedging Manager. **Corporate headquarters location:** This location. **Other U.S. locations:** FL; CA; MI; MS; PA; NY; TX. **International locations:** Canada; Mexico. **Parent Company:** Hydro Aluminum. **President:** Martin Carter. **Sales/revenue:** Approximately $1 billion.

IBM CORPORATION
6710 Rockledge Drive, Bethesda MD 20817. **Toll-free phone:** 800/333-6705. **Contact:** IBM Staffing Services. **World Wide Web address:** http://www.ibm.com. **Description:** International Business Machines Corporation (IBM) is a developer, manufacturer, and marketer of advanced information processing products including computers and microelectronic technology products, software, and networking systems. The company also provides information technology-related services. **NOTE:** Online applications are available. **Positions advertised include:** AIX Storage Area Network Associate; BP Engineer; Client Executive; Data Modeler; Information Technology Architect; Research Program Security Consultant; Pricing Analyst; Siebel Coordinator; Subcontract Administrator; User Case Analyst. **Special programs:** Training. **Corporate headquarters location:** Armonk NY. **Other U.S. locations:** Nationwide. **International locations:** Worldwide. **Subsidiaries include:** IBM Credit Corporation; IBM Instruments, Incorporated; IBM World Trade Corporation. **Operations at this facility include:** This location is an administrative service center. **Listed on:** New York Stock Exchange. **Stock exchange symbol:** IBM. **President/CEO/Chairman:** Samuel J. Palmisano. **Sales/revenue:** Approximately $81 billion. **Number of employees worldwide:** 335,421.

IGEN INTERNATIONAL
16020 Industrial Drive, Gaithersburg MD 20877. 301/869-9800. **Toll-free phone:** 800/336-4436. **Contact:** Human Resources. **E-mail address:** recruiting@igen.com. **World Wide Web address:** http://www.igen.com. **Description:** Researches, develops, and markets diagnostic products used to detect and measure biological substances. IGEN International uses its patented ORIGEN technology, a universal diagnostic platform, to develop these products. The company tests within three markets: clinical testing, industrial, and life sciences. Founded in 1982. **Positions advertised include:** Biotech Laboratory Technician; Research Associate; General Scientist; Biochemist; Advanced Diagnostics Scientist; Polymer Chemist; Field Application Scientist; Business Development Associate; Product Manager; Sales Manager; Area Account Manager; Mechanical Engineer; Plastics Engineer; Electrical Engineer; Quality Control Inspector; Manufacturing Technician; Calibration Administrator; Process Development Associate; Web Developer; Software Tester. **Corporate headquarters location:** This location. **International locations:** Oxford, England. **Listed on:** NASDAQ. **Stock exchange symbol:** IGEN. **CEO/Chairman:** Samuel J. Wohlstadter. **Sales/revenues:** $5 - $10 million. **Number of employees at this location:** 130.

ITSI
136 Lafayette Avenue, Laurel MD 20707. 301/725-9500. **Toll-free phone:** 800/232-ITSI. **Contact:** Ann Osten, Human Resources. **World Wide Web address:** http://www.itsi-web.com. **Description:** Manufactures uniforms, linens, towels, and other textile products.

IXL CABINETS
10500 Ewing Road, Beltsville MD 20705. 301/937-5000. **Contact:** Human Resources. **World Wide Web address:** http://www.ixlcabinets.com. **Description:** IXL Cabinets is a division of Triangle Pacific Corporation, a manufacturer of kitchen cabinets. **Corporate headquarters location:** Addison TX. **Other U.S. locations:** Nationwide. **Parent company:** Armstrong World Industries, Incorporated.

INDEPENDENT CAN COMPANY
P.O. Box 370, 1300 Brass Mill Road, Belcamp MD 21017. 410/272-0090. **Fax:** 410/272-3159. **Contact:** Personnel. **E-mail address:** hrdept@independentcan.com. **World Wide Web address:** http://www.independentcan.com. **Description:** Manufactures decorative metal tins. Founded in 1929. **NOTE:** To contact Human Resources directly, call 410/272-2315. **Positions advertised include:** Can Line Machine Operator; Press Room Operator; Can Line Mechanic; Machinist; Tool and Die Maker; Technical Director of Lithography; Outside Sales Representative; Lithography Pressman; Manufacturing Line Mechanic. **Corporate headquarters location:** This location. **Other U.S. locations:** City of Industry CA; Fort Madison IA.

INFORMATION SYSTEMS & NETWORK CORPORATION (ISN)
10411 Motor City Drive, Bethesda MD 20817. 301/469-0400. **Contact:** Human Resources. **World Wide Web address:** http://www.isncorp.com. **Description:** Provides systems integration services to the U.S. government. Founded in 1980. **Corporate headquarters location:** This location.

INFORMATION SYSTEMS AND SERVICES, INC. (ISSI)
8601 Georgia Avenue, Suite 708, Silver Spring MD 20910. 301/588-3800. **Fax:** 301/588-3986. **Contact:** Human Resources. **E-mail address:** info@issinet.com. **World Wide Web address:** http://www.issinet.com. **Description:** Develops and integrates enterprise software. Founded in 1987.

INITIAL CONTRACT SERVICES
1505 Bloomfield Avenue, Baltimore MD 21227. 410/525-1800. **Fax:** 410/525-3535. **Contact:** General Manager. **World Wide Web address:** http://www.initialcontract.com. **Description:** Provides housekeeping and building maintenance services to a wide range of clientele. **Corporate headquarters location:** Norcross GA. **Other U.S. locations:** Danbury CT; Atlanta GA; New York NY. **Parent company:** Rentokil Initial PLC. **Number of employees nationwide:** Over 3,000.

INN AT THE COLONNADE
4 West University Parkway, Baltimore MD 21218. 410/235-5400. **Contact:** Human Resources. **World Wide Web address:** http://www.colonnadebaltimore.com. **Description:** A 125 room hotel located across the street from Johns Hopkins University and a short distance to the harbor that offers dining, banquet, and meeting facilities.

INTERNATIONAL MEDICAL NEWS GROUP
12230 Wilkins Avenue, Rockville MD 20852. 301/816-8700. **Fax:** 301/816-8738. **World Wide Web address:** http://www.imng.com. **Contact:** Human Resources. **Description:** A publisher of medical periodicals. **Corporate headquarters location:** Morristown NJ. **Other U.S. locations:** Mamaroneck NY. **Operations at this facility include:** This location houses the company's editorial offices.

INTERVISE CONSULTANTS, INC.
12 South Summit Avenue, Suite 100, Gaithersburg MD 20877. 240/364-9500. **Contact:** Human Resources. **E-mail address:** nc-resumes@intervise.com. **World Wide Web address:** http://www.intervise.com. **Description:** A computer systems engineering consulting firm whose clientele include commercial firms and government contractors. **Positions advertised include:** Government Professional Services Salesperson. **Corporate headquarters location:** This location. **Other U.S. locations:** Minneapolis MN; Raleigh NC; Dallas TX; McLean VA.

I.C. ISAACS & COMPANY
3840 Bank Street, Baltimore MD 21224. 410/342-8200. **Contact:** Human Resources. **World Wide Web address:** http://www.icisaacs.com. **Description:** Designs and manufactures a full line of jeans and sportswear for men and women under the brand name Marithe & Francois Girbaud. **Operations at this facility include:** This location houses the administrative offices. **Listed on:** OTC. **Stock exchange symbol:** ISAC. **President/CEO/Chairman:** Robert J. Arnot. **Sales/revenue:** Approximately $1.6 million.

J.C.J. INC.
P.O. Box 1297, Upper Marlboro MD 20773. 301/780-6420. **Physical address:** 15123 Marlboro Pike, Upper Marlboro MD 20772. **Contact:** Owner. **Description:** A sheet metal and roofing contractor. The company is also engaged in stainless steel fabrication. **Corporate headquarters location:** This location.

JOHNS HOPKINS HOSPITAL
600 North Wolfe Street, Baltimore MD 21287-1454. 410/955-6575. **Fax:** 410/ 614-2960. **Contact:** Human Resources. **E-mail address:** careers@jhmi.edu. **World Wide Web address:** http://www.hopkinsmedicine.org. **Description:** A 1,036-bed hospital that is a part of Johns Hopkins Health System, which includes Johns Hopkins Bayview Medical Center, an outpatient center, a geriatrics center, and Johns Hopkins Home Care Group. Johns Hopkins offers programs in AIDS and cancer treatment, cardiology, endocrinology, gastroenterology, geriatrics, gynecology, neurology, orthopedics, otolaryngology, rheumatology, urology, ophthalmology, pediatrics, and psychiatry. **NOTE:** Resumes should be mailed to: The Johns Hopkins Hospital, Department of Human Resources, Office of Career Services, 98 North Broadway, 3rd Floor, Baltimore MD 21231. Online applications are also available. **Positions advertised include:** Addiction Therapist; Administrative Coordinator; Assistant Director; Case Manager Nursing Associate; Clinical Social Worker; Clinical Technician; Credentialing Coordinator; Information Receptionist; Lab Technician; Mail Services Support Clerk; Clinical Nurse; Pharmacist; Programs Analyst. **Special programs:** Training; Tuition Reimbursement Program. **Office hours:** Monday – Friday, 9:00 a.m. – 4:00 p.m. **President:** Ronald R. Peterson. **Number of employees at this location:** 8,500.

JOHNS HOPKINS UNIVERSITY
APPLIED PHYSICS LABORATORY
11100 Johns Hopkins Road, Laurel MD 20723-6099. 240/228-3172, or 443/778-3172. **Fax:** 240/228-5274. **Contact:** Employment Office. **E-mail address:** recruiter0@jhuapl.edu. **World Wide Web address:** http://www.jhuapl.edu. **Description:** A nonprofit research and development laboratory, the Applied Physics Laboratory (APL) of Johns Hopkins University makes contributions in defense, space, and biomedicine. **NOTE:** Entry-level positions are offered. To contact the employment office directly, call 240/228-3172. **Positions advertised include:** Network Technician; Telecommunications Engineer; Network Workstation Support Engineer; Network Support Section Supervisor; Senior Administrative Specialist; Maintenance Electrician; Project Manager; Biomechanical Engineer; Aerosol Facility Test Operator; Electrical Engineer; Mechanical Engineer; Post-Doctoral Epidemiologist; Spacecraft Systems Engineer; Space/Atmospheric Physicist; Computer Science Researcher; Strike Warfare Project Manager. **Special programs:** Continuing Education Program; Scholarship Program. **Number of employees at this location:** 3,350.

JOS. A. BANK CLOTHIERS INC.
500 Hanover Pike, Hampstead MD 21074. 410/239-5728. **Fax:** 410/239-5868. **Recorded jobline:** 800/520-4473. **Contact:** Human Resources. **E-mail address:** jobs@jos-a-bank.com. **World Wide Web address:** http://www.josbank.com. **Description:** A retailer of men's clothing. Founded in 1905. **NOTE:** Entry-level and seasonal positions are offered. **Positions advertised include:** Planner; Finance and Accounting Specialist; Marketing Manager; Catalog Developer; Accounts Payable Clerk. **Office Hours:** Monday – Friday, 8:30 a.m. – 5:00 p.m. **Special programs:** Tuition Reimbursement Program. **Corporate headquarters location:** This location.

Other U.S. locations: Nationwide. **Listed on:** NASDAQ. **Stock exchange symbol:** JOSB. **President/CEO:** Robert Wildrick. **Sales/revenues:** $210 million. **Number of employees at this location:** 300. **Number of employees nationwide:** 1,400.

K&L MICROWAVE, INC.
2250 Northwood Drive, Salisbury MD 21801. 410/749-2424. **Contact:** Human Resources. **E-mail address:** hr@klmicrowave.com. **World Wide Web address:** http://www.klmicrowave.com. **Description:** Manufactures custom and general electronic components for various types of communications systems, including microwave filters used in communications lines and for satellite dishes. **Positions advertised include:** Electronics Technician; Director of Materials; Purchasing Manager; Manufacturing Manager. **Corporate headquarters location:** This location. **International locations:** China; Dominican Republic; United Kingdom. **Parent company:** Dover Corporation. **Listed on:** New York Stock Exchange. **Stock exchange symbol:** DOV. **Number of employees worldwide:** Over 500.

KCI TECHNOLOGIES, INC.
10 North Park Drive, Hunt Valley MD 21030-1846. 410/316-7800. **Fax:** 410/316-7817. **Contact:** Bob Bell, Hiring Manager. **E-mail address:** employment@kci.com. **World Wide Web address:** http://www.kci.com/tech. **Description:** Provides planning, engineering, surveying, geotechnical testing, and construction inspection services. **Positions advertised include:** CADD Designer; 3rd Party Inspector; Accounts Payable Specialist; Administrative Assistant; CADD Drafter; Civil Designer; Engineer; Environmental Scientist; Estimator; Geotechnical Engineer; Human Resources Assistant; Marketing Associate; Planner; Structural Design Clerk. **Corporate headquarters location:** This location. **Other area locations:** Laurel MD; Baltimore MD. **Other U.S. locations:** PA; OH; WV; VA; NC; DE; NC; DC; GA; FL. **Listed on:** Privately held. **President/CEO/Chairman:** Terry F. Neimeyer.

KPMG
111 South Calvert Street, Baltimore MD 21202-6174. 410/949-8500. **Contact:** Tara C. Huber, Human Resources. **E-mail address:** tchuber@kpmg.com. **World Wide Web address:** http://www.kpmgcampus.com. **Description:** KPMG delivers a wide range of value-added assurance, tax, and consulting services. **Special programs:** Internships; Training. **Corporate headquarters location:** McLean VA. **Other U.S. locations:** Nationwide. **International locations:** Worldwide. **Listed on:** NASDAQ. **Stock exchange symbol:** KCIN. **Sales/revenue:** $13.5 billion. **Number of employees at this location:** Over 200. **Number of employees worldwide:** Over 100,000.

KAYDON RING & SEAL INC.
P.O. Box 626, Baltimore MD 21203. 410/547-7700. **Contact:** Human Resources. **World Wide Web address:** http://www.kaydon.com. **Description:** A diversified manufacturer offering specialized engineering and construction capabilities to various industries. Kaydon Ring & Seal also manufactures railroad ties, road paving, roofing, and lumber products, as well as machinery for the mining, paper, packaging, and agricultural industries. **Corporate headquarters location:** Ann Arbor MI. **Parent company:** Kaydon Corporation. **Operations at this facility include:** This location produces power transmission equipment (couplings) and adjustable-speed transmission drives. **Listed on:** New York Stock Exchange. **Stock exchange symbol:** KDN.

KELLY-SPRINGFIELD TIRE COMPANY
12501 Willow Brook Road SE, Cumberland MD 21502-2599. 301/777-6000. **Contact:** Human Resources. **World Wide Web address:** http://www.kelly-springfield.com. **Description:** A manufacturer of automobile tires and inner tubes. **Corporate headquarters location:** This location. **Other U.S. locations:** Freeport IL; Fayetteville NC; Tyler TX. **International locations:** Worldwide. **Parent company:** Goodyear Tire & Rubber Company's principal business is the development, manufacture, distribution, marketing, and sale of tires for markets worldwide. Goodyear also manufactures and sells a broad range of rubber products and rubber-related chemicals for various industrial and consumer markets and also provides auto repair services. **Listed on:** New York Stock Exchange. **Stock exchange symbol:** GT.

KENNEDY KRIEGER INSTITUTE
707 North Broadway, Baltimore MD 21205. 443/923-5800. **Recorded jobline:** 443/923-5820. **Contact:** Human Resources. **World Wide Web address:** http://www.kennedykrieger.org. **Description:** Kennedy Krieger Institute began as Children's Rehabilitation Center in 1937 to serve children with cerebral palsy and from there developed in a center for research and treatment of children's neurological diseases. The Kennedy Krieger School for children with physical, emotional, and learning disabilities offers extended day programs for adolescents with severe emotional disabilities. **NOTE:** Interested jobseekers are encouraged to apply online. If submitting resume by mail, send to: KKI Processing Center, 28501-A Ryan Road, A-105, Warren MI 48092. **Positions advertised include:** Aide; Accounting Specialist; Administrative Assistant; Assistant Teacher. **Special program:** Tuition Reimbursement Program. **President:** Gary W. Goldstein, MD.

KESWICK MULTI-CARE CENTER
700 West 40th Street, Baltimore MD 21211. 410/662-4260. **Fax:** 410/662-4263. **Recorded jobline:** 410/662-4350. **Contact:** Human Resources. **E-mail address:** hr@keswick-multicare.org. **World Wide Web address:** http://www.keswick-multicare.org. **Description:** A nursing home that provides adult daycare and assisted living services. Founded in 1883. **NOTE:** Entry-level positions and second and third shifts are offered. Job seekers may apply online. **Company slogan:** We can make it happen. **Positions advertised include:** Dietitian; Floor Technician; Geriatric Nursing Assistant; Staff Registered Nurse; Licensed Practical Nurse; MDS Coordinator; Adult Day Services Driver; Building Engineer; Security Agent; Nursing Director; 1st Class Mechanic. **Special programs:** Summer Jobs; Tuition Reimbursement Program; Nursing Scholarship Program. **Office hours:** Monday – Friday, 8:00 a.m. – 5:00 p.m. **Corporate headquarters location:** This location. **Listed on:** Privately held. **CEO:** Andrea Braid. **Number of employees at this location:** 435.

JOHN J. KIRLIN, INC.
515 Dover Road, Suite 2100, Rockville MD 201850. 301/738-8856. **Fax:** 301/ 738-8888. **Contact:** Shane L. Williams, Corporate Director of Human Resources. **E-mail address:** swilliams@johnjkirlin-inc.com. **World Wide Web address:** http://www.johnjkirlin-inc.com. **Description:** Installs mechanical systems, such as HVAC, site utilities, plumbing, and process piping. **NOTE:** Online applications are available. **Positions advertised include:** Senior Project Manager; Estimator; CADD Operator; Mechanical Coordinator; Drafter. **Office hours:** Monday - Friday, 7:30 a.m. - 5:00 p.m. **Corporate headquarters location:** This location. **Other U.S. locations:** Fort Lauderdale FL; Atlanta GA; Baltimore MD; Raleigh NC. **President/CEO:** Wayne T. Day.

KOONS AUTOMOTIVE
5001 Auth Way, Suitland MD 20746. 301/702-0590. **Contact:** Human Resources. **World Wide Web address:** http://www.koons.com. **Description:** An automobile dealership selling Mazda, Nissan, Volvo, Buick, Volkswagen, BMW, and Pontiac vehicles. Founded in 1964. **NOTE:** Job seekers may apply online for specific positions or for general consideration. **President:** Jim Koons.

KOP-FLEX, INC.
EMERSON POWER TRANSMISSION
7565 Harmans Road, Hanover MD 21076. 410/787-8482. **Fax:** 410/787-8514. **Contact:** Colleen Rigatti, Employee Relations Representative. **E-mail address:** salestraining@emerson-ept.com. **World Wide Web address:** http://www.emerson-ept.com. **Description:** A manufacturer of power transmission couplings and components for use in steel mills, paper mills, and navy ships. **NOTE:** Second and third shifts are offered. **Special programs:** Co-ops; Summer Jobs; Training. **Corporate headquarters location:** This location. **Other U.S. locations:** Houston TX; Aurora IL; Valparaiso IN; Monticello IN; Florence KY; Maysville KY; Morehead KY; Chino CA; Ithaca NY. **International locations:** Canada; Mexico; Japan; Taiwan. **Operations at this facility include:** Administration; Research and Development; Sales; Service. **Sales/revenue:** $15.5 billion. **Number of employees at this location:** 370.

L-SOFT INTERNATIONAL, INC.
8100 Corporate Drive, Suite 350, Landover MD 20785-2231. 301/731-0440. **Toll-free phone:** 800/399-5449. **Fax:** 301/731-6302. **Contact:** Human Resources. **E-mail address:** jobs@lsoft.com. **World Wide Web address:** http://www.lsoft.com. **Description:** Develops mailing list management software. The company's product line includes LISTSERV, an electronic mailing list management product; LSMTP, a program for large quantity delivery of Internet mail; and EASE, which allows users to create mail lists on L-Soft's centrally maintained servers. Founded in 1994. **Positions advertised include:** Senior Custom Support Engineer. **Corporate headquarters location:** This location. **Other area locations:** Bethesda MD. **International locations:** Sweden; United Kingdom.

LAND ROVER NORTH AMERICA, INC.
P.O. Box 1503, 4371 Parliament Place, Lanham MD 20706. 301/429-3652. **Contact:** Human Resources. **World Wide Web address:** http://www.landrover.com. **Description:** Manufactures four-wheel drive, sport-utility vehicles under the names Land Rover and Range Rover. Founded in 1948. **Corporate headquarters location:** This location. **Parent company:** Ford Motor Company. **Listed on:** New York Stock Exchange. **Stock exchange symbol:** F.

LANDMARK COMMUNITY NEWSPAPERS OF MARYLAND INC.
CARROLL COUNTY TIMES
P.O. Box 346, Westminster MD 21158. 410/848-4400. **Physical address:** 201 Railroad Avenue, Westminster MD 21157. **Fax:** 410/848-9331. **Contact:** Personnel. **World Wide Web address:** http://www.carrollcountytimes.com. **Description:** Provides newspaper publishing, specialty publications, and commercial printing. **NOTE:** Entry-level positions are offered. **Positions advertised include:** Graphic Designer; Post Press Operator. **Special programs:** Apprenticeships. **Office hours:** Monday – Friday, 8:30 a.m. – 4:30 p.m. **Corporate headquarters location:** Norfolk VA. **Parent company:** Landmark Communications. **Operations at this facility include:** Manufacturing; Sales; Service. **Listed on:** Privately held. **Number of employees at this location:** 210. **Number of employees nationwide:** 5,000.

LANIER WORLDWIDE, INC.
300 Red Brook Boulevard, Suite 110, Owings Mills MD 21117. 443/394-6064. **Fax:** 443/394-6068. **Contact:** Bridgette Black. **E-mail address:** bblack@lanier.com. **World Wide Web address:** http://www.lanier.com. **Description:** A business services company that provides document management solutions. **Positions advertised include:** Collections Supervisor; Commercial Sales Representative; Senior Operations Analyst. **Corporate headquarters location:** Atlanta GA. **Other U.S. locations:** Nationwide. **International locations:** Worldwide. **President and CEO:** Nori Goto.

LEGG MASON, INC.
100 Light Street, Baltimore MD 21202-1099. 410/539-3400. **Contact:** Human Resources. **World Wide Web address:** http://www.leggmason.com. **Description:** A full-service broker-dealer that also offers investment banking services. **Parent company:** Legg Mason, Incorporated (Baltimore MD) is a holding company with subsidiaries engaged in securities brokerage and trading; investment management of mutual funds and individual and institutional accounts; underwriting of corporate and municipal securities and other investment banking activities; sales of annuities and banking services; and the provision of other financial services. The company serves its brokerage clients through 128 offices and manages $82 billion in assets for individual and institutional accounts and mutual funds. **Positions advertised include:** Accountant; Account Administrator; Administrative Assistant; Administrative Manager; Administrative Assistant; Business Analyst; Compliance Officer; Corporate Technical College; Developer Analyst; Graphic Designer; Operations Trainee; Proposal Writer; Research Associate. **Special programs include:** Internships. **Corporate headquarters location:** This location. **Listed on:** New York Stock Exchange. **Stock exchange symbol:** LM. **Chairman:** Raymond A. Mason. **Number of employees nationwide:** 4,200.

LIPPINCOTT WILLIAMS & WILKINS
351 West Camden Street, Baltimore MD 21201. 410/528-4000. **Contact:** Human Resources. **World Wide Web address:** http://www.lww.com. **Description:** Publishes and prints medical and scientific books, journals, and periodicals that are marketed and sold worldwide. LWW's primary customers are medical and scientific practitioners, libraries, and universities. **NOTE:** Online applications are available. **Positions advertised include:** Electronic Media Sales; Human Resources Manager; Media Sales Associate; Manager; Editor; Production Assistant; Production Manager; Senior Software Engineer; Software Development Manager. **Corporate headquarters location:** Philadelphia PA. **Other area locations:** Hagerstown MD. **Other U.S. locations:** Hudson NY; New York NY; Springhouse PA; Skokie IL. **International locations:** Australia; China; United Kingdom; Argentina.

LOCKHEED MARTIN
6560 Rock Spring Drive, Bethesda MD 20817-1146. 301/214-3000. **Contact:** Human Resources. **E-mail address:** jobs.lmc@lmco.com. **World Wide Web address:** http://www.lockheedmartin.com. **Description:** An aerospace and technology company engaged in the design, manufacture, and management of systems and products in the fields of space, defense, electronics, communications, information management, energy, and materials. **NOTE:** Entry-level positions are offered. **Positions advertised include:** Administrative Assistant; Engineering Technician; Environmental Remediation Analyst. **Corporate headquarters location:** Bethesda MD. **Listed on:** New York Stock Exchange. **Stock exchange symbol:** LMT. **President/COO:** Robert J. Stevens. **Sales/revenue:** $26.6 billion. **Number of employees worldwide:** 125,000.

LOCKHEED MARTIN
700 North Frederick Avenue, Gaithersburg MD 20879. 301/240-6400. **Fax:** 301/ 240-7190. **Contact:** Human Resources. **E-mail address:** jobs.lmc@lmco.com. **World Wide Web address:** http://www.lockheedmartin.com. **Description:** An aerospace and

technology company engaged for the design, manufacture, and management of systems and products in the fields of space, defense, electronics, communications, information management, energy, and materials. **Positions advertised include:** Program Manager; Systems Integration Analyst; Systems Engineer; Technical Editor. **NOTE:** Entry-level positions are offered. **Corporate headquarters location:** Bethesda MD. **Other U.S. locations:** Nationwide. **Operations at this facility include:** This location is part of the Systems Integration division of Lockheed Martin. **Listed on:** New York Stock Exchange. **Stock exchange symbol:** LMT. **President/COO:** Robert J. Stevens. **Sales/revenue:** $26.6 billion. **Number of employees at this location:** 1,200. **Number of employees worldwide:** 125,000.

LOCKHEED MARTIN
7375 Executive Place, Suite 101, Seabrook MD 20706. 301/805-0300. **Contact:** Human Resources. **E-mail address:** jobs.lmc@lmco.com. **World Wide Web address:** http://www.lockheedmartin.com. **Description** An aerospace and technology company engaged in the design, manufacture, and management of systems and products for the fields of space, defense, electronics, communications, information management, energy, and materials. **NOTE:** Entry-level positions are offered. **Positions advertised include:** Administrative Assistant. **Office hours:** Monday – Friday, 8:15 a.m. – 5:00 p.m. **Corporate headquarters location:** Bethesda MD. **Other U.S. locations:** Nationwide. **Operations at this facility include:** This location is part of the Information Support Services division of Lockheed Martin, and provides turnkey systems development, engineering services, and spaceflight mission support for civil and commercial space programs worldwide. This location also supports both space and ground-based systems, with an emphasis on command and control, data storage, and processing systems. **Listed on:** New York Stock Exchange. **Stock exchange symbol:** LMT. **President/COO:** Robert J. Stevens. **Sales/revenue:** $26.6 billion. **Number of employees at this location:** 2,100. **Number of employees worldwide:** 125,000.

LOCKHEED MARTIN
7100 Standard Drive, Hanover MD 21076. 410/796-2100. **Contact:** Human Resources. **E-mail address:** jobs.lmc@lmco.com. **World Wide Web address:** http://www.lockheedmartin.com. **Description:** An aerospace and technology company engaged in the design, manufacture, and management of systems and products for the fields of space, defense, electronics, communications, information management, energy, and materials. **NOTE:** Entry-level positions are offered. **Positions advertised include:** Cost Schedule Analyst; Systems Engineer. **Corporate headquarters location:** Bethesda MD. **Other U.S. locations:** Nationwide. **Operations at this facility include:** This location is a development lab. **Listed on:** New York Stock Exchange. **Stock exchange symbol:** LMT. **President/COO:** Robert J. Stevens. **Sales/revenue:** $26.6 billion. **Number of employees worldwide:** 125,000.

LOCKHEED MARTIN
6801 Rockledge Drive, Bethesda MD 20817. 301/897-6000. **Contact:** Human Resources. **E-mail address:** jobs.lmc@lmco.com. **World Wide Web address:** http://www.lockheedmartin.com. **Description:** An aerospace and technology company engaged in the design, manufacture, and management of systems and products for the fields of space, defense, electronics, communications, information management, energy, and materials. **NOTE:** Entry-level positions are offered. **Positions advertised include:** Administrative Assistant; Paralegal. **Corporate headquarters location:** This location. **Other U.S. locations:** Nationwide. **Operations at this facility include:** This location houses administrative offices. **Listed on:** New York Stock Exchange. **Stock exchange symbol:** LMT. **President/COO:** Robert J. Stevens. **President/COO:** Robert J. Stevens. **Number of employees worldwide:** 125,000.

LONDON FOG INDUSTRIES
1332 Londontown Boulevard, Eldersburg MD 21784. 410/549-8183. **Contact:** Human Resources. **E-mail address:** jobs@londonfog.com. **World Wide Web address:** http://www.londonfog.com. **Description:** London Fog is a manufacturer and retailer of traditional and contemporary men's and women's rainwear. The company is also a manufacturer and retailer of men's, women's, and children's outerwear and sportswear. Founded in 1923. **NOTE:** Entry-level positions are offered. **Special programs:** Tuition Reimbursement Program. **Corporate headquarters location:** Seattle WA. **Other U.S. locations:** Nationwide. **Subsidiaries include:** Pacific Trail (also at this location). **Listed on:** Privately held.

LOYOLA COLLEGE
4501 North Charles Street, Baltimore MD 211210-2699. 410/617-2000. **Toll-free phone:** 800/221-9107. **E-mail address:** humanresources@loyola.edu. **World Wide Web address:** http://www.loyola.edu. **Description:** A Jesuit Catholic University. **Note:** Human resources phone: 410/617-2354. **Positions advertised include:** Information Systems Assistant Professor; Reading Education Assistant Professor; Operations Management Assistant Professor; Art History Assistant Professor; Computer Science Visiting Faculty; Education Administrative Associate Professor; Economics Instructor; Special Gifts Assistant Director; Capital Program Director; Annual Giving Assistant; Account Affairs Vice President; Student Life Director; Alumni Relations Office Manager; Alumni Relations Administrative Assistant.

LUSTINE GM PARTS DISTRIBUTORS
4510 Longfellow Street, Hyattsville MD 20781. 301/277-7361. **Contact:** Human Resources. **World Wide Web address:** http://www.lustineparts.com. **Description:** A wholesale distributor of new and remanufactured General Motors automotive parts, engines, and transmissions. Founded in 1924. **Office hours:** Monday - Friday, 8:00 a.m. - 5:30 p.m. **Corporate headquarters location:** This location.

MACK TRUCKS INC.
13302 Pennsylvania Avenue, Hagerstown MD 21742. 301/790-5638. **Fax:** 301/790-5400. **Contact:** Personnel. **E-mail address:** job_opportunities@macktrucks.com. **World Wide Web address:** http://www.macktrucks.com. **Description:** Produces heavy and medium-duty trucks, as well as related components. Founded in 1900. **NOTE:** Entry-level positions and second and third shifts are offered. **NOTE:** Resumes submitted via e-mail must be in Microsoft Word 6.0 format. **Positions advertised include:** Project Engineer; Staff Engineer; Quality Engineer; Manufacturing Engineer; Reliability Engineer; Financial Analyst; Senior Buyer; Quality Engineer. **Special programs:** Training. **Corporate headquarters location:** Allentown PA. **Other U.S. locations:** Chicago IL; Baltimore MD; Macungie PA; Winnsboro SC. **Subsidiaries include:** Mack Canada, Incorporated; Mack Trucks Australia Pty, Limited. **Parent company:** Volvo AB. **Operations at this facility include:** This location manufactures the Mack Truck powertrain. Products include Mack engines and transmissions. In addition to the plant, this location features an Engine Development and Test laboratory. **Listed on:** NASDAQ. **Stock exchange symbol:** VOLVY. **President/CEO:** Paul Vikner. **Sales/revenue:** Approximately $18 billion. **Number of employees at this location:** 1,300. **Number of employees worldwide:** 4,314.

MANAGEMENT TECHNOLOGY INC. (MTI)
7700 Old Branch Avenue, Suite C200, Clinton MD 20735. 301/856-4840. **Toll-free phone:** 800/821-8133. **Fax:** 301/868-6227. **Contact:** Recruiting Department. **E-mail address:** personnel@mtiinc.com. **World Wide Web address:** http://www.mtiinc.com. **Description:** Develops and markets a variety of banking and financial software. **Positions advertised include:** Web Developer; Administrative Assistant; Contract Administrator; Business Development Associate; Chief Financial Aide Officer; Corporate IT Recruiter; Computer Programmer. **NOTE:** Entry-level positions are offered. Resumes may be submitted online. **Special programs:** Tuition Reimbursement Program. **Corporate headquarters location:** This location. **Other U.S. locations:** Falls Church VA; Hampton VA; New York NY. **President/CEO:** Pauline C. Brooks.

MANUGISTICS, INC.
9715 Key West Avenue, Rockville MD 20850. 301/255-5000. **Toll-free phone:** 800/331-0728. **Contact:** Human Resources. **E-mail address:** jobs@manu.com. **World Wide Web address:** http://www.manugistics.com. **Description:** Develops decision support software and provides support services for Fortune 500 manufacturing, transportation, and distribution companies. **Positions advertised include:** Accounting Manager; Business Development Manager; Database Developer; Director Industry & Alliance Marketing; Help Desk Specialist; Lead Software Developer; Financial Planning Analyst; Project Analyst; Production Manager; Applications Developer; Corporate Receptionist; Human Resources Generalist; Model Analyst; Program Manager; Proposal Writer; Software Developer C++; Software Manager; Test Manager. **Special programs:** Internships; Training. **Corporate headquarters location:** This location. **Other U.S. locations:** Nationwide. **International locations:** United Kingdom; Taiwan; Sweden; Spain; Singapore; the Netherlands; Japan; Italy; Australia; Belgium; Brazil; France; Germany; China. **Operations at this facility include:** Administration; Research and Development; Sales; Service. **Listed on:** NASDAQ. **Stock exchange symbol:** MANU. **CEO/Chairman:** Gregory J. Owens. **Sales/revenue:** $310 million. **Number of employees at this location:** 300. **Number of employees worldwide:** Approximately 2,000.

MARINER HEALTH CARE
1502 Frederick Road, Catonsville MD 21228. 410/747-3287. **Toll-free phone:** 800/929-4762. **E-mail address:** jambrose@marinerhealthcare.com. **Contact:** Human Resources Manager. **Description:** Mariner is one of the largest long term health care systems in the United States located in 20 states providing 24 hour care. **Positions advertised include:** Medical Admissions Coordinator; A/R Coordinator. **Number of employees at this location:** 260. **President:** C. Christian Winkle.

THE MARRIOTT GAITHERSBURG
9751 Washingtonian Boulevard, Gaithersburg MD 20878. 301/590-0044. **Recorded jobline:** 888/462-7746. **Contact:** Human Resources. **E-mail address:** staffing@marriott.com. **World Wide Web address:** http://www.marriott.com. **Description:** A hotel. **Positions advertised include:** Sales Manager. **NOTE:** Entry-level positions are offered. Resumes should be sent to: Marriott International, One Marriott Drive, Washington DC 20058. **Special programs:** Internships. **Corporate headquarters location:** Washington, D.C. **Other U.S. locations:** Nationwide. **International locations:** Worldwide. **Parent company:** Marriott International, Incorporated operates and franchises hotels and related lodgings. **Listed on:** New York Stock Exchange. **Stock exchange symbol:** MAR. **Sales/revenue:** $8.4 billion. **Number of employees at this location:** 4,000. **Number of employees worldwide:** 180,000.

MARTEK BIOSCIENCES CORPORATION
6480 Dobbin Road, Columbia MD 21045. 410/740-0081. **Fax:** 410/740-2985. **Contact:** Human Resources. **E-mail address:** jobs@martekbio.com. **World Wide Web address:** http://www.martekbio.com. **Description:** Engaged in the research, development, and production of nutritional supplements, food ingredients, reagents, and pharmaceuticals drawn from the ocean's microalgae supply. Founded in 1985. **Positions advertised include:** Clinical Research Associate; Clinical Research Manager; Competitive Intelligence Analyst; Molecular Bio Research Associate. **Corporate headquarters location:** This location. **Other U.S. locations:** Boulder CO; Winchester KY. **Listed on:** NASDAQ. **Stock exchange symbol:** MATK. **President:** Richard J. Radmer. **Number of employees nationwide:** 172.

MARTIN'S INC.
6821 Dogwood Road, Baltimore MD 21244. 410/265-1300. **Fax:** 410/265-1328. **Contact:** Human Resources. **E-mail address:** lmoler@martinscaterers.com. **World Wide Web address:** http://www.martinscaterers.com. **Description:** A catering company serving the Baltimore area. **Corporate headquarters location:** This location.

MARYLAND COLLEGE OF ART AND DESIGN
10500 Georgia Avenue, Silver Spring MD 20902-4111. 301/649-4454. **Contact:** Human Resources. **World Wide Web address:** http://www.mcadmd.org. **Description:** A two-year college focusing on fine arts, visual communications, and studio arts. Founded in 1954. **President:** Donald J. Smith.

MARYLAND INDEPENDENT
7 Industrial Park Drive, Waldorf MD 20602. 301/645-9480. **Contact:** Human Resources. **World Wide Web address:** http://www.chespub.com. **Description:** Publishes the *Maryland Independent* newspaper (circulation: 12,500). Founded in 1872. **Corporate headquarters location:** Elkton MD. **Other U.S. locations:** Easton MD. **Parent company:** Chesapeake Publishing Corporation publishes 50 other newspapers including *Enterprise* (circulation: 14,000); *South County Current* (circulation: 33,000); *Calvert County Recorder* (circulation: 5,500); and *Flightline* (circulation: 9,000). The company also provides commercial printing services.

MARYLAND INSTITUTE COLLEGE OF ART
1300 Mount Royal Avenue, Baltimore MD 21217-4191. 410/225-2420. **Fax:** 410/225-2557. **Contact:** Human Resources. **E-mail address:** jobs@mica.edu. **World Wide Web address:** http://www.mica.edu. **Description:** An art school that offers undergraduate, graduate, continuing education, and summer programs in various areas of art studies. Full-time undergraduate enrollment is approximately 900 students. **Positions advertised include:** Director of Annual Fund; Associate Dean of Continuing Studies; Data Processor; Assistant Director of Academics; Artist-in-Residence; Department of Environmental Design Chair; Art History Professor. **Special programs:** Tuition Remission Program.

MARYLAND PLASTICS
P.O. Box 472, Federalsburg MD 21632. 410/754-5566. **Toll-free phone:** 800/544-5582. **E-mail address:** sales@marylandplastics.com. **Physical address:** 251 East Central Avenue, Federalsburg MD 21632. **Contact:** George Weeks, Personnel Manager. **World Wide Web address:** http://www.marylandplastics.com. **Description:** Manufactures cutlery and housewares including plastic serving dishes, and offers custom molding. **Number of employees at this location:** 300.

MARYLAND PUBLIC TELEVISION
11767 Owings Mills Boulevard, Owings Mills MD 21117. 410/356-3600. **Contact:** Donna L. Blum, Phr. Director of Human Resources. **E-mail address:** dblum@mpt.org.

World Wide Web address: http://www,mpt.org. **Description:** Publicly funded television with local access for Maryland. **Positions advertised include:** Corporate Communications Director; Creative Sales Assistant; Producer; Maintenance Engineer; Transmitter Support Specialist. **President:** Dr. Rick Breitenfeild.

MARYLAND SPECIALTY WIRE COMPANY
100 Cockeysville Road, Cockeysville MD 21030. 410/785-2500. **Toll-free phone:** 800/444-7938. **Contact:** Human Resources. **E-mail address:** sales@mdspecwire.com. **World Wide Web address:** http://www.mdspecwire.com. **Description:** Produces stainless steel and alloy wire used for springs, reinforced hose, wire rope, and ball bearings. **Corporate headquarters location:** This location. **Parent company:** Handy & Harmon.

MARYLAND STATE DEPARTMENT OF HEALTH AND MENTAL HYGIENE
P.O. Box 22330, Baltimore MD 21203-4330. 410/767-5689. **Physical address:** 201 West Preston Street, Baltimore MD 21201. **Recorded jobline:** 410/767-6018. **Contact:** Joseph Elliot, Personnel Officer. **World Wide Web address:** http://www.dhmh.state.md.us. **Description:** Provides health regulatory, public health, mental health/addictions, environmental health, and medico-public health laboratory services on a statewide basis. **NOTE:** Entry-level positions and second and third shifts are offered. To contact personnel services directly, call 410/767-5700. **Positions advertised include:** Community Health Nurse Supervisor; Environmental Services; Licensed Practical Nurse; Registered Nurse; Program Administrator. **Special programs:** Training; Tuition Reimbursement Program; Employee Development Program. **Office hours:** Monday – Friday, 8:00 a.m. – 5:00 p.m. **Corporate headquarters location:** This location. **Operations at this facility include:** Administration; Divisional Headquarters; Regional Headquarters; Service. **Number of employees nationwide:** 12,000.

MASTER SECURITY INC.
10944C Beaver Dam Road, Cockeysville MD 21030. 410/584-8789. **Contact:** Human Resources. **Description:** Provides security guards for malls and private buildings including apartments and corporate offices.

McARDLE PRINTING COMPANY, INC.
800 Commerce Drive, Upper Marlboro MD 20774-8792. 301/390-8500. **Fax:** 301/390-8502. **Contact:** Human Resources Coordinator. **E-mail address:** mpchuman@bna.com. **World Wide Web address:** http://www.mcardleprinting.com. **Description:** A commercial printing firm. Founded in 1947. **Positions advertised include:** Printing Sales Representative; Electronic Pre Press Associate; Journeyman Web Press Manager; Journeyman Book Binder. **Corporate headquarters location:** This location. **Parent company:** Bureau of National Affairs. **Operations at this facility include:** Administration; Manufacturing; Sales. **Listed on:** Privately held. **Number of employees at this location:** 200.

McCORMICK & COMPANY
10950 Beaver Dam Road, Cockeysville MD 21030. 410/771-7595. **Contact:** Susan Foster, Personnel Manager. **World Wide Web address:** http://www.mccormick.com. **Description:** A diversified specialty food company engaged in the manufacturing and marketing of seasonings and flavoring products. Products are sold in 84 countries and processed at more than 40 facilities throughout the world. Principal products include spices, herbs, seeds, vegetable products, seasoning blends, food seasoning mixes, and specialty frozen foods. Trademarks of McCormick & Company include McCormick and Schilling. The company also manufactures plastic bottles and tubes used in the pharmaceutical, cosmetic, and food packaging and preparation industries, as well as operating a cogeneration facility that supplies energy to a subsidiary and is sold to utility companies. Founded in 1889. **NOTE:** Online applications are available. **Positions advertised include:** Assistant Sourcing Manager. **Special programs:** Training; Education Assistance Program. **Corporate headquarters location:** Sparks MD. **Listed on:** New York Stock Exchange. **Stock exchange symbol:** MKC. **President/CEO/ Chairman:** Robert J. Lawless. **Sales/revenue:** Approximately $2 billion. **Number of employees worldwide:** Over 8,000.

McCORMICK & COMPANY
P.O. Box 6000, 18 Loveton Circle, Sparks MD 21152. 410/771-7301. **Fax:** 410/ 771-7462. **Contact:** Karen Weatherholtz, Vice President of Human Relations. **World Wide Web address:** http://www.mccormick.com. **Description:** A diversified specialty food company engaged in the manufacturing and marketing of seasonings and flavoring products to the food industry. Products are sold in 84 countries and processed at more than 40 facilities throughout the world. Principal products include spices, herbs, seeds, vegetable products, seasoning blends, seasoning mixes, and specialty frozen foods. Trademarks of McCormick & Company include McCormick and Schilling. The company also manufactures plastic bottles and tubes used in the pharmaceutical, cosmetic, and food packaging and preparation industries, as well as operating a cogeneration facility that supplies energy to a subsidiary and is sold to utility companies. Founded in 1889. **NOTE:** Online applications are available. **Positions advertised include:** Senior Financial Analyst; Associate Counsel. **Special programs:** Training; Education Assistance Program. **Corporate headquarters location:** This location. **Listed on:** New York Stock Exchange. **Stock exchange symbol:** MKC. **President/CEO/Chairman:** Robert J. Lawless. **Sales/revenue:** Approximately $2 billion. **Number of employees worldwide:** Over 8,000.

McCREADY HEALTH SERVICES FOUNDATION
201 Hall Highway, Crisfield MD 21817. 410/968-1200. **Fax:** 410/968-3005. **Contact:** Human Resources. **E-mail address:** hr@mccreadyfoundation.org. **World Wide Web address:** http://www.mcreadyfoundation.org. **Description:** Operates the Edward W. McCready Memorial Hospital, the Alice Byrd Tawes Nursing Home, and the Peyton Center. Combined, these facilities offer emergency services; inpatient accommodations including acute medical and surgical beds, skilled nursing beds, and a comprehensive care unit; surgical services including inpatient and outpatient general, gynecological, plastic, and dental surgeries; diagnostic services; rehabilitation and extended recovery services; and social services. Founded in 1923. **NOTE:** Entry-level positions and second and third shifts are offered. Applications are available online. **Positions advertised include:** Registered Nurse; Licensed Practical Nurse; Manager Medical Surgical Unit; Patient Care Registered Nurse; Facilitator. **Special programs:** Training; Co-ops; Summer Jobs. **Corporate headquarters location:** This location. **Administrator/CEO:** Novella Bozman. **Number of employees at this location:** 300.

MCDANIEL COLLEGE
2 College Hill, Westminster MD 21157-4390. 410/848-7000. **Contact:** Thomas G. Steback, Human Resources. **E-mail address:** tsteback@mcdaniel.edu. **World Wide Web address:** http://www.mcdaniel.edu. **Description:** A private, coeducational institution offering both undergraduate and graduate programs. The college has a full-time enrollment of approximately 1,500 students. **NOTE:** To contact Human Resources directly, call 410/857-2229. **Positions advertised include:** Residential Life Coordinator; Assistant Woman's Volley Ball Coach; PC Support Technician; Administrative Secretary; Housekeeper; Grounds Maintenance Worker. **Office hours:** Monday – Friday, 8:30 a.m. – 4:30 p.m.

MEADWESTVACO
300 Pratt Street, Luke MD 21540. 301/359-3311. **Contact:** Human Resources. **World Wide Web address:** http://www.meadwestvaco.com. **Description:** A manufacturer of paper for high-quality graphic reproduction, consumer and industrial packaging, and specialty chemicals for industrial and environmental applications. The company is also one of the largest envelope manufacturers in the world. **Corporate headquarters location:** Stamford CT. **International locations:** Worldwide. **Subsidiaries include:** AMCAL, Incorporated. **Operations at this facility include:** This location manufactures paper. **Listed on:** New York Stock Exchange. **Stock exchange symbol:** MWV. **CEO/Chairman:** John A. Luke, Junior. **Sales/revenue:** $7.2 billion. **Number of employees worldwide:** Over 30,000.

MEDIMMUNE, INC.
One Medimmune Way, Gaithersburg MD 20878. 301/417-0770. **Fax:** 301/527-4215. **Contact:** Human Resources. **E-mail address:** JobOpenings@medimmune.com. **World Wide Web address:** http://www.medimmune.com. **Description:** Researches and develops biopharmaceuticals for the infectious disease and organ transplant markets. **Positions advertised include:** Clinical Data Analyst; Director of Project Planning and Alliance Management; Associate Scientist; Administrative Assistant; Clinical Liaison; Senior Project Engineer; Accounting Assistant. **Note:** Do not e-mail resumes. Only include your contact information and information request. **Special programs:** Educational Assistance Program. **Corporate headquarters location:** This location. **Other area locations:** Frederick MD. **Other U.S. locations:** CA; PA. **International locations:** United Kingdom; the Netherlands. **Subsidiaries include:** Medimmune Oncology; U.S. Bioscience; Medimmune Vaccines. **Listed on:** NASDAQ. **Stock exchange symbol:** MEDI. **Founder/Chairman:** Wayne D. Hockmeyer. **Sales/revenue:** $619 million. **Number of employees nationwide:** Over 1,500.

MEDSTAR HEALTH
5565 Sterrett Place, 5th Floor, Columbia MD 21044. 410/772-6500. **Fax:** 410/ 715-3809. **Contact:** Zipporah Williams, Human Resources Generalist. **E-mail address:** zipporah.williams@medstar.net. **World Wide Web address:** http://www.medstarhealth.org. **Description:** A healthcare organization that operates Franklin Square Hospital; Harbor Hospital Center; National Rehabilitation Hospital; Washington Hospital Center; Union Memorial Hospital; Good Samaritan Hospital; nursing centers; Ask-A-Nurse health information and physician referral; home health care services; and rehabilitation services. **NOTE:** To contact Human Resources directly, call 410/772-6751. **Positions advertised include:** Administrative Assistant; Outreach Program Director. **Corporate headquarters location:** This location. **Number of employees nationwide:** 22,000.

MELWOOD TRAINING CENTER
5606 Dower House Road, Upper Marlboro MD 20772. 301/599-8000. **Fax:** 301/599-0180. **Recorded jobline:** 866/447-1340. **Contact:** Corporate Recruiting Manager. **E-mail address:** cdougher@melwood.org. **World Wide Web address:** http://www.melwood.org. **Description:** A private, nonprofit agency providing services for individuals with disabilities. Founded in 1963. **NOTE:** Entry-level and seasonal positions, part-time jobs, and second and third shifts are offered. The Corporate Recruiting Office is located at 9666 Pennsylvania Avenue, Upper Marlboro MD 20772. To contact directly, call 301/599-7913 or fax to 301/599-7915. **Positions advertised include:** Community Support Assistant; Resident Service Counselor; Assistant Cook; Writing Assistant; Summer Life Guard; Van Driver. **Company slogan:** Growing together. **Special programs:** Internships; Training; Summer Jobs. **Office hours:** Monday - Friday, 8:00 a.m. - 5:00 p.m. **Corporate headquarters location:** This location.

MEMORIAL HOSPITAL OF EASTON
219 South Washington Street, Easton MD 21601. 410/822-1000. **Toll-free phone:** 888/463-3150. **Fax:** 410/819-0161. **Contact:** Human Resources. **World Wide Web address:** http://www.shorehealth.org. **Description:** A 137-bed, acute care hospital that offers inpatient and outpatient services. **NOTE:** Entry-level positions and second and third shifts are offered. Job seekers may apply online. **Positions advertised include:** Staff Production Therapist; Clinical Coordinator; Cardiopulmonary Service; Clinical Information Management Specialist; Editorial Specialist; Environmental Technician; Food Production Associate; Food Services Aide; Development & Operations Director; Database Administrator; Materials Management Director; Licensed Practical Nurse; Registered Nurse; Nursing Technician; Radiological Specialist; Quality Improvement Nurse. **Special programs:** Co-ops. **Other area locations:** Cambridge MD.

MERCANTILE BANKSHARES CORPORATION
2 Hopkins Plaza, P.O. Box 1477, Baltimore MD 21203. 410/237-5900. **Contact:** Human Resources. **World Wide Web address:** http://www.mercantile.net. **Description:** A multibank holding company. Affiliates of Mercantile Bankshares Corporation include 20 banks and a mortgage banking company. The affiliated banks are engaged in general, personal, and corporate banking and have 155 retail banking offices located in Maryland, Delaware, and Virginia that provide personal banking services including deposit vehicles such as checking accounts, NOW accounts, money market deposit accounts, certificates of deposit, and individual retirement accounts. Mercantile Bankshares Corporation's largest bank, Mercantile Safe Deposit & Trust Company, also provides a full range of trust services. **NOTE:** Resumes should be mailed to Mercantile Safe Deposit & Trust Company, Human Resources Manager, 750 Old Hammonds Ferry Road, Linthicum MD 21090. **Positions advertised include:** Marketing Coordinator; Field Examiner; Administrative Assistant; Credit Analyst; Teller. **Special programs:** Educational Assistance Program. **Corporate headquarters location:** This location. **Listed on:** NASDAQ. **Stock exchange symbol:** MRBK. **President/CEO/Chairman:** Edward J. Kelly III. **Sales/revenue:** $730 million. **Number of employees at this location:** 500. **Number of employees nationwide:** Approximately 3,000.

MERCANTILE PENINSULA BANK
P.O. Box 219. Princess Anne MD 21853. 410/651-2400. **Physical address:** 11738 Somerset Avenue, Princess Anne MD 21853. **Fax:** 410/651-0179. **Contact:** Human Resources. **E-mail address:** peninisula.info@mercantile.net. **World Wide Web address:** http://www.peninsulabankmd.com. **Description:** A local Maryland Bank serving Ocean City area since 1889. **Positions advertised include:** Teller; Finance Manager.

MERCANTILE SAFE DEPOSIT & TRUST COMPANY
7301 Ritchie Highway, Glen Burnie MD 21061. 410/768-5252. **Contact:** Human Resources. **World Wide Web address:** http://www.mercantile.net. **Description:** Mercantile Engaged in general personal and corporate banking providing a full range of trust services. Mercantile Safe Deposit & Trust is the largest of the 21 banking and mortgage companies owned by Mercantile Bankshares Corporation. **Positions advertised include:** IRA Clerk. **Special programs:** Educational Assistance Program.

Parent company: Mercantile Bankshares Corporation (Baltimore MD). **Listed on:** NASDAQ. **Stock exchange symbol:** MRBK. **Number of employees at this location:** 400. **Number of employees nationwide:** 3,000.

MERCURY INTERACTIVE CORPORATION
8201 Corporate Drive, Suite 600, Landover MD 20785. 301/459-2163. **Fax:** 301/459-5916. **Contact:** Human Resources. **E-mail address:** jobs@merc-int.com. **World Wide Web address:** http://www-svca.mercuryinteractive.com. **Description:** A developer of automated software quality (ASQ) tools for enterprise applications testing. The company's products are used to isolate software and system errors prior to application deployment. Founded in 1989. **NOTE:** Interested jobseekers should direct resumes to Mercury Interactive, 1325 Borregas Avenue, Sunnyvale CA 94089. **Positions advertised include:** Contract Manager. **Corporate headquarters location:** Sunnyvale CA. **Other U.S. locations:** Nationwide. **International locations:** Worldwide. **Operations at this facility include:** This location is a sales office. **Listed on:** NASDAQ. **Stock exchange symbol:** MERQ. **President/CEO:** Amnon Landan. **Sales/revenue:** $400 million. **Number of employees worldwide:** 1,822.

MERCY MEDICAL CENTER
301 St. Paul Place, Baltimore MD 21202. 410/332-9743. **Fax:** 410/783-5863. **Recorded jobline:** 866/332-9414. **Contact:** Human Resources. **E-mail address:** edaly@mercymed.com. **World Wide Web address:** http://www.mdmercy.com. **Description:** An acute care general hospital. Specialty services at Mercy Medical Center include eating disorder treatment programs, women's services, detoxification facilities, and a sexual assault and crisis center. **Positions advertised include:** AC Service Technician; Admissions Coordinator; Patient Transport Aide; Anesthesia Technician; Clinical Nurse; Billing Clerk; Director of Facilities Services; Echocardiology Sonographer; Fire Safety Technician; IT Support Technician; Medical Transcriptionist; Medical Assistant; Medical Technologist; Patient Care Coordinator; Pharmacist; Phlebotomy Supervisor; Physical Therapy Assistant; Registrar; Systems Analyst; Security Officer. **Number of employees at this location:** 1,800.

METASTORM
8825 Stanford Boulevard, Suite 200, Columbia MD 21045. 410/290-0101. **Toll-free phone:** 877/321-META (6382). **Fax:** 410/290-1171. **E-mail address:** recruitment@metastorm.com. **World Wide Web address:** http://www.metastorm.com. **Description:** Provider of business process management (BPM) software for modeling, automating, and controlling processes. **Positions advertised include:** Account Executive (AE); Technical Support Analyst/Software Support Analyst. **Corporate headquarters location:** This location. **International locations:** Künten Switzerland; Wimbledon, London.

R.E. MICHEL COMPANY INC.
One R.E. Michel Drive, Glen Burnie MD 21060. 410/760-4000. **Contact:** Human Resources. **E-mail address:** jobs@remichel.com. **World Wide Web address:** http://www.remichel.com. **Description:** A wholesale distributor of air conditioning, heating, and refrigeration parts and supplies. **Positions advertised include:** Counter Sales Representative; Driver; Information Systems Help Desk Associate; Sales Representative; Warehouse Worker. **Office hours:** Monday – Friday, 8:00 a.m. – 4:00 p.m. – 11:00 a.m. **Other area locations:** Statewide. **Other U.S. locations:** Nationwide. **Operations at this facility include:** This location is a central distribution center.

MICROLOG CORPORATION OF MARYLAND
20270 Goldenrod Lane, Germantown MD 20876. 301/540-5500. **Fax:** 301/540-5557. **Contact:** Human Resources. **E-mail address:** human.resources@mlog.com. **World Wide Web address:** http://www.mlog.com. **Description:** Designs, assembles, and supports a line of interactive communications systems and application solutions software for customers worldwide. **Corporate headquarters location:** This location. **International locations:** The Netherlands. **Listed on:** OTC. **Stock exchange symbol:** MLOG. **Number of employees at this location:** 105. **Number of employees nationwide:** 300.

MICROS SYSTEMS, INC.
7031 Columbia Gateway Drive, Columbia MD 21046-2289. 443/285-6000. **Fax:** 443/285-0650. **Contact:** Personnel. **E-mail address:** employment@micros.com. **World Wide Web address:** http://www.micros.com. **Description:** Engaged in enterprise systems integration for the leisure and entertainment industries. **NOTE:** Entry-level positions are offered. **Positions advertised include:** Customer Care Account Specialist; Implementation Specialist; Network Specialist; Production Support Specialist; Project Specialist; Credit Representative; Payroll Analyst; Implementation Specialist; Product Specialist; Application Solutions Specialist; Restaurant Director POS Sales; Inside Sales Representative; Sales Executive; Account Executive. **Special programs:** Internships. **Office hours:** Monday – Friday, 8:00 a.m. – 5:00 p.m. **Corporate headquarters location:** This location. **Other U.S. locations:** Nationwide. **International locations:** Worldwide. **Subsidiaries include:** Fidelio Software Corporation; Fidelio Software GmbH. **Operations at this facility include:** Administration; Manufacturing; Regional Headquarters; Research and Development; Sales; Service. **Listed on:** NASDAQ. **Stock exchange symbol:** MCRS. **President/CEO:** Tom Giannopoulos. **Number of employees at this location:** 700. **Number of employees nationwide:** 900. **Number of employees worldwide:** 1,100.

MID-ATLANTIC COCA-COLA BOTTLING COMPANY
9770 Patuxent Woods Drive, Columbia MD 21046. 410/381-7800. **Contact:** Human Resources. **World Wide Web address:** http://www.cocacola.com. **Description:** Coca-Cola Enterprises Incorporated is one of the world's largest producers, marketers, and distributors of bottled products of The Coca-Cola Company. The company also bottles several other national and regional beverages such as Barq's and Dr. Pepper. **NOTE:** Must apply online at http://www.cokecce.com/careers. **Special programs:** Internships. **Corporate headquarters location:** Atlanta GA. **Other U.S. locations:** Nationwide. **International locations:** Worldwide. **Operations at this facility include:** Division Headquarters; Sales. **Listed on:** New York Stock Exchange. **Stock exchange symbol:** CCE. **CEO/Chairman:** Lowry F. Kline. **Sales/revenue:** Approximately $17 billion. **Number of employees worldwide:** 72,000.

MID-ATLANTIC MEDICAL SERVICES, INC. (MAMSI)
4 Taft Court, Rockville MD 20850. 301/294-5057. **Fax:** 301/545-5389. **Contact:** Human Resources. **E-mail address:** rockvilleresume@mamsi.com. **World Wide Web address:** http://www.mamsi.com. **Description:** A holding company whose subsidiaries are active in managed health care. MAMSI operates two health maintenance organizations: Maryland Individual Practice Association, Incorporated and Optimum Choice, Incorporated, a nonfederally qualified HMO that serves commercial and other specialized markets such as Medicare and Medicaid. Other MAMSI subsidiaries include Alliance PPO, Incorporated, a preferred provider organization marketing its provider network products to self-insured employers, indemnity carriers, and other health care purchasing groups; Mid-Atlantic Psychiatric Services, Incorporated, which provides specialized nonrisk mental health services; and FirstCall and HomeCall, which provide nursing and care to patients who are confined to their homes. **Positions advertised include:** Web Designer; Web Developer; ARS Sales Representative; Actuate; Developer Representative; Sales Analyst; Applications Developer; Programming Analyst; SQV Database Analyst; Staff Accountant; Implementation Specialist; Program Manager; Benefits Consultant. **Corporate headquarters location:** This location. **Listed on:** New York Stock Exchange. **Stock exchange symbol:** MME. **Number of employees nationwide:** 2,025.

MILES & STOCKBRIDGE
10 Light Street, Baltimore MD 21202-1487. 410/385-3563. **Fax:** 410/385-3700. **Contact:** Randi Lewis, Director of Diversity and Professional Development. **E-mail address:** lewis@milesstockbridge.com. **World Wide Web address:** http://www.milesstockbridge.com. **Description:** A law firm that operates on a regional level in the practice areas of business, litigation, and commercial law. Founded in 1932. **NOTE:** To contact Human Resources directly, call 410/385-3563. **Positions advertised include:** Senior Business Lawyer; Senior Estate Planning and Probate Lawyer; Corporate Lawyer; Litigation Associate; Paralegal. **Special programs:** Summer Associate Program. **Other area locations:** Cambridge MD; Columbia MD; Easton MD; Frederick MD; Rockville MD; Towson MD. **Other U.S. locations:** Tysons Corner VA; Washington DC.

MILLENNIUM CHEMICALS
20 Wight Avenue, Suite 100, Hunt Valley MD 21030. 410/229-4400. **Fax:** 410/229-5003. **Contact:** Human Resources. **World Wide Web address:** http://www.millenniumchem.com. **Description:** A chemical company whose products include paints, coatings, resins, lacquers, and other chemicals for commodity, industrial, performance, and specialty applications. **NOTE:** Apply online only. **Positions advertised include:** Accounting Manager; Information Technology Analyst; Accountant Policies Control Associate; Technical Service Marketing Manager; Chemist Technical Support Analyst. **Special programs:** Educational Assistance Program; Fitness Reimbursement Program. **Corporate headquarters location:** Red Bank NJ. **Other U.S. locations:** Nationwide. **International locations:** Worldwide. **Operations at this facility include:** This location produces specialized titanium dioxide pigments for industrial and related uses. **Listed on:** New York Stock Exchange. **Stock exchange symbol:** MCH. **Number of employees nationwide:** 1,500. **Number of employees worldwide:** Over 4,000.

MILLER & LONG COMPANY, INC.
4824 Rugby Avenue, Bethesda MD 20814. 301/657-8000. **Contact:** Miles Gladstone, Personnel Director. **E-mail address:** hr@millerandlong.com. **World Wide Web address:** http://www.millerandlong.com. **Description:** A construction firm specializing in high-rise concrete construction. Founded in 1947. **NOTE:** Resumes may be submitted via e-mail. **Corporate headquarters location:** This location. **Other area locations:** Baltimore MD. **Other U.S. locations:** Garner NC.

MINE SAFETY APPLIANCES COMPANY (MSA)
38 Loveton Circle, Sparks MD 21152. 410/472-7700. **Contact:** Human Resources. **E-mail address:** msa.jobs.1@msanet.com. **World Wide Web address:** http://www.msanet.com. **Description:** MSA manufactures a variety of gas masks and respiratory protection products, protective headgear, and gas and vapor sensors for supply to the fire service, mining, construction, and industrial subcontracting industries. The company is divided into two major operating groups. The Safety Products Division designs and manufactures full face pieces for self-contained breathing apparatuses, respirators, communication equipment for breathing apparatuses, cooling vests designed to combat heat stress, and a hand-held infrared heat detector. The Instrument Division makes a variety of monitors and sensors. MSA's international affiliates manufacture a wide array of equipment ranging from thermal imaging cameras to air supply units. **Positions advertised include:** Buyer; Planner; Internal Staff Auditor. **Corporate headquarters location:** Pittsburgh PA. **Other U.S. locations:** Nationwide. **International locations:** Worldwide. **Operations at this facility include:** Manufacturing. **Listed on:** American Stock Exchange. **Stock exchange symbol:** MSA. **Number of employees at this location:** 30.

MONARCH SERVICES
4517 Harford Road, Baltimore MD 21214. 410/254-9200. **Contact:** Human Resources. **Description:** Publishes *Girls' Life* magazine and *Adam* magazine. The company also owns and operates a food court and tobacco and coffee shop. **Corporate headquarters location:** This location. **Listed on:** NASDAQ. **Stock exchange symbol:** MAHI. **President/CEO:** Jackson Dott. **Sales/revenue:** $2.2 billion. **Number of employees at this location:** 23.

MONTGOMERY COMMUNITY TELEVISION
7548 Standish Place, Rockville MD 20855. 301/424-1730. **Fax:** 301/294-7476. **Contact:** Human Resources Department. **E-mail address:** dwillett@Montgomerycommunity.com. **World Wide Web address:** http://www.Montgomerycommunitytv.com. **Description:** Operates two cable channels, produces original programming, and provides production training and facilities for residents of Montgomery County. **Positions advertised include:** Post Production Assistant- Access Facilities; Network Manager- Web Master; Production Technician. **Special programs:** Internships. **Office hours:** Monday – Friday, 9:00 a.m. – 5:30 p.m. **Corporate headquarters location:** This location. **Number of employees at this location:** 70.

MONTGOMERY COUNTY COMMUNITY CORRECTIONS PRE-RELEASE CENTER
11651 Nebel Street, Rockville MD 20852. 301/468-4200. **Fax:** 301/468-4720. **Contact:** Human Resources. **World Wide Web address:** http://www.montgomercountymd.gov. **Description:** Provides community correctional alternatives between probation/parole supervision and security confinement for male and female offenders. **Positions advertised include:** Correctional Dietary Officer; Correctional Specialist; Resident Supervisor. **Special programs:** Internships.

MONTGOMERY GENERAL HOSPITAL
18101 Prince Philip Drive, Olney MD 20832. 301/774-8666. **Fax:** 301/774-7389. **Recorded jobline:** 301/774-8787. **Contact:** Human Resources. **World Wide Web address:** http://www.montgomerygeneral.com. **Description:** A 229-bed, nonprofit, acute care, community hospital. **Positions advertised include:** Administrative Supervisor; Addiction and Mental Health Center Counselor; Cardiovascular/Radiology Nurse; Charge Nurse; Director of Performance Improvement Risk Management; Environmental Assistant; Field Psychiatric Registered Nurse; Home Care Aide; LPN; Nursing Technician; Phlebotomy Clerk; Occupational Therapist; Performance Improvement Specialist; Physical Therapist; Radiologic Technologist; Security Officer; Special Procedures Technician; Speech/Language Pathologist; Unit Clerk; Ultrasound Technologist. **Office hours:** Monday - Friday, 9:00 a.m. - 5:00 p.m. **Operations at this facility include:** Administration. **Listed on:** Privately held. **President/CEO:** Peter W. Monge. **Number of employees at this location:** Over 1,000.

MONTGOMERY VILLAGE FOUNDATION
10120 Apple Ridge Road, Montgomery Village MD 20886. 301/949-0110. **Toll-free phone:** 800/215-1784. **Fax:** 301//990-7071. **E-mail address:** mvinfo@mvf.org. **Contact:** William Koarid, Human Resources. **World Wide Web address:** http://www.mvf.org. **Description:** A planned living community with 35,000 residents living in Montgomery County. **Positions advertised include:** Aquatics Assistant; Facilities Manager; Part Time Receptionist; Seasonal Receptionist.

MORGAN STATE UNIVERSITY
1700 East Cold Spring Lane, Baltimore MD 21251. 443/885-3333. **Contact:** Kenneth Johnson, Human Resources. **E-mail address:** jobs@moac.morgan.edu. **World Wide Web address:** http://www.morgan.edu. **Description:** Morgan State University is an African-American institution conferring degrees to the doctoral level. The university offers programs through the College of Arts and Sciences; the School of Education and Urban Studies; and the School of Engineering. **NOTE:** To contact Human Resources directly, call 443/885-3195. Applications are available online. **Positions advertised include:** Program Contract Manager; Grants Associate; Assistant to Assistant Vice President; Administrative Assistant; Office Secretary; Architecture CADD Technician; Broadcast Engineer; Director of Financial Aide. **Special programs:** Internships. **President:** Earl Richardson.

MOSAIC COMMUNITY SERVICES, INC.
1925 Greenspring Drive, Timonium MD 21093. 410/453-9553 ext. 102. **Contact:** Human Resources. **World Wide Web address:** http://www.mosaicinc.org. **Description:** A mental health care provider offering a variety of services and community programs. **Positions advertised include:** Accounting Clerks; Accountant; Administrative Assistants; Licensed Mental Health Professionals; Program Coordinators; Program Specialists; Rehabilitation Counselors; Residential Service Coordinators.

MOTOROLA COMMUNICATIONS & ELECTRONICS, INC.
7230 Parkway Drive, Hanover MD 21076. 410/712-6881. **Contact:** Human Resources. **World Wide Web address:** http://www.mot.com. **Description:** Manufactures electronic equipment and components. **Positions advertised include:** Project Manager. **Other U.S. locations:** Nationwide. **International locations:** Worldwide. **Parent company:** Motorola, Incorporated, provides integrated communications and embedded electronic solutions. The company's products include microwave, satellite, and wireless communications systems and equipment. **Operations at this facility include:** This location is a regional sales office. **Listed on:** New York Stock Exchange. **Stock exchange symbol:** MOT.

MULTIMAX, INC.
1441 McCormick Drive, Largo MD 20774. 301/925-8222. **Toll-free phone:** 800/339-8828. **Fax:** 301/925-2956. **Contact:** Human Resources Department. **E-mail address:** hrmd@multimax.com. **World Wide Web address:** http://www.multimax.com. **Description:** Provides LAN/WAN design and networking services to customers in the government and commercial sectors. **Positions advertised include:** Business Developer; Account Manager; Federal Information Technology Services Associate; Computer Sales Associate. **Corporate headquarters location:** This location. **Other U.S. locations:** Beavercreek OH; Tinton Falls NJ; Atlantic City NJ; Montgomery AL; Indialantic FL; Nashua NH; Virginia Beach VA; Alexandria VA.

MURRY'S INC.
8300 Pennsylvania Avenue, Upper Marlboro MD 20772-2673. 301/967-5593x593. **Toll-free phone:** 800/782-1516. **Contact:** Human Resources. **E-mail address:** hr@murrys.com. **World Wide Web address:** http://www.murrys.com. **Description:** Engaged in the manufacture, distribution, retail, and wholesale of frozen meats and specialty food items. **Positions advertised include:** General Manager; Produce Specialist; Cashier; District Manager; Store Manager; Warehouse Supervisor. **Corporate headquarters location:** This location. **Other U.S. locations:** Washington DC; Baltimore MD.

NSGDATA.COM, INC.
7435 New Technology Way, Frederick MD 21703-9401. 301/662-5926. **Contact:** Human Resources. **E-mail address:** info@nsgdata.com. **World Wide Web address:** http://www.nsgdata.com. **Description:** Designs and markets data communications (packet switching and radio frequency) equipment on a worldwide basis. **Corporate headquarters location:** This location. **President:** Dr. Graham King.

NVR, INC.
7601 Lewinsville Road, Suite 300, McLean VA 22102. 703/761-2000. **Fax:** 703/761-2030. **Contact:** Human Resources. **E-mail address:** elresumes@nvrinc.com. **World Wide Web address:** http://www.nvrinc.com. **Description:** A homebuilding and mortgage banking company. **Positions advertised include:** Loan Processor; Regional Manager; Unified Construction System (UCS) Group Administrator. **Corporate headquarters location:** This location. **Other area locations:** Statewide. **Other U.S. locations:** Nationwide.

THE NATIONAL AQUARIUM
501 East Pratt Street, Baltimore MD 21202. 410/576-3800. **Contact:** Human Resources. **E-mail address:** jobs@aqua.com. **World Wide Web address:** http://www.aqua.org. **Description:** An aquarium institute focused on environmental conservation. **Positions advertised include:** Publications Manager; Sales Associate; Security Officer; Veterinary Associate; Visitor Advocate. **Special programs:** Internships. **Executive Director:** David M. Pittenger.

NATIONAL ARCHIVES AND RECORDS ADMINISTRATION
8601 Adelphi Road, Room 1200, College Park MD 20740-6001. 301/837-3670. **Contact:** Human Resources. **World Wide Web address:** http://www.nara.gov. **Description:** Manages federal records and makes these records readily available for public use and research purposes. **Positions advertised include:** Archives Information Technologies Specialist; Application Management Analyst; Manager; Program Analyst; Microphotographic Technician; Records Analyst; Motor Vehicle Operator. **Special programs:** Internships; Training. **Corporate headquarters location:** This location. **Other U.S. locations:** Nationwide.

NATIONAL ASSOCIATION OF BLACK ACCOUNTANTS
7249-A Hanover Parkway, Greenbelt MD 20770. 301/474-6222. **Fax:** 301/474-3114. **Contact:** Challenge Okiwe, Program Coordinator. **World Wide Web address:** http://www.nabainc.org. **Description:** A nonprofit membership organization for accounting and business professionals and students. The association has nationwide chapters. Founded in 1969. **Special programs:** Internships. **Corporate headquarters location:** This location. **Operations at this facility include:** Administration. **Listed on:** Privately held. **President:** Kim Griffin-Hunter. **Number of employees at this location:** 10.

NATIONAL FEDERATION OF THE BLIND
NATIONAL CENTER FOR THE BLIND
1800 Johnson Street, Baltimore MD 21230. 410/659-9314. **Contact:** Human Resources. **World Wide Web address:** http://www.nfb.org. **Description:** An organization geared toward helping blind people. The organization provides literature and public education about blindness; equipment to assist the blind; and offers the Job Opportunities for the Blind program that helps blind persons who are seeking employment. Founded in 1940.

NATIONAL GYPSUM COMPANY
2301 South Newkirk Street, Baltimore MD 21224. 410/631-4900x4920. **Contact:** Sue Tyber, Personnel Director. **World Wide Web address:** http://www.national-gypsum.com. **Description:** National Gypsum is an integrated, diversified manufacturer of products for building, construction, and shelter markets. The company specializes in gypsum wallboard and joint compounds. **NOTE:** Interested job seekers may apply online. **Positions advertised include:** Market Development Representative. **Corporate headquarters location:** Charlotte NC. **Other U.S. locations:** Nationwide. **International locations:** Canada. **Operations at this facility include:** Manufacturing. **Listed on:** Privately held. **Number of employees at this location:** 150.

THE NELSON COMPANY
2116 Sparrows Point Road, Baltimore MD 21219-1798. 410/477-3000. **Fax:** 410/388-0246. **Contact:** Human Resources. **World Wide Web address:** http://www.nelsoncompany.com. **Description:** Produces wooden boxes, pallets, crates, angleboard, and corrugated boxes. The Nelson Company also recycles pallets. Founded in 1921. **Corporate headquarters location:** This location. **Other U.S. locations:** New Castle PA; Raleigh NC; Conyers GA; Jackson MI; Memphis TN; Walton KS.

NEVAMAR CORPORATION
8339 Telegraph Road, Odenton MD 21113. 410/551-5000. **Contact:** Human Resources. **World Wide Web address:** http://www.internationalpaper.com. **Description:** Manufactures decorative surfacing materials marketed to the furniture, fixtures, cabinets, and graphic arts industries. **Corporate headquarters location:** Hanover MD. **Other U.S. locations:** Charlotte NC; Portland OR; Dallas TX; Westampton NJ; Aurora IL; Cerritos CA; Hampton SC. **International locations:** Singapore.

NEWROADS, INC.
2 North Maple Avenue, Ridgely MD 21660. 410/634-2060. **Contact:** Human Resources. **E-mail address:** info@newroads.com. **World Wide Web address:** http://www.newroads.com. **Description:** Provides outsourced operations solutions to companies engaged in one-to-one direct commerce. **NOTE:** Resumes should be mailed to NewRoads, Incorporated, 75 Holy Hill Lane, Greenwich CT 06830, or faxed to 203/625-4767. **Corporate headquarters location:** Greenwich CT. **President/CEO:** Fred Forsyth.

NORTH ARUNDEL HOSPITAL
301 Hospital Drive, Glen Burnie MD 21061. 410/787-4000. **Fax:** 410/553-0671. **Recorded jobline:** 410/787-4270. **Contact:** Human Resources. **World Wide Web address:** http://www.northarundel.org. **Description:** A full-service hospital that offers care in the ambulatory surgery, cardiology, community health and wellness programs, comprehensive rehabilitation care, emergency, endoscopy, home care, laboratory, nursing, oncology, orthopedic, primary care, pediatrics, psychiatry, radiology, and respiratory and pulmonary fields. **Positions advertised include:** Registered Nurse; Nurse Practitioner; Nurse Manager. **NOTE:** Online applications are available. Part-time positions and second and third shifts are offered. **Office hours:** Monday – Friday, 9:00 a.m. – 3:00 p.m.

NORTHROP GRUMMAN
7501 Greenway Center Drive, Suite 1000, Greenbelt MD 20770. 301/446-3100. **Fax:** 301/446-3322. **Contact:** Personnel. **World Wide Web address:** http://www.northropgrummanit.com. **Description:** Northrop Grumman's Computing Systems division specializes in custom software development and systems integration. **Positions advertised include:** Administrative Assistant; Account Manager; Inside Sales Representative; Sales Director; Enterprise Software Consultant; Lease Operations Analyst; Alliance Partner Manager; Strategic Operations Planning Manager; General Security Representative; Accounts Receivable Clerk; Quality Assurance Analyst; Team Leader Systems Engineer; Civilian Sales Manager. **Corporate headquarters location:** Los Angeles CA. **Other U.S. locations:** Nationwide. **Operations at this facility include:** This location is part of the Information Technology sector of Northrop Grumman Corporation. **Listed on:** New York Stock Exchange. **Stock exchange symbol:** NOC.

NORTHROP GRUMMAN ADVANCED SYSTEMS
dba DENRO SYSTEMS
9318 Gaither Road, Gaithersburg MD 20877. 301/840-1597. **Contact:** Human Resources. **World Wide Web address:** http://www.denro.com. **Description:** Designs, manufactures, and services electronic communications equipment primarily for the air traffic control industry. **Special programs:** Internships. **Corporate headquarters location:** Los Angeles CA. **Parent company:** Northrop Grumman Corporation. **Operations at this facility include:** Manufacturing; Research and Development; Sales; Service. **Listed on:** New York Stock Exchange. **Stock exchange symbol:** NOC.

NORTHROP GRUMMAN CORPORATION
895 Oceanic Drive, Annapolis MD 21401. 410/260-5000. **Contact:** Human Resources. **E-mail address:** jobs_esss@md.northgrum.com. **World Wide Web address:** http://www.northgrum.com. **Description:** Northrop Grumman manufactures military aircraft, commercial aircraft, radar equipment, and other electronic systems. Northrop Grumman has developed the B-2 Stealth Bomber, parts for the F/A-18 and the 747. Other operations include computer systems developed for management and scientific applications. **Positions advertised include:** Controlled Material Monitor; Designer; Senior Structural Engineer. **Corporate headquarters location:** Los Angeles CA. **Operations at this facility include:** This location is part of the Electronic Systems sector of Northrop Grumman Corporation. **Listed on:** New York Stock Exchange. **Stock exchange symbol:** NOC.

NORTHROP GRUMMAN ELECTRONIC SENSORS & SYSTEMS SECTOR
1580-A West Nursery Road, Linthicum MD 21090. 410/765-1000. **Contact:** Human Resources. **E-mail address:** Jobs_ESSS@ngc.com. **World Wide Web address:** http://www.es.northropgrumman.com/index.html. **Description:** Northrop Grumman manufactures military aircraft, commercial aircraft, and electronic systems. Northrop Grumman has developed the B-2 Spirit Stealth Bomber and parts for the F/A-18 and the 747. Other operations include computer systems developed for management and scientific applications. **NOTE:** Entry-level positions and part-time jobs are offered. **Positions advertised include:** Manager NGAD East; Technology Auditor Specialist; Product Support Representative. **Special programs:** Internships; Training; Summer Jobs. **Internship information:** Summer internship opportunities are offered for college

juniors and seniors in electrical engineering, computer science, mechanical engineering, and industrial engineering. An overall GPA of 3.5/4.0 is required. Resumes and transcripts must be received by March 1. **Corporate headquarters location:** Los Angeles CA. **Other U.S. locations:** Nationwide. **International locations:** Worldwide. **Subsidiaries include:** Norden Systems (Norwalk CT); Xetron Corporation (Cincinnati OH). **Parent company:** Northrop Grumman Corporation. **Operations at this facility include:** This location is the divisional headquarters of the Electronic Systems sector of Northrop Grumman Corporation. This company is engaged in the research and development, design, integration, and manufacture of advanced electronic sensors and systems for the U.S. government, its allies, and other industrial and commercial customers. Major products include airborne and ground-based radar; electronic countermeasures; air traffic control and air defense systems; electro-optical sensors; solid-state devices; sonar and antisubmarine warfare systems; and advanced imaging systems. **Listed on:** New York Stock Exchange. **Stock exchange symbol:** NOC. **Number of employees at this location:** 6,000. **Number of employees nationwide:** 14,000. **Number of employees worldwide:** Over 22,000.

NORTHROP GRUMMAN INFORMATION TECHNOLOGY
4800 Hampden Lane, Suite 1100, Bethesda MD 20814. 301/986-0800. **Contact:** Human Resources. **World Wide Web address:** http://www.northropgrummanit.com. **Description:** Provides information technology services and solutions. **Positions advertised include:** Web Software Designer; Multimedia Designer; Help Desk Associate; Contracts Administrator; Media Producer; Photographer; Graphic Artist; Media Script Writer; Viideographer; Network Manager Engineer. **Special programs:** Internships; Training; Summer Jobs. **Corporate headquarters location:** Herndon VA. **Other U.S. locations:** Nationwide. **International locations:** Germany; Korea. **Listed on:** New York Stock Exchange. **Stock exchange symbol:** NOC.

NORTHWEST HOSPITAL CENTER
5401 Old Court Road, Baltimore MD 21133-5103. 410/521-2200. **Contact:** Human Resources. **World Wide Web address:** http://www.lifebridgehealth.org. **Description:** Northwest Hospital Center is a 240-bed, private, nonprofit hospital with more than 500 doctors specializing in a range of fields. The hospital serves the health care needs of the northwest Baltimore metropolitan area. The hospital is accredited by the Joint Commission on Accreditation of Healthcare Organizations, the American Association of Blood Banks, and the College of American Pathologists. Northwest Hospital Center is affiliated with Cherrywood Manor Extended Care Centre, a 161-bed nursing home. Northwest Hospital Center is also a member of the SunHealth Network, the Preferred Health Network of Maryland, and the Maryland Hospital Association. **NOTE:** Online applications are available. **Positions advertised include:** Registered Nurse; Licensed Practical Nurse; Clinical Nurse; Nurse Manager; Nursing Director; Emergency Room Technician; Sitter; CAT Scan Technician; Medical Radiation Technician; Nuclear Medicine Technologist; Physical & Occupational Therapist; Respiratory Therapist. **Special programs:** Tuition Reimbursement Program.

OCEAN CITY MD RECREATION & PARKS
P.O. Box 15. Ocean City MD 21842. 410/250-0125. **Physical address:** 200 125th Street, Ocean City MD 21842. **Contact:** Human Resources Manager. **E-mail address:** dcockrell@ococean.com. **World Wide Web address:** http://www.ococean.com. **Description:** Recreation and parks information for Ocean City. **Positions advertised include:** Special Events Operations Manager.

ORFG OPERATIONS
7200 Wisconsin Avenue, Suite 1100, Bethesda MD 20814. 301/654-3100. **Contact:** Human Resources. **Description:** Manages apartment complexes.

ONGUARD INDUSTRIES, L.L.C.
1850 Clark Road, Harve De Grace MD 21078. 410/272-2000. **Fax:** 410/272-3346. **Contact:** Human Resources. **World Wide Web address:** http://www.onguardindustries.com. **Description:** A manufacturer and marketer of industrial protective footwear, safety boots, and related products. **Positions advertised include:** Production Worker. **Office Hours:** Monday – Friday, 8:00 a.m. – 4:00 p.m.

OPTELECOM, INC.
12920 Cloverleaf Center Drive, Germantown MD 20874. 301/444-2200. **Toll-free phone:** 800/293-4237. **Contact:** Diane Mortazavi, Human Resources Manager. **E-mail address:** humanresources@optelecom.com. **World Wide Web address:** http://www.optelecom.com. **Description:** Designs and manufactures various communication products such as modems and interface cards for video, audio, and data transmission. Optelecom also performs coil windings. **NOTE:** To contact Human Resources directly, call 301/444-2223. **Corporate headquarters location:** This location. **International locations:** Worldwide. **Listed on:** NASDAQ. **Stock exchange symbol:** OPTC. **President/CEO:** Edmund D. Ludwig.

ORBITAL SCIENCES CORPORATION
7160 Riverwood Drive, Columbia MD 21046. 443/259-7000. **Contact:** Human Resources. **World Wide Web address:** http://www.orbital.com. **Description:** Designs, develops, and produces space electronics and other spacecraft systems; digital avionics equipment; communication and intelligence systems; and components and subsystems for aerospace applications. The company is composed of five business units: Space Technical Services, Transportation Management Systems, Launch Vehicle Systems, Missile Defense Systems, and Satellites and Space Systems. Founded in 1982. **Positions advertised include:** Associate Software Designer; Principal Software Tester; Test Engineer; Software Engineer. **Corporate headquarters location:** Dulles VA. **Other area locations:** Greenbelt MD. **Other U.S. locations:** Pomona CA; Houston TX; Chandler AZ; Vandenberg AFB CA. **Operations at this facility include:** Administration; Manufacturing; Research and Development; Service. This location is part of the Transportation Management Systems Division. **Listed on:** New York Stock Exchange. **Stock exchange symbol:** ORB. **CEO/Chairman:** David W. Thompson. **Number of employees at this location:** 1,000. **Number of employees worldwide:** 5,200.

OSIRIS THERAPEUTICS, INC.
2001 Aliceanna Street, Baltimore MD 21231-3043. 410/522-5005. **Fax:** 410/522-5519. **Contact:** Human Resources. **E-mail address:** hr@osiristx.com. **World Wide Web address:** http://www.osiristx.com. **Description:** Osiris Therapeutics is a clinical stage biotechnology company founded for the purpose of commercializing stem cell products harvested from a readily available but non-controversial source (adult bone marrow). **Positions advertised include:** Manufacturing Associate/Cell Technician. **Corporate headquarters location:** This location.

PHH ARVAL
940 Ridgebrook Drive, Sparks MD 21152. 410/771-3600. **Fax:** 410/771-2962. **Contact:** Human Resources. **World Wide Web address:** http://www.phh.com. **Description:** PHH Arval offers vehicle management services consisting primarily of the management, purchase, leasing, and resale of vehicles for corporate clients and government agencies including fuel and expense management programs and other fee-based services for clients' vehicle fleets. Founded in 1946. **NOTE:** Apply online. **Positions advertised include:** Business Development Executive; D&A Specialist; Fuel Auditor; Client Liaison; Title Associate; Damage Specialist; Administration Assistant; Regional Director; MSO Associate; Service Specialist; Vehicle Accident Services Director; Process Implementation Project Leader; East Coast Member Benefits Manager. **Special programs:** Tuition Assistance Program; Adoption Assistance Program. **Office hours:** Monday – Friday, 9:00 a.m. – 5:00 p.m. **Corporate headquarters location:** This location. **Other U.S. locations:** Nationwide. **International locations:** Worldwide. **Parent company:** Cendant Corporation. **Listed on:** New York Stock Exchange. **Stock exchange symbol:** CD. **President/CEO:** George J. Kilroy.

PALL CORPORATION
FILTERITE DIVISION
2118 Green Spring Drive, Timonium MD 21093. 410/252-0800. **Fax:** 410/560-3044. **Contact:** Human Resources. **World Wide Web address:** http://www.filterite.com. **Description:** Produces filters, filtration equipment, strainers, and related items for water and wastewater treatment and management. USFilter also operates research and development facilities. **Positions advertised include:** Maintenance Worker. **Special programs:** Internships; Apprenticeships; Training; Tuition Reimbursement Program. **Corporate headquarters location:** This location. **International locations:** United Kingdom; Singapore; France; Italy; Germany; Japan; Australia. **Parent company:** Pall Corporation. **Operations at this facility include:** Administration; Manufacturing; Research and Development; Sales; Service. **Listed on:** New York Stock Exchange. **Stock exchange symbol:** PLL. **President:** Ronald T. Riley. **Number of employees at this location:** 400.

PARADISE PLAZA INN
9th Street, Ocean City Maryland 21842. 410/289-6381. **Fax:** 410/289-1303. **Toll-free phone:** 888/678-4111. **Contact:** Human Resources. **World Wide Web address:** http://www,paradiseplazainn.com. **Description:** An AAA approved hotel on the boardwalk in Ocean City Maryland. **Positions advertised include:** Maintenance Manager.

PATTON ELECTRONICS COMPANY
7622 Rickenbacker Drive, Gaithersburg MD 20879. 301/975-1000. **Contact:** Human Resources. **E-mail address:** employment@patton.com. **World Wide Web address:** http://www.patton.com. **Description:** Manufactures computer hardware including modems, surge protectors, and interface converters. Founded in 1984. **Positions advertised include:** National Account Representative; Regional Account Representative; Outside Sales; Nuclear Medicine Technician; Respiratory Monitor; Buyer; Respiratory Therapist; Mortgage Banker; Purchasing Assistant; Human Resource Manager. **Corporate headquarters location:** This location. **International locations:** Worldwide. **Listed on:** Privately held. **Annual sales/revenues:** $11 - $20 million. **CEO:** Robert E. Patton. **Number of employees worldwide:** Over 170.

PENINSULA REGIONAL MEDICAL CENTER
100 East Carroll Street, Salisbury MD 21801 410/546-6400. **Contact:** Human Resources. **World Wide Web address:** http;//www.peninsula.org. **Description:** A 106 year old Care facility with 322 acute & 36 sub acute care beds. **Positions advertised include:** Environmental Services Aide; Licensed Practical Nurse; Clinical Technician; Registered Nurse; Personal Care Assistant; Inventory Control Coordinator; Security Police; Nurse Assistant; Health Care Center Manager; Radiology Registered Nurse; Medical Lab Technician; Cat Scan Technician; Console Operator; Clinical Dietitian; Hospitalist.

PERDUE FARMS, INC.
P.O. Box 1537, Salisbury MD 21802-1537. 410/543-3000. **Physical address:** 31149 Old Ocean City Road, Salisbury MD 21804. **Fax:** 410/860-4329. **Contact:** Human Resources. **World Wide Web address:** http://www.perdue.com. **Description:** One of the largest suppliers of fresh and processed poultry products in the United States. The company's products are sold in supermarkets, small grocery stores, warehouse clubs, and butcher shops. Perdue Farms is a fully-integrated operation, from overseeing breeding and hatching to delivering packaged goods to market. **Positions advertised include:** Logistics Customer Accountant; Breeder; Accounting Specialist; Foot Technologist Supervisor; Network Design Engineer; Manager; Logistics Analyst; Food Technologist; Systems Analyst; Purchasing Manager; Instructional Finance Director; Application Systems Project Leader; Information System Finance Manager; Windows Administrator. **Special programs:** Internships. **Corporate headquarters location:** This location. **Other U.S. locations:** Nationwide. **Operations at this facility include:** Administration; Logistics; Marketing; Research and Development; Sales. **CEO/Chairman:** Jim Perdue. **Sales/revenue:** Over $2.7 billion. **Number of employees at this location:** 550. **Number of employees nationwide:** 20,000.

PERKINELMER FLUID SCIENCES
11600 Old Baltimore Pike, Beltsville MD 20705-1294. 301/937-4010. **Fax:** 301/902-3414. **Toll-free phone:** 800/775-6786. **Contact:** Human Resources. **World Wide Web address:** http://www.perkinelmer.com. **Description:** A manufacturer of mechanical components and subsystems for aerospace and industrial applications. Products include valves, seals, and bellows. **Positions advertised include:** Accountant; Manufacturing Engineer. **Corporate headquarters location:** Wellesley MA. **Other U.S. locations:** Nationwide. **Parent company:** PerkinElmer is a diversified technology company that operates through four business units: Life Sciences, Optoelectronics, Instruments, and Fluid Sciences. **Listed on:** New York Stock Exchange. **Stock exchange symbol:** PKI. **President:** Robert A. Barrett.

POLK AUDIO
5601 Metro Drive, Baltimore MD 21215. 410/358-3600. **Fax:** 410/764-4812. **Contact:** Human Resources. **World Wide Web address:** http://www.polkaudio.com. **Description:** Designs, manufactures, and markets audio speaker systems under the brand names Polk Audio and Eosone for use in homes and automobiles. Founded in 1972. **Corporate headquarters location:** This location.

POLY-SEAL BERRY PLASTICS CORPORATION
1810 Portal Street, Baltimore MD 21224. 410/633-1990. **Fax:** 410/631-1344. **Contact:** Human Resources. **E-mail address:** pscapinfo@berryplastics.com. **World Wide Web address:** http://www.poly-seal.com. **Description:** Manufactures plastic caps for pharmaceutical and personal health care product bottles including lotion and shampoo bottles. **Corporate headquarters location:** Evansville IN. **Parent company:** Berry Plastics Corporation.

POWERCON CORPORATION
1551 Florida Avenue, P.O. Box 477, Severn MD 21144. 410/551-6500. **Contact:** Human Resources. **E-mail address:** info@powerconcorp.com. **World Wide Web address:** http://www.powerconcorp.com. **Description:** Manufactures medium voltage electrical switchgears for use by electric, gas, and private companies.

THE PRESIDIO CORPORATION
5100-J Philadelphia Way, Lanham MD 20706. 301/459-2200. **Fax:** 301/955-3554. **Contact:** Human Resources. **E-mail address:** jobs@presido.com. **World Wide Web address:** http://www.presidio.com. **Description:** Provides applications and systems integration that enable electronic mail, file exchanges, shared peripherals, and a wide range of group applications. **NOTE:** Mail resumes to 7601 Ora Glen Drive, Suite 100, Greenbelt MD 20770. Resumes sent via e-mail must be formatted in ASCII text. **Company slogan:** Delivering unified solutions. **Corporate headquarters location:** This location. **Other U.S. locations:** CA; FL; GA; VA; TX; NC. **CEO/Chairperson:** Kristine Cruikshank. **Listed on:** Privately held.

PRICEWATERHOUSECOOPERS
250 West Pratt Street, Suite 2100, Baltimore MD 21201-2304. 410/783-7600. **Contact:** Human Resources. **World Wide Web address:** http://www.pwcglobal.com. **Description:** A certified public accounting firms with worldwide operations. PricewaterhouseCoopers provides public accounting, business advisory, management consulting, and taxation services. **NOTE:** Online applications area available. **Positions advertised include:** Senior Associate Auditor; GRMS Internal Audit Associate; HCP Experienced Associate; Middle Market Tax Senior Associate; Middle Market Tax Manager; Business Solutions Development Manager. **Corporate headquarters location:** New York NY. **Other U.S. locations:** Nationwide. **International locations:** Worldwide. **Global Chairman:** Andrew Ratcliffe. **Sales/revenue:** Approximately $14 billion. **Number of employees worldwide:** 125,000.

THE PRINCE GEORGE'S PUBLICK PLAYHOUSE FOR THE PERFORMING ARTS
5445 Landover Road, Cheverly MD 20784-1225. 301/277-1711. **Contact:** Hiring Manager. **World Wide Web address:** http://www.pgparks.com/places/artsfac/publick.html. **Description:** A theater offering dramatic, dance, and musical performances year-round. Founded in 1947. **Corporate headquarters location:** This location.

PROCTER & GAMBLE
COSMETIC AND FRAGRANCE SALES
11050 York Road, Cockeysville MD 21030-2098. 410/785-4600. **Contact:** Human Resources. **World Wide Web address:** http://www.pg.com. **Description:** Procter & Gamble manufactures over 300 laundry, cleaning, paper, beauty, health care, food, and beverage products in more than 140 countries. Brand name products include Cover Girl, Max Factor, Vidal Sassoon, Clearasil, and Noxzema health and beauty products; Pepto-Bismol, Vicks, and NyQuil health care products; Bounce, Downy, Tide, Comet, and Mr. Clean cleaning products; Luvs, Pampers, Always, Tampax, Bounty, Charmin, and Puffs paper products; and Crisco, Folgers, Millstone, Sunny Delight, and Pringles food and beverage products. **Positions advertised include:** External Relations Manager; Finance & Accounting Manager; Human Resource Manager; Market Research Manager; Pharmaceutical Representative; Tax Analyst; Analytical Lab Research; R&D Engineer. **Special programs:** Internships; Co-ops. **Corporate headquarters location:** Cincinnati OH. **Other U.S. locations:** Nationwide. **International locations:** Worldwide. **Operations at this facility include:** Manufacturing; Research and Development; Sales; Logistics; Customer Service. Both Max Factor and Cover Girl cosmetics are produced at this location. **Listed on:** New York Stock Exchange. **Stock exchange symbol:** PG. **President/CEO/Chairman:** Alan G. Lafley. **Sales/revenue:** Over $40 billion. **Number of employees nationwide:** 2,500. **Number of employees worldwide:** Over 100,000.

PROFESSIONAL MAILING AND DISTRIBUTION SERVICES (PMDS)
9050 Junction Drive, Annapolis Junction MD 20701-1150. 301/604-3305. **Fax:** 301/953-2838. **Contact:** Human Resources. **E-mail address:** info@pmds.com. **World Wide Web address:** http://www.pmds.com. **Description:** PMDS offers complete turnkey services that include publications and subscription processing; membership database maintenance; meeting registration and planning; automated mailing services; and additional support services. The company's client base is composed of membership associations and nonprofit organizations. **NOTE:** Entry-level positions are offered. **Corporate headquarters location:** This location. **Listed on:** Privately held. **President:** Rita Hope Counts. **Number of employees at this location:** Over 200.

PROVIDENT BANK OF MARYLAND
P.O. Box 1661, HR-432, Baltimore MD 21203-1661. 410/277-7000. **Physical address:** 114 East Lexington Street, Baltimore MD 21202. **Fax:** 410/277-2664. **Recorded jobline:** 800/722-2367x2885. **Contact:** Human Resources. **E-mail address:** mycareer@provbank.com. **World Wide Web address:** http://www.providentbankmd.com. **Description:** A full-service, commercial bank. Founded in 1886. **NOTE:** Part-time positions are offered. **Positions advertised include:** Branch Manager; Customer Service Representative; Financial Services Representative; Traditional Summer Teller. **Special programs:** Tuition Reimbursement Plan; Summer Jobs. **Corporate headquarters location:** This location. **Parent company:** Provident Bankshares Corporation. **Listed on:** NASDAQ. **Stock exchange symbol:** PBKS. **CEO/Chairman:** Peter M. Martin.

QUANTA SYSTEMS CORPORATION
213 Perry Parkway, Gaithersburg MD 20877-2145. 301/590-3300. **Fax:** 301/590-3325. **Contact:** Human Resources. **World Wide Web address:** http://www.quantasystems.com. **Description:** A research and development engineering company that also manufactures high-technology products and commercial communications equipment. **Positions advertised include:** Business Development Director. **Corporate headquarters location:** Hanover MD. **Parent company:** Compudyne Corporation. **Listed on:** NASDAQ. **Stock exchange symbol:** CDCY.

QUEST DIAGNOSTICS INCORPORATED
1901 Sulphur Spring Road, Baltimore MD 21227. 410/247-9100. **Fax:** 410/536-1667. **Contact:** Bonnie Cohen-Finch, Personnel. **World Wide Web address:** http://www.questdiagnostics.com. **Description:** Provides a broad range of clinical laboratory services to health care clients that include physicians, hospitals, clinics, dialysis centers, pharmaceutical companies, and corporations. The company performs tests on blood, urine, and other bodily fluids and tissues to provide information for health and well-being. **NOTE:** Apply online. **Positions advertised include:** Quality Assurance; Sales Associate; Marking Associate; Specimen Processor; Medical Operator; Administrative Assistant; Laboratory Management; Accounts Receivable; Human Resources Manager. **Corporate headquarters location:** Teterboro NJ. **Other U.S. locations:** Nationwide. **Operations at this facility include:** This location is a laboratory facility. **Listed on:** New York Stock Exchange. **Stock exchange symbol:** DGX.

QUEST INTERNATIONAL FLAVORING AND FOOD INGREDIENTS, INC.
10 Painters Mill Road, Owings Mills MD 21117-3686. 410/363-2550. **Contact:** Human Resources. **World Wide Web address:** http://www.questintl.com. **Description:** A flavorings, food ingredients, and fragrances company. **NOTE:** Mail resumes to 400 International Drive, Mount Olive NJ 07828. **Other U.S. locations:** Norwich NY; Rochester NY; Hoffman States IL; Itasca IL; Silverton OR. **International locations:** Worldwide. **Operations at this facility include:** This location is part of the Flavors and Food Ingredients division of Quest International. **Number of employees worldwide:** Over 4,600.

RWD TECHNOLOGIES, INC.
5521 Research Park Drive, Baltimore MD 21228. 410/869-1000. **Toll-free phone:** 888/RWD-TECH. **Fax:** 410/869-3002. **Contact:** Lisa Heslin, Human Resources. **E-mail address:** jobs@rwd.com. **World Wide Web address:** http://www.rwd.com. **Description:** An engineering consulting firm that offers a broad range of integrated business solutions to increase worker effectiveness and productivity. **NOTE:** Resumes sent via e-mail must be formatted in ASCII text. **Office hours:** Monday – Friday, 8:30 a.m. – 5:15 p.m. **Other area locations:** Baltimore MD. **Other U.S. locations:** Nationwide. **International locations:** Germany; United Kingdom; Belgium; Canada. **Subsidiaries include:** Deutschland GmbH; RWD Technologiens; RWD Technologies Canada; RWD Technologies UK, Limited; RWD Technologies Belgium, B.V.B.A.; Sap Learning Solutions Pte, Limited; SAP Learning Solutions Australia Pty, Limited. **Listed on:** NASDAQ. **Stock exchange symbol:** RWDT. **President/Founder/CEO/Chairman:** Dr. Robert W. Deutsch. **Number of employees worldwide:** Over 900.

RANDOM HOUSE, INC.
400 Hahn Road, Westminster MD 21157. 410/848-1900. **Contact:** Jim Welkos, Human Resources. **E-mail address:** jobs@randomhouse.com. **World Wide Web address:** http://www.randomhouse.com. **Description:** One of the largest trade book publishers in the United States. Trade divisions include Villard Books, Vintage, Times Books, Pantheon/Schocken, and Knopf. Crown Publishing Group includes Crown Adult Books, Clarkson N. Potter, Fodor's Travel Guides, and Orion Books. Ballantine, Fawcett, Del Rey, and Ivy are mass-market imprints. **NOTE:** Resumes may be sent to 400 Bennett Surf Drive, Westminster MD 21157 or faxed to 410/386-7268. **Positions advertised include:** Telemarketing Sales Manager. **Special programs:** Internships; Associates Program. **Corporate headquarters location:** New York NY. **Other U.S. locations:** Chicago IL. **International locations:** Japan; Australia; Hong Kong; New Zealand; South Africa; United Kingdom. **Parent company:** Bertelsmann, AG. **Listed on:** Privately held. **Number of employees nationwide:** 1,200.

RAYTHEON COMPANY IDENTIFICATION SYSTEMS
1300 East Joppa Road, Towson MD 21286. 410/583-4000. **Contact:** Human Resources. **World Wide Web address:** http://www.raytheon.com. **Description:** A leader in the design of military tactical communications, electronic combat, command and control, and antisubmarine warfare products and systems for the U.S. armed forces and its allies. **Positions advertised include:** Quality Assurance Manager; Mechanical Design Engineer; Export Licensing & Compliance Advertising Associate; Six Sigma Expert; IFF Systems Engineer; Software Engineer Manager; Digital Design Engineer. **NOTE:** Entry-level positions are offered. **Special programs:** Co-ops; Internships. **Office hours:** Monday – Friday, 7:30 a.m. – 4:00 p.m. **Corporate headquarters location:** Lexington MA. **Other U.S. locations:** Nationwide. **Listed on:** New York Stock Exchange. **Stock exchange symbol:** RTN. **CEO/Chairman:** Daniel P. Burnham. **Sales/revenue:** $16.9 billion. **Number of employees worldwide:** 77,500.

REYNOLDS & REYNOLDS
14600 York Road, Suite E, Sparks MD 21152. 410/771-9211. **Contact:** Human Resources. **E-mail address:** hr@reyrey.com. **World Wide Web address:** http://www.reyrey.com. **Description:** Provides systems integration and analysis for the automotive and health care industries. The company also supplies these industries with business forms. **NOTE:** Apply online. **Special programs:** Internships; Co-ops. **Corporate headquarters location:** Dayton OH. **Other U.S. locations:** Nationwide. **International locations:** Worldwide. **Operations at this facility include:** Manufacturing; Sales; Service. **Listed on:** New York Stock Exchange. **Stock exchange symbol:** REY. **President/CEO/Chairman:** Lloyd G. Waterhouse. **Sales/revenue:** Over $990 million. **Number of employees worldwide:** Over 5,000.

ROCK CREEK FOUNDATION
700 Roeder Road, 6th Floor, Silver Spring MD 20910-4457. 301/589-8303. **Fax:** 301/887-8724. **Contact:** Human Resources. **World Wide Web address:** http://www.ddmaryland.org/rockcreek.htm. **Description:** A national training site engaged in creating opportunities for disabled adults. Individuals are aided in community integration through avenues such as educational, volunteer, and employment opportunities.

ROCKY GORGE ANIMAL HOSPITAL
7515 Brooklyn Bridge Road, Laurel MD 20707. 301/776-7744. **Fax:** 301/776-1575. **Contact:** Personnel. **World Wide Web address:** http://www.rockygorgevet.com. **Description:** Provides general medical and surgical services to domestic animals. **NOTE:** Online applications are available. **Positions advertised include:** Veterinary Receptionist/Assistant. **Office hours:** Monday – Friday, 8:00 a.m. – 8:00 p.m., Saturday, 9:00 a.m. – 2:00 p.m.

RODMAN'S DISCOUNT FOOD & DRUG
4301 Randolph Road, Silver Spring MD 20906. 301/230-8930. **Contact:** Human Resources. **World Wide Web address:** http://www.rodmans.com. **Description:** A retailer of drugs, appliances, cameras, health and beauty aids, beer, and wine. **Corporate headquarters location:** This location. **Other area locations:** Rockville MD; Wheaton MD. **Other U.S. locations:** Washington DC.

THE ROUSE COMPANY
10275 Little Patuxent Parkway, Columbia MD 21044. 410/992-6000. **Fax:** 410/ 964-3436. **Contact:** Human Resources. **E-mail address:** careers@therousecompany.com. **World Wide Web address:** http://www.therousecompany.com. **Description:** Develops, acquires, owns, and manages commercial real estate projects, primarily large regional retail centers. The Rouse Company manages approximately 250 properties across the United States including Faneuil Hall Marketplace (Boston MA), South Street Seaport (New York NY), Harborplace (Baltimore MD), Bayside Marketplace (Miami FL), Arizona Center (Phoenix AZ), Pioneer Place (Portland OR), and Westlake Center (Seattle WA). Founded in 1939. **NOTE:** Online applications are available. **Positions advertised include:** Group Secretary; Retail Marketing Manager. **Corporate headquarters location:** This location. **Listed on:** New York Stock Exchange. **Stock exchange symbol:** RSE. **CEO/Chairman:** Anthony W. Deering.

ROYAL GLASS COMPANY
9241 Hampton Overlook, Capitol Heights MD 20743. 301/336-5010. **Toll-free phone:** 800/787-0404. **Fax:** 301/808-0623. **Contact:** Human Resources. **World Wide Web address:** http://www.royalglass.com. **Description:** Installs automobile glass. **Positions advertised include:** Auto Glass Installers; Flat Glass Installers; Manager Trainees. **Office hours:** Monday – Saturday, 8:00 a.m. – 5:00 p.m. **Corporate headquarters location:** This location. **Other area locations:** Statewide. **Other U.S. locations:** Fairfax VA; Alexandria VA.

S&S GRAPHICS
14880 Sweitzer Lane, Laurel MD 20707. 301/206-7777. **Fax:** 301/206-5436. **Contact:** Human Resources. **E-mail address:** president@snsgraphics.com. **World Wide Web address:** http://www.snsgraphics.com. **Description:** A printing company that offers high-quality sheetfed and half-web printing as well as many additional services (full web, variable data digital printing, fulfillment, POP, etc.) through a network of 65 affiliated companies under Consolidated Graphics. **Positions advertised include:** Accounts Payable Clerk; Billing/Estimating; Bindery Operators; Receptionist/Administrative Assistant; Scanner Operator.

SFA, INC.
9315 Largo Drive West, Suite 200, Largo MD 20774. 301/350-0938. **Fax:** 301/350-5153. **Contact:** Lisa Broome, Human Resources. **E-mail address:** lbroome@sfa.com. **World Wide Web address:** http://www.sfa.com. **Description:** A diversified international supplier of products and services aimed at helping clients capitalize on leading edge systems and technologies. SFA conducts advanced research studies; designs and develops state-of-the-art prototypes; and produces customized hardware and software systems for defense, communications, and other commercial applications. **NOTE:** Fax resume or apply online. **Corporate headquarters location:** This location. **Other area locations:** Columbia MD; Frederick MD; Landover MD; Lexington Park MD. **Other U.S. locations:** Washington DC; San Diego CA; Charleston SC. **Subsidiaries include:** SFA DataComm, Incorporated; SFA SACOM. **Listed on:** Privately held. **President/CEO:** Jerry D. Robinson. **Number of employees at this location:** 300.

SI INTERNATIONAL
2099 Gaither Road, 3rd Floor, Rockville MD 20850. 240/778-1200. **Fax:** 240/778-1400. **Contact:** Human Resources. **E-mail address:** jobs@si-intl.com. **World Wide Web address:** http://www.si-intl.com. **Description:** Provides computer systems engineering consulting services and information technology network solutions. The company's primary customer is the federal government. **Positions advertised include:** Application Designer; EPSS Developer; Project Manager; Technical Manager; Material Handler. **Special programs:** Tuition Reimbursement Program. **Corporate headquarters location:** Reston VA. **Other area locations:** Hanover MD. **Other U.S. locations:** Denver CO; Colorado Springs CO; Arlington VA; Bakersville CA. **Listed on:** NASDAQ. **Stock exchange symbol:** SINT. **CEO/Chairman:** Ray J. Oleson.

ST SERVICES
1134 Marine Road, Salisbury MD 21801. 410/742-2204. **Fax:** 410/742-2205. **Contact:** Human Resources. **World Wide Web address:** http://www.stservices.net. **Description:** A petroleum products and specialty liquids terminaling company. **Corporate headquarters location:** Dallas TX. **Other area locations:** Baltimore MD; Andrews AFB MD; Piney Point MD. **Other U.S. locations:** Nationwide. **International locations:** District of Columbia; United Kingdom. **Parent company:** Kaneb Pipeline Partners, L.P.

STV GROUP
7125 Ambassador Road, Suite 200, Baltimore MD 21244. 410/944-9112. **Contact:** Human Resources. **E-mail address:** careers@stvinc.com. **World Wide Web address:** http://www.stvinc.com. **Description:** STV Group provides engineering and architectural consulting and design services for a variety of projects. The company operates four business segments including civil engineering, which provides services for the construction of highways, bridges, airports, and marine ports; defense systems engineering, which serves the U.S. Department of Defense regarding the development of equipment and special hardware; industrial process engineering, which consists of services for the development of manufacturing equipment and process systems; and transportation engineering, which involves consulting, design, and construction supervision services for transportation facilities. **Corporate headquarters location:** Douglasville PA. **Other U.S. locations:** Nationwide. **Subsidiaries include:** STV Environmental; STV International; STV Architects; STV Incorporated. **Number of employees at this location:** 120. **Number of employees nationwide:** 1,300.

A.J. SACKETT & SONS COMPANY
1701 South Highland Avenue, Baltimore MD 21224. 410/276-4466. **Contact:** Human Resources. **E-mail address:** sales@ajsackett.com. **World Wide Web address:** http://www.ajsackett.com. **Description:** An engineering services company that also manufactures handling and processing equipment. **President:** Larry Taylor.

SAFEWAY, INC.
7595 Greenbelt Road, Greenbelt MD 20770. 301/345-0150. **Contact:** Employment Supervisor. **World Wide Web address:** http://www.safeway.com. **Description:** A regional food store with approximately 1,700 locations in North America. **Positions advertised include:** Shopper Administrator; Staff Pharmacist; Auditor. **Corporate headquarters location:** Pleasanton CA. **Other U.S. locations:** Nationwide. **International locations:** Canada. **Subsidiaries include:** Randall's Food Markets, Incorporated; Carr-Gottstein Foods Company; Dominick's Supermarkets, Incorporated; The Vons Companies, Incorporated. **Operations at this facility include:** Regional Headquarters. **President/Chairman/CEO:** Steve Burd. **Listed on:** New York Stock Exchange. **Stock exchange symbol:** SWY.

ST. JOSEPH MEDICAL CENTER
7601 Osler Drive, Towson MD 21204-7582. 410/337-1288. **Fax:** 410/337-1203. **Contact:** Human Resources. **E-mail address:** stjosmedhr@chi-east.org. **World Wide Web address:** http://www.sjmcmd.org. **Description:** A member of the Franciscan Health System and a regional medical center providing comprehensive acute care with diversified specialty services. The medical center is sponsored by the Sisters of St. Francis of Philadelphia. **NOTE:** Interested job seekers may apply online. **Positions advertised include:** Clinical Unit Clerk; Medical Technician; Occupational Therapist; Physical Therapist; Respiratory Therapist; Certified Nurses Aide; Nurse Practitioner; Registered Nurse; Maintenance Engineer; Physical Therapy Assistant; Radiological Technician; Case Management Director; Medical Records Technologist; Phlebotomist; Data Analyst; Social Worker; Data Entry Clerk; Medical Transcriptionist; Executive Assistant; Case Manager. **President/CEO:** John K. Tolmie.

ST. PAUL TRAVELERS
ALLFIRST INSURANCE
25 South Charles St, Baltimore MD 21201. 410/244-4622. **Contact:** Human Resources. **World Wide Web address:** http://www.stpaultravelers.com. **Description:** Provides a wide variety of insurance lines including property, casualty, and life insurance. Founded in 1863. **Special programs:** Internships. **Positions advertised include:** Financial and Professional Services Associate; Claims Staff Attorney. **Corporate headquarters location:** Saint Paul MN. **International locations:** London, England. **Listed on:** New York Stock Exchange. **Stock exchange symbol:** STA.

SAFENET, INC.
4690 Millenium Drive, Belcamp MD 21017. 410/931-7500. **Fax:** 410/931-7524. **Contact:** Human Resources. **E-mail address:** humanresources@safenet-inc.com. **World Wide Web address:** http://www.safenet-inc.com. **Description:** Develops encryption software to ensure secure transactions. **Positions advertised include:** Software Engineer; Product Line Manager; Contracts Administrator; Corporate Tax Manager; Accountant; Corporate Tax Manager; OEM Sales & Hardware Channel Manager; Sales Director; Account Manager; Marketing Manager; Quality Manager; Configuration Analyst; Purchasing Manager; Trainer; Desktop Support Technologists. **Corporate headquarters location:** This location. **Other U.S. locations:** Los Gatos CA; Danvers MA. **International locations:** The Netherlands; Switzerland. **Listed on:** NASDAQ. **Stock exchange symbol:** SFNT.

SAKS FIFTH AVENUE
5555 Wisconsin Avenue, Chevy Chase MD 20815. 301/657-9000. **Contact:** Personnel Director. **World Wide Web address:** http://www.saksincorporated.com. **Description:** A 62-store chain emphasizing soft-goods products, primarily apparel for men, women, and children. **Parent company:** Saks Incorporated is a department store holding company that operates approximately 360 stores in 36 states. The company's stores include Saks Fifth Avenue, Parisian, Proffit's, Younker's, Herberger's, Carson Pirie Scott, Boston Store, Bergner's, and Off 5th, the company's outlet store. Saks Incorporated also operates two retail catalogs and several retail Internet sites. **Special programs:** Scholarship Program; Wellness Program. **Corporate headquarters location:** Birmingham AL. **Description: Operations at this facility include:** This location is a part of the nationwide specialty department store chain. **Listed on:** New York Stock Exchange. **Stock exchange symbol:** SKS.

SALISBURY UNIVERSITY
1101 Camden Avenue, Salisbury MD 21801. 410/543-6000. **Contact:** Human Resources. **E-mail address:** lashull@salibury.edu. **World Wide Web address:** http://www.ssu.edu. **Description:** Offers a traditional liberal arts curriculum and a variety of preprofessional and professional programs on both the graduate and undergraduate levels. The university's 5,200 full-time undergraduates can also earn their degrees from the Franklin P. Perdue School of Business, the Richard A. Henson School of Science and Technology, the School of Education and Professional Studies, or the Charles R. and Martha N. Fulton School of Liberal Arts. **NOTE:** To reach Human Resources directly, call 410/543-6035. **Positions advertised include:** Electronic Resources Librarian; Spanish Associate Professor; Developing Psychology Associate Professor; Film and Literature Associate Professor; Health Psychology Associate Professor; Medieval Associate Professor; Executive Chief; University Registrar; Business Consultant.

SATURN OF SALISBURY
30275 Winner Boulevard, Delmar MD 21875. **Toll-free phone:** 800/297-0857. **Contact:** Human Resources Manager. **World Wide Web address:** http;//www.saturnofsalisbury.com. **Description:** Saturn auto dealer for Salisbury Maryland. **Positions advertised include:** Finance Manager; New Vehicle Sales Associate; Lot Porter; Sales Manager.

SAUL EWING LLP
100 South Charles Street, 15th Floor, Baltimore MD 21201-2773. 410/332-8600. **Fax:** 410/332-8862. **Contact:** Human Resources. **World Wide Web address:** http://www.saul.com. **Description:** A general practice law firm with over 222 lawyers nationwide in more than 12 fields including business, contracts, employment, estates and trusts, intellectual property, and real estate. **Special programs:** Summer Program. **Other U.S. locations:** Wilmington DE; Princeton NJ; New York NY; Berwyn PA; Harrisburg PA; Philadelphia PA.

S. SCHWAB COMPANY
P.O. Box 1742, Cumberland MD 21502-1742. 301/729-4488. **Fax:** 301/729-0065. **Contact:** Human Resources. **E-mail address:** lmhr@sschwab.com. **World Wide Web address:** http://www.sschwab.com. **Description:** Manufactures Little Me and Ralph Lauren brand children's playwear. **Corporate headquarters location:** This location.

SCIENCE APPLICATIONS INTERNATIONAL CORPORATION (SAIC)
P.O. Box B, Building 371, Frederick MD 21701-1201. 301/846-1146. **Contact:** Human Resources. **World Wide Web address:** http://www.saic.com. **Description:** A research and engineering firm offering technology development, computer systems integration, technical support, and computer hardware and software products. Services are aimed at the energy, environment, health care, information technology, Internet, maritime, national security, space, telecommunications, transportation, and logistics fields. **NOTE:** Must apply online. Part-time and temporary positions are offered. **Positions advertised include:** Subcontracts Supervisor; Public Legislative Affairs Analyst; Biology Tech Writer; Systems Engineer; Regulatory Affairs; Scientist; Biomedical R&D Support Specialist; Document Specialist; Finance Analyst; Budget Analyst; Conference Administration Assistant; Word Processing Assistant; Clinical Quality Assurance Associate; Research Associate; Webmaster; Logistic Specialist; Clinical Project Manager; Post Doctoral Fellow; Visiting Scientist; Quality Assurance Manager. **Corporate headquarters location:** San Diego CA. **Operations at this facility include:** This location is engaged in cancer research. The company provides operations and technical support services to the National Cancer Institute-Frederick Research and Development Center including scientific resources; safety, medical, and security programs; and business administrative services. **Listed on:** Privately held. **President/CEO:** J.R. Beyster. **Sales/revenue:** $6.1 billion. **Number of employees nationwide:** 1,100. **Number of employees worldwide:** Over 41,000.

SEARS, ROEBUCK & CO.
7103 Democracy Boulevard, Bethesda MD 20817. 301/469-4000. **Contact:** Human Resources. **World Wide Web address:** http://www.sears.com. **Description:** A diversified company that is divided into three groups: Sears Merchandise Group, Allstate Insurance Group, and Corporate Business. With its network of mall-based stores, Sears, Roebuck & Co. is a retailer of apparel, home, and automotive products and related services for families throughout North America, serving more than 50 million households. **Positions advertised include:** Sales Manager; Project Manager; Call Center Team Manager; Pricing & Signing Lead; Custom Window Designer; Technical Manager; Auto Center Manager; Repair Team Manager; Repair Services Requisition. **Corporate headquarters location:** Hoffman Estates IL. **Other U.S. locations:** Nationwide. **Subsidiaries include:** Allstate Insurance Group is one of the nation's largest publicly held property and casualty insurance companies, with more than 20 million customers and approximately 14,600 full-time agents in the United States and Canada. Founded in 1931 by Sears, Roebuck & Co., which owns 80 percent, Allstate is also a major life insurer. Allstate Insurance Group offers automobile insurance, homeowners insurance, life insurance, annuity and pension products, business insurance (insurance for small- and mid-size businesses, as well as reinsurance for other insurers), and mortgage guaranty insurance (through Allstate's wholly-owned subsidiary, PMI Mortgage Insurance Company). Sears, Roebuck & Co. also operates or holds interests in related businesses in real estate, computer, and information services that extend or support its core businesses. Homart, a wholly-owned subsidiary of Sears, Roebuck & Co., is one of the country's leading developers, owners, and managers of regional shopping malls and community centers. Prodigy, a Sears/IBM partnership, is a

home computer network providing a wide variety of interactive personal services including news, shopping, bulletin boards, travel ticketing, brokerage, banking, and e-mail services. Advantis, another partnership formed by Sears and IBM, is a networking technology company that provides businesses with data, voice, and multimedia services. **Operations at this facility include:** This is a location of the nationwide retail department store chain. **Listed on:** New York Stock Exchange. **Stock exchange symbol:** S. **CEO/Chairman:** Alan J. Lacy. **Sales/revenue:** Approximately $41 billion. **Number of employees nationwide:** 289,000.

SEMMES, BOWEN & SEMMES
250 West Pratt Street, 16th Floor, Baltimore MD 21201. 410/539-5040. **Fax:** 410/576-4868. **Contact:** Human Resources. **E-mail address:** semmes@mail.semmes.com. **World Wide Web address:** http://www.semmes.com. **Description:** A general civil law firm. Founded in 1887. **Special programs:** Summer Jobs. **Corporate headquarters location:** This location. **Other area locations:** Hagerstown MD; Salisbury MD; Towson MD. **Other U.S. locations:** Washington DC; McLean VA.

SERTA MATTRESS/AW INDUSTRIES & COMPANY
8415 Ardmore Road, Landover MD 20785. 301/322-1000. **Fax:** 240/487-1044. **Contact:** Human Resources. **World Wide Web address:** http://www.serta.com. **Description:** Manufactures Serta and private-label mattresses and box springs. Serta Mattress/AW Incorporated also distributes bedding related items such as bunk beds, bed frames, headboards, electric beds, and futons. **Office hours:** Monday - Friday, 9:00 a.m. - 5:00 p.m. **Corporate headquarters location:** This location. **Other U.S. locations:** Nationwide. **International locations:** Worldwide. **Parent company:** Serta, Incorporated. **Listed on:** Privately held. **President/CEO:** Edward F. Lilly. **Sales/revenue:** $870 million. **Number of employees at this location:** 250. **Number of employees worldwide:** 4,800.

SHEPPARD PRATT HEALTH SYSTEM
P.O. Box 6815, 6501 North Charles Street, Baltimore MD 21285-6815. 410/938-3000. **Contact:** Georgia Coleman, Director of Human Resources. **E-mail address:** recruitment@sheppardpratt.org. **World Wide Web address:** http://www.sheppardpratt.org. **Description:** A nonprofit health system, Sheppard Pratt is a provider of managed behavioral health care services. Sheppard Pratt Health System offers integrated EAP/managed mental health programs, case management, claims processing, and at-risk or fee-for-service contracting. **NOTE:** To contact Human Resources directly, call 410/938-3315. **Positions advertised include:** Chemical Dependency Counselor; Quality Director; Educational Aide; Mental Health Worker; Office Assistant; Patient Accounts Representative; Plant Operations Mechanic; Recreation Therapist; Resource Specialist; School Records Technician; Secretary; Teacher Social Studies; Unit Secretary. **Corporate headquarters location:** This location. **President/CEO:** Dr. Steven S. Sharfstein.

SHERWIN-WILLIAMS COMPANY
2325 Hollins Ferry Road, Baltimore MD 21230. 410/625-8257. **Contact:** Human Resources. **E-mail address:** Darlene.Bergeron@sherwin.com. **World Wide Web address:** http://www.sherwin.com. **Description:** Manufactures, sells, and distributes coatings and related products. Coatings are produced for original equipment manufacturers in various industries, as well as for the automotive aftermarket, the industrial maintenance market, and the traffic paint market. Sherwin-Williams labeled architectural and industrial coatings are sold through company-owned specialty paint and wallcovering stores. The Sherwin-Williams Company also manufactures paint under the Acme, Dutch Boy, Kem-Tone, Lucas, Martin-Senour, Minwax, Pratt & Lambert, Rogers, and Thompson brand names, as well as private labels, and markets its products to independent dealers, mass merchandisers, and home improvement centers. **Special programs:** Internships; Training. **Corporate headquarters location:** Cleveland OH. **Listed on:** New York Stock Exchange. **Stock exchange symbol:** SHW. **CEO/Chairman:** Chris Conner. **Sales/revenue:** Over $5 billion.

SMITHS DETECTION
2202 Lakeside Boulevard, Edgewood MD 21040. 410/510-9100. **Fax:** 410/510-9490. **Contact:** Human Resources. **World Wide Web address:** http://www.smithsdetection.com. **Description:** Specializes in trace detection technology. The company is divided into three business segments: transportation security, military, and facilities security, and services customers in the government, military, and commercial sectors. **Other U.S. locations:** Warren NJ. **International locations:** West Sussex, UK; Herts, UK; Roissy CDG, France; Kuala Lumpur, Malaysia. **Listed on:** Privately held. **Number of employees at this location:** 100.

SMURFIT-STONE CONTAINER CORPORATION
725 Pittman Road, Baltimore MD 21226. **Toll-free phone:** 877/772-2999. **Contact:** Human Resources. **World Wide Web address:** http://www.smurfit-stone.com. **Description:** A paper-based packaging company whose main products include corrugated containers, folding cartons, and multiwall industrial bags. The company is also one of the world's largest collectors and processors of recycled products that are then sold to a worldwide customer base. In addition, Smurfit-Stone Container Corporation operates several paper tube, market pulp, and newsprint production facilities. **Corporate headquarters location:** Chicago IL. **Other U.S. locations:** Nationwide. **International locations:** Dublin, Ireland. **Operations at this facility include:** This location manufactures corrugated boxes. **Listed on:** NASDAQ. **Stock exchange symbol:** SSCC.

SODEXHO
9801 Washingtonian Boulevard, Gaithersburg MD 20878. 877/560-4084. **Toll-free phone:** 800/763-3946. **Contact:** Human Resources. **E-mail address:** careers@sodexhousa.com. **World Wide Web address:** http://www.sodexhousa.com. **Description:** A contract service management company that provides food services to health care facilities, schools, and corporate dining areas. **NOTE:** Job seekers may apply online for specific positions or for general consideration. **Positions advertised include:** Finance Manager; Food Service Manager; Administrative Assistant; Staff Accountant; Nutrition Manager; Benefits Administrator; Buyer; Design Coordinator. **Special programs:** Internships. **Corporate headquarters location:** This location. **Other U.S. locations:** Nationwide. **International locations:** Canada. **Listed on:** New York Stock Exchange. **Stock exchange symbol:** SDX. **President/CEO:** Michael Landel. **Number of employees worldwide:** 100,000.

SOUTHERN MARYLAND OIL
P.O. Box 2130, La Plata MD 20646. 301/932-3600. **Physical address:** 6355 Crain Highway, La Plata MD 20646. **Toll-free phone:** 800/492-3420. **Contact:** Human Resources. **E-mail address:** info_smo@twgi.net. **World Wide Web address:** http://www.southernmdoil.com. **Description:** A distributor of petroleum products. Southern Maryland Oil also owns and operates a chain of 50 convenience stores throughout Maryland, Delaware, and Virginia. **NOTE:** Online applications are available. **Special programs:** Internships. **Corporate headquarters location:** This location. **Parent company:** The Wills Group. **Operations at this facility include:** Administration.

SPHERIX INC.
12051 Indian Creek Court, Beltsville MD 20705. 301/419-3900. **Fax:** 301/623-2330. **Contact:** Human Resources. **E-mail address:** hrdept@spherix.com. **World Wide Web address:** http://www.spherix.com. **Description:** Develops and maintains hotlines for public and professional inquiries about the health care and government industries. Spherix also provides information technology services and develops biotech products. **Positions advertised include:** National Pharmaceutical Account Manager; National Government Account Manager; Customer Service Call Center Representative. **Office hours:** Monday - Friday, 8:00 a.m. - 5:30 p.m. **Corporate headquarters location:** This location. **Other area locations:** Cumberland MD. **Listed on:** NASDAQ. **Stock exchange symbol:** SPEX. **President:** David Affeldt. **Number of employees at this location:** 300. **Number of employees nationwide:** 500.

SPIRENT COMMUNICATIONS HEKIMIAN DIVISION
15200 Omega Drive, Rockville MD 20850-3240. 301/590-3600. **Contact:** Director of Human Resources. **E-mail address:** info@spirentcom.com. **World Wide Web address:** http://www.spirentcom.com. **Description:** Designs, manufactures, and markets equipment that provides testing, access, and performance monitoring services for telecommunications networks. **Positions advertised include:** Interoperability Specialist; Electronic Assembler; Inventory Control Clerk; Manufacturing Engineer; Operations Support & Quality Engineer; Professional Services Marketing Engineer; Marketing Communications Engineer; Marketing Analyst; Marketing Communications Director; Channel Sales Director; Sales Support Specialist; Inside Sales Director; Sales Engineer; Software Engineer; Software Test Engineer; Chief Architect; Systems Engineer Director; Hardware Technical Writer. **Note:** Applicants can apply online. **Special programs:** Tuition Reimbursement Program. **Corporate headquarters location:** This location. **Other U.S. locations:** Sunnyvale CA; Calabasas CA; Honolulu HI; Eatontown NJ. **International locations:** Glasglow, Scotland; Paignton, England; Ottawa, Canada. **Listed on:** New York Stock Exchange. **Stock exchange symbol:** SPM. **President:** Jim Schleckser.

THE STATIONERY HOUSE INC.
1000 Florida Avenue, Hagerstown MD 21740. 301/739-4487. **Toll-free phone:** 800/638-3033. **Fax:** 301/739-7981. **Contact:** Human Resources Director. **E-mail address:** hrdirector@stationaryhouse.com. **World Wide Web address:** http://www.stationaryhouse.com. **Description:** A catalog retailer of a wide range of holiday greeting cards for corporations. **Corporate headquarters location:** This location.

STATTON FURNITURE MANUFACTURING
P.O. Box 530, Hagerstown MD 21741. 301/739-0360. **Physical address:** 504 East First Street, Hagerstown MD 21740. **Contact:** Human Resources. **World Wide Web address:** http://www.statton.com. **Description:** Manufactures solid cherry wood bedroom and dining room furniture as well as tables and bookcases.

STEWART ENTERPRISES, INC.
7800 Park Heights Avenue, Baltimore MD 21208. 410/486-5300. **Contact:** Human Resources. **E-mail address:** hrinfo@stei.com. **World Wide Web address:** http://www.stewartenterprises.com. **Description:** A funeral service provider. The company is one of the first in the industry to integrate funeral home and cemetery operations through combined facilities. Through its subsidiaries, the company operates 134 funeral homes and 95 cemeteries worldwide. **Positions advertised include:** Sales Associate; Management Assistants. **Special programs:** Educational Assistance Program; Internships. **Corporate headquarters location:** Metairie LA. **Other U.S. locations:** Nationwide. **International locations:** Australia; Mexico. **Listed on:** NASDAQ. **Stock exchange symbol:** STEI. **President/CEO:** William E. Rowe. **Sales/revenue:** $581 million. **Number of employees worldwide:** 6,500.

STONE INDUSTRIAL
9207 51st Avenue, College Park MD 20740. 301/474-3100. **Fax:** 301/345-2367. **Contact:** Human Resources. **E-mail address:** sales@stoneindustries.net. **World Wide Web address:** http://www.stoneindustrial.com. **Description:** A manufacturing company with operations in three industry segments: packaging items (metal and plastic containers, metal tubes, composite containers, and various specialty chemicals); filters (oil, air, fuel, coolant, hydraulic fluid, and chemical solution filters used in a variety of products and industries); and paper and plastic tubes. Stone Industrial specializes in spiral-winding technology and thermoplastic extrusion. **Corporate headquarters location:** This location. **Operations at this facility include:** Administration; Production.

STORAGE TECHNOLOGY CORPORATION (STORAGETEK)
12200 Tech Road, Silver Spring MD 20904. 301/622-7070. **Contact:** Human Resources. stkjobs@storagetek.com. **World Wide Web address:** http://www.stortek.com. **Description:** Manufactures high-performance computer information storage and retrieval systems for mainframe and mid-frame computers and networks. Products include automated cartridge systems, random access subsystems, and fault-tolerant disk arrays. The company also distributes equipment; sells new peripherals, software, and hardware; and offers support services. **Positions advertised include:** Financial Sales Manager; Product Sales Specialist; Sales Executive; Strategic Executive; Systems Engineer. **Special programs:** Internships. **Corporate headquarters location:** Louisville CO. **Other area locations:** Elkridge MD; Hunt Valley MD; Baltimore MD. **Other U.S. locations:** Nationwide. **International locations:** Worldwide. **Listed on:** New York Stock Exchange. **Stock exchange symbol:** STK. **Sales/revenue:** $2.04 billion. **Number of employees worldwide:** Over 7,000.

SUNTRUST BANK
120 East Baltimore Street, Baltimore MD 21202. 410/986-1545. **Contact:** Human Resources. **World Wide Web address:** http://www.suntrust.com. **Description:** A full-service commercial bank offering checking and savings accounts; NOW accounts; Christmas clubs; certificates of deposit; All-Savers certificates; IRA and Keogh accounts; safe-deposit boxes; travelers' checks; personal money orders; credit cards; commercial, construction, mortgage, consumer, and check credit loans; and money market investment services. **NOTE:** Entry-level positions are offered. Resumes may be submitted online. **Positions advertised include:** Assistant Branch Manager; Business Banking Marketing Team Leader; Commercial Banking Specialist; In Store Service Representative; Operations Manager; Recruiting Associate; Wealth Strategist; Wholesale Equity Account Executive. **Special programs:** Associate Training Program. **Office hours:** Monday – Thursday, 9:00 a.m. – 3:00 p.m., Friday, 8:30 a.m. – 4:00 p.m. **Corporate headquarters location:** Atlanta GA. **Other area locations:** Statewide. **Other U.S. locations:** AL; FL; GA; TN; VA; D.C. **Listed on:** New York Stock Exchange. **Stock exchange symbol:** STI.

SWEETHEART CUP COMPANY, INC.
10100 Reisterstown Road, Owings Mills MD 21117. 410/363-1111. **Contact:** Human Resources. **E-mail address:** hr@sweetheart.com. **World Wide Web address:**

http://www.sweetheart.com. **Description:** Manufactures and distributes paper and plastic cups, containers, bowls, plates, lids, cutlery, and drinking straws. Sweetheart Cup also produces ice cream cones. Two divisions manufacture packaging and production machinery. **Positions advertised include:** Electrician; Distribution Center Shift Supervisor; Technical Trainer; Plant Manager. **Special programs:** Tuition Reimbursement Program. **Corporate headquarters location:** Chicago IL. **Other U.S. locations:** Nationwide. **Operations at this facility include:** Manufacturing; Sales.

SYBASE, INC.
6550 Rock Spring Drive, Suite 700, Bethesda MD 20817. 301/896-1600. **Fax:** 301/896-1111. **Contact:** Human Resources. **E-mail address:** mdresumes@sybase.com. **World Wide Web address:** http://www.sybase.com. **Description:** Develops, markets, and supports a full line of relational database management software products and services for integrated, enterprise-wide information management systems. **NOTE:** Resumes should be mailed to Sybase, Incorporated, 5000 Hacienda Drive, Dublin CA 94568 or faxed to 301/896-1774. **Positions advertised include:** Federal Security Specialist; Federal Security Operations Manager; Practice Manager; Consultant; Channel Account Manager; Strategic Account Manager. **Corporate headquarters location:** Dublin CA. **Other U.S. locations:** Nationwide. **International locations:** Worldwide. **Operations at this facility include:** This location is a sales office that also provides education services. **Listed on:** New York Stock Exchange. **Stock exchange symbol:** SY.

SYMANTEC CORPORATION
1375 Piccard Drive, Suite 360, Rockville MD 20850. 301/670-1813. **Toll-free phone:** 800/298-2620. **Contact:** Human Resources. **World Wide Web address:** http://www.symantec.com. **Description:** Provides content and network security software and appliance solutions to individual, corporate, and computer service customers. Founded in 1984. **Positions advertised include:** Agency Account Manager; National Account Manager; Systems Engineer; Sales Manager. **Corporate headquarters:** Cupertino CA. **International locations:** Worldwide. **Listed on:** NASDAQ. **Stock exchange symbol:** SYMC. **CEO/Chairman:** John W. Thompson. **Sales/revenue:** $1,071 million. **Number of employees worldwide:** Over 4,000.

SYMPHONY HEALTH SERVICES
910 Ridgebrook Road, Sparks MD 21152. 410/773-2555. **Toll-free phone:** 800/ 359-5971. **Fax:** 410/773-2390. **Contact:** Human Resources. **World Wide Web address:** http://www.sresp-inc.com. **Description:** Provides physical, occupational, respiratory, and speech therapy services. The company's operates through four divisions: Respiratory Services, Rehabilitation Works, Mobilex, and Consulting Services. **Other U.S. locations:** Nationwide. **Operations at this facility include:** This location is home to the company's Respiratory Services division. Symphony's Respiratory Services offers management and administrative services, as well as equipment and staffing, to hospitals and nursing facilities.

SYNERGICS
191 Main Street, 3rd Floor, Annapolis MD 21401. 410/268-8820. **Contact:** Human Resources. **World Wide Web address:** http://www.synergicsenergyservices.com. **Description:** A developer, builder, owner, and operator of independent power generating plants, with an emphasis on hydroelectric power. **Corporate headquarters location:** This location.

SYSTEMS ALLIANCE, INC.
34 Loveton Circle, Suite 102, Sparks MD 21152. 410/584-0595. **Toll-free phone:** 877/797-2554. **Fax:** 410/584-0594. **Contact:** Human Resources: **E-mail address:** bambrose@systemsalliance.com. **World Wide Web address:** http://www.systemsalliance.com. **Description:** An information technology solutions company. **Positions advertised include:** Business Analyst; Network Administrator; Network/LAN Administrator; Product Support Technician.

SYTEL, INC.
6430 Rockledge Drive, Suite 400, Bethesda MD 20817. 301/530-1000. **Contact:** Matt Smith, Human Resources. **E-mail address:** resumes@sytel.com. **World Wide Web address:** http://www.sytel.com. **Description:** An information technology consulting firm with specializations in the areas of e-business and network infrastructure support and solutions. **Positions advertised include:** LAN Support Technician; Network Security Analyst; Web Developer. **Special programs:** Educational Assistance Program. **Other U.S. locations:** Herndon VA. **President/CEO:** Jeannette Lee White.

TATE ACCESS FLOORS, INC.
P.O. Box 278, Jessup MD 20794. 410/799-4200. **Fax:** 717/246-3437. **Physical address:** 7510 Montevideo Road, Jessup MD 20794. **Contact:** Human Resources. **E-mail address:** joybise@tateaccessfloors.com. **World Wide Web address:** http://www.tateaccessfloors.com **Description:** Manufactures access flooring and accessories. Founded in 1962. **NOTE:** Mail resumes to 52 Springdale Road, Red Lion PA 17356. **Corporate headquarters location:** This location. **Other U.S. locations:** Nationwide. **Subsidiaries include:** Floating Floors; Innocrete; USG Access Floor Division Assets. **Parent company:** Kingspan Group plc. **Operations at this facility include:** Manufacturing. **Sales/revenue:** Over $150 million.

TECHNICAL AND MANAGEMENT SERVICES CORPORATION (TAMSCO)
4041 Powder Mill Road, Suite 700, Calverton MD 20705. 301/595-0710. **Toll-free phone:** 800/282-6727. **Fax:** 301/937-5236. **Contact:** Director of Human Resources. **E-mail address:** tamscojobs@tamscohq.com. **World Wide Web address:** http://www.tamsco.com. **Description:** Offers a variety of ADP-oriented and telecommunications system development, manufacturing, and integration services. These products and services include requirements definition; systems engineering; systems and telecommunications network design; software development; electronics and telecommunications equipment; hardware development and manufacturing; and systems integration and implementation. **Positions advertised include:** Billing Specialist; Accountant Representative; Marketing Specialist. **Corporate headquarters location:** This location. **Other area locations:** Abingdon MD; Lexington Park MD. **Other U.S. locations:** Dayton OH; Warner Robins GA; Fort Gordon GA; Elizabeth City NC; San Diego CA; Ogden UT; Polson MO. **Operations at this facility include:** Administration. **Listed on:** Privately held. **President/CEO:** David R. Gust. **Number of employees at this location:** 40. **Number of employees nationwide:** 500.

TECORE WIRELESS SYSTEMS
7165 Columbia Gateway Drive, Columbia MD 21046. 410/872-6000. **Fax:** 410/872-6010. **Contact:** Human Resources. **E-mail address:** info@tecore.com. **World Wide Web address:** http://www.tecore.com. **Description:** A wireless telecommunications systems company that provides feature-rich, cost-effective and scalable wireless mobility solutions to network operators in emerging markets worldwide. **Positions advertised include:** Configuration Engineer; Entry Level Engineer; Network Administrator; Sales Account Associate; Staff Accountant; System Test Engineer; Technical Support/Implementation Engineer; Wireless Telecom Real-Time Engineer. **Corporate headquarters location:** This location.

TECTURA CORPORATION
11350 McCormick Road, Suite 801, Hunt Valley MD 21031. 410/229-9898. **Contact:** Human Resources. **World Wide Web address:** http://www.us.tectura.com. **Description:** Tectura provides software, consulting, and IT implementation services to clients in the distribution, manufacturing, healthcare, and service-based industries. **Positions advertised include:** Account Executive; Great Plains Consultant I. **Corporate headquarters location:** Redwood City CA. **Other U.S. locations:** Nationwide. **International locations:** Worldwide.

TELECOMMUNICATION SYSTEMS, INC.
275 West Street, Suite 400, Annapolis MD 21401. 410/263-7616. **Fax:** 410/263-7617. **Contact:** Human Resources. **E-mail address:** jobs@telecomsys.com. **World Wide Web address:** http://www.telecomsys.com. **Description:** Develops prepaid wireless and short message service applications. Founded in 1988. **Positions advertised include:** Communications Network Engineer; Customer Care Specialist; Program Manager; Software Engineer; Systems Engineer; Test Engineer; USAT Programs Manager. **Corporate headquarters location:** This location. **Other U.S. locations:** Tampa FL; Atlanta GA; Arlington VA; Newington VA. **International locations:** London, UK. **Listed on:** NASDAQ. **Stock exchange symbol:** TSYS. **President/CEO/Chairman:** Maurice B. Tose. **Number of employees at this location:** 100. **Number of employees nationwide:** 270.

TENDER LOVING CARE/STAFF BUILDERS
1830 Caton Center Drive, Suite A-B Baltimore MD 21227. 410/734-0400. **Contact:** Human Resources. **World Wide Web address:** http://www.tlcathome.com. **Description:** A home health care agency. Founded in 1967. **NOTE:** Interested job seekers may submit resumes online for specific positions or for general consideration. **Positions advertised include:** Assistant Director of Clinical Services; Dietitian; Home Care Nurse; Occupational Therapist; Performance Improvement Clinician; Physical Therapist; Speed Language Pathologist. **Corporate headquarters location:** Lake Success NY. **Other area locations:** Silver Springs MD. **Other U.S. locations:** Nationwide. **CEO:** James Happ. **Number of employees nationwide:** 20,000.

TENDER LOVING CARE/STAFF BUILDERS
4000 Blackburn Lane, Suite 150, Burtonsville MD 20866. 301/421-9091. **Contact:** Human Resources. **World Wide Web address:** http://www.tlcathome. com. **Description:** A home health care agency. **NOTE:** Interested job seekers may submit resumes online for specific positions or for general consideration. **Positions advertised include:** Care Team Manager; Dietitian; Home Care Nurse; Home Health Aide; Performance Improvement Clinician; Physical Therapist; Social Worker; Speech Language Pathologist. **Special programs:** Training; Tuition Assistance Program. **Corporate headquarters location:** Lake Success NY. **Other area locations:** Baltimore MD. **Other U.S. locations:** Nationwide. **CEO:** James Happ. **Number of employees nationwide:** 20,000.

TETRA TECH NUS, INC.
20251 Century Boulevard, Suite 200, Germantown MD 20874-7114. 301/528-5552. **Fax:** 301.528-2000. **Contact:** Human Resources **World Wide Web address:** http://www.tetratech.com. **Description:** Provides engineering and environmental waste services. **Corporate headquarters location:** Pasadena CA. **Other area locations:** Bel Air MD; Annapolis MD; Edgewater MD; Laurel MD; Owings Mills MD. **Other U.S. locations:** Nationwide. **Parent company:** Tetra Tech, Incorporated is an environmental management, consulting, and technical services group. **Listed on:** NASDAQ. **Stock exchange symbol:** TTEK. **President:** James M. Jaska. **Sales/revenue:** $740 million. **Number of employees worldwide:** Over 7,000.

THALES COMMUNICATIONS, INC.
22605 Gateway Center Drive, Clarksburg MD 20871. 240/864-7000. **Toll-free phone:** 800/258-4420. **Fax:** 240/864-7249. **Contact:** Human Resources. **World Wide Web address:** http://www.racalcomm.com. **Description:** Manufactures military tactical and strategic radio and communications equipment with clients in over 140 countries. Products include communication systems for electronic warfare, security, simulation, and training; electro-acoustic and ground-sensor systems; and satellite communications equipment. Other services include design automation, instrumentation, and health and safety. **NOTE:** Entry-level positions are offered. **Positions advertised include:** Embedded Software Engineer; Digital Signal Processing Engineer; RF Engineer; Embedded Engineer; Engineering Project Manager; Principal Engineer; Principal Engineer Embedded Software; Principal Engineer Systems; Principal Engineer Tactical Communication; Senior Engineer; Mechanical Engineer; Supervisor; SCM Builds Position; Designer; Business Development Manager; VP of Business Development; Organizational Process Group.

THINQ LEARNING SOLUTIONS, INC.
300 East Lombard Street, 15th floor, Baltimore MD 21202. 410/727-5112. **Fax:** 410/837-7903. **Contact:** Human Resources. **World Wide Web address:** http://www.thinq.com. **Description:** Provides innovative enterprise learning management software to its clients. **Positions advertised include:** Technical Support Engineer. **Corporate Headquarters:** This location.

THOMSON FINANCIAL
1455 Research Boulevard, Rockville MD 20850. 301/545-4000. **Contact:** Human Resources. **World Wide Web address:** http://www.thomsonfinancial.com. **Description:** Provides financial information to the investment industry through its four business units: the Investment Banking Group, the Investment Management Group, the Sales and Trading Group, and the Corporate Group. **Positions advertised include:** Administrative Assistant; Database Engineer; FDR Research Specialist; Financial Data Analyst; Inside Sales Representative; Product Manager; Senior Product Specialist; SQL Systems Administrator; Systems Operator; Technical Account Specialist. **Corporate headquarters location:** New York NY. **Other U.S. locations:** San Francisco CA; Chicago IL; Boston MA. **International locations:** Worldwide. **Parent company:** The Thomson Corporation. **CEO:** David H. Shaffer.

THE TITAN CORPORATION
22290 Exploration Drive, Lexington Park MD 20653-1397. 301/862-3509. **Fax:** 240/725-0015. **Contact:** Human Resources. **World Wide Web address:** http://www.titansystemscorp.com/groups/cgsg. **Description:** Titan Corporation provides information solutions, system support and products for national defense and civilian agencies. **Positions advertised include:** Acoustic Test Engineer; Administrative Assistant; Avionics Components Engineer; Communication Systems Manager; Test Analyst; Engineering Support; Mechanical Engineer; Network Administrator; Public Safety Communications Engineer; Business Analyst; Software Systems Analyst; Software Engineer. **Corporate headquarters:** San Diego CA. **Other U.S. locations:** Nationwide. **International locations:** Worldwide. **Operations at this facility include:** This location is part of the Systems Technology division of The Titan Corporation, specializing in ship and aviation engineering. **Listed on:** New York Stock Exchange. **Stock exchange symbol:** TTN. **CEO/Chairman:** Gene W. Ray. **Sales/revenue:** $2 billion. **Number of employees worldwide:** 12,000.

TOWSON UNIVERSITY
8000 York Road, Towson MD 21252-0001. 410/830-2000. **Fax:** 410/704-2891. **Recorded jobline:** 410/704-2161. **Contact:** Philip Ross III, Human Resources. **World Wide Web address:** http://www.towson.edu. **Description:** Offers undergraduate programs of study through the College of Allied Health Sciences and Physical Education, the College of Education, the College of Fine Arts and Communication, the College of Liberal Arts, the College of Natural and Mathematical Sciences, and the School of Business and Economics. Founded in 1866. **NOTE:** To contact Human Resources directly, call 410/704-2162. **Positions advertised include:** Administrative Assistant; Executive Assistant; Finisher- Bindery Assistant; Geographical Information Systems Student Coordinator; Geographical Information Systems Technician; Program Director; Consultant Trainer; Athletic Director; Admission Director; Event Planning Director; Field Work Director; Business Counselor; Admissions Recruitment; Parking Director; Service Worker; Campus Police Officer. **Office hours:** Monday – Friday, 8:00 a.m. – 4:30 p.m.

TRANDES CORPORATION
4601 President's Drive, Suite 360, Lanham MD 20706. 301/459-0200. **Fax:** 301/459-1069. **Contact:** Janine Carran, Director of Human Resources. **E-mail address:** jcarran@trandes.com. **World Wide Web address:** http://www.trandes.com. **Description:** An engineering contractor providing services to the federal government. Founded in 1972. **Special programs:** Tuition Assistance Program. **Corporate headquarters location:** This location. **Other area locations:** Lexington Park MD. **Other U.S. locations:** Nationwide. **Sales/revenue:** Over $16 million. **Number of employees nationwide:** Over 220.

TRANS-TECH INC.
P.O. Box 369, 5520 Adamstown Road, Adamstown MD 21710. 301/695-9400. **Fax:** 301/662-5204. **Contact:** Joanne Sheldon, Human Resources. **E-mail address:** joanne.sheldon@sktworksinc.com. **World Wide Web address:** http://www.trans-techinc.com. **Description:** Manufactures a number of electronic-grade ceramic materials used in microwave electronic components, such as link telephones. **Parent company:** Alpha Industries (Woburn MA). **Positions advertised include:** Supply Chain Manager; Inside Sales Representative; Production Worker. **Operations at this facility include:** Administration; Manufacturing; Research and Development; Sales. **Listed on:** NASDAQ. **Stock exchange symbol:** AHAA. **Number of employees nationwide:** 500.

TRI-COR INDUSTRIES, INC.
4600 Forbes Boulevard, Suite 205, Lanham MD 20706. 301/731-6140. **Fax:** 301/306-6742. **Contact:** Stafford DeWitt, Personnel. **E-mail address:** resumes@tricorind.com. **World Wide Web address:** http://www.tricorind.com. **Description:** Provides contractual computer services to the federal government. Services include networking, software development, operations, and security. Founded in 1983. **Note:** Can download employment applications on website. **Positions advertised include:** Proposal Manager. **Corporate headquarters location:** This location. **Other U.S. locations:** Nationwide. **President/CEO:** Louis Gonzalez. **Sales/revenue:** Over $50 million. **Number of employees nationwide:** Over 350.

TYDINGS & ROSENBERG LLP
100 East Pratt Street, 26th Floor, Baltimore MD 21202. 410/752-9700. **Contact:** Diane Castello, Hiring Coordinator. **E-mail address:** dcastello@tydingslaw.com. **World Wide Web address:** http://www.tydingslaw.com. **Description:** A general practice law firm with over 60 lawyers in fields including corporate law, commercial and business litigation, family law, employment law, and environmental litigation. **NOTE:** To reach Human Resources directly, call 410/752-9816. **Special programs:** Summer Associate Program. **Other U.S. locations:** Washington DC.

U.S. DEPARTMENT OF VETERANS AFFAIRS
BALTIMORE VETERANS ADMINISTRATION MEDICAL CENTER
10 North Greene Street, Baltimore MD 21201-1524. 410/605-7000. **Recorded jobline:** 800/463-6295x7211. **Contact:** Human Resources. **World Wide Web address:** http://www.vamchs.med.va.gov. **Description:** A medical center operated by the U.S. Department of Veterans Affairs (VA). From 54 hospitals in 1930, the VA health care system has grown to include 171 medical centers; more than 364 outpatient, community, and outreach clinics; 130 nursing home care units; and 37 domiciliary residences. VA operates at least one medical center in each of the 48 contiguous states, Puerto Rico, and the District of Columbia. With approximately 76,000 medical center beds, VA treats nearly 1 million patients in VA hospitals; 75,000 in nursing home care units; and 25,000 in domiciliary residences. **Positions advertised include:** Social Worker; Diagnostic Technician; Physical Therapist; Physical Account Supervisor; Medical Records Administrator; Medical Support Assistant.

U.S. FOOD AND DRUG ADMINISTRATION
Parklawn Building Room 7B-44, 5600 Fishers Lane, Rockville MD 20857. 301/827-4070. **Toll-free phone:** 888/463-6332. **Contact:** Office of Human Resources. **World Wide Web address:** http://www.fda.gov. **Description:** Monitors the manufacture, transport, storage, and sale of U.S. consumer products. FDA responsibilities include checking wharves for the illegal import of food, drugs, cosmetics, medical devices, and radiation-emitting products. **Positions advertised include:** Supervisory Medical Officer; Secretary; Management Analyst; Engineer; Information Technology Specialist; Biologist; Consumer Safety Officer; Pharmacologist; Chemist; Math Statistician; Microbiologist. **Corporate headquarters location:** This location.

U.S. FOODSERVICE
9755 Patuxent Woods Drive, Columbia MD 21046. 410/312-7100. **Fax:** 410/312-7591. **Contact:** Heather Sweet, Human Resources Department. **E-mail address:** heather.sweet@usfood.com. **World Wide Web address:** http://www.usfoodservice.com. **Description:** Distributes food products, fresh meats, dairy products, and cleaning supplies to restaurants and other institutional food service establishments. **Positions advertised include:** Delivery Driver; Business Analyst; Territory Manager; Vendor Coordinator; Web Designer. **Corporate headquarters location:** This location. **Other area locations:** Severn MD. **Other U.S. locations:** Nationwide. **Number of employees nationwide:** Over 34,000.

U.S. FOODSERVICE
P.O. Box 728, Severn MD 21144. 410/551-2000. **Physical address:** 8024 Telegraph Road, Severn MD 21144. **Toll-free phone:** 800/638-9402. **Contact:** Personnel. **World Wide Web address:** http://www.usfoodservice.com. **Description:** Distributes food products, fresh meats, dairy products, and cleaning supplies to restaurants and other institutional food service establishments. **Corporate headquarters location:** Columbia MD. **Other U.S. locations:** Nationwide. **Sales/revenue:** Over $19 billion. **Number of employees nationwide:** Over 34,000.

UNITED STATES GYPSUM COMPANY
5500 Quarantine Road, Baltimore MD 21226. 410/355-6600. **Contact:** Human Resources. **World Wide Web address:** http://www.usg.com. **Description:** A manufacturer of building materials, producing a complete range of products for use in new building construction, repair, and remodeling. **NOTE:** Job seekers may apply online for consideration. **Positions advertised include:** Manufacturing Services Position; Plant Department Manager; Plant Manager; Production Manager; Product Engineer; Manufacturing Management; Subsidiary Engineering Position. **Corporate headquarters location:** Chicago IL. **Other U.S. locations:** Nationwide. **International locations:** Canada; Mexico; England. **Subsidiaries include:** L&W Supply. **Parent company:** USG Corporation. **Operations at this facility include:** This location produces a wide range of gypsum building products. **Listed on:** New York Stock Exchange. **Stock exchange symbol:** USG. **President/CEO/Chairman:** William C. Foote. **Number of employees worldwide:** 14,000.

UNIVERSITY OF BALTIMORE
1420 North Charles Street, Baltimore MD 21201. 410/837-4200. **Contact:** Karen Drake, Human Resources Employment Specialist. **E-mail address:** kdrake@ubalt.edu. **World Wide Web address:** http://www.ubalt.edu. **Description:** A state university composed of a School of Business, a School of Law, and a Liberal Arts School. The university offers both graduate and undergraduate programs. Full-time enrollment is approximately 5,000 students. **Positions advertised include** Law Library Director; People Soft Systems Administrator; Cabinet Maker; Golf Driving Range Manager; Golf Driving Range Attendants; Admissions Counselor; Campus Web Master; Executive Administrative Assistant; Academic Program Specialist. **Special programs:** Tuition Waiver Program. **Office hours:** Monday – Friday, 8:30 a.m. – 4:30 p.m. **Parent company:** University System of Maryland. **President:** Robert L. Bogomolny.

UNIVERSITY OF MARYLAND AT BALTIMORE COUNTY
1000 Hilltop Circle, 532 Administration Building, Baltimore MD 21250. 410/ 455-2337. **Recorded jobline:** 410/455-1100. **Contact:** Human Resources. **World Wide Web address:** http://www.umbc.edu. **Description:** A research university with an enrollment of more than 10,500 students, serving the Baltimore metropolitan region. The university places special emphasis on its undergraduate programs, offering 30 majors. Founded in 1966. **Note:** http://www.umbc.edu/hr/employment is the University's employment web page. **Positions advertised include:** HVAC Mechanic; Accounting Associate; Librarian Technician. **Special programs:** Tuition Remission Program. **Office hours:** Monday – Friday, 8:00 a.m. – 5:00 p.m. **Parent company:** University System of Maryland. **Operations at this facility include:** Administration; Research and Development; Service. **President:** Freeman A. Hrabowski III. **Number of employees at this location:** 1,800.

UNIVERSITY OF MARYLAND AT COLLEGE PARK
COOPERATIVE EXTENSION SERVICE
Symons Hall, Room 2119, College Park MD 20742. 301/405-5679. **Contact:** Personnel Services Department. **E-mail address:** personnel@accmail.umd.edu. **World Wide Web address:** http://www.umd.edu. **Description:** A university offering 117 undergraduate and 84 graduate programs. **Positions advertised include:** Assistant Director of Special Events; Information Technology Coordinator; Web Communications Manager; Assistant Director; Registrar Analyst; Admissions Coordinator; Auditor; Business Manager; Program Coordinator; Registered Nurse; Resident Director; Science Editor. **President:** C.D. Mote, Junior. **Number of employees at this location:** 12,478.

UNIVERSITY OF MARYLAND BALTIMORE
737 West Lombard Street, Baltimore MD 21201. 410/706-7171. **Recorded jobline:** 410/706-5562. **Contact:** Human Resources. **E-mail address:** resume@hr.umaryland.edu. **World Wide Web address:** http://www.umaryland.edu. **Description:** The University of Maryland Baltimore specializes in health and human service programs. The 32-acre campus is a leader in medical research and education and is affiliated with the University of Maryland Medical System. **NOTE:** Applications are available online. **Positions advertised include:** Database Engineer; People Soft Functional Specialist; Information Systems Engineer; Information Technology Specialist; People Soft Functional Analyst. **Office hours:** Monday – Friday, 8:30 a.m. – 4:30 p.m. **Parent company:** University System of Maryland. **Operations at this facility include:** Administration; Research and Development. **Number of employees at this location:** 4,500.

VIPS, INC.
One West Pennsylvania Avenue, Suite 700, Baltimore MD 21204. 410/832-8300. **Fax:** 410/832-8315. **Contact:** Human Resources Specialist. **E-mail address:** career@vips.com. **World Wide Web address:** http://www.vips.com. **Description:** Offers computer consulting services and business solutions for the health care industry. **Positions advertised include:** A Web Applications Programmer; Unix System Administrator; Clinical Analyst; System Analyst; Programming Analyst. **Corporate headquarters location:** This location. **Other U.S. locations:** Washington DC; Minneapolis MN; Los Angeles CA. **CEO:** Jenny Morgan.

VENABLE ATTORNEYS AT LAW
2 Hopkins Plaza, Suite 1800, Baltimore MD 21201. 410/244-7400. **Fax:** 410/244-7742. **Contact:** Human Resources. **E-mail address:** careeropp@venable.com. **World Wide Web address:** http://www.venable.com. **Description:** A law firm with over 25 practice areas including corporate law and litigation. **NOTE:** Part-time and temporary positions are offered. **Positions advertised include:** Bankruptcy Associate; Staff Attorney; Paralegal; Employment Associate; Products Paralegal. **Other area locations:** Rockville MD; Towson MD. **Other U.S. locations:** Washington DC; McLean VA.

VERIZON CONNECTED SOLUTIONS
11750 Beltsville Drive, 3rd Floor, Beltsville MD 20705. 301/586-1100. **Contact:** Human Resources. **World Wide Web address:** http://www.baccsi.com. **Description:** Designs and installs communications products and solutions for audio, data, video, and voice applications for home entertainment, home networks, home offices, ADSL, LAN and WAN networks, and Internet access. **Positions advertised include:** Accounts Payable Specialist; Auto Equipment Technician; Accounting Specialist. **Corporate headquarters location:** This location. **Parent company:** Verizon Communications is a full-service communications services provider. Verizon offers residential local and long distance telephone services and Internet access; wireless service plans, cellular phones, and data services; a full-line of business services including Internet access, data services, and telecommunications equipment and services; and government network solutions including Internet access, data services, telecommunications equipment and services, and enhanced communications services. **Listed on:** New York Stock Exchange. **Stock exchange symbol:** VZ. **CEO:** Ivan Seidenburg. **Sales/revenue:** $67 billion. **Number of employees worldwide:** Over 229,000.

VULCAN HART COMPANY
3600 North Point Boulevard, Baltimore MD 21222. 410/284-0660. **Contact:** Human Resources. **World Wide Web address:** http://www.vulcanhart.com. **Description:** A manufacturer of commercial cooking equipment including gas and electric ovens, ranges, broilers, and fryers. **Corporate headquarters location:** Louisville KY. **Other U.S. locations:** Compton CA; St. Louis MO. **President:** Mark Whalen.

WDCA-TV
UPN/CHANNEL 20
5202 River Road, Bethesda MD 20816. 301/986-9322. **Contact:** Human Resources. **World Wide Web address:** http://www.wdca.com. **Description:** A television station. **Positions advertised include:** Accounting Coordinator; Assignment Editor; Meteorologist; Writer Fill-in Technician; General Assignment Reporter; Broadcast Designer; Research Analyst; Technician; Traffic Coordinator; Sales Assistant; Assignment Editor. **Special programs:** Internships. **Corporate headquarters location:** New York NY. **Parent company:** Fox Television Stations, Incorporated. **Operations at this facility include:** Administration; Production; Sales. **Listed on:** New York Stock Exchange. **Stock exchange symbol:** FOX.

WMDT- ABC DELMAR
P.O. BOX 4009, 202 Downtown Plaza, Salisbury MD 21803. 410/742-4747. **Fax:** 410/742-5767. **E-mail address:** dawn_mitchell@wmdt.com. **Contact:** Dawn Mitchell Human Resources. **World Wide Web address:** http://www.wmdt.com. **Description:** Delmar's ABC affiliate. **Positions advertised include:** General Assignment Reporter; Sport's Anchor Reporter.

WIYY- FM 98 ROCK
3800 Hooper Avenue, Baltimore MD 21211. 410/889-0098. **Fax:** 410/675-7946. **Contact:** Hugues Jean, General Sales Manager. **E-mail address:** hjean@hearst.com. **World Wide Web address:** http://www.98online.com. **Description:** Baltimore's Rock Station. **Positions advertised include:** Sales & marketing Executive. **Internship information:** Internships available. **Office Hours:** Monday – Friday 9:00 a.m. – 5:30 p.m.

THE WALTERS ART MUSEUM
600 North Charles Street, Baltimore MD 21201-5188. 410/547-9000. **Contact:** Human Resources. **E-mail address:** jobs@thewalters.org. **World Wide Web address:** http://www.thewalters.org. **Description:** Holds the private collections of William and Henry Walters. The Walters Art Gallery sponsors traveling and special exhibitions to supplement the Walters' original collections. **Positions advertised include:** Rentals Events Assistant; Special Events Security Officer. **Special programs:** Internships.

WARWICK MANOR
3680 Warwick Road, East New Market MD 21631. 410/943-8108. **Contact:** Human Resources. **Description:** Provides behavioral health care and substance abuse services.

WASHINGTON COUNTY HOSPITAL
1101 Jefferson Boulevard, Hagerstown MD 21742. 301/790-8000. **Contact:** Human Resources. **World Wide Web address:** http://www.wchsys.org. **Description:** An acute care, nonprofit, regional medical center. Washington County Hospital serves a tri-state region including western Maryland, southern Pennsylvania, and northern West Virginia. Washington County Hospital includes facilities totaling 371 beds; intensive care, coronary care, and progressive care units; a cardiac catheterization lab; a family birthing center; a full range of radiologic/diagnostic services; a pediatric unit; inpatient and outpatient mental health units/services; a certified oncology program; extended care facilities; Alzheimer's disease and related disorders programs; cardiac rehabilitation; community education programs; physician practices; and home health care. **NOTE:** To contact Human Resources directly, call 301/790-8500. **Positions advertised include:** Patient Accounts Representative; Washing Machine Assistant; Registered Nurse; Home Health Aide Therapist; Out Patient Speech Therapist; Ortho Physical Therapist; Neuro Physical Therapist; Occupational Physical Therapist; Day House Keeper; Linen Assistant; Environmental Services Assistant; Licensed Practical Nurse; Utilization Revenue Specialist; Certified Nursing Assistant; Pharmaceutical Technician; Ultrasonographer. **Number of employees at this location:** 1,500.

WASTE MANAGEMENT, INC.
8101 Beechcraft Avenue, Gaithersburg MD 20879. 301/340-0833. **Contact:** Human Resources. **World Wide Web address:** http://www.wastemanagement.com. **Description:** An international provider of comprehensive waste management services, as well as engineering and construction, industrial, and related services. **Positions advertised include:** Safety Quality Specialist; Sales Representative; Outside Sales Representative. **Corporate headquarters location:** Houston TX. **Other U.S. locations:** Nationwide. **Listed on:** New York Stock Exchange. **Stock exchange symbol:** WMI. **President/CEO/Chairman:** A. Maurice Myers.

WEYERHAEUSER COMPANY
3400 East Biddle Street, Baltimore MD 21213. 410/327-7376. **Contact:** Human Resources. **World Wide Web address:** http://www.weyerhaeuser.com. **Description:** A company whose principal businesses are the growing and harvesting of timber; the manufacture, distribution, and sale of forest products including logs, wood chips, and building products; real estate development and construction; and financial services. Weyerhaeuser Company is one of the world's largest private owners of marketable softwood timber and also one of the largest producers of softwood lumber and pulp. The company is also one of North America's largest producers of forest products and recyclers of office wastepaper, newspaper, and corrugated boxes. Weyerhaeuser Company also sells electricity to utility companies generated from its 15 trash-to-energy plants and 6 small cogeneration or recycling plants. The Water Division manufactures and operates facilities and systems for water purification, water treatment, and managed by-products. The Air Division designs, manufactures, and integrates air pollution emission control and measurement systems and related equipment. **Positions advertised include:** Sales Representative; Drafting Associate; Designing Associate; Trading Associate; Technical Designing Associate. **Special programs:** Tuition Reimbursement Program; Training; Mentorship. **Corporate headquarters location:** Tacoma WA. **Other U.S. locations:** Nationwide. **International locations:** Worldwide. **Operations at this facility include:** This location is a container plant. **Listed on:** New York Stock Exchange. **Stock exchange symbol:** WY. **President/CEO/Chairman:** Steven Rogel. **Sales/revenue:** $18.5 billion. **Number of employees worldwide:** 47,000.

WILCOXON RESEARCH, INC.
21 Firstfield Road, Gaithersburg MD 20878. 301/330-8811. **Toll-free phone:** 800/WILCOXON. **Fax:** 301/527-9761. **Contact:** Human Resources. **E-mail address:** wrjobs@wilcoxon.com. **World Wide Web address:** http://www.wilcoxon.com. **Description:** A designer and producer of a variety of electromechanical devices for use in machinery maintenance, predictive maintenance programs, and laboratory research. Products include electromagnetic vibration generators and underwater accelerometers. **NOTE:** Resumes may be submitted online. **Positions advertised include:** Human Resources Generalist. **Special programs:** Tuition Reimbursement Program; Internal Training Program. **Office hours:** Monday - Friday, 8:00 a.m. - 4:30 p.m. **Corporate headquarters location:** This location. **Listed on:** Privately held. **President/CEO:** Fred Wilcoxon. **Number of employees at this location:** 110.

M.S. WILLETT, INC.
220 Cockeysville Road, Cockeysville MD 21030. 410/771-0460. **Fax:** 410/771-8434. **Contact:** Erik Benzer, Human Resources. **E-mail address:** hr@mswillett.com. **World Wide Web address:** http://www.mswillett.com. **Description:** A tool and die manufacturer, engaged in metal stamping and punch-press automation services. **NOTE:** Second and third shifts are offered. Resumes can be sent to: resumes@mswillett.com. **Positions advertised include:** Tool and Die Maker; Machinist; Tool and Die Salesperson. **Special programs:** Apprenticeships. **Corporate headquarters location:** This location. **Number of employees at this location:** 100.

WILLIAMS SCOTSMAN
8211 Town Center Drive, Baltimore MD 21236. 800/782-1500. **Fax:** 410/931-6063. **Contact:** Human Resources. **E-mail address:** hr@willscot.com. **World Wide Web address:** http://www.willscot.com. **Description:** A national provider of mobile and modular building solutions for the construction, education, commercial, healthcare and government markets. **Corporate headquarters locations:** This location. **Other U.S. locations:** Nationwide.

XPEDX
7445 New Ridge Road, Hanover MD 21076. 410/694-8500. **Contact:** Personnel. **E-mail address:** recruiting@xpedx.com. **World Wide Web address:** http://www.xpedx.com. **Description:** Manufactures paper primarily used by local printing companies. The company also distributes packaging supplies and equipment, graphic imaging prepress supplies and equipment, and other facility supplies. **Corporate headquarters location:** Covington KY. **Other U.S. locations:** Nationwide. **President:** Richard B. Lowe. **Sales/revenue:** Approximately $7 billion.

ZENTECH MANUFACTURING, INC.
6980 Tudsbury Road, Baltimore MD 21244. 443/348-4500. **Fax:** 443/348-4505. **Contact:** Human Resources. **E-mail address:** jobs@zentechman.com. **World Wide Web address:** http://www.zentechman.com. **Description:** Electronics manufacturing company. **Positions advertised include:** Program Manager; Receptionist; Surface Mount Technicians; Soldering; Quality Control Inspectors. **Operations at this facility include:** Administrative; Production.

ZURICH NORTH AMERICA SURETY & FINANCIAL ENTERPRISES
P.O. Box 1227, Baltimore MD 21203. 410/366-1000. **Physical address:** 3910 Keswick Road, Baltimore MD 21203. **Toll-free phone:** 800/821-4635. **Contact:** Human Resources. **World Wide Web address:** http://www.zurichna.com. **Description:** Specializes in surety bonds and insurance. **Positions advertised include:** Claims Specialist; Claims Counsel; Coverage Counsel; Marketing Assistant; Operations Supervisor; Operations Technician; Risk Engineering Consultant; Underwriter; Quality Assurance Manager. **NOTE:** Resumes may be submitted online for advertised positions or for general consideration. **Special programs:** Internships. **Corporate headquarters location:** This location. **Parent company:** Zurich North America.

A-AFFORDABLE AUTO INSURANCE
480 Forest Avenue, Brockton MA 02301. 508/588-4333. **Fax:** 508/588-2958. **Contact:** Human Resources. **World Wide Web address:** http://www.a-affordableinsurance.com. **Description:** Provides automobile insurance and some commercial insurance policies.

AAA AUTO CLUB
900 Hingham Street, Rockland MA 02370. 781/871-5880. **Contact:** Human Resources. **E-mail address:** humanresources@aaasne.com. **World Wide Web address:** http://www.aaasne.com. **Description:** Provides insurance, travel, and related services to motorists through a network of over 50 branch offices. **Positions advertised include:** Dispatcher Road Services Call Center; Call Counselor; Auto Travel Call Counselor; Insurance Customer Service Representative; Travel Agent; Membership Processor; Security Guard; Auto Travel Route Marker; Human Resource Assistant; Non Radio Dispatcher; Executive Assistant.

ABT ASSOCIATES INC.
55 Wheeler Street, Cambridge MA 02138. 617/492-7100. **Fax:** 617/492-5219. **Contact:** Human Resources. **E-mail address:** abtassoc@rpc.webhire.com. **World Wide Web address:** http://www.abtassoc.com. **Description:** One of the largest government and business consulting and research firms in the country. The company offers policy analysis, technical assistance, program evaluation, and program operation services to governmental clients and provides organizational development, service quality measurement and management, strategic planning, management consulting, and new product development services to business clients. ABT Associates conducts its business through four main practice areas: international economic policy research; business research and consulting; and ABT Associates Clinical Trials. Founded in 1965. **Positions advertised include:** Analyst; Research Assistant; Medical Associate; MIS Director; Programmer Analyst; Research Project Manager; Accounts Payable Clerk; Informational Payroll Manager; Administrative Assistant; Principal Associate; Biostatistician. **NOTE:** Applicants can mail resumes with appropriate source code found on website to this address for consideration: Abt Associates Inc., Source Code, P.O. Box 369 Burlington MA 01803. **Corporate headquarters location:** This location. **Other area locations:** Lexington MA; Hadley MA. **Other U.S. locations:** Washington DC; Chicago IL; Bethesda MD. **International locations:** Egypt; South Africa. **Operations at this facility include:** Administration; Research and Development. **Annual sales/revenues:** More than $100 million. **Number of employees worldwide:** 1,000.

ACS DEVELOPMENT
80 Everett Avenue, Suite 319, Chelsea MA 02150. 617/889-6900. **Fax:** 617/889-6255. **Contact:** Patricia Simboli, Principal. **Description:** A real estate corporation with assets in the metropolitan Boston and Florida markets. Properties include retail, office, and industrial locations. **Corporate headquarters location:** This location. **Operations at this facility include:** Administration; Sales.

ADE CORPORATION
80 Wilson Way, Westwood MA 02090. 781/467-3500. **Fax:** 781/467-0500. **Contact:** Human Resources. **World Wide Web address:** http://www.ade.com. **Description:** Develops and manufactures measurement and automation equipment for the instrumentation, electronics, and semiconductor markets. **Positions advertised include:** Application Engineering Manager. **NOTE:** Entry-level positions are offered. **Special programs:** Internships. **Corporate headquarters location:** This location. **Other area locations:** Newton MA. **Other U.S. locations:** Tuscon AZ. **Operations at this facility include:** Administration; Divisional Headquarters; Manufacturing; Research and Development; Sales; Service. **Listed on:** NASDAQ. **Stock exchange symbol:** ADEX. **Annual sales/revenues:** $51 - $100 million. **Number of employees at this location:** 200. **Number of employees worldwide:** 600.

AGFA CORPORATION
200 Ballardvale Street, Wilmington MA 01887. 978/658-5600. **Contact:** Human Resources. **World Wide Web address:** http://www.agfa.com. **Description:** AGFA operates through several divisions: the Photographic Division produces films, printing papers, cameras, film projectors, lenses, and other related products used in X-ray and nondestructive testing applications; the Office Systems Division produces office duplicators and printers, a wide range of microfiche and microfilm products, and related supplies; and the Magnetic Tape Division produces professional audio products and amateur videocassette products. **Corporate headquarters location:** This location. **Other U.S. locations:** Nationwide. **International locations:** Worldwide. **Operations at this facility include:** This location manufactures phototypesetting equipment including fonts, parts, supplies, and output devices.

AM-PM CLEANING CORPORATION
1560 Trapelo Road, Waltham MA 02451. 781/622-1444. **Contact:** Human Resources. **Description:** Provides cleaning and maintenance service. **NOTE:** Entry-level positions and part-time jobs are offered. **Company slogan:** Maintaining an atmosphere of excellence. **Corporate headquarters location:** This location. **General Manager:** J. Kenneth Fosealdo. **Sales Manager:** Karen Perkins. **Annual sales/revenues:** $11 - $20 million. **Number of employees at this location:** 650.

ASA INTERNATIONAL LTD.
10 Speen Street, Framingham MA 01701. 508/626-2727. **Fax:** 508/626-0645. **Contact:** Human Resources. **World Wide Web address:** http://www.asaint.com. **Description:** Designs, develops, and installs proprietary vertical market software. **Special programs:** Internships. **Corporate headquarters location:** This location. **Other U.S. locations:** Nashua NH; Blue Bell PA. **Subsidiaries include:** ASA Legal Systems; ASA Tire Systems. **Listed on:** NASDAQ. **Stock exchange symbol:** ASAA. **Annual sales/revenues:** $21 - $50 million. **Number of employees at this location:** 85. **Number of employees nationwide:** 190.

ABBOT BUILDING RESTORATION COMPANY, INC.
28 Allerton Street, Boston MA 02119. 617/445-0274. **Contact:** Human Resources Department. **Description:** Specializes in building restoration. Services include brick masonry and concrete repair.

ABBOTT BIORESEARCH CENTER
100 Research Drive, Worcester MA 01605. 508/849-2500. **Fax:** 508/755-8511 **Contact:** Human Resources. **E-mail address:** abcjobs@abbott.com. **World Wide Web address:** http://www.abbott.com. **Description:** Engaged in immunology and oncology research for the development of pharmaceuticals. **Positions advertised include:** Process Engineer; Director of Translation; Validation Specialist; Research Associate; Scientist; Quality Assurance Specialist. **Corporate headquarters location:** Abbott Park IL. **Parent company:** Abbott Laboratories. **Other U.S. locations:** Nationwide. **International locations:** Worldwide.

ABBOTT LABORATORIES
4A Crosby Drive, Bedford MA 01730. 781/276-6000. **Contact:** Human Resources. **World Wide Web address:** http://www.abbott.com. **Description:** Develops, manufactures, and markets blood-glucose monitoring systems that enable diabetics to manage their disease more effectively. **Positions advertised include:** Site Director; Engineer; Program Coordinator; Scientist; Material Handler; Label Editor. **Corporate headquarters location:** Abbott Park IL. **Other U.S. locations:** Nationwide. **International locations:** Worldwide.

ABERDEEN GROUP
260 Franklin Street Suite 1700, Boston MA 02108. 617/723-7890. **Toll-free phone:** 800/577-7897. **Contact:** Human Resources. **E-mail address:** inquiry@Aberdeen.com. **World Wide Web address:** http://www.aberdeen.com. **Description:** A computer systems, software, and communications consulting and research firm. Aberdeen Group provides strategic management solutions for domestic and international clients. **Positions advertised include:** Sales Account Manager; Product Marketing Manager; Curriculum Director.

ABINGTON SAVINGS BANK
536 Washington Street, Abington MA 02351. 781/982-3200. **Fax:** 781/682-8777. **Contact:** Human Resources. **E-mail address:** hradmin@abingtonsavings.com. **World Wide Web address:** http://www.abingtonsavings.com. **Description:** A full-service bank. **Corporate headquarters location:** This location. **Other U.S. locations:** Halifax MA; Hanover MA; Holbrook MA; Hull MA; Kingston MA; Pembroke MA; Whitman MA. **Listed on:** NASDAQ. **Stock exchange symbol:** ABBK.

ABIOMED, INC.
22 Cherry Hill Drive, Danvers MA 01923. 978/777-5410. **Fax:** 978/777-8411. **Contact:** Human Resources. **E-mail address:** staffing@abiomed.com. **World Wide Web address:** http://www.abiomed.com. **Description:** Develops, manufactures, and markets cardiovascular, medical, and dental products. The company is also engaged in the research and development of heart support systems. **Positions advertised include:** Clinical Manager, Field Operations; Clinical Research Manager; Product Manager; Scientist. **Corporate headquarters location:** This location. **Subsidiaries include:** Abiodent; Abiomed B.V., Abiomed Cardiovascular; Abiomed R&D. **Operations at this facility include:** Administration; Manufacturing; Research and Development; Sales; Service. **Listed on:** NASDAQ. **Stock exchange symbol:** ABMD. **Number of employees at this location:** 140. **Number of employees nationwide:** 170.

ACADIAN ASSET MANAGEMENT INC.
10 Post Office Square, 8th Floor, Boston MA 02109. 617/946-3500. **Fax:** 617/946-3501. **Contact:** Human Resources. **World Wide Web address:** http://www.acadian-asset.com. **Description:** A money management firm specializing in international stocks. **Positions advertised include:** Investment Operations Specialist; Portfolio Associate; Database Systems Engineer. **NOTE:** Summer internships available. Search for current positions on website.

ACAMBIS INC.
38 Sidney Street, 4th Floor, Cambridge MA 02139. 617/761-4200. **Fax:** 617/494-1741. **Contact:** Human Resources. **World Wide Web address:** http://www.acambis.com. **Description:** Discovers and develops oral vaccines and noninjected antibody products to prevent and treat diseases that infect the human body at its mucous membranes. These tissues include the linings of the gastrointestinal, respiratory, and genitourinary tracts and the surfaces of the eyes. Acambis is pursuing three principal product development programs that target diseases that have high rates of incidence including viral pneumonia in children, peptic ulcer disease, and antibiotic-associated diarrhea and colitis. **Positions advertised include:** Accounting Manager; Network Engineer; IT Manager; Clinical Regulatory Manager; Clinical Trial Manager. **Corporate headquarters location:** Cambridge, England. **Listed on:** NASDAQ. **Stock exchange symbol:** ACAM.

ACCENTURE
100 William Street, Wellesley MA 02481. 617/454-4000. **Contact:** Human Resources. **World Wide Web address:** http://www.accenture.com. **Description:** A management and technology consulting firm. Accenture offers a wide range of services including business re-engineering, customer service system consulting, data system design and implementation, Internet sales systems research and design, and strategic planning. **Positions advertised include:** Oracle Operations Consultant; PeopleSoft Financials Functional Consultant; SAP Technical Architect; Credit & Collections Solutions Consultant; Service Attendant; Transaction Attorneys; Finance Professional; Executive Assistant; Project Administrator. **Corporate headquarters location:** Chicago IL. **Other area locations:** Boston MA. **Other U.S. locations:** Nationwide. **International locations:** Worldwide. **Listed on:** New York Stock Exchange. **Stock exchange symbol:** ACN.

ACME PRINTING COMPANY
30 Industrial Way, Wilmington MA 01887. 978/658-0800. **Contact:** Human Resources. **World Wide Web address:** http://www.acmeprinting.com. **Description:** A commercial printer.

ACTION FOR BOSTON COMMUNITY DEVELOPMENT (ABCD)
178 Tremont Street, Boston MA 02111. 617/357-6000. **Contact:** Human Resources. **E-mail address:** hr@bostonabc.org. **NOTE:** When sending in applications please have them in Microsoft Word format only. **World Wide Web address:** http://www.bostonabcd.org. **Description:** A nonprofit, community action, human services agency helping low-income residents make the transition from poverty to self-sufficiency. ABCD provides programs and services including job training, education, weatherization, housing services, fuel assistance, the Urban College Program, child care including Head Start and daycare, and elder service programs. **Positions advertised include:** Receptionist; Program Assistant. **Corporate headquarters location:** This location. **Operations at this facility include:** Administration; Research and Development.

ACTON MEDICAL ASSOCIATES, PC
321 Main Street, Acton MA 01720. 978/263-1425. **Fax:** 978/263-1562. **Contact:** Human Resources. **E-mail address:** hr@actonmedical.com. **World Wide Web address:** http://www.actonmedical.com. **Description:** Offices of a primary care medical group that include laboratory and X-ray facilities. Founded in 1958. **NOTE:** Entry-level positions are offered. **Positions advertised include:** Medical Technologist; PA Diabetes Management; Phlebotomist; Registered Nurse; Licensed Practical Nurse; Internal Medicine. **Special programs:** Internships; Summer Jobs. **Listed on:** Privately held. **Number of employees at this location:** 170.

ACUSHNET COMPANY
333 Bridge Street, Fairhaven MA 02719. 508/979-2000. **Contact:** Human Resources. **World Wide Web address:** http://www.acushnet.com. **Description:** Manufactures a wide range of golf equipment including golf balls, clubs, and shoes. Products are sold under the Titleist, Foot-Joy, Pinnacle, and Cobra brand names. **Positions advertised include:** Interactive Marketing Manager. **Parent company:** Fortune Brands, Inc. **Listed on:** New York Stock Exchange. **Stock exchange symbol:** FO.

ACUSHNET RUBBER COMPANY
744 Belleville Avenue, New Bedford MA 02745. 508/998-4000. **Contact:** Human Resources. **World Wide Web address:** http://www.acushnet.com. **Description:** Manufactures and markets rubber and elastomeric products worldwide.

ADAMS MEDIA, AN F+W PUBLICATIONS COMPANY
57 Littlefield Street, Avon MA 02322. 508/427-7100. **Toll-free phone:** 800/872-5627. **Fax:** 800/872-5628. **Contact:** Human Resources. **E-mail address:** hr@adamsmedia.com. **World Wide Web address:** http://www.adamsmedia.com. **Description:** A rapidly growing publisher of nonfiction books in a wide range of categories. Major book series include the Everything® series, Cup of Comfort®, JobBank, Knock 'em Dead, and Polka Dot Press. The company's line of business books includes the Adams Small Business series, the Adams Streetwise® series, and Platinum Press. Other nonfiction categories include self-help, weddings, humor, personal finance, parenting, and reference. Founded in 1980. **Positions advertised include:** Associate Editor; Editorial Assistant; Manufacturing Coordinator; Production Artist; Production Editor. **NOTE:** Refer to http://www.fwpublications.com for current employment opportunities. **Special programs:** Internships. **Internship information:** Adams Media's internship program runs throughout the year. **Office hours:** Monday - Friday, 8:00 a.m. - 5:00 p.m. **Corporate headquarters location:** Cincinnati OH. **Parent Company:** F&W Publications, Inc. **Operations at this facility include:** Accounting/Auditing; Administration; Customer Service; Editorial - Reference; Editorial - Trade; Marketing; Operations; Production; Publishing; Sales. **Listed on:** Privately held.

ADAMS/CHESHIRE HEADSTART PROJECT
46 Howland Avenue, Adams MA 01220. 413/743-5150. **Contact:** Human Resources. **Description:** A state- and federally funded daycare program for low-income families with children between the ages of three and five.

ADDISON WESLEY
75 Arlington Street, Suite 300, Boston MA 02116. 617/848-6000. **Contact:** Human Resources. **World Wide Web address:** http://www.awl.com. **Description:** Publishes and distributes educational materials for use in elementary and high schools, universities, and certain businesses. Addison Wesley publications cover all of the major disciplines. The company also publishes professional, reference, and nonfiction trade books. The company operates in three divisions: Higher Education; School; and General Books. **Positions advertised include:** Page Formatter; Project Manager; Sales Representative; Webmaster; Associate Media Producer; Designer; Development Editor; Editorial Assistant; Education Consultant; Executive Assistant; Managing Editor; Marketing Manager; Production Editor; Math Content Writer. **Corporate headquarters location:** Upper Saddle River NJ. **International locations:** England, Hong Kong. **Parent company:** Pearson Education

ADESA BOSTON
63 Western Avenue, Framingham MA 01702. 508/626-7000. **Contact:** Human Resources. **E-mail address:** email_careers@adesa.com. **World Wide Web address:** http://www.adesa.com. **Description:** Auctions used cars and other vehicles to franchised auto dealerships. Adesa also provides auto reconditioning and vehicle transport services. **NOTE:** Entry-level positions and part-time jobs are offered. **Positions advertised include:** Application Technician; NT Analyst; Senior Financial Analyst. **Office hours:** Monday - Friday, 8:30 a.m. - 5:00 p.m. **Number of employees at this location:** 380. **Number of employees nationwide:** 4,000.

ADHESIVE PACKAGING SPECIALTIES, INC.
103 Foster Street P.O. Box 31, Peabody MA 01960. 978/531-3300. **Toll-free phone:** 800/222-1117. **Fax:** 978/532-8901. **Contact:** Human Resources. **E-mail address:** humanresources@adhesivepackaging.com. **World Wide Web address:** http://www.adhesivepackaging.com. **Description:** A custom repackager of resins and adhesives.

ADVANCED MAGNETICS, INC.
61 Mooney Street, Cambridge MA 02138. 617/497-2070. **Fax:** 617/547-2445. **Contact:** Human Resources. **E-mail address:** contactus@advancedmagnets.com. **World Wide Web address:** http://www.advancedmagnetics.com. **Description:** Engaged in the development and manufacture of MRI contrast agents for the detection of cancer and other diseases. **Listed on:** American Stock Exchange. **Stock exchange symbol:** AVM.

ADVEST
100 Federal Street, 29th Floor, Boston MA 02110. 617/348-2200. **Contact:** Human Resources. **World Wide Web address:** http://www.advest.com. **Description:** Provides stock brokerage services. **Positions advertised include:** Financial Analyst.

ADVIZEX TECHNOLOGIES
128 Wheeler Road, Burlington MA 01803. 781/229-2419. **Toll-free phone:** 800/366-6096. **Fax:** 781/229-9991. **Contact:** Human Resources. **E-mail address:** jobs@advizex.com. **World Wide Web address:** http://www.advizex.com. **Description:** Provides open systems technology integration along with other business services including IT planning and developing, and computer reselling. **Positions advertised include:** Oracle Apps Data Base Administrator; Project Manager; Storage Consultant; Oracle Solution Architect; Unix Consultant; Account Executive.

AEGIS ASSOCIATES, INC.
98 Galen Street, Watertown MA 02472. 617/923-2500. **Fax:** 617/926-7050. **Contact:** Marie Stefanik, Human Resources Coordinator. **E-mail address:** hr2@aegis-inc.com. **World Wide Web address:** http://www.aegis-inc.com. **Description:** A computer reseller and network integrator that provides custom computer systems, networks, and related services. This location also hires seasonally. Founded in 1989. **NOTE:** Entry-level positions are offered. **Company slogan:** Your technology experts. **Positions advertised include:** Account Executive; Inside sales Representative. **Special programs:** Training. **Office hours:** Monday - Friday, 8:30 a.m. - 5:00 p.m. **Corporate headquarters location:** This location. **Annual sales/revenues:** $5 - $10 million.

AEROVOX, INC.
167 John Vertente Boulevard, New Bedford MA 02745-1221. 508/994-9661. **Fax:** 508/995-3000. **Contact:** Human Resources. **E-mail address:** sales@aerovox.com. **World Wide Web address:** http://www.aerovox.com. **Description:** A manufacturer of capacitors for electrical and electronic applications. **Operations at this facility include:** Manufacturing; Research and Development. **Number of employees nationwide:** 1,300.

AGGREGATE INDUSTRIES
1715 Broadway, Saugus MA 01906. 781/941-7200. **Fax:** 781/941-7228. **Contact:** Human Resources. **World Wide Web address:** http://www.aggregate.com. **Description:** A leading producer of crushed stone, bituminous and ready-mixed concrete, and liquid asphalt. Aggregate Industries also engages in a variety of general construction, asphalt and concrete recycling, and soil remediation activities. **Corporate headquarters location:** Bethesda MD. **Other area locations:** Stoughton MA.

AGGREGATE INDUSTRIES
1101 Turnpike Street, Stoughton MA 02072. 781/344-1100. **Contact:** Human Resources. **World Wide Web address:** http://www.aggregate.com. **Description:** A leading producer of crushed stone, bituminous and ready-mixed concrete, and liquid asphalt. Aggregate Industries also engages in a variety of general construction, asphalt and concrete recycling, and soil remediation activities. **Corporate headquarters location:** Bethesda MD. **Other area locations:** Saugus, MA.

AIDS ACTION COMMITTEE
294 Washington Street 5th Floor, Boston MA 02108. 617/437-6200. **Fax:** 617/437-6445. **Recorded jobline:** 617/450-1435. **Contact:** Human Resources. **E-mail address:** resumes@aac.org. **World Wide Web address:** http://www.aac.org. **Description:** A nonprofit organization providing services to people living with HIV, and their families; combating the AIDS epidemic through education; and advocating fair and effective AIDS policy and funding. The AIDS Action Committee is the largest AIDS service organization in New England. Founded by a small group of volunteers, the organization now includes a full-time professional staff supported by several thousand volunteers. The group operates through several segments, all of which offer employment and volunteer opportunities. They include clinical services, housing, financial and legal, counseling, education, training, development, fundraising, public policy, government relations, communications, grant writing, administration and finance, AR/AP, human resources, MIS, computer operations, and facilities. Founded in 1983. **Positions advertised include:** Clinical Specialist; Associate Director of Major Gifts; Bilingual Hotline Coordinator; Field Interviewer. **NOTE:** Please call the jobline for current openings. Indicate the position of interest in your cover letter. **Special programs:** Internships. **Corporate headquarters location:** This location. **Operations at this facility include:** Administration. **Number of employees at this location:** 100.

AIR COMPRESSOR ENGINEERING COMPANY INC.
P.O. Box 738, Westfield MA 01806. 413/568-2884. **Physical Address:** 17 Meadow Street, Westfield MA 01085-3221. **Contact:** Human Resources. **Description:** Engaged in the wholesale of new and used metalworking machinery.

AIRVANA, INC.
19 Alpha Road, Chelmsford MA 01824. 866/344-7437. **Fax:** 978/250-3910. **Contact:** Human Resources. **E-mail address:** information@airvananet.com. **World Wide Web address:** http://www.arivananet.com. **Description:** Develops All-IP 3G Radio Access Network infrastructure equipment for wireless carriers and global infrastructure suppliers such as Nortel Networks and Ericsson. **Positions advertised include:** Automation Test Engineer; Consulting Systems Engineer; Customer Network Engineer; General Counsel; Marketing Manager; Mobile IP Architect; QA Engineer.

ALKERMES, INC.
64 Sidney Street, Cambridge MA 02139. 617/494-0171. **Contact:** Peter Maguire, Director of Human Resources. **World Wide Web address:** http://www.alkermes.com. **Description:** A pharmaceutical company that produces drug delivery systems for pharmaceutical agents. Alkermes produces four proprietary delivery systems including Cereport blood-brain permeabilizer, ProLease and Medisorb injectable sustained-release systems, RingCap and Dose Sipping oral delivery systems, and AIR pulmonary delivery systems. **Positions advertised include:** Clinical Manager; Drug Safety Associate; Medical Director; Statistical Programmer; Development Engineer; Scientist; Quality Control Microbiologist Supervisor; Regulatory Affairs Director; Regulatory Affairs Manager; Strategic Procurement Manager. **NOTE:** Apply and submit resumes online. Resumes should be sent to Peter Maguire at 840 Memorial Drive, Cambridge MA 02139. **Corporate headquarters location:** This location. **Other U.S. locations:** Cincinnati OH. **Listed on:** NASDAQ. **Stock exchange symbol:** ALKS.

ALL CARE VISITING NURSE ASSOCIATION
16 City Hall Square, Lynn MA 01901. 781/598-2454. **Toll-free phone:** 800/287-2454. **Fax:** 781/586-1636. **Contact:** Ray Felice, Human Resources Representative. **E-mail address:** professional@allcarevna.org. **World Wide Web address:** http://www.allcarevna.org. **Description:** A nonprofit, certified, home health care agency. The agency's services include HIV/AIDS, mental health, pediatric, oncology, rehab nursing, home nursing, and paraprofessional care. **NOTE:** Entry-level positions and second and third shifts are offered. **Company slogan:** A tradition of caring. **Positions advertised include:** Community Health Nurse; Physical Therapist. **Special programs:** Training; Summer Jobs. **Office hours:** Monday - Friday, 8:00 a.m. - 5:00 p.m. **Corporate headquarters location:** This location. **Subsidiaries include:** All Care Resources provides private-duty nurses and companion care to the elderly. **Number of employees nationwide:** 650.

ALL WORLD TRAVEL
COOPERS LIMOUSINE SERVICE
54 Canal Street, Suite 1, Boston MA 02114. 617/720-2000. **Contact:** Human Resources. **Description:** All World Travel is a travel agency. Coopers Limousine Service (also at this location) provides limousine transportation services.

ALLEGRO MICROSYSTEMS
115 Northeast Cutoff, P.O. Box 15036, Worcester MA 01615. 508/853-5000. **Contact:** Human Resources. **E-mail address:** allegro@rpc.webhire.com. **World Wide Web address:** http://www.allegromicro.com. **Description:** Manufactures mixed-signal integrated circuits. **Positions advertised include:** Design Engineer; Failure Analysis Engineer; Product Design Engineer; Process Technician; Buyer; .NET Programmer; Analyst; Product Applications Engineer; Product Supervisor.

ROBERT ALLEN FABRICS
55 Cabot Boulevard, Mansfield MA 02048. 508/339-9151. **Fax:** 508/339-4057. **Contact:** Human Resources. **E-mail address:** careers@robertallendesign.com. **World Wide Web address:** http://www.robertallendesign.com. **Description:** Robert Allen Fabrics is a fabric retailer. **Office hours:** Monday - Friday, 8:30 a.m. - 5:00 p.m. **Corporate headquarters location:** This location. **Other U.S. locations:** Nationwide. **Operations at this facility include:** This location houses the corporate offices.

ALLIANCE IMAGING
600 Federal Street, Andover MA 01810. 978/658-5357. **Contact:** Human Resources. **World Wide Web address:** http://www.allianceimaging.com. **Description:** Alliance Imaging provides magnetic resonance imaging systems and services. The company schedules and screens patients; maintains medical and administrative records; and operates both mobile and fixed MRI systems. **Positions advertised include:** Medical Records Clerk; Scheduling Coordinator. **NOTE:** Search and apply for jobs online. **Corporate headquarters location:** Anaheim CA. **Other U.S. locations:** Nationwide. **Listed on:** New York Stock Exchange. **Stock exchange symbol:** AIQ.

ALLIED ADVERTISING
545 Boylston Street, 11th Floor, Boston MA 02116. 617/859-4800. **Contact:** Human Resources. **Description:** An advertising agency. **Other U.S. locations:** Washington DC; St. Louis MO; New York City NY; Syracuse NY; Cleveland OH; Philadelphia PA. **International locations:** Toronto.

ALLMERICA FINANCIAL
440 Lincoln Street, Worcester MA 01653. 508/855-1000. **Fax:** 508/853-5351. **Contact:** Human Resources. **World Wide Web address:** http://www.allmerica.com. **Description:** A major provider of insurance and financial services and products. Allmerica Financial operates through two business groups, asset accumulation and risk management. The asset accumulation group is comprised of Allmerica Financial Services, which provides insurance and retirement plans to individuals and businesses, and Allmerica Asset Management Inc., which provides investment management services to businesses. As part of the risk management group, Hanover Insurance and Citizens Insurance provide property and casualty insurance to individuals and businesses. The other subsidiaries that operate as part of the risk management group are Sterling Risk Management Services and Citizens Management, both of which offer claims services and benefits administration services. Founded in 1844. **NOTE:** Entry-level positions are offered. **Positions advertised include:** Shipper Receiver; Service Support Manager; Administrative Assistant; Business Analyst; Inside Adjuster; Program Manager; CAD Administrative Assistant; Researcher; Actuarial Trainee; Inside Property Adjuster; Business Analyst; Accountant; Program Underwriting Manager. **Special programs:** Internships; Training; Summer Jobs. **Office hours:** Monday - Friday, 8:00 a.m. - 5:00 p.m. **Corporate headquarters location:** This location. **Other U.S. locations:** Nationwide. **Listed on:** New York Stock Exchange. **Stock exchange symbol:** AFC. **President/CEO:** John O'Brien. **Annual sales/revenues:** More than $100 million. **Number of employees at this location:** 2,900. **Number of employees nationwide:** 6,000.

ALPHA SOFTWARE CORPORATION
83 Cambridge Street, Suite 3B, Burlington MA 01803. 781/229-4500. **Fax:** 781/272-4876. **Contact:** Human Resources. **E-mail address:** jobs@alphasoftware.com. **World Wide Web address:** http://www.alphasoftware.com. **Description:** Develops and markets business software for IBM personal computers and compatibles. The company distributes its products to Canada and Europe. **Positions advertised include:** Customer Service Representatives.

ALTMAN & ALTMAN
675 Massachusetts Avenue, 11th Floor, Cambridge MA 02139. 617/492-3000. **Contact:** Human Resources. **Description:** A law firm specializing in personal injury, divorce and family, and criminal defense law.

ALVIN HOLLIS
One Hollis Street, South Weymouth MA 02190. 781/335-2100. **Toll-free phone:** 800/649-5090. **Contact:** Human Resources. **World Wide Web address:** http://www.alvinhollis.com. **Description:** A leading supplier of fuel and home heating oil to South Shore Massachusetts homes and businesses. **Corporate headquarters location:** This location.

AMERICAN BILTRITE INC.
57 River Street, Wellesley Hills MA 02481. 781/237-6655. **Fax:** 781/237-6880. **Contact:** Human Resources. **E-mail address:** info@ambilt.com. **World Wide Web address:** http://www.ambilt.com. **Description:** Manufactures hard floor coverings including asphalt felt-based linoleum. **NOTE:** Hiring is conducted through a subsidiary of American Biltrite. Please forward all inquiries to Bonnie Posnak, Vice President of Human Resources, Ideal Tape, 1400 Middlesex Street, Lowell MA 01851. **Listed on:** American Stock Exchange. **Stock exchange symbol:** ABL.

AMERICAN EXPRESS TRAVEL RELATED SERVICES
One State Street, Ground Level, Boston MA 02109. 617/723-8400. **Contact:** Human Resources. **World Wide Web address:** http://www.americanexpress.com. **Description:** A full-service travel agency. Founded in 1850. **Corporate headquarters location:** Cambridge MA. **Parent company:** American Express is a diversified travel and financial services company operating in 160 countries. The company offers consumers the Personal, Gold, and Platinum credit cards, as well as revolving credit products such as Optima Cards, which allow customers to extend payments. Other products include the American Express Corporate Card, which helps businesses manage their travel and entertainment expenditures; and the Corporate Purchasing Card, which helps businesses manage their expenditures on supplies, equipment, and services. American Express Financial Advisors provides a variety of financial products and services to help individuals, businesses, and institutions establish and achieve their financial goals. American Express Financial Advisors employs more than 8,000 financial advisors in the United States and offers products and services that include financial planning; annuities; mutual funds; insurance; investment certificates; and institutional investment advisory trust, tax preparation, and retail securities brokerage services. American Express Bank seeks to meet the financial services needs of wealthy entrepreneurs and local financial service institutions through a global network of offices in 37 countries. **Positions advertised include:** Administrative Assistant; Team Leader Consumer Travel. **NOTE:** Submit resumes and apply online. **Listed on:** Privately held. **Number of employees nationwide:** 3,700.

AMERICAN FLAT GLASS DISTRIBUTORS, INC. (AFGD)
575 Currant Road, Fall River MA 02720. 508/675-9220. **Toll-free phone:** 800/666-2343. **Contact:** Branch Manager. **World Wide Web address:** http://www.afgd.com. **Description:** Specializes in the manufacture of architectural insulated units and custom tempering services. The firm manufactures a complete line of insulated units for commercial and residential applications including clear, tint, and reflective float glass; laminated, low-emissivity, tempered, acrylic, mirror, obscure, insulated and polished wire glass; and a complete line of glass handling, storage, and transportation equipment. **Positions advertised include:** Inside Sales Representative. **Corporate headquarters location:** Atlanta GA. **Other U.S. locations:** Nationwide. **Subsidiaries include:** AFGD Canada. **Parent company:** AFG Industries, Inc. **Listed on:** Privately held. **Number of employees at this location:** 150. **Number of employees nationwide:** 1,000.

AMERICAN HOSPITALITY CONCEPTS
703 Granite Street, Braintree MA 02184. 781/380-3100. **Contact:** Human Resources. **World Wide Web address:** http://www.ahconcepts.com. **Description:** A restaurant company operating the Ground Round chain of family-oriented restaurants.

AMERICAN INK JET CORPORATION
13 Alexander Road, Billerica MA 01821. 978/667-0600. **Fax:** 978/667-0200. **Contact:** Human Resources. **E-mail address:** info@amjet.com. **World Wide Web address:** http://www.amjet.com. **Description:** Manufactures ink, cartridges, and paper for ink jet printers. American Ink Jet provides retailers with ink jet supplies for a wide range of printers.

AMERICAN INTERNATIONAL COLLEGE
1000 State Street, Springfield MA 01109. 413/737-7000. **Contact:** Human Resources. **World Wide Web address:** http://www.aic.edu. **Description:** A private, independent, coeducational college with approximately 1,200 undergraduate and 800 graduate and part-time students. The college offers more than 35 majors within the schools of Arts and Sciences, Business Administration, Psychology and Education, and Health Sciences. **Positions advertised include:** Non Credit Program Manager; Student Activities Director; Political Science Assistant Professor.

AMERICAN MEDICAL RESPONSE (AMR)
4 Tech Circle, P.O. Box 3720, Natick MA 01760. 508/650-5600. **Toll-free phone:** 800/950-9266. **Fax:** 508/650-5656. **Contact:** Human Resources. **E-mail address:** snorton@amr-ems.com. **World Wide Web address:** http://www.amr-inc.com. **Description:** Provides emergency medical transportation. **Other U.S. locations:** Nationwide.

AMERICAN OVERSEAS MARINE CORPORATION
116 East Howard Street, Quincy MA 02169. 617/786-8300. **Contact:** Human Resources. **E-mail address:** hr@gdamsea.com. **World Wide Web address:** http://www.gdamsea.com. **Description:** Provides supplies and support to ships for the U.S. Navy and maritime academies. **Positions advertised include:** Port Engineer; Program Manager. **Corporate headquarters location:** Falls Church VA. **Other U.S. locations:** CT; IL; MI; NJ; RI; SC. **Parent company:** General Dynamics is a major producer of nuclear submarines and land systems. The company has two main divisions: the Electric Boat Division designs and builds nuclear submarines including the Seawolf class attack submarine and the New Attack submarine; The Land Systems Division designs and builds armored vehicles such as the M1 Series of battle tanks for the U.S. Army, the U.S. Marine Corps, and a number of international customers. General Dynamics also has coal mining operations, provides ship management services for the U.S. government on prepositioning and ready reserve ships, and leases liquefied natural gas tankers. **Listed on:** New York Stock Exchange. **Stock exchange symbol:** GD.

AMERICAN REF-FUEL
257 Ivory Street, Braintree MA 02184. 781/843-6209. **Contact:** Human Resources. **World Wide Web address:** http://www.ref-fuel.com. **Description:** American Ref-Fuel accepts municipal solid waste from residents and commercial haulers and transfers the waste to an incinerator site in Wareham MA. **NOTE:** Please forward all resumes to Jerry Croufford, Human Resources Manager, 141 Cranberry Highway, Wareham MA 02576-1504. **Positions advertised include:** Operating Technician; Fuel Plant Service Technician. **Corporate headquarters location:** Houston TX. **Operations at this facility include:** This location is a transfer station. **Subsidiaries include:** Duke Energy North America; United American Energy Corp.

AMERICAN REPERTORY THEATRE
Loeb Drama Center, 64 Brattle Street, Cambridge MA 02138. 617/495-2668. **Contact:** Robert Orchard, Managing Director. **E-mail address:** info@amrep.org. **World Wide Web address:** http://www.amrep.org. **Description:** A nonprofit theater. **Special programs:** Internships. **Office hours:** Monday - Friday, 9:00 a.m. - 5:00 p.m.

AMERICAN SCIENCE & ENGINEERING, INC.
829 Middlesex Turnpike, Billerica MA 01821. 978/262-8700. **Fax:** 978/262-8896. **Contact:** Human Resources. **E-mail address:** service@as-e.com. **World Wide Web address:** http://www.as-e.com. **Description:** Researches, develops, produces, and sells instrumentation for X-ray research for use in government space science programs and other scientific applications. The company also manufactures and sells a load management and automatic remote meter-reading system for public utilities; and develops, manufactures, and markets X-ray equipment. **Positions advertised include:** Corporate Counsel; Field Service Engineer; Project Manager; Project Cost Accountant. **Corporate headquarters location:** This location. **Operations at this facility include:** Administration; Manufacturing; Research and Development; Sales; Service. **Listed on:** American Stock Exchange. **Stock exchange symbol:** ASE.

AMERICAN SUPERCONDUCTOR CORPORATION
Two Technology Drive, Westborough MA 01581. 508/836-4200. **Fax:** 508/836-4248. **Contact:** Human Resources. **E-mail address:** resumes@amsuper.com. **World Wide Web address:** http://www.amsuper.com. **Description:** Manufactures flexible high-temperature superconductor wires, wire products, and systems. Products are incorporated in compact, cost-effective electric power and magnet systems such as power transmission cables, motors, generators, transformers, energy storage devices, and magnetic resonance imaging systems. **Positions advertised include:** Chief Engineer. **Corporate headquarters location:** This location. **Other U.S. locations:** Madison WI; Milwaukee WI. **Subsidiaries include:** American Superconductor Europe GmbH, Germany. **Listed on:** NASDAQ. **Stock exchange symbol:** AMSC. **Number of employees nationwide:** 100.

AMES ON-DEMAND
12 Tyler Street, Somerville MA 02143. 617/776-3360x1126. **Contact:** Human Resources. **World Wide Web address:** http://www.amesondemand.com. **Description:** A large commercial printer. **Parent company:** Ames Safety Envelope Company.

AMES SPECIALTY PACKAGING
12 Tyler Street, Somerville MA 02143. 617/776-3360. **Fax:** 617/776-6269. **Contact:** Human Resources. **E-mail address:** jobs@amespage.com. **World Wide Web address:** http://www.amespage.com. **Description:** Manufactures a variety of paper products including file folders and X-ray jackets. **Positions advertised include:** Master Development Scheduler; Master Code Writer; Digital Print Sales Representative. **Parent company:** Ames Safety Envelope Company.

AMETEK, INC.
50 Fordham Road, Wilmington MA 01887. 978/988-4101. **Contact:** Human Resources. **E-mail address:** corps.jobs@ametek.com. **World Wide Web address:** http://www.ametek.com. **Description:** AMETEK is a global manufacturing company that serves a variety of industrial and commercial markets. The company produces and sells its products through its Electromechanical, Precision Instruments, and Industrial Materials groups. The Electromechanical Group manufactures electric motors for vacuum cleaners and floor care equipment and technical motor products for computer, medical, and other markets. **Corporate headquarters location:** Philadelphia PA. **International locations:** Denmark; England; Italy; Mexico. **Operations at this facility include:** This location manufactures aircraft parts and auxiliary equipment. **Listed on:** New York Stock Exchange. **Stock exchange symbol:** AME. **Number of employees worldwide:** 6,000.

AMPAD CORPORATION
75 Appleton Street, Holyoke MA 01040. 413/536-3511. **Fax:** 972/578-3364. **NOTE:** Fax # for Plano Office. **Contact:** Human Resources Manager. **World Wide Web address:** http://www.ampad.com. **Description:** A paper converting company that

manufactures school and office supplies. **NOTE:** Resumes should be sent to Plano Texas office, American Pad & Paper, Attention: Human Resources. 3000 East Plano Parkway, Plano Texas, 75074. **Corporate headquarters location:** Dallas TX. **Other U.S. locations:** Atlanta GA; Mattoon IL; Marion IN; North Salt Lake City UT. **Parent company:** American Pad & Paper Company. **Operations at this facility include:** Manufacturing. **Listed on:** Privately held. **Number of employees at this location:** 350. **Number of employees nationwide:** 900.

ANALOG DEVICES, INC.
One Technology Way, P.O. Box 9106, Norwood MA 02062-9106. 781/329-4700. **Contact:** Human Resources. **World Wide Web address:** http://www.analog.com. **Description:** Designs, manufactures, and markets a broad line of high-performance analog, mixed-signal, and digital integrated circuits (ICs) that address a wide range of real-world signal processing applications. The company's principal products include system-level ICs and general purpose, standard linear ICs. Other products include devices manufactured using assembled product technology such as hybrids, which combine unpackaged IC chips and other chip-level components in a single package. Analog Device's system-level ICs are used predominately in communications and computer applications. The company's largest communications application is the pan-European GSM (Global System for Mobile Communications) digital cellular telephone system. **Positions advertised include:** Corporate US Business Analyst; Human Resources Director; Layout Engineering Specialist; NT Web Security Project Leader; PC Support Specialist; Product Development Engineer; Benefits Analyst; Design Engineer; Development Engineer; Software Engineer. **Corporate headquarters location:** This location. **Other U.S. locations:** Nationwide. **International locations:** Worldwide. **Operations at this facility include:** Administration; Manufacturing; Research and Development. **Listed on:** New York Stock Exchange. **Stock exchange symbol:** ADI.

ANALOGIC CORPORATION
8 Centennial Drive, Peabody MA 01960. 978/977-3000. **Fax:** 978/977-6810. **Contact:** Human Resources. **World Wide Web address:** http://www.analogic.com. **Description:** Designs, manufactures, and sells a broad line of high-precision data-conversion and signal-processing equipment. Principal customers are original equipment manufacturers who incorporate products into systems for medical, industrial, and telecommunications applications. The company's products include measurement, display, and control instruments, consisting of digital panel instruments, digital test instruments, and industrial digitizing systems; data acquisition and conversion products, consisting of A/D and D/A converters, supporting modules, data acquisition systems, and subsystems; and computer-based products, consisting of medical imaging equipment and array processors. Founded in 1969. **Company slogan:** The world resource for precision signal technology. **Positions advertised include:** Corporate US Business Analyst; Human Resource Director; Layout Engineering Specialist; PC Support Specialist; Product Development Engineer; Benefits Analyst; Design Engineer; Development Engineer; Software Engineer. **Special programs:** Co-ops. **Corporate headquarters location:** This location. **Other U.S. locations:** WI. **Subsidiaries include:** Anatel Communications Corporation; B-K Medical A/S; Camtronics Medical Systems; International Security Systems; SKY Computers. **Listed on:** NASDAQ. **Stock exchange symbol:** ALOG. **Annual sales/revenues:** More than $100 million. **Number of employees at this location:** 1,150. **Number of employees nationwide:** 1,400.

ANALYSIS AND COMPUTER SYSTEMS INC.
One Van de Graaff Drive, Burlington MA 01803. 781/272-8841. **Contact:** Human Resources. **World Wide Web address:** http://www.acsi1.com. **Description:** Offers software consulting. Analysis and Computer Systems provides support services to the U.S. government and commercial organizations.

ANDERSON GREENWOOD CROSBY
43 Kendrick Street, Wrentham MA 02093. 508/384-3121. **Contact:** Human Resources. **World Wide Web address:** http://www.andersongreenwood.com. **Description:** Manufacturers and marketers of safety and relief valves for power generation and petrochemical industries. **Parent Company:** Tyco International.

ANDERSON POWER PRODUCTS
13 Pratts Junction Road, P.O. Box 579, Sterling MA 01564. 978/422-3600. **Fax:** 978/422-3700. **Contact:** Human Resources. **E-mail address:** employment@andersonpower.com. **World Wide Web address:** http;//www.andersonpower.com. **Description:** Designs, manufactures, and markets high power interconnects and accessories.

ANDOVER CONTROLS CORPORATION
300 Brickstone Square, Andover MA 01810. 978/470-0555. **Fax:** 978/470-0946. **Contact:** Human Resources. **World Wide Web address:** http://www.andovercontrols.com. **Description:** Manufactures building automation systems. **Positions advertised include:** Project Engineer; Service Technician. **International locations:** Worldwide. **Parent company:** Balfour Beatty.

ANGELL MEMORIAL ANIMAL HOSPITAL
350 South Huntington Avenue, Boston MA 02130. 617/522-7400. **Fax:** 617/989-1601. **Contact:** Recruiter/Trainer. **E-mail address:** recruiter@mspca.org. **World Wide Web address:** http://www.angell.org. **Description:** A veterinary hospital that offers general medical care as well as specialized services including heart catheterization facilities, kidney transplant procedures, and radiology treatments. **Parent company:** Massachusetts Society for the Prevention of Cruelty to Animals (MSPCA).

ANIKA THERAPEUTICS
236 West Cummings Parkway, Woburn MA 01801. 781/932-6616. **Fax:** 781/935-4120. **Contact:** Personnel. **World Wide Web address:** http://www.anikatherapeutics.com. **Description:** Develops and commercializes products using hyaluronic acid (HA) for medical and therapeutic applications. Products include AMVISC, a high molecular weight HA product that is used as a viscoelastic agent in ophthalmic surgical procedures including cataract extraction and intraocular lens implantation; HYVISC, a high molecular weight HA product used for the treatment of joint dysfunction in horses due to noninfectious synovitis associated with equine osteoarthritis; ORTHOVISC, a high molecular weight, injectable HA product for the symptomatic treatment of osteoarthritis of the knee; and INCERT, a chemically modified, cross-linked form of HA designed to prevent the formation of post-surgical wound adhesions. Founded in 1993. **Positions advertised include:** Process Development Engineer; Quality Engineer; Scientist. **NOTE:** Entry-level positions and second and third shifts are offered. **Special programs:** Internships. **Corporate headquarters location:** This location. **Listed on:** NASDAQ. **Stock exchange symbol:** ANIK. **CEO:** Douglas R. Potter.

THE ANIMAL CARE CENTER
678 Brookline Avenue, Brookline MA 02445. 617/277-2030. **E-mail address:** careers@healthypet.org. **World Wide Web address:** http://www.healthypet.org. **Contact:** Human Resources. **Description:** An animal hospital providing medical and surgical services. The Center also runs a pet adoption service for the city of Boston.

ANIMED PET HOSPITAL
918 Providence Highway, Dedham MA 02026. 781/329-5333. **Contact:** Human Resources. **Description:** A full-service pet hospital.

ANNA MARIA COLLEGE
50 Sunset Lane, Paxton MA 01612-1198. 508/849-3398. **Toll-free phone:** 800/344-4586. **Fax:** 508/849-3319. **Contact:** Lisa Driscoll, Human Resources. **E-mail address:** ldriscoll@annamaria.edu. **World Wide Web address:** http://www.annamaria.edu. **Description:** A nonprofit, private, liberal arts college for women offering both undergraduate and graduate degrees. Founded in 1947. **NOTE:** Entry-level positions and part-time jobs are offered. **Special programs:** Internships; Summer Jobs. **Office hours:** Monday - Friday, 8:30 a.m. - 4:30 p.m. **President:** William McGarry. **Facilities Manager:** Paul Chenevert. **Information Systems Manager:** John Price. **Purchasing Manager:** Susan Lynch. **Number of employees at this location:** 165.

ANTHONY'S PIER FOUR
140 Northern Avenue, Boston MA 02210. 617/482-6262. **Contact:** Anthony Athanas, Owner. **E-mail address:** pier4@pier4.com. **World Wide Web address:** http://www.pier4.com. **Description:** A restaurant. **NOTE:** Jobseekers must apply in person at the restaurant.

ANTIGENICS INC.
3 Forbes Road, Lexington MA 02421-7305. 781/674-4400. **Fax:** 781/674-4200. **Contact:** Human Resources. **E-mail address:** recruiter@antigenics.com. **World Wide Web address:** http://www.antigenics.com. **Description:** Develops diagnostic and vaccine products to fight AIDS, cancer, and other diseases. **Positions advertised include:** Research Associate; Paralegal; Process Development; Scientist; Research Associate; Web Producer; Payroll Specialist. **Corporate headquarters location:** New York City NY. **Other area locations:** Woburn, MA. **International locations:** The Netherlands. **Listed on:** NASDAQ. **Stock exchange symbol:** AGEN.

APOGEE TECHNOLOGY INC.
129 Morgan Drive, Norwood MA 02062. 781/551-9450. **Fax:** 781/440-9528. **Contact:** Human Resources. **World Wide Web address:** http://www.apogeeddx.com. **Description:** A silicon based semiconductor manufacturer specializing in audio technology.

APPLESEED'S
30 Tozer Road, Beverly MA 01915. 978/922-2040. **Fax:** 978/922-7001. **Contact:** Human Resources. **E-mail address:** jobs@appleseeds.com. **World Wide Web address:** http://www.appleseeds.com. **Description:** A retailer of women's clothing through its stores and catalog.

APPLIED EXTRUSION TECHNOLOGIES, INC.
3 Centennial Drive, Peabody MA 01960. 978/538-1500. **Contact:** Human Resources. **World Wide Web address:** http://www.aetfilms.com. **Description:** A leading manufacturer of a broad range of plastic films, nets, and webs used primarily in packaging, health care, and environmental settings. The Packaging Films Division develops, manufactures, and sells oriented polypropylene film for flexible packaging applications, primarily for the snack food, soft drink, and confectionery markets. The Specialty Nets and Profiles Divisions develop, manufacture, and sell oriented aperture film or nets, as well as non-net thermoplastic products to a number of markets such as health care, environmental, packaging, and home products. **Corporate headquarters location:** This location. **Listed on:** NASDAQ. **Stock exchange symbol:** AETC.

APPLIED SCIENCE LABORATORIES
175 Middlesex Turnpike, Bedford MA 01730. 781/275-4000. **Fax:** 781/275-3388. **Contact:** Human Resources. **E-mail address:** asl@a-s-l.com. **World Wide Web address:** http://www.a-s-l.com. **Description:** Develops and manufactures eye tracking systems and technology. The company also provides contract research. **Corporate headquarters location:** This location. **Parent company:** Applied Science Group, Inc.

APPLIX, INC.
289 Turnpike Road, Westborough MA 01581. 508/870-0300. **Contact:** Human Resources. **E-mail address:** jobs@applix.com. **World Wide Web address:** http://www.applix.com. **Description:** Develops and markets software applications for the UNIX market. **Positions advertised include:** Localization Engineer; Systems Engineer. **Corporate headquarters location:** This location. **Other U.S. locations:** Warren NJ; Vienna VA. **International locations:** Worldwide. **Listed on:** NASDAQ. **Stock exchange symbol:** APLX.

AQUA-LEISURE INDUSTRIES
525 Bodwell Street, P.O. Box 239, Avon MA 02322. 508/587-5400. **Contact:** Human Resources. **World Wide Web address:** http://www.aqualeisure.com. **Description:** A manufacturer of water sport products and inflatable water toys and pools.

ARAMARK UNIFORM SERVICES
P.O. Box 568, Lawrence MA 01842. 978/685-1936. **Physical Address:** 110 Glenn Street, Lawrence MA 01843. **Contact:** Human Resources. **World Wide Web address:** http://www.aramark-uniform.com. **Description:** Offers uniforms to reinforce corporate identities or to meet specialized demands for static control and flame resistance. The company also provides a variety of products including walk-off mats, cleaning cloths, disposable towels, and other environmental control items. **Parent company:** ARAMARK (Philadelphia PA) is one of the world's leading providers of managed services. The company operates in all 50 states and 10 foreign countries, offering a broad range of services to businesses of all sizes including many *Fortune* 500 companies and thousands of universities, hospitals, and municipal, state, and federal government facilities. The company is employee-owned.

ARBOR NETWORKS
430 Bedford Street, Suite 160, Lexington MA 02420. 781/684-0900. **Toll-free phone:** 866/212-7267. **Fax:** 781/768-3299. **Contact:** Human Resources. **World Wide Web address:** http://www.arbornetworks.com. **Description:** Develops network integrity systems for enterprises and service providers. **Positions advertised include:** Consulting Engineer; Staff Accountant. **Corporate headquarters location:** This location. **Other U.S. locations:** Ann Arbor MI.

ARBOUR SENIOR CARE & COUNSELING SERVICES
100 Ledgewood Place, Suite 202, Rockland MA 02370. 781/871-6550. **Contact:** Human Resources. **Description:** Provides behavioral health services delivered by mobile multidisciplinary teams of clinicians at outpatient service sites. The company offers therapeutic, psychiatric, neurological, and diagnostic imaging services. **Corporate headquarters location:** This location. **Number of employees at this location:** 100.

ARCADD, INC.
1185 Washington Street, West Newton MA 02465. 617/332-1200. **Fax:** 617/969-3362. **Contact:** Employment. **E-mail address:** arcaddinc@aol.com. **World Wide Web address:** http://www.arcadd.com. **Description:** An architectural design firm.

ARCH WIRELESS, INC.
1800 West Park Drive, Suite 250, Westborough MA 01581-3912. 508/898-0962. **Contact:** Human Resources. **World Wide Web address:** http://www.arch.com. **Description:** Provides telephone paging services. **Positions advertised include:** Senior Auditor; Senior Benefits Administrator. **Corporate headquarters location:** This location.

ARIAD PHARMACEUTICALS, INC.
26 Landsdowne Street, Cambridge MA 02139. 617/494-0400. **Contact:** Human Resources. **E-mail address:** human.resources@ariad.com. **World Wide Web address:** http://www.ariad.com. **Description:** A biopharmaceutical company that uses gene regulation and signal transduction to develop therapeutic products. Founded in 1991. **Positions advertised include:** Medical Director; Pharmaceutical Affairs Manager; Quality Assurance Manager; Quality Assurance Manager; Quality Control Specialist; Research Associate; Analytical Chemistry; Research Associate. **NOTE:** When mailing resumes, address to Job Code:___ before the above address. Job codes can be found on the website. **Corporate headquarters location:** This location. **Listed on:** NASDAQ. **Stock exchange symbol:** ARIA.

ARK-LES CORPORATION
95 Mill Street, Stoughton MA 02072. 781/297-6000. **Fax:** 781/297-6160. **Contact:** Human Resources. **World Wide Web address:** http://www.ark-les.com. **Description:** ARK-LES manufactures electrical components and switches. **Corporate headquarters location:** This location. **Other area locations:** Stoughton MA (Manufacturing); Gloucester MA. **Other U.S. locations:** Raleigh NC; New Berlin WI. **International locations:** Guandong, China; Juarez, Mexico.

ARLEY CORPORATION
1115 West Chestnut Street, Brockton MA 02301-7501. 508/580-4245. **Contact:** Human Resources. **World Wide Web address:** http://www.arley.com. **Description:** A curtain and drapery manufacturer.

ARMATRON INTERNATIONAL INC.
15 Highland Avenue, Malden MA 02148. 781/321-2300. **Contact:** Cindie McCue, Human Resources Director. **Description:** Operates through two segments: The Consumer Products segment manufactures and distributes bug killers, chipper/shredders, and leaf-eaters; and The Industrial Products segment imports and sells radios to large automobile manufacturers. **Corporate headquarters location:** This location.

ARNOLD WORLDWIDE
101 Huntington Avenue, Boston MA 02199. 617/587-8000. **Fax:** 617/587-8070. **Contact:** Human Resources. **World Wide Web address:** http://www.arn.com. **Description:** An advertising, marketing, and public relations firm.

HH ARNOLD COMPANY
529 Liberty Street, Rockland MA 02370. 781/878-0346. **Fax:** 781/878-7944. **Contact:** Human Resources. **World Wide Web address:** http://www.hharnold.com. **Description:** A manufacturing company providing quality machine parts & machine assemblers for over 90 years.

ARROW INTERNATIONAL, INC.
9 Plymouth Street, Everett MA 02149. 617/389-6400. **Contact:** Human Resources. **E-mail address:** staffing.manager@arrowintl.com. **World Wide Web address:** http://www.arrowintl.com. **Description:** Arrow International develops, manufactures, and markets central vascular access catheterization products. The company's products are also used for patient monitoring, diagnosis, pain management, and treating patients with heart and vascular disease. **Corporate headquarters location:** Reading PA. **Operations at this facility include:** This location manufactures intra-aortic balloons. **Listed on:** NASDAQ. **Stock exchange symbol:** ARRO.

ARTESYN TECHNOLOGIES
125 Newbury Street, Framingham MA 01701. 508/628-5600. **Fax:** 508/424-2752. **Contact:** Human Resources. **E-mail address:** Jackie.kallman@artsesyn.com. **World Wide Web address:** http://www.artesyn.com. **Description:** Offers repair services for computer and peripheral manufacturers. The company also manufactures power conversion products. **Positions advertised include:** Engineering Manager; Key Account Manager for Medical Industry; Design Engineer; SAP Control Lead; SAP Sales & Distributor; Electrical Design Engineer. **Other international locations:** Worldwide. **Listed on:** NASDAQ. **Stock exchange symbol:** ATSN.

ARTISOFT, INC.
5 Cambridge Center, 3rd Floor, Cambridge MA 02142. 617/354-0600. **Fax:** 617/354-7744. **Contact:** Personnel. **E-mail address:** jobs@artisoft.com. **World Wide Web address:** http://www.artisoft.com. **Description:** A provider of networking solutions for businesses. The company offers the LANtastic network operating system as well as network management, backup, and multiplatform connectivity systems. **Positions advertised include:** Channel Development Representative. **Corporate headquarters location:** This location. **Listed on:** NASDAQ. **Stock exchange symbol:** ASFT.

ASCENTIAL SOFTWARE
50 Washington Street, Westborough MA 01581. 508/366-3888. **Fax:** 508/389-8955. **Contact:** Human Resources Manager. **E-mail address:** staffing@ascentialsoftware.com. **World Wide Web address:** http://www.ascentialsoftware.com. **Description:** Manufactures a wide range of software products including database systems and warehouse development tools. Ascential serves government and business customers in the manufacturing, health care, telecommunications, aerospace, defense, financial services, and utilities industries. **Positions advertised include:** Solutions Architect; SQA Engineer; Software Engineering Web Services; Software Engineer; Tax Analyst; Manager of Marketing Communication & Services; Account Development Representative; Help Desk Analyst; Account Executive; District Sales Manager; IBM Alliance Director. **Corporate headquarters location:** This location. **Other U.S. locations:** CA; CO; GA; IL; NC; NJ; TX; WA. **International locations:** Australia; Brazil; Canada; France; Germany; Hong Kong; Japan; South Africa; United Kingdom. **Listed on:** NASDAQ. **Stock exchange symbol:** ASCL.

ASLANIS SEAFOODS
10 Granite Street, Quincy MA 02169. 617/479-0500. **Contact:** Personnel. **World Wide Web address:** http://www.aslanis.com. **Description:** A wholesale processor and packager of seafood.

ASPENTECH
10 Canal Park, Cambridge MA 02141-2201. 617/949-1000. **Fax:** 617/949-1030. **Contact:** Human Resources. **World Wide Web address:** http://www.aspentech.com. **Description:** Supplies chemical engineering software to the chemicals, petroleum, pharmaceuticals, metals, minerals, food products, consumer products, and utilities industries. **Positions advertised include:** Oil & Gas Solutions Director; Software Quality Engineer; Accounts Receivable Clerk; Collections Specialist; Accountant; Director Computer & Network Operations; Sales Operations Director. **Corporate headquarters location:** This location. **Other U.S. locations:** Nationwide. **International locations:** Worldwide. **Listed on:** NASDAQ. **Stock exchange symbol:** AZPN.

ASSUMPTION COLLEGE
P.O. Box 15005, Worcester MA 01615-0005. 508/767-7000. **Fax:** 508/756-1780. **Contact:** Human Resources. **E-mail address:** resumes@assumption.edu. **World Wide Web address:** http://www.assumption.edu. **Description:** A Catholic college with an undergraduate enrollment of approximately 1,600 students. Approximately 1,200 students are enrolled in graduate and continuing education programs. The college also offers a Center for Continuing and Professional Education, which grants associate's and bachelor's degrees on a part-time basis; The French Institute, an academic research facility and a center for French cultural activities; and the Institute for Social and Rehabilitation Services. Founded in 1904. **Positions advertised include:** Annual Giving Director; Graduate Assistant for Student Activities; Resident Director; Area Coordinator; Assistant Director of Athletics for Sports Medicine. **Corporate headquarters location:** This location.

ASTRAZENECA
50 Otis Street, Westborough MA 01581. 508/366-1100. **Contact:** Human Resources. **World Wide Web address:** http://www.astrazeneca.com. **Description:** Develops pharmaceuticals to fight infections, cardiovascular and gastrointestinal diseases, cancer, and asthma and other respiratory problems. Other products developed by AstraZeneca are used as anesthetics and to control pain. **Positions advertised include:** Research Associate; Pharmaceutical Sales; Principal Scientist; Purchasing Manager; Administrative Coordinator; Facilities Technician; Product Operation; Machine Adjuster; CAD Leader; Patent Attorney; Chemist; Training Specialist; Scientist.

ATARI INC.
50 Dunham Road, Beverly MA 01915. 978/921-3700. **Contact:** Human Resources. **World Wide Web address:** http://www.iatari.com. **Description:** Develops, manufactures, and sells a line of interactive computer and video games and educational materials. **Corporate headquarters location:** New York NY. **Other U.S. locations:** Santa Monica CA; Sunnyvale CA; Beverly MA; Plymouth MN; Bothell WA. **International locations:** Worldwide. **Operations at this facility include:** Administration; Divisional Headquarters; Research and Development; Sales.

ATEX MEDIA SOLUTIONS
15 Crosby Drive, Bedford MA 01730. 781/275-2323. **Fax:** 781/276-1254. **Contact:** Human Resources. **E-mail address:** jobs.bedford@atexmediacommand.com. **World Wide Web address:** http://www.atex.com. **Description:** Designs, develops, and sells computer software products for the newspaper, magazine, and prepress publishing markets worldwide. **Positions advertised include:** Vice President of Customer Support Services. **Corporate headquarters location:** This location. **Other U.S. locations:** Nationwide. **International locations:** Worldwide. **Operations at this facility include:** Administration; Research and Development; Sales; Service. **Listed on:** Privately held. **Number of employees at this location:** 240. **Number of employees nationwide:** 400.

ATHENA DIAGNOSTICS, INC.
4 Biotechnology Research Park, 377 Plantation Street, Worcester MA 01605. 508/756-2886. **Toll-free phone:** 800/394-4493. **Fax:** 508/753-5601. **Contact:** Human Resources. **E-mail address:** employment@athenadiagnostics.com. **World Wide Web address:** http://www.athenadiagnostics.com. **Description:** A reference laboratory that develops and commercializes diagnostics and therapeutics for neurological and neurogenic disorders. **Corporate headquarters location:** South San Francisco CA. **Parent company:** Elan Pharmaceuticals, Inc. **Operations at this facility include:** Administration; Manufacturing; Research and Development; Sales; Service. **Listed on:** NASDAQ. **Annual sales/revenues:** $11 - $20 million. **Number of employees at this location:** 65.

ATHOL MEMORIAL HOSPITAL
2033 Main Street, Athol MA 01331. 978/249-3511. **Fax:** 978/249-5658. **E-mail address:** eamparo@atholhospital.org. **Contact:** Human Resources. **World Wide Web address:** http://www.atholhospital.org. **Description:** An acute care hospital. **Positions advertised include:** MLT; Respiratory Therapist; Physical Therapist.

ATLANTIC DATA SERVICES
One Batterymarch Park, Quincy MA 02169. 617/770-3333. **Contact:** Director of Human Resources. **E-mail address:** joinourteam@adsfs.com. **World Wide Web address:** http://www.atlanticdataservices.com. **Description:** A professional services firm providing computer consulting and project management services to the banking and financial industries. **Positions advertised include:** Project Consultant; Business Development Manager. **Corporate headquarters location:** This location. **Other U.S. locations:** Nationwide. **Listed on:** NASDAQ. **Stock exchange symbol:** ADSC. **Annual sales/revenues:** $21 - $50 million. **Number of employees nationwide:** 200.

AU BON PAIN CORPORATION
19 Fid Kennedy Avenue, Boston MA 02210-2497. 617/423-2100. **Contact:** Human Resources. **E-mail address:** kris_broe@aubonpain.com. **World Wide Web address:** http://www.aubonpain.com. **Description:** Owns and operates a chain of 280 French bakery cafes worldwide. **NOTE:** Entry-level positions are offered. **Company slogan:** The French Bakery Cafe. **Positions advertised include:** General Manager; Baker; Customer Service Representative; Catering Call Center Representative; Shift Supervisor; Associate Manager; District Manager. **Special programs:** Internships. **Corporate headquarters location:** This location. **Other U.S. locations:** Nationwide. **Parent company:** Compass plc. **Listed on:** Privately held. **Number of employees nationwide:** 3,500.

AUTOMATIC DATA PROCESSING (ADP)
225 Second Avenue, Waltham MA 02454. 781/890-2500. **Contact:** Human Resources. **World Wide Web address:** http://www.adp.com. **Description:** A data processing and computing services firm that provides commercial services such as payroll, accounts receivable, accounts payable, financial statement preparation, tax services, and unemployment compensation management; financial services including general and specialized management oriented online services to major corporations, large financial institutions, and the government; dealer services in the auto, truck, and industrial equipment trade; collision estimating services; and pension services. **Positions advertised include:** Consultant; Driver; Night Coordinator; National Sales Manager; Implementation Specialist; Resource Manager; Sales Administrator; New Account

Coordinator; Telephone Data Representative; Customer Service Representative; Inventory Control Clerk; Billing Specialist; eTechnical Support. **Corporate headquarters location:** Roseland NJ. **Operations at this facility include:** Service. **Listed on:** New York Stock Exchange. **Stock exchange symbol:** ADP.

AUTOMATIC SPECIALTIES, INC.
422 Northboro Road, Marlboro MA 01752. 508/481-2370. **Toll-free phone:** 800/445-2370. **Fax:** 508/485-6276. **Contact:** Human Resources. **Description:** A leading manufacturer of a variety of metal products including wire and strip forms, metal stampings, and welded wire assemblies.

AVANT IMMUNOTHERAPEUTICS, INC.
119 Fourth Avenue, Needham MA 02194-2725. 781/433-0771. **Fax:** 781/433-3113. **Contact:** Human Resources. **E-mail address:** info@avantimmune.com. **World Wide Web address:** http://www.avantimmune.com. **Description:** A biopharmaceutical company specializing in the understanding and treatment of diseases caused by misregulation of the body's natural defense systems. **Positions advertised include:** Document Control Manager; Manufacturing Manager. **Corporate headquarters location:** This location. **Other area locations:** Fall River MA. **Listed on:** NASDAQ. **Stock exchange symbol:** AVAN.

AVERY DENNISON CORPORATION
P.O. Box 7057, Chicopee MA 01022. 413/593-3963. **Physical address:** One Better Way, Chicopee MA 02021. **Fax:** 413/593-3445. **Contact:** Human Resources. **World Wide Web address:** http://www.averydennison.com. **Description:** A manufacturer of stationery and office products. **Positions advertised include:** Associate Project Manager; Director of Marketing; Financial Analyst. **Corporate headquarters location:** Pasadena CA. **Operations at this facility include:** Administration; Manufacturing. **Listed on:** New York Stock Exchange. **Stock exchange symbol:** AVY. **Number of employees at this location:** 300.

AVID TECHNOLOGY, INC.
Avid Technology Park, 1925 Andover Street (Building 2), Tewksbury MA 01876. 978/640-6789. **Contact:** Human Resources. **World Wide Web address:** http://www.avid.com. **Description:** A leading provider of digital audio and video tools. Products include digital editing systems and networking and shared storage systems. The company's products are used for various media and entertainment applications. Founded in 1987. **Positions advertised include:** Customer Service & Technical Support Representative; Broadcast Engineer; Post Engineer; Workgroup & Storage Engineer; Finance & Accounting Representative; Human Resources Representative; Information Systems Representative; Manufacturing Representative; Marketing Representative; Product Marketing Representative. **Corporate headquarters location:** This location. **International locations:** Worldwide. **Listed on:** NASDAQ. **Stock exchange symbol:** AVID.

AVOCENT CORPORATION
4 Meeting House Road, Chelmsford MA 01824. 978/244-2000. **Toll-free phone:** 800/264-9443. **Fax:** 978/244-0334. **Contact:** Human Resources. **World Wide Web address:** http://www.avocent.com. **Description:** Develops and markets connectivity solutions for businesses, data centers, service providers, and financial institutions. Avocent Corporation's products include KVM switching, remote access, and video display solutions. **Positions advertised include:** Software Engineer. **NOTE:** Jobseekers should send resumes to: Human Resources, 4991 Corporate Drive, Huntsville AL 35805. **Corporate headquarters location:** Huntsville AL. **Other U.S. locations:** Huntsville AL; Sunrise FL; Austin TX; Redmond WA. **International locations:** Canada; Germany; Hong Kong; Ireland. **Listed on:** NASDAQ. **Stock exchange symbol:** AVCT.

AWARE INC.
40 Middlesex Turnpike, Bedford MA 01730. 781/276-4000. **Fax:** 781/276-4001. **Contact:** Human Resources. **E-mail address:** jobs@aware.com. **World Wide Web address:** http://www.aware.com. **Description:** A world leader in the development of xDSL technology for high-speed, broadband modems. Founded in 1986. **Other U.S. locations:** Lafayette CA. **Listed on:** NASDAQ. **Stock exchange symbol:** AWRE. **Annual sales/revenues:** $5 - $10 million. **Number of employees at this location:** 80.

AXCELIS TECHNOLOGIES
108 Cherry Hill Drive, Beverly MA 01915. 978/921-0750. **Contact:** Human Resources. **World Wide Web address:** http://www.axcelis.com. **Description:** Manufactures ion implanters. **Positions advertised include:** Documentation Contest Specialist; Eco Planner; Electronics Engineer; Group Manager Software; Marketing Analyst; Packaging Engineer; Section Coordinator; Tax Accountant; Telecom Analyst. **Corporate headquarters location:** This location. **Other U.S. locations:** Nationwide. **Listed on:** NASDAQ. **Stock exchange symbol:** ACLS. **Number of employees worldwide:** 64,000.

AXIS COMPUTER SYSTEMS
201 Boston Post Road West, Marlborough MA 01752. 508/481-9600. **Toll-free phone:** 800/370-AXIS. **Contact:** Human Resources. **E-mail address:** hr@axiscomp.com. **World Wide Web address:** http://www.axiscomp.com. **Description:** Develops software for manufacturing facilities in the metals industry. **Positions advertised include:** Software Developer; Development Manager; Software Quality Assurance Manager; Customer Service Consultant; Product Support Specialist; Sales Professional; Support Specialist.

AYRE REAL ESTATE COMPANY, INC.
701 Main Street, Agawam MA 01001. 413/789-0812. **Fax:** 413/789-2427. **Contact:** Human Resources. **E-mail address:** ayrerealestate@ayrerealestate.com. **World Wide Web address:** http://www.ayrerealestate.com. **Description:** A commercial and residential real estate company serving the greater Springfield area.

B & E TOOL COMPANY, INC.
P.O. Box 40, Southwick MA 01077. 413/569-5585. **Physical address:** 10 Hudson Drive, Southwick MA 01077. **Fax:** 413/569-6543. **Contact:** Human Resources. **E-mail address:** info@betool.com. **World Wide Web address:** http://www.betool.com. **Description:** Manufactures aircraft components and parts for aircraft engines and controls. Founded in 1954. **Corporate headquarters location:** This location.

BAE SYSTEMS
2 Forbes Road, Lexington MA 02421-7306. 781/862-6222. **Contact:** Human Resources. **E-mail:** careers@baesystems.com. **World Wide Web address:** http://www.na.baesystems.com. **Description:** A business unit of the Information and Electronic Systems Integration Sector within BAE SYSTEMS North America. They are a major producer of aircraft self-protection systems and tactical surveillance and intelligence systems. Their products are supplied to all branches of the armed forces. BAE SYSTEMS also produces missile and space electronics; infrared imaging; and automated mission planning systems. **Corporate headquarters location:** Bethesda MD. **Other U.S. locations:** Pomona CA; Hudson NH; Nahua NH; Merrimack NH; Yonkers NY; Arlington VA; Manassas VA. **Number of employees nationwide:** 4,400.

BBK COMMUNICATIONS
320 Needham Street, Suite 150, Newton MA 02464. 617/630-4477. **Contact:** Human Resources. **World Wide Web address:** http://www.bbkweb.com. **Description:** BBK is an integrated advertising and public relations firm serving the health policies, technologies, managed care, and pharmaceutical fields. **NOTE:** Please indicate the department to which you are applying. **Corporate headquarters location:** This location. **Listed on:** Privately held. **Number of employees at this location:** 30.

BDO SEIDMAN, LLP
40 Broad Street, Suite 500, Boston MA 02109. 617/422-7576. **Fax:** 617/422-7570. **Contact:** Katie Rojik, Office Manager. **World Wide Web address:** http://www.bdo.com. **Description:** A public accounting and consulting firm. **Positions advertised include:** Administrative Assistant; Senior Tax Consultant.

BJ'S WHOLESALE CLUB
One Mercer Road, Natick MA 01760. 508/651-7400. **Contact:** Human Resources. **World Wide Web address:** http://www.bjs.com. **Description:** Membership club retailer of bulk merchandise from grocery items to electronics, automotive accessories and vacations. **Corporate headquarters location:** This location. **Listed on:** New York Stock Exchange. **Stock exchange symbol:** BJ.

BMC SOFTWARE
Waltham Woods, 880 Winter Street, Building 4, Waltham MA 02454. 781/891-0000. **Contact:** Human Resources. **World Wide Web address:** http://www.bmc.com. **Description:** Manufactures, sells, and supports software used for MIS and business productivity. The integrated software is written for IBM, IBM compatible VAX/VMS mainframes and RS/6000 workstations, new applications, and network performance management. The company distributes its products across North America, South America, Europe, the Middle East, and the Pacific Rim. **Positions advertised include:** Software Consultant; Administrative Support Assistant. **Other U.S. locations:** Nationwide. **International locations:** Worldwide. **Listed on:** New York Stock Exchange. **Stock exchange symbol:** BMC. **Number of employees at this location:** 180.

BOC EDWARDS
301 Ballardvale Street, Wilmington MA 01887. 978/658-5410x3154. **Toll-free phone:** 800/848-9800. **Fax:** 978/988-9360. **Contact:** Zena Gerolimato, Human Resources Manager. **E-mail address:** zina.gerolimato@Edwards.boc.com. **World Wide Web address:** http://www.bocedwards.com. **Description:** Supplies high vacuum manufacturing and process control equipment, industrial freeze dryers, and thin-film coating systems used in a variety of applications including pharmaceutical processing, microchip manufacturing, and vacuum packaging. Founded in 1919. **NOTE:** Entry-level positions are offered. **Office hours:** Monday - Friday, 8:30 a.m. - 5:00 p.m. **Corporate headquarters location:** This location. **Other U.S. locations:** Fairfield CA; Tonawanda NY. **International locations:** Worldwide. **Parent company:** BOC Group. **Listed on:** London Stock Exchange. **President:** Mark Rosenzweig. **Annual sales/revenues:** More than $100 million. **Number of employees at this location:** 200. **Number of employees nationwide:** 700. **Number of employees worldwide:** 2,000.

BT CONFERENCING
25 Braintree Hill Park, Suite 200, Braintree MA 02184. 781/843-2002. **Fax:** 781/849-8136. **Contact:** Recruiter. **E-mail address:** jobs@btna.com. **World Wide Web address:** http://www.btconferencing.com. **Description:** Provides communications services to businesses. **Positions advertised include:** Client Relations; Call Center Team Leader; Billing Applications Engineer; Partner Integration Engineer; Customer Service Representative; Inside Sales Manager.

BTU INTERNATIONAL
23 Esquire Road, North Billerica MA 01862. 978/667-4111. **Contact:** Human Resources. **E-mail address:** btuhr@btu.com. **World Wide Web address:** http://www.btu.com. **Description:** A manufacturer of thermal processing systems used in electronics packaging, metals and ceramics sintering, nuclear fuel sintering, and various nonelectronics applications. **Positions advertised include:** Electrical Wirer; Final Test Technician; Mechanical Assembler; Plumber. **Corporate headquarters location:** This location. **Operations at this facility include:** Administration; Manufacturing; Research and Development; Sales; Service. **Listed on:** NASDAQ. **Stock exchange symbol:** BTUI.

BABSON COLLEGE
Nichols Hall, Babson Park MA 02457. 781/239-4121. **Contact:** Human Resources. **E-mail address:** jobs@babson.edu. **World Wide Web address:** http://www.babson.edu. **Description:** A four-year business college with an enrollment of approximately 1,700 undergraduate students and 1,730 graduate students. **Positions advertised include:** Undergraduate Student Accounts Coordinator; Financial Accounting Coordinator; Corporate Outreach Manager; Reserve Librarian.

BACK BAY RESTAURANT GROUP, INC.
284 Newbury Street, Boston MA 02115. 617/536-2800. **Fax:** 617/236-4175. **Contact:** Human Resources. **E-mail address:** cbradley@bbrginc.com. **World Wide Web address:** http://www.backbayrestaurantgroup.com. **Description:** Owns several Boston-based restaurant chains including Joe's American Bar & Grill, PapaRazzi, Atlantic Fish Company, and Charlie's Saloon. The company also owns a racetrack in New Hampshire. **Special programs:** Internships. **Corporate headquarters location:** This location. **Parent company:** Westwood Group. **Operations at this facility include:** Administration. **Listed on:** NASDAQ. **Number of employees at this location:** 60. **Number of employees nationwide:** 4,500.

BACK CHANNEL MEDIA
107 South Street, 2nd Floor, Boston MA 02116. 617/728-3626. **Fax:** 617/728-0511. **Contact:** Human Resources. **E-mail address:** info@backchannelmedia.com. **World Wide Web address:** http://www.backchannelmedia.com. **Description:** Secures full-time cable channel positions on behalf of emerging cable programmers. Back Channel Media also tracks per inquiry sales, and offers interactive television consulting services. Founded in 2000. **Office hours:** Monday - Friday, 9:00 a.m. - 5:00 p.m. **Corporate headquarters location:** This location. **Listed on:** Privately held. **President:** Michael Kokernak. **Annual sales/revenues:** $11 - $20 million. **Number of employees at this location:** 30.

BAIN & COMPANY, INC.
131 Dartmouth Street, Boston MA 02116. 617/572-2000. **Contact:** Human Resources. **World Wide Web address:** http://www.bain.com. **Description:** An international management consulting firm that helps major companies achieve higher levels of competitiveness and profitability. Founded in 1973. **Corporate headquarters location:** This location. **Other U.S. locations:** Nationwide. **International locations:**

Worldwide. **Number of employees nationwide:** 1,000. **Number of employees worldwide:** 2800.

BAKER COMMODITIES INC.
P.O. Box 132, North Billerica MA 01862-0132. 978/454-8811. **Physical address:** 134 Billerica Avenue, North Billerica MA 01862. **Contact:** Human Resources. **Description:** Processes grease, tallow, and bone meal.

BALCO INC.
306 Northern Avenue, Boston MA 02210. 617/482-0100. **Contact:** Human Resources. **Description:** A heating, ventilation, air conditioning, and refrigeration contractor engaged in construction and residential building maintenance services. **Corporate headquarters location:** This location. **Other U.S. locations:** Birmingham AL; Rockville MD; Harrisburg PA. **Parent company:** Energy Systems, Inc. **Operations at this facility include:** Administration; Sales; Service. **Number of employees at this location:** 500.

BANK OF AMERICA
11 Center Street, Burlington MA 01803. 781/273-3783. **Contact:** Human Resources. **World Wide Web address:** http://www.bankofamerica.com. **Description:** A full-service bank. **Positions advertised include:** Premier Client Manager; Teller. **Corporate headquarters location:** Charlotte NC.

BANK OF AMERICA
460 West Broadway, South Boston MA 02127. 617/268-1936. **Contact:** Joe Lynch, Branch Manager. **World Wide Web address:** http://www.bankofamerica.com. **Description:** A full-service bank. **Positions advertised include:** Premier Client Manager; Teller. **Corporate headquarters location:** Charlotte NC.

BANK OF AMERICA
100 Federal Street, Boston MA 02110. 617/434-2200. **Fax:** 617/434-1941. **Contact:** Human Resources. **World Wide Web address:** http://www.bankofamerica.com. **Description:** Operates a full-service bank, serving the commercial and consumer banking needs of individuals, corporations, institutions, and government in the Northeast. **Positions advertised include:** Branch Manager; F/A Invest Operator Assistant; Premium Client Manager; Sales & Service Representative; Regional Sales Director; Administrative Assistant. **Corporate headquarters location:** Charlotte NC. **Note:** Please send resumes to: One Federal Street, Boston MA 02110.

BANKNORTH MASSACHUSETTS
153 Merrimack Street, Haverhill MA 01830. 978/374-1911. **Contact:** Human Resources. **Description:** Operates a full-service bank providing residential mortgage lending, commercial lending, construction lending, and savings. **Other U.S. locations:** MA; NH. **Parent company:** Banknorth, N.A.

BARNES & NOBLE BOOKSTORES
395 Washington Street, Boston MA 02108. 617/426-5184. **Contact:** Manager. **World Wide Web address:** http://www.bn.com. **Description:** A discount bookstore chain. **Corporate headquarters location:** New York NY. **Other U.S. locations:** Nationwide.

BARNES & NOBLE BOOKSTORES
150 Granite Street, Braintree MA 02184. 781/380-3655. **Fax:** 781/380-0665. **Contact:** Manager. **World Wide Web address:** http://www.bn.com. **Description:** A discount bookstore chain. **Corporate headquarters location:** New York NY. **Other U.S. locations:** Nationwide.

BARRY CONTROLS
40 Guest Street, Brighton MA 02135. 617/787-1555. **Fax:** 617/254-7381. **Contact:** Human Resources. **E-mail address:** resume@bcdi.com. **World Wide Web address:** http://www.barrycontrols.com. **Description:** Engaged in the design, manufacture, and sale of shock, noise, and vibration isolation and absorption products used in a wide variety of industrial applications. **Other U.S. locations:** Nationwide. **International locations:** Worldwide. **Parent company:** Hutchinson Worldwide. **Operations at this facility include:** Administration; Divisional Headquarters; Manufacturing; Research and Development; Sales.

BATTENFELD GLOUCESTER ENGINEERING COMPANY, INC.
Blackburn Industrial Park, P.O. Box 900, Gloucester MA 01931. 978/281-1800. **Contact:** Human Resources. **World Wide Web address:** http://www.battenfeld.com. **Description:** A manufacturer of plastics, processing machinery, and related components. **Other area locations:** Rockport MA. **Other U.S. locations:** Santa Ana CA; Woodstock GA; Algonquin IL; Medina OH; Frisco TX. **International locations:** Worldwide. **Parent company:** Battenfeld (Germany).

BAY STATE GAS COMPANY
300 Friberg Parkway, Westborough MA 01581-5039. 508/836-7000. **Contact:** Human Resources. **World Wide Web address:** http://www.baystategas.com. **Description:** A gas distribution utility. The company furnishes gas to 300,000 customers in more than 60 eastern Massachusetts communities. Through its subsidiary, Northern Utilities, Inc. it also serves 41 communities in New Hampshire and Maine. **Corporate headquarters location:** Merrillville IN. **Subsidiaries include:** Northern Utilities, Inc. **Parent company:** NiSource Inc.

BAY STATE MILLING COMPANY
100 Congress Street, Quincy MA 02169. 617/328-4400. **Toll-free phone:** 800/553-5687. **Fax:** 617/479-8910. **Contact:** Human Resources. **E-mail address:** info@bsm.com. **World Wide Web address:** http://www.baystatemilling.com. **Description:** A flour milling company with nationwide manufacturing facilities. **Corporate headquarters location:** This location. **Other U.S. locations:** Tolleson AZ; Platteville CO; Indiantown FL; Minneapolis MN; Winona MN; Clifton NJ; Mooresville NC.

BAY STATE SCHOOL OF TECHNOLOGY
225 Turnpike Street, Canton MA 02021. 781/828-3434. **Toll-free phone:** 888/828-3434. **Fax:** 781/575-0089. **Contact:** Human Resources. **E-mail address:** bssanet@ultranet.com. **World Wide Web address:** http://users.rcn.com/bssanet. **Description:** A technical institute offering programs in electronics, HVAC, and computers. **Positions advertised include:** Electronics Instructor; Major Appliance Instructor.

BAYER DIAGNOSTICS
63 North Street, Medfield MA 02052. 508/359-7711. **Contact:** Human Resources. **World Wide Web address:** http://www.bayerds.com. **Description:** Develops, manufactures, and sells clinical diagnostic systems. Bayer Diagnostics specializes in critical care, laboratory, and point-of-care testing. **International locations:** Worldwide. **Parent company:** Bayer Group. **Number of employees nationwide:** 4,500.

BAYSTATE FINANCIAL SERVICES
699 Boylston Street One Exeter Plaza, Suite 1400, Boston MA 02116. 617/585-4500. **Contact:** Human Resources. **World Wide Web address:** http://www.baystatefinancial.com. **Description:** A life insurance company.

BEACON PRESS
25 Beacon Street, Boston MA 02108. 617/742-2110. **Fax:** 617/723-3097. **Contact:** Human Resources. **World Wide Web address:** http://www.beacon.org. **Description:** An independent publisher of nonfiction and fiction books. Founded in 1854. **Special programs:** Internships. **Corporate headquarters location:** This location. **Parent company:** Unitarian Universalist Association. **Number of employees at this location:** 25.

BEALS & THOMAS, INC.
144 Turnpike Road, Southborough MA 01772-2104. 508/786-5431. **Fax:** 508/366-4391. **Contact:** Human Resources. **E-mail address:** hr@btiweb.com. **World Wide Web address:** http://www.btiweb.com. **Description:** A civil engineering firm offering a variety of services including surveying, site planning, and landscape architecture. **Positions advertised include:** Geographic Information Systems Manager; Land Surveyor; Staff Level Civil Engineer; Civil Engineer. **NOTE:** Users can submit resume online.

BEAR, STEARNS & COMPANY, INC.
One Federal Street, 29th Floor, Boston MA 02110. 617/654-2800. **Toll-free phone:** 800/333-2327. **Fax:** 617/654-2329. **Contact:** Human Resources. **World Wide Web address:** http://www.bearstearns.com. **Description:** A leading worldwide investment banking, securities trading, and brokerage firm. The firm's business includes corporate finance, mergers and acquisitions, public finance, institutional equities, fixed income sales and trading, private client services, foreign exchange, future sales and trading, derivatives, and asset management. **Corporate headquarters location:** New York NY. **Other U.S. locations:** Nationwide. **International locations:** Worldwide. **Parent company:** The Bear Stearns Companies Inc. also operates Bear, Stearns Securities Corporation, providing professional and correspondent clearing services, including securities lending; and Custodial Trust Company, providing master trust, custody, and government securities services. **Listed on:** New York Stock Exchange. **Stock exchange symbol:** BSC. **Annual sales/revenues:** More than $100 million. **Number of employees nationwide:** 7,800.

R.W. BECK, INC.
P.O. Box 9344, Framingham MA 01701-9344. 508/935-1600. **Fax:** 508/935-1888. **Physical address:** 550 Cochituate Road, Framingham MA. **Fax:** 508/935-1666. **Contact:** William G. LaBonte, Director of Administration and Human Resources. **E-mail address:** boston@rwbeck.com. **World Wide Web address:** http://www.rwbeck.com. **Description:** A diversified professional, technical, and management consulting firm. The company provides construction, environmental, technical, energy, solid waste, and water/wastewater services nationwide. Founded in 1942. **Positions advertised include:** Senior Water Practice Consultant. **Corporate headquarters location:** Seattle WA. **Other area locations:** Waltham MA. **Operations at this facility include:** Divisional Headquarters; Regional Headquarters. **Listed on:** Privately held. **Number of employees at this location:** 100. **Number of employees nationwide:** 500.

BECKER COLLEGE
61 Sever Street, Box 15071, Worcester MA 01609-2195. 508/791-9241. **Toll-free phone:** 877/5 BECKER. **Fax:** 508/849-5275. **Contact:** Kathy Garvey, Director of Human Resources. **E-mail address:** kgarvey@becker.edu. **World Wide Web address:** http://www.beckercollege.com. **Description:** Offers a variety of associate's and bachelor's degrees, and certificate programs in business, law, computers, health, education, and social sciences. **Positions advertised include:** Nursing Faculty; Library Supervisor; Adjunct Faculty.

BENTLEY COLLEGE
175 Forest Street, Waltham MA 02452-4705. 781/891-3427. **Fax:** 781/891-2494. **Contact:** Joseph Salvucci, Senior Human Resources Business Partner. **World Wide Web address:** http://www.bentley.edu. **Description:** A business college offering undergraduate and graduate programs, as well as professional development certificates. The college offers associate's, bachelor's, and master's (including MBAs) degrees. **Positions advertised include:** Associate Director of Corporate Relations; Communication Designer; Assistant Director of Development; Receptionist; Campus Police Officer; Dispatcher; Records Coordinator; Work Order Control Assistant; Behavioral & Political Sciences Faculty; CIS Faculty; English Faculty; History Faculty; International Studies Faculty; Media Studies Faculty; Philosophy Faculty.

BERKLEE COLLEGE OF MUSIC
1140 Boylston Street, Boston MA 02215. 617/266-1400. **Fax:** 617/247-0166. **Contact:** Employee Relations Manager. **World Wide Web address:** http://www.berklee.edu. **Description:** An independent music college offering four-year programs of study in composition, film scoring, music business/management, music education, music production and engineering, music synthesis, music therapy, and performance. The college enrolls 3,000 students. **Positions advertised include:** Assistant Chair; Stage Manager; Assistant Vice President for Berklee Media; Course Developer; Continuing Education Registrar; Lab Monitor; Harmony Department Chair; Front Desk Supervisor. **Corporate headquarters location:** This location. **Number of employees at this location:** 170.

BERKSHIRE BANK
P.O. Box 1308, Pittsfield MA 01202. 413/443-5601. **Toll-free phone:** 800/773-5601. **Fax:** 413/447-1830. **Physical address:** 24 North Street, Pittsfield MA 01201. **Contact:** Human Resources. **E-mail address:** resumes@berkshirebank.com. **World Wide Web address:** http;//www.berkshirebank.com. **Description:** A full-service mutual savings bank. **Corporate headquarters location:** This location. **Operations at this facility include:** Administration. **Number of employees at this location:** 150.

THE BERKSHIRE GAS COMPANY
115 Cheshire Road, Pittsfield MA 01201. 413/445-0252. **Contact:** Human Resources. **World Wide Web address:** http://www.berkshiregas.com. **Description:** A public gas utility operating in western Massachusetts, eastern New York, and southern Vermont. The Berkshire Gas Company distributes natural gas to approximately 30,000 people in its service area. The Berkshire Propane Division sells and leases related gas-burning appliances, and markets liquefied petroleum. **NOTE:** Entry-level positions are offered. **Company slogan:** Energy you can count on. People you can trust. **Special programs:** Internships; Summer Jobs. **Corporate headquarters location:** This location. **Listed on:** NASDAQ. **Stock exchange symbol:** BGAS. **President/CEO:** Scott Robinson. **Information Systems Manager:** Joseph Bosworth. **Annual sales/revenues:** $21 - $50 million. **Number of employees at this location:** 130.

BERKSHIRE LIFE INSURANCE COMPANY
700 South Street, Pittsfield MA 01201. 413/499-4321. **Contact:** Human Resources. **E-mail address:** carreers@theberkshire.com. **World Wide Web address:** http://www.theberkshire.com. **Description:** Offers a wide range of life insurance and insured pension plans.

WILLIAM A. BERRY & SON, INC.
99 Conifer Hill Drive, Suite 410, Danvers MA 01923. 978/774-1057. **Toll-free phone:** 877/774-1057. **Fax:** 978/777-9024. **Contact:** Human Resources. **E-mail address:** contactus@berry.com. **World Wide Web address:** http://www.waberry.com. **Description:** A construction management firm. Founded in 1857. **Positions advertised include:** Senior Project Manager; Project Manager; Project/Lead Estimator; HVAC Project Engineer; Project Coordinator.

BETA GROUP, INC.
1420 Providence Highway, Suite 117, Norwood MA 02062. 781/255-1982. **Contact:** Human Resources. **E-mail address:** tgarro@beta-inc.com. **World Wide Web address:** http://www.beta-inc.com. **Description:** An engineering firm specializing in environmental engineering and site remediation; highway engineering; water/wastewater engineering; and landfill closures. **Positions advertised include:** Civil Transportation Engineer; Structural Engineer; Geographic Information Systems Project Manager.

CHANNING L. BETE COMPANY INC.
One Community Place, South Deerfield MA 01373-0200. 413/665-7611. **Toll-free phone:** 800/477-4776. **Fax:** 413/665-6397. **Contact:** Human Resources. **World Wide Web address:** http://www.channing-bete.com. **Description:** Publishers and printers of educational booklets, calendars, videos, coloring books, and posters. **Positions advertised include:** Copywriter; Advertising Direct Marketer; Product Manager; Market Research Specialist; Programming Analyst. **Corporate headquarters location:** This location. **Operations at this facility include:** Administration; Manufacturing; Research and Development; Sales. **Listed on:** Privately held. **Number of employees at this location:** 275.

BETH ISRAEL DEACONESS MEDICAL CENTER
330 Brookline Avenue, Boston MA 02215. 617/667-8000. **Contact:** Human Resources. **World Wide Web address:** http://www.bidmc.harvard.edu. **Description:** A hospital that also supports a network of primary care physicians. **NOTE:** Applicants should send resumes to The Talent Bank at: CareGroup, 21 Autumn Street, Boston MA 02215. **Positions advertised include:** Procurement Manager; Food Service Worker; Director of Human Resources Information Systems; Ultrasonographer; Clinical Research Coordinator; Research Student; Customer Service Representative; Administrative Assistant; Financial Analyst; Materials Handler.

THE BETTER BUSINESS BUREAU, INC.
235 Central Street, Suite 1, Natick MA 01760. 508/652-4800. **Fax:** 508/652-4833. **Contact:** Human Resources. **World Wide Web address:** http://www.bosbbb.org. **Description:** The Better Business Bureau provides information to consumers and businesses about companies so that they are better informed before entering into a business relationship. **Special programs:** Internships. **Operations at this facility include:** This office is the regional headquarters serving eastern Massachusetts, Maine, and Vermont.

BEVERLY HOSPITAL
85 Herrick Street, Beverly MA 01915. 978/922-3000. **Contact:** Human Resources. **World Wide Web address:** http://www.nhs-healthlink.org. **Description:** A hospital. Beverly Hospital is part of the Northeast Health System. **Positions advertised include:** Access Representative; Administrative Associate; Admissions Registered Nurse; Clinical Associates; Coder; Data Manager; Employment Manager; Executive Assistant; Human Resources Clerk; Lab Associate; Registered Nurse; Security Guard.

BICKFORD'S FAMILY RESTAURANTS
1330 Soldiers Field Road, Boston MA 02135. 617/782-4010. **Contact:** Human Resources. **World Wide Web address:** http://www.bickfordsrestaurants.com. **Description:** Operates the Bickford's Family Restaurants chain in the New England area. **Positions advertised include:** Waiter; Hostess; Utility Person. **Corporate headquarters location:** This location. **Other area locations:** Statewide. **Other U.S. locations:** CT; RI; VT. **Operations at this facility include:** Administration.

BICKFORD'S FAMILY RESTAURANTS
135 Union Street, Braintree MA 02184. 781/848-7045. **Contact:** Manager. **World Wide Web address:** http://www.bickfordsrestaurants.com. **Description:** One location of the restaurant chain. **NOTE:** This location hires for much of the South Shore area outside of Boston. **Positions advertised include:** Waiter; Hostess; Utility Person. **Corporate headquarters location:** Boston MA.

BIG BROTHERS ASSOCIATION
55 Summer Street, 8th Floor, Boston MA 02110. 617/542-9090. **Contact:** Human Resources. **Description:** Provides a mentor program for underprivileged children by pairing them with an adult volunteer.

BIG Y FOODS INC.
2145 Roosevelt Avenue, Springfield MA 01102. 413/784-0600. **Fax:** 413/732-7350. **Contact:** Human Resources. **World Wide Web address:** http://www.bigy.com. **Description:** Operates a chain of over 40 supermarkets. **Positions advertised include:** Staff Accountant; Financial Representative Support; HVAC/R Technician; General Maintenance Mechanic; Food Service Equipment Technician; Computer Operator; Loss Prevention Representative. **NOTE:** Users may apply for positions online. **Special programs:** Internships. **Other area locations:** Statewide. **Other U.S. locations:** CT. **Corporate headquarters location:** This location. **Operations at this facility include:** Administration. **Listed on:** Privately held. **Number of employees nationwide:** 7,200.

BIOGEN CORPORATION
14 Cambridge Center, Cambridge MA 02142. 617/252-9200. **Fax:** 617/679-2546. **Contact:** Human Resources. **E-mail address:** resumes@biogen.com. **World Wide Web address:** http://www.biogen.com. **Description:** Develops and commercializes drugs produced by genetic engineering. Products include alpha interferon, sold by Schering-Plough, and Hepatitis B vaccines, sold by Merck and SmithKline Beecham. **Positions advertised include:** Associate Customer Service Director; Manufacturing Associate; Commodity Analyst; Medical Coder; Sales Analyst; Data Support Administrator; Web Architect; Associate Scientist; Business Analyst; Business Project Manager; Development Engineer; Documentation Specialist. **Special programs:** Internships. **Corporate headquarters location:** This location. **Other U.S. locations:** Research Triangle Park NC. **International locations:** France. **Operations at this facility include:** Administration; Manufacturing; Research and Development. **Listed on:** NASDAQ. **Stock exchange symbol:** BGEN. **Number of employees nationwide:** 430.

BIOPURE CORPORATION
11 Hurley Street, Cambridge MA 02141. 617/234-6500. **Contact:** Personnel. **E-mail address:** hr@biopure.com. **World Wide Web address:** http://www.biopure.com. **Description:** A pharmaceutical company that develops oxygen-based therapeutic products. **Positions advertised include:** Biostatistics Data Manager; Clinical Project Manager; Clinical Operations Director; Regulatory Affairs Drug Safety Specialist. **Listed on:** NASDAQ. **Stock exchange symbol:** BPUR.

BIOSPHERE MEDICAL INC.
1050 Hingham Street, Rockland MA 02370. 781/681-7900. **Fax:** 781/792-2745. **Contact:** Human Resources. **World Wide Web address:** http://www.biospheremed.com. **Description:** Biomedical company focused on embolotherapy. **Other locations:** France.

BIOTRANSPLANT, INC.
Building 75, Third Avenue, Charlestown Navy Yard, Charlestown MA 02129. 617/241-5200. **Contact:** Human Resources. **World Wide Web address:** http://www.biotransplant.com. **Description:** Engaged in the research and development of pharmaceuticals. Products are designed to help the human body to accept transplants; to increase the potential for more nonhuman to human transplants; and to treat rejection of transplanted organs and tissues. **Listed on:** NASDAQ. **Stock exchange symbol:** BTRN.

BIRD MACHINE COMPANY
100 Neponset Street, South Walpole MA 02071. 508/668-0400. **Fax:** 508/660-1385. **Contact:** Human Resources. **World Wide Web address:** http://www.bakerhughes.com. **Description:** Designs, develops, and manufactures centrifuges, filters, and other solid/liquid separation equipment systems for process industries. **Other U.S. locations:** Houston TX; Salt Lake City UT. **International locations:** Worldwide. **Parent company:** Baker Hughes Inc. **Annual sales/revenues:** More than $100 million. **Number of employees at this location:** 360. **Number of employees nationwide:** 500. **Number of employees worldwide:** 15,000.

BITSTREAM, INC.
245 First Street 17th Floor, Cambridge MA 02142. 617/497-6222. **Contact:** Human Resources. **E-mail address:** careers@bitstream.com. **World Wide Web address:** http://www.bitstream.com. **Description:** Develops and markets digital font software packages for original equipment manufacturers and end users. Products include fonts used in graphic arts image setters, printers, and screen displays for both personal computer and Macintosh platforms. Founded in 1981.

BLACK & VEATCH
230 Congress Street, Suite 802, Boston MA 02110. 617/451-6900. **Contact:** Human Resources. **World Wide Web address:** http://www.bv.com. **Description:** An environmental/civil engineering and construction firm serving utilities, commerce, and government agencies in more than 40 countries worldwide. Black & Veatch provides a broad range of study, design, construction management, and turnkey capabilities to clients in the water and wastewater fields. The firm is one of the leading authorities on drinking water treatment through the use of activated carbon, ozone, and other state-of-the-art processes. Black & Veatch is also engaged in wastewater treatment work including reclamation and reuse projects and the beneficial use of wastewater residuals. Other services are provided for solid waste recycling and disposal, transportation, and storm water management. In the energy field, Black & Veatch is a leader in providing engineering procurement and construction for electric power plants. The firm's areas of expertise include coal-fueled plants, simple and combined-cycle combustion turbines, fluidized bed combustion, waste-to-energy facilities, hydroelectric plants, and cogeneration facilities. Black & Veatch's capabilities also include nuclear power projects, advanced technology, air quality control, performance monitoring, plant life management, and facilities modification. In addition, Black & Veatch operates in the transmission and distribution field. In the industrial sector, Black & Veatch focuses on projects involving cleanrooms, industrial processes and planning, utility systems, and cogeneration. In addition to engineering, procurement, and construction, Black & Veatch offers a variety of management and financial services including institutional strengthening, privatization, strategic financial planning, and information management. **Positions advertised include:** Communication Specialist; Document Associate; Civil Engineer; Consultant; Electrical Engineer; Engineering Technician; Associate Estimator; Programming Analyst; Human Resources Division Director; Mechanical Engineer; Planning Specialist; Engineer; Procurement Specialist. **Special programs:** Co-ops. **Corporate headquarters location:** Kansas City MO. **Other U.S. locations:** Nationwide. **International locations:** Worldwide. **Listed on:** Privately held. **Number of employees worldwide:** 10,000.

BLACKWELL PUBLISHERS
350 Main Street, Malden MA 02148. 781/388-8200. **Fax:** 781/388-8210. **Contact:** Human Resources. **World Wide Web address:** http://www.blackwellpub.com. **Description:** Publishes books and journals on a variety of subjects including history, linguistics, and air pollution. **Positions advertised include:** Conference Services Marketing Manager; Telemarketing Coordinator; Journal Editor; Associate Publisher; Production Assistant; Conference Assistant; Editorial Coordinator. **International locations:** England.

ARTHUR BLANK & COMPANY
225 Rivermoor Street, Boston MA 02132. 617/325-9600. **Toll-free phone:** 800/776-7333. **Fax:** 617/327-1235. **Contact:** Human Resources. **E-mail address:** abco@abco.com. **World Wide Web address:** http://www.abco.com. **Description:** Manufactures a wide variety of flat plastic products including calling cards, access cards, and rulers.

BLUE CROSS AND BLUE SHIELD OF MASSACHUSETTS
100 Summer Street, Boston MA 02110. 617/832-5000. **Toll-free phone:** 800/262-BLUE. **Contact:** Human Resources. **World Wide Web address:** http://www.bcbsma.com. **Description:** A nonprofit health care insurance organization providing managed health care plans to both individuals and groups. Blue Cross and Blue Shield offers Point-of-Service, individual health, PPO, and HMO plans, as well as life, dental, vision, and disability insurance. **Positions advertised include:** Office Administrator; Medical Analyst; Data Architect; Cost Accounting Analyst; Administrative Assistant; Reimbursement Analyst; Project Manager; Secretary; Web Support Analyst; Network Infrastructure Manager; Dental Director; Underwriting Consultant. **Operations at this facility include:** Administration; Sales; Service.

BLUESTONE ENERGY
871 Washington Street, Braintree MA 02184. 781/356-8865. **Fax:** 781/356-8864. **Contact:** Human Resources. **E-mail address:** blu@bluestoneenergy.com. **World Wide Web address:** http://www.bluestoneenergy.com. **Description:** Specializes in identifying and implementing products that improve energy efficiency.

THE BOEING COMPANY
81 Hartwell Avenue, Lexington MA 02141. 781/863-5454. **Toll-free phone:** 800/254-1591. **Contact:** Human Resources. **E-mail address:** employmentoperations@boeing.com. **World Wide Web address:** http://www.boeing.com. **Description:** The Boeing Company is one of the largest aerospace firms in the United States, one of the nation's top exporters, and one of the world's leading manufacturers of commercial jet transports. The company is a major U.S. government contractor, with capabilities in missile and space, electronic systems, military aircraft, helicopters, and information systems management. Boeing is divided into four business segments: Commercial Aircraft, Space & Communications, Military Aircraft and Missiles, and Shared Services. **Corporate headquarters location:** Chicago IL. **Operations at this facility include:** This location is a marketing office. **Subsidiaries include:** Boeing Information Services, Inc. (Vienna VA) develops and manages large-scale information systems for selected agencies of the federal government. **Listed on:** New York Stock Exchange. **Stock exchange symbol:** BA.

BOISE CASCADE CORPORATION
P.O Box 130, Nutting Lake Massachusetts 01865. 978/670-3800. **Physical Address:** 32 Manning Road, Billerica MA 01821. **Contact:** Human Resources. **Description:** A wholesale lumber company.

BORDER CAFE
32 Church Street, Cambridge MA 02138. 617/864-6100. **Contact:** Manager. **Description:** A restaurant and bar specializing in Mexican and Cajun food.

BORDERS BOOKS & MUSIC
10-24 School Street, Boston MA 02108. 617/557-7188. **Fax:** 617/557-4476. **Contact:** Hiring Manager. **World Wide Web address:** http://www.borders.com. **Description:** One location of the discount bookstore chain offering over 200,000 book titles, as well as music and videos. Borders also provides year-round events including live musical performances, author readings, kids programs, book groups, and art exhibitions.

BORDERS BOOKS & MUSIC
255 Grossman Drive, Braintree MA 02184. 781/356-5111. **Contact:** Hiring Manager. **World Wide Web address:** http://www.borders.com. **Description:** One location of the discount bookstore chain offering over 200,000 book titles, as well as music and videos. Borders also provides year-round events including live musical performances, author readings, kids programs, book groups, and art exhibitions.

BRODEUR PORTER NOVELLI
855 Boylston Street, 8th Floor, Boston MA 02116. 617/587-2800. **Contact:** Human Resources. **World Wide Web address:** http://www.brodeur.com. **Description:** A public relations firm. **Office hours:** Monday - Friday, 8:30 a.m. - 5:30 p.m.

ROBERT BOSCH CORPORATION
101 First Avenue, Waltham MA 02451. 781/890-8282. **Contact:** Human Resources. **World Wide Web address:** http://www.boschusa.com. **Description:** Robert Bosch Corporation operates in three groups: Automotive-Original Equipment, Industrial Group, and Sales-Automotive Aftermarket. The largest segment of the company's business is the Automotive Group, which includes products such as antilock braking systems (ABS), airbag electronics, fuel injectors, and oxygen sensors. The Industrial Group consists of the Packaging Machinery Division, which sells high-technology packaging equipment, primarily to the food processing and pharmaceutical industries; the Surftran Division, which offers a range of deburring services, as well as manufacturing, selling, and servicing cleaning equipment; Weldun International, Inc. manufactures flexible assembly systems and automation products and assembles machinery for the Packaging Machinery Division; and Robert Bosch Fluid Power Corporation, which designs, produces, and markets hydraulic pumps, valves, and power units, and sells a full line of pneumatic products. The Sales Group handles automotive aftermarket, mobile communications, and household goods. Robert Bosch Corporation also participates in three joint ventures. Diesel Technology Company produces electronic and mechanical unit injectors. S-B Power Tool Company markets portable electric power tools and accessories to the industrial, contractor, and do-it-yourself markets. Automotive Electronic Controls Systems, Inc. manufactures parts for fuel-injection systems and automotive transmissions. **Corporate headquarters location:** Broadview IL. **Other U.S. locations:** Nationwide. **Operations at this facility include:** This location provides automotive sales, engineering, and administration as part of Robert Bosch Corporation's Automotive Group.

BOSE CORPORATION
The Mountain, Framingham MA 01701-9168. 508/766-1099. **Toll-free phone:** 800/999-BOSE. **Contact:** Human Resources. **World Wide Web address:** http://www.bose.com. **Description:** Designs and manufactures audio-related consumer electronics products including speakers, stereos, and related stereo components. **Positions advertised include:** Program Manager; Administrative Assistant; Channel Marketing Manager; Research Technologist; Mechanical Engineer; DRP Planner; Product Marketing Specialist. **Corporate headquarters location:** This location. **Other U.S. locations:** Yuma AZ; Hillsdale MI; Columbia SC. **International locations:** Canada; Ireland; Mexico. **Operations at this facility include:** Administration; Research and Development.

BOSTIK FINDLEY, INC.
211 Boston Street, Middleton MA 01949. 978/777-0100. **Fax:** 978/750-7249. **Contact:** Human Resources. **E-mail address:** careers@bostikfindley.com. **World Wide Web address:** http://www.bostik.com. **Description:** Bostik, Inc. and Ato Findley, Inc. merged in the Fall of 2000 to become Bostik Findley, Inc. Bostik Findley produces more than 2,000 formulations of rubber-based, polymer, water-borne, and epoxy adhesives. Bostik Findley also manufactures sealants, aerosol, engineering adhesives, maintenance aerosols, and construction grouts and mastics. Founded in 1889. **Positions advertised include:** Hardwood Product Manager; Process Specialist. **Corporate headquarters location:** This location. **Other U.S. locations:** Long Beach CA; Conyers GA; Marshall MI; Cleveland OH; Huntingdon Valley PA. **International locations:** Australia; England; France; Germany; Korea; Mexico; New Zealand; Portugal; Spain; Sweden. **Parent company:** TotalFinaElf. **Operations at this facility include:** Administration; Divisional Headquarters; Manufacturing; Research and Development; Sales; Service. **Listed on:** Privately held. **Number of employees at this location:** 350. **Number of employees worldwide:** 4500.

BOSTON BALLET
19 Clarendon Street, Boston MA 02116. 617/695-6950. **Fax:** 617/695-6995. **Contact:** Human Resources. **E-mail address:** diane@bostonballet.com. **World Wide Web address:** http://www.bostonballet.org. **Description:** One of the largest dance companies in the United States. Boston Ballet performs a mix of classic story ballets, contemporary ballets, and avant-garde works. Founded in 1965. **Positions advertised include:** Major Gifts Officer; Data Coordinator; Managing Director; Male Principal Dancer; Resident Director.

BOSTON BEER WORKS
61 Brookline Avenue, Boston MA 02215. 617/536-2337. **Contact:** Manager. **Description:** A restaurant and brewery with a diverse menu serving the area near Fenway Park.

BOSTON BIOMEDICA, INC.
375 West Street, West Bridgewater MA 02379. 508/580-1900. **Contact:** Human Resources. **World Wide Web address:** http://www.bbii.com. **Description:** A clinical laboratory that provides diagnostic testing specifically for HIV-1 (AIDS), HTLV-1, HIV-2, and Viral Hepatitis. **Other U.S. locations:** Garden Grove CA; Gaithersburg MD. **Listed on:** NASDAQ. **Stock exchange symbol:** BBII.

BOSTON BRUINS
One Fleet Center Place, Suite 250, Boston MA 02114. 617/624-1050. **Contact:** Human Resources. **World Wide Web address:** http://www.bostonbruins.com. **Description:** Administrative and publicity offices for the National Hockey League team. **Corporate headquarters location:** This location.

BOSTON BUSINESS JOURNAL
200 High Street, Suite 4B, Boston MA 02110. 617/330-1000. **Fax:** 617/330-1015. **Contact:** Personnel. **E-mail address:** boston@bizjournals.com. **World Wide Web address:** http://www.amcity.com/boston. **Description:** Publishes a weekly business journal serving the Boston area. **Publisher:** James C. Menneto.

BOSTON COLLEGE
140 Commonwealth Avenue, More Hall, Room 315, Chestnut Hill MA 02467. 617/552-3330. **Contact:** Human Resources. **World Wide Web address:** http://www.bc.edu/. **Description:** A private, four-year, Jesuit college offering bachelor's and master's degree programs. **Positions advertised include:** Administrative Secretary; Administrative Coordinator; General Service Worker; Development Secretary; Staff Assistant; Research Director; Sales Assistant; Second Cook; Digital Media Producer; Associate Dean; Gate Attendant; Classroom Technology Specialist.

BOSTON COMMON PRESS
17 Station Street, Brookline MA 02445. 617/232-1000. **Contact:** David Mack, Circulation Director. **World Wide Web address:** http://www.cooksillustrated.com. **Description:** Publishes *Natural Health Magazine, Cooks Illustrated,* and *Handcraft* magazines.

THE BOSTON COMPANY
One Boston Place, Boston MA 02108. 617/722-7000. **Contact:** Human Resources. **World Wide Web address:** http://www.thebostoncompany.com. **Description:** A bank and mutual fund management company. **NOTE:** Please send resumes to: The Boston Company, Human Resources, 135 Santelli Highway, Everett MA 02149. **Special programs:** Internships. **Corporate headquarters location:** Pittsburgh PA. **Other U.S. locations:** CA; DE; MD; PA. **Subsidiaries include:** Boston Safe Deposit & Trust Company (also at this location.) **Parent company:** Mellon Bank Corporation. **Operations at this facility include:** Regional Headquarters. **Listed on:** New York Stock Exchange. **Stock exchange symbol:** MEL. **Number of employees at this location:** 3,000. **Number of employees nationwide:** 3,200.

BOSTON CONCESSIONS GROUP INC.
55 Cambridge Parkway, Cambridge MA 02141. 617/499-2700. **Fax:** 617/679-0800. **Contact:** Human Resources. **E-mail address:** joberlander@bostonconcessionsgroup.com. **World Wide Web address:** http://www.bostonconcessionsgroup.com. **Description:** Provides food services and related products to a wide range of customers. Boston Concessions operates in 15 states. **Corporate headquarters location:** This location.

BOSTON FEDERAL SAVINGS BANK
17 New England Executive Park, Burlington MA 01803. 781/273-0300. **Fax:** 781/229-0282. **Contact:** Human Resources. **World Wide Web address:** http://www.bfsb.com. **Description:** A full-service federal savings bank with several branch locations throughout the greater Boston area. **Positions advertised include:** Loan Services Representative; Teller; Assistant Branch Manager; Loan Investment Specialist; Floating Assistant Manager; Floating Assistant Manager; Construction Loan Services; Brand Administrative Specialist. **Corporate headquarters location:** This location. **Other area locations:** Arlington MA; Bedford MA; Billerica MA; Boston MA; Lexington MA; Peabody MA; Wellesley MA; Woburn MA. **Operations at this facility include:** Administration.

BOSTON FINANCIAL DATA SERVICES, INC.
2 Heritage Drive, North Quincy MA 02171. 617/483-5000. **Toll-free phone:** 888/772-BFDS. **Contact:** Human Resources. **E-mail address:** jobs@bostonfinancial.com. **World Wide Web address:** http://www.bostonfinancial.com. **Description:** A service agent for State Street Bank & Trust Company specializing in the mutual fund, corporate stock transfer, and insurance services industries. **Positions advertised include:** Mutual Fund Correspondence Specialist; Customer Services Representative; Operations Representative; Audit Specialist. **Special programs:** Internships. **Parent company:** State Street Bank & Trust and DST Systems. **Operations at this facility include:** Administration; Service.

THE BOSTON GLOBE
P.O. Box 2378, Boston MA 02107-2378. 617/929-2000. **Physical address:** 135 Morrissey Boulevard, Boston MA 02125. **Fax:** 617/929-3376. **Contact:** Human Resources. **World Wide Web address:** http://www.boston.com/. **Description:** One of New England's largest daily newspapers. Founded in 1872. **Special programs:** Internships; Co-ops. **Internship information:** The Boston Globe offers a Business Summer internship program to college sophomores and juniors. There are two internship positions available: one in advertising and one in accounting. The accounting intern is assigned to the Controller's Office and works on specific projects for the Credit, Accounting, and Payroll departments. The advertising intern is responsible for selling advertising space and servicing existing accounts. Summer interns work from June 1 through Labor Day and are paid approximately $550.00 per week. The deadline for applications (including resume and personal statement) is February 28. Questions about application procedures should be addressed to Human Resources. **Parent company:** New York Times Company. **Listed on:** New York Stock Exchange. **Stock exchange symbol:** NYT. **Number of employees at this location:** 2,400.

BOSTON HERALD
P.O. Box 2096, Boston MA 02106. 617/426-3000. **Contact:** Human Resources. **World Wide Web address:** http://www.bostonherald.com. **Description:** One of New England's largest daily newspapers.

BOSTON MAGAZINE
300 Massachusetts Avenue, Boston MA 02115. 617/262-9700. **Contact:** Human Resources. **World Wide Web address:** http://www.bostonmagazine.com.

Description: A monthly magazine focusing on local interest stories, politics, entertainment, theater, and dining. **Corporate headquarters location:** This location. **Parent company:** MetroCorp (Philadelphia PA).

BOSTON MARRIOTT NEWTON
2345 Commonwealth Avenue, Newton MA 02466. 617/969-1000. **Fax:** 617/630-3578. **Contact:** Human Resources. **World Wide Web address:** http://www.marriott.com. **Description:** A 430-room hotel. **Positions advertised include:** Director of Housekeeping; Night Manager; Business Transient Sales Manager; Marketing Executive. **Special programs:** Internships. **Corporate headquarters location:** Washington DC. **Parent company:** Marriott International. **Operations at this facility include:** Administration; Sales; Service. **Listed on:** New York Stock Exchange. **Stock exchange symbol:** MAR. **Number of employees at this location:** 400.

BOSTON MEDICAL CENTER
88 East Newton Street, Boston MA 02118. 617/638-8585. **Fax:** 617/638-8577. **Contact:** Human Resources. **World Wide Web address:** http://www.bmc.org. **Description:** A private, nonprofit, 277-bed hospital. The center provides a full range of medical services and offers specialty care units that include psychiatric care, coronary care, metabolic care, medical intensive care, surgical intensive care, the Northeast Regional Center for Brain Injury, the New England Regional Spinal Cord Injury Center, the Breast Health Center, the Cancer Center, the Center for Minimal Access Surgery, the Center for Lung Disease, the Voice Center, the Wald Neurological Unit, the New England Male Reproductive Center, and the University Continence Center. As a major teaching hospital, Boston Medical Center ENC specializes in heart care, the neurosciences, emergency medicine and critical care, elderly care, cancer care, and women's health. The center serves approximately 10,000 admissions and 153,000 outpatient and emergency visits annually. Founded in 1855. **NOTE:** Please send resumes to: Human Resources Department, 88 East Newton Street, Boston MA 02118. **Positions advertised include:** Medical Staff Assistant; Medical Technologist; Radiology Technologist; Respiratory Therapist; Certified Nurses Assistant; Nurse Manager; Registered Nurse; Unit Coordinator; Accounts Receivable Clerk; Administrative Assistant; Administrative Coordinator; Billing Assistant; Patient Access Representative; Research Assistant; Medical Staff Assistant; Residency Coordinator; Payment Processor; General Cleaner; Dietary Aide; Central Processing Technician; Lab Support Technician; Clinical Pharmacist; Budget Manager; Dietician; Record Assistant; Team Leader.

BOSTON MUTUAL LIFE INSURANCE COMPANY
120 Royall Street, Canton MA 02021. 781/828-7000. **Toll-free phone:** 800/669-2668x372. **Fax:** 781/770-0975. **Contact:** Human Resources. **E-mail address:** hr@bostonmutual.com. **World Wide Web address:** http://www.bostonmutual.com. **Description:** Provides life insurance. **Positions advertised include:** Actuarial Assistant; Telephone Representative. **NOTE:** Apply in person Monday – Friday 8:00 a.m. – 3:00 p.m. **Corporate headquarters location:** This location. **Operations at this facility include:** Administration; Sales; Service. **Number of employees at this location:** 300. **Number of employees nationwide:** 500.

BOSTON 128 COMPANIES, INC.
3 University Office Park, 95 Sawyer Road, Suite 110, Waltham MA 02453. 781/642-0777. **Contact:** Human Resources. **World Wide Web address:** http://www.boston128companies.com. **Description:** A full-service financial company. Boston 128 Companies specializes in deferred compensation plans for corporate and individual clients. **Positions advertised include:** Account Manager; Brokerage Relationship Manager.

BOSTON POLICE DEPARTMENT
One Schroeder Plaza, Boston MA 02120. 617/343-4200. **Contact:** Human Resources. **World Wide Web address:** http://www.ci.boston.ma.us/police/default.asp. **Description:** This location serves as the headquarters for Boston's police department.

BOSTON PUBLIC HEALTH COMMISSION
1010 Massachusetts Avenue, 6th Floor, Boston MA 02118. 617/534-5395. **Fax:** 617/534-2418. **Contact:** Patty Hall, Staffing Specialist. **E-mail address:** patty_hall@bphc.org. **World Wide Web address:** http://www.bphc.org. **Description:** A nonprofit agency whose mission is to protect, preserve, and promote the well-being of all Boston residents. Boston Public Health Commission provides community-based public health programs including tobacco control, domestic violence prevention, environmental health, communicable disease awareness, maternal/child health, addictions services, homeless services, and AIDS services. **NOTE:** All positions with Boston Public Health Commission require residency in the city of Boston or a willingness to move to Boston if hired. Entry-level positions and second and third shifts are offered. **Positions advertised include:** Research Assistant; Administrative Assistant; Project Manager; Head Administrative Clerk; Project Manager; Administrative Assistant; Social Worker; Program Coordinator; Counselor; Staffing Coordinator; Resource Clerk; Medical Director; Custodian; Data Analyst. **Number of employees at this location:** 1,100.

BOSTON PUBLIC WORKS DEPARTMENT
One City Hall Plaza Room 714, Boston MA 02118. 617/635-4900. **Fax:** 617/635-7499. **Contact:** Human Resources. **World Wide Web address:** http://www.cityofboston.gov/publicworks. **Description:** Performs street repairs, snow plowing, street light replacement, trash pickup, and recycling services for the city of Boston.

BOSTON RED SOX BASEBALL CLUB
Fenway Park, 4 Yawkey Way, Boston MA 02215. 617/267-9440. **Contact:** Human Resources. **World Wide Web address:** http://boston.redsox.mlb.com. **Description:** Operates the Boston Red Sox, an American League professional baseball franchise.

BOSTON RESTAURANT ASSOCIATES, INC.
999 Broadway, Suite 400, Saugus MA 01906. 781/231-7575. **Fax:** 781/231-3225. **Contact:** Human Resources. **World Wide Web address:** http://www.pizzariaregina.com. **Description:** Boston Restaurant Associates owns and operates a chain of seven pizzerias under the name Pizzeria Regina; two Italian/American, family style restaurants under the name Polcari's North End; and three full-service, Italian restaurants under the names Bel Canto and Cappuccino's.

BOSTON SAND & GRAVEL COMPANY
169 Portland Street, P.O. Box 9187, Boston MA 02114. 617/227-9000. **Contact:** Human Resources. **Description:** Produces ready-mixed concrete. **Corporate headquarters location:** This location. **Operations at this facility include:** Administration; Sales. **Listed on:** Privately held. **Number of employees at this location:** 30. **Number of employees nationwide:** 250.

BOSTON SCIENTIFIC CORPORATION
480 Pleasant Street, Watertown MA 02172. 617/972-4000. **Contact:** Human Resources. **World Wide Web address:** http://www.bostonscientific.com. **Description:** Boston Scientific Corporation is a worldwide developer, manufacturer, and marketer of medical devices used in a broad range of interventional medical procedures including cardiology, gastroenterology, pulmonary medicine, and vascular surgery. **Positions advertised include:** R&D Engineer; Project Manager; APO Supply Planning Manager. **Corporate headquarters location:** Natick MA. **Other area locations:** Quincy MA. **Other U.S. locations:** CA; FL; IN; MN; NJ; NY. **International locations:** Argentina; Brazil; Mexico; Uruguay; Venezuela. **Operations at this facility include:** This location manufactures balloon catheters used in surgery. **Listed on:** New York Stock Exchange. **Stock exchange symbol:** BSX. **Number of employees at this location:** 1,200.

BOSTON SCIENTIFIC CORPORATION
One Boston Scientific Place, Natick MA 01760-1537. 508/650-8000. **Contact:** Human Resources. **World Wide Web address:** http://www.bostonscientific.com. **Description:** A worldwide developer, manufacturer, and marketer of medical devices used in a broad range of interventional procedures including cardiology, gastroenterology, pulmonary medicine, and vascular surgery. **Positions advertised include:** Research Director; Human Resources Manager; Database Administrator; Software Quality Assurance Specialist; Clinical Data Specialist; Principal Engineer; Safety Coordinator; Project Manager; Administrative Assistant; Clinical Counsel; Strategic Sourcing Manager; Associate Scientist; Medical Research Associate; Tax Analyst; Benefits Analyst; Quality Engineer; Human Resource Process Analyst; Database Specialist; Quality Engineer; Assistant Medical Director; Product Manager; Marketing Communication Specialist; Product Manager. **Corporate headquarters location:** This location. **Other area locations:** Quincy MA. **Other U.S. locations:** CA; FL; IN; MN; NJ; NY. **International locations:** Argentina; Brazil; Mexico; Uruguay; Venezuela. **Listed on:** New York Stock Exchange. **Stock exchange symbol:** BSX.

BOSTON SPORTS CLUB
201 Brookline Avenue, Boston MA 02215. 617/266-7400. **Contact:** Human Resources. **Description:** A fully equipped fitness center with free weights, nautilus equipment, a pool, massage therapy, and exercise classes including sports conditioning, aerobics, and yoga.

BOSTON STOCK EXCHANGE
100 Franklin Street, Boston MA 02110. 617/235-2000. **Fax:** 617/235-2200. **Contact:** Human Resources. **World Wide Web address:** http://www.bostonstock.com. **Description:** A stock exchange. **Positions advertised include:** Sales; Staff Accountant.

BOSTON SYMPHONY ORCHESTRA, INC.
301 Massachusetts Avenue, Boston MA 02115. 617/266-1492. **Contact:** Human Resources. **World Wide Web address:** http://www.bso.org. **Description:** Administrative offices for the Boston Symphony Orchestra.

BOSTON UNIVERSITY
25 Buick Street, Boston MA 02215. 617/353-2380. **Contact:** Human Resources. **World Wide Web address:** http://www.bu.edu/. **Description:** A private, four-year university offering both undergraduate and graduate degrees. **Positions advertised include:** Administrative Assistant; Patient Coordinator; Research Administrative Assistant; Data Technician; Admissions Officer; Clinical Operations Manager; Program Manager; Research Administrator; Community Liaison; Project Coordinator; Data Manager; Executive Secretary; Program Coordinator. **Corporate headquarters location:** This location.

BOWDITCH & DEWEY
P.O. Box 15156, Worcester MA 01615-0156. 508/791-3511. **Fax:** 508/929-3195. **Physical address:** 311 Main Street, Worcester MA 01615. **Contact:** Human Resources. **E-mail address:** recruiting@bowditch.com. **World Wide Web address:** http://www.bowditch.com. **Description:** A 50-attorney law firm practicing a variety of law disciplines including environmental, labor, real estate, and litigation. **Other area locations:** Framingham MA.

BOWNE OF BOSTON
411 D Street, Boston MA 02210. 617/542-1926. **Fax:** 617/542-5790. **Contact:** Human Resources. **World Wide Web address:** http://www.bowne.com. **Description:** Engaged in financial and commercial printing services. Founded in 1775. **Positions advertised include:** Reprographic Associate; Hospitality Associate; Records Manager; Receptionist; Office Service Associate; Client Services Shift Supervisor; Estimator. **Corporate headquarters location:** New York NY. **Parent company:** Bowne & Company, Inc. is a financial printer. **Other area locations:** Cambridge MA. **Other U.S. locations:** Nationwide. **International locations:** Worldwide. **Listed on:** New York Stock Exchange. **Stock exchange symbol:** BNE.

BRANDEIS UNIVERSITY
Mail Stop 118, P.O. Box 9110, Waltham MA 02454-9110. 781/736-4473. **Fax:** 781/736-4466. **Contact:** Employment Administrator. **World Wide Web address:** http://www.brandeis.edu. **Description:** A four-year university offering both undergraduate and graduate programs of study. **Positions advertised include:** Assistant Controller; Executive Director of Intellectual Properties; Director of Athletics; Advancement Services Director; Research Analyst; Lab Coordinator; Lab Technician; Administrative Assistant; Cashier; University Police Officer. **Corporate headquarters location:** This location. **Number of employees at this location:** 1,300.

BRAUN NORTH AMERICA
400 Unicorn Park Drive, Woburn MA 01801. 781/939-8300. **Toll-free phone:** 800/BRA-UN11. **Contact:** Human Resources. **World Wide Web address:** www.braun.com. **Description:** Distributes a variety of consumer products including coffee makers, juicers, and razors, all of which are manufactured by Braun in Germany. **Parent company:** The Gillette Company.

BREWER & LORD LLP
P.O. Box 9146, Norwell MA 02061-9146. 781/792-3200. **Physical address:** 600 Longwater Drive, Norwell MA 02061. **Fax:** 781/792-3434. **Contact:** Human Resources. **World Wide Web address:** http://www.brewerlord.com. **Description:** One of the largest insurance agencies in New England, providing commercial and personal lines of insurance. **Positions advertised include:** Accounting Manager; Assistant Account Representative; Marketing Representative; Account Manager; Account Representative; Regional Account Representative. **Other area locations:** Abington MA; Acton MA; Cambridge MA; Danvers MA; Falmouth MA; Framingham MA; Lexington MA; Marshfield MA. **Other U.S. locations:** Providence RI.

THE BRICK COMPUTER COMPANY
80 Turnpike Road, Ipswich MA 01938. 978/356-1228. **Contact:** Human Resources. **World Wide Web address:** http://www.brickcomputers.com. **Description:** Sells laptops through a mail-order catalog.

BRIDGEWATER STATE COLLEGE
Boyden Hall, Room 103, Offices of Human Resources, Bridgewater MA 02325. 508/697-1324. **Fax:** 508/531-1725. **Contact:** Human Resources. **E-mail address:** humres@bridgew.edu. **World Wide Web address:** http://www.bridgew.edu. **Description:** A four-year state college offering a variety of undergraduate and graduate degree programs. **Positions advertised include:** Vice President Student Affairs; Head Women's Tennis Coach; Bookkeeper; Clerk. **Special programs:** Internships. **Number of employees at this location:** 900.

BRIGHAM & WOMEN'S HOSPITAL
75 Francis Street, Boston MA 02115. 617/732-5790. **Fax:** 617/277-1263. **Contact:** Human Resources. **World Wide Web address:** http://www.brighamandwomens.org. **Description:** A 750-bed, nonprofit hospital. Brigham & Women's houses one of New England's largest birthing centers and a regional center for high-risk obstetrics and neonatology. The hospital is nationally recognized for its transplant programs; joint replacement and orthopedic surgery; and the treatment of arthritis, rheumatic disorders, and cardiovascular disease. **Positions advertised include:** Access Facilitator; Administrative Secretary; Admitting Officer; Nurse Manager; Licensed Practical Nurse; Clinical Dietician; Coding Specialist; Data Coordinator; Environmental Services Aide; Exercise Psychologist; Programmer Analyst; Medical Technologist; Nurse Practitioner; Personal Care Assistant; Processing Technician; Research Assistant; Registered Nurse; Social Worker; Unit Coordinator. **Parent company:** Partners HealthCare System Inc. **Number of employees at this location:** 8,500.

BRIGHAM'S INC.
30 Mill Street, Arlington MA 02476. 781/648-9000. **Fax:** 781/646-0509. **Contact:** Jessica Olson, Human Resources. **E-mail address:** jolson@brighams.com. **World Wide Web address:** http://www.brighams.com. **Description:** Operates a chain of more than 60 restaurants and ice cream parlors throughout New England, New York, and New Jersey. **Positions advertised include:** Sundae Party Coordinator; On Site Special Events Manager; Special Events Staff. **Corporate headquarters location:** This location. **Operations at this facility include:** Administration; Manufacturing; Regional Headquarters; Sales.

BRISTOL-MYERS SQUIBB COMPANY
331 Treble Cove Road, Building 300-2, Billerica, MA 01862. 978/667-9531. **Contact:** Human Resources. **World Wide Web address:** http://www.bms.com. **Description:** Manufactures pharmaceuticals including Coumadin, Sinemet, Cardiolite, Thallium, and I.V. Persantine. **Positions advertised include:** International Brand Manager Cardiolite; Research Scientist Assistant; Technical Transfer Representative; Accounts Receivable Representative; Process Engineer; Technician Principal; Principal Quality Scientist; Planner; Buyer; Assistant Vet Services Technician; Occupational Health; Purchase Agent; Customer Service Representative; Lead Person; Project Custodian. **Corporate headquarters location:** New York NY. **Listed on:** New York Stock Exchange. **Stock exchange symbol:** BMY.

BROADVISION
400 Fifth Avenue, Waltham MA 02451. 781/290-0710. **Contact:** Human Resources. **World Wide Web address:** http://www.broadvision.com. **Description:** BroadVision creates communications and marketing applications for business and governmental entities. **Positions advertised include:** Sales Representative. **Special programs:** Internships. **Corporate headquarters location:** Redwood City CA. **Other U.S. locations:** Nationwide. **International locations:** Brazil; Canada; Mexico. **Operations at this facility include:** This location develops document management systems and solutions software. **Listed on:** NASDAQ. **Stock exchange symbol:** BVSN.

BROCKTON HOSPITAL
680 Centre Street, Brockton MA 02302. 508/941-7000. **Fax:** 508/941-6204. **Contact:** Human Resources. **World Wide Web address:** http://www.brocktonhospital.com. **Description:** A 250-bed, acute care hospital. **Positions advertised include:** Case Manager; Centralized Scheduler; Certified Nurses Assistant; Clerk; Clinical Care Assistant; Mental Health Worker; Physical Therapist; Registered Nurse; Speech Pathologist; Staff Accountant; Switch Board Operator; Unit Secretary.

BROOKFIELD ENGINEERING LABORATORIES, INC.
11 Commerce Boulevard, Middleborough MA 02346-1031. 508/946-6200. **Toll-free phone:** 800/628-8139. **Fax:** 508/946-6262. **Contact:** Human Resources. **E-mail address:** hr@brookfieldengineering.com. **World Wide Web address:** http://www.brookfieldengineering.com. **Description:** Designs, manufactures, sells, and services electromechanical instrumentation, viscometers, and accessories for a broad range of industries. Founded in 1934. **NOTE:** Second and third shifts are offered. **Special programs:** Co-ops; Summer Jobs. **Office hours:** Monday - Friday, 8:00 a.m. - 5:00 p.m. **Corporate headquarters location:** This location. **Subsidiaries include:** Brookfield Viscometers Ltd. (England); Brookfield Engineering Laboratories Vertriebs, GmbH (Germany). **Listed on:** Privately held.

BROOKLINE SAVINGS BANK
P.O. Box 470469, Brookline MA 02477. 617/730-3500. **Toll-free phone:** 877/668-2265. **Physical address:** 24 Webster Place, Brookline MA 02477. **Contact:** Jack Nealon, Personnel Director. **World Wide Web address:** http://www.brooklinesavings.com. **Description:** A full-service savings bank. **Positions advertised include:** Teller; Customer Service Representative. **Corporate headquarters location:** This location.

BROOKS AUTOMATION, INC.
15 Elizabeth Drive, Chelmsford MA 01824. 978/262-2400. **Contact:** Human Resources. **E-mail address:** hr@brooks-pri.com. **World Wide Web address:** http://www.brooks-pri.com. **Description:** Manufactures robotic arms, wafer disks, vacuum cassette elevators, and other electronic devices. **Positions advertised include:** Accounts Payable Specialist; Product Marketing Manager; Product Manager; Mechanical Engineer; Mechanical Systems Engineer; Quality Engineer; Sales Account Manager; Software Support Engineer; Software Engineer. **Corporate headquarters location:** This location. **Other U.S. locations:** Nationwide. **International locations:** Worldwide. **Subsidiaries include:** AutoSimulations, Inc.; Auto-Soft Corporation; CCS Technology, Inc.; Daifuku Co., Ltd. Business Unit; Domain Manufacturing Corporation; e-Diagnostics; FASTech Integration, Inc.; Hanyon Technology; INFAB; Irvine Optical Company; MiTeX; Progressive Technologies, Inc.; SEMY Engineering Inc.; SimCon Engineering Inc.; Smart Machines; Techware Systems Corporation. **Listed on:** NASDAQ. **Stock exchange symbol:** BRKS.

BROOKTROUT TECHNOLOGY, INC.
250 First Avenue, Needham MA 02494. 781/449-4100. **Fax:** 781/433-9596. **Contact:** Human Resources. **E-mail address:** hr@brooktout.com. **World Wide Web address:** http://www.brooktrout.com. **Description:** Designs, manufactures, and markets software, hardware, and systems solutions for electronic messaging applications in telecommunications and networking environments worldwide. These products help integrate voice, fax, and data communications across networks. **Positions advertised include:** Principal Hardware Engineer; Principal Engineer; Product Manager. **Corporate headquarters location:** This location. **Other U.S. locations:** Nationwide. **International locations:** Worldwide. **Subsidiaries include:** Brooktrout Networks Group, Inc. (Texas); Brooktrout Securities Corporation; Brooktrout Technology Europe, Ltd. **Listed on:** NASDAQ. **Stock exchange symbol:** BRKT. **Number of employees nationwide:** 60.

BROWN, RUDNICK, FREED & GESMER
One Financial Center, Boston MA 02111. 617/330-9000. **Contact:** Human Resources. **World Wide Web address:** http://www.brownrudnick.com. **Description:** A 150-attorney law firm specializing in a variety of legal disciplines including bankruptcy, corporate, international, tax, government, and estate law. **Positions advertised include:** Audio Visual Specialist; Support Specialist; Financial Analyst; Intellectual Property & Litigation Partner. **Corporate headquarters location:** This location. **Other U.S. locations:** Hartford CT; Providence RI. **International locations:** London, England. **Number of employees at this location:** 300.

BRYANT ASSOCIATES, INC.
160 North Washington Street, Suite 700, Boston MA 02114-2127. 617/248-0300. **Fax:** 617/248-0212. **Contact:** Human Resources. **E-mail address:** jobs@bryant-engrs.com. **World Wide Web address:** http://www.bryant-engrs.com. **Description:** An engineering and surveying firm. Founded in 1976. **Positions advertised include:** Operations Manager. **Other U.S. locations:** New Ipswich NH; Syracuse NY; Lincoln RI.

BRYLANE, INC.
35 United Drive, West Bridgewater MA 02379. 508/583-8110. **Fax:** 508/588-7994. **Contact:** Human Resources. **E-mail address:** chadwicksjobs@brylane.com. **World Wide Web address:** http://www.brylane.com. **Description:** A specialty catalog retailer. **Positions advertised include:** Control Buyer; Rebuyer; Collateral Projects Coordinator; Maintenance Mechanic Coordinator. **Corporate headquarters location:** New York NY.

BRYLEY SYSTEMS INC.
12 Main Street, Hudson MA 01749. 978/562-6077. **Fax:** 978/562-5680. **Contact:** Human Resources. **E-mail address:** humanresources@bryley.com. **World Wide Web address:** http://www.bryley.com. **Description:** A network systems integrator that provides computer network/telephone solutions to businesses throughout New England. The company provides analysts, consulting, design, and installation services. **Positions advertised include:** Account Executives.

BULKLEY, RICHARDSON AND GELINAS, LLP
1500 Main Street, Suite 2700, Springfield MA 01115-5507. 413/781-2820. **Fax:** 413/785-5060. **Contact:** Michael Burke, Hiring Partner. **World Wide Web address:** http://www.bulkley.com. **Description:** A law firm specializing in a variety of legal disciplines including environmental, employment, health, and intellectual property law. **Other area locations:** Boston MA.

BULL HN INFORMATION SYSTEMS INC.
300 Concord Road, Billerica MA 01821-4199. 978/294-6000. **Fax:** 978/294-6601. **Contact:** Human Resources. **E-mail address:** job.opportunities@bull.com. **World Wide Web address:** http://www.bull.com. **Description:** Bull HN Information Systems is a major systems and technologies integrator with a comprehensive range of solutions, services, and support capabilities. Bull's strategy, the Distributed Computing Model, allows users to integrate multivendor systems in a flexible, open environment. **Corporate headquarters location:** This location. **International locations:** Worldwide. **Parent company:** Groupe Bull (France).

BURLE ELECTRO-OPTICS
Sturbridge Business Park, P.O. Box 1159, Sturbridge MA 01566-1159. 508/347-4000. **Contact:** Human Resources. **E-mail address:** rabens@burle.com. **World Wide Web address:** http://www.burle.com. **Description:** Manufactures microchannel plates, flexible fiber optics, and amplifiers. **Corporate headquarters location:** Lancaster PA. **International locations:** England; Germany.

BUTLER AUTOMATIC INC.
41 Leona Drive, Middleboro MA 02346. 781/828-5450. **Toll-free phone:** 800/544-0070. **Fax:** 508/923-0885. **Contact:** Marilyn Kujala, Director of Personnel. **World Wide Web address:** http://www.butlerautomatic.com. **Description:** Manufactures automatic web-handling equipment for sale to the printing and corrugating industries. **Positions advertised include:** Field Services Representative. **Corporate headquarters location:** This location. **International locations:** Australia; France; Japan; Mexico.

BYTEX CORPORATION
495 Commerce Park, 113 Cedar Street, Suite 2, Milford MA 01757. 508/422-9422. **Fax:** 508/422-9410. **Contact:** Human Resources. **E-mail address:** personell@bytex.com. **World Wide Web address:** http://www.bytex.com. **Description:** A data communications and internetworking company providing manufacturing, sales, and service of an intelligent switching hub used in both local and wide area computer networks. **Other U.S. locations:** Columbia MD; Minnetonka MI. **Operations at this facility include:** Engineering and Design; Manufacturing; Marketing; Service. **Number of employees at this location:** 200. **Number of employees nationwide:** 1,300.

CB RICHARD ELLIS INVESTORS
800 Boylston Street, Suite 1475, Boston MA 02199. 617/425-2800. **Fax:** 617/425-2801. **Contact:** Personnel. **World Wide Web address:** http://www.cbrichardellis.com. **Description:** Provides real estate services. **Positions advertised include:** Real Estate Analyst; Research Analyst; Network Engineer; Production Officer. **Corporate headquarters location:** Los Angeles CA. **Other U.S. locations:** Nationwide. **International locations:** Worldwide. **Listed on:** New York Stock Exchange. **Stock exchange symbol:** CBG.

CB RICHARD ELLIS/WHITTIER PARTNERS
Federal Reserve Building, 600 Atlantic Avenue, Boston MA 02210. 617/912-7000. **Fax:** 617/912-7001. **Contact:** Human Resources. **World Wide Web address:** http://www.cbrichardellis.com. **Description:** Provides real estate services. **Positions advertised include:** Real Estate Analyst; Research Analyst; Network Engineer;

Production Officer, **Corporate headquarters location:** Los Angeles CA. **Other U.S. locations:** Nationwide. **International locations:** Worldwide. **Listed on:** New York Stock Exchange. **Stock exchange symbol:** CBG.

CDC IXIS ASSET MANAGEMENT NORTH AMERICA
399 Boylston Street, Boston MA 02116. 617/449-2100. **Contact:** Human Resources. **World Wide Web address:** http://www.cdcixis-amna.com. **Description:** An investment management company. **Parent company:** CDC IXIS Asset Management (France). **Corporate headquarters location:** This location.

C.E.A. (CORPORATE ENVIRONMENTAL ADVISORS)
127 Hartwell Street, West Boylston MA 01583. 508/835-8822. **Contact:** Human Resources **Description:** An environmental consulting firm engaged in contract consulting projects.

CGI INFORMATION SYSTEMS
600 Federal Street, Andover MA 01810. 978/682-5500. **Contact:** Human Resources. **World Wide Web address:** http://www.cgi.ca. **Description:** Provides systems integration, outsourcing, consulting, and business solutions to the financial, telecommunications, manufacturing, government, health care, and utilities industries. **Other U.S. locations:** Nationwide. **International locations:** Worldwide. **Listed on:** New York Stock Exchange. **Stock exchange symbol:** GIB.

CGM FUNDS
P.O. Box 8511, Boston MA 02266 **Physical address:** 222 Berkeley Street, Suite 1013, Boston MA 02116. 617/859-7714. **Toll-free phone:** 800/345-4048. **Fax:** 617/226-1838. **Contact:** Tony Figueiredo, Human Resources. **World Wide Web address:** http://www.cgmfunds.com. **Description:** Manages mutual funds for investors.

CH2M HILL
25 New Chardon Street, Suite 500, Boston MA 02114. 617/523-2260. **Fax:** 617/723-9036. **Contact:** Human Resources. **World Wide Web address:** http://www.ch2m.com. **Description:** An environmental engineering company specializing in water and remediation projects. **Positions advertised include:** NEPA Expert; Process Engineer; Air Water Process Project Manager; Construction Manager. **NOTE:** Jobseekers should address resumes to the attention of the manager of the group to which they are applying. Please contact this location for further information. **Corporate headquarters location:** Greenwood Village CO. **Other U.S. locations:** Nationwide. **International locations:** Worldwide.

CMGI
100 Brickstone Square, Andover MA 01810. 978/684-3600. **Contact:** Human Resources. **World Wide Web address:** http://www.cmgi.com. **Description:** Develops and integrates a variety of advanced Internet and database management technologies. **Corporate headquarters location:** This location. **Other area locations:** Wilmington MA. **International locations:** Worldwide. **Subsidiaries Include:** AltaVista; CMGion; Engage, Inc.; Equilibrium; NaviSite; SalesLink; Tallan; uBid.com; yesmail.com. **Listed on:** NASDAQ. **Stock exchange symbol:** CMGI.

CSC CONSULTING & SYSTEMS
275 Second Avenue, Waltham MA 02451. 781/890-7446. **Fax:** 781/890-1208. **Contact:** Patricia Bleheen, Recruiting Manager. **World Wide Web address:** http://www.csc.com. **Description:** A consulting firm specializing in systems integration, systems design, and applications development for the commercial and private sectors. Founded in 1959. **Positions advertised include:** Business Process Architect; Application Developer; Business Analyst; Network Engineer; System Administrator; Application Manager; Application Designer; Enterprise Package Solution Specialist; Application Designer; Payroll Specialist; Accountant. **Corporate headquarters location:** El Segundo CA. **Other U.S. locations:** Nationwide. **Parent company:** Computer Sciences Corporation. **Listed on:** New York Stock Exchange. **Stock exchange symbol:** CSC. **Annual sales/revenues:** More than $100 million. **Number of employees at this location:** 300. **Number of employees worldwide:** 44,000.

CSL INTERNATIONAL
55 Tozer Road, Beverly MA 01915. 978/922-1300. **Fax:** 978/922-1772. **Contact:** Human Resources. **World Wide Web address:** http://www.csl.ca. **Description:** A bulk freight shipping company that specializes in self-unloading bulk carriers. **Parent company:** Canada Steamship Lines (Montreal, Quebec, Canada). **International locations:** Manitoba; Nova Scotia; Ontario; Singapore.

CSN STORES
Two Copley Place, Floor 4, Boston MA 02116. 617/532-6100. **Fax:** 617/236-4761. **Contact:** Recruiting. **E-mail address:** jobs@csnstores.com. **World Wide Web address:** http://www.csnstores.com. **Description:** An online retailer. **Positions advertised include:** Customer Care Representative. **NOTE:** Mail resume to: CSN Stores, Attention Recruiting, Two Copley Place Floor 4, Boston MA, 02116.

CSPI
43 Manning Road, Billerica MA 01821. 978/663-7598. **Toll-free phone:** 800/325-3110. **Fax:** 978/663-0150. **E-mail address:** hr@cspi.com. **Contact:** Karen Lacroix, Human Resources Manager. **World Wide Web address:** http://www.cspi.com. **Description:** CSPI designs, manufactures, and markets digital signal processing, high-performance, multiprocessing systems for real-time applications. These low-power, special purpose computers enhance a system's ability to perform high-speed arithmetic and are primarily used for defense, medical, industrial, and real-time applications. **Special programs:** Co-ops. **Corporate headquarters location:** This location. **Other U.S. locations:** CA; FL; MD; VA. **Subsidiaries include:** MODCOMP, Inc. sells real-time process control systems and legacy solutions; Scanalytics, Inc. is focused on hardware and software products for scientific imaging. **Listed on:** NASDAQ. **Stock exchange symbol:** CSPI. **Number of employees at this location:** 60. **Number of employees nationwide:** 150.

CTC COMMUNICATIONS
220 Bear Hill Road, Waltham MA 02451. 781/466-8080. **Contact:** Human Resources. **World Wide Web address:** http://www.ctcnet.com. **Description:** CTC Communications is an independent sales agent for the Regional Bell Operating Companies. The company markets discounted telephone calling plans, 800-number services, Centrex systems, and data transport networks to mid-sized commercial accounts. The company operates 15 branch offices in the Northeast. **Corporate headquarters location:** This location. **Listed on:** NASDAQ. **Stock exchange symbol:** CPTL. **Number of employees nationwide:** 180.

CABOT CORPORATION
2 Seaport Lane, Suite 1300, Boston MA 02210. 617/345-0100. **Contact:** Human Resources. **World Wide Web address:** http://www.cabot-corp.com. **Description:** A supplier of liquefied natural gas; and Distrigas Corporation, which imports liquefied natural gas from Algeria. **Positions advertised include:** Corporate Accountant. **Corporate headquarters location:** This location. **Other area locations:** Billerica MA; Woburn MA. **Other U.S. locations:** Alpharetta GA; Tuscola IL; Franklin LA; Ville Platte LA; Midland MI; Pampa TX; The Woodlands TX; Waverly WV. **International locations:** Worldwide. **Listed on:** New York Stock Exchange. **Stock exchange symbol:** CBT.

THE CACTUS CLUB
939 Boylston Street, Boston MA 02115. 617/236-0200. **Fax:** 617/236-0419. **Contact:** Manager. **E-mail address:** resumes@bestmarguitas.com. **World Wide Web address:** http://www.cactusclubboston.com. **Description:** A restaurant and bar with a diverse menu including Mexican, South American, and Cuban entrees.

CADENCE DESIGN SYSTEMS, INC.
270 Billerica Road, Chelmsford MA 01824. 978/262-6000. **Contact:** Human Resources. **World Wide Web address:** http://www.cadence.com. **Description:** Develops automation software for wireless computers and telecommunication devices. **Positions advertised include:** Marketing Program Manager; Sales Technical Leader. **Corporate headquarters location:** San Jose CA. **Other U.S. locations:** Nationwide. **International locations:** Worldwide. **Listed on:** New York Stock Exchange. **Stock exchange symbol:** CDN.

THE CADMUS GROUP, INC.
57 Water Street, Watertown MA 02472. 617/673-7000. **Contact:** Human Resources. **World Wide Web address:** http://www.cadmusgroup.com. **Description:** An environmental consulting and engineering firm. **Positions advertised include:** Analyst; Environmental Professional; Research Analyst.

CALIPER LIFE SCIENCES
68 Elm Street, Hopkinton MA 01748. 508/435-9500. **Fax:** 508/497-2685. **Contact:** Human Resources. **World Wide Web address:** http://wwwcaliperts.com. **Description:** Designs and manufactures robots and robotic systems for use in laboratories to speed the discovery process in the biotechnological and pharmaceutical industries. Founded in 1981. **NOTE:** Entry-level positions are offered. **Positions advertised include:** Project Manager; Consumables Business Line Manager. **Special programs:** Internships; Co-ops; Summer Jobs. **Office hours:** Monday - Friday, 8:00 a.m. - 5:00 p.m. **Corporate headquarters location:** This location.

CAMBEX CORPORATION
115 Flanders Road, Westborough MA 01581. 508/983-1200. **Toll-free phone:** 800/325-5565. **Fax:** 508/983-0255. **Contact:** Human Resources. **World Wide Web address:** http://www.cambex.com. **Description:** Cambex Corporation develops, manufactures, and markets a variety of direct access storage products that improve the performance of large- and mid-size IBM computers. These products include central and expanded memory, controller cache memory, disk array systems, disk and tape subsystems, and related software products. **Positions advertised include:** Sales Executive; Regional Sales Manager; Telemarketing Representative. **Corporate headquarters location:** This location. **Other U.S. locations:** Scottsdale AZ; Thousand Oaks CA; Walnut Creek CA; Westport CT; Clearwater FL; Roswell GA; Schaumburg IL; Troy MI; Chesterfield MO; Charlotte NC; Clark NJ; Cincinnati OH; Blue Bell PA; Dallas TX; Reston VA. **Operations at this facility include:** Administration; Manufacturing; Research and Development; Sales; Service.

CAMBRIDGE COLLEGE
1000 Massachusetts Avenue, Cambridge MA 02138. 617/873-0100. **Toll-free phone:** 888/868-1002. **Contact:** Human Resources. **World Wide Web address:** http://www.cambridgecollege.edu. **Description:** A college offering bachelor's and master's degrees for adult psychology students.

CAMBRIDGE HEALTH ALLIANCE
1493 Cambridge Street, Cambridge MA 02139. 617/498-1000. **Contact:** Human Resources. **World Wide Web address:** http://www.challiance.org. **Description:** An alliance made up of Cambridge Hospital, Somerville Hospital, a nursing home and several neighborhood health centers. Cambridge Hospital, also at this location, is a 170-bed, full-service hospital owned by the city of Cambridge and affiliated with Harvard and Tufts Medical Schools. **Positions advertised include:** Administrative Assistant; Applications Analyst; Buyer; Clerk; Cardiac Sonographer; Central Processing Department Technician; Clerk & Typist; Computerized Tomography Technologist; Dental Hygienist; Marketing Specialist; Medical Technician; Medical Assistant; Physical Therapist; Dietary Trainee; Case Management Director; General Data Manager; Hospital Aide.

CAMBRIDGE SAVINGS BANK
P.O. Box 380206, Cambridge MA 02238-0206. 617/864-8700. **Physical Address:** 1374 Massachusetts Avenue, Cambridge MA 02138. **Fax:** 617/441-4171. **Contact:** Human Resources. **E-mail address:** jobs@csb.usa.com. **World Wide Web address:** http://www.cambridgesavings.com. **Description:** Operates a full-service savings bank. **Positions advertised include:** Teller; Corporate Lending Administrator; Messenger/Driver; Underwriter; WebBank Product Manager. **Special programs:** Internships. **Corporate headquarters location:** This location. **Operations at this facility include:** Administration; Sales; Service. **Number of employees at this location:** 265.

CAMBRIDGE SOUNDWORKS, INC.
311 Needham Street, Newton MA 02464. 617/332-5936. **Fax:** 617/244-3743. **Contact:** Human Resources. **World Wide Web address:** http://www.hifi.com. **Description:** A factory-direct retailer that designs and manufactures stereo and home theater speakers under the Cambridge SoundWorks brand name. **Listed on:** NASDAQ. **Stock exchange symbol:** HIFI.

CAMBRIDGE TECHNOLOGY PARTNERS
8 Cambridge Center, Cambridge MA 02142. 617/374-9800. **Contact:** Human Resources. **World Wide Web address:** http://www.ctp.com. **Description:** Provides information technology consulting and software development services to organizations with large-scale information processing and distribution needs that are utilizing or migrating to open systems computing environments. **Positions advertised include:** Technical Account Manager. **Corporate headquarters location:** This location. **Other U.S. locations:** Nationwide. **International locations:** Worldwide. **Parent company:** Novell, Inc.

CAMBRIDGE-LEE INDUSTRIES, INC.
500 Lincoln Street, Allston MA 02134. 617/783-3100. **Contact:** Human Resources. **World Wide Web address:** http://www.cambridgelee.com. **Description:** A distributor of copper, brass, and other industrial metals. Founded in 1939. **Subsidiaries include:** IUSA; Reading Tube Corporation.

CAMBRIDGEPORT BANK
1380 Soldiers Field Road, Brighton MA 02135. 617/779-2900. **Fax:** 617/779-2729. **Contact:** Human Resources. **E-mail address:** HumanResource@Cambridgeport.com. **World Wide Web address:** http://www.host.theeditors.com/cp-bank. **Description:** A full service community bank providing personal and business financial services. **Other area locations:** Arlington MA; Newton MA; Lexington MA; Wellesley MA; Needham MA; Winchester MA; Natick MA; Westwood MA.

CAMP DRESSER & McKEE, INC. (CDM)
One Cambridge Place, 50 Hampshire Street, Cambridge MA 02139. 617/452-6000. **Contact:** Human Resources. **World Wide Web address:** http://www.cdm.com. **Description:** A worldwide provider of environmental engineering, scientific, planning, and management services. The company focuses on professional activities for the management of wastewater, drinking water, water resources, hazardous waste, solid waste, infrastructure, and environmental systems. **Positions advertised include:** Geotechnical Engineer; Environmental Scientist; Environmental Engineer; Instrumentation Control Engineer; O&M Specialist; Marketing Coordinator; Planner; Air Quality Scientist or Engineer; Administrative Assistant. **Special programs:** Internships. **Corporate headquarters location:** This location. **Other U.S. locations:** Nationwide. **International locations:** Worldwide.

CANAM STEEL CORPORATION
P.O. Box 1245, Easton MA 02334-1245. 508/238-4500. **Physical address:** 50 Eastman Street, Easton MA 02334. **Fax:** 508/238-8253. **Contact:** Paul Lestrange, Controller. **World Wide Web address:** http://www.canammanac.com. **Description:** A fabricator of structural steel and steel commodities including joists and metal deck. **Corporate headquarters location:** Point of Rocks MD. **Parent company:** Canam Manac Group (Saint George's, Quebec, Canada). **Operations at this facility include:** Administration; Engineering and Design; Sales. **Number of employees at this location:** 50.

CANDELA CORPORATION
530 Boston Post Road, Wayland MA 01778. 508/358-7400. **Contact:** Human Resources. **World Wide Web address:** http://www.clzr.com. **Description:** Designs, manufactures, markets, and services lasers for a variety of medical applications. The company also licenses medical products and sells them through its worldwide distribution network. Products include Vbeam, which treats vascular lesions; AlexLAZR, which removes tattoos; and GentleLASE Plus, which removes unwanted hairs and also treats vascular lesions. **Corporate headquarters location:** This location. **Number of employees at this location:** 200.

CANNON DESIGN
One Center Plaza, Boston MA 02108. 617/742-5440. **Contact:** Human Resources. **World Wide Web address:** http://www.cannondesign.com. **Description:** An architectural, interior design, and engineering firm. **Positions advertised include:** Engineer; Project Architect; Educational Planner. **Corporate headquarters location:** Grand Island NY. **Other U.S. locations:** Los Angeles CA; Washington DC; Jacksonville FL; Chicago IL; Baltimore MD; St. Louis MO.

CAPE AIR/NANTUCKET AIRLINES
660 Barnstable Road, Hyannis MA 02601. 508/771-6944. **Toll-free phone:** 800/352-0714. **Contact:** Personnel. **World Wide Web address:** http://www.flycapeair.com. **Description:** An air transportation company with direct service to Cape Cod and the islands.

CAPE COD COMMUNITY COLLEGE
2240 Iyanough Road, West Barnstable MA 02668. 508/362-2131. **Toll-free phone:** 877/846-3672. **Fax:** 508/362-3988. **Contact:** Human Resources. **E-mail address:** info@capecod.mass.edu. **World Wide Web address:** http:///www.capecod.mass.edu. **Description:** A two-year college offering associate degrees. **Positions advertised include:** Program Assistant; Special Program Coordinator; Part Time Faculty; Associate Academic Dean.

CAPE COD FIVE CENTS SAVINGS BANK
P.O. Box 10, Orleans MA 02653. 508/240-0555. **Contact:** Human Resources. **World Wide Web address:** http://www.capecodfive.com. **Description:** A full-service savings bank.

CAPE COD HOSPITAL
27 Park Street, Hyannis MA 02601. 508/771-1800. **Fax:** 508/790-7964. **Contact:** Personnel. **World Wide Web address:** http://www.capecodhealth.org. **Description:** A nonprofit, 258-bed, general acute care, regional hospital. **Positions advertised include:** Assessment Team Clinician; CAT Scan Technologist; Clinical Dietician; Environmental Service Aide; Food Service Assistant; Occupational Therapist. **Number of employees at this location:** 1,400.

CAPE COD TIMES
319 Main Street, Hyannis MA 02601. 508/775-1200. **Contact:** Human Resources. **World Wide Web address:** http://www.capecodtimes.com/cctimes. **Description:** A daily newspaper serving Cape Cod. **Parent company:** Ottaway Newspapers, Inc. (Campbell Hall NY). **Operations at this facility include:** Administration; Manufacturing; Sales; Service. **Number of employees at this location:** 300.

THE CAPITAL THEATRE
204 Massachusetts Avenue, Arlington MA 02174. 781/648-6022. **Contact:** Manager. **Description:** An independently owned, six-screen movie theater. Founded in 1925. **Corporate headquarters location:** This location.

CAREY LIMOUSINE OF BOSTON
161 Broadway, Somerville MA 02145. 617/623-8700. **Contact:** Kevin Muldenatto, General Manager. **Description:** A limousine service and executive travel specialist. Carey Limousine offers services for business meetings, airport transfers, dinner/theater events, weddings, and sightseeing activities. **Positions advertised include:** Accountant/Auditor. **Corporate headquarters location:** This location. **Parent company:** Carey International. **Operations at this facility include:** Administration; Sales; Service. **Listed on:** Privately held. **Number of employees at this location:** 50.

CARLSON ASSOCIATES, INC.
959 Concord Street, 2nd Floor, Framingham MA 01701. 508/370-0100. **Fax:** 508/626-2390. **Contact:** Ms. Saroj Patel, Personnel Manager. **Description:** Provides a variety of architectural services. **Corporate headquarters location:** This location. **Other U.S. locations:** CA; FL; NC. **Subsidiaries include:** Carlson Design/Construction Corporation. **Parent company:** Carlson Holdings Company. **Operations at this facility include:** Administration. **Number of employees at this location:** 40. **Number of employees nationwide:** 95.

CASS INFORMATION SYSTEMS, INC.
P.O. Box 6540, Chelmsford MA 01824-0940. 978/446-0101. **Fax:** 978/323-6624. **Contact:** John A. Luciano, Human Resources. **E-mail address:** humanresourcesbos@cassinfo.com. **World Wide Web address:** http://www.cassinfo.com. **Description:** Cass Information Services is a provider of information services. These logistics-related services include the processing and payment of freight charges, preparation of transportation management reports, auditing of freight charges, and rating of freight shipments. Cass Information Systems operations are divided between its Payment Systems Group and its Software Systems Group. **NOTE:** Jobseekers should send resumes to: Human Resources, 900 Chelmsford Street, Lowell MA 01851-8101. **Subsidiaries include:** Cass Bank & Trust is a bank that provides a full range of banking services to individual, corporate, and institutional customers. **Parent company:** Cass Commercial Corporation. **Other U.S. locations:** Bridgeton MO; Columbus OH. **Operations at this facility include:** This location operates as part of the Payment Systems Group. **Listed on:** NASDAQ. **Stock exchange symbol:** CASS.

CASUAL MALE CORPORATION
555 Turnpike Street, Canton MA 02021. 781/828-9300. **Contact:** Human Resources. **World Wide Web address:** http://www.casualmale.com. **Description:** Engaged in the retail sale of footwear and apparel. Casual Male Corporation sells footwear through self-service licensed shoe departments in mass merchandising department stores, through full- and semiservice licensed shoe departments in department and specialty stores, on a wholesale basis, and through its Fayva and Parade of Shoes chains of shoe stores. The company is also involved in the retail sale of apparel through its chain of Casual Male Big & Tall men's stores and also through its chain of Work 'n Gear work clothing stores. **Special programs:** Internships. **Corporate headquarters location:** This location. **Operations at this facility include:** Administration; Service.

CATHOLIC CHARITIES
75 Kneeland Street, 8th Floor, Boston MA 02111. 617/482-5440. **Fax:** 617/482-9737. **Contact:** Human Resources. **E-mail address:** resumes@ccab.org. **World Wide Web address:** http://www.ccab.org. **Description:** A social service agency. Services include career counseling, alternative education, immigration refugee services and relief, family guidance, shelter and ministry programs, substance abuse services, and English-as-a-Second-Language (ESL) programs. **Positions advertised include:** Administrative Assistant; Payroll Assistant; Outreach Family Therapy.

CATHOLIC CHARITIES
EL CENTRO DEL CARDENAL
76 Union Park Street, Boston MA 02118. 617/542-9292. **Contact:** Human Resources. **Description:** A social service agency. Services include career counseling, alternative education, immigration refugee services and relief, family guidance, shelter and ministry programs, substance abuse services, and English-as-a-Second-Language (ESL) programs.

CATHOLIC MEMORIAL HOME
2446 Highland Avenue, Fall River MA 02720-4599. 508/679-0011. **Contact:** Human Resources. **World Wide Web address:** http://www.dhfo.org. **Description:** A 300-bed nursing home with a unit specializing in caring for those with Alzheimer's disease. **Positions advertised include:** Registered Nurse; Certified Nursing Aide; Licensed Practical Nurse. Parent **company:** Diocesan Health Facilities Office (Fall River MA) operates five nursing homes throughout southeastern Massachusetts.

CENTER FOR BLOOD RESEARCH LABORATORIES, INC.
800 Huntington Avenue, Boston MA 02115. 617/731-6470. **Contact:** Human Resources. **World Wide Web address:** http://www.cbrlabs.com. **Description:** Provides molecular diagnostic and genetic typing services for the purpose of identity testing, matching potential donors for patients, and diagnosis of inherited diseases. The company also provides blood testing services to detect diseases for early treatment, as well as the testing new medical treatments and diagnostic products. **Special programs:** Internships. **Corporate headquarters location:** This location. **Parent company:** The Center for Blood Research (CBR) is a nonprofit organization affiliated with Harvard Medical School that conducts research on the functions and uses of components of blood and other tissue and trains medical and scientific personnel in research. **Operations at this facility include:** Research and Development. **Number of employees at this location:** 150.

CENTURY BANK
400 Mystic Avenue, Medford MA 02155. 781/393-4613. **Toll-free phone:** 800/442-1859. **Fax:** 781/393-4220. **Contact:** Kathleen McGillicuddy, Human Resources. **E-mail address:** kmcgillicuddy@century-bank.com. **World Wide Web address:** http://www.century-bank.com. **Description:** A bank holding company. Founded in 1969. **NOTE:** Entry-level positions and part-time jobs are offered. This location also hires seasonally. **Positions advertised include:** Head Teller; Assistant Manager; Branch Manager; Service Counselor; Item Process Supervisor; Customer Service Representative; Accounts Receivable Specialist; Balance & Reconciliation Specialist; Sorter Operator. **Office hours:** Monday - Friday, 8:30 a.m. - 5:00 p.m. **Corporate headquarters location:** This location. **Other area locations:** Beverly MA; Boston MA; Braintree MA; Brighton MA; Brookline MA; Burlington MA; Cambridge MA; Everett MA; Lynn MA; Malden MA; Medford MA; Newton MA; Peabody MA; Quincy MA; Salem MA; Somerville MA. **Subsidiaries include:** Century Bank and Trust Company offers a full range of banking services to individuals, businesses, and municipal customers. The bank operates through 16 branches in the greater Boston area. **Listed on:** NASDAQ. **Stock exchange symbol:** CNBKA. **Chairman/President/CEO:** Marshall Sloane. **Number of employees at this location:** 150. **Number of employees nationwide:** 300.

CENTURY 21 ANNEX REALTY
49 Beale Street, Quincy MA 02170. 617/472-4330. **Toll-free phone:** 800/345-4614. **Contact:** Human Resources. **World Wide Web address:** http://www.c21annex.com. **Description:** A real estate company. **Other area locations:** Hanover MA.

CENTURY 21 CAPE SAILS, INC.
133 Route 6A, Sandwich MA 02563. 508/888-2121. **Contact:** Human Resources. **World Wide Web address:** http://www.c21capesails.com. **Description:** A residential real estate company serving the Cape Cod area.

CEREBRAL PALSY OF THE SOUTH SHORE
CHILDREN'S DEVELOPMENTAL DISABILITIES CENTER
43 Old Colony Avenue, Quincy MA 02170. 617/479-7443. **Contact:** Human Resources. **Description:** An outpatient rehabilitation and treatment center for children from birth to eight years old who have disabilities. The onsite treatment facilities also include a school and a daycare center. **Positions advertised include:** Nurse; Social Worker; Therapist.

CERIDIAN EMPLOYER SERVICES
401 Edgewater Place, Suite 220, Wakefield MA 01880. 781/213-8000. **Contact:** Human Resources. **World Wide Web address:** http://www.ceridian.com. **Description:** An accounting and auditing services company. **Positions advertised include:** Client Service Analyst. **Parent company:** Ceridian Corporation (Minneapolis MN.)

CHAMPAGNE/LAFAYETTE COMMUNICATIONS
7 Strathmore Road, Natick MA 01760. 508/651-0400. **Contact:** Human Resources. **World Wide Web address:** http://www.chamlaf.com. **Description:** Provides graphic design services. Champagne/Lafayette Communications is also involved in commercial printing and direct mail marketing. Founded in 1967. **Positions advertised include:** Sales; Prepress Supervisor.

CHANNEL 1 INTERNET
P.O. Box 338, Cambridge MA 02238. 617/864-0100. **Fax:** 617/354-3100. **Physical address:** 14 Arrow Street, Cambridge MA 02138. **Contact:** Human Resources. **World Wide Web address:** http://www.channel1.com. **Description:** Designs Websites and virtual stores.

CHARLES RIVER LABORATORIES
251 Ballardvale Street, Wilmington MA 01887. 978/658-6000. **Contact:** Human Resources Manager. **E-mail address:** jobs@criver.com. **World Wide Web address:** http://www.criver.com. **Description:** A commercial supplier of laboratory animals including mice, rats, and guinea pigs for use in medical and scientific research. Users include chemical and pharmaceutical companies, government agencies, universities, commercial testing laboratories, hospitals, and others. **Positions advertised include:** Manager, Computer Operations & Operating Systems; Product Marketing Administrator, Transgenics; Sr. Analyst, Corporate Accounting; Sr. Technologist, Diagnostic Support; Administrator, Corporate Engineering. **Corporate headquarters location:** This location. **Operations at this facility include:** Administration; Manufacturing; Research and Development; Sales; Service. **Listed on:** New York Stock Exchange. **Stock exchange symbol:** CRL. **Number of employees nationwide:** 1,100.

CHARLES SCHWAB & CO., INC.
127 Congress Street, Boston MA 02110. **Toll-free phone:** 800/435-4000. **Fax:** 617/210-7418. **Contact:** Branch Manager. **World Wide Web address:** http://www.schwab.com. **Description:** A leading provider of discount brokerage services and no-transaction fee mutual funds. The company provides a wide range of services for individuals, institutions, financial advisors, and retirement plans, and has over 4 million investor accounts. Charles Schwab & Co., Inc. also provides online brokerage services. **Positions advertised include:** Account Representative; Branch Manager. **Corporate headquarters location:** San Francisco CA. **Other U.S. locations:** Nationwide. **Operations at this facility include:** Sales; Service. **Listed on:** New York Stock Exchange. **Stock exchange symbol:** SCH. **Number of employees worldwide:** 10,400.

CHARLES SCHWAB & CO., INC.
Liberty Square, 1220 Iyanough Road, Route 132, Suite G, Hyannis MA 02601. 508/778-5050. **Toll-free phone:** 800/435-4000. **Contact:** Branch Manager. **World Wide Web address:** http://www.schwab.com. **Description:** A leading provider of discount brokerage services and no-transaction fee mutual funds. The company provides a wide range of services for individuals, institutions, financial advisors, and retirement plans, and has over 4 million investor accounts. Charles Schwab & Co., Inc. also provides online brokerage services. **Corporate headquarters location:** San Francisco CA. **Number of employees worldwide:** 10,400.

CHARLES SCHWAB & CO., INC.
1262 Boylston Street, Chestnut Hill MA 02467. **Toll-free phone:** 800/435-4000. **Contact:** Branch Manager. **World Wide Web address:** http://www.schwab.com. **Description:** A leading provider of discount brokerage services and no-transaction fee mutual funds. The company provides a wide range of services for individuals, institutions, financial advisors, and retirement plans, and has over 4 million investor accounts. Charles Schwab & Co., Inc. also provides online brokerage services. **Corporate headquarters location:** San Francisco CA. **Stock exchange symbol:** SCH. **Number of employees worldwide:** 10,400.

CHARLES SCHWAB & CO., INC.
54 Mall Road, Burlington MA 01803. 781/270-7475. **Contact:** Branch Manager. **World Wide Web address:** http://www.schwab.com. **Description:** A leading provider of discount brokerage services and no-transaction fee mutual funds. The company provides a wide range of services for individuals, institutions, financial advisors, and retirement plans, and has over 4 million investor accounts. Charles Schwab & Co., Inc. also provides online brokerage services. **Corporate headquarters location:** San Francisco CA. **Number of employees worldwide:** 10,400.

CHARLESBRIDGE PUBLISHING
85 Main Street, Watertown MA 02472. 617/926-0329. **Toll-free phone:** 800/225-3214. **Fax:** 617/926-5720. **Contact:** Personnel. **E-mail address:** books@ charlesbridge.com. **World Wide Web address:** http://www.charlesbridge.com. **Description:** Publisher of educational materials for the classroom and both fiction and nonfiction books for children. Picture books cover a wide range of topics including math, nature, multiculturalism, animals, history, geography, and nursery rhymes. Charlesbridge Publishing also has two fiction imprints (Talewinds and Whispering Coyotes) as well as a diversity imprint (Shakti). **Special programs:** Internships. **Internship information:** Internship applications should be directed to Ms. Elena Wright in the School Department. **Corporate headquarters location:** This location. **President:** Brent Farmer. **Number of employees at this location:** 25.

CHARRETTE CORPORATION
P.O. Box 4010, Woburn MA 01888-4010. 781/935-6000. **Physical address:** 31 Olympia Avenue, Woburn MA 01801. **Fax:** 781/933-6104. **Contact:** Lawrence Mansfield, Director of Human Resources. **E-mail address:** csullivan@charette.com. **World Wide Web address:** http://www.charrette.com. **Description:** Offers a variety of products and services to design professionals. Products include a wide range of art, design, and office products from mat boards and paints, to furniture and software. Services include digital imaging, offset printing, reprographics, and blueprinting. **NOTE:** Entry-level positions are offered. **Special programs:** Internships. **Corporate headquarters location:** This location. **Other U.S. locations:** Nationwide. **Operations at this facility include:** Administration; Sales; Service. **Listed on:** Privately held. **Annual sales/revenues:** $51 - $100 million. **Number of employees at this location:** 350. **Number of employees nationwide:** 750.

CHASE & SONS
19 Highland Avenue, Randolph MA 02368. 781/963-2600. **Contact:** Human Resources. **World Wide Web address:** http://www.chasecorp.com. **Description:** Produces shielding and binding tapes for electronic and telecommunication cables. **Corporate headquarters location:** Bridgewater MA. **Other U.S. locations:** Webster MA. **Parent company:** Chase Corporation is involved in the manufacture of insulating products. The company's divisions produce and market products worldwide to insulated electric, electronic, and telecommunications cable manufacturers, producers of electronic parts, and to contractors involved in the construction of underground gas and oil pipelines and highway and bridge construction and repairs.

CHASE & SONS
Goya Industrial Park, Cudworth Road, Webster MA 01570. 508/949-6006. **Contact:** Human Resources. **World Wide Web address:** http://www.chasecorp.com. **Description:** Produces shielding and binding tapes for electronic and telecommunication cables. **Corporate headquarters location:** Bridgewater MA. **Other U.S. locations:** Randolph MA. **Parent company:** Chase Corporation is involved in the manufacture of insulating products. The company's divisions produce and market products worldwide to insulated electric, electronic, and telecommunications cable manufacturers, producers of electronic parts, and to contractors involved in the construction of underground gas and oil pipelines and highway and bridge construction and repairs.

CHASE CORPORATION
26 Summer Street, Bridgewater MA 02324. 508/279-1789. **Contact:** Human Resources. **World Wide Web address:** http://www.chasecorp.com. **Description:** Manufactures insulating products. **Corporate headquarters location:** This location. **Subsidiaries include:** Chase & Sons produces shielding and binding tapes for electronics and telecommunications cables; Chase Canada manufactures tapes for electronics, telecommunications, and fiber optic cables as well as specialty tapes and laminates for packaging and industrial applications; Fluid Polymers (Pittsburgh PA) provides sealants, adhesives coating, and dielectric materials for fluid purification and other processes; Sunburst EMS (West Bridgewater MA) manufactures electronics; HumiSeal (Woodside NY) provides insulating conformal coatings, potting compounds, and ancillary products for electronic applications; and Royston (Pittsburgh PA) offers insulating and protective mastics, coatings, and tapes for pipelines, highways, and bridges as well as waterproofing membranes for commercial and residential construction. **Number of employees nationwide:** 145.

CHECKPOINT ENVIRONMENTAL, INC.
12 Linden Street, Hudson MA 01749. 978/562-4300. **Contact:** Personnel. **Description:** An environmental engineering firm specializing in the drilling of small diameter wells.

CHELSEA CLOCK COMPANY
284 Everett Avenue, Chelsea MA 02150. 617/884-0250. **Fax:** 617/884-8639. **Contact:** Human Resources. **World Wide Web address:** http://www.chelseaclock.com. **Description:** Manufactures, sells, and repairs clocks.

A.W. CHESTERTON COMPANY
225 Fallon Road, Stoneham MA 02180. 781/438-7000. **Fax:** 781/481-2530. **Contact:** Human Resources. **E-mail address:** jobs@Chesterton.com. **World Wide Web address:** http://www.chesterton.com. **Description:** Manufactures polishing and cleaning goods. **Corporate headquarters location:** This location. **Other area locations:** Groveland MA; Winchester MA. **Other U.S. locations:** Elmhurst IL; Baton Rouge LA; North Smithfield RI; Pasadena TX. **International locations:** Australia; Canada; Germany; Hungary; Mexico; Poland; Slovakia.

CHILDREN'S HOSPITAL
333 Longwood Avenue, 2nd Floor, Boston MA 02115. 617/355-7780. **Contact:** Human Resources. **Note:** Please send all resumes to: P.O. Box 549252, Suite 227, Waltham MA 02454-9252. **Fax:** 781/663-3722. **World Wide Web address:** http://www.childrenshospital.org/jobs. **Description:** A full-service pediatric hospital. **Positions advertised include:** Research Technician; Speech Language Pathologist; Application Development Specialist; Staff Nurse; Patient Access Representative; Audiologist; Physician Assistant.

CHOATE, HALL & STEWART
Exchange Place, 53 State Street, Boston MA 02109. 617/227-5020. **Contact:** Human Resources. **World Wide Web address:** http://www.choate.com. **Description:** A law firm whose legal specialties include business, energy and telecommunications, government enforcement and compliance, health care, real estate, and trusts and estates. **Positions advertised include:** Team Leader; Tax Attorney; Bankruptcy Associate; Probate Paralegal.

CHRISTIAN SCIENCE MONITOR
Christian Science Center, One Norway Street, Boston MA 02115-3195. 617/450-2000. **Contact:** Human Resources. **World Wide Web address:** http://www.csmonitor.com. **Description:** A daily newspaper focusing primarily on national and international news. Founded in 1908. **Corporate headquarters location:** This location. **Operations at this facility include:** Publishing.

CITIGATE CUNNINGHAM INC.
One Memorial Drive, 9th Floor, Cambridge MA 02142. 617/494-8202. **Contact:** Human Resources. **E-mail address:** careers@citigatecunningham.com. **World Wide Web address:** http://www.citigatecunningham.com. **Description:** A public relations firm that also offers organization strategies, research, and brand positioning. **Parent company:** Incepta Group plc.

CITIZENS BANK
28 State Street, Boston MA 02108. 617/725-5500. **Contact:** Human Resources. **World Wide Web address:** http://www.citizensbank.com. **Description:** A commercial bank holding company. Citizens Bank maintains more than 700 branch locations and more than 1,490 ATMs in Connecticut, Massachusetts, New Hampshire, Rhode Island, Pennsylvania, and Delaware. **Corporate headquarters location:** Providence RI. **Other area locations:** Brighton, Chestnut Hill, Arlington, Braintree, Concord, Groton, Littleton, Brookline, Framingham, Newton, Newton Centre, Quincy, Norwell and many other locations. **Parent company:** Citizens Financial Group, Inc. **Number of employees nationwide:** 12,500.

CITIZENS ENERGY CORPORATION
530 Atlantic Avenue, Boston MA 02210. 617/338-6300. **Contact:** Controller. **E-mail address:** inform@citizensenergy.com. **World Wide Web address:** http://www.citizensenergy.com. **Description:** A nonprofit organization aimed at providing needy families with affordable home heating oil.

DAVID CLARK COMPANY, INC.
360 Franklin Street, Box 15054, Worcester MA 01615-0054. 508/751-5800. **Fax:** 508/751-5827. **Recorded jobline:** 508/751-5861. **Contact:** Personnel. **E-mail address:** humanresc@davidclark.com. **World Wide Web address:** http://www.davidclark.com. **Description:** Manufacturers of air crew protective

clothing, communication headsets, hearing protectors, and antishock trousers. Founded in 1935. **Positions advertised include:** Mechanical Designer. **NOTE:** Entry-level positions are offered. **Special programs:** Summer Jobs. **Office hours:** Monday - Friday, 8:00 a.m. - 4:30 p.m. **Corporate headquarters location:** This location. **Listed on:** Privately held. **President:** Robert Vincent. **Facilities Manager:** Vin Klimas. **Information Systems Manager:** James Grigos. **Purchasing Manager:** Gerry Leach. **Number of employees at this location:** 350.

CLARK CONSTRUCTION
263 Summer Street, Boston MA 02210. 617/439-0073. **Contact:** Human Resources. **World Wide Web address:** http://www.clarkus.com. **Description:** A general construction contractor. Founded in 1906. **Positions advertised include:** Project Manager; Superintendent; Field Engineer; Office Engineer. **Corporate headquarters location:** Bethesda MD. **Other U.S. locations:** Irvine CA; Oakland CA; Tampa FL; Chicago IL.

CLARK UNIVERSITY
950 Main Street, Worcester MA 01610. 508/793-7294. **Fax:** 508/793-8809. **Contact:** Human Resources Department. **E-mail address:** resumes@clarku.edu. **World Wide Web address:** http://www.clarku.edu. **Description:** A four-year research university offering bachelor's, master's, and doctoral degrees. The student body consists of approximately 2,200 graduate and undergraduate students. During the summer the College of Professional and Continuing Education (C.O.P.A.C.E.) program offers select classes for credit or personal enrichment. **NOTE:** Entry-level positions and part-time jobs are offered. **Positions advertised include:** Assistant Director of Admissions; Office Assistant; Assistant Director; Area Coordinator; Director of Major Gifts. **Office hours:** Monday - Friday, 8:30 a.m. - 4:30 p.m. **Other area locations:** Framingham MA.

CLARK UNIVERSITY
COMPUTER CAREER INSTITUTE
10 California Avenue, Framingham MA 01701. 508/620-5904. **Toll-free phone:** 800/568-1776. **Fax:** 508/875-7285. **Contact:** Human Resources. **Description:** Offers a variety of computer-related courses designed to help people reentering the workforce. Certificates are awarded at the end of 9 to 12 week daytime class sessions, or 6 to 7 month evening class sessions.

CLEAN HARBORS, INC.
530 East First Street, South Boston MA 02127. 617/269-5830. **Contact:** Personnel. **World Wide Web address:** http://www.cleanharbors.com. **Description:** Through its subsidiaries, Clean Harbors, Inc. provides comprehensive environmental services in 35 states in the Northeast, Midwest, Central, and Mid-Atlantic regions. Clean Harbors provides a wide range of hazardous waste management and environmental support services to a diversified customer base from 40 locations. The company's hazardous waste management services include treatment, storage, recycling, transportation, risk analysis, site assessment, laboratory analysis, site closure, and disposal of hazardous materials through environmentally sound methods. Environmental remediation services include emergency response, surface remediation, groundwater restoration, industrial maintenance, and facility decontamination. Customers include nearly 300 *Fortune* 500 companies; regional utilities; oil, pharmaceutical, and chemical companies; small businesses; and the high-tech and biotech industries. **Positions advertised include:** Accountant; Transportation Compliance Manager; Container Business Development Manager; Web Developer; Technician Services Representative; Purchase Order Administrator; Billing Clerk; Credit Request Check; T&D Order Placement Representative; Billing Supervisor; Tech Services. **NOTE:** Interested jobseekers should direct resumes to: Human Resources, 1501 Washington Street, Braintree MA 02184. **Corporate headquarters location:** Braintree MA. **Other area locations:** Kingston MA; Natick MA; North Grafton MA: West Springfield MA; Weymouth MA; Woburn MA. **Other U.S. locations:** Nationwide. **Listed on:** NASDAQ. **Stock exchange symbol:** CLHB. **Number of employees nationwide:** 1,400.

CLEAN HARBORS, INC.
P.O. Box 859048, Braintree MA 02185-9048. 781/849-1800. **Fax:** 781/356-1363. **Contact:** Personnel. **World Wide Web address:** http://www.cleanharbors.com. **Description:** Through its subsidiaries, Clean Harbors, Inc. provides comprehensive environmental services in 35 states in the Northeast, Midwest, Central, and Mid-Atlantic regions. Clean Harbors provides a wide range of hazardous waste management and environmental support services. The company's hazardous waste management services include treatment, storage, recycling, transportation, risk analysis, site assessment, laboratory analysis, site closure, and disposal of hazardous materials through environmentally sound methods. Environmental remediation services include emergency response, surface remediation, groundwater restoration, industrial maintenance, and facility decontamination. Customers include regional utilities; oil, pharmaceutical, and chemical companies; small businesses; and the high-tech and biotech industries. **Positions advertised include:** Accountant; Transportation Compliance Manager; Container Business Development Manager; Web Developer; Technician Services Representative; Purchase Order Administrator; Billing Clerk; Credit Request Check; T&D Order Placement Representative Billing Supervisor; Tech Services. **NOTE:** Interested jobseekers should direct resumes to: Human Resources, 1501 Washington Street, Braintree MA 02184. **Corporate headquarters location:** This location. **Other area locations:** Kingston MA; Natick MA; North Grafton MA: West Springfield MA; Weymouth MA; Woburn MA. **Other U.S. locations:** Nationwide. **Listed on:** NASDAQ. **Stock exchange symbol:** CLHB. **Number of employees nationwide:** 1,400.

COCA-COLA BOTTLING COMPANY OF CAPE COD
P.O. Box 779, Sandwich MA 02563-0779. 508/888-0001. **Contact:** Human Resources. **World Wide Web address:** http://www.cocacola.com. **Description:** A bottling plant for Coca-Cola, one of the world's largest soft drink makers. Brand names include Coca-Cola, Diet Coke, Coca-Cola light (international), Sprite, Diet Sprite, Mr. PiBB, Mello Yello, Fanta, TAB, Fresca, Fruitopia, Powerade, and Minute Maid. **Parent company:** The Coca-Cola Company owns 100 supporting brands around the world including Aquarius, Hi-C, Georgia (canned coffee, sold in Japan), Thums Up & Limca (India), Sparletta Brands (South Africa), Nestea (distributed by Coca-Cola Enterprises Inc.), and Seiryusabo (Japan). The Coca-Cola Company has owning interest in many bottlers including 44 percent of Coca-Cola Enterprises Inc., as well as Coca-Cola Foods, the world's largest seller of juice and juice-related products under brands such as FiveAlive, Hi-C, Bright & Early, and Bacardi.

COCA-COLA BOTTLING COMPANY OF NEW ENGLAND
9 B Street, Needham Heights MA 02494. 781/449-4300. **Contact:** Human Resources. **World Wide Web address:** http://www.cocacola.com. **Description:** A bottling plant for Coca-Cola, one of the world's largest soft drink makers. Brand names include Coca-Cola, Diet Coke, Coca-Cola light (international), Sprite, Diet Sprite, Mr. PiBB, Mello Yello, Fanta, TAB, Fresca, Fruitopia, Powerade, and Minute Maid. **Corporate headquarters location:** Atlanta GA. **Parent company:** The Coca-Cola Company owns 100 supporting brands around the world including Aquarius, Hi-C, Georgia (canned coffee, sold in Japan), Thums Up & Limca (India), Sparletta Brands (South Africa), Nestea (distributed by Coca-Cola Enterprises Inc.), and Seiryusabo (Japan). The Coca-Cola Company has owning interest in many bottlers including 44 percent of Coca-Cola Enterprises Inc., as well as Coca-Cola Foods, the world's largest seller of juice and juice-related products under brands such as FiveAlive, Hi-C, Bright & Early, and Bacardi.

COGNEX CORPORATION
One Vision Drive, Natick MA 01760. 508/650-3000. **Fax:** 508/650-3340. **Recorded jobline:** 508/650-3232. **Contact:** Human Resources. **E-mail address:** human.resources@cognex.com. **World Wide Web address:** http://www.cognex.com. **Description:** Designs, develops, manufactures, and markets machine vision systems used to automate a wide range of manufacturing processes. Cognex machine vision systems are used in the electronics, semiconductor, pharmaceutical, health care, aerospace, automotive, packaging, and graphic arts industries to gauge, guide, inspect, and identify products in manufacturing operations. Founded in 1981. **NOTE:** Entry-level positions and part-time jobs are offered. **Company slogan:** To preserve and enhance vision. **Positions advertised include:** End User Sales; Cost Accounting Manager; Principal Product Marketing Manager; HW Engineer; PC Specialist; Account Specialist; Credit Collection Specialist; Project Engineer. **Special programs:** Internships; Training; Co-ops; Summer Jobs. **Office hours:** Monday - Friday, 8:00 a.m. - 5:00 p.m. **Corporate headquarters location:** This location. **Other U.S. locations:** Alameda CA; Mountain View CA; Naperville IL; Novi MI; Portland OR; Wayne PA; Austin TX; West Allis WI. **International locations:** Worldwide. **Listed on:** NASDAQ. **Stock exchange symbol:** CGNX. **President/CEO:** Dr. Robert Shillman. **Number of employees at this location:** 300. **Number of employees nationwide:** 450. **Number of employees worldwide:** 600.

COGNOS CORPORATION
15 Wayside Road, Burlington MA 01803. 781/229-6600. **Toll-free phone:** 800/426-4667. **Fax:** 781/229-9844. **Contact:** Human Resources. **World Wide Web address:** http://www.cognos.com. **Description:** Develops a line of business management software. **Positions advertised include:** Accounting Manager; Account Executive; Commission System Supervisor; Business Analyst; Business Development Representative; Service Operations Advisor; Solutions Architect. **Corporate headquarters location:** This location. **Other U.S. locations:** Nationwide. **International locations:** Worldwide. **Listed on:** NASDAQ. **Stock exchange symbol:** COGN.

COLER & COLANTONIO
101 Accord Park Drive, Norwell MA 02061. 781/982-5400. **Contact:** Human Resources. **World Wide Web address:** http://www.col-col.com. **Description:** A civil and environmental engineering firm. Coler & Colantonio specializes in a variety of engineering projects including pipeline, transportation, and water projects. **Positions advertised include:** Waste Water Treatment Operator; Project Engineer; Drafter; Civil Engineer. **Other area locations:** South Deerfield MA; South Easton MA. **Other U.S. locations:** Houston TX.

COLONIAL SAW
P.O. Box A 122 Pembroke Street, Kingston MA 02364. 781/585-4364. **Fax:** 781/585-9375. **Contact:** Human Resources: **E-mail address:** info@csaw.com. **World Wide Web address:** http://www.csaw.com. **Description:** Produces the worlds most advanced woodworking and tool grinding technology.

COLUMBIA MOTORS
1817 Washington Street, Hanover MA 02339. 781/826-8300. **Contact:** Human Resources. **E-mail address:** sales@columbiamotors.com. **World Wide Web address:** http://www.columbiamotors.com. **Description:** A Pontiac, GMC, Buick, car dealership.

THE COLONNADE HOTEL
120 Huntington Avenue, Boston MA 02116. 617/424-7000. **Fax:** 617/424-1717. **Contact:** Human Resources. **E-mail address:** careers@colonnadehotel.com. **World Wide Web address:** http://www.colonnadehotel.com. **Description:** An independently-owned, luxury hotel featuring dining and on-premise parking facilities. **Positions advertised include:** Banquet Line Cook; Line Cook; Lifeguard; Server; Bell Attendant; Turn Down Attendant.

COMMERCE INSURANCE COMPANY
211 Main Street, Webster MA 01570. 508/943-9000. **Toll-free phone:** 800/922-8276. **Fax:** 508/949-4921. **Contact:** Carolyn Burke, Human Resources. **World Wide Web address:** http://www.commerceinsurance.com. **Description:** Underwrites personal and commercial property and casualty insurance such as motor vehicle insurance covering personal automobiles; offers homeowners inland/marine, fire, general liability, and commercial multiperil insurance; and provides residential and commercial mortgage loans. Founded in 1972. **NOTE:** Fill out online application. **Positions advertised include:** Physical Damage Coordinator; D/L Auto Service Supervisor; Material Damage Appraiser; SIU Adjuster; Litigation Consultant; Mail Clerk; File Clerk; Underwriter Specialist; Property Services Supervisor; Data Entry Specialist; Programmer Analyst; Cash Analyst; General Claims Representative. **Special programs:** Training. **Corporate headquarters location:** This location. **Subsidiaries include:** American Commerce Insurance Company (Columbus OH); Commerce West Insurance Company (Pleasanton CA); Bay Finance (Webster MA). **Listed on:** New York Stock Exchange. **Stock exchange symbol:** CGI. **Annual sales/revenues:** More than $100 million. **Number of employees at this location:** 1,300.

COMMONWEALTH CREATIVE ASSOCIATES
345 Union Avenue, Framingham MA 01702. 508/620-6664. **Contact:** Human Resources. **World Wide Web address:** http://www.commcreative.com. **Description:** A full-service advertising agency. **Corporate headquarters location:** This location. **Operations at this facility include:** Administration; Sales. **Listed on:** Privately held. **Number of employees at this location:** 10.

COMMONWEALTH HEMATOLOGY-ONCOLOGY
10 Willard Street, Quincy MA 02169. 617/479-3550. **Contact:** Human Resources. **World Wide Web address:** http://www.chomed.com. **Description:** A private practice outpatient facility specializing in the treatment of cancer and blood disorders. **Other area locations:** Brighton MA; Dorchester MA; Lawrence MA; Malden MA; Milton MA; South Weymouth MA.

COMMUNITY HEALTHLINK
72 Jaques Avenue, Worcester MA 01610. 508/860-1000. **Contact:** Human Resources. **World Wide Web address:** http://www.umassmemorial.org. **Description:** A multifaceted community service center whose programs include substance abuse treatment, outpatient services, geriatric services, medical day treatment, and services for the homeless. Community Healthlink is a member of the UMass Memorial Behavioral Health System.

COMMUNITY NEWSPAPER COMPANY
72 Cherry Hill Drive, Beverly MA 01915. 978/739-1300. **Contact:** Human Resources. **Description:** Owns and operates several weekly newspapers in communities north of Boston. Publications include *Ipswich Chronicle.*

COMPASSBANK
141 North Main Street, Fall River MA 02720. 508/994-5000. **Toll-free phone:** 800/322-9313. **Fax:** 508/646-3425. **Contact:** Linda Empoliti, Director of Human Resources. **E-mail address:** hresources@compassbank.com. **World Wide Web address:** http://www.compassbank.com. **Description:** Operates a full-service savings bank. Founded in 1855. **Corporate headquarters location:** New Bedford MA. **Other area locations:** Assonet MA; Buzzards Bay MA; Carver MA; Cedarville MA; Chatham MA; Chilmark MA; Dartmouth MA; Edgartown MA; Fairhaven MA; Falmouth MA; Hyannis MA; Mattapoisett MA; Oak Bluffs MA; Orleans MA; Plymouth MA; Pocasset MA; Sandwich MA; Seekonk MA; Somerset MA; South Dennis MA; South Sandwich MA; South Yarmouth MA; Swansea MA; Vineyard Haven MA; Wareham MA; West Tisbury MA; Westport MA. **Parent company:** Seacoast Financial Services Corporation. **Listed on:** NASDAQ. **Stock exchange symbol:** SCFS.

COMPUREX SYSTEMS
P.O. Box 2000, Easton MA 02334. 508/230-3700. **Fax:** 508/238-8250. **Contact:** Human Resources. **World Wide Web address:** http://www.compurex.com. **Description:** Rents, sells, and leases new and used Compaq and Digital Equipment Corporation systems, peripherals, and compatibles.

COMPUTER ASSOCIATES INTERNATIONAL, INC.
100 Staples Drive, Framingham MA 01702. 508/628-8000. **Contact:** Human Resources. **World Wide Web address:** http://www.cai.com. **Description:** Computer Associates International, Inc. is one of the world's leading developers of client/server and distributed computing software. The company develops, markets, and supports enterprise management, database and applications development, business applications, and consumer software products for a broad range of mainframe, midrange, and desktop computers. The company serves major business, government, research, and educational organizations. **Positions advertised include:** Development Manager; Principal Consultant; Systems Engineer. **Corporate headquarters location:** Islandia NY. **Other U.S. locations:** Nationwide. **International locations:** Worldwide. **Operations at this facility include:** This location develops software. **Listed on:** New York Stock Exchange. **Stock exchange symbol:** CA.

COMPUTER CORPORATION OF AMERICA, INC.
500 Old Connecticut Path, Framingham MA 01701. 508/270-6666. **Contact:** Human Resources. **World Wide Web address:** http://www.cca-int.com. **Description:** Develops high-speed database software. **Corporate headquarters location:** This location. **International locations:** Canada; England.

COMPUTER HORIZONS CORPORATION
35 Braintree Hill Park, Suite 108, Braintree MA 02184. 781/356-7800. **Toll-free phone:** 800/773-3496. **Fax:** 781/356-8899. **Contact:** Human Resources. **World Wide Web address:** http://www.computerhorizons.com. **Description:** A full-service technology solutions company offering contract staffing, outsourcing, re-engineering, migration, downsizing support, and network management. The company has a worldwide network of 33 offices. Founded in 1969. **Corporate headquarters location:** Mountain Lakes NJ. **Other U.S. locations:** Nationwide. **International locations:** Canada. **Listed on:** NASDAQ. **Stock exchange symbol:** CHRZ. **Number of employees nationwide:** 1,500. **Number of employees worldwide:** 3,000.

THE COMPUTER MERCHANT, LTD.
95 Longwater Circle, Norwell MA 02061. 781/878-1070. **Toll-free phone:** 800/617-6172. **Fax:** 781/878-4712. **Contact:** Human Resources. **World Wide Web address:** http://www.tcml.com. **Description:** Provides software consulting services. **NOTE:** Part-time jobs are offered. **Positions advertised include:** Tester; Engineer; Project Manager; Business Analyst; Programmer; Database Administrator; Network Service Support Technician. **Special programs:** Internships; Summer Jobs. **Listed on:** Privately held. **CEO:** John Danieli. **Information Systems Manager:** Donna Cash. **Annual sales/revenues:** More than $100 million. **Number of employees at this location:** 80.

COMPUTERWORLD INC.
500 Old Connecticut Path, Framingham MA 01701. 508/879-0700. **Contact:** Human Resources. **World Wide Web address:** http://www.computerworld.com. **Description:** Publishes *Computerworld,* a weekly newspaper devoted to the computer industry, with a special emphasis on the Internet; and *ROI,* a magazine for CIOs.

COMVERSE NETWORK SYSTEMS
100 Quannapowitt Parkway, Wakefield MA 01880. 781/246-9000. **Contact:** Human Resources. **E-mail address:** careeropportunities@comverse.com. **World Wide Web address:** http://www.comverse.com. **Description:** Manufactures and designs networking equipment for the telecommunications industry. **Corporate headquarters location:** This location. **Other U.S. locations:** Alpharetta GA; Park Ridge IL; Overland Park KS; Florissant MO; New York NY; Woodbury NY; Charlotte NC; Addison TX; Chantilly VA; Bellevue WA; Gig Harbor WA. **International locations:** Worldwide.

CONCENTRA MANAGED CARE SERVICES
130 Second Avenue, Waltham MA 02451. 781/290-5350. **Contact:** Human Resources. **World Wide Web address:** http://www.concentramc.com. **Description:** A full-service cost containment company that focuses on workers' compensation costs, and offers various consulting services. **Positions advertised include:** .NET Developer; Business Analyst; Quality Assurance Analyst; Business Report Analyst; Customer Service Representative; Operation Business Analyst; Pricing Analyst; Release Support Engineer; Vice President of Sales. **Other U.S. locations:** Nationwide.

CONCERTO SOFTWARE
6 Technology Park Drive, Westford MA 01886. 978/952-0200. **Contact:** Human Resources. **World Wide Web address:** http://www.concerto.com. **Description:** Develops, markets, implements, supports, and services outbound and inbound/outbound management systems for call center operations. These systems consist mainly of predictive dialing products and related autodialing systems responsible for important business applications including credit/collections, customer service, and telephone sales. Concerto Software provides unified call center solutions to banks, consumer finance organizations, retailers, and utilities. **Positions advertised include:** Technical Support Services; New Product Integration; Engineer. **Special programs:** Internships. **Corporate headquarters location:** This location. **Other U.S. locations:** Santa Clara CA; Norcross GA; Newtown PA; Dallas TX. **Listed on:** NASDAQ. **Stock exchange symbol:** DAVX. **Number of employees at this location:** 100. **Number of employees nationwide:** 160.

CONCORD COMMUNICATIONS, INC.
400+600 Nickerson Road, Marlboro MA 01752. 508/460-4646. **Contact:** Human Resources. **World Wide Web address:** http://www.concord.com. **Description:** Manufactures telecommunications equipment. **Positions advertised include:** Director of Sales Engineering; Commission Accountant; Services Product Marketing Specialist; Technical Support Engineer; Global Sales Representative. **Other U.S. locations:** Atlanta GA (formerly Empire Technologies). **Listed on:** NASDAQ. **Stock exchange symbol:** CCRD.

CONE INC.
90 Canal Street, 6th Floor, Boston MA 02114. 617/227-2111. **Contact:** Human Resources. **E-mail address:** hr@coneinc.com. **World Wide Web address:** http://www.conenet.com. **Description:** A strategic marketing communications firm. **Positions advertised include:** Crisis Prevention Planning & Management Position; Cause Branding Account Director.

CONSOLIDATED SERVICES GROUP
661 Pleasant Street, Norwood MA 02062. 781/769-4316. **Toll-free phone:** 800/742-7240. **Fax:** 781/769-2144. **Contact:** Human Resources. **E-mail address:** lsalvia@constar.com. **World Wide Web address:** http://www.constar.com. **Description:** A telecommunications and voice data firm. Founded in 1993. **NOTE:** Entry-level positions are offered. **Corporate headquarters location:** This location. **Other U.S. locations:** Nationwide. **Parent company:** Constar International, Inc. **Annual sales/revenues:** $21 - $50 million. **Number of employees at this location:** 100. **Number of employees nationwide:** 175.

CONTINENTAL RESOURCES, INC.
175 Middlesex Turnpike, P.O. Box 9137, Bedford MA 01730-9137. 781/275-0850. **Toll-free phone:** 800/937-4688. **Fax:** 781/533-0212. **Contact:** Human Resources. **World Wide Web address:** http://www.conres.com. **Description:** Configures, integrates, sells, services, and supports computer systems and electronic test equipment. **NOTE:** Entry-level positions are offered. **Special programs:** Internships. **Corporate headquarters location:** This location. **Other U.S. locations:** Milpitas CA; Torrance CA; Orlando FL; Wood Dale IL; Silver Spring MD; Mount Laurel NJ; Somerset NJ; New York NY. **Subsidiaries include:** Wall Industries manufactures AC/DC power sources and DC/DC converters; Continental Leasing is a lease financing company. **Operations at this facility include:** Administration; Manufacturing; Sales; Service. **Annual sales/revenues:** More than $100 million. **Number of employees at this location:** 120. **Number of employees nationwide:** 275.

CONTRAVISORY RESEARCH & MANAGEMENT CORPORATION
99 Derby Street, Suite 302, Hingham MA 02043. 781/749-3380. **Contact:** Human Resources. **E-mail address:** info@contravisory.com. **World Wide Web address:** http://www.contravisory.com. **Description:** An investment advisory firm whose services include mutual funds.

CONVERSE, INC.
1 High Street, Andover MA 01845. 978/983-3300. **Fax:** 978/664-7472. **Contact:** Human Resources. **E-mail address:** jobs@converse.com. **World Wide Web address:** http://www.converse.com. **Description:** Manufactures men's, women's, and children's footwear. **Positions advertised include:** Application Programmer; Creative Director; Designer; Marketing Communications Manager; Public Relations Manager. **Special programs:** Internships. **Corporate headquarters location:** This location. **Other U.S. locations:** Nationwide. **Operations at this facility include:** Administration; Research and Development; Sales; Service. **Number of employees at this location:** 400. **Number of employees nationwide:** 2,000.

CORE, INC.
88 Black Falcon Avenue, Suite 353, Boston MA 02210-2414. 617/375-7700. **Fax:** 617/375-7777. **Contact:** Human Resources. **World Wide Web address:** http://www.coreinc.com. **Description:** A national provider of physician-intensive, specialty-matched, health care utilization management programs. Health care utilization management is a system of reviewing, evaluating, and monitoring the medical necessity and appropriateness of health care services prescribed for participants in health care plans. Services include independent physician review, behavioral health review, medical resource management, comprehensive case management, rehabilitation review, and disability review. **Corporate headquarters location:** Portland ME. **Parent company:** Fortis, Inc. **Number of employees at this location:** 180.

CORNING INC.
Life Sciences, 45 Nagog Park, Acton MA 01720-3413. 978/635-2200. **Contact:** Human Resources. **World Wide Web address:** http://www.corning.com. **Description:** Corning's Science Products Division is engaged in the design, development, manufacture, and sale of disposable plastic research labware. **Positions advertised include:** Business Development Manager; Midwest Area Sales Manager. **NOTE:** Summer internships are available, search the website for more information and apply online. **Other U.S. locations:** Nationwide. **International locations:** Worldwide. **Operations at this facility include:** This location houses the company's administrative offices. **Listed on:** New York Stock Exchange. **Stock exchange symbol:** GLW.

COURIER EPIC, INC.
COURIER CORPORATION
15 Wellman Avenue, North Chelmsford MA 01863. 978/251-6000. **Contact:** Human Resources. **World Wide Web address:** http://www.courier.com. **Description:** As a division of Courier Corporation, Courier EPIC coordinates material for electronic publishers and software companies. Courier Corporation (also at this location) offers a full range of book production and distribution services. Publishing markets served include educational, religious, reference, medical, financial, trade, and software. Founded in 1824. **Positions advertised include:** Staff Accountant. **Corporate headquarters location:** This location. **Other area locations:** Stoughton MA; Westford MA. **Other U.S. locations:** Hayward CA; Buffalo Creek CO; Chicago IL; Kendallville IN; North Bergen NJ; North Caldwell NJ; Mineola NY; New York NY; Philadelphia PA. **Listed on:** NASDAQ. **Stock exchange symbol:** CRRC.

COURIER STOUGHTON, INC.
100 Alpine Circle, Stoughton MA 02072. 781/341-1800. **Contact:** Human Resources. **World Wide Web address:** http://www.courier.com. **Description:** Offers a full-range of book production and distribution services. Publishing markets served include educational, religious, reference, medical, financial, trade, and software. Founded in 1824. **Positions advertised include:** Bindery Cutter Operator. **Corporate headquarters location:** North Chelmsford MA. **Other area locations:** Hayward CA; Buffalo Creek CO; Chicago IL; Kendallville IN; North Bergen NJ; North Caldwell NJ; Mineola NY; New York NY; Philadelphia PA. **Listed on:** NASDAQ. **Stock exchange symbol:** CRRC. **Other U.S. locations:** Kendallville IN; Philadelphia PA. **Parent company:** Courier Corporation.

COURIER WESTFORD, INC.
22 Town Farm Road, Westford MA 01886. 978/692-6321. **Fax:** 978/692-7292. **Contact:** Human Resources. **World Wide Web address:** http://www.courier.com. **Description:** Offers a full-range of book production and distribution services. Publishing markets served include educational, religious, reference, medical, financial, trade, and software. Founded in 1824. **Positions advertised include:** Human Resources Manager; Casebinder Operator; Web Press Operator; Skidder; General Worker. **Corporate headquarters location:** North Chelmsford MA. **Other area locations:** Stoughton MA. **Other U.S. locations:** Hayward CA; Buffalo Creek CO; Chicago IL; Kendallville IN; North Bergen NJ; North Caldwell NJ; Mineola NY; New York NY; Philadelphia PA. **Listed on:** NASDAQ. **Stock exchange symbol:** CRRC. **Parent company:** Courier Corporation.

COX ENGINEERING COMPANY
35 Industrial Drive, Canton MA 02021. 781/302-3300. **Contact:** Human Resources. **Description:** Engaged in mechanical engineering and sheetmetal work for the aerospace industry.

CRANBERRY VALLEY GOLF COURSE
183 Oak Street, Harwich MA 02645. 508/430-5234. **Contact:** Human Resources. **World Wide Web address:** http://www.cranberryvalley.com. **Description:** A town owned and operated golf course.

THE CREDIT NETWORK
59 Howard Street, Framingham MA 01702. 508/875-5266. **Contact:** Human Resources. **World Wide Web address:** http://www.tcnlink.com. **Description:** A credit reporting service catering to the mortgage industry. **Positions advertised include:** National Account Manager.

CREO AMERICAS, INC.
8 Oak Park Drive, Bedford MA 01730. 781/275-5150. **Fax:** 781/275-3430. **Contact:** Human Resources. **E-mail address:** resume.america@creo.com. **World Wide Web address:** http://www.creo.com. **Description:** Designs, develops, manufactures, markets, and services electronic prepress systems for the printing and publishing industries. These systems automate the labor- and materials-intensive prepress process of converting graphic design specifications for color slides, text, and graphics into final color separation films. **Positions advertised include:** Marketing Manager; Product Marketing Engineer; Professional Success Team Lead; Manager Market Development. **Listed on:** NASDAQ. **Stock exchange symbol:** CREO.

CUBIST PHARMACEUTICALS
65 Hayden Avenue, Lexington MA 02421. 781/860-8660. **Fax:** 781/861-0566. **Contact:** Human Resources. **E-mail address:** hr@cubist.com. **World Wide Web address:** http://www.cubist.com. **Description:** Pharmaceutical company focused on the production of antiinfective drugs. **Corporate headquarters location:** This location.

CUMBERLAND ENGINEERING LLC
BROWN PLASTIC MACHINERY LLC
100 Roddy Avenue, South Attleboro MA 02703. 508/399-6400. **Fax:** 508/399-3057. **Contact:** Donna Welch, Director of Human Resources. **World Wide Web address:** http://www.cumberland-plastics.com. **Description:** Manufactures industrial and commercial machinery. **Corporate headquarters location:** This location. **Number of employees at this location:** 200. **Number of employees nationwide:** 1,250.

CUMBERLAND FARMS, INC.
777 Dedham Street, Canton MA 02021. 781/828-4900. **Fax:** 781/828-9012. **Contact:** Human Resources. **World Wide Web address:** http://www.cumberlandfarms.com. **Description:** Cumberland Farms operates a chain of retail convenience stores and gas stations. **Positions advertised include:** Multi Unit Area Manager; Equipment Operator. **Corporate headquarters location:** This location. **Operations at this facility include:** Manufacturing; Sales. **Listed on:** Privately held. **Number of employees at this location:** 700. **Number of employees nationwide:** 8,000.

CURRY COLLEGE
1071 Blue Hill Avenue, Milton MA 02186. 617/333-0500. **Contact:** Human Resources. **World Wide Web address:** http://www.curry.edu. **Description:** A four-year liberal arts college with programs for undergraduate and graduate students. **Positions advertised include:** Graduate Education Faculty; Assistant Director Financial Aide; Enrollment Representative; Assistant Director Admissions; Public Safety Officer

CUTTING EDGE TECHNOLOGIES
250 Nicks Rock Road, Plymouth MA 02360. 508/746-6900. **Toll-free phone:** 800/233-9956. **Fax:** 508/747-4339. **Contact:** Human Resources. **E-mail address:** toolsales@cetdirect.com. **World Wide Web address:** http://www.cetdirect.com. **Description:** 1SO 9002 certified company to make cutting tools that meet standard or special tolerances.

CYN ENVIRONMENTAL
P.O. Box 119, Stoughton MA 02072. 781/341-1777. **Toll-free phone:** 800/242-5818. **Fax:** 781/341-6246. **Physical address:** 100 Tosca Drive, Stoughton MA 02072. **Contact:** Chuck Klinger, Human Resources. **E-mail address:** cklinger@cynenv.com. **World Wide Web address:** http://www.cynenv.com. **Description:** Provides hazardous waste removal and remediation. **Positions advertised include:** Environmental Project Manager. **Other area locations:** Wilbraham MA. **Other U.S. locations:** Dover NH; Johnston RI.

CYRK, INC.
201 Edgewater Drive, Suite 225, Wakefield MA 01880. 781/876-5800. **Fax:** 360/805-2671. **Contact:** Human Resources. **E-mail address:** careers@cyrk.com. **World Wide Web address:** http://www.cyrk.com. **Description:** Designs, develops, manufactures, and distributes products for promotional programs. The company also provides integrated marketing services to national and international clients. Founded in 1976. **Positions advertised include:** Account Manager; Field Sales Representative. **Corporate headquarters location:** This location. **Other U.S. locations:** Nationwide. **Annual sales/revenues:** More than $100 million.

DM COMMUNICATIONS, INC.
651 Clapboardtree Street, Westwood MA 02090. 781/329-7799. **Fax:** 781/461-8266. **Contact:** Human Resources. **World Wide Web address:** http://www.ad-pr-dm.com. **Description:** A marketing and public relations firm.

DS GRAPHICS INC.
120 Stedman Street, Lowell MA 01851-2797. 978/970-1359. **Toll-free phone:** 800/536-8283. **Fax:** 978/970-1253. **Contact:** Human Resources. **World Wide Web address:** http://www.dsgraphics.com. **Description:** A commercial printer engaged in the printing of books, software documentation, and direct mail marketing materials. Founded in 1974. **Corporate headquarters location:** This location.

DAILY EVENING ITEM
38 Exchange Street, Lynn MA 01901. 781/593-7700. **Contact:** Allan Kort, Managing Editor. **World Wide Web address:** http://www.thedailyitem.com. **Description:** Publishes a daily newspaper with a weekday circulation of more than 20,000. **Parent company:** Ottaway Newspapers, Inc.

DANA FARBER CANCER INSTITUTE
44 Binney Street, Boston MA 02115. 617/732-3000. **Contact:** Human Resources. **World Wide Web address:** http://www.dfci.havard.edu. **Description:** A cancer research institute and hospital. **Positions advertised include:** Administrative Assistant; Administrative Specialist; Lab Systems Coordinator; Office Support Specialist; Child Life Specialist; Clinic Assistant; Facilitator; Level II Pharmacist; New Patient Coordinator; Human Resources Specialist; Program Administrator; Clinical Research Audit manager; Intranet Specialist; Health Educator; Intervention Coordinator; Survey Assistant; Research Associate; Research Fellow; Credit Collection Officer; Statistician; Transcription Assistant; Application Analyst; Research Scientist; Nurse Practitioner; Registered Nurse; Research Nurse; Social Worker.

D'ANGELO SANDWICH SHOPS
49 River Street, Waltham MA 02154. 781/893-0034. **Contact:** Human Resources. **World Wide Web address:** http://www.dangelos.com/. **Description:** One location of a chain of 200 quick-service sandwich shops. **Parent company:** Papa Gino's of America Inc. **Positions advertised include:** Assistant Manager; General Manager.

DATA DIRECT, INC.
27 Charles Street, Needham Heights MA 02494. 781/444-9290. **Contact:** Human Resources. **Description:** Distributes products and services for the software manufacturing industry including software duplication systems, data recording media, and CD-ROMs. The company offers data recording products from suppliers including 3M, Maxell, and Sony.

DATA SET CABLE COMPANY
ADD-ON DATA
323 Andover Street, Wilmington MA 01887. 978/988-1900. **Contact:** Human Resources. **Description:** Data Set Cable Company manufactures custom computer cable assemblies. Add-On Data (also at this location) resells computers.

DATA TRANSLATION
100 Locke Drive, Marlborough MA 01752-1192. 508/481-3700. **Fax:** 508/481-5670. **Contact:** Human Resources. **E-mail address:** hresources@datx.com. **World Wide Web address:** http://www.datatranslation.com. **Description:** Designs, develops, and manufactures high-performance digital media, data acquisition, and imaging products. The company's principal products are digital signal processing boards and software, which use personal computers to receive analog signals, convert them to digital form, and process the digital data. One product, Media 100, enables video producers to produce broadcast quality videos on a Macintosh computer. **Positions advertised include:** Test Operator. **Corporate headquarters location:** This location. **Subsidiaries include:** Data Translation, GmbH (Germany); Data Translation Ltd. (England). **Listed on:** NASDAQ. **Stock exchange symbol:** DATX.

DATACUBE, INC.
300 Rosewood Drive, Danvers MA 01923. 978/777-4200. **Fax:** 978/777-3117. **Contact:** Human Resources. **World Wide Web address:** http://www.datacube.com. **Description:** A manufacturer of board- and system-level hardware for image processing. **NOTE:** Entry-level positions are offered. **Positions advertised include:** Principal/Senior Software Engineer. **Corporate headquarters location:** This location. **Listed on:** Privately held. **Annual sales/revenues:** $11 - $20 million. **Number of employees at this location:** 140.

DATAMARINE INTERNATIONAL, INC.
4 Barlows Landing Road, Pocasset MA 02559-1984. 508/563-7151. **Contact:** Human Resources. **Description:** Manufactures and markets electronics including ocean depth sounders, and radio and telephone systems for land and ocean applications.

DATAWATCH CORPORATION
175 Cabot Street, Suite 503, Lowell MA 01854. 978/441-2200. **Contact:** Human Resources. **World Wide Web address:** http://www.datawatch.com. **Description:** Designs, manufactures, markets, and supports personal computer software including Monarch, which provides data access, translation, and reporting capability to users of network PCs, and VIREX, which detects, repairs, and monitors virus infections for Macintosh computers. **Positions advertised include:** Sales Executive; Product Manager. **Subsidiaries include:** Datawatch Europe Ltd. (England); Datawatch GmbH (Germany); Datawatch International Ltd. (England); Datawatch Pty Ltd. (Australia); Datawatch Sarl (France). **Listed on:** NASDAQ. **Stock exchange symbol:** DWCH.

DATEL INC.
11 Cabot Boulevard, Mansfield MA 02048. 508/339-3000. **Contact:** Human Resources. **World Wide Web address:** http://www.datel.com. **Description:** Manufactures electronic components used in data acquisition. **International locations:** England; France; Germany; Japan.

DAVOL INC.
160 New Boston Street, Woburn MA 01801. 781/932-5900. **Fax:** 781/932-4125. **Contact:** Human Resources. **E-mail address:** arlene.andreozzi.@crbard.com. **World Wide Web address:** http://www.davol.com. **Description:** Develops, manufactures, and markets specialty medical products for use in surgical and nonsurgical procedures. Davol specializes in products relating to hernia repair, laparascopy, and orthopedics. **Positions advertised include:** Product Manager; Cost Supervisor; Manufacturing Engineer. **Corporate headquarters location:** Cranston RI. **Parent company:** C.R. Bard, Inc. **Number of employees at this location:** 45.

DAY, BERRY & HOWARD LLP
260 Franklin Street, 21st Floor, Boston MA 02110. 617/345-4600. **Contact:** Human Resources. **E-mail address:** lnotarangelo@dbh.com. **World Wide Web address:** http://www.dbh.com. **Description:** One of New England's largest law firms. Day, Berry & Howard LLP specializes in more than 60 legal disciplines including banking, construction, insurance, torts, and venture capital. **Positions advertised include:** Trust & Estate Paralegal; Paralegal; Associate Employment Litigator; Attorney. **Other U.S. locations:** Greenwich CT; Hartford CT; Stamford CT; New York NY.

DEC-TAM CORPORATION
50 Concord Street, North Reading MA 01864. 978/470-2860. **Contact:** Human Resources. **World Wide Web address:** http://www.dectam.com. **Description:** Provides lead paint and asbestos removal.

DECHERT
10 Post Office Square South, Boston MA 02109-4603. 617/728-7100. **Fax:** 617/426-6567. **Contact:** Human Resources Department. **World Wide Web address:** http://www.dechert.com. **Description:** A law firm specializing in intellectual property, taxation, and litigation. The firm operates 10 offices throughout the United States and Europe. **Other U.S. locations:** Hartford CT; Washington DC; Princeton NJ; New York NY; Harrisburg PA; Philadelphia PA; Newport RI. **International locations:** Belgium; England; France; Luxembourg.

DEER ISLAND TREATMENT PLANT
P.O. Box 100, Winthrop MA 02152. 617/846-5800. **Contact:** Human Resources. **Description:** A wastewater treatment facility run by the Massachusetts Water Resources Authority (MWRA).

DEFENSE CONTRACT MANAGEMENT DISTRICT EAST
10 Causeway Street, Boston MA 02222. 617/565-6850. **Contact:** Human Resources. **Description:** The defense contract management center for the Northeast.

DELPHI FORUMS INC.
1030 Massachusetts Avenue, Cambridge MA 02138. 617/576-3690. **Fax:** 617/995-3032. **Contact:** Human Resources. **E-mail address:** jobs@delphi.com. **World Wide Web address:** http://www.delphiforums.com. **Description:** Manages a Website that hosts online forums and supports thousands of special interest communities including free do-it-yourself message boards, chat rooms, and personal home pages. Delphi Forums has more than 2 million registered users of approximately 80,000 forums. **Corporate headquarters location:** This location.

DEMOULAS SUPERMARKETS INC.
875 East Street, Tewksbury MA 01876. 978/851-8000. **Contact:** President of Operations. **Description:** Operates a grocery store chain with locations throughout northern and eastern Massachusetts. **Corporate headquarters location:** This location.

DEPUY ACROMED
325 Paramount Drive, Raynham MA 02767. 508/880-8100. **Toll-free phone:** 800/227-6633. **Contact:** Personnel. **E-mail address:** careers_acromed@dpyus.jnj.com. **World Wide Web address:** http://www.depuyacromed.com. **Description:** Manufactures and supplies a broad line of surgical products including instruments, equipment, implants, surgical disposables, and electronic pain control stimulators and electrodes. **Positions advertised include:** Product Director; Clinical Research Manager; Clinical Research Associate; Corporate Account Manager; Senior Scientist. **Subsidiaries include:** DePuy International Ltd. (England). **Parent company:** Johnson & Johnson.

DEVINE & PEARSON COMMUNICATIONS
300 Congress Street, Suite 201, Quincy MA 02169. 617/472-2700. **Contact:** Charlotte Delaney, Office Manager. **World Wide Web address:** http://www.devine-pearson.com. **Description:** An advertising and public relations agency that also offers design and consulting services.

DEWBERRY & GOODKIND
31 St. James Avenue, 3rd Floor, Boston MA 02116. 617/695-3400. **Fax:** 617/695-3310. **Contact:** Personnel. **World Wide Web address:** http://www.dewberry.com. **Description:** An engineering firm specializing in architectural design, environmental consulting, and construction administration. Founded in 1922. **Positions advertised include:** Architectural Project Manager; Senior Traffic Engineer; Structural Project Engineer.

DEWOLFE NEW ENGLAND
326 Washington Street, Wellesley Hills MA 02481. 781/235-6885. **Contact:** Human Resources. **World Wide Web address:** http://www.dewolfenewengland.com. **Description:** An integrated residential real estate service company that provides sales and marketing services to residential real estate consumers. In addition, the company originates, processes, and closes residential mortgage loans; provides corporate and employee relocation services; and provides asset management services to a variety of clients. In residential real estate and marketing, the company acts as a broker or agent in transactions through independent sales associates. **Corporate headquarters location:** This location. **Other U.S. locations:** CT; NH. **Subsidiaries include:** DeWolfe Relocation Services, Inc. offers employers a variety of specialized services primarily concerned with facilitating the resettlement of transferred employees. **Listed on:** American Stock Exchange. **Stock exchange symbol:** DWL. **Number of employees nationwide:** 275.

DEXTER SHOE COMPANY
1230 Washington Street, West Newton MA 02465-2129. 617/332-4300. **Contact:** Office Manager. **E-mail address:** jobs@dextershoe.com. **World Wide Web address:** http://www.dextershoe.com. **Description:** Manufactures men's and women's footwear. **Corporate headquarters location:** Dexter ME. **Parent company:** Berkshire Hathaway. **Operations at this facility include:** Administration.

DIEBOLD, INC.
261 Cedar Hill Road, Marlborough MA 01752. 508/480-6400. **Contact:** Personnel. **E-mail:** hrinfo@diebold.com. **World Wide Web address:** http://www.diebold.com. **Description:** Diebold is engaged in the sale, manufacture, installation, and service of automated teller machines, physical and electronic security systems, and software for the financial and commercial industries. Other products include vaults, vault doors, lockers, safes, alarms, video surveillance systems, and data line security systems. Founded in 1859. **NOTE:** Resumes should be sent to: Human Resources, 5995 Mayfair Road, P.O. Box 3077, North Canton OH 44720-8077. **Corporate headquarters location:** North Canton OH. **Operations at this facility include:** This location is a sales office for the company's MedSelect product line. **Listed on:** New York Stock Exchange. **Stock exchange symbol:** DBD.

DIELECTRICS INDUSTRIES, INC.
300 Burnett Road, Chicopee MA 01020. 413/594-8111. **Toll-free phone:** 800/472-7286. **Fax:** 413/594-2343. **Contact:** Personnel. **World Wide Web address:** http://www.dielectrics.com. **Description:** As the medical division of Dielectrics Industries, DMC designs and fabricates a variety of sophisticated medical devices for the laparoscopic, orthopedic, and blood fluid delivery markets. Overall, Dielectrics Industries is a leading designer, developer, fabricator, and supplier of air cell and other bladder technologies. Markets served include medical, aerospace, automotive, recreational, and industrial. Products include laparoscopic surgical devices, inflatable vests, in-line skate inserts, and lumbar support systems. **Corporate headquarters location:** This location.

DIOCESAN HEALTH FACILITIES
368 North Main Street, Fall River MA 02720. 508/679-8154. **Contact:** Human Resources. **World Wide Web address:** http://www.dhfo.org. **Description:** Operates nonprofit nursing homes including Catholic Memorial Home (Fall River MA), Our Lady's Haven (Fairhaven MA), Madonna Manor (North Attleboro MA), Sacred Heart (New Bedford MA), and Marian Manor (Taunton MA). **Corporate headquarters location:** This location.

DIVERSIFIED VISITING NURSE ASSOCIATION (DVNA)
316 Nichols Road, Fitchburg MA 01420. 978/342-6013. **Contact:** Human Resources. **Description:** Provides home care to residents of north central Massachusetts and south central New Hampshire. Nursing care services include antibiotic and nutritional infusions, wound care, cardiac care, and care of ventilator patients. Rehabilitation services include physical, occupational, and speech therapy. **Corporate headquarters location:** Leominster MA. **Parent company:** HealthAlliance also operates a number of other subsidiaries, which include Burbank Hospital; Diversified Medical Equipment Services; Leominster Hospital; Fairlawn Nursing Home; The Highlands; and Coordinated Primary Care.

DOBLE ENGINEERING COMPANY
85 Walnut Street, Watertown MA 02472. 617/926-4900. **Fax:** 617/926-0528. **Contact:** Human Resources. **E-mail address:** hr@doble.com. **World Wide Web address:** http://www.doble.com. **Description:** Manufactures and repairs circuit breakers and test transformers for utility companies.

DOE & INGALLS INC.
P.O. Box 560, Medford MA 02155. 781/391-0090. **Physical address:** 25 Commercial Street, Medford MA 02155. **Contact:** Peter Liebman, President. **World Wide Web address:** http://www.doeingalls.com. **Description:** Manufactures and distributes chemicals. Founded in 1921. **Other U.S. locations:** Tampa FL; Durham NC.

R.R. DONNELLEY FINANCIAL
20 Custom House Street, Suite 650, Boston MA 02110. 617/345-4300. **Contact:** Human Resources. **World Wide Web address:** http://www.rrdonnelley.com. **Description:** R.R. Donnelley & Sons is a world leader in managing, reproducing, and distributing print and digital information for publishing, merchandising, and information technology customers. The company is one of the largest commercial printers in the world, producing catalogs, inserts, magazines, books, directories, computer documentation, and financial materials. R.R. Donnelley has more than 180 sales offices and production facilities worldwide. Principal services offered by the company are conventional and digital prepress operations; computerized printing and binding; sophisticated pool shipping and distribution services for printed products; information repackaging into multiple formats including print, magnetic, and optical media; database management, list rental, list enhancement, and direct mail production services; turnkey computer documentation services including outsourcing, translation, printing, binding, diskette replication, kitting, licensing, republishing, and fulfillment; reprographics and facilities management; creative design and communication services; and digital and conventional map creation and related services. Founded in 1864. **Corporate headquarters location:** Chicago IL. **Other U.S. locations:** Nationwide. **International locations:** Worldwide. **Operations at this facility include:** This location prints financial materials. **Parent company:** R.R. Donnelley & Sons. **Listed on:** New York Stock Exchange. **Stock exchange symbol:** DNY. **Number of employees worldwide:** 35,000.

DORANCO INC.
200 Gilbert Street, Mansfield MA 02048. 508/261-1200. **Fax:** 508/237-6965. **Contact:** Human Resources. **E-mail address:** info@doranco.com. **World Wide Web address:** http://www.doranco.com. **Description:** A manufacturer of decorative metal parts, primarily for the consumer audio electronics and telecommunications industries. Products include floor stands for speakers and faceplates for audio and computer components as well as nameplates for consumer products ranging from automobiles to household appliances. **Corporate headquarters location:** This location. **Other U.S. locations:** Phoenix AZ; Attleboro Falls MA. **International locations:** South Korea. **Number of employees worldwide:** 200.

CHARLES STARK DRAPER LABORATORY, INC.
555 Technology Square, Mail Stop 44, Cambridge MA 02139-3563. 617/258-1000. **Contact:** Personnel. **E-mail address:** hr@draper.com. **World Wide Web address:** http://www.draper.com. **Description:** A private, nonprofit corporation dedicated to scientific research, development, and education. **Positions advertised include:** Test Engineer; Systems Engineer; Communications Engineer; Software Engineer. **Corporate headquarters location:** This location.

DUKE ENERGY ALGONQUIN
1284 Soldiers Field Road, Brighton MA 02135. 617/254-4050. **Toll-free phone:** 800/USE-DUKE. **Contact:** Personnel. **World Wide Web address:** http://www.duke-energy.com. **Description:** A natural gas transmission company. The company pipes natural gas to utility companies. **Listed on:** New York Stock Exchange. **Stock exchange symbol:** DUK.

DUN & BRADSTREET, INC.
1800 West Park Drive, Suite 300, Westborough MA 01581. 508/871-8000. **Contact:** Human Resources. **E-mail:** hrsourcing@dnb.com. **World Wide Web address:** http://www.dnb.com. **Description:** Provides business-to-business credit, marketing, and investment management services. **Corporate headquarters location:** Murray Hill NJ. **Parent company:** The Dun & Bradstreet Corporation. **Listed on:** New York Stock Exchange. **Stock exchange symbol:** DNB. **CEO:** Allan Loren. **Number of employees worldwide:** 9,000.

DUNKIN' DONUTS OF AMERICA INC.
P.O. Box 317, Randolph MA 02368. 781/961-4000. **Physical address:** 14 Pacella Park Drive, Randolph MA 02368. **Contact:** Human Resources. **World Wide Web address:** http://www.dunkindonuts.com. **Description:** Develops and franchises Dunkin' Donuts shops that sell coffee, donuts, and baked goods. **Corporate headquarters location:** This location. **Subsidiaries include:** Togo; Baskin Robbins. **Parent company:** Allied Domecq Retailing USA.

DYAX CORPORATION
One Kendall Square, Building 600, Suite 623, Cambridge MA 02139. 617/225-2500. **Contact:** Human Resources. **World Wide Web address:** http://www.dyax.com. **Description:** Engaged in producing protein and peptide separations as well as screening technology products. Dyax Corporation also develops nuclear medicine to help alleviate clotting problems. **Positions advertised include:** Procurement Manager; Program Management Director; System Administrator. Subsidiaries include: Dyax s.a. (Belgium); Biotage Division (Charlottesville VA); Biotage UK (England). Listed on: New York Stock Exchange. Stock exchange symbol: DYAX.

DYNAGRAF, INC.
5 Dan Road, Canton MA 02021. 781/575-1700. **Contact:** Human Resources. **World Wide Web address:** http://www.dynagraf.com. **Description:** A printing company. Dynagraf prints annual reports, educational materials, and financial documents.

DYNAMICS RESEARCH CORPORATION (DRC)
60 Frontage Road, Andover MA 01810. 978/475-9090. **Fax:** 978/470-0201. **Contact:** Human Resources. **World Wide Web address:** http://www.drc.com. **Description:** Provides systems engineering and analysis, operations research, logistics, and database systems support for the Department of Defense. Applications include acquisition management, inertial navigation and guidance, human resources requirements analyses, software systems, and logistic support analyses. The company also manufactures rotary and linear optical incremental encoders and precision patterned glass and metal products including precision measuring scales, reticles, and optical pick-offs for computer peripheral and optical equipment OEMs. **Positions advertised include:** Compensation Administrator; Credit Collection Manager; Accounting Assistant; EBS Business Analyst. **Corporate headquarters location:** This location. **Other area locations:** Bedford MA; West Newton MA; Wilmington MA. **Other U.S. locations:** Nationwide. **Operations at this facility include:** Administration; Research and Development; Sales; Service. **Listed on:** NASDAQ. **Stock exchange symbol:** DRCO.

DYNAMICS RESEARCH CORPORATION (DRC)
60 Concord Street, Wilmington MA 01887. 978/658-6100. **Contact:** Human Resources. **World Wide Web address:** http://www.drc.com. **Description:** As part of the Encoder Division, this location designs and manufactures a wide range of encoders, from rotary and hollow shaft to modular and linear. Overall, Dynamics Research Corporation operates through six divisions and four subdivisions: Encoders; Mediagraphics Systems, which is broken down into Information Technology Services, Logistics, Systems Engineering, and Systems Engineering and Technical Assistance (SETA); Tactical Communications; Telecommunications; and Test Equipment. **Positions advertised include:** Administrative Assistant; Software Developer; Database Specialist. **Corporate headquarters location:** Andover MA. **Other area locations:** Bedford MA; West Newton MA. **Other U.S. locations:** Nationwide. **Listed on:** NASDAQ. **Stock exchange symbol:** DRCO.

E INK CORPORATION
733 Concord Avenue, Cambridge MA 02138. 617/499-6000. **Fax:** 617/234-8450. **Contact:** Human Resources. **E-mail address:** jobs@eink.com. **World Wide Web address:** http://www.eink.com. **Description:** A growth-stage company that commercialized the invention of electronic ink. Founded in 1987. **Positions advertised include:** Polymeric Materials Engineer; Device Performance Scientist/Engineer; Chemical Technician; Utility Technician. **International locations:** Japan.

EAD SYSTEMS CORPORATION
300 Congress Street #304, Quincy MA 02169. 617/328-5258. **Fax:** 617/328-4941. **Contact:** Human Resources. **World Wide Web address:** http://www.ead.com. **Description:** Repairs computer monitors. **Other U.S. locations:** Fremont CA.

EDS (ELECTRONIC DATA SYSTEMS CORPORATION)
5 Clock Tower Place, Suite 300, Maynard MA 01754. 781/487-1000. **Contact:** Human Resources. **World Wide Web address:** http://www.eds.com. **Description:** EDS serves cellular carriers on over 500 U.S. and international markets, specifically in the areas of billing and rating, real-time networking and switching, and new technologies. **Corporate headquarters location:** Plano TX. **Parent company:** General Motors Corporation. **Operations at this facility include:** Divisional Headquarters. **Listed on:** New York Stock Exchange. **Stock exchange symbol:** EDS. **Number of employees at this location:** 390. **Number of employees nationwide:** 77,000. **Number of employees worldwide:** 140,000.

EMC CORPORATION
P.O. Box 9103, Hopkinton MA 01748-9103. 508/435-1000. **Fax:** 508/435-8884. **Contact:** Human Resources. **E-mail address:** resumes@emc.com. **World Wide Web address:** http://www.emc.com. **Description:** EMC designs, manufactures, markets, and supports high-performance data storage products. The company also provides related services for selected mainframe and mid-range computer systems primarily manufactured by IBM and Unisys. **Positions advertised include:** District Administration; Functional Program Manager; Software Release Administrator; Speechwriter; PR Specialist; Corporate Systems Engineer; Lead Corporation Systems Engineer; Product Manager; Controller; Financial Analyst; Cost Accounting Supervisor; Global Solutions; Mechanical Engineer; Materials Quality Engineer; HR Operation Manager; IT Program Research; Paralegal. **NOTE:** Applicants should mail their resumes to: EMC Corporation, Attn: Employment Opportunities, 5 Technology Drive, Milford, MA 01757. **Corporate headquarters location:** This location. **Listed on:** New York Stock Exchange. **Stock exchange symbol:** EMC. **Annual sales/revenues:** More than $100 million. **Number of employees at this location:** 1,500.

EMJ METALS
59 South Street, Hopkinton MA 01748. 508/435-6854. **Toll-free phone:** 800/336-5365. **Fax:** 508/435-2520. **Contact:** Human Resources. **World Wide Web address:** http://www.emjmetals.com. **Description:** A metal services center offering a diverse stock of metal products. Products include various forms of tubing and bars as well as steel and aluminum products. **Corporate headquarters location:** Brea CA. **Other U.S. locations:** Nationwide. **Operations at this facility include:** Manufacturing; Sales; Service. **Number of employees at this location:** 45.

ENSR INTERNATIONAL
2 Technology Park Drive, Westford MA 01886-3140. 978/589-3000. **Toll-free phone:** 800/722-2440. **Contact:** Human Resources. **World Wide Web address:** http://www.ensr.com. **Description:** An environmental consulting and engineering services firm. Services include pollution prevention, risk assessment, property transfer assessment, environmental permitting, environmental communication, remedial design, and engineering and construction management. ENSR has over 1,000 scientists, engineers, communications professionals, construction managers, regulatory specialists, and health and safety experts nationwide. **Positions advertised include:** Proposal Coordinator; Staff Specialist; Technician; Project Specialist; Engineer; Administrative Assistant; Training Specialist; Project Manager; Program Manager; Fisheries Biologist. **Corporate headquarters location:** This location. **Other U.S. locations:** Nationwide. **International locations:** Worldwide.

EARTHTECH
196 Baker Avenue, Concord MA 01742. 978/371-4000. **Contact:** Human Resources. **World Wide Web address:** http://www.earthtech.com. **Description:** An environmental engineering compliance firm. **Positions advertised include:** Administrative Assistant; Project Professional. **Corporate headquarters location:** Long Beach CA. **Other area locations:** Middleboro MA. **Other U.S. locations:** Nationwide. **International locations:** Worldwide.

EAST BOSTON NEIGHBORHOOD HEALTH CENTER
10 Gove Street, East Boston MA 02128. 617/569-5800. **Contact:** Human Resources. **Description:** A community health clinic supporting area urgent care, home care, and physician services.

EAST CAMBRIDGE NEIGHBORHOOD HEALTH CENTER
163 Gore Street, Cambridge MA 02141. 617/665-3000. **Contact:** Human Resources. **Description:** A community-based clinic offering general care on an outpatient basis. **Parent company:** Cambridge Hospital is a 170-bed, full-service hospital owned by the city of Cambridge and affiliated with Harvard and Tufts Medical Schools.

EASTERN BANK
195 Market Street, Lynn MA 01901. 781/598-7899. **Contact:** Human Resources. **World Wide Web address:** http://www.easternbank.com. **Description:** Operates a full-service savings bank. **Corporate headquarters location:** This location. **Other area locations:** Beverly MA; Boston MA; Braintree MA; Brockton MA; Burlington MA; Canton MA; Danvers MA; Hanover MA; Hingham MA; Lynnfield MA; Malden MA; Marblehead MA; Marshfield MA; Medford MA; Melrose MA; Newburyport MA; Norwell MA; Peabody MA; Quincy MA; Randolph MA; Reading MA; Salem MA; Saugus MA; South Boston MA; Stoneham MA; Stoughton MA; Swampscott MA; Wakefield MA; Weymouth MA. **Positions advertised include:** Data Entry Clerk; Quality Control Clerk; Teller; Human Resources Officer; Mortgage Production Specialist.

EASTMAN KODAK COMPANY
900 Chelmsford Street, Lowell MA 01851. 978/323-7600. **Contact:** Human Resources. **World Wide Web address:** http://www.kodak.com. **Description:** Develops color management software. **Subsidiaries include:** Eastman Software (Billerica MA).

EASTWOOD CARE CENTER
1007 East Street, Dedham MA 02026. 781/329-1520. **Contact:** Human Resources. **Description:** A 145-bed medical center focusing on long-term care and rehabilitation.

EAT WELL, INC.
19 North Street, Hingham MA 02043. 781/741-5100. **Contact:** Human Resources. **World Wide Web address:** http://www.eatwellinc.com. **Description:** Operates 13 dining and recreational facilities including Waterworks, a large outdoor bar overlooking the ocean with a volleyball court, pool tables, a TV/bar, a mixed drink bar, concert area and dance floor, and a sit-down food court.

EATON VANCE CORPORATION
255 State Street, Boston MA 02109. 617/482-8260. **Toll-free phone:** 800/225-6265. **Contact:** Mora O'Brien, Recruiting Manager. **World Wide Web address:** http://www.eatonvance.com. **Description:** An investment firm. **CEO/President:** James Hawkes.

ECKLAND CONSULTANTS
131 Tremont Street, Boston MA 02111. 617/423-1100. **Fax:** 617/423-1188. **Contact:** Human Resources. **World Wide Web address:** http://www.eckland.com. **Description:** An architecture and engineering consulting firm that specializes in property and environmental assessments for real estate agencies and banks. **Other U.S. locations:** Nationwide.

EDUCATION DEVELOPMENT CENTER, INC.
55 Chapel Street, Newton MA 02458. 617/969-7100. **Contact:** Human Resources. **World Wide Web address:** http://www.edc.org. **Description:** One of the world's leading educational nonprofit research and development firms specializing in early childhood development, K-12 education, health promotion, learning technologies, and institutional reform. Founded in 1958. **Company slogan:** Promoting human development through education. **Positions advertised include:** Office Assistant; Project Coordinator. **Corporate headquarters location:** This location. **Other U.S. locations:** Washington DC; New York NY; Newport RI. **International locations:** The Netherlands. **Listed on:** Privately held. **Annual sales/revenues:** $21 - $50 million. **Number of employees at this location:** 310. **Number of employees nationwide:** 400.

EDWARDS & ANGELL
101 Federal Street, Boston MA 02110. 617/439-4444. **Contact:** Human Resources. **World Wide Web address:** http://www.ealaw.com. **Description:** A law firm specializing in intellectual property law. **Positions advertised include:** Litigation Legal Secretary; support Staff Supervisor. **Corporate headquarters location:** This location. **Listed on:** Privately held. **Number of employees at this location:** 50.

EDWARDS & KELCEY
The Schrafft Center, 529 Main Street, Suite 203, Boston MA 02129. 617/242-9222. **Contact:** Human Resources. **E-mail address:** corphr@ekmail.com. **World Wide Web address:** http://www.ekcorp.com. **Description:** An engineering firm specializing in road/highway, traffic, and structural projects. **Positions advertised include:** Marketing Coordinator; Structural Engineer. **Corporate headquarters location:** Morristown NJ. **Other U.S. locations:** Nationwide. **International locations:** The Netherlands; Puerto Rico.

ELCOM INTERNATIONAL INC.
10 Oceana Way, Norwood MA 02062. 781/762-0202. **Contact:** Human Resources. **E-mail address:** hr@elcon.com. **World Wide Web address:** http://www.elcom.com. **Description:** Elcom International Inc. produces products for the electronic commerce software market. The company's software is designed to support the sales of computer products, as well as aid companies in the production of electronic catalogs and ordering systems. **Corporate headquarters location:** This location. **Other U.S. locations:** San Diego CA; Washington DC; Tampa FL; Chicago IL; New York NY. **International locations:** Brazil; England; India; South Africa. **Operations at this facility include:** This location resells computers.

EMERSON COLLEGE
120 Boylston Street, Boston MA 02116. 617/824-8500. **Contact:** Human Resources. **World Wide Web address:** http://www.emerson.edu. **E-mail address:** employment@emerson.edu. **Description:** A four-year communications college offering both undergraduate and graduate degrees to approximately 2,000 students. **Positions advertised include:** Associate Vice President; College Counsel; Assistant Director; Head Women's Soccer Coach; Social Worker; Education Technologist; Loading Dock Supervisor; Public Safety Officer; Journalism Technology Manager; Student Service Advisor; Multi-cultural Student Affairs Director. **Special programs:** Internships. **Corporate headquarters location:** This location. **Operations at this facility include:** Administration. **Number of employees at this location:** 350.

EMMANUEL COLLEGE
400 The Fenway, Boston MA 02115. 617/735-9991. **Fax:** 617/735-9877. **Contact:** Human Resources. **E-mail address:** jobs@emauneul.edu. **World Wide Web address:** http://www.emmanuel.edu. **Description:** A four-year undergraduate college. **Positions advertised include:** Site Coordinator; Director of the Annual Fund; Assistant Director of Corporate; Development Assistant; Web Designer; Graphic Designer; Assistant Professor.

THE ENTERPRISE
60 Main Street, P.O. Box 1450, Brockton MA 02303. 508/586-6200. **Contact:** Caroline Darosa, Personnel Director. **Description:** Publishes the *Enterprise,* a daily newspaper that is distributed throughout southeastern Massachusetts and has a daily circulation of over 60,000. **Parent company:** Newspaper Media LLC.

ENVIROGEN, INC.
480 Neponset Street, Canton MA 02021. 781/821-5560. **Contact:** Human Resources. **E-mail address:** employment@envirogen.com. **World Wide Web address:** http://www.envirogen.com. **Description:** Provides a variety of environmental services including remediation and engineering. **Corporate headquarters location:** Lawrenceville NJ. **Other U.S. locations:** San Diego CA; St. Charles IL; Lansing MI; Ashwaubenon WI; Onalaska WI; Mosinee WI; Pewaukee WI. **Listed on:** NASDAQ. **Stock exchange symbol:** ENVG.

ENVIRONMENTAL SCIENCE SERVICES, INC.
888 Worcester Street, Suite 240, Wellesley MA 02482. 781/431-0500. **Contact:** Human Resources. **World Wide Web address:** http://www.essgroup.com. **Description:** An environmental consulting and engineering firm offering a variety of services including soil sampling, water sampling, and hazardous materials services. **Other U.S. locations:** Providence RI. **Positions advertised include:** Environmental Engineer; Engineer; Geologist; Civil Engineer.

ENVIRONMENTAL STRATEGIES CORPORATION
1740 Massachusetts Avenue, Boxborough MA 01719. 978/635-9600. **Contact:** Human Resources. **E-mail address:** envtl-recruit@escva.com. **World Wide Web address:** http://www.envstratcorp.com. **Description:** An environmental engineering firm. **Positions advertised include:** Environmental Engineer; Geologist; Environmental Professional; Environmental Compliance Auditor; Industrial Hygienist Safety Specialist. **Corporate headquarters location:** Reston VA. **Other U.S. locations:** San Jose CA; Denver CO; Minneapolis MN; Somerset NJ; Albany NY; Cazenovia NY; Durham NC; Pittsburgh PA; Houston TX.

EPIX MEDICAL INC.
71 Rogers Street, Cambridge MA 02142. 617/250-6000. **Fax:** 617/250-6041. **Contact:** Human Resources. **E-mail address:** careers@epixmed.com. **World Wide Web address:** http://www.epixmed.com. **Description:** Engaged in the development of advanced imaging agents. The company's initial products in development are for magnetic resonance imaging. **Positions advertised include:** Biophysics Intern; Synthetic Organic Chemist; Director of Pharmacology. **Corporate headquarters location:** This location. **Operations at this facility include:** Administration; Research and Development. **Listed on:** NASDAQ. **Stock exchange symbol:** EPIX. **Number of employees at this location:** 30.

EPOXY TECHNOLOGY
14 Fortune Drive, Billerica MA 01821. 978/667-3805. **Fax:** 978/663-9782. **Contact:** Human Resources. **World Wide Web address:** http://www.epotek.com. **Description:** Develops conductive epoxies, adhesives, and coatings for a wide range of industrial uses. Industries served include electronics, optical, medical, and metals.

EPSILON
50 Cambridge Street, Burlington MA 01803. 781/273-0250. **Fax:** 781/685-0807. **Contact:** Human Resources. **E-mail address:** jobs@epsilon.com. **World Wide Web address:** http://www.epsilon.com. **Description:** Designs, implements, and supports database marketing programs in a variety of industries including financial services, retail, health care, technology, telecommunications, and nonprofit. Founded in 1970. **NOTE:** Entry-level positions and second and third shifts are offered. **Special programs:** Internships; Summer Jobs. **Office hours:** Monday - Friday, 8:30 a.m. - 5:30 p.m. **Corporate headquarters location:** This location. **Other U.S. locations:** Timonium MD; Earth City MO; Carrollton TX; Dallas TX; Salt Lake City UT; Arlington VA. **Operations at this facility include:** Administration; Divisional Headquarters; Research and Development; Sales; Service. **Listed on:** Privately held. **Annual sales/revenues:** More than $100 million. **Number of employees at this location:** 600. **Number of employees nationwide:** 700.

EQUISERVE
150 Royall Street, Canton MA, 02021. 781/575-2508. **Contact:** Human Resources. **World Wide Web address:** http://www.equiserve.com. **Description:** A stock trading transfer agency. **Positions advertised include:** Account Administrator; Accountant; Business Operations Specialist; Business Systems Analyst; Conversion Analyst; Mail Distribution Associate; Processing Associate; Unit Leader, Transfer Operation.

EQUITY OFFICE PROPERTIES
100 Summer Street, 2nd Floor, Boston MA 02110. 617/425-7500. **Contact:** Human Resources. **World Wide Web address:** http://www.equityoffice.com. **Description:** Operates as a self-administered and self-managed real estate investment trust (REIT). The company specializes in property acquisitions, management, leasing, design, construction, and development. In addition to its own locations, the company manages properties for several third-party property owners. **Corporate headquarters location:** Chicago IL. **Other U.S. locations:** Atlanta GA. **Operations at this facility include:** Administration. **Listed on:** New York Stock Exchange. **Stock exchange symbol:** EOP.

ERNST & YOUNG LLP
200 Clarendon Street, Boston MA 02116. 617/266-2000. **Contact:** Personnel Manager. **World Wide Web address:** http://www.ey.com. **Description:** A certified public accounting firm that also provides management consulting services. Services include data processing, financial modeling, financial feasibility studies, production planning and inventory management, management sciences, health care planning, human resources, cost accounting, and budgeting systems. **Other U.S. locations:** Nationwide. **International locations:** Worldwide. **Number of employees worldwide:** 77,000.

EROOM TECHNOLOGY, INC.
725 Concord Avenue, Cambridge MA 02138. 617/497-6300. **Contact:** Human Resources. **World Wide Web address:** http://www.eroom.com. **Description:** A leading Web-based project management application. **Corporate headquarters location:** This location.

ESSEX COUNTY NEWSPAPERS, INC.
SALEM EVENING NEWS
32 Dunham Road, Beverly MA 01915. 978/922-1234. **Fax:** 978/927-1020. **Contact:** Kathy Melanson, Director of Human Resources. **World Wide Web address:** http://www.ecnnews.com. **Description:** Publishes the *Salem Evening News, Gloucester Daily Times,* and the *Daily News* of Newburyport. **NOTE:** Second and third shifts are offered. **Special programs:** Internships. **Corporate headquarters location:** Campbell Hall NY. **Parent company:** Ottaway Newspapers, Inc. (a subsidiary of Dow Jones & Company.) **Operations at this facility include:** Administration; Manufacturing; Regional Headquarters; Sales; Service. **Listed on:** New York Stock Exchange. **Stock exchange symbol:** DJ. **Annual sales/revenues:** $11 - $20 million. **Number of employees at this location:** 350.

EVERGREEN FUNDS
200 Berkeley Street, Boston MA 02116. 617/338-3200. **Fax:** 617/210-3234. **Contact:** Human Resources. **World Wide Web address:** http://www.evergreenfunds.com. **Description:** A mutual fund and retirement management company. Founded in 1932. **Positions advertised include:** Financial Advisor.

EXPONENT, INC.
21 Strathmore Road, Natick MA 01760. 508/652-8500. **Contact:** Human Resources Department. **E-mail address:** hr@exponent.com. **World Wide Web address:** http://www.exponent.com. **Description:** A technical consulting firm dedicated to the investigation, analysis, and prevention of accidents and failures of an engineering or scientific nature. The company provides a multidisciplinary approach to analyze how failures occur. The company specializes in accident reconstruction, biomechanics, construction/structural engineering, aviation and marine investigations, environmental assessment, materials and product testing, warning and labeling issues, accident statistical data analysis, and risk prevention/mitigation. Founded in 1967. **Positions advertised include:** Engineer; Managing Scientist Engineer; Lab Technician; Managing Engineer. **NOTE:** All hiring is conducted through corporate headquarters. Please send resumes to: Exponent, Inc., Human Resources, 149 Commonwealth Drive, Menlo Park CA 94025. **Other U.S. locations:** Nationwide. **Parent company:** Exponent, Inc. **Listed on:** NASDAQ. **Stock exchange symbol:** EXPO.

EXTRUSION TECHNOLOGY, INC.
80 Trim Way, Randolph MA 02368. 781/963-7200. **Contact:** Human Resources. **E-mail address:** careers@extrutech.com. **World Wide Web address:** http://www.extrutech.com. **Description:** Manufactures fabricated aluminum extrusions including electronic enclosures and rack systems. **Positions advertised include:** Sales Program Manager; Materials Service Manager; Computer Numerical Control Operator; Lead Mechanical Assembler; Shipper Supervisor; Environmental & Supply Specialist; Customer Support Representative; Junior Accountant; Manager.

FEI COMPANY
One Corporation Way, Peabody MA 01960. 978/538-6700. **Fax:** 978/531-9648. **Contact:** Human Resources. **World Wide Web address:** http://www.feic.com. **Description:** Designs, develops, manufactures, and markets focused ion and electron beam technology for the semiconductor, thin film head, life science, and material science industries. **Positions advertised include:** Mask Repair Applications Engineer; Fib Systems Engineer. **Corporate headquarters location:** Hillsboro OR. **Other U.S. locations:** Sunnyvale CA. **International locations:** Czech Republic; The Netherlands. **Listed on:** NASDAQ. **Stock exchange symbol:** FEIC. **Number of employees worldwide:** 1,500.

FAIRLAWN NURSING HOME
370 West Street, Leominster MA 01453. 978/537-0771. **Fax:** 978/534-0824. **Contact:** Human Resources. **Description:** Offers long-term care services to the elderly and other adults who need 24-hour nursing and personal care. **Parent company:** HealthAlliance operates a number of other subsidiaries, which include Burbank Hospital, Coordinated Primary Care, Diversified Medical Equipment Services, Diversified Visiting Nurse Association, The Highlands, and Leominster Hospital.

FAIRMONT COPLEY PLAZA HOTEL
138 St. James Avenue, Boston MA 02116. 617/267-5300. **Fax:** 617/859-8836. **Recorded jobline:** 617/867-8500. **Contact:** Human Resources. **E-mail address:** fcphr@aol.com. **World Wide Web address:** http://www.fairmont.com. **Description:** A 376-room, four-star, luxury hotel. Founded in 1907. **Positions advertised include:** Staff Accountant; Banquet Manager; Fairmont Gold Manager; Front Office; Guest Service Manager; Housekeeping; Room Attendant; PT Turn Down Attendant; Refreshment Order Taker; Kitchen Cook. **NOTE:** Entry-level positions and second and third shifts are offered. **Office hours:** Monday - Friday, 8:00 a.m. - 6:00 p.m. **Corporate headquarters location:** San Francisco CA. **Other U.S. locations:** Nationwide. **Parent company:** Fairmont. **Operations at this facility include:** Administration; Sales; Service. **Listed on:** New York Stock Exchange. **Stock exchange symbol:** FHR. **CEO:** Robert Small. **Facilities Manager:** John Unwin. **Number of employees at this location:** 440.

FARBERWARE HOME PRODUCTS, INC.
175 McClellan Highway, P.O. Box 9114, East Boston MA 02128. 617/561-2200. **Contact:** Human Resources. **World Wide Web address:** http://www.farberware.com. **Description:** This location houses administrative offices. Overall, Farberware manufactures and sells silverware, flatware, crystal, and water filtration systems. **Corporate headquarters location:** This location.

FAULKNER HOSPITAL
1153 Centre Street, Boston MA 02130. 617/522-5800. **Recorded jobline:** 617/983-7426. **Contact:** Human Resources Department. **World Wide Web address:** http://www.faulknerhospital.org. **Description:** A hospital. **Positions advertised include:** Registration Office; Community Benefits Associate; Health Information Systems; Receptionist; Rehab Services; Switch Board Operator; Safety Security Shift Operator; Security Officer.

FAY, SPOFFORD & THORNDIKE, INC.
5 Burlington Woods, Burlington MA 01803. 781/221-1000. **Fax:** 781/221-1025. **Contact:** Human Resources. **E-mail:** hr@fstinc.com. **World Wide Web address:** http://www.fstinc.com. **Description:** Engaged in civil, electrical, environmental, and mechanical engineering. **Corporate headquarters location:** This location. **Other U.S. locations:** Cromwell CT; Boston MA; Bedford NH; West Caldwell NJ; Melville NY; New York NY; Whippany NY; Fort Washington PA. **Number of employees at this location:** 175.

FEDERATED DORCHESTER NEIGHBORHOOD HOUSES
450 Washington Street, Dorchester MA 02124. 617/282-5034. **Fax:** 617/265-6020. **Contact:** Brigette Henry, Human Resources Director. **E-mail address:** hrfdnh@thecia.net. **World Wide Web address:** http://www.fdnh.org. **Description:** A nonprofit, human service agency with eight locations. **NOTE:** Entry-level positions and part-time jobs are offered. **Positions advertised include:** Case Manager; Operations and Administration Coordinator; Community Outreach Coordinator; Teen Recreation Worker. **Special programs:** Internships; Summer Jobs. **Corporate headquarters location:** This location. **Number of employees at this location:** 450.

FENWAL SAFETY SYSTEMS
700 Nickerson Road, Marlborough MA 01752-4602. 508/481-5800. **Contact:** Human Resources. **World Wide Web address:** http://www.fenwalsafety.com. **Description:** Manufactures aircraft explosion protection equipment.

FIDELITY INVESTMENTS
82 Devonshire Street, Boston MA 02109. 617/563-7000. **Fax:** 617/476-4262. **Contact:** Human Resources. **World Wide Web address:** http://www.fidelity.com/employment. **Description:** One of the nation's leading investment counseling and mutual fund/discount brokerage firms. **Positions advertised include:** Quantitative Analyst; Report Developer; Business Analyst; Benefits Specialist; Team Manager; Fund Accounting Manager. **Corporate headquarters location:** This location. **Other U.S. locations:** Nationwide. **International locations:** Worldwide. **Operations at this facility include:** Administration; Regional Headquarters; Research and Development; Sales. **Listed on:** Privately held. **Number of employees at this location:** 9,000.

FIDELITY INVESTMENTS
300 Puritan Way, Mail Zone MM1H, Marlborough MA 01752. 508/787-7000. **Contact:** Human Resources. **World Wide Web address:** http://www.fidelity.com. **Description:** Fidelity Investments is one of the nation's leading investment counseling and mutual fund/discount brokerage firms. **Corporate headquarters location:** Boston MA. **Operations at this facility include:** This location is an investor center. **Number of employees at this location:** 3,500.

FIDELITY INVESTMENTS
300 Granite Street, Suite 102, Braintree MA 02184. **Toll-free phone:** 800/544-9797. **Contact:** Human Resources. **World Wide Web address:** http://www.fidelity.com. **Description:** Fidelity Investments is one of the nation's leading investment counseling and mutual fund/discount brokerage firms. **Positions advertised include:** Benefits Manager; Pension Manager. **Corporate headquarters location:** Boston MA. **Operations at this facility include:** This location is an investor center.

FIDELITY INVESTMENTS
155 Congress Street, Boston MA 02109. **Toll-free phone:** 800/544-9797. **Contact:** Human Resources. **World Wide Web address:** http://www.fidelity.com. **Description:** Fidelity Investments is one of the nation's leading investment counseling and mutual fund/discount brokerage firms. **Corporate headquarters location:** Boston MA. **Operations at this facility include:** This location is an investor center.

THE FIELD COMPANIES
P.O. Box 78, Watertown MA 02471-0078. 617/926-5550. **Toll-free phone:** 800/369-1593. **Physical address:** 385 Pleasant Street, Watertown MA 02472. **Fax:** 617/924-9011. **E-mail address:** info@fieldcompanies.com. **World Wide Web address:** http://www.fieldcompanies.com. **Contact:** Mr. J. McDonald, Human Resources Representative. **Description:** Provides direct mail services such as list procurement and post office delivery. **NOTE:** Entry-level positions are offered. **Corporate headquarters location:** This location. **Listed on:** Privately held. **Number of employees at this location:** 70.

FILENE'S
426 Washington Street, Boston MA 02108. 617/357-2100. **Contact:** Human Resources. **World Wide Web address:** http://www.filenes.com. **Description:** A fashion department store with locations in the New England and New York areas. **NOTE:** Visit http://www.mayco.com for employment information. **Special programs:** Internships. **Corporate headquarters location:** St. Louis MO. **Parent company:** May Department Stores Company. **Other locations:** Hanover MA; Braintree MA; Kingston MA; Taunton MA; Framingham MA; Manchester NH; Middletown NY. Additional locations in CT, ME, & VT. **Operations at this facility include:** Administration; Divisional Headquarters. **Listed on:** New York Stock Exchange. **Stock exchange symbol:** MAY.

FILENE'S BASEMENT CORPORATION
12 Gill Street, Woburn MA 01801. 617/348-7075. **Fax:** 617/348-7159. **Contact:** David Abelson, Personnel. **World Wide Web address:** http://www.filenesbasement.com. **Description:** Operates specialty stores offering assortments of fashionable, nationally recognized brands and private-label family apparel and accessories. **Corporate headquarters location:** This location. **Other U.S. locations:** CT; DC; IL; ME; MN; NH; NJ; NY; PA; RI; VA.

FIRST INVESTORS CORPORATION
305 Second Avenue, Waltham MA 02451. 781/890-9201. **Fax:** 781/890-8817. **Contact:** Human Resources. **World Wide Web address:** http://www.firstinvestors.com. **Description:** Offers investment programs, life insurance, retirement planning, and other tax-deferred programs. Founded in 1930. **NOTE:** Entry-level workers begin as Registered Representative/Management Trainees after successfully completing the National Association of Securities Dealers Licensing Course and passing examinations administered by First Investors Corporation. **Corporate headquarters location:** New York NY. **Other U.S. locations:** Nationwide. **Operations at this facility include:** Regional Headquarters.

FIRST WINTHROP CORPORATION
P.O. Box 9507, Boston MA 02114. 617/234-3000. **Contact:** Human Resources. **Description:** A real estate agency specializing in commercial properties. Founded in 1978. **Corporate headquarters location:** This location. **Listed on:** Privately held. **Number of employees at this location:** 30. **Number of employees nationwide:** 110.

THE FIRST YEARS
One Kiddie Drive, Avon MA 02322-1171. 508/588-1220. **Contact:** Human Resources. **World Wide Web address:** http://www.thefirstyears.com. **Description:** A leading manufacturer and marketer of products for infants and toddlers. The First Years supplies its products to toy stores, mass merchandising chains, drug stores, grocery chains, and individual retailers worldwide. **Positions advertised include:** Assistant Controller; Associate Business Unit Manager; New Product Manager; Product Development Manager; Project Manager; Insight Manager. **Listed on:** NASDAQ. **Stock exchange symbol:** KIDD.

FISH & RICHARDSON, P.C.
225 Franklin Street, Boston MA 02110-2804. 617/542-5070. **Fax:** 617/542-8906. **Contact:** Betsy Butler, Office Manager. **E-mail address:** work@fr.com. **World Wide Web address:** http://www.fr.com. **Description:** A law firm with various areas of practice including patents, copyrights, and trademarks. **Other U.S. locations:** Redwood City CA; San Diego CA; Wilmington DE; Washington DC; Minneapolis MN; New York NY; Dallas TX.

FISHER COLLEGE
118 Beacon Street, Boston MA 02116. 617/536-4647. **Contact:** Human Resources. **World Wide Web address:** http://www.fisher.edu. **Description:** A private junior college. **Positions advertised include:** Administrative Assistant; Associate Registrar; Dean of Student Affairs; Campus Safety Officer; Director for Annual Giving. **Other in-state locations:** Fall River; New Bedford; Attleboro Falls.

FITCHBURG STATE COLLEGE
160 Pearl Street, Fitchburg MA 01420. 978/345-2151. **Contact:** Human Resources. **E-mail address:** resumes@fsc.edu. **World Wide Web address:** http://www.fsc.edu. **Description:** A state college offering bachelor's and master's degrees. **Positions advertised include:** Assistant Professor, Special Education; Assistant/Associate Professor, Criminal Justice; Assistant Professor, Industrial Technology.

FLIR SYSTEMS
16 Esquire Road, North Billerica MA 01862. 978/901-8000. **Fax:** 978/901-8367. **Contact:** Human Resources. **World Wide Web address:** http://www.flir.com. **Description:** A manufacturer of infrared systems. **Positions advertised include:** Business Development Representative; Customer Service Representative; Administration Assistant; Systems Engineer; Buyer Planner; Commodity Manager. **Other U.S. locations:** Portland OR. **International locations:** Sweden. **Listed on:** NASDAQ. **Stock exchange symbol:** FLIR.

FOLEY, HOAG & ELIOT, L.L.P.
165 Seaport Boulevard, Boston MA 02210. 617/832-1000. **Contact:** Dina Wreede, Director of Legal Recruiting. **E-mail address:** hiring@foleyhoag,com. **World Wide Web address:** http://www.fhe.com. **Description:** A law firm covering a broad range of practice areas including litigation, labor, business, international, and intellectual property. **Positions advertised include:** Legal Secretary. **Other U.S. locations:** Washington DC.

FOREST CITY DEVELOPMENT
38 Sidney Street, Cambridge MA 02139. 617/225-0310. **Contact:** Human Resources. **World Wide Web address:** http://www.fceboston.com. **Description:** A real estate developer.

FORRESTER RESEARCH
400 Technology Square, Cambridge MA 02139. 617/497-7090. **Contact:** Human Resources. **World Wide Web address:** http://www.forrester.com. **Description:** An independent research firm that provides technology consulting services to business. **Positions advertised include:** Corporate Communication Manager; Editing Manager; Web Developer; Client Care Specialist; Financial Services Analyst; Research Advisor; Healthcare Analyst; Sales Associate; Healthcare Associate; Applications Analyst; Business Development Director; Account Executive; Research Associate. **Corporate headquarters location:** This location. **Other U.S. locations:** San Francisco CA. **International locations:** England; Germany; The Netherlands. **Listed on:** NASDAQ. **Stock exchange symbol:** FORR.

THE FORUM CORPORATION
One Exchange Place, 3rd Floor, Boston MA 02109. 617/523-7300. **Toll-free phone:** 800/367-8611. **Fax:** 617/973-2005. **Contact:** Human Resources. **E-mail address:** careers@forum.com. **World Wide Web address:** http://www.forum.com. **Description:** An international training and consulting firm. Founded in 1971. **Special programs:** Internships. **Office hours:** Monday - Friday, 9:00 a.m. - 5:30 p.m. **Corporate headquarters location:** This location. **Other U.S. locations:** San Francisco CA; Wilmington DE; Chicago IL; Landover MD; New York NY. **International locations:** Australia; Canada; England; Hong Kong; Korea; New Zealand; Singapore. **CEO:** Pippa Wicks. **Number of employees at this location:** 115. **Number of employees nationwide:** 260.

FOSTER WHEELER ENVIRONMENTAL CORPORATION
133 Federal Street, 6th Floor, Boston MA 02110. 617/451-1201. **Contact:** Human Resources. **World Wide Web address:** http://www.fwec.com. **Description:** An environmental engineering firm.

FOUR STAR PRINTING COMPANY, INC.
P.O. Box 301, Lynn MA 01903-0301. 781/599-8772. **Physical address:** 82 Sanderson Avenue, Lynn MA 01902-1937. **Fax:** 781/581-3930. **Contact:** Doug Stewart, President. **Description:** A commercial printer. **Number of employees at this location:** 15.

THE FOXBORO COMPANY
38 Neponset Avenue, Foxboro MA 02035. 508/543-8750. **Contact:** Human Resources. **World Wide Web address:** http://www.foxboro.com. **Description:** Designs, builds, and markets instruments and systems for process management and control. Products include pneumatic and electronic instruments, and analog and digital control systems. The company also offers a range of engineering services, education and training, and post-sales technical support. **Parent company:** Invensys Systems, Inc.

FRAMATOME AWP
400 Donald Lynch Boulevard, Marlborough MA 01752. 508/229-2100. **Contact:** Human Resources. **World Wide Web address:** http://www.framatome-awp.com. **Description:** A nuclear engineering company. **Parent company:** Areva.

FRAMINGHAM STATE COLLEGE
100 State Street, Framingham MA 01701-9101. 508/626-4530. **Fax:** 508/626-4592. **Contact:** Human Resources. **World Wide Web address:** http://www.framingham.edu. **Description:** Founded as the first public teacher's college in the country, Framingham State has grown to include 28 majors in undergraduate, graduate, and continuing education programs with an emphasis on business administration, and elementary and early childhood education. Framingham State's nationally recognized faculty is involved in many community and professional organizations. Learning resources include an advising center, the MetroWest Economic Research Center, modern computer facilities, and a planetarium. Founded in 1839. **Positions advertised include:** Director of Health Services; Distance Education Program Clerical; Office of Residential Life Maintainer; Office of Residential Life Trade Worker; Steam Firemen; Skilled Laborer; HVAC Mechanic; Communications Dispatcher.

FRANCISCAN CHILDREN'S HOSPITAL AND REHABILITATION CENTER
30 Warren Street, Brighton MA 02135. 617/254-3800. **Contact:** Human Resources. **E-mail address:** aeponte@fchrc.org. **World Wide Web address:** http://www.fchrc.org. **Description:** A hospital and rehabilitation center for children. The hospital also operates the Kennedy Day School for children with special needs. **Positions advertised include:** Certified Nurses Assistant; Care Manager; Home Health Registered Nurse; Nurse Practitioner; Registered Nurse; Family Therapist; Mental Health Specialist; Psychologist; Impatient Clinical Supervisor; Respiratory Therapist; Teaching Assistant; Fiscal Administrative Coordinator; Registration Manager; Admissions Clerk; Dental Assistant; Pediatric Dietician; Van Driver.

FRANKLIN ENVIRONMENTAL SERVICES, INC.
P.O. Box 617, Wrentham MA 02093. 508/384-6151. **Physical address:** 185 Industrial Road, Wrentham MA 02093. **Contact:** Human Resources. **Description:** Engaged in hazardous waste remediation and transportation services. Founded in 1977.

FREEDOM CAPITAL
One Beacon Street, 5th Floor, Boston MA 02108. 617/725-2300. **Contact:** Human Resources. **Description:** A security brokerage firm.

FRESENIUS MEDICAL CARE NORTH AMERICA
2 Ledgemont Center, 95 Hayden Avenue, Lexington MA 02420. 781/402-9000. **Toll-free phone:** 800/662-1237. **Fax:** 781/402-9005. **Contact:** Human Resources. **E-mail address:** resumes@fmc-na.com. **World Wide Web address:** http://www.fmcna.com. **Description:** One of the nation's leading manufacturers and distributors of renal dialysis products and services. The company also provides dialysis treatment, diagnostic testing, blood testing, and home health programs. Fresenius Medical Care's dialysis services include outpatient hemodialysis, peritoneal dialysis, and support for home dialysis patients. **Positions advertised include:** Financial Analyst; Staff Auditor; Secretary; Switchboard Operator; Clinical Quality Manager; Documentation Coordinator; Real Estate Specialist; Treasury Analyst; Employment Coordinator; Human Resources Secretary; Research Assistant; Benefits Analyst; Legal Secretary; Regulatory Affairs Specialist; Clinical Applications Programmer; Manager NT Services; Manager or Desktop PC; Network Security; Specialist; Program Analyst. **Special programs:** Co-ops. **Corporate headquarters location:** This location. **Parent company:** Fresenius Medical Care AG (Germany) **Listed on:** New York Stock Exchange. **Stock exchange symbol:** FMS. **Number of employees at this location:** 600. **Number of employees nationwide:** 21,000. **Number of employees worldwide:** 24,000.

FRESH POND ANIMAL HOSPITAL
15 Flanders Road, Belmont MA 02478. 617/484-1555. **Fax:** 617/484-2509. **Contact:** Human Resources. **World Wide Web address:** http://www.fpah.com. **Description:** An animal hospital offering surgical, dental, and medical services.

FRIENDLY'S ICE CREAM CORPORATION
1855 Boston Road, Wilbraham MA 01095. 413/543-2400. **Contact:** Human Resources. **World Wide Web address:** http://www.friendlys.com. **Description:** Operates approximately 535 Friendly's restaurants serving hamburgers, sandwiches, salads, and ice cream. **Corporate headquarters location:** This location. **Listed on:** American Stock Exchange. **Stock exchange symbol:** FRN. **Number of employees nationwide:** 35,000.

DR. SOLOMON CARTER FULLER MENTAL HEALTH CENTER
85 East Newton Street, Boston MA 02118. 617/626-8700. **Contact:** Human Resources. **Description:** A psychiatric hospital.

FUNK SOFTWARE, INC.
222 Third Street, Suite 2163, Cambridge MA 02142. 617/497-6339. **Fax:** 617/547-1031. **Contact:** Human Resources. **E-mail address:** hr@funk.com. **World Wide Web address:** http://www.funk.com. **Description:** Develops remote access and LAN-based communications software. Products include Steel-Belted Radius for NetWare which provides centralized authentication for dial-in users; WanderLink remote access software for NetWare; Proxy remote control software, which allows remote operation of PCs; and AppMeter II, a software usage metering product. Founded in 1982. **Positions advertised include:** SBR Engineer; Quality Assurance Project Lead; Software Engineer; Radius Territory Manager; Renewal Sales Representative. **Corporate headquarters location:** This location. **Listed on:** Privately held.

GCC PRINTERS, INC.
209 Burlington Road, Bedford MA 01730. 781/275-5800. **Contact:** Human Resources. **World Wide Web address:** http://www.gcctech.com. **Description:** Manufactures printers for use with personal computers. GCC also does research in the areas of computer graphics, VLSI design, consumer robotics, and digital sound generation. **NOTE:** Applicants must show proven ability in one or more of the following areas: real-time programming for microprocessors; applications software for personal computers; or computer graphics. **Positions advertised include:** Direct Sales Representative; Education Account Manager; Administrative Assistant; PCB Repair & Test Technician; Hardware Engineer; Software Engineer; Networking Software Engineer. **Corporate headquarters location:** This location. **Operations at this facility include:** Administration; Manufacturing; Research and Development; Sales; Service. **Number of employees at this location:** 150.

GEI CONSULTANTS, INC.
1021 Main Street, Winchester MA 01890. 781/721-4000. **Contact:** Human Resources. **World Wide Web address:** http://www.geiconsultants.com. **Description:** An environmental and geo-technical engineering firm. **Positions advertised include:** Accounting Assistant; Geotechnical Engineer; Civil Engineer; Drafter; Environmental Engineer; Geologist; Human Resources Generalist; Laboratory & Field Technician; Project Manager; Staff Engineer; Technician. **Corporate headquarters location:** This location. **Other U.S. locations:** Carlsbad CA; Oakland CA; Colchester CT; Englewood CO; Concord NH; St. Louis MO.

GPC BIOTECH
610 Lincoln Street, Waltham MA 02451. 781/890-9007. **Fax:** 781/890-9005. **Contact:** Human Resources. **E-mail address:** hr.waltham@gpc-biotech.com. **World Wide Web address:** http://www.gpc-biotech.com. **Description:** A transatlantic genomics drug discovery company that specializes in proprietary genomics, proteomics, and drug discovery technologies designed to improve the process of drug development. Founded in 1992. **Positions advertised include:** Scientist; Chemist. **Office hours:** Monday - Friday, 8:30 a.m. - 5:00 p.m. **Listed on:** Privately held. **Number of employees at this location:** 75.

GSI LUMONICS INC.
39 Manning Road, Billerica MA 01821. 978/439-5511. **Contact:** Human Resources. **World Wide Web address:** http://www.gsilumonics.com. **Description:** Produces laser-based, automated manufacturing systems, instrumentation, and components for a wide range of industries. **Positions advertised include:** Internal Audit Director; Principal Development Engineer; Human Resources Representative; Principal Supply Quality Engineer; Customer Support Manager; Financial Reporting Accountant; supply Chain Specialist; Machinist. **Corporate headquarters location:** Kanata, Ontario. **Other U.S. locations:** Wilmington MA. **Listed on:** NASDAQ. **Stock exchange symbol:** GSLI.

GSI LUMONICS INC.
60 Fordham Road, Wilmington MA 01887. 978/661-4300. **Fax:** 978/998-8798. **Contact:** Human Resources. **World Wide Web address:** http://www.gsilumonics.com. **Description:** Produces laser-based, automated manufacturing systems, instrumentation, and components for a wide range of industries. **Positions advertised include:** Manufacturing Technician; Engineering Technician; Principal Hardware Engineer; Technical Support Engineer; Principal Software Engineer; Buyer; Planner; Manufacturing Engineer. **Corporate headquarters location:** Kanata, Ontario. **Other U.S. locations:** Billerica MA. **Listed on:** NASDAQ. **Stock exchange symbol:** GSLI.

GZA GEOENVIRONMENTAL TECHNOLOGIES
One Edgewater Drive, Norwood MA 02062. 781/278-3700. **Contact:** Human Resources. **World Wide Web address:** http://www.gza.com. **Description:** Provides consulting, remediation, and geo-technical services, principally in the Northeast and the Midwest. The company also maintains its own drilling, laboratory, and instrumentation facilities to support environmental and geo-technical activities. Environmental services range from initial assessment and evaluation of contaminated sites to design, construction, and operation of remediation systems. **Corporate headquarters location:** This location. **Other U.S. locations:** CT; ME; MA; MI; NH; NJ; NY; PA; RI; VT; WI. **Subsidiaries include:** Environmental Real Estate Investors, Inc. (EREI); GZA Drilling, Inc. provides drilling services; GZA GeoEnvironmental, Inc. provides environmental consulting and geo-technical services; Soil and Rock Instrumentation Division (SRI). **Number of employees nationwide:** 450.

GALAXY INTERNET SERVICES
188 Needham Street, Suite 110R, Newton MA 02164. 617/558-0909. **Contact:** Human Resources. **World Wide Web address:** http://www.gis.net. **Description:** Offers services including Web page design, technical support, and business connectivity. **Positions advertised include:** Director of Sales; Broadband Sales; Dialup Sales Representatives; Technical Support Specialist

GALE ASSOCIATES, INC.
163 Libbey Parkway, P.O. Box 890189, Weymouth, MA 02189. 781/335-6465. **Toll-free phone:** 800/659-4753. **Fax:** 781/335-6467. **Contact:** Kathleen A. Forrand, Human Resources Manager. **E-mail address:** kaf@gainc.com. **World Wide Web address:** http://www.gainc.com. **Description:** A national architecture and engineering firm that specializes in the improvement of existing buildings, sites, and infrastructures for both public and private clients. This location also hires seasonally. Founded in 1964. **NOTE:** Entry-level positions and part-time jobs are offered. **Positions advertised include:** Corporate Inspector; Civil Engineer; Project Manager; Structural Engineer; Engineer; Architect. **Special programs:** Training; Co-ops; Summer Jobs. **Office hours:** Monday - Friday, 8:00 a.m. - 5:00 p.m. **Corporate headquarters location:** This location. **Other U.S. locations:** Mountain View CA; Oakland CA; Winter Park FL; Baltimore MD; Bedford NH. **Operations at this facility include:** Divisional Headquarters. **Listed on:** Privately held. **President:** Harold E. Flight. **Accounting Manager:** Bruce P. White. **Annual sales/revenues:** $5 - $10 million. **Number of employees at this location:** 60. **Number of employees nationwide:** 100.

GAMBRO HEALTHCARE
660 Harrison Avenue, Boston MA 02118. 617/859-7000. **Contact:** Human Resources. **World Wide Web address:** http://www.usa-gambro.com. **Description:** Provides renal dialysis services to patients suffering from chronic kidney failure, primarily in its freestanding outpatient dialysis centers. The company also provides dialysis in patients' homes or at hospitals on a contractual basis; urine and blood testing at its centers; and independent physicians at its clinical labs. **Positions advertised include:** Center Director; Clinical Nurse Manager; Registered Nurse; Patient Care Technician. **Number of employees nationwide:** 1,240.

GANNETT FLEMING
150 Wood Road, Braintree MA 02184. 781/380-7750. **Contact:** Donald B. Nicholas, Human Resources. **E-mail address:** dnicholas@gfnet.com. **World Wide Web address:** http://www.gannettfleming.com. **Description:** An engineering firm offering a wide variety of services including structural, geo-technical, environmental, hazardous waste, bridge design, and tunnel design. **Positions advertised include:** Environmental Engineer; Resident Engineer. **Other U.S. locations:** Nationwide.

GANNETT OFFSET BOSTON
565 University Avenue, Norwood MA 02062. 781/762-0277. **Contact:** Human Resources. **World Wide Web address:** http://www.gannett.com. **Description:** A full-service newspaper printer. **Corporate headquarters locations:** Springfield VA. **Parent company:** Gannett Company, Inc. is a nationwide news and information company that publishes 92 newspapers including *USA Today*, and is one of the largest outdoor advertising companies in North America. Gannett is also involved in marketing, television news and program production, and research satellite information systems. **Listed on:** New York Stock Exchange. **Stock exchange symbol:** GCI.

GARBER TRAVEL
660 Beacon Street, Boston MA 02215. 617/353-2100. **Contact:** Paul Woods, Human Resources. **E-mail address:** pwoods@garbertravel.com. **World Wide Web address:** http://www.garber.com. **Description:** A travel agency. **Other U.S. locations:** Nationwide.

GARELICK FARMS
626 Lynnway, Lynn MA 01905. 781/599-1300. **Fax:** 781/595-9862. **Contact:** Human Resources. **Description:** A manufacturer and distributor of dairy and related food items. **Other area locations:** Franklin MA. **Number of employees nationwide:** 15,000.

GEERLINGS & WADE
960 Turnpike Street, Canton MA 02021. 781/821-4152. **Toll-free phone:** 800/782-WINE. **Contact:** Human Resources Department. **World Wide Web address:** http://www.geerwade.com. **Description:** Provides personal wine-buying services to consumers through direct marketing. The company purchases imported and domestic wines and delivers them directly to the customer's home or office. **Corporate headquarters location:** This location.

GENERAL DYNAMICS
77 A Street, Needham MA 02494. 781/449-2000. **Contact:** Human Resources Department. **World Wide Web address:** http://www.generaldynamics.com. **Description:** Provides secure communication systems and information solutions to both commercial and military markets. The Communications Systems division also develops broadband data communications, digital network management systems, and PCS base stations. **Corporate headquarters location:** Taunton MA.

GENERAL DYNAMICS
400 John Quincy Adams Road, Taunton MA 02780. 508/880-4000. **Contact:** Human Resources. **World Wide Web address:** http://www.generaldynamics.com. **Description:** Provides secure communication systems and information solutions to both commercial and military markets. The Communications Systems division also develops broadband data communications, digital network management systems, and PCS base stations. **Corporate headquarters location:** This location.

GENERAL ELECTRIC COMPANY
1000 Western Avenue, Building 174AD, Mail Drop 14515, Lynn MA 01910. 781/594-0100. **Fax:** 781/594-1917. **Contact:** Mary Welsh, Personnel Technician. **World Wide Web address:** http://www.ge.com. **Description:** General Electric operates in the following areas: aircraft engines including jet engines, replacement parts, and repair services for commercial, military, executive, and commuter aircraft; appliances; broadcasting (NBC); industrial through lighting products, electrical distribution and control equipment, transportation systems products, electric motors and related products, a broad range of electrical and electronic industrial automation products, and a network of electrical supply houses; materials including plastics, ABS resins, silicones, superabrasives, and laminates; power systems including products for the generation, transmission, and distribution of electricity; technical products and systems including medical systems and equipment, as well as a full range of computer-based information and data interchange services for both internal use and external commercial and industrial customers; and capital services including consumer services; financing; and specialty insurance. **Corporate headquarters location:** Fairfield CT. **Operations at this facility include:** This facility manufactures aircraft engines and engine parts. **Listed on:** New York Stock Exchange. **Stock exchange symbol:** GE. **Number of employees worldwide:** 230,000.

GE FANUC AUTOMATION
325 Foxboro Boulevard, Foxboro MA 02035. 508/698-3322. **Fax:** 508/698-8391. **Contact:** Human Resources. **World Wide Web address:** http://www.gefanucautomation.com/. **Description:** Develops industrial automation solutions software. **Parent company:** Emerson Process Management (St. Louis MO).

GENOME THERAPEUTICS CORPORATION
100 Beaver Street, Waltham MA 02453-8443. 781/398-2300. **Fax:** 781/893-9535. **Contact:** Personnel. **World Wide Web address:** http://www.genomecorp.com. **Description:** Engaged in the research, analysis, and commercial development of genetic information. Founded in 1961. **NOTE:** Entry-level positions and second and third shifts are offered. **Positions advertised include:** Accounts Payable Administrator; Vice President Corporate Capability Registration Compliance; Vice President Drug Safety; Clinical Trials Manager; Product Manager; Associate Director. **Office hours:** Monday - Friday 8:30 a.m. - 5:00 p.m. **Corporate headquarters location:** This location. **Operations at this facility include:** Administration; Research and Development. **Listed on:** NASDAQ. **Stock exchange symbol:** GENE. **President/CEO:** Steven Rauscher. **Annual sales/revenues:** $21 - $50 million. **Number of employees at this location:** 200.

GENVEC INC.
Building 96, 13th Street, Charlestown Navy Yard, Charlestown MA 02129. 617/242-9100. **Fax:** 617/242-0070. **Contact:** Human Resources. **E-mail address:** resume@genvec.com. **World Wide Web address:** http://www.genvec.com. **Description:** A biotechnology company that specializes in cell transplantation technology designed to treat diseases characterized by cell dysfunction or cell death. Founded in 1989. **Positions advertised include:** Research Scientist; Research Assistant; Research Assistant Biochemistry. **Special programs:** Co-ops. **Office hours:** Monday - Friday, 8:00 a.m. - 5:30 p.m.

GENZYME BIOSURGERY
64 Sidney Street, Cambridge MA 02139-4136. 617/494-8484. **Contact:** Human Resources. **World Wide Web address:** http://www.genzyme.com. **Description:** Develops tissues grown from human cells for medical use. **Corporate headquarters location:** Cambridge MA. **Other U.S. locations:** Nationwide. **International locations:** Worldwide. **Parent company:** Genzyme Corporation (Cambridge MA). **Listed on:** NASDAQ. **Stock exchange symbol:** GENZ. **Annual sales/revenues:** $51 - $100 million. **Number of employees nationwide:** 3,140. **Number of employees worldwide:** 3,700.

GENZYME CORPORATION
One Kendall Square, Building 1400, Cambridge MA 02139-1562. 617/252-7500. **Contact:** Human Resources. **World Wide Web address:** http://www.genzyme.com. **Description:** An international, diversified health care products company focused on developing and delivering practical solutions to specific medical needs. The company's activities and products are organized into six primary business areas: Therapeutics, Surgical Products, Genetics, Pharmaceuticals, Diagnostic Services, and Tissue Repair. Founded in 1981. **Special programs:** Internships; Co-ops; Summer Jobs. **Office hours:** Monday - Friday, 8:30 a.m. - 5:00 p.m. **Corporate headquarters location:** This location. **Other U.S. locations:** Nationwide. **International locations:** Worldwide. **Listed on:** NASDAQ. **Stock exchange symbol:** GENZ. **Annual sales/revenues:** $51 - $100 million. **Number of employees nationwide:** 3,140. **Number of employees worldwide:** 3,700.

GENZYME CORPORATION
One Mountain Road, P.O. Box 9322, Framingham MA 01701-9322. 508/872-8400. **Contact:** Human Resources. **World Wide Web address:** http://www.genzyme.com. **Description:** Genzyme Corporation is an international, diversified health care products company dedicated to developing and delivering practical solutions to specific medical needs. **Corporate headquarters location:** Cambridge MA. **Other U.S. locations:** Nationwide. **International locations:** Worldwide. **Operations at this facility include:** This location is engaged in the application of transgenic technology to the development and production of recombinant proteins for therapeutic and diagnostic uses. . **Listed on:** NASDAQ. **Stock exchange symbol:** GENZ. **Annual sales/revenues:** $51 - $100 million. **Number of employees nationwide:** 3,140. **Number of employees worldwide:** 3,700.

GEOLABS, INC.
45 Johnson Lane, Braintree MA 02184. 781/848-7844. **Toll/free phone:** 800/298-7060. **Fax:** 781/848-7811. **Contact:** Human Resources. **E-mail address:** geolabs@attbi.net. **World Wide Web address:** http://www.geolabs.com. **Description:** Provides analytical environmental testing of soil, ground water, wastewater, and air. Founded in 1995. **NOTE:** Entry-level positions are offered. **Company slogan:** Quick service without sacrificing. **Special programs:** Internships; Training; Co-ops; Summer Jobs. **Office hours:** Monday - Friday, 8:00 a.m. - 5:00 p.m. **Corporate headquarters location:** This location. **Listed on:** Privately held. **President/Owner:** David J. Kahler. **Annual sales/revenues:** Less than $5 million. **Number of employees at this location:** 20.

GEOLOGIC SERVICES CORPORATION
15 Robert Bonazzoli Avenue, Hudson MA 01749. 978/568-8740. **Contact:** Human Resources. **Description:** Provides underground storage tank evaluation services.

THE GILLETTE COMPANY
Prudential Tower Building, 40th Floor, Boston MA 02199. 617/421-7000. **Contact:** Personnel Director. **World Wide Web address:** http://www.gillette.com. **Description:** Manufactures consumer products for the personal care market. Products include razors and blades including Trac II, Atra, Sensor, Mach 3, MicroTrac, Daisy, and Platinum Plus; toiletries, cosmetics, and deodorants such as Right Guard, and Dry Idea; hair care products including White Rain and Silkience; skin care and shaving cream products; dental accessories including toothbrushes, toothpaste, rinses, and related items; and Duracell alkaline batteries. **NOTE:** Please check the Website for available positions before applying. **Corporate headquarters location:** This location. **Subsidiaries include:** Braun AG (Germany) manufactures household appliances. **Parent company:** Procter & Gamble. **Listed on:** New York Stock Exchange. **Stock exchange symbol:** G.

GLOBAL PETROLEUM CORPORATION
P.O. Box 9161, Waltham MA 02454-9161. 781/894-8800. **Physical address:** 800 South Street, Suite 200, Waltham MA 02454. **Contact:** Human Resources. **Description:** Wholesale retailer of refined petroleum products and marketer of natural gas. **Corporate headquarters location:** This location.

GLOBALWARE SOLUTIONS
200 Ward Hill Avenue, Haverhill MA 01835. 978/469-7500. **Fax:** 979/469-7555. **Contact:** Personnel. **E-mail address:** jobs@globalwaresolutions.com. **World Wide Web address:** http://www.globalwaresolutions.com. **Description:** Develops e-business solutions for the delivery and management of digital content products. **Positions advertised include:** Sales Executive; Web Applications Developer.

GODDARD VALVE
P.O. Box 765, Worcester MA 01613-0765. 508/852-2435. **Physical address:** 705 Plantation Street, Worcester MA 01605. 508/852-2435. **Contact:** Human Resources. **World Wide Web address:** http://www.goddardvalve.com. **Description:** Designs and manufactures cryogenic gate, globe, and check valves and control devices required for the handling of liquefied natural gas, liquid oxygen, and other liquefied gases. **Corporate headquarters location:** This location. **International locations:** Australia; England. **Parent company:** Goddard Industries, Inc.

GOODRICH CORPORATION
5 Omni Road, Chelmsford MA 01824. 978/250-2325. **Contact:** Human Resources. **World Wide Web address:** http://www.goodrich.com. **Description:** A research and development firm involved in the technologies of optics, electro-optics, and imaging systems. These technologies are applied to the fields of surveillance and reconnaissance, mapping, and remote sensing. **Positions advertised include:** Software Engineer; Field Service Engineer; Facilities Operations Specialist; Manager Facility Maintenance; Electrical Engineer; Mechanical Engineer; Systems Engineer; Hardware Configuration Management Specialist; Quality Engineer. **Corporate headquarters location:** Charlotte NC. **Listed on:** New York Stock Exchange. **Stock exchange symbol:** GR.

GOODWIN PROCTER, LLP
53 State Street, Boston MA 02109. 617/570-1000. **Contact:** Human Resources. **World Wide Web address:** http://www.gph.com. **Description:** A general practice law firm. **Corporate headquarters location:** This location. **Other U.S. locations:** Washington DC; Roseland NJ; New York NY.

GORDON COLLEGE
255 Grapevine Road, Wenham MA 01984. 978/927-2300. **Contact:** Human Resources. **World Wide Web address:** http://www.gordon.edu. **Description:** A four-year liberal arts college offering Bachelor of Science, Bachelor of Arts, Bachelor of Music, and Master of Education degrees. **Positions advertised include:** Head Women's Soccer Coach; Director of Communications; Public Safety Officer.

JAMES GORMAN INSURANCE
One Exeter Plaza, 3rd Floor, Boston MA 02116. 617/266-4100. **Contact:** Jim Gorman, President. **Description:** Specializes in insurance and risk management services.

GORTON'S, INC.
128 Rogers Street, Gloucester MA 01930-6019. 978/283-3000. **Contact:** Personnel. **E-mail:** careers@gortons.com. **World Wide Web address:** http://www.gortons.com. **Description:** Processes frozen and canned seafood products. Founded in 1849. **Positions advertised include:** Project Engineer; Financial Management Associate. **Special programs:** Internships. **Corporate headquarters location:** This location. **Operations at this facility include:** Administration; Manufacturing; Research and Development; Sales. **Number of employees at this location:** 1,000.

GOULSTON & STORRS, P.C.
400 Atlantic Avenue, Boston MA 02110-3333. 617/482-1776. **Contact:** Nancy Needle, Recruiting Director. **World Wide Web address:** http://www.goulstorrs.com. **Description:** A law firm with a variety of practice areas including corporate law and litigation. **Other U.S. locations:** Washington DC.

GRACE CONSTRUCTION PRODUCTS
62 Whittemore Avenue, Cambridge MA 02140. 617/876-1400. **Contact:** Human Resources. **E-mail address:** careers@grace.com. **World Wide Web address:** http://www.grace.com. **Description:** As part of W.R. Grace & Company, Grace Construction Products manufactures concrete additives, waterproofing products and systems, and fire protection products. The company has more than 125 plants and sales offices worldwide. **NOTE:** Entry-level positions are offered. **Special programs:** Internships. **Corporate headquarters location:** Columbia MD. **Subsidiaries include:** Darex Container Products (Belgium; Lexington MA); Davison Chemicals (Canada; Columbia MD); Performance Chemicals (Cambridge MA). **Listed on:** New York Stock Exchange. **Stock exchange symbol:** GRA. **CEO:** Paul Norris.

GRADIENT CORPORATION
238 Main Street, Cambridge MA 02142. 617/395-5000. **Contact:** Laura Gordon, Human Resources. **E-mail address:** lgordon@gradientcorp.com. **World Wide Web address:** http://www.gradcorp.com. **Description:** An environmental consulting firm. **Positions advertised include:** Technologist; Environmental Engineer. **Other U.S. locations:** Mercer Island WA. **Annual sales/revenues:** $5 - $10 million. **Number of employees at this location:** 50.

GRANT THORNTON LLP
98 North Washington Street, Boston MA 02114-1913. 617/723-7900. **Contact:** Human Resources. **World Wide Web address:** http://www.grantthornton.com. **Description:** An international certified public accounting organization offering consulting and accounting services as well as strategic and tactical planning assistance to a diversified client base. Founded in 1924. **Positions advertised include:** Auditor; Experienced Tax Manager; Tax Associate; State & Local Tax Manager. **Corporate headquarters location:** Chicago IL. **Other U.S. locations:** Nationwide. **International locations:** Worldwide.

GRAY RAMBUSCH, INC.
One Washington Mall, 10th Floor, Boston MA 02108-2603. 617/367-0100. **Contact:** Human Resources. **Description:** An advertising firm.

GREATER BOSTON CHAMBER OF COMMERCE
75 State Street, 2nd Floor, Boston MA 02109. 617/227-4500. **Contact:** Human Resources. **World Wide Web address:** http://www.gbcc.org. **Description:** Attracts and promotes businesses in the greater Boston area.

GREATER MEDIA, INC.
55 Morrissey Boulevard, Boston MA 02125. 617/822-9600. **Contact:** Human Resources. **World Wide Web address:** http://www.greaterbostonradio.com. **Description:** Operates several Boston-area radio broadcasting stations with a variety of formats. Stations include WROR, WBOS, WKLB, WMJX, and WTKK.

GROSSMAN'S INC.
90 Hawes Way, Stoughton MA 02072. 781/297-3300. **Contact:** Human Resources. **Description:** Sells lumber, building materials, doors and windows, hardware, paint, plumbing, and electrical supplies. Grossman's Inc. operates five retail warehouse stores and has over 70 locations in nine states. **Subsidiaries include:** Builder's Mart and Contractors' Warehouse have large, drive-thru lumber yards and focus on the needs of contractors, remodelers, tradespeople, and other building professionals; Mr. 2nd's Bargain Outlet offers close-outs, seconds, and overstocks in a wide range of building materials; The Project-Pros provides materials and design and building services for a variety of home improvement projects including fencing, decks, windows and doors, siding and roofing, electric and alarms, painting, kitchens and baths, plumbing, landscaping, masonry, and additions.

GROUNDWATER & ENVIRONMENTAL SERVICES, INC.
364 Littleton Road, Suite 4, Westford MA 01886. 978/392-0090. **Contact:** Human Resources. **World Wide Web address:** http://www.gesonline.com. **Description:** An environmental engineering firm specializing in groundwater and remediation. **Corporate headquarters location:** Wall NJ. **Other U.S. locations:** CT; IL; MD; MI; NJ; NY; OH; PA; TN; VA; WV. **Listed on:** Privately held.

GULF OF MAINE RESEARCH CENTER
204 Lafayette Street, Salem MA 01970. 978/745-6618. **Contact:** Human Resources. **Description:** An environmental consulting firm specializing in a variety of areas including wetlands projects and hazardous waste remediation.

H&R BLOCK
77 Main Street, Andover MA 01810. 978/686-1371. **Contact:** Human Resources. **World Wide Web address:** http://www.hrblock.com. **Description:** Engaged in consumer tax preparation. H&R Block operates more than 9,500 offices nationwide, and prepares more than 10 million tax returns each year. The company has offices in over 750 Sears stores in both the United States and Canada. Many offices operate as franchises, and some operate on a seasonal basis. H&R Block is also engaged in a number of other tax-related activities, including group tax programs, premium tax service, tax training schools, and real estate tax awareness seminars. **Corporate headquarters location:** Kansas City MO. **Other U.S. locations:** Nationwide. **Listed on:** New York Stock Exchange. **Stock exchange symbol:** HRB. **President/CEO:** Mark Ernst.

H&R BLOCK
157 Centre Street, Malden MA 02148. 781/322-7453. **Contact:** Human Resources. **World Wide Web address:** http://www.hrblock.com. **Description:** Engaged in consumer tax preparation. H&R Block operates more than 9,500 offices nationwide, and prepares more than 10 million tax returns each year. The company has offices in over 750 Sears stores in both the United States and Canada. Many offices operate as franchises, and some operate on a seasonal basis. H&R Block is also engaged in a number of other tax-related activities, including group tax programs, premium tax service, tax training schools, and real estate tax awareness seminars. **Corporate headquarters location:** Kansas City MO. **Other U.S. locations:** Nationwide. **Listed on:** New York Stock Exchange. **Stock exchange symbol:** HRB. **President/CEO:** Mark Ernst.

H&R BLOCK
1515 Dorchester Avenue, Fields Corner, Dorchester MA 02122. 617/825-4514. **Contact:** Human Resources. **World Wide Web address:** http://www.hrblock.com. **Description:** Engaged in consumer tax preparation. H&R Block operates more than 9,500 offices nationwide, and prepares more than 10 million tax returns each year. The company has offices in over 750 Sears stores in both the United States and Canada. Many offices operate as franchises, and some operate on a seasonal basis. H&R Block is also engaged in a number of other tax-related activities, including group tax programs, premium tax service, tax training schools, and real estate tax awareness seminars. **Corporate headquarters location:** Kansas City MO. **Other U.S. locations:** Nationwide. **Listed on:** New York Stock Exchange. **Stock exchange symbol:** HRB. **President/CEO:** Mark Ernst.

HCPRO
100 Hoods Lane, P.O. Box 1168, Marblehead MA 01945. 781/639-1872. **Fax:** 781/639-2982. **Contact:** Human Resources. **E-mail address:** hcprocustomerservice@hcpro.com. **World Wide Web address:** http://www.hcpro.com. **Description:** A publisher of health care newsletters and related materials.

HDR ENGINEERING, INC.
7 Winthrop Square, Boston MA 02111. 617/357-7700. **Contact:** Human Resources. **E-mail address:** careers@hdrinc.com. **World Wide Web address:** http://www.hdrinc.com. **Description:** HDR Engineering, Inc. provides water, transportation, waste, and energy services including studies, design, and implementation for complex projects. **Positions advertised include:** Civil Section Manager; Civil Roadway Engineer; Rail Engineer; Civil Engineer. **Corporate headquarters location:** Omaha NE. **Operations at this facility include:** This location specializes in a variety of transportation-related engineering projects including bridges, roads, and tunnels. **Parent company:** HDR, Inc.

HNTB CORPORATION
75 State Street, Boston MA 02109. 617/542-6900. **Contact:** Human Resources. **World Wide Web address:** http://www.hntb.com. **Description:** An architectural engineering firm specializing in the design of highways and bridges. **Corporate headquarters location:** Kansas City MO. **Other U.S. locations:** Nationwide.

HABITAT FOR HUMANITY BOSTON
455 Arborway, Jamaica Plain MA 02130. 617/524-8891. **Contact:** Human Resources. **World Wide Web address:** http://www.habitatboston.org. **Description:** A nonprofit organization that builds homes for the homeless. **Corporate headquarters location:** Americus GA. **Other U.S. locations:** Nationwide.

HAEMONETICS CORPORATION
400 Wood Road, Braintree MA 02184. 781/848-7100. **Toll-free phone:** 800/225-5242. **Fax:** 781/848-9959. **Contact:** Human Resources. **World Wide Web address:** http://www.haemonetics.com. **Description:** Designs, manufactures, markets, and services blood processing systems and related sterile, disposable items used for the processing of human blood for transfusion and other therapeutic medical purposes. The company sells its products to blood banks, hospitals, and commercial plasma centers. **Positions advertised include:** Contract Agent; Supply Chain Integration Manager; Project Manager; Planning Analyst. **Corporate headquarters location:** This location. **Other U.S. locations:** Leetsdale PA; Union SC. **Operations at this facility include:** Administration; Divisional Headquarters; Manufacturing; Research and Development; Sales; Service. **Listed on:** New York Stock Exchange. **Stock exchange symbol:** HAE. **Number of employees at this location:** 700. **Number of employees nationwide:** 1,000.

HALEY & ALDRICH INC.
465 Medford Street, Suite 2200, Charlestown MA 02129. 617/886-7300. **Contact:** Human Resources. **E-mail address:** info@haleyaldrich.com. **World Wide Web address:** http://www.haleyaldrich.com. **Description:** An environmental and geotechnical engineering firm. **Positions advertised include:** Geotechnical Engineer; Tunnel Engineer; Structural Engineer; Environmental Scientist; Environmental Engineer; Chemical Engineer; Environmental Health & Safety Specialist; Industrial Hygienist; Geologist; Information Technology Specialist; Scientific Visualization Specialist.

HAMMERSMITH HOUSE NURSING CARE CENTER
73 Chestnut Street, Saugus MA 01906. 781/233-8123. **Fax:** 781/231-2918. **Contact:** Human Resources. **Description:** A 103-bed nursing home and rehabilitation center. Hammersmith House also operates a 47-bed special care unit for Alzheimer's patients. **Positions advertised include:** Certified Nurses Aide; Licensed Practical Nurse.

J.L. HAMMETT COMPANY
P.O. Box 859057, Braintree MA 02185. 781/848-1000. **Toll-free phone:** 800/955-2200. **Physical address:** One Hammett Place, Braintree MA 02184. **Fax:** 781/848-3869. **Contact:** Human Resources. **World Wide Web address:** http://www.hammett.com. **Description:** Distributes educational supplies and equipment through catalog and retail stores. **Corporate headquarters location:** This location. **Operations at this facility include:** Administration; Regional Headquarters; Sales; Service.

HANSCOM AIR FORCE BASE
20 Schilling Circle, Building 1305, Hanscom MA 01731-2135. 781/377-2280. **Contact:** Personnel. **World Wide Web address:** http://www.hanscom.af.mil. **Description:** An Air Force base. This location also offers seasonal hiring. **NOTE:** Entry-level positions and part-time jobs are offered. **Special programs:** Training; Co-ops; Summer Jobs. **Number of employees at this location:** 2,200.

HARD ROCK CAFE
131 Clarendon Street, Boston MA 02116. 617/353-1400. **Contact:** Manager. **World Wide Web address:** http://www.hardrock.com. **Description:** A casual dining restaurant decorated with rock and roll memorabilia. Hard Rock Cafe serves American cuisine and operates a gift shop. **Other U.S. locations:** Nationwide. **International locations:** Worldwide.

HARODITE INDUSTRIES, INC.
66 South Street, Taunton MA 02780. 508/824-6961. **Contact:** Human Resources. **E-mail address:** jjardin@harodite.com. **World Wide Web address:** http://www.harodite.com. **Description:** One of the oldest textile manufacturing companies in New England. Products include a complete range of woven and nonwoven fabrics. Founded in 1908. **Corporate headquarters location:** This location. **Other U.S. locations:** Taylors SC. **Operations at this facility include:** Administration; Manufacturing. **Listed on:** Privately held. **Annual sales/revenues:** $5 - $10 million. **Number of employees at this location:** 130.

HARTE-HANKS DATA TECHNOLOGIES
25 Linnell Circle, Billerica MA 01821. 978/436-8981. **Fax:** 978/663-3576. **Contact:** David Lobley, Human Resources Representative. **World Wide Web address:** http://www.harte-hanks.com. **Description:** A leading provider of database marketing services and software for database marketing uses. Harte-Hanks Data Technologies supports corporations in banking, insurance, retail, and technology. Founded in 1968. **Company slogan:** Directly ahead. **Positions advertised include:** Account Executive; Business Developer; Business Development Director; Database Marketing Practice Leader; Database Marketing RFP manager; Director of Information & Network Security; Education Consultant; Field Marketing Manager; Product Marketing Manager; Quality Assurance Engineer; Technical Writer; Web Marketing Manager. **Special programs:** Internships; Training. **Corporate headquarters location:** San Antonio TX. **Other U.S. locations:** Nationwide. **International locations:** Asia; Australia; Canada; South America; United Kingdom. **Parent company:** Harte-Hanks Communications. **Listed on:** New York Stock Exchange. **Stock exchange symbol:** HHS. **Annual sales/revenues:** More than $100 million. **Number of employees at this location:** 550. **Number of employees nationwide:** 6,000. **Number of employees worldwide:** 7,000.

HARVARD BUSINESS SCHOOL PUBLISHING CORPORATION
60 Harvard Way, Boston MA 02163. 617/783-7400. **Physical address:** 300 North Beacon Street, Watertown MA 02472. **Fax:** 617/783-7485. **Contact:** Human Resources. **World Wide Web address:** http://www.hbsp.harvard.edu. **Description:** Publishes *Harvard Business Review, Harvard Management Update,* and many books on business management. The company also produces videos and interactive CD-ROMs. **NOTE:** Entry-level positions are offered. **Number of employees at this location:** 190.

THE HARVARD COOPERATIVE SOCIETY
1400 Massachusetts Avenue, Cambridge MA 02138. 617/499-2000. **Contact:** Human Resources. **World Wide Web address:** http://www.thecoop.com. **Description:** A member-owned, collegiate department store selling a broad range of merchandise from clothing, books, and music, to housewares, electronics, and prints. **Corporate headquarters location:** This location.

HARVARD PILGRIM HEALTHCARE
1600 Crowne Colony Park, Quincy MA 02169. 617-745-1001. **Contact:** Human Resources. **World Wide Web address:** http://www.harvardpilgrim.org. **Description:** The oldest non-profit healthcare available in New England. **Positions advertised**

include: Nurse Care Manager; Account Services Coordinator; Clinical Trainer; Account Services Manager. **NOTE:** Apply online.

HARVARD UNIVERSITY
11 Holyoke Street, Harvard Square, Cambridge MA 02138. 617/495-2771. **Contact:** Personnel. **World Wide Web address:** http://www.hr.harvard.edu/employment. **Description:** A private, four-year, Ivy League university. Harvard University collaborates with nearby Radcliffe College, allowing graduate and undergraduate students to take certain classes at Radcliffe and vice versa. **Positions advertised include:** Special Assistant to the President; Facility Manager; Payroll Accountant; Staff Assistant. **NOTE:** Harvard University posts listings for all support and professional job openings. Please check these listings in the employment office or on Harvard University's website and respond directly to the department that is hiring. **Office hours:** Monday, Tuesday, Wednesday, Friday, 11:00 a.m. - 4:00 p.m.; Thursday, 8:30 a.m. - 6:00 p.m.

HARVARD UNIVERSITY PRESS
79 Garden Street, Cambridge MA 02138. 617/495-2600. **Contact:** Human Resources. **World Wide Web address:** http://www.hup.harvard.edu. **Description:** A publisher of scholarly books and journals. **Corporate headquarters location:** This location.

HARVEY INDUSTRIES, INC.
400 Main Street, Waltham MA 02451-9180. 781/899-3500. **Toll-free phone:** 800/9HARVEY. **Contact:** Human Resources. **E-mail address:** jobs@harveyind.com. **World Wide Web address:** http://www.harveyind.com. **Description:** Manufactures windows and doors. The company is also a wholesale distributor of building materials. **Positions advertised include:** Administrative Assistant; New Business Sales Representative.

HASBRO GAMES
443 Shaker Road, East Longmeadow MA 01028. 413/525-6411. **Contact:** Human Resources. **World Wide Web address:** http://www.hasbro.com. **Description:** Develops, manufactures, and sells a line of games, toys, and educational materials including board and card games; puzzles; skill and action games; electronic games and toys; and activity items. **Other area locations:** Fall River MA; Ludlow MA. **Parent company:** Hasbro, Inc. **Listed on:** New York Stock Exchange. **Stock exchange symbol:** HAS.

HAYES ENGINEERING
603 Salem Street, Wakefield MA 01880. 781/246-2800. **Fax:** 781/246-7596. **Contact:** Human Resources. **E-mail address:** jogren@hayeseng.com. **World Wide Web address:** http://www.hayeseng.com. **Description:** A civil and environmental engineering firm that also provides land surveying services.

HEAD START PROJECT
62 First Street, Pittsfield MA 01201. 413/499-0137. **Contact:** Human Resources. **E-mail address:** lmcallops@nhsa.org. **World Wide Web address:** http://www.nhsa.org. **Description:** A state- and federally-funded program for low-income families with young children.

HEALTH AND RETIREMENT PROPERTIES TRUST
400 Centre Street, Newton MA 02458. 617/332-3990. **Fax:** 617/332-2261. **E-mail address:** ifno@hrpreit.com. **World Wide Web address:** http://www.hrpreit.com. **Contact:** Joyce Silver, Human Resources. **Description:** A real estate investment trust that invests primarily in retirement communities, assisted living centers, nursing homes, and other long-term care facilities. **Corporate headquarters location:** This location.

HEALTHALLIANCE/BURBANK HOSPITAL
275 Nichols Road, Fitchburg MA 01420. 978/343-5000. **Contact:** Human Resources. **World Wide Web address:** http://www.healthalliance.com. **Description:** An acute care medical facility. The hospital provides inpatient and outpatient services including medical, surgical, and subspecialty care, as well as same-day surgery and 24-hour emergency coverage. The hospital also offers a psychiatric center, speech and hearing center, and regional trauma center. A 25-bed inpatient rehabilitation center affiliated with the Spaulding Rehabilitation Hospital in Boston is also at this location. The center offers a rehabilitation program for patients who have suffered from strokes and patients with arthritis, amputations, neurological disorders, orthopedic conditions, spinal cord injuries, brain injuries, and complex medical conditions. **Corporate headquarters location:** Leominster MA. **Subsidiaries include:** Coordinated Primary Care; Diversified Medical Equipment Services; Diversified Visiting Nurse Association; Fairlawn Nursing Home; The Highlands; and Leominster Hospital.

HEALTHALLIANCE/LEOMINSTER HOSPITAL
60 Hospital Road, Leominster MA 01453. 978/466-2000. **Fax:** 978/466-2189. **Contact:** Human Resources. **World Wide Web address:** http://www.healthalliance.com. **Description:** An acute care medical facility. The hospital provides inpatient and outpatient services including medical, surgical, and subspecialty care, as well as same-day surgery and 24-hour emergency coverage. The hospital also offers the Center for Cancer Care and Blood Disorders, diagnostic services including mobile MRIs, cardiac catheterization labs, and a diagnostic lab for the diagnostic study of sleep disorders. **NOTE:** Entry-level positions are offered. **Positions advertised include:** Certified Nurses Aide; Certified Occupational Therapy Assistant; Clinical Lab Technician; Computer Operator; Computer Programmer; EEG Technologist; EKG Technician; Home Health Aide; Licensed Practical Nurse; Medical Records Technician; Network/Systems Administrator; Nuclear Medicine Technologist; Occupational Therapist; Physical Therapist; Physical Therapy Assistant; Radiological Technologist; Recreational Therapist; Registered Nurse; Respiratory Therapist; Social Worker; Speech-Language Pathologist. **Operations at this facility include:** Administration; Service. **Annual sales/revenues:** More than $100 million. **Number of employees at this location:** 750. **Number of employees nationwide:** 2,000.

HEALTHALLIANCE/THE HIGHLANDS
335 Nichols Road, Fitchburg MA 01420. 978/343-4411. **Contact:** Human Resources. **World Wide Web address:** http://www.healthalliance.com. **Description:** Offers subacute and long-term care in a residential setting for adults. One unit is devoted to people with Alzheimer's disease. The subacute care unit helps people complete the transition from a hospital or a rehabilitation facility to their home following surgery, accident, or illness. A long-term care unit provides nursing and personal care for residents who need full-time care. HealthAlliance/The Highlands also provides an adult daycare health center. **NOTE:** Entry-level positions are offered. **Positions advertised include:** Accountant/Auditor; Dietician/Nutritionist; Health Services Manager; Licensed Practical Nurse; Occupational Therapist; Physical Therapist; Registered Nurse; Social Worker. **Special programs:** Training. **Corporate headquarters location:** Leominster MA. **Subsidiaries include:** Burbank Hospital; Coordinated Primary Care; Diversified Medical Equipment Services; Diversified Visiting Nurse Association; Fairlawn Nursing Home; Leominster Hospital. **Operations at this facility include:** Service. **Annual sales/revenues:** $5 - $10 million.

HEALTHSOUTH BRAINTREE HOSPITAL
P.O. Box 859020, Braintree MA 02185-9020. 781/848-5353. **Physical address:** 250 Pond Street, Braintree MA 02184. **Contact:** Human Resources. **World Wide Web address:** http://www.healthsouth.com. **Description:** A rehabilitation hospital. Founded in 1984. **Other U.S. locations:** Nationwide. **Listed on:** New York Stock Exchange. **Stock exchange symbol:** HRC.

HEBREW COLLEGE
160 Herrick Street, Newton Centre MA 02459. 617/559-8600. **Toll-free phone:** 800/866-4814. **Fax:** 617/559-8601. **Contact:** Human Resources Department. **E-mail address:** hr@hebrewcollege.edu. **World Wide Web address:** http://www.hebrewcollege.edu. **Description:** A college offering courses in the Hebrew language and literature, Rabbinics, and Jewish music and culture. The college offers courses in cooperation with Boston University, Northeastern University, Simmons College, Boston College, Brandeis University, and University of Massachusetts Boston. **Positions advertised include:** Vice President of Institutional Achievement; Database Depart Writer.

HEILIND ELECTRONICS INC.
58 Jonspin Road, Wilmington MA 01887. 978/657-4870. **Fax:** 978/657-7905. **Contact:** Human Resources. **World Wide Web address:** http://www.heilind.com. **Description:** Distributes internal electric components for computer systems and other computer-related products. **Positions advertised include:** Northeast Regional Product Manager. **Other U.S. locations:** Wallingford CT; Orlando FL; Norcross GA; Arlington Heights IL; Eden Prairie MN; Hudson NH; Mountain Lakes NJ; Binghamton NY; Raleigh NC; Highland Heights OH; King of Prussia PA.

HELIX TECHNOLOGY CORPORATION
Mansfield Corporate Center, 9 Hampshire Street, Mansfield MA 02048. 508/337-5500. **Fax:** 508/337-5169. **Contact:** Human Resources. **E-mail address:** careers@helixtechnology.com. **World Wide Web address:** http://www.ctihelix.com. **Description:** Manufactures vacuum technology products for the semiconductor industry. **Positions advertised include:** Global Service Supply Chain Manager; Services Marketing Director; Corporate Accountant; Director of Product Marketing; Quality Systems Manager; Buyer Planner. **Special programs:** Internships; Training; Co-ops. **Corporate headquarters location:** This location. **Other U.S. locations:** Tempe AZ; Santa Clara CA; Longmont CO; Austin TX. **International locations:** France; Germany; Japan; Scotland; Taiwan. **Subsidiaries include:** GPC. **Listed on:** NASDAQ. **Stock exchange symbol:** HELX. **Annual sales/revenues:** More than $100 million. **Number of employees at this location:** 300. **Number of employees worldwide:** 500.

HEWLETT PACKARD
200 Forest Street, Marlborough MA 01752. 978/493-5111. **Contact:** Human Resources. **World Wide Web address:** http://www.hp.com. **Description:** Designs, manufactures, sells, and services computers and associated peripheral equipment, and related software and supplies. Applications and programs include scientific research, computation, communications, education, data analysis, industrial control, time sharing, commercial data processing, graphic arts, word processing, health care, instrumentation, engineering, and simulation. **Positions advertised include:** Sales Representative; Direct Deployment Specialist; Pre Sales Consultant; Director Client Manager; Lead Solutions Architect; Inbound Operation Manager; Web Manager; End User Sales Representative; Director Client Manager; Business Systems Analyst; Information Technology Technical Lead; Logistics Individual Contributor; Market Researcher; HP Services Tax Manager. **Other U.S. locations:** Nationwide.

HIGH VOLTAGE ENGINEERING CORP.
401 Edgewater Place, Suite 680, Wakefield MA 01880. 781/224-1001. **Fax:** 781/224-1011. **Contact:** Human Resources. **World Wide Web address:** http://www.asirobicon.com. **Description:** Owns and operates a diversified group of technology-based, middle market, industrial manufacturing businesses.

HILL, HOLLIDAY
200 Clarendon Street, Boston MA 02116. 617/437-1600. **Contact:** Director of Human Resources. **E-mail address:** careers@hhcc.com. **World Wide Web address:** http://www.hhcc.com. **Description:** An advertising agency. **Other U.S. locations:** New York NY; San Francisco CA.

HITACHI AMERICA, LTD.
200 Lowder Brook Drive, Suite 2200, Westwood MA 02090. 781/461-8300. **Toll-free phone:** 800/441-4832. **Fax:** 781/461-8664. **Contact:** Human Resources. **World Wide Web address:** http://www.hitachidisplays.com. **Description:** This location is a sales office and imports and distributes computer monitors. **NOTE:** Entry-level positions are offered. **Annual sales/revenues:** $51 - $100 million. **Number of employees at this location:** 30. **Number of employees nationwide:** 155.

HITACHI COMPUTER PRODUCTS
1601 Trapelo Road, 3rd Floor, Waltham MA 02451. 781/890-0444. **Toll-free phone:** 800/745-4056. **Fax:** 781/890-4998. **Contact:** Human Resources. **E-mail address:** cssc@hitachisoftware.com. **World Wide Web address:** http://www.hi.com. **Description:** Develops electronic commerce software. **International locations:** England; Japan.

BERNARD HODES ADVERTISING
215 First Street, Cambridge MA 02142. 617/576-2131. **Contact:** Human Resources. **World Wide Web address:** http://www.hodes.com. **Description:** An advertising agency specializing in recruitment and employee communications. **Corporate headquarters location:** New York NY. **Other U.S. locations:** Nationwide. **International locations:** Worldwide. **Parent company:** Omnicom.

HOLIDAY INN
55 Ariadne Road, Dedham MA 02026. 781/329-1000. **Contact:** Human Resources. **World Wide Web address:** http://www.holiday-inn.com. **Description:** One location of the hotel chain. **Other U.S. locations:** Nationwide.

HOLIDAY INN LOGAN AIRPORT
225 McClellan Highway, East Boston MA 02128. 617/569-5250. **Contact:** Human Resources. **Description:** Operates a hotel, restaurant, and entertainment facility, primarily for the business traveler.

HOLLAND & KNIGHT
10 St. James Avenue, Boston MA 02116. 617/523-2700. **Fax:** 617/523-6850. **Contact:** Hiring Partner. **World Wide Web address:** http://www.hklaw.com. **Description:** A general practice law firm. **Other U.S. locations:** Nationwide. **International locations:** Worldwide.

HOLLINGSWORTH & VOSE COMPANY
112 Washington Street, East Walpole MA 02032. 508/668-0295. **Fax:** 508/668-3057. **Contact:** Human Resources. **E-mail address:** info@hovo.com. **World Wide Web address:** http://www.hollingsworth-vose.com. **Description:** Manufactures high-tech specialty filtration papers including nonwovens, battery separators, and engine filtration products. Founded in 1843. **NOTE:** Entry-level positions are offered. **Special programs:** Co-ops. **Corporate headquarters location:** This location. **Other area locations:** West Groton MA. **Other U.S. locations:** Concord CA; Hawkinsville GA; Hillsdale IL; Easton NY; Greenwich NY; Charlotte NY; Brentwood TN; Floyd VA. **International locations:** Belgium; Brazil; England; Germany; India; Italy; Japan; Korea; Mexico. **Operations at this facility include:** Administration; Manufacturing; Research and Development; Sales; Service. **Listed on:** Privately held. **Annual sales/revenues:** More than $100 million. **Number of employees at this location:** 200. **Number of employees nationwide:** 750. **Number of employees worldwide:** 900.

HOLOGIC INC.
35 Crosby Drive, Bedford MA 01730. 781/999-7300. **Fax:** 781/275-7090. **Contact:** Human Resources. **E-mail address:** hr@hologic.com. **World Wide Web address:** http://www.hologic.com. **Description:** Manufactures quantitative digital radiography X-ray bone densitometers that are used for the precise measurement of bone density to assist in the diagnosis and monitoring of metabolic bone diseases. **Positions advertised include:** Application Support Specialist; Regulatory Affairs Manager. **Corporate headquarters location:** This location. **Other area location:** Littleton MA. **Other U.S. locations:** Danbury CT; Newark DE. **International locations:** Belgium; France. **Listed on:** NASDAQ. **Stock exchange symbol:** HOLX.

COLLEGE OF THE HOLY CROSS
One College Street, Worcester MA 01610. 508/793-3756. **Fax:** 508/793-3575. **Contact:** Director of Personnel. **E-mail address:** resumes@holycross.edu. **World Wide Web address:** http://www.holycross.edu. **Description:** A private, four-year college offering bachelor's and master's degree programs. **Positions advertised include:** Dining Room Manager; Assistant Director; Community Development Coordinator; Applications Administrator; Vice President Administrative & Finance. **Special programs:** Internships. **Operations at this facility include:** Administration; Sales; Service. **Number of employees at this location:** 800.

HOLYOKE HOSPITAL, INC.
575 Beech Street, Holyoke MA 01040. 413/534-2547. **Fax:** 413/534-2635. **Recorded jobline:** 413/534-2639. **Contact:** Anne Barrett, Human Resources Administrator. **World Wide Web address:** http://www.holyokehealth.com. **Description:** A 225-bed, acute care, community hospital that serves an aggregate population of 145,000 and admits nearly 7,000 patients annually. **Positions advertised include:** Audiologists; Head Research Processor; Medical Transcriber; Nursing Division; Radiological Technology; Speech Pathologist. **Number of employees at this location:** 1,000.

HOME HEALTH AND CHILDCARE SERVICES
P.O. Box 640, Brockton MA 02303-0640. 508/588-6070. **Fax:** 508/587-3560. **Physical address:** 15 Jonathan Drive, Brockton MA 02301. **Contact:** Human Resources. **E-mail address:** ccrr@hhcc.org. **World Wide Web address:** http://www.hhcc.org. **Description:** A private, nonprofit family care services agency providing in-home health care for the elderly and childcare services.

HONEYWELL CONSUMER PRODUCTS GROUP
250 Turnpike Road, Southborough MA 01772. 508/490-7000. **Contact:** Human Resources. **World Wide Web address:** http://www.honeywell.com. **Description:** Honeywell is engaged in the research, development, manufacture, and sale of advanced technology products and services in the fields of chemicals, electronics, automation, and controls. The company's major businesses are home and building automation and control, performance polymers and chemicals, industrial automation and control, space and aviation systems, and defense and marine systems. **Corporate headquarters location:** Morristown NJ. **Operations at this facility include:** This location develops, manufactures, and markets a broad range of consumer household products including fans, heaters, humidifiers, vaporizers, and air cleaners. **Listed on:** New York Stock Exchange. **Stock exchange symbol:** HON.

HONEYWELL SENSING AND CONTROL
100 Discovery Way, Acton MA 01720. 978/264-9550. **Contact:** Human Resources. **World Wide Web address:** http://content.honeywell.com/sensing/. **Description:** Honeywell is engaged in the research, development, manufacture, and sale of advanced technology products and services in the fields of chemicals, electronics, automation, and controls. The company's major businesses are home and building automation and control, performance polymers and chemicals, industrial automation and control, space and aviation systems, and defense and marine systems. **Corporate headquarters location:** Morristown NJ. **Operations at this facility include:** This location manufactures transducers and safety equipment for presses. **Listed on:** New York Stock Exchange. **Stock exchange symbol:** HON.

H.P. HOOD INC.
90 Everett Avenue, Chelsea MA 02150. 617/887-3000. **Contact:** Employment Manager. **World Wide Web address:** http://www.hphood.com. **Description:** One of New England's largest food products firms, engaged in the processing and distribution of dairy products. **Positions advertised include:** Assistant Marketing Manager; Claims Manager; Retail Area Manager; Sales Manager. **Corporate headquarters location:** This location. **Operations at this facility include:** Administration; Manufacturing; Research and Development; Service. **Other U.S. locations:** Suffield CT; Portland ME; Agawam MA; Oneida NY; Vernon NY; Barre VT; Winchester VA.

HORIZON GROUP
7232 Garden Street, Needham MA 02492. 781/444-4141. **Contact:** Human Resources. **Description:** Acquires and operates long-term care facilities throughout the United States; provides health care services such as nursing care, rehabilitation, and other therapies; provides institutional pharmacy services; provides specialty care to Alzheimer's patients; and offers subacute care. Horizon Group operates approximately 280 facilities in 25 states.

HOUGHTON MIFFLIN COMPANY
222 Berkeley Street, Boston MA 02116. 617/351-5180. **Fax:** 617/351-1106. **Contact:** Human Resources. **World Wide Web address:** http://www.hmco.com. **Description:** A publisher of school textbooks; fiction, nonfiction, and reference works; educational software; and related multimedia products. **NOTE:** Entry-level positions are offered. **Positions advertised include:** Administrative Coordinator; Editor; Editorial Project Manager; Associate Editor Dictionaries; Image Producer; Designer; Editorial Project Manager; Lead Desktop Analyst; Project Manager; Helpdesk Supervisor; Sales & Service Coordinator. **Special programs:** Internships. **Corporate headquarters location:** This location. **Listed on:** New York Stock Exchange. **Stock exchange symbol:** HTN. **Annual sales/revenues:** More than $100 million. **Number of employees at this location:** 850. **Number of employees nationwide:** 2,300.

HUMAN SERVICE OPTIONS, INC.
35 Braintree Hill Park, Suite 307, Braintree MA 02184. 781/356-0710. **Fax:** 781/356-0748. **Contact:** Human Resources. **Description:** A home health care agency that provides staffing to schools, group homes, and workshops. The firm also provides a home health service for elderly and homebound individuals, and community residences for adults with developmental disabilities.

RODNEY HUNT COMPANY
46 Mill Street, Orange MA 01364. 978/544-2511. **Fax:** 978/544-7209. **Contact:** David Broghum, Manager of Human Resources. **World Wide Web address:** http://www.rodneyhunt.com. **Description:** Manufactures water control valves and related components. **Positions advertised include:** Design Hydraulic Engineer. **Parent company:** GA Industries.

HYATT REGENCY BOSTON
One Avenue de Lafayette, Boston MA 02111. 617/422-5414. **Fax:** 617/422-5416. **Contact:** Human Resources. **World Wide Web address:** http://www.hyatt.com. **Description:** Operates a 500-room luxury hotel with full convention and dining services. **Positions advertised include:** Customer Service Representative; Services Sales Representative. **Other U.S. locations:** Nationwide.

HYATT REGENCY CAMBRIDGE
575 Memorial Drive, Cambridge MA 02139. 617/492-1234. **Fax:** 617/491-6906. **Contact:** Human Resources. **World Wide Web address:** http://www.hyatt.com. **Description:** A 460-room hotel and function facility. **NOTE:** Entry-level positions and second and third shifts are offered. **Corporate headquarters location:** Chicago IL. **Other U.S. locations:** Nationwide. **International locations:** Worldwide. **Parent company:** Hyatt Hotels Corporation. **Number of employees at this location:** 480. **Number of employees nationwide:** 40,000.

HYBRIDON, INC.
345 Vassar Street, Cambridge MA 02139. 617/679-5500. **Contact:** Human Resources. **E-mail address:** hr@hybridon.com. **World Wide Web address:** http://www.hybridon.com. **Description:** A pharmaceutical research and development company focused on the treatment of viral diseases, cancer, and diseases of the eye. **Positions advertised include:** Manager Clinical Research.

I-LOGIX, INC.
3 Riverside Drive, Andover MA 01810. 978/682-2100. **Toll-free phone:** 888/BILOGIX. **Fax:** 978/682-5995. **Contact:** Human Resources. **E-mail address:** info@ilogix.com. **World Wide Web address:** http://www.ilogix.com. **Description:** Manufactures software for high-technology applications. **International locations:** England; France; Germany; Israel.

IDX SYSTEMS CORPORATION
116 Huntington Avenue, Boston MA 02116. 617/424-6800. **Fax:** 617/266-5419. **Contact:** Human Resources. **World Wide Web address:** http://www.idx.com. **Description:** Develops medical software for hospitals. IDX Systems Corporation provides health care information to physician groups and academic medical centers across the country. **Positions advertised include:** Project Manager; Implementation Lead; eCommerce Software Engineer; Project Manager; Technical Writer. **NOTE:** Entry-level positions are offered. **Office hours:** Monday - Friday, 8:30 a.m. - 5:15 p.m. **Corporate headquarters location:** Burlington VT. **Other U.S. locations:** San Francisco CA; Deerfield Beach FL; Atlanta GA; Chicago IL; Louisville KY; Dallas TX; Arlington VA; Seattle WA. **Listed on:** NASDAQ. **Stock exchange symbol:** IDXC. **Annual sales/revenues:** More than $100 million. **Number of employees at this location:** 550. **Number of employees nationwide:** 3,600.

ITG INC.
44 Farnsworth Street, 9th Floor, Boston MA 02210. 617/728-2800. **Toll-free phone:** 800/983-4484. **Contact:** Human Resources. **E-mail address:** itg_hr@itginc.com. **World Wide Web address:** http://www.itginc.com. **Description:** Provides automated securities trade execution and analysis services to institutional equity investors. ITG's two main services are POSIT, the largest automated stock crossing system operated during trading hours; and QuantEX, a proprietary software that enhances customers' trading efficiencies, access to market liquidity, and portfolio analysis capabilities. **Corporate headquarters location:** New York NY. **Other U.S. locations:** Los Angeles CA. **International locations:** London, England. **Parent company:** Investment Technology Group. **Listed on:** New York Stock Exchange. **Stock exchange symbol:** ITG.

ITT INDUSTRIES CANNON
57 Stanley Avenue, Watertown MA 02472. 617/926-6400. **Contact:** Human Resources. **World Wide Web address:** http://www.ittcannon.com. **Description:** Manufactures switchgear and switchboard apparatus. **Positions advertised include:** E-learning Coordinator. **Corporate headquarters location:** White Plains NY. **Other U.S. locations:** Santa Ana CA: Loveland CO; Cromwell CT; Eden Prairie MN; Newport News VA. **International locations:** Worldwide. **Listed on:** New York Stock Exchange. **Stock exchange symbol:** ITT.

ITW DEVCON PLEXUS
30 Endicott Street, Danvers MA 01923. 978/777-1100. **Toll-free phone:** 800/851-6692. **Fax:** 978/777-9871. **Contact:** Human Resources. **E-mail address:** jdelisle@devcon.com. **World Wide Web address:** http://www.itwplexus.com. **Description:** Manufactures structural adhesives for the transportation, marine, and engineering construction industries. **Positions advertised include:** Production Worker.

ITW FOILMARK
5 Malcolm Hoyt Drive, Newburyport MA 01950. 978/462-7300. **Toll-free phone:** 800/468-7826. **Fax:** 978/462-0831. **Contact:** Human Resources. **E-mail address:** corporate@foilmark.com. **World Wide Web address:** http://www.foilmark.com. **Description:** Manufactures metallized, pigmented, and diffraction foils; and packaging films. **Office hours:** Monday - Friday, 8:00 a.m. - 5:00 p.m. **Corporate headquarters location:** This location.

IKON OFFICE SOLUTIONS
204 Second Avenue, Waltham MA 02451. 781/487-5100. **Contact:** Human Resources. **World Wide Web address:** http://www.ikon.com. **Description:** A wholesaler and distributor of copy machines, fax machines, and related office supplies. **Positions advertised include:** Associate Sales Representative; On-Site Support Specialist; Major Account Representative; Associate Sales Representative; Account Executive; Operations Manager; Field Support Specialist; Production Manager; Receptionist; Customer Service Representative. **Other U.S. locations:** Nationwide. **International locations:** Worldwide. **Listed on:** New York Stock Exchange. **Stock exchange symbol:** IKN.

IMARKET, INC.
460 Totten Pond Road, 7th Floor, Waltham MA 02451. 781/672-9200. **Toll-free phone:** 800/590-0085. **Fax:** 781/672-9290. **Contact:** Personnel. **World Wide Web address:** http://www.imarketinc.com. **Description:** Develops desktop marketing software that allows companies to computerize their marketing efforts. Products include MarketPlace, which gives the user desktop access to the Dun & Bradstreet marketing database.

IMMUNOGEN INC.
128 Sidney Street, Cambridge MA 02139. 617/995-2500. **Fax:** 617/995-2510. **Contact:** Human Resources. **E-mail address:** resume@immunogen.com. **World Wide Web address:** http://www.immunogen.com. **Description:** ImmunoGen Inc. is engaged in the research and development of pharmaceuticals, primarily for the treatment of cancer. The company's product line consists of proprietary toxins or drugs coupled with highly specific targeting agents. **Positions advertised include:** Patent Agent; Validation Engineer; Principal Development Director; Analytical Development Scientist/ Chemistry Scientist; Chemistry Research Associate; Process Development Research Associate. **Corporate headquarters location:** This location. **Operations at this facility include:** This location is a research facility. **Listed on:** NASDAQ. **Stock exchange symbol:** IMGN.

IMMUNOGEN INC.
333 Providence Highway, Norwood MA 02062. 781/769-4242. **Fax:** 781/255-1489. **Contact:** Human Resources. **E-mail address:** resume@immunogen.com. **World Wide Web address:** http://www.immunogen.com. **Description:** ImmunoGen is engaged in the research and development of pharmaceuticals, primarily for the treatment of cancer. The company's product line consists of proprietary toxins or drugs coupled with highly specific targeting agents. The drugs, called immunoconjugates, are designed to identify, bind to, and destroy target cells. **Positions advertised include:** Patent Agent; Validation Engineer; Principal Development Director; Analytical Development Scientist/ Chemistry Scientist; Chemistry Research Associate; Process Development Research Associate. **Other U.S. locations:** Cambridge MA. **Operations at this facility include:** This location is a manufacturing facility. **Listed on:** NASDAQ. **Stock exchange symbol:** IMGN.

IMTRAN FOILMARK
25 Hale Street, Newburyport MA 01950. 978/462-2722. **Contact:** Human Resources. **World Wide Web address:** http://www.foilmark.com. **Description:** Manufactures pad printing equipment and supplies, dies, tooling, and silicone rubber products. **Corporate headquarters location:** This location. **Parent company:** Foilmark, Inc. **Listed on:** NASDAQ. **Stock exchange symbol:** FLMK.

INC. MAGAZINE
38 Commercial Wharf, Boston MA 02110. 617/248-8000. **Contact:** Personnel Department. **E-mail address:** mail@inc.com. **World Wide Web address:** http://www.inc.com. **Description:** Publishes a financial and business news magazine that is distributed worldwide. **Special programs:** Internships. **Corporate headquarters location:** This location.

INFINIUM SOFTWARE
25 Communication Way, P.O. Box 6000, Hyannis MA 02601. 508/778-2000. **Contact:** Human Resources. **World Wide Web address:** http://www.infinium.com. **Description:** Develops software for business applications. **Corporate headquarters location:** This location. **Other area locations:** Marlboro MA. **Other U.S. locations:** Irvine CA; Alpharetta GA; Lisle IL; Las Vegas NV; Bend OR. **International locations:** Mexico. **Listed on:** NASDAQ. **Stock exchange symbol:** INFMC.

INSTRON CORPORATION
100 Royall Street, Canton MA 02021. 781/828-2500. **Toll-free phone:** 800/877-6674. **Fax:** 781/575-5776. **Contact:** Human Resources. **E-mail address:** careers@instron.com. **World Wide Web address:** http://www.instron.com. **Description:** Manufactures, markets, and services materials testing instruments, systems, software, and accessories used to evaluate the mechanical properties and performance of metals, plastics, composites, textiles, ceramics, rubber, adhesives, and other materials. Instron's applications technology is used by research scientists, design engineers, and quality control managers in industry, academia, and government. The systems include electromechanical and servohydraulic instruments, structural components, computer software, temperature chambers, and hardness testers. **Positions advertised include:** Field Service Engineer; Product Manager. **Corporate headquarters location:** This location. **Other U.S. locations:** Nationwide. **International locations:** Worldwide. **Subsidiaries include:** Laboratory Microsystems (Troy NY). **Listed on:** American Stock Exchange. **Stock exchange symbol:** INSTRN. **Number of employees at this location:** 400.

INSTRUMENTATION LABORATORY
101 Hartwell Avenue, Lexington MA 02421. 781/861-0710. **Contact:** Human Resources. **World Wide Web address:** http://www.ilww.com. **Description:** Manufactures medical instruments used in blood gas analysis. **Positions advertised include:** Administrative Support; Marketing Product Specialist; Principal Software Engineer.

INTEGRATED IT SOLUTIONS
290 Vanderbilt Avenue, Norwood MA 02494. 781/453-5100. **Fax:** 781/449-7897. **Contact:** Human Resources. **E-mail address:** jobs@integratedit.com. **World Wide Web address:** http://www.integratedit.com. **Description:** A full-service consulting firm. Integrated IT Solutions offers information and consultation on system choice, network configurations, the Internet, and e-business solutions. **Positions advertised include:** Sales Engineer; Field Service Engineer; Account Executive. **Corporate headquarters location:** This location.

INTEL NETWORK SYSTEMS
75 Reed Road, Hudson MA 01749. 978/553-4000. **Contact:** Human Resources. **World Wide Web address:** http://www.intel.com. **Description:** Produces a line of direct-dial products and remote access servers. **NOTE:** Apply online. **Other area locations:** Boston MA; Framingham MA; Lowell MA; Shrewsbury MA; Waltham MA; Springfield MA. **Other U.S. location:** Nationwide. **International locations:** Worldwide.

INTERNATIONAL DATA GROUP (IDG)
5 Speen Street, Framingham MA 01701. 508/872-8200. **Contact:** Human Resources Department. **World Wide Web address:** http://www.idg.com. **Description:** Publishes periodicals that primarily focus on computer-related topics. **Positions advertised include:** Advertising Sales Associate; Client Services Representative; Conference Coordinator; Premium Content Services Director; Editor in Chief; Features Writer; Graphic Designer; Staff Accountant; Market Development Manager; Managing Editor; Marketing Communications Coordinator; Program Manager; Research Analyst; Research Manager; Account Executive; Inquiry Analyst; Training & Development Coordinator; Vice President Interactive Products & Services.

INTERNATIONAL EQUIPMENT COMPANY
300 Second Avenue, Needham Heights MA 02494-2811. 781/449-8060. **Fax:** 781/453-3381. **Contact:** Manager of Human Resources. **World Wide Web address:** http://www.labcentrifuge.com. **Description:** Manufactures and distributes laboratory equipment including centrifuges and cryostats. **Parent company:** Thermo Electron. **Operations at this facility include:** Administration; Manufacturing; Research and Development; Sales; Service. **Number of employees at this location:** 175.

INTERNEURON PHARMACEUTICALS, INC.
One Ledgemont Center, 99 Hayden Avenue, Suite 200, Lexington MA 02421. 781/861-8444. **Contact:** Human Resources, Tessa Cooper. **E-mail address:** hr@interneuron.com. **World Wide Web address:** http://www.interneuron.com. **Description:** Develops medical products to treat neurological and behavioral disorders. **Corporate headquarters location:** This location. **Subsidiaries include:** Intercardia, Inc.; Progenitor, Inc.; and Transcell Technologies, Inc. develop products and technologies that treat cardiovascular disease, and are used for gene therapy, stem cell production, oligosaccharide synthesis, and drug transport. **Listed on:** NASDAQ. **Stock exchange symbol:** IPIC.

INTRANET, INC.
One Gateway Center, Suite 700, Newton MA 02458. 617/527-7020. **Contact:** Human Resources. **World Wide Web address:** http://www.intranet.com. **Description:** Manufactures networking software. **Positions advertised include:** Senior Technical Writer. **NOTE:** Search and apply for open positions online. **Parent company:** Transaction Systems Architects, Inc.

INVACARE SUPPLY GROUP
75 October Hill Road, Holliston MA 01746. 508/429-1000. **Fax:** 508/429-6669. **Contact:** Human Resources. **Description:** A wholesale distributor of medical supplies including ostomy dressings, wound care products, respiratory products, and enteral feeding products. **NOTE:** Entry-level positions and part-time jobs are offered. **Positions advertised include:** Account Representative; Consumer Services Representative; Distribution Center Associate. **Special programs:** Training; Summer Jobs. **Office hours:** Monday - Friday, 8:00 a.m. - 5:30 p.m. **Corporate headquarters location:** Elyria OH. **Parent company:** Invacare Corporation. **Listed on:** New York Stock Exchange. **Stock exchange symbol:** IVC. **Number of employees at this location:** 100.

IONICS INC.
P.O. Box 9131, Watertown MA 02472. 617/926-2500. **Physical address:** 65 Grove Street, Watertown MA 02472. **Contact:** Brenda Madden, Recruiter. **World Wide Web address:** http://www.ionics.com. **Description:** Designs, manufactures, and sells four groups of products: Water Processing Systems are used for water desalination, food processing, chemical manufacturing, and biological separations that include ion-exchange membranes and electrochemical cells. Membrane Cell Products include products used in food processing, the manufacture of chlorination chemicals, and products used by the food, pharmaceutical, and chemical industries for special process problems; Energy Related & Other Fabricated Products include products used in nuclear or fossil fuel power plants and heat recuperating systems; and Instruments & Medical Products include laboratory and process control instruments and medical products. **Positions advertised include:** Purchasing Agent. **NOTE:** Visit http://www.monster.com to search for open positions. **Corporate headquarters location:** This location. **Other U.S. locations:** Nationwide. **International locations:** Worldwide. **Operations at this facility include:** Administration; Manufacturing; Research and Development; Sales; Service. **Listed on:** New York Stock Exchange. **Stock exchange symbol:** ION. **Number of employees nationwide:** 800.

IRON MOUNTAIN INC.
745 Atlantic Avenue, Boston MA 02111. 617/357-4455. **Fax:** 617/ **Contact:** Human Resources. **Fax:** 617/368-9117. **E-mail address:** jobs@ironmountain.com. **World Wide Web address:** http://www.ironmountain.com. **Description:** One of the nation's largest record management companies. Iron Mountain provides businesses with storage facilities for their records. **Positions advertised include:** Telemarketing Representative; Seibel Design Engineer; Corporate Staff Accountant; Marketing Specialist; Marketing Administration; Systems Engineer; Quality Assurance Manager. **Corporate headquarters location:** This location. **Other U.S. locations:** Nationwide. **Listed on:** NASDAQ. **Stock exchange symbol:** IRM.

THE ITALIAN HOME FOR CHILDREN
1125 Center Street, Jamaica Plain MA 02130. 617/524-3116. **Contact:** Director. **E-mail address:** hr@italianhome.org. **World Wide Web address:** http://www.italianhome.org. **Description:** A residential treatment center for emotionally disturbed children. The Italian Home for Children provides counseling and schooling for approximately 60 youths, aged six to 13. **Positions advertised include:** Childcare Worker; Quality Improvement Associate; Director of Child Care Training Services. **Number of employees at this location:** 100.

THE J. JILL GROUP, INC.
4 Batterymarch Park, Quincy MA 02169. 617/376-4300. **Fax:** 617/376-4479. **Contact:** Human Resources. **E-mail address:** jobs@jjillgroup.com. **World Wide Web address:** http://www.jjillgroup.com. **Description:** A leading retailer of women's apparel, shoes, gifts, and accessories. The company sells its products through catalogs, retail stores, and an e-commerce Website. Founded in 1987. **Office hours:** Monday - Friday, 8:30 a.m. - 5:00 p.m. **Corporate headquarters location:** This location. **Listed on:** NASDAQ. **Stock exchange symbol:** JILL. **Number of employees nationwide:** 825.

JACO, INC.
140 Constitution Boulevard, Franklin MA 02038. 508/553-1000. **Fax:** 508/553-1061. **Contact:** Human Resources. **E-mail address:** info@jaco.com. **World Wide Web address:** http://www.jacoinc.com. **Description:** Manufactures housings for computers and medical equipment. **Positions advertised include:** Assembler; Press Brake Operator; Grinder; Packer.

JACOB'S PILLOW DANCE FESTIVAL, INC.
P.O. Box 287, Lee MA 01238-0287. 413/637-1322. **Fax:** 413/243-4744. **Contact:** Connie Chin, Company Manager. **E-mail address:** info@jacobspillow.org. **World Wide Web address:** http://www.jacobspillow.org. **Description:** One of America's oldest dance festivals, presenting 10 weeks of dance performances and conducting a professional dance school each summer. Founded in 1942. **Positions advertised include:** Director of Marketing & PR; Audience Engagement Liaison; Development Manager for Institutional Support; Nurse; Emergency Medical Technician; Housekeeper; Driver. . **Special programs:** Internships. **Internship information:** Internships are offered in the following areas: archives/preservation; business office;

development; documentation; education; marketing/press; operations; programming; technical/theatre production; and ticket services. Applicants are asked to send a resume, two work-related references with phone numbers, two letters of recommendation, and a cover letter. The cover letter should indicate a primary area of interest and describe goals and expectations for the internship. Applicants for marketing, development, education, and programming must include at least two writing samples, maximum two pages in length each. Please call the organization to find out deadline information.

JACOBS SVERDRUP
2 Center Plaza, 7th Floor, Boston MA 02108. 617/742-8060. **Contact:** Human Resources. **World Wide Web address:** http://www.sverdrup.com. **Description:** A civil engineering firm engaged in the operation of environmental, transportation, and water resources projects.

JANE DOE INC.
MA COALITION AGAINST SEXUAL ASSAULT & DOMESTIC VIOLENCE
14 Beacon Street, Suite 507, Boston MA 02108. 617/248-0922. **Fax:** 617/248-0902. **Contact:** Human Resources. **E-mail address:** jobs@janedoe.org. **World Wide Web address:** http://www.janedoe.org. **Description:** A nonprofit public education and advocacy organization. Jane Doe Inc. operates more than 30 programs across the state.

JANNELL MOTORS
2000 Washington Street, Hanover MA 02339. 781/982-4500. **Fax:** 781/982-4535. **Contact:** Human Resources. **E-mail address:** sales@jannell.com. **World Wide Web address:** http://www.jannell.com. **Description:** A Ford dealership on the South Shore.

JEFFERIES & COMPANY, INC.
One Post Office Square, 40th Floor, Boston MA 02109. 617/342-7800. **Contact:** Human Resources. **World Wide Web address:** http://www.jefco.com. **Description:** Engaged in equity, convertible debt, taxable fixed income securities brokerage and trading, and corporate finance. Jefferies is one of the leading national firms engaged in the distribution and trading of blocks of equity securities and conducts such activities primarily in the third market. Founded in 1962. **Corporate headquarters location:** Los Angeles CA. **Other U.S. locations:** San Francisco CA; Stamford CT; Atlanta GA; Chicago IL; New Orleans LA; Jersey City NJ; Short Hills NJ; New York NY; Nashville TN; Dallas TX; Richmond VA. **International locations:** Australia; Hong Kong; London; Paris; Tokyo; Zurich. **Listed on:** New York Stock Exchange. **Stock exchange symbol:** JEF. **Parent company:** Jefferies Group, Inc. is a holding company that, through Jefferies & Company and its three other primary subsidiaries, Investment Technology Group, Inc., Jefferies International Limited, and Jefferies Pacific Limited, is engaged in securities brokerage and trading, corporate finance, and other financial services.

JET AVIATION OF AMERICA
380 Hanscom Drive, Hanscom Field, Bedford MA 01730. 781/274-0030. **Fax:** 781/274-6573. **Contact:** Human Resources. **World Wide Web address:** http://www.jetaviation.com. **Description:** Manages a fleet of 100 aircraft and provides a wide range of aviation services including airframe and engine maintenance, and FBO services to business aircraft. **Corporate headquarters location:** West Palm Beach FL. **Other U.S. locations:** Burbank CA; Chicago IL; Teterboro NJ; Dallas TX. **International locations:** Bermuda.

JOAN FABRICS CORPORATION
100 Vesper Executive Park, Tyngsboro MA 01879-2710. 978/649-5626. **Contact:** Human Resources. **World Wide Web address:** http://www.joanfabrics.com. **Description:** Engaged in the manufacturing of woven and knitted fabrics for furniture and automotive manufacturers. The company also operates retail fabric stores nationwide. **Corporate headquarters location:** This location. **Other U.S. locations:** Hickory NC; Troy MI.

JOHN HANCOCK FINANCIAL SERVICES
John Hancock Place, Box 111, Boston MA 02117. 617/572-4500. **Fax:** 617/572-4539. **Contact:** Human Resources. **E-mail address:** employment@jhancock.com. **World Wide Web address:** http://www.jhancock.com. **Description:** An insurance and financial services firm operating through two divisions: The Retail Sector offers protection and investment products to middle- and upper-income markets; The Investment & Pension Group is involved in bond and corporate finance services as well as in real estate and mortgage loans. Founded in 1862. **NOTE:** Entry-level positions are offered. **Special programs:** Internships; Training. **Corporate headquarters location:** This location. **International locations:** Worldwide. **Annual sales/revenues:** More than $100 million. **Number of employees at this location:** 4,100. **Number of employees nationwide:** 11,000.

KHJ INTEGRATED MARKETING
One Constitution Plaza, Boston MA 02129-2025. 617/241-8000. **Contact:** Diana Richards, Human Resources. **E-mail address:** drichards@khj.com. **World Wide Web address:** http://www.khj.com. **Description:** An advertising and public relations firm.

KLA-TENCOR
200 Friberg Parkway, Westborough MA 01581. 508/616-0412. **Contact:** Human Resources. **World Wide Web address:** http://www.kla-tencor.com. **Description:** Manufactures electron scanning microscopes.

KPMG
99 High Street, Boston MA 02110-2371. 617/988-1000. **Contact:** Human Resources. **World Wide Web address:** http://www.kpmg.com. **Description:** Delivers a wide range of value-added assurance, tax, and consulting services. **Positions advertised include:** Tax Associate; Transactions Services Manager; Internal Auditor; IT Audit Associate; Corporate Tax Associate; Corporate Tax Associate; Office Services Supervisor; Auditor; Corporate Recovery Associate. **Corporate headquarters location:** Montvale NJ. **Other U.S. locations:** Nationwide. **International locations:** Worldwide. **Parent company:** KPMG International is a leader among professional services firms engaged in capturing, managing, assessing, and delivering information to create knowledge that will help its clients maximize shareholder value. **Number of employees worldwide:** 100,000.

KATHARINE SCHOOL
126 Newbury Street, Boston MA 02116. 617/578-7100. **Toll-free phone:** 800/6SK-ILLS. **Contact:** Human Resources. **World Wide Web address:** http://www.katharinegibbs.com. **Description:** One of the nation's foremost business instruction schools. Founded in 1911. **Other U.S. locations:** Nationwide.

KEANE, INC.
10 City Square, Boston MA 02129. 617/241-9200. **Contact:** Human Resources. **World Wide Web address:** http://www.keane.com. **Description:** Designs, develops, and manages software for corporations and health care facilities. Keane, Inc.'s services enable clients to leverage existing information systems and develop and manage new software applications more rapidly and proficiently. Founded in 1965. **Positions advertised include:** Web Developer; Web Applications Developer; Technical Recruiter; Administrative Assistant; Proposal Writer; Technical Support Manager; Business Analyst; Client Server Developer; Recruiting Associate; Quality Assurance Analyst; Sales Associate. **Corporate headquarters location:** This location. **Other U.S. locations:** Nationwide. **Listed on:** American Stock Exchange. **Stock exchange symbol:** KEA. **Number of employees at this location:** 100.

A.T. KEARNEY, INC.
One Memorial Drive, 14th Floor, Cambridge MA 02142-1301. 617/374-2600. **Contact:** Human Resources. **World Wide Web address:** http://www.atkearney.com. **Description:** A general management consulting firm. **NOTE:** Visit website for more information concerning recruiting process. **Parent company:** EDS.

KELLAWAY TRANSPORTATION
One Kellaway Drive, P.O. Box 750, Randolph MA 02368. 781/961-8200. **Contact:** Human Resources. **E-mail address:** kellaway@kellaway.com. **World Wide Web address:** http://www.kellaway.com. **Description:** An intermodal distribution company. **Corporate headquarters location:** This location. **Parent company:** RoadLink USA.

KEMA
3 Burlington Woods, Burlington MA 01803-4543. 781/273-5700. **Fax:** 781/229-4867. **Contact:** Paula LaRue, Director of Human Resources. **World Wide Web address:** http://www.kema.com. **Description:** Develops software products for utilities and energy companies.

KEN-WELD COMPANY, INC.
P.O. Box 15021, Worcester MA 01615-0021. 508/798-8756. **Physical address:** 68 Albany Street, Worcester MA 01604. **Fax:** 508/798-3785. **Contact:** Human Resources. **E-mail address:** kenweld@compuserve.com. **World Wide Web address:** http://www.kenweld.com. **Description:** Engaged in metal fabrication and machining. Founded in 1945.

KENNAMETAL GREENFIELD IPG
34 Sanderson Street, Greenfield MA 01301. 413/772-3200. **Contact:** Esther M. Johnson, CPS/Human Resources Specialist. **World Wide Web address:** http://www.gfii.com. **Description:** Kennametal Greenfield IPG is also one of North America's leading producers of rotary cutting tools and suppliers of circuit board drills to the Far East. The company operates in four divisions: Industrial, Electronics, Oil Field Equipment, and Consumer. The company distributes its products to manufacturers, the federal government, electronic OEMs, electronic subcontractors, oil field pump manufacturers, do-it-yourself customers, and contractors. The company's product lines are sold under an array of national brand names. **Corporate headquarters location:** Augusta GA. **Other U.S. locations:** Nationwide. **Operations at this facility include:** This location manufactures cutting tools. **Listed on:** New York Stock Exchange. **Stock exchange symbol:** KMT. **Annual sales/revenues:** More than $100 million. **Number of employees at this location:** 160. **Number of employees nationwide:** 4,700.

KEVLIN CORPORATION
596 Lowell Street, Methuen MA 01844 978/557-2400. **Contact:** Human Resources. **World Wide Web address:** http://www.kevlin.com. **Description:** Kevlin Corporation designs, manufactures, and sells microwave rotary couplers, connectors, cable assemblies, and microwave components. These products are used in air traffic control radars, satellite communications systems, airborne weather radars, and surveillance radars for drug interdiction. **Positions advertised include:** Contract Administrator; Engineer; Antenna Design Engineer; Microwave Manufacturing Engineer; Assembler; Bonder; Machinist Assistant; Program Manager; Sales Engineer; Test Technician; Antenna Technician.

KEYSPAN ENERGY DELIVERY
201 Rivermoor Street, West Roxbury MA 02132. 617/742-8400. **Fax:** 617/327-2865. **Contact:** Personnel. **World Wide Web address:** http://www.keyspanenergy.com. **Description:** The largest distributor of natural gas in the Northeast, serving residential, commercial, and industrial customers throughout eastern and central Massachusetts, New Hampshire, New York City, and Long Island. **Listed on:** New York Stock Exchange. **Stock exchange symbol:** KSE.

KIRKPATRICK & LOCKHART LLP
75 State Street, Boston MA 02109. 617/261-3100. **Contact:** Jeffrey King, Hiring Partner. **E-mail address:** bmorrissey@kl.com. **World Wide Web address:** http://www.kl.com. **Description:** A law firm with a broad range of practice areas including international law and intellectual property. **Positions advertised include:** Legal Assistant; Clerk; Legal Secretary; Administration. **Other U.S. locations:** Los Angeles CA; San Francisco CA; Washington DC; Miami FL; Newark NJ; New York NY; Harrisburg PA; Pittsburgh PA; Dallas TX.

KOHL'S
125 Church Street, Pembroke MA 02359. 781/826-3696. **Fax:** 781/982-4535. **Contact:** Human Resources. **World Wide Web address:** http://www.kohls.com. **Description:** A clothing department store. **Positions advertised include:** Cash Office Associate; Customer Service Associate; Department Supervisor; Housekeeper; Loss Prevention Associate; Register Operator; Sales Associate.

KOLLMORGEN CORPORATION
347 King Street, Northampton MA 01060. 413/586-2330. **Fax:** 413/586-1324. **Contact:** Human Resources. **Description:** Kollmorgen operates in three business segments: Industrial Drives, Motors and Controls, and Electro-Optical Instruments. Founded in 1916. **NOTE:** Entry-level positions are offered. **Other U.S. locations:** VT. **International locations:** Italy. **Operations at this facility include:** This location designs and supplies advanced submarine periscopes, weapon directors, and military optics for the U.S. armed forces and its allies. Products allow the operator to search, detect, and identify targets anytime during the day or night using thermal imaging, high-resolution TV, lasers, direct-viewing channels, and video tracking and processing technologies. **Annual sales/revenues:** $21 - $50 million. **Number of employees at this location:** 230.

KONICA BUSINESS TECHNOLOGIES
175 Great Road, Bedford MA 01730. 781/275-4643. **Contact:** Human Resources. **E-mail address:** philbins@kmbs.konicaminolta.com. **World Wide Web address:** http://www.konicabt.com. **Description:** Sells and services copier machines, duplicator equipment, and facsimile machines.

KOPIN CORPORATION
200 John Hancock Road, Taunton MA 02780. 508/824-6696. **Fax:** 508/822-1381. **Contact:** Human Resources. **E-mail address:** info@kopin.com. **World Wide Web address:** http://www.kopin.com. **Description:** Kopin Corporation is a developer of

advanced flat-panel display products. The company's products include compact projectors and head-mounted display systems featuring higher resolution, lighter weight, and greater portability as well as large-screen monitors offering higher definition and streamlined dimensions. Kopin's proprietary wafer engineering has a broad range of computer, entertainment, business product, medical imaging, avionics, and industrial applications. **Positions advertised include:** Process Engineer; Cleanroom Operator; Equipment Maintenance Technician; Test Technician. **Corporate headquarters location:** This location. **Other area locations:** Westborough MA. **Other U.S. locations:** Los Gatos CA. **Listed on:** NASDAQ. **Stock exchange symbol:** KOPN.

KOPIN CORPORATION
125 North Drive, Westborough MA 01581. 508/870-5959. **Fax:** 508/870-0660. **Contact:** Human Resources. **E-mail address:** info@kopin.com. **World Wide Web address:** http://www.kopin.com. **Description:** Kopin Corporation is a developer of advanced flat-panel display products. The company's products include compact projectors and head-mounted display systems featuring higher resolution, lighter weight, and greater portability as well as large-screen monitors offering higher definition and streamlined dimensions. Kopin's proprietary wafer engineering has a broad range of computer, entertainment, business product, medical imaging, avionics, and industrial applications. **Corporate headquarters location:** Taunton MA. **Other U.S. locations:** Los Gatos CA. **Listed on:** NASDAQ. **Stock exchange symbol:** KOPN.

KRONOS INC.
297 Billerica Road, Chelmsford MA 01824. 978/250-9800. **Contact:** Human Resources. **World Wide Web address:** http://www.kronos.com. **Description:** Designs, develops, and markets labor management software and computerized systems that measure employee attendance and schedules. Founded in 1977. **Positions advertised include:** Information Systems Manager; Software Quality Assurance Engineer; Software Engineer; Prospect Marketing Representative; Marketing Writer; Solutions Consultant; Financial Analyst; Enterprise Account Manager; Vice President of Marketing; Network Security Officer; Technical Support Engineer; Events Specialist; Software Product Manager. **Special programs:** Internships. **Corporate headquarters location:** This location. **Other U.S. locations:** Nationwide. **International locations:** Worldwide. **Operations at this facility include:** Administration; Research and Development; Sales; Service. **Listed on:** NASDAQ. **Stock exchange symbol:** KRON. **Annual sales/revenues:** More than $100 million. **Number of employees at this location:** 900.

KUBOTEK USA
100 Locke Drive, Marlborough MA 01752. 508/229-2020. **Fax:** 508/229-2121. **Contact:** Human Resources. **World Wide Web address:** http://www.kubotekusa.com. **Description:** A developer of 3-D mechanical design software for CAD systems. **Corporate headquarters location:** This location.

LKM INDUSTRIES
44 Sixth Road, Woburn MA 01801. 781/935-9210. **Contact:** Human Resources. **World Wide Web address:** http://www.lkm.com. **Description:** Manufactures parts for aircraft engines and cooling systems.

LTX CORPORATION
50 Rosemount Road, Westwood MA 02090. 781/461-1000. **Contact:** Human Resources. **World Wide Web address:** http://www.ltx.com. **Description:** Manufactures and markets testing equipment for semiconductors and electronic assemblies. The company's semiconductor test systems include digital test systems, which test digital ICs such as microprocessors and microcontrollers; linear/mixed signal test systems, which test a wide range of linear and mixed signal ICs; and discrete component test systems. The company also provides applications support for its test systems. Founded in 1976. **Positions advertised include:** Research & Development; Software Engineer; Hardware Engineer; Manufacturing Engineer; Sales Associate; Marketing Representative; Product Manufacturing Representative; Information Services Representative; Finance Accountant. **Corporate headquarters location:** This location. **Other U.S. locations:** AZ; CA; IN; PA; TX. **International locations:** England; France; Germany; Israel; Italy; Japan; Korea; Singapore; Taiwan. **Listed on:** NASDAQ. **Stock exchange symbol:** LTXX.

LAHEY AT ARLINGTON MEDICAL CENTER
Hospital Road, Arlington MA 02474. 781/646-1500. **Contact:** Human Resources. **World Wide Web address:** http://www.lahey.org. **Description:** Part of the Lahey Clinic's network of health care services. This location provides emergency, acute, transitional, subacute, and intensive care. **Positions advertised include:** Clinical Nurse; Medical Office Secretary; Physician.

LANGUAGE ENGINEERING CORPORATION
385 Concord Avenue, Belmont MA 02478. 617/489-4000. **Fax:** 617/489-3850. **Contact:** Human Resources. **E-mail address:** info@hq.lec.com. **World Wide Web address:** http://www.lec.com. **Description:** Develops Logovista Internet software that translates English Web pages into Japanese.

LANTANA
43 Scanlon Drive, Randolph MA 02368. 781/961-4660. **Contact:** Human Resources. **World Wide Web address:** http://www.thelantana.com. **Description:** A restaurant. **NOTE:** Interested jobseekers must apply in person.

LAWRENCE MEMORIAL HOSPITAL
170 Governors Avenue, Medford MA 02155. 781/306-6000. **Fax:** 781/306-6573. **Contact:** Human Resources. **World Wide Web address:** http://www.lmh.org. **Description:** A hospital that serves as a teaching facility for Tufts University School of Medicine. **Positions advertised include:** Registered Nurse; Clinical Associate; Licensed Practical Nurse; Clinical Nurse Educator; Medical Transcriptionist; Application Analyst; Desktop Technician; Director; Registered Respiratory Therapist. **Parent company:** Hallmark Health.

LAWYERS TITLE INSURANCE CORPORATION
77 Franklin Street, 7th Floor, Boston MA 02110. 617/619-4500. **Contact:** Human Resources. **World Wide Web address:** http://www.landam.com. **Description:** Lawyers Title Insurance Corporation provides title insurance and other real estate-related services on commercial and residential transactions in the United States, Canada, the Bahamas, Puerto Rico, and the U.S. Virgin Islands. Lawyers Title Insurance Corporation also provides search and examination services and closing services for a broad-based customer group that includes lenders, developers, real estate brokers, attorneys, and homebuyers. **Corporate headquarters location:** Richmond VA. **Other U.S. locations:** Nationwide. **Operations at this facility include:** This location covers Connecticut, Maine, Massachusetts, New Hampshire, Rhode Island, Vermont, and Canada. **Subsidiaries include:** Datatrace Information Services Company, Inc. (Richmond VA) markets automated public record information for public and private use; Genesis Data Systems, Inc. (Englewood CO) develops and markets computer software tailored specifically to the title industry; Lawyers Title Exchange Company functions as an intermediary for individual and corporate investors interested in pursuing tax-free property exchanges. **Parent company:** LandAmerica Financial Group, Inc. **Listed on:** NASDAQ. **Stock exchange symbol:** LFG.

LE MERIDIEN BOSTON
250 Franklin Street, Boston MA 02110. 617/451-1900. **Fax:** 617/422-5169. **Recorded jobline:** 617/422-5180. **Contact:** Human Resources. **World Wide Web address:** http://www.lemeridien.com. **Description:** A 326-bed luxury hotel offering extensive conference and banquet facilities. Le Meridien Boston has two restaurants, a seasonal outdoor cafe, a piano bar, nine meeting rooms, a full-service business center, an indoor health club, and a swimming pool. **Positions advertised include:** Cook; On Call Bell Person.

LEGAL SEAFOODS, INC.
1 Seafood Way, Boston MA 02210. 617/783-8084. **Fax:** 617/782-4479. **Contact:** Human Resources. **E-mail address:** careers@legalseafoods.com. **World Wide Web address:** http://www.legalseafoods.com. **Description:** Operates a chain of seafood restaurants. **Special programs:** Internships. **Corporate headquarters location:** This location. **Operations at this facility include:** Administration; Research and Development; Sales.

LEMESSURIER CONSULTANTS
675 Massachusetts Avenue, Cambridge MA 02139. 617/868-1200. **Fax:** 617/661-7520. **Contact:** Peter Cheevers, Personnel Director. **World Wide Web address:** http://www.lemessurier.com. **Description:** Provides structural engineering consulting services. Founded in 1961. **Positions advertised include:** Experienced CAD Operators.

LENOX SAW
301 Chestnut Street, East Longmeadow MA 01028. 413/525-3961. **Contact:** Human Resources. **World Wide Web address:** http://www.lenoxsaw.com. **Description:** A manufacturer of cutting tools and related products. **Corporate headquarters location:** This location. **Listed on:** Privately held. **Number of employees at this location:** 600.

THE LENOX HOTEL
61 Exeter Street at Boylston Back Bay, Boston MA 02116. 617/536-5300. **Fax:** 617/267-1237. **Contact:** Human Resources. **World Wide Web address:** http://www.lenoxhotel.com. **Description:** A 222-room, full-service hotel.

LESLEY UNIVERSITY
29 Everett Street, Cambridge MA 02138-2890. 617/349-8787. **Toll-free phone:** 800/999-1959. **Contact:** Maryanne Gallagher, Associate Director of Human Resources. **World Wide Web address:** http://www.lesley.edu. **Description:** A private, four-year university offering an undergraduate liberal arts program and a variety of graduate and doctoral degree programs including arts, education, management, and social sciences. **Positions advertised include:** Assistant Director of Financial Aide; Assistant Professor of Mathematics; Conference Assistant; Administrative Assistant; Director of Health Services; Certification Officer; Graphic Design Faculty; Customer Care Coordinator; Administrative Assistant. **Listed on:** Privately held. **Number of employees at this location:** 400. **Number of employees nationwide:** 450.

LIANT SOFTWARE CORPORATION
354 Waverly Street, Framingham MA 01702. 508/872-8700. **Fax:** 508/626-2221. **Contact:** Human Resources. **World Wide Web address:** http://www.liant.com. **Description:** A developer of network-based programming and software development tools that enhance client/server systems and architectures. **Corporate headquarters location:** This location. **Other U.S. locations:** Austin TX. **International locations:** London, England. **Listed on:** Privately held. **Number of employees worldwide:** 60.

LIBERTY MUTUAL INSURANCE COMPANY
175 Berkeley Street, Boston MA 02117. 617/357-9500. **Fax:** 617/574-5616. **Contact:** Human Resources. **World Wide Web address:** http://www.libertymutual.com. **Description:** A full-line insurance firm offering life, medical, and business insurance, as well as investment and retirement plans. **Positions advertised include:** Customer Service Representative; Assistant Service Manager. **Special programs:** Internships; Training. **Corporate headquarters location:** This location. **Other U.S. locations:** Nationwide. **International locations:** Worldwide. **Subsidiaries include:** Wausau Insurance Company. **Operations at this facility include:** Administration; Research and Development; Sales; Service. **Annual sales/revenues:** More than $100 million. **Number of employees at this location:** 1,800. **Number of employees nationwide:** 23,000.

LIFELINE SYSTEMS, INC.
111 Lawrence Street, Framingham MA 01702-8156. 508/988-1000. **Fax:** 508/988-1384. **Contact:** Personnel. **World Wide Web address:** http://www.lifelinesys.com. **Description:** Manufactures personal emergency response systems and provides monitoring and related services. The company's services consist of 24-hour, at-home assistance and personalized support for elderly and physically challenged individuals. The company's principal product is LIFELINE, which consists of equipment manufactured by the company combined with a monitoring service. The equipment includes a personal help button, worn or carried by the individual subscriber, and a communicator that connects to the phone line in the subscriber's home. **Positions advertised include:** Marketing Communications Manager; Personal Response Associate; Inside Sales Account; Customer & Referral Sales Manager; Employment Manager; Equipment Product Manager. **Corporate headquarters location:** This location. **Subsidiaries include:** Lifeline Systems Canada. **Listed on:** NASDAQ. **Stock exchange symbol:** LIFE. **Number of employees at this location:** 735.

LIGHTOLIER
631 Airport Road, Fall River MA 02720. 508/679-8131. **Fax:** 508/646-3357. **Contact:** Human Resources. **World Wide Web address:** http://www.lightolier.com. **Description:** A manufacturer of lighting fixtures. Founded in 190. **Positions advertised include:** Sourcing Material Analyst; Quotations Analyst. **Special programs:** Training; Co-ops; Summer Jobs. **Corporate headquarters location:** This location. **Other U.S. locations:** Nationwide. **Parent company:** Genlyte Thomas Group. **Operations at this facility include:** Divisional Headquarters; Manufacturing. **Listed on:** NASDAQ. **Stock exchange symbol:** GLYT. **Annual sales/revenues:** More than $100 million. **Number of employees at this location:** 500. **Number of employees nationwide:** 5,000.

LILY TRANSPORTATION CORPORATION
145 Rosemary Street, Needham MA 02494. 781/449-8811. **Toll-free phone:** 800/248-LILY. **Contact:** Human Resources. **E-mail address:** hr@lilytransportation.com. **World Wide Web address:** http://www.lily.com. **Description:** A truck rental and leasing company. **Positions advertised include:** CDL Class A Truck Driver; CDL

Class B Truck Driver; Truck Mechanic. **Corporate headquarters location:** This location. **Other U.S. locations:** CT; ME; NH; NJ; NY; RI; VT.

ERICH LINDEMANN MENTAL HEALTH CENTER
25 Staniford Street, Boston MA 02114. 617/626-8000. **Contact:** Human Resources. **Description:** A residential mental health center. **Number of employees at this location:** 300.

ARTHUR D. LITTLE, INC.
25 Acorn Park, Cambridge MA 02140. 617/498-5290. **Fax:** 617/498-7005. **Contact:** Human Resources. **E-mail address:** careers.mc@adlittle.com. **World Wide Web address:** http://www.adl.com. **Description:** An employee-owned international management and technology consulting firm. The company offers services in three areas: management consulting; technology and product development; and environmental, health, and safety consulting. Services include cost reduction, total quality management consulting, market assessments, logistics management, telecommunications management, auditing, safety programs, software development, and toxicology. Clients operate in a variety of industries including aerospace, automobiles, telecommunications, electronics, and consumer products. Founded in 1886. **Positions advertised include:** Business Analyst; Consultant. **Corporate headquarters location:** This location. **Other U.S. locations:** Cupertino CA; Irvine CA; Palo Alto CA Ventura CA; Philadelphia PA; Charleston SC; Houston TX; Arlington VA. **International locations:** Asia; Europe; Middle East; South America. **Operations at this facility include:** Administration; Manufacturing; Research and Development. **Number of employees at this location:** 1,000. **Number of employees nationwide:** 2,500.

LITTLE, BROWN AND COMPANY
3 Center Plaza, Boston MA 02108. 617/227-0730. **Contact:** Human Resources. **World Wide Web address:** http://www.littlebrown.com. **Description:** The publishing house has printed works by such well-known authors as Louisa May Alcott, Emily Dickinson, Oliver Wendell Holmes, Jr., J.D. Salinger, and Norman Mailer. Little, Brown and Company operates through two divisions: The Professional Division produces law and medical textbooks for students, and reference books and journals for professionals; The Trade Division consists of Adult Trade, and Children's Books including Joy Street Books, Bulfinch Press, and Arcade. In total, the company produces and publishes close to 400 new titles each year. The number of titles in print of all the divisions at any one time is approximately 3,000. Founded in 1837. **Other U.S. locations:** New York NY. **Parent company:** AOL Time Warner.

LO-JACK CORPORATION
200 Lowder Brook Drive, Suite 1000, Westwod MA 02090. 781/326-4700. **Contact:** Human Resources. **World Wide Web address:** http://www.lojack.com. **Description:** Manufactures electronic recovery systems for stolen automobiles. **Positions advertised include:** Automotive Installation Technician; Installation Supervisor; Field Specialist; Quality Control Specialist; Manager of Commercial Sales Division; Customer Service Representative. **NOTE:** Marketing and PR Internships available. **International locations:** Worldwide. **Number of employees at this location:** 190.

LOCKHEED ENVIRONMENTAL SYSTEMS
175 Cabot Street, Suite 415, Lowell MA 01854. 978/275-9730. **Contact:** Personnel. **Description:** Engaged in contract environmental analysis work for the Environmental Protection Agency (EPA).

LOGICA NORTH AMERICA, INC.
32 Hartwell Avenue, Lexington MA 02421. 617/476-8000. **Contact:** Andrea Merurio, Human Resources. **World Wide Web address:** http://www.logica.com. **Description:** Provides computer programming systems, design, and consulting services for the banking, insurance, and telecommunications industries. **Other U.S. locations:** San Francisco CA; New York NY; Dearborn MI; Pittsburgh PA; Dallas TX; Houston TX; Bellevue WA. **International locations:** Worldwide.

LOTUS DEVELOPMENT CORPORATION
One Rogers Street, Cambridge MA 02142. 617/577-8500. **Toll-free phone:** 800/796-9876. **Contact:** Personnel. **World Wide Web address:** http://www.lotus.com/jobs. **Description:** Lotus develops, manufactures, and markets applications software and services that meet the evolving technology and business application needs for individuals, work groups, and entire organizations. Products include Lotus Notes, a software application that provides groupware links allowing workers to share information. **Positions advertised include:** Associate Project Manager; Lead Consultant. **NOTE:** Visit: http://www-1.ibm.com/employment/ for current positions. **Corporate headquarters location:** This location. **Parent company:** IBM. **Number of employees nationwide:** 4,400.

LOURIE & CUTLER
60 State Street, Boston MA 02109. 617/742-6720. **Contact:** David Andelman, Esq., Hiring Partner. **Description:** A law firm specializing in estate planning and taxation.

LOWE GROB HEALTH & SCIENCE
200 Clarendon Street 42nd Floor, Boston MA 02138. 617/876-9300. **Fax:** 617/859-4233. **Contact:** Human Resources. **E-mail address:** info@lowegrob.com. **World Wide Web address:** http://www.lowegrob.com. **Description:** Provides advertising, consulting, market research, and public relations services to companies primarily in the biotechnical, health, medical, and scientific industries. **Positions advertised include:** Art Director Supervisor. **NOTE:** Entry-level positions are offered. **Special programs:** Internships. **Number of employees at this location:** 25.

LOWELL GENERAL HOSPITAL INC.
295 Varnum Avenue, Lowell MA 01854. 978/937-6000. **Contact:** Human Resources. **World Wide Web address:** http://www.lowellgeneral.org. **Description:** A 200-bed hospital that offers a variety of specialized services including the Special Care Nursery, the Cancer Center, and the Children's Place. **Positions advertised include:** 2nd Cook; ACR Mechanic; Clinical Manager; CT Technician; Development Assistant; Endoscopy Coordinator; Financial Specialist; Medical Technologist; Registered Nurse.

LOWELL SUN PUBLISHING COMPANY
P.O. Box 1477, Lowell MA 01853. 978/458-7100. **Contact:** Carmen Bellrose, Controller. **World Wide Web address:** http://www.newschoice.com. **Description:** Publishes the *Lowell Sun,* a daily newspaper with a weekday circulation of more than 56,000.

LUCENT TECHNOLOGIES INC.
1600 Osgood Street, North Andover MA 01845. 978/960-2000. **Contact:** Human Resources. **World Wide Web address:** http://www.lucent.com. **Description:** Manufactures communications products including switching, transmission, fiber-optic cable, wireless systems, and operations systems. **Positions advertised include:** Security Consultant; Project Manager. **Corporate headquarter location:** Murray Hill NJ. **Other U.S. locations:** Nationwide. **Listed on:** New York Stock Exchange. **Stock exchange symbol:** LU.

LUCENT TECHNOLOGIES INTERNETWORKING SYSTEMS
One Robbins Road, Westford MA 01886. 978/952-1600. **Fax:** 978/392-9682. **Contact:** Human Resources. **World Wide Web address:** http://www.lucent.com. **Description:** Develops, manufactures, markets, and supports a family of high performance, multiservice wide area network (WAN) switches that enable public carrier providers and private network managers to provide cost-effective, high-speed, enhanced data communications services. These products direct and manage data communications across wide area networks that utilize different network architectures and services, and are designed to support, on a single platform, the major high-speed packet data communications services. These services include frame relay, switched multimegabit data service, and asynchronous transfer mode. The company markets its products to public network providers, including interexchange carriers, local exchange carriers, competitive access providers, other public network providers, and private network managers. **Positions advertised include:** Security Consultant; Logistics Strategy Manager; EMEA Regional PEC Leader; CALA Regional PEC Leader. **Corporate headquarters location:** Murray Hill NJ. **Other U.S. locations:** Nationwide. **Listed on:** New York Stock Exchange. **Stock exchange symbol:** LU. **Number of employees at this location:** 650.

LUMBER INSURANCE COMPANIES
One Speen Street, P.O. Box 9165, Framingham MA 01701. 508/872-8111. **Fax:** 508/872-9711. **Contact:** Human Resources Department. **Description:** Provides commercial property and casualty insurance. **Corporate headquarters location:** This location. **Number of employees at this location:** 225. **Number of employees nationwide:** 325.

LUXTEC CORPORATION
99 Hartwell Street, West Boylston MA 01583. 508/856-9454. **Toll-free phone:** 800/325-8966. **Contact:** Human Resources. **World Wide Web address:** http://www.luxtec.com. **Description:** Designs, develops, manufactures, and markets illumination and vision products utilizing fiber-optic technology for the medical and dental industries. These products are designed to produce high-quality light delivered directly to the operative site. Products include fiber-optic headlights and headlight television camera systems for audio/video recordings of surgical procedures; light sources; cables; retractors; loupes; surgical telescopes; and other custom-made surgical specialty instruments. **Corporate headquarters location:** This location. **Subsidiaries include:** Cathtec, Inc.; Fiber Imaging Technologies, Inc.; Luxtec Fiber Optics B.V. **Parent company:** PrimeSource Healthcare (Tuscon AZ). **Number of employees nationwide:** 50.

LYCOS, INC.
400-2 Totten Pond Road, Waltham MA 02451-2000. 781/370-2700. **Contact:** Human Resources. **World Wide Web address:** http://www.lycos.com. **Description:** An Internet search engine that finds, indexes, and filters information from the World Wide Web. **Corporate headquarters location:** This location. **Listed on:** NASDAQ. **Stock exchange symbol:** LCOS.

M/A-COM, INC.
1011 Pawtucket Boulevard, Lowell MA 01854. 978/442-5000. **Contact:** Human Resources. **World Wide Web address:** http://www.macom.com. **Description:** Designs, develops, and manufactures microwave semiconductors and subsystems for commercial wireless, cellular, satellite, and automotive communications, and for government and defense applications. **Positions advertised include:** Electronics Engineer; Accountant; Manufacturing Engineer; Reliability Engineer. **Corporate headquarters location:** This location. **Other area locations:** Burlington MA. **Other U.S. locations:** San Jose CA; Torrance CA; Harrisburg PA; Lynchburg VA; Roanoke VA. **International locations:** Canada; England; Ireland. **Parent company:** Tyco Electronics.

MCI
800 Boylston Street, 7th Floor, Boston, MA 02199. 617/867-7400. **Contact:** Human Resources. **World Wide Web address:** http://www.mci.com. **Description:** One of the world's largest suppliers of local, long distance, and international telecommunications services, and a global Internet service provider. MCI services more than 150 countries. **NOTE:** Submit resume and search for positions online. **Positions advertised include:** SBS Account Representative. **Corporate headquarters location:** Ashburn VA.

MELMARK NEW ENGLAND
50 Tower Office Park, Woburn MA 01801. 781/932-9211. **Fax:** 781/932-0189. **Contact:** Recruiting Department. **E-mail address:** recruiter@melmarkne.org. **World Wide Web address:** http://www.melmarkne.org. **Description:** A non-profit organization, serving children with autism, neurological disorders, and acquired brain injuries. **Positions advertised include:** ABA Counselor; Classroom Teacher; Speech Language Pathologist.

MFS INVESTMENT MANAGEMENT
500 Boylston Street, Boston MA 02116. 617/954-5000. **Contact:** Human Resources. **E-mail address:** jobs@mfs.com. **World Wide Web address:** http://www.mfs.com. **Description:** A full-service investment management firm. Founded in 1924. **Positions advertised include:** Divisional Director; Administrative Assistant; Regional Vice President; Regional Sales Representative; Office Associate; Lead RFP Writer; Programmer; Financial Systems Analyst; Corporate Tax Manager; Tax Analyst; Equity Trader; Asset Controller; Fund Administrator; Fund Team Manager. **NOTE:** Entry-level positions are offered. **Corporate headquarters location:** This location. **Other U.S. locations:** Phoenix AZ. **Parent company:** Sun Life Assurance. **Operations at this facility include:** Administration; Research and Development; Sales; Service. **Number of employees at this location:** 1,500.

MIT (MASSACHUSETTS INSTITUTE OF TECHNOLOGY)
400 Main Street, 2nd Floor, Cambridge MA 02142. 617/253-4251. **Contact:** Human Resources. **World Wide Web address:** http://web.mit.edu/personnel. **Description:** A private, four-year academic and research institution with an enrollment of approximately 4,300 undergraduate students and 5,600 graduate students. **Positions advertised include:** Administrative Assistant; Associate Counsel; Chief Radiological Technician; Circulation Assistant; Computational Biologist; Departmental Liaison; Mechanic; Member Relations Representative; Post Doctoral Associate; Research Scientist; Software Engineer; Staff Accountant; Technical Assistant. **Office hours:** Monday - Friday, 9:00 a.m. - 5:00 p.m. **NOTE:** Send resumes to P.O. Box 391229, Cambridge MA 02139.

MIT LINCOLN LABORATORY
244 Wood Street, Lexington MA 02420-9108. 781/981-7066. **Fax:** 781/981-7086. **Contact:** Human Resources Department. **E-mail address:** resume@ll.mit.edu. **World Wide Web address:** http://www.ll.mit.edu. **Description:** A federally funded, nonprofit

research center of the Massachusetts Institute of Technology (MIT). Lincoln Laboratory applies science, by means of advanced technology, to critical problems of national security. Problems focus on space surveillance, tactical systems, free space and terrestrial optical communications, and air traffic control systems. Founded in 1951. **NOTE:** Resumes must be in a scannable format and may be e-mailed (ASCII text file) or faxed. **Positions advertised include:** Engineer; Analyst; Laboratory Assistant; Biologist. **Office hours:** Monday - Friday, 8:30 a.m. - 5:00 p.m. **Corporate headquarters location:** This location. **Operations at this facility include:** Research and Development. **Number of employees at this location:** 2,200.

MIT PRESS
5 Cambridge Center, 4th Floor, Cambridge MA 02142-1493. 617/253-5646. **Contact:** Human Resources. **World Wide Web address:** http://www.mitpress.mit.edu. **Description:** Publishes scholarly books. Founded in 1962. **Corporate headquarters location:** This location.

MKS-ASTEX PRODUCTS
90 Industrial Way, Wilmington MA 01887-4610. 978/284-4000. **Contact:** Human Resources. **World Wide Web address:** http://www.astex.com. **Description:** A manufacturer of systems and components used in the production of advanced semiconductors and chemical vapor deposition (CVD) diamond. ASTeX components are used in a number of semiconductor fabrication steps such as stripping, etching, CVD, and physical vapor deposition. The company's CVD diamond production systems are used to develop and manufacture tool coatings, optics and optical coatings, thermal management substrates for high performance electronics, and bearing seals and wear parts for a variety of applications. ASTeX markets its systems to producers of CVD diamond, while its microwave power generators, plasma sources, and ozone generators and subsystems are marketed to semiconductor capital equipment manufacturers. **Positions advertised include:** Electrical Engineer; Engineer; Employment Relations Manager; Advanced Manufacturing Engineer. **Corporate headquarters location:** Andover MA. **Listed on:** NASDAQ. **Stock exchange symbol:** MKSI.

MRO SOFTWARE, INC.
100 Crosby Drive, Bedford MA 01730. 781/280-2000. **Contact:** Human Resources. **World Wide Web address:** http://www.mro.com. **Description:** Develops, markets, and supports enterprisewide client/server applications software used to assist in maintaining and developing high-value capital assets such as facilities, systems, and production equipment. The company's products enable customers to reduce downtime, control maintenance expenses, cut spare parts inventories, improve purchasing efficiency, shorten product development cycles, and deploy productive assets and personnel more effectively. **Positions advertised include:** Consultant Information Technology Asset Management. **Corporate headquarters location:** This location. **International locations:** Worldwide. **Listed on:** NASDAQ. **Stock exchange symbol:** MROI.

MRV COMMUNICATIONS
295 Foster Street, Littleton MA 01460. 978/952-4700. **Contact:** Tracy Flory, Human Resources. **E-mail address:** hr@mrv.com. **World Wide Web address:** http://www.mrv.com. **Description:** Designs, manufactures, markets, and supports high-performance data communications network systems. **Listed on:** NASDAQ. **Stock exchange symbol:** MRVC.

MWH
12 Farnsworth Street, Boston MA 02110. 617/338-7100. **Contact:** Human Resources. **World Wide Web address:** http://www.mw.com. **Description:** An environmental engineering firm specializing in water and wastewater projects. **Corporate headquarters location:** Broomfield CO. **Other U.S. locations:** Nationwide.

MWRA (MASSACHUSETTS WATER RESOURCES AUTHORITY)
100 First Avenue, Charlestown Navy Yard, Boston MA 02129. 617/242-6000. **Contact:** Human Resources. **World Wide Web address:** http://www.mwra.com. **Description:** Manages the quality of water throughout Massachusetts, including the cleanup of Boston Harbor and other large projects.

MACROCHEM CORPORATION
110 Hartwell Avenue, Lexington MA 02421-3134. 781/862-4003. **Fax:** 781/862-4338. **Contact:** Human Resources. **E-mail address:** hr@macrochem.com. **World Wide Web address:** http://www.macrochem.com. **Description:** Engaged in the development and commercialization of advanced drug delivery systems for the transdermal delivery of enzyme, protein, and drug compounds for therapeutic, over-the-counter, and cosmetic applications. SEPA, MacroChem's worldwide-patented compound, accelerates the passage of drugs through the skin and other biomembranes. **Corporate headquarters location:** This location. **Listed on:** NASDAQ. **Stock exchange symbol:** MCHM.

MACROMEDIA, INC.
275 Grove Street, Newton MA 02466. 617/219-2000. **Fax:** 617/219-2100. **Contact:** Human Resources. **World Wide Web address:** http://www.macromedia.com. **Description:** Develops and supports application development and server software that allow businesses to develop e-commerce systems. **Corporate headquarters location:** San Francisco.

MACY'S
450 Washington Street, Boston MA 02111. 617/357-3000. **Recorded jobline:** 800/603-6229. **Contact:** Human Resources. **World Wide Web address:** http://www.macys.com. **Description:** One location of the department store chain. **Positions advertised include:** Beauty Advisor; Bridal Consultant; Cosmetic Business Manager; Counter Manager; Fine Jewelry Service Associate; Furniture Service Associate Selling Specialist; Women's Shoe Service Specialist; Department Sales Manager; Group Sales Manager; Human Resources Coordinator; Merchandise Manager. **Corporate headquarters location:** New York City.

MAGUIRE GROUP, INC.
225 Foxborough Boulevard, Foxborough MA 02035. 508/543-1700. **Contact:** Jan Washburn, Human Resources Manager. **World Wide Web address:** http://www.maguiregroup.com. **Description:** An architectural, engineering, and planning firm, serving domestic and international clients. Maguire Group, Inc. is engaged in the design and construction management of industrial commercial buildings; environmental facilities including sewers and treatment plants; hydroelectric power plants; highways, bridges, airports, and mass transit projects; and port and marine facilities. **Positions advertised include:** Environmental Specialist. **Corporate headquarters location:** This location. **Other U.S. locations:** New Britain CT; Portland ME; Portsmouth NH; Atlantic City NJ; Lawrenceville NJ; Harrisburg PA; Philadelphia PA; Pittsburgh PA; State College PA; Providence RI. **International locations:** St. Croix, U.S. Virgin Islands.

MAIL COMPUTER SERVICE INC. (MCS)
321 Manly Street, West Bridgewater MA 02379. 508/584-6490. **Contact:** Human Resources. **E-mail address:** 508/584-2890. **World Wide Web address:** http://www.mailcompserv.com. **Description:** A full-service mail house. Mail Computer Service Inc.'s mass-mailing services include data processing, mail processing, digitizing, lasering, and printing.

MAINTENANCE CHEMICAL SUPPLIERS INC.
101 Messina Drive, Braintree MA 02184. 781/849-6168. **Contact:** Human Resources. **Description:** Provides maintenance and janitorial services. The company is also involved in the direct sale of industrial chemical products. **Corporate headquarters location:** This location. **Number of employees at this location:** 10.

B.L. MAKEPEACE, INC.
125 Guest Street, Brighton MA 02135-2083. 617/782-3800. **Fax:** 617/782-9768. **Contact:** Human Resources. **E-mail address:** personel@makepeace.com. **World Wide Web address:** http://www.makepeace.com. **Description:** A firm specializing in supplying drafting room equipment and supplies. **Corporate headquarters location:** This location. **Other area locations:** Hopkinton MA.

THE MARINO CENTER FOR PROGRESSIVE HEALTH
2500 Massachusetts Avenue, Cambridge MA 02140. 617/661-6225. **Fax:** 617/492-2002. **Contact:** Human Resources. **E-mail address:** contact@marinocenter.org. **World Wide Web address:** http://www.marinocenter.org. **Description:** A medical center with a full-service health store specializing in family medicine, acupuncture, health education, prevention programs, and complementary therapies. The Marino Center for Progressive Health includes: The Center for Men's Health is devoted to diagnosing and treating sexual dysfunction, prostate disease, and incontinence; The Center for Women's Health is devoted to gynecological care, birth control, sexually transmitted diseases, PMS, menstrual disorders, and menopause; The UroCare Clinic is devoted to addressing the needs of women with urinary incontinence. Also provided are classes, therapy groups, workshops, and free lectures. Areas of specialization include general medicine, psychology, psychotherapy, stress-reduction, urology, neurology, chiropractic, acupuncture, traditional Chinese medicine, nutrition, massage therapy, infusion therapy, chelation therapy, biofeedback, coping with cancer, yoga, meditation, and fitness. **Positions advertised include:** Primary Care Physician; Nurse Practitioner; Physicians Assistant. **Other area locations:** Dedham MA; Wellesley MA.

MARKET FORGE INDUSTRIES, INC.
35 Garvey Street, Everett MA 02149. 617/387-4100. **Toll-free phone:** 800/227-2659. **Fax:** 617/387-4456. **Contact:** Human Resources. **E-mail address:** custserv@mfii.com. **World Wide Web address:** http://www.mfii.com. **Description:** Manufactures restaurant equipment including ranges, ovens, convection ovens, shelving, and tilting skillets.

W.B. MASON
P.O. Box 111, Brockton MA 02303-0111. 508/586-3434. **Physical address:** 59 Centre Street, Brockton MA 02301. **Contact:** Human Resources. **World Wide Web address:** http://www.wbmason.com. **Description:** Distributes a wide range of office supplies, primarily to businesses. **Positions advertised include:** Driver; Picker Packer Warehouse Associate; Customer Service Representative; 3rd Shift Supply Warehouse Worker; Desktop Publishing Marketing Department. **Corporate headquarters location:** This location. **Other area locations:** Auburn MA; Boston MA; Hyannis MA; Woburn MA. **Other U.S. locations:** North Haven CT; Secaucus NJ; Cranston RI.

MASS BUYING POWER (MBP)
1076 Washington Street, Hanover MA 02339. 781/829-4900. **Contact:** Human Resources. **E-mail address:** massbuy@massbuy.com. **World Wide Web address:** http://www.massbuy.com. **Description:** Provides discount purchasing benefits for employees of member companies. Mass Buying Power offers discounts on a wide variety of products and services including automobiles, major household appliances, furniture, consumer loans, and home improvements. Mass Buying Power also operates a full-service travel agency specializing in discount travel packages. Founded in 1967. **Corporate headquarters location:** This location. **Listed on:** Privately held.

MASSACHUSETTS ATTORNEY GENERAL'S OFFICE
One Ashburton Place, Boston MA 02108. 617/727-2200. **Contact:** Human Resources. **World Wide Web address:** http://www.ago.state.ma.us. **Description:** Provides legal services for all state entities and represents the state in legal cases.

MASSACHUSETTS AUDOBON SOCIETY
MOOSE HILL WILDLIFE SANCTUARY
Moosehill Sanctuary, 293 Moose Hill Street, Sharon MA 02067. 781/784-5691. **Contact:** Director. **World Wide Web address:** http://www.massaudubon.org. **Description:** A nonprofit organization involved in educating the community about the environment and promoting conservation efforts. The sanctuary offers a wide range of programs including Owl Prowls, family camp-outs, summer camp for children, and maple sugaring tours. The sanctuary also has its own art gallery featuring bimonthly exhibits of works by local artists. **NOTE:** Moose Hill Wildlife Sanctuary welcomes applicants for volunteer positions. **Positions advertised include:** Development Officer; Administrative Assistant. **NOTE:** For either of these positions send resume to: Mass Audubon Society, 208 South Great Road, Lincoln MA, 01773. Attention: Karen O'Neil. E-mail koneill@massaudubon.org. Education Coordinator: For this position mail resume to Rebecca Taylor, Felix Neck Wildlife Sanctuary, P.O. Box, 494, Vineyard Haven MA, 02568. **Corporate headquarters location:** Lincoln MA.

MASSACHUSETTS BAY TRANSPORTATION AUTHORITY (MBTA)
10 Park Plaza, Boston MA 02116. 617/222-5000. **Contact:** Human Resources. **World Wide Web address:** http://www.mbta.com. **Description:** Operates the subways, trolleys, buses, and commuter train lines.

MASSACHUSETTS COLLEGE OF ART
621 Huntington Avenue, Boston MA 02115. 617/232-1555. **Fax:** 617/879-7911. **Contact:** Human Resources. **World Wide Web address:** http://www.massart.edu. **Description:** An art school offering multimedia courses in a variety of disciplines including photography and painting.

MASSACHUSETTS DEPARTMENT OF BUSINESS AND TECHNOLOGY
One Ashburton Place, Room 2101, Boston MA 02108. 617/727-8380. **Fax:** 617/727-4426. **Contact:** Personnel. **E-mail address:** econ@state.ma.us. **World Wide Web address:** http://www.state.ma.us/econ. **Description:** Dedicated to improving the job market and long-term economic growth of the state. **Director:** Carolyn E. Boviard.

MASSACHUSETTS DEPARTMENT OF ENVIRONMENTAL MANAGEMENT BUREAU OF RECREATION
251 Causeway Street, Boston MA 02114. 617/626-1250. **Contact:** Human Resources. **World Wide Web address:** http://www.state.ma.us/dem. **Description:** Responsible

for the maintenance and improvement of Massachusetts state parks and reservations. The department also offers a variety of educational programs.

MASSACHUSETTS DEPARTMENT OF INDUSTRIAL ACCIDENTS
600 Washington Street, 7th Floor, Boston MA 02111. 617/727-4900. **Toll-free phone:** 800/323-3249. **Contact:** Human Resources. **World Wide Web address:** http://www.state.ma.us/dia. **Description:** Responsible for the administration and management of workers' compensation claims. The Department of Industrial Accidents is part of the Massachusetts Department of Labor and Workforce Development.

MASSACHUSETTS DEPARTMENT OF MENTAL RETARDATION
500 Harrison Avenue, Boston MA 02118. 617/727-5608. **Fax:** 617/624-7577. **Contact:** Human Resources. **World Wide Web address:** http://www.dmr.state.ma.us. **Description:** The Department of Mental Retardation provides support and services to Massachusetts residents with mental retardation. Services include assistance with transportation, job placement, and treatment. **Operations at this facility include:** This location houses the administrative offices of the Department of Mental Retardation.

MASSACHUSETTS DEPARTMENT OF PUBLIC HEALTH
250 Washington Street, 1st Floor, Boston MA 02108-4619. 617/624-5700. **Contact:** Human Resources. **World Wide Web address:** http://www.state.ma.us/dph. **Description:** Responsible for ensuring quality health care and safe living conditions to the people of Massachusetts.

MASSACHUSETTS DEPARTMENT OF REVENUE
51 Sleeper Street, Boston MA 02210. 617/626-3400. **Contact:** Human Resources. **World Wide Web address:** http://www.dor.state.ma.us. **Description:** Massachusetts Department of Revenue processes all Massachusetts residents' income tax returns and provides tax forms, state tax information, and tax publications.

MASSACHUSETTS DEPARTMENT OF TELECOMMUNICATIONS AND ENERGY
One South Station, Boston MA 02110. 617/305-3500. **Contact:** Human Resources. **World Wide Web address:** http://www.mass.gov/dte. **Description:** A regulatory agency for utility companies in the state.

MASSACHUSETTS ELECTRIC COMPANY
55 Bearfoot Road, Northborough MA 01532. 508/421-7000. **Toll-free phone:** 800/322-3223. **Contact:** Personnel. **World Wide Web address:** http://www.masselectric.com. **Description:** An electric utility company. **Listed on:** New York Stock Exchange. **Stock exchange symbol:** NGG. **Parent company:** National Grid.

MASSACHUSETTS ELECTRIC CONSTRUCTION COMPANY
180 Guest Street, Boston MA 02135-2028. 617/254-1015. **Contact:** Human Resources. **World Wide Web address:** http://www.masselec.com. **Description:** An electrical contractor. Services include construction management, value engineering, design, and consultation. **Other U.S. locations:** Nationwide.

MASSACHUSETTS GENERAL HOSPITAL
55 Fruit Street, Boston MA 02114. 617/726-2000. **Fax:** 617/724-2266. **Contact:** Human Resources. **World Wide Web address:** http://www.mgh.harvard.edu. **Description:** An 820-bed, nonprofit, teaching hospital. As part of the Harvard Medical School, MGH offers diagnostic and therapeutic care in virtually every specialty of medicine. This location also hires seasonally. **NOTE:** Please direct resumes to Partners HealthCare System Inc., Human Resources, 101 Merrimac Street, 5th Floor, Boston MA 02114. 617/726-2210. Entry-level positions are offered. **Positions advertised include:** Administrative Assistant; Admissions Coordinator; Admissions Interviewer; Beautician. **Special programs:** Internships; Training; Co-ops; Summer Jobs. **Office hours:** Monday - Friday, 8:30 a.m. - 4:30 p.m. **Parent company:** Partners HealthCare System Inc. **Operations at this facility include:** Administration; Research and Development; Service. **Number of employees at this location:** 10,000.

MASSACHUSETTS HIGHWAY DEPARTMENT
10 Park Plaza, Room 3510, Boston MA 02116-3973. 617/973-7500. **Contact:** Human Resources. **World Wide Web address:** http://www.state.ma.us/mhd. **Description:** Provides highway maintenance and repair services as part of the Public Works Department.

MASSACHUSETTS HOSPITAL ASSOCIATION
5 New England Executive Park, Burlington MA 01803. 781/272-8000. **Contact:** Lisa Bales, Human Resources. **World Wide Web address:** http://www.mhalink.org. **World Wide Web address:** http://www.mhalink.org. **Description:** A trade association for professionals in the hospital industry, providing such services as continuing education and information on new developments within the industry.

MASSACHUSETTS MUTUAL LIFE INSURANCE COMPANY
1295 State Street, Springfield MA 01111. 413/788-8411. **Contact:** Human Resources. **World Wide Web address:** http://www.massmutual.com. **Description:** One of the largest insurers in the United States, with over 500 offices nationwide. MassMutual Life Insurance Company provides both individual and group insurance coverage. **Positions advertised include:** Customer Service Representative; Data Management Technician; Internal Sales Manager; Financial Reporting Analyst; Accountant; Relationship Manager. **Special programs:** Internships. **Corporate headquarters location:** This location. **Parent company:** MassMutual Financial Group. **Operations at this facility include:** Administration; Service. **Number of employees nationwide:** 10,000.

MASSACHUSETTS OFFICE OF TRAVEL AND TOURISM
State Transportation Building, 10 Park Plaza, Suite 4510, Boston MA 02116. 617/973-8500. **Toll-free phone:** 800/227-MASS. **Contact:** Director of Operations. **World Wide Web address:** http://www.mass-vacation.com. **Description:** Promotes the state of Massachusetts as a vacation destination. **Special programs:** Internships. **Office hours:** Monday - Friday, 8:45 a.m. - 5:00 p.m. **Number of employees at this location:** 30.

MASSACHUSETTS PORT AUTHORITY (MASSPORT)
One Harborside Drive, Suite 200S, East Boston MA 02128-2909. 617/428-2800. **Contact:** Human Resources. **World Wide Web address:** http://www.massport.com. **Description:** Owns and operates Logan International Airport and the public terminals of the Port of Boston. The Massachusetts Port Authority operates an engineering department and environmental unit at this facility.

MASSACHUSETTS TRADE OFFICE
State Transportation Building, 10 Park Plaza, Suite 3720, Boston MA 02116. 617/367-1830. **Contact:** Personnel. **World Wide Web address:** http://www.state.ma.us/moiti. **Description:** Assists local businesses in their dealings with international companies. Services include export counseling and trade seminars. Founded in 1983.

MASSASOIT COMMUNITY COLLEGE
One Massasoit Boulevard, Brockton MA 02302. 508/588-9100. **Toll-free phone:** 800/CAR-EERS. **Contact:** Personnel. **World Wide Web address:** http://www.massasoit.mass.edu. **Description:** A community college offering a variety of two-year programs. **Other area locations:** Canton MA, **NOTE:** Call 781/821-2222 for Canton Campus.

MASSBANK CORPORATION
123 Haven Street, Reading MA 01867. 781/662-0100. **Contact:** Human Resources. **World Wide Web address:** http://www.massbank.com. **Description:** A savings and loan corporation. **NOTE:** Please send resumes to: Human Resources, MASSBANK Corporation, 50 Central Street, Lowell MA 01852. **Number of employees at this location:** 150.

MATEC INSTRUMENT COMPANIES
56 Hudson Street, Northborough MA 01532. 508/393-0155. **Fax:** 508/393-5476. **Contact:** Ed Antolino, Human Resources. **E-mail address:** eantolino@matec.com. **World Wide Web address:** http://www.matec.com. **Description:** Designs, manufactures, imports, and sells quartz crystals and oscillators; develops and manufactures computer-controlled, ultrasonic test equipment to perform real-time measurements and analysis; and produces and sells instruments to evaluate the stability of colloidal dispersions. **Corporate headquarters location:** This location. **Subsidiaries include:** Valpey-Fisher Corporation. **Listed on:** American Stock Exchange. **Stock exchange symbol:** MXC. **CEO:** Ted Valpey, Jr.

MATH WORKS
3 Apple Hill Drive, Natick MA 01760. 508/647-7000. **Fax:** 508/647-7001. **Contact:** Human Resources. **World Wide Web address:** http://www.mathworks.com. **Description:** Develops mathematical software packages. **Positions advertised include:** Applications Support Engineer; FPC Manager; MATLAB Software Developer; Software Engineer; Release Engineer; Principal Tools Engineer; Business Systems Administration; Physical Modeling Developer; Communications Quality Engineer; Applications Engineer.

MATHSOFT ENGINEERING & EDUCATION, INC.
101 Main Street, 16th Floor, Cambridge MA 02142. 617/577-1017. **Fax:** 617/444-8001. **Contact:** Human Resources. **E-mail address:** hrjobs@mathsoft.com. **World Wide Web address:** http://www.mathsoft.com. **Description:** A leading developer of mathematical software and electronic books for desktop computers. Products include Mathcad, a live interactive environment for mathematics work in a wide variety of fields including engineering, science, and education. MathSoft also publishes the Mathcad Library of Electronic Books, Maple V symbolic computation software, and other third-party mathematical software. Founded in 1984. **Positions advertised include:** Math CAD Author; Math CAD Reviewer. **Corporate headquarters location:** This location. **International locations:** England; Germany. **Annual sales/revenues:** $11 - $20 million. **Number of employees at this location:** 60. **Number of employees nationwide:** 150.

MATRITECH, INC.
330 Nevada Street, Newton MA 02460. 617/928-0820. **Toll-free phone:** 800/320-2521. **Fax:** 617/928-0821. **Contact:** Human Resources. **World Wide Web address:** http://www.matritech.com. **Description:** A biotechnology company using proprietary nuclear matrix protein technology to develop and commercialize innovative serum-, cell-, and urine-based NMP diagnostics that enable physicians to detect and monitor the presence of bladder, breast, colorectal, cervical, and prostate cancers. The company's other primary focus is the development of additional serum assays for lung, liver, pancreatic, stomach, and renal cancer. Founded in 1987. **NOTE:** Entry-level positions are offered. **Positions advertised include:** Biochemist; Research Assistant. **Corporate headquarters location:** This location. **Listed on:** NASDAQ. **Stock exchange symbol:** NMPS. **CEO:** Stephen D. Chubb. **Annual sales/revenues:** Less than $5 million. **Number of employees at this location:** 55.

MAXWELL SHOE COMPANY INC.
P.O. Box 37, Hyde Park MA 02137-0037. 617/364-5090. **Physical address:** 101 Sprague Street, Hyde Park MA 02136. **Toll-free phone:** 800/326-6687. **Fax:** 617/364-9058. **Contact:** Human Resources. **E-mail address:** hr@maxwellshoe.com. **World Wide Web address:** http://www.maxwellshoe.com. **Description:** Designs, develops, and markets moderately priced casual and dress footwear for women under the A Line Anne Klein, Anne Klein2, Mootsies Tootsies, Sam & Libby, J.G. Hook, and Dockers brand names and for children under the Mootsies Kids brand name. The company also designs and develops private label footwear for selected retailers. **Corporate headquarters location:** This location. **Listed on:** NASDAQ. **Stock exchange symbol:** MAXS. **Chairman and CEO:** Mark J. Cocozza.

McDERMOTT, WILL & EMERY
28 State Street, Boston MA 02109-1775. 617/535-4000. **Contact:** Human Resources. **World Wide Web address:** http://www.mwe.com. **Description:** A law firm with concentrations in health care, corporate law, and litigation.

McDONALD'S CORPORATION
690 Canton Street, Suite 310, Westwood MA 02090. 781/329-1450. **Contact:** Personnel Manager. **World Wide Web address:** http://www.mcdonalds.com. **Description:** McDonald's develops, operates, franchises, and services a worldwide system of restaurants that process, package, and sell a limited menu of fast foods. One of the largest restaurant operations in the United States and one of the largest food service organizations in the world, McDonald's operates more than 30,000 McDonald's restaurants in all 50 states and in 119 countries. **NOTE:** Entry-level positions are offered. **Positions advertised include:** Management Trainee. **Corporate headquarters location:** Oak Brook IL. **Other U.S. locations:** Nationwide. **Operations at this facility include:** This location houses regional management offices for the international fast food chain. **Listed on:** New York Stock Exchange. **Stock exchange symbol:** MCD.

McGRAW-HILL COMPANIES, INC.
24 Hartwell Avenue, Lexington MA 02421. 781/863-5100. **Contact:** Human Resources. **World Wide Web address:** http://www.mcgraw-hill.com. **Description:** McGraw-Hill Companies, Inc. provides computer-accessible economic information, models, forecasts, analyses, software, and consulting services to clients in industry, government, and business. **Positions advertised include:** Market Research Analyst; Economic Analyst; Bid News Coordinator. **Corporate headquarters location:** New York NY. **Listed on:** New York Stock Exchange. **Stock exchange symbol:** MHP.

McKESSONHBOC
3 Bridle Road, Chelmsford MA 01824. 978/256-1655. **Contact:** Human Resources. **World Wide Web address:** http://www.hboc.com. **Description:** An information solutions company that provides information systems and technology to health care enterprises including hospitals, integrated delivery networks, and managed care

organizations. McKesson HBOC's primary products are Pathway 2000, a family of client/server-based applications that allows for the integration and uniting of health care providers; STAR, Series, and HealthQuest transaction systems; TRENDSTAR decision support system; and QUANTUM enterprise information system. The company also offers outsourcing services that include strategic information systems planning, data center operations, receivables management, business office administration, and major system conversions. **Positions advertised include:** Night Warehouse Supervisor; Sales Manager; Vice President Business Solutions; Radiology Information Systems; Department Liaison; Driver. **Corporate headquarters location:** San Francisco CA.

MEADWESTVACO
40 Willow Street, South Lee MA 01260. 413/243-1231. **Contact:** Human Resources Manager. **World Wide Web address:** http://www.meadwestvaco.com. **Description:** Manufactures papers for decorative and industrial laminates, and papers made from various materials including mica, cotton, metal, and carbon. **Corporate headquarters location:** Stamford CT. **Other U.S. locations:** Nationwide. **Listed on:** New York Stock Exchange. **Stock exchange symbol:** MWV. **Number of employees worldwide:** 30,000.

MED TAC CORPORATION
P.O. Box 9111, Newtonville MA 02460. 617/244-5333. **Fax:** 617/244-5111. **Contact:** Human Resources. **E-mail address:** hr@medtac.com. **World Wide Web address:** http://www.medtac.com. **Description:** Offers medical and dental insurance. **Positions advertised include:** Claims Manager; Regional Sales Representative.

MEDIEVAL MANOR
246 East Berkeley Street, Boston MA 02118. 617/423-4900. **Contact:** Manager. **World Wide Web address:** http://www.medievalmanor.com. **Description:** A dinner/theater restaurant with a medieval theme.

MEDITECH (MEDICAL INFORMATION TECHNOLOGY, INC.)
One MEDITECH Circle, Westwood MA 02090. 781/821-3000. **Contact:** Human Resources. **E-mail address:** jobs@meditech.com. **World Wide Web address:** http://www.meditech.com. **Description:** Develops, sells, installs, and supports computer software designed to help the medical community share critical information. **NOTE:** Entry-level positions are offered. **Positions advertised include:** Marketing Consultant; Marketing Consultant Nursing; Marketing Support Representative; Application Specialist; Programmer; Accounts Receivable Specialist. **Office hours:** Monday - Friday, 9:00 a.m. - 5:30 p.m. **Corporate headquarters location:** This location. **Other U.S. locations:** Canton MA; Framingham MA; Norwood MA. **Operations at this facility include:** Administration; Research and Development; Sales; Service. **Number of employees nationwide:** 1,900.

MEDITRUST CORPORATION
197 First Avenue, Needham Heights MA 02494. 781/433-6000. **Contact:** Human Resources. **Description:** A health care real estate investment trust. Meditrust invests primarily in health care facilities providing subacute and long-term care services. The company has investments in more than 400 health care facilities in 38 states. **Corporate headquarters location:** This location. **Other U.S. locations:** Palm Beach FL. **Parent company:** The Meditrust Companies (also at this location) also consists of Meditrust Operating Company. **Number of employees at this location:** 50.

MEDSOURCE TECHNOLOGIES
150 California Street, Newton MA 02458. 617/964-9100. **Fax:** 617/964-2660. **Contact:** Human Resources. **World Wide Web address:** http://www.medsourcetech.com. **Description:** Designs and manufactures disposable medical devices such as endoscopic catheters, safety needles, balloon catheters, ligation devices, and laser delivery devices. **NOTE:** Entry-level positions are offered. **Positions advertised include:** Design Engineer. **Special programs:** Internships; Training. **Corporate headquarters:** Minneapolis MN. **Other U.S. locations:** Nationwide. **Listed on:** Privately held. **Annual sales/revenues:** $11 - $20 million. **Number of employees at this location:** 120.

THE MEDSTAT GROUP
125 Cambridge Park Drive, Cambridge MA 02140. 617/576-3237. **Contact:** Human Resources. **E-mail address:** recruiting@medstat.com. **World Wide Web address:** http://www.medstat.com. **Description:** Provides information that helps manage the purchasing and administration of health benefits and services. **Positions advertised include:** Senior Consultant. **Corporate headquarters location:** Ann Harbor MI. **Parent Company:** Thompson Financial.

MEDTRONIC/AVE
37A Cherry Hill Drive, Danvers MA 01923. 978/777-0042. **Contact:** Human Resources Department. **World Wide Web address:** http://www.medtronic.com. **Description:** Manufactures a line of minimally invasive devices for use in treating patients with coronary artery and peripheral vascular disease. **Positions advertised include:** Packaging Engineer; Manufacturing Engineer; RaD Engineer; Production Scheduler; Supplier Quality Manager. **Corporate headquarters location:** Minneapolis MN. **Listed on:** New York Stock Exchange. **Stock exchange symbol:** MDT.

MELICK PORTER & SHEA
28 State Street, 22nd Floor, Boston MA 02109-1775. 617/523-6200. **Fax:** 617/523-8130. **Contact:** Human Resources. **E-mail address:** jobs@melicklaw.com. **World Wide Web address:** http://www.melicklaw.com. **Description:** A law firm consisting mainly of defense attorneys. **Positions advertised include:** Associate; Summer Intern; Legal Secretary; Paralegal.

MENTOR GRAPHICS
300 Nickerson Road, Suite 200, Marlborough MA 01752. 508/480-0881. **Toll-free phone:** 800/592-2210. **Contact:** Human Resources. **World Wide Web address:** http://www.mentor.com. **Description:** A leader in electronic hardware and software design solutions, providing products, consulting services and support for electronics and semiconductor companies. **Positions advertised include:** Director of Marketing; Product Marketing Manager; Technical Marketing Engineer; Software Development Engineer; Financial Analyst. **Special programs:** Internships.

MERCURY AIR CENTER
180 Hanscom Drive, Bedford MA 01730. 781/274-0010. **Contact:** Human Resources. **World Wide Web address:** http://www.mercuryairgroup.com. **Description:** Sells and maintains aircraft and parts, and provides ground support services.

MERCURY COMPUTER SYSTEMS, INC.
199 Riverneck Road, Chelmsford MA 01824. 978/256-1300. **Contact:** Human Resources. **World Wide Web address:** http://www.mc.com. **Description:** A leading provider of high-performance, real-time, embedded solutions for diverse applications including medical imaging, defense electronics, and shared storage configurations. **NOTE:** Entry-level positions are offered. **Positions advertised include:** Component Engineer; Director of Systems Architecture; Engineer. **Special programs:** Internships; Co-ops; Summer Jobs. **Corporate headquarters location:** This location. **Listed on:** NASDAQ. **Stock exchange symbol:** MRCY. **Annual sales/revenues:** $51 - $100 million. **Number of employees nationwide:** 370.

MERCURY INTERACTIVE CORPORATION
25 Burlington Mall Road, Burlington MA 01803. 800/837-8911. **Contact:** Personnel. **World Wide Web address:** http://www.mercuryinteractive.com. **Description:** Mercury Interactive Corporation is a developer of automated software quality (ASQ) tools for enterprise applications testing. The company's products are used to isolate software and system errors prior to application deployment. **Positions advertised include:** Product Marketing Manager; Product Manager; Brand Manager; ITG Applications Engineer; Technical Support Application Engineer; Commercial Counsel; Contract Negotiation; Stock Administrator; Financial Analyst; Treasury Operations Manager; Accountant. **NOTE:** Resumes should be sent to: Human Resources, 1325 Borregas Avenue, Sunnyvale CA 94089. **Corporate headquarters location:** Sunnyvale CA. **Operations at this facility include:** This location is a sales office. **Listed on:** NASDAQ. **Stock exchange symbol:** MERQ. **Annual sales/revenues:** More than $100 million.

MERRILL LYNCH
2 Batterymarch Park, Quincy MA 02169. 617/745-5500. **Contact:** Human Resources. **World Wide Web address:** http://www.ml.com. **Description:** One of the largest securities brokerage firms in the United States. Merrill Lynch provides securities, extensive insurance, and real estate and related services. The company also brokers commodity futures, commodity options, and corporate and municipal securities. In addition, Merrill Lynch is engaged in investment banking activities. **Positions advertised include:** Manager Assistant; Financial Advisor. **Special programs:** Internships. **Office hours:** Monday - Friday, 8:30 a.m. - 5:00 p.m. **Corporate headquarters location:** New York NY. **Other U.S. locations:** Nationwide. **International locations:** Worldwide. **Listed on:** New York Stock Exchange. **Stock exchange symbol:** MER. **President/CEO:** E. Stanley O'Neal. **Annual sales/revenues:** More than $100 million. **Number of employees worldwide:** 63,800.

MERRIMACK VALLEY CHAMBER OF COMMERCE
264 Essex Street, Lawrence MA 01840. 978/686-0900. **Fax:** 978/794-9953. **Contact:** Personnel. **World Wide Web address:** http://www.merrimackvalleychamber.com. **Description:** Attracts and promotes businesses in the Merrimack Valley area.

MESTEK INC.
260 North Elm Street, Westfield MA 01085. 413/568-9571. **Fax:** 413/562-7630. **Contact:** Karen Chartier, Personnel Manager. **E-mail address:** kchartier@mestek.com. **World Wide Web address:** http://www.mestek.com. **Description:** Manufactures industrial refrigeration and heating equipment. **Corporate headquarters location:** This location. **Listed on:** New York Stock Exchange. **Stock exchange symbol:** MCC. **Number of employees nationwide:** 2,000.

META ENVIRONMENTAL, INC.
49 Clarendon Street, Watertown MA 02472. 617/923-4662. **Fax:** 617/923-4610. **Contact:** Human Resources. **Description:** An environmental engineering firm. This location also houses a research laboratory. **NOTE:** Entry-level positions are offered. **Special programs:** Co-ops. **Corporate headquarters location:** This location. **Listed on:** Privately held. **Annual sales/revenues:** Less than $5 million. **Number of employees at this location:** 15.

META SOFTWARE CORPORATION
125 Cambridge Park Drive, Cambridge MA 02140. 617/576-6920. **Toll-free phone** 800/227-4106. **Fax:** 617/661-2008. **Contact:** Human Resources. **E-mail address:** resumes@metasoft.com. **World Wide Web address:** http://www.metasoftware.com. **Description:** Develops business process re-engineering software and provides consulting services. Founded in 1985. **Positions advertised include:** Senior Consultant; Technical Support Specialist; Programmer/Analyst. **Corporate headquarters location:** This location. **President/CEO:** Robert Seltzer.

METCALF & EDDY, INC.
30 Harvard Mill Square, P.O. Box 4071, Wakefield MA 01880-5371. 781/246-5200. **Fax:** 781/245-6293. **Contact:** Human Resources. **World Wide Web address:** http://www.m-e.com. **Description:** An environmental engineering firm offering professional consulting services for water, wastewater, hazardous waste, and landfills. Metcalf & Eddy, Inc. specializes in design engineering. The firm's projects include wastewater treatment facilities, waterworks projects, industrial and hazardous waste treatment, environmental modeling, and solid waste treatment. **Positions advertised include:** Human Resources Generalist; Production Architect; Librarian; Project Director. **Other U.S. locations:** Nationwide. **Parent company:** AECOM.

METLIFE FINANCIAL SERVICES
1601 Trapelo Road, 1st Floor, Waltham MA 02451. 781/672-2800. **Contact:** Human Resources. **World Wide Web address:** http://www.metlife.com. **Description:** MetLife is a financial services company that offers a wide range of individual and group insurance policies including life, annuity, disability, and mutual funds. **Positions advertised include:** Recruiting Selection Consultant; Corporate Compliance Consultant; Systems Consultant; Team Manager; Business Systems Analyst; Marketing Consultant; Communications Director; Recruiting Director; Supervisor; Service Representative; Financial Consultant. **Corporate headquarters location:** New York NY. **Other U.S. locations:** Nationwide. **Operations at this facility include:** This location is a sales and service office. **Number of employees nationwide:** 13,500.

METROPOLITAN LIFE INSURANCE COMPANY
99 High Street, 32nd Floor, Boston MA 02110. 617/338-1300. **Contact:** Human Resources. **World Wide Web address:** http://www.metlife.com. **Description:** Offers a wide range of individual and group insurance policies including life, annuity, disability, and mutual funds. **Corporate headquarters location:** New York NY. **Other U.S. locations:** Nationwide. **Number of employees nationwide:** 13,500.

METROWEST BANK
420 Franklin Street, Framingham MA 01702. 508/879-7525. **Contact:** Human Resources. **World Wide Web address:** http://www.metrowestbank.com. **Description:** A full-service savings bank. **Parent company:** Banknorth, N.A.

METSO AUTOMATION
P.O. Box 8044, Shrewsbury MA 01545. 508/852-0200. **Physical address:** 44 Bowditch Street, Shrewsbury MA 01545. **Contact:** Marcia Siart, Employment Manager. **World Wide Web address:** http://www.metsoautomation.com. **Description:** Manufactures valves and controls for the process control industry. **Positions advertised include:** Machinist; Industrial Controls Technician. **NOTE:** Entry-level positions and second and third shifts are offered. **Special programs:** Summer Jobs. **International locations:** Brazil; Finland; Singapore. **Parent company:** Metso

Corporation. **Listed on:** New York Stock Exchange. **Stock exchange symbol:** MX. **Annual sales/revenues:** More than $100 million. **Number of employees at this location:** 450. **Number of employees nationwide:** 500. **Number of employees worldwide:** 750.

MICROCAL LLC.
222 Industrial Drive East, Northampton MA 01060-2327. 413/586-7720. **Toll-free phone:** 800/633-3115. **Fax:** 413/586-0149. **Contact:** Bill Plumley. **E-mail address:** billplumley@microcalorimetry.com. **World Wide Web address:** http://www.microcalorimetry.com. **Description:** A high-tech manufacturer. **Positions advertised include:** Accountant; Human Resources Specialist.

MICRO NETWORKS INTEGRATED CIRCUIT SYSTEMS ANDERSEN LABORATORIES
324 Clark Street, Worcester MA 01606. 508/852-5400. **Fax:** 508/853-8296. **Contact:** Human Resources. **E-mail address:** humanresources@mnc,com. **World Wide Web address:** http://www.mnc.com. **Description:** Micro Networks supplies microelectronic circuits to OEMs. These circuits are used for frequency control and data conversion in the information technology field. Founded in 1969. **Positions advertised include:** Applications Engineer. **Corporate headquarters location:** This location. **Other U.S. locations:** Bloomfield CT; Auburn NY. **International locations:** England; The Netherlands. **Subsidiaries include:** Andersen Laboratories (also at this location) manufactures acoustic signal processing products for use in the commercial communications market. **Listed on:** Privately held. **Number of employees at this location:** 95.

MICROCUT
18 Plymouth Drive, South Easton MA 02375. 508/230-9389. **Fax:** 508/230-0387. **Contact:** Human Resources. **E-mail address:** info@microcutusa.com. **World Wide Web address:** http://www.microcutusa.com. **Description:** A manufacturer of premium carbide end mills and special application rotary cutting tools.

MICROFLUIDICS INTERNATIONAL CORPORATION
30 Ossipee Road, Newton MA 02464. 617/969-5452. **Contact:** Human Resources. **World Wide Web address:** http://www.microfluidics.com. **Description:** Manufactures and distributes high-performance mixing equipment primarily for the chemical, pharmaceutical, biotechnology, food, and personal care products industries. **Corporate headquarters location:** This location.

MICROSEMI CORPORATION
580 Pleasant Street, Watertown MA 02472-2408. 617/926-0404. **Fax:** 617/924-1235. **Contact:** Human Resources. **World Wide Web address:** http://www.microsemi.com. **Description:** Microsemi Corporation manufactures and markets semiconductors and similar products and provides related services, principally for the military, aerospace, medical, computer, and telecommunications industries. Major products include high-reliability silicon rectifiers and zener diodes; low-leakage and high-voltage diodes; temperature-compensated zener diodes; and a family of subminiature high-power transient suppresser diodes. **Positions advertised include:** Water Process Technician; Water Process Operator; Data Entry Clerk; In Process Inspector. **Corporate headquarters location:** Irvine CA. **Other area locations:** Lawrence MA; Lowell MA; Melrose MA. **Other U.S. locations:** Scottsdale AZ; Carlsbad CA; Garden Grove CA; Los Angeles CA; Broomfield CO; Riveria Beach FL; Montgomery PA. **International locations:** Hong Kong; India; Ireland. **Operations at this facility include:** This location is a manufacturing facility. **Listed on:** NASDAQ. **Stock exchange symbol:** MSCC. **Number of employees at this location:** 315.

MICROSEMI MICROWAVE PRODUCTS
75 Technology Drive, Lowell MA 01851. 978/442-5600. **Contact:** Human Resources. **World Wide Web address:** http://www.microsemi.com. **Description:** Manufactures and markets semiconductors and similar products and provides related services, principally for the military, aerospace, medical, computer, and telecommunications industries. Major products include high-reliability silicon rectifiers and zener diodes; low-leakage and high-voltage diodes; temperature-compensated zener diodes; and a family of subminiature high-power transient suppresser diodes. **Corporate headquarters location:** Irvine CA. **Other area locations:** Lawrence MA; Melrose MA; Watertown MA. **Other U.S. locations:** Scottsdale AZ; Carlsbad CA; Garden Grove CA; Los Angeles CA; Broomfield CO; Riveria Beach FL; Montgomery PA. **International locations:** Hong Kong; India; Ireland. **Listed on:** NASDAQ. **Stock exchange symbol:** MSCC.

MICROTIME COMPUTER DISTRIBUTION, INC.
300 Wildwood Avenue, Woburn MA 01801. 781/938-6699. **Fax:** 781/938-5599. **Contact:** Human Resources. **Description:** Wholesales and distributes computer peripherals and components to the reseller market. The company also assembles custom-built PCs.

MICROWAY, INC.
Plymouth Industrial Park 12 Richards Road, Plymouth MA 02360. 508/746-7341. **Fax:** 508/746-4678. **Contact:** Human Resources. **E-mail address:** info@microway.com. **World Wide Web address:** http://www.microway.com. **Description:** Designs state-of-the-art, high quality Linux clusters, servers, and RAID storage solutions for universities, life sciences, Fortune 500 companies and research agencies worldwide. **NOTE:** Check http://www.monster.com for latest job postings.

MIDDLESEX SAVINGS BANK
6 Main Street, Natick MA 01760. 508/653-0300. **Toll-free phone:** 877/463-6287. **Fax:** 508/651-9026. **Contact:** Personnel. **E-mail address:** careers@middlesexbank.com. **World Wide Web address:** http://www.middlesexbank.com. **Description:** A savings bank. **Positions advertised include:** Commercial Banking Officer; Commercial Real Estate Analyst; Vice President Commercial Real Estate. **Corporate headquarters location:** This location. **Other U.S. locations:** Acton MA; Ashland MA; Concord MA; Framingham MA; Groton MA; Holliston MA; Hopkinton MA; Littleton MA; Maynard MA; Medfield MA; Millis MA; Natick MA; Southborough MA; Sudbury MA; Wayland MA; Wellesley MA; Westford MA.

MIDDLETON AEROSPACE CORPORATION
206 South Main Street, Middleton MA 01949. 978/774-6000. **Fax:** 978/777-5640. **Contact:** Human Resources. **E-mail address:** sales@midaero.com. **World Wide Web address:** http://www.midaero.com. **Description:** Manufactures aircraft engine components.

MIKRON BOSTOMATIC CORPORATION
150 Hopping Brook Road, Holliston MA, 01746. 508/474-1100. **Fax:** 508/474-1111. **Contact:** Human Resources. **E-mail address:** info@mikronus.com. **World Wide Web address:** http://www.bostomatic.com. **Description:** A manufacturer of vertical and horizontal machining centers; modular machining centers for stand-alone and cellular applications; and CNC controls marketed under the Bostomatic trademark. **International locations:** France; Germany.

MILHENCH SUPPLY COMPANY
121 Duchaine Road, New Bedford MA 02745. 508/995-8331. **Toll-free phone:** 800/642-7570. **Fax:** 508/995-4187. **Contact:** Human Resources. **World Wide Web address:** http://www.milhench.com. **Description:** A supplier of janitorial & maintenance, industrial packaging, safety & material handling & storage supplies.

MILLENNIUM PHARMACEUTICALS, INC.
640 Memorial Drive, Cambridge MA 02139. 617/679-7000. **Toll-free phone:** 800/390-566.3. **Fax:** 617/663-3735. **Contact:** Human Resources. **E-mail:** info@minm.com. **World Wide Web address:** http://www.mlnm.com. **Description:** Engaged in genomics research and development. **Other U.S. locations:** San Diego CA. **International locations:** England; Japan. **Listed on:** NASDAQ. **Stock exchange symbol:** MLNM.

MILLIPORE CORPORATION
17 Cherry Hill Drive, Danvers MA 01923. 978/777-3622. **Contact:** Human Resources. **World Wide Web address:** http://www.millipore.com. **Description:** Manufactures microporous filters and filtration devices used for the analysis, separation, and purification of fluids. Products are used in the fields of health care, pharmaceuticals, micro-electronics, biological sciences, and genetic engineering. **Positions advertised include:** Product & Process Development Engineer; Product Manager. **Corporate headquarters location:** Bedford MA. **International locations:** Canada; Japan. **Operations at this facility include:** District Headquarters; Manufacturing. **Listed on:** New York Stock Exchange. **Stock exchange symbol:** MIL. **Number of employees worldwide:** 4,200.

MILLIPORE CORPORATION
80 Ashby Road, Bedford MA 01730. 781/533-6000. **Contact:** Employment Manager. **World Wide Web address:** http://www.millipore.com. **Description:** Manufactures microporous filters and filtration devices used for the analysis, separation, and purification of fluids. Products are used in the fields of health care, pharmaceuticals, micro-electronics, biological sciences, and genetic engineering. **Positions advertised include:** Process Engineer; Software Engineer; Development Engineer. **Corporate headquarters location:** This location. **Listed on:** New York Stock Exchange. **Stock exchange symbol:** MIL. **Number of employees worldwide:** 4,200.

MILTON HOSPITAL
92 Highland Street, Milton MA 02186. 617/696-4600. **Fax:** 617/698-4730. **Contact:** Human Resources. **E-mail address:** humanresources@miltonhospital.org. **World Wide Web address:** http://www.miltonhospital.org. **Description:** A general hospital. Milton Hospital offers free health screenings, support groups, and lectures for the public, as well as free vaccinations for public safety workers. **Positions advertised include:** Admitting Representative; Care Manager; Environmental Services Assistant; Human Resources Manager; PP&D Supervisor; Medical Technician; Records Clerk; Dietary Aide; Secretary; Pharmacist; Radiological Technician; CT Technician; Ultrasound Technician; Physical Therapist; Registered Nurse; Licensed Practical Nurse; Nurse Assistant; Ward Clerk; Nurse Manager. **Special programs:** Internships.

MINTZ, LEVIN, COHN, FERRIS, GLOVSKY & POPEO
One Financial Center, 40th Floor, Boston MA 02111. 617/542-6000. **Contact:** Julie Zammuto, Manager of Attorney Recruiting & Training. **World Wide Web address:** http://www.mintz.com. **Description:** A law firm with a wide range of practice areas including trade regulation, real estate, and technology. **Other U.S. locations:** Los Angeles CA; New Haven CT; Washington DC; New York NY; Reston VA.

MIRICK, O'CONNELL, DEMALLIE & LOUGEE
100 Front Street, 17th Floor, Worcester MA 01608. 508/791-8500. **Fax:** 508/791-8502. **Contact:** Human Resources. **World Wide Web address:** http://www.modl.com. **Description:** A law firm with many areas of practice including intellectual property, banking and commercial lending, labor and employment, and biotechnology. **Other area locations:** Westborough MA; Worcester MA.

MITEK PRODUCTS
60 Glacier Drive, Westwood MA 02090. 781/251-2700. **Toll-free phone:** 800/35M-ITEK. **Fax:** 781/278-9578. **Contact:** Human Resources. **World Wide Web address:** http://www.mitek.com. **Description:** Develops, manufactures, and markets minimally-invasive proprietary surgical implants that facilitate the reattachment of damaged tendons, ligaments, and other soft tissue to bones. These devices reduce tissue trauma, speed patient recovery, and shorten operating time. Primary products consist of a line of suture anchors utilizing nitinol, a highly elastic nickel titanium alloy, as well as related surgical instruments such as drill guides and inserters. **NOTE:** Second and third shifts are offered. All mail should be sent to: Human Resources, 249 Vanderbilt Avenue, Norwood MA 02062. **Corporate headquarters location:** This location. **Parent company:** Ethicon, Inc. **Number of employees at this location:** 275.

MITRE CORPORATION
202 Burlington Road, Bedford MA 01730-1420. 781/271-2000. **Contact:** Human Resources. **World Wide Web address:** http://www.mitre.org. **Description:** An international, nonprofit high-technology electronics and communications firm that produces large-scale command, control, and communications (C3) systems for the U.S. Air Force. **Positions advertised include:** Office Support Staff; Associate Section Leader; Global Positioning Systems Engineer; Database & Data Mining Researcher; Lead Software Systems Engineer; Radar Systems Engineer; Office Support Staff; Database Developer; Information Systems Engineer; Budget Analysis; Sensors System Engineer. **Corporate headquarters location:** This location. **Other U.S. locations:** Ft. Huachuca AZ; Colorado Springs CO; Ft. Monmouth NJ; San Antonio TX; McLean VA. **Operations at this facility include:** Research and Development.

MORGAN CONSTRUCTION COMPANY
15 Belmont Street, Worcester MA 01605. 508/755-6111. **Contact:** Human Resources. **World Wide Web address:** http://www.morganco.com. **Description:** Engineers and manufactures heavy machinery, ferrous and nonferrous rolling mills, and wire drawing machinery. **Positions advertised include:** Process Metallurgist. **Special programs:** Internships. **Other U.S. locations:** Chicago IL; Pittsburgh PA. **International locations:** Brazil; China; England; France; Japan; India. **Operations at this facility include:** Administration; Manufacturing; Sales.

MORGAN MEMORIAL GOODWILL INDUSTRIES, INC.
1010 Harrison Avenue, Boston MA 02119-2540. 617/541-1400. **Fax:** 617/541-1495. **Contact:** Toni Preston, Director of Human Resources. **World Wide Web address:** http://www.goodwillmass.org. **Description:** A nonprofit human services agency. Programs include training, employment, and career services for persons with disabilities and others who face barriers to employment; and youth services including a live-in summer camp in central Massachusetts for inner-city youth, ages 7 through 16.

The organization also operates nine retail stores. **NOTE:** Volunteer opportunities are offered. **Positions advertised include:** Human Resources Benefits Coordinator; Accounts Payable Specialist; Manager of Career Counseling; Community Job Placement Specialist; Reporting and Analysis Specialist; Training Instructor; Case Manager. **Special programs:** Internships. **President/CEO:** Joanne K. Hilferty.

MORGAN STANLEY DEAN WITTER & COMPANY
125 High Street, 24th Floor, Boston MA 02110. 617/478-6400. **Contact:** Human Resources. **World Wide Web address:** http://www.msdw.com. **Description:** Offers diversified financial services including equities, fixed income securities, commodities, money market instruments, and investment banking services. **Office hours:** Monday - Friday, 8:30 a.m. - 5:00 p.m. **Corporate headquarters location:** New York NY.

MORGAN STANLEY DEAN WITTER & COMPANY
6 Park Avenue, Worcester MA 01605. 508/849-5500. **Contact:** Human Resources. **World Wide Web address:** http://www.msdw.com. **Description:** Offers diversified financial services including equities, fixed income securities, commodities, money market instruments, and investment banking services. **Corporate headquarters location:** New York NY.

MOUNT HOLYOKE COLLEGE
50 College Street, South Hadley MA 01075. **Contact:** Human Resources. **World Wide Web address:** http://www.mtholyoke.edu. **Description:** A private, four-year college offering a variety of programs for undergraduate and graduate students. **Positions advertised include:** Director of Administrative Computing; Public Safety Officer; Director of Financial Assistance; Class Dean; Administrative Assistant; Coordinator of Educational Opportunities Abroad; Academic Computer Support Specialist; Director of Residential Life; Counseling Service Postdoctoral Clinician; Research Assistant in Educational Psychology; Laboratory Director Introductory Physics; Coordinator of Multicultural Affairs; Director of Equestrian Center; Payroll Specialist.

MULLEN AGENCY
36 Essex Street, Wenham MA 01984. 978/468-1155. **Contact:** Human Resources. **E-mail address:** jobs@mullen.com. **World Wide Web address:** http://www.mullen.com. **Description:** A leading advertising and public relations firm. **Positions advertised include:** Interactive Account Executive; Mullen Media; Direct Account Executive; Direct Resource Art Director. **Other U.S. locations:** Detroit MI; Winston-Salem NC; Pittsburgh PA.

MUSEUM OF FINE ARTS - BOSTON
465 Huntington Avenue, Boston MA 02115. 617/267-9300. **Contact:** Sandra Matthews, Human Resources. **World Wide Web address:** http://www.mfa.org. **Description:** One of the largest museums in New England, with a wide spectrum of permanent and featured exhibits. **Positions advertised include:** Assistant Curator for Chinese Art; Registrar Assistant, Exhibitions and Loans; Grants Officer; Director of Marketing; MFA Fund Officer. **Positions advertised include:** Curatorial Specialist. **Corporate headquarters location:** This location.

NMS COMMUNICATIONS
100 Crossing Boulevard, Framingham MA 01702. 508/620-9300. **Contact:** Human Resources. **E-mail address:** resumes@nmss.com. **World Wide Web address:** http://www.nmss.com. **Description:** Designs, manufactures, and markets enabling technology products for the call processing market. These products permit others to efficiently develop and implement high performance, PC-based call processing systems that provide applications in one or a combination of areas such as automated attendant, voicemail, and interactive voice response. Product applications include telephone banking, medical alert services, pay-per-view cable services, and telemarketing. **Positions advertised include:** Principal NT Server & Network Analyst; Principal Hardware Engineer. **Corporate headquarters location:** This location. **Other U.S. locations:** Los Gatos CA. **International locations:** Worldwide. **Listed on:** NASDAQ. **Stock exchange symbol:** NMSS.

NSTAR
One NSTAR Way, SUMSE 150, Westwood MA 02090. 781/441-8000. **Toll-free phone:** 800/592-2000. **Fax:** 781/441-8886. **Recorded jobline:** 781/441-8091. **Contact:** Human Resources. **E-mail address:** resumes@nstaronline.com. **World Wide Web address:** http://www.nstaronline.com. **Description:** A public utility engaged in the generation, purchase, transmission, distribution, and sale of electric energy. The company supplies electricity to the city of Boston and 39 surrounding communities. The company also wholesales electricity to other utilities and municipal electric departments for resale. **Corporate headquarters location:** Boston MA. **Subsidiaries include:** NSTAR Communications, Inc.; Advanced Energy Systems, Inc.; NSTAR Steam Corporation; Hopkinton LNG Corp. **Listed on:** New York Stock Exchange. **Stock exchange symbol:** NST.

NX NETWORKS
9 Technology Drive, Westborough MA 01581. 508/898-2800. **Contact:** Human Resources. **E-mail address:** hr@nsgdata.com. **World Wide Web address:** http://www.nxnetworks.com. **Description:** Provides secure voice and data networking products to corporations, government agencies, and service providers worldwide. **Corporate headquarters location:** Herndon VA. **International locations:** England; Hong Kong.

NANTUCKET BANK
104 Pleasant Street, Nantucket Island MA 02554. 508/228-0580. **Toll-free phone:** 800/533-9313. **Fax:** 508/228-1322. **Contact:** Human Resources. **E-mail address:** lmccandless@nantucketbank.com. **World Wide Web address:** http://www.nantucketbank.com. **Description:** A local island bank.

NATIONAL AMUSEMENTS INC.
200 Elm Street, Dedham MA 02026. 781/461-1600. **Fax:** 781/407-0052.**Contact:** Maureen Dixon, Personnel Manager. **E-mail address:** mdixon@nationalamusements.com. **World Wide Web address:** http://www.nationalamusements.com. **Description:** National Amusements operates the Showcase and Multiplex movie theater chains. **Positions advertised include:** Cashier; Usher; Concession Attendant. **Parent company:** Viacom is a diversified entertainment and communications company with operations in four principal segments: Viacom Networks operates three advertiser-supported basic cable television program services: MTV, VH-1, and Nickelodeon/Nick at Nite; and three premium subscription television services, SHOWTIME, The Movie Channel, and FLIX; Viacom Entertainment distributes television series, feature films, made-for-television movies, miniseries, and movies for prime time broadcast network television. Viacom Entertainment also acquires and distributes television series for initial exhibition on a first-run basis; and develops, produces, distributes, and markets interactive software for the stand-alone and other multimedia marketplaces; Viacom Cable Television owns and operates cable television systems in California, the Pacific Northwest, and Midwest; Viacom Broadcasting owns and operates 5 network-affiliated television stations and 14 radio stations. **Operations at this facility include:** This location houses administrative offices.

NATIONAL DATACOMPUTER, INC.
900 Middlesex Turnpike, Building 5, Billerica MA 01821. 978/663-7677. **Fax:** 978/667-1869. **Contact:** Human Resources. **E-mail:** tferra@ndcomputer.com. **World Wide Web address:** http://www.ndcomputer.com. **Description:** Designs, manufactures, and markets computerized systems used to automate the collection, processing, and communication of information related to product sales, distribution, and inventory control. The company's products and services include data communication networks, application-specific software, hand-held computers and related peripherals, and associated training and support services. The company's products facilitate rapid and accurate data collection, data processing, and two-way communication of information with a customer's host information system.

NATIONAL DENTEX CORPORATION
526 Boston Post Road, Suite 207, Wayland MA 01778. 508/358-4422. **Contact:** Human Resources. **World Wide Web address:** http://www.nationaldentex.com. **Description:** National Dentex Corporation is one of the largest operators of dental laboratories in the United States. These dental laboratories provide a full range of custom-made dental prosthetic appliances, divided into three main groups: restorative products including crowns and bridges; reconstructive products including partial and full dentures; and cosmetic products including porcelain veneers and ceramic crowns. **Positions advertised include:** Dental Lab Trainee; Maintenance; Janitorial Associate; Driver; Office Representative; Scheduler Associate; Department Manager; Shipping & Receiving Clerk; Skilled Technician; Corporate Support Specialist. **Corporate headquarters location:** This location. **Other U.S. locations:** Nationwide. **Subsidiaries include:** Dodd Dental Laboratories; H&O Associated Dental Laboratories; H&O Eliason; Lakeland Dental; Massachusetts Dental Associates. **Listed on:** NASDAQ. **Stock exchange symbol:** NADX.

NATIONAL ENGINEERING SERVICE CORPORATION
10 Cedar Street, Suite 27, Woburn MA 01801. 781/938-4747. **Contact:** Human Resources. **Description:** A contract engineering firm engaged primarily in civil engineering projects.

NATIONAL EVALUATION SYSTEMS
30 Gatehouse Road, Amherst MA 01002. 413/256-0444. **Contact:** Personnel Director. **E-mail address:** personnel@nesinc.com. **World Wide Web address:** http://www.nesinc.com. **Description:** A contract-based company providing educational products and services in a variety of areas including professional licensing and certification testing programs, large-scale pupil assessment, and print-based educational materials. Clients include state departments of education and professional licensing boards. **Positions advertised include:** Project Director; Statistical Programmer/Analyst; Project Assistant. **Corporate headquarters location:** This location. **Other U.S. locations:** Sacramento CA; Austin TX. **Operations at this facility include:** Administration; Research and Development; Service.

NATIONAL GRID
25 Research Drive, Westborough MA 01582. 508/389-2000. **Contact:** Human Resources. **World Wide Web address:** http://www.ngtgroup.com. **Description:** A public utility holding company. Founded in 1947. **Positions advertised include:** Analyst; Engineer; Information Technologist Engineer. **Corporate headquarters location:** This location. **Other U.S. locations:** NH; NY; RI. **Subsidiaries include:** Massachusetts Electric Company, Narragansett Electric Company, Nantucket Electric Company, Niagara Mohawk, and Granite State Electric Company are retail electric companies that provide electricity and related services to 1.3 million customers in 197 communities; New England Power Company is a wholesale electric generating company that operates 5 thermal generating systems, 14 hydroelectric generating stations, a pumped storage station, and 2,400 miles of transmission lines; New England Electric Resources, Inc. is an independent project development and consulting company; New England Electric Transmission Corporation, New England Hydro-Transmission Corporation, and New England Hydro-Transmission Electric Company, Inc. are electric transmission companies that develop, own, and operate facilities associated with high-voltage, direct current interconnection; Narragansett Energy Resources Company is a wholesale electric generating company; New England Energy Inc. is an oil and gas exploration and development company; and New England Power Services Company is a service company that provides administrative, legal, engineering, and other support to the subsidiaries. **Parent company:** National Grid USA. **Listed on:** New York Stock Exchange. **Stock exchange symbol:** NGG. **Number of employees at this location:** 1,200. **Number of employees nationwide:** 5,200.

NATIONAL NONWOVENS
P.O. Box 150, Easthampton MA 01027. 413/527-3445. **Physical address:** 180 Pleasant Street, Easthampton MA 01027. **Toll-free phone:** 800/333-3469. **Fax:** 413/527-9570. **Contact:** Personnel. **World Wide Web address:** http://www.nationalnonwovens.com. **Description:** Develops, markets, and manufactures needle punch and other nonwoven textiles. **Corporate headquarters location:** This location. **Operations at this facility include:** Administration; Manufacturing; Research and Development; Sales. **Listed on:** Privately held. **Annual sales/revenues:** $21 - $50 million. **Number of employees at this location:** 200.

NECCO (NEW ENGLAND CONFECTIONERY COMPANY)
HAVILAND CANDY, INC.
135 American Legion Highway, Revere MA, 02151. 617/876-4700. **Fax:** 781/485-4519. **Contact:** Personnel. **E-mail:** njobs@necco.com. **World Wide Web address:** http://www.necco.com. **Description:** NECCO is a manufacturer of a wide variety of candy including NECCO Wafers, Conversation Hearts, and Mary Janes. **Other U.S. locations:** Thibodaux LA; Watertown MA; Pewaukee WI. **Operations at this facility include:** Administration; Manufacturing.

NEIGHBORHOOD HEALTH PLAN
253 Summer Street, Boston MA 02210. 617/772-5500. **Fax:** 617/478-7198. **Contact:** Alessandra DeVaca, Director of Human Development and Employee Systems. **E-mail:** careers@nhp.com. **World Wide Web address:** http://www.nhp.org. **Description:** A nonprofit HMO serving approximately 46,000 members through 116 community health centers and medical groups across Massachusetts. Founded in 1986. **Company slogan:** Make us part of your plan. **Positions advertised include:** Accountant; Administrative Assistant; Appeals Coordinator; Care Manager; Chief Manager; Chief Actuary; Claims Customer Service Representative; Clinical Outcomes Coordinator; Data Analyst; Healthcare Audit Analyst; Information Technologist Security Manager; Nurse Practitioner; Registered Nurse. **Corporate headquarters location:** This location. **Annual sales/revenues:** More than $100 million. **Number of employees at this location:** 200.

NETEGRITY INC.
201 Jones Road, Waltham MA 02451. 781/890-1700. **Fax:** 781/487-7791. **Contact:** Human Resources. **E-mail address:** swjobs@netegrity.com. **World Wide Web address:** http://www.netegrity.com. **Description:** Designs and markets data and voice intra and extranet security products. **Other U.S. locations:** New York NY; Reston VA; San Mateo CA; Los Angeles CA; Rosemount IL. **International locations:** Worldwide. **Parent company:** Computer Associates.

NETEZZA CORPORATION
200 Crossing Boulevard, 5th Floor, Framingham MA 01702. 508/665-6800. **Fax:** 508/665-6811. **Contact:** Human Resources. **World Wide Web address:** http://www.netezza.com. **Description:** A provider of enterprise-class data warehouse solutions that integrate database, server, and storage in one appliance. **Positions advertised include:** Software Engineer, Storage Manager; Sr. Software Engineer, Project Leader; Sr. Customer Service Engineer; System Product Manager; Sr. Software Quality Engineer; Channels Manager.

NETSILICON
411 Waverley Oaks Road, Suite 304, Waltham MA 02452. 781/647-1234. **Toll-free phone:** 800/243-2333. **Fax:** 781/893-1338. **Contact:** Personnel. **E-mail address:** staffing@netsilicon.com. **World Wide Web address:** http://www.netsilicon.com. **Description:** Develops and markets hardware and software that allows copiers, fax machines, printers, and scanners to communicate over internal and external networks. NETsilicon also offers technical support and consulting services. **Corporate headquarters location:** This location. **International locations:** Germany; Japan; Korea. **Listed on:** NASDAQ. **Stock exchange symbol:** NSIL.

NEW BALANCE ATHLETIC SHOE INC.
Brighton Landing, 20 Guest Street, Brighton MA 02135. 617/783-4000. **Contact:** Human Resources. **World Wide Web address:** http://www.newbalance.com. **Description:** Manufactures and distributes running and other athletic shoes. **Positions advertised include:** Administrative Assistant; Billing Specialist; Lead Programming Analyst; Network Engineer; Associate Product Manager; Marketing Manager; Designer; Retail Sales Associate. **Corporate headquarters location:** This location. **International locations:** Worldwide. **Number of employees worldwide:** 2,400.

NEW ENGLAND AQUARIUM
Central Wharf, Boston MA 02110. 617/973-5200. **Contact:** Human Resources. **World Wide Web address:** http://www.neaq.org. **Description:** An aquarium offering a variety of educational programs, outdoor shows, whale watching trips, and the Aquarium Medical Center. Founded in 1969. **Positions advertised include:** Visitor Assistant; Sales Associate; Lead Sales Associate; Alternate Lead Visitor Attendant; IMAX Theatre Host; Reservation Assistant; Administrative Assistant.

NEW ENGLAND BAPTIST HOSPITAL
125 Parker Hill Avenue, Boston MA 02120. 617/754-5800. **Contact:** Human Resources. **World Wide Web address:** http://www.nebh.org. **Description:** A 150-bed, surgical hospital providing specialty services in cardiology, sports medicine, occupational medicine, and musculoskeletal care. Founded in 1893. **Positions advertised include:** Administrative Assistant; Central Support Operator; Coding Supervisor; File Clerk; Registered Nurse; Groundskeeper; Head Therapist; Quality Manager; Nurse Assistant; Unit Aide; Unit Secretary.

NEW ENGLAND BIOLABS, INC.
32 Tozer Road, Beverly MA 01915. 978/927-5054. **Contact:** Human Resources. **E-mail address:** kong@neb.com. **World Wide Web address:** http://www.neb.com. **Description:** A medical research laboratory that manufactures products for molecular biology research with a specialization in restriction endonucleases. **Positions advertised include:** Executive Director; Organic Chemist; Post Doctoral Fellow.

NEW ENGLAND BUSINESS SERVICE INC. (NEBS)
500 Main Street, Groton MA 01471. 978/448-6111. **Fax:** 978/449-3841. **Contact:** Human Resources. **E-mail address:** hr@nebs.com. **World Wide Web address:** http://www.nebs.com. **Description:** A supplier of business forms and software for small businesses. The company's product line consists of over 1,000 standardized imprinted manual and computer business forms including billing forms, work orders, job proposals, and purchase orders; stationery including letterheads, envelopes, and business cards; checks and check writing systems; and marketing products including advertising labels, pricing tags and labels, signage, and greeting cards. The company offers a line of software that includes check writing, billing, and mailing applications, as well as a variety of simpler form-filling software; and One-Write Plus, a line of accounting software that integrates accounting and payroll functions with basic word processing, mail merge, a spreadsheet link, a backup utility, and a menu organizer. The computer forms are compatible with over 3,500 personal computer software packages developed by third parties and used by small businesses. **Positions advertised include:** Call Center Supervisor; Composition Artist; Corporate Legal Manager; Corporate Legal Manager; Corporate Paralegal; Customer Sales Consultant; Field Sales Support Representative; Field Sales Support Representative; Human Resources Director; Inbound Sales Representative; Data Mining Analyst. **Corporate headquarters location:** This location. **Other area locations:** Sudbury MA; Townsend MA; Woburn MA. **Other U.S. locations:** Flagstaff AZ; Maryville MO; Nashua NH; Peterborough NH. **International locations:** Canada; England; France. **Operations at this facility include:** Administration; Sales; Service. **Listed on:** New York Stock Exchange. **Stock exchange symbol:** NEB. **Number of employees at this location:** 800. **Number of employees nationwide:** 2,600.

NEW ENGLAND COLLEGE OF FINANCE
One Lincoln Plaza, 89 South Street, Boston MA 02111. 617/951-2350. **Fax:** 617/951-2533. **Contact:** Personnel. **E-mail address:** info@finance.edu. **World Wide Web address:** http://www.finance.edu. **Description:** A college offering associate's degrees, bachelor's degrees, and certificate courses in the areas of finance, banking, and insurance. Founded in 1909.

NEW ENGLAND CONSERVATORY OF MUSIC
290 Huntington Avenue, Boston MA 02115. 617/585-1230. **Contact:** Human Resources. **World Wide Web address:** http://www.newenglandconservatory.edu. **Description:** A music school. New England Conservatory of Music also operates a preparatory school and offers continuing education classes for students of all levels. **Positions advertised include:** Composition Faculty; Music Theory Faculty; Academic Training; Executive Director of Development; Office Manager; Major Gifts Officer; Technology Support Specialist.

NEW ENGLAND FINANCIAL
501 Boylston Street, Boston MA 02116. 617/578-2000. **Toll-free phone:** 800/627-6806. **Fax:** 617/578-3088. **Contact:** Personnel Department. **World Wide Web address:** http://www.nefn.com. **Description:** Provides a variety of financial services including mutual funds, investment advice, IRAs, 401(k)s, and individual and group health insurance. **Positions advertised include:** Sales Representative.

NEW ENGLAND GAS COMPANY
155 North Main Street, Fall River MA 02720. 508/679-5271. **Toll-free phone:** 800/936-7000. **Contact:** Human Resources. **World Wide Web address:** http://www.negasco.com. **Description:** A public utility company selling natural gas at retail in Fall River, Somerset, Swansea, and Westport. **Corporate headquarters location:** This location.

NEW ENGLAND MANAGEMENT
375 Harvard Street, Brookline MA 02134. 617/566-5571. **Contact:** Human Resources. **Description:** Acquires, develops, operates, and sells residential and commercial real estate. **Corporate headquarters location:** This location.

NEW ENGLAND MEDICAL CENTER
750 Washington Street, New England Medical Center #795, Boston MA 02111. 617/636-5666. **Fax:** 617/636-4658. **Contact:** Human Resources. **World Wide Web address:** http://www.nemc.org. **Description:** New England Medical Center is the major teaching hospital for Tufts University Medical School. One branch of the New England Medical Center is the Floating Hospital for Children, which provides treatment for children suffering from various kinds of cancer, leukemia, and arthritis. **Positions advertised include:** Administrative Assistant; Admitting Representative; Assistant Nurse Manager; Business Operations Manager; Clinical Nutritionist; Clinical Pharmacist; Clinical Research Coordinator; Coder; CT Scanner; Lab Technologist; Medical Assistant; Nursing Technologist; Physical Therapist. **Operations at this facility include:** Administration. **Number of employees at this location:** 6,000.

NEW ENGLAND PATRIOTS FOOTBALL CLUB
60 Washington Street, Foxboro MA 02035. 508/543-8200. **Contact:** Human Resources. **World Wide Web address:** http://www.patriots.com. **Description:** Houses the executive offices of the New England Patriots, a member of the National Football League.

NEW ENGLAND SINAI HOSPITAL AND REHABILITATION CENTER
150 York Street, Stoughton MA 02072. 781/344-0600. **Contact:** Human Resources. **Description:** A hospital and rehabilitation center providing a variety of services including physical therapy, occupational therapy, and pulmonary rehabilitation, as well as special areas dealing specifically with back, feet, vision, and speech problems.

NEW HARBOUR INC.
1 West Street, Fall River MA 02720. 508/678-3202. **Fax:** 508/673-4887. **Contact:** Human Resources. **World Wide Web address:** http://www.newharbour.com. **Description:** A manufacturer of home accessories. **Positions advertised include:** Customer Service Manager; Showroom Manager.

NEWSEDGE CORPORATION
80 Blanchard Road, Burlington MA 01803. 781/229-3000. **Contact:** Human Resources. **World Wide Web address:** http://www.newsedge.com. **Description:** Provides customized, real-time news and information delivered to knowledge workers over their organizations' local area networks. The company's NewsEDGE service delivers more than 480 news and information sources, in real-time, to users' personal computers; automatically monitors and filters the news according to pre-established personal interest profiles; and alerts users to stories matching their profiles. The NewsEDGE service is used by executives, salespeople, marketers, lawyers, accountants, consultants, bankers, and financial professionals. News and information sources available on NewsEDGE include newswire from AFP/Extel News Limited; The Associated Press; Dow Jones; Knight-Ridder/Tribune Information Services; and the text of stories in the *Financial Post, Financial Times,* the *New York Times* News Service, *USA Today,* and the *Wall Street Journal.* Also available on NewsEDGE are the business sections of over 100 North American newspapers; periodicals such as *Forbes, Fortune, InfoWorld, MacWeek,* and *PC Week*; and newsletters such as those distributed by American Banker and Philips Business Information Services, Inc. **Positions advertised include:** Business Development Executive; Inside Sales Representative. **Corporate headquarters location:** This location. **Other U.S. locations:** Irvine CA; San Francisco CA; Washington DC; Miami FL; Chicago IL; Iselin NJ; New York NY; Addison TX; Burlington VT. **International locations:** Canada; England; France; Germany; Japan; The Netherlands; Switzerland. **Parent company:** The Thomson Corporation.

NEWTON-WELLESLEY HOSPITAL
2014 Washington Street, Newton MA 02462. 617/243-6000. **Fax:** 617/243-6876. **Contact:** Human Resources. **World Wide Web address:** http://www.nwh.org. **Description:** A hospital serving as a teaching facility for Tufts School of Medicine. **Positions advertised include:** Administrative Assistant; Assistant Cook; CT Technologist; Clinical Social Worker; Executive Assistant; Food Service Worker; Human Resources Coordinator; Image Service Representative; Medical Lab Assistant; Pharmacist; Registered Nurse; Ultrasound Technologist; Unit Coordinator

NICHOLS COLLEGE
P.O. Box 5000, Dudley MA 01571-5000. 508/943-2055. **Toll-free phone:** 800/470-3379. **Contact:** Rick Woods, Director of Human Resources. **E-mail address:** rick.woods@nichols.edu. **World Wide Web address:** http://www.nichols.edu. **Description:** A private, coeducational, liberal arts college known for business education with an enrollment of 700 undergraduates. Founded in 1815. **Positions advertised include:** Office Assistant.

NIDEC/POWER GENERAL
100 River Ridge Drive, Norwood MA 02062. 781/769-0619. **Fax:** 781/551-6825. **Contact:** Human Resources. **E-mail address:** jobs@nidecpg.com. **World Wide Web address:** http://www.nidec.com. **Description:** Develops, manufactures, and markets axial fans and motors, power supplies, and AC/DC converters. **Positions advertised include:** Administration Assistant; Engineer; Manufacturer; Sales. **Corporate headquarters location:** Torrington CT. **Parent company:** Nidec Corporation (Japan).**Operations at this facility include:** Manufacturing; Research and Development; Sales. **Number of employees at this location:** 300.

NIXON PEABODY LLP
100 Summer Street, Boston MA 02110. 617/345-1280 **Fax:** 866/743-2439. **Contact:** Layla Callahan, Hiring Coordinator. **E-mail address:** ctaylor@nixonpeabody.com. **Wide Web address:** http://www.nixonpeabody.com. **Description:** A law firm covering several areas of practice through its commercial, corporate, estate, litigation, real estate, and syndication groups.

NORFOLK RAM GROUP
One Roberts Road, Plymouth MA 02360. 508/822-5500. **Fax:** 508/747-3658. **Contact:** Human Resources. **World Wide Web address:** http://www.norfolkenvironmental.com.

Description: An environmental and civil engineering firm. **Positions advertised include:** Civil Engineer.

NORTEL NETWORKS
8 Federal Street, Billerica MA 01821. 978/670-8888. **Contact:** Human Resources. **World Wide Web address:** http://www.nortel.com. **Description:** Designs, produces, and supports multimedia access devices for use in building corporate, public and Internet networks. The primary focus of the company's services is the consolidation of voice, fax, video, and data and multimedia traffic into a single network link. **Positions advertised include:** Software Engineer; Technical Support Engineer; Account Manager; Product Line Manager; Software Routing Manager; Shasta Routing Project Lead; Service Delivery GSM, BTS Engineer. **Other U.S. locations:** Nationwide. **International locations:** Worldwide. **Listed on:** New York Stock Exchange. **Stock exchange symbol:** NT.

NORTH SHORE MEDICAL CENTER
SALEM HOSPITAL
81 Highland Avenue, Salem MA 01970. 978/741-1200. **Recorded jobline:** 978/741-1215x4365. **Contact:** Personnel. **World Wide Web address:** http://www.partners.org. **Description:** Salem Hospital is a 322-bed teaching hospital that operates as part of North Shore Medical Center. North Shore Medical Center is a nonprofit health care system consisting of several hospitals and health organizations. Services range from primary, emergency/trauma, and advanced levels of acute care to rehabilitation and long-term care. A program of ambulatory health care includes walk-in medical centers and one of the region's largest occupational and preventative health companies. North Shore Medical Center's facilities include Salem Hospital; Shaughnessy-Kaplan Rehabilitation Hospital, a 160-bed rehabilitation facility; North Shore Children's Hospital, one of only four pediatric hospitals in the state; Work Venture, a comprehensive industrial rehabilitation program geared toward returning injured workers to their jobs; and the Visiting Nurse Association of Greater Salem, consisting of various private duty services. **Positions advertised include:** Clinical Lab Technician; Dietician/Nutritionist; Medical Records Technician; Nuclear Medicine Technologist; Occupational Therapist; Pharmacist; Physical Therapist; Physician; Registered Nurse. **Parent company:** Partners HealthCare System Inc. **Number of employees at this location:** 3,000.

NORTHEAST CONCRETE PRODUCTS
P.O. Box 2189, Plainville MA 02762. 508/695-1737. **Fax:** 508/695-7596. **Physical address:** 24 Cross Street, Plainville MA 02762. **Contact:** Human Resources. **World Wide Web address;** http://www.necp.net. **Description:** Manufactures concrete products for use in the building of parking lots and bridges.

NORTHEAST PUBLISHING COMPANY
FALL RIVER HERALD NEWS
207 Pocasset Street, Fall River MA 02721. 508/676-8211. **Contact:** Dan Goodrich, Publisher. **World Wide Web address:** http://www.heraldnews.com. **Description:** Publishes a daily newspaper with a weekday circulation of more than 39,000.

NORTHEASTERN UNIVERSITY
360 Huntington Avenue, 250 Columbus Place, Boston MA 02115. 617/373-2230. **Contact:** Human Resources. **World Wide Web address:** http://www.neu.edu. **Description:** A university operating through several colleges and programs including the College of Arts and Science, the Boston Bouve College of Pharmacy and Health Professions, the Graduate School of Business Administration, a law school, part-time evening programs, and graduate, professional, and continuing education courses. **Positions advertised include:** Spanish Instructor; Math Instructor; Science Instructor; Math SAT Instructor; Decision Making Instructor; Recreational Coordinator; Current Events Instructor; English SAT Instructor; English Instructor; Assistant Residential Director; Administration Coordinator; Grants & Contract Specialist; Carpentry & Lockshop Supervisor. **Corporate headquarters location:** This location. **Other area locations:** Burlington MA; Dedham MA.

NORTH RIVER REALTY
228 R. Columbia Road Suite #11, Hanover MA 02339. 781/829-9441. **Fax:** 781/829-9427. **Contact:** Paul Bourque, President. **E-mail address:** pbourque@northriverrealty.com. **World Wide Web address:** http://www.northriverrealty.com. **Description:** A full service real estate agency. **Positions advertised include:** Experienced Broker.

NORTHWESTERN MUTUAL FINANCIAL NETWORK
55 William Street Suite 110, Wellesley MA, 02481. 781/237-7070. **Contact:** Steve Tipton, Director of Training & Development. **World Wide Web address:** http://www.nmfn.com. **Description:** A financing network with home offices in Milwaukee WI.

NORTON COMPANY
P.O. Box 15008, Worcester MA 01615-0008. 508/795-5000. **Physical address:** One New Bond Street, Worcester MA 01606. **Fax:** 508/795-2828. **World Wide Web address:** http://www.nortonabrasives.com. **Contact:** Human Resources. **Description:** The Norton Company is one of the world's largest manufacturers of abrasives. Founded in 1885. **Positions advertised include:** Accountant; Application Engineer; Application Developer; Customer Service Representative; Financial Analyst; Human Resources Specialist; Industrial Engineer; Manufacturing Engineer; Network Specialist; Quality Engineer; Process Engineer; Product Engineer; Purchasing Agent; Research & Development Engineer; Technical Sales Representative. **International locations:** Worldwide. **Parent company:** Saint-Gobain Corporation (Valley Forge PA) consists of Certainteed Corporation, Norton Company, and all of their subsidiaries. **Operations at this facility include:** This location is the headquarters for the Abrasives Branch. The Abrasives Branch is one of the only worldwide manufacturers to produce the three major types of abrasives: bonded abrasives including grinding wheels, coated abrasives including sandpaper, and superabrasives. The products of the Abrasives Branch are sold under several names including Amplex, Carborundum Abrasives, Clipper, Norton, Penhall, and Procut.

NOVA BIOMEDICAL
200 Prospect Street, Waltham MA 02454. 781/647-3700. **Fax:** 781/899-6259. **Contact:** Human Resources. **E-mail address:** hr@novabio.com. **World Wide Web address:** http://www.novamanufacturing.com. **Description:** Develops and manufactures blood analyzers. **Positions advertised include:** Program Manager; Clinical Applications Training Specialist; Inside Sales Representative; Regional Sales Representative; Clinical Product Specialist; Operator.

NUTRAMAX PRODUCTS INC.
51 Blackburn Drive, Gloucester MA 01930. 978/283-1800. **Fax:** 978/282-3794. **Contact:** Human Resources. **E-mail address:** hr@nutramax.com. **World Wide Web address:** http://www.nutramax.com. **Description:** Manufactures pharmaceutical and personal care products. **Positions advertised include:** Domestic Sales Representative; International Sales Representative. **Corporate headquarters location:** This location. **Operations at this facility include:** Administration; Manufacturing; Sales. **Number of employees at this location:** 250. **Number of employees nationwide:** 525.

NUTTER, McCLENNEN & FISH, LLP
155 Seaport Boulevard, Boston MA 02210. 617/439-2000. **Fax:** 617/310-9000. **Contact:** Terese M. Cunningham, Human Resources. **E-mail address:** tcunningham@nutter.com. **World Wide Web address:** http://www.nutter.com. **Description:** A law firm offering a variety of legal specialties including litigation, intellectual property, environmental, labor and employment, and trusts and estates. **Other area locations:** Hyannis MA.

NYPRO, INC.
101 Union Street, P.O. Box 2005, Clinton MA 01510. 978/365-9721. **Fax:** 978/368-0236. **Contact:** Human Resources. **World Wide Web address:** http://www.nypro.com. **Description:** Manufactures custom injection moldings. **Other U.S. locations:** Nationwide. **International locations:** Worldwide.

OFS FITEL
50 Hall Road, Sturbridge MA 01566. 508/347-2261. **Fax:** 508/347-8668. **Contact:** Human Resources. **Description:** Manufactures communications products including switching, transmission, fiber-optic cable, wireless systems, and operations systems to fulfill the needs of telephone companies and other communications services providers.

OCEAN SPRAY CRANBERRIES, INC.
One Ocean Spray Drive, Lakeville MA 02349. 508/946-1000. **Contact:** Human Resources. **World Wide Web address:** http://www.oceanspray.com. **Description:** A food processor engaged in the packaging, processing, and marketing of fresh cranberries, cranberry sauces, and fruit juices. **Positions advertised include:** Business Development Manager; Customer Development Coordinator; Deduction Collection Analyst; Manager of Consumer Insights; Manager of Internal Audits; Manager of Unsaleables; Financial Analyst; Sensory Scientist. **Corporate headquarters location:** This location. **Other area locations:** Middleborough MA. **Other U.S. locations:** Vero Beach FL; Bordenton NJ; Sulphur Springs TX; Markham WA; Kenosha WI.

OLD COLONY ELDERLY SERVICES, INC.
P.O. Box 4469 Brockton MA 02301 508/584-1561. **Physical address:** 144 Main Street, Brockton MA 02301. **Contact:** Human Resources. **Description:** Provides various services to the elderly including transportation and in-home care.

OLD MUTUAL ASSET MANAGERS (U.S.)
200 Clarendon Street, 53rd Floor, Boston MA 02116. 617/369-7300. **Contact:** Lucy Stinson, Human Resources. **World Wide Web address:** http://www.omam.com. **Description:** Provides investment management services primarily to institutional investors through 42 operating firms. **Corporate headquarters location:** This location. **Subsidiaries include:** Acadian Asset Management; Analytic Investment Management; Barrow, Hanley, Mewhinney & Strauss; C.S. McKee & Company; Cambiar Investors; Chicago Asset Management Company; Cooke & Bieler; Dewey Square Investors Corporation; Dwight Asset Management Company; Fiduciary Management Associates; First Pacific Advisors; GSB Investment Management; Hagler, Mastrovita & Hewitt; Hamilton, Allen & Associates; Hanson Investment Management Company; Heitman Financial; Hellman, Jordan Management Company; Investment Counselors of Maryland; Investment Research Company; Murray Johnstone Limited; Nelson, Benson & Zellmer; Newbold's Asset Management; Northern Capital Management; NWQ Investment Management Company; Olympic Capital Management; Pell, Rudman & Co.; Provident Investment Counsel; Regis Retirement Plan Services; Rice, Hall, James & Associates; Rothschild/Pell, Rudman & Co.; Sirach Capital Management; Spectrum Asset Management; Sterling Capital Management Company; Suffolk Capital Management; The Campbell Group; The L&B Group; Thompson, Siegel & Walmsley; Tom Johnson Investment Management; UAM Investment Services. **Number of employees nationwide:** 1,500.

OLD STURBRIDGE VILLAGE
One Old Sturbridge Village Road, Sturbridge MA 01566. 508/347-3362. **Fax:** 508/347-0254. **Contact:** Human Resources. **World Wide Web address:** http://www.osv.org. **Description:** An outdoor history museum representing rural New England during the 1830s. Old Sturbridge Village operates a working farm, a mill, blacksmith and pottery shops, and a variety of other exhibits on 200 acres of land. Old Sturbridge Village also offers a wide range of events including apple cider tasting, archaeology programs, and concerts. **President:** Alberta Sebolt George.

OLYMPUS SPECIALTY HOSPITAL
2001 Washington Street, Braintree MA 02184. 781/848-2600. **Contact:** Human Resources. **Description:** A hospital specializing in the treatment of respiratory diseases.

OMNI PARKER HOUSE HOTEL
60 School Street, Boston MA 02108. 617/227-8600. **Fax:** 617/725-1645. **Recorded jobline:** 617/725-1627. **Contact:** Human Resources. **World Wide Web address:** http://www.omnihotels.com. **Description:** A four-star hotel with 550 rooms. **NOTE:** Entry-level positions are offered. **Positions advertised include:** Night Auditor; Housekeeping Manager. **Special programs:** Internships; Summer Jobs. **Corporate headquarters location:** Irving TX. **Other U.S. locations:** Nationwide. **International locations:** Canada; Mexico. **Operations at this facility include:** Service. **Number of employees at this location:** 300.

ONE SOURCE INFORMATION SERVICES, INC.
300 Baker Avenue, Concord MA 01742. 978/318-4300. **Toll-free phone:** 800/333-8036. **Contact:** Human Resources. **E-mail address:** info@corptech.com. **World Wide Web address:** www.corptech.com. **Description:** Publishes company information in print and electronic formats. **Corporate headquarters location:** This location. **Listed on:** NASDAQ. **Stock exchange symbol:** ONES. **Number of employees at this location:** 60.

ONEBEACON INSURANCE
One Beacon Street, Boston MA 02108. 617/725-6000. **Contact:** Human Resources. **World Wide Web address:** http://www.onebeacon.com. **Description:** A carrier of property, casualty, and life insurance. **Positions advertised include:** Underwriting Assistant; Administrative Assistant; Legal Administrator; Financial Analyst; Human Resources Consultant; Inspector; Actuarial Manager. **NOTE:** Apply online. **Corporate headquarters location:** This location.

OPTA FOOD INGREDIENTS, INC.
25 Wiggins Avenue, Bedford MA 01730. 781/276-5100. **Toll-free phone:** 800/353-OPTA. **Contact:** Human Resources. **World Wide Web address:** http://www.opta-food.com. **Description:** Develops food ingredients including fiber-based texturizers, starch-based texturizers, and protein-based coatings. These products improve the

nutrition, texture, and taste of food products and are targeted at the baking, dairy, and meat industries. Founded in 1991. **Positions advertised include:** Technical Support Representative. **Corporate headquarters location:** This location. **Other U.S. locations:** Galesburg IL; Louisville KY. **Listed on:** NASDAQ. **Stock exchange symbol:** OPTS. **President/CEO:** Arthur McEvily, Ph.D. **Annual sales/revenues:** $11 - $20 million. **Number of employees at this location:** 40. **Number of employees nationwide:** 80.

ORACLE CORPORATION
10 Van De Graaff Drive, Burlington MA 01803. 781/744-0000. **Contact:** Human Resources. **World Wide Web address:** http://www.oracle.com. **Description:** Designs and manufactures database and information management software for businesses. The company also provides consulting services. **Positions advertised include:** Staff Sales Consultant; Contracts Administrator; Product Manager; Telesales Representative; Contracts Manager; Field Support Sales; Applications Developer; Technical Writer; Quality Assurance Engineer; Manager Business Development. **Corporate headquarters location:** Redwood Shores CA. **Other U.S. locations:** Nationwide. **Listed on:** NASDAQ. **Stock exchange symbol:** ORCL.

ORBOTECH LTD.
44 Manning Road, Billerica MA 01821. 978/667-6037. **Fax:** 978/667-9969. **Contact:** Human Resources. **E-mail address:** jobsusa@orbotech.com. **World Wide Web address:** http://www.orbotech.com. **Description:** Orbotech, Ltd. designs, develops, manufactures, and services computerized, electro-optical systems for automated inspection and identification of flaws in printed circuit boards, multichip modules, and flat panel displays, and sells CAD/CAM systems for electronic design and preparation of printed circuit board artwork masters and tooling. **Listed on:** NASDAQ. **Stock exchange symbol:** ORBK.

ORGANOGENESIS INC.
150 Dan Road, Canton MA 02021. 781/575-0775. **Fax:** 781/401-1299. **Contact:** Human Resources. **World Wide Web address:** http://www.organogenesis.com. **Description:** Designs, develops, and manufactures medical therapeutics containing living cells and/or natural connective tissue components. The company's products are designed to promote the establishment and growth of new tissues to restore, maintain, or improve biological function. Organogenesis's product development focus includes living tissue replacements, organ assist treatments, and guided tissue regeneration scaffolds. **Positions advertised include:** Product Associate; Facilities Technician; Quality Control Microbiologist; Human Resources Director. **Corporate headquarters location:** This location. **Listed on:** AMEX. **Stock exchange symbol:** ORG.

OVID TECHNOLOGIES
100 River Ridge Drive, Norwood MA 02062. 781/769-2599. **Fax:** 781/769-8763. **Contact:** Amy Narcotta, Human Resources. **E-mail address:** resumes@ovid.com. **World Wide Web address:** http://www.ovid.com. **Description:** Publishes and distributes over 225 authoritative databases. Ovid Technologies also publishes CD-ROMs and develops software systems for data retrieval and full text linking. Founded in 1985. **NOTE:** Entry-level positions are offered. **Positions advertised include:** Database Design Analyst; Technical Support Specialist. **Corporate headquarters location:** New York NY. **Other U.S. locations:** New York NY; Salt Lake City UT. **International locations:** Berlin, Germany; Bologna, Italy; Hong Kong; London, England; Paris, France; Sydney, Australia. **Listed on:** Privately held. **Annual sales/revenues:** $51 - $100 million. **Number of employees at this location:** 200. **Number of employees nationwide:** 240.

PCD (PRODUCT DEVELOPMENT CONSULTING, INC.)
2 Technology Drive, Centennial Park, Peabody MA 01960. 978/532-8800. **Fax:** 978/532-6800. **Contact:** Human Resources. **E-mail address:** info@amphenolpcd.com. **World Wide Web address:** http://www.pcdinc.com. **Description:** Manufactures electronic connector devices. **Listed on:** NASDAQ. **Stock exchange symbol:** PCDI.

PFPC
101 Federal Street, Boston MA 02110. 617/535-0300. **Contact:** Human Resources. **World Wide Web address:** http://www.pfpc.com. **Description:** Provides a broad range of financial services including accounting, global fund services, retirement services, securities lending services, and fund custody services.

PLC MEDICAL SYSTEMS, INC.
10 Forge Park, Franklin MA 02038. 508/541-8800. **Fax:** 781/326-6048. **Contact:** Jeanne Watkins, Personnel. **E-mail address:** kpapa@insightperformance.com. **World Wide Web address:** http://www.plcmed.com. **Description:** Develops cardiovascular products used to perform transmocardia revascularization (TMR). **Positions advertised include:** Quality Engineer; Principal Engineer. **Corporate headquarters location:** This location. **Parent company:** PLC Systems Inc. **Listed on:** American Stock Exchange. **Stock exchange symbol:** PLC.

PNC ADVISORS
99 High Street, Oliver Tower, 27th Floor, Boston MA 02110. 617/334-6030. **Contact:** Human Resources. **World Wide Web address:** http://www.pncadvisors. com. **Description:** An investment firm that provides financial planning, customized credit solutions, brokerage services, mutual funds, and customized investment portfolios. **Positions advertised include:** Administrative Assistant. **NOTE:** Apply online. **Parent company:** PNC Bank Corporation (Pittsburgh, PA).

PSG
775 South Street, Holbrook MA 02343. 781/767-3670. **Contact:** Human Resources. **Description:** An environmental engineering firm offering professional consulting services for water, wastewater, hazardous waste, and landfills.

PALMER AND DODGE LLP
111 Huntington Avenue, Boston MA 02199-7613. 617/239-0100. **Contact:** Kathy Von Mehren, Human Resources. **E-mail address:** pdhiring@palmerdodge.com. **World Wide Web address:** http://www.palmerdodge.com. **Description:** A general practice law firm. **Positions advertised include:** Patent Group Associate; Municipal Finance Associate.

PALOMAR MEDICAL TECHNOLOGIES, INC.
82 Cambridge Street, Burlington MA 01803. 781/993-2300. **Fax:** 781/993-2330. **Contact:** Human Resources. **E-mail address:** hr@palmed.com. **World Wide Web address:** http://www.palmed.com. **Description:** Palomar Medical Technologies designs, manufactures, and markets lasers, delivery systems, and related disposable products for use in medical and surgical procedures. The company operates in two business segments. The Medical Product segment develops and manufactures pulsed dye and diode medical lasers for use in clinical trials and is engaged in the research and development of additional medical and surgical products. The Electronic Products segment manufactures high-density, flexible, electronic circuitry for use in industrial, military, and medical devices. **Positions advertised include:** Clinical Research Manager; Accounting Manager; Programming Specialist; Optical Assembler; Laser Technician. **NOTE:** This company also has distribution opportunities. **Corporate headquarters location:** This location. **Listed on:** NASDAQ. **Stock exchange symbol:** PMTI.

PAN COMMUNICATIONS INC.
300 Brickstone Square, Andover MA 01810. 978/474-1900. **Fax:** 978/474-1903. **Contact:** Personnel. **E-mail address:** info@pancomm.com. **World Wide Web address:** http://www.pancommunications.com. **Description:** A full-service public relations agency specializing in four portfolios: business-to-business, high-technology, fashion and consumer products, and trade shows. Founded in 1995. **NOTE:** Entry-level positions offered. **Company slogan:** Partners in public relations. **Positions advertised include:** Associate; Junior Associate; Account Manager; Senior Account Manager; Director. **Special programs:** Internships. **Corporate headquarters location:** This location. **Annual sales/revenues:** Less than $5 million. **Number of employees at this location:** 45.

PAPA GINO'S OF AMERICA INC.
600 Providence Highway, Dedham MA 02026. 781/461-1200. **Toll-free phone:** 800/PAPA-GINO. **Fax:** 781/461-1896. **Contact:** Human Resources. **E-mail address:** hr@papaginos.com. **World Wide Web address:** http://www.papaginos.com. **Description:** Operates an Italian restaurant chain with over 200 restaurants in New England specializing in pizza and pasta. **Positions advertised include:** Restaurant/Food Service Manager. **Operations at this facility include:** Regional Headquarters. **Number of employees nationwide:** 5,500.

PARAMETRIC TECHNOLOGY CORPORATION
140 Kendrick Street, Needham MA 02494. **Fax:** 781/370-6000. **Contact:** Human Resources. **World Wide Web address:** http://www.ptc.com. **Description:** Designs and develops fully integrated software products for mechanical engineering and automated manufacturing based upon a parametric solids modeling system. **Positions advertised include:** Inside Sales Representative; Strategic Account Representative; Administrative Assistant; Corporate Visiting Center Coordinator; Product Development Consultant; French Localization Specialist; Korean Localization Specialist; German Localization Specialist; Business Systems Analyst; Associate Technologist Support Engineer. **Corporate headquarters location:** This location. **International locations:** Worldwide. **Listed on:** NASDAQ. **Number of employees at this location:** 500. **Number of employees nationwide:** 1,600.

PARKER HANNIFIN NICHOLS AIRBORNE DIVISION
14 Robbins Pond Road, Ayer MA 01432-5641. 978/784-1200. **Contact:** Human Resources. **World Wide Web address:** http://www.parker.com. **Description:** Parker Hannifin Corporation makes motion control products including fluid power systems, electromechanical controls, and related components. The Motion and Control Group manufactures hydraulic pumps, power units, control valves, accumulators, cylinders, actuators, and automation devices to remove contaminants from air, fuel, oil, water, and other fluids. The Fluid Connectors Group manufactures connectors, tube and hose fittings, hoses, and couplers that transmit fluid. The Seal Group manufactures sealing devices, gaskets, and packing that insure leak-proof connections. The Automotive and Refrigeration Group manufactures components for use in industrial and automotive air conditioning and refrigeration systems. **Operations at this facility include:** This location manufactures fuel systems and components for aircraft. **Listed on:** New York Stock Exchange. **Stock exchange symbol:** PH.

PARKS CORPORATION
One West Street, Fall River MA 02720-1336. 508/679-5939. **Toll-free phone:** 800/225-8543. **Fax:** 508/674-8404. **Contact:** Human Resources. **World Wide Web address:** http://www.parkscorp.com. **Description:** Manufactures solvents, cleaners, paint remover, and finish remover. The company markets its products under the brand names Carver Tripp and Parks.

PARLEX CORPORATION
One Parlex Place, Methuen MA 01844. 978/685-4341. **Fax:** 978/685-8809. **Contact:** Joyce Collins, Human Resources. **E-mail address:** flexcircuits@parlex.com. **World Wide Web address:** http://www.parlex.com. **Description:** Manufactures flexible and rigid printed circuits, multilayer boards, flat cable products, and other electronic components. **Positions advertised include:** Regional Sales Engineer; Product Line Manager; Director of Sales & Marketing. **Corporate headquarters location:** This location. **Listed on:** NASDAQ. **Stock exchange symbol:** PRLX.

PARSONS
30 Dan Road, Canton MA 02021. 781/401-3200. **Contact:** Human Resources. **World Wide Web address:** http://www.parsons.com. **Description:** An engineering and construction company specializing in power generation and utilities, general industrial engineering, and environmental engineering. Founded in 1944. **Other U.S. locations:** Nationwide. **International locations:** Worldwide.

PARSONS BRINCKERHOFF INC.
75 Arlington Street, Boston MA 02116. 617/348-2950. **Contact:** Human Resources. **World Wide Web address:** http://www.pbworld.com. **Description:** An engineering and design firm engaged in the design of bridges, tunnels, rapid transit systems, hydroelectric facilities, water supply systems, and marine facilities. **Positions advertised include:** Architectural Inspector. **Other U.S. locations:** Nationwide.

PASSKEY INTERNATIONAL INC.
180 Old Colony Avenue, Quincy MA 02170. 617/237-8200. **Fax:** 617/328-12121. **Contact:** Human Resources. **E-mail address:** hr@passkey.com. **World Wide Web address:** http://www.passkey.com. **Description:** Provides web-based solutions for processing group hotel reservations. **Corporate headquarters location:** This location.

THE PATRIOT LEDGER
400 Crown Colony Drive, P.O. Box 699159, Quincy MA 02269-9159. 617/786-7246. **Fax:** 617/786-7259. **Contact:** Cynthia Papil, Human Resources Manager. **World Wide Web address:** http://www.southofboston.com. **Description:** Publishes a suburban daily newspaper, with a weekday circulation of more than 90,000. **NOTE:** Entry-level positions are offered. **Special programs:** Internships; Apprenticeships. **Corporate headquarters location:** This location. **Parent company:** Newspaper Media LLP. **Listed on:** Privately held. **Number of employees at this location:** 575.

PEABODY & ARNOLD LLP
30 Rowes Wharf, Boston MA 02110-3342. 617/951-2100. **Fax:** 617/951-2125.**Contact:** Human Resources. **World Wide Web address:** http://www.peabodyarnold.com. **Description:** A law firm that operates through three legal groups: The Personal Law Group provides tax and estate planning services; The Business Law Group specializes in securities, corporate, banking and finance, and health care; and The Litigation Group specializes in antitrust and trade regulation, employment, environmental, surety, and workers' compensation.

PEARSON EDUCATION
160 Gould Street, Needham Heights MA 02494. 781/455-1200. **Contact:** Human Resources. **World Wide Web address:** http://www.pearsoned.com. **Description:** Publishes educational textbooks in the following divisions: elementary school reading and math, junior high school social studies, and college. **Positions advertised include:** Marketing Assistant. **Corporate headquarters location:** New York NY.

PEGASYSTEMS INC.
101 Main Street, Cambridge MA 02142-1590. 617/374-9600. **Fax:** 617/374-9620. **Contact:** Personnel. **World Wide Web address:** http://www.pegasystems.com. **Description:** Develops software for the financial industry. **Listed on:** NASDAQ. **Stock exchange symbol:** PEGA.

PEPSI-COLA BOTTLING COMPANY
261 Neck Road, Haverhill MA 01835. 978/521-3923. **Contact:** Human Resources. **World Wide Web address:** http://www.pepsico.com. **Description:** An independent franchise that is a bottling facility for the international soft drink company.

PEPSI-COLA BOTTLING COMPANY
111 Eames Street, Wilmington MA 01887. 978/657-8022. **Fax:** 978/658-9647. **Contact:** Human Resources. **World Wide Web address:** http://www.pepsico.com. **Description:** A bottling facility and a division of the international soft drink manufacturer. **Parent company:** PepsiCo, Inc. (Purchase NY) consists of Frito-Lay Company, Pepsi-Cola Company, and Tropicana Products, Inc. **Listed on:** New York Stock Exchange. **Stock exchange symbol:** PBG.

PEPSI-COLA BOTTLING COMPANY
130 Western Avenue, Allston MA 02134. 617/254-2400. **Contact:** Human Resources. **World Wide Web address:** http://www.pepsico.com. **Description:** A bottling facility and a division of the international soft drink manufacturer. **Parent company:** PepsiCo, Inc. (Purchase NY) consists of Frito-Lay Company, Pepsi-Cola Company, and Tropicana Products, Inc. **Listed on:** New York Stock Exchange. **Stock exchange symbol:** PBG.

PEPSI-COLA BOTTLING COMPANY
620 Myles Standish Boulevard, Taunton MA 02780. 508/823-1500. **Contact:** Human Resources. **World Wide Web address:** http://www.pepsico.com. **Description:** A bottling facility and a division of the international soft drink manufacturer. **Parent company:** PepsiCo. **Listed on:** New York Stock Exchange. **Stock exchange symbol:** PBG.

PERCUSSION SOFTWARE, INC.
600 Unicorn Park Drive, Woburn MA 01801. 781/438-9900. **Toll-free phone:** 800/283-0800. **Fax:** 781/438-9955. **Contact:** Human Resources. **World Wide Web address:** http://www.percussion.com. **Description:** Develops enterprise content management software. **NOTE:** See website for positions and contact information. **Positions advertised include:** QA Engineer; Software Engineer; Technical Trainer; JAVA/Domino Consultant; Content Management Consultant; Pre-Sales Manager.

PERINI CORPORATION
73 Mt. Wayte Avenue, Framingham MA 01701. 508/628-2000. **Fax:** 508/628-2960. **Contact:** Human Resources. **E-mail address:** dtanner@perini.com. **World Wide Web address:** http://www.perini.com. **Description:** One of the largest heavy and building construction firms in the United States. Worldwide projects include bridges and roads, mass transportation and airport construction, and commercial building construction. Perini also provides engineering and consulting services. Founded in 1894. **Positions advertised include:** Scheduler; Estimator; Project Engineer. **Corporate headquarters location:** This location. **Operations at this facility include:** Administration. **Listed on:** American Stock Exchange. **Stock exchange symbol:** PCR.

PERKINELMER
35 Congress Street, Salem MA 01970. 978/745-3200. **Contact:** Human Resources. **World Wide Web address:** http://www.perkinelmer.com. **Description:** Operates four separate business units. The Instruments Unit designs and manufactures products for detecting, measuring, and testing purposes, and markets them to the pharmaceuticals, food, chemical, plastics, and environmental industries. The Life Sciences Unit designs and manufactures bioanalytic and diagnostic instrument systems and markets them to medical research facilities, hospitals, and clinics. The Fluid Sciences Unit manufactures sealing systems, advanced pneumatic components, and static and dynamic valves for use by OEMs and end users. The Optoelectronics Unit produces silicon-based sensor products, imaging technology, and a range of light sources. **Positions advertised include:** Global Risk Manager; Manager of Technical Accounting & Controls. **Other area locations:** Boston MA. **Other U.S. locations:** Beltsville MD; Norton OH. **International locations:** Belgium; Canada; England; Finland. **Listed on:** New York Stock Exchange. **Stock exchange symbol:** PKI.

PERKINELMER LIFE SCIENCES INC.
549 Albany Street, Boston MA 02118. 617/482-9595. **Toll-free phone:** 800/446-0035. **Fax:** 617/338-9758. **Contact:** Human Resources. **World Wide Web address:** http://las.perkinelmer.com/. **Description:** Provides radioactive, chemilluminescent and fluorescent labeling and detection products for life science and drug discovery. **Special programs:** Internships; Co-ops. **Other area locations:** Billerica MA; Wellesley MA. **Other U.S. locations:** Beltsville MD; Norton OH. **International locations:** Belgium; Canada; England; Finland. **Number of employees at this location:** 400.

PERMA INC.
605 Springs Road, Bedford MA 01730. 978/667-5161. **Fax:** 978/670-5797. **Contact:** Human Resources. **World Wide Web address:** http://www.perma.com. **Description:** Manufactures specialty chemicals for commercial cleaning applications.

PHILIPS ANALYTICAL
12 Michigan Drive, Natick MA 01760. 508/647-1100. **Contact:** Human Resources. **World Wide Web address:** http://www.philips.com. **Description:** Sells and services analytical X-ray systems. **Positions advertised include:** Applications Engineer; Application Group Leader; Assembly Technician; Technology Group Leader. **Corporate headquarters location:** New York NY. **Other U.S. locations:** Tempe AZ; Fremont CA; Alpharetta GA; Roselle IL; Columbia MD; Bellaire TX. **Parent company:** Philips Electronics North America, one of the larger industrial companies in the United States, is a multimarket manufacturing organization with nationwide locations and various subsidiaries. Philips concentrates its efforts primarily in the fields of consumer electronics, consumer products, electrical and electronics components, and professional equipment.

F.C. PHILLIPS
471 Washington Street, Stoughton MA 02072. 781/344-9400. **Contact:** Human Resources. **World Wide Web address:** http://www.fcphillips.com. **Description:** Manufactures screw machines and cleat spikes for athletic shoes.

PHILIPS MEDICAL SYSTEMS
3000 Minuteman Road, Andover MA 01810. 978/687-1501. **Contact:** Human Resources. **World Wide Web address:** http://www.medical.phillips.com. **Description:** Produces stethoscopes, electrolytes, and disposable ECG monitoring electrodes for adults and infants, as well as blood-pressure transducers and disposable transducer domes, chart papers, and disposable pressure kits.

PHOENIX CONTROLS CORPORATION
55 Chapel Street, Newton MA 02458. 617/964-6670. **Fax:** 617/965-9450. **Contact:** Human Resources. **E-mail address:** hr@pheonixcontrols.com. **World Wide Web address:** http://www.phoenixcontrols.com. **Description:** A manufacturer of air-flow control devices for hospitals and laboratories.

PHOENIX MEDIA/COMMUNICATIONS GROUP
126 Brookline Avenue, Boston MA 02215. 617/859-3339. **Fax:** 617/425-2615. **Contact:** Joe Goss, Human Resources. **E-mail address:** jobs@phx.com. **World Wide Web address:** http://www.bostonphoenix.com. **Description:** Publishes the *Boston Phoenix*, a weekly newspaper focusing on the art and entertainment industries in the greater Boston area. **Parent company:** Phoenix Media Group.

PHOENIX TECHNOLOGIES LTD.
320 Norwood Park South, Norwood MA 02062. 781/792-4760. **Fax:** 781/551-4000. **Contact:** Human Resources. **World Wide Web address:** http://www.phoenix.com. **Description:** Designs, develops, and markets systems software and end user software products. The Peripherals Division designs, develops, and supplies printer emulation software, page distribution languages, and controller hardware designs for the printing industry. The PhoenixPage imaging software architecture enables printer manufacturers to offer products that are compatible with the PostScript language, the PCL printer language, and other imaging standards. Phoenix Technologies' PC Division works with leading vendors and standards committees to ensure that Phoenix products enable manufacturers to develop and deploy next-generation PCs quickly and cost effectively. The company's Package Products Division is a single-source publisher of MS-DOS, Windows, and other software packages. **Corporate headquarters location:** San Jose CA. **Listed on:** NASDAQ. **Stock exchange symbol:** PTEC. **Number of employees at this location:** 330.

PIERCE BOSTON TECHNOLOGY CENTER
30 Commerce Way, Woburn MA 01801-1059. 781/937-0890. **Fax:** 781/937-3096. **Contact:** Human Resources. **World Wide Web address:** http://www.endogen.com. **Description:** Develops, manufactures, and markets diagnostic test kits that test for HIV and cancer. Products are sold in the United States to private and government institutions, university hospitals, medical centers, and large commercial laboratories via a direct sales force. **Positions advertised include:** Research Associate; Technical Marketing Assistant. **Corporate headquarters location:** Rockford IL. **Parent Company:** Pierce Chemical Corporation. **NOTE:** Please send all resumes to: Pierce Chemical Corporation, P.O. Box 117, Rockford IL 61105.

PILGRIM NUCLEAR POWER PLANT
600 Rocky Hill Road, Plymouth MA 02360. 508/830-7000. **Contact:** Human Resources. **Description:** A 670-megawatt plant supplying energy to New England.

PINE STREET INN, INC.
434 Harrison Avenue, Boston MA 02118. 617/521-7621. **Fax:** 617/521-7667. **Contact:** Human Resources. **World Wide Web address:** http://www.pinestreetinn.org. **Description:** Provides shelter, transitional programs, and housing for men, women, and children. **Operations at this facility include:** Administration; Service. **Number of employees at this location:** 650.

PIONEER BEHAVIORAL HEALTH
200 Lake Street, Suite 102, Peabody MA 01960. 978/536-2777. **Toll-free phone:** 800/543-2447. **Fax:** 978/536-2677. **Contact:** Human Resources. **E-mail address:** info@phc-inc.com. **World Wide Web address:** http://www.phc-inc.com. **Description:** Operates a variety of mental health, chemical dependency, and dual diagnosis programs throughout the country that provide inpatient and outpatient services, partial hospitalization, residential care, aftercare, and employee assistance programs. Founded in 1976. **Subsidiaries include:** Behavioral Stress Center (Elmhurst NY); Harbor Oaks Hospital (New Baltimore MI); Harmony Healthcare (Las Vegas NV); Highland Ridge Hospital (Salt Lake City UT); Mount Regis Center (Salem VA); Pioneer Counseling Centers of Michigan (Farmington Hills MI); Pioneer Counseling of Virginia (Salem VA); Pioneer Development & Support Services (Salt Lake City UT). **President/CEO:** Bruce A. Shear. **Number of employees at this location:** 300.

THE PIONEER GROUP, INC.
60 State Street, 19th Floor, Boston MA 02109. 617/742-7825. **Contact:** Human Resources. **World Wide Web address:** http://www.pioneerfunds.com. **Description:** Offers individual investment, institutional investment management, real estate advisory, venture capital, and emerging market services. **Corporate headquarters location:** This location.

PLEXUS NPI PLUS
4 Copeland Drive, Ayer MA 01432. 978/784-1500. **Contact:** Human Resources. **World Wide Web address:** http://www.plexus.com. **Description:** Manufactures circuit boards. **Positions advertised include:** Engineer. **Corporate headquarters location:** Neenah WI. **Parent Company:** Plexus Corporation. **Listed on:** NASDAQ. **Stock exchange symbol:** PLXS.

PLIMOTH PLANTATION
P.O. Box 1620, Plymouth MA 02362. 508/746-1622. **Fax:** 508/746-3407. **Contact:** Susan Haverstock, Human Resources. **E-mail address:** shaverstock@plimoth.org. **World Wide Web address:** http://www.plimoth.org. **Description:** An outdoor authentic re-creation of the seventeenth-century Plymouth Colony. The staff plays the parts of the villagers and tour guides. Plimoth Plantation is open seven days a week, 9:00 a.m. - 5:00 p.m. from April through November. Founded in 1947. **Positions advertised include:** Mayflower II Security Officer; Stockroom Supervisor; Wompanoag Food-ways Supervisor; Industrial Advancement Writer; Director of Development.

PLYMOUTH RUBBER COMPANY, INC.
104 Revere Street, Canton MA 02021. 781/828-0220. **Contact:** Human Resources. **World Wide Web address:** http://www.plymouthrubber.com. **Description:** Manufactures and markets rubber and vinyl products. The company serves the automotive, electrical supply, and utilities industries. **Listed on:** American Stock Exchange. **Stock exchange symbol:** PLRa.

PLYMOUTH SAVINGS BANK
151 Campanelli Drive, P.O. Box 1439, Middleboro MA 02346. 508/946-3000. **Contact:** Personnel. **World Wide Web address:** http://www.plymouthsavings.com.

Description: A full-service savings bank with 17 branch offices. **Positions advertised include:** Teller; Mortgage Officer; Assistant Manager. **Corporate headquarters location:** This location. **Other area locations:** Duxbury MA; Falmouth MA; Lakeville MA; Marion MA; Mashpee MA; Mattapoisett MA; Raynham MA; Sandwich MA. **Parent company:** Plymouth Bancorp, Inc.

POHLY & PARTNERS
27 Melcher Street, 2nd Floor, Boston MA 02210. 617/451-1700. **Toll-free phone:** 877/687-6459. **Fax:** 617/338-7767. **Contact:** Human Resources. **World Wide Web address:** http://www.pohlypartners.com. **Description:** A full-service provider of end-to-end custom publishing services in the production of books, magazines, newsletters, and Websites. **Parent company:** Cadmus Communications Corporation is a graphic communications company offering specialized products and services in three broad areas: printing, marketing, and publishing. Cadmus is one of the largest graphic communications companies in North America. Product lines include annual reports, catalogs, direct marketing financial printing, point-of-sale marketing, promotional printing, publishing, research journals, specialty magazines, and specialty packaging. Subsidiaries of Cadmus Communications include Cadmus Color Center, Inc. (Sandston VA); Cadmus Consumer Publishing (Richmond VA); Cadmus Direct Marketing, Inc. (Charlotte NC); Cadmus Interactive (Tucker GA); Cadmus Journal Services (Linthicum MD; Easton MD; and Richmond VA); Cadmus Marketing Services (Atlanta GA); Central Florida Press, L.C. (Orlando FL); Expert Brown (Sandston VA); Graftech Corporation (Charlotte NC); 3Score, Inc. (Tucker GA); Washburn Graphics, Inc. (Charlotte NC); and The William Byrd Press (Richmond VA).

POLLAK
195 Freeport Street, Boston MA 02122. 617/282-9550. **Contact:** Human Resources. **World Wide Web address:** http://www.pollak.com. **Description:** Pollak designs, develops, and produces integral components and systems for virtually every area of the transportation industry. The company creates electronic instrumentation including analog and digital clusters, drive information displays, power supplies, and warning light bars. Pollak manufactures electronic modules including light and HVAC control, panel seat memory, window control, brake monitoring, data acquisition, engine oil life monitor, multiplexing, and network interface. Founded in 1909. **Parent company:** Stoneridge, Inc. (Warren OH). **Operations at this facility include:** This location manufactures actuated automotive parts. **Listed on:** New York Stock Exchange. **Stock exchange symbol:** SRI.

POLLAK
300 Dan Road, Canton MA 02021. 781/830-0340. **Contact:** Human Resources. **World Wide Web address:** http://www.pollak.com. **Description:** Pollak designs, develops, and produces integral components and systems for virtually every area of the transportation industry. The company creates electronic instrumentation including analog and digital clusters, drive information displays, power supplies, and warning light bars. Pollak manufactures electronic modules including light and HVAC control, panel seat memory, window control, brake monitoring, data acquisition, engine oil life monitor, multiplexing, and network interface. Founded in 1909. **Parent company:** Stoneridge, Inc. (Warren OH). **Operations at this facility include:** This location manufactures a variety of automotive parts. **Listen on:** New York Stock Exchange. **Stock exchange symbol:** SRI.

POLYCOM, INC.
100 Minuteman Road, Andover MA 01810. 978/292-5000. **Toll-free phone:** 800/POL-YCOM. **Contact:** Personnel. **World Wide Web address:** http://www.polycom.com. **Description:** Develops, manufactures, and markets visual communications systems using advanced video and audio compression technology. Founded in 1984. **Positions advertised include:** Network Engineer; Product Support Technologist; Staff Engineer; Technical Support Engineer; Web Content Manager. **Corporate headquarters location:** Milipitas CA. **Listed on:** NASDAQ. **Stock exchange symbol:** PLCM. **Number of employees at this location:** 670.

POLYMEDICA CORPORATION
11 State Street, Woburn MA 01801. 781/933-2020. **Fax:** 781/933-7992. **Contact:** Human Resources. **World Wide Web address:** http://www.polymedica.com. **Description:** A leading provider of targeted medical products and services focusing primarily on the diabetes and consumer health care markets. Founded in 1988. **Special programs:** Co-ops. **Corporate headquarters location:** This location. **Other U.S. locations:** Golden CO; Palm City FL. **Subsidiaries include:** Liberty Medical Supply is one of the largest direct-mail distributors of diabetes supplies covered by Medicare. Liberty distributes more than 200,000 diabetes products to over 70,000 customers. PolyMedica Healthcare, Inc. holds leading positions in the urinary health and over-the-counter medical device markets by distributing a broad range of products to food, drug, and mass retailers nationwide. PolyMedica Pharmaceuticals (USA), Inc. manufactures, distributes, and markets prescription urological and suppository products. **Listed on:** NASDAQ. **Stock exchange symbol:** PLMD. **CEO:** Steven J. Lee. **Annual sales/revenues:** More than $100 million. **Number of employees at this location:** 30. **Number of employees nationwide:** 345.

PRECISION OPTICS CORPORATION
22 East Broadway, Gardner MA 01440. 978/630-1800. **Fax:** 978/630-1487. **Contact:** Human Resources. **E-mail address:** info@poci.com. **World Wide Web address:** http://www.poci.com. **Description:** Designs, develops, manufactures, and sells specialized optical systems and components and optical thin film coatings. The products and services are used in the medical and advanced optical systems industries. Medical products include endoscopes and image couplers, beamsplitters, and adapters that are used as accessories to endoscopes. Advanced optical design and developmental services provide advanced lens design, image analysis, optical system design, structural design and analysis, prototype production and evaluation, optics testing, and optical system assembly. **Corporate headquarters location:** This location. **Listed on:** NASDAQ. **Stock exchange symbol:** POCI.

PRICEWATERHOUSECOOPERS LLP
160 Federal Street, Boston MA 02110. 617/439-4390. **Contact:** Director of Recruiting. **World Wide Web address:** http://www.pwcglobal.com. **Description:** One of the largest certified public accounting firms in the world. PricewaterhouseCoopers provides public accounting, business advisory, management consulting, and taxation services. **Positions advertised include:** Data Quality Manager; Manager; Executive Assistant; Actuarial Life Manager; Service Center Clerk; Instructor Trainee; Information Technology Manager. **Special programs:** Internships. **Corporate headquarters location:** New York NY. **Other U.S. locations:** Nationwide. **Number of employees at this location:** 540.

PRIMUS MANAGED HOSTING SOLUTIONS
330 Lynnway, Lynn MA 01901. 781/586-6100. **Fax:** 781/593-6858. **Contact:** Human Resources. **World Wide Web address:** http://www.shore.net. **Description:** Provides Internet access and other online services including dial-up networking, Web design, and scripting. **Positions advertised include:** Customer Account Manager; Agent Channel Marketing; Help Desk Technician; Inside Accounting Representative; Internal Auditor; Legal Secretary; Manager Training Quality Assistant.

PRINCESS HOUSE, INC.
470 Myles Standish Boulevard, Taunton MA 02780. 508/823-0711. **Contact:** Human Resources. **World Wide Web address:** http://www.princesshouse.com. **Description:** A national direct sales company specializing in crystal and china. **Corporate headquarters location:** This location. **Parent company:** Colgate-Palmolive Company. **Operations at this facility include:** Administration; Service.

PROGRESS SOFTWARE CORPORATION
14 Oak Park, Bedford MA 01730. 781/280-4000. **Contact:** Human Resources. **World Wide Web address:** http://www.progress.com. **Description:** Manufactures and supplies application development software to business and government customers worldwide. Products include PROGRESS, a complete, integrated environment for developing and deploying mission-critical applications that are scalable, portable, and reconfigurable across a wide range of computing environments including client/server, host-based, and mixed. **Positions advertised include:** Data Integration; Facilities Manager; Inside Sales Representative; International Accounting Supervisor; International Financial Analyst; Research Assistant. **Listed on:** NASDAQ. **Stock exchange symbol:** PRGS. **Number of employees nationwide:** 630.

PROJECT BREAD
WALK FOR HUNGER
145 Border Street, Boston MA 02128. 617/723-5000. **Contact:** Human Resources. **World Wide Web address:** http://www.projectbread.org. **Description:** Supports nearly 500 food pantries, soup kitchens, homeless shelters, food banks, and other emergency feeding programs in 119 Massachusetts communities. Project Bread's Technical Assistance Program trains over 200 volunteers and staff, provides over 100 programs with one-on-one management assistance, and holds training series. Project Bread's transportation program, Food Drive for the Hungry, operated jointly with the American Red Cross, provides transportation to pick up low-cost or donated food. Since it began in 1969, the Walk for Hunger has become one of the nation's largest annual, one-day fundraisers for the hungry.

PROVIDENCE AND WORCESTER RAILROAD COMPANY
75 Hammond Street, Worcester MA 01610. 508/755-4000. **Contact:** Human Resources. **World Wide Web address:** http://www.pwrr.com. **Description:** Providence and Worcester Railroad Company is an interstate freight carrier conducting railroad operations in Massachusetts, Rhode Island, and Connecticut. The railroad operates on approximately 470 miles of track. Freight traffic is interchanged with Consolidated Rail Corporation (ConRail) at Worcester MA and New Haven CT; with Springfield Terminal Railway Company at Gardner MA; and with New England Central Railroad at New London CT. Through its connections, Providence and Worcester Railroad links approximately 78 communities through its lines. Founded in 1847. **Corporate headquarters location:** This location. **Other U.S. locations:** Plainfield CT; Cumberland RI. **Operations at this facility include:** This location is the main freight classification yard and the locomotive and car maintenance facility. **Listed on:** American Stock Exchange. **Stock exchange symbol:** PWX. **Number of employees nationwide:** 140.

PSYCHEMEDICS CORPORATION
1280 Massachusetts Avenue, Suite 200, Cambridge MA 02138. 617/868-7455. **Fax:** 617/864-1639. **Contact:** Human Resources Department. **World Wide Web address:** http://www.psychemedics.com. **Description:** A biotechnology company concentrating on diagnostics through the detection and measurement of substances in the body using hair samples. The first commercial product, a testing service for the detection of drugs, is provided principally to private sector companies. This test identifies traces of cocaine, marijuana, opiates, methamphetamines, and PCP. Psychemedics's testing methods use patented technology for performing immunoassays on enzymatically dissolved hair samples with confirmation testing by gas chromatography or mass spectrometry. **Corporate headquarters location:** This location. **Other U.S. locations:** Los Angeles CA; Fort Lauderdale FL; Atlanta GA; Chicago IL; Las Vegas NV; Dallas TX. **Listed on:** American Stock Exchange. **Stock exchange symbol:** PMD. **Number of employees nationwide:** 95.

PUBLISHERS CIRCULATION FULFILLMENT
P.O. Box 537, Waltham MA 02454. 781/466-1800. **Physical address:** 60 First Avenue, Waltham MA 02454. **Contact:** Human Resources. **Description:** Contracts home delivery of newspapers such as the *Wall Street Journal, Boston Globe,* and *New York Times.*

PUTNAM INVESTMENTS
One Post Office Square, Boston MA 02109. 617/292-1000. **Contact:** Human Resources. **World Wide Web address:** http://www.putnaminv.com. **Description:** A money management firm. **Positions advertised include:** Business Data Analyst; Strategic Relationship Analyst; Mail Clerk; Investment Reporting Analyst; Portfolio Analyst; Financial Engineer. **Corporate headquarters location:** This location. **Other U.S. locations:** Andover MA; Franklin MA; Quincy MA.

QRS CORPORATION
17 Rogers Street, Gloucester MA 01930. 978/283-9505. **Contact:** Human Resources. **E-mail address:** careers@qrs.com. **World Wide Web address:** http://www.qrs.com. **Description:** Develops supply chain management software. **Corporate headquarters location:** Richmond CA. **Listed on:** NASDAQ. **Stock exchange symbol:** QRSI.

QUADTECH INC.
5 Clock Tower Place, Suite 210 East, Maynard MA 01754. 978/461-2100. **Toll-free phone:** 800/253-1230. **Fax:** 978/461-4295. **Contact:** Human Resources Department. **World Wide Web address:** http://www.quadtechinc.com. **Description:** Engaged in the sale of electronic test equipment. **Positions advertised include:** Applications Engineer; Electronics Technician; Documentation Control Specialist; Customer Service Representative.

QUAKER FABRIC CORPORATION
941 Grinnell Street, Fall River MA 02721. 508/678-1951. **Fax:** 508/646-2429. **Contact:** Personnel. **World Wide Web address:** http://www.quakerfabric.com. **Description:** Manufactures textile upholstery fabrics and yarn. **Positions advertised include:** Textile Designer; Process Engineer; Lab Manager; Quality Engineer; Entry Level Engineer; Health & Wellness Specialist; Employee Development Specialist; Human Resources Representative; Benefits Coordinator; Manufacturing Supervisor; Marketing Professional. **Corporate headquarters location:** This location. **Operations at this facility include:** Administration; Divisional Headquarters; Manufacturing; Regional Headquarters; Research and Development; Service. **Listed on:** NASDAQ. **Stock exchange symbol:** QFAB. **Number of employees at this location:** 1,500.

QUEBECOR WORLD BOOK SERVICES DIVISION
1133 County Street, Taunton MA 02780. 508/823-4581. **Fax:** 508/828-4356. **Contact:** Human Resources. **World Wide Web address:** http://www.quebecorworld.com. **Description:** One of the largest commercial printers in the world. **Positions advertised include:** Production Worker. **NOTE:** Entry-level positions and second and third shifts are offered. **Special programs:** Co-ops. **Office hours:** Monday - Friday, 8:00 a.m. - 5:00 p.m. **Other U.S. locations:** Nationwide. **Listed on:** New York Stock Exchange. **Stock exchange symbol:** IQW. **Annual sales/revenues:** More than $100 million. **Number of employees at this location:** 450. **Number of employees nationwide:** 12,000. **Number of employees worldwide:** 16,000.

QUEST DIAGNOSTICS INCORPORATED
415 Massachusetts Avenue, Cambridge MA 02139-4102. 617/547-8900. **Fax:** 617/868-7962. **Contact:** Human Resources. **World Wide Web address:** http://www.questdiagnostics.com. **Description:** One of the largest clinical laboratories in North America, providing a broad range of clinical laboratory services to health care clients that include physicians, hospitals, clinics, dialysis centers, pharmaceutical companies, and corporations. The company offers and performs tests on blood, urine, and other bodily fluids and tissues to provide information for health and well-being. **Positions advertised include:** Phlebotomy Services Representative; Account Manager; Medical Technologist; Billing Supervisor; Processing Associate.

QUINCY COLLEGE
34 Coddington Street, Quincy MA 02169. 617/984-1600. **Contact:** Steve McGrath, Human Resources. **E-mail address:** smcgrath@quincycollege.edu. **World Wide Web address:** http://www.quincycollege.edu. **Description:** A two-year commuter college. Quincy College's combined full-time and part-time student enrollment is 5,000.

QUINCY MEDICAL CENTER
114 Whitwell Street, Quincy MA 02169. 617/773-6100. **Contact:** Human Resources. **World Wide Web address:** http://www.quincymc.com. **Description:** A hospital offering a variety of services including a 24-hour emergency room, surgery, OB/GYN services, radiology, and a center for women's health. **Positions advertised include:** Cafeteria Helper; CT Technologist; Occupational Therapist; Physical Therapist; Radiological Therapist; Registered Nurse; Respiratory Therapist; Security Officer; Ultrasonographer.

RSA SECURITY, INC.
20 Crosby Drive, Bedford MA 01730. 781/687-7000. **Contact:** Human Resources. **World Wide Web address:** http://www.rsasecurity.com. **Description:** Develops and markets software for security applications. **Positions advertised include:** Systems Engineer; Inside Sales Representative; Account Manager; Executive Assistant; Accountant; Business Analyst; Administrative Assistant; Quality Assurance Performance Test Engineer; Product Manager; Financial Analyst; Strategic Web Manager; Programming Analyst. **Corporate headquarters location:** This location. **Listed on:** NASDAQ. **Stock exchange symbol:** RSAS.

RVSI ACUITY CIMATRIX
5 Shawmut Road, Canton MA 02021. 781/821-0830. **Toll-free phone:** 800/646-6664. **Fax:** 781/828-8942. **Contact:** Human Resources. **World Wide Web address:** http://www.rvsi.com. **Description:** RVSI Acuity CiMatrix is a leader in the development of bar code and symbology solutions that automatically capture, analyze, and communicate identification information in industrial, material handling, and manufacturing environments. The company also manufactures machine vision systems, industrial controllers, data entry technicals, and LANs. **Positions advertised include:** Embedded Software Engineer; Applications Engineer; Software Engineer. **Corporate headquarters location:** This location. **Other U.S. locations:** Mission Viejo CA; San Jose CA; West Hartford CT; Roswell GA; Schaumburg IL; Southfield MI; Raleigh NC; Cincinnati OH; Irving TX. **Parent company:** Robotic Vision Systems, Inc. **Listed on:** NASDAQ. **Stock exchange symbol:** ROBV.

RADCLIFFE INSTITUTE FOR ADVANCED STUDY
10 Garden Street, Faye House, Room 106, Cambridge MA 02138. 617/495-8608. **Fax:** 617/496-0255. **Contact:** Human Resources. **E-mail address:** info@radcliffe.edu. **World Wide Web address:** http://www.radcliffe.edu. **Description:** A college offering both graduate and undergraduate programs. Radcliffe Institute for Advanced Study was established as a result of the merger of Radcliffe College with Harvard University.

RADICI SPANDEX CORPORATION
125 Hartwell Street, Fall River MA 02721. 508/674-3585. **Fax:** 508/674-3580. **Contact:** Personnel. **World Wide Web address:** http://www.radicispandex.com. **Description:** A manufacturer and worldwide marketer of rubber threads and synthetic spandex fibers. Customers include apparel, textile, and nonwoven manufacturers. **Corporate headquarters location:** This location.

RANSOM ENVIRONMENTAL CONSULTANTS, INC.
Brown's Wharf, Newburyport MA 01950. 978/465-1822. **Fax:** 978/465-2986. **Contact:** Human Resources. **World Wide Web address:** http://www.ransomenv.com. **Description:** An environmental consulting firm specializing in remediation design and environmental risk assessment. **Positions advertised include:** Project Geologist; Project Manager; Engineer Geologist; Manager Engineer. **Corporate headquarters location:** This location. **Other U.S. locations:** Bristol RI.

RATIONAL SOFTWARE CORPORATION
20 Maguire Road, Lexington MA 02421. 781/676-2400. **Contact:** Human Resources. **World Wide Web address:** http://www.rational.com. **Description:** Rational Software develops, markets, and supports embedded software products for Web and e-commerce applications. The company's products operate on both Windows and UNIX systems. **Positions advertised include:** Air Force C2 Systems Engineer; Contracts Negotiator; Financial Planning & Analysis; Quality Assurance Engineer; Principal Budget Analyst; Systems Engineer; Environmental Test Engineer; Supply Chain Source Specialist; Process Working Group Lead; Communication Systems Engineer; Field Engineer. **International locations:** Worldwide. **Operations at this facility include:** This location is the North American sales center. **Listed on:** NASDAQ. **Stock exchange symbol:** RATL.

RAYTHEON COMPANY
141 Spring Street, Lexington MA 02421. 781/862-6600. **Contact:** Human Resources. **World Wide Web address:** http://www.raytheon.com. **Description:** Raytheon Company is a diversified, international, multi-industry technology-based company ranked among the 100 largest U.S. industrial corporations. Raytheon has facilities in 42 states and the District of Columbia. Overseas facilities and representative offices are located in 34 countries. The company's two business segments include Defense and Commercial Electronics, and Business Aviation and Special Mission Aircraft. **Corporate headquarters location:** This location. **Other U.S. locations:** Nationwide. **International locations:** Worldwide. **Listed on:** New York Stock Exchange. **Stock exchange symbol:** RTN.

RAYTHEON SYSTEMS COMPANY
1001 Boston Post Road, Marlborough MA 01752. 508/490-1000. **Contact:** Human Resources. **World Wide Web address:** http://www.raytheon.com. **Description:** Manufactures search, detection, navigation, guidance, aeronautical, and nautical systems and instruments. **Parent company:** Raytheon Company is a diversified, international, multi-industry, technology-based company ranked among the 100 largest U.S. industrial corporations. The company has four business segments: Electronics, Major Appliances, Aircraft Products, and Energy and Environmental. Raytheon has over 100 facilities in the United States.

RAYTHEON TECHNICAL SERVICES
2 Wayside Road, Burlington MA 01801. 781/238-3000. **Contact:** Human Resources. **World Wide Web address:** http://www.raytheon.com. **Description:** Provides electrical engineering services. **Positions advertised include:** Software Engineer; Program Manager; Project Manager; Logistics Engineer; Civil Engineer; ATM Transitional Implementation Manager; Technical Recruiter; Web Project Manager; Support Assistant; Media Production Specialist; Electrical Engineer; Subcontract Administrator. **Corporate headquarters location:** Lexington MA. **Parent company:** Raytheon Company is a diversified, international, multi-industry, technology-based company ranked among the 100 largest U.S. industrial corporations. The company has four business segments: Electronics, Major Appliances, Aircraft Products, and Energy and Environmental. Raytheon has over 100 facilities in the United States. Overseas facilities and representative offices are located in 26 countries, principally in Europe, the Middle East, and the Pacific Rim.

REEBOK INTERNATIONAL LTD.
1895 J.W. Foster Boulevard, Canton MA 02021. 781/401-5000. **Contact:** Human Resources. **World Wide Web address:** http://www.reebok.com. **Description:** A leading worldwide designer, marketer, and distributor of sports, fitness, and casual footwear, apparel, and equipment. Principal operating units include the Reebok Division, Avia Group International, Inc., and The Rockport Company, Inc. **Positions advertised include:** Human Resources Assistant; Apparel Designer; Creative Director; Designer; Product Planning Manager; Technical Designer; Associate Product Line Manager; Production Manager. **Corporate headquarters location:** This location. **Listed on:** New York Stock Exchange. **Stock exchange symbol:** RBK.

REED BUSINESS INFORMATION
275 Washington Street, Newton MA 02458-1630. 617/964-3030. **Contact:** Human Resources. **World Wide Web address:** http://www.reedbusiness.com. **Description:** A publisher whose offerings include over 50 magazines in both business and consumer markets. They also provide a variety of marketing and publishing services including direct mail, economic forecasting, and marketing research.

REED & BARTON
144 West Brittania Street, Taunton MA 02780. 508/824-6611. **Toll-free phone:** 800/343-1383. **Contact:** Human Resources. **E-mail address:** information@reedbarton.com. **World Wide Web address:** http://www.reedbarton.com. **Description:** A manufacturer of sterling, silver plate, pewter, and stainless steel silverware. Reed & Barton also produces a line of jewelry products. **Corporate headquarters location:** This location.

REED & PRINCE
8 Mohawk Drive, Leominster MA 01453. 508/753-2931. **Fax:** 978/466-6980. **Contact:** Human Resources. **Description:** A manufacturer and packager of metal fasteners and fastening systems including high-precision fittings for use in spacecraft, recessed and slotted screws, nuts, bolts, rivets, and screwdrivers. **Corporate headquarters location:** This location.

REED-RICO
18 Industrial Drive, Holden MA 01520. 508/829-4491. **Contact:** Human Resources. **Description:** Produces thread-rolling machines, die attachments, thread rolls, and knurls. Reed-Rico has more than 2,000 registered trademarks, and more than 5,000 U.S. and foreign patents or patent applications. **Corporate headquarters location:** Portland OR. **Other U.S. locations:** Bristol RI; Gaffney SC. **Parent company:** Precision Castparts Corporation. **Listed on:** New York Stock Exchange. **Stock exchange symbol:** PCP. **Number of employees at this location:** 345.

REGIS COLLEGE
Box 4, 235 Wellesley Street, Weston MA 02493. 781/768-7210. **Contact:** Human Resources. **World Wide Web address:** http://www.regiscollege.edu. **Description:** A private liberal arts and sciences college for women. Founded in 1927.

GT REILLY & COMPANY
424 Adams Street, Milton MA 02186-4358. 617/696-8900. **Fax:** 617/698-1803. **Contact:** Director of Personnel. **E-mail address:** pjf@gtreilly.com. **World Wide Web address:** http://www.gtreilly.com. **Description:** A 45 year old growing regional accounting firm. **Positions advertised include:** Public Accounting Professional.

REPLIGEN CORPORATION
41 Seyon Street Building #1, Suite 100, Waltham MA 02453. 781/250-0111. **Toll-free phone:** 800/622-2259. **Fax:** 781/259-0015. **Contact:** Human Resources. **World Wide Web address:** http://www.repligen.com. **Description:** Researches and manufactures pharmaceutical products. **Positions advertised include:** Associate Medical Director; Analytical Biochemist; Quality Affairs Associate; Regulatory Affairs Manager; Clinical Research Associate.

RITZ CAMERA
South Shore Plaza, 250 Granite Street, Braintree MA 02184. 781/843-4619. **Contact:** Hiring Manager. **World Wide Web address:** http://www.ritzcamera.com. **Description:** One location of the camera shop and photo developer chain.

RIVERSIDE HEALTH CENTER
205 Western Avenue, Cambridge MA 02139. 617/498-1109. **Contact:** Human Resources. **Description:** An outpatient clinic providing services that include general medical care for adults, prenatal, family planning, nutrition, psychiatric treatment, and pediatric care. **Parent company:** Cambridge Hospital is a 170-bed, full-service hospital owned by the city of Cambridge and affiliated with Harvard and Tufts Medical Schools.

RIZZO ASSOCIATES, INC.
P.O. Box 9005, One Grant Street, Framingham MA 01701-9005. 508/903-2000. **Fax:** 508/903-2001. **Contact:** Human Resources. **E-mail address:** hr@rizzo.com. **World Wide Web address:** http://www.rizzo.com. **Description:** An engineering and

environmental consulting firm. The company provides engineering, environmental compliance, hazardous waste management, transportation, and water/wastewater services. **NOTE:** Entry-level positions and part-time jobs are offered. **Positions advertised include:** Civil Engineer; Site Engineer; Engineer. **Special programs:** Internships; Co-ops. **Office hours:** Monday - Friday, 9:00 a.m. - 5:30 p.m. **Parent company:** Tetra Tech, Inc. **Listed on:** Privately held. **Annual sales/revenues:** $21 - $50 million.

ROBINS, KAPLAN, MILLER & CIRESI LLP
111 Huntington Avenue, Suite 1300, Boston MA 02199-7610. 617/267-2300. **Fax:** 617/267-8288. **Contact:** Human Resources. **World Wide Web address:** http://www.rkmc.com. **Description:** A law firm covering many practice areas including insurance law, business and commercial litigation, and intellectual property law. Founded in 1938. **Corporate headquarters location:** Minneapolis MN. **Other U.S. locations:** Los Angeles CA; San Francisco CA; Washington DC; Atlanta GA; Chicago IL. **Number of employees at this location:** 37. **Number of employees nationwide:** 650.

ROCKBESTOS-SURPRENANT CABLE CORPORATION
172 Sterling Street, Clinton MA 01510. 978/365-6331. **Toll-free phone:** 800/444-3792. **Fax:** 978/365-3287. **Contact:** Peter Stephan, Human Resources Manager. **World Wide Web address:** http://www.r-scc.com. **Description:** A major manufacturer of quality-assured, specialty purpose insulated wire and cable products. **Special programs:** Internships. **Office hours:** Monday - Friday, 8:00 a.m. - 5:00 p.m. **Corporate headquarters location:** This location. **Other U.S. locations:** New Haven CT. **Operations at this facility include:** Administration; Manufacturing; Research and Development; Sales. **Listed on:** Privately held. **President:** Fred Schwelm. **Annual sales/revenues:** More than $100 million. **Number of employees at this location:** 300. **Number of employees nationwide:** 600.

ROCKLAND TRUST
288 Union Street, Rockland MA 02370. 781/878-6100. **Fax:** 781/982-6424. **Contact:** Paul McDonough, Employment Manager. **World Wide Web address:** http://www.rocklandtrust.com. **Description:** Rockland Trust is a commercial bank with 44 offices offering retail and commercial banking services, trust and estate planning, investment, and employee benefit services. Founded in 1907. **NOTE:** Entry-level positions are offered. **Positions advertised include:** Customer Service Agent; Mortgage Originator. **Special programs:** Training. **Corporate headquarters location:** This location. **Other area locations:** Statewide. **Parent company:** Independent Bank Corp. **Listed on:** NASDAQ. **Stock exchange symbol:** INDB. **Number of employees at this location:** 570.

THE ROCKPORT COMPANY, LLC
1895 J.W. Foster Boulevard, Canton MA 02021. 781/401-5000. **Toll-free phone:** 800/ROCKPORT. **Contact:** Human Resources. **World Wide Web address:** http://www.rockport.com. **Description:** Designs, markets, and sells men's and women's shoes. **Corporate headquarters location:** This location. **Parent company:** Reebok International Ltd. **Operations at this facility include:** Administration; Research and Development; Sales; Service. **Annual sales/revenues:** More than $100 million.

ROCKWELL AUTOMATION
ALLEN-BRADLEY COMPANY
2 Executive Drive, Chelmsford MA 01824. 978/441-9500. **Contact:** Human Resources. **World Wide Web address:** http://www.automation.rockwell.com. **Description:** Designs, manufactures, and markets electronic controls and control systems for industrial markets. Principal products are photoelectric controls, inductive proximity controls, sensing products, and mechanical limit switches for the automation of industrial processes. Founded in 1904. **Positions advertised include:** Product Manager; Electrical Engineer. **Corporate headquarters location:** Milwaukee WI. **Other U.S. locations:** Manchester NH. **Parent company:** Rockwell International. **Listed on:** New York Stock Exchange. **Stock exchange symbol:** ROK. **Number of employees at this location:** 115. **Number of employees nationwide:** 900. **Number of employees worldwide:** 26,000.

ROLLS ROYCE NAVAL MARINE
110 Norfolk Street, Walpole MA 02081. 508/668-9610. **Fax:** 508/668-5638. **Contact:** Human Resources. **Description:** Manufactures marine propulsion systems.

ROPES & GRAY
One International Place, Boston MA 02110-2624. 617/951-7000. **Contact:** Human Resources. **World Wide Web address:** http://www.ropesgray.com. **Description:** A law firm specializing in corporate law.

ROYAL SONESTA HOTEL
5 Cambridge Parkway, Cambridge MA 02142. 617/491-3600. **Fax:** 617/806-4183. **Contact:** June Oppedisano, Employment Manager. **E-mail address:** joppedisano@sonesta-boston.com. **World Wide Web address:** http://www.sonesta.com. **Description:** Royal Sonesta Hotel offers 400 guest rooms, 15 function rooms, and dining in the Gallery Cafe. **Positions advertised include:** Catering Sales Manager; Shift Engineer; Engineering Office Coordinator; Front Desk Agent. **NOTE:** Entry-level positions are offered. **Corporate headquarters location:** Boston MA. **Other U.S. locations:** Key Biscayne FL; New Orleans LA. **Parent company:** Sonesta International Hotels Corporation. **Operations at this facility include:** Administration; Sales; Service. **Listed on:** NASDAQ. **Stock exchange symbol:** SNSTA. **Number of employees at this location:** 300.

SAP AMERICA, INC.
950 Winter Street, Suite 3800, Waltham MA 02451. 781/672-6500. **Fax:** 781/672-6683. **Contact:** Human Resources. **World Wide Web address:** http://www.sap.com. **Description:** Develops a variety of client/server computer software packages including programs for finance, human resources, and materials management applications. Founded in 1972. **Positions advertised include:** Administrative Assistant. **Special programs:** Internships; Summer Jobs. **Corporate headquarters location:** Newtown Square PA. **Other U.S. locations:** Nationwide. **International locations:** Germany. **Parent company:** SAP AG. **Annual sales/revenues:** More than $100 million. **Number of employees at this location:** 200. **Number of employees nationwide:** 3,000. **Number of employees worldwide:** 13,000.

SEA CONSULTANTS, INC.
485 Massachusetts Avenue, Cambridge MA 02139. 617/497-7800 **Contact:** Human Resources. **World Wide Web address:** http://www.seacon.com. **Description:** A multifunctional engineering firm offering a wide variety of engineering services including civil, structural, scientific, and environmental engineering. **Positions advertised include:** Accounts Payable Coordinator.

SEA CORPORATION
20 Vernon Street, Norwood MA 02062. 781/762-9252. **Contact:** Human Resources. **World Wide Web address:** http://www.seacorp.com. **Description:** Provides systems integration and networking services under government contract.

SPSS INC.
One Alewife Center, Cambridge MA 02140. 617/665-9200. **Contact:** Human Resources. **World Wide Web address:** http://www.spss.com. **Description:** Develops software that allows businesses to analyze and predict online consumer behavior. **Positions advertised include:** Business Development Manager; Product Manager. **NOTE:** Apply online. **Other U.S. locations:** San Francisco CA; Miami FL; Newton MA; New York NY; Cincinnati OH; Arlington VA.

ST. ELIZABETH'S MEDICAL CENTER
736 Cambridge Street, Brighton MA 02135. 617/789-3000. **Contact:** Human Resources. **World Wide Web address:** http://www.semc.org. **Description:** A hospital. **Positions advertised include:** Nursing Administration; Administrative Assistant; Ambulatory Scheduling Coordinator; Benefits Manager; Billing Coordinator; Care Manager; Counselor; Dietician; Housekeeper; Licensed Practical Nurse; Medical Technician; Nursing Assistant; Secretary; Registered Nurse.

ST. PAUL FIRE & MARINE INSURANCE COMPANY
P.O. Box 8848, Boston MA 02114. 617/227-7890. **Contact:** Human Resources. **Description:** A multiline insurance company providing fire, extended coverage, inland marine, and workers' compensation insurance. **Corporate headquarters location:** St. Paul MN. **Listed on:** New York Stock Exchange. **Stock exchange symbol:** SPC. **Number of employees at this location:** 60. **Number of employees nationwide:** 11,000.

ST PAUL TRAVELERS
300 Crown Colony Drive, Quincy MA 02169. 617/984-1000. **Contact:** Human Resources. **World Wide Web address:** http://www.stpaultravelers.com. **Description:** Provides commercial property-casualty insurance, personal property-casualty insurance and asset management services. **Positions advertised include:** Risk Control Consultant; Account Executive. **Corporate headquarters location:** St Paul MN. **Other area locations:** Boston MA, Worcester MA.

SAINT-GOBAIN CONTAINERS
One National Street, Milford MA 01757. 508/478-2500. **Contact:** Human Resources. **Description:** Manufactures glass bottles.

SAKS FIFTH AVENUE
Prudential Center, Boston MA 02199. 617/262-8500. **Contact:** Human Resources. **World Wide Web address:** http://www.saksincorporated.com. **Description:** Saks Fifth Avenue is a 62-store chain emphasizing soft-goods products, primarily apparel for men, women, and children. **Corporate headquarters location:** New York NY. **Parent company:** Saks Incorporated is a department store holding company that operates approximately 360 stores in 36 states. The company's stores include Saks Fifth Avenue, Parisian, Proffit's, Younker's, Herberger's, Carson Pirie Scott, Boston Store, Bergner's, and Off 5th, the company's outlet store. Saks Incorporated also operates two retail catalogs and several retail Internet sites. **Listed on:** New York Stock Exchange. **Stock exchange symbol:** SKS.

SALEM CHAMBER OF COMMERCE
63 Wharf Street, Salem MA 01970. 978/744-0004. **Fax:** 978/745-3855. **Contact:** Denise Flynn, Executive Director. **E-mail address:** scc@salem-chamber.org. **World Wide Web address:** http://www.salem-chamber.org. **Description:** Attracts and promotes businesses in the city of Salem.

SALEM STATE COLLEGE
352 Lafayette Street, Salem MA 01970. 978/542-6000. **Contact:** Human Resources. **E-mail address:** eo-hr@salemstate.edu. **World Wide Web address:** http://www.salemstate.edu. **Description:** A state college.

SALOMON SMITH BARNEY
53 State Street, 39th Floor, Boston MA 02109. 617/589-3500. **Contact:** Human Resources. **World Wide Web address:** http://www.salomonsmithbarney.com. **Description:** An international investment banking, market making, and research firm serving corporations, state and local governments, sovereign and provincial governments and their agencies, central banks, and other financial institutions. **Other area locations:** Brockton; Hingham; Pittsfield; Waltham; State Street Boston; Danvers; Hyannis; Springfield; Worcester. **Corporate headquarters location:** New York NY.

THE SALVATION ARMY
187 Columbus Avenue, Boston MA 02116-5197. 617/542-5420. **Fax:** 617/338-7990. **Contact:** Divisional Personnel Secretary. **World Wide Web address:** http://www.salvationarmy.org. **Description:** A nonprofit organization providing several service programs including day-care centers, programs for people with disabilities, substance abuse programs and tutoring for at-risk students. The Salvation Army targets its programs to assist alcoholics, battered women, drug addicts, the elderly, the homeless, people with AIDS, prison inmates, teenagers, and the unemployed. **Corporate headquarters location:** Alexandria VA. **Other U.S. locations:** Nationwide. **Operations at this facility include:** Administration; Divisional Headquarters. **Number of employees at this location:** 50.

THE SALVATION ARMY
402 Massachusetts Avenue, P.O. Box 647, Cambridge MA 02139. 617/547-3400. **Contact:** Personnel. **World Wide Web address:** http://www.salvationarmy.org. **Description:** A nonprofit organization providing several service programs including day-care centers, programs for people with disabilities, substance abuse programs and tutoring for at-risk students. The Salvation Army targets its programs to assist alcoholics, battered women, drug addicts, the elderly, the homeless, people with AIDS, prison inmates, teenagers, and the unemployed. **Corporate headquarters location:** Alexandria VA. **Other U.S. locations:** Nationwide.

A.R. SANDRI, INC.
P.O. Box 1578, Greenfield MA 01302-1578. 413/773-3658. **Physical address:** 400 Chapman Street, Greenfield MA 01301. **Contact:** Human Resources. **World Wide Web address:** http://www.sandrisunoco.com. **Description:** One of the largest regional distributors of Sunoco brand gasoline, heating oil, lubricants, and other petroleum products. **Corporate headquarters location:** This location.

SANKATY HEAD GOLF CLUB
100 Sankaty Road, Siasconsett MA 02564. 508/257-6655. **Fax:** 508/257-4265. **Contact:** Human Resources. **Description:** A private golf club on Nantucket Island known for its signature hole next to Sankaty Head Light House.

SAPIENT CORPORATION
One Memorial Drive, 3rd Floor, Cambridge MA 02142. 617/621-0200. **Contact:** Director of Hiring. **World Wide Web address:** http://www.sapient.com. **Description:** Provides systems integration, consulting, and software integration services. Founded in 1991. **Positions advertised include:** Billing Associate; Payroll Associate; Finance Manager; Technology Developer; Internal Audit Finance Manager; Technology Associate; People Strategy Manager. **Corporate headquarters location:** This location. **Other U.S. locations:** Los Angeles CA; San Francisco CA; Denver CO; Washington DC; Atlanta GA; Chicago IL; Portland ME; Minneapolis MN; Jersey City NJ; Austin TX; Dallas TX. **International locations:** Australia; England; Germany; India; Italy; Japan. **Listed on:** NASDAQ. **Stock exchange symbol:** SAPE. **Annual sales/revenues:** More than $100 million.

SASAKI ASSOCIATES, INC.
64 Pleasant Street, Watertown MA 02472. 617/926-3300. **Fax:** 617/924-2748. **Contact:** Human Resources. **World Wide Web address:** http://www.sasaki.com. **Description:** An architectural and design firm that specializes in architecture, civil engineering, graphic design, interior design, landscape architecture, and urban design. Founded in 1953. **Positions advertised include:** Interior Design; Marketing Coordinator. **Corporate headquarters location:** This location. **Other U.S. locations:** San Francisco CA; Dallas TX. **Number of employees at this location:** 155. **Number of employees nationwide:** 200.

SATCON TECHNOLOGY CORPORATION
161 First Street, Cambridge MA 02142. 617/661-0540. **Fax:** 617/661-3373. **Contact:** Human Resources. **World Wide Web address:** http://www.satcon.com. **Description:** Designs, develops, manufactures, and markets active motion control systems. These systems use magnetic forces, coupled with precision sensors and specialized electronics, to control both linear and rotary motion. The company has developed revolutionary technologies for applications that affect large segments of global industries, from ground and air transportation to CFC-free refrigeration and air conditioning systems. **Listed on:** NASDAQ. **Stock exchange symbol:** SATC.

SAUCONY, INC.
P.O. Box 6046, Peabody MA 01961. 978/532-9000. **Fax:** 978/538-3080. **Physical address:** 13 Centennial Drive, Peabody MA 01960. **Fax:** 978/538-3080. **Contact:** Kerry Smith, Director of Human Resources. **World Wide Web address:** http://www.sauconyinc.com. **Description:** Engaged in the design, manufacture, import, export, development, and marketing of a wide range of athletic footwear and recreational products. **Positions advertised include:** Account Development Manager; Technical Product Developer. **Special programs:** Internships. **Corporate headquarters location:** This location. **Other area locations:** Cambridge MA; East Brookfield MA; Fall River MA. **Other U.S. locations:** Bangor ME. **Operations at this facility include:** Administration; Research and Development; Sales; Service. **Listed on:** NASDAQ. **Stock exchange symbol:** SCNYA. **Number of employees at this location:** 140. **Number of employees nationwide:** 415.

SCANSOFT, INC.
9 Centennial Drive, Peabody MA 01960. 978/977-2000. **Toll-free phone:** 800/248-6550. **Fax:** 978/977-2129. **Contact:** Human Resources. **World Wide Web address:** http://www.scansoft.com. **Description:** Manufactures TextBridge and Pagis scanning software and OCR (Optical Character Recognition) software. **NOTE:** Entry-level positions are offered. **Positions advertised include:** Internal Audit & Compliance Director; Telecommunications Manager; Product Marketing Manager; Inside Sales Representative; Outbound Sales Representative. **Special programs:** Internships; Training; Co-ops; Summer Jobs. **Corporate headquarters location:** This location. **Other U.S. locations:** Nationwide. **Operations at this facility include:** Divisional Headquarters. **Listed on:** NASDAQ. **Stock exchange symbol:** SSFT. **President/CEO:** Mike K. Tivnan. **Annual sales/revenues:** $21 - $50 million. **Number of employees at this location:** 120.

SCHNEIDER AUTOMATION
One High Street, North Andover MA 01845. 978/794-0800. **Contact:** Human Resources. **World Wide Web address:** http://www.modicon.com. **Description:** Manufactures industrial instruments for measurement, display, and control of process variables and related products. **Positions advertised include:** Principal Product Leader.

SEACOAST CAPITAL PARTNERS
55 Ferncroft Road, Suite 110, Danvers MA 01923-4001. 978/750-1351. **Fax:** 978/750-1301. **Contact:** Human Resources. **World Wide Web address:** http://www.seacoastcapital.com. **Description:** A personal credit institution. **Other U.S. location:** San Francisco CA.

SEAPORT GRAPHICS
12 Channel Street, Suite 802, Marine Industrial Park, Boston MA 02210. 617/330-1200. **Contact:** Human Resources. **E-mail address:** employment@seaportgraphics.com. **World Wide Web address:** http://www.seaportgraphics.com. **Description:** Manufactures presentation graphics software and workstation products. Seaport Graphics also creates imaging systems for personal computers and Macintosh desktop packages, color electronic prepress systems, and overnight slide services. **Positions advertised include:** Sales Representative; Account Manager.

SEARS, ROEBUCK & CO.
Route 6 and 118, Swansea Mall Drive, Swansea MA 02777. 508/324-6500. **Contact:** Human Resources. **World Wide Web address:** http://www.sears.com. **Description:** One location of the department chain store. **Listed on:** NYSE. **Stock exchange symbol:** S.

SECURITAS USA
575 Boylston Street, 6th Floor, Boston MA 02116. 617/437-9119. **Contact:** Human Resources. **World Wide Web address:** http://www.securitasusa.com. **Description:** A contract security agency providing uniformed security officers, investigative services, and security system installation.

SELECT, INC.
31 Dartmouth Street, Westwood MA 02090. 781/326-8600. **Toll-free phone:** 800/634-1806. **Contact:** Human Resources. **World Wide Web address:** http://www.select.com. **Description:** Manufactures and sells network servers.

SEPRACOR, INC.
111 Locke Drive, Marlborough MA 01752. 508/481-6700. **Fax:** 508/357-7490. **Contact:** Human Resources. **World Wide Web address:** http://www.sepracor.com. **Description:** Develops new and improved versions of prescription drugs. Sepracor's products are known as Improved Chemical Entities (ICE Pharmaceuticals) and are used in the allergy, asthma, gastroenterology, neurology, psychiatry, and urology markets. **Positions advertised include:** Principal Application Support Center; Validation Support Specialist; Project Coordinator; Purchasing Administrator; Medical Information Manager; Information Technology Administration Assistant; Financial Systems Support Specialist; Human Resources Associate Director; Project Manager; Technical Business Analyst. **Corporate headquarters location:** This location. **Listed on:** NASDAQ. **Stock exchange symbol:** SEPR.

SERONO, INC.
One Technology Place, Rockland MA 02370. 781/982-9000. **Toll-free phone:** 800/283-8088. **Contact:** Human Resources. **World Wide Web address:** http://www.seronousa.com. **Description:** Manufactures prescription pharmaceuticals for the treatment of a variety of diseases including multiple sclerosis and cancer. **Positions advertised include:** Systems Engineer; Managed Marketing Manager; National Account Manager; Postdoctoral Fellow; Accounts Payable Specialist; General Counsel; Distributor; Facilities Operations Manager. **Corporate headquarters location:** This location. **Operations at this facility include:** Administration; Manufacturing; Research and Development; Sales; Service. **Listed on:** Privately held. **Number of employees at this location:** 150. **Number of employees nationwide:** 370.

SHAW ENVIRONMENTAL & INFRASTRUCTURE
88C Elm Street, Hopkinton MA 01748-1656. 508/435-9561. **Contact:** Human Resources. **World Wide Web address:** http://www.shawgrp.com. **Description:** Develops advanced technologies for the environmental restoration of contaminated sites. One of the largest environmental consulting, engineering, and remediation firms in the world, the company operates 70 locations worldwide. **Positions advertised include:** Engineer Technician.

SHAW'S SUPERMARKETS
P.O. Box 600, East Bridgewater MA 02333-0600. 508/378-7211. **Physical address:** 750 West Center Street, East Bridgewater MA. **Contact:** Human Resources. **World Wide Web address:** http://www.shaws.com. **Description:** Administrative offices of the New England supermarket chain. Shaw's Supermarkets has locations throughout New England. **Corporate headquarters location:** This location. **Other U.S. locations:** CT; ME; MA; NH; RI; VT. **Subsidiaries include:** Star Markets; Wild Harvest. **Parent company:** J Sainsbury plc.

SHERATON COLONIAL HOTEL
One Audubon Road, Wakefield MA 01880. 781/245-9300. **Contact:** Human Resources. **World Wide Web address:** http://www.sheraton.com. **Description:** A full-service hotel complete with restaurant and entertainment facilities, an 18-hole PGA golf course, and a health club. **Corporate headquarters location:** White Plains NY. **Parent company:** Starwood Hotels & Resorts Worldwide, Inc. **Number of employees at this location:** 300.

SHERATON FERNCROFT RESORT
50 Ferncroft Road, Danvers MA 01923. 978/777-2500. **Fax:** 978/750-7959. **Contact:** Joanne Sweeney, Human Resources. **World Wide Web address:** http://www.sheraton.com. **Description:** Operates a 367-room luxury hotel with a wide range of recreational services including a PGA tour country club, USTA tour tennis courts, and a full-service health club. **Special programs:** Internships. **Corporate headquarters location:** White Plains NY. **Parent company:** Starwood Hotels & Resorts Worldwide, Inc. **Operations at this facility include:** Sales; Service. **Number of employees at this location:** 300. **Number of employees nationwide:** 5,000.

SIEBEL SYSTEMS, INC.
One Apple Hill, Suite 301, Natick MA 01760. 508/652-8600. **Fax:** 508/652-8601. **Contact:** Human Resources. **World Wide Web address:** http://www.siebel.com. **Description:** Siebel Systems is a leading provider of customer relationship management (CRM) solutions and applications for business intelligence and standards-based integration.

SIEMENS BUSINESS SERVICES
45 Shawmut Road, Canton MA 02021-1408. 781/830-2200. **Contact:** Human Resources. **World Wide Web address:** http://www.sbs-usa.siemens.com. **Description:** A manufacturer of computer systems, software, and peripherals. The company also offers consulting, planning, and implementation services. **Positions advertised include:** Program Director. **Corporate headquarters location:** Rye Brook NY. **Other U.S. locations:** Nationwide. **International locations:** Worldwide.

SIEMENS BUSINESS SERVICES
200 Wheeler Road, Burlington MA 01803. 781/273-0480. **Fax:** 781/313-4231. **Contact:** Human Resources. **World Wide Web address:** http://www.sbs-usa.siemens.com. **Description:** A manufacturer of computer systems, software, and peripherals. The company also offers consulting, planning, and implementation services. **Corporate headquarters location:** Rye Brook NY. **Other U.S. locations:** Nationwide. **International locations:** Worldwide.

SIGNATRON TECHNOLOGY CORPORATION
29 Domino Drive, Concord MA 01742. 978/371-0550. **Fax:** 978/371-7414. **Contact:** Human Resources. **E-mail address:** jobs@signatron.com. **World Wide Web address:** http://www.signatron.com. **Description:** Engaged in research and development for advanced communication systems and precision radio location systems. **Positions advertised include:** Software Engineer. **Corporate headquarters location:** This location. **Number of employees at this location:** 20.

SIMMONS COLLEGE
300 The Fenway, Boston MA 02115-5898. 617/521-2000. **Contact:** Human Resources. **World Wide Web address:** http://www.simmons.edu. **Description:** A private, four-year, liberal arts and sciences college for women. The college also offers 12 graduate programs for both men and women. The total graduate enrollment is approximately 2,000.

SINNOTT SCHOOL
210 Winter Street, Suite 204, Weymouth MA 02188. 781/331-6769. **Contact:** Human Resources. **World Wide Web address:** http://www.sinnottschool.com. **Description:** A computer training school offering classes in Microsoft Office and other applications. Clients are both individuals and corporations. The Microsoft Office curriculum includes Windows, NT, Microsoft Word, Excel, Access, and PowerPoint. Classes are held both on-site as well as at corporate locations. Sinnott School offers long-term day courses as well as half- and full-day courses.

SIPEX CORPORATION
22 Linnell Circle, Billerica MA 01821. 978/667-8700. **Fax:** 978/671-9502. **Contact:** Human Resources. **E-mail address:** maresume@sipex.com. **World Wide Web address:** http://www.sipex.com. **Description:** Manufactures analog integrated circuits, microchips, and semiconductors. **Positions advertised include:** Design Engineer; Product Application Engineer.

SIPPICAN, INC.
7 Barnabas Road, Marion MA 02738. 508/748-1160. **Contact:** Human Resources. **World Wide Web address:** http://www.sippican.com. **Description:** Manufacturers of radar, infrared, and electro-optical expendable countermeasure systems for ships, aircraft, and ground vehicles. **Positions advertised include:** Components Engineer; Purchasing Agents; Security Engineer; Engineer Manager; Program Administrator; Software Engineer; Configuration Manager; Production Control; Electronics Design Engineer.

SIX FLAGS NEW ENGLAND
P.O. Box 307, Agawam MA 01001. 413/786-9300. **Fax:** 413/821-0038. **Contact:** Human Resources. **World Wide Web address:** http://www.sixflags.com. **Description:** A 160-acre amusement park with over 100 rides and attractions. Founded in 1940. **NOTE:** Apply online. Applicants must be available to work weekends April and May, daily June though Labor Day, and weekends in September and October. Must be at least 16 years old. Applicants may apply in person or mail in an application. **Parent company:** Premier Parks (OK) owns and operates 35 theme parks nationwide. **CEO:** Kieran Burke.

SKADDEN, ARPS, SLATE, MEAGHER & FLOM
One Beacon Street, 31st Floor, Boston MA 02108. 617/573-4800. **Fax:** 617/573-4822. **Contact:** Human Resources. **World Wide Web address:** http://www.skadden.com. **Description:** One of the world's largest law firms. Skadden, Arps, Slate, Meagher & Flom specializes in more than 40 practice areas through 21 worldwide offices.

SKY COMPUTERS INC.
27 Industrial Avenue, Chelmsford MA 01824. 978/250-1920. **Fax:** 978/250-0959. **Contact:** Human Resources Department. **E-mail address:** resumes@skycomputers.com. **World Wide Web address:** http://www.skycomputers.com. **Description:** Manufactures high-speed processing computer components including compilers, daughterboards, and accelerators.

SKYWORKS SOLUTIONS, INC.
20 Sylvan Road, Woburn MA 01801. 781/935-5150. **Contact:** Human Resources. **World Wide Web address:** http://www.skyworksinc.com. **Description:** A manufacturer of integrated circuits and microwave semiconductor devices including gallium arsenide microwave monolithic integrated circuits; microwave ferrite and other microwave ceramic materials; microwave solid state switches, oscillators, gallium arsenide field effect transistor amplifiers; and millimeter wave components, subsystems, and antennas. **Positions advertised include** Applications Staff Engineer; Electrical Principal Engineer; ESD Quality Engineer; Senior Director Operations; Photolithography Equipment/Process Engineer; Power Amplifier Design Engineer; I/C Layout Designer. **Corporate headquarters location:** This location. **Other U.S. locations:** Irvine CA; Santa Rosa CA; Hillsboro OR; Cedar Rapids IA. **Operations at this facility include:** Administration; Manufacturing; Research and Development; Sales. **Listed on:** NASDAQ. **Stock exchange symbol:** SWKS.

SLADE'S FERRY BANCORP
SLADE'S FERRY BANK
P.O Box 390, Somerset MA 02726. 508/675-2121. **Physical address:** 100 Slade's Ferry Avenue, Somerset MA 02726. **Fax:** 508/675-1751. **Contact:** Charlene Jarest, Vice President of Human Resources. **World Wide Web address:** http://www.sladesferry.com. **Description:** A holding company. This location also houses a branch of Slade's Ferry Bank. Founded in 1989. **Positions advertised include:** Teller; Assistant Branch Manager. **Corporate headquarters location:** This location. **Other area locations:** Fairhaven MA; Fall River MA; New Bedford MA; Seekonk MA; Swansea MA. **Subsidiaries include:** Slade's Ferry Trust Company. **Listed on:** NASDAQ. **Stock exchange symbol:** SFBC. **President/CEO:** James Carey. **Number of employees nationwide:** 250.

SMART MODULAR TECHNOLOGIES, INC.
7 Lopez Road, Wilmington MA 01887. 978/988-8848. **Contact:** Human Resources. **World Wide Web address:** http://www.smartm.com. **Description:** Designs, manufactures, and sells personal computer cards used in portable computers and industrial applications and font cartridges used in laser printers. The PC cards enhance the utility of portable computers and electronic equipment by adding memory, data/fax capabilities, and custom applications. The company's laser printer font cartridges broaden the capabilities of laser printers with applications in desktop publishing, word processing, and spreadsheet preparation. **Corporate headquarters location:** This location.

SOCIETY FOR THE PRESERVATION OF NEW ENGLAND ANTIQUITIES
141 Cambridge Street, Boston MA 02114. 617/227-3956. **Fax:** 617/227-9204. **Contact:** Human Resources. **World Wide Web address:** http://www.spnea.org. **Description:** A nonprofit society founded to preserve New England's domestic buildings and artifacts. It is among the country's largest regional preservation organizations, owning 43 historic properties, 34 of which are open as house museums. Founded in 1910. **Special programs:** Internships. **Corporate headquarters location:** This location. **Other U.S. locations:** CT; ME; NH; RI. **Number of employees at this location:** 45. **Number of employees nationwide:** 100.

SODEXHO
45 Hayden Avenue, Lexington MA 02420. 781/372-6000. **Contact:** Human Resources. **World Wide Web address:** http://www.sodexhousa.com. **Description:** A contract service management company that provides food services to health care facilities, schools and colleges, and corporate dining areas. **Number of employees at this location:** 200. **Number of employees nationwide:** 6,350.

SOFTECH, INC.
2 Highwood Drive, Tewksbury MA 01876. 978/640-6222. **Fax:** 978/858-0440. **Contact:** Human Resources. **E-mail address:** hr-tewks@softech.com. **World Wide Web address:** http://www.softech.com. **Description:** Manufacturers, markets, and maintains product life-cycle software. Founded in 1969. **Positions advertised include:** Senior Software Engineer. **NOTE:** Apply online.

SOLDIERS' HOME
110 Cherry Street, Holyoke MA 01040. 413/532-9475. **Contact:** Human Resources. **Description:** A hospital and nursing home for veterans offering both inpatient and outpatient care.

SONAMED CORPORATION
1250 Main Street, Waltham MA 02451. 781/899-6499. **Fax:** 781/899-8318. **Contact:** Human Resources. **E-mail address:** sonamed@sonamed.com. **World Wide Web address:** http://www.sonamed.com. **Description:** Sells equipment for detecting long-term hearing problems in infants. **Positions advertised include:** Sales and Marketing Representative.

SONESTA INTERNATIONAL HOTELS CORPORATION
116 Huntington Avenue, Boston MA 02116. 617/421-5400. **Fax:** 617/421-5402. **Contact:** Human Resources. **World Wide Web address:** http://www.sonesta.com. **Description:** Operates hotels including the Royal Sonesta Hotels in Cambridge MA and New Orleans LA. **Corporate headquarters location:** This location. **Listed on:** NASDAQ. **Stock exchange symbol:** SNSTA.

SOVEREIGN BANK
One Harvard Street, Brookline Village MA 02446. 617/232-0467. **Toll-free phone:** 877/768-2265. **Contact:** Human Resources. **World Wide Web address:** http://www.sovereignbank.com. **Description**: A $55 billion financial institution with nearly 600 community banking offices and 1,000 ATMs in Connecticut, Massachusetts, New Hampshire, New Jersey, New York, Pennsylvania, and Rhode Island. **Parent company:** Sovereign Bancorp, Inc. **Listed on:** New York Stock Exchange. **Stock exchange symbol:** SOV. **Number of employees nationwide:** 9,500.

SOVEREIGN BANK
75 State Street, Boston MA 02109. 617/757-3410. **Toll-free phone:** 877/768-2265. **Contact:** Human Resources. **World Wide Web address:** http://www.sovereignbank.com. **Description:** A $55 billion financial institution with nearly 600 community banking offices and 1,000 ATMs in Connecticut, Massachusetts, New Hampshire, New Jersey, New York, Pennsylvania, and Rhode Island. **Positions advertised include:** Anti – Money Laundering Analyst; Community Banking Manager; Customer Service Representative; Teller; Deposit Manager; Executive Assistant; Financial Assistant. **Parent company:** Sovereign Bancorp, Inc. **Listed on:** New York Stock Exchange. **Stock exchange symbol:** SOV. **Number of employees nationwide:** 9,500.

SPALDING SPORTS WORLDWIDE
425 Meadow Street, Chicopee MA 01021. 413/536-1200. **Contact:** Human Resources. **World Wide Web address:** http://www.spalding.com. **Description:** Manufactures performance athletic footwear specializing in golf, tennis, soccer, and basketball shoes. **Annual sales/revenues:** More than $100 million. **Number of employees at this location:** 80.

SPAULDING & SLYE COLLIERS
255 State Street, 4th Floor, Boston MA 02109. 617/523-8000. **Fax:** 617/531-4281. **Contact:** Catherine Spritca, Human Resources. **World Wide Web address:** http://www.spauldslye.com. **Description:** Corporate offices of a national, full-service real estate development firm. Services include development, construction, brokerage and property management, and advisory services. **Positions advertised include:** Project Manager; Property Manager; Associate; Administrative Assistant; Assistant Construction Manager; Graphic Designer; Tenant Coordinator; Superintendent; Construction Manager; Marketing Associate. **Other area locations:** Burlington MA. **Other U.S. locations:** Washington DC. **Operations at this facility include:** Administration; Sales. **Listed on:** Privately held. **Number of employees at this location:** 170. **Number of employees nationwide:** 235.

SPAULDING REHABILITATION HOSPITAL
125 Nashua Street, Boston MA 02114. 617/720-6400. **Contact:** Human Resources. **World Wide Web address:** http://spauldingrehab.org. **Description:** A 296-bed, rehabilitation hospital. Spaulding is one of the largest rehabilitation facilities nationwide. **Positions advertised include:** Case Manager; Clinical Director; Liaison Representative; Registered Nurse; Nurse Practitioner; Occupational Therapist; Paramedic; Speech Pathologist; Physical Therapist.

SPECTEL
200 Minuteman Road, Andover MA 01810. 978/552-6200. **Toll-free phone:** 800/685-8454. **Contact:** Personnel. **World Wide Web address:** http://www.spectel.com. **Description:** Manufactures audio- and videoconferencing products. **Positions advertised include:** Senior Software Engineer. **Corporate headquarters location:** This location. **Other U.S. locations:** Denver CO; Atlanta GA; Chicago IL; New York NY. **International locations:** England; Ireland; Singapore.

SPIRE CORPORATION
One Patriots Park, Bedford MA 01730-2396. 781/275-6000. **Fax:** 781/275-7470. **Contact:** Human Resources. **E-mail address:** hr@spirecorp.com. **World Wide Web address:** http://www.spirecorp.com. **Description:** Provides products and services to customers in the solar photovoltaics, opto-electronics, and biomedical markets. The company's products include compound semiconductor wafers and devices, photovoltaic manufacturing equipment and production lines, and ion beam-based processing services for medical components. **Positions advertised include:** Production & Inventory Control Coordinator; Biomaterials Coatings Technician; Lead Process Engineer. **Corporate headquarters location:** This location. **Listed on:** NASDAQ. **Stock exchange symbol:** SPIR. **Number of employees at this location:** 150.

SPYGLASS INTEGRATION
55 Hayden Avenue, Lexington MA 02421. 781/372-4600. **Contact:** Human Resources. **World Wide Web address:** http://www.spyglassintegration.com. **Description:** Spyglass Integration is a leading provider of software and services to make non-PC devices including TVs, phones, faxes, and PDAs work with the Web. **Positions advertised include:** Software Engineer; Quality Assurance Engineer. **Corporate headquarters location:** Mountain View CA. **Operations at this facility include:** This location is a research center focused on content conversion, collaborative applications, and an HTML engine. **Parent company:** OpenTV. **Listed on:** NASDAQ. **Stock exchange symbol:** OPTV.

STADIUM AUTO BODY, INC.
305 Western Avenue, Brighton MA 02134. 617/254-6163. **Contact:** Human Resources. **World Wide Web address:** http://www.stadiumauto.com. **Description:** Provides a wide variety of auto body and car repair services. The company also offers 24-hour towing services. **Corporate headquarters location:** This location.

STANDARD-THOMSON CORPORATION
152 Grove Street, Waltham MA 02453-8325. 781/894-7310. **Contact:** Louis Mollinedo, Human Resources. **E-mail address:** hr@Schrader-bridgeport.net. **World Wide Web address:** http://www.schrader-bridgeport.net. **Description:** Engaged in the production of original equipment and replacement engine temperature control devices. The company is also a producer of automotive electronic and fuel control devices. Other products include a specialized fuel heater for diesel truck and off-highway equipment. **Parent company:** Schrader-Bridgeport/Standard Thomson.

THE STANDARD-TIMES PUBLISHING COMPANY
25 Elm Street, New Bedford MA 02740. 508/997-7411. **Contact:** Human Resources. **World Wide Web address:** http://www.s-t.com. **Description:** Publishes a daily newspaper with a circulation of more than 48,000.

STAPLES, INC.
500 Staples Drive, Framingham MA 01702. 508/253-5000. **Contact:** Human Resources. **World Wide Web address:** http://www.staples.com. **Description:** Staples is a leading retailer of discount office products. The company operates over 350 high-volume office superstores in 18 states and the District of Columbia. **Positions advertised include:** Recruiting Specialist; Loss Prevention Manager; Senior Business Analyst; Business Development Associate; Customer Relations Manager. **Corporate headquarters location:** This location. **Other U.S. locations:** Nationwide. **Operations at this facility include:** Administration. **Listed on:** NASDAQ. **Stock exchange symbol:** SPLS. **Number of employees at this location:** 850. **Number of employees nationwide:** 15,700.

L.S. STARRETT COMPANY
121 Crescent Street, Athol MA 01331. 978/249-3551. **Fax:** 978/249-3457. **Contact:** Human Resources. **World Wide Web address:** http://www.starrett.com. **Description:** Manufactures industrial, professional, and consumer products. Among the items produced are precision tools, tape measures, levels, electronic gages, dial indicators, gage blocks, digital-readout measuring tools, granite surface plates, optical measuring projectors, and coordinate measuring vises. Much of the company's production is concentrated in hand measuring tools and precision instruments. These products are sold throughout the United States and in over 100 foreign countries. **Corporate headquarters location:** This location. **Other U.S. locations:** NC; OH; PA; SC. **International locations:** Brazil; England; Puerto Rico; Scotland. **Listed on:** New York Stock Exchange. **Stock exchange symbol:** SCX.

STATE STREET CORPORATION
225 Franklin Street, Boston MA 02110. 617/786-3000. **Contact:** Human Resources. **World Wide Web address:** http://www.statestreet.com. **Description:** Provides securities and recordkeeping services to nearly 2,000 mutual funds and manages a large number of tax-exempt assets. State Street is a major manager of international index assets and provides corporate banking services, specialized lending, and international banking services. **Corporate headquarters location:** This location. **Parent company:** State Street Boston Corporation. **Number of employees worldwide:** 17,400.

STATE STREET RESEARCH
One Financial Center, 22nd Floor, Boston MA 02111. 617/482-3920. **Contact:** Human Resources. **World Wide Web address:** http://www.statestreetresearch.com. **Description:** A financial services organization primarily involved in the management of corporate funds.

STERIS-ISOMEDIX SERVICES
435 Whitney Street, Northborough MA 01532. 508/393-9323. **Contact:** Human Resources. **World Wide Web address:** http://www.steris.com. **Description:** Provides contract sterilization services to manufacturers of prepackaged products such as health care and certain consumer products. The company uses gamma radiation and ethylene oxide in these operations. **Positions advertised include:** Field Service Representative. **Corporate headquarters location:** Mentor OH.

STEVENS LINEN ASSOCIATES, INC.
P.O. Box 95, Dudley MA 01571. 508/943-0813x38. **Fax:** 800/339-1569. **Contact:** Human Resources. **E-mail address:** info@stevenslinen.com. **World Wide Web address:** http://www.stevenslinen.com. **Description:** Engaged in linen screen-printing. Products include calendar towels, tea towels, pot holders, and other domestic goods. Founded in 1846. **NOTE:** Entry-level positions are offered. **Office hours:** Monday - Friday, 8:00 a.m. - 5:00 p.m. **Corporate headquarters location:** This location. **Listed on:** Privately held. **President:** Greg Kline. **Facilities Manager:** Michael Burzynski. **Number of employees at this location:** 100.

STOCKCROSS
One Washington Mall, Boston MA 02108. 617/367-5700. **Toll-free phone:** 800/225-6196. **Fax:** 617/367-6399. **Contact:** Human Resources. **E-mail address:** info@stockcross.com. **World Wide Web address:** http://www.stockcross.com. **Description:** A discount stock brokerage.

J. STONE & SON INC.
23 Turcotte Memorial Drive, Rowley MA 01969. 978/948-7276. **Contact:** Human Resources. **Description:** Manufactures and distributes custom packaging including boxes, cups, and microwavable containers.

STONE & WEBSTER ENGINEERING CORPORATION
100 Technology Center Drive, Stoughton MA 02072. 617/589-5111. **Fax:** 617/589-1587. **Contact:** Human Resources Department. **World Wide Web address:** http://www.shawgrp.com/stonewebster. **Description:** Provides construction, consulting, engineering, environmental, and procurement services to a variety of industries worldwide. **Positions advertised include:** Principal Mechanical Engineer; Lead Mechanical Engineer. **NOTE:** Apply online. **Office hours:** Monday - Friday, 8:00 a.m. - 4:45 p.m. **Corporate headquarters location:** This location. **Other U.S. locations:** Denver CO; Cherry Hill NJ; New York NY; Chattanooga TN; Houston TX. **Parent company:** The Shaw Group, Inc. **Listed on:** New York Stock Exchange. **Stock exchange symbol:** SGR. **Number of employees at this location:** 1,200. **Number of employees nationwide:** 6,000.

STONEHILL COLLEGE
320 Washington Street, Easton MA 02357. 508/565-1000. **Contact:** Human Resources. **E-mail address:** employment_ervices@stonehill.edu. **World Wide Web address:** http://www.stonehill.edu. **Description:** A private, four-year, Catholic college. Stonehill offers liberal arts programs to approximately 2,000 undergraduate students.

THE STOP & SHOP COMPANIES, INC.
1385 Hancock Street, Quincy MA 02169. 781/380-8000. **Contact:** Human Resources. **World Wide Web address:** http://www.stopandshop.com. **Description:** A national supermarket retail chain. **Corporate headquarters location:** This location.

STORAGETEK
230 Third Avenue, 3rd Floor, Waltham MA 02451. 781/890-2650. **Fax:** 781/890-9106. **Contact:** Human Resources. **World Wide Web address:** http://www.stortek.com. **Description:** Storage Technology Corporation manufactures high-performance computer information storage and retrieval systems for mainframe and mid-frame computers and networks. Products include automated cartridge systems, random access subsystems, and fault-tolerant disk arrays. The company also distributes equipment; sells new peripherals, software, and hardware; and offers support services. **Corporate headquarters location:** Louisville CO. **Operations at this facility include:** This location sells computer data storage systems.

STRATUS TECHNOLOGIES
111 Powdermill Road, Maynard MA 01754. 978/461-7000. **Contact:** Human Resources. **World Wide Web address:** http://www.stratus.com. **Description:** Stratus Technologies offers a broad range of computer systems, application solutions, middleware, and professional services for critical online operations. **Corporate headquarters location:** This location. **Subsidiaries include:** Shared Systems Corporation provides software and professional services to the financial services, retail, and health care industries. SoftCom Systems, Inc. provides data communications middleware and related professional services that bridge the gap between open distributed systems and legacy mainframe and midrange systems used for online applications. Isis Distributed Systems, Inc. develops advanced messaging middleware products that enable businesses to develop reliable, high-performance distributed computing applications involving networked desktop computers and shared systems.

STREAM INTERNATIONAL
85 Dan Road, Canton MA 02021. 781/575-6800. **Contact:** Human Resources. **World Wide Web address:** http://www.stream.com. **Description:** Resells computer software and offers support services. **Other locations:** Beaverton Oregon, Watertown New York.

STRIDE-RITE CORPORATION
191 Spring Street, P.O. Box 9191, Lexington MA 02421. 617/824-6000. **Contact:** Mary Kuconis, Human Resources Director. **World Wide Web address:** http://www.striderite.com. **Description:** Manufactures and distributes children's footwear. The company also operates retail stores. **Corporate headquarters location:** This location. **Listed on:** New York Stock Exchange. **Stock exchange symbol:** SRR.

SUFFOLK DOWNS
111 Waldemar Avenue, East Boston MA 02128. 617/567-3900. **Contact:** Human Resources. **World Wide Web address:** http://www.suffolkdowns.com. **Description:** A thoroughbred racetrack and entertainment facility offering live racing June through September. In the off-season, the track offers simulcasted broadcasts of races throughout the country.

SUFFOLK UNIVERSITY
8 Ashburton Place, Boston MA 02108. 617/573-8415. **Fax:** 617/367-2250. **Contact:** Judy Minardi, Director of Human Resources. **E-mail address:** jobs@suffolk.edu. **World Wide Web address:** http://www.suffolk.edu. **Description:** A four-year university. Suffolk University's Frank Sawyer School of Management offers an Executive MBA program. Suffolk University also houses a law school. **Positions advertised include:** Assistant Director; Leadership Giving Officer.

SULLIVAN & WORCESTER
One Post Office Square, Boston MA 02109. 617/338-2800. **Fax:** 617/338-2880. **Contact:** Janet Brussard, Legal Recruiting. **E-mail address:** hrdepartment@sandw.com. **World Wide Web address:** http://www.sandw.com. **Description:** A law firm that practices all areas of law including intellectual property and international law.

SUNCOR STAINLESS
70 Armstrong Road, Plymouth MA 02360. 508/732-9191. **Fax:** 508/732-9798. **Contact:** Human Resources. **E-mail address:** sales@suncorstainless.com. **World Wide Web address:** http://www.suncorstainless.com. **Description:** A stainless steel and titanium products manufacturer. **Other U.S. Locations:** California, Florida & New Mexico. **International location:** Ontario Canada.

SUN LIFE ASSURANCE COMPANY OF CANADA
One Sun Life Executive Park, Wellesley Hills MA 02481. 781/237-6030. **Contact:** Human Resources. **World Wide Web address:** http://www.sunlife.com. **Description:** Offers a wide range of life, health, and dental insurance products, as well as a variety of other financial services. **Positions advertised include:** Marketing Consultant; Business Systems Analyst; Investment Analyst; Regional Vice President Individual Insurance; Product Services Administrator; Operations Coordinator; Compensation Director; Customer Service Representative; Underwriting Specialist. **Corporate headquarters location:** Toronto, Canada. **Parent company:** Sun Life Financial Services of Canada Inc. **Operations at this facility include:** Administration; Divisional Headquarters; Regional Headquarters; Service.

SUN MICROSYSTEMS, INC.
One Network Drive, Burlington MA 01803. 978/442-6200. **Contact:** Human Resources. **World Wide Web address:** http://www.sun.com. **Description:** Produces high-performance computer systems, workstations, servers, CPUs, peripherals, and operating system software. The company developed its own microprocessor called SPARC. **Positions advertised include:** Programming Analyst; Web Design Administration; Mission Critical Technical Support; Technical Training Development & Delivery; Customer Services; Application Development; GUI Design; Test Engineer; Product Engineer; Product Management. **Corporate headquarters location:** Palo Alto CA. **Subsidiaries include:** Forte Software Inc. manufactures enterprise application integration software. **Listed on:** NASDAQ. **Stock exchange symbol:** SUNW.

SWANK, INC.
6 Hazel Street, Attleboro MA 02703. 508/222-3400. **Contact:** Human Resources. **World Wide Web address:** http://www.swankaccessories.com. **Description:** Manufactures men's and women's jewelry, gift items, and leather products including wallets and key chains.

SYBASE, INC.
561 Virginia Road, Concord MA 01742. 978/287-1500. **Fax:** 978/369-3175. **Contact:** Human Resources. **World Wide Web address:** http://www.sybase.com. **Description:** Develops, markets, and supports a full line of relational database management software products and services for integrated, enterprisewide information management systems. Founded in 1984. **Positions advertised include:** Software Engineer. **Special programs:** Internships; Co-ops. **Corporate headquarters location:** Emeryville CA. **Other U.S. locations:** Nationwide. **Operations at this facility include:** Divisional Headquarters. **Listed on:** NASDAQ. **Stock exchange symbol:** SYBS. **President/CEO:** Michael Kietzman. **Annual sales/revenues:** More than $100 million. **Number of employees at this location:** 800. **Number of employees worldwide:** 5,600.

SYRATECH CORPORATION
175 McClellan Highway, East Boston MA 02128. 617/561-2200. **Fax:** 617/568-1528. **Contact:** Katie Ventura, Human Resources Director. **World Wide Web address:** http://www.syratech.com. **Description:** Manufactures housewares, cookware, and gift items. **NOTE:** Entry-level positions are offered. Use http:///www.monster.com for searching for current job postings for this company. **Special programs:** Internships. **Corporate headquarters location:** This location. **Operations at this facility include:** Administration; Sales. **Listed on:** New York Stock Exchange. **Stock exchange symbol:** SYR. **Annual sales/revenues:** More than $100 million. **Number of**

employees at this location: 350. **Number of employees nationwide:** 1,800. **Number of employees worldwide:** 2,300.

SYSTEMS ENGINEERING, INC.
657 Main Street, Waltham MA 02451-0602. 781/736-9100. **Fax:** 781/736-6969. **Contact:** Human Resources. **E-mail address:** info@sengi.com. **World Wide Web address:** http://www.sengi.com. **Description:** A computer consulting firm. **Positions advertised include:** Microsoft Software Designer/Developer; Sales Professional.

SYSTEMSOFT CORPORATION
275 Grove Street, Suite 1-300, Newton MA 02466-2273. 617/614-4315. **Fax:** 508/651-4138. **Contact:** Recruiter. **World Wide Web address:** http://www.systemsoft.com. **Description:** Supplies PCMCIA (Personal Computer Memory Card International Association) and other system-level software to the rapidly growing market of mobile computers, comprised of laptops, notebooks, subnotebooks, and personal computing devices. System-level software provides both a connectivity layer, which facilitates the addition, configuration, and use of peripheral devices; and a hardware adaptation layer including the communication link between a computer operating system and hardware. **Corporate headquarters location:** This location. **Parent company:** Rocket Software. **Number of employees nationwide:** 250.

TECH-ETCH, INC
45 Aldrin Road, Plymouth MA 02360. 508/747-0300. **Fax:** 508/746-9639. **Contact:** Human Resources. **E-mail address:** hr@tech-etch.com. **World Wide Web address:** http://www.tech-etch.com. **Description:** A manufacturing company producing precision parts. **Positions advertised include:** Process Engineer; Product Engineer; Tool & Die Maker; Tool Designer; CAD Drafter; Technician. **Number of employees:** 600.

THE TJX COMPANIES, INC.
770 Cochituate Road, Framingham MA 01701. 508/390-1000. **Fax:** 508/390-2650. **Recorded jobline:** 888/JOB-S597. **Contact:** Staffing Specialist. **E-mail address:** jobs@tjx.com. **World Wide Web address:** http://www.tjx.com. **Description:** The TJX Companies, Inc. is one of the world's largest off-price retailers. It consists of T.J. Maxx, Marshall's, Home Goods, A.J. Wright, Winners Apparel Ltd. in Canada, and T.K. Maxx in Europe. **NOTE:** Entry-level positions, part-time jobs, and second and third shifts are offered. **Positions advertised include:** Administrative Assistant; Domestics Buyer. **Special programs:** Internships; Training; Co-ops; Summer Jobs. **Corporate headquarters location:** This location. **Other U.S. locations:** Nationwide. **International locations:** Canada; Europe. **Listed on:** New York Stock Exchange. **Stock exchange symbol:** TJX. **Annual sales/revenues:** More than $100 million. **Number of employees at this location:** 2,000. **Number of employees nationwide:** 60,000.

TLC STAFF BUILDERS HOME HEALTH
175 Cabot Street, Suite 100, Lowell MA 01853. 978/458-4357. **Toll-free phone:** 800/698-1535. **Contact:** Human Resources. **World Wide Web address:** http://www.tlcathome.com. **Description:** A home health care agency. **Positions advertised include:** Assistant Director of Clinical Services; General Manager; Home Care Nurse; Home Health Aide. **Corporate headquarters location:** Lake Success NY. **Other U.S. locations:** Nationwide. **Number of employees nationwide:** 20,000.

TMP WORLDWIDE
63 Kendrick Street, Suite 201, Needham MA 02494. 978/461-5999. **Contact:** Human Resources. **World Wide Web address:** http://www.tmpw.com. **Description:** An advertising agency specializing in human resources and employee communications. **Other U.S. locations:** Santa Monica CA; Sausalito CA. **Listed on:** NASDAQ. **Stock exchange symbol:** TMPW.

TNCO, INC.
15 Colebrook Boulevard, Whitman MA 02382. 781/447-6661. **Fax:** 781/447-2132. **Contact:** Human Resources. **E-mail address:** info@tnco-inc.com. **World Wide Web address:** http://www.tnco-inc.com. **Description:** Manufactures surgical instruments. Founded in 1964. **NOTE:** Part-time jobs are offered. **Company slogan:** Passion for precision. **Special programs:** Co-ops. **Office hours:** Monday - Friday, 7:00 a.m. - 3:30 p.m. **Corporate headquarters location:** This location. **Listed on:** Privately held. **Annual sales/revenues:** $5 - $10 million. **Number of employees at this location:** 65.

TAGE INN CORPORATION
131 River Road, Andover MA 01810. 978/683-0232. **Fax:** 978/687-2454. **Contact:** Human Resources. **World Wide Web address:** http://www.tageinn.com. **Description:** Operates three hotels in the Greater Boston area. **Corporate headquarters location:** This location. **Other area locations:** Boston/Somerville MA; Milford MA.

TALBOTS INC.
One Talbots Drive, Hingham MA 02043. 781/749-7600. **Contact:** Human Resources. **World Wide Web address:** http://www.talbots.com. **Description:** Talbots is a leading specialty retailer and cataloger of women's classic apparel, shoes, and accessories. Talbots operates more than 330 stores in North America and has 23 different catalogs with a total annual circulation of approximately 60 million. The company also operates a chain of Talbots for Kids stores. Founded in 1947. **Other U.S. locations:** Nationwide. **Listed on:** New York Stock Exchange. **Stock exchange symbol:** TLB.

TAXWARE INTERNATIONAL, INC.
27 Congress Street, Salem MA 01970. 978/741-0101. **Contact:** Lisa Burns, Human Resources Manager. **World Wide Web address:** http://www.taxware.com. **Description:** Develops a line of tax software. **Positions advertised include:** Business Development Director Systems Analyst; Marketing Director; Ohio Regional Sales Manager; Telemarketer; New England Regional Sales Manager; Database Administrator; Software Engineer; Research Lead Tax Counsel.

TECH/OPS SEVCON, INC.
155 Northboro Road, Southborough MA 01772. 508/281-5500. **Fax:** 508/281-5341. **Contact:** Human Resources. **E-mail address:** hr@sevcon.com. **World Wide Web address:** http://www.sevcon.com. **Description:** A world leader in the design, manufacture, and marketing of microcomputer-based solid-state controls for electric vehicles. These controllers vary the speed of vehicles, improve performance, and prolong the shift life of batteries. The company's customers include manufacturers of forklift trucks, mining vehicles, airport tractors, aerial lifts, sweepers, and other battery-powered vehicles.

TECHNICAL COMMUNICATIONS CORPORATION (TCC)
100 Domino Drive, Concord MA 01742. 978/287-5100. **Fax:** 978/287-4475. **Contact:** Personnel. **E-mail address:** tccjobs@tccsecure.com. **World Wide Web address:** http://www.tccsecure.com. **Description:** Technical Communications Corporation designs, manufactures, and sells communications security devices and systems. Products include the Cipher family of encryption devices, which protect computer terminals with an encryption key that needs to be changed on a regular basis; and KEYNET key management system, which is an advanced system that permits geographically dispersed data networks to be managed economically and safely from a single secured site. The KEYNET system provides an electronic courier to distribute the keys automatically, securely, cost effectively, and invisibly. KEYNET protects and manages the sensitive data traveling between U.S. government agencies on government networks. **Positions advertised include:** Embedded Software Engineer. **Corporate headquarters location:** This location. **Annual sales/revenues:** $11 - $20 million. **Number of employees at this location:** 65.

TELCO SYSTEMS
2 Hampshire Street, Suite 3A, Foxboro MA 02035-2897. 781/551-0300. **Contact:** Human Resources. **World Wide Web address:** http://www.telco.com. **Description:** Develops, manufactures, and markets fiber-optic transmission products, customer premises network access products, and LAN/WAN internetworking products. Applications include voice, data, and video communication networks. Primary customers are independent telephone companies, resellers, competitive access providers, interexchange carriers, and corporate end users. **Positions advertised include:** Design Engineer; Verification Engineer; Automotive Design Engineer; Commercial Manager; Country Manager; Customer Support Engineer; Database Software Engineer; Marketing Communication Director; Elearning Developer; Financial Analyst; GUI Software Developer. **Corporate headquarters location:** This location.

TELLABS
30 North Avenue, Burlington MA 01803. 781/273-1400. **Fax:** 781/273-4160. **Contact:** Human Resources. **World Wide Web address:** http://www.tellabs.com. **Description:** Supplies wideband base-station products for wireless communication applications including cellular products and personal computers. **Listed on:** NASDAQ. **Stock exchange symbol:** TLAB. **Annual sales/revenues:** More than $100 million.

TELLUS INSTITUTE
11 Arlington Street, Boston MA 02116. 617/266-5400. **Fax:** 617/266-8303. **Contact:** David McAnulty, Human Resources. **E-mail address:** dmac@tellus.org. **World Wide Web address:** http://www.tellus.org. **Description:** An environmental research and consulting agency. Much of the Tellus Institute's work is under government contract in the fields of energy, gas, and solid waste. **Corporate headquarters location:** This location.

TEMPTRONIC CORPORATION
4 Commercial Street, Sharon MA 02067. 781/688-2300. **Fax:** 781/688-2301. **Contact:** Human Resources. **E-mail address:** info@temptronic.com. **World Wide Web address:** http://www.temptronic.com. **Description:** Produces controlled temperature test equipment. **NOTE:** Entry-level positions are offered. **Special programs:** Internships. **Corporate headquarters location:** This location. **Listed on:** Privately held. **Annual sales/revenues:** $11 - $20 million. **Number of employees at this location:** 100.

TERADYNE, INC.
321 Harrison Avenue, Boston MA 02118. 617/482-2700. **Contact:** Human Resources. **E-mail address:** jobs@teradyne.com. **World Wide Web address:** http://www.teradyne.com. **Description:** Designs and manufactures a variety of automatic test equipment. **NOTE:** Apply online or e-mail resume. Please refer to the company's Website for instructions about where resumes for each available position should be directed. If no applicable jobs are available, resumes may be directed to this location and will be entered into a searchable database. **Positions advertised include:** Administrative Assistant; Test Development Engineer; Project Manager; Application Engineer; Financial Analyst; Financial Manager; Human Resources Representative; Information Technology Manager; Attorney; Product Manager; Calibration Technologist; Business Analyst. **Corporate headquarters location:** This location. **Listed on:** New York Stock Exchange. **Stock exchange symbol:** TER.

TETRA TECH, INC.
55 Jonstin Road, Wilmington MA 01887. 978/658-7500 **Contact:** Human Resources. **World Wide Web address:** http://www.tetratech.com. **Description:** An environmental engineering firm.

TEXAS INSTRUMENTS, INC.
34 Forest Street, Attleboro MA 02703. 508/236-3800. **Fax:** 508/236-1322. **Contact:** Human Resources. **World Wide Web address:** http://www.ti.com. **Description:** Texas Instruments (TI) is one of the world's largest suppliers of semiconductor products. TI's defense electronics business is a leading supplier of avionics, infrared, and weapons guidance systems to the U.S. Department of Defense and U.S. allies. The company is also a technology leader in high-performance notebook computers and model-based software development tools. TI sensors monitor and regulate pressure and temperature in products ranging from automobiles to air conditioning systems. **Positions advertised include:** Product Marketing Developer; Electro Mechanical Technician. **NOTE:** Apply online. **Corporate headquarters location:** Dallas TX. **Operations at this facility include:** This location manufactures controls and sensors. **Listed on:** New York Stock Exchange. **Stock exchange symbol:** TXN. **Annual sales/revenues:** More than $100 million. **Number of employees at this location:** 4,000. **Number of employees nationwide:** 5,000.

THERMEDICS POLYMER PRODUCTS
207 Lowell Street, Wilmington MA 01887. 978/642-5000. **Fax:** 978/657-4371. **Contact:** Human Resources. **E-mail address:** edelehanty@thermadics.com. **World Wide Web address:** http://www.thermedics.com. **Description:** Thermedics Polymer Products is a leading supplier of custom manufactured thermoplastic polyurethanes.

THERMO BLH
75 Shawmut Road, Canton MA 02021. 781/821-2000. **Contact:** Human Resources. **World Wide Web address:** http://www.blh.com. **Description:** An electronics manufacturer that produces strain gauges, transducers, and instrumentation controls. **Corporate headquarters location:** This location. **Operations at this facility include:** Manufacturing.

3COM CORPORATION
350 Campus Drive, Marlborough MA 01752. 508/323-5000. **Contact:** Human Resources. **World Wide Web address:** http://www.3com.com. **Description:** 3Com is a *Fortune* 500 company delivering global data networking solutions to organizations around the world. 3Com designs, manufactures, markets, and supports a broad range of ISO 9000-compliant global data networking solutions including routers, hubs, remote access servers, switches, and adapters for Ethernet, Token Ring, and high-speed networks. These products enable computers to communicate at high speeds and share resources including printers, disk drives, modems, and minicomputers. **Corporate headquarters location:** This location. **Listed on:** NASDAQ. **Stock exchange symbol:**

COMS. **Annual sales/revenues:** More than $100 million. **Number of employees worldwide:** 1,800.

3M TOUCH SYSTEMS
501 Griffin Brook Park Drive, Methuen MA 01844. 978/659-9000. **Fax:** 978/659-9100. **Contact:** Human Resources Manager. **World Wide Web address:** http://www.3mtouch.com. **Description:** 3M Touch Systems is a manufacturer of touch-screen systems. Products are used in a broad range of applications including point-of-sale terminals, self-service kiosks, gaming machines, industrial systems, ATMs, multimedia applications, and many other computer-based systems. MicroTouch also manufactures and markets TouchPen, a touch- and pen-sensitive digitizer used for pen-based and whiteboarding applications; TouchMate, a pressure-sensitive pad that makes any monitor placed on it touch-sensitive; and ThruGlass, a product that can sense a touch through up to two inches of glass, allowing kiosks to be placed behind store windows for 24-hour access. **Listed on:** New York Stock Exchange. **Stock exchange symbol:** MMM.

THYSSENKRUPP ELEVATOR
665 Concord Avenue, Cambridge MA 02138. 617/547-9000. **Contact:** Human Resources. **World Wide Web address:** http://www.thyssenkruppelevator.com. **Description:** Manufactures and installs elevators.

TIGHE & BOND
53 Southampton Road, Westfield MA 01085. 413/562-1600. **Contact:** April Lassard, Administrative Assistant. **E-mail address:** alassard@tighebond.com. **World Wide Web address:** http://www.tighebond.com. **Description:** Offers environmental and civil engineering consulting services. **Positions advertised include:** Site Civil Engineer; Geotechnical Engineer; Structural Engineer.

TIGHE WAREHOUSING & DISTRIBUTION, INC.
45 Holton Street, Winchester MA 01890. 781/729-5440. **Fax:** 781/721-5862. **Contact:** Human Resources. **E-mail address:** personnel@tighe-co.com. **World Wide Web address:** http://www.tighe-co.com. **Description:** Provides warehousing, transportation, and related distribution services. **Positions advertised include:** Class A CDL Driver; Warehouse Forklift Operations.

TILLOTSON CORPORATION
59 Waters Avenue, Everett MA 02149. 617/387-9400. **Contact:** Human Resources. **World Wide Web address:** http://www.thcnet.com. **Description:** Manufactures rubber-based products including molds and gloves.

TITAN CORPORATION
12 Oak Park Drive, Bedford MA 01730. 781/266-5550. **Contact:** Human Resources. **World Wide Web address:** http://www.titan.com. **Description:** Provides software systems, services, and products to a broad base of customers around the world. The company specializes in language design and programmer productivity tools; digital signal processing tools and application; hardware and system simulation; computer and network security; guidance, navigation, and control; and information systems integration.

TORTO WHEATON RESEARCH
200 High Street, 3rd Floor, Boston MA 02110. 617/912-5200. **Fax:** 617/912-5240. **Contact:** Frank Moynihan, Human Resources Department. **E-mail address:** fmoyniham@tortowheatonresearch.com. **World Wide Web address:** http://www.twr.com. **Description:** Provides real estate services. **Corporate headquarters location:** Los Angeles CA. **Parent company:** CB Richard Ellis. **Stock exchange symbol:** CBG.

TRANSKARYOTIC THERAPIES, INC.
700 Main Street, Cambridge MA 02139. 617/349-0200. **Contact:** Human Resources. **World Wide Web address:** http://www.tktx.com. **Description:** Engaged in the research and development of gene therapy. **Positions advertised include:** Research & Design Specialist; Quality Control Analyst; Bioengineer; Staff Scientist; Warehouse Manager; Inventory Control Coordinator; Material Planner; Operations Analysis Manager; Financial Planning Analyst; Regulatory Documentation Coordinator. **Listed on:** NASDAQ. **Stock exchange symbol:** TKTX.

TUFTS HEALTH PLAN
333 Wyman Street, P.O. Box 9112, Waltham MA 02154. 781/466-9400. **Contact:** Human Resources. **World Wide Web address:** http://www.tufts-healthplan.com. **Description:** A health maintenance organization offering hospital coverage, doctors in private practice, emergency coverage, and coverage for student dependants. Tufts Health Plan also offers a range of fitness benefits. **Positions advertised include:** Accounts Representative; Administrative Assistant; Appeals Analyst; Application Developer; Application Engineer; Benefits Analyst; Claims Specialist; Computer Operator; Executive Assistant; Graphic Designer; Inside Sales Representative; Member Relations Associate; Mental Health Services Representative; Notes Developer; Project Manager; Registered Nurse; Resource Specialist. **Corporate headquarters location:** This location. **Other U.S. locations:** NH.

TUFTS NEW ENGLAND VETERINARY MEDICAL CENTER
200 Westborough Road, North Grafton MA 01536. 508/839-5395. **Contact:** Human Resources. **World Wide Web address:** http://www.tufts.edu/vet. **Description:** An animal hospital that offers a broad range of services including cardiology, dermatology, neurology, nutrition, oncology, and surgical procedures.

TUFTS UNIVERSITY
169 Holland Street, Somerville MA 02144. 617/627-3272. **Fax:** 617/627-3725. **Contact:** Human Resources. **World Wide Web address:** http://www.tufts.edu. **Description:** Offers both undergraduate and graduate programs through the schools of arts and sciences; Fletcher School of Law and Diplomacy; medical, dental, and veterinary schools; and a human nutrition research center. **Other area locations:** Boston MA.

TURBINE INC.
60 Glazier Drive, Westwood MA 02090. 781/320-8222. **Fax:** 781/329-5463. **Contact:** Human Resources. **World Wide Web address:** http://www.turbine.com. **Description:** A leading producer and publisher of multiplayer online games. **Other U.S. locations:** Santa Monica CA.

TYCO HEALTHCARE KENDALL
15 Hampshire Street, Mansfield MA 02048. 508/261-8000. **Toll-free phone:** 800/962-9888. **Fax:** 508/261-8105. **Contact:** Human Resources. **E-mail address:** jobs@kendallhq.com. **World Wide Web address:** http://www.kendallhq.com. **Description:** Manufactures and markets disposable medical supplies and adhesives for general medical and industrial uses. The company sells its products to hospitals and to alternative health care facilities worldwide, and also markets products to pharmacies and retail outlets. Products include wound care, vascular therapy, urological care, incontinence care, anesthetic care, and adhesives and tapes. Founded in 1903. **NOTE:** Entry-level positions are offered. **Positions advertised include:** Accountant; Associate General Counsel; Patent & Trademarks Attorney; Customer Accounts Representative; Marketing Director. **Special programs:** Internships; Co-ops. **Corporate headquarters location:** This location. **Other U.S. locations:** Nationwide. **International locations:** Worldwide. **Parent company:** Tyco International Inc. **Listed on:** New York Stock Exchange. **Stock exchange symbol:** TYC. **CEO/Chairman:** L. Dennis Kozlowski. **Annual sales/revenues:** More than $100 million. **Number of employees at this location:** 600. **Number of employees nationwide:** 5,000. **Number of employees worldwide:** 19,000.

UBS PAINEWEBBER INC.
100 Federal Street, 27th Floor, Boston MA 02110. 617/261-1000. **Contact:** Human Resources. **World Wide Web address:** http://www.ubspainewebber.com. **Description:** A full-service securities firm with over 300 offices nationwide. Services include investment banking, asset management, merger and acquisition consulting, municipal securities underwriting, estate planning, retirement programs, and transaction management. Clients include corporations, governments, institutions, and individuals. Founded in 1879. **Corporate headquarters location:** New York NY. **Other U.S. locations:** Nationwide. **Listed on:** New York Stock Exchange. **Stock exchange symbol:** UBS. **Annual sales/revenues:** More than $100 million.

UBS PAINEWEBBER INC.
265 Franklin Street, Boston MA 02110. 617/439-8000. **Contact:** Human Resources. **World Wide Web address:** http://www.ubspainewebber.com. **Description:** A full-service securities firm with over 300 offices nationwide. Services include investment banking, asset management, merger and acquisition consulting, municipal securities underwriting, estate planning, retirement programs, and transaction management. Clients include corporations, governments, institutions, and individuals. Founded in 1879. **Corporate headquarters location:** New York NY. **Other U.S. locations:** Nationwide. **Listed on:** New York Stock Exchange. **Stock exchange symbol:** UBS. **Annual sales/revenues:** More than $100 million.

UFP TECHNOLOGIES, INC.
172 East Main Street, Georgetown MA 01833. 978/352-2200. **Fax:** 978/352-5616. **Contact:** Human Resources. **E-mail address:** hr@ufpt.com. **World Wide Web address:** http://www.ufpt.com. **Description:** Specializes in custom engineered packaging and specialty solutions that are produced by converting a wide range of foam, rigid plastic, fabric, fiber, and other composite materials. Packaging products and services include custom thermoforming plastics and foams; designing and manufacturing precision, 100-percent recycled protective packaging and multimaterial solutions for durable, reusable inter- and intra-plant product shipment; producing interior packaging; manufacturing complex product handling devices; and clean room manufacturing capabilities, which enable particulate, temperature, and humidity controlled manufacturing. Specialty products include precision-molded foams, performance products, laminating and molding, custom footbeds, and medical components. **Positions advertised include:** Packaging Engineer; Manufacturing Engineer; Quality Management; Field Service Engineer; Inside Sales Representative. **Corporate headquarters location:** This location. **Listed on:** NASDAQ. **Stock exchange symbol:** UFPT.

U.S. DEPARTMENT OF VETERANS AFFAIRS
BROCKTON VETERANS ADMINISTRATION MEDICAL CENTER
940 Belmont Street, Building 1, Brockton MA 02301. 508/583-4500. **Contact:** Craig Polucha, Human Resources Manager. **World Wide Web address:** http://www.va.gov. **Description:** A medical center operated by the U.S. Department of Veterans Affairs. From 54 hospitals in 1930, the VA health care system has grown to include 171 medical centers; more than 364 outpatient, community, and outreach clinics; 130 nursing home care units; and 37 domiciliaries. The VA operates at least one medical center in each of the 48 contiguous states, Puerto Rico, and the District of Columbia. With approximately 76,000 medical center beds, the VA treats nearly 1 million patients in VA hospitals; 75,000 in nursing home care units; and 25,000 in domiciliaries. The VA's outpatient clinics register approximately 24 million visits per year.

U.S. DEPARTMENT OF VETERANS AFFAIRS
EDITH NOURSE ROGERS MEMORIAL VETERANS HOSPITAL
200 Springs Road, Bedford MA 01730-1114. 781/687-2490. **Contact:** Human Resources. **World Wide Web address:** http://www.visn1.med.va.gov/bedford. **Description:** A medical center operated by the U.S. Department of Veterans Affairs. From 54 hospitals in 1930, the VA health care system has grown to include 171 medical centers; more than 364 outpatient, community, and outreach clinics; 130 nursing home care units; and 37 domiciliaries. VA operates at least one medical center in each of the 48 contiguous states, Puerto Rico, and the District of Columbia. With approximately 76,000 medical center beds, VA treats nearly one million patients in VA hospitals; 75,000 in nursing home care units; and 25,000 in domiciliaries. VA's outpatient clinics register approximately 24 million visits per year.

U.S. ENVIRONMENTAL PROTECTION AGENCY (EPA)
One Congress Street, Boston MA 02114-2023. 617/918-1111. **Contact:** Human Resources. **World Wide Web address:** http://www.epa.gov. **Description:** The EPA is dedicated to improving and preserving the quality of the environment, both nationally and globally, and protecting human health and the productivity of natural resources. The agency is committed to ensuring that federal environmental laws are implemented and enforced effectively; U.S. policy, both foreign and domestic, encourages the integration of economic development and environmental protection so that economic growth can be sustained over the long term; and public and private decisions affecting energy, transportation, agriculture, industry, international trade, and natural resources fully integrate considerations of environmental quality. Founded in 1970. **Special programs:** Internships. **Corporate headquarters location:** Washington DC. **Other U.S. locations:** San Francisco CA; Denver CO; Atlanta GA; Chicago IL; Kansas City KS; New York NY; Philadelphia PA; Dallas TX; Seattle WA. **Number of employees nationwide:** 19,000.

U.S. FEDERAL RESERVE BANK OF BOSTON
600 Atlantic Avenue, Employment Unit T-3, Boston MA 02106. 617/973-3518. **Contact:** Human Resources. **World Wide Web address:** http://www.bos.frb.org. **Description:** One of 12 regional Federal Reserve banks that, along with the Federal Reserve Board of Governors (Washington DC) and the Federal Open Market Committee, comprise the Federal Reserve System. As the nation's central bank, the Federal Reserve is charged with three major responsibilities: monetary policy, banking supervision and regulation, and processing payments.

U.S. FISH AND WILDLIFE SERVICE
300 Westgate Center Drive, Hadley MA 01035. 413/253-8200. **Contact:** Human Resources. **World Wide Web address:** http://www.fws.gov. **Description:** Protects

fish and wildlife in national parks and recreation areas. **Corporate headquarters location:** Washington DC.

U.S. FOOD AND DRUG ADMINISTRATION (FDA) NORTHEAST REGION/BOSTON DISTRICT
One Montvale Avenue, 4th Floor, Stoneham MA 02180. 781/279-1675. **Contact:** Human Resources. **World Wide Web address:** http://www.fda.gov. **Description:** Monitors the manufacture, import, transport, storage, and sale of consumer products. Responsibilities include checking wharves for imports of food, drugs, cosmetics, medical devices, and radiation emitting products. **Other area locations:** Winchester MA.

U.S. FOODSERVICE
201 Beacham Street, Everett MA 02149. 617/389-3300. **Toll-free phone:** 800/732-3350. **Fax:** 617/381-6929. **Contact:** Human Resources. **World Wide Web address:** http://www.usfoodservice.com. **Description:** Distributes food products, fresh meats, dairy products, and cleaning supplies to restaurants and other institutional food service establishments. **Corporate headquarters location:** Columbia MD.

U.S. FOODSERVICE CONTRACT AND DESIGN DIVISION
8 Carnegie Row, Norwood MA 02062. 781/551-3145. **Toll-free phone:** 888/374-8774. **Fax:** 781/551-3294. **Contact:** Human Resources. **World Wide Web address:** http://www.usfoodservice.com. **Description:** The Contract and Design Division installs and designs commercial kitchens, dining areas, and hotel/motel rooms. It is also a national distributor of kitchen, hotel, and restaurant equipment. Overall, U.S. Foodservice distributes food products, fresh meats, dairy products, and cleaning supplies to restaurants and other institutional food service establishments. **NOTE:** Entry-level positions and part-time jobs are offered. **Corporate headquarters location:** Columbia MD. **Number of employees at this location:** 30. **Number of employees worldwide:** 14,000.

U.S. HEALTH AND HUMAN SERVICES
JFK Federal Building, Room 2100, Boston MA 02203. 617/565-1500. **World Wide Web address:** http://www.os.dhhs.gov. **Description:** A government health and human services facility.

U.S. POSTAL SERVICE
59 West Dedham Street, Boston MA 02118. **Toll-free phone:** 800/275-8777. **Contact:** Human Resources. **World Wide Web address:** http://www.usps.com. **Description:** A post office.

USA TODAY
100 Unicorn Park Drive, Woburn MA 01801. 781/932-0660. **Contact:** Kathi Bakas, Assistant to General Manager. **World Wide Web address:** http://www.usatoday.com. **Description:** Publishes *USA Today,* a nationally distributed newspaper. **Parent company:** Gannett Company, Inc. (Arlington VA). **Operations at this facility include:** Administration; Regional Headquarters; Sales; Service. **Number of employees at this location:** 45.

USFILTER
P.O. Box 36, Sturbridge MA 01566-0036. 508/347-7344. **Physical address:** 441 Main Street, Sturbridge MA 01518. **Contact:** Human Resources. **World Wide Web address:** http://www.usfilter.com. **Description:** Manufactures water pollution control pumps. **Positions advertised include:** Business Unit Sales Manager; Administrative Assistant; Plant Operator; Maintenance Specialist. **Parent company:** Vivendi.

THE UNION GROUP
648 Alden Street, P.O. Box 3160, Fall River MA 02722. 508/675-4545. **Fax:** 508/677-0130. **Contact:** Human Resources. **E-mail address:** info@theuniongroup.com. **World Wide Web address:** http://www.theuniongroup.com. **Description:** Manufactures custom loose-leaf ring binders, indexes, software, binder/slipcases, and audio/visual cassette holders. **Subsidiaries include:** Elbe-Cesco.

UNISYS CORPORATION
154 Middlesex Turnpike, Burlington MA 01803. 781/238-1300. **Contact:** Human Resources. **World Wide Web address:** http://www.unisys.com. **Description:** Provides information services, technology, and software. Unisys Corporation specializes in developing critical business solutions based on open information networks. The company's Enabling Software Team creates a variety of software projects that facilitate the building of user applications and the management of distributed systems. The company's Platforms Group is responsible for UNIX Operating Systems running across a wide range of multiple processor server platforms including all peripheral and communication drivers. The Unisys Commercial Parallel Processing Team develops microkernel-based operating systems, I/O device drivers, ATM hardware, diagnostics, and system architectures. The System Management Group is in charge of the overall management of development programs for UNIX desktop and entry-server products. **Positions advertised include:** System Architect. **Corporate headquarters location:** Blue Bell PA. **Other U.S. locations:** Nationwide. **Listed on:** New York Stock Exchange. **Stock exchange symbol:** UIS.

UNITED ELECTRIC CONTROLS
P.O. Box 9143, Watertown MA 02471. 617/926-1000. **Fax:** 617/926-8076. **Contact:** Human Resources. **World Wide Web address:** http://www.ueonline.com. **Description:** Manufactures temperature control devices for many industries.

UNITED LIQUORS LTD.
One United Drive, West Bridgewater MA 02379. 617/323-0500. **Contact:** Human Resources. **E-mail address:** hr@unitedliqours.com. **World Wide Web address:** http://www.unitedliquors.com. **Description:** A beverage wholesaler. **Corporate headquarters location:** This location. **Operations at this facility include:** Administration; Sales; Service. **Listed on:** Privately held. **Number of employees at this location:** 750.

UNITED LITHOGRAPH
48 Third Avenue, Somerville MA 02143. 617/629-3200. **Contact:** Human Resources. **World Wide Web address:** http://www.unitedlithograph.com. **Description:** A commercial printer.

UNITED RENTALS
133 Southampton Street, Boston MA 02118. 617/445-6750. **Contact:** Human Resources. **E-mail address:** careerinfo@ur.com. **World Wide Web address:** http://www.unitedrentals.com. **Description:** Rents construction equipment and supplies. **Positions advertised include:** District Manager. **Corporate headquarters locations:** Greenwich CT. **Other U.S. locations:** Nationwide. **Listed on:** NYSE. **Stock exchange symbol:** URI.

UNITED WAY OF MASSACHUSETTS BAY
245 Summer Street, Suite 1401, Boston MA 02210. 617/624-8000. **Fax:** 617/624-9114.**Contact:** Human Resources. **World Wide Web address:** http://www.uwmb.org. **Description:** Through a vast network of volunteers and local charities, the United Way helps to meet the health and human-care needs of millions of people. The United Way is comprised of approximately 1,900 organizations. **Other U.S. locations:** Nationwide.

UNIVERSITY OF MASSACHUSETTS/AMHERST
167 Whitmore Administration Building, Amherst MA 01003. 413/545-1396. **Contact:** Employment Office. **World Wide Web address:** http://www.umass.edu/humres. **Description:** The main campus of the four-year, state university. **Other U.S. locations:** Boston MA; North Dartmouth MA; Lowell MA.

UNIVERSITY OF MASSACHUSETTS/BOSTON
100 Morrissey Boulevard, Boston MA 02125-3393. 617/287-5150. **Fax:** 617/287-5179. **Contact:** Human Resources. **World Wide Web address:** http://www.umb.edu. **Description:** A campus of the four-year, state university offering approximately 90 fields of study to over 12,000 students. **Other area locations:** Amherst MA; North Dartmouth MA; Lowell MA. **Number of employees at this location:** 1,800.

UNIVERSITY OF MASSACHUSETTS/DARTMOUTH
285 Old Westport Road, North Dartmouth MA 02747-2300. 508/999-8060. **Contact:** Todd Swarts, Director of Human Resources. **World Wide Web address:** http://www.umassd.edu. **Description:** A campus of the four-year, state university offering graduate and undergraduate programs to approximately 6,000 students. **Other area locations:** Amherst MA; Boston MA; Lowell MA.

UNIVERSITY OF MASSACHUSETTS/LOWELL
883 Broadway Street, Room 101, Lowell MA 01854. 978/934-3555. **Contact:** Human Resources. **World Wide Web address:** http://www.uml.edu. **Description:** A campus of the four-year, state university. University of Massachusetts/Lowell offers undergraduate majors in a variety of disciplines including engineering, computer technology, sales, business, sciences, education, health professions, human services, liberal arts, and music. The college also offers post-graduate certificate programs in paralegal studies, electronics technology, packaging, data/telecommunications, technical writing, purchasing management, quality assurance, and wastewater treatment. **NOTE:** Each fall (and sometimes in the spring) UMass/Lowell hosts a business and technology career fair. For more information, visit the UMass/Lowell Career Services Website at http://ocs.uml.edu. **Other area locations:** Amherst MA; Boston MA; North Dartmouth MA.

UNO RESTAURANT CORPORATION
100 Charles Park Road, Boston MA 02132. 617/323-9200. **Fax:** 617/469-3949. **Contact:** Human Resources. **E-mail address:** resume@unos.com. **World Wide Web address:** http://www.pizzeriauno.com. **Description:** Uno Restaurant Corporation operates and franchises a chain of casual dining, full-service restaurants under the name Pizzeria Uno. **NOTE:** Entry-level positions are offered. **Positions advertised include:** Restaurant/Food Service Manager. **Special programs:** Training. **Corporate headquarters location:** This location. **Other U.S. locations:** Nationwide. **Operations at this facility include:** Service. **Listed on:** New York Stock Exchange. **Stock exchange symbol:** UNORST. **Annual sales/revenues:** More than $100 million. **Number of employees at this location:** 100. **Number of employees nationwide:** 5,000.

UNUMPROVIDENT
18 Chestnut Street, Worcester MA 01608. 508/799-4441. **Contact:** Human Resources. **World Wide Web address:** http://www.unumprovident.com. **Description:** A life insurance carrier with a broad range of group and individual coverages. **Positions advertised include:** Disability Claims Examiner; Orthopedic Clinic Consultant; Clinical Consultant; Registered Nurse. **Corporate headquarters:** Chattanooga TN. **Listed on:** New York Stock Exchange. **Stock exchange symbol:** UNM.

VCA SOUTH SHORE ANIMAL HOSPITAL
595 Columbian Street, South Weymouth MA 02190. 781/337-6622. **Contact:** Human Resources. **World Wide Web address:** http://www.vca.com. **Description:** A full-service pet hospital providing medical, nursing, and surgical services.

VARIAN VACUUM TECHNOLOGIES
121 Hartwell Avenue, Lexington MA 02421. 781/861-7200. **Contact:** Human Resources. **World Wide Web address:** http://www.varianinc.com. **Description:** Produces vacuum products used in leak detection. **Positions advertised include:** Customer Care Supervisor; Technical Product Manager. **Corporate headquarters location:** Palo Alto CA. **Parent company:** Varian Associates has manufacturing facilities in seven nations and has sales and service offices worldwide. The company is organized around the following core businesses: Health Care Systems, Instruments, Electronic Devices, and Semiconductor Equipment. The company is a leading supplier of X-ray tubes for imaging systems of all types. Leading semiconductor chip manufacturers worldwide rely on Varian's manufacturing systems. The company's instruments also aid physicians and researchers in the fight against diseases such as AIDS. Varian is also a worldwide leader in the manufacture of devices that generate, amplify, and define signals for radio and television broadcasting and satellite communications. These are also essential elements in air traffic control, navigation, radar, fusion energy, and other scientific research applications. **Listed on:** NASDAQ. **Stock exchange symbol:** VARI. **Number of employees nationwide:** 6,500.

VERIZON INFORMATIONAL SERVICES
35 Village Road, Middleton MA 01949. 978/762-0350. **Contact:** Human Resources. **World Wide Web address:** http://www.bigyellow.com. **Description:** Verizon provides a wide variety of communications services ranging from local telephone services for the home and office to highly complex voice and data services for governments and commercial industries. **Operations at this facility include:** This location is engaged in Yellow Pages publishing.

VERTEX PHARMACEUTICALS INCORPORATED
40 Allston Street, Cambridge MA 02139-4242. 617/576-3111. **Fax:** 617/577-6444. **Contact:** Human Resources. **World Wide Web address:** http://www.vpharm.com. **Description:** Develops drugs for viral, autoimmune, inflammatory, and neurodegenerative diseases. Vertex Pharmaceuticals also develops oral active pharmaceuticals for drug-resistant cancer and hemoglobin disorders. **Positions advertised include:** Biochemistry Investigator; Principal Biostatistician; Associate Scientist; Staff Investigator; Administrative Assistant; Accountant; Financial Analyst; Compensation Director; Human Resources Manager; Human Resources Administrative Assistant; System Analyst; Staff Investigator; Logistics Manager; Document Management Specialist; Quality Assurance Specialist; Staff Investigator Toxicity. **Corporate headquarters location:** This location. **Subsidiaries include:** Altus Biologics Inc. (Cambridge MA); Versal Technologies, Inc. (Cambridge MA); Vertex

Pharmaceuticals (Europe) Limited (United Kingdom); Vertex Securities Corporation (Cambridge MA). **Listed on:** NASDAQ. **Stock exchange symbol:** VRTX.

VICOR CORPORATION
25 Frontage Street, Andover MA 01810. 978/470-2900. **Fax:** 978/749-7700. **Contact:** Human Resources. **E-mail address:** hr@vicr.com. **World Wide Web address:** http://www.vicr.com. **Description:** Develops, manufactures, and markets components for modular power systems and complete power systems using a patented, high-frequency, electronic power conversion technology called zero current switching. Components are used in electronic products to convert power from a primary power source into the direct current required by most contemporary electronic circuits. **Positions advertised include:** Front End Manufacturing Engineering Manager; Engineering Aide; Design Engineer; Layout Design Engineer. **Corporate headquarters location:** This location. **Other U.S. locations:** Sunnyvale CA; Lombard IL. **International locations:** France; Gemany; Hong Kong; Italy; Japan; United Kingdom. **Operations at this facility include:** Administration; Manufacturing; Research and Development; Sales; Service. **Listed on:** NASDAQ. **Stock exchange symbol:** VICR. **Number of employees at this location:** 700.

VICTORY SUPERMARKETS
75 North Main Street, Leominster MA 01453. 978/840-2200. **Contact:** Human Resources. **World Wide Web address:** http://www.victorysupermarkets.com. **Description:** A grocery store chain with 20 outlets located in Massachusetts and New Hampshire. **Parent company:** Hannaford Supermarkets. **Other area locations:** Clinton MA; Fitchburg MA; Gardner MA; Marlborough MA; Uxbridge MA.

VIRYANET
2 Willow Street, Southborough MA 01745. 508/490-8600. **Contact:** Human Resources Department. **E-mail address:** jobs@viryanet.com. **World Wide Web address:** http://www.viryanet.com. **Description:** Develops field management system software for large organizations. **Positions advertised include:** Sales; Pre Sales; Sales Engineering; Product Management; Project Management; Software Engineer; Product Marketer.

VISION-SCIENCES INC.
9 Strathmore Road, Natick MA 01760. 508/650-9971. **Fax:** 508/650-9976. **Contact:** Human Resources. **E-mail address:** info@visionsciences.com. **World Wide Web address:** http://www.visionsciences.com. **Description:** Manufactures a flexible endoscopy system that utilizes single-use protective sheaths designed to reduce reprocessing time and infection concerns. Founded in 1990. **NOTE:** Entry-level positions are offered. **Office hours:** Monday - Friday, 8:00 a.m. - 5:00 p.m. **Corporate headquarters location:** This location. **Other U.S. locations:** Orangeburg NY. **International locations:** Israel. **Listed on:** NASDAQ. **Stock exchange symbol:** VSCI. **President/CEO:** Katsumi Oneda. **Annual sales/revenues:** $5 - $10 million. **Number of employees at this location:** 35. **Number of employees nationwide:** 70.

VULCAN INDUSTRIES, INC.
P.O. Box 166, 4 Cabot Road, Hudson MA 01749. 978/562-0003. **Fax:** 978/562-0285. **Contact:** Personnel. **E-mail address:** metalman@vulcanindustries.com. **World Wide Web address:** http://www.vulcanindustry.com. **Description:** A leading fabricator of precision sheet metal. **Positions advertised include:** Engineering Associate; Shearing Associate.

WAAF 107.3 FM
P.O. Box 1073, Boston MA 02215. 617/931-1223. **Contact:** Station Manager. **World Wide Web address:** http://www.waaf.com. **Description:** A radio station with a hard rock format.

WBCN 104.1 FM
1265 Boylston Street, Boston MA 02215. 617/266-1111. **Contact:** Dawn McNeil, Business Manager. **World Wide Web address:** http://www.wbcn.com. **Description:** A rock and roll format FM radio station.

WBZ-TV, CHANNEL 4
1170 Soldiers Field Road, Boston MA 02134. **Contact:** Station Manager. **World Wide Web address:** http://www.wbz.com. **Description:** A television station broadcasting to metropolitan Boston and portions of southern New England.

WCVB-TV, CHANNEL 5
5 TV Place, Needham MA 02494. 781/449-0400. **Fax:** 781/449-6682. **Contact:** Human Resources. **World Wide Web address:** http://www.thebostonchannel.com. **Description:** An ABC-affiliated television station. **Special programs:** Internships. **Corporate headquarters location:** New York NY.

WFXT-TV, CHANNEL 25
dba FOX 25
25 Fox Drive, P.O. Box 9125, Dedham MA 02027-9125. 781/326-8825. **Fax:** 781/467-7212. **Contact:** Director of Human Resources. **World Wide Web address:** http://www.fox25.com. **Description:** A television station affiliated with the Fox Broadcasting Network. **Positions advertised include:** Director; Studio Technician; Local Sales Manager; Account Executive; Sales Assistant; Traffic Assistant. **Special programs:** Internships. **Corporate headquarters location:** This location. **Parent company:** Boston Celtics Broadcasting. **Operations at this facility include:** Administration; Sales. **Number of employees at this location:** 60.

WHDH-TV, CHANNEL 7
7 Bulfinch Place, Boston MA 02114. 617/725-0777. **Contact:** Human Resources. **World Wide Web address:** http://www.whdh.com. **Description:** An NBC-affiliated television station.

WLVI-TV, CHANNEL 56 (WB-56)
75 Morrissey Boulevard, Boston MA 02125. 617/265-5656 **Contact:** Human Resources. **World Wide Web address:** http://www.wb56.com. **Description:** A television station offering a variety of programming. WLVI-TV is part of the WB Network.

WSBK-TV, CHANNEL 38 (UPN-38)
83 Leo Birmingham Parkway, Brighton MA 02135. 617/787-7000. **Contact:** Manager. **World Wide Web address:** http://www.upn38.com. **Description:** A television broadcasting station serving metropolitan Boston and parts of southern New England. WSBK-TV's programming format includes entertainment, news, and sports.

WTE CORPORATION
7 Alfred Circle, Bedford MA 01730. 781/275-6400. **Contact:** Human Resources. **World Wide Web address:** http://www.wte.com. **Description:** Recycles plastics and metals. **Corporate headquarters location:** This location.

WASHINGTON GROUP INTERNATIONAL, INC.
One Broadway, Cambridge MA 02142. 617/494-7000. **Contact:** Human Resources. **World Wide Web address:** http://www.wgint.com. **Description:** Provides design, engineering, and construction services to chemical, petroleum, and other related industrial customers. **Positions advertised include:** Engineer.

WASTE MANAGEMENT, INC.
256 New Lancaster Road, Leominster MA 01453. 978/840-9557. **Contact:** Human Resources. **World Wide Web address:** http://www.wastemanagement.com. **Description:** Engaged in hauling trash and waste.

WATERS CORPORATION
34 Maple Street, Milford MA 01757. 508/478-2000. **Fax:** 508/482-2413. **Recorded jobline:** 508/482-3332. **Contact:** Human Resources. **World Wide Web address:** http://www.waters.com. **Description:** Produces a range of instruments, information management systems, and chromatography products for high-performance liquid chromatography and related applications. Waters Corporation's products are also used in fundamental research directed toward a better understanding of the chemical, physical, and biological composition of compounds, as well as in the detection, measurement, and identification of compounds of interest across a wide range of industries. Founded in 1958. **NOTE:** Entry-level positions and second and third shifts are offered. **Positions advertised include:** Administrative & Support; Chemistry; Electrical Engineer. **NOTE:** Apply Online. **Office hours:** Monday - Friday, 8:00 a.m. - 4:30 p.m. **Corporate headquarters location:** This location. **Other U.S. locations:** Nationwide. **International locations:** Worldwide. **Operations at this facility include:** Regional Headquarters. **Listed on:** New York Stock Exchange. **CEO/President:** Douglas Berthiaume. **Facilities Manager:** William Stares. **Annual sales/revenues:** More than $100 million. **Number of employees at this location:** 950. **Number of employees worldwide:** 2,000.

WATTS REGULATOR COMPANY
815 Chestnut Street, North Andover MA 01845. 978/688-1811. **Fax:** 978/794-1848. **Contact:** Human Resources. **World Wide Web address:** http://www.wattsind.com. **Description:** Designs, manufactures, and sells an extensive line of valves for the plumbing and heating, water quality, municipal water, steam, industrial, and oil and gas markets. The company has 28 manufacturing plants worldwide. Major products include relief valves; water pressure regulators; backflow preventers; ball valves; hydronic heating valves; butterfly valves; steam specialty products; automatic control valves; drainage products; water supply stops; tubular and specialty water supply products; flexible water supply connectors, fittings, and tubing products; float valves; and water conditioning valves. **Listed on:** New York Stock Exchange. **Stock exchange symbol:** WTS.

WAYSIDE YOUTH & FAMILY SUPPORT NETWORK
118 Central Street, Waltham MA 02453. 781/891-0555. **Toll-free phone:** 800/564-4010. **Fax:** 781/647-1432. **Contact:** Human Resources Director. **E-mail address:** wayside_info@waysideyouth.org. **World Wide Web address:** http://www.waysideyouth.org. **Description:** A childcare center and children's mental health clinic. **Positions advertised include:** Classroom Behavioral Assistant; Overnight Counselor; Case Manager; Clinician; Floating Counselor; Day Counselor; Shift Supervisor.

WEARGUARD CORPORATION
141 Longwater Drive, Norwell MA 02061. 781/871-4100. **Contact:** Kathy Gillis, Director of Training. **E-mail address:** employment@wearguard.com. **World Wide Web address:** http://www.wearguard.com. **Description:** WearGuard is a leading direct marketer of work clothing serving over 2 million businesses and individuals and, in association with Sears Shop at Home, markets Workwear and Big and Tall Men's Clothing catalogs under the Sears name. **Parent company:** ARAMARK (Philadelphia PA) is one of the world's leading providers of quality managed services. The company operates in all 50 states and 10 foreign countries, offering a broad range of services to businesses of all sizes including most *Fortune* 500 companies and thousands of universities, hospitals, and municipal, state, and federal government facilities. ARAMARK's major businesses include Food, Leisure & Support Services, including Campus Dining Services, School Nutrition Services, Leisure Services, Business Dining Services, International Services, Healthcare Support Services, Conference Center Management, and Refreshment Services; Facility Services, Correctional Services, and Industrial Services; Uniform Services, which includes Uniform Services and WearGuard; Health & Education Services, which includes Spectrum Healthcare Services and Children's World Learning Centers; and Book & Magazine Services, of which ARAMARK is one of the largest distributors in the country. **Positions advertised include:** Corporate Financial Officer; Business Sales Group Director; QSR Director; Program Manager; Staff Accountant; Human Resources Generalist; Account Coordinator Supervisor; Regional Sales Representative; Sales Representative; Market Center Developer; Business Sales Group Representative; Print Production Artist; Account Coordinator; Administrative Assistant; Sales Associate; Machine Operator; Trainer; Computerized Machine Operator; Incentive Packer; Quality Auditor. **NOTE:** Download latest job postings in Adobe Acrobat PDF format online. **Operations at this facility include:** This location is a retail store and catalog marketer.

WEB INDUSTRIES
1700 West Park Drive, Suite 110, Westborough MA 01581. 508/898-2988. **Toll-free phone:** 800/932-3213. **Fax:** 508/898-3329. **Contact:** Alan Harrington, Director of Human Resources. **World Wide Web address:** http://www.webconverting.com. **Description:** A custom contractor that converts various foils (including aluminum), plastics, and woven and nonwoven materials into different forms for use by other companies. **Corporate headquarters location:** This location. **Subsidiaries include:** Web Converting, 2272 Park Central Boulevard, Decatur GA 30035, 770/593-2004.

WEBHIRE, INC.
91 Hartwell Avenue, Lexington MA 02421. 781/869-5000. **Fax:** 781/869-5050. **Contact:** Human Resources. **World Wide Web address:** http://www.webhire.com. **Description:** Manufactures and sells software that sorts and ranks resumes by criteria selected by the resume screener. **Positions advertised include:** Staff Accountant; Strategic Process Consultant; Vice President Client Services & Operations; Lead Development Representative. **Corporate headquarters location:** This location. **Listed on:** Privately held.

WEBSTER INDUSTRIES
58 Pulaski Street, Peabody MA 01960. 978/532-2000. **Fax:** 978/531-3354. **Contact:** Human Resources. **World Wide Web address:** http://www.websterindustries.com. **Description:** Manufactures a variety of plastic bags including garbage and sandwich bags.

THE WEETABIX COMPANY, INC.
20 Cameron Street, Clinton MA 01510. 978/368-0991. **Contact:** Human Resources. **World Wide Web address:** http://www.weetabix.com. **Description:** A cereal

manufacturer. **Corporate headquarters location:** This location. **Operations at this facility include:** Administration; Manufacturing; Research and Development; Sales; Service.

WELCH FOODS, INC.
3 Concord Farm, 575 Virginia Road, Concord MA 01742. 978/371-1000. **Contact:** Human Resources. **World Wide Web address:** http://www.welchs.com. **Description:** Produces canned fruits, vegetables, and preserves.

WELLESLEY COLLEGE
106 Central Street, Wellesley MA 02481. 781/235-0320. **Contact:** Human Resources. **World Wide Web address:** http://www.wellesley.edu. **Description:** A private liberal arts college for women. **Positions advertised include:** Vice President for Finance Treasurer; Director of Admission; Campus Police Office; Science Librarian; Director of International Studies; Residential Director.

WENTWORTH INSTITUTE OF TECHNOLOGY
550 Huntington Avenue, Boston MA 02115-5998. 617/989-4590. **Fax:** 617/989-4195. **Contact:** Anne Gill, Associate Vice President of Human Resources. **World Wide Web address:** http://www.wit.edu. **Description:** A technical university noted for its strengths in engineering, science, technology, and design. Total student enrollment is approximately 3,000. Founded in 1904. **Positions advertised include:** Student Services Representative; Assistant Director of Alumni Relations; Provost; Architecture Faculty; Laboratory Technician; Academic Department Head; Career Planning Coordinator; Co-op Coordinator; Assistant Director of Student Undergraduate Program HVAC B Level Mechanic. **Special programs:** Internships. **Corporate headquarters location:** This location. **Number of employees at this location:** 380.

WESTERBEKE CORPORATION
150 John Hancock Road, Taunton MA 02780. 508/823-7677. **Fax:** 508/884-9688. **Contact:** Monica Corbeio, Human Resources Manager. **World Wide Web address:** http://www.westerbeke.com. **Description:** Designs, manufactures, and markets marine engine and air conditioning products. The company's products consist of diesel and gasoline engine-driven electrical generator sets; inboard propulsion engines; self-contained, reverse cycle air-conditioners; and associated spare parts and accessories. Westerbeke's generator sets are installed in powerboats, houseboats, large sailboats, and other types of pleasure and commercial boats to provide electricity for operating, safety, and convenience needs. The company's propulsion engines are installed as auxiliary power systems for sailboats. In addition, the company manufactures and markets a limited number of electrical generator sets for use in nonmarine applications. Westerbeke's products are marketed through a nationwide and international network of 54 distributors and approximately 400 dealers and through the company's direct sales personnel. Founded in 1930. **NOTE:** Entry-level positions are offered. **Special programs:** Co-ops. **Office hours:** Monday - Friday, 8:15 a.m. - 5:00 p.m. **Listed on:** NASDAQ. **Stock exchange symbol:** WTBK. **President:** Jack Westerbeke. **Facilities Manager:** Bob Bisanti. **Purchasing Manager:** Dennis Durkee. **Sales Manager:** Tom Sutherland. **Number of employees at this location:** 150.

WESTIN WALTHAM-BOSTON
70 Third Avenue, Waltham MA 02451. 781/290-5600. **Fax:** 781/290-5626. **Contact:** Director of Human Resources. **World Wide Web address:** http://www.starwood.com. **Description:** A Four Star/Four Diamond, 346-room hotel. **Positions advertised include:** Assistant Controller; Director of Group Sales. **NOTE:** Entry-level positions, part-time jobs, and second and third shifts are offered. **Special programs:** Internships. **Office hours:** Monday - Friday, 9:00 a.m. - 5:00 p.m. **Corporate headquarters location:** White Plains NY. **Parent company:** Starwood Hotels and Resorts. **Listed on:** New York Stock Exchange. **Stock exchange symbol:** HOT. **CEO:** Barry Sternlicht. **Number of employees at this location:** 250. **Number of employees nationwide:** 80,000. **Number of employees worldwide:** 135,000.

WESTON & SAMPSON ENGINEERS INC.
5 Centennial Drive, Peabody MA 01960. 978/532-1900 **Toll-free phone:** 800/SAM-PSON. **Fax:** 978/977-0100. **Contact:** Colleen Manning, Human Resources Manager. **World Wide Web address:** http://www.wseinc.com. **Description:** Specializes in infrastructure and environmental engineering. The company provides services in the areas of water, wastewater, transportation, solid waste, and geo-technical. Founded in 1899. **Positions advertised include:** Construction Inspector; Project Manager; Environmental Scientist; Engineer; Waste Water Treatment Operator; Water Operator.

WHEATON COLLEGE
26 East Main Street, Norton MA 02766. 508/285-7722. **Fax:** 508/286-8262. **Recorded jobline:** 508/286-3547. **Contact:** Barbara Lema. Director of Human Resources. **E-mail address:** hr@wheatoncollege.edu. **World Wide Web address:** http://www.wheatonma.edu. **Description:** A private, coed, four-year college. **Positions advertised include:** Program Coordinator; Communications Officer; Grounds Helper; Writing Teacher; Quantitative Analysis Instructor.

WHEELOCK COLLEGE
200 The Riverway, Boston MA 02215. 617/734-5200. **Fax:** 6177/879-2000. **Contact:** Human Resources. **E-mail address:** opportunities@wheelock.edu. **World Wide Web address:** http://www.wheelock.edu. **Description:** A small liberal arts college offering both graduate and undergraduate courses of study. **Positions advertised include:** Assistant Professor of Human Development; Associate Professor in Juvenile Justice; Department Chair; Head Field Coach; HVAC Maintenance Mechanic.

WHITE HEN PANTRY, INC.
41 Montvale Avenue, Stoneham MA 02180. 781/438-1140. **Fax:** 781/438-9354. **Contact:** General Manager. **World Wide Web address:** http:://www.whitehenpantry.com. **Description:** White Hen Pantry operates a chain of convenience food stores. **Corporate headquarters location:** Elmhurst IL. **Parent company:** Clark Retail Enterprises, Inc. **Operations at this facility include:** This location houses administrative offices.

WHITEHEAD INSTITUTE FOR BIOMEDICAL RESEARCH
9 Cambridge Center, Cambridge MA 02142-1479. 617/258-5000. **Fax:** 617/258-6294. **Contact:** Human Resources **E-mail address:** resumes@wi.mit.edu. **World Wide Web address:** http://www.wi.mit.edu. **Description:** A nonprofit research and teaching institution that specializes in programs regarding AIDS and cancer research, developmental biology, genetics, infectious diseases, and structural biology. **Positions advertised include;** Research Scientist; Programmer; Technical Assistant. **Corporate headquarters location:** This location.

WINCHESTER HOSPITAL
41 Highland Avenue, Winchester MA 01890. 781/729-9000. **Fax:** 781/756-2908. **Contact:** Personnel. **World Wide Web address:** http://www.winchesterhospital.org. **Description:** A community hospital offering a variety of medical services including emergency, pediatrics, surgery, maternity, intensive care, and telemetry. Winchester Hospital also supports wellness and home health care programs. **Positions advertised include:** Accountant; Administrative Assistant; Billing Representative; Cat Scan Technologist; Child Life Coordinator; Clinical Associate; Diet Technician; Message Therapist; Medical Records Clerk; MRI Technologist; Patient Registrar; Radiology Technologist; Registered Nurse; Sleep Lab Technician; Team leader; Ultrasound Technologist.

THE WINDHOVER VETERINARY CENTER
944-A Main Street, Walpole MA 02081. 508/668-4520. **Contact:** Human Resources. **World Wide Web address:** http://www.windhovervet.com. **Description:** A veterinary center providing basic care for small pets with an emphasis on treating birds.

WINDSOR STREET HEALTH CENTER
119 Windsor Street, Cambridge MA 02139. 617/665-3600. **Contact:** Human Resources. **Description:** A community-based health clinic providing general medicine and care. **Parent company:** Cambridge Hospital is a 170-bed, full-service hospital owned by the city of Cambridge and affiliated with Harvard and Tufts Medical Schools.

WINTHROP PRINTING COMPANY
235 Old Colony Avenue, South Boston MA 02127. 617/268-9660. **Fax:** 617/268-6735. **Contact:** Human Resources. **World Wide Web address:** http://www.winprint.com. **Description:** A commercial printer. **Positions advertised include:** Sales Executive;.

WOLF, GREENFIELD & SACKS
Federal Reserve Plaza, 600 Atlantic Avenue, Boston MA 02210. 617/720-3500. **Fax:** 617/720-2441. **Contact:** Sheila LeDuc, Director of Human Resources. **E-mail address:** sleduc@wolfgreenfield.com. **World Wide Web address:** http://www.wolfgreenfield.com. **Description:** A leading intellectual property law firm. Areas of specialization include patent, trademark, and copyright law.

WOODS HOLE OCEANOGRAPHIC INSTITUTION
Mail Stop 15, 14 Maury Lane, Woods Hole MA 02543-1120. 508/457-2000. **Fax:** 508/457-2173. **Contact:** Human Resources. **E-mail address:** hr@whoi.edu. **World Wide Web address:** http://www.whoi.edu. **Description:** A private, nonprofit oceanography research institute. **Positions advertised include:** Assistant Scientist; Chief Scientist; Engineering Assistant; Part Time Helper; Postdoctoral Investigator; Research Assistant; Security Guard; Electrician.

WOODWORKERS WAREHOUSE
126 Oxford Street, Lynn MA 01901. 781/598-6393. **Contact:** Human Resources. **World Wide Web address:** http://www.woodworkerswarehouse.com. **Description:** A distributor of woodworkers tools and accessories. Products are sold through Woodworkers Warehouse retail stores, with 100 Northeast locations. Founded in 1981. **Corporate headquarters location:** This location.

WORCESTER POLYTECHNIC INSTITUTE
100 Institute Road, Worcester MA 01609. 508/831-5000. **Fax:** 508/831-5715. **Contact:** Human Resources. **E-mail address:** human-resources@wpi.edu. **World Wide Web address:** http://www.wpi.edu. **Description:** A technical college offering both undergraduate and graduate programs. Founded in 1865. **Positions advertised include:** Instructional Technologist; Accounting Manager; Assistant Director of Annual Giving; Web Applications Director; Assistant Football Coach; Magazine Editor.

WORCESTER TELEGRAM & GAZETTE
P.O. Box 15012, Worcester MA 01615-0012. 508/793-9260. **Physical address:** 20 Franklin Street, Worcester MA 01615. **Contact:** Victor A. DiNardo, Director of Human Resources. **World Wide Web address:** http://www.telegram.com. **Description:** Publishes the *Worcester Telegram & Gazette* with a daily circulation of over 107,000 and a Sunday circulation of over 133,000, and several weekly and semiweekly newspapers. The company also provides the *Telegram & Gazette* online, an Internet access service, and a wide range of online community information directories. **Parent company:** The New York Times Company.

WORLD TIMES INC.
225 Franklin Street 26th Floor, Boston MA 02110. 617/439-5400. **Fax:** 617/439-5415. **Contact:** Human Resources. **E-mail address:** info@worldtimes.com. **World Wide Web address:** http://www.worldtimes.com. **Description:** Publishes the monthly *WorldPaper,* an international newspaper. Founded in 1978. **Corporate headquarters location:** This location.

WORLDTEACH
Center for International Development, Harvard University, 79 JFK Street, Cambridge MA 02138. 617/495-5527. **Toll-free phone:** 800/4TE-ACH0. **Fax:** 617/495-1599. **Contact:** Director of Recruiting. **E-mail address:** info@worldteach.org. **World Wide Web address:** http://www.worldteach.org. **Description:** A nonprofit organization, based at Harvard University, which places volunteers overseas as teachers in developing countries. Volunteers have served in Asia, Africa, Central America, and Central Europe. Volunteers make a commitment of either six months or one year and pay a program fee of approximately $4,800. Volunteers must have a bachelor's degree, but no previous teaching or foreign language is required. WorldTeach also runs a summer teaching program in China for undergraduate and graduate students. **Positions advertised include:** Ecuador Summer Field Director.

WILLIAM E. WRIGHT LIMITED PARTNERSHIP
85 South Street, West Warren MA 01092. 413/436-7732. **Toll-free phone:** 877/597-4445. **Fax:** 413/436-9510. **Contact:** Human Resources. **E-mail address:** pgancorz@wrights.com. **World Wide Web address:** http://www.wrights.com. **Description:** Manufactures and markets fashion trimmings for its home sewing, home furnishing, and decorative packaging customers. **Positions advertised include:** Assembly Machine Operator; Winder; Order Packer; Material Handler; Associate; Buyer; Inventory Return Clerk.

WYETH GENETICS INSTITUTE
35 Cambridge Park Drive, Cambridge MA 02140. 617/876-1170. **Contact:** Human Resources. **World Wide Web address:** http://www.wyeth.com. **Description:** Performs biotechnology research contributing to the application and creation of recombinant DNA technology. **Positions advertised include:** Staff Engineer; Associate Director; Plant Engineer; Senior Maintenance Mechanic; Project Specialist; Process Technician. **Other area locations:** Andover MA. **Other U.S. locations:** St. Louis MO. **International locations:** Germany. **Parent company:** American Home Products Corporation (Madison NJ).

WYMAN-GORDON COMPANY
244 Worcester Street, Box 8001, North Grafton MA 01536-8001. 508/839-4441. **Contact:** Human Resources. **World Wide Web address:** http://www.wyman-

gordon.com. **Description:** Wyman-Gordon uses forging and investment casting technologies to produce components for applications such as jet turbine engines and airframes, and designs and produces prototype products using composite technologies. **Corporate headquarters location:** This location. **Subsidiaries include:** Wyman-Gordon Investment Castings, Inc. uses automated, high-volume production equipment and both air-melt and vacuum-melt furnaces to produce a wide variety of complex investment castings. WGIC investment castings are made from a range of metal alloys including aluminum and magnesium, steel, titanium, and high-temperature-based alloys. The company's composites operation, Scaled Composites, Inc., plans, proposes, designs, fabricates, and tests prototypes for aerospace, automotive, and other customers. **Operations at this facility include:** This location manufactures metal components for aerospace applications. **Number of employees at this location:** 725. **Number of employees nationwide:** 2,600. **Number of employees worldwide:** 3,000.

XERIUM TECHNOLOGIES, INC.
1 Technology Drive, Westborough Technology Park, Westborough MA 01581. 508/616-9468. **Fax:** 508/616-9487. **Contact:** Human Resources. **World Wide Web address:** http://www.xerium.com. **Description:** A leading global manufacturer and supplier of consumable products used in the production of paper. Operates 39 manufacturing facilities in 15 countries. **Corporate headquarters location:** This location. **Listed on:** New York Stock Exchange. **Stock exchange symbol:** XRM. **Number of employees worldwide:** 4,000.

XPEDX
613 Main Street, Wilmington MA 01887. 978/988-7447. **Fax:** 978/988-8595. **Contact:** Human Resources. **World Wide Web address:** http://www.xpedx.com. **Description:** Distributes office and printing papers. **Corporate headquarters location:** Denver CO. **Other U.S. locations:** City of Industry CA; Detroit MI.

XYVISION ENTERPRISE SOLUTIONS, INC.
30 New Crossing Road, Reading MA 01867. 781/756-4400. **Fax:** 781/756-4330. **Contact:** Diane Lambas, Human Resources. **World Wide Web address:** http://www.xyvision.com. **Description:** Develops and supports software for document management, publishing, and prepress applications worldwide. The company combines its software with standard computer hardware, selected third-party software, and support services to create integrated systems that improve productivity and strategic position. Xyvision's color electronic prepress applications are marketed to commercial trade shops, printers, prepress service organizations, consumer goods companies, advanced design firms, and packaging manufacturers. **Corporate headquarters location:** This location.

YANKEE AVIATION SERVICES INC.
246 South Meadow Road, Box 11, Plymouth Airport, Plymouth MA 02360. 508/746-5511. **Contact:** Human Resources Department. **World Wide Web address:** http://www.yankeeaviation.com. **Description:** Services and maintains aircraft.

YANKEE CANDLE COMPANY
P.O. Box 110, South Deerfield MA 01373. 413/664-8306. **Fax:** 413/665-0158. **Recorded jobline:** 800/830-6038. **Contact:** Employment Department. **E-mail address:** jobs@yankeecandle.com. **World Wide Web address:** http://www.yankeecandle.com. **Description:** Manufactures premium scented candles. **Positions advertised include:** Associate Brand Manager; Database Administrator; Business Unit Manager; Electrician; Warehouse Management Systems Specialist.

YOUVILLE HOSPITAL
1575 Cambridge Street, Cambridge MA 02138-4398. 617/876-4344. **Fax:** 617/234-7996. **Contact:** Jack Carrol, Human Resources Director. **World Wide Web address:** http://www.youville.org. **Description:** A nonprofit hospital and nursing home offering rehabilitation and medical care. **Positions advertised include:** Occupational Therapist; Pharmacist; Physical Therapist; Recreational Therapist; Registered Nurse; Respiratory Therapist.

ZIFF-DAVIS PUBLISHING COMPANY
500 Unicorn Park Drive, Woburn MA 01801. 781/938-2600. **Fax:** 781/393-3038. **World Wide Web address:** http://www.zdnet.com. **Contact:** Human Resources. **Description:** A publisher of over 22 computer industry magazines in the United States and abroad. Titles published by Ziff-Davis include *PC Week* and *Computer Shopper*. **Positions advertised include:** Editor; Reporter.

ZOLL MEDICAL CORPORATION
32 Second Avenue, Burlington MA 01803. 781/229-0020. **Contact:** Human Resources. **World Wide Web address:** http://www.zoll.com. **Description:** Designs, manufactures, and markets an integrated line of proprietary, noninvasive, cardiac resuscitation devices and disposable electrodes. **Positions advertised include:** Hospital Territory Manager; Sales Development Specialist; Administrative Assistant; Clinical Nurse Specialist.

ZOOM TELEPHONICS INC.
207 South Street, Boston MA 02111. 617/423-1072. **Fax:** 617/423-2836. **Contact:** Karen Player, Director of Human Resources. **E-mail address:** hr@zoom.com. **World Wide Web address:** http://www.zoomtel.com. **Description:** Designs, produces, and markets internal, external, and PCMCIA modems and fax modems. **Positions advertised include:** Accountant/Auditor; Design Engineer; Industrial Engineer; Mechanical Engineer; MIS Specialist; Software Engineer; Technical Writer/Editor. **Corporate headquarters location:** This location. **Listed on:** NASDAQ. **Stock exchange symbol:** ZOOM. **Annual sales/revenues:** $51 - $100 million. **Number of employees at this location:** 320.

ZURICH SCUDDER INVESTMENTS
2 International Place, Boston MA 02110. 617/295-1000. **Contact:** Human Resources. **World Wide Web address:** www.scudder.com. **Description:** An investment firm.

AAA MICHIGAN
One Auto Club Drive, Dearborn MI 48126. 313/336-1598. **Fax:** 313/436-7188. **Contact:** Human Resources. **E-mail address:** jobs@aaamich.com. **World Wide Web address:** http://www.aaamich.com. **Description:** Provides insurance, travel, and a wide variety of services to motorists through a network of over 50 branch offices. **NOTE:** Part-time positions are offered. **Positions advertised include:** Travel Agent; Life Insurance Agent; Actuarial Analyst; Senior Actuarial Analyst; Senior Information Technology Auditor; Senior Support Specialist; Sales Compliance Manager; Business Consultant; Senior Marketing Research Consultant; Business Consultant. **Special programs:** Internships; Tuition Reimbursement Program. **Corporate headquarters location:** This location. **Other area locations:** Statewide. **Number of employees nationwide:** 4,000.

ABB FLEXIBLE AUTOMATION
1250 Brown Road, Auburn Hills MI 48326. 248/393-4600. **Fax:** 248/393-4602. **Contact:** Alison Worsely, Human Resources Professional. **E-mail address:** alison.m.worsely@us.abb.com. **World Wide Web address:** http://www.abb.com. **Description:** Engaged in the manufacture of testing and powertrain assembly equipment. **Positions advertised include:** Account Executive. **Special programs:** Training; Internships. **Corporate headquarters location:** This location. **International locations:** Worldwide. **Parent company:** ABB Group (Zurich, Switzerland). **Listed on:** New York Stock Exchange. **Stock exchange symbol:** ABB. **Annual sales/revenues:** Approximately $5 billion. **Number of employees worldwide:** 33,343.

ABL ELECTRONIC SERVICE, INC.
314 East 14 Mile Road, Madison Heights MI 48071. 248/588-6663. **Fax:** 248/588-0851. **Contact:** Personnel. **World Wide Web address:** http://www.ablserv.com. **Description:** Services computer hardware for individuals and businesses. ABL Electronic Service repairs CPUs, monitors, printers, and other peripherals for IBM, IBM compatibles, and some Apple units. **Positions advertised include:** T.V. Repair Bench Technician; T.V. Repair Road Technician. **Corporate headquarters location:** This location. **Other area locations:** Dearborn Heights MI; Southfield MI.

ACO HARDWARE INC.
23333 Commerce Drive, Farmington Hills MI 48335-2764. 248/471-0100. **Fax:** 248/615-2696. **Contact:** Director of Personnel. **E-mail address:** hmrs@acohardware.com. **World Wide Web address:** http://www.acohardware.com. **Description:** Operates over 60 hardware stores throughout southeast Michigan. **NOTE:** Entry-level positions are offered. **Positions advertised include:** Store Management Trainee. **Corporate headquarters location:** This location. **Other area locations:** Statewide. **Listed on:** Privately held. **Number of employees at this location:** 200. **Number of employees worldwide:** 1,300.

A.M.P. INDUSTRIES
42050 Executive Drive, Harrison Township MI 48045-1311. 586/469-4100. **Fax:** 586/463-8650. **Contact:** Shannon Hensley, Human Resources Manager. **E-mail address:** sales@theamericanteam.com. **World Wide Web address:** http://www.theamericanteam.com. **Description:** Supplies plastic injection molding and tool building services to OEM automotive and recreational vehicle manufacturers. **Positions advertised include:** Machine Operator; Quality Auditor. **Special programs:** Internships. **Office hours:** Monday – Friday, 9:00 a.m. – 4:00 p.m. **Corporate headquarters location:** This location. **President:** Karl Blankenburg. **Number of employees at this location:** 260.

ASC INC.
One ASC Center, Southgate MI 48195. 734/285-4911. **Fax:** 734/246-2609. **Contact:** Human Resources. **E-mail address:** hr@ascglobal.com. **World Wide Web address:** http://www.ascglobal.com. **Description:** An original equipment manufacturer that engineers and develops convertible systems, exterior enhancement programs, sunroofs, and interior trim for cars and trucks. ASC Incorporated also converts imported and domestic sedans into convertibles. Founded in 1965. **Positions advertised include:** Product Planning Specialist; Purchasing Manager; Account Financial Manager; Program Manager. **Special programs:** Internships. **Corporate headquarters location:** This location. **Other area locations:** Gibraltar MI; Lansing MI; Livonia MI. **Other U.S. locations:** Long Beach CA; Bowling Green KY; Statesville NC; Columbus OH; Dublin VA; Vancouver WA. **Parent company:** Questor. **International locations:** Germany; Japan; Korea. **Listed on:** Privately held. **CEO:** Paul Wilbur. **Number of employees at this location:** 500. **Number of employees nationwide:** 2,500.

ACCIDENT FUND COMPANY
232 South Capitol Avenue, P.O. Box 40790, Lansing MI 48901. 517/342-4200. **Contact:** Human Resources. **E-mail address:** careers@accidentfund.com. **World Wide Web address:** http://www.accidentfund.com. **Description:** A workers' compensation insurance company. **NOTE:** Resumes may be submitted online. **Positions advertised include:** Business Development Manager; Regional Assistant; Account Service Technician. **Special programs:** Internships; Tuition Reimbursement Program. **Corporate headquarters location:** This location. **Parent company:** Blue Cross Blue Shield of Michigan. **President/CEO:** James C. Epolito.

ACE TEX ENTERPRISES
7601 Central Avenue, Detroit MI 48210. 313/834-4000. **Toll-free phone:** 800/444-3800. **Fax:** 313/834-0260. **Contact:** Personnel Director. **World Wide Web address:** http://www.ace-texplastics.com. **Description:** Manufactures textile goods including cotton wiping cloths, disposable paper wipers, and other specialty items. Founded in 1946. **Corporate headquarters location:** This location. **Number of employees nationwide:** 650.

ACHESON COLLOIDS COMPANY
1600 Washington Avenue, Port Huron MI 48060. 810/984-5581. **Toll-free phone:** 800/255-1908. **Fax:** 810/984-1446. **Contact:** Business Manager. **World Wide Web address:** http://www.achesoncolloids.com. **Description:** A high-tech firm engaged in the production of electrically conductive coatings and dry film lubricants. **Corporate headquarters location:** This location. **Other U.S. locations:** Brookfield OH. **International locations:** Singapore; France; Germany; Japan; the Netherlands; Korea; Spain; Australia; Brazil; Great Britain; Canada. **Parent company:** ICI plc. **Listed on:** New York Stock Exchange. **Stock exchange symbol:** ICI.

THE ACME GROUP
301 Arch Avenue, Hillsdale MI 49242. 517/437-8940. **Fax:** 517/437-8942. **Contact:** Joan Pulford, Personnel Director. **World Wide Web address:** http://www.fairway-products.com. **Description:** Engaged in the wholesale distribution of automobile parts, seats, and supplies. **Corporate headquarters location:** This location. **Number of employees nationwide:** 100.

ACME MANUFACTURING COMPANY
4240 North Atlantic Boulevard, Auburn Hills MI 48326. 248/393-7300. **Fax:** 248/393-4060. **Contact:** Fritz Carlson, President. **E-mail address:** merrimanc@acmemfg.com. **World Wide Web address:** http://www.acmemfg.com. **Description:** Designs and manufactures automated machines including polishing, buffing, and grinding equipment. **Corporate headquarters location:** This location. **International locations:** Worldwide. **Operations at this facility include:** Administration; Manufacturing; Research and Development; Sales; Service.

ADVANCE ENGINEERING COMPANY
12025 Dixie Avenue, Redford MI 48239. 313/537-3500. **Contact:** Personnel Department. **Description:** A manufacturer of deep drawn, eyelet-type stampings. **Corporate headquarters location:** Belleville MI. **Parent company:** L&W Engineering Company. **Operations at this facility include:** Manufacturing. **Number of employees at this location:** 100. **Number of employees nationwide:** 700.

ADVANCED ENGINEERING SOLUTIONS, INC.
5860 North Canton Center Road, Suite 380, Canton MI 48187. 734/459-9948. **Fax:** 734/459-7590. **Contact:** Human Resources. **E-mail address:** eds@erpsinfo.com. **World Wide Web address:** http://www.aes-inc.com. **Description:** An engineering and information technology consulting firm. **Positions advertised include:** Embedded Systems Engineer; Industrial Engineer; Manufacturing Process Engineer; Quality Engineer; Test Engineer; Database Administrator; Network Administrator; Java Programmer; C++ Programmer; Peoplesoft Consultant; Cold Fusion Expert. **Corporate headquarters location:** This location.

ADVANTAGE COMPUTING SYSTEMS, INC.
3850 Ranchero Drive, Ann Arbor MI 48108. 734/327-3600. **Fax:** 734/327-3620. **Contact:** Personnel Manager. **E-mail address:** jobs@advantagecs.com. **World Wide Web address:** http://www.advantagecs.com. **Description:** Markets Publisher's Advantage Computing System brand software to special interest publishers. The company also resells a wide range of hardware options. Founded in 1980. **NOTE:** If submitted via e-mail, resumes must be formatted in Microsoft Word or plain text. **Corporate headquarters location:** This location. **Operations at this facility include:** Administration; Manufacturing; Research and Development; Sales; Service. **Listed on:** Privately held. **Number of employees at this location:** 75.

AFLAC
4565 Wilson Street, Suite 5, Grandville MI 49418. 616/538-6400. **Fax:** 616/538-6500. **Contact:** Dianna Atchison. **E-mail address:** dianna_atchison@us.aflac.com. **World Wide Web address:** http://www.aflac.com. **Description:** Aflac is a leading provider of insurance sold on a voluntary basis at the worksite in the United States and the largest foreign insurer in Japan.

AGILISYS INC.
41780 Six Mile Road, Northville MI 48167. 248/697-3200. **Toll-free phone:** 800/442-2488. **Fax:** 248/697-3484. **Contact:** Debbie Templeton, Human Resources. **E-mail address:** hr@agilisys.com. **World Wide Web address:** http://www.agilisys.com. **Description:** Develops software for the automotive industry. **NOTE:** To reach Human Resources directly call: 248/697-3332. **Corporate headquarters location:** Alpharetta GA. **Operations at this facility include:** This location is the North American Headquarters of the company's Automotive Division. **President:** Ken Walters. **Number of employees worldwide:** 800.

AIR GAGE CORPORATION
12170 Globe Road, Livonia MI 48150. 734/591-9220. **Contact:** Human Resources. **World Wide Web address:** http://www.airgage.com. **Description:** Develops and manufactures air gages and statistical process control software that allow manufacturers to monitor, regulate, and collect data on their manufacturing processes. **Corporate headquarters location:** This location. **Parent company:** SPX Corporation. **Listed on:** New York Stock Exchange. **Stock exchange symbol:** SPW.

AJAY SPORTS, INC.
32751 Middlebelt Road, Suite B, Farmington Hills MI 48334. 248/851-5651. **Contact:** Human Resources. **Description:** Designs, manufactures, and markets golf and billiard accessories through its wholly owned subsidiary, Ajay Leisure Products, Incorporated. Ajay's products are sold nationwide to discount stores, department stores, catalog showrooms, and other mass merchandise outlets primarily under the Ajay, Pro Classic, Private Pro, and Spalding brand names. **Corporate headquarters location:** This location. **Subsidiaries include:** Leisure Life, Incorporated manufactures and markets outdoor and indoor casual living furniture. Leisure Life's products are sold through independent retailers and larger chains of home and garden stores. **Listed on:** OTC. **Stock exchange symbol:** AJAY. **President/COO:** Joseph J. White. **Number of employees at this location:** 33.

AKZO NOBEL COATINGS
30 Brush Street, Pontiac MI 48341. 248/334-7010. **Fax:** 248/253-7799. **Contact:** Maryanne Hagan, Human Resources Department. **World Wide Web address:** http://www.akzonobel.com. **Description:** A diversified company that produces salt and chemicals, coatings, health care products, and fibers. Business activities are conducted in four units: Chemicals, Coatings, Pharma, and Fibers. The Chemicals Group produces polymer chemicals, rubber chemicals, catalysts, detergents, surfactants, functional chemicals, salt, chlor-alkali, and industrial chemicals. The Coatings Group produces decorative coatings, car refinishes, industrial coatings, industrial wood finishes, aerospace finishes, automotive finishes, and resins. The Pharma Group includes the production of ethical drugs, hospital supplies, nonprescription products, raw materials for the pharmaceutical industry, generics, and veterinary products. The Fibers Group produces textile, industrial, and high-performance fibers; industrial nonwovens; and membranes for medical, technical, and industrial uses. **NOTE:** Second and third shifts are offered. **Special programs:** Summer Jobs; Internships. **Corporate headquarters location:** Dobbs Ferry NY. **Other U.S. locations:** Nationwide. **International locations:** Worldwide. **Operations at this facility include:** This location is engaged in the manufacture and distribution of transportation coatings. **Listed on:** NASDAQ. **Stock exchange symbol:** AKZOY.

ALLIED VAUGHN
11923 Brookfield Street, Livonia MI 48150. 734/462-5543. **Toll-free phone:** 800/462-5543. **Fax:** 734/462-4004. **Contact:** Human Resources. **E-mail address:** human.resources@alliedvaughn.com. **World Wide Web address:** http://www.alliedvaughn.com. **Description:** An independent multimedia manufacturing company that offers CD-audio and CD-ROM mastering and replication, videocassette and audiocassette duplication, laser video disc recording, off-line and online video editing, motion picture film processing, film-to-tape and tape-to-film transfers and complete finishing, packaging, warehousing, and fulfillment services. Founded in 1942. **Corporate headquarters location:** Minneapolis MN. **Other U.S. locations:** Nationwide. **Subsidiaries include:** TangibleData, Incorporated.

ALTARUM
3520 Green Court, Suite 300, P.O. Box 134001, Ann Arbor MI 48113-4001. 734/302-4600. **Contact:** Recruiting Manager. **World Wide Web address:**

http://www.altarum.org. **Description:** A private, nonprofit research and development organization engaged in the design and development of radar and electro-optical sensors and imaging systems. **NOTE:** Resumes may be submitted online. **Positions advertised include:** Analyst; Operations Research Analyst; Principal Investigator; Practice Area Leader; Project Scientist/Researcher; Research Engineer; Senior Software Analyst; Senior Supply Chain Analyst. **Special programs:** Internships. **Corporate headquarters location:** This location. **Other U.S. locations:** Orange Park FL; Arlington VA. **Operations at this facility include:** Research and Development. **President/CEO:** Kenneth R. Baker. **Number of employees at this location:** 850.

AMERICAN AXLE MANUFACTURING
1 Dauch Drive, Detroit MI 48211. 313/974-2000. **Fax:** 800/343-6045. **Contact:** Human Resources. **E-mail address:** human.resources@aam.com. **World Wide Web address:** http://www.aam.com. **Description:** A manufacturer of axles and other vehicle parts. **Special programs:** Co-ops; Internships; Tuition Assistance Program. **Corporate headquarters location:** This location. **Other U.S. locations:** OH; NY. **International locations:** Brazil; United Kingdom; Mexico. **Listed on:** New York Stock Exchange. **Stock exchange symbol:** AXL. **President/CEO:** Joel D. Robinson. **Number of employees nationwide:** 4,300. **Number of employees worldwide:** Approximately 12,000.

AMERICAN EXPRESS FINANCIAL ADVISORS
352 12th Street, Plainwell MI 49080. 269/685-6417. **Contact:** Human Resources. **World Wide Web address:** http://www.americanexpress.com. **Description:** Provides a variety of financial products and services to help individuals, businesses, and institutions establish and achieve their financial goals. American Express Financial Advisors has a field of more than 8,000 financial advisors in the United States and offers financial planning, annuities, mutual funds, insurance, and investment certificates. Other services include institutional investment advisory trust, tax preparation, and retail securities brokerage. **Corporate headquarters location:** Minneapolis MI. **Other U.S. locations:** Nationwide. **Listed on:** New York Stock Exchange. **Stock exchange symbol:** AXP. **President:** James M. Cracchiolo. **Annual sales/revenues:** $5.6 billion. **Number of employees nationwide:** Approximately 10,000.

AMERICAN PLASTIC TOYS INC.
799 Ladd Road, P.O. Box 100, Walled Lake MI 48390-0100. 248/624-4881. **Toll-free phone:** 800/521-7080. **Contact:** Diane Saltzman, Manager of Human Resources Department. **World Wide Web address:** http://www.americanplastictoys.com. **Description:** Engaged in the manufacture of plastic-injection molded toys. **NOTE:** Second and third shifts are offered. **Positions advertised include:** Assembly Operators; Forklift Operators. **Office hours:** Monday – Friday, 7:30 a.m. – 4:30 p.m. **Corporate headquarters location:** This location. **Other U.S. locations:** Olive Branch MS. **Operations at this facility include:** Administration; Manufacturing; Sales. **Number of employees nationwide:** 500.

AMERICAN SHOWER AND BATH
693 South Court Street, Lapeer MI 48446. 810/664-8501. **Contact:** Human Resources. **World Wide Web address:** http://www.asbcorp.com. **Description:** Manufactures products for showers and bathtubs, including wall surrounds, shower enclosure kits, and bathtub and shower doors. **Special programs:** Internships. **Corporate headquarters location:** Moorestown NJ. **Parent company:** Masco Corporation. **Operations at this facility include:** Manufacturing; Sales. **Number of employees at this location:** 100.

AMFAB INC.
1446 South 35th Street, Galesburg MI 49053-9679. 269/665-6703. **Contact:** Alan Anderson, Human Resources. **Description:** Manufactures and sells physical therapy and orthopedic products. **Parent company:** Bissell, Incorporated.

ANALYSTS INTERNATIONAL CORPORATION (AIC)
3252 University Drive, Suite 200, Auburn Hills MI 48326. 248/299-2660. **Fax:** 248/299-4830. **Contact:** Human Resources. **E-mail address:** jobs@analysts.com. **World Wide Web address:** http://www.analysts.com. **Description:** An international computer consulting firm. The company assists clients in developing systems in a variety of industries using different programming languages and software. **NOTE:** Interested job seekers may apply online. **Corporate headquarters location:** Minneapolis MN. **Other U.S. locations:** Nationwide. **International locations:** Canada; United Kingdom. **Listed on:** NASDAQ. **Stock exchange symbol:** ANLY. **President/CEO:** Mike LaVelle. **Number of employees worldwide:** 3,000.

ANN ARBOR COMPUTER
34375 West Twelve Mile Road, Farmington Hills MI 48331-5624. 248/553-5200. **Fax:** 248/553-5292. **Contact:** Human Resources. **World Wide Web address:** http://www.annarborcomputer.com. **Description:** Designs software for automated inventory systems used by warehouses. Founded in 1965. **Corporate headquarters location:** This location. **Parent company:** Jervis B. Webb Company.

ANN ARBOR PUBLIC SCHOOLS
2555 South State Street, Ann Arbor MI 48104. 734/994-2200. **Fax:** 734/994-1792. **Contact:** Human Resources. **World Wide Web address:** http://.aaps.k12.mi.us. **Description:** Coordinates information, resources, and services for the Ann Arbor public school district. The district serves over 16,000 students and employs over 3,000 full and part-time staff members. **Positions advertised include:** Speech Therapist; Behavioral Specialist; Early Childhood Special Education Teacher; Substitute Teacher; Bus Mechanic; Communications Classroom Assistant; Varsity Girl's Lacrosse Coach; Substitute Teacher Assistant.

APPLIED INDUSTRIAL TECHNOLOGIES
11677 Wayne Road, Suite 112, Romulus MI 48174. 734/840-9000. **Contact:** Human Resources. **World Wide Web address:** http://www.smp.applied.com. **Description:** A manufacturer and distributor of bearings, power transmission products, V-belts, hoses, plastics, chains, and sprockets. **Corporate headquarters location:** Cleveland OH. **Other area locations:** Statewide. **Other U.S. locations:** Nationwide. **International locations:** Canada; Puerto Rico; Mexico. **Operations at this facility include:** Administration; Sales; Service. **Listed on:** New York Stock Exchange. **Stock exchange symbol:** AIT. **President/COO:** Bill L. Purser. **Annual sales/revenues:** $1.6 billion. **Number of employees nationwide:** 4,300.

AQUINAS COLLEGE
1607 Robinson Road SE, Grand Rapids MI 49506-1799. 616/459-8281. **Fax:** 616/459-2563. **Contact:** Human Resources. **E-mail address:** humanresources@aquinas.edu. **World Wide Web address:** http://www.aquinas.edu. **Description:** A Catholic liberal arts college offering undergraduate and graduate programs in over 40 majors. Founded by the Dominican Sisters of Grand Rapids in 1886. **NOTE:** Resumes are accepted by mail, fax, or e-mail. **Positions advertised include:** Associate Professor, Business Management. **President:** Harry J. Knopke, Ph.D.

ARCADIS GIFFELS
25200 Telegraph Road, Southfield MI 48034. 248/936-8000. **Fax:** 248/936-8111. **Contact:** Human Resources Administrator. **World Wide Web address:** http://www.arcadis-us.com. **Description:** An engineering, architectural, and surveying firm that services clients in the communications, environmental, infrastructure, and buildings business sectors. **Positions advertised include:** Scientist. **Corporate headquarters location:** Denver CO. **Other U.S. locations:** Nationwide. **International locations:** Worldwide. **Parent company:** Arcadis NV (the Netherlands). **Listed on:** NASDAQ. **Stock exchange symbol:** ARCAD. **CEO:** Stephen B. Blake. **Number of employees at this location:** 500. **Number of employees worldwide:** 8,500.

ARGUS CORPORATION
12540 Beech Daly Road, Redford MI 48329. 313/937-2900. **Contact:** Human Resources. **World Wide Web address:** http://www.arguscorporation.com. **Description:** A full service automotive supplier. Argus Corporation supports automotive development projects and manufactures material handling equipment and custom fabrication and machining services for automobile manufacturers and suppliers around the world. **Positions advertised include:** CAD Designer; CMM Operator; Cost Estimator; Maintenance Painter; Sales Representative; Sheet Metal Model Maker.

ARVIN MERITOR
2135 West Maple Road, Troy MI 48084. 248/435-1000. **Fax:** 248/435-7571. **Contact:** Human Resources. **E-mail address:** job.opportunities@arvinmeritor.com. **World Wide Web address:** http://www.arvinmeritor.com. **Description:** Operates in three business segments: Heavy Vehicle Systems, Light Vehicle Systems, and Light Vehicle Aftermarket. Heavy Vehicle Systems supplies drivetrain components and systems for commercial vehicles. Light Vehicle Systems' products include automotive electronic controls, electric motors, and suspension systems for light trucks and passenger cars. The Light Vehicle Aftermarket supplies exhaust systems, air, oil, and fuel filters, and ride-control products to the automotive market. **NOTE:** Entry-level positions are offered. Interested candidates can search and apply for positions online. **Positions advertised include:** Benefit Analyst; Project Management Specialist; International Tax Manager; Materials Engineer; Financial Analyst; Staff Accountant; Noise Vibration Engineer. **Special programs:** Internships; Co-ops. **Corporate headquarters location:** This location. **Operations at this facility include:** Administration; Divisional Headquarters; Research and Development; Sales; Service. **Listed on:** New York Stock Exchange. **Stock exchange symbol:** ARM. **CEO/Chairman:** Larry Yost. **Annual sales/revenues:** $8 billion.

ATTWOOD CORPORATION
1016 North Monroe Street, Lowell MI 49331. 616/897-9241. **Fax:** 616/897-2247. **Contact:** Thomas Powell, Director of Personnel. **World Wide Web address:** http://www.attwoodmarine.com. **Description:** Manufactures components of molded plastics for its parent company, Steelcase, Incorporated. Attwood is also engaged in chrome plating and manufactures a proprietary product line for the pleasure marine industry. Manufacturing processes include diecast, injection molding, light assembly, and chrome plating. **Corporate headquarters location:** Grand Rapids MI. **Parent company:** Steelcase Incorporated. **Listed on:** New York Stock Exchange. **Stock exchange symbol:** SCS.

ATWELL-HICKS, INC.
500 Avis Drive, Suite 100, Ann Arbor MI 48108. 734/994-4000. **Fax:** 734/994-1590. **Contact:** Human Resources. **E-mail address:** careers@atwell-hicks.com. **World Wide Web address:** http://www.atwell-hicks.com. **Description:** A land development consulting firm. AHI provides a wide range of services for commercial and residential land development projects. **Positions advertised include:** Project Engineer; Survey CAD Technician. **Corporate headquarters location:** This location. **Other area locations:** Brighton MI; Washington MI; Grand Rapids MI. **Other U.S. locations:** Naperville IL. **President:** Bob Macomber.

AUSABLE VALLEY COMMUNITY MENTAL HEALTH
511 Griffin Road, West Branch MI 48661. 989/345-5540. **Fax:** 989/345-4111. **Contact:** Human Resources. **Description:** Provides mental health and substance abuse treatment services on an outpatient basis. **Office hours:** Monday – Friday, 8:00 a.m. – 5:00 p.m.

AUTOALLIANCE INTERNATIONAL, INC.
One International Drive, Flat Rock MI 48134-9401. 734/782-7800. **Contact:** Human Resources. **World Wide Web address:** http://www.autoalliance.com. **Description:** A manufacturer of automobiles. AutoAlliance International is a joint venture between the Ford and Mazda motor companies. **Corporate headquarters location:** This location. **Operations at this facility include:** Administration; Manufacturing. **President/CEO:** Deborah S. Coleman. **Number of employees at this location:** 1,900.

AUTOMATIC DATA PROCESSING (ADP)
175 Jackson Plaza, Ann Arbor MI 48106. 734/769-6800. **Contact:** Human Resources. **World Wide Web address:** http://www.adp.com. **Description:** A computer software and data processing firm specializing in software development, sales, and support; remote computing services; and telecommunications. There are four divisions of Automatic Data Processing at this complex: Automotive Claims Services; Dealer Services; Interactive Personnel and Payroll; and Network Services-Division Headquarters. **Positions advertised include:** Autosource Service Representative; Technical Support Representative; Database Administrator; Internet Administrator. **Corporate headquarters location:** Roseland NJ. **Other U.S. locations:** Nationwide. **International locations:** Worldwide. **Operations at this facility include:** Divisional Headquarters; Service. **Listed on:** New York Stock Exchange. **Stock exchange symbol:** ADP. **CEO/Chairman:** Arthur F. Weinbach. **Number of employees worldwide:** Over 40,000.

AUTOMOBILE MAGAZINE
120 East Liberty Street, Ann Arbor MI 48104. 734/994-3500. **Contact:** Human Resources. **World Wide Web address:** http://www.automobilemag.com. **Description:** Produces the monthly periodical *Automobile Magazine*. **Parent company:** PRIMEDIA, Incorporated. (New York NY). **Listed on:** New York Stock Exchange. **Stock exchange symbol:** PRM. **Editor-in-Chief:** Jean Jennings.

AVON RUBBER & PLASTICS, INC.
805 West 13th Street, Cadillac MI 49601. 231/775-6571. **Fax:** 231/775-7304. **Contact:** Dale Rosser, Corporate Human Resources Manager. **World Wide Web address:** http://www.avon-rubber.com. **Description:** Produces rubber extrusions and profiles, as well as plastic injection-molded components and assembles vacuum emission harnesses for the automotive industry. **Corporate headquarters location:** This location. **Other area locations:** Statewide. **Other U.S. locations:** WI; CA; MI; NJ. **International locations:** United Kingdom; France; Czech Republic; Germany; Portugal; Mexico; India; Turkey.

AWREY BAKERIES INC.
12301 Farmington Road, Livonia MI 48150. 734/522-1100. **Toll-free phone:** 800/950-BAKE. **Contact:** Personnel Department. **E-mail address:** personnel@awrey.com. **World Wide Web address:** http://www.awrey.com. **Description:** A producer of bread, pies, pastries, and other bakery products. **Corporate headquarters location:** This location. **Other U.S. locations:** Nationwide. **Number of employees nationwide:** 600.

BASF CORPORATION
1609 Biddle Avenue, Wyandotte MI 48192. 734/324-6000. **Contact:** Human Resources. **World Wide Web address:** http://www.basf.com. **Description:** BASF Corporation is an international chemical products organization doing business in five operating groups: Agricultural Chemicals; Chemicals; Colors and Auxiliaries; Pigments and Organic Specialties; and Polymers. **NOTE:** Entry-level positions are offered. Resumes must be submitted online. **Company slogan:** We don't make a lot of products you buy. We make a lot of the products you buy better. **Positions advertised include:** Senior Technical Service Representative. **Special programs:** Internships; Professional Development Program; Tuition Reimbursement Program. **Corporate headquarters location:** Mount Olive NJ. **Other U.S. locations:** Nationwide. **International locations:** Worldwide. **Operations at this facility include:** This location manufactures industrial inorganic chemicals. **Listed on:** New York Stock Exchange; also, major stock exchanges in Frankfurt, London, Paris, and Zurich. **Stock exchange symbol:** New York (BF); Frankfurt (BAS); London (BFA); Paris (BA); Zurich (BAS). **CEO/Chairman:** Klaus Peter Lobbe. **Annual sales/revenues:** $9 billion. **Number of employees at this location:** 800. **Number of employees nationwide:** 11,000. **Number of employees worldwide:** Over 93,000.

BAKER BOOK HOUSE
6030 East Fulton Street, Ada MI 49301. 616/676-9185. **Contact:** Human Resources Department. **E-mail address:** jobs@bakerbooks.com. **World Wide Web address:** http://www.bakerbooks.com. **Description:** A publisher of religious books. **Corporate headquarters location:** This location. **Parent company:** Baker Publishing Group.

BAKER COLLEGE
1903 Marquette Avenue, Muskegon MI 49442. 231/777-8800. **Contact:** Rosemary Zawacki, Vice President of Human Resources. **E-mail address:** humanresources@baker.edu. **World Wide Web address:** http://www.baker.edu. **Description:** A business college offering both graduate and undergraduate programs of study. **NOTE:** Baker College's Human Resources office is located at 1050 West Bristol Road, Flint MI 48507. Phone: 810/766-4028. Fax: 810/766-4279. **Positions advertised include:** Financial Aid Officer; Residence Life Director. **Other area locations:** Statewide. **President/CEO:** F. James Cummins.

BARRONCAST INC.
215 Plexus Drive, P.O. Box 138, Oxford MI 48371. 248/628-4300. **Fax:** 248/628-3810. **Contact:** Human Resources. **E-mail address:** mbarron@barroncast.com. **World Wide Web address:** http://www.barroncast.com. **Description:** Supplies ferrous investment castings to a variety of industries. **Positions advertised include:** Hourly Production Employee; Machine Shop Supervisor. **Corporate headquarters location:** This location. **Chairman:** Paul Barron. **Number of employees at this location:** 100.

BARTON MALOW COMPANY
26500 American Drive, Southfield MI 48034. 248/436-5000. **Fax:** 248/436-5001. **Contact:** Jose Herrera, Recruiting Manager. **E-mail address:** jose.herrera@bartonmalow.com. **World Wide Web address:** http://www.bmco.com. **Description:** A construction management, program management, and general contracting company engaged in the construction of health facilities and commercial and industrial buildings. **NOTE:** To contact Human Resources directly, call 248/436-5024. **Positions advertised include:** Director of Marketing. **Special programs:** Internships. **Corporate headquarters location:** This location. **Other area locations:** Detroit MI; Oak Park MI. **Other U.S. locations:** Columbus OH; Phoenix AZ; Chantilly VA; Charlottesville VA; Norcross GA; Linthicum MD. **Operations at this facility include:** Administration. **President:** Ben Maibach III. **Annual sales/revenues:** Over $1 billion. **Number of employees nationwide:** 1,550.

BATTLE CREEK HEALTH SYSTEM
300 North Avenue, Battle Creek MI 49016. 616/966-8060. **Fax:** 616/966-8366. **Contact:** Jill Cardenas, Human Resources. **E-mail address:** cardenaj@trinity-health.org. **World Wide Web address:** http://www.bchealth.com. **Description:** A multi-campus health care provider comprised of two hospitals, which offers a comprehensive range of services. **NOTE:** Resumes may be submitted online. **Positions advertised include:** CT Technologist; Outcomes Specialist; Radiation Therapist; Registered Nurse. **Special programs:** Internships. **Corporate headquarters location:** Farmington Hills MI. **Parent company:** Mercy Health Services and Community Hospital Association. **Operations at this facility include:** Service. **Number of employees at this location:** 1,800.

BECTON DICKINSON BIOSCIENCES
920 Henry Street, Detroit MI 48201. 313/442-8800. **Toll-free phone:** 800/638-8663. **Contact:** Human Resources Manager. **World Wide Web address:** http://www.bdbiosciences.com. **Description:** Engaged in the manufacture of microbiological products such as dehydrated culture media, diagnostic reagents, and capital equipment. **Special programs:** Scholarship Programs. **Corporate headquarters location:** Franklin Lakes NJ. **Other U.S. locations:** Nationwide. **International locations:** Worldwide. **Parent company:** Becton, Dickinson and Company. **Listed on:** New York Stock Exchange. **Stock exchange symbol:** BDX. **Number of employees at this location:** 300. **Number of employees worldwide:** Approximately 3,000.

BERRY MOORMAN P.C.
535 Griswold, Suite 1900, Detroit MI 48226-3679. 313/496-1200. **Fax:** 313/496-1300. **Contact:** Human Resources. **E-mail address:** susan@berrymoorman.com. **World Wide Web address:** http://www.berrymoorman.com. **Description:** A law firm specializing in corporate law, taxation, securities regulations, estate planning, and labor law. **Corporate headquarters location:** This location. **Other area locations:** Birmingham MI; Ann Arbor MI. **International locations:** St. Petersburg, Russia.

BIL MAR FOODS/SARA LEE CORPORATION
8300 96th Avenue, Zeeland MI 49464. 616/875-8131. **Fax:** 616/875-3328. **Contact:** Jodi Ciolek, Human Resources. **World Wide Web address:** http://www.saralee.com. **Description:** A meat processing company affiliated with Sara Lee Corporation, a manufacturer and marketer of branded packaged goods. **Corporate headquarters location:** Chicago IL. **Parent company:** Sara Lee. **Operations at this facility include:** Administration; Divisional Headquarters; Manufacturing; Regional Headquarters; Research and Development; Sales. **Listed on:** New York Stock Exchange. **Stock exchange symbol:** SLE. **Sales/revenue:** $17.6 billion. **Number of employees at this location:** 2,400. **Number of employees nationwide:** 3,100. **Number of employees worldwide:** 145,800.

BISSELL INC.
P.O. Box 1888, Grand Rapids MI 49501. 616/453-4451. **Physical address:** 2345 Walker Avenue, Grand Rapids MI 49544. **Fax:** 616/453-3485. **Contact:** Renee Griffen, Human Resources Representative. **E-mail address:** renee.griffen@bissell.com. **World Wide Web address:** http://www.bissell.com. **Description:** Manufactures vacuums, steam cleaners, sweepers, and related parts, accessories, and cleaning formulas. Founded in 1876. **Note:** Interested job seekers may apply online. **Positions advertised include:** Web Communications Specialist; Manufacturing Engineer. **Special programs:** Internships. **Corporate headquarters location:** This location. **Other U.S. locations:** Butler PA. **Subsidiaries include:** Bissell Graphics; Bissell Healthcare. **Operations at this facility include:** Administration; Manufacturing; Research and Development; Sales; Service. **Listed on:** Privately held. **Number of employees at this location:** 800. **Number of employees nationwide:** 2,700.

BIXBY MEDICAL CENTER
818 Riverside Avenue, Adrian MI 49221. 517/263-0711. **Recorded jobline:** 517/265-0920. **Contact:** Human Resources. **E-mail address:** hr@lhanet.org. **World Wide Web address:** http://www.promedica.org. **Description:** A 140-bed, acute care medical center. **NOTE:** To contact Human Resources directly, call 517/424-3464. **Positions advertised include:** Physical Therapist; Switchboard Operator; Registration Clerk. **Office hours:** Monday – Friday, 7:00 a.m. – 4:30 a.m. **Parent company:** ProMedica Health System.

BLISS CLEARING NIAGARA
1004 East State Street, Hastings MI 49058. 269/948-3300. **Fax:** 269/948-3310. **Contact:** Human Resource Manager. **E-mail address:** info@bcn-usa.com. **World Wide Web address:** http://www.bcn-usa.com. **Description:** Manufactures metal stamping presses. **Corporate headquarters location:** This location.

BLUE CROSS AND BLUE SHIELD OF MICHIGAN
600 East Lafayette Street, Detroit MI 48226. 313/225-9000. **Contact:** Human Resources. **World Wide Web address:** http://www.bcbsm.com. **Description:** A nonprofit health care insurance organization providing managed health care plans to both individuals and groups. Blue Cross and Blue Shield offers Point-of-Service, individual health, and HMO plans, as well as dental and vision insurance. **Positions advertised include:** Auditor; Customer Service Representative; Building and Industrial Engineer. **Office hours:** Monday – Friday, 8:30 a.m. – 4:30 p.m. **Corporate headquarters location:** This location. **Other area locations:** Statewide. **President/CEO:** Richard E. Whitmer.

BORDERS GROUP, INC.
100 Phoenix Drive, Ann Arbor MI 48108. 734/477-1100. **Contact:** Human Resources Department. **E-mail address:** jobsr1@bordersstores.com. **World Wide Web address:** http://www.bordersgroup.com. **Description:** One of the nation's largest retail bookselling chains. Borders Group also operates Waldenbooks. Founded in 1933. **NOTE:** Interested job seekers may apply online. **Positions advertised include:** Marketing Systems Specialist; Replenishment Manager; Category Manager, Multimedia; Senior Tax Specialist; Accounts Payable Representative; Copy Editor; Content Editor; Allocation Analyst; Café Buyer; Storage Administrator. **Corporate headquarters location:** This location. **Listed on:** New York Stock Exchange. **Stock exchange symbol:** BGP. **Annual sales/revenues:** $3.4 billion. **Number of employees worldwide:** Over 32,000.

BORGWARNER AUTOMOTIVE
11955 East Nine Mile Road, Warren MI 48089. 586/497-4000. **Contact:** Personnel. **World Wide Web address:** http://www.bwauto.com. **Description:** An automotive company specializing in powertrain components and business solutions. **Corporate headquarters location:** Chicago IL. **International locations:** Worldwide. **Operations at this facility include:** This location is the divisional headquarters and is engaged in the manufacture of automotive components including throttle bodies, fuel injections, and transmission solenoids. **Listed on:** New York Stock Exchange. **CEO/Chairman:** John F. Fiedler. **Annual sales/revenues:** $2.7 billion. **Stock exchange symbol:** BWA. **Number of employees nationwide:** 2,200. **Number of employees worldwide:** 14,300.

ROBERT BOSCH CORPORATION
38000 Hills Tech Drive, Farmington Hills MI 48331. 248/553-9000. **Contact:** Personnel. **World Wide Web address:** http://www.boschusa.com. **Description:** Robert Bosch Corporation operates in three groups: Automotive-Original Equipment, Industrial, and Sales-Automotive Aftermarket. The largest segment of the company's business is the Automotive Group, which supplies products such as antilock braking systems (ABS), airbag electronics, fuel injectors, and oxygen sensors. The Industrial Group consists of the Packaging Machinery Division (selling high-technology packaging equipment, primarily to the food processing and pharmaceutical industries); the Surftran Division (offering a range of deburring services, as well as manufacturing, selling, and servicing cleaning equipment); Weldun International, Inc. (manufactures flexible assembly systems and automation products and assembles machinery for the Packaging Machinery Division); and Robert Bosch Fluid Power Corporation (a subsidiary that designs, produces, and markets hydraulic pumps, valves, and power units, and sells a full line of pneumatic products). The Sales Group handles automotive aftermarket, mobile communications, and household goods. **NOTE:** Interested job seekers may apply online. **Positions advertised include:** Senior Applications Engineer; Calibration Engineer; Sales Account Manager; Hardware Engineer; Resident Quality Engineer. **Corporate headquarters location:** Broadview IL. **Other U.S. locations:** Nationwide. **Parent company:** Bosch Group (Stuttgart, Germany). **Operations at this facility include:** This location provides automotive sales, engineering, and administration as part of Robert Bosch Corporation's Automotive Group. **Annual sales/revenues:** $6.2 billion. **Number of employees at this location:** 1,000. **Number of employees nationwide:** Approximately 21,750.

ROBERT BOSCH PACKAGING
9890 Red Arrow Highway, Bridgman MI 49106. 616/466-4000. **Contact:** Sally Schweha, Manager of Human Resources Department. **World Wide Web address:** http://www.boschpackaging.com. **Description:** Manufactures products including a wide range of equipment used in the packaging of pharmaceuticals and drugs, foods and beverages, confectionery products, cosmetics and toiletries, and industrial and chemical products. **Other U.S. locations:** Minneapolis MN. **Parent company:** Bosch Group (Stuttgart, Germany) is a manufacturer of automotive components, household appliances, cine camera technology, medical technology, heating technology, and assembly line technology. **Number of employees at this location:** 200.

BRASSCRAFT MANUFACTURING COMPANY
39600 Orchard Hill Place, Novi MI 48375. 248/305-6001. **Fax:** 248/305-6011. **Contact:** Human Resources. **World Wide Web address:** http://www.brasscraft.com.

Description: Engaged in the manufacture of plumbing supplies including valves, drainage tubes, copper water inlet tubes, flexible appliance connectors, brass fittings, and accessories. **Corporate headquarters location:** This location. **Other U.S. locations:** CA; NC; TX. **Parent company:** Masco Corporation. **Operations at this facility include:** Administration. **Listed on:** New York Stock Exchange. **Stock exchange symbol:** MAS. **Number of employees nationwide:** 1,100.

BRENCAL CONTRACTORS INC.
6686 East McNichols Street, Detroit MI 48212. 313/365-4300. **Fax:** 313/365-4739. **Contact:** Anne Colo, Personnel Director. **Description:** A contracting company specializing in concrete and industrial construction. **Corporate headquarters location:** This location. **Number of employees at this location:** 200.

BRIGHTON ELECTRONIC SUPPLY COMPANY
2452 West Hill Road, Flint MI 48507. 810/234-2000. **Contact:** Human Resources. **Description:** A wholesale distributor of electrical apparatus and equipment including service panels. **Corporate headquarters location:** This location. **Operations at this facility include:** Administration; Sales. **Listed on:** Privately held. **Number of employees at this location:** 50.

BRONSON HEALTHCARE GROUP
BRONSON METHODIST HOSPITAL
601 John Street, Box G, Kalamazoo MI 49007. 269/341-7654. **Fax:** 269/341-7644. **Recorded jobline:** 269/341-6800. **Contact:** Human Resources. **World Wide Web address:** http://www.bronsonhealth.com. **Description:** Bronson Healthcare Group is a community-owned, nonprofit health care provider. The group operates Bronson Methodist Hospital, a 414-bed medical center that provides both inpatient and outpatient services. The hospital specializes in trauma, burn care, women's and children's health, prenatal care, and pediatrics. Comprehensive care is also offered in a number of areas including cardiology, critical care, neurosciences, home health care, and rehabilitation. **NOTE:** Entry-level positions and second and third shifts are offered. Interested job seekers may apply online. **Positions advertised include:** Clinical Dietician; Ultrasound Technician; CT Technologist; Licensed Practical Nurse; Medical Assistant; MRI Technologist; Occupational Therapist; Occupational Therapy Assistant; Paramedic; Pharmacist; Physical Therapist; Radiologic Technologist; Registered Nurse. **Special programs:** Internships. **Office hours:** Monday - Friday, 8:30 a.m. - 3:30 p.m. **Corporate headquarters location:** This location. **Subsidiaries include:** Bronson Health Foundation; Bronson Home Health Care; Bronson Medical Group; Bronson Outpatient Surgery; Bronson Vicksburg Hospital; IBA Health and Life Assurance Company; Physicians Health Plan of Southwest Michigan. **Number of employees at this location:** 2,750.

BRUNSWICK INDOOR RECREATION GROUP
525 West Laketon Avenue, Muskegon MI 49441. 231/725-3300. **Contact:** Human Resources. **World Wide Web address:** http://www.brunswickbowling.com. **Description:** Brunswick Indoor Recreation Group manufactures assorted sporting equipment, with a special emphasis on bowling facilities and supplies. **Corporate headquarters location:** Lake Forest IL. **Other area locations:** Statewide. **Operations at this facility include:** This location manufactures bowling balls.

THE BUDD COMPANY
12141 Charlevoix Avenue, Detroit MI 48215. 313/823-9100. **Contact:** Human Resources. **World Wide Web address:** http://www.buddcompany.com. **Description:** An automotive supplier specializing in body stampings. **Office hours:** Monday – Friday, 7:30 a.m. – 4:00 p.m. **Corporate headquarters location:** Troy MI. **Parent company:** ThyssenKrupp Budd.

BUTZEL LONG
150 West Jefferson Avenue, Suite 100, Detroit MI 48226. 313/225-7000. **Contact:** Diane Maguire, Human Resources Director. **E-mail address:** maguire@butzel.com. **World Wide Web address:** http://www.butzel.com. **Description:** A law firm specializing in corporate law. **NOTE:** Interested job seekers may apply online. Candidates interested in attorney positions should contact Christine Scurto, Recruiting Coordinator. E-mail address: scurto@butzel.com. **Positions advertised include:** Legal Records Clerk; Research and Intranet Librarian; Library Clerk. **Special programs:** Summer Associate Program. **Corporate headquarters location:** This location. **Other area locations:** Holland MI; Lansing MI; Bloomfield Hills MI; Ann Arbor MI. **Other U.S. locations:** FL. **CEO/Chairman:** Richard E. Rassel.

CMS ENERGY CORPORATION
One Energy Plaza, Jackson MI 49201. 517/788-0550. **Fax:** 517/768-3366. **Contact:** Human Resources Director. **E-mail address:** oliverrecruiter@cmsenergy.com. **World Wide Web address:** http://www.cmsenergy.com. **Description:** An electric and gas utility holding company conducts its business through five segments: Gas Transmission, Independent Power Production, Liquefied Natural Gas Services, Electric Utility, and Gas Utility. **NOTE:** Entry-level positions are offered. CMS strongly encourages candidates to apply online. **Positions advertised include:** Accountant; International Accounting Manager; IT Analyst; Oracle Support Analyst. **Corporate headquarters location:** This location. **Subsidiaries include:** Consumers Energy Company; CMS Enterprises. **Listed on:** New York Stock Exchange. **Stock exchange symbol:** CMP. **CEO/Chairman:** Kenneth Whipple.

CTG (COMPUTER TASK GROUP)
2851 Charlevoix Drive, Suite 203, Grand Rapids MI 49546. 616/956-0131. **Fax:** 616/956-0048. **Contact:** Human Resources. **World Wide Web address:** http://www.ctg.com. **Description:** A computer consulting firm that performs programming and networking services for corporate clients. **NOTE:** Submit resumes online. **Corporate headquarters location:** Buffalo NY. **Other U.S. locations:** Nationwide. **International locations:** United Kingdom; the Netherlands; Germany; Canada; Belgium. **Listed on:** New York Stock Exchange. **Stock exchange symbol:** CTG. **CEO/Chairman:** James R. Boldt. **Number of employees worldwide:** 2,800.

CADILLAC PRODUCTS INC.
5800 Crooks Road, Troy MI 48098. 248/879-5000. **Contact:** Human Resources. **E-mail address:** cipchr@cadprod.com. **World Wide Web address:** http://www.cadprod.com. **Description:** Cadillac Products Company is organized into three business units: Automotive Products, Film and Flexible Packaging, and Thermoformed Products, which are composed of plastic materials and supplied for industrial use. **Special programs:** Internships. **Corporate headquarters location:** This location. **Other area locations:** Rogers City MI. **Other U.S. locations:** Dallas GA; Paris IL. **Operations at this facility include:** Administration; Divisional Headquarters; Research and Development; Sales. **Listed on:** Privately held. **Number of employees at this location:** 100. **Number of employees nationwide:** 1,000.

CAMPBELL-EWALD COMPANY
30400 Van Dyke Avenue, Warren MI 48093. 586/574-3400. **Contact:** Human Resources. **World Wide Web address:** http://www.campbell-ewald.com. **Description:** An advertising agency. **NOTE:** Interested job seekers may submit resumes online. **Positions advertised include:** Senior Media Planner; Senior Account Executive; Junior Database Analyst; New Business Administrator; Copywriter; Attorney; Production Artist; Account Supervisor; Recruiter. **Special programs:** Internships. **Corporate headquarters location:** This location. **Other area locations:** Southfield MI. **Other U.S. locations:** Los Angeles CA; New York NY. **International locations:** Frankfurt, Germany. **Parent company:** The Interpublic Group of Companies, Incorporated. **Listed on:** New York Stock Exchange. **Stock exchange symbol:** IPG. **Number of employees at this location:** 800.

CARBOLOY, INC.
11177 East Eight Mile Road, Warren MI 48089. 586/497-5000. **Fax:** 586/497-5318. **Contact:** Human Resources. **E-mail address:** jwilson@carboloy.com. **World Wide Web address:** http://www.carboloy.com. **Description:** Engaged in the manufacture of carbide cutting tools. Founded in 1928. **Positions advertised include:** Technical Specialist. **Corporate headquarters location:** This location. **Other U.S. locations:** Nationwide. **International locations:** Canada; Mexico; Sweden. **Operations at this facility include:** Administration; Manufacturing; Sales; Service. **Number of employees at this location:** 500.

CARHARTT INC.
5750 Mercury Drive, P.O. Box 600, Dearborn MI 48126. 313/271-8460. **Toll-free phone:** 800/833-3118. **Fax:** 313/749-6441. **Contact:** Human Resources. **E-mail address:** careers@carhartt.com. **World Wide Web address:** http://www.carhartt.com. **Description:** Manufactures casual and work clothing for men, women, and children. **NOTE:** Candidates can search and apply for positions online. Resumes are also accepted by e-mail, fax, or mail. **Positions advertised include:** International Business Coordinator; Retail Merchandiser. **Corporate headquarters location:** This location. **Listed on:** Privately held. **President/CEO:** Mark Valade.

CENTER FOR CREATIVE STUDIES
COLLEGE OF ART AND DESIGN
201 East Kirby Street, Detroit MI 48202. 313/872-3118. **Fax:** 313/872-7505. **Contact:** Human Resources. **E-mail address:** hr@ccscad.edu. **World Wide Web address:** http://www.ccscad.edu. **Description:** A four-year college specializing in professional arts programs. **Positions advertised include:** Chairperson, Interior Design; Professor, Graphic Design/Interactive Design ; Professor, Transportation Design; Adjunct Professors, Various Disciplines; Director, Marketing and Communications. **President:** Rick Rogers.

CENTRAL MICHIGAN UNIVERSITY
109 Rowe Hall, Mount Pleasant MI 48859. 989/774-3753. **Fax:** 989/774-3256. **Recorded jobline:** 989/774-7195. **Contact:** Human Resources. **E-mail address:** http://www.cmu.jobs@cmich.edu. **World Wide Web address:** http://www.cmich.edu. **Description:** A four-year university with an enrollment of approximately 28,000 undergraduate and graduate students. **NOTE:** As of 2003, the recorded job hotline is for service and maintenance positions only. Consult website for professional and administrative listings. **Positions advertised include:** Assistant Professor, Broadcast and Cinematic Arts; Adjunct Professor, Business; Assistant Professor, Community Health/Health Administration; Assistant Football Coach; Head Women's Volleyball Coach; Academic Advisor; Assistant Manager, Bookstore; Communications Coordinator; Graphic Designer; Residence Hall Director; Writer/Editor; Radio Producer. **President:** Michael Rao.

CENTRAL TRANSPORT INTERNATIONAL
1225 Stephens Road, Warren MI 48089. 586/939-7000. **Toll-free phone:** 800/334-4883. **Contact:** Personnel Director. **E-mail address:** careers@centraltransportint.com. **World Wide Web address:** http://www.centraltransportint.com. **Description:** A trucking company serving the United States, Canada, and Mexico. **Positions advertised include:** Accountant; Telemarketer; Administrative Assistant; Billing Specialist; Accountant; Operations Coordinator; Sales Account Executive; National Sales Representative. **Special programs:** Tuition Assistance Program. **Corporate headquarters location:** This location. **Other U.S. locations:** Nationwide. **International locations:** Canada; Mexico. **Number of employees at this location:** 700. **Number of employees worldwide:** 4,000.

CHAMPS SPORTS
Southland Mall, 23000 Eureka Road, Space 102, Taylor MI 48180. 734/287-9092. **Contact:** Store Manager. **World Wide Web address:** http://www.champssports.com. **Description:** A specialty/sporting goods retailer. Products include hardgoods, apparel, footwear, and accessories. **Corporate headquarters location:** Bradenton FL. **Other U.S. locations:** Nationwide. **International locations:** Canada; Puerto Rico. **Parent company:** Foot Locker, Incorporated Group.

CHILDREN'S HOSPITAL OF MICHIGAN
3901 Beaubien Street, Detroit MI 48201. 313/5778-3930. **Contact:** Human Resources. **World Wide Web address:** http://www.chmkids.org/chm. **Description:** One of the nation's largest pediatric hospitals. Founded in 1886. **NOTE:** Interested job seekers may apply online. **Positions advertised include:** Staff Nurse; Patient Services Clerk; Student Nurse Associate; Pediatrics Administrative Coordinator; Pharmacy Technician; Patient Management Clerical Associate; Dietary Aide; Surgical Technician; Coordinator, Pastoral Education; Care Management Specialist; Surgical Technician; Radiologic Technologist; Registration/Insurance Assistant; Respiratory Therapist; MRI Technologist; Speech Language Pathologist; Imaging Research Assistant; Coordinator, Child Life Services. **Office hours:** Monday – Friday, 8:00 a.m. – 4:30 p.m. **Parent company:** The Detroit Medical Center. **Number of employees at this location:** Approximately 1,900.

CHIVAS INDUSTRIES
42555 Merrill Road, Sterling Heights MI 48314. 586/254-3535. **Contact:** Mary Iannucci, Corporate Personnel Director. **Description:** Manufactures interior automotive products including lighting systems, instrument panel components, floor consoles, and overhead system components. **Corporate headquarters location:** This location. **Operations at this facility include:** Administration; Manufacturing; Research and Development; Sales. **Listed on:** Privately held. **Number of employees at this location:** 450.

CIBER, INC.
30 Oak Hollow, Suite 340, Southfield MI 48034. 248/352-8650. **Fax:** 248/352-3010. **Contact:** Human Resources. **E-mail address:** jobs@ciber.com. **World Wide Web address:** http://www.ciber.com. **Description:** Provides consulting for client/server development, mainframe and legacy systems, industry-specific analysis, application-specific analysis, and network development. Founded in 1974. **Corporate headquarters location:** Englewood CO. **Other U.S. locations:** Nationwide. **International locations:** Canada; the Netherlands. **Listed on:** New York Stock Exchange. **Stock exchange symbol:** CBR. **President/CEO:** Mac J. Slingerlend. **Annual sales/revenues:** $692 million. **Number of employees worldwide:** 5,750.

CITATION CORPORATION
3559 Kraft Avenue, Grand Rapids MI 49512. 616/949-2002. **Contact:** Human Resources. **World Wide Web address:** http://www.citationcorp.com. **Description:** Operates precision machining, manufacturing, and die-casting facilities serving the automotive, appliance, and furniture industries. **Positions advertised include:** Engineering Manager; Process Engineer; Quality Engineer. **Corporate headquarters location:** Birmingham AL. **Other U.S. locations:** CA; TX; TN; NC; IL; IN; WI. **Operations at this facility include:** This location is comprised of a machining facility, a casting plant, and a warehouse. **Listed on:** Privately held. **President/CEO:** Ed Buker. **Number of employees at this location:** 475.

CITIZENS BANKING CORPORATION
CITIZENS BANK
328 South Saginaw Street, Flint MI 48502. 810/766-7500. **Toll-free phone:** 800/806-1692. **Contact:** Human Resources. **E-mail address:** hr@cbcf-net.com. **World Wide Web address:** http://www.cbclientsfirst.com. **Description:** Citizens Banking Corporation is the holding company for Citizens Bank (also at this location), a full-service banking institution. **NOTE:** Online applications are available. **Positions advertised include:** Personal Banker; Business Loan Servicer; Project Analyst; Consumer Credit Operations Manager; Loan Review Officer; Audit Manager; Portfolio Manager. **Corporate headquarters location:** This location. **Subsidiaries include:** Citizen Bank – Illinois; F&M Bank. **Listed on:** NASDAQ. **Stock exchange symbol:** CBCF. **President/CEO:** William R. Hartman.

COCA-COLA BOTTLING COMPANY OF MICHIGAN
100 Coca-Cola Drive, Belleville MI 48111. 734/397-2700. **Recorded jobline:** 734/397-3995. **Fax:** 734/397-3454. **Contact:** Human Resources. **E-mail address:** michhreast@na.cokecce.com. **World Wide Web address:** http://www.cokecce.com/careers. **Description:** A bottling company for Coca-Cola, Barq's, and Dr. Pepper. **NOTE:** Resumes may e-mail, fax, or mail. Resumes submitted via e-mail must be in text format. Attachments will not be opened. Please indicate job requisition number and title when applying. **Positions advertised include:** Rebate Analyst. **Corporate headquarters location:** Charlotte NC. **Other U.S. locations:** Nationwide. **Operations at this facility include:** Division Headquarters. **Listed on:** NASDAQ. **Stock exchange symbol:** COKE. **Number of employees at this location:** 800. **Number of employees nationwide:** 6,200.

COLDWELL BANKER
SCHWEITZER REAL ESTATE
901 Tower Drive, Suite 150, Troy MI 48098. 248/879-3400. **Contact:** Ronald Moore, Sales Manager. **E-mail address:** career@cbschweitzer.com. **World Wide Web address:** http://www.cbschweitzer.com. **Description:** A real estate firm specializing in residential properties. **Special programs:** Training. **Corporate headquarters location:** Parsippany NJ. **President:** Paul Schweitzer. **Number of employees at this location:** 400. **Number of employees nationwide:** Over 600.

COMCAST
7200 West Saginaw, Suite 3, Lansing MI 48917. 517/703-0791. **Contact:** Human Resources. **World Wide Web address:** http://www.comcast.com. **Description:** One of the nation's largest cable television and broadband services companies. **NOTE:** Search and apply for positions online. **Positions advertised include:** Business Account Executive. **Corporate headquarters location:** Philadelphia PA. **Other U.S. locations:** Nationwide. **Parent company:** Comcast. **Listed on:** NASDAQ. **Stock exchange symbol:** CMCSA.

COMERICA INC.
Comerica Tower at Detroit Center, 500 Woodward Avenue, Detroit MI 48226. 248/371-5000. **Toll-free phone:** 800/521-1190. **Contact:** Staffing Department. **World Wide Web address:** http://www.comerica.com. **Description:** A bank holding company whose primary businesses include individual banking, which consists of consumer banking and lending, mortgage banking, small business banking, and private banking; investment banking, which offers investment services; and business banking, which provides corporate, global, and asset-based banking. Comerica Incorporated operates a network of 350 branch offices and 770 ATMs, supermarket branches, and PC and telephone banking services. Founded in 1849. **NOTE:** Entry-level positions and part-time jobs are offered. **Positions advertised include:** Associate Marketing Manager; Business Development Officer; Corporate Investment Banker; Senior Human Resources Consultant/Generalist; System Support Analyst; Treasury Analyst. **Special programs:** Internships; Summer Jobs. **Corporate headquarters location:** This location. **Other U.S. locations:** CA; CO; FL; IL; IN; NY; TN; TX. **International locations:** Canada; Mexico. **Subsidiaries include:** Comerica Community Development Corporation; Comerica Corporate Banking; Comerica Investment Services, Inc. **Listed on:** New York Stock Exchange. **Stock exchange symbol:** CMA. **Number of employees nationwide:** 11,800.

COMPUNETICS
3863 Rochester Road, Troy MI 48083. 248/524-6376. **Fax:** 248/524-6374. **Contact:** Human Resources. **World Wide Web address:** http://www.compuneticsinc.com. **Description:** A manufacturer of surface-mounted circuits used in the prototype circuit boards contained in the electronics systems of Ford automobiles. **Corporate headquarters location:** This location.

COMPUTER DECISIONS INTERNATIONAL INC.
23933 Research Drive, Farmington Hills MI 48355. 248/347-4600. **Fax:** 248/347-1567. **Contact:** Human Resources. **World Wide Web address:** http://www.cdi-usa.com. **Description:** A computer hardware and software reseller. Founded in 1981. **Office hours:** Monday - Friday, 8:00 a.m. - 5:30 p.m. **Corporate headquarters location:** This location.

COMPUTER METHODS CORPORATION
13740 Merriman Road, Livonia MI 48150. 734/522-5187. **Fax:** 734/522-2705. **Contact:** Jennifer Llanto, Recruiter. **E-mail address:** jllanto@cmethods.com. **World Wide Web address:** http://www.cmethods.com. **Description:** Develops software and provides computer consulting services. Computer Methods Corporation's staff includes software engineers with knowledge of C, C++, and other programming languages; business consultants with skills in COBOL and client/server environments; and individuals with Microsoft certification. **NOTE:** Interested job seekers may submit resumes online. **Special programs:** Healthcare Reimbursement Program; Tuition Assistance Program. **Corporate headquarters location:** This location.

COMPUWARE CORPORATION
One Campus Martius, Detroit MI 48226. 313/227-7300. **Toll-free phone:** 800/521-9353. **Fax:** 877/873-6784. **Contact:** Corporate Recruiting. **E-mail address:** compuware.recruiting@compuware.com. **World Wide Web address:** http://www.compuware.com. **Description:** Develops, markets, and supports an integrated line of systems software products that improve the productivity of programmers and analysts in application program testing, test data preparation, error analysis, and maintenance. Compuware also provides a broad range of professional data processing services including business systems analysis, design, and programming, and systems planning and consulting. **Positions advertised include:** Software Developer; Product Consultant; Services Account Manager; Customer Support Analyst; System Administrator; Global Channel Manager; Director of Marketing. **Special programs:** Training; Continued Career Development Program. **Corporate headquarters location:** This location. **Other U.S. locations:** Nationwide. **International locations:** Worldwide. **Listed on:** NASDAQ. **Stock exchange symbol:** CPWR. **CEO:** Peter Karmanos Jr. **Number of employees worldwide:** Approximately 10,000.

CONLEE OIL COMPANY
815 South Mill Street, Clio MI 48420. 810/686-5600. **Contact:** Jeff Conlee, Personnel Director. **Description:** Conlee Oil Company operates a chain of gasoline service stations and convenience stores. **Corporate headquarters location:** This location. **Operations at this facility include:** This location houses administrative offices. **Number of employees at this location:** 100.

CONSUMERS ENERGY COMPANY
212 West Michigan Avenue, Jackson MI 49201. 517/788-1351. **Fax:** 517/768-3366. **Contact:** Staffing. **World Wide Web address:** http://www.consumersenergy.com. **Description:** A gas and electric utility company. **NOTE:** Interested candidates can search and apply for a position online. Resumes are also accepted by mail or fax and should be addressed to the corporate headquarters office: Consumers Energy Company, Attention: Staffing, One Energy Plaza, Jackson MI 49201. **Parent company:** CMS Energy Corporation. **Listed on:** New York Stock Exchange. **Stock exchange symbol:** CMS. **President/CEO:** John G. Russel. **Annual sales/revenues:** $4 billion. **Number of employees nationwide:** 9,000.

CONTINENTAL PAPER AND SUPPLY
6400 East Eight Mile Road, Detroit MI 48234. 313/892-7600. **Fax:** 313/892-7618. **Contact:** Dave Marshall, Controller. **World Wide Web address:** http://www.hpproducts.com. **Description:** Engaged in the wholesale trade of industrial and personal service paper products. **Corporate headquarters location:** Indianapolis IN. **Parent company:** HP Products. **Number of employees at this location:** 100.

COOPER-STANDARD AUTOMOTIVE
THE STANDARD PRODUCTS COMPANY
P.O. Box 8034, Novi MI 48376. **Physical address:** 39550 Orchard Hill Place Drive, Novi MI 48375. 248/596-5900. **Contact:** Anne Marie Hooey, Human Resources Department. **E-mail address:** recruiter@cooperstandard.com. **World Wide Web address:** http://www.cooperstandard.com. **Description:** Manufactures sealing, trimming, and vibration control systems for the automotive original equipment industry. **NOTE:** Entry-level positions and part-time jobs are offered. **Special programs:** Internships; Co-ops; Summer Jobs. **Corporate headquarters location:** This location. **Other U.S. locations:** Nationwide. **International locations:** Worldwide. **Subsidiaries include:** Helen Industries; Oliver Rubber. **Parent company:** Cooper Tire and Rubber Company. **Operations at this facility include:** Administration; Research and Development; Sales. **Listed on:** New York Stock Exchange. **Stock exchange symbol:** CTB. **President:** James S. McElya. **Sales/revenue:** $1.6 billion. **Number of employees at this location:** 400. **Number of employees nationwide:** 10,000.

CORE TECHNOLOGY CORPORATION
7435 Westshire Drive, Lansing MI 48917. 517/627-1521. **Fax:** 517/627-8944. **Contact:** Human Resources. **E-mail address:** jobs@ctc-core.com. **World Wide Web address:** http://www.ctc-core.com. **Description:** Provides connectivity solutions for companies in a variety of markets. **Positions advertised include:** Sales Representative; Software Developer; Software Support Representative; Marketing Representative. **Corporate headquarters location:** This location. **President/CTO:** David A. Hadsall.

COUNTRY FRESH
609 Chavez Drive, Flint MI 48503. 810/232-9193. **Contact:** Personnel. **World Wide Web address:** http://www.deanfoods.com. **Description:** Produces milk and other dairy products. **Parent company:** Dean Foods company operates in five business divisions: Dairy Group, Morningstar Foods, White Wave Specialty Foods, and International. **Listed on:** New York Stock Exchange. **Stock exchange symbol:** DF. **Number of employees at this location:** 200.

COVANSYS
32605 West 12 Mile Road, Suite 250, Farmington Hills MI 48334. 248/488-2088. **Toll-free phone:** 800/688-2088. **Contact:** Faye Silva, Personnel Department. **E-mail address:** fsilva@covansys.com. **World Wide Web address:** http://www.cbsinc.com. **Description:** An international systems integration consulting firm specializing in strategic systems development, systems integration, software application development, projects, contracts, and business process/system re-engineering. **NOTE:** Interested job seekers may apply online. **Corporate headquarters location:** This location. **Other area locations:** Okemos MI. **Other U.S. locations:** Nationwide. **International locations:** Worldwide. **Listed on:** NASDAQ. **Stock exchange symbol:** CVNS. **President/CEO:** Martin C. Clague. **Number of employees worldwide:** 4,700.

COVENANT MEDICAL CENTER
1447 North Harrison Street, Saginaw MI 48602. 989/583-4080. **Fax:** 989/583-4816. **Contact:** Human Resources. **World Wide Web address:** http://www.covenanthealthcare.com. **Description:** A 700-bed hospital that offers comprehensive inpatient and outpatient care. **Positions advertised include:** Food Service Worker; HIM Transcriptionist; Clerical Medical Assistant; Clinical Documentation Specialist; Mammographer; Nuclear Medicine Technologist; Office Support Associate; Occupational Therapist; Patient Placement Specialist; Pharmacist; Nursing Care Assistant; Radiographer; Registered Nurse. **Corporate headquarters location:** This location. **Parent company:** Covenant Healthcare. **Number of employees at this location:** 4,000.

CRAIN COMMUNICATIONS INC.
1155 Gratiot Avenue, Detroit MI 48207-2997. 313/446-6000. **Fax:** 313/259-8454. **Contact:** Human Resources Department. **E-mail address:** detroit_jobs@crain.com. **World Wide Web address:** http://www.crain.com. **Description:** A publishing company that produces business, trade, and consumer newspapers and magazines. **Positions advertised include:** Reporter; Administrative Assistant. **Special programs:** Internships. **Corporate headquarters location:** This location. **Other U.S. locations:** Chicago IL; New York NY; Akron OH; Cleveland OH; Boston MA; Washington DC; San Francisco CA; Los Angeles CA; Costa Mesa CA; Nashville TN; Denver CO; Florida Keys FL. **International locations:** Mexico; England; Germany; Japan. **Operations at this facility include:** This location houses the company's administrative offices, and also functions as the headquarters for the publications *Automotive News*, *Autoweek*, *Crain's Detroit Business*, and *Crain Custom Publishing*. **President:** Rance E. Crain.

CRANKSHAFT MACHINE COMPANY
314 North Jackson Street, P.O. Box 1127, Jackson MI 49201. 517/787-3791. **Fax:** 517/787-7677. **Contact:** Plant Manager. **E-mail address:** info@crankshaft.net. **World Wide Web address:** http://www.crankshaft.net. **Description:** Designs and manufactures industrial machines that are used to make crankshafts, camshafts, and other related products. **Parent company:** Crankshaft Machine Group (also at this location) is composed of Swisher Finishing Systems, U.S. Broach Company, Lindberg Hydraulic Systems, and Crankshaft Machine Company. **Number of employees at this location:** 100.

CREATIVE FOAM CORPORATION
300 North Alloy Drive, Fenton MI 48430. 810/629-4149. **Fax:** 810/750-7613. **Contact:** Human Resources. **E-mail address:** hr@creativefoam.com. **World Wide Web address:** http://www.creativefoam.com. **Description:** A fabricator and manufacturer of OEM foam products and foam packaging for a wide range of applications. Founded in 1969. **Corporate headquarters location:** This location. **Other U.S. locations:** IN. **Operations at this facility include:** Administration; Manufacturing; Research and Development; Sales. **Chairman:** Peter T. Swallow. **Annual sales/revenues:** Approximately $84 million. **Number of employees nationwide:** Over 600.

CREATIVE SOLUTIONS
7322 Newman Boulevard, Dexter MI 48130. 734/426-5860. **Contact:** Human Resources Department. **E-mail address:** recruiting@creativesolutions.com. **World Wide Web address:** http://www.creativesolutions.com. **Description:** Develops, markets, and supports accounting and tax software. **NOTE:** Interested job seekers may submit resumes online. **Positions advertised include:** Project Support Representative; Account Representative; Associate Account Representative; Tax Development Analyst. **Special programs:** Internships; Co-ops. **Corporate headquarters location:** This location.

CROTTY CORPORATION
854 East Chicago Road, P.O. Box 37, Quincy MI 49082. 517/639-8787. **Fax:** 517/639-4309. **Contact:** Human Resources. **World Wide Web address:** http://www.crottycorp.com. **Description:** Manufactures automotive parts, including gaskets and sun visors, for clients such as General Motors, DaimlerChrysler, Subaru, Isuzu, and Saturn. Founded in 1946. **Corporate headquarters location:** This location. **Other U.S. locations:** Celina TN; Gainesboro TN. **Operations at this facility include:** This location houses the administrative offices, the engineering department, and the Michigan Manufacturing Divisions. **President:** Keith Boyle.

THE CROWN GROUP, INC.
2111 Walter Reuther Drive, Warren MI 48091. 586/575-9800. **Contact:** Personnel. **Description:** An automotive manufacturing company specializing in electroplating. **Corporate headquarters location:** This location.

CUNNINGHAM-LIMP COMPANY
39300 West 12 Mile Road, Suite 200, Farmington Hills MI 48331. 248/489-2300. **Fax:** 248/489-1247. **Contact:** Personnel. **E-mail address:** info@cunninghamlimp.com. **World Wide Web address:** http://www.cunninghamlimp.com. **Description:** An engineering, architectural, and surveying services company. **Corporate headquarters location:** This location.

CYBERNET SYSTEMS CORPORATION
727 Airport Boulevard, Ann Arbor MI 48108. 734/668-2567. **Fax:** 734/668-8780. **Contact:** Human Resources. **E-mail address:** jobs@cybernet.com. **World Wide Web address:** http://www.cybernet.com. **Description:** A technology research and development company that specializes in virtual reality, force feedback, robotics, human/computer interactions, electromechanical systems, computer vision, and real-time systems. Cybernet Systems Corporation also provides integrated network client/server services. Founded in 1988. **Positions advertised include:** Mathematician and Computer Programmer Research Engineer; Aerospace Engineer; Electrical Engineer; Computer Scientist. **Office hours:** Monday – Friday, 9:00 a.m. – 5:00 p.m. **Corporate headquarters location:** This location.

D.A. STUART COMPANY
9100 Freeland Avenue, Detroit MI 48228. 313/273-7374. **Contact:** Human Resources. **World Wide Web address:** http://www.d-a-stuart.com. **Description:** Engaged in the manufacture and distribution of lubricating oil and grease products. **Corporate headquarters location:** Warrenville IL. **Other U.S. locations:** Batavia NY; Philadelphia PA; Los Angeles CA. **International locations:** Worldwide. **Number of employees nationwide:** 100.

DLZ CORPORATION
1425 Keystone Avenue, Lansing MI 48911. 517/393-6800. **Fax:** 517/272-7390. **Contact:** Human Resources. **E-mail address:** hrdept@dlzcorp.com. **World Wide Web address:** http://www.dlzcorp.com. **Description:** A professional consulting firm providing complete architectural, engineering, and environmental services to public and private sector clients. **NOTE:** Interested candidates can apply online, via e-mail (must be in ASCII text format), or by sending a resume to: DLZ Corporation, Attention: Human Resources, Job Code: #, 6121 Huntley Road, Columbus OH 43229-1003. Indicate the job code number on cover letter and on the outside of the mailing envelope. **Positions advertised include:** Civil Engineer; Entry Level Biologist; Highway Project Manager; Landscape Architect; Registered Surveyor; Survey Crew Chief; Transportation Planner/NEPA Specialist; Wastewater Engineer. **Corporate headquarters location:** Columbus OH. **Other area locations:** Detroit MI; Gaylord MI; Niles MI. **Other U.S. locations:** IN; IL; MA; WV. **Number of employees nationwide:** Over 700.

D-M-E COMPANY
P.O. Box 64155, Detroit MI 48264-0155. 248/398-6000. **Physical address:** 29111 Stephenson Highway, Madison Heights MI 48071. **Toll-free phone:** 800/626-6653. **Fax:** 888/808-4363. **Contact:** Human Resources. **E-mail address:** human_resources@dme.net. **World Wide Web address:** http://www.dme.net. **Description:** Manufactures and supplies tooling and electronic control systems for the plastics injection molding industry. **Corporate headquarters location:** This location. **International locations:** Worldwide. **Number of employees nationwide:** 1,000.

DOC OPTICS CORPORATION
19800 West Eight Mile Road, Southfield MI 48075. 248/354-7100. **Contact:** Personnel Director. **World Wide Web address:** http://www.docoptics.com. **Description:** Manufactures prescription glasses and contacts. DOC Optics operates over 100 retail locations in six states offering eye care products and laser eye surgery. Founded in 1946. **Special programs:** Training. **Positions advertised include:** Retail Manager; Assistant Retail Manager; Lab Manager; Assistant Lab Manager; Optician; Service Coordinator; Optometric Technician. **Corporate headquarters location:** This location. **Other area locations:** Statewide. **Other U.S. locations:** FL; MO; OH; WI; IL. **Number of employees at this location:** 800.

DTE ENERGY
2000 Second Avenue, Detroit MI 48226. 313/235-8000. **Contact:** Human Resources. **World Wide Web address:** http://www.dteenergy.com. **Description:** Offers energy products and services including light fixtures and environmental analysis. **Corporate headquarters location:** This location. **Subsidiaries include:** Detroit Edison; MichCon; Plug Power; Midwest Energy Sources. **Listed on:** New York Stock Exchange. **Stock exchange symbol:** DTE. **President/CEO/Chairman:** Anthony F. Earley, Junior. **Annual sales/revenues:** $6.7 billion. **Number of employees nationwide:** Over 11,000.

DAIMLERCHRYSLER CORPORATION
CIMS 485-01-99, 1000 Chrysler Drive, Auburn Hills MI 48326. 248/576-5741. **Recorded jobline:** 248/512-2187. **Contact:** Employment Operations. **E-mail address:** resume@daimlerchrysler.com. **World Wide Web address:** http://www.daimlerchrysler.com. **Description:** Manufactures cars, trucks, minivans, and sport-utility vehicles for customers in more than 100 countries. **Special programs:** Internships. **Corporate headquarters location:** This location. **Other U.S. locations:** Nationwide. **International locations:** Worldwide. **Listed on:** New York Stock Exchange. **Stock exchange symbol:** DAJ. **Annual sales/revenues:** $171.9 billion. **Number of employees worldwide:** 362,100.

DAIMLERCHRYSLER CORPORATION
38111 Van Dyke Avenue, Sterling Heights MI 48312. 586/978-6032. **Contact:** Human Resources. **World Wide Web address:** http://www.daimlerchrysler.com. **Description:** DaimlerChrysler produces cars, trucks, minivans, and sport-utility vehicles for customers in more than 100 countries. **NOTE:** All hiring for this plant is done through the Auburn Hills office. Please send resumes to: CIMS 485-01-99, 1000 Chrysler Drive, Auburn Hills MI 48326. **Special programs:** Internships. **Corporate headquarters location:** Auburn Hills MI. **Other U.S. locations:** Nationwide. **International locations:** Worldwide. **Operations at this facility include:** This location assembles Chrysler automobiles. **Listed on:** New York Stock Exchange. **Stock exchange symbol:** DAJ. **Sales/revenue:** $171.9 billion. **Number of employees worldwide:** 362,100.

DAIMLERCHRYSLER CORPORATION
800 Chrysler Drive, Auburn Hills MI 48326. 248/576-5741. **Contact:** Human Resources. **World Wide Web address:** http://www.daimlerchrysler.com. **Description:** Provides automotive and dealer leasing and other related financial services. **Special programs:** Internships. **Corporate headquarters location:** This location. **Other U.S. locations:** Nationwide. **International locations:** Worldwide. **Listed on:** New York Stock Exchange. **Stock exchange symbol:** DAJ. **Sales/revenue:** $171.9 billion. **Number of employees worldwide:** 362,100.

DAIRY FRESH FOODS INC.
21405 Trolley Industrial Drive, Taylor MI 48180. 313/295-6300. **Contact:** Operations Manager. **Description:** A wholesale distributor of dairy and deli products. **Special programs:** Training. **Corporate headquarters location:** This location. **Listed on:** Privately held. **Number of employees at this location:** 200.

DANA CORPORATION
916 West State Street, St. Johns MI 48879. 989/224-2384. **Contact:** Human Resources. **World Wide Web address:** http://www.dana.com. **Description:** Engineers, manufactures, and markets products and systems for the worldwide vehicular, industrial, and mobile off-highway original equipment markets and is a major supplier to the related aftermarkets. Dana also provides lease financing services in selected markets. The company's products include drivetrain components such as axles, driveshafts, clutches, and transmissions; engine parts such as gaskets, piston rings, seals, pistons, and filters; chassis products such as vehicular frames and cradles and heavy-duty side rails; fluid power components such as pumps, motors, and control valves; and industrial products such as electrical and mechanical brakes and clutches, drives, and motion control devices. Dana's vehicular components and parts are used on automobiles, pickup trucks, vans, minivans, sport utility vehicles, medium and heavy trucks, and off-highway vehicles. The company's industrial products include mobile off-highway and stationary equipment applications. **Corporate headquarters location:** Toledo OH. **Other U.S. locations:** Nationwide. **International locations:** Worldwide. **Operations at this facility include:** This location manufactures piston rings for use in the assembly of automobiles. **Listed on:** New York Stock Exchange. **Stock exchange symbol:** DCN. **Annual sales/revenues:** $7.9 billion. **Number of employees worldwide:** Approximately 45,000.

DATA SYSTEMS NETWORK CORPORATION
34705 West 12 Mile Road, Suite 300, Farmington Hills MI 48331. 248/489-7117. **Contact:** Human Resources. **Description:** Provides data management systems and computer network integration services. **Listed on:** OTC. **Stock exchange symbol:** DSYS.

DAVENPORT UNIVERSITY
4801 Oakman Boulevard, Dearborn MI 48126. 313/581-4400. **Toll-free phone:** 800/585-1479. **Contact:** Director of Human Resources. **World Wide Web address:** http://www.davenport.edu. **Description:** A four-year college specializing in business. Davenport College also offers programs in medical, travel, and paralegal studies. **Positions advertised include:** Career and Education Advisor. **Other area locations:** Statewide. **Other U.S. locations:** TN. **President:** Randolph K. Flechsig.

DAVENPORT UNIVERSITY
4123 West Main Street, Kalamazoo MI 49006. 269/382-2835. **Toll-free phone:** 800/632-8928. **Contact:** Human Resources. **E-mail address:** personnel@davenport.edu. **World Wide Web address:** http://www.davenport.edu. **Description:** A four-year college specializing in business. Davenport College also offers programs in medical, travel, and paralegal studies. **Other area locations:** Statewide. **Other U.S. locations:** TN. **President:** Randolph K. Flechsig.

DAVENPORT UNIVERSITY
415 East Fulton Street, Grand Rapids MI 49503. 616/451-3511. **Toll-free phone:** 800/632-9569. **Contact:** Personnel Department. **E-mail address:** personnel@davenport.edu. **World Wide Web address:** http://www.davenport.edu. **Description:** A four-year college specializing in business. Davenport College also offers programs in medical, travel, and paralegal studies. **Positions advertised include:** Accounts Receivable Clerk. **Other area locations:** Statewide. **Other U.S. locations:** TN. **President:** Randolph K. Flechsig.

DAVIS DENTAL LABORATORY
5830 Crossroads Commerce Parkway, Wyoming MI 49509. 616/261-9191. **Fax:** 616/261-9889. **Contact:** Ms. Christine Bainbridge, Human Resources Administrator.

E-mail address: jgerace@dentalservices.com. **World Wide Web address:** http://www.dentalservices.net. **Description:** A full-service dental laboratory that manufactures and supplies various restorative dental products. **NOTE:** Entry-level positions are offered. For career opportunities, call 800/253-9227. **Corporate headquarters location:** Minneapolis MN. **Special programs:** Internships; Co-ops. **Number of employees at this location:** 130.

DAVIS TOOL AND ENGINEERING INC.
19250 Plymouth Road, Detroit MI 48228. 313/835-6000. **Contact:** Human Resources Director. **Description:** A Tier One supplier of metal stampings and welded assemblies to the automotive industry. **Corporate headquarters location:** Plymouth MI. **Parent company:** Davis Industries. **Listed on:** Privately held. **Number of employees at this location:** 350.

DE-STA-CO
P.O. Box 2800, Troy MI 48007-2800. 248/589-2008. **Physical address:** 31791 Sherman Drive, Madison Heights MI 48071. **Contact:** Human Resources Director. **World Wide Web address:** http://www.destaco.com. **Description:** Provides workplace automation products such as robotic grippers, rotary actuators, and collision control devices. The company also manufactures fans and blowers. **Corporate headquarters location:** This location. **Other area locations:** Birmingham MI; Canton MI; Plymouth MI; Charlevoix MI. **Other U.S. locations:** Dallas TX; Monroe CT. **International locations:** Worldwide.

DELPHI AUTOMOTIVE SYSTEMS CORPORATION
1441 West Long Lake Road, Troy MI 48098. 248/813-2000. **Contact:** Human Resources. **World Wide Web address:** http://www.delphi.com. **Description:** Delphi is one of the world's largest suppliers of automotive components and parts. **NOTE:** Interested candidates cans search and apply for positions online. **Positions advertised include:** Electrical Systems Integration Engineer; Budget Analyst; Product Development Manager; Marketing Manager; National Account Manager; Regional Account Manager. **Special programs:** Tuition Assistance Program; On-Site Education Program. **Corporate headquarters location:** This location. **International locations:** Worldwide. **Number of employees nationwide:** Over 61,000. **Number of employees worldwide:** 190,000.

DENSO INTERNATIONAL AMERICA, INC.
24777 Denso Drive, Southfield MI 48034. 248/350-7500. **Fax:** 248/213-2337. **Contact:** Human Resources. **E-mail address:** southfieldhr@denso-diam.com. **World Wide Web address:** http://www.densocorp-na.com. **Description:** Denso International America, Incorporated sells air conditioners, electrical automotive equipment, heaters, radiators, instrument clusters, and automotive electronic products; and provides engineering services, design, testing, and R&D. **Positions advertised include:** Senior Accounting Analyst; Senior Software Analyst; Application Engineer; Senior Tax Specialist. **Special programs:** Internships; Co-ops. **Parent company:** Denso Company, Limited supplies automotive components and systems to the several U.S. automakers, as well as to most of the Japanese and European automakers. The company manufactures its products at 34 plants in 13 countries. Denso is a leader in automotive electronics, as well as in systems for electronic fuel injection, braking control, and navigation. The company is one of the world's largest manufacturers of automobile heaters and air conditioners. Other products include hand-held bar code readers, factory automation systems, and portable telephones. **Operations at this facility include:** This location is the U.S. regional headquarters of Denso Corporation (Japan). **Listed on:** OTC. **Stock exchange symbol:** DNZOY. **Annual sales/revenues:** $19.4 billion. **Number of employees at this location:** 395. **Number of employees worldwide:** 89,000.

DENSO MANUFACTURING MICHIGAN, INC.
One Denso Road, Battle Creek MI 49015-1083. 269/965-3322. **Fax:** 269/965-8399. **Contact:** Human Resources. **E-mail address:** dmmi_recruiter@denso-diam.com. **World Wide Web address:** http://www.densocorp-na.com. **Description:** Manufactures and sells automotive radiators, heaters, blowers, air-conditioners, and other automotive components. **Positions advertised include:** Facilities Project Section Leader; Human Resources Manager; Systems Integration; Cost Planning Specialist; Team Leader. **Special programs:** Internships; Co-ops. **Corporate headquarters location:** Southfield MI. **Parent company:** Denso Corporation (Japan) supplies automotive components and systems to the Big Three U.S. automakers, as well as most of the Japanese and European automakers. The company manufactures its products at 34 plants in 13 nations. Denso is a leader in automotive electronics, as well as in systems for electronic fuel injection, braking control, and navigation. The company is one of the world's largest manufacturers of automobile heaters and air conditioners. Other products include hand-held bar-code readers, factory automation systems, and portable telephones. **Listed on:** OTC. **Stock exchange symbol:** DNZOY. **Number of employees at this location:** 2,400.

DENTON ENTERPRISES
22003 Harper Avenue, St. Clair Shores MI 48080. 313/884-5530. **Contact:** Human Resources. **Description:** A contracting company specializing in the construction of streets and highways. **Corporate headquarters location:** This location.

DETREX CORPORATION
24901 Northwestern Highway, Suite 500, Southfield MI 48075. 248/358-5800 ext.108. **Fax:** 248/358-5803. **Contact:** Human Resources. **World Wide Web address:** http://www.detrex.com. **Description:** Engaged in the manufacture of industrial inorganic chemicals. Products also include PVC and CPVC pipe, ducts, fitting, and specialty extrusions. **Corporate headquarters location:** This location. **Subsidiaries include:** Harvel Plastics, Incorporated; The Elco Corporation. **Listed on:** NASDAQ. **Stock exchange symbol:** DTRX. **Sales/revenue:** $60 million. **Number of employees at this location:** 250.

DETROIT DIESEL CORPORATION
13400 West Outer Drive, Detroit MI 48239-4001. 313/592-7155. **Contact:** Personnel. **E-mail Address:** DDCINFO@detroitdiesel.com. **World Wide Web address:** http://www.detroitdiesel.com. **Description:** Designs, manufactures, and sells heavy-duty diesel engines. Founded in 1988. **NOTE:** Resumes should be submitted online. **Special programs:** Internships. **Internship information:** Summer internships are offered. Interested students should send a resume, transcript, and cover letter. **Corporate headquarters location:** This location. **Other U.S. locations:** Nationwide. **International locations:** Worldwide. **Parent company:** DaimlerChrysler AG. **Operations at this facility include:** Administration; Research and Development; Sales; Service. **Listed on:** New York Stock Exchange. **Stock exchange symbol:** DDC. **CEO:** Ludvik F. Koci. **Number of employees at this location:** 3,500. **Number of employees worldwide:** 6,200.

THE DETROIT INSTITUTE OF ARTS
5200 Woodward Avenue, Detroit MI 48202. 313/833-7900. **Contact:** Human Resources. **E-mail address:** hrjobs@dia.org. **World Wide Web address:** http://www.dia.org. **Description:** Preserves, collects, and displays works of art and generally furthers the understanding and appreciation of the visual arts. Founded in 1885. **Positions advertised include:** Donor Relations Manager. **Corporate headquarters location:** This location.

DETROIT NEWSPAPERS
615 West Lafayette Boulevard, Detroit MI 48226. 313/222-2085. **Fax:** 313/223-3209. **Recorded jobline:** 313/222-6050. **Contact:** Human Resources Department. **E-mail address:** employment@dnps.com. **World Wide Web address:** http://www.detroitnewspapers.com. **Description:** A business operating unit for the *Detroit News* and *Detroit Free Press.* **Positions advertised include:** Account Executive; Electronic Technician; Customer Service Representative. **Special programs:** Internships. **Parent company:** Gannett/Knight-Ridder (Arlington VA). **Operations at this facility include:** Administration; Sales. **Listed on:** New York Stock Exchange. **Stock exchange symbol:** GCI. **Number of employees at this location:** 3,500.

DETROIT PUMP & MANUFACTURING COMPANY
18943 John R. Street, Detroit MI 48203. 313/893-4242. **Toll-free phone:** 800/686-1662. **Fax:** 313/893-7139. **Contact:** Human Resources. **World Wide Web address:** http://www.detroitpump.com. **Description:** A manufacturer and distributor of industrial pumps, machinery, and related equipment. **Corporate headquarters location:** This location. **Other area locations:** Grand Rapids MI; Flint MI. **Number of employees at this location:** 38.

DETROIT REGIONAL CHAMBER
One Woodward Avenue, Suite 1900, P.O. Box 33840, Detroit MI 48232-0840. 313/596-0303. **Fax:** 866/891-6401. **Contact:** Elisa Stevenson, Human Resources. **E-mail address:** estevens@detroitchamber.com. **World Wide Web address:** http://www.detroitchamber.com. **Description:** The mission of the Detroit Regional Chamber of Commerce is to retain and attract jobs and investment in metropolitan Detroit, improve the economic vitality of the region, and assist member firms in competing in local, national, and international markets. **Positions advertised include:** Membership Development Manager; Marketing Opportunities Account Executive; Member Relations Account Representative. **Other area locations:** Lansing MI; Oakland County MI. **Number of employees at this location:** 95.

DETROIT STOKER COMPANY
P.O. Box 732, Monroe MI 48161-0732. 734/241-9500. **Physical address:** 1510 East First Street, Monroe MI 48161. **Fax:** 734/241-7126. **Contact:** Human Resources Department. **World Wide Web address:** http://www.detroitstoker.com. **Description:** An international manufacturer of metal industrial furnace parts for heating, industrial, and electric power generation applications. **Corporate headquarters location:** This location. **Other U.S. locations:** Nationwide. **Number of employees at this location:** 300.

DIVERSIFIED DATA PRODUCTS
1995 Highland Drive, Suite D, Ann Arbor MI 48108. 734/677-7878. **Fax:** 734/677-0938. **Contact:** Human Resources. **Description:** Supplies individuals and businesses with consumable parts for computer printers including ribbons and drums. **Corporate headquarters location:** This location. **President:** Joseph Hollenshead.

DODGE CITY/WARREN TRUCK DIVISION
21500 Mound Road, Warren MI 48091. 586/497-2400. **Contact:** Human Resources. **Description:** A manufacturer of motor vehicles. **Corporate headquarters location:** Auburn Hills MI. **Number of employees nationwide:** 4,700.

DOMINO'S PIZZA, INC.
30 Frank Lloyd Wright Drive, P.O. Box 997, Ann Arbor MI 48106-0997. 734/930-3030. **Contact:** Human Resources. **E-mail address:** recruiter1@dominos.com. **World Wide Web address:** http://www.dominos.com. **Description:** Operates a franchised home-delivery pizza chain. Founded in 1960. **NOTE:** Part-time positions are offered. **Positions advertised include:** Cash Accountant; Executive Assistant; Senior Graphic Designer; Print Marketing Manager. **Special programs:** Education Assistance Program; Internships. **Corporate headquarters location:** This location. **Other U.S. locations:** Worldwide. **Number of employees at this location:** 525. **Number of employees worldwide:** Over 140,000.

DOMTAR
P.O. Box 5003, Port Huron MI 48061. 810/982-0191. **Physical address:** 1700 Washington Avenue, Port Huron MI 48060. **Fax:** 810/982-7124. **Contact:** Human Resources. **E-mail address:** careers@domtar.com. **World Wide Web address:** http://www.domtar.com. **Description:** A forest products company comprised of three divisions: Papers, Wood, and Packaging. **Positions advertised include:** Safety and Health Manager. **Corporate headquarters location:** Montreal, Canada. **Operations at this facility include:** As part of the company's paper segment, this location manufactures paper rolls for printing, specialty, and packaging purposes. E.B. Eddy Specialty Paper, Incorporated is also at this location. **Listed on:** New York Stock Exchange. **Stock exchange symbol:** DTC. **Annual sales/revenues:** $5.5 billion. **Number of employees at this location:** 310. **Number of employees worldwide:** 12,500.

THE DOW CHEMICAL COMPANY
P.O. Box 1655, Midland MI 48641-1655. 989/636-1000. **Physical address:** 2030 Dow Center, Midland MI 48642. **Contact:** Applicant Center. **World Wide Web address:** http://www.dow.com. **Description:** One of the largest chemical companies in the United States, Dow manufactures industrial and consumer products. Consumer products include Saran Wrap, Spray 'N Wash, Dow bathroom cleaners, prescription drugs, and over-the-counter health care products. Industrial chemicals are used in the food processing, pharmaceuticals, and utilities markets. Plastics are manufactured for the automotive, electronics, packaging, and recreation markets. Other operations include cogeneration and steam power for the utility market and petrochemical production. **NOTE:** Candidates can search and apply for positions online. **Corporate headquarters location:** This location. **Other area locations:** Auburn Hills MI; Ludington MI. **Other U.S. locations:** Nationwide. **International locations:** Worldwide. **Operations at this facility include:** Administration; Research and Development; Manufacturing. **Listed on:** New York Stock Exchange. **Stock exchange symbol:** DOW. **President/CEO/Chairman:** William S. Stravropoulos. **Number of employees worldwide:** 46,000. **Annual sales/revenues:** $33 billion.

DRAW-TITE INC.
40500 Van Born Road, Canton MI 48188. 734/722-7800. **Contact:** Human Resources Director. **World Wide Web address:** http://www.draw-tite.com. **Description:** A manufacturer of trailer hitches. **Corporate headquarters location:** This location. **Other U.S. locations:** Corona CA; Marysville CA; Starke FL; Burlington NJ; Arlington TX; Fife WA. **International locations:** Canada; Mexico. **Number of employees at this location:** 400.

DUPONT COMPANY
400 Groesbeck Highway, Mount Clemens MI 48043. 586/468-9000. **Contact:** Human Resources. **World Wide Web address:** http://www.dupont.com. **Description:** A diversified chemicals company. **Operations at this facility include:** This location manufactures paint for the automotive industry. **Special programs:** Internships; Co-ops. **Corporate headquarters location:** Wilmington DE. **Other U.S. locations:** Nationwide. **International locations:** Worldwide. **Listed on:** New York Stock Exchange. **Stock exchange symbol:** DD. **CEO/Chairman:** Charles O. Holliday, Jr. **Annual sales/revenues:** $27 billion. **Number of employees at this location:** 450. **Number of employees worldwide:** 78,000.

DURA CONVERTIBLE SYSTEMS
1365 East Beecher Street, Adrian MI 49221. 517/263-7864. **Contact:** Robin Linville, Director of Human Resources. **World Wide Web address:** http://www.collinsaikman.com. **Description:** Designs and manufactures convertible tops. Dura Convertible Systems also assembles hydraulic power units and other miscellaneous automobile parts. **Corporate headquarters location:** Southfield MI. **Parent company:** Collins & Aikman Corporation. **Listed on:** New York Stock Exchange. **Stock exchange symbol:** CKC.

DURAKON INDUSTRIES INC.
2101 North Lapeer Road, Lapeer MI 48446. 810/664-0850. **Fax:** 865/457-6486. **Contact:** Kathy Richard, Human Resources Director. **E-mail address:** human.resources@durakon.com. **World Wide Web address:** http://www.durakon.com. **Description:** Engaged in the manufacture and wholesale trade of pickup truck bedliners. **NOTE:** To contact Human Resources directly, call 865/457-8244. **Corporate headquarters location:** This location. **Other area locations:** Farmington Hills, MI. **Other U.S. locations:** Clinton TN. **International locations:** Lerma, Mexico. **Parent company:** Littlejohn and Company. **Number of employees nationwide:** 600.

DURR AUTOMATION, INC.
31077 Durr Drive, Wixom MI 48393. 248/960-4630. **Fax:** 248/960-4633. **Contact:** Human Resources Department. **World Wide Web address:** http://www.durrautomation.com. **Description:** A manufacturer of assembly systems, automation equipment, and industry parts washers. **Corporate headquarters location:** This location. **International locations:** Germany; Brazil. **Operations at this facility include:** Administration; Manufacturing; Sales; Service. **Number of employees at this location:** 100.

DURR ENVIRONMENTAL INC.
40600 Plymouth Road, Plymouth MI 48170. 734/459-6800. **Contact:** Diana Thomas, Payroll Supervisor. **E-mail address:** hr@durrusa.com. **World Wide Web address:** http://www.durrenvironmental.com. **Description:** Manufactures paint finishing systems, automated metal cleaning technology, robot systems, and related environmental equipment. **Parent company:** The Durr Group. **Operations at this facility include:** Regional Headquarters.

DYKEMA & GOSSETT
400 Renaissance Center, Detroit MI 48243-1668. 313/568-6800. **Fax:** 313/568-6691. **Contact:** Sarah Staup, Human Resources. **E-mail address:** sstaup@dykema.com. **World Wide Web address:** http://www.dykema.com. **Description:** A law firm specializing in corporate law. Dykema & Gossett is one of the largest law firms in the Midwest. **NOTE:** For administrative and support personnel positions, contact the Human Resources Department at the following e-mail address: hr@dykema.com. **Positions advertised include:** Legal Specialist; Floating Administrative Assistant. **Special programs:** Summer jobs. **Corporate headquarters location:** This location. **Other area locations:** Ann Arbor MI; Bloomfield Hills MI; Lansing MI; Grand Rapids MI. **Other U.S. locations:** Washington DC; Chicago IL. **Chairman:** Rex E. Schlaybaugh, Jr. **Number of employees nationwide:** 600.

E&L CONSTRUCTION GROUP
P.O. Box 418, Flint MI 48501. 810/744-4300. **Physical address:** 2830 Lippincott Boulevard, Flint MI 48506. **Fax:** 810/744-1735. **Contact:** Human Resources. **E-mail address:** mark@eandlgroup.com. **World Wide Web address:** http://www.eandlgroup.com. **Description:** A contracting company specializing in the construction of industrial buildings and warehouses. **NOTE:** Entry-level positions are offered. **Other area locations:** Marie MI. **President/CEO:** Bob Root. **Number of employees at this location:** 120.

EDS PLM SOLUTIONS
800 Tower Drive, Troy MI 48098. 248/874-2702. **Contact:** Human Resources. **E-mail address:** careers@eds.com. **World Wide Web address:** http://www.eds.com. **Description:** The product lifecycle management segment of EDS offers technological consulting, deployment, and support services. **Special programs:** Internships. **Corporate headquarters location:** Plano TX. **Other U.S. locations:** Nationwide. **International locations:** Worldwide. **Parent company:** Electronic Data Systems. **Operations at this facility include:** This location is a sales office and also develops dimensional management software for engineering applications. **Listed on:** New York Stock Exchange. **Stock exchange symbol:** EDS. **President:** Jeff Heller. **Sales/revenue:** $21.5 billion. **Number of employees worldwide:** Over 130,000.

EDS PLM SOLUTIONS
2600 Green Road, Suite 100, Ann Arbor MI 48105. 734/995-6000. **Contact:** Personnel. **E-mail address:** careers@eds.com. **World Wide Web address:** http://www.eds.com. **Description:** The product lifecycle management segment of EDS offers technological consulting, deployment, and support services. **Special programs:** Internships. **Corporate headquarters location:** Plano TX. **Other U.S. locations:** Nationwide. **International locations:** Worldwide. **Parent company:** Electronic Data Systems. **Operations at this facility include:** This location manufactures CAD/CAM software. **Listed on:** New York Stock Exchange. **Stock exchange symbol:** EDS. **Sales/revenue:** $21.5 billion. **Number of employees worldwide:** Over 130,000.

EAGLE-PICHER AUTOMOTIVE GROUP
2424 John Daly Road, Inkster MI 48141. 313/278-5956. **Contact:** Personnel. **E-mail address:** career.automotive@eaglepicher.com. **World Wide Web address:** http://www.epcorp.com. **Description:** Eagle-Picher is a diversified manufacturer of raw materials serving industrial clients. **Parent company:** Eagle-Picher Industry, Incorporated. **Corporate headquarters location:** This location. **Other U.S. locations:** Blacksburg VA; Leesburg FL. **Operations at this facility includes:** This is the Wolverine Gasket Division headquarters. As part of the company's Automotive Group, this location develops, markets, and manufactures automotive components. **International locations:** Germany; Korea; Japan.

EAGLE-PICHER AUTOMOTIVE GROUP
135 East South Street, Hillsdale MI 49242. 517/439-9381. **Contact:** Human Resources. **World Wide Web address:** http://www.epcorp.com. **E-mail address:** career.automotive@eaglepicher.com. **Description:** Eagle-Picher is a diversified manufacturer of raw materials serving industrial clients. **Other area locations:** Inkster MI; Mount Pleasant MI; Traverse City MI; Vassar MI. **Other U.S. locations:** Manchester TN; Hamilton IN; **International locations:** Mexico; United Kingdom; Germany; France; Italy; Brazil; Korea; Japan. **Parent company:** Eagle-Picher Industry, Incorporated. **Operations at this facility include:** This is the Hillsdale Division headquarters. As part of the company's Automotive Group, this location designs and manufactures automotive parts including dampers and crankshafts.

EASTERN MICHIGAN UNIVERSITY
204 Bowen, Ypsilanti MI 48197. 734.487-3430. **Fax:** 734/487-7995. **Recorded jobline:** 734/487-0016. **Contact:** Employment and Recruiting Office. **E-mail address:** employee@emich.edu. **World Wide Web address:** http://www.emich.edu. **Description:** A public, comprehensive university with an enrollment of 25,000 students. Founded in 1849. **NOTE:** For faculty positions, apply to: Posting #, Eastern Michigan University, 202 Boone Hall, Ypsilanti MI 48197. See EMU's website for more detailed application procedures. **Positions advertised include:** Area Complex Director; Academic Advisor; Principal Plant Engineer; Mathematics Professor; Business Librarian. **Office hours:** Monday – Friday, 8:00 a.m. – 4:45 p.m. **President:** Samuel A. Kirkpatrick, Ph.D. **Number of employees at this location:** 2,000.

EATON CORPORATION
315 South First Street, Ann Arbor MI 48104. 734/761-7666. **Contact:** Personnel. **World Wide Web address:** http://www.eaton.com. **Description:** Eaton Corporation is a worldwide manufacturer of hydraulic products, fluid connectors, electrical power distribution equipment, engine components, and truck drivetrain systems. The company serves a variety of industries including automotive, aerospace, industrial, and semiconductor. **Positions advertised include:** Senior Product Engineer; Product Senior Designer; Assembly Technician. **NOTE:** Applications for available positions may be submitted through website. **Corporate headquarters location:** Cleveland OH. **Operations at this facility include:** This location is an automotive controls plant that manufactures valves and screw machine parts. **Listed on:** New York Stock Exchange. **Stock exchange symbol:** ETN. **President/CEO/Chairman:** Alexander M. Cutler. **Annual sales/revenues:** $7.2 billion. **Number of employees worldwide:** 51,000.

EATON CORPORATION
300 South East Avenue, Jackson MI 49203-1973. 517/787-8121. **Contact:** Chris Lewless, Personnel Manager. **World Wide Web address:** http://www.eaton.com. **Description:** Eaton Corporation is a worldwide manufacturer of hydraulic products, fluid connectors, electrical power distribution equipment, engine components, and truck drivetrain systems. The company serves a variety of industries including automotive, aerospace, industrial, and semiconductor. **NOTE:** Applications for available positions may be submitted through website. **Positions advertised include:** Customer Service Manager; Customer Program Manager; Lead Engineer. **Corporate headquarters location:** Cleveland OH. **Operations at this facility include:** This location manufactures aerospace hosing and cutlinks. **Listed on:** New York Stock Exchange. **Stock exchange symbol:** ETN. **President/CEO/Chairman:** Alexander M. Cutler. **Annual sales/revenues:** $7.2 billion. **Number of employees worldwide:** 51,000.

EATON CORPORATION
6825 Beatrice Drive, Kalamazoo MI 49009. 616/375-4090. **Contact:** Human Resources Manager. **World Wide Web address:** http://www.eaton.com. **Description:** Eaton Corporation is a worldwide manufacturer of hydraulic products, fluid connectors, electrical power distribution equipment, engine components, and truck drivetrain systems. The company serves a variety of industries including automotive, aerospace, industrial, and semiconductor. **NOTE:** Applications for available positions may be submitted through website. **Corporate headquarters location:** Cleveland OH. **Operations at this facility include:** This location is the Trucks Components Operations remanufacturing headquarters and plant. **Listed on:** New York Stock Exchange. **Stock exchange symbol:** ETN. **President/CEO/Chairman:** Alexander M. Cutler. **Annual sales/revenues:** $7.2 billion. **Number of employees worldwide:** 51,000.

EDGCOMB METALS COMPANY
30360 Edison Drive, Roseville MI 48066. 586/779-7950. **Toll-free phone:** 800/359-1333. **Contact:** Human Resources Manager. **World Wide Web address:** http://www.macsteelusa.com. **Description:** Engaged in the processing, sale, and storage of steel products. **Parent company:** Mac Steel USA.

EMHART AUTOMOTIVE
P.O. Box 868, Mount Clemens MI 48046. 586/949-0440. **Fax:** 586/949-0443. **Contact:** Director of Human Resources. **E-mail address:** emhart.technologies@bdk.com. **World Wide Web address:** http://www.emhart.com. **Description:** A manufacturer of plastic fasteners and clips for the automotive industry. **Special programs:** Internships. **Corporate headquarters location:** New Haven CT. **Other area locations:** Farmington Hills MI. **Other U.S. locations:** Shelton CT; Irving CA. **Parent company:** Black & Decker (Towson MD). **Operations at this facility include:** Administration; Manufacturing; Research and Development; Sales; Service. **Listed on:** New York Stock Exchange. **Stock exchange symbol:** BDK. **Number of employees at this location:** 500.

ENGINEERING SERVICE, INC.
21556 Telegraph Road, Southfield MI 48034. 248/357-3800. **Contact:** Human Resources. **Description:** An engineering firm specializing in CAD design for powertrain, electrical, and tooling applications in the automotive and aerospace industries. Engineering Service also offers services project management. **Corporate headquarters location:** This location. **Other U.S. locations:** Dearborn MI. **Number of employees nationwide:** 200.

ENTERPRISE AUTOMOTIVE SYSTEMS
21445 Hoover Road, Warren MI 48089-4031. 586/755-3180. **Fax:** 586/759-3540. **Contact:** Personnel Department. **E-mail address:** info@think-eas.com. **World Wide Web address:** http://www.think-eas.com. **Description:** A manufacturer of various engine components. Formerly known as Machining Enterprises, EAS is a Tier One and Tier Two supplier to the automotive industry. **Corporate headquarters location:** This location. **Other area locations:** Saginaw MI. **President/CEO:** Jerrel Vickers. **Number of employees at this location:** 300. **Number of employees nationwide:** 400.

ENTERTAINMENT PUBLICATIONS, INC.
1414 East Maple Road, Troy MI 48083. 248/637-8400. **Fax:** 248/404-1915. **Contact:** Corporate Recruiter. **World Wide Web address:** http://www.entertainment.com. **Description:** Develops and markets discount programs, directories, and promotions. Founded in 1962. **NOTE:** Temporary positions available. **Positions advertised include:** Recruiting Specialist; PeopleSoft Administrator; Division Support Coordinator; Logistics Analyst; Vice President, Merchant Marketing. **Corporate headquarters location:** This location. **Parent company:** Cendant Corporation. **Operations at this facility include:** Administration; Sales; Service. **Listed on:** New

York Stock Exchange. **Stock exchange symbol:** CD. **President/CEO:** Alan Bittker. **Number of employees at this location:** 300. **Number of employees nationwide:** 1,300.

ETKIN SKANSKA CONSTRUCTION COMPANY
30445 Northwestern Highway, Suite 250, Farmington Hills MI 48333. 248/737-5800. **Contact:** Controller. **E-mail address:** michigancareers@skanskausa.com. **World Wide Web address:** http://www.skanskausa.com. **Description:** Engaged in the construction of commercial, educational, retail, and hospital buildings. **Corporate headquarters location:** Parsippany NJ. **Other area locations:** Grand Rapids MI; Kalamazoo MI. **Other U.S. locations:** Nationwide. **Sales/revenue:** $5 billion. **Number of employees at this location:** 200. **Number of employees nationwide:** 5,300.

EVANS INDUSTRIES
200 Renaissance Center, Suite 3150, Detroit MI 48243. 313/259-2266. **Contact:** Human Resources. **Description:** Manufactures various industrial products including casters, wheels, glue, and other rubber and plastic parts. **Corporate headquarters location:** This location.

EVANS-SHERRATT COMPANY
13050 Northend Avenue, Oak Park MI 48237-3405. 248/584-5500. **Fax:** 248/584-5510. **Contact:** John H. Lyngklip, President. **E-mail address:** esoakpark@evans-sherratt.com. **World Wide Web address:** http://www.evans-sherratt.com. **Description:** Engaged in the wholesale trade and servicing of professional office and consumer equipment and supplies. **Corporate headquarters location:** This location. **Other area locations:** Petosky MI; Grand Rapids MI. **Other U.S. locations:** OH; WV; PA. **Number of employees at this location:** 100.

EVER FRESH LACROIX
6600 East Nine Mile Road, Warren MI 48091. 586/755-9500. **Contact:** Personnel Manager. **E-mail address:** humanresources@nationalbeverage.com. **World Wide Web address:** http://www.nationalbeverage.com. **Description:** Produces fruit juices. **Corporate headquarters location:** Fort Lauderdale FL. **Parent company:** National Beverage Corporation. **Listed on:** American Stock Exchange. **Stock exchange symbol:** FIZ. **Number of employees at this location:** 100.

EXECUTONE BUSINESS SYSTEMS
30927 Schoolcraft Road, Livonia MI 48150. 248/649-9100. **Fax:** 248/649-5558. **Contact:** Human Resources. **E-mail address:** employment@executone.biz. **World Wide Web address:** http://www.executone-michigan.com. **Description:** Engaged in the sale, installation, and service of complete communications systems including telephone, voicemail, data, and video conferencing for corporate and industrial customers. **Corporate headquarters location:** Milford CT. **Operations at this facility include:** Administration; Sales; Service. **Number of employees at this location:** 90.

EXOTIC AUTOMATION AND SUPPLY
P.O. Box 395, Farmington MI 48332-0395. 248/477-2122. **Physical address:** 34700 Grand River Avenue, Farmington Hills MI 48335. **Fax:** 248/473-7972. **Contact:** Human Resources. **E-mail address:** jobs@erpc.com. **World Wide Web address:** http://www.exoticautomation.com. **Description:** Manufactures and distributes plastic and rubber products including rollers, o-rings, and die strippers. Founded in 1962. **Positions advertised include:** Inside Sales Representative. **Special programs:** Internships. **Corporate headquarters location:** This location. **Other area locations:** Flint MI; Lansing MI; Rochester Hills MI; Southgate MI; Freeland MI; Jackson MI. **Other U.S. locations:** Indianapolis IN; Franklin OH. **Operations at this facility include:** Administration; Manufacturing; Sales; Service. **Listed on:** Privately held.

EXPONENT, INC.
39100 Country Club Drive, Farmington Hills MI 48331. 248/324-9100. **Contact:** Human Resources. **E-mail address:** hr@exponent.com. **World Wide Web address:** http://www.exponent.com. **Description:** A technical consulting firm dedicated to the investigation, analysis, and prevention of accidents and failures of an engineering or scientific nature. The company specializes in accident reconstruction, biomechanics, construction/structural engineering, aviation and marine investigations, environment assessment, materials and product testing, warning and labeling issues, accident statistic data analysis, and risk prevention/mitigation. Founded in 1967. **NOTE:** All hiring for Exponent, Incorporated is conducted through the main offices. Forward resumes to Human Resources, 149 Commonwealth Drive, Menlo Park CA 94025. **Positions advertised include:** Managing Engineer. **Corporate headquarters location:** Menlo Park CA. **Other U.S. locations:** Nationwide. **International locations:** United Kingdom; Germany. **Parent company:** Exponent. **Listed on:** NASDAQ. **Stock exchange symbol:** EXPO. **President/CEO:** Michael R. Gaulke.

FM GLOBAL
39555 Orchard Hill Place, Suite 400, Novi MI 48375. 734/344-0340. **Contact:** Human Resources Department. **E-mail address:** jobs@fmglobal.com. **World Wide Web address:** http://www.fmglobal.com. **Description:** A loss control service organization. The company helps policyholders protect their properties against fire, wind, flood, and explosion, as well as many other hazards. **NOTE:** Interested job seekers may submit resumes online. **Corporate headquarters location:** Johnston RI. **Other U.S. locations:** Nationwide. **International locations:** Worldwide.

FNT INDUSTRIES, INC.
927 First Street, Menominee MI 49858. 906/863-5531. **Toll-free phone:** 800/338-9860. **Contact:** Human Resources. **E-mail address:** kathy@fnt-victory.net. **World Wide Web address:** http://www.fnt-victory.net. **Description:** Manufactures sport and fish netting. **Office hours:** Monday – Friday, 8:00 a.m. – 4:30 p.m. **Listed on:** Privately held. **Number of employees at this location:** 60.

FANUC ROBOTICS NORTH AMERICA, INC.
3900 West Hamlin Road, Rochester Hills MI 48309. 248/377-7000. **Fax:** 248/377-7362. **Recorded jobline:** 248/377-7677. **Contact:** Department of Human Resources. **E-mail address:** resume@fanucrobotics.com. **World Wide Web address:** http://www.fanucrobotics.com. **Description:** Engaged in the business of automation intelligence and solutions for assembling, cutting, dispensing, laser processing, material handling and removing, painting, palletizing, and welding processes. **Positions advertised include:** Process Engineer; Financial Analyst. **Special programs:** Tuition Reimbursement Program. **Corporate headquarters location:** This location. **Other U.S. locations:** Los Angeles CA; Chicago IL; Cincinnati OH; Charlotte NC. **International locations:** Japan; Mexico; Canada; Brazil; Luxembourg. **Parent company:** Fanuc Limited. **Operations at this facility include:** Administration; Manufacturing; Research and Development; Sales; Service. **President/CEO:** Rick Schneider. **Number of employees at this location:** 500. **Number of employees nationwide:** 600. **Number of employees worldwide:** Over 1,100.

FAYGO BEVERAGES, INC.
3579 Gratiot Avenue, Detroit MI 48207. 313/925-1600. **Fax:** 313/925-0932. **Contact:** Human Resources Manager. **World Wide Web address:** http://www.faygo.com. **Description:** A bottler and canner of soft drinks. **Positions advertised include:** Warehouse Loader; Sales Representative; Oiler Mechanic; Machine Operator; Maintenance Supervisor; Delivery Driver. **Special programs:** Tuition Reimbursement Program. **Parent company:** National Beverage Corporation. **Corporate headquarters location:** Fort Lauderdale FL. **Listed in:** New York Stock Exchange. **Stock exchange symbol:** FIZ. **Number of employees at this location:** 400.

FEDERAL APD, INC.
42775 Nine Mile Road, Novi MI 48375-4113. 248/374-9600. **Contact:** Human Resources Administrator. **E-mail address:** jobs@fedsig.com. **World Wide Web address:** http://www.federalapd.com. **Description:** Manufactures facility management system software used for parking, access, and revenue control. Products include the self-park, microprocessor-based barrier gate. **NOTE:** Entry-level positions are offered. Resumes should be forwarded to the Corporate Recruiting Department at 1550 Wall Street, Suite 243, St. Charles MO 6330, or faxed to 636/916-3266. **Positions advertised include:** Manufacturing Engineer; Mechanical Design Engineer; Sales Manager. **Corporate headquarters location:** This location. **Other U.S. locations:** Nationwide. **International locations:** Hong Kong; Brazil. **Parent company:** Federal Signal Corporation.

FEDERAL SCREW WORKS
20229 Nine Mile Road, Saint Clair Shores MI 48080. 586/443-4222. **Fax:** 586/443-4220. **Contact:** Personnel. **E-mail address:** fsw@federalscrew.com. **World Wide Web address:** http://www.federalscrew.com. **Description:** Manufactures bolts, nuts, and screws. **Office hours:** Monday – Friday, 8:15 a.m. – 5:00 p.m. **Corporate headquarters location:** This location. **Listed on:** NASDAQ. **Stock exchange symbol:** FSCR. **Number of employees at this location:** 500.

FEDERAL-MOGUL CORPORATION
26555 Northwestern Highway, Southfield MI 48034. 248/354-7700. **Contact:** Corporate Human Resources Staffing. **World Wide Web address:** http://www.federal-mogul.com. **Description:** Manufactures engine components and transportation products. Founded in 1899. **Special programs:** Training. **Corporate headquarters location:** This location. **Other U.S. locations:** Nationwide. **International locations:** Worldwide. **Listed on:** OTC. **Stock exchange symbol:** FDMLQ. **CEO:** Chip McClure. **Annual sales/revenues:** $5.5 billion. **Number of employees worldwide:** 45,000.

FELDER COMMUNICATIONS GROUP
50 Louis Street NW, 600 Trade Center, Grand Rapids Michigan 49503. Contact: Mike Schurr. **E-mail address:** mike@felder.com. **World Wide Web address:** http://www.felder.com. **Description:** Felder Communications provides Brand elevation campaigns whose clients include engineering firms, hospitals, airports, and websites.

FERRIS STATE UNIVERSITY
420 Oak Street, Prakken 150, Big Rapids MI 49307-2031. 231/591-2000. **Fax:** 231/591-2978. **Recorded jobline:** 231/591-JOBS. **Contact:** Human Resources. **World Wide Web address:** http://www.ferris.edu. **Description:** A university with approximately 9,500 students offering a wide range of educational programs, including doctoral, master's, bachelor's and associate's degrees. **NOTE:** Part-time and temporary positions are offered. To contact Human Resources directly, call 231/591-2150. **Positions advertised include:** Assistant Secretary; Biology Professor; Dental Hygienist; Database Administrator; History Professor; Educational Counselor; Residence Hall Director; Nuclear Medicine Technology Instructor. **Number of employees at this location:** Approximately 1,800.

FIEGER, FIEGER, KENNEY AND JOHNSON P.C.
19390 West Ten Mile Road, Southfield MI 48075. 248/355-5555. **Contact:** Human Resources. **E-mail address:** info@fiegerlaw.com. **World Wide Web address:** http://www.fiegerlaw.com. **Description:** A law firm specializing in medical malpractice and complex litigation. Geoffrey Fieger's list of well-known clients includes Dr. Jack Kevorkian. **Corporate headquarters location:** This location. **Operations at this facility include:** Service. **Number of employees at this location:** 50.

FIFTH THIRD BANCORP
18800 Hall Road, Clinton Township MI 48038. 586/226-4690. **Recorded jobline:** 800/552-4350. **Contact:** Human Resources. **World Wide Web address:** http://www.53.com. **Description:** A financial services institution that, through its subsidiaries, provides mortgage loans and traditional banking services. Founded in 1853. **NOTE:** Entry-level positions, part-time jobs, and second and third shifts are offered. **Positions advertised include:** Securities Retail Investment Consultant; Credit Analyst. **Office hours:** Monday – Thursday, 9:00 a.m. – 5:00 p.m., Friday, 9:00 a.m. – 6:00 p.m., Saturday 9:00 a.m. – 1:00 p.m. **Corporate headquarters location:** Cincinnati OH. **Other area locations:** Statewide. **Other U.S. locations:** Nationwide. **Subsidiaries include:** Fifth Third Bank Processing Solutions; Fifth Third Securities, Incorporated; Fifth Third Leasing Company. **Listed on:** NASDAQ. **Stock exchange symbol:** FITB. **Number of employees nationwide:** Over 19,000.

FIFTH THIRD BANCORP
4468 Cascade Road SE, Grand Rapids MI 49546. 616/653-6226. **Recorded jobline:** 800/552-4350. **Contact:** Human Resources. **World Wide Web address:** http://www.53.com. **Description:** A financial services institution that, through its subsidiaries, provides mortgage loans and traditional banking services. Founded in 1853. **NOTE:** Entry-level positions, part-time jobs, and second and third shifts are offered. **Positions advertised include:** Customer Service Representative; Financial Analyst; Structured Finance Banker; Associate Education Consultant. **Office hours:** Monday-Thursday, 9:30 a.m. – 5:00 p.m., Friday, 9:30 a.m. – 5:30 p.m., Saturday, 9:30 a.m. – 12:00 p.m. **Corporate headquarters location:** Cincinnati OH. **Other area locations:** Statewide. **Other U.S. locations:** Nationwide. **Subsidiaries include:** Fifth Third Bank Processing Solutions; Fifth Third Securities, Incorporated; Fifth Third Leasing Company. **Operations at this facility include:** Sales; Service. **Listed on:** NASDAQ. **Stock exchange symbol:** FITB. **Number of employees nationwide:** Over 19,000.

FIRST AMERICAN TITLE
1650 West Big Beaver Road, P.O. Box 1289, Troy MI 48084. 248/643-4000. **Contact:** Personnel Manager. **World Wide Web address:** http://www.firstam.com. **Description:** An insurance company specializing in title abstracts. **Corporate headquarters location:** Santa Ana CA. **Other area locations:** Statewide. **Other U.S. locations:** Nationwide. **Parent company:** First American Corporation. **Listed on:** New York Stock Exchange. **Stock exchange symbol:** FAF.

FIRST FEDERAL OF MICHIGAN
1001 Woodward Avenue, Detroit MI 48226. 313/965-1400. **Fax:** 800/972-9614. **Contact:** Human Resources. **E-mail address:** cofhr@charteronebank.com. **World Wide Web address:** http://www.charterone.com. **Description:** A bank with 82 branch offices in Michigan. Founded in 1934. **Company slogan:** First in the U.S. **NOTE:** Interested job seekers may submit resumes online. **Positions advertised include:** Customer Service Team Leader; Financial Consultant; Senior Project Assistant. **Special programs:** Tuition Reimbursement Program. **Office hours:** Monday – Thursday, 9:30 a.m. – 4:30 p.m., Friday, 9:30 a.m. – 5:30 p.m. **Parent company:** Charter One Financial, Incorporated (Cleveland OH) is one of the largest thrifts in the country. In addition to First Federal of Michigan, the company also operates Charter One Bank, with 100 branch offices in Ohio; Rochester Community Savings Bank, with 38 branch offices in western New York; Charter One Investments, Michigan; Real Estate Appraisal Services; and Equity One Credit Corporation. **Listed on:** New York Stock Exchange. **Stock exchange symbol:** CF. **Number of employees nationwide:** 2,000.

FISHBECK, THOMPSON, CARR & HUBER, INC.
1515 Arboretum Drive SE, Grand Rapids MI 4956. 616/575-3824. **Fax:** 616/464-3995. **Contact:** Human Resources. **E-mail address:** humanres@ftch.com. **World Wide Web address:** http://www.ftch.com. **Description:** A firm providing a full range of civil engineering, architectural/engineering, and environmental services to public and private sector clients. **Positions advertised include:** Project Architect; Mechanical CAD Technician; Programmer. **Corporate headquarters location:** This location. **Other area locations:** Farmington Hills MI; Kalamazoo MI; Lansing MI. **President:** James D. Townley. **Number of employees nationwide:** 260.

FISHER/UNITECH INC.
1150 West Stevenson Highway, Troy MI 48083. 248/577-5100. **Toll-free phone:** 800/816-8314. **Fax:** 248/577-8524. **Contact:** Human Resources Department. **E-mail address:** info@funtech.com. **World Wide Web address:** http://www.funtech.com. **Description:** An engineering technologies firm. **Corporate headquarters location:** This location. **Other area locations:** Grand Rapids MI. **Other U.S. locations:** Chicago IL; Cleveland OH; Milwaukee WI.

FLAGSTAR BANK
301 West Michigan Avenue, Jackson MI 49201. 517/787-9700. **Contact:** Personnel. **World Wide Web address:** http://www.flagstar.com. **Description:** A full-service savings and loan institution. **Positions advertised include:** Licensed Banker; Call Center Representative; Teller. **Corporate headquarters location:** Troy MI. **Subsidiaries include:** Flagstar Capital Corporation; Flagstar Trust. **Listed on:** New York Stock Exchange. **Stock exchange symbol:** FBC. **President/CEO:** Mark Hammond.

FLEX-N-GATE
4336 Coolidge Highway, Royal Oak MI 48073. 248/549-3800. **Contact:** Human Resources. **World Wide Web address:** http://www.flex-n-gate.com. **Description:** A metal stampings facility for the Big Three U.S. automakers. **Corporate headquarters location:** Urbana IL. **Other area locations:** New Baltimore MI. **Other U.S. locations:** Celina TN. **International locations:** Canada.

FOCUS HOPE
1355 Oakman Boulevard, Detroit MI 48238. 313/494-4775. **Fax:** 313/494-4287. **Contact:** Human Resources. **E-mail address:** hr@focushope.edu. **World Wide Web address:** http://www.focushope.edu. **Description:** An organization providing civil rights advocacy and operating a food center. **Number of employees statewide:** Over 800.

FOOTE HOSPITAL
205 North East Avenue, Jackson MI 49201. 517/796-6400. **Fax:** 517/789-5933. **Contact:** Human Resources Manager. **E-mail address:** hrinfo@wafoote.org. **World Wide Web address:** http://www.footehealth.org. **Description:** A 411-bed hospital offering comprehensive services. **NOTE:** Interested job seekers may apply online. **Positions advertised include:** Clinical Nurse Manager; Registered Nurse; Licensed Practical Nurse; Physical Therapist; Respiratory Therapist; Ultrasound Supervisor; Sleep Technologist; MRI Technologist; Human Resources Recruiter. **Operations at this facility include:** Service. **Number of employees at this location:** 1,900.

FORD MOTOR COMPANY
37625 Michigan Avenue, Wayne MI 48184. 734/467-0200. **Contact:** Human Resources. **World Wide Web address:** http://www.ford.com. **Description:** Ford Motor Company is engaged in the design, development, manufacture, and sale of cars, trucks, tractors, and related components and accessories. Ford is also one of the largest providers of financial services in the United States. Ford's two core businesses are the Automotive Group and the Financial Services Group (Ford Credit, The Associates, USL Capital, and First Nationwide). Ford is also engaged in a number of other businesses, including electronics, glass, electrical and fuel-handling products, plastics, climate-control systems, automotive service and replacement parts, vehicle leasing and rental, and land development. **NOTE:** Ford Motor no longer accepts paper resumes. Please apply online on the Website. **Special programs:** Summer Internship Program; Co-ops. **Corporate headquarters location:** Dearborn MI. **Other U.S. locations:** Nationwide. **Operations at this facility include:** This location primarily manufactures the Ford Focus. **Listed on:** New York Stock Exchange. **Stock exchange symbol:** F. **CEO/Chairman:** William Clay Ford, Jr. **Annual sales/revenues:** $164 billion. **Number of employees nationwide:** 150,000. **Number of employees worldwide:** Approximately 328,000.

FORD MOTOR COMPANY
One American Road, Building 49, Dearborn MI 48126. 313/322-7500. **Toll-free phone:** 800/248-4444. **Contact:** Salaried Recruiting Office. **World Wide Web address:** http://www.ford.com. **Description:** Engaged in the design, development, manufacture, and sale of cars, trucks, tractors, and related components and accessories. Ford Motor Company is also one of the largest providers of financial services in the United States. The company's two core businesses are the Automotive Group and the Financial Services Group (Ford Credit, The Associates, USL Capital, and First Nationwide). Ford is also engaged in other businesses including electronics, glass, electrical and fuel-handling products, plastics, climate-control systems, automotive service and replacement parts, vehicle leasing and rental, and land development. **NOTE:** Ford Motor no longer accepts paper resumes. Please apply online on the Website. **Special programs:** Summer Internship Program; Co-ops. **Corporate headquarters location:** This location. **Other U.S. locations:** Nationwide. **Listed on:** New York Stock Exchange. **Stock exchange symbol:** F. **CEO/Chairman:** William Clay Ford, Jr. **Annual sales/revenues:** $164 billion. **Number of employees nationwide:** 150,000. **Number of employees worldwide:** Approximately 328,000.

FORD MOTOR COMPANY
7700 East Michigan Avenue, Saline MI 48176-9778. 734/429-4911. **Contact:** Personnel Department. **World Wide Web address:** http://www.ford.com. **Description:** Ford Motor Company is engaged in the design, development, manufacture, and sale of cars, trucks, tractors, and related components and accessories. Ford is also one of the largest providers of financial services in the United States. Ford's two core businesses are the Automotive Group and the Financial Services Group (Ford Credit, The Associates, USL Capital, and First Nationwide). Ford is also engaged in a number of other businesses, including electronics, glass, electrical and fuel-handling products, plastics, climate-control systems, automotive service and replacement parts, vehicle leasing and rental, and land development. **NOTE:** Ford Motor no longer accepts paper resumes. Please apply online on the Website. **Special programs:** Summer Internship Program; Co-ops. **Corporate headquarters location:** Dearborn MI. **Other U.S. locations:** Nationwide. **Operations at this facility include:** This location manufactures vehicle parts. **Listed on:** New York Stock Exchange. **Stock exchange symbol:** F. **CEO/Chairman:** William Clay Ford, Jr. **Annual sales/revenues:** $164 billion. **Number of employees nationwide:** 150,000. **Number of employees worldwide:** Approximately 328,000.

FOREST COMPUTER INC.
1749 Hamilton Road, Okemos MI 48864. 517/349-4700. **Toll-free phone:** 800/951-3135. **Fax:** 517/349-2947. **Contact:** Human Resources. **E-mail address:** info@forest.com. **World Wide Web address:** http://www.forest.com. **Description:** Develops network software. Founded in 1981.

FORWARD INDUSTRIES
15150 Cleat Street, Plymouth MI 48170. 734/354-2785. **Toll-free phone:** 800/860-5301. **Fax:** 734/354-2786. **Contact:** Human Resources Department. **World Wide Web address:** http://www.forwardind.com. **Description:** A manufacturer of cylinders, manifolds, and special dies and tools. **Parent company:** Livernois Engineering Company (also at this location). **Operations at this facility include:** Administration; Manufacturing; Research and Development; Sales; Service. **Listed on:** NASDAQ. **Stock exchange symbol:** FORD.

FRANCO PUBLIC RELATIONS GROUP
400 Renaissance Center, Suite 1000, Detroit MI 48243. 313/567-2300. **Fax:** 313/567-4486. **Contact:** Human Resources. **E-mail address:** info@franco.com. **World Wide Web address:** http://www.franco.com. **Description:** A public relations firm. Founded in 1964. **Special programs:** Internships. **Corporate headquarters location:** This location. **Subsidiaries include:** Brightlines Creative; The Comark Group Incorporated. **President:** Maria Leonhauser Rosenau. **Number of employees at this location:** 25.

FRANKLIN BANK, N.A.
24725 West 12 Mile Road, Southfield MI 48034. 248/358-4710. **Contact:** Human Resources. **E-mail address:** mat@franklinbank.com. **World Wide Web address:** http://www.franklinbank.com. **Description:** An independently owned commercial bank. **Corporate headquarters location:** This location. **Other area locations:** Birmingham MI; Grosse Pointe Woods MI; Troy, MI. **Subsidiaries include:** Franklin Finance Corporation; Franklin Home Lending Group. **Listed on:** NASDAQ. **Stock exchange symbol:** FBCP. **President/CEO:** Craig L. Johnson.

FRITO-LAY, INC.
1000 Enterprise Drive, Allen Park MI 48101. 313/271-3000. **Contact:** Human Resources. **World Wide Web address:** http://www.fritolay.com. **Description:** A worldwide manufacturer and wholesaler of snack products including the brand names Fritos Corn Chips, Doritos Tortilla Chips, Lays Potato Chips, and Smartfood Popcorn. **NOTE:** Applicants may apply for positions at http://www.fritolayjobs.com. **Positions advertised include:** Inventory Control System Coordinator; Human Resource Manager; Technical Manager; Maintenance Business Unit Leader. **Special programs:** Internships. **Corporate headquarters location:** Plano TX. **Parent company:** PepsiCo, Incorporated (Purchase NY) consists of Frito-Lay Company, Pepsi-Cola Company, and Tropicana Products, Incorporated. **Operations at this facility include:** Administration; Manufacturing; Sales. **Listed on:** New York Stock Exchange. **Stock exchange symbol:** PEP. **CEO/Chairman:** Abelardo E. Bru. **Sales/revenue:** $14 billion. **Number of employees at this location:** 500. **Number of employees nationwide:** 28,000.

GKN AUTOMOTIVE INC.
3300 University Drive, Auburn Hills MI 48326. 248/377-1200. **Contact:** Michelle Fournier, Human Resources. **World Wide Web address:** http://www.us.add.gknplc.com. **Description:** A leading manufacturer of systems for automotive drive assemblies and automotive components. **Special programs:** Internships. **Office hours:** Monday – Friday, 8:00 a.m. – 4:30 p.m. **Corporate headquarters location:** Timberlake NC. **Other U.S. locations:** Columbia SC; Medane NC; Sanford NC. **Parent company:** GKN plc. **CEO:** Thomas R. Stone.

GM POWERTRAIN
12200 Middlebelt Road, Livonia MI 48150. 734/523-0200. **Contact:** Administrator. **World Wide Web address:** http://www.gm.com. **Description:** Manufactures motor vehicle engines and components for General Motors Corporation. Founded in 1908. **NOTE:** Interested candidates can search and apply for positions online. **Special Programs:** Internships; Co-ops. **Corporate headquarters location:** Pontiac MI. **Other U.S. locations:** Nationwide. **International locations:** Worldwide. **Parent company:** General Motors Corporation is one of the world's largest full-line vehicle manufacturers, and also has substantial interests in information technology, electronics, and finance. GM conducts business through the following sectors: North American Automotive Operations, Delphi Automotive Systems, International Operations, General Motors Acceptance Corporation (GMAC), Electronic Data Systems Corporation (EDS), and GM Hughes Electronics Corporation. North American Automotive Operations includes Sales/Service Groups (Buick, Cadillac, Chevrolet, GMC Truck, Oldsmobile, Pontiac, and Saturn) and Vehicle Development Groups (Powertrain, Truck Group, Small Car Group, and Midsize/Luxury Car Group). Delphi Automotive Systems, formerly known as Automotive Components Group, consists of Delphi Chassis Systems; Delphi Packard Electric Systems; Delphi Energy & Engine Management Systems; Delphi Saginaw Steering Systems; Delphi Harrison Thermal Systems; Delphi Interior & Lighting Systems; Delphi Automotive Systems European Region; Delphi Automotive Systems Asia/Pacific Region; and Delphi Automotive Systems South America. International Operations include GM Europe; Asia Pacific Operations; and Latin America, Africa, Middle East Operations. GMAC provides financing and insurance to GM customers and dealers, and consists of North American Operations, International Operations, Motors Insurance Corporation, and GMAC Mortgage Group. EDS applies information technologies to more than 8,000 customers globally in the communications, energy/chemical, insurance, public sector, travel and transportation, financial services, manufacturing, and retail industries. GM Hughes Electronics Corporation is involved in automotive electronics, telecommunications and space electronics, and defense electronics. **Listed on:** New York Stock Exchange. **Stock exchange symbol:** GM.

G.T.N. INDUSTRIES, INC.
13320 Northend, Oak Park MI 48237. 248/548-2500. **Fax:** 248/548-8614. **Contact:** Kathleen Dargel, Director of Human Resources. **E-mail address:** kdargel@gtninc.com.

World Wide Web address: http://www.gtninc.com. Description: A global production, post production, and new media company. Special programs: Internships. Internship information: Internships are offered in various departments including: Audio Post; Post Production; Film Transfer; Information Technology; Visual Effects; and Operations. Corporate headquarters location: This location. Other area locations: Troy MI.

THE GALE GROUP
27500 Drake Road, Farmington Hills MI 48331. 248/699-4253. **Contact:** Corporate Recruiter. **World Wide Web address:** http://www.galegroup.com. **Description:** Offers complete business information solutions with various data delivery methods such as print, CD-ROM, database, and online services. The company's electronic information incorporates indexes, charts, photographs, glossaries, sound bites, video clips, and hypertext links to customize their business-related information. **Corporate headquarters location:** This location. **Other U.S. locations:** Foster City CA; Beachwood OH; Woodbridge CT. **International locations:** United Kingdom; Malaysia; Australia; Germany; Switzerland. **Parent company:** Thomson Corporation. **Listed on:** New York Stock Exchange; Toronto Stock Exchange. **Stock exchange symbol:** TOC. **President:** Allen W. Paschal. **Number of employees worldwide:** 39,000.

GALLAGHER-KAISER CORPORATION
13710 Mount Elliott Street, Detroit MI 48212. 313/368-3100. **Fax:** 313/368-3109. **Contact:** Human Resources. **E-mail address:** gkemployment@mail.gkcorp.com. **World Wide Web address:** http://www.gkcorp.com. **Description:** Manufactures paint finishing systems and air pollution control equipment. **Special programs:** Training. **Corporate headquarters location:** This location. **President:** Bob Kaiser.

GEAC COMSHARE
555 Briarwood Circle, Ann Arbor MI 48108. 734/994-4800. **Toll-free phone:** 800/922-7979. **Fax:** 734/668-7277. **Contact:** Bruce Harrison, Director of Human Resources. **World Wide Web address:** http://www.performance.geac.com. **Description:** Develops financial applications software for mid-sized companies and international enterprises. **Positions advertised include:** Media Writer. **Corporate headquarters location:** Markham Ontario. **Other U.S. locations:** Nationwide. **International locations:** Worldwide. **Listed on:** NASDAQ; Toronto Stock Exchange. **Stock exchange symbol:** GEAC; GAC. **Number of employees worldwide:** 2,400.

GEDAS, INC.
3499 Hamlin Road, Rochester Hills MI 48309. 248/273-8100. **Fax:** 248/273-8130. **Contact:** Human Resources. **E-mail address:** careers@gedas.com. **World Wide Web address:** http://www.gedasusa.com. **Description:** A worldwide information technology company. **Positions advertised include:** Account Executive; Executive Director of SCM/ERP; Network Manager/Infrastructure Architect; Principal Consultant; SAP HR/Payroll Functional Consultant; SAP FI/CO Consultant; SAP Solution Manager; SAP Project Manager. **Corporate headquarters location:** Berlin, Germany. **International locations:** Worldwide. **CEO:** Axel Knobe.

GENERAL DYNAMICS LAND SYSTEMS
76 South Getty Street, Muskegon MI 49442. 231/724-2151. **Fax:** 231/724-2723. **Contact:** Human Resources. **E-mail address:** jobs@gdls.com. **World Wide Web address:** http://www.gdls.com. **Description:** General Dynamics is a diversified producer of armored weapons systems, industrial and aviation machines, machine tools, aviation and electronics equipment, specialty metals, and consumer products. **Positions advertised include:** Family Representative. **Corporate headquarters location:** Sterling Heights MI. **Other area locations:** Shelby Township MI. **Other U.S. locations:** Groton CT; Lima OH; Eynon PA; Tallahassee FL; Westminster MD; Imperial Valley CA; Woodbridge VA. **Parent company:** General Dynamics Corporation (Falls Church VA). **Operations at this facility include:** This location is a propulsion systems center and manufactures engines and related parts used in industrial equipment. **Listed on:** New York Stock Exchange. **Stock exchange symbol:** GD. **President:** Charles M. Hall. **Number of employees nationwide:** 7,400.

GENERAL DYNAMICS LAND SYSTEMS
38500 Mound Road, Sterling Heights MI 48310. 586/825-4000. **Contact:** Human Resources Department. **E-mail address:** jobs@gdls.com. **World Wide Web address:** http://www.gdls.com. **Description:** General Dynamics is a diversified producer of armored weapons systems, industrial and aviation machines, machine tools, aviation and electronics equipment, specialty metals, and consumer products. **NOTE:** Only experienced professionals should apply for positions at this location. **Positions advertised include:** International Human Resources Representative; Family Engineer. **Corporate headquarters location:** This location. **Other area locations:** Shelby Township MI; Muskogee MI. **Other U.S. locations:** Groton CT; Lima OH; Eynon PA; Tallahassee FL; Westminster MD; Imperial Valley CA; Woodbridge VA. **International locations:** Canada; Switzerland; Australia. **Parent company:** General Dynamics Corporation (Falls Church VA). **Operations at this facility include:** Administration; Divisional Headquarters; Research and Development. This location manufactures and assembles the MIAI Main Battle Tank for the U.S. Army. Products of other General Dynamics divisions include the F-16 aircraft, the Trident nuclear submarine, and the Stinger shoulder-launch missile. **Listed on:** New York Stock Exchange. **Stock exchange symbol:** GD. **President:** Charles M. Hall. **Number of employees at this location:** Over 1,500. **Number of employees nationwide:** 7,400.

GENERAL MOTORS CORPORATION
300 Renaissance Center, Detroit MI 48265. 313/556-5000. **Contact:** Human Resources. **World Wide Web address:** http://www.gm.com. **Description:** General Motors Corporation is one of the world's largest full-line vehicle manufacturers, and has substantial interests in information technology, electronics, and finance. GM conducts business through the following sectors: North American Automotive Operations, International Operations, General Motors Acceptance Corporation (GMAC), Electronic Data Systems Corporation (EDS), and GM Hughes Electronics Corporation. North American Automotive Operations includes Sales/Service Groups (Buick, Cadillac, Chevrolet, GMC Truck, Oldsmobile, Pontiac, and Saturn) and Vehicle Development Groups (Powertrain, Truck Group, Small Car Group, and Midsize/Luxury Car Group). International Operations includes GM Europe; Asia Pacific Operations; and Latin America, Africa, Middle East Operations. GMAC, which provides financing and insurance to GM customers and dealers, consists of North American Operations, International Operations, Motors Insurance Corporation, and GMAC Mortgage Group. EDS applies information technologies to customers globally in the communications, energy/chemical, insurance, public sector, travel and transportation, financial services, manufacturing, and retail industries. GM Hughes Electronics Corporation is involved in automotive electronics, telecommunications and space electronics, and defense electronics. Founded in 1908. **NOTE:** Search and apply for positions online. **Positions advertised include:** Staff Assistant; Administrative Assistant; Purchasing Agent; Manufacturing Engineer; Information Technology Manager. **Corporate headquarters location:** This location. **Other U.S. locations:** Nationwide. **International locations:** Worldwide. **Operations at this facility include:** This location houses the administrative offices. **Listed on:** New York Stock Exchange. **Stock exchange symbol:** GM. **President/CEO:** G. Richard Wagoner, Jr. **Annual sales/revenues:** $186 billion. **Number of employees worldwide:** 325,000.

GENERAL MOTORS CORPORATION
One General Motors Road, Milford MI 48380. 248/685-5000. **Contact:** Personnel Department. **World Wide Web address:** http://www.gm.com. **Description:** General Motors Corporation is one of the world's largest full-line vehicle manufacturers, and also has substantial interests in information technology, electronics, and finance. GM conducts business through the following sectors: North American Automotive Operations, International Operations, General Motors Acceptance Corporation (GMAC), Electronic Data Systems Corporation (EDS), and GM Hughes Electronics Corporation. North American Automotive Operations includes Sales/Service Groups (Buick, Cadillac, Chevrolet, GMC Truck, Oldsmobile, Pontiac, and Saturn) and Vehicle Development Groups (Powertrain, Truck Group, Small Car Group, and Midsize/Luxury Car Group). International Operations includes GM Europe; Asia Pacific Operations; and Latin America, Africa, Middle East Operations. GMAC, which provides financing and insurance to GM customers and dealers, consists of North American Operations, International Operations, Motors Insurance Corporation, and GMAC Mortgage Group. EDS applies information technologies to more than 8,000 customers globally in the communications, energy/chemical, insurance, public sector, travel and transportation, financial services, manufacturing, and retail industries. GM Hughes Electronics Corporation is involved in automotive electronics, telecommunications and space electronics, and defense electronics. Founded in 1908. **NOTE:** Search and apply for positions online. **Positions advertised include:** Senior Project Engineer; Associate Engineer. **Corporate headquarters location:** Detroit MI. **Other U.S. locations:** Nationwide. **International locations:** Worldwide. **Operations at this facility include:** This location is the automotive proving grounds. **Listed on:** New York Stock Exchange. **Stock exchange symbol:** GM. **President/CEO/Director:** G. Richard Wagoner, Junior. **Sales/revenue:** $186 billion. **Number of employees at this location:** 4,100. **Number of employees worldwide:** 325,000.

GENERAL MOTORS CORPORATION
23500 Mound Road, Warren MI 48091. 313/252-0964. **Contact:** Salaried Personnel. **World Wide Web address:** http://www.gm.com. **Description:** General Motors Corporation is one of the world's largest full-line vehicle manufacturers, and also has substantial interests in information technology, electronics, and finance. GM conducts business through the following sectors: North American Automotive Operations, International Operations, General Motors Acceptance Corporation (GMAC), Electronic Data Systems Corporation (EDS), and GM Hughes Electronics Corporation. North American Automotive Operations includes Sales/Service Groups (Buick, Cadillac, Chevrolet, GMC Truck, Oldsmobile, Pontiac, and Saturn) and Vehicle Development Groups (Powertrain, Truck Group, Small Car Group, and Midsize/Luxury Car Group). International Operations includes GM Europe; Asia Pacific Operations; and Latin America, Africa, Middle East Operations. GMAC, which provides financing and insurance to GM customers and dealers, consists of North American Operations, International Operations, Motors Insurance Corporation, and GMAC Mortgage Group. EDS applies information technologies to more than 8,000 customers globally in the communications, energy/chemical, insurance, public sector, travel and transportation, financial services, manufacturing, and retail industries. GM Hughes Electronics Corporation is involved in automotive electronics, telecommunications and space electronics, and defense electronics. Founded in 1908. **Positions advertised include:** Project Engineer; Senior Project Engineer; Senior Administrator; Sculptor; Staff Research Scientist; Senior Designer. **Corporate headquarters location:** Detroit MI. **Other U.S. locations:** Nationwide. **International locations:** Worldwide. **Operations at this facility include:** This location manufactures automotive transmissions. **Listed on:** New York Stock Exchange. **Stock exchange symbol:** GM. **President/CEO:** G. Richard Wagoner, Jr. **Sales/revenue:** $186 billion. **Number of employees at this location:** 4,000. **Number of employees worldwide:** 325,000.

GENERAL MOTORS TECHNICAL CENTER
30400 Mound Road, 3rd Floor, Warren MI 48090-9055. 313/556-5000. **Contact:** Personnel. **World Wide Web address:** http://www.gm.com. **Description:** Performs research and development for the transportation industry. Founded in 1908. **Special programs:** Internships. **Corporate headquarters location:** Detroit MI. **Parent company:** General Motors Corporation is one of the world's largest full-line vehicle manufacturers, and also has substantial interests in information technology, electronics, and finance. GM conducts business through the following sectors: North American Automotive Operations, Delphi Automotive Systems, International Operations, General Motors Acceptance Corporation (GMAC), Electronic Data Systems Corporation (EDS), and GM Hughes Electronics Corporation. North American Automotive Operations includes Sales/Service Groups (Buick, Cadillac, Chevrolet, GMC Truck, Oldsmobile, Pontiac, and Saturn) and Vehicle Development Groups (Powertrain, Truck Group, Small Car Group, and Midsize/Luxury Car Group). Delphi Automotive Systems, formerly known as Automotive Components Group, consists of Delphi Chassis Systems; Delphi Packard Electric Systems; Delphi Energy & Engine Management Systems; Delphi Saginaw Steering Systems; Delphi Harrison Thermal Systems; Delphi Interior & Lighting Systems; Delphi Automotive Systems European Region; Delphi Automotive Systems Asia/Pacific Region; and Delphi Automotive Systems South America. International Operations includes GM Europe; Asia Pacific Operations; and Latin America, Africa, Middle East Operations. EDS applies information technologies to more than 8,000 customers globally in the communications, energy/chemical, insurance, public sector, travel and transportation, financial services, manufacturing, and retail industries. GM Hughes Electronics Corporation is involved in automotive electronics, telecommunications and space electronics, and defense electronics. **Other U.S. locations:** Nationwide. **International locations:** Worldwide. **Operations at this facility include:** Research and Development. **Listed on:** New York Stock Exchange. **Stock exchange symbol:** GM. **President/CEO:** G. Richard Wagoner, Jr. **Annual sales/revenues:** $186 billion. **Number of employees at this location:** 6,000. **Number of employees worldwide:** 325,000.

GENESEE COUNTY COMMUNITY MENTAL HEALTH SERVICES
420 West Fifth Avenue, 1st Floor, Flint MI 48503. 810/257-3705. **Contact:** Sheila Mason, Director of Human Resources. **World Wide Web address:** http://www.gencmh.org. **Description:** Involved in the development and administration of public health programs. **Positions advertised include:** Clinical Therapist; Psychiatric Nurse; Nurse Practitioner. **Office hours:** Monday – Friday, 8:00 a.m. – 5:00 p.m. **Corporate headquarters location:** This location.

GENOVA PRODUCTS
7034 East Court Street, P.O. Box 309, Davison MI 48423-0309. 810/744-4500. **Toll-free phone:** 800/521-7488. **Contact:** Personnel. **World Wide Web address:** http://www.genovaproducts.com. **Description:** Engaged in the manufacture of PVC. Products include plumbing materials, vinyl rainware products, and fencing. **Corporate headquarters location:** This location. **Other U.S. locations:** Sparks NV; Fort Wayne

IN; Hazelton PA; New Boston TX; Faribault MN. **International locations:** England; Lithuania.

GENTEX CORPORATION
600 North Centennial Street, Zeeland MI 49464. 616/772-1800. **Fax:** 616/772-7348. **Contact:** Manager of Human Resources. **E-mail address:** hr@gentex.com. **World Wide Web address:** http://www.gentex.com. **Description:** Designs, develops, manufactures, and markets proprietary products employing electro-optical technology. The company has two primary product lines: automatic rearview mirrors for automobiles and fire protection products for commercial applications. **NOTE:** Interested candidates can write to Human Resources at the following address: 58 East Riley Street, Zeeland MI 49464. **Positions advertised include:** Manufacturing Process Technician; Product Development Technician; Electrical Engineering Program Manager; Electrical Patent Attorney; Technical Team Leader; Product Line Workers. **Special programs:** Internships. **Corporate headquarters location:** This location. **Other area locations:** Livonia MI. **International locations:** Japan; Korea; United Kingdom; Germany; France. **Operations at this facility include:** Administration; Manufacturing; Research and Development. **Listed on:** NASDAQ. **Stock exchange symbol:** GNTX. **CEO/Chairman:** Fred Bauer. **Number of employees nationwide:** Approximately 2,000.

GEORGIE BOY MANUFACTURING INC.
69950 M-62, Edwardsburg MI 49112. 269/663-3415. **Fax:** 269/663-2065. **Contact:** Controller. **World Wide Web address:** http://www.georgieboy.com. **Description:** Manufactures recreational vehicles such as motorhomes. **Corporate headquarters location:** This location.

GERBER PRODUCTS COMPANY
445 State Street, Fremont MI 49413. 231/928-2000. **Contact:** Human Resources Manager. **World Wide Web address:** http://www.gerber.com. **Description:** Manufactures baby food. **Corporate headquarters location:** Parsippany NJ. **Parent company:** Novartis. **Listed on:** New York Stock Exchange. **Stock exchange symbol:** NVS.

GILL INDUSTRIES
5271 Plainfield NE, Grand Rapids MI 49525. 616/559-2714. **Fax:** 616/559-9518. **Contact:** Rick Foster. **E-mail address:** rfoster@gill-industries.com. **World Wide Web address:** http://www.gill-industries.com. **Description:** Gill Industries specializes in mechanism design and development.

GOODWILL INDUSTRIES OF GREATER DETROIT
3111 Grand River Avenue, Detroit MI 48208. 313/964-3900 ext.348. **Fax:** 313/964-3972. **Contact:** Nykia Daniels, Human Resources. **E-mail address:** ndaniels@goodwilldetroit.com. **World Wide Web address:** http://www.goodwilldetroit.org. **Description:** Besides operating 1,400 thrift stores nationwide, Goodwill is a nonprofit provider of employment training for the disabled and the poor. **Positions advertised include:** Support Coordination Specialist. **Corporate headquarters location:** This location. **Other U.S. locations:** Nationwide.

GORDON FOOD SERVICE
P.O. Box 1787, Grand Rapids MI 49501. 616/530-7000. **Physical address:** 333 50th Street SW, Grand Rapids MI 49548. **Fax:** 616/717-9162. **Contact:** Employment Coordinator. **World Wide Web address:** http://www.gfs.com. **Description:** One of the largest family-owned food distributors in the nation. **NOTE:** Interested job seekers may submit resumes online. **Positions advertised include:** Product Development Specialist; Human Resource Analyst; Product Development Specialist; Sales Representative. **Corporate headquarters location:** This location. **Other U.S. locations:** IL; IN; OH; PA; WV. **International locations:** Canada. **Operations at this facility include:** Administration; Sales; Service. **Listed on:** Privately held. **Number of employees at this location:** 700. **Number of employees worldwide:** 5,750.

GRACE & WILD STUDIOS, INC.
23689 Industrial Park Drive, Farmington Hills MI 48335. 248/471-6010. **Contact:** Human Resources. **World Wide Web address:** http://www.gracewild.com. **Description:** Engaged in film and videotape production, film transfer, and related services. **Special programs:** Internships. **Corporate headquarters location:** This location. **Subsidiaries include:** Postique; Griot Editorial; Detroit Power & Light; Projections; IN-GEAR Equipment Rental; Film Craft Lab; Grace & Wild Interactive Development; Grace & Wild Digital Studios. **President:** Steven D. Wild.

GRAND HOTEL
P.O. Box 286, Mackinac Island MI 49797. 906/847-9201. **Fax:** 906/847-3259. **Contact:** Human Resources. **World Wide Web address:** http://www.grandhotel.com. **Description:** A summer resort hotel. **NOTE:** Seasonal positions are open from mid-May until late October. Interested jobseekers should write to the address listed above for an employment application or apply online. **Positions advertised include:** Pantry Cook; Pastry Cook; Dishwasher; Bar Porter; Cocktail Server; Waiter/Waitress; Storeroom Clerk; Cashier; Recreation Attendant; Pool Attendant; Desk Clerk; Convention Porter; Maintenance Worker; Laundry Attendant; Uniform Valet Attendant.

GRAND RAPIDS CONTROLS, INC.
825 Northland Drive, P.O. Box 360, Rockford MI 49341. 616/866-9551. **Fax:** 616/866-1373 **Contact:** Human Resources. **E-mail address:** loug@grcontrols.com. **World Wide Web address:** http://www.grcontrols.com. **Description:** Manufactures cable assembly products for automotive and furniture manufacturers. **NOTE:** Online applications are available. **Corporate headquarters location:** This location. **Operations at this facility include:** Administration; Manufacturing. **Listed on:** Privately held. **Number of employees at this location:** 250.

JOHN E. GREEN COMPANY
220 Victor Avenue, Highland Park MI 48203. 313/868-2400. **Fax:** 313/868-0011. **Contact:** Personnel Director. **World Wide Web address:** http://www.johnegreen.com. **Description:** A plumbing and heating contracting firm specializing in mechanical and fire protection systems. **Corporate headquarters location:** This location. **Other area locations:** Ann Arbor MI; Lansing MI; Saginaw MI; Petoskey MI; Negaunee MI. **Other U.S. locations:** Nashville TN. **President:** Peter J. Green. **Number of employees at this location:** 200.

HHA SERVICES
22622 Harper Avenue, St. Clair Shores MI 48080. 586/771-3040. **Toll-free phone:** 800/442-1140. **Fax:** 810/771-3044. **Contact:** Jennifer Fedderson, Recruiting Manager. **E-mail address:** jfedderson@hhaservices.com. **World Wide Web address:** http://www.hhaservices.com. **Description:** Offers contract services for maintenance, food service, transportation, security, clinical engineering, housekeeping, laundry, and linen supply. Founded in 1974. **Positions advertised include:** Regional Director of Sales; Regional Director of Operations; Director of Facilities Management; Senior Area Manager; Director of Environmental Services/Housekeeping. **Special programs:** Training; Tuition Reimbursement Program; Relocation Assistance Program. **Corporate headquarters location:** This location. **Other U.S. locations:** Austin TX. **Listed on:** Privately held. **President/CEO:** Paul Fayad.

HAHN ELASTOMER
14601 Keel Street, Plymouth MI 48170. 734/455-3300. **Fax:** 734/455-0546. **Contact:** Human Resources Department. **World Wide Web address:** http://www.hahnelastomer.com. **Description:** Manufactures molded and extruded plastic materials for the automotive industry. **Corporate headquarters location:** Plymouth MI. **Number of employees at this location:** 200.

HANDLEMAN COMPANY
500 Kirts Boulevard, Troy MI 48084. 248/362-4400. **Contact:** Vice President of Personnel. **E-mail address:** careers@handleman.com. **World Wide Web address:** http://www.handleman.com. **Description:** Engaged in the wholesale distribution of prerecorded music, books on tape, and videos. The company is comprised of two segments: Handleman Entertainment Resources and Northcoast Entertainment. **NOTE:** Interested job seekers may submit resumes online. **Special programs:** Executive Candidate Training Program; Mentor Program; Educational Assistance Program. **Corporate headquarters location:** This location. **Other area locations:** Romulus MI. **Other U.S. locations:** Nationwide. **International locations:** Canada; Mexico; Brazil; Argentina; United Kingdom. **Subsidiaries include:** Anchor Bay Entertainment; Madacy Entertainment; Entertainment Company. **Listed on:** New York Stock Exchange. **Stock exchange symbol:** HDL. **Annual sales/revenues:** Over $1 billion. **Number of employees worldwide:** 2,300.

HARLAN ELECTRIC COMPANY
2695 Crooks Road, Rochester Hills MI 48309. 248/853-4601. **Contact:** Human Resources. **E-mail address:** employment@myrgroup.com. **World Wide Web address:** http://www.myrgroup.com. **Description:** A company providing engineering, architectural, and surveying services. **NOTE:** Resumes should be mailed to the parent company's corporate headquarters: MYR Group, Inc., Attention: Human Resources, Three Continental Towers, 1701 West Golf Road,-Suite 1012, Rolling Meadows IL 60008-4270. Resumes are also accepted via e-mail. **Corporate headquarters location:** This location. **Other U.S. locations:** Bloomfield CT; Carlisle PA. **Parent company:** MYR Group. **Number of employees at this location:** 1,900.

HARLEYELLIS ASHVILLE
26913 Northwestern Highway, Suite 200, Southfield MI 48034. 248/262-1500. **Fax:** 248/262-1552. **Contact:** Michelle Kaye or Karen Szostack, Human Resources. **E-mail address:** careers@harleyellis.com. **World Wide Web address:** http://www.harleyellis.com. **Description:** A multidivisional architectural and engineering firm providing comprehensive planning, design, and problem-solving services to commercial, governmental, industrial, and institutional clients. Founded in 1962. **Corporate headquarters location:** This location. **Other U.S. locations:** Cincinnati OH; Chicago IL; Los Angeles CA. **Subsidiaries include:** ENG/6A. **Listed on:** Privately held. **Number of employees at this location:** 100. **Number of employees nationwide:** Over 350.

HARPER UNIVERSITY HOSPITAL
3990 John R. Street, Detroit MI 48201. 313/745-8040. **Contact:** Director of Human Resources. **World Wide Web address:** http://www.dmc.org. **Description:** A hospital affiliated with the Wayne State University School of Medicine that specializes in teaching, cardiology, and oncology. **NOTE:** To contact Human Resources directly, call 313/578-3930. **Positions advertised include:** Transplant Services Director; Surgical Technician; Staff Nurse; Clinical Pharmacist; Radiologic Technologist; Vascular Surgical Technologist; ; Respiratory Therapist; Ultrasound Technologist; Special Procedures Nurse; MRI Technologist; Adjunct Chaplain; Research Assistant. **Special programs:** Internships. **Parent company:** Detroit Medical Center.

HASTINGS MANUFACTURING COMPANY
325 North Hanover, Hastings MI 49017. 269/945-2491. **Fax:** 269/945-4667. **Contact:** Barb Randall, Personnel Department. **E-mail address:** brandall@hastingsmfg.com. **World Wide Web address:** http://www.hastingsmfg.com. **Description:** Manufactures automotive parts, piston rings, and oil filters. **Special programs:** Internships. **Corporate headquarters location:** This location. **International locations:** Canada; Mexico. **Subsidiaries include:** Hastings, Inc. (Barrie Ontario). **Operations at this facility include:** Administration; Manufacturing; Research and Development; Sales; Service. **Listed on:** American Stock Exchange. **Stock exchange symbol:** HMF. **Number of employees nationwide:** 413.

HASTINGS MUTUAL INSURANCE COMPANY
404 East Woodlawn Avenue, Hastings MI 49058. 269/945-3405. **Toll-free phone:** 800/442-8277. **Fax:** 269/945-4095. **Contact:** Dana Walters, Vice President of Human Resources Department. **E-mail address:** humanresources@hastingsmutual.com. **World Wide Web address:** http://www.hastingsmutual.com. **Description:** Sells property and casualty insurance through independent agents to policyholders in Michigan, Indiana, Illinois, Ohio, and Wisconsin. **Positions advertised include:** Senior Claims Supervisor; Quality Services Supervisor; Commercial Underwriter. **Special programs:** Internships; Training. **Corporate headquarters location:** This location. **Operations at this facility include:** Administration. **President/CEO:** William H. Wallace. **Number of employees at this location:** 290.

HAWORTH INC.
One Haworth Center, Holland MI 49423. 269/393-3000. **Fax:** 269/393-1551. **Contact:** Claudia Wilkinson, Human Resources. **E-mail address:** claudia.wilkinson@haworth.com. **World Wide Web address:** http://www.haworth.com. **Description:** Manufactures office furniture. Founded in 1948. **NOTE:** Entry-level positions and second and third shifts are offered. **Positions advertised include:** Remedy Programmer Analyst; Packaging Engineer; Sales Training Consultant; Corporate Project Manager; Senior Systems Analyst. **Special programs:** Internships; Apprenticeships; Training; Summer Jobs. **Corporate headquarters location:** This location. **Other U.S. locations:** Nationwide. **International locations:** Worldwide. **Operations at this facility include:** Administration; Manufacturing; Research and Development. **Listed on:** Privately held. **Number of employees at this location:** 3,400. **Number of employees worldwide:** 10,000.

HAYES LEMMERZ INTERNATIONAL, INC.
1500 Fourth Avenue, Cadillac MI 49601-1399. 231/779-9600. **Contact:** Human Resources Department. **E-mail address:** hr@hayes-lemmerz.com. **World Wide Web address:** http://www.hayes-lemmerz.com. **Description:** Hayes Lemmerz International manufactures metal automobile components. **NOTE:** Resumes may be submitted online for general consideration. **Corporate headquarters location:** Northville MI. **Other area locations:** Montague MI; Homer MI; Howell MI; Au Gres MI; Southfield MI. **Other U.S. locations:** Sedalia MO; Bowling Green OH; Akron OH; Gainesville GA; Berea KY; Huntington IN; Wabash IN; Bristol IN. **International locations:**

Worldwide. **Subsidiaries include:** CMI International Incorporated. **Operations at this facility include:** This location manufactures exhaust manifolds, and steering knuckles. **Listed on:** OTC. **Stock exchange symbol:** HLMMQ. **President/CEO/Chairman:** Curtis J. Clawson.

HELM INC.
14310 Hamilton Avenue, Highland Park MI 48203. 313/865-5000. **Toll-free phone:** 800/782-4356. **Fax:** 313/865-5927. **Contact:** Kristin Kostan, Human Resources Manager. **E-mail address:** kkostan@helminc.com. **World Wide Web address:** http://www.helminc.com. **Description:** Engaged in the packing and distribution of literature. Founded in 1943. **NOTE:** To contact Human Resources directly, call 313/733-3435. **Corporate headquarters location:** This location. **Other U.S. locations:** Laguna Hills, CA. **President:** Dennis Gusick. **Number of employees at this location:** 265.

HEMLOCK SEMICONDUCTOR CORPORATION
12334 Geddes Road, P.O. Box 80, Hemlock MI 48626. 989/642-5201. **Contact:** Human Resources Manager. **World Wide Web address:** http://www.hscpoly.com. **Description:** Produces and markets polycrystalline silicon and related chemicals. **NOTE:** Applications for open positions available at website. **Corporate headquarters location:** This location. **Parent company:** Dow Corning Corporation. **Number of employees nationwide:** 500.

HENKEL SURFACE TECHNOLOGIES
32100 Stephenson Highway, Madison Heights MI 48071. 248/583-9300. **Fax:** 248/589-4837. **Contact:** Human Resources. **E-mail address:** hst.resume@hstna.com. **World Wide Web address:** http://www.henkelsurftechna.com. **Description:** A manufacturer of surface treatment chemicals. **NOTE:** Interested job seekers may submit resumes online. **Special programs:** Co-ops; Educational Assistance Program. **Corporate headquarters location:** This location. **Other U.S. locations:** Nationwide. **International locations:** Worldwide. **Parent company:** Henkel Corporation (Dusseldorf, Germany). **Operations at this facility include:** Administration; Research and Development; Sales; Service. **Number of employees at this location:** 650. **Number of employees nationwide:** Over 4,000. **Number of employees worldwide:** 56,600.

HERMAN MILLER INC.
855 East Main Avenue, P.O. Box 302, Zeeland MI 49464. 616/654-3000. **Toll-free phone:** 888/443-4357. **Recorded jobline:** 616/654-3771. **Contact:** Human Resources Department. **E-mail address:** jobs@hermanmiller.com. **World Wide Web address:** http://www.hermanmiller.com. **Description:** A manufacturer of interior systems, furnishings, and seating products for offices, public areas, and health care facilities. **Positions advertised include:** Test Engineer; Custom Website Publisher; Market Development Leader. **Special programs:** Internships. **Office hours:** Monday – Friday, 8:00 a.m. – 5:00 p.m. **Corporate headquarters location:** This location. **International locations:** Worldwide. **Subsidiaries include:** Meridan; Milcare; Miltech; Phoenix Designs. **Operations at this facility include:** Administration; Manufacturing; Research and Development. **Listed on:** NASDAQ. **Stock exchange symbol:** MLHR. **Number of employees worldwide:** 6,300.

HILGRAEVE INC.
P.O. Box 941, Monroe MI 48161-0941. 734/243-0576. **Physical address:** 111 Conant Avenue, Suite A, Monroe MI 48161. **Contact:** Human Resources. **E-mail address:** resume@hilgraeve.com. **World Wide Web address:** http://www.hilgraeve.com. **Description:** Develops and manufactures asynchronous communications software for IBM-compatible desktop computers and portable PCs. **Positions advertised include:** Vice President of Marketing; Web Developer; Corporate Sales Representative. **Corporate headquarters location:** This location.

HOBAN FOODS, INC.
1599 East Warren Avenue, Detroit MI 48207-1035. 313/833-1500. **Fax:** 313/833-0629. **Contact:** Human Resources. **World Wide Web address:** http://www.hobanfoods.com. **Description:** Distributes frozen foods to restaurants and nursing homes. **Corporate headquarters location:** This location. **Operations at this facility include:** Administration; Sales; Service. **Listed on:** Privately held. **President:** John Van Tiem. **Number of employees at this location:** 35.

HOLCIM US, INC.
P.O. Box 122, Dundee MI 48131-0122. 734/529-2411. **Physical address:** 6211 North Ann Arbor Road, Dundee MI 48131. **Contact:** Sharon Patchett, Human Resources. **E-mail address:** sharon.patchett@holcim.com. **World Wide Web address:** http://www.holcim.com/us. **Description:** A manufacturer and distributor of hydraulic cement and related products. **NOTE:** Interested job seekers may submit resumes online. **Positions advertised include:** Information Technology Auditor; Administrative Assistant; Computer Operations Analyst; Network Analyst; Accountant; Senior Logistics Analyst. **Special programs:** Co-ops; Internships; Training; Education Assistance Program. **Corporate headquarters location:** This location. **Other U.S. locations:** Nationwide. **Parent company:** Holcim Limited. **Annual sales/revenues:** Approximately $1.1 billion. **Number of employees nationwide:** 2,400.

HOLIDAY INN
5801 Southfield Service Drive, Detroit MI 48228. 313/336-3340. **Contact:** Personnel. **World Wide Web address:** http://www.holiday-inn.com. **Description:** A hotel with 347 rooms. **Corporate headquarters location:** Cincinnati OH. **Other U.S. locations:** Nationwide. **International locations:** Worldwide. **Parent company:** Six Continents Hotels. **Listed on:** New York Stock Exchange. **Stock exchange symbol:** SXC.

HONEYWELL
375 North Lake Street, Boyne City MI 49712. 231/582-6526. **Contact:** Human Resources. **World Wide Web address:** http://www.honeywell.com. **Description:** Honeywell is engaged in the research, development, manufacture, and sale of advanced technology products and services in the fields of chemicals, electronics, automation, and controls. The company's major businesses are home and building automation and control, performance polymers and chemicals, industrial automation and control, space and aviation systems, and defense and marine systems. **Special programs:** Internships. **Corporate headquarters location:** Morristown NJ. **Other U.S. locations:** Nationwide. **International locations:** Worldwide. **Operations at this facility include:** This location is engaged in the manufacture of aircraft and missile systems instruments. **Listed on:** New York Stock Exchange; also, the London, Chicago, and Pacific Stock Exchanges. **Stock exchange symbol:** HON. **CEO/Chairman:** David M. Cote.

HOWMET CORPORATION
One Misco Drive, Whitehall MI 49461. 231/894-5686. **Contact:** Human Resources. **World Wide Web address:** http://www.howmet.com. **Description:** Manufactures high-temperature engines for the automotive and aerospace industries. **Corporate headquarters location:** Darien CT. **Other U.S. locations:** TN; CA; NJ; VA; OH; TX. **International locations:** England; France; Japan. **Parent company:** Alcoa. **President/CEO:** Mario Longhi. **Number of employees at this location:** 1,600. **Number of employees worldwide:** 11,000.

THE HUNTINGTON NATIONAL BANK
101 East Main, Zeeland MI 49464. 616/355-9019. **Contact:** Director of Human Resources. **World Wide Web address:** http://www.huntington.com. **Description:** A full-service commercial bank. **NOTE:** Hiring is conducted through the regional headquarters. Interested jobseekers may search and apply for positions online. Resumes may also be mailed to: Hudson National Bank Human Resources, 50 Monroe Street. Grand Rapids MI 49503. **Corporate headquarters location:** Columbus OH. **Other U.S. locations:** OH; IN; KY; WV. **Parent company:** Huntington Bancshares, Incorporated. **Listed on:** NASDAQ. **Stock exchange symbol:** HBAN. **CEO:** Tom Hoaglin.

HURLEY MEDICAL CENTER
One Hurley Plaza, Flint MI 48503. 810/257-9140. **Fax:** 810/762-6513. **Contact:** Human Resources. **E-mail address:** resume@hurleymc.com. **World Wide Web address:** http://www.hurleymc.com. **Description:** A 463-bed publicly owned teaching hospital affiliated with Michigan State University's College of Human Medicine, the University of Michigan Medical School, and the Henry Ford Health System. **NOTE:** Entry-level positions are offered. **Positions advertised include:** Assistant Head Nurse; Registered Nurse; Nurse Manager; Licensed Practical Nurse; Certified Hand Therapist; Clinical Nurse Specialist; Clinical Practitioner; Director of Environmental Services; Director of Facilities Management; Echocardiographer; EEG Technician; House Director; Medical Secretary; Occupational Therapist; Physical Therapist; Respiratory Therapist; Registered Dietitian; Medical Technologist; Pharmacy Technician; Surgical Technician; Special Procedures Technician; Reimbursement Analyst; Public Safety Officer. **Special programs:** Internships. **Operations at this facility include:** Administration; Research and Development; Service. **Number of employees at this location:** 2,700.

HUTZEL HOSPITAL
4707 St. Antoine Boulevard, Detroit MI 48201. 313/745-7555. **Recorded jobline:** 313/745-JOBS. **Contact:** Employment Center. **E-mail address:** jobs@dmc.org. **World Wide Web address:** http://www.hutzel.org. **Description:** A 244-bed hospital specializing in obstetrics, orthopedics, and ophthalmology. **NOTE:** The hospital is part of the Detroit Medical Center; applicants should contact the Employment Center at One Orchestra Place, 3663 Woodward Avenue, Suite 200, Detroit MI 48201. **Positions advertised include:** Clinical Nurse Manager; Physician Assistant; Nurse Practitioner; Clinical Improvement Specialist; Research Nurse; Lactation Consultant; Staff Nurse. **Parent company:** Detroit Medical Center. **Operations at this facility include:** Service. **Number of employees at this location:** 2,500.

IBM CORPORATION
1800 West Nine Mile Road, Southfield MI 48075. 248/552-4200. **Contact:** Human Resources. **World Wide Web address:** http://www.ibm.com. **Description:** IBM is a leading provider of enterprise architecture and open solutions for large corporations. The company's Enterprise Division provides architectural consulting, professional services, and industry-leading servers that enable customers to migrate successfully from host-based, proprietary computer environments to open, client/server architectures. Working closely with leading hardware and software partners, the Enterprise Division helps customers design and implement enterprisewide architectures and systems for online transaction processing, decision support, and workgroup computing. IBM's Platform Division develops high-performance, Intel-based, symmetric, multiprocessing servers that run on the UNIX and Microsoft Windows NT operating systems and support enterprisewide applications and information services. The Platform Division's products are sold by the Enterprise Division and through a variety of indirect channels, including OEM resellers, value-added resellers, and distributors. Founded in 1983. **Positions advertised include:** Client Representative; Content Management Specialist; Information Technology Specialist; Information Technology Consultant; Mainframe Developer; Technical Representative. **Corporate headquarters location:** Armonk NY. **Other U.S. locations:** Nationwide. **International locations:** Worldwide. **Operations at this facility include:** This location is a sales office. **Listed on:** New York Stock Exchange. **Stock exchange symbol:** IBM. **President/CEO/Chairman:** Samuel J. Palmisano. **Annual sales/revenues:** $89 billion. **Number of employees worldwide:** Over 255,000.

ICA CINETIC AUTOMATION CORPORATION
23400 Halstead Road, Farmington Hills MI 48335. 248/477-0800. **Contact:** Gerry Makuch, Vice President of Human Resources. **E-mail address:** recruiter@cineticusa.com. **World Wide Web address:** http://www.cineticautomation.com. **Description:** A manufacturer of industrial cleaning, washing, and finishing equipment. **NOTE:** Applications are available online. **Positions advertised include:** Program Manager; Engineer; Validation Technician. **Corporate headquarters location:** This location. **Other U.S. locations:** Nationwide. **International locations:** Mexico; United Kingdom. **Operations at this facility include:** Administration; Manufacturing; Sales; Service.

INDIANHEAD MOUNTAIN RESORT
500 Indianhead Road, Wakefield MI 49968. 906/229-5181. **Contact:** Human Resources. **E-mail address:** Julie@indianheadmtn.com. **World Wide Web address:** http://www.indianheadmtn.com. **Description:** A full-service year-round resort. The resort offers skiing with 18 trails, as well as a health and racquet club. **NOTE:** Seasonal positions are offered.

INDUCTOHEAT INC.
32251 North Avis Drive, Madison Heights MI 48071. 248/585-9393. **Toll-free phone:** 800/624-6297. **Fax:** 248/589-1062. **Contact:** Human Resources. **World Wide Web address:** http://www.inductoheat.com. **Description:** Engaged in the manufacture of industrial furnaces. **Office hours:** Monday – Friday, 8:00 a.m. – 5:00 p.m. **Corporate headquarters location:** This location. **Other area locations:** Ray Township MI. **Other U.S. locations:** Columbus OH; Rancocas NJ; Edgewood NY; Fort Worth TX; Milwaukee WI. **International locations:** Worldwide. **Number of employees at this location:** 500.

INDUSTRIAL TECTONICS INC.
7222 West Huron River Drive, Dexter MI 47270. 734/426-4681. **Contact:** Human Resources. **World Wide Web address:** http://www.itiball.com. **Description:** Engaged in the manufacture of high-precision ball products. **Corporate headquarters location:** Ann Arbor MI. **Parent company:** Kadon. **Listed on:** New York Stock Exchange. **Stock exchange symbol:** KDN.

INFOR
d.b.a. AGILYSIS AUTOMOTIVE
3855 Sparks Drive SE, Suite 201, Grand Rapids MI 49546. 616/957-4444. **Fax:** 616/957-8954. **Contact:** Human Resources. **E-mail address:** hr@brainna.com. **World**

Wide Web address: http://www.agilisys.com. **Description:** Develops software for the automotive industry. **Corporate headquarters location:** Atlanta GA.

INSITUFORM TECHNOLOGIES
1950 Sequoia Trail, Owosso MI 48867-0250. 989/725-9525. **Contact:** Human Resources Department. **E-mail address:** careers@insituform.com. **World Wide Web address:** http://www.insituform.com. **Description:** Manufactures casting pipe. **Parent company:** Insituform Mid-America, Incorporated uses various trenchless technologies for restoration, new construction, and improvements of pipeline systems including sewers; gas lines; industrial waste lines; water lines; and oil field, mining and industrial process pipelines. The company's trenchless technologies require little or no excavation and eliminate the need to replace deteriorating pipe. Insituform Mid-America provides a wide variety of technologies including Insituform, PALTEM, Tite Liner, tunneling, and many others. **NOTE:** Jobseekers should send resumes to: Insituform Technologies, Human Resources, 702 Spirit 40 Parkway, Chesterfield MO 63005. **Special programs:** Superintendent Development Program. **Corporate headquarters location:** Chesterfield MO. **Other U.S. locations:** Nationwide. **International locations:** Worldwide. **Listed on:** NASDAQ. **Stock exchange symbol:** INSUA. **President:** Thomas S. Rooney, Junior. **Annual sales/revenues:** $487 million. **Number of employees worldwide:** 2,176.

INTEGRAL VISION INC.
38700 Grand River Avenue, Farmington Hills MI 48335. 248/471-2660. **Fax:** 248/615/2971. **Contact:** Human Resources. **E-mail address:** tsimmerman@iv-usa.com. **World Wide Web address:** http://www.iv-usa.com. **Description:** Manufactures machine vision-based inspection systems and resistance welding controls. Integral's machine vision-based inspection systems are designed for the automatic inspection of compact discs, glass containers, and other manufacturing processes. The company's resistance welding controls provide important data about the welding process in order to assure quality. **Special programs:** Educational Assistance Program. **Corporate headquarters location:** This location.

INTERMET CORPORATION
5445 Corporate Drive, Suite 200, Troy MI 48098. 248/952/2500. **Fax:** 248/952-1512. **Contact:** Human Resources. **E-mail address:** bmills@intermet.com. **World Wide Web address:** http://www.intermet.com. **Description:** Designs and manufactures cast-metal components for automotive and industrial applications. **Corporate headquarters location:** This location. **Other U.S. locations:** GA; IL; WI; VA. **International locations:** Portugal. **Listed on:** NASDAQ. **Stock exchange symbol:** INMT. **Annual sales/revenues:** $731 million. **Number of employees worldwide:** Approximately 5,600.

INTERTAPE POLYMER GROUP
317 Kendall Avenue, Marysville MI 48040. 810/364-9000. **Fax:** 810/364-4733. **Contact:** Human Resources Department. **World Wide Web address:** http://www.intertapepolymer.com. **Description:** A manufacturer and distributor of masking tape, reinforced tape, fiberglass tape, and paper packaging products. **Corporate headquarters location:** Bradenton FL. **Other U.S. locations:** IL; GA; SC; VA; WI; CA. **International locations:** Canada; Mexico; Portugal. **Listed on:** New York Stock Exchange. **Stock exchange symbol:** ITP. **Number of employees worldwide:** 2,800.

JSP INTERNATIONAL
13889 West Chicago Boulevard, Detroit MI 48228. 313/935-1856. **Fax:** 313/834-0213. **Contact:** Human Resources. **E-mail address:** jill.parker@jsp.com. **World Wide Web address:** http://www.jsp.com. **Description:** A plastic foams manufacturer. Engineers from JSP work closely with molders and OEM design teams to help create solutions to product design problems. **Positions advertised include:** Production Supervisor. **International locations:** Worldwide.

JABIL CIRCUIT COMPANY
3800 Giddings Road, Auburn Hills MI 48326. 248/392-6000. **Fax:** 248/292-6901. **Contact:** Human Resources. **E-mail address:** hr_auburnhills@jabil.com. **World Wide Web address:** http://www.jabil.com. **Description:** Produces circuit boards and provides other manufacturing services and solutions to clients in the electronic industry. **Special programs:** Internships. **NOTE:** Interested candidates can search and apply for positions online. **Positions advertised include:** Configuration Management Analyst; Process Quality Engineer; Material Planner; Buyer. **Corporate headquarters location:** St. Petersburg FL. **Other U.S. locations:** Billerica MA; Louisville KY; McAllen TX; Memphis TN; San Jose CA; St. Petersburg FL; Tampa FL. **International locations:** Worldwide. **Listed on:** New York Stock Exchange. **Stock exchange symbol:** JBL. **President/CEO:** Timothy L. Main. **Annual sales/revenues:** $4.7 billion. **Number of employees at this location:** 1,000. **Number of employees worldwide:** Approximately 26,000.

JACKSON NATIONAL LIFE INSURANCE COMPANY
One Corporate Way, Lansing MI 48951. 517/367-4237. **Fax:** 517/367/4237. **Contact:** Human Resources Department. **E-mail address:** staffing@jnli.com. **World Wide Web address:** http://www.jnl.com. **Description:** Involved in the underwriting of life insurance and annuity policies. **Positions advertised include:** Administrative Assistant; Director, Government Relations; Java Programmer; Mainframe Programmer; UNIX Administrator; Senior Applications Database Administrator; Client Service Associate. **Special programs:** Summer Internships. **Corporate headquarters location:** This location. **Other U.S. locations:** Denver CO; Santa Monica CA. **Parent company:** Prudential Place of England.

JAY DEE CONTRACTORS INC.
38881 Schoolcraft Road, Livonia MI 48150. 734/591-3400. **Fax:** 734/464-6868. **Contact:** Human Resources Department. **E-mail address:** careers@jaydeecontr.com. **World Wide Web address:** http://www.jaydeecontractors.com. **Description:** A tunneling contractor for underground construction projects. **Positions advertised include:** Project Manager; Project Superintendent; Project Engineer; Surveyor; Civil Engineer; Estimator; Experienced Tunnel Laborers; Experienced Operating Engineers; Administrative and Accounting Support Staff. **Special programs:** Internships. **Corporate headquarters location:** This location. **Other area locations:** Detroit MI. **Number of employees at this location:** 100.

JOHNSON CONTROLS, INC.
49200 Halyard Drive, Plymouth MI 48170. 734/254-5000. **Contact:** Human Resources Department. **World Wide Web address:** http://www.johnsoncontrols.com. **Description:** The company is comprised of two divisions: the Automotive Systems Group and the Controls Group. The Automotive Systems Group is an independent supplier of automotive and light truck seating systems and components. Founded in 1885. **Special programs:** Internships; Co-ops. **Corporate headquarters location:** Milwaukee WI. **Operations at this facility include:** This location is the division headquarters for the company's Automotive Systems Group. Research and development are also conducted here. **Listed on:** New York Stock Exchange. **Stock exchange symbol:** JCI. **President/CEO:** John M. Barth. **Annual sales/revenues:** $22.6 billion. **Number of employees at this location:** 1,200. **Number of employees worldwide:** 118,000.

KALAMAZOO PUBLIC SCHOOLS
1220 Howard Street, Kalamazoo MI 49008. 269/337-0177. **Fax:** 269/377-0185. **Contact:** Kathleen J. Thompson, Human Resources. **E-mail address:** thompsonkj@kalamazoo.k12.mi.us. **World Wide Web address:** http://www.kalamazoopublicschools.com. **Description:** Coordinates information, resources, and services for the Kalamazoo public school district. Kalamazoo Public Schools serve over 11,000 students. **Positions advertised include:** Head Football Coach; Substitute Teacher; Substitute Paraprofessional; Substitute Secretary; Bus Driver. **Office hours:** Monday – Friday, 8:00 a.m. – 5:00 p.m.

KAMAX
500 West Long Lake Road, Troy MI 48098. 248/879-0200. **Contact:** Human Resources. **World Wide Web address:** http://www.kamax.com. **Description:** Designs and manufactures fasteners for cold heading thread rolling and heat treatment operations. Founded in 1939. **NOTE:** Second and third shifts are offered. **Special programs:** Internships; Training; Management Development Program; Exchange Program. **Corporate headquarters location:** This location. **Other U.S. locations:** Nationwide. **International locations:** Germany; Spain; Czech Republic. **Listed on:** Privately held.

KASLE STEEL CORPORATION
P.O. Box 33536, Detroit MI 48232. 313/943-2500. **Physical address:** 4343 Wyoming, Dearborn MI 48126. **Fax:** 313/943-2597. **Contact:** Human Resources Manager. **World Wide Web address:** http://www.kaslesteel.com. **Description:** Kasle Steel Corporation operates a chain of metal service centers that provide numerous steel processing services, such as blanking, splitting, and pickling. **Corporate headquarters location:** This location. **Other area locations:** Woodhaven MI; Flint MI. **International locations:** Windsor Ontario. **Operations at this facility include:** This location houses the administrative offices. **President/CEO:** Michael Limauro. **Annual sales/revenues:** $100 million. **Number of employees at this location:** 400.

KAYDON CORPORATION
315 East Eisenhower Parkway, Suite 300, Ann Arbor MI 48108. 734/747-7025. **Contact:** Human Resources. **World Wide Web address:** http://www.kaydon.com. **Description:** Manufactures ball bearings, filtration systems, and fluid power products. **Corporate headquarters location:** This location. **Listed on:** New York Stock Exchange. **Stock exchange symbol:** KDN. **President/CEO:** Brian P. Campbell. **Annual sales/revenues:** $294 million. **Number of employees nationwide:** 1,850.

KELLOGG COMPANY
P.O. Box 3599, Battle Creek MI 49016. 269/961-2000. **Physical address:** One Kellogg Square, Battle Creek MI 49017. **Toll-free phone:** 800/962-1413. **Fax:** 269/961-9047. **Contact:** Human Resources. **World Wide Web address:** http://www.kelloggs.com. **Description:** Kellogg Company is the world's leading producer of ready-to-eat cereal products and a leading producer of other grain-based convenience foods including toaster pastries, frozen waffles, and cereal bars. The company's products are manufactured on six continents and sold in more than 160 countries around the world. Founded in 1906. **Company slogan:** A healthy life is within your reach. **Positions advertised include:** Electrical Technician; Business Unit Leader; Product Development Scientist; Food Technologist; Compensation Manager; Communications Specialist; Nutrition Communications Director; Financial Analyst; Senior Auditor; Senior Tax Accountant; Corporate Public Relations Manager. **Special programs:** Training; Mentoring Program. **Office hours:** Monday - Friday, 8:00 a.m. - 4:45 p.m. **Corporate headquarters location:** This location. **Other U.S. locations:** Nationwide. **International locations:** Worldwide. **Subsidiaries include:** Keebler Foods Company. **Operations at this facility include:** Administration; Manufacturing; Research and Development. **Listed on:** New York Stock Exchange. **Stock exchange symbol:** K. **CEO/President:** Carlos Gutierrez. **Annual sales/revenues:** $8.8 billion. **Number of employees at this location:** 3,500. **Number of employees worldwide:** Over 25,000.

KENWAL STEEL CORPORATION
8223 West Warren Avenue, Dearborn MI 48129. 313/739-1000. **Contact:** Diane Chmura, Personnel Manager. **E-mail address:** dchmura@kenwal.com. **World Wide Web address:** http://www.kenwalsteel.com. **Description:** Kenwal Steel Corporation operates a chain of metal service centers. **Corporate headquarters location:** This location. **Other U.S. locations:** Gary IN. **International locations:** Canada. **Operations at this facility include:** This location houses the administrative offices. **Number of employees at this location:** 100. **CEO:** Kenneth Eisenberg.

KEY SAFETY SYSTEMS, INC.
7000 Nineteen Mile Road, Sterling Heights MI 48314. 586/726-3800. **Fax:** 863/726-4222. **Contact:** Human Resources. **World Wide Web address:** http://www.keysafetyinc.com. **Description:** Manufactures safety restraint products such as seat belts and airbags. **Special programs:** Continuing Education Programs. **Corporate headquarters location:** This location. **Other U.S. locations:** TN; WI; TX; CA; AL. **International locations:** Mexico; Italy; England; Germany; Hungary; Romania; South Korea; China; Thailand; Japan. **Number of employees at this location:** 430.

KMART CORPORATION
3100 West Big Beaver Road, Troy MI 48084. 248/643-1000. **Contact:** Human Resources. **E-mail address:** hireme@kmart.com. **World Wide Web address:** http://www.kmartcorp.com. **Description:** One of the largest retailers in the United States. Kmart Corporation operates approximately 1,000 discount general merchandise department stores throughout the United States, Puerto Rico, the U.S. Virgin Islands, and Guam. **Special programs:** Internships. **Corporate headquarters location:** This location. **Other U.S. locations:** Nationwide. **Listed on:** OTC. **Stock exchange symbol:** KMRTQ. **President/CEO:** Julian C. Day. **Annual sales/revenues:** $30 billion. **Number of employees nationwide:** 212,000.

KNOVALENT
17187 North Laurel Park Place, Suite 225, Livonia MI 48152. 734/779-0001. **Contact:** Human Resources. **World Wide Web address:** http://www.knovalent.com. **Description:** A diversified consulting services and solutions company that specializes in designing inventory software for the automotive industry. **Corporate headquarters location:** Ann Arbor MI. **CEO:** Jim Heaton.

KOENIG FUEL & SUPPLY
500 East Seven Mile Road, Detroit MI 48203. 313/368-1870. **Contact:** Tim Moelker, Controller. **Description:** A manufacturer of ready-mix concrete and a supplier of home heating oil. **Number of employees at this location:** 100.

KOLENE CORPORATION
12890 Westwood Avenue, Detroit MI 48223-3472. 313/273-9220. **Toll-free phone:** 800/521-4182. **Contact:** Human Resources. **World Wide Web address:** http://www.kolene.com. **Description:** Engaged in the sale of metal cleaning chemicals and related equipment to clients in the automotive, aerospace, and manufacturing industries. **Corporate headquarters location:** This location. **Operations at this facility include:** Administration; Manufacturing; Research and Development; Sales; Service.

KOLTANBAR ENGINEERING COMPANY
P.O. Box 3456, Troy MI 48007-3456. 248/362-2400. **Physical Address:** 950 West Maple Road, Troy MI 48084. **Fax:** 248/362-2316. **Contact:** Personnel Department. **E-mail address:** jobs@koltanbar.com. **World Wide Web address:** http://www.koltanbar.com. **Description:** Provides manufacturing engineering, process development, and planning services. **Special programs:** Internships. **Corporate headquarters location:** This location.

KOREX CORPORATION
5000 West Pontiac Trail, P.O. Box 930339, Wixom MI 48393-0339. 248/624-0000. **Fax:** 248/624-0506. **Contact:** Human Resources. **World Wide Web address:** http://www.korex-us.com. **Description:** A custom manufacturer of household products including laundry detergent, dish detergent, and all-fabric bleach. **Corporate headquarters location:** This location. **International locations:** Toronto Canada. **Number of employees worldwide:** Over 500.

KRAFT FOODS, INC.
275 Cliff Street, Battle Creek MI 49014. 269/966-1000. **Contact:** Human Resources. **World Wide Web address:** http://www.kraft.com/corporate. **Description:** Kraft Foods is one of the largest producers of packaged grocery products in North America. Major brands include Jell-O, Post, Kool-Aid, Crystal Light, Entenmann's, Miracle Whip, Stove Top, and Shake 'n Bake. Kraft markets a number of products under the Kraft brand name including natural and processed cheeses and dry packaged dinners. The Oscar Mayer unit markets processed meats, poultry, lunch combinations, and pickles under the Oscar Mayer, Louis Rich, Lunchables, and Claussen brand names. Kraft is also one of the largest coffee companies with principal brands including Maxwell House, Sanka, Brim, and General Foods International Coffees. Kraft Foods Ingredients Corporation manufactures private-label and industrial food products for sale to other food processing companies. **Corporate headquarters location:** Northfield IL. **International locations:** Worldwide. **Parent company:** Philip Morris Companies (now Altria Group) is a company whose principal wholly-owned subsidiaries are Philip Morris Inc. (Philip Morris USA), Philip Morris International Inc., Kraft Foods Inc., and Philip Morris Capital Corporation. In the tobacco industry, Philip Morris U.S.A. and Philip Morris International together form one of the largest international cigarette operations in the world. U.S. brand names include Marlboro, Parliament, Virginia Slims, Benson & Hedges, and Merit. Philip Morris Capital Corporation is engaged in financial services and real estate. **Operations at this facility include:** This location is part of the Post division and manufactures cereal. **Listed on:** New York Stock Exchange. **Stock exchange symbol:** KFT. **President:** Betsy D. Holden. **Number of employees worldwide:** 106,000.

KUX GRAPHIC SYSTEMS
12675 Burt Road, Detroit MI 48223. 313/255-6460. **Fax:** 313/255-3303. **Contact:** Human Resources. **World Wide Web address:** http://www.kux.com. **Description:** A manufacturer of decals for automobiles, trucks, and industrial vehicles; building and window graphics; and corporate identification signage. Founded in 1952. **Corporate headquarters location:** This location. **Number of employees at this location:** 100.

LA-Z-BOY INC.
1284 North Telegraph Road, Monroe MI 48162. 734/242-1444. **Contact:** Human Resources. **World Wide Web address:** http://www.lazboy.com. **Description:** A leading manufacturer of upholstered seating and residential furniture. La-Z-Boy operates 24 plants in the United States and Canada and sells its products through over 10,000 retail locations. The company operates in five divisions. La-Z-Boy Residential produces stationary chairs, sofas, loveseats, recliners, reclining sofas, sleeper sofas, and modular seating groups, which it sells in a national network of La-Z-Boy proprietary stores, and in department stores, furniture stores, and regional furniture chains. La-Z-Boy Canada manufactures residential seating and markets La-Z-Boy residential products in Canada, and is also initiating a Canadian network of La-Z-Boy proprietary retail stores. Hammary produces high-tables, living room cabinets, wall entertainment units, and upholstered furniture sold in furniture and department stores, as well as CompaTables occasional tables, which are featured in La-Z-Boy proprietary stores. Kincaid makes solid-wood bedroom, dining room, and occasional furniture sold through in-store Kincaid Galleries, select La-Z-Boy Furniture Galleries stores, and better-quality furniture stores nationally. La-Z-Boy Contract Furniture Group includes La-Z-Boy Business Furniture, La-Z-Boy Healthcare Furniture (hospital chairs, recliners, and special mobile recliners marketed through contract dealers and medical sales companies), and La-Z-Boy Hospitality Furniture (specially engineered La-Z-Boy recliners that are sold directly to hotel and motel chains and through hospitality sales companies). Founded in 1929. **NOTE:** Entry-level positions are offered. **Positions advertised include:** Interior Designer; Procurement Department Manager; Packaging Engineer; Administrative Coordinator; Purchasing Agent; Public Relations Manager. **Special programs:** Internships. **Corporate headquarters location:** This location. **Other U.S. locations:** Nationwide. **Operations at this facility include:** Administration; Research and Development; Sales; Service. **Listed on:** New York Stock Exchange; Pacific Stock Exchange. **Stock exchange symbol:** LZB. **President/CEO/Director:** Kurt L. Darrow. **Annual sales/revenues:** $2 billion. **Number of employees nationwide:** 10,000. **Number of employees worldwide:** 17,000.

LAFARGE CORPORATION
4000 Town Center, Suite 2000, Southfield MI 48075. 248/354-9050. **Contact:** Human Resource **World Wide Web address:** http://www.lafargecorp.com. **Description:** Produces cement, concrete, aggregates, and related products in the United States and in Canada through its subsidiary, Lafarge Canada Incorporated. The company operates 16 full-production cement plants and 420 construction materials facilities. **NOTE:** Interested job seekers may submit resumes online. **Positions advertised include:** Regional Marketing Analyst; Regional Product Manager. **Corporate headquarters location:** Herndon VA. **Other U.S. locations:** Nationwide. **International locations:** Canada. **Subsidiaries include:** Systech Environmental Corporation processes and recycles industrial waste products into fuel for the cement kilns. **Operations at this facility include:** Regional Headquarters; Sales. **Listed on:** New York Stock Exchange. **Stock exchange symbol:** LAF. **Number of employees worldwide:** 15,500.

LAKE SUPERIOR STATE UNIVERSITY
650 West Easterday Avenue, Sault Ste. Marie MI 49783. 906/635-2213. **Fax:** 906/635-2111. **Contact:** Human Resources Office. **E-mail address:** humanresources@lssu.edu. **World Wide Web address:** http://www.lssu.edu. **Description:** A four-year, comprehensive state university with an enrollment of approximately 3,400 students. **NOTE:** Candidates must indicate the specific search committee to which they are applying when addressing application materials. See job postings for more information. **Positions advertised include:** Professor, Marketing; Professor, Electrical and Computer Engineering; Professor, Exercise Science; Electrician; Director, University Safety; Director, Admissions; Webmaster. **President:** Betty J. Youngblood.

LAPEER GRAIN/EAST
155 South Saginaw, Lapeer MI 48446. 810/664-2907. **Contact:** General Manager. **Description:** Engaged in the wholesale trade of grain, fertilizer, and chemicals. **Corporate headquarters location:** This location. **Number of employees at this location:** 100.

LAWRENCE TECHNOLOGICAL UNIVERSITY
21000 West Ten Mile Road, Southfield MI 48075-1058. 248/204-4000. **Fax:** 248/204-2119. **Contact:** Stacie Thorton, Human Resources Generalist. **E-mail address:** thorton@ltu.edu. **World Wide Web address:** http://www.ltu.edu. **Description:** An independent university specializing in technology and management. Approximately 5,000 students are enrolled in the university. **NOTE:** To contact Human Resources directly, call 248/204-2151. **Positions advertised include:** Business Services Director; Program Manager; Internal Auditor; Research Assistant; Help Desk Technician; Admissions Counselor; Recruitment Coordinator; Clerical Assistant; Campus Safety Officer; Senior Lecturer, Developmental Mathematics; Management Professor.

LAWYERS TITLE INSURANCE CORPORATION
1050 Wilshire Drive, Suite 303, Troy MI 48084. 248/649-0755. **Toll-free phone:** 800/848-9039. **Fax:** 248/649-6980. **Contact:** Human Resources. **World Wide Web address:** http://www.landam.com. **Description:** Provides title insurance and other real estate-related services for commercial and residential transactions in the United States, Canada, the Bahamas, Puerto Rico, and the U.S. Virgin Islands. Lawyers Title Insurance Corporation also provides search and examination services and closing services for a broad-based customer group that includes lenders, developers, real estate brokers, attorneys, and home buyers. Founded in 1925. **Corporate headquarters location:** Richmond VA. **Other area locations:** Statewide. **Other U.S. locations:** Nationwide. **Subsidiaries include:** Datatrace Information Services Company, Inc. (Richmond VA) markets automated public record information for public and private use; Genesis Data Systems, Inc. (Englewood CO) develops and markets computer software tailored specifically to the title industry; and Lawyers Title Exchange Company operates out of 10 of the Lawyers Title Insurance Corporation's regional offices and functions as an intermediary for individual and corporate investors interested in pursuing tax-free property exchanges. **Parent company:** LandAmerica Financial Group, Incorporated.

LEAR CORPORATION
2998 Waterview Drive, Rochester Hills MI 48309. 248/853-3040. **Contact:** Personnel. **E-mail address:** hrtech@lear.com. **World Wide Web address:** http://www.lear.com. **Description:** Lear Corporation is a worldwide supplier of automotive seat systems and interiors. Founded in 1917. **Special programs:** Internships. **Corporate headquarters location:** Southfield MI. **Other U.S. locations:** GA; IL; OH; SC; TN; WI. **International locations:** Worldwide. **Operations at this facility include:** Designs and manufactures interior trim systems and blow-molded plastic parts including gas tank shields, radiator coolant overflow reservoirs, and complete door panel assemblies. **Listed on:** New York Stock Exchange. **Stock exchange symbol:** LEA. **CEO/Chairman:** Robert E. Rossiter. **Annual sales/revenues:** $15.7 billion. **Number of employees at this location:** 2,930. **Number of employees nationwide:** Approximately 35,000. **Number of employees worldwide:** 110,000.

LEAR CORPORATION
4425 Purks Drive, Auburn Hills MI 48326. 248/276-8484. **Contact:** Personnel. **E-mail address:** hrtech@lear.com. **World Wide Web address:** http://www.lear.com. **Description:** A worldwide supplier of automotive seat systems and interiors. Founded in 1917. **Special programs:** Internships. **Corporate headquarters location:** Southfield MI. **Other U.S. locations:** GA; IL; OH; SC; TN; WI. **International locations:** Worldwide. **Listed on:** New York Stock Exchange. **Stock exchange symbol:** LEA. **CEO/Chairman:** Robert E. Rossiter. **Annual sales/revenues:** $15.7 billion. **Number of employees nationwide:** Approximately 35,000. **Number of employees worldwide:** 110,000.

LEAR CORPORATION
5200 Auto Club Drive, Dearborn MI 48126. 313/240-3000. **Contact:** Human Resources. **E-mail address:** hrtech@lear.com. **World Wide Web address:** http://www.lear.com. **Description:** A worldwide supplier of automotive seat systems and interiors. Founded in 1917. **Special programs:** Internships. **Other U.S. locations:** Nationwide. **International locations:** Worldwide. **Operations at this facility include:** Administration; Divisional Headquarters; Research and Development; Sales; Service. **Listed on:** New York Stock Exchange. **Stock exchange symbol:** LEA. **CEO/Chairman:** Robert E. Rossiter. **Annual sales/revenues:** $15.7 billion. **Number of employees at this location:** 1,800. **Number of employees nationwide:** Approximately 35,000. **Number of employees worldwide:** 110,000.

LEAR CORPORATION
21557 Telegraph Road, P.O. Box 5008, Southfield MI 48034. 248/447-1500. **Fax:** 248/447-1722. **Contact:** Human Resources Representative. **E-mail address:** hrtech@lear.com. **World Wide Web address:** http://www.lear.com. **Description:** A worldwide supplier of automotive seat systems, floor and acoustic systems, instrument panel systems, overhead systems, and door and interior trim systems. Founded in 1917. **Special programs:** Internships. **Corporate headquarters location:** This location. **Other U.S. locations:** Atlanta GA; IL; OH; SC; Louisville TN; WI. **International locations:** Worldwide. **Listed on:** New York Stock Exchange. **Stock exchange symbol:** LEA. **CEO/Chairman:** Robert E. Rossiter. **Annual sales/revenues:** $15.7 billion. **Number of employees nationwide:** Approximately 35,000. **Number of employees worldwide:** 110,000.

LETICA CORPORATION
52585 Dequindre Road, P.O. Box 5005, Rochester MI 48308-5005. 248/652-0557. **Fax:** 248/608-2153. **Contact:** Director of Personnel. **E-mail address:** leticahr@letica.com. **World Wide Web address:** http://www.letica.com. **Description:** Manufactures plastic and paper packaging materials. **Corporate headquarters location:** This location. **Other U.S. locations:** Nationwide.

LETTS INDUSTRIES INC.
1111 Bellevue Avenue, Detroit MI 48207. 313/579-1100. **Contact:** Human Resources. **E-mail address:** info@letts.com. **World Wide Web address:** http://www.letts.com. **Description:** A manufacturer of machining and forging equipment. Letts Industries also sells construction equipment parts. **Corporate headquarters location:** This location. **Listed on:** Privately held. **CEO:** C.E. Letts, Jr. **Annual sales/revenues:** $93 million. **Number of employees nationwide:** 560.

LIFETIME DOORS INC.
30700 Northwestern Highway, Farmington Hills MI 48334. 248/851-7700. **Fax:** 248/851-8534. **Contact:** Human Resources Department. **World Wide Web address:** http://www.lifetimedoors.com. **Description:** A privately held manufacturer of a variety of flush doors. Founded in 1947. **Corporate headquarters location:** This location. **Other U.S. locations:** Los Banos CA; Sacramento CA; Hearne TX; Watseka IL; Easton PA; Denmark SC. **Number of employees nationwide:** Approximately 500.

LITTLE CAESAR'S
2211 Woodward Avenue, Detroit MI 48201. 313/983-6000. **Fax:** 313/983-6428. **Recorded jobline:** 888/456-2752. **Contact:** Nancy Iatrow, Human Resources. **E-mail address:** hrresume@lcecorp.com. **World Wide Web address:** http://www.littlecaesars.com. **Description:** Little Caesar's is a pizza restaurant chain. **Positions advertised include:** Franchise Real Estate Director; Credit Coordinator. **Corporate headquarters location:** This location. **Other U.S. locations:** Nationwide. **Operations at this facility include:** This location houses administrative offices.

LIVING ALTERNATIVES
8054 Ortonville Road, P.O. Box 965, Clarkston MI 48347. 248/625-3870. **Contact:** Human Resources Department. **World Wide Web address:** http://www.laddinc.net. **Description:** Establishes group homes for developmentally disabled adults. Founded in 1978. **Positions advertised include:** Professional Care Technician; Assistant Manager; Manager; Area Supervisor; Quality Assurance Supervisor; Office Coordinator; Director of Operations; Administrator. **Corporate headquarters location:** This location.

LOUISIANA-PACIFIC CORPORATION
P.O. Box 100, Sagola MI 49881. 906/542-7101. **Contact:** Human Resources Department. **World Wide Web address:** http://www.lpcorp.com. **Description:** A forest products firm that harvests timber and converts it into a wide range of wood products including lumber, panel products, doors, and other goods. Louisiana-Pacific operates more than 100 manufacturing facilities and 20 distribution centers in the United States and Canada. **Corporate headquarters location:** Portland OR. **Other U.S. locations:** Nationwide. **International locations:** Canada; Chile. **Listed on:** New York Stock Exchange. **Stock exchange symbol:** LPX. **CEO/Chairman:** Mark Suwyn. **Annual sales/revenues:** $2.3 billion. **Number of employees worldwide:** 7,100.

LOWRY COMPUTER PRODUCTS
9420 Maltby Road, Brighton MI 48116. 810/229-7200. **Fax:** 810/227-8155. **Contact:** Human Resources. **E-mail address:** hr@lowrycomputer.com. **World Wide Web address:** http://www.lowrycomputer.com. **Description:** A leading national systems integrator and distributor specializing in bar code printing, automatic data collection, wireless data communications, and time accounting systems. The company serves the manufacturing, distribution, logistics, health care, and government markets with over 35 offices nationwide. Founded in 1974. **NOTE:** Part-time jobs are offered. To contact Human Resources directly, call 800/733-0210. **Positions advertised include:** Account Executive; Printing Systems Sales Representative; Parts Sales Representative. **Special programs:** Internships. **Corporate headquarters location:** This location. **Other U.S. locations:** Nationwide.

MNP CORPORATION
P.O. Box 189002, Utica MI 48318. 586/254-1320. **Physical address:** 44225 Utica Road, Utica MI 48318-9002. **Contact:** Randy Allison, Director of Human Resources. **E-mail address:** human.resources@mnp.com. **World Wide Web address:** http://www.mnp.com. **Description:** Manufactures bolts, nuts, and screws. **Corporate headquarters location:** This location. **Subsidiaries include:** Michigan Wire Die; VMC Industries, Incorporated; Highland Bolt & Nut. **CEO:** Larry Berman. **Number of employees at this location:** 400.

MPI INTERNATIONAL, INC.
2129 Austin Avenue, Rochester Hills MI 48309. 248/853-9010. **Contact:** Vice President of Operations. **E-mail address:** humanresources@mpi-int.com. **World Wide Web address:** http://www.mpi-int.com. **Description:** Manufactures metal stampings. **Positions advertised include:** Tool Design Engineer; Manufacturing Engineer; Product Engineer; Tool and Die Maker; Tool and Die Designer; Die Setter; Machinist. **Special programs:** Tuition Reimbursement Program. **Corporate headquarters location:** This location. **Other U.S. locations:** Deerfield WI; Lake Mills WI; Cowpens SC; Knox IN; Dayton OH. **Parent company:** Klockner Capital Corporation. **Annual sales/revenues:** $135 million. **Number of employees at this location:** 25. **Number of employees nationwide:** Over 950.

MRC INDUSTRIAL GROUP, INC.
13201 Stephens Road, Warren MI 48089. 586/754-5100. **Fax:** 586/754-2750. **Contact:** Human Resources. **World Wide Web address:** http://www.michriv.com. **Description:** Manufactures bolts, nuts, and fasteners. **Special programs:** Internships. **Corporate headquarters location:** This location. **President/CEO:** Steven E. Engelman. **Number of employees at this location:** 150.

MTS SYSTEMS CORPORATION
14000 Technology Drive, Eden Prairie MN 55344. 800/328-2255. **Fax:** 952/974-8546. **E-mail address:** employment@mts.com. **World Wide Web address:** http://www.mts.com. **Description:** Supplier of mechanical testing and simulation equipment. Their equipment helps customers accelerate and improve their design, development and manufacturing processes. **Positions advertised include:** Electro-Mechanical Assembler; Electronic Design Engineer; Senior Software Engineer. **Corporate headquarters location:** Eden Prairie, Minnesota. **Chairman, CEO, & President:** Sidney W. Emery, Jr.

MAC VALVES INC.
30569 Beck Road, Wixom MI 48393-7011. 248/624-7700. **Fax:** 248/624-0549. **Contact:** Personnel. **World Wide Web address:** http://www.macvalves.com. **Description:** Manufactures pneumatic valves. **Corporate headquarters location:** This location. **Other area locations:** Dundee MI. **International locations:** Belgium; New Zealand; Taiwan. **Number of employees worldwide:** Approximately 1,000.

MACLEAN VEHICLE SYSTEMS
3200 West 14 Mile Road, Royal Oak MI 48073. 248/280-0880x200. **Contact:** Denise Ballinger, Personnel Manager. **World Wide Web address:** http://www.mfmvs.com. **Description:** Engaged in the manufacture of wheel nuts, capped wheel nuts, and specialty nuts. The company is an OEM, Tier One supplier. **Positions advertised include:** Manufacturing Engineer; Accounting Clerk; Production Supervisor. **Corporate headquarters location:** Mundelein IL. **Other area locations:** Rochester Hills MI; Chesterfield MI. **Other U.S. locations:** WI; UT; IL; AR. **International locations:** Mexico; Canada; Germany; United Kingdom; Taiwan. **Parent company:** MacLean-Fogg Company. **Number of employees at this location:** 110.

MADISON ELECTRIC COMPANY
31855 Van Dike Avenue, Warren MI 48093-1047. 586/825-0200. **Fax:** 586/825-0225. **Contact:** Ben Rosenthal, Personnel Director. **World Wide Web address:** http://www.madisonelectric.com. **Description:** A wholesaler of electrical apparatus and equipment. **Office hours:** Monday – Friday, 7:30 a.m. – 5:00 p.m. **Corporate headquarters location:** This location. **Other area locations:** Statewide. **Listed on:** NASDAQ. **Stock exchange symbol:** MDSN. **Number of employees at this location:** 200.

MAGNA DONNELLY CORPORATION
49 West Third Street, Holland MI 49423. 616/786-7000. **Fax:** 616/786-6236. **Contact:** Human Resources. **E-mail address:** recruitment@magnadon.com. **World Wide Web address:** http://www.donnelly.com. **Description:** Supplies systems, assemblies, components, and various products for the automotive industry. The company specializes in manufacturing rearview mirrors. **Positions advertised include:** Advance Purchasing Buyer; Human Resources Generalist; Quality Manager. **Special programs:** Internships; Co-ops. **Corporate headquarters location:** Troy MI. **International locations:** Worldwide. **Parent company:** Magna International Inc (Aurora Ontario). **Listed on:** New York Stock Exchange; Toronto Stock Exchange. **Stock exchange symbol:** MGA; MG.A. **CEO/Chairman:** Carlos E. Mazzorin. **Number of employees worldwide:** 8,200.

MAGNA DONNELLY CORPORATION
P.O. Box 96, Alto MI 49302. 616/868-6122. **Physical address:** 6151 Bancroft Avenue SE, Alto MI 49302. **Fax:** 616/868-0084. **Contact:** Human Resources Manager. **E-mail address:** recruitment@magnadon.com. **World Wide Web address:** http://www.magnadon.com. **Description:** Manufactures exterior automobile mirrors. **NOTE:** Second and third shifts are offered. Address resumes and inquiries to: Magna Donnelly, Recruitment, 49 West Third Street, Troy MI 49423-2813. Phone: 616/786-7000. Fax: 616/786-6124. **Special programs:** Training. **Corporate headquarters location:** Troy MI. **Other U.S. locations:** Nationwide. **International locations:** Worldwide. **Parent company:** Magna International Incorporated. **Listed on:** New York Stock Exchange. **Stock exchange symbol:** MGA. **Number of employees worldwide:** 8,000.

MALLOY LITHOGRAPHING, INC.
5411 Jackson Road, Ann Arbor MI 48103-1865. 734/665-6113. **Toll-free phone:** 800/722-3231. **Fax:** 734/665-2326. **Contact:** Human Resources Department. **World Wide Web address:** http://www.malloy.com. **Description:** A lithographing company that specializes in the printing of books. **NOTE:** Second and third shifts are offered. To reach Human Resources directly call: 877/MALLOY1. **Special programs:** Tuition Reimbursement Program. **Office hours:** Monday – Friday, 8:00 a.m. – 5:00 p.m. **Corporate headquarters location:** This location. **Annual sales/revenues:** Approximately $40 million. **Number of employees at this location:** 350.

MANATRON INC.
510 East Milham Avenue, Portage MI 49002. 269/567-2900. **Toll-free phone:** 800/666-5300. **Fax:** 269/567-2912. **Contact:** Human Resources. **E-mail address:** recruiter@manatron.com. **World Wide Web address:** http://www.manatron.com. **Description:** Develops software for government agencies. **Positions advertised include:** Sales Executive. **Office hours:** Monday – Friday, 8:00 a.m. – 5:00 p.m. **Corporate headquarters location:** This location. **Other area locations:** Escanaba MI. **Other U.S. locations:** Miamisburg OH; Springfield OH; Canton OH; Indianapolis IN; Greenville NC; Excelsior Springs MO; Tampa FL. **Listed on:** NASDAQ. **Stock exchange symbol:** MANA.

MARTINREA INDUSTRIES INC.
2319 Bishop Circle East, Dexter MI 48130. 734/426-4376. **Fax:** 734/426-8160. **Contact:** Human Resources. **E-mail address:** hr@martinrea.com. **World Wide Web address:** http://www.martinrea.com. **Description:** Manufactures automotive and nonautomotive components, primarily focusing on the development of fuel-carrying systems. Founded in 1977. **NOTE:** Resumes may be submitted by e-mail or fax. Fax resumes to: 905/264-0574. **Positions advertised include:** Automotive Engineer; Fork Lift Operator; Welder; Electrician; Press Operator; Tool and Die Maker; Maintenance Worker. **Corporate headquarters location:** This location. **Other area locations:** Clare MI; Reed City MI. **Other U.S. locations:** North Vernon IN. **International locations:** Canada; The Netherlands; United Kingdom; Mexico. **Operations at this facility include:** Administration; Manufacturing; Research and Development; Sales. **Listed on:** Toronto Stock Exchange. **Stock exchange symbol:** MRE. **Number of employees worldwide:** 3,000.

McKESSON SURGICAL
38150 Plymouth Road, Livonia MI 48150. 734/632-6400. **Contact:** Human Resources. **World Wide Web address:** http://www.mckhboc.com. **Description:** A wholesale distributor of medical equipment and supplies. **NOTE:** Interested job seekers may view current positions and apply online. **Positions advertised include:** Account Manager; Marketing Manager; Warehouse Supervisor. **Corporate headquarters locations:** San Francisco CA. **Other U.S. locations:** Nationwide. **Operations at this facility include:** Administration. **Listed on:** New York Stock Exchange. **Stock exchange symbol:** MCK. **CEO/Chairman:** John H. Hammergren. **Annual sales/revenues:** $50 billion. **Number of employees worldwide:** 24,000.

McNAUGHTON-McKAY ELECTRIC
1357 East Lincoln Avenue, Madison Heights MI 48071. 248/399-7500. **Fax:** 248/572-5033. **Contact:** Kathy Gollin, Vice President of Human Resources. **E-mail address:** gollink@mc-mc.com. **World Wide Web address:** http://www.mc-mc.com. **Description:** Engaged in the wholesale trade of electrical appliances and equipment. **NOTE:** To contact Human Resources directly, call 248/582-2343. **Office hours:** Monday – Friday, 7:30 a.m. – 5:30 p.m. **Corporate headquarters location:** This location. **Other area locations:** Ann Arbor MI; Flint MI. **Other U.S. locations:** OH; NC; SC; GA. **President:** David J. Beattie. **Number of employees nationwide:** 850.

MEADWESTVACO
7100 County Road 426, Escanaba MI 49829. 906/786-1660. **Contact:** Human Resources. **World Wide Web address:** http://www.meadwestvaco.com. **Description:** Manufactures and markets coated and specialty papers, packaging materials, office products and specialty chemicals. **Corporate headquarters location:** Stamford CT. **International locations:** Worldwide. **Parent company:** Mead Corporation manufactures, sells, and markets pulp, paper, paperboard, shipping containers, packaging, lumber, school and office supplies, stationery products, and electronic publishing and information retrieval systems. **Listed on:** New York Stock Exchange. **Stock exchange symbol:** MWV. **CEO/Chairman:** John A. Luke, Jr. **Annual sales/revenues:** $7.5 billion.

THE MEDSTAT GROUP, INC.
777 East Eisenhower Parkway, 10th Floor, Ann Arbor MI 48108. 734/913-3000. **Contact:** Human Resources. **World Wide Web address:** http://www.medstat.com.

Description: A health care information, software, and consulting firm that designs and builds database systems for use in analyzing health care claims and benefits for large employers, insurance companies, and the research industry. **NOTE:** Interested job seekers may apply online. **Positions advertised include:** Collections Accountant; Data Management Analyst; Data Management Consultant; Marketing Director; Sales Director; Project Manager; Sales Support Consultant. **Corporate headquarters location:** This location. **Other U.S. locations:** San Francisco CA; Sacramento CA; Rocklin CA; Santa Barbara CA; Atlanta GA; Boston MA; Franklin TN; Cambridge MA; Washington DC. **Parent company:** The Thomson Corporation. **Operations at this facility include:** Administration; Research and Development; Sales; Service.

MEIJER INC.
2929 Walker Avenue NW, Grand Rapids MI 49544. 269/453-6711. **Fax:** 616/735-7569. **Contact:** Employment Manager. **E-mail address:** careers@meijer.com. **World Wide Web address:** http://www.meijer.com. **Description:** One of the largest privately owned retail companies in the Midwest. The company operates 99 hypermarkets throughout Michigan, Ohio, Indiana, and Illinois. Hypermarkets are combination stores that allow customers to purchase general merchandise products as well as grocery items through one central checkout area. Founded in 1934. **NOTE:** To contact Human Resources directly, call 800/219-9150. **Positions advertised include:** Internal Auditor; Deployment Coordinator; Performance Measurement Analyst; Pharmacy Team Leader; Staff Pharmacist. **Corporate headquarters location:** This location. **Other area locations:** Statewide. **Other U.S. locations:** IN; IL; KY; NJ; OH. **Number of employees nationwide:** 75,000.

MELODY FARMS, INC.
31111 Industrial Road, Livonia MI 48150. 734/525-4000. **Fax:** 734/525-5735. **Contact:** Human Resources. **E-mail address:** careers@melodyfarms.com. **World Wide Web address:** http://www.melodyfarms.com. **Description:** A distributor of ice cream and other dairy products. **Corporate headquarters location:** This location. **Other area locations:** Detroit MI; Lansing MI. **Operations at this facility include:** Administration; Sales; Service. **President/CEO:** Rodney George. **Number of employees at this location:** 200. **Number of employees nationwide:** 500.

MESCO (MANUFACTURERS EQUIPMENT AND SUPPLY COMPANY)
2401 Lapeer Road, Flint MI 48503. 800/373-2173. **Fax:** 810/239-5360. **Contact:** John Kurtz. **E-mail address:** johnk@mescosys.com. **World Wide Web address:** http://www.mescosys.com. **Description:** Automotive parts supply and service provider specializing in die room products, fasteners, power transmission, and cutting tools. **Positions advertised include:** CAD Software Developer. **Corporate headquarters location:** This location. **Other area locations:** Grand Blanc MI.

METALDYNE PRECISION FORMING
47603 Halyard Drive, Plymouth MI 48170. 734/207-6200. **Contact:** Personnel Department. **World Wide Web address:** http://www.metaldyne.com. **Description:** Manufactures products for the construction, home improvement, and consumer industries such as faucets, plumbing supplies, kitchen and bathroom cabinets, bathroom and spa equipment, locks, and hardware. The company also manufactures home furnishing products including furniture, upholstery and fabrics, mirrors, lamps, and decorative treatments and accessories. **Positions advertised include:** Shared Services Director; Fixed Asset Manager; International Tax Manager; Senior Cost Analyst; Supplier Quality Engineer. **Corporate headquarters location:** This location. **Other area locations:** Statewide. **Other U.S. locations:** IN; PA; OH; IL; GA; NC. **International locations:** Worldwide. **President/CEO/Chairman:** Tim Leuliette. **Annual sales/revenue:** $1.8 billion. **Number of employees worldwide:** 7,100.

METALDYNE PRECISION FORMING
19001 Glendale Avenue, Detroit MI 48223. 313/270-1700. **Fax:** 313/270-1725. **Contact:** Human Resources. **World Wide Web address:** http://www.metaldyne. com. **Description:** Engaged in the manufacture and metal extrusion of vehicle parts. **Corporate headquarters location:** Plymouth MI. **Other area locations:** Statewide. **Other U.S. locations:** IN; PA; OH; IL; GA; NC. **International locations:** Worldwide. **Parent company:** Metaldyne Corporation manufactures diverse industrial products including specialized component parts for transportation related industries; manufactures architectural, energy-related, and other specialty products including steel doors, door frames, pumping engines, valves, and projectiles and casings for rocket motors; and provides auto design and engineering services. **Operations at this facility include:** Manufacturing; Research and Development; Sales. **President/CEO/Chairman:** Tim Leuliette. **Annual sales/revenues:** $1.8 billion. **Number of employees at this location:** 270. **Number of employees worldwide:** 7,100.

METRO PLANT SERVICES
19648 Purlington Street, Livonia MI 48152. 248/426-3000. **Contact:** Human Resources. **E-mail address:** mpfflorist@aol.com. **Description:** Provides houseplants and offers related interior plant arrangement services. Metro Plant Services' facilities include greenhouses.

MICHIGAN CAT
24800 Novi Road, Novi MI 48375. 248/349-4800. **Toll-free phone:** 888/MIC-HCAT. **Contact:** Wes Winn, Human Resources Manager. **World Wide Web address:** http://www.michigancat.com. **Description:** Sells and services Caterpillar construction equipment and engines. Founded in 1944. **NOTE:** Entry-level positions, part-time jobs, and second and third shifts are offered. Interested job seekers may apply online. To reach Human Resources directly call: 248/348-6520. **Positions advertised include:** Service Technician; Heavy Equipment Service Technician. **Special programs:** Internships; Apprenticeships; Training; Co-ops; Summer Jobs. **Corporate headquarters location:** Wixom MI. **Other area locations:** Statewide. **Listed on:** New York Stock Exchange. **Stock exchange symbol:** CAT. **President/CEO:** Jerry Jung. **Annual sales/revenues:** $400 million.

MICHIGAN DEPARTMENT OF COMMUNITY HEALTH
320 South Walnut Street, Lansing MI 48193. 517/373-2057. **Contact:** Human Resources. **World Wide Web address:** http://www.michigan.gov/mdch. **Description:** Manages Michigan's publicly funded health services system. **Operations at this facility include:** This location is responsible for the storage and research of birth, death, divorce, marriage, and adoption records for the city of Lansing. The agency also provides information about health care facilities and issues concerning occupational and environmental health. **Director:** Janet Olszewski.

MICHIGAN LUMBER COMPANY
P.O. Box 766, Flint MI 48501. 810/232-4108. **Physical address:** 1919 Clifford Street, Flint MI 48503. **Toll-free phone:** 800/282-5707. **Fax:** 810/232-7169. **Contact:** Personnel Department. **World Wide Web address:** http://www.michiganlumber.com. **Description:** A retailer of lumber and related materials. **Corporate headquarters location:** This location. **Number of employees at this location:** 100.

MICHIGAN MILK PRODUCERS, INC.
41310 Bridge Street, P.O. Box 8002, Novi MI 48376. 248/474-6672. **Fax:** 248/474-0924. **Contact:** Human Resources. **World Wide Web address:** http://www.mimilk.com. **Description:** A milk cooperative that markets milk and dairy products for 400 area dairy farmers. Founded in 1916. **Corporate headquarters location:** This location. **Other U.S. locations:** OH; IN; WI.

MICHIGAN RUBBER PRODUCTS
1200 Eighth Avenue, Cadillac MI 49601. 231/775-1316. **Fax:** 231/775-3160. **Contact:** Human Resources. **World Wide Web address:** http://www.michigan-rubber.com. **Description:** Manufactures hoses and related products for the automotive industry. Founded in 1972. **NOTE:** Second and third shifts are offered. **Special programs:** Tuition/Education Reimbursement Program. **Corporate headquarters location:** This location. **Parent company:** ATP Automotive. **Number of employees at this location:** 400.

MICHIGAN STATE UNIVERSITY
1407 South Harrison Road, Nisbet Building Room 110, East Lansing MI 48823-5294. 517/353-3720. **Contact:** Human Resources. **World Wide Web address:** http://www.msu.edu. **Description:** A state university offering more than 200 programs of study. MSU is comprised of 14 degree-granting colleges as well as an affiliated law college. MSU has an enrollment of approximately 44,500 students. **NOTE:** Applications are available in the Human Resources office as well as online. Consult website for detailed application procedures. **Positions advertised include:** Accountant; Development Officer; Information Technologist; Research Assistant, Genomic Technology; Instructor, Linguistics and Languages; Lecturer, Chemistry; Police Officer. **Office hours:** Monday – Friday, 8:00 a.m. – 5:00 p.m. **President:** Peter McPherson.

MICHIGAN TECHNOLOGICAL UNIVERSITY
1400 Townsend Drive, Houghton MI 49931-1295. 906/487-2280. **Fax:** 906/487-3220. **Contact:** Human Resources. **World Wide Web address:** http://www.mtu.edu. **Description:** A university offering undergraduate and graduate degree programs. MTU is divided into two colleges and three schools: The College of Engineering; The College of Sciences and Arts; The Schoo of Business and Economics; The School of Forest Resources and Environmental Science; and The School of Technology. **Positions advertised include:** Administrative Assistant; Office Assistant; Executive Secretary; Alumni Outreach Coordinator; Contract Analyst; Coordinator, Student Orientation and Parent Programs; System Administrator. **President:** Curtis J. Tompkins.

THE MIDLAND CENTER FOR THE ARTS
1801 West St. Andrews Road, Midland MI 48640. 989/631-5930. **Fax:** 989/631-7890. **Contact:** Human Resources. **World Wide Web address:** http://www.mcfta.org. **Description:** Provides various types of entertainment including musical comedy, jazz bands, dance groups, and pop artists. Founded in 1943. **Special programs:** Internships. **Internship information:** The company offers summer internships. Applications are accepted year-round.

MIDLAND MENTAL HEALTH CENTER
2603 West Wackerly Street, Suite A, Midland MI 48640. 989/631-2320. **Contact:** Human Resources. **Description:** Provides outpatient therapy, case management services, and children's intensive services.

MIDMICHIGAN MEDICAL CENTER
4005 Orchard Drive, Midland MI 48670. 989/839-3000. **Contact:** Human Resources. **E-mail address:** recruitment@midmichigan.org. **World Wide Web address:** http://www.midmichigan.org. **Description:** An 250-bed acute care hospital that provides comprehensive health-care services. **NOTE:** Interested job seekers may apply online. **Positions advertised include:** Registered Nurse; Licensed Practical Nurse; Paramedic; Home Care Coordinator; Respiratory Therapist; System Administrator; Transcriptionist. **Special programs:** Tuition Reimbursement Program; Mentorship Program. **Parent company:** MidMichigan Regional Health System. **Operations at this facility include:** Administration. **Number of employees at this location:** 1,670.

MIDWEST MANAGEMENT
950 Corporate Office Drive, Suite 100, Milford MI 48381. 248/529-2020. **Fax:** 248/529-2001. **Contact:** Human Resources. **World Wide Web address:** http://www.midwest-mgmt.com. **Description:** A property management company. Founded in 1973. **Positions advertised include:** Regional Property Manager; Property Manager; Leasing Consultant; Financial Manager; Office Manager; Maintenance Technician; Janitorial Worker. **Corporate headquarters location:** This location. **Other area locations:** Lansing MI; Kentwood MI. **Other U.S. locations:** Chicago IL. **President:** Michael G. McGhie. **Number of employees nationwide:** 1,400.

THE MILLGARD CORPORATION
12822 Stark Road, Livonia MI 48150. 734/425-8550. **Fax:** 734/425-0624. **Contact:** Human Resources. **World Wide Web address:** http://www.millgard.com. **Description:** A contractor specializing in caissons, piles, and slurrywall construction. **Corporate headquarters location:** This location. **Other U.S. locations:** Boston MA. **Operations at this facility include:** Administration; Divisional Headquarters. **Listed on:** Privately held. **Number of employees at this location:** 100.

MIRACLE SOFTWARE
23800 West Ten Mile Road, Suite 260, Southfield MI 48034. 248/350-1515. **Fax:** 248/350-2575. **Contact:** Human Resources. **E-mail address:** detroit@miraclesoft.com. **World Wide Web address:** http://www.miraclesoft.com. **Description:** A worldwide business consulting company. **Positions advertised include:** Java/J2EE consultants; WBI/MB/ICS consultants. **Corporate headquarters location:** This location. **Other U.S. locations:** CA; GA; MA; OH. **International locations:** Worldwide. **CEO, President & Chief Architect:** Prasad V. Lokam. **Number of employees worldwide:** 1217.

MODERN ENGINEERING INC.
130 Town Center Drive, Suite 100, Troy MI 48084. 248/528-2888. **Fax:** 248/689-2117. **Contact:** Human Resources. **E-mail address:** staffing@menet.com. **World Wide Web address:** http://www.menet.com. **Description:** A full-service design engineering firm primarily serving the automotive industry. Founded in 1939. **NOTE:** Entry-level positions are offered. **Positions advertised include:** Senior Lead Manufacturing Consultant; Project Manager; Manufacturing Program Manager. **Special programs:** Apprenticeships. **Corporate headquarters location:** Rochester Hills MI. **Other area locations:** Madison Heights MI; Dearborn MI; Grand Rapids MI; Pontiac MI. **Other U.S. locations:** Anniston AL; Huntsville AL; Mesa AZ; Baltimore MD. **Listed on:** Privately held. **Number of employees at this location:** 150.

MORBARK INDUSTRIES
8507 South Winn Street, P.O. Box 1000, Winn MI 48896-1000. 989/866-2381. **Toll-free phone:** 800/831-0042. **Contact:** Personnel. **World Wide Web address:** http://www.morbark.com. **Description:** Manufactures industrial machinery for the forestry industry including chippers, shredders, sawmill equipment, and debarkers. **Corporate headquarters location:** This location. **Number of employees at this location:** 500.

MORGAN OLSON
1801 South Nottawa Street, Sturgis MI 49091-2005. 269/659-0200. **Toll-free phone:** 800/624-9005. **Contact:**, Human Resources. **World Wide Web address:** http://www.mstruckbody.com. **Description:** Formerly known as Grumman Olson, this company was acquired by the Morgan Corporation in August of 2003. Morgan Olson is a manufacturer of aluminum bodies for trucks, such as the delivery vehicles used by the United Parcel Service and Roadway Package System. **Corporate headquarters location:** Morgantown PA. **Other U.S. locations:** Tulare CA.

MUNSON MEDICAL CENTER
1105 Sixth Street, Traverse City MI 49684-2386. 231/935-6490. **Toll-free phone:** 800/713-3206. **Fax:** 231/935-7191. **Contact:** Gina Ranger, Recruiter. **E-mail address:** employment@mhc.net. **World Wide Web address:** http://www.mhc.net. **Description:** A 368-bed, acute care, regional referral center. Founded in 1915. **NOTE:** Second and third shifts are offered. **Company slogan:** Expertise, when and where you need it most. **Positions advertised include:** Admitting Representative; Certified Athletic Trainer; Licensed Practical Nurse; Registered Nurse; Nurse Assistant; Medical Transcriptionist; Human Resources Director; Pharmacist; Physical Therapist; Radiologic Technologist; Surgical Technologist; Speech Pathologist; Ultrasonographer. **NOTE:** Part-time and Temporary positions are available. **Special programs:** Summer jobs. **Office hours:** Monday - Friday, 7:00 a.m. - 4:30 p.m. **Corporate headquarters location:** This location. **Parent company:** Munson Healthcare System. Other subsidiaries of the parent company include Kalkaske Memorial Hospital and Paul Oliver Memorial Hospital. **Operations at this facility include:** Administration; Service. **Number of employees at this location:** 3,000.

MUSKEGON COMMUNITY COLLEGE
221 South Quarterline Road, Muskegon MI 49442. 231/773-9131. **Fax:** 231/777-0601. **Contact:** Human Resources. **E-mail address:** hr@muskegoncc.edu. **World Wide Web address:** http://www.muskegon.cc.mi.us. **Description:** A community college. **NOTE:** To contact Human Resources directly, call 231/777-0407. **Positions advertised include:** Adjunct Instructors, Various Disciplines; Machining Technology Instructor; Psychology Instructor; Associate Director of Financial Aid. **President:** Dr. Frank M. Marczak.

NSK CORPORATION
P.O. Box 134007, Ann Arbor MI 48113-4007. 734/913-7500. **Physical address:** 4200 Goss Road, Ann Arbor MI 48105. **Toll-free phone:** 877/NSK-JOBS. **Fax:** 734/913-7740. **Contact:** Employment Representative. **E-mail address:** jobs@nsk-corp.com. **World Wide Web address:** http://www.nsk-corp.com. **Description:** Engaged in the design, manufacture, and marketing of ball bearings. **Special programs:** Tuition Reimbursement Program. **Office hours:** Monday - Friday, 8:00 a.m. - 5:00 p.m. **Corporate headquarters location:** This location. **International locations:** Worldwide. **Parent company:** NSK Tokyo. **Operations at this facility include:** Administration; Research and Development. **Number of employees nationwide:** 1,700. **Number of employees worldwide:** 18,000.

NTB
6601 Sloan Highway, Lansing MI 48917. 517/322-2252. **Fax:** 616/878-5587. **Contact:** Kristin Donbrock. **E-mail address:** hr@ntbtrk.com. **World Wide Web address:** http://www.ntbtrk.com. **Description:** A trucking company. **Positions advertised include:** Dispatcher.

NABCO INC.
591 East Church Avenue, Reed City MI 49677. 231/832-2001. **Contact:** Human Resources. **Description:** Remanufactures starters and alternators for use in automobiles. **Corporate headquarters location:** This location.

NARTRON CORPORATION
5000 North US-131, Reed City MI 49677. 231/832-5525. **Contact:** Human Resources. **World Wide Web address:** http://www.nartron.com. **Description:** Manufactures sensors and switches for use by the military and the automotive industry. Founded in 1967. **Corporate headquarters location:** This location. **Other area locations:** Bloomfield Hills MI; Traverse City MI.

NATIONAL CITY BANK
108 East Michigan Avenue, Kalamazoo MI 49007. 269/376-9010. **Contact:** Human Resources. **World Wide Web address:** http://www.national-city.com. **Description:** A bank. **Positions advertised include:** Collateral Administrator; Corporate Banking Representative; Field Examiner; Private Banker. **Corporate headquarters location:** Cleveland OH. **Other U.S. locations:** Nationwide. **Parent company:** National City Corporation (Cleveland OH) is a major bank holding company with subsidiaries engaging in full-service banking, trust, mortgage banking, merchant banking, insurance, and item processing products and services. **Listed on:** New York Stock Exchange. **Stock exchange symbol:** NCC. **CEO/Chairman:** David A. Daberko. **Annual sales/revenues:** $9.5 billion. **Number of employees nationwide:** Over 33,000.

NATIONAL CITY BANK
1001 South Worth, Birmingham MI 48009. 248/901-2200. **Description:** A bank. **Positions advertised include:** Business Systems Analyst; Market Financial Advisor; Operations Specialist. **Corporate headquarters location:** Cleveland OH. **Other U.S. locations:** Nationwide. **Parent company:** National City Corporation (Cleveland OH) is a major bank holding company with subsidiaries engaging in full-service banking, trust, mortgage banking, merchant banking, insurance, and item processing products and services. **Listed on:** New York Stock Exchange. **Stock exchange symbol:** NCC. **CEO/Chairman:** David A. Daberko. **Annual sales/revenues:** $9.5 billion. **Number of employees nationwide:** Over 33,000.

NATIONAL TECH TEAM, INC.
27335 West Eleven Mile Road, Southfield MI 48034. 248/357-2866. **Toll-free phone:** 800/522-4451. **Fax:** 248/357-2570. **Contact:** Human Resources. **E-mail address:** jobs@techteam.com. **World Wide Web address:** http://www.techteam.com. **Description:** Provides computer network design, programming, and training services. **Positions advertised include:** Support Technician. **Special programs:** Training. **Corporate headquarters location:** This location. **Other area locations:** Dearborn MI. **Other U.S. locations:** Davenport IA. **International locations:** Germany; Sweden; Belgium; United Kingdom. **Listed on:** NASDAQ. **Stock exchange symbol:** TEAM. **Annual sales/revenues:** $88 million. **Number of employees worldwide:** 1,600.

NATIONWIDE ADVERTISING SERVICE INC.
34405 West Twelve Mile Road, Suite 224, Detroit MI 48331. 248/489-8875. **Fax:** 248/489-9118. **Contact:** Regional Manager. **World Wide Web address:** http://www.hrads.com. **Description:** An independent, full-service advertising agency specializing in human resource communications, promotions, and advertising. The company offers consultation, campaign planning, ad placement, research, and creative production. **Corporate headquarters location:** Cleveland OH. **Other U.S. locations:** Nationwide. **International locations:** Canada. **Parent company:** McCann-Erikson Worldgroup.

NEMATRON CORPORATION
5840 Interface Drive, Ann Arbor MI 48103. 734/214-2000. **Fax:** 734/994-8074. **Contact:** Human Resources. **E-mail address:** jobs@nematron.com. **World Wide Web address:** http://www.nematron.com. **Description:** Manufactures rugged computers with touch screen interfaces. **Positions advertised include:** Software Technical Designer; Technical Writer; Shipping Clerk. **Corporate headquarters location:** This location. **Other area locations:** Auburn Hills MI. **Other U.S. locations:** Huntsville AL. **International locations:** United Kingdom. **Listed on:** American Stock Exchange. **Stock exchange symbol:** NMN. **President/CEO:** Matthew S. Galvez. **Annual sales/revenues:** Approximately $3.3 million.

NEW HUDSON CORPORATION
57077 Pontiac Trail, New Hudson MI 48165. 248/437-1701. **Fax:** 248/437-0420. **Contact:** Lynn Seamark, Personnel Director. **World Wide Web address:** http://www.newhudson.com. **Description:** Manufactures precision rolls for the float glass and flexographic print industries. **Corporate headquarters location:** This location. **Other area locations:** Milford MI. **International locations:** France; Japan. **President:** Van R. Sandstrom. **Number of employees at this location:** 200.

NORGREN AUTOMOTIVE
44831 Groesbeck Highway, P.O. Box 787, Mount Clemens MI 48046-0787. 586/463-3000. **Fax:** 586/465-2840. **Contact:** Personnel. **World Wide Web address:** http://www.norgren.com. **Description:** Manufactures material handling products including clamps, grippers, and supporting actuators and valves for the automotive industry. **Corporate headquarters location:** Littleton CO. **International locations:** Worldwide. **Parent company:** Norgren. **Operations at this facility include:** This location is part of the company's automotive division.

NORTHERN MICHIGAN UNIVERSITY
1401 Presque Isle Avenue, 202 Cohodas, Marquette MI 49855. 906/227-2330. **Fax:** 906/227-2334. **Recorded jobline:** 906/227-2562. **Contact:** Human Resources. **Description:** A four-year public university offering undergraduate and graduate degrees in 180 academic programs. NMU has an enrollment of 9,300 students. Founded in 1899. **NOTE:** Application materials are not accepted by e-mail. Application forms are available online. **Positions advertised include:** Gifts Officer; Director, Development Fund Operations; Political Science Instructor; Assistant Professor, Nursing; Professor, Secondary Education; Assistant Professor, Sociology.

NUMATICS INC.
1450 North Milford Road, Highland MI 48357. 248/887-4111. **Fax:** 248/887-0046. **Contact:** Human Resources Department. **E-mail address:** humanresources@numatics.com. **World Wide Web address:** http://www.numatics.com. **Description:** Manufactures pneumatic air valves, controls, cylinders, dryers, and all types of ancillary equipment associated with the fluid power industry. **Positions advertised include:** CAD Detailer; Quality Engineer; Engineer. **Office hours:** Monday – Friday, 8:00 a.m. – 5:00 p.m. **Corporate headquarters location:** This location. **Operations at this facility include:** Administration; Manufacturing; Research and Development; Sales. **Listed on:** Privately held. **Number of employees at this location:** 200.

OAKLAND PRESS COMPANY
48 West Huron Street, Pontiac MI 48342. 248/332-8181. **Contact:** Sandra Groves, Director of Personnel. **World Wide Web address:** http://www.theoaklandpress.com. **Description:** Publishes the *Oakland Press,* a daily newspaper. Circulation is 85,000 weekdays and 100,000 Sundays. **Number of employees at this location:** 300.

OAKLAND UNIVERSITY
140 North Foundation Hall, Rochester MI 48309-4401. 248/370-3840. **Fax:** 248/370-3044. **Recorded jobline:** 248/370-4500. **Contact:** Human Resources. **E-mail address:** uhr@oakland.edu. **World Wide Web address:** http://www.oakland.edu. **Description:** A university with approximately 14,000 students that offers 114 bachelor degrees and graduate and certificate programs in 72 academic areas. **NOTE:** Faculty hiring is handled by the Office of the Vice President of Academic Affairs and Provost: 205 Wilson Hall, Rochester MI 48309-4401. Phone: 248/370-2190. Fax: 248/370-4475. E-mail: provost@Oakland.edu. **Positions advertised include:** Visiting Assistant Professor, Music Education; Senior Accountant; Academic Advisor, Health Sciences; Publicist; Information Technology Specialist. **Office hours:** Monday – Friday, 8:00 a.m. – 5:00 p.m. **President:** Gary D. Russi.

OAKWOOD HOSPITAL MEDICAL CENTER
18101 Oakwood Boulevard. P.O. Box 2500, Dearborn MI 48124. 313/593-7000. **Contact:** Human Resources. **World Wide Web address:** http://www.oakwood.org. **Description:** A 615-bed, full-service teaching hospital serving southeast Michigan. **Positions advertised include:** Staff Nurse; Nursing Assistant; Radiology Technologist; Security Officer; Dietary Clerk; Clinical Dietitian; Physical Therapist; Staff Attorney; Surgical Technologist; Medical Technologist; Laboratory Support Specialist. **Parent company:** Oakwood Healthcare System operates seven area hospitals and 25 area ambulance services.

H.J. OLDENKAMP COMPANY
P.O. Box 865, Warren MI 48090. 586/756-0600. **Physical address:** 4669 East Eight Mile Road, Warren MI 48090. **Toll-free phone:** 800/462-6047. **Fax:** 586/756-1045. **Contact:** Personnel. **World Wide Web address:** http://www.oldenkamp.com. **Description:** Engaged in the wholesale trade of materials including Formica, laminates, and cabinets. Founded in 1946. **Corporate headquarters location:** This location. **Other area locations:** Highland Parks MI. **Number of employees at this location:** 100.

OPPENHEIMER
300 River Place, Suite 4000, Detroit MI 48207. 313/259-2600. **Toll-free phone:** 800/795-4366. **Contact:** Human Resources Director. **World Wide Web address:** http://www.opco.com. **Description:** An investment banking corporation and one of Michigan's leading brokerage firms. Formerly known as Fahnestock, this company took on the name of the company it acquired, Oppenheimer. **Corporate headquarters location:** New York NY. **Other area locations:** Statewide. **Other U.S. locations:** Nationwide. **International locations:** Worldwide. **Subsidiaries include:** Freedom Investments, Incorporated. **Operations at this facility include:** Administration; Sales.

Listed on: New York Stock Exchange; Toronto Stock Exchange. **Stock exchange symbol:** New York Stock Exchange (OPY); Toronto Stock Exchange (OPY). **Number of employees nationwide:** 3,000.

OVERHEAD CONVEYOR COMPANY
1330 Hilton Road, Ferndale MI 48220. 248/547-3800. **Contact:** Human Resources. **E-mail address:** occ@occ-conveyer.com. **World Wide Web address:**http://www.occ-conveyor.com. **Description:** Engaged in the manufacture of conveyor systems and related equipment. Founded in 1945. **Corporate headquarters location:** This location. **Subsidiaries include:** J.L. Peters Company; Spurgeon Company. **Number of employees at this location:** 100.

PM ENVIRONMENTAL
3340 Ranger Road, Lansing MI 48906. 517/485-3333. **Fax:** 517/323-7228. **Contact:** Human Resources. **E-mail address:** pme@pmenv.com (subject: Job Application). **World Wide Web address:** http://www.pmenv.com. **Description:** An environmental consulting firm. **Other area locations:** Hazel Park MI. **Other U.S. locations:** Decatur AL.

POH MEDICAL CENTER
50 North Perry Street, Pontiac MI 48342-2253. 248/338-5662. **Fax:** 248/338-5174. **Recorded jobline:** 248/338-5647. **Contact:** Human Resources. **E-mail address:** human.resources@pohmedical.org. **World Wide Web address:** http://www.pohmedical.org. **Description:** An osteopathic teaching hospital. **NOTE:** Online applications are available. **Positions advertised include:** Registered Nurse; Licensed Practical Nurse; Medical Technologist; Patient Care Associate; Financial Analyst; Information Clerk; X-Ray Technologist; Telemetry Technician. **Other U.S. locations:** Oxford MI. **Listed on:** Privately held. **Number of employees at this location:** 1,500.

PPG INDUSTRIES, INC.
AUTOMOTIVE TECHNICAL CENTER
5875 New King Court, Troy MI 48098. 248/641-2000. **Fax:** 248/641-2111. **Contact:** Human Resources Manager. **World Wide Web address:** http://www.ppg.com. **Description:** A diversified global producer of coatings and resins, continuous-strand fiberglass, flat and fabricated glass, and chemicals. The company supplies products for numerous industries including automotive, construction, industrial, aerospace, electronics, and manufacturing. Founded in 1883. **Special programs:** Education Assistance Program; Adoption Assistance Reimbursement Program. **Corporate headquarters location:** Pittsburgh PA. **Other U.S. locations:** Nationwide. **International locations:** Worldwide. **Operations at this facility include:** This location houses the company's Automotive Technical Center and sales offices. **Listed on:** New York Stock Exchange. **Stock exchange symbol:** PPG. **Number of employees at this location:** 180. **Number of employees nationwide:** 17,000. **Number of employees worldwide:** Over 35,000.

PALL LIFE SCIENCES INC.
674 South Wagner Road, Ann Arbor MI 48103-9109. 734/665-0651. **Contact:** Human Resources. **World Wide Web address:** http://www.pall.com. **Description:** Engaged in the manufacture of microfiltration devices. **NOTE:** Interested candidates may submit a resume online. **Corporate headquarters location:** East Hills NY. **Other U.S. locations:** NY; MA; PA; CA; MD. **International locations:** Worldwide. **Parent company:** Pall Corporation is organized into two markets: Life Sciences and Industrial. **Operations at this facility include:** Administration; Manufacturing; Research and Development; Service. **Listed on:** New York Stock Exchange. **Stock exchange symbol:** PLL. **Annual sales/revenues:** $1.6 billion. **Number of employees at this location:** 625. **Number of employees worldwide:** 11,000.

PANGBORN DESIGN LTD.
275 Iron Street, Detroit MI 48207. 313/259-3400. **Fax:** 313/259-5690. **Contact:** Human Resources. **E-mail address:** jobs@pangborndesign.com. **World Wide Web address:** http://www.pangborndesign.com. **Description:** A graphic communications firm specializing in the design of brochures and pamphlets. **Corporate headquarters location:** This location. **Other U.S. locations:** Chicago IL. **President:** Dominic Pangborn.

PARAMETRIC TECHNOLOGY CORPORATION
3310 West Big Beaver Road, Suite 100, Troy MI 48084. 248/458-7700. **Contact:** Human Resources. **World Wide Web address:** http://www.ptc.com. **Description:** Parametric Technology Corporation is engaged in the design and development of fully integrated software products for mechanical engineering and automated manufacturing based upon a parametric solids modeling system. **NOTE:** Resumes submitted by e-mail are preferred, however, e-mail addresses may vary according to specific positions or areas of employment. See website for detailed application procedures. **Positions advertised include:** Implementation Consultant; Strategic Account Sales Representative. **Special programs:** Training; Tuition Reimbursement Program. **Corporate headquarters location:** Needham MA. **Other area locations:** Grand Rapids MI. **Other U.S. locations:** Nationwide. **International locations:** Worldwide. **Operations at this facility include:** This location is a sales and technical support office. **Listed on:** NASDAQ. **Stock exchange symbol:** PMTC. **Number of employees worldwide:** 3,200.

PARKER ABEX NWL
2220 Palmer Avenue, Kalamazoo MI 49001. 269/384-3400. **Contact:** Brent Butler, Senior Manager of Employee Services. **E-mail address:** hrabexnwl@parker.com. **World Wide Web address:** http://www.parker.com. **Description:** As part of the company's aerospace division, Parker Abex designs and manufactures flight, missile, and engine controls for both commercial and military programs. The product lines consist of electronics, hydraulics, and electrohydraulic components. Founded in 1904. **Positions advertised include:** Laboratory Technician; Information Technology Analyst; Customer Service Administrator. **Special programs:** Internships. **Corporate headquarters location:** Cleveland OH. **International locations:** Worldwide. **Parent company:** Parker Hannifin Corporation is a diversified manufacturer of motion control products and systems. **Operations at this facility include:** Administration; Divisional Headquarters; Manufacturing; Research and Development. **Listed on:** New York Stock Exchange. **Stock exchange symbol:** PH. **Annual sales/revenues:** Over $6 billion. **Number of employees at this location:** 820. **Number of employees worldwide:** 48,000.

PEERLESS STEEL COMPANY
2450 Austin, Troy MI 48083. 248/528-3200. **Toll-free phone:** 800/482-3947. **Fax:** 248/528-3971. **Contact:** Cindy Slessor, Human Resources Manager. **E-mail address:** cvar@peerlesssteel.com. **World Wide Web address:** http://www.peerlesssteel.com. **Description:** A metal service center that stores and distributes steel. **Corporate headquarters location:** This location. **Other area locations:** Saginaw MI; Grandville MI. **Subsidiaries include:** Peerless Steel of Grand Rapids; Peerless Steel of Saginaw; Sterling Metal Services. **Operations at this facility include:** Administration; Sales. **Listed on:** Privately held. **Number of employees at this location:** 100.

PERINI BUILDING COMPANY
535 Griswold, Suite 1818, Detroit MI 48226. 313/965-4888. **Contact:** Personnel Department. **World Wide Web address:** http://www.periniwest.com. **Description:** A contracting company engaged in the construction of industrial buildings and warehouses. **Other U.S. locations:** Atlantic City NJ; Las Vegas NV; Phoenix AZ; Framingham MA. **Number of employees at this location:** 200. **President:** Craig W. Shaw.

PERRIGO COMPANY
515 Eastern Avenue, Allegan MI 49010. 269/673-8451. **Contact:** Employment Specialist. **World Wide Web address:** http://www.perrigo.com. **Description:** Manufactures and sells pharmaceuticals, vitamins, and personal care products. These products are sold under individual store brand names such as Tylenol, Advil, and One-A-Day. **Positions advertised include:** Quality Assurance Auditor; Regulatory Affairs Project Manager; Automated Systems Engineer; Research Scientist; Facilities Engineer; Sourcing Manager; Analytical Senior Chemist; Marketing Information Manager. **Corporate headquarters location:** This location. **Other area locations:** Holland MI; Montague MI; **Other U.S. locations:** SC; NJ; CA. **International locations:** England; Mexico. **Operations at this facility include:** Administration; Divisional Headquarters; Manufacturing; Research and Development; Sales. **Listed on:** NASDAQ. **Stock exchange symbol:** PRGO. **Annual sales/revenues:** Over $800 million. **Number of employees worldwide:** Approximately 4,000.

PFIZER GLOBAL RESEARCH AND DEVELOPMENT
2800 Plymouth Road, Ann Arbor MI 48105. 734/622-7000. **Fax:** 734/622-3310. **Contact:** Human Resources. **World Wide Web address:** http://www.pfizer.com. **Description:** The world's largest research-based pharmaceutical company. This segment of Pfizer researches and manufactures pharmaceutical products for human and animal healthcare. **Positions advertised include:** Administrative Specialist; Scientist; Corporate Counsel; Patent Counsel; Financial Analyst; Marketing Manager; Clinical Pharmacometrician. **Special programs:** Internships; Co-ops. **Corporate headquarters locations:** New York NY. **Other U.S. locations:** Cambridge MA; New London CT; Groton CT; La Jolla CA. **International locations:** Canada; France; Japan; United Kingdom. **Operations at this facility include:** Administration; Divisional Headquarters; Research and Development. **Listed on:** New York Stock Exchange; London Stock Exchange; Swiss Euronext. **Stock exchange symbol:** New York Stock Exchange (PFE); London and Swiss Stock Exchanges (PFZ). **CEO/Chairman:** Henry A. McKinnel, Ph.D. **Annual sales/revenues:** $45.2 billion. **Number of employees worldwide:** 122,000.

PFIZER INC.
188 Howard Avenue, Holland MI 49424-6517. 616/392-2375. **Contact:** Human Resources. **World Wide Web address:** http://www.pfizer.com. **Description:** The world's largest research-based pharmaceutical company. Pfizer researches, develops, manufactures, and markets pharmaceutical products for human and animal healthcare. **Positions advertised include:** Senior Development Scientist; Human Resources Generalist; Associate Chemist; Manufacturing Engineer; Validation Associate; Compliance Engineer; Web Developer. **Special programs:** Internships; Co-ops. **Corporate headquarters locations:** New York NY. **Other U.S. locations:** Natiowide. **International locations:** Worldwide. **Listed on:** New York Stock Exchange; London Stock Exchange; Swiss Euronext. **Stock exchange symbol:** New York Stock Exchange (PFE); London and Swiss Stock Exchanges (PFZ). **CEO/Chairman:** Henry A. McKinnel, Ph.D. **Annual sales/revenues:** $45.2 billion. **Number of employees worldwide:** 122,000.

PFIZER INC.
7000 Portage Road, Kalamazoo MI 49001. 616/833-4000. **Contact:** Human Resources. **World Wide Web address:** http://www.pfizer.com. **Description:** Formerly known as the Pharmacia Corporation, this company was recently acquired by Pfizer Inc. Pfizer researches, develops, manufactures and markets pharmaceuticals for human and animal healthcare. **Positions advertised include:** Principal Scientist; Research Scientist; Production Engineer; Facilities Engineer; Maintenance Engineer; Project Engineer; Aviation Director; Laboratory Professional; Animal Technician. **Special programs:** Internships; Co-ops. **Corporate headquarters location:** New York NY. **Other U.S. locations:** Nationwide. **International locations:** Worldwide. **Listed on:** New York Stock Exchange. **Stock exchange symbol:** PFE. **CEO/Chairman:** Henry A. McKinnel, Ph.D. **Annual sales/revenues:** $45.2 billion. **Number of employees worldwide:** 122,000.

PHILIPS DISPLAY COMPONENTS COMPANY
300 West Morgan Road, Ann Arbor MI 48108. 734/996-9400. **Contact:** Human Resources. **World Wide Web address:** http://www.lgphilips-displays.com. **Description:** Manufactures and sells cathode ray tubes for TV sets. The company also sells and markets high-resolution data-display tubes (color and monochrome), wire-wound components, and television/satellite tuners. **Corporate headquarters location:** This location. **Parent company:** Philips Display is a joint venture between Philips Electronics and LG Electronics (Korea). Philips Electronics (the Netherlands) is a multimarket manufacturing organization with locations throughout the United States. The company concentrates its efforts primarily in the fields of consumer electronics, consumer products, electrical and electronics components, and professional equipment. **International locations:** Worldwide. **CEO/Chairman:** Jeong Il Son. **Annual sales/revenues:** $4 billion. **Number of employees worldwide:** Approximately 27,000.

PLANTE & MORAN, LLP
P.O. Box 307, Southfield MI 48037-0307. 248/352-2500. **Physical address:** 27400 Northwestern Highway, Southfield MI 48034. **Contact:** Human Resources Department. **E-mail address:** pmcareers@plante-moran.com. **World Wide Web address:** http://www.plantemoran.com. **Description:** Provides accounting, tax, financial planning, and corporate finance services. **Positions advertised include:** Advanced General Accountant; Tax Professional; Technical Standard Manager; Lotus Notes/PDA Support Specialist. **Special programs:** Internships. **Corporate headquarters location:** This location. **Other area locations:** Statewide. **Other U.S. locations:** Cleveland OH; Dublin OH; Lancaster OH; Toledo OH. **Number of employees nationwide:** Over 1,300.

PLASTECH
2500 Executive Hills Drive, Auburn Hills MI 48326. 248/858-2800. **Contact:** Karrie Labadie, Human Resources. **E-mail address:** hr@plastecheng.com. **World Wide Web address:** http://www.plastecheng.com. **Description:** In February of 2004, LDM Technologies was acquired by Plastech Engineered Products, Inc. The two companies now function as one entity under the name Plastech. Plastech manufactures plastic injection moldings for the automotive industry. **Corporate headquarters location:** Dearborn MI. **Other U.S. locations:** Nationwide. **International locations:** Germany. **Operations at this facility include:** This location houses administrative offices.

PLASTOMER CORPORATION
37819 Schoolcraft Road, Livonia MI 48150. 734/464-0700. **Fax:** 734/464-4792. **Contact:** David P. Groenewoud, Director of Human Resources Department. **World Wide Web address:** http://www.plastomer.com. **Description:** Manufactures polyurethane foam. **Corporate headquarters location:** This location. **Operations at this facility include:** Manufacturing. **Listed on:** Privately held. **Number of employees at this location:** 320.

THE POLK COMPANY
26955 Northwestern Highway, Southfield MI 48034. 248/728-7000. **Toll-free phone:** 800/464-7655. **Fax:** 248/728-7680. **Contact:** Human Resources. **E-mail address:** careers@polk.com. **World Wide Web address:** http://www.polk.com. **Description:** Publishers of city directories, book directories, and statistical information. The Polk Company also offers direct mail marketing and specialty advertising services. **Positions advertised include:** Customer Development Executive; Business Systems Director; Business Development Manager; Project Coordinator; Inside Sales Account Director; Security Specialist; Account Group Manager; Data Control Analyst; Research Analyst. **Corporate headquarters location:** This location. **Other U.S. locations:** Long Beach CA; Cincinnati OH; Woodcliff Lake NJ. **International locations:** Worldwide. **President/CEO/Chairman:** Steven Polk. **Number of employees worldwide:** 1,600.

PREMARC CORPORATION
4950 White Lake Road, Clarkston MI 48346. 800/968-2662. **Fax:** 248/625-0978. **Contact:** Human Resources. **E-mail address:** resumes@premarc.com. **World Wide Web address:** http://www.premarc.com. **Description:** The Premarc Corporation is a leading manufacturer of concrete products for the construction industry. **Positions advertised include:** Maintenance Manager; Maintenance Technician. **Other area locations:** Cadillac MI; Clarkston MI; Durand MI; Grand Rapids MI. **Chief Operating Officer:** Thomas Hager.

PREMIERE VIDEO INC.
35455 Veronica, Livonia MI 48150. 734/464-8939. **Contact:** Personnel. **World Wide Web address:** http://www.premierevideo.com. **Description:** A videotape duplicating company. Founded in 1984. **Corporate headquarters location:** This location.

PRESTIGE STAMPING, INC.
23513 Groesbeck Highway, Warren MI 48089. 586/773-2700. **Fax:** 586/773-2298. **Contact:** James Leo, Human Resources Manager. **World Wide Web address:** http://www.prestigestamping.com. **Description:** A manufacturer of washers and shims, primarily for the automotive industry. **Corporate headquarters location:** This location. **Listed on:** Privately held. **CEO:** Robert J. Rink. **Number of employees at this location:** 100.

PRINTEK, INC.
1517 Townline Road, Benton Harbor MI 49022. 616/925-3200. **Fax:** 616/925-8539. **Contact:** Human Resources Administrator. **E-mail address:** hr@printek.com. **World Wide Web address:** http://www.printek.com. **Description:** Designs and manufactures mobile and desktop printers. Founded in 1980. **Positions advertised include:** Software/Application Engineer; Engineering Clerk; Engineering Technician; National Sales Manager. **Office hours:** Monday - Friday, 8:00 a.m. - 5:00 p.m. **Corporate headquarters location:** This location. **Other U.S. locations:** Wheaton IL. **Listed on:** Privately held. **Number of employees at this location:** 100.

PRODUCTION TOOL SUPPLY
8655 East Eight Mile Road, Warren MI 48089. 586/755-5258. **Fax:** 586/755-4921. **Contact:** Human Resources. **World Wide Web address:** http://www.pts-tools.com. **Description:** A distributor of industrial tools, including precision measuring instruments, fasteners, tool room machinery, hand tools, power tools, and carbide inserts. **Office hours:** Monday – Friday, 8:00 a.m. – 5:00 p.m., Saturday, 8:00 a.m. – 12:00 p.m. **Corporate headquarters location:** This location. **Other area locations:** Lansing MI; Novi MI; Grand Rapids MI; Redford MI; Madison Heights MI; Roseville MI; Jackson MI. **Other U.S. locations:** Cleveland OH. **Listed on:** Privately held. **Number of employees at this location:** 260. **Number of employees nationwide:** 600.

PROGRESSIVE ARCHITECTURE ENGINEERING
1811 Four Mile Road NE, Grand Rapids MI 49525. 616/361-2664. **Contact:** Human Resources. **E-mail address:** foxj@progressiveae.com. **World Wide Web address:** http://www.progressiveae.com. **Description:** A full-service architectural and engineering firm. **Positions advertised include:** Director of Design. **Special programs:** Medical Reimbursement Program; Tuition Reimbursement Program. **Corporate headquarters location:** This location. **Number of employees at this location:** 150.

PRONATIONAL INSURANCE COMPANY
2600 Professionals Drive, P.O. Box 150, Okemos MI 48864. 517/349-6500. **Toll-free phone:** 800/292-1036. **Fax:** 517/349-8977. **Contact:** Human Resources Department. **World Wide Web address:** http://www.proassurance.com. **Description:** Provides professional liability insurance and reinsurance for professionals and institutions in the Midwest. **Corporate headquarters location:** Birmingham AL. **Other U.S. locations:** Mobile AL; Columbus OH; Cleveland OH; Carlisle PA; Indianapolis IN; Lisle IL; Charleston WV; Springfield MO; Miramar FL; Tampa FL. **Parent company:** ProAssurance Corporation. **Listed on:** New York Stock Exchange. **Stock exchange symbol:** PRA. **CEO/Chairman:** A. Derrill Crowe, M.D.

PULLMAN INDUSTRIES INC.
820 Kirts Boulevard, Suite 400, Troy MI 48084. 248/273-5000. **Fax:** 248/244-9708. **Contact:** Personnel. **World Wide Web address:** http://www.pullmanind.com. **Description:** Manufactures automotive roll form products, automobile and truck doorframes, and metal stampings. **Corporate headquarters location:** This location. **Other area locations:** South Haven MI. **Other U.S. locations:** Butler IN. **International locations:** Mexico. **Operations at this facility include:** Administration; Sales.

PULTE HOME CORPORATION
100 Bloomfield Hills Parkway, Suite 200, Bloomfield Hills MI 48304. 248/644-7300. **Toll-free phone:** 800/777-8683. **Contact:** Renee Belanger, Human Resources Manager. **World Wide Web address:** http://www.pulte.com. **Description:** One of the largest independent, publicly owned, homebuilding companies in the United States. The principal business of Pulte Home Corporation is the construction and sale of moderately priced, single-family homes. **Positions advertised include:** 401(k) Administrator; Assistant Superintendent; Corporate Audit Manager; Risk Finance Manager; Production Assistant. **Corporate headquarters location:** This location. **Other U.S. locations:** Nationwide. **Subsidiaries include:** Builders Supply and Lumber; ICM Mortgage Corporation. **Parent company:** Pulte Corporation. **Listed on:** New York Stock Exchange. **Stock exchange symbol:** PHM. **President/CEO:** Richard J. Dugas, Jr. **Number of employees nationwide:** 10,800.

QAD INC.
1188 East Paris Avenue, Suite 100, Grand Rapids MI 49546. 616/285-9400. **Contact:** Tom Adam, Corporate Recruiter. **E-mail address:** careers@qad.com. **World Wide Web address:** http://www.qad.com. **Description:** QAD develops software including MFG/PRO, a software package designed to aid in supply and distribution management for large companies. **NOTE:** Interested job seekers may apply online for posted positions or submit a profile for future consideration. **Corporate headquarters location:** Carpinteria CA. **Other U.S. locations:** Hoffman Estates IL; Mt. Laurel NJ. **International locations:** Worldwide. **Operations at this facility include:** This location develops software for the automotive industry. **Listed on:** NASDAQ. **Stock exchange symbol:** QADI.

R&B PLASTICS MACHINERY LLC
1605 Woodland Drive, P.O. Box 100, Saline MI 48176. 734/429-9421. **Contact:** Human Resources Director. **World Wide Web address:** http://www.rbmachine.com. **Description:** A manufacturer of metal cutting machinery. **Corporate headquarters location:** This location. **Parent company:** Lamb Technicon. **Operations at this facility include:** Administration; Research and Development; Sales; Service. **Listed on:** NASDAQ. **Stock exchange symbol:** RBINC. **Number of employees at this location:** 270.

RS ELECTRONICS
34443 Schoolcraft Road, Livonia MI 48150. 734/525-1155. **Toll-free phone:** 800/555-5312. **Fax:** 734/525-1184. **Contact:** Maureen Beatty, Human Resources Department. **E-mail address:** rselectronics@rselectronics.com. **World Wide Web address:** http://www.rselectronics.com. **Description:** A wholesale distributor of electrical parts and equipment including measurement equipment. Founded in 1929. **NOTE:** Resumes may be sent to the above e-mail address. To contact Human Resources directly, call 734/525-1155. **Special programs:** Internships; Summer Jobs. **Office hours:** Monday - Friday, 8:00 a.m. - 5:00 p.m. **Corporate headquarters location:** This location. **Other area locations:** Grand Rapids MI. **Other U.S. locations:** Cleveland OH; Holtsville NY; Greenville SC; Overland Park KS; Maryland Heights MO; Norcross GA; Melbourne FL; Huntsville AL. **International locations:** Canada; Mexico. **President:** Howard Taxe. **Annual sales/revenues:** $65.7 million. **Number of employees nationwide:** 175.

RANDERS ENGINEERS AND CONSTRUCTORS
3597 Henry Road, Suite 200, Muskegon MI 49441. 231/780-1200. **Fax:** 231/780-0211. **Contact:** Human Resources. **World Wide Web address:** http://www.randers.com. **Description:** A full-service architectural, construction, development, engineering, and environmental firm. The company also provides turnkey modular systems for complex process operations. **Corporate headquarters location:** This location. **Other U.S. locations:** Cincinnati OH. **Subsidiaries include:** Clark-Trombley Consulting Engineers, Incorporated; Randers Engineering, Incorporated; Randers Group Property Corporation; Randers-EPC Incorporated; Redeco Incorporated.

RANIR DCP
4701 East Paris Southeast, Grand Rapids MI 49512. 616/698-8880. **Fax:** 616/222-0710. **Contact:** Human Resources. **E-mail address:** employment@ranir.com. **World Wide Web address:** http://www.ranir-dcp.com. **Description:** Manufactures private label oral health care products including toothbrushes and dental floss. **Office hours:** Monday – Friday, 8:00 a.m. – 5:00 p.m. **Corporate headquarters location:** West Orange NJ. **Other U.S. locations:** Richmond VA. **Operations at this facility include:** Administration; Manufacturing. **Listed on:** Privately held. **Number of employees at this location:** 350.

RAYMOND JAMES INVESTMENT BANK
One Griswold Street, Detroit MI 48226. 313/963-6700. **Fax:** 313/442-1600. **Contact:** Director of Human Resources. **E-mail address:** employment@hr.rjf.com. **World Wide Web address:** http://www.raymondjames.com. **Description:** A regional, full-service investment banking and securities brokerage firm. Products and services include mutual funds, insurance, corporate bonds, investment management services, and retirement planning. **Positions advertised include:** Support Analyst; Supervisor. **Special programs:** Internships; Co-ops. **Corporate headquarters location:** St. Petersburg FL. **Other U.S. locations:** FL; TX; IL; NY; GA; TN; CA. **International locations:** Turkey; Switzerland; France; England; India; Germany; Canada; Belgium; Italy; Argentina. **Listed on:** New York Stock Exchange. **Stock exchange symbol:** RJF. **CEO/Chairman:** Tom James. **Annual sales/revenues:** Over $1 billion.

RAYTECH AUTOMOTIVE
44600 Merrill Road, Sterling Heights MI 48314. 586/731-6300. **Contact:** Human Resources Manager. **World Wide Web address:** http://www.raytechautomotive.com. **Description:** Manufactures transmission parts including clutch plates and transmission bands. **Corporate headquarters location:** Shelton CT. **Listed on:** New York Stock Exchange. **Stock exchange symbol:** RAY. **President/CEO/Chairman:** Albert A. Canosa. **Annual sales/revenues:** Over $200 million. **Number of employees nationwide:** Over 1,500.

REPROGRAPHICS ONE INC.
36060 Industrial Road, Livonia MI 48150. 734/542-8800. **Fax:** 734/542-8480. **Contact:** Kathy Charest, Human Resource Director. **World Wide Web address:** http://www.reprographicsone.com. **Description:** Supplies reproduction, plotting, art, and drafting products and services to corporate entities. **Corporate headquarters location:** This location.

REPTRON MANUFACTURING SERVICES
1746 O'Rourke Boulevard, Gaylord MI 49735. 989/732-6244. **Contact:** Human Resources. **E-mail address:** recruiting@kbyte.net. **World Wide Web address:** http://www.reptronmfg.com. **Description:** Reptron Electronics manufactures and distributes a wide array of electronic products, as well as providing logistics and supply chain services and engineering services. **Corporate headquarters location:** Tampa FL. **Other U.S. locations:** MN. **International locations:** China. **Parent company:** Reptron Electronics. **Operations at this facility include:** This location is a manufacturing plant that produces electronic circuit boards for computers. **Listed on:** NASDAQ. **Stock exchange symbol:** REPT. **President/CEO:** Paul Plante. **Annual sales/revenues:** $171.4 million. **Number of employees nationwide:** 1,139.

REPUBLIC DIE AND TOOL COMPANY
45000 Van Born Road, P.O. Box 339, Belleville MI 48112. 734/699-3400. **Contact:** Personnel. **Description:** A manufacturer of special dies and tools. **Corporate headquarters location:** This location. **Number of employees at this location:** 400.

REQUEST FOODS, INC.
P.O. Box 2577, Holland MI 49422-2577. 616/786-0900. **Physical address:** 3460 John F. Donnelly Drive, Holland MI 49424. **Fax:** 616/786-9180. **Contact:** Bill Teisman, Human Resources Director. **E-mail address:** biltei@requestfoods.com. **World Wide Web address:** http://www.requestfoods.com. **Description:** A producer of frozen food

entrees. **Corporate headquarters location:** This location. **Other U.S. locations:** Chicago IL. **Operations at this facility include:** Administration; Manufacturing; Research and Development; Sales. **Listed on:** Privately held. **President:** Jack DeWitt. **Number of employees at this location:** 300.

RICHFIELD INDUSTRIES
3020 Airpark Drive South, Flint MI 48507. 810/233-0440. **Fax:** 810/233-0231. **Contact:** Ernie Hlinsky, Personnel Director. **E-mail address:** ehlinsky@richind.com. **World Wide Web address:** http://www.richind.com. **Description:** Richfield Industries manufactures fabricated metal shipping and storage racks and containers. **Corporate headquarters location:** This location. **Other area locations:** Holly MI. **Other U.S. locations:** Edinburgh IN. **International locations:** Ontario Canada. **Operations at this facility include:** This location houses administrative offices. **Listed on:** Privately held. **Number of employees at this location:** 30. **Number of employees nationwide:** Over 450.

RIETER AUTOMOTIVE NORTH AMERICA
38555 Hills Tech Drive, Farmington Hills MI 48331. 248/848-0100. **Contact:** Human Resources. **World Wide Web address:** http://www.rieter.ch. **Description:** Manufactures sound-deadening materials, thermal insulation products, and interior trim for the automotive industry. **Corporate headquarters location:** This location. **Other area locations:** St Joseph MI. **Other U.S. locations:** Lowell IN; Oregon OH; Aiken SC. **International locations:** Worldwide. **Parent company:** The Rieter Group. **President:** Hartmut Reuter. **Number of employees worldwide:** 8,629.

RITE-ON INDUSTRIES INC.
24400 Plymouth Road, Redford MI 48239. 313/387-1111. **Fax:** 313/387-1289. **Contact:** Personnel. **World Wide Web address:** http://www.rite-on.net. **Description:** A manufacturer of metal cutting machinery. **Corporate headquarters location:** This location.

ROLLS-ROYCE & BENTLEY MOTOR CARS INC.
3800 Hamlin Road, Auburn Hills MI 48326. 248/340-6464. **Fax:** 248/340-6455. **Contact:** Human Resources. **World Wide Web address:** http://www.rollsroycemotorcars.com.uk. **Description:** Manufactures and markets refined motors cars. **Corporate headquarters location:** England. **Other U.S. locations:** Boca Raton FL; Cranford NJ; West Lake Village CA. **International locations:** Worldwide. **Operations at this facility include:** This location serves as the North American sales headquarters. All Rolls-Royce cars and parts are manufactured in England.

ROSS CONTROLS
P.O. Box 7015, Troy MI 48007-7015. 248/764-1800. **Physical address:** 1250 Kirts Boulevard, Troy MI 48084. **Fax:** 248/764-1850. **Contact:** Human Resources. **E-mail address:** humanresources@rosscontrols.com. **World Wide Web address:** http://www.rosscontrols.com. **Description:** A manufacturer of directional air control devices and related pneumatic products. Founded in 1921. **Positions advertised include:** Accountant. **Corporate headquarters location:** This location. **Other area locations:** Madison Heights MI. **Other U.S. locations:** Lavonia GA. **International locations:** Worldwide. **Subsidiaries include:** Ross Asia; Ross Europa; Ross Great Britain. **Operations at this facility include:** Administration; Financial Offices; Manufacturing; Sales. **Number of employees at this location:** 45.

ROUSH INDUSTRIES
11916 Market Street, Livonia MI 48150. 734/779-7270. **Fax:** 734/779-7804. **E-mail address:** careers@roushind.com. **World Wide Web address:** http://www.roushind.com. **Description:** A premier provider of full service automotive engineering and design services. **Positions advertised include:** Automotive Technician; CNC Machinist; Development Engineer; Maintenance Technician; Powertrain Development Engineer; Program Manager; Recruiting Manager; Tool Room Attendant; Test Coordinator.

SER SOLUTIONS, INC.
811 South Boulevard East, Suite 220, Rochester Hills MI 48307. 248/293-0332. **Fax:** 248/293-0340. **Contact:** Human Resources. **E-mail address:** jobs.usa@ser.com. **World Wide Web address:** http://www.ser.com. **Description:** A systems integrator offering both hardware and software solutions. SER Solutions assembles tape and disk storage subsystems for mainframe and open systems. The company also develops computer imaging systems. **Corporate headquarters location:** Dulles VA. **Other U.S. locations:** Norfolk CT. **International locations:** United Kingdom. **CEO:** Carl E. Mergele.

SMZ ADVERTISING
900 Wilshire Drive, Suite 102, Troy MI 48084. 248/362-4242. **Fax:** 248/362-2014. **Contact:** Personnel. **World Wide Web address:** http://www.smz.com. **Description:** Develops and produces advertising and marketing communications materials. **Special programs:** Internships. **Corporate headquarters location:** This location. **Listed on:** Privately held. **President:** Jim Michelson. **Number of employees at this location:** 60.

SPX CORPORATION
28635 Mound Road, Warren MI 48092-3499. 586/574-2332. **Toll-free phone:** 800/962-8734. **Fax:** 586/582-5850. **Contact:** Human Resources. **E-mail address:** hrww@servicesolutions.spx.com. **World Wide Web address:** http://www.spx.com. **Description:** SPX manufactures specialty tools and components for the automotive industry. Products include gauges, hand tools, battery testers, air conditioning and antifreeze recycling systems, and diagnostic and emissions testing equipment. Subsidiaries are involved in the production of valves, die casting, filters, piston rings, and cylinder liners for the automotive, commercial, and manufacturing industries. Founded in 1925. **Positions advertised include:** Internal Controls Specialist; Financial Analyst; Customer Service Supervisor. **Corporate headquarters location:** Charlotte NC. **Other area locations:** Bridgeport MI; Novi MI. **Other U.S. locations:** Nationwide. **International locations:** Worldwide. **Operations at this facility include:** This location designs, manufactures, and distributes specialty service tools and equipment for the repair of automobiles, trucks, and off-road vehicles. **Listed on:** New York Stock Exchange; Pacific Stock Exchange. **Stock exchange symbol:** SPW. **President/CEO/Chairman:** John B. Blystone. **Annual sales/revenues:** $5 billion. **Number of employees at this location:** 225. **Number of employees worldwide:** 22,200.

SPX CONTECH METAL FORGE
8001 Angling Road, Suite 100, Portage MI 49024. 616/327-9990. **Fax:** 616/327-9958. **Contact:** Mike Coolican, Director of Human Resources. **E-mail address:** hremail@contech.spx.com. **World Wide Web address:** http://www.spxcontech.com. **Description:** Manufactures cold-forged solid and tubular metal components and assemblies for automobiles and bicycles. **Positions advertised include:** Sales Manager. **Corporate headquarters location:** This location. **Other area locations:** Walled Lake MI; Dowagiac MI; Alma MI. **Other U.S. locations:** Pierceton IN; Mishawaka IN; Clarksville TN; Auburn IN; Albermarle NC. **Parent company:** SPX Corporation provides technical, industrial, and automotive products and services to various markets. **Listed on:** New York Stock Exchange. **Stock exchange symbol:** SPW. **President:** James Peters.

SAINT JOSEPH MERCY LIVINGSTON HOSPITAL
620 Byron Road, Howell MI 48843. 517/545-6000. **Recorded jobline:** 517/545-6606. **Contact:** Human Resources. **World Wide Web address:** http://www.sjmh.com. **Description:** A 136-bed full-service hospital. Founded in 1928. **NOTE:** Entry-level positions and second and third shifts are offered. To contact Human Resources directly, call 517/545-6295. **Positions advertised include:** Physical Therapist; Radiologic Technologist; Registered Nurse; Speech Language Pathologist; Mental Health Clinician; Environmental Aide; Surgical Technician; Nurse Anesthetist; Medical Assistant; Patient Care Assistant. **Corporate headquarters location:** Ann Arbor MI. **Parent company:** Saint Joseph Mercy Health System.

ST. JOSEPH'S MERCY OF MACOMB
15855 Nineteen Mile Road, Clinton Township MI 48038. 586/263-2800. **Fax:** 586/263-2803. **Contact:** Lisa Renaud, Recruitment. **E-mail address:** renaudl@trinity-health.org. **World Wide Web address:** http://www.stjoe-macomb.com. **Description:** A hospital. **Positions advertised include:** Certified Occupational Therapy Assistant; Field Service Specialist; Pharmacy Technician; Lead Clinical Pharmacist; Nurse Technician; Respiratory Therapist; Speech and Language Pathologist; Registered Nurse. **Parent company:** Trinity Health. **Operations at this facility include:** Administration. **Number of employees at this location:** 2,600.

SATURN CORPORATION
P.O. Box 7025, Troy MI 48007-7025. 248/524-5000. **Physical address:** 1400 Stephenson Highway, Troy MI 48083. **Contact:** Human Resources Department. **E-mail address:** resume@saturn.com. **World Wide Web address:** http://www.saturn.com. **Description:** Develops, manufactures, and sells cars. **NOTE:** Please send resumes to Human Resources, Saturn Corporation, 100 Saturn Parkway, Mail Drop 371999E21, P.O. Box 1500, Spring Hill TN 37174. **Corporate headquarters location:** This location. **Other U.S. locations:** Nationwide. **Parent company:** General Motors Corporation. **Operations at this facility include:** Administration; Manufacturing; Regional Headquarters; Research and Development; Service. **Listed on:** New York Stock Exchange. **Stock exchange symbol:** GM. **President:** Annette K. Clayton.

SATURN ELECTRONICS AND ENGINEERING, INC.
575 Glaspie Street, Oxford MI 48371. 248/628-8831. **Fax:** 248/628-4618. **Contact:** Human Resources Department. **E-mail address:** hr@saturnee.com. **World Wide Web address:** http://www.saturnee.com. **Description:** Provides a wide range of contract manufacturing services and solutions for customers in the OEM industry. **NOTE:** To reach Human Resources directly call: 248/299-8546. **Corporate headquarters location:** Auburn Hills MI. **Other area locations:** Coopersville MI. **Other U.S. locations:** Rocky Mount NC; Tustin CA. **International locations:** Mexico; Singapore; the Philippines. **Parent company:** Saturn Corporation. **Operations at this facility include:** This location manufactures body controllers and relays for the automotive industry. **Number of employees at this location:** 132. **Number of employees worldwide:** Over 4,000.

SATURN ELECTRONICS AND ENGINEERING, INC.
323 Skeels Street, Coopersville MI 49404 616/837/9711. **Fax:** 616/837-7054. **Contact:** Human Resources Department. **E-mail address:** hr@saturnee.com. **World Wide Web address:** http://www.saturnee.com. **Description:** Provides a wide range of contract manufacturing services and solutions for customers in the OEM industry. **NOTE:** To reach Human Resources directly call: 248/299-8546. **Corporate headquarters location:** Auburn Hills MI. **Other area locations:** Oxford MI. **Other U.S. locations:** Rocky Mount NC; Tustin CA. **International locations:** Mexico; Singapore; the Philippines. **Operations at this facility include:** This location assembles electronic PCB boards mainly for automotive applications. **Number of employees at this location:** 166. **Number of employees worldwide:** Over 4,000.

SCOTT MANAGEMENT COMPANY
26100 Northwestern Highway, Suite 1913, Southfield MI 48076. 248/354-9900. **Fax:** 248/351-4887. **Contact:** Personnel. **World Wide Web address:** http://www.smcliving.com. **Description:** A real estate brokerage firm specializing in apartment rentals. **NOTE:** Online applications are available. **Corporate headquarters location:** This location.

SECOR INTERNATIONAL
2321 Club Meridian Drive, Suite E, Okemos MI 48864. 517/349-9499. **Contact:** Marguerite Shuffleton, Human Resources. **E-mail address:** mshuffleton@secor.com. **World Wide Web address:** http://www.secor.com. **Description:** An environmental engineering firm. **Corporate headquarters location:** Redmond WA. **Other area locations:** Detroit MI. **Other U.S. locations:** Nationwide. **International locations:** Canada; United Kingdom. **Listed on:** Privately held. **President/CEO:** Jim Vais. **Annual sales/revenues:** $100 million. **Number of employees worldwide:** 700.

SEMCO ENERGY
405 Water Street, Port Huron MI 48060. 810/987-2200. **Fax:** 810/987-7286. **Contact:** Human Resources. **E-mail address:** careers@semcoenergy.com. **World Wide Web address:** http://www.semcoenergy.com. **Description:** A regional producer and distributor of natural gas. The company is comprised of two segments: SEMCO Energy Gas Company and SEMCO Energy Ventures. **Positions advertised include:** Electrical Engineer. **Special programs:** Tuition and Book Reimbursement Program. **Corporate headquarters location:** Farmington Hills MI. **Other U.S. locations:** WI; TX; NJ; NE; LA; KS; GA; IA. **Listed on:** New York Stock Exchange. **Stock exchange symbol:** SEN. **President/CEO:** George A. Schreiber, Jr.

SENSYTECH
300 Parkland Plaza, P.O. Box 1869, Ann Arbor MI 48106. 734/769-5649. **Contact:** Human Resources. **E-mail address:** hr@sensytech.com. **World Wide Web address:** http://www.sensytech.com. **Description:** An electronics and technology services company with clientele in the commercial, military, and industrial markets. **NOTE:** Resumes may be mailed to Human Resources, SenSyTech, Incorporated, P.O. Box 1430, Newington VA 22122-1430, or faxed to: 703/550-7470. **Corporate headquarters location:** Newington VA. **Other U.S. locations:** Lemont Furnace PA; Farmingdale NJ; Camarillo CA. **Operations at this facility include:** This location manufactures optical equipment including infrared airborne scanning equipment. **Listed on:** NASDAQ. **Stock exchange symbol:** STST. **Annual sales/revenues:** $53 million. **Number of employees nationwide:** 220.

SERVICE STEEL CORPORATION
P.O. Box 12579, Detroit MI 48212. 313/365-3600. **Physical address:** 13700 Sherwood Avenue, Detroit MI 48212-2060. **Fax:** 313/365-2828. **Contact:** Personnel. **World

Wide Web address: http://www.servicesteel.com. **Description:** A metal service center engaged in the storage and wholesale distribution of steel. Founded in 1920. **Corporate headquarters location:** This location. **Other U.S. locations:** Cincinnati OH; East Moline IL; Tonawanda NY. **Chairman:** David B. Van Pelt. **Number of employees at this location:** 200.

SINAI-GRACE HOSPITAL
6071 West Outer Drive, Detroit MI 48235. 313/966-3300. **Contact:** Human Resources. **World Wide Web address:** http://www.dmc.org. **Description:** A 500-bed hospital offering comprehensive patient care. **NOTE:** Interested job seekers may apply online. To contact Human Resources directly, call 313/966-3101. **Positions advertised include:** Patient Care Associate; Staff Nurse; Paramedic; Licensed Practical Nurse; Surgical Physician Assistant; Speech Language Pathologist; Physical Therapist Assistant; Mental Health Associate; Clinical Pharmacist; Radiologic Technologist; Respiratory Therapist; Clinical Social Worker. **Parent company:** Detroit Medical Center. **Number of employees at this location:** Over 3,000.

SLIGH FURNITURE
1201 Industrial Avenue, Holland MI 49423. 616/392-7101. **Contact:** Human Resources Department. **World Wide Web address:** http://www.sligh.com. **Description:** Manufactures desks, credenzas, grandfather clocks, and other furniture. **Corporate headquarters location:** This location.

SMITHGROUP INC.
500 Griswold Street, Suite 1700, Detroit MI 48226. 313/983-3600. **Contact:** Human Resources. **E-mail address:** hr@dt.smithgroup.com. **World Wide Web address:** http://www.smithgroup.com. **Description:** A multifaceted architectural and engineering firm engaged in construction, facility management, historic preservation, landscaping, telecommunications, and real estate consulting. **Special programs:** Internships. **Corporate headquarters location:** This location. **Other area locations:** Ann Arbor MI. **Other U.S. locations:** Phoenix AZ; San Francisco CA; Santa Monica CA; Washington DC; Madison WI; Chicago IL. **Operations at this facility include:** Service. **Number of employees at this location:** 250.

SMITHS INDUSTRIES AEROSPACE
3290 Patterson Avenue SE, Grand Rapids MI 49512. 616/241-7000. **Contact:** Human Resources. **E-mail address:** techjobs@smiths-aerospace.com. **World Wide Web address:** http://www.smithsind-aerospace.com. **Description:** An aerospace engineering facility involved in aerospace avionics and weapons management. **Positions advertised include:** Senior Mechanical Designer; Navigation Database Engineer; Program Quality Engineer; Senior Application Developer; Avionic Systems Analysis Engineer; Technical Training Manager. **Special programs:** Internships; Co-ops. **Corporate headquarters location:** This location. **Other U.S. locations:** Nationwide. **International locations:** United Kingdom; Singapore; Russian Federation; the Netherlands; Malaysia; Germany; France; Denmark; China; Canada; Australia. **Annual sales/revenues:** Approximately $2 billion. **Number of employees worldwide:** Over 12,000.

SOFTECH
40701 Woodward Avenue, Bloomfield Hills MI 48304. 248/203-6930. **Contact:** Human Resources. **E-mail address:** careers@softech.com. **World Wide Web address:** http://www.softech.com. **Description:** Designs customized, automated, engineering software that assists in a variety of industrial process. Clients include tool and die companies and molding companies. **Corporate headquarters location:** Tewksbury MA. **Other area locations:** Troy MI. **International locations:** France; Germany; Italy. **President/CEO:** Joe Mullaney.

SPARROW HEALTH SYSTEM
SPARROW HOSPITAL
1215 East Michigan Avenue, Lansing MI 48912. 517/364-5858. **Fax:** 517/364-5818. **Contact:** Human Resources. **E-mail address:** hr@sparrow.org. **World Wide Web address:** http://www.sparrow.com. **Description:** A community hospital engaged in inpatient and outpatient health care services. **Positions advertised include:** Health Unit Coordinator; Patient Care Technician; Registered Nurse; Licensed Practical Nurse; Respiratory Therapist; Health Record Analyst; Paramedic; Clinical Pharmacist; Health Desk Specialist; Customer Service Supervisor; Physical Therapy Assistant; Phlebotomy Technician; Medical Technologist. **Corporate headquarters location:** This location.

SPARTAN MOTORS
1165 Reynolds Road, Charlotte MI 48813. 517/543-6400. **Contact:** Human Resources. **World Wide Web address:** http://www.spartanmotors.com. **Description:** Produces custom-designed heavy truck chassis for specialized applications. The company sells to three principal markets: fire truck, motor home, and bus specialty. **Corporate headquarters location:** This location. **Other U.S. locations:** Alabama; Minnesota; South Carolina; South Dakota. **Listed on:** NASDAQ. **Stock exchange symbol:** SPAR. **CEO:** John E. Sztykiel. **Number of employees nationwide:** 750.

SPARTAN STORES INC.
850 76th Street SW, P.O. Box 8700, Grand Rapids MI 49518-8700. 616/878-2000. **Contact:** Human Resources. **E-mail address:** human_resources@spartanstores.com. **World Wide Web address:** http://www.spartanstores.com. **Description:** Owns and operates a chain of grocery stores. **Positions advertised include:** Inventory Control Clerk; Technical Analyst; Category Manager. **Special programs:** Tuition Reimbursement Program. **Corporate headquarters location:** This location. **Other area locations:** Statewide. **Other U.S. locations:** OH. **Listed on:** NASDSAQ. **Stock exchange symbol:** SPTN. **Number of employees nationwide:** 7,400.

STANDARD FEDERAL BANK
2600 West Big Beaver Road, Troy MI 48084. 800/643-9600. **Fax:** 248/637-2759. **Contact:** Human Resources. **World Wide Web address:** http://www.standardfederalbank.com. **Description:** One of the largest banks in the Midwest with assets of over $50.5 billion and 273 branch locations in Michigan and Indiana. **NOTE:** Human Resources contacts vary according to the Business Unit to which one is applying. Consult website or contact the Human Resources Department for more information. **Corporate headquarters location:** This location. **Other area locations:** Statewide. **Other U.S. locations:** Indiana. **Parent company:** ABN AMRO Bank N.V. (Netherlands). **CEO:** Scott K. Heitmann. **Number of employees nationwide:** Over 4,000.

I I STANLEY CO., INC.
1500 Hill Brady Road, Battle Creek MI 49017. 269/660-7777. **Fax:** 269/660-7756. **Contact:** Jim Brown, Human Resources. **E-mail address:** jim_brown@iistanleybc.com. **World Wide Web address:** http://www.iistanleybc.com. **Description:** Manufactures automotive lighting and electronic office automation products. **NOTE:** Online applications are available. **Corporate headquarters location:** This location. **Other area locations:** Farmington Hills MI. **Other U.S. locations:** Ohio. **International locations:** China; Taiwan; Japan; Vietnam; Thailand; France. **Parent company:** Stanley Electric Company, Limited. **Operations at this facility include:** Administration; Manufacturing; Research and Development; Sales. **Listed on:** Privately held. **Number of employees at this location:** 720. **Number of employees nationwide:** 1,200.

STAR CUTTER COMPANY
P.O. Box 376, Farmington MI 48332. 248/474-8200. **Physical address:** 23461 Industrial Park Drive, Farmington Hills MI 48335. **Contact:** Tim Zoia, Human Resources Manager. **E-mail address:** hr@starcutter.com. **World Wide Web address:** http://www.starcutter.com. **Description:** A manufacturer of machine tools. Founded in 1927. **NOTE:** Resumes should be mailed to Star Cutter Company, Human Resources, 2083 West M-55, West Branch MI 48661, or faxed to: 989/345-3719. **Corporate headquarters location:** This location. **Operations at this facility include:** Administration; Manufacturing; Research and Development; Sales. **Listed on:** Privately held. **Number of employees at this location:** 750. **Number of employees nationwide:** Approximately 1,000.

STARR COMMONWEALTH
13725 Starr Commonwealth Road, Albion MI 49224. 517/629-5593. **Contact:** Dennis Eddy, Human Resources. **E-mail address:** eddyd@starr.org. **World Wide Web address:** http://www.starr.org. **Description:** An organization for troubled youth offering long-term residential care, alternative education, and foster care. **NOTE:** Summer jobs and temporary positions are offered. Interested job seekers may apply online. **Positions advertised include:** Public Relations Specialist; Youth Specialist; Marketing Services Coordinator; Teacher/Counselor. **Other area locations:** Battle Creek MI; Detroit MI. **Other U.S. locations:** Van Wert OH. **President/CEO:** Arlin Ness. **Number of employees nationwide:** Over 500.

STEELCASE INC.
1901 44th Street SE, Grand Rapids MI 49508. 616/247-2710. **Contact:** Tom Dryer, Employee Relations Manager. **World Wide Web address:** http://www.steelcase.com. **Description:** Manufactures office furniture. **Positions advertised include:** Internal Audit Consultant. **Office hours:** Monday – Friday, 8:00 a.m. – 5:00 p.m. **Corporate headquarters location:** This location. **Other area locations:** Statewide. **International locations:** Worldwide. **Listed on:** New York Stock Exchange. **Stock exchange symbol:** SCS. **Annual sales/revenues:** $2.3 billion. **President/CEO:** James P. Hackett. **Number of employees worldwide:** Approximately 19,000.

STELLAR ENGINEERING INC.
5505 Thirteen Mile Road, Warren MI 48092. 586/978-8444. **Fax:** 586/978-2315. **Contact:** Human Resources Manager. **E-mail address:** hr@stellar-eng.com. **World Wide Web address:** http://www.stellareng.com. **Description:** Designs automated assembly and welding systems for the automotive industry. **NOTE:** Interested job seekers may apply online. **Corporate headquarters location:** This location. **Other area locations:** Sterling Heights MI. **Listed on:** Privately held. **President:** Les Jones.

STERICYCLE, INC.
1040 Market Avenue SW, Grand Rapids MI 49503. 616/454-9405. **Contact:** Human Resources. **E-mail address:** careers@stericycle.com. **World Wide Web address:** http://www.stericycle.com. **Description:** The largest provider of medical waste management services in the United States. **Positions advertised include:** Driver. **Corporate headquarters location:** Lake Forest IL. **Other U.S. locations:** Nationwide. **Listed on:** NASDAQ. **Stock exchange symbol:** SRCL. **Number of employees nationwide:** Approximately 2,900.

STONE AND SIMONS ADVERTISING INC.
24245 Northwestern Highway, Southfield MI 48075. 248/358-4800. **Fax:** 248/358-0128. **Contact:** Human Resources. **E-mail address:** humanresources@stonesimons.com. **World Wide Web address:** http://www.stonesimons.com. **Description:** An advertising agency. Founded in 1958. **Corporate headquarters location:** This location. **Number of employees at this location:** 40.

STRYKER CORPORATION
P.O. Box 4085, Kalamazoo MI 49003-4085. 269/385-2600. **Physical address:** 2725 Fairfield Road, Kalamazoo MI 49002. **Toll-free phone:** 800/726-2725. **Fax:** 269/385-2659. **Contact:** Personnel. **World Wide Web address:** http://www.strykercorp.com. **Description:** Develops, manufactures, and markets specialty surgical and medical products including endoscopic systems, orthopedic implants, powered surgical instruments, and patient care and handling equipment for the global market. Stryker also provides outpatient physical therapy services in the United States. Founded in 1941. **NOTE:** Interested candidates can search and apply for positions online. **Special programs:** Internships. **Office hours:** Monday - Friday, 8:00 a.m. - 5:00 p.m. **Corporate headquarters location:** This location. **Other U.S. locations:** Nationwide. **International locations:** Worldwide. **Subsidiaries include:** Howmedica Osteonics. **Listed on:** New York Stock Exchange. **Stock exchange symbol:** SYK. **CEO/President:** John W. Brown. **Number of employees worldwide:** Over 14,000.

SULZER METCO
1972 Meijer Drive, Troy MI 48084. 248/288-1200. **Contact:** Human Resources Department. **E-mail address:** hr-us@sulzermetco.com. **World Wide Web address:** http://www.sulzermetco.com. **Description:** Manufactures primary metal products. Sulzer Metco specializes in the production of powders for coating and brazing jet engine parts. Founded in 1961. **Corporate headquarters location:** Switzerland. **Other U.S. locations:** Hicksville NY; Westbury NY. **International locations:** Worldwide. **Operations at this facility include:** Manufacturing; Distribution. **Number of employees worldwide:** Over 1,500.

SUPERIOR ENVIRONMENTAL
1128 Franklin Street, Marne MI 49435. 616/667-4000. **Fax:** 616/667-3666. **Contact:** Human Resources. **E-mail address:** resumes@superiorenvironmental.com. **World Wide Web address:** http://www.superiorenvironmental.com. **Description:** Provides environmental assessment, soil testing, remediation, underground storage tank removal, and other environmental services. **Positions advertised include:** Environmental Driller. **Corporate headquarters location:** This location. **Other area locations:** Detroit MI; Bay City MI. **Other U.S. locations:** Indianapolis IN; Rochelle IL; Springfield IL; Hartford CT.

SYSTEMS INTEGRATION SPECIALISTS COMPANY, INC. (SISCO)
6605 19½ Mile Road, Sterling Heights MI 48314-1408. 586/254-0020. **Fax:** 586/254-0053. **Contact:** Human Resources. **World Wide Web address:** http://www.sisconet.com. **Description:** A privately held company founded in 1983 that is dedicated to applying standards to address real-world problems in the electric utility, manufacturing, and automation industries. SISCO offers real-time communications and application integration products and services that are used worldwide in many industries by leading OEMs, system integrators, and end users. **Positions advertised include:** Software Engineer. **Other U.S. locations:** Hartselle AL.

TCF BANK
401 East Liberty Street, Ann Arbor MI 48104. 734/769-8300. **Fax:** 734/930-6199. **Recorded jobline:** 888/823-2554. **Contact:** Human Resources Department. **E-mail address:** recruit@tcfbank.com. **World Wide Web address:** http://www.tcfbank.com. **Description:** A bank holding company with 63 branches in Michigan. **NOTE:** Part-time positions are offered. To contact Human Resources directly, call 734/669-5331. **Positions advertised include:** Operations Specialist; Proof Operator; Residential Team Leader; Teller; Senior Closer; Commercial Banker; Banking Sales Representative; Credit Analyst; Loan Processor; File Review Manager. **Corporate headquarters location:** This location. **Other area locations:** Statewide. **Other U.S. locations:** IN; CO; WI; MN; IL. **Parent company:** TCF Financial Corporation (MN). **Listed on:** New York Stock Exchange. **Stock exchange symbol:** TCB.

TI AUTOMOTIVE
12345 East Nine Mile Road, Warren MI 48090. 586/758-4511. **Fax:** 586/758-1131. **Contact:** Human Resources. **World Wide Web address:** http://www.tiautomotive.com. **Description:** A manufacturer and supplier of fuel storage, fluid carrying, and delivery systems for the automotive industry. **Corporate headquarters location:** This location. **Other area locations:** Statewide. **Other U.S. locations:** Nationwide. **International locations:** Worldwide. **CEO:** William J. Laule. **Annual sales/revenues:** $2.3 billion. **Number of employees nationwide:** 2,900. **Number of employees worldwide:** Over 20,000.

TRMI, INC.
100 Hill Brady Road, Battle Creek MI 49015. 269/966-0100. **Fax:** 269/966-0818. **Contact:** Human Resources Generalist. **World Wide Web address:**http://www.tokai-rika-usa.com. **Description:** Assembles electric automotive switches. Founded in 1986. **NOTE:** Jobs for this company are posted on www.monster.com. **Positions advertised include:** Plastic Injection Molding Team Leader; Cost Accountant; Quality Engineer; Maintenance Technician; New Products Coordinator. **Office hours:** Monday - Friday, 7:30 a.m. - 4:00 p.m. **Corporate headquarters location:** This location. **Other area locations:** Jackson MI; Plymouth MI. **Other U.S. locations:** Ashley IN. **Parent company:** Tokai Rika (Japan). **Number of employees at this location:** 560.

TRW AUTOMOTIVE
12025 Tech Center Drive, Livonia MI 48150. 734/855-2600. **Fax:** 734/266-5702. **Contact:** Human Resources. **World Wide Web address:** http://www.trw.com. **Description:** Provides systems for engine controls, power generation, flight controls, and cargo handling to the aerospace industry. TRW also supplies diesel fuel injection and electrical and electronic systems for the automotive industry. **Positions advertised include:** Senior Human Resources Generalist; Program Coordinator. **Corporate headquarters location:** This location. **Other U.S. locations:** Nationwide. **International locations:** Worldwide. **Parent company:** Northrup Grumman. **Listed on:** New York Stock Exchange. **Stock exchange symbol:** TRW. **President/CEO:** John C. Plant. **Annual sales/revenues:** Approximately $10.6 billion. **Number of employees worldwide:** 61,000.

TRW AUTOMOTIVE ELECTRONICS GROUP
23855 Research Drive, Farmington Hills MI 48335. 248/478-7210. **Fax:** 248/426-3953. **Contact:** Human Resources. **World Wide Web address:** http://www.trwauto.com. **Description:** Manufactures electronic controls, sensors, and displays for passenger cars, trucks and buses. **NOTE:** Interested job seekers may apply online. **Positions advertised include:** Buyer; Product Development Manager; Senior Project Engineer; Senior Human Resources Representative; Software Development Team Leader. **Corporate headquarters location:** Livonia MI. **Other U.S. locations:** Nationwide. **International locations:** Worldwide. **Parent company:** Northrup Grumman. **Operations at this facility include:** Administration; Divisional Headquarters; Research and Development. **Listed on:** New York Stock Exchange. **Stock exchange symbol:** TRW. **President/CEO:** John C. Plant. **Annual sales/revenues:** Approximately $10.6 billion. **Number of employees at this location:** 500. **Number of employees worldwide:** 61,000.

TRW STEERING & SUSPENSION SYSTEMS
P.O. Box 8008, Sterling Heights MI 48311. 586/977-1000. **Physical address:** 34201 Van Dyke Avenue, Sterling Heights MI 48312. **Fax:** 586/977-1278. **Contact:** Human Resources Manager. **World Wide Web address:** http://www.trw.com. **Description:** Manufactures steering linkage; suspension ball joints and assemblies; and manual and power rack and pinion steering gears. **Positions advertised include:** Commodity Buyer. **Corporate headquarters location:** Livonia MI. **Other U.S. locations:** Nationwide. **International locations:** Worldwide. **Parent company:** Northrup Grumman. **Listed on:** New York Stock Exchange. **Stock exchange symbol:** TRW. **President/CEO:** John C. Plant. **Annual sales/revenues:** Approximately $10.6 billion. **Number of employees worldwide:** 61,000.

TRW VEHICLE SAFETY SYSTEMS INC.
4505 West 26 Mile Road, Washington MI 48094. 586/781-7200. **Contact:** Human Resources. **World Wide Web address:** http://www.trw.com. **Description:** Manufactures automotive occupant restraint systems including seat belts and inflatable restraints. **Positions advertised include:** Operations Program Manager; Application Engineer. **Corporate headquarters location:** Livonia MI. **Other U.S. locations:** Nationwide. **International locations:** Worldwide. **Parent company:** Northrup Grumman. **Listed on:** New York Stock Exchange. **Stock exchange symbol:** TRW. **President/CEO:** John C. Plant. **Annual sales/revenues:** Approximately $10.6 billion. **Number of employees worldwide:** 61,000.

TECHSMITH CORPORATION
2405 Woodlake Drive, Okemos MI 48864-5910. 517/381-2300. **Toll-free phone:** 800/517-3001. **Fax:** 517/381-2336. **Contact:** Amy Walsh, Human Resources. **E-mail address:** personnel@techsmith.com. **World Wide Web address:** http://www.techsmith.com. **Positions advertised include:** Corporate Sales Consultant; C++ Programmer; Receptionist. **Special programs:** Internships. **Description:** Develops SnagIt screen capture software; Camtasia, a desktop camcorder and DubIt, an audio editing utility. Founded in 1988. **Corporate headquarters location:** This location. **Listed on:** Privately held. **Number of employees at this location:** Over 70.

TECUMSEH PRODUCTS COMPANY
100 East Patterson Street, Tecumseh MI 49286. 517/423-8411. **Fax:** 517/423-8853. **Contact:** Human Resources. **E-mail address:** careers.corp@tecumseh.com. **World Wide Web address:** http://www.tecumseh.com. **Description:** Manufactures a variety of hermetic compressors for air conditioning and refrigeration systems, gas engines for lawn and garden uses, and pumps. The company markets its compressor products for use in commercial devices, household appliances, room air conditioners, and central air systems for commercial and residential buildings. Pumps are sold under the brand names Little Giant, Jaeger, and MP Pump. **Positions advertised include:** Cost Accountant. **Corporate headquarters location:** This location. **Other area locations:** Ann Arbor MI; Clinton MI; Dundee MI. **Other U.S. locations:** Atlanta GA; Corinth MS; Tupelo MS; Dunlap TN: Grafton WI; New Holstein WI. **International locations:** Worldwide. **Listed on:** NASDAQ. **Stock exchange symbol:** TECUA. **Number of employees worldwide:** Approximately 20,000.

TETRA TECH MPS
710 Avis Drive, Ann Arbor MI 48108. 734/665-6000. **Fax:** 734/665-2570. **Contact:** Human Resources. **E-mail address:** careers@ttmps.com. **World Wide Web address:** http://www.ttmps.com. **Description:** An engineering, architectural, and surveying firm. **Positions advertised include:** Civil Engineer. **Special programs:** Internships. **Corporate headquarters location:** This location. **Other area locations:** Statewide. **Other U.S. locations:** Toledo OH. **International locations:** Worldwide. **Subsidiaries include:** McNamee Industrial Services, Incorporated. **Parent company:** Tetra Tech, Incorporated. **Listed on:** NASDAQ. **Stock exchange symbol:** TTEK. **Number of employees nationwide:** 400.

THETFORD CORPORATION
P.O. Box 1285, Ann Arbor MI 48106. 734/769-6000. **Physical address:** 7101 Jackson Road, Ann Arbor MI 48103. **Toll-free phone:** 800/521-3032. **Fax:** 734/769-2023. **Contact:** Personnel Department. **World Wide Web address:** http://www.thetford.com. **Description:** Produces and markets sanitation products for customers in the RV, marine, and truck industries. **Corporate headquarters:** This location. **Other area locations:** Dexter MI. **Other U.S. locations:** Elkhart IN. **International locations:** Canada; England; France; Germany; The Netherlands; Sweden. **President/CEO:** Michael Harris. **Number of employees at this location:** 300.

THOMPSON-McCULLY COMPANY
5905 Belleville Road, Belleville MI 48111. 734/397-2050. **Fax:** 734/397-8480. **Contact:** Personnel Department. **World Wide Web address:** http://www.thompsonmccully.com. **Description:** A company engaged in both the manufacture of asphalt and the construction of streets and highways. **Corporate headquarters location:** This location. **Other area locations:** Statewide.

THYSSENKRUPP INFORMATION MANAGEMENT
3155 West Big Beaver Road, Troy MI 48007. 248/643-3929. **Contact:** Human Resources. **World Wide Web address:** http://www.thyssenkrupp.com. **Description:** A national chain of nonferrous metals service centers. **NOTE:** Hiring is conducted through the corporate headquarters. Interested jobseekers should direct resumes to: ThyssenKrupp Materials Group, NA Inc., Attention: Human Resources, 22355 West Eleven Mile Road, Southfield MI 48034. Phone: 248/233-5600. Fax: 248/233-5677. **Corporate headquarters location:** Southfield MI. **Other U.S. locations:** Nationwide.

TITAN INSURANCE COMPANY
901 Wilshire Drive, Suite 550, Troy MI 48084. 248/244-9770. **Toll-free phone:** 800/347-7930. **Fax:** 248/244-6121. **Contact:** Human Resources Department. **E-mail address:** careers@titanauto.com. **World Wide Web address:** http://www.titanauto.com. **Description:** Underwrites private passenger, nonstandard automobile insurance for individuals in Michigan. **NOTE:** Entry-level positions are offered. **Corporate headquarters location:** This location. **Other U.S. locations:** AZ; CO; FL; IN; NM; NV. **Parent company:** Nationwide Mutual Insurance Company. **CEO:** John Burkhalter. **Number of employees at this location:** 150. **Number of employees nationwide:** 400.

TOTAL PLASTICS COMPANY, INC.
1661 Northfield Drive, Rochester Hills MI 48309. 248/299-9500. **Fax:** 248/299-4330. **Contact:** Chris Brierly, Human Resources. **E-mail address:** jobs@totalplastics.com. **World Wide Web address:** http://www.totalplastics.com. **Description:** Fabricates and distributes plastic products (sheet, rod, tube, and film), as well as some adhesives. **NOTE:** Resumes may be faxed to the Rochester Hills office. Interested candidates may also direct resumes to: Human Resources, 2810 North Burdick Street, Kalamazoo MI 49004. Fax: 269/344-0711. **Corporate headquarters location:** Kalamazoo MI. **Other area locations:** Grand Rapids MI. **Other U.S. locations:** Sales offices are located throughout Mid-America. **Operations at this facility include:** Administration; Manufacturing; Research and Development; Sales; Service. **Listed on:** Privately held. **Number of employees at this location:** 50.

TOWER AUTOMOTIVE
27175 Haggerty Road, Novi MI. 248/675-6000. **Fax:** 248/675-6200. **Contact:** Personnel. **World Wide Web address:** http://www.towerautomotive.com. **Description:** A Tier One supplier to the automotive industry. Products include precision light stampings and related assemblies. **NOTE:** Interested job seekers may apply online. **Positions advertised include:** Administrative Assistant; Business Process Analyst; Financial Analyst; General Ledger Accountant; Hyperion Administrator; Global Cash Manager; Account Receivable Analyst; Accounts Payable Analyst; Buyer. **Corporate headquarters location:** This location. **Other area locations:** Statewide. **Other U.S. locations:** IL; IN; KY; MD; OH; TN; VA; WI. **Operations at this facility include:** Administration; Manufacturing. **Listed on:** New York Stock Exchange. **Stock exchange symbol:** TWR. **Annual sales/revenues:** $2.5 billion. **Number of employees worldwide:** Over 12,000.

TOWER AUTOMOTIVE
P.O. Box 1251, Traverse City MI 49686. 231/946-2520. **Physical address:** 280 Hughes Drive, Traverse City MI 49686. **Fax:** 231/941-6814. **Contact:** Clay Cronin, Human Resources Manager. **E-mail address:** info@towerautomotive.com. **World Wide Web address:** http://www.towerautomotive.com. **Description:** A Tier One supplier to the automotive industry. Products include precision light stampings and related assemblies. **NOTE:** Interested job seekers may apply online. **Positions advertised include:** Environmental Health and Safety Specialist. **Corporate headquarters location:** Novi MI. **Other area locations:** Statewide. **Other U.S. locations:** IL; IN; KY; MD; OH; TN; VA; WI. **International locations:** Worldwide. **Operations at this facility include:** Manufacturing; Regional Headquarters. **Listed on:** New York Stock Exchange. **Stock exchange symbol:** TWR. **Annual sales/revenues:** $2.5 billion. **Number of employees at this location:** 450. **Number of employees worldwide:** Over 12,000.

TOWER AUTOMOTIVE
81 Drettmann Drive, Elkton MI 48731. 989/375-2201. **Contact:** Personnel. **World Wide Web address:** http://www.towerautomotive.com. **Description:** Engaged in the manufacture and distribution of automotive stampings. **NOTE:** Interested job seekers may apply online. **Corporate headquarters location:** Novi MI. **Other area locations:** Statewide. **Other U.S. locations:** IL; IN; KY; MD; OH; TN; VA; WI. **International locations:** Worldwide. **Operations at this facility include:** Manufacturing. **Listed on:** New York Stock Exchange. **Stock exchange symbol:** TWR. **Annual sales/revenues:** $2.5 billion. **Number of employees worldwide:** Over 12,000.

TRANS-INDUSTRIES INC.
2637 North Adams Road, Rochester Hills MI 48306. 248/852-1990. **Fax:** 248/852-1211. **Contact:** Human Resources. **E-mail address:** inquiries@transindustries.com.

World Wide Web address: http://www.transindustries.com. **Description:** Produces signs, advertising displays, and lighting and environmental systems for highways, as well as for automotive and commercial applications. **Corporate headquarters location:** This location. **Other area locations:** Bad Axe MI; Waterford MI. **Other U.S. locations:** Wilmington NC. **Subsidiaries include:** Transign, Inc.; Vultron, Inc.; Transmatic, Inc. **Listed on:** NASDAQ. **Stock exchange symbol:** TRNI. **Annual sales/revenues:** $34.5 million. **Number of employees at this location:** Approximately 250.

TRENDWAY CORPORATION
P.O. Box 9016, Holland MI 49422. 616/399-3900. **Fax:** 616/399-8410. **Contact:** Connie Vanderzwag, Human Resources Director. **E-mail address:** cvanderzwaag@trendway.com. **World Wide Web address:** http://www.trendway.com. **Description:** A manufacturer of office systems furniture, floor-to-floor ceiling partitions, and seating. **NOTE:** Online applications are available. Resumes are also accepted by mail, e-mail, or fax. **Positions advertised include:** Credit Specialist; Customer Service Representative. **Corporate headquarters location:** This location. **Other U.S. locations:** Nationwide. **Operations at this facility include:** Administration; Manufacturing; Research and Development; Sales; Service. **Listed on:** Privately held. **Number of employees nationwide:** 350.

H.O. TRERICE COMPANY
12950 West Eight Mile Road, Oak Park MI 48237-3288. 248/399-8000. **Fax:** 248/399-7246. **Contact:** Human Resources. **E-mail address:** info@trerice.com. **World Wide Web address:** http://www.hotrericeco.com. **Description:** Engaged in the manufacture of industrial instruments for temperature and pressure control. Founded in 1923. **Corporate headquarters location:** This location. **Other U.S. locations:** Regional Sales and Marketing Centers are located throughout the U.S. **International locations:** Mexico. **Number of employees at this location:** 300.

U.S. EQUIPMENT INC.
20580 Hoover Road, Detroit MI 48205. 313/526-8300. **Fax:** 313/526-5303. **Contact:** Human Resources Department. **E-mail address:** resume@usequipment.com. **World Wide Web address:** http://www.usequipment.com. **Description:** Rebuilds and remanufactures machine tools and machinery. Founded in 1946. **Positions advertised include:** Sales Engineer; Office Manager; Machine Builder; Electrical Technician. **Parent company:** U.S. Group Incorporated. **Number of employees at this location:** 300.

U.S. MANUFACTURING CORPORATION
28201 Van Dyke Avenue, Warren MI 48093. 586/467-1600. **Contact:** Human Resources. **World Wide Web address:** http://www.usmfg.com. **Description:** Manufactures axles for the automotive industry. Founded in 1964. **Corporate headquarters location:** This location. **International locations:** Silao, Mexico. **President/CEO:** Brian A. Simon.

USFILTER
6575 23 Mile Road, Utica MI 48316. 586/323-8800. **Contact:** Human Resources. **World Wide Web address:** http://www.usfilter.com. **Description:** A water company that provides comprehensive treatment and management services for customers in the commercial, industrial, municipal, and residential sectors. **Corporate headquarters location:** Palm Desert CA. **Other U.S. locations:** Nationwide. **International locations:** Canada. **Parent company:** Veolia Environnement. **President/CEO:** Andrew D. Seidel. **Annual sales/revenues:** $4 billion. **Number of employees at this location:** 100. **Number of employees worldwide:** 15,000.

UNIQUE FABRICATING INC.
800 Standard Parkway, Auburn Hills MI 48326. 248/853-2333. **Fax:** 248/853-7720. **Contact:** Human Resources Department. **World Wide Web address:** http://www.uniquefab.com. **Description:** Manufactures gaskets and seals for General Motors and Ford. **NOTE:** Entry-level positions are offered. **Special programs:** Internships; Training. **Corporate headquarters location:** This location. **Other U.S. locations:** LaFayette GA. **Operations at this facility include:** Administration; Manufacturing; Sales; Service. **Listed on:** Privately held. **President:** Doug Stahl. **Number of employees at this location:** 500.

UNISYS CORPORATION
41100 Plymouth Road, Plymouth MI 48170. 734/737-4000. **Fax:** 734/737-4616. **Contact:** Human Resources Department. **World Wide Web address:** http://www.unisys.com. **Description:** Unisys Corporation provides information services, technology, and software. Unisys specializes in developing critical business solutions based on open information networks. The company's Enabling Software Team creates a variety of software projects that facilitate the building of user applications and the management of distributed systems. The company's Platforms Group is responsible for UNIX Operating Systems running across a wide range of multiple processor server platforms including all peripheral and communication drivers. The Unisys Commercial Parallel Processing Team develops microkernel-based operating systems, I/O device drivers, ATM hardware, diagnostics, and system architectures. The System Management Group is in charge of the overall management of development programs for UNIX desktop and entry-server products. **NOTE:** Search and apply for positions online. **Corporate headquarters location:** Blue Bell PA. **Other area locations:** Grand Rapids MI; Okemos MI. **Other U.S. locations:** Nationwide. **International locations:** Worldwide. **Operations at this facility include:** Engineering assembly and marketing. **Listed on:** New York Stock Exchange. **Stock exchange symbol:** UIS. **President/CEO/Chairman:** Lawrence A. Weinbach. **Number of employees worldwide:** 37,000.

UNITED AMERICAN HEALTHCARE
P.O. Box 07309, Detroit MI 48207. 313/259-4000. **Physical address:** 1155 Brewery Park Boulevard, Suite 250, Detroit MI 48207. **Fax:** 313/393-7944. **Contact:** Human Resources. **E-mail address:** jobpostings@ochp.com. **World Wide Web address:** http://www.ochp.com. **Description:** Provides management consulting services to health care companies. **Corporate headquarters location:** This location. **Listed on:** NASDAQ. **Stock exchange symbol:** UAHC.

UNITED BANK OF MICHIGAN
900 East Paris Avenue SE, Suite 100, Grand Rapids MI 49546. 616/559-7000. **Contact:** Brenda Johnston, Human Resources Representative. **World Wide Web address:** http://www.unitedbankofmichigan.com. **Description:** A full-service banking institution. **NOTE:** Interested candidates can download an application from the website. **Office hours:** Monday – Friday, 8:00 a.m. – 5:00 p.m., Saturday, 9:30 a.m. – 1:00 p.m. **Corporate headquarters location:** This location. **Other area locations:** Statewide. **CEO/Chairman:** Arthur C. Johnson.

UNITED SOLAR SYSTEMS CORPORATION
3800 Lapeer Road, Auburn Hills MI 48326. 248/475-0100. **Toll-free phone:** 800/843-3892. **Contact:** Human Resources. **World Wide Web address:** http://www.uni-solar.com. **Description:** A leading developer and manufacturer of photovoltaic products and solar panels under the brand name UNI-SOLAR. Founded in 1990. **NOTE:** Entry-level positions are offered. **Corporate headquarters location:** This location. **Other U.S. locations:** San Diego CA. **International locations:** Mexico. **Listed on:** Privately held. **Number of employees at this location:** 80.

UNITED STATES GYPSUM COMPANY
10090 West Jefferson, River Rouge MI 48218. 313/842-4455. **Contact:** Human Resources. **World Wide Web address:** http://www.usg.com. **Description:** Engaged in the manufacture of gypsum products and ceiling suspension systems. **NOTE:** Entry-level positions are offered. Interested job seekers may apply online. **Corporate headquarters location:** Chicago IL. **Other U.S. locations:** Nationwide. **Parent company:** USG Corporation. **Operations at this facility include:** Manufacturing. **Subsidiaries include:** L&W Supply. **Listed on:** New York Stock Exchange. **Stock exchange symbol:** USG. **Number of employees at this location:** 150. **Number of employees worldwide:** 14,000.

UNITED WAY COMMUNITY SERVICES
1212 Griswold Street, Detroit MI 48226. 313/226-9200. **Fax:** 313/226-9210. **Contact:** Human Resources. **E-mail address:** resume@uwcs.org. **World Wide Web address:** http://www.unitedway.org. **Description:** Through a vast network of volunteers and local charities, the United Way helps to meet the health and human-care needs of millions of people. The United Way includes approximately 1,900 organizations. **Positions advertised include:** Special Events Director; Grants Manager; Director of Diversity Relationships; Editorial Associate; Editorial Service Manager; Graphich Design Associate. **Corporate headquarters location:** Alexandria VA.

UNIVERSAL FOREST PRODUCTS, INC.
2801 East Beltline Avenue NE, Grand Rapids MI 49525. 616/364-6161. **Contact:** Human Resources. **E-mail address:** jobs@ufp.com. **World Wide Web address:** http://www.ufpinc.com. **Description:** Manufactures and distributes trusses, deck panels, and lattice work. **Positions advertised include:** Senior Benefits Analyst. **Corporate headquarters location:** This location. **Other U.S. locations:** Nationwide. **International locations:** Canada; Mexico. **Listed on:** NASDAQ. **Stock exchange symbol:** UFPI. **Chairman:** Peter F. Secchia.

UNIVERSAL SYSTEMS
1401 East Stewart Avenue, Flint MI 48505-3698. 810/785-7970. **Fax:** 810/785-7990. **Contact:** Human Resources. **World Wide Web address:** http://www.universalsys.com. **Description:** Provides a variety of services including the design, manufacture, and installation of electrical and control systems. **Corporate headquarters location:** This location. **President:** Gene Dennis.

UNIVERSITY OF DETROIT MERCY
8200 West Outer Drive, Administrative Building, Room 104, Detroit MI 48219-0900. 313/993-6400. **Recorded jobline:** 313/993-6404. **Fax:** 313/993-6408. **Contact:** Human Resources. **World Wide Web address:** http://www.udmercy.edu. **Description:** A Catholic university with an enrollment of approximately 6,900 students. UDM was formed in 1990 when the University of Detroit and Mercy College of Detroit consolidated. **NOTE:** Resumes are accepted via mail or fax. **Positions advertised include:** Director, Gift Planning; Head Women's Golf Coach; Patient Care Coordinator; Faculty Legal Secretary; Director, International Programs; Library Technician. **President:** Maureen A. Fay.

UNIVERSITY OF MICHIGAN
3003 South State Street, Room G250 Wolverine Tower, Ann Arbor MI 48109. 734/764-6580. **Contact:** Employment Services. **World Wide Web address:** http://www.umich.edu. **Description:** A public university comprised of 19 schools and colleges, a comprehensive health system, and various affiliated research institutes. The University of Michigan serves approximately 50,000 students, and has 5,000 faculty and 30,000 staff members. This location is the main campus; regional campuses are located in Dearborn and Flint. Founded in 1817. **NOTE:** Entry-level positions and second and third shifts are offered. **Positions advertised include:** Chair, Microbiology and Immunology; Chair and Professor, Neurosurgery; Financial Clerk; Research Secretary; Administrative Assistant; Associate Hall Director; Student Services Assistant; Director of Sales; Editor; Business Analyst; Data Analyst; Treasury Manager; Clinical Professor, Urology; Clinical Professor, General Medicine; Clinical Professor, Emergency Medicine; Lecturer, Romance Languages. **Special programs:** Apprenticeships; Summer Jobs. **Office hours:** Monday – Friday, 8:00 a.m. – 5:00 p.m. **President:** Mary Sue Coleman. **Number of employees at this location:** 21,000.

UNIVERSITY OF MICHIGAN-DEARBORN
1050 Administration Building, 4901 Evergreen Road, Dearborn MI 48128. 313/593-5190. **Contact:** Personnel. **World Wide Web address:** http://www.umd.umich.edu. **Description:** A location of the state university with approximately 8,300 students. **Positions advertised include:** Teacher, Child Development Center; Program Coordinator, Student Activities; Associate Professor, Electrical Engineering; Assistant Professor, Industrial Engineering. **Office hours:** Monday – Friday, 8:00 a.m. – 5:00 p.m.

UNIVERSITY OF MICHIGAN-FLINT
219 University Center Building, Flint MI 48502-2186. 810/762-3150. **Contact:** Human Resources. **World Wide Web address:** http://www.flint.umich.edu. **Description:** A location of the state university. **Positions advertised include:** Dean, School of Education; Director, Health Profession Studies; Senior Executive Secretary; Director of Admissions; Assistant Professor, Chemistry; Assistant Professor, Special Education; Professor, Early Childhood Education; Assistant Professor, Nursing; Assistant Professor, Psychology; Lecturer, Communications. **Office hours:** Monday – Friday, 8:00 a.m. – 5:00 p.m.

UPCAP SERVICES
2501 14th Avenue South, P.O. Box 606, Escanaba MI 49829. 906/786-4701. **Contact:** Human Resources. **World Wide Web address:** http://www.upcapservices.com. **Description:** An agency on aging. UPCAP contracts and manages services for the elderly including personal care, meal delivery, and homemaker aid. Founded in 1961. **Corporate headquarters location:** This location. **Other area locations:** Marie MI; Munising MI; Marquette MI; Manistique MI; Ironwood MI; Iron Mountain MI; Houghton MI.

VALASSIS COMMUNICATIONS, INC.
19975 Victor Parkway, Livonia MI 48152. 734/591-3000. **Toll-free phone:** 800/437-0479. **Fax:** 734/591-4994. **Contact:** Human Resources. **World Wide Web address:** http://www.valassis.com. **Description:** A printer and publisher of four-color coupon newspaper inserts. The company also arranges the publication of promotions and offers design, printing, and distribution of promotional items including calendars, posters, and die-cuts. Founded in 1972. **NOTE:** Interested job seekers may apply online. **Positions advertised include:** Data Development Representative; Credit and Collections

Supervisor; IT Systems Administrator; Account Coordinator; Production Workflow Developer. **Special programs:** Internships. **Corporate headquarters location:** This location. **Other U.S. locations:** Nationwide. **International locations:** Canada; France. **Subsidiaries include:** NCH Marketing Services, Inc.; Valassis Canada; PreVision Marketing, LLC; Coupons, Inc.; Valassis Relationship Marketing Systems, LLC. **Operations at this facility include:** Administration; Manufacturing; Sales; Service. **Listed on:** New York Stock Exchange. **Stock exchange symbol:** VCI. **Number of employees at this location:** 550. **Number of employees worldwide:** 4,000.

VALENITE, INC.
P.O. Box 9636, Madison Heights MI 48071. 248/589-1000. **Physical address:** 31700 Research Park Drive, Madison Heights MI 48071. **Contact:** Tamara Bieth, Human Resources Administrator. **World Wide Web address:** http://www.valenite.com. **Description:** A manufacturer of pressed and extruded carbide products. **Corporate headquarters location:** This location. **Other area locations:** Oak Park MI; Clawson MI; Troy MI; Muskegon MI. **Other U.S. locations:** NY; OH; PA; SC; TX. **Number of employees nationwide:** 3,500.

VALENITE, INC.
21101 Fern Avenue, Oak Park MI 48237. 248/589-7401. **Contact:** Joe Syler, Human Resources Administrator. **World Wide Web address:** http://www.vdww.com. **Description:** Valenite is a manufacturer of pressed and extruded carbide products. **Corporate headquarters location:** Madison Heights MI. **Other U.S. locations:** Seneca SC; Gainesville TX. **Parent company:** Milacron, Inc. **Operations at this facility include:** Steel Manufacturing; Product Development; Sales; Research and Development. **Number of employees at this location:** 200. **Number of employees nationwide:** 3,500.

VALIANT INTERNATIONAL INC.
1511 East Fourteen Mile Road, Troy MI 48083. 248/588-4510. **Fax:** 248/588-3910. **Contact:** Human Resources. **World Wide Web address:** http://www.valiantcorp.com. **Description:** Performs automotive design, engineering, and Auto/CAD services for major U.S. automakers. **Special programs:** Internships. **Corporate headquarters location:** Windsor Ontario. **Parent company:** Valiant Machine & Tool Incorporated. **Number of employees at this location:** 70.

VIRTUAL SERVICES
25307 Dequindre Road, Madison Heights MI 48071. 248/545-3100. **Fax:** 248/546-8404. **Contact:** Carol Taylor, Human Resources Coordinator. **E-mail address:** cmt@virtualgrp.com. **World Wide Web address:** http://www.virtualautomotive.com. **Description:** Sells, leases, repairs, and services various types of computer hardware and software. Founded in 1983. **Positions advertised include:** Computer Field Service Engineer; Sales Account Manager. **Corporate headquarters location:** This location. **Other area locations:** Troy MI. **Number of employees at this location:** 60.

VISIONEERING, INC.
P.O. Box 127, Fraser MI 48026. 586/293-1000. **Physical address:** 31985 Groesbeck Highway, Fraser MI 48026. **Contact:** Diane Thoel, Human Resources Director. **World Wide Web address:** http://www.vistool.com. **Description:** Produces tooling for major automotive and aerospace manufacturers around the world. The company uses the latest CAD/CAM, machining, and material technologies in model and tooling techniques. **Corporate headquarters location:** This location. **International locations:** United Kingdom. **Operations at this facility include:** Administration; Manufacturing; Sales.

VISTEON CORPORATION
One Village Center Drive, Van Buren Township MI 48111. 734/710-2000. **Contact:** Human Resources Department. **World Wide Web address:** http://www.visteon.com. **Description:** Visteon Corporation is one of the largest automotive suppliers in the world. **NOTE:** Entry-level positions are offered. **NOTE:** Interested candidates can submit a resume to the company's online database. **Corporate headquarters location:** This location. **International locations:** Canada; Mexico; Germany; Argentina; Brazil; United Kingdom. **Special programs:** Internships. **Listed on:** New York Stock Exchange. **Stock exchange symbol:** VC. **CEO/Chairman:** Peter J. Pestillo. **Annual sales/revenues:** $17.7 billion. **Number of employees worldwide:** 72,000.

VOLKSWAGEN OF AMERICA
3800 Hamlin Road, Auburn Hills MI 48326. 248/340-5000. **Contact:** Human Resources. **World Wide Web address:** http://www.vw.com. **Description:** Engaged in the manufacture and wholesale distribution of automobiles. **Positions advertised include:** Customs Analyst; Retail-Integrated Marketing Leader; Warranty Auditor. **Special programs:** Training. **Corporate headquarters location:** This location. **Other U.S. locations:** Nationwide. **International locations:** Canada. **Parent company:** Volkswagen AG. **President/CEO:** Gerd Klauss

W.B. DONER & COMPANY
25900 Northwestern Highway, Southfield MI 48075. 248/354-9700. **Fax:** 248/827-8375. **Contact:** Director of Human Resources. **E-mail address:** jkingsley@donerus.com. **Description:** An advertising agency specializing in print and television campaigns. **NOTE:** Submit resumes by e-mail or fax. **Special programs:** Internships. **Other U.S. locations:** Tampa FL; Baltimore MD; Boston MA; Cleveland OH; Dallas TX. **International locations:** Brussels; London; Melbourne; Montreal; Sydney; Toronto. **Number of employees worldwide:** 930.

WKZO
4200 West Main Street, Kalamazoo MI 49006. 269/345-7121. **Contact:** Personnel. **E-mail address:** 590info@wzko.com. **World Wide Web address:** http://www.wkzo.com. **Description:** A radio broadcasting company. **Parent company:** Fairfield Broadcasting. **Corporate headquarters location:** This location.

WXYZ-CHANNEL 7
20777 West Ten Mile Road, Southfield MI 48037. 248/827-7777. **Fax:** 248/827-4983. **Contact:** Debbie Suminski, Human Resources. **E-mail address:** wxyzjobs@scripps.com. **World Wide Web address:** http://www.wxyztv.com. **Description:** A television broadcasting company. **NOTE:** Entry-level positions and second and third shifts are offered. Job postings for WXYZ-Channel 7 are listed on the parent company's website: http://www.scripps.com. **Positions advertised include:** Assignment Editor; General Assignment Reporter; Investigative Producer; Managing Editor; Weekend Assignment Editor. **Special programs:** Internships. **Internship information:** Questions regarding internships should be directed to Marlene Corsault. Phone: 248/827-9202. E-mail: mcorsault@wxyztv.com. **Corporate headquarters location:** Cincinnati OH. **Parent company:** The E.W. Scripps Company. **Operations at this facility include:** Administration; Sales. **Listed on:** New York Stock Exchange. **Stock exchange symbol:** SSP. **Number of employees at this location:** 250.

WACKER SILICONES CORPORATION
3301 Sutton Road, Adrian MI 49221-9397. 517/264-8500. **Toll-free phone:** 800/248-0063. **Fax:** 517/264-8520. **Contact:** Human Resources Department. **E-mail address:** hr@wacker.com. **World Wide Web address:** http://www.wackersilicones.com. **Description:** A manufacturer of silicone that is used in a variety of applications including car waxes, paper coating, paints, textiles, sealants, and caulking. **Corporate headquarters location:** Germany. **Other U.S. locations:** CA; IA; KY; OR; SC. **International locations:** Worldwide. **Parent company:** Wacker Chemie, GMBH. **Operations at this facility include:** Administration; Manufacturing; Regional Headquarters; Research and Development; Sales. **Listed on:** Privately held. **Number of employees at this location:** 500. **Number of employees worldwide:** Over 16,000.

WADE-TRIM
400 Monroe Street, Suite 310, Detroit MI 48226. 313/961-3650. **Fax:** 313/961-0898. **Contact:** Tammy Forney, Human Resources. **E-mail address:** tforney@wadetrim.com. **World Wide Web address:** http://www.wadetrim.com. **Description:** A firm providing a full range of engineering, planning, surveying and landscape architecture services for government and industry. **NOTE:** Resumes are accepted by e-mail and regular mail. Address resumes to: Wade-Trim Associates, Inc., Attention: Employment Manager, P.O. Box 10, Taylor MI 48180. **Positions advertised include:** Civil Engineer; GIS Analyst; Construction Technician. **Corporate headquarters location:** This location. **Other area locations:** Bay City MI; Cadillac MI; Flint MI; Gaylord MI; Grand Rapids MI; Taylor MI; Troy MI. **Other U.S. locations:** Tampa FL; Cleveland OH; Pittsburgh PA. **Subsidiaries include:** Facilities Management; Municipal Systems Consulting. **Number of employees nationwide:** Over 400.

WAGON ENGINEERING
25900 West Eleven Mile Road, Southfield MI 48034. 248/262-2020. **Fax:** 248/262-3488. **Contact:** Human Resources. **World Wide Web address:** http://www.wagon-usa.com. **Description:** Provides automotive design and engineering services. **NOTE:** Interested candidates can search and apply for positions online. **Positions advertised include:** CAE Engineer; Design Release Engineer; CATIA Designer. **Corporate headquarters location:** This location. **Other area locations:** Pontiac MI; Sterling Heights MI; Wixom MI. **Parent company:** Wagon plc. is a worldwide automotive supplier based in Warwick, England. **Operations at this facility include:** Administration; Divisional Headquarters. **Listed on:** Privately held. **Number of employees at this location:** 250. **Number of employees nationwide:** 875.

WALSH COLLEGE
3838 Livernois Road, P.O. Box 7006, Troy MI 48007-7006. 248/689-8282. **Contact:** Robin Benvenuti, Human Resources. **E-mail address:** rbenvenu@walshcollege.edu. **World Wide Web address:** http://www.walshcollege.edu. **Description:** A business college with approximately 4,000 undergraduate and graduate students. **NOTE:** To apply for adjunct faculty positions, contact Lynne Ciemochowski. E-mail: lciemoch@walshcollege.edu. Adjunct faculty applications are accepted throughout the year. **Corporate headquarters location:** This location. **Other area locations:** Novi MI. **Number of employees at this location:** 200.

WAR MEMORIAL HOSPITAL
500 Osborn Boulevard, Sault Sainte Marie MI 49783. 906/635-4652. **Fax:** 906/635-4423. **Contact:** Jan Holt, Recruiter. **E-mail address:** jmholt@wmhos.org. **World Wide Web address:** http://www.warmemorialhospital.org. **Description:** An 82-bed, full-service hospital that also offers a long-term care center. **Positions advertised include:** Radiology Technologist; Registered Nurse. **Office hours:** Monday – Friday, 7:30 a.m. – 4:30 p.m. **Corporate headquarters location:** This location. **President/CEO:** Wm. David Rencher. **Number of employees at this location:** 400.

WAYNE COUNTY COMMUNITY COLLEGE
801 West Fort Street, Detroit MI 48226. 313/496-2765. **Fax:** 313/963-5816. **Contact:** Human Resources Director. **E-mail address:** jobs@wccc.edu. **World Wide Web address:** http://www.wccc.edu. **Description:** A multi-campus community college offering liberal arts and occupational courses and programs. **NOTE:** Applications for adjunct faculty positions are accepted throughout the year. **Positions advertised include:** Learning Resource Center Assistant; General Clerk; Math Instructor; Nursing Instructor; English Instructor; Surgical Technology Instructor; Welding Instructor. **Office hours:** Monday – Friday, 8:30 a.m. – 4:30 p.m. **Corporate headquarters location:** This location. **Other area locations:** Taylor MI; Belleville MI. **Chancellor:** Dr. Curtis L. Ivery.

WAYNE STATE UNIVERSITY
5700 Cass Avenue, Suite 1900 A/AB, Detroit, MI 48202. 313/577-2010. **Fax:** 313/577-7508. **Contact:** Department of Employment Services. **E-mail address:** jobs@wayne.edu. **World Wide Web address:** http://www.wayne.edu. **Description:** A university with 14 colleges and schools offering 128 bachelor's, 136 master's, and 61 doctoral degrees. WSU has an enrollment of 33,000 undergraduate and graduate students. **NOTE:** Interested candidates should apply for positions via the university's new online hiring system. **Positions advertised include:** Research Assistant, Various Disciplines; Lecturer, Communications; Associate Professor, Computer Science; Associate Dean, Science; Academic Services Officer; Development Officer; Research Scientist, Neurology; Professor, Internal Medicine; University Counselor; Information Officer; Assistant Professor, Music. **Office hours:** Monday – Friday, 8:30 a.m. – 4:30 p.m.

WAYNE STATE UNIVERSITY PRESS
4809 Woodward Avenue, Detroit MI 48201. 313/577-6120. **Contact:** Human Resources Department. **World Wide Web address:** http://www.wsupress.wayne.edu. **Description:** A publisher of scholarly and regional interest books. Founded in 1941. **Special programs:** Internships. **Parent company:** Wayne State University. **Number of employees at this location:** 20.

JERVIS B. WEBB COMPANY
34375 West Twelve Mile Road, Farmington Hills MI 48331. 248/553-1220. **Fax:** 248/553-1228. **Contact:** Human Resources. **E-mail address:** careers@jerviswebb.com. **World Wide Web address:** http://www.jervisbwebb.com. **Description:** Engaged in the design, fabrication, and installation of material handling systems. Custom engineered products include conveyors, driverless vehicles, and automated storage and retrieval systems. The firm maintains sales offices and plant locations. Founded in 1919. **NOTE:** Resumes may be submitted online. **Corporate headquarters location:** This location. **Other U.S. locations:** Nationwide. **International locations:** Worldwide. **Listed on:** Privately held. **President/CEO:** Susan M. Webb. **Annual sales/revenues:** $250 million. **Number of employees worldwide:** 1,200.

WESTERN MICHIGAN UNIVERSITY
1300 Seibert Administration Building, 1903 Western Michigan Avenue, Kalamazoo MI 49008-5217. 269/387-3620. **Fax:** 269/387-3441. **Contact:** Krista Cekola, Human Resources Analyst. **E-mail address:** krista.cekola@wmich.edu. **World Wide Web address:** http://www.wmichedu. **Description:** A four-year university offering undergraduate and graduate programs of study. **Positions advertised include:** Fitness

Programs Coordinator; Director, Marketing and Communications; Medical Office Assistant; Research Fellow, Chemistry. **Operations at this facility include:** Administration. **Number of employees at this location:** 3,000.

WHIRLPOOL CORPORATION
2000 North M-63, Benton Harbor MI 49022. 269/923-5000. **Contact:** Dave Binkley, Senior Vice President of Human Resources. **E-mail address:** careers@email.whirlpool.com. **World Wide Web address:** http://www.whirlpoolcorp.com. **Description:** Whirlpool Corporation manufactures and markets home appliances under brand names such as Whirlpool, KitchenAid, Roper, Estate, Bauknecht, Ignis, Laden, and Inglis. Whirlpool is also manufactures and supplies major home appliances to Sears, Roebuck and Company under the Kenmore brand name. **NOTE:** Interested candidates can search and apply for position online. **Positions advertised include:** Visual Designer; Master Black Belt. **Special programs:** Internships. **Corporate headquarters location:** This location. **Other U.S. locations:** Nationwide. **International locations:** Worldwide. **Operations at this facility include:** Administration; Manufacturing. **Listed on:** New York Stock Exchange. **Stock exchange symbol:** WHR. **Number of employees at this location:** 2,000. **Number of employees worldwide:** 68,000.

WILLIAMS INTERNATIONAL CORPORATION
2280 West Maple Road, P.O. Box 200, Walled Lake MI 48390. 248/624-5200. **Fax:** 248/669-9172. **Contact:** Human Resources Department. **E-mail address:** hr@williams-int.com. **World Wide Web address:** http://www.williams-int.com. **Description:** Engaged in the research, development, and manufacture of small gas turbine engines for military and commercial applications. Founded in 1955. **Positions advertised include:** Security Assistant. **Corporate headquarters location:** This location. **Other U.S. locations:** Ogden UT. **Listed on:** Privately held. **President:** Gregg G. Williams. **Number of employees at this location:** 440. **Number of employees nationwide:** Over 900.

WIRTZ MANUFACTURING COMPANY INC.
1105 24th Street, P.O. Box 5006, Port Huron MI 48061. 810/987-4700. **Fax:** 810/987-8135. **Contact:** Human Resources Director. **World Wide Web address:** http://www.wirtzusa.com. **Description:** Manufactures industrial machinery designed to produce batteries. **Corporate headquarters location:** This location. **Other U.S. locations:** Charlotte NC; Atlanta GA; Brandon MS. **Annual sales/revenues:** Over $25 million. **Number of employees nationwide:** Approximately 300.

F.B. WRIGHT COMPANY
9999 Mercier Avenue, P.O. Box 770, Dearborn MI 48121. 313/843-8250. **Fax:** 313/843-8450. **Contact:** Human Resources. **World Wide Web address:** http://www.fbwright.com. **Description:** A distributor of a variety of hoses, gaskets, and fittings. **Corporate headquarters location:** This location. **Other area locations:** Grand Rapids MI; Saginaw MI. **Other U.S. locations:** Toledo OH. **Number of employees at this location:** 100.

X-RITE CORPORATION, INC.
3100 44th Street SW, Grandville MI 49418. 616/534-7663. **Fax:** 616/534-5832. **Contact:** Human Resources. **E-mail address:** hr@xrite.com. **World Wide Web address:** http://www.x-rite.com. **Description:** Designs, engineers, and manufactures quality control instruments, which are marketed worldwide to companies in the paint, plastic, textile, packaging, photographic, graphic arts, and medical industries. **Positions advertised include:** Corporate Development Manager; Customer Service Associate; Global Accounts Manager; Human Resources Manager; Product Support Engineer. **Office hours:** Monday – Friday, 8:00 a.m. – 6:30 p.m. **Corporate headquarters location:** This location. **Other U.S. locations:** Andover MA; Hollywood FL. **International locations:** Worldwide. **Subsidiaries include:** Labsphere; Optronik; Coherix; XR Ventures. **Listed on:** NASDAQ. **Stock exchange symbol:** XRIT.

XPEDX
3101 South Gulley Road, Unit F, Dearborn MI 48124. 313/563-7333. **Fax:** 313/563-7552. **Contact:** Human Resources. **E-mail address:** xpedx.recruiting@xpedx.com. **World Wide Web address:** http://www.xpedx.com. **Description:** Engaged in the wholesale distribution of printing and writing paper. **Corporate headquarters location:** Covington KY. **Other area locations:** Statewide. **Other U.S. locations:** Nationwide. **Operations at this facility include:** This location is a business store.

XYCOM AUTOMATION
750 North Maple Road, Saline MI 48176. 734/429-4971. **Fax:** 734/492-8206. **Contact:** Human Resources. **E-mail address:** hrdept@xycom.com. **World Wide Web address:** http://www.xycom.com. **Description:** Develops, manufactures, and sells industrial microcomputers. Applications include the regulation and monitoring of continuous batch processes, and the control and monitoring of material handling equipment. **Positions advertised include:** National Channel Partner Manager; Area Sales Manager; Application Engineer. **Corporate headquarters location:** This location. **International locations:** Canada.

YMCA OAK PARK
900 Long Boulevard, Lansing MI 48911. 517/694-3901. **Contact:** Tiffeny Forrest, Associate Executive Director. **E-mail address:** tforrest@ymcaoflansing.org. **World Wide Web address:** http://www.ymcaoflansing.org. **Description:** One of the nation's largest and most comprehensive service organizations. The YMCA provides health and fitness; social and personal development; sports and recreation; education and career development; and camps and conferences to children, youths, adults, the elderly, families, the disabled, refugees and foreign nationals, YMCA residents, and community residents, through a broad range of specific programs. **Corporate headquarters location:** Chicago IL. **Other U.S. locations:** Nationwide. **International locations:** Worldwide.

YAMAHA CORPORATION OF AMERICA
3445 East Paris Avenue, Grand Rapids MI 49512. 616/940-4900. **Fax:** 616/949-7721. **Contact:** Human Resources. **World Wide Web address:** http://www.yamaha.com/band. **Description:** Manufactures musical instruments. **Corporate headquarters location:** Buena Park CA. **Other U.S. locations:** Nationwide. **Parent company:** Yamaha Corporation. **President:** Yoshihiro Doi. **Annual sales/revenues:** $705 million.

YOUNG & RUBICAM, INC.
550 Town Center Drive, Suite 300, Dearborn MI 48126. 313/583-8000. **Contact:** Cathy Coraci, Director of Human Resources. **World Wide Web address:** http://www.yr.com. **Description:** An international advertising agency. Founded in 1923. **NOTE:** Entry-level positions are offered. **Special programs:** Internships. **Office hours:** Monday - Friday, 9:00 a.m. - 5:00 p.m. **Corporate headquarters location:** New York NY. **Other U.S. locations:** Nationwide. **International locations:** Worldwide. **Parent company:** WPP Group. **Operations at this facility include:** This location houses Young & Rubicam Advertising, Wunderman Cato Johnson, Burson-Marsteller, and Capital Consulting & Research. **Listed on:** New York Stock Exchange. **Stock exchange symbol:** YNR. **CEO/Chairwoman:** Ann M. Fudge. **Annual sales/revenues:** Approximately $1 billion. **Number of employees at this location:** 260. **Number of employees nationwide:** Over 11,000.

ZENACOMP
17187 North Laurel Park Drive, Suite 351, Livonia MI 48152. 734/464-3700. **Toll-free phone:** 800/639-5967. **Fax:** 734/464-3730. **Contact:** Consulting Manager. **E-mail address:** recruiter@zenacomp.com. **World Wide Web address:** http://www.zenacomp.com. **Description:** Provides computer consulting services. **Corporate headquarters location:** This location. **President/CEO:** Mark Lichtman.

ZIEBART INTERNATIONAL CORPORATION
P.O. Box 1290, Troy MI 48007-1290. 248/588-4100. **Physical address:** 1290 East Maple Road, Troy MI 48083. **Fax:** 248/588-1444. **Contact:** Personnel. **E-mail address:** info@ziebart.com. **World Wide Web address:** http://www.ziebart.com. **Description:** Operates a network of franchised automotive service locations. Founded in 1959. **Corporate headquarters location:** This location. **International locations:** Worldwide. **President/CEO/Chairman:** Thomas E. Wolfe. **Number of employees at this location:** 250.

ZONDERVAN PUBLISHING HOUSE
5300 Patterson Avenue SE, Grand Rapids MI 49512. 616/698-6900. **Contact:** Human Resources. **E-mail address:** zjobs@zondervan.com. **World Wide Web address:** http://www.zondervan.com. **Description:** Publishes Christian-oriented books, audio books, eBooks, videos, CD-ROMs, and gifts. **Positions advertised include:** Media Relations Director; Bookkeeper; National Accounts Director; Internet Marketing Manager; Corporate Librarian. **Special programs:** Internships. **Corporate headquarters location:** This location. **President/CEO:** Bruce Ryskamp. **Number of employees at this location:** 330.

A&E PRODUCTS CATERING
900 Apollo Road, Eagan MN 55121. 651/229-5300. **Toll-free phone:** 800/752-7462. **Fax:** 800/328-1819. **Contact:** Human Resources. **World Wide Web address:** http://www.plastics-inc.com. **Description:** Manufactures plastic disposable serviceware and kitchen storage containers. **Parent company:** Tyco International Ltd.

ADC TELECOMMUNICATIONS
13625 Technology Drive, Eden Prairie MN 55344. 952/938-8080. **Toll-free phone:** 800/366-3889. **Fax:** 952/917-1717. **Contact:** Human Resources. **World Wide Web address:** http://www.adc.com. **Description:** Supplies voice, video, and data systems for high-speed transmissions. ADC Telecommunications serves the broadcast, cable television, Internet, telephone, and wireless communications industries worldwide. **NOTE:** Search and apply for positions or submit resume online. **Positions advertised include:** Stock Program Analyst; Principal Web Designer; Manager, Sarbanes Oxley; Sr. Production Designer. **Corporate headquarters location:** This location. **Listed on:** NASDAQ. **Stock exchange symbol:** ADCT.

APA CABLES & NETWORKS
5480 Nathan Lane, Suite 120, Plymouth MN 55442. 952/942-3800. **Contact:** Human Resources. **E-mail address:** apacn-hr@apacn.com. **World Wide Web address:** http://www.apacn.com. **Description:** Designs and manufactures a complete line of passive fiber optic connectivity solutions. **Parent company:** APA Optics.

ASI DATAMYTE, INC.
2800 Campus Drive, Suite 60, Plymouth MN 55441. 763/553-1040. **Toll-free phone:** 800/207-5631. **Fax:** 763/553-1041. **Contact:** Human Resources. **E-mail address:** hr@asidatamyte.com. **World Wide Web address:** http://www.asidatamyte.com. **Description:** Develops products for quality planning and control, data collection, precision measurement, analysis and reporting, and gage management for the manufacturing marketplace. **Corporate headquarters location:** This location. **Annual sales/revenues:** $5 - $10 million. **Number of employees at this location:** 50.

ATK
5050 Lincoln Drive, Edina MN 55436. 952/351-3000. **Fax:** 952/351-3009. **Contact:** Human Resources. **E-mail address:** atk.corporate@atk.com. **World Wide Web address:** http://www.atk.com. **Description:** A provider of advanced weapons and space systems. The core of their businesses is conventional munitions and rocket motors. **NOTE:** Search and apply for jobs online. **Positions advertised include:** Administrative Positions; Mission Research; Plant Managers. **Corporate headquarters location:** This location. **Other U.S. locations:** Nationwide. **Listed on:** New York Stock Exchange. **Stock exchange symbol:** ATK. **President and CEO:** Dan Murphy. **Annual sales:** $2.4 billion. **Number of employees worldwide:** 14,000.

ATS MEDICAL, INC.
3905 Annapolis Lane, Suite 105, Minneapolis MN 55447. 763/553-7736. **Toll-free phone:** 800/399-1381. **Fax:** 763/557-2244. **Contact:** Human Resources. **E-mail address:** hr@atsmedical.com. **World Wide Web address:** http://www.atsmedical.com. **Description:** Manufactures and markets medical devices including aortic valve graft prosthesis, mechanical heart valves, and related cardiovascular devices. Founded in 1991. **Positions advertised include:** Sr. Research Engineer. **Corporate headquarters location:** This location. **Subsidiaries include:** ATS Medical, Ltd. (Glasgow, Scotland). **Listed on:** NASDAQ. **Stock exchange symbol:** ATSI.

ABDO PUBLISHING COMPANY
4940 Viking Drive, Suite 622, Edina MN 55435. **Toll-free phone:** 800/800-1312. **Fax:** 952/831-1632. **Contact:** Personnel Director. **E-mail address:** info@abdopub.com. **World Wide Web address:** http://www.abdopub.com. **Description:** Publishes children's books.

ABBOTT NORTHWESERN HOSPITAL
800 East 28th Street, Minneapolis MN 55407. 612/863-4000. **World Wide Web address:** http://www.abbottnorthwestern.com. **Description:** The largest not-for-profit hospital in the Twin Cities area. **NOTE:** Search and apply for positions online. **Positions advertised include:** Business Analyst; Cardiac Sonographer; Director, Planned Giving; EMT; Film Librarian; Nursing Manager; Practice Manager; Operations Coordinator; Perinatal Ultrasonographer; Physical Therapist; RN's; Speech Pathologist. **Parent company:** Allina Hospitals & Clinics.

ABELCONN, LLC
9210 Science Center Drive, New Hope MN 55428. 763/533-3533. **Fax:** 763/536-0349. **Contact:** Human Resources. **World Wide Web address:** http://www.abelconn.com. **Description:** AbelConn manufactures electronic connectors, circuit boards, and other electronic products.

ACME TAG AND LABEL COMPANY
2838 Fremont Avenue South, Minneapolis MN 55408. 612/872-0333. **Fax:** 612/872-0022. **E-mail address:** info@acmetag.com. **World Wide Web address:** http://www.acmetag.com. **Contact:** Human Resources. **Description:** Manufactures tags, printed gum labels, and printed pressure-sensitive labels.

ACROMETAL COMPANIES INC.
210 NE 10th Avenue, P.O. Box 408, Brainerd MN 56401. 218/829-4719. **Fax:** 218/828-6620. **Contact:** Human Resources. **World Wide Web address:** http://www.acrometal.com. **Description:** A manufacturer of metal spools and reels, wire handling and packaging equipment, and other industrial products. **NOTE:** Hiring is done through Acrometal's sister company. Please send resumes to Sue Hilgard, Human Resources Manager, ATEK, P.O. Box 403, Brainerd MN 56401 and note the location to which you are applying. **Corporate headquarters location:** Plymouth MN.

ADOLFSON AND PETERSON INC.
6701 West 23rd Street, Minneapolis MN 55426. 952/544-1561. **Fax:** 952/525-2333. **Contact:** Personnel. **E-mail address:** ehermanek@a-p.com. **World Wide Web address:** http://www.adolfsonpeterson.com. **Description:** A construction company. **Positions advertised include:** Facilities Maintenance Manager; Project Manager; Superintendent. **Other U.S. locations:** CO; AZ; WI; TX.

ADVANTEK
5801 Clearwater Drive, Minnetonka MN 55343. 952/938-6800. **Fax:** 952/938-1800. **Contact:** Human Resources. **World Wide Web address:** http://www.advantek.com. **Description:** A manufacturer of packing products including carrier tape, cover tapes, shipping reels, and bags for the electronics industry. **Corporate headquarters location:** This location. **Other U.S. locations:** CA; MA; TX; ID.

ADVO SYSTEM INC.
4216 Park Glen Road, Minneapolis MN 55416. 952/929-1441. **Contact:** Human Resources. **World Wide Web address:** http://www.advo.com. **Description:** A direct mail company. Advo distributes ShopWise branded programs and missing children alert cards through the mail. **Positions advertised include:** District Sales Manager. **Corporate headquarters location:** Windsor CT.

AERATION INDUSTRIES INTERNATIONAL
4100 Peavey Road, P.O. Box 59144, Minneapolis MN 55459-0144. 952/448-6789. **Toll-free phone:** 800/328-8287. **Contact:** Personnel. **World Wide Web address:** http://www.aireo2.com. **Description:** Provides products and systems to treat industrial and municipal wastewater, restore lakes, rivers and harbors, increase production yields in aquaculture, and improve water quality on golf courses and recreational water areas.

AERO SYSTEMS ENGINEERING
358 East Fillmore Avenue, St. Paul MN 55107. 651/227-7515. **Fax:** 651/227-0519. **Contact:** Sharon Dibb, Human Resources Director. **E-mail address:** sdibb@aerosysengr.com. **World Wide Web address:** http://www.aerosysengr.com. **Description:** An aerospace engineering firm serving both defense and commercial clients.

AFFILIATED COMPUTER SERVICES (ACS)
2901 Third Street South, Waite Park MN 56387. 320/253-2170. **Contact:** Human Resources. **World Wide Web address:** http://www.acs-inc.com. **Description:** Develops business process and assessment software for commercial and government clients. **Corporate headquarters location:** Dallas TX. **Other U.S. locations:** Nationwide. **Listed on:** New York Stock Exchange. **Stock exchange symbol:** ACS.

AFFINITY PLUS FEDERAL CREDIT UNION
175 West Lafayette Road, St. Paul MN 55107. 651-312-9342. **Toll-free phone:** 800/322-7228. **Contact:** Human Resources. **E-mail address:** hr@affinityplus.org. **World Wide Web address:** http://www.affinityplus.org. **Description:** Affinity Plus is a not-for-profit member-owned financial institution/credit union. **NOTE:** Search for open positions online. **Positions advertised include:** Accounting Manager; Assistant Manager; Branch Manager; Financial Service Officer; IT Help Desk Associate; Member Relations Specialist; Member Service Representative; Mortgage Specialist; Operations Service Representative; Records Service Representative; Systems Administrator. **Corporate headquarters location:** This location. **Other area locations:** Statewide.

AG-CHEM EQUIPMENT COMPANY, INC.
202 Industrial Park, Jackson MN 56143. 507/847-2690. **Fax:** 507/847-7482. **Contact:** Karen Cross, Human Resources Manager. **E-mail address:** HR.Jackson@agcocorp.com. **World Wide Web address:** http://www.agchem.com. **Description:** Manufactures equipment for the agricultural and industrial markets. **Corporate headquarters location:** Minnetonka MN. **Parent company:** AGCO Corporation. **Number of employees at this location:** 600. **Number of employees nationwide:** 1,200.

AG-CHEM EQUIPMENT COMPANY, INC.
5720 Smetana Drive, Suite 300, Minnetonka MN 55343. 952/933-9006. **Contact:** Personnel. **World Wide Web address:** http://www.agchem.com. **Description:** Manufactures equipment for the agricultural and industrial markets. **Corporate headquarters location:** This location. **Parent company:** AGCO Corporation. **Number of employees nationwide:** 1,200.

AGRIBANK, FCB
375 Jackson Street, St. Paul MN 55101. 651/282-8800. **Fax:** 651/282-8671. **Contact:** Human Resources Manager. **E-mail address:** hr@agribank.com. **World Wide Web address:** http://www.agribank.com. **Description**: Provides wholesale funds and services to Farm Credit Services organizations serving 15 states. **Corporate headquarters location:** This location. **Positions advertised include:** Manager, Organizational Effectiveness; Employee Benefits Manager; Business Process Analyst.

ALBANY HOSPITAL MEDICAL CENTER
300 Third Avenue, Albany MN 56307. 320/845-6104. **Fax:** 320/845-6127. **Contact:** Renee Thelen, Human Resources. Manager **E-mail address:** reneethelen@catholichealth.net. **World Wide Web address:** http://www.albanyareahospital.com. **Description:** A hospital offering acute care services. **NOTE:** Outpatient services are provided at the hospital's clinic, located at 320 Third Avenue, Albany MN.

ALLETE
30 West Superior Street, Duluth MN 55802. 218/279-5000. **Contact:** Human Resources. **World Wide Web address:** http://www.allete.com. **Description:** Generates, transmits, distributes and markets electrical power for retail and wholesale customers in the Upper Midwest. ALLETE also owns a significant portfolio of real estate in Florida. Affiliate companies mine lignite coal and provide telecommunications services. **NOTE:** Search and apply for positions online. **Positions advertised include:** Accounting Specialist; Network/IPT Engineer; Sales Representative; Telecom Assistant; Temporary Attendant. **Corporate headquarters location:** This location. **Listed on:** New York Stock Exchange. **Stock exchange symbol:** ALE.

ALLIANZ LIFE INSURANCE COMPANY OF NORTH AMERICA
P.O. Box 1344, Minneapolis MN 55416-1297. 800/950-5872. **Fax:** 763/582-6400. **Contact:** Human Resources. **World Wide Web address:** http://www.allianzlife.com. **Description:** One of the world's largest integrated financial services organizations with operations in 70 countries, offering annuities, universal life insurance, and long-term care for individuals. Allianz also provides specialized healthcare products and services to HMO's, businesses with self-insured employee benefit plans, and PPO's. **NOTE:** Search and apply for positions online. Resumes may be mailed to: Employee Support Services, 5701 Golden Hills Drive, Minneapolis MN 55416-1297. **Positions advertised include:** Accountant; Assistant Actuary; Claims Manager; Employee Relations Specialist; Sr. Programmer Analyst; Sr. Web Analyst. **Corporate headquarters location:** This location. **Parent company:** Allianz AG (Germany). **Listed on:** New York Stock Exchange. **Stock exchange symbol:** AZ.

ALLINA HOSPITALS & CLINICS
710 East 24th Street, Minneapolis MN 55404. 612/775-5000. **Contact:** Lynda Laskow, Director of Human Resources. **World Wide Web address:** http://www.allina.com. **Description:** Owns 11 and manages two hospitals, and operates 42 clinics in Minnesota and western Wisconsin. **Number of employees nationwide:** 22,000.

ALTRON INC.
6700 Industry Avenue NW, Anoka MN 55303-4595. 763/427-7735. **Fax:** 763/427-3773. **Contact:** Personnel. **E-mail address:** info@altronmfg.com. **World Wide Web address:** http://www.altronmfg.com. **Description:** Contract manufacturer of electronic and electro-mechanical assemblies and products. Founded in 1974.

AMERICAN CRYSTAL SUGAR COMPANY
101 North Third Street, Moorhead MN 56560. 218/236-4400. **Fax:** 218/236-4485. **Contact:** Sharon Connell, Human Resources. **E-mail address:** sconnell@crystalsugar.com. **World Wide Web address:** http://www.crystalsugar.com. **Description:** American Crystal Sugar Company, an agricultural cooperative, processes and markets sugar, sugar beet pulp, molasses, and seed. Customers are primarily American companies in the food processing industry. American Crystal is a partner in Midwest Agri-Commodities with Minn-Dak Farmers Cooperative and Southern Minnesota Beet Sugar Cooperative. **Corporate headquarters location:** This location. **Other U.S. locations:** Crookston MN; East Grand Forks MN; Drayton ND; Hillsboro ND. **Number of employees nationwide:** 1,100.

AMERICAN HARDWARE INSURANCE GROUP
P.O. Box 435, Minneapolis MN 55440. 952/939-4615. **Physical address:** 5605 Green Circle Drive, Minnetonka MN 55343. **Toll-free phone:** 800/544-8400. **Fax:** 800/841-5339. **Recorded jobline:** 952/939-4545. **Contact:** Human Resources. **E-mail address:** mmic@rpc.webhire.com. **World Wide Web address:** http://www.american-hardware.com. **Description:** A property and casualty insurance company. **Positions advertised include:** Customer Service Representative. **Corporate headquarters location:** This location. **Other U.S. locations:** Nationwide. **Parent company:** Motorist Insurance Group Inc. **Number of employees at this location:** 200.

AMERICAN MEDICAL SYSTEMS, INC.
10700 Bren Road West, Minnetonka MN 55343. 952/933-4666. **Toll-free phone:** 800/328-3881. **Fax:** 952/930-6514. **Contact:** Human Resources. **E-mail address:** careers@AmericanMedicalSystems.com. **World Wide Web address:** http://www.visitams.com. **Description:** Manufactures and distributes medical devices for the diagnosis and treatment of a variety of illnesses including prostate diseases, severe fecal incontinence, urethral strictures, and urinary incontinence. **NOTE:** Resumes accepted only for open positions. **Positions advertised include:** Clinical Documentation Coordinator; CNC Analyst; Director of Clinical Programs; Director of Information Technology; Director of Quality Engineering Systems and Services; Director, Healthcare Affairs Director, Project Management; Product Manager. **Listed on:** NASDAQ. **Stock exchange symbol:** AMMD.

AMERIPRIDE SERVICES
10801 Wayzata Boulevard, Minnetonka MN 55305. 612/371-4200. **Contact:** Personnel Director. **World Wide Web address:** http://www.ameripride.com. **Description:** A linen and uniform rental and supply company. **Other U.S. locations:** Nationwide. **International locations:** Canada.

ANALYSTS INTERNATIONAL CORPORATION (AIC)
3601 West 76th Street, Minneapolis MN 55435-3000. 952/835-5900. **Toll-free phone:** 800/800-5044. **Fax:** 952/897-4555. **Contact:** Senior Staffing Assistant. **E-mail address:** jobs@analysts.com. **World Wide Web address:** http://www.analysts.com. **Description:** Analysts International is an international computer consulting and staffing firm. The company assists clients in analyzing, designing, and developing systems using different programming languages and software. **NOTE:** A minimum of one to two years of programming experience is required. **Corporate headquarters location:** This location. **Other U.S. locations:** Nationwide. **Listed on:** NASDAQ. **Stock exchange symbol:** ANLY. **Annual sales/revenues:** More than $100 million. **Number of employees at this location:** 400.

ANDERSEN CORPORATION
100 Fourth Avenue North, Bayport MN 55003-1096. 651/264-5150. **Contact:** Human Resources. **World Wide Web address:** http://www.andersenwindows.com. **Description:** Manufactures windows and doors. **NOTE:** Search and apply for positions online. **Positions advertised include:** Product Development Engineer; Engineer; Project Manager; Quality Engineer; Production Supervisor; Design Engineer; Pilot Plant Engineering Manager.

AON RISK SERVICES INC. OF MINNESOTA
8300 Norman Center Drive, Suite 400, Minneapolis MN 55437. 952/656-8000. **Fax:** 952/656-8601. **Contact:** Department of Human Resources. **World Wide Web address:** http://www.aon.com. **Description:** Provides risk management solutions for commercial and industrial enterprises, insurance organizations, and individuals worldwide. **NOTE:** Search and apply for positions online. **Positions advertised include:** Relationship Assistant; Syndicator. **Corporate headquarters location:** Chicago IL.

APPLIANCE RECYCLING CENTER OF AMERICA, INC.
7400 Excelsior Boulevard, Minneapolis MN 55426. 952/930-9000. **Contact:** Human Resources Manager. **World Wide Web address:** http://www.arcainc.com. **Description:** Provides a full range of environmentally sound appliance collection, processing, and recycling services and reclaims hazardous substances for reuse. **Number of employees at this location:** 280.

ARBY'S/FRANCHISE ASSOCIATES INC.
5354 Parkdale Drive, Suite 100, Minneapolis MN 55416. 952/546-3391. **Contact:** Staffing and Communications Manager. **E-mail address:** fai@arbys-sbarro.com. **Description:** Operates a franchise of several national restaurant chains including Arby's and Sbarro. **Corporate headquarters location:** This location. **Parent company:** Triarc Restaurant Group. **Operations at this facility include:** Regional Headquarters.

ARCHITECTURE TECHNOLOGY CORPORATION
9971 Valley View Road, Eden Prairie MN 55344. 952/829-5864. **Fax:** 952/829-5871. **Contact:** Human Resources. **E-mail address:** es.resume@atcorp.com. **World Wide Web address:** http://www.atcorp.com. **Description:** A computer architectural and networking technologies consulting firm. Founded in 1981. **NOTE:** Search and apply for positions online. Forward resumes for research positions to: r&d.resume@atcorp.com. **Positions advertised include:** Systems Engineer; Research Staff. **Other U.S. locations:** Washington DC; Ithaca NY.

ARCON CONSTRUCTION COMPANY
43249 Frontage Road, P.O. Box 159, Harris MN 55032. 651/674-4474. **Contact:** Controller/Secretary. **Description:** A contracting firm specializing in highway and street construction.

ARCTIC CAT, INC.
601 Brooks Avenue South, Thief River Falls MN 56701. 218/681-8558. **Fax:** 218/681-3162. **Contact:** Human Resources. **World Wide Web address:** www.arcticcat.com. **Description:** Designs, engineers, manufactures and markets snowmobiles and all-terrain vehicles (ATVs) under the Arctic Cat brand name, as well as related parts, garments and accessories. The Company markets its products through a network of independent dealers located throughout the contiguous United States and Canada, and through distributors representing dealers in Alaska, Europe, the Middle East, Asia and other international markets. **NOTE:** Search and apply for jobs online. **Positions advertised include:** Accounts payable clerk; Accounts Payable Supervisor; Area Assembly Supervisor; Design Engineer-Electrical; Executive Director of MIS; Field Engineer-Engine Development; Manufacturing Engineer; Senior Graphic Stylist. **Corporate headquarters location:** This location. **Listed on:** National Association of Securities Dealers Automated Quotation (NASDAQ). **Stock exchange symbol:** ACAT. **CEO:** Christopher A. Twomey.

ARIZANT HEALTHCARE, INC.
10393 West 70th Street, Eden Prairie MN 55344. 952/947-1214. **Fax:** 952/947-1400. **Contact:** Carolyn Kassebaum, Human Resources Director. **Description:** Manufactures convective warming blankets and fluid warmers for the health care industry.

ARTESYN TECHNOLOGIES
1425 East Bridge Street, Redwood Falls MN 56283. 507/644-2966. **Fax:** 507/644-3737. **Contact:** Human Resources. **World Wide Web address:** http://www.artesyn.com. **Description:** The company supplies power conversion products and communications subsystems to the communications industry. **Corporate headquarters location:** Boca Raton FL.

ARTHUR, CHAPMAN, KETTERING, SMETAK & PIKALA, P.A.
500 Young Quinlan Building, 81 South Ninth Street, Minneapolis MN 55402. 612/339-3500. **Fax:** 612/339-7655. **Contact:** Human Resources Manager. **E-mail address:** info@arthurchapman.com. **World Wide Web address:** http://www.arthurchapman.com. **Description:** A law firm specializing in insurance, liability, product liability, and workers' compensation cases. Founded in 1974.

ASHLAND ENVIRONMENTAL SERVICES
ASHLAND CHEMICAL COMPANY
4471 Valley Industrial Boulevard, P.O. Box 520, Shakopee MN 55379. 952/403-5151. **Contact:** District Manager. **World Wide Web address:** http://www.ashchem.com. **Description:** Provides hazardous waste removal services. Ashland Chemical Company (also at this location) is a distribution center for the company's manufactured industrial chemicals and solvents. **Parent company:** Ashland Oil Company, Inc.

A-TEK
Highway 210 East, Brainerd MN 56401. 218/829-4719. **Toll-free phone:** 866/879-2835. **Fax:** 218/825-2299. **Contact:** Human Resources. **World Wide Web address:** http://www.atekmanufacturing.com. Description: A contract manufacturer, assembler, and distributor.

AUGSBURG COLLEGE
2211 Riverside Avenue, CB #79, Minneapolis MN 55454. 612/330-1000. **Recorded jobline:** 612/330-1317. **Contact:** Human Resources Department. **E-mail address:** jobs@augsburg.edu. **World Wide Web address:** http://www.augsburg.edu. **Description:** A private, four-year college, affiliated with the Evangelical Lutheran Church in America, offering undergraduate degrees in 50 areas of study and five graduate programs. Enrollment is approximately 3,000 students. **NOTE:** Search and apply for positions online.

AUGSBURG FORTRESS PUBLISHERS
P.O. Box 1209, Minneapolis MN 55440-1209. 612/330-3300. **Physical address:** 100 South Fifth Street, Suite 700, Minneapolis MN 55402. **Fax:** 612/330-3387. **Contact:** Human Resources Manager. **E-mail address:** jobs@augsburgfortress.org. **World Wide Web address:** http://www.augsburgfortress.org. **Description:** A publishing house for the Evangelical Lutheran Church in America. Augsburg Fortress operates retail stores nationwide and in Canada. **Positions advertised include:** Print Buyer; Development Editor; Customer Service Associate. **Corporate headquarters location:** This location. **Operations at this facility include:** Administration; Manufacturing; Research and Development; Sales; Service. **Number of employees at this location:** 320. **Number of employees nationwide:** 570.

AULT INC.
7105 Northland Terrace, Minneapolis MN 55428. 763/592-1900. **Fax:** 763/592-1911. **Contact:** Judy Sand, Benefits and Compensation Administrator. **E-mail address:** info@aultinc.com. **World Wide Web address:** http://www.aultinc.com. **Description:** A designer, manufacturer, and marketer of power conversion products for electronics OEM's. **NOTE:** Entry-level positions are offered. **Corporate headquarters location:** This location. **Listed on:** NASDAQ. **Stock exchange symbol:** AULT. **Annual sales/revenues:** $21 - $50 million. **Number of employees at this location:** 145.

AVEDA CORPORATION
4000 Pheasant Ridge Drive, Blaine MN 55449. 763/783-4000. **Fax:** 763/783-6850. **Contact:** Human Resources. **E-mail address:** jobs@aveda.com. **World Wide Web address:** http://www.aveda.com. **Description:** Manufactures perfume, makeup, and other beauty products. Aveda Corporation also operates salons and retail stores. **NOTE:** Search and apply for positions online. **Positions advertised include:** Analytical Phytochemist; Chemist; Marketing Director; Material Handler; Packager. **Special programs:** Internships. **Internship information:** Candidates should check the company's Website for application procedures. **Corporate headquarters location:** This location. **Other U.S. locations:** New York NY. **International locations:** Worldwide. **Parent company:** Estee Lauder Companies, Inc.

BFI WASTE SYSTEMS, INC.
9813 Flying Cloud Drive, Eden Prairie MN 55347. 952/941-5174. **Contact:** Human Resources. **Description:** Engaged primarily in the collection and disposal of solid waste for commercial, industrial, and residential customers. Services provided by BFI include landfill services, waste-to-energy programs, hazardous waste removal, and liquid waste removal. The company has operations at more than 500 facilities worldwide. **Parent company:** Allied Waste Industries. **Listed on:** New York Stock Exchange. **Stock exchange symbol:** AW.

BLM TECHNOLOGIES INC.
14755 27th Avenue North, Minneapolis MN 55447. 763/559-5100. **Fax:** 763/551-4319. **Contact:** Katy Bentrott, Operations Manager. **World Wide Web address:** http://www.blmtechnology.com. **Description:** Provides information technology products and services to corporate and government entities. **NOTE:** Entry-level positions are offered.

BMC INDUSTRIES INC.
7000 Sunwood Drive, Ramsey MN 55303. 763/576-3930. **Fax:** 763/576-5127. **Contact:** Human Resources. **World Wide Web address:** http://www.bmcind.com. **Description:** Designs, manufactures and distributes eyewear lenses. **Listed on:** New York Stock Exchange. **Stock exchange symbol:** BMM.

BACHMAN'S INC.
6010 Lyndale Avenue South, Minneapolis MN 55419. 612/861-7600. **Fax:** 612/861-7748. **Recorded jobline:** 612/861-9242. **Contact:** Personnel. **E-mail address:**

jobs@bachmans.com. **World Wide Web address:** http://www.bachmans.com. **Description:** A retail florist, landscaper, garden center, nursery, and greenhouse with 20 retail locations. **Positions advertised include:** Boiler Operator. **Special programs:** Internships. **Corporate headquarters location:** This location. **Number of employees at this location:** 1,000.

BAILEY NURSERIES, INC.
1325 Bailey Road, St. Paul MN 55119. 651/459-9744. **Fax:** 651/459-5100. **Contact:** Joe Bailey, Personnel Manager. **World Wide Web address:** http://www.baileynursery.com. **Description:** A large wholesale grower of nursery products including evergreens, trees, shrubs, bedding plants, annuals, and perennials. **Corporate headquarters location:** This location. **Listed on:** Privately held. **Number of employees at this location:** 210. **Number of employees nationwide:** 400.

BANKERS SYSTEMS, INC.
6815 Saukview Drive, P.O. Box 1457, St. Cloud MN 56302-1457. 320/251-3060. **Toll-free phone:** 800/397-2341. **Contact:** Human Resources. **E-mail address:** hr@bankerssystems.com. **World Wide Web address:** http://www.bankerssystems.com. **Description:** Develops marketing, operations, regulatory compliance, and training software for the financial services industry. **Positions advertised include:** Pricing Specialist. **Parent company:** WoltersKluwer.

BANNER ENGINEERING CORPORATION
9714 10th Avenue North, Minneapolis MN 55441. 763/544-3164. **Toll-free phone:** 800/809-7043. **Fax:** 763/544-3213. **Contact:** Human Resources. **World Wide Web address:** http://www.bannerengineering.com. **Description:** Designs and manufactures photoelectric control systems. Founded in 1966. **Corporate headquarters location:** This location. **Listed on:** Privately held. **Number of employees at this location:** 200. **Number of employees nationwide:** 550. **Number of employees worldwide:** 600.

BANTA BOOK GROUP
7000 Washington Avenue South, Eden Prairie MN 55344. 952/826-3500. **Contact:** Human Resources. **E-mail address:** apply@banta.com. **World Wide Web address:** http://www.banta.com. **Description:** Prints books and manuals, and handles fulfillment orders. **Parent company:** Banta Corporation (Menasha WI) is a technology and market leader in printing and digital imaging. The corporation serves publishers of educational and general interest books, special interest magazines, consumer and business catalogs, and direct marketing materials. In addition to printing and digital imaging, Banta offers multimedia and software packages, interactive media, point-of-purchase materials, and single-use products. Banta operates through the following groups: Banta Book Group; Banta Catalog Group; Banta Digital Group; Banta Direct Marketing Group; Banta Information Services Group; Banta Publications Group; Signs, Displays, Labels & Stamps; and Single-Use Products. **Listed on:** New York Stock Exchange. **Stock exchange symbol:** BN.

BANTA CATALOG MINNEAPOLIS
7401 Kilmer Lane, Maple Grove MN 55369-5699. 763/315-8100. **Contact:** Human Resources. **E-mail address:** apply@banta.com. **World Wide Web address:** http://www.banta.com. **Description:** The company is part of the Banta Catalog Group, whose products and services include consumer catalogs, primarily full-color specialty catalogs; advertising inserts; electronic prepress services; selective binding; inkjet addressing and messaging; zip code sorting; mail list processing and maintenance services; computerized distribution services; and dealer and franchise personalization programs. **Parent company:** Banta Corporation (Menasha WI) is a technology and market leader in printing and digital imaging. The corporation serves publishers of educational and general interest books, special interest magazines, consumer and business catalogs, and direct marketing materials. In addition to printing and digital imaging, Banta offers multimedia and software packages, interactive media, point-of-purchase materials, and single-use products. Banta operates through the following groups: Banta Book Group; Banta Catalog Group; Banta Digital Group; Banta Direct Marketing Group; Banta Information Services Group; Banta Publications Group; Signs, Displays, Labels & Stamps; and Single-Use Products. **Operations at this facility include:** This location is a printer of catalogs and inserts. **Listed on:** New York Stock Exchange. **Stock exchange symbol:** BN.

BANTA DIGITAL
18790 West 78th Street, Chanhassen MN 55317. 952/937-5005. **Contact:** Human Resources. **E-mail address:** apply@banta.com. **World Wide Web address:** http://www.banta.com. **Description:** Provides data management for the creation of film and printing plates (electronic and conventional prepress services); preparation and storage of customers' digital electronic files containing text and images; high-speed transmission of digitized text and graphics; digital photography; electronic layout and design; one- and four-color digital printing; television identity campaigns; corporate image videos; and interactive and alternative media programming. **Parent company:** Banta Corporation (Menasha WI) is a technology and market leader in printing and digital imaging. The corporation serves publishers of educational and general interest books, special interest magazines, consumer and business catalogs, and direct marketing materials. In addition to printing and digital imaging, Banta offers multimedia and software packages, interactive media, point-of-purchase materials, and single-use products. Banta operates through the following groups: Banta Book Group; Banta Catalog Group; Banta Digital Group; Banta Direct Marketing Group; Banta Information Services Group; Banta Publications Group; Signs, Displays, Labels & Stamps; and Single-Use Products. **Listed on:** New York Stock Exchange. **Stock exchange symbol:** BN.

BANTA DIRECT MARKETING
18780 West 78th Street, Chanhassen MN 55317. 952/937-9764. **Contact:** Human Resources. **E-mail address:** apply@banta.com. **World Wide Web address:** http://www.banta.com. **Description:** This location provides direct marketing services. Overall, the company is part of the Banta Direct Marketing Group, whose products include direct mail products such as brochures, publication and package inserts, coupons, reply cards, return envelopes, and specialty booklets. The group serves national advertisers, direct marketers, publishers, and ad agencies. **Parent company:** Banta Corporation (Menasha WI) is a technology and market leader in printing and digital imaging. The corporation serves publishers of educational and general interest books, special interest magazines, consumer and business catalogs, and direct marketing materials. In addition to printing and digital imaging, Banta offers multimedia and software packages, interactive media, point-of-purchase materials, and single-use products. Banta operates through the following groups: Banta Book Group; Banta Catalog Group; Banta Digital Group; Banta Direct Marketing Group; Banta Information Services Group; Banta Publications Group; Signs, Displays, Labels & Stamps; and Single-Use Products. **Listed on:** New York Stock Exchange. **Stock exchange symbol:** BN.

BANTA PUBLICATIONS
100 Banta Road, Long Prairie MN 56347. 320/732-2121. **Contact:** Duane Byers, Human Resources. **E-mail address:** apply@banta.com. **World Wide Web address:** http://www.banta.com. **Description:** Prints a variety of special interest magazines. **Parent company:** Banta Corporation (Menasha WI) is a technology and market leader in printing and digital imaging. The corporation serves publishers of educational and general interest books, special interest magazines, consumer and business catalogs, and direct marketing materials. In addition to printing and digital imaging, Banta offers multimedia and software packages, interactive media, point-of-purchase materials, and single-use products. Banta operates through the additional following groups: Banta Book Group; Banta Catalog Group; Banta Digital Group; Banta Direct Marketing Group; Banta Information Services Group; Signs, Displays, Labels & Stamps; and Single-Use Products. **Listed on:** New York Stock Exchange. **Stock exchange symbol:** BN.

BARNA, GUZY & STEFFEN LTD.
400 Northtown Financial Center, 200 Coon Rapids Boulevard, Minneapolis MN 55433-5894. 763/780-8500. **Toll-free phone:** 800/422-3486. **Fax:** 763/780-1777. **Contact:** Heidi Burmif, Director of Human Resources. **World Wide Web address:** http://www.bgslaw.com. **Description:** A law firm covering a variety of areas.

BASSFORD, LOCKHART, TRUESDELL & BRIGGS
33 South Sixth Street, Suite 3800, Minneapolis MN 55402-3707. 612/333-3000. **Fax:** 612/333-8829. **Contact:** Administrator. **E-mail address:** info@bassford.com. **World Wide Web address:** http://www.bassford.com. **Description:** A law firm specializing in litigation. Founded in 1882. **Positions advertised include:** Legal Assistant. **Office hours:** Monday - Friday, 8:00 a.m. - 5:00 p.m. **Number of employees at this location:** 70.

BECKMAN COULTER, INC.
1000 Lake Hazeltine Drive, Chaska MN 55318-1084. 612/448-4848. **Fax:** 612/368-1140. **Contact:** Personnel Manager. **E-mail address:** chaskahr@beckman.com. **World Wide Web address:** http://www.beckman.com. **Description:** Sells and services a diverse range of scientific instruments, reagents, and related equipment. Products include DNA synthesizers, robotics workstations, centrifuges, electrophoresis systems, detection and measurement equipment, data processing software, and specialty chemical and automated general chemical systems. Many of the company's products are used in research and development and diagnostic analysis. **NOTE:** Search and apply for positions online. **Positions advertised include:** Sr. Quality Assurance Scientist; Production Scientist; Sr. Software Development Engineer; Technical Support Engineer. **Operations at this facility include:** Administration; Manufacturing; Research and Development; Sales; Service. **Listed on:** New York Stock Exchange. **Stock exchange symbol:** BEC. **Number of employees worldwide:** 10,000.

BELL INDUSTRIES
580 Yankee Doodle Road, Suite 1200, Eagan MN 55121. 651/450-9020. **Fax:** 651/450-0844. **Contact:** Human Resources. **E-mail address:** dmccord@bellind.com. **World Wide Web address:** http://www.bellrpg.com. **Description:** A wholesaler of parts and equipment for recreational vehicles, ATVs, boats, and mobile homes. **Other U.S. locations:** Germantown WI; Grand Rapids MI. **Parent company:** Bell Industries.

BEMIS COMPANY INC.
222 South Ninth Street, Suite 2300, Minneapolis MN 55402. 612/376-3000. **Contact:** Mr. Gene Seashore, Vice President of Human Resources. **World Wide Web address:** http://www.bemis.com. **Description:** Bemis is a diversified producer of consumer and industrial packaging materials, film products, and business products. Packaging products include tapes and paper bags for pharmaceuticals, candy, toilet paper, and detergents. The company also produces sheetprint stock, roll labels, laminates, and adhesive products. **Corporate headquarters location:** This location. **Operations at this facility include:** Administration. **Listed on:** New York Stock Exchange. **Stock exchange symbol:** BMS.

BERKLEY RISK ADMINISTRATORS COMPANY
222 South Ninth Street, Suite 2300, Minneapolis MN 55402-3332. 612/376-3000. **Toll-free phone:** 800/618-0484. **Fax:** 612/766-3099. **Contact:** Human Resources Manager. **World Wide Web address:** http://www.berkleyrisk.com. **Description:** Provides third-party administration for workers' compensation policies. **Positions advertised include:** Financial Analyst; Internal Auditor. **Parent company:** W.R. Berkley Corporation.

BERMO INC.
4501 Ball Road NE, Circle Pines MN 55014. 763/786-7676. **Fax:** 763/785-2159. **Contact:** Human Resources. **World Wide Web address:** http://www.bermo.com. **Description:** A manufacturer of sheet metals, metal stampings, and injection-molded parts.

BERNAFON-MAICO INC.
9675 West 76th Street, Eden Prairie MN 55344. 952/941-4200. **Toll-free phone:** 888/941-4200. **Fax:** 952/903-4200. **Contact:** Human Resources. **World Wide Web address:** http://www.bernafon.com. **Description:** Produces and sells hearing aides and audiometer equipment. The company also provides support services and resources for the hearing impaired. Founded in 1936. **Office hours:** Monday - Friday, 8:00 a.m. - 5:00 p.m. **Corporate headquarters location:** This location. **Parent company:** Bernafon AG (Switzerland). **Operations at this facility include:** Administration; Manufacturing; Research and Development; Sales; Service. **Annual sales/revenues:** $5 - $10 million.

BEST BUY COMPANY, INC.
7601 Penn Avenue South, Richfield MN 55423. 612/291-1000. **Recorded jobline:** 952/947-2555. **Contact:** Human Resources. **World Wide Web address:** http://www.bestbuy.com. **Description:** A national retailer of consumer electronics, appliances, and home office products. **NOTE:** Search and apply for positions online. **Corporate headquarters location:** This location. **Other U.S. locations:** Nationwide. **Operations at this facility include:** Administration. **Listed on:** New York Stock Exchange. **Stock exchange symbol:** BBY. **Annual sales/revenues:** More than $100 million. **Number of employees at this location:** 1,500. **Number of employees nationwide:** 100,000.

BIOSCRIP
10900 Red Circle Drive, Minnetonka MN 55343. 800/444-5951. **Fax:** 952/979-3713. **Contact:** Human Resources. **E-mail address:** hr@bioscrip.com. **World Wide Web address:** http://www.bioscrip.com. **Description:** Provides specialty pharmacy services, including clinical management and specialty medication distribution, as well as infusion medications for patients with complex health conditions. BioScrip serves patients with a broad range of complex health conditions, including HIV/AIDS, Transplantation, Oncology, Hepatitis C, Arthritis, Multiple Sclerosis and more. **NOTE:** Search and apply for positions online. **Positions advertised include:** A/R Specialist; Accountant-Retail Revenue & A/R; Director, Customer Service; Traditional Customer Service Representative; Pharmacist (Traditional). **Corporate headquarters location:** Elmsford NY. **Other U.S. locations:** Nationwide. **Listed on:** National Association of Securities Dealers Automated Quotation (NASDAQ). **Stock exchange symbol:** BIOS.

BLACKBOURN MEDIA PACKAGING
200 Fourth Avenue North, Edgerton MN 56128. **Toll-free phone:** 800/842-7550. **Fax:** 507/442-4313. **Contact:** Human Resources. **World Wide Web address:** http://www.blackbourn.com. **Description:** Manufactures vinyl packaging systems. **Corporate headquarters location:** This location. **Operations at this facility include:** Administration; Manufacturing; Sales. **Parent company:** Fey Industries, Inc.

BORN
301 Carlson Parkway, Minnetonka MN 55305. 952/258-6000. **Toll-free phone:** 877/446-2676. **Fax:** 952/258-6001. **Contact:** Human Resources. **World Wide Web address:** http://www.born.com. **Description:** A national IT consulting firm offering a broad portfolio of technology and business solutions. **NOTE:** Search and apply for positions online. **Positions advertised include:** PeopleSoft Enterprise Asset Management; BizTalk Consultant; Business Intelligence Developer; Microsoft Solutions Practice Leader; Business Intelligence Technical Architect.

BOSTON SCIENTIFIC SCIMED, INC.
One Scimed Place, Maple Grove MN 55311-1506. 763/494-1700. **Contact:** Human Resources. **World Wide Web address:** http://www.bostonscientific.com. **Description:** A medical equipment manufacturer primarily engaged in the production of catheters. **NOTE:** Search and apply for positions online. **Positions advertised include:** Sr. Process Engineer; Patent Attorney; Manufacturing Engineer; Global Director, Design Assurance; Vice President Cardiology; Principal Pharmaceutical Scientist. **Corporate headquarters location:** Natick MA. **Listed on:** New York Stock Exchange. **Stock exchange symbol:** BSX. **Number of employees worldwide:** 15,000.

BOWNE BUSINESS SOLUTIONS
333 South 7th Street, Suite 2110, Minneapolis MN 55402. 612/375-8884. **Contact:** Human Resources. **World Wide Web address:** http://www.bowne.com. **Description:** A leader in the outsourcing industry for financial institutions and law firms. **Positions advertised include:** Project Coordinator.

BOZELL KAMSTRA
100 North Sixth Street, Suite 800-A, Minneapolis MN 55403. 612/371-7500. **Contact:** President. **World Wide Web address:** http://www.bozell.com. **Description:** An advertising agency.

BREMER FINANCIAL SERVICES INC.
445 Minnesota Street, Suite 2000, St. Paul MN 55101. 651/227-7621. **Contact:** Human Resources. **E-mail address:** hrtwincities@bremer.com. **World Wide Web address:** http://www.bremer.com. **Description:** A financial services company offering banking, investment, trust and insurance solutions in more than 100 locations in Minnesota, North Dakota, and Wisconsin. **NOTE:** Search for positions and download application online. **Positions advertised include:** Trust Analyst. **Number of employees nationwide:** 1,700.

BRIGGS & MORGAN PROFESSIONAL ASSOCIATION
2200 First National Bank Building, 332 Minnesota Street, St. Paul MN 55101. 651/808-6600. **Fax:** 651/808-6450. **Contact:** Human Resources. **World Wide Web address:** http://www.briggs.com. **Description:** A business law and trial law firm. Founded in 1882. **Corporate headquarters location:** This location. **Other U.S. locations:** Minneapolis MN. **Listed on:** Privately held. **Number of employees at this location:** 165. **Number of employees nationwide:** 330. **Positions advertised include:** Employee Benefits Attorney; Franchise Attorney; Litigation Associate Attorney.

BROADVIEW MEDIA
4455 West 77th Street, Minneapolis MN 55435. 952/835-4455. **Fax:** 952/835-0971. **Contact:** Red White, Operations Director. **World Wide Web address:** http://www.broadviewmedia.com. **Description:** A full-service production company in film, video, audio, and interactive media. **Other U.S. locations:** Chicago IL.

BROOKDALE PLASTICS INC.
9909 South Shore Drive, Plymouth MN 55441. 612/797-1000. **Toll-free phone:** 800/383-7092. **Fax:** 763/797-5252. **Contact:** Jane Schneider, Human Resources. **E-mail address:** jschneider@brookdaleplastics.com. **World Wide Web address:** http://www.brookdaleplastics.com. **Description:** Manufactures plastic packing and display products for the medical, retail, and industrial markets. Founded in 1963. **NOTE:** Entry-level positions are offered **Positions advertised include:** Thermoforming Machine Set-up Specialist. **Corporate headquarters location:** This location. **Parent company:** Ameristar Packaging. **Listed on:** Privately held. **Annual sales/revenues:** $5 - $10 million. **Number of employees at this location:** 60.

BROWN AND BIGELOW INC.
345 Plato Boulevard East, St. Paul MN 55107. 651/293-7000. **Contact:** Personnel. **World Wide Web address:** http://www.brownandbigelow.com. **Description:** Manufactures promotional products including calendars, greetings, foil certificates, leather books, and playing cards. **Number of employees at this location:** 400.

BRUTGER EQUITIES, INC.
P.O. Box 399, St. Cloud MN 56302-0399. 320/529-2837. **Contact:** Thomas Etienne, Vice President of Human Resources. **Description:** Engaged in real estate development and management of properties including hotels. **Special programs:** Internships. **Corporate headquarters location:** This location. **Other U.S. locations:** AZ; CO; ID; MT; ND; SD; WY. **Listed on:** Privately held. **Number of employees at this location:** 25. **Number of employees nationwide:** 325.

BUCA INC.
1300 Nicollet Mall, Suite 5003, Minneapolis MN 55403. 612/288-2382. **Fax:** 612/225-3340. **Contact:** Human Resources. **World Wide Web address:** http://www.bucainc.com. Description: Operates Buca de Beppo and Vinny T's of Boston restaurants. **Positions advertised include:** Accounts Payable Specialist; Accounting Manager. **Number of employees nationwide:** 6,000.

BUFFETS, INC.
dba OLD COUNTRY BUFFET
1460 Buffet Way, Eagan MN 55121. 651/994-8608. **Fax:** 651/365-2356. **Recorded jobline:** 800/388-6506. **Contact:** Human Resources. **World Wide Web address:** http://www.buffet.com. **Description:** Operates a chain of 399 restaurants in 36 states. **NOTE:** Search and apply for positions online. **Positions advertised include:** Project Planning Manager; Manager of Application Development; Employee Relations Representative; Market Research Specialist. **Corporate headquarters location:** This location. **Other U.S. locations:** Nationwide. **Number of employees at this location:** 150. **Number of employees nationwide:** 27,000.

BUHLER INC.
1100 Xenium Lane, Minneapolis MN 55441. 763/847-9900. **Contact:** Human Resources. **World Wide Web address:** http://www.buhler.com. **Description:** Designers and manufacturers of grain milling machinery and other agricultural equipment.

BULLETIN NEWSPAPERS
7584 80th Street South, Cottage Grove MN 55016. 651/459-3434. **Fax:** 651/459-9491. **Contact:** Jeff Patterson, General Manager. **World Wide Web address:** http://www.swcbulletin.com. **Description:** Publishes a weekly newspaper, the *South Washington County Bulletin*. **Special programs:** Internships. **Parent company:** RiverTown Newspaper Group. **Operations at this facility include:** Administration; Sales. **Listed on:** Privately held. **Number of employees at this location:** 20.

THE BUREAU
3400 Technology Drive, Minneapolis MN 55418. 612/788-1000. **Contact:** Gary Minlschmidt, Director of Human Resources. **World Wide Web address:** http://www.thebureau.com. **Description:** A diversified printer and engraver. **Number of employees nationwide:** 1,000.

BURLINGTON NORTHERN AND SANTA FE RAILWAY
176 East Fifth Street, 1st Floor, St. Paul MN 55101. 651/298-2121. **Contact:** James Dailey, Placement Center. **World Wide Web address:** http://www.bnsf.com. **Description:** Operates a railroad system that transports coal, agricultural commodities, and industrial products. **NOTE:** Search and apply for positions or submit resume online. **Special programs:** Internships. **Corporate headquarters location:** Fort Worth TX. **Operations at this facility include:** Administration. **Listed on:** New York Stock Exchange. **Stock exchange symbol:** BNI.

BURNSVILLE, CITY OF
100 Civic Center Parkway, Burnsville MN 55337. 952/895-4470. **Recorded jobline:** 952/895-4475. **Contact:** Human Resources. **World Wide Web address:** http://www.burnsville.org. **Description:** Administrative offices of the city of Burnsville. **Special programs:** Internships. **Operations at this facility include:** Administration; Service. **Number of employees at this location:** 250.

CAMPBELL MITHUN
222 South Ninth Street, Minneapolis MN 55402. 612/347-1326. **Contact:** K.C. Foley, Human Resources Director. **E-mail address:** careers@campbellmithun.com. **World Wide Web address:** http://www.campbellmithun.com. **Description:** An advertising agency.

CANNON EQUIPMENT
15100 Business Parkway, Rosemont MN 55068. 651/322-6300. **Toll-free phone:** 800/533-2071. **Contact:** Human Resources Manager. **World Wide Web address:** http://www.cannonequipment.com. **Description:** A manufacturer, merchandiser, and distributor of metal products ranging from steel curtain rods to wire racks.

CARDINAL GLASS INDUSTRIES
7201 West Lake Street, Minneapolis MN 55426. 952/929-3134. **Contact:** Human Resources. **World Wide Web address:** http://www.cardinalcorp.com. **Description:** Manufactures insulated glass for window units. **Corporate headquarters location:** Eden Prairie MN.

CARDINAL GLASS INDUSTRIES
775 Prairie Center Drive, Eden Prairies MN 55344. 952/935-1722. **Fax:** 952/935-5538. **Contact:** Human Resources Manager. **World Wide Web address:** http://www.cardinalcorp.com. **Description:** Manufactures insulated glass for window units. **Corporate headquarters location:** This location.

CARGILL INC.
P.O. Box 9300, Minneapolis MN 55440-9300. 952/742-7575. **Contact:** Selection Department, #10. **E-mail address:** employment@cargill.com. **World Wide Web address:** http://www.cargill.com. **Description:** Cargill, with its subsidiaries and its affiliates, is involved in nearly 50 individual lines of business. The company deals in commodity trading, handling, transporting, processing, and risk management. Cargill is a major trader of grains and oilseeds, as well as a marketer of other agricultural and nonagricultural commodities. As a transporter, the company moves bulk commodities using a network of rail and road systems, inland waterways, and ocean-going routes combining its own fleet and transportation services purchased from outside sources. Agricultural products include a wide variety of feed, seed, fertilizers, and other goods and services for producers worldwide. Cargill is also a leader in producing and marketing seed varieties and hybrids. Cargill Central Research (also at this location) aims to develop new agricultural products to address the needs of customers around the world. Cargill's Financial Markets Division supports Cargill and its subsidiaries through financial instrument trading, emerging markets instrument trading, value investing, and money management. Cargill's worldwide food processing businesses supply products ranging from basic ingredients used in food production to name brands. The company also operates a number of industrial businesses including the production of steel, industrial-grade starches, ethanol, and salt products. **NOTE:** Entry-level positions and second and third shifts are offered. **Positions advertised include:** Administrative Assistant; Logistics Specialist; Tax Consultant; Human Resources Generalist; Payroll Specialist; Marketing Analyst; Chemical Engineer. **Special programs:** Internships; Training; Co-ops; Summer Jobs. **Corporate headquarters location:** This location. **International locations:** Worldwide. **Listed on:** Privately held. **Annual sales/revenues:** More than $100 million. **Number of employees worldwide:** 80,000.

CARLETON COLLEGE
One North College Street, Northfield MN 55057. 507/646-5424. **Contact:** Human Resources. **World Wide Web address:** http://www.carleton.edu. **Description:** A private, four-year, liberal arts college.

CARLSON COMPANIES, INC.
CARLSON MARKETING GROUP
P.O. Box 59159, Mail Stop 8246, Minneapolis MN 55459. 763/212-5000. **Contact:** Human Resources. **World Wide Web address:** http://www.carlson.com. **Description:** A highly diversified corporation doing business through a variety of subsidiaries. Business areas include hotels, restaurant operations, and retail and wholesale travel. Carlson Marketing Group (also at this location) provides a variety of marketing services for sporting events and airlines; incentive programs for employees of other companies; and strategic consulting services to help client companies create customer/brand loyalty. **Corporate headquarters location:** This location. **Number of employees nationwide:** 50,000.

CARMICHAEL LYNCH
800 Hennepin Avenue, Minneapolis MN 55403. 612/334-6000. **Fax:** 612/334-6171. **Contact:** Julie Sprint, Director of Human Resources. **World Wide Web address:** http://www.carmichaellynch.com. **Description:** A full-service advertising agency. Carmichael-Lynch Advertising offers a variety of services including direct marketing,

public relations, new media design, and market research. Founded in 1962. **NOTE:** Entry-level positions are offered. **Special programs:** Internships; Training. **Corporate headquarters location:** This location. **Listed on:** Privately held. **Annual sales/revenues:** More than $100 million. **Number of employees at this location:** 200.

CARTER-DAY INDUSTRIES
500 73rd Avenue NE, Minneapolis MN 55432. 763/571-1000. **Fax:** 763/571-3012. **Contact:** Tim Ryan, Human Resources. **World Wide Web address:** http://www.carterday.com. **Description:** Engineers, designs, and manufactures seed grains and plastic pellets for the agricultural processing and petrochemical industries.

CARVER, COUNTY OF
Carver County Government Center, Administration Building, 600 East Fourth Street, Chaska MN 55318. 952/361-1525. **Fax:** 952/361-1536. **Recorded jobline:** 952/361-1522. **Contact:** Personnel. **World Wide Web address:** http://www.co.carver.mn.us. **Description:** The administrative offices of Carver County. **Special programs:** Internships. **Office hours:** Monday - Friday, 8:00 a.m. - 4:30 p.m. **Corporate headquarters location:** This location.

CATERPILLAR PAVING PRODUCTS
9401 85th Avenue North, Brooklyn Park MN 55445. 763/425-4100. **Contact:** Bill Jetson, Manager of Personnel. **World Wide Web address:** http://www.cat.com. **Description:** Caterpillar is one of the world's largest manufacturers of construction and mining equipment, natural gas engines, and industrial gas turbines; and a leading global supplier of diesel engines. Products include track-type tractors, hydraulic excavators, backhoe loaders, motor graders, and off-highway trucks. Products are used in the construction, road building, mining, forestry, energy, transportation, and material-handling industries. Caterpillar products and components are manufactured in 38 plants in the United States and 33 plants worldwide. **Corporate headquarters location:** Peoria IL. **Operations at this facility include:** This location manufactures road construction equipment.

CELESTICA
4300 Round Lake Road, Arden Hills MN 55112. 651/604-2400. **Contact:** Sue Bergman, Human Resources. **World Wide Web address:** http://www.manserv.com. **Description:** A manufacturer of circuit boards and other electronic products.

CENEX HARVEST STATES COOPERATIVES
P.O. Box 64089, St. Paul MN 55164-0089. 651/451-5151. **Physical address:** 5600 Cenex Drive, Inver Grove Heights MN 55077. **Toll-free phone:** 800/232-3639. **Recorded jobline:** 800/325-6826. **Contact:** Human Resources Generalist. **World Wide Web address:** http://www.chsinc.com. **Description:** A grain marketing company. **Special programs:** Internships. **Corporate headquarters location:** This location. **Operations at this facility include:** Administration. **Number of employees at this location:** 400. **Number of employees nationwide:** 2,800.

CENTER FOR DIAGNOSTIC IMAGING
5775 Wayzata Blvd, Suite 400, St. Louis Park MN 55416. 952/543-6500. **Toll-free phone:** 877-566-6500. **Fax:** 952/513-6879. **E-mail address:** jobs@cdirad.com. **World Wide Web address:** http://www.cdirad.com. **Description:** A physician-led national radiology practice with 26 centers in six states. **Positions advertised include:** Staff Accountant; Accounts Payable Associate; Scheduling Specialist.

CENTERPOINT ENERGY MINNEGASCO
800 LaSalle Avenue, P.O. Box 59038, Minneapolis MN 55459-0038. 612/372-4664. **Contact:** Human Resources. **World Wide Web address:** http://www.minnegasco.com. **Description:** Serves customers in Minnesota with natural gas and home products and services **NOTE:** Search and apply for positions or submit resume online. Advance C&M Mechanic Operator; Inventory Control Supervisor; Lead GIS Specialist. **Parent company:** CenterPoint Energy.

CENTURY COLLEGE
3300 Century Avenue, White Bear Lake MN 55110. 651/779-5804. **Toll-free phone:** 800/228-1978. **Fax:** 651/779-5757. **Contact:** Betty Mayer, Human Resources Director. **World Wide Web address:** http://www.century.cc.mn.us. **Description:** A community college offering associate's degrees, as well as diplomas and certificates. **Positions advertised include:** Mathematics Instructor.

CERIDIAN CORPORATION
3311 East Old Shakopee Road, Minneapolis MN 55425. 952/853-8100. **World Wide Web address:** http://www.ceridian.com. **Contact:** Human Resources. **Description:** Provides information services for human resources, transportation, and retailing. **NOTE:** Search and apply for positions online. **Positions advertised include:** Account Services Representative; Channel Development Manager; Financial Analyst; Network Analyst; Sales Contract Analyst; Tax Specialist. **Listed on:** New York Stock Exchange. **Stock exchange symbol:** CEN.

CERTAINTEED CORPORATION
3303 Fourth Avenue East, Shakopee MN 55379. 612/445-6450. **Contact:** Human Resources. **World Wide Web address:** http://www.certainteed.com. **Description:** Certainteed Corporation manufactures and distributes building materials, fiberglass products, and piping products. Principal products are used in residential, commercial, and industrial construction; repair and remodeling; fiberglass reinforcement applications; water and sewer systems; and other underground utility systems. Other products include roofing, acoustical insulation, fiberglass thermal insulation, air handling products, glass fiber, vinyl siding, and PVC piping. **Corporate headquarters location:** Valley Forge PA. **Operations at this facility include:** This location manufactures shingles.

CHILDREN'S HOSPITALS & CLINICS - MINNEAPOLIS
Mailstop 32-H190, 2525 Chicago Avenue South, Minneapolis MN 55404. 612/813-6111. **Contact:** Human Resources. **E-mail address:** hrrecruiting@childrenshc.org. **World Wide Web address:** http://www.childrenshc.org. **Description:** A children's hospital and medical center with 147 beds.

CHILDREN'S HOSPITALS & CLINICS - ST. PAUL
Mailstop 32-H190, 2525 Chicago Avenue South, Minneapolis MN 55404. 651/220-6000. **Physical address:** 345 North Smith Avenue, St. Paul MN 55102. **Contact:** Human Resources. **E-mail address:** hrrecruiting@childrenshc.org. **World Wide Web address:** http://www.childrenshc.org. **Description:** A 105-bed pediatric hospital. Founded in 1920.

THE CHILDREN'S THEATRE COMPANY
2400 Third Avenue South, Minneapolis MN 55404. 612/874-0500. **Fax:** 612/874-8119. **Contact:** Human Resources Representative. **World Wide Web address:** http://www.childrenstheatre.org. **Description:** Offers professional theater performances and evening and weekend acting classes. **Positions advertised include:** Janitor; Ticket Reservationist; Usher.

CHIQUITA PROCESSED FOODS
900 North Cedar Avenue, Owatonna MN 55060. 507/446-7700. **Contact:** Human Resources. **World Wide Web address:** http://www.chiquita.com. **Description:** Chiquita Processed Foods is one of the largest private-label canneries in the western United States. The comprehensive product line includes corn, asparagus, peas, diced peas and carrots, green beans, spinach, dry-soaked beans, and meat products.

CIBER, INC.
2222 18th Avenue NW, Suite 100, Rochester MN 55901. 507/280-9267. **Toll-free phone:** 888/232-4237. **Fax:** 507/280-0833. **Contact:** Recruiter. **World Wide Web address:** http://www.ciber.com. **Description:** Provides consulting for client/server development, mainframe and legacy systems, industry-specific analysis, application-specific analysis, and network development. **Corporate headquarters location:** Greenwood Village CO.

CIM SOFTWARE CORPORATION
5735 Lindsay Street, Minneapolis MN 55422. 763/544-1752. **Fax:** 763/544-5768. **Contact:** Human Resources. **E-mail address:** employment@cimsoftware.com. **World Wide Web address:** http://www.cimsoftware.com. **Description:** Develops networking software for systems integration.

CIMA LABS INC.
10000 Valley View Road, Eden Prairie MN 55344. 952/947-8725. **Fax:** 952/947-8770. **Contact:** Human Resources. **E-mail address:** hr@cimalabs.com. **World Wide Web address:** http://www.cimalabs.com. **Description:** Develops, formulates, and manufactures a pharmaceutical drug delivery system. CIMA LABS INC.'s main product is a fast-dissolving tablet for individuals who have difficulty swallowing pills. Founded in 1986. **NOTE:** Entry-level positions are offered. **Corporate headquarters location:** This location. **Listed on:** NASDAQ. **Stock exchange symbol:** CIMA. **President/CEO:** John Siebert, Ph.D. **Annual sales/revenues:** Less than $5 million. **Number of employees at this location:** 70.

CIPRICO, INC.
17400 Medina Road, Minneapolis MN 55447. 763/551-4797. **Fax:** 763/551-4002. **Contact:** Jeanne Vincill, Director of Human Resources. **World Wide Web address:** http://www.ciprico.com. **Description:** A designer and manufacturer of intelligent disk and tape controller boards. **Corporate headquarters location:** This location.

CIRRUS DESIGN
4515 Taylor Circle, Duluth MN 55811. 218/727-2737. **Fax:** 218/727-2148. **Contact:** Human Resources. **World Wide Web address:** http://www.cirrusdesign.com. **Description:** Manufactures aircraft.

CITY PAGES, INC.
401 North Third Street, Suite 550, Minneapolis MN 55401. 612/375-1015. **Fax:** 612/372-3737. **Contact:** Human Resources Manager. **World Wide Web address:** http://www.citypages.com. **Description:** Publishes a weekly alternative newspaper. **Special programs:** Internships. **Corporate headquarters location:** This location. **Operations at this facility include:** Administration; Sales; Service. **Listed on:** Privately held. **Publisher:** Mark Bartel. **Number of employees at this location:** 90.

CLORE AUTOMOTIVE
9231 Penn Avenue South, Minneapolis MN 55431. 952/884-3211. **Toll-free phone:** 800/328-2921. **Fax:** 952/886-6405. **Contact:** Human Resources Generalist. **Description:** Manufactures battery chargers and testers, portable power supplies, automotive refrigerant and coolant recyclers, arc and MIG welders, plasma cutters, and welding accessories. Brand names include Century, Solar, Booster Pac, Viper, and Cobra. Century Manufacturing serves the automotive aftermarket and retail channels for professional and do-it-yourself automotive and body repair. **NOTE:** Entry-level positions and second and third shifts are offered. **Special programs:** Internships; Co-ops; Summer Jobs. **Internship information:** Internships are offered in the areas of engineering and marketing. **Other U.S. locations:** Bloomington MN; Pierre SD. **International locations:** St. Jean-sur-Richelieu, Quebec, Canada. **Parent company:** Pentair, Inc. (St. Paul MN) is a diversified industrial manufacturer comprised of nine businesses that serve the construction, woodworking, electronics, water conditioning, automotive, and industrial markets. Primary products are electrical and electronic closures, professional tools and equipment, and water and fluid technologies. The company has 54 locations in North America, Europe, and Asia. **President:** Steve Bentson. **Annual sales/revenues:** $51 - $100 million. **Number of employees at this location:** 320. **Number of employees worldwide:** 445.

COLD SPRING GRANITE COMPANY
202 South Third Avenue, Cold Spring MN 56320. 320/685-3621. **Contact:** Chuck Goores, Human Resources Manager. **World Wide Web address:** http://www.coldspringgranite.com. **Description:** Mines, quarries, and sells granite.

COLDWELL BANKER BURNET
7550 France Avenue South, Suite 300, Edina MN 55435. 952/844-6400. **Fax:** 952/844-6407. **Contact:** Human Resources. **World Wide Web address:** http://www.coldwellbanker.com. **Description:** A real estate agency. Coldwell Banker also provides relocation services to businesses worldwide.

COLEMAN POWERMATE COMPRESSORS
118 West Rock Street, Springfield MN 56087. 507/723-6211. **Contact:** Human Resources. **World Wide Web address:** http://www.colemanpowermate.com. **Description:** A manufacturer of power compressors for use in various industries.

COLLE & McVOY MARKETING COMMUNICATIONS
8500 Normandale Lake Boulevard, Suite 2400, Bloomington MN 55437-3800. 952/852-7500. **Fax:** 952/852-8128. **Contact:** Phil Johnson, Recruiting Manager. **World Wide Web address:** http://www.collemcvoy.com. **Description:** An advertising agency. Founded in 1935. **Company slogan:** Connect/compel. **Office hours:** Monday - Friday, 8:00 a.m. - 5:00 p.m. **Subsidiaries include:** Sable Advertising Systems. **Parent company:** MDC Corporation. **Listed on:** Privately held. **CEO:** Jim Bergeson. **Facilities Manager:** Jim Heinz. **Information Systems Manager:** Britt Morries. **Annual sales/revenues:** $21 - $50 million. **Number of employees at this location:** 280.

COLLEGE OF SAINT BENEDICT
37 College Avenue South, St. Joseph MN 56374. 320/363-5500. **Contact:** Herb Trenz, Director of Human Resources. **World Wide Web address:** http://www. csbsju.edu. **Description:** A private, four-year, liberal arts college for women.

COLOR SPECIALTIES INC.
6405 Cedar Avenue South, Richfield MN 55423. 612/861-1555. **Contact:** Personnel Manager. **Description:** A manufacturer and distributor of chemicals, bonds, and dyes used in automobile refinishing. **Special programs:** Training.

COLWELL INDUSTRIES INC.
123 North Third Street, Suite 702, Minneapolis MN 55401. 612/340-0365. **Contact:** Human Resources. **World Wide Web address:** http://www.colwellind.com. **Description:** Colwell Industries is involved in the printing of brochures, albums, and color cards. **Corporate headquarters location:** This location. **Operations at this facility include:** This location houses administrative offices.

COMDISCO, INC.
5468 Feltl Road, Minnetonka MN 55343. 952/931-9966. **Contact:** Human Resources. **World Wide Web address:** http://www.comdisco.com. **Description:** Provides computer equipment leasing, remarketing, and refurbishing; business continuity; consulting; strategic and financial planning; asset management software tools; data center moving services; and consolidations. Comdisco has more than 100 locations worldwide, and serves customers in North and South America, Europe, the Pacific Rim, and Australia. **Corporate headquarters location:** Rosemont IL.

COMMUNITY HOSPITAL & HEALTH CARE CENTER
1900 North Sunrise Drive, St. Peter MN 56082. 507/931-2200. **Contact:** Human Resources. **E-mail address:** valk@mctcnet.net. **World Wide Web address:** http://www.stpeterhealth.org. **Description:** A medical center offering acute care and outpatient services as well as a wide variety of diagnostic testing. **Positions advertised include:** Registered Nurse; Volunteer EMT.

COMMUNITY MEMORIAL HOSPITAL
855 Mankato Avenue, Winona MN 55987-0600. 507/454-3650. **Contact:** Melissa Gerry, Human Resources Representative. **E-mail address:** jobs@winonahealth.org. **World Wide Web address:** http://www.winonahealthonline.org. **Description:** A hospital offering various social service programs in order to promote the welfare of the community. **Positions advertised include:** Executive Assistant; Health Unit Coordinator; Nursing Assistant; Charge Nurse; Licensed Practical Nurse.

COMPUTER ASSOCIATES INTERNATIONAL, INC.
7760 France Avenue, Suite 810, Bloomington MN 55435. 952/835-4200. **Contact:** Human Resources. **World Wide Web address:** http://www.cai.com. **Description:** One of the world's leading developers of client/server and distributed computing software. The company develops, markets, and supports enterprise management, database and applications development, business applications, and consumer software products for a broad range of mainframe, midrange, and desktop computers. Computer Associates serves major business, government, research, and educational organizations. **Corporate headquarters location:** Islandia NY. **Other U.S. locations:** Nationwide. **Listed on:** New York Stock Exchange. **Stock exchange symbol:** CA.

COMPUTER NETWORK TECHNOLOGY CORPORATION
6000 Nathan Lane North, Plymouth MN 55442. 763/541-9575. **Fax:** 763/541-1921. **Contact:** Human Resources. **World Wide Web address:** http://www.cnt.com. **Description:** Designs, manufactures, markets, and supports channel networking products that enable the high-speed transmission of information among local and geographically dispersed computing systems, primarily IBM and IBM-compatible, as well as related peripheral devices.

COMPUWARE CORPORATION
505 North Highway 169, Suite 750, Plymouth MN 55441. 763/541-9575. **Fax:** 763/541-1921. **Contact:** Human Resources. **World Wide Web address:** http://www.compuware.com. **Description:** Provides technology-based consulting solutions in the areas of software engineering, business applications development, and network architecture and security. **Positions advertised include:** Sales Representative; Product Account Manager.

CONAGRA FOODS
P.O. Box 508, St. James MN 56081. 507/375-3124. **Contact:** Human Resources. **World Wide Web address:** http://www.conagra.com. **Description:** This location is a meat packaging and processing plant.

CONAGRA SNACK FOODS
7450 Metro Boulevard, Edina MN 55439. 952/835-6900. **Contact:** Personnel. **World Wide Web address:** http://www.conagrafoods.com. **Description:** A producer of microwave foods including breakfast foods and popcorn. **Parent company:** ConAgra, Inc.

CONKLIN COMPANY
551 Valley Park Drive, P.O. Box 155, Shakopee MN 55379. 952/445-6010. **Contact:** Human Resources. **World Wide Web address:** http://www.conklin.com. **Description:** Manufactures lubricants, fertilizers, and cleaning products.

CONSECO FINANCIAL CORPORATION
600 Landmark Towers, 345 St. Peter Street, St. Paul MN 55102-1639. 651/293-3500. **Fax:** 651/293-3622. **Recorded jobline:** 651/293-5825. **Contact:** Human Resources. **World Wide Web address:** http://www.conseco.com. **Description:** Aggregates and secures conventional manufactured home, motorcycle, and home improvement contracts and sells securities through public offerings and private placements. Conseco's FHA-insured and VA-guaranteed manufactured home contracts are converted into GNMA certificates and are sold in the secondary market. The company also markets homeowners and life insurance. Founded in 1976. **Special programs:** Internships. **Corporate headquarters location:** This location. **Parent company:** Conseco, Inc. (Carmel IN) is a leading provider of insurance and financial products. **Number of employees at this location:** 1,200. **Number of employees nationwide:** 4,000.

CRAY INC.
1340 Mendota Heights Road, Mendota Heights MN 55120. 651/605-9000. **Fax:** 651/605-9001. **Contact:** Human Resources. **World Wide Web address:** http://www.cray.com. **Description:** Cray designs, develops, markets, and services high performance computer systems, commonly known as supercomputers. **Corporate headquarters location:** Seattle WA. **Other U.S. locations:** WI. **Number of employees nationwide:** 900.

CRENLO, INC.
1600 Fourth Avenue NW, Rochester MN 55901. 507/287-3610. **Contact:** Human Resources. **E-mail address:** hr@crenlo.com. **World Wide Web address:** http://www.crenlo.com. **Description:** A manufacturer of metal fabrications ranging from simple sheet metal panels to large, complex weldings. Crenlo is also a supplier of off-highway vehicle cabs, electronic cabinets, metal enclosures, and subcontract metal fabrications. Founded in 1951. **Special programs:** Internships. **Corporate headquarters location:** This location. **Number of employees at this location:** 875.

CRESTLINER INC.
609 13th Avenue NE, Little Falls MN 56345. 320/632-6686. **Contact:** Human Resources. **World Wide Web address:** http://www.crestliner.com. **Description:** Manufactures pleasure boats.

CRYSTAL CABINET WORKS, INC.
1100 Crystal Drive, Princeton MN 55371. 763/389-4187. **Contact:** Human Resources. **World Wide Web address:** http://www.ccworks.com. **Description:** Manufactures custom-made kitchen cabinets.

CRYSTEEL MANUFACTURING
P.O. Box 178, Lake Crystal MN 56055. 507/726-2728. **Contact:** Human Resources. **World Wide Web address:** http://www.crysteel.com. **Description:** Manufactures truck bodies and hoists.

CUMMINS NORTH CENTRAL
3030 Centre Pointe Drive, Suite 500, St. Paul MN 55113. 651/636-1000. **Contact:** Margene Duffy, Human Resources Representative. **World Wide Web address:** http://www.cummins.com. **Description:** A distributor of diesel engines.

CYBEROPTICS CORPORATION
5900 Golden Hills Drive, Minneapolis MN 55416. 763/542-5000. **Toll-free phone:** 800/746-6315. **Fax:** 763/542-5103. **Contact:** Human Resources. **E-mail address:** hr@cyberoptics.com. **World Wide Web address:** http://www.cyberoptics.com. **Description:** Designs, develops, and manufactures optical process control sensors and intelligent, laser-based sensor systems that are used for electronics inspections and related applications. **Positions advertised include:** Receptionist; Senior Accountant/Cost Analyst; Software Test Engineer; NPI Sourcing Specialist. **Corporate headquarters location:** This location.

CYTEC FIBERITE INC.
501 West Third Street, Winona MN 55987. 507/452-8038. **Fax:** 507/454-3611. **Contact:** Donald Schneider, Employee Resources Manager. **World Wide Web address:** http://www.cytec.com. **Description:** Manufactures advanced composite and adhesives for aerospace, industrial, recreational, and other applications. **NOTE:** Entry-level positions and second and third shifts are offered. **Positions advertised include:** Accountant; Cost Accountant; Library Supervisor; Legal Coordinator; Marketing Administrator. **Special programs:** Internships; Training. **Corporate headquarters location:** This location. **Other U.S. locations:** Tempe AZ; Orange CA; Delano PA; Greenville TX. **Parent company:** Cytec Industries. **Number of employees at this location:** 250.

DAIRY FARMERS OF AMERICA
1313 North Star Drive, Zumbrota MN 55992. 507/732-5124. **Contact:** Human Resources. **World Wide Web address:** http://www.dfamilk.com. **Description:** A producer of cheddar cheese. **Corporate headquarters location:** Kansas City KS. **Operations at this facility include:** Manufacturing.

JOHN A. DALSIN AND SON, INC.
2830 20th Avenue South, Minneapolis MN 55407. 612/729-9334. **Fax:** 612/729-9330. **Contact:** Don Wagner, Human Resources. **World Wide Web address:** http://www.dalsin.com. **Description:** A roofer and sheet metal contractor. Founded in 1912.

DART TRANSIT COMPANY
P.O. Box 64110, St. Paul MN 55164-0110. **Toll-free phone:** 800/366-9000. **Fax:** 651/683-1650. **Contact:** Katy Carter, Human Resources Representative. **E-mail address:** kcarter@dartadvantage.com. **World Wide Web address:** http://www.dartadvantage.com. **Description:** A trucking company with land-based transportation services throughout the United States, Canada, and Mexico. **NOTE:** Entry-level positions, part-time jobs, and second and third shifts are offered. **Positions advertised include:** Assistant Revenue Specialist; Accounting Coordinator; Compliance Technician; Regional Account Manager. **Special programs:** Internships; Summer Jobs. **Corporate headquarters location:** Eagan MN. **Other U.S. locations:** Sellersburg IN; Dallas TX. **Annual sales/revenues:** More than $100 million. **Number of employees at this location:** 225. **Number of employees nationwide:** 1,000.

DATA RECOGNITION CORPORATION
13490 Bass Lake Road, Maple Grove MN 55311. 763/268-2000. **Fax:** 763/268-3003. **Recorded jobline:** 763/268-3009. **Contact:** Human Resources. **E-mail address:** resumes@datarecognitioncorp. **World Wide Web address:** http://www.drc-mn.com. **Description:** Processes educational tests and surveys. **NOTE:** Entry-level positions and second and third shifts are offered. **Positions advertised include:** Associate Software Developer; Senior Software Developer; Quality Assurance Analyst; Test Development Specialist. **Special programs:** Internships. **Corporate headquarters location:** This location. **Listed on:** Privately held. **Number of employees at this location:** 150.

DATACARD CORPORATION
11111 Bren Road West, Minnetonka MN 55343. 952/988-2000. **Contact:** Human Resources. **E-mail address:** datacard_jobs@datacard.com. **World Wide Web address:** http://www.datacard.com. **Description:** A world leader in the development and manufacture of plastic card personalization equipment. Products meet industry needs for conducting transactions, exchanging information, and identification. Customers include financial institutions, health care providers, retailers, oil companies, government agencies, and other industries. **Special programs:** Internships. **Corporate headquarters location:** This location. **Other U.S. locations:** Nationwide. **Operations at this facility include:** Administration; Manufacturing; Research and Development; Sales; Service. **Listed on:** Privately held. **Number of employees at this location:** 750. **Number of employees nationwide:** 1,400.

DAYCO PRODUCTS
4079 Pepin Avenue, Red Wing MN 55066. 651/388-0771. **Contact:** Becky Turner, Director of Personnel. **E-mail address:** dayco_employment@markivauto.com. **World Wide Web address:** http://www.daycoproducts.com. **Description:** A manufacturer of rubber belts for the automotive and machinery industries.

DELTAK
2905 Northwest Boulevard, Suite 150, Minneapolis MN 55441. 763/557-7440. **Fax:** 763/557-4700. **Contact:** Human Resources. **E-mail address:** resumes@deltak.com. **World Wide Web address:** http://www.deltak.com. **Description:** Custom designs, manufactures, and constructs heat recovery systems worldwide. **Corporate headquarters location:** This location. **Annual sales/revenues:** $51 - $100 million. **Number of employees nationwide:** 350.

DELUXE CORPORATION
3680 Victoria Street North, Shoreview MN 55126. 651/787-2759. **Contact:** Susan Pierre-Zilles, Personnel. **World Wide Web address:** http://www.deluxe.com. **Description:** Provides check printing, electronic funds transfer processing services, and related services to the financial industry; check authorization and collection services to retailers; and electronic benefit transfer services to state governments. Deluxe also produces forms, specialty papers, and other products for small businesses, professional practices, and medical/dental offices; and provides tax forms and electronic tax filing services to tax preparers. Through the direct mail channel, Deluxe sells greeting cards, gift-wrap, and related products to households. Founded in 1915. **Positions advertised include:** Call Center Traffic and Scheduling Analyst; Compensation Manager; Customer Management Representative; Finance Manager; Lead Financial Analyst. **Corporate headquarters location:** This location. **Other U.S. locations:** Nationwide. **International locations:** Canada; United Kingdom. **Listed on:** New York Stock Exchange. **Stock exchange symbol:** DLX. **Number of employees at this location:** 3,000. **Number of employees nationwide:** 18,000.

DEPARTMENT OF LABOR & INDUSTRY
443 Lafayette Road North, St. Paul MN 55155. 651/284-5000. **Contact:** Human Resources. **World Wide Web address:** http://www.state.mn.us/ebranch/doli. **Description:** Sets labor standards and wages, provides workers' compensation, and houses offices for OSHA (Occupational Safety and Health Administration).

DESPATCH INDUSTRIES
P.O. Box 1320, Minneapolis MN 55440. 612/781-5363. **Physical address:** 63 St. Anthony Parkway, Minneapolis MN 55418. **Fax:** 612/781-5353. **Contact:** Human Resources Representative. **World Wide Web address:** http://www.despatch.com. **Description:** A designer and manufacturer of standard and custom industrial heat processing and environmental test equipment including industrial ovens, environmental simulation chambers, and custom-engineered turnkey systems. **Corporate headquarters location:** This location. **Other area locations:** Lakeville MN. **Number of employees at this location:** 100.

DETECTOR ELECTRONICS CORPORATION (DET-TRONICS)
6901 West 110th Street, Bloomington MN 55438. 952/941-5665. **Toll-free phone:** 800/765-FIRE. **Fax:** 952/829-8728. **Contact:** Human Resources Manager. **E-mail address:** human.resources@detronics.com. **World Wide Web address:** http://www.detronics.com. **Description:** An international leader in manufacturing electronic flame and gas detection equipment and systems. Founded in 1973. **NOTE:** Entry-level positions and second and third shifts are offered. **Positions advertised include:** Regional Sales Manager; Production Planner. **Office hours:** Monday - Friday, 7:30 a.m. - 5:30 p.m. **Corporate headquarters location:** This location. **International locations:** Worldwide. **Parent company:** Kidde, PLC. **Listed on:** Privately held. **Annual sales/revenues:** $21 - $50 million. **Number of employees at this location:** 200. **Number of employees worldwide:** 260.

DIAMETRICS MEDICAL, INC.
2658 Patton Road, St Paul MN 55113. 651/639-8035. **Contact:** Dede Lebens, Human Resources. **E-mail address:** dlebens@diametrics.com. **World Wide Web address:** http://www.diametrics.com. **Description:** Develops, manufactures, and markets patient testing kits that enable a range of tests including blood gas analyses to be done during emergency air transports and home health care visits. **Positions advertised include:** Technical Support Specialist; Associate Quality Control Technician; Senior Accounting Manager.

DIAMOND PRODUCTS COMPANY
St. Paul Manufacturing Center, 310 East Fifth Street, St. Paul MN 55105. 651/292-2900. **Contact:** Human Resources. **Description:** This location manufactures shampoos, conditioners, and Liquid Paper.

DIASORIN INC.
1951 Northwest Avenue, P.O. Box 285, Stillwater MN 55082-0285. 651/439-9710. **Contact:** Human Resources. **E-mail address:** hr@diasorin.com. **World Wide Web address:** http://www.diasorin.com. **Description:** Manufactures medical testing kits. **Special programs:** Internships; Summer Jobs. **Office hours:** Monday - Friday, 8:00 a.m. - 5:00 p.m. **International locations:** Worldwide. **Number of employees at this location:** 325.

DIGI INTERNATIONAL INC.
11001 Bren Road East, Minnetonka MN 55343. 952/912-3444. **Contact:** Human Resources. **World Wide Web address:** http://www.dgii.com. **Description:** Provides data communications hardware and software that enable connectivity solutions for multi-user environments, remote access, and LAN connectivity markets. These products support most major microcomputer and workstation architectures and most popular single- and multi-user systems. Digi International also provides cross-platform compatibility and software and technical support services. The company's products are marketed to a broad range of worldwide distributors, system integrators, value-added resellers, and OEMs. **Positions advertised include:** Technical Writer; Senior Web Designer. **Corporate headquarters location:** This location. **International locations:** Worldwide. **Listed on:** NASDAQ. **Stock exchange symbol:** DGII. **President/CEO:** Jerry A. Dusa.

DIVERSIFOAM PRODUCTS
9091 County Road 50, Rockford MN 55373. 763/477-5854. **Fax:** 763/477-5863. **Contact:** Personnel. **World Wide Web address:** http://www.diversifoam.com. **Description:** A manufacturer of polystyrene insulation and protective packaging. **Corporate headquarters location:** This location. **Operations at this facility include:** Administration; Manufacturing.

DONALDSON COMPANY INC.
P.O. Box 1299, Minneapolis MN 55440-1299. 952/887-3131. **Fax:** 952/887-3555. **Contact:** Human Resources. **World Wide Web address:** http://www.donaldson.com. **Description:** A manufacturer of filtration systems and noise abatement products. **Positions advertised include:** Senior Bookkeeper; After Markets Account Representative; Sales Assistant. **Corporate headquarters location:** This location. **Operations at this facility include:** Administration; Research and Development; Sales. **Listed on:** New York Stock Exchange. **Stock exchange symbol:** DCI. **Number of employees at this location:** 700. **Number of employees nationwide:** 4,000.

DORSEY & WHITNEY
50 South Sixth Street, Suite 1500, Minneapolis MN 55402-1498. 612/340-2600. **Fax:** 612/340-2868. **Contact:** Joan Oyaff, Director of Human Resources. **World Wide Web address:** http://www.dorseylaw.com. **Description:** A law firm specializing in a variety of areas including insurance, real estate, environmental, and tax law.

DOUBLETREE GUEST SUITES HOTEL
1101 LaSalle Avenue South, Minneapolis MN 55403. 612/332-6800. **Contact:** Human Resources. **World Wide Web address:** http://www.doubletree.com. **Description:** An all-suite hotel.

DOUGLAS MACHINE, LLC
3404 Iowa Street, Alexandria MN 56308. 320/763-6587. **Fax:** 320/763-5754. **Contact:** Human Resources. **World Wide Web address:** http://www.douglas-machine.com. **Description:** A manufacturer of packaging equipment for case packing, palletizing and depalletizing, shrink wrapping, and tray forming.

DOWNTOWN PONTIAC JAGUAR
222 Hennepin Avenue, Minneapolis MN 55401. 612/371-1400. **Contact:** Stacy Droun, Controller. **E-mail address:** info@downtownjaguar.com. **World Wide Web address:** http://www.downtownpontiac.com. **Description:** A new and used automobile dealership. **Parent company:** Luther Automobile Dealerships.

THE DUFFY DESIGN GROUP
900 Marquette Avenue South, Suite 3000, Minneapolis MN 55402. 612/321-2333. **Contact:** Joe Duffy, President. **World Wide Web address:** http://www.duffy.com. **Description:** An advertising agency.

DULUTH ENTERTAINMENT CONVENTION CENTER
350 Harbor Drive, Duluth MN 55802. 218/722-5573. **Contact:** Human Resources. **E-mail address:** bfrench@decc.org. **World Wide Web address:** http://www.decc.org. **Description:** A convention center that hosts a variety of sports and entertainment events.

DULUTH-MISSABE AND IRON RANGE RAILWAY COMPANY
227 West First Street, Room 400, Missabe Building, Duluth MN 55802. 218/723-2138. **Fax:** 218/723-2160. **Contact:** Human Resources. **World Wide Web address:** http://www.gltx.com. **Description:** A railroad company.

DURA SUPREME
300 Dura Drive, Howard Lake MN 55349. 320/543-3872. **Contact:** Sharon Bargel, Human Resources Manager. **World Wide Web address:** http://www.durasupreme.com. **Description:** Manufactures cabinets. **Positions advertised include:** Woodworker; Builder; Machine Operator; Material Handler. **Special programs:** Internships. **Corporate headquarters location:** This location. **Operations at this facility include:** Administration; Manufacturing. **Listed on:** Privately held. **Number of employees at this location:** 300.

EMA SERVICES, INC.
1970 Oakcrest Avenue, Suite 100, St. Paul MN 55113. 651/639-5600. **Toll-free phone:** 800/800-2110. **Fax:** 651/639-5635. **Contact:** Human Resources. **E-mail address:** hrinfo@ema-inc.com. **World Wide Web address:** http://www.ema-inc.com. **Description:** A specialized consulting firm that works with utilities and selected manufacturers to help clients develop and implement operational strategies for improving work practices, addressing organizational development, and leveraging technology. Services focus on helping clients improve productivity and long-term performance in competitive business environments. Founded in 1975. **NOTE:** Entry-level positions are offered. **Company slogan:** Linking people and technology for business results. **Positions advertised include:** Network Support Analyst. **Office hours:** Monday - Friday, 8:00 a.m. - 5:00 p.m. **Corporate headquarters location:** This location. **Other U.S. locations:** Phoenix AZ; Tucson AZ; Los Angeles CA; Sacramento CA; San Francisco CA; Orlando FL; Boston MA; Philadelphia PA. **International locations:** Canada. **Listed on:** Privately held. **CEO:** Alan Manning. **Annual sales/revenues:** $21 - $50 million. **Number of employees at this location:** 80. **Number of employees nationwide:** 180. **Number of employees worldwide:** 185.

ECM PUBLISHERS, INC.
4101 Coon Rapids Boulevard, Coon Rapids MN 55443. 763/712-2420. **Toll-free phone:** 877/691-4171. **Fax:** 763/712-2482. **Contact:** Human Resources. **World Wide Web address:** http://www.ecm-inc.com. **Description:** Publishes 17 community weekly newspapers including *Anoka County Union, Elk River Star News, Mille Lacs County Times,* and *Princeton Union-Eagle,* and seven shopper publications. **Corporate headquarters location:** This location. **Operations at this facility include:** Administration; Manufacturing; Sales; Service. **Listed on:** Privately held. **Number of employees at this location:** 70.

EFI
1340 corporate Center Curve, Egan MN 55121. 651/365-5200. **Fax:** 651/365-5346. **Contact:** Human Resources. **E-mail address:** hr@efi.com. **World Wide Web address:** http://www.printcafe.com. **Description:** Develops management software for the graphic arts industry. **NOTE:** Search for positions online. **Corporate headquarters locations:** Pittsburgh PA. **Other U.S. locations:** Chandler AZ; Rosemont IL; Hanover MA; Lebanon NH.

EPC (ENGINEERED POLYMERS CORPORATION)
1020 East Maple Avenue, Mora MN 55051. 320/679-3232. **Contact:** Jim Forde, Human Resources Manager. **Description:** Produces custom injection-molded plastics. **Corporate headquarters location:** London, England. **Operations at this facility include:** Manufacturing; Sales.

ECO WATER SYSTEMS
P.O. Box 64420, St. Paul MN 55164. 651/739-5330. **Physical address:** 1890 Woodlane Drive, Woodbury MN 55125. **Contact:** Human Resources Manager. **World Wide Web address:** http://www.ecowater.com. **Description:** Develops, manufactures, and markets water conditioning equipment, drinking water purifiers, chemical feed pumps, and commercial and industrial water systems. **Corporate headquarters location:** Chicago IL. **Operations at this facility include:** Administration; Manufacturing; Regional Headquarters; Research and Development; Sales; Service.

ECOLAB INC.
370 North Wabasha Street, St. Paul MN 55102-2233. 651/293-2233. **Contact:** Vice President of Corporate Human Resources. **World Wide Web address:** http://www.ecolab.com. **Description:** Ecolab provides cleaning, sanitizing, and maintenance products and services for the food service, lodging, health care, laundry, dairy, and food and beverage processing markets in the United States, Canada, Latin America, Asia, and Europe. Products include dispensers, kitchen supplies, cleaners, sanitizers, janitorial products, textile care products, and commercial pest control items. **Listed on:** New York Stock Exchange. **Stock exchange symbol:** ECL.

EGAN MECHANICAL CONTRACTORS INC.
7100 Medicine Lake Road, Minneapolis MN 55427. 612/591-5578. **Contact:** Director of Human Resources. **World Wide Web address:** http://www.eganco.com.

Description: Mechanical and electrical contractors specializing in commercial and industrial projects.

ELECTRIC MACHINERY
800 Central Avenue, Minneapolis MN 55413. 612/378-8000. **Fax:** 612/378-8050. **Contact:** Personnel. **World Wide Web address:** http://www.electricmachinery.com. **Description:** Custom manufacturers of heavy industrial electric motors and generators and related equipment. **Number of employees at this location:** 240.

ELECTROLUX HOME PRODUCTS
701 33rd Avenue North, St. Cloud MN 56303. 320/253-1212. **Contact:** Human Resources. **World Wide Web address:** http://www.electrolux-usa.com. **Description:** This location manufactures freezers. Overall, Electrolux manufactures household appliances including laundry machines, ranges, dishwashers, refrigerators, freezers, air conditioners, and disposals. **Parent company:** AB Electrolux has four business areas: Household Appliances, Commercial Appliances, Outdoor Products, and Industrial Products. The main operation in Household Appliances is white goods. Other operations of Household Appliances include floor care products, absorption refrigerators for caravans and hotel rooms, room air conditioners, and sewing machines, as well as kitchen and bathroom cabinets. The main operations in Commercial Appliances are food-service equipment for restaurants and institutions, and equipment for such applications as apartment-house laundry rooms and commercial laundries. Other operations of Commercial Appliances include refrigeration equipment and freezers for shops and supermarkets, as well as vacuum cleaners and wet/dry cleaners for commercial use. Outdoor Products include garden equipment, chain saws, and other equipment for forestry operations. Garden equipment refers to portable products such as lawn trimmers and leaf blowers, as well as lawn mowers and garden tractors. Industrial Products comprise the Group's second-largest business area. Over 40 percent of sales in this business area come from profiles and other half-finished goods in aluminum, manufactured by Granges. Other main operations in Industrial Products include car safety belts and other products for personal safety in cars, as well as materials-handling equipment.

ELECTRONICS FOR IMAGING
1340 Corporate Center Curve, Eagan MN 55121. 651/365-5200. **Contact:** Human Resources. **World Wide Web address:** http://www.efi.com. **Description:** Develops graphics systems for computers and applicable software.

ELLERBE BECKET
800 LaSalle Avenue, Minneapolis MN 55402-2014. 612/376-2000. **Fax:** 612/376-2271. **Contact:** Human Resources. **E-mail address:** jobs@ellerbebecket.com. **World Wide Web address:** http://www.ellerbebecket.com. **Description:** An architectural and engineering firm engaged in the design of industrial, commercial, corporate, public assembly, educational, and medical buildings nationwide. Founded in 1908. **NOTE:** Entry-level positions are offered. **Corporate headquarters location:** This location. **Annual sales/revenues:** More than $100 million. **Number of employees at this location:** 425. **Number of employees nationwide:** 700.

EMPI, INC.
599 Cardigan Road, St. Paul MN 55126-4099. 651/415-9000. **Fax:** 651/415-8406. **Contact:** Human Resources. **E-mail address:** employspecialist@empi.com. **World Wide Web address:** http://www.empi.com. **Description:** Manufactures and markets products for incontinence, physical rehabilitation, and orthopedics. Major products include neuromuscular stimulators, braces and splints, drug administering devices, and cervical traction devices. **Positions advertised include:** Senior Oracle Developer; Assistant Controller; Business Systems Analyst; Senior Accountant. **Corporate headquarters location:** This location. **Listed on:** NASDAQ. **Stock exchange symbol:** EMPI.

ENDOCARE
6585 City West Parkway, Eden Prairie MN 55344. 952/947-9410. **Contact:** Human Resources. **World Wide Web address:** http://www.endocare.com. **Description:** Manufactures medical equipment used for the treatment of impotence.

EPICOR SOFTWARE CORPORATION
2000 Interchange Tower, 600 South Highway 169, Minneapolis MN 55426. 952/417-5000. **Fax:** 952/544-8253, **Contact:** Human Resources. **World Wide Web address:** http://www.epicor.com. **Description:** Provides integrated enterprise software to midmarket companies. Founded in 1984. **Positions advertised include:** Technical Support Analyst. **Corporate headquarters location:** Irvine CA. **Number of employees worldwide:** 950.

ERNST & YOUNG LLP
220 South Sixth Street, Suite 1400, Minneapolis MN 55402. 612/343-1000. **Contact:** Recruiter. **World Wide Web address:** http://www.ey.com. **Description:** A certified public accounting firm that also provides management consulting services. Services include data processing, financial modeling, financial feasibility studies, production planning and inventory management, management sciences, health care planning, human resources, cost accounting, and budgeting systems. **Other U.S. locations:** Nationwide. **International locations:** Worldwide.

FSI INTERNATIONAL, INC.
3455 Lyman Boulevard, Chaska MN 55318. 952/448-5440. **Contact:** Mark Almond, Human Resources Representative. **World Wide Web address:** http://www.fsi-intl.com. **Description:** A worldwide leader in producing automated silicon wafer processing equipment used by semiconductor manufacturers. The company offers three types of products: microlithography clusters, surface conditioning products, and spin-on dielectrics. Microlithography clusters apply and develop photosensitive materials to the surface of silicon wafers. Surface conditioning products are used to prepare silicon wafers for the processing of integrated circuits. Spin-on dielectrics produces systems for etching dielectric film. **Corporate headquarters location:** This location. **Subsidiaries include:** Semiconductor Systems. **Operations at this facility include:** Administration; Manufacturing; Research and Development; Sales; Service.

FAEGRE & BENSON LLP
2200 Wells Fargo Center, 90 South Seventh Street, Minneapolis MN 55402-3901. 612/336-3000. **Fax:** 612/766-1763. **Contact:** Director of Human Resources. **World Wide Web address:** http://www.faegre.com. **Description:** A corporate law firm.

FAIR, ISAAC AND CO., INC.
4295 Lexington Avenue North, St. Paul MN 55126. 651/482-8593. **Contact:** Human Resources. **World Wide Web address:** http://www.fairisaac.com. **Description:** A leading developer of data management systems and services for the consumer credit, personal lines insurance, and direct marketing industries. Fair, Isaac and Co. employs various tools such as database enhancement software, predictive modeling, adaptive control, and systems automation. **Corporate headquarters location:** San Rafael CA. **Other U.S. locations:** Nationwide. **International locations:** Worldwide. **Listed on:** New York Stock Exchange. **Stock exchange symbol:** FIC.

FAIRVIEW HEALTH SERVICES
2450 Riverside Avenue, Minneapolis MN 55454. 612/672-4545. **Fax:** 612/672-6337. **Contact:** Human Resources. **E-mail address:** corpres@fairview.org. **World Wide Web address:** http://www.fairview.org. **Description:** A nonprofit, regionally integrated health care network of primary, specialty, acute, long-term, and home care services. Fairview Health Services consists of seven hospitals, over 96 primary and specialty care clinics, 20 retail pharmacies, and long-term care facilities. **NOTE:** Entry-level positions are offered. **Special programs:** Internships. **Corporate headquarters location:** This location. **Parent company:** Fairview Health Services. **Operations at this facility include:** Service. **Listed on:** Privately held. **President/CEO:** David R. Page. **Number of employees nationwide:** 15,000.

FALLON McELLIGOTT
50 South Sixth Street, Suite 2800, Minneapolis MN 55402. 612/321-2345. **Contact:** Human Resources. **World Wide Web address:** http://www.fallon.com. **Description:** An advertising firm.

FARGO ELECTRONICS, INC.
6533 Flying Cloud Drive, Eden Prairie MN 55344. 952/941-9470. **Toll-free phone:** 800/459-5636. **Fax:** 952/941-7836. **Contact:** Human Resources. **World Wide Web address:** http://www.fargo.com. **Description:** Manufactures plastic card printers. **Corporate headquarters location:** This location.

FARLEY'S AND SATHER'S CANDY COMPANY
One Sather Plaza, P.O. Box 28, Round Lake MN 56167. 507/945-8181. **Contact:** Human Resources. **World Wide Web address:** http://www.phillipmorris.com. **Description:** Manufactures candy. **Parent company:** Phillip-Morris Companies Inc.

FASTENAL COMPANY
2001 Theurer Boulevard, P.O. Box 978, Winona MN 55987. 507/454-5374. **Contact:** Human Resources. **E-mail address:** great2b@fastenal.com. **World Wide Web address:** http://www.fastenal.com. **Description:** Markets and distributes threaded fasteners such as bolts, nuts, screws, studs, and washers, as well as other related construction supplies such as cutting tools, paints, chains, pins, machinery keys, concrete anchors, masonry drills, flashlights, batteries, sealants, metal framing systems, wire rope, and related accessories through company-operated stores. **Positions advertised include:** Customer Service Representative; Sales Support Representative; Store Manager. **Listed on:** NASDAQ. **Stock exchange symbol:** FAST. **Number of employees nationwide:** 870.

FEDERAL BEEF PROCESSORS
2817 Blaisdell Avenue, Minneapolis MN 55408. 612/870-8078. **Contact:** Human Resources Manager. **Description:** A beef packing plant. **Corporate headquarters location:** This location. **Other U.S. locations:** Rapid City SD.

FEDERAL CARTRIDGE COMPANY
900 Ehlen Drive, Anoka MN 55303. 763/323-2300. **Fax:** 763/323-2506. **Contact:** Human Resources Manager. **World Wide Web address:** http://www.federalcartridge.com. **Description:** Manufactures ammunition for sporting use and law enforcement.

FEDERATED INSURANCE
P.O. Box 328, Owatonna MN 55060-0328. 507/455-5200. **Fax:** 507/455-5452. **Contact:** Recruiting and Staffing. **E-mail address:** iemployment@fedins.com. **World Wide Web address:** http://www.federatedinsurance.com. **Description:** A multiline insurance company specializing in commercial business insurance for small and medium-sized companies. **Positions advertised include:** Actuarial; Field Services Representative. **Corporate headquarters location:** This location. **Other U.S. locations:** Phoenix AZ; Atlanta GA. **Number of employees nationwide:** 2,700.

FINGERHUT COMPANY INC.
4400 Baker Road, Minnetonka MN 55343. 952/932-3100. **Contact:** Human Resources. **World Wide Web address:** http://www.fingerhut.com. **Description:** Markets general merchandise including electronics, home furnishings, household goods, women's and men's apparel, and jewelry through catalogs and other direct mail solicitations. Fingerhut Company also operates a specialty food gifts mail order business; rents customer lists; markets various insurance products; and offers and services credit cards.

FLINT HILL RESOURCES
12555 Clayton Avenue, Rosemont MN 55068. 651/437-0700. **Contact:** Human Resources. **World Wide Web address:** http://www.fhr.com. **Description:** An oil refinery. **Positions advertised include:** Instrument Reliability Engineer. **Corporate headquarters location:** Wichita KS. **Parent company:** Koch Industries.

FLOUR CITY PACKAGING
12220 Lund Boulevard, Anoka MN 55303. 612/378-2100. **Contact:** Human Resources. **Description:** A manufacturer of paperboard boxes.

S.B. FOOT TANNING COMPANY
805 Bench Street, Red Wing MN 55066. 651/388-4731. **Contact:** Human Resources. **Description:** A leather tanning and finishing company. **Special programs:** Internships. **Corporate headquarters location:** This location. **Parent company:** Red Wing Shoe Company.

FORD MOTOR COMPANY
966 South Mississippi River Boulevard, St. Paul MN 55116. 651/699-1321. **Contact:** Personnel. **World Wide Web address:** http://www.ford.com. **Description:** Ford Motor Company is engaged in the design, development, manufacture, and sale of cars, trucks, tractors, and related components and accessories. Ford is also one of the largest providers of financial services in the United States. The company has manufacturing, assembly, and sales affiliates in 29 countries outside the United States. The company's two core businesses are the Automotive Group and the Financial Services Group (Ford Credit, The Associates, USL Capital, and First Nationwide). Ford is also engaged in a number of other businesses including electronics, glass, electrical and fuel-handling products, plastics, climate control systems, automotive service and replacement parts, vehicle leasing and rental, and land development. **Corporate headquarters location:** Dearborn MI. **Operations at this facility include:** This location is an automobile assembly plant. **Number of employees worldwide:** 300,000.

FOURTH SHIFT CORPORATION
2 Meridian Crossings, Minneapolis MN 55423. 612/851-1500. **Fax:** 612/851-1560. **Contact:** Human Resources. **World Wide Web address:** http://www.fs.com. **Description:** Develops and sells software used for billing, tracking, and production in manufacturing facilities. **International locations:** Worldwide.

FREDRIKSON & BYRON, P.A.
4000 Pillsbury Center, 200 South Sixth Street, Minneapolis MN 55402-1425. 612/492-7000. **Fax:** 612/492-7077. **Contact:** Personnel. **World Wide Web address:** http://www.fredlaw.com. **Description:** A business and trial law firm with 140 attorneys. **Corporate headquarters location:** This location. **Number of employees at this location:** 275.

H.B. FULLER COMPANY
1200 Willow Lake Boulevard, P.O. Box 64683, St. Paul MN 55164-0683. 651/236-5900. **Fax:** 651/236-5100. **Contact:** Human Resources Department. **World Wide Web address:** http://www.hbfuller.com. **Description:** A worldwide manufacturer of adhesives, sealants, coatings, and specialty chemicals. **Positions advertised include:** Financial Analyst; Business Support Analyst; Corporate Human Resources Manager; Seasonal Maintenance Worker. **Special programs:** Internships. **Corporate headquarters location:** This location. **Other U.S. locations:** Nationwide. **Number of employees at this location:** 300. **Number of employees nationwide:** 2,000. **Number of employees worldwide:** 6,000.

FUTURE PRODUCTS INC.
2100 Minnesota Avenue, Benson MN 56215. 320/843-4614. **Fax:** 320/843-2900. **Contact:** Don Lenz, Human Resources Representative. **World Wide Web address:** http://www.futureproductsinc.com. **Description:** Manufactures sewing and embroidery products.

G&K SERVICES INC.
5995 Opus Parkway, Suite 500, Minnetonka MN 55343. 952/912-5500. **Contact:** Human Resources. **World Wide Web address:** http://www.gkcares.com. **Description:** A linen supply service. **Positions advertised include:** Territory Sales Representative; Accounts Receivable Representative. **Corporate headquarters location:** This location. **Listed on:** NASDAQ. **Stock exchange symbol:** GKSRA.

GE CAPITAL FLEET SERVICES
3 Capital Drive, Eden Prairie MN 55344. 952/828-1000. **Contact:** Human Resources. **World Wide Web address:** http://www.ge.com. **Description:** One of the largest vehicle leasing companies in the United States and Canada, providing fleet financing and related management services to corporate clients. **Parent company:** General Electric Company (Fairfield CT) operates in the following areas: aircraft engines (jet engines, replacement parts, and repair services for commercial, military, executive, and commuter aircraft); appliances; broadcasting (NBC); industrial (lighting products, electrical distribution and control equipment, transportation systems products, electric motors and related products, a broad range of electrical and electronic industrial automation products, and a network of electrical supply houses); materials (plastics, ABS resins, silicones, superabrasives, and laminates); power systems (products for the generation, transmission, and distribution of electricity); technical products and systems (medical systems and equipment, as well as a full range of computer-based information and data interchange services for both internal use and external commercial and industrial customers); and capital services (consumer services, financing, and specialty insurance).

GE OSMONICS
5951 Clearwater Drive, Minnetonka MN 55343. 952/933-2277. **Fax:** 952/988-6698. **Contact:** Human Resources. **World Wide Web address:** http://www.gewater.com. **Description:** Designs, manufactures, and markets fluid processing machines, systems, and components. **NOTE:** Search and apply for positions at: http://www.gecareers.com. **Positions advertised include:** HR Manager; Buyer, Black Belt; Planner; Design Engineer Process Controls; Associate Research Scientist. **Parent company:** GE Water Technologies. **Number of employees at this location:** 600

GFI PREMIUM FOODS, INC.
2815 Blaisdell Avenue South, Minneapolis MN 55408. 612/872-6262. **Fax:** 612/870-4955. **Contact:** Josefina Duran, Human Resources Manager. **E-mail address:** jayo@gfiamerica.com. **World Wide Web address:** http://www.gfiamerica.com. **Description:** A premium meat products company that processes, packages, and distributes wholesale and retail beef, pork, and veal products. GFI Premium Foods distributes to large national and local markets. **NOTE:** Second and third shifts are offered. **Listed on:** Privately held. **President:** Robert Goldberger.

GMAC-RFC
8400 Normandale Lake Boulevard, Suite 250, Minneapolis MN 55437. 952/832-7000. **Contact:** Human Resources. **World Wide Web address:** http://www.rfc.com. **Description:** A secondary mortgage provider. **Positions advertised include:** Account Executive; Accounts Receivable Senior Associate; Administrative Assistant; Associate Counsel; Business Continuity Program Manager. **Special programs:** Internships. **Corporate headquarters location:** This location. **Parent company:** GMAC Mortgage Corporation. **Operations at this facility include:** Administration; Sales; Service. **Number of employees nationwide:** 500.

GABBERTS INC.
3501 Galleria, Minneapolis MN 55435. 952/828-8500. **Contact:** Human Resources. **Description:** A retail furniture store. **Corporate headquarters location:** This location. **Other U.S. locations:** Dallas TX; Fort Worth TX. **Number of employees nationwide:** 700.

GAGE MARKETING GROUP
10000 Highway 55, Minneapolis MN 55441-6365. 763/595-3800. **Contact:** Human Resources. **World Wide Web address:** http://www.gage.com. **Description:** Provides a wide range of integrated marketing services through the following five divisions: Gage Marketing Communications, Gage In-Store Marketing, Gage Print Services, Gage Trade Support Services, and Gage Automotive. **Corporate headquarters location:** This location. **Other area locations:** Howard Lake MN; Long Lake MN; Maple Plain MN; New Brighton MN; Roseville MN; Wayzata MN. **Other U.S. locations:** Newport Beach CA; Kankakee IL; Plymouth MI; El Paso TX. **International locations:** Mexico.

GANDER MOUNTAIN COMPANY
180 East Fifth Street, Suite 1300, Saint Paul MN 55101. 651/325-4300. **Toll-free phone:** 800/282-5993. **Contact:** Human Resources. **E-mail address:** greatjobs@gandermountain.com. **World Wide Web address:** http://www.gandermountain.com. **Description:** Retailer that serves the needs of outdoor lifestyle enthusiasts, with a particular focus on hunting, fishing and camping. **NOTE:** Search and apply for positions online. **Positions advertised include:** District Loss Control Manager; HR Field Manager; IS Manager; Operations Auditor; Senior Payroll Specialist; Treasury Analyst. **Corporate headquarters location:** This location. **Listed on:** New York Stock Exchange. **Stock exchange symbol:** GMTN.

GENERAL MILLS, INC.
8000 Audubon Road, Chanhassen MN 55317. 952/474-7444. **Fax:** 952/474-9319. **Contact:** Personnel. **World Wide Web address:** http://www.generalmills.com. **Description:** A producer of bakery goods for food service distribution. **Corporate headquarters location:** Minneapolis MN. **Other U.S. locations:** Los Angeles CA; Cedar Rapids IA; Eden Prairie MN; Joplin MO; Martel OH. **Operations at this facility include:** Administration; Manufacturing; Research and Development. **Listed on:** New York Stock Exchange. **Stock exchange symbol:** GIS.

GENERAL MILLS, INC.
One General Mills Boulevard, Minneapolis MN 55426. 612/330-4966. **Contact:** Personnel. **World Wide Web address:** http://www.generalmills.com. **Description:** Manufactures and markets food products for consumers and industrial customers worldwide. **Positions advertised include:** Internal Auditor. **Special programs:** Internships. **Corporate headquarters location:** This location. **Listed on:** New York Stock Exchange. **Stock exchange symbol:** GIS.

GENERAL MILLS, INC.
P.O. Box 1113, Minneapolis MN 55440-1113. 612/540-2311. **Contact:** Personnel. **World Wide Web address:** http://www.generalmills.com. **Description:** Produces and markets consumer foods. Food products include Cheerios, Wheaties, and Total cereals; Betty Crocker desserts, frostings, and baking mixes; Pop Secret microwave popcorn; Gorton's frozen seafood; Yoplait yogurt; Bisquik pancake mix; and Gold Medal flour. General Mills is also engaged in the full-service dinnerhouse restaurant business, operating over 1,000 company-owned Red Lobster and Olive Garden restaurants in North America. Founded in 1928. **Listed on:** New York Stock Exchange. **Stock exchange symbol:** GIS.

GENMAR INC.
100 South Fifth Street, Suite 2400, Minneapolis MN 55402. 612/339-7900. **Contact:** David Vigdal, Senior Vice President of Operations. **World Wide Web address:** http://www.genmar.com. **Description:** A holding company for boat manufacturers.

GEORGIA-PACIFIC CORPORATION
P.O. Box 16267, Duluth MN 55816. 218/720-8200. **Contact:** Human Resources. **World Wide Web address:** http://www.gp.com. **Description:** Manufactures, wholesales, and distributes building products, industrial wood products, pulp, paper, packaging, and related chemicals. The company is one of the world's largest manufacturers of forest products, with facilities in 48 states and overseas. **Corporate headquarters location:** Atlanta GA.

GOPHER ELECTRONICS COMPANY
222 Little Canada Road, St. Paul MN 55117. 651/490-4900. **Toll-free phone:** 800/592-9519. **Fax:** 651/490-4911. **Contact:** Human Resources. **World Wide Web address:** http://www.gopherelectronics.com. **Description:** Distributes passive and electromechanical components.

GRACO INC.
P.O. Box 1441, Minneapolis MN 55440-1441. 612/623-6000. **Physical address:** 4050 Olson Memorial Highway, Golden Valley MN 55422-2322. **Fax:** 612/623-6640. **Contact:** Employment. **E-mail address:** hr@graco.com. **World Wide Web address:** http://www.graco.com. **Description:** Designs, manufactures, and markets fluid handling systems and equipment for both industrial and commercial applications. Graco's products are used by companies in the manufacturing, processing, construction, and maintenance industries. Founded in 1926. **Positions advertised include:** Manufacturing Engineer; Design Engineer; Technician; Designer. **Corporate headquarters location:** This location. **Other U.S. locations:** Plymouth MI; Rogers MN; Sioux Falls SD. **International locations:** Belgium; China; Japan; Korea. **Listed on:** New York Stock Exchange. **Stock exchange symbol:** GGG. **CEO:** George Aristides. **Number of employees nationwide:** 2,080.

GRANT THORNTON LLP
200 South Sixth Street, Suite 500, Minneapolis MN 55402. 612/332-0001. **Fax:** 612/332-8361. **Contact:** Michelle Montan, Human Resources Director. **World Wide Web address:** http://www.grantthornton.com. **Description:** An international, certified public accounting organization offering a comprehensive scope of consulting and accounting services as well as strategic and tactical planning assistance to a diverse clientele. **Other U.S. locations:** Nationwide.

GREAT NORTHERN IRON ORE PROPERTIES
332 Minnesota Street, Suite W-1290, St. Paul MN 55101. 651/224-2385. **Contact:** Human Resources. **Description:** A trust company engaged in the leasing of land for use in mining iron ore.

GREAT RIVER ENERGY
P.O. Box 800, Elk River MN 55330. 763/441-3121. **Physical address:** 17845 East Highway 10, Elk River MN 55330. **Fax:** 763/241-6187. **Contact:** Human Resources. **E-mail address:** careers@greatriverenergy.com. **World Wide Web address:** http://www.greatriverenergy.com. **Description:** An electric utility company. **Positions advertised include:** Material Handler; System Administrator. **Corporate headquarters location:** This location. **Number of employees at this location:** 200. **Number of employees nationwide:** 400.

GUARDIAN BUILDING PRODUCTS
5110 Main Street, Fridley MN 55421. 763/571-5100. **Toll-free phone:** 800/643-5678. **Fax:** 763/571-5186. **Contact:** Human Resources. **E-mail address:** WebResume@GuardX.com. **World Wide Web address:** http://www.gbpd.com. **Description:** A wholesaler of building supplies including ceiling tiles, coatings, gutters, nails, roofing, screws, siding, and ventilation equipment. **NOTE:** Submit application online or forward resume in ASCII format to e-mail address above. **Corporate headquarters location:** Greer SC. **Parent company:** Guardian Industries.

GUIDANT CRM CORPORATION
4100 Hamline Avenue North, St. Paul MN 55112-5798. 651/582-4000. **Toll-free phone:** 800/227-3422. **Fax:** 651/582-4166. **Contact:** Human Resources Manager. **World Wide Web address:** http://www.guidant.com. **Description:** Develops, manufactures, and sells a wide range of products used in the treatment of cardiac arrhythmias. The company's products are both implantable and external electronic devices and accessories that are sold to hospitals and other health care providers worldwide. **NOTE:** Search and apply for positions online. **Positions advertised include:** Electrical Engineer; Electronic Engineer; Mechanical Engineer; Process/Quality Engineer; Systems Engineer; Business Analyst; Contract Administrator; Clinical Consultant. **Corporate headquarters location:** Indianapolis IN.

GUTHRIE THEATER
725 Vineland Place, Minneapolis MN 55403. 612/347-1100. **Fax:** 612/347-0451. **Contact:** Human Resources Department. **E-mail address:** search@guthrietheater.org. **World Wide Web address:** http://www.guthrietheater.org. **Description:** A theater featuring a resident professional repertory company that presents ensemble productions

of classical and modern drama. **Positions advertised include:** Associate Properties Manager; Director of Corporate and Foundation Giving.

GYRUS MEDICAL CORPORATION
6655 Wedgwood Road, Suite #105, Osseo MN 55311-3602. 763/416-3000. **Fax:** 763/416-3001. **Contact:** Human Resources Department. **E-mail address:** hr@gyrusmedical.com. **World Wide Web address:** http://www.gyrusmedical.com. **Description:** Manufactures tissue management surgical instruments. **Corporate headquarters location:** This location.

HEI INC.
1495 Steiger Lake Lane, Victoria MN 55386. 952/443-2500. **Fax:** 952/443-2668. **Contact:** Human Resources. **E-mail address:** jobs@heii.com. **World Wide Web address:** http://www.heii.com. **Description:** Develops and manufactures components, medical software, medical devices, and non-medical products. **NOTE:** Search and apply for positions online. **Positions advertised include:** Production Supervisor; Test Engineer. **Other area locations:** Chanhassen MN. **Other U.S. locations:** Boulder CO; Tempe AZ.

HANS HAGEN HOMES
941 NE Hillwind Road, Suite 300, Fridley MN 55432. 763/252-1500. **Contact:** Personnel Director. **E-mail address:** info@hanshagenhomes.com. **World Wide Web address:** http://www.hanshagenhomes.com. **Description:** A construction company specializing in townhouses and single-family homes.

HAMLINE UNIVERSITY
1536 Hewitt Avenue, St. Paul MN 55104. 651/523-2210. **Recorded jobline:** 651/523-3046. **Contact:** Dixie Lindsley, Director of Human Resources. **World Wide Web address:** http://www.hamline.edu. **Description:** A private, Methodist university with an enrollment of 3000. **NOTE:** Search for positions online. **Positions advertised include:** Program Assessment Coordinator; Literacy Faculty; Assistant University Chaplain; Assistant Director, Office of Safety and Security.

HAMMEL GREEN & ABRAHAMSON, INC.
701 Washington Avenue North, Minneapolis MN 55401. 612/758-4000. **Fax:** 612/758-4199. **Contact:** Human Resources Director. **E-mail address:** recruiting@hga.com. **World Wide Web address:** http://www.hga.com. **Description:** An architectural engineering firm. **Positions advertised include:** Architect. **Other area locations:** Rochester MN. **Other U.S. locations:** Milwaukee WI; San Francisco CA; Los Angeles CA; Sacramento CA.

HARDRIVES INC.
P.O. Box 579, St. Cloud MN 56302. 320/251-7376. **Physical address:** 1892 74th Avenue South, St. Cloud MN 56301. **Fax:** 320/251-5178. **Contact:** Human Resources. **E-mail address:** stcloud@hardrivesinc.com. **World Wide Web address:** http://www.hardrivesinc.com. **Description:** Engaged in road construction and the manufacture of paving mixes and associated material.

HARDRIVES INC.
14475 Quiram Drive, Rogers MN 55374-9461. 763/428-8886. **Fax:** 763/428-8868. **Contact:** Human Resources. **E-mail address:** mpls@hardrivesinc.com. **World Wide Web address:** http://www.hardrivesinc.com. **Description:** Engaged in road construction and the manufacture of paving mixes and associated material. **NOTE:** When sending a resume, please indicate the department of interest.

THE HARTFORD LIFE AND ANNUITY INSURANCE COMPANY
505 North Highway 169, Minneapolis MN 55441. 763/765-3000. **Fax:** 612/595-4635. **Contact:** Human Resources. **World Wide Web address:** http://www.thehartford.com. **Description:** A provider of investment products, life insurance and group and employee benefits; automobile and homeowners products; and business insurance. **NOTE:** Search and apply for positions online. **Corporate headquarters location:** Hartford CT. **Number of employees at this location:** 400. **Number of employees worldwide:** 29,000.

HAUENSTEIN & BURMEISTER, INC.
2629 30th Avenue South, Minneapolis MN 55406. 612/721-5031. **Fax:** 612/721-1665. **Contact:** Renee Schmitt, Human Resources. **E-mail address:** career@handbinc.com. **World Wide Web address:** http://www.handbinc.com. **Description:** A manufacturer of elevator entrances and cabs, partitions and ceiling systems, hollow metal and other metal specialties, a complete school equipment line, and telephone and sound systems.

HAWKINS CHEMICAL, INC.
3100 East Hennepin Avenue, Minneapolis MN 55413. 612/331-6910. **Fax:** 612/331-5304. **Contact:** Human Resources Representative. **World Wide Web address:** http://www.hawkinschemical.com. **Description:** A manufacturer, distributor, and sales agent for over 500 industrial chemicals and 600 reagent-grade laboratory chemicals.

HEALTH OUTCOME MANAGEMENT INC.
2331 University Avenue SE, Suite 100, Minneapolis MN 55414. 612/378-3053. **Contact:** Human Resources. **World Wide Web address:** http://www.homi.com. **Description:** Develops, markets, and maintains software for health care providers including long-term care facilities, retail pharmacies, and hospitals. **Parent company:** Quality Business Solutions.

HEARTLAND HEALTH, INC.
2250 County Road C, Roseville MN 55113. 651/633-6522. **Fax:** 816/271-7534. **Contact:** Human Resources. **E-mail address:** careerhelp@mail.heartland-health.com. **World Wide Web address:** http://www.heartlandhomehealth.com. **Description:** Heartland Health provides comprehensive health care and home-making services to clients in their residences. Services are provided through a network of over 40 offices and two infusion pharmacies in more than 20 geographic markets. **NOTE:** Search and apply for positions online. **Positions advertised include:** Director of Professional Services; Hospice Administrator; Patient Care Coordinator. **Corporate headquarters location:** St. Joseph MO.

HEAT-N-GLO CORPORATION
20802 Kensington Boulevard, Lakeville MN 55044. **Toll-free phone:** 888/427-3973. **Contact:** Human Resources. **E-mail address:** info@heatnglo.com. **World Wide Web address:** http://www.heatnglo.com. **Description:** Manufactures and installs gas, wood, and electric fireplaces, stoves, and related accessories. **NOTE:** Send resumes to: Hearth & Home Technologies, 800 West Jefferson, Lake City MN 55041, or fax to: 651-437-5121. **Positions advertised include:** Quality Manager. **Corporate headquarters location:** This location.

HEWITT ASSOCIATES
45 South Seventh Street, Suite 2100, Minneapolis MN 55402. 612/339-7501. **Fax:** 612/339-3517. **Contact:** Personnel. **World Wide Web address:** http://www.hewitt.com. **Description:** Hewitt Associates is an international human resources outsourcing and consulting firm delivering a range of human capital management services. **NOTE:** Search and apply for positions online. **Corporate headquarters location:** Lincolnshire IL.

HITCHCOCK INDUSTRIES, INC.
8701 Harriet Avenue South, Bloomington MN 55420-2787. 952/881-1000. **Fax:** 952/887-7790. **Contact:** Human Resources. **E-mail address:** hr@hitchcockusa.com. **World Wide Web address:** http://www.hitchcock-ind.com. **Description:** A nonferrous foundry that manufactures aluminum and magnesium castings for aerospace and industrial companies. Founded in 1916. **NOTE:** Search and apply for positions online. **Positions advertised include:** Production Manager; Production Supervisor. **Corporate headquarters location:** This location.

HOBART CORPORATION
1610 Broadway Street NE, Minneapolis MN 55413. 612/379-7544. **Fax:** 612/331-1051. **Contact:** Human Resources. **World Wide Web address:** http://www.hobartcorp.com. **Description:** Sells and services commercial food preparation equipment used in the food service industry and in the retail food/supermarket industry. **Corporate headquarters location:** Troy OH. **Parent company:** Premark International. **Operations at this facility include:** Administration; Regional Headquarters; Sales; Service.

HOFFMAN ENGINEERING
2100 Hoffman Way, Anoka MN 55303. 763/421-2240. **Contact:** Human Resources. **World Wide Web address:** http://www.hoffmanonline.com. **E-mail address:** careers@hoffmanonline.com. **Description:** Manufactures and distributes electrical and electronic enclosures. **NOTE:** Search and apply for positions online. **Positions advertised include:** Application Developer. **Corporate headquarters location:** This location. **Parent company:** Pentair, Inc. (Minneapolis MN). **Operations at this facility include:** Administration; Manufacturing; Research and Development; Sales; Service. **Listed on:** New York Stock Exchange. **Stock exchange symbol:** PNR.

HOIGAARD'S
3550 South Highway 100, St. Louis Park MN 55416. 952/929-1351. **Contact:** Personnel. **World Wide Web address:** http://www.hoigaards.com. **Description:** A retailer of sporting goods.

HOLDEN GRAPHIC SERVICES
607 Washington Avenue North, Minneapolis MN 55401. 612/339-0241. **Fax:** 952/929-2669. **Contact:** Human Resources. **World Wide Web address:** http://www.holdengraphics.com. **Description:** Produces custom business forms. **Corporate headquarters location:** This location. **Other U.S. locations:** Rockford IL; Arlington TX; Dallas TX. **Operations at this facility include:** Administration; Manufacturing; Sales. **Listed on:** Privately held. **Number of employees at this location:** 60. **Number of employees nationwide:** 280.

HOLIDAY INN HOTEL & SUITES
200 West First Street, Duluth MN 55802. 218/722-1202. **Fax:** 218/722-0233. **Contact:** Personnel Director. **World Wide Web address:** http://www.ichotelsgroup.com. **Description:** A 353-room, full-service hotel with three restaurants, conference facilities, and meeting space. **NOTE:** Entry-level positions, part-time jobs, and second and third shifts are offered. **Annual sales/revenues:** Less than $5 million. **Number of employees at this location:** 240.

HOLIDAY STATIONSTORES
4567 West 80th Street, Bloomington MN 55437. 952/832-8530. **Toll-free phone:** 800/745-7411. **Fax:** 952/832-8551. **Recorded jobline:** 952/832-8585. **Contact:** Recruiting Department. **E-mail address:** jobs@holidaystationstores.com. **World Wide Web address:** http://www.holidaystationstores.com. **Description:** Operates retail convenience stores/gas stations with over 300 locations in 11 states. **Positions advertised include:** Assistant Manager; Sales Associate; Night Manager. **Special programs:** Internships; Training. **Corporate headquarters location:** This location. **Other U.S. locations:** IA; ID; MI; MT; ND; NE; SD; WA; WI; WY. **Parent company:** Holiday Companies. **Operations at this facility include:** Administration. **Listed on:** Privately held. **Annual sales/revenues:** More than $100 million. **Number of employees at this location:** 500. **Number of employees nationwide:** 6,000.

HOMETIME
4275 Norex Drive, Chaska MN 55318. 612/448-9912. **Contact:** Plant Manager. **World Wide Web address:** http://www.hometime.com. **Description:** Produces a television show. Duplication Factory (also at this location) is a provider of video duplication services.

HORMEL FOODS CORPORATION
One Hormel Place, Austin MN 55912. **Toll-free phone:** 800/533-2000. **Fax:** 507/437-5171. **Contact:** Lynelle E. Topp, Supervisor of Professional Recruitment. **E-mail address:** careers@hormel.com. **World Wide Web address:** http://www.hormel.com. **Description:** Hormel Foods is one of the leading processors and marketers of branded meat and food products. Principal products of the company are processed meat and food entrees that are sold fresh, frozen, cured, smoked, and cooked; and canned foods including sausages, hams, franks, bacon, luncheon meats, shelf-stable microwaveable entrees, stews, chili, hash, meat spreads, and frozen processed products. The majority of the company's products are sold under the Hormel brand name. Other trademarks include Farm Fresh, Little Sizzlers, Quick Meal, Kid's Kitchen, Chi-Chi's, House of Tsang, Mary Kitchen, Dinty Moore, Light & Lean, Chicken by George, Black Label, and SPAM. Founded in 1891. **NOTE:** Search and apply for positions online. **Positions advertised include:** Associate software Engineer; Bilingual Production Supervisor; food Process Engineer. **Special programs:** Internships. **Office hours:** Monday - Friday, 7:00 a.m. - 4:00 p.m. **Corporate headquarters location:** This location. **Other U.S. locations:** Nationwide. **International locations:** Worldwide. **Subsidiaries include:** Dan's Prize, Inc.; Dubuque Foods; Jennie-O Foods. **Listed on:** New York Stock Exchange. **Stock exchange symbol:** HRL. **Annual sales/revenues:** More than $100 million. **Number of employees at this location:** 2,400. **Number of employees nationwide:** 10,500. **Number of employees worldwide:** 15,600.

HUTCHINSON TECHNOLOGY INC.
40 West Highland Park, Hutchinson MN 55350. 320/587-3797. **Fax:** 320/587-1290. **Contact:** Human Resources. **World Wide Web address:** http://www.htch.com. **Description:** Manufactures suspension assemblies for disk drives. **NOTE:** Search and apply for positions online. **Positions advertised include:** Sr. Instructional Designer; Materials Contract Analyst; Process Engineer; Machine Design Engineer; Data Architect; Systems Integration Architect; Engineering Supervisor. **Special programs:** Internships. **Corporate headquarters location:** This location. **Other area locations:** Plymouth MN. **Other U.S. locations:** Sioux Falls SD; Eau Claire WI. **Operations at this facility include:** Administration; Manufacturing; Research and Development; Sales. **Listed on:** NASDAQ. **Stock exchange symbol:** HTCH.

HYATT REGENCY MINNEAPOLIS
1300 Nicollet Mall, Minneapolis MN 55403. 612/370-1234. **Fax:** 612/370-1463. **Recorded jobline:** 612/370-1202. **Contact:** Employment Manager. **World Wide Web address:** http://www.careers.hyatt.com. **Description:** A downtown hotel with over 500 rooms and suites. The hotel's restaurants include Spike's Sports Bar and Grille, and Taxxi, an American bistro. **Special programs:** Internships. **Corporate headquarters location:** Chicago IL. **Other U.S. locations:** Nationwide. **Parent company:** Hyatt Hotels Corporation. **Operations at this facility include:** Administration; Sales; Service. **Listed on:** Privately held. **Number of employees at this location:** 335. **Number of employees nationwide:** 40,000.

IBM CORPORATION
3605 Highway 52 North, Rochester MN 55901-7829. 507/253-4011. **Toll-free phone:** 800/796-9876. **Contact:** IBM Staffing Services. **World Wide Web address:** http://www.ibm.com. **Description:** IBM is a developer, manufacturer, and marketer of advanced information processing products including computers and microelectronic technology, software, networking systems, and information technology-related services. **NOTE:** Search and apply for positions online. **Positions advertised include:** Facility Management/Construction; Physical Design Integrator; Software Developer; Software Engineer. **Corporate headquarters location:** Armonk NY. **Operations at this facility include:** This location is a manufacturing facility. **Subsidiaries include:** IBM Credit Corporation; IBM Instruments, Inc.; IBM World Trade Corporation. **Number of employees worldwide:** 319,000.

I.C. SYSTEM
444 Highway 96 East, St. Paul MN 55127-2557. 800/685-0595. **Contact:** Human Resources. **World Wide Web address:** http://www.icsystem.com. **Description:** An accounts receivable/collections services management company founded in 1938. **NOTE:** Search and apply for jobs online. **Positions advertised include:** Account Executive; Developer; Operations Manager; SQL Database Administrator; Web Dialer Administrator. **Other U.S. locations:** Nationwide. **Number of Employees:** 900.

ING
20 Washington Avenue South, Minneapolis MN 55401. 612/372-1178. **Contact:** Human Resources. **World Wide Web address:** http://www.ing-usa.com. **Description:** One of the largest integrated financial services companies in the world, providing insurance, banking, and asset management products. **NOTE:** Second and third shifts are offered. **Positions advertised include:** Senior Enterprise Architect; Account Representative; TPA Relationship Manager; Office Support Clerk; Paralegal; Business Analyst. **Special programs:** Internships. **Corporate headquarters location:** This location. **Other U.S. locations:** Nationwide. **Parent company:** ING Groep N.V. (Amsterdam). **Operations at this facility include:** Administration; Sales; Service. **Number of employees at this location:** 2,000. **Number of employees nationwide:** 10,000.

IDENTIX INC.
5600 Rowland Road, Minnetonka MN 55343. 952/932-0888. **Fax:** 952/945-3393. **Contact:** Human Resources. **E-mail address:** mnrecruit@identix.com. **World Wide Web address:** http://www.Identix.com. **Description:** A manufacturer of computerized fingerprint identification and facial identification systems. **Positions advertised include:** Engineering Documentation Specialist; Product Management Specialist; Reseller Channel Manager; Internal Audit Manager; Sr. Sales Support Engineer.

IKON OFFICE SOLUTIONS
1800 Commerce Drive, North Mankato MN 56003. 507/625-7440. **Contact:** Human Resources. **World Wide Web address:** http://www.ikon.com. **Description:** Resells computers, fax machines, and other office equipment. **NOTE:** Search and apply for positions online. **Positions advertised include:** Associate Order Coordination; HR Generalist; Account Manager; Sr. On-Site Services Specialist.

IMAGE SYSTEMS CORPORATION
6103 Blue Circle Drive, Minnetonka MN 55343. 952/935-1171. **Fax:** 952/935-1386. **Contact:** Ms. Laura Sorensen, Manager of Human Resources Department. **E-mail address:** lauras@imagesystemscorp.com. **World Wide Web address:** http://www.imagesystemscorp.com. **Description:** Develops, markets, and supports LCD and CRT displays, controllers, calibration, and display accessory products. **NOTE:** Second and third shifts are offered. **Positions advertised include:** Software Engineer. **Special programs:** Internships. **Corporate headquarters location:** This location. **Listed on:** NASDAQ. **Stock exchange symbol:** IMSG. **Annual sales/revenues:** $5 - $10 million. **Number of employees at this location:** 40.

IMATION CORPORATION
One Imation Place, Oakdale MN 55128-3414. 651/704-4000. **Toll-free phone:** 888/466-3456. **Fax:** 651/704-4171. **Contact:** Human Resources. **E-mail address:** info@imation.com. **World Wide Web address:** http://www.imation.com. **Description:** Develops and manufactures magnetic and optical removable data storage media. **NOTE:** Search and apply for positions online. **Positions advertised include:** Application Developer; FA/DA Engineer; Sr. Synthetic Chemist; . **Corporate headquarters location:** This location. **Listed on:** Chicago Stock Exchange; New York Stock Exchange. **Stock exchange symbol:** IMN. **Annual sales/revenues:** More than $100 million. **Number of employees worldwide:** 2,800.

IMMANUEL-ST. JOSEPH'S HOSPITAL
1025 Marsh Street, P.O. 8673, Mankato MN 56002-8673. 507/345-2632. **Fax:** 507/389-4750. **Recorded jobline:** 866/488-8736. **Contact:** Human Resources Department. **World Wide Web address:** http://www.isj-mhs.org. **Description:** Immanuel-St. Joseph's Hospital serves as south central Minnesota's regional medical center. Specialized care includes birthing suites for expectant mothers; a fully staffed emergency room; the assessment, diagnosis, and treatment of behavioral health problems; a cancer center; home health care; and a hospice for terminally ill patients and their families. **Positions advertised include:** Clinical Coordinator; Clinical Dietitian; Coordinator, New Hire Support; Internist; Lead Registered Nurses; LPN's; Manager, Facilities Project; Medical Oncologist; Polysomnography Technologist; Pulmonologist; RN's. **Subsidiaries include:** Waseca Area Memorial Hospital. **Parent company:** Mayo Health Systems. **Number of employees at this location:** 900.

IMMUNOCHEMISTRY TECHNOLOGIES, LLC
9401 James Avenue South, Suite 155, Bloomington MN 55431. 952/888-8788. **Fax:** 952/888-8988. **Contact:** Personnel. **E-mail address:** hr@immunochemistry.com. **World Wide Web address:** http://www.immunochemistry.com. **Description:** Develops, manufactures, and optimizes custom-designed immunoassays in kit form. Immunochemistry Technologies also provides protein purification, modification, and conjugation services, as well as antibody production. Founded in 1994. **NOTE:** Entry-level positions are offered. **Corporate headquarters location:** This location. **Listed on:** Privately held. **President:** Gary L. Johnson. **Annual sales/revenues:** Less than $5 million. **Number of employees at this location:** 15.

INDUSTRIES INC.
500 South Walnut Street, Mora MN 55051. 320/679-2354. **Contact:** Human Resources. **Description:** Provides job training and placement services for individuals who are mentally challenged.

INNOVEX, INC.
5540 Pioneer Creek Drive, Maple Plain MN 55359. 763/479-5300. **Fax:** 763/479-5395. **Contact:** Personnel. **World Wide Web address:** http://www.innovexinc.com. **Description:** Designs and manufactures flexible circuitry and chemically machined components. **NOTE:** Search and apply for positions online. **Positions advertised include:** Six Sigma Black Belt; Chemical Lab Technician; Production Trainer; Laser Engineer; Global IT Director. **Corporate headquarters location:** This location. **Other area locations:** Litchfield MN. **International locations:** Thailand. **Listed on:** NASDAQ. **Stock exchange symbol:** INVX.

INTEGRIS METALS
455 85th Avenue NW, Minneapolis MN 55433. 763/717-9000. **Toll-free phone:** 800/328-7800. **Fax:** 763/717-7112. **Contact:** John Oldendorf, Director of Human Resources. **World Wide Web address:** http://www.integrismetals.com. **Description:** A distributor of ferrous and nonferrous metals. **Corporate headquarters location:** This location. **Other U.S. locations:** Nationwide.

INTERNATIONAL ASSESSMENT NETWORK
7400 Metro Boulevard, Suite 350, Edina MN 55439. 952/921-9368. **Fax:** 952/844-9025. **Contact:** Human Resources. **World Wide Web address:** http://www.assessment.com. **Description:** Develops software and products for the application of advanced science and mathematics.

INTERNATIONAL DAIRY QUEEN INC.
7505 Metro Boulevard, Minneapolis MN 55439-0286. 952/830-0200. **Contact:** Human Resources. **World Wide Web address:** http://www.dairyqueen.com. **Description:** A restaurant chain with 5,900 restaurants in 22 countries, specializing in burgers and ice cream. International Dairy Queen operates 11 regional offices. **Corporate headquarters location:** This location. **Subsidiaries include:** Karmelkorn Shoppes, Inc.; Orange Julius of America. **Parent company:** Berkshire Hathaway Inc. **Number of employees at this location:** 330. **Number of employees nationwide:** 2,450.

INTERNATIONAL MULTIFOODS
110 Cheshire Lane, Suite 300, Minnetonka MN 55305. 952/594-3300. **Fax:** 952/594-3570. **Contact:** Human Resources. **E-mail address:** jobs@multifoods.com. **World Wide Web address:** http://www.multifoods.com. **Description:** An international processor and distributor of food products. Segments of International Multifoods include U.S. Food Services, which prepares food products for a variety of industries; Canadian Foods, which produces consumer, institutional, and industrial flour, mixes, cereals, and condiments; and Venezuelan Foods, which provides foods and animal feeds. **NOTE:** Search and apply for positions online. Resumes accepted only for advertised positions. **Positions advertised include:** Trade Marketing Analyst; Sales Specialist; Marketing Manager; Sr. Financial Analyst. **Corporate headquarters location:** This location. **Parent company:** J.M. Smucker Company. **Listed on:** New York Stock Exchange. **Stock exchange symbol:** IMC.

INTERPLASTIC CORPORATION
1225 Willow Lake Boulevard, St. Paul MN 55110-5145. 651/481-6860. **Fax:** 651/481-9836. **Contact:** George McMurray, Human Resources Manager. **World Wide Web address:** http://www.interplastic.com. **Description:** Produces synthetic resins and companion items, polyethylene containers, and sheet molding compound. **NOTE:** Search and apply for positions online. **Positions advertised include:** VP of Research & Technology; Quality Control Technician. **Corporate headquarters location:** This location. **Operations at this facility include:** Administration; Sales. **Listed on:** Privately held. **Number of employees at this location:** 60. **Number of employees nationwide:** 350.

INTERSTATE BRANDS CORPORATION
5130 Winnetka Avenue North, New Hope MN 55428. 763/533-2221. **Contact:** Donna Braun, Personnel Manager. **Description:** Manufactures and distributes a line of bread and cake products. **Corporate headquarters location:** Kansas City MO. **Operations at this facility include:** Distribution; Sales. **Sales Manager:** Mike Heiss.

INVER HILLS COMMUNITY COLLEGE
2500 80th Street East, Inver Grove Heights MN 55076. 651/450-8500. **Fax:** 651/450-8677. **Contact:** Human Resources Representative. **World Wide Web address:** http://www.inverhills.mnscu.edu. **Description:** A state community college offering two-year associate degrees, as well as vocational certificates and professional development certificates. **NOTE:** Applicants for open positions must submit an employment application, which may be downloaded online. Search for positions online.

ION CORPORATION
1311 South Fifth Street, Hopkins MN 55343. 952/936-9490. **Fax:** 952/936-7527. **Contact:** Human Resources. **World Wide Web address:** http://www.ioncorp.com. **Description:** Manufactures electronic products including circuit boards, cables, and harnesses. **Corporate headquarters location:** This location. **Other U.S. locations:** Huntsville AL. **Operations at this facility include:** Administration; Manufacturing; Sales. **Number of employees at this location:** 100.

JAPS-OLSON COMPANY
7500 Excelsior Boulevard, St. Louis Park MN 55426-4519. 952/932-9393. **Fax:** 952/912-1900. **Contact:** Mike Murphy, President. **World Wide Web address:** http://www.japsolson.com. **Description:** A commercial printer and **Listed on:** Privately held. **Annual sales/revenues:** $51 - $100 million. **Number of employees at this location:** 550.

JASC SOFTWARE
7905 Fuller Road, P.O. Box 44997, Eden Prairie MN 55344. 952/934-8888. **Toll-free phone:** 800/622-2793. **Fax:** 952/937-1732. **Contact:** Human Resources. **E-mail address:** jobs@jasc.com. **World Wide Web address:** http://www.corel.com. **Description:** Develops Windows-based graphics and multimedia software. Jasc's product line includes Paint Shop Pro, Jasc Media Center, and Professional Capture Systems. Founded in 1991. **Special programs:** Internships. **Annual sales/revenues:** $5 - $10 million. **Number of employees at this location:** 25.

JCPENNEY COMPANY, INC.
Miller Hill Mall, 1600 A Miller Trunk Highway, Duluth MN 55811. 218/727-8111. **Contact:** Human Resources. **World Wide Web address:** http://www.jcpenney.net. **Description:** JCPenney sells apparel, home furnishings, and leisure lines in catalogs and 1,100 stores. **NOTE:** Search and apply for positions online. **Corporate headquarters location:** Plano TX. **Operations at this facility include:** This location is a department store.

JEFFERSON PARTNERS L.P.
2100 East 26th Street, Minneapolis MN 55404-4101. 612/332-8745. **Recorded jobline:** 800/767-5333x495. **Contact:** Human Resources Manager. **World Wide Web address:** http://www.jefferson.com. **Description:** An intercity bus line and travel company. **Corporate headquarters location:** This location. **Other U.S. locations:** Fort Smith AR; Des Moines IA; Kansas City MO; Oklahoma City OK; Tulsa OK. **Operations at this facility include:** Administration; Sales; Service. **Listed on:** Privately held. **Number of employees at this location:** 65. **Number of employees nationwide:** 265.

JENNIE-O FOODS, INC.
1202 SW Willmar Avenue, P.O. Box 778, Willmar MN 56201. 320/235-2622. **Fax:** 320/214-2885. **Contact:** Manager, Corporate Human Resources. **E-mail address:** jocareer@j-ots.com. **World Wide Web address:** http://www.jennie-o.com. **Description:** One of the nation's largest turkey processors. Jennie-O Foods grows, processes, and markets turkey products nationally and internationally. Founded in 1949. **NOTE:** Entry-level positions are offered. **Positions advertised include:** QA Engineer; Manufacturing Engineer; Production Supervisor. **Special programs:** Internships. **Corporate headquarters location:** This location. **Subsidiaries include:** Heartland Foods; West Central Turkeys. **Parent company:** Hormel Foods. **Annual sales/revenues:** More than $100 million. **Number of employees at this location:** 100. **Number of employees nationwide:** 7,000.

E.F. JOHNSON COMPANY
299 Johnson Avenue, P.O. Box 1249, Waseca MN 56093. 507/835-6222. **Toll-free phone:** 800/328-3911. **Fax:** 507/835-6415. **Contact:** Human Resources. **E-mail address:** hjones@efjohnson.com. **World Wide Web address:** http://www.efjohnson.com. **Description:** Manufactures interoperable wireless communications systems for federal, state, and local agencies involved with homeland security and public safety. **Corporate headquarters location:** Washington DC. **Parent company:** Transcrypt International. **Number of employees nationwide:** 600.

JOSTENS, INC.
5501 American Boulevard West, Minneapolis MN 55437. 952/830-3300. **Fax:** 952/838-8020. **Contact:** Staffing. **World Wide Web address:** http://www.jostens.com. **Description**: A leading provider of products, programs and services that celebrate important moments or recognize achievements. The company's products include yearbooks, class rings, graduation products, school photography and products for athletic champions and their fans. **NOTE:** Search and apply for positions online. **Positions advertised include:** Sr. Financial Analyst; Marketing Analysis Manager. **Corporate headquarters location:** This location. **Other U.S. locations:** Nationwide. **International locations:** Worldwide. **Operations at this facility include:** Administration; Sales; Service. **Number of employees at this location:** 330. **Number of employees nationwide:** 10,000.

K&G MANUFACTURING, INC.
226 Park Avenue NW, P.O. Box 187, Faribault MN 55021. 507/334-5501. **Contact:** Human Resources. **Description:** A machine shop and precision-parts manufacturer of various components for the automotive, airline, and medical industries.

K-TEL INTERNATIONAL (USA), INC.
2655 Cheshire Lane North, Plymouth MN 55447. 763/268-0226. **Fax:** 763/559-5505. **Contact:** Manager of Human Resources. **World Wide Web address:** http://www.k-tel.com. **Description:** Distributes recorded music products. **Corporate headquarters location:** This location. **Parent company:** K-Tel International, Inc. **Listed on:** NASDAQ. **Stock exchange symbol:** KTEL.

KPMG
4200 Wells Fargo Center, 90 South Seventh Street, Minneapolis MN 55402. 612/305-5000. **Fax:** 612/305-5100. **Contact:** Catherine Goset, Recruiting Coordinator. **World Wide Web address:** http://www.kpmg.com. **Description:** KPMG delivers a wide range of assurance, tax, and consulting services. **NOTE:** Search and apply for positions online. **Positions advertised include:** Sr. Associates, Audit; Tax Manager; Director, Investigative & Integrity Advisory Services; Sr. Associate, Information Risk Management. **Special programs:** Internships. **Corporate headquarters location:** Montvale NJ. **Parent company:** KPMG International has more than 100,000 employees in 150 countries worldwide. **Operations at this facility include:** Service.

KSTP-TV
HUBBARD BROADCASTING, INC.
3415 University Avenue SE, St. Paul MN 55114. 651/646-5555. **Contact:** Human Resources. **World Wide Web address:** http://www.kstp.com. **Description:** A television station affiliated with the ABC network. **Parent company:** Hubbard Broadcasting, Inc. (also at this location).

KEMPS, LLC
2929 University Avenue SE, Minneapolis MN 55414. 612/331-3775. **Toll-free phone:** 800/322-9566. **Contact:** Human Resources Director. **World Wide Web address:** http://www.kemps.com. **Description:** A producer of ice cream and related products. **Corporate headquarters location:** This location.

KINNEY & LANGE, P.A.
312 South Third Street, Minneapolis MN 55415. 612/339-1863. **Fax:** 612/339-6580. **Contact:** Recruitment. **E-mail address:** info@kinney.com. **World Wide Web address:** http://www.kinney.com. **Description:** A patent law firm. **Corporate headquarters location:** This location. **Operations at this facility include:** Legal/Legal Research. **Number of employees at this location:** 55.

KMART STORES
1734 Mall Drive, Duluth MN 55811. 218/727-0816. **Contact:** Human Resources. **World Wide Web address:** http://www.kmart.com/corp. **Description:** Kmart is one of the nation's largest owners and operators of general merchandising stores. The company operates 1,500 Kmart outlets in 49 states, Puerto Rico, and the Virgin Islands. **NOTE:** Submit resume online. **Corporate headquarters location:** Troy MI. **Operations at this facility include:** This location is a retail store. **Number of employees worldwide:** 144,000.

KNOWLAN'S SUPER MARKETS
111 East County Road F, Vadnais Heights MN 55127. 651/483-9242. **Contact:** Chris Thinnes, Human Resources Director. **World Wide Web address:** http://www.knowlans.com. **Description:** Operates a chain of retail grocery stores. **Corporate headquarters location:** This location.

KOHL'S DEPARTMENT STORE
2115 Miller Trunk Highway, Duluth MN 55811. 218/722-9699. **Contact:** Human Resources. **World Wide Web address:** http://www.kohls.com. **Description:** Kohl's sells apparel, shoes, accessories, home products, and housewares through 500 locations nationwide. **Corporate headquarters location:** Menomonee Falls WI. **Number of employees nationwide:** 50,000.

KROLL ONTRACK INC
9023 Columbine Road, Eden Prairie MN 55347. **Toll-free phone:** 800/347-6105. **Contact:** Human Resources. **E-mail address:** hr@krollontrack.com. **World Wide Web address:** http://www.krollontrack.com. **Description:** Kroll Ontrack provides computer software and services to help companies and computer users worldwide manage, recover, and discover their valuable data. **Corporate headquarters location:** This location.

KURT MANUFACTURING COMPANY
5280 Main Street NE, Minneapolis MN 55421. 763/572-1500. **Toll-free phone:** 800/458-7855. **Fax:** 763/574-8344. **Recorded jobline:** 763/572-4505. **Contact:** Mr. Kern Walker, Vice President of Human Resources. **E-mail address:** kernw@kurt.com. **World Wide Web address:** http://www.kurt.com. **Description:** A manufacturer of a variety of industrial products including gauging and motion control systems, hydraulic products, precision gears, and workholding devices. Kurt Manufacturing Company also performs die casting, industrial precision machining, and screw machining. **Corporate headquarters location:** This location.

LAND O'LAKES, INC.
P.O. Box 64101, St. Paul MN 55164-0101. 651/481-2222. **Contact:** Human Resources. **World Wide Web address:** http://www.landolakesinc.com. **Description:** A large agricultural cooperative of farmers and ranchers involved in the processing and distribution of dairy-related food products including deli cheeses, butter, milk, sour cream, yogurt, ice cream, dips, sauces, and butter blends. The company provides management, research, advisory, lobbying, and other farm-related services for its members. Founded in 1921. **NOTE:** Search and apply for positions online. **Positions advertised include:** Procurement/Risk Manager; Corporate Account Manager; Applications Analyst/Programmer; Technologist; Director, Executive Compensation and Retirement. **Special programs:** Internships. **Corporate headquarters location:** This location. **Other U.S. locations:** Nationwide. **President/CEO:** John E. Gherty. **Annual sales/revenues:** More than $100 million. **Number of employees nationwide:** 6,000.

LARKIN, HOFFMAN, DALY & LINDGREN
1500 Wells Fargo Plaza, 7900 Xerxes Avenue South, Bloomington MN 55431. 952/835-3800. **Fax:** 952/896-3333. **Contact:** Human Resources. **E-mail address:** hr@larkinhoffman.com. **World Wide Web address:** http://www.lhdl.com. **Description:** A law firm specializing in a wide variety of areas including corporate, franchise, international, and tax law. **Special programs:** Internships. **Corporate headquarters location:** This location.

GUSTAVE A. LARSON COMPANY
13200 10th Avenue North, Plymouth MN 55441. 612/546-7175. **Contact:** Human Resources Department. **World Wide Web address:** http://www.galarson.com. **Description:** A wholesaler of heating and air conditioning systems. **Positions advertised include:** Inside Sales Rep. **Corporate headquarters location:** Pewaukee WI. **Operations at this facility include:** Sales.

LASER DESIGN INC.
9401 James Avenue South, Suite 132, Minneapolis MN 55431. 952/884-9648. **Fax:** 952/884-9653. **Contact:** Personnel. **World Wide Web address:** http://www.laserdesign.com. **Description:** Designs software for three-dimensional laser digitizers. **Positions advertised include:** Application Engineer.

LAWSON SOFTWARE
380 St. Peter Street, St. Paul MN 55102-1302. 651/767-7000. **Contact:** Human Resources. **World Wide Web address:** http://www.lawson.com. **Description:** Provides business process software. **Positions advertised include:** Revenue Analyst; Payroll Supervisor; Senior Systems Implementation Consultant. **NOTE:** Search and apply for positions online. **Positions advertised include:** Sr. Project Manager; Strategic Finance Analyst; Sr. Accountant; PSA Application Consultant; Engagement Manager; Database Administrator; Sr. Emerging Technology Web Developer; Manager, Marketing Operations; Sr. Application Development Manager. **Corporate headquarters location:** This location. **Listed on:** NASDAQ. **Stock exchange symbol:** LWSN.

LEGGETTE BRASHEARS & GRAHAM
Northpark Corporate Center, 1210 8 Pine Tree Drive, Suite 250, St. Paul MN 55112. 651/490-1405. **Fax:** 651/490-1006. **Contact:** Kevin Powers, Vice President. **E-mail address:** kevin.powers@lbgmn.com. **World Wide Web address:** http://www.lbgweb.com. **Description:** A consulting company that tests soil and groundwater samples and recommends environmentally sound cleanup procedures. **Positions advertised include:** Hydrogeologist; Remediation Engineer.

LESTER BUILDING SYSTEMS
1111 Second Avenue South, Lester Prairie MN 55354. 320/395-2531. **Fax:** 320/395-5393. **Contact:** Human Resources. **E-mail address:** hr@lesterbuildings.com. **World Wide Web address:** http://www.lesterbuildings.com. **Description:** A manufacturer and retailer of pre-engineered wood-frame buildings. **NOTE:** Entry-level positions are offered. Search and apply for positions online. **Positions advertised include:** Carpenter; Crew Leader. **Corporate headquarters location:** This location. **Parent company:** Butler Manufacturing Company.

LIBERTY DIVERSIFIED INDUSTRIES (LDI)
5600 North Highway 169, New Hope MN 55428. 763/536-6600. **Fax:** 763/536-6813. **Contact:** Human Resources. **E-mail address:** hr@libertydiversified.com. **World Wide Web address:** http://www.libertydiversified.com. **Description:** LDI is a diversified organization consisting of nine companies located throughout the United States. Products include corrugated boxes; metal fabricated products; and plastic extruded products. Other subsidiaries include a paper mill and a manufacturer/wholesaler of office and industrial supplies. Founded in 1918. **NOTE:** Entry-level positions and part-time jobs are offered. Search and apply for positions online. **Positions advertised include:** Sr. Business Trainer; General Manager; National/Key Account Rep. **Special programs:** Internships; Apprenticeships; Training; Summer Jobs. **Corporate headquarters location:** This location. **Other U.S. locations:** Baldwyn MS; Haltom City TX. **Annual sales/revenues:** More than $100 million. **Number of employees at this location:** 350. **Number of employees nationwide:** 1,400.

LIEBERMAN COMPANIES, INC.
9549 Penn Avenue South, Bloomington MN 55431. 952/887-5299. **Toll-free phone:** 800/879-0321. **Fax:** 952/887-5656. **Contact:** Personnel. **E-mail address:** jobs@liebermancompanies.com. **World Wide Web address:** http://www.liebermanmusic.com. **Description:** A distributor of gaming, amusement, and vending equipment. **Special programs:** Internships. **Corporate headquarters**

location: This location. **Parent company:** LIVE. **Operations at this facility include:** Administration; Sales; Service. **Listed on:** Privately held. **Number of employees at this location:** 60.

LIFECORE BIOMEDICAL INC.
3515 Lyman Boulevard, Chaska MN 55318. 952/368-4300. **Fax:** 952/368-3411. **Contact:** Human Resources. **E-mail address:** careers@lifecore.com. **World Wide Web address:** http://www.lifecore.com. **Description:** Manufactures and markets implantable biomaterials and medical devices. Lifecore Biomedical's products are used in the fields of dentistry, drug delivery, general surgery, ophthalmology, and wound care management. **NOTE:** Search and apply for positions online. **Positions advertised include:** Director, Clinical & Regulatory Affairs; Marketing Communications Manager; Mechanical Drafter; Mechanical Engineer. **Corporate headquarters location:** This location.

LIGHTHOUSE FOR THE BLIND
4505 West Superior Street, Duluth MN 55807. 218/624-4828. **Toll-free phone:** 800/422-0833. **Fax:** 218/624-4479. **Contact:** Human Resources. **World Wide Web address:** http://www.lighthousefortheblind-duluth.org. **Description:** Provides sight-impaired and blind people with rehabilitative services such as Braille instruction and teaching daily living skills.

LINDQUIST & VENNUM P.L.L.P.
4200 IDS Center, 80 South Eighth Street, Minneapolis MN 55402. 612/371-3211. **Fax:** 612/371-3207. **Contact:** Lisanne Weisz, Director of Legal Recruiting. **E-mail address:** lweisz@lindquist.com. **World Wide Web address:** http://www.lindquist.com. **Description:** A law firm specializing in a variety of areas including banking, bankruptcy, corporate, employee benefits, family, and real estate. **Other area locations:** St. Paul MN. **Other U.S. locations** Denver CO.

LOCKHEED MARTIN MARITIME SYSTEMS & SENSORS
P.O. Box 64525, St. Paul MN 55164. 651/456-2222. **Physical address:** 3333 Pilot Knob Road, St Paul MN 55121. **Contact:** Human Resources. **World Wide Web address:** http://www.lockheedmartin.com. **Description:** Lockheed Martin Tactical Defense Systems designs and builds 16-bit and 32-bit technical computing systems used in mil-spec environments. Applications include electronic warfare, signal intelligence, radar, sonar, and imaging where digital signal processing or general purpose computing is required. The company also provides systems engineering, software development tools, rugged computer systems, and integrated workstations of commercial architectures for proof-of-concept program phases. **NOTE:** Search and apply for positions online. **Positions advertised include:** Business Development Analysis Manager; Computer System Design Engineer; Cost-Schedule Analysis. **Corporate headquarters location:** Bethesda MD. **Operations at this facility include:** This location designs computer systems for the defense industry. **Parent company:** Lockheed Martin Corporation.

LOSSING ORTHOPEDIC
P.O. Box 6224, Minneapolis MN 55406. 612/724-2669. **Physical address:** 3230 Snelling Avenue South, Minneapolis MN 55406. **Fax:** 612/724-5089. **Contact:** Human Resources. **World Wide Web address:** http://www.losingorthopedic.com. **Description:** A manufacturer of medical supplies, specializing in the production and marketing of back and neck devices. **Operations at this facility include:** Administration; Manufacturing; Sales; Service. **Number of employees at this location:** 15. **Number of employees nationwide:** 60.

LUND FOOD HOLDINGS
BYERLY'S INC.
4100 West 50th Street, Suite 2100, Edina MN 55424-1204. 952/927-3663. **Contact:** Human Resources. **World Wide Web address:** http://www.byerlys.com. **Description:** Lund Food Holdings owns and operates Byerly's, a retail grocery store chain with 12 stores in the Minneapolis-St. Paul region. **Corporate headquarters location:** This location.

LUTHERAN BROTHERHOOD COMPANY
625 Fourth Avenue South, Minneapolis MN 55415-1624. 612/340-7054. **Contact:** Human Resources. **World Wide Web address:** http://www.luthbro.com. **Description:** A financial institution providing life, health, and disability insurance, in addition to annuities and mutual funds. **NOTE:** Search and apply for positions online. **Positions advertised include:** Field Development Analyst; Sr. Financial Writer; Associate General Counsel, Product Development; Application Analyst; Information Architecture Analyst; Marketing Strategist; Investment Accountant. Corporate **headquarters location:** This location.

LYMAN LUMBER COMPANY
300 Morse Avenue, P.O. Box 40, Excelsior MN 55331. 952/474-0844. **Fax:** 952/470-3666. **Contact:** Human Resources. **Description:** A lumber and building materials company with several divisions in the Twin Cities metropolitan area, two in Wisconsin, and one in North Carolina. **Corporate headquarters location:** This location. **Operations at this facility include:** Administration.

M.E. GLOBAL
3901 University Avenue Northeast, Minneapolis MN 55421. 763/788-1651. **Fax:** 763/788-8300. **Contact:** Human Resources. **World Wide Web address:** http://www.meglobal.com. **Description:** A foundry that produces steel castings for the mining industry. **Corporate headquarters location:** This location. **Other area locations:** Duluth MN. **Other U.S. locations:** Tempe AZ.

M & I MARSHALL & ILSLEY CORPORATION
6625 Lyndale Avenue South, Richfield MN 55423. 612/798-3400. **Fax:** 612/798-3191. **Contact:** Human Resources Representative. **E-mail address:** careers@mibank.com. **World Wide Web address:** http://www.richfieldbank.com. **Description:** One location of a banking chain. **Corporate headquarters location:** Milwaukee WI. **Other U.S. locations:** AZ; NV; FL; IL.

MTS SYSTEMS CORPORATION
14000 Technology Drive, Eden Prairie MN 55344-2290. 952/937-4000. **Fax:** 952/974-8546. **Contact:** Human Resources. **E-mail address:** employment@mts.com. **World Wide Web address:** http://www.mts.com. **Description:** Manufactures mechanical testing and simulation equipment. **NOTE:** Search and apply for positions online. **Positions advertised include:** Applications Engineer; Electrical Engineer; Manager, Internal Assurance & Accounting Services; Sr. Buyer; Product Manager; Worldwide Sales Director. **Other U.S. locations:** Ann Arbor MI; Madison Heights MI; Cary NC; Milford OH; Oak Ridge TN. **International locations:** Japan; Germany.

MACALESTER COLLEGE
1600 Grand Avenue, St. Paul MN 55105. 651/696-6000. **Fax:** 651/696-6612. **Contact:** Ms. Terry Bailey, Human Resources Representative. **E-mail address:** hr@macalester.edu. **World Wide Web address:** http://www.macalester.edu. **Description:** A private, four-year, liberal arts college with an enrollment of 1,850. Founded in 1874. **Positions advertised include:** Admissions Officer; Web Programmer.

MACDERMID COLORSPAN INC.
7090 Shady Oak Road, Eden Prairie MN 55344. 952/944-9330. **Fax:** 952/943-3339. **Contact:** Corporate Staffing. **E-mail address:** recruiter@colorspan.com. **World Wide Web address:** http://www.colorspan.com. **Description:** A designer and manufacturer of wide format digital inkjet printers for the pay-for-print segment of the graphic communications market. **Positions advertised include:** Mechanical Designer; District Account Sales Representative. **Special programs:** Internships. **Corporate headquarters location:** This location. **International locations:** The Netherlands. **Parent company:** MacDermid Printing Solutions. **Number of employees nationwide:** 400.

MACKAY ENVELOPE CORPORATION
2100 Elm Street SE, Minneapolis MN 55414-2597. 612/331-9311. **Toll-free phone:** 800/622-5299. **Contact:** Human Resources. **World Wide Web address:** http://www.mackayenvelope.com. **Description:** Manufactures envelopes. **Corporate headquarters location:** This location. **Other U.S. locations:** Mount Pleasant IA; Portland OR. **Listed on:** Privately held. **Number of employees at this location:** 250. **Number of employees nationwide:** 350.

MALLINCKRODT, INC.
2200 University Avenue West, Suite 170, St Paul MN 55114. 651/646-7229. **Contact:** Human Resources. **World Wide Web address:** http://www.mallinckrodt.com. **Description:** Manufactures and markets health care products through three main specialty groups. The Imaging Group provides contrast media and delivery systems, radiopharmaceuticals, and urology imaging systems for the diagnosis and treatment of disease in many imaging procedures. **NOTE:** Search and apply for positions online. **Special programs:** Internships; Co-ops. **Corporate headquarters location:** St. Louis MO. **Other U.S. locations:** Nationwide. **International locations:** Worldwide. **Parent company:** Tyco Healthcare. **Listed on:** NASDAQ. **Stock exchange symbol:** MKG. **Number of employees at this location:** 350. **Number of employees worldwide:** 12,000.

MALT-O-MEAL
701 West Fifth Street, Northfield MN 55057. 507/645-6681. **Toll-free phone:** 800/743-3029. **Fax:** 507/663-6203. **Recorded jobline:** 507/645-6681x4415. **Contact:** Human Resources. **E-mail address:** human_resources@malt-o-meal.com. **World Wide Web address:** http://www.malt-o-meal.com. **Description:** A manufacturer of breakfast cereals.

MANKATO REHABILITATION CENTER (MRCI)
15 Map Drive, Mankato MN 56001. 507/386-5600. **Fax:** 507/345-5991. **Contact:** Human Resources. **World Wide Web address:** http://www.mrcifoundation.org. **Description:** A sheltered workshop for mentally and physically challenged individuals.

MANN THEATRES
711 Hennepin Avenue, #300, Minneapolis MN 55403. 612/332-3303. **Contact:** Human Resources. **Description:** Operates a chain of movie theaters throughout Minnesota. **Corporate headquarters location:** This location.

MARATHON ASHLAND PETROLEUM COMPANY
459 Third Street, St. Paul Park MN 55071. 651/459-9771. **Contact:** Angela Chen, Human Resources. **World Wide Web address:** http://www.mapllc.com. **Description:** Marathon Ashland Petroleum Company is a large, diversified petroleum corporation with a group of nonrefining operations. Operations include retail marketing, motor oil marketing, chemicals, engineering and construction, and oil and gas exploration and production. **Operations at this facility include:** This location operates a refinery for fuel oil, gasoline, diesel, kerosene, propane, jet fuel, and asphalt.

MARRIOTT CITY CENTER HOTEL
30 South Seventh Street, Minneapolis MN 55402. 612/349-4000. **Fax:** 612/332-7165. **Contact:** Susan Mattson, Personnel Director. **World Wide Web address:** http://www.marriott.com. **Description:** A 31-floor glass tower hotel, linked to the city's skyway system. **NOTE:** Search and apply for positions online. **Positions advertised include:** Human Resource Generalist; Restaurant Supervisor.

MARSDEN BUILDING MAINTENANCE COMPANY
1717 University Avenue West, St. Paul MN 55104. 651/641-1717. **Fax:** 641/641-0523. **Contact:** Human Resources. **E-mail address:** mbn-apls@marsden.com. **World Wide Web address:** http://www.marsden.com. **Description:** Provides contract janitorial services. **Corporate headquarters location:** This location. **Other area locations:** Hopkins MN; Rochester MN. **Other U.S. locations:** Des Moines IA; Omaha NE; Phoenix AZ; Stevens Point WI; Milwaukee WI; Madison WI; Green Bay WI; Sheboygan WI; Racine WI; Appleton WI.

THE MARSHALL GROUP
150 South Fifth Street, Suite 3000, Minneapolis MN 55402. 612/376-1500. **Fax:** 612/692-5150. **Contact:** Carol Anderson, Personnel Director. **E-mail address:** canderson@marshallgroupinc.com. **World Wide Web address:** http://www.marshallgroupinc.com. **Description:** The Marshall Group specializes in the origination, structuring, placement, and servicing of commercial loans and fixed income securities nationwide. **Other U.S. locations;** Dallas TX; Atlanta GA; St. Louis MO; Chicago IL; San Diego CA. **Number of employees at this location:** 250.

MARTIN WILLIAMS ADVERTISING INC.
60 South Sixth Street, Suite 2800, Minneapolis MN 55402. 612/340-0800. **Contact:** Tena Murphy, Director of Human Resources. **E-mail address:** human@martinwilliams.com. **World Wide Web address:** http://www.martinwilliams.com. **Description:** An advertising agency. **NOTE:** Search for positions online. **Positions advertised include:** Production Biller. **Special programs:** Internships. **Corporate headquarters location:** This location.

McGLADREY & PULLEN, LLP
801 Nicollet Avenue, Suite 1300, Minneapolis MN 55402. 612/332-4300. **Fax:** 612/376-9876. **Contact:** Kathy Pedersen, Human Resources Director. **World Wide Web address:** http://www.mcgladrey.com. **Description:** A certified public accounting firm providing audit, tax, management, data processing, and cost systems services. **NOTE:** Search and apply for positions online. **Positions include:** Audit, Sr. Associate; Audit Associate; Tax Manager; Internal Audit Associate. **Corporate headquarters location:** This location. **Other area locations:** Bloomington MN; Duluth MN; Rochester MN; St. Paul MN.

McGLYNN BAKERIES, INC.
3090 North Shore Drive, Orono MN 55391. 763/574-2222. **Toll-free phone:** 800/624-5966. **Fax:** 763/574-2210. **Contact:** Amy Delis, Human Resources. **World Wide Web address:** http://www.mcglynn.com. **Description:** A producer of cookies and other baked goods. **Corporate headquarters location:** This location.

McGOUGH CONSTRUCTION COMPANY
2737 North Fairview Avenue, St. Paul MN 55113-1372. 651/633-5050. **Fax:** 651/633-5673. **Contact:** Human Resources. **E-mail address:** info@mcgough.com. **World Wide Web address:** http://www.mcgough.com. **Description:** A contractor specializing in industrial buildings and warehouses. **Other area locations:** Rochester MN. **Other U.S. locations:** Phoenix AZ.

McKESSON PROVIDER TECHNOLOGIES
2700 Snelling Avenue North, Roseville MN 55113. 651/697-5900. **Contact:** Human Resources. **Email address:** jobs.infosolutions@mckesson.com. **World Wide Web address:** http://www.mckesson.com. **Description:** Provides information system solutions for the healthcare industry. **NOTE:** Search and apply for positions online. **Positions advertised include:** Product Manager/Development Manager. **Office hours:** Monday - Friday, 8:00 a.m. - 5:00 p.m.

McKESSONHBOC RED LINE EXTENDED CARE
8121 10th Avenue North, Golden Valley MN 55427-9824. **Toll-free phone:** 800/328-8111. **Fax:** 763/595-6677. **Contact:** Human Resources. **E-mail address:** hr@redline.mckhboc.com. **World Wide Web address:** http://www.redline.com. **Description:** Distributes medical equipment to nursing homes. **Positions advertised include:** Pricing Coordinator; Rebate Coordinator; Business Analyst.

McQUAY INTERNATIONAL
13600 Industrial Park Boulevard, Minneapolis MN 55441. **Toll-free phone:** 800/432-1342. **Fax:** 763/553-5177. **Recorded jobline:** 763/595-6776. **Contact:** Colleen Anderson, Human Resources. **E-mail address:** colleen.anderson@mcquay.com. **World Wide Web address:** http://www.mcquay.com. **Description:** McQuay is an international company that engineers, manufactures, sells, and services commercial heating, ventilating, and air conditioning equipment. **Corporate headquarters location:** This location. **Operations at this facility include:** This location houses administrative offices only.

MEDICAL GRAPHICS CORPORATION
350 Oak Grove Parkway, St. Paul MN 55127. 651/484-4874. **Fax:** 651/484-8941. **Contact:** Ms. Sheryl Raphael, Director of Human Resources Department. **E-mail address:** hr@medgraphics.com. **World Wide Web address:** http://www.medgraphics.com. **Description:** A manufacturer of computerized medical testing equipment for the health care industry. Products include diagnostic systems that test and treat lung and heart disorders. **Listed on:** NASDAQ. **Stock exchange symbol:** MGCC.

MEDTOX LABORATORIES
402 West County Road D, St. Paul MN 55112-3522. 651/636-7466. **Toll-free phone:** 800/832-3244. **Fax:** 651/628-6160. **Contact:** Personnel. **World Wide Web address:** http://www.medtox.com. **Description:** A drug testing and toxicology laboratory.

MEDTRONIC ENERGY & COMPONENT CENTER
6700 Shingle Creek Parkway, Brooklyn Center MN 55430. 763/514-1000. **Contact:** Human Resources Director. **World Wide Web address:** http://www.medtronic.com. **Description:** Researches, designs, and manufactures medical equipment used in cardiac rhythm management, neurological, spinal, ENT, cardiac, and vascular surgery. Founded in 1949. **NOTE:** Search and apply for positions online. **Positions advertised include:** Manufacturing Engineer; Sr. Manufacturing Engineer; Sr. Project Engineer; Sr. Assembler; Principle Health and Safety Specialist. **Corporate headquarters location:** Minneapolis MN. **Operations at this facility include:** This location manufactures implantable, cardiac pacemakers. **Listed on:** New York Stock Exchange. **Stock exchange symbol:** MDT. **Number of employees nationwide:** 10,000.

MEDTRONIC, INC.
710 Medtronic Parkway, Minneapolis MN 55432-5604. 763/514-4000. **Fax:** 763/514-4879. **Recorded jobline:** 763/514-7724. **Contact:** Human Resources. **E-mail address:** employment@medtronic.com. **World Wide Web address:** http://www.medtronic.com. **Description:** Researches, designs, and manufactures medical equipment used in cardiac rhythm management, neurological, spinal, ENT, cardiac, and vascular surgery. Founded in 1949. **NOTE:** Search and apply for positions online. **Positions advertised include:** Perfusion Systems Sales Manager; Sr. Manufacturing Engineer; Sr. QA Engineer; Sr. Competitive Intelligence Specialist. **Office hours:** Monday - Friday, 8:00 a.m. - 5:00 p.m. **Corporate headquarters location:** This location. **Other U.S. locations:** Nationwide. **International locations:** Worldwide. **Operations at this facility include:** Manufacturing; Research and Development. **Listed on:** New York Stock Exchange. **Stock exchange symbol:** MDT. **President:** Bill George. **Annual sales/revenues:** More than $100 million. **Number of employees at this location:** 4,000. **Number of employees nationwide:** 10,000. **Number of employees worldwide:** 22,000.

MEREEN-JOHNSON MACHINE COMPANY
4401 Lyndale Avenue North, Minneapolis MN 55412. 612/529-7791. **Fax:** 612/529-0120. **Contact:** Human Resources Manager. **World Wide Web address:** http://www.mereenjohnson.com. **Description:** Manufactures woodworking production machinery.

MERRILL CORPORATION
One Merrill Circle, St. Paul MN 55108-5267. 651/646-4501. **Toll-free phone:** 800/688-4400. **Fax:** 651/646-5332. **Contact:** Human Resources. **E-mail address:** resumes@merrillcorp.com. **World Wide Web address:** http://www.merrillcorp.com. **Description:** provides electronic and paper document and information management services. **NOTE:** Search and apply for positions online. **Positions advertised include:** Associate Accountant; Sr. Financial Business Analyst; Integration Engineer. **Corporate headquarters locations:** This location. **Other U.S. locations:** Nationwide. **Number of employees worldwide:** 4,200.

MESABA AIRLINES
1000 Blue Gentian Road, Suite 200, Eagan MN 55121. 651/367-5000. **Fax:** 651/367-5392. **Contact:** Human Resources. **E-mail address:** employment@mesaba.com. **World Wide Web address:** http://www.mesaba.com. **Description:** A scheduled passenger airline carrier that provides service to 103 U.S. and Canadian cities. Operates as a Northwest Airlink affiliate. **Positions advertised include:** Pilot. **Corporate headquarters location:** This location. **Other U.S. locations:** Detroit MI; Memphis TN. **Parent company:** Mesaba Holdings, Inc. **Listed on:** NASDAQ. **Stock exchange symbol:** MAIR. **Number of employees at this location:** 300. **Number of employees nationwide:** 1,400.

METAFILE INFORMATION SYSTEMS INC.
2900 43rd Street NW, Rochester MN 55901-5895. 507/286-9232. **Fax:** 507/286-9065. **Contact:** Human Resources. **E-mail address:** jobs@metafile.com. **World Wide Web address:** http://www.metafileweb.com. **Description:** A software and systems integration company. Founded in 1979.

METHODIST HOSPITAL
6500 Excelsior Boulevard, Saint Louis Park MN 55426. 952/993-5000. **Fax:** 952/993-1638. **Contact:** Human Resources Representative. **World Wide Web address:** http://www.methodisthospital.com. **Description:** A 426-bed, full-service hospital. **NOTE:** Mail resumes to: Human Resources, 3800 Park Nicollet Boulevard, St. Louis Park MN 55416-2699. **NOTE:** Search and apply for positions online. **Number of employees at this location:** 4,650.

METRIS COMPANIES INC.
10900 Wayzata Boulevard, Minnetonka MN 55305. 952/525-5020. **Contact:** Human Resources. **E-mail address:** staffing@metriscompanies.com. **World Wide Web address:** http://www.metriscompanies.com. **Description:** A holding company whose subsidiaries offer credit card, travel, and fraud services. **NOTE:** Search and apply for positions online. **Positions advertised include:** Accounts Payable Analyst; Business Analyst; Director, Business Development; Human Resources ESC Administrator; Marketing Operations Project Manager; Recruitment Operations Coordinator; Sr. Java Developer. **Corporate headquarters location:** This location. **Other area locations:** Duluth MN. **Other U.S. locations:** Scottsdale AZ; Jacksonville FL; Orlando FL; White Marsh MD; Tulsa OK. **Listed on:** New York Stock Exchange. **Stock exchange symbol:** MXT. **Annual sales/revenues:** More than $100 million.

METRO TRANSIT
570 Sixth Avenue North, Minneapolis MN 55411. 612/349-7550. **Contact:** Joe Richardson, Director of Human Resources. **E-mail address:** joe.richardson@metc.state.mn.us. **World Wide Web address:** http://www.metrotransit.org. **Description:** The metropolitan transportation authority. **Positions advertised include:** Budget and Evaluation Manager; Assistant Business Unit Manager.

MICHELINAS
525 Lake Avenue South, Duluth MN 55802. 218/723-5555. **Contact:** Human Resources. **World Wide Web address:** http://www.michelinas.com. **Description:** Produces frozen Italian and Chinese entrees under the brand names Michelina's and Yu Sing.

MICHAEL FOODS, INC.
301 Carlson Parkway, Suite 400, Minnetonka MN 55305. 952/258-4000. **Toll-free phone:** 800/EGG-LINE. **Fax:** 952/258-4731. **Contact:** Human Resources. **E-mail address:** hr.mgwcorpmfi@michaelfoods.com. **World Wide Web address:** http://www.michaelfoods.com. **Description:** Processes and distributes food products including dairy, egg, and refrigerated grocery and potato products. **NOTE:** Entry-level positions are offered. **Positions advertised include:** Strategic Sourcing Manager; E-sourcing/Operating Supply Sourcing Manager. **Special programs:** Internships; Summer Jobs. **Corporate headquarters location:** This location. **Annual sales/revenues:** More than $100 million. **Number of employees at this location:** 150. **Number of employees nationwide:** 4,000.

MICRO COMPONENT TECHNOLOGY INC.
2340 West County Road C, St. Paul MN 55113-2528. 651/697-4000. **Fax:** 651/697-4200. **Contact:** Human Resources. **E-mail address:** info@mct.com. **World Wide Web address:** http://www.mct.com. **Description:** Manufactures test handling and automation solutions for the semiconductor industry. **Other U.S. locations:** Santa Clara CA; Tempe AZ. **Subsidiaries include:** Aseco Corporation.

MIDWEST ELECTRIC PRODUCTS, INC.
P.O. Box 910, Highway 22 North, Mankato MN 56002-0910. 507/625-4414. **Fax:** 507/345-2529. **Contact:** Human Resources. **E-mail address:** hr@midwestelectric.com. **World Wide Web address:** http://www.midwestelectric.com. **Description:** A manufacturer of outdoor waterproof and weatherproof electrical equipment including junction boxes, meter sockets, power outlets, RV products, and transfer switches. **Corporate headquarters location:** This location.

MIDWEST PLASTIC COMPONENTS
7309 West 27th Street, St. Louis Park MN 55426. 952/929-3312. **Fax:** 952/929-8404. **Contact:** Human Resources. **World Wide Web address:** http://www.mpc-mn.com. **Description:** A manufacturer of injection-molded plastics. **Corporate headquarters location:** This location.

MILLER ARCHITECTS AND BUILDERS
P.O. Box 1228, St. Cloud MN 56302. 320/251-4109. **Physical address:** 3335 West St. Germain, St. Cloud MN 56301. **Toll-free phone:** 800/772-1758. **Fax:** 320/251-4693. **Contact:** Personnel Department. **E-mail address:** mab@cloudnet.com. **World Wide Web address:** http://www.millerab.com. **Description:** A construction contractor.

MINCO PRODUCTS, INC.
7300 Commerce Lane, Minneapolis MN 55432-3177. 763/571-3121. **Fax:** 763/571-9142. **Contact:** Jane Stoner, Human Resources Director. **E-mail address:** hr@minco.com. **World Wide Web address:** http://www.minco.com. **Description:** Minco Products is a manufacturer of temperature sensors, heaters, and flexible interconnecting devices. **Positions advertised include:** Business Intelligence Manager/Analyst; Marketing Manager. **Special programs:** Internships. **Corporate headquarters location:** This location.

MINNEAPOLIS GRAIN EXCHANGE
400 South Fourth Street, Minneapolis MN 55415. 612/338-6212. **Contact:** Human Resources. **E-mail address:** resume@mgex.com. **World Wide Web address:** http://www.mgex.com. **Description:** The Minneapolis Grain Exchange trades on futures and options contracts.

MINNEAPOLIS HILTON & TOWERS
1001 Marquette Avenue South, Minneapolis MN 55403-2440. 612/397-1000. **Fax:** 612/397-4872. **Contact:** Tracy Schultz, Director of Human Resources. **World Wide Web address:** http://www.hilton.com. **Description:** An 814-room convention hotel with both full-service and fine-dining restaurants. **NOTE:** Search for positions online. Fax resumes to above number. **Special programs:** Internships. **Corporate headquarters location:** Beverly Hills CA. **Other U.S. locations:** Nationwide. **Number of employees at this location:** 600.

THE MINNEAPOLIS INSTITUTE OF ARTS
2400 Third Avenue South, Minneapolis MN 55404. 612/870-3014. **Fax:** 612/870-3263. **Recorded jobline:** 612/870-3239. **Contact:** Human Resources. **E-mail address:**

miajobs@artsmia.org. **World Wide Web address:** http://www.artsmia.org. **Description:** An art museum that stresses the collection of master works of art in the areas of painting; sculpture; decorative arts; prints; drawings; photography; textiles; and Asian, African, Oceanic, and Native American arts. Founded in 1883.

MINNESOTA COACHES
322 West 59 1/2 Street, Minneapolis MN 55419. 612/866-6628. **Fax:** 612/866-5691. **Contact:** Human Resources. **World Wide Web address:** http://www.minnesotacoaches.com. **Description:** Provides school bus and charter motor coach services. **NOTE:** Download application form online and mail to 425 East 31st Street, Hastings MN 55033-3691, or fax to: 651/437-1302.

MINNESOTA POWER, INC.
30 West Superior Street, Duluth MN 55802. 218/722-2641. **Recorded jobline:** 218/723-3949. **Contact:** Human Resources. **World Wide Web address:** http://www.mnpower.com. **Description:** An electric utility for 135,000 customers in northeastern Minnesota. **Positions advertised include:** Telephony Engineer. **Parent company:** ALLETE. **Listed on:** New York Stock Exchange. **Stock exchange symbol:** MPL.

MINNESOTA RUBBER
3630 Wooddale Avenue, Minneapolis MN 55416. 952/927-1400. **Fax:** 952/927-2192. **Contact:** John Camp, Director of Personnel. **World Wide Web address:** http://www.mnrubber.com. **Description:** Produces precision-molded rubber and plastic parts. **Corporate headquarters location:** This location. **Parent company:** Quadion Corporation.

MINNESOTA STATE UNIVERSITY MANKATO
228 Wiecking Center, Mankato MN 56001. 507/389-2015. **Fax:** 507/389-2960. **Contact:** Mary Ellen Kamas, Human Resources. **E-mail address:** mary.ellen.kamas@mnsu.edu. **World Wide Web address:** http://www.mnsu.edu. **Description:** A four-year, state university offering undergraduate and graduate degrees in arts and humanities; business; education; allied health and nursing; science, engineering, and technology; and social and behavioral sciences. Approximately 14,000 students attend Minnesota State University Mankato. **Number of employees at this location:** 1,300.

MINNESOTA STATE UNIVERSITY MOORHEAD
1104 Seventh Avenue South, Moorhead MN 56563. 218/236-2157. **Fax:** 218/236-3127. **Contact:** Human Resources. **E-mail address:** employ@mnstate.edu. **World Wide Web address:** http://www.mnstate.edu/home. **Description:** A four-year, state university offering bachelor's and master's degrees in over 100 majors, as well as preprofessional programs in 20 disciplines. Approximately 7,800 students attend Moorhead State University. **NOTE:** Search for positions online. **Positions advertised include:** Alumni foundation Executive Director; Assistant Professor, Various Disciplines. **Number of employees at this location:** 790.

MINNESOTA SUN PUBLICATIONS
10917 Valley View Road, Eden Prairie MN 55344. 952/829-0797. **Fax:** 952/941-3588. **Contact:** Human Resources. **World Wide Web address:** http://www.mnsun.com. **Description:** A publisher of 41 weekly newspapers reaching over 428,000 homes in the suburbs of Minneapolis and St. Paul, Minnesota. **Corporate headquarters location:** This location.

MINNESOTA TIMBERWOLVES
Target Center, 600 First Avenue North, Minneapolis MN 55403. 612/673-1600. **Contact:** Human Resources. **E-mail address:** hr@timberwolves.com. **World Wide Web address:** http://www.timberwolves.com. **Description:** Operates an NBA basketball team. **Positions advertised include:** Accounting Manager; Marketing Coordinator.

MINNESOTA TWINS
34 Kirby Puckett Place, Minneapolis MN 55415. 612/375-1366. **Contact:** Ms. Raenell Dorn, Vice-President of Human Resources. **World Wide Web address:** http://www.mntwins.com. **Description:** Operates a Major League Baseball franchise.

MINNESOTA VIKINGS
9520 Viking Drive, Eden Prairie MN 55344. 952/828-6500. **Contact:** Senior Vice President of Football Operations. **World Wide Web address:** http://www.vikings.com. **Description:** Operates the National Football League team. **Corporate headquarters location:** This location.

MINUTE MAN PRESS
8043 Lewis Road, Golden Valley MN 55427. 763/553-1630. **Fax:** 763/553-1562. **Contact:** General Manager. **World Wide Web address:** http://www.mmp-plymouth.com. **Description:** A national corporation that publishes magazines and is also engaged in commercial printing and mailing. **Special programs:** Internships. **Corporate headquarters location:** This location. **Operations at this facility include:** Manufacturing; Sales. **Number of employees at this location:** 15.

MOCON
7500 Boone Avenue North, Minneapolis MN 55428. 763/493-6370. **Fax:** 763/493-6358. **Contact:** Human Resources. **World Wide Web address:** http://www.mocon.com. **Description:** Develops instruments that test packages and packaging materials for the pharmaceutical market. **Corporate headquarters location:** This location. **Listed on:** NASDAQ. **Stock exchange symbol:** MOCO.

MOORE NORTH AMERICA
100 Washington Avenue South, Suite 1000, Minneapolis MN 55411. 612/661-1500. **Contact:** Human Resources. **World Wide Web address:** http://www.mgservices.com. **Description:** Provides commercial printing and electronic, on-demand, and database publishing to *Fortune* 500 companies. **Corporate headquarters location:** Bannockburn IL. **Other U.S. locations:** Nationwide. **Parent company:** R.R. Donnelley. **Operations at this facility include:** Manufacturing. **Listed on:** New York Stock Exchange. **Stock exchange symbol:** RRD. **Number of employees at this location:** 100.

M.A. MORTENSON COMPANY
P.O. Box 710, Minneapolis MN 55440-0710. 763/522-2100. **Fax:** 763/287-5339. **Contact:** Mr. Dan Haag, Human Services Director. **E-mail address:** jobs@mortenson.com. **World Wide Web address:** http://www.mortenson.com. **Description:** A general construction firm that provides construction management, design-build, general contracting, maintenance and operations, turnkey construction, and project development services. **Positions advertised include:** Assistant Safety Trainer; Design-Build Manager; Field Engineer; Learning and Development Facilitator; Project Accountant; Project Director; Project Engineer. **Special programs:** Internships. **Corporate headquarters location:** This location. **Other U.S. locations:** CO; WA; AZ; HI; WI; TX; IL; NC. **Operations at this facility include:** Administration. **Number of employees nationwide:** 1,800.

MOSS & BARNETT, P.A.
4800 Wells Fargo Center, 90 South Seventh Street, Minneapolis MN 55402-4129. 612/347-0300. **Fax:** 612/339-6686. **Contact:** Julie Donaldson, Hiring Coordinator. **World Wide Web address:** http://www.moss-barnett.com. **Description:** A law firm specializing in a variety of areas, excluding criminal law.

MULTI-TECH SYSTEMS INC.
2205 Woodale Drive, Mounds View MN 55112. 763/785-3500. **Toll-free phone:** 800/328-9717. **Fax:** 763/785-9874. **Contact:** Human Resources. **World Wide Web address:** http://www.multitech.com. **Description:** Manufactures Voice over IP, Internet access, remote access, and modem products.

MUSICLAND GROUP, INC.
10400 Yellow Circle Drive, Minnetonka MN 55343-9012. 952/931-8000. **Fax:** 952/931-8286. **Contact:** Human Resources. **World Wide Web address:** http://www.musicland.com. **Description:** This location houses the corporate headquarters for the chain of retail specialty music stores operating under the names: Sam Goody, Suncoast, and Media Play. **Parent company:** Sun Capital Partners.

NAPCO INTERNATIONAL INC.
11055 Excelsior Boulevard, Hopkins MN 55343. 952/931-2400. **Fax:** 952/931-2402. **Contact:** Judy Winkler, Human Resources Administrator. **E-mail address:** judyw@napcointl.com. **World Wide Web address:** http://www.napcointl.com. **Description:** A manufacturer of defense-related products. **Corporate headquarters location:** This location. **Parent company:** Venturian Corporation. **Operations at this facility include:** Sales; Service. **Number of employees at this location:** 85.

NASH FINCH COMPANY
P.O. Box 355, Minneapolis MN 55440-0355. 952/832-0534. **Physical address:** 7600 France Avenue South, Edina MN 55435. **Fax:** 952/844-1237. **Contact:** Personnel Administration. **E-mail address:** careers@nashfinch.com. **World Wide Web address:** http://www.nashfinch.com. **Description:** Engaged in wholesale distribution, retail distribution, and produce marketing. The wholesale distribution segment supplies products to supermarkets, military bases, convenience stores, and other customers in 27 states. The retail distribution segment consists of approximately 100 company-owned retail stores. Nash Finch's corporate stores operate under names such as AVANZA, Econofoods, Buy-n-Save, Sun Mart. **Positions advertised include:** Contract Analyst; Financial Analyst; Benefits Manager; Sr. Human Resources Manager; Manager, Retail Technology; Sr. Auditor; Corporate Safety and Environmental Manager; Director, Training and Development. **Corporate headquarters location:** This location. **Listed on:** NASDAQ. **Stock exchange symbol:** NAFC.

NAVARRE CORPORATION
7400 49th Avenue North, New Hope MN 55428. 763/535-8333. **Fax:** 763/533-2156. **E-mail address:** info@navarre.com. **World Wide Web address:** http://www.navarre.com. **Description:** A leading distributor of propriety and non-propriety home entertainment PC software, music and DVD. The company's customers include a wide spectrum of national and regional retailers. This customer base includes mass merchants, specialty stores, wholesalers, e-tailers. The company operates a business-to-business web site, navarre.com providing product fulfillment to both traditional and e-commerce retailers. **NOTE:** Search and apply for jobs online. **Positions advertised include:** College Music Marketing Representative; Custodian; Internal Auditor; Talent Management; Warehouse. **Corporate headquarters location:** This location. **Other U.S. locations:** Nationwide. **Listed on:** National Association of Securities Dealers Automated Quotation (NASDAQ). **Stock exchange symbol:** NAVR.

NETASPX
1200 Washington Avenue South, Minneapolis MN 55415. 612/337-0200. **Fax:** 612/337-3400. **Contact:** Personnel Department. **World Wide Web address:** http://www.netaspx.com. **Description:** Provides Lawson managed applications for finance, human resources, accounting, payroll, and supply chain management. **NOTE:** Search and apply for positions online. **Positions advertised include:** Systems Programmer; Desktop/Server Systems Administrator. **Corporate headquarters location:** Herndon VA. **Other U.S. locations:** New York NY.

NEW MECH CONSTRUCTION
1633 Eustis Street, St. Paul MN 55108. 651/645-0451. **Fax:** 651/642-5591. **Contact:** Wayne Henquinet, Human Resources Manager. **World Wide Web address:** http://www.newmech.com. **Description:** A heating, plumbing, and air conditioning contractor involved primarily in large commercial or government projects.

NILFISK-ADVANCE INC.
14600 21st Avenue North, Plymouth MN 55447-3408. 763/745-3500. **Fax:** 763/745-3718. **Contact:** Director of Human Resources. **World Wide Web address:** http://www.nilfisk-advance.com. **Description:** Manufactures professional floor maintenance equipment. **Parent company:** Nilfisk-Advance A/S (Denmark). **Operations at this facility include:** Administration; Manufacturing; Research and Development; Sales; Service. **Number of employees at this location:** 650.

NORCRAFT COMPANIES, INC.
3020 Denmark Avenue, Suite 100, Eagan MN 55121. 651/234-3300. **Fax:** 651/234-3398. **Contact:** Brenda Lee Lally, Manager of Benefits & Payroll. **World Wide Web address:** http://www.norcraftcompanies.com. **Description:** Manufactures wooden kitchen and bath cabinets. **Corporate headquarters location:** This location. **Other U.S. locations:** Nationwide. **Number of employees at this location:** 50. **Number of employees nationwide:** 1,700.

NORDIC WARE
Highway 7 & 100, Minneapolis MN 55416-2274. 952/920-2888. **Toll-free phone:** 800/328-4310. **Fax:** 952/924-9655. **Contact:** Human Resources Manager. **World Wide Web address:** http://www.nordicware.com. **Description:** Produces aluminum cookware and related products. Founded in 1946. **NOTE:** Second and third shifts are offered. **Office hours:** Monday - Friday, 8:00 a.m. - 5:00 p.m. **Corporate headquarters location:** This location. **Parent company:** Northland Aluminum Products, Inc. **Operations at this facility include:** Administration; Manufacturing; Research and Development; Sales; Service. **Listed on:** Privately held. **Number of employees at this location:** 140.

NORSTAN, INC
5101 Shady Oak Road, Minnetonka MN 55343. 952/352-4000. **Fax:** 952/352-4191. **Contact:** Human Resources. **E-mail address:** greatjobs@norstan.com. **World Wide Web address:** http://www.norstan.com. **Description:** Provides voice and data technologies and services, and remanufactured equipment to select corporate end-users

and channel partners. **NOTE:** Search and apply for positions online. **Positions advertised include:** Sr. Consultant; Sr. Telesales Account Rep; IS Professional; Managing Partner; Convergence Manager.

NORTH STAR STEEL MINNESOTA
1678 Red Rock Road, St. Paul MN 55119. 651/735-2110. **Contact:** Human Resources. **World Wide Web address:** http://www.cargillsteel.com. **Description:** A manufacturer of steel bars used for roadway construction. **Positions advertised include:** Engineer Manager Trainee. **Parent company:** Cargill Steel. **Number of employees at this location:** 400.

NORTHERN ITASCA HEALTH CARE CENTER
258 Pinetree Drive, Bigfork MN 56628. 218/743-3177. **Fax:** 218/743-3559. **Contact:** Faye Reigel, Human Resources Manager. **World Wide Web address:** http://www.nihcc.com. **Description:** A nonprofit medical facility consisting of a 20-bed hospital, a 40-bed long-term care unit, and 30 apartments attached to an outpatient clinic. The center also offers adult daycare and pharmacy services. **NOTE:** Entry-level positions and second and third shifts are offered. **Special programs:** Training. **Corporate headquarters location:** This location. **Administrator:** Richard Ash. **Number of employees at this location:** 150.

NORTHWEST AIRLINES
5101 Northwest Drive, Mail Stop A-1415, St. Paul MN 55111-3034. 612/726-3600. **Fax:** 612/726-2524. **Recorded jobline:** 612/726-3600. **Contact:** Personnel. **E-mail address:** nwajobs@nwa.com. **World Wide Web address:** http://www.nwa.com. **Description:** The world's fourth largest airline and one of America's oldest carriers. Northwest Airlines serves more than 750 cities in 120 countries on 6 continents. The U.S. system spans 49 states and the District of Columbia. Hub cities are located in Amsterdam, Detroit, Minneapolis/St. Paul, Memphis, and Tokyo. Maintenance bases are in Duluth, Minneapolis/St. Paul, and Tokyo. The company maintains a fleet of over 400 aircraft. Founded in 1926. **NOTE:** Search and apply for positions online. **Positions advertised include:** Avionics Engineer; Electrical Engineer; Powerplant Engineer; Systems Engineer; Information Technology Auditor; Commodity Manager; Reporting Manager; Sr. Sourcing Analyst Sr. Specialist Inflight Technical Communication. **Special programs:** Co-ops. **Corporate headquarters location:** This location. **Other U.S. locations:** Nationwide. **Operations at this facility include:** Administration; Divisional Headquarters; Sales. **Listed on:** NASDAQ. **Stock exchange symbol:** NWA. **Number of employees worldwide:** 40,000.

NORWOOD PROMOTIONAL PRODUCTS, INC.
1000 Third Avenue SW, Sleepy Eye MN 56085. 507/794-8000. **Contact:** Human Resources. **World Wide Web address:** http://www.norwood.com. **Description:** Imprints and distributes over 6,000 promotional items to distributors nationwide. Product lines include badges, business gifts, buttons, headwear, mugs and glassware, paper products, sporting goods, electronic accessories, packet specialties, recognition and award items, and writing instruments. **Corporate headquarters location:** Indianapolis IN. **Number of employees worldwide:** 3,000.

NOVUS AUTO GLASS REPAIR & REPLACEMENT
10425 Hampshire Avenue South, Minneapolis MN 55438. **Toll-free phone:** 800/328-1117. **Fax:** 952/946-0481. **Contact:** Human Resources. **World Wide Web address:** http://www.novusglass.com. **Description:** Operates franchises that provide auto glass and windshield repair and replacement services. **Corporate headquarters location:** This location. **International locations:** Canada.

OCCUPATIONAL DEVELOPMENT CENTER
1520 Highway 32 South, P.O. Box 730, Thief River Falls MN 56701. 218/681-4949. **Contact:** Human Resources. **World Wide Web address:** http://www.odcmn.com. **Description:** Provides disabled people with an environment where they can enhance job skills, and aids them in finding employment.

OLD DUTCH FOODS
P.O. Box 64627, St. Paul MN 55164. 651/633-8810. **Contact:** Human Resources. **World Wide Web address:** http://www.olddutchfoods.com. **Description:** Produces a variety of foods including Old Dutch brand potato chips and other snack items.

OLD REPUBLIC NATIONAL TITLE INSURANCE COMPANY
400 Second Avenue South, Minneapolis MN 55401-2499. 612/371-1111. **Toll-free phone:** 800/328-4441. **Fax:** 612/371-1191. **Contact:** Human Resources Representative. **World Wide Web address:** http://www.oldrepublictitle.com. **Description:** Provides title insurance. **Corporate headquarters location:** This location. **Parent company:** Old Republic Title Insurance Group. **Operations at this facility include:** Administration; Regional Headquarters; Sales.

OLSON & COMPANY
1625 Hennepin Avenue, Minneapolis MN 55403. 612/215-9800. **Fax:** 612/215-9801. **Contact:** Human Resources. **E-mail address:** info@oco.com. **World Wide Web address:** http://www.oco.com. **Description:** An advertising agency focusing on corporate advertising.

ONAN CORPORATION
1400 73rd Avenue NE, Minneapolis MN 55432. 763/574-5000. **Contact:** Katie Pearson, Director of Personnel. **World Wide Web address:** http://www.onan.com. **Description:** Manufactures generators. **Corporate headquarters location:** This location. **Parent company:** Cummins Inc.

OPPENHEIMER WOLFF & DONNELLY
Plaza VII, Suite 3300, 45 South Seventh Street, Minneapolis MN 55402. 612/607-7000. **Fax:** 612/607-7100. **Contact:** Jacalyn Gunstad, Attorney Recruiting Coordinator. **E-mail address:** jgunstad@oppenheimer.com. **World Wide Web address:** http://www.oppenheimer.com. **Description:** A law firm specializing in a variety of areas including commercial, health care, intellectual property, and tax law. **Positions advertised include:** Commercial Real Estate Attorney; Lateral Attorney; Real Estate Paralegal. **Special programs:** Internships. **Number of employees at this location:** 400.

OPTICAL SENSORS INCORPORATED
7615 Golden Triangle Drive, Suite C, Minneapolis MN 55344. 952.944.5857. **Fax:** 952/944-6022. **Contact:** Human Resources. **World Wide Web address:** http://www.opsi.com. **Description:** Optical Sensors Incorporated (OSI) is a technology development and manufacturing company specializing in low-cost, miniature sensors and optical instruments.

ORLUCK INDUSTRIES
17171 113th Avenue North, Suite B, Maple Grove MN 55369. 763/428-3175. **Contact:** Mark Orluck, President. **Description:** A metalworking shop that performs machining services on a subcontract basis.

OTTER TAIL POWER COMPANY
215 South Cascade, Fergus Falls MN 56537. 218/739-8200. **Contact:** Human Resources. **World Wide Web address:** http://www.otpco.com. **Description:** Produces, transmits, distributes, and sells electricity to 128,000 customers in Minnesota, North Dakota, and South Dakota. Founded in 1907. **Corporate headquarters location:** This location. **Listed on:** NASDAQ. **Stock exchange symbol:** OTTR. **Number of employees nationwide:** 750.

PC SOLUTIONS
3839 Washington Avenue North, Minneapolis MN 55412. 612/588-7501. **Contact:** Controller. **Description:** Custom-designs, distributes, installs, and maintains networking systems, primarily for corporate customers.

PC WHOLESALE
1295 Bandana Boulevard, Suite 310, Saint Paul MN 55108-5116. 651/632-5600. **Toll-free phone:** 800/801-6285. **Fax:** 651/632-5601. **Contact:** Human Resources. **World Wide Web address:** http://www.pcwholesale.com. **Description:** Distributes computer systems, peripherals, supplies, and services to an international client base. Founded in 1989. **Corporate headquarters location:** Bloomingdale IL. **Other U.S. locations:** West Berlin NJ; East Ellijay GA.

PCI (PROGRESSIVE CONTRACTORS INC.)
14123 42nd Street NE, St. Michael MN 55376-9563. 763/497-6100. **Fax:** 763-497-6101. **Contact:** Human Resources. **E-mail address:** brosso@progressivecontractors.com. **World Wide Web address:** http://www.progressivecontractors.com. **Description:** A contractor specializing in highway and street construction.

PACESETTER
2015 Gateway Boulevard, Arden Hills MN 55112-2785. 651/631-3040. **Toll-free phone:** 800/666-8581. **Contact:** Personnel Department. **World Wide Web address:** http://www.pacesetteronline.com. **Description:** Manufactures and sells a wide variety of home improvement products including windows and cabinet refacing. Pacesetter also sells siding manufactured by other companies. **NOTE:** Search for positions online. **Corporate headquarters location:** Omaha NE.

PACKAGING CORPORATION OF AMERICA (PCA)
1821 Marshall Street NE, Minneapolis MN 55418. 612/789-3511. **Fax:** 612/782-2571. **Contact:** Human Resources. **Description:** Manufactures paper, corrugated paper, paperboard, aluminum, and plastic packaging material. Products are used in the packaging of food, paper and paper products, metal products, rubber and plastics, automotive products, and point-of-purchase displays; the packaging of soap, detergent, and food products; and residential construction. **NOTE:** Job seekers may contact Steve Calhoun, VP, Human Resources at 847/482-2111, or via fax: 847/482-2238 concerning employment opportunities. **Other area locations:** Golden Valley MN; Fridley MN.

PADDOCK LABORATORIES, INC.
3940 Quebec Avenue North, New Hope MN 55427. 763/546-4676. **Toll-free phone:** 800/328-5113. **Fax:** 763/546-4842. **Contact:** Human Resources. **E-mail address:** employment@paddocklabs.com. **World Wide Web address:** http://www.paddocklabs.com. **Description:** Manufactures generic pharmaceuticals. Founded in 1977. **NOTE:** Search and apply for positions online. **Positions advertised include:** Lab Tech; Regulatory Affairs Analyst; Director of Regulatory Affairs; Stability Chemist. **Number of employees at this location:** 225.

PADELFORD PACKET BOAT COMPANY
Harriet Island, St. Paul MN 55107. 651/227-1100. **Toll-free phone:** 800/543-3908. **Fax:** 651/227-0543. **Contact:** Human Resources. **E-mail address:** info@riverrides.com. **World Wide Web address:** http://www.riverrides.com. **Description:** Padelford Packet Boat Company provides Mississippi riverboat cruises in St. Paul and Minneapolis. Operations include sightseeing cruises, dinner cruises, and private charters from April through October. **Positions advertised include:** Boat Crew Member; Boat Crew Chief; Office Crew Member; Photographer. **Operations at this facility include:** Administration; Service.

PAM COMPANIES
1105 Xenium Lane North, Suite 200, Plymouth MN 55441. 612/591-5827. **Contact:** Personnel. **World Wide Web address:** http://www.pam-companies.com. **Description:** Distributes automotive parts to retailers and wholesalers in the midwest. **Corporate headquarters location:** Sioux Falls SD. **Other U.S. locations:** Denver CO; Boise ID; Fargo ND; Salt Lake City UT; Omaha NE. **Listed on:** Privately held. **Number of employees nationwide:** 325.

PAPER, CALMENSON & COMPANY
P.O. Box 64432, St. Paul MN 55164-0432. 651/631-1111. **Contact:** Human Resources. **World Wide Web address:** http://www.pacal.com. **Description:** Manufactures fabricated steel products for industrial use. **Corporate headquarters location:** This location.

PARK CONSTRUCTION COMPANY
7900 Beech Street NE, Minneapolis MN 55432-1795. 763/786-9800. **Fax:** 651/631-9076. **Contact:** Personnel. **Description:** A contractor specializing in the construction of bridges and tunnels.

PARK NICOLLET HEALTH SERVICES
3800 Park Nicollet Boulevard, St. Louis Park MN 55416-2699. 952/993-1600. **Fax:** 952/993-1638. **Contact:** Human Resources. **World Wide Web address:** http://www.parknicollet.com. **Description:** Operates Methodist Hospital, a 426-bed, full-service hospital, and Park Nicollet Clinic, one of the largest multispecialty clinics in the United States, with 25 neighborhood clinics. **NOTE:** Search and apply for positions online. **Number of employees nationwide:** 7,500.

PARKER HANNIFIN CORPORATION – COMPUMOTOR
3650 Chestnut Street North, Chaska MN 55318. 952/448-9800. **Fax:** 952/448-9321. **Contact:** Human Resources. **World Wide Web address:** http://www.parker.com. **Description:** Parker Hannifin Corporation makes motion control products including fluid power systems, electromechanical controls, and related components. Products are sold through direct sales employees and more than 4,900 distributors. The Motion and Control Group manufactures hydraulic pumps, power units, control valves, accumulators, cylinders, actuators, and automation devices to remove contaminants from air, fuel, oil, water, and other fluids. The Fluid Connectors Group manufactures connectors, tube and hose fittings, hoses, and couplers that transmit fluid. The Seal Group makes sealing devices, gaskets, and packing that ensure leak-proof connections. The Automotive and Refrigeration Groups manufacture components for use in industrial and automotive air conditioning and refrigeration systems. Principal products of the aerospace segment are hydraulic and pneumatic fuel systems and components. **Corporate headquarters location:** Cleveland OH. **Listed on:** New York Stock

Exchange. **Stock exchange symbol:** PH.

PARKER HANNIFIN CORPORATION – QUICK COUPLING
8145 Lewis Road, Minneapolis MN 55427. 763/544-7781. **Fax:** 763/544-3418. **Contact:** Human Resources. **World Wide Web address:** http://www.parker.com. **Description:** Parker Hannifin Corporation makes motion control products including fluid power systems, electromechanical controls, and related components. Products are sold through direct sales employees and more than 4,900 distributors. The Motion and Control Group manufactures hydraulic pumps, power units, control valves, accumulators, cylinders, actuators, and automation devices to remove contaminants from air, fuel, oil, water, and other fluids. The Fluid Connectors Group manufactures connectors, tube and hose fittings, hoses, and couplers that transmit fluid. The Seal Group makes sealing devices, gaskets, and packing that ensure leak-proof connections. The Automotive and Refrigeration Groups manufacture components for use in industrial and automotive air conditioning and refrigeration systems. Principal products of the aerospace segment are hydraulic and pneumatic fuel systems and components. **Corporate headquarters location:** Cleveland OH. **Listed on:** New York Stock Exchange. **Stock exchange symbol:** PH.

PARKER HANNIFIN CORPORATION - OILDYNE
5520 North Highway 169, Minneapolis MN 55428-3602. 763/533-1600. **Fax:** 763/533-0082. **Contact:** Human Resources. **World Wide Web address:** http://www.parker.com. **Description:** Parker Hannifin Corporation makes motion control products including fluid power systems, electromechanical controls, and related components. Products are sold through direct sales employees and more than 4,900 distributors. The Motion and Control Group manufactures hydraulic pumps, power units, control valves, accumulators, cylinders, actuators, and automation devices to remove contaminants from air, fuel, oil, water, and other fluids. The Fluid Connectors Group manufactures connectors, tube and hose fittings, hoses, and couplers that transmit fluid. The Seal Group makes sealing devices, gaskets, and packing that ensure leak-proof connections. The Automotive and Refrigeration Groups manufacture components for use in industrial and automotive air conditioning and refrigeration systems. Principal products of the aerospace segment are hydraulic and pneumatic fuel systems and components. **Corporate headquarters location:** Cleveland OH. **Operations at this facility include:** This location produces hydraulic pumps, motors, valves, and filters for various industrial uses. **Listed on:** New York Stock Exchange. **Stock exchange symbol:** PH.

PARSONS BRINCKERHOFF & QUADE INC.
510 First Avenue North, Suite 550, Minneapolis MN 55403. 612/371-0443. **Fax:** 612/371-4410. **Contact:** Human Resources. **World Wide Web address:** http://www.pbworld.com. **Description:** Provides complete engineering and construction management services including the development of major bridges, tunnels, highways, marine facilities, buildings, industrial complexes, and railroads. **Corporate headquarters location:** New York NY.

PATTERSON DENTAL COMPANY
2930 Waters Road, Suite 100, Eagan MN 55121. 651/688-6054. **Toll-free phone:** 800/328-5536. **Contact:** Director of Human Resources. **E-mail address:** jobs@pattersondental.com. **World Wide Web address:** http://www.pattersondental.com. **Description**: A distributor serving the dental supply, companion-pet veterinarian supply and rehabilitation supply markets. **Positions advertised include:** Technology Service Technician.

PEARSON NCS
5601 Green Valley Drive, Bloomington MN 55437. 952/829-3000. **Toll-free phone:** 800/328-6172. **Contact:** Human Resources. **E-mail address:** jobs@ncs.com. **World Wide Web address:** http://www.pearsonncs.com. **Description:** A global information services company providing software, service, and systems for the collection, management, and interpretation of data. **NOTE:** Search and apply for positions online. **Positions advertised include:** Director, Scanning Products. **Special programs:** Internships. **Corporate headquarters location:** This location. **Other U.S. locations:** Nationwide. **Annual sales/revenues:** More than $100 million. **Number of employees nationwide:** 3,000.

PEARSON NCS
1313 Lone Oak Road, Eagan MN 55121-1334. **Toll-free phone:** 800/336-3426. **Contact:** Personnel. **E-mail address:** jobs@ncs.com. **World Wide Web address:** http://www.ncspearson.com. **Description:** This location manufactures scanner software. Overall, Pearson NCS is a global information services company providing software, service, and systems for the collection, management, and interpretation of data. **NOTE:** Search and apply for positions online. **Positions advertised include:** Project Manager; Senior Accountant. **Corporate headquarters location:** Bloomington MN. **Other U.S. locations:** Nationwide. **Number of employees nationwide:** 3,000.

PEMSTAR
3535 Technology Drive NW, Rochester MN 55901. 507/288-6720. **Fax:** 507/280-0838. **Contact:** Human Resources. **E-mail address:** HR@pemstar.com. **World Wide Web address:** http://www.pemstar.com. **Description:** Provides a comprehensive range of engineering, product design, automation and test, manufacturing and fulfillment services and solutions to customers in the communications, computing and data storage, industrial equipment and medical industries. **NOTE:** Search and apply for positions online. **Positions advertised include:** Accounting Manager; Controller; Human Resources Generalist; IS Operations Technician. **Corporate headquarters location:** This location. **International locations:** Worldwide. **Listed on:** National Association of Securities Dealers Automated Quotation (NASDAQ). **Stock exchange symbol:** PMTR. **CEO:** Allen J. Berning.

PENTAIR, INC.
5500 Wayzata Boulevard, Suite 800, Golden Valley MN 55416-1259. 763/545-1730. **Fax:** 763/656-5400. **Contact:** Amy Crews, Human Resources Department. **E-mail address:** amy_crews@pentair.com. **World Wide Web address:** http://www.pentair.com. **Description:** Pentair Industries is a diverse firm with core operations in tools, water technologies, and enclosures. **Corporate headquarters location:** This location. **Listed on:** New York Stock Exchange. **Stock exchange symbol:** PNR. **Number of employees at this location:** 40. **Number of employees nationwide:** 12,000.

PEPSI-COLA COMPANY
1300 East Cliff Road, Burnsville MN 55337. 952/890-8940. **Contact:** Human Resources. **World Wide Web address:** http://www.pepsico.com. **Description:** This location houses administrative offices. Overall, Pepsi-Cola Company produces and distributes a variety of beverages including the brand names Pepsi-Cola, Mountain Dew, Mug Root Beer, and Slice. **NOTE:** Search and apply for positions online. **Parent company:** PepsiCo, Inc. (Purchase NY) consists of Frito-Lay Company, Pepsi-Cola Company, and Tropicana Products, Inc. **Operations at this facility include:** Administration; Manufacturing; Regional Headquarters; Sales; Service. **Listed on:** New York Stock Exchange. **Stock exchange symbol:** PEP.

PERSONNEL DECISIONS INTERNATIONAL (PDI)
2000 Plaza VII Tower, 45 South Seventh Street, Minneapolis MN 55402. 920/997-6995. **Fax:** 612/337-8217. **Contact:** Human Resources Representative. **E-mail address:** resumes@pdi-corp.com. **World Wide web address:** http://www.personneldecisions.com. **Description:** A worldwide consulting firm specializing in talent management. PDI applies behavioral sciences to help organizations define successful performance; measure capabilities and potential; and develop the skills and abilities of individuals, teams and organizations. **NOTE:** Search and apply for positions online. **Positions advertised include:** Account Executive; Content Developer; Project Coordinator; Regional Financial Specialist; Sr. Consultant; Vice President of Technology. **Corporate headquarters location:** This location. **Other U.S. locations:** Atlanta GA; Boston MA; Chicago IL; Dallas TX; Denver CO; Detroit MI; Houston TX; Los Angeles CA; New York NY; San Francisco CA; Washington DC.

PHYSICAL ELECTRONICS, INC.
18725 Lake Drive East, Chanhassen MN 55317. 952/828-6200. **Fax:** 952/828-6176. **Contact:** Human Resources. **World Wide Web address:** http://www.phi.com. **Description:** Manufacturers of surface analysis instrumentation. **Corporate headquarters location:** This location. **Parent company:** ULVAC-PHI. **Operations at this facility include:** Administration; Manufacturing; Research and Development; Sales; Service. **Listed on:** Privately held. **Number of employees at this location:** 300.

PLASMON IDE
9625 West 76th Street, Suite 100, Eden Prairie MN 55344. 952/946-4100. **Fax:** 952/946-4141. **Contact:** Human Resources. **World Wide Web address:** http://www.plasmon.com. **Description:** Engaged in the manufacture of optical and media storage products. **NOTE:** Resumes accepted only for open positions. Search and apply for positions online. **Operations at this facility include:** Sales and marketing.

PLASTECH CORPORATION
56 East Broadway, Suite 210, Forest Lake MN 55025. 651/407-5700. **Fax:** 651/407-5650. **Contact:** Kari Bauer, Personnel Manager. **Description:** A manufacturer of assorted plastic products including injection moldings. Founded in 1963. **Special programs:** Internships. **Corporate headquarters location:** This location. **Operations at this facility include:** Administration; Manufacturing. **Listed on:** Privately held. **Number of employees at this location:** 360.

PLASTIC PRODUCTS INC.
30355 Akerson Street, Lindstrom MN 55045. 651/257-5980. **Contact:** Jacquie Stendahl, Personnel. **Description:** A plastics company producing a wide range of injection-molded products. **Number of employees at this location:** 200.

PLYMOLD SEATING
615 Centennial Drive, Kenyon MN 55946. 507/789-5111. **Toll-free phone:** 800/759-6653. **Fax:** 800/544-0480. **Contact:** Human Resources. **World Wide Web address:** http://www.plymold.com. **Description:** A manufacturer of seating and furniture for the restaurant industry.

POLARFAB
2800 East Old Shakopee Road, Bloomington MN 55425-1350. 952/876-3000. **Toll-free phone:** 800/882-3472. **Fax:** 952/876-2350. **Contact:** Robert Rousseau, Director of Human Resources. **E-mail address:** info@polarfab.com. **World Wide Web address:** http://www.polarfab.com. **Description:** Manufactures semiconductors and integrated circuits. **Positions advertised include:** Device Development Engineer; Fab Operator; Process Development Engineer. **Listed on:** Privately held.

POLARIS INDUSTRIES INC.
2100 Highway 55, Medina MN 55340. 763/542-0500. **Contact:** Human Resources. **World Wide Web address:** http://www.polarisindustries.com. **Description:** A worldwide manufacturer and marketer of motorized products for recreational and utility use. Products include snowmobiles, all-terrain vehicles, and personal watercraft. Polaris also manufactures garments and accessories such as snowmobile suits and leathers, wet suits, helmets, goggles, activewear, and tennis shoes. **NOTE:** Search and apply for positions online. **Positions advertised include:** ATV Marketing Manager; Business Unit Controller; Lead Industrial Designer; Sr. Purchasing Agent. **Corporate headquarters location:** This location. **Other U.S. locations:** Spirit Lake IA; Roseau MN; Osceola WA; Vermillion SD. **International locations:** Worldwide. **Listed on:** New York Stock Exchange; Pacific Stock Exchange. **Stock exchange symbol:** PII. **Number of employees nationwide:** 3,500.

POLARIS INDUSTRIES INC.
301 Fifth Avenue SW, Roseau MN 56751. 218/463-2312. **Contact:** Terri Larson, Personnel Supervisor. **World Wide Web address:** http://www.polarisindustries.com. **Description:** Polaris Industries manufactures and markets recreational vehicles. Other company products include personal watercraft garments and accessories such as snowmobile suits and leathers, wet suits, helmets, goggles, activewear, and tennis shoes. Polaris products are sold around the world through a network of nearly 2,000 dealers in North America and 55 distributors covering 82 countries worldwide. **NOTE:** Search and apply for positions online. **Positions advertised include:** Design Engineer; Engineering Manager; Fabricator Technician; Intellectual Property Specialist; Inventory Control Coordinator; Project Design Engineer; Quality Engineer; Sr. Development Engineer; Snowmobile Program Leader. **Corporate headquarters location:** Medina MN. **Other U.S. locations:** Spirit Lake IA; Medina MN; Osceola WI; Vermillion SD. **International locations:** Worldwide. **Operations at this facility include:** This location manufactures ATVs and snowmobiles. **Listed on:** New York Stock Exchange; Pacific Stock Exchange. **Stock exchange symbol:** PII. **Number of employees at this location:** 1,800. **Number of employees nationwide:** 3,500.

PREMIUMWEAR, INC.
5500 Feltl Road, Minnetonka MN 55343. 952/979-1700. **Contact:** Susan Workman, Personnel Manager. **World Wide Web address:** http://www.premiumwear.com. **Description:** A manufacturer of apparel and accessories for the promotional apparel industry. **Other U.S. locations:** Clarksville TN.

PRESBYTERIAN HOMES OF MINNESOTA
3220 Lake Johanna Boulevard, Arden Hills MN 55112. 651/631-6126. **Fax:** 651/631-6108. **Recorded jobline:** 877/747-4473. **Contact:** Angie Pearson, Human Resources Representative. **World Wide Web address:** http://www.preshomes.com. **Description:** Offers a broad range of residential and support services to the elderly. Services include apartment living, long-term nursing care, and home health respite programs. **NOTE:** Entry-level positions and second and third shifts are offered. Search for positions online. **Positions advertised include:** Clinical Coordinator; Physical Therapist; RN.

Special programs: Summer Jobs. **Corporate headquarters location:** This location. **CEO:** Daniel Lindh. **Number of employees at this location:** 1,500.

PRIORITY PUBLICATIONS
6700 France Avenue South, Suite 200, Edina MN 55435. 952/920-9928. **Contact:** Human Resources. **World Wide Web address:** http://www.prioritypub.com. **Description:** Publishes financial and health articles for inclusion in newsletters. **Corporate headquarters location:** This location.

PROSPECT FOUNDRY INC.
1225 Winter Street NE, Minneapolis MN 55413-2697. 612/331-9282. **Fax:** 612/331-4122. **Contact:** Human Resources Representative. **World Wide Web address:** http://www.prospectfoundry.com. **Description:** An iron foundry primarily engaged in the manufacture of gray and ductile iron castings.

PROTEIN DESIGN LABS, INC.
3955 Annapolis Lane, Plymouth MN 55447. 763/551-1778. **Fax:** 763/551-1780. **Contact:** Human Resources. **World Wide Web address:** http://www.pdl.com. **Description:** A research and development company focused on the development of humanized and human monoclonal antibodies for the treatment and prevention of various diseases. **NOTE:** Search and apply for positions online. **Positions advertised include:** Maintenance Technician; Application Analyst; Business Analyst; Metrology Technician; Scientist, Cell Culture; Scientist, Purification; Manufacturing Supervisor: Manager, Quality Assurance. **Corporate headquarters location:** Fremont CA. **Other area locations:** Brooklyn Park MN.

PROVELL, INC.
11100 Wayzata Boulevard, Suite 680, Minneapolis MN 55305. 952/258-2000. **Fax:** 952/258-2100. **Contact:** Human Resources. **World Wide Web address:** http://www.provell.com. **Description:** Markets general merchandise through catalogs. Products include computers, home office, home decor, consumer electronics, home improvements, and sporting/fitness goods. **Number of employees at this location:** 750. **Listed on:** NASDAQ. **Stock exchange symbol:** PRVL.

PURINA MILLS, INC.
3901 Hiawatha Avenue South, Minneapolis MN 55406. 612/721-0738. **Fax:** 612/721-0706. **Contact:** Personnel. **World Wide Web address:** http://www.purinamills.com. **Description:** A feed manufacturing plant specializing in the production of animal and poultry feeds. **NOTE:** Entry-level positions are offered. **Corporate headquarters location:** St. Louis MO. **Other U.S. locations:** Nationwide. **Operations at this facility include:** Administration; Manufacturing; Sales. **Listed on:** Privately held. **Annual sales/revenues:** More than $100 million. **Number of employees at this location:** 100. **Number of employees nationwide:** 2,500.

QUALITY PARK PRODUCTS
2520 Como Avenue, St. Paul MN 55108. 651/645-0251. **Toll-free phone:** 800/328-2990. **Fax:** 651/659-3680. **Contact:** Mr. Ron Rebeck, Vice President of Human Resources. **World Wide Web address:** http://www.qualitypark.com. **Description:** An envelope and paper manufacturer and wholesaler.

QUEBECOR WORLD, INC.
660 Mayhew Lake Road NE, Saint Cloud MN 56304. 320/654-2400. **Fax:** 320/252-0067. **Contact:** Human Resources. **World Wide Web address:** http://www.quebecorworldinc.com. **Description:** Quebecor Printing Inc. is o the world's largest commercial printer with 160 printing and related facilities in 17 countries. The company's major product categories include inserts and circulars, magazines, books, catalogs, directories, checks, bonds and bank notes, specialty printing, and newspapers. Quebecor Printing also offers web offset, gravure, and sheetfed printing capacity, plus related services that include advanced electronic prepress and imaging, database and list management, shipping and distribution, and CD-ROM mastering and replicating. **Parent company:** Quebecor Inc. (Canada). **Operations at this facility include:** This location prints a variety of catalogs and magazines. **Listed on:** New York Stock Exchange. **Stock exchange symbol:** IQW. **Number of employees worldwide:** 37,000.

QUEST DIAGNOSTICS INCORPORATED
600 West County Road D, Suite 11, St. Paul MN 55112. 651/635-1500. **Contact:** Personnel. **World Wide Web address:** http://www.questdiagnostics.com. **Description:** One of the largest clinical laboratories in North America, providing a broad range of clinical laboratory services to health care clients that include physicians, hospitals, clinics, dialysis centers, pharmaceutical companies, and corporations. The company offers and performs tests on blood, urine, and other bodily fluids and tissues to provide information for health and well-being. **Positions advertised include:** Phlebotomy Service Floater; Cyto Tech Assistant;

QUESTAR DATA SYSTEMS, INC.
2905 West Service Road, Eagan MN 55121. 651/688-0089. **Toll-free phone:** 800/959-8755. **Fax:** 651/688-0546. **Contact:** Human Resources. **E-mail address:** careers@questarweb.com. **World Wide Web address:** http://www.questarweb.com. **Description:** A full-service survey research and consulting firm that works with clients to develop, conduct, and analyze surveys in the areas of public sector research, organizational consulting, and service quality research. **NOTE:** Search for positions online. **Positions advertised include:** Market Research Project Manager; Vice President of Sales and Marketing; Consultant. **Office hours:** Monday - Friday, 8:00 a.m. - 5:00 p.m. **Corporate headquarters location:** This location.

R&D SYSTEMS
TECHNE CORPORATION
614 McKinley Place NE, Minneapolis MN 55413. 612/379-2956. **Toll-free phone:** 800/343-7475. **Fax:** 612/656-4400. **Contact:** Lea Simoane, Human Resources Manager. **World Wide Web address:** http://www.rndsystems.com. **Description:** R&D Systems is a supplier of cytokine and related reagents to research institutions. Founded in 1976. **Positions advertised include:** Planning Associate; Scientist; Quality Control Technician; Research Associate. **Corporate headquarters location:** This location. **Parent company:** Techne Corporation (also at this location) is a holding company whose subsidiaries manufacture hematology control products, biotech products, and biological products. **Number of employees at this location:** 190.

RBC DAIN RAUSCHER
Dain Rauscher Plaza, 60 South Sixth Street, Minneapolis MN 55402-4422. 612/371-2711. **Toll-free phone:** 800/678-3246. **Contact:** Human Resources. **World Wide Web address:** http://www.rbcdain.com. **Description:** A financial consulting and securities firm. The company also provides real estate syndication and property investment services, as well as data processing services. **NOTE:** Search and apply for positions online. **Positions advertised include:** Sr. Associate, Margins; Sr. Associate, Annuity Operations; Supervisor, Margins; Associate General Counsel; Sr. Compliance Officer. **Corporate headquarters location:** This location. **Parent company:** Royal Bank of Canada.

RSM McGLADREY, INC.
227 West First Street, Suite 700, Duluth MN 55802. 218/727-8253. **Fax:** 218/727-1438. **Contact:** Human Resources. **E-mail address:** jobs@rsmi.com. **World Wide Web address:** http://www.rsmmcgladrey.com. **Description:** Provides accounting and auditing services, business planning, taxation, and consulting services. **NOTE:** Search and apply for positions online. **Corporate headquarters location:** Minneapolis MN. **Other U.S. locations:** Nationwide. **Number of employees nationwide:** 4,000.

RTI PLASTICS
1260 Red Fox Road, Arden Hills MN 55112. 651/636-9770. **Fax:** 651/636-9503. **Contact:** Human Resources. **World Wide Web address:** http://www.rti-corp.com. **Description:** A manufacturer of injection-molded plastic products including components for hearing aids for the health care industry. **Corporate headquarters location:** This location.

RTP COMPANY
580 East Front Street, P.O. Box 5439, Winona MN 55987-0439. 507/454-6900. **Toll-free phone:** 800/433-4787. **Fax:** 507/454-2041. **Contact:** Human Resources. **E-mail address:** employment@rtpcompany.com. **World Wide Web address:** http://www.rtpcompany.com. **Description:** Manufactures reinforced and modified thermoplastics. **Other U.S. locations:** Indianapolis IN; South Boston VA; Fort Worth TX. **Parent company:** Miller Waste Mills (also at this location).

RADISSON HOTEL
505 West Superior Street, Duluth MN 55802. 218/727-8981. **Contact:** Human Resources. **World Wide Web address:** http://www.radisson.com. **Description:** A 268-room hotel.

RED WING SHOE COMPANY
314 Main Street, Riverfront Center, Red Wing MN 55066. 651/388-8211. **Toll-free phone:** 888/873-5546. **Fax:** 651/385-0897. **Contact:** Human Resources. **World Wide Web address:** http://www.redwing.com. **Description:** A manufacturer of men's footwear.

REGIONS HOSPITAL
640 Jackson Street, St. Paul MN 55101. 651/254-4784. **Toll-free phone:** 800/332-5720. **Fax:** 651/254-3450. **Recorded jobline:** 651/254-0855. **Contact:** Human Resources. **World Wide Web address:** http://www.regionshospital.com. **Description:** A full-service private hospital with a Level I trauma center.. **NOTE:** Human Resources Department is located at: 690 North Robert Street, St. Paul MN 55101. **Positions advertised include:** Infection Control Manager; Manager of Benefits and Compensation; Orthopedic Practice Manager; Chemical Health Counselor; Cytotechnologist; Neurodiagnostic Technologist; Pharmacists; Polysomnographic Technologist; LPN's; RN's. **Special programs:** Internships. **Office hours:** Monday - Friday, 8:00 a.m. - 4:30 p.m. **Corporate headquarters location:** This location. **Number of employees at this location:** 500.

REGIS CORPORATION
7201 Metro Boulevard, Minneapolis MN 55439. 952/947-7777. **Contact:** Human Resources. **World Wide Web address:** http://www.regiscorp.com. **Description:** The world's largest company in the hair salon industry. REGIS Corporation has salon franchise locations all over the world. **NOTE:** Search and apply for both franchise and corporate positions online. **Positions advertised include:** Accounts Payable Specialist; Advertising Manager; Architectural Designer; Beauty School Coordinator; Benefit Staff Accountant; Data Entry Clerk; Hair Stylists; JDE Programmer/Analyst; Lease Payables Analyst; Merchandise Buyer. **Corporate headquarters location:** This location. **Other U.S. locations:** Nationwide. **International locations:** Worldwide. **Listed on:** New York Stock Exchange. **Stock exchange symbol:** RGS.

REM, INC.
6921 York Avenue South, Edina MN 55435. 952/925-5067. **Toll-free phone:** 800/896-8814. **Fax:** 952/925-0739. **Contact:** Human Resources Manager. **World Wide Web address:** http://www.reminc.com. **Description:** A provider of community-based health care and related services, with locations in Minnesota and Wisconsin. **Positions advertised include:** RN; LPN. **Special programs:** Training; Summer Jobs. **Corporate headquarters location:** This location. **Parent company:** The Mentor Network. **Listed on:** Privately held. **Annual sales/revenues:** $11 - $20 million. **Number of employees at this location:** 1,000.

REMMELE ENGINEERING
10 Old Highway 8 SW, New Brighton MN 55112. 651/635-4100. **Toll-free phone:** 800/222-7737. **Fax:** 651/635-4168. **Contact:** Human Resources. **World Wide Web address:** http://www.remmele.com. **Description:** Operates a machine shop for large industrial equipment. **Positions advertised include:** Manager of Manufacturing Engineering; Manufacturing Engineer. **Corporate headquarters location:** This location.

RESEARCH, INC.
7128 Shady Oak Road, Eden Prairie MN 55344. 952/941-3300. **Fax:** 952/941-3628. **Contact:** Human Resources Department. **World Wide Web address:** http://www.researchinc.com. **Description:** Designs and manufactures electric infrared heating components and integrated heating systems. **Positions advertised include:** Mechanical Design Engineer. **Corporate headquarters location:** This location. **Operations at this facility include:** Administration; Manufacturing; Research and Development; Sales; Service. **Listed on:** NASDAQ. **Stock exchange symbol:** RESR. **Annual sales/revenues:** $21 - $50 million. **Number of employees at this location:** 160.

RESISTANCE TECHNOLOGY, INC.
1260 Red Fox Road, Arden Hills MN 55112. 651/636-9770. **Fax:** 651/636-8944. **Contact:** Cari Sather, Human Resources Coordinator. **World Wide Web address:** http://www.rti-corp.com. **Description:** A worldwide producer of medical hearing products including ultraminiature volume controls, CIC faceplates, and programmable hearing systems. **NOTE:** Entry-level positions and second and third shifts are offered. **Corporate headquarters location:** This location. **Parent company:** Selas. **Annual sales/revenues:** $21 - $50 million. **Number of employees at this location:** 260.

RETEK
950 Nicollet Mall, Minneapolis MN 55403. 612/587-5000. **Toll-free phone:** 877/517-3835. **Fax:** 612/587-5100. **Contact:** Human Resources. **World Wide Web address:** http://www.retek.com. **Description:** Retek is a worldwide provider of mission-critical software and services to the retail industry. Founded in 1986. **NOTE:** Search and apply for positions online. Do not submit resumes via e-mail. **Positions advertised include:**

Software Engineer; Business Consultant; Technical Consultant; Revenue Recognition Director. **Corporate headquarters location:** This location. **Other U.S. locations:** Atlanta GA. **Parent company:** Oracle. **Number of employees worldwide:** 525.

RICE MEMORIAL HOSPITAL
301 Becker Avenue SW, Willmar MN 56201. 320/235-4543. **Toll-free phone:** 800/537-4677. **Fax:** 320/231-4940. **Contact:** Human Resources. **E-mail address:** nski@rice.willmar.mn.us. **World Wide Web address:** http://www.ricehospital.com. **Description:** A 136-bed hospital offering both acute care and outpatient services. **Positions advertised include:** RN's; Security Officer; Dietary Aide. **Number of employees at this location:** 900.

RIDGEVIEW MEDICAL CENTER
500 South Maple Street, Waconia MN 55387-1714. 952/442-2191. **Toll-free phone:** 800/967-4620. **Contact:** Human Resources. **World Wide Web address:** http://www.ridgeviewmedical.org. **Description:** A medical center with 129 beds offering both acute care and outpatient services. **NOTE:** Search and apply for positions online. **Positions advertised include:** Medical Language Specialist; Pharmacist; Radiology Technologist; Home Medical Equipment Services Director; Clinical Informatics Coordinator; RN's..

RIMAGE CORPORATION
7725 Washington Avenue South, Minneapolis MN 55439. 952/944-8144. **Fax:** 952/946-4576. **Contact:** Human Resources. **E-mail address:** hr@rimage.com. **World Wide Web address:** http://www.rimage.com. **Description:** Designs and manufactures CD-R/DVD-R duplication equipment. **Positions advertised include:** Manufacturing Engineer.

RISDALL ADVERTISING AGENCY
550 Main Street, New Brighton MN 55112. 651/286-6700. **Fax:** 651/631-2561. **Contact:** John Risdall, Chairman. **World Wide Web address:** http://www.risdall.com. **Description:** An advertising firm specializing in environmental, high-tech, industrial, and business-to-business advertising. Founded in 1972.

ROBINS, KAPLAN, MILLER & CIRESI
2800 LaSalle Plaza, 800 LaSalle Avenue, Minneapolis MN 55402. 612/349-8500. **Fax:** 612/339-4181. **Contact:** Human Resources. **World Wide Web address:** http://www.rkmc.com. **Description:** A law firm specializing in medical malpractice, product liability, and similar areas. **NOTE:** Search and apply for positions online. **Positions advertised include:** Business Litigation Attorney Insurance Litigation Staff Attorney; Intellectual Property Litigation Associate. **Special programs:** Internships. **Corporate headquarters location:** This location. **Other U.S. locations:** Atlanta GA; Boston MA; Los Angeles CA; Naples FL; Washington DC. **Number of employees nationwide:** 600.

C.H. ROBINSON WORLDWIDE, INC.
8100 Mitchell Road, Eden Prairie MN 55344. 952/937-8500. **Contact:** Human Resources. **World Wide Web address:** http://www.chrobinson.com. **Description:** A worldwide transportation, logistics, and sourcing company founded in 1905. **NOTE:** Search and apply for positions online at http://www.chrwjobs.com. **Positions advertised include:** Business Analyst; Data Architect; IT Project Manager; Order Entry Clerk; Produce Sales; Senior Retail Business Analyst; Transportation Sales; Transportation Support. **Corporate headquarters location:** This location. **Other U.S. locations:** Nationwide. **International locations:** Worldwide. **Listed on:** National Association of Securities Dealers Automated Quotation (NASDAQ). **Stock exchange symbol:** CHRW. **Number of employees worldwide:** 4,800.

ROCHESTER METHODIST HOSPITAL
201 West Center Street, Rochester MN 55902-3003. 507/286-7890. **Contact:** Human Resources. **World Wide Web address:** http://www.mayo.org. **Description:** A 794-bed hospital offering acute care and outpatient services through its Epilepsy Monitoring Unit; a perinatal care center for high-risk pregnancies; a psoriasis and dermatology program; an intraoperative radiation surgical suite; transplant programs for bone marrow, kidney, liver, and pancreas diseases; and a women's cancer center. Rochester Methodist Hospital is an affiliate of the Mayo Clinic. **NOTE:** Search and apply for positions online. **Positions advertised include:** Administrator; Administrator, health Information Operations; Application Analyst; Biomedical Engineer; Cardiac Monitor Technician; Clinical Nurse Specialist; Contract Manager; Creative Services Director; Cytogenetics Education Specialist.

ROCK-TENN COMPANY
2250 Wabash Avenue, St. Paul MN 55114. 651/641-4938. **Fax:** 651/641-4469. **Contact:** Human Resources. **World Wide Web address:** http://www.rocktenn.com. **Description:** Rock-Tenn Company is a leading manufacturer of packaging products, merchandising displays and recycled paperboard. **Corporate headquarters location:** Norcross GA. **Operations at this facility include:** This location is a paperboard mill.

ROCKWELL AUTOMATION
6950 Washington Avenue South, Eden Prairie MN 55344. 952/942-3600. **Contact:** Human Resources. **World Wide Web address:** http://www.rockwellautomation.com. **Description:** The company has three operating segments: control systems including motor starters, relays and signaling devices; power systems, which includes power transmission products; and FirstPoint Contact, which includes call center systems, computer telephony integration software and management systems. **Positions advertised include:** Product Marketing Manager; Application Engineer. **Corporate headquarters location:** Milwaukee WI.

ROSEMOUNT INC.
8200 Market Boulevard, Chanhassen MN 55317. 952/941-5560. **Recorded jobline:** 952/828-3513. **Contact:** Human Resources. **E-mail address:** rmdhr@emersonprocess.com. **World Wide Web address:** http://www.rosemount.com. **E-mail address:** rmdhr@emersonprocess.com. **Description:** Engaged in the design and manufacture of precision measurement and control instrumentation for the aerospace and process control industries. Rosemount's process instrumentation products are used to control flow, level, pressure, and temperature. **NOTE:** Search and apply for positions online. **Positions advertised include:** Human Resources Analyst; Production Supervisors; Project Software Engineer. **Parent company:** Emerson

RYAN COMPANIES U.S., INC.
50 South 10th Street, Suite 300, Minneapolis MN 55403-2012. 612/492-4000. **Fax:** 612/492-3000. **Contact:** Director of Human Resources. **E-mail address:** opportunity@ryancompanies.com. **World Wide Web address:** http://www.ryancompanies.com. **Description:** Engaged in the design and construction of commercial projects including corporate office, manufacturing, industrial, product distribution, high-tech, medical and retail buildings. The company also provides property management and turnkey development services. **NOTE:** Entry-level positions and part-time jobs are offered. **Positions advertised include:** Project Manager. **Special programs:** Internships; Training; Co-ops. **Corporate headquarters location:** This location. **Other U.S. locations:** Chicago IL; Phoenix AZ; Cedar Rapids IA; Des Moines IA. **Listed on:** Privately held. **Annual sales/revenues:** More than $100 million. **Number of employees nationwide:** 300.

S-T INDUSTRIES, INC.
301 Armstrong Boulevard North, P.O. Box 517, St. James MN 56081-0517. 507/375-3211. **Toll-free phone:** 800/326-2039. **Fax:** 507/375-4503. **Contact:** Melanie Minehan, Personnel. **World Wide Web address:** http://www.stindustries.com. **Description:** Manufactures and sells precision measuring instruments, optical comparators, and video inspection systems. **NOTE:** Entry-level positions are offered. **Corporate headquarters location:** This location. **Operations at this facility include:** Administration; Manufacturing; Research and Development; Sales; Service. **Listed on:** Privately held. **President:** Michael J. Smith. **Annual sales/revenues:** $5 - $10 million. **Number of employees at this location:** 125.

SPX CORPORATION
655 Eisenhower Drive, Owatonna MN 55060. 507/455-7000. **Fax:** 507/455-7300. **Contact:** Desiree Walsh, Personnel Manager. **World Wide Web address:** http://www.spx.com. **Description:** SPX conducts business in five segments: technical products and systems, industrial products and services, flow technology, cooling technologies, and services and service solutions **NOTE:** Entry-level positions and second and third shifts are offered. Search and apply for positions at: Monster.com. **Positions advertised include:** Buyer; Production Supervisor; Supplier Quality Engineer. **Special programs:** Internships. **Corporate headquarters location:** Charlotte NC. **Listed on:** New York Stock Exchange. **Stock exchange symbol:** SPW. **Number of employees at this location:** 550. **Number of employees worldwide:** 22,200.

SPX VALVES & CONTROLS
250 Riverside Avenue North, Sartell MN 56377. 320/259-2000. **Fax:** 320/259-2227. **Contact:** Human Resources. **World Wide Web address:** http://www.spxvalves.com. **Description:** An international manufacturer, seller, and servicer of industrial valves and flow control products for process industries such as municipal, HVAC, pulp and paper, chemical, power, and mining. **Positions advertised include:** Regional Sales Manager. **Special programs:** Internships. **Corporate headquarters location:** This location. **Other U.S. locations:** Nationwide. **Parent company:** SPX Corporation. **Operations at this facility include:** Administration; Manufacturing; Research and Development; Sales; Service. **Listed on:** New York Stock Exchange. **Stock exchange symbol:** SPW. **Number of employees at this location:** 600. **Number of employees nationwide:** 1,000.

SAGEBRUSH CORPORATION
3601 Minnesota Drive, Suite 550, Minneapolis MN 55435. 952/656-2999. **Toll-free phone:** 800/328-2923. **Fax:** 952/656-2993. **Contact:** Human Resources. **E-mail address:** hr@sagebrushcorp.com. **World Wide Web address:** http://www.sagebrushcorp.com. **Description:** A developer of software for libraries. Products are used by librarians as well as by library patrons. **NOTE:** Search and apply for positions online. **Positions advertised include:** Learning Resources Product Manager; Analytics Technical Specialist.

ST. BENEDICT'S SENIOR COMMUNITY
1810 Minnesota Boulevard SE, St. Cloud MN 56304. 320/654-2355. **Fax:** 320/252-8311. **Contact:** Melissa Baker, Recruitment Coordinator. **World Wide Web address:** http://www.centracare.com/stben/stben_stcloud.html. **Description:** Offers nonprofit health care and housing for older adults. St. Benedict's Senior Community provides nursing services to over 220 individuals who require 24-hour care. Saint Benedict's Senior Community also offers a subacute care unit, a special care unit, hospice care, and respite care. The center also operates a retirement community, an assisted living facility, income-based senior housing, a residential center for those in the early stages of Alzheimer's disease or memory loss, home care services, and a senior dining program for the residents of southeast St. Cloud. Founded in 1978. **NOTE:** Entry-level positions, part-time jobs, and second and third shifts are offered. **Positions advertised include:** Registered Nurse; Licensed Practical Nurse; Certified Nursing Assistant; Registered Dietician; Recreational Therapist. **Special programs:** Internships; Summer Jobs. **Internship information:** Unpaid internships are offered during the fall and spring. Opportunities are available in Human Resources, working with people suffering from cognitive disorders, and social services. For more information or to volunteer, call the Volunteer Coordinator at 320/252-0010. **Office hours:** Monday - Friday, 8:00 a.m. - 4:30 p.m. **Parent company:** CentraCare Health Systems. **Number of employees at this location:** 525.

ST. CLOUD HOSPITAL
1406 Sixth Avenue North, St. Cloud MN 56303. 320/251-2700. **Fax:** 320/255-5711. **Contact:** Employment Department. **E-mail address:** hrs@centracare.com. **World Wide Web address:** http://www.centracare.com. **Description:** A regional medical center offering a variety of medical specialties. **NOTE:** Search and apply for positions online. **Positions advertised include:** Community Initiatives Specialist; Diagnostic Medical Sonographer; Disease Management/Wellness Specialist; Pharmacist; Physical Therapist; Recruiter; Staff Psychotherapist; RN's. **Special programs:** Internships. **Operations at this facility include:** Health Care; Service. **Number of employees at this location:** 3,600.

ST. CLOUD STATE UNIVERSITY
204 Administrative Services, St. Cloud MN 56301. 320/308-3203. **Fax:** 320/308-1607. **Contact:** Human Resources. **E-mail address:** hr@condor.stcloudstate.edu. **World Wide Web address:** http://www.stcloudstate.edu. **Description:** A four-year state university offering 175 programs of study, with an enrollment of 16,000. **Positions advertised include:** Director of Affirmative Action and Social Equity; University Assessment Director; Dean of Undergraduate Studies; Alumni Director; Alumni Communications Specialist; Coordinator of Business Operations/Marketing; Various Faculty Positions. **Number of employees at this location:** 1,450.

ST. FRANCIS REGIONAL MEDICAL CENTER
1455 St. Francis Avenue, Shakopee MN 55379-3380. 952/403-3000. **Contact:** Human Resources. **World Wide Web address:** http://www.stfrancis-shakopee.com. **Description:** A non-profit hospital. **NOTE:** Search and apply for positions online. **Positions advertised include:** Cardiac Sonographer; CRNA's; Diagnostic Imaging Tech; Maintenance Engineer; Medical Lab Tech: MRI Tech; RN's; Surgical Tech. **Parent company:** Benedictine Health System, Park Nicollet Health Services, and Allina Hospitals and Clinics.

ST. JUDE MEDICAL, INC.
One Lillehei Plaza, St. Paul MN 55117-9983. 651/483-2000. **Fax:** 651/766-3045. **Contact:** Human Resources. **World Wide Web address:** http://www.sjm.com. **Description:** A world leader in the development of cardiovascular medical devices. The company operates through three divisions: Cardiac Surgery, which develops

mechanical heart valve devices; the Cardiac Rhythm Management Division, which manufactures cardiac rhythm products; and Daig, which specializes in the manufacture of catheters. **NOTE:** Search and apply for positions or submit resume online. **Positions advertised include:** Director, Global Application Services; Manager, R&D; marketing Manager; Principal Engineer; Sr. Business Analyst: Senior Information Technology Security & Control Analyst; Sr. Software Developer; Sr. Clinical Research Associate. **Corporate headquarters location:** This location. **International locations:** Worldwide. **Listed on:** New York Stock Exchange. **Stock exchange symbol:** STJ. **Annual sales/revenues:** More than $100 million. **Number of employees worldwide:** 7,400.

ST. MARIE'S GOPHER NEWS COMPANY
4918 Lightning Drive, Duluth MN 55811. 218/729-8746. **Contact:** Human Resources. **Description:** A distributor of periodicals, paperback books, trade books, audiotapes, videotapes, and children's toys. **Number of employees at this location:** 105.

ST. PAUL BAR AND RESTAURANT SUPPLY
655 Payne Avenue, St. Paul MN 55101. 651/774-0361. **Contact:** Human Resources. **Description:** Manufactures and distributes restaurant equipment. **NOTE:** Interested jobseekers should address all inquiries to Human Resources, Palm Brothers, 1031 Madeira Avenue, Minneapolis MN 55408.

ST. PAUL LINOLEUM & CARPET COMPANY
2956 Center Court, Eagan MN 55121. 651/686-7770. **Contact:** Clemment J. Commers, Owner/President. **World Wide Web address:** http://www.stpaullinocpt.com. **Description:** A floor-covering contractor and acoustical products distributor.

ST. PAUL PIONEER PRESS
345 Cedar Street, St. Paul MN 55101. 651/228-5002. **Recorded jobline:** 651/228-5008. **Contact:** Employee Relations Office. **E-mail address:** resumes@pioneerpress.com. **World Wide Web address:** http://www.pioneerplanet.com. **Description:** A newspaper publisher. **Special programs:** Internships. **Parent company:** Knight-Ridder, Inc. (Miami FL). **Operations at this facility include:** Manufacturing.

ST. PAUL TRAVELERS
385 Washington Street, St. Paul MN 55102. 651/310-7911. **Contact:** Human Resources. **World Wide Web address:** http://www.stpaul.com. **Description:** Provides property-liability and life insurance services. **NOTE:** Search and apply for positions online. **Positions advertised include:** Manager, Corporate Audit; HR Operations Staffing Manager; Claim Rep; Sr. Corporate Accounting Manager; Sr. Tax Specialist; Investigator; Director, Financial Analysis. **Corporate headquarters location:** This location. **Annual sales/revenues:** More than $100 million.

ST. THERESE HOME
8000 Bass Lake Road, New Hope MN 55428. 763/531-5000. **Fax:** 763/531-5004. **Contact:** Rand Brugger, Director of Human Resources. **Description:** A religious-sponsored nonprofit organization that provides long-term health care to the elderly. The company consists of a 302-bed care center, 220 units of senior housing, home care services, and a rehabilitation agency. **NOTE:** Entry-level positions and second and third shifts are offered. **Special programs:** Internships; Summer Jobs. **Corporate headquarters location:** This location. **Listed on:** Privately held. **Annual sales/revenues:** $11 - $20 million. **Number of employees at this location:** 600.

SARA LEE
2745 Long Lake Road, Roseville MN 55113. 651/636-8400. **Contact:** Personnel. **World Wide Web address:** http://www.saralee.com. **Description:** Produces bread and a variety of other wholesale bakery products. **Corporate headquarters location:** Chicago IL. **Listed on:** New York Stock Exchange. **Stock exchange symbol:** SLE.

SAXTON FERRIS
11900 Wayzata Boulevard, Suite 114, Minnetonka MN 55305-2010. 952/544-9300. **Fax:** 952/544-7911. **Contact:** June Ferris, General Manager. **World Wide Web address:** http://www.saxton-ferris.com. **Description:** A national Yellow Pages advertising agency. **NOTE:** Entry-level positions are offered. **Corporate headquarters location:** This location. **Parent company:** Ferris Marketing, Inc. **Operations at this facility include:** Service. **Annual sales/revenues:** $5 - $10 million.

SCHECHTER DOKKEN KANTER
100 Washington Avenue South, Suite 1600, Minneapolis MN 55401. 612/332-5500. **Fax:** 612/332-1529. **Contact:** Chuck Selcer, Shareholder. **E-mail address:** cselcer@sdkcpa.com. **World Wide Web address:** http://www.sdkcpa.com. **Description:** A regional accounting and management consulting firm performing audits, accounting, tax, employee benefits plan consulting, litigation support, and management consulting services. **Corporate headquarters location:** This location. **Operations at this facility include:** Service. **Number of employees at this location:** 50.

SCHOTT CORPORATION
1000 Parkers Lake Road, Wayazata MN 55391. 952/475-1173. **Fax:** 952/475-1786. **Contact:** Human Resources. **E-mail address:** denisev@schottcorp.com. **World Wide Web address:** http://www.schottcorp.com. **Description:** A manufacturer of electronic transformers, inductors, and magnetic components for telecommunications, measurement and control equipment, military and aerospace, and medical instrumentation and devices. **NOTE:** An application may be downloaded online and mailed to Human Resources, 1210 East College Drive, Marshall MN 56258, or faxed to: 507/532-4290.

SCICOM DATA SERVICES
10101 Bren Road East, Minnetonka MN 55343. 952/933-4200. **Toll-free phone:** 800/488-9087. **Contact:** Human Resources. **E-mail address:** inquire@scicom.com. **World Wide Web address:** http://www.scicom.com. **Description:** Provides document and mail processing services, marketing publication services, and information management. **Positions advertised include:** Laser Printer Operator.

SCIENCE MUSEUM OF MINNESOTA
120 West Kellogg Boulevard, St. Paul MN 55102. 651/221-2532. **Fax:** 651/221-4777. **Recorded jobline:** 651/221-4548. **Contact:** Human Resources. **E-mail address:** humanresources@smm.org. **World Wide Web address:** http://www.smm.org. **Description:** Science Museum of Minnesota is a private, nonprofit, educational and research institution organized to collect, study, and preserve objects of scientific significance and to interpret the objects, discoveries, and insights of science for the general public through its exhibits and education programs. The museum has exhibits in anthropology, biology, geography, paleontology, technology, cultural history, and natural history. Additionally, the museum houses a collection of over 1.5 million scientific objects and an Omnitheater that produces and distributes OMNIMAX films shown around the world. **NOTE:** Advanced degrees in the natural sciences are required for curatorial positions. **Positions advertised include:** Interpretive Naturalist. **Corporate headquarters location:** This location. **Operations at this facility include:** Administration. **Number of employees at this location:** 600.

SCIMED LIFE SYSTEMS, INC.
One SciMed Place, Maple Grove MN 55311-1566. 763/494-1700. **Fax:** 763/494-2290. **Contact:** Personnel. **World Wide Web address:** http://www.bostonscientific.com. **Description:** SciMed Life Systems, Inc. develops, manufactures, and markets disposable medical devices principally for the nonsurgical diagnosis and treatment of coronary, peripheral, and neurovascular disease. **NOTE:** Search and apply for positions online. **Positions advertised include:** Technical Team Leader; Revenue Analyst; Sr. Financial Analyst; Quality Engineer; Sr. Process Engineer; Manufacturing Engineer; Principal Pharmaceutical Scientist; Quality Engineer. **Corporate headquarters location:** This location. **Parent company:** Boston Scientific. **Operations at this facility include:** Administration; Manufacturing; Research and Development. **Listed on:** NASDAQ. **Number of employees at this location:** 1,400.

SEAGATE TECHNOLOGY
7801 Computer Avenue South, Mail Station MRW-100, Bloomington MN 55435-5489. 952/844-8000. **Fax:** 952/402-7008. **Contact:** Human Resources. **World Wide Web address:** http://www.seagate.com. **Description:** Seagate Technology is a designer and manufacturer of data storage devices and related products including hard disk drives, tape drives, software, and systems for many different computer-related applications and operating systems. These products include 2.5 and 3.5 inch drives with memory storage capacity between 150 megabytes and one gigabyte. **NOTE:** Search and apply for positions online. **Special programs:** Training. **Corporate headquarters location:** Scotts Valley CA. **Other U.S. locations:** OK. **Operations at this facility include:** This location is a manufacturing facility. **Annual sales/revenues:** More than $100 million. **Number of employees at this location:** 3,500. **Number of employees nationwide:** 89,000.

SECURITAS
5810 West 78th Street, Suite 100, Bloomington MN 55420. 952/844-9015. **Contact:** Human Resources. **World Wide Web address:** http://www.securitasgroup.com. **Description:** Securitas offers a full range of specialized protective services including premier property/high-rise services, health care/hospital services, special event services, ATM services, and patrol services. The company provides thousands of companies worldwide with investigation services, threat assessment services, and executive protection. **Positions advertised include:** Account Manager. **International locations:** Worldwide. **Operations at this facility include:** This location is a district office of the international investigation and security company. **Number of employees at this location:** 300. **Number of employees nationwide:** 100,000.

SENECA FOODS CORPORATION
P.O. Box 35, Blue Earth MN 56013. 507/526-2131. **Physical address:** 710 East Seventh Street, Blue Earth MN. **Contact:** Human Resources. **World Wide Web address:** http://www.senecafoods.com. **Description:** This location is a vegetable canning plant. Overall, Seneca Foods Corporation's products include canned and frozen vegetables and bottled, canned, and frozen fruit juice drinks. Brand names include Seneca, Libby's, and Tree Sweet. **Corporate headquarters location:** Marion NY.

SENECA FOODS CORPORATION
101 West Eighth Street, Glencoe MN 55336. 320/864-3151. **Fax:** 320/864-5779. **Contact:** Human Resources Manager. **World Wide Web address:** http://www.senecafoods.com. **Description:** Seneca Foods Corporation's products include canned and frozen vegetables and bottled, canned, and frozen fruit juice drinks. Brand names include Seneca, Libby's, and Tree Sweet. Seneca also offers air charter service through Seneca Flight Operations. **Corporate headquarters location:** Marion NY. **Other area locations:** Arlington MN; Blue Earth MN; LeSueur MN; Montgomery MN; Rochester MN. **Operations at this facility include:** This location is a vegetable canning plant.

SHELDAHL INC.
1150 Sheldahl Road, Northfield MN 55057. 507/663-8000. **Fax:** 507/663-8535. **Contact:** Tammy Krienke, Human Resources. **E-mail address:** hr@sheldahl.com. **World Wide Web address:** http://www.sheldahl.com. **Description:** Manufactures advanced laminates, high performance tapes, flexible printed circuitry for automotive and datacommunication markets. **Positions advertised include:** Product Engineer; Product Manager.

SHOP NBC
6740 Shady Oak Road, Eden Prairie MN 55344. 952/943-6000. **Contact:** Barry Schwerr, Personnel Director. **World Wide Web address:** http://www.shopnbc.com. **Description:** Operates a home shopping cable television channel. **NOTE:** Search and apply for positions online. **Positions advertised include:** Assistant Buyer; Data Architect; Business Development Manager; Graphic Designer; Interactive Merchandise Coordinator; Line Producer; Manager of System Administration; Risk Manager; Unix System Administrator.

SPSS INC.
4115 Highway 52 North, Suite 300, Rochester MN 55901. 507/288-5922. **Contact:** Human Resources. **World Wide Web address:** http://www.showcasecorp.com. **Description:** Provides predictive analytics software and solutions. **NOTE:** Search and apply for positions online. **Positions advertised include:** Global Support Center Specialist. **Corporate headquarters location:** Chicago IL.

SICO INC.
7525 Cahill Road, Edina MN 55439-2745. 952/941-1700. **Toll-free phone:** 800/328-6138. **Fax:** 952/941-6688. **Contact:** Human Resources. **World Wide Web address:** http://www.sicoinc.com. **Description:** A manufacturer of a diverse line of products including room-service centers, stages, tables, wall-beds, and other related products. Clients include schools and hotels.

SIGNATURE DINING
6300 Penn Avenue South, Richfield MN 55423-1139. 612/866-0041. **Contact:** Human Resources Manager. **Description:** This location houses administrative offices. Overall, Signature Dining provides vending machine and cafeteria services. **Corporate headquarters location:** This location. **Operations at this facility include:** Administration; Sales; Service.

SIGNATURE FLIGHT SUPPORT
3800 East 70th Street, Minneapolis MN 55450-1107. 612/726-5700. **Fax:** 612/726-5032. **Contact:** Human Resources Representative. **World Wide Web address:** http://www.signatureflight.com. **Description:** A fixed-base aviation operator at the Minneapolis-St. Paul International Airport. Signature Flight Support provides fuel, hangar, avionics, maintenance, and parts services to the corporate aircraft market.

SILGAN CONTAINERS
755 North Prior Avenue, St. Paul MN 55104. 651/643-3200. **Contact:** John Faltesek, Human Resources Manager. **World Wide Web address:** http://www.silgan.com. **Description:** Manufactures metal food cans, aluminum food containers, and convenience ends for food cans. **Corporate headquarters location:** Stamford CT.

SMEAD MANUFACTURING COMPANY
600 Smead Boulevard, Hastings MN 55033-2219. 651/437-4111. **Fax:** 800/959-9134. **Contact:** Director of Human Resources. **E-mail address:** jobs@smead.com. **World Wide Web address:** http://www.smead.com. **Description:** Manufactures die-cut paper. **Corporate headquarters location:** This location. **Operations at this facility include:** Manufacturing.

SMITHS MEDICAL MD, INC.
1265 Grey Fox Road, St. Paul MN 55112. 651/633-2556. **Fax:** 651/628-7153. **Contact:** Human Resources. **E-mail address:** hr@deltec.com. **World Wide Web address:** http://www.deltec.com. **Description:** Manufactures and markets ambulatory infusion systems, large-volume infusion pumps, and vascular access systems. **Corporate headquarters location:** This location.

SNYDER DRUG STORES
14525 Highway Seven, Minnetonka MN 55345. 952/935-5441. **Fax:** 952/936-2512. **Contact:** Lisa Kraft, Manager of Human Resources Development. **World Wide Web address:** http://www.snyderdrug.com. **Description:** Operates a chain of 120 retail drug stores in Minnesota, Wisconsin, and Montana. **Corporate headquarters location:** This location. **Listed on:** Privately held. **Parent company:** Katz Group (Canada). **Annual sales/revenues:** More than $100 million. **Number of employees at this location:** 125. **Number of employees nationwide:** 1,300.

SOFITEL HOTEL
5601 West 78th Street, Bloomington MN 55439. 952/835-1900. **Fax:** 952/835-2696. **Recorded jobline:** 952/835-1900x5959. **Contact:** Jeanne Bursch, Human Resources Director. **World Wide Web address:** http://www.sofitel.com. **Description:** The first North American location of the French hotel chain, offering 282 rooms.

SOFTWARE AG AMERICAS
1650 West 82nd Street, Suite 750, Bloomington MN 55431. 952/948-3500. **Fax:** 952/885-5979. **Contact:** Recruiting. **E-mail address:** jobs@softwareagusa.com. **World Wide Web address:** http://www.softwareagusa.com. **Description:** Provides system software and high-performance databases to allow customers to run cross-platform applications, and to simplify the exchange of data between systems. **Corporate headquarters location:** Reston VA. **International locations:** Germany. **Parent company:** Software AG (Germany). **Operations at this facility include:** This location develops software products and serves as a regional sales office for Software AG Americas.

SOLVAY PHARMACEUTICALS
210 Main Street West, Baudette MN 56623. 218/634-3500. **Fax:** 218/634-3540. **Contact:** Human Resources. **E-mail address:** careers@solvay.com. **World Wide Web address:** http://www.solvaypharmaceuticals-us.com. **Description:** Develops a variety of prescription pharmaceuticals used to treat psychiatric, hormonal, and gastrointestinal disorders. **NOTE:** Search and apply for positions online. **Other U.S. locations:** Marietta GA. **Number of employees worldwide:** 30,000.

SOUTHWEST STATE UNIVERSITY
1501 State Street, Marshall MN 56258. 507/537-7021. **Contact:** Office of Human Resources. **E-mail address:** okrinab@southwest.msus.edu. **World Wide Web address:** http://www.southwest.msus.edu. **Description:** A four-year, state university with approximately 2,400 students. The university offers graduate programs in education and management. **Positions advertised include:** Assistant/Associate Professor, Various Disciplines; Athletic Director.

SPECTRASCIENCE
14405 21st Avenue North, Suite 111, Minneapolis MN 55447. 763/745-4120. **Contact:** Office Administrator. **Description:** Designs, manufactures, and markets laser-based medical devices for the treatment of heart and blood vessel diseases.

SPECTRUM COMMUNITY HEALTH, INC.
1831 24th Street NW, Rochester MN 55901. 507/282-8052. **Contact:** Marilyn Hanson, Human Resources. **Description:** A home health care provider that offers nursing, rehabilitation, and personal care assistance to individuals of all ages.

SPEEDWAY SUPERAMERICA LLC
2060 Centre Point Boulevard, Suite 1, Mendota Heights MN 55120. **Toll-free phone:** 800/328-2927. **Recorded jobline:** 800/328-2927 ext. 146. **Contact:** Human Resources Manager. **World Wide Web address:** http://www.speedway.com. **Description:** Operates a chain of over 1,700 convenience store/gas stations in 9 states in the Midwest. **NOTE:** Entry-level positions are offered. **Special programs:** Internships. **Office hours:** Monday - Friday, 8:00 a.m. - 4:30 p.m. **Corporate headquarters location:** Enon OH. **Parent company:** Marathon Ashland Petroleum, LLC. **Operations at this facility include:** Administration; Regional Headquarters. **Number of employees at this location:** 100. **Number of employees nationwide:** 10,000.

STAR TRIBUNE
425 Portland Avenue South, Minneapolis MN 55488. 612/673-4000. **Recorded jobline:** 612/673-4075. **Contact:** Human Resources. **World Wide Web address:** http://www.startribune.com. **Description:** A daily newspaper with a weekday circulation of 412,400 and a Sunday circulation of 696,100. The paper's employees are divided into four components: one to serve reader customers, one to serve marketer customers (primarily advertisers), a production and distribution function, and support services. **Positions advertised include:** Sr. Financial Analyst; Retirement Benefits Administrator. **Parent company:** McClatchey Newspapers. **Number of employees at this location:** 3,300.

STEARNS INC.
1100 Stearns Drive, Sauk Rapids MN 56379. 320/252-1642. **Fax:** 320/252-4425. **Recorded jobline:** 800/783-2767. **Contact:** Human Resources. **E-mail address:** jobs@stearnsnet.com. **World Wide Web address:** http://www.stearnsinc.com. **Description:** Manufactures life jackets and other flotation devices. **Positions advertised include:** Sewing Machine Operator; Buyer; Product Manager; Sales Manager. **Special programs:** Internships. **Corporate headquarters location:** This location. **Parent company:** K2. **Operations at this facility include:** Administration; Divisional Headquarters; Manufacturing; Sales.

STERION, INC.
13828 Lincoln Street NE, Minneapolis MN 55304-6949. 763/755-9516. **Fax:** 763/755-9466. **Contact:** Human Resources. **Description:** Assembles medical devices and manufactures closed-suction wound drainage products. **Corporate headquarters location:** This location. **Listed on:** NASDAQ. **Stock exchange symbol:** STEN. **Annual sales/revenues:** Less than $5 million.

STEVENS COMMUNITY MEDICAL CENTER
400 East First Street, Box 660, Morris MN 56267. 320/589-1313. **Fax:** 320/589-3533. **Contact:** Personnel. **World Wide Web address:** http://www.scmcmorris.com. **Description:** A nonprofit, multispecialty clinic and hospital serving the west central Minnesota region. Founded in 1951. **Company slogan:** Caring is our reason for being. **Corporate headquarters location:** This location. **President/CEO:** John Rau.

STORAGETEK
33 South Sixth Street, 4130 Multifoods Tower, Suite 4130, Minneapolis MN 55402. 612/339-6161. **Fax:** 612/321-5718. **Contact:** Human Resources Manager. **World Wide Web address:** http://www.stortek.com. **Description:** Manufactures high-performance computer information storage and retrieval systems for mainframe and mid-frame computers and networks. Products include automated cartridge systems, random access subsystems, and fault-tolerant disk arrays. The company also distributes equipment; sells new peripherals, software, and hardware; and offers support services. Founded in 1969. **NOTE:** Search and apply for positions online. **Other U.S. locations:** Nationwide. **Number of employees worldwide:** 7,000.

STORK TWIN CITY TESTING
662 Cromwell Avenue, St. Paul MN 55114. 651/645-3601. **Toll-free phone:** 888/645-8378. **Fax:** 651/659-7348. **Contact:** Human Resources. **World Wide Web address:** http://www.twincitytesting.com. **Description:** Provides environmental consulting, geotechnical engineering, specialty testing, and chemistry services.

STREATER STORE FIXTURES
411 South First Avenue, Albert Lea MN 56007-1779. 507/373-0611. **Fax:** 507/373-7630. **Contact:** Human Resources. **World Wide Web address:** http://www.streater.com. **Description:** A manufacturer of furniture and shelving fixtures for use in retail stores. **Parent company:** Marmon Retail Services.

SUNRISE PACKAGING
9937 Goodhue Street NE, Blaine MN 55449. 763/785-2505. **Fax:** 763/785-2210. **Contact:** Mr. James Hartley, Controller. **World Wide Web address:** http://www.sunpack.com. **Description:** Manufactures three-ring binders and storage albums for software, audio, and video use.

SUPERVALU INC.
P.O. Box 990, Minneapolis MN 55440. 952/828-4000. **Fax:** 952/828-4803. **Contact:** Michael Overline, General Director of Human Resources. **E-mail address:** super.careers@supervalu.com. **World Wide Web address:** http://www.supervalu.com. **Description:** One of the nation's largest food retailers and distribution companies, supplying grocery, health and beauty aids, and general merchandise products. In the corporate retail sector, SUPERVALU operates over 1,400 stores in 39 states under the following names: bigg's, Cub Foods, Shop 'n Save, Save-A-Lot, Scott's Foods, Deals, Shoppers Food Warehouse, and Hornbachers. **Positions advertised include:** Buyer; Category Manager; Risk Control Manager; Staff Accountant. **Corporate headquarters location:** This location. **Other U.S. locations:** Nationwide. **Subsidiaries include:** Hazelwood Farms Bakeries manufactures frozen bakery products. **Listed on:** New York Stock Exchange. **Stock exchange symbol:** SVU. **Annual sales/revenues:** More than $100 million. **Number of employees nationwide:** 57,000.

SYNGENTA SEEDS
7500 Olsen Memorial Highway, Golden Valley MN 55427. 763/593-7333. **Contact:** Human Resources. **World Wide Web address:** http://www.syngenta.com. **Description:** A researcher, producer, and marketer of agricultural seeds and products. **Parent company:** Syngenta AG. **Listed on:** New York Stock Exchange. **Stock exchange symbol:** SYT.

SYNTEGRA, INC.
4201 Lexington Avenue North, Arden Hills MN 55126. 651/415-2999. **Contact:** Katy Adams, Vice President of Human Resources. **World Wide Web address:** http://www.us.syntegra.com. **Description:** Provides a range of services including design consulting, program management, application development, network integration, and life cycle support. **Positions advertised include:** Sr. Solutions Architect, Provisioning; Project Manager, Network Services; Solutions Architect, Lotus Notes; VoIP Integration Engineer, Vocera.

TCF FINANCIAL CORPORATION
TCF BANK F.S.B.
801 Marquette Avenue, Minneapolis MN 55402. 612/661-8450. **Fax:** 612/661-8277. **Recorded jobline:** 612/661-8989. **Contact:** Human Resources. **World Wide Web address:** http://www.tcfbank.com. **Description:** A bank holding company. **Positions advertised include:** Business Systems Analyst; Proof Operator; Graphic Design Specialist; Region Manager; Administrative Assistant; Collector; Mail Clerk; Underwriter; Operations Specialist. **Corporate headquarters location:** This location. **Other U.S. locations:** Oakbrook IL; Ann Arbor MI; Pontiac MI; Milwaukee WI. **Subsidiaries include:** TCF Bank (also at this location) is a thrift and banking institution that operates 395 retail branches in Colorado, Illinois, Minnesota, Wisconsin, Indiana, and Michigan. Other subsidiaries provide consumer lending, insurance, mutual funds, title insurance, and mortgage banking products and services. **Listed on:** New York Stock Exchange. **Number of employees at this location:** 2,500. **Number of employees nationwide:** 3,500.

TRW AUTOMOTIVE ELECTRONICS
5676 Industrial Park Road, Winona MN 55987. 507/457-3750. **Fax:** 507/454-5977. **Contact:** Paula Brown, Human Resources Recruiter. **World Wide Web address:** http://www.trw.com. **Description:** A full-service contract manufacturer of switches and controls, primarily for the automotive industry. **NOTE:** Search and apply for positions online. **Positions advertised include:** Sr. Software Engineer. **Special programs:** Internships. **Parent company:** Northrop Grumman.

TSI INC.
P.O. Box 64394, St. Paul MN 55164. 651/483-0900. **Physical address:** 500 Cardigan Road, Shore View MN 55126. **Fax:** 651/490-2748. **Contact:** Human Resources Manager. **Description:** Engaged in the production of particle research instruments, wire-hot film anemometry, laser velocimetry, and mass flow transconductors. **NOTE:** Resumes accepted only for open positions. **Positions advertised include:** SAP Business Analyst; Project Manager; Mechanical Engineer; Mechanical Designer; Electrical Engineer.

TARGET STORES
1000 Nicollet Mall, Minneapolis MN 55403. 612/304-6073. **Physical address:** 33 South Sixth Street, Minneapolis MN 55402. **Fax:** 612/696-3731. **Contact:** Human

Resources. **World Wide Web address:** http://www.targetcorp.com. **Description:** Operates a retail chain of discount department stores. **NOTE:** Search and apply for positions online. **Positions advertised include:** IT Auditor; Specialist Copywriter; Business Analyst; Sr. CAD Designer; Sr. Systems Engineer; Technical Architect; Electronic Production Artist; Sr. Manager, Marketing Planning; Director, Creative Services; Human Resources Representative; Sr. Measurement Analyst. **Corporate headquarters location:** This location.

TELEX COMMUNICATIONS, INC.
12000 Portland Avenue South, Burnsville MN 55337. 952/884-4051. **Fax:** 952/884-0043. **Contact:** Kathy Curran, Vice President of Human Resources. **E-mail address:** humanresources@telex.com. **World Wide Web address:** http://www.telex.com. **Description:** Manufactures electronic components for intercom systems and related communications products. **Positions advertised include:** Director, Strategic Marketing; Manager, Engineering Services; Product Manager. **Corporate headquarters location:** This location. **Other U.S. locations:** Nationwide.

TELEX COMMUNICATIONS, INC.
1720 East 14th Street, Glencoe MN 55336. 320/864-3177. **Fax:** 952/886-3225. **Contact:** Judy Graupmann, Human Resources Manager. **World Wide Web address:** http://www.telex.com. **Description:** Manufactures electronic components for intercom systems and related communications products. **Special programs:** Internships. **Corporate headquarters location:** Minneapolis MN. **Other U.S. locations:** Nationwide. **Listed on:** Privately held. **Number of employees nationwide:** 3,000.

TENNANT COMPANY
701 North Lilac Drive, P.O. Box 1452, Minneapolis MN 55440. 763/540-1200. **Fax:** 763/513-1754. **Contact:** Human Resources. **E-mail address:** info@tennantco.com. **World Wide Web address:** http://www.tennantco.com. **Description:** Manufactures floor maintenance equipment including industrial sweepers and scrubbers, floor coating machinery, and commercial equipment. **NOTE:** Visit monster.com to search for current positions. **Corporate headquarters location:** This location. **Operations at this facility include:** Administration; Engineering and Design; Manufacturing; Research and Development; Sales. **Listed on:** New York Stock Exchange. **Stock exchange symbol:** TNC. **Number of employees at this location:** 1,000.

THERMO KING CORPORATION
314 West 90th Street, Bloomington MN 55429. 952/887-2200. **Fax:** 952/885-3404. **Contact:** Human Resources Manager. **World Wide Web address:** http://www.thermoking.com. **Description:** Serves the refrigeration and air conditioning needs of buses and tractor-trailer centers. Thermo King is a world leader in temperature-controlled transport. **Corporate headquarters location:** This location. **Other U.S. locations:** Montgomery AL; Louisville GA; Hastings NE. **Subsidiaries include:** I.C.C. **Parent company:** Westinghouse. **Operations at this facility include:** Administration; Divisional Headquarters; Manufacturing; Regional Headquarters; Research and Development; Sales; Service. **Number of employees at this location:** 850. **Number of employees nationwide:** 2,000.

THERMO RAMSEY
501 90th Avenue NW, Minneapolis MN 55433. 763/783-2500. **Fax:** 763/783-2525. **Contact:** Human Resources. **World Wide Web address:** http://www.thermo.com. **Description:** Manufactures industrial instruments for the measurement, display, and control of process variables. **NOTE:** Search and apply for positions online. **Positions advertised include:** Product Marketing Manager. **Corporate headquarters location:** Waltham MA. **Parent company:** Thermo Electron. **Operations at this facility include:** Administration; Divisional Headquarters; Research and Development; Sales; Service. **Number of employees at this location:** 255.

3M
3M Center, Building 224-1W-02, St. Paul MN 55144-1000. 651/733-0694. **Contact:** Staffing Resources. **World Wide Web address:** http://www.3m.com. **Description:** Manufactures products in three sectors: Industrial and Consumer; Information, Imaging, and Electronic; and Life Sciences. The Industrial and Consumer Sector includes a variety of products under brand names including 3M, Scotch, Post-it, Scotch-Brite, and Scotchgard. The Information, Imaging, and Electronic Sector is a leader in several high-growth global industries including telecommunications, electronics, electrical, imaging, and memory media. The Life Sciences Sector serves two broad market categories: health care, and traffic and personal safety. In the health care market, 3M produces medical and surgical supplies, drug delivery systems, and dental products; in traffic and personal safety, 3M is a leader in products for transportation safety, worker protection, vehicle and sign graphics, and out-of-home advertising. **Corporate headquarters location:** This location. **International locations:** Worldwide. **Listed on:** New York Stock Exchange. **Stock exchange symbol:** MMM. **Number of employees nationwide:** 33,000. **Number of employees worldwide:** 67,000.

3M COTTAGE GROVE
P.O. Box 33131, St. Paul MN 55133. 651/458-2000. **Physical address:** 10746 Innovation Road, Cottage Grove MN 55016-4600. **Contact:** Human Resources Manager. **World Wide Web address:** http://www.3m.com. **Description:** 3M manufactures products in three sectors: Industrial and Consumer; Information, Imaging, and Electronic; and Life Sciences. The Industrial and Consumer Sector includes a variety of products under brand names including 3M, Scotch, Post-it, Scotch-Brite, and Scotchgard. The Information, Imaging, and Electronic Sector is a leader in several high-growth global industries including telecommunications, electronics, electrical, imaging, and memory media. The Life Science Sector serves two broad market categories: health care, and traffic and personal safety. In the health care market, 3M is a leading provider of medical and surgical supplies, drug delivery systems, and dental products; in traffic and personal safety, 3M is a leader in products for transportation safety, worker protection, vehicle and sign graphics, and out-of-home advertising. **Corporate headquarters location:** St. Paul MN. **Operations at this facility include:** This location manufactures photographic chemicals and supplies. **Listed on:** New York Stock Exchange. **Stock exchange symbol:** MMM.

THRIFTY WHITE STORES
6901 East Fishlake Road, Suite 118, Maple Grove MN 55369. 763/513-4300. **Contact:** Shannon Kadlec, Human Resources. **E-mail address:** skadlec@thriftywhite.com. **World Wide Web address:** http://www.thriftywhite.com. **Description:** Operates a retail drugstore chain with over 50 rural locations in Minnesota, the Dakotas, Iowa, and Montana. **Positions advertised include:** Sales Associate. **Corporate headquarters location:** This location. **Operations at this facility include:** Administration; Sales. **Number of employees at this location:** 60. **Number of employees nationwide:** 1,150.

TOM THUMB FOOD MARKETS, INC.
POLKA DOT DAIRY, INC.
110 East 17th Street, Hastings MN 55033. 651/437-9023. **Fax:** 651/438-2638. **Contact:** Todd Huffman, Director of Human Resources. **World Wide Web address:** http://www.randalls.com. **Description:** Tom Thumb Food Markets operates an area grocery and convenience store chain. Polka Dot Dairy (also at this location) is a distributor of bottled milk. **Corporate headquarters location:** This location. **Parent company:** Randalls. **Operations at this facility include:** Administration; Regional Headquarters; Sales; Service.

THE TORO COMPANY
8111 Lyndale Avenue South, Bloomington MN 55420. 952/888-8801. **Contact:** Dave Tourville, Corporate Human Resources Manager. **World Wide Web address:** http://www.toro.com. **Description:** Engaged in the manufacture and marketing of outdoor power products for consumer, irrigation, and commercial industries. Products include lawn mowers, snowblowers, tractors, trimmers, irrigation systems and components, and appliances marketed under the brand names Toro, Wheel Horse, and Lawn-Boy. The company distributes its products through 10,800 independent retailers worldwide. **Positions advertised include:** Hydraulics Design Engineer; Retail Finance Program Manager; Sales Tax Accountant; Designer/Sr. Designer; Engineering Administrative Coordinator. **Corporate headquarters location:** This location. **Listed on:** New York Stock Exchange. **Stock exchange symbol:** TTC.

TOWERS PERRIN
8000 Norman Center Drive, Suite 1200, Minneapolis MN 55437-1097. 952/842-5600. **Contact:** Kathy Halverson, Office Administrator. **World Wide Web address:** http://www.towers.com. **Description:** A management consulting firm. **NOTE:** Search and apply for positions online. **Positions advertised include:** Senior Retirement Consultant. **Other U.S. locations:** Nationwide.

THE TRANE COMPANY
4833 White Bear Parkway, St. Paul MN 55110. 651/407-4199. **Contact:** Human Resources. **E-mail address:** whitebearjobs@trane.com. **World Wide Web address:** http://www.trane.com. **Description:** Manufactures and markets heating and air conditioning products for residential, commercial, and industrial buildings. **NOTE:** Search and apply for positions online. **Positions advertised include:** Construction Project Manager; Engineering Manager; Financial Manager; Marketing Communications Specialist. **Corporate headquarters location:** Piscataway NJ. **Parent company:** American Standard, Inc. **Operations at this facility include:** Administration; Divisional Headquarters; Financial Offices; Manufacturing; Policy Development; Sales; Service.

TRANSITION NETWORKS
6475 City West Parkway, Eden Prairie MN 55344. 952/941-7600. **Fax:** 952/941-2322. **Contact:** Human Resources. **E-mail address:** hr@transition.com. **World Wide Web address:** http://www.transition.com. **Description:** Provides network connectivity solutions that allow for the conversion of different media types. **Positions advertised include:** Project Manager. **Corporate headquarters location:** This location.

TRANSPORT CORPORATION OF AMERICA, INC.
1715 Yankee Doodle Road, Eagan MN 55121. 651/686-2500. **Toll-free phone:** 800/345-0479. **Fax:** 651/994-5785. **Contact:** Human Resources. **E-mail address:** humanresources@transportamerica.com. **World Wide Web address:** http://www.transportamerica.com. **Description:** An irregular route truckload motor carrier, covering 48 states. Founded in 1984. **NOTE:** Entry-level positions are offered. **Positions advertised include:** Cargo Claims Supervisor; Fleet Manager; Planner; Director of Safety; ERS Coordinator. **Corporate headquarters location:** This location. **Operations at this facility include:** Administration; Sales; Service. **Listed on:** NASDAQ. **Stock exchange symbol:** TCAM. **President/CEO:** Robert Meyers. **Annual sales/revenues:** Less than $5 million. **Number of employees at this location:** 275. **Number of employees nationwide:** 1,150. **Number of employees worldwide:** 2,700.

TRAVELERS EXPRESS COMPANY
1550 Utica Avenue South, Suite 100, St Louis Park MN 55416-5301. 952/591-3000. **Toll-free phone:** 800/328-5678. **Fax:** 952/591-3121. **Contact:** Human Resources Manager. **Description:** Sells money orders and automated dispensers to convenience store chains, grocery store chains, and oil companies with 20 or more outlets. **Parent company:** Viad.

TREEV, INC.
6 Pine Tree Drive, Suite 150, Arden Hills MN 55112. 651/486-7901. **Toll-free phone:** 800/229-5430. **Fax:** 651/486-7911. **Contact:** Human Resources. **E-mail address:** hr@treev.com. **World Wide Web address:** http://www.treev.com. **Description:** Provides software and consulting services to financial institutions. **NOTE:** Search and apply for positions or submit application online. **Corporate headquarters location:** Herndon VA.

TRIMIN SYSTEMS, INC.
3030 Center Point Drive, Suite 100, St. Paul MN 55113. 651/636-7667. **Fax:** 651/636-9932. **Contact:** Staffing. **World Wide Web address:** http://www.triminsystems.com. **Description:** Provides MAPICS manufacturing solutions. Founded in 1986.

TRUTH HARDWARE
700 West Bridge Street, Owatonna MN 55060. 507/451-5620. **Toll-free phone:** 800/866-7884. **Fax:** 507/451-5655. **Contact:** Human Resources Manager. **E-mail address:** awalter@truth.com. **World Wide Web address:** http://www.truth.com. **Description:** Manufactures hardware for windows, doors, and skylights.

TWIN CITY FAN COMPANIES
5959 Trenton Lane North, Minneapolis MN 55442-3237. 763/551-7600. **Fax:** 763/551-7601. **Contact:** Human Resources Department. **E-mail address:** hr@tcf.om. **World Wide Web address:** http://www.tcf.com. **Description:** Twin City Fan Companies is a leader in the design and manufacture of air-moving equipment. The company has a complete line of fans and blowers from 1/6 HP to over 1,000 HP for various commercial and industrial uses. Products include airfoil design ventilating fans, packaged ventilating sets, material handling fans, high-pressure and induced draft fans, axial fans, propeller fans, and custom designs and accessories. Each fan and blower produced is manufactured to the customer's specifications. The company operates manufacturing facilities in Mitchell and Brookings SD and maintains a nationwide network of sales representatives. **Positions advertised include:** Sr. Buyer; Design Engineer; Sales Application Engineer. **Corporate headquarters location:** This location. **Subsidiaries include:** Azen Manufacturing; Clarage; TCF Aerovent, Inc.; TC Axial; Twin City Fan & Blower Company.

TYCO PLASTICS, INC.
1401 West 94th Street, Minneapolis MN 55431. 952/884-7281. **Toll-free phone:** 800/873-3941. **Contact:** Diane Gibson, Director of Personnel. **World Wide Web address:** http://www.tycoplastics.com. **Description:** Manufactures and markets plastic products including Film-Gard brand plastic sheeting; a full line of sheeting products including construction film for building and remodeling; do-it-yourself products such

as drop cloths and landscape films; and agricultural products for farm applications. Tyco Plastics also makes private label products including garbage, waste, and tall kitchen household bags; lawn and leaf bags; sandwich bags; and reclosable bags. **Positions advertised include:** Outside Sales Representative; Program Director; Regional Sales Manager; Senior Engineering Technician. **Corporate headquarters location:** Phoenix AZ. **Parent company:** Tyco International, Ltd. **Operations at this facility include:** Divisional Headquarters; Manufacturing; Sales. **Listed on:** New York Stock Exchange. **Stock exchange symbol:** TYC. **Number of employees at this location:** 150. **Number of employees nationwide:** 2,100.

UFE INC.
1850 South Greeley Street, P.O. Box 7, Stillwater MN 55082-0007. 651/351-4273. **Fax:** 651/351-4287. **Recorded jobline:** 651/351-4397. **Contact:** Janet Ziebell, Human Resources. **E-mail address:** janet.ziebell@ufeinc.com. **World Wide Web address:** http://www.ufeinc.com. **Description:** A leader in the design and production of precision-molded plastic components. Founded in 1953. **NOTE:** Entry-level positions are offered. **Special programs:** Internships; Apprenticeships; Training; Co-ops. **Corporate headquarters location:** This location. **Other U.S. locations:** El Paso TX; Dresser WI; River Falls WI. **Operations at this facility include:** Administration; Manufacturing; Regional Headquarters; Research and Development; Sales; Service. **Listed on:** Privately held. **Annual sales/revenues:** $51 - $100 million. **Number of employees at this location:** 200. **Number of employees worldwide:** 800.

URS CORPORATION
Thresher Square, 700 South Third Street, Minneapolis MN 55415-1199. 612/370-0700. **Fax:** 612/370-1378. **Contact:** Personnel. **World Wide Web address:** http://www.urscorp.com. **Description:** A fully-integrated engineering and architectural organization that specializes in the project management, design, and construction management of industrial, private, and government facilities. URS Corporation also provides process and environmental engineering, architectural design, and total support services. **Positions advertised include:** CADD Technician; Project Administrator; Project Architect/Designer; Project Environmental Engineer; Regional Controller. **Corporate headquarters location:** San Francisco CA. **Other U.S. locations:** Nationwide. **International locations:** Worldwide. **Listed on:** New York Stock Exchange. **Stock exchange symbol:** URS.

U.S. BANCORP
U.S. BANK
800 Nicollet Mall, Minneapolis MN 55402. 612/973-1111. **Contact:** Human Resources. **World Wide Web address:** http://www.usbank.com. **Description:** U.S. Bancorp is one of the largest bank holding companies in the Northwest. **NOTE:** Search and apply for positions online. **Corporate headquarters location:** This location.

U.S. BANCORP PIPER JAFFRAY
800 Nicollet Mall, Suite 800, Minneapolis MN 55402. 612/303-6000. **Toll-free phone:** 800/333-6000. **Fax:** 612/303-1311. **Contact:** Erica Tulay, Recruiter. **World Wide Web address:** http://www.piperjaffray.com. **Description:** A securities firm that offers individual investors and businesses a full array of investment services through 73 branch offices in 17 Midwest, Mountain, and Pacific Northwest states. The company also provides capital markets and investment management services.

U.S. DEPARTMENT OF HOUSING & URBAN DEVELOPMENT
Kinnard Financial Center, 920 Second Street South, Suite 1300, Minneapolis MN 55402. 612/370-3000. **Fax:** 612/370-3220. **Contact:** Human Resources. **World Wide Web address:** http://www.hud.gov/local/min. **Description:** Acquires foreclosed housing in order to sell it back to the general public. Department of Housing & Urban Development provides mortgage/loan management services, subsidized housing, and assistance to homeless people.

U.S. FEDERAL RESERVE BANK OF MINNEAPOLIS
90 Hennepin Avenue, Minneapolis MN 55401. 612/204-5000. **Fax:** 612/204-5339. **Recorded jobline:** 877/766-8533. **Contact:** Human Resources. **World Wide Web address:** http://www.minneapolisfed.org. **Description:** One of 12 regional Federal Reserve banks that, along with the Federal Reserve Board of Governors in Washington DC and the Federal Open Market Committee, form the Federal Reserve System. As the nation's central bank, the Federal Reserve System is charged with three major responsibilities: monetary policy, banking supervision and regulation, and processing payments. **Positions advertised include:** Audit manager; Community Affairs Specialist; Lead Database Administrator. **Operations at this facility include:** Administration; Regional Headquarters; Research and Development. **Number of employees at this location:** 1,150.

UNITED DEFENSE
Armament Systems Division, 4800 East River Road, Minneapolis MN 55421-1498. 763/572-7615. **Fax:** 763/572-3300. **Contact:** Human Resources. **World Wide Web address:** http://www.udlp.com. **Description:** Designs, develops, an produces combat vehicles, artillery, naval guns, missile launchers, and precision munitions for the U.S. Department of Defense and allies worldwide. **NOTE:** Search and apply for positions online. **Positions advertised include:** CDM Specialist; Principal Field Service Engineer; Sr. Project Specialty Engineer; Testability Project Engineer; Sr. Contracts Representative. **Special programs:** Internships. **Corporate headquarters location:** Arlington VA. **Parent company:** The Carlyle Group. **Operations at this facility include:** Divisional Headquarters. **Listed on:** New York Stock Exchange. **Stock exchange symbol:** UDI. **Number of employees at this location:** 1,500. **Number of employees worldwide:** 7,000.

UNITED HARDWARE DISTRIBUTION COMPANY
5005 Nathan Lane North, Plymouth MN 55442. 763/559-1800. **Contact:** Lisa Hoey, Human Resources. **World Wide Web address:** http://www.unitedhardware.com. **Description:** United Hardware Distribution Company operates the Hardware Hank and Trustworthy Hardware chains of hardware stores, and the Golden Rule Lumber chain of retail lumber stores. **Corporate headquarters location:** This location.

UNITEDHEALTH GROUP
P.O. Box 1459, Minneapolis MN 55440-1459. **Toll-free phone:** 800/328-5979. **Contact:** Personnel. **World Wide Web address:** http://www.unitedhealthgroup.com. **Description:** A managed health care company with a nationwide network of owned/managed health plans and integrated specialty companies (pharmaceutical, mental health/substance abuse, and workers' compensation). **NOTE:** Search and apply for positions online. **Positions advertised include:** Sr. PeopleSoft Developer; Compensation Consultant; Manager, Information Systems; Sr. Accountant. **Corporate headquarters location:** This location.

UNIVERSAL CO-OP INC.
1300 Corporate Center Curve, Eagan MN 55121. 651/239-1000. **Fax:** 651/239-1123. **Contact:** Human Resources. **World Wide Web address:** http://www.ucoop.com. **Description:** An interregional farm supply cooperative providing manufacturing, distribution and purchasing services for it's members in the United States, Canada and Europe.

UNIVERSITY OF MINNESOTA DULUTH
Darland Administration Building 255, 1049 University Drive, Duluth MN 55812-2496. 218/726-7161. **Contact:** Jeanne Lukkarila, Assistant Director of Human Resources. **E-mail address:** umdhr@d.umn.edu. **World Wide Web address:** http://www.d.umn.edu. **Description:** A branch of the four-year, state university offering undergraduate and graduate degrees. Enrollment is 10,000. students. **Positions advertised include:** Associate Program Director, College of Pharmacy; Departmental Director, School of Fine Arts; Assistant Business Development Specialist, School of Business and Economics. **Corporate headquarters location:** Minneapolis MN. **Number of employees at this location:** 1,700.

UNIVERSITY OF MINNESOTA MORRIS
Office of the Chancellor, 309 Behmler Hall, 600 East Fourth Street, Morris MN 56267. 320/589-6021. **Fax:** 218/726-7505. **Contact:** Sarah Mattson, Human Resource Director. **E-mail address:** mattsosj@mrs.umn.edu. **World Wide Web address:** http://www.mrs.umn.edu. **Description:** A public, liberal arts college offering bachelor's degrees and preprofessional programs. Enrollment is 1,900 students. **Positions advertised include:** Professor, Various Disciplines; Associate Professor, Various Disciplines; Division Director, Medical School. **Corporate headquarters location:** Minneapolis MN. **Number of employees at this location:** 380.

UNIVERSITY OF MINNESOTA TWIN CITIES
Suite 170 Donhowe Building, 319 15th Avenue SE, Minneapolis MN 55455. 612/625-2000. **Fax:** 612/624-6037. **Contact:** Human Resources. **E-mail address:** acadjobs@ohr.umn.edu. **World Wide Web address:** http://www.umn.edu/twincities. **Description:** A branch of the four-year, state university offering 161 bachelor's degrees, 218 master's degrees, 114 doctoral degrees, and five professional degrees. **Positions advertised include:** Professor, Various Disciplines; Associate Professor, Various Disciplines. **Corporate headquarters location:** This location. **Operations at this facility include:** Administration; Research and Development; Service.

UNIVERSITY OF ST. THOMAS
Mail Number AQU217, 2115 Summit Avenue, St. Paul MN 55105. 651/962-6510. **Fax:** 651/962-6905. **Contact:** Human Resources Department. **E-mail address:** employment@stthomas.edu. **World Wide Web address:** http://www.stthomas.edu. **Description:** A Catholic, four-year, liberal arts college with 11,000 undergraduate and graduate students. **Positions advertised include:** Dean, College of Engineering; Sr. Development Officer; Director, Theological Librarian.

UPSHER-SMITH LABORATORIES
6701 Evenstad Drive, Maple Grove MN 55369. 612/475-3023. **Toll-free phone:** 800/654-2299. **Contact:** Human Resources Department. **E-mail address:** uslhr@Upsher-Smith.com. **World Wide Web address:** http://www.upsher-smith.com. **Description:** Manufactures prescription and nonprescription pharmaceuticals. **NOTE:** Search and apply for positions online. **Positions advertised include:** Quality Assurance Validation Specialist; Territory Sales Representative; Sr. Scientist, Pharmaceutical Development; Computer Validation Administrator; Sr. Counsel.

THE VALSPAR CORPORATION
P.O. Box 1461, Minneapolis MN 55440. 612/375-7740. **Physical address:** 1101 Third Street South, Minneapolis MN 55415. **Contact:** Paul Mason, Human Resources Representative. **World Wide Web address:** http://www.valspar.com. **Description:** Manufactures paints, varnishes, lacquers, and related products. **Special programs:** Internships. **Corporate headquarters location:** This location. **Other U.S. locations:** Nationwide. **Operations at this facility include:** Administration; Research and Development; Sales; Service. **Listed on:** New York Stock Exchange. **Stock exchange symbol:** VAL. **Number of employees worldwide:** 7,000.

VARITRONIC SYSTEMS, INC.
6835 Winnetka Circle, Brooklyn Park MN 55428. 763/536-6400. **Toll-free phone:** 800/637-5461. **Fax:** 763/536-0769. **Contact:** Human Resources. **World Wide Web address:** http://www.varitronicsystems.com. **Description:** Develops, produces, and sells business graphics products for communication materials. The products are made to satisfy presentation, labeling, and signage in a variety of markets including general office, manufacturing, and education. Varitronic sells lettering and labeling systems that generate print in a variety of styles, in sizes ranging from one-half inch to four inches, using thermal transfer technology. **NOTE:** Search and apply for positions online. **Positions advertised include:** Sr. Mechanical Design Engineer. **Corporate headquarters location:** This location. **Parent company:** Brady Worldwide. **Number of employees at this location:** 100. **Number of employees nationwide:** 290.

VELOS, INC.
7101 West 78th Street, Suite 200, Bloomington MN 55439. 952/833-9700. **Contact:** Human Resources. **E-mail address:** humanresources@velos.com. **World Wide Web address:** http://www.velos.com. **Description:** Develops and markets application, Internet, and wireless device infrastructure software for the healthcare industry. **Corporate headquarters location:** Fremont CA.

VIRACON
800 Park Drive, Owatonna MN 55060. 507/451-9555. **Toll-free phone:** 800/533-2080. **Fax:** 507/444-5162. **Contact:** Jim Wendorff, Human Resources Director. **E-mail address:** jobs@viracon.com. **World Wide Web address:** http://www.viracon.com. **Description:** Manufactures high-performance glass products such as insulating, laminated, security, silk-screened, and tempered coatings. **Corporate headquarters location:** This location. **Parent company:** Apogee Enterprises, Inc. **Number of employees at this location:** 1,200.

VIRATEC THIN FILMS, INC.
2150 Airport Drive, Faribault MN 55021-7798. 507/334-0051. **Fax:** 507/334-0059. **Contact:** Human Resources. **World Wide Web address:** http://www.viratec.com. **Description:** Manufactures high-performance, optical, thin film coatings for glass and plastic. Founded in 1988. **Corporate headquarters location:** This location. **Other U.S. locations:** San Diego CA. **Parent company:** Apogee Enterprises, Inc.

VIROMED LABORATORIES
6101 Blue Circle Drive, Minnetonka MN 55343. 952/563-3300. **Fax:** 952/563-4152. **Contact:** Jackie Williams, Human Resources. **E-mail address:** hr@viromed.com. **World Wide Web address:** http://www.viromed.com. **Description:** A medical laboratory that provides laboratory testing services to the healthcare, transplant medicine, pharmaceutical, and biotechnology industries.

VISION-EASE LENS, INC.
700 54th Avenue North, P.O. Box 969, St. Cloud MN 55303. 763/576-3930. **Fax:** 763/576-5127. **Contact:** Lori Wallace, Human Resources. **World Wide Web address:**

http://www.vision-ease.com. **Description:** Manufactures polycarbonate lenses for eyeglasses. **NOTE:** Entry-level positions and second and third shifts are offered. **Special programs:** Internships; Training; Summer Jobs. **Corporate headquarters location:** This location. **Other U.S. locations:** St. Cloud MN. **Parent company:** BMC Industries. **Listed on:** New York Stock Exchange. **Stock exchange symbol:** BMC. **CEO:** Paul Burke. **Annual sales/revenues:** More than $100 million. **Number of employees at this location:** 160.

WCCO-TV
90 South 11th Street, Minneapolis MN 55403. 612/339-4444. **Fax:** 612/330-2603. **Contact:** Ann Ouellette, Controller. **World Wide Web address:** http://www.wcco.com. **Description:** A television broadcasting company. **Positions advertised include:** Reporter, Photojournalist; Web Producer. **Corporate headquarters location:** New York NY. **Parent company:** CBS, Inc. **Number of employees at this location:** 200.

WAGNER SPRAY TECH
1770 Fernbrook Lane North, Plymouth MN 55447. 763/553-7000. **Fax:** 763/519-3563. **Contact:** Human Resources. **World Wide Web address:** http://www.wagnerspraytech.com. **Description:** A manufacturer of paint sprayers.

WAL-MART STORES, INC.
4740 Mall Drive, Hermantown MN 55811. 218/727-1310. **Contact:** Human Resources. **World Wide Web address:** http://www.walmart.com. **Description:** Wal-Mart Stores is one of the largest retail merchandise chains in the country, operating full-service discount department stores, combination grocery and discount stores, and warehouse stores requiring membership. Founded in 1962. **Corporate headquarters location:** Bentonville AR.

WALKER ART CENTER
725 Vineland Place, Minneapolis MN 55403. 612/375-7600. **Fax:** 612/375-7590. **Recorded jobline:** 612/375-7588. **Contact:** Human Resources. **E-mail address:** work@walkerart.org. **World Wide Web address:** http://www.walkerart.org. **Description:** An international contemporary art museum with exhibition, film/video, and performing arts programming. **Special programs:** Internships. **Corporate headquarters location:** This location. **Number of employees at this location:** 150.

WALMAN OPTICAL COMPANY
801 12th Avenue North, Minneapolis MN 55411. 612/520-6000. **Fax:** 612/520-6096. **Contact:** Human Resources. **E-mail address:** humanresources@walman.com. **World Wide Web address:** http://www.walman.com. **Description:** An employee-owned manufacturer of ophthalmic products with 40 offices in 19 states. **Positions advertised include:** Customer Service Representative. **Other U.S. locations:** Nationwide. **Operations at this facility include:** Administration; Manufacturing; Sales; Service.

WATEROUS COMPANY
125 Hardman Avenue South, South St. Paul MN 55075-2456. 651/450-5000. **Fax:** 651/450-5241. **Recorded jobline:** 651/450-5299. **Contact:** Human Resources. **World Wide Web address:** http://www.waterousco.com. **Description:** Manufactures and assembles parts for fire hydrants, underground valves for the waterworks industry, and pumps for fire services. **NOTE:** Entry-level positions, part-time jobs, and second and third shifts are offered. **Positions advertised include:** Helper; Assembler. **Office hours:** Monday - Friday, 8:00 a.m. - 4:30 p.m. **Corporate headquarters location:** This location. **Parent company:** American Cast Iron Pipe Company (ACIPCO). **Listed on:** Privately held. **Number of employees at this location:** 360.

WEATHERFORD/JOHNSON SCREENS
1950 Old Highway 8 NW, New Brighton MN 55112. 651/636-3900. **Toll-free phone:** 800/833-9473. **Fax:** 651/638-3132. **Contact:** Human Resources. **World Wide Web address:** http://www.weatherford.com. **Description:** Manufactures screens used in industrial, oil and gas, and mining applications. Founded in 1902. **NOTE:** Entry-level positions as well as second and third shifts are offered. **Positions advertised include:** Field Service Technician; Sales Engineer; General Manager. **Other U.S. locations:** Nationwide. **International locations:** Worldwide. **Parent company:** Weatherford. **Operations at this facility include:** Divisional Headquarters. **Number of employees at this location:** 300.

WEIGH-TRONIX INC.
1000 Armstrong Drive, Fairmont MN 56031. 507/238-4461. **Toll-free phone:** 800/533-0456. **Fax:** 507/238-8258. **Contact:** Human Resources. **E-mail address:** employment@weigh-tronix.com. **World Wide Web address:** http://www.weigh-tronix.com. **Description:** Manufactures scales for industrial and agricultural use. **Positions advertised include:** Cost Accounting Manager; Industrial Controls & Communication Specialist.

THE FREDERICK R. WEISMAN ART MUSEUM
University of Minnesota, 333 East River Road, Minneapolis MN 55455. 612/625-9494. **Contact:** Carol Stafford, Human Resources. **World Wide Web address:** http://hudson.acad.umn.edu. **Description:** A museum of contemporary American art.

WELLS FARGO & COMPANY
401 Second Avenue South, Minneapolis MN 55401. 612/667-0081. **Contact:** Human Resources. **World Wide Web address:** http://www.wellsfargo.com. **Description:** A diversified financial institution with over $397 billion in assets. Wells Fargo serves over 17 million customers through 5,900 independent locations worldwide. The company also maintains several stand-alone ATMs and branches within other retail outlets. Services include community banking, credit and debit cards, home equity and mortgage loans, online banking, student loans, and insurance. Wells Fargo also offers a complete line of commercial and institutional financial services. Founded in 1852. **Corporate headquarters location:** San Francisco CA. **Other U.S. locations:** Nationwide. **International locations:** Worldwide. **Listed on:** New York Stock Exchange. **Stock exchange symbol:** WFC. **Annual sales/revenues:** More than $100 million. **Number of employees worldwide:** 143,000.

WELLS FARGO MORTGAGE INC.
3601 Minnesota Drive, Suite 100, Bloomington MN 55435. 952/844-2200. **Contact:** Personnel Department. **World Wide Web address:** http://www.wellsfargo.com. **Description:** Wells Fargo is a diversified financial institution with over $397 billion in assets. Wells Fargo serves over 17 million customers through 5,900 independent locations worldwide. The company also maintains several stand-alone ATMs and branches within other retail outlets. Services include community banking, credit and debit cards, home equity and mortgage loans, online banking, student loans, and insurance. Wells Fargo also offers a complete line of commercial and institutional financial services. Founded in 1852. **Corporate headquarters location:** San Francisco CA. **Other U.S. locations:** Nationwide. **International locations:** Worldwide. **Operations at this facility include:** This location offers home equity and mortgage services. **Listed on:** New York Stock Exchange. **Stock exchange symbol:** WFC. **Annual sales/revenues:** More than $100 million. **Number of employees worldwide:** 143,000.

WEST GROUP
610 Opperman Drive, Eagan MN 55123. 651/687-7000. **Contact:** Human Resources. **World Wide Web address:** http://www.westgroup.com. **Description:** Publishes legal research information in CD-ROM and book formats for law practitioners and the judiciary. **Positions advertised include:** Account Manager; Acquisition Editor; Attorney Editor; Business Analyst; Database Marketing Analyst; Director, Global Strategy; Editor; EPS Sr. Coordinator; Financial Analyst. **Parent company:** Thomson Corporation.

WESTERN LAKE SUPERIOR SANITARY DISTRICT
2626 Courtland Street, Duluth MN 55806. 218/722-3336. **Contact:** Personnel. **Description:** Operates a landfill and collects household hazardous waste.

AMHERST H. WILDER FOUNDATION
919 Lafond Avenue, St. Paul MN 55104. 651/642-4000. **Fax:** 651/642-4033. **Contact:** Human Resources. **E-mail address:** jobs@wilder.org. **World Wide Web address:** http://www.wilder.org. **Description:** A nonprofit, health and human services organization operating over 100 programs. **NOTE:** Entry-level positions are offered. **Positions advertised include:** Administrative Specialist; Assistant Teacher; Program Service Aide; Counselor; Social Worker. **Special programs:** Internships. **Corporate headquarters location:** This location. **Operations at this facility include:** Administration; Service. **Number of employees at this location:** 1,300.

WINMARK CORPORATION
4200 Dahlberg Drive, Suite 100, Minneapolis MN 55422-4837. **Toll-free phone:** 800/567-6600. 763/520-8500. **Fax:** 763/520-8410. **Contact:** Personnel. **E-mail address:** hr@winmarkcorporation.com. **World Wide Web address:** http://www.winmarkcorporation.com. **Description:** A retail franchiser that sells a variety of new and used merchandise. **Positions advertised include:** Account Services Representative; Configuration Specialist; Field Operations Manager. **Corporate headquarters location:** This location. **Subsidiaries include:** Music Go Round; Once Upon A Child; Play It Again Sports; Plato's Closet.

WINONA STATE UNIVERSITY
P.O. Box 5838, Winona MN 55987-5838. 507/457-5005. **Fax:** 507/457-5054. **Contact:** Human Resources. **World Wide Web address:** http://www.winona.msus.edu. **Description:** A four-year, state university offering undergraduate, graduate, and preprofessional programs through Winona State University's five colleges: business, education, liberal arts, nursing and health sciences, and science and engineering. Approximately 8,000 students attend the university.

XATA CORPORATION
151 East Cliff Road, Suite 10, Burnsville MN 55337. 952/894-3680. **Fax:** 952/894-2463. **Contact:** Human Resources. **E-mail address:** hr@xata.com. **World Wide Web address:** http://www.xata.com. **Description:** Manufactures onboard computers and software for the transportation and logistics segments of the fleet trucking industry. Founded in 1985. **Office hours:** Monday - Friday, 7:30 a.m. - 5:30 p.m. **Corporate headquarters location:** This location. **Other U.S. locations:** Peoria IL. **Listed on:** NASDAQ. **Stock exchange symbol:** XATA. **President/CEO:** Dennis Johnson. **Number of employees at this location:** 75. **Number of employees nationwide:** 90.

XCEL ENERGY
414 Nicollet Mall, Minneapolis MN 55401-1993. **Toll-free phone:** 800/328-8226. **Contact:** Human Resources. **World Wide Web address:** http://www.xcelenergy.com. **Description:** Xcel Enegy was formed in the merger of Northern States Power Company and New Century Energies in August 2000. Xcel Energy generates, transmits, and distributes electric energy in 11 states. The company also transports and distributes natural gas. **Number of employees nationwide:** 13,000.

XERXES CORPORATION
7901 Xerxes Avenue South, Minneapolis MN 55431. 952/887-1890. **Fax:** 952/887-1882. **Contact:** Barbara J. Meyer, Supervisor of Payroll and Accounting. **World Wide Web address:** http://www.xerxescorp.com. **Description:** Manufactures fiberglass structural products including multicompartment tanks, oil and water separators, and underground storage tanks for the petroleum, chemical, water, and wastewater markets.

ZELLE, HOFMANN, VOELBEL & GETTE LLP
500 Washington Avenue South, Suite 4000, Minneapolis MN 55415. **Toll-free phone:** 800/899-5291. **Fax:** 612/336-9100. **Contact:** Human Resources. **E-mail address:** zelleweb@zelle.com. **World Wide Web address:** http://www.zelle.com. **Description:** A law firm that specializes in insurance litigation.

ZIMMER SPINE
7375 Bush Lake Road, Minneapolis MN 55439. 952/832-5600. **Fax:** 952/832-5620. **Contact:** Human Resources. **World Wide Web address:** http://www.zimmerspine.com. **Description:** Products include spinal implants to help the fusion of vertebrae in order to stabilize the spine. **Positions advertised include:** Director of Logistics; Finance Director; Clinical Research Associate; Product Development Engineer; Quality Systems Specialist.

ZOMAX INCORPORATED
5353 Nathan Lane, Plymouth MN 55442. 763/553-9300. **Fax:** 763/553-0826. **Contact:** Human Resources. **World Wide Web address:** http://www.zomax.com. **Description:** Engaged in the authoring, mastering, replicating, production, and distribution of CD/DVD products for software and entertainment companies. **Corporate headquarters location:** This location. **Other U.S. locations:** Fremont CA; Concord CA; Indianapolis IN. **International locations:** Canada; Germany; Ireland. **Listed on:** NASDAQ. **Stock exchange symbol:** ZOMX. **Annual sales/revenues:** $100. million.

ABMB ENGINEERS, INC.
700 North State Street, Suite 300, Jackson MS 39202. 601/354-0696. **Contact:** Human Resources. **E-mail address:** hr@abmb.com. **World Wide Web address:** http://www.abmb.com. **Description:** Provides engineering services nationwide, specializing in highway and traffic engineering, bridges and other structures, site civil and surveying, and civil works. **NOTE:** Send resume to ABMB Engineers, Inc., 500 Main Street, Baton Rouge LA 70801; fax to: 225-765-7244; or e-mail to address above. **Positions advertised include:** Civil Engineer. **Corporate headquarters location:** Baton Rouge LA. **Other area locations:** Vicksburg MS.

ACT ELECTRONICS, INC.
1801 Fulton Drive, Corinth MS 38834. 662/287-3771. **Fax:** 662/665-3495. **Contact:** Director of Employee Relations. **World Wide Web address:** http://www.actmfg.com. **Description:** Manufactures telecommunications equipment and systems and performs contract manufacturing services to both the telecommunications and computer electronics industries. Manufactured products include telecommunications equipment, computer peripherals and subassemblies, and printed circuit board (PCB) assemblies. ACT's manufacturing capabilities range from plastic injection molding to wire and cable assembly to final unit assembly and testing. The company's turnkey manufacturing services include component procurement and testing, PCB assembly using both advanced SMT and PTH technologies, post assembly board testing, in-circuit test development, assembly of PCBs and other components into final products, and product design and engineering support services. **Corporate headquarters location:** Hudson MA. **Other U.S. locations:** San Jose CA; Hudson MA. **Listed on:** NASDAQ. **Stock exchange symbol:** ACTM.

AFFILIATED COMPUTER SERVICES, INC.
2847 Virlilia Road, Flora MS 39071. 601/879-8211. **Contact:** Human Resources. **E-mail Address:** info@acs-inc.com. **World Wide Web address:** http://www.acs-inc.com. **Description:** Provides information management and storage services. **NOTE:** Apply online. **Company Slogan:** People Making Technology Work. **Positions advertised include:** Micro Systems Analyst; Documentation Specialist; Operations Manager; Power Builder Developer; Security Guard; Custodian. **Corporate headquarters location:** Dallas TX. **Listed on:** New York Stock Exchange. **Stock exchange symbol:** ACS.

AIRCAP INDUSTRIES CORPORATION
P.O. Box 2120, Tupelo MS 38803. 662/566-2332. **Fax:** 662-566-2872. **Physical address:** 5484 Route 145 South, Verona MS 38879. **Contact:** Human Resources. **Description:** Aircap Industries Corporation manufactures snow blowers and lawn mowers.

ALLEN & HOSHALL LTD.
4270 I-55 North, Suite 103, Jackson MS 39211. 601/366-3388. **Fax:** 601/366-2802. **Contact:** Human Resources. **E-mail address:** employment@allenhoshall.com. **World Wide Web address:** http://www.allenhoshall.com. **Description:** Allen & Hoshall Ltd. provides architectural, structural, and civil engineering services. **NOTE:** Corporate hiring is done through the Memphis, Tennessee headquarters location: 1661 International Drive, Suite 100, Memphis TN 38120. 901/820-0820. **Fax:** 901/683-1001. **Other area locations:** Nashville TN; Knoxville TN; Hernando MS.

AMERICAN TROUSER
P.O. Box 391, Columbus MS 39703. 662/329-8100. **Fax:** 662/329-8115. **Physical address:** 605 17th Street South, Columbus MS 39701. **Contact:** Charles Powell, Personnel Director. **World Wide Web address:** http://www.american-trouser.com. **Description:** American Trouser is an apparel manufacturer. **Other U.S. Locations:** New York, NY. **Parent company:** Interco is a broadly based manufacturer and retailer of consumer products and services with operations in apparel manufacturing, retailing, footwear manufacturing, and home furnishings.

AMERISTAR CASINO VICKSBURG
4116 South Washington Street, Vicksburg MS 39180. 601/638-1000. **Toll-free phone:** 800/700-7770. **Recorded Jobline:** 601/630-3696. **Contact:** Human Resources. **World Wide Web address:** http://www.ameristarcasinos.com. **Description:** Operates a riverboat casino in central Mississippi. Ameristar features 1,003 slot machines, 53 table games, and the three-tiered Delta Grand Showroom which hosts nationally-known entertainers. **Positions advertised include:** Public Relations Manager. **Corporate headquarters location:** 3773 Howard Hughes Parkway Suite 490 South Las Vegas NV 89109 702/567-7000 **Other U.S. locations:** St. Charles MO; Kansas City MO; Council Bluffs IA; Jackpot NV. **Parent company:** Ameristar Casinos, Inc., through its wholly-owned subsidiary Cactus Pete's, owns and operates Cactus Pete's Resort Casino and The Horseshu Hotel and Casino, two casino-hotels in Jackpot, Nevada. Ameristar Casino Council Bluffs, Inc., a wholly-owned subsidiary of Ameristar, was awarded one of two riverboat gaming licenses in Council Bluffs, Iowa. Ameristar's wholly-owned subsidiary Ameristar Casino Lawrenceburg, Inc. is one of seven applicants seeking a single gaming license in Lawrenceburg, Indiana.

ARCH ALUMINUM & GLASS COMPANY
2030 NW Progress Parkway, Jackson MS 39213. 601/713-0302. **Fax:** 601/713-0302. **Toll-free phone:** 800/815-5658. **Contact:** Human Resources. **E-mail address:** information@archaluminum.net. **World Wide Web address:** http://www.arch.amarlite.com. **Description:** Arch Aluminum & Glass Co. is one of North America's largest architectural glass and aluminum fabricators and distributors. **NOTE:** Hiring is done through the Corporate Headquarters location: 10200 NW 67th St. Tamarac, FL 33321. 800/432-8132. Fax: 954/724-9293. **Positions advertised include:** Estimator/Project Coordinator; Inside Technical Sales; Product Design & Development. **Other U.S. locations:** NC; FL; OR; GA; OH; AZ; NJ; WI; IN; TX; KS; CA.

BANCORPSOUTH
P.O. Box 789, Tupelo MS 38802. 662/680-2577. **Fax:** 662/680-2513. **Physical address:** 1 Mississippi Plz, Tupelo MS 38804 **Contact:** Personnel Department. **World Wide Web address:** http://www.bancorpsouthonline.com. **Description:** A bank offering a vast array of financial services from checking and savings to insurance, investments, and wealth management, including online services. **Other U.S. locations:** TX; AS; LA; AL; TN. **Listed on:** New York Stock Exchange. **Stock exchange symbol:** BXS. **Number of employees at this location:** 600.

BARKLEY FILING SYSTEMS
5370 Highway 42, Hattiesburg MS 39401. 601/545-2200. **Fax:** 800/423-7589. **Toll-free phone:** 800/647-3070. **Contact:** Human Resources. **E-mail address:** barkley@infiling.com. **World Wide Web address:** http://www.barkleyfiling.com. **Description:** A stationery and office supplies manufacturer.

BARNES & NOBLE BOOKSTORES
1057 East County Line Road, Jackson MS 39211-1851. 601/991-3835. **Contact:** Manager. **World Wide Web address:** http://www.bn.com. **Description:** A bookstore chain operating nationwide. This location has a cafe in addition to its comprehensive book departments. **NOTE:** Apply for positions online. **Office hours:** 9-11 everyday. **Corporate headquarters location:** 76 Ninth Ave., 9th Floor New York NY 10011.

BAXTER HEALTHCARE CORPORATION
911 North Davis Avenue, Cleveland MS 38732. 662/843-9421. **Contact:** Human Resources Manager. **World Wide Web address:** http://www.baxter.com. **Description:** This facility is a manufacturer of intravenous solutions and sterile disposable hospital devices. Baxter Healthcare, through its subsidiaries, is a producer, developer, and distributor of medical products and technologies for use in hospitals and other health care settings. **NOTE:** Baxter no longer accepts paper resumes. **Positions advertised include:** Quality Associate; Engineer; Manufacturing Supervisor; Microbiologist; Maintenance Supervisor. **Special Programs:** Internships. **Corporate headquarters location:** Deerfield IL. **Operations at this facility include:** Administration; Manufacturing. **Number of employees at this location:** 1,200. **Number of employees worldwide:** 35,000.

BAY TECHNICAL ASSOCIATES
5239 A Avenue, Long Beach MS 39560. **Toll-free phone:** 800/523-2702. **Fax:** 228/563-7335. **Contact:** Human Resources. **World Wide Web address:** http://www.baytechdcd.com. **Description:** Designs, manufactures, and markets data communication components and equipment. Founded in 1976. **Operations at this facility include:** Administration; Manufacturing; Research and Development; Sales; Service.

BILOXI REGIONAL MEDICAL CENTER
150 Reynoir Street, Biloxi MS 39530. 228/432-1571. **Recorded jobline:** 228/436-1232. **Contact:** Human Resources. **E-mail address:** human.resources@brmc.hma-corp.com. **World Wide Web address:** http://www.hmabrmc.com. **Description:** A 152-bed, acute care private hospital, with a 24 hour emergency room and patient oriented programs with an emphasis on elderly, women's and children's healthcare. **Positions advertised include:** Registered Nurse; Housekeeper; Operating Room Surgical Technician; Nursing Assistant; LPN. **Special Programs:** Volunteer Opportunities. **Corporate headquarters location:** Naples FL. **Parent company:** Health Management Associates, Inc. **Operations at this facility include:** Administration; Service. **Number of employees at this location:** 600. **Number of employees nationwide:** 12,000.

BLACK WARRIOR WIRELINE CORPORATION
P.O. Box 9188, Columbus MS 39705. 662/329-1047. **Fax:** 662/329-1089. **Physical address:** 100 Rosecrest Lane, Columbus MS 39701. **Contact:** Cheryl Hicks, Office Manager. **World Wide Web address:** http://www.bwwc.com. **Description:** Provides services to oil and gas well operators primarily in the Black Warrior Basin in Alabama and Mississippi and the Permian Basin in Texas. Businesses include electric wireline services; completion and workover services; and the sale, rental, and service of wireline and drilling/completion tools and equipment. Black Warrior provides services to both the nonconventional (coalbed methane gas) and conventional fuel sectors (all sources other than coalbed methane).. **Number of employees at this location:** 90.

BOOMTOWN BILOXI CASINO
P.O. Box 369, Biloxi MS 39533. 228/435-7000. **Toll-free phone:** 800/627-0777. **Fax:** 228/435-5104. **Physical address:** 676 Bayview Ave. Biloxi MS 39530. **Contact:** General Manager. **World Wide Web address:** http://www.boomtownbiloxi.com. **Description:** A western-themed casino serving the Mississippi Gulf Coast. The structure contains over 900 slot machines and 35 table games such as dice, roulette, Caribbean Stud poker, and Pai Gow. The complex features two restaurants (Longhorn's and Stagecoach Deli), an arcade, and the Dynamic Motion Theater. **Positions advertised include:** Custodian; Table Games Dealer; Buffet Attendant; Steward; Restaurant Supervisor; Food Server; Baker; Hostess/Cashier; Barback; Slots Floor Person; Booth Cashier. **Parent company:** Boomtown, Inc.

BORG-WARNER AUTOMOTIVE
P.O. Box 727, Water Valley MS 38965. 662/473-3100. **Physical address:** 600 Highway 32 East, Water Valley MS 38965. **Contact:** Personnel Department. **World Wide Web address:** http://www.bwauto.com. **Description:** A manufacturer of advanced products and technologies for powertrain components and systems. Founded in 1928. **Number of employees at this location:** 1,000. **Stock exchange symbol:** BWA. **CEO:** John Fiedler.

BOYS & GIRLS CLUBS OF CENTRAL MISSISSIPPI
1450 West Capital, Jackson MS 39203. 601/969-7088. **Contact:** Personnel. **World Wide Web address:** http://www.bgccm.net. **Description:** Serves children ages 6 to 18 in programs emphasizing youth development, based on principles of behavioral guidance. **Corporate headquarters location:** Atlanta GA. **Parent company:** United Way.

BRITTON & KOONTZ FIRST NATIONAL BANK
500 Main Street, P.O. Box 1407, Natchez MS 39121. 601/445-5576. **Fax:** 601/445-2488. **Contact:** Personnel. **World Wide Web address:** http://www.bkbank.com. **Description:** A bank holding company that performs commercial banking operations and other financial services. **Other area locations:** Vicksburg MS. **Other U.S. locations:** Baton Rouge LA. **Stock exchange symbol:** BKBK. **Listed on:** NASDAQ. **Number of employees at this location:** 70.

BROOKWOOD FURNITURE
263 Brookwood Drive, P.O. Box 540, Pontotoc MS 38863. 662/489-1100. **Fax:** 662/489-0916. **Contact:** Mr. B.J. Shamblee, Human Resources Director. **World Wide Web address:** http://www.brookwoodsofa.com. **Description:** Brookwood Furniture manufactures and distributes tables, bookcases, and other furniture items for domestic use.

CAGY INDUSTRIES, INC.
P.O. Box 1109, Columbus MS 39703. 662/329-7732. **Fax:** 662/329-7729. **Contact:** Human Resources. **E-mail address:** cagy@cagy.com. **World Wide Web address:** http://www.cagy.com. **Description:** A holding company for various railroads and railroad services corporations. **Subsidiaries include:** Columbus & Greenville Railway Company, Chattooga & Chickamauga Railway Company, Railway Management, Inc. & Luxapalila Valley Railroad Company. **Number of employees at this location:** 90.

CAL MAINE FOODS, INC.
P.O. Box 2960, Jackson MS 39209. 601/948-6813. **Fax:** 601/969-0905. **Physical address:** 3320 West Woodrow Wilson Avenue, Jackson MS 39209-3409. **Contact:** Personnel. **World Wide Web address:** http://www.calmainefoods.com. **Description:** Producers of eggs and poultry feeds. **Number of employees nationwide:** 1,700.

CALSONICKANSEI NORTH AMERICA, INC.
101 Calsonic Way, Vicksburg MS 39183. 601/661-5000. **Fax:** 601/661-5050. **Contact:**

Human Resources. **World Wide Web address:** http://www.calsonic.com. **Description:** Manufactures automotive components including HVAC systems. **NOTE:** Search and apply for positions online. **Positions advertised include:** Benefits And Compensation Specialist; Cost Accountant Ii; Maintenance Technician; Manufacturing Process Engineer; Organizational Development And Training Manager; Product Data Management Specialist; Production Planner; Production Supervisor; Site Supervisor, Manufacturing.

CASINO MAGIC CORPORATION
711 Casino Magic Drive, P.O. Box 8003, Bay Saint Louis MS 39520. 228/467-9257. **Fax:** 228/463-4089. **Toll-free phone:** 800/562-4425. **Contact:** Human Resources Department. **World Wide Web address:** http://www.casinomagic.com. **Description:** A holding company that operates casinos. **Subsidiaries include:** Atlantic-Pacific Corporation (Deadwood SD) leases and operates a limited-stakes gaming establishment. Biloxi Casino Corporation (Biloxi MS) operates a three-level dockside casino. Casino Magic Neuquen SA operates casinos in the Argentine province of Neuquen in the cities of Neuquen City and San Martin de los Andes. Mardi Gras Casino Corporation (Bay Saint Louis MS) operates a bi-level dockside casino. **Number of employees at this location:** 3,150.

CENTRAL SERVICE ASSOCIATION
P.O. Box 3480, Tupelo MS 38803-3480. 662/842-5962. **Fax:** 662/840-1329. **Physical address:** 93 South Coley Road, Tupelo MS 38801. **Contact:** Human Resources. **E-mail address:** bclark@csa1.com. **World Wide Web address:** http://www.csa1.com. **Description:** Provides billing services for electric and water utilities. Founded in 1938. **Positions advertised include:** Information Systems Representative/Accounting.

CHEMFIRST, INC.
P.O. Box 1249, Jackson MS 39215-1240. 601/948-7550. **Contact:** Human Resources. **World Wide Web address:** http://www.chemfirst.com. **Description:** ChemFirst is a global supplier of electronic chemicals and materials to the semiconductor industry and specialty intermediates for polyurethanes and other applications. **Parent company:** DuPont. **Listed on:** New York Stock Exchange. **Stock exchange symbol:** CEM.

CHEVRON PRODUCTS CO.
P.O. Box 1300, Pascagoula MS 39568-1300. 228/938-4600. **Contact:** Human Resources. **E-mail address:** comment@chevrontexaco.com. **World Wide Web address:** http://www.chevrontexaco.com. **Description:** A petroleum refining company. **Corporate headquarters location:** San Ramon CA. **Parent company:** ChevronTexaco Corporation is an international oil firm with operations in more than 90 countries, engaged in worldwide integrated petroleum operations, including the exploration and production of crude oil and natural gas reserves; the transportation of crude oil, natural gas, and petroleum products by pipeline, tanker, and motor equipment; the operation of oil-refining complexes; and the wholesale and retail marketing of hundreds of petroleum products. **Number of employees at this location:** 1,000. **Number of employees worldwide:** 53,000.

THE CLARION-LEDGER
201 South Congress Street, Jackson MS 39201. 601/961-7000. **Toll-free phone:** 800/222-8015. **Fax:** 601/961-7329. **Contact:** Lindsay Carter, Human Resources Director. **E-mail address:** lcarter@jackson.gannett.com. **World Wide Web address:** http://www.clarionledger.com. **Description:** Publishes the *Clarion-Ledger,* a daily newspaper that is circulated statewide. **Positions advertised include:** Editorial Assistant; Consumer Marketing Manager; Material Handler; Advertising Account Executive. **Corporate headquarters location:** Arlington VA. **Parent company:** Gannett Corporation is a nationwide news and information company that publishes 81 newspapers including *USA Today,* and is the largest outdoor advertising company in North America. Gannett is also involved in marketing, television news and program production, and research satellite information systems and owns a national group of commercial printing facilities. Gannett has operations in 41 states, the District of Columbia, Guam, the Virgin Islands, Canada, Great Britain, Hong Kong, Singapore, and Switzerland. **Operations at this facility include:** Manufacturing; Sales; Service. **Listed on:** New York Stock Exchange. **Stock exchange symbol:** GCI.

COOKE DOUGLASS FARR LEMONS/LTD.
3780 I-55 North, Suite 101, Jackson MS 39211. 601/366-3110. **Fax:** 601/366-3181. **Contact:** Human Resources. **E-mail address:** cdfl@cdfl.com. **World Wide Web Address:** http://www.cdfl.com. **Description:** Provides architectural, engineering, and interior design services. Founded in 1961.

COOPER INDUSTRIES
P.O. Box 820824, 5035 Highway 61 South, Vicksburg MS 39182-0824. 601/638-1522. **Contact:** Personnel. **E-mail address:** vicksburg.recruit@cooperlighting.com. **World Wide Web address:** http://www.cooperindustries.com. **Description:** Provides industrial lighting products, fixtures, and related products. **Positions advertised include:** Design Engineer. **Corporate headquarters location:** Houston TX. **Other U.S. locations:** Nationwide. **Parent company:** Cooper Industries Inc. **Operations at this facility include:** Administration; Research and Development; Sales. **Listed on:** New York Stock Exchange. **Stock exchange symbol:** CBE. **Number of employees at this location:** 580. **Number of employees worldwide:** 29,000.

CREATIVE CONTROLLERS INC.
128 Kendrick Lane, Picayune MS 39466. 601/798-0577. **Toll-free phone:** 800/950-6224. **Fax:** 601/798-0656. **Contact:** General Manager. **Description:** Manufactures boards that interface with IBM computers, enabling compatibility with printers.

CROFT METALS INC.
P.O. Box 826, McComb MS 39649. 601/684-6121. **Physical address:** 107 Oliver Emmerich Drive, McComb MS 39648. **Toll-free phone:** 800/222-3195. **Fax:** 601/684-0537. **Contact:** Victor C. Donati, Jr., Corporate Human Resources Director. **E-mail address:** donativ@croftmetals.com. **World Wide Web address:** http://www.croftmetals.com. **Description:** A national manufacturer of aluminum and vinyl building products. Products include windows, doors, patio doors, and bath and shower enclosures. **Office hours:** Monday-Friday 7am-5:15pm CST. **Other U.S. locations:** Oviedo FL; Newton MS; Lumber Bridge NC. **Number of employees at this location:** 105. **Number of employees nationwide:** 2,500.

DAY-BRITE CAPRI OMEGA
776 South Green Street, Tupelo MS 38804. 662/842-7212. **Fax:** 662/680-6619. **Contact:** Personnel Manager. **World Wide Web address:** http://www.daybritelighting.com. **Description:** Manufactures a wide variety of lighting products for commercial, industrial, and institutional applications including use in schools, warehouses, office buildings, hospitals, hotels, restaurants, and retail stores.

DELPHI PACKARD ELECTRIC SYSTEMS
925 Industrial Park Road, Brookhaven MS 39601. 601/833-0112. **Contact:** Gwen Gayden, Personnel Director. **World Wide Web address:** http://www.delphi.com. **Description:** Manufactures automotive wiring harnesses. **Parent company:** General Motors Corporation is one of the world's largest full-line vehicle manufacturers, and also has substantial interests in information technology, electronics, and finance. GM conducts business through the following sectors: North American Automotive Operations, Delphi Automotive Systems, International Operations, General Motors Acceptance Corporation (GMAC), Electronic Data Systems Corporation (EDS), and GM Hughes Electronics Corporation. North American Automotive Operations includes Sales/Service Groups (Buick, Cadillac, Chevrolet, GMC Truck, Oldsmobile, Pontiac, and Saturn) and Vehicle Development Groups (Powertrain, Truck Group, Small Car Group, and Midsize/Luxury Car Group). Delphi Automotive Systems consists of Delphi Chassis Systems, Delphi Packard Electric Systems, Delphi Energy & Engine Management Systems, Delphi Saginaw Steering Systems, Delphi Harrison Thermal Systems, Delphi Interior & Lighting Systems, Delphi Automotive Systems European Region, Delphi Automotive Systems Asia/Pacific Region, and Delphi Automotive Systems South America. International Operations include GM Europe; Asia Pacific Operations; and Latin America, Africa, Middle East Operations. GMAC, which provides financing and insurance to GM customers and dealers, consists of North American Operations, International Operations, Motors Insurance Corporation, and GMAC Mortgage Group. EDS applies information technologies to more than 8,000 customers globally in the communications, energy/chemical, insurance, public sector, travel and transportation, financial services, manufacturing, and retail industries. GM Hughes Electronics Corporation is involved in automotive electronics, telecommunications and space electronics, and defense electronics. **Corporate headquarters location:** Troy MI. **Number of employees worldwide:** 216,000.

DELPHI PACKARD ELECTRIC SYSTEMS
1001 Industrial Park Drive, Clinton MS 39056-3211. 601/924-7411. **Contact:** Human Resources Manager. **World Wide Web address:** http://www.delphiauto.com. **Description:** Manufactures automotive wiring harnesses. **Parent company:** General Motors Corporation is one of the world's largest full-line vehicle manufacturers, and also has substantial interests in information technology, electronics, and finance. GM conducts business through the following sectors: North American Automotive Operations, Delphi Automotive Systems, International Operations, General Motors Acceptance Corporation (GMAC), Electronic Data Systems Corporation (EDS), and GM Hughes Electronics Corporation. North American Automotive Operations includes Sales/Service Groups (Buick, Cadillac, Chevrolet, GMC Truck, Oldsmobile, Pontiac, and Saturn) and Vehicle Development Groups (Powertrain, Truck Group, Small Car Group, and Midsize/Luxury Car Group). Delphi Automotive Systems consists of Delphi Chassis Systems, Delphi Packard Electric Systems, Delphi Energy & Engine Management Systems, Delphi Saginaw Steering Systems, Delphi Harrison Thermal Systems, Delphi Interior & Lighting Systems, Delphi Automotive Systems European Region, Delphi Automotive Systems Asia/Pacific Region, and Delphi Automotive Systems South America. International Operations include GM Europe; Asia Pacific Operations; and Latin America, Africa, Middle East Operations. GMAC, which provides financing and insurance to GM customers and dealers, consists of North American Operations, International Operations, Motors Insurance Corporation, and GMAC Mortgage Group. EDS applies information technologies to more than 8,000 customers globally in the communications, energy/chemical, insurance, public sector, travel and transportation, financial services, manufacturing, and retail industries. GM Hughes Electronics Corporation is involved in automotive electronics, telecommunications and space electronics, and defense electronics. **Corporate headquarters location:** Troy MI. **Number of employees worldwide:** 216,000.

DELTA PRIDE CATFISH, INC.
P.O. Box 850, 1301 Industrial Park Drive, Indianola MS 38751. 662/887-5401. **Toll-free phone:** 800/421-1045. **Contact:** Human Resources. **World Wide Web address:** http://www.deltapride.com. **Description:** A catfish farming and processing company. Founded in 1981.

DICKTEN & MASCH MS INC.
977 Sullivan Drive, Hattiesburg MS 39401. 601/545-2882. **Fax:** 601/545-2884. **Contact:** Debbie Thompson. **E-mail address:** debbiet@dickten.com. **World Wide Web address:** http://www.dickten.com. **Description:** Produces tooling and custom molded plastic parts. Founded in 1941. **Positions advertised include:** Press Operator. **Corporate headquarters location:** Nashotah WI.

DIVERSIFIED TECHNOLOGY, INC.
P.O. Box 748, Ridgeland MS 39158. 601/856-4121. **Physical address:** 476 Highland Colony Parkway, Ridgeland MS 39157. **Toll-free phone:** 800/443-2667. **Fax:** 601/856-2888. **Contact:** Personnel Department. **E-mail address:** personnel@dtims.com. **World Wide Web address:** http://www.dtims.com. **Description:** Manufactures computers that are used in a wide array of industrial applications. **Parent company:** Ergon. **President:** Barrie McArthur

R.R. DONNELLEY & SONS COMPANY
121 Matthews Drive, Senatobia MS 38668-2304. 662/562-5252. **Contact:** Human Resources Manager. **World Wide Web address:** http://www.rrdonnelley.com. **Description:** This location specializes in trade journal printing. R.R. Donnelley & Sons is a world leader in managing, reproducing, and distributing print and digital information for publishing, merchandising, and information technology customers. The company is one of the largest commercial printers in the world, producing catalogs, inserts, magazines, books, directories, computer documentation, and financial printing. R.R. Donnelley has more than 180 strategically located sales offices and production facilities. Principal services offered by the company are conventional and digital prepress operations, computerized printing and binding, and sophisticated pool shipping and distribution services for printed products; information repackaging into multiple formats (print, magnetic, and optical media); database management, list rental, list enhancement, and direct mail production services; turnkey computer documentation services (outsourcing, translation, printing, binding, diskette replication, licensing, republishing, and fulfillment); reprographics and facilities management; creative design and communication services; and digital and conventional map creation and related services. Founded in 1864. **Corporate headquarters location:** Chicago IL. **Other U.S. locations:** Nationwide. **International locations:** Worldwide. **Listed on:** New York Stock Exchange. **Stock exchange symbol:** DNY. **Annual sales/revenues:** More than $100 million. **Number of employees nationwide:** 30,000. **Number of employees worldwide:** 35,000.

ECO SYSTEMS, INC.
6360 I55 North, Suite 330, Jackson MS 39211. 601/936-4440. **Fax:** 601/936-4463. **Contact:** Operations Manager. **World Wide Web address:** http://www.eco-systemsinc.com. **Description:** An environmental consulting company providing consulting services to large and small companies seeking assistance with complex environmental problems. These services include contamination assessments, remedial planning and design, disposal site engineering, groundwater plans, air quality, water quality, ecological assessments, environmental audits, regulatory compliance assistance, facility permitting, health and safety training, and OSHA compliance.

Founded in 1993. **Other U.S. locations:** Little Rock AR; Houston TX. **Number of employees at this location:** 15.

EDISON WALTHALL HOTEL
225 East Capitol Street, Jackson MS 39201. 601/948-6161. **Contact:** Human Resources Department. **Toll-free phone:** 800/932-6161. **Fax:** 601/948-0088. **World Wide Web address:** http://www.edisonwalthallhotel.com. **Description:** A moderately priced hotel. The hotel features 208 guest rooms with six suites including two hospitality suites; hotel dining room and bar; recreation center with heated swimming pool, hot-tub, and fitness center; over 7,200 square feet of meeting and banquet space; and special guest services including room service, same-day valet dry-cleaning and laundry, gift and book shop, barbershop, airline reservations, complimentary van, and an indoor, security-monitored parking garage. Founded in 1928. **Parent company:** Edison Hotels and Resorts Company.

ENTERGY MISSISSIPPI
P.O. Box 1640, Jackson MS 39286-1995. 601/368-5000. **Recorded jobline:** 800/231-4481. **Contact:** Human Resources. **World Wide Web address:** http://www.entergy-mississippi.com. **Description:** Entergy Corporation is an energy company engaged primarily in electric power production, retail distribution operations, energy marketing and trading, and gas transportation. **Positions advertised include:** HR Representative. **Special programs:** Co-ops; Internships. **Number of employees at this location:** 1,235. **CEO:** Carolyn Shanks.

ERGON, INC.
P.O. Box 1639, Jackson MS 39215-1639. 601/933-3000. **Physical address:** 2829 Lakeland Drive, Ste 2000, Jackson MS 39232-7611. **Fax:** 601/933-3373. **Contact:** Ricky Allen, Human Resources Director. **E-mail address:** ricky.allen@ergon.com. **World Wide Web address:** http://www.ergon.com. **Description:** Produces and transports oil and gas. **Number of employees nationwide:** 2,300.

FLEXIBLE FLYER TOYS
P.O. Box 1296, West Point MS 39773. 662/494-4732. **Physical address:** 100 Tubb Avenue, West Point MS 39773. 662/494-4732. **Contact:** Human Resources Manager. **World Wide Web address:** http://www.flexible-flyer.com. **Description:** Manufactures outdoor recreational gear including bicycles, tricycles, junior riding products for children's swing sets, and fitness equipment. Since 1889.

GEORGIA-PACIFIC RESINS, INC.
Highway 28 West, Taylorsville MS 39168. 601/785-4721. **Fax:** 601/785-6560. **Contact:** Human Resources. **World Wide Web address:** http://www.gp.com. **Description:** A manufacturer of formaldehyde and wood adhesives. **Parent company:** Georgia-Pacific Corporation.

GRAND CASINO GULFPORT
3215 West Beach Boulevard, Gulfport MS 39501. 228/870-7777. **Toll-free phone:** 800/946-7777. **Fax:** 228/867-5589. **Contact:** Human Resources. **World Wide Web address:** http://www.grandcasinos.com. **Description:** One of the largest dockside casinos on the Mississippi Gulf Coast. Founded in 1993. **Advertised positions include:** Banquet Chef; Fine Dining Manager. **Parent company:** Caesars Entertainment Inc. **Listed on:** New York Stock Exchange. **Stock exchange symbol:** CZR. **Number of employees at this location:** 2,100.

GULF STATES MANUFACTURERS
P.O. Box 1128, Starkville MS 39760. 662/323-8021. **Physical address:** 101 Airport Road, Starkville MS 39759. **Fax:** 662/323-4225. **Contact:** Gary Mitchell, Director of Human Resources. **E-mail address:** gmitchell@gulfstatesmanufacturers,com **World Wide Web address:** http://www.gulfstatesmanufacturers.com. **Description:** Manufactures pre-engineered metal buildings. Founded in 1968. **Number of employees at this location:** 400.

HANCOCK FABRICS, INC.
1 Fashion Way, Baldwin MS 38824. 662/842-2834 **Fax:** 662/365-6348. **Contact:** Personnel. **World Wide Web address:** http://www.hancockfabrics.com. **Description:** Hancock Fabrics, Inc. operates retail and wholesale fabric businesses offering a wide selection of clothing fabrics, notions, patterns, decorative fabrics, craft items, and related supplies. **Corporate headquarters location:** This location. **Subsidiaries include:** Minnesota Fabrics, Inc. **Listed on:** New York Stock Exchange. **Stock exchange symbol:** HKF. **Number of employees nationwide:** 7,000.

HATTIESBURG CLINIC
415 South 28th Avenue, Hattiesburg MS 39401-7283. 601/264-6000. **Fax:** 601/579-5152. **Recorded jobline:** 601/268-5803. **Contact:** Human Resources Manager. **World Wide Web address:** http://www.hattiesburgclinic.com. **Description:** One of Mississippi's largest multispecialty clinics with over 80 physicians representing almost every medical specialty. **NOTE:** Direct line to Human Resources: 601/268-5737. **Fax:** 601-579-5152. **Positions advertised include:** Registered Nurse; Licensed Practical Nurse; CT Technician; Manager; Administrative Assistant; Contract Accountant Clerks; Receptionist; Patient Account Representative; Cashier; Data Entry Claims Processor; Workman's Comp Clerk; Patient Representative. **Number of employees at this location:** 720.

HATTIESBURG PAPER CORPORATION
One W.L. Runnels Drive, Hattiesburg MS 39401. 601/545-3400. **Contact:** Human Resources. **Description:** A manufacturer of paper products for use in various applications including, consumer tissue, personal care, and business-to-business. **Office hours:** Monday through Friday 8-4. **Number of employees at this location:** 175.

HAZCLEAN ENVIRONMENTAL CONSULTANTS, INC.
P.O. Box 16485, 160 Upton Drive, Jackson MS 39236-6485. 601/922-0766. **Fax:** 601/922-7927. **Contact:** Human Resources. **E-mail address:** info@hazclean.com. **World Wide Web address:** http://www.hazclean.com. **Description:** A multidisciplined environmental engineering and hazardous waste management consulting firm. Hazclean Environmental Consultants, Inc. serves a diverse range of businesses, as well as federal, state, and local governments throughout the southeastern United States. Its clients include *Fortune* 500 companies, many of whom use Hazclean's professionals to conduct or verify formal audit compliance procedures. Services to industrial clients include air quality services, industrial wastewater, emergency planning and Community Right-to-Know Act, process design/modification, hazardous materials management, remediation services, pollution prevention program, and strategic and tactical environmental planning. Services to commercial, financial, and real estate clients include audit and assessment programs, site investigations, indoor air quality, and wetlands. Services to petroleum marketers include underground and aboveground storage tanks.

HEATCRAFT INC.
3984 Highway 51 South, P.O. Box 948, Grenada MS 38901. 662/229-2000. **Fax:** 662/229-2618. **Contact:** Andy Carter, Director of Human Resources. **E-mail address:** andycarter@heatcraft.com. **World Wide Web address:** http://www.heatcraft.com. **Description:** Engaged in the manufacture of industrial air conditioning and heating systems. **Number of employees nationwide:** 1,300.

HERCULES INC.
613 West Seventh Street, Hattiesburg MS 39401. 601/545-3450. **Fax:** 601/584-3226. **Contact:** Human Resources. **World Wide Web address:** http://www.herc.com. **Description:** Manufactures cellulose and natural gum thickeners; flavors and fragrances; natural and hydrocarbon rosins and resins; polypropylene fibers and films; graphite fibers; and aerospace products. **Corporate headquarters located:** Wilmington DE. **Number of employees at this location:** 185.

HIGH TECH, INC.
1390 29th Avenue, Gulfport MS 39501. 228/868-6632. **Contact:** Human Resources. **E-mail address:** hightechinc@worldnet.att.net. **World Wide Web address:** http://www.hightechinc.com. **Description:** Manufacturers of custom acoustic sensors data acquisition systems for rugged underwater and other environments. Founded in 1989. **Positions advertised include:** Electronic Design Engineer.

HOODINDUSTRIES, INC.
15 Professional Parkway, P.O. Box 17317, Hattiesburg MS 39402. 601/264-2559. **Contact:** Human Resources. **E-mail address:** alford@hoodindustries.com. **World Wide Web address:** http://www.hoodindustries.com. **Description:** A lumber company specializing in Southern Yellow Pine lumber and plywood.. **Other area locations:** Beaumont MS; Waynesboro MS; Wiggins MS. **Other U.S. locations:** Choshatta LA.

HORNE CPA GROUP
P.O. Box 22964, Jackson MS 39225-2964. 601/948-0940. **Physical address:** 200 East Capitol Street, Suite 1400, Jackson MS 39201. **Contact:** Robert Spring, Personnel Manager. **E-mail address:** bob.spring@horne-llp.com. **World Wide Web address:** http://www.hcpag.com. **Description:** An accounting firm. **Positions advertised include:** Employee Benefit Audit Manager; Financial Institutions Audit Manager; HR Manager. **Other area locations:** Grenada MS; Gulfport MS; Hattiesburg MS; Laurel MS; Lucedale MS; Oxford MS. **Other U.S. locations:** Nashville TN.

HOWARD INDUSTRIES, INC.
P.O. Box 1588, Laurel MS 39441. 601/425-3151. **Fax:** 601/422-1483. **Contact:** Human Resources Manager. **E-mail address:** HumanResources@Howard-Ind.com. **World Wide Web address:** http://www.howard-ind.com. **Description:** A manufacturer of oil-filled distribution transformers, personal computers and servers, electronic and magnetic fluorescent ballasts and HID ballasts, industrial and commercial lighting products, and is a provider of full-load long-haul transportation services. **Positions advertised include:** Electrical Engineer; Mechanical Engineer; Truck Driver; Hardware Engineer; Software Engineer.

HUFFMAN & COMPANY, CPA
P.O. Box 321330, Flowood MS 39232. 601/355-6104. **Physical address:** 497 Keywood Circle, Suite A, Flowood MS 39232. **Fax:** 601/944-0548. **Contact:** Ginger Carter, Office Manager. **E-mail address:** cpahuff@aol.com. **Description:** Huffman & Company provides individual and small business accounting and tax services.

INTERNATIONAL PAPER COMPANY
Highway 3 N, P.O. Box 950, Vicksburg MS 39181. 601/638-3665. **Contact:** Human Resources. **World Wide Web address:** http://www.internationalpaper.com. **Description:** International Paper is a manufacturer of pulp and paper, packaging, and wood products as well as a range of specialty products. The company is organized into five business segments including Printing Papers with principal products including uncoated papers, coated papers, bristles, and pulp; Packaging, which includes industrial packaging, consumer packaging, and kraft and specialty papers; Distribution, which includes sales of printing papers, graphic arts equipment and supplies, packaging materials, industrial supplies, and office products; Specialty Products, which include imaging products, specialty panels, nonwovens, chemicals, and minerals; and Forest Products, including logs and wood products. **Corporate headquarters location:** Stamford CT. **Operations at this location include:** This location manufactures unbleached kraftliner board. **Listed on:** New York Stock Exchange. **Stock exchange symbol:** IP. **Number of employees worldwide:** 72,500.

INTERNATIONAL PAPER COMPANY
61 Carthage Point Road, P.O. Box 311, Natchez MS 39120. 601/445-1000. **Contact:** Human Resources. **World Wide Web address:** http://www.internationalpaper.com. **Description:** International Paper Company manufactures pulp and paper, packaging, wood products, and a range of specialty products. The company is organized into five business segments: Printing Papers, whose principal products include uncoated papers, coated papers, bristles, and pulp; Packaging, which includes industrial packaging, consumer packaging, and kraft and specialty papers; Distribution, including the sale of printing papers, graphic arts equipment and supplies, packaging materials, industrial supplies, and office products; Specialty Products, which includes imaging products, specialty panels, nonwovens, chemicals, and minerals; and Forest Products, which includes logging and wood products. **Corporate headquarters location:** Stamford CT. **Operations at this location include:** This location is engaged in the process of dissolving paper pulp. **Listed on:** New York Stock Exchange. **Stock exchange symbol:** IP. **Number of employees worldwide:** 72,500.

IRBY CONSTRUCTION COMPANY
815 South State Street, P.O Box 1819, Jackson MS 39215-1819. 601/960-7304.. **Fax:** 601/960-7377. **Contact:** Leslie Sumners, Human Resources Director. **E-mail address:** resumes@irby.com. **World Wide Web address:** http://www.irby.com. **Description:** A construction company specializing in powerline and transmission line construction. Irby Construction also has a telecommunications division. **Positions advertised include:** Counter Sales; Short Haul Driver; Inside/Outside Sales; Warehouse Receiving Clerk. **Other area locations:** Hattiesburg MS; Pascagoula MS; Tupelo MS; Vicksburg MS; Ridgeland MS. **Other U.S. locations:** Nationwide.

THE ISLE OF CAPRI CASINOS, INC.
1641 Popps Ferry Road, Suite B-1, Biloxi MS 39532. 228/396-7000. **Toll-free phone:** 800/843-4753. **Fax:** 228/396-2634. **Contact:** Erica Spencer, Human Resources Department. **World Wide Web address:** http://www.theislecorp.com. **Description:** Develops, owns, and operates riverboat, dockside casinos, and related facilities.

IVEY MECHANICAL COMPANY, LLC
514 North Wells Street, P.O. Box 610, Kosciusko MS 39090. 662/289-3646. **Fax:** 662/289-8602. **Contact:** Danny Brunt, Human Resources. **E-mail address:** danny.brunt@iveymechanical.com. **World Wide Web address:**

http://www.iveymechanical.com. **Description:** A mechanical contracting company that provides piping, plumbing, and HVAC services primarily to the correctional, healthcare, commercial, entertainment, industrial, and manufacturing industries. **Other U.S. locations:** GA; Al; NC; KY; TN. **CEO & President:** Larry Terrell.

JACKSON STATE UNIVERSITY
Administration Tower, 3rd Floor, P.O. Box 17028, Jackson MS 39217. 601/979-2015. **Toll-free phone:** 866/578-8648. **Fax:** 601/968-8644. **Contact:** Lester Pourciau, Director of Human Resources. **E-mail address:** l.pourciau@jsmus.edu. **World Wide Web address:** http://www.jsums.edu. **Description:** A state university. Founded in 1877. **Positions advertised include:** Capital Improvement Assistant Director; Clinical and Community Director; Center for Business Development Director; Director of Institutional Research; Master of Social Work Program Director; Admissions Advisor; Capacity Building Coordinator; Community Director; Games Area Manager; Graphic Artist; Production Coordinator; Special Events Coordinator; Remote Sensing Technician; Receptionist; Carpenter; Cook; Custodian. **Special programs:** Internships. **Operations at this facility include:** Administration; Research and Development. **Number of employees at this location:** 1,165.

JESCO INC.
2020 McCullough Boulevard, Tupelo MS 38801. 662/842-3240. **Toll-free phone:** 800/280-1792. **Contact:** President, Jerry Stubblefield. **World Wide Web address:** http://www.jescoinc.net. **Description:** An industrial contracting company engaged in the construction of buildings, mill work, agricultural buildings, and steel fabrication. Jesco also provides mechanical and electrical services, and industrial maintenance. Established in 1941. **Other area locations:** Fulton MS. **Other U.S. locations:** AL; GA; TN.

J.M. JONES LUMBER
P.O. Box 1368, Natchez MS 39120. 601/442-7471. **Physical Address:** 136 Government Fleet Road, Natchez MS 39120. **Fax:** 601/446-7448. **Contact:** Human Resources. **Description:** A lumber processor. The company manages in excess of 125,000 acres of prime southern forestland with a present timber inventory of more than 250 million board feet. Species include red oak, ash, elm, hackberry, poplar, cottonwood, pecan, willow, sycamore, and other southern hardwoods. Founded in 1911. **NOTE:** Send resumes to the P.O. Box address.

K.L.L.M. TRANSPORT SERVICES INC.
P.O. Box 6098, Jackson MS 39288 **Physical address:** 135 Riverview Drive, Richland MS 39218. 601/939-2545. **Toll-free phone:** 800-925-5556. **Contact:** Human Resources. **World Wide Web address:** http://www.kllm.com. **Description:** K.L.L.M. transports truckload quantities of various commodities, specializing in temperature-controlled shipments. **Number of employees at this location:** 2,000.

KELLWOOD COMPANY
P.O. Box 970, McComb MS 39649. 601/276-9331. **Physical address:** 1401 Old Highway 51 North, Summit MS 39666. **Fax:** 601/276-5016. **Contact:** Mr. L.H. Gibson, Personnel Director. **World Wide Web address:** http://www.kwdco.com. **Description:** Kellwood is a manufacturer, marketer, and merchandiser of apparel, home fashions, and recreational camping soft goods. The company operates many business units including AJ Brandon and California Ivy, a manufacturer of women's knitwear and sportswear; Crowntuft Manufacturing, whose products include loungewear, beachwear, and lingerie; En Chante, a manufacturer of sportswear, dresses, and casual wear; Kellwood Sportswear, a manufacturer of sportswear and outerwear for men, women, and children; Sag Harbor, whose products include women's career and dress casual related separates; Smart Shirts, Ltd., a manufacturer of men's dress and sports shirts, women's woven shirts and blouses, men's and women's pants and shorts, babywear, and men's boxer shorts; American Recreation Products, Inc., a manufacturer of tents, sleeping bags, backpacks, and related camping accessories; Cape Cod-Cricket Lane, a manufacturer of women's sportswear; Decorp, a manufacturer of dresses and women's sportswear; Goodman Knitting, a manufacturer of women's, men's, and girls' knitwear and sportswear; Kellwood Lingerie and Activewear, a manufacturer of underwear, daywear, and sleepwear for women, as well as activewear and swimwear; Melrose, a manufacturer of career clothing and separates; and SBH Group, a manufacturer of women's sportswear. **Corporate headquarters location:** St Louis MO. **Other U.S. locations:** Nationwide. **Operations at this facility include:** This location manufactures women's underwear, daywear, and sleepwear. **Listed on:** New York Stock Exchange. **Stock exchange symbol:** KWD. **Number of employees at this location:** 1,450. **Number of employees worldwide:** 24,000.

KELLWOOD COMPANY
P.O. Box 89, Calhoun City MS 38916. 662/628-5155. **Physical address:** 306 North Madison, Calhoun City MS 38916. **Contact:** Mary Allen, Human Resources. **E-mail address:** maryallen@kellwood.com. **World Wide Web address:** http://www.kwdco.com. **Description:** Kellwood is a manufacturer, marketer, and merchandiser of apparel, home fashions, and recreational camping soft goods. The company operates many business units including AJ Brandon and California Ivy, a manufacturer of women's knitwear and sportswear; Crowntuft Manufacturing, whose products include loungewear, beachwear, and lingerie; En Chante, a manufacturer of sportswear, dresses, and casual wear; Kellwood Sportswear, a manufacturer of sportswear and outerwear for men, women, and children; Sag Harbor, whose products include women's career and dress casual related separates; Smart Shirts, Ltd., a manufacturer of men's dress and sports shirts, women's woven shirts and blouses, men's and women's pants and shorts, babywear, and men's boxer shorts; American Recreation Products, Inc., a manufacturer of tents, sleeping bags, backpacks, and related camping accessories; Cape Cod-Cricket Lane, a manufacturer of women's sportswear; Decorp, a manufacturer of dresses and women's sportswear; Goodman Knitting, a manufacturer of women's, men's, and girls' knitwear and sportswear; Kellwood Lingerie and Activewear, a manufacturer of underwear, daywear, and sleepwear for women, as well as activewear and swimwear; Melrose, a manufacturer of career clothing and separates; and SBH Group, a manufacturer of women's sportswear. **Corporate headquarters location:** St Louis MO. **Operations at this location include:** This location manufactures men's and boys' pants. **Listed on:** New York Stock Exchange. **Stock exchange symbol:** KWD. **Number of employees worldwide:** 24,000.

KOCH FOODS
4688 Highway 80 East, Morton MS 39117. 601/732-8911. **Toll-free phone:** 800/837-2778. **Fax:** 601/732-1228. **Contact:** Dale Duncan, Human Resources. **E-mail address:** daledun@kochfoods.com. **World Wide Web address:** http://www.kochfoods.com. **Description:** A poultry processor.

LA-Z-BOY CHAIR COMPANY
Route 2, Box 500, Leland MS 38756. 662/686-5749. **Contact:** Human Resources. **World Wide Web address:** http://www.la-z-boy.com. **Description:** A leading manufacturer of upholstered seating and one of the nation's largest overall manufacturers of residential furniture. La-Z-Boy specializes in upholstered recliners. The company has grown into a complete furniture resource for family rooms, living rooms, bedrooms, and dining rooms. La-Z-Boy operates 24 plants in the United States and Canada. Its products are sold through over 10,000 retail locations. The company operates in five divisions. La-Z-Boy Residential produces stationary chairs, sofas and loveseats, recliners, reclining sofas, sleeper sofas, and modular seating groups, which it sells in a national network of La-Z-Boy proprietary stores and in department stores, furniture stores, and regional furniture chains. La-Z-Boy Canada manufactures residential seating and markets La-Z-Boy residential products in Canada, and is initiating a Canadian network of La-Z-Boy proprietary retail stores. Hammary produces occasional tables, living room cabinets, wall entertainment units, and upholstered furniture sold in furniture and department stores, as well as CompaTables occasional tables, which are featured in La-Z-Boy proprietary stores. Kincaid makes solid-wood bedroom, dining room, and occasional furniture sold through in-store Kincaid Galleries, select La-Z-Boy Furniture Galleries stores, and stores nationally. La-Z-Boy Contract Furniture Group includes La-Z-Boy Business Furniture, La-Z-Boy Healthcare Furniture (hospital chairs, recliners, and special mobile recliners, marketed through contract dealers and medical sales companies), and La-Z-Boy Hospitality Furniture (specially engineered La-Z-Boy recliners that are sold directly to major hotel and motel chains and through hospitality sales companies). **Corporate headquarters location:** Monroe MI. **Listed on:** New York Stock Exchange. **Stock exchange symbol:** LZB. **Number of employees nationwide:** 9,370. **Number of employees worldwide:** 10,000.

LANDAU UNIFORMS, INC.
P.O. Box 516, Olive Branch MS 38654. 662/895-7200. **Physical address:** 8410 West Sandidge Road, Olive Branch MS 38654. **Fax:** 662/893-9289. **Contact:** Don Coleman, Personnel Manager. **E-mail address:** resumes@landau.com. **World Wide Web address:** http://www.landau.com. **Description:** A manufacturer of health care uniforms. Founded in 1938. **Corporate headquarters location:** This location. **Other U.S. locations:** New Albany MS. **Operations at this facility include:** Administration; Manufacturing; Sales. **Listed on:** Privately held. **Number of employees at this location:** 400. **Number of employees nationwide:** 600.

LANE INDUSTRIES INC.
P.O. Box 1628, Tupelo MS 38802. 662/566-7211. **Fax:** 662/566-3474. **Contact:** Human Resources. **E-mail address:** humanresources@lanefurniture.com. **World Wide Web address:** http://www.lanefurniture.com. **Description:** A manufacturer of upholstered wooden household furniture under the brand name Lane. Founded in 1912. **Positions advertised include:** Product Designer; Accountant; Cost Accountant/Plant Controller; Executive Sales Trainee; Programmer/Analyst; Systems Programmer; Professional Driver. **Number of employees at this location:** 1,500.

LEXTRON CORPORATION
P.O. Box 23971, Jackson MS 39225. 601/713-8350. **Fax:** 601/713-8380. **World Wide Web address:** lextroncorporation.com. **Description:** A small manufacture of electrical and electronic assemblies for the telecommunications and automotive industries. **Positions advertised include:** Engineer, Maintenance, Assembly Line Workers. **President and CEO:** Charles Doty.

MCH TRANSPORTATION CO.
3180 Utica Street, Jackson MS 39209. 601/353-9382. **Toll-free phone:** 800/824-5142. **Fax:** 601/355-9055. **Contact:** Helen Boler. **World Wide Web address:** http://www.mchtrans.com. **Description:** A specialized trucking company. Founded in 1986. **Other area locations:** Tupelo MS; Olive Branch MS.

MS DIVERSIFIED CORPORATION
1501 Lakeland Dr., Jackson MS 39216. 601/420-4909. **Contact:** Human Resources. **World Wide Web address:** http://www.assurant.com. **Description:** Provides a wide range of products and services to automotive dealers and financial institutions. Products and services include credit life insurance; accident and health insurance; vehicle extended service contracts; administrative services; automobile financing; and financial services. MS Diversified serves a strong base of auto dealers with approximately 400 dealership agreements throughout the South, and provides products and services to more than 700 financial institutions. **Corporate headquarters location:** Miami FL. **Parent company:** Assurant Group. **Listed on:** Privately held. **Annual sales/revenues:** $51 - $100 million. **Number of employees at this location:** 100.

MAGNOLIA REGIONAL HEALTH CENTER
611 Alcorn Drive, Corinth MS 38834. 662/293-1000. **Fax:** 662/293-4285. **Contact:** Human Resources. **E-mail address:** info@mrhc.org. **World Wide Web address:** http://www.mrhc.org. **Description:** A 165-bed medical center. **Positions advertised include:** Social worker. **Operations at this facility include:** Administration. **Number of employees at this location:** 700.

MAXXIM MEDICAL
P.O. Box 2425, Columbus MS 39704. 662/327-8011. **Physical address:** 549 Yorkville Park Square, Columbus MS 39702. **Toll-free phone:** 888/462-9922. **Contact:** Carie Moore, Human Resources. **E-mail address:** maxximhelp@medline,com. **World Wide Web address:** http://www.maxximmedical.com. **Description:** One of the largest makers of customized clinical and surgical procedure trays in the United States. The company assembles, packages, and sterilizes ready-to-use custom procedure trays for hospitals, outpatient surgery centers, and medical clinics. All of the items included in the company's trays are disposable. Typical items include drapes, gowns, and other instruments such as sutures, needles, gloves, tubing, sponges, towels, and gauze. Customers consist primarily of hospitals and outpatient surgery centers. **Corporate headquarters location:** Mundeleine IL. **Parent company:** Medline.

THE MCC GROUP, L.L.C.
24101 Spyder Dr., Pass Christian MS 39571. 228/452-0502. **Contact:** Tara Schott. **E-mail address:** tara@mccgroup.com. **World Wide Web address:** http://www.mccgroup.com. **Description:** The MCC Group, L.L.C., founded in 1958, is a complete M.E.P. contractor, offering customers total mechanical, electrical and plumbing pre-construction and construction services. **NOTE:** Resumes must be sent to P.O. Box 7460, Metairie LA 70010. **Positions advertised include:** Plumber, Plumber Foreman.

MCLAN ELECTRONICS, INC.
1339 Wooddell Drive, Jackson MS 39212. **Physical Address:** 7770 Jackson Raymond Road, Raymond MS 39154. 601/373-2392. **Fax:** 601/372-4229. **Contact:** Human Resources. **E-mail address:** mclan@mclan.com. **World Wide Web address:** http://www.mclan.com. **Description:** Design and installation of photovoltaic systems, and remote communications systems.

MISSISSIPPI BUSINESS JOURNAL
5120 Galaxie Drive, Jackson MS 39206. 601/364-1000. **Toll-free phone:** 800/283-4625. **Contact:** Human Resources. **E-mail address:** mbj@msbusiness.com. **World Wide Web address:** http://www.msbusiness.com. **Description:** Publishes a monthly business journal. Founded in 1979. **Parent company:** Venture Publications.

MISSISSIPPI PHOSPHATES CORPORATION
601 Industrial Road, P.O. Box 848, Pascagoula MS 39567. 228/762-3210. **Fax:** 228/762-4173. **Contact:** Tommy McKiernon, Human Resources. **E-mail address:** hr@missphosphates.com. **World Wide Web address:** http://www.misschem.com. **Description:** Produces and distributes diammonium phosphate. **Parent company:** Mississippi Chemical Corporation, a major manufacturer of fertilizers, produces and markets three primary crop nutrients which include diammonium phosphate fertilizer, nitrogen fertilizer, and potash fertilizer.

MISSISSIPPI POWER COMPANY
2992 West Beach Boulevard, P.O. Box 4079, Gulfport MS 39501. 228/864-1211. **Toll-free phone:** 800/353-9777. **Contact:** Personnel Department. **World Wide Web address:** http://careers.southerncompany.com. **Description:** A utility company providing electric services. **NOTE:** The general website is http://www.mspower.com. **Positions advertised include:** Part-Time Administrative Assistant; Communications Co-op; Customer Service Representative; Apprentice Lineman. **Number of employees nationwide:** 1,590.

MISSISSIPPI STATE UNIVERSITY
P.O. Box 9603, Starkville MS 39762. 662/325-3713. **Physical address:** 150 McArthur Hall, Barr Avenue, Mississippi State MS 39762. **Fax:** 662/325-8395. **Contact:** Ann Bell, Director of Human Resources. **E-mail address:** bell@hrm.msstate.edu. **World Wide Web address:** http://www.msstate.edu. **Description:** One of Mississippi's largest universities, with over 13,800 students and 840 faculty members. The university offers a wide range of bachelor's degrees and pre-professional programs, as well as master's and doctoral degree programs. **NOTE:** Applicants must apply online at http://www.jobs.msstate.edu. **Number of employees at this location:** 4,240.

MISSISSIPPI VALLEY GAS COMPANY
P.O. Box 3348, Jackson MS 39207. 601/961-6900. **Physical address:** 4155 Industrial Drive, Jackson MS 39207. **Contact:** Human Resources. **World Wide Web address:** http://www.mvgas.com. **Description:** A natural gas utility company. **Corporate headquarters location:** Dallas TX. **Parent company:** Atmos Energy. **Listed on:** New York Stock Exchange. **Stock exchange symbol:** ATO.

MODERN LINE PRODUCTS
2nd Street, P.O. Box 110, Indianola MS 38751. 662/887-4151. **Contact:** Personnel Director. **World Wide Web address:** http://www.mtdproducts.com. **Description:** A company engaged in the manufacture of lawn mowers, tractors, and other garden equipment. **Positions advertised include:** Production Supervisor; Product Engineer; Financial Analyst; Purchasing Agent; Shipping Clerk. **Parent company:** MTD.

NEEL-SCHAFFER, INC.
666 North Street, Suite 201, Jackson MS 39202. 601/948-3071. **Fax:** 601/948-3178. **Contact:** Human Resources Department. **World Wide Web address:** http://www.neel-schaffer.com. **Description:** Neel-Schaffer, Inc. is one of the largest privately held engineering firms in the Southeast. A multi-disciplined engineering and planning firm, it has offices in Alabama, Florida, Georgia, Louisiana, Mississippi, and Tennessee. Founded in 1983.

NISSAN NORTH AMERICA
152 Watford Parkway Drive, P.O. Box 1606, Canton MS 39046. 601/855-8050. **Fax:** 601/855-8055. **Contact:** Employment Department. **E-mail address:** canton.careers@nmm.nissan-usa.com. **World Wide Web address:** http://www.nissanusa.com. **Description:** Automotive manufacturer. **NOTE:** Search and apply for positions online. **Positions advertised include:** Industrial Maintenance Technician; Maintenance Technician; Safety Engineer.

NORTHROP GRUMMAN SHIP SYSTEMS
P.O. Box 149, Pascagoula MS 39568-0149. 228/935-1122. **Physical address:** 1000 Access Road, Pascagoula MS 39567. **Contact:** Employment Department. **World Wide Web address:** http://www.ss.northropgrumman.com. **Description:** A ship building and repair company. **Positions advertised include:** Compensation Specialist; Section Manager Engineer; Design Program Integration Manager; Engineering Specialist; Naval Architect; Engineering Project Supervisor; Life Cycle Support Engineer; Subcontract Management Specialist. **Corporate headquarters location:** Los Angeles CA. **Parent company:** Northrop Grumman Corporation is a global aerospace and defense company. Northrop Grumman provides services and solutions in defense and commercial electronics, systems integration, information technology, and non-nuclear shipbuilding systems. **Listed on:** New York Stock Exchange. **Stock exchange symbol:** NOC. **Annual sales/revenues:** $15 billion. **Number of employees nationwide:** 12,000. **Number of employees worldwide:** 100,000.

OLIVE BRANCH CATFISH COMPANY
9659 Highway 178, Olive Branch MS 38654. 662/895-9494. **Fax:** 662/893-4123. **Contact:** Human Resources. **Description:** A catfish processor. When the fish reach 18 months old, they are harvested and hauled to the processing plants by live-haul trucks. The company then cleans, processes, and freezes the fish. Finished products include whole fish, steaks, fillets, nuggets, strips, and marinated and breaded catfish, as well as precooked frozen dinners and entrees. The two major channels for distribution of the catfish are retail grocery store outlets and the food service sector.

ORECK MANUFACTURING
21180 Oreck Avenue, Long Beach MS 39560. 228/863-7112. **Toll-free phone:** 800/989-3535. **Contact:** Director of Human Resources. **E-mail address:** ddesporte@oreck.com. **World Wide Web address:** http://www.oreck.com. **Description:** Manufactures electronic machinery such as vacuum cleaners. **NOTE:** Entry-level positions and second and third shifts are offered. **Special programs:** Apprenticeships; Training; Co-ops. **President:** James McCain. **Number of employees at this location:** 465.

PEAVEY ELECTRONICS CORPORATION
711 A Street, Meridian MS 39301. 601/483-5365. **Fax:** 601/486-1198. **Contact:** Human Resources. **E-mail address:** humanresources@peavy.com. **World Wide Web address:** http://www.peavey.com. **Description:** Peavey Electronics Corporation manufactures sound equipment including power amplifiers, mixing consoles, speakers, and microphones. Peavey's products under the Audio Media Research (AMR) name are designed specifically for the recording studio environment. Products under the Architectural Acoustics (AA) name are found in a wide range of places including supermarkets and theme parks. **Operations at this facility include:** Administration; Manufacturing; Research and Development; Sales; Service. **Listed on:** Privately held. **Number of employees at this location:** 2,000.

PEOPLE LEASE
P.O. Box 3303, 689-B Towne Center, Ridgeland MS 39158-3303. 601/987-3025. **Toll-free phone:** 800/723-3025. **Fax:** 601/987-3029. **Contact:** Human Resources. **E-mail address:** mail@peoplelease.com. **World Wide Web address:** http://www.peoplelease.com. **Description:** People Lease provides payroll and other business services. **Company slogan:** The leader in employee administrative services.

REED MANUFACTURING COMPANY INC.
P.O. Box 650, Tupelo MS 38801. 662/842-4472. **Physical address:** 1321 South Veteran's Road, Tupelo MS 38801. **Contact:** Personnel Director. **Description:** A clothing company engaged in the manufacture of men's work clothes. **Number of employees at this location:** 700.

RIVER REGION HEALTH SYSTEM
2100 Highway 61 North, Vicksburg MS 39183. 601/883-5900. **Toll-free phone:** 800/548-2419. **Fax:** 601/883-5014. **Recorded jobline:** 601/631-2749. **Contact:** Human Resources. **E-mail address:** human.resources@riverregion.com. **World Wide Web address:** http://www.riverregion.com. **Description:** A 227-bed medical center. **Positions advertised include:** Clinical Therapist; Recreational Therapist; Bariatric Coordinator; Clinical Supervisor; Nursing Supervisor; Physical Therapist; Radiologic Technologist; Sonographer. **Office hours:** Monday through Friday 8-5. **Corporate headquarters location:** Nashville TN. **Operations at this facility include:** Administration; Service. **Number of employees at this location:** 750.

SAKS INCORPORATED
P.O. Box 10327, Jackson MS 39289. 601/968-4400. **Contact:** Human Resources. **World Wide Web address:** http://www.saksincorporated.com. **Description:** A department store holding company that operates a total of approximately 360 stores in 36 states. The company's stores include Saks Fifth Avenue, Parisian, Proffit's, Younker's, Herberger's, Carson Pirie Scott, Boston Store, Bergner's, and Off 5th, the company's outlet store. Saks Incorporated also operates two retail catalogs and several retail Internet sites. **Corporate headquarters location:** Birmingham AL. **Operations at this facility include:** Divisional Headquarters.

SANDERSON FARMS, INC.
225 North 13th Avenue, P.O. Box 988, Laurel MS 39441-0988. 601/649-4030. **Toll-free phone:** 800/844-4030. **Fax:** 601/426-1461. **Contact:** Human Resources. **World Wide Web address:** http://www.sandersonfarms.com. **Description:** Produces, processes, markets, and distributes fresh, frozen and further processed chicken, as well as over 100 frozen prepared entrees and other specialty food products. Founded in 1955. **NOTE:** Submit inquiry online or contact local state employment agency. Do not forward resume. **Listed on:** NASDAQ. **Stock exchange symbol:** SAFM. **Number of employees nationwide:** 8,300.

SARA LEE FOODS INC.
P.O. Box 1177, West Point MS 39773. 662/494-3741. **Fax:** 662/495-4439. **Physical address:** 100 Church Hill Road, West Point MS 39773. **Contact:** Human Resources. **World Wide Web address:** http://www.saralee.com. **Description:** A manufacturer and marketer of household, food and beverage, and branded apparel products for consumers. **Corporate Headquarters:** Chicago IL. **Number of employees worldwide:** 150,400.

SEVERN TRENT SERVICES
3810 I-55 South, P.O. Box 7578, Jackson MS 39212. 601/372-3439. **Fax:** 601/371-2453. **World Wide Web address:** http://www.severntrentservices.com. **Description:** A leading supplier of water and wastewater treatment solutions. **Corporate headquarters location:** Fort Washington PA.

THE SHERWIN-WILLIAMS COMPANY
10136 Magnolia Drive, Olive Branch MS 38654. 662/895-5594. **Fax:** 662/893-5019. **Contact:** Human Resources. **World Wide Web address:** http://www.sherwin.com. **Description:** Manufactures, sells, and distributes coatings and related products. Coatings are produced for original equipment manufacturers in various industries, as well as for the automotive aftermarket, the industrial maintenance market, and the traffic paint market. Sherwin-Williams labeled architectural and industrial coatings are sold through company-owned specialty paint and wallcovering stores. The Sherwin-Williams Company also manufactures paint under the Acme, Dutch Boy, Kem-Tone, Lucas, Martin-Senour, Minwax, Pratt & Lambert, Rogers, and Thompson brand names, as well as private labels, and markets its products to independent dealers, mass merchandisers, and home improvement centers. **Corporate headquarters location:** Upper Saddle River NJ. **Other U.S. locations:** Flora IL; Memphis TN. **Operations at this facility include:** Manufacturing. **Listed on:** Privately held. **Annual sales/revenues:** More than $100 million. **Number of employees at this location:** 275. **Number of employees nationwide:** 1,200.

SKYTEL COMMUNICATIONS
P.O. Box 2469 Jackson MS 39225-2469. 601/944-1300. **Physical address:** 515 East Amite Street, Jackson MS 39201. **Fax:** 601/460-8736. **Toll-free phone:** 800/552-6835. **Contact:** Personnel. **World Wide Web address:** http://www.skytel.com. **Description:** A telecommunications company specializing in global wireless data communications. Products and services include SkyPager, a nationwide numeric paging service; SkyTalk, a full-featured voicemail system with instant notification of messages via the SkyTel System; and SkyWord, a nationwide wireless text messaging service. Integration with services and computer software features SkyNews, a wireless information service that provides Reuters news headlines to SkyWord subscribers. **NOTE:** Application may be done on-line through the parent company. **Corporate headquarters location:** This location. **Parent company:** MCI.

SOUTH CENTRAL REGIONAL MEDICAL CENTER
P.O. Box 607, Laurel MS 39441. 601/399-0517. **Fax:** 601/425-7535. **Recorded jobline:** 601/399-0510. **Contact:** Lorrie Smith, Personnel Coordinator. **E-mail address:** lsmith@scrmc.com. **World Wide Web address:** http://www.scrmc.com. **Description:** A 285-bed medical center. **Positions advertised include:** Diagnostic Technician; Physical Therapist; Occupational Therapist; Paramedic; Speech Therapist; Registered Nurse; Admissions Clerk; Accounting Clerk; Secretary; Pharmacy Technician. **Operations at this facility include:** Administration; Service. **Number of employees at this location:** 1,100.

SOUTHEASTERN FREIGHT LINES
130 Riverview Drive, Richland MS 39218. 601/420-0465. **Toll-free phone:** 866/700-7335. **Fax:** 601/939-3556. **Contact: World Wide Web address:** http://www.sefl.com. **Description:** A trucking company that provides assembly and distribution services throughout the south. **NOTE:** Online application is available. **Company Slogan:** "Quality without Question". **Positions advertised include:** Account Manager; Freight Handler; Pick-up and Delivery Driver. **Corporate headquarters:** Lexington SC. **Other area locations:** Tupelo MS. **Other U.S. locations:** VA; NC; SC; TN; GA; FL; AL; LA; TX.

STRATTFORD AND SIMMONS COMPANY
1201 West Bankhead Street, New Albany MS 38652. 662/534-4762. **Contact:** Gala Jolly, Human Resources. **World Wide Web address:** http://www.simmons.com.

Description: A furniture company engaged in the manufacture of sofas, recliners, and other upholstered household furniture. **Number of employees nationwide:** 1,400.

SUNBEAM-OSTER HOUSEHOLD PRODUCTS
224 Russell Drive, P.O. Box 469, Waynesboro MS 39367. 601/671-2200. **Contact:** Human Resources. **World Wide Web address:** http://www.sunbeam.com. **Description:** Sunbeam-Oster is a designer, manufacturer, and marketer of consumer products. The company is divided into four business groups: Outdoor Products, Household Products, Specialty Products, and International. Outdoor Products include propane, natural gas, electric, and charcoal barbecue grills; aluminum lawn and patio furniture and related accessories; and wrought iron and wood furniture. Small kitchen appliances include stand mixers, hand mixers, blenders, food processors, juice extractors, toasters, can openers, waffle makers, and other culinary accessories. Sunbeam also produces barber and beauty products, personal care products, and pet and large animal products, as well as clocks, timers, thermometers, and weather instruments. The company operates in over 60 countries through its international unit, primarily throughout Latin America and Canada, with manufacturing facilities in Mexico and Venezuela. **Positions advertised include:** Computer Operator; Graphic Designer; Program Manager. **Corporate headquarters location:** Boca Raton FL. **Parent company:** Sunbeam Corporation **Operations at this facility include:** This location manufactures electric blankets.

SUPER SAGLESS CORPORATION
1961 South Green Street, P.O. Box 197, Tupelo MS 38801. 662/842-5704. **Fax:** 662/791-7187. **Contact:** Human Resources Manager. **Description:** Super Sagless Corporation manufactures and assembles hardware and mechanisms for hide-a-beds and recliners. **Corporate headquarters location:** Carthage MO. **Other U.S. locations:** Pomona CA; Hickory NC. **Parent company:** Leggett & Platt. **Operations at this facility include:** Administration; Manufacturing; Research and Development; Sales; Service. **Listed on:** New York Stock Exchange. **Stock exchange symbol:** LEG.

TECUMSEH PRODUCTS
P.O. Box 527, Tupelo MS 38802. 662/566-2231. **Physical address:** 5424 Highway 145 South, Verona MS 38879. **Contact:** Human Resources Director. **World Wide Web address:** http://www.tecumseh.com. **Description:** A manufacturer of compressors for use in industrial and residential air-conditioning and heating systems. Founded in 1934. **Company slogan:** Better right from the start. **Other area locations:** Corinth MS. **Other U.S. locations:** GA; MI; TN; WI. **Number of employees at this location:** 700.

TERRA INDUSTRIES, INC.
P.O. Box 388, Yazoo City MS 39194. 662/746-4131. **Fax:** 662/751-2478. **Contact:** Human Resources. **World Wide Web address:** http://www.terraindustries.com. **Description:** Poduces and markets three primary crop nutrients, which include diammonium phosphate fertilizer, nitrogen fertilizer, and potash fertilizer. **Positions advertised include:** Machine Operator; Maintenance Mechanic; User Support Analyst; Network Operations Analyst; Accountant; Auditor; Financial Analyst. **Special Programs:** Internships available. **Corporate headquarters location:** Sioux City, Iowa. **Subsidiaries include:** Mississippi Phosphates Corporation (Pascagoula MS) produces diammonium phosphate fertilizer. Mississippi Potash, Inc. (Carlsbad NM) produces potash fertilizer at its mines and refinery. Triad Nitrogen, Inc. (Donaldsonville LA) produces nitrogen fertilizer. **Operations at this location include:** This location houses administrative offices and also produces nitrogen fertilizer. **Listed on:** New York Stock Exchange. **Stock exchange symbol:** TRA. **President/CEO:** Mike Bennett. **Number of employees worldwide:** 1,250.

THE THERMOS COMPANY
355 Thermos Road, Batesville MS 38606. 662/563-7691. **Toll-free phone:** 800/831-9242. **Fax:** 662/563-2175. **Contact:** Human Resources Manager. **World Wide Web address:** http://www.thermos.com. **Description:** A manufacturer of cooler and thermos products, as well as school lunch kits. Since 1904. **Corporate headquarters location:** Rolling Meadows IL. **Other U.S. locations:** Nationwide. **Parent company:** Nippon Sanso. **Operations at this facility include:** Administration; Manufacturing; Service: Product Returns. **Annual sales/revenues:** More than $100 million. **Number of employees at this location:** 370. **Number of employees nationwide:** 850.

THOMAS & BETTS CORPORATION
8735 Hamilton Road, P.O. Box 100, Southaven MS 38671. 662/342-1545. **Fax:** 662/342-0246. **Contact:** Personnel. **World Wide Web address:** http://www.thomasandbetts.com. **Description:** Engaged in the design, manufacture, and marketing of electrical and electronic components and systems for connecting, fastening, protecting, and identifying wires, components, and conduits. The company's products include fittings and accessories for electrical raceways; solderless terminals for small wires and heavy power cables, wire fastening devices and markers; insulation products, flat cable, connectors, and IC sockets for electronic applications; ceramic chip capacitors for electronic circuitry, fiber-optic connectors and accessories, and wire management systems; and customer-specific products for major original equipment manufacturers. Most of the products are used in numerous markets, from power generating plants to telecommunications to transportation equipment. This location manufactures street lighting equipment. **Corporate headquarters location:** Memphis TN. **Listed on:** New York Stock Exchange. **Stock symbol exchange:** TNB.

TIME WARNER CABLE
5375 Executive Place, Jackson MS 39206. 601/982-0922. **Fax:** 601/321-3888. **Contact:** Human Resources. **World Wide Web Address:** http://www.twcjam.com. **Description:** Provides cable services. **Positions advertised include:** HSD Commercial Product Specialist; Direct Sales Representative.

THE TRAVEL COMPANY
605 North Park Dr., Suite D, Ridgeland MS 39157. 601/981-1133. **Toll-free phone:** 800/844-1133. **Fax:** 601/991-1865. **Contact:** Human Resources. **World Wide Web address:** http://www.thetravelcoinc.com. **Description:** A travel agency. Founded in 1983. **Corporate headquarters location:** This location. **Operations at this facility include:** Sales; Service. **Listed on:** Privately held. **Number of employees at this location:** 15. **Number of employees nationwide:** 35.

TRUSTMARK NATIONAL BANK
P.O. Box 291, Jackson MS 39205. 601/208-5111. **Physical address:** 248 East Capitol Street, Jackson MS 39201-2582. **Toll-free phone:** 800/844-2000. **Contact:** Personnel Department. **World Wide Web address:** http://www.trustmark.com. **Description:** A banking institution. **Positions advertised include:** Asset Review Examiner; Head Teller; Loan Adjuster; Commercial Banker. **Number of employees at this location:** 1,400. **Other area locations:** FL; TN; TX. **Listed on:** NASDAQ. **Stock symbol exchange:** TRMK.

TYSON FOODS, INC.
P.O. Box 577, 3865 Highway 35 North, Carthage MS 39051. 601/298-5300. **Contact:** Human Resources. **World Wide Web address:** http://www.tyson.com. **Description:** A poultry processing company. **NOTE:** Entry-level positions and second and third shifts are offered. **Positions advertised include:** Debone Supervisor; Maintenance Supervisor. **Special programs:** Internships. **Operations at this facility include:** Administration; Manufacturing; Sales; Service. **Annual sales/revenues:** More than $100 million. **Number of employees at this location:** 2,200.

TYSON FOODS, INC.
P.O. Box 433, 305 Cleveland Street, Forest MS 39074. 601/469-1712. **Contact:** Personnel. **World Wide Web address:** http://www.tyson.com. **Description:** An integrated poultry processing company producing fresh, ice packed, and frozen poultry products. **Corporate headquarters location:** Springdale AR. **Operations at this facility include:** Administration. **Number of employees nationwide:** 3,600.

TYSON FOODS, INC.
P.O. Box 2579, Jackson MS 39207-2579. 601/372-7441. **Physical address:** 238 Wilmington Street, Jackson MS. **Contact:** Human Resources. **World Wide Web address:** http://www.tyson.com. **Description:** An integrated poultry processing company producing fresh, ice packed, and frozen poultry products. **Corporate headquarters location:** Springdale AR. **Number of employees nationwide:** 3,600.

THE UNITED WAY OF THE CAPITAL AREA
P.O. Box 23169, Jackson MS 39225. 601/948-4725. **Physical address:** 843 North President Street, Jackson MS 39202. **Contact:** Administrative Assistant. **World Wide Web address:** http://www.myunitedway.com. **Description:** The United Way provides community and emergency services to families and children, health and rehabilitation services, and youth development services. Community and living services include daily living needs, aid for the homeless, HIV/AIDS education, housing, 24-hour crisis counseling, disaster relief, emergency assistance, military family services, elderly services, and services for victims of sexual assault. Services to families and children include counseling in areas of teen pregnancy, family violence, illiteracy, child abuse, adoption, speech and hearing, and emergency shelter for children. Health and Rehabilitation Services include drug/alcohol treatment, health research, health screening, mental illness, medication assistance, training and employment for the handicapped, and developmental services for mentally and physically handicapped individuals. Youth Development Services assist in dropout prevention, tutoring, child care, after school care, water safety, safe places, recreational activities, camping opportunities, and character building. **Corporate headquarters location:** Alexandria VA.

UNIVERSAL LIGHTING TECHNOLOGIES
19120 Highway 51, P.O. Box 128, Harrisville MS 39082. 601/892-2534. **Fax:** 601/892-2076. **Contact:** Director of Human Resources. **E-mail address:** hr@universalballast.com. **World Wide Web address:** http://www.universalballast.com. **Description:** A designer, producer, and marketer of electrical, electronic, and industrial components and products. The company also offers services and repair support for its components. Principal products include ballasts and transformers for lighting; motors; and control components for motors and generators, systems, and controls. The company's service group rebuilds and repairs large motors, generators, and transformers primarily for utility companies and industrial manufacturers. **Corporate headquarters location:** Nashville TN. **Other U.S. locations:** Nationwide. **Parent company:** MagneTek, Inc. **Number of employees at this location:** 1,300.

UNIVERSITY OF MISSISSIPPI
P.O. Box 1848, University MS 38677-1848. 662/915-5690. **Fax:** 662/915-5836. **Contact:** Clay Jones, Director Human Resources. **E-mail address:** employ@olemiss.edu. **World Wide Web address:** http://www.olemiss.edu. **Description:** A state university with an undergraduate and graduate enrollment of approximately 12,400 students. The University of Mississippi offers more than 100 programs of study through the College of Liberal Arts, Medical Center, School of Accountancy, School of Business Administration, School of Education, School of Engineering, School of Law, and School of Pharmacy. Founded in 1848. **NOTE:** Check Website for whom to contact in regards to specific positions. **Positions advertised include:** Assistant Professor of Pharmacy Administration; Assistant Professor of Bands; Assistant Professor of Hospitality Management; Assistant Professor of Family and Consumer Science; Chair and Professor or Associate Professor of Political Science; Dean of University Libraries and Professor; Alumni Center Hotel Assistant Manager; Assistant Director of Marketing; Assistant Research and Development Chemist; Coordinator of Corporate Relations; Assistant to the Dean of Advancement; Research Scientist; Director of Aquatics; Custodian; Property Control Auditor; Records Coordinator; University Police; Senior Secretary; Plumber. **Special programs:** Internships; Apprenticeships. **Corporate headquarters location:** This location. **Other area locations:** Jackson MS; Southaven MS; Tupelo MS. **Number of employees at this location:** 2,800.

UNIVERSITY OF SOUTHERN MISSISSIPPI
118 College Drive, Box 5111, Hattiesburg MS 39406. 601/266-4050. **Physical location:** Room 317, Forest County Hall. **Contact:** Human Resources. **Fax:** 601/266-4541. **E-mail address:** hr@usm.edu. **World Wide Web address:** http://www.usm.edu. **Description:** A university made up of colleges in the Arts, Business Administration, Education and Psychology, Health and Human Sciences, International and Continuing Education, Liberal Arts, Nursing, Science and Technology, Marine Sciences, Graduate Studies and Honors. Founded in 1910. **NOTE:** Human Resources Website is: http://www.hr.usm.edu. Must use standard application, which can be downloaded. **Positions advertised include:** Chief Information Technology Enterprise Architect; Chair of the Department of Economic Development and Planning; HVAC Mechanic; Speech-Language Pathologist; Music Professor; Assistant Medical Director; Assistant Geology Professor; Chief Financial Officer of the Office of Development; Coordinator of Post-Secondary Programs. **Number of employees at this location:** 1,900.

VALLEY FRESH
P.O. Box 708, Water Valley MS 38965. 209/668-3695. **Contact:** Terry McMinn, Human Resources Director. **Description:** A producer of poultry products. **Common positions include:** Buyer; Health Services Manager; Human Resources Manager. **Operations at this facility include:** Sales.

VALLEY INNOVATIVE SERVICES
P.O. Box 5454, Jackson MS 39288-5454. 601/664-3100. **Toll-free phone:** 800/541-3805 ext. 168. **Fax:** 601/664-3368. **Contact:** Heather Bean, Recruiting. **E-mail address:** jobs@valleyservicesi.com. **World Wide Web address:** http://www.valleyservicesi.com. **Description:** A food service management and consulting firm. Primary customers include health care facilities, schools, country clubs, and large businesses. Founded in 1960. **NOTE:** Entry-level positions are offered. **Positions advertised include:** Clinical Dietitian; Dietitian; Chef; Vending Manager; Foodservice Director; Direct Sales Manager; Clinical Research Manager; Catering Manager. **Special programs:** Internships; Training. **Annual sales/revenues:** More than $100 million. **Number of employees nationwide:** 1,500.

EATON AEROSPACE
VICKERS FLUID POWER
5353 Highland Drive, Jackson MS 39206-3449. 601/981-2811. **Fax:** 601/987-3268. **Contact:** Steve Szabo, Human Resources. **E-mail address:** steveszabo@eaton.com. **World Wide Web address:** http://www.eaton.com. **Description:** A manufacturer of hydraulic pumps and motors. **NOTE:** Human Resources direct line is 601/987-3417. **Positions Advertised include:** Quality Systems Manager; Quality Manager; Cost Accounting Manager; General Accountant; Materials Planner; Commodity Manager. **Special Programs:** Co-ops; Summer Internships. **Corporate headquarters location:** Cleveland OH. **Parent company:** Eaton Corporation. **Listed on:** New York Stock Exchange. **Stock exchange symbol:** ETN. **Annual sales/revenues:** More than $100 million. **Number of employees at this location:** 700.

WXVT-TV 15
3015 East Reed Road, Greenville MS 38703. 662/334-1500. **Fax:** 662/378-8122. **Contact:** Leigh D. McDowell, Personnel. **E-mail address:** ldm@tecinfo.com. **World Wide Web address:** http://www.wxvt.com. **Description:** A CBS television affiliate. Founded in 1980. **Special programs:** Internships.

WATKINS LUDLAM WINTER & STENNIS, P.A.
633 North State Street, Jackson MS 39202. 601/949-4900. **Fax:** 601/949-4804. **Contact:** Angie Artman, Recruiting Coordinator. **E-mail address:** aartman@watkinsludlam.com. **World Wide Web address:** http://www.wlwslaw.com. **Description:** A legal services firm. **Special programs:** Internships; Summer Associate Programs. **Office hours:** Monday through Friday, 8:30 a.m. - 5:00 p.m. **Chairman of the Board:** Alveno Castilla. **Annual sales/revenues:** $11 - $20 million. **Number of employees at this location:** 140.

WESLEY MEDICAL CENTER
5001 Hardy Street, Hattiesburg MS 39402. 601/268-8106. **Recorded jobline:** 800/246-1675. **Contact:** Human Resources. **World Wide Web address:** http://www.wesley.com. **Description:** A medical center. **Positions advertised include:** Admissions Coordinator; Cook; Rehabilitation Services Director; Environmental Technician; Medical Technologist; Occupational Therapist; Phlebotomist; Special Procedures Technologist; Ultrasonographer; LPN; Registered Nurse. **Office hours:** Monday through Friday 9-4. **Number of employees at this location:** 725.

WEYERHAEUSER COMPANY
P.O. Box 708, Philadelphia MS 39350. 601/656-5300. **Physical address:** 1016 Weyerhaeuser Road, Philadelphia MS 39350. **Contact:** Bernadette in Human Resources. **World Wide Web address:** http://www.weyerhaeuser.com. **Description:** This location produces pine lumber and plywood. Weyerhaeuser Company is a manufacturer of forest products. Its principal businesses are the growing and harvesting of timber; the manufacture, distribution, and sales of forest products including logs, wood chips, building products, pulp, paper, and packaging products; real estate development and construction; and financial services. The company is one of the world's largest private owners of marketable softwood timber and a large producer of softwood lumber and market pulp. **NOTE:** Unsolicited resumes receive no response. Open positions are advertised in local newspapers.

WEYERHAEUSER COMPANY
P.O. Box 2288, Columbus MS 39704-2288. 662/245-5000. **Physical address:** 29 Tom Rose Road, Columbus MS 39701. **Contact:** Personnel. **World Wide Web address:** http://www.weyerhaeuser.com. **Description:** Weyerhaeuser Company's principal businesses are the growing and harvesting of timber; the manufacture, distribution, and sale of forest products including logs, wood chips, and building products; real estate development and construction; and financial services. Weyerhaeuser Company is one of the world's largest private owners of marketable softwood timber and also one of the largest producers of softwood lumber and pulp. The company is also one of North America's largest producers of forest products and recyclers of office wastepaper, newspaper, and corrugated boxes. **Corporate headquarters location:** Tacoma WA. **Other area locations:** Philadelphia MS. **Other U.S. locations:** Nationwide. **Operations at this location include:** This location manufactures lightweight paper. **Listed on:** New York Stock Exchange. **Stock exchange symbol:** WY. **Number of employees worldwide:** 37,000.

WINSTON MEDICAL CENTER
562 East Main Street, P.O. Box 967, Louisville MS 39339. 662/773-6211. **Fax:** 662/773-6223. **Contact:** Human Resources Department. **E-mail address:** info@winstonmedical.org. **World Wide Web address:** http://www.winstonmedical.org. **Description:** A 65-bed acute care hospital that also operates a 120-bed nursing home and home health care agency. Founded in 1958. **NOTE:** Human Resources direct line is: 662/779-5102. **Company slogan:** Professional care close to home. **Number of employees at this location:** 250.

WORLDCOM
500 Clinton Center Drive, Clinton MS 39056. 601/460-5600. **Contact:** Human Resources. **World Wide Web address:** http://www.wcom.com. **Description:** One of the world's largest suppliers of local, long-distance, and international telecommunications services, and a global Internet service provider. **NOTE:** All hiring is done through the corporate headquarters location. **Corporate headquarters location:** 22001 Loudon County Parkway, Ashburn. VA 20147, 703/416-0760. **International locations:** Worldwide. **Parent company:** MCI **Listed on:** NASDAQ. **Stock exchange symbol:** WCOM. **Annual sales/revenues:** More than $100 million.

YMCA
840 East River Place, Suite 503, Jackson MS 39202-3488. 601/948-0818. **Fax:** 601/968-3874. **Contact:** Tina Voltz, Human Resources. **E-mail address:** tina@jacksony.org. **World Wide Web address:** http://www.jacksony.org. **NOTE:** Employment information also available at http://www.ymca.com. **Description:** The YMCA provides health and fitness; social and personal development; sports and recreation; education and career development; and camps and conferences to children, youths, adults, the elderly, families, the disabled, refugees and foreign nationals, YMCA residents, and community residents, through a broad range of specific programs. **Other U.S. locations:** Nationwide.

AAA
12901 North 40 Drive, St. Louis MO 63141-8699. 314/523-7350. **Fax:** 314/523-6973. **Contact:** Personnel Department. **E-mail address:** personnel@aaamissouri.com. **World Wide Web address:** http://www.ouraaa.com. **Description:** Provides insurance, travel advice, and a wide variety of services to motorists through a network of over 50 branch offices. **Positions advertised include:** Corporate Travel Counselor; Customer Care Representative; Executive Secretary; Marketing Database Analyst; Member Service Counselor; Programmer Analyst; Sales Agent; Sales Assistant; Travel Counselor; Ticket Coordinator; Travel Accounting Clerk. **Corporate headquarters location:** Heathrow FL. **Other U.S. locations:** Nationwide. **Operations at this facility include:** Administration; Regional Headquarters; Service. **Number of employees at this location:** 400. **Number of employees nationwide:** 850.

ACF INDUSTRIES INC.
AMERICAN RAILCAR INDUSTRIES
620 North 2nd Street, St. Charles MO 63301-2075. 636/940-6000. **Contact:** Recruitment Officer. **World Wide Web address:** http://www.americanrailcar.com. **Description:** Manufactures, leases, and sells railroad freight and tank cars; acquires, owns, leases, and sells to industrial corporations special purpose freight and tank cars and provides maintenance for such cars in its lease fleet; and manufactures certain freight and tank car parts, piggy-back trailer hitches, and tank car valves.

ACS
1015 Locust Street, St. Louis MO 63101. 314/231-5002. **Contact:** Human Resources. **World Wide Web address:** http://www.acs-inc.com. **Description:** A provider of diversified business process and information technology outsourcing solutions to commercial and government clients. **NOTE:** Search and apply for positions online. **Positions advertised include:** Parking Consultant. **Corporate headquarters location:** Dallas TX. **Listed on:** New York Stock Exchange. **Stock exchange symbol:** ACS. **Number of employees worldwide:** 40,000.

AMC ENTERTAINMENT INC.
P.O. Box 219615, Kansas City MO 64121-9615. 816/221-4000. **Fax:** 816/480-4625. **Contact:** Human Resources. **E-mail address:** human_resources@amctheatres.com. **World Wide Web address:** http://www.amctheatres.com. **Description:** AMC Entertainment Inc. is one of the largest motion picture exhibitors in the United States. AMC's theater technology ranges from computerized box offices to High Impact Theatre Systems. The company operates 214 theaters with 2,906 screens in 23 states and the District of Columbia. **Corporate headquarters location:** This location. **Subsidiaries include:** American Multi-Cinema Inc. (AMC).

AOS GLOBAL SOLUTIONS
403 Axminister Drive, St. Louis MO 63026. 636/343-200. **Contact:** Thatcher Alexander, Human Resources. **E-mail address:** thatchera@aos5.com **World Wide Web address:** http://www.globalsolutionsgroup.com. **Description:** Develops IT solutions through consultation, design, and implementation. **Positions advertised include:** Sr. Microsoft Systems Engineer; Account Manager; Scheduler; Web Developer; Computer Operator.

ACCENTURE
1010 Market Street, St. Louis, Missouri 63101. 314/345-3000. **Fax:** 314/345-3505. **Contact:** Human Resources. **World Wide Web address:** http://www.accenture.com. **Description:** Accenture is a global management consulting, technology services, and outsourcing company. The company helps clients identify and enter new markets, increase revenues in existing markets, improve operational performance, and deliver their products and services more effectively and efficiently. Founded in 1989. **NOTE:** Search and apply for positions online. **Positions advertised include:** JAVA/J2EE Sr. Programmer/Analyst Programmer; Cobol Sr. Programmer; Cobol Systems Analyst.

AJILON SERVICES INC.
425 South Woodsmill Road, Suite 400, Town & Country MO 63017-3441. 314/434-5003. **Fax:** 314/434-7441. **Contact:** Human Resources Department. **E-mail address:** recruit@stlouis.ajilon.com. **World Wide Web address:** http://www.ajilon.com. **Description:** Offers computer consulting services, project support, and end user services. **Other U.S. locations:** Nationwide. **Parent company:** Adecco

ALCO CONTROLS
11911 Adie Road, Maryland Heights MO 63043. 314/569-4500. **Contact:** Manager of Human Resources. **World Wide Web address:** http://www.alcocontrols.com. **Description:** Manufactures flow controls. **Positions advertised include:** Business Unit Leader; Sales Director. **Parent company:** Emerson Electric Company manufactures environmental and building systems, tools, and service equipment; commercial control systems and components; and industrial automation, process control, and electronic systems. **Number of employees at this location:** 400.

ALL STAR GAS CORPORATION
119 West Commercial Street, Lebanon MO 65536. 417/532-3103. **Fax:** 417/532-8529. **Contact:** Human Resources Manager. **World Wide Web address:** http://www.allstargas.com. **Description:** Engaged in the retail sale of propane. **Corporate headquarters location:** This location. **Other U.S. locations:** CO; AZ; AR; OK; WY. **Operations at this facility include:** Divisional Headquarters.

ALLEGIANCE HEALTHCARE CORPORATION
5 Sunnen Drive, St. Louis MO 63143. 314/647-0700. **Contact:** Human Resources. **World Wide Web address:** http://www.cardinal.com. **Description:** Allegiance Healthcare, through its subsidiaries, produces, develops, and distributes medical products and technologies for use in hospitals and other health care settings. The company operates in two industry segments: medical specialties and medical/laboratory products and distribution. **Parent company:** Cardinal Health Company.

ALLIED HEALTHCARE PRODUCTS, INC.
1720 Sublette Avenue, St. Louis MO 63110-1968. 314/771-2400. **Toll-free phone:** 800/444-3954. **Contact:** Human Resources. **World Wide Web address:** http://www.alliedhpi.com. **Description:** A manufacturer of medical gas construction equipment, respiratory therapy equipment, home health care products, and emergency medical equipment. **Corporate headquarters location:** This location. **Number of employees at this location:** 830.

ALLIED SECURITY INC.
1910 Pine Street, Suite 400, St. Louis MO 63103. 314/241-4220. **Toll-free phone:** 800/609-9673. **Fax:** 314/241-6899. **Contact:** Personnel Director. **World Wide Web address:** http://www.alliedsecurity.com. **Description:** Provides contract security guard services. **NOTE:** Apply for positions online. **Positions advertised include:** Manager; Security Officer; Sales Representative. **Office hours:** Monday - Friday, 8:00 a.m. - 4:00 p.m. **Corporate headquarters location:** King of Prussia PA. **Other U.S. locations:** Nationwide. **Operations at this facility include:** Administration; Sales. **Listed on:** Privately held. **Number of employees at this location:** 400.

ALLTEL MISSOURI INC.
1394A State Highway 24B, Branson MO 65616. 417/335-5220. **Contact:** Personnel. **World Wide Web address:** http://www.alltel.com. **Description:** Provides telecommunications equipment and services. **NOTE:** Search and apply for positions online. **Corporate headquarters location:** Little Rock AR.

AMEREN CORPORATION
One Ameren Plaza, 1901 Chouteau Avenue, St. Louis MO 63103. 314/554-2119. **Contact:** Johnetta Carver, Staffing Supervisor. **World Wide Web address:** http://www.ameren.com. **Description:** A holding company operating through subsidiaries that generate, transmit, distribute, and sell electric energy; and purchase, distribute, transport, and sell natural gas to over 1 million customers in Illinois and Missouri. NOTE: Search and apply for positions online. **Positions advertised include:** Compensation Specialist; Engineer; Financial Specialist; Lead Data Architect; Strategic Sourcing Consultant; eProcurement Business Consultant. **Corporate headquarters location:** This location. **Subsidiaries include:** AmerenCIPS; AmerenUE. **Listed on:** New York Stock Exchange. **Stock exchange symbol:** AEE. **Number of employees nationwide:** 8,000.

AMERICAN INGREDIENTS COMPANY
3947 Broadway, Kansas City MO 64111. 816/561-9050. **Toll-free phone:** 800/669-4092. **Contact:** Personnel. **World Wide Web address:** http://www.americaningredients.com. **Description:** A manufacturer and processor of specialty chemicals and food ingredients. **NOTE:** Search and apply for positions online. **Positions advertised include:** Customer Account Representative; Director of Accounting.

AMERICAN RECREATION PRODUCTS INC.
1224 Fern Ridge Parkway, St. Louis MO 63141. 314/576-8000. **Fax:** 314/576-8072. **Contact:** Courtney Strautz, Director of Human Resources. **World Wide Web address:** http://www.slumberjack.com. **Description:** American Recreation Products manufactures tents, sleeping bags, backpacks, outdoor technical clothing, and related clothing and camping accessories for family campers, recreational vehicle campers, and experienced backpackers. Brand names include Kelty, Ridgeway, Sierra Designs, Slumberjack, Everest Elite, Wenzel, Traversak, and TREKK. **Operations at this facility include:** This location manufactures and distributes tents, sleeping bags, and other camping equipment. **Parent company:** Kellwood Company manufactures and sells apparel and home fashion products including accessories for bedrooms and bathrooms. Subsidiaries of the parent company include: AJ Brandon (Minneapolis MN); California Ivy (Vernon CA); Cape Cod-Cricket Lane (West Bridgewater MA); Crowntuft Manufacturing (New York NY); David Dart (Chatsworth CA); Decorp (Carrollton TX); Goodman Knitting (Brockton MA); Halmode Apparel, Inc. (New York); Kellwood Lingerie/Activewear (Summit MS); Kellwood Sportswear (Rutherford TN); Melrose (Chatsworth CA); Sag Harbor (New York NY); SBH Group (Dedham MA); Smart Shirts, Ltd. (Hong Kong).

AMERICAN RECREATION PRODUCTS INC.
302 Hawthorn Drive, Glasgow MO 65254. 660/338-2273. **Contact:** Human Resources. **World Wide Web address:** http://www.slumberjack.com. **Description:** This location manufactures sleeping bags. Overall, American Recreation Products manufactures tents, sleeping bags, backpacks, outdoor technical clothing, and related clothing and camping accessories for family campers, recreational vehicle campers, and backpackers. Brand names include Kelty, Ridgeway, Sierra Designs, Slumberjack, Everest Elite, Wenzel, Traversak, and TREKK. **NOTE:** Search and apply for positions at: http://www.kellwood.com/careers. **Parent company:** Kellwood Company is a marketer of apparel and consumer soft goods.

AMERICAN RECREATION PRODUCTS INC.
502 Orchard Street, New Haven MO 63068. 573/237-4200. **Contact:** Human Resources. **World Wide Web address:** http://www.slumberjack.com. **Description:** This location manufactures boat covers and awnings. Overall, American Recreation Products manufactures tents, sleeping bags, backpacks, outdoor technical clothing, and related clothing and camping accessories for family campers and hunters, recreational vehicle campers, and experienced backpackers. Brand names include Kelty, Ridgeway, Sierra Designs, Slumberjack, Everest Elite, Wenzel, Traversak, and TREKK. **NOTE:** Search and apply for positions at: http://www.kellwood.com/careers. **Parent company:** Kellwood Company is a marketer of apparel and consumer soft goods.

AMERICO LIFE, INC.
P.O. Box 410288, West 11th Street, Kansas City MO 64141. 816/391-2000. **Contact:** Human Resources. **E-mail address:** careerskc@americo.com. **World Wide Web address:** http://www.americo.com. **Description:** Americo Life, Inc. is a holding company with subsidiaries that sell life insurance and annuity products, and finance property and casualty insurance premiums. **NOTE:** Search and apply for positions online. **Positions advertised include:** Bilingual Customer Service Providers; Policy Accounting Team Leader; LAN Administration; client Support Specialist; Underwriter. **Corporate headquarters location:** Dallas TX.

ANALYSTS INTERNATIONAL CORPORATION (AIC)
Broadway Summit, 3101 Broadway, Suite 550, Kansas City MO 64111-2416. 816/531-5050. **Toll-free phone:** 800/530-5259. **Fax:** 888/442-4122. **Contact:** Human Resources Department. **E-mail address:** kc.jobs@analysts.com. **World Wide Web address:** http://www.analysts.com. **Description:** AiC is an international computer consulting firm. The company assists clients in developing systems in a variety of industries using different programming languages and software. **NOTE:** Search and apply for positions online. **Positions advertised include:** Natural Adabase Programmer. **Corporate headquarters location:** Minneapolis MN. **Other area locations:** St. Louis MO. **Other U.S. locations:** Nationwide. **Listed on:** NASDAQ. **Stock exchange symbol:** ANALY. **Annual sales/revenues:** More than $100 million.

ANALYSTS INTERNATIONAL CORPORATION (AIC)
1066 Executive Parkway, Suite 203, St. Louis MO 63141. 314/469-4900. **Toll-free phone:** 800/998-5995. **Contact:** Human Resources Department. **World Wide Web address:** http://www.analysts.com. **Description:** AiC is an international computer consulting firm. The company assists clients in developing systems in a variety of industries using different programming languages and software. **NOTE:** Search and apply for positions online. **Positions advertised include:** Deployment Manager. **Corporate headquarters location:** Minneapolis MN. **Other area locations:** Kansas City MO. **Other U.S. locations:** Nationwide. **Listed on:** NASDAQ. **Stock exchange symbol:** ANALY. **Annual sales/revenues:** More than $100 million.

ANGELICA CORPORATION
424 South Woods Mill Road, Chesterfield MO 63017. 314/854-3800. **Toll-free phone:** 800/235-8410. **Contact:** Human Resources. **World Wide Web address:** http://www.angelica-corp.com. **Description:** Angelica Corporation provides textile rental and laundry services; manufactures and markets healthcare apparel; and operates specialty retail stores primarily for nurses and other health care professionals.

Corporate headquarters location: This location. **Operations at this facility include:** This location houses the general offices for the Angelica Healthcare Services Group, Inc., a health care uniform rental store. **Number of employees nationwide:** 9,500.

ANGELICA CORPORATION
LIFEUNIFORM AND SHOE SHOPS
2132 Kratky Road, St. Louis MO 63114. 314/824-2900. **Toll-free phone:** 800/325-8033. **Contact:** Human Resources. **World Wide Web address:** http://www.angelica-corp.com. **Description:** Provides apparel needs of healthcare employees through retail locations nationwide, and on-premise hospital and clinic stores. **Positions advertised include:** Payroll Clerk. **Corporate headquarters location:** Chesterfield MO. **Number of employees nationwide:** 9,500.

ANHEUSER-BUSCH COMPANIES
One Busch Place, St. Louis MO 63118. 314/577-0701. **Contact:** Corporate Employment Services. **E-mail address:** buschjobs@anheuser-busch.com. **World Wide Web address:** http://www.anheuser-busch.com. **Description:** Anheuser-Busch is a diverse company involved in the entertainment, brewing, baking, and manufacturing industries. The company operates 13 breweries throughout the United States and distributes through over 900 independent wholesalers. Beer brands include Budweiser, Michelob, Busch, and King Cobra, as well as O'Doul's (nonalcoholic). Related businesses include can manufacturing, paper printing, and barley malting. Anheuser-Busch is also one of the largest operators of amusement parks in the United States, with locations in Florida, Virginia, Texas, Pennsylvania, and California. **NOTE:** Search and apply for positions online. **Corporate headquarters location:** This location. **Subsidiaries include:** Campbell Taggart Inc. is one of the largest commercial baking companies in the United States, producing foods under the Colonial brand name, among others. **Listed on:** New York Stock Exchange. **Stock exchange symbol:** BUD.

AON CONSULTING WORLDWIDE
1000 Walnut Street, Kansas City MO 64106-2123. 816/391-1000. **Fax:** 816/391-1129. **Contact:** Human Resources. **World Wide Web address:** http://www.aon.com. **Description:** Offers human capital consulting services. **NOTE:** Search and apply for positions online. **Positions advertised include:** Health and Welfare Consultant; Communication Consultant. **Other area locations:** Clayton MO. **Other U.S. locations:** Nationwide.

AON RISK SERVICES
8182 Maryland Avenue, Suite 1500, St. Louis MO 63105. 314/721-5100. **Fax:** 314/721-8212. **Contact:** Human Resources Manager. **World Wide Web address:** http://www.aon.com. **Description:** A provider of insurance services. **NOTE:** Search and apply for positions online. **Positions advertised include:** Administrative Associate; Relationship Manager. **Corporate headquarters location:** New York NY. **Number of employees at this location:** 200.

AQUILA
20 West Ninth Street, Kansas City MO 64105. 816/421-6600. **Contact:** Human Resources. **World Wide Web address:** http://www.aquila.com. **Description:** An investor-owned utility that operates electricity and natural gas distribution networks serving customers in seven U.S. states and in Canada. Aquila also owns and operates power generation assets. Founded in 1883. **NOTE:** Applications accepted only online. **Positions advertised include:** Technical Consultant IT. **Corporate headquarters location:** This location. **Parent company:** Ameren. **Listed on:** New York Stock Exchange. **Stock exchange symbol:** ILA.

ARCH COAL, INC.
One CityPlace Drive, Suite 300, St. Louis MO 63141-7306. 314/994-2700. **Contact:** Jane C. Fox, Director of Personnel. **E-mail address:** careers@archcoal.com. **World Wide Web address:** http://www.archcoal.com. **Description:** Arch Coal Corporation is one of the country's largest bituminous coal exploration and processing companies, operating 13 mining complexes. **NOTE:** Search and apply for positions online. **Positions advertised include:** Administrative Assistant; Financial Reporting Analyst. **Special programs:** Internships. **Corporate headquarters location:** This location. **Other U.S. locations:** KY; WV; WY; VA; CO; UT. **Operations at this facility include:** This location houses administrative and sales offices. **Subsidiaries include:** Apogee Coal Company; Catenary Coal Holdings, Inc. **Listed on:** Privately held. **Number of employees at this location:** 100. **Number of employees nationwide:** 2,300.

ARCHER DANIELS MIDLAND COMPANY
5020 Shreve Avenue, St. Louis MO 63115. 314/385-9100. **Contact:** Personnel. **World Wide Web address:** http://www.admworld.com. **Description:** Archer Daniels Midland is engaged in the business of procuring, transporting, storing, processing, and merchandising agricultural commodities. The company processes agricultural products, such as corn, soybeans, dry-milled grains (wheat, rice, and masa), cottonseed, and canola. The company produces a variety of products, including vegetable oils (lecithin, cooking oil, and margarine); vitamin E; protein (soy flour, soy isolates, soy protein, soy milk, and TVP); high-fructose corn syrup; sorbitol; starch; ethanol; xanthan gum; tryptophan; vitamin C; fermentation products (lysine, threonine, lactic acid, citric acid, and MSG); pasta; and cottonseed flour products. **NOTE:** Search and apply for positions online. **Corporate headquarters location:** Decatur IL. **Listed on:** New York Stock Exchange. **Stock exchange symbol:** ADM.

ARGOSY CASINO
777 Northwest Argosy Parkway, Riverside MO 64150-1512. 816/741-7568. **Fax:** 816/741-5423. **Recorded jobline:** 816/746-3160. **Contact:** Human Resources. **World Wide Web address:** http://www.casinocity.com. **Description:** A river boat casino that features 1,750 slots and forty-two table games. The property has seven restaurants.

ARMSTRONG TEASDALE LLP
One Metropolitan Square, Suite 2600, 211 North Broadway, St. Louis MO 63102-2740. 314/621-5070. **Contact:** Personnel. **World Wide Web address:** http://www.armstrongteasdale.com. **Description:** A general practice law firm. **Other area locations:** Kansas City MO; Jefferson City MO. **Number of employees at this location:** 290.

ARNOLD WORLDWIDE
701 Market Street, Suite 200, St. Louis MO 63101. 314/421-6610. **Fax:** 314/491-5627. **Contact:** Human Resources. **E-mail address:** jobs@arn.com. **World Wide Web address:** www.arnoldworldwide.com. **Description:** An international advertising agency whose client roster includes several nationally advertised brands. **Corporate headquarters:** Boston, MA. **Other U.S. locations:** Boston MA, Los Angeles CA, New York NY, Washington D.C.

ASCHINGER ELECTRIC COMPANY
877 Horan Drive, P.O. Box 26322, Fenton MO 63026. 636/343-1211. **Fax:** 636/343-9658. **Contact:** Donna L. Kebel, Controller/Office Manager. **E-mail address:** info@aschinger.com. **World Wide Web address:** http://www.aschinger.com. **Description:** An electrical contracting firm specializing in industrial and commercial applications. **Office hours:** Monday - Friday, 8:00 a.m. - 5:00 p.m. **Corporate headquarters location:** This location. **Listed on:** Privately held. **President:** Eric D. Aschinger. **Annual sales/revenues:** $21 - $50 million. **Number of employees at this location:** 200.

ASSOCIATED ELECTRIC COOPERATIVE, INC.
P.O. Box 754, Springfield MO 65801-0754. 417/881-1204. **Fax:** 417/885-9252. **Contact:** Human Resources Representative. **E-mail address:** employment@aeci.org. **World Wide Web address:** http://www.aeci.org. **Description:** Associated Electric Cooperative, Inc. is owned by and provides wholesale power to six regional and 51 local electric cooperative systems in Missouri, northeast Oklahoma and southeast Iowa, which serve over 750,000 homes and businesses, representing 1.95 million individual consumers. NOTE: Search and apply for positions online. **Positions advertised include:** C#/.Net Developer; Corporate Tax Accountant. **Special programs:** Internships. **Corporate headquarters location:** This location. **Number of employees at this location:** 150.

AUDRAIN MEDICAL CENTER
201 East Monroe Street, Mexico MO 65265. 573/581-1760. **Fax:** 573/582-3725. **Contact:** Manager of Human Resources Department. **World Wide Web address:** http://www.audrainmedicalcenter.com. **Description:** A private, nonprofit health care center providing a nursery, as well as cancer, cardiology, emergency, and home care services. **NOTE:** Search for positions and download application online. **Positions advertised include:** Therapist; Computer Operator; Director of Medical Imaging Services; Registered Nurse; Licensed Practical Nurse. **Special programs:** Internships. **Listed on:** Privately held. **Number of employees at this location:** 830.

AUTOMATIC DATA PROCESSING (ADP)
12200 Webber Hill Road, St. Louis MO 63127. 314/525-3000. **Contact:** Human Resources Manager. **World Wide Web address:** http://www.adp.com. **Description:** Automatic Data Processing (ADP) helps clients improve their business performance by providing computerized transaction processing, data communications, and information services. The company processes paychecks for over 17 million wage earners and issues 32 million W-2s to employees annually. The company's services include payroll, payroll tax, and human resource information management; brokerage industry market data; back-office and proxy services; industry-specific services to auto and truck dealers; and computerized auto repair and replacement estimating for auto insurance companies and body repair shops. **NOTE:** Search and apply for positions online. **Positions advertised include:** Field Engineer; Associate AE; SBS Outside Sales Associate; Associate Implementation Specialist. **Corporate headquarters location:** Roseland NJ.

AUTOZONE
9710 Page Avenue, Overland MO 63132. 314/428-9955. **Contact:** Human Resources. **World Wide Web address:** http://www.autozone.com. **Description:** A do-it-yourself retail auto parts chain specializing in foreign and domestic parts. The company operates over 2,700 stores in 40 states. **Corporate headquarters location:** Memphis TN.

AUXI HEALTH OF ST. LOUIS
9312 Olive Street Road, St. Louis MO 63132. 314/993-2273. **Toll-free phone:** 888/758-4200. **Fax:** 314/993-1196. **Contact:** Director of Administration. **Description:** A home health care agency offering private duty nursing services, supplemental staffing, live-in companions, short-term respite, therapy services, social work, and in-home support services. Founded in 1976. **NOTE:** Entry-level positions and second and third shifts are offered. Search and apply for positions online. **Positions advertised include:** CNA; Branch Manager. **Special programs:** Summer Jobs. **Office hours:** Monday - Friday, 8:00 a.m. - 5:30 p.m. **Corporate headquarters location:** This location. **Other area locations:** Hillsboro MO; St. Charles MO. **Parent company:** Auxi Health, Inc.

AVAX TECHNOLOGIES, INC
4520 Main Street, Suite 930, Kansas City MO 64111. 816/960-1333. **Fax:** 816/960-1334. **Contact:** Human Resources. **World Wide Web address:** http://www.avax-tech.com. **Description:** AVAX Technologies is a biotechnology company involved in research and development of therapeutic products. Founded in 1990. **Corporate headquarters location:** Overland Park KS. Public **Listed on:** NASDAQ. **Stock exchange symbol:** AVXT.

AVENTIS PHARMACEUTICALS
10236 Marion Park Drive, Kansas City MO 64137-1405. 816/966-5100. **Contact:** Human Resources. **World Wide Web address:** http://www.aventis.com. **Description:** Manufactures prescription pharmaceuticals. **NOTE:** Search and apply for positions online. **Positions advertised include:** Diabetes Scientific Manager/Specialist; External Manufacturing Specialist; Sales Representative. **Corporate headquarters location:** Strasbourg, France.

BHA COMPANY
Route 1, Box 123, Holbrook Drive, Salisbury MO 65281-9640. 660/388-6412. **Contact:** Human Resources. **World Wide Web address:** http://www.bhagroup.com. **Description:** A leading manufacturer of quality replacement parts and accessories. BHA also provides engineering services for fabric filter air-pollution control equipment used in various industries. Products include industrial and utility coal-fired boilers, incinerators, cement, hot-mix asphalt, and metals along with chemical and carbon black processors. **NOTE:** Search and apply for positions online. **Corporate headquarters location:** Kansas City MO. **Parent company:** BHA Group, Inc. designs, manufactures, and sells replacement parts and accessories for the types of industrial air pollution control equipment known as baghouses and electrostatic precipitators, and provides rehabilitation and conversion services for the types of industrial air pollution control equipment the company produces. **Listed on:** NASDAQ. **Stock exchange symbol:** BHAG.

BHA GROUP, INC.
8800 East 63rd Street, Kansas City MO 64133. 816/356-8400. **Contact:** Human Resources Department. **E-mail address:** hr@bha.com. **World Wide Web address:** http://www.bhagroup.com. **Description:** Designs, manufactures, and sells replacement parts and accessories for electrostatic precipitators and baghouses, and provides rehabilitation and conversion services for the types of industrial air pollution control equipment it produces. As a fully-integrated company, BHA Group manufactures mechanical and electrical products and has a full range of engineering and service capabilities. **NOTE:** Search and apply for positions online. **Positions advertised include:** Sales Rep; Marketing Manager; Latin America Sales Rep; Marketing Communication Specialist; Application Engineer. **Corporate headquarters location:** This location. **Listed on:** NASDAQ. **Stock exchange symbol:** BHAG.

BHA GROUP, INC.
225 Industrial Boulevard, Slater MO 65349. 660/529-3208. **Contact:** Human Resources. **World Wide Web address:** http://www.bhagroup.com. **Description:** BHA Group designs, manufactures, and sells replacement parts and accessories for the types of industrial air pollution control equipment known as baghouses and electrostatic precipitators, and provides rehabilitation and conversion services for the types of industrial air pollution control equipment it produces. **NOTE:** Search and apply for positions online. **Listed on:** NASDAQ. **Stock exchange symbol:** BHAG.

BSI CONSTRUCTORS INC.
6767 Southwest Avenue, St. Louis MO 63143. 314/781-7820. **Contact:** Joseph M. Kaiser, Executive Vice President. **World Wide Web address:** http://www.bsistl.com. **Description:** A general contracting and construction management firm. **Corporate headquarters location:** This location. **Number of employees at this location:** 100.

EDWARD L. BAKEWELL, INC.
7716 Forsyth Boulevard, St. Louis MO 63105. 314/721-5555. **Toll-free phone:** 800/341-4791. **Contact:** Human Resources Department. **E-mail address:** info@bakewellinc.com. **World Wide Web address:** http://www.bakewellinc.com. **Description:** A real estate agency. **Number of employees at this location:** 100.

BANK OF AMERICA
One Bank of America Plaza, 800 Market Street, St. Louis MO 63101. 314/466-6117. **Contact:** Centralized Resume Database. **World Wide Web address:** http://www.bankofamerica.com. **Description:** Bank of America is a full-service banking and financial institution. The company operates through four business segments: Global Corporate and Investment Banking, Principal Investing and Asset Management, Commercial Banking, and Consumer Banking. **NOTE:** Search and apply for positions online. **Positions advertised include:** Credit Products Sr. Underwriter; Streamlined Approval Officer; Teller; Operations Representative; Banking Center Service Manager; Recruiter. **Corporate headquarters location:** Charlotte NC. **Other U.S. locations:** Nationwide.

BARNES-JEWISH HOSPITAL NORTH
One Barnes-Jewish Hospital Plaza, St. Louis MO 63110. 314/454-7025. **Contact:** Human Resources. **World Wide Web address:** http://www.barnesjewish.org. **Description:** An 887-bed general hospital. **NOTE:** Search and apply for positions online. **Positions advertised include:** Admitting Representative; Assistant Professor; Biomedical Electronic Technician; Cardiac Sonographer; Case Coordinator; Clinical Manager; Nurse Practitioner; Doula; Nursing Practice Manager; Orderly; Pharmacist; Physical Therapist; Registered Respiratory Therapist; Resource Nurse. **Special programs:** Internships. **Parent company:** BJC Health System. **Number of employees at this location:** 9,250.

BARNES-JEWISH ST. PETERS HOSPITAL
10 Hospital Drive, St. Peters MO 63376. 314/278-5900. **Fax:** 636/916-9127. **Recorded jobline:** 636/916-9734. **Contact:** Recruiting Department. **World Wide Web address:** http://www.bjsph.org. **Description:** A 111-bed acute-care community hospital. The hospital offers general care, intensive care, obstetric, and pediatric services. **NOTE:** Search and apply for positions online. **Positions advertised include:** Medical Imaging Technologist; Nuclear Medicine Technologist; Staff Nurse; Phlebotomist; Sonographer; Speech Pathologist; Registered Polysomnographic Technician. **Corporate headquarters location:** St. Louis MO. **Parent company:** BJC Health System. **Number of employees at this location:** 700.

BARNES-JEWISH WEST COUNTY HOSPITAL
12634 Olive Boulevard, St. Louis MO 63141. 314/996-8000. **Fax:** 314/996-8436. **Contact:** Personnel. **World Wide Web address:** http://www.bjc.org/bjwch.html. **Description:** A 113-bed general hospital. The hospital specializes in cosmetic surgery, dermatology, sports medicine, and urology. **NOTE:** Search and apply for positions online. **Positions advertised include:** Medical Imaging Technologist; Charge Nurse; Occupational Therapist; Staff RN; Patient Care Technician. **Corporate headquarters location:** This location. **Number of employees at this location:** 625.

BAUSCH & LOMB SURGICAL
3365 Tree Court Industrial Boulevard, St. Louis MO 63122. 636/225-7782. **Contact:** Employment Department. **World Wide Web address:** http://www.bausch.com. **Description:** A manufacturer and distributor of micro-surgical instruments and diagnostic medical equipment. **NOTE:** Search and apply for positions online. **Positions advertised include:** Contract Administrator; Associate Product Manager; Marketing Coordinator; Manager, Mechanical Design; Sr. Marketing Coordinator. **Special programs:** Internships. **Corporate headquarters location:** Rochester NY. **Parent company:** Bausch & Lomb, Inc.

BAYER CORPORATION
8400 Hawthorn Road, Kansas City MO 64120. 816/242-2000. **Contact:** Human Resources. **World Wide Web address:** http://www.bayerus.com. **Description:** Bayer's four operating business areas, HealthCare, CropScience, Polymers and Chemicals, produce a broad range of products that help diagnose and treat diseases, purify water, preserve local landmarks, protect crops, and advance automobile safety and durability. **NOTE:** Search and apply for positions online. **Corporate headquarters location:** Pittsburgh PA. **Parent company:** Bayer Group (Germany). **Operations at this facility include:** This location produces pesticides and other agricultural chemicals. **Number of employees nationwide:** 21,000. **Number of employees worldwide:** 115,400.

BELDEN INC.
7701 Forsyth Boulevard, Suite 800, St. Louis MO 63105. 314/854-8000. **Fax:** 314/854-8001. **Contact:** Personnel. **World Wide Web address:** http://www.belden.com. **Description:** A manufacturer of advanced wire, cable, and fiber optic products through the Belden Electronics Division (Richmond IN) and Belden Communications Division (Phoenix AZ). **Corporate headquarters location:** This location. **Stock exchange symbol:** BWC. **Number of employees at this location:** 10. **Number of employees nationwide:** 2,730.

BERNADETTE BUSINESS FORMS INC.
8950 Pershall Road, Hazelwood MO 63042. 314/522-1700. **Fax:** 314/524-6161. **Contact:** Personnel Director. **World Wide Web address:** http://www.bbf.com. **Description:** A printing company. **Number of employees at this location:** 100.

BERNSTEIN-REIN ADVERTISING, INC.
4600 Madison Avenue, Suite 1500, Kansas City MO 64112. 816/756-0640. **Toll-free phone:** 800/571-6246. **Fax:** 816/531-5708. **Contact:** Human Resources. **E-mail address:** human_res@bradv.com. **World Wide Web address:** http://www.bradv.com. **Description:** A national advertising agency. **NOTE:** Search and apply for positions online. **Positions advertised include:** Account Executive; Group Account Director; Print Production Manager; Media Buyer. **Corporate headquarters location:** This location. **Number of employees at this location:** 300.

BIG BEN WOODS
110 Highland Avenue, Valley Park MO 63088. 636/225-5144. **Fax:** 636/225-8427. **Contact:** Staff Development. **Description:** A nursing home providing rehabilitation, physical, speech, and occupational therapy services. **Operations at this facility include:** Administration. **Number of employees at this location:** 120.

BLACK & VEATCH
P.O. Box 8405 Ward Parkway, Kansas City MO 64114. 913/458-2000. **Contact:** Hiring Manager. **World Wide Web address:** http://www.bv.com. **Description:** Black & Veatch Corporation is a global engineering, consulting and construction company specializing in infrastructure development in the fields of energy, water and information. Black & Veatch offers conceptual and preliminary engineering services, engineering design, procurement, construction, financial management, asset management, information technology, environmental, security design and consulting, and management consulting services. Founded in 1915. **NOTE:** Search and apply for positions online. **Positions advertised include:** Communications Specialist; Electrical Engineer; **Corporate headquarters location:** Overland Park KS. **Other area locations:** St. Louis MO. **Other U.S. locations:** Nationwide. **International locations:** Worldwide.

BLACK & VEATCH
15450 South Outer Forty Drive, Chesterfield MO 63017-8522. 636/532-7940. **Fax:** 636/532-1465. **Contact:** Recruiting Department. **World Wide Web address:** http://www.bv.com. **Description:** Black & Veatch Corporation is a global engineering, consulting and construction company specializing in infrastructure development in the fields of energy, water and information. Black & Veatch offers conceptual and preliminary engineering services, engineering design, procurement, construction, financial management, asset management, information technology, environmental, security design and consulting, and management consulting services. Founded in 1915. **NOTE:** Search and apply for positions online. **Corporate headquarters location:** Overland Park KS. **Other area locations:** Kansas City MO. **Other U.S. locations:** Nationwide. **International locations:** Worldwide.

BLUE CROSS & BLUE SHIELD OF MISSOURI
1831 Chestnut Street, St. Louis MO 63103. 314/923-4444. **Fax:** 314/923-8907. **Contact:** Human Resources Manager. **E-mail address:** resumes@bcbsmo.com. **World Wide Web address:** http://www.bcbsmo.com. **Description:** A prepaid health care benefits company providing hospitalization and medical coverage to individuals and groups. **Corporate headquarters location:** This location. **Operations at this facility include:** Service. **Number of employees at this location:** 1,000.

BOASBERG WHEELER COMMUNICATIONS
4700 Belleview, Suite 100, Kansas City MO 64112. 816/531-2100. **Contact:** Sharen Hasted, Office Manager. **World Wide Web address:** http://www.bwcom.com. **Description:** A public relations firm. **Parent company:** Valentine-Radford, Inc.

THE BOEING COMPANY
P.O. Box 516, Mail Stop S276-1740, St. Louis MO 63166-0516. 314/232-0232. **Contact:** Employee Office. **E-mail address:** stljobs@mw.boeing.com. **World Wide Web address:** http://www.boeing.com. **Description:** Boeing is one of the largest aerospace firms in the United States, one of the nation's top exporters, and one of the world's leading manufacturers of commercial jet transports. The company is a major U.S. government contractor, with the manufacturing and service capabilities including missile and space; electronic systems; military aircraft; helicopters; and information systems management. **NOTE:** Search and apply for positions online. **Positions advertised include:** Marketing and Sales Rep; Program Integration Engineer; Procurement Analyst Military Effectiveness Analyst. **Corporate headquarters location:** Chicago IL. **Operations at this facility include:** This location manufactures military aircraft.

BRICK NETWORK
1000 Macklind Avenue, Lower Level, St. Louis MO 63100. 314/645-5550. **Fax:** 314/638-7814. **Toll-free phone:** 888/999-7540. **Contact:** Human Resources. **E-mail address:** job@brick.net. **World Wide Web address:** http://www.brick.net. **Description:** A local network service provider for St. Louis area businesses.

BROWN SHOE COMPANY
8300 Maryland Avenue, St. Louis MO 63166-0029. 314/854-4000. **Contact:** Director of Human Resources. **E-mail address:** resumes@brownshoe.com. **World Wide Web address:** http://www.brownshoe.com. **Description:** A footwear company with worldwide operations in the manufacturing, marketing, and retailing of footwear for women, men, and children. The company's Footwear Retail Operations include Famous Footwear, one of the nation's largest chains of branded family shoe stores. Brown Shoe also owns and operates the Naturalizer brand in the United States and Canada, and the F.X. LaSalle chain of shoe stores in Canada. Footwear Wholesale Operations include Pagoda, leading marketers of brand name footwear throughout the world. Major brand names include Naturalizer, Life Stride, NaturalSport, Penaljo, Air Step, and Connie for women; Dr. Scholl's for men and women; and a wide variety of children's brands including Disney, Barbie, Buster Brown, Playskool, and Candie's. **NOTE:** Search and apply for positions online. **Positions advertised include:** Associate Merchandiser; Auditor; consumer Services Associate; Customer Relationship Marketing Manager; Sr. Financial Analyst. **Corporate headquarters location:** This location. **Number of employees nationwide:** 14,500.

BRYAN CAVE LLP
One Metropolitan Square, 211 North Broadway, Suite 3600, St. Louis MO 63102-2750. 314/259-2000. **Fax:** 314/259-2020. **Recorded jobline:** 314/259-2022. **Contact:** Mary B. Featherstone, Recruiter. **E-mail address:** mbfeatherstone@bryancave.com. **World Wide Web address:** http://www.bryancavellp.com. **Description:** An international law firm. **NOTE:** Entry-level positions are offered. **Positions advertised include:** Corporate Associate; Legal Assistant. **Special programs:** Internships; Training; Summer Jobs. **Corporate headquarters location:** This location. **Other U.S. locations:** Phoenix AZ; Los Angeles CA; Washington DC; Kansas City MO; New York NY. **International locations:** China; Kuwait; England; Saudi Arabia; United Arab Emirates. **Number of employees at this location:** 675. **Number of employees worldwide:** 1,380.

BUNGE CORPORATION
11720 Borman Drive, P.O. Box 28500, St. Louis MO 63146-1000. 314/872-3030. **Contact:** Director of Human Resources. **E-mail address:** recruiter@bunge.com. **World Wide Web address:** http://www.bunge.com. **Description:** Bunge Corporation handles and processes grains and oilseeds. The company also manufactures and markets food ingredients. The company does business through the Bunge Commodities Group and the Bunge Foods Group. The Bunge Commodities Group, the company's largest component, is formed around the company's original agricultural commodity businesses and includes the Grain, Soybean Processing, and Lauhoff Milling Divisions. The Soybean Processing Division produces soybean meal and soybean oil for both

export and domestic customers. The meal is sold as a feed ingredient for poultry, hogs, cattle, and fish. The oil is sold to refineries, including the company's own, to make shortenings and cooking oils. With numerous plants located throughout the Midwest and South, Bunge is one of the largest soybean processors in the United States. The Grain Division operates in the United States and Canada, and markets bulk sorghum, oats, and barley. **Corporate headquarters location:** This location. **Operations at this facility include:** This location houses the Grain and Soybean Divisions.

BURNS & McDONNELL
9400 Ward Parkway, Kansas City MO 64114. 816/333-9400. **Fax:** 816/333-3690. **Contact:** Human Resources. **E-mail address:** recruiter@burnsmcd.com. **World Wide Web address:** http://www.burnsmcd.com. **Description:** A consulting firm specializing in architectural and environmental engineering. **Positions advertised include:** Senior Architect; Structural Engineer; Project Assistant. **Corporate headquarters location:** This location. **Other U.S. locations:** Denver CO; Chicago IL; St. Louis MO. **Listed on:** Privately held.

BUTLER MANUFACTURING COMPANY
1540 Genessee Street, Kansas City MO 64102. 816/559-0546. **Fax:** 816/968-3720. **Contact:** Human Resources. **E-mail address:** recruiting@butlermfg.com. **World Wide Web address:** http://www.butlermfg.com. **Description:** Supplies steel and wood frame pre-engineered building systems for a wide variety of commercial, community, industrial, and agricultural applications. The company designs, manufactures, and markets component systems for nonresidential construction including aluminum curtain wall, storefront entrances and doors, and roof accessories. Butler also provides comprehensive design and construction planning, execution, and management services for major purchasers of construction. In addition, the company designs, manufactures, and sells commercial and on-farm grain storage units. **Number of employees nationwide:** 3,065.

BUTTERBALL TURKEY COMPANY
411 North Main Street, Carthage MO 64836. 417/358-5914. **Fax:** 417/358-7535. **Contact:** Human Resources. **World Wide Web address:** http://www.butterball.com. **Description:** Processes fresh and frozen poultry. **Special programs:** Internships. **Corporate headquarters location:** Omaha NE. **Other U.S. locations:** Nationwide. **Parent company:** ConAgra, Inc. **Number of employees at this location:** 1,100.

CMP (CENTRAL MISSOURI PIZZA, INC.)
dba DOMINO'S PIZZA
1350 Elbridge Payne Road, Suite 208, Chesterfield MO 63017. 636/537-1120. **Fax:** 636/537-1265. **Contact:** Human Resources Manager. **World Wide Web address:** http://www.dominos.com. **Description:** CMP is one of the largest franchisees of Domino's Pizza, with locations in Missouri and Kentucky. **Corporate headquarters location:** This location. **Number of employees at this location:** 600.

CPI CORPORATION
1706 Washington Avenue, St. Louis MO 63103. 314/231-1575. **Fax:** 314/231-2398. **Contact:** Christina Ellis, Employment Manager. **World Wide Web address:** http://www.cpicorp.com. **Description:** CPI Corporation is a holding company with subsidiaries operating professional portrait studios, photographic finishing laboratories, electronic publishing stores, and wall decor stores. **Positions advertised include:** Cash Manager; Digital Imaging Retoucher; Merchandise Manager; Marketing Manager; Benefits Specialist. **Corporate headquarters location:** This location. **Number of employees at this location:** 1,000.

CANAM STEEL CORPORATION
2000 West Main Street, Washington MO 63090-1008. 636/239-6716. **Fax:** 636/239-1588. **Contact:** Human Resources. **World Wide Web address:** http://www.canammanac.com. **Description:** Manufactures steel and other fabricated metal alloys. **Corporate headquarters location:** Point of Rocks MD. **Parent company:** The Canam Manac Group (Saint-Georges, Quebec, Canada).

CARAUSTAR CUSTOM PACKAGING
10750 Baur Boulevard, St. Louis MO 63132. 314/994-7600. **Fax:** 314/994-7609. **Contact:** Human Resources. **World Wide Web address:** http://www.caraustar.com. **Description:** Manufactures folding cartons and other products including shipping containers and containerboard products, molded pulp products, and solid wood products. **Corporate headquarters location:** Charlotte NC.

CARDINAL RITTER INSTITUTE
7601 Watson Road, St. Louis MO 63119. 314/961-8000. **Fax:** 314/962-7140. **Contact:** Human Resources. **E-mail address:** jkohlberg@ccstl.org. **World Wide Web address:** http://www.ccstl.org/cri. **Description:** An organization that specializes in providing home health care, housing, social services, employment programs, and volunteer programs to the elderly. **Corporate headquarters location:** This location. **Number of employees at this location:** 350.

CARDIOVASCULAR CONSULTANTS, PC
4330 Wornall Road, Suite 2000, Kansas City MO 64111. 816/931-1883. **Fax:** 816/931-7714. **Contact:** Human Resources. **World Wide Web address:** http://www.cc-pc.com. **Description:** A 20-physician cardiology practice providing patient care and research services in the fields of nuclear cardiology, preventive cardiology, and EP/rhythm. Offices in Missouri and Kansas. **Positions advertised include:** Clinical Technician; Administrative Assistant; Receptionist; Scheduler; Clinical Technician; Charge Entry Clerk. **Office hours:** Monday - Friday, 8:00 a.m. - 5:00 p.m. **Corporate headquarters location:** This location. **Number of employees at this location:** 125.

CARLISLE CONNECT
2601 West Battlefield Street, Springfield MO 65807-4009. 417/881-7440. **Contact:** Director of Human Resources. **World Wide Web address:** http://www.cptbelts.com. **Description:** A worldwide manufacturer and distributor of a wide range of highly-engineered rubber and plastic products, many of which are used for replacement purposes. Principal markets include the agricultural, automotive, construction, energy, printing, mining, textile, and transportation industries.

CARONDELET CORPORATION
8600 Commercial Boulevard, Pevely MO 63070. 636/479-4499. **Fax:** 636/479-7476. **Contact:** Human Resources. **Description:** Manufacturers of gray, alloy iron, and alloy steel castings. **Number of employees at this location:** 100.

CASS INFORMATION SYSTEMS, INC.
13001 Hollenberg Drive, Bridgeton MO 63044. 314/506-5500. **Fax:** 314/506-5955. **Contact:** Human Resources. **E-mail address:** cassrecruiter@cassbank.com. **World Wide Web address:** http://www.cassinfo.com. **Description:** Provides a full range of banking services to individual, corporate, and institutional customers. Cass Information Services (also at this location) processes payments for freight and utility services. **Other U.S. locations:** Columbus OH; Lowell MA. **Parent company:** Cass Commercial Corporation.

CASSENS TRANSPORT COMPANY, INC.
2000 Mraz Lane, Fenton MO 63026. 636/343-2161. **Fax:** 636/343-4268. **Contact:** Recruiter. **Description:** Engaged in a variety of trucking services, excluding local trucking. **Number of employees at this location:** 600.

THE CATHOLIC HEALTH ASSOCIATION OF THE U.S.
4455 Woodson Road, St. Louis MO 63134-3797. 314/427-2500. **Fax:** 314/427-0029. **Contact:** Personnel Director. **World Wide Web address:** http://www.chausa.org. **Description:** Engaged in a wide variety of administrative services for member hospitals and organizations across the United States. **Other U.S. locations:** Washington DC.

CENTRAL COAL & COKE CORPORATION
911 Main Street, Suite 1710, Kansas City MO 64105. 816/842-2430. **Contact:** Human Resources. **Description:** Central Coal & Coke leases properties and mineral interests to operating lessees.

CENTRAL INSTITUTE FOR THE DEAF
4560 Clayton Avenue, St. Louis MO 63110. 314/977-0000. **Fax:** 314/977-0025. **Contact:** Personnel Manager. **World Wide Web address:** http://www.cid.wustl.edu. **Description:** A specialized educational agency that operates speech and hearing clinics, professional education programs, research facilities, and an elementary school for deaf children. **Corporate headquarters location:** This location.

CENTRAL MINE EQUIPMENT COMPANY
4215 Rider Trail North, St. Louis MO 63045-1106. 314/291-7700. **Toll-free phone:** 800/325-8827. **Fax:** 314/291-4880. **Contact:** Human Resources. **E-mail address:** info@cmeco.com. **World Wide Web address:** http://www.cmeco.com. **Description:** A manufacturer of drilling rigs and related tools for mining and industry. Founded in 1928. **Number of employees at this location:** 100.

CENTRAL MISSOURI STATE UNIVERSITY
P.O. Box 800, Warrensburg MO 64093. 660/543-4255. **Recorded jobline:** 660/543-8300. **Contact:** Office of Human Resources. **World Wide Web address:** http://www.cmsu.edu. **Description:** Offers over 150 undergraduate and graduate programs and has an enrollment of approximately 11,000 students. Founded in 1871. **NOTE:** Search and apply for positions online.

CENTRIFUGAL AND MECHANICAL INDUSTRIES, INC. (CMI)
201 President Street, St. Louis MO 63118. 314/776-2848. **Fax:** 314/776-2918. **Contact:** Personnel Director. **World Wide Web address:** http://www.cmi-centrifuges.com. **Description:** CMI manufactures a wide range of centrifuges and process equipment for a diverse group of industries, including coal preparation, mineral and chemical processes, general manufacturing, and automotive manufacturing. **Parent company:** Elgin National Industries, Inc. **Number of employees at this location:** 100.

CERNER CITATION, INC.
424 South Woods Mill Road, Suite 200, Chesterfield MO 63017. 314/579-7900. **Contact:** Vice President of Human Resources. **World Wide Web address:** http://www.cita.com. **Description:** Designs, develops, markets, and services cost-effective proprietary networking systems for laboratories, financial/administrative departments, and order communications/results reporting areas. These systems are marketed to hospitals, group practices, clinics, reference laboratories, and nursing homes. **Positions advertised include:** Test Analyst. **NOTE:** Search and apply for positions online. **Parent Company:** Cerner Corporation. **Listed on:** NASDAQ. **Stock exchange symbol:** CERN. **Number of employees at this location:** 110. **Number of employees nationwide:** 185.

CERNER CORPORATION
2800 Rockcreek Parkway, Kansas City MO 64117. 816/221-1024. **Fax:** 816/474-1742. **Contact:** Human Resources. **World Wide Web address:** http://www.cerner.com. **Description:** Cerner designs, installs, and supports software systems for the health care industry including hospitals, HMOs, clinics, physicians' offices, and integrated health organizations. **NOTE:** Search and apply for positions online. **Positions advertised include:** Business Analyst; Human Resources Operations Support; Graphic Designer; Sr. Software Engineer; Legal Specialist; Technology Engineer; Operations Analyst; Java Architect. **Corporate headquarters location:** This location. **Other U.S. locations:** Nationwide. **Operations at this facility include:** This location develops software. **Listed on:** NASDAQ. **Stock exchange symbol:** CERN. **Annual sales/revenues:** More than $100 million. **Number of employees worldwide:** 5,100.

CHASE GENERAL CORPORATION
3600 Leonard Road, P.O. Box 698, St. Joseph MO 64502. 816/279-1625. **Toll-free phone:** 800/786-1625. **Fax:** 816/279-1997. **Contact:** Barry Yantis, President. **World Wide Web address:** http://www.cherrymash.com. **Description:** Manufactures confectionery products including candy bars and other coconut, peanut, chocolate, and fudge candy.

CHATEAU GIRARDEAU
3120 Independence Street, Cape Girardeau MO 63701. 573/335-1281. **Toll-free phone:** 800/428-0069. **Contact:** Administrative Secretary. **World Wide Web address:** http://www.chateaugirardeau.com. **Description:** A retirement center for senior citizens. Chateau Girardeau offers four levels of care: a health center/nursing home providing complete health care services; an assisted living option; apartments providing an opportunity for a more independent lifestyle; and private houses.

CHRISTIAN BOARD OF PUBLICATIONS
P.O. Box 179, St. Louis MO 63133-0179. 314/231-8500. **Physical address:** 1221 Locust Street, Suite 1200, St. Louis MO 63103. **Contact:** Personnel Director. **World Wide Web address:** http://www.cbp21.com. **Description:** A book and magazine publisher that specializes in religious material.

CIBER INFORMATION SERVICES
12312 Olive Boulevard, Suite 175, St. Louis MO 63141. 314/434-7900. **Toll-free phone:** 800/878-1596. **Fax:** 314/434-1117. **Contact:** Recruiter. **World Wide Web address:** http://www.ciber.com. **Description:** Provides consulting for client/server development, mainframe and legacy systems, industry-specific analysis, application-specific analysis, and network development. Founded in 1974. **NOTE:** Search and apply for positions online. **Positions advertised include:** Java Middleware Developer; Information Architect; JAVA Developer; Sr. ABAP Programmer/Analyst; QA Software Tester. **Corporate headquarters location:** Greenwood Village CO. **Other U.S. locations:** Nationwide. **Listed on:** New York Stock Exchange. **Stock exchange symbol:** CBR. **Number of employees at this location:** 115. **Number of employees nationwide:** 4,000.

CLARK RICHARDSON & BISKUP CONSULTING ENGINEERS, INC.
7410 Northwest Tiffany Springs, Suite 100, Kansas City MO 64153. 816/880-9800. **Fax:** 816/880-9898 **Contact:** Human Resources. **E-mail address:** kcjobs@crbusa.com. **World Wide Web address:** http://www.crbusa.com. **Description:** A design firm primarily involved in facility and process design for high technology industries such as pharmaceutical, biotechnology, specialty chemical, and microelectronics. Founded in 1984. **NOTE:** Search and apply for positions online. **Positions advertised include:** HVAC Engineer; Mechanical Engineer; Process Utility Engineer; Sr. Pharmaceutical Process Engineer; Instrumentation & Controls Engineer; Electrical Engineer. **Other U.S. locations:** NC; PA; CA; MN; NE.

CLEAN UNIFORM COMPANY
1316 South Seventh Street, St. Louis MO 63104. 314/421-1220. **Fax:** 314/421-4902. **Contact:** Office Manager. **World Wide Web address:** http://www.cleanuniform.com. **Description:** Engaged in the rental and laundering of uniforms, dust mops, and dust mats. **Number of employees at this location:** 100.

CLEAN-TECH COMPANY
2815 Olive Street, St. Louis MO 63103. 314/652-2388. **Contact:** Vice President of Operations. **Description:** Engaged in a variety of services including janitorial and security guard services.

CLEMCO INDUSTRIES
One Cablecar Drive, Washington MO 63090. 636/239-8135. **Fax:** 800/726-7559. **Contact:** Personnel Department. **World Wide Web address:** http://www.clemcoindustries.com. **Description:** Manufacturers of blasting, peening, and finishing equipment; beverage and food tanks in stainless steel; refrigerated, dairy farm, bulk milk tanks in stainless steel; computerized feed management systems for dairy farms; and dairy farm milking machines.

CLIMATE ENGINEERING CORPORATION
152 East Kirkham Avenue, St. Louis MO 63119. 314/968-8400. **Contact:** Personnel. **Description:** Engaged in contract engineering services for plumbing, heating, and air conditioning. **Number of employees at this location:** 100.

CLIPPER CRUISE LINE
11969 Westline Industrial Drive, St. Louis MO 63146-3220. 314/655-6700. **Fax:** 314/655-6670. **Contact:** Personnel. **E-mail address:** employment.global@nwship.com. **World Wide Web address:** http://www.clippercruise.com. **Description:** A cruise line. **Parent company:** INTRAN.

COIN ACCEPTORS INC.
300 Hunter Avenue, St. Louis MO 63124-2013. 314/725-0100. **Toll-free phone:** 800/325-2646. **Fax:** 314/725-7198. **Contact:** Human Resources Director. **E-mail address:** recruiter@coinco.com. **World Wide Web address:** http://www.coinco.com. **Description:** Manufacturers of coin mechanisms for vending machines. **Positions advertised include:** Software Developer; Cost Accountant; Global Sourcing Buyer; Sr. Technician. **Corporate headquarters location:** This location. **Number of employees at this location:** 200.

COLDWELL BANKER
1505 South Big Bend Boulevard, St. Louis MO 63117. 314/647-0002. **Contact:** Human Resources. **World Wide Web address:** http://www.coldwellbanker.com. **Description:** Coldwell Banker is one of the largest residential real estate companies in the United States and Canada in terms of total home sales transactions. Coldwell Banker is also a leader in meeting corporate America's specialized relocation needs on a worldwide basis. Coldwell Banker operates Coldwell Banker Relocation Services, a corporate relocation management company. Coldwell Banker also launched Coldwell Banker Residential Affiliates, Inc., aimed at franchising select brokers who served small to medium-sized markets. **Corporate headquarters location:** Mission Viejo CA. **Parent company:** Cendant Corporation. **Number of employees at this location:** 800.

COLOR-ART, INC.
10300 Watson Road, St. Louis MO 63127. 314/966-2000. **Fax:** 314/966-4725. **Contact:** Tim Murphy, Human Resources Manager. **World Wide Web address:** http://www.color-art.com. **Description:** A commercial printing company engaged in offset and letter press printing. **Other U.S. locations:** CA; FL; NY. **Subsidiaries include:** Lake Printing; Plus Communications. **Parent company:** Mail-Well Print Group. **Operations at this facility include:** Divisional Headquarters; Manufacturing; Sales. **Number of employees at this location:** 300.

COLOR-ART OFFICE INTERIORS INC.
1325 North Warson Road, St. Louis MO 63132. 314/432-3000. **Contact:** Human Resources. **World Wide Web address:** http://www.color-art.com. **Description:** Designs and constructs office interiors and sells related products and services. **Positions advertised include:** Account Development Representative; New Business Development Representative; Showroom Manager; Designer. **Special programs:** Internships. **Number of employees at this location:** 95.

COLUMBIA COLLEGE OF MISSOURI
125 St. Clair Hall, 1001 Rogers Street, Columbia MO 65216. 573/875-7260. **Toll-free phone:** 800/231-2391. **Fax:** 573/875-7379. **Contact:** Bruce Strickland, Director of Human Resources. **World Wide Web address:** http://www.ccis.edu. **Description:** A post-secondary educational institution offering both undergraduate and graduate programs of study. Founded in 1851. **NOTE:** Search and apply for positions online. **Positions advertised include:** Nursing Instructor; Adjunct Faculty, Computer Information Systems; Visiting Professor, Biology. **Corporate headquarters location:** This location. **Number of employees at this location:** 200.

COLUMBIA REGIONAL HOSPITAL
404 Keene Street, Columbia MO 65201. 573/875-9000. **Recorded jobline:** 573/499-6499. **Contact:** Human Resources Department. **World Wide Web address:** http://www.muhealth.org/~columbiaregional. **Description:** A 219-bed medical referral center with over 200 staff physicians representing medical specialties including orthopedics, oncology, neurology, and ophthalmology. Columbia Regional Hospital is an American Medical International affiliate. Founded in 1974. **Positions advertised include:** Benefits Specialist; Clinical Dietician; Director of Development; Managed Care Specialist; Pharmacist; Medical Technologist; Neurophysiology Tech; Radiologic Technologist, Registered Respiratory Therapist; RN's; Clinical Coordinator.

COMFORT PRINTING AND STATIONERY COMPANY
COMFORT COMPANIES
1611 Locust Street, St. Louis MO 63103. 314/241-6991. **Contact:** Personnel Director. **Description:** A commercial printing and lithography company. Comfort Printing and Stationery is also engaged in the wholesale and retail sale of office supplies and furniture. **Parent company:** Comfort Companies. **Number of employees at this location:** 100.

COMPUTERIZED MEDICAL SYSTEMS, INC.
1145 Corporate Lake Drive, Suite 100, St. Louis MO 63132. 314/993-0003. **Toll-free phone:** 800/878-4267. **Fax:** 314/993-0075. **Contact:** Human Resources. **World Wide Web address:** http://www.cms-stl.com. **Description:** A developer of radiation treatment software. **NOTE:** Search and apply for positions online. **Positions advertised include:** Applications Specialist; Database Developer.

CONCORDIA PUBLISHING HOUSE
3558 South Jefferson Avenue, St. Louis MO 63118. 314/268-1252. **Fax:** 314/268-1329. **Contact:** Employment Recruiter. **E-mail address:** cphresume@cph.org. **World Wide Web address:** http://www.cph.org. **Description:** Publishers of religious curriculum, periodicals, books, pamphlets, and Bibles. **Positions advertised include:** Manager, Marketing Communications; Software Sales Representative. **Corporate headquarters location:** This location. **Operations at this facility include:** Administration; Sales; Service. **Number of employees at this location:** 335.

CONCORDIA SEMINARY
801 De Mun Avenue, St. Louis MO 63105. 314/505-7000. **Fax:** 314/505-7001. **Contact:** Employment. **E-mail address:** sumoskip@csl.edu. **World Wide Web address:** http://www.csl.edu. **Description:** A four-year seminary college that also offers a variety of graduate programs in theology. **Positions advertised include:** Director of Alumni Activities.

CONDAIRE INC.
1141 Reco Drive, St. Louis MO 63126. 314/821-8388. **Fax:** 314/821-6530. **Contact:** Malcolm Sweet, Jr., President. **World Wide Web address:** http://www.condaire.com. **Description:** A mechanical contracting firm engaged in a variety of heating, ventilating, air conditioning, plumbing, and industrial piping services. Founded in 1946. **Corporate headquarters location:** This location. **Listed on:** Privately held. **Annual sales/revenues:** $11 - $20 million. **Number of employees at this location:** 100.

CONNECTOR CASTINGS INC.
1600 North 22nd Street, St. Louis MO 63106. 314/421-5895. **Contact:** Personnel. **World Wide Web address:** http://www.connectorcastings.com. **Description:** Manufactures nonferrous grounding equipment, electrical hardware, nonferrous castings, and noncurrent-carrying wiring devices.

CONTICO INTERNATIONAL, INC.
1101 North Warson Road, St. Louis MO 63132. 314/997-5900. **Contact:** Personnel Department. **Description:** Contico International designs, manufactures, and markets a broad range of molded plastic and liquid dispensing products for consumer and industrial use including sanitary maintenance products, industrial containers, and materials handling products. **Corporate headquarters location:** This location. **Other U.S. locations:** Los Angeles CA; El Paso TX; Houston TX. **Operations at this facility include:** Administration; Manufacturing; Research and Development; Sales; Service. **Number of employees nationwide:** 2,600.

CONTINENTAL FABRICATORS
5601 West Park Avenue, St. Louis MO 63110. 314/781-6300. **Contact:** Personnel Department. **Description:** Manufactures steel plate fabrication ducts, hoppers, and pressure vessels. **Number of employees at this location:** 100.

COOPER BUSSMANN
P.O. Box 14460, St. Louis MO 63178-4460. 636/394-2877. **Contact:** Human Resources. **E-mail address:** jobs@buss.com. **World Wide Web address:** http://www.bussmann.com. **Description:** Manufactures fuses and fuse accessories. **Positions advertised include:** Marketing Manager; New Business Development Manager. **Corporate headquarters location:** Houston TX. **Other U.S. locations:** IL; KY; NC. **Parent company:** Cooper Industries. **Operations at this facility include:** Divisional Headquarters; Manufacturing. **Listed on:** New York Stock Exchange. **Stock exchange symbol:** CBE. **Number of employees at this location:** 650. **Number of employees nationwide:** 3,100.

CORRECTIONAL MEDICAL SERVICES
12647 Olive Boulevard, St. Louis MO 63141. 314/919-8500. **Toll-free phone:** 800/325-3982. **Fax:** 314/919-8903. **Recorded jobline:** 314/919-9547. **Contact:** Dorothy Henricks, Personnel. **E-mail address:** dhenricks@spectrumhealth.com. **World Wide Web address:** http://www.spectrumhealth.com. **Description:** A leading clinical management company that provides outpatient services in emergency care at over 450 facilities. Spectrum offers health care and administrative management services to hospitals, physicians, clinics, managed care programs, insurers, businesses, and government entities. **NOTE:** Entry-level positions are offered. **Special programs:** Internships; Training. **Corporate headquarters location:** This location. **Other U.S. locations:** Nationwide. **Listed on:** Privately held. **Number of employees at this location:** 500.

CORRIGAN COMPANY
3545 Gratiot Street, St. Louis MO 63103. 314/771-6200. **Fax:** 314/771-8537. **Contact:** Thomas L. Garbin, Director of Human Resources. **World Wide Web address:** http://www.corrigan.com. **Description:** A mechanical contracting company engaged in heating, air conditioning, and plumbing. Founded in 1896. **NOTE:** Entry-level positions are offered. **Special programs:** Co-ops; Summer Jobs. **President:** Thomas J. Corrigan. **Annual sales/revenues:** More than $100 million. **Number of employees at this location:** 500.

COX HEALTH SYSTEM
1423 North Jefferson Street, Springfield MO 65802. 417/269-3000. **Fax:** 417/269-3548. **Recorded jobline:** 417/269-5525. **Contact:** Human Resources. **World Wide Web address:** http://www.coxhealth.com. **Description:** Operates a multi-facility hospital. **Positions advertised include:** Business Office Representative; Clinic Office Assistant; File Specialist; Information Desk Receptionist; Support Staff Assistant; Accounting Supervisor; Community Support Worker. **Corporate headquarters location:** This location. **Subsidiaries include:** Burrell; Cox Monett; Oxford Health Care. **Operations at this facility include:** Administration; Service. **Number of employees at this location:** 4,500.

CHARLES L. CRANE AGENCY
100 South Fourth Street, Suite 800, St. Louis MO 63102. 314/241-8700. **Contact:** General Manager. **Description:** A full-service insurance agency. **Corporate headquarters location:** This location. **Parent company:** Crane Company. **Operations at this facility include:** Administration; Sales; Service. **Number of employees at this location:** 100.

CRANE MERCHANDISING SYSTEMS
12955 Enterprise Way, Bridgeton MO 63044. 314/298-3500. **Contact:** Vice President of Human Resources. **World Wide Web address:** http://www.nationalvendors.com. **Description:** Manufactures vending machines and currency products. **Positions advertised include:** Service Engineer. **Corporate headquarters location:** Stamford CT. **Parent company:** Crane Company. **Operations at this facility include:** Administration; Manufacturing; Research and Development; Sales; Service. **Listed on:** New York Stock Exchange. **Stock exchange symbol:** CR. **Number of employees nationwide:** 700.

CUMMINS GATEWAY
7210 Hall Street, St. Louis MO 63147. 314/389-5400. **Contact:** John Wagner, President. **World Wide Web address:** http://www.gateway.cummins.com. **Description:** Distributes diesel engines and parts for diesel engines. Cummins Gateway also provides service for diesel engines. **Number of employees at this location:** 100.

CUPPLES RUBBER COMPANY
9430 Page Avenue, St. Louis MO 63132. 314/426-7750. **Contact:** Personnel Director. **World Wide Web address:** http://www.cupplesrubber.cc. **Description:** Manufactures inner tubes, molded and extruded rubber products, and lathe-cut gaskets. **Number of employees at this location:** 400.

CURTIS-TOLEDO INC.
1905 Kienlen Avenue, St. Louis MO 63133. 314/383-1300. **Contact:** Diane Nemec, Personnel Administrator. **Description:** A manufacturer of machinery, specializing in the production of air compressors, pipe threading machines, and hand tools. **Number of employees at this location:** 100.

CUTLER-HAMMER, INC.
2050 Westport Center Drive, St. Louis MO 63146. 314/812-2800. **Contact:** District Manager. **World Wide Web address:** http://www.cutler-hammer.com. **Description:** Cutler-Hammer is engaged principally in the manufacture, sale, and service of equipment and components for the generation, transmission, distribution, utilization, and control of electricity both domestically and internationally. The company also offers a wide range of products and services that are unrelated to electrical manufacturing, such as broadcasting and cable television operations, land development, bottling and distribution of beverage products, transport refrigeration, and financial services. The company operates in four segments: Power Systems, Industry Products, Public Systems, and Broadcasting and Cable. **Parent company:** Eaton Corporation.

D&K HEALTHCARE RESOURCES
8235 Forsyth Boulevard, Clayton MO 63105. 314/727-3485. **Fax:** 314/727-5759. **Contact:** Human Resources. **World Wide Web address:** http://www.dkwd.com. **Description:** Distributes pharmaceuticals and health and beauty aids to retailers and hospitals. **Corporate headquarters location:** This location. **Listed on:** NASDAQ. **Stock exchange symbol:** DKWD.

DST SYSTEMS, INC.
333 West 11th Street, Kansas City MO 64105. 816/435-1000. **Contact:** Human Resources. **World Wide Web address:** http://www.dstsystems.com. **Description:** A software developer and transfer agent for the financial industry. **NOTE:** Entry-level positions are offered. **Special programs:** Internships. **Corporate headquarters location:** This location. **Subsidiaries include:** Argus Health Systems, Inc.; NFDS. **Number of employees at this location:** 6,000.

DAIMLERCHRYSLER CORPORATION
1050 Dodge Drive, Fenton MO 63026. 636/343-2424. **Contact:** Human Resources. **World Wide Web address:** http://www.daimlerchrysler.com. **Description:** This facility is an assembly plant. Overall, DaimlerChrysler Corporation manufactures cars, trucks, minivans, and sport-utility vehicles for customers in more than 100 countries. **Listed on:** New York Stock Exchange. **Stock exchange symbol:** DCX.

DAIMLERCHRYSLER CORPORATION
1001 North Highway Drive, Fenton MO 63026. 636/349-4040. **Contact:** Personnel Manager. **World Wide Web address:** http://www.daimlerchrysler.com. **Description:** DaimlerChrysler Corporation manufactures cars, trucks, minivans, and sport-utility vehicles for customers in more than 100 countries. **Operations at this facility include:** This location is an assembly plant. **Listed on:** New York Stock Exchange. **Stock exchange symbol:** DCX.

DAIRY FARMERS OF AMERICA, INC.
P.O. Box 909700, Kansas City MO 64190-9700. 816/801-6455. **Contact:** Human Resources. **World Wide Web address:** http://www.dfamilk.com. **Description:** A dairy cooperative that processes and markets numerous dairy products. **Special programs:** Internships. **Operations at this facility include:** Administration; Research and Development; Sales; Service.

THE DANIEL AND HENRY COMPANY
1001 Highlands Plaza Drive West, Suite 500, St. Louis MO 63110. 314/421-1525. **Fax:** 314/444-1990. **Contact:** Human Resources Manager. **World Wide Web address:** http://www.danielandhenry.com. **Description:** Provides all types of commercial and personal insurance, as well as brokerage services. Founded in 1921. **Corporate headquarters location:** This location. **Operations at this facility include:** Administration; Sales; Service. **Listed on:** Privately held. **Annual sales/revenues:** $11 - $20 million. **Number of employees at this location:** 190.
location: 175. **Number of employees nationwide:** 6,500.

DATA2
222 Turner Boulevard, St. Peters MO 63376. 636/278-8888. **Fax:** 636/278-2180. **Contact:** Human Resources. **World Wide Web address:** http://www.data2.com. **Description:** An electronic typesetting, data processing services bureau. The company also manufactures pressure-sensitive bar code labels.

DAUGHERTY SYSTEMS
One City Place Drive, Suite 240, St. Louis MO 63141. 314/432-8200. **Fax:** 314/432-8217. **Contact:** Human Resources. **E-mail address:** staffingstl@daugherty.com. **World Wide Web address:** http://www.daugherty.com. **Description:** A computer consulting firm. **Special programs:** Training. **Corporate headquarters location:** This location. **Other U.S. locations:** Atlanta GA; Chicago IL; Baltimore MD; Dallas TX. **Listed on:** Privately held. **Annual sales/revenues:** $21 - $50 million. **Number of employees at this location:** 190. **Number of employees nationwide:** 300.

DELOITTE & TOUCHE
100 South 4th Street, Suite 300, St. Louis MO 63102. 314/342-1801. **Fax:** 314/342-1100. **Contact:** Human Resources. **World Wide Web address:** http://www.us.deloitte.com. **Description:** An international firm of certified public accountants providing professional accounting, auditing, tax, and management consulting services to widely diversified clients. The company has a specialized program consisting of national industry groups and functional groups that cross industry lines. Groups are involved in various disciplines including accounting, auditing, taxation management advisory services, small and growing businesses, mergers and acquisitions, and computer applications.

DETROIT TOOL & ENGINEERING
P.O. Box 232, Lebanon MO 65536. 417/532-2141. **Physical address:** 441 West Elm Street, Lebanon MO 65536. **Fax:** 417/532-1039. **Contact:** Human Resources Manager. **World Wide Web address:** http://www.detroittool.com. **Description:** Designs and manufactures special machines, automated assembly systems, tooling, fixturing, and a complete line of thermoforming machines under exclusive license from Rigo. **Special programs:** Apprenticeships; Co-ops. **Office hours:** Monday - Friday, 8:00 a.m. - 5:00 p.m. **Parent company:** DT Industries (Dayton OH). **Annual sales/revenues:** $51 - $100 million. **Number of employees at this location:** 450. **Number of employees nationwide:** 2,500. **Number of employees worldwide:** 3,000.

DIAGRAPH CORPORATION
One Missouri Research Park Drive, St. Charles MO 63304-5685. **Toll-free phone:** 800/526-2531. **Contact:** Human Resources. **E-mail address:** hr@diagraph.com. **World Wide Web address:** http://www.diagraph.com. **Description:** A manufacturer of ink-jet printers.

THE DIAL CORPORATION
6901 McKissock Avenue, St. Louis MO 63147. 314/382-8535. **Contact:** Employment/Training Manager. **World Wide Web address:** http://www.dialcorp.com. **Description:** The Dial Corporation is a diverse company engaged in consumer products and financial services. Dial manufactures soap, air fresheners, detergents, bleach, ammonia, plastic containers, and canned meats. Financial services include Traveler's Express, which sells money orders; and Dobbs International, which provides airline food. The company operates 13 production facilities in the United States and one in Mexico. **Special programs:** Internships. **Corporate headquarters location:** Phoenix AZ. **Operations at this facility include:** This location manufactures laundry detergent. **Listed on:** New York Stock Exchange. **Stock exchange symbol:** DL.

DIDION AND SONS FOUNDRY COMPANY
P.O. Box 520, St. Peters MO 63376. 636/928-1130. **Fax:** 636/447-8640. **Contact:** Ferd Potthast, Personnel Director. **E-mail address:** humanresources@didionfoundry.com. **World Wide Web address:** http://www.didionfoundry.com. **Description:** Manufacturers of gray and ductile iron castings. **Office hours:** Monday - Friday, 7:30 a.m. - 4:30 p.m. **Corporate headquarters location:** This location. **Operations at this facility include:** Manufacturing. **Number of employees at this location:** 200.

DIRECTORY DISTRIBUTING ASSOCIATES, INC. (DDA)
160 Corporate Woods Court, Bridgeton MO 63044. 314/592-8600. **Contact:** Personnel Director. **World Wide Web address:** http://www.ddai.com. **Description:** Distributes telephone books. **Number of employees at this location:** 100.

DOCUMENT IMAGING SYSTEMS CORPORATION
1520 Washington Avenue, St. Louis MO 63103. 314/436-2800. **Contact:** Personnel Department. **Description:** Distributes microfilm equipment and supplies. **Corporate headquarters location:** This location. **Operations at this facility include:** Administration; Sales; Service. **Listed on:** Privately held. **Number of employees at this location:** 25.

DRUG PACKAGE INC.
901 Drug Package Lane, O'Fallon MO 63366. 636/272-6261. **Contact:** Personnel Department. **World Wide Web address:** http://www.drugpackage.com. **Description:** Manufactures boxes and labels for prescription pharmaceuticals. **Number of employees at this location:** 100.

EAST CENTRAL COLLEGE
1964 Prairie Dell Road, Union MO 63084. 636/583-5195. **Contact:** Beth Watts, Human Resources. **E-mail address:** wattsb@eastcentral.edu. **World Wide Web address:** http://www.eastcentral.edu. **Description:** A two-year college with an enrollment of approximately 3,000 students. Founded in 1968. **Number of employees at this location:** 100.

ECKADAMS
1866 Craig Road, St. Louis MO 63146. 314/576-8200. **Contact:** Human Resources. **World Wide Web address:** http://www.eckadams.com. **Description:** Manufactures office furniture and hospitality industry products such as wardrobe hangers, lockers, cabinets, and accessories. **Special programs:** Internships. **Corporate headquarters location:** This location. **Other U.S. locations:** Nationwide. **Parent company:** Acco North America. **Operations at this facility include:** Administration; Manufacturing; Research and Development; Sales; Service. **Number of employees at this location:** 200.

EDWARD JONES
201 Progress Parkway, Maryland Heights MO 63043. 314/515-2000. **Fax:** 866/860-4094. **Contact:** Personnel. **World Wide Web address:** http://www.edwardjones.com. **Description:** A securities brokerage firm. **Corporate headquarters location:** This location. **Listed on:** Privately held. **Number of employees nationwide:** 7,000.

ELDER MANUFACTURING COMPANY
999 Executive Parkway, St. Louis MO 63141. 314/469-1120. **Contact:** Human Resources. **Description:** Manufacturers of boys' clothing and furnishings and men's shirts. **Number of employees at this location:** 100.

ELSEVIER SCIENCE
11830 Westline Industrial Drive, St. Louis MO 63146. 314/872-8370. **Toll-free phone:** 800/325-4177. **Fax:** 314/432-1380. **Contact:** Human Resources. **World Wide Web address:** http://www.elsevier.com. **Description:** A publisher of books and periodicals in the field of health sciences. **Corporate headquarters location:** Philadelphia PA. **Parent company:** Reed Elsevier. **Annual sales/revenues:** More than $100 million. **Number of employees at this location:** 400. **Number of employees nationwide:** 600.

EMERSON ELECTRIC COMPANY
P.O. Box 4100, 8000 West Florissant Avenue, St. Louis MO 63136-8506. 314/553-2000. **Contact:** Director, Corporate Personnel. **World Wide Web address:** http://www.emersonelectric.com. **Description:** This location operates as part of the Electronics and Space division. Overall, Emerson Electric Company produces process control instrumentation and systems, industrial motors and drives; industrial machinery and components; computer support products; fractional horsepower motors; and components for air conditioners, heaters, and hand tools. **NOTE:** Contact Director, Corporate Personnel in writing concerning career opportunities at Emerson's Corporate Division headquarters. **Corporate headquarters location:** This location. **Operations**

at this facility include: Divisional Headquarters; Manufacturing. **Listed on:** New York Stock Exchange. **Stock exchange symbol:** EMR. **Number of employees worldwide:** 106,000.

EMPIRE DISTRICT ELECTRIC COMPANY
602 Joplin Street, Joplin MO 64802. 417/625-5100. **Contact:** Human Resources. **World Wide Web address:** http://www.empiredistrict.com. **Description:** Purchases, generates, transmits, distributes, and sells electricity. The company also provides water service. **Listed on:** New York Stock Exchange. **Stock exchange symbol:** EDE.

ENGINEERED AIR SYSTEMS INC.
201 Evans Lane, St. Louis MO 63121. 314/553-4766. **Contact:** Human Resources. **World Wide Web address:** http://www.easistl.com. **Description:** Manufactures ground support equipment for portable military air conditioning and heating units, environmental control systems, and containers. **Corporate headquarters location:** This location. **Operations at this facility include:** Administration; Manufacturing; Research and Development; Sales; Service.

ENTERPRISE RENT-A-CAR
600 Corporate Park Drive, St. Louis MO 63105. 314/512-5000. **Contact:** Human Resources. **World Wide Web address:** http://www.erac.com. **Description:** Enterprise Rent-A-Car is an automobile rental and leasing agency. **Number of employees at this location:** 100.

ERICSON VETERINARY HOSPITAL
1000 NW South Outer Road, Blue Springs MO 64015. 816/229-8255. **Contact:** Human Resources. **E-mail address:** vetinfo@bluespringsvet.com. **World Wide Web address:** http://www.bluespringsvet.com. **Description:** Ericson Veterinary Hospital provides general medical and surgical care to animals.

ERNST & YOUNG LLP
1200 Main Street, Suite 1800, Kansas City MO 64105. 816/480-5546. **Contact:** Susan Chapman, Human Resources. **World Wide Web address:** http://www.ey.com. **Description:** A certified public accounting firm that also provides management consulting services. Services include data processing, financial modeling, financial feasibility studies, production planning and inventory management, management sciences, health care planning, human resources, cost accounting, and budgeting systems. **Special programs:** Internships. **Corporate headquarters location:** New York NY. **International locations:** Worldwide.

ESCO TECHNOLOGIES
8888 Ladue Road, Suite 200, St. Louis MO 63124. 314/213-7200. **Contact:** Debbie Hanlon, Vice President of Human Resources. **World Wide Web address:** http://www.escostl.com. **Description:** Manufactures and supplies engineered filtration products to the health care, process, and transportation markets. ESCO Technologies also markets a variety of proprietary communications systems as well as RF shielding and test products. **Subsidiaries include:** Comtrak Technologies, L.C.C.; Distribution Control Systems, Inc. (DCSI); Filtertek, Inc.; Lindgren RF Enclosures; PTI Consolidated; Rantec Power Systems, Inc.; VACCO Industries.

ESSEX INDUSTRIES INC.
7700 Gravois Avenue, St. Louis MO 63123. 314/832-4500. **Contact:** Personnel Director. **World Wide Web address:** http://www.essexind.com. **Description:** Designs, develops, and manufactures aircraft systems and components including quick disconnect couplings, check valves, relief and drain valves, pressure switches, regulators, pressure vessels, cryogenics oxygen systems, solenoids and rain repellent systems, and screw machine products. **Other U.S. locations:** IL; MD; PA. **Operations at this facility include:** Administration; Manufacturing; Sales. **Number of employees at this location:** 450.

EXCHANGE NATIONAL BANCSHARES INC.
132 East High Street, Jefferson City MO 65101. 573/761-6261. **Contact:** Jenny Lamb, Human Resources Assistant. **E-mail address:** jlamb@exchangebk.com. **World Wide Web address:** http://www.exchangebk.com. **Description:** A bank holding company that performs commercial banking operations and other related financial activities. This location also hires seasonally. Founded in 1865. **NOTE:** Entry-level positions and part-time jobs are offered. **Positions advertised include:** Accounting Assistant; Investment Clerk; Assistant Manager; Bookkeeping Clerk; Branch Manager; Receptionist; Commercial Loan Officer; Credit Analyst. **Special programs:** Internships; Summer Jobs. **Office hours:** Monday - Friday, 8:00 a.m. - 5:00 p.m. **Corporate headquarters location:** This location. **CEO:** Donald L. Campbell. **Number of employees at this location:** 130.

EXEL TRANSPORTATION
5310 St. Joseph Avenue, P.O. Box 939, St. Joseph MO 64502. 816/233-3158. **Contact:** Human Resources. **World Wide Web address:** http://www.exel.com. **Description:** One of the country's leading providers of single-source transportation services to some of the largest shippers in the world. The company provides a full complement of logistics management services such as dedicated fleet, warehousing, and risk management, as well as the component services involved in these activities. With over 90 offices across North America, Exel is one of the largest transportation services companies in the United States. The company's areas of operation include Intermodal, Trucking Services; Carload, International, Dimensional Traffic; Consolidation & Distribution Services; and its newest division, Air Freight. Services include double stack, trailers, and containers on rail cars; trucks; and ocean-going transportation.

EXPRESS SCRIPTS, INC.
14000 Riverport Drive, Maryland Heights MO 63043. 314/770-1666. **Contact:** Director of Human Resources. **World Wide Web address:** http://www.express-scripts.com. **Description:** One of the largest, independent, full-service pharmacy benefit management companies in the United States, serving more than 7 million members through its integrated retail pharmacy network and mail service programs. The company's clients are health plan sponsors including HMOs, insurance companies, third-party administrators, unions, and self-insured companies. The company offers services through a nationwide network of more than 40,000 participating pharmacies with point-of-sale claims administration and two mail service pharmacies. The company also provides benefit design consultation and drug utilization review and formulates management services through its pharmacy benefit management programs. In addition, Express Scripts offers other ancillary services designed to control medical costs: IVTx offers infusion therapy through six sites in the East, Midwest, and Southwest, and OPTx offers a national vision program through a full-service vision laboratory and a network of ophthalmologists and optometrists. **Corporate headquarters location:** This location. **Other U.S. locations:** Tempe AZ; St. Louis MO. **Listed on:** NASDAQ. **Stock exchange symbol:** ESRX. **Annual sales/revenues:** More than $100 million. **Number of employees at this location:** 850.

FKI LOGISTEX
9301 Olive Boulevard, St. Louis MO 63132. 877/935-4565. **Contact:** Human Resources. **E-mail address:** careers@fkilogistex.com. **World Wide Web address:** http://www.fkilogistex.com. **Description:** Manufactures conveyors of various types including gravity conveyor belts and live roller conveyors, apron conveyors, chain conveyors, completely automated conveyor systems, pallet loaders, depalletizers, pallet-dispensing units, and related equipment. **NOTE:** Search and apply for positions online. **Number of employees at this location:** 400.

FM GLOBAL
540 Maryville Center Drive, Suite 400, St. Louis MO 63141. 314/453-9660. **Fax:** 314/453-9559. **Contact:** Human Resources Department. **World Wide Web address:** http://www.fmglobal.com. **Description:** A loss-control service organization. The company helps owner policyholders to protect their properties and occupancies from damage caused by fire, wind, flood, and explosion and from boiler, pressure vessel, and machinery accidents. **Corporate headquarters location:** Johnston RI. **Other U.S. locations:** Nationwide. **International locations:** Worldwide.

JOHN FABICK TRACTOR COMPANY
One Fabick Drive, Fenton MO 63026. 636/343-5900. **Contact:** Personnel Director. **World Wide Web address:** http://www.johnfabick.com. **Description:** Offers retail sales and service of new and used Caterpillar products including diesel engines, electric generator sets, road construction and earth moving equipment, mining equipment, materials handling equipment, and oil and gas pipe equipment. **Number of employees at this location:** 200.

FAIRBANKS SCALES
821 Locust Street, Kansas City MO 64106. 816/471-0231. **Contact:** Pam Mills, Corporate Human Resource Manager. **E-mail address:** Pam.J.Mills@Fancor.com. **World Wide Web address:** http://www.fairbanks.com. **Description:** Manufactures scales for industrial use. **NOTE:** Search for positions online. **Positions advertised include:** Director of Channel Development. **Corporate headquarters location:** This location: Other U.S. locations: St. Johnsbury VT; Meridian MS. **Number of employees nationwide:** 500.

FAIRCOM
6300 West Sugar Creek Drive, Columbia MO 65203-0100. 573/445-6833. **Fax:** 573/445-9698. **Contact:** Human Resources Department. **World Wide Web address:** http://www.faircom.com. **Description:** Develops database file handler software. Founded in 1979. **NOTE:** Entry-level positions are offered. **Office hours:** Monday - Friday, 9:00 a.m. - 5:00 p.m. **Corporate headquarters location:** This location. **International locations:** Brazil; Italy; Japan. **Listed on:** Privately held. **Number of employees worldwide:** 35.

FALCON PRODUCTS INC.
9387 Dielman Industrial Drive, St. Louis MO 63132-2219. 314/991-9200. **Fax:** 314/991-9227. **Contact:** Director of Human Resources. **World Wide Web address:** http://www.falconproducts.com. **Description:** Falcon Products manufactures and sells pedestal table bases; table tops; metal, wood, and plastic chairs; booths; folding banquet tables; wire shelving systems; wood-edge top and millwork; and sheet metal kitchen equipment. **Listed on:** New York Stock Exchange. **Stock exchange symbol:** FCP. **Number of employees at this location:** 100. **Number of employees nationwide:** 800.

FAMOUS-BARR COMPANY
601 Olive Street, St. Louis MO 63101. 314/444-3111. **Fax:** 314/444-3175. **Contact:** Bob Becherer, Executive Recruiting Manager. **World Wide Web address:** http://www.mayco.com. **Description:** Operates a retail department store chain with over 20 stores throughout Missouri, Illinois, and Indiana. **Positions advertised include:** Sales Associate. **Corporate headquarters location:** This location. **Parent company:** The May Department Store Company.

FARMLAND INDUSTRIES, INC.
P.O. Box 20111, Department 16, Kansas City MO 64116. 816/713-7000. **Physical address:** 3315 North Oak Trafficway, Kansas City MO 64116. **Fax:** 816/713-5954. **Recorded jobline:** 816/713-5056; 800/822-8263x5056 **Contact:** Human Resources Department. **E-mail address:** careers@farmland.com. **World Wide Web address:** http://www.farmland.com. **Description:** One of the largest farmer-owned agricultural food-marketing and manufacturing cooperative associations in the United States. The company is engaged in grain marketing, pork and beef processing, and manufacturing of fertilizers, livestock feeds, and petroleum products. Membership includes farmers from Iowa, Kansas, Oklahoma, South Dakota, Illinois, Nebraska, and Mexico. **Special programs:** Internships. **Corporate headquarters location:** This location. **Other U.S. locations:** Nationwide. **Operations at this facility include:** Administration; Divisional Headquarters; Manufacturing; Regional Headquarters; Research and Development; Sales. **Number of employees at this location:** 12,000.

FERGUSON COMPANY
11820 Lackland Road, St. Louis MO 63146. 314/567-3200. **Toll-free phone:** 800/422-8936. **Contact:** Personnel Director. **World Wide Web address:** http://www.ferguson-co.com. **Description:** Ferguson Company develops, manufactures, and markets indexers and related transfer and positioning products to designers, builders, and integrators of automation equipment worldwide. The company's products include custom cams, indexers, lubrication monitoring systems, part handlers, precision indexing conveyor systems, rotary tables, and torque limiters. **Corporate headquarters location:** This location. **Parent company:** UMC Industries, Inc. **Number of employees at this location:** 100.

FIKE CORPORATION
704 South 10th Street, Blue Springs MO 64015. 816/229-3405. **Fax:** 816/228-9277. **Contact:** Human Resources Department. **E-mail address:** fikehr@fike.com. **World Wide Web address:** http://www.fike.com. **Description:** manufactures fire protection systems, fire detection systems, an extensive line of rupture disc (or rupture disk) products and industrial explosion/dust explosion systems. **Positions advertised include:** Associate Quality Engineer.

FINANCIAL INFORMATION TECHNOLOGY INC.
P.O. Box 1058, Blue Springs MO 64013-1058. 816/229-8225. **Physical address:** 1504 NW Mock, Blue Springs MO 64013. **Contact:** Al Opsal, Recruiting. **Description:** Develops policy administration software packages for insurance agencies.

FIREMAN'S FUND INSURANCE COMPANY
727 Craig Road, St. Louis MO 63141. 314/569-7300. **Contact:** Human Resources. **World Wide Web address:** http://www.the-fund.com. **Description:** Underwrites all types of commercial insurance. **Corporate headquarters location:** Novato CA. **Other U.S. locations:** Nationwide. **Parent company:** Allianz AG. **Operations at this facility include:** Administration; Sales; Service. **Number of employees at this location:** 175.

FIRST BANK
11901 Olive Boulevard, Creve Coeur MO 63141. 314/995-8700. **Contact:** Human Resources Manager. **World Wide Web address:** http://www.firstbanks.com. **Description:** A full-service bank. **Corporate headquarters location:** This location. **Other U.S. locations:** CA; IL; TX. **Listed on:** Privately held. **Number of employees at this location:** 100. **Number of employees nationwide:** 1,700.

FIRST BANK
135 North Meramec Avenue, Clayton MO 63105-3751. 314/854-4600. **Contact:** Human Resources. **Description:** A banking and savings and loan holding company. The company offers a wide range of commercial banking services, savings bank services, mortgage banking services, and other related financial activities through its subsidiaries. **NOTE:** For information on professional hiring, contact the Human Resources Manager, 11901 Olive Boulevard, Creve Coeur MO 63141. 314/995-8700.

FIRST HOME SAVINGS BANK
P.O. Box 807, Mountain Grove MO 65711. 417/926-5151. **Contact:** Human Resources. **Description:** First Home Savings Bank is a stock savings and loan association. The bank provides a wide range of banking services including one- to four-family residential mortgage loans, multifamily residential, consumer, commercial, and home equity loans. First Home also invests in mortgage-backed, U.S. government and agency securities and other assets. Founded in 1911. **Other area locations:** Ava MO; Gainesville MO; Marshfield MO; Sparta MO.

FLORSHEIM FACTORY OUTLET
312 Wilson Drive, Jefferson City MO 65109. 573/635-1210. **Contact:** Personnel. **Description:** A factory outlet location for Florsheim Shoe Company, a retailer and manufacturer of footwear.

FOLLMAN PROPERTIES
ONCOR INTERNATIONAL
165 North Meramec, Suite 500, St. Louis MO 63105. 314/721-3444. **Contact:** Gary Follman, President. **World Wide Web address:** http://www.follman.com. **Description:** A full-service, commercial real estate services firm. Follman Properties is part of Oncor International, serving office, industrial, retail, and investment brokerage requirements. The company is also involved in asset and property management, consulting, appraisal, and information services. **Corporate headquarters location:** This location. **Listed on:** Privately held. **Number of employees at this location:** 40.

FONTBONNE COLLEGE
6800 Wydown Boulevard, St. Louis MO 63105. 314/719-8007. **Fax:** 314/719-8023. **Contact:** Sandy Davis, Human Resources. **E-mail address:** sdavis@fontbonne.edu. **World Wide Web address:** http://www.fontbonne.edu. **Description:** A four-year, liberal arts college. **Number of employees at this location:** 200.

FOOD FOR LESS
8985 Jennings Station Road, Jennings MO 63136. 314/867-8100. **Contact:** Human Resources. **Description:** Food For Less operates a chain of supermarkets; conducts bakery and creamery operations; and owns and operates a full-line warehouse and distribution facility.

FORD MOTOR COMPANY
6250 North Lindbergh Boulevard, Hazelwood MO 63042-2898. 314/731-6300. **Contact:** Human Resources/Salaried Personnel. **World Wide Web address:** http://www.ford.com. **Description:** Ford Motor Company is engaged in the design, development, manufacture, and sale of cars, trucks, tractors, and related components and accessories. Ford is also one of the largest providers of financial services in the United States. The company's two core businesses are the Automotive Group and the Financial Services Group (Ford Credit, The Associates, USL Capital, and First Nationwide). Ford also is engaged in a number of other businesses including electronics, glass, electrical and fuel-handling products, plastics, climate-control systems, automotive service and replacement parts, vehicle leasing and rental, and land development. **Corporate headquarters location:** Dearborn MI. **Operations at this facility include:** This location is an assembly plant. **Number of employees worldwide:** 322,000.

FOREST PHARMACEUTICALS, INC.
13600 Shoreline Drive, St. Louis MO 63045. 314/493-7000. **Contact:** Personnel Department. **World Wide Web address:** http://www.forestpharm.com. **Description:** Distributes pharmaceutical products for Forest Laboratories, Inc. **Corporate headquarters location:** New York NY. **Parent company:** Forest Laboratories, Inc. develops, manufactures, and sells both branded and generic forms of ethical drug products, as well as nonprescription pharmaceutical products sold over –the counter, which are used for the treatment of a wide range of illnesses. **Listed on:** American Stock Exchange. **Stock exchange symbol:** FRX.

FRU-CON CONSTRUCTION CORPORATION
P.O. Box 100, 15933 Clayton Road, Ballwin MO 63022. 636/391-6700. **Contact:** Human Resources. **E-mail address:** jobs@frucon.com. **World Wide Web address:** http://www.fru-con.com. **Description:** An international construction and engineering firm. **Positions advertised include:** Project Manager; Project Engineer; Estimator; Engineer. **Corporate headquarters location:** This location. **Number of employees at this location:** 1,000.

FULTON STATE HOSPITAL
600 East Fifth Street, Fulton MO 65251. 573/592-4100. **Fax:** 573/592-3000. **Contact:** Lori Hollinger, Personnel. **World Wide Web address:** http://www.modmh.state.mo.us/fulton. **Description:** A maximum-security psychiatric hospital that provides long-term residential care to mentally ill patients. **Special programs:** Internships. **Office hours:** Monday - Friday, 8:00 a.m. - 4:30 p.m. **Corporate headquarters location:** Jefferson City MO. **Operations at this facility include:** Administration; Service. **CEO:** Felix Vincenz. **Number of employees at this location:** 1,400.

FURNITURE BRANDS INTERNATIONAL
101 South Hanley Road, St. Louis MO 63105. 314/863-1100. **Fax:** 314/863-5306. **Contact:** Operations Director. **World Wide Web address:** http://www.furniturebrands.com. **Description:** Manufactures and retails dining room furniture, living room furniture, and occasional furniture. Furniture is sold under the names Lane and Broyhill. The company manufactures products in 31 furniture facilities in the United States. The company also manufactures and retails footwear including men's dress shoes and athletic shoes.

GE TRANSPORTATION SYSTEMS
321 SE County Road AA, Blue Springs MO 64014. 816/229-3345. **Contact:** Human Resources. **World Wide Web address:** http://www.ge.com. **Description:** A supplier of signal and control products to railroads throughout the world. The company sells its products to Class I and short-line freight railroads and to mass rail transit customers. Products are designed to improve the safety and productivity of railroad train operations and include a broad line of railroad signal and train control systems and related components and services, as well as customized asset management services.

GMAC INSURANCE
One GMAC Insurance Plaza, Earth City MO 63045. 314/716-5526. **Fax:** 314/493-8114. **Contact:** Human Resources. **World Wide Web address:** http://www.gmacinsurance.com. **Description:** Engaged in the direct response marketing of personal lines insurance (homeowners, automobile, and motorcycle) and data management services to sponsoring associations in 48 states. **Positions advertised include:** Application System Analyst; Business Systems Analyst; Call Center Supervisor; Enterprise Data Architect; Manager IS&S; Reissue Agent; Software Systems Engineer; Technical Architect. **Corporate headquarters location:** This location. **Parent company:** General Motors Insurance Company. **Operations at this facility include:** Administration; Sales; Service. **Number of employees at this location:** 680. **Number of employees nationwide:** 750.

GPL
A DIVISION OF CRANE MERCHANDISING SYSTEMS
12955 Enterprise Way, Bridgeton MO 63044. 314/298-0899. **Contact:** Human Resources. **World Wide Web address:** http://www.cranems.com. **Description:** Manufactures and sells vending equipment.

GENAMERICA FINANCIAL CORPORATION
13045 Tesson Ferry Road, St. Louis MO 63128. 314/843-8700. **Contact:** Human Resources. **World Wide Web address:** http://www.genamerica.com. **Description:** Offers life insurance, securities, and other related financial services to corporate and individual clients. **Corporate headquarters location:** This location.

GENERAL METAL PRODUCTS COMPANY
3883 Delor Street, St. Louis MO 63116. 314/481-0300. **Contact:** Penny Ross, Personnel Director. **Description:** Manufacturers of metal stampings, fabrications, tools, dies, and gauges. **Number of employees at this location:** 400.

GENERAL MOTORS CORPORATION
1500 East Route A, Wentzville MO 63385. 636/327-5711. **Contact:** Human Resources. **World Wide Web address:** http://www.gm.com. **Description:** General Motors Corporation is one of the world's largest full-line vehicle manufacturers and also has substantial interests in information technology and finance. GM conducts business through the following sectors: North American Automotive Operations, International Operations, General Motors Acceptance Corporation (GMAC), and Electronic Data Systems Corporation (EDS). North American Automotive Operations includes Sales/Service Groups (Buick, Cadillac, Chevrolet, GMC Truck, Oldsmobile, Pontiac, and Saturn) and Vehicle Development Groups (Powertrain, Truck Group, Small Car Group, and Midsize/Luxury Car Group). International Operations include GM Europe; Asia Pacific Operations; and Latin America, Africa, Middle East Operations. GMAC, which provides financing and insurance to GM customers and dealers, consists of North American Operations, International Operations, Motors Insurance Corporation, and GMAC Mortgage Group. EDS applies information technologies to more than 8,000 customers globally in the communications, energy/chemical, insurance, public sector, travel and transportation, financial services, manufacturing, and retail industries. Founded in 1908. **Corporate headquarters location:** Detroit MI. **Operations at this facility include:** This location manufactures and assembles automobiles. **Listed on:** New York Stock Exchange. **Stock exchange symbol:** GM. **Number of employees at this location:** 3,000.

GEOENGINEERS
5051 South National Avenue, Suites 4-10, Springfield MO 65810. 417/831-9700. **Fax:** 417/831-9777. **Contact:** Human Resources. **E-mail address:** employment@geoengineers.com. **World Wide Web address:** http://www.geoengineers.com. **Description:** Provides earth science, environmental, and technology consulting services focusing on the areas of transportation, energy, development, government services, and water and natural resources. **NOTE:** Apply online. **Positions advertised include:** Design Engineer; HDD Design Engineer. **Other locations:** Anchorage AK; Honolulu HI; Boise ID; Portland OR; Redmond WA.

GLAZER'S MIDWEST
6501 Hall Street, St. Louis MO 63147. 314/382-9990. **Fax:** 314/382-7123. **Contact:** Personnel Department. **E-mail address:** humanresources@glazers.com. **World Wide Web address:** http://www.glazers.com. **Description:** A wholesaler of wine and distilled beverages. **Corporate headquarters location:** Dallas TX.

GOEDECKE COMPANY INC.
4101 Clayton Avenue, St. Louis MO 63110. 314/652-1810. **Contact:** Human Resources. **Description:** Goedecke Company provides construction services including insulation, hard board for industrial buildings, wall systems, sealants, insulation, adhesives, waterproofing, and scaffold rental and erection. **Special programs:** Internships. **Corporate headquarters location:** This location. **Other U.S. locations:** Decatur IL; Evansville IN; Indianapolis IN; Louisville KY; Kansas City MO; Springfield MO. **Operations at this facility include:** This location houses administrative offices only. **Listed on:** Privately held. **Number of employees at this location:** 100.

GOOD HUMOR-BREYERS
2400 Rose Parkway, Sikeston MO 63801-3920. 573/472-8100. **Contact:** Human Resources. **World Wide Web address:** http://www.icecreamusa.com. **Description:** A major producer of frozen packaged ice cream and novelties distributed nationally.

GRAYBAR ELECTRIC COMPANY
34 North Meramec Avenue, St. Louis MO 63105. 314/573-9200. **Contact:** Manager of Personnel Department. **E-mail address:** opportunities@graybaronline.com. **World Wide Web address:** http://www.graybar.com. **Description:** Distributes electrical and telecommunications equipment including wire, transformers, lighting fixtures, power transmission equipment, telephone station apparatuses, and other hardware, primarily to independent telephone companies and public power utilities. Founded in 1869. **Corporate headquarters location:** This location. **Number of employees at this location:** 180. **Number of employees nationwide:** 7,100.

GREAT SOUTHERN BANK
P.O. Box 9009, Springfield MO 65808-9009. 417/895-4509. **Physical address:** 218 South Glenstone, Springfield MO 65808. **Fax:** 417/895-4595. **Contact:** Human Resources. **E-mail address:** hjbeck@greatsouthernbank.com. **World Wide Web address:** http://www.greatsouthernbank.com. **Description:** A savings and loan bank that performs savings bank operations, mortgage banking services, and other related financial activities. **Parent company:** Great Southern Bancorp.

WARREN H. GREEN, INC.
8356 Olive Boulevard, St. Louis MO 63132. 314/991-1335. **Fax:** 314/997-1788. **Contact:** Human Resources. **World Wide Web address:** http://www.whgreen.com. **Description:** Publishes books in a broad range of categories including medical, law, art, history, and philosophy. **Special programs:** Internships. **Corporate headquarters location:** This location. **Operations at this facility include:** Administration; Research and Development; Sales; Service. **Number of employees at this location:** 10.

GREENSFELDER, HEMKER & GALE, P.C.
2000 Equitable Building, 10 South Broadway, St. Louis MO 63102. 314/241-9090. **Fax:** 314/241-8624. **Contact:** Angela Schaefer, Personnel Director. **E-mail address:** ads@greensfelder.com. **World Wide Web address:** http://www.greensfelder.com. **Description:** A general practice law firm specializing in bankruptcy, construction, corporate, employee benefits, environmental, estate planning, health care, immigration, intellectual property, labor, litigation, real estate, and tax law. Founded in 1895. **Number of employees at this location:** 170.

H&R BLOCK
4400 Main Street, Kansas City MO 64111. 816/753-6900. **Contact:** Human Resources. **World Wide Web address:** http://www.hrblock.com. **Description:** Primarily engaged in consumer tax preparation. H&R Block has offices in over 750 Sears stores in both the United States and Canada. Many offices operate as franchises, and some operate on a seasonal basis. H&R Block is also engaged in a number of other tax-related activities including Group Tax Programs, Premium Tax Service, Tax Training Schools, and Real Estate Tax Awareness seminars. **Corporate headquarters location:** This location. **Listed on:** New York Stock Exchange. **Stock exchange symbol:** HRB. **Number of employees at this location:** 300. **Number of employees nationwide:** 80,000.

H.B.D. CONTRACTING INC.
5517 Manchester Avenue, St. Louis MO 63110-1975. 314/781-8000. **Fax:** 314/781-5214. **Contact:** Human Resources Department. **World Wide Web address:** http://www.hbdcontracting.com. **Description:** A general contracting firm specializing in commercial engineering. **Positions advertised include:** Civil Engineer. **Corporate headquarters location:** This location. **Operations at this facility include:** Administration. **Number of employees at this location:** 100.

HBE CORPORATION
11330 Olive Boulevard, St. Louis MO 63141. 314/567-9000. **Fax:** 314/567-0602. **Contact:** Personnel Director. **World Wide Web address:** http://www.hbecorp.com. **Description:** Engaged in the design and construction of hospitals, financial institutions, and hotels. HBE Corporation also operates and manages hotels. **World Wide Web address:** http://www.hbecorp.com. **Positions advertised include:** Architect; Engineer; Construction Manager; Sales Representative. **Corporate headquarters location:** This location. **Operations at this facility include:** Divisional Headquarters.

HMS HOST
10701 Natural Bridge Road, St. Louis MO 63145. 314/429-3400. **Recorded jobline:** 888/462-8562. **Contact:** Henrietta Mack, Human Resources Recruiter. **World Wide Web address:** http://www.hmshost.com. **Description:** Provides catering services to restaurants, bars, and airlines.

HAGER HINGE COMPANY
139 Victor Street, St. Louis MO 63104. 314/772-4400. **Toll-free phone:** 800/325-9995. **Fax:** 314/772-0744. **Contact:** Blake Earnest, Human Resources Director. **World Wide Web address:** http://www.hagerhinge.com. **Description:** Manufactures and wholesales hinges and other door hardware.

JOHN Q. HAMMONS HOTELS, INC.
300 John Q. Hammons Parkway, Suite 900, Springfield MO 65806. 417/864-4300. **Fax:** 417/873-3593. **Contact:** Human Resources. **World Wide Web address:** http://www.jqhhotels.com. **Description:** A leading owner, manager, and developer of affordable upscale hotels in secondary, tertiary, and airport market areas. The company owns and manages 31 hotels located in 16 states, containing 8,054 guest rooms or suites, and also manages six additional hotels located in four states, containing 1,345 guest rooms. The company's existing hotels operate primarily under the Holiday Inn and Embassy Suites trade names.

HANNIBAL REGIONAL HOSPITAL
Highway 36 West, Hannibal MO 63401. 573/248-1300. **Fax:** 573/248-5612. **Recorded jobline:** 573/248-5611. **Contact:** Ms. Marcia Davis, Personnel. **E-mail address:** marcia.davis@hrhonline.org. **World Wide Web address:** http://www.hrhonline.org. **Description:** A 105-bed, acute care hospital. **Positions advertised include:** Clinical Educator; Director of Hospital Operations; Monitor Technician; Occupational Therapist; Physical Therapist; Registered Nurse; Licensed Practical Nurse. **Special programs:** Internships. **Number of employees at this location:** 600.

HARCOURT BRACE & JOVANOVICH INC.
298 Academic Way, Troy MO 63379. 314/528-8110. **Contact:** Human Resources. **World Wide Web address:** http://www.harcourt.com. **Description:** Harcourt is a publishing company whose operations are divided into Elementary and Secondary Education, and University and Professional Education. Elementary and Secondary Education publishes textbooks and other instructional materials, publishes and scores achievement and aptitude tests, and manufactures and markets school and office supplies and equipment. University and Professional Education publishes textbooks and other instructional materials for higher education, scientific and medical books and journals, and general fiction and nonfiction; publishes books and conducts courses and seminars for law, accounting, and business; and provides outplacement counseling services. **Corporate headquarters location:** Orlando FL. **Operations at this facility include:** This location is a distribution center. **Parent company:** Reed Elsevier Group.

HARTMAN-WALSH PAINTING COMPANY
7144 North Market Street, St. Louis MO 63133-1899. 314/863-1800. **Fax:** 314/863-6964. **Contact:** Personnel. **World Wide Web address:** http://www.hartmanwalsh.com. **Description:** Provides commercial and industrial painting and waterproofing services.

HARVARD ELECTRONICS
HARVARD INDUSTRIES INC.
P.O. Box 370, 3000 Arnold Tenbrook Road, Arnold MO 63010. 314/291-3700. **Contact:** Personnel Director. **World Wide Web address:** http://www.harvardind.com. **Description:** Manufactures office furniture, dormitory furniture, electric bed controls, and electronic assemblies.

HAWKEYE-SECURITY INSURANCE
14567 North Outer 40 Road, Suite 300, Chesterfield MO 63017. 636/728-1090. **Fax:** 636/728-4290. **Contact:** Human Resources. **World Wide Web address:** http://www.hawkeyesecurity-ins.com. **Description:** A carrier of property, casualty, and life insurance.

HAWTHORN CHILDREN'S PSYCHIATRIC HOSPITAL
1901 Pennsylvania Avenue, St. Louis MO 63133. 314/512-7800. **Contact:** Department of Human Resources. **Description:** A psychiatric hospital for children ranging in ages from 6 to 17 years old.

HAZEL PROMOTIONAL PRODUCTS
1100 Stafford Street, Washington MO 63090. 636/239-2781. **Contact:** Debbie Stone, Personnel Manager. **World Wide Web address:** http://www.hazelpromo.com. **Description:** Manufactures vinyl and leather advertising items and record binders.

HEARTLAND TECHNOLOGY SOLUTIONS
526 South Main Street, Joplin MO 64801. 417/623-5553. **Contact:** Human Resources. **World Wide Web address:** http://www.cpoint-joplin.com. **Description:** Provides IT solutions for small and medium-sized businesses. **Other U.S. locations:** Harlan IA; Ames IA.

HELLMUTH, OBATA & KASSABAUM, INC.
1 Metropolitan Square, St. Louis MO 63102. 314/421-2000. **Contact:** Personnel Director. **World Wide Web address:** http://www.hok.com. **Description:** An architectural and structural engineering firm. **Positions advertised include:** Bookkeeper; Senior Project Manager; Interiors Technician. **Other U.S. locations:** Nationwide. **International locations:** Worldwide.

JAY HENGES ENTERPRISES, INC.
4133 Shoreline Drive, Earth City MO 63045. 314/291-6600. **Fax:** 314/291-7630. **Contact:** Personnel. **Description:** Engaged in the installation of carpet, wood, and vinyl floors; insulation and acoustical ceiling work; and the manufacture of portable buildings. **Corporate headquarters location:** This location.

JACK HENRY AND ASSOCIATES, INC.
663 West Highway 60, P.O. Box 807, Monett MO 65708-0807. 417/235-6652. **Fax:** 972/359-5609. **Contact:** Anne Puddister, Human Resources. **E-mail address:** hr@jackhenry.com. **World Wide Web address:** http://www.jackhenry.com. **Description:** Provides integrated computer systems to banks and other financial institutions for in-house data processing. The company also provides data conversion, software installation, and software customization services for the implementation of its systems, as well as customer maintenance and support services. Founded in 1976. **NOTE:** Search and apply for positions online. **Positions advertised include:** Development Programmer; Business Analyst; Programmer Analyst; Corporate Disaster Recovery Manager. **Special programs:** Internships. **Corporate headquarters location:** This location. **Other U.S. locations:** St. Paul MN; Charlotte NC; Houston TX. **Subsidiaries include:** Bankvision Software, Ltd.; Commlink Corporation; Jack Henry International, Ltd. **Annual sales/revenues:** $51 - $100 million. **Number of employees at this location:** 340. **Number of employees nationwide:** 500.

HERTZ RENT-A-CAR
THE HERTZ CORPORATION
Lambert International Airport, 9477 Aerospace Drive, St. Louis MO 63134. 314/426-7555. **Contact:** Personnel. **World Wide Web address:** http://www.hertz.com. **Description:** Area offices for one of the nation's leading transportation services organizations are at this location. Overall, the company operates nationally through several divisions: Rent-A-Car Division (car rental services); Car Leasing Division; and Equipment Rental and Leasing Division. Hertz is also engaged in joint-venture truck leasing operations with Penske Corporation (Hertz Penske Truck Leasing) at 600 locations. **Parent company:** RCA Corporation.

HEWLETT-PACKARD COMPANY
721 Emerson Road, St. Louis MO 63141. 314/991-6400. **Contact:** Human Resources. **World Wide Web address:** http://www.hp.com. **Description:** Hewlett-Packard designs, manufactures, sells, and services computers and associated peripheral equipment, and related software and supplies. Applications and programs include scientific research, computation, communications, education, data analysis, industrial control, time sharing, commercial data processing, graphic arts, word processing, health care, instrumentation, engineering, and simulation. **NOTE:** Search and apply for positions online. **Corporate headquarters location:** Palo Alto CA. **Operations at this facility include:** This location is a sales office. **Listed on:** New York Stock Exchange. **Stock exchange symbol:** HPQ.

HITCHINER MANUFACTURING COMPANY INC.
P.O. Box 280, 600 Cannonball Lane, O'Fallon MO 63366. 636/272-6176. **Fax:** 636/272-6180. **Contact:** Personnel Department. **World Wide Web address:** http://www.hitchiner.com. **Description:** Manufactures nonferrous investment castings. **Corporate headquarters location:** Milford NH.

HOLIDAY INN DOWNTOWN/CONVENTION CENTER
811 North Ninth Street, St. Louis MO 63101. 314/421-4000. **Contact:** Personnel Manager. **World Wide Web address:** http://www.holiday-inn.com. **Description:** A hotel. **Special programs:** Internships. **Parent company:** Intercontinental Hotels Group. **Number of employees at this location:** 130.

HOLIDAY INN NORTH
4545 North Lindbergh Boulevard, St. Louis MO 63044. 314/731-2100. **Contact:** Personnel. **World Wide Web address:** http://www.holiday-inn.com. **Description:** Operates a full-service hotel.

HOULIHAN'S RESTAURANT GROUP, INC.
384 Crestwood Plaza, St. Louis MO 63126. 314/963-9994. **Contact:** Thuan Nguyen, Director of Recruiting. **E-mail address:** tnguyen@houlihans.com. **World Wide Web address:** http://www.houlihans.com. **Description:** Houlihan's Restaurant Group owns, operates, and franchises 78 full-service, casual dining restaurants. **Corporate headquarters location:** Leawood KS. **Other U.S. locations:** Nationwide. **Number of employees nationwide:** 3,500.

HOWARD JOHNSON
4530 North Lindbergh Boulevard, St. Louis MO 63044. 314/731-1652. **Fax:** 314/731-1534. **Contact:** Human Resources. **World Wide Web address:** http://www.hojo.com. **Description:** A hotel with a restaurant and bar. **Operations at this facility include:** Administration; Sales; Service. **Number of employees at this location:** 200.

HUDSON SERVICES
P.O. Box 221000, St. Louis MO 63122. 314/965-1929. **Contact:** Mr. C.L. Hudson, President. **Description:** Provides building services, consulting, management, and bookkeeping.

HUMANA HEALTH CARE
10450 Holmes Road, Suite 100, Kansas City MO 64131-3471. 816/941-8900. **Toll-free phone:** 800/842-6188. **Fax:** 816/941-0879. **Contact:** Manager of Employment. **World**

Wide Web address: http://www.humana.com. **Description:** One of Kansas City's oldest and largest HMOs. The company operates through 10 medical facilities. **NOTE:** Search and apply for positions online. **Positions advertised include:** Sales Director. **Special programs:** Internships; Co-ops. **Corporate headquarters location:** Louisville KY. **Other U.S. locations:** Nationwide. **Parent company:** Prime Health Medical Center. **Listed on:** New York Stock Exchange. **Stock exchange symbol:** HUM. **Annual sales/revenues:** More than $100 million. **Number of employees at this location:** 1,200. **Number of employees nationwide:** 8,000.

HUMANE SOCIETY OF MISSOURI
1201 Macklind Avenue, St. Louis MO 63110. 314/647-8800. **Fax:** 314/647-4317. **Contact:** Human Resources. **E-mail address:** hr@hsmo.org. **World Wide Web address:** http://www.hsmo.org. **Description:** One of the oldest and largest humane societies in the United States, providing emergency field services in St. Louis County. The organization investigates cruelty and neglect to animals statewide, and operates two animal shelters and two veterinary clinics. The society provides public relations and educational programs and operates a rehabilitation farm for large animals. **Positions advertised include:** Client and Animal Service specialist; Adoption Counselor; Development Data Specialist. **Special programs:** Internships. **Corporate headquarters location:** This location. **Operations at this facility include:** Service.

HUSSMANN CORPORATION
12999 St. Charles Rock Road, Bridgeton MO 63044-2483. 314/291-2000. **Fax:** 314/298-4756. **Contact:** Human Resources. **World Wide Web address:** http://www.hussmann.com. **Description:** Manufactures refrigerated display fixtures and cases, walk-in coolers, condensing units, shelving, and refrigeration systems. **NOTE:** Search and apply for positions online at: http://www.irco.com/careers. **Positions advertised include:** Credit Manager; Director of Customer Technical Service; Director, Service Business Delivery; Director, Technology Business Development Legal Contracts Administrator; Sourcing Specialist. **Special programs:** Internships. **Corporate headquarters location:** This location. **Other area locations:** Fenton MO. **Parent company:** Ingersoll-Rand. **Operations at this facility include:** Administration; Manufacturing; Research and Development; Sales; Service.

IBM CORPORATION
325 James S Mcdonnell Boulevard, Hazelwood MO 63042. 314/731-2328. **Toll-free phone:** 800/796-9876. **Contact:** IBM Staffing Services. **World Wide Web address:** http://www.ibm.com. **Description:** IBM Corporation is a developer, manufacturer, and marketer of advanced information processing products including computers and microelectronic technology, software, networking systems, and information technology-related services. **NOTE:** Search and apply for positions online. Positions advertised include: IT Architect/Specialist. **Corporate headquarters location:** Armonk NY. **International locations:** Africa; Asia Pacific; Canada; Europe; Latin America; Middle East. **Operations at this facility include:** This location is a sales office. **Subsidiaries include:** IBM Credit Corporation; IBM Instruments, Inc.; IBM World Trade Corporation.

ISP MINERALS INC.
One Hillcrest Drive, P.O. Box 186, Annapolis MO 63620. 573/598-4235. **Contact:** Human Resources. **Description:** Manufactures granules that are then used in roofing products.

IMPACT TECHNOLOGIES, INC.
16647 Chesterfield Grove, Suite 120, St. Louis MO 63005. 314/743-1400. **Fax:** 314/763-1401. **Contact:** Human Resources. **E-mail address:** HR@impacttech.com. **World Wide Web address:** http://www.impacttech.com. **Description:** Develops software for telecommunications applications. Founded in 1990. **NOTE:** Search and apply for positions online. **Positions advertised include:** Network Engineer.

INDEECO
425 Hanley Industrial Court, St. Louis MO 63144. 314/644-4300. **Toll-free phone:** 800/243-8162. **Fax:** 314/644-5332. **Contact:** Human Resources Recruiter. **E-mail address:** recruiter@indeeco.com. **World Wide Web address:** http://www.indeeco.com. **Description:** Engaged in the design and manufacture of custom electric heating equipment for industrial and commercial applications.

INLAND PAPERBOARD & PACKAGING
1201 North Highway Drive, Fenton MO 63026. 636/225-4900. **Contact:** Tim Toma, Employee Relations Supervisor. **World Wide Web address:** http://www.myinland.com. **Description:** Manufactures shipping containers. **NOTE:** Search and apply for positions online. **Parent company:** Temple-Inland.

INSITUFORM MID-AMERICA, INC.
702 Spirit 40 Park Drive, Chesterfield MO 63005. 636/530-8000. **Toll-free phone:** 800/234-2992. **Fax:** 636/519-8010. **Contact:** Human Resources. **E-mail address:** careers@insituform.com. **World Wide Web address:** http://www.insituform.com. **Description:** Insituform Mid-America, Inc. uses various trenchless technologies for rehabilitation, new construction, and improvements of pipeline systems (sewers; gas lines; industrial waste lines; water lines; oil field mining; and industrial process pipelines). The company's trenchless technologies require little or no excavation and eliminate the need to replace deteriorating pipes. Insituform Mid-America provides a wide variety of technologies including Insituform, PALTEM, Tite Liner, and tunneling. **Listed on:** NASDAQ. **Stock exchange symbol:** INSU. **Number of employees nationwide:** 570. **Number of employees worldwide:** 2,100.

INTEGRIS METALS
2630 Metro Boulevard, Maryland Heights MO 63043. 314/344-0123. **Fax:** 314/344-0834. **Contact:** Personnel Department. **E-mail address:** info@integrismetals.com. **World Wide Web address:** http://www.integrismetals.com. **Description:** A wholesale service center for high-performance, corrosion-resistant metals. **Corporate headquarters location:** Minneapolis MN. **Parent company:** Alcoa Inc. and BHP Billiton. **Number of employees nationwide:** 3,000.

INTERMET CORPORATION
P.O. Box 278, 801 Second Street, Monroe City MO 63456. 573/735-4577. **Contact:** Human Resources. **E-mail address:** bmills@intermet.com. **World Wide Web address:** http://www.intermet.com. **Description:** Manufactures and distributes zinc, aluminum, and magnesium diecastings. Primary customers include the automotive industry, and hand-tool and computer manufacturers. Other services include complete in-house diecasting making; advanced product development; engineering support; and die design. **Corporate headquarters location:** Troy MI. **Operations at this facility include:** Administration; Management Consulting; Research and Development; Sales; Service. **Listed on:** NASDAQ. **Stock exchange symbol:** INMT. **Number of employees nationwide:** 830.

INTERSTATE BAKERIES CORPORATION
INTERSTATE BRANDS CORPORATION
P.O. Box 419627, Kansas City MO 64141-0627. 816/502-4000. **Physical address:** 12 East Armour Boulevard, Kansas City MO 64111. **Contact:** Director of Human Resources. **World Wide Web address:** http://www.irin.com/ibc. **Description:** The largest wholesale baker and distributor of fresh baked bread and sweet goods in the United States, operating 57 bakeries and distributing to 200.000 outlets. **Corporate headquarters location:** This location. **Parent company:** Interstate Brands Corporation (also at this location). **Listed on:** New York Stock Exchange. **Stock exchange symbol:** IBC. **Number of employees worldwide:** 33,000.

INTRAV INC.
11969 Westline Industrial Drive, St. Louis MO 63146. 314/655-6700. **Toll-free phone:** 800/456-8100. **Fax:** 314/655-6670. **Contact:** Human Resources Director. **E-mail address:** employment.global@nwship.com. **World Wide Web address:** http://www.intrav.com. **Description:** Intrav organizes, markets, and operates escorted, international travel programs. **NOTE:** Search and apply for positions online. **Corporate headquarters location:** This location. **Parent company:** Kuoni (Switzerland).

JBM ELECTRONICS COMPANY
4645 Laguardia Drive, St. Louis MO 63134-3100. 314/426-7781. **Toll-free phone:** 800/489-7781. **Fax:** 314/426-0007. **Contact:** Human Resources. **World Wide Web address:** http://www.jbmelectronics.com. **Description:** Manufactures network connectivity products including TC/IP, ethernet and token ring, frame relays, and ISDNs. Founded in 1975.

JCPENNEY COMPANY INC.
METRO DISTRICT OFFICE
90 West County Court, St. Louis MO 63131. 314/965-5969. **Contact:** Personnel Manager. **World Wide Web address:** http://www.jcpenney.com. **Description:** This location houses administrative offices for the major domestic retailer, with 1,100 store operations in all 50 states and Puerto Rico. The dominant portion of the company's business consists of providing merchandise and services to customers through stores and catalog operations. Overall, JCPenney operates and manages almost 600 full-line stores, and more than 1,060 small soft-line stores. **Positions advertised include:** Management Trainee. **Corporate headquarters location:** Plano TX. **Operations at this facility include:** Administration.

JACOBS FACILITIES INC.
One Financial Plaza, 501 North Broadway, St. Louis MO 63102-1826. 314/335-4000. **Fax:** 314/335-5102. **Contact:** Recruiting Manager. **World Wide Web address:** http://www.jacobs.com. **Description:** An engineering, architectural, and construction firm that provides consulting services, design services, construction management, and construction services. **NOTE:** Search and apply for positions online. Entry-level positions are offered. **Positions advertised include:** Project Hydraulic Modeling Engineer; Plumbing/Fire Protection Design Engineer. **Special programs:** Internships; Summer Jobs. **Corporate headquarters location:** Pasadena CA. **Other U.S. locations:** Nationwide. **International locations:** Worldwide. **Operations at this facility include:** Administration; Regional Headquarters; Sales; Service. **Listed on:** New York Stock Exchange. **Stock exchange symbol:** JEC. **Annual sales/revenues:** More than $100 million. **Number of employees at this location:** 580.

JEFFERSON COLLEGE
1000 Viking Drive, Hillsboro MO 63050. 636/797-3000. **Fax:** 636/789-4012. **Contact:** Director of Human Resources. **World Wide Web address:** http://www.jeffco.edu. **Description:** A two-year community college. **NOTE:** Search and apply for positions online. **Positions advertised include:** Registrar; Director of Student Development. **Corporate headquarters location:** This location. **Number of employees at this location:** 220.

JEWISH CENTER FOR AGED
13190 South Outer 40 Road, Chesterfield MO 63017. 314/434-3330. **Fax:** 314/434-9179. **Recorded jobline:** 314/434-8561. **Contact:** Human Resources. **Description:** A skilled nursing facility for the elderly. **NOTE:** Candidates for therapist and nursing positions must have applicable licenses, degrees, and certification. **Operations at this facility include:** Service.

JEWISH COMMUNITY CENTERS
2 Millstone Campus Drive, Carlyn H. Wohl Building, St. Louis MO 63146. 314/432-5705. **Contact:** Director of Personnel. **Description:** A service organization whose facilities include a swimming pool, fitness center, and racquetball courts.

JIFFY DELIVERY
6185 Olive Boulevard, St. Louis MO 63130. 314/725-3995. **Contact:** Gordie Webb, Manager. **Description:** An express package delivery service. **Positions advertised include:** Truck Driver. **Operations at this facility include:** Service.

JOHN KNOX VILLAGE
1001 Northwest Chipman Road, Lees Summit MO 64081. 816/251-8000. **Fax:** 816/246-4739. **Contact:** Human Resources. **E-mail address:** jobs@jkv.org. **World Wide Web address:** http://www.johnknoxvillage.org. **Description:** One of the nation's largest continuing care retirement communities that offers various living options and services including support groups, social, nursing, nutritional, rehabilitation, and ambulance services. Founded in 1970. **NOTE:** Entry-level positions and second and third shifts are offered. **Special programs:** Training. **Office hours:** Monday - Friday, 8:00 a.m.-4:30 p.m. **Corporate headquarters location:** This location. **Annual sales/revenues:** $21 - $50 million. **Number of employees at this location:** 950.

JOHNSON GROUP, INC.
8860 Ladue Road, Suite 200, St. Louis MO 63124. 314/862-3000. **Fax:** 314/862-1307. **Contact:** Human Resources. **World Wide Web address:** http://www.j-group.com. **Description:** A real estate and office building management firm.

JONES PHARMACEUTICALS, INC.
1945 Craig Road, St. Louis MO 63146. 314/576-6100. **Fax:** 314/469-5749. **Contact:** Human Resources. **World Wide Web address:** http://www.kingpharm.com. **Description:** A specialty pharmaceutical manufacturer that targets specific areas. The company produces endocrine products for the treatment of thyroid disease; manufactures and markets a variety of veterinary pharmaceuticals; and markets pharmaceuticals used in hospitals. **NOTE:** Search and apply for positions online. **Positions advertised include:** Quality Systems Analyst. **Parent company:** King Pharmaceuticals. **Corporate headquarters location:** Bristol TN. **Listed on:** New York Stock Exchange. **Stock exchange symbol:** KG.

JOURNAL NEWSPAPERS OF SOUTH COUNTY
SOUTH SUBURBAN PUBLICATIONS, INC.
4210 Chippewa, St. Louis MO 63116. 314/664-2700. **Contact:** Human Resources. **World Wide Web address:** http://www.yourjournal.com. **Description:** A holding company for a group of area newspapers.

JUDEVINE CENTER FOR AUTISM
1101 Olivette Executive Parkway, St. Louis MO 63132. 314/432-6200. **Fax:** 314/849-2721. **Contact:** Human Resources. **E-mail address:** hr@judevine.org. **World Wide Web address:** http://www.judevine.org. **Description:** A pioneer agency providing services to children and adults with autism and related conditions in the areas of independent living, employment, training, family support, and professional development. **Positions advertised include:** Program Manager; Supported Living Coordinator; Employment Technician; **Operations at this facility include:** Administration; Divisional Headquarters; Regional Headquarters; Research and Development; Service. **Number of employees at this location:** 400.

JUSTIN BOOT COMPANY
2236 Missouri Avenue, Carthage MO 64836. 417/358-1877. **Contact:** Hiring Manager. **World Wide Web address:** http://www.justinboots.com. **Description:** Manufactures cowboy boots, leather belts, handbags, and billfolds. **Parent company:** Justin Industries, Inc. traces its history to a company that began making boots in 1879. Today, in addition to producing western-style personal and outdoor products through Justin Boot, Justin Industries also produces building materials and evaporative coolers. **Parent company:** Berkshire Hathaway.

KMOV-TV
CBS TELEVISION CHANNEL 4
One Memorial Drive, St. Louis MO 63102. 314/621-4444. **Fax:** 314/444-6393. **Contact:** Human Resources. **E-mail address:** employment@kmov.com. **World Wide Web address:** http://www.kmov.com. **Description:** A CBS-affiliated radio and television broadcasting station. **NOTE:** Search and apply for positions online. **Positions advertised include:** Internet News Producer; Anchor/Reporter; Assistant News Director; News Writer; Meteorologist; Interactive Account Executive. **Parent company:** Viacom Inc.

KPLR-TV/CHANNEL 11
2251 Ball Drive, St. Louis MO 63146. 314/447-7211. **Contact:** Human Resources. **World Wide Web address:** http://www.wb11tv.trb.com. **Description:** A television broadcasting station.

KPMG
10 South Broadway, Suite 900, St. Louis MO 63102-1761. 314/444-1400. **Fax:** 314/444-1470. **Contact:** Human Resources Director. **World Wide Web address:** http://www.us.kpmg.com. **Description:** KPMG delivers a wide range of value-added assurance, tax, and consulting services. Founded in 1897. **NOTE:** Search and apply for positions online. **Positions advertised include:** Sr. Manager, Audit; Sr. Manager, Information Risk Management; Sr. Associate, Internal Audit; Manager, Industry Risk-Based Solutions. **Corporate headquarters location:** Montvale NJ. **Parent company:** KPMG International is a leader among professional services firms engaged in capturing, managing, assessing, and delivering information to create knowledge that will help its clients maximize shareholder value.

KV PHARMACEUTICAL COMPANY
2503 South Hanley Road, St. Louis MO 63144. 314/645-6600. **Fax:** 314/644-2419. **Contact:** Staffing Department. **E-mail address:** staffing@kvpharmaceutical.com. **World Wide Web address:** http://www.kvpharmaceutical.com. **Description:** KV Pharmaceutical Company researches, develops, produces, and sells drug delivery products. **NOTE:** Second and third shifts are offered. Search and apply for positions online. **Positions advertised include:** Packaging Supervisor; Document Control Specialist; Staffing Specialist; Research Scientist; DEA Compliance Inspector; Inspector/Auditor. **Office hours:** Monday - Friday, 8:00 a.m. - 4:30 p.m. **Corporate headquarters location:** This location. **Listed on:** New York Stock Exchange. **Stock exchange symbol:** KVA. **Annual sales/revenues:** More than $100 million. **Number of employees nationwide:** 550.

KANSAS CITY LIFE INSURANCE COMPANY
3520 Broadway, Kansas City MO 64111-2565. 816/753-7000. **Fax:** 816/753-0138. **Contact:** Human Resources. **E-mail address:** kajones@kclife.com. **World Wide Web address:** http://www.kclife.com. **Description:** Offers a variety of individual life insurance and annuity policies, group life insurance, and small life reinsurance. Founded in 1895. **NOTE:** Search and apply for positions online. **Positions advertised include:** Real Estate and Mortgage Loan Analyst; Accounting Manager; Valuation Analyst. **Number of employees at this location:** 600.

KANSAS CITY POWER AND LIGHT COMPANY
P.O. Box 418679, Kansas City MO 64141-9679. 816/556-2200. **Fax:** 816/556-2884. **Recorded jobline:** 816/556-2500. **Contact:** Personnel Department. **E-mail address:** careeropp@kcpl.com. **World Wide Web address:** http://www.kcpl.com. **Description:** A public utility engaged in the generation, transmission, distribution, and sale of electricity. The company generates and distributes electricity to approximately 1 million customers in a 4,700 square mile area located in all or portions of 23 counties in western Missouri and eastern Kansas. **NOTE:** Search and apply for positions online. **Positions advertised include:** Claims Supervisor; Claims Representative; Fuels Analyst; Credit and Collection Manager; Transmission Operations Engineer; Mapping Technician. **Parent company:** Great Plains Energy.

KELLWOOD COMPANY
600 Kellwood Parkway, Chesterfield MO 63017. 314/576-3100. **Contact:** Roberta Parker, Human Resources. **World Wide Web address:** http://www.kellwood.com. **Description:** A marketer of apparel and consumer soft goods. **NOTE:** Search and apply for positions online. **Positions advertised include:** Accountant; Accounting Manager; Accounts Payable; Sr. Internal Auditor. **Listed on:** New York Stock Exchange. **Stock exchange symbol:** KWD. **Number of employees worldwide:** 24,000.

KENRICK GLENNON SEMINARY
5200 Glennon Drive, St. Louis MO 63119-4399. 314/792-6100. **Fax:** 314/792-6500. **Contact:** Human Resources. **World Wide Web address:** http://www.kenrick.edu. **Description:** A men's seminary specializing in a four-year undergraduate college program and a five-year graduate program that prepares men for the priesthood.

KILLARK ELECTRIC MANUFACTURING COMPANY
3940 Dr. Martin Luther King Drive, St. Louis MO 63113. 314/531-0460. **Fax:** 314/531-7164. **Contact:** Director of Employee Relations. **World Wide Web address:** http://www.hubbell-killark.com. **Description:** Manufactures conduit fittings, lighting fixtures, and control housings. **Parent company:** Hubbell Incorporated.

KMART
11978 St. Charles Rock Road, Bridgeton MO 63044. 314/739-8800. **Contact:** Personnel Department. **E-mail address:** hireme@kmart.com. **World Wide Web address:** http://www.kmart.com. **Description:** Kmart is one of the nation's largest owners and operators of general merchandising stores. The company operates 1,500 Kmart outlets in 49 states, Puerto Rico, and the Virgin Islands. **NOTE:** Submit resume online. **Corporate headquarters location:** Troy MI. **Operations at this facility include:** This location is a retail store that includes a pharmacy and food court. **Number of employees worldwide:** 144,000.

KRAFT FOODS
P.O. Box 3440, Springfield MO 65808. 417/881-2701. **Physical address:** 2035 East Bennett, Springfield MO 65804. **Contact:** Human Resources Director. **World Wide Web address:** http://www.kraft.com. **Description:** Processes and distributes cheese and other food products as a division of Kraft, Inc. **Corporate headquarters location:** Northfield IL. **Parent company:** Phillip-Morris. **Number of employees at this location:** 1,300.

KUPPER PARKER COMMUNICATIONS
8301 Maryland Avenue, St. Louis MO 63105-3644. 314/290-2000. **Fax:** 314/290-2101. **Contact:** Director of Human Resources. **E-mail address:** resumes@kupperparker.com. **World Wide Web address:** http://www.kupperparker.com. **Description:** A full-service advertising agency. **NOTE:** Search for positions online.

LMI AEROSPACE, INC.
3600 Mueller Road, St. Charles MO 63302. 636/946-6525. **Fax:** 636/949-1576. **Contact:** Manager of Human Resources Department. **World Wide Web address:** http://www.lmiaerospace.com. **Description:** Manufactures a broad range of metal components for the aerospace industry. **Corporate headquarters location:** This location. **Other U.S. locations:** Wichita KS; Tulsa OK; Seattle WA. **Operations at this facility include:** Administration; Manufacturing. **Listed on:** NASDAQ. **Stock exchange symbol:** LMIA. **Annual sales/revenues:** $21 - $50 million. **Number of employees at this location:** 260. **Number of employees nationwide:** 740.

LA-Z-BOY CHAIR COMPANY
4301 Howard Bush Drive, Neosho MO 64850-9166. 417/451-5400. **Contact:** Billy Meyer, Human Resources Manager. **World Wide Web address:** http://www.la-z-boy.com. **Description:** A leading manufacturer of upholstered seating and among the nation's largest overall manufacturers of residential furniture. La-Z-Boy specializes in upholstered recliners. The company also manufactures hospitality and assisted-living contract furniture and specialized health care seating. **Corporate headquarters location:** Monroe MI. **Number of employees nationwide:** 10,000.

LACLEDE GAS COMPANY
720 Olive Street, St. Louis MO 63101. 314/342-0877. **Fax:** 314/588-0615. **Recorded jobline:** 314/342-0762. **Contact:** Human Resources. **World Wide Web address:** http://www.lacledegas.com. **Description:** Distributes and transports natural gas; transports and stores liquid propane; operates underground natural gas storage fields; and invests in nonutility operations. The company serves 2 million customers in eastern Missouri. **Positions advertised include:** Auditor; Business Analyst; Security Administrator; Engineering Assistant. **Corporate headquarters location:** This location. **Operations at this facility include:** Administration; Sales. **Number of employees at this location:** 2,000.

LAMMERT FURNITURE COMPANY
501 South Lindbergh Boulevard, St. Louis MO 63131. 314/993-1111. **Contact:** Human Resources. **Description:** A wholesaler and retailer of home and commercial furnishings. The company is also engaged in contract design.

LEEROWAN COMPANY
1901 Lee Avenue, Jackson MO 63755-3923. 636/343-0700. **Contact:** Personnel Manager. **World Wide Web address:** http://www.leerowan.com. **Description:** Manufactures wood, plastic, and metal home-storage devices. **Parent company:** Rubbermaid Newell.

LEGGETT & PLATT, INC.
Number 1 Leggett Road, P.O. Box 757, Carthage MO 64836. 417/358-8131. **Contact:** Employment Manager. **E-mail address:** resumes@leggett.com. **World Wide Web address:** http://www.leggett.com. **Description:** Manufactures and distributes furniture components used in bedding and finished furniture; manufactures and sells finished furniture including adjustable electric beds, bed frames, bunk beds, and wooden headboards; and produces and sells products for industrial and commercial uses, such as custom aluminum die-cast products, metal and wire shelving, display racks, nonwoven textile fiber products, and steel tubing and steel posts for fencing and roadway signs. **NOTE:** Search for jobs at Hotjobs. **Positions advertised include:** Capital Projects Analyst; Group Controller, Fixturing and Displays; Internal Auditors; International Systems Analyst; Manager, Planning and Operations; Manufacturing systems Analyst; Project Leader. **Corporate headquarters location:** This location. **Other U.S. locations:** Nationwide. **Listed on:** New York Stock Exchange. **Stock exchange symbol:** LEG. **Number of employees nationwide:** 11,000.

LINCOLN INDUSTRIAL
One Lincoln Way, St. Louis MO 63120. 314/679-4200. **Fax:** 314/679-4359. **Contact:** Al Adams, Vice President of Personnel. **World Wide Web address:** http://www.lincolnindustrial.com. **Description:** Manufactures automotive, industrial, and agricultural lubricating equipment.

LINDELL BANK AND TRUST COMPANY
P.O. Box 211, St. Louis MO 63166. 314/645-7700. **Physical address:** 6900 Clayton Avenue, St. Louis MO 63139. **Fax:** 314/645-0733. **Contact:** Janice M. Walton, Personnel Director. **Description:** A full-service bank.

LINDENWOOD UNIVERSITY
209 South Kingshighway, St. Charles MO 63301. 636/949-2000. **Contact:** Dr. James D. Evans, Provost and Dean of Faculty. **World Wide Web address:** http://www.lindenwood.edu. **Description:** A four-year university offering 80 undergraduate and graduate degrees with an enrollment of 12,000. **NOTE:** Address resumes for teaching and administrative positions to above contact; address resumes for staff or management positions to: Ms. Julie Mueller, Chief Operating Officer.

LION'S CHOICE
12015 Manchester Road, Suite 118, St. Louis MO 63131. 314/821-8665ext. 244. **Fax:** 314/822-7144. **Contact:** Human Resources. **E-mail address:** mgadell@lionschoice.com. **World Wide Web address:** http://www.lionschoice.com. **Description:** Owns and operates a chain of 19 fast-food restaurants in Missouri and Illinois. **Corporate headquarters location:** This location.

LOOMIS FARGO & COMPANY
2220 Mason Lane, Ballwin MO 63021. 314/835-9070. **Fax:** 314/835-0705. **Contact:** Human Resources. **World Wide Web address:** www.loomisfargo.com. **Description:** An armored car service specializing in transporting currency, serving the St. Louis area. **Other U.S. locations:** Nationwide.

LOOMIS FARGO & COMPANY
300 NW Parkway, Riverside MO 64150. 816/587-1000. **Fax:** 816/587-7441. **Contact:** Human Resources. **World Wide Web address:** www.loomisfargo.com. **Description:** An armored car service specializing in transporting currency, serving the Kansas City area. **Other U.S. locations:** Nationwide.

LOWE BOATS
2900 Industrial Drive, Lebanon MO 65536. 417/532-9101. **Contact:** Human Resources. **World Wide Web address:** http://www.loweboats.com. **Description:** A manufacturer of aluminum boats. **Parent company:** Genmar Holdings.

LOWELL MANUFACTURING COMPANY
100 Integram Drive, P.O. Box 385, Pacific MO 63069. 636/257-3400. **Contact:** Human Resources. **World Wide Web address:** http://www.lowellmfg.com. **Description:** Manufactures baffles, enclosures, masking units, cabinets, racks, and accessories. **Positions advertised include:** Audio Engineer. **Corporate headquarters location:** This location. **Operations at this facility include:** Administration; Manufacturing; Research and Development; Sales; Service. **Listed on:** Privately held. **Number of employees at this location:** 80.

MEMC ELECTRONIC MATERIALS, INC.
501 Pearl Drive, St. Peters MO 63376-0008. 636/474-5000. **Contact:** Human Resources. **World Wide Web address:** http://www.memc.com. **Description:** One of the largest silicon wafer suppliers in North America and Europe, as well as one of the largest Western suppliers to Japan. **NOTE:** Search for positions or submit resume online. **Positions advertised include:** Global Manager, Quality Systems. **Corporate headquarters location:** This location. **Listed on:** New York Stock Exchange. **Stock exchange symbol:** WFR. **Number of employees worldwide:** 4,900.

MERS/MISSOURI GOODWILL INDUSTRIES INC.
1727 Locust Street, St. Louis MO 63103. 314/241-3464. **Fax:** 314/241-9348. **Contact:** Human Resources Director. **E-mail address:** employment@mersgoodwill.org. **World Wide Web address:** http://mersgoodwill.org. **Description:** Provides vocational rehabilitation services for clients needing evaluation, work adjustment, business career training, computer training, and placement services. **Special programs:** Internships. **Operations at this facility include:** Administration. **Number of employees at this location:** 200.

MFA INCORPORATED
201 Ray Young Drive, Columbia MO 65201. 573/874-5111. **Contact:** Human Resources Manager. **E-mail address:** hr@mfa-inc.com. **World Wide Web address:** http://www.mfa-inc.com. **Description:** An agricultural cooperative supplying feed, seed, plant foods, farm supplies, agricultural chemicals, and associated services. **Positions advertised include:** Account Manager; Graphic Designer; Web Developer. **Corporate headquarters location:** This location.

MADISON WAREHOUSE CORPORATION
4300 Planned Industrial Drive, St. Louis MO 63120. 314/382-3700. **Fax:** 314/383-1909. **Contact:** Human Resources Department. **E-mail address:** hrstlouis@madisonwarehouse.com. **World Wide Web address:** http://www.madisonwarehouse.com. **Description:** A general warehousing and storage company. **Positions advertised include:** Forklift Operator; Clerk; Operation Manager.

MALLINCKRODT, INC.
16035 Swinole Ridge Road, Chesterfield MO 63017. 314/654-2000. **Contact:** Personnel. **E-mail address:** employment@tycohealthcare.com. **World Wide Web address:** http://www.mallinckrodt.com. **Description:** Manufactures and markets healthcare products through three main specialty groups. The Imaging Group provides magnetic resonance, nuclear medicine, and X-ray products. The Pharmaceuticals Group provides pharmaceutical products for addiction therapy and pain relief. The Respiratory Group manufactures airway management systems and respiratory devices. **NOTE:** Jobseekers should send resumes to Corporate Employment, 675 McDonnell Boulevard, P.O. Box 5840, St. Louis MO 63134. **Corporate headquarters location:** This location. **Parent company:** TYCO International. **Number of employees worldwide:** 13,000.

MARITZ, INC.
1375 North Highway Drive, Fenton MO 63099. 636/827-2828. **Contact:** Human Resources. **World Wide Web address:** http://www.maritz.com. **Description:** Maritz delivers a wide range of integrated, custom-designed, performance enhancement services. The company's resources include marketing services, all-employee involvement programs, and travel services. Marketing services include sales incentive programs; performance enhancement training; business communications; database marketing; customer satisfaction/surveys; business meetings; data collection/analysis; information services; marketing research; teleservices; fulfillment services; and direct marketing. Employee involvement programs include employee suggestions; cost reduction; quality improvement; safety; team building; and rewards and recognition. Travel services include group travel awards; individual travel awards; business meetings; special events travel; and corporate travel management. **Positions advertised include:** Analyst, IT; Director, IT; Programmer/Developer, IT; Sr. Research Analyst; Sr. Research Manager; Director, Client Operations; Market Development Director; Product Development Manager; Product Manager; Sr. Information Manager. **Number of employees at this location:** 2,500. **Number of employees worldwide:** 5,700.

MARLO COIL NUCLEAR COOLING INC.
6060 Highway PP, P.O. Box 171, High Ridge MO 63049. 636/677-7731. **Fax:** 636/677-1203. **Contact:** Evelyn Horkman, Human Resources Director. **E-mail address:** ehorkman@marlocoil.com. **World Wide Web address:** http://www.marlocoil.com. **Description:** Manufactures component parts (cooling for ships and submarines), air-handling equipment, cooling coils, and steam coils for hospitals, schools, and industry. **Parent company:** Engineered Support Systems, Inc.

MARQUETTE TOOL & DIE COMPANY
3185 South Kingshighway Boulevard, St. Louis MO 63139. 314/771-8509. **Fax:** 314/771-7964. **Contact:** Human Resources. **E-mail address:** info@marquettetool.com. **World Wide Web address:** http://www.marquettetool.com. **Description:** A manufacturer of metal stampings, special machining and assemblies, tools, and dies.

MARSH INC.
800 Market Street, Suite 2600, St. Louis MO 63101. 314/621-5540. **Fax:** 314/32-2600. **Contact:** Personnel Director. **World Wide Web address:** http://www.marsh.com. **Description:** Provides advice and services worldwide through an insurance brokerage and risk management firm; reinsurance intermediary facilities; and a consulting and financial services group, to clients concerned with the management of assets and risks. Specific services include insurance and risk management services, reinsurance, consulting and financial services, merchandising, and investment management. **NOTE:** Search and apply for positions online. **Positions advertised include:** Claims Support Analyst; Client Advisor; Client Representative. **Corporate headquarters location:** New York NY. **Subsidiaries include:** Marsh & McClennan Companies.

MARYVILLE UNIVERSITY
13550 Conway Road, St. Louis MO 63141. 314/529-9398. **Contact:** Jacqueline Plunkett, Director of Personnel. **World Wide Web address:** http://www.maryville.edu. **Description:** A four-year university with and enrollment of 1,450 undergraduate and 500 graduate students. Founded in 1872. **NOTE:** Search and apply for positions and download application forms online. Only resumes received for a specific opening will be accepted. **Positions advertised include:** Adjunct Instructors; Assistant director of Residential Life; Director of Multicultural Programs; Personal Counselor.

MAVERICK TUBE CORPORATION
16401 Swingley Ridge Road, Suite 700, Chesterfield MO 63017. 636/733-1600. **Fax:** 636/733-1670. **Contact:** Jill Kickham, Human Resources. **World Wide Web address:** http://www.maverick-tube.com. **Description:** Maverick Tube Corporation is one of the largest U.S. manufacturers of oil country tubular goods, the steel tubular products used in the completion of oil and gas wells. Maverick also produces line pipe for handling and transporting oil and natural gas. **NOTE:** Search for positions online. **Other U.S. locations:** GA; TN; Oh; MI; AR; TX.

THE MAY DEPARTMENT STORES COMPANY
611 Olive Street, St. Louis MO 63101. 314/342-6300. **Contact:** Liz Torres, Manager of Human Resources. **World Wide Web address:** http://www.maycompany.com. **Description:** A retail organization with 13 department store companies and a discount shoe division. These department store companies operate under various names including Filene's, Lord & Taylor, and Kaufmann's. **Corporate headquarters location:** This location. **Number of employees worldwide:** 127,000.

MAYFLOWER TRANSIT, INC.
P.O. Box 26150, One Mayflower Drive, Fenton MO 63026. 636/305-4000. **Contact:** Human Resources. **World Wide Web address:** http://www.mayflower.com. **Description:** A diversified holding company whose subsidiaries provide a variety of transportation-related services including household moving services; services for goods that require special handling; and storage and distribution, freight forwarding, and flatbed hauling of containerized shipments. Mayflower Transit also owns and operates moving and storage agencies; provides school bus service to school districts; provides on-demand transportation services for local communities; operates a school bus dealership; sells tractor trailers; operates a road equipment maintenance facility; and sells moving supplies, equipment, and uniforms to agents and owner operators. Mayflower also provides a variety of insurance services. **Positions advertised include:** Underwriting Administrator; Chief IT Architect; Data Center Operations Analyst. **Corporate headquarters location:** This location. **Parent company:** UniGroup Inc.

McBRIDE & SON
One McBride Center Drive, Chesterfield MO 63005. 636/537-2000. **Fax:** 636/537-2546. **Contact:** Director of Human Resources. **World Wide Web address:** http://www.mcbridehomes.com. **Description:** A construction company engaged in concrete foundation work, carpentry work, home building, general contracting, real estate sales, property management, and remodeling. **NOTE:** See company website for application instructions for specific openings. **Positions advertised include:** Administrative Assistant; Craftsman; Project Manager; Sales Representative; Superintendent. **Corporate headquarters location:** This location. **Operations at this facility include:** Administration; Regional Headquarters. **Number of employees at this location:** 400.

McCARTHY CONSTRUCTION COMPANY
1341 North Rock Hill Road, St. Louis MO 63124-1498. 314/968-3300. **Fax:** 314/968-4642. **Contact:** Jan Kraemer, Human Resources. **E-mail address:** jkraemer@mccarthy.com. **World Wide Web address:** http://www.mccarthy.com. **Description:** One of the nation's oldest privately held construction firms. The company provides a wide range of construction-related services under construction management, general contract, and design and building contractual arrangements, and operates a separate division for work on bridges. **Company slogan:** Our goal is to be the best builder in America. **Positions advertised include:** MEP Controls Superintendent; Project Engineer; Insurance and Risk Analyst; Superintendent. **Special programs:** Internships. **Corporate headquarters location:** This location. **Other U.S. locations:** Phoenix AZ; Newport Beach CA; Sacramento CA; San Francisco CA; Las Vegas NV; Dallas TX. **Annual sales/revenues:** More than $100 million. **Number of employees at this location:** 150. **Number of employees nationwide:** 2,000.

McDONALD'S CORPORATION
14567 North Outer 40 Drive, Suite 500, Chesterfield MO 63017. 636/537-0809. **Contact:** Human Resources. **World Wide Web address:** http://www.mcdonalds.com. **Description:** Develops, operates, franchises, and services a worldwide system of restaurants that process, package, and sell a limited menu of fast foods. One of the largest restaurant operations in the United States and one of the largest food service organizations in the world, McDonald's operates more than 30,000 McDonald's restaurants in all 50 states and in 119 other countries. **Positions advertised include:** Marketing Manager; Senior Database Analyst. **Special programs:** Internships. **Corporate headquarters location:** Oak Brook IL. **Other U.S. locations:** Nationwide. **Operations at this facility include:** Regional Headquarters. **Number of employees at this location:** 300.

MEDICAL ASSURANCE, INC.
1505 East Bradford Parkway, Springfield MO 65804-6565. 417/887-3120. **Fax:** 417/887-0300. **Contact:** Executive Assistant. **E-mail address:** personnel@maih.com. **World Wide Web address:** http://www.medicalassurance.com. **Description:** Medical Assurance operates through its subsidiaries, which provide medical malpractice insurance. **Corporate headquarters location:** Birmingham AL. **Parent company:** ProAssurance Corporation.

MEDICINE SHOPPE INTERNATIONAL INC.
1100 North Lindbergh Boulevard, St. Louis MO 63132. 314/993-6000. **Toll-free phone:** 800/325-1397. **Fax:** 314/872-5370. **Contact:** Human Resources. **World Wide Web address:** http://www.medshoppe.com. **Description:** Medicine Shoppe International operates and franchises retail drug stores.

MERAMEC GROUP
P.O. Box 279, Sullivan MO 63080. 573/468-3101. **Fax:** 573/860-3101. **Contact:** Human Resources Director. **E-mail address:** info@meramec.com. **World Wide Web**

address: http://www.meramec.com. **Description:** Manufactures footwear unit soles, furniture parts, sporting goods parts, and other specialty items.

MERIDIAN MEDICAL TECHNOLOGIES
2550 Hermelin Drive, St. Louis MO 63144. 314/236-4200. **Fax:** 314/236-4201. **Contact:** Personnel. **World Wide Web address:** http://www.meridianmeds.com. **Description:** Manufactures auto-injectors that are used for injecting medication. The company also develops, manufactures, and markets cardiopulmonary medical devices including noninvasive cardiac arrhythmia management devices. **NOTE:** Search and apply for positions online. **Positions advertised include:** Export Compliance Administrator. **Corporate headquarters location:** Rockville MD. **Parent company:** King Pharmaceuticals, Inc. **Operations at this facility include:** Administration; Manufacturing; Research and Development; Service. **Number of employees at this location:** 235. **Number of employees nationwide:** 275.

MERRILL LYNCH
800 Market Street, Suite 2400, St. Louis MO 63101. 314/982-8000. **Contact:** Personnel. **World Wide Web address:** http://www.ml.com. **Description:** Merrill Lynch is a worldwide financial firm. The company provides both traditional and innovative products and services to a broad range of individual and institutional customers. Merrill Lynch operates primarily through functional units that include individual services; capital markets; assets management; futures; international; real estate; and insurance. **NOTE:** Search and apply for positions online. **Positions advertised include:** Commercial Banking Professional; Sr. Regional Manager. **Special programs:** Internships. **Corporate headquarters location:** New York NY. **Listed on:** New York Stock Exchange. **Stock exchange symbol:** MER.

MICHAEL'S STORES
Bogey Hills Plaza, 2155 Zumbehl Road, St. Charles MO 63303. 636/947-6379. **Contact:** Human Resources. **World Wide Web address:** http://www.michaels.com. **Description:** A nationwide specialty retailer of art, crafts, and decorative items and supplies, with a wide range of products ranging from picture framing materials to seasonal and holiday merchandise. The company also offers educational programs and creative activities in home decor, art, and craft projects. **NOTE:** Search and apply for positions online. **Corporate headquarters location:** Irving TX. **Other U.S. locations:** Nationwide.

THE MICHELSON ORGANIZATION
7701 Forsyth Boulevard, Suite 900, St. Louis MO 63105. 314/862-7080. **Contact:** Mike Casey, Controller. **World Wide Web address:** http://www.michelson-realty.com. **Description:** Develops, acquires, and manages real estate investments. **Corporate headquarters location:** This location. **Subsidiaries include:** Michelson Commercial Realty and Development Company assists corporate clients with a wide range of services. **Number of employees at this location:** 40.

MIDWEST BANKCENTRE
2191 Lemay Ferry Road, St. Louis MO 63125. 314/631-5500. **Contact:** Personnel Director. **E-mail address:** hr@midwestbankcentre.com. **World Wide Web address:** http://www.midwestbankcentre.com. **Description:** A banking institution with eight locations and member of the Federal Reserve. **Positions advertised include:** Service Associate; Audit Specialist: Sr. Audit Specialist; Insurance/Escrow Specialist.

MIDWEST EMPLOYERS CASUALTY COMPANY
14755 North Outer Forty Drive, Suite 300, Chesterfield MO 63017. 636/449-7000. **Fax:** 636/449-7199. **Contact:** Tom Vonderheid, Director of Human Resources. **E-mail address:** careers@mwecc.com. **World Wide Web address:** http://www.mwecc.com. **Description:** Midwest Employers Casualty Company markets and underwrites excess workers' compensation insurance. Founded in 1986. **NOTE:** Entry-level positions and part-time jobs are offered. **Special programs:** Internships; Training; Co-ops; Summer Jobs. **Number of employees nationwide:** 100.

MIDWEST RESEARCH INSTITUTE
425 Volker Boulevard, Kansas City MO 64110-2299. 816/753-7600. **Fax:** 816/753-8420. **Contact:** Personnel. **World Wide Web address:** http://www.mriresearch.org. **Description:** Engaged in all types of scientific research in the areas of health, agricultural and food safety, national defense, engineering, and energy. **NOTE:** Applications may be submitted online (preferred method). **Other U.S. locations:** FL; MD; CO.

THE MILLER GROUP
1555 Larkin Williams Road, Fenton MO 63026. **Toll-free phone:** 800/325-3350. **Fax:** 636/326-1716. **Contact:** Human Resources. **World Wide Web address:** http://www.miller-group.com. **Description:** Manufactures store display fixtures. Founded in 1903. **NOTE:** Entry-level positions are offered. **Office hours:** Monday - Friday, 8:00 a.m. - 4:30 p.m. **Corporate headquarters location:** Richmond VA. **President:** Frank G. Grelle. **Annual sales/revenues:** $11 - $20 million. **Number of employees at this location:** 135. **Number of employees nationwide:** 385.

MILLSTONE BANGERT INC.
601 fountain Lakes Boulevard, St. Charles MO 63301. 636/949-0038. **Contact:** Human Resources. **Description:** Engaged in road and heavy construction general contracting. **Number of employees at this location:** 100.

MISS ELAINE
8430 Valcour Avenue, St. Louis MO 63123. 314/631-1900. **Contact:** Personnel. **World Wide Web address:** http://www.misselaine.com. **Description:** Manufactures a variety of sleepwear, loungewear, eveningwear, and lingerie.

MISSISSIPPI RIVER TRANSMISSION CORPORATION
9900 Clayton Road, St. Louis MO 63124. 314/991-9900. **Contact:** Human Resources. **Description:** Transports natural gas through a system of pipelines. **Corporate headquarters location:** This location. **Parent company:** NorAm Energy Corporation. **Number of employees at this location:** 80.

MISSOURI AMERICAN WATER COMPANY
535 North New Ballas Road, St. Louis MO 63141. 314/991-3404. **Fax:** 314/432-7824. **Contact:** Manager of Personnel. **World Wide Web address:** http://www.mawc.com. **Description:** A water utility company.

MISSOURI ATHLETIC CLUB
405 Washington Avenue, St. Louis MO 63102-2183. 314/231-7220. **Fax:** 314/213-2327. **Recorded jobline:** 314/539-4437. **Contact:** Human Resources. **World Wide Web address:** http://www.mac-stl.com. **Description:** A private club offering a full gymnasium, heated swimming pool and solarium, multiple private dining rooms and a la carte outlets, a pro shop, and overnight guest accommodations. This location also hires seasonally. Founded in 1903. **NOTE:** Entry-level positions and second and third shifts are offered. **Special programs:** Apprenticeships; Summer Jobs. **Office hours:** Monday - Friday, 8:00 a.m. - 4:30 p.m. **Corporate headquarters location:** This location. **Other area locations:** Town and Country MO. **Number of employees at this location:** 235. **Number of employees nationwide:** 310.

MISSOURI BAPTIST COLLEGE
One College Park Drive, St. Louis MO 63141. 314/434-1115. **Contact:** Human Resources. **World Wide Web address:** http://www.mobap.edu. **Description:** A four-year Baptist college with an enrollment of approximately 3,600 at four locations around St. Louis.

MISSOURI BAPTIST MEDICAL CENTER
3015 North Ballas Road, St. Louis MO 63131. 314/996-5525. **Fax:** 314/996-6974. **Contact:** Human Resources. **World Wide Web address:** http://www.missouribaptistmedicalcenter.org. **Description:** A 400-bed, acute care hospital. **NOTE:** Search and apply for positions online. **Positions advertised include:** Pharmacist; Asst. Nurse, PRN; Biomedical Electronic Technician; Coder; Case Coordinator; Director, Oncology and Digestive Disease Service Line; Director, Facility Services; Dosimetrist; DRG Coordinator; Integrated Clinical Specialist Technician; Manager, Financial Services; Medical Technologist; Nurse; Occupational Therapist; Registered Nurse; Nuclear Medicine Technologist. **Special programs:** Internships. **Parent company:** BJC HealthCare. **Operations at this facility include:** Administration; Service. **Number of employees at this location:** 2,000.

MISSOURI BOTANICAL GARDEN
2345 Tower Grove Avenue, St. Louis MO 63110. 314/577-9400. **Fax:** 314/577-9597. **Recorded jobline:** 314/577-9401. **Contact:** Human Resource Management. **E-mail address:** jobs@mobot.org. **World Wide Web address:** http://www.mobot.org. **Description:** A nonprofit cultural organization that promotes the preservation and enrichment of plant life and the environment. Missouri Botanical Garden has been internationally recognized for its botanical research, education programs, and horticulture display. Founded in 1859. **NOTE:** Part-time jobs are offered. Applications may be downloaded and mailed or e-mailed to Human Resource Management. Resumes accepted only for current job openings. Search for openings online. **Special programs:** Internships; Summer Jobs; Volunteer Positions. **Office hours:** Monday - Friday, 9:00 a.m. - 5:00 p.m. **Corporate headquarters location:** This location. **Director:** Dr. Peter H. Raven. **Number of employees at this location:** 370.

MISSOURI INFORMATION SOLUTIONS
8333 East 350 Highway, Kansas City MO 64133. 816/358-5545. **Fax:** 816/358-5546. **Contact:** Human Resources. **World Wide Web address:** http://www.moinfo.com. **Description:** A provider of hardware, software, voice, data, and video networking that also provides service and support. **NOTE:** Apply online.

MONSANTO COMPANY
800 North Lindbergh Boulevard, St. Louis MO 63167. 314/694-1000. **Contact:** Personnel Director. **World Wide Web address:** http://www.monsanto.com. **Description:** Manufactures and markets agricultural products, performance chemicals used in consumer products, prescription pharmaceuticals, and food ingredients. **NOTE:** Search and apply for positions online. **Positions advertised include:** Sr. Research Scientist; Agronomist; Biologist; SAP Developer; Technical Services & Compliance Manager; Director, Regulatory Affairs; Antitrust Attorney; Litigation Attorney; MIDAS Technical Lead. **Corporate headquarters location:** This location. **Parent company:** Pharmacia. **Listed on:** New York Stock Exchange. **Stock exchange symbol:** MON.

MORGAN WIGHTMAN SUPPLY COMPANY
739 Goddard Avenue, Chesterfield MO 63005. 314/995-9990. **Fax:** 314/995-9781. **Contact:** Mr. Ken Gudeman, Personnel Department. **World Wide Web address:** http://www.morgan-wightman.com. **Description:** A distributor of wholesale building materials including windows, doors, moldings, and cabinets. **Corporate headquarters location:** This location. **Operations at this facility include:** Administration.

MOTEL 6
6500 South Lindbergh Boulevard, St. Louis MO 63123. 314/892-3664. **Contact:** Human Resources. **World Wide Web address:** http://www.motel6.com. **Description:** One location of the motel chain. Overall, the company operates more than 800 motels in the U.S. and Canada. **Corporate headquarters location:** Carrollton TX. **Parent company:** Accor (Paris, France).

MOTOR APPLIANCE CORPORATION
555 Spirit of St. Louis Boulevard, Chesterfield MO 63005. 636/532-3406. **Toll-free phone:** 800/622-3406. **Fax:** 636/532-4609. **Contact:** Human Resources. **World Wide Web address:** http://www.macmc.com. **Description:** Manufactures battery chargers, motors, and generators. **Number of employees at this location:** 100.

PAUL MUELLER COMPANY
P.O. Box 828, Springfield MO 65801. 417/831-3000. **Physical address:** 1514 South Glenstone Street, Springfield MO 65802. **Fax:** 417/575-9669. **Contact:** Mike Young, Human Resources. **E-mail address:** myoung@muel.com. **World Wide Web address:** http://www.muel.com. **Description:** Manufactures stainless steel equipment for the dairy, food, brewery, beverage, pure water, and pharmaceutical industries. Founded in 1940. **Positions advertised include:** Heat Transfer Specialist. **Subsidiaries include:** Mueller International Sales Corporation.

MULTIDATA SYSTEMS INTERNATIONAL CORPORATION
9801 Manchester Road, St. Louis MO 63119. 314/968-6880. **Contact:** Human Resources. **E-mail address:** jobs@multidata-systems.com. **World Wide Web address:** http://www.multidata-systems.com. **Description:** Provider of radiation oncology products and systems. Founded in 1979. **NOTE:** Search and apply for positions online. **Positions advertised include:** Sr. Delphi Programmer; Product Design Engineer; Application Support Specialist.

MUNICIPAL THEATRE ASSOCIATION OF ST. LOUIS
The Muny, Forest Park, St. Louis MO 63112. 314/361-1900. **Fax:** 314/361-0009. **Contact:** Employment. **World Wide Web address:** http://www.muny.com. **Description:** A nonprofit theatrical production company that operates a large outdoor theater. Founded in 1919. **Special programs:** Internships; Summer Jobs. **Corporate headquarters location:** This location. **Operations at this facility include:** Sales. **Number of employees at this location:** 20.

NABISCO BRANDS INC.
13411 Lake Front Drive, Earth City MO 63045. 314/209-4600. **Toll-free phone:** 877/454-2305. **Fax:** 314/209-4699. **Recorded jobline:** 888/807-7419. **Contact:** Operations Manager. **World Wide Web address:** http://www.kraft.com. **Description:** The warehouse, delivery, and sales office of the manufacturer of crackers, packaged food products, and wholesale bakery products. As one of the largest food companies in the United States, Nabisco has a strong market position in such areas as cookies,

margarine, hot cereals, and pet snacks. **Other U.S. locations:** Nationwide. **Parent company:** Kraft Foods Inc. (Phillip Morris). **Listed on:** New York Stock Exchange. **Stock exchange symbol:** KFT. **Number of employees nationwide:** 69,000.

NATIONAL LINEN SERVICE
P.O. Box 14467, St. Louis MO 63178. 314/865-4500. **Physical address:** 315 Lynch Street, St. Louis MO 63118. **Fax:** 314/773-3828. **Contact:** Human Resources. **World Wide Web address:** http://www.national-linen.com. **Description:** A linen rental service. Primary customers include restaurants, hospitals, hotels, and catering companies. **Corporate headquarters location:** Atlanta GA. **Parent company:** National Services Industries. **Number of employees at this location:** 120. **Number of employees nationwide:** 12,000.

NATIONWIDE ADVERTISING SERVICE INC.
1023 Executive Parkway, Suite 16, St. Louis MO 63141. 314/579-0050. **Fax:** 314/579-0575. **Contact:** Regional Manager. **World Wide Web address:** http://www.hrads.com. **Description:** With offices in 37 major U.S. and Canadian cities, Nationwide Advertising Service is one of the largest and oldest independent, full-service advertising agencies specializing in human resource communications, promotions, and advertising. Nationwide Advertising Service offers consultation, campaign planning, ad placement, research, and creative production. **NOTE:** Search and apply for positions online. **Corporate headquarters location:** Cleveland OH. **Other U.S. locations:** Nationwide. **Parent company:** McCann-Erickson WorldGroup.

NEIMAN MARCUS
100 Plaza Frontenac, St. Louis MO 63131. 314/567-9811. **Contact:** Human Resources Manager. **E-mail address:** slcareers@neimanmarcus.com. **World Wide Web address:** http://www.neimanmarcus.com. **Description:** A retail department store. **Positions advertised include:** Buyer; Merchandiser; Designer. **Special programs:** Internships. **Corporate headquarters location:** Dallas TX. **Parent company:** The Neiman Marcus Group, Inc. operates three specialty retailing businesses: Neiman Marcus, Bergdorf Goodman, and Contempo Casuals. Combined, these three chains offer high-quality men's and women's apparel, fashion accessories, precious jewelry, fine china, and moderately priced crystal and silver. Neiman Marcus has 27 stores nationwide. Contempo Casuals has 247 contemporary shops featuring young women's clothing and accessories. NM Direct, another subsidiary, is a direct marketing company that advertises primarily through the use of specialty catalogs such as Neiman Marcus and Horchow. **Operations at this facility include:** Sales; Service. **Listed on:** New York Stock Exchange. **Stock exchange symbol:** NMG.

NESTLE PURINA PETCARE
200 Checkerboard Square, Gray Summit MO 63039. 314/982-3232. **Contact:** Director of Human Resources. **World Wide Web address:** http://www.purina.com. **Description:** Nestle Purina Company is one of the world's largest producers of dry dog and soft-moist cat foods, with 26 manufacturing facilities worldwide. Founded in 1894. **NOTE:** Search and apply for positions online. **Positions advertised include:** Advanced Accounting Associate; Associate Creative Director; Brand Manager; Business Analyst; Customer Supply Chain Manager; Manager, Veterinary Communications. **Operations at this facility include:** This location manufactures pet food. **Corporate headquarters location:** This location. **Parent company:** Nestle Purina.

NETTIE'S FLOWER GARDEN INC.
3801 South Grand Boulevard, St. Louis MO 63118. 314/771-9600. **Contact:** Personnel Office. **Description:** A retail florist specializing in fresh and artificial flowers, supplies, and custom decorating.

NEW GROUND
13537 Barrett Parkway Drive, Suite 200, Manchester MO 63021. 314/821-2265. **Fax:** 314/821-6443. **Contact:** Personnel. **E-mail address:** jobs@newground.com. **World Wide Web address:** http://www.newground.com. **Description:** A national design and building firm that also provides consulting and planning services. **Operations at this facility include:** Administration; Regional Headquarters. **Other U.S. locations:** IL; CA; NH. **International locations:** Canada.

THE NEWBERRY GROUP
94 Executive Parc, 2440 Executive Drive, Suite 208, St. Charles MO 63303. 636/928-9944. **Fax:** 636/928-8899. **Contact:** Human Resources. **World Wide Web address:** http://thenewberrygroup.com. **Description:** Specializes in IT and systems consulting services. **NOTE:** Search and apply for positions online. **Positions advertised include:** Sr. Data Security Analyst; Sr. IT Client/Server Developer/Programmer. **Other U.S. locations:** Stroudsburg PA; Arlington VA.

NIEHAUS CONSTRUCTION SERVICES INC.
4151 Sarpy Avenue, St. Louis MO 63110. 314/533-8434. **Fax:** 314/533-1448. **Contact:** Director of Personnel. **World Wide Web address:** http://www.ncs-stl.com. **Description:** Engaged in terrazzo, tile, marble, and mosaic construction.

NIES/ARTCRAFT
5900 Berthold Avenue, St. Louis MO 63110-1384. 314/647-3400. **Fax:** 314/951-0498. **Contact:** Personnel Department. **World Wide Web address:** http://www.nies.com. **Description:** A commercial printing company.

NORTH KANSAS CITY HOSPITAL
2800 Clay Edwards Drive, North Kansas City MO 64116. 816/691-2060. **Fax:** 816/691-2065. **Contact:** Personnel. **E-mail address:** human.resources@nkch.org. **World Wide Web address:** http://www.nkch.org. **Description:** A 360-bed, nonprofit, acute care hospital with a medical staff of over 300 physicians representing 44 medical specialties. **Positions advertised include:** Registered Nurse; Licensed Practical Nurse; CS Technician; Teacher; Environmental Services Worker; Food Service Worker; Health Information Services Clerk; Physical Therapist; Lab Assistant; Unit Secretary; Orderly; Supervisor; Respiratory Therapist. **Number of employees at this location:** 1,400.

NORTHWEST MISSOURI STATE UNIVERSITY
800 University Drive, Maryville MO 64468-6001. 660/562-1127. **Fax:** 660/562-1034. **Contact:** Michelle Drake, Personnel. **E-mail address:** mmattso@mail.nwmissouri.edu. **World Wide Web address:** http://www.nwmissouri.edu. **Description:** A four-year, state university offering bachelor's, master's, and specialist in education degrees with an enrollment of 6,500. Founded in 1905. **NOTE:** Search and apply for positions online. **Positions advertised include:** Assistant Professor; Teaching Assistant; Accounting Manager; Counselor. **Number of employees at this location:** 855.

O'REILLY OZARK
233 South Patterson, Springfield MO 65802. 417/862-6708. **Contact:** Director of Human Resources. **E-mail address:** resume@oreillyauto.com. **World Wide Web address:** http://www.oreillyauto.com. **Description:** O'Reilly Ozark operates 1000 automotive supply stores in 17 states offering aftermarket parts, tools, supplies, equipment, and accessories. Founded in 1957. **NOTE:** Apply online or via e-mail. **Other U.S. locations:** Midwest. **Listed on:** NASDAQ. **Stock exchange symbol:** ORLY.

ORTHOBAND BARNHART INDUSTRIES INC.
3690 Highway M, Imperial MO 63052. 636/942-3133. **Toll-free phone:** 800/325-9973. **Fax:** 636/948-3152. **Contact:** Human Resources. **World Wide Web address:** http://www.orthoband.com. **Description:** Manufacturers of feminine hygiene products, garters, elastic notions, sewing accessories, surgical garments, hospital accessories, advertising novelties, and orthodontic appliances. **Corporate headquarters location:** This location. **Operations at this facility include:** Administration; Manufacturing; Sales. **Number of employees at this location:** 50.

ORSCHELN INDUSTRIES
1177 North Morley, Moberly MO 65270. 660/269-3934. **Fax:** 660/269-3934. **Contact:** HR Manager. **E-mail address:** kgittemeier@orscheln.com. **World Wide Web address:** http://www.orscheln.com. **Description:** A manufacturer of mechanical and electromechanical automotive and industrial equipment components; sealants; and adhesives for the automotive and construction industries. Orscheln also operates approximately 115 retail outlets. Founded in 1946. **NOTE:** Entry-level positions and second and third shifts are offered. **Positions advertised include:** Department Administrator. **Special programs:** Training. **Office hours:** Monday - Friday, 8:00 a.m. - 5:00 p.m. **Corporate headquarters location:** This location. **International locations:** Canada; Australia; England. **Listed on:** Privately held. **Annual sales/revenues:** More than $100 million. **Number of employees at this location:** 750. **Number of employees nationwide:** 6,000.

O'SULLIVAN INDUSTRIES HOLDINGS INC.
1900 Gulf Street, Lamar MO 64759-1899. 417/682-8218. **Contact:** Brenda Caruthers, Human Resources. **E-mail address:** brenda.caruthers@osullivan.com. **World Wide Web address:** http://www.osullivan.com. **Description:** Manufactures and markets ready-to-assemble home office electronics and residential furniture.

OZARKS MEDICAL CENTER
1100 Kentucky Avenue, P.O. Box 1100, West Plains MO 65775. 417/287-6730. **Fax:** 417/257-5804. **Contact:** Joann Blackburn, Personnel Manager. **E-mail address:** omchrdept1@townsqr.com. **World Wide Web address:** http://www.ozarksmedicalcenter.com. **Description:** A 114-bed, not-for-profit medical center. **Positions advertised include:** Cardiologist; Clinic LPN; CRNA; Emergency Dept. Physician; Family Nurse Practitioner; ICU Nurse Manager; LPN; OB/GYN Physician; Occupational Therapist; Phlebotomist; Physical Therapist; Psychiatrist; Radiation Oncologist; Radiation Technologist; RN's. **Number of employees at this location:** 1,100.

PM RESOURCES
13001 St. Charles Rock Road, Bridgeton MO 63044. 314/291-6720. **Fax:** 314/291-2657. **Contact:** Plant Manager. **Description:** Formulates and distributes animal health products including feed additives, medicated treatments, anthelmintics, nutritional supplements, cleaners and disinfectants, and pest control products. **Parent company:** Agri-Nutritional Group.

PARK UNIVERSITY
8700 North West River Park Drive, Parkville MO 64152-3795. 816/741-2000. **Contact:** Director of Human Resources. **E-mail address:** careers@park.edu. **World Wide Web address:** http://www.park.edu. **Description:** An independent, four-year liberal arts college with an enrollment of 21,000 on 40 campus centers in 20 states, 34 of which are located on military bases. Founded in 1875. **NOTE:** Search and apply for positions online. **Positions advertised online:** Multimedia Application Developer; Assistant VP for Academic Affairs; Dean, College of Liberal Arts and Sciences; Visiting Assistant Professor of Spanish; Adjunct Faculty; Online Instructor.

PARSONS BRINCKERHOFF INC.
1831 Chestnut Street, 7th Floor, St. Louis MO 63103-2225. 314/421-1476. **Fax:** 314/421-1741. **Contact:** Director of Personnel. **World Wide Web address:** http://www.pbworld.com. **Description:** Provides total engineering and construction management services, from project conception through completion, through a worldwide staff of 9,000 professionals and support personnel. Services include the development of major bridges, tunnels, highways, marine facilities, buildings, industrial complexes, and railroads. **NOTE:** Search and apply for positions online. **Positions advertised include:** Sr. CADD Designer; Sr. Supervising Engineer. **Corporate headquarters location:** New York NY. **Other U.S. locations:** Nationwide. **International locations:** Worldwide.

PAULO PRODUCTS COMPANY
5711 West Park Avenue, St. Louis MO 63110. 314/647-7500. **Fax:** 314/647-7518. **Contact:** Human Resources. **World Wide Web address:** http://www.paulo.com. **Description:** A commercial heat-treating and copper brazing, and metal finishing services company. **NOTE:** Search and apply for positions online. **Other area locations:** Kansas City MO. **Other U.S. locations:** Cleveland OH; Murfreesboro TN; Nashville TN.

PEA RIDGE IRON ORE COMPANY
HC65 Box 110, Sullivan MO 63080-9200. 573/468-4111. **Fax:** 573/468-7202. **Contact:** Director of Employee Relations. **World Wide Web address:** http://www.pearidgeiron.com. **Description:** Engaged in the mining and processing of customized iron ore pellet and high-grade iron oxide powders. **Corporate headquarters location:** St. Louis MO. **Parent company:** Big River Minerals Corporation. **Operations at this facility include:** Administration; Manufacturing.

PEABODY ENERGY
701 Market Street, St. Louis MO 63101. 314/342-3400. **Contact:** Human Resources. **World Wide Web address:** http://www.peabodyenergy.com. **Description:** A private-energy coal company. **Positions advertised include:** Business Analyst. **Corporate headquarters location:** This location. **Subsidiaries include:** Peabody Coal Company is engaged in coal mining, production, and processing. **Operations at this facility include:** Administration; Sales. **Listed on:** New York Stock Exchange. **Stock exchange symbol:** BTU. **Number of employees nationwide:** 6,900.

PERKINELMER OPTOELECTRONICS
10900 Page Boulevard, St. Louis MO 63132. 314/423-4900. **Fax:** 314/423-3956. **Contact:** Personnel. **World Wide Web address:** http://www.perkinelmer.com. **Description:** A manufacturer of photocells, phototransistors, photodiedes, opto-isolators, infrared interrupter switches, and retro-reflective switches. **NOTE:** Search and apply for positions online. **Corporate headquarters location:** Wellesley MA. **Other U.S. locations:** Nationwide. **Listed on:** New York Stock Exchange. **Stock exchange symbol:** PKI.

PFIZER
One Pfizer Way, Lees Summit MO 64081. 816/524-5580. **Contact:** Human Resources. **World Wide Web address:** http://www.pfizer.com. **Description:** A leading pharmaceutical company that distributes products concerning cardiovascular health, central nervous system disorders, infectious diseases, and women's health worldwide. The company's brand-name products include Benadryl, Ben Gay, Cortizone, Desitin, Halls, Listerine, Sudafed, and Zantac 75.

PHOENIX SCIENTIFIC INC.
3915 South 48th Street Terrace, St. Joseph MO 64503. 816/364-3777. **Fax:** 816/364-3778. **Contact:** Human Resources. **E-mail address:** tkarr@psiqv.com. **World Wide Web address:** http://www.psiqv.com. **Description:** A manufacturer of generic animal pharmaceuticals.

POTTER ELECTRIC SIGNAL COMPANY
2081 Craig Road, St. Louis MO 63146. 314/878-4321. **Toll-free phone:** 800/325-3936. **Fax:** 800/768-8377. **Contact:** Human Resources Director. **E-mail address:** potter@pottersignal.com. **World Wide Web address:** http://www.pottersignal.com. **Description:** Manufacturers of fire sprinklers and security products.

PREMCOR INC.
8182 Maryland Avenue, Suite 600, St. Louis MO 63105. 314/854-9696. **Fax:** 314/854-1580. **Contact:** Paula Novak, Human Resources. **World Wide Web address:** http://www.premcor.com. **Description:** Through its subsidiaries the company is a leading independent refiner and marketer of petroleum products in the central United States. The company's principal activities consist of crude oil marketing, wholesale marketing of refined petroleum products, and retail marketing of gasoline and convenience products through its company-operated retail network. Premcor operates its business on a decentralized basis through a refining division and a marketing division. The refining division operates four refineries, 16 product distribution terminals, an LPG storage terminal, a crude oil terminal, and pipeline interests. The marketing division consists of approximately 840 retail locations selling gasoline and convenience products in 12 midwestern states as well as a wholesale marketing group selling gasoline, diesel, jet fuel, and other petroleum products currently on an unbranded basis. In addition, a corporate service division provides centralized administrative, business, financial, and human resources support systems for the refining and marketing divisions. **Positions advertised include:** Process Engineer. **Corporate headquarters location:** Old Greenwich CT. **Other U.S. locations:** Blue Island IL; Hartford IL; Lima OH; Port Arthur TX. **Subsidiaries include:** Port Arthur Coker Company; Premcor Refining Group. **Listed on:** Privately held.

PREMIER TURBINES
3551 Doniphan Drive, Neosho MO 64850. 417/451-1810. **Fax:** 417/451-7245. **Contact:** Personnel. **World Wide Web address:** http://www.premierturbines.com. **Description:** Premier Turbines is engaged in the production of aircraft parts and auxiliary equipment. **Parent company:** BBA Aviation.

PRESIDENT CASINO LACLEDE'S LANDING
800 North First Street, St. Louis MO 63102. 314/622-3000. **Fax:** 314/622-3029. **Recorded jobline:** 314/622-3159. **Contact:** Human Resources. **E-mail address:** careers@presidentcasino.com. **World Wide Web address:** http://www.presidentcasino.com. **Description:** A riverboat casino with over 1,200 slots and 46 table games. Founded in 1907. **Positions advertised include:** Assistant Engineer; Dealer. **Other U.S. locations:** Biloxi MS. **Parent company:** President Casinos, Inc. (St. Louis MO) operates President Casino & Blackhawk Hotel, President Casino Laclede's Landing, and President Casino Broadwater Resort. **Number of employees nationwide:** 2,000.

PRICEWATERHOUSECOOPERS
P.O. Box 1097, St. Louis MO 63188. 314/206-8500. **Physical address:** 800 Market Street, St. Louis MO 63101-2695. **Fax:** 314/206-8514. **Contact:** Human Resources. **World Wide Web address:** http://www.pwcglobal.com. **Description:** One of the largest certified public accounting firms in the world. PricewaterhouseCoopers provides public accounting, business advisory, management consulting, and taxation services. **NOTE:** Search and apply for positions online. **Positions advertised include:** Tax Manager; Audit Associate; Audit Manager, Financial Services; Sr. Associate, IT Audit; Data Management Associate. **Corporate headquarters location:** New York NY. **Other U.S. locations:** Nationwide.

PURINA MILLS, INC.
P.O. Box 66812, St. Louis MO 63166-6812. 314/317-5100. **Physical address:** 555 Maryville University Drive, Suite 440 and 500, St. Louis MO 63141. **Toll-free phone:** 800/227-8941. **Fax:** 314/317-5280. **Contact:** Human Resources. **E-mail address:** employment@purina-mills.com. **World Wide Web address:** http://www.purina-mills.com. **Description:** A holding company with operating subsidiaries that develop, manufacture, and market animal nutrition products for dairy and beef cattle, hogs, and horses; and develop, manufacture, and sell poultry feeds and specialty feeds for rabbits, zoo animals, birds, and fish. **NOTE:** Search and apply for positions online.

QUALEX
2838 Market Street, St. Louis MO 63103. 314/652-1300. **Contact:** Human Resources Department. **Description:** Wholesalers of photographic supplies and retailers of photo-finishing services. **Number of employees at this location:** 100.

QUALITY SOFTWARE ENGINEERING, INC.
10820 Sunset Office Drive, Suite 302, St. Louis MO 63127-1037. 314/965-7800. **Fax:** 314/965-7802. **Contact:** Human Resources. **E-mail address:** resumes@qse.com. **World Wide Web address:** http://www.qse.com. **Description:** An information technology consulting and services firm. The Information Systems Consulting Division provides services to professionals including application system development and maintenance, database administration, system installation and management, network installation and management, technical writing, training, quality assurance, project management, and management consulting. The Information Technologies Division provides services for clients who outsource those functions, including hardware and software evaluation and selection, installation, systems integration, project development services, training, and end user support. **NOTE:** Search and apply for positions online. **Positions advertised include:** Technical Resource Planner; Process Improvement Specialist; Project Managers; Business Objects Developer; Client/Server Programmer/Analyst; Java Application Team Lead/Developer. **Corporate headquarters location:** This location.

QUEST DIAGNOSTICS INCORPORATED
11636 Administration Drive, St. Louis MO 63146. 314/567-3905. **Contact:** Human Resources Department. **World Wide Web address:** http://www.questdiagnostics.com. **Description:** One of the largest clinical laboratories in North America, providing a broad range of clinical laboratory services to health care clients that include physicians, hospitals, clinics, dialysis centers, pharmaceutical companies, and corporations. The company offers and performs tests on blood, urine, and other bodily fluids and tissues to provide information for health and well-being. **NOTE:** Search and apply for positions online. **Other U.S. locations:** Nationwide.

RADIOSHACK
371 South County Center Way, P.O. Box 515371, St. Louis MO 63129. 314/892-1800. **Contact:** Store Manager. **World Wide Web address:** http://www.radioshack.com. **Description:** A store location of the national consumer electronics retailer. Overall, RadioShack operates through more than 7,000 stores worldwide. **Corporate headquarters location:** Fort Worth TX. **Parent company:** InterTAN, Inc. (Fort Worth TX). **Listed on:** New York Stock Exchange. **Stock exchange symbol:** RSH.

RALCORP HOLDINGS, INC.
P.O. Box 618, St. Louis MO 63188-0618. 314/877-7000. **Physical address:** 800 Market Street, St. Louis MO 63101. **Fax:** 314/877-7663. **Contact:** Human Resources. **World Wide Web address:** http://www.ralcorp.com. **Description:** Manufactures and sells branded and store brand cereals, baby food, cracker and cookie products. **Positions advertised include:** Director, Order Life Cycle; Logistics Management Trainee.

RAMADA INN BRANSON
1700 West Highway 76, Branson MO 65616. 417/334-1000. **Fax:** 417/339-3046. **Toll-free:** 800/641-4106. **Contact:** Human Resources. **World Wide Web address:** www.ramada.com. **Description:** A 296-room hotel on 22 acres in the Ozark Mountains. **Other U.S. locations:** Nationwide.

RAWLINGS SPORTING GOODS COMPANY, INC.
1859 Bowles Avenue, Fenton MO 63026. 636/349-3500. **Contact:** Human Resources. **World Wide Web address:** http://www.rawlings.com. **Description:** A leading manufacturer and supplier of team sports equipment in North America and, through its licensee, of baseball equipment and uniforms in Japan. It offers a wide range of quality products for baseball and softball (gloves, baseballs, bats, helmets, protective gear, team uniforms, and accessories); basketball (balls, team uniforms, warm-ups, and accessories); football (balls, shoulder pads, protective gear, and team uniforms); and other sports. The company operates five manufacturing facilities in the United States and Latin America. **Corporate headquarters location:** This location.

RECKITT BENCKISER
30 Arrowhead Industrial Boulevard, St. Peters MO 63376. 636/397-5211. **Contact:** Cindy Landrum, Human Resources Manager. **World Wide Web address:** http://www.reckitt.com. **Description:** Manufactures a variety of nationally marketed detergents and air fresheners. **International locations:** Worldwide. **Number of employees at this location:** 100.

REGAL RIVERFRONT HOTEL
200 South Fourth Street, St. Louis MO 63102. 314/241-9500. **Fax:** 314/516-8156. **Contact:** Director of Human Resources. **Description:** A downtown convention hotel with 780 rooms, extensive banquet facilities, and two restaurants. **Corporate headquarters location:** Denver CO. **Parent company:** Richfield Hotel Management. **Listed on:** Privately held. **Number of employees at this location:** 600. **Number of employees nationwide:** 18,000.

RELIV INTERNATIONAL INC.
P.O. Box 405, Chesterfield MO 63006. 636/537-9715. **Physical address:** 136 Chesterfield Industrial Boulevard, Chesterfield MO 63006. **Fax:** 636/537-8910. **Contact:** Manager of Human Resources. **World Wide Web address:** http://www.reliv.com. **Description:** Manufactures and markets a line of nutritional supplements, weight control products, fruit and fiber bars, and sports drink mixes.

REYNOLDS & REYNOLDS
2388 Schuetz Road, St. Louis MO 63146. 314/569-3345. **Contact:** Human Resources. **E-mail address:** hr@reyrey.com. **World Wide Web address:** http://www.reyrey.com. **Description:** Reynolds & Reynolds provides systems integration and analysis for the automotive industry. **Corporate headquarters location:** Dayton OH. **Operations at this facility include:** This location serves as a regional sales office. **Number of employees worldwide:** 4,500.

THE RIVAL COMPANY
THE HOLMES GROUP
800 East 101 Terrace, Suite 100, Kansas City MO 64131. 816/943-4100. **Contact:** Human Resources. **World Wide Web address:** http://www.rivco.com. **Description:** The Rival Company is a leading designer, manufacturer, and marketer of small household appliances, personal care appliances, and sump, well, and utility pumps. The company's product lines are sold to major retail outlets in the United States and Canada, hardware stores, home centers, department stores, catalog showrooms, and warehouse clubs. **NOTE:** Search and apply for positions at: http://www.theholmesgroup.com. **Corporate headquarters location:** This location. **Parent company:** The Holmes Group.

THE RIVAL COMPANY
THE HOLMES GROUP
1001 Golden Drive, Clinton MO 64735. 660/885-5564. **Contact:** Human Resources. **World Wide Web address:** http://www.rivco.com. **Description:** The Rival Company is a leading designer, manufacturer, and marketer of small household appliances; personal care appliances; and sump, well, and utility pumps. The company's product lines are sold to major retail outlets in the United States and Canada, hardware and home centers, department stores, catalog showrooms, and warehouse clubs. **NOTE:** Search and apply for positions at: http://www.theholmesgroup.com. **Corporate headquarters location:** Kansas City MO. **Operations at this facility include:** This location manufactures electric cooking pots. **Parent company:** The Holmes Group.

ROADWAY EXPRESS INC.
205 Soccer Park Road, Fenton MO 63026. 636/349-5300. **Contact:** Personnel Manager. **World Wide Web address:** http://www.roadway.com. **Description:** Operates a freight consolidation and distribution terminal for one of the largest common carriers in the United States, with terminals in more than 633 cities nationwide. **NOTE:** All candidates follow the same career path: Management Trainee, 10 weeks; Dock Supervisor, one to five years. All hiring is done through the Missouri Department of Employment. Please contact this location for more information. **Corporate headquarters location:** Akron OH. **Other U.S. locations:** Nationwide. **Parent company:** Roadway Services is a transportation holding company with subsidiaries involved in long-haul, airfreight, small package, and custom logistics services. Subsidiaries of Roadway Services include Roadway Global Air with worldwide airfreight service through 230 service centers; Roadway Package System with 271 terminals in the United States and a dozen in Canada; and four regional short-haul freight carriers. The company also offers indirect service to Latin America, Guam,

Europe, the Middle East, and the Pacific Rim. **Number of employees worldwide:** 25,000.

RUBIN, BROWN, GORNSTEIN & CO. LLP
One North Brentwood Boulevard, St. Louis MO 63105. 314/290-3300. **Fax:** 314/290-3400. **Contact:** Human Resources. **E-mail address:** recruiting@rbg.com. **World Wide Web address:** http://www.rbg.com. **Description:** A public accounting firm operating primarily in the St. Louis metropolitan area. Services and specialties include accounting, audit, and tax services; and computer, employee benefit plan, legal support management, personal financial, and acquisition consulting services. The company provides services to accounting firms, automotive dealerships, financial services firms including financial institutions and mortgage banks, government agencies, health care companies, hospitality firms, law firms, manufacturing companies, international business consultants, nonprofit organizations, real estate and construction firms, and retailers. **Positions advertised include:** Health Care Audit Management Professional; Small Business Group Accountant; Internal Auditor. **Special programs:** Internships. **Corporate headquarters location:** This location. **Operations at this facility include:** Administration; Sales; Service. **Number of employees at this location:** 200.

SSM CARDINAL GLENNON CHILDREN'S HOSPITAL
1465 South Grand Boulevard, St. Louis MO 63104-1003. 314/577-5600. **Fax:** 314/268-4188. **Contact:** Kathleen A. Morris, Human Resources Services Representative. **E-mail address:** kathleen_a_morris@ssmhc.com. **World Wide Web address:** http://www.cardinalglennon.com. **Description:** A pediatric hospital. **Positions advertised include:** Staff Nurses; LPN's; RN's; Administrative Director; Clinical Dietitian; Cytogenetics Technologist; Emergency Technician; Information Specialist; Medical Technologist. **Number of employees at this location:** 1,600.

SSM REHABILITATION INSTITUTE
St. Mary's Health Center, 6420 Clayton Road, Suite 600, St. Louis MO 63117. 314/768-5207. **Fax:** 314/768-5342. **Contact:** Human Resources. **World Wide Web address:** http://www.ssmrehab.com. **Description:** A specialty hospital providing rehabilitation for persons with head injuries, spinal cord injuries, and general rehabilitation needs. **Positions advertised include:** Occupational Therapist; Physical Therapist; Registered Nurse; Social Worker; Speech-Language Pathologist. **Special programs:** Internships. **Other area locations:** Bridgeton MO; St. Charles MO; Kirkwood MO. **Number of employees nationwide:** 450.

SABRELINER CORPORATION
7733 Forsyth Boulevard, Suite 1500, St. Louis MO 63105-1821. 314/863-6880. **Contact:** Human Resources. **World Wide Web address:** http://www.sabreliner.com. **Description:** Sabreliner Corporation manages sophisticated aviation products, services, and training programs; repairs, modifies, and remanufactures aircraft; maintains and overhauls aircraft engines and specialized industrial engines; and sells aircraft parts.

ST. ALEXIUS HOSPITAL, BROADWAY CAMPUS
3933 South Broadway, St. Louis MO 63118. 314/865-7910. **Fax:** 314/865-7934. **Contact:** Human Resources. **E-mail address:** jobs@st-alexius-hospital.com. **World Wide Web address:** http://www.stalexiushospital.com. **Description:** St. Alexius Hospital, Broadway Campus, formerly Alexian Brothers Hospital, is a 203-bed community hospital. Founded in 1869. **NOTE:** Search and apply for positions or submit resume online. **Positions advertised include:** Occupational Therapist; LPN's; Pharmacist; RN's; CNA; Respiratory Tech; Nuclear Med Tech. **Corporate headquarters location:** Dallas TX. **Parent company:** Tenet Healthcare Corporation. **Listed on:** New York Stock Exchange. **Stock exchange symbol:** THC.

ST. ALEXIUS HOSPITAL, JEFFERSON CAMPUS
2639 Miami Street, St. Louis MO 63118. 314/577-5860. **Fax:** 314/577-5805. **Recorded jobline:** 314/268-6262. **Contact:** Manager of Human Resources Department. **World Wide Web address:** http://www.sohospital.com. **Description:** A general, 408-bed acute care medical center. **Positions advertised include:** Registered Nurse; Licensed Practical Nurse; Recreation Therapist; Security Officer; Social Worker; Pharmacist; Chart Auditor. **Corporate headquarters location:** Dallas TX. **Parent company:** Tenet Healthcare Corporation. **Listed on:** New York Stock Exchange. **Stock exchange symbol:** THC.

ST. ANTHONY'S MEDICAL CENTER
10010 Kennerly Road, St. Louis MO 63128. 314/525-1010. **Contact:** Personnel. **World Wide Web address:** http://www.stanthonysmedcenter.com. **Description:** A 292-bed health care facility consisting of St. Anthony's Hospital and St. Clare's Hospital. **NOTE:** Online applications are the preferred method of employment inquiry. **Positions advertised include:** Certified Nursing Assistant; Cardiac Ultrasonographer; Clinical Dietician; Cook; CT/MRI Technologist; Food Service Aide; Housekeeper; Imaging Clerk; Licensed Practical Nurse; Nurse Assistant; Nutrition Services Assistant; Physical Therapist; Registered Nurse; Rehabilitation Technician; Speech Therapist; Therapy Attendant; Transport Technician; Unit Secretary.

SAINT-GOBAIN CALMAR INC
1001 South 291 Highway, Lees Summit MO 64081. 816/524-4160. **Toll-free phone:** 800/599-2124. **Fax:** 816/246-3820. **Contact:** Human Resources Director. **E-mail address:** info@calmar.com. **World Wide Web address:** http://www.calmar.com. **Description:** A leading producer of high-performance mechanical (nonaerosol) dispensing systems. Calmar also develops child-resistant and tamper-evident caps that are widely used by pharmaceutical firms. **Other U.S. locations:** Nationwide. **International locations:** Worldwide.

ST. JOHN'S BANK & TRUST COMPANY
8924 St. Charles Rock Road, St. Louis MO 63114-4258. 314/428-1000. **Fax:** 314/298-1479. **Recorded jobline:** 314/428-1059 ext. 2000. **Contact:** Human Resources. **E-mail address:** info@stjohnsbank.com. **World Wide Web address:** http://www.stjohnsbank.com. **Description:** A full-service bank with seven locations. **Positions advertised include:** Teller; Loan Services Clerk: SJFS Administrative Sales Assistant.

ST. JOSEPH HOSPITAL
525 Couch Avenue, Kirkwood MO 63122. 314/966-1551. **Fax:** 314/822-6340. **Recorded jobline:** 877/916-7300. **Contact:** Human Resources. **World Wide Web address:** http://www.stjosephkirkwood.com. **Description:** An acute-care hospital. **NOTE:** Search and apply for positions online. **Positions advertised include:** Cardiovascular Coordinator; Certified Nurse Assistant; Coding Specialist; Communications Coordinator; Director, Revenue integrity; Director of Health Information Management; Echo Technician; EMS Liaison; Nursing Supervisor; Nuclear Medicine Technologist; Radiologic Technologist; RN's. **Special programs:** Internships; Training. **Corporate headquarters location:** St. Louis MO. **Parent company:** SSM Health Care.

THE ST. LOUIS ART MUSEUM
One Fine Arts Drive, Forest Park, St. Louis MO 63110-1380. 314/721-0072. **Fax:** 314/721-6172. **Contact:** Human Resources. **E-mail address:** jhawkins@slam.org. **World Wide Web address:** http://www.slam.org. **Description:** A comprehensive, free, public art museum with diverse collections from cultures worldwide, along with strong educational programs and a regular schedule of special exhibitions. Founded in 1879.

ST. LOUIS CHILDREN'S HOSPITAL
One Children's Place, St. Louis MO 63110. 314/454-6000. **Physical address:** 4444 Forrest Park Avenue, 2nd Floor, St. Louis MO 63178. **Fax:** 314/454-4775. **Recorded jobline:** 314/863-5627. **Contact:** Human Resources Department. **World Wide Web address:** http://www.stlouischildrens.org. **Description:** A 235-bed hospital that specializes in pediatrics. **NOTE:** Only online applications are accepted. Set up profile to search for non-physician positions. **Positions advertised include:** Neonatologist; Pediatric Emergency Medicine Physician; Pediatric Pulmonologist; Pediatric Allergist; **Parent company:** BJC Health Systems. **Operations at this facility include:** Administration; Service. **Number of employees at this location:** 2,000.

ST. LOUIS CHRISTIAN COLLEGE
1360 Grandview Drive, Florissant MO 63033. 314/837-6777. **Fax:** 314/837-8291. **Contact:** Manager of Human Resources Department. **World Wide Web address:** http://www.slcconline.edu. **Description:** A college offering two- and four-year undergraduate degrees.

ST. LOUIS COLLEGE OF PHARMACY
4588 Parkview Place, St. Louis MO 63110-1088. 314/367-8700. **Toll-free phone:** 800/278-5267. **Contact:** Human Resources. **E-mail address:** HR@stlcop.edu. **World Wide Web address:** http://www.stlcop.edu. **Description:** A private, nonsectarian college of pharmaceutical study. Degrees offered are Bachelor of Science in Pharmacy, Master of Science in Pharmacy Administration, and Doctor of Pharmacy. Founded in 1864.

ST. LOUIS LITHOGRAPHING COMPANY
6880 Heege Road, St. Louis MO 63123. 314/352-1300. **Fax:** 314/352-4941. **Contact:** Personnel Director. **Description:** A lithography company specializing in the manufacture of a variety of liquor labels and packaging.

ST. LOUIS MARRIOTT PAVILION HOTEL
One South Broadway, St. Louis MO 63102. 314/421-1776. **Fax:** 314/331-9029. **Contact:** Rhonda Ross, Human Resources. **World Wide Web address:** http://www.marriotthotels.com. **Description:** A hotel with 672 guest rooms and 11 suites. The hotel offers a variety of recreation facilities, restaurants, and lounges. **NOTE:** Search and apply for positions online. **Special programs:** Internships. **Corporate headquarters location:** Bethesda MD. **Other U.S. locations:** Nationwide. **Number of employees at this location:** 400. **Number of employees nationwide:** 128,000.

THE ST. LOUIS POST-DISPATCH
900 North Tucker Boulevard, St. Louis MO 63101-1069. 314/340-8000. **Fax:** 314/340-3005. **Contact:** Director of Human Resources. **World Wide Web address:** http://www.stltoday.com. **Description:** Publishes a daily newspaper.

ST. LOUIS REHABILITATION CENTER
5300 Arsenal Street, St. Louis MO 63139. 314/644-8000. **Fax:** 314/644-8115. **Contact:** Director of Human Resources. **E-mail address:** hrmail@dmh.mo.gov. **World Wide Web address:** http://www.dmh.missouri.gov. **Description:** A long-term, psychosocial rehabilitation hospital. The facility provides treatment and rehabilitation services to forensic patients committed to the Department of Mental Health as the result of a criminal offense and the diagnosis of a serious mental disorder. Specific rehabilitation programs are available for individuals with severe and persistent mental illnesses, individuals with personality disorders, and individuals requiring restoration of competence to stand trial. **NOTE:** View open positions for DMH facilities at: http://www.dmh.missouri.gov/offices/hr/jobs. Contact facility directly to apply. **Corporate headquarters location:** Jefferson City MO. **Parent company:** Missouri Department of Mental Health.

ST. LOUIS SYMPHONY COMMUNITY MUSIC SCHOOL
560 Trinity Street, University City MO 63130. 314/863-3033. **Contact:** Director. **Description:** An educational institution with an emphasis on the study of the performing arts.

ST. LOUIS SYMPHONY ORCHESTRA
718 North Grand Boulevard, St. Louis MO 63103. 314/533-2500. **Contact:** Personnel Department. **E-mail address:** resume@slso.org. **World Wide Web address:** http://www.slso.org. **Description:** Houses the administrative offices for one of the oldest orchestras in the United States. Founded in 1880. **Positions advertised include:** Network Administrator.

SAINT LOUIS UNIVERSITY
221 North Grand Boulevard, St. Louis MO 63103. 800/758-3678. **Fax:** 314/977-8598. **Recorded jobline:** 314/977-2265. **Contact:** Sandy Cox, Human Resources. **World Wide Web address:** http://www.slu.edu. **Description:** Saint Louis University is a Catholic, Jesuit university and leading research institution, offering undergraduate, graduate and professional degree programs. Founded in 1818. Enrollment is 11,000 students on campuses in St. Louis and Madrid, Spain. **Number of employees at this location:** 6,237.

SAINT LOUIS UNIVERSITY HOSPITAL
3635 Vista Avenue, St. Louis MO 63110. 314/577-8000. **Contact:** Human Resources. **World Wide Web address:** http://www.sluhospital.com. **Description:** A 356-bed, teaching hospital for the Saint Louis University School of Medicine. The hospital is a certified Level I Trauma Center in both Missouri and Illinois. **NOTE:** Search and apply for positions or submit resume online. **Parent company:** Tenet HealthSystem.

SAINT LOUIS UNIVERSITY SCHOOL OF MEDICINE
1402 South Grand Blvd, St. Louis MO 63104. 314/977-9853. **Contact:** Human Resources. **World Wide Web address:** http://medschool.slu.edu. **Description:** Saint Louis University School of Medicine trains physicians and biomedical scientists, conducts medical research, and provides health services on a local, national and international level. Founded in 1836. The School of Medicine is a pioneer in geriatric medicine, organ transplantation, chronic disease prevention, cardiovascular disease, neurosciences and vaccine research, among others. **NOTE:** Search for positions online.

SAINT LUKE'S HOSPITAL
232 South Woods Mill Road, Chesterfield MO 63017. 314/434-1500. **Recorded jobline:** 314/205-6677. **Contact:** Human Resources Department. **E-mail address:**

jobs@stlukes-stl.com. **World Wide Web address:** http://www.stlukes-stl.com. **Description:** A general hospital. **NOTE:** Search and apply for positions online. **Positions advertised include:** Associate Head Nurse; Certified Nurse Assistant; Occupational Therapist; Perfusionist; Licensed Practical Nurse; Registered Nurse; Pharmacist; Physical Therapist; Speech Language Pathologist.

ST. PAUL TRAVELERS
940 West Port Plaza, Suite 450, St. Louis MO 63136. 314/994-2200. **Contact:** Human Resources. **World Wide Web address:** http://www.stpaultravelers.com. **Description**: The second-largest commercial U.S. property-liability insurance company, St. Paul Travelers offers insurance to a wide variety of businesses and other organizations, as well as individuals, through independent insurance agents and brokers. The company also holds a nearly 80 percent majority interest in Nuveen Investments. **NOTE:** Search and apply for positions online. **Positions advertised include:** Loss Control Engineer. **Corporate headquarters location:** Saint Paul MN. **Other U.S. locations:** Nationwide. **Listed on:** New York Stock Exchange. **Stock exchange symbol:** STA.

SAKS FIFTH AVENUE
One Plaza Frontenac, Frontenac MO 63131. 314/567-9200. **Fax:** 314/567-3339. **Contact:** Personnel Director. **World Wide Web address:** http://www.saksincorporated.com. **Description:** This location houses the business offices. Overall, Saks Fifth Avenue is a 62-store chain emphasizing soft-goods products, primarily apparel for men, women, and children. **Parent company:** Saks Incorporated is a department store holding company that operates approximately 379 stores in 39 states. The company's stores include Saks Fifth Avenue, Parisian, Proffit's, Younker's, Herberger's, Carson Pirie Scott, Boston Store, Bergner's, McRae's, Boston Store, and Off 5th, the company's outlet store. Saks Incorporated also operates two retail catalogs and several retail Internet sites.

SATELLITE ENGINEERING GROUP INC.
P.O. Box 33475, 6050 Connecticut Avenue, Kansas City MO 64120-3475. 816/231-8080. **Fax:** 816/483-5811. **Toll-free phone:** 800/932-1555. **Contact:** Mike Lloyd. **E-mail address:** mlloyd@sateng.com. **World Wide Web address:** http://www.sateng.com. **Description:** A leading distributor of satellite, cable, and broadcast equipment. Also designs and installs equipment for apartment complexes and hotels.

L.E. SAUER MACHINE COMPANY
3535 Tree Court Industrial Boulevard, St. Louis MO 63122. 636/225-5358. **Toll-free phone:** 800/745-4107. **Fax:** 636/225-3438. **Contact:** Human Resources. **World Wide Web address:** http://www.sauermachine.com/lesauer. **Description:** Manufactures rotary die-cutting equipment, scorers, and associated parts for paper cutting. Also performs CNC machining, laser cutting, and heat-treating.

SAVVIS COMMUNICATIONS INC.
1 Savvis Parkway, Town & Country MO 63017. 314/628-7000. **Contact:** Human Resources. **World Wide Web address:** http://www.savvis.net. **Description:** An IT utility provider that delivers secure and reliable hosting, network, and application services. **Positions advertised include:** Billing Analyst; Revenue Assurance Analyst; Collection Analyst; Fixed Asset Accountant; Sr. Analyst Carrier Management; Metrics Sr. Analyst; Sr. Procurement Manager. **Other U.S. locations:** Atlanta GA; Waltham MA; Chicago IL; Dallas TX; Denver CO; Santa Clara CA; Miami FL; New York NY; San Francisco CA.

SCHNEITHORST'S
1600 South Lindbergh Boulevard, St. Louis MO 63131. 314/993-5600. **Fax:** 314/993-1069. **Contact:** Jim Schneithorst, Jr., Owner. **E-mail address:** info@schneithorst.com. **World Wide Web address:** http://www.schneithorst.com. **Description:** Owns and operates restaurants and catering services. **Annual sales/revenues:** $5 - $10 million. **Number of employees at this location:** 175.

SCHNUCK MARKETS, INC.
11420 Lackland Road, St. Louis MO 63146-6928. 314/994-9900. **Toll-free phone:** 800/459-HIRE. **Contact:** Employment Manager. **World Wide Web address:** http://www.schnucks.com. **Description:** Operates a chain of 100 supermarkets. **Positions advertised include:** Pharmacists. **Corporate headquarters location:** This location. **Other U.S. locations:** IL; IN; WI; MS; TN. **Number of employees nationwide:** 2,530.

SEMCO PLASTIC COMPANY INC.
5301 Old Baumgartner Road, St. Louis MO 63129. 314/487-4557. **Fax:** 314/487-4724. **Contact:** Personnel. **World Wide Web address:** http://www.semcoplastics.com. **Description:** Manufactures plastic injection molders, blow molders, plastic items, boxes, and wall anchors. The company also manufactures packaging for hardware, electrical, and plumbing contractors.

SENSIENT COLOR GROUP
2526 Baldwin Street, St. Louis MO 63106-1903. 314/889-7600. **Toll-free phone:** 800/325-8110. **Fax:** 314/658-7318. **Contact:** Personnel. **E-mail address:** employment@sensient-tech.com. **World Wide Web address:** http://www.sensient-tech.com. **Description:** Manufacturers and distributors of colored dyes for the food, drug, and cosmetics industries. Founded in 1904. **Parent company:** Sensient Technologies Corporation.

SERVCO EQUIPMENT COMPANY
3189 Jamieson Avenue, St. Louis MO 63139. 314/781-3189. **Contact:** Human Resources. **Description:** A manufacturer of food service equipment for cafeterias, restaurants, and hospitals.

SEVERN TRENT LABORATORIES, INC.
13715 Rider Trail North, Earth City MO 63045. 314/298-8566. **Fax:** 314/298-8757. **Contact:** Personnel Department. **World Wide Web address:** http://www.stl-inc.com. **Description:** Provides a complete range of environmental testing services to private industry, engineering consultants, and government agencies in support of federal and state environmental regulations. The company also possesses analytical capabilities in the fields of air toxins, field analytical services, radiochemistry/mixed waste, and advanced technology. **Positions advertised include:** Project Manager; Analyst; **Other U.S. locations:** Nationwide.

SHERATON WESTPORT INN
900 Westport Plaza Tower Drive, St. Louis MO 63146. 314/878-1500. **Fax:** 314/434-0140. **Contact:** Jim Grant, Personnel Department. **World Wide Web address:** http://www.startwoodhotels.com. **Description:** One of several area locations of the international hotel chain, specializing in accommodations for business travelers. **Corporate headquarters location:** Boston MA. **Parent company:** Starwood Hotels and Resorts Worldwide, Inc.

SHRINERS HOSPITAL FOR CHILDREN
2001 South Lindbergh Boulevard, St. Louis MO 63131. 314/432-3600. **Fax:** 314/872-7873. **Recorded jobline:** 314/872-7852. **Contact:** Jean Anton, Human Resources Manager. **E-mail address:** janton@shrinenet.org. **World Wide Web address:** http://www.shriners.com. **Description:** An 80-bed nonprofit hospital providing free care, inpatient services, and outpatient services for orthopedically handicapped children. **NOTE:** Entry-level positions, part-time jobs, and second and third shifts are offered. Search and apply for positions online. **Positions advertised include:** Nurse Practitioner; RN; Orthotics Technician; Respiratory Therapist. **Corporate headquarters location:** Tampa FL. **Listed on:** Privately held. **Number of employees at this location:** 300. **Number of employees nationwide:** 3,000.

SIEGEL-ROBERT INC.
8645 South Broadway, St. Louis MO 63111. 314/638-8300. **Contact:** Personnel Department. **World Wide Web address:** http://www.srob.com. **Description:** Manufactures injection moldings. The company is also engaged in the electroplating and decoration of plastics. Founded in 1946.

SIGMA-ALDRICH
3050 Spruce Street, St. Louis MO 63103. 314/771-5765. **Toll-free phone:** 800/521-8956. **Fax:** 314/771-5757. **Contact:** Human Resources. **World Wide Web address:** http://www.sigmaaldrich.com. **Description:** Manufactures and distributes a broad range of biochemical and organic chemical products and kits used in scientific and genomic research, biotechnology, pharmaceutical development, the diagnosis of disease, and chemical manufacturing. **NOTE:** Search and apply for positions online. **Positions advertised include:** Distribution Supervisor; Product Manager; Sr. Project Manager, Process Improvement; Manager of Tact Marketing and Sales Development; Sr. Design Engineer; R&D Associate Scientist. **Special programs:** Internships. **Corporate headquarters location:** This location. **Operations at this facility include:** Manufacturing. **Annual sales/revenues:** More than $100 million. **Number of employees at this location:** 1,800. **Number of employees nationwide:** 3,000.

SIRSI CORPORATION
1276 North Warson Road, St. Louis MO 63132-1806. 314/432-1100. **Toll-free phone:** 800/325-0888. **Fax:** 314/993-8927. **Contact:** Human Resources. **E-mail address:** hr-stl@sirsi.com. **World Wide Web address:** http://www.sirsi.com. **Description:** An automation systems integrator for libraries and other information providers. Sirsi's products and services improve efficiency in traditional library operations and give libraries networking capabilities. Sirsi's automation systems and networking services are adaptable for use in libraries of various sizes. Sirsi's customer base includes more than 10,000 libraries worldwide. Founded in 1975. **Positions advertised include:** Data Conversion Specialist; JAVA Developer; Software Trainer. **Corporate headquarters location:** Huntsville AL.

SIX FLAGS ST. LOUIS
I-44 & Six Flags Road, Eureka MO 63025. 636/938-4800. **Contact:** Human Resources Manager. **E-mail address:** jljohnson@sftp.com. **World Wide Web address:** http://www.sixflags.com/stlouis. **Description:** An amusement park. **Positions advertised include:** Cash Control Agent; Food Service Attendant; Host; Hostess; Laborer; Loss Prevention Officer. **Special programs:** Internships. **Other U.S. locations:** Nationwide. **Parent company:** Premier Parks (OK) owns and operates 35 theme parks nationwide. **Operations at this facility include:** Divisional Headquarters; Sales.

SKYWALKER COMMUNICATIONS
9390 Veterans Memorial Parkway, O'Fallon MO 63366. 636/272-8025. **Toll-free phone:** 800/844-9555. **Contact:** Human Resources. **E-mail address:** jobs@skywalker.com. **World Wide Web address:** http://www.skywalker.com. **Description:** Distributes satellite systems and computer products including mice, modems, and scanners. **Corporate headquarters location:** This location.

SMURFIT-STONE CONTAINER CORPORATION
577 Goddard Avenue, Chesterfield MO 63005. 636/532-3492. **Contact:** Personnel. **World Wide Web address:** http://www.smurfit-stone.com. **Description:** Smurfit-Stone Container Corporation is one of the world's leading paper-based packaging companies. The company's main products include corrugated containers, folding cartons, and multiwall industrial bags. The company is also one of the world's largest collectors and processors of recycled products that are then sold to a worldwide customer base. Smurfit-Stone Container Corporation also operates several paper tube, market pulp, and newsprint production facilities. **Positions advertised include:** Customer Service Representative. **Corporate headquarters location:** Chicago IL. **Other U.S. locations:** Nationwide. **International locations:** Dublin, Ireland. **Operations at this facility include:** This location manufactures corrugated fiberboard boxes. **Listed on:** NASDAQ. **Stock exchange symbol:** SSCC. **Annual sales/revenues:** More than $100 million. **Number of employees worldwide:** 35,000.

SMURFIT-STONE CONTAINER CORPORATION
5505 Natural Bridge Road, St. Louis MO 63120. 314/383-4930. **Contact:** Personnel Director. **World Wide Web address:** http://www.smurfit-stone.com. **Description:** One of the world's leading paper-based packaging companies. Smurfit-Stone Container Corporation's main products include corrugated containers, folding cartons, and multiwall industrial bags. The company is also one of the world's largest collectors and processors of recycled products that are then sold to a worldwide customer base. Smurfit-Stone Container Corporation also operates several paper tube, market pulp, and newsprint production facilities. **Corporate headquarters location:** Chicago IL. **Other U.S. locations:** Nationwide. **Operations at this facility include:** Recycling. **Listed on:** NASDAQ. **Stock exchange symbol:** SSCC. **Annual sales/revenues:** More than $100 million.

SMURFIT-STONE CONTAINER CORPORATION
9150 Latty Avenue, St. Louis MO 63134-1029. 314/522-6600. **Contact:** Human Resources. **World Wide Web address:** http://www.smurfit-stone.com. **Description:** Smurfit-Stone Container Corporation is one of the world's leading paper-based packaging companies. The company's main products include corrugated containers, folding cartons, and multiwall industrial bags. The company is also one of the world's largest collectors and processors of recycled products that are then sold to a worldwide customer base. Smurfit-Stone Container Corporation also operates several paper tube, market pulp, and newsprint production facilities. **Corporate headquarters location:** Chicago IL. **Other U.S. locations:** Nationwide. **Operations at this facility include:** This location manufactures cardboard boxes. **Listed on:** NASDAQ. **Stock exchange symbol:** SSCC. **Annual sales/revenues:** More than $100 million.

SMURFIT-STONE CONTAINER CORPORATION
8182 Maryland Avenue, Clayton MO 63105. 314/746-1100. **Fax:** 314/746-1331. **Contact:** Bob Hardie, Manager of Human Resources. **World Wide Web address:** http://www.smurfit-stone.com. **Description:** One of the world's leading paper-based

packaging companies. Smurfit-Stone Container Corporation's main products include corrugated containers, folding cartons, and multiwall industrial bags. The company is also one of the world's largest collectors and processors of recycled products that are then sold to a worldwide customer base. The company also operates several paper tube, market pulp, and newsprint production facilities. **Corporate headquarters location:** Chicago IL. **Other U.S. locations:** Nationwide. **International locations:** Dublin, Ireland. **Listed on:** NASDAQ. **Stock exchange symbol:** SSCC. **Annual sales/revenues:** More than $100 million.

SOCKET INTERNET
810 Cherry Street, Columbia MO 65201. 816/393-5222. **Fax:** 573/875-5812. **Toll-free phone:** 800/762-5383. **Contact:** Human Resources. **E-mail address:** joinsocket@socket.net. **World Wide Web address:** http://www.socket.net. **Description:** An internet service provider for homes and businesses. **Positions advertised include:** Major Account Representative; Sales Representative; Customer Service Representative; Technical Support Agent.

SOLUTIA, INC.
P.O. Box 66760, St. Louis MO 63166-6760. 314/674-5375. **Physical address:** 575 Maryville Centre Drive, St. Louis MO 63141. **Contact:** Human Resources. **E-mail address:** scresu@solutia.com. **World Wide Web address:** http://www.solutia.com. **Description:** Solutia manufactures chemicals for a broad range of industries including agriculture, food, and printing. **NOTE:** Resumes accepted for open positions only. **Corporate headquarters location:** This location.

SOUTHEAST MISSOURI STATE UNIVERSITY
One University Plaza, Cape Girardeau MO 63701. 573/651-2206. **Contact:** Personnel Director. **World Wide Web address:** http://www.semo.edu. **Description:** A state university offering 150 areas of study. Founded in 1873.

SOUTHWEST BANK
2301 South Kingshighway Boulevard, St. Louis MO 63110. 314/776-5200. **Contact:** Human Resources. **E-mail address:** hr@swbank-stl.com. **World Wide Web address:** http://www.mysouthwestbank.com. **Description:** A bank with six locations in St. Louis, and one in Belleville IL. **NOTE:** Search and apply for positions online. **Special programs:** Internships. **Corporate headquarters location:** This location. **Parent company:** Marshall & Ilsley Corporation. **Operations at this facility include:** Service. **Number of employees at this location:** 190.

SOUTHWEST MISSOURI STATE UNIVERSITY
901 South National Avenue, Springfield MO 65804. 417/836-5000. **Contact:** Human Resources. **World Wide Web address:** http://www.smsu.edu. **Description:** A state university offering 150 undergraduate and 43 graduate academic programs. **NOTE:** Search and apply for positions online. **Positions advertised include:** Assistant/Associate Professors; Associate Dean of Agricultural Sciences; Lecturers; Distance Learning Media Production Specialist; Financial and System Administrator; Videographer/Editor.

SPANN BUILDING MAINTENANCE COMPANY
3130 Gravois Avenue, St. Louis MO 63118. 314/241-1975. **Contact:** Quintin Clemmons, Personnel. **Description:** A janitorial service. **Corporate headquarters location:** This location. **Operations at this facility include:** Administration; Sales; Service.

THE SPORTING NEWS
10176 Corporate Square Drive, Suite 200, St. Louis MO 63122. 314/997-7111. **Contact:** Human Resources. **E-mail address:** tsnjobs@sportingnews.com. **World Wide Web address:** http://www.sportingnews.com. **Description:** A national newspaper, covering a wide range of sports-related news. **Corporate headquarters location:** This location. **Parent company:** Vulcan Inc.

SQUARE D COMPANY
13515 Barrett Parkway Drive, Suite 170, Baldwin MO 63021. 314/821-8181. **Contact:** Human Resources Manager. **World Wide Web address:** http://www.squared.com. **Description:** A manufacturer of electrical distribution products for the construction industry. Products are used in commercial and residential construction, industrial facilities, machinery, and original equipment manufacturers' products. **Corporate headquarters location:** Palatine IL. **Other U.S. locations:** AZ; CA; KY; NE; OH; SC; TN. **Parent company:** Groupe Schneider offers electrical contracting, industrial engineering, and construction services. Its five major operating companies are Jeumont-Schneider Industrie, Merlin Gerin, Spie Batignolles, Square D, and Telemecanique. The companies are organized into two operational sectors. Schneider Industrie designs, manufactures, and markets electrical products and systems for the distribution and control of electricity. Through Spie Batignolles, Groupe Schneider serves as a general contractor for large-scale industrial and government construction projects around the world.

STANDARD MACHINE & MANUFACTURING COMPANY
10014 Big Bend Boulevard, St. Louis MO 63122. 314/966-4500. **Contact:** Personnel Director. **Description:** An industrial manufacturer specializing in the production of water, oil, and air filters; refrigerant filters and valves; and industrial controls.

STAR MANUFACTURING INTERNATIONAL, INC.
10 Sunnen Drive, P.O. Box 430129, St. Louis MO 63143-3800. 314/781-2777. **Toll-free phone:** 800/264-7827. **Contact:** Human Resources. **World Wide Web address:** http://www.star-mfg.com. **Description:** Manufacturers of commercial food service and concession equipment. **Corporate headquarters location:** This location. **Other U.S. locations:** TN. **Operations at this facility include:** Administration; Research and Development; Sales; Service. **Number of employees at this location:** 50. **Number of employees nationwide:** 180.

JOHN STARK PRINTING COMPANY INC.
12969 Manchester Road, St. Louis MO 63131. 314/966-6800. **Contact:** Personnel Department. **World Wide Web address:** http://www.jsprint.com. **Description:** A commercial lithographer, specializing in offset printing. **Parent company:** Cliff Kelley.

STERIS CORPORATION
7501 Page Avenue, St. Louis MO 63133. 314/290-4600. **Contact:** Human Resources. **World Wide Web address:** http://www.steris.com. **Description:** Develops, manufactures and markets infection prevention, contamination prevention, microbial reduction and surgical support systems, products, technologies and services for healthcare, scientific, food, research and industrial customers. **NOTE:** Search and apply for positions online. **Positions advertised include:** Associate Scientist. **Corporate headquarters location:** Mentor OH. **Listed on:** New York Stock Exchange. **Stock exchange symbol:** STE. **Number of employees worldwide:** 5,100.

STIFEL, NICOLAUS & COMPANY
501 North Broadway, St. Louis MO 63102. 314/342-2000. **Fax:** 314/342-2051. **Recorded jobline:** 314/342-2900. **Contact:** Human Resources. **World Wide Web address:** http://www.stifel.com. **Description:** A full-service regional investment firm. Services include fixed income securities, corporate finance, public finance, syndicate participation, trading, broker-dealer services, options, research, mutual funds, asset management, and estate planning. Founded in 1890. **Corporate headquarters location:** This location. **Parent company:** Stifel Financial Corporation. **Number of employees at this location:** 275. **Number of employees nationwide:** 1,000.

WILLIAM A. STRAUB INC.
8282 Forsyth Boulevard, St. Louis MO 63105. 314/725-2121. **Toll-free phone:** 866/725-2121. **Fax:** 314/725-2123. **Contact:** Paul Poe, General Manager. **Description:** Owners and operators of a chain of retail grocery stores. **President:** Jack Straub, Jr.

J.D. STREETT & COMPANY INC.
144 Weldon Parkway, Maryland Heights MO 63043. 314/432-6600. **Contact:** Personnel. **World Wide Web address:** http://www.jdstreett.com. **Description:** Retailers and wholesale marketers of petroleum products. **Corporate headquarters location:** This location.

STRUCTURAL SYSTEMS INC.
816 South Kirkwood Road, Kirkwood MO 63122. 314/966-5920. **Fax:** 314/966-6267. **Contact:** Human Resources. **Description:** An architectural and construction firm specializing in fabricated buildings, general contracting, and design/build contracting.

SUBSURFACE CONSTRUCTORS
110 Angelica Street, St. Louis MO 63147. 314/421-2460. **Fax:** 314/421-2479. **Contact:** Personnel Director. **World Wide Web address:** http://www.subsurfaceconstructors.com. **Description:** A foundation contracting firm that provides pile driving and core drilling services.

SUMNER GROUP, INC.
2121 Hampton Avenue, St. Louis MO 63139. 314/645-0769. **Fax:** 314/633-8005. **Contact:** Personnel Department. **Description:** A wholesale supplier of office equipment and an authorized Canon dealer, specializing in the sale of copying and duplicating equipment. **Corporate headquarters location:** This location. **Other U.S. locations:** Little Rock AR. **Number of employees at this location:** 300. **Number of employees nationwide:** 450.

SUNNEN PRODUCTS COMPANY
7910 Manchester Avenue, St. Louis MO 63143. 314/781-2100. **Fax:** 314/951-2775. **Contact:** Kathy Cherry, Human Resources. **World Wide Web address:** http://www.sunnen.com. **Description:** Manufacturers of precision honing equipment, internal gauges, and a variety of automotive tools. **Positions advertised include:** Sales and Application Engineer. **Number of employees at this location:** 650.

SUNSET LIFE INSURANCE COMPANY
3520 Broadway Boulevard, Kansas City MO 64111. 816/753-0034. **Toll-free phone:** 800/678-6898. **Contact:** Human Resources. **World Wide Web address:** http://www.sunsetlife.com. **Description:** Provides insurance services and handles advertising and other operations for the company. **Parent company:** Kansas City Life Insurance Company.

SUNTRUP FORD CITY
10700 Page Boulevard, St. Louis MO 63132. 314/428-8329. **Contact:** Personnel Director. **World Wide Web address:** http://www.dealernet.com. **Description:** A dealer of new and used automobiles.

SUPERVALU INC.
7100 Hazelwood Avenue, Hazelwood MO 63042. 314/524-4000. **Contact:** Human Resources. **E-mail address:** super.careers@supervalu.com. **World Wide Web address:** http://www.supervalu.com. **Description:** One of the nation's largest food retailers and distribution companies, supplying grocery, health and beauty aids, and general merchandise products to over 3,100 customers. In the corporate retail sector, SUPERVALU operates over 1,500 stores in 39 states under the following names: bigg's, Cub Foods, Shop 'n Save, Save-A-Lot, Scott's Foods, Laneco, and Hornbachers. **Corporate headquarters location:** Eden Prairie MN. **Subsidiaries include:** Hazelwood Farms Bakeries manufactures frozen bakery products. **Listed on:** New York Stock Exchange. **Stock exchange symbol:** SVU.

SWANK MOTION PICTURES
211 South Jefferson Avenue, St. Louis MO 63103-2579. 314/534-6300. **Toll-free phone:** 800/876-3322. **Contact:** Human Resources. **E-mail address:** humanres@swank.com. **World Wide Web address:** http://www.swankav.com. **Description:** A nontheatrical film distribution and audiovisual equipment rental company. **Special programs:** Internships. **Corporate headquarters location:** This location. **Other U.S. locations:** Nationwide. **Operations at this facility include:** Administration; Regional Headquarters; Sales. **Listed on:** Privately held. **Number of employees at this location:** 100. **Number of employees nationwide:** 900.

SWIFT PRINT COMMUNICATIONS
1248 Research Boulevard, St. Louis MO 63132. 314/991-4300. **Toll-free phone:** 800/545-1141. **Fax:** 314/991-3080. **Contact:** Bryan Swift, President. **World Wide Web address:** http://www.swiftprint.com. **Description:** A printing, lithography, and offsetting company.

SWING-A-WAY MANUFACTURING COMPANY
4100 Beck Avenue, St. Louis MO 63116. 314/773-1487. **Contact:** Personnel. **Description:** Manufactures a variety of consumer items including can openers, ice crushers, and jar openers.

SYSTEMS & ELECTRONICS INC.
201 Evans Lane, St. Louis MO 63121-1126. 314/553-4901. **Fax:** 314/553-4215. **Contact:** Human Resources. **E-mail address:** employment@seistl.com. **World Wide Web address:** http://www.seistl.com. **Description:** Designs and manufactures tactical mobility systems, tactical bridging, automated test equipment, airborne radar, materials handling devices, and commercial communications systems. **Positions advertised include:** Contact Administrator; Sr. Engineering Specialist; Engineering Technical Specialist; Sr. Technician; Sr. Planner/Scheduler. **Other area locations:** West Plains MO. **Parent company:** Engineered Support Systems, Inc.

TALX CORPORATION
1850 Borman Court, Maryland Heights MO 63146. 314/214-7000. **Toll-free phone:** 800/888-8277. **Fax:** 314/214-7588. **Contact:** Human Resources Manager. **E-mail address:** hr@talx.com. **World Wide Web address:** http://www.talx.com. **Description:** A business process outsourcer of payroll and HR functions. **NOTE:**

Search and apply for positions online. **Positions advertised include:** Claims Service Representative; Director of Training; Equipment Technician; Payroll Data Analyst. **Other U.S. locations:** Hilliard OH; Richardson TX. **Listed on:** NASDAQ. **Stock exchange symbol:** TALX. **Number of employees nationwide:** 1,000.

TARLTON CORPORATION
5500 West Park Avenue, St. Louis MO 63110. 314/633-3300. **Fax:** 314/647-1940. **Contact:** Human Resources. **Wide Web address:** http://www.tarltoncorp.com. **Description:** A general contractor and construction company. **Special programs:** Internships. **Corporate headquarters location:** This location. **Operations at this facility include:** Administration. **Listed on:** Privately held. **Number of employees at this location:** 45.

TENET HEALTHCARE
15450 South Outer 40 Drive, Suite 120, Chesterfield MO 63017. 636/537-7950. **Contact:** Human Resources. **World Wide Web address:** http://www.tenethealth.com. **Description:** Tenet Health owns or operates 97 acute care hospitals and medical centers in 14 states. Missouri operations include DePeres Hospital, Forest Park Hospital, St. Alexius Hospital, St. Alexius Hospital Jefferson Campus, and St. Louis University Hospital. **NOTE:** Entry-level positions and second and third shifts are offered. **Positions advertised include:** Regional Director, Managed Care. **Corporate headquarters location:** Dallas TX. **Operations at this facility include:** Regional management.

THERMADYNE HOLDINGS CORPORATION
16052 Swingley Ridge Road, Suite 300, St. Louis MO 63107. 636/728-3000. **Contact:** Employee Relations. **World Wide Web address:** http://www.thermadyne.com. **Description:** A diversified industrial holding company that engages in the manufacture of cutting and welding equipment. **NOTE:** Managerial/administrative positions are based in St. Louis. Sales positions are offered nationwide. **Positions advertised include:** National Accounts Manager; Graphic Services Coordinator. **Special programs:** Internships. **Corporate headquarters location:** This location. **Subsidiaries include:** C&G Systems, Inc.; Stoody Company; Thermal Arc; Thermal Dynamics Corporation; Tweco Arcair; Victor Equipment Company; Thermadyne Welding Products Canada. **Listed on:** OTC Bulletin Board. **Stock Exchange symbol:** THMD.

THOMPSON COBURN LLP
One U.S. Bank Plaza, St. Louis MO 63101-1693. 314/552-6000. **Fax:** 314/552-7000. **Contact:** Personnel. **World Wide Web address:** http://www.thompsoncoburn.com. **Description:** A corporate law firm. **NOTE:** Search and apply for positions online. **Special programs:** Summer Associate Program. **Corporate headquarters location:** This location. **Other U.S. locations:** Washington DC; Belleville IL. **Number of employees nationwide:** 300.

TOASTMASTER, INC.
1801 North Stadium Boulevard, Columbia MO 65202. 573/445-8666. **Contact:** Human Resources. **World Wide Web address:** http://www.toastmaster.com. **Description:** Toastmaster designs, manufactures, markets, and services a wide array of electrical consumer appliances and timepieces including kitchen counter-top appliances, electric fans, heaters, and clocks. **Corporate headquarters location:** This location. **Parent company:** Salton Inc.

TOASTMASTER, INC.
708 South Missouri Street, Macon MO 63552. 660/385-3136. **Contact:** Human Resources. **World Wide Web address:** http://www.toastmaster.com. **Description:** Toastmaster designs, manufactures, markets, and services a wide array of electrical consumer appliances and timepieces including kitchen counter-top appliances, electric fans, heaters, and clocks. **Corporate headquarters location:** Columbia MO. **Operations at this facility include:** This location is a distribution center.

TOMKINS INDUSTRIES INC.
RUSKIN DIVISION
3900 Doctor Greaves Road, Grandview MO 64030. 816/761-7476. **Fax:** 816/765-8955. **Contact:** Human Resources. **E-mail address:** hr@ruskin.com. **World Wide Web address:** http://www.ruskin.com. **Description:** Manufactures sheet metal and provides related services.

TONY'S INC.
410 Market Street, St. Louis MO 63102. 314/231-7007. **Fax:** 314/231-4740. **Contact:** Human Resources. **World Wide Web address:** http://www.tonysstlouis.com. **Description:** Owners and operators of a restaurant specializing in continental Italian cuisine. **Number of employees at this location:** 90.

TRADCO, INC.
1701 West Main Street, Washington MO 63090. 636/239-7816. **Fax:** 636/239-3214. **Contact:** George Schrecengost, President and General Manager. **World Wide Web address:** http://www.tradco-inc.com. **Description:** Manufacturers and processors of titanium sheets; economy blanking dies; and aircraft component parts and assemblies. Tradco, Inc. is also engaged in titanium hot forming and blanking.

TRIPOS INC.
1699 South Hanley Road, Suite 303, St. Louis MO 63105. 314/647-1099. **Toll-free phone:** 800/323-2960. **Fax:** 314/647-9241. **Contact:** Human Resources Manager. **E-mail address:** hr@tripos.com. **World Wide Web address:** http://www.tripos.com. **Description:** A provider of discovery chemistry, integrated discovery software products, software consulting services, and discovery research services to the pharmaceutical, biotechnology, agrochemical, and other life sciences industries. **NOTE:** Search and apply for positions online. **Positions advertised include:** Controller; Database Application Developer. **Corporate headquarters location:** This location. **Listed on:** NASDAQ. **Stock exchange symbol:** TRPS.

TRUMAN MEDICAL CENTER LAKEWOOD
7900 Lees Summit Road, Kansas City MO 64139. 816/373-4485. **Fax:** 816/478-7500. **Contact:** Human Resources. **World Wide Web address:** http://www.trumed.org. **Description:** A medical center with 92 acute care beds and 212 long-term care beds. Truman Medical Center Lakewood provides medical care and education under the direction of the Department of Community and Family Medicine. **NOTE:** Search and apply for positions online.

TRUMAN MEDICAL CENTER HOSPITAL HILL
2301 Holmes Street, Kansas City MO 64108. 816/404-1000. **Fax:** 816/556-4124. **Contact:** Corporate Director of Personnel. **World Wide Web address:** http://www.trumed.org. **Description:** The primary teaching hospital for the University of Missouri-Kansas City School of Health Sciences. Inpatient and outpatient services include the hospital's Level I trauma center; pregnancy and childbirth services; radiology services, which include an on-site MRI and a fully-accredited mammography program; and The Eye Foundation, which provides care for the eye. Truman Medical Center West also provides complete dental care, inpatient services, a skilled nursing unit, and a wide variety of outpatient clinics. **NOTE:** Search and apply for positions online.

TRUMAN STATE UNIVERSITY
106 McClain Hall, 100 East Normal Street, Kirksville MO 63501-4221. 660/785-4301. **Fax:** 660/785-7520. **Contact:** Human Resources Department. **E-mail address:** hrstaff@truman.edu. **World Wide Web address:** http://www.truman.edu. **Description:** A liberal-arts university with an undergraduate enrollment of 5,500 and 200 graduate students. Founded in 1867. **NOTE:** Search for positions online.

TUBULAR STEEL INC.
1031 Executive Parkway Drive, St. Louis MO 63141-6351. 314/851-9200. **Fax:** 314/851-9336. **Contact:** Human Resources. **E-mail address:** careers@tubularsteel.com. **World Wide Web address:** http://www.tubularsteel.com. **Description:** A nationwide distributor of carbon, alloy and stainless steel pipe, tubing and bar products. Founded in 1953. **NOTE:** Part-time jobs and second and third shifts are offered. Search and apply for positions online. **Positions advertised include:** Account Manager; Logistics Coordinator; Senior Level Operations and Logistics Manager. **Corporate headquarters location:** This location. **Other U.S. locations:** IL; OH; TX; CA; PA; WA: GA; MO. **Operations at this facility include:** Administration; Sales; Service. **Listed on:** Privately held. **President:** John C. Hauck. **Number of employees at this location:** 130. **Number of employees nationwide:** 300.

URS CORPORATION
1001 Highlands Drive West, Suite 300, St. Louis MO 63110. 314/429-0100. **Fax:** 314/429-0462. **Contact:** Human Resources. **World Wide Web address:** http://www.urscorp.com. **Description:** An architectural, engineering, and environmental consulting firm that specializes in air transportation, environmental solutions, surface transportation, and industrial environmental and engineering concerns. URS operates 300 offices in 20 countries. **NOTE:** Search and apply for positions online. **Positions advertised include:** Graduate Civil-Geotechnical Engineer; Inspector/Field Technician. **Corporate headquarters location:** San Francisco CA. **Number of employees worldwide:** 26,000.

U.S. BANK
202 East McPherson Street, Kirksville MO 63501. 660/665-8374. **Contact:** Human Resources. **World Wide Web address:** http://www.usbank.com. **Description:** A savings bank with 2,100 locations in 24 states. **NOTE:** Search and apply for positions online.

U.S. DEPARTMENT OF VETERANS AFFAIRS
VETERANS ADMINISTRATION MEDICAL CENTER
IRM Service, 915 North Grand, St. Louis 63106. 314/652-4100. **Physical address:** One Jefferson Barracks Drive, St. Louis MO 63125. **Contact:** Human Resources. **World Wide Web address:** http://www.va.gov/stlouis. **Description:** The VA health care system includes 171 medical centers; more than 364 outpatient, community, and outreach clinics; 130 nursing home care units; and 37 domiciliary residences. VA operates at least one medical center in each of the 48 contiguous states, Puerto Rico, and the District of Columbia. With approximately 76,000 medical center beds, VA treats nearly 1 million patients in VA hospitals, 75,000 in nursing home care units, and 25,000 in domiciliary residences. **Special programs:** Internships. **Corporate headquarters location:** Washington DC. **Operations at this facility include:** This location is a tertiary care, teaching medical center. **Parent company:** U.S. Department of Veterans Affairs.

U.S. FEDERAL RESERVE BANK OF ST. LOUIS
P.O. Box 442, St. Louis MO 63166. 314/444-8444. **Physical address:** 411 Locust Street, St. Louis MO 63102. **Contact:** Personnel. World Wide Web address: http://www.stls.frb.org. **Description:** One of 12 regional Federal Reserve banks that, along with the Federal Reserve Board of Governors in Washington DC and the Federal Open Market Committee, comprise the Federal Reserve System, the nation's central bank. As the nation's central bank, the Federal Reserve is charged with three major responsibilities: managing the nation's supply of money and credit, regulating certain banking institutions to ensure their safety and soundness, and serving as a bank for depository institutions and the federal government. **NOTE:** Search and apply for positions online. **Positions advertised include:** Recruiter; Strategic Consultant; Operations Analyst; Sr. Java Developer; Programmer Analyst; Sr. Programmer Analyst; Sr. Project Manager. **Operations at this facility include:** Regional Headquarters. **Number of employees at this location:** 800.

U.S. PAINT CORPORATION
831 South 21st Street, St. Louis MO 63103. 314/621-0525. **Fax:** 314/621-0722. **Contact:** Personnel Department. **World Wide Web address:** http://www.uspaint.com. **Description:** Manufactures a wide variety of industrial finishes. **Corporate headquarters location:** This location. **Operations at this facility include:** Administration; Manufacturing; Research and Development; Sales. **Number of employees at this location:** 110.

UNILEVER
4720 Scruggs Station Road, Jefferson City MO 65109. 573/638-7249. **Contact:** Human Resources. **World Wide Web address:** http://www.unilever.com. **Description:** A manufacturer of soaps and detergents. **Number of employees worldwide:** 247,000.

UNION PACIFIC RAILROAD
210 North 13th Street, St. Louis MO 63103. 314/992-2000. **Contact:** Human Resources. **World Wide Web address:** http://www.up.com. **Description:** the largest railroad in North America, covering 23 states. **NOTE:** Search and apply for positions online. **Parent company:** Union Pacific Corporation is a diversified conglomerate including railroad, holding companies, oil and petroleum exploration and development, real estate, waste management, and other operations. Through its subsidiaries, the company owns over 22 million acres of undeveloped property for oil production, interest in the Black Butte mine, industrial waste facilities, three landfills in Oklahoma and Utah, and 17,835 miles of rail, which link the Pacific and Gulf Coasts with the Midwest. Subsidiaries include Skyway Freight Systems and USPCI, Inc. **Number of employees nationwide:** 47,000.

UNITED HEALTH CARE OF THE MIDWEST
13655 Riverport Drive, P.O. Box 2560, Maryland Heights MO 63043. 314/592-7000. **Contact:** Human Resources. **World Wide Web address:** http://www.unitedhealthcare.com. **Description:** United Health Care of the Midwest operates closely related managed health and dental care plans that provide comprehensive health services to its members. **NOTE:** Search and apply for positions online. **Positions advertised include:** Pharmacy Business Development Manager; Market Medical Expense Management Specialist. **Parent company:** UnitedHealth Group.

UMB FINANCIAL CORPORATION
1010 Grand Boulevard, Kansas City MO 64108. 816/860-7000. **Contact:** Human Resources. **World Wide Web address:** http://www.umb.com. **Description:** A diverse banking and financial services company with 165 banking centers in Missouri, Illinois, Colorado, Kansas, Oklahoma, and Nebraska. **NOTE:** Search and apply for positions online. **Positions advertised include:** Group Audit Director; Sr. Auditor. **Subsidiaries include:** UMB Bank.

UMB BANK
2 South Broadway, St. Louis MO 63102-1713. 314/621-1000. **Contact:** Human Resources Department. **World Wide Web address:** http://www.umb.com. **Description:** A national bank doing business as a member of the Federal Reserve. **NOTE:** Search and apply for positions online. **Parent company:** UMB Financial Corporation.

UNITED VAN LINES INC.
One United Drive, Fenton MO 63026. 636/343-3900. **Fax:** 636/349-8794. **Contact:** Human Resources. **E-mail address:** hr@unigroupin.com. **World Wide Web address:** http://www.unitedvanlines.com. **Description:** Offices of the international household goods moving service. **Parent company:** UniGroup Inc., also at this location.

UNIVERSITY OF MISSOURI/COLUMBIA
201 South Seventh Street, 130 Heinkel Building, Columbia MO 65211. 573/882-7976. **Recorded jobline:** 573/884-9675. **Contact:** Human Resources. **World Wide Web address:** http://www.missouri.edu. **Description:** A university offering 278 degree programs with an enrollment of 20,000 undergraduate and 6,300 graduate students. Founded in 1839. **NOTE:** Search and apply for positions online. **Positions advertised include:** Assistant Manager, University Club; Manager, Business/Fiscal Operations; Manager, Network Security; Project Director; Academic Advisor; Director of Development; Database Administrator; Programmer/Analyst; Health Physicist; Research Specialist; Sr. Veterinary Technician. **Special programs:** Internships. **Corporate headquarters location:** This location. **Number of employees nationwide:** 11,000.

UNIVERSITY OF MISSOURI/ST. LOUIS
222 General Services Building, 8001 Natural Bridge Road, St. Louis MO 63121-4499. 314/516-5804. **Fax:** 314/516-6463. **Recorded jobline:** 314/516-5926. **Contact:** Human Resource Services. **World Wide Web address:** http://www.umsl.edu. **Description:** A university offering 88 degree programs with an enrollment of 16,000 students. **NOTE:** Search and apply for positions online. **Positions advertised include:** Admissions counselor; Associate Vice Chancellor for Information Technology; System Administrator Specialist;

UNLIMITED WATER PROCESSING, INC.
6701 Lillian Avenue, St. Louis MO 63136. 314/381-8591. **Toll-free phone:** 888/381-4466. **Fax:** 314/381-8648. **Contact:** Human Resources. World Wide Web address: http://unlimitedwater.net. **Description:** Processes, bottles, and sells processed drinking water in eight-ounce, one-gallon, and five-gallon bottles. The company also rents and sells coolers for five-gallon bottled water.

VF JEANSWEAR
1900 Industrial Drive, Lebanon MO 65536. 417/588-3281. **Fax: 417/532-7821. Contact:** Human Resources Department. **World Wide Web address:** http://www.vfc.com. **Description:** Manufactures and distributes jeans and related apparel. **Corporate headquarters location:** Greensboro NC. **Parent company:** VF Corporation.

VML
250 Richards Road, Kansas City MO 64116. 816/283-0700. **Fax:** 816/283-0954. **Contact:** Human Resources. **World Wide Web address:** http://www.vml.com. **Description:** An advertising firm that blends marketing and technology through strategic campaigns, web interaction, and software design. **Positions advertised include:** Lead Project Manager; Sr. Account Manager; Experience Architect; Research Analyst. **Other U.S. locations:** Dallas TX; White Salmon WA; Jacksonville FL; New York NY.

VALENTINE-RADFORD, INC.
P.O. Box 13407, Kansas City MO 64199. 816/842-5021. **Physical address:** 911 Main Street, Suite 1000, Kansas City MO 64105. **Contact:** Human Resources. **World Wide Web address:** http://www.valrad.com. **Description:** An advertising agency.

VALLEY FARM DAIRY COMPANY INC.
P.O. Box 78039, St. Louis MO 63178. 314/535-0800. **Contact:** Personnel Department. **Description:** Producers, processors, retailers, and wholesalers of fluid milk, cream, and related products.

VANGUARD PLASTICS INC.
1780 Belt Way Drive, St. Louis MO 63114. 314/428-3020. **Toll-free phone:** 800/969-2247. **Fax:** 314/423-7251. **Contact:** Human Resources. **World Wide Web address:** http://www.vplast.com. **Description:** A manufacturer of blow-molded custom and stock plastic containers.

CHARLES F. VATTEROTT & COMPANY
10449 St. Charles Rock Road, St. Louis MO 63114. 314/427-4000. **Contact:** Personnel Department. **Description:** A residential construction firm.

VI-JON LABORATORIES, INC.
8515 Page Avenue, St. Louis MO 63114. 314/427-1000. **Fax:** 314/427-1010. **Contact:** Human Resources Manager. **E-mail address:** hr@vijon.com. **World Wide Web address:** http://www.vijon.com. **Description:** Wholesalers of a variety of pharmaceuticals and cosmetics. **NOTE:** Search for positions online. **Positions advertised include:** Buyer; Sr. Buyer; Material Planning Coordinator; Chemical Processing Manager; **Corporate headquarters location:** This location. **Operations at this facility include:** Manufacturing. **Listed on:** Privately held. **Number of employees at this location:** 100.

VIACOM OUTDOOR
6767 North Hanley Road, St. Louis MO 63134. 314/524-0800. **Fax:** 314/524-5047. **Contact:** Personnel Department. **World Wide Web address:** http://www.viacomoutdoor.com. **Description:** An advertising agency specializing in the design of billboards and billposters. **Other U.S. locations:** Nationwide. **Parent company:** Viacom, Inc.

VIATECH PUBLISHING SOLUTIONS
424 North Cedarbrook, Springfield MO 65802-2576. 417/866-0822. **Toll-free phone:** 800/888-0823. **Fax:** 417/866-8459. **Contact:** Human Resources Department. **World Wide Web address:** http://www.viatechpub.com. **Description:** Offers print-on-demand and book binding services. ViaTech Publishing Solutions also manufactures loose-leaf catalog binders and plastic tab indexes.

VISITING NURSE ASSOCIATION OF GREATER ST. LOUIS
9450 Manchester Road, Suite 206, St. Louis MO 63119. 314/918-7171. **Fax:** 314/918-8053. **Contact:** Human Resources Department. **World Wide Web address:** http://www.vnastl.com. **Description:** Provides in-home health services and support to terminally-ill patients and their family. Services include nursing, physical therapy, occupational therapy, speech pathology, nutritional therapy, mental health and enterostomal therapy, medical social services, and hospice care. **Office hours:** Monday - Friday, 8:00 a.m. - 4:15 p.m. **Operations at this facility include:** Service. **Number of employees at this location:** 45.

WALGREEN CO.
440 North Highway 67, Florissant MO 63031. 314/837-5500. **Contact:** Personnel Department. **World Wide Web address:** http://www.walgreens.com. **Description:** Walgreen's is one of the largest retail drug store chains in the United States, which sells prescription and nonprescription drugs, cosmetics, toiletries, liquor and beverages, tobacco, and general merchandise. **NOTE:** Search and apply for positions online. **Operations at this facility include:** This location is the district office.

WASHINGTON UNIVERSITY IN ST. LOUIS
7425 Forsyth Boulevard, Box 1178, St. Louis MO 63105. 314/935-5990. **Fax:** 314/935-9780. **Contact:** Personnel. **E-mail address:** human_resources@aismail.wustl.edu. **World Wide Web address:** http://www.wustl.edu. **Description:** A four-year university that offers 90 programs and has an enrollment of 6,500 undergraduate and 5,500 graduate students. Founded in 1853. **NOTE:** Search and apply for positions online. **Positions advertised include:** Associate Director of Development; Contract Manager; Director, donor Relations and Major Gifts; Hazardous Materials Manager; LAN Engineer; Research Statistician; Summer School and Special Sessions Coordinator. **Number of employees at this location:** 10,500.

WATERLOO INDUSTRIES
1500 Waterloo Road, P.O. Box 1501, Sedalia MO 65301. 660/826-0960. **Contact:** Human Resources. **World Wide Web address:** http://www.waterlooindustries.com. **Description:** Manufactures tool cabinets and related products including metal saw stands. **Corporate headquarters location:** Waterloo IA. **Parent company:** Fortune Brands, Inc.

WATLOW ELECTRIC MANUFACTURING COMPANY
12001 Lackland Road, St. Louis MO 63146. 314/878-4600. **Contact:** Personnel Department. **E-mail address:** info@watlow.com. **World Wide Web address:** http://www.watlow.com. **Description:** Manufactures industrial electric heating elements and other electric apparatus. **Positions advertised include:** Strategic Marketing Manager; VP Marketing.

WAVE THOMSON LEARNING
WestChase Park, 10845 Olive Boulevard, Suite 250, St. Louis MO 63141. 314/692-1933. **Fax:** 314/995-3886. **Contact:** Human Resources. **World Wide Web address:** http://www.wavetech.com. **Description:** Offers help desk support, courseware products, and computer training programs.

FRED WEBER INC.
2320 Creve Coeur Mill Road, P.O. Box 2501, Maryland Heights MO 63043-8501. 314/344-0070. **Fax:** 314/344-0970. **Contact:** Jackie O'Leary, VP Human Resources. **E-mail address:** jsoleary@fredweberinc.com. **World Wide Web address:** http://www.fredweberinc.com. **Description:** A contractor specializing in highway construction, stone quarries, asphalt plants, sand plants, and commercial construction.

WEBSTER UNIVERSITY
470 East Lockwood Avenue, St. Louis MO 63119. 314/968-7192. **Recorded jobline:** 314/968-7114. **Contact:** Julie Dreiling, Human Resources. **E-mail address:** dreilija@webster.edu. **World Wide Web address:** http://www.webster.edu. **Description:** A four-year university offering undergraduate and graduate programs. **NOTE:** Search and apply for positions online. **Positions advertised include:** Assistant Director, Employment Services; Development Officer for Alumni Programs; Network Coordinator; Director of Academic Assessment.

THE WESTERN GROUP
1637 North Warson Road, St. Louis MO 63132. 314/427-6733. **Toll-free phone:** 800/325-2801. **Fax:** 314/427-6199. **Contact:** Human Resources. **E-mail address:** hr1@westerngroup. com. **World Wide Web address:** http://www.westerngroup.com. **Description:** A contractor engaged in masonry and concrete restoration and preventive waterproofing. The Western Group is also involved in exterior coating, epoxy injection, pedestrian and vehicle traffic systems, and specialty roofing construction. **Number of employees nationwide:** 1,000.

WESTERN LITHOTECH
2625 North Neergard Avenue, Springfield MO 65803. 417/831-4949. **Contact:** Personnel Coordinator/Benefits Administrator. **World Wide Web address:** http://www.westernlithotech.com. **Description:** Manufactures lithographic plates, chemicals, and high-speed exposure/processing systems. **Corporate headquarters location:** This location. **Other U.S. locations:** Springfield MO; Jacksonville TX. **Parent company:** Lastra America Corporation. **Operations at this facility include:** Administration; Manufacturing; Research and Development; Sales; Service. **Number of employees at this location:** 145.

WESTERN MISSOURI MEDICAL CENTER
403 Burkarth Road, Warrensburg MO 64093-3101. 660/747-2500. **Fax:** 660/747-8455. **Contact:** Human Resources. **E-mail address:** aowens@wmmconline.org. **World Wide Web address:** http://www.wmmconline.org. **Description:** A 104-bed acute care hospital with a 14-bed skilled nursing facility. **Positions advertised include:** RN's; LPN's; CNA's; Director of Quality/Risk; Compliance Coordinator; Physical Therapist. **Operations at this facility include:** Administration; Service. **Number of employees at this location:** 315.

WESTERN SUPPLIES COMPANY
2920 Cass Avenue, St. Louis MO 63106. 314/531-0100. **Fax:** 314/531-0126. **Contact:** Human Resources. **Description:** A manufacturer of cutting dies and shoe machinery. The company is engaged in machine shop work and specializes in dies and machinery for heat-sealing thermoplastics.

WESTERN UNION FINANCIAL SERVICES INC.
13022 Hollenberg Drive, P.O. Box 4430, Bridgeton MO 63044-2409. 314/291-8000. **Toll-free phone:** 800/325-6000. **Contact:** Anne Barrett, Manager of Personnel and Training. **World Wide Web address:** http://www.westernunion.com. **Description:** A

customer service center that provides money transfer and message services to the public. Founded in 1851. **NOTE:** Entry-level positions, part-time jobs, and second and third shifts are offered. **Company slogan:** The fastest way to send money worldwide. **Special programs:** Training; Co-ops; Summer Jobs. **Corporate headquarters location:** Greenwood Village CO. **International locations:** Worldwide. **Parent company:** First Data Corporation. **Operations at this facility include:** Service. **Listed on:** New York Stock Exchange. **Stock exchange symbol:** FDC. **Number of employees at this location:** 750. **Number of employees nationwide:** 36,000.

WHELAN SECURITY COMPANY INC.
1750 South Hanley Road, St. Louis MO 63144. 314/644-1974. **Contact:** Human Resources. **World Wide Web address:** http://www.transnationalsecurity.com. **Description:** Provides contract security guard services. **Special programs:** Internships. **Corporate headquarters location:** This location. **Other U.S. locations:** LA; IL; KS; TX. **Operations at this facility include:** Administration; Regional Headquarters; Service. **Listed on:** Privately held. **Number of employees nationwide:** 1,500.

WILLERT HOME PRODUCTS INC.
4044 Park Avenue, St. Louis MO 63110. 314/772-2822. **Fax:** 314/772-3506. **Contact:** Personnel Director. **E-mail address:** hr@willert.com. **World Wide Web address:** http://www.willert.com. **Description:** A consumer products manufacturer specializing in the production of such items as household deodorants, moth preventatives, plastic ashtrays, and potpourri products. **Corporate headquarters location:** This location. **Operations at this facility include:** Administration; Manufacturing; Regional Headquarters; Research and Development; Sales; Service. **Number of employees at this location:** 300.

WILLIAMS PATENT CRUSHER & PULVERIZER COMPANY
2701 North Broadway, St. Louis MO 63102. 314/621-3348. **Fax:** 314/436-2639. **Contact:** Personnel. **World Wide Web address:** http://www.williamscrusher.com. **Description:** Manufactures crushing and pulverizing equipment, air moving equipment, and material conveyors.

WINNTECH
7023 East 12th Terrace, Kansas City MO 64125. 816/241-4002. **Fax:** 816/241-1288. **Contact:** Theresa Lusk, Director of Human Resources. **E-mail address:** theresal@winntech.com. **World Wide Web address:** http://www.winntech.com. **Description:** A full-service design and marketing firm with in-house production capabilities.

WONDERBREAD/HOSTESS CAKES
6301 North Broadway, St. Louis MO 63147. 314/385-1600. **Contact:** Personnel Department. **Description:** Manufactures bread, cake, and other bakery products. **Corporate headquarters location:** This location.

WORLD WIDE TECHNOLOGY INC.
127 Weldon Parkway, St. Louis MO 63043. 314/569-7000. **Fax:** 314/919-1441. **Contact:** Human Resources. **E-mail address:** careers@wwt.com. **World Wide Web address:** http://www.wwt.com. **Description:** Provides information technology solutions for e-commerce supply chains. **Positions advertised include:** Contract Administrator; Maintenance Coordinator; Price Analyst; Business Systems Analyst; Lab Manager. **Other U.S. locations:** Phoenix AZ; Livermore CA; Los Angeles CA; Detroit MI; Reno NV; Nashville TN; Austin TX; Plano TX; San Antonio TX; Mclean VA.

WYETH
4766 LaGuardia Drive, St. Louis MO 63134. 314/426-5000. **Fax:** 314/426-6229. **Contact:** Human Resources. **E-mail address:** wyeth@trackcareers.com. **World Wide Web address:** http://www.wyeth.com. **Description:** Performs biotechnology research contributing to the application and creation of recombinant DNA technology. **Corporate headquarters location:** Madison NJ. **Other U.S. locations:** Nationwide. **Operations at this facility include:** Administration; Manufacturing. **Number of employees worldwide:** 52,000.

XTRA LEASE
1801 Park 270 Drive, Suite 400, St. Louis MO 63146. 314/579-9300. **Toll-free phone:** 800/325-1453. **Fax:** 314/542-2150. **Contact:** Human Resources. **E-mail address:** humanresources@xtra.com. **World Wide Web address:** http://www.xtralease.com. **Description:** Leases trailers, containers, and chassis to railroads as well as trailers for over-the-road use. Operates 90 locations in North America. **NOTE:** Complete job profile form online. **Corporate headquarters location:** This location. **Parent company:** XTRA Corporation.

XYQUAD INC.
2921 South Brentwood Boulevard, St. Louis MO 63144-2700. 314/961-5995. **Toll-free phone:** 800/228-3168. **Fax:** 314/961-8094. **Contact:** Human Resources. **World Wide Web address:** http://www.xyquad.com. **Description:** A computer integration firm, specializing in systems automation and providing a variety of computer related services to financial, industrial and government clients nationwide. **Corporate headquarters location:** This location.

YMCA OF GREATER ST. LOUIS
1528 Locust Street, St. Louis MO 63103-1816. 314/436-4100. **Contact:** Jean Hubler, Vice President of Human Resources. **World Wide Web address:** http://www.ymca.com. **Description:** The YMCA provides health and fitness, social and personal development, Provides health and fitness, social and personal development, sports and recreation, education and career development, and camps and conferences to children, youths, adults, the elderly, families, the disabled, refugees and foreign nationals. **NOTE:** Search for positions online.

YMCA OF SPRINGFIELD
417 South Jefferson Avenue, Springfield MO 65806. 417/862-7456. **Contact:** Human Resources. **World Wide Web address:** http://www.ymca.com. **Description:** Provides health and fitness, social and personal development, sports and recreation, education and career development, and camps and conferences to children, youths, adults, the elderly, families, the disabled, refugees and foreign nationals.

YELLOW FREIGHT SYSTEMS, INC.
400 Barton Street, St. Louis MO 63104. 314/772-2905. **Fax:** 314/865-7201. **Contact:** Personnel Department. **World Wide Web address:** http://www.myyellow.com. **Description:** A national long-haul truckload carrier, with over 585 terminal locations in 50 states, Puerto Rico, and many Canadian provinces. **NOTE:** Search for positions online. Submit resume and letter of interest to local facility. **Corporate headquarters location:** Overland Park KS. **Parent company:** Yellow Corporation. **Number of employees worldwide:** 28,000.

THE YOUNG GROUP, LTD.
1054 Central Industrial Drive, St. Louis MO 63110. 314/771-3080. **Fax:** 314/771-1842. **Contact:** Human Resources. **World Wide Web address:** http://www.theyounggroup.com. **Description:** A sheet metal fabricator and contractor. **Corporate headquarters location:** This location. **Operations at this facility include:** Administration; Manufacturing; Sales.

ZENITH AIRCRAFT COMPANY
P.O. Box 650, Mexico Municipal Airport, Mexico MO 65265. 573/581-9000. **Fax:** 573/581-0011. **Contact:** Personnel. **E-mail address:** info@zenithair.com. **World Wide Web address:** http://www.zenithair.com. **Description:** A company that designs and produces a line of all metal kit aircraft.

ZURHEIDE-HERRMANN INC.
4333 Clayton Avenue, St. Louis MO 63110. 314/652-6805. **Contact:** Ronald Dahman, President. **Description:** Provides engineering and architectural services. **Special programs:** Internships. **Corporate headquarters location:** This location. **Other U.S. locations:** Champaign IL. **Operations at this facility include:** Service. **Number of employees at this location:** 35.

ASARCO INC.
P.O. Box 1230, East Helena MT 59635. 406/227-4098. **Contact:** Human Resources. **World Wide Web address:** http://www.asarco.com. **Description:** A producer of nonferrous metals, principally copper, lead, zinc, and silver, from its own mines and through its interest in Southern Peru Copper Corporation. Asarco also produces specialty chemicals and construction aggregates and provides environmental services. Asarco's copper operations are conducted through its Mission and Ray mines in Arizona; smelters in Hayden, Arizona, and El Paso, Texas; and a refinery in Amarillo, Texas. In Missouri, the company operates an integrated lead circuit consisting of West Fork and Sweetwater mines which provide over 90 percent of the feed for the nearby Glover smelter and refinery. The Tennessee mines division accounts for 57 percent of the zinc concentrates produced by the company. The remaining 43 percent is produced as a co-product at the West Fork and Sweetwater lead mines in Missouri and at the Leadville mine in Colorado. **Corporate headquarters location:** Phoenix AZ. **Parent company:** Grupo Mexico S.A. de C.V. **Operations at this facility include:** This location processes lead and zinc oxide. **Number of employees at this location:** 19

ASH GROVE CEMENT COMPANY
100 Highway 518, Clancy MT 59634-9701. 406/442-8855. **Contact:** Office Manager. **World Wide Web address:** http://www.ashgrove.com. **Description:** Ash Grove Cement Company produces cement, lime, ready-mixed concrete, and crushed stone. **Positions advertised include:** Plant Manager; Production Manager; Maintenance Manager; Process Engineer; Plant Engineer; Chief Chemist; Environmental and Safety Manager; Quarry Superintendent; Human Resources Manager; Sales Representative; Traffic Manager; Geologist; Corporate Attorney. **Special programs:** Manufacturing Development Program; Summer Program. **Corporate headquarters location:** Overland Park KS. **Operations at this facility include:** This location produces cement.

BIG HORN COUNTY MEMORIAL HOSPITAL
200 North Mitchell, Hardin MT 59034. 406/665-2310. **Fax:** 406/665-9238 **Physical address:** 17 North Miles Avenue, Hardin MT 59034. **Contact:** Human Resources. **Description:** A not-for-profit general medical and surgical hospital with 16 beds. Big Horn County Memorial Hospital also operates a nursing home with 37 beds. **Annual sales/revenues:** $5 - $10 million. **Number of employees at this location:** 59

THE BIG MOUNTAIN SKI & SUMMER RESORT
WINTER SPORTS, INC. (WSI)
P.O. Box 1400, Whitefish MT 59937. 406/862-1937. **Toll-free phone:** 800/858-3930. **Fax:** 406/862-1998. **Contact:** Director of Human Resources. **E-mail address:** jobs@bigmtn.com. **World Wide Web address:** http://www.bigmtn.com. **Description:** A full-service resort featuring 3000 acres of skiable terrain, 11 ski lifts, 11 food and beverage operations, nine retail shops, child care, ski and snowboard school, and slopeside lodging for over 1600 guests. **NOTE:** Entry-level positions are offered. **Special programs:** Internships. **Office hours:** Monday - Friday, 8:00 a.m. - 4:30 p.m. **Corporate headquarters location:** This location. **Subsidiaries include:** Big Mountain Water Company furnishes the domestic water supply to the resort and adjacent properties. Big Mountain Development Corporation oversees and coordinates the planning and development of certain parcels owned by Winter Sports, Inc. **Operations at this facility include:** Administration; Sales; Service. **Annual sales/revenues:** $11 - $20 million. **Number of employees at this location:** 450.

BILLINGS GAZETTE
P.O. Box 36300, Billings MT 59107-6300. 406/657-1478. **Contact:** Jay Strever. **E-mail address:** bghr@billingsgazette.com. **World Wide Web address:** http://www.billingsgazette.com. **Description:** Publishes a daily newspaper with a circulation of 50,000. **Parent company:** Lee Enterprises.

BLUE CROSS BLUE SHIELD OF MONTANA, INC.
P.O. Box 4309, Helena MT 59604. 800/447-7828 x3410. **Physical address:** 560 North Park Avenue, Helena MT 59604. **Recorded jobline:** 800/821-0264. **Contact:** Human Resources. **E-mail address:** hr@bcbsmt.com. **World Wide Web address:** http://www.bcbsmt.com. **Description:** The company combines the financing and delivery of health care services into a single system. Participating physicians, hospitals, and other health care providers are directly involved in controlling the cost of health care. **Positions advertised include:** Customer Service and Claims Representative; Clerical Support Team Member; Individual Underwriter. **Other area locations:** Billings MT; Bozeman MT; Butte MT; Great Falls MT; Helena MT; Kalispell MT; Missoula MT. **Operations at this facility include:** Member Services and Marketing.

CENTURYTEL, INC.
290 North Main Street, Kalispell MT 59901. 406/758-1000. **Contact:** Personnel Department. **E-mail address:** staffing@centurytel.com. **World Wide Web address:** http://www.centurytel.com. **Description:** A regional integrated telephone communications company that provides local exchange, long-distance, wireless communications, operator, and data services in 22 states. **Corporate headquarters location:** Monroe LA. **Listed on:** New York Stock Exchange. **Stock exchange symbol:** CTL. **Chairman/CEO:** Glen Post III. **Annual sales/revenues:** $2 billion. **Number of employees nationwide:** 6,720.

COLUMBIA FALLS ALUMINUM COMPANY
2000 Aluminum Drive, Columbia Falls MT 59912. 406/892-8400. **Contact:** Human Resources. **World Wide Web address:** http://www. cfaluminum.com. **Description:** An aluminum producer. **Parent company:** Glencore International AG. **Operations at this facility include:** Administration; Manufacturing; Mechanical and Environmental Engineering.

CORIXA CORPORATION
553 Old Corvallis Road, Hamilton MT 59840. 406/363-6214. **Contact:** Human Resources. **E-mail address:** employment@corixa.com. **World Wide Web address:** http://www.corixa.com. **Description:** Involved in the research and development of immunotherapeutics to prevent or treat cancer, autoimmune diseases, and infectious diseases. **Positions advertised include:** Development Assistant/Associate. **Corporate headquarters location:** Seattle WA. **Other U.S. locations:** San Francisco CA. **Operations at this facility include:** Manufacturing and Adjuvant Development. **Listed on:** NASDAQ. **Stock exchange symbol:** CRXA. **Number of employees nationwide:** 380.

D.A. DAVIDSON & COMPANY
P.O. Box 5015, Great Falls MT 59403. 406/791-7467. **Physical address:** 8 Third Street North, Great Falls MT 59401. **Contact:** Dan McLaughlin. **World Wide Web address:** http://www.dadco.com. **Description:** A financial services holding company, security broker, and travel agency. Founded in 1935. **Positions advertised include:** Account Supervisor; IT Technician. **Corporate headquarters location:** This location. **Other U.S. locations:** ID; OR; UT; WA; WY. **Operations at this facility include:** Full-service investment firm. **Number of employees at this location:** 200. **Number of employees nationwide:** 750.

DEACONESS BILLINGS CLINIC
P.O. Box 37000, Billings MT 59107. 406/657-4000. **Physical address:** 2800 10th Avenue North, Billings MT 59101. **Recorded jobline:** 800/332-7156 x4600. **Contact:** Human Resources. **E-mail address:** careers@billingsclinic.org. **World Wide Web address:** http://www.billingsclinic.com. **Description:** A full-service, nonprofit, 272-bed regional medical center. Affiliates include Billings Clinic, a 140-physician multispecialty medical clinic with six locations; Deaconess Research Institute; Deaconess Foundation; and Deaconess Psychiatric Billings Clinic Services, which includes the Psychiatric Center and Behavioral Health Clinic, providing adults and youth with a continuum of comprehensive mental health care. Long-term care is provided through Aspen Meadows, a skilled nursing facility, and Deaconess Hospital's Transitional Care Unit. Cardiology services are provided at the Deaconess Medical Center and the Billings Clinic. Deaconess also provides a series of educational programs and a women's resource center. Three hundred physicians have hospital privileges. **Note:** Largest employer in Billings.

EMPIRE STEEL MANUFACTURING CO.
P.O. Box 2565, Billings MT 59103-2565. 406/252-0101. **Fax:** 406/252-9922. **Physical address:** 501 North 18th Street. **Contact:** Human Resources. **World Wide Web address:** http://www.empiresteel.com. **Description:** Manufacturer of corrugated steel culverts, steel plates, and steel tanks. **Corporate headquarters location:** This location. **Number of employees at this location:** 50.

FALLON MEDICAL COMPLEX
P.O. Box 820, Baker MT 59313-0820. 406/778-3331. **Toll-free phone:** 800/676-7161. **Fax:** 406/778-2488. **Physical address:** 202 South Fourth Street West, Baker MT 59313. **Contact:** Human Resources. **Description:** Fallon Medical Complex consists of three main divisions: a 40-bed nursing home; a 12-bed, acute care hospital providing general medical services, cardiac rehabilitation, chemotherapy, and outpatient surgery; and a clinic with two general practitioners and one physician's assistant.

FIRST INTERSTATE BANCSYSTEM, INC.
P.O. Box 30918, Billings MT 59116. 406/255-5375. **Physical address:** 401 North 31st Street, Billings MT 59101. **Fax:** 406/255-5213. **Recorded jobline:** 888/833-3449. **Contact:** Human Asset Management Group. **World Wide Web address:** http://www.firstinterstatebank.com. **Description:** A commercial banking holding company operating 59 branches throughout Montana and Wyoming offering depository and brokerage services, trust services, agricultural, commercial, real estate and consumer loans. Founded in 1968. **NOTE:** Applications are accepted on the company website. **Positions advertised include:** Administrative Assistant; Payroll Clerk; Accountant. **Corporate headquarters location:** This location. **Other U.S. locations:** WY. **Listed on:** Privately held. **Number of employees:** 1,600.

FIRST SECURITY BANK
P.O. Box 910, Bozeman MT 59771. 406/556-3760. **Fax:** 406/329-1993. **Physical address:** 208 East Main Street, Bozeman MT 59715. **Contact:** Cynthia Cheney. **World Wide Web address:** http://www.ourbank.com. **Description:** A full-service, locally owned, community bank with branches throughout southwest Montana.

5 STAR BUSINESS TECHNOLOGY GROUP
1515 Wyoming Street, Missoula MT 59801. 406/532-5454. **Fax:** 406/721-2744. **Contact:** Theodore Weber, Human Resources. **World Wide Web address:** http://www.cp4g.com. **Description:** Provides networking services for a variety of systems including Compaq and Hewlett-Packard. **Corporate headquarters location:** This location. **Annual sales/revenues:** Less than $5 million.

GLACIER BANCORP, INC.
49 Commons Loop, Kalispell MT 59901. 406/756-4200. **Toll-free phone:** 800/735-4371. **Fax:** 406/756-3518. **World Wide Web address:** http://www. glacierbancorp.com. **Description:** A multibank holding company with assets of more than $2.6 billion. **Corporate headquarters location:** This location. **Subsidiaries include:** Glacier Bank of Kalispell, Glacier Bank of Whitefish, First Security Bank of Missoula, Valley Bank of Helena, Big Sky Western Bank, Western Security Bank, Community First, Inc., Glacier Capital Trust I, and Mountain West Bank in Idaho and Utah. **Listed on:** NASDAQ. **Stock exchange symbol:** GBCI. **Chairman:** John MacMillan. **Annual sales/revenues:** $134 million. **Number of employees nationwide:** 642.

GREAT FALLS TRIBUNE COMPANY
P.O. Box 5468, Great Falls MT 59401. 406/791-1434. **Physical address:** 205 River Drive South, Great Falls MT 59405. **Toll-free phone:** 800/438-6600. **Contact:** Human Resources. **World Wide Web address:** http://www. greatfallstribune.com. **Description:** Regional newspaper with a daily circulation of 33,000 and Sunday circulation of 38,000. **Positions advertised include:** Advertising Sales Representative; Single Copy Sales Representative; Circulation. **Parent company:** Gannett Company, Inc. **Number of employees:** 185.

HKM ENGINEERING INC.
222 N 32nd Street, Billings MT 59101. 406/723-8213. **Fax:** 406/723-8328. **Contact:** Diane Beck, Personnel Director. **E-mail address:** dbeck@hkminc.com. **World Wide Web address:** http://www.hkminc.com. **Description:** Provides technology development, demonstration, and fabrication services to government agencies. The company operates in a variety of areas including plasma-based systems for the treatment of hazardous materials and waste; civil engineering design and project management; biological treatment, thermal spraying technologies; and specialized technology development and research services. **Positions advertised include:** Civil CAD Technician; Water Resources Project Manager; Senior Water/Wastewater Treatment Engineer; Transportation Engineer; Water Engineer. **Special programs:** Internships. **Corporate headquarters location:** This location. **Other area locations:** Bozeman MT; Butte MT; Miles City MT. **Other U.S. locations:** Rapid City SD; Sheridan WY. **Operations at this facility include:** Administration; Divisional Headquarters; Regional Headquarters; Research and Development. **Listed on:** Privately held. **Number of employees at this location:** 250. **Number of employees nationwide:** 360.

HOLCIM (US) INC.
4070 Trident Road, Three Forks MT 59752. 406/285-3241. **Contact:** Personnel Manager. **E-mail address:** holcim@aip.e-cruiter.com. **World Wide Web address:** http://www.holcim.com. **Description:** Manufactures and distributes portland cement. **Corporate headquarters location:** Dundee MI. **Other U.S. locations:** Nationwide. **Parent company:** Holcim Ltd. **Operations at this facility include:** Sales; Administration; Manufacturing. **Number of employees at this location:** 85. **Number of employees nationwide:** 2,400. **Number of employees worldwide:** 50,000.

HOLLY SUGAR
P.O. Box 1168, Sidney MT 59270. 406/433-3303. **Contact:** State Employment Office. **World Wide Web address:** http://www.imperialsugar.com. **Description:** Holly Sugar

produces sugar and related products such as beet pulp and molasses. **NOTE:** All employment inquiries should be directed to the State Employment Office, 211 North Central Avenue, Sidney MT 59270. 406/482-1204. **Corporate headquarters location:** Sugar Land TX. **Parent company:** Imperial Sugar Corporation.

HOLY ROSARY HEALTH CENTER
2600 Wilson Street, Miles City MT 59301-5094. 406/233-2600. **Contact:** Human Resources. **E-mail address:** sheryl.kron@hrh-mt.org. **World Wide Web address:** http://www.hrh-mt.org. **Description:** Holy Rosary Health Center consists of an acute care hospital with 44 beds, offering general medical and surgical services, chemotherapy treatments, and a 5-bed intensive care unit. The health center also operates a nursing home with 120 beds, 18 of which are in the skilled care unit and are devoted to physical rehabilitation. Opened in 1910. **Positions advertised include:** Director of Human Resources; Physician (various specialties); Registered Nurse; Surgical Services Nurse Manager. **Number of employees at this location:** 375

ILX LIGHTWAVE CORP.
P.O. Box 6310, Bozeman MT 59771. 406/586-1244. **Physical address:** 31950 East Frontage Road, Bozeman MT 59715. 406/586-1244. **Toll-free phone:** 800/459-9459. **Fax:** 406/586-9405. **Contact:** Human Resources. **E-mail address:** hr@ilxlightwave.com. **World Wide Web address:** http:// www.ilxlightwave.com. **Description:** Manufactures test and measurement equipment for fiber optic telecommunications specializing in laser diode instrumentation and equipment. Affiliates in Europe and Asia. Founded in 1986. **Positions advertised include:** Project Manager; Analog Development Engineer; Customer Service Engineer; Electronics Test Technician; Manufacturing Engineer; Optical Physicist Product Manager; Sales Engineer; Software Engineer; Firmware Engineer. **Corporate headquarters location:** This location. **Other U.S. locations:** Boulder CO. **International locations:** Japan; United Kingdom. **Listed on:** Privately held. **President/CEO:** Lawrence A. Johnson.

INSTY-PRINTS
39 South Tracy Avenue, Bozeman MT 59715. 406/586-7007. **Contact:** Store Manager. **World Wide Web address:** http://www.instybozeman. com. **Description:** Commercial printing, photocopying, and binding, as well as lithograph, prepress and offset printing operating two dozen outlets throughout Montana. **Other area locations:** Belgrade MT; Livingston MT; Billings MT; Hamilton MT; Polson MT; Kalispell MT; Great Falls MT; Missoula MT; Butte MT; Glasgow MT; Helena MT.

KALISPELL REGIONAL MEDICAL CENTER
310 Sunnyview Lane, Kalispell MT 59901. 406/752-1760. **Fax:** 406/257-5430. **Recorded jobline:** 406/756-4405. **Contact:** Human Resources Recruiter. **E-mail address:** human_resources@krmc.org. **World Wide Web address:** http://www.krmc.org. **Description:** A medical center that is also the primary referral center for northwest Montana. Facilities include a 100-bed hospital, a long-term care facility, a cancer center, a medical library, a birthing center, a chemical treatment center, the Brenden House, a nursing and rehabilitation facility, and Pathways Treatment Center, which offers behavioral health, psychiatric, and substance abuse treatment. The Center also offers emergency, home health, diabetes, diagnostic imaging, hospice, private care, nutritional, and helicopter rescue services. **Positions advertised include:** Licensed Practical Nurse; Certified Nurses Aide; Restorative Aide; Operating Room Technician; Home Health Aide; Respiratory Therapist; Registered Nurse; Infection Control; Patient Coordinator; Dietary Aide. **Number of employees at this location:** 1,300.

KIDS BEHAVIORAL HEALTH OF MONTANA, INC.
55 Basin Creek Road, Butte MT 59701-9704. 406/494-4183. **Toll-free phone:** 800/447-1067. **Contact:** Kristine Carpenter, Human Resources. **E-mail address:** kcarpenter@kidsbh.com. **World Wide Web address:** http://www.kidsofmontana.com. **Description:** An 85-bed child and adolescent psychiatric hospital that provides services on inpatient, outpatient, and day program bases. **Positions advertised include:** Mental Health Associate. **Number of employees at this location:** 200.

LATTICE MATERIALS CORPORATION
516 East Tamarack Street, Bozeman MT 59715. 406/586-2122. **Fax:** 406/587-9055. **Contact:** Human Resources. **E-mail address:** careers@latticematls.com. **World Wide Web address:** http://www.latticematerials.com. **Description:** Manufacturer and worldwide supplier of silicon and germanium products for infrared optics, sputter targets, as well as specialty parts for night vision, surgical instruments, precision cameras, and mirrors for lasers. Affiliate distributors in United Kingdom, France, Liechtenstein, Israel, South Korea, and South Africa. Founded in 1989. **Number of employees:** 35.

LOGISTICS SYSTEMS INC.
3000 Palmer Street, Missoula MT 59808. 406/728-0921. **Fax:** 406/728-8754. **Contact:** Human Resources. **E-mail address:** careers@logistic-systems.com. **World Wide Web address:** http://www.logistic-systems.com. **Description:** Develops logistics and inventory management software used by police and fire departments. **Positions advertised include:** Project Manager; Programmer; UNIX Trainer; Technical Support Troubleshooter; Software Tester; Information Technology Specialist; Network Administrator.

MEISSNER TRACTORS, INC.
P.O. Box 1111, Havre MT 59501. 406/265-5457. **Physical address:** US Hwy 2 West & US Hwy 87 North, Havre MT 59501. **Toll-free phone:** 800/800-3113. **Fax:** 406/265-4062. **Contact:** Arnold Lalum, General Manager. **World Wide Web address:** http://www.meissners.com. **Description:** Manufactures scrapers for construction machinery and large farm tractors. **Positions advertised include:** Accountant/Auditor; Draftsperson; Industrial Designer; Industrial Engineer; Manufacturer's/Wholesaler's Sales Representative; Mechanical Engineer; Quality Control Supervisor; Technical Writer/Editor. **Corporate headquarters location:** This location. **Other area locations:** Denton MT. **Operations at this facility include:** Administration; Manufacturing; Research and Development.

MIDWEST TECHNOLOGIES, INC.
90 West Central Avenue, Belgrade MT 59714. 406/586-2658. **Contact:** Human Resources. **World Wide Web address:** http://mid-tech.com. **Description:** Manufactures electronic chemical applicator controls for agricultural applications and produces direct injected sprayer control technologies using internally expandable systems compatible with GPS/GIS technology and handles both liquid and granular applications as well as applications and record keeping of chemical and fertilizer applications for site-specific farming. **Corporate headquarters location:** Springfield IL.

MILK RIVER COOPERATIVE
P.O. Box 990, Havre MT 59501. 406/265-2296. **Physical address:** 5 First Street, Havre MT 59501. **Fax:** 406/265-5651. **Contact:** Human Resources. **Description:** An agricultural cooperative that provides a variety of products and services. Products include petroleum and feeds, and services include wheat milling; food manufacturing and distribution; and oilseed processing and refining. **Corporate headquarters location:** St. Paul MN.

THE MISSOULIAN
P.O. Box 8029, Missoula MT 59807. 406/523-5200. **Physical address:** 500 South Higgins Avenue, Missoula MT 59801. **Toll-free phone:** 800/366-7102. **Fax:** 406/523-5221. **Contact:** HR Manager. **World Wide Web address:** http://www.missoulian.com. **Description:** Regional newspaper with a daily circulation of 30,000 and Sunday circulation of 35,000. **Parent company:** Lee Enterprises.

MISSOURI RIVER MANOR
1130 17th Avenue, South Great Falls MT 59405. 406/771-4507. **Fax:** 406/761-6020. **Contact:** Peak Medical Corporation Human Resources, P.O. Box 94060, Albuquerque NM 87199. **World Wide Web address:** http://www.peakmedicalcorp.com/facility/mt/missouri/missouri.html. **Description:** A nursing home with 278 beds offering nursing care, restorative programs, and physical rehabilitation. **Positions advertised include:** Facility Administrator; Director of Nursing. **Parent company:** Peak Medical Corporation.

MONTANA DEPARTMENT OF ENVIRONMENTAL QUALITY
P.O. Box 200901, Helena MT 59620. 406/444-4218. **Physical address:** 1520 East Sixth Avenue, Helena MT 59601. **Fax:** 406/444-4386. **Contact:** Diane Neff, Personnel Department. **E-mail address:** dineff@state.mt.us. **World Wide Web address:** http://www.deq.state.mt.us. **Description:** The environmental management agency for the state of Montana with divisions for enforcing water quality regulations, issuing permits, and assessing environmental impact compliance. **NOTE:** Application materials can be found on http://www.employmontana.com. **Positions advertised include:** Contracts Officer; Data Management Section Supervisor; Project Manager; Special Projects Manager; Systems Analyst; Water Quality Specialist. **Other area locations:** Billings; Kalispell; Ronan; Missoula.

MONTANA STATE HOSPITAL
P.O. Box 300, Warm Springs MT 59756. 406/693-7000. **Physical Address:** 300 Garnet Way, Warm Springs MT 59756. **Contact:** Human Resources. **Description:** A state psychiatric hospital with 200 beds that provides inpatient care for adults. **Positions advertised include:** Director of Human Resources; Physician Assistant; Psychiatric Nurse; Licensed Practical Nurse; Recreation Therapist.

MONTANA STATE UNIVERSITY/BILLINGS
1500 University Drive, Billings MT 59101-0298. 406/657-2278. **Fax:** 406/657-2120. **Recorded jobline:** 406/657-2116. **Contact:** Patty Rukstad, Interim Director. **E-mail address:** employment@msubillings.edu. **World Wide Web address:** http://www.msubillings.edu. **Description:** Montana State University/Billings consists of a graduate studies program and four undergraduate programs: Arts and Sciences; Business; Education; and Human Services; and a separately located two-year College of Technology. Unique within the university system are undergraduate and graduate programs in special education, human services, and rehabilitation counseling. The Center for Continuing Education, Summer Session, and Community Services provides a wide variety of professional courses, workshops, seminars, and conferences across the state. A faculty of about 190 serves a student body of approximately 4,000. Founded in 1927. **Positions advertised include:** Administrative Associate; Assistant Professor; Associate Professor; Full Professor; University Lecturer; Instructor. **Chancellor:** Dr. Ronald P. Sexton. **Number of employees at this location:** 500.

MONTANA STATE UNIVERSITY - NORTHERN
P.O. Box 7751, Havre MT 59501. 406/265-3700. **Toll-free phone:** 800/662-6132. **Fax:** 406/265-3777. **Contact:** Employee Relations Specialist. **E-mail address:** emprel@msun.edu. **World Wide Web address:** http://www.msun.edu. **Description:** Montana State University - Northern is a comprehensive university serving approximately 1,640 students seeking technical and liberal arts educations. The university offers certificate, associate's, bachelor's, and master's degrees. **Other area locations:** Great Falls MT; Lewistown MT. **Chancellor:** Alexander Capdeville.

MONTANA TECH OF THE UNIVERSITY OF MONTANA
1300 West Park, Butte MT 59701. 406/496-4280. **Toll-free phone:** 800/445-7324. **Contact:** Personnel Office. **E-mail address:** cisakson@mtech.edu. **World Wide Web address:** http://www. mtech.edu. **Description:** Montana Tech of the University of Montana is an engineering, science, and computer science institution offering degrees that specialize in mineral and energy-related engineering education and in related areas in the arts and sciences. Montana Tech offers 13 undergraduate degree programs (with 18 concentrations available) and 11 graduate degree programs. Founded in 1900. **Positions advertised include:** Director of Nursing Programs; Assistant Professor; Team Leader; Training Specialist; Research Assistant.

MSE TECHNOLOGY APPLICATIONS, INC.
P.O. Box 4078, Butte MT 59702. 406/494-7385. **Physical address:** 200 Technology Way, Butte MT 59701. **Fax:** 406/494-7230. **Contact:** Leslie Clark, Human Resources Manager. E-mail address: lesliec@mse-ta.com. **World Wide Web address:** http://www.mse-ta.com. **Description:** An advanced technology development firm that manages federal government technology research and development. The company develops, tests, evaluates, and deploys technologies for the energy and aerospace sector. The company maintains a Tetragenics Division, which manufactures communications software and hardware for monitoring and control systems used in hydroelectric plants. **Corporate headquarters location:** This location. **Other area locations:** Bozeman MT. **Other U.S. locations:** Sacramento CA; Washington DC; Idaho Falls ID; Fort Bragg NC; Pittsburgh PA; Richland WA; Morgantown WV. **Subsidiaries include:** Tetragenics Division. **Number of employees nationwide:** 206.

NORTHROP GRUMMAN MISSION SYSTEMS
2401 Colonial Drive, Helena MT 59601. 406/443-8600. **Contact:** Human Resources. **World Wide Web address:** http://www.Northropgrumman.com. **Description:** This is the former TRW Systems location that develops software. Overall, the company is an information technology services firm whose operating subsidiaries provide research and development and contract support to clients in the following industries: aerospace, automotive markets, national defense, communications, energy, transportation, environmental, and other areas. **Sector headquarters:** Reston VA. **Positions advertised include:** Systems Engineer; IS Technologist. **Corporate headquarters:** Los Angeles CA. **Other U.S. locations:** Nationwide. **International locations:** Worldwide. **Parent company:** TRW/Mission Systems remains a wholly owned subsidiary of the Northrop Grumman Corporation. **Listed on:** New York Stock Exchange. **Stock exchange symbol:** NOC. **Number of employees nationwide:** 15,000.

NORTHWESTERN ENERGY
40 East Broadway, Butte MT 59701. 406/497-2587. **Contact:** Human Resources Northwestern Corporation, 125 South Dakota Avenue, Sioux Falls SD 57104. **E-mail**

address: careers@northwestern.com. **World Wide Web address:** http://www.northwesternenergy.com. **Description:** Supplies electricity, natural gas, oil, and coal to customers throughout the state, and provides energy and telecommunications services. **Positions advertised include:** Relay Engineer; Apprentice Gas Serviceman; Apprentice Lineman; Journeyman Gas Serviceman. **Corporate headquarters location:** Sioux Falls SD. **Other area locations:** Billings MT; Bozeman MT; Butte MT; Great Falls MT; Havre MT; Helena MT; Kalispell MT; Lewistown MT; Missoula MT. **Parent Company:** Northwestern Corporation. **Listed on:** New York Stock Exchange. **Stock exchange symbol:** NOR. **Number of employees nationwide:** 8,500.

PACIFIC STEEL & RECYCLING
P.O. Box 1549, Great Falls MT 59403. 406/727-6222. **Physical address:** 1401 Third Street NW, Great Falls MT 59404. **Fax:** 406/727-9833. **Contact:** Personnel Department. **World Wide Web address:** http://www.pacific-recycling.com. **Description:** One of the largest steel suppliers and recycling companies in the North Rocky Mountains and inland Pacific Northwest. Branches include nine large steel service centers supported by 16 additional steel stocking facilities. The company's steel processing provides plate burning, sharing, press braking, punching, and drilling. In addition to a full range of steel products, several facilities stock aluminum and stainless steel. Nonferrous recycling includes aluminum cans, scrap aluminum, brass, copper, radiators, and stainless steel. The company also recycles cardboard, newspaper, computer paper, office ledger, and other commodities. **Other U.S. locations:** ID; OR; SD; UT; WA; WY.

PHARMERICA
1130 17th Avenue South, Great Falls MT 59405. 406/452-3713. **Toll-free phone:** 800/237-7676. **Contact:** Human Resources. **World Wide Web address:** http://www.pharmerica.com. **Description:** A supplier of pharmaceuticals and related products to long-term care facilities, hospitals, and assisted living communities. PharMerica also provides nurse consultant services, infusion therapy and training, medical records consulting, and educational programs. **Corporate headquarters location:** Tampa FL. **Other U.S. locations:** Nationwide. **Parent company:** AmerisourceBergen Corporation. **Listed on:** New York Stock Exchange. **Stock exchange symbol:** ABC.

RIGHTNOW TECHNOLOGIES, INC.
40 Enterprise Boulevard, P.O. Box 9300, Bozeman MT 59718. 406/522-4200. **Toll-free phone:** 877/363-5678. **Fax:** 406/522-4227. **Contact:** Human Resources. **World Wide Web address:** http://www.rightnow.com. **Description:** A provider of customer service solutions offering unified, online customer service operations, plus tools for online surveys, data analysis, call center management and marketing. Products feature quick installation, Web hosting, and professional support services. Founded in 1997. **NOTE:** Online application available on company Website. **Positions advertised include:** Linux System Administrator; Marketing Project Manager; Senior Quality Assurance Engineer; Software Developer; Technical Writer; Implementation Specialist; Pro Services Integration Architect; Direct Response Rep. **Corporate headquarters location:** This location. **Other U.S. locations:** Dallas TX. **International locations:** Australia; Germany; Japan; United Kingdom. **Number of employees worldwide:** 260.

SGM BIOTECH, INC.
10 Evergreen Drive, Suite E, Bozeman MT 59715. 406/585-9535. **Fax:** 406/585-9219. **Contact:** Human Resources. **World Wide Web address:** http://www.sgmbiotech.com. **Description:** Manufactures biological indicators and products that visually indicate when sterilization is complete by evaluating the common sterilization processes of ethylene oxide gas, steam, and dry heat.

ST. MARY LODGE & RESORT
Browning MT 59417. 406/732-4431. **Physical address:** East Gateway to Glacier National Park, St Mary MT 59417. **Fax:** 406/732-9265. **Contact:** Human Resources. **E-mail address:** jobs@glcpark.com. **World Wide Web address:** http://www.glcpark.com. **Description:** A full service, family owned, guest facility located at the East Gateway of Glacier National Park with a wide variety of accommodations in the lodge and cottages as well as a 250-seat dining room. Founded in 1932. **NOTE:** Low-cost housing and food is provided for managers and staff. **Positions advertised include:** Resort Manager; Chef; Restaurant Manager; Assistant Controller; Retail Manager; Assistant General Manager; Front Office/Reservations Manager; Executive Secretary/ Administrative Assistant. **Internship information:** Those studying hotel-restaurant, accounting, business and retail management may be eligible to receive summer credit for business related experience. **Winter address:** The Resort at Glacier, P.O. Box 1808, Sun Valley ID 83353 (Oct. 15 – April 15) 800/368/3689. **Number of employees:** 200.

ST. PATRICK HOSPITAL & HEALTH SCIENCES CENTER
P.O. Box 4587, Missoula MT 59807. 406/543-7271. **Physical address:** 500 West Broadway, Missoula MT 59802. **Fax:** 406/329-5856. **Recorded jobline:** 406/329-5885. **Contact:** Human Resources. **World Wide Web address:** http://www.saintpatrick.org. **Description:** A nonprofit, 213-bed, acute care hospital. Founded in 1873. **NOTE:** Entry-level positions and second and third shifts are offered. **Positions advertised include:** Registered Nurse; Radiation Therapist; File Room Tech; Pharmacy Tech. **Special programs:** Internships. **Internship information:** Internships are unpaid. **Corporate headquarters location:** Spokane WA. **Parent company:** Sisters of Providence. **Operations at this facility include:** Administration; Research and Development. **Number of employees at this location:** 1,400.

ST. PETER'S COMMUNITY HOSPITAL
2475 East Broadway, Helena MT 59601. 406/442-2480. **Fax:** 406/447-2609. **Contact:** Carla in Human Resources. **E-mail address:** csisk@stpetes.org. **World Wide Web address:** http://www.stpetes.org. **Description:** St. Peter's Community Hospital is a 99-bed, acute-care facility. St. Peter's Community Hospital services include general medical and surgical services, pediatrics, a psychiatric unit, intensive/cardiac care, emergency services, OB/nursery, same-day surgery, a regional dialysis unit, a pharmacy, oncology, respiratory therapy, cardiac catheterization, and neuroscience and physician medicine. **Positions advertised include:** Registered Nurse; Licensed Practical Nurse; MRI Technician; Radiological Technologist; Transcriptionist; Physical Therapist; Accountant; Aide.

SLETTEN CONSTRUCTION COMPANY
P.O. Box 2467, Great Falls MT 59403. 406/761-7920. **Physical address:** 1000 25th Street North, Great Falls MT 59401. **Fax:** 406/761-0923. **Contact:** Fred Dahlman, Personnel Director. **World Wide Web address:** http://www.slettencompanies.com. **Description:** A general construction contractor with operations in bridge, dam, medical center, light and heavy industrial, and multi-unit housing construction. Sletten Construction is licensed to perform construction in Montana, Wyoming, Washington, Idaho, Nevada, Oregon, California, Arizona, Utah, North and South Dakota, and Colorado. **Special programs:** Internships. **Other U.S. locations:** Phoenix AZ; Las Vegas NV; Boise ID; Cody WY. **Operations at this facility include:** Administration; Regional Headquarters. **Listed on:** Privately held. **Number of employees at this location:** 30. **Number of employees nationwide:** 350.

STEEL ETC. LLP
P.O. Box 1279, Great Falls MT 59403. 406/761-4848. **Physical address:** 302 3rd Avenue South, Great Falls MT 59405. **Contact:** Human Resources. **Description:** Steel Inc. operates an automotive parts store, an industrial hardware store, a steel company, and a scrap yard. **Other U.S. locations:** WY.

STILLWATER MINING COMPANY
P.O. Box 1330, Columbus MT 59019-1330. 406/322-8766. **Physical address:** 536 East Pike Avenue, Columbus MT 59019. **Fax:** 406/322-9985. **Contact:** Human Resources. **World Wide Web address:** http://www.stillwatermining.com. **Description:** A mining company specializing in extraction, development, and processing of platinum and palladium metals. Operating mines near Nye and Big Timber with smelter and refining operations in Columbia. **Corporate headquarters location:** This location. **Other area locations:** Big Timber MT; Nye MT. **Listed on:** New York Stock Exchange. **Stock exchange symbol:** SWC. **Annual sales/revenues:** $276 million. **Number of employees at this location:** 820. **Number of employees nationwide:** 1,600.

STIMSON LUMBER
P.O. Box 1120, Bonner MT 59823. 406/258-2100. **Physical address:** Highway 200, Bonner MT 59823. **Contact:** Human Resources. **World Wide Web address:** http://www.stimsonlumber.com. **Description:** Manufactures building materials including plywood, dimension lumber, and studs. **Corporate headquarters location:** Portland OR. **Other area locations:** Libby MT. **Other U.S. locations:** ID; OR; WA. **Number of employees nationwide:** 2,300.

STOCKMAN BANK – GREAT FALLS
P.O. Box 2327, Great Falls MT 59403-2327. 406/771-2740. **Physical address:** 711 Third Street NW, Great Falls MT 59404. **Contact:** Branch Manager. **World Wide Web address:** http://www.stockmanbank.com. **Description:** Branch office of a full-service bank with numerous branches throughout Montana, northern Wyoming, and western North Dakota. **Corporate headquarters location:** Miles City MT.

STOCKMAN BANK – MILES CITY
P.O. Box 250, Miles City MT 59301. 406/234-8420. **Physical address:** 700 Main Street, Miles City MT 59301. **Contact:** Branch Manager. **World Wide Web address:** http://www.stockmanbank.com. **Description:** Branch office of a full-service bank with numerous branches throughout Montana, northern Wyoming, and western North Dakota. **Corporate headquarters location:** This location.

TAMSCO MANUFACTURING
P.O. Box 1449, Polson MT 59860. 406/883-8520. **Physical address:** 219 First Street East, Polson MT 59860. **Fax:** 406/883-8530. **Contact:** Human Resources. **E-mail address:** tamscojobs@tamscohq.com. **World Wide Web address:** http://www.tamsco.com. **Description:** Provides and installs cables, circuit boards, and other electrical equipment under government contracts as well as a limited amount of work for private companies. **NOTE:** The Human Resources Department is in the Calverton MD location. **Corporate headquarters location:** Calverton MD. **Other U.S. locations:** Nationwide.

THATCHER COMPANY OF MONTANA
3200 Raser Drive, Missoula MT 59801. 406/721-3479. **Fax:** 801/972-4606. **Contact:** Diane Barlow, Human Resources. **E-mail address:** DBarlow@thatchercompany.com. **World Wide Web address:** http://www.tchem.com. **Description:** Manufactures and distributes various chemicals and pharmaceuticals throughout the northwest United States. **NOTE:** Thatcher Company prefers that applicants apply in person between 8:00 a.m. and 4:00 p.m. at 1905 West Fortune Road (1250 South) and fill out an application. Faxed or emailed resumes are acceptable. **Positions advertised include:** Truck Driver; Quality Control; Manufacturing Operator; Warehouse Worker; Customer Service Representative; Dispatch Clerk.

TOWN PUMP, INC. AND AFFILIATES
P.O. Box 6000, Butte MT 59702. 406/497-6700. **Physical address:** 600 South Main Street, Butte MT 59701. **Fax:** 406/497-6702. **Recorded jobline:** 800/823-3252. **Contact:** Human Resources Director. **E-mail address:** townpump@townpump.com. **World Wide Web address:** http://www.townpump.com. **Description:** Owns and operates 62 convenience stores, truck stops, car washes, restaurants, 58 casinos, and eight motels throughout Montana. The company also operates a petroleum transportation and delivery division. Founded in 1954. **NOTE:** Entry-level positions, part-time jobs, and second and third shifts are offered. **Company slogan:** Montana owned and operated. **Positions advertised include:** Car Wash Manager; Convenience Store Manager. **Special programs:** Internships; Training; Summer Jobs. **Office hours:** Monday - Friday, 8:00 a.m. - 5:00 p.m. **Corporate headquarters location:** This location. **Subsidiaries include:** Northwest Petroleum; Town Pump Food Stores; Town Pump Car Wash; Town Pump 5600; Lucky Lil's Casino; Magic Diamond Casino. **Listed on:** Privately held. **Annual sales/revenues:** More than $100 million. **Number of employees at this location:** 100. **Number of employees nationwide:** 1,500.

UNIVERSITY OF MONTANA
Emma B. Lommasson Center, Missoula MT 59812. 406/243-6766. **Fax:** 406/243-6095. **Recorded jobline:** 406/243-6760. **Contact:** Human Resource Services. **World Wide Web address:** http://www.umt.edu. **Description:** A university offering undergraduate and graduate degrees in a variety of disciplines as well as continuing education and summer programs. The university maintains schools of law, business and journalism, and offers Arts and Sciences degrees in technology, education, fine arts, forestry, and pharmacy. **Company slogan:** The discovery continues. **Positions advertised include:** Assistant Professor; Professor; Associate Dean; Director; Lecturer; Fiscal Officer; Administrative Associate; Research Assistant.

VLC (VIDEO LOTTERY CONSULTANTS)
2311 South Seventh Avenue, Bozeman MT 59715. 406/585-6600. **Contact:** Ed Neuman, Human Resources Director. **World Wide Web address:** http://www.igt.com. **Description:** Provides online lottery and video lottery gaming systems, terminals, and services to governments and off-track betting authorities around the world. **Special programs:** Internships. **Corporate headquarters location:** Reno NV. **Other area locations:** Billings MT. **Other U.S. locations:** Clifton NJ; Las Vegas NV. **Operations at this facility include:** Administration; Manufacturing; Research and Development; Sales; Service. **Parent company:** IGT. **Number of employees at this location:** 300. **Number of employees worldwide:** 6,250.

VALLEY BANK OF HELENA
P.O. Box 5269, Helena MT 59604. 406/495-2400. **Physical address:** 3030 North Montana Avenue, Helena MT 59601. **Fax:** 406/443-1586. **Contact:** Human Resources. **World Wide Web address:** http://www.valleybankhelena.com. **Description:** A full-

service bank with several branches in the Helena area. **Corporate headquarters location:** This location. **Parent company:** Glacier Bancorp, Inc.

WELLS FARGO BANK
1400 North 19th Street, Bozeman MT 59718. 406/586-3839. **Contact:** Human Resources. **World Wide Web address:** http://www.wellsfargo.com. **Description:** A diversified financial institution with $388 billion in assets. Wells Fargo serves over 17 million customers through 5,900 independent locations worldwide. The company also maintains several stand-alone ATMs and branches within other retail outlets. Services include community banking, credit and debit cards, home equity and mortgage loans, on-line banking, student loans, and insurance. Wells Fargo also offers a complete line of commercial and institutional financial services. Founded in 1852. **Corporate headquarters location:** San Francisco CA. **Other U.S. locations:** Nationwide. **International locations:** Worldwide. **Listed on:** New York Stock Exchange. **Stock exchange symbol:** WFC. **Annual sales/revenues:** More than $100 million. **Number of employees worldwide:** 144,000.

WESTERN SECURITY BANK
P.O. Box 5269, Billings MT 59104. 406/238-8100. **Physical address:** 2929 3rd Avenue, Billings MT 59101. **Contact:** Branch Manager. **World Wide Web address:** http://www.westernsecuritybank.com. **Description:** Branch office of a full-service bank with several branches in the Billings area. **Corporate headquarters location:** This location. **Other area locations:** Lewistown MT; Laurel MT. **Parent company:** Glacier Bancorp, Inc.

WESTERN SUGAR COMPANY
3020 State Avenue, Billings MT 59101. 406/245-6393. **Fax:** 406/248-3677. **Contact:** Ken Bennet, Factory Manager. **E-mail address:** HR@westernsugar.com. **World Wide Web:** http://www. westernsugar.com. **Description:** Produces sugar and sugar beet products such as molasses and pulp pellets. **Corporate headquarters location:** Denver CO. **Other U.S. locations:** CO; NE; WY. **Parent company:** Western Sugar Cooperative. **Number of employees nationwide:** 5,000.

ACI WORLDWIDE
330 South 108th Avenue, Omaha NE 68154-2602. 402/390-7600. **Fax:** 402/330-1528. **Contact:** Lauralee Neubauer, Personnel. **World Wide Web address:** http://www.aciworldwide.com. **Description:** Manufactures the BASE24 family of software. Products include electronic payment, wire transfer, and clearing software solutions. ACI supports customers operating over 900 systems in more than 71 countries on six continents including some of the world's largest financial institutions, retailers, petroleum companies, and data processing service bureaus. The company also offers a suite of networking, connectivity, transaction delivery, and system software tools that help customers maximize the value of their operations. Founded in 1975. **Positions advertised include:** Division Controller; Engineer/Sr.; Engineer; Executive Assistant; Sr./Pre-Sales Support Analyst; Sr./Tax Analyst; Sr./Product Manager; Sr. Manager of Finance. **Corporate headquarters location:** This location. **Parent company:** Transaction Systems Architects, Inc. **Listed on:** NASDAQ. **Stock exchange symbol:** TSAI. **Annual sales/revenues:** More than $100 million. More than $100 million. **Number of employees at this location:** 600. **Number of employees nationwide:** 650. **Number of employees worldwide:** 1,000.

AGP
P.O. Box 2047, Omaha NE 68103-2047. 402/496-7809. **Physical Address:** 12700 West Dodge Road, Omaha NE 68154. **Toll-free phone:** 900/247-1345. **Fax:** 402/498-5548. **Contact:** Human Resources. **E-mail address:** jobs@agp.com. **World Wide Web address:** http://www.agp.com. **Description:** Processes soybean and soy flour. AGP is also engaged in vegetable oil refinement; grain merchandising and storage; and livestock feed production, sales, and research and development. Founded in 1983. **Positions advertised include:** Environmental/Safety Supervisor (Plant Supervisor). **Corporate headquarters location:** This location. **Other U.S. locations:** IA; MN; MO. **Operations at this facility include:** Administration; Divisional Headquarters; Research and Development; Sales. **Number of employees at this location:** 2,200.

ACHALA CREATIVE SOLUTIONS
3141 North 93rd Street, Omaha NE 68134. 402/343-0920. **Fax:** 402/343-1004. **Contact:** Recruitment. **E-mail address:** jobs@achala.com. **World Wide Web address:** http://www.achala.com. **Description:** Provides IT consulting, Internet development, and website creation.

AIRGAS
8427 Madison Street, Omaha NE 68127. 402/339-8080. **Toll-free phone:** 800/255-2165. **Fax:** 402/339-4155. **Contact:** Human Resources. **E-mail address:** jobs@airgas.com. **World Wide Web address:** http://www.airgas.com. **Description:** Airgas is one of the largest suppliers of gases in the U.S., handling everything from industrial and medical gases to safety and welding products. The company offers catalogs and telesales channels through which to buy its products. **Corporate headquarters location:** Radnor, PA. **Other U.S. locations:** Nationwide. **Listed on:** New York Stock Exchange. **Stock exchange symbol:** ARG. **Employees nationwide:** 8,500.

AMERITAS LIFE INSURANCE CORPORATION
P.O. Box 81889, Lincoln NE 68501-1889. 402/467-7377. **Physical address:** 5900 O Street, Lincoln NE 68510. **Toll-free phone:** 800/745-6665. **Fax:** 402/467-7935. **Recorded jobline:** 402/467-7199. **Contact:** Human Resources. **World Wide Web address:** http://www.ameritas.com. **Description:** A mutual life insurance company chartered by the state of Nebraska. The company offers life and health insurance and annuity and pension contracts. Ameritas Life Insurance Company's sister company, The Acacia Group, is headquartered in Bethesda MD. **Positions advertised include:** Field Customer Relations Manager; Office Manager; Worksite Marketing Regional Manager; Group Communications Sales Specialist; Regional Marketing Consultant; Worksite – National Accounts Representative; Part-time Technical Assistant; Individual Sales Opportunities. **Special programs:** Internships. **Corporate headquarters location:** This location. **Subsidiaries include:** Acacia Federal Savings Bank; The Advisors Group Inc.; Ameritas Dental Group, a prepaid dental organization; Ameritas Direct; Ameritas Investment Advisors, Inc., an advisor providing investment management services to the parent company and other insurance companies; Ameritas Retirement Plans; Ameritas Variable Life Insurance Company, Calvert Group, Ltd.; First Ameritas Life Insurance Corp. of New York; Acacia Life Insurance Company; Acacia National Life Insurance Company. **Operations at this facility include:** Administration; Sales; Service. **Number of employees at this location:** 750.

AMERITRADE HOLDING CORPORATION
4211 South 102nd Street, Omaha NE 68127. 402/331-7856. **Toll-free phone:** 800/237-8692. **Contact:** Human Resources. **World Wide Web address:** http://www.ameritradeholding.com. **Description:** Provides discount brokerage and financial services including electronic trading, market data, and research services. **Positions advertised include:** Quality Assurance Manager; Apex Program Manager; Outbound Sales Associate; Training & Development Specialist; Human Resource Manager; Client Service Representative; Licensed Service Representative; Sr. Manager of Information Technology Sourcing; Enterprise Project Manager; QA Manager. **Corporate headquarters location:** This location. **Listed on:** NASDAQ. **Stock exchange symbol:** AMTD.

ANALYSTS INTERNATIONAL CORPORATION (AIC)
6610 So. 118th Street, Omaha NE 68137. 402/861-0061. **Toll-free phone:** 800/735-3300. **Fax:** 402/861-0064. **Contact:** Human Resources. **E-mail address:** jobs@analysts.com. **World Wide Web address:** http://www.analysts.com. **Description:** AIC is an international computer consulting firm. The company assists clients in developing systems in a variety of industries using different programming languages and software. **Positions advertised include:** Sr. level data administrator. **Corporate headquarters location:** Minneapolis MN. **Other U.S. locations:** Nationwide. **International locations:** Canada; United Kingdom. **Listed on:** NASDAQ. **Stock exchange symbol:** ANLY.

AUTOMATED SYSTEMS, INC.
P.O. Box 22277, Lincoln NE 68524. 402/420-6000. **Physical address:** 1201 Libra Drive, Lincoln NE 68512. **Fax:** 402/420-6006. **Contact:** Human Resources. **World Wide Web address:** http://www.asiweb.com. **Description:** Automated Systems is engaged in network design, sales, installation, management, training, and support services. Founded in 1981. **Positions advertised include:** Network Engineer; Sales Consultant; Software Support Specialist; Part-time Application Support Specialist; Account Executive; Delphi Developer/Programmer; Application Developer. **Corporate headquarters location:** This location. **Other U.S. locations:** Lenexa KS. **Operations at this facility include:** This location houses administrative offices.

BECTON DICKINSON
1329 West Highway 6, P.O. Box 860, Holdrege NE 68949-0860. 308/995-6501. **Recorded jobline:** 800/349-4726. **Contact:** Human Resources. **World Wide Web address:** http://www.bd.com. **Description:** Becton Dickinson is a medical and pharmaceutical company engaged in the manufacture of health care products, medical instrumentation, diagnostic products, and industrial safety equipment. Major medical equipment product lines include hypodermics, intravenous equipment, operating room products, thermometers, gloves, and specialty needles. The company also offers contract packaging services. Founded in 1896. **NOTE:** Entry-level positions and second and third shifts are offered. **Positions advertised include:** Sr. Quality Engineer; Finance Team Leader; Manufacturing Quality Engineer; Engineering Coordinator; Quality Engineer. **Special programs:** Internships; Apprenticeships. **Office hours:** Monday - Friday, 7:30 a.m. - 4:30 p.m. **Corporate headquarters location:** Franklin Lakes NJ. **Other U.S. locations:** Nationwide. **International locations:** Worldwide. **Operations at this facility include:** This location manufactures disposable medical devices such as syringes, pens, lancets, and pen needles for the treatment of diabetes. **Listed on:** New York Stock Exchange. **Stock exchange symbol:** BDX. **Annual sales/revenues:** More than $100 million. **Number of employees at this location:** 750. **Number of employees worldwide:** 25,000.

BED, BATH & BEYOND
2960 Pine Lake Road, Lincoln NE 68516. 402/420-6767. **Fax:** 908/688-0141. **Contact:** Human Resources. **E-mail address:** employment@bedbath.com. or careers@bedbath.com. **World Wide Web address:** http://www.bedbath.com. **Description:** Nationwide chain of domestic merchandise and furniture stores. Founded in 1971. **Positions advertised include:** Store Manager; Department Manager; Sales Associate; District Human Resources Representative. **Corporate headquarters:** Union NJ. **Other area locations:** Statewide. **Other U.S. locations:** Nationwide. **Listed on:** NASDAQ. **Stock exchange symbol:** BBBY.

BERKSHIRE HATHAWAY INC.
1440 Kiewit Plaza, Omaha NE 68131. 402/346-1400. **Contact:** Human Resources. **World Wide Web address:** http://www.berkshirehathaway.com. **Description:** Berkshire Hathaway is a diverse company involved in insurance, manufacturing, and publishing. The manufacturing units include producing and distributing footwear, candy, home cleaning products, pressure and fluid control devices, uniforms, and electrical components. The insurance division, which conducts business through the National Indemnity Company of Omaha has 14 offices. Services include property and casualty insurance. The company also has a savings and loan association. Berkshire Hathaway's publishing interests include a daily newspaper in Buffalo NY, an encyclopedia, and other educational materials. **Corporate headquarters location:** This location. **Subsidiaries include:** Dexter Shoe Company; Fechheimer Brothers Co.; H.H. Brown Shoe Co.; Scott Fetzer Co.; The Buffalo News. **Listed on:** New York Stock Exchange. **Stock exchange symbol:** BRKB.

BONNAVILLA HOMES
P.O. Box 127, Aurora NE 68818-0127. 402/694-5250. **Fax:** 402/694-5873. **Contact:** Human Resources. **World Wide Web address:** http://www.bonnavilla.chiefind.com. **Description:** A housing manufacturer. Established in 1970. **NOTE:** Entry-level positions are offered. **Special programs:** Summer Jobs. **Office hours:** Monday - Friday, 8:00 a.m. - 5:00 p.m. **Other U.S. locations:** CO, ND, SD, MT, WY, KS, MN, IA, MO. **Parent company:** Chief Industries, Inc. (Grand Island NE). **NOTE:** Contact Chief Industries at hr@chiefind.com; 3492 W. Old Highway 30 P.O. Box 2078 Grand Island, NE 68802-2078. 308/389-7200. **Operations at this facility include:** Divisional Headquarters; Manufacturing. **Number of employees at this location:** 350.

BOOZ ALLEN HAMILTON
1299 Farnam Street, Suite 1230, Omaha NE 68102. 402/522-2800. **Fax:** 308/254-4800. **Contact:** Human Resources. **World Wide Web address:** http://www.boozallen.com. **Description:** A global strategy and technology consulting firm. **NOTE:** For employment opportunities, visit website, do not call. **Positions advertised include:** Information Operations JMEN CND Analyst; Human Source Intelligence Analyst; Operational Concepts Analyst; Sr. Associate Financial Services. **Other U.S. locations:** Nationwide. **International locations:** Worldwide.

BOZELL & JACOBS
13801 FNB Parkway, Omaha NE 68154-5229. 402/965-4300. **Fax:** 402/965-4399. **Contact:** Meg Graves, Human Resources. **World Wide Web address:** http://www.bozelljacobs.com. **Description:** Bozell & Jacobs is one of the largest advertising agencies in its primary operating area of Nebraska, Iowa, Colorado, Kansas, South Dakota, and Missouri. Bozell & Jacobs also offers public relations services such as corporate relations, marketing support, employee relations, financial relations, government affairs, and community relations. The staff includes specialists in marketing, media, account service, creative work, research, public relations, finance, agriculture, and broadcast affairs. **NOTE:** Unsolicited portfolios are welcome. **Special programs:** Internships. **Corporate headquarters location:** New York NY. **Other U.S. locations:** Nationwide. **Parent company:** True North Communications.

THE BUCKLE, INC.
2407 West 24th Street, Kearney NE 68845. 308/236-8491. **Fax:** 308/236-4493. **Contact:** Human Resources. **World Wide Web address:** http://www.buckle.com. **Description:** The Buckle, Inc. is a retailer of casual apparel for young men and women. The company operates over 300 retail stores in 38 states. The company markets a wide selection of brand-name casual apparel including denims, other casual bottoms, tops, sportswear, outerwear, accessories, shoes, and children's clothes. **Positions advertised include:** Store Manager; Area Manager; District Manager; Full-time and Part-time Sales; Management Development. **Special Programs:** Internships. **Corporate headquarters location:** This location. **Other U.S. locations:** Nationwide. **Listed on:** New York Stock Exchange. **Stock exchange symbol:** BKE.

CABELA'S INC.
One Cabela Way, Sidney NE 69160. 308/254-5505. **Fax:** 308/254-4500. **Contact:** Employment Specialist. **World Wide Web address:** http://www.cabelas.com. **Description:** The largest mail-order, retail, and Internet outfitter of hunting, fishing, and outdoor gear in the world. Founded in 1961. **Positions advertised include:** Sr. Systems Architect; Financial Analyst; Retail Merchandiser; Graphic Designer; Sr. Programmer/Analyst; Copywriter; Construction Project Manager. **Corporate headquarters location:** This location. **Other U.S. locations:** Kearney NE; Owatonna MN; Prairie du Chien, WI; East Grand Forks MN, Mitchell SD; Dundee MI; Kansas City KS; Hamburg PA; Wheeling WV.

CENTURION WIRELESS TECHNOLOGIES INC.
3425 North 44th Street, Lincoln NE 68504. 402/467-0491. **Fax:** 402/465-1338. **Contact:** Human Resources. **E-mail address:** USHR@centurion.com. **World Wide Web address:** http://www.centurion.com. **Description:** A leading designer and manufacturer of antennas and batteries for the wireless communications industry. **Positions advertised include:** Customer Care Representative; Director of Engineering; Manufacturing Engineer; Quality Engineer; Mechanical Design Technician; Mechanical Engineer; RF Engineer.

COLONIAL CHEMICAL RESEARCH CORPORATION
P.O. Box 609, Norfolk NE 68702-0609. 402/379-0100. **Contact:** Human Resources. **E-**

mail address: colresch@kdsi.net. **World Wide Web address:** http://www.colonialresearch.com. **Description:** A specialty chemical producer. Manufacturers a full line of various specialty household cleaning fluids.

COMMERCIAL FEDERAL BANK
13220 California Street, 2nd Floor, Omaha NE 68154. 402/514-5400. **Toll-free phone:** 800/228-5023x15430. **Fax:** 402/514-5484. **Contact:** Human Resources. **E-mail address:** humanresources@commercialfed.com. **World Wide Web address:** http://www.comfedbank.com. **Description:** Commercial Federal Bank is a federal savings bank offering a wide range of financial services. **Positions advertised include:** Client Service Representative; Personal Banker; Latino Initiative Coordinator; Compliance Auditor; Area Sales Manager; Cash Management Assistant; Investigations Assistant – Lending and Credit. **Corporate headquarters location:** This location. **Parent company:** Commercial Federal Corporation (also at this location). **Operations at this facility include:** Administration; Divisional Headquarters; Regional Headquarters; Sales; Service. **Listed on:** New York Stock Exchange. **Stock exchange symbol:** CFB. **Number of employees nationwide:** 2,800.

COMMUNITY HOSPITAL
P.O. Box 1328, McCook NE 69001. 308/345-2650. **Physical address:** 1301 East H Street, McCook NE 69001. **Fax:** 308/345-8358. **Contact:** Human Resources Coordinator. **E-mail address:** sbeiber@chmccook.org. **World Wide Web address:** http://www.chmccook.org. **Description:** An acute care hospital. **NOTE:** Human Resources phone is 308/345-8307. Please visit website for online employment application. **Company slogan:** Better care for the good life. **Positions advertised include:** Home Health Director; Surgery RN and Surgery Tech; Home Health RN/LPN; Licensed Practical Nurse; Registered Nurse. **President:** Gary Bieganski. **Annual sales/revenues:** $5 - $10 million. **Number of employees at this location:** 185.

COMPUTER CABLE CONNECTION, INC.
P.O. Box 1269, Bellevue NE 68005-1269. 402/291-9500. **Physical address:** 2810 Harlan Drive, Bellevue NE 68005. **Toll-free phone:** 800/535-1715. **Fax:** 402/291-0179. **Contact:** Human Resources. **World Wide Web address:** http://www.cccne.com. **Description:** Installs office networking systems and provides various custom cabling services, including technological consulting, design, and installation. **President:** Eric Parks.

CONAGRA, INC.
One ConAgra Drive, Omaha NE 68102. 402/595-4000. **Contact:** Human Resources. **World Wide Web address:** http://www.conagrafoods.com. **Description:** A diversified, international food company. Products range from convenient prepared foods to farming supplies. ConAgra has major businesses in branded grocery products including shelf-stable and frozen foods, processed meats, chicken and turkey products, and cheeses. The company also has major businesses in potato products, private label grocery products, beef, pork, seafood, grain and pulse (edible beans) merchandising, grain processing, specialty trailing, crop protection chemicals, fertilizers, and animal feed. ConAgra is a family of independent operating companies operating in three industry segments: prepared foods, trading and processing, and agri-products. **Positions advertised include:** Project Manager; Director of Food Safety; Financial Analyst; Accounting Specialist; Culinary Chef; Food Technologist; Customer Service Team Supervisor. **Special programs:** Internships, College recruiting. **Corporate headquarters location:** This location. **Listed on:** New York Stock Exchange. **Stock exchange symbol:** CAG.

CREIGHTON UNIVERSITY MEDICAL CENTER
601 North 30th Street, Omaha NE 68131. 402/449-4000. **Recorded jobline:** 402/449-4451. **Contact:** Human Resources Manager. **World Wide Web address:** http://www.creightonhospital.com. **NOTE:** Please see website for online application form and to search for jobs. **Description:** A hospital. **Parent company:** Tenet HealthSystem.

CREIGHTON UNIVERSITY
2500 California Plaza, Omaha NE 68178. 402/280-2700. **Fax:** 402/280-5516. **Recorded jobline:** 402/280-2943. **Contact:** William Hill, Director of Human Resources. **E-mail address:** resume@creighton.edu. **World Wide Web address:** http://www.creighton.edu. **Description:** A Jesuit university. In addition to the College of Arts and Sciences, Creighton has a College of Business Administration; University College; Schools of Dentistry, Medicine, Law, Nursing, and Pharmacy and Allied Health Professions; and a Graduate School offering master's and doctoral degrees. Creighton operates continuing education programs and a summer session. The University College offers undergraduate degree and certificate programs for part-time students and specializes in noncredit offerings for adults. The university has an enrollment of approximately 6,340. **NOTE:** Human Resources phone is 402/280-2709. **Positions advertised include:** Administrative Assistant Cardiology; Cardiac Technician; Coordinator of Multicultural Student Affairs; Director of the Magis Program; Medical Assistant; Office Manager, Registered Sonographer; Research Fellow; Research Nurse; Senior Laboratory Technician; Staff Assistant.

DAMACREG CORPORATION
4701 Innovation Drive, Lincoln NE 68521-5330. 402/323-0700. **Fax:** 402/304-1202. **Contact:** Human Resources. **E-mail address:** jobs@damacreg.com. **World Wide Web address:** http://www.damacreg.com. **Description:** A software development company specializing in the security CCTV market. **Positions advertised include:** Marketing; Software Developers.

DUTTON-LAINSON COMPANY
451 West Second Street, Hastings NE 68902-0729. 402/462-4141. **Fax:** 402/460-4612. **Contact:** Human Resources. **World Wide Web address:** http://www.dutton-lainson.com. **Description:** A wholesaler of electrical apparatus and equipment and a metal manufacturer for the marine, hardware, and health care industries. The company also operates the Cornhusker Press, a full-service printer. **Corporate headquarters location:** This location. **Operations at this facility include:** Administration; Divisional Headquarters; Manufacturing; Regional Headquarters; Research and Development; Sales; Service. **Listed on:** Privately held.

EGS ELECTRICAL GROUP
2500 East 23rd Street, Columbus NE 68601. 402/564-0400. **Contact:** Human Resources. **World Wide Web address:** http://www.egseg.com. **Description:** Manufactures electronic components, including those meant for hazardous work situations. **Parent company:** Emerson Electric. **Operations at this facility include:** Manufacturing. **Number of employees at this location:** 700.

EATON CORPORATION
4200 Highway 30 East, Kearney NE 68847. 308/234-1841. **Contact:** Tim Krohn, Human Resources Manager. **World Wide Web address:** http://www.eaton.com. **Description:** Eaton Corporation is a manufacturer of hydraulic products, fluid connectors, electrical power distribution equipment, engine components, and truck drivetrain systems, supplying its products to more than 100 countries worldwide. The company serves a variety of industries including automotive, aerospace, industrial, and semiconductor. **Corporate headquarters location:** Cleveland OH. **Other area locations:** Hastings, NE. **Other U.S. locations:** Nationwide. **International locations:** Worldwide. **Operations at this facility include:** This location manufactures vehicle parts. **Listed on:** New York Stock Exchange. **Stock exchange symbol:** ETN. **Number of employees worldwide:** 51,000.

EX-CEL SOLUTIONS, INC.
14618 Grover Street, Omaha NE 68144. 402/333-6541. **Fax:** 402/333-3124. **Contact:** Human Resources. **E-mail address:** recruiters@excels.com. **World Wide Web address:** http://www.excels.com. **Description:** Provides customized computer sales, service, and maintenance. Ex-Cel Solutions is a systems integrator for Novell Netware and Windows NT networks. Founded in 1974. **Positions advertised include:** Visual Basic - Oracle Programmer. **NOTE:** Entry-level positions are offered. Please see website for online application form and printable application. **Office hours:** Monday - Friday, 8:00 a.m. - 5:00 p.m. **Corporate headquarters location:** This location. **Listed on:** Privately held. **President:** Glenn J. Stenger. **Annual sales/revenues:** $11 - $20 million. **Number of employees at this location:** 55.

EXPERIAN INFORMATION SOLUTIONS, INC.
901 West Bond Street, Lincoln NE 68521-3694. 402/475-4591. **Contact:** Human Resources. **E-mail address:** lincoln.resume@experian.com. **World Wide Web address:** http://www.experian.com. **Description:** Experian is a global information solutions company that supplies consumer and business credit, direct marketing, and real estate information services. Founded in 1946. **NOTE:** Part-time jobs and second and third shifts are offered. **Positions advertised include:** Client Services Analyst; Sales Supervisor. **Special programs:** Internships. **Office hours:** Monday - Friday, 8:00 a.m. - 5:00 p.m. **Corporate headquarters location:** Costa Mesa CA. **Other U.S. locations:** Nationwide. **International locations:** Worldwide. **Parent company:** GUS plc. **Operations at this facility include:** Sales. **Number of employees at this location:** 700. **Number of employees nationwide:** 4,500. **Number of employees worldwide:** 13,000.

FARMLAND FOODS INC.
P.O. Box 67, Crete NE 68333. 402/826-4381. **Physical address:** South Highway 103, Crete NE 68333. **Contact:** Human Resources. **E-mail Address:** jobs@farmland.com. **World Wide Web address:** http://www.farmlandfoods.com. **Description:** A pork processing plant. **Corporate headquarters location:** Kansas City MO.

FIRST DATA CORPORATION
7305 Pacific Street, Omaha NE 68114. 402/777-2000. **Fax:** 402/777-1738. **Contact:** Personnel. **World Wide Web address:** http://www.firstdatacorp.com. **Description:** First Data Corporation offers electronic commerce and payment services to 2 million merchant locations. **Positions advertised include:** Quality Assurance Analyst; TeleCheck Area Representative; Sales Trainer; Associate Customer Engineer; Production Machine Operator. **Corporate headquarters location:** Greenwood Village, CO. **Other U.S. locations:** Atlanta GA. **Operations at this facility include:** Administration; Divisional Headquarters; Sales; Service. **Listed on:** New York Stock Exchange. **Stock exchange symbol:** FDC. **Annual sales/revenues:** More than $100 million. **Number of employees at this location:** 7,000. **Number of employees worldwide:** 29,000.

FIRST NATIONAL BANK OF OMAHA
1620 Dodge Street, Omaha NE 68197. 402/633-3860. **World Wide Web address:** http://www.firstnational.com/fnb. **Contact:** Human Resources. **Description:** A commercial bank and financial services company. **Positions advertised include:** Lead Mail Insert Operator; Attorney; Sr. Loan Review Analyst. **Corporate headquarters location:** This location. **Other U.S. locations:** CO; KS; NE; SD; TX. **Parent company:** First National of Nebraska. **Operations at this facility include:** Administration; Divisional Headquarters; Regional Headquarters; Sales. **Number of employees at this location:** 2,500. **Number of employees nationwide:** 3,700.

THE GALLUP ORGANIZATION
1001 Gallup Drive, Omaha NE 68102. 402/451-2003. **Fax:** 888/500-8282. **Contact:** Human Resources. **World Wide Web address:** http://www.gallup.com. **Description:** A market research company founded in 1935 that uses scientific polling data to consult clients. **NOTE:** Apply online. **Corporate Headquarters location:** Washington DC.

GEORGE RISK INDUSTRIES INC. (G.R.I.)
802 South Elm Street, Kimball NE 69145. 308/235-4645. **Toll-free phone:** 800/523-1227. **Contact:** Human Resources. **World Wide Web address:** http://www.grisk.com. **Description:** A manufacturer of electronic reed switches, computer keyboards (custom or standard), security switches and magnets, wall plates, horns, and sirens. GRI is engaged in custom key cap engraving and plastic injection molding. **Corporate headquarters location:** This location.

GIBRALTAR PACKAGING GROUP, INC.
GREAT PLAINS PACKAGING DIVISION
2000 Summit Avenue, Hastings NE 68901. 402/463-1366. **Fax:** 402/463-1661. **Contact:** Human Resources. **E-mail address:** jlewis@gppkg.com. **World Wide Web address:** http://www.gppkg.com. **Description:** Gibraltar Packaging Group, Inc. designs and manufactures high-quality packaging products serving a variety of industries including the pharmaceutical, food, cosmetic, textile, toy, automotive aftermarket, specialty confectionery, and other consumer markets. The company's product line includes folding cartons, flexible polyfilm packaging, and specialty laminated boxes. **Corporate headquarters location:** This location. **Subsidiaries include:** Flashfold Carton (Fort Wayne IN); Standard Packaging & Printing (Hastings NE). **Operations at this facility include:** This location houses a box factory.

GODFATHER'S PIZZA, INC.
9140 West Dodge Road, Suite 300, Omaha NE 68114. 402/391-1452. **Toll-free phone:** 800/456-8347. **Fax:** 402/255-2687. **Contact:** Human Resources. **World Wide Web address:** http://www.godfathers.com. **NOTE:** Please see website for online application form. **Description:** A chain of pizza restaurants offering performance-based compensation. **Corporate headquarters location:** This location. **Other U.S. locations:** Nationwide.

GOODYEAR TIRE & RUBBER COMPANY
4521 Northwest 34th Street, Lincoln NE 68504. 402/466-8311. **Toll-free phone:** 800/466-3932. **Contact:** Human Resources. **World Wide Web address:** http://www.goodyear.com. **Description:** Goodyear Tire & Rubber Company's principal business is the development, manufacture, distribution, and sale of tires for most applications worldwide. Goodyear also manufactures and sells a broad spectrum of rubber products and rubber-related chemicals for various industrial and consumer markets and provides auto repair services. The company operates 32 plants in the United States, 85 plants in 28 other countries, and more than 1,800 retail tire and

service centers and other distribution facilities worldwide. Strategic business units of Goodyear Tire & Rubber include North American Tire; Kelly-Springfield; Goodyear Europe; Goodyear Latin America; Goodyear Asia; Engineered Products; Chemicals; Celeron; and Goodyear Racing. **Corporate headquarters location:** Akron OH. **Other U.S. locations:** Nationwide. **International locations:** Worldwide. **Operations at this facility include:** This location manufactures V-belts and hose products. **Listed on:** New York Stock Exchange. **Stock exchange symbol:** GT. **Annual sales/revenues:** More than $100 million. **Number of employees worldwide:** 92,000.

GORDMANS
12100 West Center Road, Omaha NE 68144. 402/691-4000. **Fax:** 402/691-4269. **Fax:** 402/691-4269. **Contact:** Human Resources Manager. **E-mail address:** hr@gordmans.com. **World Wide Web address:** http://www.gordmans.com. **Description:** Operates a chain of off-price department stores. Features brand name furniture, clothing, jewelry, accessories, and shoes. **Positions advertised include:** Store Manager; Assistant Manager; Buyer for Toys; Guest Services Manager. **Corporate headquarters location:** This location. **Other U.S. locations:** CO; IL; IA; KS; MO; ND; OK; SD, WI. **Number of employees at this location:** 200. **Number of employees nationwide:** 2,500.

GREAT PLAINS REGIONAL MEDICAL CENTER
P.O. Box 1167, 601 West Leota, North Platte NE 69101. 308/696-8000. **Toll-free phone:** 800/662-0011. **Contact:** Human Resources. **E-mail address:** recruiter@mail.gprmc.com. **World Wide Web address:** http://www.gprmc.com. **Description:** A medical center. **NOTE:** Human Resources phone is 308/535-7437. **Positions advertised include:** Blood Bank Supervisor; Director – Surgery; Histology technician; Licensed Practical Nurse; Occupational Therapist; Physical Therapist; Practitioner; Registered Nurse; Tech Assistant. **Special programs:** Internships. **Listed on:** Privately held. **Number of employees at this location:**720.

HDR, INC.
8404 Indian Hills Drive, Omaha NE 68114-4049. 402/399-1000. **Toll-free phone:** 800/366-4411. **Fax:** 402/399-1238. **Contact:** Human Resources. **E-mail address:** careers@hdrinc.com. **World Wide Web address:** http://www.hdrinc.com. **Description:** An architecture and engineering firm that operates worldwide and is employee owned. Founded in 1917. **NOTE:** Entry-level positions and part-time jobs are offered. **Company slogan:** Shaping the future through creative solutions and visionary leadership. **Special programs:** Internships; Co-ops; Summer Jobs. **Corporate headquarters location:** This location. **Other U.S. locations:** Nationwide. **Subsidiaries include:** HDR Architecture, Inc. specializes in the architectural design of health care facilities (hospitals and integrated health care networks, ambulatory care centers, oncology and cardiology centers, diagnostic and treatment centers, and strategic facilities assessment); justice facilities (courthouse and administrative facilities, adult and juvenile detention facilities, and state correctional facilities); and science and technology facilities (research facilities, advanced technology facilities, telecommunications, university science facilities, and manufacturing facilities). HDR Engineering, Inc. provides water, transportation, waste, and energy services including studies, design, and implementation for complex projects. **Listed on:** Privately held. **Chairman/CEO:** Dick Bell. **Information Annual sales/revenues:** $51 - $100 million. **Number of employees at this location:** 450. **Number of employees worldwide:**3,300.

HORMEL FOODS CORPORATION
P.O. Box 69, Fremont NE 68026-0069. 402/721-2300. **Physical address:** 900 South Platte Avenue, Fremont NE 68025. **Corporate resume fax:** 507/437-5171. **Contact:** Lynelle Topp. **E-mail:** careers@hormel.com. **World Wide Web address:** http://www.hormel.com. **Description:** Hormel, a *Fortune* 500 company, is one of the leading processors and marketers of branded, value-added meat and food products. Principal products of the company are branded, processed meat and food entrees that are sold fresh, frozen, cured, smoked, cooked, and canned. Included are sausages, hams, hot dogs, bacon, canned luncheon meats, shelf-stable microwaveable entrees, stews, chili, hash, meat spreads, and frozen processed products. The majority of the company's products are sold under the Hormel brand name. Other trademarks include Farm Fresh, Little Sizzlers, Quick Meal, Kid's Kitchen, Chi Chi's, House of Tsang, Mary Kitchen, Dinty Moore, Light & Lean, Chicken by George, Black Label, and SPAM. **NOTE:** Entry-level positions and second and third shifts are offered. **Positions advertised include:** Staff Accountant; Industrial Engineer; Associate Maintenance Engineer; Computer Analyst; Production Manager; Quality Assurance Manager; Food Technologist; Foodservice Salesperson; Grocery Products Salesperson; Meat Products Salesperson. **Corporate headquarters location:** Austin MN. **NOTE:** Resume fax number sends to corporate office. **Other U.S. locations:** Nationwide. **International locations:** Australia; England; Japan; Korea; Panama; Philippines. **Operations at this facility include:** This location is a meat processing plant. **Listed on:** New York Stock Exchange. **Stock exchange symbol:** HRL. **Number of employees at this location:** 1,200. **Number of employees nationwide:**15,600.

IMAGINE TECHNOLOGY
One Technology Place, Suite 110, 4711 Innovation Drive, Lincoln NE 68521. 402/323-0707. **Fax:** 847/357-1981. **Contact:** Human Resources. **E-mail address:** skroeker@imaginetechnology.net. **World Wide Web address:** http://www.imaginetechnology.net. **Description:** Designs and markets complex telephone solutions for businesses. **Positions advertised include:** Sr. DSP Engineer; DSP Engineer. **Parent company:** Ingenient Technologies.

INFORMATION TECHNOLOGY, INC.
P.O. Box 22705, Lincoln NE 68542-2705. **Physical address:** 1345 Old Cheney Road, Lincoln NE 68512. 402/423-2682. **Contact:** Human Resources. **NOTE:** Human Resources phone is 402/421-4269. **World Wide Web address:** http://www.itiwnet.com. **Description:** Develops financial software for companies in the banking industry. **Positions advertised include:** Sales Executive; Conversion Programmer; Customer Support Analyst; Software Development Analyst; Technical Writer. **Parent company:** Fiserv, Inc.

INFOUSA
5711 South 86th Circle, P.O. Box 27347, Omaha NE 68127. 402/596-8900 **Toll-free phone:** 800/321-0869. **Fax:** 402/592-3109. **Contact:** Jim Stultz, Recruiter. **E-mail address:** jobs@infousa.com. **World Wide Web address:** http://www.infousa.com. **Description:** Provides business and consumer marketing information services including market research services, online information services, and business directories. Information is supplied from the company's proprietary database containing information on about 10 million businesses in the United States and 1 million businesses in Canada. The database of infoUSA is compiled and updated annually from approximately 5,000 yellow page telephone directories, as well as other publicly-available sources including business white pages, directories, annual reports and other SEC filing information, press releases, business magazines, newsletters, and top newspapers. Founded in 1972. **Positions advertised include:** Sales Executive; Accounts Executive; Outbound Telemarketing; General Manager; Software Engineer; Vice resident of Sales. **Office hours:** Monday - Friday, 8:00 a.m. - 5:00 p.m. **Corporate headquarters location:** This location. **Other U.S. locations:** Nationwide. **International locations:** Canada; England. **Listed on:** NASDAQ. **Stock exchange symbol:** IUSA. **Number of employees worldwide:** 2,000.

ISCO, INC.
P.O. Box 82531, Lincoln NE 68501-2531. 402/464-0231. **Physical address:** 4700 Superior Street, Lincoln NE 68501. **Recorded jobline:** 402/465-2016. **Fax:** 402/465-3944. **Contact:** Human Resources. **E-mail address:** resumes@isco.com. **World Wide Web address:** http://www.isco.com. **Description:** A designer, manufacturer, and worldwide marketer of instruments used by scientists and engineers addressing concerns such as water pollution, biological research, environmental testing, and industrial quality control. The company's products include wastewater samplers, open channel flow meters, parameter monitoring products, liquid chromatography products, supercritical fluid extraction products, and syringe pumps. Markets served include enforcement agencies, dischargers, environmental consulting engineers, environmental analysis labs, bioseparators, food processors, plastics manufacturers, and petroleum manufacturers. Isco also collaborates with commercial and academic scientists and technicians concerned with separating and analyzing the components of a wide variety of materials. These components and materials include the fat content of food, pollutants in environmental samples, and additives in plastics. The company's separation instruments are also used by customers involved in biotechnology, pharmaceutical, life science, and medical research. Founded in 1958. **Positions advertised include:** Assembler; Swift Sales and Marketing Manager. **Corporate headquarters location:** This location. **Subsidiaries include:** STIP Isco GmbH (Gross Umstadt, Germany). **Listed on:** NASDAQ. **Stock exchange symbol:** ISKO. **Owner:** Robert W. Allington. **Annual sales/revenues:** $21 - $50 million. **Number of employees at this location:** 420.

JEFFERSON-PILOT FINANCIAL
8801 Indian Hills Drive, Omaha NE 68114-4066. 402/361-7300. **Toll-free phone:** 800/423-2765. **Fax:** 402/361-1426. **Contact:** Human Resources. **E-mail address:** jobs.jobs@jpfinancial.com. **World Wide Web address:** http://www.jpfinancial.com. **NOTE:** Please see website for online application form. **Description:** An insurance company; also offers investment and annuity products. **Special programs:** Internships. **Corporate headquarters location:** Greensboro NC. **Other U.S. locations:** Lexington KY; Concord NH. **Listed on:** New York Stock Exchange. **Stock exchange symbol:** JP. **Number of employees at this location:** 470.

THE KIEWIT COMPANIES
1000 Kiewit Plaza, Omaha NE 68131. 402/342-2052. **Fax:** 402/271-2939. **Contact:** Human Resources. **E-mail address:** human.resources@kiewit.com. **World Wide Web address:** http://www.kiewit.com. **Description:** One of the largest construction companies in the country. Kiewit's primary markets are the building, power, transportation, water resources, and mining industries. Projects include highways, bridges, high-rise buildings, office complexes, railroads, tunnels, subways, dams, airports, power plants, canals, water treatment facilities, offshore petroleum platforms, and other heavy civil projects. The company has district offices throughout North America. **Positions advertised include:** Structural Design Engineer; Engineer; Superintendent; Business Manager; Internal Auditor. **Special Programs:** Internships, Co-ops. **Corporate headquarters location:** This location. **Other U.S. locations:** Nationwide. **Operations at this facility include:** Administration. **Listed on:** Privately held. **Annual sales/revenues:** More than $100 million. **Number of employees at this location:** 300. **Number of employees nationwide:**15,000.

MARY LANNING MEMORIAL HOSPITAL
715 North St. Joseph Avenue, Hastings NE 68901. 402/463-4521. **Contact:** Human Resources. **E-mail address:** lflorian@mlmh.org. **World Wide Web address:** http://www.mlmh.org. **Description:** A general, acute care hospital. **Positions advertised include:** Controller; Director – Patient Accounts; Registered Nurse; Respiratory Therapist; Physical Therapist; Occupational Therapist; Speech Pathologist. **Number of employees at this location:** 770.

LINCOLN JOURNAL STAR
926 P Street, Lincoln NE 68508. 402/475-4200. **Contact:** Human Resources. **E-mail address:** hr@journalstar.com. **World Wide Web address:** http://www.journalstar.com. **Description:** A newspaper printing company. **Office hours:** Monday – Friday 9:00 am – 4:30 pm. **Parent company:** Lee Enterprises. **Number of employees nationwide:** 6,000.

LOZIER CORPORATION
P.O. Box 19999, Omaha NE 68119-0999. 402/457-8000. **Physical address:** 6336 Pershing Drive, Omaha NE 68110. **Toll-free phone:** 800/228-9882. **Fax:** 402/457-8297. **Contact:** Human Resources. **E-mail address:** HR@lozier.biz. **World Wide Web address:** http://www.lozier.com. **Description:** A leading manufacturer of store fixtures. **NOTE:** Second and third shifts are offered. Human Resources phone is 402/457-8240. **Positions advertised include:** Product Consultant; Maintenance Mechanic; Plant Manager; Area Manager; Scheduler/Planner. **Special programs:** Internships; Summer Jobs. **Office hours:** Monday - Friday, 8:00 a.m. - 5:00 p.m. **Other U.S. locations:** Scottsboro AL; Joplin MO; Hallmark PA; McClure PA. **Annual sales/revenues:** More than $100 million. **Number of employees at this location:** 1,700. **Number of employees nationwide:** 3,000.

MDS PHARMA SERVICES
621 Rose Street, Lincoln NE 68501-0837. 402/476-2811. **Fax:** 402/476-7598. **Contact:** Human Resources. **World Wide Web address:** http://www.mdsps.com. **Description:** Offers a complete range of clinical trials, analytical and statistical services, and consumer product research. These services are provided from facilities and offices in the United States, Europe, and Japan, and in more than 1,000 clinical investigation sites. MDS Pharma Services performs all types of Phase I studies including complete bioavailability and bioequivalence studies and pharmacokinetic/pharmacodynamic clinical studies with healthy and special populations, as well as offering data analysis and customized reporting. MDS Pharma Services also designs and manages complete Phase II, III, and IV multicenter clinical studies. **Positions advertised include:** Clinical Study Design Technician; Proposal Development Coordinator; Principal Investigator; Instrument Specialist; Regulatory Submission Coordinator; Scientific Writer; Senior Pharmacokinetiscist; Clinical Conduct Associate; Scientist; Extraction Analyst; Clinical Research Nurse; Custodian. **NOTE:** Please see website for online application form. **Other U.S. locations:** Nationwide. **International locations:** Worldwide. **Parent company:** MDS Inc. **Listed on:** New York Stock Exchange. **Stock exchange symbol:** MDZ.

MEMORIAL HEALTH CENTER
645 Osage Street, Sidney NE 69162. 308/254-5825. **Fax:** 308/254-2300. **Contact:** Carrie Trost, Director of Human Resources. **E-mail address:** mhchr@hamilton.net. **World Wide Web address:** http://www.memorialhealthcenter.org. **Description:** A nonprofit home health counseling and medical center with a 30-bed acute care unit and

a 70-bed extended care unit, as well as physical therapy and surgery departments. **NOTE:** Entry-level positions and second and third shifts are offered. Please see website for downloadable job application. Director of Human Resources phone is 877/642-8326. **Special programs:** Internships; Training; Summer Jobs. **Office Hours:** Monday – Friday 8:00 am – 5:00 pm. **CEO:** Rex Walk. **Annual sales/revenues:** Less than $5 million. **Number of employees at this location:** 240.

MID-AMERICA ENERGY COMPANY, INC.
302 South 36th Street, Suite 400, Omaha NE 68131. 402/341-4500. **Contact:** Human Resources. **E-mail address:** employment@midamerican.com. **World Wide Web address:** http://www.midamerican.com. **Description:** Mid-America Energy Company, Inc. designs, builds, owns, and operates environmentally responsible electric power production facilities. A full-service company, Mid-America Energy can provide the following services for all of its projects: reservoir engineering, modeling, and drilling; licensing and permitting; engineering and design; financial packaging; construction and project management; and operations and maintenance. **Subsidiaries include:** MidAmerican Capital Company, Midwest Capital Group. **CEO:** David Sokol. **President:** Gregory E. Abel.

MODIS
2611 South 117th Street, Omaha NE 68144. 402/333-1700. **Fax:** 402/333-2239. **Contact:** Human Resources. **E-mail address:** resume@modisit.com. **World Wide Web address:** http://www.modisit.com. **NOTE:** Please see website for online application form. **Description:** A consulting firm that specializes in software. Founded in 1987. **Corporate headquarters location:** Jacksonville FL. **Other U.S. locations:** Nationwide. **Annual sales/revenues:** $21 - $50 million.

MUTUAL OF OMAHA INSURANCE COMPANY
Mutual of Omaha Plaza, Omaha NE 68175. 402/342-7600. **Contact:** Personnel. **E-mail address:** careers@mutualofomaha.com. **World Wide Web address:** http://www.mutualofomaha.com. **Description:** Mutual of Omaha offers a full portfolio of insurance coverages and services with $25.4 billion paid in benefits to policyholders. **Positions advertised include:** Associate Financial/Operational Auditor; Contract Analyst; Care Services Coordinator; Direct to Consumer Project Leader; Underwriter, Manager – Group Contract Services; Clinical Pharmacy Assistant. **Special programs:** Internships. **Corporate headquarters location:** This location. **Operations at this facility include:** Administration; Divisional Headquarters; Regional Headquarters; Sales. **Listed on:** Privately held. **Number of employees at this location:** 5,500. **Number of employees nationwide:** 7,300.

NATIONAL INDEMNITY COMPANY
3024 Harney Street, Omaha NE 68131-3580. 402/536-3390. **Fax:** 402/536-3030. **Contact:** Human Resources. **World Wide Web address:** http://www.nationalindemnity.com. **NOTE:** Please see website to fill out a Personal Information Sheet. Human Resources will contact you if you qualify for a position. **Description:** A property and casualty insurance company. **Positions advertised include:** Senior Claim Examiner; Word Processing Technician; Processing Technician. **Corporate headquarters location:** This location. **Parent company:** Berkshire Hathaway.

NATURE TECHNOLOGY CORPORATION
4701 Innovation Drive, Lincoln NE 68521. 402/472-6530. **Fax:** 402/472-6532. **Contact:** Dr. Claude Hodgson. **E-mail address:** hodgson@natx.com. **World Wide Web address:** http://www.natx.com. **Description:** Provides vector design, development, and manufacturing assistance to the biotech and bio-pharmaceutical industries for the construction of genes in living cells and organisms.

NEBRASKA BOOK COMPANY
4700 South 19th Street, Lincoln NE 68501-0529. 402/421-7300. **Toll-free phone:** 800/869-0366. **Fax:** 800/869-0399. **Contact:** Ed Phillips, Personnel Department. **E-mail address:** ephillips@nebook.com. **World Wide Web address:** http://www.nebook.com. **NOTE:** Please see website to fill out online application form. **Description:** Nebraska Book Company provides used textbook services to colleges and universities throughout the United States. **Corporate headquarters location:** This location. **Other U.S. locations:** Nationwide. **Operations at this facility include:** This location is a wholesale book warehouse. **Number of employees nationwide:** 2,000.

NEBRASKA PUBLIC POWER DISTRICT
P.O. Box 499, Columbus NE 68602-0499. 402/564-8561. **Toll-free phone:** 877/275-6773. **Physical address:** 1414 15th Street, Columbus NE 68601. **Recorded jobline:** 402/563-5010. **Contact:** Human Resources. **World Wide Web address:** http://www.nppd.com. **Description:** A utility company. Founded 1970. **NOTE:** Entry-level positions and part-time jobs are offered. **Company slogan:** Nebraska's energy leader. **Positions advertised include:** Technical Services Assistant; Custodian; Network Applications Engineer; Lab Technician; Station Chemist; Hydrologist. **Special programs:** Internships; Apprenticeships; Training; Co-ops; Summer Jobs. **Corporate headquarters location:** This location. **Other area locations:** Statewide. **Annual sales/revenues:** More than $100 million. **Number of employees at this location:** 2,000.

NORTHERN NATURAL GAS
1111 South 103rd Street, Omaha NE 68124-1000. 402/398-7664. **Contact:** Human Resources. **World Wide Web address:** http://www.northernnaturalgas.com. **Description:** Explores for, develops, and produces natural gas and crude oil primarily in the United States and to a lesser extent, in Canada and selected international areas. Principal oil and gas properties are in the Big Piney area of Wyoming, the Matagorda Trend in the federal waters of offshore Texas, and the Canyon Trend in west Texas. **Positions advertised include:** Account Director; Air Program Manager; Financial Accountant – Operations; Manager – Applications Development. **Corporate headquarters location:** This location. **Number of employees nationwide:** 1,100.

NORTHROP GRUMMAN
1408 Fort Crook Road South, Bellevue NE 68005. 402/291-7750. **Contact:** Human Resources. **World Wide Web address:** http://www.northropgrumman.com. **NOTE:** Please see website for information on how to apply. **Description:** A developer of client/server and distributed computing software. The company develops, markets, and supports enterprise management, database and applications development, business applications, and consumer software products for a broad range of mainframe, midrange, and desktop computers. Northrop Grumman serves major business, government, research, and educational organizations. **Positions advertised include:** Software Test Lead; Contracts Administrator; PR Cis Development; Human Resources Generalist; Systems Software Engineer; Customer Service Analyst; Technical Service Engineer; Lead Engineer; Technical Writer; Software Installer/Maintainer; Software Engineer. **Corporate headquarters location:** Los Angeles, CA. **Other U.S. locations:** Nationwide. **International locations;** UK, Norway, Austria, Japan. **Operations at this facility include:** Information technology, Missions systems. **Listed on:** New York Stock Exchange. **Stock exchange symbol:** NOC. **Number of employees worldwide:**120,000.

NUCOR STEEL
P/O/ Box 94 Norfolk NE 68701. 402/644-0200. **Physical address:** 2911 East Nucor Street, Norfolk NE 68701. **Toll-free phone:** 800/228-8174. **Fax:** 402/644-8559. **Contact:** Human Resources. **World Wide Web address:** http://www.nucorne.com. **Description:** Produces bars, angles, light structural, sheet, and special steel products. In addition to selling steel on the open market, these steel mills assure an economical supply of steel for the Vulcraft, Nucor Cold Finish, Nucor Grinding Balls, Nucor Fastener, and Nucor Building Systems operations. **Corporate headquarters location:** Charlotte, NC. **Parent company:** Nucor Corporation is a manufacturer of steel products, whose other divisions include: Nucor Bearing Products, Inc., which produces steel bearings and machined steel parts; Nucor Building Systems, which produces metal buildings and components; Nucor Cold Finish, which produces cold-finished steel bars used extensively for shafting and machined precision parts; Nucor Grinding Balls, which produces steel grinding balls in Utah for the mining industry; Nucor Fastener, a steel bolt-making facility; and Vulcraft, one of the nation's largest producers of steel joists and joist girders. **Listed on:** New York Stock Exchange. **Stock exchange symbol:** NUE. **Number of employees nationwide:** 9,800.

OMAHA PUBLIC POWER DISTRICT
444 South 16th Street Mall, Omaha NE 68102-2247. 402/536-4131. **Recorded jobline:** 402/636-3046. **Toll-free phone:** 800/648-2658. **Contact:** Employment Department. **World Wide Web address:** http://www.oppd.com. **Description:** A business-managed electric utility organized in 1946 as a political subdivision of the state of Nebraska. The Power District serves 53 towns and surrounding farm areas in 13 southeastern Nebraska counties. **NOTE:** Human Resources phone is 402/636-3059. Other area locations: Ashland, Blair, Humbolt, Louisville, North Bend, Syracuse, Tecumseh. **Corporate headquarters location:** This location. **Number of employees at this location:** 2,400.

OMAHA STEAKS
10909 John Galt Boulevard, Omaha NE 68137. 402/597-3000. **Toll-free phone:** 800/960-8400. **Contact:** Human Resources Manager. **World Wide Web address:** http://www.omahasteaks.com. **NOTE:** Please see website for online application form. **Description:** A food retailing company primarily selling cuts of beef and pork through the mail. Founded 1917. **Corporate headquarters location:** This location. **Number of employees at this location:** 1,800.

OMAHA WORLD-HERALD
14th & Dodge Street, Omaha NE 68102. 402/444-1000. **Fax:** 402/444-1211. **E-mail address:** dbuscher@owh.com **Contact:** Donna Buscher, Human Resources. **World Wide Web address:** http://www.omaha.com. **Description:** Publishes a daily newspaper. The company is also engaged in advertising. **NOTE:** Entry-level positions, part-time jobs, and second and third shifts are offered. Positions advertised include: District Supervisor, Electronics Technician, Part-time PBX Operator, PT Tearsheet Clerk, Safety Director, Telemarketing Sales Representative. **Special programs:** Internships; Apprenticeships. **Office hours:** Monday – Friday 7:00 am – 6:00 pm. Saturday 7:00 am – noon. **Corporate headquarters location:** This location. **Listed on:** Privately held. **Number of employees at this location:** 900. **Number of employees nationwide:** 1,100.

PAMIDA, INC.
8800 F Street, Omaha NE 68127. 402/339-2400. **Recorded jobline:** 800/284-7270. **Contact:** Human Resources. **E-mail address:** bhackett@pamida.com **World Wide Web address:** http://www.pamida.com. **NOTE:** Please see website for online application form. **Description:** A general merchandise retailer operating nearly 160 stores in 15 Midwestern states. **NOTE:** Entry-level positions are offered. **Positions advertised include:** Pharmacist; Assistant Team Leads; Store Team Leader; Store Team Leader in Training. **Special programs:** Training. **Corporate headquarters location:** This location. **Parent company:** Shopko Stores, Inc. **Listed on:** New York Stock Exchange. **Stock exchange symbol:** SKO. **Annual sales/revenues:** More than $100 million. **Number of employees at this location:** 400. **Number of employees nationwide:** 5,000.

PARKER INDUSTRIAL HOSE
P.O. Box 1448, McCook NE 69001. 308/345-1700. **World Wide Web address:** http://www.parker.com. **Contact:** Human Resources. **Description:** A nationwide producer of rubber hoses. **Corporate headquarters location:** Cleveland OH. **Parent company:** Parker Hannifin Corporation. **Operations at this facility include:** Manufacturing. **Listed on:** New York Stock Exchange. **Stock exchange symbol:** PH. **Number of employees at this location:** 325.

PFIZER ANIMAL HEALTH
601 West Cornhusker Highway, Lincoln NE 68521. 402/475-4541. **Contact:** Human Resources. **World Wide Web address:** http://www.pfizer.com. **NOTE:** Please see website for online application form. **Description:** Manufactures veterinary biologicals and pharmaceuticals. **Corporate headquarters location:** New York, NY. **Other U.S. locations:** Nationwide. **International locations:** Worldwide. **Listed on:** New York Stock Exchange. **Stock exchange symbol:** PFE.

PHARMA CHEMIE
P.O. Box 326, 1877 Midland Street, Syracuse NE 68446-0326. 402/269-3195. **Fax:** 402/269-3196. **Contact:** Human Resources. **World Wide Web address:** http://www.pharma-chemie.com. **Description:** Produces a full line of animal nutritional supplements.

PINNACLE FOODS CORPORATION
P.O. Box 778, Omaha NE 68101-0778. 402/342-8118. **Physical address:** 1116 Capital Avenue, Omaha NE 68102. **Contact:** Human Resources. **World Wide Web address:** http://www.pinnaclefoodscorp.com. **Description:** Pinnacle Foods Corporation is the parent company of both Vlasic Foods, a producer of commercial soups, juices, pickles, frozen foods, canned beans, canned pasta products, spaghetti sauces, and baked goods, and Swanson, producer of frozen dinners such as Hungry Man. The company's products are distributed worldwide. **Corporate headquarters location:** Cherry Hill NJ. **Operations at this facility include:** This location produces frozen convenience and food service meals under the following labels: Swanson, Mrs. Paul's, Hungry Man, and Campbell's Food Service. **Number of employees at this location:** 1,600.

QUEBECOR WORLD
3700 NW 12th Street, Lincoln NE 68521. 402/474-5825. **Fax:** 402/479-1710. **Contact:** Human Resources. **E-mail address:** usa.careers@quebecorworld.com. **World Wide Web address:** http://www.quebecorworld.com. **Description:** Quebecor World is a national publication and commercial printer. **Corporate headquarters location:** Montreal, Quebec, Canada. **Other U.S. locations:** Nationwide. **International locations:** Worldwide. **Listed on:** New York Stock Exchange. **Stock exchange symbol:** IQW. **Number of employees worldwide:** 38,000.

QUILOGY
13220 Birch Drive, Suite 220, Omaha NE 68164. 402/491-3007. **Contact:** Human Resources. **E-mail address:** resumes@quilogy.com. **World Wide Web address:** http://www.quilogy.com. **Description:** Firm specializing in business solutions. Founded in 1992. **Positions advertised include:** Application Developer; Business Strategist; Database Consultor; Enterprise Architect; Graphic Designer; Multimedia Specialist; Networking Consultant; Technology Trainer; Web Technology Developer; Accountant; Contract Administrator; Marketing/Communications; Recruiter; Technical Sales; Training Sales. **Corporate headquarters:** St. Charles MO. **Other U.S. locations:** Nationwide.

RAYTHEON
1620 Wilshire Drive, Suite 301, Bellevue NE 68005. 402/291-0100. **Contact:** Human Resources. **World Wide Web address:** http://www.raytheon.com. **Description:** A defense and aerospace systems supplier. **NOTE:** Please see website for online application form and to search for job openings. **Positions advertised include:** Configuration Analyst; Quality Assurance Representative; Principle Systems Engineer. **Corporate headquarters location:** Waltham, MA. **Listed on:** New York Stock Exchange. **Stock exchange symbol:** RTN. **Annual Sales/Revenue:** More than $16 billion. **Number of employees worldwide:**78,000.

RICHARD YOUNG CENTER
P.O. Box 24424, Omaha NE 68124. 402/354-6600. **Fax:** 402/354-6648. **Physical address:** 5151 South 26th Street, Omaha NE 68105. **Contact:** Human Resources. **World Wide Web address:** http://www.unl.edu/schpsych/consortium/richard2002.htm. **Description:** A behavioral hospital providing psychiatric, chemical dependency, and behavioral health programs. Richard Young Center also provides assessments, evaluations, and a full continuum of treatment services for all age groups. **Special programs:** Internships. **Operations at this facility include:** Administration.

SANDHILLS PUBLISHING
P.O. Box 82545, Lincoln NE 68501-2545. 402/479-2181. **Physical address:** 120 W. Harvest Drive, Lincoln NE 68521. **Toll-free phone:** 800/331-1978. **Fax:** 402/479-2195. **Contact:** Human Resources. **E-mail address:** human-resources@sandhills.com. **World Wide Web address:** http://www.sandhills.com. **NOTE:** Please see website for online application form. **Description:** An information processing company that publishes six trade (advertising only) publications for buyers and sellers of heavy machinery, trucks, aircraft, and computer equipment. The company also produces two general interest computer magazines that cover personal computing fundamentals and computing options for small businesses. Sandhills Publishing also markets online services that offer instant access to nationwide dealers of personal computer parts and systems, as well as heavy equipment parts. Founded in 1978. **Positions advertised include:** Graphic Artist; Human Resources Consultant; Illustrator; Marketing Field Representative; Sales Representative; Summer Groundskeeper; Writer. **Special Programs:** Internships. **Corporate headquarters location:** This location. **Listed on:** Privately held. **Number of employees at this location:** 350.

SARA LEE BAKING GROUP
1310 Fort Crook Road North, Bellevue NE 68005. 402/731-8370. **Fax:** 402/731-8677. **Contact:** Human Resources. **World Wide Web address:** http://www.earthgrains.com/index.htm. **Description:** Produces bread and a variety of other wholesale bakery products. **Corporate headquarters location:** St. Louis MO. **Listed on:** New York Stock Exchange. **Stock exchange symbol:** SLE.

THE SCOULAR COMPANY
2027 Dodge Street, Omaha NE 68102. 402/342-3500. **Contact:** Personnel. **E-mail address:** resume@scoular.com. **World Wide Web address:** http://www.scoular.com. **Description:** A privately-owned grain and feed ingredient trading company. **Positions advertised include:** Receptionist; International Specialist; Merchandiser Assistant; Senior Merchandiser Assistant; Merchandiser Trainee; Market Specialist; Senior Business Unit Manager; Senior Manager. **Corporate headquarters location:** This location. **Other U.S. locations:** Nationwide. **Number of employees at this location:** 35. **Number of employees nationwide:** 250.

SQUARE D COMPANY
1717 Central Park Road, Lincoln NE 68512-1290. 402/423-6721. **Contact:** Human Resources. **World Wide Web address:** http://www.squared.com. **Description:** Square D Company is a leading supplier of electrical distribution, automation, and industrial control products, systems, and services for the distribution, application, and control of electrical energy. The company's products are marketed to industrial customers, the construction industry, electric utilities, individual consumers, government agencies, and other manufacturers for use in or on their products and equipment. **Other U.S. locations:** Nationwide. **International locations:** Canada; Mexico. **Parent company:** Schneider Electric. **Operations at this facility include:** This location manufactures electrical circuit breakers.

U.S. DEPARTMENT OF VETERANS AFFAIRS
VA NEBRASKA WESTERN IOWA HEALTH CARE SYSTEM
4101 Woolworth Avenue, Omaha NE 68105. 402/346-8800. **Fax:** 402/449-0618. **Contact:** Human Resources. **World Wide Web address:** http://www.va.gov/index.htm. **NOTE:** Please see website for online application form. **Description:** Provides acute medical, surgical, and psychiatric care, as well as a wide variety of outpatient services to veterans in eastern Nebraska and western Iowa. Specialized services are offered in speech pathology, ophthalmology, otolaryngology, hematology, gastroenterology, immunology, allergy, cardiology, nephrology, hypertension, endocrinology, oncology, diabetes, orthopedics, and prosthetics. The medical center is affiliated with the University of Nebraska Medical Center and Creighton University School of Medicine. **Positions advertised include:** Dentist, Nurse; Occupational Therapist; Optometrist; Pharmacist; Physical Therapist; Physician; Podiatrist; Registered Therapy Technician. **Other area locations:** Grand Island NE; Lincoln NE.

U.S. DEPARTMENT OF VETERANS AFFAIRS
VA NEBRASKA WESTERN IOWA HEALTH CARE SYSTEM
2201 North Broadwell Avenue, Grand Island NE 68803-2196. 308/382-3660. **Contact:** Human Resources. **World Wide Web address:** http://www.va.gov/index.htm. **Description:** A medical center. From 54 hospitals in 1930, the VA health care system has grown to include 171 medical centers; more than 364 outpatient, community, and outreach clinics; 130 nursing home care units; and 37 domiciliary residences. VA operates at least one medical center in each of the 48 contiguous states, Puerto Rico, and Washington DC. With approximately 76,000 medical center beds, VA treats nearly 1 million patients in VA hospitals; 75,000 in nursing home care units; and 25,000 in domiciliary residences. VA's outpatient clinics register approximately 24 million visits per year. **Positions advertised include:** Dentist; Nurse; Occupational Therapist; Optometrist; Pharmacist; Physical Therapist; Physician; Podiatrist; Registered Therapy Technician. **Other area locations:** Lincoln NE; Omaha NE.

UNION PACIFIC CORPORATION
1416 Dodge Street, Omaha NE 68179. 402/544-4000. **Toll-free phone:** 888/870-8777. **Fax:** 402/271-6408 **Contact:** Human Resources. **World Wide Web address:** http://www.up.com. **Description:** Provides transportation, computer technology, and logistics services. Union Pacific Corporation operates in three divisions: Union Pacific Railroad; Overnite Transportation; and Union Pacific Technologies. **Corporate headquarters location:** This location. **Listed on:** New York Stock Exchange. **Stock exchange symbol:** UNP. **Number of employees nationwide:** 47,000.

UNIVERSITY OF NEBRASKA AT KEARNEY
905 West 25th Street, Kearney NE 68849. 308/865-8441. **Fax:** 308/865-8630. **Contact:** Human Resources. **World Wide Web address:** http://www.unk.edu. **NOTE:** See website for available positions and corresponding direct contacts. **Description:** A state university.

UNIVERSITY OF NEBRASKA AT LINCOLN
P.O. Box 880438, Lincoln NE 68588-0438. 402/472-3101. **Physical address:** 407 Canfield Administration Building, 501 North 14th Street, Room 407, Lincoln NE 68588. **Contact:** Department of Human Resources. **World Wide Web address:** http://www.unl.edu. **Description:** A state university

UNIVERSITY OF NEBRASKA AT OMAHA
6001 Dodge Street, EAB 205, Omaha NE 68182-0263. 402/554-2321. **Fax:** 402/554--3777. **Recorded jobline:** 402/554-2959. **Contact:** Mary Sweaney, Employment Manager. **E-mail address:** msweaney@mail.unomaha.edu **World Wide Web address:** http://www.unomaha.edu. **Description:** A university. **Positions advertised include:** Computer Systems Specialist; Associate Vice President and Director of Budget; Assistant Vice President and Director of Institutional Research. **Special programs:** Internships. **Number of employees at this location:** 1,200.

UNIVERSITY OF NEBRASKA MEDICAL CENTER
44th and Emile, Omaha NE 68198-5470. 402/559-4000. **Recorded jobline:** 402/559-5443. **Contact:** Human Resources. **NOTE:** Human Resources number is 402/559-4071. Please see website for online application form and for guidelines on how to apply for any open positions. **World Wide Web address:** http://www.unmc.edu. **Description:** Provides family-focused services and supports individuals with disabilities.

VALMONT INDUSTRIES, INC.
One Valmont Plaza, Omaha NE 68154-5215. 402/963-1000. **Toll-free phone:** 800/825-6668. **Fax:** 402/359-6022. **Contact:** Human Resources. **E-mail address:** hr@valmont.com. **World Wide Web address:** http://www.valmont.com. **Description:** Manufactures irrigation equipment, steel and aluminum poles, tubing, and fluted poles. **Corporate headquarters location:** This location. **Other area locations:** McCook NE; Valley NE; Waverly NE; West Point NE. **Other U.S. locations:** Nationwide. **Listed on:** NASDAQ. **Stock exchange symbol:** VALM.

VETERINARY DIAGNOSTIC CENTER
Fair Street and East Campus Loop, P.O. Box 830907, Lincoln NE 68583-0907. 402/472-1434. **Fax:** 402/472-3094. **Contact:** Human Resources. **E-mail:** vdc@unl.edu. **World Wide Web address:** http://vbms.unl.edu/nvdls.shtml. **Description:** A veterinary diagnostic laboratory, part of the Nebraska Veterinary Diagnostic System at University of Nebraska at Lincoln, that identifies animal diseases. **NOTE:** Human Resources phone is 402/472-3101. Part of University of Nebraska at Lincoln.

VISHAY DALE ELECTRONICS
P.O. Box 609, Columbus NE 68602-0609. 402/564-3131. **Physical address:** 1122 23rd Street, Columbus NE 68601. **Fax:** 402/563-6204. **Contact:** Human Resources. **World Wide Web address:** http://www.vishay.com. **Description:** Vishay Dale Electronics is one of the largest manufacturers of fixed resistors and inductors in the United States and a producer of other passive electronic components including transformers, specialty connectors, and plasma displays. **Corporate headquarters location:** This location. **Other U.S. locations:** Norfolk NE; Yankton SD. **Parent company:** Vishay Intertechnology (Malvern PA) is a leader in passive electronic component manufacturing. Other Vishay subsidiaries include Draloric Electronic GmbH, one of the largest manufacturers of resistors in Germany and also a producer of specialty ceramic capacitors; Sfernice, S.A., one of the largest manufacturers of fixed and variable resistors (potentiometers) and printed circuit boards in France; Sprague, a leading supplier of tantalum capacitors to the commercial, industrial, military, and aerospace electronics markets, and also a manufacturer of thick film resistor networks; and Roederstein, a leading European and U.S. film capacitor manufacturer and also a producer of tantalum, aluminum, and ceramic disk capacitors, hybrids, and other passive electronic components. **Operations at this facility include:** This location manufactures wirewound resistors and plasma displays. **Listed on:** New York Stock Exchange. **Stock exchange symbol:** VSH. **Number of employees at this location:** 700.

VISHAY DALE ELECTRONICS
P.O. Box 74, Norfolk NE 68702-0074. 402/371-0080. **Physical address:** 2300 Riverside Boulevard, Norfolk NE 68701. **Contact:** Jeff Nelson, Human Resources Manager. **World Wide Web address:** http://www.vishay.com. **Description:** Vishay Dale Electronics is one of the largest manufacturers of fixed resistors and inductors in the United States and a producer of other passive electronic components including transformers, specialty connectors, and plasma displays. **Corporate headquarters location:** Columbus NE. **Parent company:** Vishay Intertechnology (Malvern PA) is a leader in passive electronic component manufacturing. **Operations at this facility include:** This location manufactures metal film resistors, thick and thin film chip resistors, and resistor networks. **Listed on:** New York Stock Exchange. **Stock exchange symbol:** VSH. **Number of employees at this location:** 730.

WERNER ENTERPRISES, INC.
P.O. Box 45308, Omaha NE 68145-0308. 402/895-6640. **Physical address:** 14507 Frontier Road, Omaha NE 68138. **Toll-free phone:** 800/228-2240. **Fax:** 402/894-3927. **Recorded jobline:** 800/937-6374. **Contact:** Human Resources. **E-mail address:** hr@werner.com. **World Wide Web address:** http://www.werner.com. **Description:** Provides transportation services. **Positions advertised include:** Customer Service Manager; Driver Recruiter; Human Resource Generalist; Night Fleet Coordinator; Safety Supervisor; Accounting Clerk; Customer Service Assistant; Health Insurance Coordinator; Security Gate Guard. **Special programs:** Internships. **Corporate headquarters location:** This location. **Listed on:** NASDAQ. **Stock exchange symbol:** WERN. **Number of employees nationwide:** 12,100.

AAA (AUTOMOBILE ASSOCIATION OF AMERICA)
3312 West Charleston, Las Vegas NV 89102. 702/870-9171. **Contact:** Personnel. **World Wide Web address:** http://www.csaa.com. **Description:** A nonprofit membership organization offering a range of automotive and travel services. **Positions advertised include:** Supervisor, Resolution Center; Tow Truck Operator; Call Center Quality Assurance Analyst; Field Stationary Engineer; Sales Representative; Claim Coordinator. **Other U.S. locations:** Nationwide.

A.B.B. INC.
2175 Lockheed Way, Carson City NV 89706. 775/883-4366. **Contact:** Human Resources. **World Wide Web address:** http://www.abb.com/us. **Description:** Manufactures pH sensors and other electronic equipment. **Corporate headquarters location:** Zurich, Switzerland. **Number of employees nationwide:** 9,500. **Number of employees worldwide:** 120,000.

ATC/VANCOM OF NEVADA, INC.
CITIZENS AREA TRANSIT
3210 Citizen Avenue, North Las Vegas NV 89032. 702/636-6790. **Fax:** 702/636-0562. **Contact:** Human Resources. **Description:** A local and suburban transportation company. Founded in 1992. **Parent company:** ATC. **Listed on:** Privately held.

ACUITY SOLUTIONS
7881 West Charleston Boulevard, Suite 165, Las Vegas NV 89117. 702/196-2000. **Contact:** Human Resources. **World Wide Web address:** http://acuitynv.com. **Description:** A technology consulting firm that designs accounting and business management software solutions.

FERN ADAIR CONSERVATORY OF THE ARTS
3265 East Patrick Lane, Las Vegas NV 89120. 702/458-7575. **Contact:** Staffing. **World Wide Web address:** http://www.fernadair.com. **Description:** A dance school offering ballet, tap, hip hop, tumbling, and jazz lessons, as well as classes in piano, voice, karate, and children's theatre.

NATHAN ADELSON HOSPICE
4141 South Swenson Street, Las Vegas NV 89119-6718. 702/796-3131. **Fax:** 702/796-3163. **Contact:** Human Resources Department. **E-mail address:** jpeasley@nah.org. World **Wide Web address:** http://www.nah.org. **Description:** A nursing home. Founded in 1978. **Positions advertised include:** Registered Nurse; Certified Nursing Assistant; Social Worker; Spiritual Care Counselor; Receptionist.

ADERA
4545 West Diablo Drive, Suite A, Las Vegas NV 89118. 702/257-2810. **Toll-free phone:** 800/650-4797. **Contact:** Human Resources. **World Wide Web address:** http://www.aderacorp.com. **Description:** Performs large-scale printing work. Formats offered include billboards, convention displays, and other signage.

AERVOE INDUSTRIES INC.
P.O. Box 485, Gardnerville NV 89410-0485. 775/783-3100. **Physical address:** 1100 Mark Circle, Gardnerville NV 89410. **Toll-free phone:** 800/548-4656. **Contact:** Human Resources. **E-mail address:** personnel@aervoe.com. **World Wide Web address:** http://www.aervoe.com. **Description:** Manufactures paints, specialty coatings, cleaners, lubricants, MRO products, and recycling equipment for industrial use. **Corporate headquarters location:** This location. **Other U.S. locations:** Nashville IL. **International locations:** Toronto, Canada. **Number of employees at this location:** 100.

AIG VALIC
2030 East Flamingo Road, Suite 145, Las Vegas NV 89119. 702/796-0047. **Contact:** Bruce Corcoran, District Manager. E-mail address: valicresumes@valic.com **World Wide Web address:** http://www.valic.com. **Description:** An insurance and financial services company. **NOTE:** When applying for positions you must fill out an online application form and attach your resume. **Corporate headquarters location:** Houston TX. **Other U.S. locations:** 1400 offices in 44 states. **Parent company:** American International Group, Incorporated. **President/CEO:** Robert P. Condon. **Number of employees nationwide:** Approximately 2,000.

AIRPORT AUTHORITY OF WASHOE COUNTY
RENO/TAHOE INTERNATIONAL AIRPORT
P.O. Box 12490, Reno NV 89510. 775/328-6450. **Physical address:** 2001 East Plum Lane, Reno NV 89502. **Fax:** 775/328-6519. **Contact:** Paul Fillo, Human Resources. **E-mail address:** pfillo@renoairport.com. **World Wide Web address:** http://www.renoairport.com. **Description:** The Airport Authority of Washoe County, comprised of Reno Cannon International and Reno Stead Airports, is an international aviation transportation center. Reno Cannon provides a full range of aviation services and facilities for the Reno-Sparks metropolitan area, as well as western Nevada and northeastern California. The airport serves major and commuter airlines, numerous charter airline flights, cargo carriers, general aviation aircraft, and military aircraft. The Reno Stead Airport provides a wide range of general aviation services and facilities for the Northern Reno/Sparks metro area.

ALARMCO INC.
2007 Las Vegas Boulevard South, Las Vegas NV 89104. 702/382-5000. **Contact:** Human Resources. **World Wide Web address:** http://www.alarmco.com. **Description:** Installs and services alarms for businesses and residences. Founded in 1950. **Corporate headquarters location:** This location. **Number of employees at this location:** 100.

ALBERTSON'S
4995 South Kietzke Lane, Reno NV 89519. 775/827-5350. **Contact:** Hiring Manager. **World Wide Web address:** http://www.albertsons.com. **Description:** A store location of one of the largest food and drug retailers in the United States. The company operates approximately 2,500 stores in 38 states. **Corporate headquarters location:** Boise ID. **Listed on:** New York Stock Exchange. **Stock exchange symbol:** ABS.

ALERE MEDICAL INC.
595 Double Eagle Court, Suite 1000, Reno NV 89521. 775/829-8885. **Fax:** 775/829-8637. **Contact:** Human Resources. **E-mail address:** jobs@alere.com. **World Wide Web address:** http://www.alere.com. **Description:** Works to improve home health care of individuals with heart failure through technology and education. **Positions advertised include:** RN; Sr. Analyst.

ALLIANCE GAMING CORPORATION
6601 South Bermuda Road, Las Vegas NV 89119. 702/896-7600. **Contact:** Human Resources. **E-mail address:** jobs@ally.com. **World Wide Web address:** http://www.ally.com. **Description:** One of the largest private gaming device route operators in the United States. In its Nevada gaming device route operations, the company selects, owns, installs, manages, and services gaming devices in third-party-owned local establishments such as taverns, supermarkets, drug stores, and convenience stores. The company also owns and operates one full-service casino and leases and operates three small casinos, one casino-hotel, and four taverns, which collectively have approximately 840 gaming devices and 10 table games. The company also has operations in Louisiana, where it has approximately 730 video poker devices. **NOTE:** Search and apply for positions online. **Corporate headquarters location:** This location. **Listed on:** NYSE. **Stock exchange symbol:** AGI. **Number of employees worldwide:** 2,300.

ALLIED SECURITY, INC.
1515 East Tropicana Avenue, Suite 395, Las Vegas NV 89119. 702/795-3317. **Contact:** Personnel. **World Wide Web address:** http://www.alliedsecurity.com. **Description:** Provides security services to a wide variety of clients including businesses, hospitals, and residential customers. **NOTE:** Apply for positions online. **Corporate headquarters location:** King of Prussia PA. **Other U.S. locations:** 60 offices nationwide. **Number of employees nationwide:** 20,000.

AMERCO
1325 Airmotive Way, Suite 100, Reno NV 89502. 775/688-6300. **Contact:** Human Resources. **World Wide Web address:** http://www.amerco.com. **Description:** Amerco is the holding company for U-Haul International, Ponderosa Holdings, and the Amerco Real Estate Company. U-Haul rents trucks, trailers, and support items to the do-it-yourself mover in the United States and Canada. U-Haul International also rents self-storage facilities in the United States. The company's distribution network includes approximately 1,100 U-Haul centers and 11,500 independent dealers. Ponderosa is a holding company for the company's two insurance businesses: Oxford Life and Republic Western Insurance. Oxford provides life and health insurance to employees; Republic Western provides auto insurance to U-Haul rental customers. Amerco Real Estate Company operates and manages nonresidential buildings. **Listed on:** New York Stock Exchange. **Stock exchange symbol:** AOPRA.

AMERICAN BUILDINGS COMPANY
2263 Mouton Drive, Carson City NV 89706. 775/882-4060. **Contact:** Human Resources. **E-mail address:** employment@americanbuildings.com. **World Wide Web address:** http://www.americanbuildings.com. **Description:** Manufactures prefabricated metal buildings. **Positions advertised include:** CAD/Drafting,; Engineering; Sales. **Corporate headquarters location:** Eufaula AL. **Parent company:** MAGNATRAX. **Number of employees nationwide:** 500. **Other U.S. locations:** Nationwide.

AMERICAN HEART ASSOCIATION (AHA)
2355 Red Rock Street, Suite 103, Las Vegas NV 89146. 702/367-1366. **Contact:** Barbara Wood, Director. **E-mail address:** opportunity@heart.org. **World Wide Web address:** http://www.americanheart.org. **Description:** The American Heart Association is one of the oldest and largest national, nonprofit, voluntary health associations dedicated to reducing disability and death from cardiovascular diseases and stroke. The AHA, also called the Heart Fund, is a community-based organization with about 2,100 state and metropolitan affiliates, divisions, and branches throughout the United States and Puerto Rico. AHA-funded research has yielded such discoveries as CPR, bypass surgery, pacemakers, artificial heart valves, microsurgery, life-extending drugs, and new surgical techniques to repair heart defects. The American Heart Association develops interactive public education programs and trains about 5 million Americans per year in emergency care procedures; these training systems are used by millions more worldwide. Founded in 1924. **Corporate headquarters location:** Dallas TX. **Other U.S. locations:** Nationwide.

AMERICAN MEDICAL RESPONSE
1200 South Martin Luther King Boulevard, Las Vegas NV 89102-2303. 702/671-6975. **Contact:** Human Resources. **E-mail address:** jose_valenzuela@amr-ems.com. **World Wide Web address:** http://www.amr.net. **Description:** The nation's leading private medical transportation company. **NOTE:** Search and apply for positions online. **Positions advertised include:** Paramedics. **Office hours:** Monday - Friday, 8:00 a.m. - 5:00 p.m. **Corporate headquarters location:** Aurora CO. **Number of employees nationwide:** 18,000.

AMERICAN PACIFIC CORPORATION
3770 Howard Hughes Parkway, Suite 300, Las Vegas NV 89109. 702/671-6975. **Fax:** 702/735-4876. **Contact:** Human Resources. **World Wide Web address:** http://www.apfc.com. **Description:** American Pacific Corporation is a specialty chemical company that produces products used primarily in space flight and defense systems, automotive airbag safety systems and fire extinguishment systems. The Company also designs and manufactures environmental protection equipment products and is involved in real estate development. **Subsidiaries include:** American Azide Corporation; Ampac Development Company; Halotron, Inc.; Pepcon Systems, Inc.; Western Electrochemical Company. **Corporate headquarters location:** This location. **Listed on:** NASDAQ. **Stock exchange symbol:** APFC.

AMERICAN RED CROSS
3672 North Rancho Drive, Las Vegas NV 89130. 702/791-3311. **Fax:** 702/791-3372. **Contact:** Personnel. **World Wide Web address:** http://www.redcross.org. **Description:** A humanitarian organization that aids disaster victims, gathers blood for crisis distribution, trains individuals to respond to emergencies, educates individuals on various diseases, and raises funds for other charitable establishments. **Corporate headquarters location:** Washington DC. **Other U.S. locations:** Nationwide.

AMERICAN RIVER PACKAGING
250 Vista Boulevard, Suite 101, Sparks NV 89434. 775/352-2000. **Fax:** 775/352-2040. **Contact:** Human Resources. **World Wide Web address:** http://www.arpkg.com. **Description:** This location manufactures corrugated containers. Founded in 1980. **Other U.S. locations:** Madera CA; Sacramento CA.

AMERICAN VANTAGE COMPANIES
4735 South Durango Avenue, Las Vegas NV 89147. 702/227-9800. **Contact:** Human Resources. **Description:** Provides consulting services to tribal gaming organizations.

AMERISTAR CASINOS, INC.
3773 Howard Hughes Parkway, Suite 490S, Las Vegas NV 89109. 702/567-7000. **Fax:** 702/866-6416. **Contact:** Human Resources/Recruiter. **E-mail address:** corporaterecruiting@ameristarcasinos.com. **World Wide Web address:** http://www.ameristarcasinos.com. **Description:** A casino holding company. **Positions advertised include:** Administrative Assistant; Assistant VP of Administration; VP of Procurement and QA; Webmaster. **Corporate headquarters location:** This location. **Subsidiaries include:** Ameristar Casino St. Charles (St. Charles MO): Ameristar Casino Hotel Council Bluffs (Council Bluffs IA); Ameristar Casino Hotel Kansas City (Kansas City MO); Ameristar Casino Hotel Vicksburg (Vicksburg MS); Cactus Pete's Resort Casino (Jackpot NV). **Listed on:** NASDAQ. **Stock exchange symbol:** ASCA.

ANGLOGOLD (JERRITT CANYON) CORPORATION
HC 31, Box 78, Elko NV 89801. 775/738-5006. **Contact:** Human Resources. **World Wide Web address:** http://www.anglogold.com. **Description:** A gold mining company. **Special programs:** Apprenticeships; Training. **Corporate headquarters location:** Denver CO. **Other U.S. locations:** Victor CO. **International locations:** Worldwide. **Listed on:** New York Stock Exchange. **Stock exchange symbol:** AU. **Annual sales/revenues:** More than $100 million. **Number of employees at this location:** 400. **Number of employees nationwide:** 700. **Number of employees worldwide:** 90,000.

ANTHEM BLUE CROSS BLUE SHIELD
6900 West Cliff Drive, Suite 600, Las Vegas NV 89145. 702/228-2583. **Contact:** Human Resources. **World Wide Web address:** http://www.anthem.com. **Description:** A nonprofit health care insurance organization providing managed health care plans to both individuals and groups. Anthem Blue Cross Blue Shield offers Point-of-Service, individual health, PPO, and HMO plans. **NOTE:** Search and apply for positions online. **Corporate headquarters location:** Indianapolis IN. **Listed on:** New York Stock Exchange. **Stock exchange symbol:** ATH.

ANTHEM BLUE CROSS BLUE SHIELD
5250 South Virginia, Reno NV 89520. 775/448-4000. **Contact:** Human Resources Manager. **World Wide Web address:** http://www.anthem.com. **Description:** A nonprofit health care insurance organization providing managed health care plans to both individuals and groups. Anthem Blue Cross Blue Shield offers Point-of-Service, individual health, PPO, and HMO plans. **NOTE:** Search and apply for positions online. **Listed on:** New York Stock Exchange. **Stock exchange symbol:** ATH.

ARAMARK LEISURE SERVICES
3150 Paradise Road, Las Vegas NV 89109. 702/791-8182. **Contact:** Human Resources. **World Wide Web address:** http://www.aramark.com. **Description:** This location provides all food and catering services for Cashman Field, a minor league baseball park. **Corporate headquarters location:** Philadelphia PA. **Parent company:** ARAMARK is one of the world's leading providers of managed services. The company operates in all 50 states and 10 foreign countries, offering a broad range of services to businesses of all sizes, including most *Fortune* 500 companies and thousands of universities; hospitals; and municipal, state, and federal government facilities. ARAMARK is employee-owned. With revenues of over $5 billion, the company is among the market leaders in all of its businesses. ARAMARK's businesses include Food, Leisure, and Support Services including Campus Dining Services, School Nutrition Services, Leisure Services, Business Dining Services, International Services, Healthcare Support Services, Conference Center Management, and Refreshment Services; Facility Services; Correctional Services; Industrial Services; Uniform Services, which includes Wearguard, a direct marketer of work clothing; Health and Education Services, including Spectrum Healthcare Services and Children's World Learning Centers; and Book and Magazine Services.

ARAMARK SPORTS & ENTERTAINMENT, INC
P.O. Box 12309, Zephyr Cove NV 89448-4309. 775/588-6644. **Physical address:** 760 Highway 50, Zephyr Cove NV 89448. **Fax:** 775/588-1792. **Contact:** Human Resources. **E-mail address:** mcconville-mary@aramark.com. **World Wide Web address:** http://www.zephyrcove.com. **Description:** Owns and operates Zephyr Cove Resort and Zephyr Cove Snowmobile Center. **Office hours:** Monday - Friday, 8:30 a.m. - 6:00 p.m. **Corporate headquarters location:** This location.

ARCATA ASSOCIATES, INC.
2588 Fire Mesa Street, Suite 110, Las Vegas NV 89128. 702/642-9500. **Fax:** 702/968-2237. **Contact:** Director of Human Resources. **E-mail address:** resumes@arcataassoc.com. **World Wide Web address:** http://www.arcataassoc.com. **Description:** Provides computer engineering and systems manufacturing services. **Positions advertised include:** Quality Assurance Engineer II; Computer Operator IV. **Corporate headquarters location:** This location. **Other area locations:** Fallon NV. **Other U.S. locations:** Huntsville AL; Barstow CA; Greenbelt MD; Las Cruces NM; Wallops Island VA.

ARISTOCRAT TECHNOLOGIES, INC.
7230 Amigo Street, Las Vegas NV 89119. 702/270-1000. **Contact:** Human Resources Manager. **World Wide Web address:** http://www.aristocrattechnologies.com. **Description:** Designs, manufactures, and distributes products including a slot machine accounting system, a player tracking system known as OASIS System II, and products that link slot machines in various locations. **NOTE:** Search and apply for positions online. **Positions advertised include:** Operations Analyst; Implementation Specialist; Technical Support Specialist; Project Manager; Program Manager. **Corporate headquarters location:** Australia. **Other U.S. locations:** Nationwide. **International locations:** Worldwide. **Number of employees nationwide:** 600.

ARIZONA CHARLIE'S, INC.
740 South Decatur Boulevard, Las Vegas NV 89107. 702/258-5200. **Contact:** Human Resources. **E-mail address:** Debra.Pingul@azcharlies.com **World Wide Web address:** http://www.azcharlies.com. **Description:** Operates two full-service gaming, entertainment, and dining facilities. **NOTE:** search and apply for positions online. **Positions advertised include:** Front Desk Clerk; Night Auditor; Security Officer; Room Attendant; Food Server; Cook; Ultimate Rewards Representative. **Parent company:** Becker Gaming is a holding company with subsidiaries that operate a gaming machine route and own and operate the Charlie's restaurant chain.

ARROW ELECTRONICS, INC.
665 Maestro Drive, Reno NV 89511. 775/334-2800. **Contact:** Human Resources. **World Wide Web address:** http://www.arrow.com. **Description:** A distributor of electronics components, systems, and related items, Arrow serves as a supply channel partner for more than 600 suppliers and over 150,000 original equipment manufacturers, contract manufacturers, and commercial customers through more than 193 sales facilities and 21 distribution centers in 40 countries. **NOTE:** Search and apply for positions online. **Corporate headquarters location:** Melville NY. **Other U.S. locations:** Nationwide. **Subsidiaries include:** CCI Electronique (France); Components Agents Ltd. (Asia); Microprocessor & Memory Distribution Limited (United Kingdom); The ATD Group (Portugal, Spain); Zeus Components (United States). **Listed on:** New York Stock Exchange. **Stock exchange symbol:** ARW. **Number of employees at this location:** 150.

ATA AIRLINES, INC.
P.O. Box 11027, Las Vegas NV 89111. 702/261-3610. **Physical address:** 5757 Wayne Newton Boulevard, Las Vegas NV 89111. **Contact:** Human Resources. **E-mail address:** jobs@iflyata.com. **World Wide Web address:** http://www.ata.com. **Description:** An air transportation company serving major business centers and popular vacation destinations through scheduled service and charter operations. **NOTE:** Search and apply for positions online. **Corporate headquarters location:** Indianapolis IN. **Listed on:** NASDAQ. **Stock exchange symbol:** ATAH. **Chairman and CEO:** J. George Mikelsons. **Number of employees nationwide:** 7,200.

AUTO DIESEL ELECTRIC
1150 Matley Lane, Reno NV 89502. 775/329-0707. **Toll-free phone:** 800/648-1810. **Contact:** Manager. **World Wide Web address:** http://www.adereno.com. **Description:** Rebuilds, repairs, services, and retails electronic automotive parts including batteries, alternators, starters, and lights. **Other U.S. locations:** Sparks NV.

BPB GYPSUM
HCR 89033, Box 2900, Las Vegas NV 89124. 702/875-4111. **Contact:** Human Resources. **E-mail address:** hr@bpb-na.com. **World Wide Web address:** http://www.bpb-na.com. **Description:** Mines gypsum.

BALLARD COMMUNICATIONS
321 North Pecos, Suite 110, Henderson NV 89074-1348. 702/836-3000. **Fax:** 702/836-3003. **Contact:** Human Resources. **E-mail address:** careers@ballardpr.com. **World Wide Web address:** http://www.ballardpr.com. **Description:** Provides creative solutions to communications challenges. An advertising agency, public relations firm, and graphic and web design firm.

BALLY'S LAS VEGAS
3645 Las Vegas Boulevard South, Las Vegas NV 89109. 702/739-4111. **Contact:** Human Resources. **World Wide Web address:** http://www.parkplace.com/ballys/lasvegas. **Description:** Operates Bally's Las Vegas, which provides convention center and casino resort hotel facilities. The hotel features 2,800 rooms. **NOTE:** Search and apply for positions online. **Parent company:** Caesars Entertainment.

BANK OF AMERICA
401 South Virginia Street, Reno NV 89501. 775/688-8630. **Contact:** Human Resources. **World Wide Web address:** http://www.bankofamerica.com. **Description:** A full-service banking and financial institution. **Positions advertised include:** Customer Service Representative, Full Time Teller. **Corporate headquarters location:** Charlotte NC. **Other area locations:** Statewide. **Other U.S. locations:** Nationwide.

BARNES & NOBLE BOOKSELLERS
5555 South Virginia Street, Reno NV 89502. 775/826-8882. **Contact:** Store Manager. **World Wide Web address:** http://www.bn.com. **Description:** One location of the bookstore chain. This location also has a cafe. **Corporate headquarters location:** New York NY. **Other U.S. locations:** Nationwide.

BARNES & NOBLE BOOKSELLERS
567 North Stephanie, Henderson NV 89014. 702/434-1533. **Contact:** Manager. **World Wide Web address:** http://www.bn.com. **Description:** One location of the bookstore chain. This location also has a cafe and music department. **Corporate headquarters location:** New York NY. **Other U.S. locations:** Nationwide.

BARNES & NOBLE BOOKSELLERS
3860 Maryland Parkway, Las Vegas NV 89119 702-734-2900. **Contact:** Manager. **World Wide Web address:** http://www.bn.com. **Description:** One location of the bookstore chain. This location also has a cafe and music department. **Corporate headquarters location:** New York NY. **Other U.S. locations:** Nationwide.

BECHTEL NEVADA
P.O. Box 98521, Las Vegas NV 89193. 702/295-0577. **Fax:** 702/295-2448. **Recorded jobline:** 702/295-0200. **Contact:** Itaska Cole, Human Resources. **E-mail address:** bnresumes@nv.doe.gov. **World Wide Web address:** http://www.bechtelnevada.com. **Description:** Provides nuclear engineering services in support of the U.S. Department of Energy. Services include hazardous chemical spill tests, emergency response training, conventional weapon testing, and environmental technology studies. **NOTE:** Entry-level positions are offered. Search and apply for positions online. **Positions advertised include:** Senior Operations Specialist; Clerk; Technical Staff Member; Administrative Staff Member; Assistant Superintendent; Scientist; Fire Fighter; Senior Engineer; Procurement Specialist; Principle Engineer. **Special programs:** Internships; Summer Jobs. **Other U.S. locations:** Pleasanton CA; Santa Barbara CA; Washington DC; Los Alamos NM. **Number of employees at this location:** 1,980. **Number of employees nationwide:** 2,500.

BENTLY NEVADA CORPORATION
1631 Bently Parkway South, Minden NV 89423. 775/782-3611. **Contact:** Personnel Department. **World Wide Web address:** http://www.bently.com. **Description:** Bently Nevada Corporation is a producer of monitoring and diagnostic systems for rotating machinery. The company's product line includes vibration transducers, monitors, and systems for predictive maintenance, as well as test equipment for the diagnostics of rotating machines. The company's services include technical training, design and installation, product, and machinery diagnostics services. **NOTE:** Co-op and intern positions available. Search and apply for positions online. **Corporate headquarters location:** This location. **Other U.S. locations:** Nationwide. **International locations:** Worldwide. **Parent company:** GE Energy.

THE LOUIS BERGER GROUP, INC.
500 Amigo Court, Suite 100, Las Vegas NV 89119. 702/736-6632. **Contact:** Human Resource Dept. **E-mail address:** recruiter@louisberger.com. **World Wide Web address:** http://www.louisberger.com. **Description:** A roadway design and engineering company. Founded in 1953. **NOTE:** Search and apply for positions online. **Corporate headquarters location:** East Orange NJ. **Other U.S. locations:** Nationwide.

BERRY PLASTICS CORPORATION
800 East Horizon Drive, Henderson NV 89015. 702/564-7770. **Fax:** 702/564-2174. **Contact:** Personnel. **World Wide Web address:** http://www.berryplastics.com. **Description:** Berry Plastics Corporation manufactures and markets plastic packaging products including caps for aerosol cans and rigid open-top containers. The company operates three manufacturing plants throughout the country. **NOTE:** Applicants must fill out the online application form for consideration. See Website for details. **Corporate headquarters location:** Evansville IL. **Other U.S. locations:** IL; IA; KS; MD; NC; OH; TX; VA. **International locations:** England; Italy. **Operations at this facility include:** This location manufactures plastic containers for food and industrial uses.

BEST WESTERN AIRPORT PLAZA HOTEL
1981 Terminal Way, Reno NV 89502-3215. 775/348-6370. **Contact:** Employment. **World Wide Web address:** http://www.bestwestern.com. **Description:** A hotel operated by Best Western International, the mid-priced hotel chain with over 3,400 hotels in 60 countries including over 1,000 in Europe. Best Western has over 1,900

meeting facilities worldwide with 900 in the United States. **NOTE:** Search and apply for positions online.

BLACK & DECKER
3585 South Decatur, Suite A, Las Vegas NV 89103. 702/889-6025. **Contact:** Human Resources. **World Wide Web address:** http://www.bdk.com. **Description:** Black & Decker is a global marketer and manufacturer of products used in and around the home and for commercial applications. The company is also a major supplier of information technology and services to governmental and commercial clients worldwide. Black & Decker is one of the world's largest producers of power tools, power tool accessories, security hardware, and electric lawn and garden tools, as well as one of the largest global suppliers of engineered fastening systems to the markets it serves. **NOTE:** Apply for positions online: **Operations at this facility include:** This location is a retail store. **Listed on:** New York Stock Exchange. **Stock exchange symbol:** BDK.

BLACK & VEATCH
4040 South Eastern Avenue, Suite 330, Las Vegas NV 89119. 702/732-0448. **Contact:** Human Resources. **World Wide Web address:** http://www.bv.com. **Description:** An environmental/civil engineering and construction firm serving utilities, commerce, industry, and government agencies in more than 40 countries throughout the world. Black & Veatch provides a broad range of study, design, construction management, and turnkey capabilities to clients in the water and wastewater fields. The firm is one of the leading authorities on drinking water treatment through the use of activated carbon, ozone, and other processes. Black & Veatch is also engaged in wastewater treatment work including reclamation and reuse projects and the beneficial use of wastewater residuals. Other services are provided for solid waste recycling and disposal, transportation, and storm water management. In the energy field, Black & Veatch is a leader in providing engineering procurement and construction for electric power plants. The firm's areas of expertise include coal-fueled plants; simple and combined-cycle combustion turbines; fluidized bed combustion; waste-to-energy facilities; hydroelectric plants; and cogeneration facilities. Black & Veatch's capabilities also include nuclear power projects, advanced technology, air quality control, performance monitoring, plant life management, and facilities modification. In addition, Black & Veatch has extensive expertise in the transmission and distribution field. These capabilities encompass substations, overhead and underground transmission, energy management systems, and communications. In the industrial sector, Black & Veatch's experience is focused primarily on projects involving cleanrooms, industrial processes and planning, utility systems, and cogeneration. In addition to engineering, procurement, and construction, Black & Veatch offers a variety of management and financial services, including institutional strengthening, privatization, strategic financial planning, and information management. **NOTE:** Search and apply for positions online. **Corporate headquarters location:** Overland Park KN. **Other U.S. locations:** Nationwide. **International locations:** Worldwide.

B'MORE SECURITY & PROTECTION AGENCY
1928 Western Avenue, Suite 5, Las Vegas NV 89102. 702/598-1941. **Contact:** Human Resources. **Description:** An agency providing armed and unarmed security services including bodyguard services, convention security, and NDOT-certified traffic control. Founded in 1989. **Corporate headquarters location:** This location. **Listed on:** Privately held. **Annual sales/revenues:** Less than $5 million. **Number of employees at this location:** 65.

THE BOARDWALK CASINO HOLIDAY INN
3750 Las Vegas Boulevard South, Las Vegas NV 89109. 702/735-2400. **Contact:** Human Resources Manager. **World Wide Web address:** http://boardwalklv.com. **Description:** Operates a hotel/casino offering gaming facilities, restaurants, meeting space, and gift shops.

BOISE CASCADE CORPORATION
3950 West Diablo Drive, Building B2, Las Vegas NV 89118. 702/740-8200. **Contact:** Human Resources. **World Wide Web address:** http://www.bc.com. **Description:** Boise Cascade Corporation is a producer and distributor of pulp and paper, a direct distributor of office products, and a manufacturer and distributor of building products. The company has more than 90 manufacturing and distribution locations in 27 states. Boise Cascade Corporation's paper is used for commercial printing and publishing, forms, envelopes, reprographics, tablets, and packaging. Boise Cascade Corporation provides customers with direct delivery of office and computer supplies. Boise Cascade Corporation also produces engineered wood products such as laminated veneer lumber and wood I-joists. Founded in 1957. **NOTE:** Search and apply for positions online: **Corporate headquarters location:** Boise ID. **Operations at this location include:** This location is a warehouse. **Listed on:** New York Stock Exchange. **Stock exchange symbol:** BCC. **Number of employees worldwide:** 24,000.

BOY SCOUTS OF AMERICA
7220 South Paradise Road, Las Vegas NV 89119. 702/736-4366. **Contact:** Joe Danizewski, Director of Field Service. **World Wide Web address:** http://www.scouting.org. **Description:** A national scouting organization for young adults. The Boy Scouts of America has 340 local councils nationwide. **Corporate headquarters location:** Irving TX.

BOYD GAMING CORPORATION
2950 South Industrial Road, Las Vegas NV 89109-1150. 702/792-7200. **Fax:** 702/792-7354. **Contact:** Personnel. **World Wide Web address:** http://www.boydgaming.com. **Description:** An owner and operator of casino entertainment properties. Boyd Gaming Corporation owns and operates seven properties in Las Vegas: California Hotel & Casino; Eldorado Casino; Fremont Hotel & Casino; Jokers Wild Casino; Main Street Station Casino, Brewery, & Hotel; Sam's Town Hotel & Gambling Hall; and Stardust Resort & Casino. In addition, the company owns and operates Blue Chip Casino & Hotel (Michigan City IN), Par-A-Dice Hotel & Casino (East Peoria IL), Sam's Town Motel & Gambling Hall (Robinson MS), and Treasure Chest Casino (Kenner LA). **Positions advertised include:** Media Coordinator; Database Manager; Slot Floor Person; Custodian; Food Server; Cocktail Waitress; Maintenance Engineer; Specialty Room Supervisor. **Corporate headquarters location:** This location. **Other U.S. locations:** IL; LA; MO; MS. **Listed on:** New York Stock Exchange. **Stock exchange symbol:** BYD. **Chairman/CEO:** William S. Boyd. **Annual sales/revenues:** More than $100 million.

BULLDOG EQUIPMENT
281 Commerce Park Court, North Las Vegas NV 89032. 702/646-4070. **Contact:** Manager. **Description:** A contractor that performs paving, excavating, sewer, and water work.

BURNS VETERINARY SUPPLY, INC.
4795 Longley Lane, Reno NV 89502. 775/828-4843. **Contact:** Personnel. **World Wide Web address:** http://www.burnsvet.com. **Description:** A distributor of veterinary pharmaceuticals and biological products. **NOTE:** Jobseekers are required to have an A.H.T. License or the equivalent for sales representatives and telemarketers. **Corporate headquarters location:** Westbury NY. **Other U.S. locations:** Nationwide. **International locations:** Worldwide. **Listed on:** Privately held. **Number of employees at this location:** 50. **President:** Kim Allen.

CH2M HILL
2285 Corporate Circle, Suite 200, Henderson NV 89014. 702/369-6175. **Contact:** Human Resources Manager. **World Wide Web address:** http://www.ch2m.com. **Description:** An engineering consulting firm. The company provides planning, engineering design, and operation and construction management services to help clients apply technology, safeguard the environment, and develop infrastructure. The staff includes specialists in environmental engineering and waste management, water management, transportation, industrial facilities, and a broad spectrum of infrastructure systems. Founded in 1946. **Corporate headquarters location:** Englewood CO. **Other U.S. locations:** Nationwide. **International locations:** Worldwide.

CH2M HILL
5370 Kietzke Lane, Reno NV 89511. 775/329-7300. **Contact:** Human Resources. **World Wide Web address:** http://www.ch2m.com. **Description:** An engineering consulting firm. The company provides planning, engineering design, and operation and construction management services to help clients apply technology, safeguard the environment, and develop infrastructure. The staff includes specialists in environmental engineering and waste management, water management, transportation, industrial facilities, and a broad spectrum of infrastructure systems. Founded in 1946. **Corporate headquarters location:** Englewood CO. **Other U.S. locations:** Nationwide. **International locations:** Worldwide.

CAESARS ENTERTAINMENT, INC
3930 Howard Hughes Parkway, Las Vegas NV 89109. 702/699-5000. **Contact:** Human Resources Manager. **World Wide Web address:** http://www.caesars.com. **Description:** Operates 29 properties including Grand Casinos, Flamingo Casinos, Bally's, and Hilton Gaming Resorts & Casinos. **NOTE:** Search and apply for positions online. **Corporate headquarters location:** This location. **Listed on:** New York Stock Exchange. **Stock exchange symbol:** CZR. **Number of employees worldwide:** 54,000.

CALIFORNIA HOTEL & CASINO
P.O. Box 630, Las Vegas NV 89125-0630. 702/385-1222. **Physical address:** 12 Ogden, Las Vegas NV 89101. **Contact:** Human Resources. **World Wide Web address:** http://www.thecal.com. **Description:** A hotel and casino. **Positions advertised include:** Prep Cook; Custodian; Database Manager; Security Guard. **Parent company:** Boyd Gaming Corporation.

CALIFORNIA POOLS & SPAS
9037 West Sahara Avenue, Las Vegas NV 89117. 702/254-2654. **Contact:** Personnel Director. **E-mail address:** careers@californiapools.com. **World Wide Web address:** http://www.californiapools.com. **Description:** Constructs spas and swimming pools. **Other U.S. locations:** AZ; CA; TX.

CAMDEN
4041 East Sunset Road, Henderson NV 89014. 702/435-9800. **Fax:** 702/435-6815. **Recorded jobline:** 866/524-3592. **Recorded jobline:** 866/524-3592. **Contact:** Human Resources. **E-mail address:** jobs@camdenliving.com. **World Wide Web address:** http://www.camdenliving.com. **Description:** A self-administered and self-managed real estate investment trust, engaged in the acquisition, development, and operation of multifamily properties in the greater Las Vegas NV area. **Corporate headquarters location:** Houston TX. **Listed on:** New York Stock Exchange. **Stock exchange symbol:** CPT.

CAPITAL CABINET CORPORATION
3645 Losee Road, North Las Vegas NV 89030-3324. 702/649-8733. **Fax:** 702/649-6512. **Contact:** Human Resources Department. **E-mail address:** employment@capitalcabinet.com. **World Wide Web address:** http://www.capitalcabinet.com. **Description:** Manufactures wooden kitchen cabinetry. Founded in 1946. **Positions advertised include:** Finish Room Technician; Cabinet Designer; Sales Representative; Installer. **International locations:** Ontario CA.

CARDINAL HEALTH LAS VEGAS
61 Spectrum Boulevard, Las Vegas NV 89101. 702/438-4494. **Contact:** Human Resources. **World Wide Web address:** http://www.cardinal.com. **Description:** Cardinal Health, Incorporated manufactures and distributes pharmaceuticals, as well as medical supplies and equipment. **NOTE:** Search and apply for positions online. **Corporate headquarters location:** Dublin OH. **Other U.S. locations:** Nationwide. **International locations:** Worldwide. **Operations at this facility include:** This location manufactures radioactive drugs that are distributed to businesses and hospitals in the Las Vegas area. **Listed on:** New York Stock Exchange. **Stock exchange symbol:** CAH. **CEO/Chairman:** Robert D. Walter. **Sales/revenue:** Over $50 billion. **Number of employees worldwide:** 55,000.

CARSON CITY, CITY OF
201 North Carson Street, Suite 4, Carson City NV 89701. 775/887-2103. **Fax:** 775/887-2067. **Recorded jobline:** 775/887-2240. **Contact:** Personnel Manager. **E-mail address:** pers@ci.carson-city.nv.us. **World Wide Web address:** http://www.carson-city.nv.us. **Description:** Administrative offices for Carson City. The city and county governments were combined in 1969 to form one government. The city has a population of approximately 52,000. This location also hires seasonally. Founded in 1969. **NOTE:** Entry-level positions, part-time positions, and second and third shifts are offered. **Positions advertised include:** Grants Administrator; Recreational Aides; Deputy Sheriff; Public Safety Communication Operator. **Special programs:** Training; Summer Jobs. **Office hours:** Monday - Friday, 8:00 a.m. - 5:00 p.m. **Annual sales/revenues:** $21 - $50 million. **Number of employees at this location:** 850.

CARSON TAYLOR HARVEY CONSTRUCTION
255 East Warm Springs Road, Las Vegas NV 89119. 702/876-6013. **Fax:** 702/876-5580. **Contact:** Human Resources. **World Wide Web address:** http://www.taylorconstrgrp.com. **Description:** A construction company specializing in commercial and industrial projects. **Corporate headquarters location:** Des Moines IA. **Parent company:** Taylor Construction Group (Des Moines IA).

CARSON-TAHOE HOSPITAL
P.O. Box 2168, Carson City NV 89702-2168. 775/882-1361. **Physical address:** 775 Fleischmann Way, Carson City NV 89703. **Fax:** 775/885-4500. **Contact:** Human Resources. **World Wide Web address:** http://www.carsontahoe.com. **Description:** A fully-accredited, nonprofit county hospital. Carson-Tahoe, maintaining a 128-bed, acute care facility, provides medical, surgical, obstetrical, neonatal, nursery, pediatric, psychiatric, intensive, cardiac, and emergency care services. The outpatient center includes laboratory, cardiopulmonary, medical imaging, physical therapy services, and cardiac rehabilitation. Founded in 1949. **NOTE:** Search and apply for positions online.

Positions advertised include: Certified Nurses Assistants; Cook; Dietitian; Lab Asst; LPN; RN; Ultrasound Technician. **Number of employees at this location:** 900.

CASTAWAYS HOTEL
P.O. Box 43117, Las Vegas NV 89116-1117. 702/385-9123. **Physical address:** 2800 Fremont Street, Las Vegas NV 89104. **Recorded jobline:** 702/385-9101. **Contact:** Human Resources. **Description:** A hotel with 447 guest rooms including four suites. Castaways Hotel also includes an 80,000 square foot casino, a 1,200-seat bingo parlor, dining and meeting facilities, and a 106-lane bowling alley.

CENTURY GRAPHICS INC.
4645 South Procyon Avenue, Suite C, Las Vegas NV 89103. 702/795-0440. **Toll-free phone:** 888/413-2240. **Contact:** Human Resources Manager. **World Wide Web address:** http://www.centurygraphicsprinting.com. **Description:** Century Graphics specializes in commercial and four-color printing. Founded in 1983. **Operations at this facility include:** This location prints magazines and catalogs.

CHAMPION CHEVROLET
P.O. Box 7277, Reno NV 89510. 775/786-3111. **Physical address:** 800 Kietzke Lane, Reno NV 89502. **Contact:** Maxine Taylor, Office Manager. **World Wide Web address:** http://www.championchev.com. **Description:** A Chevrolet Geo dealership.

CHARTER COMMUNICATIONS
9335 Prototype Drive, Reno NV 89511. 775/850-8555. **Contact:** Human Resources. **World Wide Web address:** http://www.charter.com. **Description:** A cable television and broadband services companies. **NOTE:** Search and apply for positions online. Job notification via e-mail. **Listed on:** NASDAQ. **Stock exchange symbol:** CHTR.

CHEMICAL LIME COMPANY
P.O. Box 127, Henderson NV 89015-0127. 702/565-8991. **Physical address:** 8000 West Lake Mead, Henderson NV 89015. **Contact:** Plant Manager. **E-mail address:** recruitment@lhoist.com. **World Wide Web address:** http://www.chemicallime.com. **Description:** Operates two manufacturing plants and two quarries in Clark County. The company's principal products are high-calcium limestone, dolomite limestone, dolomite glass flux, high-calcium quicklime, dolomitic quicklime, calcium hydrated lime, and dolomitic hydrated lime, which is sold widely in the western United States to the construction industry under the trade name Type S Hydrated Lime. **Corporate headquarters location:** Fort Worth TX. **Parent company:** Lhoist Group, Belgium.

CHEMICAL LIME COMPANY
P.O. Box 363068, North Las Vegas NV 89036-7068. 702/643-7702. **Contact:** Plant Manager. **E-mail address:** recruitment@lhoist.com. **World Wide Web address:** http://www.chemicallime.com. **Description:** Operates two manufacturing plants and two quarries in Clark County. The company's principal products are high-calcium limestone, dolomite limestone, dolomite glass flux, high-calcium quicklime, dolomitic quick lime, calcium hydrated lime, and dolomitic hydrated lime, which is sold widely in the western United States. to the construction industry under the trade name Type S Hydrated Lime. **Corporate headquarters location:** Fort Worth TX. **Parent company:** Lhoist Group, Belgium.

CIRCUIT CITY STORES, INC.
4811 Kietzke Lane, Reno NV 89509. 775/827-5011. **Contact:** Manager. **World Wide Web address:** http://www.circuitcity.com. **Description:** A store location of one of the largest U.S. retailers of brand name consumer electronics and major appliances, as well as personal computers and music software. **NOTE:** Apply for positions online. **Corporate headquarters location:** Richmond VA.

CIRCUS CIRCUS
2880 Las Vegas Boulevard South, Las Vegas NV 89109. 702/734-0410. **Fax:** 709/734-2051. **Contact:** Vivian Hudson, Personnel. **World Wide Web address:** http://www.circuscircus.com. **Description:** A casino and hotel with over 2,700 rooms. **NOTE:** Search and apply for positions online. **Positions advertised include:** Gaming Audit Supervisor; Slot Promotions Host; Cooks Helper; Fry Cook; Guest Room Attendant; Housekeeper; Security Guard; Booth Cashier; Floor Person; Money Runner; Investigator.

CITADEL COMMUNICATIONS CORPORATION
7201 West Lake Mead Blvd, Suite 400, Las Vegas NV. 702/804-5200. **Fax:** 702/804-5936. **Contact:** Human Resources Representative. **E-mail address:** h.r@citcomm.com. **World Wide Web address:** http://www.citadelcommunications.com. **Description:** Owns and operates 150 FM and 63 AM radio stations in 44 markets located in 25 states. **Corporate headquarters location:** This location.

CITIBANK
201 West Telegraph Street, Carson City NV 89703. **Toll-free phone:** 800/756-7047. **Fax:** 775/882-7515. **Contact:** Human Resources. **World Wide Web address:** http://www.citi.com. **Description:** A full-service bank. **NOTE:** Search and apply for positions online. **Corporate headquarters location:** Los Angeles CA.

CITIBANK
2375 South Virginia Street, Reno NV 89502. **Toll-free phone:** 800/756-7047. **Contact:** Human Resources. **World Wide Web address:** http://www.citi.com. **Description:** A full-service bank. **NOTE:** Search and apply for positions online. **Corporate headquarters location:** Los Angeles CA.

CITIBANK
593 East Prater Way, Sparks NV 89431. **Toll-free phone:** 800/756-7047. **Contact:** Human Resources. **World Wide Web address:** http://www.citi.com. **Description:** A full-service bank. **NOTE:** Search and apply for positions online. **Corporate headquarters location:** Los Angeles CA.

CLARK, COUNTY OF
500 South Grand Central Parkway, Government Center Building, 3rd Floor, Las Vegas NV 89155. 702/455-4565. **Fax:** 702/455-2253. **Recorded jobline:** 702/455-3174. **Contact:** Human Resources. **World Wide Web address:** http://www.co.clark.nv.us. **Description:** The administrative offices of Clark County. **NOTE:** Search for positions online. Applications are not accepted by email. **Positions advertised include:** Senior Business Analyst; Legal Office Specialist; Attorney; Executive Assistant; Investigator; Recreational Specialist; Departmental Systems Administrator; Director of Comprehensive Planning; Principle Civil Engineer. **Special programs:** Internships. **Number of employees at this location:** 6,000.

CLARK COUNTY CREDIT UNION
P.O. Box 36490, Las Vegas NV 89133-6490. 702/228-2228. **Contact:** Human Resources. **World Wide Web address:** http://www.ccculv.org. **Description:** A credit union serving the Clark County area. Customers include county employees and members of the medical field. **Number of employees at this location:** 75.

CLICK BOND INC.
2151 Lockheed Way, Carson City NV. 89706-0713. 775/885-8000. **Fax:** 775/883-0191. **Contact:** Human Resources. **World Wide Web address:** http://www.clickbond.com. **Description:** A manufacturer of fasteners for adhesive bonding to structures, with a focus on the airline industry.

COLLEGIATE GRAPHICS
3250 West Ali Baba Lane, Las Vegas NV 89118. 702/737-0771. **Contact:** Human Resources. **Description:** Produces screen-printed and embroidered textile products including T-shirts featuring collegiate logos and emblems.

COMGLOBAL SYSTEMS INC.
7385 Prairie Falcon Road, Suite 150, Las Vegas NV 89128. 702/856-3363. **Fax:** 702/869-9530. **Contact:** Human Resources. **E-mail address:** apply@comglobal.com. **World Wide Web address:** http://www.comglobal.com. **Description:** Provides information technology solution for the defense and other federal agencies. **Positions advertised include:** Software Engineer. **Corporate headquarters location:** San Diego CA. **Other U.S. locations:** Norfolk VA; Arlington VA; San Jose CA.

COMMUNITY SERVICES AGENCY
P.O. Box 10167, Reno NV 89510. 775/786-6023. **Physical address:** 1090 East Eighth Street, Reno NV 89512. **Contact:** Human Resources. **World Wide Web address:** http://www.csareno.org. **Description:** A human service organization whose operations include the Head Start program, a rental assistance program, and a homeownership assistance program. **NOTE:** Search for positions online. **Positions advertised include:** Site Supervisor; Head Teacher; Assistant Teacher; Substitute Teacher.

CONVERSE CONSULTANTS
731 Pilot Road, Suite H, Las Vegas NV 89119. 702/269-8336. **Contact:** Personnel. **E-mail address:** lasvegas@Converseconsultants.com. **World Wide Web address:** http://www.converseconsultants.com. **Description:** An environmental engineering consulting firm. Founded in 1946. **NOTE:** Search and apply for positions online. **Positions advertised include:** Environmental Technician; Geotechnical Technician; Soils Technician; Environmental Professional; Geologist; Geotechnical Engineer; Construction Materials Engineer. **Other U.S. locations:** CA; NJ; PA. **Number of employees nationwide:** 275.

COORS OF LAS VEGAS
1849 West Cheyenne Avenue, North Las Vegas NV 89032. 702/735-9141. **Contact:** Personnel. **World Wide Web address:** http://www.coors.com. **Description:** One of the largest brewers in the United States. The company's largest selling brand, Coors Light, is one of the best-selling beers nationwide. Other brands include Zima and Killian's Irish Red. **NOTE:** Internships available. Search and apply for positions online. **Listed on:** New York Stock Exchange. **Stock exchange symbol:** RKY.

CRUMRINE MANUFACTURING JEWELERS
145 Catron Drive, Reno NV 89512-1001. 775/786-3712. **Toll-free phone:** 800/444-3575. **Contact:** Renee Bell, Human Resources Director. **World Wide Web address:** http://www.crumrineonline.com. **Description:** A jewelry manufacturer.

CUBIX CORPORATION
2800 Lockheed Way, Carson City NV 89706. 775/888-1000. **Toll-free phone:** 800/829-0550. **Fax:** 775/888-1002. **Contact:** Human Resources Department. **E-mail address:** personnel@cubix.com. **World Wide Web address:** http://www.cubix.com. **Description:** Designs and manufactures computer networking products for use as mission-critical communication, specialty, and file servers. **Corporate headquarters location:** This location. **Other U.S. locations:** Tampa FL.

DECATUR PRESS INC.
3401 Sirius Avenue, Suite 110, Las Vegas NV 89102. 702/871-1701. **Contact:** Rosa Villarreal, Business Manager. **Description:** Handles all kinds of printing jobs including letterhead and business cards.

DELOITTE & TOUCHE
3773 Howard Hughes Parkway, Suite 490 North, Las Vegas NV 89109. 702/893-3100. **Contact:** Human Resources. **World Wide Web address:** http://www.us.deloitte.com. **Description:** An international firm of certified public accountants providing professional accounting, auditing, tax, and management consulting services to widely diversified clients. The company has a specialized program consisting of national industry groups and functional groups that cross industry lines. Groups are involved in various disciplines including accounting, auditing, taxation management advisory services, small and growing businesses, mergers and acquisitions, and computer applications. **NOTE:** Search and apply for positions online. **Other U.S. locations:** Nationwide. **Number of employees at this location:** 107. **Number of employees nationwide:** 120,000.

DELOITTE & TOUCHE
50 West Liberty Street, Suite 900, Reno NV 89501. 775/326-5900. **Contact:** Human Resources. **World Wide Web address:** http://www.us.deloitte.com. **Description:** An international firm of certified public accountants providing professional accounting, auditing, tax, and management consulting services to widely diversified clients. The company has a specialized program consisting of national industry groups and functional groups that cross industry lines. Groups are involved in various disciplines including accounting, auditing, taxation management advisory services, small and growing businesses, mergers and acquisitions, and computer applications. **NOTE:** Search and apply for positions online. **Other U.S. locations:** Nationwide. **Number of employees at this location:** 29. **Number of employees nationwide:** 120,000.

DESERT BMW OF LAS VEGAS
2333 South Decatur Boulevard, Las Vegas NV 89102. 702/871-1010. **Contact:** Mr. Dale Workman, General Sales Manager. **World Wide Web address:** http://www.autonation.com/dealers/desert/bmw-vegas. **Description:** Rents, leases, repairs, and sells new and used automobiles.

DESERT FIRE PROTECTION
505 Valley Road, Reno NV 89512. 775/329-1926. **Contact:** Manager. **Description:** Fabricates and installs automatic sprinkler systems to extinguish fires in buildings.

DESERT RADIOLOGISTS
2020 Palomino Lane, Suite 100, Las Vegas NV 89106. 702/384-5210. **Recorded jobline:** 702/384-5210. **Contact:** Kim Swift, Personnel Director. **E-mail address:** careers@desertrad.com. **World Wide Web address:** http://www.desertrad.com. **Description:** An outpatient group that performs radiology, radiation therapy, and angiography. **Positions advertised include:** Billing Representative; Payroll Administrator. **Annual sales/revenues:** $21 - $50 million. **Number of employees at this location:** 180.

DESIGN ENGINEERING CORPORATION
2900 South Rancho Drive, Las Vegas NV 89102. 702/871-9069. **Fax:** 702/456-9463. **Contact:** Personnel. **Description:** A design engineering company involved in civil surveying and electrical, structural, and mechanical engineering. **Number of employees at this location:** 50.

DILLARD'S DEPARTMENT STORES
3700 South Maryland Parkway, Las Vegas NV 89119. 702/734-2111. **Contact:** Steve Dohm, Store Manager. **World Wide Web address:** http://www.dillards.com. **Description:** A store location of the retail chain. Dillard's offers a full line of brand-name fashion apparel and home furnishings. Dillard's has 300 stores in 29 states. Founded in 1938. **Corporate headquarters location:** Little Rock AR. **Other U.S. locations:** Nationwide. **Annual sales/revenues:** More than $100 million.

DOLISOS LABORATORIES
3014 Rigel Avenue, Las Vegas NV 89102. 702/871-7153. **Contact:** Mario Gervais, Production Manager. **World Wide Web address:** http://www.dolisosamerica.com. **Description:** A manufacturer of homeopathic remedies. **NOTE:** Mario Gervais handles resumes for production positions in the laboratory. Candidates interested in other areas of employment should contact Human Resources.

R.H. DONNELLEY
2030 East Tropicana Road, Las Vegas NV 89119. 702/369-3700. **Contact:** Human Resources. **World Wide Web address:** http://www.rhdonnelley.com. **Description:** An area sales office for the national company. The company is engaged in selling advertising space in 500 Yellow Pages directories of more than 58 independent telephone companies. R.H. Donnelley also provides telemarketing services. Founded in 1886. **NOTE:** Search and apply for positions online. **Positions advertised include:** Credit Support Analyst; National Acct Manager; National Sales Rep. **Corporate headquarters location:** Purchase NY. **Listed on:** New York Stock Exchange. **Stock exchange symbol:** RHD. **Number of employees nationwide:** 1600.

R.R. DONNELLEY & SONS, INC.
6305 Sunset Corporate Drive, Las Vegas NV 89109. 702/949-8500. **Contact:** Human Resources. **World Wide Web address:** http://www.rrdonnelley.com. **Description:** R.R. Donnelley & Sons provides commercial printing, forms and labels, direct mail, financial printing, print fulfillment, business communication outsourcing, logistics, online services, digital photography, and content and database management. Founded in 1864. **NOTE:** Search and apply for positions online. **Corporate headquarters location:** Chicago IL. **Operations at this facility include:** This location prints catalogs. **Listed on:** New York Stock Exchange. **Stock exchange symbol:** RRD. **Number of employees worldwide:** 50,000.

EG&G SPECIAL PROJECTS
P.O. Box 93747, Las Vegas NV 89193. 702/361-1660. **Physical address:** 811 Grier Drive, Las Vegas NV 89119. **Contact:** Jack Pollock, Recruiter. **E-mail address:** employmentccy@egginc.com **World Wide Web address:** http://www.egginc.com. **Description:** EG&G Special Projects, a government contractor, provides electronics and systems engineering services including radar, RF microwave, video, telemetry, optics, communications, instrumentation, and data processing. **Corporate headquarters location:** Gaithersburg MD. **Other U.S. locations:** Nationwide. **Parent Company:** URS Corporation. **Operations at this facility include:** Administration; Divisional Headquarters; Service. **Number of employees at this location:** 1,250. **Number of employees nationwide:** 10,000.

EAGLE-PICHER MINERALS, INC.
P.O. Box 12130, Lovelock NV 89510-2130. 775/273-2636. **Physical address:** 150 Coal Canyon Road, Lovelock NV 89419. **Toll-free phone:** 800/228-3859. **Contact:** Human Resources. **E-mail address:** Career.Minerals@EaglePicher.com. **World Wide Web address:** http://www.epcorp.com. **Description:** Manufactures diatomaceous earth, perlite, and specialty filter aids used for filtration, fillers, and as soil amendments and conditioners.

EAGLE-PICHER MINERALS, INC.
Magnolia South Meadows Office, 9785 Gateway Drive, Suite 1000, Reno NV 89511. 775/824-7600. **Contact:** Human Resources. **E-mail address:** Career.Minerals@EaglePicher.com. **World Wide Web address:** http://www.epcorp.com. **Description:** Administrative offices for the national mining operation, which mines and processes diatomaceous earth.

ECONOMIC OPPORTUNITY BOARD OF CLARK COUNTY
P.O. Box 270880, Las Vegas NV 89127-4880. 702/647-1510. **Fax:** 702/647-6639. **Contact:** Human Resources Department. **World Wide Web address:** http://www.eobcc.org. **Description:** A social service agency that provides employment training and community outreach programs. **NOTE:** Search for positions online.

EDURUS INC.
769 Basque Way, Carson City NV 89706. 775/885-8333. **Fax:** 775/885-8334. **Contact:** Human Resources. **World Wide Web address:** http://www.edurus.com. **Description:** A full service interactive agency specializing in web-integration. Creates brochures, catalogs, and direct-mail campaigns.

ELDORADO HOTEL/CASINO
P.O. Box 3399, 345 North Virginia Street, Reno NV 89505-3399. 775/786-5700. **Recorded jobline:** 775/348-9278. **Contact:** Human Resources. **E-mail address:** jobinfo@eldoradoreno.com. **World Wide Web address:** http://www.eldoradoreno.com. **Description:** A privately-owned and family-operated hotel/casino featuring a 25-story tower, a 60,000 square-foot casino, eight restaurants, live cabaret entertainment, 24-hour room service, and a heated outdoor pool and spa. **NOTE:** Search and apply for positions online. **Positions advertised include:** A/P Clerk; Asst Front Desk Manager; Cage Cashier; Computer Operator; Dealers; Food Server; Restaurant Manager; Retail Sales Associate; Security Officer.

ELSINORE CORPORATION
FOUR QUEENS HOTEL & CASINO
P.O. Box 370, Las Vegas NV 89101-0370. 702/385-4011. **Physical address:** 202 Fremont Street, Las Vegas NV 89101. **Fax:** 702/387-5125. **Recorded jobline:** 702/385-4011x3126. **Contact:** Linda Yard, Director of Human Resources Department. **E-mail address:** employment@fourqueens.com. **World Wide Web address:** http://www.fourqueens.com. **Description:** A publicly-held casino management company that develops and operates gaming facilities throughout the country. In addition to its Las Vegas-based Four Queens Hotel & Casino, Elsinore Corporation is working with Native American tribes to develop, construct, and manage casinos on tribal lands. **Positions advertised include:** Multi-Game Dealer; Pit Clerk; Keno Writer; Reservations Clerk; Soft Count Clerk; Armed Security Guard; Casino Porter; Slot Club Supervisor. **Special programs:** Internships. **Corporate headquarters location:** This location. **Subsidiaries include:** Pinnacle Gaming. **Operations at this facility include:** Administration; Sales. **Number of employees at this location:** 1,150.

EMHISER RESEARCH INC.
P.O. Box 189, Verdi NV 89439-0189. 775/345-2705. **Physical address:** 2705 Old Highway 40 West, Verdi NV 89439. **Contact:** Personnel Manager. **E-mail address:** info@emhiser.com. **World Wide Web address:** http://www.emhiser.com. **Description:** Designs and manufactures military communication systems including transmitters, receivers, encoders, decoders, and telemetry products. **International locations:** Ontario, Canada. **Operations at this facility include:** Administration; Manufacturing; Research and Development; Sales; Service. **Number of employees at this location:** 10.

EMPLOYERS INSURANCE COMPANY OF NEVADA
2550 Paseo Verde Parkway, Henderson NV 89074-7117. 888/682-6671. **Contact:** Human Resources. **World Wide Web address:** http://www.employersinsco.com. **Description:** A full-service workers' compensation mutual insurance company, providing claims management, loss prevention consulting, underwriting and care management services to Nevada businesses. **NOTE:** Check Website for name of contact person, as it varies per position. **Positions advertised include:** Claims Examiner; Benefits Coordinator; Director, Financial Planning; Customer Service Rep. **Other area locations:** Reno NV.

ENDEAVOR
6200 West Oakey Boulevard, Las Vegas NV 89146. 702/649-7151. **Contact:** Director. **Description:** A job training and rehabilitation service for individuals with physical or emotional disabilities.

ETHEL M. CHOCOLATES, INC.
One Sunset Way, Henderson NV 89014. 702/458-8864. **Contact:** Human Resources. **World Wide Web address:** http://www.ethelm.com. **Description:** Producers of premium assorted boxed chocolates. Founded in 1911. **Other area locations:** Reno NV; Stateline NV. **Other U.S. locations:** Honolulu HI; McLean VA.

EXCALIBUR HOTEL
3850 Las Vegas Boulevard South, Las Vegas NV 89109. 702/597-7777. **Fax:** 702/597-7009. **Contact:** Human Resources Department. **World Wide Web address:** http://www.excaliburcasino.com. **Description:** A hotel and casino with over 4,000 rooms. **NOTE:** Search and apply for positions online. **Positions advertised include:** Assistant Restaurant Manager; Courtesy Host; Game Operator; Lifeguard; Microfilm Clerk; Race and Sports Writer; Surveillance Investigator.

FAIRWAY CHEVROLET
3100 East Sahara Avenue, Las Vegas NV 89104. 702/432-3530. **Contact:** Terry Hoisington, General Sales Manager. **World Wide Web address:** http://www.fairwaychevy.com. **Description:** An automotive dealership.

FIRST AMERICAN TITLE COMPANY OF NEVADA
2490 Paseo Verde Parkway, Suite 100, Henderson NV 89074. 702/731-4131. **Fax:** 702/458-5144. **Contact:** Human Resources. **World Wide Web address:** http://www.firstam.com. **Description:** Provides title insurance, escrow and loan servicing, home warranties, and lender and national escrow processing services. **NOTE:** Entry-level positions and part-time positions are offered. Search and apply for positions online. **Special programs:** Internships; Training; Summer Jobs. **Office hours:** Monday - Friday, 8:00 a.m. - 5:00 p.m. **Corporate headquarters location:** Santa Ana CA. **Other U.S. locations:** Nationwide. **Parent company:** The First American Corporation. **Listed on:** New York Stock Exchange. **Stock exchange symbol:** FAF. **Annual sales/revenues:** More than $100 million. **Number of employees at this location:** 200. **Number of employees nationwide:** 16,000.

FIRTH RIXSON VIKING
P.O. Box 339, One Elk Circle, Verdi NV 89439-0339. 775/345-0345. **Contact:** Human Resources. **E-mail address:** info@firthrixson.com. **World Wide Web address:** http://www.firthrixson.com. **Description:** Manufactures a variety of fabricated metal products for industrial applications including seamless ring and press forgings. **Corporate headquarters location:** Sheffield England.

FISHER SPACE PEN COMPANY
711 Yucca Street, Boulder City NV 89005. 702/293-3011. **Contact:** Human Resources. **World Wide Web address:** http://www.spacepen.com. **Description:** Manufactures space pens, which are pressurized pens that can write underwater, in space, in subzero temperatures, and in other harsh environments. **International locations:** Ontario, Canada. **Number of employees at this location:** 65.

FLAMINGO LAS VEGAS
3555 Las Vegas Boulevard South, Las Vegas NV 89109. 888/308-8899. **Contact:** Human Resources. **World Wide Web address:** http://www.lv-flamingo.com. **Description:** Flamingo Hilton offers over 3,600 rooms, gaming facilities, and live entertainment. **NOTE:** Search and apply for positions online. **Positions advertised include:** Retail Supervisor; Porter; Ticket Writer; Poker Dealer; Booth Cashier; Food Server; Payroll Clerk; Hotel Audit Clerk; Advertising Coordinator; Assistant Chef; Fry Cook; Bartender; Spa Masseur; Valet Attendant. **Parent company:** Caesars Entertainment.

GAMING PARTNERS INTERNATIONAL CORPORATION
1700 Industrial Road, Las Vegas NV 89102. 702/384-2425. **Contact:** Human Resources. **World Wide Web address:** http://www.gpigaming.com. **Description:** Paul-Son Gaming Corporation is a manufacturer and supplier of casino table game equipment. The company's products include casino chips, felt table layouts, playing cards, dice, gaming furniture, and miscellaneous table accessories such as chip trays, drop boxes, and dealing shoes. **Corporate headquarters location:** This location. **Listed on:** NASDAQ. **Stock exchange symbol:** GPIC.

G.E.S. EXPOSITION SERVICES
GEM CAPSTONE DIVISION
950 Grier Drive, Las Vegas NV 89119. 702/263-1500. **Contact:** Human Resources Manager. **E-mail address:** careers@gesexpo.com. **World Wide Web address:** http://www.gesexpo.com. **Description:** Designs, builds, and sets up booths and displays for exhibits and trade shows. **NOTE:** Search and apply for positions online. **Other U.S. locations:** Nationwide. **International location:** Canada.

GENERAL MOTORS CORPORATION
P.O. Box 51555, Sparks NV 89435-1555. 775/356-5000. **Physical address:** 555 Vista Boulevard, Sparks NV 89434. **Contact:** Roy Hermann, Labor Relations. **World Wide Web address:** http://www.gm.com. **Description:** General Motors Corporation is one of the world's largest full-line vehicle manufacturers. GM conducts business through the following sectors: North American Automotive Operations, International

Operations, General Motors Acceptance Corporation (GMAC), Electronic Data Systems Corporation (EDS), and GM Hughes Electronics Corporation. North American Automotive Operations includes Sales/Service Groups (Buick, Cadillac, Chevrolet, GMC Truck, Oldsmobile, Pontiac, and Saturn) and Vehicle Development Groups (Powertrain, Truck Group, Small Car Group, and Midsize/Luxury Car Group). International Operations include GM Europe (GME); Asia Pacific Operations (APO); and Latin America, Africa, Middle East Operations (LAAMO). GMAC, which provides financing and insurance to GM customers and dealers, consists of North American Operations, International Operations, Motors Insurance Corporation, and GMAC Mortgage Group. EDS applies information technologies to more than 8,000 customers globally in the communications, energy/chemical, insurance, public sector, travel and transportation, financial services, manufacturing, and retail industries. GM Hughes Electronics Corporation is involved in automotive electronics, telecommunications and space electronics, and defense electronics. Founded in 1908. **NOTE:** Search and apply for positions online. **Corporate headquarters location:** Detroit MI. **Operations at this facility include:** This location is a parts warehouse. **Listed on:** New York Stock Exchange. **Stock exchange symbol:** GM.

GEORGIA-PACIFIC CORPORATION
P.O. Box 337350, 11401 Highway 91 North, Las Vegas NV 89101. 702/643-8100. **Contact:** Robert Williams, Personnel Manager. **World Wide Web address:** http://www.gp.com. **Description:** Georgia-Pacific Corporation is a manufacturer, wholesaler, and distributor of building products, industrial wood products, pulp, paper, packaging, and related chemicals. The company is one of the world's largest manufacturers of forest products, with facilities in 48 states and overseas. Georgia-Pacific owns 6 million acres of forestland in North America. **NOTE:** Search and apply for positions online. **Corporate headquarters location:** Atlanta GA. **Operations at this facility include:** This location manufactures wallboard. **Listed on:** New York Stock Exchange. **Stock exchange symbol:** GP. **Number of employees nationwide:** 75,000.

GIRL SCOUTS OF THE UNITED STATES OF AMERICA
2941 Harris Avenue, Las Vegas NV 89101. 702/385-3677. **Contact:** Business Administrator. **World Wide Web address:** http://www.girlscouts.org. **Description:** Part of the national scouting organization for girls. **NOTE:** Apply for positions online. **Positions advertised include:** Group/School Coordinator; Drop-In Center Director. **Corporate headquarters location:** New York NY.

GLENCOE MANAGEMENT
dba BURGER KING
7432 West Sahara Avenue, Suite 103, Las Vegas NV 89117. 702/254-7400. **Fax:** 702/254-7494. **Contact:** Controller. **Description:** A franchisee of Burger King restaurants with approximately 30 locations in Nevada, Georgia, and Texas.

GOLD COAST HOTEL
4000 West Flamingo Road, Las Vegas NV 89103. 702/367-7111. **Toll-free phone:** 800/331-5334. **Contact:** Human Resources Manager. **World Wide Web address:** http://www.goldcoastcasino.com. **Description:** A hotel and casino featuring 750 rooms, a heated swimming pool, five restaurants, two show lounges, a 72-lane bowling center, free child care, and one of Nevada's largest dance halls. **NOTE:** Search and apply for positions online.

GOLDEN NUGGET HOTEL AND CASINO
129 East Fremont Street, Las Vegas NV 89101. 702/386-8245. **Fax:** 702/386-8173. **Recorded jobline:** 702/386-8181. **Contact:** Carole Knepper, Employment Manager. **World Wide Web address:** http://www.goldennugget.com. **Description:** A four-star, four-diamond hotel and casino. This location also hires seasonally. Founded in 1950. **NOTE:** Entry-level positions, part-time jobs, and second and third shifts are offered. **Positions advertised include:** Account Receivable Clerk; Assistant Front Desk Manager; Assistant Pastry Chef; Cocktail Server; Employee Relations Coordinator; Room Attendant; Guest Service Representative; Retail Cashier; Security Secretary; Revenue Audit Clerk; Security Officer; Ticket Cashier; Usher. **Special programs:** Internships; Training; Summer Jobs. **Internship information:** Internships are available to University of Las Vegas Nevada students only. **Office hours:** Monday - Friday, 9:00 a.m. - 5:00 p.m. **Corporate headquarters location:** This location. **Other U.S. locations:** Biloxi MS; Laughlin NV. **Parent company:** Mirage Resorts, Inc. **Listed on:** New York Stock Exchange. **Stock exchange symbol:** MIR. **Annual sales/revenues:** More than $100 million. **Number of employees at this location:** 3,000. **Number of employees nationwide:** 30,000.

GOLD'S GYM
3750 East Flamingo Road, Las Vegas NV 89121. 702/451-4222. **Contact:** Manager. **World Wide Web address:** http://www.goldsgym.com. **Description:** A full-service health and fitness club that offers weights and cardiovascular equipment, fitness and aerobic instruction, tanning, personal training, and child care facilities. Gold's Gym is one of the world's largest health club chains with over 650 locations. **NOTE:** Part-time jobs are offered. **Special programs:** Training; Summer Jobs. **Corporate headquarters location:** Palm Springs CA. **Other U.S. locations:** Nationwide. **Parent company:** Neste Development. **Number of employees at this location:** 40.

GOLD'S GYM
4720 West Sahara Boulevard, Las Vegas NV 89102. 702/877-6966. **Contact:** Manager. **World Wide Web address:** http://www.goldsgym.com. **Description:** A full-service health and fitness club that offers weights and cardiovascular equipment, fitness and aerobic instruction, tanning, personal training, and child care facilities. Gold's Gym is one of the world's largest health club chains, with over 650 locations. **NOTE:** Part-time jobs are offered. **Corporate headquarters location:** Palm Springs CA. **Other U.S. locations:** Nationwide. **Parent company:** Neste Development. **Number of employees at this location:** 40.

GOLD'S GYM
7501 West Lake Mead Boulevard, Suite 109, Las Vegas NV 89128. 702/360-8205. **Contact:** Manager. **World Wide Web address:** http://www.goldsgym.com. **Description:** A full-service health and fitness club that offers weights and cardiovascular equipment, fitness and aerobic instruction, tanning, personal training, and child care facilities. Gold's Gym is one of the world's largest health club chains, with over 650 locations. **Corporate headquarters location:** Palm Springs CA. **Other U.S. locations:** Nationwide. **Parent company:** Neste Development. **Number of employees at this location:** 40.

GOLD'S GYM
9310 South Eastern Avenue, Suite 110, Henderson NV 89009. 702/914-5885. **Contact:** Manager. **World Wide Web address:** http://www.goldsgym.com. **Description:** A full-service health and fitness club that offers weights and cardiovascular equipment, fitness and aerobic instruction, tanning, personal training, and child care facilities. Gold's Gym is one of the world's largest health club chains with over 650 locations. **NOTE:** Part-time jobs are offered. **Corporate headquarters location:** Palm Springs CA. **Other U.S. locations:** Nationwide. **Parent company:** Neste Development.

GOOD HUMOR-BREYERS ICE CREAM
1001 Olsen Street, Henderson NV 89015. 702/564-0020. **Contact:** Human Resources. **E-mail address:** jobs.ghbhr@unilever.com. **World Wide Web address:** http://www.icecreamusa.com. **Description:** A major producer of frozen packaged ice cream and novelties distributed nationally. **Corporate headquarters:** Green Bay WI.

GOTHIC LANDSCAPING INC.
4565 West Nevso Drive, Las Vegas NV 89103. 702/252-7017. **Contact:** Human Resources. **Description:** A landscaping company for major builders and construction companies. **Corporate headquarters location:** Los Angeles CA. **Other U.S. locations:** Phoenix AZ. **Number of employees at this location:** 100.

W.W. GRAINGER
2401 Western Avenue, Las Vegas NV 89102. 702/385-6833. **Contact:** Human Resources. **World Wide Web address:** http://www.grainger.com. **Description:** Distributes a variety of equipment and components to the industrial, commercial, contracting, and institutional markets worldwide. The company has 337 branches in all 50 states and Puerto Rico, and a catalog that lists 78,000 items. Products include equipment and components for motors, air tools, hydraulic products, refrigeration items, power and hand tools, office equipment, computer supplies, storage equipment, replacement parts, industrial products, safety items, cold weather clothing, and sanitary supplies. **NOTE:** Search and apply for positions online. **Listed on:** New York Stock Exchange. **Stock exchange symbol:** GWW.

GRANT THORNTON LLP
100 West Liberty Street, Suite 770, Reno NV 89501. 775/786-1520. **Contact:** Human Resources. **World Wide Web address:** http://www.grantthornton.com. **Description:** An international, certified public accounting organization offering a wide variety of consulting and accounting services as well as strategic and tactical planning assistance to a diverse clientele. Founded in 1924. **NOTE:** Search and apply for positions online. **Corporate headquarters location:** Chicago IL. **Other U.S. locations:** Nationwide. **Number of employees nationwide:** 3,000.

GRAY LINE TOURS OF SOUTHERN NEVADA
4020 East Long Mountain Road, Las Vegas NV 89081. 702/384-1234. **Contact:** Human Resources. **E-mail address:** info@grayline.com. **World Wide Web address:** http://www.grayline.com. **Description:** Provides guided tours of Las Vegas. **Other U.S. locations:** Nationwide. **International locations:** Worldwide.

GREAT BASIN COLLEGE
1500 College Parkway, Elko NV 89801. 775/753-2914. **Contact:** Human Resources. **World Wide Web address:** http://www.gbcnv.edu. **Description:** A two-year community college with an enrollment of approximately 5,000. The college offers certificates and associate's degrees. **NOTE:** Search and apply for positions online. **Positions advertised include:** Recruiter; Development Coordinator; Instructors; Library Director.

GREELEY & HANSEN
4625 South Polaris Avenue, Suite 210, Las Vegas NV 89103. 702/736-7062. **Contact:** Ms. Terry Woods, Human Resources. **E-mail address:** careers@greeley-hansen.com. **World Wide Web address:** http://www.greeleyhansen.com. **Description:** A national engineering consulting company specializing in water, wastewater, and solid waste management. The firm's services include technical and feasibility reports, facility design, engineering services during construction, operations assistance, and performance evaluation. **NOTE:** Search and apply for positions online. **Positions advertised include:** Project Managers; Civil Engineers; Management Consultants; Construction Engineers. **Corporate headquarters location:** Chicago IL. **Other U.S. locations:** Nationwide. **Number of employees nationwide:** 300.

HDR ENGINEERING
770 East Warm Springs Road, Suite 360, Las Vegas NV 89119. 702/938-6000. **Contact:** Human Resources. **E-mail address:** careers@hdrinc.com. **World Wide Web address:** http://www.hdrinc.com. **Description:** An architecture and engineering firm. HDR has projects in all 50 states and in 30 foreign countries. The company has 90 locations worldwide. Founded in 1917. **NOTE:** Search and apply for positions online. **Number of employees nationwide:** 1,600. **Corporate headquarters location:** Omaha NE. **Other U.S. locations:** Nationwide. **International locations:** Worldwide. **Number of employees worldwide:** 3,300.

HALE, LANE, PEEK, DENNISON, HOWARD, ANDERSON & PEARL
2300 West Sahara Boulevard, Suite 800, Las Vegas NV 89102. 702/222-2500. **Contact:** Jayne Klein, Recruiting Department. **E-mail address:** info@halelane.com. **World Wide Web address:** http://www.halelane.com. **Description:** A legal services firm specializing in transactional law and offering a wide range of other legal services. **Positions advertised include:** Commercial Litigation Lawyer. **Special Programs:** Mentoring; Internships; Summer Associate Programs. **Other area locations:** Carson City NV; Reno NV.

THE HAMILTON COMPANY
P.O. Box 10030, Reno NV 89520. 775/858-3000. **Contact:** Human Resources. **E-mail address:** afogerson@hamiltoncompany.com. **World Wide Web address:** http://www.hamiltoncomp.com. **Description:** Manufacturers of industrial measurement instruments. **NOTE:** Search and apply for positions online. **Corporate headquarters location:** This location. **International locations:** Germany; United Kingdom. **Subsidiaries include:** Hamilton Bonaduz AG (Switzerland).

HARD ROCK CAFE
4475 Paradise Road, Las Vegas NV 89109-6574. 702/733-8400. **Contact:** General Manager. **World Wide Web address:** http://www.hardrock.com. **Description:** A restaurant decorated with rock and roll memorabilia. Hard Rock Cafe serves American cuisine and operates a gift shop. **NOTE:** Search and apply for positions online. **Other U.S. locations:** Nationwide. **International locations:** Worldwide.

HARRAH'S LAS VEGAS
3475 Las Vegas Boulevard South, Las Vegas NV 89109. 702/369-5287. **Toll-free phone:** 800/392-9002. **Fax:** 702/369-5108. **Contact:** Human Resources. **World Wide Web address:** http://www.harrahs.com. **Description:** A casino featuring 2,711 tower rooms, six restaurants, convention space, a wedding chapel, five cocktail lounges, the Commander's Theatre featuring nightly entertainment, the Improv Comedy Club, a health club and Olympic-sized pool, a game room and video arcade, gift shops, and a beauty salon. **NOTE:** Search and apply for positions online. **Positions advertised include:** Security Officer. **Parent company:** Harrah's Entertainment Inc. (Memphis TN). **Listed on:** New York Stock Exchange. **Stock exchange symbol:** HET. **Number of employees at this location:** 3,000. **Number of employees nationwide:** 10,000.

HARRAH'S RENO
P.O. Box 10, Reno NV 89504-0010. 775/786-3232. **Physical address:** 219 North Center Street, Reno NV 89501. **Contact:** Human Resources Director. **World Wide Web address:** http://www.harrahs.com. **Description:** Operates hotels and casinos. **NOTE:** Search and apply for positions online. **Parent company:** Harrah's Entertainment Inc. (Memphis TN). **Listed on:** New York Stock Exchange. **Stock exchange symbol:** HET. **Number of employees nationwide:** 10,000.

HEART INSTITUTE OF NEVADA
1090 East Desert Inn Road, Suite 100, Las Vegas NV 89109-2803. 702/765-5700. **Toll-free phone:** 800/782-0088. **Fax:** 702/765-5826. **Contact:** Diane Love, Human Resources. **Description:** A medical practice specializing in cardiology. Founded in 1975. **NOTE:** Entry-level positions are offered. **Special programs:** Internships. **Office hours:** Monday - Friday, 8:00 a.m. - 5:00 p.m. **Parent company:** Cardiology Associates of Nevada. **Number of employees at this location:** 65.

HENDERSON, CITY OF
240 Water Street, Henderson NV 89015. 702/565-2070. **Fax:** 702/565-1267. **Contact:** Human Resources. **World Wide Web address:** http://www.cityofhenderson.com. **Description:** Government offices for the city of Henderson. **NOTE:** Employment application must accompany resume. **Positions advertised include:** Bus Driver; Systems Support Analyst; Fire Fighter; Paramedic; Pool Manager; Crossing Guard; Recreation Assistant; Utility Services Engineer. **Special programs:** Internships.

HIDDEN VALLEY RANCH FOOD PRODUCTS
12150 Moya Boulevard, Reno NV 89506. 775/677-0900. **Contact:** Human Resources. **World Wide Web address:** http://www.hiddenvalley.com. **Description:** This location manufactures and distributes salad dressing for the national company.

HOLIDAY INN EMERALD SPRINGS
325 East Flamingo Road, Las Vegas NV 89109. 702/732-9100. **Contact:** Human Resources. **World Wide Web address:** http://www.holidayinnlasvegas.com. **Description:** Engaged in the operation of hotels. **Parent company:** Intercontinental Hotels.

THE HOME DEPOT
861 South Rainbow Boulevard, Las Vegas NV 89145. 702/870-9600. **Contact:** Store Manager. **World Wide Web address:** http://www.homedepot.com. **Description:** Operates retail warehouse stores selling a wide assortment of building materials and home improvement products, primarily to the do-it-yourself and home remodeling markets. The company operates more than 1,500 stores (Home Depot, EXPO, and other subsidiary companies). The stores stock over 35,000 different kinds of building materials, home improvement supplies, and lawn and garden products. **NOTE:** Apply for positions online. **Corporate headquarters location:** Atlanta GA.

HOST INTERNATIONAL
2000 East Plumb Lane, Reno NV 89502-3250. 775/785-2587. **Fax:** 775/785-2590. **Contact:** Human Resources. **Description:** Provides food, beverage, and merchandise concessions in the travel and leisure industry.

A.C. HOUSTON LUMBER COMPANY
P.O. Box 337410, North Las Vegas NV 89033-7410. 702/633-5000. **Physical address:** 2912 East La Madre Way, North Las Vegas NV 89031. **Contact:** Denise Nichols, Human Resources. **E-mail address:** dnichols@achoustonlumber.com. **World Wide Web address:** http://www.achoustonlumber.com. **Description:** This is the main store location of the retailer of lumber and related products. **NOTE:** Search and apply for positions online. **Positions advertised include:** Truss Designers. **Corporate headquarters location:** This location. **Other U.S. locations:** CA; CO; ID; NM.

HUGHES SUPPLY INC
P.O. Box 270668, Las Vegas NV 89127. 702/382-6930. **Fax:** 702/968-7130. **Physical address:** 855 West Bonanza Road, Las Vegas NV 89106. **Contact:** Human Resources. **World Wide Web address:** http://www.hughessupply.com. **Description:** A wholesaler of electrical, waterworks, and plumbing supplies. **NOTE:** Job application may be downloaded and faxed.

HYTEK MICROSYSTEMS, INC.
400 Hot Springs Road, Carson City NV 89706. 775/883-0820. **Fax:** 775/883-0827. **Contact:** Human Resources. **World Wide Web address:** http://www.hytek.com. **Description:** Designs, manufactures, and markets hybrid microcircuits for medical, military, and space applications. Products are sold to original equipment manufacturers in various industries including telecommunications and industrial electronics. Founded in 1974. **NOTE:** Entry-level positions are offered. **Corporate headquarters location:** This location. **Listed on:** NASDAQ. **Stock exchange symbol:** HTEK. **Annual sales/revenues:** $5 - $10 million. **Number of employees at this location:** 100.

ITS (INTERNATIONAL TOTAL SERVICES)
3305 Spring Mountain Road, Suite 73, Las Vegas NV 89102. 702/251-7944. **Contact:** Human Resources. **Description:** A security firm offering unarmed guard services to a wide range of clients. **Number of employees at this location:** 150.

IKON OFFICE SOLUTIONS
680 Pilot Road, Las Vegas NV 89119-4441. 702/795-3366. **Contact:** Human Resources. **World Wide Web address:** http://www.ikon.com. **Description:** Distributes, sells, and repairs office equipment including photocopiers, fax machines, and printers. **NOTE:** Search and apply for positions online. **Other U.S. locations:** Nationwide. **Listed on:** New York Stock Exchange. **Stock exchange symbol:** IKN.

IMPERIAL PALACE, INC.
3535 Las Vegas Boulevard South, Las Vegas NV 89109. 702/731-3311. **Toll-free phone:** 800/634-6441. **Fax:** 702/794-3356. **Recorded jobline:** 702/794-3191. **Contact:** Richard Danzak, Personnel Director. **E-mail address:** hr@imperialpalace.com. **World Wide Web address:** http://www.imperialpalace.com. **Description:** A hotel and casino. **NOTE:** Part-time positions and second and third shifts are offered. **Positions advertised include:** Lead Cook; Bar Back; Graphic Artist; Front Desk Clerk; Security; Palace Princess; Gift Shop Sales Associate; Counter Person; Grounds Keeper; Medical Claims Processor; Maintenance Laborer; Promotions Models. **Listed on:** Privately held. **Annual sales/revenues:** More than $100 million. **Number of employees at this location:** 2,500.

INFOSCIENTIFIC.COM
2275 Corporate Circle, Suite 220, Henderson NV 89074. 702/433-8843. **Fax:** 702/433-8994. **Contact:** Human Resources. **World Wide Web address:** http://infoscientific.com. **Description:** Designs software applications for the collection of scientific data. **Other U.S. locations:** Manassas VA; Carmichael CA.

INTERNATIONAL GAME TECHNOLOGY (IGT)
9295 Prototype Drive, Reno NV 89521-8986. 775/688-0100. **Fax:** 775/448-1600. **Contact:** Human Resources. **World Wide Web address:** http://www.itg.com. **Description:** International Game Technology (IGT) is one of the world's leading designers and manufacturers of video game equipment, slot machines, and proprietary software for computerized wide-area game monitoring systems. The company offers an extensive product line including the S-Plus spinning reel slot; Player's Edge-Plus series; Game King video gaming machines; wide-area progressive products including Megabucks; and a variety of specialty casino devices such as carousel displays. Founded in 1975. **NOTE:** Search and apply for positions online. Entry-level positions, part-time jobs, and second and third shifts are offered. **Positions advertised include:** Regulatory Compliance Analyst; Trainer Systems Operator; Progressive Systems Engineer Associate; Human Resources Representative; Accountant; Security Guard; Administrative Intern; Mechanical Technician; Project Coordinator. **Special programs:** Internships; Training. **Corporate headquarters location:** This location. **Other U.S. locations:** Nationwide. **Subsidiaries include:** Barcrest Ltd. (United Kingdom); Olympic Gaming (Australia). **Operations at this facility include:** Administration; Manufacturing; Research and Development; Sales; Service. **Listed on:** New York Stock Exchange. **Stock exchange symbol:** IGT. **Annual sales/revenues:** More than $100 million. **Number of employees at this location:** 1,800. **Number of employees nationwide:** 3,300.

INTERNATIONAL MINUTE PRESS
2585 East Flamingo Road, #11, Las Vegas NV 89121. 702/451-0028. **Contact:** Human Resources. **Description:** Handles all kinds of printing jobs including letterhead and business cards. Each location is an independently owned branch of the franchise.

INTERPLEX INTERNATIONAL
P.O. Box 22031, Carson City NC 89721. 775/885-0488. **Fax:** 775/885-1946. **Contact:** Human Resources. **World Wide Web address:** http://www.interplex.biz. **Description:** A communications company that design and markets wireless connectivity technology and software for businesses. **Positions advertised include:** Web Designer; Technical Lead; Network Administrator; Controller; Marketing Research Analyst.

INTUIT INC.
1285 Financial Boulevard, Reno NV 89502. 775/332-8800. **Contact:** Human Resources. **World Wide Web address:** http://www.intuit.com. **Description:** A payroll processor. **NOTE:** Search and apply for positions online. **Corporate headquarters location:** Mountain View CA. **Other U.S. locations:** Nationwide. **International locations:** Canada; Japan; United Kingdom. **Listed on:** NASDAQ. **Stock exchange symbol:** INTU. **Number of employees worldwide:** 7,500.

JACK IN THE BOX
3703 East Flamingo Road, Las Vegas NV 89121. 702/451-0950. **Contact:** Human Resources. **World Wide Web address:** http://www.jackinthebox.com. **Description:** A restaurant with over 1600 locations throughout the western United States. **NOTE:** Search and apply for positions online. **Listed on:** New York Stock Exchange. **Stock exchange symbol:** JBX.

JACOBS CIVIL, INC.
2500 North Buffalo Drive, Suite 110, Las Vegas NV 89128. 702/870-2130. **Contact:** Human Resources. **World Wide Web address:** http://www.jacobs.com. **Description:** An environmental, architectural, and construction firm that offers consulting services, design services, and operations management to diverse clientele. **NOTE:** Search and apply for positions online. **Positions advertised include:** Construction Inspector. **Corporate headquarters location:** Pasadena CA. **Other U.S. locations:** Nationwide. **Parent company:** Jacobs Engineering. **Listed on:** New York Stock Exchange. **Stock exchange symbol:** JEC. **Number of employees worldwide:** 5,000.

JOHN DEERE CAPITAL CORPORATION
First Interstate Bank Building, One East First Street, Suite 600, Reno NV 89501. 775/786-5527. **Contact:** Human Resources. **World Wide Web address:** http://www.deere.com. **Description:** The US credit subsidiary of Deere & Company. The credit segment primarily finances sales and leases by John Deere dealers of new and used agricultural, commercial, consumer, construction, and forestry equipment. In addition, it provides wholesale financing to dealers, as well as operating loans and retail revolving charge accounts. **Corporate headquarter location:** Moline IL. **Listed on:** New York Stock Exchange. **Stock exchange symbol:** DE.

JOHNSON CONTROLS, INC.
3579 Red Rock Street, Suite B, Las Vegas NV 89103. 702/798-1979. **Contact:** Branch Manager. **World Wide Web address:** http://www.johnsoncontrols.com. **Description:** Johnson Controls is a global market leader in automotive systems and facility management and control. In the automotive market, it is a major supplier of integrated seating and interior systems, and batteries. For nonresidential facilities, Johnson Controls provides control systems and services including comfort, energy and security management. Founded in 1885. **NOTE:** Search and apply for positions online. **Corporate headquarters location:** Milwaukee WI. **Operations at this facility include:** As part of the controls segment, this location is involved in the installation and service of facility management and control systems, retrofit and service of mechanical equipment and lighting systems in nonresidential buildings, and on-site management of facility operations and management. **Listed on:** New York Stock Exchange. **Stock exchange symbol:** JCI. **Number of employees worldwide:** 119,000.

JONES VARGAS
3773 Howard Hughes Parkway, 3rd Floor South, Las Vegas NV 89109. 702/734-2220. **Contact:** Lynda Soper, Personnel. **E-mail address:** lws@jonesvargas.com. **World Wide Web address:** http://www.jonesvargas.com. **Description**: Represents local, national, and international clients in business, litigation, government relations, gaming, corporate, municipal finance, real estate, bankruptcy, estate and probate, tax, zoning, healthcare, and domestic matters. **Other area locations:** Reno NV.

JONES WEST FORD
3600 Keitzke Lane, Reno NV 89502. 775/745-0646. **Contact:** Jay Costet, Sales Manager. **World Wide Web address:** http://www.jwford.com. **Description:** An automotive dealership.

JOSTENS CLASS RINGS
2913 Mead Avenue, Las Vegas NV 89102. 702/579-0204. **Contact:** Human Resources. **World Wide Web address:** http://www.jostens.com. **Description:** The company produces recognition products and educational software. Josten's primary business segments are School Products, Recognition, and Jostens Learning. The School Products segment consists of five businesses: Printing and Publishing, Jewelry, Graduation Products, U.S. Photography, and Jostens Canada. Products include yearbooks, commercial printing, desktop publishing curriculum kits, class rings, graduation accessories, diplomas, trophies, plaques and other awards, school pictures, group photographs for youth camps and organizations, and senior graduation portraits. This

segment serves schools, colleges, and alumni associations in the United States and Canada through 1,100 independent sales representatives. Jostens also maintains an international sales force in approximately 50 countries for American schools and military installations. The Recognition segment provides products and services that reflect achievements in service, sales, quality, productivity, attendance, safety, and retirements. It also produces awards for championship team accomplishments and affinity products for associations. This segment serves companies, professional and amateur sports teams, and special interest associations, through an independent sales force of approximately 100. Jostens Learning produces educational software for kindergarten through grade 12, offering more than 7,000 hours of software-based curriculum in reading, mathematics, language arts, science programs, and early childhood instruction, as well as programs for at-risk learning and home learning. As one of the nation's largest providers of curriculum software, Jostens Learning serves more than 4 million students in 10,000 schools nationwide. **NOTE:** Search and apply for positions online. **Corporate headquarters location:** Minneapolis MN. **Operations at this facility include:** This location is engaged in selling class rings to students.

KFBT-TV WB/CHANNEL 33
3830 South Jones Boulevard, Las Vegas NV 89103. 702/873-0033. **Contact:** Rob Weisbord, General Manager. **World Wide Web address:** http://www.kfbt33.com. **Description:** A Warner Brothers network-affiliated television station. NOTE: Search and apply for positions online.

KLAS-TV/CHANNEL 8
P.O. Box 15047, Las Vegas NV 89114. 702/792-8888. **Physical address:** 3228 Channel 8 Drive, Las Vegas NV 89109. **Contact:** Dick Fraim, General Manager. **World Wide Web address:** http://www.klas-tv.com. **Description:** A television station. **NOTE:** Search and apply for positions online. **Positions advertised include:** Producer; Reporter; Account Executive; Weather Anchor/Reporter.

KTNV-TV ABC/CHANNEL 13
3355 South Valley View Boulevard, Las Vegas NV 89102. 702/876-1313. **Contact:** Administrative Assistant. **E-mail address:** jprother@journalbroadcastinggroup.com. **World Wide Web address:** http://www.ktnv.com. **Description:** An ABC-affiliated television station. **NOTE:** Search and apply for positions online. **Positions advertised include:** Assistant Manager; Reporter; Sales Assistant; Photojournalist; Account Executive; Production Specialist; Investigative Reporter.

KVBC-TV NBC/CHANNEL 3
1500 Foremaster Lane, Las Vegas NV 89101. 702/642-3333. **Contact:** Production Manager. **World Wide Web address:** http://www.kvbc.com. **Description:** An NBC-affiliated television station. **NOTE:** Search and apply for positions online. **Positions advertised include:** Writer/Producer/Editor; Photojournalist; Newscast Producer; Business Manager; Reporter; Associate Producer. **Special Programs:** Internships. **Number of employees at this location:** 200.

KVVU FOX TV/CHANNEL 5
25 TV 5 Drive, Henderson NV 89014. 702/435-5555. **Contact:** Personnel Department. **World Wide Web address:** http://www.kvvutv.com. **Description:** A Fox TV network affiliate. **NOTE:** Search and apply for positions online. **Positions advertised include:** Account Executive; News Reporter.

KVWB/ CHANNEL 21
3830 South Jones Boulevard, Las Vegas NV 89103. 702/382-2121. **Contact:** Human Resources. **Description:** A TV station. **NOTE:** Search and apply for positions online. **Positions advertised include:** Photographer; Sales Assistant; Assistant Business Manager; Accounting Assistant; Reporter/Producer; Traffic Assistant. **Corporate headquarters location:** Hunt Valley MD. **Parent company:** Sinclair Broadcast Group. **Listed on:** NASDAQ. **Stock exchange symbol:** SBGI. **Number of employees at this location:** 50.

KXNT-AM
INFINITY BROADCASTING
6655 West Sahara Avenue, Suite D-110, Las Vegas NV 89146. 702/364-8400. **Contact:** Human Resources. **World Wide Web address:** http://www.kxnt.com. **Description:** An AM talk radio station.

KAFOURY ARMSTRONG & CO.
801 South Rancho Drive, Suite E6, Las Vegas NV 89106-4828. 702/384-7717. **Contact:** Personnel. **E-mail address:** dfelder@kafoury.com. **World Wide Web address:** http://www.kafoury.com. **Description:** An accounting, auditing, and taxation specialist. Founded in 1941. **NOTE:** Entry-level positions are offered. **Positions advertised include:** Accountant; Auditor. **Corporate headquarters location:** Reno NV. **Other U.S. locations:** Elko NV; Fallon NV; Winnemucca NV; Yerington NV. **Listed on:** Privately held. **Annual sales/revenues:** $5 - $10 million. **Number of employees at this location:** 15. **Number of employees nationwide:** 140.

KAR PRODUCTS INC.
1085 Telegraph Street, Reno NV 89502. 775/786-0811. **Contact:** Human Resources. **E-mail address:** barnesjobs@bd-bgi.com. **World Wide Web address:** http://www.karproducts.com. **Description:** A distributor of nuts, bolts, and a variety of other fasteners. **NOTE:** Search and apply for positions online. **Corporate headquarters location:** Des Plaines IL. **Other U.S. locations:** Fairburn GA; Monroe Township NJ; Irving TX. **International locations:** Ontario, Canada.

KENNAMETAL INC.
347 North Taylor Street, Fallon NV 89406-5730. 775/428-6200. **Contact:** Rick Beach, Human Resources Manager. **E-mail address:** kennametal.resumes@kennametal.com. **World Wide Web address:** http://www.kennametal.com. **Description:** Manufactures, purchases, and distributes a broad range of tools, tooling systems, supplies, and services for the metalworking, mining, and highway construction industries. Kennametal specializes in developing and manufacturing metal cutting tools and wear-resistant parts using a specialized type of powder metallurgy. The company's metal cutting tools are made of cemented carbides, ceramics, cermets, and other hard materials. Kennametal manufactures a complete line of toolholders and toolholding systems by machining and fabricating steel bars and other metal alloys. The company's mining and construction cutting tools are tipped with cemented carbide and are used for underground coal mining and highway construction, repair, and maintenance. Metallurgical products consist of powders made from ore concentrates, compounds, and secondary materials. **NOTE:** Search and apply for positions online. **Corporate headquarters location:** Latrobe PA. **Other U.S. locations:** Troy MI; Henderson NC; Roanoke Rapids NC; Orwell OH; Solon OH; Bedford PA; Johnson City TN; New Market VA. **International locations:** Canada; China; England; Germany; Singapore; The Netherlands. **Listed on:** New York Stock Exchange. **Stock exchange symbol:** KMT. **Number of employees worldwide:** 13,500.

KENNY ROGERS ROASTERS
4340 South Valley View, Suite 220, Las Vegas NV 89103. 702/248-1559. **Contact:** Human Resources. **Description:** Area administrative offices for the quick-service roasted chicken restaurant chain. **Parent company:** Nathan's Famous.

KERR-McGEE CHEMICAL CORPORATION
P.O. Box 55, 8000 West Mead Drive, Henderson NV 89009-0055. 702/651-2200. **Contact:** Human Resources. **World Wide Web address:** http://www.kerr-mcgee.com. **Description:** Manufactures a variety of electro-chemicals for commercial and defense needs. Electrolytic battery active manganese dioxide is produced for use in the battery industry in the manufacturing of high-performance dry cells. Chlorates and perchlorates constitute other principal products. Kerr-McGee is a producer of ammonium perchlorate, which is chiefly used as an oxidizer material in solid propellant rocket fuel. Founded in 1929. **Corporate headquarters location:** Oklahoma City OK. **Parent company:** Kerr-McGee Corporation is a petroleum and natural gas exploration company which is also involved in the marketing and processing of petrochemicals, the mining of coal, and the refinement of crude oil. Exploration and production of oil and natural gas is conducted in the North Sea, the Gulf of Mexico, and on-shore in Canada and the United States. **Operations at this facility include:** Electrolytics. **Listed on:** New York Stock Exchange. **Stock exchange symbol:** KMG.

KINDRED HEALTHCARE
5110 West Sahara Avenue, Las Vegas NV 89146. 702/871-1418. **Contact:** Human Resources Manager. **World Wide Web address:** http://www.kindredhealthcare.com. **Description:** Specializes in providing long-term, acute care. **NOTE:** Search and apply for positions online. **Corporate headquarters location:** Louisville KY. **Other U.S. locations:** Nationwide. **Listed on:** NASDAQ. **Stock exchange symbol:** KIND.

KLEINFELDER
6380 South Polaris Avenue, Las Vegas NV 89118. 702/736-2936. **Contact:** Human Resources. **World Wide Web address:** http://www.kleinfelder.com. **Description:** An engineering consulting firm. **NOTE:** Search and apply for positions online. **Positions advertised include:** Project Professional, Geotechnical; Project Managers; Soils and Materials Technicians. **Corporate headquarters location:** San Diego CA. **Other area locations:** Reno, Carson City. **Subsidiaries include:** The Kleinfelder Group, Inc.; Kleinfelder, Inc.; Kleinfelder Mexico, S.A. de C.V.; Spectrum Exploration, Inc., Trinity Engineering/Kleinfelder, and GeoSystems, a Kleinfelder Company.

KRUMP CONSTRUCTION, INC.
825 Steneri Way, Sparks NV 89431. 775/358-5679. **Contact:** Karen Albrecht, Director, Corporate Administration. **E-mail address:** karenA@krump.com. **World Wide Web address:** http://www.krump.com. **Description:** A contracting company specializing in industrial and warehouse building construction. Founded 1967. **Positions advertised include:** Project Engineer; IT Support Analyst; Superintendent; Project Manager.

LA PETITE ACADEMY
76 North Pecos Road, Henderson NV 89014-3380. 702/897-0171. **Contact:** Personnel. **World Wide Web address:** http://www.lapetite.com. **Description:** Owns and operates a group of proprietary child care and preschool education centers. **NOTE:** Search and apply for positions online. **Corporate headquarters:** Chicago IL. **Other U.S. locations:** Nationwide. **Number of employees nationwide:** 12,800.

LABORATORY CORPORATION OF AMERICA (LABCORP)
888 Willow Street, Reno NV 89502. 775/334-3400. **Contact:** Human Resources Manager. **World Wide Web address:** http://www.labcorp.com. **Description:** One of the nation's leading clinical laboratory companies, providing services primarily to physicians, hospitals, clinics, nursing homes, and other laboratories nationwide. LabCorp performs tests on blood, urine, and other bodily fluids and tissue, aiding the prompt and accurate diagnosis of disease. **NOTE:** Search and apply for positions online. **Corporate headquarters location:** Burlington NC. **Other U.S. locations:** Nationwide. **Listed on:** New York Stock Exchange. **Stock exchange symbol:** LH. **Number of employees nationwide:** 23,000.

PARK PLAZA LAS VEGAS LADY LUCK CASINO HOTEL
206 North Third Street, Las Vegas NV 89101. 702/477-3000. **Fax:** 702/385-5540. **Contact:** Personnel. **World Wide Web address:** http://www.ladylucklv.com. **Description:** A casino/hotel operating individually themed gaming facilities. These facilities include Lady Luck Natchez, a showboat-themed dockside casino in Mississippi; Lady Luck Central City, a Las Vegas-style casino; and Lady Luck Tunica. **Parent company:** Carlson Hotels Worldwide.

LAHEY COMPUTER SYSTEMS, INC.
P.O. Box 6091, Incline Village NV 89450. 775/831-2500. **Physical address:** 865 Tahoe Boulevard, Incline Village NV 89451. **Toll-free phone:** 800/548-4778. **Fax:** 775/831-8123. **Contact:** Human Resources Department. **World Wide Web address:** http://www.lahey.com. **Description:** Develops scientific and engineering solutions software. **Corporate headquarters location:** This location.

LAND TITLE OF NEVADA, INC.
3301 North Buffalo Road, Suite 195, Las Vegas NV 89129. 702/385-5566. **Contact:** Carolyn Stokes, Personnel. **World Wide Web address:** http://www.landtitle-nv.com. **Description:** This location is the main office of the land title and escrow company. **NOTE:** Search and apply for positions online. **Positions advertised include:** Searcher; Policy Typist; Courier.

LAS VEGAS HILTON
3000 Paradise Road, Las Vegas NV 89109. 702/732-5111. **Contact:** Human Resources. **World Wide Web address:** http://www.hilton.com. **Description:** A 3,100-room hotel and casino. **NOTE:** Search and apply for positions online.

LAS VEGAS COLD STORAGE
1201 Searles Avenue, Las Vegas NV 89101. 702/649-8002. **Contact:** Human Resources. **Description:** Operates cold storage warehousing facilities for use by other companies.

LAS VEGAS PRESS
1385 Pama Lane, Suite 111, Las Vegas NV 89119. 702/871-6780. **Contact:** Human Resources Department. **World Wide Web address:** http://www.lvbusinesspress.com. **Description:** Publishes the *Las Vegas Business Press*, *CityLife*, and *Las Vegas Senior Press*.

LAS VEGAS REVIEW-JOURNAL
P.O. Box 70, 1111 West Bonanza Boulevard, Las Vegas NV 89125. 702/383-0211. **Fax:** 702/383-0435. **Contact:** Jim Hannah, Human Resources Director. **World Wide Web address:** http://www.lvrj.com. **Description:** Publishes a daily newspaper with a weekday circulation of approximately 167,000 and a Sunday circulation of more than

211,500. **NOTE:** Search and apply for positions online. **Corporate headquarters location:** Fort Smith AR. **Other U.S. locations:** Nationwide. **Parent company:** Stephens Media Group. **Listed on:** Privately held. **Number of employees at this location:** 750. **Number of employees nationwide:** 4,000.

LAS VEGAS SUN
2275 Corporate Circle Drive, Suite 300, Henderson NV 89074. 702/385-3111. **Contact:** Human Resources. **World Wide Web address:** http://www.lasvegassun.com. **Description:** The *Las Vegas Sun* is Las Vegas's only daily afternoon newspaper. The *Las Vegas Sun* is published under a joint operating agreement with the Las Vegas Review-Journal. Founded in 1950.

LAS VEGAS VALLEY WATER DISTRICT
1001 South Valley View Boulevard, Las Vegas NV 89153. 702/258-3220. **Contact:** Human Resources. **World Wide Web address:** http://www.lvvwd.com. **Description:** A major water utility company. **NOTE:** Search for positions online. **Positions advertised include:** Civil Engineer; Development Officer; Director of Education and Volunteer Programs; Electrical/Electronics Systems Technician; Environmental Planner; Project Manager. **Office hours:** Monday - Friday, 8:00 a.m. - 5:00 p.m.

LEVITZ FURNITURE CORPORATION
91 South Martin Luther King Boulevard, Las Vegas NV 89106. 702/366-9097. **Contact:** Human Resources. **E-mail address:** careers@levitz.com. **World Wide Web address:** http://www.levitz.com. **Description:** A store location of the national furniture store chain. **Corporate headquarters location:** Woodbury NY. **Other area locations:** Henderson NV.

LIONEL, SAWYER & COLLINS
1100 Bank of America Plaza, 50 West Liberty Street, Suite 1100, Reno NV 89501. 775/788-8666. **Contact:** Human Resources Department. **World Wide Web address:** http://www.lionelsawyer.com. **Description:** Lionel, Sawyer & Collins is a legal services firm specializing in corporate law. The firm's three areas of focus are commercial, administrative, and litigation. **Other area locations:** Carson City NV; Las Vegas NV. **Other U.S. locations:** Washington DC.

LLOYD'S REFRIGERATION & AIR CONDITIONING
3550 West Tompkins Avenue, Las Vegas NV 89103. 702/798-1010. **Contact:** Human Resources Manager. **E-mail address:** employment@lloydshomepage.com. **World Wide Web address:** http://www.lloydshomepage.com. **Description:** Designs and installs refrigeration systems, air conditioning and ventilation systems, and stainless steel and sheet metal work in both residential and commercial buildings.

LOCKHEED MARTIN
SYSTEMS SUPPORT & TRAINING SERVICES
4151 North Pecos Road, Suite 207, Las Vegas NV 89115-0189. 702/651-7100. **Fax:** 702/651-7188. **Contact:** Human Resources. **World Wide Web address:** http://www.lmco.com. **Description:** Operations at this location include maintaining ranges at Nellis Air Force Base. Overall, Lockheed Martin is a diversified defense contractor with businesses in engineering contracting, civil space programs, government services, commercial electronics, aeronautical systems, avionics, aerodynamics, and materials. **NOTE:** Search and apply for positions online. **Positions advertised include:** Chemist; Electronic Engineers; Environmental Technician; Network Engineer; Maintenance Worker. **Corporate headquarters location:** Bethesda MD. **Other U.S. locations:** Nationwide. **Parent company:** Lockheed Martin Corporation. **Listed on:** New York Stock Exchange. **Stock exchange symbol:** LMT. **Number of employees worldwide:** 130,000.

LONE STAR STEAKHOUSE & SALOON
1611 South Decatur Boulevard, Las Vegas NV 89102. 702/259-0105. **Contact:** General Manager. **E-mail address:** team@thesteakcompany.com. **World Wide Web address:** http://www.lonestarsteakhouse.com. **Description:** Lone Star Steakhouse & Saloon owns and operates a chain of 265 full-service, casual dining restaurants. **NOTE:** Apply for management positions online. **Corporate headquarters location:** Wichita KS. **Other U.S. locations:** Nationwide. **Listed on:** NASDAQ. **Stock exchange symbol:** STAR.

LOOMIS, FARGO & COMPANY
3370 Palm Parkway, Las Vegas NV 89104. 702/457-0105. **Contact:** Personnel. **World Wide Web address:** http://www.loomisfargo.com. **Description:** An armored security service specializing in transporting currency. **NOTE:** Applications will not be mailed to jobseekers. They must be picked up in person. **Other U.S. locations:** Nationwide. **Number of employees at this location:** 45.

LUXOR LAS VEGAS
3900 Las Vegas Boulevard South, Las Vegas NV 89119-1000. 702/262-4000. **Contact:** Doug McCombs, Human Resources Director. **World Wide Web address:** http://www.luxor.com. **Description:** A resort hotel and casino offering over 2,500 rooms. **NOTE:** Search and apply for positions online. **Parent company:** Mandalay Resort Group.

M-I LLC
P.O. Box 370, Battle Mountain NV 89820-0370. 775/635-5135. **Fax:** 775/635-2191. **Contact:** Personnel. **Description:** This location houses a mining and grinding plant for Barite products. Overall, M-I is an international oil field drilling services company providing drilling fluids, well-hole logging, and engineering. **NOTE:** Second and third shifts are offered. Search and apply for positions online. **Common positions include:** Accountant; Branch Manager; Civil Engineer; Clerical Supervisor; Construction Contractor; Electrician; Emergency Medical Technician; General Manager; Mechanical Engineer; Metallurgical Engineer; Production Manager; Secretary; Transportation/Traffic Specialist; Typist/Word Processor. **Special programs:** Summer Jobs. **Office hours:** Monday - Friday, 8:00 a.m. - 5:00 p.m. **Corporate headquarters location:** Houston TX. **Other U.S. locations:** Nationwide. **International locations:** Worldwide. **Parent company:** Smith International Inc. **Listed on:** New York Stock Exchange. **Stock exchange symbol:** SII. **Annual sales/revenues:** More than $100 million. **Number of employees at this location:** 75. **Number of employees worldwide:** 2,000.

MGM GRAND HOTEL
3799 Las Vegas Boulevard South, Las Vegas NV 89109. 702/891-1111. **Contact:** Casting Center. **World Wide Web address:** http://www.mgmgrand.com. **Description:** A hotel that includes over 5,000 guest rooms and suites, one of the world's largest casinos divided into areas with different themes, eight restaurants, a fast-food court, three entertainment lounges, and two showrooms. The complex also includes a youth center for younger guests and the Oz Midway & Arcade. The complex's theme park, MGM Grand Adventures, is set on 33 acres and features seven major rides and five shows in four theaters. **NOTE:** Search and apply for positions online. **Positions advertised include:** Food and Beverage Service Worker; Hotel/Motel Clerk; Retail Sales Worker. **Corporate headquarters location:** This location. **Parent company:** MGM Grand, Inc.

MARCH OF DIMES BIRTH DEFECTS FOUNDATION
3650 North Rancho, Suite 106, Las Vegas NV 89130. 702/732-9255. **Contact:** Director. **E-mail address:** NV411@marchofdimes.com. **World Wide Web address:** http://www.modimes.org. **Description:** The mission of the March of Dimes Birth Defects Foundation is to improve the health of babies by preventing birth defects and infant mortality. The March of Dimes carries out this mission through the Campaign for Healthier Babies, which includes programs of research, community services, education, and advocacy. Birth defects are the primary focus of March of Dimes research efforts. Every year, hundreds of grants are awarded to scientists to help find cures to over 3,000 known birth defects. March of Dimes chapters across the country work with their communities to determine and meet the needs of women, babies, and families. **NOTE:** Search and apply for positions online. **Other U.S. locations:** Nationwide.

MARSH INC.
7251 West Lake Mead Boulevard, Suite 401, Las Vegas NV 89128. 702/804-7200. **Fax:** 702/804-7300. **Contact:** Human Resources Department. **E-mail address:** employment.jobs@marsh.com. **World Wide Web address:** http://www.marsh.com. **Description:** Provides consulting services worldwide through an insurance brokerage and risk management firm, reinsurance intermediary facilities, and a consulting and financial services group, to clients concerned with the management of assets and risks. Specific services include insurance and risk management services, reinsurance, consulting and financial services, merchandising, and investment management. **NOTE:** Search and apply for positions online. **Positions advertised include:** Account Executive; Operations Manager; Sales Executive; Claims Consultant. **Other U.S. locations:** Nationwide. **International locations:** Worldwide. **Parent company:** Marsh & McLennan Companies, Inc.

MEADOW VALLEY CORPORATION
4635 Andrew Street, Suite F, North Las Vegas NV 89081. 702/643-9472. **Contact:** Human Resources. **E-mail address:** info@meadowvalley.com. **World Wide Web address:** http://www.meadowvalley.com. **Description:** Performs heavy construction services including highway and bridge construction and the paving of airport runways and highways. **NOTE:** Search for positions online. **Positions advertised include:** Entry Level Construction, Civil, or Structural Engineer; Project Construction, Civil or Structural Engineer. **Corporate headquarters location:** Phoenix AZ. **Subsidiaries include:** Meadow Valley Contractors, Inc.; Ready Mix Inc. **Listed on:** NASDAQ. **Stock exchange symbol:** MVCO.

MERIDIAN GOLD COMPANY
9670 Gateway Drive, Suite 200, Reno NV 8951. 775/850-3777. **Toll-free phone:** 800/572-4519. **Fax:** 775/850-3733. **Contact:** Human Resources. **World Wide Web address:** http://www.meridiangold.com. **Description:** A precious metals producer. The company produces over 400,000 ounces of gold yearly. Meridian Gold has reserves of 4 million ounces of gold. **NOTE:** Search for positions online. **Corporate headquarters location:** This location. **Other area locations:** Elko NV. **Other U.S. locations:** Salmon ID. **International locations:** Chile; Peru; Argentina. **Listed on:** New York Stock Exchange. **Stock exchange symbol:** MDG.

MERILLAT INDUSTRIES, INC.
6405 South Ensworth Street, Las Vegas NV 89119. 702/361-4353. **Contact:** Human Resources. **World Wide Web address:** http://www.merillat.com. **Description:** A manufacturer of cabinets and vanity furniture. **Corporate headquarters location:** Adrian MI. **Number of employees at this location:** 250. **Number of employees nationwide:** 4,200.

MERRILL LYNCH
2300 West Sahara Avenue, Suite 1200, Las Vegas NV 89102. 702/227-7000. **Contact:** Manager. **World Wide Web address:** http://www.ml.com. **Description:** A diversified financial services organization. Merrill Lynch is a major broker in securities, option contracts, commodities and financial futures contracts, and insurance. The company also deals with corporate and municipal securities and investment banking. **NOTE:** Entry-level positions are offered. Search and apply for positions online. **Corporate headquarters location:** New York NY. **Other U.S. locations:** Nationwide. **International locations:** Worldwide. **Number of employees worldwide:** Over 49,000.

MERVYN'S CALIFORNIA
3871 South Carson Street, Carson City NV 89701-5538. 775/887-8800. **Contact:** Human Relations Coordinator. **World Wide Web address:** http://www.mervyns.com. **Description:** One location of the 264-store chain. **NOTE:** Search and apply for positions online (including openings at Target and Marshall Field's). **Corporate headquarters location:** Hayward CA. **Other U.S. locations:** Nationwide. **Parent company:** Target Corporation. **President:** Diane L. Neal. **Sales/revenue:** Approximately $4 billion. **Number of employees nationwide:** 28,000.

METROPOLITAN LIFE INSURANCE COMPANY
1771 East Flamingo Road, Las Vegas NV 89119. 702/731-0257. **Contact:** Steve Trotman, General Manager. **World Wide Web address:** http://www.metlife.com. **Description:** Metropolitan Life offers a wide range of individual and group insurance including life, annuity, disability, and mutual funds. **NOTE:** Search and apply for positions online. **Special programs:** Internships; Training. **Corporate headquarters location:** New York NY. **Other U.S. locations:** Nationwide. **Operations at this facility include:** This location is a sales and service office. **Listed on:** New York Stock Exchange. **Stock exchange symbol:** MET. **Number of employees at this location:** 30. **Number of employees nationwide:** 13,500.

MIKOHN GAMING CORPORATION
920 Pilot Road, Las Vegas NV 89119. 702/896-3890. **Toll-free phone:** 800/336-8449. **Contact:** Human Resources. **E-mail address:** careers@mikohn.com. **World Wide Web address:** http://www.mikohn.com. **Description:** Develops, manufactures, and distributes progressive jackpot systems for use with gaming machines. The company also designs, manufactures, and distributes custom electrical signs for both internal and external use. The company's jackpot systems and interior casino sign products are marketed and sold both separately and together as integrated, value-added casino marketing and promotional packages. Founded in 1986. **NOTE:** Search for positions online. **Positions advertised include:** Electronics OEM Products Project Manager. **Special programs:** Training. **Corporate headquarters location:** This location. **Other U.S. locations:** MS; CO; FL; MO; NJ; WI. **International locations:** Australia; The Netherlands. **Listed on:** NASDAQ. **Stock exchange symbol:** MIKN. **Number of employees worldwide:** 500.

MONARCH CASINO & RESORT, INC.
1175 West Moana Lane, Suite 200, Reno NV 89509. 775/825-3355. **Contact:** Human Resources Department. **World Wide Web address:** http://www.monarchcasino.com. **Description:** Monarch Casino & Resort, Incorporated, through its wholly-owned

subsidiary, Golden Road Motor Inn, Incorporated, owns and operates Atlantis Resort Casino in Reno, which caters primarily to area residents and leisure travelers. Atlantis offers approximately 51,000 square feet of casino area, a hotel, seven restaurants, seven public bars, a nightclub, swimming pools and health club. The casino offers 965 slot machines and 34 table games. **Subsidiaries include:** Golden Road Motor Inn, Incorporated. **Listed on:** NASDAQ. **Stock exchange symbol:** MCRI.

MOORE BUSINESS FORMS & SYSTEMS
840 Grier Drive, Suite 310, Las Vegas NV 89119. 702/914-4300. **Contact:** Human Resources. **World Wide Web address:** http://www.rrdonnelley.com. **Description:** A manufacturer of business forms and equipment with more than 280 sales offices and branches in 39 countries. **Corporate headquarters location:** Stamford CT. **Other U.S. locations:** Nationwide. **International locations:** Worldwide. **Parent company:** RR Donnelley. **Number of employees worldwide:** 11,000.

MORGAN STANLEY DEAN WITTER & COMPANY
3800 Howard Hughes Parkway, Suite 800, Las Vegas NV 89109-0925. 702/737-7275. **Contact:** Mike Nahasa, Branch Manager. **World Wide Web address:** http://www.msdw.com. **Description:** Offers diversified financial services including equities, fixed income securities, commodities, money market instruments, and investment banking services. **Positions advertised include:** Financial Advisor Trainee. **Other U.S. locations:** Nationwide. **International locations:** Worldwide.

MR. GASKET
550 Mallory Way, Carson City NV 89701. 775/882-6600. **Contact:** Human Resources. **World Wide Web address:** http://www.mrgasket.com. **Description:** Produces assembly drawings; coils and accessories; distributors including dual point and electronic distributors; electric and mechanical fuel pumps; electronic ignition control systems; marine fuel pumps and ignition systems; racing ignition products; spark plug wire kits; tachometers and gauges; and tune-up parts and engine accessories.

NEIMAN MARCUS
3200 Las Vegas Boulevard South, Las Vegas NV 89109. 702/731-3636. **Contact:** Personnel. **World Wide Web address:** http://www.neimanmarcus.com. **Description:** A department store. Founded in 1907. **NOTE:** Entry-level positions are offered. Search and apply for positions online. **Positions advertised include:** Department Manager. **Special programs:** Training. **Corporate headquarters location:** Dallas TX. **Parent company:** Neiman Marcus Group, Incorporated operates two specialty retailing businesses: Neiman Marcus and Bergdorf Goodman. Combined, these chains offer men's and women's apparel, fashion accessories, precious jewelry, fine china, and crystal and silver. Neiman Marcus has 35 stores nationwide. NM Direct, another subsidiary, is a direct marketing company, which advertises primarily through the use of such specialty catalogues as Neiman Marcus and Horchow. **Listed on:** New York Stock Exchange. **Stock exchange symbol:** NMGA. **Number of employees at this location:** 300.

NEVADA BUSINESS JOURNAL MAGAZINE
4386 South Eastern Avenue, Suite B, Las Vegas NV 89119. 702/735-7003. **Fax:** 702/791-5921. **Contact:** Lyle E. Brennan, Human Resources. **E-mail address:** lyle@nbj.com. **World Wide Web address:** http://www.nevadabusiness.com. **Description:** Publishes a business periodical. **Positions advertised include:** Account Representative/Salesperson. **Parent company:** Business Link, LLC. **President:** Mark Keays.

NEVADA CEMENT COMPANY
P.O. Box 840, Fernley NV 89408-0840. 775/575-2281. **Contact:** Personnel. **Description:** A manufacturer of hydraulic cement. **Corporate headquarters location:** This location. **Number of employees at this location:** 132.

NEVADA POWER COMPANY
P.O. Box 98910, Las Vegas NV 89151-0001. 702/367-5000. **Physical address:** 6226 West Sahara Avenue, Las Vegas NV 89151. **Fax:** 702/367-5053. **Recorded jobline:** 800/NPC-SPPC. **Contact:** Human Resources Department. **E-mail address:** hr@nevp.com. **World Wide Web address:** http://www.nevadapower.com. **Description:** Provides electric services to over 700,000 customers in Clark and Nye Counties in southern Nevada. Nevada Power's electrical system includes one four-unit coal-fired plant, two gas-fired plants, and approximately 11,000 miles of transmission and distribution lines. Nevada Power Company is also partial owner of the Navajo Generating Station, located near Page AZ, and the Mojave Generating Station near Laughlin NV. The company purchases a large portion of its customers' power needs from other utilities and independent power producers, as well as a small amount from the Hoover Dam hydroelectric plant. **NOTE:** When emailing your resume, you must attach a completed application. Applications can be downloaded from the company's Website. Online applications are also available. **Positions advertised include:** Accountant; Automated Mapping Technician; Engineer; Quality Assurance Consultant. **Parent company:** Sierra Pacific Resources. **Number of employees nationwide:** 1,700.

NEVADA STATE BANK
2255 North Las Vegas Boulevard, North Las Vegas NV 89030. 702/649-4490. **Recorded jobline:** 702/383-4160. **Contact:** Human Resources. **World Wide Web address:** http://www.nsbank.com. **Description:** A full-service bank. This location is one of 60 branches statewide. **NOTE:** Resumes should be sent to Human Resources Manager, 750 East Warm Springs Road, 1st Floor, Las Vegas NV 89119. Interested job seekers may also call 800/797-WORK to apply for a position. Search for positions online. **Positions advertised include:** Teller; Financial Services Representative. **Corporate headquarters location:** Las Vegas NV.

NEVADA STATE BANK
4600 East Sunset Road, Henderson NV 89014. 702/456-3776. **Fax:** 702/456-3042. **Recorded jobline:** 702/383-4160. **Contact:** Human Resources. **World Wide Web address:** http://www.nsbank.com. **Description:** A full-service bank. This location is one of 60 branches statewide. **NOTE:** Resumes should be sent to Human Resources Manager, 750 East Warm Springs Road, 1st Floor, Las Vegas NV 89119. Interested job seekers may also call 800/797-WORK to apply for a position. Search for positions online. **Positions advertised include:** Financial Services Supervisor; Teller. **Corporate headquarters location:** Las Vegas NV.

NEVADA STATE BANK
4240 West Flamingo Road, 2nd Floor, Las Vegas NV 89103. 702/889-8052. **Recorded jobline:** 702/383-4160. **Contact:** Human Resources. **World Wide Web address:** http://www.nsbank.com. **Description:** A full-service bank. This location is one of 60 branches statewide. **NOTE:** Resumes should be sent to Human Resources Manager, 750 East Warm Springs Road, 1st Floor, Las Vegas NV 89121. Interested job seekers may also call 800/797-WORK to apply for a position. Search for positions online. **Positions advertised include:** Financial Services Supervisor; Teller. **Corporate headquarters location:** Las Vegas NV.

NEVADA STATE PLASTERING
3308 Meade Avenue, Las Vegas NV 89102-7893. 702/873-6110. **Contact:** Office Manager. **World Wide Web address:** http://www.thestreaker.com/nsp/nevada.html. **Description:** A plastering contractor.

NEW LIFE BAKERY, INC.
1766 Van Epps Drive, Carson City NV 89701. 775/884-3900. **Toll-free phone:** 800/407-6379. **Contact:** Human Resources Department. **Description:** A private-label bakery that produces baked goods for other companies.

NEW YORK LIFE INSURANCE COMPANY
3993 Howard Hughes Parkway, Suite 500, Las Vegas NV 89109. 702/796-2000. **Fax:** 702/796-3930. **Contact:** Managing Partner. **World Wide Web address:** http://www.newyorklife.com. **Description:** New York Life Insurance Company is one of the nation's largest financial services organizations. The company, its subsidiaries, and affiliates offer a wide variety of products and services. Services include life, health, and disability insurance; annuities; mutual funds; structured finance products; health care management services; and commercial mortgage financing. Operations are conducted in the United States, the United Kingdom, the Pacific Rim, and Mexico. The company's Asset Management operation (including pensions, mutual funds, and NYLIFE Securities) is located in Parsippany NJ. Founded in 1845. **Corporate headquarters location:** New York NY. **Other U.S. locations:** Nationwide. **Listed on:** Privately held. **CEO/Chairman:** Seymour Sternberg. **Sales/revenue:** Over $24 billion. **Number of employees nationwide:** 7,500.

NEWMONT MINING CORPORATION
P.O. Box 669, Carlin NV 89822. 775/778-4831. **Fax:** 775/778-4753. **Contact:** Human Resources. **E-mail address:** hrrecruiter@newmont.com. **World Wide Web address:** http://www.newmont.com. **Description:** Newmont Mining Corporation is a gold mining company. Operations include open-pit mines, leach operations, and milling. **Positions advertised include:** Mechanical Engineer. **Corporate headquarters location:** Denver CO. **International locations:** Worldwide. **Operations at this facility include:** Administration; Manufacturing; Research and Development. **Listed on:** New York Stock Exchange. **Stock exchange symbol:** NEM. **Number of employees nationwide:** 3,000. **Number of employees worldwide:** 14,000.

NEWMONT MINING CORPORATION
TWIN CREEKS MINE
P.O. Box 69, Golconda NV 89414-0069. 775/635-9400. **Contact:** Human Resources. **E-mail address:** hrrecruiter@newmont.com. **World Wide Web address:** http://www.newmont.com. **Description:** Newmont Mining Corporation is a gold mining company. Operations include open-pit mines, leach operations, and milling. **Corporate headquarters location:** Denver CO. **International locations:** Worldwide. **Listed on:** New York Stock Exchange. **Stock exchange symbol:** NEM. **Number of employees nationwide:** 3,000. **Number of employees worldwide:** Over 14,000.

NORTH AMERICAN MORTGAGE COMPANY
5300 West Sahara Avenue, Las Vegas NV 89102. 702/365-0476. **Contact:** Human Resources. **World Wide Web address:** http://www.namc.com. **Description:** Originates, acquires, sells, and services mortgage loans, principally first lien mortgage loans secured by single-family residences. North American Mortgage Company also sells servicing rights associated with a portion of such loans. The company operates through a network of 50 loan origination offices in 14 states. Founded in 1948. **Other U.S. locations:** Nationwide. **Parent company:** Washington Mutual Bank, FA.

NORTHERN NEVADA MEDICAL CENTER
2375 East Prater Way, Sparks NV 89434. 775/331-7000. **Fax:** 775/356-4901. **Contact:** Human Resources. **E-mail address:** pdowns@uhsinc.com. **World Wide Web address:** http://www.northernnvmed.com. **Description:** Offers health care in over 30 specialties including 24-hour emergency care; communication therapy; CT scans; diagnostic imaging/mammography; gastroenterology; geriatrics; intensive care services; kidney dialysis; laboratory services; laser surgery; nuclear medicine; occupational therapy; oncology; ophthalmic surgery; orthopedics; pediatrics; physical therapy; geriatric, inpatient, partial (day), and home care psychiatric programs; pulmonary; reconstructive plastic surgery; rehabilitation; respiratory care; sports medicine; inpatient and outpatient surgery; and telemetry services. **NOTE:** To contact Human Resources directly, call 775/356-4085. **Positions advertised include:** Chief Nurse Executive; Critical Care Unit Manager; Registered Nurses; Certified Nursing Assistants; Physical Therapist; Occupational Therapist. **Office hours:** Monday – Friday, 7:00 a.m. – 4:30 p.m.

OCEAN SPRAY CRANBERRIES, INC.
1301 American Pacific Drive, Henderson NV 89014. 702/566-7100. **Contact:** Plant Manager. **World Wide Web address:** http://www.oceanspray.com. **Description:** The company is a nationally recognized food processor engaged in the packaging, processing, and marketing of fresh cranberries, cranberry sauces, and cranberry and grapefruit juices. **NOTE:** Search and apply for positions online. **Positions advertised include:** Operations Technician; Team Leader. **Corporate headquarters location:** Lakeville MA. **Other U.S. locations:** Vero Beach FL; Middleborough MA; Bordenton NJ; Sulphur Springs TX; Markham WA; Kenosha WI. **International locations:** Worldwide. **Operations at this facility include:** This location is the West Coast distribution facility for all Ocean Spray products. **Sales/revenue:** Over $1 billion. **Number of employees worldwide:** 2,000.

OLIVE GARDEN ITALIAN RESTAURANT
6850 West Cheyenne Avenue, Las Vegas NV 89108-4590. 702/658-2144. **Contact:** Manager. **World Wide Web address:** http://www.olivegarden.com. **Description:** One location of the chain of family-style Italian restaurants. **NOTE:** Job application available for download. **Other U.S. locations:** Nationwide. **International locations:** Canada.

OMNISHORE
1700 Forrest Way, Carson City NV 89706. 775/687-2800. **Contact:** Human Resources. **Description:** Omnishore is a contract manufacturer of printed circuit assemblies, computers, subsystems, and other electronic equipment. **Corporate headquarters location:** This location.

OZBURN-HESSEY LOGISTICS
450 Lillard Drive, Sparks NV 89434. 775/355-2150. **Contact:** Human Resources. **E-mail address:** hr@ohlogistics.com. **World Wide Web address:** http://www.ohlogistics.com. **Description:** A commercial and household warehousing company. **NOTE:** Search for positions online. **Corporate headquarters location:** Nashville TN. **Other U.S. locations:** Nationwide. **CEO:** Scott McWilliams.

PPG INDUSTRIES
4375 South Valley View Boulevard, Suite C, Las Vegas NV 89101. 702/367-1313. **Contact:** Manager. **World Wide Web address:** http://www.ppg.com. **Description:**

PPG Industries is a supplier of products for manufacturing, building, automotive, processing, and other industries. The company manufactures decorative and protective coatings, flat glass and fabricated glass products, continuous-strand fiberglass, and industrial and specialty chemicals. **NOTE:** Search and apply for positions online. **Corporate headquarters location:** Pittsburgh PA. **Other U.S. locations:** Nationwide. **International locations:** Worldwide. **Operations at this facility include:** This location is a warehouse.

PACIFICARE HEALTH SYSTEMS INC.
700 East Warm Springs Road, Las Vegas NV 89119. 702/269-7500. **Contact:** Human Resources. **World Wide Web address:** http://www.pacificare.com. **Description:** Offers a full range of health care products and services to 3 million health plan members and approximately 9 million specialty plan members nationwide. Established in 1992. **NOTE:** Search and apply for positions online. **Positions advertised include:** Associate, Marketing and Sales; Program Manager. **Corporate headquarters location:** Cypress CA. **Listed on:** NASDAQ. **Stock exchange symbol:** PHSY. **Sales/revenue:** $11 billion.

PALACE STATION HOTEL AND CASINO
2411 West Sahara Avenue, Las Vegas NV 89102. 702/367-2411. **Recorded jobline:** 702/221-6789. **Contact:** Human Resources Director. **World Wide Web address:** http://www.palacestation.com. **Description:** Owns and operates a hotel and casino and provides slot machine route management, vending, and payphone services to numerous food and beverage establishments, commercial businesses, and major hotels and casinos. **NOTE:** Search for positions online. **Parent company:** Station Casinos. **Listed on:** New York Stock Exchange. **Stock exchange symbol:** STN.

PENNZOIL-QUAKER STATE
5470 Wynn Road, Suite 400, Las Vegas NV 89118-2352. 702/895-6726. **Contact:** Human Resources. **World Wide Web address:** http://www.shell.com. **Description:** A natural resource company engaged in oil and gas exploration and production; processing, refining, and marketing oil, gas, and refined petroleum products; and mining and marketing sulfur. **Corporate headquarters location:** Houston TX. **Other U.S. locations:** Nationwide. **International locations:** Worldwide. **Parent company:** Shell Oil Products U.S. **Listed on:** New York Stock Exchange. **Stock exchange symbol:** RD.

PEPSI-COLA BOTTLING COMPANY
355 Edison Way, Reno NV 89502. 775/856-1387. **Contact:** Human Resources. **World Wide Web address:** http://www.pepsico.com. **Description:** A bottling facility and a division of Pepsi-Cola Company. **NOTE:** Search and apply for positions online. **Parent company:** PepsiCo, Incorporated (Purchase NY) consists of Frito-Lay Company, Pepsi-Cola Company, and Tropicana Products, Incorporated. **Listed on:** New York Stock Exchange. **Stock exchange symbol:** PEP.

PEPSI-COLA COMPANY
FOUNTAIN & VENDING SALES
3333 West Sirius Avenue, Las Vegas NV 89102. 702/362-1884. **Contact:** Personnel. **World Wide Web address:** http://www.pepsico.com. **Description:** Pepsi-Cola Company produces and distributes a variety of beverages including the brand names Pepsi-Cola, Mountain Dew, Mug Root Beer, and Slice. **NOTE:** Search and apply for positions online. **Positions advertised include:** Sales Representative. **Office hours:** Monday – Friday, 8:00 a.m. – 4:00 p.m. **Parent company:** PepsiCo, Incorporated (Purchase NY) consists of Frito-Lay Company, Pepsi-Cola Company, and Tropicana Products, Incorporated. **Operations at this facility include:** This location is a sales facility. **Listed on:** New York Stock Exchange. **Stock exchange symbol:** PEP.

PERFECT COMMERCE, INC.
3291 North Buffalo Avenue, Suite 9, Las Vegas NV 89129. 702/316-7000. **Fax:** 702/316-7001. **Contact:** Human Resources. **E-mail address:** jobs@perfect.com. **World Wide Web address:** http://www.perfect.com. **Description:** Develops internet-based purchasing software, as well as providing related services and expertise. **Corporate headquarters location:** Kansas City MO. **Other U.S. locations:** Cupertino and San Diego CA. **President/CEO:** James McCormick.

PIONEER COMPANIES, INC.
P.O. Box 86, Henderson NV 89009-7001. 702/565-8781. **Physical address:** 8000 Lake Mead Parkway, Henderson NV 89015. **Fax:** 702/565-7145. **Contact:** Human Resources Director. **World Wide Web address:** http://www.piona.com. **Description:** Pioneer Chlor Alkali is one of the world's largest processors of chlorine and caustic soda (sodium hydroxide). **Office hours:** Monday – Friday, 7:00 a.m. – 4:00 p.m. **Corporate headquarters location:** Houston TX. **Other U.S. locations:** LA; CA; WA. **International locations:** Canada. **Operations at this facility include:** This location manufactures chlorine, caustic soda, hydrochloric acid, and bleach.

PORT OF SUBS, INC.
5365 Mae Anne Avenue, Suite A29, Reno NV 89523. 775/747-0555. **Fax:** 775/747-1510. **Contact:** Personnel. **E-mail address:** kaquino@portofsubs.com. **World Wide Web address:** http://www.portofsubs.com. **Description:** Operates a 125-unit chain of sandwich shops. **NOTE:** Search and apply for positions online. **Positions advertised include:** IT Manager; Field Marketing Assistant; Accounts Payable and Payroll Clerk. **Corporate headquarters location:** This location. **Other U.S. locations:** CA; AZ; ID; UT; WA, OR, HI.

POTLATCH CORPORATION
3901 North Donna Street, North Las Vegas NV 89030. 702/657-1707. **Contact:** Human Resources. **E-mail address:** jobs@potlatchcorp.com. **World Wide Web address:** http://www.potlatchcorp.com. **Description:** Potlatch Corporation is a diversified forest products company with 1.5 million acres of timberland in Arkansas, Idaho, and Minnesota. Products include lumber and panels, bleached pulp, paperboard, and consumer tissue. **NOTE:** Search and apply for positions online. **Positions advertised include:** Production Associate. **Corporate headquarters location:** Spokane WA. **Other U.S. locations:** AR; ID; MN; OR. **Operations at this facility include:** This location is a paper mill producing bathroom tissue, facial tissue, paper towels, and napkins. **Listed on:** New York Stock Exchange. **Stock exchange symbol:** PCH. **Sales/revenue:** $1.3 billion. **Number of employees nationwide:** 4,200.

PRECISION ROLLED PRODUCTS INC.
P.O. Box 60010, Reno NV 89506. 775/972-0272. **Contact:** Personnel Manager. **World Wide Web address:** http://www.prpusa.com. **Description:** Precision Rolled Products is an approved superalloy manufacturer and supplier to most of the world's leading gas turbine manufacturers and their subcontractors. **Corporate headquarters location:** This location. **Parent company:** Krupp VDM USA Incorporated.

PRESTIGE TRAVEL AMERICAN EXPRESS
6175 Spring Mountain Road, Las Vegas NV 89146. 702/251-5552. **Contact:** Human Resources. **Description:** A travel agency with 21 locations in the greater Las Vegas area. **Corporate headquarters location:** This location.

PRICEWATERHOUSECOOPERS
3800 Howard Hughes Parkway, Suite 550, Las Vegas NV 89109. 702/691-5400. **Contact:** Human Resources Department. **World Wide Web address:** http://www.pricewaterhousecoopers.com. **Description:** One of the largest certified public accounting firms in the world. PricewaterhouseCoopers provides public accounting, business advisory, management consulting, and taxation services. **NOTE:** Search and apply for positions online. **Positions advertised include:** Assurance Associates. **Corporate headquarters location:** New York NY. **Other U.S. locations:** Nationwide. **International locations:** Worldwide. **Number of employees worldwide:** Over 124,000.

PRIMEX PLASTICS CORPORATION
752 Turtleback Road, Mesquite NV 89027. 702/346-7100. **Fax:** 702/346-7150. **Contact:** Human Resources Manager. **E-mail address:** hr@primexplastics.com. **World Wide Web address:** http://www.primexplastics.com. **Description:** A manufacturer and extruder of sheet and rolled plastic. **Corporate headquarters location:** Richmond IN.

PRIMM VALLEY RESORTS
31900 South Las Vegas Boulevard, Prim NV 89019. 702/382-1212. **Fax:** 702/679-5633. **Recorded jobline:** 702/679-5627. **Contact:** Human Resources. **E-mail address:** positions@primm.mgmgrand.com. **World Wide Web address:** http://www.primmvalleyresorts.com. **Description:** Owns and operates hotels and casinos. **NOTE:** Search and apply for positions online. **Positions advertised include:** Assistant Casino Controller; Audit Clerk; Hard Count Clerk; Ride Associate; Cage Cashier; Assistant Payroll Manager; Payroll Clerk; Purchasing Agent; Staff Accountant; Fry Cook; Busperson; Host/Cashier; Director of Food and Beverage; Valet Attendant; Application Specialist; Convention Services Manager; EMT Officer; Slot Booth Cashier.

QUALITY WOOD PRODUCTS
3001 North Nellis Boulevard, Las Vegas NV 89115. 702/369-3008. **Contact:** Human Resources. **Description:** Manufactures and installs doors in both residential and commercial buildings.

QUEST DIAGNOSTICS
4230 Burnham Avenue, Suite 144, Las Vegas NV 89119-5410. 702/733-7866. **Toll-free phone:** 800/433-2750. **Contact:** Human Resources. **World Wide Web address:** http://www.questdiagnostics.com. **Description:** A medical testing laboratory offering over 500 diagnostic determinations. **NOTE:** Search and apply for positions online. **Positions advertised include:** Transcriptionist; Medical Technologist; Assistant Controller; Billing Coordinator; Route Service Rep; Laboratory Assistant; Specimen Technician; Phlebotomy Services Representative.

RALEY'S
2105 West Williams Avenue, Fallon NV 89406. 775/423-7114. **Contact:** Manager. **World Wide Web address:** http://www.raleys.com. **Description:** A grocery store location of the chain of supermarkets. Raley's operates more than 50 stores in Nevada and Northern California. **NOTE:** Search and apply for corporate positions online. **Corporate headquarters location:** West Sacramento CA. **Other U.S. locations:** Nationwide.

RENO, CITY OF
CIVIL SERVICE COMMISSION
P.O. Box 1900, Reno NV 89505-1900. 775/334-2223. **Physical address:** 490 South Center Street, Room 102, Reno NV 89501. **Fax:** 775/334-2573. **Recorded jobline:** 775/334-2287. **Contact:** Civil Services. **E-mail address:** crowe@ci.reno.nv.us. **World Wide Web address:** http://www.cityofreno.com. **Description:** Administrative offices for the city of Reno. **NOTE:** Search for positions online. **Positions advertised include:** Associate Civil Engineer; Code Enforcement Manager; Equipment Mechanic; Office Assistant; Public Safety Dispatcher; Reserve Police Officer; Water Conservation Consultant. **Special programs:** Internships. **Office hours:** Monday – Friday, 8:00 a.m. – 5:00 p.m. **Corporate headquarters location:** This location. **Operations at this facility include:** Administration. **Number of employees at this location:** 1,200.

RENO FAMILY YMCA
1300 Foster Drive, Reno NV 89509. 775/329-1311. **Contact:** Director. **World Wide Web address:** http://www.ymca.com. **Description:** One of the nation's largest and most comprehensive service organizations. The YMCA provides the opportunity for health and fitness; social and personal development; sports and recreation; education and career development; and camps and conferences for individuals of all ages and backgrounds. **NOTE:** Search and apply for positions online. **Corporate headquarters location:** Chicago IL. **Other U.S. locations:** Nationwide.

RENO GAZETTE-JOURNAL/USA TODAY
P.O. Box 22000, Reno NV 89520. 775/885-5561. **Toll-free phone:** 800/648-5048. **Fax:** 775/327-6756. **Contact:** Carolyn Lutts, Recruitment Manager. **E-mail address:** jobs@rgj.com. **World Wide Web address:** http://www.rgj.com. **Description:** Publishes and distributes the *Reno Gazette-Journal* newspaper and distributes *USA Today*. **NOTE:** Entry-level positions are offered. **Positions advertised include:** Accounting Representative; Assistant City Editor; Classified Advertising Manager. **Special programs:** Internships. **Parent company:** Gannett Company, Incorporated (Arlington VA). **Listed on:** New York Stock Exchange. **Stock exchange symbol:** GCI. **Number of employees at this location:** 400.

RIO ALL-SUITE HOTEL & CASINO, INC.
3700 West Flamingo Road, Las Vegas NV 89103. 702/777-7777. **Contact:** Human Resources. **E-mail address:** jobs@harrahs.com. **World Wide Web address:** http://www.playrio.com. **Description:** Owns and operates the Rio All-Suites Hotel & Casino in Las Vegas. The Rio is a 21-story hotel containing over 860 suites, 79,000 square feet of casino space, 10 restaurants and food outlets, and other related amenities. The casino has 1,950 slot machines; craps, 21, roulette, pai gow poker, and minibaccarat; other casino games such as Keno and poker; and a race and sports book. **NOTE:** Part-time positions are offered. Search and apply for positions online. **Positions advertised include:** Pit Clerk; Hard Count Attendant; Showroom Cocktail Server; Cage Cashier; Total Rewards Host; Special Events Coordinator; Food Runner; Spa Receptionist; Massage Therapist; Graphic Artist; Aesthetician; Table Games Supervisor/Dealer; Data Entry Clerk; Keno Writer/Runner; Lifeguard; Utility Cleaner; Security Secretary. **Parent company:** Harrah's Entertainment, Incorporated.

RIVERSIDE RESORT & CASINO
1650 Casino Drive, Laughlin NV 89029. 702/298-2535. **Contact:** Human Resources. **World Wide Web address:** http://www.riversideresort.com. **Description:** A hotel and casino. **Other U.S. locations:** AZ.

RIVIERA HOTEL & CASINO
2901 Las Vegas Boulevard South, Las Vegas NV 89109. 702/794-9651. **Fax:** 702/794-9668. **Contact:** Human Resources Department. **World Wide Web address:** http://www.theriviera.com. **Description:** The Riviera offers 2,075 rooms, including 158 suites and 35 rooms specially equipped to accommodate wheelchair patrons. The facility also features six restaurants, three cocktail lounges, shopping, meeting and convention facilities, a wedding chapel, award-winning entertainment, and a 100,000 square-foot casino. **Parent company:** Riviera Holdings. **Listed on:** American Stock Exchange. **Stock exchange symbol:** RIV.

ROADWAY EXPRESS INC.
1355 Spice Island Drive, Sparks NV 89431. 775/331-6061. **Contact:** Mark Nedrow, Terminal Manager. **World Wide Web address:** http://www.roadway.com. **Description:** Operates a freight consolidation and distribution terminal for one of the largest common carriers in the United States, with terminals in 371 cities nationwide. **Corporate headquarters location:** Akron OH. **Other U.S. locations:** Nationwide. **International locations:** Canada; Mexico; Puerto Rico. **Parent company:** Roadway Corporation. **Listed on:** NASDAQ. **Stock exchange symbol:** ROAD. **President:** Bob Stull. **Number of employees worldwide:** 24,800.

SBC NEVADA BELL
P.O. Box 11010, Reno NV 89520. 775/333-4811. **Recorded jobline:** 775/333-4003. **Contact:** Personnel. **World Wide Web address:** http://www.nevadabell.com. **Description:** A telephone communications company. **NOTE:** Search and apply for positions online. **Positions advertised include:** Account Executive; Sales Specialist. **Parent company:** SBC Communications. **Listed on:** New York Stock Exchange. **Stock exchange symbol:** SBC. **President/CEO:** Edward E. Whitacre. **Number of employees nationwide:** 1,200.

ST. JUDE'S RANCH FOR CHILDREN
100 St. Jude's Street, Boulder City NV 89005. 702/294-7100. **Toll-free phone:** 800/492-3562. **Contact:** Human Resources Department. **E-mail address:** hr@stjudesranch.org. **World Wide Web address:** http://www.stjudesranch.org. **Description:** A residential facility specializing in the treatment of children with emotional problems, particularly those who have suffered from neglect or abuse. **Special programs:** Internships. **Corporate headquarters location:** This location. **Other U.S. locations:** Bulverde TX; New Braunfels TX.

ST. MARY'S REGIONAL MEDICAL CENTER
235 West Sixth Street, Reno NV 89503. 775/770-3001. **Fax:** 775/770-3260. **Contact:** Human Resources. **World Wide Web address:** http://www.saintmarysreno.com. **Description:** A private, nonprofit hospital that is a complete medical and surgical facility with 367 beds. The hospital offers comprehensive radiology, laboratory, and pharmacy services; an emergency department; a full range of surgical services including an outpatient surgical center; a family birthing center and a newborn intensive care nursery; the Wiegand Heart Center, which consolidates all the equipment and services a heart patient needs in one facility; community health programs; and chemical dependency treatment programs for adults and adolescents. The hospital's home care services promote cost-effective care in the home and provide nurses, health aides, and therapists as needed. Founded in 1908. **NOTE:** Interested job seekers may apply online. **Positions advertised include:** Billing Representative; Administrative Assistant; CT Technologist; Certified Nursing Assistant; Clinical Nurse Specialist; Collector; Health Management Specialist; EMT; Food Service Worker; Intake Representative; LPN; Laboratory Assistant; Manager Cardiac Services; Medical Technologist; New Graduate Nurse; Nurse Practitioner; OB Tech; Occupational Therapist; RN. **Employees at this location:** 2,500.

ST. ROSE DOMINICAN HOSPITALS
102 East Lake Mead Parkway, Henderson NV 89015. 702/616-5000. **Recorded jobline:** 702/616-6100. **Contact:** Human Resources Representative. **E-mail address:** srdhnursingcareers@chw.edu (for nursing opportunities); srdhclinicalcareers@chw.edu (for ancillary clinical opportunities); srdhnonclinicalcareers@chw.edu (for ancillary nonclinical opportunities). **World Wide Web address:** http://www.strosecares.com. **Description:** A 214-bed hospital affiliated with the 138-bed Rose de Lima hospital. **NOTE:** Search and apply for positions online. **Positions advertised include:** Assistant Nurse Manager; Case Manager; Certified Nursing Assistant; Charge Registered Nurse; Coder; Customer Service Rep; Echocardiographer; GI Lab Technician; Imaging Technologist; Medical Technologist; Occupational Therapist; RN. **Office hours:** Monday – Friday, 7:30 a.m. – 5:00 p.m. **Parent company:** Catholic HealthcareWest.

THE SALVATION ARMY
P.O. Box 28369, Las Vegas NV 89126. 702/870-4430. **Physical address:** 2035 Yale Street, North Las Vegas NV 89030. **Contact:** Human Resources. **World Wide Web address:** http://www.salvationarmy.org. **Description:** The Salvation Army is a Christian organization that offers services such as food, medical attention, and daycare for the homeless nationwide. **Other U.S. locations:** Nationwide. **International locations:** Worldwide. **Operations at this facility include:** This location houses the main administrative offices for the Nevada branches of the charitable organization.

SANDS REGENCY HOTEL & CASINO
345 North Arlington Avenue, Reno NV 89501-1132. 775/348-2200. **Contact:** Human Resources. **World Wide Web address:** http://www.sandsregency.com. **Description:** Owns and operates an 800-room hotel and casino. **Listed on:** NASDAQ. **Stock exchange symbol:** SNDS.

SECURITAS USA
5250 Neil Road, Suite 303, Reno NV 89502. 775/828-1590. **Contact:** Human Resources. **E-mail address:** human.resources@securitassystems.com. **World Wide Web address:** http://www.pinkertons.com. **Description:** Operating for more than 130 years, Pinkerton Burns Security is one of the oldest and largest nongovernmental security service organizations in the world. The company's principal business is providing security, investigative, and consulting services to commercial, industrial, institutional, governmental, and residential clients. Major services include industrial and nuclear plant security, institutional security, commercial and residential building security, retail security, construction security, patrol and inspection services, community security, sports and special events services, K-9 patrol services, courier services, inventory services, investigation services, security consultation, and equipment evaluation. **NOTE:** Apply to local office for Security Officer positions; search and apply online for other positions. **Corporate headquarters location:** Chicago IL **Other area locations:** Statewide. **Other U.S. locations:** Nationwide. **Parent company:** Securitas Group. **Sales/revenue:** $5 billion. **Number of employees worldwide:** Over 210,000.

SECURITAS USA
2770 South Maryland Parkway, Suite 100, Las Vegas NV 89119. 702/691-3317. **Contact:** Human Resources. **E-mail address:** human.resources@securitassystems.com. **World Wide Web address:** http://www.pinkertons.com. **Description:** Operating for more than 130 years, Pinkerton Burns Security is one of the oldest and largest nongovernmental security service organizations in the world. The company's principal business is providing security, investigative, and consulting services to commercial, industrial, institutional, governmental, and residential clients. Major services include industrial and nuclear plant security, institutional security, commercial and residential building security, retail security, construction security, patrol and inspection services, community security, sports and special events services, K-9 patrol services, courier services, inventory services, investigation services, security consultation, and equipment evaluation. **NOTE:** Apply to local office for Security Officer positions; search and apply online for other positions. **Corporate headquarters location:** Chicago IL. **Other area locations:** Statewide. **Other U.S. locations:** Nationwide. **Parent company:** Securitas Group. **Sales/revenue:** $5 billion. **Number of employees worldwide:** Over 210,000.

7-UP BOTTLING COMPANY OF RENO
1000 Terminal Way, Reno NV 89502. 775/322-3456. **Contact:** Human Resources. **World Wide Web address:** http://www.7up.com. **Description:** A bottling company for 7-Up and other soft drink products. **NOTE:** Jobseekers should indicate area of interest so resumes can be forwarded to the appropriate department.

THE SHERWIN-WILLIAMS COMPANY
1606 South Commerce Street, Las Vegas NV 89102. 702/386-5700. **Contact:** Human Resources. **World Wide Web address:** http://www.sherwin.com. **Description:** Sherwin-Williams manufactures, sells, and distributes coatings and related products. Coatings are produced for original equipment manufacturers in various industries, as well as for the automotive aftermarket, the industrial maintenance market, and the traffic paint market. Sherwin-Williams labeled architectural and industrial coatings are sold through company-owned specialty paint and wallcovering stores. The Sherwin-Williams Company also manufactures paint under the Acme, Dutch Boy, Kem-Tone, Lucas, Martin-Senour, Minwax, Pratt & Lambert, Rogers, and Thompson brand names, as well as private labels, and markets its products to independent dealers, mass merchandisers, and home improvement centers. **NOTE:** Submit resume online. **Special programs:** Management Training Program; Internships. **Corporate headquarters location:** Cleveland OH. **Other U.S. locations:** Nationwide. **Operations at this facility include:** This location houses the district offices. **Listed on:** New York Stock Exchange. **Stock exchange symbol:** SHW. **Sales/revenue:** Over $5 billion.

SHUFFLE MASTER INC.
1106 Palms Airport Drive, Las Vegas NV 89119-3730. 702/897-7150. **Fax:** 702/897-2284. **Contact:** Human Resources. **World Wide Web address:** http://www.shufflemaster.com. **Description:** Designs and manufactures automatic card shufflers for the gaming industry. Also designs technology to identify gaming cheats. **NOTE:** Job openings can be viewed at jobs.shufflemaster.com.

SIERRA NEVADA CORPORATION
444 Salomon Circle, Sparks NV 89434. 775/331-0222. **Fax:** 775/331-0370. **Contact:** Human Resources. **E-mail address:** hr@sncorp.com. **World Wide Web address:** http://www.sncorp.com. **Description:** A defense electronics engineering and manufacturing firm. **Positions advertised include:** Associate Program Manager; Director of Security; Information Systems Manager; Lotus Notes Administrator; Management Analyst; Software Engineer.

SIERRA PACIFIC POWER COMPANY
P.O. Box 10100, Reno NV 89520-0026. 775/834-3600. **Physical address:** 6100 Neil Road, Reno NV 89511. **Recorded jobline:** 800/672-7772. **Contact:** Human Resources. **E-mail address:** hr@nevp.com (resumes not accepted unless part of online employment application). **World Wide Web address:** http://www.sierrapacific.com. **Description:** Provides electric service to 318,000 customers in a 50,000-square-mile region of northern Nevada and northeastern California, natural gas service to 124,000 customers, and water service to 58,000 in the Reno area. **Positions advertised include:** Accountant; Engineer; Quality Assurance Consultant. **Note:** Search and apply for positions online. **Corporate headquarters location:** This location. **Other area locations:** Statewide. **Other U.S. locations:** Portola CA; South Lake Tahoe CA. **Office hours:** Monday – Friday, 7:30 a.m. – 5:30 p.m. **Parent company:** Sierra Pacific Resources. **Listed on:** New York Stock Exchange. **Stock exchange symbol:** SRP. **President:** Jeffrey L. Ceccarelli. **Number of employees nationwide:** Over 1,400.

SIGMA GAME, INC.
7160 South Amigo Street, Las Vegas NV 89119. 702/260-3100. **Fax:** 702/260-0677. **Contact:** Human Resources Specialist. **E-mail address:** jobs@sigmagame.com. **World Wide Web address:** http://www.sigmagame.com. **Description:** Manufactures, distributes, and services electronic video and slot gaming devices. Founded in 1984. **NOTE:** Search and apply for positions online. **Positions advertised include:** Account Executive; Factory Representative; Software Engineer. **Special programs:** Education Reimbursement Program. **Office hours:** Monday - Friday, 8:00 a.m. - 5:00 p.m. **Corporate headquarters location:** This location. **Other U.S. locations:** Atlantic City NJ; Germantown TN; Green Bay WI; Kalamazoo MI; Hollywood FL. **Listed on:** Privately held. **Number of employees at this location:** 100.

SILVER LEGACY RESORT/CASINO
P.O. Box 3920, Reno NV 89505. 775/329-4777. **Physical address:** 407 North Virginia Street, Reno NV 89501. **Contact:** Human Resources. **World Wide Web address:** http://www.silverlegacy.com. **Description:** Silver Legacy Resort/Casino is one of the largest casinos in Reno. The hotel features 1,600 rooms and five restaurants including the Sweetwater Cafe. **NOTE:** Employment varies seasonally and can reach 3,800 during peak months. Search and apply for positions online. **Positions advertised include:** Reservation Agent; PBX Operator; Spokesmodel; Food Server; Saute Cook; Security Officer; National Sales Manager; Maintenance Person. **Number of employees at this location:** 2,800.

SILVER STATE INTERNATIONAL TRUCKS
P.O. Box 1680, Sparks NV 89431. 775/685-6000. **Physical address:** 2255 Larkin Circle, Sparks NV 89431. **Contact:** Manager. **World Wide Web address:** http://www.itctrucks.com. **Description:** An international truck dealership that leases and sells trucks to consumers and industrial customers. **Positions advertised include:** Service Technicians.

SILVERTON HOTEL AND CASINO
3333 Blue Diamond Road, Las Vegas NV 89139. 702/263-7777. **Recorded jobline:** 702/914-8696. **Contact:** Human Resources. **World Wide Web address:** http://www.silvertoncasino.com. **Description:** A resort facility featuring a 30,000 square-foot casino with 1,100 slot and video gaming machines and 28 table games. There is 24-hour dining in the Comstock Coffee Shop, buffets in the Chuckwagon, a

300-seat combination restaurant-theater called the Opera House, and a lounge called Rattlesnake Ricky's. **NOTE:** Search and apply for positions online. **Positions advertised include:** Inventory Control Clerk; Revenue Audit Clerk; Cage Cashier; Assistant Director of Food and Beverages; Food Server; Busperson; Kitchen Cleaner; Dealer; Retail Clerk/Cashier; Lifeguard; Vault Cashier; Coin Runner; Housekeeper. **Special programs:** Tuition Reimbursement Program. **Office hours:** Monday – Friday, 9:00 a.m. – 2:00 p.m.

SIMPLEXGRINNELL
5325 South Valley View Boulevard, Las Vegas NV 89103. 702/739-1921. **Contact:** Human Resources. **World Wide Web address:** http://www.simplexgrinnell.com. **Description:** Designs and installs fire alarm and sprinkler systems. **Positions advertised include:** Fire Alarm Inspector. **Special programs:** Training; Tuition Assistance Program. **Corporate headquarters location:** Westminster MA. **Other area locations:** Elko NV; Reno NV. **Other U.S. locations:** Nationwide. **International locations:** Canada. **Parent company:** Tyco International Limited (Exeter NH). **Number of employees worldwide:** Over 10,000.

SODEXHO CAMPUS SERVICES
4505 Maryland Parkway, Las Vegas NV 89154. 702/895-3858. **Contact:** Human Resources. **Description:** Provides all food and catering services for the University of Nevada, Las Vegas. **NOTE:** Interested job seekers should apply in person. **Positions advertised include:** Student Manager; Grill Cook; Saute Cook; Catering Cook; Line Server; Cashier; Dining Room Attendant; Expediter. **Special programs:** Tuition Reimbursement Program.

SOLO CUP COMPANY
4425 Mitchell Street, North Las Vegas NV 89181. 702/644-0980. **Contact:** Linda Waskom, Human Resources Manager. **E-mail address:** hr@sweetheart.com. **World Wide Web address:** http://www.solocup.com. **Description:** Manufactures and distributes a variety of food serviceware including plastic plates, cups, bowls, and drinking straws; ice cream cones; and paper containers for use in packaging food and dairy products. **Special programs:** Tuition Reimbursement Program. **Other U.S. locations:** Nationwide. **International locations:** Worldwide.

SOUTHERN ELECTRIC INC.
620 South 11th Street, Suite 5, Las Vegas NV 89101. 702/384-4440. **Contact:** Human Resources. **Description:** Southern Electric Incorporated provides operations and maintenance support for a 50-megawatt, gas-fired, combined-cycle cogeneration plant in North Las Vegas. The plant provides more than 45 megawatts of electric capacity to Nevada Power Company. **Office hours:** Monday – Friday, 8:00 a.m. – 4:00 p.m. **Corporate headquarters location:** This location.

SOUTHERN NEVADA PAVING, INC.
3555 South Polaris Avenue, Las Vegas NV 89103. 702/876-5226. **Fax:** 702/253-0919. **Contact:** Steve Jenson, Controller. **Description:** An aggregate, asphalt, and contracting company. **Parent company:** Aggregate Industries. **Number of employees at this location:** 500.

SOUTHWEST GAS CORPORATION
P.O. Box 98510, Las Vegas NV 89150-8510. 702/876-7300. **Physical address:** 5241 Spring Mountain Road, Las Vegas NV 89150. **Recorded jobline:** 702/365-2085. **Contact:** Human Resources. **World Wide Web address:** http://www.swgas.com. **Description:** Distributes natural gas to 1.5 million customers in Arizona, California, and Nevada. Founded in 1931. **Positions advertised include:** Coordinator; Analyst/Central Gas Dispatch Network; Analyst/Contact Administration. **Special programs:** Internships. **Office hours:** Monday – Friday, 8:30 a.m. – 4:30 p.m. **Corporate headquarters location:** This location. **Other area locations:** Carson City NV. **Other U.S. locations:** Phoenix AZ; Tucson AZ; Victorville CA. **Subsidiaries include:** Northern Pipeline. **Listed on:** New York Stock Exchange; Pacific Stock Exchange. **Stock exchange symbol:** SWX. **President/CEO:** Michael O. Maffie. **Sales/revenue:** Over $1 billion. **Number of employees nationwide:** 2,400.

SQUARE D COMPANY
1210 South Valley View Boulevard, Suite 208, Las Vegas NV 89102. 702/258-8889. **Contact:** Human Resources. **E-mail address:** uwb@schneiderelectricjobs.com. **World Wide Web address:** http://www.squared.com. **Description:** A manufacturer of electrical distribution products for the construction industry. Products are used in commercial and residential construction, industrial facilities, and machinery and original equipment manufacturers' products. **Corporate headquarters location:** Palatine IL. **Other U.S. locations:** Nationwide. **International locations:** Canada; Mexico. **Parent company:** Schneider Electric. **Listed on:** Euronext Paris. **Stock exchange symbol:** SU.

STARDUST RESORT & CASINO
3000 Las Vegas Boulevard South, Las Vegas NV 89109. 702/732-6111. **Contact:** Human Resources. **E-mail address:** stardustemployment@boydgaming.com. **World Wide Web address:** http://www.stardustlv.com. **Description:** A 2,335-room hotel and casino. **Positions advertised include:** Security Officer; Assistant Custodial Services Manager; Revenue Audit Clerk; Slot Floor Person; Catering Coordinator. **Parent company:** Boyd Gaming Corporation is one of the leading providers of casino entertainment in the United States. Boyd Gaming Corporation owns and operates five other facilities in Las Vegas: Sam's Town Hotel and Gambling Hall, the Eldorado Casino, and Jokers Wild Casino on the Boulder Strip; and California Hotel & Casino and Fremont Hotel and Casino in downtown Las Vegas. The company also owns and operates Sam's Town Hotel and Gambling Hall in Tunica County MS; owns and operates Sam's Town Casino, a riverboat gaming entertainment complex in Kansas City MO; manages Silver Star Hotel and Casino, a casino hotel property near Philadelphia MS; and manages and partly owns Treasure Chest Casino, a riverboat casino in Kenner LA. **Listed on:** New York Stock Exchange. **Stock exchange symbol:** BYD.

STATEWIDE FIRE PROTECTION
3130 Westwood Drive, Las Vegas NV 89109. 702/737-1055. **Contact:** Manager. **World Wide Web address:** http://www.statewidefire.com. **Description:** Designs and installs sprinkler systems in commercial, residential, and industrial buildings. **Parent company:** API Group, Incorporated.

STEINBERG DIAGNOSTIC MEDICAL IMAGING
P.O. Box 36900, Las Vegas NV 89133-6900. 702/732-6000. **Physical address:** 2950 South Maryland Parkway, Las Vegas NV 89109-2257. **Fax:** 702/731-5067. **Contact:** Human Resources Manager. **E-mail address:** melvionl@sdmi-lv.com. **World Wide Web address:** http://www.sdmi-lv.com. **Description:** A radiology lab. **NOTE:** Search and apply for positions online. **Positions advertised include:** Mammography Technologist; MRI Technologist; RN-Special Procedures; Ultrasound Technologist.

STRATOSPHERE HOTEL & CASINO
2121 South Las Vegas Boulevard, Las Vegas NV 89104-2507. 702/380-7777. **Fax:** 702/383-5349. **Recorded jobline:** 702/383-4800. **Contact:** Manager of Human Resources Department. **E-mail address:** jobs@stratospherehotel.com. **World Wide Web address:** http://www.stratospherehotel.com. **Description:** Operates a free-standing observation tower casino hotel. **NOTE:** Search and apply for positions online. **Positions advertised include:** Wedding Chapel Sales Manager; Cook; Host; Revenue Audit Clerk; F&B Supervisor; Food Server; Bus/Runner; Security Officer; Utility Lead Porter; Dealer; Bartender.

SUNKIST GRAPHICS
401 East Sunset Road, Henderson NV 89015. 702/566-9008. **Contact:** Thomas Hudon, Operations Manager. **World Wide Web address:** http://www.sunkistgrfx.com. **Description:** Manufactures and distributes custom slot and power machine glass used in resorts and casinos around the world.

SUNRISE HOSPITAL & MEDICAL CENTER
SUNRISE CHILDREN'S HOSPITAL
3186 South Maryland Parkway, Las Vegas NV 89109. 702/731-8898. **Toll-free phone:** 800/634-6864. **Fax:** 702/836-3813. **Recorded jobline:** 702/731-8350. **Contact:** Human Resources. **E-mail address:** sunrise.humanresources@hcahealthcare.com. **World Wide Web address:** http://www.sunrisehospital.com. **Description:** An acute care hospital and a children's hospital with over 730 beds. **NOTE:** Entry-level positions and second and third shifts are offered. Search and apply for positions online. **Positions advertised include:** Director, Cardiovascular Services; Accessioning Clerk; Medical Lab Tech; Charge Nurse; Clinical Nurse Specialist; Director, Maternal Services; LPN; RN; Director, Critical Care Services; Nurse Managers; Pharmacist; Occupational Therapist; Physical Therapist Assistant; Social Worker. **Corporate headquarters location:** Nashville TN. **Parent company:** HCA Healthcare Corporation. **Listed on:** New York Stock Exchange. **Stock exchange symbol:** HCA. **Number of employees at this location:** 2,500.

SUPERIOR TILE
4305 South Polaris Avenue, Las Vegas NV 89103-4152. 702/798-7882. **Contact:** Human Resources. **Description:** A tile and marble contracting company. **Corporate headquarters location:** Oakland CA.

SWIFT TRANSPORTATION COMPANY, INC.
1455 Hulda Way, Sparks NV 89431. 775/359-5161. **Fax:** 775/359-5155. **Contact:** Human Resources. **World Wide Web address:** http://www.swifttrans.com. **Description:** One of the largest truckload motor carriers in the United States, Swift Transportation offers a wide variety of trailers to its customers, and as well as providing full-service equipment leasing, fleet programs, and third-party logistics services for its major clientele. The company has more than 2,400 power units and 37 full-service terminals. **NOTE:** Entry-level positions are offered. Search and apply for positions online. **Corporate headquarters location:** Phoenix AZ. **Other U.S. locations:** Nationwide. **Listed on:** NASDAQ. **Stock exchange symbol:** SWFT. **Number of employees nationwide:** 6,700.

TACO BELL
1210 S Valley View Blvd, Las Vegas NV 89102. 702/880-5818. **Contact:** Sandra Bowen, Director of Human Resources. **World Wide Web address:** http://www.tacobell.com. **Description:** Taco Bell is a global franchise specializing in Mexican style fast food. **NOTE:** Recruitment events are held periodically. Search and apply for positions online. **Corporate headquarters location:** Irvine CA. **Parent company:** Yum! Brands, Incorporated operates KFC, Taco Bell, Pizza Hut, Long John Silvers, and A&W restaurants worldwide. **Operations at this facility include:** This location is a business office that manages Taco Bell restaurant franchises.

TIMET
8000 West Lake Mead Parkway, Henderson NV 89015. 702/556-4403. **Fax:** 702/564-9038. **Contact:** Human Resources. **World Wide Web address:** http://www.timet.com. **Description:** Timet is one of the largest integrated producers of titanium in the world. **Office hours:** Monday - Friday, 7:30 a.m. - 4:00 p.m. **Corporate headquarters location:** Denver CO. **Other U.S. locations:** Vallejo CA; Los Angeles CA; Denver CO; Dallas TX; St. Louis MO; Hartford CT; Morgantown PA; Toronto OH. **International locations:** Worldwide. **Operations at this facility include:** This location produces sponge titanium ingots and is also a research and development facility. **Listed on:** New York Stock Exchange. **Stock exchange symbol:** TIE. **Sales/revenue:** Over $480 million. **Number of employees at this location:** 550.

TOYS 'R US, INC.
5000 Smithridge Drive, Reno NV 89502. 775/827-8697. **Contact:** Store Manager. **World Wide Web address:** http://help.toysrus.com. **Description:** Toys 'R Us operates 1,600 retail toy stores throughout the United States and 500 stores in 27 countries. **NOTE:** Search and apply for positions online. **Corporate headquarters location:** Paramus NJ. **Other U.S. locations:** Nationwide. **Operations at this facility include:** This location is a retail outlet for the international toy store. **Listed on:** New York Stock Exchange. **Stock exchange symbol:** TOY. **President/CEO/Chairman:** John H. Eyler, Junior. **Sales/revenue:** Over $11 billion. **Number of employees worldwide:** 113,000.

TREASURE ISLAND HOTEL AND CASINO
3300 Las Vegas Boulevard South, Las Vegas NV 89109. 702/894-7111. **Recorded jobline:** 702/792-JOBS. **Contact:** Personnel. **World Wide Web address:** http://www.treasureislandlasvegas.com. **Description:** A 2,900-room hotel and casino. **NOTE:** Interested job seekers must apply in person at the Employment Center. Search for positions online at: http://www.mgmmirage.com. **Positions advertised include:** Accounts Payable Clerk; Accounts Receivable Clerk; Administrative Clerk; Apprentice Bartender; Assistant Room Service Manager; Assistant Spa Manager; Assistant Lobby Store Manager; Busperson. **Office hours:** Monday – Friday, 10:00 a.m. – 2:00 p.m. **Parent company:** Mirage Resorts Incorporated owns 12 properties. **Number of employees nationwide:** 45,000.

TROPICANA RESORT & CASINO
3801 Las Vegas Boulevard South, Las Vegas NV 89109. 702/739-2222. **Fax:** 702/739-2719. **Recorded jobline:** 702/739-2473. **Contact:** Human Resources. **E-mail address:** employment@tropicanalv.com. **World Wide Web address:** http://www.tropicanalv.com. **Description:** A hotel and casino. **NOTE:** Search and apply for positions online. **Parent company:** Aztar Corporation. **Listed on:** New York Stock Exchange. **Stock exchange symbol:** AZR. **Positions advertised include:** Employee Development Assistant; Security Officer; Claim Examiner; Casino Analyst; Promotions Representative; Paralegal.

TRUCKEE MEADOWS COMMUNITY COLLEGE (TMCC)
7000 Dandini Boulevard, RDMT 211, Reno NV 89512-3999. 775/673-7168. **Fax:**

775/674-7560. **Contact:** Human Resources. **E-mail address:** humanresources@tmcc.edu. **World Wide Web address:** http://www.tmcc.edu. **Description:** A community college with an enrollment of approximately 11,000 students. TMCC offers more than 50 degree and certificate programs in 40 academic and occupational areas. The community college is accredited by the Northwest Association of Schools and Colleges. Founded in 1971. **NOTE:** Search for positions online. Part-time positions are offered. To contact Human Resources directly, call 775/673-7168. **Positions advertised include:** Director of Nursing; Employment Specialist; Vice President of Student Services; Dental Hygiene Instructor; Nursing Instructor. **President:** Dr. Philip Ringle.

UBS FINANCIAL SERVICES INC.
3800 Howard Hughes Parkway, Suite 1200, Las Vegas NV 89109. 702/731-1121. **Contact:** David Frieden, Branch Manager. **World Wide Web address:** http://financialservicesinc.ubs.com. **Description:** A full-service securities firm with offices nationwide. Services include investment banking, asset management, merger and acquisition consulting, municipal securities underwriting, estate planning, retirement programs, and transaction management. UBS Financial Services offers its services to corporations, governments, institutions, and individuals. Founded in 1879. **NOTE:** Training program offered. Apply for positions online. **Corporate headquarters location:** New York NY. **Other U.S. locations:** Nationwide. **Parent company:** UBS AG. **Listed on:** New York Stock Exchange. **Stock exchange symbol:** UBS. **Number of employees nationwide:** Over 8,000. **Number of employees worldwide:** 66,000.

US AIRWAYS, INC.
P.O. Box 11091, Las Vegas NV 89111. 702/261-5344. **Contact:** Personnel Department. **World Wide Web address:** http://www.usairways.com. **Description:** US Airways offers service to 187 cities in the United States, Canada, Mexico, the Caribbean, France, England, Spain, Italy, The Netherlands, and Germany. The company's primary hubs are in Charlotte, Pittsburgh, Baltimore/Washington, and Philadelphia. **NOTE:** Search and apply for positions online. Unsolicited resumes not accepted. **Special programs:** Internships. **Corporate headquarters location:** Arlington VA. **Listed on:** OTC. **Stock exchange symbol:** UAWGQ. **President/CEO/Chairman:** David N. Siegel. **Sales/revenue:** Approximately $7 billion. **Number of employees nationwide:** 28,300.

U.S. BANK OF NEVADA
1525 Highway 395 North, Gardnerville NV 89410. 775/782-2268. **Contact:** Human Resources. **World Wide Web address:** http://www.usbank.com. **Description:** U.S. Bank of Nevada, one of the largest commercial banks in the state, is a commercial and consumer banking institution. U.S. Bank of Nevada provides a full range of commercial real estate products and services, cash management services and consultation, and merchant services and sales. The bank offers ATM capabilities, PC home banking, telephone bill-paying systems, loans by phone, and mortgage loans by phone. The Homepartners family of mortgage loan products provides down payment assistance, underwriting and repayment terms, and homebuyer education for first-time and low- to moderate-income buyers. All-U-Need Banking offers free checking. **NOTE:** Search and apply for positions online. **Corporate headquarters location:** Portland OR. **Parent company:** U.S. Bancorp operates 2,243 banks and 4,425 ATMs in 24 states. **Operations at this facility include:** This location is a branch of the U.S. Bank of Nevada. **Listed on:** New York Stock Exchange. **Stock exchange symbol:** USB. **Number of employees nationwide:** 12,000.

U.S. BANK OF NEVADA
4000 Kietzke Lane, Reno NV 89502. 775/689-8255. **Contact:** Human Resources. **World Wide Web address:** http://www.usbank.com. **Description:** U.S. Bank of Nevada, one of the largest commercial banks in the state, is a commercial and consumer banking institution. U.S. Bank of Nevada provides a full range of commercial real estate products and services, cash management services and consultation, and merchant services and sales. The bank offers ATM capabilities, PC home banking, telephone bill-paying systems, loans by phone, and mortgage loans by phone. The Homepartners family of mortgage loan products provides down payment assistance, underwriting and repayment terms, and homebuyer education for first-time and low- to moderate-income buyers. All-U-Need Banking offers free checking. **NOTE:** Search and apply for positions online. **Corporate headquarters location:** Portland OR. **Parent company:** U.S. Bancorp operates 2,243 banks and 4,425 ATMs in 24 states. **Operations at this facility include:** This location is a branch of the U.S. Bank of Nevada. **Listed on:** New York Stock Exchange. **Stock exchange symbol:** USB. **Number of employees nationwide:** 12,000.

U.S. BANK OF NEVADA
2203 Oddie Boulevard, Sparks NV 89431. 775/685-3600. **Contact:** Human Resources. **World Wide Web address:** http://www.usbank.com. **Description:** U.S. Bank of Nevada, one of the largest commercial banks in the state, is a commercial and consumer banking institution. U.S. Bank of Nevada provides a full range of commercial real estate products and services, cash management services and consultation, and merchant services and sales. The bank offers ATM capabilities, PC home banking, telephone bill-paying systems, loans by phone, and mortgage loans by phone. The Homepartners family of mortgage loan products provides down payment assistance, underwriting and repayment terms, and homebuyer education for first-time and low- to moderate-income buyers. All-U-Need Banking offers free checking. **NOTE:** Search and apply for positions online. **Corporate headquarters location:** Portland OR. **Parent company:** U.S. Bancorp operates 2,243 banks and 4,425 ATMs in 24 states. **Operations at his facility include:** This location is a branch of the U.S. Bank of Nevada. **Listed on:** New York Stock Exchange. **Stock exchange symbol:** USB. **Number of employees nationwide:** 12,000.

U.S. DEPARTMENT OF VETERANS AFFAIRS
SOUTHERN NEVADA HEALTHCARE SYSTEM (VASNHS)
P.O. Box 360001, North Las Vegas NV 89036. 702/636-3000. **Fax:** 702/636-4000. **Contact:** Human Resources. **E-mail address:** VHAPlacementService@hq.med.va.gov. **World Wide Web address:** http://www.las-vegas.med.va.gov. **Description:** The Department of Veterans Affairs was established in 1989 to provide federal benefits to veterans and their dependents. The department operates nationwide programs of health care, assistance services, and national cemeteries. The VA's health care system is the largest in the nation. From 54 hospitals in 1930, the system has grown to include 171 medical centers; more than 364 outpatient, community and outreach clinics; 130 nursing home care units; and 37 domiciliary residences. The VA operates at least one medical center in each of the 48 contiguous states, Puerto Rico, and the District of Columbia. With approximately 76,000 medical center beds, the VA treats nearly 1 million patients in VA hospitals, 75,000 in nursing home care units, and 25,000 in domiciliary residences. The VA's outpatient clinics register approximately 24 million visits a year. The VA is affiliated with 104 medical schools, 48 dental schools, and more than 850 other schools across the country. **NOTE:** To contact Human Resources directly, call 702/636-3033. Search and apply for positions online at http://www.vacareers.com. **Corporate headquarters location:** Washington DC.

U.S. DEPARTMENT OF VETERANS AFFAIRS
SIERRA NEVADA HEALTH CARE CENTER
1000 Locust Street, Reno NV 89502. 775/786-7200. **Contact:** Human Resources. **E-mail address:** VHAPlacementService@hq.med.va.gov. **Description:** The Reno Veterans Administration Medical Center consists of a fully-accredited, 168-bed, general medical and surgical hospital and a 60-bed nursing home care unit. Divisions include medicine, surgery, psychiatric, alcohol, and neurology. The medical center has developed geriatric health programs, providing opportunities for improved patient care to the rapidly growing group of elderly veterans. The medical center has an active affiliation with the University of Nevada School of Medicine and the Orvis School of Nursing, University of Nevada-Reno. The medical center has training programs in five allied health fields, has its own American Psychology Association accredited predoctoral psychology training program, and conducts residency training programs in internal medicine and general surgery. The Reno Veterans Administration Medical Center has active programs of medical research including brain cell changes in Alzheimer's disease; the role of fatty acids in diabetes; the effects of aging, alcohol, and diabetes on the intestines; and the measurement of past alcohol consumption through analysis of red blood cells. **NOTE:** Search and apply for positions online at http://www.vacareers.com. **Special programs:** Internships. **Corporate headquarters location:** Washington DC.

U.S. FOODSERVICE
1685 West Cheyenne Avenue, North Las Vegas NV 89032. 702/636-3663. **Toll-free phone:** 800/835-4414. **Contact:** Human Resources. **World Wide Web address:** http://www.usfoodservice.com. **Description:** Distributes food products, fresh meats, dairy products, and cleaning supplies to over 300,000 foodservice customers, including restaurants, hotels, healthcare facilities, cafeterias and schools. **NOTE:** Search and apply for positions online. **Corporate headquarters location:** Columbia MD. **Other area locations:** Sierra NV; Reno NV. **Other U.S. locations:** Nationwide. **Sales/revenue:** Over $19 billion. **Number of employees nationwide:** 28,500.

UNITED ENGINE & MACHINE COMPANY
4909 Goni Road, Carson City NV 89706. 775/882-7790. **Contact:** Nick Mercado, Personnel Manager. **World Wide Web address:** http://www.kb-silvolite.com. **Description:** Manufactures aluminum pistons for automotive engines. Founded in 1922. **Corporate headquarters location:** This location.

UNITED STATES GYPSUM COMPANY
P.O. Box 130, Highway 47, Empire NV 89405-0130. 775/557-2341. **Fax:** 775/557-2212. **Contact:** Personnel Director. **World Wide Web address:** http://www.usgcorp.com. **Description:** Manufactures gypsum wallboard, plasters, and agricultural gypsum. **NOTE:** Entry-level positions are offered. Apply for positions online. **Special programs:** Internships. **Corporate headquarters location:** Chicago IL. **International locations:** Worldwide. **Other U.S. locations:** Nationwide. **Subsidiaries include:** L&W Supply. **Parent company:** USG Corporation. **Operations at this facility include:** Manufacturing. **Listed on:** New York Stock Exchange. **Stock exchange symbol:** USG. **Sales/revenue:** Approximately $850 million. **Number of employees at this location:** 150. **Number of employees worldwide:** 14,000.

UNIVERSITY MEDICAL CENTER
1815 West Charleston Boulevard, Las Vegas NV 89102-2386. 702/383-2000. **Recorded jobline:** 702/383-2490. **Contact:** Human Resources. **World Wide Web address:** http://www.umc-cares.org. **Description:** A hospital that offers comprehensive health care services and is designated a Level One Trauma Center for southern Nevada. **NOTE:** The Human Resources Office is located at 1815 West Charleston Boulevard, Suite 3, Las Vegas NV 89102-2386. Interested job seekers may also search and apply for positions online. **Positions advertised include:** Applications Programmer; Clinical Laboratory Technologist; Clinical Manager; Data Specialist; MRI Technologist; Pharmacist; Registered Nurse; Staff Physician; Systems Programmer; Ultrasound Technologist. **Office hours:** Monday – Friday, 7:30 a.m. – 5:00 p.m. **Number of employees at this location:** Over 3,500.

UNIVERSITY OF NEVADA, LAS VEGAS
4505 South Maryland Parkway, Las Vegas NV 89154. 702/895-3504. **Contact:** Human Resources. **World Wide Web address:** http://www.unlv.edu. **Description:** A university offering more than 180 undergraduate, master's, and doctoral degree programs to 24,000 students. UNLV has 11 academic colleges and two schools: Architecture, Construction Management, and Planning; Business and Economics; Education; Engineering; Fine and Performing Arts; Graduate College; Health Sciences; Hotel Administration; Human Performance and Development; Liberal Arts; Science and Mathematics; the Greenspun School of Communication; and the School of Social Work. More than 700 full-time instructional faculty are involved in teaching, research, and community service. Founded in 1957. **NOTE:** Search and apply for positions online. **Positions advertised include:** Accountant; Assistant Professors; Associate Professors; Full Professors; Program Coordinator; Career Counselor; Computer Application Developer; Technical Administrator; Director of Annual Giving; Liberal Arts Dean.

UNIVERSITY OF NEVADA PRESS
Mail Stop 166, Reno NV 89557-0076. 775/784-6573. **Toll-free phone:** 877/682-6657. **Fax:** 775/784-6200. **Contact:** Human Resources. **World Wide Web address:** http://www.nvbooks.nevada.edu. **Description:** Publishes scholarly and popular books on Nevada; natural history; the West and the Basque people; women and the West; Native American studies; and Western literature. **Positions advertised include:** Marketing Manager.

VAL-PAK
3232 West Desert Inn Road, Las Vegas NV 89102. 702/248-9600. **Contact:** Human Resources. **World Wide Web address:** http://www.valpak.com. **Description:** Provides direct marketing services through its monthly mailing of coupons to consumer households. This location is one of 220 franchise offices in the U.S. **NOTE:** Search and apply for sales positions online. **Corporate headquarters location:** Largo FL. **Other U.S. locations:** Nationwide. **International locations:** Puerto Rico; Canada. **Parent company:** Cox Enterprises, Inc. **Number of employees worldwide:** Over 1,200.

VALENCE TECHNOLOGY
301 Conestoga Way, Henderson NV 89015. 702/558-1000. **Fax:** 702/558-1001. **Contact:** Personnel. **E-mail address:** hr@valence.com. **World Wide Web address:** http://www.valence-tech.com. **Description:** Engaged in the research and development of lithium polymer batteries for telecommunications, computer, military, consumer, industrial, and automotive markets. Founded in 1989. **Corporate headquarters location:** Austin TX. **International locations:** Mallusk, Northern Ireland. **Listed on:** NASDAQ. **Stock exchange symbol:** VLNC. **President/CEO/Chairman:** Stephan Godevais.

VERIFLO DIVISION
PARKER HANNIFIN CORPORATION
2801 Arrowhead Drive, Carson City NV 89706. 775/887-2640. **Contact:** Human Resources. **World Wide Web address:** http://www.veriflo.com. **Description:** Manufactures valves and regulators for industrial applications. Founded in 1976. **NOTE:** Resumes may be sent to the attention of Eunice Stephenson, Human Resources Training Representative at 250 Canal Boulevard, Richmond CA 94804, or faxed to 510/412-1270. **Office hours:** Monday - Friday, 7:00 a.m. - 5:00 p.m. **Corporate headquarters location:** Richmond CA. **Parent company:** Parker Hannafin Corporation. **Number of employees at this location:** 128.

VINYL PRODUCTS MANUFACTURING
10117 US Highway 50 East, Mound House NV 89706. 775/882-4472. **Contact:** Personnel. **Description:** A producer of accessories and components for waterbeds. **Corporate headquarters location:** This location.

WACHOVIA SECURITIES
3763 Howard Hughes Parkway, Suite 330, Las Vegas NV 89109. 702/796-0135. **Contact:** Human Resources. **World Wide Web address:** http://www.wachovia.com. **Description:** An international securities brokerage and investment firm. The company offers clients more than 70 investment products including stocks, options, bonds, commodities, tax-favored investments, and insurance. **NOTE:** Search and apply for positions online. **Special programs:** Financial Advisor in Training Program.

WACKENHUT SERVICES INC.
6280 South Valley View Boulevard, Suite 314, Las Vegas NV 89118. 702/227-3484. **Fax:** 702/227-5131. **Contact:** Human Resources. **E-mail address:** recruitment@wackenhut.com. **World Wide Web address:** http://www.wackenhut.com. **Description:** Provides contract services to the Department of Energy. **Corporate headquarters location:** Palm Beach Gardens FL. **Other U.S. locations:** Nationwide. **Parent company:** Wackenhut is a leading provider of contract services to major corporations, government agencies, and a wide range of industrial and commercial customers. The company's security-related services include uniformed security officers, investigations, background checks, emergency protection, and security audits and assessments. Other services include facility operations and management, fire suppression and prevention, and airport crash-fire-rescue. The Corporation's training arm, the Wackenhut Training Institute develops and conducts training programs not only for Company personnel, from security officers to managers, but also for outside proprietary security force personnel. **NOTE:** Search and apply for positions online. **Corporate headquarters location:** Palm Beach Gardens FL. **Parent company:** Group 4 Securicor. **Operations at this facility include:** Administration; Service. **Number of employees at this location:** 200. **Number of employees nationwide:** 40,000.

WELLS FARGO BANK
200 South Virginia Street, Reno NV 89501. 775/348-7030. **Contact:** Human Resources. **World Wide Web address:** http://www.wellsfargo.com. **Description:** A diversified financial institution with over $234 billion in assets. Wells Fargo serves over 17 million customers through 5,900 independent locations worldwide. The company also maintains several stand-alone ATMs and branches within retail outlets. Services include community banking, credit and debit cards, home equity and mortgage loans, online banking, student loans, and insurance. Wells Fargo also offers a complete line of commercial and institutional financial services. Founded in 1852. **NOTE:** Search and apply for positions online. **Positions advertised include:** Inbound Sales Specialist; Mortgage Consultant; Business Relationship Manager. **Corporate headquarters location:** San Francisco CA. **Other U.S. locations:** Nationwide. **International locations:** Worldwide. **Listed on:** New York Stock Exchange. **Stock exchange symbol:** WFC. **Number of employees worldwide:** 144,000.

WEST HILLS HOSPITAL
P.O. Box 30012, Reno NV 89520-0012. 775/323-0478. **Physical address:** 1240 East Ninth Street, Reno NV 89512. **Recorded jobline:** 775/789-4286. **Contact:** Henrietta Wiggins, Director of Human Resources. **World Wide Web address:** http://www.bhcwesthills.com. **Description:** A medical facility that specializes in the treatment of alcohol and chemical dependency. The hospital also offers psychiatric and mental health services. **NOTE:** Entry-level positions, part-time jobs, and second and third shifts are offered. **Positions advertised include:** Human Resources Director. **Special programs:** Internships; Apprenticeships. **Parent company:** Ardent Health Services. **Operations at this facility include:** Administration. **Number of employees at this location:** 300.

WESTPOINT STEVENS, INC.
993 Howard Hughes Parkway, Las Vegas NV 89109. 702/866-2283. **Contact:** Human Resources. **E-mail address:** wphuman.resources@wpstv.com. **World Wide Web address:** http://www.westpointstevens.com. **Description:** An outlet store for West Point Stevens, a manufacturer of bedding, bath, and kitchen towels. **Special programs:** Internships; Tuition Reimbursement Program. **Other U.S. locations:** Nationwide. **Number of employees nationwide:** 14,400.

WESTERN NEVADA COMMUNITY COLLEGE
2201 West College Parkway, Carson City NV 89703. 775/445-3000. **Recorded jobline:** 775/887-3165. **Contact:** Personnel. **E-mail address:** personnel@wncc.edu. **World Wide Web address:** http://www.wncc.edu. **Description:** A two-year, general community college with 6000 students offering 50 academic degrees and certificates. **NOTE:** Search and apply for positions online. **Positions advertised include:** Coordinator of Counseling; Dean of Instruction; Student Services Programmer/Analyst; Academic Skills Coordinator; Instructors. **Other area locations:** Douglas NV; Fallon NV.

WESTERN TECHNOLOGIES, INC.
3611 West Tompkins Avenue, Las Vegas NV 89103. 702/798-8050. **Fax:** 702/798-7664. **Contact:** Human Resources. **E-mail address:** s.allanson@wt-us.com. **World Wide Web address:** http://www.wt-us.com. **Description:** Provides engineering, consulting, and testing of environmental, geotechnical, and construction materials. Environmental services include site assessments, investigations, feasibility studies, problem solving, and remedial services with use of state-of-the-art technology. Materials Engineering and Testing provides analysis and quality assurance of materials and methods for clients. Materials Research develops methods of improving the strength and durability of conventional construction materials through research into feasibility of substituting less expensive or more available materials. Construction Quality Control provides interpretation of geotechnical reports, observation and testing of reinforced steel and concrete, visual and nondestructive evaluation of bolted and welded structural steel components, concrete and asphalt mix designs, as well as sampling and testing many other architectural and structural components. **NOTE:** Entry-level positions are available. **Positions advertised include:** Senior Geotechnical Engineer; Geotechnical Project Engineer; Environmental Scientist; Geologist; Senior Engineering Technician; Welding Inspector; Structural Steel Technician; Nuclear Gauge Technician; NAQTC or WAQTC Certified Technician; ICC/ICBO Certified Inspectors. **Special programs:** Training. **Corporate headquarters location:** Phoenix AZ. **Other U.S. locations:** AZ; CO; NM; TX; UT. **International locations:** Mexico. **Number of employees worldwide:** Over 425.

WESTERN TITLE COMPANY
241 Ridge Street, Reno NV 89501. 775/332-7100. **Contact:** Human Resources. **World Wide Web address:** http://www.westerntitle.net. **Description:** Western Title handles land title insurance and escrow contracts. Founded in 1902. **Corporate headquarters location:** This location. **Other area locations:** Carson NV; Fernley NV; Minden NV; Winnemucca NV; Yerington NV. **President:** Don Allen.

WESTRONICS
GAME MASTERS
2575 South Highland Drive, Las Vegas NV 89109. 702/732-1414. **Contact:** Human Resources. **Description:** Manufactures, distributes, sells, and leases coin-operated gaming machines. **Office hours:** Monday – Friday, 9:00 a.m. – 4:00 p.m. **Corporate headquarters location:** This location.

WET 'N WILD LAS VEGAS
2635 Paradise Road, Las Vegas NV 89109. 702/737-3819. **Contact:** Human Resources. **E-mail address:** info@wetnwildlv.com. **World Wide Web address:** http://www.wetnwildlv.com. **Description:** An amusement park featuring water slide rides. **Other U.S. locations:** Orlando FL; Greensboro NC. **International locations:** Brazil; Mexico.

WILLIAMS DETROIT DIESEL-ALLISON
2680 Losee Road, North Las Vegas NV 89030. 702/399-1890. **Contact:** Human Resources. **E-mail address:** jobslas@wddasw.com. **World Wide Web address:** http://www.wddasw.com. **Description:** Manufactures heavy-duty diesel engines for use in the transportation, construction, industrial, marine, and stationary power markets. Founded in 1912. **Positions advertised include:** Automatic Transmission Technician; Engine Diesel Technician; Front Counter Sales Associate; Warehouse Associate. **Corporate headquarters location:** Columbus OH. **Other U.S. locations:** AL; AZ; GA; MI; OH; SC.

WYMAN-GORDON COMPANY
2727 Lockheed Way, Carson City NV 89706. 775/883-3800. **Contact:** Human Resources. **World Wide Web address:** http://www.wyman-gordon.com. **Description:** A producer of highly engineered, technically advanced components, primarily for the aerospace industry. The company uses forging and investment casting technologies to produce components for technically demanding applications such as jet turbine engines and airframes, and designs and produces prototype products using composite technologies. The Forging Division melts titanium into ingot and converts ingot to billet in its cogging presses. It also produces superalloy metal powders and consolidates and extrudes these powders into billets. The company's investment casting operation, Wyman-Gordon Investment Castings, Incorporated (WGIC), uses modern, automated, high-volume production equipment and both air-melt and vacuum-melt furnaces to produce a wide variety of complex investment castings. The company's composites operation, Scaled Composites, Inc., plans, proposes, designs, fabricates, and tests prototypes for aerospace, automotive, and other customers. Founded in 1883. **Corporate headquarters location:** North Grafton MA. **Other U.S. locations:** Brighton MI; Cleveland OH; Franklin NH; Tilton NH; Houston TX; Worchester MA. **International locations:** Czech Republic; England; Scotland; Mexico; Australia. **Parent company:** Precision Castparts Corporation. **Operations at this location include:** This location manufactures investment castings for aerospace applications. **Number of employees at this location:** 225. **Number of employees nationwide:** 2,600.

WYNN LAS VEGAS
3131 Las Vegas Boulevard South, Las Vegas NV 89109. 702/770-5627. **Contact:** Human Resources. **World Wide Web address:** http://www.wynnlasvegas.com. **Description:** The newest grand-scale hotel in Las Vegas, complete with shopping, dining, and golf. **NOTE:** Paper applications are not accepted. Apply online at www.wynnjobs.com. **Positions advertised include:** Cook; Concierge; Guest Services Representative; IT Business Systems Analyst; Pit Clerk.

ASA TIRE SYSTEMS
615 Amherst Street, Nashua NH 03063-1017. 603/889-8700. **Fax:** 603/880-3438. **Contact:** Human Resources. **E-mail address:** webmaster@asaint.com. **World Wide Web address:** http://www.asatire.com/index.htm. **Description:** Designs and develops software for tire retailers. **NOTE:** Please no phone calls about employment. Please visit website to send resume via email. **Corporate headquarters location:** Framingham MA. **Subsidiaries include:** ASA Legal Systems Company, Inc.; ASA, Inc. **Parent company:** ASA International Ltd. designs and develops proprietary vertical market software and installs software on a variety of computers and networks. **Listed on:** NASDAQ. **Stock exchange symbol:** ASAA.

ATC POWER SYSTEMS INC.
45 Depot Street, Merrimack NH 03054. 603/429-0391. **Fax:** 603/429-0795. **E-mail address:** info@atcpower.com. **World Wide Web address:** http://www.atcpower.com. **Description:** Produces power supply systems used for standard commercial use, as well as for military use. **Positions advertised include:** Mechanical Engineer; Quality Assurance Inspector; Electrical Design Engineer; Electronic Assembly/Soldering; Analog Test Technician.

AAVID THERMALLOY, LLC
P.O. Box 400, Laconia NH 03247. 603/528-3400. **Physical address:** 67 Primrose Drive, Laconia NH 03246. **Fax:** 603/528-1478. **Contact:** Human Resources Recruiter. **E-mail address:** nazarenko@aavid.com. **World Wide Web address:** http://www.aavid.com. **Description:** A thermal engineering and management company that develops and markets solutions to heat-related problems. **Office hours:** Monday – Friday 8:00 a.m. – 5:00 p.m. **Corporate headquarters location:** Concord NH. **Other U.S. locations:** Santa Clara CA; Plano TX. **International locations:** Worldwide. **Parent company:** Aavid Thermal Technologies, Inc. **CEO:** Bharatan R. Patel. **Number of employees at this location:** 700. **Number of employees nationwide:** 1,800.

AHEARN & SOPER
26 South Main Street, Number 312, Concord NH 03301. 800/879-3224. **Fax:** 800/349-1476. **Contact:** Human Resources. **World Wide Web address:** http://www.ahearn.com. **Description:** Distributes various types of printers and scanners for consumer use. The company is also a systems integrator. Ahearn & Soper is comprised of four divisions: ImPrint, Advanced Barcode Systems, Video and Network Solutions, and Customer Services. **Corporate headquarters location:** Toronto, Canada. **Other U.S. locations:** Farmington Hills MI; Buffalo NY; East Syracuse NY. **Other international locations:** Canada. **Number of employees worldwide:** 150.

AMERICAN CANCER SOCIETY
360 Route 101, Unit 8 Bedford NH 03110. 603/472-8899. **Fax:** 603/472-7093. **Contact**: Patricia Trotta. **E-Mail Address**: Patricia.Trotta@cancer.org. **World Wide Web Address**: http://www.cancer.org. **Description**: With chartered divisions throughout the country and over 3, 400 local offices, the American Cancer Society is committed to fighting cancer through balanced programs of research, education, patient service, advocacy, and rehabilitation.

AMERICAN EXPLOSIVES CORP.
668 First New Hampshire Turnpike, Northwood NH 03261. 603/942-8899. **Fax:** 603/942-8558. **E-mail address:** jobapp@americanexplosives.com. **World Wide Web address:** http://www.americanexplosives.com. **Description:** American Explosives is a drilling and blasting company; its workers are contracted for jobs of all types, everything from highway work to residential neighborhoods. It is the fastest growing company in its field in Southern New Hampshire, Maine, and Vermont. **NOTE:** Please visit website for online application form. **Positions advertised include:** Blaster; Driller; Laborer; Driver. **Number of employees at this location:** 41.

AMHERST TECHNOLOGIES
40 Continental Boulevard, Merrimack NH 03054. 603/578-7668. **Fax:** 603/577-9439. **Contact:** Stephanie McDonald. **E-mail address:** hr@amherst1.com. **World Wide Web address:** http://www.amherst1.com. **Description:** Provides technology based solutions for customers. **Positions advertised include:** Collections Specialist; Account Executive Internal Sales; Account Executive External Sales; Systems Engineer.

ANDROSCOGGIN VALLEY HOSPITAL
59 Page Hill Road, Berlin NH 03570-3542. 603/752-2200. **Fax:** 603/752-3727. **Contact:** Human Resources Director. **E-mail address:** employment@avhosp.org. **World Wide Web address:** http://www.avhosp.org or http://www.avhnh.com. **Description:** Androscoggin Valley Hospital provides various medical services including inpatient and outpatient services, clinics, community programs, and emergency services. **Positions advertised include:** CT/Radiologist Technologist; Medical Technologist. **Parent company:** NorthCare (also at this location) is a nonprofit health care corporation.

ANHEUSER-BUSCH, INC.
221 Daniel Webster Highway, Merrimack NH 03054. 603/889-6631. **Contact:** Human Resources. **World Wide Web address:** http://www.budweiser.com. **Description:** A beer producer with a high-tech brewing process and high-speed packaging lines. **NOTE:** Company accepts resumes for currently open positions only. **Corporate headquarters location:** St. Louis MO. **Parent company:** Anheuser-Busch Companies is a diverse company involved in the entertainment, brewing, baking, and manufacturing industries. The company is one of the largest domestic brewers, operating 13 breweries throughout the United States and distributing through over 900 independent wholesalers. Beer brands include Budweiser, Michelob, Busch, King Cobra, and O'Doul's nonalcoholic beverages. Related businesses include can manufacturing, paper printing, and barley malting. Anheuser-Busch is also one of the largest operators of theme parks in the United States, with locations in Florida, Virginia, Texas, Ohio, and California. Through subsidiary Campbell Taggart Inc., Anheuser-Busch is also one of the largest commercial baking companies in the United States, producing foods under the Colonial brand name, among others. Anheuser-Busch also has various real estate interests. **Other U.S. locations:** Nationwide. **International locations:** Worldwide. **Operations at this facility include:** This location is a brewery.

APPLEBEE'S NEIGHBORHOOD GRILL & BAR
40 Key Road, Keene NH 03431-3925. 603/355-6300. **Fax:** 603/358-5122. **Contact:** Manager. **World Wide Web address:** http://www.applebee.com. **Description:** One franchise location of the national casual dining restaurant chain. Applebee's Neighborhood Grill & Bar offers mainly American fare. **Corporate headquarters location:** Overland Park KA. **Other U.S. locations:** Nationwide. **Other area locations:** Statewide. **Operations at this location include:** This location is a restaurant. **Listed on:** NASDAQ. **Stock exchange symbol:** APPB.

APPLEBEE'S NEIGHBORHOOD GRILL & BAR
1464 Woodbury Avenue, Portsmouth NH 03801-3239. 603/433-7400. **Fax:** 603/433-1372. **Contact:** Manager. **World Wide Web address:** http://www.applebee.com. **Description:** One franchise location of the national, casual dining restaurant chain. Applebee's Neighborhood Grill & Bar offers mainly American fare. **Corporate headquarters location:** Overland Park KA. **Other U.S. locations:** Nationwide. **Other area locations:** Statewide. **Operations at this location include:** This location is a restaurant. **President/CEO:** Lloyd L. Hill. **Listed on:** NASDAQ. **Stock exchange symbol:** APPB.

ASSOCIATED GROCERS OF NEW ENGLAND
P.O. Box 5200, Manchester NH 03108-5200. 603/669-3250. **Physical address:** 725 Gold Street, Manchester NH 03108. **Fax:** 603/669-5423. **Contact:** Human Resources. **World Wide Web address:** http://www.agne.com. **Description:** Offers wholesale grocery services and related support services. **NOTE:** Employment is extension 306. Please visit website for online application form. **Positions advertised include:** CDL – Drivers. **Number of employees at this location:** 700.

ATTITASH BEAR PEAK
Route 302, Bartlett NH 03812. 603/374-2368. **Fax:** 603/374-1960. **Contact:** Sandra Woehr, Human Resources. **E-mail address:** swoehr@attitash.com. **World Wide Web address:** http://www.attitash.com. **Description:** A four season, big mountain resort. **Positions advertised include:** Maintenance Technician; Lift Mechanic; Relief Night Auditor; Ski and Snowboard Pro; Daycare/Nursery Staff Member; Lift Operator; Lift Attendant; Rental and Repair Technician; Market Researcher; Retail Associate.

AUTOMATIC DATA PROCESSING (ADP)
105 Gay Street, Manchester NH 03103. 603/668-1291. **Contact**: Human Resources. **World Wide Web Address**: http://www.adp.com. **Description:** ADP offers benefit administration, human resource and retirement services for businesses of any size. **NOTE:** Please visit website to search for jobs and an application. **Corporate Headquarters**: Roseland, NJ

BAE SYSTEMS
65 Spit Brook Road, Nashua NH 03060. 603/885-4321. **Contact:** Human Resources. **World Wide Web address:** http://www.na.baesystems.com. **NOTE:** Please visit website to search for jobs and to apply online. **Description:** BAE SYSTEMS develops and manufactures advanced defense electronic systems. The company is a leading supplier of infrared and electronic countermeasures for aircraft protection, surveillance systems, air defense radar, mission planning, training and simulation systems, cockpit display systems, and automatic test equipment. **Positions advertised include:** Senior Principal Systems Engineer; EO/Laser Systems Engineer; Principal Test Design Engineer; Lead Optical Systems Engineer; Electron Beam Lithography Engineer; RF Countermeasures System Engineer; Senior Principal Reliability Engineer; Material Planner; Manager – Program Control; Principle QA Engineer; Electronic Technician; RF Test Technician; Data Management Specialist; Senior Engineering Writer; Electronic Assembler; Program Planner; Program Control Administrator. **Special programs:** Co-ops; Internships. **Office hours:** 7:00 a.m. – 5:30 p.m.

BICC GENERAL
345 McGregor Street, Manchester NH 03102. 603/668-1620. **Contact:** Andrea Weinhoffer, Human Resources. **E-mail address:** resumes-hr@generalcable.com; acweinhoffer@suscom.net. **World Wide Web address:** http://www.generalcable.com. **NOTE:** Please visit website to search for jobs and apply online. You may also send your resume to the corporate office at 4 Tesseneer Drive, Highland Heights, KY 41076-9753. Phone is 859/572-8000. **Description:** Company's business units include the Electrical Group, the Telecommunications and Electronics Group, the Consumer Products Group, and the Manufacturing Group. The Electrical Group operates under the following business units: General Cable/Guardian, which manufactures and distributes a full line of copper building wire, tray cable, power cable, and other cable products; Carol Cable Electrical, which manufactures industrial, power, mining, and control cable as well as THHN building wire, entertainment cable, rubber portable cord, and cordsets insulated with plastic and thermosetting compounds; and Capital Wire and Cable, which manufactures insulated wire and cable using both aluminum and copper conductors. The Telecommunications and Electronics Group operates under the business units Outside Products, which markets wire and cable designed for use in the outside plant network; Premise Products, which manufactures wire products that support the central office and commercial premise markets; and Electronics, which manufactures computer and control cables, IBM cabling products, ethernet, coaxial, twin axial, and fire alarm cables. The Consumer Products Group operates under the business units Carol Cable, which manufactures extension cords, portable lights, and home office power supplies; General/Capital Wire Retail, which sells building wire to the retail market; and the OEM Engineered Cordsets Division, which manufactures cord and cordsets for data processing equipment, tools, floor care products, and other appliances. The Manufacturing Group provides specialized support and expertise in the areas of purchasing, transportation, engineering, labor relations, manufacturing, and environmental and safety support. BICC is a brand-name product under the General Cable company. **Positions advertised include:** Materials Manager. **Corporate headquarters location:** Highland Heights KY. **Parent company:** General Cable. **Operations at this facility include:** This location of BICC General produces a variety of telecommunication cable. **International locations:** Worldwide. **Number of employees worldwide:** 5,900.

BANK OF NEW HAMPSHIRE
194 West Street, Keene NH 03431. 603/354-2040. **Contact:** Human Resources. **E-mail address:** HRnh@banknorth.com. **World Wide Web address:** http://www.banknh.com. **NOTE:** Please visit website to search employment opportunities by area of interest. **Description:** A bank holding company. **Office hours:** Monday – Friday, 8:30 a.m. – 5:00 p.m. **Other U.S. locations:** CT; MA; ME; NY; VT. **Corporate headquarters location:** Manchester NH. **Subsidiaries include:** Bank of New Hampshire is a state-chartered bank with 20 full-service banking offices located throughout Cheshire County, western Hillsborough County, southern Merrimack County, and Belknap County. **Parent company:** Banknorth Group, Inc. **Listed on:** New York Stock Exchange. **Stock exchange symbol:** BNK. **President:** R. Scott Bacon.

BANK OF NEW HAMPSHIRE CORPORATION
Center of New Hampshire, Elm Street, P.O. Box 600, Manchester NH 03105-0600. 603/624-6600. **Physical address:** 300 Franklin Street, Manchester NH 03101. **Toll-free phone:** 800/922-5705. **Fax:** 603/695-3010. **Contact:** Human Resources. **E-mail address:** HRnh@banknorth.com. **World Wide Web address:** http://www.banknh.com. **NOTE:** Please visit website to search employment opportunities by area of interest. **Description:** Bank of New Hampshire is a full-service financial institution whose operations include commercial banking operations, credit card services, and other related financial activities. **Corporate headquarters location:** This location. **Parent company:** Banknorth Group, Inc. **Operations at this facility include:** This location is a data center. **Listed on:** New York Stock Exchange. **Stock exchange symbol:** BNK. **President:** R. Scott Bacon.

BARNES & NOBLE BOOKSTORES
235 Daniel Webster Highway, Nashua NH 03060. 603/888-0533. **Contact:** Manager. **World Wide Web address:** http://www.bn.com. **Description:** A bookstore chain operating nationwide. This location has a cafe and music department in addition to its book departments. **Office hours:** 9:00 a.m. – 11:00 p.m.

BARNES & NOBLE BOOKSTORES
125 South Broadway, Route 28, Salem NH 03079. 603/898-1930. **Contact:** Manager. **World Wide Web address:** http://www.bn.com. **Description:** A bookstore chain operating nationwide. This location has a cafe in addition to its book departments. **Office hours:** 9:00 a.m. – 11:00 p.m.

BATESVILLE CASKET COMPANY
55 Palm Street, Nashua NH 03060-3212. 603/886-3600. **Fax:** 603/598-5672. **Contact:** Human Resources. **World Wide Web address:** http://www.batesville.com. **Description:** Batesville Casket Company is one of the nation's leading funeral service supply companies. Founded in 1884. **NOTE:** Entry-level positions are offered. **Corporate headquarters location:** Batesville IN. **Other U.S. locations:** Nationwide. **Parent company:** Hillenbrand Industries Inc. **Operations at this facility include:** This location manufactures protective metal and hardwood burial caskets. **Listed on:** New York Stock Exchange. **Stock exchange symbol:** HB. **Annual sales/revenues:** More than $100 million. **Number of employees at this location:** 275. **Number of employees nationwide:** 4,500. **Number of employees worldwide:** 4,900.

D.D. BEAN & SONS COMPANY
P.O. Box 348, Jaffrey NH 03452-0348. 603/532-8311. **Physical address:** 207 Peterborough Street, Jaffrey NH 03452. **Fax:** 603/532-6001. **Contact:** Human Resources Manager. **E-mail address:** info@ddbean.com. **World Wide Web address:** http://www.ddbean.com. **Description:** Designs and manufactures paper book matches and matchbook covers.

BEL-AIR NURSING HOME
29 Center Street, Goffstown NH 03045-2936. 603/497-4871. **Contact:** Robert Lenox, Human Resources. **Description:** An intermediate care nursing home. Founded in 1970. **NOTE:** Part-time jobs and second and third shifts are offered. **Special programs:** Internships. **Office hours:** Monday - Friday, 9:00 a.m. - 5:00 p.m. **Facilities Manager:** William Goldthwaite. **Purchasing Manager:** Robert W. Lenox. **Annual sales/revenues:** Less than $5 million. **Number of employees at this location:** 60.

BLACK MOUNTAIN SKI RESORT
P.O. Box B, Jackson NH 03846. 603/383-4490. **Physical address:** Black Mountain Road, Jackson NH 03846. **Contact:** Human Resources. **E-mail address:** jobs@blackmt.com. **World Wide Web address:** http://www.blackmt.com. **Description:** New Hampshire's oldest ski resort.

BOTTOMLINE TECHNOLOGIES
325 Corporate Drive, Portsmouth NH 03801. 603/436-0700. **Toll-free phone:** 800/243-2528. **Fax:** 603/427-6556. **Contact:** Human Resources. **E-mail address:** humanresources@bottomline.com. **World Wide Web address:** http://www.bottomline.com. **Description:** Designs and manufactures software that allows users to print checks from a laser printer. **Positions advertised include:** Account Manager; Customer Support Specialist; Application Developer; Java Programmer; Lotus Notes Script Programmer; Senior Software Developer; Quality Assurance Analyst; Human Resources Director; Application Support Specialist; Account Executive. **NOTE:** Please do not call about positions. **Corporate headquarters location:** This location. **Other U.S. locations:** San Francisco CA; Lakewood CO; Charlestown MA. **Listed on:** NASDAQ. **Stock exchange symbol:** EPAY. **President and CEO:** Joseph Mullen. **Number of employees worldwide:** 450.

BRONZE CRAFT CORPORATION
P.O. Box 788, Nashua NH 03061-0788. 603/883-7747. **Physical address:** 37 Will Street, Nashua NH 03060. **Toll-free phone:** 800/488-7747. **Fax:** 603/883-0222. **Contact:** Personnel Director. **World Wide Web address:** http://www.bronzecraft.com. **Description:** A sand-cast foundry, Bronze Craft Corporation manufactures architectural products including window and door hardware. The company also supplies finished products to companies like Steinway, GE, and Westinghouse. Operations at this location include machining, polishing, finishing, and assembly. Bronze Craft Corporation also provides customer support including engineering, pattern making, tooling, and repairing. **Office hours:** Monday – Friday, 8:00 a.m. – 5:00 p.m. **Corporate headquarters location:** This location. **Operations at this facility include:** Administration; Manufacturing; Research and Development; Sales; Service. **Number of employees at this location:** 150.

BROOKSTONE COMPANY
17 Riverside Street, Nashua NH 03062. 603/880-9500. **Fax:** 603/577-8004. **Contact:** Human Resources. **E-mail address:** hr@brookstone.com. **World Wide Web address:** http://www.brookstone.com. **Description:** Operates a chain over 200 specialty retail stores. **NOTE:** Please send resumes to 1 Innovation Way, Merrimack NH 03054. **Positions advertised include:** Retail Buyer; Creative Director; Art Director; Copywriter; Benefits Administrator; Mail Order Planner; General Ledger Specialist; Project Manager; Merchandise Coordinator. **Corporate headquarters location:** This location. **Listed on:** NASDAQ. **Stock exchange symbol:** BKST.

BUSINESS NEW HAMPSHIRE MAGAZINE
670 North Commerce Street, Suite 110, Manchester NH 03101. 603/626-6354. **Fax:** 603/626-6359. **Contact:** Matt Mowry, Editor. **World Wide Web address:** http://www.businessnhmagazine.com. **Description:** A monthly business magazine. Founded in 1983.

CCA GLOBAL PARTNERS
670 North Commercial Street, Manchester NH 03101. 800/450-7595. **Fax:** 603/626-3444. **Contact:** Human Resources. **World Wide Web address:** http://www.ccaglobal.com. **Description:** Engaged in the flooring, mortgage lending, lighting, formalwear, and biking industries. **Positions advertised include:** Member Relations Specialist.

C&J TRAILWAYS
185 Grafton Drive, Portsmouth NH 03801. 603/430-1100. **Toll-free phone:** 800/258-7111. **Fax:** 603/433-8960. **Contact:** Human Resources. **E-mail address:** tcolen@cjtrailways.com. **World Wide Web address:** http://www.cjtrailways.com. **Description:** Provides transportation from the seacoast to Boston MA. Offers early morning and late night transportation. Founded in 1968. **Positions advertised include:** Customer Service Provider; Driver; Fleet Mechanic.

CADEC CORPORATION
8 East Perimeter Road, Londonderry NH 03053. 603/668-1010. **Fax:** 603/668-3665; 603/623-0604. **Contact:** Human Resources. **E-mail address:** hr@cadec.com. **World Wide Web address:** http://www.cadecsystems.com. **Description:** A manufacturer of on-board computer systems for the trucking industry. **Positions advertised include:** Regional Sales Manager.

CAMPAGNE ASSOCIATES
195 McGregor Street, Suite 410, Manchester NH 03102. 603/622-4776. **Fax:** 603/622-5192. **E-mail address:** hr@campagne.com. **World Wide Web address:** http://www.campagne.com. **Description:** Offers fundraising software to non-profit organizations, to aid their fundraising organization and subsequent success. **Positions advertised include:** Controller; Software Sales Professional; Customer Support Representative. **CEO:** Ric Pratte.

CANOBIE LAKE PARK
P.O. Box 190, Salem NH 03079-0190. 603/893-3506. **Physical address:** 85 North Policy Street, Salem NH 03079. **Fax:** 603/890-2404. **Contact:** Personnel Department. **World Wide Web address:** http://www.canobie.com. **NOTE:** Please visit website to download application, or to have an application sent to you. **Description:** A family amusement park. The park offers attractions and rides including steel corkscrew and wooden rollercoasters as well as one of 12 remaining historical carousels in the nation. Founded in 1902. **Positions advertised include:** Ride Operator; Ride Attendant; Games Attendant; Cashier; Gate Attendant; Security Officer; Mechanic; Office Staff; Costume Character; Lifeguard; Midway Sweeper; Matron/Custodian; First Aid Attendant; Landscaping Grounds Crew; Food Service Worker. **Office hours:** Monday – Friday, 10:00 a.m. – 4:30 p.m.

CHANNEL MARINE
1 Channel Lane, P.O. Box 5397, Weirs Beach NH 03247. 603/366-4801. **Toll-free phone:** 800/524-BOAT. **Fax:** 603/366-4101. **Contact:** Brad Davidson, Operations Manager. **E-mail address:** brad@channelmarine.com. **World Wide Web address:** http://www.channelmarine.com. **Description:** Sells and services powerboats. Founded 1946. **Positions advertised include:** Parts Manager; Marine Service Technician; Assistant Service Manager; Fork Truck Operator.

CHESHIRE MEDICAL CENTER
580 Court Street, Keene NH 03431. 603/354-5400. **Fax:** 603/354-6519. **Contact:** Personnel. **E-mail address:** pbeardsley@Cheshire-Med.com; cstalker@cheshire-med.com. **World Wide Web address:** http://www.cheshire-med.com. **Description:** A nonprofit, 177-bed, regional medical center with medical/surgical, emergency care, women's and children's, rehabilitation, oncology, and mental health services. **NOTE:** Entry-level positions and second and third shifts are offered. Contact Personnel directly by calling 603/354-5454 Ext. 3520. **Positions advertised include:** Housekeeper; RN – Various Departments; Physical Therapist; LPN; Medical Technologist; Laundry Tech; Psychiatric Technician; Cafeteria Representative; Hostess; Vascular Technologist; Optician; Ultrasound Tech. **President/CEO:** Robert Langlais. **Facilities Manager:** Frank Werbinski. **Annual sales/revenues:** $21 - $50 million. **Number of employees at this location:** 800.

CHRISTMAS FARM INN
P.O. Box CC, Route 16B, Jackson Village NH 03846. 603/383-4313. **Toll-free phone:** 800/443-5837. **Fax:** 603/383-6495. **Contact:** General Manager. **E-mail address:** info@christmasfarminn.com. **World Wide Web address:** http://www.christmasfarminn.com. **Description:** Privately owned, traditional style inn and restaurant.

CIGNA HEALTHCARE
2 College Park Drive, Hooksett NH 03106. 603/268-7000. **Toll-free phone:** 800/531-4584. **Fax:** 603/268-7981. **Contact:** Human Resources. **World Wide Web address:** http://www.cigna.com. **Description:** CIGNA HealthCare is a health care management company that has interests in or manages seven individual practice associations and model health maintenance organizations that market and provide prepaid health care services to more than 250,000 members in New Hampshire, Maine, North Carolina, Indiana, Tennessee, and New York. The company also owns a third-party administrator that processes medical and dental claims for more than 180,000 members and has an array of managed care products that it offers to companies financing health care through self-insured indemnity plans. **NOTE:** CIGNA Healthcare prefers that jobseekers apply online to all open positions. Please visit the website to register, search for jobs, and apply online. **Corporate headquarters location:** Philadelphia PA. **Other U.S locations:** Nationwide. **Parent company:** CIGNA Companies. **Listed on:** New York Stock Exchange. **Stock exchange symbol:** CI. **CEO:** H. Edward Hanway.

CITADEL COMPUTER CORPORATION
29 Armory Road, Milford NH 03055. 603/672-5500. **Fax:** 603/672-5590. **Contact:** Human Resources. **World Wide Web address:** http://www.citadelcomputer.com. **Description:** A manufacturer of durable computers for use in warehouses and on loading docks. **Office hours:** Monday – Friday, 8:00 a.m. – 5:00 p.m.

CITIZENS BANK
587 Main Street, Laconia NH 03246. 603/527-3000. **Contact:** Human Resources. **World Wide Web address:** http://www.citizensbank.com. **Description:** Citizens Bank provides a full range of banking services, serving the retail, commercial, and fiduciary needs of individuals, businesses, and local governments. **NOTE:** Apply for a Bank Teller position by calling 877/TELLER1. Apply for an in-store supermarket position by calling 877/INAISLE. **Office hours:** Monday – Wednesday, 9:00 a.m. – 4:00 p.m.; Thursday – Friday, 9:00 a.m. – 5:00 p.m.; Saturday, 9: 00 a.m. – 12:00 p.m. **Other area locations:** Meredith; Wolfeboro; Franklin. **Corporate headquarters location:** Providence RI. **Parent company:** Citizens Financial Group, Inc. **Number of employees nationwide:** 15,000.

CLARK'S TRADING POST
U.S. Route 3, P.O. Box 1, Lincoln NH 03251. 603/745-8913. **Contact:** Human Resources. **E-mail address:** info@clarkstradingpost.com. **World Wide Web address:** http://www.clarkstradingpost.com. **Description:** A family entertainment spot. Features animal shows, train rides, and a specialty gift shop. **NOTE:** Clark's Trading Post runs on a summer season schedule – from May through October. Call for more detailed dates.

CLEAN HARBORS, INC.
20 Dunklee Road, Bow NH 03304. 603/224-6626. **Toll-free phone:** 800/645-8265. **Fax:** 603/224-6778. **Contact:** Judy Torres, Human Resources. **E-mail address:** torresj@cleanharbors.com. **World Wide Web address:** http://www.cleanharbors.com. **NOTE:** Please visit website to see a listing of all open positions. **Description:** Clean Harbors, Inc., through its subsidiaries, provides comprehensive environmental services in 35 states in the Northeast, Midwest, Central, and Mid-Atlantic regions. Clean Harbors provides a wide range of hazardous waste management and environmental support services to a diversified customer base from over 40 locations. The company's hazardous waste management services include treatment, storage, recycling, transportation, risk analysis, site assessment, laboratory analysis, site closure, and

disposal of hazardous materials through environmentally sound methods including incineration. Environmental remediation services include emergency response, surface remediation, groundwater restoration, industrial maintenance, and facility decontamination. **Positions advertised include:** Field Technician. **Corporate headquarters location:** Braintree MA. **Other U.S. locations:** Nationwide. **Listed on:** NASDAQ. **Stock exchange symbol:** CLHB. **CEO:** Alan S. McKim. **Number of employees nationwide:** 3,775.

COCA-COLA BOTTLING COMPANY OF NORTHERN NEW ENGLAND
One Executive Park Drive, Bedford NH 03110. 603/627-7871. **Fax:** 603/627-6108. **Contact:** Director of Human Resources. **World Wide Web address:** http://www.cocacola.com. **Description:** A bottling plant for Coca-Cola. **Corporate headquarters location:** Atlanta GA. **Parent company:** The Coca-Cola Company is one of the world's largest soft drink makers. Brand names include Coca-Cola, diet Coke, Coca-Cola light (international), Sprite, diet Sprite, Mr. PiBB, Mello Yello, Fanta, TAB, Fresca, Fruitopia, PowerAide, and Minute Maid. The Coca-Cola Company owns 100 supporting brands around the world including Powerade, Aquarius, Hi-C, Georgia (canned coffee, sold in Japan), Thums Up & Limca (India), Sparletta Brands (South Africa), Nestea (distributed by Coca-Cola Enterprises Inc.), and Seiryusabo (Japan). The Coca-Cola Company has owning interest in many bottlers including 44 percent of Coca-Cola Enterprises Inc., as well as Coca-Cola Foods, the world's largest seller of juice and juice-related products under brand names such as FiveAlive, Hi-C, Bright & Early, and Bacardi. **NOTE:** Coca-cola will only accept resumes through their Careers website. **Listed on:** New York Stock Exchange. **Stock exchange symbol:** KO.

COLBY-SAWYER COLLEGE
100 Main Street, New London NH 03257. 603/526-3000. **Contact:** Human Resources. **E-mail address:** welcome@colby-sawyer.edu. **World Wide Web address:** http://www.colby-sawyer.edu. **NOTE:** Electronic submissions are preferred. Contact Human Resources directly at 603/526-3740. **Description:** A four-year, coeducational liberal arts college. Major programs offered include business administration, nursing, psychology, sports science, communication studies, and graphic design. **Positions advertised include:** Assistant Professor – Various Departments; Teaching Faculty – Various Departments; Head Coach – Tennis; Assistant Athletic Trainer/Instructor; Assistant Coach – Various Sports. **Number of employees at this location:** 250.

RJ COLE SOLUTIONS
250 Commercial Street, Suite 4002A, Manchester NH 03101. 603/606-5585. **Fax:** 603/606-5586. **Contact:** Human Resources. **World Wide Web address:** http://www.rjcolesolutions.com. **Description:** Provides Information Technology services for the medical and dental practice market. **Positions advertised include:** Administrative Assistant.

COLLEGE FOR LIFELONG LEARNING
125 North State Street, Concord NH 03301. 603/228-3000. **Toll-free phone:** 800/582-7248. – New Hampshire only. **Fax:** 603/229-0964. **Contact:** Human Resources. **E-mail address:** kristie.camacho@cll.edu. **World Wide Web address:** http://www.usnh.unh.edu/cll. **Description:** A part of the University System of New Hampshire, CLL offers a bachelor's of professional studies in management, behavioral science, criminal justice, and early childhood education; bachelor's of general studies; associate's degrees in general studies, microcomputer applications, business studies, early childhood education, and behavioral sciences; certificate programs in child care, library techniques, computer applications, adult learning and development, leadership in the workplace, and paralegal studies; and professional continuing education with teacher education courses, management development training, real estate recertification, real estate appraisal, certified nurses assistant, administrative assistant programs, and computer training workshops. CLL is accredited by the New England Association of Schools and Colleges. **Positions advertised include:** Adjunct Faculty. **NOTE:** Please no phone calls regarding employment. **Corporate headquarters location:** This location. **Other area locations:** Statewide.

COLLINS & AIKMAN CORPORATION
RR 1, Box 518L, Farmington NH 03835. 603/755-4200. **Fax:** 603/755-4825. **Contact:** Patricia Slaght, Human Resources. **E-mail address:** Patricia.Slaght@colaik.com. **World Wide Web address:** http://www.colaik.com. **Description:** Manufactures air bags and glove compartments for automobiles. **NOTE:** Please do not call regarding submitted resumes. **Special programs:** Internships. **Office hours:** Monday – Friday, 8:00 a.m. – 5:00 p.m. **Corporate headquarters location:** Troy MI. **Other U.S. locations:** Nationwide. **International locations:** Worldwide. **Listed on:** New York Stock Exchange. **Stock exchange symbol:** CKC. **Number of employees worldwide:** 25,000.

COMMUNITY ALLIANCE OF HUMAN SERVICES
P.O. Box 188, 46 North Main Street, Newport NH 03773. 603/863-7708. **Contact:** Judi Deavers, Director of Fiscal and IT Services. **E-mail address:** jdeavers@communityalliance.net. **World Wide Web address:** http://www.communityalliance.net. **Description:** Provides a range of human services including residential programming, counseling, court liaisons, parental aides, diversions, and mentoring. **Positions advertised include:** Certified Nurse's Aide; Licensed Practical Nurse; Registered Nurse; Childcare Teacher.

COMPUWARE CORPORATION
9 Townsend West, Nashua NH 03063. 603/578-8400. **Fax:** 603/578-8401. **Contact:** Human Resources. **World Wide Web address:** http://www.compuware.com. **Description:** A technology and market leader in the development of Windows-based advanced error detection and debugging tools. **NOTE:** Entry-level positions are offered. Send Resumes to One Campus Martius, Detroit MI 48226. **Positions advertised include:** Software Developer; QA Testing Analyst Lead; Release Engineer; Software Developer; Products Telesales Representative. **Corporate headquarters location:** Detroit MI. **Other U.S. locations:** Nationwide. **International locations:** Worldwide. **Listed on:** NASDAQ. **Stock exchange symbol:** CPWR. **Number of employees at this location:** 85.

CONCORD ELECTRIC COMPANY
P.O. Box 2013, Concord NH 03302. 603/224-2311. **Physical address:** One Maguire Street, Concord NH 03301. **Toll-free phone:** 800/852-3339. **Contact:** Human Resources. **World Wide Web address:** http://www.unitil.com. **Description:** A power company. **Parent company:** Unitil is a public utility holding company providing electric and gas service through its subsidiaries. **Number of employees at this location:** 60.

CONCORD HOSPITAL
250 Pleasant Street, Concord NH 03301. 603/225-2711. **Fax:** 603/228-7346. **Recorded jobline:** 877/777-8444. **Contact:** Human Resources. **World Wide Web address:** http://www.concordhospital.org. **Description:** A full-service, nonprofit hospital offering both inpatient and outpatient services. **NOTE:** Second and third shifts are offered. Please visit website to apply online. **Positions advertised include:** Cafeteria Aide; Call Center Associate; Care Partner; Cashier; Central Sterile Supply Tech; Clerical Partner; Clinical Lab Assistant; Clinical Nurse Specialist; Commercial Claim Representative; Cytotechnologist; Dental Assistant; ED Technician; Exercise Instructor; Food Service Assistant; Heart Gifts Boutique Assistant Manager; Insurance Authorization Assistant; Lead Mammographer; Medical Assistant – Internal Medicine; MT/MLT; Multi-Tech Outpatient; Nurse Practitioner; Pathology Lab Assistant; Phlebotomist; Physical Therapist – Various Departments; Porter Dishwasher; Rehab Secretary; RN – Various Departments; Security Officer; Spiritual Care Counselor; Transporter. **Special programs:** Internships. **Number of employees at this location:** 1,800.

THE CONCORD MONITOR
One Monitor Drive, P.O. Box 1177, Concord NH 03302-1177. 603/224-5301. **Fax:** 603/228-5868. **Contact:** Tracie Wajer, Human Resources Manger. **E-mail address:** hr@cmonitor.com. **World Wide Web address:** http://www.concordmonitor.com. **Description:** Publishes a daily newspaper with a circulation of 22,500. The *Concord Monitor* also does press runs for other area newspapers. **Positions advertised include:** Press Operator; Motor Route Service Manager; Distribution Inserter; Retention Marketing Specialist; Weekend Delivery Assistant. **Special programs:** Internships. **Corporate headquarters location:** This location. **Listed on:** Privately held. **Number of employees at this location:** 170.

CONCRETE SYSTEMS INC.
9 Commercial Street, Hudson NH 03051. 603/889-4163. **Contact:** Human Resources. **World Wide Web address:** http://www.sheltech.com. **Description:** Manufactures precast concrete products. **Subsidiaries include:** CSI Shelter Technologies. **Number of employees at this location:** 100.

COOKSON ELECTRONICS
POLYCLAD FRANKLIN
40 Industrial Park Drive, Franklin NH 03235. 603/934-5642. **Contact:** Sherry Emerson, Director of Human Resources. **E-mail address:** semerson@cooksonelectronics.com. **World Wide Web address:** http://www.cooksonpwb.com/laminates/index.shtml. **Description:** Manufactures laminates for printed circuit boards. **Number of employees at this location:** 500.

COOKSON ELECTRONICS
144 Harvey Road, Londonderry NH 03053. 603/934-5642. **Contact:** Human Resources. **E-mail address:** info@cooksonElectronics.com. **World Wide Web address:** http://www.cooksonelectronics.com. **Description:** Offers equipment to companies who work hand-on with electronics, precious metals, and ceramics. **Other U.S. locations:** Foxboro MA; Jersey City NJ.

THE CORRIGAN COMPANY, INC.
Hills Court, 6-C Hills Avenue, Concord NH 03301. 603/225-3801. **Fax:** 603/225-0436. **E-mail address:** jwctcc.jwc@verizon.net. **World Wide Web address:** http://www.thecorrigancompany.com. **Description:** A real estate firm that specializes in the leasing/selling of land and property for commercial purposes.

COUNTRY VILLAGE GENESIS ELDER CARE
P.O. Box 441, Lancaster NH 03584. 603/788-4935. **Physical address:** 91 Country Village Road, Lancaster NH 03584. **Contact:** Human Resources. **Description:** A nursing home that offers intermediate care and has an assisted-living residential facility.

CRANMORE MOUNTAIN RESORT
1 Skimobile Road, P.O. Box 1640, North Conway NH 03860. 603/356-8500. **Toll-free phone:** 800-SUN-N-SKI. **Contact:** Human Resources. **World Wide Web address:** http://www.cranmore.com. **Description:** A ski, snowboard, and tubing resort.

CREARE INC.
P.O. Box 71, Hanover NH 03755. 603/643-3800. **Fax:** 603/643-4657. **Contact:** Human Resources. **E-mail address:** recruit@creare.com. **World Wide Web address:** http://www.creare.com. **NOTE:** Please see website and job listings for information on how to submit electronic applications. **Description:** Provides engineering services to customers worldwide. Services range from basic research to the development of prototype products. Founded in 1961. **Positions advertised include:** Design Engineer; R&D Engineer; Mechanical Detail Drafter; Mechanical Technician; Office Assistant/Receptionist. **Office hours:** Monday - Friday, 8:00 a.m. - 5:00 p.m. **Corporate headquarters location:** This location. **Operations at this facility include:** Administration; Research and Development; Sales; Service. **Number of employees at this location:** 100.

CUSTOMIZED STRUCTURES INC.
P.O. Box 884, Plains Road, Claremont NH 03743. 603/543-1236. **Toll-free phone:** 800/523-2033. **Fax:** 603/542-5650. **Contact:** Human Resources. **World Wide Web address:** http://www.custruct.com. **Description:** Manufactures modular homes and wholesales to residential builders and dealers of modular systems. Customized Structures specializes in homes of wood platform frame construction, designed for single-family housing, two-family housing, and multifamily housing. Each unit includes suggested plans for foundations. **Number of employees at this location:** 100.

DANIEL WEBSTER COLLEGE
20 University Drive, Nashua NH 03063-1300. 603/577-6600. **Fax:** 603/577-6001. **Contact:** Personnel Office. **E-mail address:** hr@dwb.edu. **World Wide Web address:** http://www.dwc.edu. **Description:** A small, private, four-year college specializing in aviation, computer science, business, and sports management. Daniel Webster College offers both bachelor's and associate's degrees. **Positions advertised include:** Database/Information Technology Manager; Director of Annual Fund; Director of Flight Operations; Assistant/Associate Professor; Campus Safety Officer; Assistant Professor - Business and Management; Assistant Professor- Sports Management; Director of Academic Resources; Assistant Registrar. **President:** Hannah McCarthy. **Number of employees at this location:** 100.

DAHLE NORTH AMERICA
375 Jaffrey Road, Petersborough NH 03458. 800/995-1379. **Contact:** Human Resources. **E-mail address:** info@dahle.com. **World Wide Web address:** http://www.dahleusa.com. **Description:** Manufactures and distributes business machines, art and craft tools, and office products. **Positions advertised include:** Service Coordinator.

DARTMOUTH COLLEGE
7 Lebanon Street, Suite 203, Hanover NH 03755. 603/646-3411. **E-mail address:** human.resources.employment@dartmouth.edu. **World Wide Web address:** http://www.dartmouth.edu. **Description:** Founded in 1769, Dartmouth is a four-year, coeducational college and graduate school of business, engineering, and medicine and sixteen graduate programs in the arts and sciences. **Positions advertised include:**

Budget Planner/Analyst; IC Coordinator Athletics; Assistant to the Director Tuck School; System Administrator.

DARTMOUTH PRINTING COMPANY
69 Lyme Road, Hanover NH 03755. 603/643-2220. **Fax:** 603/643-4062. **Contact:** Catherine Budd, Director of Human Resources. **E-mail address:** cbudd@dpc-nh.com. **World Wide Web address:** http://www.dpc-nh.com. **NOTE:** Please visit website for online application form. **Description:** A commercial printer. **Positions advertised include:** Mailhandler; Press Utility Person; Handworker; Mail Control Technician; Robot Operator. **Corporate headquarters location:** This location. **Operations at this facility include:** Administration; Manufacturing. **Annual sales/revenues:** $21 - $50 million. **Number of employees at this location:** 250.
1103 North Main Street

ALICE PECK DAY MEMORIAL HOSPITAL
125 Mascoma Street, Lebanon NH 03766-3205. 603/448-3121. **Fax:** 603/443-9501. **Contact:** Human Resources. **E-mail address:** jobs@alicepeckday.org. **World Wide Web address:** http://www.alicepeckday.org. **Description:** A hospital. **Positions advertised include:** Mammography Technologist; Radiologic Technologist; Manager, Rehab Services; Social Worker; RN – Various Departments; Patient Care Tech; Occupational Therapist; Clinic Coordinator; Housekeeper; Custodian; Public Affairs and Marketing Coordinator; Catering Cook; Wait Staff.

DESIGN CONTEMPO INC. (DCI)
265 South Main Street, Lisbon NH 03585. 603/838-6544. **Toll-free phone:** 800/552-8286. **Fax:** 603/838-6826. **Contact:** Personnel Director. **World Wide Web address:** http://www.dcifurn.com. **Description:** Manufactures furniture for college dormitories, hospitals, and government agencies. **Corporate headquarters location:** This location. **Number of employees at this location:** 250. **Other U.S. locations:** NC; CA.

DEVINE, MILLIMET & BRANCH
111 Amherst Street, Manchester NH 03101. 603/669-1000. **Fax:** 603/669-8547. **Contact:** Human Resources. **E-mail address:** careers@dmb.com. **World Wide Web address:** http://www.dmb.com. **Description:** A law firm operating through two groups. The Corporate Group's areas of focus include intellectual property/patent law, estate planning, real estate, and business and tax planning. The Litigation Group's services include insurance defense, business litigation, and commercial litigation. **Positions advertised include:** Summer Associate; First Year Associate; Lateral Associate; Lateral Shareholder; Paralegal; Secretary/Staff. **Corporate headquarters location:** This location. **Other area locations:** Concord NH; North Hampton NH. **Other U.S. locations:** Andover MA. **Number of employees at this location:** 180.

DOVER VETERINARY HOSPITAL
96 Durham Road, Dover NH 03820-4278. 603/742-6438. **Fax:** 603/742-4037. **Contact:** Human Resources. **E-mail address:** resume@dovervet.com. **World Wide Web address:** http://www.dovervet.com. **NOTE:** Please visit website to access application form. You may apply online, or print and fax or mail the application. **Description:** Dover Veterinary Hospital offers general medical, surgical, and diagnostic services for dogs and cats. The hospital specializes in orthopedic surgery. **Positions advertised include:** Small Animal Surgeon; Internist; Part Time Veterinarian; Veterinary Nurse; Animal Care Specialist; Client Care Coordinator. **Office hours:** Monday – Friday, 8:00 a.m. – 6:00 p.m.

THE DUMPSTER DEPOT
47 Rockingham Road, Londonderry NH 03053. 603/432-6333. **Toll-free phone:** 866/99-DEPOT. **Fax:** 603/537-9614. **E-mail address:** dumpsterdepot@aol.com. **World Wide Web address:** http://www.dumpsterdepot.com. **Description:** The Dumpster Depot removes waste from businesses, homes, contract sites, and commercial locations. They specialize in construction material. The company is in the process of expanding business and finding new locations. **Other area locations:** Andover NH. **Other U.S. locations:** Hull MA.

ELLIOT HOSPITAL
One Elliot Way, Manchester NH 03103. 603/669-5300. **Contact:** Personnel. **World Wide Web address:** http://www.elliothospital.com. **Description:** A 296-bed acute care hospital serving southern New Hampshire. Established in 1890, Elliot Hospital serves as the trauma center for the Manchester metropolitan area. Facilities include the Max K. Wilscher Urology Center, the Elliot Regional Cancer Center, and a level-three neonatal intensive care unit (NICU). **NOTE:** Volunteer positions also available. Online applications preferred. **Positions advertised include:** Accounting Clerk; Associate Teacher; Breast Sonographer; CT Technologist; Cardiac Ultrasonographer; Clinical Leader; Clinical Nurse; Clinical Nursing Supervisor; Cytotechnologist; Diet Aide; Director of Pharmacy Services; Environmental Services Technician; LNA – Various Departments; Mailroom Clerk; Non-Invasive Cardiac Tech; Nurse Practitioner; Occupational Therapist; Pharmacy Technician; Physical Therapist; Physician Recruiter; Project Manager; RN – Various Departments; Radiology Technologist; Respiratory Care Practitioner; Security Officer; Shuttle Driver; Social Worker; Unit Secretary.

ENTERASYS NETWORKS
P.O. Box 5005, Rochester NH 03866. 603/332-9400. **Physical address:** 35 Industrial Way, Rochester NH 03866-5005. **Contact:** Human Resources. **World Wide Web address:** http://www.enterasys.com. **Description:** Develops, manufactures, markets, installs, and supports a wide range of standards-based LAN connectivity products such as network management software, high-speed adapter cards, smart hubs, and other network interconnection equipment. **Note**: Send resumes to 50 Minuteman Road, Andover MA 01810. **Special programs:** Internships. **Corporate headquarters location:** Andover MA. **Other U.S. locations:** Nationwide. **International locations:** Nationwide. **Operations at this facility include:** Administration; Sales. **Listed on:** New York Stock Exchange. **Stock exchange symbol:** ETS. **Annual sales/revenues:** More than $100 million. **Number of employees at this location:** 2,000.

EXETER HOSPITAL
5 Alumni Drive, Exeter NH 03833. 603/778-7311. **Toll-free phone:** 800/439-3837. (For NH, ME, MA, VT.) **Fax:** 603/580-6905. **Recorded jobline:** 603/778-6660. **Contact:** Danielle Hughes, Human Resources Department. **E-mail address:** ehrjobs@ehr.org. **World Wide Web address:** http://www.ehr.org. **Description:** An acute care, 100-bed hospital. Founded in 1892. **NOTE:** Entry-level positions and second and third shifts are offered. Volunteer positions also available. **Positions advertised include:** Yoga Instructor; Vice President; Vascular Technologist; Unit Educator; Social Worker; Respiratory Therapist; Research Coordinator; Radiologic Technologist; Physical Therapist; Pharmacist; Paramedic; Pediatric Dental Receptionist; Occupational Therapist; RN – Various Departments; Medical Lab Technician; LNA – Various Departments; Dietitian; Cook; Biller. **Special programs:** Internships; Summer Jobs. **Corporate headquarters location:** This location. **Parent company:** Exeter Health Resources is a nonprofit company comprised of Exeter Hospital, an acute care, 100-bed hospital; Exeter Healthcare, a long-term care, subacute, rehabilitative hospital with 125 beds; Rockingham Visiting Nurse Association and Hospice; Synergy Health and Fitness; and CORE Physician Health Services, which offers primary care physicians and family medical services. **President/CEO:** Kevin Callahan. **Number of employees at this location:** 1,200.

FCI ELECTRICAL, INC.
47 East Industrial Park Drive, Manchester NH 03109. 603/647-5000. **Fax:** 603/647-5202. **Contact:** Human Resources. **World Wide Web address:** http://www.fciconnect.com. **NOTE:** Please visit website for online application form. **Description:** A multinational corporation serving virtually every segment of industry through the design, manufacture, and sale of a broad line of electrical and electronic connectors and allied products. **Other area locations:** Littleton NH. **Other U.S. locations:** Nationwide. **International locations:** Worldwide. **Parent company:** Areva. (Paris, France). **Operations at this facility include:** Manufacturing. **Number of employees worldwide:** 12,000.

FERROTEC CORPORATION
40 Simon Street, Nashua NH 03060-3075. 603/883-9800. **Fax:** 603/883-2308. **Contact:** Human Resources. **E-mail address:** hr@ferrotec.com. **World Wide Web address:** http://www.fero.com. **Description:** Ferrofluidics Corporation and its subsidiaries develop, manufacture, and market products that are based on or derived from the company's magnetic fluid (ferrofluids) technology. In addition to designing and manufacturing its ferrofluids, the company also designs applications; subcontracts its manufacturing; and assembles, tests, and ships products from the company's headquarters. The company concentrates in four product areas: ferrofluids used in the audio loudspeaker market, nondestructive testing and sensor applications, magnetic fluid sealing devices and subsystems that separate the manufacturing process from the environment, and crystal growing systems that facilitate the growth of silicon and other metal alloys. **Other U.S. locations:** Santa Clara CA. **International locations:** Worldwide.

FIREYE, INC.
3 Manchester Road, Derry NH 03038. 603/432-4100. **Fax:** 603/432-1570. **Contact:** Human Resources. **E-mail address:** humanresources@fireye.com. **World Wide Web address:** http://www.fireye.com. **Description:** A manufacturer of flame safeguard controls for industrial burners and furnaces. **Corporate headquarters location:** This location. **Other U.S. locations:** NC; MA; DE; NJ; OH; OK; CA. **International locations:** Canada; England; Belgium; Germany; Poland; Singapore; China.

FIRST SIGNATURE BANK & TRUST
325 Corporate Drive, Portsmouth NH 03801. 603/433-3700. **Toll-free phone:** 800/522-1776. **Contact:** Human Resources. **World Wide Web address:** http://www.firstsignature.com. **Description:** A state commercial bank offering money market accounts, certificates of deposit, IRAs, NOW accounts, instant credit, home mortgages, home equity lines of credit, and consumer loans. **Office hours:** Monday – Friday, 8:30 a.m. – 5:00 p.m. **Corporate headquarters location:** This location. **Parent company:** John Hancock Financial Services (Boston MA). **President:** Richard P. Zeloski.

FIRST STUDENT INCORPORATED
271 Derry Road, Litchfield NH 03052. 603/886-0661. **Toll-free phone:** 800/844-5588. **Fax:** 603/882-3585. **Contact:** Human Resources. **E-mail address:** kelley.newman@firstgroupamerica.com. **World Wide Web address:** http://www.firststudentinc.com. **NOTE:** Please visit website to apply online. **Description:** Provides transportation for students to and from school and for chartered trips. First Student serves Nashua, Londonderry, and the Lakes area. **Positions advertised include:** Manager in Training. **Corporate headquarters location:** Cincinnati OH. **Number of employees at this location:** 110.

FIRST VIRTUAL COMMUNICATIONS
542 Amherst Street, Nashua NH 03063. 603/886-9050. **Toll-free phone:** 800/241-7463. **Fax:** 603/886-9051. **Contact:** Human Resources. **E-mail address:** jobs@fvc.com. **World Wide Web address:** http://www.fvc.com. **Description:** A developer of computer-based information access and communications software. The company offers cross-platform desktop videoconferencing, network access, and file transfer. **Positions advertised include:** Field Marketing Specialist. **Corporate headquarters location:** Redwood City CA. **International locations:** Worldwide. **Listed on:** NASDAQ. **Stock exchange symbol:** FVCX.

FISHER SCIENTIFIC INTERNATIONAL INC.
1 Liberty Lane, Hampton NH 03842. 603/926-5911. **Fax:** 603/929-2379. **Contact:** Human Resources. **World Wide Web address:** http://www.fisherscientific.com. **Description:** One of the largest providers of instruments, equipment, and other products to the scientific community. The company offers a selection of products and services to research centers and industrial customers worldwide. Fisher Scientific serves scientists engaged in biomedical, biotechnology, pharmaceutical, chemical, and other fields of research and development in corporations, the educational and research institutions, and government agencies. The company also supplies clinical laboratories, hospitals, environmental testing centers, remediation companies, quality control laboratories, and other industrial facilities. In addition, Fisher Scientific represents its customers as a third-party purchaser of maintenance materials and other basic supplies. **Corporate headquarters location:** This location. **Other U.S. locations:** Tustin CA; Suwanee GA; Hanover Park IL; Houston TX. **International locations:** Worldwide. **Listed on:** New York Stock Exchange. **Stock exchange symbol:** FSH. **Annual sales/revenues:** More than $100 million. **Number of employees at this location:** 110. **Number of employees worldwide:** 10,000.

FOSS MANUFACTURING COMPANY, INC.
P.O. Box 5000, Hampton NH 03843-5000. 603/929-6000. **Physical address:** 380 Lafayette Road, Hampton NH 03842. **Toll-free phone:** 800/343-3277. **Fax:** 603/929-6189. **Contact:** Human Resources. **World Wide Web address:** http://www.fossmfg.com. **Description:** Foss Manufacturing is a vertically integrated producer of engineered fabrics. The Automotive Group supplies high-quality engineered fabric products and manufacturing strategies to original equipment manufacturers worldwide. **Corporate headquarters location:** This location. **Other U.S. locations:** Rancho Dominguez CA; Atlanta GA; Elkhart IN; Troy MI. **International locations:** Australia; England; France.

FOSTER'S DAILY DEMOCRAT
333 Central Avenue, Dover NH 03820. 603/742-4455. **Contact:** Human Resource. **World Wide Web address:** http://www4.fosters.com. **Description:** A newspaper publisher. **Positions advertised include:** Advertising Sales Representative. **Other area locations:** Rochester NH; Somersworth NH; Portsmouth NH; Exeter NH. **Other U.S. locations:** York ME. **Number of employees at this location:** 300.

FRANKLIN PIERCE COLLEGE
20 College Road, Rindge NH 03461-0060. 603/899-4000. **Toll-free phone:** 800/437-0048. **Fax:** 603/899-4326. **Contact:** John Mims, Director of Human Resources. **E-mail**

address: hr@fpc.efu. **World Wide Web address:** http://www.fpc.edu. **Description:** A private college offering bachelor of arts and bachelor of science degrees, as well as MBAs. Associate of arts degrees are awarded in the continuing education programs. **NOTE:** Entry-level positions are offered. Please visit website for online application form. **Positions advertised include:** Head Women's Golf Coach; Head Cheerleading Coach; Assistant Softball Coach; Dean of Undergraduate Studies; Director of Recreation; Adjunct Faculty – Various Locations; Assistant Professor – Various Departments; Application Analyst; Experience Director; Campus Safety Officer. **Operations at this facility include:** Administration; Education. **Annual sales/revenues:** $21 - $50 million. **Number of employees at this location:** 475.

FRANKLIN REGIONAL HOSPITAL
15 Aiken Avenue, Franklin NH 03235. 603/934-2060. **Fax:** 603/934-4616. **Contact:** Human Resources. **World Wide Web address:** http://www.frh.org. **Description:** A hospital. Established in 1910, Franklin Regional Hospital now employs over 300 employees. **Positions advertised include:** Environmental Services Aide; Clinical Nurse; Medical Transcriptionist; Health Unit Coordinator; Radiologic Technologist; Respiratory Therapist; Speech Language Pathologist. **NOTE:** For questions about employment, you may call 603/527-2872, or 603/524-3211 Ext. 3124.

FRISBIE MEMORIAL HOSPITAL
11 Whitehall Road, Rochester NH 03867-3439. 603/332-3100. **Fax:** 603/330-8975. **Contact:** Joe Wyman, Human Resources Department. **E-mail address:** j.wyman@fmhospital.com. **World Wide Web address:** http://www.frisbiehospital.com. **Description:** A 101-bed, acute care hospital. Frisbie is a nonprofit, community hospital that offers a broad range of services. The medical staff includes more than 140 physicians representing 28 specialties in addition to general practice. Founded in 1919. **NOTE:** Human Resources phone is 603/335-8169. Fax is 603/335-8882. **Positions advertised include:** Care Manager; Clinical Coordinator; Director of Radiology; Geriatric Psychiatrist; Medical Assistant; Nursing Care Technician; Office Nurse; Patient Account Clerk; Pharmacist; Phlebotomist; Respiratory Therapist; RN – Various Departments.

GARBER TRAVEL
111 Main Street, Nashua NH 03060. 603/883-1546. **Fax:** 603/883-4616. **Contact:** Paul Woods, Director of Human Resources. **E-mail address:** jobs@garbertravel.com. **World Wide Web address:** http://www.garber.com. **Description:** A travel agency. **NOTE:** Jobseekers should send resume or application form to: 27 Boylston Street, Chestnut Hill MA 02467. Please visit website to download application form. **Corporate headquarters location:** Chestnut Hill MA. **Other area locations:** Hanover NH; Manchester NH; Portsmouth NH. **Other U.S. locations:** CA; IL; VT; VA. **International locations:** Canada; United Kingdom. **President:** Roz Garber.

GENERAL CHEMICAL GROUP INC.
Liberty Lane, Hampton NH 03842. 603/929-2606. **Contact:** Human Resources Department. **E-mail address:** hrinfo@genchem.com. **World Wide Web address:** http://www.genchem.com. **Description:** Produces inorganic chemicals and soda ash. **NOTE:** Please send resumes, including salary history, to 90 East Halsey Road, Parsippany NJ 07054. **President/CEO:** John M. Kehoe, Jr.

GENERAL ELECTRIC COMPANY
130 Main Street, Somersworth NH 03878-3108. 603/692-2100. **Contact:** Human Resources. **World Wide Web address:** http://www.ge.com. **Description:** General Electric operates in the following areas: aircraft engines (jet engines, replacement parts, and repair services for commercial, military, executive, and commuter aircraft); appliances; broadcasting (NBC); industrial (lighting products, electrical distribution and control equipment, transportation systems products, electric motors and related products, a broad range of electrical and electronic industrial automation products, and a network of electrical supply houses); materials (plastics, ABS resins, silicones, superabrasives, and laminates); power systems (products for the generation, transmission, and distribution of electricity); technical products and systems (medical systems and equipment, as well as a full range of computer-based information and data interchange services for both internal use and external commercial and industrial customers); and capital services (consumer services, financing, and specialty insurance). **Corporate headquarters location:** Fairfield CT. **Operations at this facility include:** This location manufactures meters and transformers. **Listed on:** New York Stock Exchange. **Stock exchange symbol:** GE. **Number of employees worldwide:** 230,000.

GENERAL ELECTRIC COMPANY
AIRCRAFT ENGINE GROUP
31 Industrial Park Drive, Hooksett NH 03106. 603/666-8300. **Contact:** Human Resources. **World Wide Web address:** http://www.ge.com. **Description:** General Electric operates in the following areas: aircraft engines (jet engines, replacement parts, and repair services for commercial, military, executive, and commuter aircraft); appliances; broadcasting (NBC); industrial (lighting products, electrical distribution and control equipment, transportation systems products, electric motors and related products, a broad range of electrical and electronic industrial automation products, and a network of electrical supply houses); materials (plastics, ABS resins, silicones, superabrasives, and laminates); power systems (products for the generation, transmission, and distribution of electricity); technical products and systems (medical systems and equipment, as well as a full range of computer-based information and data interchange services for both internal use and external commercial and industrial customers); and capital services (consumer services, financing, and specialty insurance). **Corporate headquarters location:** Fairfield CT. **Operations at this facility include:** This location manufactures engines and engine parts. **Listed on:** New York Stock Exchange. **Stock exchange symbol:** GE. **Number of employees worldwide:** 230,000.

GRANITE STATE MANUFACTURING
124 Joliette Street, Manchester NH 03102. 603/668-1900. **Toll-free phone:** 800/GO-GSM-GO. **Fax:** 603/668-1906. **Contact:** Donna Losefsky, Human Resources Manager. **E-mail address:** ddlosefsky@gsmai.com. **World Wide Web address:** http://www.gsmai.com. **Description:** A contract manufacturer. Founded in 1938.

GRANITE SYSTEMS RESEARCH
1228 Elm Street, 5th Floor, Manchester NH 03101-1115. 603/625-0100. **Fax:** 603/625-4812. **Contact:** Human Resources. **E-mail address:** careers@granite.com. **World Wide Web address:** http://www.granite.com. **Description:** Develops network operations software including Xper. **Office hours:** Monday - Friday, 9:00 a.m. - 5:00 p.m. **Corporate headquarters location:** This location. **Other U.S. locations:** Denver CO; Miami FL. **International locations:** France; Germany; Italy; Singapore; United Kingdom. **Listed on:** Privately held. **President/CEO:** Jay Borden.

HACKETT HILL HEALTHCARE CENTER
191 Hackett Hill Road, Manchester NH 03102. 603/668-8161. **Fax:** 603/622-2584. **Contact:** Human Resources. **World Wide Web address:** http://www.thicare.com. **Description:** The Hackett Hill Healthcare Center is a housing facility for the care of elderly patients. Trans Healthcare Inc. is concerned with providing communities with quality services in the medical and healthcare industries. **Corporate headquarters location:** Sparks MD. **Parent company:** Trans Healthcare Inc.

ROBERT HALF TECHNOLOGY
1155 Elm Street, 7th floor, Manchester NH 03101. 603/647-6200. **Fax:** 603/641-8933. **Contact:** human resources. **E-mail address:** Manchester@roberthalftechnology.com. **World Wide Web address:** http://www.roberthalftechnology.com. **Description:** Provides staffing solutions to premier organizations worldwide that require technical expertise. Projects range from complex e-business and web development initiatives to enterprise wide application development and technical system support. **Positions advertised include:** Systems Administrator; Data Warehouse Developer; Access Developer; .net Developer, J2ee Developer.

HARVEY INDUSTRIES INC.
725 Huse Street, Manchester NH 03103. 603/669-2121. **Toll-free phone:** 800/562-6237. **Fax:** 603/669-9098. **Contact:** Shelley Holmes, Human Resources. **E-mail address:** jobs@harveyind.com. **World Wide Web address:** http://www.harveyind.com. **NOTE:** Please visit website for online application form. **Description:** Manufactures windows and doors. The company is also a wholesale distributor of building materials. **Positions advertised include:** First Shift Production Supervisor; Second Shift Production Supervisor; Administrative Clerk; Customer Service Representative; Inside Sales Representative; Second Shift Leadperson; Design Engineer – Windows and Doors. **Corporate headquarters location:** Waltham MA.

HEALTHSOUTH
254 Pleasant Street, Concord NH 03301-2551. 603/226-9800. **Fax:** 603/226-9808. **Contact:** Erika Pouliot, Human Resources. **E-mail address:** Erika.pouliot@healthsouth.com. **World Wide Web address:** http://www.healthsouth.com. **NOTE:** Please visit website for online application form. **Description:** An acute care rehabilitation center offering physical and occupational therapy services. HealthSouth also offers inpatient services. **Positions advertised include:** Physical Therapist. **Corporate headquarters location:** Birmingham AL. **Other U.S. locations:** Nationwide. **International locations:** Australia; Puerto Rico; United Kingdom. **Listed on:** OTC Pink Sheets. **Stock exchange symbol:** HLSH. **Number of employees at this location:** 200.

HEIDELBERG WEB SYSTEMS
121 Broadway, Dover NH 03820-3290. 603/749-6600. **Fax:** 603/749-3301. **Contact:** Human Resources. **World Wide Web address:** http://www.heidelberg.com. **Description:** Designs, manufactures, markets, installs, and services printing equipment worldwide for the printing and publishing industry. **Special programs:** Internships. **Corporate headquarters location:** Heidelberg Germany. **Parent company:** Heidelberg. **Operations at this facility include:** Administration; Manufacturing; Research and Development; Sales. **Number of employees at this location:** 850. **Number of employees nationwide:** 1,150. **Number of employees worldwide:** 23,400.

HENKEL LOCTITE
167 Batchelder Road, Seabrook NH 03874. 603/474-5541. **Contact:** Human Resources. **E-mail address:** hrclassifieds@loctite.com. **World Wide Web address:** http://www.loctite.com. **Description:** Produces wet formed nonwovens that are used for food packaging, medical, personal care, and specialized industrial applications. Products include tea and coffee filtration materials; medical fabrics including surgical apparel, face masks, and patient drapes; and carpet backing. **Parent company:** Henkel Loctite Corporation. **Number of employees at this location:** Approximately 100.

HITCHINER MANUFACTURING COMPANY, INC.
P.O. Box 2001, Milford NH 03055-2001. 603/673-1100. **Fax:** 603/672-0314. **Contact:** Human Resources. **E-mail address:** hr@hitchiner.com. **World Wide Web address:** http://www.hitchiner.com. **Description:** Manufactures investment castings. **NOTE:** Absolutely no phone calls regarding jobs. **Corporate headquarters location:** This location. **Other area locations:** Littleton NH. **Other U.S. locations:** O'Fallon MO. **International locations:** France; Mexico. **Operations at this facility include:** Manufacturing; Research and Development. **Number of employees at this location:** 500.

HITCHINER MANUFACTURING COMPANY, INC.
P.O. Box 679, Littleton NH 03561. 603/444-6304. **Contact:** Human Resources. **World Wide Web address:** http://www.hitchiner.com. **Description:** Manufactures investment castings. **NOTE:** Absolutely no phone calls regarding jobs. **Corporate headquarters location:** Milford NH. **Other U.S. locations:** O'Fallon MO. **International locations:** France; Mexico. **Operations at this facility include:** Manufacturing; Research and Development. **Number of employees at this location:** 500.

HOWTEK, INC.
4 Townsend West Suite 17, Nashua NH 03063. 603/882-5200. **Fax:** 603/880-3843. **World Wide Web address:** http://www.howtek.com. **Description:** Howtek, Inc. designs, engineers, and manufactures flatbed and drum scanners for the graphic arts and desktop publishing industries, densitometers for the life sciences industry, and film digitizers for the medical imaging industry. **NOTE:** Human Resources phone is 603/882-5200x204. **Corporate headquarters location:** This location. **Parent company:** iCAD, Inc. **Annual sales/revenues:** $11 - $20 million. **Number of employees at this location:** 65.

IMAGIC, INC.
235 West Road, Unit 7, Portsmouth NH 03801. 603/427-5544. **Toll-free phone:** 800/953-2459. **Contact:** Human Resources. **World Wide Web address:** http://www.imagic-inc.com. **Description:** A software and hardware engineering firm that develops products for factory automation, data acquisition, and microprocessor-based applications.

INFOR GLOBAL SOLUTIONS
500 Lafayette Road, Hampton NH 03842. 603/926-9696. **Fax:** 603/926-9698. **Contact:** Human Resources. **E-mail address:** hr@infor.com. **World Wide Web address:** http://www.infor.com. **Description:** Develops materials requirement planning (MRP) client/server software, called Visual Manufacturing, which allows managers to track all phases of production. **Positions advertised include:** Maintenance Programmer; Lead Generation Representative; Account Representative; Field Sales Representative. **Office hours:** Monday - Friday, 8:00 a.m. - 6:00 p.m. **Corporate headquarters location:** This location. **Other U.S. locations:** Miami FL; Minnetonka MN; Concord NC; Farmington NY; Bay Shore NY; Cuyahoga Falls OH; West Chester PA; Pleasant Grove UT. **International locations:** Worldwide. **President:** Richard T. Lilly.

INTERIM HEALTHCARE
PO Box 1780, 608 Chestnut Street, Manchester NH 03105. 603/668-6956. **Fax:** 603/668-6959. **Contact:** Human Resources. **World Wide Web address:**

http://www.interimhealthcare.com/newhampshire. **Description:** Provider of in-home health care. **Positions advertised include:** RN; LPN/LVN; Certified Nursing Assistants; Home Health Aides; Allied Health Professionals.

KANA COMMUNICATIONS
50 Phillipe Cote Street, Manchester NH 03101. 603/625-0070. **Fax:** 603/625-0428. **Contact:** Human Resources. **E-mail address:** jobs@kana.com. **World Wide Web address:** http://www.kana.com. **Description:** Develops and manufactures customer support software. **Positions advertised include:** Engineering Manager; Product Designer/Architect; Financial Services Industry Solutions Product Manager. **Corporate headquarters location:** Menlo Park CA. **Other U.S. locations:** Atlanta GA; Framingham MA; New York NY; Plano TX. **International locations:** Worldwide. **Listed on:** NASDAQ. **Stock exchange symbol:** KANA. **CEO:** Chuck Bay.

KEENE STATE COLLEGE
229 Main Street, Keene NH 03435. 603/352-1909. **Toll-free phone:** 800/572-1909. **Contact:** Catherine Greene, Human Resources Assistant. **E-mail address:** cgreene@keene.edu. **World Wide Web address:** http://www.keene.edu. **Description:** A four-year state college offering certificates, associate's, bachelor's, and master's degrees including an MBA. Approximately 3,500 undergraduate and 500 graduate students attend Keene State College. **NOTE:** Human Resources phone is 603/358-2485. **Positions advertised include:** Administrative Assistant; Accreditation and Assessment Coordinator; Demographic Data Processor; Funds and Stewardship Coordinator; Divisional Dean; Bursar; Tenure-track Positions – Various Departments.

KINGSBURY CORPORATION
80 Laurel Street, Keene NH 03431-4207. 603/352-5212. **Fax:** 603/352-8789. **Contact:** Human Resources. **World Wide Web address:** http://www.kingsburycorp.com. **Description:** Designs and manufactures special purpose, high-production metal cutting assembly equipment and machining centers. **NOTE:** Entry-level positions and second and third shifts are offered. **Positions advertised include:** Sales Agent; Direct Sales Agent; Mechanical Engineer; Senior Application-Proposal Engineer. **Corporate headquarters location:** This location. **Listed on:** Privately held. **Annual sales/revenues:** $51 - $100 million. **Number of employees at this location:** 280.

KOLLSMAN, INC.
220 Daniel Webster Highway, Merrimack NH 03054-4844. 603/889-2500. **Contact:** Human Resources. **E-mail address:** careers@kollsman.com. **World Wide Web address:** http://www.kollsman.com. **Description:** Designs and manufactures avionic flight instruments, high-tech weapons systems and subsystems, and diagnostic medical equipment. Founded in 1928. **Positions advertised include:** Senior Mechanical Engineer; Manager – Engineering; Program Manager – Head Up Displays; Chief Financial Officer; Principal Systems Engineer; Marketing/Business Development Manager; Software Engineer; Systems Engineer; Principal Electrical Engineer. **Corporate headquarters location:** This location. **Subsidiaries include:** KMC Systems, Inc. **Listed on:** Privately held. **President/CEO:** John S. Dehne. **Annual sales/revenues:** More than $100 million. **Number of employees at this location:** 600.

LACROSSE FOOTWEAR, INC.
401 Washington Street, Claremont NH 03743. 603/543-1266. **Contact:** Human Resources. **World Wide Web address:** http://www.lacrossefootwearinc.com. **Description:** LaCrosse Footwear, Inc. is a leading producer of premium quality protective footwear for the sporting, occupational, and recreational markets. The company markets its products primarily under the LaCrosse and Danner brands. Since 1897, the LaCrosse brand has specialized in hand-crafted rubber footwear. Danner provides a full line of hunting, hiking, and occupational leather footwear. **Corporate headquarters location:** Portland OR. **Operations at this facility include:** This location manufactures PVC footwear. Products include industrial and children's boots. **Listed on:** NASDAQ. **Stock exchange symbol:** BOOT. **Annual sales/revenues:** $51 - $100 million. **Number of employees at this location:** 185. **Number of employees nationwide:** 500.

LAKE SUNAPEE BANK
P.O. Box 29, Newport NH 03773. 603/863-0886. **Physical address:** 9 Main Street, Newport NH 03773. **Toll-free phone:** 800/281-5772 Ext. 6036. **Contact:** Fran Clow. **E-mail address:** fclow@lakesunbank.com. **World Wide Web address:** http://www.lakesunbank.com. **Description:** A federal savings bank providing financial services throughout central and western New Hampshire. **NOTE:** Please call to learn about current employment opportunities. **Other area locations:** Statewide. **Parent company:** New Hampshire Thrift Bancshares, Inc. **Listed on:** NASDAQ. **Stock exchange symbol:** NHTB.

LAW OFFICES OF WM. HOWARD DUNN
221 Broad Street, PO Box 676, Claremont NH 03743. 603/543-0111. **Fax:** 603/543-0604. **Contact:** Lisa Farley. **E-mail address:** ltemup@hotmail.com. **Description:** Provides local legal services. **Positions advertised include:** Legal Assistant/Secretary; Paralegal.

LOON MOUNTAIN RECREATION CORPORATION
Rural Route 1, Box 41, Kancamagus Highway, Lincoln NH 03251. 603/745-8111. **Toll-free phone:** 800/229-LOON. **Contact:** Human Resources. **E-mail address:** jobs.lm@boothcreek.com. **World Wide Web address:** http://www.loonmtn.com. **Description:** A ski resort. Off-season activities include biking, horseback riding, gondola rides, Mountain Man Tours, and numerous arts and crafts fairs. **NOTE:** Contact Human Resources at 603/745-6281 Ext. 5518 or 5575. Please visit website for online application form. **Positions advertised include:** Customer Service Representative; Ski Patrol Ambassador Coordinator; Lift Maintenance Mechanic; Business Plan Developer; F&B Line Worker; Cashier; Grounds and Parking Manager; Sales Manager; Equipment Rental Technician; Shuttle Bus Driver; Children Center Daycare Attendant; Children Center Ski and Snowboard Instructors; Ski and Snowboard Instructors; Custodian.

LUMINESCENT SYSTEMS INC. (LSI)
4 Lucent Drive, Lebanon NH 03766. 603/643-7766. **Fax:** 603/643-5947. **Contact:** Human Resources Director. **World Wide Web address:** http://www.lumsys.com. **Description:** Manufactures specialized lighting systems for aircraft and other applications. **Other U.S. locations:** Aurora NY. **International locations:** Quebec Canada; Bornem Belgium. **Parent company:** Astronics Corporation (Buffalo NY). **Listed on:** NASDAQ. **Stock exchange symbol:** ATRO.

MARKEM CORPORATION
P.O. Box 2100, Keene NH 03431. 603/352-1130. **Physical address:** 150 Congress Street, Keene NH 03431. **Toll-free phone:** 800/356-2375. **Fax:** 603/357-1835. **Contact:** Human Resources. **World Wide Web address:** http://www.markem.com. **Description:** An international firm providing complete specialty in-plant printing systems to industries throughout the world. Markem Corporation specializes in the design, manufacture, sale, and service of printing elements, various in-line and independent printing mechanisms, and accompanying chemical supplies. **Special programs:** Internships. **Other U.S. locations:** Reardan WA; San Jose CA. **International locations:** Worldwide. **Operations at this facility include:** Administration; Manufacturing; Research and Development; Sales; Service. **Number of employees nationwide:** 1,500.

MARKETING INITIATIVES
15 Constitution Drive, Suite 371, Bedford NH 03110. 603/645-6239. **Contact:** Human Resources. **World Wide Web address:** http://www.marketinginitiatives.com. **Description:** A marketing communications consulting group handling a broad range of clients. **Positions advertised include:** Data Warehouse Developer. **Parent company:** IMS Health. **CEO:** Thomas M. DiGiacinto.

McLANE, GRAF, RAULERSON & MIDDLETON, P.A.
P.O. Box 326, Manchester NH 03105-0326. 603/625-6464. **Fax:** 603/625-5650. **Physical address:** 900 Elm Street, Manchester NH 03105. **Contact:** Bettina Caminati, Recruitment Coordinator and Director of Human Resources. **E-mail address:** Bettina.caminati@mclane.com. **World Wide Web address:** http://www.mclane.com. **Description:** Provides statewide legal services. The practice is divided into various departments. The Corporate Department serves as counsel for national corporations headed within and outside of the state. The firm represents plaintiffs and defendants in state and federal courts. Plaintiff representation includes personal injury, medical negligence, product liability and commercial cases. Defense representation includes personal and corporate clients in civil rights, criminal defense, employment discrimination, and business litigation cases. Pro Bono work is also provided. The Commercial Lending & Real Estate Department represents banks and developers. The Trust and Estate and Tax Departments provide estate planning, corporate and individual tax planning, pension and profit sharing, corporate liquidations, mergers and acquisition representation. The Administrative Law and Environmental Practice Department provides guidance for clients through governmental regulations. Founded in 1920. **NOTE:** Entry-level positions are offered. **Positions advertised include:** Litigation Attorney; Tax Attorney. **Other area locations:** Concord NH; Portsmouth NH. **Special programs:** Summer jobs. **Office hours:** Monday - Friday, 8:30 a.m. - 5:00 p.m. **Corporate headquarters location:** This location. **Number of employees at this location:** 150. **Number of employees nationwide:** 170.

MICRONETICS
26 Hampshire Drive, Hudson NH 03051. 603/883-2900. **Fax:** 603/882-8987. **Contact:** Human Resources. **E-mail address:** marketing@micronetics.com. **World Wide Web Address:** http://www.micronetics.com. **Description:** Designs and manufactures Microwave RF building block components, integrated subassemblies, and test equipment used in defense, aerospace, and commercial applications. **Positions advertised include:** technical sales

MILLIPORE CORPORATION
11 Prescott Road, Jaffrey NH 03452. 603/532-8711. **Contact:** Susan Marble, Human Resources Manager. **World Wide Web address:** http://www.millipore.com. **NOTE:** Please visit website for online application form. **Description:** Millipore Corporation manufactures microporous filters and filtration devices used for the analysis, separation, and purification of fluids. Products are used in the fields of health care, pharmaceuticals, micro-electronics, biological sciences, and genetic engineering. **Positions advertised include:** Document Control Coordinator; Production Supervisor; Quality Supervisor; Finance Manager; Shipper/Receiver; Process Technician; Validation Engineer; Quality Assurance Inspector; HVAC Technician. **Office hours:** Monday – Thursday, 6:30 a.m. – 4:00p.m.; Friday, 6:30 a.m. – 3:00 p.m. **Corporate headquarters location:** Bellirica MA. **Operations at this facility include:** This location manufactures filtration devices for the pharmaceutical industry. **Listed on:** New York Stock Exchange. **Stock exchange symbol:** MIL. **Number of employees worldwide:** 4,200.

MOORE NORTH AMERICA
1050 Perimeter Road, Manchester NH 03103-3355. 603/314-5636. **Contact:** Human Resources Representative. **World Wide Web address:** http://www.moore.com. **Description:** Manufactures, assembles, and services forms-handling equipment. Moore also modifies forms-handling equipment for special applications. **Corporate headquarters location:** Toronto, Canada. **Other U.S. locations:** Stamford CT; Miami FL; Bannockburn IL; Columbia MD. **International locations:** Worldwide. **Operations at this facility include:** Administration; Divisional Headquarters; Manufacturing; Sales; Service. **Listed on:** New York Stock Exchange; Toronto Stock Exchange. **Stock exchange symbol:** MWI. **Number of employees at this location:** 220. **Number of employees nationwide:** 460.

MOUNT WASHINGTON OBSERVATORY
P.O. Box 2310, North Conway NH 03860. 603/356-2137. **Fax:** 603/356-0307. **Contact:** Human Resources. **World Wide Web address:** http://www.mountwashington.org. **Description:** A non-profit institution that maintains a permanently staffed observatory at the top of Mount Washington. Environmental and scientific research is continually conducted. **NOTE:** Volunteer positions also available. E-mail applications are preferred. **Special Programs:** Internships.

MUDDY MOOSE RESTAURANT AND PUB
2344 White Mountain Highway, North Conway NH 03860. 603/356-7696. **Fax:** 603/356-7702. **Contact:** Human Resources. **World Wide Web address:** http://www.muddymoose.com. **Description:** A rustic themed tourist restaurant.

NTP SOFTWARE
427 Amherst Street, Unit 381, Nashua NH 03063. 603/641-6937. **Fax:** 603/263-2375. **Contact:** Human Resources. **E-mail address:** employment@ntpsoftware.com. **World Wide Web address:** http://www.ntpsoftware.com. **Description:** Develops software products for Windows NT and UNIX add-ons, and also provides technology consulting and training. **Note:** Offers applications on website.

NASHUA CORPORATION
57 Daniel Webster Highway, Merrimack NH 03054. 603/880-1200. **Fax:** 603/880-1255. **Contact:** Human Resources. **World Wide Web address:** http://www.nashua.com. **NOTE:** Please visit website to view job listings by location. You may submit your resume directly to the Human Resources department of the location you are interested in. **Description:** Manufactures office supplies including thermal papers, specialty papers, and copier and printer supplies. **Corporate headquarters location:** Nashua NH. **Other U.S. locations:** IL; TN; NE; TX; CA; MO; MA. **International locations:** Mexico; Canada. **Operations at this facility include:** This location focuses on the company's toner products. **Listed on:** New York Stock Exchange. **Stock exchange symbol:** NSH. **President/CEO:** Andrew Albert.

NATIONAL GRANGE MUTUAL INSURANCE COMPANY
P.O. Box 2300, Keene NH 03431. 603/352-4000. **Physical address:** 55 West Street, Keene NH 03431. **Toll-free phone:** 800/258-5310. **Recorded jobline:** 866/MSA-

JOBS. **Contact:** Human Resources. **E-mail address:** ngmstaffing@msagroup.com. **World Wide Web address:** http://www.msagroup.com. **Description:** A full-service property and casualty company that writes all personal lines of insurance including homeowner and automotive, as well as a wide range of commercial products for the small business owner. National Grange Mutual Insurance Company markets these products over a 14-state area in the Northeast through 700 independent insurance agents. **NOTE:** You can contact Human Resources individuals directly by calling the recorded jobline. Please visit the website for the online application form. **Positions advertised include:** Associate Computer Operator; Business Systems Analyst; Commercial Lines Underwriting Assistant; Customer Service Representative; Data Analyst; Field Trial Attorney; Lead Testing Analyst; Manager, Organized Development; Senior Applications Programmer; Senior Business Systems Analyst. **Corporate headquarters location:** This location. **Other U.S. locations:** Nationwide. **Subsidiaries include:** MSA Group. **Operations at this facility include:** Administration; Service. **CEO:** Tom Van Berkel.

NEW ENGLAND BUSINESS SERVICE INC. (NEBS)
49 Vose Farm Road, Peterborough NH 03458. 603/924-7201. **Contact:** Human Resources. **World Wide Web address:** http://www.nebs.com. **Description:** New England Business Service is a supplier of business forms and software for small businesses. The company's product line consists of over 1,000 standardized, imprinted manual and computer business forms including billing forms, work orders, job proposals, and purchase orders; stationery including letterhead, envelopes, and business cards; checks and check-writing systems; and marketing products including advertising labels, pricing tags and labels, signage, and seasonal greeting cards. The company offers a line of NEBS software, which includes check-writing, billing, and mailing applications, as well as a variety of simpler form-filling software; and One-Write Plus, a line of accounting software that integrates accounting and payroll functions with basic word processing, mail merge, a spreadsheet link, a backup utility, and a menu organizer. **NOTE:** Visit http://www.nebscareers.com to view information on careers at New England Business Service Inc. There is also an online application form available at this website. **Corporate headquarters location:** Groton MA. **Other U.S. locations:** Flagstaff AZ; Sudbury MA; Townsend MA; Woburn MA; Maryville MO. **International locations:** Canada; England; France. **Subsidiaries include:** Chiswick Trading, Inc.; McBee Systems, Inc.; PremiumWear, Inc.; Rapidforms, Inc.; Standard Forms, Ltd. **Operations at this facility include:** Telemarketing; Printing. **Listed on:** New York Stock Exchange. **Stock exchange symbol:** NEB. **CEO:** Richard T. Riley. **Number of employees nationwide:** 3,700.

NEW ENGLAND HOMES INC.
270 Ocean Road, Greenland NH 03840. 603/436-8830. **Toll-free phone:** 800/800-8831. **Fax:** 603/431-8540. **Contact:** Human Resources. **World Wide Web address:** http://www.newenglandhomes.net. **Description:** A manufacturer of modular homes. **NOTE:** Please visit website to fill out online application form. **Positions advertised include:** Roofer; Framer; CDL-A Driver; Field Set Crew; Entry Level Sales; Estimator. **Number of employees at this location:** 120.

NEW HAMPSHIRE CORRECTIONAL INDUSTRIES
P.O. Box 14, Concord NH 03302-0014. 603/271-1875. **Physical address:** 281 North State Street, Concord NH 03302. **Fax:** 603/271-1116. **Contact:** Human Resources. **World Wide Web address:** http://www.state.nh.us/nhci. **Description:** Located at New Hampshire State Prison, New Hampshire Correctional Industries educates and trains inmates. It offers a number of school and vocational training courses to prepare inmates for work upon release. **Number of employees at this location:** 500.

NEW HAMPSHIRE TECHNICAL INSTITUTE
31 College Drive, Concord NH 03301-7412. 603/271-6484. **Fax:** 603/271-7734. **Contact:** Kilee Douglass, Human Resources. **E-mail address:** kdouglass@nhctc.edu. **World Wide Web address:** http://www.nhti.net. **Description:** A technical college. The largest programs at NHTI include nursing and engineering. Other courses of study include computer science, early childhood education, human services, and criminal justice. **NOTE:** Contact Human Resources directly at 603/271-7731. The state of New Hampshire requires an application to be filled out for any of these positions; a resume cannot be submitted instead of an application. Please visit website to download the application and to see more details on applying. **Positions advertised include:** Part-time Instructors – Various Departments; Adjunct Instructor – Various Departments; Tutor – Various Departments. **Special programs:** Internships. **Number of employees at this location:** 150.

NEW HAMPSHIRE VOCATIONAL REHABILITATION OFFICE DEPARTMENT OF EDUCATION
78 Regional Drive, Building 2, Concord NH 03301. 603/271-3471. **Toll-free phone:** 800/339-9900. **Fax:** 603/271-7095. **Contact:** Human Resources. **World Wide Web address:** http://www.ed.state.nh.us/VR. **Description:** Assists disabled persons in obtaining or maintaining employment. **Office hours:** Monday 0 Friday, 8:00 a.m. – 4:30 p.m. **Corporate headquarters location:** This location. **Other U.S. locations:** Berlin NH; Keene NH; Lebanon NH; Manchester NH; Nashua NH; Portsmouth NH.

NEW LONDON HOSPITAL
273 County Road, New London NH 03257. 603/526-2911. **Fax:** 603/526-5150. **Contact:** Shari Phetteplace, Human Resources Assistant. **E-mail address:** shari.phetteplace@nlh.crhm.org. **World Wide Web address:** http://newlondonhospital.org. **Description:** A community based, full service hospital. Founded in 1918. **NOTE:** Human Resources phone is 603/526-5307. Please apply through website. Volunteer positions are also available. **Positions advertised include:** Child Care Assistant; Controller; Courier; Emergency Department Staff RN; Financial Analyst; LNA; Night Nursing Supervisor; Occupational Therapist; Certified Surgical Tech; Physical Therapist; Respiratory Therapist; Staff Radiographer. **CEO:** Bruce King.

NINETY-NINE RESTAURANT AND PUB
1308 Hooksett Road, Hooksett NH 03106. 603/641-2999. **Fax:** 603/641-2263. **Contact:** General Manager. **World Wide Web address:** http://www.99restaurants.com. **Description:** A chain restaurant serving moderately priced American food. **Positions advertised include:** Assistant Kitchen Manager; Kitchen Manager; Assistant Manager; General Managing Partner; Dishwasher; Food Server; Prep Cook; Host; Line Cook; Bartender; First Cook; Busser. **NOTE:** Please contact location to learn more about immediate openings. **Corporate headquarters location:** Woburn MA.

NIXON PEABODY LLP
889 Elm Street, Manchester NH 03101. 603/628-4000. **Fax**: 603/628-4040. **Contact**: Human Resources. **World Wide Web Address**: www.nixonpeabody.com. **Description**: Nixon Peabody is one of the largest multipractice law firms in the United States, with offices in fourteen cities and more than six hundred attorneys collaborating across fifteen major practice areas. **Positions Advertised Include**: Attorneys, Collections Clerk, Paralegal

NORMANDEAU ASSOCIATES, INC.
25 Nashua Road, Bedford NH 03110-5500. 603/472-5191. **Fax:** 603/472-7052. **Contact:** Human Resources. **World Wide Web address:** http://www.normandeau.com. **Description:** An environmental consulting company specializing in wetland studies, air quality control, and hydrogeology. Founded in 1970. **NOTE:** Human Resources fax is 603/471-0874. **Corporate headquarters location:** This location. **Other area locations:** Hampton NH; Westmoreland NH. **Other U.S. locations:** Norfolk CT; Yarmouth ME; Plymouth MA; Point Pleasant Beach NJ; Peekskill NY; Spring City PA; Aiken SC; Lewes DE; Stevenson WA; WI. **Number of employees at this location:** 180.

NORTHEAST REHABILITATION HEALTH NETWORK
70 Butler Street, Salem NH 03079. 603/893-2900. **Fax:** 603/893-9625. **Contact:** Human Resources. **E-mail address:** jobs@northeastrehab.com. **World Wide Web address:** http://www.northeastrehab.com. **Description:** A rehabilitation hospital. Northeast Rehabilitation Hospital has both inpatient and outpatient services including acute physical rehabilitation, physical therapy, and occupational therapy. **NOTE:** Human Resources Extension is 444. **Positions advertised include:** Certified Hand Therapist; Cold Production Worker; Food and Nutritionist; Housekeeping Associate; Laundry Associate; LNA; Nursing Supervisor; Patients Account Representative; Physical Therapy Assistant; Physical Therapist; Respiratory Therapist; RN; Speech Language Pathologist. **Other U.S. locations:** MA. **Number of employees at this location:** 460.

NORTHERN FOREST HERITAGE PARK
961 Main Street, Berlin NH 03570. 603/752-7202. **Fax:** 603/752-7222. **Contact:** Human Resources Department. **E-mail address:** heritage@ncia.net. **World Wide Web address:** http://www.northernforestheritage.org. **Description:** An on-site logging museum with plans to open an authentic logging camp and hands-on exhibits for tourists. Founded in 1996. **NOTE:** The Park is open May through October.

NORTHERN UTILITIES
325 West Road, Portsmouth NH 03801. 603/436-0310. **Contact:** Human Resources. **World Wide Web address:** http://www.northernutilities.com. **Description:** An energy services company that provides natural gas to approximately 46,000 customers in New Hampshire and Maine. **Parent company:** NiSource Inc. **Number of employees nationwide:** 130.

NOYES FIBER SYSTEMS
16 Eastgate Park Road, Belmont NH 03220. 603/528-7780. **Contact:** Human Resources. **World Wide Web address:** http://www.alcoa.com. **NOTE:** You must register an e-mail address and password online to apply for jobs. **Description:** Designs and manufactures fiber-optic test equipment. Founded in 1987. **Positions advertised include:** Software Engineer – Embedded; Software Engineer – Visual Basic. **Special programs:** Internships; Co-ops. **Corporate headquarters location:** This location. **Other U.S. locations:** Nationwide. **International locations:** England; Hong Kong. **Parent company:** Alcoa FujiKura, Ltd. **Listed on:** Privately held. **Number of employees at this location:** 55.

OASIS IMAGING PRODUCTS
460 Amherst Street, Nashua NH 03063. 603/880-3991. **Toll-free phone:** 888/627-6555. **Fax:** 603/598-4277. **Contact:** Nancy Boisvert, Human Resources. **E-mail address:** nlb@oasis-imaging.com. **World Wide Web address:** http://www.oasis-imaging.com. **Description:** Repairs Canon and IBM bubble-jet printers. **Corporate headquarters location:** This location. **Other U.S. locations:** Orange CA; Oak Brook IL; Sanford NC; Memphis TN; Richardson TX. **International locations:** Netherlands; Canada.

OCEAN NATIONAL
P.O. Box 627, Keene NH 03431-0627. 603/352-1600. **Physical address:** 122 West Street, Keene NH 03431. **Toll-free phone:** 800/922-0051. **Fax:** 603/358-5707. **Contact:** Human Resources. **E-mail address:** jobs@eocean.com. **World Wide Web address:** http://www.eocean.com. **Description:** A full-service community bank with a diversified lending operation that services Cheshire, Sullivan, Hillsborough, Strafford, and Rockingham counties through eight full-service offices. Founded in 1895. **Other area locations:** Statewide. **Parent company:** Chittenden Corporation. **Operations at this facility include:** Administration; Sales; Service. **Listed on:** New York Stock Exchange. **Stock exchange symbol:** CHZ. **Number of employees at this location:** 75. **Number of employees nationwide:** 170.

OCEAN NATIONAL
35 Main Street; Peterborough NH 03458. 603/924-7111. **Contact:** Human Resources. **E-mail address:** jobs@ecean.com. **World Wide Web address:** http://www.eocean.com. **Description:** A full-service community bank with a diversified lending operation that services Cheshire, Sullivan, Hillsborough, Strafford, and Rockingham Counties through eight full-service offices. **Office hours:** Monday – Friday 8:30 a.m. – 5:00 p.m. **Other area locations:** Statewide. **Parent company:** Chittenden Corporation. **Operations at this facility include:** Administration; Sales; Service. **Listed on:** New York Stock Exchange. **Stock exchange symbol:** CHZ. **Number of employees at this location:** 75. **Number of employees nationwide:** 170.

OLIVE GARDEN ITALIAN RESTAURANT
219 Loudon Road, Concord NH 03301. 603/228-6886. **Fax:** 603/223-0871. **Contact:** Mark Connelly, General Manager. **World Wide Web address:** http://www.olivegarden.com. **Description:** One location of a chain of family-style Italian restaurants. **Positions advertised include:** Host; Server; Bartender; Line Cook; Preparation Cook; Alley Coordinator; Busser; Dishwasher. **Parent company:** Darden Restaurants.

OMTOOL
8A Industrial Way, Salem NH 03079. 603/898-8900. **Fax:** 603/890-6756. **Contact:** Human Resources. **E-mail address:** jobs@omtool.com. **World Wide Web address:** http://www.omtool.com. **Description:** Develops client/server software solutions serving the network fax, document management, and workgroup markets. **Positions advertised include:** Territory Sales Manager. **Corporate headquarters location:** This location. **Other U.S. locations:** Beaverton OR. **International locations:** England. **Listed on:** NASDAQ. **Stock exchange symbol:** OMTL.

ORACLE
One Oracle Drive, Nashua NH 03062. 603/897-3000. **Fax:** 603/897-3300. **Contact:** Personnel. **World Wide Web address:** http://www.oracle.com. **Description:** Oracle is a global IT organization, providing databases, applications, and development tools to business throughout the world. **Other U.S. locations:** Nationwide. **International locations:** Worldwide.

OSRAM-SYLVANIA, INC.
Portsmouth Avenue, Exeter NH 03833. 603/772-4331. **Fax:** 603/772-2072. **Contact:** Human Resources. **World Wide Web address:** http://www.sylvania.com. **Description:** OSRAM-SYLVANIA, Inc. operates in the following divisions: Coated Coil Operation, which involves the production of tungsten filaments coated with high-performance insulator aluminum oxide used in television electron guns; Special Refractory Products, which manufactures products made from refractory metals that are used as furnace hardware; the Ceramics Department, which produces various types of steatite ceramic electrical insulators used in bases of light bulbs; and the Quartz Department, which produces and finishes quartz crucibles for use by the semiconductor industry. **Corporate headquarters location:** Danvers MA. **Other area locations:** Hillsboro NH. **Other U.S. locations:** Nationwide. **International locations:** Worldwide. **Operations at this facility include:** Glass technologies headquarters. **Parent company:** OSRAM. **President:** Charlie Jerabek. **Number of employees worldwide:** 27,000.

OWENS-ILLINOIS
One Cellu Drive, Nashua NH 03063. 603/889-2000. **Contact:** Human Resources Manager. **World Wide Web address:** http://www.o-i.com. **Description:** Owens-Illinois produces and sells containerboard, corrugated containers, printing plates and ink, plywood and dimension lumber, blown plastic containers, plastic beverage bottles, plastic drums, metal and plastic closures, tamper-resistant closures, plastic and glass prescription containers, pharmaceutical items, labels, and multipack plastic carriers for containers. Specialized glass products made and sold by the company include Libbey Tumblers, stemware, and decorative glassware; television bulbs for picture tubes; and Kimble scientific and laboratory ware. **Corporate headquarters location:** Toledo OH. **Other U.S. locations:** Nationwide. **Operations at this facility include:** This location manufactures plastic bottles, vials, and caps. **Listed on:** New York Stock Exchange. **Stock exchange symbol:** OI.

OXFORD HEALTH PLANS, INC.
10 Tara Boulevard, Nashua NH 03062. 603/891-7000. **Contact:** Human Resources. **World Wide Web address:** http://www.oxhp.com. **Description:** Oxford Health Plans is a managed care company providing health benefit plans in New Hampshire, New York, New Jersey, and Connecticut. Oxford's product lines include traditional health maintenance organizations, a point-of-service Freedom Plan, third-party administration of employer funded benefit plans, Medicare and Medicaid plans, and dental plans. Oxford markets its health plans to employers and individuals through its direct sales force and through independent insurance agents and brokers. **NOTE:** Please visit website for online application form. **Corporate headquarters location:** Trumbull CT. **Other area locations:** Hooksett NH. **Other U.S. locations:** Iselin NJ; White Plains NY. **Listed on:** New York Stock Exchange. **Stock exchange symbol:** OHP.

PC CONNECTION
730 Milford Road, Merrimack NH 03054. 603/446-3383. **Toll-free phone:** 888/213-0260. **Contact:** Human Resources. **World Wide Web address:** http://www.pcconnection.com. **Description:** A mail-order retailer of PCs and computer peripheral equipment. **NOTE:** Please visit website for online application form. **Positions advertised include:** Senior Web Developer; Technical Architect; Account Manager. **Corporate headquarters location:** This location. **Other area locations:** Dover NH; Keene NH. **Other U.S. locations:** Marlborough MA; Fairfield CT; Rockville MD; Boca Raton FL. **Listed on:** NASDAQ. **Stock exchange symbol:** PCCC. **Number of employees nationwide:** 1,300.

L.W. PACKARD & COMPANY
P.O. Box 515, Ashland NH 03217. 603/968-3351. **Physical address:** 6 Mill Street, Ashland NH 03217. **Fax:** 603/968-7649. **Contact:** Human Resources. **E-mail address:** info@lwpackard.com. **World Wide Web address:** http://www.lwpackard.com. **Description:** Manufactures woolen fabric for the apparel industry. L.W. Packard's manufacturing processes include blending, carding, rewinding, spinning, and weaving. **Special programs:** Internships. **Corporate headquarters location:** This location. **Operations at this facility include:** Administration; Manufacturing; Research and Development. **Listed on:** Privately held. **Number of employees at this location:** 300.

PAGE BELTING COMPANY, INC.
24 Chenell Drive, Concord NH 03301. 603/225-5523. **Toll-free phone:** 800/258-3654. **Fax:** 603/226-2790. **Contact:** Mark Coen, President. **E-mail address:** info@pagebelting.com. **World Wide Web address:** http://www.pagebelting.com. **Description:** A manufacturer of leather and polyurethane products. Products include pouches, cases, and toolholders. Page also manufactures transmission belting and conveyor belts. Founded 1868. **Number of employees at this location:** 40.

PARKER CHOMERICS
16 Flagstone Drive, Hudson NH 03051. 603/880-4807. **Contact:** Human Resources. **Description:** Manufactures thermally-conducive materials and specialty laminates. **Positions advertised include:** Maintenance Mechanic; Process Engineer. **Corporate headquarters location:** Woburn MA. **Other U.S. locations:** Nationwide. **Parent company:** Parker Hannifin Corporation.

PARKLAND MEDICAL CENTER
One Parkland Drive, Derry NH 03038. 603/432-1500. **Fax:** 603/421-2074. **Recorded jobline:** 603/432-1500 Ext. 4400. **Contact:** Human Resources. **World Wide Web address:** http://www.parklandmedicalcenter.com. **Description:** A Hospital. **NOTE:** Volunteer positions also available. Please visit website for online application form. You must register before applying online. Contact Human Resources directly at 603/421-2070. **Positions advertised include:** Administrative Nursing Supervisor; Admissions Nurse; Case Manager; Floor Tech; Medical Staff Manager; Medical Technologist; Quality Coordinator; Radiology Technologist; Registered Dietician; RN – Various Departments; Speech Pathologist; Staff Physical Therapist; Surgical Tech; Switchboard Operator. **Number of employees at this location:** 800.

PENNICHUCK CORPORATION
PENNICHUCK WATER WORKS, INC.
25 Manchester Street, PO Box 1947, Merrimack NH 03054. 603/882-5191. **Toll-free phone:** 800/553-5191. **Fax:** 603/882-4125. **Contact:** Human Resources. **E-mail address:** hr@pennichuck.com. **World Wide Web address:** http://www.pennichuck.com. **Description:** A holding company. **Corporate headquarters location:** This location. **Subsidiaries include:** Pennichuck Water Works, Inc. collects, distributes, and supplies water for domestic, commercial, industrial, and fire protection purposes for Nashua and southern New Hampshire. The Southwood Corporation is a commercial and residential real estate development company with land holdings in Nashua and Merrimack. **Listed on:** NASDAQ. **Stock exchange symbol:** PNNW.

PIKE INDUSTRIES
650 Peverly Hill Road, Portsmouth NH 03802. 603/436-4432. **Fax:** 603/527-5101. **Contact:** Fran Prentice, Human Resources. **E-mail address:** fprentice@pikeindustries.com. **World Wide Web address:** http://www.pikeindustries.com. **Description:** A road paving and construction firm. Pike Industries also sells aggregates and loam. **NOTE:** Please visit website for online application form. **Corporate headquarters location:** Belmont NH. **Other area locations:** Statewide. **Other U.S. locations:** ME; MA; RI; VT.

PINKERTON ACADEMY
5 Pinkerton Street, Derry NH 03038. 603/437-5200. **Contact:** Marie Rogers, Director of Human Resources. **E-mail address:** marierogers@pinkertonacademy.org. **World Wide Web address:** http://www.mv.com/ipusers/pinkerton. **Description:** A private, regional high school serving students from the towns of Derry, Hampstead, and Chester. **NOTE:** Contact Human Resources directly at 603/437-5222 Ext. 3110. NH Certification or Certifiability required for all teaching positions. Please see website for more details on applying for specific positions. **Number of employees at this location:** 175.

PITCO MAGIKITCH'N
Route 3A, Bow NH 03304. 603/225-6684. **Toll-free phone:** 800/258-3708. **Fax:** 603/225-8472. **Contact:** Human Resources. **World Wide Web address:** http://www.blodgett.com. **Description:** A manufacturer of commercial cooking equipment. **Office hours:** Monday - Friday, 8:00 a.m. - 5:00 p.m. **Corporate headquarters location:** Burlington VT. **Parent company:** G. S. Blodgett Corporation. **Operations at this facility include:** Administration; Manufacturing; Research and Development; Sales; Service. **Annual sales/revenues:** $51 - $100 million. **Number of employees at this location:** 325.

PRECISION TECHNOLOGIES
39 Sheep Davis Road, Pembroke NH 03275. 603/225-7717. **Toll-free phone:** 800/362-7717. **Fax:** 603/225-7480. **Contact:** Cathy Lewis, Director of Human Resources. **World Wide Web address:** http://www.precisiontechnology.com. **Description:** Performs all varieties of printing services including printing, binding, scoring, and folding. Its direct mailing division, Spectrum Direct, does mailings for AT&T, Nynex, American Express, Pepsi, and others. **Number of employees at this location:** 400.

PRESIDENTIAL OAKS
200 Pleasant Street, Concord NH 03301-2599. 603/225-6644. **Toll-free phone:** 800/678-1333. **Contact:** Human Resources. **E-mail address:** jobs@presidentialoaks.com. **World Wide Web address:** http://www.presidentialoaks.org. **Description:** A home for the aged. Presidential Oaks offers three levels of care: independent living, supported residential care, and nursing care. **Positions advertised include:** MDS Coordinator. **NOTE:** Employee inquiries dial Ext. 106. **Number of employees at this location:** 200.

PRESSTEK
55 Executive Drive, Hudson NH 03051. 603/595-7000. **Fax:** 603/594-8575. **Contact:** Human Resources Manager. **E-mail address:** humanresources@presstek.com. **World Wide Web address:** http://www.presstek.com. **Description:** PRESSTEK develops, manufactures, markets, and services products utilizing its proprietary, nonphotographic, digital imaging technologies, system architectures, and consumables used primarily in the graphic arts and related imaging industries. Founded in 1987. **NOTE:** Human Resources phone is 603/594-8585. **Positions advertised include:** Logistics Coordinator; Regional Sales Manager – Midwest. **Corporate headquarters location:** This location. **Operations at this facility include:** Administration; Manufacturing; Research and Development; Sales; Service. **Listed on:** NASDAQ. **Stock exchange symbol:** PRST. **CEO:** Edward J. Marino. **Number of employees at this location:** 85.

PROFITKEY INTERNATIONAL, INC.
2 Keywaydin Street, Salem NH 03079. 603/898-9800. **Fax:** 603/898-7554. **Contact:** Human Resources. **E-mail address:** pkjobs@profitkey.com. **World Wide Web address:** http://www.profitkey.com. **Description:** A leader in the advanced planning and scheduling industry, providing manufacturers with real-time ERP systems. ProfitKey International markets Rapid Response Manufacturing Client/Server, a graphical 32-bit application. **NOTE:** Part-time jobs are offered. **Special programs:** Co-ops. **Corporate headquarters location:** This location. **Other U.S. locations:** Nationwide. **Parent company:** Platinum Equity Holdings. **Listed on:** Privately held. **Number of employees at this location:** 45.

PUBLIC SERVICE OF NEW HAMPSHIRE
P.O. Box 330, Manchester NH 03105. 603/669-4000. **Toll-free phone:** 800/662-7764. **Contact:** Elaine Dame, Human Resources. **E-mail address:** dameem@psnh.com. **World Wide Web address:** http://www.psnh.com. **Description:** The largest electrical utility in the state, supplying electricity to approximately three quarters of the population in New Hampshire. **Positions advertised include:** Assistant/Associate Engineer; Senior Engineer; Customer Service Center Representative; Field Technician Specialist; Relay Technician; Working Foreman; System Electrician. **Special programs:** Internships. **Other area locations:** Statewide. **Parent company:** Northeast Utilities. **Number of employees nationwide:** 1,200.

RDF CORPORATION
23 Elm Avenue, Hudson NH 03051-0490. 603/882-5195. **Toll-free phone:** 800/445-8367. **Contact:** Human Resources. **World Wide Web address:** http://www.rdfcorp.com. **Description:** RDF Corporation is an ISO certified producer of engineering-oriented temperature instrumentation and components for aircraft, military, aerospace, and nuclear applications. **NOTE:** Entry-level positions are offered. **Annual sales/revenues:** $5 - $10 million. **Number of employees at this location:** 90.

RMC RESEARCH CORPORATION
1000 Market Street, Portsmouth NH 03801. 603/422-8888. **Toll-free phone:** 800/258-0802. **Fax:** 603/436-9166. **Contact:** Human Research. **E-mail address:** rmc@rmcres.com. **World Wide Web address:** http://www.rmcres.com. **Description:** An educational research firm. RMC works with Chapter 1, Title 1, Head Start, and Even Start programs. **Other U.S. locations:** Denver CO; Portland OR; Arlington VA.

RVSI
486 Amherst Street, Nashua NH 03063. 603/598-8400. **Toll-free phone:** 800/729-9888. **Contact:** Human Resources. **World Wide Web address:** http://www.rvsi.com. **Description:** RVSI manufactures and markets machine vision systems that help to automate industrial applications by emulating human sight. These systems measure, determine presence, detect flaws, read and verify characters, determine product location to control motion, and inspect products for imperfections. These products and systems are commonly used in discrete part manufacturing and in the pharmaceutical and semiconductor industries. Founded in 1994. **NOTE:** No phone calls regarding employment. **Listed on:** NASDAQ. **Stock exchange symbol:** RVSI.PK.

RAGGED MOUNTAIN RESORT
620 Ragged Mountain Road, Danbury NH 03230. 603/768-3600. **Fax:** 603/768-3929. **Contact:** Human Resources. **E-mail address:** ragged@ragged-mt.com. **World Wide**

Web address: http://www.ragged-mt.com. **Description:** A four season ski and golf resort.

RIVIER COLLEGE
420 South Main Street, Nashua NH 03060-5086. 603/888-1311. **Toll-free phone:** 800/44-RIVIER. **Fax:** 603/897-8883. **Contact:** Gail M. Galipeau, Human Resources Coordinator. **E-mail address:** hr@rivier.edu. **World Wide Web address:** http://www.rivier.edu. **Description:** A college. **NOTE:** Human Resources phone is 603/897-8211. **Positions advertised include:** Assistant Professor – Various Departments; Chairperson – Nursing and Health Sciences; Clinical Adjunct – Nursing Faculty.

RIVERBEND COMMUNITY MENTAL HEALTH
P.O. Box 2032, Concord NH 03302-2032. 603/228-1551. **Contact:** Human Resources. **E-mail address:** hr@riverbendcmhc.org. **World Wide Web address:** http://www.riverbendcmhc.org. **Description:** An organization providing outpatient, group, and family therapy; case management; psychiatric treatment; 24-hour emergency and assessment services; a crisis intervention program; and supervised residential living. Founded in 1963. **NOTE:** Entry-level positions and second and third shifts are offered. **Positions advertised include:** Residential Rehabilitation Specialist; Children's Respite Care; Psychiatric Rehabilitation Case Manager; Emergency Service Clinician; Internship Director/Child Clinical Psychologist; Child and Family Therapist; Custodian; Admissions Clinical Coordinator; Clinician; Intensive Case Manager; Child and Family Therapist; Admissions Coordinator; Family Support Therapist; Residential Rehabilitation Specialist – Part-time; Substitute Van Driver – Part-time; LPN – Part-time. **NOTE:** Volunteer positions are also available. Please visit website for online application form. **Special programs:** Internships; Training. **Office hours:** Monday - Friday, 8:00 a.m. - 5:00 p.m. **Corporate headquarters location:** This location. **Other area locations:** Franklin NH; Henniker NH; Hillsboro NH. **President:** Dale K. Klatzker. **Annual sales/revenues:** $11 - $20 million. **Number of employees at this location:** 250.

SACO RIVER MEDICAL GROUP
7 Greenwood Avenue, P.O. Box 2679, Conway NH 03818. 603/447-3500. **Fax:** 603/447-5568. **Contact:** Human Resources. **World Wide Web address:** http://www.sacodocs.com. **Description:** An independent medical office that provides general practice, pediatrics, walk-in, gynecology, counseling, and acupuncture services. **Office hours:** Monday – Friday, 8:30 a.m. – 4:30 p.m.

SAINT-GOBAIN
P.O. Box 1137, Merrimack NH 03054. 603/424-9000. **Physical Address:** 701 Daniel Webster Highway, Merrimack NH 03054. **Fax:** 603/424-9012. **Contact:** Human Resources. **World Wide Web address:** http://www.saint-gobain.com/en/html. **Description:** Saint-Gobain is an international company that develops, manufactures, and markets polymer-based engineered products and materials systems for use in severe service environments. Products typically consist of fiber-reinforced flexible composites coated or laminated with fluoropolymers and specialty fluoropolymer films. **NOTE:** Please visit website for online application form. **Special programs:** Internships. **Other U.S. locations:** Nationwide. **International locations:** Worldwide. **Number of employees worldwide:** 172,000.

ST. ANSELM COLLEGE
100 Saint Anselm Drive, Manchester NH 03102. 603/641-7000. **Fax:** 603/222-4014. **Contact:** Human Resources Director. **E-mail address:** hr@anselm.edu. **World Wide Web address:** http://www.anselm.edu. **Description:** A four-year, coeducational, Catholic, liberal arts college. Approximately 1,850 full-time students are enrolled in 27 majors offered, in addition to professional and cooperative engineering programs. Saint Anselm College is accredited by the New England Association of Schools and Colleges. In recent years, *U.S. News and World Report* has ranked Saint Anselm among the top 10 liberal arts colleges in the Northeast. Founded in 1889. **NOTE:** Human Resources phone is 603/641-7020. **Positions advertised include:** Administrative Assistant; Chair/Director – Department of Nursing; Line Server/Cashier.

ST. MARY'S BANK
P.O. Box 990, Manchester NH 03105-0990. 603/669-4600. **Physical address:** 200 McGregor Street, Manchester NH 03102. **Fax:** 603/629-1592. **Contact:** Human Resources. **E-mail address:** hr@stmarysbank.com. **World Wide Web address:** http://www.stmarysbank.com. **Description:** A full-service bank with both business and personal banking services. **Positions advertised include:** Branch Sales and Service Counselor; Credit Analyst; Credit Investigator; Member Call Center Representative; Mortgage Loan Originator. **Office hours:** Monday – Friday, 9:00 a.m. – 5:00 p.m.; Saturday, 9:00 a.m. – 12:30 p.m. **Number of employees at this location:** 145.

ST. PAUL'S SCHOOL
325 Pleasant Street, Concord NH 03301. 603/229-4600. **Fax:** 603/229-4761. **Contact:** Human Resources. **E-mail address:** allhr@sps.edu. **World Wide Web address:** http://www.sps.edu. **Description:** A private, college preparatory school. **NOTE:** Human Resources phone is 603/229-4640. **Positions advertised include:** Humanities Teacher; Ballet Director; Biology Teacher; Classroom Assistant/Long-term Substitute, Infant/Toddler Classroom.

ST. VINCENT DE PAUL NURSING HOME
29 Providence Avenue, Berlin NH 03570-3199. 603/752-1820. **Fax:** 603/752-7149. **Contact:** Personnel. **World Wide Web address:** http://www.northernwhitemountains.com/stvincent. **Description:** A nursing home licensed for 80 beds.

SANMINA-SCI CORPORATION
12-A Manor Parkway, Salem NH 03079. 603/898-8000. **Contact:** Human Resources. **World Wide Web address:** http://www.sanmina.com. **Description:** Manufactures custom-designed backpanel assemblies and subassemblies; multilayer, high-density printed circuit boards; and surface mount technology assemblies used in sophisticated electronics equipment with primary customers in the telecommunication, data communications, industrial/medical, computer systems, and contract assembly business sectors. **NOTE:** Please visit website for online application form. **Positions advertised include:** Regional Quality Director – East Coast; Senior Technical Program/Project Manager. **Corporate headquarters location:** San Jose CA. **Other area locations:** Manchester NH. **Other U.S. locations:** Nationwide. **Listed on:** NASDAQ. **Stock exchange symbol:** SANM. **Annual sales/revenues:** More than $100 million. **CEO:** Jure Sola.

SCHLEICHER & SCHUELL INC.
10 Optical Avenue, Keene NH 03431. 603/352-3810. **Toll-free phone:** 800/245-4024. **Fax:** 603/357-3627. **Contact:** Human Resources. **World Wide Web address:** http://www.s-and-s.com. **Description:** Manufactures filtration and separation devices for laboratories and scientific research centers. Products include DNA purification kits, centrifugal filters, and electroelution systems. **Special programs:** Apprenticeships. **International locations:** Germany. **Number of employees at this location:** 150.

SEACOAST NEWSPAPERS
111 Maplewood Avenue, Portsmouth NH 03801. 603/418-0443. **Fax:** 603/427-0550. **Contact:** Hope Conery, Human Resources. **E-mail address:** hconery@seacoastonline.com. **World Wide Web address:** http://www.seacoastonline.com. **Description:** Publishes the *Portsmouth Herald*, a daily newspaper. **Positions advertised include:** Machine Operator; Sales Team Coordinator.

SERIF, INC.
P.O. Box 803 Nashua NH 03061-9885. 603/889-8650. **Physical address:** 13 Hampshire Drive, Suite 12, Hudson NH 03051-4948. **Fax:** 603/889-1127. **Contact:** Clare Holden, Human Resources. **E-mail address:** recruitment@serif.com. **World Wide Web address:** http://www.serif.com. **Description:** Develops and supports software products for the desktop publishing and graphics markets. **Positions advertised include:** Outbound Sales. **International locations:** England. **Number of employees worldwide:** 150.

SERVICEMASTER AAA
12 Progress Avenue, Nashua NH 03062. 603/883-4800. **Fax:** 800/443-1819. **Contact:** Human Resources. **E-mail address:** SVMAAA@aol.com. **World Wide Web address:** http://svmaaa.com. **Description:** A residential and commercial cleaning service with two specific divisions: disaster restoration due to flood or fire damage, and carpet/upholstery steam cleaning. **Office hours:** Monday - Friday, 8:00 a.m. - 5:00 p.m.

SHAW'S SUPERMARKETS
1600 Woodbury Avenue, Durgin Square Plaza, Portsmouth NH 03801. 603/436-0323. **Contact:** Human Resources. **World Wide Web address:** http://www.shaws.com. **Description:** A supermarket with multiple area locations. Founded in 1860. **Corporate headquarters location:** East Bridgewater MA. **NOTE:** There is an office located in Stratham NH. Applying through website is strongly encouraged. **Other area locations:** Statewide. **Other U.S. locations:** CT; ME; RI; VT. **Operations at this facility include:** This location is a store.

SMITHS MEDICAL
10 Bowman Drive, Keene NH 03431. 603/352-3812. **Contact:** Personnel. **E-mail address:** human.resources@portex.com. **World Wide Web address:** http://www.portex.com/index2.asp. **Description:** Manufactures disposable hospital supplies. Brand-name products include Concord Laboratory and Portex. **International locations:** United Kingdom. **Parent company:** Smiths Medical.

SOUTHERN NEW HAMPSHIRE UNIVERSITY
2500 North River Road, Manchester NH 03106. 603/668-2211. **Fax:** 603/645-9661. **Recorded jobline:** 603/629-INFO. **Contact:** Human Resources. **World Wide Web address:** http://www.snhu.edu. **Description:** Southern New Hampshire University is a private, independent college offering undergraduate, graduate, and doctoral academic programs. SNHU was founded by H.A.B. Shapiro as the New Hampshire School of Accounting and Secretarial Science. SNHU now has a day college enrollment of over 1,000 students, 1,500 in the graduate school of business, and nearly 4,000 in the division of continuing education. SNHU offers associate's degrees in culinary arts and several business-related fields; bachelor of science degrees in 20 areas of business and liberal arts; master's degrees in business administration, accounting, business education, computer information systems, community economic development, and international business; and doctoral programs in international business and community economic development. Founded in 1932. **NOTE:** Part-time positions are offered. Human Resources phone is 603/644-3125. Please visit website for details on applying for specific positions. **Company slogan:** Where the world comes to mind. **Positions advertised include:** Assistant/Associate Professor – Various Departments; Teacher Education Faculty; Vice President of Academic Affairs; Vice President of Student Affairs; Development Coordinator; Men's Head Soccer Coach; Academic Advisor; Computer Lab Assistant; Diving Server. **Office hours:** Monday – Friday, 8:00 a.m. – 4:30 p.m. **Other U.S. locations:** ME; VT. **Number of employees worldwide:** 1,500.

SPECTRA INC.
101 Etna Road, Lebanon NH 03766. 603/443-5300. **Fax:** 603/448-5402. **Contact:** Human Resources Manager. **E-mail address:** hr@spectra-inc.com. **World Wide Web address:** http://www.spectra-inc.com. **Description:** Manufactures computer printer heads and ink. **NOTE:** Entry-level positions and second and third shifts are offered. **Positions advertised include:** Mechanical Engineer; Financial Analyst; Senior HR Generalist; Documentation Specialist; Engineering Technician; Production Technician; Mechanical Design Engineer; Project Leader – Mechanical Engineering; Project Manager – Software and Electronics; General Accounting Manager. **Special programs:** Training. **Corporate headquarters location:** This location. **International locations:** The Netherlands; Japan; Korea; China. **Annual sales/revenues:** $11 - $20 million. **Number of employees at this location:** 130.

STANDEX INTERNATIONAL CORPORATION
6 Manor Parkway, Salem NH 03079. 603/893-9701. **Fax:** 603/893-7324. **Contact:** Human Resources. **World Wide Web address:** http://www.standex.com. **Description:** Standex International Corporation is divided into three main product groups: Institutional Products, Industrial Products, and Graphics/Mail Order. The Institutional Products Group (consisting of Master-Bilt, Federal Industries, Jarvis, BK Industries, Williams Healthcare Systems, and the Toastswell Company) produces such items as food service equipment, air distribution products, casters, chiropractic tables and physical therapy equipment, industrial hardware, and restaurant china. The Industrial Products Group (consisting of National Metal Industries, Snappy Air Distribution Products, H.F. Coors, Mason Candlelight Company, USECO, General Slicing, Mold-Tech, Standex Electronics, Spincraft, B.F. Perkins, Custom Hoists, Procon, and Roehlen Industries) manufactures such products as texturizing systems; pumps; converting and finishing machinery; reed switches and relays; hydraulic cylinders; inductors, connectors, and custom electronic assemblies; and performs power metal spinning. The Graphics/Mail Order Group (consisting of Standard Publishing, Doubleday Brothers and Company, James Burn International, and Crest Fruit Company) provides business forms, binding systems, office supplies, and election materials, as well as educational and religious publishing and distribution, commercial printing, and mail order gift packages. **Corporate headquarters location:** This location. **Other U.S. locations:** Nationwide. **International locations:** Worldwide. **Listed on:** New York Stock Exchange. **Stock exchange symbol:** SXI. **CEO:** Roger Fix.

STEALTH COMPONENTS
15 Rye Street, Portsmouth NH 03801. 603/501-5087. **Fax:** 603/501-5901. **Contact:** Human Resources. **E-mail address:** info@stealthcomponents.com. **World Wide Web address:** http://www.stealthcomponents.com. **Description:** Distributes semiconductors, electronic components, and integrated circuits. **Positions advertised include:** Account executive, inside sales.

STEENBEKE & SONS BUILDING SUPPLY
112 High Street, Boscawen NH 03303. 603/796-2974. **Fax:** 603/796-2106. **Contact:** Human Resources. **E-mail address:** steenbekes@aol.com. **World Wide Web address:** http://www.steenbekes.com. **Description:** Sells lumber, hardware, and building materials and supplies to contractors. The company also runs Distinctive Kitchens, and Northeastern Truss and Structural Components. **Office hours:** Monday – Friday, 7:00 a.m. – 5:00 p.m.; Saturday 8:00 a.m. – 12:00 p.m. **Other area locations:** Statewide. **President:** James Steenbeke III. **Number of employees at this location:** 100.

STOCKERYALE, INC.
32 Hampshire Road, Salem NH 03079. 603/893-8778. **Fax:** 603/893-5604. **Contact:** Human Resources. **E-mail address:** hr@stockeryale.com. **World Wide Web address:** http://www.stockeryale.com. **Description:** An independent designer and manufacturer of phase masks and specialty optical fiber. These products are used by optical equipment telecommunication integrators and manufacturers. Founded in 1946, StockerYale also develops and manufactures advanced illumination products that are used in the machine vision and industrial inspection industries. **Corporate headquarters location:** This location. **International locations:** Canada; Ireland; Singapore. **Listed on:** NASDAQ. **Stock exchange symbol:** STKR.

STONEWALL FARM
242 Chesterfield Road, Keene NH 03431. 603/357-7278. **Fax:** 603/357-6018. **World Wide Web address:** http://www.stonewallfarm.org. **Description:** Stonewell Farm began as a family farm. Over time, it change families – the few families who owned the farm passed it down to their children. In 1989, with no children to pass it on to, Norm Chase sold the farm to Michael Kidder, who transformed it into a place that would benefit the community. Today, Stonewall Farm offers horse drawn hay and sleigh rides, a hiking trail, while maintaining a dairy, sugarhouse, and garden. It is a non-profit organization. **Positions advertised include:** Grant Writer; Teamster. **Office hours:** Monday – Friday, 8:30 a.m. – 4:30 p.m. **President:** Mary Ann Kristiansen.

STORAGE COMPUTER CORPORATION
11 Riverside Street, Nashua NH 03062-1372. 603/880-3005. **Fax:** 603/889-7232. **Contact:** Human Resources. **E-mail address:** hr@storage.com. **World Wide Web address:** http://www.storage.com. **Description:** Storage Computer Corporation designs, manufactures, and sells standards-based, high-performance, fault-tolerant storage solutions for use in client/server, online transaction processing, large database, multimedia, video-on-demand, and high-volume imaging applications. **Corporate headquarters location:** This location. **Operations at this facility include:** Administration; Manufacturing; Research and Development; Sales; Service. **Listed on:** American Stock Exchange. **Stock exchange symbol:** SOS. **CEO/President:** Theodore J. Goodlander. **Number of employees at this location:** 60.

STORYLAND
Route 16, Glen NH 03838. 603/383-4186. **Contact:** Human Resources. **E-mail address:** hr@storylandnh.com. **World Wide Web address:** http://www.storylandnh.com. **Description:** A children's theme park in the White Mountains. Founded in 1954. **NOTE:** The season generally lasts from May through October. Year-round positions are available. Story Land encourages people with skills in welding, plumbing, electricity, automotive mechanics, and painting to apply. They also encourage those with interest in management, marketing, and professional staff positions to apply. **Positions advertised include:** Parking Assistant; Pet Kennel Assistant; Live Character; Stage Entertainment/Theatrics; Ride Operator; Grounds Maintenance Worker; Cashier; Sales Assistant; Cook; Food Server; Dishwasher; Greeter.

CB SULLIVAN COMPANY
15 West Alice Avenue, Hooksett NH 03106. 603/624-4752. **Toll-free phone:** 800/321-2889. **Fax:** 800/428-6954. **Contact:** Human Resources Department. **World Wide Web address:** http://www.cbsullivan.com. **Description:** Distributes supplies to beauty salons and barbershops. Distributed lines include Matrix and Sebastian. CB Sullivan also operates retail stores throughout New England. **Corporate headquarters location:** This location. **Other area locations:** Hinsdale NH; Lebanon NH; Nashua NH; Newington NH; Salem NH. **Other U.S. locations:** ME; MA; RI; TX; VT.

SQUAM LAKES NATURAL SCIENCE CENTER
P.O. Box 173, Route 113, Holderness NH 03245. 603/968-7194. **Fax:** 603/968-2229. **E-mail address:** info@nhnature.org. **World Wide Web address:** http://www.nhnature.org. **Description:** A non-profit organization featuring educational programs, wildlife trails, pond tours, and gardens. **Positions advertised include:** Ragged Island Manager. **NOTE:** Volunteer positions also available. **Special programs:** Internships.

TELEDYNE ELECTRONIC TECHNOLOGIES
110 Lowell Road, Hudson NH 03051. 603/889-6191. **Fax:** 603/882-4457. **Contact:** Human Resources. **World Wide Web address:** http://www.tet.com. **Description:** Manufactures electronic components including electronic relays, multichip modules, microwave filters, aviation data management systems, and circuit boards. **NOTE:** Please visit website for online application form. **Special programs:** Internships; Co-ops. **Corporate headquarters location:** Los Angeles CA. **Other U.S. locations:** Nationwide. **Parent company:** Teledyne Technologies, Inc. **Listed on:** New York Stock Exchange. **Stock exchange symbol:** TDY. **Number of employees worldwide:** 2,500.

TEXAS INSTRUMENTS
70 Phillippe Cote Street, Manchester NH 03101. 603/222-8500. **Contact:** Human Resources. **World Wide Web address:** http://www.ti.com. **Description:** Texas Instruments designs and manufactures high-performance power management integrated circuits. These circuits are used in switching power supplies to regulate voltages and to monitor and control outputs. In motor controls, they are used to control the speed, position, braking, and power consumption of DC motors. These products are sold worldwide for a variety of data processing, telecommunications, industrial, military, automotive, and consumer applications. Founded in 1960. **NOTE:** Entry-level positions and second and third shifts are offered. Please visit website to register and apply online. **Positions advertised include:** Applications Engineer; Engineer Supervisor. **Corporate headquarters location:** Dallas TX. **Other U.S. locations:** Nationwide. **International locations:** Worldwide. **Operations at this facility include:** Administration; Management Consulting; Research and Development; Sales. **Listed on:** New York Stock Exchange. **Stock exchange symbol:** TXN. **President/CEO:** Tom Engibous. **Annual sales/revenues:** More than $100 million. **Number of employees at this location:** 460. **Number of employees nationwide:** 490. **Number of employees worldwide:** 560.

THERMO ELECTRON CORPORATION
P.O. Box 1178, Newington NH 03802-1178. 603/436-9444. **Physical address:** 25 Nimble Hill Road, Newington NH 03801. **Toll-free phone:** 800/258-0830. **Fax:** 603/436-8411. **Contact:** Human Resources Director. **World Wide Web address:** http://www.thermo.com. **Description:** Thermo Electron provides laboratory, analytical, and scientific equipment and technology. Among their products is the Spectra-Physics brand, the first commercial laser company, founded in 1961. Their Optical Technologies remain one of their most important developments. **NOTE:** Please visit website for online application form. **Positions advertised include:** Director of Manufacturing; Sales Operations Manager; Cost Analyst; Manufacturing Engineer; Test Technician; Sheetmetal Operator; Rheology Applications Engineer; Marketing Communications Specialist. **Corporate headquarters location:** Waltham MA. **Other U.S. locations:** Nationwide. **International locations:** Worldwide. **Listed on:** New York Stock Exchange. **Stock exchange symbol:** TMO. **Number of employees at this location:** 320. **Number of employees worldwide:** 10,000.

THE TIMBERLAND COMPANY
200 Domain Drive, Stratham NH 03885. 603/772-9500. **Contact:** Human Resources Department. **World Wide Web address:** http://www.timberland.com. **Description:** The Timberland Company designs, manufactures, and markets footwear, apparel, and accessories under the Timberland brand name. Timberland products for men and women include boots, casual shoes, boat shoes, and accessories. Timberland products are sold primarily through Timberland stores, other retail specialty stores, department stores, athletic stores, and shoe stores worldwide. **NOTE:** Please visit website for online application form. **Positions advertised include:** Account Executive; Assistant Field Marketing Manager; Benefits Analyst; Business Process and Information Manager; Designer; Direct Ship Administrator; Finance Manager; Financial Analyst; Fixturing Project Manager; GBA Administrative Assistant; Men's Apparel Product Line Coordinator; Merchandise Manager; Sales Analyst Pro; Senior Auditor; Senior General Accountant; Senior Manager IT; Store Control Analyst. **Corporate headquarters location:** This location. **Other U.S. locations:** Danville KY; Ontario CA. **International locations:** Singapore; United Kingdom; Netherlands. **Operations at this facility include:** Administration. **Listed on:** New York Stock Exchange. **Stock exchange symbol:** TBL. **Annual sales/revenues:** More than $100 million. **Number of employees at this location:** 600.

TIMKEN SUPER PRECISION
MPB DIVISION
P.O. Box 547, Keene NH 03431-0547. 603/352-0310. **Physical address:** 7 Optical Avenue, Keene NH 03431. **Fax:** 603/355-4553. **Contact:** Human Resources. **World Wide Web address:** http://www.timken.com/industries/superprecision. **Description:** Manufactures ball and roller bearings. **Corporate headquarters location:** This location. **International locations:** Worldwide. **Operations at this facility include:** Manufacturing. **Listed on:** New York Stock Exchange. **Stock exchange symbol:** TKR. **Number of employees worldwide:** 26,000.

TYCO INTEGRATED CABLE SYSTEMS
P.O. Box 479, Portsmouth NH 03802-0479. 603/436-6100. **Physical address:** 2073 Woodbury Avenue, Newington NH 03801. **Fax:** 603/430-4668. **Contact:** Joe DeRoy, Human Resources. **World Wide Web address:** http://www.tycotelecom.com. **Description:** One of the world's leading suppliers of undersea optical fiber cable for telecommunications and oceanographic research. Tycom Integrated Cable Systems has also designed, built, and installed numerous underwater power cable systems. Other product areas include electromechanical cables, precise instrumentation, tow cables, umbilical cables, armored flexible pipes, and specialty ropes. **NOTE:** Out of state fax is 603/427-0701. **Corporate headquarters location:** Morristown NJ. **International locations:** Singapore; Japan; UK; France; Spain. **Parent company:** Tyco International Ltd. is a global manufacturer, installer, and distributor of products and systems for a broad spectrum of markets. Tyco has four core businesses: Fire Protection, Flow Control, Electrical and Electronic Components, and Disposable and Specialty Products. **Listed on:** New York Stock Exchange. **Stock exchange symbol:** TYC. **Number of employees worldwide:** 260,000.

TYCO INTERNATIONAL
3 Holland Way, Exeter NH 03833. 603/778-9499. Human Resources. **World Wide Web address:** http://www.tyco.com. **Description:** Tyco International Ltd. is a global manufacturer, installer, and distributor of products and systems for a broad spectrum of markets. Tyco has four core businesses: Fire Protection, Flow Control, Electrical and Electronic Components, and Disposable and Specialty Products. **Listed on:** New York Stock Exchange. **Stock exchange symbol:** TYC. **Number of employees worldwide:** 260,000.

U.S. DEPARTMENT OF LABOR
OCCUPATIONAL SAFETY & HEALTH ADMINISTRATION (OSHA)
J.C. Cleveland Federal Building, 55 Pleasant Street, Room 3901, Concord NH 03301. 603/225-1629. **Fax:** 603/225-1580. **Contact:** Human Resources. **World Wide Web address:** http://www.osha.gov. **Description:** OSHA conducts unannounced health and safety inspections of businesses to make sure they meet government regulations. **Corporate headquarters location:** Washington D.C. **Other U.S. locations:** Nationwide.

U.S. DEPARTMENT OF VETERANS AFFAIRS MEDICAL CENTER
718 Smyth Road, Manchester NH 03104. 603/624-4366. **Toll-free phone:** 800/892-8384. **Fax:** 603/626-6568. **Contact:** Human Resources Department. **World Wide Web address:** http://www.visn1.med.va.gov/manchester. **Description:** A medical center operated by the U.S. Department of Veterans Affairs. From 54 hospitals in 1930, the VA health care system has grown to include 171 medical centers; more than 364 outpatient, community and outreach clinics; 130 nursing home care units; and 37 domiciliaries. VA operates at least one medical center in each of the 48 contiguous states, Puerto Rico, and the District of Columbia. With approximately 76,000 medical center beds, VA treats nearly 1 million patients per year in VA hospitals, 75,000 in nursing home care units, and 25,000 in domiciliaries. **NOTE:** Human Resources phone is 603/626-6513. Please visit website for more information on how to search for and apply to jobs. The office only accepts resumes that have been sent in response to recent openings. Please search for jobs first. **Operations at this facility include:** Administration; Service. **Number of employees at this location:** 580.

UNION LEADER
P.O. Box 9555, Manchester NH 03108-9555. 603/668-4321. **Physical address:** 100 William Loeb Drive, Manchester NH 03109. **Fax:** 603/314-0130. **Contact:** Human Resources. **E-mail address:** ulrecruit@theunionleader.com. **World Wide Web address:** http://www.theunionleader.com. **Description:** Publishes a daily newspaper with a weekday circulation of approximately 85,000 and 102,000 on Sundays. **Positions advertised include:** Web Site Director and Sales Manager; Relief District Manager – Part-time; Delivery Personnel. **Office hours:** Monday – Friday 5:00 a.m. – 6:00 p.m.; Saturday – Sunday, 5:00 a.m. – 12:00 p.m. **Corporate headquarters location:** This location. **Number of employees at this location:** 365.

UNITED AIRLINES
Manchester Airport, Manchester NH 03103. 800/241-6522. **World Wide Web Address:** http://www.united.com. **Description:** United Airlines is the second largest

air carrier in the world. **NOTE**: Offers applications online for currently open positions. **Positions include**: Transportation, Logistics and Warehouse, Communications, Sales, Public Relations. **Parent Company**: UAL Corporation.

UNITIL CORPORATION
6 Liberty Lane West, Hampton NH 03842-1720. 603/772-0775. **Toll-free phone:** 888/8-UNITIL. **Contact:** Human Resources. **World Wide Web address:** http://www.unitil.com. **Description:** UNITIL Corporation is a public utility holding company with subsidiaries that purchase, transmit, distribute, and sell electric service in New Hampshire; distribute and sell electric and natural gas services in Massachusetts; and provide consulting services on energy-related matters. Founded 1984. **Corporate headquarters location:** This location. **Subsidiaries include:** Concord Electric Company; Exeter & Hampton Electric Company; Fitchburg Gas and Electric Light Company; UNITIL Power Corporation; UNITIL Realty Corporation; UNITIL Resources, Inc.; UNITIL Service Corporation. **Listed on:** American Stock Exchange. **Stock exchange symbol:** UTL. **Number of employees nationwide:** 316.

UNIVERSITY OF NEW HAMPSHIRE
2 Leavitt Lane, Durham NH 03824. 603/862-1234. **Fax:** 603/862-0077. **Recorded jobline:** 603/862-HIRE. **Contact:** Human Resources. **E-mail address:** Hrinfo@unh.edu. **World Wide Web address:** http://www.unh.edu. **Description:** A four-year state university. Originally founded as an agricultural school, the University of New Hampshire now encompasses a wide variety of disciplines, including the Whittemore School of Business & Economics, which provides one of the oldest Executive MBA programs in New England. Founded in 1866. **NOTE:** Please call the jobline to find out when applications are accepted. Human Resources phone is 603/862-0501. Find out more about employment opportunities at https://www.unhjobs.com – you must register on this website in order to apply for jobs at UNH. **Positions advertised include:** Accountant; Administrative Assistant; Assistant Professor – Various Departments; Athletic Coach; Boiler Attendant; Building Service Worker; Chairperson – Nursing; Clinical Coordinator; Cook; Executive Director for Alumni Affairs; Food Service Assistant; Information Support Assistant; Information Technologist; Instructor – Various Departments; Laboratory Technician; Lecturer – Various Departments; Manager of Research Administration; Nutritionist; Research Faculty; Residence Hall Director; Sedimentary Geologist; Television Producer/Director; Tenure-track Faculty. **Office hours:** Monday – Friday, 8:00 a.m. – 4:30 p.m. **Operations at this facility include:** Administration; Research and Development. **Number of employees at this location:** 2,500.

VECTRON INTERNATIONAL
267 Lowell Road, Hudson NH 03051-4916. 603/598-0070. **Toll-free phone:** 88/VECTRON. **Fax:** 603/577-6767. **E-mail address:** careers@vectron.com. **World Wide Web address:** http://www.vectron.com. **Description:** Creates and manufactures products that generate and control frequency waves. **Positions advertised include:** Business Analyst; Shipping Coordinator; Sales Account Manager; Assembly Engineer; Crystal Process Engineer. **Corporate headquarters location:** This location. **Other U.S. locations:** Norwalk CT; Cincinnati OH. **International locations:** Germany; China.

VITEX EXTRUSION
43 Industrial Park Drive, PO box 6149, Franklin NH 03235. 603/934-5275. **Fax:** 603/934-0355. **Contact:** Human Resources. **E-mail address:** alum@vitexcorp.com. **World Wide Web address:** http://www.vitexcorp.com. **Description:** Manufactures aluminum profiles for applications including automotive, building and construction, electronics, medical, lighting, and military products. **Positions advertised include:** Maintenance Mechanic.

VITRONICS SOLTEC
2 Marin Way, Stratham NH 03885. 603/772-7778. **Fax:** 603/772-7776. **Contact:** Human Resources. **E-mail address:** info@us.vitronics-soltec.com. **World Wide Web address:** http://www.vitronics-soltec.com. **Description:** Vitronics Corporation designs, engineers, manufactures, and markets thermal process and associated systems for production soldering, cleaning, and repair of surface-mounted devices to printed circuit boards. The primary market for these products is the electronics industry, although other markets include computers and peripheral office equipment; military, consumer, mechanical, and automotive electronics; telecommunications equipment; test and measurement equipment; and contract assembly. **Corporate headquarters location:** This location. **International locations:** Germany; The Netherlands; Singapore; China; Malaysia; South Korea. **Number of employees at this location:** 90.

WHEELABRATOR TECHNOLOGIES INC.
4 Liberty Lane West, Hampton NH 03842. 603/929-3000. **Toll-free phone:** 800/682-0026. **Contact:** Human Resources Department. **E-mail address:** wti-info@wm.com. **World Wide Web address:** http://www.wheelabratortechnologies.com. **Description:** Wheelabrator has more than 800 professionals involved in engineering, fabricating, operating, and maintaining clean air systems. The company's pollution control and measurement equipment, and oxidation and carbon systems operate at hundreds of power plants, industries, and water and wastewater treatment facilities. Nearly 2,000 employees at Wheelabrator deliver clean water/wastewater systems and services worldwide. In addition to process engineered systems and filtration/membrane technologies, the company offers contract treatment plant operations, biosolids management, and privatization for cities and industries. More than 1,000 employees develop, finance, own, and operate Wheelabrator's renewable energy and independent power facilities. The company has 16 trash-to-energy plants and 6 independent power facilities operating throughout the United States. **Parent company:** Waste Management, Inc. **President:** Drennan Lowell.

WHITE MOUNTAINS INSURANCE GROUP
80 South Main Street, Hanover NH 03755. 603/640-2200. **Fax:** 603/643-4592. **Contact:** Human Resources. **World Wide Web address:** http://www.whitemountains.com. **Description:** A major financial services holding company specializing in reinsurance, as well as property and casualty insurance. **Corporate headquarters location:** Hamilton Bermuda. **Subsidiaries include:** OneBeacon Insurance Group; Folksamerica Reinsurance Company; Fund American Reinsurance Company, Ltd.; White Mountains Underwriting Limited; Esurance; AutoOne Insurance. **Parent company:** Tuckerman Capital. **Listed on:** New York Stock Exchange. **Stock exchange symbol:** WTM.

WILLEY BROTHERS, INC.
10 Main Street, Rochester NH 03839. 603/335-1400. **Toll-free phone:** 800/732-3999. **Fax:** 603/332-7429. **Contact:** Human Resources. **E-mail address:** jobs@willeybrothers.com. **World Wide Web address:** http://www.willeybrothers.com. **Description:** Provides retail services. **NOTE:** No phone calls regarding employment. **Positions advertised include:** Community Bank Project Manager.

VIBRO-METER INC.
10 Ammon Drive, Manchester NH 03103. 603/669-0940. **Fax:** 603/627-9537. **Contact:** Personnel Director. **E-mail address:** hr.us@vibro-meter.com. **World Wide Web address:** http://www.vibro-meter.com. **Description:** A manufacturer of a wide variety of electronic components and systems including pressure indication instruments. **Corporate headquarters location:** Fribourg Switzerland. **International locations:** United Kingdom. **Parent company:** Meggitt PLC (England). **Number of employees worldwide:** 5,100.

YMCA CAMP BELKNAP
P.O. Box 1546 Wolfeboro NH 03894. 603/569-3475. **Physical address:** Route 109, Tuftonboro NH 03894. **Fax:** 603/569-1471. **Contact:** Gene Clark, Director. **E-mail address:** clarks@campbelknap.org. **World Wide Web address:** http://www.campbelknap.org. **Description:** YMCA-affiliated overnight summer camp, providing valuable camping, recreational, and physical skills to male campers. **Positions advertised include:** Assistant Chef/Cook; Associate Nurse.

ZETA ELECTRONIC DESIGN, INC
1461 Hooksett Road, Hooksett NH 03106. 603/644-3239. **Fax:** 603/644-3413. **E-mail address:** info@zetainc.com. **World Wide Web Address:** http://www.zetainc.com. **Description:** Develops electronic hardware and software for a range of clients. **NOTE:** Provides job listings and resume editing on website. **Corporate Headquarters:** This location.

ZYDACRON, INC.
7 Perimeter Road, Manchester NH 03103. 603/647-1000. **Fax:** 603/647-9470. **Contact:** Human Resources. **E-mail address:** info@zydacron.com. **World Wide Web address:** http://www.zydacron.com. **Description:** A designer and manufacturer of communications systems. **Positions advertised include:** National Account Manager. **Office hours:** Monday – Friday, 8:30 a.m. – 5:30 p.m. **Corporate headquarters location:** Grambach Austria. **Other U.S. locations:** Atlanta GA. **International locations:** Philippines. **Parent company:** SCOTTY.

ABB INC.
P.O. Box 6005, North Brunswick NJ 08902. **Physical Address:** 1460 Livingstone Avenue, North Brunswick NJ 08902-6005. 732/932-6000. **Contact:** Human Resources Manager. **World Wide Web address:** http://www.abb.com/us. **Description:** Provides engineering, construction, and sales support services as part of a worldwide engineering firm. Internationally, the company operates through the following business segments: oil field equipment and services; power systems; engineering and construction; process equipment; and industrial products. **Corporate headquarters location:** Norwalk CT. **Other U.S. locations:** New York NY. **Subsidiaries include:** ABB Lumus Global Inc. (Bloomfield NJ); ABB Simcom (Bloomfield NJ); ABB Susa (also at this location). **Parent company:** ABB AG (Baden, Switzerland). **Number of employees worldwide:** 220,000.

ABB LUMMUS GLOBAL INC.
1515 Broad Street, Bloomfield NJ 07003. 973/893-1515. **Fax:** 973/893-2000. **Contact:** Human Resources. **World Wide Web address:** http://www.abb.com/us. **Description:** An engineering firm serving power plants, chemical plants, and petrochemical and oil refineries, as well as other industries such as aviation and storage. **Parent company:** ABB Inc. (Norwalk CT) provides engineering, construction, and sales support services as part of the worldwide engineering firm. Another subsidiary, ABB Simcon (Bloomfield NJ), specializes in chemical engineering. Internationally, the company operates in five business segments: oil field equipment and services, power systems, engineering and construction, process equipment, and industrial products.

ACI
90 Woodbridge Center Drive, Suite 400, Woodbridge NJ 07095. 732/602-0200. **Contact:** Personnel. **World Wide Web address:** http://www.aci.com. **Description:** Provides systems integration services. **Positions advertised include:** Analyst; Help Desk Associate; Unix Administrator; DBA; Project Manager; Technical Writer; Quality Assurance Tester; Developer; Java Programmer.

ADP/OMR
101 Business Park Drive, Suite 220, Skillman NJ 08558. 609/683-9058. **Contact:** Human Resources. **World Wide Web address:** http://www.adp.com. **Description:** Develops trade-processing software for the financial services industry. **Positions advertised include:** Internal Architect; Information Technology Auditor; Network Consultant; Payroll Professional; Marketing Manager; District Sales Manager; Associate Website Developer; Project Manager; Sales Consultant; Executive Assistant; Client Account Representative.

ADT SECURITY SERVICES
21 Northfield Avenue, Edison NJ 08837. 732/225-0047. **Contact:** Personnel. **World Wide Web address:** http://www.adt.com. **Description:** Services more than 15,000 burglar, fire, and other alarm systems. ADT Security Services also manufactures a variety of alarms and monitoring equipment for use in alarm service operations and for sale to commercial and industrial users. **Positions advertised include:** Data Entry Processor. **Corporate headquarters location:** Boca Raton FL. **Other U.S. locations:** Orlando FL; St. Petersburg FL; Tampa FL; Atlanta GA; Baltimore MD; Rockville MD. **Parent company:** Tyco Fire & Security.

AM BEST COMPANY
1 AMbest Road, Oldwick NJ 08858. 908/439-2200. **Fax:** 908/439-3027. **Contact:** Human Resources. **E-mail address:** hr@ambest.com. **World Wide Web address:** http://www.ambest.com. **Description:** Manufactures products including software, CD-ROMs, and diskette support products for the insurance industry. **Positions advertised include:** Tax Analyst; Customer Service Representative; Financial Analyst; Editorial Assistant; Sales Analyst. **Corporate headquarters location:** This location.

AT&T CORPORATION
295 North Maple Avenue, Basking Ridge NJ 07920. 908/221-6035. **Contact:** Human Resources. **World Wide Web address:** http://www.att.com. **Description:** AT&T is a major long-distance telephone company that provides domestic and international voice and data communications and management services, telecommunications products, and leasing and financial services. The company manufactures data communications products, computer products, switching and transmission equipment, and components. **NOTE:** Please send resumes to the resume scanning center at 1200 Peachtree Street, Room 7075, Promenade 1, Atlanta GA 30309. **Positions advertised include:** Telecommunications Analyst. **Corporate headquarters location:** New York NY. **Other U.S. locations:** Nationwide. **Subsidiaries include:** AT&T Capital Corporation offers financing and leases and provides consumer credit through its AT&T Universal credit card. **Listed on:** New York Stock Exchange. **Stock exchange symbol:** T.

AXS-ONE INC.
301 Route 17 North, 12th Floor, Rutherford NJ 07070. 201/935-3400. **Toll-free phone:** 800/828-7660. **Fax:** 201/935-8482. **Contact:** Human Resources. **E-mail address:** careers@axsone.com. **World Wide Web address:** http://www.axsone.com. **Description:** Develops and markets various financial software products. **Positions advertised include:** Senior Consultant.

ACCENTURE
5 Spring Street, Murray Hill NJ 07974. 908/898-5000. **Contact:** Human Resources. **World Wide Web address:** http://www.accenture.com. **Description:** A management and technology consulting firm. Accenture offers a wide range of services including business re-engineering; customer service system consulting; data system design and implementation; Internet sales systems research and design; and strategic planning. **Number of employees nationwide:** 5,600.

ADMIRAL INSURANCE COMPANY
1255 Caldwell Road, Cherry Hill NJ 08034. 856/429-9200. **Contact:** Human Resources. **World Wide Web address:** http://www.admiralins.com. **Description:** Underwrites casualty and property insurance.

ADVANCED ENERGY
1007 Laurel Oak Road, Voorhees NJ 08043. 970/221-4670. **Fax:** 856/627-6159. **Contact:** Human Resources. **World Wide Web address:** http://www.advanced-energy.com. **Description:** Designs, develops, manufactures, and markets ion-beam sources, plasma abatement systems, power conversion and control system solutions, and process monitoring and control tools. Founded in 1981. **NOTE:** Apply online. **Corporate headquarters location:** Fort Collins CO.

AFFINITI GROUP
106 Apple Street, Suite 110, Tinton Falls NJ 07724. 732-747-9600. **Contact:** Human Resources. **E-mail address:** careers@affinitigroup.com. **World Wide Web address:** http://www.affinitigroup.com. **Description:** Provides systems integration and software development services. **Positions advertised include:** Sales Representative; Programmer; Unix System Administrator; Technical Support Representative; Network Engineer; Traffic Coordinator.

AGFA CORPORATION
100 Challenger Road, Ridgefield Park NJ 07660-2199. 201/440-2500. **Contact:** Human Resources. **World Wide Web address:** http://www.agfa.com. **Description:** Produces polyurethane raw materials, polymer thermoplastic resins and blends, coatings, industrial chemicals, and other related products. **Operations at this facility include:** This location manufactures photographic imaging equipment and film.

AGILENT TECHNOLOGIES
550 Clark Drive, Netcong NJ 07857. 973/448-9177. **Contact:** Employment Office. **World Wide Web address:** http://www.agilent.com. **Description:** Designs and manufactures test, measurement, and monitoring instruments, systems, and solutions. The company also designs and manufactures semiconductor and optical components. Agilent Technologies serves the communications, electronics, life sciences and health care industries. Founded in 1999. **Positions advertised include:** Field Technology Support Specialist. **NOTE:** Send employment correspondence to: Resume Processing Center, 89 Davis Road, Suite 160, Orinda CA 94563. **Corporate headquarters location:** Palo Alto CA. **Other U.S. locations:** Nationwide. **International locations:** Worldwide. **Listed on:** New York Stock Exchange. **Stock exchange symbol:** A. **Number of employees worldwide:** 46,000.

ALEXANDER HAMILTON INSTITUTE, INC.
70 Hilltop Road, Ramsey NJ 07446. 201/825-3377. **Toll-free phone:** 800/879-2441. **Fax:** 201/825-8696. **Contact:** Personnel. **World Wide Web address:** http://www.ahipubs.com. **Description:** Publishes newsletters and manuals focused on employment law.

ALPHA METALS, INC.
600 Route 440, Jersey City NJ 07304. 201/434-6778. **Fax:** 201/434-7508. **Contact:** Human Resources. **World Wide Web address:** http://www.alphametals.com. **Description:** Manufactures specialized alloys, chemicals, and instrumentation for soldering applications used by electronics OEMs throughout the world. The company's consumer division manufactures solders for plumbing and hobbyists. **Positions advertised include:** Human Resources Coordinator; Operations Coordinator.

ALPHA WIRE COMPANY
711 Lidgerwood Avenue, Elizabeth NJ 07207. 908/925-8000. **Toll-free phone:** 800/52A-LPHA. **Fax:** 908/925-6923. **Contact:** Human Resources. **E-mail address:** info@alphawire.com. **World Wide Web address:** http://www.alphawire.com. **Description:** An international distributor of high-tech and high-reliability wire, cable, tubing, and connector products including communications and control cables, shrinkable and nonshrinkable tubing and insulation, instrumentation cables, flat cable and connectors, coaxial and data cables, plenum cable, and hook-up wire used for electrical and electronic equipment. Products are sold to a network of distributors and OEMs. Founded in 1922. **Positions advertised include:** District Sales Manager. **NOTE:** Entry-level positions and part-time jobs are offered. **Special programs:** Internships. **Office hours:** Monday - Friday, 8:00 a.m. - 8:00 p.m. **Corporate headquarters location:** St. Louis MO. **Other U.S. locations:** Nationwide. **International locations:** Worldwide. **Operations at this facility include:** Administration; Research and Development; Sales; Service. **General Manager:** Brian O'Connell. **Purchasing Manager:** Ben Ochinegro. **Annual sales/revenues:** $51 - $100 million. **Number of employees at this location:** 120. **Number of employees nationwide:** 180. **Number of employees worldwide:** 185.

ALPHARMA INC.
One Executive Drive, Fort Lee NJ 07024. 201/947-7774. **Toll-free phone:** 800/645-4216. **Fax:** 201/947-6145. **Contact:** Human Resources. **World Wide Web address:** http://www.alpharma.com. **Description:** A multinational pharmaceutical company that develops, manufactures, and markets specialty generic and proprietary human pharmaceuticals and animal health products. The U.S. Pharmaceuticals Division is a market leader in liquid pharmaceuticals and a prescription market leader in creams and ointments. The International Pharmaceuticals Division manufactures generic pharmaceuticals and OTC products. Other divisions include the Animal Health Division, which manufactures and markets antibiotics and other feed additives for the poultry and swine industries; the Aquatic Animal Health Division, which serves the aquaculture industry and is a manufacturer and marketer of vaccines for farmed fish; and the Fine Chemicals Division, which is a basic producer of specialty bulk antibiotics. **Corporate headquarters location:** This location. **Listed on:** New York Stock Exchange. **Stock exchange symbol:** ALO.

ALTEON INC.
170 Williams Drive, Ramsey NJ 07446. 201/934-5000. **Fax:** 201/934-0090. **Contact:** Human Resources Director. **E-mail address:** careers@alteon.com. **World Wide Web address:** http://www.alteonpharma.com. **Description:** A pharmaceutical company engaged in the discovery and development of novel therapeutic and diagnostic products for treating complications associated with diabetes and aging. **Positions advertised include:** Clinical Research Associate; Clinical Team Manager; Regulatory & Quality Assurance Manager. **Listed on:** American Stock Exchange. **Stock exchange symbol:** ALT.

ALUMINUM SHAPES LLC
9000 River Road, Delair NJ 08110. 856/662-5500. **Fax:** 801/740-6585. **Contact:** Al DiFrancesco, Director of Personnel. **E-mail address:** adifrancesco@shapesllc.com. **World Wide Web address:** http://www.shapesllc.com. **Description:** An aluminum extrusion company serving the architectural, defense, distribution, and transportation industries. **Corporate headquarters location:** This location.

AMERADA HESS CORPORATION
One Hess Plaza, Woodbridge NJ 07095-1229. 732/636-3000. **Contact:** Human Resources. **World Wide Web address:** http://www.hess.com. **Description:** Extracts, refines, and markets petroleum. **Corporate headquarters location:** New York NY. **Listed on:** New York Stock Exchange. **Stock exchange symbol:** AHC.

AMERICAN GAS & CHEMICAL COMPANY LTD.
220 Pegasus Avenue, Northvale NJ 07647. 201/767-7300. **Toll-free phone:** 800/288-3647. **Fax:** 201/767-1741. **Contact:** Human Resources Department. **E-mail address:** hr@amgas.com. **World Wide Web address:** http://www.amgas.com. **Description:** Manufactures electronic chemical and gas leak detectors. **Corporate headquarters location:** This location. **Operations at this facility include:** Administration; Manufacturing; Research and Development; Sales. **Listed on:** Privately held. **Number of employees at this location:** 125.

AMERICAN RE-INSURANCE COMPANY
555 College Road East, Princeton NJ 08543. 609/243-4649. **Fax:** 609/243-4257. **Contact:** Virginia Zdanowicz, Recruiting Director. **World Wide Web address:** http://www.amre.com. **Description:** Underwrites property and casualty reinsurance in both the domestic and international markets. **Positions advertised include:** Actuarial Associate; Audit Risk Practice Manager; Supervising Auditor; Business Analyst;

Contracts Writer; Excess Medical Writer; IT Training Specialist; Research Analyst; Tax Administrator; Underwriting Vice President. **Corporate headquarters location:** This location. **Other U.S. locations:** Nationwide. **International locations:** Worldwide. **Parent company:** Munich Re Group. **Number of employees at this location:** 800. **Number of employees nationwide:** 1,200.

AMERICAN RED CROSS
203 West Jersey Street, Elizabeth NJ 07202. 908/353-2500. **Contact:** Human Resources. **World Wide Web address:** http://www.redcross.org. **Description:** A humanitarian organization that aids disaster victims, gathers blood for crisis distribution, trains individuals to respond to emergencies, educates individuals on various diseases, and raises funds for other charities. **Other U.S. locations:** Nationwide.

AMERICAN STANDARD COMPANIES INC.
P.O. Box 6820, Piscataway NJ 08854. 732/980-6000. **Physical address:** One Centennial Avenue, Piscataway NJ 08855. **Contact:** Human Resources. **World Wide Web address:** http://www.americanstandard.com. **Description:** A global, diversified manufacturer. The company's operations are comprised of four segments: air conditioning products, plumbing products, automotive products, and medical systems. The air conditioning products segment (through subsidiary The Trane Company) develops and manufactures Trane and American Standard air conditioning equipment for use in central air conditioning systems for commercial, institutional, and residential buildings. The plumbing products segment develops and manufactures American Standard, Ideal Standard, Porcher, Armitage Shanks, Dolomite, and Standard bathroom and kitchen fixtures and fittings. The automotive products segment develops and manufactures truck, bus, and utility vehicle braking and control systems under the WABCO and Perrot brands. The medical systems segment manufactures Copalis, DiaSorin, and Pylori-Chek medical diagnostic products and systems for a variety of diseases including HIV, osteoporosis, and renal disease. **Corporate headquarters location:** This location. **International locations:** Worldwide. **Listed on:** New York Stock Exchange. **Stock exchange symbol:** ASD. **Chairman/CEO:** Frederic M. Poses. **Number of employees worldwide:** 57,000.

AMERICAN WATER WORKS SERVICE COMPANY
1025 Laurel Oak Road, Voorhees NJ 08043. 856/346-8200. **Contact:** Stanley Smith, Director of Personnel. **World Wide Web address:** http://www.amwater.com. **Description:** Acquires, manages, and services water companies across the country.

ANALYSTS INTERNATIONAL CORPORATION (AIC)
111 Wood Avenue South, Iselin NJ 08830. 732/906-0100. **Fax:** 732/906-8808. **Contact:** Human Resources. **World Wide Web address:** http://www.analysts.com. **Description:** AiC is an international computer consulting firm. The company assists clients in analyzing, designing, and developing systems in a variety of industries using different programming languages and software. **Corporate headquarters location:** Minneapolis MN.

ANCHOR GLASS CONTAINER CORPORATION
83 Griffith Street, Salem NJ 08079. 856/935-4000. **Contact:** Personnel. **World Wide Web address:** http://www.anchorglass.com. **Description:** Engaged in the manufacture and sale of a diversified line of household, hardware, and packaging products including glassware, commercial and institutional chinaware, decorative and convenience hardware, glass containers, and metal and plastic closures. Operations encompass over 20 divisions and subsidiaries with 40 plants and distribution centers located in the United States and abroad.

ANCORA HOSPITAL
202 Spring Garden Road, Ancora NJ 08037. 609/561-1700. **Contact:** Human Resources. **Description:** A 500-bed psychiatric hospital that offers inpatient services for adults.

ANHEUSER-BUSCH, INC.
200 U.S. Highway 1, Newark NJ 07114. 973/645-7700. **Contact:** Human Resources. **World Wide Web address:** http://www.budweiser.com. **Description:** A leading producer of beer. Beer brands include Budweiser, Michelob, Busch, King Cobra, and O'Doul's (nonalcoholic) beverages. **Corporate headquarters location:** St. Louis MO. **Other U.S. locations:** Los Angeles CA; Jacksonville FL; Tampa FL; Merrimack NH; Baldwinsville NY; Columbus OH; Houston TX; Williamsburg VA. **Parent company:** Anheuser-Busch Companies is a diverse company involved in the entertainment, brewing, baking, and manufacturing industries. The company is one of the largest domestic brewers, operating 13 breweries throughout the United States and distributing through over 900 independent wholesalers. Related businesses include can manufacturing, paper printing, and barley malting. Anheuser-Busch Companies is also one of the largest operators of theme parks in the United States, with locations in Florida, Virginia, Texas, Ohio, and California. Through subsidiary Campbell Taggart Inc., Anheuser-Busch Companies is also one of the largest commercial baking companies in the United States, producing foods under the Colonial brand name, among others. Anheuser-Busch Companies also has various real estate interests. **Listed on:** New York Stock Exchange. **Stock exchange symbol:** BUD.

ANSOFT CORPORATION
669 River Drive, Suite 200, Elmwood Park NJ 07407-1361. 201/796-2003. **Contact:** Human Resources. **E-mail address:** jobs@ansoft.com. **World Wide Web address:** http://www.ansoft.com. **Description:** Develops and distributes circuit design software. **NOTE:** Send resumes and cover letters to: 4 Station Square, Suite 200, Pittsburgh PA 15219-1119. 412/261-3200. **Positions advertised include:** Customer Support Engineer; Marketing Engineer; Software Engineer; Technical Writer; Research & Development Engineer. **Corporate headquarters location:** Pittsburgh PA.

AON CONSULTING
125 Chubb Avenue, Lyndhurst NJ 07071. 201/460-6854. **Contact:** Human Resources. **World Wide Web address:** http://www.aonconsulting.com. **Description:** An international human resources consulting and benefits brokerage firm providing integrated advisory and support services in retirement planning, health care management, organizational effectiveness, compensation, human resources-related communications, and information technologies. **Corporate headquarters location:** Chicago IL.

APPLIED GRAPHICS TECHNOLOGIES (AGT)
One Kero Road, Carlstadt NJ 07072. 201/933-8585. **Fax:** 201/935-5108. **Contact:** Human Resources. **World Wide Web address:** http://www.agt.com. **Description:** Applied Graphics Technologies (AGT) is one of the largest providers of integrated graphic communications services to advertising agencies, magazine and catalog publishers, and corporate clients in various industries. The company's services include commercial printing, color separation and retouching, facilities management, photo CD and digital image archiving, electronic imaging services, flexo/packaging services, publication and catalog services, satellite transmission services, creative design services, technical support and training services, and black and white ad production. **NOTE:** All of the hiring is conducted through the corporate headquarters. Interested jobseekers should address all inquiries to Applied Graphics Technologies, 450 West 33rd Street, 11th Floor, New York NY 10001. 212/716-6600. **Corporate headquarters location:** New York NY. **Operations at this facility include:** This location offers publication and catalog services, satellite transmission services, a desktop service bureau, four-color facsimile or digital transmittal, and packaging services.

APPLIED PRINTING TECHNOLOGIES
77 Moonachie Avenue, Moonachie NJ 07074. 201/896-6600. **Fax:** 201/896-1893. **Contact:** Personnel. **World Wide Web address:** http://www.appliedprinting.com. **Description:** Offers commercial printing services, bindery services, a desktop service bureau, and advertising agency services. **Corporate headquarters location:** This location.

THE ARC OF BERGEN AND PASSAIC COUNTIES, INC.
223 Moore Street, Hackensack NJ 07601. 201/343-0322. **Fax:** 201/343-0401. **Contact:** Human Resources. **E-mail address:** arcbpc@aol.com. **World Wide Web address:** http://www.arcbergenpassaic.org. **Description:** A nonprofit organization that works with mentally disabled people to improve their quality of life.

ARCH WIRELESS
80 East Ridgewood Avenue, Paramus NJ 07652. 201/265-1130. **Contact:** Human Resources. **World Wide Web address:** http://www.arch.com. **Description:** A telecommunications service company providing a wide variety of specialized data- and message-processing and communications services. The company operates a nationwide computer-controlled network that electronically receives, processes, and transmits record and data communications. Arch Wireless also operates a radio paging business. **Positions advertised include:** Outside Sales Representative; Sales Executive.

ARIES ELECTRONICS
P.O. Box 130, 62A Trenton Ave., Frenchtown NJ 08825. 908/996-6841. **Fax:** 908/996-3891. **Contact:** Personnel. **E-mail address:** info@arieselec.com. **World Wide Web address:** http://www.arieselec.com. **Description:** Manufactures a wide variety of electronic components including pin grid array footprints, ZIF and test sockets, cable assemblies, DIP/SIP sockets/headers, display sockets, programming devices, and switches.

ARROW FASTENER COMPANY
271 Mayhill Street, Saddle Brook NJ 07663. 201/843-6900. **Contact:** Plant Manager. **World Wide Web address:** http://www.arrowfastener.com. **Description:** Produces stapling machines and similar products.

ARROW GROUP INDUSTRIES, INC.
1680 Route 23 North, P.O. Box 928, Wayne NJ 07474-0928. 973/696-6900. **Fax:** 973/696-8539. **Contact:** Joanne Trezza, Human Resources Director. **E-mail address:** assist@arrowsheds.com. **World Wide Web address:** http://www.sheds.com. **Description:** Manufactures steel storage buildings. **Corporate headquarters location:** This location. **Other U.S. locations:** Breese IL. **Listed on:** Privately held. **Number of employees at this location:** 115. **Number of employees nationwide:** 330.

THE ASBURY PARK PRESS
3601 Highway 66, P.O. Box 1550, Neptune NJ 07754. 732/922-6000. **Contact:** Human Resources. **E-mail address:** hr@app.com. **World Wide Web address:** http://www.app.com. **Description:** Publishes a daily local newspaper. **Special programs:** Internships. **Corporate headquarters location:** This location. **Other U.S. locations:** Orlando FL. **Listed on:** Privately held. **Number of employees nationwide:** 1,900.

ASCENT MEDIA EAST
235 Pegasus Avenue, Northvale NJ 07647. 201/767-3800. **Contact:** Human Resources. **World Wide Web address:** http://www.apvi.com. **Description:** Services include post-production work and audio and video restoration for a variety of networks including the Children's Television Network (CTW). **Corporate headquarters location:** New York NY. **Parent company:** International Post Ltd. provides a wide range of post-production services, primarily to the television advertising industry, and distributes television programming to the international market through its operating subsidiaries. Other subsidiaries of the parent company include Big Picture/Even Time Limited; Cabana; Manhattan Transfer, Inc.; and The Post Edge, Inc. The company's services include creative editorial services, film-to-tape transfer, electronic video editing, computer-generated graphics, duplication, and audio services, all in multiple standards and formats, as well as network playback operations. The company's services are provided in the New York metropolitan area and South Florida.

ASHLAND SPECIALITY CHEMICAL COMPANY
One Drew Plaza, Boonton NJ 07005. 973/263-7600. **Fax:** 973/263-4487. **Contact:** Personnel. **World Wide Web address:** http://www.ashchem.com. **Description:** This location supplies specialty chemicals and services to the international maritime industry and other industrial markets worldwide. Through its industrial chemical sector, the Drew Division also manufactures and markets products for water management and fuel treatment, as well as specialized chemicals for major industries. The Ameroid Marine Division provides chemical and sealing products and applications technology for these products to the maritime industry. Ashland Chemical Company provides shipboard technical service for more than 15,000 vessels in more than 140 ports around the world. **Positions advertised include:** Water Treatment Technical Sales Representative; Office Services Assistant; Office Typist. **Corporate headquarters location:** Dublin OH. **Parent company:** Ashland Inc. **Listed on:** New York Stock Exchange. **Stock exchange symbol:** ASH.

ASPECT COMPUTER CORPORATION
19 World's Fair Drive, Somerset NJ 08873. 732/563-1304. **Contact:** Human Resources. **World Wide Web address:** http://www.aspectcom.com. **Description:** Manufactures computers.

ATLANTIC CITY HILTON CASINO RESORT
P.O. Box 1737, Boston and Pacific Avenues, Atlantic City NJ 08401. 609/347-7111. **Contact:** Human Resources. **World Wide Web address:** http://www.hiltonac.com. **Description:** An 804-room hotel and casino. Atlantic City Hilton Casino Resort also features gourmet restaurants, live theater, a shopping center, and convention rooms.

ATLANTIC CITY MEDICAL CENTER
1925 Pacific Avenue, Atlantic City NJ 08401. 609/344-4081. **Contact:** Human Resources Department. **World Wide Web address:** http://www.atlanticare.org. **Description:** A full-service hospital, also providing a cancer center, neonatal intensive care unit, coronary care center, and a Level II Trauma Center. **Positions advertised include:** Patient Access Coordinator; Pool Technician; Group Teacher; Clinical

Therapist; Operations Assistant; Lab Assistant; Lab Testing Personnel; Emergency Medical Person; Administrative Associate; Dialysis Technician; Nutritional Counselor; Clinical Nurse Specialist; Registered Nurse. **Other area locations:** Pomona NJ.

ATLANTIC CITY SHOWBOAT INC.
P.O. Box 840, 801 Boardwalk, Atlantic City NJ 08401. 609/343-4000. **Contact:** Personnel. **World Wide Web address:** http://www.harrahs.com. **Description:** A hotel and casino. **Parent company:** Harrah's.

ATLANTIC METAL PRODUCTS, INC.
21 Fadem Road, Springfield NJ 07081. 973/379-6200. **Contact:** Personnel. **World Wide Web address:** http://www.atlanticmetal.com. **Description:** Manufactures custom precision sheet metal parts for the computer and office equipment industries. **Corporate headquarters location:** This location. **Other U.S. locations:** Hillside NJ.

AUTOMATIC DATA PROCESSING (ADP)
99 Jefferson Road, P.O. Box 450, Parsippany NJ 07054. 973/739-3000. **Contact:** Human Resources. **World Wide Web address:** http://www.adp.com. **Description:** One of the world's largest providers of computerized transaction processing, data communications, and information services. ADP pays over 18 million U.S. employees. The company provides payroll processing, payroll tax filing, job costing, labor distribution, automated bill payment, management reports, unemployment compensation management, human resource information, and benefits administration support to over 300,000 businesses. **Special programs:** Internships. **Corporate headquarters location:** Roseland NJ. **Operations at this facility include:** Divisional Headquarters; Research and Development. **Listed on:** New York Stock Exchange. **Stock exchange symbol:** ADP. **Annual sales/revenues:** More than $100 million. **Number of employees nationwide:** 25,000.

AUTOMATIC DATA PROCESSING (ADP)
One ADP Boulevard, Roseland NJ 07068. 973/974-5000. **Contact:** Human Resources. **World Wide Web address:** http://www.adp.com. **Description:** ADP is one of the world's largest providers of computerized transaction processing, data communications, and information services. ADP pays over 18 million U.S. employees. The company provides payroll processing, payroll tax filing, job costing, labor distribution, automated bill payment, management reports, unemployment compensation management, human resource information, and benefits administration support to over 300,000 businesses. **Corporate headquarters location:** This location. **Operations at this facility include:** This location houses administrative offices. **Listed on:** New York Stock Exchange. **Stock exchange symbol:** ADP. **Annual sales/revenues:** More than $100 million. **Number of employees nationwide:** 25,000.

AVENTIS PHARMACEUTICALS
200-400 Crossing Boulevard, Bridgewater NJ 08807. 908/304-7000. **Contact:** Human Resources. **World Wide Web address:** http://www.aventispharma-us.com. **Description:** An international pharmaceutical company working with respiratory, cardiac, and osteopathic medications. **Positions advertised include:** Animal Care Technician; Associate Chemist; Associate Scientist; Epidemiologist; Global Change Coordinator; Global Program Manager; Manager. **Operations at this facility include:** Marketing; Research and Development.

BASF CORPORATION
KNOLL PHARMACEUTICALS
100 Campus Drive, Florham Park NJ 07932. 973/245-6000. **Fax:** 973/245-6002. **Contact:** Liz Roman, Director of Human Resources. **World Wide Web address:** http://www.basf.com. **Description:** BASF Corporation is an international chemical products organization, doing business in five operating groups: Chemicals; Coatings and Colorants; Consumer Products and Life Sciences; Fiber Products; and Polymers. **Positions advertised include:** Quality Assurance Plant Specialist; Product Manager; Regulatory Supervisor; Business Process Optimization Manager; Technical Service Representative. **Corporate headquarters location:** This location. **Operations at this facility include:** This location serves as the U.S. headquarters and houses management offices and the pharmaceutical division, Knoll Pharmaceuticals. **Listed on:** New York Stock Exchange. **Stock exchange symbol:** BF. **Number of employees worldwide:** 125,000.

BJ'S WHOLESALE CLUB
1910 Deptford Center Road, Deptford NJ 08096. 856/232-8880. **Contact:** Human Resources. **E-mail address:** 44689.intjobpost.255@openhireresumes.com. **World Wide Web address:** http://www.bjswholesale.com. **Description:** A bulk distributor of merchandise from electronics to groceries. **Positions advertised include:** Assistant Store Manager; Overnight Merchandise Manager; Loss Prevention Manager; Meat Manager. **Corporate headquarters location:** Natick MA. **Parent company:** Waban Inc.

BMH CHRONOS RICHARDSON INC.
2 Stewart Place, Fairfield NJ 07004. 973/276-3692. **Contact:** Human Resources. **World Wide Web address:** http://www.bmhchronosrichardson.com. **Description:** Manufactures bagging equipment and batching systems for the food, chemical, rubber, and minerals market. **Office hours:** Monday - Friday, 8:30 a.m. - 5:00 p.m.

BMW OF NORTH AMERICA, INC.
P.O. Box 964, Hewitt NJ 07461. 201/307-4000. **Physical address:** 300 Chestnut Ridge Road, Woodcliff Lake NJ 07675. **Contact:** Employment Manager. **E-mail address:** bmwna@hreasy.com. **World Wide Web address:** http://www.bmwusa.com. **Description:** BMW of North America is responsible for U.S. marketing operations for BMW's extensive line of motorcycles and automobiles. **Parent company:** BMW-Bayerische Motoren Werke AG (Munich, Germany).

BOC GASES
575 Mountain Avenue, Murray Hill NJ 07974. 908/464-8100. **Fax:** 410/749-4073. **Contact:** Corporate Personnel. **World Wide Web address:** http://www.boc.com/gases. **Description:** BOC Gases manufactures industrial, electronic, and medical gases; and cryogenic equipment. **Corporate headquarters location:** This location. **Other U.S. locations:** Nationwide.

BAKER & TAYLOR
1120 Highway 22 East, Bridgewater NJ 08807-0885. 908/541-7000. **Contact:** Human Resources. **World Wide Web address:** http://www.btol.com. **Description:** A leading full-line distributor of books, videos, and music products. Customers include online and traditional retailers and institutional customers. Baker & Taylor also provides customers with value-added proprietary data products and customized management and outsourcing services. Founded in 1828. **NOTE:** Entry-level positions and second and third shifts are offered. **Positions advertised include:** Adaptive Cataloger; Collection Development Librarian; Publisher Services Supervisor; Support Center Representative. **Corporate headquarters location:** Charlotte NC. **Listed on:** Privately held. **Number of employees worldwide:** 2,500.

BALLY'S PARK PLACE
Park Place and Boardwalk, Atlantic City NJ 08401. 609/340-2000. **Contact:** Human Resources. **World Wide Web address:** http://www.ballysac.com. **Description:** A resort hotel and casino with 1,254 rooms, nine restaurants, a theater, retail space and convention facilities. **Subsidiaries include:** Bally's Wild Wild West casino is connected to Bally's Park Place, though it maintains separate gaming, dining and retail facilities. **Parent company:** Park Place Entertainment Corporation. **Listed on:** New York Stock Exchange. **Stock exchange symbol:** PPE.

BALTEK CORPORATION
P.O. Box 195, 10 Fairway Court, Northvale NJ 07647. 201/767-1400. **Fax:** 201/387-6631. **Contact:** Personnel. **World Wide Web address:** http://www.baltek.com. **Description:** Manufactures wood panels and other balsa wood products for marine and industrial use. **Corporate headquarters location:** This location.

BANK OF AMERICA
55 Challenger Road, Ridgefield Park NJ 07660. 201/547-7000. **Contact:** Human Resources. **World Wide Web address:** http://www.bankofamerica.com. **Description:** A full-service financial institution that serves corporate, retail, and private markets. **Corporate headquarters location:** Charlotte, NC. **Parent company:** Bank of America. **Listed on:** New York Stock Exchange. **Stock exchange symbol:** BAC.

BANK OF GLOUCESTER COUNTY
100 Park Avenue, Woodbury NJ 08096. 856/845-0700. **Fax:** 856/415-1347. **Contact:** Human Resources. **E-mail address:** humanresources@thebankofgc.com. **World Wide Web address:** http://www.thebankofgc.com. **Description:** A bank. Founded in 1989. **Positions advertised include:** Teller; Personal Banking Representative; Training & Development Specialist. **Office hours:** Monday - Friday, 8:30 a.m. - 5:00 p.m. **Corporate headquarters location:** This location. **Parent company:** Fulton Financial Corporation. **Listed on:** NASDAQ. **Stock exchange symbol:** FULT. **Number of employees at this location:** 200.

BANK OF NEW YORK
385 Rifle Camp Road, West Paterson NJ 07424. 973/357-7405. **Contact:** Personnel. **World Wide Web address:** http://www.bankofny.com. **Description:** A bank that serves individuals, corporations, foreign and domestic banks, governments, and other institutions through banking offices in New York City and foreign branches, representative offices, subsidiaries, and affiliates. **Positions advertised include:** Teller; Training & Development Specialist; Personal Banking Representative. **Corporate headquarters location:** New York NY. **Parent company:** Bank of New York Company, Inc. **Listed on:** New York Stock Exchange. **Stock exchange symbol:** BK. **Number of employees nationwide:** 12,000.

C.R. BARD, INC.
730 Central Avenue, Murray Hill NJ 07974. 908/277-8000. **Fax:** 908/277-8412. **Contact:** Human Resources. **World Wide Web address:** http://www.crbard.com. **Description:** Manufactures and distributes disposable medical, surgical, diagnostic, and patient care products. Cardiovascular products include angioplastic recanalization devices such as balloon angioplasty catheters, inflation devices, and developmental atherectomy and laser devices; electrophysiology products such as temporary pacing catheters, diagnostic and therapeutic electrodes, and cardiac mapping systems; a cardiopulmonary system; and blood oxygenators, cardiotomy reservoirs, and other products used in open heart surgery. Urological products include Foley catheters, trays, and related urine contract collection systems used extensively in postoperative bladder drainage. Surgical products include wound and chest drainage systems and implantable blood vessel replacements. **Corporate headquarters location:** This location. **Listed on:** New York Stock Exchange. **Stock exchange symbol:** BCR.

BARHAM-McBRIDE COMPANY INC.
80 Park Plaza Newark NJ 07102. 973/430-5640. **Contact:** Human Resources. **World Wide Web address:** http://www.pseg.com. **Description:** Mechanical contractors for the architecture and construction industries. **Parent company:** PSEG.

BARNERT HOSPITAL
680 Broadway, Paterson NJ 07514. 973/977-6600. **Fax:** 973/279-2924. **Recorded jobline:** 973/977-6824. **Contact:** Human Resources. **World Wide Web address:** http://www.barnerthosp.com. **Description:** A 280-bed hospital. **Positions advertised include:** Nurse Assistant; Unit Clerk; Medical Assistant; Ultrasonographer; Physical Therapist; Laboratory Technician; Medical Technologist; Pharmacy Tech; Independent Living Specialist; Mental Health Clinic; Outpatient Clinician; Resident Counselor; American Sign Language Associate; Maintenance Supervisor; Operator; Mechanic; Patient Biller; Credit Representative; House Keeper; Communications Representative; Registrar. **Special programs:** Internships. **Operations at this facility include:** Administration; Service. **Number of employees at this location:** 1,000.

BARRETT PAVING MATERIALS INC.
3 Becker Farm Road, Roseland NJ 07068-1748. 973/533-1001. **Fax:** 973/533-1020. **Contact:** Chris Kirby, Director of Human Resources. **E-mail address:** bpmicorp@aol.com. **World Wide Web address:** http://www.barrettpaving.com. **Description:** Barrett Paving Materials is engaged in the manufacture of road construction materials and the construction and paving of roads, airports, parking lots, race tracks, driveways, and bike paths. Founded in 1903. **NOTE:** Entry-level positions are offered. **Positions advertised include:** Manager; Construction Support Supervisor; Project Manager; Estimator; Equipment Support Specialist; Plant Superintendent; Quality Control Technician; Sales Associate; Accounting Associate; Administrative Associate; Plant Operator; Equipment Operator; Plant Foreman; Mechanic; Welder; Laborer; Truck Driver; Clerical Associate. **Special programs:** Training; Co-ops; Summer Jobs. **Corporate headquarters location:** This location. **Other U.S. locations:** Hebron CT; Richmond IN; Bangor ME; Ypsilanti MI; Hooksett NH; Bridgewater NJ; East Syracuse NY; Norwood NY; Utica NY; Cincinnati OH; Piqua OH. **International locations:** Worldwide. **Operations at this facility include:** This location houses administrative offices. **Parent company:** Colas Inc. **Annual sales/revenues:** More than $100 million. **Number of employees at this location:** 1,000.

BAX GLOBAL
896 Frelinghuysen Avenue, Newark NJ 07114. 973/954-2000. **Fax:** 973/954-2030. **Contact:** Human Resources. **World Wide Web address:** http://www.baxglobal.com. **Description:** Bax Global offers business-to-business freight delivery through a worldwide network of offices in 124 countries, with 155 offices in the U.S. **Other area locations:** Secaucus NJ. **Other U.S. locations:** Nationwide. **International locations:** Worldwide.

BEACON LOOMS, INC.
411 Alfred Avenue, Teaneck NJ 07666. 201/833-1600. **Contact:** Human Resources Department. **E-mail address:** contact@beaconlooms.com. **World Wide Web address:** http://www.beaconlooms.com. **Description:** Produces a wide range of textiles,

primarily for sale to retailers. **Corporate headquarters location:** This location. **Other U.S. locations:** Englewood NJ.

BEAR, STEARNS & COMPANY, INC.
115 South Jefferson Road, Whippany NJ 07981. 973/793-2600. **Fax:** 973/793-2040. **Contact:** Managing Director of Personnel. **World Wide Web address:** http://www.bearstearns.com. **Description:** An investment banking, securities trading, and brokerage firm engaged in corporate finance, mergers, and acquisitions; institutional equities and fixed income sales and trading; individual investor services; asset management; and correspondent clearing. **Corporate headquarters location:** New York NY. **Parent company:** The Bear Stearns Companies Inc. is a leading worldwide investment banking, securities trading, and brokerage firm. **Listed on:** New York Stock Exchange. **Stock exchange symbol:** BSC.

BECTON DICKINSON & COMPANY
One Becton Drive, Franklin Lakes NJ 07417. 201/847-6800. **Contact:** Human Resources. **World Wide Web address:** http://www.bd.com. **Description:** A medical company engaged in the manufacture of health care products, medical instrumentation, diagnostic products, and industrial safety equipment. Major medical equipment product lines include hypodermics, intravenous equipment, operating room products, thermometers, gloves, and specialty needles. The company also offers contract packaging services. Founded in 1896. **Positions advertised include:** Administrative Assistant; Project Leader; Customer Service Associate; Customer Service Representative; Transactional Six Sigma Black Belt; Help Desk Analyst; Product Development Engineer; Cost Analyst; Training Administrator; Project Manager; Rebate Reconciliation Analyst; Corporate Development Manager; Business Analyst; Claims Associate; Data Entry Associate. **Corporate headquarters location:** This location. **Listed on:** New York Stock Exchange. **Stock exchange symbol:** BDX. **Number of employees worldwide:** 18,000.

BEL FUSE INC.
206 Van Vorst Street, Jersey City NJ 07302. 201/432-0463. **Fax:** 201/432-9542. **Contact:** Personnel Department. **World Wide Web address:** http://www.belfuse.com. **Description:** Designs, manufactures, and sells products used in local area networking, telecommunications, business equipment, and consumer electronic applications. Magnetic components manufactured by the company fall into four major groups: pulse transformers; delay lines, filters, and AC/DC converters; power transformers, line chokes, and coils; and packaged modules. The company manufactures miniature and micro fuses for supplementary circuit protection. Bel Fuse sells its products to approximately 550 customers throughout North America, Western Europe, and the Far East. **Other U.S. locations:** CA; IN. **International locations:** France; Hong Kong; Macau. **Listed on:** NASDAQ. **Stock exchange symbol:** BELF.

BEL-RAY COMPANY, INC.
P.O. Box 526, Farmingdale NJ 07727. 732/938-2421. **Physical address:** 1201 Bowman Avenue, Wall NJ 07719. **Fax:** 732/938-4232. **Contact:** Personnel. **E-mail address:** employment@belray.com. **World Wide Web address:** http://www.belray.com. **Description:** Manufactures lubricants used in the aerospace, automotive, food, marine, mining, steel, and textiles industries. **Positions advertised include:** Research & Development Specialist; Sales Representative.

BELCO TECHNOLOGIES, INC.
7 Entin Road, Parsippany NJ 07054. 973/884-4700. **Contact:** Joseph Stehn. **E-mail address:** stehn@belcotech.com. **World Wide Web address:** http://www.belcotech.com. **Description:** A worldwide manufacturer of processes and equipment for the removal of air and water pollutants. Pollution control equipment includes electrostatic precipitators and related components. **NOTE:** Applications may be sent to above address attention: Mr. Joseph T. Stehn. **Corporate headquarters location:** This location.

BENJAMIN MOORE & COMPANY
51 Chestnut Ridge Road, Montvale NJ 07645. 201/573-9600. **Fax:** 201/573-6631. **Contact:** Personnel. **World Wide Web address:** http://www.benjaminmoore.com. **Description:** Manufactures paints, varnishes, and other coatings. **Positions advertised include:** Cost Planning & Analysis Manager; Tax Accountant; Financial Analyst; Accounts Receivable Assistant; Benefits Administrator; Human Resources Information Systems Consultant; Color Marketing Manager; Business to Business Marketing Manager; Associate Project Manager; Manager of Retail Advertising; Retail Store Design Manager; Retail Regional Manager. **Corporate headquarters location:** This location. **Other U.S. locations:** Nationwide. **Operations at this facility include:** Administration; Research and Development; Sales; Service. **Listed on:** Privately held. **Number of employees at this location:** 175. **Number of employees nationwide:** 1,800.

BERGEN COMMUNITY COLLEGE
400 Paramus Road, Paramus NJ 07652-1595. 201/447-7442. **Fax:** 201/251-4987. **Contact:** Human Resources. **World Wide Web address:** http://www.bergen.cc.nj.us. **Description:** A community college enrolling over 12,000 students. The college offers associate degrees in arts, sciences, and applied sciences. **Positions advertised include:** Director of Human Resources; Financial Aide Assistant. **NOTE:** Search for updated jobs at website. Send resumes to above address.

BERGER BROWN COMMUNICATIONS
215 Ridgedale Avenue, Florham Park NJ 07932. 973/410-0500. **Fax:** 973/410-0600. **Contact:** Human Resources. **E-mail address:** bb.info@bergerbrown.com. **World Wide Web address:** http://www.bergerbrown.com. **Description:** A nationally recognized public relations & advertising firm. **Positions advertised include:** Publicist.

THE LOUIS BERGER GROUP, INC.
100 Halsted Street, East Orange NJ 07018. 973/678-1960. **Fax:** 973/676-0532. **Contact:** Ms. Terry Williams, Human Resources Manager. **E-mail address:** recruiter@louisberger.com. **World Wide Web address:** http://www.louisberger.com. **Description:** A diversified consulting firm. The company provides cultural, environmental, and transportation-related engineering and planning services in the United States. Louis Berger also aids in urban and rural development projects in Africa, Asia, Latin America, and the Middle East. This location also hires seasonally. Founded in 1940. **NOTE:** Entry-level positions and part-time jobs are offered. **Positions advertised include:** Proposal Coordinator; Office Administrator; Corporate Security Director; Security Manager; Transportation Engineer; Cost Engineer; Engineer; Project Management & Accounting Assistant; Traffic Engineer; Air Quality Control Specialist; Geologist; Industrial Hygienist. **Special programs:** Summer Jobs. **Office hours:** Monday - Friday, 8:30 a.m. - 5:15 p.m. **Corporate headquarters location:** This location. **Other U.S. locations:** Washington DC; Chicago IL; Needham MA; Las Vegas NV. **International locations:** Worldwide. **Listed on:** Privately held. **President:** Derish Wolff. **Information Systems Manager:** Michael Stern. **Annual sales/revenues:** More than $100 million. **Number of employees at this location:** 270. **Number of employees nationwide:** 900. **Number of employees worldwide:** 2,000.

BERLEX LABORATORIES, INC.
300 Fairfield Road, Wayne NJ 07470. 973/694-4100. **Contact:** Human Resources. **World Wide Web address:** http://www.berlex.com. **Description:** Researches, manufactures, and markets ethical pharmaceutical products in the fields of cardiovascular medicine, endocrinology and fertility control, diagnostic imaging, oncology, and central nervous system disorders. Berlex Laboratories has three strategic units: Berlex Drug Development & Technology (New Jersey), Oncology/Central Nervous System (California), and Berlex Biosciences (California). The company also owns Berlex Drug Development and Technology and operates a national sales force. The sales force, which is divided into three geographic regions, markets the complete line of Berlex products including BETASERON, which is used to treat multiple sclerosis. **Positions advertised include:** Sales Administrative Assistant; Clinical Supplies Packaging Specialist; Drug Safety Specialist; Facility Systems & Services Specialist. **Corporate headquarters location:** This location. **Parent company:** Schering AG (Germany).

BERLIN & JONES COMPANY, INC.
2 East Union Avenue, East Rutherford NJ 07073. 201/933-5900. **Fax:** 201/933-4242. **Contact:** Human Resources. **Description:** Manufactures envelopes. **Corporate headquarters location:** This location.

BERLITZ INTERNATIONAL, INC.
400 Alexander Park, Princeton NJ 08540. 609/514-9650. **Contact:** Human Resources. **World Wide Web address:** http://www.berlitz.com. **Description:** A language services firm providing instruction and translation services through 298 language centers in 28 countries around the world. The company also publishes travel guides, foreign language phrase books, and home study materials. **Corporate headquarters location:** This location. **Operations at this facility include:** Administration. **Number of employees nationwide:** 3,500.

BESTFOODS BAKING COMPANY
700 Sylvan Avenue, Englewood Cliffs NJ 07632. 201/894-4000. **Contact:** Corporate Personnel. **World Wide Web address:** http://www.bestfoods.com. **Description:** Bestfoods produces and distributes a variety of food products including soups, sauces, and bouillons; dressings including Hellmann's mayonnaise; starches and syrups; bread spreads including Skippy peanut butter; desserts and baking aids; and pasta. **Corporate headquarters location:** This location. **Operations at this facility include:** This location houses the administrative and marketing offices and is also the world headquarters.

BIO-REFERENCE LABORATORIES
481B Edward H. Ross Drive, Elmwood Park NJ 07407. 201/791-2600. **Contact:** Human Resources. **World Wide Web address:** http://www.bio-referencelabs.com. **Description:** Operates a clinical laboratory. Bio-Reference offers a list of chemical diagnostic tests including blood and urine analysis, blood chemistry, hematology services, serology, radioimmunological analysis, toxicology (including drug screening), Pap smears, tissue pathology (biopsies), and other tissue analyses. Bio-Reference markets its services directly to physicians, hospitals, clinics, and other health facilities. **Corporate headquarters location:** This location. **Listed on:** NASDAQ. **Stock exchange symbol:** BRLI.

BIOSEARCH MEDICAL PRODUCTS, INC.
35A Industrial Parkway, Somerville NJ 08876. 908/722-5000. **Toll-free phone:** 800/326-5976. **Fax:** 908/722-5024. **Contact:** Human Resources. **World Wide Web address:** http://www.biosearch.com. **Description:** Manufactures specialty medical devices for the gastroenterology, endoscopy, urology, and enteral feeding markets. The company's products are sold directly to hospitals and alternative care centers through domestic and international specialty dealers. Founded in 1978. **NOTE:** Entry-level positions are offered. **Special programs:** Training. **Parent company:** Hydromer Inc. **Listed on:** NASDAQ. **Stock exchange symbol:** BMPI. **Annual sales/revenues:** $5 - $10 million. **Number of employees at this location:** 30.

BISYS GROUP, INC.
2091 Springdale Road, Cherry Hill NJ 08003. 824/424-0150. **Contact:** Human Resources. **World Wide Web address:** http://www.bisys.com. **Description:** A national, third-party provider of computing, administrative, and marketing support services to financial organizations. Services are offered through three major business units: Information Services, Loan Services, and Investment Services. The company derives a majority of its revenues from services provided through a single integrated software product, TOTAL PLUS, which includes comprehensive loan and deposit administration; branch automation and electronic banking services; operations and new business systems support; and accounting, financial management, and regulatory reporting services. **Positions advertised include:** Computer Operator; Conversion Analyst; Relationship Manager; Client Services Representative. **NOTE:** Resumes may be submitted on-line at the above Website. Job postings are listed by location in the "Careers" section. **Listed on:** New York Stock Exchange. **Stock exchange symbol:** BSG.

BLONDER TONGUE LABORATORIES, INC.
One Jake Brown Road, Old Bridge NJ 08857-1000. 732/679-4000. **Fax:** 732/679-4353. **Contact:** Human Resources. **E-mail address:** employment@blondertongue.com. **World Wide Web address:** http://www.blondertongue.com. **Description:** Designs and manufactures signal processing equipment for the television industry. Products are used for satellite communications, master antennae systems (MATV), and other systems using RF technology. **Corporate headquarters location:** This location. **Operations at this facility include:** Administration; Divisional Headquarters; Manufacturing; Regional Headquarters; Research and Development; Sales; Service. **Listed on:** American Stock Exchange. **Stock exchange symbol:** BDR. **Annual sales/revenues:** $51 - $100 million. **Number of employees at this location:** 500.

BLUEBIRD AUTO RENTAL SYSTEMS INC.
200 Mineral Springs Drive, Dover NJ 07801. 973/560-0080. **Contact:** Human Resources. **E-mail address:** info@barsnet.com. **World Wide Web address:** http://www.barsnet.com. **Description:** Designs computer applications for automobile rental agencies.

BLOOMFIELD COLLEGE
467 Franklin Street, Bloomfield NJ 07003. 973/748-9000. **Fax:** 973/743-3998. **Contact:** Human Resources. **World Wide Web address:** http://www.bloomfield.edu. **Description:** A private four year college with ties to the Presbyterian Church offering bachelors and bachelor of science degrees. **Positions advertised include:** Admissions Counselor; New Business Development Manager.

BOBST GROUP, INC.
146 Harrison Avenue, Roseland NJ 07068. 973/226-8000. **Contact:** Personnel. **World Wide Web address:** http://www.bobstgroup.com. **Description:** Produces a line of equipment for the converting, printing, and publishing industries. The company operates in the United States through three groups: Bobst, Bobst Champlain, and Bobst Registron. Products include die cutter/creasers, folder/gluers, flexo and gravure presses, electronic controls, and other sheet and web-fed equipment. The company is also a manufacturer of converting equipment for the folding carton industry. **Parent company:** Bobst S.A. (Lausanne, Switzerland).

BON SECOURS & CANTERBURY PARTNERSHIP FOR CARE
25 McWilliams Place, Jersey City NJ 07302. 201/418-2065. **Fax:** 201/418-2063. **Contact:** Personnel. **World Wide Web address:** http://www.bonsecoursnj.com. **Description:** Operates two community hospitals: St. Mary Hospital (Hoboken NJ) and St. Francis Hospital (Jersey City NJ). **Positions advertised include:** Assistant Manager; Case Manager; Clinical Nurse Specialist; Coder Analyst; Home Health Care Nurse; Lead Therapist; Occupational Therapist; Receptionist; Registration Associate; Respiratory Therapist; Registered Nurse; Social Worker; X-ray Technologist. **NOTE:** Entry-level positions are offered. **Special programs:** Internships. **Corporate headquarters location:** This location. **Annual sales/revenues:** $11 - $20 million. **Number of employees at this location:** 1,500.

BOOKAZINE COMPANY INC.
75 Hook Road, Bayonne NJ 07002. 201/339-7777. **Fax:** 201/239-7778. **Contact:** Richard Kallman, Vice President. **E-mail address:** staff@bookazine.com. **World Wide Web address:** http://www.bookazine.com. **Description:** A general trade book wholesaler serving retail bookstores with an inventory of over 100,000 titles. Founded in 1928. **Corporate headquarters location:** This location. **President/CEO:** Robert Kallman.

BOWMAN & COMPANY LLP
601 White Horse Road, Voorhees NJ 08043. 856/435-6200. **Fax:** 856/435-0440. **Contact:** Robert Biddla, Human Resources. **World Wide Web address:** http://www.bowmanllp.com. **Description:** A certified public accounting firm. Founded in 1939. **NOTE:** Fill out application online. Entry-level positions are offered. **Special programs:** Internships; Co-ops. **Corporate headquarters location:** This location. **Listed on:** Privately held. **Annual sales/revenues:** $5 - $10 million. **Number of employees at this location:** 90.

BRACCO DIAGNOSTICS INC.
107 College Road East, Princeton NJ 08540. 609/514-2200. **Toll-free phone:** 800/631-5244. **Fax:** 609/514-2452. **Contact:** Human Resources. **E-mail address:** jobsearch@bracco.com. **World Wide Web address:** http://www.bdi.bracco.com. **Description:** Researches and develops diagnostic pharmaceuticals and nuclear medicine imaging products. **NOTE:** Resumes may be submitted on-line at the above Website. Job listings provide e-mail addresses and contact information. **Positions advertised include:** Personal Manager; Product Manager; Sales Operator; Financial Planning Analysis Director; Corporate Accounts Executive. **Parent company:** Bracco S.p.A. **Number of employees worldwide:** 2,300.

BRADLEY PHARMACEUTICALS, INC.
383 Route 46 West, Fairfield NJ 07004-2402. 973/882-1505. **Fax:** 973/575-5366. **Contact:** Human Resources. **E-mail address:** personnel@bradpharm.com. **World Wide Web address:** http://www.bradpharm.com. **Description:** Manufactures and markets over-the-counter and prescription pharmaceuticals, and health-related products including nutritional, personal hygiene, and internal medicine brands. Founded in 1985. **Positions advertised include:** Product Manager; Sales Assistant Training Manager; Quality Assurance Director; Pharmaceutical Sales Representative; Telemarketing. **Corporate headquarters location:** This location. **Subsidiaries include:** Doak Dermatologics Company Inc. (Westbury NY); Kenwood Therapeutics. **Listed on:** NASDAQ. **Stock exchange symbol:** BPRX.

BREEZE-EASTERN
700 Liberty Avenue, Union NJ 07083. 908/686-4000. **Fax:** 908/686-4279. **Contact:** Ed Chestnut, Director of Human Resources. **E-mail address:** echestnut@breeze-eastern.com. **World Wide Web address:** http://www.breeze-eastern.com. **Description:** Designs, develops, manufactures, and services sophisticated lifting and restraining products, principally helicopter rescue hoist and cargo hook systems; winches and hoists for aircraft and weapon systems; and aircraft cargo tie-down systems. **Positions advertised include:** Product Support Vice President; Assistant Supervisor Overhaul & Repair; Mechanical Design Engineer. **Corporate headquarters location:** This location. **Parent company:** TransTechnology designs, manufactures, sells, and distributes specialty fasteners through several other subsidiaries including: Breeze Industrial Products (Saltsburg PA) manufactures a complete line of standard and specialty gear-driven band fasteners in high-grade stainless steel for use in highly-engineered applications; The Palnut Company (Mountainside NJ) manufactures light- and heavy-duty single and multithread specialty fasteners; Industrial Retaining Ring (Irvington NJ) manufactures a variety of retaining rings made of carbon steel, stainless steel, and beryllium copper; The Seeger Group (Somerville NJ) manufactures retaining clips, circlips, spring pins, and similar components.

BRINKS INC
481 New Jersey Railroad Avenue, Newark NJ 07114. 973/824-0778. **Fax:** 973/824-1396. **Contact:** Human Resources. **World Wide Web address:** www.brinksinc.com. **Description:** An armored security service specializing in transporting currency. **Corporate headquarters location:** Dallas TX.

BRISTOL-MYERS SQUIBB COMPANY
P.O. Box 5335, Princeton NJ 08543-5335. 609/252-4000. **Fax:** 609/897-6412. **Contact:** Employment Department. **World Wide Web address:** http://www.bms.com. **Description:** Bristol-Myers Squibb manufactures pharmaceuticals, medical devices, nonprescription drugs, toiletries, and beauty aids. The company's pharmaceutical products include cardiovascular drugs, anti-infectives, anticancer agents, AIDS therapy treatments, central nervous system drugs, diagnostic agents, and other drugs. Nonprescription products include formulas, vitamins, analgesics, remedies, and skin care products. Nonprescription drug brand names include Bufferin, Excedrin, Nuprin, and Comtrex. Beauty aids include Clairol and Ultress hair care, Nice 'n Easy and Clairesse hair colorings, hair sprays, gels, and deodorants. **Positions advertised include:** Medical Marketing Director; Global Marketing Director; Clinical Scientist Associate; Research Scientist Associate; Clinical Protocol Manager; Clinical Scientist; Research Investigator; Research Assistant; Territory Business Sales Associate; Accounting Director; Principal Accountant; Associate Manager; Administrative Assistant; Counsel Patent Associate; Director Marketing Research; Manager. **Corporate headquarters location:** New York NY. **Operations at this facility include:** This location is engaged in the research and manufacture of various pharmaceuticals and personal care products. **Listed on:** New York Stock Exchange. **Stock exchange symbol:** BMY.

BROADBEAM CORPORATION
2540 Route 130, Suite 116, Cranbury NJ 08512. 609/655-3737. **Fax:** 609/655-1282. **Contact:** Human Resources. **E-mail address:** hr@broadbeam.com. **World Wide Web address:** http://www.broadbeam.com. **Description:** Provides wireless solutions by developing platform and professional services that allow companies to develop, deploy, and manage mobile solutions. **Corporate headquarters location:** This location.

BROTHER INTERNATIONAL CORPORATION
100 Somerset Corporate Boulevard, Bridgewater NJ 08807. 908/704-1700. **Contact:** Human Resources. **World Wide Web address:** http://www.brother.com. **Description:** One of America's largest manufacturers and distributors of personal word processors and portable electronic typewriters. Brother also markets many industrial products, home appliances, and business machines manufactured by its parent company. Founded in 1954. **Corporate headquarters location:** This location. **Parent company:** Brother Industries, Ltd. (Nagoya, Japan). **Number of employees nationwide:** 1,300.

BURDETTE TOMLIN MEMORIAL HOSPITAL
2 Stone Harbor Boulevard, Cape May Court House NJ 08210. 609/463-2000. **Fax:** 609/463-2379. **Contact:** Meaghan Sterner, Employment Representative. **E-mail address:** msterner@bthosp.com. **World Wide Web address:** http://www.btmh.com. **Description:** A 242-bed, acute care, community hospital. **Positions advertised include:** Nurse Manager; Registered Nurse; Medical Technologist; Medical Transcriptionist.

BURLINGTON COAT FACTORY
1830 Route 130, Burlington NJ 08016. 609/387-7800. **Contact:** Human Resources. **E-mail address:** employment.opportunites@coat.com. **World Wide Web address:** http://www.coat.com. **Description:** An off-price apparel discounter. Product lines consist of brand name apparel including coats, sportswear, children's wear, men's wear, juvenile furniture, linens, shoes, and accessories. **Corporate headquarters location:** This location. **Listed on:** New York Stock Exchange. **Stock exchange symbol:** BCF.

BURNS AND ROE ENTERPRISES, INC.
800 Kinderkamack Road, Oradell NJ 07649. 201/265-2000. **Contact:** Human Resources. **World Wide Web address:** http://www.roe.com. **Description:** Engaged in construction, engineering, maintenance, and operation services. The company specializes in the design and engineering of complex facilities. **Special programs:** Internships. **Positions advertised include:** Principal Nuclear Engineer; Vendor Document Programmer; Utilities Supervisor Services. **Corporate headquarters location:** This location. **Listed on:** Privately held. **Number of employees at this location:** 600. **Number of employees nationwide:** 1,200. **Number of employees worldwide:** 1,250.

C/S GROUP
3 Werner Way, Lebanon NJ 08833. 908/236-0800. **Fax:** 908/236-0604. **Contact:** Susan Kizies, Director of Human Resources. **E-mail address:** careerops@c-sgroup.com. **World Wide Web address:** http://www.c-sgroup.com. **Description:** Manufactures building materials including wall protection products, sun controls, and fire vents. Founded in 1948. **NOTE:** Entry-level positions and part-time jobs are offered. **Positions advertised include:** Database Analyst Programmer. **Corporate headquarters location:** This location. **Other U.S. locations:** Garden Grove CA; Muncy PA. **International locations:** France; Spain; United Kingdom. **Listed on:** Privately held. **Annual sales/revenues:** More than $100 million.

CB RICHARD ELLIS
61 South Paramus Road, 4th Floor, Paramus NJ 07652. 201/556-9800. **Fax:** 201/556-5100. **Contact:** Human Resources. **E-mail address:** opps@cbre.com. **World Wide Web address:** http://www.cbrichardellis.com. **Description:** A real estate services company offering property sales and leasing, property and facility management, mortgage banking, and investment management services. **Positions advertised include:** Building Engineer; Assistant Manager; Real Estate Manager; Sales Professional. **Corporate headquarters location:** Los Angeles CA. **Number of employees worldwide:** 9,000.

CCA INDUSTRIES INC.
200 Murray Hill Parkway, East Rutherford NJ 07073. 201/330-1400. **Contact:** Human Resources Department. **World Wide Web address:** http://www.ccaindustries.com. **Description:** Distributes a wide variety of health and beauty products manufactured by other companies using CCA's formulations. The majority of its sales are made to retail drug and food chains and mass merchandisers. Nail treatment products are sold under the name Nutra Nail; hair treatment products are sold under the names Pro Perm, Wash 'n Curl, Wash 'n Tint, and Wash 'n Straight; depilatory products are sold under the Hair Off label; skin care products are sold under the Sudden Change name; oral hygiene products are sold under the Plus+White trademark; meal replacement products are sold under the trademark Eat 'n Lose; and diet products under the trademarks Hungrex and Permathene. **Listed on:** NASDAQ. **Stock exchange symbol:** CCAM.

CIT GROUP, INC.
650 CIT Drive, Livingston NJ 07039. 973/740-5000. **Contact:** Personnel Officer. **World Wide Web address:** http://www.citgroup.com. **Description:** A diversified financial services organization that provides flexible funding alternatives, secured business lending, and financial advisory services for corporations, manufacturers, and dealers. Founded in 1908. **Positions advertised include:** Asset Management Specialist; Regional Account Manager; Document Administrator; AVP Financial Systems; Executive Assistant; Internal Audit Manager; Risk Management Vice President; Information Security Specialist; Executive Secretary; Night Shift Operator; Manager; Tax Manager; Underwriter; Accounting Manager; Network Analyst; Information Security Specialist. **Corporate headquarters location:** New York NY. **Other U.S. locations:** Nationwide. **International locations:** Worldwide. **Number of employees nationwide:** 2,500.

CMEINFO.COM
1008 Astoria Boulevard, Suite A, Cherry Hill NJ 08033. 856/874-0010. **Contact:** Human Resources. **World Wide Web address:** http://www.cmeinfo.com. **Description:** Produces educational videotapes, audiotapes, and CD-ROMs for professionals in the medical field.

CNBC
MSNBC
One Msnbc Plaza, Secaucus NJ 07094. 201/735-2622. **Fax:** 201/346-6506. **Contact:** Personnel. **World Wide Web address:** http://www.msnbc.com. **Description:** Operates all-news networks offering current business and finance news. CNBC and MSNBC are both updated 24 hours a day, seven days a week. **Positions advertised include:**

Multimedia Producer; Interactive Producer. **NOTE:** CNBC's website is http://moneycentral.msn.com/investor/home.asp. **Corporate headquarters location:** This location. **Parent company:** NBC.

CNT
100 Mount Holly Bypass, P.O. 440, Lumberton NJ 08048. 609/518-4000. **Fax:** 609/518-4019. **Contact:** Human Resources. **World Wide Web address:** http://www.inrange.com. **Description:** Produces proprietary switching and control equipment used to increase the performance of online data communications, data processing, and information systems. The company's products help anticipate system failures. **Special programs:** Internships. **Corporate headquarters location:** Minneapolis MN. **Other U.S. locations:** Orange CT; Westford MA.

CR ENGLAND
403 Dultys Lane, Burlington NJ 08016. 609/387-2766. **Contact:** Human Resources. **World Wide Web address:** http://www.crengland.com. **Description:** A trucking company providing freight services. **Positions advertised include:** Driver.

CSM WORLDWIDE, INC.
ENVIRONMENTAL SYSTEMS DIVISION
269 Sheffield Street, Mountainside NJ 07092. 908/233-2882. **Fax:** 968/233-1064. **Contact:** Human Resources. **World Wide Web address:** http://www.csmworldwide.com. **Description:** Markets, designs, manufactures, and installs air pollution control systems containing catalysts, blowers, burners, analyzers, heat exchangers, and other treatment and monitoring components. These air pollution control systems for hydrocarbon oxidation and nitrogen oxides reduction are used in a wide variety of industrial manufacturing and chemical processing applications. Environmental regulatory compliance, turnkey installation, and after-sale maintenance services are also provided. The company is a leader in supplying controls for commercial bakeries, chemical plants, the pharmaceutical industry, and can and metal coating operations. The company also sells to worldwide markets through the combination of a direct sales force and manufacturer representatives. **Positions advertised include:** Field Engineer; Sales Engineer; Project Engineer Manager.

CAESARS ATLANTIC CITY HOTEL CASINO
2100 Pacific Avenue, Atlantic City NJ 08401. 609/348-4411. **Fax:** 609/236-4522. **Contact:** Personnel. **World Wide Web address:** http://www.caesars.com. **Description:** A 1,100-room hotel. **Parent company:** Park Place Entertainment.

CAMBREX CORPORATION
One Meadowlands Plaza, East Rutherford NJ 07073-2150. 201/804-3000. **Fax:** 201/804-9852. **Contact:** Melissa Lesko, Professional Staffing Department. **E-mail address:** human.resources@cambrex.com. **World Wide Web address:** http://www.cambrex.com. **Description:** Manufactures and markets products and provides services to the life sciences industries. Cambrex Corporation operates in four segments: Human Health; Biotechnology; Animal Health and Agriculture; and Specialty Products. Founded in 1981. **NOTE:** Apply online. **Positions advertised include:** Staff Accountant; Internal Auditor; Employee Benefits Manager; Payroll Specialist; Network Engineer; Corporate Counsel. **Office hours:** Monday - Friday, 8:30 a.m. - 5:00 p.m. **Corporate headquarters location:** This location.

CAMDEN COUNTY COLLEGE
College Road, P.O. Box 200, Blackwood NJ 08012. 856/227-7200. **Contact:** Human Resources. **E-mail address:** hr@camdencc.edu. **World Wide Web address:** http://www.camdencc.edu. **Description:** A community college with more than 11,500 students enrolled in over 80 academic areas.

CAMPBELL SOUP COMPANY
One Campbell Place, Camden NJ 08103-1799. 856/342-4800. **Contact:** Human Resources. **World Wide Web address:** http://www.campbellsoups.com. **Description:** Campbell Soup Company is a producer of commercial soups, juices, pickles, frozen foods, canned beans, canned pasta products, spaghetti sauces, and baked goods. The company's products are distributed worldwide. U.S. brand names include Campbell's, Vlasic, V8, Chunky, Home Cookin', Prego, Pepperidge Farm, Inc., LeMenu, Mrs. Paul's, and Swanson. European foods are sold under brand names such as Pleybin, Biscuits Delacre, Freshbake, Groko, Godiva, and Betis. Campbell Soup Company also owns Arnotts Biscuits of Australia. **Corporate headquarters location:** This location. **Operations at this facility include:** This location houses administrative offices. **Listed on:** New York Stock Exchange. **Stock exchange symbol:** CPB.

CANTEL INDUSTRIES, INC.
Overlook at Great Notch, 150 Clove Road, 9th Floor, Little Falls NJ 07424. 973/890-7220. **Contact:** Human Resources. **World Wide Web address:** http://www.cantelmedical.com. **Description:** A holding company. **Subsidiaries include:** Carson Group Inc. (Canada) markets and distributes medical instruments including flexible and rigid endoscopes; precision instruments including microscopes and image analysis systems; and industrial equipment including remote visual inspection devices, laser distance measurement and thermal imaging products, and online optical inspection and quality assurance systems for specialized industrial applications. Carson also offers a full range of photographic equipment and supplies for amateur and professional photographers. **Listed on:** NASDAQ. **Stock exchange symbol:** CNTL.

CANTERBURY INFORMATION TECHNOLOGY, INC.
CANTERBURY CONSULTING GROUP, INC.
352 Stokes Road, Medford NJ 08055. 609/953-0044. **Toll-free phone:** 800/873-2040. **Fax:** 609/953-0062. **Contact:** Nancy Rose, Manager of Human Resources Department **E-mail address:** jobs@canterburyconsultinggroup.com. **World Wide Web address:** http://www.canterburyconsultinggroup.com. **Description:** A corporate training company providing information technology services. Training covers entry-level vocational, managerial, executive, and technical areas. **Corporate headquarters location:** This location. **Subsidiaries include:** ATM/Canterbury Corp. is a software development and consulting firm. CALC/Canterbury Corp. is a computer software training company. MSI/Canterbury Corp. is a management, sales, and communication training company. ProSoft/Canterbury Corp. is a provider of technical staffing, applications development, and corporate training.

CAPE MAY STAR & WAVE
600 Park Boulevard Park Center #5, Cape May NJ 08204. 609/884-3466. **Contact:** Human Resources **E-mail address:** cmstarwave@comcast.net. **World Wide Web address:** http://www.starandwave.com. **Description:** A 149 year old local area newspaper.

CAPGEMINI U.S.
100 Walnut Avenue, Clark NJ 07066. 732/669-6000. **Fax:** 732/669-6205. **Contact:** Human Resources. **World Wide Web address:** http://www.us.capgemini.com. **Description:** A leading provider of information technology consulting services with offices nationwide. **Positions advertised include:** Human Resources Manager; Administrative Assistant; Government Solutions Manager; Sales Executive; Sales Associate; Pharmacist Manager. **Other U.S. locations:** Nationwide.

CAPITAL HEALTH SYSTEM
FULD CAMPUS
750 Brunswick Avenue, Trenton NJ 08638. 609/394-6000. **Fax:** 609/394-4444. **Contact:** Human Resources. **E-mail address:** employment@chsnj.org. **World Wide Web address:** http://www.capitalhealth.org. **Description:** A 589-bed, acute-care, teaching hospital. **NOTE:** Mail resumes to: Human Resources Department, 446 Bellevue Avenue, Trenton NJ 08607. **Corporate headquarters location:** This location.

CAPITAL HEALTH SYSTEM
MERCER CAMPUS
446 Bellevue Avenue, Trenton NJ 08607. 609/394-4000. **Fax:** 609/394-4444. **Contact:** Human Resources. **E-mail address:** employment@chsnj.org. **World Wide Web address:** http://www.capitalhealth.org. **Description:** A 318-bed, community-based, acute care facility. **Positions advertised include:** Assistant Store Manager; Cardiac Monitor Technician; Case Manager; Claims Manager; Coder; Cook; Dietary Aide; Emergency Medical Technician; File Clerk; Food Service Worker; Housekeeper; Licensed Practical Nurse; Registered Nurse.

CASIO INC.
570 Mount Pleasant Avenue, Dover NJ 07801. 973/361-5400. **Fax:** 973/537-8910. **Contact:** Personnel Manager. **E-mail address:** casioincjobs@casio.com. **World Wide Web address:** http://www.casio.com. **Description:** Manufactures consumer electronics and computer-based products. **NOTE:** Entry-level positions are offered. **Office hours:** Monday - Friday, 9:00 a.m. - 5:00 p.m. **Corporate headquarters location:** This location. **Other U.S. locations:** Glendale Heights IL; Little Ferry NJ. **International locations:** Worldwide. **Parent company:** Casio Computer Company, Ltd. (Tokyo, Japan). **Listed on:** Privately held. **Annual sales/revenues:** More than $100 million. **Number of employees at this location:** 150. **Number of employees nationwide:** 325.

CASTROL NORTH AMERICA, INC.
1500 Valley Road, Wayne NJ 07470. 973/633-2200. **Fax:** 973/633-5305. **Contact:** Mary Thompson, Director of Human Resources. **E-mail address:** hrjobs@cnacm.com. **World Wide Web address:** http://www.castrolna.com. **Description:** Manufactures and markets lubricants and petroleum products. **NOTE:** Apply online. **Corporate headquarters location:** This location. **Parent company:** Burmah Castrol USA, Inc. **Number of employees at this location:** 200. **Number of employees nationwide:** 2,500.

CELGENE CORPORATION
86 Morris Avenue, Summit NJ 07901. 732/271-1001. **Fax:** 732/271-4184. **Contact:** Human Resources. **E-mail address:** jobs@celgene.com. **World Wide Web address:** http://www.celgene.com. **Description:** Engaged in the development and commercialization of a broad range of immunotherapeutic drugs designed to control serious disease states. Celgene also manufactures and sells chiral intermediates, key building blocks in the production of advanced therapeutic compounds and certain agrochemical and food-related products. The focus of Celgene's immunotherapeutics program is the development of small molecule compounds that modulate bodily production of tumor necrosis factor alpha, a hormone-like protein. Elevated levels of this cytokine are believed to cause symptoms associated with several debilitating diseases such as HIV and AIDS-related conditions, sepsis, and inflammatory bowel disease. **NOTE:** Search and apply for positions online. Resumes only accepted for current openings. **Positions advertised include:** Associate Director Clinical Operations; Associate Director QC; Attorney; Manager Sales Operations; Clinical Operations Coordinator; Clinical Pharmacologist; Data Manager; Manager Scientific and Medical Writing; Medical Reviewer; Sr. SAS Programmer; QC Analyst; Product Manager Strategic Marketing. **Corporate headquarters location:** This location. **Listed on:** NASDAQ. **Stock exchange symbol:** CELG.

CELSIS LABORATORY GROUP
165 Fieldcrest Avenue, Edison NJ 08837. 732/346-5100. **Contact:** Human Resources. **E-mail address:** info@celsis.com. **World Wide Web address:** http://www.celsislabs.com. **Description:** An independent testing laboratory specializing in toxicology, microbiology, and analytical chemistry. **Number of employees at this location:** 50.

CENDANT CORPORATION
1 Sylvan Way, Parsippany NJ 07054-0642. 973/428-9700. **Fax:** 973/496-5966. **Contact:** Human Resources. **E-mail address:** cendant.jobs@cendant.com. **World Wide Web address:** http://www.cendant.com. **Description:** Provides a wide range of business services including dining services, hotel franchise management, mortgage programs, and timeshare exchanges. Cendant Corporation's Real Estate Division offers employee relocation and mortgage services through Century 21, Coldwell Banker, ERA, Cendant Mortgage, and Cendant Mobility. The Travel Division provides car rentals, vehicle management services, and vacation timeshares through brand names including Avia, Days Inn, Howard Johnson, Ramada, Travelodge, and Super 8. The Membership Division offers travel, shopping, auto, dining, and other financial services through Travelers Advantage, Shoppers Advantage, Auto Vantage, Welcome Wagon, Netmarket, North American Outdoor Group, and PrivacyGuard. **Positions advertised include;** Commercial Marketing Associate; Mortgage Processor; Staff Accountant; Financial Analyst; International Treasury Manager; Marketing Manager; Executive Assistant; Regional Business Consultant; Staff Accountant; Director; Finance Manager; Administrative Assistant; Marketing Communications Manager. **Corporate headquarters location:** New York NY. **Listed on:** New York Stock Exchange. **Stock exchange symbol:** CD. **President/CEO:** Henry Silverman. **Number of employees at this location:** 1,100. **Number of employees worldwide:** 28,000.

CENTEX HOMES
500 Craig Road, Manalapan NJ 07726. 732/780-1800. **Contact:** Human Resources. **World Wide Web address:** http://www.centexhomes.com. **Description:** Centex Homes designs, constructs, and sells homes nationwide. **Other U.S. locations:** Nationwide. **Parent company:** Centex Corporation. **Listed on:** New York Stock Exchange. **Stock exchange symbol:** CTX.

CENVEO
25 Linden Avenue East, Jersey City NJ 07305. 201/434-2100. **Toll-free phone:** 800/526-3020. **Fax:** 201/434-4048. **Contact:** Human Resources. **World Wide Web address:** http://www.cenveo.com. **Description:** Manufactures and prints envelopes and tags. Primary customers are publishing houses, insurance agencies, banks, direct mail companies, pharmaceutical companies, brokers, and jobbers. **NOTE:** A college education is required of all applicants. Sales experience with industrial accounts is preferred.

CERAMCO INC.
6 Terri Lane, Suite 100, Burlington NJ 08016. 609/386-8900. **Toll-free phone:** 800/487-0100. **Fax:** 609/386-5266. **Contact:** Ms. Pat McDade, Office Administrator. **World Wide Web address:** http://www.ceramco.com. **Description:** A leading manufacturer of dental porcelain, raw materials, and equipment. Ceramco distributes these products to dental laboratories for use in preparing crowns, bridges, and restorations. Founded in 1959. **Office hours:** Monday - Friday, 8:00 a.m. - 5:00 p.m. **Corporate headquarters location:** This location. **International locations:** England; Puerto Rico. **Parent company:** Dentsply International, Inc. **Annual sales/revenues:** $21 - $50 million. **Number of employees at this location:** 65. **Number of employees nationwide:** 90. **Number of employees worldwide:** 130.

CERTAINTEED CORPORATION
P.O. Box CN-E, Williams Junction NJ 07009. 856/767-7200. **Contact:** Human Resources. **E-mail address:** ctrecruitment@saint-gobain.com. **World Wide Web address:** http://www.certainteed.com. **Description:** Certainteed Corporation operates in two business segments: Building Materials includes roofing products, vinyl siding, and door and sash products; Fiberglass Products includes thermal and acoustical insulation, a wide range of other fiberglass products, and piping products for the industrial, irrigation, sewer, mining, construction, and manufacturing markets. **NOTE:** Interested jobseekers should address inquiries to Certainteed Corporation, Human Resources, P.O. Box 860, Valley Forge PA 19482. **Corporate headquarters location:** Valley Forge PA. **Operations at this facility include:** This location is a distribution center. **Parent company:** Compagnie de Saint-Gobain (Paris, France) operates through four branches: Abrasives, Construction Materials, Industrial Ceramics, and Insulation and Reinforcements. The Saint-Gobain companies based in North America are organized under the umbrella of the Saint-Gobain Corporation, which includes the Certainteed Corporation, the Norton Company, and all of their subsidiaries. **Number of employees nationwide:** 8,000.

CERTIFIED LABORATORIES INC.
34 Stouts Lane, Monmouth Junction NJ 08852. 732/329-8117. **Contact:** Human Resources. **World Wide Web address:** http://www.certifiedlabs.com. **Description:** Manufactures and sells industrial and maintenance supplies.

CHECKPOINT METO
101 Wolf Drive, Thorofare NJ 08086. 856/848-1800. **Fax:** 856/848-0937. **Contact:** Robert Holloway, Manager of Personnel. **E-mail address:** hresources@checkpt.com. **World Wide Web address:** http://www.checkpointsystems.com. **Description:** Develops, manufactures, and markets Electronic Article Surveillance systems to control shoplifting in retail stores and protect books and materials in libraries and universities; electronic access control systems to secure buildings and areas within buildings; and closed circuit television systems and solutions to control shoplifting and internal theft. **Corporate headquarters location:** This location.

CHEF SOLUTIONS
164 Madison Street, East Rutherford NJ 07073. 973/779-2090. **Fax:** 973/779-7338. **Contact:** Human Resources. **E-mail address:** resumes@chefsolutions.com. **World Wide Web address:** http://www.chefsolutions.com. **Description:** Manufactures and markets a line of food products, primarily salads. **Positions advertised include:** Food Service Worker; Grocer. **Corporate headquarters location:** Wheeling IL. **Operations at this facility include:** Administration; Manufacturing; Research and Development; Sales; Service. **Number of employees at this location:** 200.

CHEFS INTERNATIONAL, INC.
62 Broadway, P.O. Box 1332, Point Pleasant Beach NJ 08742. 732/295-0350. **Contact:** Office Manager. **World Wide Web address:** http://www.jackbakerslobstershanty.com. **Description:** Operates eight Lobster Shanty restaurants in New Jersey and Florida. **Corporate headquarters location:** This location.

CHELSEA PROPERTY GROUP, INC.
105 Eisenhower Parkway, Roseland NJ 07068. 973/228-6111. **Contact:** Human Resources. **E-mail address:** jobs@cpgi.com. **World Wide Web address:** http://www.cpgi.com. **Description:** A self-administered and self-managed real estate investment trust engaged in the development, leasing, marketing, and management of upscale and fashion-oriented manufacturers' outlet centers. **Positions advertised include:** Security Supervisor; Assistant General Manager. **Listed on:** New York Stock Exchange. **Stock exchange symbol:** CPG.

CHEMETALL OAKITE
50 Valley Road, Berkeley Heights NJ 07922. 908/464-6900. **Contact:** Suzanne Watson, Recruiter. **E-mail address:** resumes@oakite.com. **World Wide Web address:** http://www.oakite.com. **Description:** Manufactures and markets specialty chemical products used primarily for industrial cleaning, metal conditioning, and surface preparation. **NOTE:** Resumes must be submitted in Microsoft Word, Word Perfect, or Microsoft Publisher format. **Corporate headquarters location:** This location. **Other U.S. locations:** Nationwide. **International locations:** Canada

CHERRYROAD TECHNOLOGIES INC.
199 Cherry Hill Road, Parsippany NJ 07054. 973/402-7802. **Contact:** Human Resources. **World Wide Web address:** http://www.cherryroad.com. **Description:** A computer information technology company that provides comprehensive systems integration and consulting services that maximize enterprise performance for private and public sector as well as federal clients. **NOTE:** Job searches may search for jobs and submit resumes online. **Positions advertised include:** Management Consultant; PeopleSoft Practice Manager; PeopleSoft Technical Consultants; Practice Manager. **Corporate headquarters location:** This location. **Other U.S. locations:** Nationwide.

CHEVRON CORPORATION
1200 State Street, Perth Amboy NJ 08861. 732/738-2000. **Contact:** Human Resources. **World Wide Web address:** http://www.chevron.com. **Description:** An international oil firm with operations in more than 90 countries. Chevron Corporation is engaged in worldwide integrated petroleum operations including the exploration and production of crude oil and natural gas reserves; the transportation of crude oil, natural gas, and petroleum products by pipeline, tanker, and motor equipment; the operation of oil-refining complexes; and the wholesale and retail marketing of petroleum products. **Operations at this facility include:** This location operates as part of the asphalt division. **Parent company:** ChevronTexaco Corporation. **Listed on:** New York Stock Exchange. **Stock exchange symbol:** CVX.

THE CHUBB GROUP OF INSURANCE COMPANIES
15 Mountain View Road, Warren NJ 07059. 908/903-2000. **Contact:** Human Resources. **World Wide Web address:** http://www.chubb.com. **Description:** A property and casualty insurer with more than 115 offices in 30 countries worldwide. The Chubb Group of Insurance Companies offers a broad range of specialty insurance products and services designed for individuals and businesses, serving industries including high-technology, financial institutions, and general manufacturers. Founded in 1882. **Positions advertised include:** Property Accounting; Statistical Accounting; Investment Accounting; Accounting Systems. **NOTE:** Entry-level positions are offered. **Special programs:** Internships. **Corporate headquarters location:** This location. **Listed on:** New York Stock Exchange. **Stock exchange symbol:** CB. **Annual sales/revenues:** More than $100 million. **Number of employees worldwide:** 11,000.

CHURCH & DWIGHT COMPANY, INC.
469 North Harrison Street, Princeton NJ 08543. 609/683-5900. **Contact:** Human Resources. **E-mail address:** jobs@churchdwight.com. **World Wide Web address:** http://www.churchdwight.com. **Description:** Manufactures Arm & Hammer brand products including soaps and detergents. **Listed on:** New York Stock Exchange. **Stock exchange symbol:** CHD.

CIBER, INC.
7 Ridgedale Avenue, Cedar Knolls NJ 07927. 973/267-0088. **Fax:** 973/267-8675. **Contact:** Human Resources. **World Wide Web address:** http://www.ciber.com. **Description:** A leading systems integrator. The company's services include computer network design, installation, and administration; helpdesk support; technical education; cabling and telecommunications sales and service; computer product sales and services; and Internet services. Clients include many small and mid-range companies, national and global *Fortune* 1000 companies, and large government agencies. Founded in 1984. **Positions advertised include:** Educational Sales Consultant. **Corporate headquarters location:** This location. **Other U.S. locations:** NY; PA. **Listed on:** New York Stock Exchange. **Stock exchange symbol:** CBR. **Annual sales/revenues:** More than $100 million.

CIBER, INC.
252 Fernwood Avenue, Edison NJ 08837. 732/225-1700. **Fax:** 732/225-1973. **Contact:** Human Resources. **World Wide Web address:** http://www.ciber.com. **Description:** Provides consulting for client/server development, mainframe and legacy systems, industry-specific analysis, application-specific analysis, and network development.

CLARION OFFICE SUPPLIES INC.
101 East Main Street, Little Falls NJ 07424. 973/785-8383. **Contact:** Human Resources. **World Wide Web address:** http://www.clarionofficesupply.com. **Description:** Distributes a wide variety of office supplies including computer hardware. Clarion Office Supplies provides individuals and businesses with most major brands of CPUs and monitors.

RALPH CLAYTON & SONS
1215 East Veterans Highway, Lakewood NJ 08701. 732/363-1995. **Contact:** Human Resources. **World Wide Web address:** http://www.claytonco.com. **Description:** Manufactures concrete. **Parent company:** The Clayton Companies.

CLAYTON BRICK
2 Porete Avenue, North Arlington NJ 07032. 201/998-7600. **Contact:** Human Resources. **World Wide Web address:** http://www.claytonco.com. **Description:** Engaged in precast concrete panel construction and installation. **NOTE:** For employment information contact the central Clayton Companies office: P.O. Box 3015, 515 Lakewood-New Egypt Road, Lakewood NJ 08701, 732/363-1995, or contact Wayne Tart at 732/905-3156 or by e-mail at waynetart@netscape.com..

CLEAN HARBORS, INC.
3 Sutton Place, Edison NJ 08817. 732/248-1997. **Toll-free phone:** 800/782-8805. **Fax:** 732/248-4414. **Contact:** Human Resources. **World Wide Web address:** http://www.cleanharbors.com. **Description:** Clean Harbors, Inc., through its subsidiaries, provides comprehensive environmental services in 35 states in the Northeast, Midwest, Central, and Mid-Atlantic regions. Clean Harbors provides a wide range of hazardous waste management and environmental support services to a diversified customer base from over 40 locations. The company's hazardous waste management services include treatment, storage, recycling, transportation, risk analysis, site assessment, laboratory analysis, site closure, and disposal of hazardous materials through environmentally sound methods including incineration. Environmental remediation services include emergency response, surface remediation, groundwater restoration, industrial maintenance, and facility decontamination. **Positions advertised include:** Class B Driver; Field Technician; Class A Driver; Field Service Foreman; Pack Chemist; Apollo Chemist. **NOTE:** See Website for current job opportunities and contact information. **Corporate headquarters location:** Braintree MA. **Other U.S. locations:** Nationwide. **Number of employees nationwide:** 1,400.

CLEAN HARBORS, INC.
2301 Pennsylvania Avenue, Deptford NJ 08096. 856/589-5000. **Toll-free phone:** 800/544-3128. **Fax:** 856/227-9350. **Contact:** Human Resources. **World Wide Web address:** http://www.cleanharbors.com. **Description:** Clean Harbors, Inc., through its subsidiaries, provides comprehensive environmental services in 35 states in the Northeast, Midwest, Central, and Mid-Atlantic regions. Clean Harbors provides a wide range of hazardous waste management and environmental support services to a diversified customer base from over 40 locations. The company's hazardous waste management services include treatment, storage, recycling, transportation, risk analysis, site assessment, laboratory analysis, site closure, and disposal of hazardous materials through environmentally sound methods including incineration. Environmental remediation services include emergency response, surface remediation, groundwater restoration, industrial maintenance, and facility decontamination. **Positions advertised include:** Class B Driver; Field Technician; Class A Driver; Field Service Foreman; Pack Chemist; Apollo Chemist. **NOTE:** See Website for current job opportunities and contact information. **Corporate headquarters location:** Braintree MA. **Other U.S. locations:** Nationwide. **Number of employees nationwide:** 1,400.

CLIENTLOGIC
230 Brighton Road, Clifton NJ 07012. 973/778-5588. **Fax:** 973/778-7485. **Contact:** Human Resources. **E-mail address:** cliftonjobs@clientlogic.com. **World Wide Web address:** http://www.clientlogic.com. **Description:** A direct marketing firm. **Corporate headquarters location:** Nashville TN. **Other area locations:** Weehawken NJ. **Parent company:** Onex Corporation.

CLOFINE DAIRY PRODUCTS
P.O. Box 335, 1407 New Road, Linwood NJ 08221. 609/653-1000. **Toll-free phone:** 800/441-1001. **Fax:** 609/653-0127. **Contact:** Personnel. **World Wide Web address:** http://www.clofinedairy.com. **Description:** Provides brokerage services for dairy and other food products. Clofine Dairy Products buys directly from manufacturers and then sells to distributors.

COLGATE-PALMOLIVE COMPANY
191 East Hanover Avenue, Morristown NJ 07962-1928. 973/631-9000. **Contact:** Human Resources. **World Wide Web address:** http://www.colgate.com. **Description:** Colgate-Palmolive Company manufactures and markets a wide variety of products in the United States and around the world in two business segments: Oral, Personal, and

Household Care; and Specialty Marketing. Oral, Personal, and Household Care products include toothpastes, oral rinses and toothbrushes, bar and liquid soaps, shampoos, conditioners, deodorants and antiperspirants, baby and shaving products, laundry and dishwashing detergents, fabric softeners, cleansers and cleaners, and bleach. Specialty Marketing products include pet dietary care products, crystal tableware, and portable fuel for warming food. Principal global trademarks and brand names include Colgate, Palmolive, Mennen, Ajax, Fab, and Science Diet, in addition to various regional brand names. **Corporate headquarters location:** New York NY. **Other U.S. locations:** Kansas City KS; Cambridge MA; Piscataway NJ. **Operations at this facility include:** This location manufactures baby products and deodorant.

COLGATE-PALMOLIVE COMPANY TECHNOLOGY CENTER
909 River Road, P.O. Box 1343, Piscataway NJ 08855-1343. 732/878-7500. **Contact:** Human Resources. **World Wide Web address:** http://www.colgate.com. **Description:** Colgate-Palmolive Company manufactures and markets a wide variety of products in the United States and around the world in two business segments: Oral, Personal, and Household Care; and Specialty Marketing. Oral, Personal, and Household Care products include toothpastes, oral rinses and toothbrushes, bar and liquid soaps, shampoos, conditioners, deodorants and antiperspirants, baby and shaving products, laundry and dishwashing detergents, fabric softeners, cleansers and cleaners, and bleach. Specialty Marketing products include pet dietary care products, crystal tableware, and portable fuel for warming food. Principal global trademarks and brand names include Colgate, Palmolive, Mennen, Ajax, Fab, and Science Diet, in addition to various regional brand names. **NOTE:** When submitting resumes, please include appropriate mail codes, for engineering or research positions, use Mail Code JHO and for secretarial or administrative positions, use Mail Code MG. **Positions advertised include:** Junior SAP Security Analyst; Scientist; Senior Engineer; Account Business Manager; Professional Sales Representative. **Special programs:** Internships. **Corporate headquarters location:** New York NY. **Other U.S. locations:** Kansas City KS; Cambridge MA; Morristown NJ. **Operations at this facility include:** This location houses a research and development facility. **Number of employees at this location:** 1,000.

THE COLLEGE OF NEW JERSEY
P.O. Box 7718, Ewing NJ 08628-0718. 609/771-1855. **Contact:** Human Resources. **World Wide Web address:** http://www.tcnj.edu. **Description:** A four-year state college offering bachelor's and master's degrees to approximately 6,000 undergraduate and 1,000 graduate students. **Positions advertised include:** Assistant Professor; Psychologist; Music Media Librarian; Instructional Technology Coordinator.

COLOR OPTICS, INC.
216 Midland Avenue, Saddle Brook NJ 07663. 973/772-1007. **Fax:** 973/772-8991. **Contact:** Margaret Sapinski, Human Resources. **E-mail address:** psapinski@coloroptics.com. **World Wide Web address:** http://www.coloroptics.com. **Description:** Commercial printing company. **Positions advertised include:** Customer Service Representative; Estimator/Print Production; Machine Operators; Outside Sales; Prepress; Proofing; Scanner Operators.

COLORITE WATERWORKS COLORITE POLYMERS
101 Railroad Avenue, Ridgefield NJ 07657. 201/941-2900. **Toll-free phone:** 800/631-1577. **Fax:** 201/941-2665. **Contact:** Human Resources. **E-mail address:** info@coloritepolymers.com. **World Wide Web address:** http://www.tekni-plex.com/companies/colorpoly.html. **Description:** Manufactures plastic garden hoses. Colorite Polymers (also at this location) manufactures PVC compounds. **Parent company:** Tekni-Plex Inc.

COMMERCE BANK
17000 Horizon Way, Mount Laurel NJ 08054. 856/751-9000. **Contact:** Personnel. **World Wide Web address:** http://www.commerceonline.com. **Description:** Commerce Bank is a full-service bank offering a variety of services including Commerce Capital, an in-house stocks and bonds investment program. Commerce Bank, along with its affiliates Commerce Bank NJ, Commerce Bank Shore, Commerce Bank Harrisburg, and Independence Bank, constitutes the Commerce Network. **Operations at this facility include:** This location is the operations center. **Listed on:** New York Stock Exchange. **Stock exchange symbol:** CBH.

COMMUNITY MEDICAL CENTER
99 Highway 37 West, Toms River NJ 08755. 732/240-8000. **Contact:** Human Resources. **E-mail address:** info@sbhcs.com. **World Wide Web address:** http://www.sbhcs.com/hospitals/community_medical. **Description:** An affiliate of Saint Barnabus Health Care System, Community Medical Center is a 596-bed, general, short-term care hospital.

COMMUNITY OPTIONS INC.
16 Farber Road, Princeton NJ 08540. 609/951-9900. **Fax:** 609/499-4407. **Contact:** Recruiter. **E-mail address:** resume@comop.org. **World Wide Web address:** http://www.comop.org. **Description:** A private, nonprofit organization that works with adults who have developmental disabilities to find them housing and employment opportunities. **Positions advertised include:** Recruiter; Grant Writer; Training Specialist; Human Resources Assistant. **Corporate headquarters location:** This location. **Other area locations:** Forked River NJ; Morristown NJ; Trenton NJ; Wayne NJ.

COMMVAULT SYSTEMS
2 Crescent Place, P.O. Box 900, Oceanport NJ 07757-0900. 732/870-4000. **Contact:** Human Resources. **E-mail address:** employment@commvault.com. **World Wide Web address:** http://www.commvault.com. **Description:** Develops and sells software for businesses with computer backup systems. **Positions advertised include:** Inside Sales Representative; Product Marketing Manager; Systems Tester. **Corporate headquarters location:** This location.

COMPUTER ASSOCIATES INTERNATIONAL, INC.
Route 206 and Orchard Road, Princeton NJ 08543. 908/874-9000. **Fax:** 908/874-9420. **Contact:** Hiring Manager. **E-mail address:** joinca@ca.com. **World Wide Web address:** http://www.cai.com. **Description:** One of the world's leading developers of client/server and distributed computing software. The company develops, markets, and supports enterprise management, database and applications development, business applications, and consumer software products for a broad range of mainframe, midrange, and desktop computers. Computer Associates International serves major business, government, research, and educational organizations. Founded in 1976. **Positions advertised include:** Consultant; Database Management Administrator. **NOTE:** Search for positions online. Mail resumes to: CAI Inc., One Computer Associates Plaza, Islandia NY 11749. **Corporate headquarters location:** Islandia NY. **Other U.S. locations:** Nationwide. **Listed on:** New York Stock Exchange. **Stock exchange symbol:** CA. **Annual sales/revenues:** More than $100 million.

COMPUTER ASSOCIATES INTERNATIONAL, INC.
2 Executive Drive, Fort Lee NJ 07024. 201/592-0009. **Contact:** Hiring Manager. **E-mail address:** joinca@ca.com. **World Wide Web address:** http://www.cai.com. **Description:** Computer Associates International is one of the world's leading developers of client/server and distributed computing software. The company develops, markets, and supports enterprise management, database and applications development, business applications, and consumer software products for a broad range of mainframe, midrange, and desktop computers. Computer Associates International serves major business, government, research, and educational organizations. Founded in 1976. **NOTE:** Mail resumes to: CAI Inc., One Computer Associates Plaza, Islandia NY 11749. **Corporate headquarters location:** Islandia NY. **Other U.S. locations:** Nationwide. **Operations at this facility include:** This location sells software, offers technical support, and is home to the marketing department. **Listed on:** New York Stock Exchange. **Stock exchange symbol:** CA. **Annual sales/revenues:** More than $100 million.

COMPUTER ASSOCIATES INTERNATIONAL, INC.
2000 Midlantic Drive, Suite 300, Mount Laurel NJ 08054. 856/273-9100. **Contact:** Human Resources. **E-mail address:** joinCA@ca.com. **World Wide Web address:** http://www.cai.com. **Description:** Computer Associates International is one of the world's leading developers of client/server and distributed computing software. The company develops, markets, and supports enterprise management, database and applications development, business applications, and consumer software products for a broad range of mainframe, midrange, and desktop computers. Computer Associates International serves major business, government, research, and educational organizations. Founded in 1976. **NOTE:** Mail resumes to: CAI Inc., One Computer Associates Plaza, Islandia NY 11749. **Special programs:** Internships. **Corporate headquarters location:** Islandia NY. **Operations at this facility include:** This location sells software and offers technical support. **Other U.S. locations:** Nationwide. **Listed on:** New York Stock Exchange. **Stock exchange symbol:** CA. **Annual sales/revenues:** More than $100 million.

COMPUTER HORIZONS CORPORATION
49 Old Bloomfield Avenue, Mountain Lakes NJ 07046-1495. 973/299-4000. **Toll-free phone:** 800/321-2421. **Fax:** 973/402-7986. **Contact:** Human Resources. **E-mail address:** info@computerhorizons.com. **World Wide Web address:** http://www.computerhorizons.com. **Description:** A full-service technology solutions company offering contract staffing, outsourcing, re-engineering, migration, downsizing support, and network management. Founded in 1969. **Corporate headquarters location:** This location. **Other U.S. locations:** Nationwide. **Subsidiaries include:** Birla Horizons International Ltd.; Horizons Consulting, Inc.; Strategic Outsourcing Services, Inc.; Unified Systems Solutions, Inc. **Listed on:** NASDAQ. **Stock exchange symbol:** CHRZ. **Number of employees nationwide:** 1,500.

COMPUTER OUTSOURCING SERVICES, INC. (COSI)
2 Christie Heights Street, Leonia NJ 07605. 201/840-4753. **Fax:** 201/363-9675. **Contact:** Human Resources. **World Wide Web address:** http://www.cosi-us.com. **Description:** Provides payroll, data processing, and tax filing services to companies in book publishing, apparel, direct response marketing, and other industries. **Corporate headquarters location:** This location. **Listed on:** NASDAQ. **Stock exchange symbol:** COSI.

COMPUTER SCIENCES CORPORATION
304 West Route 38, P.O. Box 1038, Moorestown NJ 08057-0902. 856/234-1166. **Contact:** Human Resources. **World Wide Web address:** http://www.csc.com. **Description:** Computer Sciences Corporation is comprised of four sectors: the Systems Group Division designs, engineers, and integrates computer-based systems and communications systems, providing all the hardware, software, training, and related elements necessary to operate such a system; the Consulting Division includes consulting and technical services in the development of computer and communication systems to nonfederal organizations; the Industry Services Group provides service to the health care, insurance, and financial services industries, as well as providing large-scale claim processing and other insurance-related services; CSC Health Care and CSC Enterprises make up the CSC Divisions. CSC Health Care markets business systems and services to the managed health care industry, clinics, and physicians. CSC Enterprises provides consumer credit reports and account management services to credit grantors. **Positions advertised include:** Application Designer; Database Administrator. **Corporate headquarters location:** El Segundo CA. **Other U.S. locations:** Nationwide. **Operations at this facility include:** This location develops software.

COMTEC, INC.
6 Just Road, Fairfield NJ 07004. 973/882-3050. **Fax:** 973/808-4302. **Contact:** Human Resources. **E-mail address:** hr@comtecnet.com. **World Wide Web address:** http://www.comtecnet.com. **Description:** Provider of customized printing, inserting, and mailing services including graphic design, custom application programming, high-speed printing, intelligent inserting and automated mailing. **Positions advertised include:** Creative Director; Production Printer Technician.

COMTREX SYSTEMS CORPORATION
102 Executive Drive, Suite 1, Moorestown NJ 08057. 856/778-0090. **Fax:** 856/778-9322. **Contact:** Personnel. **World Wide Web address:** http://www.comtrex.com. **Description:** Designs, develops, assembles, and markets computer software electronics terminals, which provide retailers with transaction processing, in-store controls, and management information capabilities. The company primarily serves the food service and hospitality industries. Founded in 1981. **Corporate headquarters location:** This location. **Listed on:** NASDAQ. **Stock exchange symbol:** COMX.

CONGOLEUM CORPORATION
P.O. Box 3127, 3500 Quakerbridge Road, Mercerville NJ 08619. 609/584-3000. **Fax:** 609/584-3522. **Contact:** Human Resources. **World Wide Web address:** http://www.congoleum.com. **Description:** Congoleum Corporation is a diversified manufacturer and distributor, operating in the areas of home furnishings, shipbuilding, and automotive and industrial distribution. **Corporate headquarters location:** This location. **Other U.S. locations:** Cedarhurst MD; Trenton NJ; Trainor PA. **Operations at this facility include:** This location distributes vinyl floor products to wholesalers worldwide. **Listed on:** American Stock Exchange. **Stock exchange symbol:** CGM.

CONSARC CORPORATION
P.O. Box 156, 100 Indel Avenue, Rancocas NJ 08073-0156. 609/267-8000. **Fax:** 609.267-1366. **Physical address:** 100 Indel Avenue, Ranocas NJ 08073. **Contact:** Pat Vogel, Executive Secretary. **World Wide Web address:** http://www.consarc.com. **Description:** Designs, manufactures, and sells industrial melting furnaces. **Corporate headquarters location:** This location. **Parent company:** Inducto Therm Industries. **Operations at this facility include:** Administration.

CONSTRUCTION DATA CORPORATION
1911 Princeton Avenue, Lawrenceville NJ 08648. 609/394-4800. **Toll-free phone:** 800/395-1400. **Fax:** 561/299-0818. **Contact:** Human Resources. **World Wide Web address:** http://www.cdcnews.com. **Description:** A construction trade publication that provides planning news and bidding opportunities in Connecticut, Delaware, New Jersey, New York, and Pennsylvania. **NOTE:** For job opportunities in New Jersey contact the Vero Beach, Florida office: Human Resources, 2770 Indian River Boulevard, Vero Beach FL 32960. 561/770-6003. Entry-level positions are offered. **Positions advertised include:** Associate Editor; Editorial Assistant; Executive Administrative Assistant. **Special programs:** Internships. **Corporate headquarters location:** Vero Beach FL. **Other U.S. locations:** Rockland MA; Austin TX. **Listed on:** Privately held. **Annual sales/revenues:** $11 - $20 million. **Number of employees at this location:** 65. **Number of employees nationwide:** 175.

CONTINENTAL CONNECTOR COMPANY
53 La France Avenue, Bloomfield NJ 07003. 973/429-8500. **Contact:** Personnel. **World Wide Web address:** http://www.continentalconnector.com. **Description:** Continental Connector Corporation is engaged in the development, manufacture, and sale of a broad line of multiprecision rack and panel circuit connectors. Manufacturing operations consist primarily of the processing and assembly of plated metals, receptacles, and plugs of various types designed and molded from thermosetting molding compounds and other precision connector parts. **Corporate headquarters location:** Las Vegas NV. **Operations at this facility include:** This location manufactures circuit connectors. **Parent company:** ASC Group Inc.

COOPER ALLOY CORPORATION
201 Sweetland Avenue, Hillside NJ 07205. 908/688-4120. **Contact:** Personnel. **Description:** Manufactures and distributes a line of plastic pumps to OEMs.

COOPER HEALTH
1 Cooper Plaza, Suite 500, Camden NJ 08103. 856/342-2000. **Fax:** 856/968-8319. **Contact:** Human Resources. **World Wide Web address:** http://www.cooperhealth.org. **Description:** A 554-bed, nonprofit, academic medical center. Cooper Health specializes in the care of seriously-ill and critically-injured patients.

NEIL COOPER LLC
436 Ferry Street, Newark NJ 07105. 973/274-0066. **Contact:** Controller. **Description:** Imports and manufactures men's and boys' leather and cloth coats and jackets in the moderate-to-high price range. The company sells coats to department stores and private label distributors, and distributes products worldwide.

CORDIS CORPORATION
45 Technology Drive, Warren NJ 07059. 908/755-8300. **Contact:** Human Resources. **World Wide Web address:** http://www.cordis.com. **Description:** Cordis manufactures medical devices such as catheters to treat cardiovascular diseases. **NOTE:** All hiring is done through the parent company. Resumes should be sent to Johnson & Johnson Recruiting Services, Employment Management Center, Room JH-215, 501 George Street, New Brunswick NJ 08906-6597. **Operations at this facility include:** This location handles administration, research and development, and quality assurance. **Parent company:** Johnson & Johnson (New Brunswick NJ).

CORPORATE DISK COMPANY
1800 Bloomsbury Avenue, Ocean City NJ 07712. 732/431-5300. **Contact:** Controller. **World Wide Web address:** http://www.disk.com. **Description:** Provides a broad range of integrated software and information distribution options in multiple formats on disk, in print, and online to many industries including the technology, insurance, financial services, pharmaceutical, publishing, government, and transportation communities. **NOTE:** Resumes should be sent to Human Resources, Corporate Disk Company, 1226 Michael Drive, Wood Dale IL 60191.

COURIER-POST NEWSPAPER
P.O. Box 5300, Cherry Hill NJ 08034. 856/663-6000. **Physical address:** 300 Cuthbert Boulevard, Cherry Hill NJ 08002. **Contact:** Lori Trasmondi, Human Resources Director. **World Wide Web address:** http://www.courierpostonline.com. **Description:** A newspaper with a circulation of approximately 100,000.

COURTYARD PRINCETON
3815 US Route 1 at Mapleton Road, Princeton NJ 08540. 609/716-9100. **Fax:** 609/716-8745. **Contact:** Human Resources. **World Wide Web address:** http://www.marriott.com. **Description:** A location of the hotel chain close to numerous shops and restaurants offering 144 rooms. **Other U.S. locations;** Nationwide.

COVANCE INC.
210 Carnegie Center, Princeton NJ 08540. 609/452-8550. **Toll-free phone:** 888/COV-ANCE. **Fax:** 609/452-8520. **Contact:** Human Resources. **World Wide Web address:** http://www.covance.com. **Description:** One of the world's largest and most comprehensive drug development services companies. Covance Inc. provides preclinical testing, health economics consulting, biomanufacturing, and clinical support services. Founded in 1993. **NOTE:** Entry-level positions are offered. **Positions advertised include:** Business Analyst. **Office hours:** Monday - Friday, 8:30 a.m. - 5:00 p.m. **Corporate headquarters location:** This location. **Other U.S. locations:** Berkeley CA; Richmond CA; Walnut Creek CA; Washington DC; Tampa FL; Indianapolis IN; Kalamazoo MI; Research Triangle Park NC; Reno NV; Allentown PA; Denver PA; Radnor PA; Nashville TN; Alice TX; Cumberland VA; Vienna VA; Madison WI. **International locations:** Worldwide. **Subsidiaries include:** Berkeley Antibody Company, Inc. provides a variety of preclinical services. GDXI, Inc. provides electrocardiogram analysis for clinical trials. **Listed on:** New York Stock Exchange. **Stock exchange symbol:** CVD. **President/CEO:** Christopher Kuebler. **Annual sales/revenues:** More than $100 million. **Number of employees at this location:** 1,000. **Number of employees worldwide:** 7,700.

COVANTA ENERGY GROUP
40 Lane Road, Fairfield NJ 07007. 973/882-9000. **Contact:** Human Resources. **World Wide Web address:** http://www.covantaenergy.com. **Description:** A global developer, owner, and operator of independent power projects and provider of related infrastructure services. Covanta Energy also operates more large-scale waste-to-energy facilities than any company in the world. **Positions advertised include:** Estimator/Project Controls Manager; Regional/Equipment Operator. **Subsidiaries include:** Covanta Energy, Inc.; Covanta Water Systems; Covanta Waste-to-Energy, Inc. **Number of employees at this location:** 310

CRADEN PERIPHERALS CORPORATION
7860 Airport Highway, Pennsauken NJ 08109. 856/488-0700. **Fax:** 856/488-0925. **Contact:** Human Resources. **E-mail address:** info@craden.com. **World Wide Web address:** http://www.craden.com. **Description:** Manufactures and markets printers under the Craden brand name.

CREATIVE HOBBIES, INC.
900 Creek Road, Bellmawr NJ 08031-1687. 856/933-2540. **Contact:** Personnel. **World Wide Web address:** http://www.creative-hobbies.com. **Description:** A wholesale distributor of hobby ceramics supplies including clay, kilns, pottery wheels, tools, glazes, and decorating supplies.

CREST FOAM INDUSTRIES, INC.
100 Carol Place, Moonachie NJ 07074. 201/807-0809. **Fax:** 201/807-1113. **Contact:** Human Resources. **E-mail address:** info@crestfoam.com. **World Wide Web address:** http://www.crestfoam.com. **Description:** Manufactures reticulated and specialty foam for a wide variety of industries such as aerospace, electronics, and medical.

CROWN FINANCIAL GROUP
525 Washington Boulevard, P.O. Box 260, Jersey City NJ 07310. 201/459-9500. **Toll-free phone:** 800/888-8118. **Fax:** 201/459-9545. **Contact:** Human Resources. **World Wide Web address:** http://www.crownfin.com. **Description:** Markets and trades approximately 7,300 securities. The company is also an active underwriter of small and mid-sized capitalization debt and equity services.

CURTISS-WRIGHT CORPORATION
1200 Wall Street West, Lyndhurst NJ 07071. 201/896-9886. **Contact:** Human Resources. **World Wide Web address:** http://www.curtisswright.com. **Description:** A diversified, multinational manufacturing and service company that designs, manufactures, and overhauls precision components and systems and provides highly-engineered services to the aerospace, automotive, shipbuilding, oil, petrochemical, agricultural equipment, power generation, metal working, and fire and rescue industries. Curtiss-Wright's principal operations include five North American manufacturing facilities; several metal improvement service facilities located in North America and Europe; and four component overhaul facilities located in Florida, North Carolina, Singapore, and Denmark. **Positions advertised include:** Senior Sub Contracts Administrator; General Accountant; Senior Buyer. **Corporate headquarters location:** This location. **Subsidiaries include:** Curtiss-Wright Flight Systems, Inc.; Curtiss-Wright Flow Control Corporation; Metal Improvement Company, Inc. **Listed on:** New York Stock Exchange. **Stock exchange symbol:** CW. **Number of employees worldwide:** 2,350.

CYTOGEN CORPORATION
650 College Road East, Princeton NJ 08540. 609/750-8100. **Toll-free phone:** 800/833-3533. **Fax:** 609/750-8130. **Contact:** Human Resources. **E-mail address:** hrdirector@cytogen.com. **World Wide Web address:** http://www.cytogen.com. **Description:** Develops products for the targeted delivery of diagnostic and therapeutic substances directly to sites of disease, using monoclonal antibodies. Proprietary antibody linking technology is used primarily to develop specific cancer diagnostic imaging and therapeutic products. Founded in 1981. **Corporate headquarters location:** This location. **Listed on:** NASDAQ. **Stock exchange symbol:** CYTO. **Number of employees at this location:** 120.

DPT
1200 Paco Way, Lakewood NJ 08701. 732/367-9000. **Contact:** Personnel. **E-mail address:** confidence@dptlabs.com. **World Wide Web address:** http://www.dptlabs.com. **Description:** Packages and ships pharmaceutical products manufactured by other companies. **Positions advertised include:** Scientist; Line Supervisor; Manufacturing Engineer; Lab Technician.

DRS PHOTRONICS
133 Bauer Drive, Oakland NJ 07436. 201/337-3800. **Fax:** 201/337-4775. **Contact:** Human Resources. **World Wide Web address:** http://www.drs.com. **Description:** Designs, manufactures, and markets high-technology electronic products used to process, display, and store information for the U.S. Department of Defense, international defense departments, other U.S. prime defense contractors, and industrial corporations. The company's advanced signal processing, display, data storage, trainer, emulation, and electro-optical systems are utilized in numerous applications for military use and for the disk drive and television broadcast industries. Founded in 1968.

DRS TECHNOLOGIES
5 Sylvan Way, Suite 60, Parsippany NJ 07054. 973/898-1500. **Fax:** 973/898-4730. **Contact:** Ann Carcione, Human Resources. **World Wide Web address:** http://www.drs.com. **Description:** A producer of magnetic recording heads for the information processing industry. **Positions advertised include:** Advertising & Media Manager. **Corporate headquarters location:** This location.

DAICOLOR-POPE INC.
33 Sixth Avenue, Paterson NJ 07524. 973/278-5170. **Contact:** Human Resources. **Description:** Manufactures pigments used by printing companies to produce inks.

THE DAILY RECORD INC.
800 Jefferson Road, Parsippany NJ 07054. 973/428-6200. **Fax:** 973/884-5768. **Contact:** Mike Owen, Personnel. **E-mail address:** mowen@morristo.gannett.com. **World Wide Web address:** http://www.dailyrecord.com. **Description:** Publishes a morning newspaper, the *Daily Record*. Circulation is approximately 63,000 on weekdays and 72,000 on Sundays. **Corporate headquarters location:** Arlington VA. **Parent company:** Gannett Company. **Listed on:** New York Stock Exchange. **Stock exchange symbol:** GSI. **Number of employees at this location:** 300.

DASSAULT FALCON JET CORPORATION
Teterboro Airport, P.O. Box 2000, South Hackensack NJ 07606. 201/262-0800. **Physical address:** Teterboro Airport, 200 Riser Road, Little Ferry NJ 07643. **Contact:** Human Resources. **E-mail address:** resumes@falconjet.com. **World Wide Web address:** http://www.falconjet.com. **Description:** Manufactures and sells a line of two- and three-engine business aircraft. Dassault Falcon Jet also operates international jet aircraft service and maintenance centers (Falcon Jet Service Centers), engaged in the service, repair, and maintenance of a wide range of jet aircraft engines, airframes, avionics, instruments, and accessories. **Positions advertised include:** Warranty Analyst Associate; Avionics Help Desk Associate; Avionics Specifications Coordinator; Service Parts Accounts Director; Field Service Representative; System Administrator; Public Relations Manager; Receptionist; Repair Agent; Technical Help Desk Clerk. **Parent company:** Dassault Aviation.

DASSAULT FALCON JET CORPORATION
475 Wall Street, Princeton NJ 08540. 609/921-0450. **Contact:** Human Resources Department. **E-mail address:** resumes@falconjet.com. **World Wide Web address:** http://www.falconjet.com. **Description:** Dassault Falcon Jet Corporation manufactures and sells a line of two- and three-engine business aircraft. The company also operates international jet aircraft service and maintenance centers (Falcon Jet Service Centers), engaged in the service, repair, and maintenance of a wide range of jet aircraft engines, airframes, avionics, instruments, and accessories. **Operations at this facility include:** This location is a sales office. **Parent company:** Dassault Aviation.

DATA DELAY DEVICES, INC.
3 Mount Prospect Avenue, Clifton NJ 07013. 973/773-2299. **Fax:** 973/773-9672. **Contact:** Human Resources. **World Wide Web address:** http://www.datadelay.com. **Description:** Manufactures analog and digital delay lines. The company's products are used by computer, telecommunications, and aerospace firms, as well as the military.

DATA SYSTEMS & SOFTWARE INC.
200 Route 17 South, Mahwah NJ 07430. 201/529-2026. **Fax:** 201/529-3163. **Contact:** Human Resources. **E-mail address:** ir@dssinc.com. **World Wide Web address:** http://www.dssiinc.com. **Description:** A leading provider of consulting and development services for computer software and systems to high-technology companies in Israel and the United States, principally in the area of embedded real-time systems.

DATARAM CORPORATION
P.O. Box 7528, Princeton NJ 08543-7528. 609/750-0475. **Physical address:** 186 Route 571, Building 2A, West Windsor 08550. **Toll-free phone:** 800/DAT-ARAM. **Fax:** 609/897-7021. **Contact:** Dawn Craft, Human Resources Administrator. **E-mail address:** hr@dataram.com. **World Wide Web address:** http://www.dataram.com. **Description:** Designs and manufactures memory products that improve the performance of computer systems. Dataram primarily serves HP, DEC, Sun, and IBM users in the manufacturing, finance, government, telecommunications, utilities, research, and education industries. **Positions advertised include:** Sales Professional. **Corporate headquarters location:** This location. **Listed on:** American Stock Exchange. **Stock exchange symbol:** DTM. **Number of employees at this location:** 100. **Number of employees nationwide:** 150.

DATASCOPE CORPORATION
14 Phillips Parkway, Montvale NJ 07645. 201/391-8100. **Contact:** Human Resources. **E-mail address:** career_opportunities@datascope.com. **World Wide Web address:** http://www.datascope.com. **Description:** Manufactures cardiac assist systems for hospital use in interventional cardiology and cardiac surgery; and patient monitors for use in the operating room, postanesthesia care, and critical care. Datascope's VasoSeal product rapidly seals femoral arterial punctures after catheterization procedures including coronary angioplasty and angiography. Datascope also manufactures a line of collagen hemostats, which are used to control bleeding during surgery. The company's cardiac assist product is an intra-aortic balloon pumping system used for treating cardiac shock, heart failure, and cardiac arrhythmia. The pump can also be used in various procedures including cardiac surgery and coronary angioplasty. Datascope's patient monitoring products comprise a line of multifunction and stand-alone models that measure a broad range of physiological data including blood oxygen saturation, airway carbon dioxide, ECG, and temperature. **Positions advertised include:** Industrial Engineer; Electro-Mechanical Engineer; Electrical Engineer; Secretary; Lotus Notes Database Developer. **Listed on:** NASDAQ. **Stock exchange symbol:** DSCP.

DATATECH INDUSTRIES INC.
23 Madison Road, Fairfield NJ 07004. 973/808-4000. **Contact:** Human Resources. **Description:** Specializes in installing mainframes and networking hardware for businesses.

DEBORAH HEART & LUNG CENTER
200 Trenton Road, Browns Mills NJ 08015. 609/893-6611. **Contact:** Human Resources. **E-mail address:** employment@deborah.org. **World Wide Web address:** http://www.deborah.org. **Description:** A hospital providing a variety of services including cardiac and pulmonary care. **Positions advertised include:** Medical Transcriptionist; Batch Control Representative; Coder; Office Assistant; Nuclear Medical Technician; Pharmacist; Registered Nurse; Licensed Practical Nurse.

DEGUSSA CORPORATION
P.O. Box 677, 379 Interpace Parkway, Parsippany NJ 07054-0677. 973/541-8000. **Fax:** 973/541-8013. **Contact:** Personnel. **World Wide Web address:** http://www.degussa-nafta.com/internet/dh-us/. **Description:** Manufactures specialty chemicals, polymers, colorants, additives, and raw materials for the coatings industry. **Special programs:** Internships; Co-ops. **Corporate headquarters location:** This location. **Other U.S. locations:** Theodore AL; Pleasanton CA; Piscataway NJ; Lockland OH. **Parent company:** Degussa AG. **Operations at this facility include:** Divisional Headquarters; Regional Headquarters. **Annual sales/revenues:** More than $100 million. **Number of employees at this location:** 350. **Number of employees nationwide:** 875.

DELOITTE & TOUCHE
2 Hilton Court, P.O. Box 319, Parsippany NJ 07054-0319. 973/683-7000. **Fax:** 973/683-7459. **Contact:** Human Resources Department. **World Wide Web address:** http://www.us.deloitte.com. **Description:** An international firm of certified public accountants providing professional accounting, auditing, tax, and management consulting services to widely diversified clients. The company has a specialized program consisting of national industry groups and functional groups that cross industry lines. Groups are involved in various disciplines including accounting, auditing, taxation management advisory services, small and growing businesses, mergers and acquisitions, and computer applications. **Positions advertised include:** Accountant. **Corporate headquarters location:** Wilton CT. **Other U.S. locations:** Nationwide. **Parent company:** Deloitte Touche Tohmatsu International is a global leader with nearly 90,000 employees in over 130 countries.

DELUXE FINANCIAL SERVICES
105 Route 46 West, Mountain Lakes NJ 07046-1645. 973/334-8000. **Fax:** 973/334-4292. **Contact:** Russ Perry, Personnel Director. **World Wide Web address:** http://www.deluxe.com. **Description:** Engaged in the printing and selling of checks, deposit tickets, and related forms to banks and other financial institutions. The company also manufactures documents printed with magnetic ink. Printing operations are carried out at more than 15 plants throughout the United States. **Corporate headquarters location:** Shoreview MN. **Parent company:** Deluxe Corporation provides check printing, electronic funds transfer processing services, and related services to the financial industry; check authorization and collection services to retailers; and electronic benefit transfer services to state governments. Deluxe Corporation also produces forms, specialty papers, and other products for small businesses, professional practices, and medical/dental offices; and provides tax forms and electronic tax filing services to tax preparers. Through the direct-mail channel, Deluxe sells greeting cards and gift wrap. **Listed on:** New York Stock Exchange. **Stock exchange symbol:** DLX.

DENDRITE INTERNATIONAL, INC.
1200 Mount Kemble Avenue, Morristown NJ 07960. 973/425-1200. **Fax:** 973/425-2100. **Contact:** Personnel. **World Wide Web address:** http://www.dendrite.com. **Description:** Develops software and provides consulting services aimed at optimizing the sales force effectiveness of pharmaceutical and consumer packaged goods companies. **Positions advertised include:** Bilingual CSR; Production Control Programmer. **Corporate headquarters location:** This location. **International locations:** Worldwide. **Listed on:** NASDAQ. **Stock exchange symbol:** DRTE. **Annual sales/revenues:** More than $100 million.

DERMA SCIENCES, INC.
214 Carnegie Center, Suite 100, Princeton NJ 08540. 609/514-4744. **Toll-free phone:** 800/825-4325. **Fax:** 609/514-0502. **Contact:** Human Resources. **E-mail address:** info@dermasciencesinc.com. **World Wide Web address:** http://www.dermasciences.com. **Description:** Engaged in the development, marketing, and sale of proprietary sprays, ointments, and dressings for the management of certain chronic, nonhealing skin ulcerations such as pressure and venous ulcers, surgical incisions, and burns.

DESKTOP ENGINEERING INTERNATIONAL, INC.
172 Broadway, Woodcliff Lake NJ 07677. 201/505-9200. **Toll-free phone:** 800/888-8680. **Fax:** 201/505-1566. **Contact:** Human Resources. **E-mail address:** information@deiusa.com. **World Wide Web address:** http://www.deiusa.com. **Description:** Designs and manufactures software for use in mechanical and structural engineering industries.

THE DEWEY ELECTRONICS CORPORATION
27 Muller Road, Oakland NJ 07436. 201/337-4700. **Toll-free phone:** 800/888-8680. **Fax:** 201/337-3976. **Contact:** Carol Grofsik, Director of Personnel Administration. **E-mail address:** dewey@deweyelectronics.com. **World Wide Web address:** http://www.deweyelectronics.com. **Description:** Develops, designs, engineers, and manufactures electronics systems for military and civilian customers. **Corporate headquarters location:** This location.

DI GIORGIO CORPORATION
WHITE ROSE FOOD
380 Middlesex Avenue, Carteret NJ 07008. 732/541-5555. **Fax:** 732/541-3730. **Contact:** Personnel Director. **World Wide Web address:** http://www.whiterose.com. **Description:** A major area distributor of approximately 850 grocery, dairy, and frozen food items. **Corporate headquarters location:** San Francisco CA. **Other U.S. locations:** Farmingdale NY.

DOOLAN INDUSTRIES, INC.
P.O. Box 73, Berlin NJ 08091. 856/791-9250. **Contact:** Tim Stein, President/CEO. **Description:** A holding company. Founded in 1938. **Operations at this facility include:** Administration; Divisional Headquarters; Sales. **Listed on:** Privately held. **Annual sales/revenues:** $5 - $10 million. **Number of employees at this location:** 10. **Number of employees nationwide:** 45.

DOW JONES & COMPANY, INC.
P.O. Box 300, Princeton NJ 08543-0300. 609/520-4000. **Physical address:** 4300 North Route 1, South Brunswick NJ 08852. **Fax:** 609/520-7401. **Contact:** Mary Pergament, Human Resources. **World Wide Web address:** http://www.dowjones.com. **Description:** A financial news service and publishing company. Publications include the *Wall Street Journal, National Business Employment Weekly,* and Barron's educational book services. **Positions advertised include:** Accounting Clerk; Assistant Business Manager; Assistant Producer; Contacts Administrator; Customer Service Representative; Assistant Marketing Resources Manager; Assistant Marketing Manager; Financial Supervisor; Human Resources Representative; Marketing Writer; News Assistant; Newscaster Production Associate; Paginator; Project Consultant; Project Manager; Business Analyst; Comprehensive Analyst; Internal Auditor; Supervisor; System Administrator Contact; Technical Architect. **Internship information:** Summer internships are offered for undergraduate and graduate students. See the above Website for program information and application schedule.

DUN & BRADSTREET
One Diamond Hill Road, Murray Hill NJ 07974. 908/665-5000. **Contact:** Human Resources. **World Wide Web address:** http://www.dnb.com. **Description:** A holding company. **Positions advertised include:** Automotive Solutions Leader; Product Strategy Leader; Channel Management Leader; Communications Consultant; MBA Project Leader & Recruiter; Administrative Assistant Sales; Teleweb Leader; Global Marketing & Promotions Leader; New Customer Acquisitions Manager; Sales Support Coordinator; Marketing Coordinator; Financial Analyst; Director Marketing Strategy; Product Marketing Manager; Program Manager; Communications Executive Assistant; Principal Consultant; Human Resources Director. **Subsidiaries include:** Dun & Bradstreet, Inc. provides information to the business community about other companies including data on credit and marketing. Moody's Investor Services provides ratings and other financial market information to assist individuals and companies in assessing investment opportunities. **Listed on:** New York Stock Exchange. **Stock exchange symbol:** DNB. **Number of employees worldwide:** 12,000.

E.I. DUPONT DE NEMOURS & COMPANY
Route 130, Deepwater NJ 08023. 856/299-5000. **Contact:** Human Resources. **World Wide Web address:** http://www.dupont.com. **Description:** E.I. DuPont de Nemours & Company's activities include the manufacturing of biomedical, industrial, and consumer products (such as photographic, data-recording, and video devices); the production of manmade fiber products (with applications in a variety of consumer and commercial industries), polymer products (such as plastic resins, elastomers, and films), and agricultural and industrial chemicals (such as herbicides and insecticides, pigments, fluorochemicals, petroleum additives, and mineral acids); the exploration and production of crude oil and natural gas; the refining, marketing, and downstream transportation of petroleum; and the mining and distribution of steam and metallurgical coals. Industries served include aerospace, agriculture, apparel, transportation, health care, and printing and publishing. **Corporate headquarters location:** Wilmington DE. **Operations at this facility include:** This location is a chemical manufacturing plant. **Listed on:** New York Stock Exchange. **Stock exchange symbol:** DD. **Chairman/CEO:** Charles O. Holliday, Jr. **Number of employees worldwide:** 94,000.

JOHN DUSENBERY COMPANY INC.
220 Franklin Road, Randolph NJ 07869. 973/366-7500. **Contact:** Connie Krupa, Controller. **Description:** Manufactures machinery for the paper, film, and foil industries. **Corporate headquarters location:** This location.

DYNASIL CORPORATION OF AMERICA
385 Cooper Road, West Berlin NJ 08091-9145. 856/767-4600. **Fax:** 856/767-6813. **Contact:** John Kane, President. **World Wide Web address:** http://www.dynasil.com. **Description:** Manufactures synthetic fused silica and fused quartz products. Founded in 1960. **Corporate headquarters location:** This location. **Annual sales/revenues:** $5 - $10 million. **Number of employees at this location:** 35. **Number of employees nationwide:** 40.

EBI MEDICAL SYSTEMS, INC.
100 Interpace Parkway, Parsippany NJ 07054. 973/299-9300. **Toll-free phone:** 800/526-2579. **Fax:** 973/402-1396. **Contact:** Department of Human Resources. **E-mail**

address: humanresources@ebimed.com. **World Wide Web address:** http://www.ebimedical.com. **Description:** Designs, develops, manufactures, and markets products used primarily by orthopedic medical specialists in both surgical and nonsurgical therapies. Products include electrical bone growth stimulators, orthopedic support devices, spinal fixation devices for spinal fusion, external fixation devices, and cold temperature therapy. Founded in 1977. **NOTE:** Entry-level positions and part-time jobs are offered. **Special programs:** Internships; Training; Summer Jobs. **Corporate headquarters location:** This location. **Other U.S. locations:** OK. **International locations:** Puerto Rico. **Parent company:** Biomet, Inc. **Listed on:** NASDAQ. **Stock exchange symbol:** BMET. **Number of employees at this location:** 360.

EDS
25 Hanover Road, 3rd Floor, Florham Park NJ 07932-1424. 973/301-7502. **Contact:** Human Resources. **World Wide Web address:** http://www.eds.com. **Description:** Provides integrated hardware, software, and network solutions to *Fortune* 500 companies. EDS focuses primarily on international corporations in the service, wholesale, distribution, and transportation industries. **Listed on:** New York Stock Exchange. **Stock exchange symbol:** EDS.

EMR SCHLUMBERGER PHOTOELECTRIC
20 Wallace Road, Princeton Junction NJ 08550. 609/799-1000. **Contact:** Personnel. **World Wide Web address:** http://www.schlumberger.com. **Description:** EMR Schlumberger Photoelectric is a research, development, and manufacturing division of Schlumberger Ltd. **Positions advertised include:** Geologist; Geophysicist; Petrophysicist; Production Engineer; Reservoir Engineer; Field Engineer; Field Specialist; CNC Programmer; ECAD Designer; Electrical Engineer; Manufacturing Engineer; Materials Specialist. **Corporate headquarters location:** This location. **Operations at this facility include:** This location is engaged in the engineering and manufacturing of critical, high-reliability transducers and transducer systems; nuclear sources and detectors for oil field services; and sensors/transducers for high-value measurement and control. **Parent company:** Schlumberger Ltd. **Listed on:** New York Stock Exchange. **Stock exchange symbol:** SLB.

EAST COAST TECHNOLOGIES
301 Pinedge Drive, Pinedge Industrial Park, West Berlin NJ 08091. 856/753-7778. **Contact:** Personnel. **E-mail address:** gwolfe@eastcoasttech.com. World **Wide Web address:** http://www.eastcoasttech.com. **Description:** Wholesales and repairs medical equipment, primarily laser and medical imaging systems.

THE ECONOMICS PRESS, INC.
12 Daniel Road, Fairfield NJ 07004-2565. 973/227-1224. **Toll-free phone:** 800/526-2554. **Fax:** 973/227-3558. **Contact:** Human Resources. **World Wide Web address:** http://www.epinc.com. **Description:** A publisher of books, audio and video programs, and computer programs focused on employee training, motivation, and business information.

EDMUND INDUSTRIAL OPTICS
101 East Gloucester Pike, Barrington NJ 08007. 856/573-6250. **Toll-free phone:** 800/363-1992. **Fax:** 856/573-6295. **Contact:** Human Resources Manager. **World Wide Web address:** http://www.edmundoptics.com. **Description:** Edmund Scientific Company is a retail supplier of industrial optics, lasers, telescopes, and precision optical instruments through two mail-order catalogs. Founded in 1942. **NOTE:** Entry-level positions are offered. **Company slogan:** Bringing science into focus. **Special programs:** Internships. **Corporate headquarters location:** This location. **Other U.S. locations:** Tucson AZ. **International locations:** China; Japan; United Kingdom. **Listed on:** Privately held. **CEO:** Robert Edmund. **Facilities Manager:** Mike Reyes. **Annual sales/revenues:** $51 - $100 million. **Number of employees at this location:** 190.

EDUCATIONAL TESTING SERVICE (ETS)
Rosedale Road, Princeton NJ 08541. 609/921-9000. **Fax:** 609/734-5410. **Contact:** Human Resources. **World Wide Web address:** http://www.ets.org. **Description:** An educational research and evaluation service that administers many aptitude and achievement tests including the SAT, CLEP, TOEFL, GRE, GMAT, and AP. **Positions advertised include:** Client Service Coordinator; Assessment Specialist; Associate Research Scientist; Audio Visual Specialist; Information Technology Auditor; Business Systems Analyst; Call Center Telephone Analyst; Group Manager; Media Planner; Information Security; SAT Mentor; GRE Mentor

EDWARDS AND KELCEY INC.
P.O. Box 1936, 299 Madison Avenue, Morristown NJ 07962-1936. 973/267-8830. **Contact:** Harry P. Daley, Human Resources Director. **World Wide Web address:** http://www.ekcorp.com. **Description:** A consulting, engineering, planning, and communications organization whose range of services includes location and economic feasibility studies; valuations and appraisals; cost analyses; computer technology; marketing studies; traffic and transportation studies; soils and foundation analyses; environmental impact studies; master planning; structural surveys; and preliminary and final designs. Services also include preparation of contract documents and observation of construction operations for public transit systems, terminals, railroads, bus depots, parking garages, airports, ports, highways, streets, bridges, tunnels, traffic control systems, military facilities, communications systems, storm and sanitary sewers, water supply and distribution, flood control, and land development. Founded in 1946. **NOTE:** Entry-level positions are offered. **Positions advertised include:** Industrial Electrician. **Special programs:** Internships. **Corporate headquarters location:** This location. **Other U.S. locations:** Atlanta GA; Chicago IL; Baltimore MD; Boston MA; Minneapolis MN; Manchester NH; New York NY; Saratoga Springs NY; Cincinnati OH; Chadds Ford PA; West Chester PA; Providence RI; Dallas TX; Houston TX; Leesburg VA; Milwaukee WI. **International locations:** Puerto Rico. **Operations at this facility include:** Administration; Divisional Headquarters. **Listed on:** Privately held. **Annual sales/revenues:** More than $100 million. **Number of employees at this location:** 200. **Number of employees nationwide:** 730.

ELAN
89 Headquarters Plaza #1420, Morristown NJ 07960. 973/272-6755. **Fax:** 973292/6759. **Contact:** Human Resources. **World Wide Web address:** http://www.elan.com. **Description:** Develops proprietary lipid- and liposome-based pharmaceuticals for the treatment, prevention, and diagnosis of cancer, systemic fungal infections, and inflammatory and vaso-occlusive diseases. **Positions advertised include:** Senior Scientist; Formulations Manager. **Corporate headquarters location:** This location.

ELEMENTIS SPECIALITIES RHEOX, INC.
329 Wyckoffs Mill Road, P.O. Box 700, Hightstown NJ 08520. 609/443-2500. **Contact:** Human Resources. **World Wide Web address:** http://www.rheox.com. **Description:** Manufactures a variety of chemicals. **Corporate headquarters location:** This location.

ELIZABETHTOWN GAS COMPANY/NUI
P.O. Box 1450, Union NJ 07207. 908/289-5000. **Physical address:** 1085 Morris Road, Union NJ 07083. **Contact:** Human Resources. **E-mail address:** hr@nui.com. **World Wide Web address:** http://www.nui.com. **Description:** Through several area locations, Elizabethtown Gas Company is engaged in the distribution of natural gas through its subsidiaries and investments in joint ventures. The company serves more than 240,000 customers. **Subsidiaries include:** Energy Marketing Exchange. **Parent company:** NUI Corporation (Bedminster NJ).

EMCORE CORPORATION
145 Belmont Drive, Somerset NJ 08873. 732/271-9090. **Contact:** Human Resources. **World Wide Web address:** http://www.emcore.com. **Description:** Manufactures semiconductors through the metal organic chemical vapor deposition production system. **NOTE:** Entry-level positions and second and third shifts are offered. **Special programs:** Training; Co-ops. **Office hours:** Monday - Friday, 8:00 a.m. - 5:00 p.m. **Corporate headquarters location:** This location. **Listed on:** NASDAQ. **Stock exchange symbol:** EMKR. **Annual sales/revenues:** $21 - $50 million.

ENOVATION GRAPHIC SYSTEMS, INC.
15 Twinbridge Drive, Pennsauken NJ 08110. 856/488-7200. **Contact:** Personnel. **World Wide Web address:** http://www.enovationgraphics.com. **Description:** Distributes graphic arts equipment and systems.

ENVIROGEN, INC.
4100 Quakerbridge Road, Lawrenceville NJ 08648. 609/936-9300. **Fax:** 609/936-9221. **Contact:** Debbie Doud, Manager of Human Resources. **E-mail address:** employment@envirogen.com. **World Wide Web address:** http://www.envirogen.com. **Description:** A leading technology-based environmental systems and services company that provides solutions to industrial and hazardous waste remediation problems. Envirogen uses biological and bio-complementary technologies for the treatment and/or cleanup of contaminated liquids, vapors, soils, and sludges. The company also designs and implements vapor extraction systems and other integrated systems for the on-site treatment of organic contaminants from soils and groundwater.

ENVIRON INTERNATIONAL CORPORATION
214 Carnegie Center, Princeton NJ 08540. 609/452-9000. **Contact:** Margaret Breyer, Human Resources. **E-mail address:** mbreyer@environcorp.com. **World Wide Web address:** http://www.environcorp.com. **Description:** A multidisciplinary environmental and health sciences consulting firm that provides a broad range of services relating to the presence of hazardous substances found in the environment, consumer products, and the workplace. ENVIRON International provides assessment and management of chemical risk and supports private sector clients with complex, potentially high-liability concerns. **Corporate headquarters location:** Arlington VA. **Other U.S. locations:** Emeryville CA; Irvine CA; Novato CA; Houston TX. **Parent company:** Applied Bioscience International Inc. (Arlington VA).

ENZON, INC.
20 Kingsbridge Road, Piscataway NJ 08854-3998. 732/980-4500. **Fax:** 732/980-5911. **Contact:** Human Resources. **E-mail address:** hr@enzon.com. **World Wide Web address:** http://www.enzon.com. **Description:** A biopharmaceutical company that develops advanced therapeutics for life threatening diseases, primarily in the area of oncology. **Positions advertised include:** Human Resources Specialist; Manufacturing Manager; Accounting Manager; Associate Director; Quality Assurance Clerk; Validation Specialist; Application Engineer; Research Associate; Clinical Project Manager; Computer Support Specialist; Clinical Research Assistant. **Office hours:** Monday - Friday, 8:30 a.m. - 5:00 p.m. **Other area locations:** South Plainfield NJ. **Listed on:** NASDAQ. **Stock exchange symbol:** ENZN. **President/CEO:** Peter Tombros. **Annual sales/revenues:** $11 - $20 million. **Number of employees at this location:** 55. **Number of employees nationwide:** 90.

EPSTEIN, INC.
P.O. Box 902, Morristown NJ 07963-0902. 973/538-5000. **Contact:** Personnel. **Description:** A department store offering a wide range of fashions and other soft and hard goods. **Corporate headquarters location:** Cedar Knolls NJ. **Other U.S. locations:** Bridgewater NJ; Princeton NJ; Shrewsbury NJ. **Operations at this facility include:** Sales.

EQUITY NATIONAL BANK
8000 Sagemore Drive, Suite 8101, Marlton NJ 08053. 856/983-4000. **Contact:** Human Resources. **Description:** A full-service bank whose operations include commercial and investment banking services.

LAWRENCE ERLBAUM ASSOCIATES, INC.
10 Industrial Avenue, Mahwah NJ 07430–2262. 201/258–2200. **Toll-free phone:** 800/9-BOOKS-9. **Fax:** 201/236–0072. **Contact:** Human Resources. **E-mail address:** hr@erlbaum.com. **World Wide Web address:** http://www.erlbaum.com. **Description:** A publishing company specializing in higher education books in communication, education and psychology. **Positions advertised include:** Desktop Formatter; Graphic Designer.

ERNST & YOUNG LLP
125 Chubb Avenue, Lyndhurst NJ 07071. 201/872-2200. **Contact:** Human Resources. **World Wide Web address:** http://www.ey.com. **Description:** A certified public accounting firm that also provides management consulting services. Services include data processing, financial modeling, financial feasibility studies, production planning and inventory management, management sciences, health care planning, human resources, cost accounting, and budgeting systems. **Positions advertised include:** Strategic Sourcing Analyst; Balance Sheet Analyst Manager; Infrastructure Engineer; Assistant Coordinator; Software Development Specialist; Production Analyst; Help Desk Analyst; Client Services Assistant; Project Account Manager; Executive Coordinator; Financial Analyst; Information Technology Technologist; Financial Application Support. **Corporate headquarters location:** New York NY.

ETHICON, INC.
U.S. Route 22, P.O. Box 151, Somerville NJ 08876. 908/218-0707. **Contact:** Human Resources. **World Wide Web address:** http://www.ethiconinc.com. **Description:** Manufactures products for precise wound closure including sutures, ligatures, mechanical wound closure instruments, and related products. The company also makes its own surgical needles and provides needle-suture combinations to surgeons. **Corporate headquarters location:** This location. **Parent company:** Johnson & Johnson (New Brunswick NJ).

EVENTIDE, INC.
One Alsan Way, Little Ferry NJ 07643. 201/641-1200. **Contact:** Human Resources Department. **E-mail address:** catbert@eventide.com. **World Wide Web address:** http://www.eventide.com. **Description:** Manufactures electronic harmonizers. **Positions advertised include:** Hardware/Software Engineer.

EXECUTIVE IMAGING SYSTEMS INC.
Marlkress Road, 8 Allison Drive, Haddonfield NJ 08033. 856/424-5898. **Fax:** 856/424-7848. **Contact:** Human Resources Department. **World Wide Web address:** http://www.executiveimaging.com. **Description:** Resells computers, facsimiles, printers, and peripherals.

EXXONMOBIL CORPORATION
1545 US Highway 22 E, Annondale NJ 08801. 908/730-0100. **Contact:** Human Resources. **World Wide Web address:** http://www.exxonmobil.com. **Description:** An integrated oil company engaged in petroleum and chemical products marketing, refining, manufacturing, exploration, production, transportation, and research and development worldwide. Other products include fabricated plastics, films, food bags, housewares, garbage bags, and building materials. The company also has subsidiaries involved in real estate development and mining operations. **Corporate headquarters location:** Irving TX. **Listed on:** New York Stock Exchange. **Stock exchange symbol:** XOM.

EXXONMOBIL CORPORATION
P.O. Box 480, 600 Billingsport Road, Paulsboro NJ 08066. 856/224-0200. **Contact:** Human Resources. **World Wide Web address:** http://www.exxonmobil.com **Description:** This location houses a refinery. Overall, ExxonMobil is an integrated oil company engaged in petroleum and chemical products marketing, refining, manufacturing, exploration, production, transportation, and research and development worldwide. Other products include fabricated plastics, films, food bags, housewares, garbage bags, and building materials. The company also has subsidiaries involved in real estate development and mining operations. **Corporate headquarters location:** Irving TX. **Listed on:** New York Stock Exchange. **Stock exchange symbol:** XOM.

FDS INTERNATIONAL
18 West Ridgewood Avenue, Paramus NJ 07652. 201/670-1300. **Fax:** 201/670-0400. **Contact:** Human Resources Department. **E-mail address:** jobs@fdsinternational.com. **World Wide Web address:** http://www.fdsinternational.com. **Description:** Develops transportation and custom brokerage software.

FM GLOBAL
400 Interpace Parkway, Building C, 3rd Floor, Parsippany NJ 07054-1196. 973/402-2200. **Contact:** District Office. **World Wide Web address:** http://www.fmglobal.com. **Description:** A loss control services organization. The company helps owner company policyholders to protect their properties and occupancies from damage caused by fire, wind, flood, and explosion; boiler, pressure vessel, and machinery accidents; and many other insured hazards. **Corporate headquarters location:** Johnston RI. **Other U.S. locations:** Nationwide. **International locations:** Worldwide.

FAIRMOUNT CHEMICAL COMPANY, INC.
117 Blanchard Street, Newark NJ 07105. 973/344-5790. **Toll-free phone:** 800/872-9999. **Fax:** 973/690-5298. **Contact:** Human Resources. **Description:** Manufactures and distributes chemical intermediates for the imaging industry; hydrazine salts and derivatives; additives used in the manufacture of plastics; and specialty chemicals, primarily pharmaceutical intermediates.

FALSTROM COMPANY
P.O. Box 118, One Falstrom Court, Passaic NJ 07055. 973/777-0013. **Contact:** Human Resources. **Description:** Manufactures steel cabinets for various clients including the defense industry.

FAULKNER INFORMATION SERVICES
114 Cooper Center, 7905 Browning Road, Pennsauken NJ 08109-4319. 856/662-2070. **Toll-free phone:** 800/843-0460. **Fax:** 856/662-3380. **Contact:** Human Resources. **World Wide Web address:** http://www.faulkner.com. **Description:** An independent publishing and research company specializing in providing technical information to end users and communication and IT professionals. Faulkner Information Services publishes more than a dozen standard information services in both print and electronic formats. The company provides comprehensive intelligence on products, vendors, technological advancements, and management issues associated with a wide range of technologies from open systems and client/server to enterprise networking, workgroup computing, and telecommunications. Faulkner also offers custom research and publication capabilities in such areas as market studies, customer satisfaction surveys, competitive analysis reports, and custom databases. **Positions advertised include:** Freelance Author; Experienced Editor. **Corporate headquarters location:** This location. **Operations at this facility include:** Administration; Research and Development; Sales; Service. **Number of employees at this location:** 45.

FEDDERS CORPORATION
505 Martinsville Road, P.O. Box 813, Liberty Corner NJ 07938. 908/604-8686. **Fax:** 908/604-8576. **Contact:** Human Resources Department. **E-mail address:** customerservice@fedders.com. **World Wide Web address:** http://www.fedders.com. **Description:** Manufactures room air conditioners. Brand names of the corporation include Airtemp, Emerson Quiet Kool, and Fedders. **Positions advertised include:** Administrative Assistant; Human Resources Assistant; Sales Manager; Traffic Manager. **Corporate headquarters location:** This location. **Listed on:** New York Stock Exchange. **Stock exchange symbol:** FJC.

FIREMAN'S FUND INSURANCE COMPANY
110 Allen Road, Liberty Corner NJ 07938. 908/542-5600. **Contact:** Human Resources. **World Wide Web address:** http://www.the-fund.com. **Description:** A holding company for a group of property/liability insurance companies operating primarily in the United States. **Positions advertised include:** Attorney; Claim Representative; Underwriter/Assistant Underwriter. **Corporate headquarters location:** Novato CA. **Parent company:** Allianz AG.

FIRST MONTAUK FINANCIAL CORPORATION
328 Newman Springs Road, Red Bank NJ 07701. 732/842-4700. **Contact:** Human Resources. **World Wide Web address:** http://www.firstmontauk.com. **Description:** A diversified holding company that provides financial services throughout the United States to individuals, corporations, and institutions. **Subsidiaries include:** First Montauk Securities Corporation is a securities broker/dealer with a nationwide network of more than 300 registered representatives in 90 branch offices serving approximately 25,000 retail and institutional clients. Montauk Insurance Services, Inc. is an insurance agency.

FIRSTENERGY CORPORATION
300 Madison Avenue, P.O. Box 1911, Morristown NJ 07962-1911. 973/955-8200. **Contact:** Personnel. **World Wide Web address:** http://www.firstenergycorp.com. **Description:** An electric utility holding company with several operating subsidiaries. **Positions advertised include:** Purchasing Representative; Executive Assistant; Lineman; Law Clerk; Attorney; Associate Generation Specialist. **Corporate headquarters location:** Akron OH. **Operations at this facility include:** Administration. **Listed on:** New York Stock Exchange. **Stock exchange symbol:** FE.

FISHER SCIENTIFIC COMPANY
One Reagent Lane, Fair Lawn NJ 07410. 201/796-7100. **Contact:** Michelle Valvano, Personnel Manager. **World Wide Web address:** http://www.fisherscientific.com. **Description:** Fisher Scientific manufactures, distributes, and sells a wide range of products used in industrial and medical laboratories. Products include analytical and measuring instruments, apparatus, and appliances; reagent chemicals and diagnostics; glassware and plasticware; and laboratory furniture. Customers are primarily industrial laboratories, medical and hospital laboratories, and educational and research laboratories. Manufacturing operations are carried out by six operating divisions in 11 U.S. locations. **Positions advertised include:** Accountant; Facilities Manager; Office Manager; Analytical Chemist; Financial Analyst. **Operations at this facility include:** This location produces reagents. **Listed on:** New York Stock Exchange. **Stock exchange symbol:** FSH.

FLUOR DANIEL, INC.
300 Atrium Way, Mount Laurel NJ 08054. 856/222-2910. **Fax:** 856/552-6837. **Contact:** Human Resources. **E-mail address:** careers@fluor.com. **World Wide Web address:** http://www.fluordaniel.com. **Description:** A full-service engineering and construction company serving the power, industrial, hydrocarbon, and process industries, as well as the federal government. **Other U.S. locations:** Nationwide. **Parent company:** Fluor Corporation (Irvine CA) engages in engineering and construction, as well as the extraction of various natural resources. **Number of employees worldwide:** 20,000.

FOOD CITY MARKETS INC.
440 Sylvan Avenue, Suite 120, Englewood Cliffs NJ 07632. 201/569-4849. **Contact:** Barry Schwartz, Supervisor of Store Operations. **Description:** Operates a chain of supermarkets. **Corporate headquarters location:** This location.

FOODARAMA SUPERMARKETS
922 Highway 33, Building 6, Suite 1, Freehold NJ 07728. 732/462-4700. **Contact:** Human Resources. **World Wide Web address:** http://www.foodarama.com. **Description:** Foodarama operates supermarkets in the states of New Jersey, New York, and Pennsylvania. **Corporate headquarters location:** This location.

FORD MOTOR COMPANY
698 U.S. Highway 46, Teterboro NJ 07608. 201/288-9421. **Contact:** Human Resources Manager. **World Wide Web address:** http://www.ford.com/careercenter. **Description:** Ford is engaged in the manufacture, assembly, and sale of cars, trucks, and related parts and accessories. Ford is also one of the largest providers of financial services in the United States. The company's two core businesses are the Automotive Group and the Financial Services Group (Ford Credit, The Associates, USL Capital, and First Nationwide). Ford is also engaged in a number of other businesses, including electronics, glass, electrical and fuel-handling products, plastics, climate control systems, automotive service and replacement parts, vehicle leasing and rental, and land development. **Corporate headquarters location:** Dearborn MI. **Operations at this facility include:** This location is a parts distribution center. **Listed on:** New York Stock Exchange. **Stock exchange symbol:** F.

FORMATION, INC.
121 Whittendale Drive, Moorestown NJ 08057. 856/234-5020. **Toll-free phone:** 800/220-1200. **Fax:** 856/234-8543. **Contact:** Human Resources. **E-mail address:** resume@formation.com. **World Wide Web address:** http://www.formation.com. **Description:** Designs and manufactures communications products and real-time, high-performance storage and retrieval systems. The company's products are capable of integrating a number of inputs including video, audio, data/text, and radar, and can employ a variety of communications protocols. The company supplies an open systems storage system using Redundant Array of Independent Disks (RAID) technology. Formation also supplies plug-compatible data storage systems for IBM AS/400 computers, as well as data storage systems to open systems computer manufacturers and systems integrators. **Corporate headquarters location:** This location. **Operations at this facility include:** Administration; Manufacturing; Research and Development; Sales; Service. **Number of employees at this location:** 75.

FOSTER WHEELER CORPORATION
Perryville Corporate Park, Clinton NJ 08809-4000. 908/730-4000. **Fax:** 908/713-3315. **Contact:** Tom Cucchiara, Personnel. **E-mail address:** us_staffing@fwc.com. **World Wide Web address:** http://www.fwc.com. **Description:** Foster Wheeler has three business segments: Process Plants segment designs, engineers, and constructs process plants and fired heaters for oil refiners and chemical producers; the Utility and Engine segment designs and fabricates steam generators, condensers, feedwater heaters, electrostatic precipitators, and other pollution abatement equipment; the Industrial segment that supplies pressure vessels and internals, electrical copper products, industrial insulation, welding wire, and electrodes. **Positions advertised include:** Senior Programmer. **Corporate headquarters location:** This location. **International locations:** Worldwide. **Listed on:** New York Stock Exchange. **Stock exchange symbol:** FWC.

FRANKLIN ELECTRONIC PUBLISHERS
One Franklin Plaza, Burlington NJ 08016. 609/386-2500. **Toll-free phone:** 800/266-5626. **Fax:** 888/891-4844. **Contact:** Human Resources. **E-mail address:** resume@franklin.com. **World Wide Web address:** http://www.franklin.com. **Description:** A publishing company that specializes in e-books. **Positions advertised include:** Product Manager; Buyer.

THE FRESH JUICE COMPANY
280 Wilson Avenue, Newark NJ 07105. 973/465-7100. **Contact:** Human Resources. **Description:** Markets and sells frozen and fresh-squeezed Florida orange juice, grapefruit juice, apple juice, and other noncarbonated beverages under the brand name Just Pik't.

FUJITSU CONSULTING
333 Thornall Street, Edison NJ 08837. 732/549-4100. **Fax:** 732/549-2375. **Contact:** Recruiting Administrator. **World Wide Web address:** http://consulting.fujitsu.com. **Description:** Provides computer consulting services including outsourcing solutions and systems integration. **Positions advertised include:** Consultant. **Corporate headquarters location:** This location. **Parent company:** Fujitsu Limited. **Number of employees worldwide:** 8,000.

FUJITSU CORPORATION
85 Challenger Road, 3rd Floor, Ridgefield Park NJ 07660. 201/229-4400. **Contact:** Human Resources. **World Wide Web address:** http://www.fujitsu.com. **Description:** This location is engaged in sales, service, and support. Overall, Amdahl designs, develops, manufactures, markets, and services large-scale, high-performance, general

purpose computer systems including both hardware and software. Customers are primarily large corporations, government agencies, and large universities with high-volume data processing requirements. Amdahl markets more than 470 different systems. **Positions advertised include:** Field Operations Installer; Field Operations Engineer; Area Sales Manager. **NOTE:** Mail employment correspondence to: 1250 East Arques Avenue, Sunnyvale CA 94088. **Corporate headquarters location:** Sunnyvale CA.

GAB ROBINS NORTH AMERICA INC.
9 Campus Drive, Suite 7, Parsippany NJ 07054. 973/993-3400. **Fax:** 973/993-3767. **Contact:** Human Resources. **E-mail address:** answers@gabrobins.com. **World Wide Web address:** http://www.gabrobinsna.com. **Description:** Provides adjustment, inspection, appraisal, and claims management services to 15,000 insurance industry customers. Specific services include the settlement of claims following major disasters; appraisal, investigation, and adjustment of auto insurance claims; casualty claims; and fire, marine, life, accident, health, and disability claims. **Corporate headquarters location:** This location. **Parent company:** SGS North America. **Number of employees nationwide:** 3,400.

GAF MATERIALS CORPORATION
1361 Alps Road, Wayne NJ 07470. 973/628-3000. **Toll-free phone:** 800/766-3411. **Contact:** Human Resources. **E-mail address:** employment@gaf.com. **World Wide Web address:** http://www.gaf.com. **Description:** Manufactures roofing materials. **Operations at this facility include:** Administration; Manufacturing.

GARDEN STATE HOSPITALIZATION PLAN
900 U.S. Highway - 9 North, Suite 101, Woodbridge NJ 07095-1096. 732/636-0404. **Fax:** 732/636-6929. **Contact:** Human Resources. **Description:** Provides hospitalization insurance throughout New Jersey. **Corporate headquarters location:** This location.

GEMINI INDUSTRIES INC.
215 Entin Road, Clifton NJ 07014. 973/471-9050. **Fax:** 973/574-7215. **Contact:** Human Resources. **E-mail address:** hr@gemini-usa.com. **World Wide Web address:** http://www.gemini-usa.com. **Description:** Manufactures PC and cellular telephone accessories, remote controls, and cable. **Positions advertised include:** Test Engineer; Security Guard.

GENERAL CHEMICAL CORPORATION
90 East Halsey Road, Parsippany NJ 07054. 973/515-0900. **Contact:** Human Resources. **E-mail address:** hrinfor@genchem.com. **World Wide Web address:** http://www.genchem.com. **Description:** Manufactures inorganic chemicals and soda ash. **Positions advertised include:** Office Manager; Network Technician. **Corporate headquarters location:** This location. **Other U.S. locations:** Claymont DE; Syracuse NY; Pittsburgh PA; Green River WY. **Parent company:** The General Chemical Group Inc. (Hampton NH). **Operations at this facility include:** Administration; Manufacturing; Sales; Service. **Number of employees at this location:** 180. **Number of employees nationwide:** 2,000.

GENTEK BUILDING PRODUCTS, INC.
11 Cragwood Avenue, Avenel NJ 07001. **Fax:** 732/827-0163. **Contact:** Jane Hohman, Human Resources Manager. **E-mail address:** jane_hohman@gentek.ca. **World Wide Web address:** http://www.gentekinc.com. **Description:** A manufacturer of vinyl, aluminum and steel exterior building products. **Positions advertised include:** Operations Manager; Outside Sales Representative; Shipping/Warehouse Supervisor. **Other U.S. locations:** Nationwide.

GLAXOSMITHKLINE CORPORATION
257 Cornelison Avenue, Jersey City NJ 07302. 201/434-3000. **Contact:** Human Resources. **World Wide Web address:** http://www.gsk.com. **Description:** Develops, manufactures, and sells products in four general categories: denture, dental care, oral hygiene, and professional dental products; proprietary products; ethical pharmaceutical products; and household products. Dental-related products include Polident denture cleansers. **Positions advertised include:** Pharmaceutical Sales Representative. **Listed on:** New York Stock Exchange. **Stock exchange symbol:** GSK.

GLAXOSMITHKLINE CORPORATION
65 Industrial South, Clifton NJ 07012. 973/778-9000. **Contact:** Human Resources. **World Wide Web address:** http://www.gsk.com. **Description:** GlaxoSmithKline Corporation is a health care company engaged in the research, development, manufacture, and marketing of ethical pharmaceuticals, animal health products, ethical and proprietary medicines, and eye care products. The company is also engaged in many other aspects of the health care field including the production of medical and electronic instruments. **Positions advertised include:** Warehouse Technician; Validation Engineer; Systems Programmer Analyst; Staff Accountant; Production Technician. **Corporate headquarters location:** Philadelphia PA. **Operations at this facility include:** This location manufactures toothpaste and Massengill products. **Listed on:** New York Stock Exchange. **Stock exchange symbol:** GSK.

GLAXOSMITHKLINE PHARMACEUTICALS
101 Possumtown Road, Piscataway NJ 08854. 732/469-5200. **Contact:** Human Resources Manager. **World Wide Web address:** http://www.gsk.com. **Description:** Manufactures penicillin. **Positions advertised include:** Analytical Chemist; Clinical Operations Project Manager. **Corporate headquarters location:** Philadelphia PA. **Parent company:** GlaxoSmithKline Corporation is health care company engaged in the research, development, manufacture, and marketing of ethical pharmaceuticals, animal health products, ethical and proprietary medicines, and eye care products. **Listed on:** New York Stock Exchange. **Stock exchange symbol:** GSK.

GLOBE MANUFACTURING SALES, INC.
1159 U.S. Route 22, Mountainside NJ 07092. 908/232-7301. **Fax:** 908/232-0179. **Contact:** Personnel. **World Wide Web address:** http://www.globebrackets.com. **Description:** Manufactures computer brackets that hold computer chips and other plastic parts. **Parent company:** AK Stamping Company, Inc.

S. GOLDBERG & COMPANY, INC.
20 East Broadway, Hackensack NJ 07601. 201/342-1200. **Contact:** Personnel Manager. **Description:** Manufactures house slippers. **Corporate headquarters location:** This location. **Operations at this facility include:** Manufacturing.

GOODRICH CORPORATION
MOTION CONTROLS DIVISION
197 Ridgedale Avenue, Cedar Knolls NJ 07927. 973/267-4500. **Contact:** Human Resources. **World Wide Web address:** http://www.goodrich.com. **Description:** Manufactures aircraft systems and components and provides services for the aerospace industry worldwide. **Positions advertised include:** Electrical Engineer. **NOTE:** For employment information contact: Human Resources, Goodrich Corporation, 100 Panton Road, Vergennes VT 05491. 802/877-2911. **Parent company:** Goodrich Company. **Listed on:** New York Stock Exchange. **Stock exchange symbol:** GR.

STEPHEN GOULD CORPORATION
35 South Jefferson Road, Whippany NJ 07981. 973/428-1500. **Contact:** Executive Assistant. **E-mail address:** j.sales@stephengould.com. **World Wide Web address:** http://www.stephengould.com. **Description:** Designs, produces, and supplies packaging including plastic, paper, and metal for a variety of materials industries. **Corporate headquarters location:** This location. **Other U.S. locations:** Nationwide.

THE GREAT ATLANTIC & PACIFIC TEA COMPANY
2 Paragon Drive, Montvale NJ 07645. 201/573-9700. **Contact:** Personnel. **World Wide Web address:** http://www.aptea.com. **Description:** The Great Atlantic & Pacific Tea Company maintains approximately 700 retail supermarkets throughout the East Coast, the Mid-Atlantic region, and Canada. **Positions advertised include:** Benefits Coordinator; Information Systems Auditor; Payroll Operations Clerk; Compensation Analyst; Human Resources Supervisor; Accountant; Voice Analyst; Coordinator. **Corporate headquarters location:** This location. **Operations at this facility include:** This location houses administrative offices for one of the nation's largest supermarket chains. **Listed on:** New York Stock Exchange. **Stock exchange symbol:** GAP. **Number of employees at this location:** 650. **Number of employees nationwide:** 85,000.

GREATER COMMUNITY BANCORP
2 Sears Drive, Paramus NJ 07653. 973/942-1111. **Contact:** Human Resources. **World Wide Web address:** http://www.greatercommunity.com. **Description:** A holding company. **Subsidiaries include:** Greater Community Bank conducts general commercial and retail banking. **Listed on:** NASDAQ. **Stock exchange symbol:** GFLS.

GREENBAUM, ROWE, SMITH, RAVIN, DAVIS & HIMMEL LLP
Metro Corporate Campus One, 99 Wood Avenue South, P.O. Box 5600, Woodbridge NJ 07095. 732/549-5600. **Fax:** 732/549-1881. **Contact:** Victoria Martignetti, Recruitment Coordinator. **E-mail address:** vmartignetti@greenbaumlaw.com. **World Wide Web address:** http://www.greenbaumlaw.com. **Description:** A law firm with practice areas including environmental, product liability, employment, white collar criminal, real estate, corporate, tax, and estate law.

GROUNDWATER AND ENVIRONMENTAL SERVICES, INC. (GES)
P.O. Box 1750, Wall NJ 07719. 732/919-0100. **Physical address:** 1340 Campus Parkway, Wall NJ 07719. **Fax:** 732/919-0916. **Contact:** Human Resources. **E-mail address:** resume@gesonline.com. **World Wide Web address:** http://www.gesonline.com. **Description:** An environmental engineering firm specializing in groundwater remediation. Founded in 1985. **Positions advertised include:** Business Developmental Manager; Geologist; Scientist; Hydrogeologist; Environmental Engineer; Project Manager; Well Driller.

GUEST SUPPLY INC.
P.O. Box 902, Monmouth Junction NJ 08852-0902. 609/514-9696. **Physical address:** 4301 U.S. Highway One, Monmouth Junction NJ 08852-0902. **Fax:** 609-514-2692. **Contact:** Joan Constanza, Human Resources Manager. **World Wide Web address:** http://www.guestsupply.com. **Description:** Manufactures, packages, and distributes travel-size personal care products, housekeeping supplies, room accessories, and textiles to the lodging industry. The company also manufactures and packages products for major consumer products and retail companies. Founded in 1979. **NOTE:** Entry-level positions and second and third shifts are offered. **Corporate headquarters location:** This location. **Other U.S. locations:** Nationwide. **Subsidiaries include:** Brecken-Ridge-Remy; Guest Distribution; Guest Packaging. **Operations at this facility include:** Divisional Headquarters; Regional Headquarters. **Listed on:** New York Stock Exchange. **Stock exchange symbol:** GSY. **Annual sales/revenues:** More than $100 million. **Number of employees at this location:** 1,000.

HACKENSACK UNIVERSITY MEDICAL CENTER
30 Prospect Avenue, Hackensack NJ 07601. 201/996-2000. **Contact:** Human Resources. **World Wide Web address:** http://www.humc.net. **Description:** A teaching medical hospital and research center affiliated with the University of Medicine. **Positions advertised include:** Registered Nurse; Licensed Practical Nurse; OB Technician; Case Manager; Social Worker.

HARRIS INTERACTIVE
5 Independence Way, P.O. Box 5305, Princeton NJ 08543. 609/520-9100. **Fax:** 609/987-8839. **Contact:** Jane Giles, Human Resources Manager. **E-mail address:** info@harrisinteractive.com. **World Wide Web address:** http://www.harrisinteractive.com. **Description:** A full-service marketing research firm that provides information for use in strategic and tactical marketing decisions. **NOTE:** Mail employment correspondence to: Human Resources, Job Code # 76, Carlson Road, Rochester NY 14610. **Positions advertised include:** Senior Research Manager; Survey Programmer; Account Executive. **Special programs:** Internships. **Corporate headquarters location:** Rochester NY. **Other U.S. locations:** Tampa FL; Chicago IL; Detroit MI; Minneapolis MN. **International locations:** Argentina; England. **Parent company:** Harris Interactive. **Listed on:** NASDAQ. **Stock exchange symbol:** HPOL.

HCR MANOR CARE HEALTH SERVICES
1412 Marlton Pike, Cherry Hill NJ 08034. 856/428-6100. **Contact:** Human Resources. **E-mail address:** jobline@hcr.manorcare.com. **World Wide Web address:** http://www.manorcare.com. **Description:** An inpatient and outpatient rehabilitation center providing physical, occupational, and speech therapies. **Positions advertised include:** Admissions Director; Registered Nurse; Licensed Practical Nurse; Nurses Assistant; Occupational Therapist. **Special programs:** Training. **Corporate headquarters location:** Toledo OH. **Other U.S. locations:** Nationwide. **Subsidiaries include:** Milestone Healthcare. **Listed on:** New York Stock Exchange. **Stock exchange symbol:** HCR. **Number of employees nationwide:** 50,000.

HRSOFT, INC.
10 Madison Avenue, 3rd Floor, Morristown NJ 07962. 973/984-6334. **Toll-free phone:** 800/437-6781. **Fax:** 973/984-5427. **Contact:** Human Resources. **E-mail address:** jobinfo@hrsoft.com. **World Wide Web address:** http://www.hrsoft.com. **Description:** Develops and provides human resource-related business software and services.

HAMON RESEARCH-COTTRELL
58 East Main Street, Somerville NJ 08876. 908/685-4000. **Contact:** Human Resources. **E-mail address:** info.hcorp@hamonusa.com. **World Wide Web address:** http://www.hamon-researchcottrell.com. **Description:** An environmental treatment and services company that provides a comprehensive range of services and technologies directed at controlling air pollution; protecting the integrity of the nation's water resources; providing services in support of the management and remediation of hazardous waste; and providing services for the operations, maintenance, and

management of treatment facilities. **Office hours:** Monday - Friday, 8:00 a.m. - 5:00 p.m. **Parent company:** Hamon Group.

J.B. HANAUER & COMPANY
4 Gatehall Drive, Parsippany NJ 07054. 973/829-1000. **Toll-free phone:** 800/631-1094. **Fax:** 973/829-0565. **Contact:** Human Resources. **World Wide Web address:** http://www.jbh.com. **Description:** A full-service brokerage firm specializing in fixed-income investments. J.B. Hanauer & Company provides a broad range of financial products and services. Founded in 1931. **NOTE:** Entry-level positions are offered. **Special programs:** Internships; Training. **Corporate headquarters location:** This location. **Other U.S. locations:** North Miami FL; Tampa FL; West Palm Beach FL; Princeton NJ; Rye Brook NY; Philadelphia PA. **Listed on:** Privately held. **Annual sales/revenues:** More than $100 million. **Number of employees at this location:** 250. **Number of employees worldwide:** 600.

HANDEX ENVIRONMENTAL
500 Campus Drive, Morganville NJ 07751. 732/536-8500. **Contact:** Human Resources. **World Wide Web address:** http://www.handex.com. **Description:** Provides environmental remediation and educational services including comprehensive solutions to contamination of groundwater and soil resulting from leaking underground storage tanks; petroleum distribution systems; refineries; heavy industrial plants; chemical, aerospace, and pharmaceutical facilities; airports; auto and truck fleet facilities; and related contamination sources. **Positions advertised include:** Professional Engineer; Filler Press Field Engineer; Permits Coordinator; Staff Hydrologist; General Manager.

HANOVER DIRECT, INC.
115 River Road, Building 10, Edgewater NJ 07020. 201/863-7300. **Fax:** 201/272-3280. **Contact:** Personnel. **World Wide Web address:** http://www.hanoverdirect.com. **Description:** A direct marketing company that sells products manufactured by other companies through its 12 core catalogs structured into operating groups. **NOTE:** Entry-level positions are offered. **Positions advertised include:** Analyst. **Corporate headquarters location:** This location. **Other U.S. locations:** San Diego CA; San Francisco CA; Hanover PA; De Soto TX; Roanoke VA; La Crosse WI. **Operations at this facility include:** Administration; Divisional Headquarters; Sales. **Listed on:** American Stock Exchange. **Stock exchange symbol:** HNV. **Annual sales/revenues:** More than $100 million. **Number of employees at this location:** 250. **Number of employees nationwide:** 3,000.

HANOVIA/COLITE, INC.
825 Lehigh Avenue, Union NJ 07083. 908/688-0050. **Contact:** Rosemary McCann, Director of Human Resources. **World Wide Web address:** http://www.hanovia-uv.com. **Description:** Designs, develops, produces, and markets plasma arc lamps and related equipment including commercial and industrial ultraviolet products and accessories; produces various phosphorescent pigments, compounds, and films; and designs, develops, manufactures, assembles, and markets high-intensity lighting equipment. **Corporate headquarters location:** This location.

HARBOUR INTERMODAL LTD.
1177 McCarter Highway, Newark NJ 07104. 973/481-6474. **Contact:** Human Resources. **Description:** Provides local intermodal transportation services in the greater New York Harbor area. The company also develops and sells equipment for intermodal services including waterborne vessels and mobile and fixed heavy materials handling equipment for transporting and sorting containers, trailers, and general cargo.

HARRAH'S ATLANTIC CITY
777 Harris Boulevard, Atlantic City NJ 08401. 609/441-5000. **Contact:** Human Resources. **E-mail address:** jobs@harrahs.com. **World Wide Web address:** http://www.harrahs.com. **Description:** A hotel and casino providing 1,174 rooms, theaters, retail space, and seven restaurants.

HARTZ MOUNTAIN CORPORATION
400 Plaza Drive, 4th Floor, Secaucus NJ 07094. 201/271-4800. **Fax:** 201/271-0164. **Contact:** Human Resources. **E-mail address:** jobopps@hartz.com. **World Wide Web address:** http://www.hartz.com. **Description:** Engaged in the manufacture, packaging, and distribution of consumer products including pet foods, pet accessories, livestock feed and products; chemical products; home carpet-cleaning products; and equipment rentals. **Positions advertised include:** Company Website Marketing Manager; EPA Specialist; FDA Director of Regulatory Affairs; Planner. **Corporate headquarters location:** This location. **Other area locations:** Bloomfield NJ. **Subsidiaries include:** Cooper Pet Supply; Permaline Manufacturing Corporation; Sternco-Dominion Real Estate Corporation; The Pet Library Ltd.

HATCH MOTT MACDONALD, INC.
27 Bleeker Street, Millburn NJ 07041. 973/379-3400. **Toll-free phone:** 800/832-3272. **Fax:** 973/912-3354. **Contact:** Personnel. **E-mail address:** hr@hatchmott.com. **World Wide Web address:** http://www.killam.com. **Description:** An infrastructure engineering, environmental, and industrial process consulting firm that serves both public and private sectors. The company operates within a wide range of areas providing architectural, environmental, outsourcing, transportation engineering, and water resource management services. Founded in 1937. **Positions advertised include:** Asbestos Inspector; Assistant Resident Engineer; Business Development Manager, Environment; Civil Engineer, Water; Civil Engineer, Environmental; Environmental Geologist; Project Manager. **Special programs:** Internships. **Internship information:** Internships are offered May through September, as well as during December and January. **Corporate headquarters location:** This location. **Other area locations:** Cape May Court House NJ; Freehold NJ; Hackensack NJ; Randolph NJ; Toms River NJ; Whitehouse NJ. **Other U.S. locations:** Nationwide. **Subsidiaries include:** BAC Killam, Inc.; Carlan Killam Consulting Group, Inc.; E3-Killam, Inc.; Killam Associates - New England; Killam Management & Operational Services, Inc.

HAUSMANN INDUSTRIES
130 Union Street, Northvale NJ 07647. 201/767-0255. **Toll-free phone:** 877/737-3332. **Fax:** 201/767-1369. **Toll-free fax:** 877-737-33322. **Contact:** Human Resources. **E-mail address:** info@hausmann.com. **World Wide Web address:** http://www.hausmann.com. **Description:** Manufactures medical examination tables and physical therapy equipment. **Corporate headquarters location:** This location.

HAYWARD INDUSTRIES
900 Fairmount Avenue, Elizabeth NJ 07201. 908/351-5400. **Fax:** 908/351-0604. **Contact:** Human Resources. **World Wide Web address:** http://www.haywardnet.com. **Description:** Manufactures swimming pool equipment. The company is engaged in all aspects of production including design and sales. Clients use equipment in the construction, repair, and maintenance of private and commercial swimming pools. The company also manufactures and distributes a standard line of industrial pipeline strainers and valves. **Positions advertised include:** National Technical Service Manager; Product Engineer; Marketing Product Manager; Associate Product Manager; Call Center Supervisor; Marketing Communications Manager. **Corporate headquarters location:** This location. **International locations:** Belgium.

THE HERTZ CORPORATION
225 Brae Boulevard, Park Ridge NJ 07656. 201/307-2000. **Fax:** 201/307-2644. **Contact:** Director of Personnel. **World Wide Web address:** http://www.hertz.com. **Description:** A large rental company that leases new and used cars and industrial and construction equipment in 130 countries worldwide. The company also sells used cars in the United States, Australia, New Zealand, and Europe. The fleet of cars consists of 283,000 automobiles, which are leased through 5,300 offices. **Corporate headquarters location:** This location.

HEWLETT-PACKARD MIDDLEWARE
6000 Irwin Road, Mount Laurel NJ 08054-4128. 856/638-6000. **Toll-free phone:** 866/452-2318. **Fax:** 856/638-6170. **Contact:** Monique McLaughlin, Recruiter. **World Wide Web address:** http://www.hpmiddleware.com. **Description:** Develops computer technology programs and provides user training. Offers Web-based software including dynamic Web applications and GUIs. **NOTE:** Entry-level positions are offered. **Special programs:** Training. **Corporate headquarters location:** Palo Alto CA. **Other U.S. locations:** Nationwide. **Listed on:** New York Stock Exchange. **Stock exchange symbol:** HWP.

THE HIBBERT GROUP
400 Pennington Avenue, Trenton NJ 08618. 609/394-7500. **Fax:** 609/392-5946. **Contact:** Human Resources. **E-mail address:** hr@hibbertco.com. **World Wide Web address:** http://www.hibbertco.com. **Description:** Offers international direct marketing services including literature fulfillment, data services, telemarketing, and direct mail. **Positions advertised include:** Program Administration; Customer Service Representative. **Corporate headquarters location:** This location. **Other U.S. locations:** Denver CO. **Operations at this facility include:** Administration; Sales; Service. **Number of employees nationwide:** 800.

HILL INTERNATIONAL
303 Lippincott Center, Marlton NJ 08053. 856/810-6200. **Contact:** Human Resources. **World Wide Web address:** http://www.hillintl.com. **Description:** Provides construction management and consulting services. **Positions advertised include:** Executive Consultant; Accounting Manager.

HILTON OF HASBROUCK HEIGHTS
650 Terrace Avenue, Hasbrouck Heights NJ 07604. 201/288-6100. **Contact:** Human Resources. **World Wide Web address:** http://www.hilton.com. **Description:** A hotel that provides a wide range of lodging, restaurant, lounge, meeting, and banquet facilities as part of an international chain. **Positions advertised include:** Customer Service Representative; Food and Beverage Service Worker; Hotel/Motel Clerk; Housekeeper. **Operations at this facility include:** Administration.

HILTON PARSIPPANY
One Hilton Court, Parsippany NJ 07054. 973/267-7373. **Fax:** 973/984-6853. **Contact:** Human Resources. **World Wide Web address:** http://www.hilton.com. **Description:** Recently renovated location of the hotel chain. Features a Ruth's Chris Steak House and accessibility to various area attractions.

HOBOKEN FLOORS
70 Demarest Drive, Wayne NJ 07470. 973/694-2888. **Contact:** Personnel. **World Wide Web address:** http://www.hobokenfloors.com. **Description:** Manufactures hardwood flooring. **Corporate headquarters location:** This location.

HOFFMANN-LA ROCHE INC.
340 Kingsland Street, Nutley NJ 07110-0119. 973/235-5000. **Contact:** Director of Staffing. **World Wide Web address:** http://www.rocheusa.com. **Description:** An international health care organization that develops and manufactures pharmaceuticals, diagnostics, and vitamins. **NOTE:** Entry-level positions, part-time jobs, and second and third shifts are offered. **Positions advertised include:** Accounting Systems Developer; Administrative Assistant; Animal Resource Technician; Associate Clinical Director; Clinical Director; Clinical Liaison; Education Team Leader. **Corporate headquarters location:** This location. **Other U.S. locations:** Nationwide. **International locations:** Worldwide. **Subsidiaries include:** Roche Biomedical Laboratories; Roche Diagnostics (ethical pharmaceuticals); Roche Vitamins Inc. **Parent company:** F. Hoffmann-La Roche Ltd. **Operations at this facility include:** Divisional Headquarters. **Listed on:** Privately held. **Annual sales/revenues:** More than $100 million. **Number of employees at this location:** 6,000. **Number of employees nationwide:** 20,000. **Number of employees worldwide:** 80,000.

HOLOPAK TECHNOLOGIES, INC.
15 Cotters Lane, East Brunswick NJ 08816. 732/651-2292. **Fax:** 732/238-3018. **Contact:** Bonnie Eichel, Human Resources Director. **Description:** HoloPak, through its subsidiaries Transfer Print Foils, Inc. and Alubec Industries Inc., is a producer and distributor of hot stamping foils, holographic foils, metallized paper, and technical coatings. Hot stamping foils are elements of the graphics and packaging industries, and are used to decorate a wide variety of products. Holographic foils are high-precision images embossed into specialized coatings, which are used to discourage counterfeiting and provide specialty decorative effects. **Parent company:** Foilmark Inc. **Corporate headquarters location:** Newburyport MA. **Other U.S. locations:** Nationwide. **International locations:** Canada.

HOME CARE INDUSTRIES
One Lisbon Street, Clifton NJ 07013. 973/365-1600. **Contact:** Human Resources. **World Wide Web address:** http://www.homecareind.com. **Description:** Manufactures vacuum cleaner bags.

HOME NEWS TRIBUNE
35 Kennedy Boulevard, East Brunswick NJ 08816. 732/246-5500. **Contact:** Personnel Department. **World Wide Web address:** http://www.injersey.com/hnt. **Description:** A daily newspaper with a weekday circulation of more than 51,000. **Parent company:** Gannett Company, Inc.

HONEYWELL
1525 West Blancke Street, Linden NJ 07036. 908/862-9551. **Contact:** Human Resources. **World Wide Web address:** http://www.honeywell.com. **Description:** Honeywell is engaged in the research, development, manufacture, and sale of advanced technology products and services in the fields of chemicals, electronics, automation, and controls. The company's major businesses are home and building automation and control, performance polymers and chemicals, industrial automation and control, space and aviation systems, and defense and marine systems. **Operations at this facility include:** This location manufactures plastic inserts for pill bottles. **Listed on:** New York Stock Exchange. **Stock exchange symbol:** HON.

HONEYWELL
101 Columbia Road, Morristown NJ 07962-1057. 973/455-2000. **Contact:** Human Resources Director. **World Wide Web address:** http://www.honeywell.com. **Description:** Honeywell is engaged in the research, development, manufacture, and sale of advanced technology products and services in the fields of chemicals, electronics, automation, and controls. The company's major businesses are home and building automation and control, performance polymers and chemicals, industrial automation and control, space and aviation systems, and defense and marine systems. **Corporate headquarters location:** This location. **Listed on:** New York Stock Exchange. **Stock exchange symbol:** HON.

HONEYWELL
DEFENSE AND AVIONICS SYSTEMS
699 Route 46 East, Teterboro NJ 07608. 201/288-2000. **Contact:** Human Resources. **World Wide Web address:** http://www.honeywell.com. **Description:** Honeywell is engaged in the research, development, manufacture, and sale of advanced technology products and services in the fields of chemicals, electronics, automation, and controls. The company's major businesses are home and building automation and control, performance polymers and chemicals, industrial automation and control, space and aviation systems, and defense and marine systems. **Operations at this facility include:** This location develops and manufactures advanced aerospace products under government contract including instrumentation for air and guidance systems. **Listed on:** New York Stock Exchange. **Stock exchange symbol:** HON.

HOOPER HOLMES, INC.
dba PORTAMEDIC
170 Mount Airy Road, Basking Ridge NJ 07920. 908/766-5000. **Contact:** Manager of Human Resources. **E-mail address:** hres@hooperholmes.com. **World Wide Web address:** http://www.hooperholmes.com. **Description:** Performs health exams for insurance companies. Founded in 1899. **Positions advertised include:** Administrative Assistant. **Office hours:** Monday - Friday, 8:30 a.m. - 5:00 p.m. **Corporate headquarters location:** This location. **Other U.S. locations:** Nationwide. **Operations at this facility include:** Administration; Divisional Headquarters; Research and Development; Sales; Service. **Listed on:** American Stock Exchange. **Stock exchange symbol:** HH. **Annual sales/revenues:** More than $100 million. **Number of employees at this location:** 120. **Number of employees nationwide:** 2,500.

HOPE HOUSE
19-21 Belmont Avenue, Dover NJ 07801. 973/361-5555. **Fax:** 973/361-5290. **Contact:** Human Resources. **E-mail address:** information@hopehousenj.org. **World Wide Web address:** http://www.hopehouse.com. **Description:** A nonprofit organization that provides AIDS outpatient, substance abuse, and family counseling; does house cleaning for the elderly; and performs household chores for home-bound individuals. Hope House also operates a 40-bed residential facility for children and adolescents. **Positions advertised include:** Executive Director; Counselor. **NOTE:** Send resume to the following address attention Human Resources. Hope House, P.O. Box 851, Dover NJ, 07801. Fax resume to: 973/361-6586.

HOPES
124 Grand Street, Hoboken NJ 07030. 201/656-3711. **Contact:** Human Resources. **Description:** A nonprofit organization funded by the state of New Jersey that sponsors programs such as Head Start and a medical transportation program for senior citizens.

HOSOKAWA MICRON POWDER SYSTEMS
20 Chatham Road, Summit NJ 07901. 908/273-6360. **Contact:** Human Resources Administrator. **World Wide Web address:** http://www.hosokawa.com. **Description:** Develops and manufactures air pollution control and process equipment. Products are used by the primary metals, nonmetallic minerals, powder, protective coatings, paper, fertilizer, chemical, pharmaceutical, and food processing industries. **Corporate headquarters location:** New York NY. **Parent company:** Hosokawa Micron International Inc.

HOUSEHOLD INTERNATIONAL
200 Somerset Corporate Boulevard, Bridgewater NJ 08807. 908/203-2100. **Contact:** Personnel. **World Wide Web address:** http://www.household.com/corp/index.jsp. **Description:** Provides data processing services for the insurance and banking industries. **Positions advertised include:** Account Executive, Beneficial.

K. HOVNANIAN COMPANIES
10 Highway 35, Red Bank NJ 07701. 732/747-7800. **Contact:** Human Resources. **World Wide Web address:** http://www.khov.com. **Description:** Designs, constructs, and sells condominium apartments, townhouses, and single-family homes in residential communities. The company is also engaged in mortgage banking. Founded in 1959. **Positions advertised include:** Training and Development Specialist; Training and Documentation Specialist; HRIS Coordinator; Benefits Coordinator. **Corporate headquarters location:** This location. **Other U.S. locations:** CA; FL; NC; NY; PA; VA. **Subsidiaries include:** New Fortis Homes. **Listed on:** New York Stock Exchange. **Stock exchange symbol:** HOV. **Number of employees at this location:** 90. **Number of employees nationwide:** 1,150.

HOWARD PRESS
450 West First Avenue, Roselle NJ 07203. 908/245-4400. **Fax:** 908/245-1139. **Contact:** Michelle Kaplan, Human Resources. **World Wide Web address:** http://www.howardpress.com. **Description:** A large commercial printing company. **Positions advertised include:** Production Planner.

HOWMEDICA OSTEONICS
325 Corporate Drive, Mahwah NJ 07430. 201/825-4900. **Contact:** Human Resources Department. **E-mail address:** hr@howost.com. **World Wide Web address:** http://www.osteonics.com. **Description:** Manufactures medical implants including artificial knees, hips, shoulders, and elbows. **Parent company:** Stryker Corporation.

HUDSON CITY SAVINGS BANK
West 80 Century Road, Paramus NJ 07652. 201/967-1900. **Fax:** 201/967-0332. **Contact:** Human Resources. **World Wide Web address:** http://www.hudsoncitysavingsbank.com. **Description:** Operates a full-service mutual savings bank with 80 branches in Bergen, Burlington, Camden, Essex, Gloucester, Hudson, Middlesex, Monmouth, Morris, Ocean, Passaic, and Union Counties. Hudson City Savings Bank provides a wide range of traditional banking services, as well as other financial services including IRAs. **Positions advertised include:** Teller; Clerk.

HUDSON UNITED BANK
222 Haddon Avenue, Westmont NJ 08108. 856/869-7900. **Contact:** Human Resources. **E-mail address:** career@hudsonunitedbank.com. **World Wide Web address:** http://www.hudsonunitedbank.com. **Description:** A full-service bank. **Positions advertised include:** Branch Manager; Sales Associate; Assistant Branch Manager; Administrative Assistant; Call Center Representative; Branch Sales Manager; Teller; Marketing Representative. **NOTE:** Positions posted on Monster.com. Please send resumes to 1000 MacArthur Boulevard, Mahwah NJ 07430. **Parent company:** Hudson United Bancorp.

HUDSON UNITED BANK
1500 Route 202, Harding Township NJ 07920. 973/425-3000. **Contact:** Human Resources. **E-mail address:** career@hudsonunitedbank.com. **World Wide Web address:** http://www.hudsonunitedbank.com. **Description:** A full-service bank. **Positions advertised include:** Branch Manager; Sales Associate; Assistant Branch Manager; Administrative Assistant; Call Center Representative; Branch Sales Manager; Teller; Marketing Representative. **NOTE:** Positions posted on Monster.com. Please send resumes to 1000 MacArthur Boulevard, Mahwah NJ 07430. **Corporate headquarters location:** This location.

HUGO NEU SCHNITZER EAST
One Jersey Avenue, Jersey City NJ 07302. 201/333-4300. **Contact:** Barney Marsh-Gessner, Personnel Manager. **E-mail address:** humanresources@hugoneu.com. **World Wide Web address:** http://www.hugoneu.com. **Description:** A metals recycling firm, engaged primarily in the purchase, sale, and export of scrap metal. **Corporate headquarters location:** This location.

HUNTERDON DEVELOPMENTAL CENTER
P.O. Box 4003, Clinton NJ 08809-4003. 908/735-4031. **Physical address:** 40 Pittstown Road, Clinton NJ 08060. **Contact:** Human Resources. **Description:** A state-run residential facility for adults with developmental disabilities.

HUNTINGDON LIFE SCIENCES
P.O. Box 2360, Mettlers Road, East Millstone NJ 08875. 732/873-2550. **Fax:** 732/873-3992. **Contact:** Human Resources. **E-mail address:** careers@princeton.huntingdon.com. **World Wide Web address:** http://www.huntingdon.com. **Description:** Provides contract biological safety (toxicological) testing services on a worldwide basis through two laboratories in the United States and the United Kingdom. The toxicology divisions of Huntington Life Sciences conduct studies designed to test pharmaceutical products, biologicals, chemical compounds, and other substances in order to produce the data required to identify, quantify, and evaluate the risks to humans and the environment resulting from the manufacture or use of these substances. These divisions also perform analytical and metabolic chemistry services. Huntington Life Sciences also performs clinical trials of new and existing pharmaceutical and biotechnology products and medical devices. The company is engaged in the clinical development process including analytical chemistry, evaluation of clinical data, data processing, biostatistical analysis, and the preparation of supporting documentation for compliance with regulatory requirements. Founded in 1952. **NOTE:** Entry-level positions, part-time jobs, and second and third shifts are offered. **Positions advertised include:** Bioanalytical Scientist and Analyst; Animal Lab Technician; Associate Research Scientist; Necropsy Technician. **Special programs:** Summer Jobs. **Office hours:** Monday - Friday, 8:30 a.m. - 5:00 p.m. **Corporate headquarters location:** Cambridgeshire, England. **Parent company:** Huntingdon Life Sciences, Ltd. **President:** Alan Staple. **Annual sales/revenues:** $51 - $100 million. **Number of employees at this location:** 200. **Number of employees worldwide:** 1,500.

I-STAT CORPORATION
104 Windsor Center Drive, East Windsor NJ 08520. 609/443-4820. **Fax:** 609/426-3907. **Contact:** Human Resources. **E-mail address:** hr_usa@i-stat.com. **World Wide Web address:** http://www.i-stat.com. **Description:** Develops, manufactures, and markets medical diagnostic products for blood analysis. Products of i-STAT provide health care professionals with diagnostic information at the point of patient care. **NOTE:** Entry-level positions and part-time jobs are offered. **Positions advertised include:** Business Analyst; Production Supervisor; Mechanical Engineering Intern; Electrical Engineer; Electronic Technician. **Corporate headquarters location:** This location. **International locations:** Kanata, Ontario, Canada. **Listed on:** NASDAQ. **Stock exchange symbol:** STAT. **Number of employees at this location:** 120. **Number of employees worldwide:** 500.

IBM CORPORATION
1551 South Washington Avenue, 3rd Floor, Piscataway NJ 08854. 732/926-2000. **Recorded jobline:** 800/964-4473. **Contact:** IBM Staffing Services Center. **World Wide Web address:** http://www.ibm.com. **Description:** IBM develops, manufactures, and markets advanced information processing products including computers and microelectronic technology, software, networking systems, and information technology-related services. IBM operates in the United States, Canada, Europe, Middle East, Africa, Latin America, and Asia Pacific. **NOTE:** Jobseekers should send a resume to IBM Staffing Services Center, 1DPA/051, 3808 Six Forks Road, Raleigh NC 27609. **Corporate headquarters location:** Armonk NY. **Operations at this facility include:** This location is a marketing office. **Subsidiaries include:** IBM Credit Corporation; IBM Instruments, Inc.; IBM World Trade Corporation. **Number of employees at this location:** 100.

IDT CORPORATION
520 Broad Street, Newark NJ 07102. 973/438-1000. **Toll-free phone:** 800/CAL-LIDT. **Contact:** Human Resources Manager. **World Wide Web address:** http://www.idt.net. **Description:** An Internet access provider that offers dial-up services, Web hosting, and e-mail by phone. Founded in 1990. **NOTE:** Entry-level positions, part-time jobs, and second and third shifts are offered. **Special programs:** Internships; Apprenticeships; Summer Jobs. **Corporate headquarters location:** This location. **Other U.S. locations:** Nationwide. **International locations:** London, England; Mexico City, Mexico. **Subsidiaries include:** Amerimax; Net2Phone; Union Telecard Alliances. **Listed on:** NASDAQ. **Stock exchange symbol:** IDTC. **Founder:** Howard Jonas. **Annual sales/revenues:** More than $100 million. **Number of employees at this location:** 1,000. **Number of employees nationwide:** 1,200. **Number of employees worldwide:** 1,500.

IFF
1040 Broad Street, Shrewsbury NJ 07702. 732/578-6700. **Contact:** Staffing. **E-mail address:** staffing.manager@iff.com. **World Wide Web address:** http://www.iff.com. **Description:** Manufactures and distributes flavors and fragrances for use in foods, beverages, detergents, cosmetics, and other personal care items. **Positions advertised include:** Research Scientist. **Other U.S. locations:** Nationwide. **International locations:** Worldwide. **Listed on:** NASDAQ. **Stock exchange symbol:** IFF.

IGI, INC.
105 Lincoln Avenue, P.O. Box 687, Buena NJ 08310. 856/697-1441. **Contact:** Human Resources. **World Wide Web address:** http://www.askigi.com. **Description:** A diversified company engaged in three business segments: animal health products, cosmetic and consumer products, and biotechnology. The animal health products business produces and markets poultry vaccines, veterinary products, nutritional supplements, and grooming aids. The cosmetic and consumer products business

produces and markets dermatologic, cosmetic, and consumer products. The biotechnology business develops and markets various applications of IGI's lipid encapsulation technology, primarily for human medicines and vaccines. Founded in 1977. **Corporate headquarters location:** This location.

IMS HEALTH
100 Campus Road, Totowa NJ 07512. 973/790-0700. **Contact:** Human Resources. **World Wide Web address:** http://www.ims-health.com. **Description:** Conducts market research on the health care industry for pharmaceutical companies. **NOTE:** Apply online. **Positions advertised include:** Account Manager; Account Service Representative; Database Analyst; Revenue Analyst. **Special programs:** Internships. **Corporate headquarters location:** Plymouth Meeting PA. **Parent company:** Dun & Bradstreet. **Number of employees at this location:** 400.

ITT INDUSTRIES
AEROSPACE/COMMUNICATIONS DIVISION
100 Kingsland Road, Clifton NJ 07014. 973/284-0123. **Contact:** Human Resources. **World Wide Web address:** http://www.ittind.com. **Description:** Designs and engineers software for satellite communications under government contracts.

IKEGAMI ELECTRONICS INC.
37 Brook Avenue, Maywood NJ 07607. 201/368-9171. **Fax:** 201/569-1626. **Contact:** Human Resources. **World Wide Web address:** http://www.ikegami.com. **Description:** Manufactures and sells computer and broadcast monitors. **Positions advertised include:** Broadcast Field Service Engineer.

IMEDIA, INC.
745 US Highway 202/206, Bridgewater NJ, 08807. 908/725-7500. **Fax:** 908-725-7501. **Contact:** Personnel. **E-mail address:** careers@imedia.com. **World Wide Web address:** http://www.imedianet.com. **Description:** Provides public relations and technological consulting services for large companies.

IMMUNOMEDICS, INC.
300 American Road, Morris Plains NJ 07950. 973/605-8200. **Fax:** 973/605-8282. **Contact:** Human Resources. **E-mail address:** hr@immunomedics.com. **World Wide Web address:** http://www.immunomedics.com. **Description:** Manufactures products to treat and detect infectious diseases and cancer. Products include LeukoScan, a diagnostic imaging tool that can scan for cancers such as osteomyelitis. **Positions advertised include:** Clinical Research Associate. **Listed on:** NASDAQ. **Stock exchange symbol:** IMMU.

IMTEK, INC.
110 High Hill Road, Swedesboro NJ 08085. 856/467-0047. **Contact:** Human Resources Department. **E-mail address:** jobs@imtek.com. **World Wide Web address:** http://www.imtek.com. **Description:** Provides complete lithography and bookbinding services. **Positions advertised include:** Web Press Operator; Customer Service Representative; Sales Representative; Bindery Professional. **Corporate headquarters location:** This location.

INGERSOLL-RAND COMPANY
200 Chestnut Ridge Road, Woodcliff Lake NJ 07677. 201/573-0123. **Contact:** Human Resources. **World Wide Web address:** http://www.ingersoll-rand.com. **Description:** Manufactures compressors, pumps, and other nonelectrical industrial equipment and machinery. Ingersoll-Rand Company's products include air compression systems, antifriction systems, construction equipment, air tools, bearings, locks, tools, and pumps. **Positions advertised include:** Human Resources Manager. **Corporate headquarters location:** This location. **Other U.S. locations:** Nationwide. **Subsidiaries include:** IR Torrington Company. **Listed on:** New York Stock Exchange. **Stock exchange symbol:** IR.

INNODATA CORPORATION
North American Solutions Center, 3 University Plaza Drive, Hackensack NJ 07601. 201/488-1200. **Contact:** Human Resources. **E-mail address:** careers@innodata-isogen.com. **World Wide Web address:** http://www.innodata.com. **Description:** A worldwide electronic publishing company specializing in data conversion for CD-ROM, print, and online database publishers. The company also offers medical transcription services to health care providers through its Statline Division. **Positions advertised include:** Business Development Executive. **Corporate headquarters location:** Brooklyn NY. **Listed on:** NASDAQ. **Stock exchange symbol:** INOD.

INRAD INC.
181 Legrand Avenue, Northvale NJ 07647. 201/767-1910. **Fax:** 201/767-9644. **Contact:** Human Resources. **World Wide Web address:** http://www.inrad.com. **Description:** Manufactures and finishes synthetic crystals.

INSTRUCTIVISION, INC.
P.O. Box 2004, 16 Chapin Road, Pine Brook NJ 07058. 973/575-9992. **Toll-free phone:** 888/551-5144. **Fax:** 973/575-9134. **Contact:** Human Resources. **World Wide Web address:** http://www.instructivision.com. **Description:** Develops video production and education software. Instructivision also operates a full-service video production facility encompassing a production stage, an interformat digital editing suite, offline editing, 3-D animation, and audio recording equipment.

INTEGRA LIFESCIENCES CORPORATION
311C Enterprise Drive, Plainsboro NJ 08536. 609/275-0500. **Fax:** 609/275-3684. **Contact:** Human Resources. **World Wide Web address:** http://www.integra-ls.com. **Description:** Researches and develops a wide range of medical devices including artificial skin for burn victims; collagen sponges for use in surgery; dental wound and dermal ulcer dressings; and packing agents for ear, nose, and throat surgery. **Positions advertised include:** Associate Product Manager; Accountant; Product Manager; Internal Audit Manager; Project Engineer; Compliant Corporate Coordinator; Marketing Administrative Assistant; Quality Assurance Director; Finance Cost Analyst; Finance Assistant Controller. **Listed on:** NASDAQ. **Stock exchange symbol:** IART.

INTEL CORPORATION
1515 Route 10, Parsippany NJ 07054. 973/993-3000. **Contact:** Human Resources. **World Wide Web address:** http://www.intel.com. **Description:** This Intel Corporation business offers computer telephony services that provide telephone network access to computer terminals. **Other U.S. locations:** Nationwide. **International locations:** Worldwide. **Listed on:** NASDAQ. **Stock exchange symbol:** INTC.

INTERBAKE FOODS, INC.
891 Newark Avenue, Elizabeth NJ 07208-3599. 908/527-7000. **Contact:** Human Resources. **World Wide Web address:** http://www.interbake.com. **Description:** Interbake Foods operates in four business segments: Food Service; Grocery Products; Dairy Products; and Girl Scout Products. The Food Service segment offers a line of more than 160 items including crackers, cookies, tart shells, and other products to institutional customers, such as health care institutions, schools and colleges, and commercial establishments; the Dairy Products segment produces wafers for ice-cream manufacturers; the Grocery Products segment includes a wide range of cookies and crackers; and the Girl Scout Products segment manufactures Girl Scout Cookies. **Operations at this facility include:** This location is a bakery. **Parent company:** General Biscuits of America, Inc. is the American subsidiary of General Biscuit, S.A. (France).

INTERCHANGE BANK
Park 80 West/Plaza 2, Saddle Brook NJ 07663. 201/703-2265. **Fax:** 201/703-5291. **Contact:** Human Resources. **E-mail address:** humanresources@interchangebank.com. **World Wide Web address:** http://www.interchangebank.com. **Description:** A full-service bank with locations throughout Bergen County. **Positions advertised include:** Administrative Assistant; Assistant Branch Manager; Business Development Officer; Commercial Lender; Customer Services Representative; General Auditor; Investment Advisor;; Loan Operations Manager; Loan Service Associate; Mortgage Originator; Claims Specialist; Retail Branch Manager; Teller. **Parent company:** Interchange Financial Services Corporation. **Listed on:** NASDAQ. **Stock exchange symbol:** IFCJ.

INTERNATIONAL PAPER COMPANY
3 Paragon Drive, Montvale NJ 07645. 201/391-1776. **Contact:** Personnel. **World Wide Web address:** http://www.internationalpaper.com. **Description:** International Paper Company manufactures pulp and paper, packaging, wood products, and a range of specialty products. The company is organized into five business segments: Printing Papers, whose principal products include uncoated papers, coated papers, bristles, and pulp; Packaging, which includes industrial packaging, consumer packaging, and kraft and specialty papers; Distribution, including the sale of printing papers, graphic arts equipment and supplies, packaging materials, industrial supplies, and office products; Specialty Products, which includes imaging products, specialty panels, nonwovens, chemicals, and minerals; and Forest Products which includes logging and wood products. **Corporate headquarters location:** Stamford CT. **Operations at this facility include:** This location houses sales offices for paperboard and paper products. **Number of employees worldwide:** 72,500.

INTERNATIONAL SPECIALTY PRODUCTS
1361 Alps Road, Wayne NJ 07470. 973/628-4000. **Contact:** Human Resources. **E-mail address:** jobs2@ispcorp.com. **World Wide Web address:** http://www.ispcorp.com. **Description:** Manufactures specialty chemicals and building materials. Chemicals include high-pressure acetylene derivatives, industrial organic and inorganic chemicals, GAF filter systems, and GAF mineral products. Building materials include prepared roofing, roll roofing, built-up roofing systems, and single-ply roofing. **Corporate headquarters location:** This location. **Listed on:** New York Stock Exchange. **Stock exchange symbol:** ISP. **Number of employees at this location:** 700. **Number of employees nationwide:** 4,300.

INTTRA INC.
One Upper Pond Road, Morris Corporate Center II, Building E, Parsippany NJ 07054. 973/265-2221. **Fax:** 973/263-5969. **E-mail address:** jobs@inttra.com. **World Wide Web address:** http://www.inttra.com. **Description:** INTTRA creates efficiencies for the ocean transportation industry by standardizing and optimizing traditionally inefficient processes. INTTRA enables shippers, freight forwarders, third party logistics providers, brokers, importers, and industry portals to manage the scheduling, booking, documentation, Bills of Lading, and tracking of cargo and the negotiation of freight services across multiple shipping lines in a single integrated process. **Positions advertised include:** Business Analyst/Product Designer; Product Manager; Quality Assurance/EDI Analyst; Technical Support Manager; Technical Support Technician. **Corporate headquarters location:** This location.

INVERNESS MEDICAL INOVATIONS
500 Halls Mill Road, Freehold NJ 07728. 732/308-3000. **Fax:** 732/761-2837. **Contact:** Human Resources. **E-mail address:** hrresumes@invernessmedical.com. **World Wide Web address:** http://www.invernessmedical.com. **Description:** Manufactures and distributes vitamins, herbs, nonprescription drugs, and nutritional supplements under the brand names Fields of Nature, Pine Brothers throat drops, Rybutol, Nature's Wonder, Synergy Plus, and Liquafil vitamin supplements. **Corporate headquarters location:** This location. **Listed on:** NASDAQ. **Stock exchange symbol:** IVCO.

ION NETWORKS INC.
1551 South Washington Avenue, Piscataway NJ 08854. 732/529-0100. **Contact:** Human Resources. **E-mail address:** resumes@ion-networks.com. **World Wide Web address:** http://www.ion-networks.com. **Description:** Develops and markets software and hardware for computer security. **Corporate headquarters location:** This location. **International locations:** Belgium; United Kingdom. **Listed on:** NASDAQ. **Stock exchange symbol:** IONN.

ITOX
8 Elkins Road, East Brunswick NJ 08816. 732/390-2815. **Toll-free phone:** 888/200-ITOX (4869). **Fax:** 7322/390-2817. **Contact:** Human Resources. **E-mail address:** sales@itox.com. **World Wide Web address:** http://www.itox.com. **Description:** Manufactures computer components including graphics accelerator boards, motherboards, and sound cards for commercial and industrial systems.

IVAX PHARMACEUTICALS INC.
140 LeGrand Avenue, Northvale NJ 07647. 201/767-1700. **Fax:** 201/767-1700. **Contact:** Personnel. **World Wide Web address:** http://www.ivaxpharmaceuticals.com. **Description:** Produces ethical pharmaceuticals for the cardiovascular, nervous, digestive, and respiratory systems. **Corporate headquarters location:** Miami FL.

J&J SNACK FOODS CORPORATION
6000 Central Highway, Pennsauken NJ 08109. 856/665-9533. **Fax:** 856/665-6718. **Contact:** Human Resources. **World Wide Web address:** http://www.jjsnack.com. **Description:** Manufactures a line of nutritional snack foods. Its principal products include frozen soft pretzels under Superpretzel and other brand names; Icee and Arctic Blast frozen carbonated beverages; frozen juice bars and desserts under Shapeups and other brand names; Luigi's Real Italian Ice; Mama Tish's Premium Italian Ices; Tio Pepe's churros; The Funnel Cake Factory funnel cakes; and Pride O' The Farm healthy baked goods. **Listed on:** NASDAQ. **Stock Exchange Symbol:** JSJF.

JCC USA
Crossroads Corporate Center, One International Boulevard, Suite 400, Mahwah NJ 07495. 201/512-8835. **Contact:** Human Resources. **E-mail address:** feedbackeast@jccusa.com. **World Wide Web address:** http://www.jccusa.com. **Description:** Manufactures and sells computer terminals with various display screens.

JACKSON HEWITT INC.
7 Sylvan Way, Parsippany NJ 07054. 973/496-1040. **Contact:** Human Resources. **World Wide Web address:** http://www.jacksonhewitt.com. **Description:** A full-service company specializing in computerized tax preparation and electronic filing. The foundation of Jackson Hewitt's tax service is Hewtax, a proprietary software program. The company offers a number of filing options including SuperFast Refund, through which customers receive a refund anticipation loan within one to two days of filing; Accelerated Check Refund, which allows Jackson Hewitt to set up a bank account for the IRS to deposit the taxpayer's refund; and a standard electronically filed return. The company also operates a travel agency, Campbell Travel. **Positions advertised include:** Accountant; Corporate Communications Manager; Accounting Director; Vehicle Damage Claim Director; Commercial Marketing Associate; Administrative Assistant; Project Manager; Desktop Support Manager; Receptionist; Database Developer; File Clerk; Director of Security. **NOTE:** Search for current positions by location online.

JACLYN, INC.
5801 Jefferson Street, West New York NJ 07093. 201/868-9400. **Contact:** Eric Gailing. **E-mail address:** eric.gailing@jaclyninc.com. **World Wide Web address:** http://www.jaclyninc.com. **Description:** Designs, manufactures, and sells women's and children's handbag fashions, accessories, specialty items, and ready-to-wear apparel. **Corporate headquarters location:** This location. **Operations at this facility include:** Administration; Manufacturing; Research and Development; Sales; Service.

JANSSEN PHARMACEUTICA INC.
1125 Trenton-Harbourton Road, Titusville NJ 08560. 609/730-2000. **Contact:** Human Resources. **World Wide Web address:** http://www.janssen.com. **Description:** A pharmaceutical research company that specializes in prescription drugs for use in a range of fields including dermatology and psychiatry. **NOTE:** Check current job postings and apply on-line at the Johnson & Johnson career Website: http://www.jnj.com/careers. **Parent company:** Johnson & Johnson (New Brunswick NJ).

JEFFERIES & COMPANY, INC.
51 JFK Parkway, 3rd Floor, Short Hills NJ 07078. 973/912-2900. **Fax:** 310/971-1066. **Contact:** See NOTE. **World Wide Web address:** http://www.jefco.com. **Description:** Engaged in equity, convertible debt and taxable fixed income securities brokerage and trading, and corporate finance. Jefferies & Company is one of the leading national firms engaged in the distribution and trading of blocks of equity securities and conducts such activities primarily in the third market, which refers to transactions in listed equity securities effected away from national securities exchanges. Founded in 1962. **NOTE:** Fax or email resumes for non-banking opportunities to Mel Locke (310/914-1066; mlocke@jefco.com), and for banking opportunities to Eastcoastrecruiting@jefco.com. **Parent company:** Jefferies Group, Inc. is a holding company which, through Jefferies & Company and its three other primary subsidiaries, Investment Technology Group, Inc., Jefferies International Limited, and Jefferies Pacific Limited, is engaged in securities brokerage and trading, corporate finance, and other financial services.

JEFFERSON INSURANCE GROUP
525 Washington Boulevard, Jersey City NJ 07310. 201/222-8666. **Fax:** 201/222-9161. **Contact:** Supervisor of Recruitment and Training. **World Wide Web address:** http://www.jeffgroup.com. **Description:** A property and casualty insurance company. Member companies include Jefferson Insurance Company of New York, Monticello Insurance Company, and Jeffco Management Company, Inc. **Corporate headquarters location:** This location. **Parent company:** Allianz (Germany). **Listed on:** Privately held.

THE JERSEY JOURNAL
30 Journal Square, Jersey City NJ 07306. 201/653-1000. **Contact:** Managing Editor. **World Wide Web address:** http://www.nj.com/jjournal/today. **Description:** Publishes a daily morning newspaper with a circulation of more than 55,000. **Parent company:** Newhouse Newspapers Group.

JEVIC TRANSPORTATION INC.
600-700 Creek Road, Delanco NJ 08075. 856/461-7111. **Toll-free phone:** 800/257-0427. **Fax:** 856/764-7224. **Contact:** Human Resources. **World Wide Web address:** http://www.jevic.com. **Description:** Jevic Transportation is a trucking company providing freight services. **Corporate headquarters location:** This location. **Operations at this facility include:** This location houses a dispatching center.

JOHNSON & JOHNSON
One Johnson & Johnson Plaza, New Brunswick NJ 08933. 732/524-0400. **Contact:** Human Resources. **World Wide Web address:** http://www.jnj.com. **Description:** A health care products company. Products include pain relievers, contact lenses, pharmaceuticals, bandages, toothbrushes, and surgical instruments under brand names including Reach, Band-Aid, and Acuvue. **NOTE:** Resumes should be sent to Johnson & Johnson Recruiting Services, Employment Management Center, Room JH-215, 501 George Street, New Brunswick NJ 08906-6597. **Corporate headquarters location:** This location. **International locations:** Worldwide.

JOHNSON & JOHNSON CONSUMER PRODUCTS, INC.
199 Grandview Road, Skillman NJ 08558. 908/874-1000. **Contact:** Employment Management Center. **World Wide Web address:** http://www.jnj.com. **Description:** A large and diverse health care products company. Products include pain relievers, contact lenses, pharmaceuticals, bandages, toothbrushes, and surgical instruments under brand names including Reach, Band-Aid, and Acuvue. **NOTE:** Search and apply for positions online. **Positions advertised include:** Pension Administrator; Auditor; Financial Analyst; Executive Director, Health Care Compliance-Consumer. **Corporate headquarters location:** New Brunswick NJ.

K-TRON INTERNATIONAL INC.
P.O. Box 888, Routes 55 and 553, Pitman NJ 08071. 856/589-0500. **Fax:** 856/582-7968. **Contact:** Human Resources. **E-mail address:** ktii@ktron.com. **World Wide Web address:** http://www.ktron.com. **Description:** Produces industrial feeders and blenders.

KPMG
3 Chestnut Ridge Road, Montvale NJ 07645. 201/307-7000. **Contact:** Human Resources. **World Wide Web address:** http://www.kpmgcareers.com. **Description:** KPMG delivers a wide range of value-added assurance, tax, and consulting services. **Corporate headquarters location:** This location. **Other U.S. locations:** Nationwide. **Operations at this facility include:** This location houses the company's administrative offices. **Parent company:** KPMG International is a leader among professional services firms engaged in capturing, managing, assessing, and delivering information to create knowledge that will help its clients maximize shareholder value.

KEAN UNIVERSITY
1000 Morris Avenue, Union NJ 07083. 908/527-2150. **Contact:** Human Resources. **World Wide Web address:** http://www.kean.edu. **Description:** A university offering more than 60 programs of study for graduates and undergraduates. The university has an enrollment of over 12,000 students. Founded in 1855.

KEANE, INC.
100 Walnut Avenue, Suite 202, Clark NJ 07066. 732/396-4321. **Contact:** Human Resources. **World Wide Web address:** http://www.keane.com. **Description:** Keane offers businesses a variety of computer consulting services. Keane also develops, markets, and manages software for its clients and assists in project management. **Positions advertised include:** Project Manager; Programming Analyst; Mainframe Programming Analyst. **Corporate headquarters location:** Boston MA. **Other U.S. locations:** Nationwide. **Operations at this facility include:** This location designs, develops, and manages software for corporations and health care facilities. **Listed on:** American Stock Exchange. **Stock exchange symbol:** KEA. **Number of employees worldwide:** 7,800.

KEARFOTT GUIDANCE & NAVIGATION CORPORATION
150 Totowa Road, Mail Code HWA01, Wayne NJ 07474. 973/785-6459. **Fax:** 973/785-6255. **Contact:** Personnel. **E-mail address:** humanresources@kearfott.com. **World Wide Web address:** http://www.kearfott.com. **Description:** Manufactures precision electromechanical and electronic components used to generate, sense, control, and display motion such as synchros, resolvers, cant angle sensors, and servo motors. Founded in 1917. **Corporate headquarters location:** This location. **Parent company:** Astronautics Corporation of America. **Listed on:** Privately held. **Number of employees at this location:** 1,300.

KEM MANUFACTURING COMPANY INC.
18-35 River Road, Fair Lawn NJ 07410. 201/796-8000. **Toll-free phone:** 800/536-5366. **Fax:** 201/796-3277. **Contact:** Personnel. **World Wide Web address:** http://www.kemparts.com. **Description:** Manufactures and markets a wide range of products for distribution to the automotive aftermarket. KEM also produces Perfect Part, a complete general service line. **Corporate headquarters location:** This location. **Operations at this facility include:** Manufacturing.

KEPNER-TREGOE, INC.
P.O. Box 704, Princeton NJ 08542. 609/921-2806. **Toll-free phone:** 800/537-6378. **E-mail address:** kt-us@kepner-tregoe.com. **Physical address:** 17 Research Road, Princeton NJ 08558. **Contact:** Human Resources. **World Wide Web address:** http://www.kepner-tregoe.com. **Description:** A worldwide management consulting firm. Product categories include strategy formulation, systems improvement, skill development, and specific issue resolution. Industry markets served include automotive, information technology, chemicals, financial services, and natural resources. Founded in 1958. **Positions advertised include:** Consultant; Inside Sales Representative. **Corporate headquarters location:** This location. **International locations:** Worldwide. **Number of employees worldwide:** 225.

KMART CORPORATION
7401 Tonnelle Avenue, North Bergen NJ 07047. 201/868-1960. **Contact:** Human Resources. **World Wide Web address:** http://www.kmartcorp.com. **Description:** One of the largest nonfood retailers in the United States. The company operates over 2,000 stores nationwide under the Kmart name, with more than 50 Kmart stores located in the New York metropolitan area. All stores offer a broad range of discounted general merchandise, both soft and hard goods. **Corporate headquarters location:** Troy MI. **Operations at this facility include:** Administration; Divisional Headquarters; Service. **Listed on:** New York Stock Exchange. **Stock exchange symbol:** KM. **Number of employees at this location:** 1,700. **Number of employees nationwide:** 330,000.

KOHL & MADDEN PRINTING INK CORP.
222 Bridge Plaza South, Suite 701, Fort Lee NJ 07024. 201/886-1203. **Toll-free phone:** 800/793-0022. **Contact:** Human Resources Manager. **World Wide Web address:** http://www.kohlmadden.com. **Description:** Produces printing inks, compounds, and varnishes. **Corporate headquarters location:** This location. **Parent company:** Sun Chemical Corporation. **Operations at this facility include:** Administration; Divisional Headquarters; Sales. **Listed on:** Privately held. **Number of employees at this location:** 25. **Number of employees nationwide:** 450.

KREMENTZ & COMPANY
P.O. Box 94, Newark NJ 07101. 973/621-8300. **Contact:** Grace Reed, Human Resources Director. **World Wide Web address:** http://www.krementzgemstones.com. **Description:** A manufacturer and distributor of fine jewelry and related items.

KROLL DIRECT MARKETING
101 Morgan Lane, Suite 120, Plainsboro NJ 08536. 609/275-2900. **Fax:** 609/275-6606. **Contact:** Personnel Manager. **World Wide Web address:** http://www.krolldirect.com. **Description:** A telemarketing company.

KULITE SEMICONDUCTOR PRODUCTS
One Willow Tree Road, Leonia NJ 07605. 201/461-0900. **Contact:** Karen Birdsall, Human Resources Manager. **E-mail address:** karen@kulite.com. **World Wide Web address:** http://www.kulite.com. **Description:** Manufactures computerized metering systems for medical applications and for use in aircraft. Sales offices are located throughout the United States. **Corporate headquarters location:** This location.

KYOCERA MITA AMERICA, INC.
225 Sand Road, Fairfield NJ 07004. 973/808-8444. **Contact:** Human Resources. **World Wide Web address:** http://www.kyoceramita.com. **Description:** One of the world's largest manufacturers of copy machines. Kyocera MITA also offers computer peripherals such as fax machines, imaging systems, and laser printers. **Corporate headquarters location:** This location.

LG ELECTRONICS USA, INC.
1000 Sylvan Avenue, Englewood Cliffs NJ 07632. 800/243-0000. **Contact:** Human Resources. **World Wide Web address:** http://www.us.lge.com. **Description:** The North American wireless division of LGE, a business unit of LG Electronics, a global manufacturer of electronics products. **Positions advertised include:** Accounts Payable Coordinator; Business Development Manager; Credit Analyst; Field Quality Manager; Inside Sales Coordinator; Junior Industrial Designer; National Account Manager; Planning Assistant Manager; Senior Financial Analyst; Western Sales Director. **Corporate headquarters location:** Seoul, Korea.

LABORATORY CORPORATION OF AMERICA (LABCORP)
116 Millburn Avenue, Suite 211, Millburn NJ 07041. 973/912-8617. **Contact:** Human Resources. **World Wide Web address:** http://www.labcorp.com. **Description:** The company is one of the nation's leading clinical laboratory companies, providing services primarily to physicians, hospitals, clinics, nursing homes, and other clinical

labs nationwide. LabCorp performs tests on blood, urine, and other body fluids and tissue, aiding the diagnosis of disease. **NOTE:** Direct employment correspondence to: LabCorp Human Resources, 309 East Davis Street, Burlington NC 27215. **Corporate headquarters location:** Burlington NC. **Operations at this facility include:** This location is a blood-drawing facility.

LAIDLAW TRANSIT
LAIDLAW EDUCATIONAL SERVICES
3349 Highway 138, Building 1, Unit D, Wall NJ 07719. 732/556-0255. **Contact:** Human Resources. **World Wide Web address:** http://www.laidlaw.com. **Description:** Laidlaw Educational Services provides school bus transportation services. **NOTE:** Entry-level positions and part-time jobs are offered. **Company slogan:** Laidlaw - we carry the nation's future. **Special programs:** Apprenticeships; Training. **Corporate headquarters location:** Lawrenceville NJ. **Other U.S. locations:** Nationwide. **Operations at this facility include:** This location houses administrative offices. **Listed on:** New York Stock Exchange. **Annual sales/revenues:** $21 - $50 million. **Number of employees nationwide:** 60,000.

LAMBDA EMI
405 Essex Road, Neptune NJ 07753. 732/922-9300. **Contact:** Human Resources. **World Wide Web address:** http://www.lambda-emi.com. **Description:** Manufactures DC power supplies. **Parent company:** Lambda Electronics.

LEBOEUF, LAMB, GREENE & MACRAE LLP
One Riverfront Plaza, Newark NJ 07102. 973/643-8000. **Contact:** Recruiting. **World Wide Web address:** http://www.llgm.com. **Description:** A law firm specializing in corporate law, international law, and litigation. The firm primarily serves the insurance and utilities industries.

LEHIGH PRESS
7001 North Park Drive, Pennsauken NJ 08109. 856/665-5200. **Contact:** Human Resources. **World Wide Web address:** http://www.lehigh-press.com. **Description:** A commercial lithograph printer.

LENOX INC.
100 Lenox Drive, Lawrenceville NJ 08648. 609/896-2800. **Fax:** 609/844-1554. **Contact:** Human Resources. **E-mail address:** lenox_hr@lenox.com. **World Wide Web address:** http://www.lenox.com. **Description:** Lenox is a manufacturer, wholesaler, and retailer of china, crystal dinnerware, and tableware. **Special programs:** Internships; Summer Jobs. **Office hours:** Monday - Friday, 8:30 a.m. - 5:00 p.m. **Corporate headquarters location:** This location. **Other U.S. locations:** Oxford CA; Hagerstown MD; Cranbury NJ; Pomona NJ; Mt. Pleasant PA; Smithfield RI. **Operations at this facility include:** This location houses administrative offices, staff functions, product management, and logistics. **Parent company:** Brown-Forman Corporation. **President:** Stan Krangel. **Annual sales/revenues:** More than $100 million. **Number of employees at this location:** 205. **Number of employees nationwide:** 3,500.

LEONE INDUSTRIES
P.O. Box 400, Bridgeton NJ 08302. 856/455-2000. **Fax:** 856/455-3491. **Physical address:** 443 Southeast Avenue, Bridgeton NJ 08302. **Contact:** Human Resources Department. **E-mail address:** corporate@leoneglass.com. **World Wide Web address:** http://www.leoneindustries.com. **Description:** Manufactures glass containers. **Corporate headquarters location:** This location. **Operations at this facility include:** Manufacturing.

LIFECELL CORPORATION
One Millennium Way, Branchburg NJ 08876. 908/947-1100. **Fax:** 908/947-1200. **Contact:** Human Resources. **E-mail address:** hr@lifecell.com. **World Wide Web address:** http://www.lifecell.com. **Description:** Designs, manufactures, and produces products dealing with skin grafts for burn patients and with the preservation of transfusable blood platelets (blood cells that control clotting). LifeCell's main product, AlloDerm, removes the cells in allograft skin (from a cadaveric donor) that the patient's own immune system would normally reject. This technology enables the AlloDerm to become populated with the patient's own skin cells and blood vessels. Founded in 1986. **Listed on:** NASDAQ. **Stock exchange symbol:** LIFC.

LINENS 'N THINGS
6 Brighton Road, Clifton NJ 07015. 973/778-1300. **Fax:** 973/815-2990. **Contact:** Personnel. **World Wide Web address:** http://www.lnthings.com. **Description:** A specialty retailer selling linens, home furnishings, and domestics. Linens 'n Things operates over 230 stores nationwide. **Positions advertised include:** Analyst; Tax Analyst; Inventory Analyst; Store Support Coordinator. **Corporate headquarters location:** This location.

LIPINSKI LANDSCAPING
P.O. Box 1340, Marlton NJ 08053. 856/797-8000. **Physical address:** 100 Sharp Road, Marlton NJ 08053. **Fax:** 856/983-0500. **Contact:** Human Resources. **Description:** Provides landscaping services to commercial and residential clients. This location also hires seasonally. **NOTE:** Entry-level positions are offered. **Special programs:** Internships; Apprenticeships; Summer Jobs. **Corporate headquarters location:** This location. **Other U.S. locations:** Princeton NJ. **Annual sales/revenues:** $21 - $50 million. **Number of employees at this location:** 320.

LOHMANN ANIMAL HEALTH INTERNATIONAL
111 Highland Avenue, Vineland NJ 08361. 856/696-9994. **Fax:** 856/691-4392. **Contact:** Patti Murphy. **E-mail address:** pmurphy@lahinternational.com. **World Wide Web address:** http://www.lah.de. **Description:** Manufacturer of avian vaccines. LAH belongs to the PHW-Group, which today embraces more than 35 companies working in the field of agriculture and nutrition. The PHW-Group focuses on promoting animal and human nutrition and health. **Positions advertised include:** Poultry Veterinarian; Production Coordinator; Production Manager.

LOOMIS FARGO & COMPANY
701 Kingstand Avenue, Lyndhurst NJ 07071. 201/939-2700. **Fax:** 201/939-1934. **Contact:** Personnel. **World Wide Web address:** http://www.loomisfargo.com. **Description:** An armored security service specializing in transporting currency. **NOTE:** Applications will not be mailed to jobseekers. They must be picked up in person. **Other U.S. locations:** Nationwide.

LOOMIS FARGO & COMPANY
1601 Hylton Road, Pennsauken NJ 08110. 856/317-2600. **Fax:** 856/488-8419. **Contact:** Personnel. **World Wide Web address:** http://www.loomisfargo.com. **Description:** An armored security service specializing in transporting currency. **NOTE:** Applications will not be mailed to jobseekers. They must be picked up in person. **Other U.S. locations:** Nationwide.

L'OREAL USA
222 Terminal Avenue, Clark NJ 07066. 732/499-2838. **Contact:** Human Resources. **World Wide Web address:** http://www.loreal.com. **Description:** Manufactures personal care products including hair dyes and shampoo.

LUCENT TECHNOLOGIES INC.
67 Whippany Road, Whippany NJ 07981. 973/386-3000. **Contact:** Employment Manager. **World Wide Web address:** http://www.lucent.com. **Description:** Manufactures communications products including switching, transmission, fiber-optic cable, wireless systems, and operations systems to fulfill the needs of telephone companies and other communications services providers. **Positions advertised include:** Accounting Policy Manager; Internal Audit Manager; Government Solutions Director; Recruiter; Transaction Manager; Corporate Counsel; Government Recruiter; Global Sales Manager; Client Manager; Manager; Conference Planner. **Corporate headquarters location:** This location.

LUCENT TECHNOLOGIES INC.
283 King George Road, Room B2C36, Warren NJ 07059. 908/559-5000. **Contact:** Human Resources. **World Wide Web address:** http://www.lucent.com. **Description:** This location is a research and development center. Overall, Lucent Technologies Inc. manufactures communications products including switching, transmission, fiber-optic cable, wireless systems, and operations systems to fulfill the needs of telephone companies and other communications services providers. **Positions advertised include:** Business Management Intern; Director of Human Resources for Managed Services. **Special programs:** Summer Jobs. **Corporate headquarters location:** Murray Hill NJ.

LYNTON AVIATION
3 Airport Road, Morristown Municipal Airport, Morristown NJ 07960-4624. 973/292-9000. **Fax:** 973/539-6657. **Contact:** Sue Lemen, Human Resources Director. **Description:** Performs aviation services including the management, charter, maintenance, and refueling of corporate helicopters and fixed-wing aircraft, and helicopter support services for industrial and utility applications. Lynton Group also provides aircraft sales and brokerage services worldwide. **Corporate headquarters location:** This location.

M&M/MARS INC.
800 High Street, Hackettstown NJ 07840. 908/852-1000. **Contact:** Human Resources. **World Wide Web address:** http://www.mmmars.com. **Description:** M&M/Mars produces a variety of candy and snack foods. **Corporate headquarters location:** This location. **Other U.S. locations:** Albany GA; Burr Ridge IL. **Operations at this facility include:** This location houses administrative offices.

MCT DAIRIES, INC.
15 Bleeker Street, Millburn NJ 07041. 973/258-9600. **Toll-free phone:** 877/258-9600. **Fax:** 973/258-9222. **Contact:** Human Resources. **E-mail address:** info@mctdairies,com. **World Wide Web address:** http://www.mctdairies.com. **Description:** Buys and sells cheeses and other industrial dairy products including bulk domestic and imported cheeses, whey powders, dairy flavorings, and buttermilk. **Corporate headquarters location:** This location.

MDY ADVANCED TECHNOLOGIES
21-00 Route 208 South, Fair Lawn NJ 07410. 201/797-6676. **Fax:** 201/797-6852. **Contact:** Human Resources. **E-mail address:** jobs@mdy.com. **World Wide Web address:** http://www.mdy.com. **Description:** Provides computer networking and record management services. **Positions advertised include:** New York Account Executive; Sales Accountant Executive Inside Sales; Telemarketing Representative.

MAERSK-SEALAND
Giralda Farms, Madison Avenue, P.O. Box 880, Madison NJ 07940-0880. 973/514-5000. **Contact:** Human Resources Department. **World Wide Web address:** http://www.maersksealand.com. **Description:** Maersk-Sealand ships large containers. **Operations at this facility include:** This location houses the northeast regional headquarters operations. **Parent company:** A.P. Moller Group.

MAGLA PRODUCTS INC.
P.O. Box 1934, Morristown NJ 07962-1934. 973/377-0500. **Physical address:** 159 South Street, Morristown NJ 07962. **Contact:** Human Resources. **World Wide Web address:** http://www.magla.com. **Description:** Manufactures kitchen and domestic household products including ironing-board covers, dish towels, oven mitts, rubber gloves, disposable wipe cloths, and cling sheets. **Corporate headquarters location:** This location.

MAGNETIC TICKET & LABEL CORPORATION
151 Cortlandt Avenue, Belleville NJ 07109. 973/759-6500. **Fax:** 973/450-4703. **Contact:** Human Resources. **World Wide Web address:** http://www.magticket.com. **Description:** Manufactures plastic and paper airline baggage tags. **Other U.S. locations:** Los Angeles CA; San Francisco CA; Nashville TN; Dallas TX. **Operations at this facility include:** Manufacturing. **Listed on:** Privately held. **Number of employees at this location:** 80. **Number of employees nationwide:** 4,000.

MAINTECH
39 Paterson Avenue, Wallington NJ 07057. 973/614-1700. **Toll-free phone:** 800/426-8324. **Contact:** Personnel. **World Wide Web address:** http://www.maintech.com. **Description:** Provides on-site computer maintenance services.

GREG MANNING AUCTIONS, INC.
775 Passaic Avenue, West Caldwell NJ 07006. 973/882-0004. **Fax:** 973/882-3499. **Contact:** Personnel. **E-mail address:** info@gregmanning.com. **World Wide Web address:** http://www.gregmanning.com. **Description:** Conducts public auctions of rare stamps, stamp collections, and stocks. Items included in the auctions are rare stamps; sports trading cards and sports memorabilia; rare glassware and pottery; pre-Colombian art objects; Egyptian, Middle Eastern, and Far Eastern antiquities; and rare coins. **Corporate headquarters location:** This location. **Listed on:** NASDAQ. **Stock exchange symbol:** GMAI.

MANNINGTON MILLS INC.
P.O. Box 30, Salem NJ 08079-0030. 856/935-3000. **Physical address:** 75 Mannington Mills Road, Salem NJ 08079. **Contact:** Human Resources. **World Wide Web address:** http://www.mannington.com. **Description:** Manufactures and wholesales various floor coverings including vinyl, wood, and carpet.

MARATHON ENTERPRISES INC.
66 East Union Avenue, East Rutherford NJ 07073. 201/935-3330. **Contact:** Personnel Manager. **Description:** Manufactures Sabrett brand hot dogs. **Corporate headquarters location:** This location.

MARCAL PAPER MILLS, INC.
One Market Street, Elmwood Park NJ 07407. 201/796-4000. **Fax:** 201/798-0670. **Contact:** James H. Nelson, Director of Human Resources Department. **World Wide Web address:** http://www.marcalpaper.com. **Description:** Manufactures and distributes a broad range of nationally advertised paper products including paper towels, toilet tissue, and napkins. **Corporate headquarters location:** This location. **Operations at this facility include:** Administration; Manufacturing; Research and Development; Sales.

MAROTTA SCIENTIFIC CONTROLS INC.
P.O. Box 427, Montville NJ 07045-0427. 973/334-7800. **Fax:** 973/334-1219. **Physical address:** 78 Boonton Avenue, Montville NJ 07045. **Contact:** Robert Cooper, Personnel Manager. **E-mail address:** bcooper@marrota.com. **World Wide Web address:** http://www.marotta.com. **Description:** Manufactures high-pressure valves for pneumatic and hydraulic equipment. The company is also a custom manufacturer of fluid control products. **Positions advertised include:** Technician; Assembler. **Corporate headquarters location:** This location.

MATHEMATICA POLICY RESEARCH, INC.
P.O. Box 2393, Princeton NJ 08543-2393. 609/799-3535. **Contact:** Personnel Department. **E-mail address:** researchrecruiting@mathematica-mpr.com. **World Wide Web address:** http://www.mathematica-mpr.com. **Description:** An employee-owned company that conducts social policy research (both data collection and data analysis) for government agencies, foundations, and private sector clients. The company specializes in health, labor, welfare, education, child care, and food and nutrition. **Positions advertised include:** Public Health Researcher; Education Researcher; Research Assistant; Human Services Policy Analyst; Health Policy Analyst; Survey Division Secretary; Survey Researcher; Statistician; Survey Specialist. **Corporate headquarters location:** This location. **Other U.S. locations:** Washington DC. **Operations at this facility include:** Service. **Number of employees at this location:** 200.

THE MATHENY SCHOOL AND HOSPITAL
P.O. Box 339, Peapack NJ 07977. 908/234-0011. **Fax:** 908/234-9496. **Contact:** Human Resources. **World Wide Web address:** http://www.matheny.org. **Description:** A licensed hospital and school for people with severe physical disabilities such as cerebral palsy and spina bifida. **NOTE:** Entry-level positions and second and third shifts are offered. **Positions advertised include:** Nurse; Occupational Therapist; Physical Therapist; Social Worker; Speech Therapist; Research Therapist; Rehab Technologist. **Special programs:** Internships; Apprenticeships; Training. **President:** Robert Schonhorn.

MATTEL INC.
6000 Midlantic Drive, Mount Laurel NJ 08054. 856/234-7400. **Contact:** Personnel Manager. **E-mail address:** mattel@rpc.webhire.com. **World Wide Web address:** http://www.mattel.com. **Description:** Mattel manufactures and distributes toys, electronic products, games, books, hobby products, and family entertainment products. **Corporate headquarters location:** El Segundo CA. **Operations at this facility include:** This location performs marketing activities for the toy manufacturer.

MAXIM HEALTHCARE
622 George's Road, North Brunswick NJ 08902. 732/246-1687. **Toll-free phone:** 800/697-2247. **Contact:** Manager. **World Wide Web address:** http://www.maxhealth.com. **Description:** A home health care agency. **Positions advertised include:** Sales Recruiter. **Corporate headquarters location:** Lake Success NY. **Other U.S. locations:** Nationwide. **Number of employees nationwide:** 20,000.

McBEE SYSTEMS, INC.
205 US Highway 46, Totoway NJ 07512. 973/256-6047. **Fax:** 973/263-8165. **Contact:** Personnel. **World Wide Web address:** http://www.mcbeesystems.com. **Description:** Manufactures business forms designed specifically for small businesses and professional offices. **Corporate headquarters location:** This location. **Parent company:** Romo Corporation. **Operations at this facility include:** Administration. **Number of employees nationwide:** 530.

McCARTER THEATRE
CENTER FOR THE PERFORMING ARTS
91 University Place, Princeton NJ 08540. 609/258-6500. **Fax:** 609/497-0369. **Contact:** General Manager. **E-mail address:** admin@mccarter.org. **World Wide Web address:** http://www.mccarter.org. **Description:** A performing arts center that produces and presents artists in dramatic, musical, dance, and special events. Established in 1963. **Special programs:** Internships. **Corporate headquarters location:** This location. **Number of employees at this location:** 200.

THE McGRAW-HILL COMPANIES
148 Princeton Hightstown Road, Hightstown NJ 08520. 609/426-5000. **Fax:** 609/426-5170. **Contact:** Human Resources. **World Wide Web address:** http://www.mcgraw-hill.com. **Description:** McGraw-Hill is a provider of information and services through books, magazines, newsletters, software, CD-ROMs, and online data, fax, and TV broadcasting services. The company operates four network-affiliated TV stations and also publishes *Business Week* magazine and books for college, medical, international, legal, and professional markets. McGraw-Hill also offers financial services including Standard & Poor's, commodity items, and international and logistics management products and services. **Company slogan:** Keeping the world up to speed. **Positions advertised include:** Financial Audit Manager; Administrative Assistant; Customer Support Specialist; Inside Sales Representative; Account Representative; Control Analyst; Cost Analyst; Technical Support Representative; News Technician; Royalty Correspondent. **Special programs:** Internships; Co-ops; Summer Jobs. **Corporate headquarters location:** New York NY. **Other U.S. locations:** Nationwide. **International locations:** Worldwide. **Operations at this facility include:** This location performs business services including accounts receivable and payroll. **Listed on:** New York Stock Exchange. **Stock exchange symbol:** MHP. **CEO:** Harold W. McGraw III. **Annual sales/revenues:** More than $100 million. **Number of employees at this location:** 1,300. **Number of employees nationwide:** 11,000. **Number of employees worldwide:** 13,000.

McKESSONHBOC
700 East Gate Drive, Suite 500, Mount Laurel NJ 08054-3808. 856/234-4041. **Contact:** Human Resources. **E-mail address:** job.infosolutions@mckesson.com. **World Wide Web address:** http://www.hboc.com. **Description:** McKessonHBOC provides networking solutions and software by supplying physicians, hospitals, and other health care facilities with network service and support. **Positions advertised include:** Route Sales Representative. **NOTE:** All resumes should be sent to Human Resources, McKesson InfoSolutions, 5995 Windward Parkway, Alpharetta GA 30005. 404/338-6000. **Corporate headquarters location:** San Francisco CA. **Operations at this facility include:** This location offers sales and technical support. **Listed on:** New York Stock Exchange. **Stock exchange symbol:** MCK.

McMASTER-CARR SUPPLY COMPANY
473 Ridge Road, Dayton NJ 08810. 732/329-6666. **Contact:** Recruiting Department. **E-mail address:** recruiting@mcmaster.com. **World Wide Web address:** http://www.mcmaster.com. **Description:** Distributes industrial products and supplies primarily through catalog sales. Products are sold worldwide. **NOTE:** Mail employment correspondence to: Recruiting, McMaster Supply Company, P.O. Box 4355, Chicago IL 60680-4355. **Positions advertised include:** Customer Service Representative. **Corporate headquarters location:** Elmhurst IL. **Operations at this facility include:** Service.

MEDAREX, INC.
707 State Road #206, Princeton NJ 08540-1437. 609/430-2880. **Fax:** 609/430-2850. **Contact:** Human Resources. **World Wide Web address:** http://www.medarex.com. **Description:** Researches and develops antibody-based pharmaceutical products to be used for the treatment of AIDS and other infectious diseases; cancers (including breast, ovarian, prostate, colon, and pancreatic); autoimmune diseases; and cardiovascular disease. These products bind to cells in the immune system and to the diseased cells, then stimulate the immune system to destroy the diseased cells. Founded in 1987. **Positions advertised include:** Accountant; Research Analyst. **NOTE:** Submit resume and search for current opportunities online. **Corporate headquarters location:** Princeton NJ.

MEDICAL RESOURCES, INC.
125 State Street, Suite 200, Hackensack NJ 07601. 201/488-6230. **Fax:** 201/488-8455. **Contact:** Human Resources. **World Wide Web address:** http://www.mrii.com. **Description:** Owns and manages medical diagnostic imaging centers nationwide. The centers offer magnetic resonance imaging (MRI), computerized tomography (CT), nuclear medicine, mammography, ultrasound, and X-ray. **Positions advertised include:** Data Analyst; Ultrasound Technologist; MRI Technologist; CT Technologist. **Listed on:** NASDAQ. **Stock exchange symbol:** MRII. **Annual sales/revenues:** More than $100 million.

MEDIQ/PRN
One Mediq Plaza, Pennsauken NJ 08110. 856/665-9300. **Toll-free phone:** 800/257-7477. **Fax:** 856/661-0223. **Contact:** Personnel. **E-mail address:** resumes@mediq.net. **World Wide Web address:** http://www.mediqprn.com. **Description:** Rents moveable life-support equipment such as ventilators, monitors, and incubators to hospitals, nursing homes, and home-care companies. **Positions advertised include:** Director of Financial Reporting and Analysis. **Corporate headquarters location:** This location.

MEDPOINTE INC.
265 Davidson Avenue, Somerset NJ 08873. 732/561-2200. **Contact:** Human Resources. **World Wide Web address:** http://www.medpointe.com. **Description:** A major manufacturer of ethical drugs and consumer products. Health care products include tranquilizers, laxatives, antibacterials, analgesics, decongestants, and cold and cough remedies. The company also manufactures tests for pregnancy, mononucleosis, rubella, and meningitis. Consumer products include Arrid antiperspirants and deodorants, Trojan condoms, hair lotions, and pet care items. **NOTE:** Entry-level positions and second and third shifts are offered. **Corporate headquarters location:** This location. **Other U.S. locations:** Decatur IL. **Number of employees nationwide:** 2,200.

MELARD MANUFACTURING CORPORATION
2 Paulison Avenue, Passaic NJ 07055-5703. 973/472-8888. **Contact:** Personnel. **World Wide Web address:** http://www.masco.com. **Description:** Manufactures a broad range of hardware products including bath accessories and plumbing equipment. **Positions advertised include:** Assistant Controller. **Corporate headquarters location:** This location. **Parent company:** Masco Corporation.

MELCOR CORPORATION
1040 Spruce Street, Trenton NJ 08648-4534. 609/393-4178. **Fax:** 609/393-9771. **Contact:** Human Resources. **World Wide Web address:** http://www.melcor.com. **Description:** Manufactures a variety of thermal, thermoelectric, and electronic products. **Positions advertised include:** Quality Incoming Inspector; Maintenance Faculty Mechanic; Customer Service Representative.

MERCEDES-BENZ USA, LLC
1 Mercedes Drive, Montvale NJ 07645. 201/573-0600. **Fax:** 201/573-6791. **Contact:** Human Resources. **E-mail address:** careers@mbusa.com. **World Wide Web address:** http://www.mercedesbenzcareers.com. **Description:** An importer of the complete line of Mercedes-Benz automobiles and related components. Mercedes-Benz of North America distributes Mercedes products to dealers throughout the United States. **Corporate headquarters location:** This location. **Parent company:** DaimlerChrysler. **Operations at this facility include:** Administration. **Number of employees nationwide:** 1,500.

MERCER HUMAN RESOURCE CONSULTING
212 Carnegie Center, 4th Floor, Princeton NJ 08543. 609/520-2500. **Fax:** 503/273-5999. **Contact:** Human Resources. **World Wide Web address:** http://www.mercerhr.com. **Description:** One of the world's largest actuarial and human resources management consulting firms, providing advice to organizations on all aspects of employee/management relationships. Services include retirement, health and welfare, performance and rewards, communication, investment, human resources administration, risk, finance and insurance, and health care provider consulting. **Positions advertised include:** Actuarial Analyst; Actuarial Consultant. **Corporate headquarters location:** New York NY. **Other U.S. locations:** Nationwide. **International locations:** Worldwide. **Parent company:** Marsh & McClennan Companies. **Listed on:** New York Stock Exchange. **Stock exchange symbol:** MMC.

MERCK & COMPANY, INC.
126 East Lincoln Avenue, P.O. Box 2000, Rahway NJ 07065. 732/594-4000. **Contact:** Human Resources. **World Wide Web address:** http://www.merck.com. **Description:** A worldwide organization engaged in discovering, developing, producing, and marketing products for health care and the maintenance of the environment. Products include human and animal pharmaceuticals and chemicals sold to the health care, oil exploration, food processing, textile, paper, and other industries. Merck also runs an ethical drug mail-order marketing business. **Positions advertised include:** Staff Biologist; Associate Director; Hospital Sales Representative; Facilities Director; Spectroscoptist; Chemist. **NOTE:** Applicants should indicate position of interest. **Corporate headquarters location:** Whitehouse Station NJ. **Other U.S. locations:** Albany GA; Montvale NJ; Whitehouse Station NJ; Wilson NC; West Point PA; Elkton VA. **Listed on:** New York Stock Exchange. **Stock exchange symbol:** MRK.

MERCK & COMPANY, INC.
P.O. Box 100, One Merck Drive, Whitehouse Station NJ 08889-0100. 908/423-1000. **Contact:** Human Resources. **World Wide Web address:** http://www.merck.com. **Description:** A worldwide organization engaged in discovering, developing,

producing, and marketing products for health care and the maintenance of the environment. Products include human and animal pharmaceuticals and chemicals sold to the health care, oil exploration, food processing, textile, paper, and other industries. Merck also runs an ethical drug mail-order marketing business. **Corporate headquarters location:** This location. **Other U.S. locations:** Albany GA; Montvale NJ; Rahway NJ; Wilson NC; West Point PA; Elkton VA. **Listed on:** New York Stock Exchange. **Stock exchange symbol:** MRK.

MERCK-MEDCO MANAGED CARE, L.L.C.
100 Parsons Pond Drive, Franklin Lakes NJ 07417. 201/269-3400. **Contact:** Human Resources. **World Wide Web address:** http://www.merck-medco.com. **Description:** Manages pharmaceutical benefits through contracts with HMOs. **Parent company:** Merck & Company, Inc. (Whitehouse Station NJ) is a worldwide organization engaged in research, development, production, and marketing of products for health care and the maintenance of the environment. Products include human and animal pharmaceuticals and chemicals sold to the health care, oil exploration, food processing, textile, paper, and other industries. **Positions advertised include:** Production Manager; Administrative Assistant; Application Architect; Associate Analyst; Business Manager; Clear Case Administrator; Client Auditor; Contracts Manager; Technology Director; Financial Analyst; Inventory Accountant; File Manager; Plan Manager; System Manager; Paralegal; Project Specialist; Client Auditor; Proposal Writer; Technical Consultant; Manager; Websphere Administrator. **Listed on:** New York Stock Exchange. **Stock exchange symbol:** MRK. **Number of employees nationwide:** 10,000.

MERRIMAC INDUSTRIES, INC.
41 Fairfield Place, West Caldwell NJ 07006. 973/575-1300. **Fax:** 973/882-5984. **Contact:** Human Resources. **E-mail address:** hrdept@merrimacind.com. **World Wide Web address:** http://www.merrimacind.com. **Description:** An international manufacturer of high-reliability signal-processing components. Products include IF-baseband components (used by electronics and military electronics OEMs); RF-microwave components (for military electronics and fiber optics users); high-reliability space and missile products (electronic components used in military satellite and missile programs); integrated microwave products (for the military and commercial communications markets); and satellite reception products (products for the CATV and satellite master antenna systems). **Corporate headquarters location:** This location. **Operations at this facility include:** Administration; Manufacturing; Research and Development; Sales.

METEX CORPORATION
970 New Durham Road, Edison NJ 08817. 732/287-0800. **Fax:** 732/248-8739. **Contact:** Human Resources. **E-mail address:** hr@metexcorp.com. **World Wide Web address:** http://www.metexcorp.com. **Description:** Manufactures and sells knitted wire mesh and products made from these materials. The company designs and manufactures knitted wire products and components through its Technical Products Division. Products are used in applications that include adverse environment protective materials used primarily as high-temperature gaskets; seals; shock and vibration isolators; noise reduction elements and shrouds; and phase separation devices used as air, liquid, and solid filtering devices. Metex is also an OEM for the automobile industry, supplying automobile manufacturers with exhaust seals and components for use in exhaust emission control devices. **Positions advertised include:** Sales Manager. **NOTE:** Search and apply for jobs directly online. **Corporate headquarters location:** Great Neck NJ. **Parent company:** United Capital Corporation. **Operations at this facility include:** Administration; Manufacturing; Research and Development; Sales. **Number of employees at this location:** 380.

METROPOLITAN LIFE INSURANCE COMPANY (METLIFE)
501 U.S. Highway 22 West, Bridgewater NJ 08807. 908/253-1000. **Contact:** Human Resources. **World Wide Web address:** http://www.metlife.com. **Description:** A national insurance and financial services company that offers a wide range of individual and group insurance including life, annuity, disability, and mutual finds. **Positions advertised include:** Quality Consultant; Middleware Administrator; Information Systems Consultant; Sales Executive; Secretary to Officer; Managing Consultant; Financial Analyst; Training Coordinator; Market Research Consultant; Human Resources Generalist; Operations Consultant; Business Systems Administrator; Procurement Sourcing Consultant; Project Manager; Client Service Analyst; Underwriting Consultant; Director. **Listed on:** New York Stock Exchange. **Stock exchange symbol:** MET.

MICRO WAREHOUSE INC.
1690 Oak Street, Lakewood NJ 08701. 732/370-3801. **Fax:** 732/886-0567. **Contact:** Kathy Hopkins, Human Resources. **E-mail address:** careers@mwhse.com. **World Wide Web address:** http://www.warehouse.com. **Description:** A catalog retailer of brand-name Macintosh and IBM-compatible personal computer software, accessories, and peripherals. **Positions advertised include:** Account Manager. **Corporate headquarters location:** South Norwalk CT. **Other U.S. locations:** Gibbsboro NJ; Wilmington OH. **International locations:** Canada; England; France; Germany; Mexico; Sweden; The Netherlands. **Operations at this facility include:** Sales; Service. **Number of employees at this location:** 600. **Number of employees nationwide:** 2,400.

MIDCO RESIDENTIAL SERVICES
11 Harmich Road, South Plainfield NJ 07080. 908/561-8380. **Contact:** Human Resources. **Description:** Provides integrated solid waste management services to residential customers concentrated in the Midwestern and mid-South regions of the United States and in Costa Rica.

MIKRON INSTRUMENT COMPANY, INC.
16 Thornton Road, Oakland NJ 07436. 201/891-7330. **Toll-free phone:** 800/631-0176. **Fax:** 201/405-6090. **Contact:** Human Resources. **World Wide Web address:** http://www.mikroninst.com. **Description:** Develops, manufactures, markets, and services equipment and instruments for noncontact temperature measurement. The company's products are typically used to measure the temperature of moving objects; of stationary objects in environments or situations where contact temperature measurement would be difficult, hazardous, or impractical; and wherever rapid temperature changes must be accurately tracked instantaneously. The company also manufactures and/or markets calibration sources and a variety of accessories and optional equipment for its infrared thermometers. **Listed on:** NASDAQ. **Stock exchange symbol:** MIKR.

MIKROS SYSTEMS CORPORATION
707 Alexander Road, Building 2, Suite 208, Princeton NJ 08540. 609/987-1513. **Fax:** 609/987-1513. **Contact:** Personnel. **E-mail address:** info@mikrossytems.com. **World Wide Web address:** http://www.mikrossystems.com. **Description:** Develops communications products for the transmission of digital data over AM and FM radio frequencies.

MILLENNIUM CHEMICALS, INC.
230 Half Mile Road, Red Bank NJ 07701. 732/933-5000. **Contact:** Human Resources. **E-mail address:** careers@millenniumchem.com. **World Wide Web address:** http://www.millenniumchem.com. **Description:** Produces a range of chemical products including detergents and fragrances. **Corporate headquarters location:** This location. **Subsidiaries include:** Millennium Petrochemicals Inc. **Listed on:** New York Stock Exchange. **Stock exchange symbol:** MCH.

MINOLTA CORPORATION
101 Williams Drive, Ramsey NJ 07446. 201/825-4000. **Fax:** 201/825-7567. **Contact:** Human Resources. **World Wide Web address:** http://www.minoltausa.com. **Description:** Markets, sells, and distributes photographic and business equipment, as well as document imaging systems. **Positions advertised include:** Asset Inventory Administrator; Special Events Assistant. **Corporate headquarters location:** This location. **Parent company:** Minolta Co., Ltd. (Osaka, Japan). **Operations at this facility include:** Administration; Sales; Service. **Listed on:** Privately held. **Number of employees at this location:** 500.

MOKRYNSKI & ASSOCIATES
401 Hackensack Avenue, 2nd Floor, Hackensack NJ 07601. 201/488-5656. **Contact:** Human Resources. **World Wide Web address:** http://www.mokrynski.com. **Description:** A direct mailing company that manages, acquires, and sells mailing lists for client companies.

MONMOUTH-OCEAN HOSPITAL SERVICE CORPORATION
4806 Megill Road, Wall Township, Neptune NJ 07753. 732/919-3045. **Fax:** 732-919-2699. **Contact:** Human Resources. **E-mail address:** http://www.jobs@monoc.org. **World Wide Web address:** http://www.monoc.org. **Description:** The Monmouth Ocean Hospital Service Corporation, is a non-profit company consisting of nineteen acute-care hospitals located in Monmouth, Ocean, Atlantic, Begen, Cape May, Hudson, Essex and Union Counties, New Jersey. **NOTE:** Search for open positions online. **Positions advertised include:** Control Center Supervisor; Emergency Medical Dispatcher; Emergency Medical Technician; EMS Supervisor (Clinical/QA); Medical Collector; Paramedic; Registered Nurse. **Number of employees nationwide:** 850.

MONMOUTH UNIVERSITY
400 Cedar Avenue, West Long Branch NJ 07764-1898. 732/571-3470. **Recorded jobline:** 732/571-3513. **Contact:** Human Resources. **E-mail address:** mujobs@monmouth.edu. World **Wide Web address:** http://www.monmouth.edu. **Description:** A private four-year university offering 26 undergraduate programs & many graduate & certificate degrees. **Positions advertised include:** Assistant Dean of Advising; Head Coach; Director of Tennis; Assistant Director of Residential Life; Assistant to the Dean; Electrician.

MONTCLAIR STATE UNIVERSITY
One Normal Avenue, Box CO 316, Upper Montclair NJ 07043. 973/655-4398. **Fax:** 973/655-7210. **Contact:** Division of Human Resources. **E-mail address:** hr@mail.monclair.edu. **World Wide Web address:** http://www.montclair.edu. **Description:** A state university with an enrollment of 13,500. The university offers over 70 programs of study. The university is located about 30 minutes south of New York City **Positions advertised include:** Adjunct Instructor; Admissions Counselor; Assistant Director; Assistant Professor; Contract Administrator; Project Coordinator; Project Director; Department Chair Person; Mail Clerk; Head Coach; Pro Award Officer. **NOTE:** E-mail applications can only be accepted in text format in Microsoft Word or Adobe Acrobat.

MONTCLAIR TIMES
114 Valley Road, Montclair NJ 07042. 973/233-5000. **Fax:** 973/233-5031. **Contact:** Human Resources. **E-mail address:** contactus@montclairtimes.com. **World Wide Web address:** http://www.montclairtimes.com. **Description:** A newspaper serving northern New Jersey.

MORETRENCH AMERICAN CORPORATION
P.O. Box 316, 100 Stickle Avenue, Rockaway NJ 07866. 973/627-2100. **Fax:** 973/627-3950. **Contact:** Personnel. **E-mail address:** lobrzut@mtac.com. **NOTE:** E-mail resume for current information about positions available. **World Wide Web address:** http://www.moretrench.com. **Description:** A nationwide engineering and contracting firm specializing in groundwater control and hazardous waste removal. **Corporate headquarters location:** This location.

MOTOROLA, INC.
85 Harristown Road, Glenrock NJ 07452. 201/447-7500. **Contact:** Human Resources. **World Wide Web address:** http://www.motorola.com. **Description:** A leading supplier of corporate networking solutions including data, voice, and video interfaces. Motorola also provides platform software and Internet connectivity services.

MOUNTAIN CREEK
200 Route 94, Vernon NJ 07462. 973/827-2000. **Contact:** Human Resources. **World Wide Web address:** http://www.mountaincreek.com. **Description:** Operates as a water amusement park in the summer and a ski resort in the winter.

JOS. L. MUSCARELLE, INC.
99 West Essex Street, Route 17, Maywood NJ 07607. 201/845-8100. **Contact:** Joseph Muscarelle, Jr., President. **Description:** Engaged in construction and real estate development.

MYERS POWER PRODUCTS INC.
P.O. Box 893, Somerville NJ 08876. **Physical address:** 80 Readington Road, Somerville NJ 08876. **Toll-free phone:** 888/222-2287. **Fax:** 908/526-6866. **Contact:** Personnel. **World Wide Web address:** http://www.myerscpi.com. **Description:** Manufactures frequency converters and uninterrupted power supplies.

MYRON MANUFACTURING CORPORATION
205 Maywood Avenue, Maywood NJ 07607. 201/843-6464. **Fax:** 201/587-1905. **Contact:** Human Resources Department. **World Wide Web address:** http://www.myron.com. **Description:** Manufactures a line of custom-made vinyl products including pocket calendars for the office and business markets. This location also hires seasonally. Founded in 1949. **NOTE:** Entry-level positions and second and third shifts are offered. **Special programs:** Internships; Training. **Office hours:** Monday - Friday, 8:00 a.m. - 5:00 p.m. **Corporate headquarters location:** This location. **Operations at this facility include:** Administration; Manufacturing; Sales; Service. **President:** Marie Adler-Kravecas. **Facilities Manager:** Dan Hurtubise. **Information Systems Manager:** Bruce Kalten. **Purchasing Manager:** Jim Ragucci. **Sales Manager:** Terrence Flynn. **Annual sales/revenues:** More than $100 million. **Number of employees at this location:** 600.

NABISCO FAIR LAWN BAKERY
22-11 State Route 208, Fair Lawn NJ 07410. 201/794-4000. **Contact:** Personnel. **World Wide Web address:** http://www.kraftfoods.com/careers. **Description:** Nabisco is one of the largest consumer foods operations in the country. The company markets a broad line of cookie and cracker products including brand names such as Oreo, Ritz, Premium, Teddy Grahams, Chips Ahoy!, and Wheat Thins. The company operates 10 cake and cookie bakeries, a flourmill, and a cheese plant. The bakeries produce over 1 billion pounds of finished products each year. Over 150 biscuit brands reach the consumer via one of the industry's largest distribution networks. **Operations at this facility include:** This location is a bakery. **Parent company:** Kraft Foods. **Listed on:** New York Stock Exchange. **Stock exchange symbol:** KFT. **Number of employees at this location:** 1,200.

NABISCO GROUP HOLDINGS
7 Campus Drive, P.O. Box 311, Parsippany NJ 07054-0311. 973/682-5000. **Contact:** Human Resources. **World Wide Web address:** http://www.kraft.com. **Description:** Nabisco is one of the largest consumer foods operations in the country. The company markets a broad line of cookie and cracker products including brand names such as Oreo, Ritz, Premium, Teddy Grahams, Chips Ahoy!, and Wheat Thins. The company operates 10 cake and cookie bakeries, a flourmill, and a cheese plant. The bakeries produce over 1 billion pounds of finished products each year. Over 150 biscuit brands reach the consumer via one of the industry's largest distribution networks. **Operations at this facility include:** This location houses administrative offices. **Parent company:** Kraft Foods. **Listed on:** New York Stock Exchange. **Stock exchange symbol:** KFT. **Annual sales/revenues:** More than $100 million.

NABISCO INC.
100 DeForest Avenue, East Hanover NJ 07936. 973/503-2000. **Contact:** Staffing Center. **World Wide Web address:** http://www.kraft.com. **Description:** One of the largest consumer foods operations in the country. The company markets a broad line of cookie and cracker products including brand names such as Oreo, Ritz, Premium, Teddy Grahams, Chips Ahoy!, and Wheat Thins. The company operates 10 cake and cookie bakeries, a flourmill, and a cheese plant. The bakeries produce over 1 billion pounds of finished products each year. Over 150 biscuit brands reach the consumer via one of the industry's largest distribution networks. **Special programs:** Internships. **Corporate headquarters location:** Northfield IL. **Parent company:** Kraft Foods. **Listed on:** New York Stock Exchange. **Stock exchange symbol:** KFT.

NAPP TECHNOLOGIES
401 Hackensack Avenue, Hackensack NJ 07601. 201/843-4664. **Fax:** 201/843-4737. **Contact:** Personnel. **E-mail address:** tom.smith@napptech.com. **World Wide Web address:** http://www.napptech.com. **Description:** Produces bulk pharmaceuticals, cosmetic raw materials, and fine chemicals. **Corporate headquarters location:** This location.

NATIONAL STARCH AND CHEMICAL COMPANY
10 Finderne Avenue, P.O. Box 6500, Bridgewater NJ 08807. 908/685-5000. **Toll-free phone:** 800/366-4031. **Fax:** 908/685-6956. **Contact:** Human Resources. **E-mail address:** nstarch.jobs@nstarch.com. **World Wide Web address:** http://www.nationalstarch.com. **Description:** Manufactures industrial chemicals including adhesives, resins, starches, and specialty chemicals for the packaging, textile, paper, food, furniture, electronic materials, and automotive markets. **NOTE:** Entry-level positions are offered. **Positions advertised include:** Administrative Coordinator; Chemist Nutritional Application Specialist; Global Network Technology Manager; Human Resources Technology Support Manager; Principal Chemist; Research Associate; Chemist; Technical Services Technician. **Special programs:** Internships; Co-ops. **Corporate headquarters location:** This location. **Other U.S. locations:** Nationwide. **International locations:** Worldwide. **Parent company:** The ICI Group. **Annual sales/revenues:** More than $100 million. **Number of employees nationwide:** 8,500. **Number of employees worldwide:** 10,000.

NETWORK SPECIALISTS INC.
dba NSI SOFTWARE
Baker Waterfront Plaza, 2 Hudson Place, Suite 700, Hoboken NJ 07030. 201/656-2121. **Toll-free phone:** 800/775-4674. **Fax:** 201/656-3865. **Contact:** Human Resources. **E-mail address:** info@nsisoftware.com. **World Wide Web address:** http://www.nsisw.com. **Description:** Develops network performance and fault-tolerant software tools. Products are compatible with Novell NetWare, Microsoft Windows NT, and UNIX. **Positions advertised include:** HP Overlay Sales Executive; Product Manager; Software Developer; Implementation Systems Engineer.

NEW JERSEY CITY UNIVERSITY
2039 Kennedy Boulevard, Hepburn Hall 105, Jersey City NJ 07305. 201/200-2335. **Fax:** 201/200-2219. **Contact:** Robert Piaskowsky, Director of Human Resources. **World Wide Web address:** http://www.njcu.edu. **Description:** A state university with approximately 10,000 students enrolled in undergraduate, graduate, and continuing education programs. **Positions advertised include:** Director; Dean of Students; Assistant Dean; Nurse; Criminal Justice Professor; Fitness Exercise Specialist; Information Technology Specialist; Health Science Professor; Business Administration; Special Education; Learning Disabilities Teachers Consultant; Early Childhood Education; Education Technology; Elementary Technology; Literacy Education; Speech Language Specialist; Therapeutic Services Supervisor; Typist Clerk.

NEW JERSEY DEPARTMENT OF LABOR
John Fitch Plaza, P.O. Box 110, Trenton NJ 08625. 609/292-2313. **Contact:** Human Resources. **E-mail address:** cmycoff@dol.state.nj.us. **World Wide Web address:** http://www.state.nj.us/labor. **Description:** Responsible for enforcing wage and hour laws, child labor laws, occupational health and safety regulations, unemployment, and disability insurance. The New Jersey Department of Labor also administers employment training and workers' compensation programs.

NEW JERSEY DEPARTMENT OF TRANSPORTATION
1035 Parkway Avenue, P.O. Box 602, Trenton NJ 08625-0600. 609/530-2953. **Contact:** Personnel. **World Wide Web address:** http://www.state.nj.us/ transportation. **Description:** State headquarters of the agency responsible for designing, building, and maintaining roads and highways throughout the state of New Jersey.

NEW JERSEY DEPARTMENT OF TRANSPORTATION
REGION 3 CONSTRUCTION
100 Daniels Way, Freehold NJ 07728. 732/409-3263. **Contact:** Human Resources. **Description:** Designs, builds, and maintains roads and highways throughout the state of New Jersey.

NEW JERSEY INSTITUTE OF TECHNOLOGY
323 Martin Luther King Jr. Boulevard, Cullimore Hall, Room 211, Newark NJ 07102. 973/596-3140. **Fax:** 973/642-4056. **Contact:** Human Resources. **World Wide Web address:** http://www.njit.edu. **Description:** A technical institute of higher learning offering undergraduate and graduate degrees in engineering, architecture, liberal arts/sciences, management, and education. **Positions advertised include:** Academic Advisor; Academic Coordinator; Accounts Payable Clerk; Administrative Assistant; Assistant Physical Education Specialist; Assistant Theatre Technician; Assistant Trainer; Associate Dean; Control Specialist; Academic Computing Director; University Information Systems Director; University Learning Director; Facility Engineer; HVAC Mechanic; Library Assistant; Provost; Receptionist; Security Officer; Recycler.

NEW JERSEY MANUFACTURERS INSURANCE COMPANY
301 Sullivan Way, West Trenton NJ 08628. 609/883-1300. **Fax:** 609/771-0384. **Contact:** Personnel. **World Wide Web address:** http://www.njminsurance.com. **Description:** An insurance provider. **Positions advertised include:** Communications Specialist; Building Systems Technologist; Staff Accountant; Claim Service Representative; Staff Appraiser; Inside Property Damage Representative; Cafeteria Aide; Cash Remittance Processor; Records Retrieval Clerk; Policy Rater; Receptionist; Business Analyst; Communications Technologist; Medical Case Manager; Project Coordinator; Helpdesk Analyst; Personal Lines Associate; Premium Auditor; Typist.

NEW JERSEY RESOURCES CORPORATION
1415 Wyckoff Road, Wall NJ 07719. 732/938-1480. **Recorded jobline:** 732/938-1000. **Contact:** Human Resources. **E-mail address:** careers@njresources.com. **World Wide Web address:** http://www.njresources.com. **Description:** A holding company for natural gas and energy companies. **Subsidiaries include:** New Jersey Natural Gas Company distributes natural gas to over 400,000 customers in Monmouth and Ocean Counties, and parts of Morris and Middlesex Counties. Other subsidiaries are engaged in exploration for natural gas and oil, real estate development, and the development of cogeneration projects.

NEW JERSEY SHAKESPEARE FESTIVAL
36 Madison Avenue, Madison NJ 07940. 973/408-3278. **Fax:** 973/408-3361. **Contact:** Joseph Discher, Artistic Associate. **E-mail address:** njsf@njshakespeare.org. **World Wide Web address:** http://www.njshakespeare.org. **Description:** A nonprofit professional theater devoted to producing the works of Shakespeare and other classic masterworks. Founded in 1962. **NOTE:** Entry-level positions are offered. **Positions advertised include:** Box Office Associate; Casting Internship; Sales Manager; Assistant Production Manager; Scenic Charge Artist. **Special programs:** Internships; Apprenticeships; Training.

NEW JERSEY SPORTS & EXPOSITION AUTHORITY
50 Route 120, East Rutherford NJ 07073. 201/935-8500. **Recorded jobline:** 201/460-4265. **Contact:** Gina Klein, Director of Human Resources. **E-mail address:** hr@njsea.com. **World Wide Web address:** http://www.njsea.com. **Description:** A state-appointed agency responsible for coordinating and running sports and entertainment activities at the Meadowlands Sports Complex, which includes Meadowlands Racetrack (harness and thoroughbred racing, as well as other events), Giants Stadium (New York Giants, New York Jets, concerts, and other events), and Continental Airlines Arena (New Jersey Nets, New Jersey Devils, tennis, track, concerts, and other events). **Corporate headquarters location:** This location.

NEW JERSEY STATE POLICE HEADQUARTERS
P.O. Box 7068, West Trenton NJ 08628-0068. 609/882-2000. **Contact:** Personnel Services. **World Wide Web address:** http://www.njsp.org. **Description:** Provides recruitment and testing information for state troopers and civilian positions including clerical staff and laboratory scientists.

NEW JERSEY TURNPIKE AUTHORITY
P.O. Box 1121, New Brunswick NJ 08903. 732/247-0900. **Contact:** Human Resources. **World Wide Web address:** http://www.state.nj.us/turnpike. **Description:** A state mandated, unsubsidized organization responsible for construction, maintenance, repair, and operation on New Jersey Turnpike projects.

NEW LISBON DEVELOPMENTAL CENTER
P.O. Box 130, Rural Route 72, New Lisbon NJ 08064. 609/894-4000. **Contact:** Human Resources. **Description:** A residential treatment facility for adolescents and adults with developmental disabilities.

NEXTEL COMMUNICATIONS
2 Industrial Road, Fairfield NJ 07004. 973/276-0283. **Contact:** Human Resources. **World Wide Web address:** http://www.nextel.com. **Description:** Nextel Communications is engaged in the specialized mobile radio (SMR) wireless communications business. These services permit the company's customers to dispatch fleets of vehicles and place calls using their two-way mobile radios to or from any telephone in North America through interconnection with the public switched telephone network. Nextel Communications also sells and rents two-way mobile radio equipment and provides related installation, repair, and maintenance services. **Corporate headquarters location:** Reston VA. **Operations at this facility include:** This location provides customer service for cellular phones. **Listed on:** NASDAQ. **Stock exchange symbol:** NXTL.

NIELSEN & BAINBRIDGE
40 Eisenhower Drive, Paramus NJ 07652. 201/845-6100. **Contact:** Dorothy Uhler, Personnel Director. **E-mail address:** info@nielson-brainbridge.com. **World Wide Web address:** http://www.nielsen-bainbridge.com. **Description:** Produces and distributes picture frames. **Operations at this facility include:** Administration; Divisional Headquarters; Service.

NOISE COM
25 Eastmans Road, Parsippany NJ 07054. 201/261-8797. **Fax:** 201/261-8339. **Contact:** Human Resources. **E-mail address:** jobs@noisecom.com. **World Wide Web address:** http://www.noisecom.com. **Description:** Manufactures test equipment for the wireless telecommunications industry. **Parent company:** Wireless Telecom Group. **Listed on:** American Stock Exchange. **Stock exchange symbol:** WTT.

NOVARTIS PHARMACEUTICALS CORPORATION
556 Morris Avenue, Summit NJ 07901. 908/277-5000. **Contact:** Human Resources. **World Wide Web address:** http://www.novartis.com. **Description:** Novartis Pharmaceuticals Corporation is one of the largest life science companies in the world. The company has three major divisions: health care, agribusiness, and nutrition. The health care division specializes in pharmaceuticals, both proprietary and generic, and ophthalmic health care. The agribusiness division is involved in seed technology, animal health, and crop protection. The nutrition sector includes medical, health, and infant nutrition. **Positions advertised include:** Communications Associate; Communications Operations Representative; Finance Business Administration Services Representative; Human Resources; Information Technologist Representative; Pharmaceutical Operations Representative; Sales Associate; State Government Affairs Representative; Transportation Tissue Engineer. **NOTE:** Resumes should be sent to Human Resources, Novartis Pharmaceuticals Corporation, 59 Route 10, East Hanover

NJ 07936. **Corporate headquarters location:** East Hanover NJ. **Operations at this facility include:** This location manufactures pharmaceuticals.

NOVARTIS PHARMACEUTICALS CORPORATION
59 Route 10, East Hanover NJ 07936. 973/503-7500. **Contact:** Human Resources. **World Wide Web address:** http://www.novartis.com. **Description:** Novartis Pharmaceuticals Corporation is one of the largest life science companies in the world. The company has three major divisions: health care, agribusiness, and nutrition. The health care division specializes in pharmaceuticals, both proprietary and generic, and ophthalmic health care. The agribusiness division is involved in seed technology, animal health, and crop protection. The nutrition sector includes medical, health, and infant nutrition. **Corporate headquarters location:** This location. **Other area locations:** Summit NJ. **Operations at this facility include:** This location houses administrative offices and Novartis Pharmaceuticals' primary research facility.

NOVO NORDISK PHARMACEUTICALS INC.
100 College West, Princeton NJ 08540. 609/987-5800. **Fax:** 609/987-3915. **Contact:** Human Resources. **World Wide Web address:** http://www.novo-nordisk.com. **Description:** One of the world's largest producers of industrial enzymes and insulin for the treatment of diabetes. **Positions advertised include:** Customer Care Administrator; Clinical Administrator; Medical Writer; Medical Information Scientist; Clinical Project Manager; Technical Rate Administrator; E-business Manager; Tax Accountant; Brand Manager; Clinical Administrator; Human Resources Generalist; Clinical Project Manager; Project Associate; Strategic Information Manager. **Parent company:** Novo Nordisk A/S (Baysvaerd, Denmark).

OAK VALLEY FARMS
P.O. Box 778, Voorhees NJ 08043. 856/435-0900. **Contact:** Julia O'Connor, Personnel Director. **World Wide Web address:** http://www.oakvalleyfarms.com. **Description:** Processes turkey products for correctional facilities, distributors, food service companies, government agencies, and schools. **Parent company:** El Jay Corporation.

OCEAN CITY GAZETTE
2087 South Shore Road 2nd Floor, Seaville NJ 08230. 609/624-8900. **Contact:** Human Resources. **World Wide Web address:** http://www.oceancitygazette.com. **Description:** A southern New Jersey newspaper with 100,000 circulation.

OCEAN COUNTY VETERINARY HOSPITAL
838 River Avenue, Lakewood NJ 08701. 732/363-7202. **Fax:** 732/370-4176. **Contact:** Human Resources. **World Wide Web address:** http://www.ocvh.com. **Description:** Provides health care services to dogs, cats, and exotic pets including surgery, hospitalization, and diagnostic testing. **Positions advertised include:** Technician; Receptionist.

OCEAN SPRAY CRANBERRIES, INC.
104 East Park Street, P.O. Box 31, Bordentown NJ 08505. 609/298-0905. **Fax:** 609/298-8353. **Contact:** Human Resources. **World Wide Web address:** http://www.oceanspray.com. **Description:** Manufactures cranberry juices and sauces. **Positions advertised include:** Continuous Improvement Manager; Customer Development Coordinator; Information Technologies Support Technician; Plant Manager. **Special programs:** Internships. **Corporate headquarters location:** Lakeville MA. **Other U.S. locations:** Vero Beach FL; Middleboro MA; Las Vegas NV; Sulphur Springs TX; Kenosha WI. **Parent company:** Ocean Spray is a food processor engaged in the packaging, processing, and marketing of fresh cranberries, cranberry sauces, and cranberry and grapefruit juices. **Operations at this facility include:** Manufacturing. **Listed on:** Privately held. **Number of employees at this location:** 300. **Number of employees nationwide:** 2,000.

OHAUS CORPORATION
29 Hanover Road, Florham Park NJ 07058. 973/377-9000. **Contact:** Human Resources. **E-mail address:** hr@ohaus.com. **World Wide Web address:** http://www.ohaus.com. **Description:** One of the world's largest manufacturers of precision weighing equipment for use in laboratory, education, and specialty markets. **Corporate headquarters location:** This location.

OKI DATA AMERICAS, INC.
2000 Bishops Gate Boulevard, Mount Laurel NJ 08054. 856/235-2600. **Contact:** Human Resources. **World Wide Web address:** http://www.okidata.com. **Description:** Manufactures computer printers and fax machines. **Positions advertised include:** Human Resources Business Partner. **Corporate headquarters location:** This location. **International locations:** Worldwide.

OKONITE COMPANY
102 Hilltop Road, P.O. Box 340, Ramsey NJ 07446. 201/825-0300. **Fax:** 201/825-2672. **Contact:** Paulette Vita, Personnel Manager. **World Wide Web address:** http://www.okonite.com. **Description:** Manufactures power cable for large-scale users. **Corporate headquarters location:** This location. **Other area locations:** Passaic NJ; Paterson NJ.

ORACLE CORPORATION
517 Route 1 South, Iselin NJ 08830. 732/636-2000. **Contact:** Human Resources. **World Wide Web address:** http://www.oracle.com. **Description:** Oracle Corporation designs and manufactures database and information management software for businesses and provides consulting services. **Corporate headquarters location:** Redwood Shores CA. **Other U.S. locations:** Nationwide. **Operations at this facility include:** This location designs and manufactures business software programs for small companies. **Listed on:** NASDAQ. **Stock exchange symbol:** ORCL. **Number of employees worldwide:** 42,000.

ORGANON INC.
375 Mount Pleasant Avenue, West Orange NJ 07052. 973/325-4500. **Toll-free phone:** 800/241-8812. **Fax:** 973/669-6144. **Contact:** Human Resources. **E-mail address:** wohr@organon-usa.com. **World Wide Web address:** http://www.organon-usa.com. **Description:** A worldwide leader in pharmaceutical research and development in the fields of reproductive medicine, anesthesiology, central nervous system disorders, thrombosis, and immunology. **NOTE:** Entry-level positions and part-time jobs are offered. **Positions advertised include:** Pharmaceutical Scientist. **Special programs:** Internships; Summer Jobs. **Office hours:** Monday - Friday, 8:00 a.m. - 4:30 p.m. **Corporate headquarters location:** This location. **Parent company:** Akzo Nobel. **Annual sales/revenues:** More than $100 million. **Number of employees at this location:** 1,200.

ORTHO-McNEIL PHARMACEUTICAL
1000 Route 202 North, P.O. Box 300, Raritan NJ 08869-0602. 908/218-6000. **Contact:** Human Resources. **World Wide Web address:** http://www.ortho-mcneil.com. **Description:** Develops and sells pharmaceutical products including women's health, infectious disease, and wound healing products. **Positions advertised include:** National Account Manager; Clinical Research Associate. **NOTE:** All hiring is done out of the corporate offices. Resumes should be sent to Johnson & Johnson Recruiting Services, Employment Management Center, Room JH-215, 501 George Street, New Brunswick NJ 08906-6597. **Parent company:** Johnson & Johnson (New Brunswick NJ).

OSTEOTECH INC.
51 James Way, Eatontown NJ 07724. 732/542-2800. **Fax:** 732/542-9312. **Contact:** Human Resources. **E-mail address:** hr@osteotech.com. **World Wide Web address:** http://www.osteotech.com. **Description:** Processes human bone and connective tissue for transplantation and develops and manufactures biomaterial and device systems for musculoskeletal surgery. Osteotech is a leader in volume and quality of tissue processing for the American Red Cross and the Musculoskeletal Tissue Foundation. Founded in 1986. **NOTE:** Entry-level positions and second and third shifts are offered. **Company slogan:** Innovators in musculoskeletal tissue science. **Positions advertised include:** Clinical Research Technician; Clinical Research Associate; Auditor Associate; Processing Technology. **Special programs:** Training. **Office hours:** Monday - Friday, 8:00 a.m. - 5:00 p.m. **Corporate headquarters location:** This location. **Other U.S. locations:** Nationwide. **International locations:** The Netherlands. **Listed on:** NASDAQ. **Stock exchange symbol:** OSTE. **President:** Richard Bauer. **Annual sales/revenues:** $21 - $50 million. **Number of employees at this location:** 180. **Number of employees nationwide:** 200. **Number of employees worldwide:** 225.

OVERLOOK HOSPITAL
P.O. Box 220, Summit NJ 07902-0220. 908/522-2241. **Physical address:** 99 Beauvoir Avenue, Summit NJ 07901. **Contact:** Human Resources. **World Wide Web address:** http://www.overlookfoundation.org. **Description:** A part of Atlantic Health Systems, Overlook Hospital is a 490-bed, public hospital with extensive facilities for pediatrics, oncology, cardiology, and same-day surgery.

PNY TECHNOLOGIES, INC.
299 Webro Road, Parsippany NJ 07054. 973/515-9700. **Toll-free phone:** 800/234-4597. **Fax:** 973/560-5283. **Contact:** Human Resources. **E-mail address:** hr@pny.com. **World Wide Web address:** http://www.pny.com. **Description:** Manufactures and designs computer memory products. Founded in 1985. **NOTE:** Entry-level positions are offered. **Positions advertised include:** Buyer; End of the Line Inspector; Memory Marketing Manager; Test Technician; Traffic Coordinator. **Corporate headquarters location:** This location. **Listed on:** Privately held. **Annual sales/revenues:** More than $100 million. **Number of employees at this location:** 250. **Number of employees nationwide:** 320. **Number of employees worldwide:** 420.

PPI ENTERTAINMENT
88 St. Francis Street, Newark NJ 07105. 973/344-4214. **Contact:** Personnel. **World Wide Web address:** http://www.peterpan.com. **Description:** Manufactures and distributes records, tapes, videos, and CD-ROMs. **Corporate headquarters location:** This location. **Listed on:** Privately held.

P.S.A. HEALTHCARE
4900 Route 33, Suite 100, Neptune NJ 07753-6804. 732/938-5550. **Fax:** 732/938-6535. **Contact:** Human Resources. **World Wide Web address:** http://www.psakids.com. **Description:** Provides infusion therapy, nursing, and other home health care services to clients. **Positions advertised include:** Clinical Care Coordinator; Registered Nurse; Field Nurse Recruiter.

PVC CONTAINER CORPORATION
2 Industrial Way West, Eatontown NJ 07724-2202. 732/542-0060. **Toll-free phone:** 800/975-2784. **Fax:** 732/544-8007. **Contact:** Personnel. **E-mail address:** mpelich@pvcc.com. **World Wide Web address:** http://www.novapakcorp.com. **Description:** Designs and manufactures plastic bottles and polyvinyl chloride compounds. **Positions advertised include:** Quality Engineer; South East Regional Sales Manager; Machine Operator; Plastics Lab Technician.

PANASONIC INDUSTRIAL COMPANY
One Panasonic Way, Mailstop 3A-5, Secaucus NJ 07094. 201/348-7000. **Fax:** 201/392-6007. **Contact:** Kisha Rand-Hudson, Human Resources. **E-mail address:** hudsonk@panasonic.com. **World Wide Web address:** http://www.panasonic.com. **Description:** Panasonic is one of the world's largest manufacturers of consumer and industrial electronic equipment and components. Brand names include Panasonic, Technics, and Quasar. **Positions advertised include:** Legal Secretary; Category Planning Analyst; Demand Specialist; Marketing Manager; Account Manager; Compensation Analyst; Technical Support Specialist; Product Development Engineer; Programmer; Technical Repair Specialist; Account Manager; Sales Manager; Instructor; Account Executive. **Other U.S. locations:** Nationwide. **Operations at this facility include:** This location houses the U.S. headquarters. **Parent company:** Matsushita Electronics Corporation of America. **Number of employees at this location:** 300. **Number of employees nationwide:** 10,000.

PANTONE
590 Commerce Boulevard, Carlstadt NJ 07072. 201/935-5500. **Fax:** 201/804-9219. **Contact:** Human Resources. **World Wide Web address:** http://www.pantone.com. **Description:** Produces color charts and color specification materials. **Positions advertised include:** Sales Representative; Marketing Assistant. **Corporate headquarters location:** This location. **Operations at this facility include:** Administration; Manufacturing; Research and Development; Sales.

PARAGON COMPUTER PROFESSIONALS INC.
20 Commerce Drive, Suite 226, Cranford NJ 07016. 908/709-6767. **Toll-free phone:** 800/462-5582. **Contact:** Human Resources Administrative Assistant. **World Wide Web address:** http://www.paracomp.com. **Description:** Offers computer consulting services to a variety of businesses. **Positions advertised include:** E-business Strategist; E-business Architect; Infrastructure Architect; Project Manager; Lead Developer; Interface Developer; Client Side Developer; Server Side Developer; Legacy Integration; Database Administrator; Business Systems Analyst; Systems Analyst; Quality Analyst. **Corporate headquarters location:** This location.

PARIS BUSINESS PRODUCTS, INC.
800 Highland Drive, Westhampton NJ 08060. 609/265-9200. **Fax:** 609/387-2114. **Contact:** Human Resources. **World Wide Web address:** http://www.pariscorp.com. **Description:** Produces business forms. Founded in 1964. **Corporate headquarters location:** This location.

PASSAIC VALLEY WATER COMMISSION
1525 Main Avenue, Clifton NJ 07011. 973/349-4309. **Contact:** Jim Gallagher, Personnel Director. **World Wide Web address:** http://www.pvwc.com. **Description:** Provides water utility services. **Corporate headquarters location:** This location.

PATENT CONSTRUCTION SYSTEMS
One Mack Centre Drive, Paramus NJ 07652. 201/986-1290. **Fax:** 201/261-5544. **Contact:** Human Resources and Labor Relations. **E-mail address:** jobs@pcshd.com. **World Wide Web address:** http://www.pcshd.com. **Description:** Manufactures and markets scaffolding as well as concrete forming and shoring products. Founded in 1909. **Positions advertised include:** Sales Representative. **Parent company:** Harsco Corporation.

PATHMARK STORES INC.
200 Milik Street, Carteret NJ 07008. 732/499-3000. **Fax:** 732/499-4250. **Contact:** Human Resources. **E-mail address:** employment@pathmark.com. **World Wide Web address:** http://www.pathmark.com. **Description:** A diversified retailer engaged primarily in the operation of large supermarket/drug stores. The company operates one of the largest supermarket chains in the country. Its Rickel Home Center division is among the largest do-it-yourself home center chains in the nation. The company's retail stores are located in the Mid-Atlantic and New England. **Positions advertised include:** Store Clerk; Store Engineer; Store Maintenance Mechanic; Merchandiser; Cashier; Night Crew Associate; Cart People; Maintenance Clerk; Cake Decorator. **Corporate headquarters location:** This location.

PEARSON EDUCATION
PRENTICE HALL INC.
One Lake Street, Upper Saddle River NJ 07458. 201/236-7000. **Contact:** Human Resources. **World Wide Web address:** http://www.pearsoneducation.com. **Description:** Pearson Education publishes consumer, educational, and professional books. Prentice Hall (also at this location) specializes in business and professional books, as well as college-level resource materials. **Positions advertised include:** Administrative Coordinator; Change Management Director; Editorial Assistant; Human Resource Manager; Image Coordinator; Accounting Manager; Staff Accountant. **Operations at this facility include:** This location houses corporate offices. **Subsidiaries include:** Macmillan. **Parent company:** Viacom. **Number of employees nationwide:** 4,000.

PEPSI-COLA
NATIONAL BRAND BEVERAGES LTD.
8275 U.S. Route 130, Pennsauken NJ 08110. 856/665-6200. **Contact:** Human Resources. **World Wide Web address:** http://www.pepsi.com. **Description:** Pepsi-Cola Company produces and distributes a variety of beverages including the brand names Pepsi-Cola, Mountain Dew, Mug Root Beer, and Slice. **Operations at this facility include:** This location bottles Canada Dry products.

PERMACEL
671 US Highway 1, North Brunswick NJ 08902. 732/418-2550. **Fax:** 732/418-2457. **Contact:** Human Resources Department. **E-mail address:** human_resources@permacel.com. **World Wide Web address:** http://www.permacel.com. **Description:** Manufactures pressure-sensitive tape. **Positions advertised include:** Financial Account Manager. **Corporate headquarters location:** This location. **Operations at this facility include:** Administration; Manufacturing; Research and Development; Sales; Service. **Listed on:** Privately held. **Number of employees at this location:** 500.

PERMANENT LABEL
790 Bloomfield Avenue, Clifton NJ 07012. 973/471-6617. **Contact:** Human Resources. **Description:** Engaged in decorating and printing labels for plastic products, primarily bottles. **Corporate headquarters location:** This location.

PERSHING
One Pershing Plaza, 9th Floor, Jersey City NJ 07399. 201/413-2000. **Contact:** Personnel Department. **World Wide Web address:** http://www.pershing.com. **Description:** A securities brokerage firm. **Positions advertised include:** Brokerage Operations Associate; International Clearance Associate; International Clearance Fall Control Associate; International Clearance Trade; Processing Associate; Margin Specialist; Compliance Associate; Account Manager; International Account Manager; Trainer; Client Services Associate; Graphic Designer; Marketing Manager; Business Analyst; Compliance Specialist. **Parent company:** Donaldson, Lufkin & Jenrette Securities Corporation.

PFIZER
201 Tabor Road, Morris Plains NJ 07950. 973/385-2000. **Contact:** Corporate Human Resources. **World Wide Web address:** http://www.pfizer.com. **Description:** A leading pharmaceutical company that distributes products concerning cardiovascular health, central nervous system disorders, infectious diseases, and women's health worldwide. The company's brand-name products include Benadryl, Ben Gay, Cortizone, Desitin, Halls, Listerine, Sudafed, Viagra, and Zantac 75. **Positions advertised include:** Executive Assistant; Buyer; Scientist; Regional Area Manager; Maintenance Craft Worker; Financial Analyst; Administrative Associate; Marketing Communications Manager; Business Development Manager; Associate Director; Data Management Specialist; Meteorologist; Scientist Chemistry Project Team Leader.

PFIZER
100 Route 206 North, Peapack NJ 07977. 908/901-8000. **Contact:** Human Resources. **World Wide Web address:** http://www.pfizer.com. **Description:** Pfizer manufactures and markets agricultural products, performance chemicals used in consumer products, prescription pharmaceuticals, and food ingredients. **Corporate headquarters location:** This location. **Operations at this facility include:** This location houses administrative offices. **Number of employees worldwide:** 60,000.

PHARMACEUTICAL FORMULATIONS, INC.
P.O. Box 1904, 460 Plainfield Avenue, Edison NJ 08818-1904. 732/985-7100. **Fax:** 732/819-3330. **Contact:** Human Resources. **E-mail address:** pfiresumes@pfiotc.com. **World Wide Web address:** http://www.pfiotc.com. **Description:** Manufactures and distributes over-the-counter, solid-dosage pharmaceutical products in tablet, caplet, and capsule forms. **Corporate headquarters location:** This location. **Operations at this facility include:** Administration; Manufacturing; Research and Development; Sales; Service. **Number of employees at this location:** 320.

PHELPS DODGE HIGH PERFORMANCE CONDUCTORS
48 Broadway Avenue, Elizabeth NJ 07006. 908/351-3200. **Fax:** 908/351-9475. **Contact:** Marge Engel, Human Resources Manager. **World Wide Web address:** http://www.phelpsdodge.com. **Description:** One of the world's leading suppliers of conductive wire. **Corporate headquarters location:** Inman SC. **Operations at this facility include:** Administration; Manufacturing; Sales. **Number of employees at this location:** 175. **Number of employees nationwide:** 400.

PHILLIPS PETROLEUM COMPANY
1400 Park Avenue, Linden NJ 07036. 908/523-5000. **Contact:** Professional Employment. **World Wide Web address:** http://www.phillips66.com. **Description:** Refines oil. **NOTE:** Mail employment correspondence to: Professional Employment, 180 Plaza Office Building, Bartlesville OK 74004.

PHILLIPS-VAN HEUSEN CORPORATION
1001 Frontier Road, Suite 100, Bridgewater NJ 08807-2955. 908/685-0050. **Contact:** Human Resources Department. **E-mail address:** hr@pvh.com. **World Wide Web address:** http://www.pvh.com. **Description:** Engaged in the manufacture, wholesale, and retail of men's and women's apparel. **NOTE:** Search for current up-to-date opportunities online. **Positions advertised include:** Administrative Assistant; Office Service Manager; Receptionist; Design Director; Product Development Director; Designer; Technical Designer; Graphic Artist; Design Assistant; CAD Operator; Merchandise Coordinator; Warehouse Manager; Picking Supervisor; Shipping Supervisor; Traffic Manager; Traffic Assistant; Assistant Controller; Financial Analyst. **Corporate headquarters location:** New York NY. **Other U.S. locations:** AL. **Listed on:** New York Stock Exchange. **Stock exchange symbol:** PVH. **Number of employees nationwide:** 14,000.

PIONEER INDUSTRIES
171 South Newman Street, Hackensack NJ 07601. 201/933-1900. **Contact:** Personnel Director. **World Wide Web address:** http://www.pioneer-industries.com. **Description:** Produces industrial doors, fireproof and theft-proof doors, and other sheet metal specialties. **Corporate headquarters location:** Bloomfield Hills MI. **Parent company:** Core Industries. **Operations at this facility include:** Manufacturing.

PNC BANK
P.O. Box 6000, Bridgewater NJ 08807. 908/429-2200. **Physical address:** 1130 Route 22 East, Bridgewater NJ 08807. **Fax:** 908/707-8329. **Contact:** Human Resources Department. **World Wide Web address:** http://www.pncbank.com. **Description:** Operates a full-service commercial bank offering a wide range of traditional banking, trust, and other financial services. **Corporate headquarters location:** This location.

POLAND SPRINGS OF AMERICA
170 West Commercial Avenue, Moonachie NJ 07074. 201/531-2044. **Contact:** Human Resources. **World Wide Web address:** http://www.polandspring.com. **Description:** Distributes bottled spring and distilled drinking water for home and industrial use. The company also provides water coolers, microwave ovens, and similar equipment for installation in commercial and industrial locations. **Parent company:** Perrier Group of America (Greenwich CT).

POLYONE CORPORATION
P.O. Box 400, Pedricktown NJ 08067. 856/838-8659. **Fax:** 856/299-8635. **Physical address:** Route 130 & Porcupine Road, Pedricktown NJ 08067. **Contact:** Human Resources. **World Wide Web address:** http://www.polyone.com. **Description:** Manufactures and develops thermoplastic compounds, specialty resins, engineered films, color and additive systems, specialty polymers, rubber compounding, and vinyl compounds. **Corporate headquarters location:** Cleveland OH. **Other U.S. locations:** Nationwide. **International locations:** Worldwide. **Listed on:** New York Stock Exchange. **Stock exchange symbol:** POL. **Annual sales/revenues:** More than $100 million.

POPULAR CLUB PLAN
22 Lincoln Place, Garfield NJ 07026. 973/471-4300. **Contact:** Human Resources. **World Wide Web address:** http://www.popularclub.com. **Description:** Operates a full-service, mail-order catalog operation offering apparel, housewares, personal care products, jewelry and related items. **Office hours:** Monday – Friday. 8:00 a.m. – 8:30 p.m. **Corporate headquarters location:** This location.

POWER BATTERY COMPANY
25 McLean Boulevard, Paterson NJ 07514-1507. 973/523-8630. **Fax:** 973/523-3023. **Contact:** Human Resources. **E-mail address:** custserv@powbat.com. **World Wide Web address:** http://www.powerbattery.com. **Description:** Manufactures batteries for use in automobiles, computers, and small electronic appliances.

POWERTECH, INC.
0-02 Fair Lawn Avenue, Fair Lawn NJ 07410. 201/791-5050. **Fax:** 201/791-6805. **Contact:** Human Resources. **World Wide Web address:** http://www.power-tech.com. **Description:** Manufactures silicon power transistors.

PRESERVER GROUP, INC.
95 Route 17 South, Paramus NJ 07653-0931. 201/291-2000. **Contact:** Human Resources. **E-mail address:** humanresources@preserver.com. **World Wide Web address:** http://www.preserver.com. **Description:** Provides automobile, homeowner, and commercial insurance. Founded in 1926. **Positions advertised include:** Lead Computer Operator. **Corporate headquarters location:** This location. **Listed on:** NASDAQ. **Stock exchange symbol:** PRES. **Number of employees at this location:** 95.

PRESS OF ATLANTIC CITY
1000 West Washington Avenue, Pleasantville NJ 08232. 609/272-7000. **Fax:** 609/272-7413. **Contact:** Human Resources. **E-mail address:** pryan@pressofac.com. **World Wide Web address:** http://www.pressofac.com. **Description:** A southern New Jersey online newspaper. **Positions advertised include:** Marketing Development Manager; Online Project Manager; Advertising Sales Account Executive.

PRIME HOSPITALITY CORPORATION
700 Route 46 East, Fairfield NJ 07007. 973/882-1010. **Contact:** Human Resources. **E-mail address:** recruiter@primehospitality.com. **World Wide Web address:** http://www.primehospitality.com. **Description:** An independent hotel operating company with ownership and management of 86 full- and limited-service hotels in 19 states and one resort hotel in the U.S. Virgin Islands. Hotels typically contain 100 to 200 guest rooms or suites and operate under franchise agreements with national hotel chains or under the company's Wellesley Inns or AmeriSuites trade names. Founded in 1961. **Corporate headquarters location:** This location. **Other U.S. locations:** Nationwide. **Operations at this facility include:** Administration. **Listed on:** New York Stock Exchange. **Stock exchange symbol:** PDQ. **Annual sales/revenues:** More than $100 million. **Number of employees at this location:** 190. **Number of employees nationwide:** 6,050.

PRINCE SPORTS
One Advantage Court, Bordentown NJ 08505-9630. 609/291-5800. **Toll-free phone:** 800/283-6647. **Fax:** 609/291-5791. **Contact:** Director of Human Resources. **World Wide Web address:** http://www.raquettech.com. **Description:** Manufactures sports equipment and related accessories.

PRINCETON FINANCIAL SYSTEMS INC.
600 College Road East, Princeton NJ 08540. 609/987-2400. **Fax:** 609/514-4798. **Contact:** Human Resource. **World Wide Web address:** http://www.pfs.com.

Description: Develops and supports investment management software. Founded in 1969. **NOTE:** Entry-level positions are offered. **Positions advertised include:** Client Support Analyst; Applications Developer; Implementation Manager. **Special programs:** Apprenticeships. **Corporate headquarters location:** This location. **International locations:** London; Toronto. **Parent company:** State Street Boston Corporation. **Number of employees at this location:** 150. **Number of employees nationwide:** 185. **Number of employees worldwide:** 200.

PRINCETON INFORMATION
399 Thornall Street, 4th Floor, Edison NJ 08837-2246. 732/906-5660. **Contact:** Human Resources. **E-mail address:** newjersey@princetoninformation.com. **World Wide Web address:** http://www.princetoninformation.com. **Description:** Offers computer consulting services. **Positions advertised include:** Developer.

PRINCETON SOFTECH
111 Campus Drive, Princeton NJ 08540. 609/627-5500. **Toll-free phone:** 800/457-7060. **Fax:** 609/457-7060. **Contact:** Human Resources. **World Wide Web address:** http://www.princetonsoftech.com. **Description:** Provides IT professionals with software solutions. Develops, researches, sells, and markets software products that are focused on intelligent data migration and database synchronization. The company offers data and program synchronization tools to solve application development and database problems. Founded in 1989. **Positions advertised include:** Oracle Application Representative; Product Integration Engineer; Professional Services Consultant. **Corporate headquarters location:** This location. **International locations:** Worldwide. **Parent company:** Computer Horizons Corporation.

PRINCETON UNIVERSITY
Office of Human Resources, One New South, Princeton NJ 08544. 609/258-3300. **Contact:** Human Resources. **E-mail address:** jobs@princeton.edu. **World Wide Web address:** http://www.princeton.edu/hr. **Description:** A private, four-year university offering bachelor of arts and science degrees, as well as master's and doctoral degrees. Approximately 4,500 undergraduate and 1,800 graduate students attend Princeton. **NOTE:** Current lists of positions can be found online. **Positions advertised include:** Administrative Support; Data Management Support; Departmental Office Support; Field Electrician; Production Supervisor; Retail Food Service Worker; Planner; Shift Supervisor.

PRUDENTIAL INSURANCE COMPANY OF AMERICA
23 Main Street, Holmdel NJ 07733. 732/946-5000. **Contact:** Human Resources. **World Wide Web address:** http://www.prudential.com. **Description:** One of the largest insurance and diversified financial services organizations in the world. The company's primary business is to offer a full range of products and services in three areas: insurance, investment, and home ownership for individuals and families; health care management and other benefit programs for employees of companies and members of groups; and asset management for institutional clients and their associates. The company insures or provides other financial services to more than 50 million people worldwide. **Positions advertised include:** Investment Analyst. **NOTE:** Jobseekers should send resumes to the corporate headquarters located at 751 Broad Street, Newark NJ 07102. **Corporate headquarters location:** Newark NJ. **Other area locations:** Iselin NJ; Roseland NJ. **Other U.S. locations:** Woodland Hills CA; Jacksonville FL; Minneapolis MN; Philadelphia PA; Houston TX. **Listed on:** New York Stock Exchange. **Stock exchange symbol:** PRU. **Annual sales/revenues:** More than $100 million. **Number of employees worldwide:** 100,000.

PRUDENTIAL INSURANCE COMPANY OF AMERICA
751 Broad Street, Newark NJ 07102. 973/802-8348. **Fax:** 973/802-5825. **Contact:** Human Resources. **World Wide Web address:** http://www.prudential.com. **Description:** One of the largest insurance companies in North America and one of the largest diversified financial services organizations in the world. The company offers a full range of products and services in three areas: insurance, investment, and home ownership for individuals and families; health care management and other benefit programs for employees of companies and members of groups; and asset management for institutional clients and their associates. The company insures or provides financial services to more than 50 million people worldwide. **Positions advertised include:** Accounting Associate; Security Manager Associate; Audit Manager; Business Analyst; Compliance Director; Process Management Director; Executive Assistant. **Special programs:** Internships. **Corporate headquarters location:** This location. **Other area locations:** Holmdel NJ; Iselin NJ; Roseland NJ. **Other U.S. locations:** Woodland Hills CA; Jacksonville FL; Minneapolis MN; Philadelphia PA; Houston TX. **Listed on:** New York Stock Exchange. **Stock exchange symbol:** PRU. **Annual sales/revenues:** More than $100 million. **Number of employees worldwide:** 100,000.

PRUDENTIAL INSURANCE COMPANY OF AMERICA
200 Wood Avenue South, Iselin NJ 08830. 732/632-7000. **Contact:** Human Resources. **World Wide Web address:** http://www.prudential.com. **Description:** Prudential Insurance Company of America is one of the largest insurance companies in North America and one of the largest diversified financial services organizations in the world. The company's primary business is to offer a full range of products and services in three areas: insurance, investment, and home ownership for individuals and families; health care management and other benefit programs for employees of companies and members of groups; and asset management for institutional clients and their associates. The company insures or provides other financial services to more than 50 million people worldwide. **NOTE:** Jobseekers should send resumes to the corporate headquarters located at 751 Broad Street, Newark NJ 07102. company insures or provides financial services to more than 50 million people worldwide. **Corporate headquarters location:** Newark NJ. **Other area locations:** Holmdel NJ; Roseland NJ. **Other U.S. locations:** Woodland Hills CA; Jacksonville FL; Minneapolis MN; Philadelphia PA; Houston TX. **Operations at this facility include:** This location manages health care policies. **Listed on:** New York Stock Exchange. **Stock exchange symbol:** PRU. **Annual sales/revenues:** More than $100 million. **Number of employees worldwide:** 100,000.

PRUDENTIAL INSURANCE COMPANY OF AMERICA
80 Livingston Avenue, Roseland NJ 07068. 973/716-6834. **Contact:** Human Resources. **World Wide Web address:** http://www.prudential.com. **Description:** One of the largest insurance companies in North America and one of the largest diversified financial services organizations in the world. The company's primary business is to offer a full range of products and services in three areas: insurance, investment, and home ownership for individuals and families; health care management and other benefit programs for employees of companies and members of groups; and asset management for institutional clients and their associates. With a sales force of approximately 19,000 agents, 3,400 insurance brokers, and 6,000 financial advisors, the company insures or provides other financial services to more than 50 million people worldwide. **Positions advertised include:** Accounting Associate; Investment Analyst; Process Management Analyst. **NOTE:** Jobseekers should send resumes to the corporate headquarters located at 751 Broad Street, Newark NJ 07102. **Corporate headquarters location:** Newark NJ. **Other area locations:** Holmdel NJ; Iselin NJ. **Other U.S. locations:** Woodland Hills CA; Jacksonville FL; Minneapolis MN; Philadelphia PA; Houston TX. **Listed on:** New York Stock Exchange. **Stock exchange symbol:** PRU. **Annual sales/revenues:** More than $100 million. **Number of employees worldwide:** 100,000.

PUBLIC SERVICE ENTERPRISE GROUP (PSEG)
80 Park Plaza, Newark NJ 07101. 973/430-7000. **Contact:** Human Resources. **World Wide Web address:** http://www.pseg.com. **Description:** An electric and gas utility holding company. **Positions advertised include:** Business Continuity Planner; Power Generation Manager; Power Accounting Manager; Global Accounting Director; Staff Engineer; Administration Associate; Consultant; Lead Associate. **Corporate headquarters location:** This location. **Other area locations:** Hancock's Bridge NJ. **Subsidiaries include:** Public Service Electric & Gas Company provides nuclear, coal, gas, oil, and purchased and interchanged power to industrial and commercial customers. **Listed on:** New York Stock Exchange. **Stock exchange symbol:** PEG.

QAD INC.
10000 Midlantic Drive, Suite 200, Mount Laurel NJ 08054. 856/273-1717. **Contact:** Human Resources. **World Wide Web address:** http://www.qad.com. **Description:** QAD develops MFG/PRO, a software package designed to aid in supply and distribution management for large companies. **Positions advertised include:** Customer Service Regional Director. **Corporate headquarters location:** Carpinteria CA. **Operations at this facility include:** This location serves as a technical support branch and regional sales office. **Listed on:** NASDAQ. **Stock exchange symbol:** QADI.

QMED, INC.
25 Christopher Way, Eatontown NJ 07724. 732/544-5544. **Fax:** 732/544-5404. **Contact:** Human Resources. **E-mail address:** jobs@qmedinc.com. **World Wide Web address:** http://www.qmedinc.com. **Description:** Designs, manufactures, and markets testing devices that enable medical professionals to perform minimally invasive diagnostic procedures for certain illnesses, such as silent myocardial ischemia, venous blood flow insufficiencies, and diabetic neuropathy. **Positions advertised include:** Licensed Practical Nurse; Patient Education Nurse; Help Desk Manager; Information Technology Developer; Registered Nurse; Operations Program Analyst; Accounting Manager; Medical Assistant; Customer Service Specialist; Account Manager. **Listed on:** NASDAQ. **Stock exchange symbol:** QEKG.

QUALEX, INC.
16-31 Route 208, Fair Lawn NJ 07410. 201/797-0600. **Contact:** Karen Mergenthaler, Senior Personnel Manager. **World Wide Web address:** http://www.kodak.com. **Description:** A photofinishing company providing processing services for print and reversal type films. **Corporate headquarters location:** Durham NC. **Parent company:** Eastman Kodak Company. **Operations at this facility include:** Administration; Customer Service; Sales; Service.

QUALITY SOFTWARE SYSTEMS INC.
200 Centennial Avenue, Suite 110, Piscataway NJ 08854. 732/885-1919. **Fax:** 732-885-1872. **Contact:** Human Resources. **E-mail address:** emtrojanello@qssi-wns.com. **World Wide Web address:** http://www.qssi-wns.com. **Description:** Develops software to aid in warehouse management and development. **Positions advertised include:** Sales; Implementation Consultant.

QUEST DIAGNOSTICS INCORPORATED
One Malcolm Avenue, Teterboro NJ 07608. 201/393-5000. **Fax:** 201/462-4715. **Contact:** Personnel. **World Wide Web address:** http://www.questdiagnostics.com. **Description:** One of the largest clinical laboratories in North America, providing a broad range of clinical laboratory services to health care clients that include physicians, hospitals, clinics, dialysis centers, pharmaceutical companies, and corporations. The company offers and performs tests on blood, urine, and other bodily fluids and tissues to provide information for health and well-being. **Positions advertised include:** Technologist; Histotechnologist; Assistant Administrator; Phlebotomy Service Representative; Pathologist Representative; Group Leader; Field Operations Manager; Customer Service Representative; Dispatcher; Imaging Clerk. **Corporate headquarters location:** This location. **Other U.S. locations:** Nationwide. **Listed on:** New York Stock Exchange. **Stock exchange symbol:** DGX.

QUEST INTERNATIONAL FRAGRANCES COMPANY
400 International Drive, Mount Olive NJ 07828. 973/691-7100. **Contact:** Human Resources. **World Wide Web address:** http://www.questintl.com. **Description:** Develops cosmetic fragrances. **Positions advertised include:** Marketing Manager; Graduate Trainee; Regional Marketing Manager; Process Development Manager; Sales Manager; Account Manager. **Corporate headquarters location:** This location. **Operations at this facility include:** Administration; Manufacturing; Marketing; Sales.

R-V METAL FABRICATING INC.
20 Sand Park Road, Cedar Grove NJ 07009. 973/239-8100. **Fax:** 973/239-2323. **Contact:** Linda Calderio, Customer Service or Human Resources. **E-mail address:** lcalderio@rvmetal.com. **World Wide Web address:** http://www.rvmetal.com. **Description:** Supplies fabricated sheet metal detail parts and assemblies for primarily the aerospace industry.

RCN CORPORATION
105 Carnegie Center, Princeton NJ 08540. 609/734-3700. **Toll-free phone:** 800/746-4726. **Fax:** 609/734-3789. **Contact:** Employment Administrator. **World Wide Web address:** http://www.rcn.com. **Description:** A full-service communications company that provides customers with cable, Internet, long-distance telephone, and local telephone services. **NOTE:** Entry-level positions and second and third shifts are offered. **Positions advertised include:** Applications Architect; Director of Product Management Bundles; Director of Accounting and Reporting; Director of Advertising; Financial Analyst; Marketing Analyst. **Special programs:** Co-ops. **Corporate headquarters location:** This location. **Other U.S. locations:** DC; MA; NY; PA; VA. **Subsidiaries include:** Starpower LLC. **Listed on:** NASDAQ. **Stock exchange symbol:** RCNC. **Annual sales/revenues:** $51 - $100 million. **Number of employees at this location:** 200. **Number of employees nationwide:** 1,400.

RFL ELECTRONICS INC.
353 Powerville Road, Boonton Township NJ 07005-9151. 973/334-3100. **Fax:** 973/334-3863. **Contact:** Human Resources. **E-mail address:** hrmanager@rflelect.com. **World Wide Web address:** http://www.rflelect.com. **Description:** Designs and manufactures a wide range of telecommunication and teleprotection products for the electric, water, gas, and telephone utilities; railroads; mines; pipelines; airlines; oil drilling and refining firms; private contractors; OEMs; and government agencies. **Positions advertised include:** Senior Software Engineer; Order Entry Administrator.

RARITAN COMPUTER INC.
400 Cottontail Lane, Somerset NJ 08873. 732/764-4600. **Fax:** 732/764-8887. **Contact:** Human Resources. **E-mail address:** hr@raritan.com. **World Wide Web address:** http://www.raritan.com. **Description:** Designs and manufactures a line of products for

sharing PCs and peripherals. Products include MasterConsole, a keyboard/video/mouse switch; CompuSwitch, a KVM switch allowing central control for up to four PCs; and Guardian, a virtual keyboard and mouse device that emulates keyboard and mouse signals. Founded in 1985. **Positions advertised include:** Software Group Consultant; System Tester; Software Engineer; Assistant Controller; Network Communication Director; Marketing Communication Launch Manager; Material Planner; Product Marketing Manager; Product Manager; Sales Engineer; Business Marketing Manager; Technical Support Representative; National Account Manager; Territory Sales Manager. **Corporate headquarters location:** This location. **Number of employees at this location:** 40. **Number of employees nationwide:** 100.

RECKITT BENCKISER
Morris Corporate Center IV, 399 Interpace Parkway, Parsippany NJ 07054-0225. 973/404-2600. **Toll-free phone:** 800/333 3899. **Fax:** 973/404-5700. **Contact:** Staffing Supervisor. **E-mail address:** human.resources@reckitt.com. **World Wide Web address:** http://www.reckitt.com. **Description:** Manufactures cleaning and specialty food products including the brand names Easy-Off oven cleaner, French's mustard, Lysol, and Woolite detergent.

THE RECORD
NORTH JERSEY MEDIA GROUP
150 River Street, Hackensack NJ 07601-7172. 201/646-4000. **Contact:** Human Resources. **World Wide Web address:** http://www.bergen.com. **Description:** A daily newspaper with a circulation of 150,000 and 203,000 for the Sunday edition. **Positions advertised include:** Post Press Production Coordinator; Press Operator; Sales Representative; Classified Sales Representative; Editorial Assistant; Reporter; Staff Accountant; Administrative Assistant; Help Desk Operator; Technical Support Supervisor; Purchasing Agent; District Manager; Customer Service Specialist; Account Executive; Receptionist; Sales Associate; Sales Support.

RECOVERY TECHNOLOGIES GROUP
7000 Boulevard East, Guttenberg NJ 07093. 201/854-7777. **Fax:** 201/854-1771. **Contact:** Office Manager. **E-mail address:** contactus@rtginc.com. **World Wide Web address:** http://www.rtginc.com. **Description:** Develops and owns waste-to-energy facilities that provide a means of disposal of nonhazardous municipal solid waste. **Corporate headquarters location:** This location.

RED DEVIL, INC.
2400 Vauxhall Road, Union NJ 07083. 908/688-6900. **Fax:** 908/688-8872. **Contact:** Maria Janeira, Director of Human Resources. **World Wide Web address:** http://www.reddevil.com. **Description:** Manufactures and distributes paint sundries; hand tools; and a full-line of caulks, sealants, and adhesives for home and professional use. **Corporate headquarters location:** This location. **Number of employees at this location:** 150. **Number of employees nationwide:** 250.

REED ELSEVIER NEW PROVIDENCE
121 Chanlon Road, New Providence NJ 07974. 908/464-6800. **Contact:** Human Resources. **World Wide Web address:** http://www.reed-elsevier.com. **Description:** A reference publisher of marketing, advertising, and corporate directories. **Subsidiaries include:** LexisNexis Business Information Services; Marquis Who's Who; Martindale-Hubbel.

REEDY INTERNATIONAL
25 East Front Street, Suite 200, Key Port NJ 07735. 732/264-1777. **Fax:** 732/264-1189. **Contact:** Human Resources. **E-mail address:** info@readyintl.com. **World Wide Web address:** http://www.reedyintl.com. **Description:** Produces chemical components for items such as Styrofoam and car parts.

REITMAN INDUSTRIES
10 Patton Drive, West Caldwell NJ 07006. 973/228-5100. **Contact:** Human Resources. **World Wide Web address:** http://www.rrmarketing.com. **Description:** Engaged in the wholesale importation and distribution of liquors and wines. **Corporate headquarters location:** This location.

RESORTS CASINO HOTEL
1133 Boardwalk, Atlantic City NJ 08401. 609/344-6000. **Fax:** 609/340-7751. **Recorded jobline:** 609/340-6756. **Contact:** Employment Office. **E-mail address:** employment@resortsinc.com. **World Wide Web address:** http://www.resortsac.com. **Description:** Atlantic City's first casino hotel, with more than 800 deluxe rooms and suites. The hotel also houses a fine dining restaurant, a full-service beauty salon, and several shops and boutiques. **Positions advertised include:** Beverage Manager; Environmental Services Supervisor; PC Programmer; Cashier; Surveillance Supervisor.

REVLON, INC.
IMPLEMENT DIVISION
196 Coit Street, Irvington NJ 07111-1490. 973/373-5803. **Contact:** Personnel Manager. **World Wide Web address:** http://www.revlon.com. **Description:** Manufactures nail files, scissors, tweezers, and other manicure and pedicure products. **Positions advertised include:** Store Clerk; Warehouse Assistant. **Corporate headquarters location:** New York NY. **Listed on:** New York Stock Exchange. **Stock exchange symbol:** REV.

RHODIA INC.
CN7500, Cranbury NJ 08512-7500. 609/860-4000. **Physical address:** 259 Prospect Plains Road, Cranbury NJ 08512. **Contact:** Human Resources. **E-mail address:** rhodia@rpc.webhire.com. **World Wide Web address:** http://www.rhodia.com. **Description:** Rhodia supplies specialty and intermediate chemicals for consumer and industrial applications. **Operations at this facility include:** This location houses administrative offices. **Other U.S. locations:** Nationwide. **Parent company:** Rhone-Poulenc.

ROBERT PLAN OF NEW JERSEY
200 Metroplex Drive, Edison NJ 08817-2600. 732/777-5300. **Fax:** 516/393-6592. **Contact:** Human Resources. **E-mail address:** drivein@rpc.com. **World Wide Web address:** http://www.rpc.com. **Description:** Robert Plan of New Jersey provides personal lines of insurance. **Positions advertised include:** Underwriting Technician. **Corporate headquarters location:** Bethpage NY. **Operations at this facility include:** This location houses an automobile claims office.

ROCHE VITAMINS INC.
45 Waterview Boulevard, Parsippany NJ 07054-1298. 973/257-1063. **Fax:** 800/526-0189. **Contact:** Human Resources. **E-mail address:** michael-j.malecki@dsm.com. **World Wide Web address:** http://www.roche-vitamins.com. **Description:** A pharmaceutical company that manufactures pharmaceutical drugs, diagnostic kits, and vitamins for dietary, pharmaceutical, and cosmetic use. **Corporate headquarters location:** This location.

ROWAN UNIVERSITY
201 Mullica Hill Road, Linden Hall, 1st Floor, Glassboro NJ 08028. 856/256-4134. **Contact:** Human Resources. **World Wide Web address:** http://www.rowan.edu. **Description:** A four-year, state college offering bachelor's and master's degrees (including MBAs). Approximately 9,000 students attend Rowan University. **Positions advertised include:** Assistant Dean of Students; Director of Judicial Affairs; Assistant Director, Graduate Assistantships.

ROYAL CONSUMER INFORMATION PRODUCTS INC
379 Campus Drive, Somerset NJ 08805. **Toll-free phone:** 888/261-4555. **Fax:** 800/232-9799. **Contact:** Human Resources. **E-mail address:** info@royalsupplies.com. **World Wide Web address:** http://www.royal.com. **Description:** Manufactures and distributes a broad line of electronic office products including typewriters, calculators, word processors, cash registers, copiers, personal and small computers, business computers, complete data processing systems, teleprinters, video terminals, telephone-switching systems, minicomputers, automatic tellers, and associated equipment.

RUSS BERRIE & COMPANY, INC.
111 Bauer Drive, Oakland NJ 07436. 201/337-9000. **Contact:** Human Resource Department. **E-mail address:** careers@russberrie.com. **World Wide Web address:** http://www.russberrie.com. **Description:** Designs and markets a line of more than 10,000 gift items in the United States and abroad. Products include toys, stuffed animals, novelties, and cards. A diverse customer base includes florists, pharmacies, party shops, and stationery stores, as well as hotel, airport, and hospital gift shops. **Positions advertised include:** Product Development Representative; Design Art Representative; Customer Service Representative; Credit & Collections Representative; Finance Representative; Information Technology Representative. **Corporate headquarters location:** This location. **Operations at this facility include:** Administration. **Listed on:** New York Stock Exchange. **Stock exchange symbol:** RUS. **Number of employees nationwide:** 2,000.

RUTGERS STATE UNIVERSITY OF NEW JERSEY
56 Bevier Road, Piscataway NJ 08854. 732/445-3020. **Fax:** 732/445-3087. **Contact:** Personnel Department. **E-mail address:** info@hr.Rutgers.edu. **World Wide Web address:** http://www.rutgers.edu. **Description:** A four-year, state university offering undergraduate and graduate programs in a wide variety of disciplines. **Positions advertised include:** Administrative Director; Administrative Assistant; Area Director; Assistant to the Dean; Director Athletics; Editorial Media Specialist; Unit Computing Specialist. **Other U.S. locations:** Camden NJ; Newark NJ.

RUTGERS STATE UNIVERSITY OF NEW JERSEY
UNIVERSITY COLLEGE-NEWARK
249 University Avenue, Room 202, Newark NJ 07102. 973/353-5500. **Contact:** Irma Mendoza, Human Resources. **E-mail address:** angelis@newark.rutgers.edu. **World Wide Web address:** http://www.rutgers.edu. **Description:** A campus of the state university. **Positions advertised include:** Administrative Director; Administrative Assistant; Area Director; Assistant to the Dean; Director Athletics; Editorial Media Specialist; Unit Computing Specialist. **Other U.S. locations:** Brunswick NJ; Camden NJ.

SGS U.S. TESTING COMPANY INC.
291 Fairfield Avenue, Fairfield NJ 07004. 973/575-5252. **Toll-free phone:** 800/777-8378. **Fax:** 973/575-1071. **Contact:** Personnel. **E-mail address:** hrustc@yahoo.com. **World Wide Web address:** http://www.ustesting.sgsna.com. **Description:** An independent laboratory specializing in the testing of a variety of industrial and consumer products. Services include biological, chemical, engineering/materials, environmental, electrical, paper/packaging, textiles, certification programs, and inspections. **Positions advertised include:** Account Executive, Outside Sales. **Corporate headquarters location:** This location. **Other U.S. locations:** Los Angeles CA; Tulsa OK. **Parent company:** SGS North America. **Operations at this facility include:** Administration; Sales; Service.

SJ NURSES
850 Hamilton Avenue, Trenton NJ 08629. 609/396-7100. **Toll-free phone:** 800/727-2476. **Fax:** 609/396-7559. **Contact:** Human Resources. **E-mail address:** application@sjnurses.com. **World Wide Web address:** http://www.sjnurses.com. **Description:** Provides home health care services. **Corporate headquarters location:** This location.

SQN BANKING SYSTEMS
65 Indel Avenue, P.O. Box 423, Rancocas NJ 08073. 609/261-5500. **Toll-free phone:** 888/744-7266. **Contact:** Human Resources. **E-mail address:** info@sqnbankingsystems.com. **World Wide Web address:** http://www.sqnbankingsystems.com. **Description:** Develops signature verification software for the banking industry.

SAINT BARNABAS HEALTH CARE SYSTEM
368 Lakehurst Road, Suite 203, Toms River NJ 08755. 888/724-7123. **Contact:** Human Resources. **E-mail address:** info@sbhcs.com. **World Wide Web address:** http://www.sbhcscareers.com. **Description:** A health care delivery system that spans the state of New Jersey and includes eight acute care hospitals, nine nursing and rehabilitation centers, three assisted living facilities, geriatric centers, and ambulatory care centers. **NOTE:** Search and apply for positions online. **Positions advertised include:** Administrative Assistant; Case Coordinator; Certified Nursing Assistant (CNA); CM Director of Nursing; Coder; Compliance Associate; Endo Technician; General Clerical; Housekeeper; Licensed Practical Nurse; Payroll Coordinator; Respiratory Therapist; Respiratory Therapy Coordinator; Staff Registered Nurse. **Other area locations:** Statewide.

ST. FRANCIS MEDICAL CENTER
601 Hamilton Avenue, Trenton NJ 08629. 609/599-5000. **Contact:** Human Resources. **World Wide Web address:** http://www.stfrancismedical.com. **Description:** A medical center that provides health care services to Trenton and the surrounding areas, with a particular emphasis on the needs of the poor. **Positions advertised include:** Registered Nurse; Licensed Practical Nurse; Medical Records Clerk; Secretary; Medical Records Clerk; Outreach Worker; ER Clerk; Support Associate; Security Guard; Maintenance Mechanic; Customer Service Representative.

SAINT-GOBAIN PERFORMANCE PLASTICS
150 Dey Road, Wayne NJ 07470. 973/696-4700. **Contact:** Anne Ginestre, Human Resources Manager. **World Wide Web address:** http://www.nortonplastics.com. **Description:** Manufactures a wide range of plastic products and shapes including pipes, rods, sheet, tape, rectangular stock, insulated wire, and coaxial cable core; finished plastic products such as laboratory wire; and nylon products such as rods, tubes, slabs, and custom castings. **Special programs:** Internships.

KURT SALMON ASSOCIATES, INC.
103 Carnegie Center, Suite 205, Princeton NJ 08540. 609/452-8700. **Contact:** Director of Recruiting. **World Wide Web address:** http://www.kurtsalmon.com. **Description:** Provides management consulting to logistics and consumer products companies.

SANDS CASINO & HOTEL
136 South Kentucky Avenue, Atlantic City NJ 08401. 609/441-4000. **Fax:** 609/441-4470. **Contact:** Personnel. **World Wide Web address:** http://www.acsands.com. **Description:** A 532-room resort hotel with extensive gaming facilities, five restaurants, and live entertainment. **Positions advertised include:** Security Officer; Casino Host; Casino Cage Supervisor; Shift Manager; Dealer; Slot Attendant Supervisor; Security Manager; Food Server; Bartender; Bus Person; Heavy Porter; Bus Porter; EMT; Valet Parking Attendant; Warehouse Supervisor; Showroom Captain; General Ledger Accountant.

SAVIENT PHARMACEUTICALS, INC.
One Tower Center 14th Floor, East Brunswick NJ 08816. 732/418-9300. **Fax:** 732/418-9235. **Contact:** Human Resources. **E-mail address:** hr@btgc.com. **World Wide Web address:** http://www.savientpharma.com. **Description:** Develops, manufactures, and markets novel therapeutic products. The company specializes in preclinical studies, research and development, and biotechnology derived products. **Positions advertised include:** Area Manager; Controller; Sales Manager; Director of Marketing. **Corporate headquarters location:** This location. **International locations:** Rehovot, Israel.

SCHERING-PLOUGH CORPORATION
2000 Galloping Hill Road, Kenilworth NJ 07033. 908/298-4000. **Contact:** Human Resources Department. **World Wide Web address:** http://www.schering-plough.com. **Description:** Engaged in the discovery, development, manufacture, and marketing of pharmaceutical and consumer products. Pharmaceutical products include prescription drugs, over-the-counter medicines, eye care products, and animal health products promoted to the medical and allied health professions. The consumer products group consists of proprietary medicines, toiletries, cosmetics, and foot care products. Brand names include Coricidin, Maybelline, Claritin, Coppertone, and Dr. Scholl's. **Positions advertised include:** Associate Manager; Compliance Manager; Computer Systems Validation Specialist; Mechanical Supervisor; Porter; Premium Buyer; CAD Operator; Validation Engineer; Computer Systems Administrator; Staff Validation Specialist; Publishing Technician; Medical Writer. **Note:** Current positions are updated on the website. **Corporate headquarters location:** This location. **Other area locations:** Statewide. **International locations:** Worldwide.

SCHERING-PLOUGH CORPORATION
One Giralda Farms, Madison NJ 07940-1000. 973/822-7000. **Contact:** Human Resources Department. **World Wide Web address:** http://www.schering-plough.com. **Description:** Engaged in the discovery, development, manufacture, and marketing of pharmaceutical and consumer products. Pharmaceutical products include prescription drugs, over-the-counter medicines, eye care products, and animal health products. The consumer products group consists of proprietary medicines, toiletries, cosmetics, and foot care products. Brand names include Coricidin, Maybelline, Claritin, Coppertone, and Dr. Scholl's. **Positions advertised include:** Associate Manager; Compliance Manager; Computer Systems Validation Specialist; Mechanical Supervisor; Porter; Premium Buyer; CAD Operator; Validation Engineer; Computer Systems Administrator; Staff Validation Specialist; Publishing Technician; Medical Writer. **Note:** Current positions are updated on the website. **Corporate headquarters location:** Kenilworth NJ. **Other area locations:** Statewide. **International locations:** Worldwide.

SCHIAVONE CONSTRUCTION CO.
150 Meadowlands Parkway, 3rd Floor, Secaucus NJ 07094. 201/867-5070. **Contact:** Recruiting. **Description:** A heavy construction firm engaged in large-scale projects such as highways, tunnels, and bridges. Clients include city, state, and federal governments.

SCHIFFENHAUS INDUSTRIES
2013 McCarter Highway, Newark NJ 07104. 973/484-5000. **Fax:** 973/268-4908. **Contact:** Human Resources. **World Wide Web address:** http://www.schifpack.com. **Description:** Manufactures corrugated boxes and flexographic, preprinted liner board. **Positions advertised include:** Sales Representative. **Corporate headquarters location:** This location. **Number of employees at this location:** 165.

SCIENCE MANAGEMENT LLC
SMC CONSULTING
745 Routes 202/206, Bridgewater NJ 08807. 908/722-0300. **Fax:** 908/722-0421. **Contact:** Personnel. **E-mail address:** info@smcmgmt.com. **World Wide Web address:** http://www.smcmgmt.com. **Description:** Works with IBM to provide disaster recovery services to large corporations. SMC Consulting (also at this location) provides management consulting services. **Corporate headquarters location:** This location.

SEALED AIR CORPORATION
Park 80 East, Saddle Brook NJ 07663. 201/791-7600. **Contact:** Manager of Employee Benefits. **World Wide Web address:** http://www.sealedaircorp.com. **Description:** Sealed Air Corporation is a diversified worldwide enterprise consisting of specialty and agricultural chemicals, energy production and services, retailing, restaurants, and other businesses. The firm operates over 2,500 facilities worldwide. **Corporate headquarters location:** This location. **Other U.S. locations:** Danbury CT; Holyoke MA; Scotia NY. **Operations at this facility include:** This location produces specialized protective packaging materials and systems that reduce or eliminate the damage to products that may occur during shipping. **Listed on:** New York Stock Exchange. **Stock exchange symbol:** SEE. **Number of employees at this location:** 35. **Number of employees nationwide:** 2,000.

SELECTIVE INSURANCE COMPANY OF AMERICA
40 Wantage Avenue, Branchville NJ 07890-1000. 973/948-3000. **Fax:** 973/948-0292. **Contact:** Tom Magistro. **E-mail address:** tom.magistro@selective.com. **World Wide Web address:** http://www.selectiveinsurance.com. **Description:** Engaged in fire, marine, and casualty insurance. **Positions advertised include:** Processing Support.

SETON COMPANY
849 Broadway, Newark NJ 07104. 973/485-4800. **Contact:** Human Resources. **E-mail address:** hr@setonco.com. **World Wide Web address:** http://www.setonleather.com. **Description:** Company operations are conducted primarily through two business segments. The Leather Division's operations include tanning, finishing, and distributing whole-hide cattle leathers for the automotive and furniture upholstery industries, cattle hide side leathers for footwear, handbag, and other markets, and cattle products for collagen, rawhide pet items, and other applications. The Chemicals and Coated Products Division is engaged in the manufacture and distribution of epoxy and urethane chemicals, specialty leather finishes, industrial and medical tapes, foams, films, and laminates. Other manufacturing facilities are located in Wilmington DE (epoxy, urethane chemicals, leather finishes); Toledo OH (cattle hide processing); Malvern PA (industrial coated products); and Saxton PA (cutting of finished leathers). **Corporate headquarters location:** This location. **Subsidiaries include:** Radel Leather Manufacturing Company; Seton Leather Company.

SETON HALL UNIVERSITY
400 South Orange Avenue, Stafford Hall, South Orange NJ 07079. 973/761-9178. **Fax:** 973/761-9007. **Contact:** Aisha Agee, Human Resources Specialist. **E-mail address:** ageeaiash@shu.edu. **World Wide Web address:** http://www.shu.edu. **Description:** A Catholic university offering a wide range of undergraduate and graduate programs. **Positions advertised include:** Secretary; Assistant Psychology Professor; Assistant Professor of Philosophy; Assistant Professor of Spanish; Physiologist; Web Services Applications Developer; Technology Budget Manager.

SHARP ELECTRONICS CORPORATION
Sharp Plaza, Mahwah NJ 07430. 201/529-8200. **Fax:** 201/529-8425. **Contact:** Human Resources. **World Wide Web address:** www.sharpusa.com. **Description:** An electronics company that produces appliances, office equipment, and entertainment products. **Other U.S. locations:** Camas WA; Memphis TN; Romeoville IL; Huntington Beach CA; Miami FL. **International locations:** Worldwide.

THE SHAW GROUP
200 Horizon Center Boulevard, Trenton NJ 08691. 609/584-8900. **Contact:** Recruiter. **World Wide Web address:** http://www.shawgrp.com. **Description:** Provides environmental engineering, consulting, and construction services to a variety of public and private sector clients. Shaw Group is a leader in the design and remediation of solid and hazardous waste, transfer, storage, and disposal facilities. The company's waste facility services include site selection and evaluation, facility design, development of preprocessing and operating plans, assistance in regulatory compliance and permitting, final closures, and end use planning and design. Services also include the development of programs dealing with environmental assessments and remediation of contaminated sites, as well as services related to applied sciences such as marine fate-and-effect studies and fuel spill and natural resource damage assessments. **Positions advertised include:** Cost Schedule Engineer; Field Technician; Project Director.

SHERATON CROSSROADS
1 International Boulevard, Rt. 17 North, Mahwah NJ 07495. 201/529-1660. **Fax:** 201/529-4709. **Contact:** Human Resources. **World Wide Web address:** http://www.starwoodhotels.com. **Description:** A 227-room hotel, 40 minutes from New York City, offering a view of the Ramapo Valley and 23,000 ft of meeting space capable of accommodating 1,200 people. **Other U.S. locations:** Nationwide.

SHOPPER'S GUIDE INC.
8 Ranoldo Terrace, Cherry Hill NJ 08034. 856/616-4900. **Contact:** Human Resources Manager. **E-mail address:** shoppersguide@advc.com. **World Wide Web address:** http://www.theshoppersguide.com. **Description:** One of the Northeast's largest, free, weekly, shopper's newspapers. **Positions advertised include:** Account Executive; Telemarketing Sales. **Parent company:** Newport Media, Inc.

SHORE MEMORIAL HOSPITAL
One East New York Avenue, Somers Point NJ 08244-2387. 609/653-3500. **Fax:** 609/926-1987. **Contact:** Human Resources Department **World Wide Web address:** http://www.shorememorial.org. **Description:** A 350-bed, nonprofit medical center providing medical, surgical, pediatric, and obstetrical services. Shore Memorial Hospital joined with Shore Care Home Health Services and Ocean Point Health Care Center to form Shore Memorial Health Care System. **Positions advertised include:** Radiation Therapist; Care Manager; Registered Nurse; Staff Technologist; MRI Technician; Chart Clerk; CT Technologist; Special Procedures Technologist. **Number of employees at this location:** 1,400.

SIBSON CONSULTING
600 Alexander Park, Suite 208, Princeton NJ 08540. 609/520-2700. **Contact:** Human Resources. **World Wide Web address:** http://www.segalco.com/sibson. **Description:** A management consulting firm. **Positions advertised include:** Associate Consultant; Consultant; Senior Consultant; Principal. **Corporate headquarters location:** This location. **Parent company:** Segal.

SIEMENS
DEMAG DELAVAL TURBOMACHINERY CORPORATION
P.O. Box 8788, 840 Nottingham Way, Trenton NJ 08650-0788. 609/890-5324. **Fax:** 609/890-5328. **Contact:** Cheryl Pedersen, Human Resources Administrator. **World Wide Web address:** http://www.siemens.com. **Description:** Manufactures steam turbines and compressors. **Operations at this facility include:** Administration; Manufacturing; Regional Headquarters; Research and Development; Sales; Service. **Number of employees at this location:** 540.

SIEMENS MEDICAL
186 Wood Avenue South, Iselin NJ 08830. 732/321-4500. **Contact:** Personnel Office. **World Wide Web address:** http://www.siemensmedical.com. **Description:** Develops, manufactures, and sells medical systems including digital X-rays and 3-D ultrasound equipment. Products are used in a variety of areas including cardiology, audiology, surgery, critical care, and oncology. **Positions advertised include:** Advanced Consultant; Business & Product Development Manager; Repair Operating Manager; Technical Competence Center Representative; New Units Vice President. **Corporate headquarters location:** This location.

SIKA CORPORATION
P.O. Box 297, 201 Polito Avenue, Lyndhurst NJ 07071. 201/933-8800. **Fax:** 201/933-6166. **Contact:** Personnel. **E-mail address:** resume@sika-corp.com. **World Wide Web address:** http://www.sikausa.com. **Description:** Manufactures specialty chemicals including sealants and adhesives for the construction and transportation industries. Founded in 1937. **Positions advertised include:** Area Sales Manager; Area Transportation Manager; Chemist; Sales Representative. **NOTE:** Search website for updated job listings. **Corporate headquarters location:** This location. **Parent company:** Sika Finanz AG. **Operations at this facility include:** Administration; Manufacturing; Regional Headquarters; Research and Development; Sales; Service. **Listed on:** Privately held. **Annual sales/revenues:** More than $100 million. **Number of employees at this location:** 200. **Number of employees nationwide:** 700.

SIMON & SCHUSTER, INC.
100 Front Street, Riverside NJ 08075. 856/461-6500. **Fax:** 856/824-2406. **Contact:** Human Resources. **World Wide Web address:** http://www.simonandschuster.com. **Description:** Simon & Schuster publishes consumer, educational, and professional books. **Other U.S. locations:** CA; MA; NY; OH. **Operations at this facility include:** This location is a distribution center. **Subsidiaries include:** Macmillan; Prentice Hall Inc. **Parent company:** Viacom. **Number of employees nationwide:** 4,000.

SLACK INCORPORATED
6900 Grove Road, Thorofare NJ 08086-9447. 856/848-1000. **Toll-free phone:** 800/257-8290. **Fax:** 856/848-6091. **Contact:** Human Resources Manager. **E-mail address:** resume@slackinc.com. **World Wide Web address:** http://www.slackinc.com. **Description:** SLACK Incorporated is a provider of information, education, and event management services focusing mainly in the healthcare marketplace. A leader in the healthcare information industry SLACK publishes over 25 journals and medical newspapers distributed worldwide; over 125 medical and allied health books worldwide; conducts major publication-related conferences and trade shows; provides exhibit sales, management services, and advertising sales representation for association clients; produces dozens of periodical special projects each year, including supplements, monographs, satellite symposia, and industry-sponsored symposia, and customized CD-ROMs; and designs and manages customized Websites for resident training and continuing education. SLACK is certified by the Accreditation Council for Continuing Medical Education to sponsor continuing education events and periodical-based Continuing Medical Education activities. **Positions advertised include:** Advertising Sales Administrator; Assistant Associate Editor; Customer Service Representative; Help Desk Representative; Copywriter; Sales Representative; Inside Sales Representative; Staff Writer; Web Editor **Corporate headquarters location:** This location.

SMITH, STRATTON, WISE, HEHER & BRENNAN
600 College Road East, Princeton NJ 08540. 609/924-6000. **Contact:** Janet M. Derr, Personnel. **E-mail address:** kbymes@smithstratton.com. **World Wide Web address:** http://www.sswhb.com. **Description:** A law firm serving the needs of businesses, the investment community, and entrepreneurs. Founded in 1948.

SMITHS AEROSPACE
110 Algonquin Parkway, Whippany NJ 07981. 973/428-9898. **Fax:** 973//884-2277. **Contact:** Human Resources. **E-mail address:** aerospace@jobpositive.com. **World Wide Web address:** http://www.smiths-aerospace.com. **Description:** Engineers and manufactures electro-mechanical actuation control systems for the aerospace and commercial industries. **Positions advertised include:** Lead Project Engineer. **Parent company:** Smiths Group. **Operations at this facility include:** Divisional Headquarters; Manufacturing; Research and Development; Sales. **Number of employees at this location:** 250.

SNOWBALL FOODS, INC.
1051 Sykes Lane, Williamstown NJ 08094. 856/629-4081. **Contact:** Robert Thompson, Human Resources Manager. **World Wide Web address:** http://www.snowballfoods.com. **Description:** Engaged in poultry processing. **Positions advertised include:** General Plant & Utility Technician; Maintenance Associate; Supervisor; Accounting Representative; Sales Associate; Quality Assurance Manager. **Special programs:** Internships. **Corporate headquarters location:** This location. **Operations at this facility include:** Administration; Manufacturing; Research and Development; Sales; Service. **Number of employees at this location:** 250.

SONY ELECTRONICS, INC.
One Sony Drive, Park Ridge NJ 07656. 201/930-1000. **Contact:** Human Resources. **World Wide Web address:** http://www.sony.com. **Description:** Sony's U.S. operations include manufacturing, engineering, design, sales, marketing, product distribution, and customer services. **Positions advertised include:** Database Marketing Manager; Account Manager; Sales Support Engineer. **Other area locations:** Moonachie NJ; Paramus NJ; Teaneck NJ. **Other U.S. locations:** New York NY. **Operations at this facility include:** This location houses the U.S. headquarters for the international electronics manufacturer. **Number of employees nationwide:** 24,000.

SONY MUSIC
400 North Woodbury Road, Pitman NJ 08071. 856/589-8000. **Contact:** Human Resources. **World Wide Web address:** http://www.sony.com. **Description:** Sony Music is a major recording company. **Operations at this facility include:** This location manufactures CDs and DVDs.

SOUTH JERSEY HEALTH SYSTEM
SOUTH JERSEY HOSPITAL
333 Irving Avenue, Bridgeton NJ 08302-2123. 856/451-6600. **Fax:** 856/575-4500. **Contact:** Personnel. **World Wide Web address:** http://www.sjhs.com. **Description:** Provides extensive medical services throughout southern New Jersey. **NOTE:** Mail employment correspondence to: 65 South State Street, Vineland NJ 08360. **Positions advertised include:** Accountant; Case Manager; Corporate Compliance Specialist; Environmental Services Aide; Food Service Aide; Human Resources Representative; Marketing and Press Release Specialist; Nurse Manager; Pharmacist; Radiological Technician; Registrar; Registered Nurse. **Subsidiaries include:** Elmer Community Hospital has 91 beds. Millville Hospital has 109 beds. Newcomb Medical Center has 235 beds. South Jersey Hospital (also at this location) has 224 beds.

SOUTH JERSEY PUBLISHING COMPANY
1000 West Washington Avenue, Pleasantville NJ 08232. 609/272-7000. **Fax:** 609/272-7135. **Contact:** Kathleen Leonard, Human Resources Director. **E-mail address:** pryan@pressofac.com. **World Wide Web address:** http://www.pressofatlanticcity.com. **Description:** Publishes the *Atlantic City Press*, a newspaper. **Positions advertised include:** Marketing Development Manager; Online Project Manager; Advertising Sales Account Executive. **Special programs:** Internships. **Corporate headquarters location:** Pittsburgh PA. **Parent company:** Abarta Inc. **Operations at this facility include:** Administration; Manufacturing; Sales; Service. **Listed on:** Privately held. **Number of employees at this location:** 360. **Number of employees nationwide:** 430.

SOVEREIGN BANK
100 Berlin Road, Clementon NJ 08021. 856/566-3283. **Contact:** Human Resources. **E-mail address:** tms-nj@sovereignbank.com. **World Wide Web address:** http://www.sovereignbank.com. **Description:** A bank. **Parent company:** Sovereign Bancorp is one of the largest thrift holding companies, with community banking and loan offices serving New England, eastern Pennsylvania, New Jersey, and northern Delaware.

SPENCER GIFTS INC.
6826 Black Horse Pike, Egg Harbor Township NJ 08234. 609/645-3300. **Contact:** Human Resources. **World Wide Web address:** http://www.spencergifts.com. **Description:** A retailer of novelty, joke, and gift items. **Operations at this facility include:** Administration; Sales; Service. **Number of employees nationwide:** 4,000.

SPHERION
9 Polito Avenue, 9th Floor, Lyndhurst NJ 07071. 201/392-0800. **Contact:** Human Resources. **World Wide Web address:** http://www.spherion.com. **Description:** A nationwide computer outsourcing service company, providing short-run supplemental and long-term contractual support for computer operations, communications operations, PC help desks, local area networks, computer programming, and technology training. The company's computer services are provided from offices strategically located throughout the United States. The company also provides the expertise for meeting applications and systems development objectives within information systems organizations. Capabilities extend beyond evaluating computer software and hardware to providing technically qualified professionals for any task in the systems development life cycle -- from conception through feasibility analysis, system design, programming, testing, implementation, and full systems maintenance and support. **Positions advertised include:** Dispatcher. **Corporate headquarters location:** Fort Lauderdale FL. **Other U.S. locations:** Nationwide. **International locations:** Worldwide. **Listed on:** New York Stock Exchange. **Stock exchange symbol:** SFN.

SPRINGFIELD PRECISION INSTRUMENTS
76 Passaic Street, Wood-Ridge NJ 07075. 973/777-2900. **Contact:** Personnel Manager. **Description:** Manufactures thermometers and barometers for consumer use. **Corporate headquarters location:** This location.

STAR-GLO INDUSTRIES L.L.C.
2 Carlton Avenue, East Rutherford NJ 07073. 201/939-6162. **Fax:** 201/939-4054. **Contact:** Personnel. **World Wide Web address:** http://www.starglo.com. **Description:** Manufactures precision-molded rubber and plastic parts, often bonded to metal. Sales are made primarily to original equipment manufacturers in the business machine and computer, welding, food packaging equipment, chemical, and aerospace industries. **Corporate headquarters location:** This location.

THE STAR-LEDGER
One Star Ledger Plaza, Newark NJ 07102. 973/877-4141. **Contact:** Human Resources. **World Wide Web address:** http://www.nj.com/starledger. **Description:** Publishes a large circulation daily newspaper covering local news. **Positions advertised include:** Recruitment Category Specialist.

STEPAN COMPANY
100 West Hunter Avenue, Maywood NJ 07607. 201/845-3030. **Contact:** Human Resources. **E-mail address:** stepanhr@stepan.com. **World Wide Web address:** http://www.stepan.com. **Description:** Produces specialty chemicals and food additives. **Corporate headquarters location:** Northfield IL. **Operations at this facility include:** Administration; Manufacturing; Research and Development; Sales. **Listed on:** New York Stock Exchange. **Stock exchange symbol:** SCL. **Number of employees at this location:** 100. **Number of employees nationwide:** 1,300.

STORAGE ENGINE, INC.
One Sheila Drive, Tinton Falls NJ 07724. 732/747-6995. **Fax:** 732/747-6542. **Contact:** Human Resources. **E-mail address:** hr@storageengine.com. **World Wide Web address:** http://www.eccs.com. **Description:** Designs and configures computer systems. Storage Engine's mass storage enhancement products include RAID (Redundant Array of Independent Disks) products and technology; external disk, optical, and tape systems; internal disk and tape storage devices; and RAM. The company also provides related technical services. **Corporate headquarters location:** This location.

STRAUSS DISCOUNT AUTO
9A Brick Plant Road, South River NJ 08882. 732/390-9000. **Contact:** Human Resources Administrator. **World Wide Web address:** http://www.straussauto.com. **Description:** Engaged in the retail trade of automotive aftermarket products. **Positions advertised include:** Store Manager; Assistant Store Manager; Service Department Manager; Auto Technician; Service Writer. **Corporate headquarters location:** This location. **Listed on:** Privately held. **Number of employees at this location:** 200. **Number of employees nationwide:** 2,200.

SUBARU OF AMERICA
2235 Route 70 West, Cherry Hill NJ 08046. 856/488-8500. **Fax:** 856/488-3196. **Contact:** Scott Mogren, Vice President of Human Resources. **World Wide Web address:** http://www.subaru.com. **Description:** Subaru of America manufactures cars and trucks. **Operations at this facility include:** This location houses administrative offices.

SUN MICROSYSTEMS, INC.
400 Atrium Drive, Somerset NJ 08873. 732/469-1000. **Contact:** Human Resources. **World Wide Web address:** http://www.sun.com. **Description:** Sun Microsystems produces high-performance computer systems, workstations, servers, CPUs, peripherals, and operating systems software. The company developed its own microprocessor called SPARC. **Positions advertised include;** Systems Engineer. **Note:** Submit resume online. **Corporate headquarters location:** Palo Alto CA. **Operations at this facility include:** This location is a sales office. **Subsidiaries include:** Forte Software Inc. manufactures enterprise application integration software. **Listed on:** NASDAQ. **Stock exchange symbol:** SUNW.

SUN NATIONAL BANK
525 Route 72 East, Manahawkin NJ 08050. 609/597-1800. **Contact:** Director of Human Resources. **World Wide Web address:** http://www.sunnb.com. **Description:** A bank. **NOTE:** Interested jobseekers should address all inquiries to: Human Resources, Sun National Bank, 226 Landis Avenue, Vineland NJ 08360.

SYBRON CHEMICALS INC.
P.O. Box 66, Birmingham Road, Birmingham NJ 08011. 609/893-1100. **Contact:** Human Resources. **World Wide Web address:** http://www.ion-exchange.com. **Description:** An international specialty chemical company that supplies chemicals and related technology to two markets: environmental products and services, primarily related to water and waste treatment; and textile processing. The company's chemical specialties are used to enhance the aesthetic and physical characteristics of textiles during textile preparation, printing, dyeing, and finishing. Sybron's environmental products soften and demineralize water, purify drinking water for safe consumption, and biologically break down waste matter into harmless components. **Corporate headquarters location:** This location. **Parent company:** Bayer. **Listed on:** New York Stock Exchange. **Stock exchange symbol:** BAY.

SYMS CORPORATION
One Syms Way, Secaucus NJ 07094. 201/902-9600. **Fax:** 201/902-0758. **Contact:** John Tyzbir, Personnel Director. **E-mail address:** hr@syms.com. **World Wide Web address:** http://www.syms.com. **Description:** Syms Corporation operates a chain of over 45 off-price apparel stores located throughout the Northeast, Midwest, Southeast, and Southwest. All stores offer men's tailored clothing; women's dresses, suits, and separates; and children's apparel. **Corporate headquarters location:** This location. **Operations at this facility include:** This location houses a retail location and a distribution center.

SYNAPTIC PHARMACEUTICAL CORPORATION
215 College Road, Paramus NJ 07652. 201/261-1331. **Contact:** Human Resources. **World Wide Web address:** http://www.synapticcorp.com. **Description:** Synaptic Pharmaceutical Corporation researches and develops pharmaceuticals. Founded in 1987. **NOTE:** For current job postings and on-line contact information, see the above Website. Part-time jobs are offered. **Positions advertised include:** Scientist. **Corporate headquarters location:** This location. **Operations at this facility include:** This location houses administrative offices and is not involved in the manufacturing process. **Listed on:** NASDAQ. **Stock exchange symbol:** SNAP. **Number of employees at this location:** 130.

SYNCSORT
50 Tice Boulevard, Woodcliff Lake NJ 07677. 201/930-8200. **Fax:** 201/930-8281. **Contact:** Human Resources. **World Wide Web address:** http://www.syncsort.com. **Description:** Develops operating systems software for businesses. **NOTE:** Submit resume online. **Positions advertised include:** Software Designer; Software Developer; Sales Representative.

TEAM STAFF, INC.
300 Atrium Drive, Somerset NJ 08873. 732/748-1700. **Toll-free phone:** 800/565-8303. **Fax:** 732/748-3220. **Contact:** Human Resources. **E-mail address:** peo@teamstaff.com. **World Wide Web address:** http://www.teamstaff.com. **Description:** A full-line provider of human resource management services to employers in a wide variety of industries. Services include professional employer organization (employee leasing) services, placement of temporary and permanent staffing, and payroll and payroll tax service preparation. **Corporate headquarters location:** This location.

TELCORDIA TECHNOLOGIES
One Telcordia Drive, Piscataway NJ 08854. 732/699-2000. **Contact:** Human Resources. **World Wide Web address:** http://www.telcordia.com. **Description:** Develops, provides, and maintains telecommunications information networking software, and professional services for businesses, governments, and telecommunications carriers. **Positions advertised include:** Applied Research; Business Processing Consultant; Corporate Marketing Communication; Contract Management; Systems Engineer; Accounting Representative; Human Resources Representative; Product Manager; Account Executive; Finance Representative; Applied Research Representative.

TEVA PHARMACEUTICALS USA
18-01 River Road, Fair Lawn NJ 07410. 201/703-2553. **Fax:** 201/703-9491. **Contact:** Human Resources. **World Wide Web address:** http://www.tevapharmusa.com. **Description:** Manufactures and markets generic pharmaceuticals. The company focuses on therapeutic medicines for the analgesic, cardiovascular, dermatological, and anti-inflammatory markets. **Corporate headquarters location:** This location. **Other area locations:** Elmwood Park NJ; Fairfield NJ; Paterson NJ; Waldwick NJ. **Other U.S. locations:** Mexico MO. **Number of employees nationwide:** 790.

L.P. THEBAULT COMPANY
249 Pomeroy Road, P.O. Box 169, Parsippany NJ 07054. 973/884-1300. **Toll-free phone:** 800/848-1702. **Contact:** Human Resources. **E-mail address:** jobs@thebault.com. **World Wide Web address:** http://www.thebault.com. **Description:** One of the largest commercial printing companies in the United States. The company specializes in the print-buying market, with projects ranging from annual reports to promotional pieces. **Positions advertised include:** Sales Executive. **Special programs:** Internships. **Corporate headquarters location:** This location. **Other U.S. locations:** Detroit MI; New York NY. **Subsidiaries include:** LPT Express Graphics. **Operations at this facility include:** Administration; Manufacturing; Sales. **Number of employees nationwide:** 400.

THERMO ELECTRIC COMPANY, INC.
109 North Fifth Street, Saddle Brook NJ 07663. 201/843-5800. **Fax:** 201/843-4568. **Contact:** Human Resources. **E-mail address:** info@te-direct.com. **World Wide Web address:** http://www.thermo-electric-direct.com. **Description:** An international leader in industrial temperature instrumentation. Thermo Electric Company, Inc. provides solutions for temperature control needs worldwide. Products include temperature sensors, instrumentation, and specialty wire and cable. **Corporate headquarters location:** This location. **Operations at this facility include:** Administration; Manufacturing; Research and Development; Sales; Service. **Listed on:** Privately held. **Number of employees at this location:** 200. **Number of employees nationwide:** 225.

THOMAS EDISON STATE COLLEGE
315 West State Street, Trenton NJ 08608. 609/984-1114. **Fax:** 609/984-1115. **Contact:** Human Resources. **E-mail address:** hr@tesc.edu. **World Wide Web address:** http://www.tesc.edu. **Description:** An adult education college offering associate's, bachelor's, and master's degree programs. **Positions advertised include:** Assistant Director of Financial Aide; Assistant To Prior Learning Assessment Specialist; Dean; Director of Learning Assessment; Information Center Representative; Program Assistant. **Corporate headquarters location:** This location.

THOMAS ELECTRONICS, INC.
100 Riverview Drive, Wayne NJ 07470. 973/696-5200. **Fax:** 973/696-8298. **Contact:** Personnel. **World Wide Web address:** http://www.thomaselectronics.com. **Description:** Manufactures cathode ray tubes and liquid crystal displays for use by military and industrial OEMs. **Corporate headquarters location:** This location.

THOMSON MEDICAL ECONOMICS COMPANY
5 Paragon Drive, Montvale NJ 07645. 201/358-7500. **Fax:** 201/722-2668. **Contact:** Human Resources. **E-mail address:** hr_postings@medec.com. **World Wide Web address:** http://www.medec.com. **Description:** Publishes medical books and journals. **Positions advertised include:** Human Resources Generalist; Program Manager; Customer Service Representative; Business Unit Advocate; Program Director; Marketing Director. **Special programs:** Internships. **Corporate headquarters location:** This location. **Other U.S. locations:** DC; IL; KS. **Operations at this facility include:** Administration; Divisional Headquarters; Research and Development; Sales; Service. **Number of employees at this location:** 425. **Number of employees nationwide:** 510.

TICONA
86-90 Morris Avenue, Summit NJ 07901. 908/598-4000. **Fax:** 908/598-4165. **Contact:** Human Resources. **World Wide Web address:** http://www.ticona.com. **Description:** Produces and markets chemicals and manufactured fibers for industrial and textile uses. **Parent company:** Hoechst Group.

TINNERMAN PALNUT ENGINEERED PRODUCTS
152 Glen Road, Mountainside NJ 07092. 908/233-3300. **Fax:** 908/233-6566. **Contact:** Human Resources Manager. **E-mail address:** careers@tinnermanpalnut.com. **World Wide Web address:** http://www.palnut.com. **Description:** Manufactures light- and heavy-duty single and multithread specialty fasteners. **Positions advertised include:** Sales Engineer; Manufacturing Engineer; Global Sourcing Analyst; Product Engineer. **Corporate headquarters location:** Brunswick OH.

TITAN GLOBAL TECHNOLOGIES, LTD.
85 Chestnut Ridge Road, P.O. Box 617, Montvale NJ 07645. 201/930-0300. **Contact:** Human Resources. **World Wide Web address:** http://www.titan-global.com. **Description:** Designs, manufactures, and installs monorail transportation systems. **Corporate headquarters location:** This location. **Operations at this facility include:** Administration; Research and Development.

TOYS 'R US
1 Geoffrey Way, Paramus NJ 07652. 201/262-7800. **Contact:** Director of Employment. **World Wide Web address:** http://www.toysrus.com. **Description:** One of the largest children's specialty retailers in the world. The company operates over 1,450 stores worldwide. Founded in 1948. **NOTE:** Entry-level positions are offered. **Special programs:** Training. **Corporate headquarters location:** This location. **Other U.S. locations:** Nationwide. **Subsidiaries include:** Babies 'R Us; Kids 'R Us. **Listed on:** New York Stock Exchange. **Stock exchange symbol:** TOY. **Annual sales/revenues:** More than $100 million. **Number of employees at this location:** 1,400. **Number of employees worldwide:** 94,000.

TRADER JOE'S
186 Columbia Turnpike, Florham Park NJ 07932. 973/514-1511. **Contact:** Human Resources, **E-mail address:** midatjobs@traderjoes.com. **World Wide Web address:** http://www.traderjoes.com. **Description:** A grocery store offering a variety of unique items and having a wide selection of fine wines. **Positions advertised include:** Grocery Store Supervisor. **Other area locations:** Marlton; Wayne; Westfield; Westwood.

TRANSTECHNOLOGY CORPORATION
150 Allen Road, Liberty Corner NJ 07938. 908/903-1600. **Contact:** Human Resources. **World Wide Web address:** http://www.transtechnology.com. **Description:** Designs, manufactures, sells, and distributes specialty fasteners. **Corporate headquarters location:** This location. **Subsidiaries include:** Breeze-Eastern (Union NJ) designs, develops, manufactures, and services sophisticated lifting and restraining products, principally helicopter rescue hoist and cargo hook systems, winches and hoists for aircraft and weapon systems, and aircraft cargo tie-down systems. Breeze Industrial Products (PA) manufactures a complete line of standard and specialty gear-driven band fasteners in high-grade stainless steel for use in highly-engineered applications. Industrial Retaining Ring (Irvington NJ) manufactures a variety of retaining rings made of carbon steel, stainless steel, and beryllium copper. The Palnut Company (Mountainside NJ) manufactures light- and heavy-duty single- and multithread specialty fasteners. The Seeger Group (Somerville NJ) manufactures retaining clips, circlips, spring pins, and similar components.

TRINITAS HOSPITAL
18-20 South Broad Street, Elizabeth NJ 07201. 908/994-5325. **Fax:** 908/527-0195. **Contact:** Human Resources. **World Wide Web address:** http://www.trinitashospital.org. **Description:** A hospital providing treatments for a variety of illnesses including cardiovascular diseases and cancer. **Positions advertised include:** Telephone Operator; Receptionist; Secretary; Lead Cashier; Registrar Trainee; Registrar; Insurance Bill Representative; Radiation Therapist; Van Driver; Diet Aide; Medical Technologist; Registered Nurse; Licensed Practical Nurse; Certified Nurses Aide; Occupational Therapist; Physical Therapist; Medical Technologist; Physicist; Mental Health Worker; Fitness Aide.

TROPICANA CASINO AND RESORT
2831 Brighton Avenue and the Boardwalk, Atlantic City NJ 08401. 609/340-4000. **Toll-free phone:** 800/843-8767. **Fax:** 609/340-4457. **Contact:** Donald Hoover, Director of Recruiting. **World Wide Web address:** http://www.tropicana.net. **Description:** A large casino and hotel that offers casino gaming, gourmet dining, hotel facilities, and an indoor amusement park. **Positions advertised include:** Security Officer; Poker Dealer; Slot Technician; Marketing Operation Supervisor; Beverage Server; Public Area Attendants; Public Area Manager; Front Desk Clerk; Cook; Food Services Attendant; Housekeeper; Hotel Cashier; Limo Dispatcher; Fleet Dispatcher; Valet Parking Attendant. **Special programs:** Internships. **Corporate headquarters location:** Phoenix AZ. **Other U.S. locations:** Las Vegas NV; Laughlin NV. **Parent company:** Aztar. **Operations at this facility include:** Administration; Service. **Number of employees at this location:** 5,000.

TRUMP HOTEL AND CASINO RESORTS
151 South Pennsylvania Avenue, Atlantic City NJ 08401. 609/441-6500. **Toll-free phone:** 877TRUMPJOB. **Fax:** 609/441-6067. **Contact:** Employment Office. **World Wide Web address:** http://www.trumpemployment.com. **Description:** Operates the Trump Marina, Trump's Taj Mahal, and Trump Plaza casino hotels. **NOTE:** All hiring for subsidiaries is done through this location. **Positions advertised include:** Banquet Server; Bar Porter; Beverage Meter Room Technician; Beverage Service Shift Manager; Bus Person; Cook; Food Server; Coin Bank Cashier; Security Officer; Slot Cashier; Compliance Accounting Clerk; Hotel Accounting Clerk; National Marketing Director; Staff Internal Auditor.

TRUST COMPANY BANK
35 Journal Square, Jersey City NJ 07306. 973/442-9131. **Toll-free phone:** 800/233-BANK. **Contact:** Human Resources. **E-mail address:** humanresources@tcofnj.com. **World Wide Web address:** http://www.tcofnj.com. **Description:** A bank serving New Jersey. **Company Slogan:** The bank with heart since 1896. **Positions advertised include:** Teller. **Office hours:** Monday – Friday, 8:00 a.m. – 5:30 p.m. **Listed on:** NASDAQ. **Stock Exchange Symbol:** TCNJ. **President:** Alan Wilzig.

TUSCAN DAIRY FARM
750 Union Avenue, Union NJ 07083. 908/686-1500. **Contact:** Human Resources. **Description:** Produces and distributes milk and related products throughout northern New Jersey and adjacent areas. **Corporate headquarters location:** This location.

U.S. CAN COMPANY
669 River Drive, Suite 340, Elmwood Park NJ 07407. 201/794-4441. **Contact:** Human Resources. **World Wide Web address:** http://www.uscanco.com. **Description:** Manufactures a wide range of steel container products. Principal clients include paint and ink manufacturers. **Corporate headquarters location:** Oak Brook IL. **Operations at this facility include:** Manufacturing.

U.S. DEPARTMENT OF TRANSPORTATION
FEDERAL AVIATION ADMINISTRATION (FAA)
FAA Technical Center, Atlantic City International Airport NJ 08405. 609/485-4000. **Contact:** Human Resources. **World Wide Web address:** http://www.faa.gov.

Description: The Federal Aviation Administration is responsible for the development and maintenance of air navigation and air traffic control systems for both civil and military aircraft, the security of airports and stability of aircraft structures, and the certification of airports that meet certain safety requirements. **Positions advertised include:** Secretary. **Operations at this facility include:** This location is a testing facility.

U.S. FILTER WALLACE & TIERNAN
1901 West Garden Road, Vineland NJ 08360. 856/507-9000. **Fax:** 856/507-4125. **Contact:** Personnel Administrator. **E-mail address:** hr@usfwt.com. **World Wide Web address:** http://www.usfwt.com. **Description:** A manufacturer of chlorinates for water and wastewater treatment. **Corporate headquarters location:** This location.

U.S. FOODSERVICE
2255 High Hill Road, Bridgeport NJ 08014. 856/467-4900. **Fax:** 856/467-7819. **Contact:** Personnel. **World Wide Web address:** http://www.usfoodservice.com. **Description:** An institutional food production and distribution company with clients in the restaurant and health care industries. **Corporate headquarters location:** Columbia MD. **Number of employees worldwide:** 12,000.

U.S. FOODSERVICE
300 Berkeley Drive, Swedesboro NJ 08085. 856/241-4000. **Contact:** Personnel. **World Wide Web address:** http://www.usfoodservice.com. **Description:** Processes and distributes a wide variety of frozen and cultured dairy products. **Office hours:** Monday - Friday, 8:00 a.m. - 5:00 p.m. **Corporate headquarters location:** Columbia MD. **Number of employees worldwide:** 12,000.

U.S. POSTAL SERVICE
46 Grove Street, Passaic NJ 07055. 973/779-0277. **Contact:** Human Resources. **World Wide Web address:** http://www.usps.com. **Description:** A post office for the city of Passaic.

U.S. POSTAL SERVICE
NEW JERSEY INTERNATIONAL BULK MAIL
80 County Road, Jersey City NJ 07097-9998. 201/714-6390. **Contact:** Human Resources. **Description:** A United States Post Office that processes foreign, military, and general bulk mail for distribution throughout the world.

USA DETERGENTS
1735 Jersey Avenue, North Brunswick NJ 08902. 732/828-1800. **Fax:** 732/246-7733. **Contact:** Human Resources. **Description:** Manufactures laundry detergents, household cleaners, and scented candles.

ULTICOM INC.
1020 Briggs Road, Mount Laurel NJ 08054. 856/787-2700. **Toll-free phone:** 888/295-6664. **Fax:** 856/866-2033. **Contact:** Human Resources. **World Wide Web address:** http://www.ulticom.com. **Description:** Develops Signal Ware brand telecommunications software and hardware. **Positions advertised include:** Product Manager; Marketing Communications Manager; Sales Administrator.

UNDERWOOD MEMORIAL HOSPITAL
509 North Broad Street, Woodbury NJ 08096. 856/845-0100. **Recorded jobline:** 856/853-2050. **Contact:** Personnel. **E-mail address:** humanresources@umhospital.org. **World Wide Web address:** http://www.umhospital.org. **Description:** A hospital.

UNIGENE LABORATORIES, INC.
110 Little Falls Road, Fairfield NJ 07004. 973/882-0860. **Fax:** 973/227-6088. **Contact:** Human Resources. **World Wide Web address:** http://www.unigene.com. **Description:** A biopharmaceutical research and manufacturing company that has developed a patented method to produce calcitonin, a leading drug for treating osteoporosis. Founded in 1980. **Corporate headquarters location:** This location. **Other U.S. locations:** Boonton NJ. **Listed on:** NASDAQ. **Stock exchange symbol:** UGNE. **President:** Warren P. Levy, Ph.D. **Annual sales/revenues:** $5 - $10 million. **Number of employees at this location:** 65.

UNILEVER FOODS
800 Sylvan Avenue, Englewood Cliffs NJ 07632. 201/567-8000. **Contact:** Personnel Administrator. **World Wide Web address:** http://www.unileverna.com. **Description:** An international consumer products firm manufacturing a wide range of soaps, toiletries, and foods. **Other U.S. locations:** Flemington NJ.

UNILEVER HOME & PERSONAL CARE USA
45 River Road, Edgewater NJ 07020. 201/943-7100. **Contact:** Human Resources. **World Wide Web address:** http://www.unilever.com. **Description:** Researches and develops household and personal care products. **Corporate headquarters location:** Greenwich CT. **Annual sales/revenues:** More than $100 million. **Number of employees at this location:** 500.

UNIMAC GRAPHICS
350 Michele Place, Carlstadt NJ 07072. 201/372-1000. **Fax:** 201/372-1241. **Contact:** Personnel. **E-mail address:** info@unimacgraphics.com. **World Wide Web address:** http://www.unimacgraphics.com. **Description:** Provides a full range of commercial printing services.

UNITED AIR LINES, INC.
Newark International Airport, Newark NJ 07114. 973/624-6925. **Toll-free phone:** 800/241-6522. **Contact:** Human Resources. **World Wide Web address:** http://www.ual.com. **Description:** An air carrier that provides transportation of people and goods through more than 1,100 daily scheduled flights at 100 airports in the United States, Canada, and Mexico. **NOTE:** Resumes should be sent to United Air Lines-WHQES, P.O. Box 66100, Chicago IL 60666. **Corporate headquarters location:** Elk Grove Township IL. **Parent company:** UAL, Inc. **Listed on:** New York Stock Exchange. **Stock exchange symbol:** UAL.

UNITED PARCEL SERVICE (UPS)
One Clover Place, Edison NJ 08837. **Toll-free phone:** 800/622-3593. **Contact:** Human Resources. **World Wide Web address:** http://www.upsjobs.com. **Description:** UPS provides package delivery services nationwide. **Positions advertised include:** Principal; Automotive Mechanic; Regional Account Manager. **Operations at this facility include:** This location is a package-handling center.

UNITED RETAIL GROUP, INC.
365 West Passaic Street, Rochelle Park NJ 07662. 201/845-0880. **Toll-free phone:** 800/963-2744. **Contact:** Human Resources Manager. **World Wide Web address:** http://www.unitedretail.com. **Description:** A leading nationwide specialty retailer of plus-size women's apparel and accessories. The company operates 502 stores in 36 states, principally under the names The Avenue and Sizes Unlimited. New/remodeled stores will bear the name Avenue Plus. Founded in 1987. **Positions advertised include:** Regional Sales Director; District Sales Manager; Store Manager; Assistant Manager; Sales Associate. **Corporate headquarters location:** This location. **Subsidiaries include:** United Retail Incorporated. **CEO:** Raphael Benaroya.

UNITED WATER RESOURCES, INC.
200 Old Hook Road, Harrington Park NJ 07640. 201/784-9434. **Fax:** 201/767-7142. **Contact:** Carol Ike, Recruiting Department. **E-mail address:** recruiting@unitedwater.com. **World Wide Web address:** http://www.unitedwater.com. **Description:** A holding company for regulated water utilities. **Subsidiaries include:** United Water New Jersey supplies water service to over 750,000 customers in 60 communities in Hudson County and Bergen County NJ.

UNITEDAUTO GROUP, INC.
One Harmon Plaza, 9th Floor, Union NJ 07087. 201/974-0869. **Contact:** Human Resources. **World Wide Web address:** http://www.unitedauto.com. **Description:** Operates car dealerships. **Corporate headquarters location:** This location. **Listed on:** New York Stock Exchange. **Stock exchange symbol:** UAG.

UNIVERSITY HOSPITAL
30 Bergen Street, Building 8, Newark NJ 07107. 973/972-0012. **Recorded jobline:** 973/972-6740. **Contact:** Human Resources. **World Wide Web address:** http://www.theuniversityhospital.com. **Description:** A 466-bed teaching hospital of the University of Medicine and Dentistry of New Jersey. **Positions advertised include:** Transport Customer Service; Principal Lab Assistant; Food Service Worker; Program Support Specialist; Research Associate; Patient Accounts Clerk; Research Teaching Specialist; Advanced Practical Nurse; Management Assistant; Case Management Coordinator.

URBAN LEAGUE OF HUDSON COUNTY
253 Martin Luther King Jr. Drive, Jersey City NJ 07305. 201/451-8888. **Contact:** Human Resources. **World Wide Web address:** http://www.urbanleaguehudsonnj.org. **Description:** A nonprofit organization that sponsors a variety of social programs including employment services and parenting programs.

VALLEY NATIONAL BANK
1455 Valley Road, Wayne NJ 07470. 973/696-4020. **Contact:** Peter Verbout, Director of Human Resources. **World Wide Web address:** http://www.valleynationalbank.com. **Description:** Operates a commercial bank offering a wide range of traditional banking services. **Positions advertised include:** Business Development Officer. **Corporate headquarters location:** This location. **Parent company:** Valley National Bancorp. **Operations at this facility include:** Administration.

VAN LEEUWEN
777 Alexander Road, Princeton NJ 08540. 609/580-0088. **Contact:** Human Resources. **World Wide Web address:** http://www.vanleeuwen.com. **Description:** Distributes pipes, valves, and fittings, serving both domestic and overseas customers. **NOTE:** If applying for a warehouse position, please contact Martin Curley, Operations Manager; for an office position, contact Jim Gallagher, Regional Manager. **Corporate headquarters location:** This location.

VENICE MAID FOODS, INC.
P.O. Box 1505, Vineland NJ 08362-1505. 856/691-2100. **Physical address:** 270 North Mill Road, Vineland NJ 08360. **Toll-free phone:** 800/257-7070.**Fax:** 856/696-1295. **Contact:** Human Resources. **World Wide Web address:** http://www.venicemaid.com. **Description:** One of the nation's largest food manufacturers for private brands. The company produces over 375 institutional and retail products. Founded in 1927. **NOTE:** Entry-level positions and second and third shifts are offered. **Operations at this facility include:** Administration; Manufacturing; Research and Development; Sales. **Parent company:** Hanover Foods Corporation. **Number of employees at this location:** 190.

VERIZON COMMUNICATIONS
540 Broad Street, Newark NJ 07101. 973/649-9900. **Contact:** Human Resources. **World Wide Web address:** http://www.verizon.com. **Description:** A full-service communications services provider. Verizon offers residential local and long distance telephone services and Internet access; wireless service plans, cellular phones, and data services; a full-line of business services including Internet access, data services, and telecommunications equipment and services; and government network solutions including Internet access, data services, telecommunications equipment and services, and enhanced communications services. **Positions advertised include:** Strategic Account Manager. **Corporate headquarters location:** New York NY. **Listed on:** New York Stock Exchange. **Stock exchange symbol:** VZ.

VICTORY/YSI INC.
118 Victory Road, P.O. Box 710, Springfield NJ 07081. 973/379-5900. **Fax:** 973/379-5982. **Contact:** Personnel. **E-mail address:** veco@ysi.com. **World Wide Web address:** http://www.ysi.com/veco. **Description:** Manufactures and distributes thermistors, varistors, and specialty temperature sensing assemblies. **Corporate headquarters location:** This location. **Parent company:** YSI Incorporated.

VILLAGE SUPERMARKET, INC.
733 Mountain Avenue, Springfield NJ 07081. 973/467-2200. **Contact:** John Jay Sumas, Personnel Director. **Description:** Operates 20 supermarkets, 17 of which are located in north central New Jersey and three of which are in eastern Pennsylvania. Village Supermarket offers traditional grocery, meat, produce, dairy, frozen food, bakery, and delicatessen departments, as well as health and beauty aids, housewares, stationery, and automotive and paint supplies. Six stores contain prescription pharmacy departments, and the company also owns and operates two retail package liquor stores and one variety store. **Corporate headquarters location:** This location. **Other area locations:** Bernardsville NJ; Chester NJ; Florham Park NJ; Livingston NJ; Morristown NJ; The Orchards NJ; Union NJ. **Parent company:** Wakefern Food Corporation.

VINELAND DEVELOPMENTAL CENTER
1676 East Landis Avenue, P.O. Box 1513, Vineland NJ 08362-1513. 856/696-6000. **Contact:** Human Resources. **Description:** A residential treatment facility for females who have mental retardation.

VISITING NURSE SERVICE SYSTEM, INC.
150 East 9th Avenue, P.O. Box 250, Runnemede NJ 08078. 856/939-9000. **Fax:** 856/939-9010. **Contact:** Human Resources. **E-mail address:** hr@vnss.com. **World Wide Web address:** http://www.vnss.com. **Description:** Provides home-based health care services including nursing, physical therapy, occupational therapy, speech pathology, nutritional therapy, mental health and enterostomal therapy, medical social services, and hospice care. **Other U.S. locations:** Nationwide.

VITAL SIGNS, INC.
20 Campus Road, Totowa NJ 07512. 973/790-1330. **Toll-free phone:** 800/932-0760. **Fax:** 973/790-4271. **Contact:** Human Resources. **E-mail address:** humanresources@vital-signs.com. **World Wide Web address:** http://www.vital-signs.com. **Description:** Manufactures disposable medical products such as face masks, manual resuscitators, anesthesia kits, and other respiratory-related critical care products. **Corporate headquarters location:** This location. **Operations at this facility include:** Administration; Manufacturing; Research and Development; Service. **Number of employees at this location:** 350. **Number of employees nationwide:** 450.

VOLVO CARS OF NORTH AMERICA, INC.
7 Volvo Drive, Rockleigh NJ 07647. 201/768-7300. **Contact:** Human Resources. **World Wide Web address:** http://www.volvo.com. **Description:** Supports the sale and service of Volvo automobiles and related parts and accessories for approximately 400 dealers. **Corporate headquarters location:** This location.

WACHOVIA BANK
One Maple Street, Summit NJ 07901. 908/277-7750. **Contact:** Human Resources. **World Wide Web address:** http://www.wachovia.com. **Description:** Wachovia is one of the nation's largest bank holding companies with subsidiaries that operate over 4,500 ATM's and over 1,330 full-service bank branches in the south Atlantic states. These subsidiaries provide retail banking, retail investment, and commercial banking services. The corporation provides other financial services including mortgage banking, home equity lending, leasing, insurance, and securities brokerage services from more than 222 branch locations. **Subsidiaries include:** CoreStates Financial Corporation; The Money Store, Inc. **Operations at this facility include:** Regional Headquarters. **Listed on:** New York Stock Exchange. **Stock exchange symbol:** WB. **Number of employees worldwide:** 87,000.

WACHOVIA BANK
220 South Broad Street, Woodbury NJ 08096. 856/845-3000. **Contact:** Human Resources Department. **World Wide Web address:** http://www.wachovia.com. **Description:** Wachovia is one of the nation's largest bank holding companies with subsidiaries that operate over 4,500 ATM's and over 1,330 full-service bank branches in the south Atlantic states. These subsidiaries provide retail banking, retail investment, and commercial banking services. The corporation provides other financial services including mortgage banking, home equity lending, leasing, insurance, and securities brokerage services from more than 222 branch locations. **Positions advertised include:** Financial Specialist; Bank Officer/Manager; Bank Teller; Branch Manager; Customer Service Representative; Loan Officer. **Listed on:** New York Stock Exchange. **Stock exchange symbol:** WB. **Number of employees at this location:** 800. **Number of employees worldwide:** 87,000.

WACHOVIA BANK
120 Albany Street Plaza, New Brunswick NJ 08901. 732/843-4200. **Contact:** Human Resources. **World Wide Web address:** http://www.wachovia.com. **Description:** Wachovia is one of the nation's largest bank holding companies with subsidiaries that operate over 4,500 ATM's, and over 1,330 full-service bank branches in the south Atlantic states. These subsidiaries provide retail banking, retail investment, and commercial banking services. The corporation provides other financial services including mortgage banking, home equity lending, leasing, insurance, and securities brokerage services from more than 222 branch locations. **Subsidiaries include:** CoreStates Financial Corporation; The Money Store, Inc. **Listed on:** New York Stock Exchange. **Positions advertised include:** Loss Specialist; Cons Credit Decision Maker. **Stock exchange symbol:** WB. **Number of employees worldwide:** 87,000.

WAKEFERN FOOD CORPORATION
600 York Street, Elizabeth NJ 07207. 908/527-3300. **Contact:** Human Resources. **World Wide Web address:** http://www.shoprite.com. **Description:** Operates a retailer-owned, nonprofit food cooperative. The company provides purchasing, warehousing, and distribution services to various grocery retailers throughout the metropolitan area. Many products are distributed under the Shop-Rite name. **Special programs:** Internships.

WASHINGTON MUTUAL HOME LOANS CENTER
One Garret Mountain Plaza, 3rd Floor, West Paterson NJ 07424. 973/881-2360. **Contact:** Human Resources. **World Wide Web address:** http://www.wamu.com. **Description:** A full-service mortgage banking company that originates, acquires, and services residential mortgage loans. **Positions advertised include:** Assistant Financial Center Manager; Mortgage Sales Assistant; Financial Center Manager. **Corporate headquarters location:** Pittsburgh PA. **Other U.S. locations:** KY; OH. **Parent company:** PNC Financial Services Group. **Operations at this facility include:** Regional Headquarters. **Listed on:** New York Stock Exchange. **Stock exchange symbol:** WM. **Number of employees nationwide:** 6,000.

WATSON PHARMACEUTICALS
360 Mount Kemble Avenue, Morristown NJ 07962. 973/355-8300. **Contact:** Human Resources. **World Wide Web address:** http://www.watsonpharm.com. **Description:** Manufactures generic drugs. **Positions advertised include:** Meeting & Travel Services Manager; System Analyst Developer; Associate Director Regulatory Affairs; Sales Automation Manager; Accountant; Administrative Assistant; Analytics & Sales Information Director. **Corporate headquarters location:** This location. **Listed on:** New York Stock Exchange. **Stock exchange symbol:** WPI. **Number of employees nationwide:** 1,500.

WEGMANS
724 Route 202 South, Bridgewater NJ, 08807. 908/243-9600. **Fax:** 609/243-0349. **Contact:** Human Resources. **E-mail address:** employment@wegmans.com. **World Wide Web Address:** http://www.wegmans.com. **Description:** Operates grocery stores in New York, Pennsylvania, New Jersey, and Virginia. **Positions advertised include:** Seafood Manager; Service Desk Associate; Producer Associate; Meat Associate; Deli Associate; Bakery Associate; Grocery Associate; Overnight Associate; Dairy Associate. **NOTE:** Mail resumes to: 29 Emmons Drive Suite 630, Princeton NJ, 03540, or apply online. **Number of employees nationwide:** 32,000.

WEICHERT REALTORS
1625 Route 10 East, Morris Plains NJ 07950. 973/267-7777. **Contact:** Human Resources. **World Wide Web address:** http://www.weichert.com. **Description:** A commercial real estate agency. **NOTE:** Jobseekers should specify a department of interest when applying. **Corporate headquarters location:** This location.

WEISS-AUG COMPANY INC.
P.O. Box 520, East Hanover NJ 07936. 973/887-7600. **Fax:** 973/887-6924. **Contact:** Mary Dante, Director of Personnel. **World Wide Web address:** http://www.weiss-aug.com. **Description:** Manufactures stampings, moldings, insert moldings, and assemblies. Industries served include automotive, telecommunications, electronic and electrical connector, medical, and several specialty markets. Services include design, tooling, production, and quality control. Founded in 1972. **NOTE:** Part-time jobs and second and third shifts are offered. **Special programs:** Apprenticeships; Training; Co-ops. **Corporate headquarters location:** This location. **Operations at this facility include:** Administration; Manufacturing; Regional Headquarters; Sales; Service. **Listed on:** Privately held. **President:** Dieter Weissenrieden. **Annual sales/revenues:** $21 - $50 million. **Number of employees at this location:** 200.

WESTERN UNION CORPORATION
436 Forest Avenue, Paramus NJ 07652. 201/261-4641. **Contact:** Personnel. **World Wide Web address:** http://www.westernunion.com. **Description:** Provides telecommunications systems and services to businesses, government agencies, and consumers. The company operates a nationwide communications network that includes Westar satellites in orbit. **Positions advertised include:** Account Executive.

WFPG 96.9 FM LITE ROCK
950 Tilton Road Suite 200, Northfield NJ 08225. 609/645-9797. **Contact:** Human Resources. **E-mail address:** lite@literock969.com. **World Wide Web address:** http://www.literock969.com. **Description:** Atlantic City area light rock station.

WHEATON USA
1101 Wheaton Avenue, Millville NJ 08332. 856/825-1400. **Contact:** Personnel. **World Wide Web address:** http://www.wheaton.com. **Description:** Manufactures glass and plastic tubes and containers used in the pharmaceutical and cosmetic industries. **Parent company:** Alcan Packaging.

WILENTZ, GOLDMAN & SPITZER
90 Woodbridge Center Drive, Suite 900, Woodbridge NJ 07095. 732/636-8000. **Contact:** Kimberly Curtis, Personnel Director. **E-mail address:** kcurtis@wilentz.com. **World Wide Web address:** http://www.newjerseylaw.com. **Description:** A law firm specializing in corporate, employment, environmental, and tax law.

JOHN WILEY & SONS, INC.
One Wiley Drive, Somerset NJ 08875. 732/469-4400. **Toll-free phone:** 800/225-5945. **Contact:** Human Resources. **World Wide Web address:** http://www.wiley.com. **Description:** This location houses the U.S. distribution center. Overall, John Wiley & Sons, Inc. is an international publishing house that publishes in four categories: Educational; Professional; Trade; and Scientific, Technical, and Medical (STM). In Educational, Wiley publishes textbooks and instructional packages for undergraduate and graduate students in the United States and internationally. Publishing programs focus on the physical and life sciences, mathematics, engineering, and accounting, with an increasing emphasis on economics, finance, business, MIS/CIS, and foreign languages. In Professional, Wiley publishes books and subscription products for lawyers, architects, accountants, engineers, and other professionals. In Trade, Wiley publishes nonfiction books in areas such as business, computers, science, and general interest. In STM, Wiley publishes approximately 260 scholarly and professional journals, as well as encyclopedias, other major reference works, and books for the research and academic communities. Major subject areas include chemistry, the life sciences, and technology. **Corporate headquarters location:** New York NY. **Other U.S. locations:** Colorado Springs CO. **Number of employees nationwide:** 1,200.

WILLIAM PATERSON UNIVERSITY OF NEW JERSEY
358 Hamburg Turnpike, College Hall-Room 150, Wayne NJ 07470. 973/720-2723. **Fax:** 973/720-2090. **Contact:** Human Resources. **World Wide Web address:** http://www.wpunj.edu. **Description:** A public university with approximately 9,000 students. Programs include liberal arts, nursing, sciences, English, history, and music. **Positions advertised include:** Assistant Director of Financial Aide; Assistant Director of Counsel; Associate Director Career Development Center; Director of the Honors College; Grant Writer; Accounting Manager.

WILSHIRE OIL COMPANY
921 Bergen Avenue, Jersey City NJ 07306. 201/420-2796. **Contact:** Human Resources. **Description:** A diversified corporation engaged in oil and gas exploration and production, real estate operations, and investment activities. **Corporate headquarters location:** This location.

WOMEN'S GOLF UNLIMITED
18 Gloria Lane, Fairfield NJ 07004. 973/227-7783. **Contact:** Personnel. **E-mail address:** eforce@wguinc.com. **World Wide Web address:** http://www.womensgolfunlimited.com. **Description:** Manufactures and markets a proprietary line of golf equipment including golf clubs, golf bags, golf balls, and accessories. The company markets these products under the trademarks Square Two, S2, PCX, XGR, ZCX, ONYX, Totally Matched, and Posiflow. Square Two Golf is also the exclusive golf club licensee of the LPGA. **Corporate headquarters location:** This location. **Listed on:** NASDAQ. **Stock exchange symbol:** GOLF.

WOODBINE DEVELOPMENTAL CENTER
1175 DeHirsch Avenue, Woodbine NJ 08270. 609/861-2164. **Contact:** Human Resources. **Description:** A residential treatment facility for adult males with mental disabilities.

WOODBRIDGE DEVELOPMENTAL CENTER
Rahway Avenue, P.O. Box 189, Woodbridge NJ 07001. 732/499-5525. **Contact:** Human Resources. **Description:** A residential treatment facility for adolescents and adults with developmental disabilities.

WORRALL COMMUNITY NEWSPAPERS INCORPORATED
P.O. Box 3109, 1291 Stuyvesant Avenue, Union NJ 07083. 908/686-7700. **Fax:** 908/686/4169. **World Wide Web address:** http://www.localsource.com. **Contact:** Human Resources. **Description:** A publisher of 18 weekly newspapers in Union and Essex Counties with a total circulation of over 40,000.

WYETH CORPORATION
5 Giralda Farms, Madison NJ 07940. 973/660-5000. **Contact:** Human Resources. **World Wide Web address:** http://www.wyeth.com. **Description:** Manufactures and markets prescription drugs and medical supplies, packaged medicines, food products, household products, and housewares. Each division operates through one or more of Wyeth Corporation's subsidiaries. Prescription Drugs and Medical Supplies operates through: Wyeth-Ayerst Laboratories (produces ethical pharmaceuticals, biologicals, nutritional products, over-the-counter antacids, vitamins, and sunburn remedies); Fort Dodge Animal Health (veterinary pharmaceuticals and biologicals); Sherwood Medical (medical devices, diagnostic instruments, test kits, and bacteria identification systems); and Corometrics Medical Systems (medical electronic instrumentation for obstetrics and neonatology). The Packaged Medicines segment operates through Whitehall-Robins Healthcare (produces analgesics, cold remedies, and other packaged medicines). The Food Products segment operates through American Home Foods (canned pasta, canned vegetables, specialty foods, mustard, and popcorn). The Household Products

and Housewares segment operates through: Boyle-Midway (cleaners, insecticides, air fresheners, waxes, polishes, and other items for home, appliance, and apparel care); Dupli-Color Products (touch-up, refinishing, and other car care and shop-use products); Ekco Products (food containers, commercial baking pans, industrial coatings, food-handling systems, foilware, and plasticware); Ekco Housewares (cookware, cutlery, kitchen tools, tableware and accessories, and padlocks); and Prestige Group (cookware, cutlery, kitchen tools, carpet sweepers, and pressure cookers). **Positions advertised include:** Administrative Assistant; Regional Manager; Clinical Research Associate; Executive Assistant; Manager of Information Management; Project Manager; Human Resources Assistant; Forecasting Analyst; Trade Promotion Manager; Category Manager. **Corporate headquarters location:** This location. **Number of employees worldwide:** 53,000.

XENOGEN BIOSCIENCES
5 Cedarbrook Drive, Cranbury NJ 08512. 609/860-0806. **Fax:** 609/860-8977. **Contact:** Human Resources. **E-mail address:** employment@xenogen.com. **World Wide Web address:** http://www.xenogen.com. **Description:** Offers real-time in vivo imaging services. Xenogen's in vivo biophotonic imaging system assists pharmaceutical companies in drug discovery and development. **Corporate headquarters location:** Alameda CA.

ZALLIE SUPERMARKETS
1230 Blackwood-Clementon Road, Clementon NJ 08021. 856/627-7585. **Contact:** Vice President of Human Resources. **Description:** This location houses administrative offices for the chain of six Shop-Rite supermarkets. **Corporate headquarters location:** This location.

A TO Z TIRE & BATTERY, INC.
P.O. Box 25603, Albuquerque NM 87125. 505/247-0134. **Physical address:** 613 Broadway Street, Albuquerque NM 87102. **Contact:** Jessica Henry. **E-mail address:** jhenry@atoztire.com. **World Wide Web address:** http://www.atoztire.com. **Description:** A retailer and wholesaler of batteries, tires, and automotive services with 21 locations in five states. Brand names include Firestone, National Tire, Carlisle, Dayton, and Titan. Founded in 1926. **NOTE:** Application available for download online. **Corporate headquarters location:** Amarillo TX. **Number of employees nationwide:** 200.

ASCG INCORPORATED
6501 Americas Parkway NE, Suite 400, Albuquerque NM 87110. 505/247-0294. **Fax:** 505/242-4845. **Contact:** Human Resources Manager. **E-mail address:** jobs@ascg.com. **World Wide Web address:** http://www.ascg.com. **Description:** An engineering firm specializing in hydrology, structural, airport design, civil, mechanical, and environmental disciplines. **Other U.S. locations:** AK; CO; ID; NM. **Corporate headquarters location:** Anchorage AK. **Parent company:** Arctic Slope Regional Corporation.

ADDUS HEALTHCARE
1100 Paseo De Onate, Suite C, Espanola NM 87532. 505/753-2284. **Contact:** Human Resources. **E-mail address:** personell@addus.com. **World Wide Web address:** http://www.addus.com. **Description:** Provides home health care services including respiratory therapy, skilled nursing, medical equipment, and rehabilitation from 127 offices in 23 states. Addus HealthCare also provides disease management programs and supplemental staffing. Founded in 1977. **NOTE:** Send resumes to: Addus Healthcare, Personnel, 2401 South Plum Grove Road, Palatine IL 60067 or to e-mail address. **Corporate headquarters location:** Palatine IL.

AEROTEK
6700 Jefferson, Building E, Albuquerque NM 87109. 505/342-5000. **Toll-free phone:** 800/298-0534. **Fax:** 505/342-5052. **Contact:** Angelo Turiciano. **E-mail address:** aturicia@aerotek.com. **World Wide Web address:** http://www.aerotek.com. **Description:** Provides commercial, industrial, and technical recruiting and staffing services. **Positions advertised include:** C programmer.

AIRPORT SHUTTLE
2200 Sunport Blvd SE, Albuquerque NM 87106. 505/765-1234. **Contact:** Human Resources Department. **Description:** An airport shuttle service providing transportation to and from airports across New Mexico.

AKAL SECURITY
7 Infinity Loop, Espanola NM 87532. 505/753-7832. **Toll-free phone:** 888/325-2527. **Fax:** 505/753-8689. **Contact:** Human Resources. **World Wide Web address:** http://www.akalsecurity.com. **Description:** Provides security services to businesses, private homes, and government facilities. Founded in 1980. **NOTE:** Search and apply for positions online. **Positions advertised include:** Security Officers; Court Security Officers. **Corporate headquarters:** This location. **Other area locations:** Albuquerque NM; Santa Fe NM. **Other U.S. locations:** Nationwide.

ALAMOGORDO PUBLIC SCHOOLS
P.O. Box 650, Alamogordo NM 88311. 505/439-3200. **Physical address:** 1211 Hawaii Ave, Alamogordo NM 88310. **Contact:** Susan Nichols, Human Resources Director. **E-mail address:** susann@aps4kids.org. **World Wide Web address:** http://www.aps4kids.org. **Description:** Administrative offices of the Alamogordo public school system, which includes nine elementary, three middle, one intermediate, one primary, and two high schools. **Positions advertised include:** High School Principal; Itinerant Gifted Teacher; Elementary Teacher; Special Education parent Liaison; Transition Specialist; Instructional Assistant; Speech/Language Pathologist; Food Worker; Substitutes.

ALBUQUERQUE ACADEMY
6400 Wyoming Boulevard NE, Albuquerque NM 87109-3899. 505/828-3200. **Fax:** 505/858-8809. **Contact:** Human Resources. **E-mail address:** humanresources@aa.edu. **World Wide Web address:** http://www.aa.edu. **Description:** A private school serving approximately 1,000 students from the sixth through twelfth grades. Founded in 1955. **NOTE:** For faculty positions contact: Andrew T. Watson, Head of School. For Staff Positions contact: Mary Jo Carrier, Head of Human Resources.

ALBUQUERQUE BOLT & FASTENER
2926 Second Street NW, Albuquerque NM 87107. 505/345-5869. **Contact:** Human Resources. **Description:** A retailer and wholesaler of bolts and fasteners for various industries.

ALBUQUERQUE, CITY OF
400 Marquette Northwest, 7th Floor, Suite 703, Albuquerque NM 87103. 505/768-3700. **Fax:** 505/768-3777. **Recorded jobline:** 505/768-4636. **Contact:** Patricia Miller, Director of Human Resources. **E-mail address:** pmiller@cabq.gov. **World Wide Web address:** http://www.cabq.gov. **Description:** The administrative offices of the city of Albuquerque. **NOTE:** Application forms are available online. **Positions advertised include:** HVAC Technician; Electrician; Vehicle Servicer; Telecommunication Operator; Office Assistant; Systems Analyst; Library Manager; Convention and Tourism Contracts Compliance Manager; Assistant City Clerk; Senior Engineer; Accountant; Security Officer. **Special Programs:** Part-Time, Temporary, and Summer/Seasonal work available.

ALBUQUERQUE INTERNATIONAL BALLOON FIESTA
4401 Alameda, Albuquerque NM 87113. 505/821-1000. **Fax:** 505/828-2887. **Contact:** Human Resources. **World Wide Web address:** http://www.balloonfiesta.com. **Description:** The Albuquerque International Balloon Fiesta is held annually during the first week of October. The Fiesta is one of the largest hot air ballooning events in the world with attendance reaching totals of over 1 million.

ALBUQUERQUE MANOR
P.O. Box 8448, Albuquerque NM 87198. 505/255-1717. **Physical address:** 500 Louisiana Boulevard, Albuquerque NM 87108. **Contact:** Human Resources Director. **E-mail address:** career@abqmanor.com. **World Wide Web address:** http://www.abqmanor.com. **Description:** One of New Mexico's largest long-term nursing care facilities. Albuquerque Manor has an on-site medical clinic, pharmacy, and rehabilitative care center for physical, occupational, speech, and respiratory therapy. A child development center, which is open to the general public, offers an Intergenerational Program. Founded in 1986. **Positions advertised include:** Nursing Manager; Registered Nurse; Licensed Practical Nurse; Certified Nurses Assistant; Housekeeper. **Internship information:** GN, GPN, and Social Services internships are available on a limited basis. **Listed on:** Privately held.

ALBUQUERQUE MARRIOTT HOTEL
2101 Louisiana Boulevard NE, Albuquerque NM 87110. 505/881-6800. **Contact:** Human Resources Department. **World Wide Web address:** http://www.marriott.com. **Description:** A 411-room, full-service hotel featuring 18 meeting rooms, an onsite restaurant, and a full business center. **Parent company:** Marriott International has more than 2,600 lodging properties, with operations and franchises in 50 states and 68 countries. The company operates lodging facilities and is the franchiser under 17 separate brand names, including: Marriott Hotels, Resorts, and Suites, Courtyard Inns, Residence Inn, Ritz-Carlton Hotels, and Fairfield Inn. **Number of employees worldwide:** 128,000.

ALBUQUERQUE PUBLIC SCHOOLS
725 University Boulevard Southeast, Albuquerque NM 87106. 505/842-3581. **Recorded jobline:** 505/842-3737. **Contact:** Human Resources. **World Wide Web address:** http://ww2.aps.edu. **Description:** The administrative offices of the Albuquerque school district, which includes 80 elementary, 26 middle, 10 alternative, and 11 high schools with more than 86,000 students. **Positions advertised include:** Coaches; Clerks; Counselors; Educational Assistants; Instructional Manager; Librarian; Principal; Secretaries; Plumbers; Speech Language Pathologists; Teachers.

ALBUQUERQUE PUBLISHING COMPANY
P.O. Drawer J-T, Albuquerque NM 87103. 505/823-7777. **Toll-free phone:** 800/641-3451. **Recorded jobline:** 505/823-3259. **Contact:** Human Resources. **E-mail address:** hr@abqpubco.com. **World Wide Web address:** http://www.abqpubco.com. **Description:** Publishes a daily morning newspaper, The *Albuquerque Journal,* and a daily evening newspaper, The *Albuquerque Tribune,* with a combined edition on Sundays. **Other area locations:** Santa Fe NM. **Employees at this location:** 650.

ALBUQUERQUE REGIONAL MEDICAL CENTER
601 Dr. Martin Luther King Jr. Avenue NE, Albuquerque NM 87102. 505/727-8000. **Contact:** Human Resources. **World Wide Web address:** http://www.lovelace.com. **Description:** A medical center with 254 beds. Part of Lovelace Sandia Health System. **NOTE:** Search and apply for positions online. **Positions advertised include:** Patient Transporter; Scheduler; Director, Case Management; Diet Technician; Nutrition Assistant; Housekeeping Supervisor; Phlebotomist; HIM Coding Manager; Mental Health Tech; RN; Charge Nurse; House Supervisor; Director of Pharmacy; Pharmacist. **Parent company:** Ardent Health Services.

ALBUQUERQUE TECHNICAL VOCATIONAL INSTITUTE
525 Buena Vista Drive SE, Albuquerque NM 87106. 505/224-4600. **Recorded jobline:** 505/224-4601. **Contact:** Karen Willis, Human Resources Director. **World Wide Web address:** http://www.tvi.cc.nm.us. **Description:** A two-year community college offering certificates, associate degrees, college transfer credit, and development education to approximately 20,000 students on four campuses. **NOTE:** Search and apply for positions online. **Positions advertised include:** Quality Assurance Analyst; Business Development Manager; Instructional Technician; Tutor; Security Dispatcher; Clerical Specialist; Instructor; Program Director; Security Officer.

ALLSUP'S CONVENIENCE STORES
P.O. Box 1907, 2112 Thornton Street, Clovis NM 88101. 505/769-2311. **Fax:** 505/769-2564. **Contact:** Human Resources. **Description:** Operates more than 300 convenience stores throughout New Mexico, Texas, and Oklahoma. Founded in 1956. Family owned and operated. **Positions advertised include:** Accountant. **Corporate headquarters location:** This location.

AMERICAN GENERAL FINANCE
2500 El Paseo Road, Suite B, Las Cruces NM 88001. 505/527-8539. **Fax:** 505/527-0653. **Contact:** Human Resources. **World Wide Web address:** http://www.agfinance.com. **Description:** One of the country's largest consumer finance companies, focusing on consumer lending, mortgages, home equity lines of credit, retail sales financing, and credit insurance. Operates more than 1400 branches in 44 states, Puerto Rico and the U.S. Virgin Islands. **NOTE:** Submit resume to local branch. **Positions advertised include:** Management Trainee; Customer Account Administrator; Customer Account Specialist. **Corporate headquarters location:** Evansville IN. **Parent company:** American General Corporation.

AMERICAN GYPSUM COMPANY
P.O. Box 90820, Albuquerque NM 87199-0820. 505/823-2022. **Physical address:** 7850 Jefferson North East, Suite 300, Albuquerque NM 87109. **Toll-free phone:** 800/545-6302. **Contact:** Ken White, Operations Administrator. **World Wide Web address:** http://www.americangypsum.com. **Description:** A two-plant operation that manufactures gypsum wallboard for the construction industry. **Corporate headquarters location:** This location. **Parent company:** Centex Construction Products, Inc. **Operations at this facility include:** Manufacturing; Regional Headquarters; Sales.

AMERICAN RED CROSS
192 Monroe NE, Albuquerque NM 87108. 505/265-8514. **Fax:** 505/265-5389. **Contact:** Chapter Manager. **E-mail address:** midriochapter@usa.redcross.org. **World Wide Web address:** http://www.redcrossalbq.org. **Description:** A humanitarian organization that aids disaster victims, gathers blood for crisis distribution, trains individuals to respond to emergencies, educates individuals on various diseases, and raises funds for other charitable establishments. **Positions advertised include:** PT Receptionist. **Other U.S. locations:** Nationwide.

AMERIWEST BUILDING SERVICE
P.O. Box 80086, Albuquerque NM 87198. 505/265-6636. **Contact:** Human Resources. **Description:** AmeriWest Building Service operates a maintenance and janitorial service.

AMREP SOUTHWEST INC.
333 Rio Rancho Drive NE, Rio Rancho NM 87124. 505/892-9200. **Fax:** 505/896-9180. **Contact:** Human Resources. **Description:** A construction and homebuilding company that is involved in both commercial and residential construction.

ARBY'S ROAST BEEF RESTAURANT
1711 Seventh Street, Las Vegas NM 87701. 505/425-5448. **Contact:** Manager. **World Wide Web address:** http://www.arbys.com. **Description:** One of the 3000 fast-food restaurants in the national chain. Founded in 1964. **NOTE:** Contact local restaurant for job information. **Other area locations:** Statewide.

ARMSTRONG CONSTRUCTION COMPANY
P.O. Box 1873, Roswell NM 88202. 505/623-6377. **Physical address:** 3300 South Sunset Avenue, Roswell NM 88201. **Contact:** Charles Yslas, Human Resources. **E-mail address:** info@armstrongcontruction.com. **World Wide Web address:** http://www.armstrongconstruction.com. **Description:** A contracting company

specializing in highway, heavy, and utility construction. Founded in 1922. **Other area locations:** Hobbs NM.

THE ASSOCIATED PRESS
5130 San Francisco Road NE, Suite A, Albuquerque NM 87109. 505/822-9022. **Contact:** Human Resources. **E-mail address:** apjobs@ap.org. **World Wide Web address:** http://www.ap.org. **Description:** An office of one of the largest independent news gathering organizations in the world. **NOTE:** Applicants interested in print, photo, or the internship program should apply to the nearest bureau. Applicants interested in radio or video should apply to Broadcast News Center, 1825 K St. NW, Washington DC 20006. All other inquires should be sent to AP Headquarters, 50 Rockefeller Plaza, New York NY 10020. 212/621-1500. **Special programs:** Internships. **Corporate headquarters location:** New York NY. **Other area locations:** Santa Fe NM. **International locations:** Worldwide.

AVONITE COMPANY
1945 Highway 304, Belen NM 87002. 505/864-3800. **Fax:** 505/864-7790. **Contact:** Human Resources Manager. **World Wide Web address:** http://www.avonite.com. **Description:** A fabricator of solid polyester acrylic counter tops and sinks for kitchen and bath use. **Positions advertised include:** Process Engineer. **Corporate headquarters location:** Florence KY.

AZTEC PUBLIC SCHOOLS
1118 West Aztec Boulevard, Aztec NM 87410. 505/334-9474. **Fax:** 505/334-9861. **Contact:** Dr. Linda Paul, Associate Superintendent. **E-mail address:** aztecpersonnel@yahoo.com. **World Wide Web address:** http://www.aztecschools.com. **Description:** Administrative office of the Aztec public school system. **NOTE:** Entry-level positions are offered. Search and apply for positions online. **Positions advertised include:** Technology Educational Assistant; Speech Language Pathologist; Head Football Coach; Physical Ed Teacher.

BANDELIER EFX
6808 Academy Parkway East NE, Suite B-1, Albuquerque NM 87109. 505/345-8021. **Fax:** 505/345-8023. **Contact:** Human Resources. **E-mail address:** allans@bandelier.com. **World Wide Web address:** http://www.bandelier.com. **Description:** A television production company that specializes in live-action and 30-second animated commercials.

BANK OF AMERICA
2720 North Prince Street, Clovis NM 88101. 505/769-2238. **Contact:** Human Resources Manager. **World Wide Web address:** http://www.bankofamerica.com. **Description:** Bank of America is a full-service banking and financial institution. The company operates through four business segments: Global Corporate and Investment Banking, Principal Investing and Asset Management, Commercial Banking, and Consumer Banking with 4,500 branches and 13,000 ATMs nationwide. **NOTE:** Search and apply for positions online. **Positions advertised include:** Teller Manager: PT Teller. **Corporate headquarters location:** Charlotte NC.

BANK OF AMERICA
4401 Central Avenue NE, Albuquerque NM 87108. 505/282-2531. **Contact:** Manager of Employment. **World Wide Web address:** http://www.bankofamerica.com. **Description:** Bank of America is a full-service banking and financial institution. The company operates through four business segments: Global Corporate and Investment Banking, Principal Investing and Asset Management, Commercial Banking, and Consumer Banking with 4,500 branches and 13,000 ATMs nationwide. **NOTE:** Search and apply for positions online. **Positions advertised include:** Teller; Operations Representative; Sales Officer. **Corporate headquarters location:** Charlotte NC.

BANK OF AMERICA
2601 Coors Boulevard NW, Albuquerque NM 87114. 505/839-2130. **Contact:** Human Resources. **World Wide Web address:** http://www.bankofamerica.com. **Description:** Bank of America is a full-service banking and financial institution. The company operates through four business segments: Global Corporate and Investment Banking, Principal Investing and Asset Management, Commercial Banking, and Consumer Banking with 4,500 branches and 13,000 ATMs nationwide. **NOTE:** Search and apply for positions online. **Positions advertised include:** Teller; Operations Representative; Sales Officer. **Corporate headquarters location:** Charlotte NC.

BANK OF AMERICA
5600 Lomas Boulevard NE, Albuquerque NM 87108. 505/282-2359. **Contact:** Manager. **World Wide Web address:** http://www.bankofamerica.com. **Description:** Bank of America is a full-service banking and financial institution. The company operates through four business segments: Global Corporate and Investment Banking, Principal Investing and Asset Management, Commercial Banking, and Consumer Banking with 4,500 branches and 13,000 ATMs nationwide. **NOTE:** Search and apply for positions online. **Positions advertised include:** Teller; Operations Representative; Sales Officer. **Corporate headquarters location:** Charlotte NC.

BANK OF AMERICA
2308 Cerrillos Road, Santa Fe NM 87505. 505/473-8875. **Contact:** Human Resources Manager. **World Wide Web address:** http://www.bankofamerica.com. **Description:** Bank of America is a full-service banking and financial institution. The company operates through four business segments: Global Corporate and Investment Banking, Principal Investing and Asset Management, Commercial Banking, and Consumer Banking with 4,500 branches and 13,000 ATMs nationwide. **NOTE:** Search and apply for positions online. **Positions advertised include:** Teller; Financial Advisor. **Corporate headquarters location:** Charlotte NC.

BANK OF AMERICA
2200 East Main Street, Farmington NM 87401. 505/599-3600. **Contact:** Human Resources Department. **World Wide Web address:** http://www.bankofamerica.com. **Description:** Bank of America is a full-service banking and financial institution. The company operates through four business segments: Global Corporate and Investment Banking, Principal Investing and Asset Management, Commercial Banking, and Consumer Banking with 4,500 branches and 13,000 ATMs nationwide. **NOTE:** Search and apply for positions online. **Positions advertised include:** Teller. **Corporate headquarters location:** Charlotte NC.

BARKER REALTY, INC.
530 South Guadalupe Street, Santa Fe NM 87501. 505/982-9836. **Contact:** David Barker, Broker/Owner. **E-mail address:** info@barkerrealtyinc.com. **World Wide Web address:** http://www.barkerrealtyinc.net. **Description:** A full-service realty firm specializing in commercial, residential, and income property, as well as vacant land. Coverage area includes Northern New Mexico.

BARNES & NOBLE BOOKSTORES
3701 Ellison Drive NW, Suite A, Albuquerque NM 87114. 505/792-4234. **Contact:** Manager. **World Wide Web address:** http://www.bn.com. **Description:** A bookstore chain operating nationwide. This location has a cafe in addition to its book departments. **Corporate headquarters location:** New York NY.

BELEN SCHOOL DISTRICT
520 North Main Street, Belen NM 87002. 505/966-1000. **Contact:** Ron Marquez, Human Resources. **E-mail address:** marquezr@belen.k12.nm.us. **World Wide Web address:** http://www.belen.k12.nm.us. **Description:** This location houses the administrative offices for the Belen school district, responsible for staffing at eight area schools including one high school, one middle school, and seven elementary schools. **NOTE:** Search for positions online. **Positions advertised include:** Truancy Home Liaison; Secretary; Special Education Assistants; Custodian.

BERNALILLO, COUNTY OF
One Civic Plaza NW, 4th Floor, Albuquerque NM 87102. 505/768-4010. **Recorded jobline:** 505/768-4887. **Contact:** Human Resources. **World Wide Web address:** http://www.bernco.gov. **Description:** Provides all types of city and county services including clerical, firefighting, park work, and custodial. **NOTE:** Application forms may be downloaded. If applying for more than one position, applicant must submit a separate application for each position. Valid New Mexico driver's license by employment date is required for all positions. Typing tests are required for all clerical positions. Call for a test appointment at 505/841-9300. **Positions advertised include:** Administrative Assistant; Avionics Mechanic; Building Maintenance Worker; Buyer; Clerical Specialist; Clinical Social Worker; Construction Inspector; Custodian; Network Engineer; Helicopter Pilot; Programmer Analyst; Security Specialist; Youth Program Officer.

BEST WESTERN ADOBE INN
1501 Will Rogers Drive, P.O. Drawer 410, Santa Rosa NM 88435. 505/472-3446. **Fax:** 505/472-5759. **Contact:** Human Resources Department. **World Wide Web address:** http://www.bestwestern.com. **Description:** A 58-room hotel featuring an outdoor heated pool, queen-sized beds in all rooms, a restaurant, and free parking.

BEST WESTERN ROYAL HOLIDAY
1903 West Highway 66, Gallup NM 87301. 505/722-4900. **Fax:** 505/863-9952. **Contact:** Human Resources. **World Wide Web address:** http://www.bestwestern.com. **Description:** A 50-room, full-service hotel featuring a pool, sauna, Jacuzzi, restaurant and lounge, and fitness center and spa. One of Best Western International's 4,000 hotels in 80 countries. **Corporate headquarters location:** Phoenix AZ.

BLOCKBUSTER VIDEO
4411 San Mateo NE, Suite A, Albuquerque NM 87109. 505/888-4777. **Fax:** 505/888-4172. **Contact:** Manager. **World Wide Web address:** http://www.blockbuster.com. **Description:** A video retail store operating as part of the nationwide chain. Blockbuster operates approximately 8,500 stores nationwide and in 28 countries. **NOTE:** Search and apply for positions online or at local store. **Corporate headquarters location:** Dallas TX. **Parent company:** Viacom Inc.

BLUE CROSS AND BLUE SHIELD OF NEW MEXICO
P.O. Box 27630, Albuquerque NM 87125. 505/291-3500. **Physical address:** 12800 Indian School Road NE, Albuquerque NM 87112. **Fax:** 505/816-5102. **Contact:** Human Resources. **E-mail address:** staffing@bcbsnm.com. **World Wide Web address:** http://www.bcbsnm.com. **Description:** A nonprofit health care insurance organization providing managed health care plans to both individuals and groups. Blue Cross Blue Shield offers Point-of-Service, individual health, managed indemnity, PPO, and HMO plans. **Positions advertised include:** Administrative Assistant; Administrative Services Coordinator; Clerk; Case Management Coordinator; Direct Sales Representative; Entry Operator; Major Accounts Sales Executive. **Number of employees at this location:** 800.

BORDER FOODS, INC.
451 Pioneer Place, Las Cruces NM 88005. 505/523-6959. **Contact:** Human Resources. **E-mail address:** border@borderfoodsinc.com. **World Wide Web address:** http://www.borderfoodsinc.com. **Description:** Processes green chili and jalapeno peppers. Border Foods primarily serves three market areas: Ingredient Sales, Food Service, and Retail/Private Label. Founded in 1974. **Corporate headquarters location:** Farmers Branch TX. **Listed on:** Privately held.

BORDER FOODS, INC.
4065 J Street Southeast, Deming NM 88030. 505/546-8863. **Fax:** 505/546-8676. **Contact:** Human Resources Manager. **E-mail address:** border@borderfoodsinc.com. **World Wide Web address:** http://www.borderfoodsinc.com. **Description:** Processes green chile and jalapeno peppers and manufactures an assortment of Mexican food products. Border Foods primarily serves three market areas: Ingredient Sales, Food Service, and Retail/Private Label. Founded in 1974. **NOTE:** Second and third shifts are offered. **Office hours:** Monday - Friday, 8:00 a.m. - 5:00 p.m. **Corporate headquarters location:** Farmers Branch TX. **Other area locations:** Las Cruces NM. **Operations at this facility include:** Administration; Manufacturing; Sales. **Listed on:** Privately held.

BUENO FOODS
P.O. Box 293, Albuquerque NM 87103-0293. 505/243-2722. **Contact:** Human Resources. **E-mail address:** info@buenofoods.com. **World Wide Web address:** http://www.buenofoods.com. **Description:** A producer, wholesaler, and retailer of frozen Mexican foods, family owned and operated.

BURN CONSTRUCTION COMPANY, INC.
P.O. Drawer 1869, Las Cruces NM 88004. 505/526-4421. **Contact:** Personnel Director. **Description:** A construction company that provides a variety of services including dirt work, paving, and concrete services. The company also works with utilities and water and wastewater treatment plants. **Corporate headquarters location:** This location.

CSR
RINKER PRESTRESS
P.O. Box 1609, Albuquerque NM 87103. 505/247-3725. **Physical address:** 2800 Second Street, Albuquerque NM 87102. **Contact:** Operations. **World Wide Web address:** http://www.rinker.com. **Description:** Manufactures and sells a variety of concrete products. Products include water transmission tubing; concrete pipe; and reinforced concrete pipe. **Corporate headquarters location:** Houston TX. **Parent company:** Rinker Materials Corporation.

CASA REAL NURSING FACILITY
1650 Galisteo Street, Santa Fe NM 87505. 505/984-8313. **Contact:** Office Manager. **Description:** A 118-room nursing facility. Casa Real has four different units including an Alzheimer's unit.

CHAVES, COUNTY OF
P.O. Box 1817, Roswell NM 88202-1817. 505/624-6557. **Physical address:** 401 North Main Street, Roswell NM 88201. **Fax:** 505/624-6631. **Contact:** Director of Personnel. **E-mail address:** hr@co.chaves.nm.us. **World Wide Web address:** http://co.chaves.nm.us. **Description:** The administrative offices of Chaves County. The office is responsible for staffing of all county departments. **Positions advertised include:** Dispatcher; Adult Detention Officers; Deputy Sheriff;

CHILD AND FAMILY SERVICES, INC. OF LEA COUNTY
950 East Snyder Street, Hobbs NM 88240. 505/397-7336. **Fax:** 505/393-0420. **Contact:** Laurie Pellissier, Human Resources Coordinator. **Description:** A nonprofit, full-service, Head Start preschool and daycare program that sponsors the summer food program in Lea County and coordinates with the Foster Grandparent Program. **NOTE:** Entry-level positions are offered. **Special programs:** Internships; Apprenticeships; Training. **Corporate headquarters location:** This location. **Other U.S. locations:** Lovington NM.

CIRCLE K CORPORATION
397 Alameda Boulevard NW, Albuquerque NM 87113. 505/898-6492. **Toll-free phone:** 800/861-8614. **Contact:** Store Manager. **Description:** Circle K Corporation operates approximately 2,000 convenience stores in 18 states and 4,000 international locations. **NOTE:** Apply for positions online. **Corporate headquarters location:** Phoenix AZ. **Parent company:** Alimentation Couche-Tard Inc., Quebec, Canada.

CITADEL COMMUNICATIONS CORPORATION
500 Fourth Street NW, Albuquerque NM 87102. 505/767-6700. **Fax:** 505/767-6767. **Contact:** Human Resources Representative. **E-mail address:** h.r@citcomm.com. **World Wide Web address:** http://www.citadelcommunications.com. **Description:** Owns and operates 150 FM and 63 AM radio stations in 44 markets located in 25 states. **Corporate headquarters location:** Las Vegas NV.

CITIBANK-CITICORP CREDIT SERVICES INC
9511 San Mateo Blvd NE, Albuquerque, NM 87113-2237. 505/797-6100. **Contact:** Human Resources. **World Wide Web address:** http://www.citi.com **Description:** Citibank delivers an array of banking, lending, and investment services to individual consumers, as well as to small businesses. Also offered are financial services products for small and large corporations, governments, and institutional and individual investors. **NOTE:** Search and apply for positions online.

CLIFFS AMUSEMENT PARK
4800 Osuna Road NE, Albuquerque NM 87109. 505/881-9373. **Contact:** Human Resources. **World Wide Web address:** http://www.cliffsamusementpark.com. **Description:** An amusement park.

CLOVIS, CITY OF
P.O. Box 760, Clovis NM 88102. 505/769-7827. **Contact:** Human Resources. **World Wide Web address:** http://www.cityofclovis.org. **Description:** The administrative offices for the city of Clovis. The office is responsible for staffing of all municipal departments. **NOTE:** Search for positions online. Application forms may be downloaded. **Positions advertised include:** Circulation Assistant-Library; Transit Driver; Dispatcher; Police Officer; Firefighter; Wastewater Treatment Plant Operator.

CLOVIS MUNICIPAL SCHOOLS
1009 Main Street, P.O. Box 19000, Clovis NM 88101 505/769-4300. **Fax:** 505/769-4333. **Contact:** Jim McDaniel, Assistant Superintendent for Personnel. **World Wide Web address:** http://www.cms.k12.nm.us. **Description:** Houses the administrative offices for the Clovis public school system, which serves 8,500 students with one high school, three junior high schools, 13 elementary schools, one pre-school, and one evening high school. **NOTE:** Part-time jobs are offered. Applications may be downloaded. **Positions advertised include:** Administrative Intern; Assistant Director of Finance; Swim Coach; Custodian; Elementary Principal; Secretary; Special Ed Teacher; Speech Language Pathologist.

COLDWELL BANKER TAYLOR & TAYLOR REALTORS
P.O. Box 344, Roswell NM 88202-0344. 505/622-1490. **Physical address:** 400 West Second Street, Roswell NM 88201. **Fax:** 505/622-1506. **Contact:** Paul Taylor III, Manager. **World Wide Web address:** http://www.coldwellbanker.com. **Description:** Coldwell Banker is one of the largest residential real estate companies in the United States and Canada. Coldwell Banker is also a leader in meeting Corporate America's specialized relocation needs on a worldwide basis. **Subsidiaries include**: Coldwell Banker Relocation Services provides corporate relocation services; Coldwell Banker Residential Affiliates, Inc. franchises select brokers who serve small to medium-sized markets.

COLDWELL BANKER TRAILS WEST
2000 Old Pecos Trail, Santa Fe NM 87505. 505/988-7285. **Contact:** Human Resources. **E-mail address:** broker@cbsantafe.com. **World Wide Web address:** http://www.cbsantafe.com. **Description:** Coldwell Banker is one of the largest residential real estate companies in the United States and Canada. Coldwell Banker is also a leader in meeting Corporate America's specialized relocation needs on a worldwide basis. **Corporate headquarters location:** Mission Viejo CA. **Subsidiaries include**: Coldwell Banker Relocation Services provides corporate relocation services; Coldwell Banker Residential Affiliates, Inc. franchises select brokers who serve small to medium-sized markets.

COLLEGE OF SANTA FE
1600 Saint Michael's Drive, Santa Fe NM 87505-7634. 505/473-6133. **Fax:** 505/473-6251. **Toll-free phone:** 800/456-2673**Contact:** Human Resources Manager. **E-mail address:** mskasik@csf.edu. **World Wide Web address:** http://www.csf.edu. **Description:** A four-year liberal arts college with 800 traditional and 1000 evening students. Operates degree-granting programs at Albuquerque campus. **Positions advertised include:** Collections Representative; Director of Evening and Weekend Degree Programs; Assistant Professor; Systems Administrator; Director of Facilities Management; Dean of Enrollment Management; VP for Development; Tenure-Track Faculty Position. **Number of employees at this location:** 200.

COLLEGE OF THE SOUTHWEST
6610 North Lovington Highway, Hobbs NM 88240. 505/392-6561. **Fax:** 505/392-6006. **Contact:** Dr. Marilyn Smith, Vice President. **World Wide Web address:** http://www.csw.edu. **Description:** An independent, Christian, five-year, liberal arts college that also offers master's programs in education and education administration. Approximately 700 students attend College of the Southwest.

COMMUNITY CABLE CHANNEL 27
P.O. Box 26206, Albuquerque NM 87125. 505/243-0027. **Contact:** Steve Ranieri, Executive Director. **E-mail address:** ccc27@quote-unquote.org. **World Wide Web address:** http://www.quote-unquote.org. **Description:** A public access television station.

COMPUTER ASSETS
805 South Riverside Drive, Espanola NM 87532. 877/448-9386. **Fax:** 505/753-6347. **Contact:** Human Resources. **World Wide Web address:** http://www.computerassets.com. **Description:** Provides communications solutions for state agencies and schools. **Positions advertised include:** Regional Account Manager; Data Network Installation Manager; Server Engineer; Network/Server Engineer; Data Network Technician; Software Specialist; Design Engineer; Internal Server Support Engineer.

COMPUTER MAINTENANCE CENTER
6105 Coronado Avenue NE, Albuquerque NM 87109. 505/345-8800. **Contact:** Owner. **Description:** Specializes in repairing a wide variety of computer hardware and software problems.

CONCENTRA MEDICAL CENTER
801 Encino Place, Suite E-12, Albuquerque NM 87102. 505/842-5151. **Contact:** Human Resources Department. **World Wide Web address:** http://www.concentra.com. **Description:** Performs drug screenings and physical examinations for corporations. Concentra Medical Center also provides medical services for individuals collecting workers' compensation. **Positions advertised include:** Staff Physician. **Corporate headquarters location:** Addison TX. **Other area locations:** Santa Fe NM. **Other U.S. locations:** Nationwide.

COOPER'S INC.
dba WESTERN WAREHOUSE
11205 Montgomery Boulevard NE, Albuquerque NM 87111-2648. 505/559-5000. **Toll-free phone:** 800/532-4888. **Fax:** 505/296-0278. **Contact:** Human Resources Administrator. **World Wide Web address:** http://www.westernwarehouse.com. **Description:** A retailer of western apparel. This location also hires seasonally. Founded in 1961. **NOTE:** Part-time jobs are offered. Search and apply for positions online. **Corporate headquarters location:** This location. **Other U.S. locations:** AZ; CA; CO. **Listed on:** Privately held.

COOPERATIVE EDUCATIONAL SERVICES
4216 Balloon Park Road NE, Albuquerque NM 87109. 505/344-5470. **Contact:** Human Resources Department. **World Wide Web address:** http://www.ces.org. **Description:** A cooperative of school districts that provide a variety of educational services. **NOTE:** Search and apply for positions in New Mexico public schools through website link to New Mexico Regional Education Applicant and Placement Program.

CREAMLAND DAIRIES INC.
P.O. Box 25067, Albuquerque NM 87125. 505/247-0721. **Physical address:** 501 Mountain Road, Albuquerque NM 87125. **Recorded jobline:** 505/248-9678. **Contact:** Linda Shores, Human Resources Director. **World Wide Web address:** http://www.creamland.com. **Description:** A regional dairy that produces milk, cream, and ice cream. **Positions advertised include:** Merchandiser; Cold Storage Warehouse; Lab Tech. **Corporate headquarters location:** This location. **Parent company:** Dean Foods.

CREATIVE PULTRUSIONS, INC.
16 East Earl Cummings Loop, Roswell NM 88201. 505/347-2226. **Contact:** Human Resources. **World Wide Web address:** http://www.pultrude.com. **Description:** A plastics manufacturer. Established in 1973. **NOTE:** Search for positions online. **Corporate headquarters location:** Alum Bank PA. **Number of employees at this location:** 35.

D.L.R. GROUP
5288 Daybreak Drive, Farmington NM 87401. 505/327-6068. **Contact:** George Trosky, Partner. **E-mail address:** Farmington@dlrgroup.com. **World Wide Web address:** http://www.dlrgroup.com. **Description:** An architectural design firm that specializes in educational, judicial, medical, and recreational projects with 15 offices nationwide. Founded in 1977. **Office hours:** Monday - Friday, 8:00 a.m. - 5:00 p.m. **Corporate headquarters location:** Omaha NE. **Number of employees nationwide:** 545.

DAVIS & ASSOCIATES
5312 Jaguar Drive, Santa Fe NM 87505. 505/473-2727. **Contact:** Human Resources. **Description:** A general contractor. Davis & Associates engages in both commercial and residential construction.

DAYS INN
1310 North Main Street, Roswell NM 88201. 505/623-4021. **Fax:** 505/623-0079. **Contact:** General Manager. **World Wide Web address:** http://www.daysinn.com. **Description:** A 62-room hotel featuring meeting and banquet facilities, outdoor pool, restaurant, and room service. There are 1900 hotels worldwide.

DEMING PUBLIC SCHOOL DISTRICT
501 West Florida Street, Deming NM 88030. 505/546-8841. **World Wide Web address:** http://www.demingps.org. **Contact:** Dr. Cory Butler, Director of Human Resources. **Description:** This location serves as the administrative offices of the Deming school system, which includes seven elementary, one middle, one middle high, and one high school. The office is responsible for staffing municipal schools. **Positions advertised include:** Elementary Health Assistant; Coach.

DOUBLETREE HOTEL
201 Marquette Boulevard NW, Albuquerque NM 87102. 505/247-3344. **Contact:** Human Resources. **World Wide Web address:** http://www.doubletreehotels.com. **Description:** A hotel and convention center. Chain includes 160 hotels. **NOTE:** Search and apply for positions online. **Parent company:** Hilton Hotels.

EASTERN NEW MEXICO MEDICAL CENTER
405 West Country Club Road, Roswell NM 88201. 505/622-8170. **Fax:** 505/624-8797. **Contact:** Beth Irizarry. **E-mail address:** beth_irizarry@hq.chs.net. **World Wide Web address:** http://www.enmmc.com. **Description:** A 162-bed acute-care hospital. **NOTE:** Direct Human Resource phone number is: 505/624-8789. **Positions Advertised Include:** Clinic RN/LPN; Coder; Controller; Patient Account Rep; Transcriptionist. **Number of employees at this location:** 630.

EASTERN NEW MEXICO UNIVERSITY
ENMU Station 21, 1500 South Avenue K, Portales NM 88130. 505/562-2115. **Contact:** Personnel Office. **World Wide Web address:** http://www.enmu.edu.

Description: A university offering 50 undergraduate major and several pre-professional programs as well as 19 masters degree programs. ENMU has campuses in Roswell and Ruidoso. **NOTE:** Support, professional, and administrative positions are listed online; call the Personnel Office at 505/562-2115 concerning faculty positions. **Positions advertised include:** Nurse; Admissions Manager; Webmaster; Broadcast Engineer; Coordinator for Prospective Students;

EASTERN NEW MEXICO UNIVERSITY-ROSWELL (ENMU)
P.O. Box 6000, Roswell NM 88202-6000. 505/624-7412. **Contact:** Human Resources. **World Wide Web address:** http://www.roswell.enmu.edu. **Description:** A branch location of Eastern New Mexico University. This location, which enrolls 4,000 students, is a community college offering programs in business, science, developmental studies, health, liberal arts, and vocational education. **Positions advertised include:** Financial Aid Data Specialist; Case Manager; Test Lab Supervisor.

ECONOMIC DEVELOPMENT DEPARTMENT
Joseph M. Montoya Building, P.O. Box 20003, Santa Fe NM 87504-5003. 505/827-0300. **Contact:** Human Resources Department. **World Wide Web address:** http://www.newmexicodevelopment.com. **Description:** A state-run agency that promotes economic development by providing services including publications and research for New Mexico businesses and communities as well as information for corporations considering a relocation or expansion to the state.

ECOSENSORS
P.O. Box 5960, Santa Fe NM 87502. 505/988-1421. **Fax:** 505/988-1315. **Contact:** Human Resources. **World Wide Web address:** http://www.ecosensors.com. **Description:** Eco Sensors manufactures low cost ozone and VOC instruments. **Positions advertised include:** Programmer.

ELASTIMOLD
6625 Bluewater Road NW, Albuquerque NM 87121. 505/836-2020. **Contact:** Human Resources Manager. **World Wide Web address:** http://www.tnb.com. **Description:** Produces high-voltage electrical connectors used by the utility industry for underground power distribution. The manufacturing process involves rubber injection molding. **Corporate headquarters location:** Chicago IL. **Other U.S. locations:** Hackettstown NJ. **Parent company:** Thomas & Betts Corporation.

ELDORADO HOTEL
309 West San Francisco Street, Santa Fe NM 87501. 505/988-4455. **Fax:** 505/995-4555. **Contact:** Personnel. **E-mail address:** rez@eldoradohotel.com. **World Wide Web address:** http://www.eldoradohotel.com. **Description:** A four-star/four-diamond, 219-room hotel. This location also hires seasonally. Founded in 1986. **NOTE:** Entry-level positions, part-time jobs, and second and third shifts are offered. **Positions advertised include:** Front Desk Agent; Garage Parking Valet; Hostperson/Cashier; Human Resources Clerk; Line Cook; Sales Administration Assistant; Banquet Manager; Catering Sales Manager; Executive Steward; Property Controller; Rooms Division Manager. **Special programs:** Summer Jobs. **Office hours:** Monday - Friday, 7:00 a.m. - 6:00 p.m. **Corporate headquarters location:** Englewood CO. **Parent company:** Richfield Hospitality Services.

EXAGEN DIAGNOSTICS
801 University Boulevard SE, Suite 209, Albuquerque NM 87106. 505/272-7966. **Fax:** 505/272-7965. **Contact:** Human Resources. **E-mail address:** info@exagendiagnostics.com. **World Wide Web address:** http://www.exagendiagnostics.com. **Description:** Exagen Diagnostics discovers, validates, and commercializes small sets of genomic markers, providing prognostic reagents for commercial laboratory testing and for pharmaceutical use in clinical trials. **Positions advertised include:** Molecular Biology Technician.

EXPLORA! SCIENCE CENTER & CHILDREN'S MUSEUM
1700 Mountain Road NW, Albuquerque NM 87104. 505/224-8300. **Contact:** Human Resources. **World Wide Web address:** http://www.explora.mus.nm.us. **Description:** An interactive science exhibit center that features 250 science, technology, and art exhibits.

EXPRESS SCRIPTS
4500 Alexander Boulevard NE, Albuquerque NM 87107. 505/345-8080. **Contact:** Human Resources. **Description:** A pharmacy benefit management company that serves 50 million members in managed care organizations, insurance carriers, third-party administrators, employers, and union-sponsored benefit plans through facilities in eight states and Canada. **NOTE:** Search and apply for positions online. **Listed on:** NASDAQ. **Stock exchange symbol:** ESRX. **Number of employees worldwide:** 7,500.

FARMINGTON DAILY TIMES
201 North Allen, Farmington NM 87401. 505/325-4545. **Contact:** Elecia Rothlisperger, Classified Advertising Manager. **World Wide Web address:** http://www.daily-times.com. **Description:** The *Farmington Daily Times* is a comprehensive newspaper that covers all towns in the San Juan Basin area. **Parent company:** Gannett Co.

FARMINGTON MUNICIPAL SCHOOL DISTRICT
2001 North Dustin, P.O. Box 5850, Farmington NM 87401. 505/324-9840. **Contact:** Bill Walz, Human Resources. **World Wide Web address:** http://www.fms.k12.nm.us. **Description:** The administrative offices of the Farmington school system, which includes 11 elementary, four middle, and three high schools. The office is responsible for staffing at all municipal schools. **NOTE:** Search and apply for positions online. **Positions advertised include:** Speech Language Pathologist; Indian Education Counselor; Spanish Bilingual Instructor; Coach; Secretary.

FIRESTONE TIRE & SERVICE CENTER
4250 Cerrillos Road, Santa Fe NM 87505. 505/438-0605. **Contact:** Manager. **Description:** One location in a chain of tire and automotive service centers.

FIRST STATE BANCORPORATION
8100 Lang Avenue NE, Albuquerque NM 87109. 505/241-7500. **Contact:** Teresa Gabel, Human Resources. **E-mail address:** tgabel@fsbnm.com. **World Wide Web address:** http://www.fsbnm.com. **Description:** A bank holding company, with offices in New Mexico, Utah, and Colorado.

FRENCH & FRENCH FINE PROPERTIES, INC.
231 Washington Avenue, Santa Fe NM 87501. 505/988-8088. **Fax:** 505/984-5191. **Contact:** Linda Varela, Office Manager. **World Wide Web address:** http://www.french-french.com. **Description:** A real estate agency.

FURR'S SUPERMARKET
Big Rock Shopping Center, Espanola NM 87532. 505/753-7333. **Contact:** Human Resources. **Description:** Operates a supermarket chain. Each location also has a video rental department, a floral department, and a pharmacy. **Other U.S. locations:** TX.

FURR'S SUPERMARKET
10701 Coors Boulevard NW, Albuquerque NM 87121. 505/899-3331. **Contact:** Human Resources Department. **Description:** One location of the supermarket chain. Each of the Furr's Supermarket locations also has a video rental department, a floral department, and a pharmacy. **Other U.S. locations:** TX.

GCR TRUCK TIRE CENTERS, INC.
1912 Second Street NW, Albuquerque NM 87102. 505/243-2876. **Contact:** Store Manager. **World Wide Web address:** http://www.gcrtires.com. **Description:** A nationwide commercial truck tire company catering to the commercial truck industry. **Corporate headquarters location:** Austin TX.

GALLUP INDEPENDENT
P.O. Box 1210, Gallup NM 87305. 505/863-6811. **Contact:** Bob Zollinger, Publisher. **World Wide Web address:** http://www.gallupindependent.com. **Description:** Publishes a daily newspaper with a circulation of 18,000.

GALLUP-McKINLEY COUNTY PUBLIC SCHOOLS
P.O. Box 1318, Gallup NM 87305-1318. 505/722-7711. **Physical address:** 700 S, Boardman Avenue, Gallup NM 87305. **Toll-free phone:** 800/842-5587. **Fax:** 505/722-9630. **Recorded jobline:** 800/842-5587. **Contact:** Ethan Manuelito, Director of Personnel. **World Wide Web address:** http://www.gmcs.k12.nm.us. **Description:** A public school district serving 14,500 students in grades K-12 in northwestern New Mexico. **NOTE:** Resumes must be in regards to a specific position. Search for positions online. **Positions advertised include:** Principal; Special Education Director; Food Services Director; Assistant Principal; Social Worker; Office Assistant; Educational Interpreter; Nurse; Teacher; Counselor; Coach; Librarian.

THE GARDNER-ZEMKE COMPANY
6100 Indian School Road, Albuquerque NM 87110. 505/881-0555. **Fax:** 505/884-2191. **Contact:** Nancy Reisbeck, Human Resources Manager. **Wide Web address:** http://www.gardnerzemke.com. **Description:** An electrical and mechanical contractor for commercial buildings. **Corporate headquarters location:** This location.

GARDUNO'S OF SANTA FE
130 Lincoln Avenue, Santa Fe NM 87501. 505/983-9797. **Contact:** Manager. **E-mail address:** charlotte@ gardunosrestaurants.com. **World Wide Web address:** http://www.gardunosrestaurants.com. **Description:** One location in a chain of 14 Mexican restaurants in New Mexico, Arizona, and Nevada. **NOTE:** Apply at restaurants between two and four PM, Monday through Thursday. **Corporate headquarters:** Albuquerque NM.

GENZYME GENETICS
2000 Vivigen Way, Santa Fe NM 87505. 505/438-1111. **Contact:** Priscilla Ornelas, Human Resources. **World Wide Web address:** http://www.genzyme.com/genetics. **Description:** A diagnostic laboratory specializing in prenatal and oncology testing as well as prenatal genetic counseling services. **NOTE:** Search and apply for positions online. **Positions advertised include:** Pathologist. **Other U.S. locations:** Nationwide. **Parent company:** Genzyme Corporation. **Number of employees nationwide:** 700.

GILMORE, GANNAWAY, ANDREWS, SMITH & COMPANY
P.O. Drawer 1517, Roswell NM 88202-1517. 505/622-5200. **Physical address:** 2724 Wilshire Boulevard, Roswell NM 88201. **Toll-free phone:** 800/748-3662. **Toll-free phone:** 800/748-3662. **Fax:** 505/622-5206. **Contact:** Office Manager. **World Wide Web address:** http://www.ggas.com. **Description:** A certified public accounting firm.

GLORIETA CONFERENCE CENTER
P.O. Box 8, Glorieta NM 87535. 505/757-6161. **Contact:** Administrative Services. **World Wide Web address:** http://www.lifeway.com/glorieta/. **Description:** A full-service conference center that provides accommodations for up to 2,000 guests.

GOODRICH CORPORATION OPTICAL & SPACE SYSTEMS
6600 Gulton Court NE, Albuquerque NM 87109. 505/345-9031. **Fax:** 505/344-9879. **Contact:** Human Resources. **World Wide Web address:** http://www.oss.goodrich.com. **Description:** Produces aerospace telemetry equipment and aerospace instrumentation. **NOTE:** Search and apply for positions online. **Positions advertised include:** Parts/Component Engineer. **Corporate headquarters location:** Charlotte NC.

GOODWILL INDUSTRIES OF NEW MEXICO
5000 San Mateo NE, Albuquerque NM 87109. 505/881-6401. **Fax:** 505/884-3157. **Contact:** Human Resources Manager. **World Wide Web address:** http://www.goodwillnm.org. **Description:** Besides operating 1,400 thrift stores nationwide, Goodwill is a nonprofit provider of employment training for the disabled and the poor. Goodwill found work for more than 100,000 jobseekers between 1990 and 1995.

GREAT RIVER TECHNOLOGY
6121 Indian School Road NE, Suite 220, Albuquerque NM 87110. 505/881-6262. **Contact:** Human Resources. **E-mail address:** jalexand@greatrivertech.com. **World Wide Web address:** http://www.greatrivertech.com. **Description:** Specializes in high performance digital video solutions for aerospace and the military. **Positions advertised include:** marketing manager.

HALL MACHINE & WELDING COMPANY
102 West Mermod, Carlsbad NM 88220. 505/887-1143. **Contact:** Human Resources. **World Wide Web address:** http://www.hallmachine.com. **Description:** A machining company involved in steel fabrication and industrial supplies. Founded in 1928. **NOTE:** Employment application available online.

HILTON LAS CRUCES
705 South Telshor Boulevard, Las Cruces NM 88011. 505/522-4300. **Contact:** Human Resources. **World Wide Web address:** http://www.hilton.com. **Description:** An independent franchise, Hilton Las Cruces is a luxury hotel located near the White Sands National Monument. The hotel offers exercise facilities, a Jacuzzi, and a pool. **NOTE:** Entry-level positions and second and third shifts are offered. **Special programs:** Internships. **Corporate headquarters location:** Albuquerque NM. **Other U.S. locations:** Nationwide. **International locations:** Worldwide. **Parent company:** American Property. **Operations at this facility include:** Divisional Headquarters; Regional Headquarters.

HINKLE, HENSLEY, SHANOR & MARTIN
P.O. Box 10, Roswell NM 88202. 505/622-6510. **Fax:** 505/623-9332. **Physical address:** 400 Penn Plaza, Suite 700, Roswell NM 88201. **Contact:** Office Manager. **Description:** A law firm specializing in a wide range of areas including oil and gas, and probate law.

HOBBS HEALTHCARE CENTER
5715 North Lovington Highway, Hobbs NM 88240-9131. 505/392-6845. **Contact:** Human Resources Department. **Description:** A 118-bed nursing home providing both short- and long-term care for elderly residents.

HOLIDAY INN
4048 Cerrillos Road, Santa Fe NM 87501. 505/473-4646. **Contact:** Human Resources Department. **E-mail address:** gmsfe@lodgian.com. **World Wide Web address:** http://www.holiday-inn.com. **Description:** A 116-room, 14-suite hotel with dining room and swimming pool available. **Corporate headquarters location:** Atlanta GA. **Other U.S. locations:** Nationwide. **International locations:** Worldwide.

HOLIDAY INN MOUNTAIN VIEW
2020 Menaul Boulevard, Albuquerque NM 87107. 505/884-2511. **Fax:** 505/881-4806. **Contact:** Human Resources. **E-mail address:** hi-albuquerque-mtnvw@ichotelsgroup.com. **World Wide Web address:** http://www.holiday-inn.com. **Description:** A 363-room hotel. **NOTE:** Entry-level positions are offered. **Corporate headquarters location:** Atlanta GA. **Other U.S. locations:** Nationwide. **International locations:** Worldwide.

HOLMAN'S
6201 Jefferson Street NE, Albuquerque NM 87109. **Contact:** Gretchen Knapp. **E-mail address:** jobs@holmans.com. **World Wide Web address:** http://www.holmans.com. **Description:** Provides advanced solution-oriented technologies for professionals in the fields of GIS, engineering, surveying, construction, government, education, and business. **Positions advertised include:** Cad/Survey Sales Coordinator; Cad/Survey Technical Support Specialist; Order Fulfillment Specialist.

HOLSUM INC.
P.O. Box 2527, Roswell NM 88202-2527. 505/622-7163. **Physical address:** 723 North Main Street, Roswell NM 88201. **Contact:** Human Resources Department. **Description:** Holsum produces wholesale baked goods. **Corporate headquarters location:** This location.

HONEYWELL
8500 Bluewater Road NW, Albuquerque NM 87101. 505/844-2887. **Contact:** Human Resources. **World Wide Web address:** http://www.honeywell.com. **Description:** Honeywell is engaged in the research, development, manufacture, and sale of aerospace products and services; control technologies for buildings, homes, and industry; automotive products; power generation systems; specialty chemicals; fibers; plastics and advanced materials. **Positions advertised include:** Mission Commander; Senior or Principal Engineer; Engineer. **Operations at this facility include:** This location builds heating and lighting controls and thermostats for commercial applications. **Corporate headquarters location:** Morris Township NJ. **Listed on:** New York Stock Exchange. **Stock exchange symbol:** HON. **Number of employees worldwide:** 100,000.

HONEYWELL
DEFENSE AVIONICS SYSTEMS DIVISION
9201 San Mateo Boulevard NE, Albuquerque NM 87113. 505/828-5000. **Contact:** Human Resources. **World Wide Web address:** http://www.honeywell.com. **Description:** Honeywell is engaged in the research, development, manufacture, and sale of aerospace products and services; control technologies for buildings, homes, and industry; automotive products; power generation systems; specialty chemicals; fibers; plastics and advanced materials. **Positions advertised include:** Mission Commander; Senior or Principal Engineer; Engineer. **Operations at this facility include:** This location manufactures search, detection, navigation, guidance, aeronautical, and nautical systems and instruments. **Corporate headquarters location:** Morris Township NJ. **Listed on:** New York Stock Exchange. **Stock exchange symbol:** HON. **Number of employees worldwide:** 100,000.

HORACE NISSAN & HYUNDAI INC.
4300 East Main Street, Farmington NM 87402. 505/327-0366. **Fax:** 505/327-0879. **Contact:** Owner/Manager. **Description:** A new and used car dealership.

HOTEL LORETTO
211 Old Santa Fe Trail, Santa Fe NM 87501. 505/988-5531. **Fax:** 505/984-7961. **Contact:** Donna Weiss, Director of Human Resources. **E-mail address:** dweiss@hotelloretto.com. **World Wide Web address:** http://www.hotelloretto.com. **Description:** A 140-room, full-service hotel located in historic Santa Fe. Founded in 1996. **NOTE:** Entry-level positions are offered. **Positions advertised include:** Conference Services Manager; Line Cook; Host Person; Busperson; Guest Service Agent; Reservation Sales Agent; Sales Manager. **Corporate headquarters location:** Seattle WA. **Other U.S. locations:** Scottsdale AZ; Daytona FL; Dallas TX. **Parent company:** Noble House. **Listed on:** Privately held.

HYATT REGENCY ALBUQUERQUE HOTEL
330 Tijeras Avenue NW, Albuquerque NM 87102. 505/842-1234. **Contact:** Human Resources Director. **World Wide Web address:** http://www.hyatt.com. **Description:** Operates a 395-room luxury hotel with complete dining and entertainment facilities. Hyatt Regency Albuquerque Hotel is part of the international hospitality firm that operates hotels and recreational facilities throughout the world. **NOTE:** Apply online.

IBM CORPORATION
2155 Louisiana Boulevard NE, 10th Floor, Albuquerque NM 87110. **Toll-free phone:** 800/426-4968. **Recorded jobline:** 800/964-4473. **Contact:** IBM Staffing Services. **World Wide Web address:** http://www.ibm.com. **Description:** A developer, manufacturer, and marketer of advanced information processing products including computers and microelectronic technology, software, networking systems, and information technology-related services. **NOTE:** Search and apply for positions online. **Positions advertised include:** Systems Service Representative. **Corporate headquarters location:** Armonk NY. **Other area locations:** Farmington NM; Santa Fe NM. **Subsidiaries include:** IBM Credit Corporation; IBM Instruments, Inc.; IBM World Trade Corporation.

IMC KALIUM
P.O. Box 71, Carlsbad NM 88220. 505/887-2871. **Physical address:** 1361 Potash Mine Road, Carlsbad NM 88220. **Contact:** Human Resources. **E-mail address:** rfgroff@imcglobal.com. **World Wide Web address:** http://www.imcglobal.com. **Description:** IMC Kalium and its subsidiaries produce oil, natural gas, sulfur deposits, and uranium oxide, a chemical that is used in nuclear power plant fuel. **Corporate headquarters location:** Lake Forest IL. **Operations at this facility include:** The production of phosphate rock and related surface mining activities.

INSTITUTE FOR ENGINEERING RESEARCH AND APPLICATIONS
901 University Boulevard SE, Albuquerque NM 87106. 505/272-7200. **Fax:** 505/272-7203. **Contact:** Human Resources Manager. **World Wide Web address:** http://iera.nmt.edu. **Description:** IERA is a nonprofit, interdisciplinary university contract research center and part of the Research & Economic Development Division of the New Mexico Institute of Mining and Technology (aka New Mexico Tech)., IERA's areas of expertise include the environment, power and energy, and homeland defense. **NOTE:** Employment opportunities are posted online.

INTEL CORPORATION
4100 Sara Road, Rio Rancho NM 87124. 505/893-7000. **Contact:** Human Resources. **World Wide Web address:** http://www.intel.com. **Description:** Intel is one of the largest semiconductor manufacturers in the world. Other operations include supercomputers; embedded control chips and flash memories; video technology software; multimedia hardware; personal computer enhancement products; and designing, manufacturing, and marketing microcomputer components, modules, and systems. **NOTE:** Search and apply for positions online. **Positions advertised include:** Process/Yield/Assembly/Test Engineer. **Other U.S. locations:** Nationwide. **Operations at this facility include:** This location manufactures microchips. **Number of employees at this location:** 5,200. **Number of employees worldwide:** 80,000.

INTROBOTICS CORPORATION
4208 Balloon Park Road NE, Albuquerque NM 87109. 505/345-7785. **Fax:** 505/792-8508. **Contact:** Human Resources. **E-mail address:** info@introbotics.com. **World Wide Web address:** http://www.introbotics.com. **Description:** Provides controlled impedance testing research and a leading supplier of testing equipment and services to the circuit board industry. **Positions advertised include:** electromechanical technician.

ISLETA CASINO & RESORT
11000 Broadway SE, Albuquerque NM 87105. 505/724-3907. **Contact:** Georgia Quintana, Personnel Manager. **World Wide Web address:** http://www.isletacasinoresort.com. **Description:** A gambling casino featuring video gaming, poker, keno, and other games. **NOTE:** Application form may be downloaded. **Positions advertised include:** Count Manager; Beverage Server; Buffet Attendant; Buffet Cook; Hostess: Transportation Lead; Valet Attendant; Chip Runner; Dealer; Delivery Clerk; Floor Technician; Change Clerk; Agent; Floor Supervisor; Pit Clerk.

JAYNES CORPORATION
P.O. Box 26841, Albuquerque NM 87125. 505/345-8591. **Physical address:** 2906 Broadway North East, Albuquerque NM 807107. **Contact:** Human Resources. **E-mail address:** info@jaynescorp.com. **World Wide Web address:** http://www.jaynescorp.com. **Description:** A construction services company with nearly 50 years of experience offering design and building, construction management, and expertise in concrete. Privately owned since 1946. **NOTE:** Search for positions online.

EDWARD JONES
One Grand Avenue Plaza, Suite 1, Roswell NM 88201. 505/624-2963. **Contact:** Human Resources. **World Wide Web address:** http://www.edwardjones.com. **Description:** A brokerage firm. **NOTE:** Internships and co-ops available. Submit resume or application online. **Corporate headquarters location:** St. Louis Mo. **Other U.S. locations:** Nationwide. **International locations:** Worldwide.

KCHF-TV 11
216 TV West Frontage Road, Santa Fe NM 87505. 505/473-1111. **Contact:** Mary Kay Gonzales, Production Manager. **World Wide Web address:** http://www.kchf.com. **Description:** An independent Christian television station associated with CBN. **Parent company:** Son Broadcasting.

KFC
2424 North Main Street, Las Cruces NM 88001-1135. 505/523-0662. **Contact:** Manager. **World Wide Web address:** http://www.kfc.com. **Description:** A worldwide fast-food chain specializing in chicken. **NOTE:** Search and apply for positions at http://www.yumcareers.com. **Parent company:** Yum! Brands.

KNME-TV
1130 University Boulevard NE, Albuquerque NM 87131. 505/277-2121. **Fax:** 505/277-2191. **Recorded jobline:** 505/272-5627. **Contact:** Sue Kurman, Office Manager. **World Wide Web address:** http://www.knmetv.org. **Description:** A public television station providing a comprehensive educational format. KNME-TV programs have been broadcast nationwide and honored with both Emmy and Peabody awards. Founded in 1958. **NOTE:** KNME-TV is considered a department of the University of New Mexico and all hiring is done through the university's Human Resources office. **Special programs:** Internships. **Internship information:** Unpaid internships can be used toward UNM credit. **Parent company:** University of New Mexico.

KOB-TV 4
4 Broadcast Plaza SW, Albuquerque NM 87104. 505/243-4411. **Contact:** Diane Brown. **World Wide Web address:** http://www.kobtv.com. **Description:** An NBC-affiliated television station. **NOTE:** Search for positions online. **Positions advertised include:** Commercial Producer/Director; Broadcast Maintenance Technician; Reporter/Photographer/Fill-in Anchor; Production Technician; Reporter.

KPMG
P.O. Box 3939, Albuquerque NM 87190. 505/884-3939. **Physical address:** 6565 Americas Parkway North East, Albuquerque NM 87110. **Contact:** Human Resources. **World Wide Web address:** http://www.kpmg.com. **Description:** KPMG delivers a wide range of value-added assurance, tax, and consulting services. **NOTE:** Search and apply for positions online. **Positions advertised include:** Associate, State and Local Tax Associate. **Corporate headquarters location:** Montvale NJ. **Parent company:** KPMG International is a leader among professional services firms engaged in capturing, managing, assessing, and delivering information to create knowledge that will help its clients maximize shareholder value. KPMG International has more than 100,000 employees worldwide including 6,500 partners and 60,000 professional staff, serving clients in 844 cities in 155 countries.

KRQE-TV 13
13 Broadcast Plaza SW, Albuquerque NM 87104. 505/243-2285. **Contact:** Human Resources. **World Wide Web address:** http://www.krqe.com. **Description:** A CBS-affiliated television station. **Positions advertised include:** News Anchor; Commercial Producer Manager; Reporter; Account Manager; Meteorologist/Reporter; Producer; Traffic Assistant.

KAMAN INDUSTRIAL TECHNOLOGIES CORPORATION
4901-E Paseo Del Norte NE, Albuquerque NM 87113. 505/247-0222. **Fax:** 505/242-8205. **Contact:** Branch Manager. **E-mail address:** KIT HR-KIT@kaman.com. **World Wide Web address:** http://www.kaman-ind-tech.com. **Description:** An industry supply house with 200 branches and distribution centers providing products and systems related to mechanical and electrical power transmission, motion control, material handling, and fluid power. **NOTE:** Resumes accepted via e-mail. **Corporate headquarters location:** Windsor CT. **Parent company:** Kaman Corporation.

KARLER PACKING COMPANY
P.O. Box 1005, Albuquerque NM 87105. 505/877-3550. **Physical address:** 9111 Broadway Boulevard South East, Albuquerque NM 87105. **Contact:** Human Resources. **Description:** Engaged in meat packing operations.

KELLY CABLE CORPORATION OF NEW MEXICO
3744 Hawkins Street NE, Albuquerque NM 87109. 505/343-1144. **Contact:** Human Resources. **World Wide Web address:** http://www.kellycorporation.com. **Description:** A cable television contractor. Kelly Cable Corporation specializes in burying phone cable, as well as installing aerial phone cable. The company also provides construction contracting for utilities. Founded in 1988. **NOTE:** Apply for positions through headquarters, at 7000 North Broadway, Bldg. 4, Suite 400, Denver CO 80221. Information at 303/430-1414 x408. **Positions advertised include:** CATV Technicians; Phone Technicians; Post/Pre-Wire Technicians; Laborers/Operators. **Corporate headquarters location:** Denver CO. **Listed on:** Privately held.

KEY ENERGY SERVICES
2625 West Marland Street, Hobbs NM 88240. 505/393-9171. **Contact:** Operations Manager. **World Wide Web address:** http://www.keyenergy.com. **Description:** One of the largest well servicing and drilling contractors in the world. Key Energy Services provides maintenance, workover, completion, plugging, and abandonment services for the worldwide oil and gas industry. The company also performs contract drilling services. **NOTE:** Entry-level positions are offered. **Number of employees nationwide:** 8,000.

KEYTRONICEMS CORPORATION
4201 North Del Rey Boulevard, Las Cruces NM 88012. 505/382-6600. **Fax:** 505/382-6642. **Contact:** Human Resources. **World Wide Web address:** http://www.keytronic.com. **Description:** A contract manufacturer for the computer, telecommunications, medical device, and automotive industries. **Corporate headquarters location:** Spokane WA. **Stock exchange symbol:** KTCC.

KLINGER CONSTRUCTORS LLC
P.O. Box 90850, Albuquerque NM 87199. 505/822-9990. **Physical address:** 8701 Washington Street NE, Albuquerque NM 87113. **Fax:** 505/821-0439. **Contact:** Office Manager. **World Wide Web address:** http://www.klinger-const.com. **Description:** A construction company in commercial, industrial, and institutional markets. **NOTE:** Search for positions online. **Parent company:** Klinger Companies, Inc.

KMART STORES
9500 Montgomery Boulevard NE, Albuquerque NM 87111. 505/293-9200. **Contact:** Store Manager. **E-mail address:** hireme@kmart.com. **World Wide Web address:** http://www.kmart.com. **Description:** Kmart is one of the nation's largest owners and operators of general merchandising stores. The company operates 1,500 Kmart discount stores in 49 states Puerto Rico and the Virgin Islands. **NOTE:** Search and apply for corporate positions online. **Corporate headquarters location:** Troy MI. **Number of employees worldwide:** 157,000.

KMART STORES
2100 Carlisle Boulevard NE, Albuquerque NM 87110. 505/265-5911. **Contact:** Store Manager. **E-mail address:** hireme@kmart.com. **World Wide Web address:** http://www.kmart.com. **Description:** Kmart is one of the nation's largest owners and operators of general merchandising stores. The company operates 1,500 Kmart discount stores in 49 states, Puerto Rico, and the Virgin Islands. **NOTE:** Search and apply for corporate positions online. **Corporate headquarters location:** Troy MI. **Number of employees worldwide:** 157,000.

KTECH CORPORATION
1300 Eubank Boulevard SE, Albuquerque NM 87123-3336. 505/998-5830. **Fax:** 505/998-5848. **Contact:** Human Resources Department. **E-mail address:** resumes@ktech.com. **World Wide Web address:** http://www.ktech.com. **Description:** An employee-owned technical services and products firm engaged in scientific and engineering services, manufacturing industrial equipment, specialty gauges and sensors, information technology products and services, and communications media including web design, exhibits, technical writing and publications.

LA PETITE ACADEMY
1361 Rufina Circle, Santa Fe NM 87505. 505/473-9525. **Contact:** Human Resources. **World Wide Web address:** http://www.lapetite.com. **Description:** A preschool and daycare center for children ages six weeks to 12 years. The chain includes 673 early childhood education centers in 36 states. **NOTE:** Search for positions online. Submit application online. **Positions advertised include:** Maintenance Technician. **Corporate headquarters location:** Chicago IL.

LAGUNA INDUSTRIES
P.O. Box 1001, One Mesita Industrial Parkway, Laguna NM 87026. 505/552-6041. **Fax:** 505/552-7642. **Contact:** Human Resources Manager. **World Wide Web address:** http://www.laguna-industries.com. **Description:** A Native American owned and operated business specializing in the design, manufacture, integration, and support of electro-mechanical systems for military and commercial applications. **Number of employees at this location:** 300.

LAKEVIEW CHRISTIAN HOME
1905 West Pierce Street, Carlsbad NM 88220. 505/887-3947. **Fax:** 505/234-1901. **Contact:** Human Resources. **World Wide Web address:** http://www.lakeviewchristian.com. **Description:** A long-term care facility for the elderly. Lakeview Christian Home provides a wide range of nursing care services to residents including restorative care; speech, physical, and occupational therapy; and counseling.

LAKEVIEW CHRISTIAN HOME
1300 North Canal Street, Carlsbad NM 88220-4610. 505/887-0551. **Contact:** Human Resources. **World Wide Web address:** http://www.lakeviewchristian.com. **Description:** A long-term care facility for the elderly. Lakeview Christian Home provides a wide range of nursing care services to residents including restorative care; speech, physical, and occupational therapy; and counseling. Founded in 1960.

LAS CRUCES PUBLIC SCHOOLS
505 South Main, Suite 249, Las Cruces NM 88001. 505/527-5973. **Fax:** 505/527-6658. **Contact:** Charles W. White, Associate Superintendent for Human Resources. **World Wide Web address:** http://www.lcps.k12.nm.us. **Description:** The administrative offices for the Las Cruces public school system, which includes 22,700 students, 23 elementary, seven middle, four high schools, and a special education training center. The office is responsible for staffing all municipal schools. **NOTE:** Search for positions online. Application packet may be requested online. **Positions advertised include:** Bilingual Teacher; Special Education Teacher; Physical Therapist; Speech Language Pathologist; Sign Language Interpreter; Professional Development Teacher; Coach; Assistant Comptroller; Campus Security Guard; Educational Assistant; Kitchen Staff Member; Food Service Cashier.

LAS CRUCES SUN-NEWS
P.O. Box 1749, 256 West Las Cruces Road, Las Cruces NM 88004. 505/523-6464. **Fax:** 505/541-54978. **Contact:** Human Resources. **E-mail address:** jluna@lcsun-news.com. **World Wide Web address:** http://www.lcsun-news.com. **Description:** Publishes a daily newspaper with a circulation of more than 24,000. **Special programs:** Internships. **Parent company:** Gannett Co., Inc.

LECTROSONICS
P.O. Box 15900, Rio Rancho NM 87174. 505/892-4501. **Physical address:** 581 Laser Road, Rio Rancho NM 87124. **Fax:** 505/892-6243. **Contact:** Human Resources. **World Wide Web address:** http://www.lectrosonics.com. **Description:** A manufacturer of wireless microphones and professional audio systems. **NOTE:** Search for positions online. **Positions advertised include:** SR RF Design Engineer.

LIFTS WEST CONDOMINIUM RESORT HOTEL
P.O. Box 330, Red River NM 87558. 505/754-2778. **Contact:** Bob Bullington, General Manager. **E-mail address:** lifts@redriver.org. **World Wide Web address:** http://www.liftswest.com. **Description:** Houses 75 condominium units that can be rented nightly. Units are complete with kitchen, living room, and variety of bedrooms. Laundry facilities are also available.

LOCKHEED MARTIN
1155 University Boulevard SE, Albuquerque NM 87106. 505/843-4000. **Contact**: Human Resources. **World Wide Web address:** http://www.lockheedmartin.com. **Description**: Lockheed Martin is an advanced technology company involved in Aeronautics, Electronic Systems, Information and Technology services, and Space Systems. **NOTE:** Applicants may apply for positions through company website. **Positions advertised include:** PC Tech Support Analyst; Systems Engineer; Software Quality Engineer; Administrative Assistant; Cost-Schedule Analyst; Mechanical Engineer.

LOOMIS FARGO & COMPANY
624 Industrial Avenue NE, Albuquerque NM 87107. 505/344-9444. **Fax:** 505/344-5305. **Contact:** Human Resources. **World Wide Web address:** www.loomisfargo.com. **Description:** An armored car service specializing in transporting currency. **Other U.S. locations:** Nationwide.

LOS ALAMOS NATIONAL LABORATORY
P.O. Box 1663, Los Alamos NM 87545. 505/667-8622. **Physical address:** Bikini Atoll Road, Los Alamos NM 87545. **Fax:** 505/665-5419. **Contact:** Resume Service Center. **E-mail address:** jobs@lanl.gov. **World Wide Web address:** http://www.lanl.gov. **Description:** A national laboratory engaged in research and development in a wide range of areas including quality and planning; energy and environment; materials science; nuclear materials and security; biotechnology and biomedicine; instrumentation; sensors and transducers; physics; and high-performance computing, modeling, and simulation. Operated by the University of California for the National Nuclear Security Administration of the U.S. Department of Energy. **NOTE:** Entry-level positions are offered. **Positions advertised include:** Administrative Specialist; Associate Director; Auditor; Biochem Lab Tech; Chief of Staff; Staff Member; Project Leader; Deputy Group Leader; Group Leader; Division Leader; Program Manager; Security Specialist; Team Leader; Computer Technician. **Number of employees at this location:** 10,700.

LOVELACE MEDICAL CENTER
5400 Gibson Boulevard SE, Albuquerque NM 87108. 505/262-7000. **Contact:** Human Resources. **World Wide Web address:** http://www.lovelace.com. **Description:** A large medical center with 221 acute-care beds and a multi-specialty outpatient center with over 40 medical specialties. **Parent company:** Ardent Health Services.

LOVELACE HEALTHCARE CENTER
440 St. Michael's Drive, Santa Fe NM 87505. 505/995-2400. **Contact:** Clinic Manager. **World Wide Web address:** http://www.lovelace.com. **Description:** A walk-in health care clinic. This is one of 16 locations.

LOVELACE RESPIRATORY RESEARCH INSTITUTE
2425 Ridgecrest Drive SE, Albuquerque NM 87108. 505/348-9400. **Fax:** 505/348-4976. **Contact:** Human Resources. **E-mail address:** hrmail@lrri.org. **World Wide Web address:** http://www.lrri.org. **Description:** A private not-for-profit biomedical research institute that is focused solely on respiratory disease research. **NOTE:** Include job number when applying for a position. **Positions advertised include:** Institute Compliance Manager; Sr. Research Technologists; Laboratory Technician; Senior Buyer; Word Processor; Science Camp Counselor. **Internship information:** Postdoctoral positions are available year-round. Please call for more information. **Corporate headquarters location:** This location. **Number of employees at this location:** 320.

LOVELACE SANDIA HEALTH SYSTEM
P.O. Box 25555, Albuquerque NM 87125. 505/727-7200. **Fax:** 505/262-7987. **Contact:** Recruiting. **E-mail address:** recruiter@lovelacesandia.com. **World Wide Web address:** http://www.sjhs.org. **Description:** A fully integrated health care system that operates four acute care hospitals, a rehabilitation hospital, the Lovelace Health Plan, S.E.D. Medical Laboratories, two physician groups, and 15 neighborhood health care centers in Albuquerque, Rio Rancho, and Santa Fe. **NOTE:** Search and apply for positions online. **Positions advertised include:** Financial Analyst; Patient Financial Services Director; Case Management Coordinator. **Parent Company:** Ardent Health Services.

MCBRIDE & ASSOCIATES
5555 McLeod Road NE, Albuquerque NM 87109. 505/837-7500. **Fax:** 505/837-7501. **Contact:** Human Resources. **World Wide Web address:** http://www.mcbride.com. **Description:** Provider of information technology products and services.

MEDICARE SERVICES
6301 Indian School Road, Suite 990, Albuquerque NM 87110. 505/872-2551. **Contact:** Human Resources. **Description:** Processes forms for Medicare Part B claims. **NOTE:** Resumes should be sent to Human Resources, 701 NW 63rd Street, Oklahoma City OK 73116.

MEGA CORPORATION
P.O. Box 26146, 700 Osuna Road, Albuquerque NM 87125-6146. 505/345-2661. **Contact:** Production Supervisor. **World Wide Web address:** http://www.megacorpinc.com. **Description:** Producer of mobile water distribution equipment for the construction and mining industry.

MEMORIAL MEDICAL CENTER
2450 South Telshor Boulevard, Las Cruces NM 88011-5065. 505/556-5833. **Contact:** Sandra Miramontes, Employment Specialist. **E-mail address:** Sandra.miramontes@prhc.com. **World Wide Web address:** http://www.mmclc.org. **Description:** Memorial Medical Center is a not-for-profit, 286-bed, acute care hospital, providing health care services to the people of southern New Mexico. Services include a cardiovascular lab for diagnostic procedures, a lithotripsy unit offering a nonsurgical technique for treating kidney stones, and the Ikard/Memorial Cancer Treatment Center, which provides radiation therapy to complement a multidisciplinary approach for the treatment of cancer. Founded in 1950. **NOTE:** Search and apply for positions online. **Positions advertised include:** Business Analyst; Inventory Coordinator; Surgical Tech; RN; Director, Surgical Services; Behavioral Health Therapist; LPN.

MERRILL LYNCH
P.O. Box 1946, 123 East Marcy Street, Santa Fe NM 87504. 505/982-4651. **Contact:** Human Resources Department. **World Wide Web address:** http://www.ml.com. **Description:** Offices for the worldwide financial services company, organized to provide both traditional and innovative products and services to a broad range of individual and institutional customers. Merrill Lynch operates primarily through functional units that include Individual Services; Capital Markets; Assets Management; Futures; International; and Real Estate and Insurance. Offices are in 35 countries.

MERRILL LYNCH
P.O. Box 2128, Roswell NM 88202-1357. 505/622-1642. **Physical address:** 400 North Pennsylvania Avenue, Suite 150, Roswell NM 88201. **Fax:** 505/623-1202. **Contact:** Charlie Murphy, Office Manager. **World Wide Web address:** http://www.ml.com. **Description:** Offices for the worldwide financial services company, organized to provide both traditional and innovative products and services to a broad range of individual and institutional customers. Merrill Lynch operates primarily through functional units that include Individual Services; Capital Markets; Assets Management; Futures; International; and Real Estate and Insurance. Offices are in 35 countries.

MESA AIRLINES, INC.
1300 West Navajo Street, Farmington NM 87401. 505/327-0271. **Contact:** Personnel Assistant. **World Wide Web address:** http://www.mesa-air.com. **Description:** Provides regularly scheduled commuter and cargo airline services to 161 cities, 41 states, Canada, Mexico, and the Bahamas. **NOTE:** Search and apply for positions online. **Corporate headquarters location:** This location.

MESILLA VALLEY HOSPITAL
3751 Del Rey Boulevard, Las Cruces NM 88012. 505/382-3500. **World Wide Web address:** http://www.mesillavalleyhospital.com. **Description:** A private psychiatric hospital for adolescents and adults. **NOTE:** Search and apply for positions online. **Parent company:** Ardent Health Services.

MIMBRES MEMORIAL HOSPITAL & NURSING HOME
P.O. Box 710, Deming NM 88031. 505/546-2761. **Physical address:** 900 West Ash Street, Deming NM 88030. **Fax:** 505/546-5410. **Recorded jobline:** 505/546-5806. **Contact:** Human Resources. **World Wide Web address:** http://www.chs.net/where.we.serve/hospitals/mimbres1.htm. **Description:** A full-service, 49-bed acute-care hospital and 69-bed long-term care nursing home. **Positions advertised include:** Registered Nurse. **NOTE:** Entry-level positions and part-time jobs are offered. **Special programs:** Internships; Training. **Corporate headquarters location:** Brentwood TN. **Parent company:** Community Health System.

MORGAN STANLEY COMPANY
6701 Uptown Boulevard NE, Albuquerque NM 87110. 505/883-6262. **Contact:** Human Resources Department. **World Wide Web address:** http://www.msdw.com. **Description:** Offers diversified financial services including equities, fixed income securities, commodities, money market instruments, and investment banking services.

MORNING SUN
P.O. Box 3488, Albuquerque NM 87190. 505/884-3484. **Fax:** 505/883-6613. **Contact:** Olga Giorgi, Vice President. **Description:** A jewelry manufacturer that supplies necklaces, earrings, bracelets, and rings to retailers.

MUTUAL OF OMAHA INSURANCE COMPANY
6000 Uptown NE, Suite 410, Albuquerque NM 87110. 505/889-9545. **Contact:** Human Resources Department. **E-mail address:** careers@mutualofomaha.com. **World Wide Web address:** http://www.mutualofomaha.com. **Description:** Offers a full portfolio of insurance coverages and services. **NOTE:** Internships available. A Human Resources Recruiter for nationwide sales management opportunities can be reached at 877/351-4680.

NAMBE MILLS
2891 Cooks Road, Santa Fe NM 87507. 505/471-2912. **Contact:** Human Resources. **World Wide Web address:** http://www.nambe.com. **Description:** A manufacturer of tabletop accessories. **Number of employees at this location:** 200.

NEW MEXICO INSTITUTE OF MINING & TECHNOLOGY
801 Leroy Place, Socorro NM 87801. 505/835-5206. **Fax:** 505/835-5337. **Contact:** Salina A. Lopez, Human Resources. **World Wide Web address:** http://www.nmt.edu. **Description:** An undergraduate and graduate university with an enrollment of 1800 specializing in science and engineering education and research. **NOTE:** E-mail applications are not accepted. **Positions advertised include:** Lab Associate; Assistant/Associate Professor; Community College Lecturer; Ordnance Technician; Petroleum Geologist; Admission Counselor; Senior Engineer; Postdoctoral Researcher; Seismological Staff Scientist; Data Specialist; Distance Education Administrator; Heavy Equipment Operators; Accounting Technician.

NEW MEXICO MILITARY INSTITUTE
101 West College, Roswell NM 88201-5173. 505/624-8080. **Contact:** Col. Judy Collins, Deputy Superintendent for Business/Personal. **E-mail address:** Carmen@nmmi.edu. **World Wide Web address:** http://www.nmmi.cc.nm.us. **Description:** A co-ed residential, college preparatory high school and two-year junior college in a military setting with a total enrollment of 970. Founded in 1891. **NOTE:** Employment application may be downloaded online. **Positions advertised include:** Business Administration Faculty; Custodian; Director of Grounds; Teacher; Lifeguard; Science Lab Technician; Secretary; Sports Information Officer; Superintendent.

NEW MEXICO MUSEUM OF NATURAL HISTORY AND SCIENCE
1801 Mountain Road NW, Albuquerque NM 87104. 505/841-2800. **Contact:** Alicia Borrego, Human Resources Manager. **E-mail address:** aborrego@nmmnh.state.nm.us. **World Wide Web address:** http://www.nmmnh-abq.mus.nm.us. **Description:** A museum focusing on nature, artifacts, and prehistoric fossils. **NOTE:** The Museum is a division of the State of New Mexico Department of Cultural Affairs. Employment opportunities can be found at the State Personnel Office web site: http://www.state.nm.us/spo/recruit.htm. **Positions advertised include:** Summer Camp Counselor. **Number of employees at this location:** 100.

NEW MEXICO STATE UNIVERSITY
P.O. Box 30001, MSC Department 5273, Las Cruces NM 88003-8001. 505/646-2420. **Contact:** Bob Howell, Personnel Director. **E-mail address:** personnel@nmsu.edu. **World Wide Web address:** http://www.nmsu.edu. **Description:** The state university's main campus with an enrollment of 16,000 offers 73 bachelor's, 51 master's, three Specialist, and 24 doctoral programs. Founded in 1888. **NOTE:** Open positions and application instructions available online. **Positions advertised include:** Electrical Technician; Assistant Conference Coordinator; Director of Financial Aid and Scholarship Services; Sr. Electrical Engineer; Director of Black Programs; Director of Campus Activities; Assistant Professor; Instructor; Animal Nutritionist; Electrician; Research Assistant; Teacher Assistant; Secretary; Program Facilitator.

NEW MEXICO STATE UNIVERSITY AT ALAMOGORDO
2400 North Scenic Drive, Alamogordo NM 88310. 505/439-3720. **Contact:** Human Resources. **E-mail address:** bobbi@nmsua.nmsu.edu. **World Wide Web address:** http://alamo.nmsu.edu. **Description:** A two-year branch campus of New Mexico State University with 2,000 students. **Positions advertised include:** Instructor of Emergency Medicine; Professor or Associate Professor and Division Head.

NEW MEXICO VA HEALTH CARE SYSTEM
1501 San Pedro Drive, SE, Albuquerque NM 87108-5153. 505/265-1711. **Fax:** 505/265-2855. **Contact:** Human Resources. **Description:** A comprehensive health care system consisting of a Level 1 tertiary referral center in Albuquerque with 217 beds, and a system of community based outpatient clinics in 21 locations throughout New Mexico and southwest Colorado. Affiliated with the University of New Mexico School of Medicine. **NOTE:** Nationwide openings in the Veterans Health Administration may be searched at: http://www.vacareers.com.

NEW YORK LIFE INSURANCE
6565 Americas Parkway NE, Suite 500, Albuquerque NM 87110. 505/883-4428. **Contact:** Human Resources. **World Wide Web address:** http://www.newyorklife.com. **Description:** An insurance and financial services firm. Present activities are in the areas of life, health, and disability insurance; annuities; and a wide range of new products and services combining investment and term life insurance protection into one package. Services are provided to individuals, families, and businesses. **NOTE:** Submit resume and cover letter online. Training programs and internships available. **Corporate headquarters location:** New York NY.

NORSAM TECHNOLOGIES, INC.
852 Gilmore, Santa Fe NM 87501. 505/984-1133. **Contact:** Human Resources. **World Wide Web address:** http://www.norsam.com. **Description:** Provides services and products in the fields of nano technology, microtooling, archival preservation, and gemstone marking.

NORTHEAST HEIGHTS MEDICAL CENTER
4701 Montgomery Boulevard NE, Albuquerque NM 87109. 505/727-6145. **Contact:** Recruiting. **E-mail address:** recruiter@lovelacesandia.com. **World Wide Web address:** http://www.lovelacesandia.com. **Description:** a 114-bed acute care hospital providing general medical and surgical services, intensive care, pediatric care, and physical therapy services. Part of the Lovelace Sandia Health System. **NOTE:** Search and apply for positions online. **Positions advertised include:** Charge Nurse; RN; House Supervisor; LPN; OR Tech; Pharmacist; Physical Therapist; X-Ray Tech.

NORTHERN NAVAJO MEDICAL CENTER
P.O. Box 160, Shiprock NM 87420. 505/368-6001. **Fax:** 505/368-6260. **Contact:** Human Resources. **Description:** A 55-bed medical center that also operates specialty outpatient clinics. This is a facility of the Navajo Area Indian Health Service, one of the administrative units of the Indian Health Service, an agency of the U.S. Public Health Service Department of Human Health Services.

NORTHROP GRUMMAN
101 Sun Avenue NE, Albuquerque NM 87109. 505/858-3460. **Contact:** Personnel Department. **World Wide Web address:** http://www.northropgrumman.com. **Description:** An information technology services firm whose operating subsidiaries provide research and development and contract support to clients in the following industries: national defense, communications, energy, transportation, environmental, and other areas. **NOTE:** Search and apply for positions online. **Positions advertised include:** Contracts Administrator; Engineer; Intern; Software Engineer.

NOVA BUS INC.
P.O. Box 5670, Roswell NM 88202. 505/347-2011. **Physical address:** 42 Earl Cummings Loop West, Roswell NM 88203. **Contact:** Ms. Cori Moore, Director of Human Resources. **World Wide Web address:** http://www.novabus.com. **Description:** A manufacturer of buses. **Parent company:** Prevost Car Inc.

OCULAR SCIENCES, INC.
6805 Academy Parkway West NE, Albuquerque NM 87109. 505/345-7967. **Contact:** Human Resources. **World Wide Web address:** http://www.ocularsciences.com. **Description:** One of the world's largest producers of ophthalmic products, specializing in soft contact lenses including sphericals, multifocals, and torics. **Corporate headquarters location:** Concord CA. **Number of employees worldwide:** 4,000.

OFFICE DEPOT, INC.
350 Eubank Boulevard NE, Albuquerque NM 87123. 505/237-1040. **Contact:** Human Resources. **World Wide Web address:** http://www.officedepot.com. **Description:** Office Depot, Inc. is one of the nation's leading office products dealers with more than 1,000 stores in 11 countries. The company offers over 11,000 different business products, from basic supplies such as copy and printer paper to high-tech business furniture. Founded in 1986. **NOTE:** Search and apply for positions online. **Corporate headquarters location:** Delray Beach FL.

OFFICEMAX
3301 Mineaul Boulevard NE, Suite A, Albuquerque NM 87107. 505/889-9696. **Contact:** Store Manager. **World Wide Web address:** http://www.officemax.com. **Description:** A retail store specializing in the sale of office supplies and equipment with more than 1,000 stores. **NOTE:** Search and apply for positions online. **Corporate headquarters location:** Shaker Heights OH. **Parent company:** Boise Cascade Corporation.

OFFICEMAX
40 Hotel Circle, Albuquerque NM 87123. 505/292-1400. **Contact:** Store Manager. **World Wide Web address:** http://www.officemax.com. **Description:** Another location of the retail store chain specializing in the sale of office supplies and equipment. **NOTE:** Search and apply for positions online. **Corporate headquarters location:** Shaker Heights OH. **Parent company:** Boise Cascade Corporation.

OLIVE GARDEN ITALIAN RESTAURANT
601 Juan Tebo Boulevard NE, Albuquerque NM 87123. 505/275-9948. **Contact:** Manager. **World Wide Web address:** http://www.olivegarden.com. **Description:** One location of the chain of family-style Italian restaurants. **NOTE:** Applicants should apply in person. Application forms are available online. **Parent company:** Darden Restaurants.

OSOGRANDE TECHNOLOGIES INC.
5921 Jefferson Court NE, Albuquerque NM 87109. 505/345-6555. **Contact:** Human Resources. **E-mail address:** jobs@osogrande.com. **World Wide Web address:** http://www.osogrande.com. **Description:** An Internet access provider working through partnerships with national laboratories, state government, and universities to provide easier access to public information. Founded in 1984. **Number of employees at this location:** 45.

PNM RESOURCES
Alvarado Square, Mail Stop 3002, Albuquerque NM 87158-0001. 505/241-4919. **Contact:** Human Resources. **World Wide Web address:** http://www.pnm.com. **Description:** An energy holding company providing electricity and natural gas to more than 1.3 million people in 100 communities. **NOTE:** Search and apply for positions online. **Positions advertised include:** Record Center Clerk; Business Consultant; IT Project Management; Customer Service Representative; Computer Systems Specialist; Sr. Engineer; Record Conversion Tech; Software Quality Assurance and Training Tech. **Corporate headquarters location:** This location. **Number of employees nationwide:** 2,700.

PEERLESS TYRE COMPANY
3010 Cerrillos Road, Santa Fe NM 87505. 505/473-0900. **Contact:** Dale Brown, Division Manager. **World Wide Web address:** http://www.peerlesstyreco.com. **Description:** Provides tires, shocks, and batteries to both the general public and area dealers. **Other area locations:** Albuquerque NM; Farmington NM.

PEERLESS TYRE COMPANY
5504 Menaul NE, Albuquerque NM 87110. 505/884-5773. **Toll-free phone:** 800/999-7810. **Contact:** Division Manager. **E-mail address:** peerless@peerlesstyreco.com. **World Wide Web address:** http://www.peerlesstyreco.com. **Description:** Operates 55 stores that provide tires, shocks, and batteries to both the general public and area dealers. **Other area locations:** Santa Fe NM; Farmington NM. **Number of employees nationwide:** 250.

PEPSI-COLA COMPANY
212 Claremont Avenue NE, Albuquerque NM 87107-1722. 505/880-5000. **Fax:** 505/883-4138. **Contact:** Human Resources. **World Wide Web address:** http://www.pepsico.com. **Description:** Pepsi-Cola Company produces and distributes a variety of beverages including the brand names Pepsi-Cola, Mountain Dew, Mug Root Beer, and Slice. **NOTE:** Search and apply for positions online. **Positions advertised include:** District Sales Leader. **Parent company:** PepsiCo, Inc. (Purchase NY) consists of Frito-Lay Company, Pepsi-Cola Company, Quaker Oats, and Tropicana Products, Inc. **Operations ad this facility include:** This location houses regional offices. **Listed on:** New York Stock Exchange. **Stock exchange symbol:** PEP.

PHARMERICA
2720 Broadbent Parkway NE, Suite A, Albuquerque NM 87107. 505/343-1113. **Contact:** Human Resources. **World Wide Web address:** http://www. pharmerica.com. **Description:** A supplier of pharmaceuticals and related products to long-term care facilities, hospitals, and assisted living communities through 83 pharmacies in 35 states. PharMerica also provides nurse consultant services, infusion therapy and training, medical records consulting, and educational programs. **NOTE:** Search and apply for positions online or contact local facility. **Corporate headquarters location:** Tampa FL. **Parent company:** AmerisourceBergen Corporation. **Number of employees nationwide:** 5,000.

PHELPS DODGE MINING COMPANY
110 W 11th Street, Silver City NM. 505/538-3553. **Contact:** Human Resources. **World Wide Web address:** http://www.phelpsdodge.com. **Description:** Phelps Dodge Mining Company is one of North America's largest producers of copper. The company produces silver, gold, and molybdenum as by-products of its copper operations and fluorspar, gold, silver, lead, zinc, and copper from mines abroad. It also explores for metals and minerals in the United States and abroad. NOTE: Search and apply for positions online. **Positions advertised include:** Pump Technician; Engineering Technician; Mine Administrative Assistant; Plant Maintenance Helper; Cost Coordinator; Mechanic; Equipment Operator; Electrical Supervisor. **Parent company:** Phelps Dodge Corporation. **Operations at this facility include:** Open-pit copper mining. (Tyrone mine). **Number of employees worldwide:** 8,700.

PHILIPS SEMICONDUCTOR
9201 Pan American Freeway NE, Albuquerque NM 87113. 505/822-7000. **Fax:** 505/822-7494. **Contact:** Human Resources Department. **World Wide Web address:** http://www.semiconductors.philips.com. **Description:** Manufactures and distributes integrated circuits for semiconductors. **NOTE:** Search and apply for jobs online at: http://www.careers.philips.com. **Positions advertised include:** Field Service Engineer. **Corporate headquarters location:** Sunnyvale CA. **Parent company:** Philips Electronics North America Corporation. **Operations at this facility include:** Manufacturing.

PHYSICAL SCIENCE LABORATORY
P.O. Box 30002, Las Cruces NM 88003-8002. 505/522-9100. **Contact:** Regina Galvan, Personnel Manager. **E-mail address:** personnel@psl.nmsu.edu. **World Wide Web address:** http://www.psl.nmsu.edu. **Description:** A part of New Mexico State University provides a wide range of research and development services in geothermal and wind energy, as well as providing contract services to the Department of Defense. **NOTE:** Search for positions online. **Positions advertised include:** Research Chemist; Atmospheric Scientist; Administrative Assistant; Instructional Coordinator; Jr. Computer Software Engineer; Sr. Computer Software Engineer. **Corporate headquarters location:** This location.

PIZZA HUT
111 Coors E9 Boulevard NW, Albuquerque NM 87121. 505/831-1133. **Contact:** Store Manager. **World Wide Web address:** http://www.pizzahut.com. **Description:** A casual pizza restaurant. There are 6,600 restaurants in the U.S. and more than 4,000 in 100 other countries. **NOTE:** Search and apply for positions online. **Parent company:** Yum! Brands, Inc.

PLAINS REGIONAL MEDICAL CENTER
2100 Dr. Martin Luther King Jr. Boulevard, Clovis NM 88101. 505/769-2141. **Fax:** 505/769-7227. **Recorded jobline:** 505/841-1720. **Contact:** Victor Jensen, Human Resources. **E-mail address:** vjensen@phs.org. **World Wide Web address:** http://www.phs.org/facilities/facclovis.htm. **Description:** A 106-bed general medical center offering both inpatient and outpatient services. Operated by Presbyterian Healthcare Services. **NOTE:** Search and apply for positions online. **Positions advertised include:** Administrative Staff Support; LPN; Nursing Tech; Cook; Nursing Supervisor; Patient Services Coordinator; Physical Therapist; Radiation Therapist; Radiographer; RN; Ultrasound Specialist; Transcriptionist.

POD ASSOCIATES, INC.
5971 Jefferson NE, Suite 101, Albuquerque NM 87109. 505/243-2287. **Fax:** 505/243-4677. **Contact:** Personnel. **E-mail address:** pod@podassoc.com. **World Wide Web address:** http://www.podassoc.com. **Description:** Provides solutions for the development, maintenance, and support of information systems. POD Associates specializes in network setup and support, database creation and support, and Web development and support. Founded in 1988. **Company slogan:** Stay connected. **Special programs:** Internships; Apprenticeships; Co-ops. **Other U.S. locations:** Phoenix AZ; Port St. Joe FL.

POJOAQUE VALLEY SCHOOL DISTRICT
P.O. Box 3468, Santa Fe NM 87501. 505/455-2284. **Contact:** Human Resources. **E-mail address:** vta@pvs.k12.nm.us. **World Wide Web address:** http://pvs.k12.nm.us. **Description:** Personnel offices for the Pojoaque Valley School District. The office is responsible for staffing at all public schools, grades K-12. **Positions advertised include:** Spanish Teacher; Library Assistant; Substitute Teachers; Custodian; Coach. **Number of employees at this location:** 200.

PRESBYTERIAN MEDICAL SERVICES
P.O. Box 2267, Santa Fe NM 87504. 505/982-5565. **Contact:** Dianne Martinez, Human Resources Manager. **World Wide Web address:** http://www.pms-inc.org. **Description:** Presbyterian Medical Services operates health care clinics throughout New Mexico. **NOTE:** Search for positions online. Download employment application. **Operations at this facility include:** This location houses administrative offices.

PRESTO PRODUCTS MANUFACTURING COMPANY
1301 Lavelle Road, Alamogordo NM 88310. 505/437-7626. **Contact:** Plant Manager. **Description:** Manufactures electric appliances and housewares. **Corporate headquarters location:** This location.

PUBLIC SERVICE COMPANY OF NEW MEXICO
Alvarado Square, Albuquerque NM 87158-0001. 505/241-4627. **Contact:** People Services. **World Wide Web address:** http://www.pnm.com. **Description:** A combined gas and electric utility serving more than 1.1 million people in approximately 100 communities in the New Mexico area. In addition to providing service to 323,000 retail electric customers and 382,000 retail gas customers, Public Service Company of New Mexico also sells electric power in the wholesale market to customers in New Mexico, California, Texas, and elsewhere in the western United States. **Positions advertised include:** Customer Service Representative; Director, Corporate Communications; Accountant; Professional Engineer; Benefits Manager; Sr. Accountant. **Corporate headquarters location:** This location. **Operations at this facility include:** Administration; Service.

PUBLIC SERVICE COMPANY OF NEW MEXICO
P.O. Box 227, Waterflow NM 87421-0027. 505/598-7200. **Contact:** Human Resources. **World Wide Web address:** http://www.pnm.com. **Description:** Branch office of a combined gas and electric utility. **Parent company:** PNM Resources.

QUAIL RUN ASSOCIATION
3101 Old Pecos Trail, Santa Fe NM 87505. 505/986-2200. **Fax:** 505/986-2257. **Contact:** Human Resources. **E-mail address:** info@qrsf.com. **World Wide Web address:** http://www.quailrunsantafe.com. **Description:** A residential community and resort. Quail Run has 260 residential units. The resort facilities include an indoor pool, weight room, sauna, massage therapy, executive golf course, and tennis courts. **Positions advertised include:** Clubhouse Manager; Human Resources Assistant; Housekeeper; Evening Line Cook; Waitstaff; Table Busser; Banquet Captain.

QUALITY PONTIACBUICK GMC
7901 Lomas Boulevard NE, Albuquerque NM 87110. 505/765-1300. **Contact:** Marcia Paz, Business Manager. **World Wide Web address:** http://www.qualitydeal.com. **Description:** A new- and used-car dealership selling Pontiac, GMC, and Buick automobiles.

QUEST DIAGNOSTICS INCORPORATED
7510 Montgomery NE, Suite 10, Albuquerque NM 87109. 505/889-7144. **Contact:** Ms. Kathy Lanman, Operations Manager. **World Wide Web address:** http://www.questdiagnostics.com. **Description:** Quest Diagnostics is one of the largest clinical laboratories in North America, providing a broad range of clinical laboratory services to health care clients that include physicians, hospitals, clinics, dialysis centers, pharmaceutical companies, and corporations. The company offers and performs tests on blood, urine, and other bodily fluids and tissues to provide information for health and well-being. **Positions advertised include:** Courier. **Corporate headquarters location:** Teterboro NJ. **Other U.S. locations:** Nationwide. **Operations at this facility include:** This location takes blood samples. **Listed on:** New York Stock Exchange. **Stock exchange symbol:** DGX.

QWEST COMMUNICATIONS INTERNATIONAL, INC.
400 Tijeras NW, Suite 510, Albuquerque, NM 87102. 505/245-7500. **Contact:** Human Resources. **E-mail address:** staffing@qwest.com. **World Wide Web Address:** http://www.qwest.com. **Description:** Provides voice, Internet, data, and video solutions for residential, business, and government customers in 14 western and mid-western states. **NOTE:** Search and apply for positions online. **Corporate headquarters location:** Denver CO. **Listed on:** New York Stock Exchange. **Stock exchange symbol:** Q. **Number of employees worldwide:** 47,000.

QYNERGY
3800 Osuna Road NE, Suite 2, Albuquerque NM 87109. 505/890-6887. **Fax:** 505/792-8508. **Contact:** Human Resources. **E-mail address:** resume@qynergy.com. **World Wide Web address:** http://www.qynergy.com. **Description:** Designs and manufactures small power devices and related sensors, including the proprietary QynCell, which directly converts the energy of ionizing radiation into electricity through non-thermal methods. **Positions advertised include:** Senior Electronics Technician.

RADIOSHACK
1625 Rio Bravo Boulevard SW, Suite 23, Albuquerque NM 87105. 505/877-0110. **Contact:** Human Resources. **World Wide Web address:** http://www. radioshack.com. **Description:** Part of the 7,000-unit retail store chain specializing in the sale of electronic and computer products. **NOTE:** Search for corporate positions online. Apply for all jobs online. **Corporate headquarters location:** Fort Worth TX. **Parent company:** InterTAN, Inc. **Listed on:** New York Stock Exchange. **Stock exchange symbol:** RSH.

RADISSON HOTEL & CONFERENCE CENTER
2500 Carlisle Boulevard NE, Albuquerque NM 87110. 505/888-3311. **Contact:** Human Resources. **World Wide Web address:** http://www.radisson.com. **Description:** A 366-room, full-service hotel featuring an amphitheatre, meeting and exhibition facilities, a restaurant, and catering services. Radisson operates 400 properties in 50 countries. **Corporate headquarters location:** Minneapolis MN. **Parent company:** Carlson Hotels Worldwide.

RADISSON SANTA FE
750 North St. Francis Drive, Santa Fe NM 87501. 505/992-5800. **Fax:** 505/992-5865. **Contact:** Human Resources. **World Wide Web address:** http://www.radisson.com. **Description:** A hotel with 160 rooms, suites, and condos featuring meeting and banquet facilities, a restaurant and bar, and catering services. Radisson operates 400 properties in 50 countries. **Corporate headquarters location:** Minneapolis MN. **Parent company:** Carlson Hotels Worldwide.

RAMADA INN
2803 West Second, Roswell NM 88201. 505/623-9440. **Fax:** 505/622-9708. **Contact:** Manager. **World Wide Web address:** http://www.ramada.com. **Description:** A 58-room hotel featuring meeting and banquet facilities, heated and outdoor pools, and a restaurant. Ramada operates 1,000 hotels nationwide. **Other area locations:** Albuquerque, Farmington, Gallup, Rio Rancho, Santa Fe, Taos NM.

RANCHO VALMORA
HCR 50 Box 1, Valmora NM 87750. 505/425-6057. **Contact:** Human Resources. **World Wide Web address:** http://www.ranchovalmora.com. **Description:** A non-profit, long-term residential treatment center for adolescents ages 12 through 18. The facility specializes in the treatment of behavioral and mental disorders.

RELIANCE METAL CENTER
6718 Jefferson Street NE, Albuquerque NM 87109-4319. 505/345-0959. **Fax:** 505/345-1187. **Contact:** Ken Bizzell, Human Resources. **E-mail address:** kbizzell@rsac.com. **World Wide Web address:** http://www.rsac.com. **Description:** Reliance is one of the largest metals service center companies in the United States. Through a network of 100 metals processing and distribution facilities in 30 states, Belgium, France, and South Korea, the company distributes a full line of more than 85,000 metal products including galvanized, hot-rolled and cold-finished steel; stainless steel; aluminum; brass; copper; titanium, and alloy steel. Founded in 1939. **Corporate headquarters location:** Los Angeles CA. **Listed on:** New York Stock Exchange. **Stock exchange symbol:** RS.

RHINOCORPS
1128 Pennsylvania Avenue, Suite 100, Albuquerque NM 87110. 505/323-9836. **Fax:** 505/323-9863. **Contact:** Human Resources. **World Wide Web address:** http://www.rhinocorps.com. **Description:** Provides specialized professional engineering and software services with an emphasis in Modeling and Simulation, Software Development, Web-based Application Development, and Specialized Scientific and Engineering services. **Positions advertised include:** programmer.

RICO MOTOR COMPANY
220 South Fifth Street, Gallup NM 87301. 505/722-2271. **Fax:** 505/863-3538. **Contact:** Human Resources. **World Wide Web address:** http://www.ricoautocomplex.com. **Description:** An automobile dealership selling Pontiac, GMC, and Buick brand vehicles.

ROBERT HALF TECHNOLOGY
6501 Americas Parkway NE, Albuquerque NM 87110. 505/888-6225. **Fax:** 505/884-4559. **Contact:** Human Resources. **E-mail address:** Albuquerque@roberthalftechnology.com. **Description:** Provides flexible staffing solutions to premier organizations worldwide that require technical expertise on demand. Projects range from complex e-business and web development initiatives to enterprise wide application development and technical system support. **Positions advertised include:** Technical Sales Representative; C Developer; IT Systems and Database Configuration Manager; Network Manager.

ROSWELL, CITY OF
P.O. Drawer 1838, Roswell NM 88202. 505/624-6700. **Physical address:** 425 North Richardson Avenue, Roswell NM 88201. **Fax:** 505/624-6709. **Contact:** Human Resources. **World Wide Web address:** http://www.roswell-usa.com. **Description:** The administrative offices of the city of Roswell. This office is responsible for staffing municipal departments. **Special programs:** Summer Jobs.

ROSWELL DAILY RECORD
P.O. Box 1897, Roswell NM 88201. 505/622-7710. **Physical address:** 2301 North Main, Roswell NM. **Fax:** 505/625-0421. **Contact:** Human Resources. **World Wide Web address:** http://www.roswell-record.com. **Description:** A daily newspaper with a circulation of 15,000 daily, and 20,000 on Sundays.

ROSWELL INDEPENDENT SCHOOL DISTRICT
P.O. Box 1437, Roswell NM 88202. 505/627-2500. **Physical address:** 300 Kentucky Street, Roswell NM 88201. **Fax:** 505/627-2524. **Contact:** Alma Aguilar, Human Resources Specialist. **World Wide Web address:** http://www.risd.k12.nm.us. **Description:** The administrative offices of the Roswell school system, responsible for staffing municipal schools, which includes 15 elementary, four middle, and three high schools. **NOTE:** Search and apply for positions online. **Positions advertised include:** Assistant Superintendent for Instruction; Interpreter for the Deaf; Community Service Teacher; Nurse Special Education Resource Teacher; IEP Facilitator; English Teacher; Head Girls Softball Coach; Kitchen Manager.

ROSWELL MUSEUM AND ART CENTER
100 West 11th Street, Roswell NM 88201. 505/624-6744. **Contact:** Human Resources. **World Wide Web address:** http://www.roswellmuseum.org. **Description:** A leading museum of Southwestern art featuring works by such artists as Georgia O'Keefe.

RUIDOSO DOWNS RACING, INC.
P.O. Box 449, Ruidoso Downs NM 88346. 505/378-4431. **Physical address:** 1461 Highway 70 West, Ruidoso Downs NM 88246. **Contact:** Vicki McCabe, Human Resources. **World Wide Web address:** http://ruidownsracing.com. **Description:** A horse racing facility featuring simulcast racing, a casino, and dining areas. The season begins in late May and runs through early September.

RUIDOSO NEWS
P.O. Box 128, Ruidoso NM 88355. 505/257-4001. **Physical address:** 104 Park Avenue, Ruidoso NM 88345. **Fax:** 505/257-7053. **Contact:** Brad Treptow, Publisher. **E-mail address:** ruidosonews@zianet.com. **World Wide Web address:** http://www.ruidosonews.com. **Description:** Publishes the Ruidoso News, a biweekly newspaper covering all of Lincoln County NM. **Parent company:** Gannett Co, Inc.

SBS TECHNOLOGIES, INC.
2400 Louisiana Boulevard NE, AFC Building 5, Suite 600, Albuquerque NM 87110. 505/875-0600. **Fax:** 505/875-0400. **Contact:** Human Resources. **E-mail address:** jobs@sbs.com. **World Wide Web address:** http://www.sbs.com. **Description:** Builds embedded computer solutions for more than 1,000 customers with over 4,000 products including processor boards, input/output modules, networking devices, and complete computer systems for both commercial and rugged environments. **NOTE:** Search for positions and submit resume online. **Positions advertised include:** Director, Avionic Products; Product Manager; Software Engineer; Engineering Planner; Help Desk Support Specialist; Programmer; Program Support Administrator. **Corporate headquarters location:** This location. **Other U.S. locations:** MA, CA, NC, MN. **International locations:** Germany.

S.P. PHARMACEUTICALS LLC
4272 Balloon Road NE, Albuquerque NM 87109. 505/345-0500. **Fax:** 505/761-9250. **Contact:** Human Resources. **World Wide Web address:** http://www.sppharma.com. **Description:** Researches, develops, and manufactures liquid and lyophilized parenterals. Services include system and equipment validations, calibration, quality assurance, and laboratory services. **Parent company:** Cardinal Health.

ST. JOHN'S COLLEGE
1160 Camino De La Cruz Blanca, Santa Fe NM 87505. 505/984-6141. **Contact:** Ted Gonzales, Director of Human Resources. **E-mail address:** ted.gonzales@sjcsf.edu. **World Wide Web address:** http://www.sjcsf.edu. **Description:** A co-ed, four-year liberal arts college with approximately 400 undergraduate students. St. John's College also has a graduate program. **Positions advertised include:** Associate Librarian for Technical Services and College Archives; Communications Coordinator. **Other U.S. locations:** Annapolis MD.

ST. VINCENT HOSPITAL
P.O. Box 2107, Santa Fe NM 87504-2107. 505/820-5629. **Physical address:** 455 St. Michael's Drive, Santa Fe NM 87505. **Recorded jobline:** 800/475-4578. **Contact:** Human Resources. **World Wide Web address:** http://www.stvin.org. **Description:** A 268-bed, non-affiliated, nonprofit acute care facility. St. Vincent Hospital is JCAHO-accredited. Founded in 1865. **NOTE:** Telephone application line: 800/475-4578. Hearing impaired: 800/360-7904. **Positions advertised include:** Executive Assistant; Billing Specialist; Patient Services Specialist; Counselor; Cath Lab Tech; Pulmonary Rehab Specialist; ESD Tech; Nursing Assistant; Surgical Tech; Staff Pharmacist; Radiologic/Diagnostic Tech; Occupational Therapist; Speech Language Pathologist; RN; LPN. **Office hours:** Monday - Friday, 8:00 a.m. - 4:30 p.m.

SAGEBRUSH TECHNOLOGY
5911 Jefferson Street NE, Albuquerque NM 87109. 505/299-6623. **Fax:** 505/298-2072. **Contact:** Human Resources. **E-mail address:** rossbachd@sagebrushtech.com. **World Wide Web address:** http://www.sagebrushtech.com. **Description:** Engineering and manufacturing company specializing in providing innovative motion control systems. **Positions advertised include:** Control Systems Engineer.

SAM GOODY
6600 Menaul Boulevard NE, Suite 331, Albuquerque NM 87110. 505/883-2961. **Contact:** Manager. **World Wide Web address:** http://www.samgoody.com. **Description:** One of the 500 unit chain of specialty retail music stores. **Parent company:** Musicland Group Inc.

SAN FELIPE'S CASINO HOLLYWOOD
25 Hagan Road, San Felipe NM 87001. 505/867-6700. **Fax:** 505/867-6627. **Contact:** Dennis Garcia, Manager. **World Wide Web address:** http://www. sanfelipecasino.com. **Description:** A Las Vegas-style casino featuring a variety of games including slots, craps, black jack, and roulette. Founded in 1995. **NOTE:** Search and apply for positions online. **Positions advertised include:** Gift Shop Attendant.

SAN JUAN COLLEGE
4601 College Boulevard, Farmington NM 87402. 505/326-3311. **Fax:** 505/566-3521. **Contact:** Director of Human Resources. **World Wide Web address:** http://www.sjc.cc.nm.us. **Description:** A comprehensive community college offering vocational, industrial, and academic transfer programs. Enrollment at San Juan College is approximately 7,300. **NOTE:** Search for positions online. **Positions advertised include:** Early Childhood Ed Instructor; Psychology Instructor; Computer Science Instructor; Physical Therapy Assistant Program Instructor; Financial Aid Advisor; Bookstore Cashier; Security Officer; Administrative Assistant.

SAN JUAN POWER PLANT
P.O. Box 227, Waterflow NM 87421. 505/598-7200. **Physical address:** County Highway North 6800, Waterflow NM 87421. **Contact:** Human Resources. **World Wide Web address:** http://www.pnm.com. **Description:** A coal-fired electrical generating station. **Number of employees at this location:** 435.

SANDERS, BRUIN, COLL & WORLEY
P.O. Box 550, Roswell NM 88202-0550. 505/622-5440. **Fax:** 505/622-5853. **Physical address:** 701 West Country Club Road, Roswell NM 88201. **Contact:** Office Manager. **World Wide Web address:** http://www.sbcw-law.com. **Description:** A law firm offering a wide range of legal specialties including agriculture, bankruptcy, commercial law, criminal law, family law, wills, and workers' compensation. Founded in 1945.

SANDIA CASINO
P.O. Box 10188, Albuquerque NM 87184. 800/526-9366. **Physical address:** 30 Rainbow Road, Albuquerque NM 87113. **Fax:** 505/796-7551. **Contact:** Human Resources. **World Wide Web address:** http://www.sandiacasino.com. **Description:** A

casino featuring a wide variety of games including poker, black jack, roulette, and craps. Sandia Casino is open 24 hours per day, seven days per week. **NOTE:** Search and apply for positions online. **Positions advertised include:** Player Development Manager; Bus Manager; Marketing Manager; Cage/Vault Manager; Driver; Table Games Floor Supervisor; Table Games Box Person; Baker; Cook; Administrative Support Clerk; Maintenance; Chief Financial Officer; Business Development Specialist; Waste Water Treatment Operator; Staff Accountant; Lifeguard. **Number of employees at this location:** 1,200.

SANDIA NATIONAL LABORATORIES
P.O. Box 5800, MS 1023, Albuquerque NM 87105-1023. 505/844-3441. **Contact:** Human Resources. **World Wide Web address:** http://www.sandia.gov. **Description:** A research facility. Areas of focus include nuclear energy research and maintaining and securing nuclear weaponry. Funded by the U.S. Department of Energy and managed by Lockheed Martin Corp. **NOTE:** Search and apply for positions online. **Positions advertised include:** Attorney; Bayesian Statistician; Cataloging Librarian; Complex Systems Engineer; Computer Software Research/Development; Economist; Electronic Engineer; Explosives Engineer; Mechanical Engineer; Medical Administrative Support; Operations Research Analyst; Optical Modeling; Project Staff; Pulsed Power Designer; Software Developer; Systems Engineer; Vulnerability Analyst. **Other U.S. locations:** CA, HI. **Number of employees nationwide:** 8,300.

SANTA FE, CITY OF
P.O. Box 909, 200 Lincoln Avenue, Santa Fe NM 87504-0909. 505/955-6597. **Contact:** Human Resources. **World Wide Web address:** http://www.santafenm.gov. **Description:** The administrative offices of the city of Santa Fe, responsible for staffing of all municipal departments. **NOTE:** Search for positions online. **Positions advertised include:** Emergency Communication Specialist; Secretary; Housing and Economic Development Division Director; Planning and Land Use Department; Police Officer; Recreation Aide; Recreation Coordinator; Transit Operator.

SANTA FE, COUNTY OF
P.O. Box 276, Santa Fe NM 87504. 505/986-6200. **Physical address:** 102 Grant Avenue, Santa Fe NM 87501. **Contact:** Artudo Rodriguez, Personnel Director. **World Wide Web address:** http://www.co.santa-fe.nm.us. **Description:** The administrative offices of the county of Santa Fe, responsible for all county staffing. **NOTE:** Search for positions and obtain employment application online. **Positions advertised include:** Transfer Station Caretaker; Assistant County Attorney; Firefighter/Paramedic; Deputy Cadet; Deputy Sheriff; Court Security and Transport Officer.

SANTA FE INDIAN SCHOOL
1501 Cerrillos Road, P.O. Box 5340, Santa Fe NM 87502. 505/989-6304. **Fax:** 505/989-6317. **Contact:** Leona Chavez, Personnel Specialist. **World Wide Web address:** http://www.sfis.k12.nm.us. **Description:** A private educational institution consisting of a secondary school, with grades seven and eight, and a high school.

SANTA FE OPERA
P.O. Box 2408, Santa Fe NM 87504-2408. 505/986-5955. **Contact:** Director of Human Resources. **E-mail address:** humanresources@santafeopera.org. **World Wide Web address:** http://www.santafeopera.org. **Description:** An opera company that offers summer performances in its outdoor theater. **NOTE:** Hiring is seasonal, with staff reaching approximately 600 during July and August. Some year round positions available. **NOTE:** Search and apply for positions online. **Positions advertised include:** Manager of Individual Giving; Summer Maintenance and Grounds Positions; Usher; Opera Shop Cashier; Customer Service Rep; Database Application Specialist.

SANTA FE PROPERTIES
644 Paseo de Peralta, Santa Fe NM 87501. 505/988-3688. **Fax:** 505/984-1003. **Contact:** Susan Bennett, Associate Broker. **World Wide Web address:** http://www.realtor.com/santafe/sfproperties. **Description:** A real estate company.

SANTA FE PUBLIC SCHOOLS
610 Altavista Street, Santa Fe NM 87505. 505/982-2631. **Fax:** 505/995-3302. **Contact:** Human Resources. **World Wide Web address:** http://www.sfps.k12.nm.us. **Description:** Administrative offices of the Santa Fe public school system, which includes 29 schools with 13,000 students. **NOTE:** Search for positions online. **Positions advertised include:** Bilingual Educational Assistants; Speech and Language Pathologist; School Counselor; Manager for Extended School Year Program; Director of Technology; Library Media Specialist; Coaches/Assistant Coaches; Occupational Therapist; Plumber; Welder; High School Principal; Elementary School Principal.

SANTA FE SKI AREA
2209 Brothers Road, Suite 220, Santa Fe NM 87505. 505/982-4429. **Contact:** Human Resources. **World Wide Web address:** http://www.skisantafe.com. **Description:** This ski area is located in the Sangre de Christo mountain range. The Santa Fe Ski Area has 44 trails. **NOTE:** The majority of the positions here are seasonal temporary positions, running from Thanksgiving to Easter. A job fair for the winter skiing season is held every November when approximately 200 positions are filled. There is usually another hiring session during the Christmas season.

SARA LEE BAKERY GROUP
111 Montano NE, Albuquerque NM 87107. 505/345-3481. **Contact:** Ms. Jackie Metcalf, Personnel Manager. **World Wide Web address:** http://www.earthgrains.com. **Description:** A national producer of a wide range of bakery products including bread and rolls. **Corporate headquarters location:** St. Louis MO. **Operations at this facility include:** Administration; Manufacturing; Sales.

SEARS, ROEBUCK & CO.
1000 South Main Street, Roswell NM 88201. 505/627-5215. **Contact:** Manager. **World Wide Web address:** http://www.sears.com. **Description:** One of 870 Sears, Roebuck & Co. stores, a retailer of apparel, home, and automotive products and related services. **NOTE:** Search and apply for positions online. **Corporate headquarters location:** Chicago IL. **Listed on:** New York Stock Exchange. **Stock exchange symbol:** S.

7-ELEVEN FOOD STORES
12801 Menaul Boulevard NE, Albuquerque NM 87112. 505/292-6922. **Contact:** Betty Gregson, District Manager. **World Wide Web address:** http://www.seveneleven.com. **Description:** This location is the district office of the convenience store chain that includes 24,000 stores worldwide. There are more than 20 stores in Albuquerque and one store in Rio Rancho. **Corporate headquarters location:** Dallas TX. **Operations at this facility include:** District Headquarters.

SIERRA PEAKS CORPORATION
8436 Washington Place NE, Albuquerque NM 87113. 505/345-5577. **Fax:** 505/345-2056. **Contact:** Human Resources. **E-mail address:** hr@spz.biz. **World Wide Web address:** http://www.spc.biz. **Description:** Provides design, manufacturing, and packaging of electromechanical systems. **Positions advertised include:** Electronics Engineer

SILVER CITY SCHOOLS
2810 North Swan Street, Silver City NM 88061. 505/388-1527. **Fax:** 505/956-2039. **Contact:** Dick Pool, Superintendent. **Description:** The administrative offices of the Silver City school system, responsible for staffing municipal schools.

SMITH ENGINEERING
P.O. Box 2565, Roswell NM 88202. 505/622-8866. **Physical address:** 210 North Main Street, Roswell NM 88201. **Contact:** Human Resources. **World Wide Web address:** http://www.secnm.com. **Description:** An engineering consulting firm providing civil, structural, and environmental engineering, as well as materials testing services. **Other area locations:** Albuquerque NM.

SMITH'S FOOD AND DRUG STORES
4700 Tramway Boulevard NE, Albuquerque NM 87111. 505-292-5484. **Contact:** Human Resources. **Description:** Operates a chain of 126 supermarkets/pharmacies in seven southwestern states. **NOTE:** Apply for positions online. **Corporate headquarters location:** Salt Lake City UT. **Parent company:** Kroger Company.

SOUTHWEST AIRLINES COMPANY
P.O. Box 9358, Albuquerque NM 87119. 505/842-1337. **Contact:** Frank Stockton, Station Manager. **World Wide Web address:** http://www.southwest.com. **Description:** A national airline company with service to 58 cities in the United States. **NOTE:** Job application information available online. **Corporate headquarters location:** Dallas TX. **Number of employees nationwide:** 34,000.

SOUTHWEST SECURITY
6565 Americas Parkway, Suite 950, Albuquerque NM 87190-0990. 505/889-7777. **Contact:** Branch Manager. **E-mail address:** careers@onlinepreferred.com. **World Wide Web address:** http://www.onlinepreferred.com. **Description:** Provides securities brokerage and other financial management services. **Positions advertised include:** Registered Sales Assistant. **Corporate headquarters location:** Dallas TX. **Other U.S. locations:** Santa Fe NM; Tulsa OK; Kerrville TX; Lufkin TX; San Antonio TX. **Operations at this facility include:** Sales; Service.

SPECIALTY BRANDS INC.
5801 Jefferson Street NE, Albuquerque NM 87109. 505/344-4590. **Contact:** Human Resources. **World Wide Web address:** http://www.specialtybrandsinc.com. **Description:** A producer and packager of a variety of frozen foods. Most of the company's products are Mexican-style foods including miniburritos and other appetizers. **Corporate headquarters location:** CA.

SUD-CHEMIE PERFORMANCE PACKAGING
101 Christine Drive, Belen NM 87002. 505/864-6691. **Toll-free phone:** 800/989-3374. **Fax:** 505/864-9296. **Contact:** Human Resources. **E-mail address:** info@s-cpp.com. **World Wide Web address:** http://www.sud-chemie.com. **Description:** Fabricator and packager of desiccants, chemicals that absorb humidity and odor. **Parent company:** Sud-Chemie AG.

SUMMIT ELECTRIC SUPPLY, INC.
2900 Stanford NE, Albuquerque NM 87107. 505/346-9000. **Fax:** 505/346-1611. **Contact:** Human Resources. **E-mail address:** Estrathdee@summit.com. **World Wide Web address:** http://www.summit.com. **Description:** Carries all types of electrical supplies including light fixtures, furnished wires, and breakers. Operates 20 service centers in four states plus an export division. **NOTE:** Search for positions online. **Positions advertised include:** Risk Management Coordinator; Regional Credit Manager. **Corporate headquarters location:** This location. **Number of employees nationwide:** 500.

SUN HEALTHCARE GROUP, INC.
101 Sun Avenue NE, Albuquerque NM 87109. 505/821-3355. **Contact:** Human Resources. **World Wide Web address:** http://www.sunh.com. **Description:** One of the nation's largest nursing home operators. Sun Healthcare Group is a comprehensive health care system that provides skilled nursing, pharmaceutical services, rehabilitation therapy, home health care services, and medical supplies. Founded in 1993. **NOTE:** Search and apply for positions online. **Corporate headquarters location:** This location. **Subsidiaries include:** SunAlliance Healthcare Services; SunBridge Healthcare Corporation; SunCare Respiratory Services, Inc.; SunChoice Medical Supply, Inc.; SunDance Rehabilitation Corporation; SunFactors, Inc.; SunPlus Home Health Services; SunScript Pharmacy Corporation. **Number of employees nationwide:** 16,800.

SUNLAND PARK RACETRACK & CASINO
P.O. Box 1, 1200 Futurity Drive, Sunland Park NM 88063. 505/874-5200. **Contact:** General Manager. **World Wide Web address:** http://www.sunland-park.com. **Description:** Offers live and simulcast horse racing, slot machines, five restaurants, and meeting rooms. **NOTE:** Search for positions online.

SUNRISE SENIOR LIVING
4910 Tramway Ridge Drive NE, Albuquerque NM 87111. 505/271-9600. **Contact:** Human Resources. **World Wide Web address:** http://www.sunriseassistedliving.com. **Description:** Operates 370 senior living communities in 34 states, Canada, and the United Kingdom. Founded in 1981. **Number of employees worldwide:** 30,000.

TALBOT FINANCIAL SERVICES
P.O. Box 90756, Albuquerque NM 87199-0756. 505/828-4000. **Physical address:** 7770 Jefferson NE, Suite 200, Albuquerque NM 87109. **Contact:** Human Resources. **E-mail address:** employmentrs@talbotcorp.com. **World Wide Web address:** http://www.talbotcorp.com. **Description:** An insurance company. Talbot Financial Services specializes in group and life insurance and annuities. Operates 60 offices in 20 states. **NOTE:** Search and apply for positions online. **Positions advertised include:** SW Regional Accounting Manager; Accountant; Securities Licensing Administrator; Assistant Licensing Administrator.

TAOS, CITY OF
400 Camino de la Placita, Taos NM 87571. 505/751-2000. **Fax:** 505/751-2026. **Contact:** Patricia Trujillo, Director of Human Resources. **World Wide Web address:** http://www.taosgov.com. **Description:** The administrative offices of the city of Taos, responsible for staffing municipal departments. **NOTE:** Search for jobs and obtain employment applications online. **Positions advertised include:** Communications Equipment Operator; Police Officer.

TAOS MOCCASIN COMPANY
P.O. Box 708, Taos NM 87571. 505/758-4276. **Fax:** 505/758-5444. **Contact:** Tom Powell, Manager. **World Wide Web address:** http://www.taosmocs.com.

Description: Manufactures a wide variety of Native American leathercraft products. **Corporate headquarters location:** This location.

TAOS MUNICIPAL SCHOOLS
213 Paseo del Canon, Taos NM 87571. 505/758-5205. **Fax:** 505/758-5298. **Contact:** Robert Romero, Human Resources. **E-mail address:** bob@taosschools.org. **World Wide Web address:** http://www.taosschools.org. **Description:** The administrative office of the Taos school system, which is responsible for staffing municipal schools. **NOTE:** Part-time jobs are offered. **Special programs:** Internships; Summer Jobs. **Office hours:** Monday - Friday, 8:00 a.m. - 4:30 p.m. **Superintendent:** Dr. Mark Space

TAOS SKI VALLEY, INC.
P.O. Box 90, Taos Ski Valley NM 87525. 505/776-2291. **Fax:** 505/776-8596. **Contact:** Hanna Levitz, Human Resources Department. **E-mail address:** melia@newmex.com. **World Wide Web address:** http://www.skitaos.org. **Description:** One of the top resort skiing areas in North America. The ski area has more than 72 trails and features one of the top-ranked ski schools in the country. **NOTE:** Most positions are entry level and seasonal. Summer and full-time, year round positions are filled from within the company. Download employment application. **Positions advertised include:** Childcare; Bussers; Cashiers; Dishwashers; Lift Operations; Line Servers; Parking Lot Shuttle Drivers; Retail Sales.

TARGET STORES
2725 North Main Street, Roswell NM 88201. 505/623-0445. **Contact:** Human Resources. **World Wide Web address:** http://www.target.com. **Description:** Target Corporation is a leading general merchandise retail company offering its products through divisions: Target, Marshall Field's, and Mervyn's. **NOTE:** Search and apply for positions online. **Positions advertised include:** Store Team Leader. **Corporate headquarters location:** Minneapolis MN.

TAYLOR PRECISION PRODUCTS
P.O. Box 1240, Las Cruces NM 88004. 505/526-0944. **Physical address:** 2220 Entrada Del Sol, Las Cruces NM 88001. **Contact:** Human Resources Department. **World Wide Web address:** http://www.taylorusa.com. **Description:** A manufacturer of bathroom scales, thermometers, and related measurement products. **Corporate headquarters location:** Oak Brook IL.

TECH REPS, INC.
1300 Eubank Boulevard SE, Albuquerque NM 87123. 505/266-5678. **Fax:** 505/988-5844. **Contact:** Human Resources. **E-mail address:** resumes@ktech.com. **World Wide Web address:** http://www.ktech.com. **Description:** A full-service communications company that provides technical documentation and visual media services for commercial firms and government agencies. Services include technical writing, production, and illustration and graphic design. Founded in 1974. **Positions advertised include:** Component Characterization Specialist; Mechanical Technician; Administrative Assistant; Environmental Scientist; Graphic Artist; Software Developer; Technical Writer. **Corporate headquarters location:** This location. **Parent company:** Ktech Corporation.

THERMO EBERLINE
P.O. Box 2108, Santa Fe NM 87504. 505/471-3232. **Contact:** Human Resources. **World Wide Web address:** http://www.thermo.com. **Description:** Manufactures radiation and environmental monitors. Thermo Eberline also develops a line of thermo-bioanalysis devices for medical applications. **NOTE:** Search and apply for positions online. **Positions advertised include:** Product Sales Support Manager; Engineering Manager. **Parent company:** Thermo Electron Corporation.

THORNBURG MORTGAGE ASSET CORPORATION
150 Washington Street, Suite 302, Santa Fe NM 87532. 505/989-1900. **Contact:** Human Resources. **World Wide Web address:** http://www.thornburgmortgage.com. **Description:** A special purpose financial institution that invests in adjustable-rate mortgage securities and provides capital to the single-family housing market. The company leverages its equity capital using borrowed funds, invests in adjustable-rate mortgage securities, and generates income based on earnings that are greater than what it pays for its borrowings. Thornburg Mortgage is a real estate investment trust and pays out its taxable earnings in the form of dividends. **Listed on:** New York Stock Exchange. **Stock exchange symbol:** TMA.

TORTILLA, INC.
dba GARDUNO'S OF MEXICO/YESTERDAVE'S
10555 Montgomery NE, Suite 90, Albuquerque NM 87111. 505/298-5514. **Fax:** 505/298-5549. **Contact:** Human Resources. **World Wide Web address:** http://www.gardunosrestaurants.com. **Description:** Operates two restaurant chains. Garduno's are Mexican restaurants with entertainment and YesterDaves is a '50s-style diner. **Special programs:** Internships. **Corporate headquarters location:** This location. **Operations at this facility include:** Administration. **Listed on:** Privately held.

TOWN & RANCH, INC.
505 Don Gaspar Avenue, Santa Fe NM 87505. 505/988-3700. **Contact:** Human Resources. **Description:** A realty firm.

TRAFFICDEVELOPER
1809 Arroyo Chamiso, Santa Fe NM 87505. 505/988-5055. **Contact:** Human Resources. **E-mail address:** chris@trafficdeveloper.com. **World Wide Web address:** www.trafficdeveloper.com. **Description:** Full service SEO company whose focus is to increase online business revenue through search engine optimization, pay per click, and website promotion. **Positions advertised include:** Perl Programmer.

UBS FINANCIAL SERVICES INC.
2155 Louisiana Boulevard NE, Suite 3000, Albuquerque NM 87110. 505/881-1700. **Contact:** Personnel. **World Wide Web address:** http://www.financialservicesinc.ubs.com. **Description:** A full-service securities firm with over 300 offices nationwide. Services include investment banking, asset management, merger and acquisition consulting, municipal securities underwriting, estate planning, retirement programs, and transaction management. Clients include corporations, governments, institutions, and individuals. Founded in 1879. **Corporate headquarters location:** New York NY. **Other U.S. locations:** Nationwide.

U.S. COTTON
590 Laser Road, Rio Rancho NM 87124. 505/892-2269. **Fax:** 505/892-0977. **Toll-free phone:** 800/888-0747. **Contact:** Human Resources. **Description:** U.S. Cotton manufactures private label and branded health, beauty aide, pharmaceutical, and industrial cotton fiber products. **NOTE:** Search and apply for positions online. **Corporate headquarters location:** This location. **Other U.S. locations:** NC; OH; NV; CT. **International locations:** Canada; Puerto Rico; Chile.

U.S. DEPARTMENT OF ENERGY
P.O. Box 3090, Carlsbad NM 88221. 505/234-7200. **Physical address:** 4021 National Parks Highway, Carlsbad NM 88221. **Contact:** Human Resources Department. **E-mail address:** infocntr@wipp.ws. **World Wide Web address:** http://www.wipp.carlsbad.nm.us. **Description:** This location is the world's first underground repository licensed to dispose of radioactive waste left from the research and production of nuclear weapons. The U.S. Department of Energy is concerned with scientific and technological development as well as economic diversification.

U.S. DEPARTMENT OF VETERANS AFFAIRS
ALBUQUERQUE REGIONAL OFFICE
Danis Chavez Federal Building, 500 Gold Avenue SW, Albuquerque NM 87102. 800/827-1000. **Contact:** Human Resources. **World Wide Web address:** http://www.va.gov. **Description:** Regional office of the U.S. Department of Veterans Affairs.

U.S. POSTAL SERVICE
1135 Broadway NE, Room 231, Albuquerque NM 87102-9421. **Toll-free phone:** 800/ASK-USPS. **Recorded jobline:** 505/346-8780. **Contact:** Human Resources. **World Wide Web address:** http://www.usps.com. **Description:** A full-service post office serving the Albuquerque area. This location is the main branch. **NOTE:** A U.S. Postal Service exam is required. Please call the jobline for details.

U.S. SOCIAL SECURITY ADMINISTRATION
4300 Cutler Avenue, Albuquerque NM 87110. 505/346-6694. **Toll-free phone:** 800/772-1213. **Contact:** Human Resources Department. **World Wide Web address:** http://www.ssa.gov. **Description:** Administers the social security program and provides benefits and services to the people residing in the state of New Mexico. **NOTE:** To be considered for a position, you must apply for a specific vacancy announcement. Unsolicited applications are not accepted. Search and apply for positions online.

UNITED WAY OF CENTRAL NEW MEXICO
302 Eighth Street NW, Albuquerque NM 87102. 505/247-3671. **Fax:** 505/242-3576. **Contact:** Human Resources. **World Wide Web address:** http://www.uwcnm.org. **Description:** Through a network of volunteers and local charities, local United Way organizations throughout America help meet the health and human care needs of millions of people. The United Way system includes approximately 1,900 community-based organizations. United Way of America operates a national service and training center, supporting its members with national services that include advertising, training, corporate relations, research, networks, and government relations.

UNIVERSITY OF NEW MEXICO
1717 Roma NE, Albuquerque NM 87131. 505/277-6947. **Fax:** 505/277-2456. **Contact:** Human Resources. **World Wide Web address:** http://www.unm.edu. **Description:** A four-year university offering associate's, bachelor's, master's, certificate, professional, and doctoral degree programs to nearly 25,000 students on the main campus and 7,000 on branch campuses and education centers. Founded in 1889. **NOTE:** Search and apply for positions online. **Positions advertised include:** Systems Analyst; Case Manager; Library Info Specialist; Enrollment Representative; Editor; Administrative Assistant; Director, Employee Assistance Programs; Dean; Visiting Professor; Lecturer.

UNIVERSITY OF NEW MEXICO/VALENCIA
280 La Entrada, Los Lunas NM 87031. 505/925-8530. **Fax:** 505/925-8501. **Contact:** Human Resources Department. **World Wide Web address:** http://www.unm.edu/~unmvc. **Description:** This location of the University of New Mexico offers associate degrees and certificate and credential programs to approximately 1,600 students. **NOTE:** Search and apply for positions online. **Positions advertised include:** Asst Professor of Developmental English.

UNIVERSITY OF NEW MEXICO HOSPITAL
2211 Lomas Boulevard NE, Albuquerque NM 87106. 505/272-2111. **Contact:** Human Resources. **World Wide Web address:** http://hospitals.unm.edu. **Description:** A 384-bed acute, tertiary care hospital offering services including pulmonary, psychiatric, neurosurgical, pediatric, and emergency care. UNM Hospital is the primary teaching hospital for the University of New Mexico's School of Medicine, and is part of the University of New Mexico Health Sciences Center. The hospital also features the Children's Hospital of New Mexico and the Senior Health Center. **NOTE:** Search and apply for positions online.

UNIVERSITY OF PHOENIX
7471 Pan American Freeway NE, Albuquerque NM 87109. 505/821-4800. **Contact:** Human Resources. **World Wide Web address:** http://www.phoenix.edu. **Description:** This location of the university offers undergraduate and graduate programs. **NOTE:** Search and apply for positions online. **Positions advertised include:** Campus College Chair. **Parent company:** Apollo Group, Inc.

VALENCIA COUNTY NEWS-BULLETIN
P.O. Box 25, Belen NM 87002. 505/864-4472. **Physical address:** 1837 Camino del Llano, Belen NM 87002. **Fax:** 505/864-3549. **Contact:** Publisher. **World Wide Web address:** http://www.news-bulletin.com. **Description:** Publishes the twice-weekly newspaper *Valencia County News-Bulletin*, with a circulation of 23,000 on Wednesdays and Saturdays. Founded in 1911. **NOTE:** Entry-level positions, part-time jobs, and second and third shifts are offered. **Special programs:** Internships; Apprenticeships; Training; Co-ops; Summer Jobs. **Office hours:** Monday - Friday, 8:00 a.m. - 5:00 p.m., Saturday 8:00 a.m. - 12:00 p.m. **Parent company:** WorldWest. **Listed on:** Privately held.

VERDE STUDIOS
2400 Louisiana NE, AFC 3, Albuquerque NM 87502. 505/348-9777. **Fax:** 505/348-9787. **Contact:** Human Resources. **E-mail address:** hr@verdestudios.com. **World Wide Web Address:** http://www.verdestudios.com. **Description:** Provides high-end creative design, back end web development, and online marketing to a growing customer base in both the commercial and government sectors. **Positions advertised include:** Illustrator; Animator; Storyboard Artist; Freelance Programmer.

WAL-MART STORES, INC.
4501 North Main, Roswell NM 88201. 505/623-2062. **Contact:** Human Resources. **World Wide Web address:** http://www.walmart.com. **Description:** Wal-Mart Stores is one of the largest retail merchandise chains in the country, operating full-service discount department stores, combination grocery and discount stores, and warehouse stores requiring membership. Founded in 1962. **NOTE:** Obtain job information and submit resume online. **Corporate headquarters location:** Bentonville AR.

WALGREENS DRUG STORE
333 Montano Road NW, Albuquerque NM 87107. 505/345-9059. **Contact:** Manager. **World Wide Web address:** http://www.walgreens.com. **Description:** Operates one of the largest retail drug store chains in the United States, selling prescription and

nonprescription drugs, cosmetics, toiletries, liquor and beverages, tobacco, and general merchandise. **NOTE:** Information online for applications in areas of pharmacy, retail management, technology, corporate, full and part-time store, managed care, and distribution center positions.

WALGREENS DRUG STORE
902 West Pierce Street, Carlsbad NM 88220. 505/887-0380. **Contact:** Manager. **World Wide Web address:** http://www.walgreens.com. **Description:** Walgreen's operates one of the largest retail drug store chains in the United States, selling prescription and nonprescription drugs, cosmetics, toiletries, liquor and beverages, tobacco, and general merchandise. **NOTE:** Information online for applications in areas of pharmacy, retail management, technology, corporate, full and part-time store, managed care, and distribution center positions.

WALGREENS DRUG STORE
895 North White Sands Boulevard, Alamogordo NM 88310. 505/434-4112. **Contact:** Store Manager. **World Wide Web address:** http://www.walgreens.com. **Description:** Operates one of the largest retail drug store chains in the United States, selling prescription and nonprescription drugs, cosmetics, toiletries, liquor and beverages, tobacco, and general merchandise. **NOTE:** Information online for applications in areas of pharmacy, retail management, technology, corporate, full and part-time store, managed care, and distribution center positions.

WASTE MANAGEMENT OF NEW MEXICO, INC.
402 Industrial Park Loop NE, Rio Rancho NM 87124. 505/892-1200. **Contact:** Human Resources. **World Wide Web address:** http://www.wm.com. **Description:** One of the nation's largest waste management companies. Waste Management of New Mexico provides hazardous waste management services and recycling and waste collection for residential customers and businesses. The company operates land disposal sites, collection facilities, transfer stations, and trash-to-energy plants. **NOTE:** Search and apply for positions online. **Corporate headquarters location:** Houston TX.

WASTE MANAGEMENT OF NEW MEXICO, INC.
101 Spruce Street, Farmington NM 87401. 505/327-6284. **Contact:** Human Resources Department. **World Wide Web address:** http://www.wm.com. **Description:** One of the nation's largest waste management companies. Waste Management of New Mexico provides hazardous waste management services and recycling and waste collection for residential customers and businesses. The company operates land disposal sites, collection facilities, transfer stations, and trash-to-energy plants. **NOTE:** Search and apply for positions online. **Corporate headquarters location:** Houston TX.

WELLS FARGO BANK
P.O. Box 2027, Santa Fe NM 87504. 505/984-0402. **Physical address:** 241 Washington Avenue, Santa Fe NM 87501. **Contact:** Human Resources. **Description:** Provides banking, insurance, investments, mortgage, and consumer finance from 5,900 locations across North America and internationally. **NOTE:** Search and apply for positions online. **Corporate headquarters location:** San Francisco CA. **Listed on:** New York Stock Exchange. **Stock exchange symbol:** WFC.

WENDY'S INTERNATIONAL, INC.
4900 Central Avenue SE, Albuquerque NM 87109. 505/268-8017. **Contact:** Personnel. **World Wide Web address:** http://www.wendysintl.com. **Description:** One of the world's largest restaurant franchising companies with 6,000 restaurants worldwide. Wendy's International includes Wendy's, a fast-food restaurant chain, and Tim Horton's, a coffee and baked goods restaurant chain. **NOTE:** Search and apply for corporate, field office, and restaurant operator jobs online. **Corporate headquarters location:** Columbus OH. **Listed on:** New York Stock Exchange. **Stock exchange symbol:** WEN.

WESTERN NEW MEXICO UNIVERSITY
Room 110 Juan Chacon, P.O. Box 680, Silver City NM 88062. 505/538-6328. **Fax:** 505/538-6338. **Contact:** Human Resources Manager. **World Wide Web address:** http://www.wnmu.edu. **Description:** A four-year university that offers graduate and undergraduate programs to approximately 2,500 students. Founded in 1893. **NOTE:** Search and apply for positions online. **Positions advertised include:** Accounts Payable Clerk; Adjunct Faculty; Cashier; Faculty Positions; Cross Country Coach; Assistant Woman's Basketball Coach; Teacher.

WESTERN TECHNOLOGIES, INC.
8305 Washington Place NE, Albuquerque NM 87113. 505/823-4488. **Fax:** 505/821-2963. **Contact:** Human Resources. **E-mail address:** s.allanson@wt-us.com. **World Wide Web address:** http://www.wt-us.com. **Description:** Provides engineering, consulting, and testing of environmental, geotechnical, and construction materials. Twenty offices in six states and Mexico. Founded in 1955. **Positions advertised include:** Senior Geotechnical Engineer; Geotechnical Project Engineer; Senior Environmental Project Manager; Geologist; Industrial Hygienist; Welding Inspector. **Corporate headquarters location:** Phoenix AZ. **Number of employees nationwide:** 425.

WHITES CITY, INC.
P.O. Box 128, Whites City NM 88268. 505/785-2294. **Contact:** Personnel Director. **Description:** Owns and operates several hotels, restaurants, gas stations, grocery stores, RV parks, and gift shops catering to tourists in the Whites City NM area.

WILD OATS MARKET
1090 St. Francis Drive, Santa Fe NM 87501. 505/983-5333. **Fax:** 505/986-6087. **Contact:** Human Resources. **World Wide Web address:** http://www.wildoats.com. **Description:** A natural food stores featuring massage therapists and coffee and juice bars. Founded in 1987. **NOTE:** For more information on what positions are currently open, inquire at the customer service desk. An application is required, and a response is usually given within a few days. **Corporate headquarters location:** Boulder CO.

WIRED NATION
3600 Cerillos Road, Suite 711, Santa Fe NM 87507. 505/471-2820. **Contact:** Human Resources. **E-mail address:** info@wirednation.com. **World Wide Web Address:** http://www.wirednation.com. **Description:** Provides computer consulting services. **NOTE:** Please apply for positions through company website. **Positions advertised include:** Programmer; Consultant.

XEROX CORPORATION
5600 Wyoming Boulevard NE, Suite 200, Albuquerque NM 87109. 505/822-5200. **Contact:** Human Resources. **World Wide Web address:** http://www.xerox.com. **Description:** Designs, develops, manufactures, markets, and services a complete range of document processing products and systems including copiers, duplicators, electronic scanners, facsimile machines, networks, multifunction publishing machines and related products, software, and supplies. **Corporate headquarters location:** Stamford CT. **Operations at this facility include:** This location is a regional sales and service office.

XILINX
7801 Jefferson Street NE, Albuquerque NM 87109. 505/828-2032. **Fax:** 505/858-3106. **Contact:** Human Resources. **World Wide Web address:** http://www.xilinx.com. **Description:** Xilinx is a provider of programmable logic devices. Develops, manufactures, and markets a broad line of advanced integrated circuits, software design tools and intellectual property. **Positions advertised include:** Design Engineer; Software engineer.

ZUNI PUBLIC SCHOOL DISTRICT
PO Drawer A, Zuni NM 87327. 505/782-5511 ext 20045. Fax: 505/782-5870. **Contact:** Human Resources Department. **World Wide Web address:** http://www.zuni.k12.nm.us. **Description:** A public school district serving more than 2,000 students. **Positions advertised include:** Elementary Principal; Counselor; Permanent Substitute Instructor; Special Education Teacher; Speech Language Pathologist; Early Childhood Instructor; Language Arts Instructor.

A&E TELEVISION NETWORKS
235 East 45th Street, New York NY 10017. 212/210-1400. **Fax:** 212/907-9402. **Contact:** Human Resources. **World Wide Web address:** http://www.aande.com/corporate. **Description:** A joint venture of The Hearst Corporation, ABC, Inc., and NBC, the company is a media corporation that provides magazine and book publishing services, distributes home videos, and operates Websites and the A&E and History Channel cable stations. **NOTE:** The company prefers resumes to be faxed to the above number along with the position to which applying and salary requirements. **Positions advertised include:** Affiliate Sales Administration Manager; Inventory Analyst; Legal & Business Affairs Assistant; Traffic Services Assistant; Account Executive. **Corporate headquarters location:** This location. **Subsidiaries include:** The History Channel; Biography Channel; History Channel International; Genealogy.com; Military.com; Mysteries.com.

ABB SSAC INC.
P.O. Box 1000, Baldwinsville NY 13027. 315/638-1300. **Physical address:** 8220 Loop Road, Baldwinsville NY 13027. **Fax:** 315/638-0333. **Contact:** Sandy Lisi, Human Resources Director. **E-mail address:** info@ssac.com. **World Wide Web address:** http://www.ssac.com. **Description:** A manufacturer of a variety of electrical components. Common products include timer modules; obstruction and lighting controls; and heating, ventilation, and air conditioning control devices. **Parent company:** ABB Inc. ATLV (Wichita Falls TX).

ABC, INC.
77 West 66th Street, New York NY 10023. 212/456-7777. **Contact:** Human Resources. **World Wide Web address:** http://www.abc.go.com. **Description:** Engaged in television and radio broadcasting, providing cable television service to subscribers, and specialized newspaper publishing. Broadcasting operations include ABC Television Network Group, the Broadcast Group, the Cable and International Broadcast Group, and the Multimedia Group. In addition to its network operation, the Broadcasting segment consists of 8 network-affiliated television stations, 10 radio stations, cable television systems providing service to subscribers in 16 states, and the developing of multimedia video-by-wire business. Publishing operations consist of 8 daily newspapers, 78 weekly newspapers, 63 shopping guides, and other specialized publications. **Positions advertised include:** Senior Promotions Manager; Manager of Sales Administration; Copy Editor; Manager of Network Promotions; Communications Manager; Retail Manager; Learning Editor. **Parent company:** The Walt Disney Company.

ACC BUSINESS, INC.
400 West Avenue, Rochester NY 14611. 585/987-3000. **Contact:** Human Resources. **World Wide Web address:** http://www.accbusiness.com. **Description:** ACC Corporation, through its subsidiaries, provides worldwide long-distance telecommunications services to customers in the United States, Canada, and the United Kingdom. ACC provides domestic and international long-distance telephone services to business and residential customers, as well as specialized programs for colleges, universities, and hospitals. **Parent company:** AT&T Corporation.

ACTV INC.
1270 Avenue of the Americas, New York NY 10020. 212/217-1600. **Contact:** Human Resources. **E-mail address:** jobs@actv.com. **World Wide Web address:** http://www.actv.com. **Description:** Engaged in individual television programming. The company's primary markets are in-home entertainment and education. **Corporate headquarters location:** This location. **Other U.S. locations:** San Francisco CA; Lexington MA. **Operations at this facility include:** Administration; Production; Research and Development; Sales; Service. **Listed on:** NASDAQ. **Stock exchange symbol:** IATV. **Annual sales/revenues:** $13.7 million. **Number of employees:** 143.

ADT SECURITY SERVICES
335 West 16th Street, New York NY 10011. 646/336-2300. **Contact:** Human Resources. **World Wide Web address:** http://www.adt.com. **Description:** Designs, programs, markets, and installs protective systems to safeguard life and property from hazards such as burglary, hold-up, and fire. ADT Security Services has over 180,000 customers in the United States, Canada, and Western Europe. Founded in 1874. **Positions advertised include:** Commercial Sales Representative. **Corporate headquarters location:** Boca Raton FL. **Parent company:** Tyco International Ltd. **Listed on:** New York Stock Exchange. **Stock exchange symbol:** TYC.

AFP IMAGING CORPORATION
250 Clearbrook Road, Elmsford NY 10523. 914/592-6100. **Fax:** 914/592-6148. **Contact:** Human Resources Manager. **E-mail address:** afp@afpimaging.com. **World Wide Web address:** http://www.afpimaging.com. **Description:** Provides medical equipment utilized by radiologists, cardiologists, and other medical professionals for generating, recording, processing, and viewing hard copy diagnostic images. The company's products are applied in medical diagnostics X-ray inspection. Products are marketed under the AFP, DENT-X, and SENS-A-RAY 2000 brand names. **International locations:** Geilenkirchen, Germany. **Listed on:** Over The Counter. **Stock exchange symbol:** AFPC. **Chairman:** David Vozick. **Annual sales/revenues:** $24 million. **Number of employees:** 106.

AFS INTERCULTURAL PROGRAMS, INC.
71 West 23rd Street, 17th Floor, New York NY 10010. 212/807-8686. **Fax:** 212/807-1001. **Contact:** Human Resources. **E-mail address:** jobs@afs.org. **World Wide Web address:** http://www.afs.org. **Description:** An international exchange organization that provides intercultural learning opportunities for high school students, families, and teachers. The agency operates programs in approximately 55 countries via an international network of volunteers. **Positions advertised include:** Youth Ambassadors Program Coordinator; Development Associate; Admissions Advisor; Administrative Assistant; Regional Coordinator. **Other locations:** Worldwide.

ALS INTERNATIONAL
18 John Street, Suite 300, New York NY 10038. 212/766-4111. **Toll-free phone:** 800/788-0450. **Fax:** 212/349-0964. **Contact:** Human Resources Supervisor. **E-mail address:** hr@alsintl.com. **World Wide Web address:** http://www.alsintl.com. **Description:** A translation and interpreting company serving a worldwide, diversified clientele. **Positions advertised include:** Language Specialist; Translator; On-site Technician; Studio Engineer; Software Engineer/Programmer.

AMEC
1633 Broadway, 24th Floor, New York NY 10019. 212/484-0300. **Fax:** 212/484-0580. **Contact:** Human Resources. **World Wide Web address:** http://www.amec.com. **Description:** One of the largest construction management companies in the world offering a wide range of services including construction management, contracting program management, consulting, and design and construction. Founded in 1936. **Special programs:** Internships. **Corporate headquarters location:** London, United Kingdom. **Subsidiaries include:** AMEC Construction Management, Inc.; Spie S.A. **Operations at this facility include:** Divisional Headquarters; Regional Headquarters. **Listed on:** London Stock Exchange. **Stock exchange symbol:** AMEC. **Annual sales/revenues:** $5 billion. **Number of employees at this location:** 140. **Number of employees nationwide:** 500. **Number of employees worldwide:** 45,000.

AMI (ADVANCED MEDIA INC.)
80 Orville Drive, Bohemia NY 11716. 631/244-1616. **Fax:** 631/244-3209. **Contact:** Office Manager. **World Wide Web address:** http://www.advancedmedia.com. **Description:** Provides professional multimedia development products, services, and proprietary technologies to corporate accounts. AMI's services include Website designing and redesigning. **Listed on:** Over The Counter. **Stock exchange symbol:** AVMJ. **Annual sales/revenues:** $1.26 million. **Number of employees:** 7.

AOL TIME WARNER, INC.
75 Rockefeller Plaza, New York NY 10019. 212/484-8000. **Fax:** 212/489-6183. **Contact:** Human Resources. **World Wide Web address:** http://www.aoltimewarner.com. **Description:** Publishes and distributes books and magazines including the weekly *Time* magazine. Time Warner also produces, distributes, licenses, and publishes recorded music; owns and administers music copyrights; produces, finances, and distributes motion pictures and television programming; distributes videocassettes; produces and distributes pay television and cable programming; and operates and manages cable television systems. **Positions advertised include:** Executive Secretary; Marketing & Business Development Manager; Ad Operations Manager; Associate Finance Manager; Human Resources Director; Articles Editor; Research Analyst; National Account Executive; Advertising Sales Assistant; Sales Assistant; Financial Analyst; Team Assistant; Network Specialist; Manager of Sales; Brand Manager; Technician; International Artist Promotion Assistant; Ad Sales Assistant; High Speed Online Sale Engineer; Manager of Licensing; Business Associate; Accounts Payable Clerk; Financial Operations and Reporting Manager; Bilingual News Assistant; Contract Administrator; Promotions Marketing Director; Special Book Sales Manager; Financial Capital Analyst. **Corporate headquarters location:** This location. **Subsidiaries include:** America Online, Inc.; AOL Time Warner Interactive Video; Columbia House Company; CompuServe; Time Inc.; Time Warner Cable; Time Warner Entertainment Company, L.P.; Time Warner Telecom Inc.; Turner Broadcasting System, Inc.; Warner Bros.; Warner Music Group. **Listed on:** New York Stock Exchange. **Stock exchange symbol:** AOL. **Chairman/CEO:** Richard (Dick) D Parsons. **Annual sales/revenues:** $41 billion. **Number of employees:** 89,300.

API AIR-TECH
91 North Street, P.O. Box 68, Arcade NY 14009. 585/496-5755. **Fax:** 585/496-5776. **Contact:** Human Resources Department. **E-mail address:** hr@apiheattransfer.com. **World Wide Web address:** http://www.apiheattransfer.com. **Description:** This division designs, engineers, and manufactures a broad range of heat transfer products that are used in a variety of applications including the cooling of oil, air, and other gases; steam condensing; vapor recovery; and many other processing requirements. **NOTE:** Resumes may be sent to the Human Resources Department of the company's headquarters address: Human Resources, API Heat Transfer, 2777 Walden Avenue, Buffalo NY 14225. **Corporate headquarters location:** Buffalo NY. **Other locations:** Bretten, Germany. **Parent company:** API Heat Transfer Inc. (Buffalo NY). **Operations at this facility include:** Air Cooled Heat Exchanger Division.

API HEAT TRANSFER INC.
2777 Walden Avenue, Buffalo NY 14225. 716/684-9700. **Fax:** 716/684-2129. **Contact:** Human Resources Department. **E-mail address:** hr@apiheattransfer.com. **World Wide Web address:** http://www.apiheattransfer.com. **Description:** API Heat Transfer manufactures industrial heat exchangers and heat transfer systems. **Corporate headquarters location:** This location. **Other locations:** Arcade NY; Bretten, Germany.

ATC ASSOCIATES INC.
104 East 25th Street, 10th Floor, New York NY 10010-2917. 212/353-8280. **Fax:** 212/353-8306. **E-mail address:** atcjobs@atc-enviro.com. **Contact:** Human Resources. **World Wide Web address:** http://www.atc-enviro.com. **Description:** An environmental consulting firm operating 65 offices in the U.S. providing asbestos, lead, water, and soil testing. Founded in 1985. **Positions advertised include:** Project Manager. **Corporate headquarters location:** Woburn MA. **Other locations:** Nationwide. **Number of employees nationwide:** 1,800.

ABERDEEN SPORTSWEAR, INC.
350 Fifth Avenue, Suite 2828, New York NY 10118. 212/244-5100. **Fax:** 212/629-4298. **Contact:** Joel Stolz, Controller. **Description:** Manufactures a line of sport jackets. **Corporate headquarters location:** This location. **Other locations:** Trenton NJ. **President/CEO:** Harold I. Berk.

ACETO CORPORATION
One Hollow Lane, Suite 201, Lake Success NY 11042-1215. 516/627-6000. **Fax:** 516/627-6093. **Contact:** Kevin Carraher, Human Resources Director. **E-mail address:** hr@aceto.com. **World Wide Web address:** http://www.aceto.com. **Description:** Manufactures chemicals for a wide variety of uses in agricultural markets, color producing industries, and pharmaceutical and health care industries. The chemicals are used to synthesize colors used in photography, textiles, plastics, paints, and printing inks. In the pharmaceutical industry, the company supplies bulk pharmaceuticals and specialty chemicals for use as raw materials to synthesize pharmaceuticals and antibiotics. Aceto also manufactures plastics, surface coatings, and other specialty performance chemicals including antioxidants for plastics, adhesion promoters for automotive finishes, and catalysts for use in the manufacture of certain resins. Founded in 1947. **Corporate headquarters location:** This location. **Other locations:** Worldwide. **Listed on:** NASDAQ. **Stock exchange symbol:** ACET. **Chairman/President/CEO:** Leonard S. Schwartz. **Annual sales/revenue:** $229 million. **Number of employees:** 240.

ACME ARCHITECTURAL PRODUCTS, INC.
dba ACME STEEL PARTITION COMPANY, INC.
513 Porter Avenue, Brooklyn NY 11222. 718/384-7800. **Contact:** Human Resources. **World Wide Web address:** http://www.acmesteel.com. **Description:** The company manufactures commercial interior products including hollow metal steel doors and frames, steel and glass partitions, toilet partitions, and office panels and furniture, as well as distributing builder's hardware and architectural wood doors.

ACU-RITE INC.
One Precision Way, Jamestown NY 14701-9699. 716/661-1700. **Fax:** 716/661-1888. **Contact:** Sally Overend, Human Resources Manager. **E-mail address:** sallyo@acu-rite.com. **World Wide Web address:** http://www.acu-rite.com. **Description:** Manufactures a variety of measuring systems for machine tools. **Corporate headquarters location:** This location. **Other U.S. locations:** CA. **International locations:** France; Germany; Italy; Korea; United Kingdom.

R.P. ADAMS COMPANY INC.
P.O. Box 963, Buffalo NY 14240-0963. 716/877-2608. **Physical address:** 225 East Park Drive, Tonawanda NY 14150-7813. **Toll-free phone:** 800/896-8869. **Fax:** 716/877-9385. **Contact:** David R. Henning, Vice President of Personnel Management. **World Wide Web address:** http://www.rpadams.com. **Description:** A manufacturer of heat exchange and strainer/filtration equipment. **NOTE:** The company requests resumes and cover letters are sent to the above mailing address to the attention of DRH; no e-mails. **Positions advertised include:** Sales Representative; Industrial Engineer; Mechanical Engineer; Administrative Assistant; Welder; Machine Operator. **Special programs:** Internships. **Number of employees:** 100.

ADDISON PRECISION MFG.
500 Avis Street, Rochester NY 14615. 585/254-1386. **Fax:** 585/254-5342. **Contact:** Human Resources Department. **World Wide Web address:** http://www.addisonprec.com. **Description:** manufactures precision-machined components for the aircraft, aerospace, medical, and research industries. **Positions advertised include:** Model Maker; CNC Setup and Run; Quality Engineer.

ADECCO SA
175 Broad Hollow Road, Melville NY 11747. 631/844-7800. **Fax:** 631/844-7022. **Contact:** Human Resources. **World Wide Web address:** http://www.adecco.com. **Description:** Provides a wide variety of job search and placement services, from temporary placements to executive recruitment. **Corporate headquarters location:** Zurich, Switzerland. **Other locations:** Worldwide. **Subsidiaries include:** Lee Hecht Harrison. **Operations at this facility include:** North American headquarters. **Listed on:** New York Stock Exchange; Swiss Exchange. **Stock exchange symbol:** ADO; ADEN. **Annual sales/revenues:** $18 million. **Number of employees worldwide:** 700,000.

ADELPHI UNIVERSITY
One South Avenue, 2 Levermore Hall, Garden City NY 11530. 516/877-3220. **Toll-free phone:** 800/ADELPHI. **Fax:** 516/877-4970. **Contact:** Lisa S Araujo, Assistant Vice President Human Resources & Labor Relations. **E-mail address:** humanres@adelphi.edu. **World Wide Web address:** http://www.adelphi.edu. **Description:** A private university with approximately 7,000 undergraduate and graduate students enrolled. Founded in 1896. **NOTE:** Entry-level positions are offered. Human Resources phone: 516/877-3224. **Positions advertised include:** Administrative Assistant; Secretary; Teacher/Professor. **Corporate headquarters location:** This location. **Number of employees at this location:** 1,300.

ADEMCO GROUP
(ALARM DEVICE MANUFACTURING COMPANY)
165 Eileen Way, Syosset NY 11791. 516/921-6704. **Fax:** 516/364-5344. **Contact:** Human Resources Department. **E-mail address:** opportunities@ademco.com. **World Wide Web address:** http://www.ademco.com/ademco. **Description:** Ademco manufactures alarm and security products. Products include smoke detectors, glass break detectors, and other home invasion alarms. Ademco's automated manufacturing facility processes more than 4 million printed circuit boards per year. The company also runs a quality service laboratory that conducts UL certified testing. Founded in 1929. **Positions advertised include:** Marketing Service Representative; Group Leader; Security & Fire Manager; Director of National Accounts; Contracts Manager; Sales Representative. **International locations:** Worldwide. **Corporate headquarters location:** This location. **Parent company:** Honeywell International. **Subsidiaries include:** ADEMCO Video Systems.

ADVANCE CIRCUIT TECHNOLOGY, INC.
19 Jet View Drive, Rochester NY 14624. 585/328-2000. **Fax:** 585/328-2019. **Contact:** Human Resources Department. **World Wide Web address:** http://www.advcircuit.com. **Description:** A contract manufacturer of hybrid circuits and printed circuit board assemblies.

ADVANCE INTERNATIONAL INC.
1200 Zerega Avenue, Bronx NY 10462. 718/892-3460. **Fax:** 718/409-2385. **Contact:** Human Resources. **Description:** Produces, imports, and exports holiday lighting sets, craft items, and other plastic products. **Positions advertised include:** Collections Agent; Customer Service Representative; Data Entry Clerk.

ADVANCE PUBLICATIONS INC.
950 Fingerboard Road, Staten Island NY 10305. 718/981-1234. **Fax:** 718/981-1456. **Contact:** Human Resources. **World Wide Web address:** http://www.advance.net. **Description:** A media publishing company that owns over 25 daily newspapers nationwide including *The Star Ledger*, *The Cleveland Plain Dealer*, and *Staten Island Advance* – a local New York daily newspaper. Advance has interests in cable television and Internet sites related to its publications and the company's subsidiaries publish 41 weekly newspapers as well as magazines including *Allure*, *Glamour*, *Vanity Fair*, *Parade Magazine* Sunday insert, and *Women's Wear Daily*. Founded in 1886. **Positions advertised include:** Marketing Coordinator; Account Executive; Internet Advertising Coordinator. **Corporate headquarters location:** This location. **Subsidiaries include:** American City Business Journals, Inc.; Condé Nast Publications Inc.; Discovery Communications, Inc.; Fairchild Publications, Inc.; Parade Publications; The Golf Digest Companies. **Chairman/CEO/Owner:** Samuel (Si) I. Newhouse Jr. **Annual sales/revenues:** $4.2 billion. **Number of employees at this location:** 450. **Number of employees nationwide:** 22,785.

ADVION BIOSCIENCES, INC.
15 Catherwood Road, Ithaca NY 14850. 607/266-0665. **Fax:** 607/266-0749. **Contact:** Human Resources. **E-mail address:** careers@advion.com. **Description:** A developer of automated, chip-based technology designed to boost the sensitivity, data quality and sample throughput for electrospray mass spectrometers. Founded in 1993. **Positions advertised include:** Assistant Scientist; Research Scientist.

AEROFLEX INCORPORATED
35 South Service Road, Plainview NY 11807. 516/694-6700. **Fax:** 516/694-4823. **Contact:** Bridget DiFalco, Human Resources Director. **World Wide Web address:** http://www.aeroflex.com. **Description:** Manufactures custom-designed hybrid microcircuits for use in applications including electrical systems used in aircraft maintenance, flight and navigational systems, sonar systems, satellite experimentation systems, missile firing systems, power supply systems, computer testing systems, television camera and radio receiver systems, and other applications using miniaturized components. Founded in 1937. **Positions advertised include:** Avionics Technical and Business Development Manager; PXI Marketing Engineer; Technical Writer; Customer Liaison Officer; Production Planner; Principle Product Engineer. **Corporate headquarters location:** This location. **Subsidiaries include:** IFR Systems, Inc. **Listed on:** NASDAQ. **Stock exchange symbol:** ARXX. **Chairman/CEO:** Harvey R. Blau. **Annual sales/revenues:** $202 million. **Number of employees:** 2,030.

AIR FRANCE
142 West 57th Street, New York NY 10019. 212/830-4000. **Fax:** 212/830-4191. **Contact:** Air France Recruitment. **E-mail address:** mail.resume@airfrance.fr. **World Wide Web address:** http://www.airfrance.com. **Description:** An international airline serving 20 U.S. cities. Founded in 1933. **NOTE:** Part-time, seasonal, second shift and third shift jobs are offered. Electronic copies of resumes/applications are only accepted in Word format, and if the position applied for is indicated. **Positions advertised include:** Manager of National Account Sales; Account Representative; Accountant; Administrative Assistant; Sales Executive. **Office hours:** Monday - Friday, 9:00 a.m. - 5:15 p.m. **Corporate headquarters location:** Paris, France. **Other area locations:** JFK Airport NY; Newark Airport NJ. **Other locations:** Worldwide. **Number of employees at this location:** 830. **Number of employees worldwide:** 49,000.

AIR INDIA
570 Lexington Avenue, 15th Floor, New York NY 10022. 212/407-1300. **Fax:** 212/838-9533. **Contact:** Human Resources Department. **World Wide Web address:** http://www.airindia.com. **Description:** An international airline with routes to major cities throughout the world. **NOTE:** Most positions are only open to Indian citizens belonging to certain caste levels who meet the company's stated requirements. **Corporate headquarters location:** Mumbai, India. **Listed on:** Government owned.

AJILON SERVICES INC.
625 Madison Avenue, New York NY 10022. 212/224-0220. **Contact:** Human Resources. **World Wide Web address:** http://www.ajilon.com. **Description:** Offers computer consulting services, staffing services, project support, and end user services with 450 offices in 17 countries. **Corporate headquarters location:** Towson MD. **Other U.S. locations:** Worldwide.

AJILON SERVICES INC.
507 Plum Street, Syracuse NY 13204. 315/422-2480. **Toll-free phone:** 800/298-5242. **Fax:** 315/478-5214. **Contact:** Sue Simms, Technical Recruiting Manager. **E-mail address:** ssimms@syra.ajilon.com. **World Wide Web address:** http://www.ajilon.com. **Description:** Offers computer consulting services, staffing services, project support, and end user services with 450 offices in 17 countries. **Corporate headquarters location:** Towson MD. **Other U.S. locations:** Worldwide.

ALBANY INTERNATIONAL CORPORATION
P.O. Box 1907, Albany NY 12201-1907. 518/445-2200. **Physical address:** 1373 Broadway, Albany NY 12204. **Toll-free phone:** 800/833-3836. **Fax:** 518/445-2265. **Contact:** Michele Dzembo, Human Resources. **World Wide Web address:** http://www.albint.com. **Description:** The company manufactures textiles used on paper making machines. **Corporate headquarters location:** This location. **Other area locations:** East Greenbush NY; Homer NY; Menands NY. **Other locations:** Worldwide. **Listed on:** New York Stock Exchange. **Stock exchange symbol:** AIN. **Chairman/CEO:** Frank R. Schmeler. **Annual sales/revenues:** $816 million. **Number of employees:** 6,200.

ALBANY MEDICAL CENTER
43 New Scotland Avenue, MC-56, Albany NY 12208-3478. 518/262-3125. **Physical address:** 411 Myrtle Avenue, Albany NY 12208. **Fax:** 518/262-4487. **Contact:** Cathy Halakan, Vice President of Human Resources. **World Wide Web address:** http://www.amc.edu. **Description:** An academic health science center. The facility specializes in inpatient and outpatient tertiary and general medical care, biomedical research, and education. **NOTE:** Employment Office phone: 518/262-8414. Resumes may be submitted online. **Positions advertised include:** Registered Nurse; Licensed Practical Nurse; Clinical Dietitian; Organ Procurement Coordinator; Cytogenetic Technologist; Genetic Counselor; Research Associate; Research Technician; Client Services Manager; Practice Operations Director; Research Director; Microbiology Director; Nursing Supervisor; Assistant Nurse Manager; Research Coordinator; Auditor; Administrative Coordinator; Cancer Registrar; Teacher Assistant; Security Officer; Parking Attendant; Driver/Courier; Food Service Worker; Housekeepers; Plant Maintenance Custodian.

ALCOHOLICS ANONYMOUS (A.A.)
P.O. Box 459, Grand Central Station, New York NY 10163. 212/870-3400. **Physical address:** 475 Riverside Drive, 11th Floor, New York NY 10115. **Contact:** Human Resources. **World Wide Web address:** http://www.alcoholics-anonymous.org. **Description:** Alcoholics Anonymous (A.A.) is a fellowship of men and women who share their experiences with each other so that they may work on their common problems and help others to recover from alcoholism. A.A. consists of 89,000 local groups in 141 countries. Founded in 1935. **Corporate headquarters location:** This location. **Subsidiaries include:** A.A. World Services, Inc. operates at this location with 100 employees coordinating with local groups, with A.A. groups in treatment and correctional facilities, and with members and groups overseas. A.A. literature is prepared, published, and distributed through this office. The A.A. Grapevine, Inc. publishes the *A.A. Grapevine,* the fellowship's monthly international journal. The magazine has a circulation of about 119,000 in the United States, Canada, and other countries. A.A. Grapevine, Inc. also produces a selection of cassette tapes and anthologies of magazine articles.

ALFRED UNIVERSITY
Saxon Drive, Greene Hall, Alfred NY 14802. 607/871-2118. **Fax:** 607/871-2318. **Contact:** Kelly Floyd, Director of Human Resources. **E-mail address:** humanresources@alfred.edu. **World Wide Web address:** http://www.alfred.edu. **Description:** This nonsectarian university is comprised of the privately endowed College of Business, the College of Engineering and Professional Studies, the College of Liberal Arts and Sciences, and the New York State College of Ceramics (School of Ceramic Engineering and Sciences) and School of Art and Design. Bachelors, masters, and doctoral degrees are offered. Approximately 2,350 undergraduate and graduate students attend Alfred University. Founded in 1836. **NOTE:** Human Resources phone: 607/871-2118. **Positions advertised include:** College of Business Dean; School of Engineering Dean; Museum of Ceramic Art Director; Raw Materials Technician; Biomedical Materials Engineering Science Professor; Photonic Materials Professor.

ALL METRO HEALTH CARE
50 Broadway, Lynbrook NY 11563. 516/887-1200. **Toll-free phone:** 800/225-1200. **Fax:** 516/593-2848. **Contact:** Human Resources. **E-mail address:** all-metro@aol.com. **Description:** A home health care provider. Plaza Domestic Agency and Caregivers on Call also operate out of this facility. Founded in 1955. **Positions advertised include:** Certified Nurses Aide; Clerical Supervisor; Home Health Aide; Licensed Practical Nurse; Marketing Manager; Occupational Therapist; Physical Therapist; Registered Nurse. **Office hours:** Sunday - Saturday, 8:30 a.m. - 8:30 p.m. **Corporate headquarters location:** This location. **Other area locations:** Statewide. **Other U.S. locations:** FL; MO; NJ. **Parent company:** All Metro Aids Inc. **Annual sales/revenues:** $50 million. **Number of employees at this location:** 2,000. **Number of employees nationwide:** 5,000.

ALLIANCE FINANCIAL CORPORATION
dba ALLIANCE BANK
65 Main Street, P.O. Box 5430, Cortland NY 13045. 607/758-2831. **Fax:** 607/758-1300. **Contact:** Human Resources. **E-mail:** humanresources@alliancebankna.com. **World Wide Web address:** http://www.alliancebankna.com. **Description:** Alliance Financial Corporation, formerly Cortland First Financial and Oneida Valley Bancshares, in the holding company for Alliance Bank, an independent commercial bank delivering financial services from 20 branches in central New York State for individuals and small businesses. **Positions advertised include:** Teller; Residential Mortgage Originator; Director of Trust and Investment Services; Branch Manager; Branch Operations Associate; Sales Program Specialist. **Corporate headquarters location:** This location. **Other locations:** Statewide. **Subsidiaries include:** Alliance Leasing, Inc.; Alliance Bank. **Listed on:** NASDAQ. **Stock exchange symbol:** ALNC. **Chairman/President/CEO:** Jack H. Webb. **Annual sales/revenues:** $50 million. **Number of employees:** 300.

ALLIANCE BANK
14 East Main Street, P.O. Box 279, Marathon NY 13803. 607/849-3275. **Contact:** Joan Coombs, Branch Manager. **World Wide Web address:** http://www.alliancebankna.com. **Description:** An independent commercial bank delivering financial services from 20 branches in central New York State for individuals and small businesses. **NOTE:** Jobseekers should send resumes to Alliance Bank, Human Resources, 65 Main Street, P.O. Box 5430, Cortland NY 13045. **Corporate headquarters location:** Cortland NY. **Other locations:** Statewide. **Parent company:** Alliance Financial Corporation.

ALLIANCE BANK
2743 NYS Route 26, P.O. Box 176, Cincinnatus NY 13040. 607/863-4100. **Contact:** Human Resources. **World Wide Web address:** http://www.alliancebankna.com. **Description:** An independent commercial bank delivering financial services from 20 branches in central New York State for individuals and small businesses. **NOTE:** Jobseekers should send resumes to Alliance Bank, Human Resources, 65 Main Street, P.O. Box 5430, Cortland NY 13045. **Corporate headquarters location:** Cortland NY. **Other locations:** Statewide. **Parent company:** Alliance Financial Corporation.

ALLIANCE BANK
Route 80 at I-81, P.O. Box 627, Tully NY 13159. 315/696-6333. **Contact:** Linda McHerron, Branch Manager. **World Wide Web address:** http://www.alliancebankna.com. **Description:** An independent commercial bank delivering financial services from 20 branches in central New York State for individuals and small businesses. **NOTE:** Jobseekers should send resumes to Alliance Bank, Human Resources, 65 Main Street, P.O. Box 5430, Cortland NY 13045. **Corporate headquarters location:** Cortland NY. **Other locations:** Statewide. **Parent company:** Alliance Financial Corporation.

ALLIANCE CAPITAL MANAGEMENT L.P.
1345 Avenue of the Americas, New York NY 10105. 212/969-1000. **Fax:** 212/969-2229. **Contact:** Human Resources. **World Wide Web address:** http://www.alliancecapital.com. **Description:** Alliance Capital Management manages mutual funds for corporations and individual investors operating 36 offices in 19 countries. **Positions advertised include:** Fixed Income Software Developer; Applications Support Specialist. **Corporate headquarters location:** This location. **Other locations:** Worldwide. **Chairman/CEO:** Bruce W. Calvert. **Annual sales/revenues:** $2.75 billion. **Number of employees worldwide:** 4,200.

ALLIED SECURITY, INC.
14 East 39th Street, 2nd Floor, New York NY 10016. 212/532-1744. **Fax:** 212/689-7521. **Contact:** Human Resources. **World Wide Web address:** http://www.alliedsecurity.com. **Description:** A full-service corporate security firm that provides contract guard services, electronic security, and investigative services. **Positions advertised include:** Security Guard. **Corporate headquarters location:** King of Prussia PA. **Other area locations:** Albany NY; Hudson NY; Mineola NY; Yonkers NY. **Other U.S. locations:** Nationwide. **Subsidiaries/Affiliates include:** Spectaguard Inc. **Parent company:** MacAndrews & Forbes. **Operations at this facility include:** Divisional Office. **Annual sales/revenues:** $500 million. **Number of employees:** 19,000.

ALLOU HEALTH & BEAUTY CARE, INC.
50 Emjay Boulevard, Brentwood NY 11717. 631/273-4000. **Fax:** 631/851-2699. **Contact:** Kathy Calzente, Personnel Manager. **World Wide Web address:** http://www.allou.com. **Description:** Distributes health and beauty products such as fragrances, cosmetics, and food items to independent retailers in the metropolitan New York area. **NOTE:** Entry-level positions and second and third shifts are offered. **Corporate headquarters location:** This location. **Listed on:** American Stock Exchange. **Stock exchange symbol:** ALU. **Chairman:** Victor Jacobs. **Annual sales/revenues:** $564 million. **Number of employees:** 300.

ALSTOM TRANSPORT
1025 John Street, West Henrietta NY 14586. 585/783-2000. **Fax:** 585/783-8777. **Contact:** Personnel. **World Wide Web address:** http://www.transport.alstom.com. **Description:** This location is an administration and engineering facility. Overall, ALSTOM Transport is a leader in providing rail signal and control systems worldwide. These systems are designed for diverse applications in mainline railways, heavy rail transit, light rail transit, commuter rail, high-speed rail, and automated guideway transit. The company's equipment is used in advancing automated control systems. These systems can comprise elements of control from the wayside including vital processors, track circuits, relays, signals, switch machines, equipment housings, and vital timers; from the vehicle including relay- and microprocessor-based automatic train control and cab signaling equipment and operator consoles; from a central area such as PC-based or workstation-based systems, code system emulators, SCADA, mosaic panels, and projection screens; or from any combination of these. **Corporate headquarters location:** Hornell NY. **Other area locations:** Hornell NY; New York NY; Rochester NY. **Other U.S. locations:** CA; CT; District of Columbia; NJ; VA; WA. **Parent company:** Alstom (Paris, France). **Operations at this facility include:** Alstom Signaling Inc. – Administration; Transport Information Solutions.

ALTRIA GROUP, INC.
120 Park Avenue, New York NY 10017. 212/880-5000. **Contact:** Human Resources Department. **World Wide Web address:** http://www.philipmorris.com. **Description:** A holding company. Its principal wholly-owned subsidiaries are Philip Morris Incorporated (also at this location), Philip Morris U.S.A., Philip Morris International Incorporated, Kraft Foods, Incorporated, and Philip Morris Capital Corporation. In the tobacco industry, Philip Morris U.S.A. and Philip Morris International together form one of the largest international cigarette operations in the world. U.S. brand names include Marlboro, Parliament, Virginia Slims, Benson & Hedges, and Merit. In the food industry, Kraft Foods, Inc. is one of the largest producers of packaged grocery products in North America. Major brands include Jell-O, Post, Kool-Aid, Crystal Light, Entenmann's, Miracle Whip, Stove Top, and Shake 'n Bake. Kraft markets a number of products under the Kraft brand including natural and process cheeses and dry packaged dinners. The Oscar Mayer unit markets processed meats, poultry, lunch combinations, and pickles under the Oscar Mayer, Louis Rich, Lunchables, and Claussen brand names. Kraft is also one of the largest coffee companies with principal brands including Maxwell House, Sanka, Brim, and General Foods International Coffees. Kraft Foods Ingredients Corporation manufactures private-label and industrial food products for sale to other food processing companies. Philip Morris Capital Corporation is engaged in financial services and real estate. **Positions advertised include:** Associate Manager of Security; Field Auditor; Customer Service Administrator; Administrative Assistant. **Special programs:** Summer Internships. **Corporate headquarters location:** This location. **Other area locations:** Rye Brook NY. **Other U.S. locations:** Stamford CT; Richmond VA. **International locations:** Australia; Brazil; Hong Kong; Japan; Switzerland. **Listed on:** New York Stock Exchange. **Stock exchange symbol:** MO. **Number of employees nationwide:** 155,000. **Number of employees worldwide:** 166,000.

ALTX INC.
150 Spring Street Road, P.O. Box 91, Watervliet NY 12189. 518/273-4110. **Fax:** 518/273-4128. **Contact:** Human Resources. **E-mail address:** altx@altxinc.com. **Description:** A steel manufacturing company. **Parent company:** Grupo Tubacex (Llodio, Alava, Spain). **Operations at this facility include:** A Steel Mill.

AMALGAMATED LIFE INSURANCE COMPANY
730 Broadway, New York NY 10003-9511. 212/473-5700. **Fax:** 212/780-4104. **Contact:** Human Resources Recruiter. **E-mail address:** hr@amalgamatedlife.com. **World Wide Web address:** http://www.amalgamatedlife.com. **Description:** Originally a nonprofit insurance firm specializing in handling claims service and group medical, life, and health maintenance policies for the national textile workers union, in 1992 the company was authorized by the State of New York to sell life, health, and disability insurance commercially outside its traditional non-profit base. The company is an insurance company, a third party administrator, a medical utilization service provider, a computer services company, an insurance brokerage, a union printer, and the administrator of the "Patron Funds" employee benefit plans. Founded in 1944. **Positions advertised include:** Senior Underwriter; Help Desk Coordinator; Property and Casualty Insurance Coordinator; Retiree Programs and Advocacy Coordinator; Sales Executive; Accountant; Technical Writer. **Corporate headquarters location:** This location. **Other locations:** District of Columbia; IL; KY; MA; NH; NJ; NV; NY. **Subsidiaries include:** Alicomp, Inc.; Alicare, Inc.; Amalgamated Agency, Inc.; Alicare Medical Management, Inc. **President/CEO:** Ronald L. Minikes. **Number of employees at this location:** 400. **Number of employees nationwide:** 500.

AMBAC FINANCIAL GROUP INC.
One State Street Plaza, 15th Floor, New York NY 10004. 212/668-0340. **Fax:** 212/509-9190. **Contact:** Gregg Bienstock, Human Resources. **World Wide Web address:** http://www.ambac.com. **Description:** AMBAC Inc. is a holding company that provides, through its affiliates, financial guarantee insurance, financial services, and health care information services to both public and private clients worldwide. **Positions advertised include:** Underwriter; Financial Services Specialist; Legal Counselor; Risk Management Associate; Investment Manager; Operations Manager; Internal Auditor; Information Technology Specialist. **Corporate headquarters location:** This location. **Other locations:** London, England; Tokyo, Japan; Sydney, Australia. **Subsidiaries include:** Ambac Assurance; Cadre Financial; Ambac Indemnity Corporation, a leading financial guarantee insurance company; Ambac Capital Management, Inc., a provider of municipal investment contracts; Ambac Financial Services, L.P., a provider of interest rate swaps to municipalities; HCIA Inc., a health care information company. **Listed on:** New York Stock Exchange. **Stock exchange symbol:** ABK. **Chairman/CEO:** Phillip B. Lassiter. **Annual sales/revenues:** $740.5 million. **Number of employees:** 370.

AMERADA HESS CORPORATION
1185 Avenue of the Americas, 38th Floor, New York NY 10036. 212/997-8500. **Fax:** 212/536-8318. **Recorded jobline:** 800/947-HESS; (800/947-4377). **Contact:** Human Resources. **E-mail address:** employeerelations@hess.com. **World Wide Web address:** http://www.hess.com. **Description:** An integrated petroleum company engaged in exploration and production with oil and gas reserves in the U.S., the UK, and the North Sea, as well as North and West Africa and Southeast Asia. In addition to a refinery in Venezuela, the company has extensive storage capacity and terminals on the East Coast from Boston to Florida. The company's retail outlets, Hess Express stores, provide food service (Godfathers Pizza, Blimpies, and TCBY yogurt), its proprietary Mountain Top coffee, fountain service, and convenience items. **NOTE:** For retail positions apply at a local Hess Express location. **Positions advertised include:** Accountant; Chemical Engineer; Financial Analyst; Marketing Specialist; Mechanical Engineer; Sales Representative; Cashier; Head Cashier; General Manager; Site Manager; Manager Trainee; Food Service Supervisor; Assistant Manager; Sales Associate; Food Service Associate. **Corporate headquarters location:** This location. **Other locations:** Woodbridge NJ; Houston TX. **International locations:** Worldwide. **Subsidiaries include:** Premier Oil; United Kingdom Energy. **Listed on:** New York Stock Exchange. **Stock exchange symbol:** AHC. **Chairman/CEO:** John B. Hess. **Annual sales/revenues:** $13 billion. **Number of employees:** 11,700.

AMERIC DISC
17 Gaigal Drive, Nesconset NY 11767. 631/360-2300. **Contact:** Human Resources. **World Wide Web address:** http://www.americdisc.com. **Description:** Americ Disc is one of the nation's leading independent multimedia manufacturing companies offering CD-audio and CD-ROM mastering and replication; videocassette and audiocassette duplication; laser video disc recording; off-line and online video editing; motion picture film processing; film-to-tape and tape-to-film transfers; and finishing, packaging, warehousing, and fulfillment services. **Corporate headquarters location:** Quebec, Canada. **Other area locations:** Forest Hills NY. **Other locations:** Worldwide.

AMERICAN ARBITRATION ASSOCIATION
335 Madison Avenue, 10th Floor, New York NY 10017-4605. 212/716-5800. **Fax:** 212/716-5905. **Contact:** Human Resources. **World Wide Web address:** http://www.adr.org. **Description:** A private, nonprofit organization dedicated to establishing and maintaining fair and impartial procedures of dispute resolution as an effective alternative to the court system. The association helps parties with disputes by encouraging them to settle differences through friendly negotiations, mediation, or arbitration. Founded in 1926. **Other U.S. locations:** Nationwide.

AMERICAN BANK NOTE HOLOGRAPHICS, INC.
399 Executive Boulevard, Elmsford NY 10523. 914/592-2355. **Fax:** 914/592-3248. **Contact:** Susan Herbert. **World Wide Web address:** http://www.abnh.com. **Description:** Produces laser-generated, three-dimensional images that appear on credit cards and products requiring proof of authenticity. The company operates 10 active mastering labs with the ability to create a variety of holograms including 3-D models, flat art, computer-generated animation, cinematography, dot matrix, Microline, and

diffractive mercurial. **Corporate headquarters location:** This location. **Other locations:** Elmsford NY; Huntingdon Valley PA. **Operations at this facility include:** Corporate administration; Production. **Listed on:** Over The Counter. **Stock exchange symbol:** ABHH. **President/CEO:** Kenneth H. Traub. **Annual sales/revenues:** $26.5 billion. **Number of employees:** 120.

AMERICAN BIBLE SOCIETY
1865 Broadway, 6th Floor, New York NY 10023. 212/408-1200. **Contact:** Human Resources. **E-mail address:** hrinbox@americanbible.org. **World Wide Web address:** http://www.americanbible.org. **Description:** Translates, publishes, and distributes the Bible and portions of the Scriptures, without doctrinal note or comment, in more than 180 nations. Founded in 1816. **Positions advertised include:** Acquisition & Renewal Projects Manager; Marketing Fullfillment Assistant; Latino Affairs Distribution Representative; Editor; Production Manager. **Corporate headquarters location:** This location. **Other locations:** CO; FL; MO; NJ; VA. **Operations at this facility include:** Administration; Manufacturing; Sales; Service. **Number of employees at this location:** 300.

AMERICAN CENTURION LIFE ASSURANCE
20 Madison Avenue Extension, P.O. Box 5550, Albany NY 12205. 518/452-4150. **Toll-free phone:** 800/633-3565. **Fax:** 518/452-3857. **Contact:** Human Resources. **Description:** Administers insurance and fixed and variable annuity products in the State of New York on behalf of American Express Financial Advisors. **Office hours:** Monday - Friday, 8:00 a.m. - 4:30 p.m. **Corporate headquarters location:** This location. **Parent company:** American Express Company.

AMERICAN CLAIMS EVALUATION, INC.
One Jericho Plaza, 3rd Floor, Wing B, Jericho NY 11753. 516/938-8000. **Fax:** 516/938-0405. **Contact:** Gary J. Knauer, CFO, Treasurer, Secretary, & Human Resources VP. **Description:** American Claims Evaluation, Inc. provides a full range of vocational rehabilitation and disability management services through its wholly owned subsidiaries. The company is a health care cost containment services company that verifies the accuracy of hospital bills submitted to its clients for payment. Such clients include commercial health insurance companies, third-party administrators, health maintenance organizations, and self-insured corporate clients. **Corporate headquarters location:** This location. **Subsidiaries include:** RPM Rehabilitation & Associates, Inc. **Listed on:** NASDAQ. **Stock exchange symbol:** AMCE. **Chairman/President/CEO:** Gary Gelman. **Annual sales/revenues:** $1.3 million. **Number of employees:** 22.

AMERICAN EXPRESS COMPANY
822 Lexington Avenue, New York NY 10021. 212/640-2000. **Contact:** Ursula F. Fairbairn, Staffing Department. **World Wide Web address:** http://www.americanexpress.com. **Description:** American Express Company is a diversified travel and financial services company. Founded in 1850. **NOTE:** Applicants are encouraged to use the company's online Resume Builder to create a resume profile account to apply to positions as well as using the automated Job Search Agent. **Positions advertised include:** Travel Support Counselor; Senior Marketing Manager; Corp Services Operations Team Leader; Senior Risk Management Manager; Purchasing/Training Manager; Acquisition Manager; Senior Marketing Manager; Cardmember Cross-Sell Senior Manager; Account Management Representative; Contracts Manager; Treasury Manager; Interactive Education Manager; Senior Customer Information Manager; Senior Marketing Manager; Training & Syndication Manager; Special Security Agent; Senior Prospect Marketing Capabilities/Information Manager; Executive Assistant; Information & Analysis Manager; Business Development Manager; Receptionist; Senior Product Development Manager; Senior Marketing Analyst; Finance Manager; Creative Services Manager; Commodities Manager; Sales Effectiveness Manager; Business Planning & Financial Analysis Manager; Administrative Assistant; Customer Information Manager; New Industry Development Vice President; Interactive Marketing Manager; Assistant Style Editor. **Corporate headquarters location:** This location. **Other U.S. locations:** Nationwide. **International locations:** Worldwide. **Subsidiaries include:** American Express Publishing Corporation; American Express Sharepeople; American Express Tax and Business Services Inc.; American Express Travel Related Services offers consumers the Personal, Gold, and Platinum Cards, as well as revolving credit products such as Optima Cards, which allow customers to extend payments. Other products include the American Express Corporate Card, which helps businesses manage their travel and entertainment expenditures; and the Corporate Purchasing Card, which helps businesses manage their expenditures on supplies, equipment, and services. American Express Travel Related Services also offers American Express Traveler's Cheques and travel services including trip planning, reservations, ticketing, and management information. American Express Financial Advisors provides a variety of financial products and services to help individuals, businesses, and institutions meet their financial goals. American Express Financial Advisors has a staff of more than 8,000 in the United States and offers products and services that include financial planning; annuities; mutual funds; insurance; investment certificates; and institutional investment advisory trust, tax preparation, and retail securities brokerage services. **Listed on:** New York Stock Exchange. **Stock exchange symbol:** AXP. **Chairman/CEO:** Kenneth I. Chenault. **Annual sales/revenues:** $24 billion. **Number of employees at this location:** 5,000. **Number of employees nationwide:** 84,400.

AMERICAN FELT & FILTER COMPANY, INC.
361 Walsh Road, New Windsor NY 12553. 845/561-3560. **Fax:** 845/561-0967. **Contact:** Scott Ryan, Director of Personnel. **World Wide Web address:** http://www.affco.com. **Description:** Manufactures a line of filter products including bags, cartridges, pressure filters, molded filter media, and nonwoven filter media for air, gas, and liquid filtration. Founded in 1899. **Positions advertised include:** Electrician; Industrial Engineer; Machinist; Sales Representative; Mechanical Engineer. **Corporate headquarters location:** This location. **Operations at this facility include:** Administration; Manufacturing; Research and Development; Sales. **Listed on:** Privately held. **President/Owner:** Wilson (Bill) H. Pryne. **Number of employees:** 225.

AMERICAN FLAT GLASS DISTRIBUTORS, INC. (AFGD)
803 Corporations Park, Scotia NY 12302. 518/374-3812. **Toll-free phone:** 800/766-2341. **Fax:** 518/372-2133. **Contact:** Greg Way, Branch Manager. **World Wide Web address:** http://www.afgd.com. **Description:** American Flat Glass Distributors specializes in architectural insulated units and custom tempering with over 50 locations nationwide. The firm manufactures a line of insulated units for commercial and residential applications. The product line includes clear, tinted, and reflective float glass; laminated, low-emissivity, tempered, acrylic, mirror, obscure, insulated, and polished wire glass; as well as a line of glass handling, storage, and transportation equipment. **NOTE:** Resumes may be sent to the company's headquarters to the attention of: HR Generalist, AFGD Glass, 1600 Parkwood Circle SE, Suite 300, Atlanta GA 30339; or fax: 770/951-9100. **Positions advertised include:** Inside Sales Representative; Industrial Engineer; Production Manager; Mechanical Engineer. **Corporate headquarters location:** Atlanta GA. **Other U.S. locations:** Nationwide. **Parent company:** AFG Industries, Inc. **Operations at this facility include:** Manufacturing; Sales. **Number of employees at this location:** 75. **Number of employees nationwide:** 1,000.

AMERICAN FOUNDATION FOR THE BLIND
11 Penn Plaza, Suite 300, New York NY 10001. 212/502-7600. **Toll-free phone:** 800/AFB-LINE. **Fax:** 212/502-7777. **Contact:** Kelly Bleach, Director of Personnel. **E-mail address:** afbinfo@afb.net. **World Wide Web address:** http://www.afb.org. **Description:** A nonprofit organization. The American Foundation for the Blind (AFB) is a leading national resource for people who are blind or visually impaired, the organizations that serve them, and the general public. AFB operates through four primary areas of activity: development, collection, and dissemination of information; identification, analysis, and resolution of critical issues; education of the public and policymakers on the needs and capabilities of people who are blind or visually impaired; and production and distribution of talking books and other audio materials. Founded in 1921.

AMERICAN INTERNATIONAL GROUP, INC.
70 Pine Street, New York NY 10270. 212/770-7000. **Fax:** 212/509-9705. **Contact:** Axel I. Freudmann, Human Resources Director. **E-mail address:** aig.hr@aig.com. **World Wide Web address:** http://www.aig.com. **Description:** American International Group, Inc. (AIG) is a leading U.S.-based international insurance organization and one of the nation's largest underwriters of commercial and industrial coverage. Member companies write property, casualty, marine, life, and financial services insurance in approximately 130 countries and jurisdictions. The company is also engaged in a broad range of financial businesses. AIG's General Insurance operations group is composed of Domestic General-Brokerage, which markets property and casualty insurance products through brokers to large corporate buyers and other commercial customers; Domestic Personal Lines, which is in the business of U.S. personal lines, principally personal auto; and Foreign General, which comprises AIG's overseas property and casualty operations. **NOTE:** The company requests job seekers to post resumes online via the company's Website. **Positions advertised include:** Senior Auditor; Collection Accountant; Staff Auditor; Accountant; Collection Representative; Corporate Comptroller; Senior Business Analyst; Treasury Operations Director; Corporate Receivables Manager; Senior Accountant; Asset Manager; Financial Analyst; Direct Marketing Actuary; Actuarial Analyst. **Subsidiaries include:** 21st Century Insurance Group; AIG Global Investment Group; American General Corporation; American Life Insurance Company; HSB Group, Inc.; International Lease Finance Corporation; John McStay Investment Counsel, L.P.; SunAmerica Inc.; United Guaranty Corporation; AIG International Services; AccessAIG; American International Technology Enterprises; American International Underwriters. **Corporate headquarters location:** This location. **Listed on:** New York Stock Exchange. **Stock exchange symbol:** AIG. **Chairman/CEO:** Maurice (Hank) R. Greenberg. **Annual sales/revenues:** $55.5 billion. **Number of employees:** 81,000.

THE AMERICAN KENNEL CLUB
260 Madison Avenue, 4th Floor, New York NY 10016. 212/696-8200. **Recorded jobline:** 919/816-3896. **Contact:** Vicki Lane Rees, Human Resources Director. **World Wide Web address:** http://www.akc.org. **Description:** An independent, nonprofit organization devoted to the advancement of purebred dogs. The American Kennel Club adopts and enforces rules and regulations governing dog shows, obedience trials, and field trials, and fosters and encourages interest in the health and welfare of purebred dogs. The club also offers a wide range of books and magazines for national distribution. Founded in 1884. **NOTE:** Entry-level positions are offered. Resumes should be sent to: AKC Human Resources Department, P.O. Box 37905, Raleigh NC 27627-7905; or fax: 919/816-4282. **Positions advertised include:** Computer Support Specialist; Administrative Assistant; Desktop Publishing Specialist; Editorial Assistant. **Office hours:** Monday - Friday, 8:30 a.m. - 4:15 p.m. **Corporate headquarters location:** This location. **Other U.S. locations:** Raleigh NC. **Listed on:** Privately held, Not-for-Profit company. **President/CEO:** Al Cheaure. **Number of employees at this location:** 75. **Number of employees nationwide:** 450.

AMERICAN MEDICAL ALERT CORPORATION
3265 Lawson Boulevard, P.O. Box 40, Oceanside NY 11572. 516/536-5850. **Toll-free phone:** 800/286-2622. **Fax:** 516/536-5276. **Contact:** Human Resources. **E-mail address:** info@amac.com. **World Wide Web address:** http://www.amacalert.com. **Description:** A manufacturer and distributor of the Personal Emergency Response System for the home health industry. The Personal Emergency Response System is an in-home safety device used by the chronically ill or physically impaired allowing them to communicate with emergency care providers using digital-wireless technology. Founded in 1981. **NOTE:** Entry-level positions are offered. **Positions advertised include:** Administrative Assistant; Sales Representative. **Corporate headquarters location:** This location. **Other U.S. locations:** Parker CO; Decatur GA; Tinley Park IL. **Operations at this facility include:** Administration; Sales; Service. **Listed on:** NASDAQ. **Stock exchange symbol:** AMAC. **Annual sales/revenues:** $14 million. **Number of employees:** 183

AMERICAN MUSEUM OF NATURAL HISTORY
Central Park West at 79th Street, New York NY 10024-5192. 212/769-5000. **Contact:** Human Resources. **World Wide Web address:** http://www.amnh.org. **Description:** A museum of anthropology, astronomy, mineralogy, and zoology. The museum has a research library and 38 exhibition halls and offers educational and research programs. The museum also publishes several in-house and nationally distributed magazines based on research conducted there. Founded in 1869. **Corporate headquarters location:** This location.

AMERICAN RED CROSS OF NENY
33 Everett Road, Albany NY 12205. 518/458-8111. **Fax:** 518/459-8268. **Contact:** Human Resources. **E-mail address:** nunnally@redcrossneny.org. **World Wide Web address:** http://www.redcrossneny.org. **Description:** The American Red Cross of Northeastern New York is part of the national humanitarian organization that aids disaster victims, gathers blood for crisis distribution, trains individuals to respond to emergencies, educates individuals on various diseases, and raises funds for other charitable establishments. **NOTE:** Human Resources phone extension: x3016. **Positions advertised include:** Volunteer Coordinator. **Special programs:** Internships. **Corporate headquarters location:** Washington DC. **Other U.S. locations:** Nationwide.

AMERICAN SOCIETY FOR THE PREVENTION OF CRUELTY TO ANIMALS
424 East 92nd Street, New York NY 10128. 212/876-7700. **Fax:** 212/876-0014. **Contact:** Human Resources. **E-mail address:** hr@aspca.org. **World Wide Web address:** http://www.aspca.org. **Description:** The society is involved in six primary areas: animals as pets; humane education; animals for sport and entertainment; experimentation on animals; animal industries; and protection of wild animals and endangered species. Founded in 1866. **NOTE:** Human Resources phone: 212/876-0014. **Positions advertised include:** Director of Medicine; Veterinarian; Custodian; Executive Assistant to COO; Assistant Director; Animal Behavior Counselor.

AMERICAN SOCIETY OF COMPOSERS, AUTHORS & PUBLISHERS (ASCAP)
One Lincoln Plaza, New York NY 10023. 212/621-6000. **Fax:** 212/724-9064. **Contact:** Human Resources Services. **E-mail address:** jobline@ascap.com. **World Wide Web address:** http://www.ascap.com. **Description:** An international service organization serving the music, publishing, and other creative industries. The organization provides a wide range of services to members including the supervision and enforcement of copyrights. **Positions advertised include:** Radio Analyst; Cable/PBS Analyst; Assistant Area Licensing Manager; International Services Representative; International Distribution Analyst; Executive Assistant; TV Service Representative.

AMERICAN STANDARDS TESTING BUREAU INC.
P.O. Box 583, New York NY 10274-0583. 212/943-3160. **Physical address:** 40 Water Street, New York NY 10004. **Toll-free phone:** 800/221-5170. **Fax:** 212/825-2250. **Contact:** John Zimmerman, Director, Professional Staffing. **Description:** Offers lab consulting and forensic services to the government and various industries. The company specializes in biotechnology, environmental sciences, forensics, engineering, failure analysis, and products liability. **Positions advertised include:** Aerospace Engineer; Biomedical Engineer; Chemical Engineer; Clerical Supervisor; Chemist; Environmental Engineer. **Corporate headquarters location:** This location. **Other U.S. locations:** Nationwide. **Operations at this facility include:** Administration; Divisional Headquarters; Research and Development; Sales. **Annual sales/revenues:** $50 million. **Number of employees at this location:** 430.

AMERICAN STOCK EXCHANGE LLC
86 Trinity Place, New York NY 10006. 212/306-1215. **Fax:** 212/306-1218. **Contact:** Catherine M. Casey, Senior Vice President of Human Resources. **E-mail address:** career@amex.com. **World Wide Web address:** http://www.amex.com. **Description:** One of the nation's largest stock exchanges, the American Stock Exchange is one of the only primary marketplaces for both stocks and derivative securities. The American Stock Exchange also handles surveillance, legal, and regulatory functions that are related to the stock exchange. **NOTE:** Human Resources phone: 212/306-1239. **Positions advertised include:** Assistant General Counsel; Chief Sales Officer; Business Strategy and Equity Order Flow Vice President; Exchange Traded Funds Analyst; Exchange Traded Funds Marketing Specialist; Building Operations Manager; Compliance Analyst; Financial Analyst; Public Relations Specialist. **Special programs:** Internships. **Parent company:** NASD (District of Columbia). **Chairman/CEO:** Salvatore F. Sodano. **Annual sales/revenues:** $287 million. **Number of employees at this location:** 700.

AMERICAN STUDENT LIST COMPANY, LLC
330 Old Country Road, Mineola NY 11501-4143. 516/248-6100. **Fax:** 516/248-6364. **Contact:** Human Resources. **World Wide Web address:** http://www.americanstudentlist.com. **Description:** A leading provider of direct marketing information of preschool children and students from elementary schools, high schools, colleges, and post-graduate schools throughout the United States. Lists are rented primarily to various colleges, educational institutions, financial institutions, magazine publishers, and national organizations. Lists are available for all geographic areas of the United States and are provided to customers in the form of mailing labels, magnetic tape, or computer diskettes. **Other U.S. locations:** Boca Raton FL. **Parent company:** Havas Advertising (Levallois-Perret Cedex, France).

AMERICAN SYMPHONY ORCHESTRA LEAGUE
33 West 60th Street, 5th Floor, New York NY 10023. 212/262-5161. **Fax:** 212/262-5198. **Contact:** Hilary Field, Human Resources Assistant. **E-mail address:** hfield@symphony.org or hr@symphony.org. **World Wide Web address:** http://www.symphony.org. **Description:** A national service organization for America's professional, symphony, chamber, youth, and college orchestras. Founded in 1942. **Positions advertised include:** Executive Assistant to the President; Secretary to the Board of Directors. **Office hours:** Monday - Friday, 9:00 a.m. - 5:30 p.m. **Other U.S. locations:** Washington DC.

AMERTAC
25 Robert Pitt Drive, Monsey NY 10952. 845/352-2400. **Fax:** 845/425-3554. **Contact:** Human Resources. **E-mail address:** jobs@amertac.com. **World Wide Web address:** http://www.amertac.com. **Description:** Formerly American Tack & Hardware Company Inc., AmerTac manufactures a broad range of decorative hardware and electrical items. Founded in 1937. **Positions advertised include:** Senior Staff Accountant; Quality Control Inspector; Electrical Engineer; Machinist; Mechanical Engineer; Tool and Die Maker. **Corporate headquarters location:** This location. **Operations at this facility include:** Administration; Manufacturing; Marketing; Sales. **Number of employees at this location:** 225.

AMERICAN TECHNICAL CERAMICS CORPORATION (ATC)
One Norden Lane, Huntington Station NY 11746. 631/622-4700. **Fax:** 631/622-4673. **Contact:** Susan McNally, Human Resources. **E-mail address:** hr@atceramics.com. **World Wide Web address:** http://www.atceramics.com. **Description:** American Technical Ceramics Corporation (ATC) is a high-technology firm engaged in the design, development, and manufacture of ceramic and porcelain capacitors. ATC's processing technology creates high-performance capacitors for critical applications in both the commercial and military markets including missile systems, satellite broadcasting equipment, mobile telephones, medical electronics, and aircraft radar and navigation systems. **NOTE:** Human Resources phone: 631/622-4774. **Positions advertised include:** Metals Engineer; Process Engineer. **Corporate headquarters location:** This location. **Other U.S. locations:** Jacksonville FL. **International locations:** Worldwide. **Listed on:** American Stock Exchange. **Stock exchange symbol:** AMK. **President/CEO/Director:** Victor Insetta. **Annual sales/revenues:** $49.6 million. **Number of employees:** 479.

AMERICAN TROUSER, INC.
350 Fifth Avenue, Suite 3200, New York NY 10118. 212/244-0900. **Fax:** 2121/695-3796. **Contact:** Human Resources. **World Wide Web address:** http://www.american-trouser.com. **Description:** American Trouser manufactures men's pants. **Corporate headquarters location:** Columbus MS. **Operations at this facility include:** Sales; Administration.

AMERICUS DENTAL LABS LP
150-15 Hillside Avenue, Jamaica NY 11432. 718/658-6655. **Fax:** 718/657-8389. **Contact:** Human Resources. **E-mail address:** info@americuslab.com. **World Wide Web address:** http://www.americuslab.com. **Description:** A dental lab that manufactures crowns, bridges, and other dental products. **Positions advertised include:** Ceramist; Die Trimmer. **Corporate headquarters location:** This location. **Other locations:** New York NY. **Number of employees:** 150.

AMERIGAS PARTNERS, L.P.
dba AMERIGAS PROPANE
69 Denton Avenue South, New Hyde Park NY 11040. 516/352-6500. **Contact:** Employment Manager. **E-mail address:** hr1@amerigas.com. **World Wide Web address:** http://www.amerigas.com. **Description:** Formerly the Columbia Propane Corporation, AmeriGas serves over one million customers from 650 locations in 46 states distributing throughout the U.S. and Canada as well as selling supplies and equipment, and exchanging empty tanks for full ones. **NOTE:** For consideration, contact Human Resources at the company's headquarters: Robert Brantley, AmeriGas, 2250 Butler Pike, Suite 150, Plymouth Meeting PA 19462; phone: 610/337-1000; fax: 610/768-7647; e-mail: brantley@amerigas.com. **Positions advertised include:** Industrial Sales Representative. **Corporate headquarters location:** King of Prussia PA. **Other locations:** Nationwide. **Parent company:** UGI Corporation (King of Prussia PA). **Listed on:** New York Stock Exchange. **Stock exchange symbol:** APU. **Annual sales/revenues:** $1.3 billion. **Number of employees:** 6,300.

AMMANN AND WHITNEY
96 Morton Street, New York NY 10014-3326. 212/462-8500. **Contact:** Ruth Darvie, Director of Human Resources. **E-mail address:** rdarvie@ammann-whitney.com. **World Wide Web address:** http://www.ammann-whitney.com. **Description:** An engineering firm specializing in structural, civil, architectural, mechanical and electrical engineering, as well as construction inspection services. **Positions advertised include:** Resident Engineer; Construction Inspector; Office Engineer; Senior Architect; Architect; Site Civil Engineer; Structural Drafter; Computer-aided Design Operator; Senior Structural Engineer; Construction Engineer; Design Engineer;. **Other U.S. locations:** Wethersfield CT; Washington DC; Boston MA; Hoboken NJ; Philadelphia PA; Richmond VA.

AMPHENOL CORPORATION
dba AMPHENOL AEROSPACE OPERATIONS
40-60 Delaware Avenue, Sidney NY 13838-1395. 607/563-5011. **Fax:** 607/563-5764. **Contact:** Sheri Youngs, Personnel Director. **World Wide Web address:** http://www.amphenol-aerospace.com. **Description:** The company designs, manufactures, and markets electrical, electronic and fiber optic connectors, coaxial and flat-ribbon cable, and interconnect systems specializing in aerospace connectors. **Positions advertised include:** Manufacturing Process Engineer; Advance Quality Engineer; Network Analyst; Process Engineer; Senior Financial Analyst; Sales Engineer; Assistant Product Manager; Sustaining/Process Engineer. **Corporate headquarters location:** Wallingford CT. **Other U.S. locations:** Danbury CT; Hamden CT. **International locations:** Worldwide. **Subsidiaries/Affiliates include:** Amphenol-Tuchel Electronics; Times Fiber. **Operations at this facility include:** Amphenol Aerospace Operations division manufacturing aerospace connectors. **Listed on:** New York Stock Exchange. **Stock exchange symbol:** APH. **Chairman/President/CEO:** Martin H. Loeffler. **Annual sales/revenues:** $1.06 billion. **Number of employees at this location:** 1,200. **Number of employees worldwide:** 10,300.

AMREP CORPORATION
641 Lexington Avenue, 6th Floor, New York NY 10022. 212/705-4700. **Fax:** 212/705-4740. **Contact:** Andrea Passes, Human Resources. **Description:** AMREP Corporation is a real estate developer and housing builder; a national distributor of magazines; and a provider of subscription fulfillment services for publishers with businesses operated by subsidiaries. AMREP Southwest Inc. is a real estate company in New Mexico and Kable operates the fulfillment services and magazine distribution company. **Corporate headquarters location:** This location. **Subsidiaries include:** Kable News Company, Inc.; Kable Distribution Services, Inc.; AMREP Southwest Inc. **Listed on:** New York Stock Exchange. **Stock exchange symbol:** AXR. **Annual sales/revenues:** $75 million. **Number of employees:** 925.

AMSTERDAM MEMORIAL HEALTH CARE SYSTEM
AMSTERDAM MEMORIAL HOSPITAL
4988 State Highway 30, Amsterdam NY 12010. 518/841-3539. **Fax:** 518/841-3749. **Contact:** Human Resources. **World Wide Web address:** http://www.amsterdammemorial.org. **Description:** A network of community health care programs and facilities providing a full range of services for residents of Fulton, Montgomery, Hamilton, Schoharie, Schenectady, and Saratoga counties which includes primary care centers, a pharmacy, the Wilkinson Center, therapy services, diagnostic imaging, and dozens of other services. Amsterdam Community Hospital offers a variety of services including primary care, rehabilitation, CT scanning, MRI, hemodialysis, ambulatory surgery, orthopedics, and women's and children's services.

AMSTERDAM PRINTING AND LITHO CORPORATION
166 Wallins Corners Road, P.O. Box 701, Amsterdam NY 12010-0701. 518/842-6000. **Fax:** 518/843-5204. **Contact:** Shirley McAuliff, Human Resources. **World Wide Web address:** http://www.amsterdamprinting.com. **Description:** A printing company that sells advertising specialties and business forms. Founded in 1898.

AMETEK POWER INSTRUMENTS
255 North Union Street, Rochester NY 14605. 585/263-7700. **Fax:** 585/238-4980. **Contact:** Human Resources. **World Wide Web address:** http://www.rochester.com. **Description:** Manufactures electrical monitoring equipment used in power plants and manufacturing facilities. Products include alarms and enunciators to monitor system malfunctions. **Corporate headquarters location:** Wilmington MA. **International locations:** United Kingdom; Singapore. **Parent company:** Ametek, Incorporated. **Operations at this facility include:** Administration; Manufacturing; Regional Headquarters; Research and Development; Sales; Service. **Listed on:** New York Stock Exchange. **Stock exchange symbol:** AME. **Number of employees at this location:** 200.

ANALYSTS INTERNATIONAL CORPORATION
16 West Main Street, Suite 731, Rochester NY 14614-1601. 716/325-6640. **Toll-free phone:** 800/864-6816. **Fax:** 716/325-6273. **Contact:** Recruiting Department. **E-mail address:** jobs@analysts.com. **World Wide Web address:** http://www.analysts.com. **Description:** AIC is an international computer consulting firm. The company assists clients in developing systems in a variety of industries using different programming languages and software. Founded in 1966. **Positions advertised include:** Applications Consultant; Computer Programmer; Information Systems Consultant; Software Engineer. **Office hours:** Monday - Friday, 8:30 a.m. - 5:00 p.m. **Corporate headquarters location:** Minneapolis MN. **Other U.S. locations:** Nationwide. **International locations:** Toronto, Canada; Cambridge, England. **Listed on:** NASDAQ. **Stock exchange symbol:** ANLY. **Annual sales/revenues:** $426 million. **Number of employees:** 3,200.

ANALYSTS INTERNATIONAL CORPORATION
7 Penn Plaza, Suite 300, New York NY 10001. 212/465-1660. **Fax:** 212/465-1724. **Contact:** Recruiter. **World Wide Web address:** http://www.analysts.com. **Description:** AIC is an international computer consulting firm. The company assists clients in developing systems in a variety of industries using different programming languages and software. **Corporate headquarters location:** Minneapolis MN. **Other U.S. locations:** Nationwide. **International locations:** Cambridge, England; Toronto, Canada. **Listed on:** NASDAQ. **Stock exchange symbol:** ANLY. **Annual sales/revenues:** $426 million. **Number of employees:** 3,200.

ANAREN, INC.
dba ANAREN MICROWAVE, INC.
6635 Kirkville Road, East Syracuse NY 13057. 315/432-8909. **Fax:** 315/432-9121. **Contact:** Dave Allen, Human Resources. **E-mail address:** hr3@anaren.com. **World Wide Web address:** http://www.anaren.com. **Description:** Anaren Microwave, Inc. is a government contracting defense facility. The company designs and manufactures microwave components, subsystems, and receiver systems for use in the electronic defense of ships, airplanes, and tactical land vehicles. **Positions advertised include:** Human Resources Assistant; Chemical Processing Equipment Operator; RF Testers. **Corporate headquarters location:** This location. **Other area locations:** Bohemia NY. **Other U.S. locations:** CA; MA; NC. **International locations:** China; England; The Netherlands. **Listed on:** NASDAQ. **Stock exchange symbol:** ANEN. **Chairman/President/CEO:** Lawrence A Sala. **Annual sales/revenues:** $73.6 million. **Number of employees:** 643.

ANDREA ELECTRONICS CORPORATION
45 Melville Park Road, Melville NY 11747. 631/719-1800. **Fax:** 631/719-1950. **Contact:** Heather Hinkley, Human Resources Manager. **World Wide Web address:** http://www.andreaelectronics.com. **Description:** Andrea Electronics Corporation designs, develops, and produces electronic audio systems, intercommunication systems, and related equipment for military and industrial companies. **Corporate headquarters location:** This location. **Other locations:** UT. **International locations:** Hong Kong; Israel. **Listed on:** American Stock Exchange. **Stock exchange symbol:** AND. **Chairman:** Douglas J. Andrea. **Annual sales/revenues:** $10 million. **Number of employees:** 88.

ANHEUSER-BUSCH, INC.
2885 Belgium Road, P.O. Box 200, Baldwinsville NY 13027. 315/635-4000. **Contact:** James McGrane, Senior Assistant Manager of Human Resources. **World Wide Web address:** http://www.anheuser-busch.com. **Description:** A diverse company involved in the entertainment, brewing, baking, and manufacturing industries. The company is the largest domestic beer brewer, operating 13 breweries throughout the United States and distributing through over 900 independent wholesalers. Beer brands include Budweiser, Michelob, Busch, King Cobra, and O'Doul's nonalcoholic beverages. Related businesses include can manufacturing, paper printing, and barley making. Anheuser-Busch is also one of the largest operators of theme parks in the United States, with locations in Florida, Virginia, Texas, Ohio, and California. Through subsidiary Campbell Taggart Inc., the company is one of the largest commercial bakers, producing foods under the Colonial brand name, among others. Anheuser-Busch also has various real estate interests. **NOTE:** Resumes may be submitted online via the company Website: http://www.buschjobs.com. **Positions advertised include:** Operations Manager; Process Support Supervisor. **Corporate headquarters location:** St. Louis MO. **Parent company:** Anheuser-Busch Companies Inc. (St Louis MO). **Operations at this facility include:** Brewery.

ANIMAL MEDICAL CENTER
THE E&M BOBST HOSPITAL
510 East 62nd Street, New York NY 10021. 212/838-8100. **Fax:** 212/758-8157. **Contact:** Human Resources. **E-mail address:** careers@amcny.org. **World Wide Web address:** http://www.amcny.org. **Description:** A full-service, nonprofit animal hospital with a staff of over 80 veterinarians. Founded in 1910. **Positions advertised include:** Staff Accountant; Stockroom Clerk; Pet Outreach Coordinator; Public Relations Administrative Assistant; Receptionist Medical Records; Veterinary Technician.

ANN TAYLOR STORES CORPORATION
142 West 57th Street, New York NY 10019. 212/541-3300. **Fax:** 212/536-4410. **Contact:** Human Resources. **E-mail address:** recruitment@anntaylor.com. **World Wide Web address:** http://www.anntaylor.com. **Description:** Ann Taylor is a leading national specialty retailer of women's apparel, shoes, and accessories sold primarily under the Ann Taylor brand name. The company operates 585 stores nationwide. Ann Taylor stores offer a collection of career and casual separates, dresses, tops, weekend wear, shoes, and accessories. **Corporate headquarters location:** This location. **Other locations:** Nationwide. **Subsidiaries include:** Ann Taylor Stores; Ann Taylor Loft; Ann Taylor Factory Stores. **Listed on:** New York Stock Exchange. **Stock exchange symbol:** ANN. **Chairman/CEO:** J. Patrick Spainhour. **Annual sales/revenues:** $1.4 billion. **Number of employees:** 10,900.

ANSEN CORPORATION
100 Chimney Point Drive, Ogdensburg NY 13669-2289. 315/393-3573. **Fax:** 315/393-7638. **Contact:** Human Resources. **E-mail address:** info@ansencorp.com. **World Wide Web address:** http://www.ansencorp.com. **Description:** Formerly Aimtronics, Ansen manufactures electronic products and componets for the microelectronic and computer industry including computer parts and hybrid circuits. The company provides services including printed circuit board surface mounting and assembles chip-on board and multi-chip modules. **Corporate headquarters location:** This location. **International locations:** Kanata, Ontario, Canada. **Parent company:** Ansen Group (Kanata, Ontario, Canada).

AON CORPORATION
dba AON RISK SERVICES
685 Third Avenue, New York NY 10017. 212/792-9200. **Contact:** Human Resources Department. **World Wide Web address:** http://www.aon.com. **Description:** An insurance brokerage that specializes in property and casualty insurance. **NOTE:** Resumes may be sent to the company's headquarters address: Aon Risk Services, 200 East Randolph Street, 12th Floor, Chicago IL 60601; or fax: 877/860-9251. **Positions advertised include:** Associate Risk Specialist; Surety Analyst; Client Specialist; Production Specialist; Senior Production Specialist; Senior Client Specialist; Account Representative; Financial Analyst; Senior Financial Analyst; Risk Consultant; Assistant Legal Director; Claims Coordinator; Assistant Director; Associate Production Specialist; Associate Client Specialist; Senior Client Specialist; Technical Staff Broker. **Corporate headquarters location:** Chicago IL. **Parent company:** Aon Corporation. **Listed on:** New York Stock Exchange. **Stock exchange symbol:** AOC.

APOLLO THEATRE
253 West 125th Street, New York NY 10027. 212/531-5300. **Fax:** 212/749-2743. **Contact:** Human Resources. **World Wide Web address:** http://www.apollotheater.com. **Description:** A nonprofit performing arts theater with performances year-round. **Parent company:** The Apollo Theater Foundation, Inc.

APPLE BANK FOR SAVINGS
122 East 42nd Street, New York NY 10168. 212/224-6400. **Toll-free phone:** 800/722-6888. **Fax:** 212/224-6592. **Contact:** Human Resources. **World Wide Web address:** http://www.theapplebank.com. **Description:** Operates a full-service savings bank serving New York City, Long Island, and Westchester with a total of 46 branches. Founded in 1836. **NOTE:** Entry-level positions are offered. **Positions advertised include:** Mortgage Underwriter; Bank Teller; Assistant Manager; Customer Service Representative. **Corporate headquarters location:** This location. **Other locations:** Greater New York City metropolitan area. **Number of employees at this location:** 900.

APPLIED ENERGY SOLUTIONS
One Technology Place, Caledonia NY 14423. 585/538-4421. **Fax:** 585/538-6345. **Contact:** Human Resources. **World Wide Web address:** http://appliedenergysol.com. **Description:** Manufactures battery chargers, power suppliers, and other electrical-related equipment. Founded in 1949.

APPLIED GRAPHICS TECHNOLOGIES, INC.
450 West 33rd Street, 11th Floor, New York NY 10001. 917/339-7320. **Fax:** 212/716-6776. **Contact:** Human Resources. **World Wide Web address:** http://www.agt.com. **Description:** Applied Graphics Technologies, Inc. along with its subsidiaries is one of the largest providers of integrated graphic communications services to advertising agencies, magazine and catalog publishers, and corporate clients in various industries worldwide. The company's services include commercial printing, color separation and retouching, facilities management, photo CD and digital image archiving, electronic imaging services, flexo/packaging services, publication and catalog services, satellite transmission services, creative design services, technical support and training services, and black and white ad production. **Corporate headquarters location:** This location. **Other area locations:** Rochester NY. **Other U.S. locations:** Nationwide. **Parent company:** Kohlberg & Company. **Subsidiaries include:** Black Dot Graphics, Inc.; Seven Worldwide, Inc. (also at this location). **Listed on:** American Stock Exchange. **Stock exchange symbol:** AGD. **Chairman/CEO:** Fred Drasner. **Annual sales/revenues:** $507 million. **Number of employees:** 4,000.

APPLIED GRAPHICS TECHNOLOGIES
1775 Broadway, 12th Floor, New York NY 10019. 212/333-4111. **Fax:** 212/333-7921. **Contact:** Human Resources. **World Wide Web address:** http://www.agt.com. **Description:** This location provides publication and catalog services, four-color facsimile or digital transmittal, desktop service bureau, satellite transmission services, and advertising agency services. Overall, Applied Graphics Technologies (AGT)/Seven is one of the largest providers of integrated graphic communications services to advertising agencies, magazine and catalog publishers, and corporate clients in various industries worldwide. The company's services include commercial printing, color separation and retouching, facilities management, photo CD and digital image archiving, electronic imaging services, flexo/packaging services, publication and catalog services, satellite transmission services, creative design services, technical support and training services, and black and white ad production. **NOTE:** All hiring is conducted through the corporate headquarters. Interested jobseekers should address all inquiries to Applied Graphics Technologies/Seven, 450 West 33rd Street, 11th Floor, New York NY 10001. 212/716-6600. **Corporate headquarters location:** New York NY. **Listed on:** American Stock Exchange. **Stock exchange symbol:** AGD.

APPLIED GRAPHICS TECHNOLOGIES
AGT – SEVEN ASSET MANAGEMENT SERVICES
450 West 33rd Street, 11th Floor, New York NY 10001. 212/716-6600. **Fax:** 585/277-1776. **Contact:** Human Resources. **World Wide Web address:** http://www.agtseven.com. **Description:** One of the largest providers of integrated graphic communications services to advertising agencies, magazine and catalog publishers, and corporate clients in various industries worldwide. Applied Graphics Technologies/Seven's services include commercial printing, color separation and retouching, facilities management, photo CD and digital image archiving, electronic imaging services, flexo/packaging services, publication and catalog services, satellite transmission services, creative design services, technical support and training services, and black and white ad production. **Corporate headquarters location:** This location. **Listed on:** American Stock Exchange. **Stock exchange symbol:** AGD.

ARCADIS G&M, INC.
88 Duryea Road, Melville NY 11747. 631/249-7600. **Contact:** Human Resources. **World Wide Web address:** http://www.arcadis-us.com. **Description:** A consulting firm that provides environmental and engineering services. The company focuses on the environmental, building, and infrastructure markets. Founded in 1888. **NOTE:** Interested jobseekers are encouraged to apply online. **Positions advertised include:** Engineering Technician. **Special programs:** Internships. **Corporate headquarters location:** Arnhem, Netherlands. **Other U.S. locations:** Nationwide. **Listed on:** NASDAQ. **Stock exchange symbol:** ARCAF. **Annual sales/revenues:** $502 million. **Number of employees worldwide:** 8,000.

ARIS INDUSTRIES, INC.
463 Seventh Avenue, New York NY 10018. 646/473-4200. **Fax:** 646/473-4242. **Contact:** Human Resources. **Description:** Engaged in the licensing and sale of men's and young men's sportswear and outerwear, as well as ladies' sportswear. **Annual sales/revenues:** $19.4 million. **Number of employees:** 71.

ARISTA INVESTORS CORPORATION
dba ARISTA INSURANCE COMPANY
116 John Street, New York NY 10038. 212/964-2150. **Fax:** 212/608-6473. **Contact:** Peter J. Norton, Human Resources Manager. **Description:** Through its subsidiary, Arista Insurance Company, the company is engaged in the sale and underwriting, as well as acting as a third-party administrator of statutory disability insurance for corporations and other insurance companies. **Listed on:** Over The Counter. **Stock exchange symbol:** ARINA. **Chairman:** Bernard Kooper. **Annual sales/revenues:** $4 million. **Number of employees:** 38.

ARISTA RECORDS
6 West 57th Street, 2nd Floor, New York NY 10019. 212/489-7400. **Fax:** 212/830-2107. **Contact:** Human Resources. **World Wide Web address:** http://www.arista.com. **Description:** Provides sales, promotional, and artist and repertoire activities for Arista Records and its contracted artists. Founded in 1974. **Corporate headquarters location:** This location. **Parent company:** BMG Entertainment. **Operations at this facility include:** Corporate Administration; Sales.

ARK RESTAURANTS CORPORATION
85 Fifth Avenue, 14th Floor, New York NY 10003. 212/206-8800. **Fax:** 212/206-8845. **Contact:** Marilyn Guy, Personnel Manager. **World Wide Web address:** http://www.arkrestaurants.com. **Description:** Ark Restaurants Corporation and its subsidiaries own, operate, or manage 27 restaurants nationwide. **Corporate headquarters location:** This location. **Listed on:** NASDAQ. **Stock exchange symbol:** ARKR. **Chairman:** Ernest Bogen. **Annual sales/revenues:** $115 million. **Number of employees:** 2,000.

ARKWIN INDUSTRIES, INC.
686 Main Street, Westbury NY 11590. 516/333-2640. **Contact:** Personnel Manager. **E-mail address:** humanresources@arkwin.com. **World Wide Web address:** http://www.arkwin.com. **Description:** Designs and manufactures fluid power control components, including hydraulics, for a wide range of industries. Founded in 1951.

Positions advertised include: Aerospace Engineer; Draftsperson; Industrial Engineer; Mechanical Engineer; Operations Manager; Systems Analyst. **Number of employees:** 300.

ARLEN CORPORATION
505 Eighth Avenue, Suite 300, New York NY 10018. 212/736-8100. **Contact:** Human Resources. **Description:** Manufactures and distributes steering wheels, physical security devices, interior accessories, and composite plastic and acrylic molded styling accessories for the automotive aftermarket and for automotive and marine original equipment manufacturers. The company also manufactures and distributes metal trim and accessories for the light-truck and sport-utility market.

AROTECH CORPORATION
250 West 57th Street, Suite 310, New York NY 10107. 212/258-3222. **Fax:** 212/258-3281. **Contact:** Human Resources. **E-mail address:** info@arotech.com. **World Wide Web address:** http://www.arotech.com. **Description:** Formerly Electric Fuel Corporation, Arotech, through its subsidiaries is engaged in training simulators for military and law enforcement applications; ceramic armor and ballistic glass for military and passenger vehicles; and zinc-air batteries and fuel cells for military, homeland security, electric vehicle, lifejacket, and safety device products. Founded in 1990. **Corporate headquarters location:** This location. **Subsidiaries include:** IES Interactive Training; M.D.T. Protective Industries; Electric Fuel Batteries. **Listed on:** NASDAQ. **Stock exchange symbol:** ARTX. **Chairman/CEO:** Robert S. Ehrlich. **Annual sales/revenues:** $6.4 million. **Number of employees:** 127.

ARROW ELECTRONICS, INC.
dba ARROW/ZEUS ELECTRONICS
2900 Westchester Avenue, Suite 401, Purchase NY 10577-2508. 914/701-7400. **Fax:** 914/701-4283. **Contact:** Human Resources Department. **World Wide Web address:** http://www.arrow.com. **Description:** Arrow Electronics distributes electronic components and computer products including semiconductors, computer peripherals, passive components, and interconnect products from over 600 suppliers to over 150,000 manufacturers with 225 sales offices and 20 distribution centers in 39 countries. The Arrow/Zeus division specializes in supplying electronic components to military and aerospace contractors with parts and solutions tailored to specific needs. **Positions advertised include:** Marketing Specialist; Sales Representative. **Corporate headquarters location:** Melville NY. **Other locations:** Brookhaven NY. **Subsidiaries/Affiliates include:** Microtronica; Marubun/Arrow; Spoerle; Sasco Semiconductor; CCI Electronique. **Operations at this facility include:** Sales. **Listed on:** New York Stock Exchange. **Stock exchange symbol:** ARW. **Annual sales:** $7.4 billion. **Number of employees at this location:** 65. **Number of employees worldwide:** 11,700.

ART LEATHER
GROSS NATIONAL PRODUCT
45-10 94th Street, Elmhurst NY 11373. 718/699-9696. **Fax:** 718/699-9621. **Contact:** Julio C. Barreneche, Human Resources Director. **World Wide Web address:** http://www.artleather.com. **Description:** A manufacturer of photo albums, displays, and folios. Partnered with Art Leather, Gross National Product manufactures photo image box display cases. Founded in 1925. **Positions advertised include:** Advertising Clerk; Clerical Supervisor; Customer Service Representative. **Corporate headquarters location:** This location. **Operations at this facility include:** Administration; Manufacturing; Sales; Service. **Number of employees at this location:** 540.

ASSOCIATED MERCHANDISING CORPORATION (AMC)
500 Seventh Avenue, New York NY 10018. 212/819-6600. **Fax:** 212/819-6701. **Contact:** Personnel. **World Wide Web address:** http://www.theamc.com. **Description:** Performs retail product development and international apparel sourcing services for retail clients operating 53 offices worldwide. Founded in 1916. **Positions advertised include:** Commercial Artist; Customer Service Representative; Product Manager. **Corporate headquarters location:** This location. **Other locations:** Worldwide. **Parent company:** Target Corporation (Minneapolis MN). **President/CEO:** Richard J. Kuzmich. **Number of employees:** 1,200.

THE ASSOCIATED PRESS
50 Rockefeller Plaza, 7th Floor, New York NY 10020. 212/621-1500. **Fax:** 212/621-5447. **Contact:** Human Resources. **E-mail address:** apjobs@ap.org. **World Wide Web address:** http://www.ap.org. **Description:** One of the largest independent news-gathering organizations in the world. Founded in 1848. **Corporate headquarters location:** This location. **Other U.S. locations:** Nationwide. **International locations:** Worldwide.

ASSOCIATED TEXTILE RENTAL SERVICE INC.
6700 Old Collamer Road, East Syracuse NY 13052. 315/414-0444. **Fax:** 315/797-1612. **Contact:** Robert Evans, Vice President of Finance. **Description:** This location is the corporate office for the business rental company. Associated Textile Rental Service deals primarily in linens, tablecloths, and uniforms for restaurants. **Corporate headquarters location:** This location. **Other locations:** East Syracuse NY; Fort Lauderdale FL; Rochester NY. **Number of employees at this location:** 10.

ASTORIA FEDERAL SAVINGS BANK
1150 Franklin Avenue, Garden City NY 11530. 516/746-0700. **Contact:** Human Resources. **E-mail address:** hr@astoriafederal.com. **World Wide Web address:** http://www.astoriafederal.com. **Description:** Provides a full range of banking and related financial services. **NOTE:** Hiring is conducted through the parent company. Interested jobseekers should address all inquiries to Manager of Human Resources, Astoria Financial Corporation, One Astoria Federal Plaza, Lake Success NY 11042-1085. **Positions advertised include:** Assistant Bank Office Manager; Teller. **Parent company:** Astoria Federal Savings & Loan Association (Lake Success NY).

ASTORIA FEDERAL SAVINGS BANK
451 Fifth Avenue, Brooklyn NY 11215. 718/965-7500. **Contact:** Human Resources Department. **E-mail address:** hr@astoriafederal.com. **World Wide Web address:** http://www.astoriafederal.com. **Description:** A savings bank offering a complete range of traditional banking and mortgage services. **NOTE:** Hiring is conducted through the parent company. Interested jobseekers should address all inquiries to Manager of Human Resources, Astoria Financial Corporation, One Astoria Federal Plaza, Lake Success NY 11042-1085. **Positions advertised include:** Assistant Bank Office Manager; Teller. **Parent company:** Astoria Federal Savings & Loan Association (Lake Success NY).

ASTORIA FINANCIAL CORPORATION
ASTORIA FEDERAL SAVINGS & LOAN ASSOCIATION
One Astoria Federal Plaza, Lake Success NY 11042-1085. 516/327-3000. **Toll-free phone:** 800/ASTORIA. **Fax:** 516/327-7610. **Contact:** Recruiting. **E-mail address:** hr@astoriafederal.com. **World Wide Web address:** http://www.astoriafederal.com. **Description:** AFC is the holding company for the Astoria Federal Savings and Loan Association operating 100 branches in the New York City metropolitan region as well as originating mortgages in the Northeast. The company offers complete banking services including offering CDs; checking, savings, and money market accounts; and NOW accounts. Founded in 1888. **NOTE:** See website for employment open house schedules. **Positions advertised include:** Internal Auditor; Assistant Banking Office Manager; Bank Office Manager; Personal Banker; Teller; Operations Supervisor; Telephone Banking Specialist. **Corporate headquarters location:** This location. **Subsidiaries include:** A.F. Insurance Agency; Astoria Federal Savings & Loan Association. **Listed on:** NASDAQ; New York Stock Exchange. **Stock exchange symbol:** ASFC; AF. **Chairman/President/CEO:** George L. Engelke, Jr. **Annual sales/revenues:** $1.4 billion. **Number of employees at this location:** 400. **Number of employees nationwide:** 2,000.

ASTREX, INC.
205 Express Street, Plainview NY 11803. 516/433-1700. **Toll-free phone:** 800/633-6360. **Fax:** 516/433-1796. **Contact:** Victoria Gagliardo, Human Resources. **World Wide Web address:** http://www.astrex.net. **Description:** Distributes electronic components used to connect, control, regulate, or store electricity in equipment. Products assembled and sold by Astrex include connectors, relays, switches, and LEDs. Founded in 1960. **Positions advertised include:** Inside Sales Representative; Strategic Account Manager; Credit Manager; Customer Service Representative; Sales Representative. **Corporate headquarters location:** This location. **Other U.S. locations:** Nationwide. **Annual sales/revenues:** $17 million. **Number of employees at this location:** 30. **Number of employees nationwide:** 60.

ASTRONICS CORPORATION
130 Commerce Way, East Aurora NY 14052. 716/805-1599. **Fax:** 716/805-1286. **Contact:** Human Resources. **World Wide Web address:** http://www.astronics.com. **Description:** Astronics Corporation operates in two divisions. The Customized Printing and Packaging division involves the design, manufacture, and marketing of proprietary paperboard and paper products. The major product lines include specialty folding boxes, invitations, and accessories to the confectionery, gift, wedding and social markets. The Electronic Systems division designs, manufactures, and markets advanced technology products. Major product lines include electroluminescent lamps and high-reliability keyboards. Major applications include aircraft crewstation and formation lighting, LCD backlighting, and keyboards for computer systems used under harsh environmental conditions. **Corporate headquarters location:** This location. **Subsidiaries include:** Luminescent Systems Incorporated; Krepe-Kraft Inc.; MOD-PAC CORP. **Listed on:** NASDAQ. **Stock exchange symbol:** ATRO. **Chairman:** Kevin T Keane. **Annual sales/revenues:** $43 million. **Number of employees:** 412.

ATALANTA SOSNOFF CAPITAL CORPORATION
101 Park Avenue, 6th Floor, New York NY 10178-0002. 212/867-5000. **Fax:** 212/922-1820. **Contact:** Human Resources Director. **E-mail address:** ksk@atalantasosnoff.com. **World Wide Web address:** http://www.atalantasosnoff.com. **Description:** Atalanta Sosnoff Capital Corporation provides discretionary investment management and brokerage services. **Corporate headquarters location:** This location. **Other locations:** Cardiff CA. **Listed on:** New York Stock Exchange. **Stock exchange symbol:** ATL. **Chairman/CEO:** Martin T. Sosnoff. **Annual sales/revenues:** $15.4 million. **Number of employees:** 46.

ATARI, INC.
417 Fifth Avenue, 8th Floor, New York NY 10016. 212/726-6500. **Fax:** 212/726-6533. **Contact:** Human Resources. **E-mail address:** recruiter@atari.com. **World Wide Web address:** http://www.infogrames.com. **Description:** Creates, wholesales, and markets a wide variety of software including interactive games. **Positions advertised include:** Policies & Procedures Manager; Associate Buyer. **Corporate headquarters location:** This location. **Other U.S. locations:** CA; MA; MN; VA; WA. **International locations:** France. **Listed on:** NASDAQ. **Stock exchange symbol:** ATAR.

ATELIER ESTHETIQUE INC.
386 Park Avenue South, Suite 1409, New York NY 10016. 212/725-6130. **Contact:** Human Resources. **World Wide Web address:** http://www.aeinstitute.net. **Description:** A wholesaler of cosmetic products and equipment. This location also houses a beauty school.

ATLANTIC MUTUAL COMPANIES
140 Broadway, 33rd Floor, New York NY 10005-1101. 212/943-1800. **Fax:** 212/428-6566. **Contact:** Human Resources Department. **World Wide Web address:** http://www.atlanticmutual.com. **Description:** Operates two multiple-line insurance companies that write property, liability, and marine insurance. **Subsidiaries include:** Atlantic Mutual Insurance Company and its wholly owned subsidiary, Centennial Insurance Company, share the same offices and staff. Services are sold primarily through independent insurance agents and brokers. Another subsidiary is Atlantic Lloyd's Insurance Company of Texas. **Other U.S. locations:** Nationwide. **International locations:** Canada; England. **Chairman/CEO:** Klaus G. Dorfi. **Annual sales/revenues:** $837 million. **Number of employees:** 1,800.

AUBURN MEMORIAL HOSPITAL
17 Lansing Street, Auburn NY 13021. 315/255-7225. **Fax:** 315/255-7018. **Contact:** Colleen McLaughlin, Employment Specialist. **E-mail address:** ahmjobs@dreamscape.com. **World Wide Web address:** http://www.auburnhospital.com. **Description:** A 226-bed hospital. **NOTE:** Human Resources phone: 315/255-7225. **Positions advertised include:** Registered Nurse; Nursing Supervisor; Licensed Practical Nurse; Certified Nursing Assistant. **Parent company:** Auburn Hospital System Foundation, Inc. (also at this location).

AUDIOVOX CORPORATION
150 Marcus Boulevard, Hauppauge NY 11788. 631/231-7750. **Fax:** 631/231-2968. **Contact:** Human Resources. **E-mail address:** employment@audiovox.com. **World Wide Web address:** http://www.audiovox.com. **Description:** Engaged in the sale and distribution of a variety of automotive electronic components including car radios, speakers, alarm systems, and cellular phones. **Positions advertised include:** Returns Clerk; Parts Clerk; Warehouse Clerk; Assembler; Project Engineers; Security Products Project Engineer; Video Products Project Engineer. **Special programs:** Internships. **Corporate headquarters location:** This location. **Other U.S. locations:** CA; FL; GA; IL; KY; LA; NC; OH; PA; SC; TN; VA. **Subsidiaries include:** Quintex Mobile Communications. **Operations at this facility include:** Administration; Divisional Headquarters; Regional Headquarters; Research and Development; Sales; Service. **Listed on:** NASDAQ. **Stock exchange symbol:** VOXXE. **Number of employees at this location:** 350. **Number of employees nationwide:** 1,000.

AUTHENTIDATE HOLDING CORPORATION
2 World Financial Center, 225 Liberty Street, 43rd Floor, New York NY 10281. 212/329-1100. **Fax:** 212/329-1101. **Contact:** Human Resources. **World Wide Web address:** http://www.authentidate.com. **Description:** The company's main subsidiary,

AuthentiDate, Inc., is engaged in the manufacture and distribution of document imaging systems, computer systems and related peripheral equipment, components, and accessories and network and Internet services. **Corporate headquarters location:** This location. **Subsidiaries include:** AuthentiDate, Inc.; Computer Professionals International; DocSTAR; Authentidate Sports Edition; Trac Medical Solutions, Inc.; DJS Marketing Group, Inc.; WebCMN, Inc. **Listed on:** NASDAQ. **Stock exchange symbol:** ADAT. **President/CEO:** John H. Botti. **Annual sales/revenues:** $16 million. **Number of employees:** 41.

AVANT SERVICES CORPORATION
686 Lexington Avenue, New York NY 10022. 212/755-7320. **Fax:** 212/370-1452. **Contact:** Personnel Manager. **Description:** A delivery company. **NOTE:** Entry-level positions, part-time jobs, and second and third shifts are offered. **Positions advertised include:** Administrative Assistant; Assistant Manager; Driver. **Special programs:** Summer Jobs.

AVNET, INC.
390 Rabro Drive, Hauppauge NY 11788. 631/582-8638. **Contact:** Human Resources. **E-mail address:** talent.acquisition@avnet.com. **World Wide Web address:** http://www.avnet.com. **Description:** One of the nation's largest distributors of electronic components and computer products for industrial and military customers. The company also manufactures and distributes other electronic, electrical, and video communications products. **NOTE:** Resumes must be sent to Avnet, Inc., Human Resources, 2211 South 47th Street, Phoenix AZ 85034. Resumes can be faxed to 602/643-4670. **Corporate headquarters location:** Phoenix AZ. **Other locations:** Worldwide. **Subsidiaries include:** Avnet Applied Computing; Avnet Direct; Avnet Electronics Marketing; Avnet Hall-Mark; Avnet Computer Marketing Avnet Enterprise Solutions. **Listed on:** New York Stock Exchange. **Stock exchange symbol:** AVT. **Annual sales/revenues:** $8.9 billion. **Number of employees:** 11,000.

AVON PRODUCTS INC.
1345 Avenue of the Americas, New York NY 10105. 212/282-5000. **Fax:** 212/282-5941. **Contact:** Staffing Manager. **E-mail address:** jobs@avon.com. **World Wide Web address:** http://www.avon.com. **Description:** A direct seller of beauty care products, fashion jewelry, gifts, fragrances, and decorative products, marketing its products through a network of almost three million independent sales representatives in 135 countries worldwide. **NOTE:** Salespeople are considered independent contractors or dealers and most work part-time. If you are interested in becoming a sales representative, please call 800/FOR-AVON, or visit the company's Website. **Positions advertised include:** Supply Manager; Product Manager; Business Analyst. **Corporate headquarters location:** This location. **Other U.S. locations:** Nationwide. **Listed on:** New York Stock Exchange. **Stock exchange symbol:** AVP.

AXIOHM TRANSACTION SOLUTIONS, INC.
950 Danby Road, Ithaca NY 14850. 607/274-2500. **Fax:** 607/274-2567. **Contact:** Personnel. **World Wide Web address:** http://www.axiohm.com. **Description:** One of the world's largest designers, manufacturers, and marketers of transaction printers. Axiohm Transaction Solutions also designs and manufactures bar code printers, magstripe and smartcard readers and writers, card printers, dot matrix impact printheads, magnetic heads, print and apply labeling systems, and consumables. Founded in 1988. The company is comprised of 2 divisions: TPG, Inc. and Cognitive. **Special programs:** Internships; Co-ops. **Corporate headquarters location:** This location. **Other U.S. locations:** CA; CO; WY. **Parent company:** Axiohm SA (France). **Number of employees at this location:** 400. **Number of employees nationwide:** 800. **Number of employees worldwide:** 1,600.

BAE SYSTEMS
One Hazelteen Way, Greenlawn NY 11740. 631/261-7000. **Contact:** Human Resources. **World Wide Web address:** http://www.baesystems.com. **Description:** Designs, develops, and manufactures information electronics systems that acquire, protect, enhance, communicate, and display information for the defense and technically related markets. **NOTE:** Applications may be done on-line. **Positions advertised include:** Material Clerk; Legal Counsel/Attorney; Antenna Design Engineering Manger; Engineering Manager; Radio Frequency Systems Department Engineer; Senior Technical/Antenna Staff Member; Staff Contract Administrator; Senior Electro-Optic Systems Engineer; Senior Servo Systems Engineer; Digital Servo Systems Engineer; Reliability & Maintainability Engineer; Principal Electromagnetic Interference Engineer; Principal Systems Engineer; Truck Driver; Senior Staff Engineer; Business Development Director; Staff Project Engineer; Senior Electronic Assembler; Citation Project Engineer; Micro-Electronic Assembler. **Corporate headquarters location:** Hampshire, United Kingdom. **Other area locations:** Johnson City NY; Syosset NY; Yonkers NY. **Other U.S. locations:** Nationwide. **International locations:** Worldwide. **Subsidiaries include:** Airbus S.A.S.; Saab AB. **Operations at this facility include:** BAE's Advanced Systems Division. **Listed on:** Over The Counter. **Stock exchange symbol:** BAESY. **Annual sales/revenues:** $13.1 billion. **Number of employees at this location:** 925. **Number of employees nationwide:** 22,000. **Number of employees worldwide:** 70,100.

BAE SYSTEMS
600 Main Street, Johnson City NY 13790. 607/770-2000. **Fax:** 607/770-3524. **Contact:** Human Resources. **World Wide Web address:** http://www.baesystems.com. **Description:** A global supplier of integrated control systems and subsystems for air, space, and ground vehicles for civilian and military markets. Controls designs, develops, produces, and supports subsystems including fly-by-wire flight controls, digital autopilots and flight directrors, full-authority digital engine controls, launch vehicle controls, UAV systems, low-visibility precision landing systems, and integrated avionics as well as provides hybrid-electric drive systems for intra-city transit buses and other medium and large vehicles. **NOTE:** Applications may be done on-line. **Positions advertised include:** Program Manager; Director of Engineering; Information Technology Hardware Infrastructure Manager; Embedded Real-Time Operating System Software Engineer; Lead Software Engineer; Software Design Engineer; V-22 Software Engineer; Actuation Systems Engineer; Principal Lead Circuit Design Engineer; Rotorcraft Systems Engineer; Contracts Administration Manager; Principal Systems Engineer. **Corporate headquarters location:** Hampshire, United Kingdom. **Other area locations:** Greenlawn NY; Syosset NY; Yonkers NY. **Other U.S. locations:** Nationwide. **International locations:** Worldwide. **Subsidiaries include:** Airbus S.A.S.; Saab AB. **Operations at this facility include:** BAE's Controls Systems Division; BAE's Engine Controls Division; BAE's Power & Drive Systems Division. **Listed on:** Over The Counter. **Stock exchange symbol:** BAESY. **Annual sales/revenues:** $13.1 billion. **Number of employees at this location:** 925. **Number of employees nationwide:** 22,000. **Number of employees worldwide:** 70,100.

BAE SYSTEMS
One Ridge Hill, Mail Stop 9, Yonkers NY 10710-5598. 914/964-2500. **Fax:** 914/964-3913. **Contact:** Human Resources Department. **World Wide Web address:** http://www.baesystems.com. **Description:** Designs, manufactures, and sells flight simulators, weapon systems, tactical air defense systems, small arms, and training devices for the U.S. government, as well as commercial and international customers. BAE Systems also develops simulation-based devices for the entertainment industry. The company also provides a variety of simulator-related training services at customer-owned facilities, its Tampa training center, and the British Aerospace-owned Dulles training facility. BAE Systems conducts business through its three primary operating segments: Training Devices, Training Services, and Systems Management. **Positions advertised include:** Program Manager; Calibration Lab Technician. **Corporate headquarters location:** Hampshire, United Kingdom. **Other area locations:** Greenlawn NY; Johnson City NY; Syosset NY. **Other U.S. locations:** Nationwide. **International locations:** Worldwide. **Subsidiaries include:** Airbus S.A.S.; Saab AB. **Operations at this facility include:** BAE's Information & Electronic Warfare Systems Division. **Listed on:** Over The Counter. **Stock exchange symbol:** BAESY. **Annual sales/revenues:** $13.1 billion. **Number of employees at this location:** 925. **Number of employees nationwide:** 22,000. **Number of employees worldwide:** 70,100.

BBDO WORLDWIDE INC.
1285 Avenue of the Americas, New York NY 10019. 212/459-5000. **Fax:** 212/459-6645. **Recorded jobline:** 212/459-5627. **Contact:** Human Resources Department. **E-mail address:** nyhrmanagerrecruiting@bbdo.com. **World Wide Web address:** http://www.bbdo.com. **Description:** Operates a worldwide network of advertising agencies in 300 offices in 45 countries with related businesses in public relations, direct marketing, sales promotion, graphic design, graphic arts, and printing. BBDO Worldwide operates 83 subsidiaries, affiliates, and associates in advertising and related operations. Since 1891. **Positions advertised include:** Assistant Media Planner; Assistant National TV Buyer; Corporate Computer Systems Manager; Media Supervisor; National TV Buyer; Media Planner; Assistant Account Executive; Budget Coordinator; Systems Engineer; Administrative Assistant; Accounting Clerk; Finance Manager; Control Coordinator; Print Estimator; Art Director; Copy Editor; Audio-Visual Technician; Business Affairs Manager; Media Producer; Traffic Coordinator. **Special programs:** Interships. **Corporate headquarters location:** This location. **Other U.S. locations:** Nationwide. **International locations:** Worldwide. **Subsidiaries include:** BBDO Detroit. **Parent company:** Omnicom Group Inc. (New York NY). **Chairman/CEO:** Allen Rosenshine. **Annual sales/revenues:** $1.6 billion. **Number of employees worldwide:** 16,600.

BP INDEPENDENT REPROGRAPHICS
853 Broadway, New York NY 10003. 212/777-1110. **Fax:** 212/777-0880. **Contact:** Human Resources. **World Wide Web address:** http://www.bpirepro.com. **Description:** Provides blueprinting services, blueprint supplies, printing services, and photo services. **Other locations:** Elmsford NY; New York NY; White Plains NY. **Subsidiaries include:** B&B Independent. **Parent company:** American Reprographics Company (Glendale CA).

BSB BANCORP, INC.
BSB BANK & TRUST
58-68 Exchange Street, P.O. Box 1056, Binghamton NY 13902-1056. 607/779-2525. **Fax:** 607/779-2486. **Contact:** Human Resources Department. **World Wide Web address:** http://www.bsbbank.com. **Description:** BSB Bancorp is the bank holding company for BSB Bank & Trust. The bank provides diversified financial services to individuals and businesses from 20 branches serving the counties of Broome, Chenango, Onondaga, and Tioga in central New York State. Services include retail banking; commercial, mortgage, and consumer loans; and investment banking. **Positions advertised include:** Accountant; Teller; Accounting Services Representative; Credit Analysis Representative; Executive Assistant; Human Resources Services Representative; Item Process Representative; Special Assets Officer; Staff Accountant; Trust Investor Officer. **Corporate headquarters location:** This location. **Other locations:** Statewide. **Subsidiaries include:** BSB Financial Services, Inc.; INVEST Financial Corporation. **Listed on:** NASDAQ. **Stock exchange symbol:** BSBN. **Chairman:** William C. Craine. **Annual sales/revenues:** $147 million. **Number of employees:** 600.

BSB BANK & TRUST COMPANY
100 Kasson Road, Camillus NY 13031. 315/487-1518. **Contact:** Human Resources. **World Wide Web address:** http://www.bsbbank.com. **Description:** Provides diversified financial services to individuals and businesses including retail banking; commercial, mortgage, and consumer loans; and investment banking. **NOTE:** You may call the customer service center for employment information at 607/779-2345. **Other locations:** Statewide. **Parent company:** BSB Bancorp Inc. (Binghamton NY). **Operations at this facility include:** A local branch office.

BALCHEM CORPORATION
2007 NY State Route 284, P.O. Box 175, Slate Hill NY 10973-0175. 845/355-5300. **Fax:** 845/355-6314. **Contact:** Human Resources. **E-mail address:** bcphr@balchem.com. **World Wide Web address:** http://www.balchem.com. **Description:** A leader in the manufacturing and marketing of encapsulated food ingredients for a variety of industries. The company is also a leading supplier of ethylene oxide, a packaging sterilant. Founded in 1967. **NOTE:** Resumes should be sent to the company's headquarters location to the attention of: JoAnne Fernandez, Balchem Corporation, P.O. Box 600, New Hampton NY 10958; or by fax: 845/326-5734; or to the above e-mail address. **Positions advertised include:** Senior Research Scientist; Western Regional Technical Sales Representative; Applications Specialist. **Corporate headquarters location:** New Hampton NY. **Other locations:** Green Pond SC; New Hampton NY; Verona MO. **Subsidiaries include:** BCP Ingredients, Inc; ARC Specialty Products. **Operations at this facility include:** Manufacturing. **Listed on:** American Stock Exchange. **Stock exchange symbol:** BCP. **President/CEO/CFO/Director:** Dino A. Rossi. **Annual sales/revenues:** $60 million. **Number of employees nationwide:** 220.

BANCTEC SYSTEMS, INC.
888 Veterans Memorial Highway, Suite 515, Hauppauge NY 11788. 631/234-5353. **Contact:** Human Resources. **E-mail address:** jobs@banctec.com. **World Wide Web address:** http://www.banctec.com. **Description:** BancTec is engaged in systems integration and specializes in document management solutions. The company also provides network support services and develops image management software. Founded in 1972. **NOTE:** Resumes should be sent to P.O. Box 660204, Dallas TX 75266-0204. **Corporate headquarters location:** Dallas TX. **Other locations:** Worldwide. **Number of employees worldwide:** 4,000.

BANK OF AMERICA
69 State Street, Albany, NY 12207. 518/447-4300. **Fax:** 518/626-2554. **Contact:** Human Resources. **World Wide Web address:** http://www.bankofamerica.com. **Description:** The bank provides commercial and consumer banking services to individuals, corporations, institutions, and governments of the Genesee, Finger Lakes, Southern Tier, and western regions of upstate New York. **NOTE:** Applications accepted online through the company Website. **Positions advertised include:** Emerging Markets/Outside Loan Officer; Applications Development Analyst; Infrastructure Specialist; Senior Relation Manager; Large Government Account

Officer; Associate Staff Auditor; Technical Project Analyst; Infrastructure Engineer. **Corporate headquarters location:** Charlotte NC. **Other U.S. locations:** Nationwide.

BANK OF AMERICA
29 Broadway, New York NY 10004. 212/563-7625. **Contact:** Human Resources. **World Wide Web address:** http://www.bankofamerica.com. **Description:** A nationwide securities brokerage firm serving retail customers and institutional investors. **Positions advertised include:** Personal Financial Consultant; Investment Center Manager. **Other U.S. locations:** Nationwide.

BANK OF NEW YORK
101 Barclay Street, Floor 1-E, New York NY 10286. 212/815-4984. **Contact:** Human Resources. **World Wide Web address:** http://www.bankofny.com. **Description:** A bank that serves individuals, corporations, foreign and domestic banks, governments, and other institutions through banking offices in New York City and foreign branches, representative offices, subsidiaries, and affiliates. **Corporate headquarters location:** New York NY. **Parent company:** The Bank of New York Company, Inc. (New York NY). **Number of employees nationwide:** 12,000.

BANK OF NEW YORK
One Wall Street, 13th Floor, New York NY 10286. 212/635-6790. **Fax:** 212/809-9528. **Contact:** Human Resources. **World Wide Web address:** http://www.bankofny.com. **Description:** A bank that serves individuals, corporations, foreign and domestic banks, governments, and other institutions through banking offices in New York City and foreign branches, representative offices, subsidiaries, and affiliates. **Special programs:** Internships. **Corporate headquarters location:** This location. **Parent company:** Bank of New York Company, Inc. (also at this location). **Number of employees nationwide:** 12,000.

BANK OF TOKYO MITSUBISHI
1251 Sixth Avenue, New York NY 10020-1104. 212/782-4000. **Fax:** 782-6415. **Contact:** Human Resources. **World Wide Web address:** http://www.btmny.com. **Description:** One of the 50 largest commercial banks in the United States. The company operates five offices throughout the New York metropolitan area, as well as in London and the Bahamas. **Corporate headquarters location:** This location. **Parent company:** The Bank of Tokyo Ltd. (Tokyo, Japan).

BARCLAYS BANK PLC
222 Broadway, 10th Floor, New York NY 10038. 212/412-4000. **Contact:** Human Resources. **World Wide Web address:** http://www.barclays.com. **Description:** An international banking institution with more than 5,000 offices in 60 countries including most international trade centers. International banking services include commercial loans, foreign exchange services, drafts and money transfers, foreign collections, leasing, stock and security custodial services, and economic information and publications. Barclays Bank also operates a global investment bank through its BZW Group subsidiary. **Parent company:** Barclays plc (London, United Kingdom). **Corporate headquarters location:** London, United Kingdom. **Other U.S. locations:** San Francisco CA.

C.R. BARD, INC.
289 Bay Road, P.O. Box 787, Queensbury NY 12804-2045. 518/793-2531. **Contact:** Human Resources. **E-mail address:** shaune.toomey@crbard.com. **World Wide Web address:** http://www.crbard.com. **Description:** This location manufactures catheters and critical care devices. Overall, C.R. Bard manufactures and distributes disposable medical, surgical, diagnostic, and patient care products. Cardiovascular products include angioplastic recanalization devices such as balloon angioplasty catheters, inflation devices, and developmental atherectomy and laser devices; electrophysiology products such as temporary pacing catheters, diagnostic and therapeutic electrodes, and cardiac mapping systems; a cardiopulmonary system; and blood oxygenators, cardiotomy reservoirs, and other products used in open heart surgery. Urological products include Foley catheters, trays, and related urine contract collection systems used extensively in postoperative bladder drainage. Surgical products include wound and chest drainage systems and implantable blood vessel replacements. **Corporate headquarters location:** Murray Hill NJ. **International locations:** Worldwide. **Listed on:** New York Stock Exchange. **Stock exchange symbol:** BCR. **Annual sales/revenues:** $1.3 billion. **Number of employees worldwide:** 7,700.

BARKSDALE HEALTH CARE SERVICES INC.
BARKSDALE HOME CARE SERVICES CORP.
BARKSDALE SERVICES CORP.
327 Fifth Avenue, Pelham NY 10803. 914/738-5600. **Fax:** 914/738-0658. **Contact:** Rosa K. Barksdale, CEO. **World Wide Web address:** http://www.barksdaleathome.com. **Description:** A home health care agency providing health care services to private homes, hospitals, and institutions in Westchester County and the Bronx NY. **Positions advertised include:** Nurses Aide; Personal Care Aide; Certified Nurses Aide; Medical Social Worker; Live-in Companion; Home Health Aide; Licensed Practical Nurse; Registered Nurse. **Corporate headquarters location:** This location. **Other locations:** Riverdale NY.

BARNARD COLLEGE
3009 Broadway, New York NY 10027-6598. 212/854-2551. **Fax:** 212/854-2454. **Contact:** Employment Manager. **World Wide Web address:** http://www.barnard.edu. **Description:** An independent college of liberal arts and sciences for women, affiliated with Columbia University. Barnard College has an enrollment of approximately 2,200 undergraduates from more than 40 countries. Barnard offers approximately 50 majors in the humanities, social sciences, arts, and natural sciences. Double- and joint-degree programs with Columbia (dentistry, engineering, international and public policy, law, and administration), Juilliard, and the Jewish Theological Seminary are offered. Founded in 1889. **Positions advertised include:** Psychological Counselor; Web/Oracle Programmer; Teacher; Housekeeping and Custodial Services Manager; Student Health Services Director; Room Reservation Specialist; Administrative Assistant; Assistant to the Director; English Poetry Lecturer; Philosophy Lecturer; Migration and Diaspora Studies Lecturer; Dance Department Chairperson; Anthropology Lecturer; Asian and Middle Eastern Cultures Lecturer; Biology Lab Associate; Biology Lecturer; Economics Lecturer; Assistant Physics Professor; Architecture & Urban Studies Lecturer; Art History Lecturer; Sociology Lecturer; Slavic Professor; Spanish Professor; Theater Professor; Security Guard.

BARNES & NOBLE BOOKSTORES
1400 Old Country Road, Westbury NY 11590. 516/338-8000. **Contact:** Human Resources. **E-mail address:** careerswestbury@bn.com. **World Wide Web address:** http://www.barnesandnobleinc.com. **Description:** A bookstore chain operating 900 stores nationwide. **NOTE:** Resumes may be either sent to the above e-mail address; posted on the company Website (http://www.barnesandnobleinc.com/jobs/index.html); sent to the company's headquarters address: Barnes & Noble, Inc., Human Resources, 122 Fifth Avenue, New York NY 10011; or faxed to: 212/463-5640. **Positions advertised include:** Accounts Payables Administrator; Expense Payables Administrator; Specialty Payables Administrator; Human Resources Representative; General Accounting Manager; Staff Accountant; AJB Programmer/Analyst. **Corporate headquarters location:** New York NY. **Other locations:** Nationwide. **Operations at this facility include:** Financial offices. **Listed on:** New York Stock Exchange. **Stock exchange symbol:** BKS. **Chairman:** Leonard S. Riggio. **Annual sales/revenues:** $5.2 billion. **Number of employees worldwide:** 37,000.

BARNES & NOBLE CORPORATION
122 Fifth Avenue, 2nd Floor, New York NY 10011. 212/633-3300. **Fax:** 212/463-5640. **Contact:** Human Resources. **E-mail address:** careersnyc@bn.com. **World Wide Web address:** http://www.barnesandnobleinc.com. **Description:** A bookstore chain operating 900 stores nationwide. **NOTE:** Resumes may be either sent to the above mailing address, e-mail address, fax, or posted on the company Website: http://www.barnesandnobleinc.com/jobs/index.html. **Positions advertised include:** Director of Financial Planning and Analysis; Human Resources Manager; Store Operations Administrative Assistant; Marketing Coordinator; Database Administrator; Web Production Engineer; Product Development Engineer. **Corporate headquarters location:** This location. **Other locations:** Nationwide. **Operations at this facility include:** Corporate administration. **Listed on:** New York Stock Exchange. **Stock exchange symbol:** BKS. **Chairman:** Leonard S. Riggio. **Annual sales/revenues:** $5.2 billion. **Number of employees worldwide:** 37,000.

BARNEYS NEW YORK, INC.
575 Fifth Avenue, New York NY 10017. 212/229-7300. **Fax:** 212/450-8489. **Contact:** Human Resources. **E-mail address:** hr@barneys.com. **World Wide Web address:** http://www.barneys.com. **Description:** A national specialty retailer offering upscale men's and women's apparel collections from both American and international designers operating eight full-price stores and 12 outlets nationwide. Founded in 1923. **NOTE:** For retail positions, contact the appropriate store. **Positions advertised include:** Buyer; Customer Service Representative. **Corporate headquarters location:** This location. **Operations at this facility include:** Administration; Sales; Service. **Listed on:** Over The Counter. **Stock exchange symbol:** BNNY. **Annual sales:** $371 million. **Number of employees:** 1,300.

BARR LABORATORIES, INC.
2 Quaker Road, P.O. Box 2900, Pomona NY 10970-0519. 845/362-1100. **Fax:** 845/362-2774. **Contact:** Human Resources. **World Wide Web address:** http://www.barrlabs.com. **Description:** Barr Laboratories is a leading independent developer, manufacturer, and marketer of off-patent pharmaceuticals. **Positions advertised include:** R&D Documentation Specialist; Senior Validation Engineer; Quality Control Manager; Quality Control Chemist; Technical Group Leader Quality Control; External Auditor. **Corporate headquarters location:** This location. **Other locations:** NJ; OH; PA; OH. **Operations at this facility include:** Development and production laboratories; Administration; Manufacturing; Research & Development; Pharmacy operations. **Listed on:** New York Stock Exchange. **Stock exchange symbol:** BRL. **Chairman/CEO:** Bruce L. Downey. **Annual sales/revenues:** $1.2 billion. **Number of employees:** 1,075.

BARRISTER GLOBAL SERVICES NETWORK, INC.
186 Exchange Street, Buffalo NY 14204-2026. 716/845-5033. **Toll-free phone:** 800/786-2472. **Fax:** 716/845-1867. **Contact:** Human Resources. **World Wide Web address:** http://www.barrister.com. **Description:** Barrister Global Services Network provides multivendor computer equipment maintenance services. Founded in 1972. **Positions advertised include:** Technical Support Specialist. **Corporate headquarters location:** New Orleans LA. **Subsidiaries include:** Barrister Advantage Services LLC. **Listed on:** American Stock Exchange. **Stock exchange symbol:** BIS. **President/CEO:** Henry (Hank) P. Semmelhack. **Annual sales/revenues:** $12.8 million. **Number of employees:** 122.

BARUCH COLLEGE
THE CITY UNIVERSITY OF NEW YORK (CUNY)
One Bernard Baruch Way, Box D-0202, New York NY 10010. 212/802-2740. **Fax:** 212/802-2745. **Contact:** Human Resources. **World Wide Web address:** http://www.baruch.cuny.edu. **Description:** A college offering undergraduate and graduate programs through its School of Business, School of Liberal Arts and Sciences, and School of Public Affairs. **Positions advertised include:** Accountancy Instructor; Black & Hispanic Studies Instructor; Career Counseling Instructor; Communication Studies Instructor; Computer Information Systems Instructor; Economics & Finance Instructor; English Instructor; Fine and Performing Arts Instructor; History Instructor; Law Instructor; Management Instructor; Marketing Instructor; Mathematics Instructor; Modern Languages Instructor; Comparative Literature Instructor; Natural Sciences Instructor; Philosophy Instructor; Political Science Instructor; Psychology Instructor; Public Affairs Instructor; Sociology and Anthropology Instructor; Statistics Instructor; Computer Information Systems Assistant Instructor; College Assistant; Continuing and Professional Studies Instructor; CUNY Custodial Assistant; CUNY Office Assistant. **Other area locations:** Bronx NY; Brooklyn NY; Flushing NY; Jamaica NY; Staten Island NY. **Operations at this facility include:** Administration; Research and Development; Service. **Number of employees at this location:** 1,800.

BATES USA
498 Seventh Avenue, New York NY 10018. 212/297-7000. **Fax:** 212/297-8888. **Contact:** Human Resources. **E-mail address:** hr@batesww.com. **World Wide Web address:** http://www.batesusa.com. **Description:** One of the largest advertising and public relations agencies in the United States. **Positions advertised include:** Account Manager; Account Planner; Creative Designer; Media Specialist. **Corporate headquarters location:** This location. **Other locations:** Worldwide.

BAUSCH & LOMB, INC.
One Bausch & Lomb Place, Rochester NY 14604-2701. 585/338-6000. **Toll-free phone:** 800/344-8815. **Fax:** 585/338-6007. **Contact:** Centralized Staffing. **World Wide Web address:** http://www.bausch.com. **Description:** Manufactures eye care products, pharmaceuticals, and surgical equipment including contact lenses; lens care solutions; premium sunglasses (sold under Ray-Ban and Revo brands) prescription and over-the-counter ophthalmic drugs; and equipment used for cataract and ophthalmic surgery. **NOTE:** You may apply online through the company Website. **Positions advertised include:** Network Specialist; Sales Support Representative; Senior Purchasing Agent; Regulatory Affairs Director; Senior Clinical Specialist; Clinical Programs Manager; Sales Materials Clerk; Commercial Procurement Clerk; Finance Clerk; Human Resources Specialist; Quality Director; Professional Relations Manager; Senior Clinical Consultant; Professional Services Manager; Audit Manager; Professional Communications Manager; Procurement Manager. **Special programs:** Summer Internships. **Corporate headquarters location:** Rochester NY. **Other area locations:** Pearl River NY. **Other U.S. locations:** Nationwide. **Operations at this facility include:** Manufacturing. **Listed on:** New York Stock Exchange. **Stock exchange symbol:** BOL. **Chairman/CEO:** Ronald L. Zarrella. **Annual sales/revenues:** $1.8 billion. **Number of employees:** 11,600.

BAX GLOBAL
19 Ransier Drive, Building-B, West Seneca NY 14224. 716/677-2041. **Fax:** 716/677-2043. **Contact:** Human Resources. **World Wide Web address:** http://www.baxglobal.com. **Description:** A business-to-business shipping service operating on an international level. **Other U.S. locations:** Nationwide. **Other international locations:** Worldwide.

BAYER DIAGNOSTICS DIVISION
BAYER HEALTHCARE
511 Benedict Avenue, Tarrytown NY 10591-5097. 914/631-8000. **Fax:** 914/333-6536. **Contact:** Kim MacNeil, Human Resources. **E-mail address:** hr.grp@bayer.com or kim.macneil.b@bayer.com. **World Wide Web address:** http://www.bayerdiag.com. **Description:** Develops, manufactures, and sells clinical diagnostic systems. Bayer Diagnostics specializes in critical care, laboratory, and point-of-care testing. **NOTE:** See http://www.monster.com for current job listings. **Positions advertised include:** Reimbursement & Public Affairs Director; Diabetes Sales Specialist; FDA/Regulatory Counselor; Finished Goods Supply Chain Manager; Training Specialist; Senior Training Specialist; Product Engineer; Clinical Account Specialist; Telehealthcare Specialist; Marketing Manager; Multistix PRO Senior Marketing Manager; Service and Support Engineer; Laboratory Automation Engineer; Health Care Professional/Manager; Research Scientist; Staff System Engineer; Senior Financial Analyst; Sales Trainer; National Advertising Division Marketing Manager; Managed Care Manager; Hematology Sales Specialist. **Corporate headquarters location:** Pittsburgh PA. **Other area locations:** Middletown NY; Nyack NY. **Other U.S. locations:** IL; LA; MA; OH; PA. **International locations:** Worldwide. **Parent company:** Bayer Corporation (Pittsburgh PA). **Operations at this facility include:** Administration; Divisional Headquarters; Manufacturing; Research and Development; Sales; Service. **Listed on:** New York Stock Exchange. **Stock exchange symbol:** BAY. **Number of employees at this location:** 800. **Number of employees nationwide:** 8,000.

BEAR, STEARNS & COMPANY, INC.
THE BEAR STEARNS COMPANIES INC.
383 Madison Avenue, 30th Floor, New York NY 10179. 212/272-2000. **Fax:** 2212/272-4785. **Contact:** Human Resources. **World Wide Web address:** http://www.bearstearns.com. **Description:** A leading worldwide investment banking, securities trading, and brokerage firm. **NOTE:** The company does not accept hard copy resumes and requests that resumes be submitted online via the company Website. **Corporate headquarters location:** This location. **Other U.S. locations:** Nationwide. **International locations:** Worldwide. **Subsidiaries include:** Bear, Stearns & Company, Inc. is an investment banking and brokerage firm; Bear, Stearns Securities Corporation provides professional and correspondent clearing services including securities lending; Custodial Trust Company provides master trust, custody, and government securities services; Bear Sterns Asset Management Inc. provides financial management services; Global Clearing Services. **Listed on:** New York Stock Exchange. **Stock exchange symbol:** BSC. **Chairman/CEO:** James E. Cayne. **Annual sales/revenues:** $6.9 billion. **Number of employees nationwide:** 10,600.

BEDFORD STUYVESANT RESTORATION CORPORATION
1368 Fulton Street, Brooklyn NY 11216-2630. 718/636-6900. **Fax:** 718/636-0511. **Contact:** Human Resources. **E-mail address:** info@restorationplaza.org. **World Wide Web address:** http://www.restorationplaza.org. **Description:** A nonprofit community development corporations promoting the economic revitalization of the Bedford Stuyvesant section of Brooklyn since 1967.

MATTHEW BENDER & COMPANY
1275 Broadway, Albany NY 12204. 518/487-3000. **Fax:** 518/487-3573. **Contact:** Human Resources. **E-mail address:** lexisnexis@hiresystems.com. **World Wide Web address:** http://www.bender.com. **Description:** A publisher of technical and reference books for law firms, real estate organizations, and industries. Recent titles include books covering modern estate planning, banking law, deposition practice, advocacy, bankruptcy, state-specific, immigration law, international business, courtroom science, criminal law, natural resources, and taxes. The company also offers an online interactive legal practice data system, as well as other electronic publishing services. **Positions advertised include:** Administrative Assistant; Legal Editor. **Special programs:** Internships. **Corporate headquarters location:** Newark NJ. **Other area locations:** Conklin NY. **Other locations:** Nationwide. **Parent company:** LexisNexis. **Number of employees at this location:** 250.

SANFORD C. BERNSTEIN & CO., LLC
dba BERNSTEIN INVESTMENT RESEARCH & MANAGEMENT
1345 Avenue of the Americas, New York NY 10105. 212/486-5800. **Fax:** 212/756-4455. **Contact:** Human Resources. **E-mail address:** resumes@bernstein.com. **World Wide Web address:** http://www.bernstein.com. **Description:** An investment management research company that conducts research on specific companies and provides investment-banking services for both private and institutional clients. **Positions advertised include:** Financial Advisor. **Corporate headquarters location:** This location. **Other U.S. locations:** Nationwide. **Parent company:** Alliance Capital Management L.P. (also at this location).

BERNZOMATIC CORPORATION
One Bernzomatic Drive, Medina NY 14103. 716/798-4949. **Contact:** Human Resources. **World Wide Web address:** http://www.bernzomatic.com. **Description:** Manufactures torches and similar equipment including propane cylinders. The company also sells wholesale to businesses. Founded in 1876. **Corporate headquarters location:** Freeport IL. **Parent company:** Newell Rubbermaid Inc.(Freeport IL). **Number of employees at this location:** 240.

BESICORP GROUP INC.
1151 Flatbush Road, Kingston NY 12401. 845/336-7700. **Fax:** 845/226-7172. **Contact:** Human Resources. **World Wide Web address:** http://www.besicorp.com. **Description:** A leading alternative energy and independent power generation company. **Corporate headquarters location:** This location.

BEST MANUFACTURING, INC.
1633 Broadway, 18th Floor, New York NY 10019-6708. 212/974-1100. **Fax:** 212/262-9840. **Contact:** Human Resources. **World Wide Web address:** http://www.bestmfg.com. **Description:** A manufacturer of textiles and washable service apparel. Founded in 1914. **Positions advertised include:** Customer Service Representative. **Corporate headquarters location:** This location. **Other U.S. locations:** Nationwide. **Operations at this facility include:** Administration. **Number of employees at this location:** 85. **Number of employees nationwide:** 1,100.

BETH ISRAEL HEALTH CARE SYSTEM
First Avenue at 16th Street, New York NY 10003. 212/420-2000. **Contact:** Human Resources. **World Wide Web address:** http://www.bethisraelny.org. **Description:** An integrated health care system providing a full continuum of primary, acute, tertiary, and long-term care. The system also operates New York HealthCare/Doctors' Walk In, the Japanese Medical Practice, Schnurmacher Nursing Home of Beth Israel Medical Center, Robert Mapplethorpe Residential Treatment Facility, Phillips Beth Israel School of Nursing, Karpas Health Information Center, and D-O-C-S, a multisite, private, group medical practice in the suburbs. **NOTE:** Resumes should be sent to Human Resources, 555 West 57th Street, New York NY 10019; or faxed to: 212/523-7193. **Positions advertised include:** Registered Dietician; Director of Safety; Cathode Laboratory Expediter; Senior Credentialing Analyst; Patient Advocate; Medical Biller; Medical Administrative Assistant; Senior Systems Analyst; Cardiovascular Technician; Radiological Technician; Registered Nurse; Cardiology Nurse; Nurse Recruiter. **Corporate headquarters location:** This location. **Other locations:** Throughout the New York City metropolitan region. **Subsidiaries include:** Beth Israel Medical Center; St Luke's-Roosevelt Hospital Center. Long Island College Hospital; New York Eye and Ear Infirmary. **Parent company:** Continuum Health Partners Inc.

BINGHAMTON PRESS COMPANY
P.O. Box 1270, Binghamton NY 13902-1270. 607/798-1234. **Physical address:** 4421 Vestal Parkway, Vestal NY 13850. **Contact:** Catherine Reeve, Director of Human Resources Department. **World Wide Web address:** http://www.pressconnects.com. **Description:** Publisher of *The Press & Sun-Bulletin*, with a circulation of 65,000 weekday and 82,000 Sunday serving the counties of Broome, Tioga, Chenango, Delaware, and Otsego in New York and Susquehanna and Bradford counties in Pennsylvania. **NOTE:** Entry-level positions and second and third shifts are offered. Human Resources phone: 607/798-1107. **Positions advertised include:** Carrier Route Driver; Marketing Operations Coordinator; Customer Service Representative; Classified Sales Representative. **Parent company:** Gannett Satellite Information Network, Inc. (Rockford IL).

BIOSPECIFICS TECHNOLOGIES CORPORATION
35 Wilbur Street, Lynbrook NY 11563. 516/593-7000. **Fax:** 516/593-7039. **Contact:** Human Resources. **World Wide Web address:** http://www.biospecifics.com. **Description:** An industry leader in the production and development of enzyme pharmaceuticals used for wound healing, tissue regeneration, and tissue remodeling. Biospecifics Technologies Corporation produces Collagenase Santyl ointment, an enzyme used for the treatment of chronic wounds and dermal ulcers. **NOTE:** Resumes should be mailed or faxed to the above address. **Positions advertised include:** Clinical Lab Technician. **Office hours:** Monday - Friday, 9:00 a.m. - 5:00 p.m. **Listed on:** NASDAQ. **Stock exchange symbol:** BSTC. **President/CEO:** Edwin H. Wegman. **Annual sales/revenues:** $8.2 million. **Number of employees:** 48.

BIRDS EYE FOODS, INC.
P.O. Box 20670, Rochester NY 14602-0670. 585/383-1850. **Physical address:** 90 Linden Oaks, Rochester NY 14625. **Fax:** 585/383-9153. **Contact:** Mary Turcotte, Human Resources. **World Wide Web address:** http://www.birdseyefoods.com. **Description:** Formerly Agrilink Foods, Birds Eye processes and markets a variety of food product lines of regional branded, private label, and food service products through 30 facilities located throughout the United States. Products include pie fillings, pretzels, cookies, and salad dressings. **NOTE:** Online application is preferred. **Positions advertised include:** Senior Cash Application Clerk; Benefits Analyst; Marketing Manager; Associate Marketing Manager; Senior Marketing Manager; Marketing Research Manager; Specifications & Technical Support Manager; Marketing Director. **Corporate headquarters location:** This location. **Other area locations:** Bergen NY; Oakfield NY; Shortsville NY. **Other U.S. locations:** DE; IL; MN; PA; TN. **Chairman/President/CEO:** Dennis M. Mullen. **Annual sales/revenues:** $1 billion. **Number of employees nationwide:** 4,000.

BIRDS EYE FOODS, INC.
40 Stevens Street, Oakfield NY 14125. 585/948-5252. **Contact:** Human Resources. **World Wide Web address:** http://www.birdseyefoods.com. **Description:** Formerly Agrilink Foods, Birds Eye processes and markets a variety of food product lines of regional branded, private label, and food service products through 30 facilities located throughout the United States. Products include pie fillings, pretzels, cookies, and salad dressings. **NOTE:** Resumes may be submitted online via the company's Website; or sent to the company's headquarters by fax: 585/383-9153; by mail: Human Resources, Birdseye Foods, Inc., 90 Linden Oaks, Rochester NY 14625. **Positions advertised include:** Maintenance Supervisor; Production Supervisor; Marketing Manager. **Corporate headquarters location:** Rochester NY. **Other area locations:** Bergen NY; Rochester NY; Shortsville NY. **Other U.S. locations:** DE; IL; MN; PA; TN. **Chairman/President/CEO:** Dennis M. Mullen. **Annual sales/revenues:** $1 billion. **Number of employees nationwide:** 4,000.

BLACK CLAWSON CO.
46 North First Street, Fulton NY 13069. 315/598-7121. **Fax:** 315/593-0499. **Contact:** Donna Cook, Human Resources Director. **E-mail address:** hr@bccmi.com. **World Wide Web address:** http://www.blkclawson.com. **Description:** Manufactures converting equipment including extruders and laminators. **Operations at this facility include:** Corporate headquarters of Black Clawson Converting Machinery, Inc.

BLOOMINGDALE'S, INC.
1000 Third Avenue, New York NY 10022. 212/705-2000. **Fax:** 212/705-2805. **Contact:** Human Resources. **World Wide Web address:** http://www.bloomingdales.com. **Description:** Operates a chain of 25 department stores in 10 states, mostly in New York and California. Founded in 1872. **NOTE:** You may apply online. **Positions advertised include:** At-His Service Manager; Bridal Registrar/Consultant; Chanel Business Manager; Cosmetics Department Manager; Director of Technical Support; Sales Associate; Women's Shoes Associate; Fragrance Specialist; Shoes Sales Associate; Graphic Designer; Gross Margin Planner; Line Cook; Marketing Analyst; Designer Apparel Sales Associate; Vendor Selling Specialist; Fine Jewelry Sales Associate; Juniors Sales Associate. **Corporate headquarters location:** This location. **Other U.S. locations:** Washington DC; Boca Raton FL; Miami FL; Palm Beach FL; Chicago IL; Boston MA; Minneapolis MN; Philadelphia PA. **Parent company:** Federated Department Stores Inc. (Cincinnati OH). **Operations at this facility include:** Administration; Regional Headquarters; Research and Development; Sales; Service. **Chairman/CEO:** Michael Gould. **Annual sales/revenues:** $1.7 billion. **Number of employees:** 9,800.

BOMBARDIER TRANSPORTATION
100 Orchard Street, Auburn NY 13021. 315/255-7800. **Contact:** Human Resources Manager. **World Wide Web address:** http://www.transportation.bombardier.com. **Description:** Bombardier Transportation, formerly Auburn Technology, specializes in rail equipment manufacturing, machine diesel welding, and tubing for aerospace as well as manufacturing aircraft sub-assembly, undercarriage trucks for subway cars, subway car ventilation units, and engine blocks for off-road vehicles. **Positions advertised include:** Six Sigma Master Agent; Electrical Technician; General Manager. **Corporate headquarters location:** Montreal, Canada. **Other area locations:** Plattsburgh NY. **Parent company:** Bombardier, Inc. (Montreal, Canada). **Number of employees at this location:** 50. **Number of employees worldwide:** 5,450.

BOSCH SECURITY SYSTEMS
130 Perinton Parkway, Fairport NY 14450-9199. 585/223-4060. **Fax:** 585/223-9180. **Contact:** Human Resources. **World Wide Web address:** http://www.boschsecurity.com. **Description:** Bosch Security Systems, formerly Detection Systems and Radionics, designs, manufactures, and markets electronic detection control and signaling equipment for the security and fire protection industries. The company's product line includes electronic intrusion detectors, fire detectors, microprocessor-based alarm control systems, and emergency call systems. **Positions advertised include:** Technical Support Representative. **Parent company:** Robert Bosch GmbH (Gerlingen-Schillerhöhe, Germany).

BOWNE & CO., INC.
345 Hudson Street, 10th Floor, New York NY 10014. 212/924-5500. **Fax:** 212/229-3400. **Contact:** Ellen McLynch, Human Resources Manager. **E-mail address:** jobs.bowne@bowne.com. **World Wide Web address:** http://www.bowne.com. **Description:** Provides nationwide information management and compliance documentation services through principal business segments. Printing activities are divided into four segments: financial, corporate, commercial, and legal printing. Services in the legal printing segment include the typesetting and printing of compliance documentation relating to corporate and municipal financing, mergers, and acquisitions; the dissemination of information by companies through annual and interim reports and proxy material; and the printing of materials unrelated to compliance such as business forms and reports, newsletters, promotional aids, market letters, sales literature, and legal printing products. Founded in 1775. **NOTE:** Entry-level positions and second and third shifts are offered. **Company slogan:** Empowering your information. **Positions advertised include:** Account Operations Manager; Project Manager; Administrative Assistant; Manager Human Resources; Assistant Controller; Learning Development Manager. **Special programs:** Internships; Training; Co-ops; Summer Jobs. **Corporate headquarters location:** This location. **Other U.S. locations:** Nationwide. **International locations:** Worldwide. **Listed on:** New York Stock Exchange. **Stock exchange symbol:** BNE. **CEO:** Robert M. Johnson. **Annual sales/revenues:** $1 billion. **Number of employees at this location:** 1,000. **Number of employees nationwide:** 6,000. **Number of employees worldwide:** 8,000.

THE BOYS' CLUB OF NEW YORK (BCNY)
287 East 10th Street, New York NY 10009. 212/677-1109. **Contact:** Hiring. **World Wide Web address:** http://www.bcny.org. **Description:** Provides a variety of services to young men in the New York City area. BCNY's educational program has helped hundreds of young men to attend leading prep schools and colleges, offering support and counseling to help them succeed. BCNY's job training program offers teenage members their first work experience in top-flight New York companies. The club offers a year-round program serving boys between 6 and 17 years old. Founded in 1876. **Corporate headquarters location:** This location.

BOZELL WORLDWIDE
40 West 23rd Street, New York NY 10010. 212/727-5000. **Fax:** 212/463-8419. **Contact:** Human Resources. **E-mail address:** bozellhr@newyork.bozell.com. **World Wide Web address:** http://www.bozell.com. **Description:** A full-service advertising agency. Bozell also offers public relations services such as corporate relations, marketing support, employee relations, financial relations, government affairs, and community relations. **Corporate headquarters location:** This location. **Other U.S. locations:** Nationwide. **International locations:** Worldwide.

BRIDGE BANCORP, INC.
dba BRIDGEHAMPTON NATIONAL BANK
2200 Montauk Highway, P.O. Box 3005, Bridgehampton NY 11932-3005. 631/537-1001 ext. 297. **Contact:** Deborah McGrory, Human Resources Officer. **E-mail address:** dmcgror@bridgenb.com. **World Wide Web address:** http://www.bridgenb.com. **Description:** A bank holding company engaged in commercial banking through wholly owned subsidiary Bridgehampton National Bank operating full-service banking offices located on Eastern Long Island, as well as a residential mortgage and loan center. Founded in 1910. **Positions advertised include:** Credit Analyst; Loan and Credit Assistant; Loan Representative; Customer Service Representative; Teller; Accounts Payable Staff Accountant; Electrical Delivery Systems Assistant. **Listed on:** Over The Counter. **Stock exchange symbol:** BDGE. **Annual sales/revenues:** $26.5 million. **Number of employees:** 115.

BRINKS INC
652 Kent Avenue, Brooklyn NY 11211. 718-643-3200. **Contact:** Personnel. **World Wide Web address:** http://www.brinksinc.com. **Description:** An armored security service specializing in transporting currency. **Other U.S. locations:** Nationwide.

BRISTOL-MYERS SQUIBB COMPANY
345 Park Avenue, New York NY 10154-0037. 212/546-4000. **Fax:** 212/546-4020. **Contact:** Stephen E. Bear, Human Resources Director. **World Wide Web address:** http://www.bms.com. **Description:** Manufacturer of pharmaceuticals, medical devices, nonprescription drugs, toiletries, and beauty aids. The company's pharmaceutical products include cardiovascular drugs, anti-infective agents, anticancer agents, AIDS therapy treatments, central nervous system drugs, diagnostic agents, and other drugs. The company's line of nonprescription products includes formulas, vitamins, analgesics, remedies, and skin care products sold under the brand names Bufferin, Excedrin, Nuprin, and Comtrex. Beauty aids include Clairol and Ultress hair care, Nice 'n Easy hair colorings, hair sprays, gels, and deodorants. **NOTE:** Resumes may be sent to the company's human resources address: Bristol-Myers Squibb Company, P.O. Box 5335, Princeton NY 08543-5335; or by fax to: 609/897-6412. **Positions advertised include:** Chemist. **Corporate headquarters location:** This location. **Subsidiaries include:** ConvaTec; Mead Johnson & Company. **Listed on:** New York Stock Exchange. **Stock exchange symbol:** BMY. **Chairman/CEO:** Peter R. Dolan. **Annual sales/revenues:** $18.1 billion. **Number of employees:** 46,000.

BRISTOL-MYERS SQUIBB COMPANY
100 Forest Avenue, Buffalo NY 14213. 716/887-3400. **Contact:** Human Resources. **World Wide Web address:** http://www.bms.com. **Description:** Manufacturer of pharmaceuticals, medical devices, nonprescription drugs, toiletries, and beauty aids. The company's pharmaceutical products include cardiovascular drugs, anti-infective agents, anticancer agents, AIDS therapy treatments, central nervous system drugs, diagnostic agents, and other drugs. The company's line of nonprescription products includes formulas, vitamins, analgesics, remedies, and skin care products sold under the brand names Bufferin, Excedrin, Nuprin, and Comtrex. Beauty aids include Clairol and Ultress hair care, Nice 'n Easy hair colorings, hair sprays, gels, and deodorants. **NOTE:** Resumes may be sent to the company's human resources address: Bristol-Myers Squibb Company, P.O. Box 5335, Princeton NY 08543-5335; or by fax to: 609/897-6412. **Positions advertised include:** Chemist. **Corporate headquarters location:** New York NY. **Subsidiaries include:** ConvaTec; Mead Johnson & Company. **Listed on:** New York Stock Exchange. **Stock exchange symbol:** BMY. **Chairman/CEO:** Peter R. Dolan. **Annual sales/revenues:** $18.1 billion. **Number of employees:** 46,000.

BROADWAY VIDEO INC.
1619 Broadway, 10th Floor, New York NY 10019. 212/265-7600. **Contact:** Vice President of Operations. **E-mail address:** info@broawayvideo.com. **World Wide Web address:** http://www.broadwayvideo.com. **Description:** An entertainment production company offering editing, design, sound, and related services for all types of media. **Corporate headquarters location:** This location. **Founder:** Mr. Lorne Michaels.

BROOKLYN ACADEMY OF MUSIC
30 Lafayette Avenue, Brooklyn NY 11217. 718/636-4111. **Fax:** 718/636-4179. **Contact:** Sarah Weinstein, Director of Human Resources. **E-mail address:** hrresumes@bam.org. **World Wide Web address:** http://www.bam.org. **Description:** A nonprofit arts showcase offering dance, opera, and theatrical performances, as well as performances by the Brooklyn Philharmonic Orchestra. Founded in 1859. **NOTE:** Job openings can be found at the stage door located at 116 St. Felix Street. **Positions advertised include:** Marketing Intern; Summer Concerts Intern; BA Mart Internship; Membership Coordinator; Director Human Resources; Marketing Manager E-media. **Special programs:** Internships.

BROOKLYN BOTANIC GARDEN
1000 Washington Avenue, Brooklyn NY 11225-1099. 718/623-7200. **Fax:** 718/622-7826. **Contact:** Director of Human Resources Department. **E-mail address:** personnel@bbg.org. **World Wide Web address:** http://www.bbg.org. **Description:** Exhibits over 10,000 plants in the Steinhardt Conservatory. Brooklyn Botanic Garden also offers programs teaching hands-on gardening to children ages three to 17. Brooklyn Botanic Garden offers special events such as the Cherry Blossom Festival, student art exhibitions, tours of the Japanese Hill-and-Pond Garden, and the Annual Spring Plant Sale. Founded in 1910. **Positions advertised include:** Grants Writer; Education Coordinator; Gardening Instructor; Vice President of Horticulture; Arborist; Maintainer; Security Guard.

BROOKS BROTHERS
346 Madison Avenue, New York NY 10017. 212/682-8800. **Fax:** 212/985-1854. **Contact:** BB Employment Specialist. **E-mail address:** jdesmar@brooksbrothers.com. **World Wide Web address:** http://www.brooksbrothers.com. **Description:** Operates over 160 retail stores and factory outlets in the United States and 75 in Southeast Asia. Founded in 1818. **NOTE:** Resumes may be sent to the human resources office at 100 Phoenix Avenue, Enfield CT 06083. 800/249-6947 ext. 2324. Fax: 860/741-3171. **Positions advertised include:** Advertising Clerk; Architect; Branch Manager; Buyer; Claim Representative; Computer Programmer; Customer Service Representative; Department Manager; Draftsperson; Editor; General Manager; Human Resources Manager; Management Trainee; Operations/Production Manager; Purchasing Agent/Manager; Receptionist; Reporter; Secretary; Stock Clerk; Systems Analyst. **Corporate headquarters location:** This location. **Parent company:** Retail Brand Alliance, Inc. (Enfield CT). **Operations at this facility include:** Administration; Divisional Headquarters; Regional Headquarters; Sales; Service. **Annual sales/revenues:** 635 million.

BROOKS MEMORIAL HOSPITAL
529 Central Avenue, Dunkirk NY 14048. 716/366-1111 ext. 7262. **Fax:** 716/363-7239. **Contact:** Human Resources. **E-mail address:** hrstaffing@brookshospital.org. **World Wide Web address:** http://www.brookshospital.org. **Description:** A nonprofit, 133-bed primary acute care hospital serving the Chautauqua County community. The hospital is JCAHO accredited. Founded in 1898. **NOTE:** Entry-level positions, part-time jobs, and second and third shifts are offered. **Company slogan:** Building a Healthy Community. **Positions advertised include:** Director of Patient Accounting; Registered Nurse; Nursing Supervisor; Licensed Practical Nurse; Physical Therapist; Respiratory Therapist. **Special programs:** Internships. **President:** Richard Ketcham. **Number of employees:** 500.

BROOME COMMUNITY COLLEGE
103 Wales Administration Building, P.O. Box 1017, Binghamton NY 13902-1017. 607/778-5319. **Fax:** 607/778-5482. **Contact:** Elizabeth Wood, Human Resources. **E-mail address:** jobs@mail.sunybroome.edu. **World Wide Web address:** http://www.sunybroome.edu. **Description:** A two-year community college. **Positions advertised include:** Financial Aid Staff Assistant.

BROWN BROTHERS HARRIMAN & COMPANY
140 Broadway, New York NY 10005. 212/483-1818. **Fax:** 212/493-8545. **Contact:** Human Resources. **E-mail address:** jobs@bbh.com. **World Wide Web address:** http://www.bbh.com. **Description:** Operating some 40 partnerships and 16 offices in seven countries worldwide, the company provides commercial banking, brokerage, and investment advisory services. Founded in 1818. **Positions advertised include:** Human Resources Assistant; Domestic Banking Officer; Event Planner; Operations Specialist; Relationship Manager. **Corporate headquarters location:** This location. **Other locations:** Boston MA; Jersey City NJ; Palm Beach FL. **Number of employees:** 3,000.

DAYTON T. BROWN INC.
1175 Church Street, Bohemia NY 11716. 631/589-6300. **Toll-free phone:** 800/232-6300. **Fax:** 631/589-0046. **Contact:** Personnel Department. **World Wide Web address:** http://www.daytontbrown.com. **Description:** Engaged in sheet metal fabrication. Dayton T. Brown also offers engineering and testing services for industrial and commercial companies. **Positions advertised include:** Senior Business Development Manager; Metallurgical Technician; Electromagnetic Interference/Electromagnetic Compatibility Technician; Production Manager. **Corporate headquarters location:** This location.

THE BUFFALO NEWS
One News Plaza, P.O. Box 100, Buffalo NY 14240. 716/849-3434. **Contact:** Dan Farberman, Senior Vice President/Employee Relations Director. **World Wide Web address:** http://www.buffalo.com. **Description:** Buffalo's largest daily newspaper. The *Buffalo News* publishes morning and evening editions with a circulation of approximately 285,000 daily and 365,000 Sundays. **Special programs:** Internships.

BUFFALO POLICE DEPARTMENT
74 Franklin Street, Buffalo NY 14202. 716/851-4444. **Contact:** Employment Office. **World Wide Web address:** http://www.city-buffalo.com/Police/My Webs/Buffalo Police Home Page.htm. **Description:** Headquarters for the city of Buffalo Police Department. **NOTE:** All employment inquiries should be directed to the Civil Service Commission, Buffalo City Hall, 65 Niagara Square, Buffalo NY 14202. 716/851-5011. **Positions advertised include:** Police Officer.

BULOVA CORPORATION
One Bulova Avenue, Woodside NY 11377-7874. 718/204-3384. **Fax:** 718/204-3300. **Contact:** Human Resources. **World Wide Web address:** http://www.bulova.com. **Description:** Manufactures and sells a wide variety of watches, clocks, and jewelry for the consumer market. **Corporate headquarters location:** This location. **Operations at this facility include:** Administration; Divisional Headquarters; Manufacturing;

Regional Headquarters; Service. **Listed on:** Over The Counter. **Stock exchange symbol:** BULV. **Chairman:** Andrew H. Tisch. **Number of employees at this location:** 400. **Number of employees nationwide:** 560.

BURSON-MARSTELLER
230 Park Avenue South, New York NY 10003. 212/614-4141. **Fax:** 212/598-6999. **Contact:** Kay Fynmore, Human Resources Director. **E-mail address:** kay_fynmore@nyc.bm.com. **World Wide Web address:** http://www.bm.com. **Description:** A full-service public relations agency with 75 offices in 34 countries. Founded in 1953. **Positions advertised include:** Public Relations Specialist. **Special programs:** Internships. **Corporate headquarters location:** This location. **Other U.S. locations:** Los Angeles CA; Sacramento CA; San Diego CA; San Francisco CA; Washington DC; Miami FL; Chicago IL; Pittsburgh PA; Dallas TX. **Subsidiaries include:** Cohn & Wolfe, Public Relations. **Parent company:** WPP Group PLC (London, United Kingdom). **Founding Chairman:** Harold Burson. **Annual sales/revenues:** $175 million. **Number of employees at this location:** 340. **Number of employees worldwide:** 1,600.

BUSH INDUSTRIES, INC.
dba BUSH FURNITURE NORTH AMERICA
One Mason Drive, P.O. Box 460, Jamestown NY 14702-0460. 716/665-2000. **Toll-free phone:** 800/727-2874. **Fax:** 716-665-2510. **Contact:** Human Resources. **E-mail address:** resumes@bushindustries.com. **World Wide Web address:** http://www.bushfurniture.com. **Description:** Bush Furniture North America markets furniture under four brand names: Bush Furniture, Eric Morgan, Bush Business Furniture and Röhr. The company designs and manufactures ready-to-assemble and assembled furniture products. Entertainment furniture, home theater furniture, home and commercial office products and ensembles, bedroom furniture, storage armoires, and other utility pieces are included in the product line sold through multiple distribution channels. Founded in 1959. **Corporate headquarters location:** This location. **Other locations:** Erie PA; Little Valley NY; St. Paul VA. **International locations:** Tijuana, Mexico. **Listed on:** New York Stock Exchange. **Stock exchange symbol:** BSH. **Chairman/CEO:** Paul S. Bush. **Annual sales/revenues:** $340 million. **Number of employees:** 3,050.

BUTTERICK MCCAL PATTERN COMPANY
11 Penn Plaza, New York NY 10001. 212/465-6800. **Contact:** Human Resources. **World Wide Web address:** http://www.butterick.com. **Description:** Manufactures two lines of clothing patterns for the home sewing market and produces related fashion publications including *Weddings*, *Butterick Home Catalog*, *Vogue Patterns Magazine*, *and Vogue Knitting Magazine*. **Positions advertised include:** Editorial Assistant; Fashion Designer; Public Relations Specialist. **Special programs:** Internships. **Corporate headquarters location:** This location. **Operations at this facility include:** Administration; Financial Offices; Research and Development; Sales; Service.

CBS BROADCASTING INC.
51 West 52nd Street, 19th Floor, New York NY 10019. 212/975-4321. **Contact:** Human Resources Department. **E-mail address:** cbsrecruitment@cbs.com. **World Wide Web address:** http://www.cbs.com. **Description:** A broad-based entertainment and communications company that operates one of the country's major commercial television networks and two nationwide radio networks. **Positions advertised include:** Audio/Video Broadcast Engineer; Executive Assistant; Affiliate System Engineering Manager; Human Resources Coordinator. **Special programs:** Internships. **Internship information:** The company offers unpaid, full-time, summer internship positions for students. **Corporate headquarters location:** This location. **Parent company:** Viacom Inc. (New York NY).

C-COR.NET CORPORATION
100 Fairgrounds Drive, Manlius NY 13104-9990. 315/682-9105. **Fax:** 315/682-1022. **Contact:** Human Resources. **World Wide Web address:** http://www.c-cor.net. **Description:** Designs, manufactures, and supplies broadband communications equipment for cable television and telecommunications worldwide. **Corporate headquarters location:** State College PA. **Other U.S. locations:** Nationwide. **International locations:** Mexico; the Netherlands. **Listed on:** NASDAQ. **Stock exchange symbol:** CCBL. **CEO/Chairman:** David A. Woodle. **Number of employees worldwide:** 1,400.

CH ENERGY GROUP, INC.
dba CENTRAL HUDSON GAS AND ELECTRIC CORPORATION
284 South Avenue, Poughkeepsie NY 12601. 845/452-2000. **Fax:** 845/486-5415. **Contact:** Human Resources. **World Wide Web address:** http://www.chenergygroup.com. **Description:** An investor-owned utility, supplying power to some 300,000 customers in the southern Hudson River valley. Main subsidiary Central Hudson Gas and Electric (also at this location) generates, purchases, and distributes electric energy, and purchases and distributes natural gas. The company's other interests include retail and wholesale energy marketing; petroleum product distribution; and energy management services in the Northeast and mid-Atlantic region. Since 1900. **Subsidiaries include:** Central Hudson Enterprises Corporation; Central Hudson Energy Services; Central Hudson Gas and Electric Corporation. **Listed on:** New York Stock Exchange. **Stock exchange symbol:** CHG. **Chairman/President/CEO:** Paul J. Ganci. **Annual sales/revenues:** $695 million. **Number of employees:** 870.

CHF INDUSTRIES, INC.
One Park Avenue, 9th Floor, New York NY 10016. 212/951-7800. **Contact:** Human Resources. **World Wide Web address:** http://www.chfindustries.com. **Description:** Engaged in the production, export, and import of home fashion products including comforters, curtains, towels, and other textile goods. **Corporate headquarters location:** This location. **Other locations:** Charlotte NC; Chicago IL; Dallas TX; Fall River MA; Kaufman TX; Loris SC; Clinton SC. **Number of employees:** 1,200.

CIT GROUP, INC.
1211 Avenue of the Americas, 12th Floor, New York NY 10036. 212/382-7000. **Contact:** Human Resources. **World Wide Web address:** http://www.citgroup.com. **Description:** This division provides factoring services to a wide range of customers as a subsidiary of CIT Financial Services. Overall, CIT Group is a diversified financial services organization providing flexible funding alternatives, secured business lending, and financial advisory services for corporations, manufacturers, and dealers. Founded in 1908. **Positions advertised include:** Executive Assistant; Verification Examiner; Collateral Analyst Supervisor; Contracts Associate; Field Examiner; Underwriter; Credit Officer; Attorney; District Sales Manager. **Corporate headquarters location:** This location. **Other locations:** Worldwide. **Subsidiaries include:** Capital Finance; CIT Commercial Finance Group; CIT Equipment Financing; CIT Specialty Finance Group; CIT Structured Finance. **Listed on:** New York Stock Exchange. **Stock exchange symbol:** CIT. **Annual sales/revenues:** $3.5 billion. **Number of employees nationwide:** 2,500.

CMP INDUSTRIES LLC
413 North Pearl Street, Albany NY 12201. 518/434-3147. **Toll-free phone:** 800/833-2343. **Fax:** 518/434-1288. **Contact:** Phyll Tabone, Director of Administration. **E-mail address:** info@cmpindustries.com. **World Wide Web address:** http://www.cmpindustry.com. **Description:** A manufacturer of dental materials, dental equipment, and other dental supplies. Founded in 1889. **Corporate headquarters location:** This location. **Operations at this facility include:** Manufacturing. **Number of employees at this location:** 65.

CMP MEDIA LLC
600 Community Drive, Manhasset NY 11030. 516/562-5000. **Fax:** 516/562-5993. **Contact:** Maria Huddleston, Staffing Department. **E-mail address:** mhuddleston@cmp.com or careers@cmp.com. **World Wide Web address:** http://www.cmp.com. **Description:** Publishes high-tech, computer-related magazines and trade publications. **NOTE:** Unsolicited resumes are not accepted. **Positions advertised include:** Editorial Assistant; Audience Development Manager; Senior Writer; Associate Editor; Director of Research; Financial Analyst; Tax Accountant. **Special programs:** Internships. **Corporate headquarters location:** This location. **Other U.S. locations:** CA; GA; KS; MA; NH. **Subsidiaries include:** CMP Publications; CMP Websites. **Parent company:** United Business Media (London, United Kingdom). **Operations at this facility include:** Sales. **President/CEO:** Gary Marshall. **Annual sales/revenues:** $530 million. **Number of employees at this location:** 1,000. **Number of employees nationwide:** 1,400.

CNA INSURANCE COMPANIES
40 Wall Street, New York NY 10005. 212/440-3000. **Contact:** Human Resources Manager. **World Wide Web address:** http://www.cna.com. **Description:** A property and casualty insurance writer offering commercial and personal policies. Since 1897. **Positions advertised include:** Actuarial Supervisor; Senior Actuarial Analyst; Regulatory Filings Technician; Underwriting Technician; Claims Consultant; Claims Specialist; Workers Compensation Specialist; Medical Case Manager. **Corporate headquarters location:** Chicago IL.

CNB FINANCIAL CORPORATION
20 Mohawk Street, Canajoharie NY 13317. 518/673-3243. **Contact:** Human Resources. **World Wide Web address:** http://www.bankcnb.com. **Description:** CNB Financial Corporation is the parent company of Central National Bank. Central National Bank provides commercial banking services to individuals, businesses, and government entities in central and western Pennsylvania. Bank offerings include deposit products, loan products, and trust and financial services. Central National Bank operates 17 full-service offices located throughout Montgomery, Fulton, Herkimer, Otsego, Schoharie, and Schenectady counties. **Corporate headquarters location:** Clearfield PA. **Listed on:** NASDAQ. **Stock exchange symbol:** CCNE. **President/CEO:** William F. Falger. **Annual sales/revenues:** $45.8 million. **Number of employees:** 239.

CNN NEWS GROUP (CABLE NEWS NETWORK)
5 Penn Plaza, 20th Floor, New York NY 10001. 212/714-7800. **Contact:** Human Resources. **World Wide Web address:** http://www.cnn.com. **Description:** A cable news network. CNN has 43 bureaus worldwide and provides 24-hour news programming worldwide. Programming includes international, domestic, and business news; sports; weather; special reports; and topical programming. **NOTE:** Current job openings are listed at http://www.turnerjobs.com. **Corporate headquarters location:** Atlanta GA. **Other locations:** Worldwide. **Parent company:** Turner Broadcasting Systems, Inc. (Atlanta GA). **Number of employees:** 4,000.

CPAC, INC.
2364 Leicester Road, P.O. Box 175, Leicester NY 14481. 585/382-3223. **Fax:** 585/382-3031. **Contact:** Human Resources. **E-mail address:** cpacinfo@cpac.com. **World Wide Web address:** http://www.cpac-fuller.com. **Description:** CPAC is a leader in the production of specialty chemicals used in the imaging industry and the cleaning and personal care markets. The Cleaning and Personal Care Division offers hundreds of household and commercial cleaning products sold through a direct sales force, retail outlet stores, and mail order. The Imaging Division serves commercial customers in photo labs, dental offices, X-ray facilities, and printing houses. Founded in 1969. **Corporate headquarters location:** This location. **International locations:** Belgium; Italy; South Africa; Thailand. **Subsidiaries include:** Comprising the Imaging segment are Allied Diagnostic Imaging Resources, Inc. (Irwindale CA; Norcross GA), a producer of processing chemicals for medical, dental, graphic arts, microfilm, and industrial applications; CPAC Equipment Division (also at this location), a manufacturer of silver recovery/chemical recycling systems and chemical mixers for all imaging markets; Fuller Brush; PRS, Inc. (also at this location), a U.S. marketing and sales organization for CPAC Equipment, Trebla products, and silver refining services; Stanley Home Products; and Trebla Chemical Company (St. Louis MO), a manufacturer of processing formulas for the color photography market. The Cleaning and Personal Care segment consists of The Fuller Brush Company, Inc. and Stanley Home Products. **Listed on:** NASDAQ. **Stock exchange symbol:** CPAK. **President/CEO:** Thomas N. Hendrickson. **Annual sales/revenues:** $100 million. **Number of employees:** 600.

CPI AEROSTRUCTURES, INC.
200-A Executive Drive, Edgewood NY 11717. 631/586-5200. **Fax:** 631/586-5814. **Contact:** Personnel Manager. **World Wide Web address:** http://www.cpiaero.com. **Description:** Engaged in contract production of structural aircraft parts and subassemblies for the commercial and military sectors of the aircraft industry. The company also provides engineering, technical, and program management services. **Corporate headquarters location:** This location. **Listed on:** American Stock Exchange. **Stock exchange symbol:** CVU. **Chairman:** Arthur August. **Annual sales/revenues:** $24 million. **Number of employees:** 50.

CT CORPORATION SYSTEM
111 Eighth Avenue, 13th Floor, New York NY 10011. 212/894-8940. **Fax:** 212/894-8710. **Contact:** Human Resources. **E-mail address:** info@ctadvantage.com. **World Wide Web address:** http://www.ctcorporation.com. **Description:** C.T. Corporation provides research and accounting services for attorneys. **Positions advertised include:** Staff Accountant; Service Team Leader; Internal Support Analyst; Accounts Receivable Maintenance Clerk; Associate Customer Specialist; Quality Assurance Professional; Receptionist; Project Manager; Desktop Support Analyst; Information Technology Manager; Senior Product Manager; Associate Customer Specialist; Operations Process Management Director; Licensing Support Specialist. **Parent company:** Wolters Kluwer U.S. **Number of employees:** 1,100.

CVD EQUIPMENT CORPORATION
1881 Lakeland Avenue, Ronkonkoma NY 11779. 631/981-7081. **Fax:** 631/981-7095. **Contact:** Human Resources. **E-mail address:** hr@cvdequipment.com. **World Wide Web address:** http://www.cvdequipment.com. **Description:** CVD manufactures chemical vapor deposition equipment, customized gas control systems, and hydrogen

annealing and brazing furnaces. These products are primarily used to produce semiconductors and other electronic components. **Positions advertised include:** Electrical Engineer; Mechanical Draftsperson; Mechanical Engineer; Electrical and Systems Engineer; Manufacturing Buyer/Planner; Inventory Control Manager; Parts Kitting Clerk; Shipping/Receiving Clerk; Mechanical Machine Assembler; Electrical Machine Assembler; Harness Wirer. **Listed on:** American Stock Exchange. **Stock exchange symbol:** CVV. **President/CEO/Director:** Leonard A. Rosenbaum. **Annual sales/revenues:** $9.2 million. **Number of employees:** 80.

CVS PROCARE
80 Air Park Drive, Ronkonkoma NY 11779. 631/981-0034. **Fax:** 631/981-0722. **Contact:** Human Resources. **World Wide Web address:** http://www.cvsprocare.com. **Description:** A national provider of outpatient drug therapies and a broad array of distribution, case management, and support services to meet the ongoing needs of patients with chronic medical conditions, the health professionals who care for them, and the third-party payers responsible for such care. The company's services include distribution of prescription drug therapies, drug utilization review programs, patient compliance monitoring, psychosocial support services, and assistance in insurance investigation, verification, and reimbursement. **Parent company:** CVS Corporation (Woonsocket RI). **Other U.S. locations:** Nationwide.

CABLEVISION SYSTEMS CORPORATION
1111 Stewart Avenue, Bethpage NY 11714. 516/803-2300. **Fax:** 516/803-3065. **Contact:** Human Resources. **E-mail address:** careers@cablevision.com. **World Wide Web address:** http://www.cablevision.com. **Description:** Owns and operates cable television systems serving customers in the New York metropolitan region. **Positions advertised include:** Customer Relations Coordinator; Field Telecommunications Technician; Cablevision Sales Representative; Outbound Telephone Sales Representative. **Special programs:** Internships. **Corporate headquarters location:** This location. **Other locations:** Statewide. **Subsidiaries include:** CCG Holdings, Inc.; Rainbow Media Holdings, Inc.; Clearview Cinema Group; Lightpath; Madison Square Garden; New York Knickerbockers; New York Rangers; The Wiz; Radio City Music Hall; New York Liberty. **Operations at this facility include:** Administration. **Listed on:** New York Stock Exchange. **Stock exchange symbol:** CVC. **Chairman:** Charles F. Dolan. **Annual sales/revenues:** $4 billion. **Number of employees at this location:** 700. **Number of employees nationwide:** 21,000.

CACHÉ, INC.
1460 Broadway, 15th Floor, New York NY 10036-7306. 212/575-3200. **Fax:** 212/944-2842. **Contact:** Margarita Croasdaile, Human Resources Manager. **World Wide Web address:** http://www.cache.com. **Description:** Owns and operates 220 upscale women's apparel specialty stores. **Corporate headquarters location:** This location. **Other locations:** Nationwide. **Listed on:** NASDAQ. **Stock exchange symbol:** CACH. **Chairman/CEO:** Brian P. Woolf. **Annual sales/revenues:** $200 million. **Number of employees:** 2,000.

CADWALADER WICKERSHAM & TAFT LLP
One World Financial Center, New York NY 10281. 212/504-6000. **Fax:** 212/504-6666. **Contact:** Human Resources. **E-mail address:** cwtinfo@cwt.com. **World Wide Web address:** http://www.cwt.com. **Description:** A law firm specializing in corporate law, tax, real estate, trusts, and estates. **NOTE:** Lateral Hiring phone: 212/504-5650. **Positions advertised include:** Banking Regulatory Associate; Financial Products Associate; Commercial Mortgage Backed Securities Associate; Residential Mortgage Backed Securities Attorney; Financial Restructuring Attorney; Corporate Healthcare Associate; Healthcare Litigator; General Litigator; Reinsurance Litigator; Real Estate Associate; Tax Associate. **Other U.S. locations:** Washington DC; Charlotte NC. **International locations:** London, England.

CAHILL GORDON & REINDEL
80 Pine Street, 17th Floor, New York NY 10005-1702. 212/701-3000. **Contact:** Joyce Hilly, Hiring Coordinator. **E-mail address:** jhilly@cahill.com. **World Wide Web address:** http://www.cahill.com. **Description:** A corporate law firm also specializing in real estate, trusts, and estates. **Corporate headquarters location:** This location.

CAM GRAPHICS COMPANY INC.
206 New Highway, Amityville NY 11701. 631/842-3400. **Fax:** 631/842-1005. **Contact:** Human Resources. **E-mail address:** info@camgraphics.com. **World Wide Web address:** http://www.camgraphics.com. **Description:** CAM Graphics Company supplies businesses and manufacturers with assorted memory-related devices.

CAMBRIDGE UNIVERSITY PRESS
40 West 20th Street, New York NY 10011-4211. 212/924-3900. **Fax:** 212/691-3239. **Contact:** Deborah Chick, Personnel Associate. **E-mail address:** jobs@cup.org. **World Wide Web address:** http://www.cup.org. **Description:** Cambridge University Press publishes an average of 1,300 nonfiction books a year. **Positions advertised include:** Journals Acquisitions Editor; Journals Assistant; Development Editor; Production Manager; Project Editor.

CAMERON ASSOCIATES
640 Fifth Avenue, 15th Floor, New York NY 10019. 212/245-8800. **Contact:** Human Resources. **E-mail address:** careers@cameronassociates.com. **World Wide Web address:** http://www.cameronassociates.com. **Description:** An investor relations firm providing financial services for public companies. Cameron Associates also offers corporate communications services. **Corporate headquarters location:** Toronto, Canada.

CAMP DRESSER & McKEE, INC. (CDM)
500 Federal Street, Suite 202, Troy NY 12180. 518/266-9620. **Fax:** 518/266-0717. **Contact:** Human Resources Department. **E-mail address:** hr@cdm.com. **World Wide Web address:** http://www.cdm.com. **Description:** Camp Dresser & McKee, Inc. is a worldwide provider of environmental engineering, scientific, planning, and management services. The company focuses on professional activities for the management of water resources, hazardous and solid wastes, wastewater, infrastructure, and environmental systems for industry and government. **NOTE:** Resumes should be sent to CDM, One Cambridge Place, 50 Hampshire Street, Cambridge MA 02139. **Positions advertised include:** Geotechnical Engineer; Electrical Engineer; Project Manager; Environmental Engineer; Senior Project Manager. **Corporate headquarters location:** Cambridge MA. **Other area locations:** Massena NY; New York NY; Syracuse NY; Rochester NY; Woodbury NY. **Other U.S. locations:** Nationwide. **International locations:** Worldwide.

CAMP DRESSER & McKEE, INC. (CDM)
16 West Main Street, Suite 114, Rochester NY 14614. 585/262-6070. **Fax:** 585/262-6065. **Contact:** Human Resources Department. **E-mail address:** hr@cdm.com. **World Wide Web address:** http://www.cdm.com. **Description:** Camp Dresser & McKee is a worldwide provider of environmental engineering, scientific, planning, and management services. The company focuses on professional activities for the management of water resources, hazardous and solid wastes, wastewater, infrastructure, and environmental systems for industry and government. **NOTE:** Resumes should be sent to CDM, One Cambridge Place, 50 Hampshire Street, Cambridge MA 02139. **Positions advertised include:** Mechanical Engineer; Environmental Engineer. **Corporate headquarters location:** Cambridge MA. **Other area locations:** Massena NY; New York NY; Syracuse NY; Troy NY; Woodbury NY. **Other U.S. locations:** Nationwide. **International locations:** Worldwide.

CAMP SYSTEMS INC. (CSI)
Long Island MacArthur Airport, 999 Marconi Avenue, Ronkonkoma NY 11779-7299. 631/588-3200. **Toll-free phone:** 877/411-2267. **Contact:** Human Resources. **E-mail address:** careers@campsys.com. **World Wide Web address:** http://www.campsys.com. **Description:** Camp Systems Inc. (CSI) performs computerized aircraft maintenance and management services. **Positions advertised include:** Aircraft Analyst. **Corporate headquarters location:** This location. **Subsidiaries include:** CAMP Europe SAS; Daniel Systems.

CANANDAIGUA WINE COMPANY, INC.
116 Buffalo Street, Canandaigua NY 14424. 585/394-7600. **Contact:** Personnel Manager. **E-mail address:** staffing@cwine.com. **World Wide Web address:** http://www.cwine.com. **Description:** A leading producer and marketer of more than 125 national and regional alcoholic beverage brands, distributed by more than 1,000 wholesalers, as well as state alcoholic beverage control agencies, throughout the United States and in selected international markets. The company is one of the largest U.S. producers of wines in the three categories of table wines, sparkling wines, and dessert wines. Products include Inglenook, Almaden Vineyards, and Paul Mason. The company is also one of the largest importers of international beer brands, with three of the top 20 imported beer brands in the United States. Products include Corona and St. Pauli Girl. The company is also one of the largest suppliers of distilled spirits in the United States, with products including bourbon, whiskey, gin, and vodka. **NOTE:** Resumes can be sent to human resources at 235 North Bloomfield Road, Canandaigua NY 14424. **Corporate headquarters location:** Fairport NY. **Subsidiaries include:** Barton Beers, Ltd.; Barton Brands of California, Inc.; Barton Brands of Georgia, Inc.; Barton Brands, Ltd.; Barton Distillers Import Corporation; Barton Financial Corporation; Barton Inc.; Batavia Wine Cellars, Inc.; Canandaigua West, Inc.; Monarch Import Company; Stevens Point Beverage Company; The Viking Distillery, Inc. **Parent company:** Constellation Brands Inc. (Fairport NY). **Annual sales/revenues:** $869 million. **Number of employees:** 1,700.

CANON U.S.A., INC.
One Canon Plaza, Lake Success NY 11042-1198. 516/328-5000. **Fax:** 516/328-4669. **Contact:** Human Resources Administrator. **World Wide Web address:** http://www.usa.canon.com. **Description:** A manufacturer of consumer and business imaging systems products including copy machines, facsimiles, printers, computers, cameras, camcorders, broadcasting lenses, and medical equipment. **NOTE:** To be considered for positions job seekers are requested to access the company's online application through the company Website. **Positions advertised include:** Planning Analylst; Credit Representative; Marketing Programs Specialist; Bid Specialist; Software Development Engineer; Staff Auditor; Advertising Associate; Marketing Programs Specialist; Sales Administrative Assistant; Technical Marketing Analyst. **Special programs:** Internships. **Corporate headquarters location:** This location. **Other U.S. locations:** Nationwide. **International locations:** Worldwide. **Parent company:** Canon Inc. (Tokyo, Japan). **President/CEO:** Kinya Uchida. **Annual sales/revenues:** $7.5 billion. **Number of employees at this location:** 800. **Number of employees nationwide:** 12,000.

CANTON-POTSDAM HOSPITAL
50 Leroy Street, Potsdam NY 13676-1786. 315/265-3300. **Contact:** Human Resources. **E-mail address:** human.resources@cphospital.net. **World Wide Web address:** http://www.cphospital.org. **Description:** CPH provides comprehensive acute medical-surgical care and emergency care, as well as programs in chemical dependency treatment, cardiac care, obstetrics, and physical rehabilitation services. The hospital operates the Warner Cancer Treatment Center with the main hospital campus in Potsdam, and provides services in Canton, Norfolk, and Richville. **Positions advertised include:** Respiratory Therapist; Respiratory Technician; Respiratory Registered Nurse; Allied Health Professional; Building Attendant; Central Supply Aide; Endoscopy Registered Nurse; Nurse Practitioner; Physician Assistant; Medical Technologist; Nurses Aide; Ward Clerk; Certified Nursing Assistant; Licensed Practical Nurse; Patient Representative; Occupational Therapy Assistant; Physical Therapist; Radiologic Technologist; Transcriptionist.

CANTOR FITZGERALD SECURITIES CORPORATION
135 East 57th Street, New York NY 10022. 212/938-5000. **Contact:** Human Resources Department. **World Wide Web address:** http://www.cantor.com. **Description:** An institutional brokerage firm dealing in fixed income securities, equities, derivatives, options, eurobonds, and emerging markets. Founded in 1945. **NOTE:** You may see the website for the appropriate web address for forward resumes. **Positions advertised include:** Computer Programmer. **Special programs:** Summer Internships (you may e-mail internshipopportunities@cantor.com). **Corporate headquarters location:** This location. **Other U.S. locations:** Los Angeles CA; Chicago IL; Boston MA; Dallas TX. **International locations:** Germany; China; England; Italy; France; Japan.

CAPGEMINI U.S.
5 Times Square, 9th Floor, New York NY 10036. 917/934-8000. **Fax:** 917/934-8001. **Contact:** Human Resources. **World Wide Web address:** http://www.us.cgey.com. **Description:** Provider of management consulting services including business strategy, operations, and people and information management. Services include systems integration; application design, development, and documentation; systems conversions and migrations; and information technology consulting. **NOTE:** Jobseekers are encouraged to apply online. **Positions advertised include:** Oracle Planner; Graphic Designer; JD Edwards Planner; Patient Financial Services Manager; Supply Chain Health Manager; Health Information Manager; Health Revenue Manager; Tech Direct Sales Executive; Business Transformation Manager; Campus Health Providers Consultant; Clinical Health Integrator. **Corporate headquarters location:** This location. **Other U.S. locations:** Nationwide. **International locations:** Worldwide. **Parent company:** Cap Gemini Ernst & Young (Paris, France). **Annual sales/revenues:** $2.6 billion. **Number of employees:** 10,000.

CAPITAL DISTRICT YMCA
P.O. Box 12640, Albany NY 12212-2640. 518/869-3500. **Physical address:** 151 Vly Road, Albany NY 12212-5005. **Contact:** Human Resources Manager. **World Wide Web address:** http://www.cdymca.org. **Description:** One of the nation's largest and most comprehensive service organizations. The YMCA provides health and fitness, social and personal development, sports and recreation, education and career development, and camps and conferences to children, youths, adults, and the elderly, families, the disabled, refugees and foreign nationals, YMCA residents, and community residents, through a broad range of specific programs. **Positions advertised include:**

Member Service Representative; Lifeguard; Childcare Associate; Maintenance Custodian; Swimming Instructor; Head Toddler Teacher; Fitness Coach; Membership Receptionist; Teen Program Assistant; Group Exercise Coordinator.

CAPLUGS LLC
2150 Elmwood Avenue, Buffalo NY 14207-1984. 716/876-9855. **Contact:** Human Resources. **E-mail address:** info@caplugs.com. **World Wide Web address:** http://www.caplugs.com. **Description:** Caplugs manufactures plastic and vinyl plugs for industrial use. Founded in 1948. **Corporate headquarters location:** This location. **Other locations:** CA. **Parent company:** Protective Industries LLC. **Number of employees at this location:** 290.

CARDINAL HEALTH
500 Neely Town Road, Montgomery NY 12549. 845/457-2000. **Contact:** Human Resources. **World Wide Web address:** http://www.cardinal.com. **Description:** A producer, developer, and distributor of medical products and technologies for use in hospitals and other health care settings such as surgical apparel, surgical drapes, surgical instruments, and respiratory care products. The company operates through two industry segments: medical specialties, and medical/laboratory products and distribution. **Corporate headquarters location:** Dublin OH. **Operations at this facility include:** Administration; distribution point of medical supplies and equipment to hospitals.

THE CARLYLE HOTEL
35 East 76th Street, New York NY 10021. 212/744-1600. **Fax:** 212/717-4682. **Contact:** Human Resources. **E-mail address:** carlylejobs@rosewoodhotels.com. **World Wide Web address:** http://www.rosewoodhotels.com. **Description:** A luxury hotel offering 180-rooms, three restaurants, and banquet/meeting facilities. **Corporate headquarters location:** This location. **Parent company:** Rosewood Hotels & Resorts.

CARRIAGE HOUSE COMPANIES, INC.
196 Newton Street, Fredonia NY 14063. 716/673-1000. **Toll-free phone:** 800/828-8915. **Fax:** 716/679-7702. **Contact:** Human Resources. **World Wide Web address:** http://www.carriagehousecos.com. **Description:** A food manufacturer. Products include spoonable and pourable salad dressings, mayonnaise, ketchup, peanut butter, sweet and sour sauce, spaghetti sauce, Bloody Mary mix, and jams and jellies. **Corporate headquarters location:** This location. **Subsidiaries include:** American Maid; Jero; Major Peters'. **Parent company:** Ralcorp Holdings Inc. (St. Louis MO). **President/CEO:** James A. Nichols. **Annual sales/revenues:** $450 million.

CARRIER CORPORATION
Building ARC, P.O. Box 4808, Carrier Parkway, Syracuse NY 13221-4808. 315/432-6000. **Contact:** Diversity and Staffing. **E-mail address:** great.jobs@carrier.utc.com. **World Wide Web address:** http://www.global.carrier.com. **Description:** Manufactures heating, ventilating, and air conditioning units. Carrier Corporation produces and sells these units for both commercial and residential use. **Positions advertised include:** Mechanical Engineer. **Corporate headquarters location:** Farmington CT. **Parent company:** United Technologies (Hartford CT). **Annual sales/revenues:** $8.8 billion. **Number of employees:** 45,000.

CARROLS CORPORATION
P.O. Box 6969, Syracuse NY 13217. 315/424-0513. **Physical address:** 968 James Street, Syracuse NY 13203. **Fax:** 315/479-8018. **Contact:** Judy Rosello, Human Resource Manager. **E-mail address:** jrosello@carrols.com. **World Wide Web address:** http://www.carrols.com. **Description:** Owns and operates fast-food restaurants and franchises including 350 Burger King restaurants, 126 Taco Caban restaurants, and 82 Pollo Tropical restaurants. Founded in 1968. **NOTE:** Applicants must fill out the standard application form to be considered. **Positions advertised include:** Lease Accounting Manager; Assistant Manager. **Corporate headquarters location:** This location. **Other U.S. locations:** Nationwide. **Annual sales/revenues:** $657 million. **Number of employees nationwide:** 16,100

CARTER, LEDYARD & MILBURN LLP
2 Wall Street, New York NY 10005. 212/238-8744. **Fax:** 212/732-3232. **Contact:** June Chotoo, Recruitment Manager & Attorney Development. **E-mail address:** recruit@clm.com. **World Wide Web address:** http://www.clm.com. **Description:** A law firm specializing in business, litigation, real estate, tax, and trust and estate law. Founded in 1854. **NOTE:** Recruitment Manager phone: 212/238-8744. **Positions advertised include:** Attorney; Paralegal. **Other U.S. locations:** Washington DC; New York NY. **Number of employees:** 250.

CASCADE LINEN SERVICES
835 Myrtle Avenue, Brooklyn NY 11206. 718/963-9600. **Contact:** Human Resources. **Description:** Provides commercial linen supply and rental services for hotels, restaurants, and medical institutions. **Corporate headquarters location:** This location.

CATHOLIC CHARITIES OF THE DIOCESE OF BROOKLYN & QUEENS
191 Joralemon Street, Brooklyn NY 11201. 718/722-6002. **Fax:** 718/722-6096. **Contact:** Sister Ellen Patricia Finn. **World Wide Web address:** http://www.ccbq.org. **Description:** A network of private social service organizations that provides food, shelter, and clothing to disadvantaged individuals. **Positions advertised include:** Social Worker; Case Aid; Staff Psychiatrist; Service Clinician; Case Manager; Social Service Assistant; Driver; Administrative Assistant; Program Coordinator. **Other locations:** Brooklyn NY; Queens NY.

CAYUGA BANK
115 Genesee Street, Auburn NY 13021. 315/252-9521. **Contact:** Human Resources. **World Wide Web address:** http://www.cayugabank.com. **Description:** Provides banking services to individuals and small to medium-sized businesses. The bank provides a variety of financial services including residential mortgage loans, consumer and commercial loans, credit cards, insurance and investment brokerage services, trust services, and safe deposit facilities. **Parent company:** First Niagara Financial Group, Inc. (Lockport NY).

CAYUGA BANK
283 Genesee Street, Utica NY 13501. 315/797-1350. **Contact:** Human Resources. **World Wide Web address:** http://www.cayugabank.com. **Description:** Provides banking services to individuals and small to medium-sized businesses. The bank provides a variety of financial services including residential mortgage loans, consumer and commercial loans, credit cards, insurance and investment brokerage services, trust services, and safe deposit facilities. **NOTE:** Interested jobseekers should send resumes to Human Resources, 115 Genesee Street, Auburn NY 13021. **Parent company:** First Niagara Financial Group, Inc. (Lockport NY).

CELANESE ACETATE TEXTILES
3 Park Avenue, 37th Floor, New York NY 10016. 212/251-8000. **Fax:** 212/251-8037. **Contact:** Ellen Sweeney. **E-mail address:** ellen.sweeney@celaneseacetate.com. **World Wide Web address:** http://www.celanese.com. **Description:** Manufactures acetate products including acetate yarn and Micro Safe fiber. Primary customers include the apparel, furnishings, and industrial markets. **NOTE:** Jobseekers are requested to use the company's Online Application Tool. For questions regarding the Champs trainee program contact: Nadia Soliz, Celanese Chemicals, 1601 West LBJ Freeway, Dallas TX 75234-6034; by phone: 361/242-4312; by e-mail: nsoliz@celanese.com. **Special programs:** Internships; Champs Training Program. **Parent company:** Celanese AG (Kronberg im Taunus, Germany) is an industrial chemical company.

CENDANT CORPORATION
9 West 57th Street, 37th Floor, New York NY 10019. 212/413-1800. **Fax:** 212/413-1918. **Contact:** Terence P. Conley, Human Resources. **World Wide Web address:** http://www.cendant.com. **Description:** Provides a wide range of business services including dining services, hotel franchise management, mortgage programs, and timeshare exchanges. Cendant Corporation's Real Estate Division offers employee relocation and mortgage services through Century 21, Coldwell Banker, ERA, Cendant Mortgage, and Cendant Mobility. The Travel Division provides car rentals, vehicle management services, and vacation timeshares through brand names including Avia, Days Inn, Howard Johnson, Ramada, Travelodge, and Super 8. The Membership Division offers travel, shopping, auto, dining, and other financial services through Travelers Advantage, Shoppers Advantage, Auto Vantage, Welcome Wagon, Netmarket, North American Outdoor Group, and PrivacyGuard. Founded in 1997. **NOTE:** Paper resumes are no longer accepted. **Positions advertised include:** International Relocation Consultant; Partner Marketing Manager; Hotel Manager; Field Auditor. **Corporate headquarters location:** This location. **Subsidiaries include:** Avis Group Holdings, Inc.; Budget Group, Inc.; Century 21 Real Estate Corporation; Coldwell Banker Real Estate Corporation; Days Inn Worldwide Inc.; Fairfield Resorts, Inc.; Galileo International, Inc.; Howard Johnson International Inc.; Jackson Hewitt Inc.; NRT Incorporated; PHH Arval; Ramada Franchise Systems Inc.; Super 8 Motels, Inc.; Travelodge Hotels, Inc.; Trendwest Resorts, Inc. **Listed on:** New York Stock Exchange. **Stock exchange symbol:** CD. **Chairman/President/CEO:** Henry R. Silverman. **Annual sales/revenues:** $14 billion. **Number of employees worldwide:** 85,000.

CENTER FOR VETERINARY CARE
236 East 75th Street, New York NY 10021. 212/734-7480. **Contact:** Human Resources. **Description:** A full-service animal hospital offering medical and surgical procedures.

CENTRAL COOPERATIVE INSURANCE CO.
P.O. Box 539, Baldwinsville NY 13027. 315/635-7606. **Contact:** David Fraser, President & Claims Manager. **World Wide Web address:** http://www.centralco-op.com. **Description:** An insurance company specializing in property and casualty insurance.

CENTRAL PARKING SYSTEMS
360 West 31st Street, 12th Floor, New York NY 10001. 212/502-5475. **Contact:** Human Resources. **World Wide Web address:** http://www.parking.com. **Description:** Operates parking garages and lots throughout New York. **Positions advertised include:** Area Manager; Field Auditor; Night Area Manager; Project Manager; Paralegal; Staff Accountant. **Corporate headquarters location:** This location. **Other U.S. locations:** Nationwide. **Parent company:** Central Parking Corporation (Nashville TN).

THE CENTRE GROUP
One Chase Manhattan Plaza, New York NY 10005. 212/898-5300. **Fax:** 212/898-5400. **Contact:** Human Resources. **World Wide Web address:** http://www.entercentre.com. **Description:** A reinsurance company that offers finite risk reinsurance, insurance, and financial solutions ranging from workers' compensation and product liability coverage to managed environmental impairment liabilities and post-closure reclamation. **International locations:** Australia; China; France; Ireland; Switzerland; United Kingdom. **Parent company:** Zurich Financial Services Group.

CERTILMAN BALIN ADLER & HYMAN, LLP
90 Merrick Avenue, East Meadow NY 11554. 516/296-7000. **Fax:** 516/296-7111. **Contact:** Laura Gole, Human Resources. **World Wide Web address:** http://www.certilmanbalin.com. **Description:** A law firm with over 100 attorneys practicing in all areas of law. **Positions advertised include:** Litigation Secretary; Foreclosure Attorney; Legal Secretary. **Corporate headquarters location:** This location. **Other locations:** Hauppauge NY.

THE CHALLENGE GROUP
1195 Atlantic Avenue, Brooklyn NY 11216. 718/636-9500. **Fax:** 718/857-9115.**Contact:** Thomas H. Watkins, Publisher. **E-mail address:** challengegroup@yahoo.com. **World Wide Web address:** http://www.challenge-group.com. **Description:** Publishes several nationally distributed, weekly newspaper (circulation of 130,000) primarily covering cultural, political, and social news of interest to African Americans. Publications include *The New American, Afro Times,* and *The Daily Challenge.* **Special programs:** Internships. **Corporate headquarters location:** This location.

CHARTER ONE BANK
833 Broadway, Albany NY 12207-2774. 518/445-2010. **Contact:** Human Resources. **World Wide Web address:** http://www.charterone.com. **Description:** Charter One Bank is one of the oldest operating savings banks in New York State. With operations in several Northeast and Midwest states, the bank operates a network of 45 branch offices in New York state. Charter One Bank is a federally chartered savings bank that, along with its brokerage and insurance subsidiary, offers a full range of financial products and services. **Positions advertised include:** Customer Service Representative; Customer Service Team Leader; Encoder I. **Other area locations:** Statewide. **Parent company:** Charter One Financial Inc. (Cleveland OH).

CHARTER ONE BANK
40 Franklin Street, Rochester NY 14604. 585/258-3105. **Fax:** 585/232-2029. **Contact:** Personnel. **World Wide Web address:** http://www.charterone.com. **Description:** Charter One Bank is one of the oldest operating savings banks in New York State. With operations in several Northeast and Midwest states, the bank operates a network of 45 branch offices in New York state. Charter One Bank is a federally chartered savings bank that, along with its brokerage and insurance subsidiary, offers a full range of financial products and services. **Positions advertised include:** Accounting Manager; Loan Adjuster; Administrative Assistant; Customer Service Representative; Dealer Credit Manager; Financial Services Representative; General Clerk; Sales Associate; Loan Processor; Community Lending Manager; Receptionist. **Other area locations:** Statewide. **Parent company:** Charter One Financial Inc. (Cleveland OH).

BERNARD CHAUS, INC.
dba JOSEPHINE CHAUS, INC.
530 Seventh Avenue, 18th Floor, New York NY 10018. 212/354-1280. **Fax:** 201/863-6307. **Contact:** Human Resources Director. **World Wide Web address:** http://www.bernardchaus.com. **Description:** Designs, manufactures, and markets women's apparel. Career casual sportswear is marketed under the Chaus, Chaus Woman, and Chaus Petite labels and blouses are marketed under the Josephine label. Weekend casual sportswear bears the Chaus Sport and Chaus Jeanswear labels. Dresses are marketed under the Chaus Dresses, Chaus Woman Dresses, and Chaus Petite Dresses labels. Founded in 1976. **Listed on:** Over The Counter. **Stock exchange symbol:** CHBD. **Chairwoman/CEO:** Josephine Chaus. **Annual sales/revenues:** $145.5 million. **Number of employees:** 242.

CHEMPRENE INC.
483 Fishkill Avenue, P.O. Box 471, Beacon NY 12508. 845/831-2800. **Fax:** 845/831-4639. **Contact:** Human Resources. **Description:** Chemprene produces a wide range of specialty industrial diaphragms, belting, and coated fabrics by spread coating, dip coating, and calendering methods. **Positions advertised include:** Draftsperson; Mechanical Engineer. **Operations at this facility include:** Administration; Manufacturing; Research and Development; Sales. **Number of employees at this location:** 180.

CHILDREN'S AID SOCIETY
105 East 22nd Street, New York NY 10010. 212/949-4800. **Contact:** Human Resources Manager. **E-mail address:** jobs@childrensaidsociety.org. **World Wide Web address:** http://www.childrensaidsociety.org. **Description:** Provides early, intensive, and long-term support to thousands of city children and their families through various programs and services including medical and dental care, foster care, group homes, adoption, homemakers, emergency assistance, food distribution, Head Start, tutoring, mentors, community centers, community schools, counseling, court diversion programs, camps, sports, arts, dance, theater, chorus, internships, jobs, teen pregnancy prevention, leadership projects, college and prep/college scholarships, and services to the homeless. Founded in 1853. **NOTE:** Jobseekers may submit an application online. **Positions advertised include:** Accounts Payable Supervisor; Purchasing Manager; Clinical Nurse Administrator; Summer Camp Group Leader; Lifeguard; Social Worker; Medical Receptionist; Senior Social Worker; Gym/Recreation Specialist; Nutritionist; Nurse; Head Teacher; Violence Prevention Coordinator; Center Director; Family Services Director; Foster Care Social Worker; Homefinding Supervisor; Substance Abuse Specialist; Education Coordinator. **Corporate headquarters location:** This location. **Other locations:** Throughout the New York City metropolitan area. **Operations at this facility include:** Administration; Regional Headquarters.

CHILDREN'S HOSPITAL OF BUFFALO
219 Bryant Street, Buffalo NY 14222. 716/878-7000. **Fax:** 716/862-6631. **Contact:** Human Resources. **E-mail address:** kaleidajobs@kaleidahealth.org. **World Wide Web address:** http://www.chob.edu. **Description:** A hospital specializing in the treatment and care of children. **NOTE:** Interested jobseekers should send resumes to 2900 Main Street, Buffalo NY 14214. **Parent company:** Kaleida Health Systems.

CHILDREN'S VILLAGE
Westmore Hall, 1st Floor, Dobbs Ferry NY 10522. 914/693-0600 ext. 1214. **Fax:** 914/674-4512. **Contact:** Human Resources Department. **E-mail address:** recruiter@childrensvillage.org. **World Wide Web address:** http://www.childrensvillage.org. **Description:** A nonprofit organization that operates a residential treatment center for emotionally disturbed children. **Positions advertised include:** Social Worker; Assistant Director; Registered Nurse; Financial Analyst; Administrative Assistant; Child Care Worker; Sociotherapist; Cyber Café Supervisor. **Corporate headquarters location:** This location. **Other locations:** Harlem NY.

CHOICE ONE COMMUNICATIONS
100 Chestnut Street, Suite 700, Rochester NY 14604. 585/697-3400. **Fax:** 716/530-2738. **Contact:** Human Resources. **World Wide Web address:** http://www.choiceonecom.com. **Description:** Choice One Communications is an Integrated Communications Provider (ICP) offering an array of local, long distance, high-speed data (including DSL), web hosting, design and development services to small and medium sized companies in the Northeast and Midwest United States. **Positions advertised include:** Associate Design Engineer; Data Delivery Coordinator; HR Communications Specialist; Payroll Coordinator; Sr. Software Engineer; Software Engineer; Software Quality Assurance Engineer.

CHYRON CORPORATION
5 Hub Drive, Department WWW, Farmingdale NY 11735. 631/845-2000. **Fax:** 631/845-2090. **Contact:** Human Resources. **E-mail address:** careers@chyron.com. **World Wide Web address:** http://www.chyron.com. **Description:** Designs, manufactures, and markets worldwide digital equipment, software, systems, and solutions that facilitate the production and enhance the presentation of live and programmed television content. Chyron also provides comprehensive solutions that address the management and routing of video and data signals prior to transmission. **NOTE:** Entry-level positions are offered. Jobseekers may apply online. **Positions advertised include:** Test Engineer. **Special programs:** Internships. **Corporate headquarters location:** This location. **International locations:** Reading, United Kingdom (Chyron Pro-Bel). **Operations at this facility include:** Chyron Graphics – Manufacturing; Corporate Administration; Research and Development; Sales; Service. **Listed on:** Over The Counter. **Stock exchange symbol:** CYRO. **Chairman/President/CEO:** Michael I. Wellesley-Wesley. **Annual sales/revenues:** $46 million. **Number of employees:** 200.

CIBA SPECIALTY CHEMICALS
540 White Plains Road, Tarrytown NY 10591-9005. 914/785-2000. **Fax:** 914/785-2183. **Contact:** Loretta Czernecki, Human Resources Manager. **E-mail address:** Loretta.cznecki@cibasc.com or careers@cibasc.com. **World Wide Web address:** http://www.cibasc.com. **Description:** Ciba manufactures specialty chemicals through five divisions: additives, colors, consumer care, performance polymers, and water treatments. **NOTE:** Human Resources phone: 914/785-3828. **Corporate headquarters location:** Basel, Switzerland. **Operations at this facility include:** NAFTA regional headquarters. Coating Effects and Plastic Additives business segment headquarters, marketing, and technical operations. Research & Development center for new product development, analytical and technical service support for Ciba's light stabilizer, antioxidant, process chemicals, imaging/coating additives, process/lubricant additives, and water/paper treatment businesses. **Listed on:** New York Stock Exchange. **Stock exchange symbol:** CSB. **Annual sales/revenues:** $5 billion. **Number of employees nationwide:** 3,000. **Number of employees worldwide:** 19,000.

CINE MAGNETICS VIDEO & DIGITAL LABORATORIES
100 Business Park Drive, Armonk NY 10504-1750. 914/273-7500. **Fax:** 914/273-7575. **Contact:** Human Resources. **E-mail address:** cminfo@cinemagnetics.com. **World Wide Web address:** http://www.cinemagnetics.com. **Description:** Cine Magnetics is involved in video and film duplication and photo finishing. **Corporate headquarters location:** This location. **Other U.S. locations:** Studio City CA.

CITIBANK (NEW YORK STATE)
One EAB Plaza, Uniondale NY 11555. 516/627-3999. **Contact:** Human Resources. **World Wide Web address:** http://www.citibank.com. **Description:** A full-service commercial bank offering a range of services through more than 80 branch banking offices in metropolitan New York and Long Island. **Positions advertised include:** Wire & Proof Clerk; Consumer Markets Group Relationship Manager; Loan Administrator; Senior Unit Manager; Financial Associate; Teller; Sales Relationship Manager; Financial Center Operations Manager; Financial Executive; Mortgage Specialist; Client Financial Analyst; Business Banking Officer; Financial Center Manager; Branch Manager; Small Business Manager. **Parent company:** Citigroup, Inc. (New York NY).

CITIBANK, N.A.
399 Park Avenue, New York NY 10043-0001. 212/559-1000. **Contact:** Search and Staffing. **World Wide Web address:** http://www.citibank.com. **Description:** Operates a global, full-service consumer franchise encompassing branch banking, credit and charge cards, and private banking. In branch banking, Citibank services almost 20 million accounts in 41 countries and territories. In global card products, Citibank is one of the world's largest bankcard and charge card issuers. In addition, Citibank issues and services approximately 5 million private-label cards for department stores and retail outlets. Citibank Private Bank offices in 31 countries and territories provide a full-range of wealth management services and serve as a window that gives clients access to the full range of Citibank's global capabilities. **Positions advertised include:** Financial Associate; Teller; Financial Center Manager; Branch Manager; Business Banking Officer; Litigation Support Specialist; Service Officer. **Parent company:** Citigroup, Inc. (New York NY).

CITIGROUP INC.
399 Park Avenue, New York NY 10043. 212/559-1000. **Fax:** 212/793-3946. **Contact:** Human Resources. **World Wide Web address:** http://www.citigroup.com. **Description:** A holding company offering a wide range of financial services through its subsidiaries. **Positions advertised include:** Financial Analyst; Data Privacy/Information Security Specialist; Administrative Assistant; Data Analyst; Area Sales Manager; GI Analyst & Liaison; Event Planner; Senior Reviewer; Senior Contract Recruiter. **Corporate headquarters location:** This location. **Subsidiaries include:** Citibank; CitiFinancial; Global Corporate & Investment Banking; Primerica Financial Services; Salomon Smith Barney; SSB Citi Asset Management Group; Travelers Life & Annuity; Travelers Property Casualty Corp. **Listed on:** New York Stock Exchange. **Stock exchange symbol:** C. **Chairman/CEO:** Sanford (Sandy) I. Weill. **Annual sales/revenues:** $92.6 billion. **Number of employees:** 255,000.

CITY CENTER OF MUSIC AND DRAMA INC. (CCMD)
70 Lincoln Center Plaza, 4th Floor, New York NY 10023-6580. 212/870-4266. **Fax:** 212/870-4286. **Contact:** Cynthia Herzegovitch, Human Resources Administrator. **Description:** Organizational and management offices for the nonprofit cultural organization with activities that include plays, ballets, and operas. The center operates the New York State Theater, the New York City Opera, the New York Ballet, and City Center Special Productions. **Positions advertised include:** Clerical Supervisor. **Corporate headquarters location:** This location. **Operations at this facility include:** Administration. **Number of employees:** 2,000.

THE CITY COLLEGE OF NEW YORK
THE CITY UNIVERSITY OF NEW YORK (CUNY)
Convent Avenue at 138th Street, New York NY 10031. 212/650-7000. **Contact:** Human Resources Department. **World Wide Web address:** http://www.ccny.cuny.edu. **Description:** A public, coeducational college offering both undergraduate and graduate programs of study in a wide variety of disciplines. **Positions advertised include:** Associate Architecture Professor; Education Teacher; Assistant Physics Professor; Economics Professor; Medical Lecturer; Associate Film & Video Production Professor; Advertising & Public Relations Professor; Film & Video Full Professor; Associate Biomedical Engineering Professor; Administrative Coordinator; Associate Biology Professor; Medical School Research Assistant; Medical School Postdoctoral Fellow; Postdoctoral Research Associate – Laser Institute; Chemistry Research Associate; Asian Studies Assistant Professor; Information Systems Assistant; Custodial Assistant; Office Assistant; Maintenance Worker. **Other area locations:** Bronx NY; Brooklyn NY; Flushing NY; Jamaica NY; Staten Island NY.

CLARKSON UNIVERSITY
8 Clarkson Avenue, P.O. Box 5542, Potsdam NY 13699. 315/268-6497. **Fax:** 315/268-4437. **Contact:** Human Resources. **World Wide Web address:** http://www.clarkson.edu. **Description:** A four-year, liberal arts college of 3,000 undergraduates and 350 graduate students with specialization in engineering sciences. **Positions advertised include:** Assistant Civil and Environmental Engineering Professor; Bioengineering/Rehabilitation Engineering Director; Assistant Chemistry Professor; Assistant Physics Professor; Assistant Cardiopulmonary Physical Therapy Professor; Safety Manager; Analytical Laboratory Director; Women's Ice Hockey Assistant Coach; Director of Gift Planning; Maintenance Mechanic.

CLEAN HARBORS, INC.
32 Bask Road, Glenmont NY 12077. 518/434-0149. **Fax:** 518/434-9118. **Contact:** Human Resources. **World Wide Web address:** http://www.cleanharbors.com. **Description:** Clean Harbors, Inc., through its subsidiaries, provides comprehensive environmental services in 35 states in the Northeast, Midwest, Central, and Mid-Atlantic regions. Clean Harbors provides a wide range of hazardous waste management and environmental support services to a diversified customer base from over 40 locations. The company's hazardous waste management services include treatment, storage, recycling, transportation, risk analysis, site assessment, laboratory analysis, site closure, and disposal of hazardous materials through environmentally sound methods including incineration. Environmental remediation services include emergency response, surface remediation, groundwater restoration, industrial maintenance, and facility decontamination. Customers include nearly 300 of the Fortune 500 companies; regional utilities; oil, pharmaceutical, and chemical companies; small businesses; and the high-tech and biotech industries. **Positions advertised include:** Class A Driver; Field Technician; Field Service Foreman; Class B Driver. **Corporate headquarters location:** Braintree MA. **Other U.S. locations:** Nationwide. **Listed on:** NASDAQ. **Stock exchange symbol:** CLHB. **Chairman/President/CEO:** Alan S. McKim. **Annual sales/revenues:** $252 million. **Number of employees nationwide:** 1,500.

CLEAR CHANNEL ENTERTAINMENT
220 West 42nd Street, New York NY 10036. 917/421-4000. **Fax:** 917/421-5673. **Contact:** Human Resources. **World Wide Web address:** http://www.cc.com. **Description:** This subsidiary of Clear Channel Communications produces and promotes live entertainment by booking 135 venues worldwide averaging 29,000

events annually. **Positions advertised include:** Legal and Business Affairs Assistant; Booking Specialist; Event Associate; Promotions Assistant; Finance Assistant. **Corporate headquarters location:** This location. **Parent company:** Clear Channel Communications, Inc. (San Antonio TX). **Chairman/CEO:** Brian Becker. **Annual sales/revenues:** $2.5 billion.

CLEARY GOTTLIEB STEEN & HAMILTON
One Liberty Plaza, New York NY 10006. 212/225-2000. **Fax:** 212/225-3999. **Contact:** Nancy Roberts, Director of Administration & Personnel. **E-mail address:** nyrecruit@cgsh.com. **World Wide Web address:** http://www.cgsh.com. **Description:** One of the nation's largest law firms, focusing on a variety of different practice areas. **Corporate headquarters location:** This location. **Other U.S. locations:** Nationwide. **International locations:** Worldwide.

CLIENTLOGIC
699 Hertel Avenue, Suite 390, Buffalo NY 14207. 716/871-6400. **Fax:** 716/871-2157. **Contact:** Human Resources. **E-mail address:** buffalojobs@clientlogic.com. **World Wide Web address:** http://www.clientlogic.com. **Description:** Provides outsourcing services to a variety of Fortune 2000 companies. **Positions advertised include:** Customer Service Representative; Telesales Representative. **Corporate headquarters location:** Nashville TN. **Other U.S. locations:** Nationwide. **International locations:** Austria; France; Germany; Ireland; Spain; United Kingdom. **Number of employees:** 12,000.

CLIFFSTAR CORPORATION
One Cliffstar Avenue, Dunkirk NY 14048. 716/366-6100. **Fax:** 716/366-6599. **Contact:** Janice Szymanski, Human Resources. **World Wide Web address:** http://www.cliffstar.com. **Description:** A producer and distributor of private label juices and juice products. Customers include grocery stores, mass merchandisers, and drug stores. **Positions advertised include:** Distribution Supervisor; Logistics Specialist; Manager of Plant Engineering and Maintenance. **Corporate headquarters location:** This location. **Other U.S. locations:** Joplin MO. **Operations at this facility include:** Administration; Manufacturing; Research and Development; Sales; Service. **Number of employees at this location:** 550. **Number of employees nationwide:** 620.

CLIFTON SPRINGS HOSPITAL & CLINIC
2 Coulter Road, Clifton Springs NY 14432. 315/462-1327. **Fax:** 716/924-4160. **Contact:** Human Resources. **E-mail address:** humanresources@cshop.com. **World Wide Web address:** http://www.cliftonspringshospital.com. **Description:** A 262-bed hospital with several units including a nursing home, medical/surgical floor, ICU, psychiatry wing, and an alcohol recovery unit. **NOTE:** Human Resources phone: 315/462-1327. **Positions advertised include:** Occupational Therapist; Radiology Technologist; Addictions Counselor; Behavioral Counselor; Psychiatric Technician; Crisis Specialist; Registered Nurse; Licensed Practical Nurse; Certified Nursing Assistant; Hemotologist; Oncologist. **Subsidiaries include:** Finger Lakes Community Cancer Center. **Operations at this facility include:** Administration. **Number of employees at this location:** 800.

CLIMAX MANUFACTURING COMPANY
7840 State Route 26, Lowville NY 13367-1290. 315/376-8000. **Fax:** 315/376-2034. **Contact:** Andrew Lowe, Human Resources. **E-mail address:** corporate@climaxpkg.com. **World Wide Web address:** http://www.climaxpkg.com. **Description:** A manufacturer of paperboard, paperboard packaging, custom packaging, and boxes. **Corporate headquarters location:** This location. **Other locations:** Carthage NY; Castorland NY; Syracuse NY. **Operations at this facility include:** Packaging Division manufacturing.

THE CLOISTERS
Fort Tryon Park, New York NY 10040. 212/923-3700. **Contact:** Assistant Museum Educator. **World Wide Web address:** http://www.metmuseum.org. **Description:** A museum devoted to the art of medieval Europe. The collection includes architectural fragments, sculptures, frescoes, illuminated manuscripts, tapestries, stained glass, and paintings. Established in 1938. **Special programs:** Internships. **Parent company:** The Metropolitan Museum of Art.

CLOUGH HARBOUR & ASSOCIATES LLP
III Winners Circle, P.O. Box 5269, Albany NY 12205-0269. 518/453-4500. **Fax:** 518/458-1735. **Contact:** Human Resources Department. **E-mail address:** infosys@cha-llp.com. **World Wide Web address:** http://www.cha-llp.com. **Description:** An engineering firm with 20 offices nationwide. Specialties include civil engineering, environmental engineering, highway planning, landscape architecture, communications infrastructure design, urban planning, and geotechnical engineering. **Positions advertised include:** Engineer; Geographic Information System Analyst; Human Resources Manager; Senior Civil Engineer; Senior Planner; Water/Wastewater Engineer. **Corporate headquarters location:** This location. **Other locations:** Nationwide. **Number of employees:** 550.

COLDWELL BANKER
151 North Main Street, New City NY 10956. 845/634-0400. **Contact:** Human Resources. **World Wide Web address:** http://www.coldwellbanker.com. **Description:** This location is one of the 3,500 independently owned and operated franchised brokerages engaged in residential and commercial real estate transactions with 106,000 Sales Associates worldwide. **Corporate headquarters location:** Parsippany NJ. **Other locations:** Worldwide. **Parent company:** Cendant Corporation (New York NY). **Operations at this facility include:** Sales.

COLDWELL BANKER PRIME PROPERTIES, INC.
1621 Central Avenue, Albany NY 12205. 518/640-4234. **Fax:** 518/383-6225. **Contact:** Jeanne Warzek, Director Human Resources. **E-mail address:** jwarzek@cbpp.com. **World Wide Web address:** http://www.coldwellbankerprime.com. **Description:** Prime Properties is an affiliate of international real estate corporation, Coldwell Banker. Prime Properties serves Central and Western New York State as well as the Capital Region. Founded in 1906. **Corporate headquarters location:** This location. **Other locations:** Statewide. **Parent company:** Cendant Corporation (New York NY). **Number of employees:** 320.

COLGATE UNIVERSITY
13 Oak Drive, Hamilton NY 13346. 315/228-1000. **Fax:** 315/228-7171. **Contact:** Amy Barnes, Associate Vice President of Human Resources. **E-mail address:** humres@mail.colgate.edu. **World Wide Web address:** http://www.colgate.edu. **Description:** A four-year, liberal arts college located in central New York with 2,700 students. Founded in 1819. **NOTE:** Human Resources phone: 315/228-7411. **Positions advertised include:** Art History Professor; Assistant Football Coach; Fitness Center Coach; Greek & Latin Professor; Computer Science Lecturer; Geography Lecturer; East Asian History Lecturer; Music Composition Professor; Peace Studies Chairperson; Sociology/Anthropology Lecturer; Admissions Counselor; Career Services Assistant Director; Leadership Center Assistant Director; Communications Assistant Director; Catholic Chaplain; Cultural Center Director; Fraternities/Sororities Director; Regional Development Director; Customer Service Associate; Cashier; Receptionist; Campus Safety Officer; Assistant Technical Director. **Special programs:** Apprenticeships. **Number of employees at this location:** 700.

COLGATE-PALMOLIVE COMPANY
300 Park Avenue, New York NY 10022. 212/310-2000. **Fax:** 212/310-2475. **Contact:** Human Resources. **World Wide Web address:** http://www.colgate.com. **Description:** Colgate-Palmolive Company manufactures and markets a wide variety of products in the United States and around the world in two distinct business segments: Oral, Personal, and Household Care; and Specialty Marketing. Oral, Personal, and Household Care products include toothpastes, oral rinses, toothbrushes, bar and liquid soaps, shampoos, conditioners, deodorants and antiperspirants, baby products, shaving products, laundry and dishwashing detergents, fabric softeners, cleansers and cleaners, and bleach. Specialty Marketing products include pet dietary care products, crystal tableware, and portable fuel for warming food. Principal global trademarks and tradenames include Colgate, Palmolive, Mennen, Ajax, Fab, and Science Diet. **Positions advertised include:** Cost Analyst; Legal Accountant; Home Care Buyer; Internet Marketing Associate Manager; Human Resources Information Systems Specialist. **Special programs:** Internships. **Corporate headquarters location:** This location. **Other locations:** Worldwide. **Subsidiaries include:** Hill's Pet Nutrition, Inc. **Listed on:** New York Stock Exchange. **Stock exchange symbol:** CL. **Chairman/CEO:** Reuben Mark. **Annual sales/revenues:** $9.3 billion. **Number of employees:** 37,700.

COLIN SERVICE SYSTEMS, INC.
One Brockway Place, White Plains NY 10601. 914/328-0800. **Fax:** 914/328-3385. **Contact:** Judy Archer, Human Resources Director. **World Wide Web address:** http://www.colin.com. **Description:** A housekeeping and mechanical maintenance company providing administrative, safety, and training services for commercial clients covering 10 states from six regional offices specializing in cleaning services. **Positions advertised include:** Customer Service Representative; Environmental Engineer; Custodian; Housekeeper. **Corporate headquarters location:** This location. **President:** Richard Marteo. **Annual sales/revenues:** $100 million. **Number of employees:** 4,000.

COLLEGE OF SAINT ROSE
432 Western Avenue, Albany NY 12203-1419. 518/454-5111. **Contact:** Human Resources. **World Wide Web address:** http://www.strose.edu. **Description:** A four-year college with 4,500 students offering 41 undergraduate and 28 masters degrees as well as six graduate certificates. **Positions advertised include:** Alumni Relations Assistant Director: Building Maintenance Mechanic; Building Maintenance Worker; Custodian; Educational Technologist; Registered Nurse; Security Officer; Neighborhood Patrol Officer; Student Loans Collections Coordinator; Art History Lecturer; Biology Lecturer; Computer Information Systems Lecturer; Counseling Lecturer; Educational Psychology Lecturer; English Lecturer; History Lecturer; Literacy Lecturer; Marketing Lecturer; Mathematics Lecturer; Political Science Lecturer; School Psychology Lecturer; Social Work Lecturer; Teacher Education Lecturer.

COLUMBIA MEMORIAL HOSPITAL
71 Prospect Avenue, Hudson NY 12534. 518/828-7601. **Fax:** 518/828-8243. **Contact:** Human Resources. **World Wide Web address:** http://www.healthyconnect.net/cmh. **Description:** A nonprofit, community-based hospital operating nine satellite facilities serving central New York. **NOTE:** Entry-level positions and second and third shifts are offered. **Company slogan:** Making a Difference! **Positions advertised include:** Certified Nurses Aide; Computer Programmer; Dietician/Nutritionist; Licensed Practical Nurse; Medical Records Technician; Nurse Practitioner; Occupational Therapist; Pharmacist; Physical Therapist; Physician; Project Manager; Radiological Technologist; Registered Nurse; Respiratory Therapist. **Special programs:** Internships. **Number of employees:** 1,000.

COLUMBIA UNIVERSITY
2960 Broadway, New York NY 10027. 212/854-1754. **Contact:** Department of Human Resources. **World Wide Web address:** http://www.columbia.edu. **Description:** A private university comprised of 15 schools and 71 academic departments and divisions. The university is affiliated with Barnard College, Teachers College, and Union Theological Seminary. There are approximately 20,000 students enrolled at the university including 11,800 graduate and professional, 5,600 undergraduate, and 2,500 nondegree students. Founded in 1754. **NOTE:** Interested jobseekers are strongly encouraged to apply online via the company Website, but may send Scannable resumes to: Columbia University, P.O. Box 920, Burlington MA 01803. **Positions advertised include:** Facilities Porter; Computer Science Technology Director; Library Assistant; Financial Services Assistant; Earth Institute Associate Director; Facilities Handy Person; Real Estate Building Superintendent; Financial Assistant; Administrative Assistant; Law School Development Assistant; Earth Institute Research Analyst; Facilities Groundskeeper; HelpDesk Support Specialist; Law School Director; School of Business Associate Director; Allumni Relations Manager; Facilities Project Manager; Security Officer; Heavy Cleaner; First Cook; Bibliographic Assistant; Dining Retail Worker;

COMBE INC.
1101 Westchester Avenue, White Plains NY 10604. 914/694-5454. **Fax:** 914/694-1926. **Contact:** John Alberto, Employee Relations Manager. **World Wide Web address:** http://www.combe.com. **Description:** A manufacturer of over-the-counter personal care products including hair care and color products, feminine hygiene products, lotions, and creams. Brand names include Just for Men, Odor Eaters, and Sea Bond. Combe also manufactures some dog care and veterinary products. Founded in 1949. **Corporate headquarters location:** This location. **Other locations:** IL; PR. **Chairman/President/CEO:** Christopher (Chris) Combe. **Annual sales/revenues:** $250 million. **Number of employees:** 620.

COMEDY CENTRAL
1775 Broadway, 9th Floor, New York NY 10019. 212/767-8600. **Contact:** Human Resources. **World Wide Web address:** http://www.comedycentral.com. **Description:** Operator of the Comedy Central cable television network, which produces such shows as The Daily Show and South Park. **NOTE:** The company's stated policy is to not accept postal mail for any reason – apply online through the company Website. However, resumes for production positions will not be considered without reels/tapes. **Positions advertised include:** Writer; Producer; Sales Operations Analyst. **Special programs:** Internships. **Parent company:** Comedy Central is a joint venture between Viacom, Inc., and Time Warner Entertainment Company.

COMMAND SECURITY CORPORATION
Route 55, Lexington Park, P.O. Box 340, LaGrangeville NY 12540. 845/454-3703. **Fax:** 845/454-0075. **Contact:** Debra Miller, Office Manager. **E-mail address:** dmiller@commandsecurity.com. **World Wide Web address:** http://www.cscny.com. **Description:** CSC principally provides uniformed and nonuniformed security services

from its 16 operating offices to commercial, financial, industrial, aviation, and government clients. Security services include providing guards for access control, theft prevention, surveillance, vehicular and foot patrol, and crowd control. **Positions advertised include:** Security Guard. **Corporate headquarters location:** This location. **Other U.S. locations:** CA; CT; FL; IL; MA; NJ; PA. **Subsidiaries include:** COMGUARD. **Listed on:** Over The Counter. **Stock exchange symbol:** CMMD. **Chairman/President/CEO:** William C. Vassell. **Annual sales/revenues:** $84 million. **Number of employees nationwide:** 3,600.

COMMODORE APPLIED TECHNOLOGIES, INC.
150 East 58th Street, Suite 3238, New York NY 10155-0035. 212/308-5800. **Fax:** 212/753-0731. **Contact:** Human Resources. **World Wide Web address:** http://www.commodore.com. **Description:** Develops technologies to destroy PCBs, chemical weapons, dioxins, and pesticides. Commodore Applied Technologies also salvages and resells cross-contaminated CFCs, and acquires and cleans up environmentally distressed properties. **Corporate headquarters location:** Alexandria VA. **Subsidiaries include:** Commodore Advanced Sciences, Inc.; Commodore Separation Technologies, Inc.; Commodore Solution Technologies, Inc.; Teledyne-Commodore LLC. **Listed on:** Over The Counter. **Stock exchange symbol:** CXII. **Annual sales/revenues:** $10 million.

COMMUNITY BANK SYSTEM INC.
dba COMMUNITY BANK, N.A.
5790 Widewaters Parkway, DeWitt NY 13214-1883. 315/445-2282. **Fax:** 315/445-2997. **Contact:** Personnel Director. **World Wide Web address:** http://www.communitybankna.com. **Description:** Community Bank System operates a full-service banking network under its wholly-owned national banking subsidiary, Community Bank, N.A., which operates 120 branches in upstate New York and Pennsylvania. Another subsidiary, CBNA, provides individual, business, agricultural, and government customers with a complete range of banking services including qualified retirement plan administration, investment management, and personal trust services; retail and commercial loan and deposit products; and annuities and investment products. **Positions advertised include:** Trust Officer; Verification Representative; Paid-out Loan Representative; Financial Analyst; Branch Service Representative; Branch Sales And Service Representative. **Corporate headquarters location:** This location. **Other locations:** Throughout New York and Pennsylvania. **Listed on:** New York Stock Exchange. **Stock exchange symbol:** CBU. **Chairman:** James A Gabriel. **Annual sales/revenues:** $237.5 million. **Number of employees:** 1,115.

COMMUNITY COUNSELING SERVICES COMPANY
461 Fifth Avenue, New York NY 10117. 212/695-1175. **Fax:** 212/967-6451. **Contact:** Human Resources Department. **E-mail address:** careers@ccsfundraising.com. **World Wide Web address:** http://www.ccsfundraising.com. **Description:** A nationwide fundraising company that organizes campaigns for nonprofit clients. **Positions advertised include:** Capital Campaign Director.

COMMUNITY GENERAL HOSPITAL/GREATER SYRACUSE
4900 Broad Road, Syracuse NY 13215-4208. 315/492-5011. **Fax:** 315/492-5275. **Contact:** Sandy Juchem, Human Resources. **World Wide Web address:** http://www.cgh.org. **Description:** Community General Hospital is a 365- bed acute care hospital offering emergency services, medical and surgical care, intensive care, maternity services, inpatient psychiatric care, and testing and community health education service. The hospital operates a 50-bed skilled nursing unit and primary care medical office in Onondaga County. **Positions advertised include:** Security Officer; Telephone Operator; Registered Nurse; Nuclear Medicine Technologist; Licensed Practical Nurse.

COMMUNITY GENERAL HOSPITAL/SULLIVAN COUNTY
P.O. Box 800, Bushville Road, Harris NY 12742-0800. 845/794-3300. **Contact:** Human Resources. **Description:** A 300-bed hospital. Community General Hospital's services include oncology, treatment of biochemical dependence, mental health services, a diabetes unit, a cardiac care unit and a maternity ward. **Number of employees at this location:** 800.

COMMUNITY MEMORIAL HOSPITAL
150 Broad Street, Hamilton NY 13346. 315/824-1100. **Contact:** Human Resources. **World Wide Web address:** http://www.communitymemorial.org. **Description:** A regional hospital operating six Family Health Centers and a 120-bed community center and a 40-bed skilled nursing facility all serving the lower Hudson Valley region. **Positions advertised include:** Registered Nurse; Licensed Practical Nurse; Certified Nursing Assistant.

COMMUNITY SERVICE SOCIETY OF NEW YORK
105 East 22nd Street, New York NY 10010. 212/254-8900. **Fax:** 212/614-5336. **Contact:** Personnel Manager. **E-mail address:** cssemployment@cssny.org. **World Wide Web address:** http://www.cssny.org. **Description:** A nonprofit, social advocacy organization that conducts policy analysis and research, provides training and technical assistance to strengthen community-based organizations, and develops service programs that respond to the complex problems faced by the poor in New York City. **Positions advertised include:** Volunteer Program Coordinator; Training Manager; Program Manager; Program Specialist; Contract Coordinator; Experience Corps Program Coordinator.

COMPUTER ASSOCIATES INTERNATIONAL, INC.
One Computer Associates Plaza, Islandia NY 11749. 631/342-5224. **Fax:** 631/342-5329. **Contact:** Global Recruiting Department. **E-mail address:** joinca@ca.com. **World Wide Web address:** http://www.ca.com. **Description:** A developer of client/server and computer software, the company develops, markets, and supports enterprise management, database and applications development, business applications, and consumer software products for a broad range of mainframe, midrange, and desktop computers. Computer Associates International serves major business, government, research, and educational organizations. Founded in 1976. **Positions advertised include:** Account Manager; Accountant; Assistant Teacher; Business Development Owner; Business Manager; Channel Marketing Manager; Channel Program Manager; Collections Representative; Contract Representative; Database Manager; Product Management Director; Sales Accountant; Finance Manager; Procurement Coordinator; Unicenter Product Manager; Project Manager; Proposal Specialist; Quality Assurance Engineer; Regional Legal Manager; Sales Specialist; Software Engineer. **Special programs:** Internships. **Corporate headquarters location:** This location. **Other U.S. locations:** Nationwide. **Subsidiaries include:** ACCPAC International, Inc. **Operations at this facility include:** Administration; Research and Development; Sales. **Listed on:** New York Stock Exchange. **Stock exchange symbol:** CA. **Chairman/President/CEO:** Sanjay Kumar. **Annual sales/revenues:** $3 billion. **Number of employees at this location:** 2,500. **Number of employees worldwide:** 16,600.

COMPUTER HORIZONS CORPORATION
747 Third Avenue, 15th Floor, New York NY 10017. 212/371-9600. **Toll-free phone:** 800/321-2421. **Fax:** 973/402-7986. **Contact:** Recruiting. **E-mail address:** info@computerhorizons.com. **World Wide Web address:** http://www.computerhorizons.com. **Description:** A full-service technology solutions company offering contract staffing, outsourcing, re-engineering, migration, downsizing support, and network management. The company has a worldwide network of 33 offices. Founded in 1969. **Positions advertised include:** Systems Analyst. **Corporate headquarters location:** Mountain Lakes NJ. **Other U.S. locations:** Nationwide. **Subsidiaries include:** Birla Horizons International Ltd.; Horizons Consulting, Inc.; Strategic Outsourcing Services, Inc.; Unified Systems Solutions, Inc. **Listed on:** NASDAQ. **Stock exchange symbol:** CHRZ. **Annual sales/revenues:** $279 million. **Number of employees nationwide:** 1,400. **Number of employees worldwide:** 2,800

COMTECH TELECOMMUNICATIONS CORPORATION
105 Baylis Road, Melville NY 11747-3833. 631/777-8900. **Fax:** 631/777-8877. **Contact:** Human Resources. **E-mail address:** jobs@comtechpst.com. **World Wide Web address:** http://www.comtechtel.com. **Description:** Manufactures and markets high-tech microwave and telecommunications products and systems including antennas, frequency converters, and VSAT transceivers and modems. Products are used worldwide in satellite, tropospheric scatter, and wireless communications systems. The company also manufactures high-power amplifiers that are used to test electronic systems for electromagnetic compatibility and susceptibility; for defense systems; and for high power testing of electronic components and systems. Comtech, through its subsidiaries, offers products to customers including domestic and foreign common carriers and telephone companies, defense contractors, medical and automotive suppliers, oil companies, private and wireless networks, broadcasters, utilities, and government entities. **Corporate headquarters location:** This location. **Subsidiaries include:** Comtech Antenna Systems; Comtech EF Data; Comtech Mobile Datacom; Comtech PST; Comtech Systems. **Operations at this facility include:** Comtech PST Corporation; Corporate Administration. **Listed on:** NASDAQ. **Stock exchange symbol:** CMTL. **Chairman/President/CEO:** Fred V. Kornberg. **Annual sales/revenues:** $119 million. **Number of employees:** 626.

COMVERSE TECHNOLOGY INC.
170 Crossways Park Drive, Woodbury NY 11797-2048. 516/677-7200. **Fax:** 516/677-7355. **Contact:** Human Resources. **E-mail address:** resumes@comverse.com. **World Wide Web address:** http://www.cmvt.com. **Description:** Manufactures, markets, and supports specialized telecommunications systems for multimedia communications and information processing applications. The company's systems are used in a broad range of applications by fixed and wireless telephone network operators, government agencies, financial institutions, and other public and commercial organizations worldwide. Products include AUDIODISK, which is a multimedia digital monitoring system; and the ULTRA series, which is a variety of multimedia recording systems. **Corporate headquarters location:** This location. **Other U.S. locations:** Nationwide. **International locations:** Worldwide. **Subsidiaries include:** Comverse Network Systems; Comverse Infosys; Ulticom, Inc.; Starhome; Verint Systems Inc.; and Startel. **Listed on:** NASDAQ. **Stock exchange symbol:** CMVT. **Chairman:** Kobi Alexander. **Annual sales/revenues:** $736 million. **Number of employees:** 5,650.

CONCORD FABRICS INC.
462 Seventh Avenue, New York NY 10018. 212/760-0300. **Fax:** 212/563-3746. **Contact:** Human Resources Manager. **World Wide Web address:** http://www.concordfabrics.com. **Description:** Designs, develops, and manufactures woven and knitted fabrics for sale to manufacturers and retailers. Concord Fabrics is one of the nation's largest independent textile converters. **Positions advertised include:** Designer. **Special programs:** Internships. **Corporate headquarters location:** This location. **Subsidiaries include:** Andover Fabrics; Mackower UK. **Chairman:** Alvin Weinstein. **Annual sales/revenues:** $50 million. **Number of employees:** 100.

CONDE NAST PUBLICATIONS INC.
4 Times Square, New York NY 10036. 212/286-2860. **Fax:** 212/286-5960. **Contact:** Human Resources Department. **World Wide Web address:** http://www.condenast.com. **Description:** Publishes a broad range of nationally distributed award-winning lifestyle-oriented magazines covering food, travel, fashion, and more which include: *Mademoiselle, Glamour, House & Garden, Vogue, Self, Gentleman's Quarterly, Allure, Wired, Modern Bride, The New Yorker, Vanity Fair,* and *Lucky Magazine.* **Subsidiaries include:** Ideas Publishing Group, Inc.; Epicurious; Concierge; Swoon. **Parent company:** Advance Publications (Staten Island NY).

CONIFER PARK
79 Glenridge Road, Glenville NY 12302. 518/399-6446. **Toll-free phone:** 800/989-6446. **Fax:** 518/399-6842. **Contact:** Jenna Bongermino, Human Resources Manager. **E-mail address:** resumes@libertymgt.com. **World Wide Web address:** http://www.libertymgt.com. **Description:** An inpatient and outpatient alcohol and drug abuse rehabilitation center. **NOTE:** Resumes should be sent to: Liberty Management Corporation, Corporate Human Resources Department, 70 Glenridge Road, Glenville NY 12302; or fax: 518/384-1394. **Positions advertised include:** Accounts Payable Clerk. **Parent company:** Liberty Management Group, Inc. (Ramsey NJ). **Number of employees at this location:** 400.

CONMED CORPORATION
525 French Road, Utica NY 13502. 315/797-8375. **Fax:** 315/735-1523. **Contact:** Human Resources. **E-mail address:** info@conmed.com. **World Wide Web address:** http://www.conmed.com. **Description:** Develops, manufactures, and markets advanced electrosurgical and single-use medical products for surgeons and other critical care providers located throughout the world. The company offers complete electrosurgical systems that include generators and disposable electrosurgical pencils, instruments, and ground pads. Patient care products include disposable electrocardiogram electrodes to monitor the heart, a disposable stabilization device for intravenous therapy, electrodes for neuromuscular stimulation, and various cable and wire products used in medical telemetry. **Positions advertised include:** Machine Operator; Mechanical Engineer; Quality Engineer; Process Technician. **Corporate headquarters location:** This location. **Other area locations:** Rome NY; Utica NY. **Other locations:** CA; CO; FL; TX. **Operations at this facility include:** Administration; Manufacturing; Research and Development. **Listed on:** NASDAQ. **Stock exchange symbol:** CNMD. **Chairman/CEO:** Eugene R. Corasanti. **Annual sales/revenues:** $453 million. **Number of employees at this location:** 200. **Number of employees nationwide:** 2,560.

CONSOLIDATED EDISON, INC.
4 Irving Place, Room 2215, New York NY 10003-3598. 212/460-4600. **Fax:** 212/228-9439. **Contact:** Human Resources Director. **E-mail address:** opportunities@coned.com. **World Wide Web address:** http://www.conedison.com. **Description:** Through its subsidiaries, Consolidated Edison supplies electricity to New York City and most of Westchester County; supplies gas to Manhattan, the Bronx, and parts of Queens and Westchester; and serves over 400,000 electric and gas customers in

the tri-state area. The company is also engaged in energy marketing, fiber-optic telecommunications, and merchant power plant development. **Positions advertised include:** Associate Engineer; Engineer; Environmental Engineer; Instrument Controls Specialist; Junior Designer; Project Specialist; Section Manager; Senior Engineer; Technical Analyst; Production Technician; Asbestos Administrator; Safety Specialist; Scientist; Senior Scientist; Senior Environmental Engineer; Senior Specialist; Human Resource Generalist; Supervisor; Bi-Lingual Korean Customer Service Representative; Electrical Mechanic; Welder Mechanic; Operating Mechanic. **Subsidiaries include:** Consolidated Edison Communications; Consolidated Edison Company of New York; Consolidated Edison Development; Consolidated Edison Energy; Consolidated Edison Solutions; Orange and Rockland Utilities. **Corporate headquarters location:** This location. **Listed on:** New York Stock Exchange. **Stock exchange symbol:** ED. **Chairman/President/CEO:** Eugene R. McGrath. **Annual sales/revenues:** $8.5 billion. **Number of employees:** 14,300.

CONSTELLATION BRANDS, INC.
300 Willowbrook Office Park, Fairport NY 14450. 585/218-2169. **Contact:** Human Resources. **E-mail address:** hr@cbrands.com. **World Wide Web address:** http://www.cbrands.com. **Description:** A leading producer and distributor of wine, beer, spirits, cider, and bottled water. The company services 17,000 customers worldwide. **NOTE:** Jobseekers can find a current listing of job openings at http://www.monster.com. **Corporate headquarters location:** This location. **Other locations:** Canandaigua NY; St. Helena CA; Chicago IL; Bristol, England. **Listed on:** New York Stock Exchange. **Stock exchange symbol:** STZ. **President/CEO:** Richard Sands. **Annual sales/revenues:** $3.6billion. **umber of employees:** 5,000.

CONTEC CORPORATION
1023 State Street, Schenectady NY 12307-1511. 518/382-8000. **Fax:** 518/382-8141. **Contact:** Human Resources. **Description:** Performs converter box repairs for cable customers. Founded in 1978. **NOTE:** Each department hires separately; call first to obtain contact names. **Corporate headquarters location:** This location. **Other locations:** AZ; FL; IN; WA.

COOPER CROUSE-HINDS
P.O. Box 4999, Syracuse NY 13221-4999. 315/477-5531. **Fax:** 315/477-5279. **Contact:** Brian Rayl, Vice President of Human Resources. **E-mail address:** recruit@cooperindustries.com. **World Wide Web address:** http://www.cooperindustries.com. **Description:** A manufacturer of various electrical components such as explosion-proof receptacles, industrial lighting, and conduits operating 21 facilities worldwide. **Positions advertised include:** Product Line Manager. **Corporate headquarters location:** This location. **Parent company:** Cooper Industries (Houston TX). **Number of employees at this location:** 1,000. **Number of employees worldwide:** 4,000.

COOPER POWER SYSTEMS
1648 Dugan Road, P.O. Box 388, Olean NY 14760-0388. 716/375-7100. **Contact:** Personnel Department. **E-mail address:** recruit@cooperpower.com. **World Wide Web address:** http://www.cooperpower.com. **Description:** Manufacturer of electrical equipment, components, and systems for distributing and managing electrical energy by utility companies in residential and commercial applications. **Corporate headquarters location:** Waukesha WI. **Other locations:** Nationwide. **Parent company:** Cooper Industries (Houston TX). **Operations at this facility include:** Components & Protective Equipment manufacturing arresters and fuses.

COOPER TOOLS
45 Cleveland Street, Cortland NY 13045. 607/756-2821. **Contact:** Human Resources. **E-mail address:** cortland.recruit@coopertools.com. **Wide Web address:** http://www.coopertools.com. **Description:** Manufactures and forges miscellaneous tools including wire rope clips and other similar small industrial items. **Corporate headquarters location:** Raleigh NC. **Parent company:** Cooper Industries (Houston TX).

COOPER TURBO COMPRESSOR, INC.
3101 Broadway, Buffalo NY 14225-0209. 716/896-6600. **Fax:** 716/896-1233. **Contact:** Human Resources. **World Wide Web address:** http://www.turbocompressor.com. **Description:** A worldwide manufacturer and distributor of turbo compressors. **Corporate headquarters location:** This location. **Other locations:** Worldwide. **Parent company:** Cooper Cameron Corporation (Houston TX). **Number of employees at this location:** 485.

COOPER WIRING DEVICES
45-31 Court Square, Long Island City NY 11101. 718/937-8000. **Contact:** Human Resources. **E-mail address:** jobs@cooperwiringdevices.com. **World Wide Web address:** http://www.cooperwiringdevices.com. **Description:** Manufactures electrical wiring devices. **Positions advertised include:** Customer Service Supervisor. **Corporate headquarters location:** This location. **Parent company:** Cooper Industries (Houston TX).

COPYTELE, INC.
900 Walt Whitman Road, Suite 203C, Melville NY 11747. 631/549-5900. **Fax:** 631/549-5974. **Contact:** Anne Rotondo, Corporate Secretary. **World Wide Web address:** http://www.copytele.com. **Description:** Designs, develops, and markets encryption products, multifunctional telecommunications products, high-resolution flat panel displays, and specialty printers. **Listed on:** Over The Counter. **Stock exchange symbol:** COPY. **Chairman/CEO:** Denis A. Krusos. **Annual sales/revenues:** $5 million. **Number of employees:** 48.

CORNELL UNIVERSITY
337 Pine Tree Road, Ithaca NY 14850. 607/254-8370. **Fax:** 607/255-4943. **Contact:** Recruitment and Employment Center. **E-mail address:** employment_svcs@cornell.edu. **World Wide Web address:** http://www.cornell.edu. **Description:** An Ivy-league university offering both undergraduate and graduate degree programs through 13 colleges and schools. The university enrolls approximately 13,600 undergraduates and over 5,000 graduate students. Founded in 1865. **Positions advertised include:** Earth & Atmospheric Sciences Assistant Professor; Associate Population Medicine & Diagnostic Sciences Professor; Research Aide; Technical Services Supervisor; Administrative Assistant; Administrative Manager; Director of Rooms/Operations; Botannical Collections Photographer; Financial Research Director; Finance Manager; Grant & Contract Administrator; Diesel Mechanic; Transit Service Worker; Maintenance Mechanic; Records Coordinator; Web Master; Student Services Associate Director; Human Ecology Registrar; Accelerator Operator; Physics Particle Systems Operator. **Number of employees:** 9,200.

CORNING INC.
One Riverfront Plaza, Corning NY 14831. 607/974-9000. **Fax:** 607/974-5927. **Contact:** Manager of Recruiting. **World Wide Web address:** http://www.corning.com. **Description:** A diverse manufacturer of specialty glass and glass ceramic products in specialty materials, environmental products, and fiber-optic cable. Brand names include Corning and Pyrex kitchenware. The company produces over 60,000 products through 45 plants in 8 countries. Corning also offers medical laboratory services through 62 facilities in 10 countries. **Positions advertised include:** Administrative Assistant; Equipment Engineer; Molecular Biology Technician; Quality Systems Engineer; Senior Research Scientist; Team Leader. **Special programs:** Internships. **Corporate headquarters location:** This location. **Other U.S. locations:** Nationwide. **International locations:** Worldwide. **Subsidiaries include:** Dow Corning Corporation; Teleco Cavi S.p.A. **Operations at this facility include:** Corporate Administration; Technical Services; Sullivan Park Research Center. **Listed on:** New York Stock Exchange. **Stock exchange symbol:** GLW. **Chairman/CEO:** James R. Houghton. **Number of employees nationwide:** 16,000. **Number of employees worldwide:** 23,200.

CORNING INC.
334 County Route 16, Canton NY 13617. 315/379-3200. **Fax:** 315/379-3211. **Contact:** Manager of Recruiting. **World Wide Web address:** http://www.corning.com. **Description:** Manufactures specialty glass and glass ceramic products in specialty materials, consumer products, and fiber-optic cable. Brand names include Corning and Pyrex kitchenware. The company produces over 60,000 products through 45 plants in 8 countries. Corning also offers medical laboratory services through 62 facilities in 10 countries. **NOTE:** Interested jobseekers should send resumes to: Corning Inc., One Riverfront Plaza, Corning NY 14831. **Corporate headquarters location:** Corning NY. **Operations at this facility include:** Canton Plant Manufacturing. **Listed on:** New York Stock Exchange. **Stock exchange symbol:** GLW.

CORNING NATURAL GAS CORPORATION
330 West William Street, P.O. Box 58, Corning NY 14830-0058. 607/936-3755. **Contact:** Human Resources. **World Wide Web address:** http://www.corninggas.com. **Description:** A natural gas utility serving the southern tier of central New York state.

CORTLAND MEMORIAL HOSPITAL
134 Homer Avenue, P.O. Box 2010, Cortland NY 13045. 607/756-3780. **Fax:** 607/756-3375. **Contact:** Human Resources Department. **E-mail address:** hr@cortlandhospital.org. **World Wide Web address:** http://www.cortlandhospital.org. **Description:** A 180-bed, community-based, nonprofit, acute care hospital. Cortland Memorial Hospital's residential geriatric care facility has 80 beds, offering such services as long-term home health care and a psychiatric unit. Founded in 1891. **NOTE:** Entry-level positions and second and third shifts are offered. **Positions advertised include:** Nuclear Medical Technologist; Registered Nurse; Physical Therapist; Registered Dietician; Medical Technologist. **Subsidiaries include:** CMH Services.

COUCH WHITE, LLP
540 Broadway, P.O. Box 22222, Albany NY 12201-2222. 518/426-4600. **Fax:** 518/426-0376. **Contact:** Linda M. Haskell, Hiring Manager. **E-mail address:** lhaskell@couchwhite.com. **World Wide Web address:** http://www.couchwhite.com. **Description:** A law firm specializing in the areas of electricity and natural gas, health care, public utility regulation, and real estate. **Corporate headquarters location:** This location. **Other locations:** Washington DC.

COUDERT BROTHERS LLP
1114 Avenue of the Americas, New York NY 10036-7794. 212/626-4400. **Fax:** 212/626-4120. **Contact:** Mary Simpson, Director of Legal Personnel. **E-mail address:** simpsonm@coudert.com. **World Wide Web address:** http://www.coudert.com. **Description:** A law firm with 650 lawyers at 30 offices in 18 countries specializing in international business transactions and dispute resolution. **Corporate headquarters location:** This location. **International locations:** Worldwide.

COURTROOM TELEVISION NETWORK LLC
600 Third Avenue, 2nd Floor, New York NY 10016. 212/973-2800. **Fax:** 240/337-8569. **Contact:** Human Resources. **World Wide Web address:** http://www.courttv.com. **Description:** Court TV is a cable television network providing coverage of publicized legal battles and couret proceedings. **Positions advertised include:** Copy Editor; Administrative Assistant; Junior Web Designer; Senior Staff Writer; Production Assistant; Executive Director. **Corporate headquarters location:** This location. **Parent company:** Turner Broadcasting System, Inc. (Atlanta GA).

COURTESY BUS COMPANY
107 Lawson Boulevard, Oceanside NY 11572. 516/766-6740. **Fax:** 516/678-0253. **Contact:** Personnel Office. **Description:** Provides bus service to local school districts, as well as a range of charter services through several area locations. **Positions advertised include:** Automotive Mechanic; Driver.

COURTYARD BY MARRIOTT
475 White Plains Road, Tarrytown NY 10591. 914/631-1122. **Contact:** General Manager. **World Wide Web address:** http://www.courtyard.com. **Description:** A hotel with 139 guest rooms and two meeting rooms. **Positions advertised include:** Senior Account Executive. **Parent company:** Marriott International, Inc. (Washington DC).

COX & COMPANY, INC.
200 Varick Street, New York NY 10014. 212/366-0265 ext. 509. **Fax:** 212/366-0284. **Contact:** Human Resources. **E-mail address:** hrresources@coxandco.com. **World Wide Web address:** http://www.coxandco.com. **Description:** Manufactures heating and cooling temperature control systems. **NOTE:** Human Resources telephone extension: x509. **Positions advertised include:** Electrical Engineer; Manufacturing Engineer; Composite Manufacturing Engineer; Production Control Planner.

CRAVATH, SWAINE & MOORE
825 Eighth Avenue, New York NY 10019-7475. 212/474-1000. **Fax:** 212/474-3095. **Contact:** Employment Manager. **World Wide Web address:** http://www.cravath.com. **Description:** A corporate law firm specializing in litigation, trusts and estates, and taxation. **Positions advertised include:** Attorney; Legal Assistant; Legal Secretary. **Corporate headquarters location:** This location. **Other locations:** London, United Kingdom. **Number of employees at this location:** 1,200.

CRAWFORD FURNITURE MANUFACTURING CORPORATION
P.O. Box 668, Jamestown NY 14702-0668. 716/661-9100. **Physical address:** 1021 Allen Street, Jamestown NY 14701. **Contact:** Joe Scoma, Human Resources Manager. **Description:** A furniture manufacturing company. **Number of employees at this location:** 300.

CREDIT SUISSE FIRST BOSTON CORPORATION
11 Madison Avenue, New York NY 10010-3629. 212/325-2000. **Fax:** 212/325-6665. **Contact:** Recruiting. **World Wide Web address:** http://www.csfb.com. **Description:**

A diversified financial services firm serving as underwriters, distributors, and investment dealers. **NOTE:** Apply online. **Corporate headquarters location:** This location. **International locations:** Switzerland; United Kingdom. **Parent company:** Credit Suisse Group (Zurich, Switzerland). **Subsidiaries include:** Credit Suisse First Boston (USA), Inc.; Imagyn Medical Technologies, Inc.; Sprout Group. **CEO:** John J. Mack. **Annual sales/revenues:** $13.7 billion. **Number of employees:** 28,415.

CRESCENT TELEPHONE COMPANY
6 Nevada Drive, Building C, Lake Success NY 11042. 516/326-0517. **Fax:** 516/437-0807. **Contact:** Human Resources Department. **Description:** Provides telecommunication services for operator-assisted and long-distance telephone calls.

CREST OFFICE PRODUCTS
448 West 16th Street, 5th Floor, New York NY 10011. 212/271-2065. **Contact:** Human Resources. **Description:** Provides commercial printing services and offset lithography.

CROSCILL, INC.
dba CROSCILL HOME FASHIONS
261 Fifth Avenue, 25th Floor, New York NY 10016. 212/689-7222. **Fax:** 252/431-0470. **Contact:** Human Resources. **E-mail address:** jobapps@croscill.com. **World Wide Web address:** http://www.croscill.com. **Description:** Manufactures curtains, draperies, and other textile products at five manufacturing plants in North Carolina. Founded in 1945. **NOTE:** Resumes should be sent to: P.O. Box 930, Durham NC 27702. **subsidiaries include:** Royal Home Fashions. **Annual sales/revenues:** $309 million. **Number of employees:** 1,500.

CROWNE PLAZA
66 Hale Avenue, White Plains NY 10601. 914/682-0050. **Toll-free phone:** 800/752-4672. **Fax:** 914/682-0405. **Contact:** Human Resources. **World Wide Web address:** http://www.crowneplaza.com. **Description:** A 401-room hotel with 13 meeting rooms. **Parent company:** Six Continents PLC (London, United Kingdom).

CRUCIBLE MATERIALS
5639 West Genesee Street, Camillus NY 13031-0991. 315/487-0800. **Toll-free phone:** 800/365-1185. **Fax:** 315/487-4028. **Contact:** Sue Walsh, Director of Human Resources. **E-mail address:** swalsh@crucibleservice.com. **World Wide Web address:** http://www.crucibleservice.com. **Description:** A specialty service steel distributor with 24 service centers throughout the United States and Canada. Founded in 1989. **Positions advertised include:** Sales Representative. **Corporate headquarters location:** This location.

CUMMINS ENGINE COMPANY, INC.
4720 Baker Street Extension, Lakewood NY 14750. 716/456-2111. **Fax:** 716/456-2541. **Contact:** Human Resources. **World Wide Web address:** http://www.cummins.com. **Description:** Manufacturer of diesel engines that are placed in heavy-duty trucking units. Cummins Engine also manufactures generators. **NOTE:** Jobseekers must apply online, paper resumes and faxes are not accepted. **Parent company:** Cummins Inc. (Columbus IN).

CURATIVE HEALTH SERVICES, INC.
150 Motor Parkway, 4th Floor, Hauppauge NY 11788. 631/232-7000. **Fax:** 631/232-9322. **Contact:** Michelle, LeDell, Director of Human Resources. **World Wide Web address:** http://www.curative.com. **Description:** Curative Health Services primarily manages, on behalf of hospital clients, a nationwide network of wound-care centers. Most of the wound-care centers managed by Curative Health Services are outpatient, although, a small portion are inpatient. The company is also engaged in the research and development of therapeutic products for wound-healing applications. **NOTE:** Jobseekers can see http://www.monster.com for a current the job listing. **Corporate headquarters location:** This location. **Other U.S. locations:** Nationwide. **Listed on:** NASDAQ. **Stock exchange symbol:** CURE. **Chairman:** Joseph L. Feshbach. **Annual sales/revenues:** $139 million. **Number of employees:** 340.

CUSHMAN & WAKEFIELD, INC.
51 West 52nd Street, 8th Floor, New York NY 10019-6178. 212/841-7500. **Fax:** 212/841-5039. **Contact:** Human Resources. **E-mail address:** recruiting@cushwake.com. **World Wide Web address:** http://www.http://www.cushmanwakefield.com. **Description:** An international commercial and industrial real estate services firm with 44 offices in 20 states. The company is engaged in appraisals, financial services, project development, research services, and the management and leasing of commercial office space, as well as providing assessment services, corporate services, brokerage services, financial and general administration, research, sales, and valuation advisory services. **Positions advertised include:** Asset Services Administrator; Executive Assistant; Marketing Coordinator; Accounting Supervisor; Payroll Coordinator; Purchasing Assistant; Broker Compensation Supervisor; New York Area Operations Manager; Administrative Assistant; Hospitality Valuation Professional. **Office hours:** Monday - Friday, 8:30 a.m. - 5:30 p.m. **Corporate headquarters location:** This location. **Other U.S. locations:** Los Angeles CA; San Francisco CA; Chicago IL. **International locations:** Worldwide. **Parent company:** The Rockefeller Group Inc. **Chairman:** John C. Cushman. **Annual sales/revenues:** $870 million. **Number of employees at this location:** 500. **Number of employees nationwide:** 11,000.

CYBER DIGITAL, INC.
400 Oser Avenue, Suite 1650, Hauppauge NY 11788-3641. 631/231-1200. **Fax:** 631/231-1446. **Contact:** Personnel. **E-mail address:** cybd@cyberdigitalinc.com. **World Wide Web address:** http://www.cyberdigitalinc.com. **Description:** Cyber Digital designs, develops, manufactures, and markets digital switching and networking systems that enable simultaneous communication of voice and data to a large number of users. The company's systems are based on its proprietary software technology that permits the modem-less transmission of data between a variety of incompatible and dissimilar end user equipment including computers, printers, workstations, and data terminals over standard telephone lines. **Corporate headquarters location:** This location. **Listed on:** Over The Counter. **Stock exchange symbol:** CYBD.

CYBERCHRON CORPORATION
P.O. Box 160, 2700 Route 9, Cold Spring NY 10516. 845/265-3700 ext. 243. **Fax:** 845/265-2909. **Contact:** Ms. Gerry Maroulis, Human Resources. **E-mail address:** gmaroulis@cyberchron.com. **World Wide Web address:** http://www.cyberchron.com. **Description:** Cyberchron manufactures computers that are made to withstand environmental extremes. The U.S. military is one user of Cyberchron's products as well as foreign defense departments. **NOTE:** Human Resources telephone extension: x243. **Positions advertised include:** Regional Sales Representative.

CYBERDATA, INC.
20 Max Avenue, Hicksville NY 11801. 516/942-8000. **Fax:** 516/942-0800. **Contact:** Job Opportunities Department. **E-mail address:** jobs@cyberdata.com. **World Wide Web address:** http://www.cyberdata.com. **Description:** Provides an array of information-based services for client companies including information management, storage, and dissemination. CyberData, Inc. offers a mass fax service through a large number of modems. **Positions advertised include:** Computer Programmer; Sales Representative.

CYGNE DESIGNS INC.
1410 Broadway, Suite 1002, New York NY 10018. 212/997-7767. **Fax:** 212/245-7724. **Contact:** Office Manager. **Description:** Cygne Designs is a private-label designer, merchandiser, and manufacturer of women's apparel, serving retailers including Ann Taylor, The Limited Stores, Express, Lane Bryant, Victoria's Secret Stores, Lerner, and Casual Corner. The company's products include a broad range of woven and knit career, casual, and intimate women's apparel. **Listed on:** Over The Counter. **Stock exchange symbol:** CYDS. **Chairman/CEO:** Bernard M. Manuel. **Annual sales/revenues:** $41 million. **Number of employees:** 1,441.

DDB WORLDWIDE COMMUNICATIONS GROUP, INC.
437 Madison Avenue, New York NY 10022. 212/415-2000. **Fax:** 212/415-3414. **Contact:** James Best, Chief People Officer. **World Wide Web address:** http://www.ddb.com. **Description:** A full-service, international advertising agency operating 200 offices in 100 countries. **Positions advertised include:** Advertising Executive; Media Specialist. **Special programs:** Internships. **Corporate headquarters location:** This location. **Other U.S. locations:** Los Angeles CA; Chicago IL. **Parent company:** Omnicom Group, Inc. (also at this location). **Chairman:** Keith L. Reinhard. **Annual sales/revenues:** $1.2 billion. **Number of employees:** 11,900.

DHB INDUSTRIES, INC.
400 Post Avenue, Suite 303, Westbury NY 11590. 516/997-1155 **Fax:** 516/997-1144. **Contact:** Human Resources. **World Wide Web address:** http://www.dhbt.com. **Description:** DHB Industries is a diversified holding company operating in two divisions: DHB Armor Group and DHB Sports Group. Through its subsidiaries, the Armor Group develops, manufactures, and distributes technically advanced bullet resistant garments, bullet-proof vests, bomb projectile blankets, and body armor from materials such as Kevlar and other related ballistic accessories for the military and law enforcement. The Sports Group manufactures and distributes protective athletic apparel and equipment including pads and braces as well as other therapy products. **Subsidiaries include:** Protective Apparel Corporation of America manufactures and distributes bullet-, bomb-, and projectile-resistant garments; NDL Products manufactures and distributes protective sports apparel and fitness products and related items; Intelligent Data Corporation develops sophisticated telecommunications systems for remote document signature and authentication; Zydacron designs and manufactures video teleconferencing codecs; Darwin Molecular Corporation develops novel drugs to treat cancer and AIDS; Point Blank Body Armor; Point Blank International; Dr. Bone Savers. **Corporate headquarters location:** This location. **Listed on:** American Stock Exchange. **Stock exchange symbol:** DHB. **Chairman/CEO:** David H. Brooks. **Annual sales/revenues:** $130 million. **Number of employees:** 500.

DSA COMMUNITY PUBLISHING
250 Miller Place, Hicksville NY 11801. 516/393-9300. **Contact:** Human Resources. **World Wide Web address:** http://www.dsapub.com. **Description:** A regional publisher involved in the publishing, printing, and distribution of weekly free-circulation newspapers, as well as circulars and other promotional and printed material. DSA's publications include *The Pennysaver*, *Shoppers Guide*, *Yankee Trader*, *Marketeer*, *Pocket Mailer*, and *Value Mailer*. **Operations at this facility include:** Administration; Manufacturing; Sales; Service.

DVL INC.
70 East 55th Street, 7th Floor, New York NY 10022. 212/350-9900. **Fax:** 212/350-9911. **Contact:** Human Resources. **Description:** Acquires and develops retirement and resort properties; purchases, collects, and services installment sales contacts originated by national tool companies for automobile mechanics' tools; and manages and services existing real estate properties. **Listed on:** Over The Counter. **Stock exchange symbol:** DVLN. **Chairman:** Frederick E. Smithline. **Annual sales/revenues:** $9.1 million. **Number of employees:** 11.

DAEMEN COLLEGE
4380 Main Street, Amherst NY 14226-3592. 716/839-3600. **Fax:** 716/839-8362. **Contact:** Pamela R. Neumann, Personnel Director. **E-mail address:** pneumann@daemen.edu or personnel@deamen.edu. **World Wide Web address:** http://www.daemen.edu. **Description:** A four-year, private college primarily offering undergraduate courses. As a liberal arts school, Daemen College offers majors including education, nursing, psychology, business and commerce, physical therapy, and physician's assistant. Graduate programs are offered in physical therapy and nursing. Founded in 1947. **NOTE:** Part-time positions offered. Human Resources phone: 716/839-8325. **Positions advertised include:** Assistant Biology Professor; Assistant English Professor; Assistant Spanish Professor; Assistant History Professor; Assistant Theatre Professor; Assistant Graphic Design Professor; Housekeeper; Dean of Student Affairs; Master's Initial Certification Program Director; West Side Community Partnership – Community Coordinator; Community Relations Coordinator.

D'AGOSTINO SUPERMARKETS, INC.
1385 Boston Post Road, Larchmont NY 10538-3904. 914/833-4000. **Contact:** Human Resources. **World Wide Web address:** http://www.dagnyc.com. **Description:** A supermarket chain offering a full line of grocery, produce, and meats. The company operates more than 23 stores serving Westchester County, and New York City. Founded in 1932. **NOTE:** Employment inquiries should be directed to: Frank Tucciarone, Director of Associate Development, 257 West 17th Street, New York NY 10011; phone: 917/606-0280; fax: 917/606-0367; email: ftucciarone@dagnyc.com. **Positions advertised include:** Cashier; Department Manager; Management Trainee; Retail Sales Worker. **Special programs:** Internships. **Corporate headquarters location:** This location. **Chairman/President/CEO:** Nicholas (Nick) D'Agostino Jr. **Annual sales/revenues:** $175 million. **Number of employees at this location:** 50. **Number of employees statewide:** 1,150.

DAL-TILE INTERNATIONAL INC.
103 South Clark Street, Olean NY 14760. 716/372-4300. **Contact:** Tom Blair, Human Resources. **World Wide Web address:** http://www.daltile.com. **Description:** Manufactures, distributes, and markets high-quality ceramic and mosaic tile products for commercial and residential use operating nine manufacturing facilities in the U.S. and Mexico. Since 1947. **Corporate headquarters location:** Dallas TX. **Other locations:** Nationwide. **Parent company:** Mohawk Industries. **Operations at this facility include:** Manufacturing of unglazed ceramic mosaic tiles. **Annual sales/revenues:** $900 million. **Number of employees:** 7,900.

DAN RIVER INC.
1325 Avenue of the Americas, New York NY 10019. 212/554-5555. **Contact:** Human Resources. **World Wide Web address:** http://www.danriver.com. **Description:**

Manufactures and markets textile products for the home fashions and apparel fabrics markets including a coordinated line of home fashions consisting of packaged bedroom furnishings such as comforters, sheets, pillowcases, shams, bedskirts, decorative pillows, and draperies. The company also manufactures a broad range of woven and knit cotton and cotton-blend apparel fabrics, and is a domestic supplier of men's dress shirt fabrics, primarily oxford and pinpoint oxford cloth. **NOTE:** Resumes should be sent to the company's headquarters: LuAnn Long, Manager of Recruiting, Dan River Inc., P.O. Box 261, Danville VA 24543; phone: 434/799-7044; email: luanne.long@danriver.com. **Positions advertised include:** Administrative Manager; Clerical Supervisor; Customer Service Representative; Merchandiser; Product Manager; Sales Manager. **Corporate headquarters location:** Danville VA. **Other U.S. locations:** Nationwide. **Subsidiaries include:** Dan River Factory Stores, Inc. operates 12 factory outlet stores in the Midwest and the Southeast. **Operations at this facility include:** Sales and Marketing headquarters. **Listed on:** New York Stock Exchange. **Stock exchange symbol:** DRF. **Annual sales/revenues:** $613 million. **Number of employees at this location:** 90. **Number of employees nationwide:** 7,000.

DANSKIN, INC.
530 Seventh Avenue, Floor M1, New York NY 10018. 212/764-4630. **Fax:** 212/764-7265. **Contact:** Human Resources. **E-mail address:** hr_new_york@danskin.com. **World Wide Web address:** http://www.danskin.com. **Description:** Danskin designs, manufactures, and markets several brands of women's activewear, dancewear, tights, and sheer hosiery. Brand names include Danskin, Dance France, Round-the-Clock, Givenchy, and Anne Klein. The company operates two manufacturing facilites and retail operations nationwide. **Positions advertised include:** Account Executive. **Corporate headquarters location:** This location. **Other U.S. locations:** Grenada MS; York PA. **Subsidiaries include:** Pennaco (Grenada MS). **Listed on:** Over The Counter. **Stock exchange symbol:** DANS. **Chairman:** Donald Schupak. **Annual sales/revenues:** $82 million. **Number of employees:** 1,000.

DARBY GROUP COMPANIES, INC.
865 Merrick Avenue, Westbury NY 11590. 516/683-1800. **Fax:** 516/832-7101. **Contact:** Debra Leff, Human Resources Department. **World Wide Web address:** http://www.darbygroup.com. **Description:** A manufacturer and distributor of over-the-counter drugs, pharmaceuticals, and vitamins operating 12 distribution facilities nationwide. **Corporate headquarters location:** This location. **Other U.S. locations:** Nationwide. **Subsidiaries include:** Dental Division; Medical Division; Burns Veterinary Supply; Darby Corporate Solutions. **Chairman:** Michael Ashkir. **Annual sales/revenues:** $625 million. **Number of employees:** 1,500.

DARLINGTON FABRICS CORPORATION
1359 Broadway, Suite 1404, New York NY 10018. 212/279-7733. **Contact:** Human Resources. **World Wide Web address:** http://www.darlingfabrics.com. **Description:** Darlington Fabrics Corporation is a wide-warp knit elastic knitting company. **NOTE:** Resumes should be sent to: Human Resources, 36 Beach Street, Westerly RI 02891. 401/596-2816. **Parent company:** Moore Corporation Limited (Mississuga, Ontario, Canada). **Operations at this facility include:** Sales office.

DAVIS POLK & WARDELL
450 Lexington Avenue, New York NY 10017. 212/450-4000. **Fax:** 212/450-3800. **Contact:** Recruiting Manager. **World Wide Web address:** http://www.dpw.com. **Description:** One of the nation's largest law firms, focusing in a variety of different practice areas. **Special programs:** Summer Internships.

DATA DEVICE CORPORATION
105 Wilbur Place, Bohemia NY 11716. 631/567-5600. **Fax:** 631/567-6357. **Contact:** Ada Villanuvea, Human Resources Supervisor. **World Wide Web address:** http://www.ddc-web.com. **Description:** A manufacturer of high-performance microelectronic components and data conversion products for military, aerospace, and industrial applications for distribution in North America and Europe. **Positions advertised include:** Material Control Stock Clerk; Sales/Marketing Manager. **Special programs:** Internships. **Corporate headquarters location:** This location. **Subsidiaries/affiliates include:** ILC Dover, Inc. **Parent company:** ILC Industries, Inc. (also at this location). **Operations at this facility include:** Manufacturing; Research and Development.

DAXOR CORPORATION
The Empire State Building, 350 Fifth Avenue, Suite 7120, New York NY 10118. 212/244-0555. **Fax:** 212/244-0806. **Contact:** Human Resources. **World Wide Web address:** http://www.daxor.com. **Description:** Promotes the safety of the American Blood Banking System. The company's Idant Division also researches cryobiology for artificial insemination purposes and operates one of the largest sperm banks in the United States. **Subsidiaries include:** IDANT Laboratories. **Listed on:** American Stock Exchange. **Stock exchange symbol:** DXR. **Chairman/President/CEO:** Joseph Feldschuh. **Annual sales/revenues:** 2.7 million. **Number of employees:** 30.

DEBEVOISE & PLIMPTON
919 Third Avenue, New York NY 10022. 212/909-6657. **Fax:** 212/909-6836. **Contact:** Sandra Herbst, Director of Legal Recruitment. **E-mail address:** recruit@debevoise.com. **World Wide Web address:** http://www.debevoise.com. **Description:** An international law partnership specializing in corporate litigation, tax, trust, estates, and real estate law with over 500 lawyers in two U.S. offices and five overseas offices. Founded in 1931. **Corporate headquarters location:** This location. **Other locations:** Washington DC; London, United Kingdom; Paris, France; Frankfurt, Germany; Moscow, Russia; Hong Kong, China; Shanghai, China. **Presiding Partner:** Martin (Rick) F. Evans. **Annual sales/revenues:** $326 million.

DEL GLOBAL TECHNOLOGIES CORPORATION
One Commerce Park, Valhalla NY 10595. 914/686-3600. **Fax:** 914/686-5424. **Contact:** Human Resources. **World Wide Web address:** http://www.delglobaltech.com. **Description:** Del Global Technologies Corporation is comprised of five operations that are engaged in the design, manufacture, and distribution of electronic components, assemblies, and systems for medical, industrial, and defense markets. Products are sold throughout the world to a broad range of OEM customers, distributors, radiologists, and defense agencies. The Dynarad subsidiary manufactures and markets mobile medical imaging systems, mammography equipment, portable dental X-ray units, and advanced neonatal imaging systems. Del Medical Systems markets medical diagnostic products on a worldwide basis. The Power Conversion Division provides standard and custom high-voltage power supplies, transformers, and custom low-voltage power supplies. The Bertan subsidiary designs and manufactures precision high-voltage power supplies and high-voltage instrumentation. The RFI subsidiary designs and manufactures electronic noise suppression filters, high-voltage capacitors, pulse transformers, and specialty magnetics. **Positions advertised include:** Manufacturing Technician; Quality Engineer; Electrical Engineer. **Listed on:** Over The Counter. **Stock exchange symbol:** DGTC. **President/CEO/Director:** Samuel E. Park. **Annual sales/revenues:** $101 million. **Number of employees:** 540.

DEL LABORATORIES, INC.
178 EAB Plaza, West Tower, 8th Floor, Uniondale NY 11556. 516/844-2020. **Fax:** 631/293-7091. **Contact:** Patty Tramposch, Human Resources. **E-mail address:** resume@dellabs.com. **World Wide Web address:** http://www.dellabs.com. **Description:** A fully integrated manufacturer and marketer of packaged consumer products including cosmetics, toiletries, beauty aids, and proprietary pharmaceuticals. Products are distributed to chain and independent drug stores, mass merchandisers, and supermarkets. Divisions include Commerce Drug Company, Del International, Natural Glow, La Cross, La Salle Laboratories, Nutri-Tonic, Naturistics, Rejuvia, and Sally Hansen. **NOTE:** Entry-level positions and second and third shifts are offered. **Positions advertised include:** Administrative Support; Business Account Manager; Category Development Manager; Operations; Regional Account Manager; Scientific Affairs; Space Management Administrator. **Corporate headquarters location:** This location. **Other area locations:** Farmingdale NY. **Other U.S. locations:** Rocky Point NC. **Operations at this facility include:** Administration; Divisional Headquarters; Manufacturing; Regional Headquarters; Research and Development; Service. **Listed on:** American Stock Exchange. **Stock exchange symbol:** DLI. **Chairman/President/CEO:** Dan K. Wassong. **Annual sales/revenues:** $350 million. **Number of employees:** 1,800.

E.J. DEL MONTE CORPORATION
909 Linden Avenue, Rochester NY 14625. 716/586-3121. **Contact:** Human Resources. **World Wide Web address:** http://www.delmontelodge.com. **Description:** E.J. Del Monte Corporation builds, owns, and operates 18 Marriott hotels as a franchisee in the greater Rochester area. In addition to hotels, the company is engaged in construction and develops patented equipment used in the production of pre-cast concrete rooms. Originally a generator manufacturer for military aircraft and guided missiles, the company specializes in building systems incorporating precision, monolithic concrete room castings. Founded in 1953. **Chairman:** Ernest J. Del Monte.

DELAWARE OTSEGO CORPORATION
One Railroad Avenue, Cooperstown NY 13326-1110. 607/547-2555. **Fax:** 607/547-9834. **Contact:** Barbara Rogers, Human Resources. **Description:** Delaware Otsego Corporation is a nonrail holding company. The principal asset is the New York, Susquehanna, and Western Railway Corporation, which provide rail transportation service to customers in New York, New Jersey, and Pennsylvania. The company is also engaged in a real estate project to further develop the traffic base of the railroad. **Corporate headquarters location:** This location.

DELOITTE TOUCHE TOHMATSU
dba DELOITTE & TOUCHE LLP
1633 Broadway, New York NY 10019-6754. 212/492-4000. **Fax:** 212/492-3990. **Contact:** Human Resources. **World Wide Web address:** http://www.deloitte.com. **Description:** An international auditing partnership of certified public accountants providing professional accounting, auditing, tax, and management consulting services to widely diversified clients from offices in 140 countries. The company has a specialized program consisting of national industry groups and functional groups that cross industy lines. Groups are involved in various disciplines including accounting, auditing, taxation management advisory services, small and growing businesses, mergers and acquisitions, and computer applications. **NOTE:** Apply online. **Positions advertised include:** Senior Industry Knowledge Manager; Administrative Assistant; Administrative Floater; Executive Assistant; Scheduling Manager; Information Technology Recruiting Manager; Tax Recruiting Manager; Client Advisory Associate; Business Development Manager; Relationship Development Manager; Assurance & Compliance Consultant. **Corporate headquarters location:** This location. **Other locations:** Worldwide. **Subsidiaries include:** Deloitte Consulting. **Chairman:** Piet Hoogendoorn. **Annual sales/revenues:** $12.5 billion. **Number of employees:** 98,000.

DERIDDER INC.
175 Humboldt Street, Rochester NY 14610-1099. 858/482-1500. **Contact:** Shaun O'Heaney. **E-mail address:** soheaney@deridder.com. **World Wide Web address:** http://www.deridder.com. **Description:** A mounting, dye-cutting, and foil-stripping facility. Deridder Inc. also designs boxes. **Corporate headquarters location:** This location.

DESIGN STRATEGY CORPORATION
600 Third Avenue, 25th Floor, New York NY 10016. 212/370-0000. **Fax:** 212/949-3648. **Contact:** Human Resources. **World Wide Web address:** http://www.designstrategy.com. **Description:** Develops and markets inventory control software. **Positions advertised include:** SAS Programmer/Analyst; Network Engineer; Egenera Systems Administrator. **Corporate headquarters location:** This location. **Other locations:** Upper Marlboro MD; Cranford NJ.

DEUTSCH RELAYS INC.
55 Engineers Road, Hauppauge NY 11788. 631/342-1700. **Fax:** 631/342-9455. **Contact:** Diane Goerz, Human Resources Manager. **E-mail address:** info@deutschrelays.com. **World Wide Web address:** http://www.deutschrelays.com. **Description:** Manufactures and designs miniature electronic relays, electro-mechanical hermetically sealed relays, time delay devices, and mating sockets for use in harsh environments.

DEUTSCHE BANK AG
31 West 52nd Street, New York NY 10019. 212/250-2500. **Contact:** Human Resources. **World Wide Web address:** http://www.deutsche-bank.com. **Description:** A merchant investment bank. Deutsche Bank also manages index funds. **Corporate headquarters location:** Frankfurt, Germany. **Subsidiaries include:** DWS Group; Deutsche Bank, S.A.E.; Deutsche Financial Services Corporation; BPT Limited; Coral Eurobet plc; Deutsche Banc Alex, Brown Incorporated; The Laurel Pub Company Limited; Piaggio SpA; RREEF; Taunus Corporation. **Listed on:** New York Stock Exchange. **Stock exchange symbol:** DB. **Annual sales/revenues:** $66.5 billion. **Number of employees:** 95,000.

DEWEY BALLANTINE LLP
1301 Avenue of the Americas, New York NY 10019. 212/259-8000. **Fax:** 212/259-6333. **Contact:** Recruiting Manager. **E-mail address:** nyrecruitment@deweyballantine.com. **World Wide Web address:** http://www.deweyballantine.com. **Description:** An international law partnership with a range of law specialties including corporate, estates groups, litigation, real estate, tax, and trust with 500 lawyers in a dozen offices worldwide. **Positions advertised include:** Attorney; Paralegal. **Special programs:** Internships; Summer Jobs. **Corporate headquarters location:** This location. **Other U.S. locations:** Los Angeles CA; Washington DC. **International locations:** Budapest, Hungary; Hong Kong, China; London, United Kingdom; Prague, Czech Republic; Warsaw, Poland. **Annual sales/revenues:** $328 million. **Number of employees at this location:** 645. **Number of employees nationwide:** 920. **Number of employees worldwide:** 950.

DICE INC.
3 Park Avenue, 33rd Floor, New York NY 10016. 212/725-6550. **Fax:** 212/725-6559. **Contact:** Jeff Deese, Human Resources Director. **World Wide Web address:** http://www.dice.com. **Description:** Provides online services to IT companies and operates a job board Website for technology professionals. The technical resources offered include hundreds of technical books, a retail store, and information on the newest technologies. Founded in 1994. **NOTE:** Mail Resumes to: Human Resources, 4101 NW Urbandale Drive, Urbandale IA 50322. **Corporate headquarters location:** This location. **Other locations:** Urbandale IA; Alpharetta GA; Augustine FL. **Subsidiaries include:** MeasureUp; dice.com. **Listed on:** Over The Counter. **Stock exchange symbol:** DICEQ. **Chairman/President/CEO/Director:** Scot W. Melland. **Annual sales/revenues:** $56 million. **Number of employees:** 153.

DIEBOLD, INCORPORATED
1133 Corporate Drive, Farmington NY 14425-9570. 585/742-7100. **Toll-free phone:** 800/999-3600. **Contact:** Human Resources. **E-mail address:** hrinfo@diebold.com. **World Wide Web address:** http://www.diebold.com. **Description:** Diebold designs, manufactures, and markets microcomputer systems and identification cards specializing in the sale, manufacture, installation, and service of automated teller machines, physical and electronic security systems, and software for the financial and commercial industries. Other products include vaults, vault doors, lockers, safes, alarms, video surveillance systems, and data line security systems. Founded in 1859. **NOTE:** Please forward any inquiries to: Diebold, Incorporated, 5995 Mayfair Drive, North Canton, OH 44720-8077. **Positions advertised include:** Associate Customer Service Engineer; Card Systems Project Manager. **Corporate headquarters location:** North Canton OH. **Subsidiaries include:** Diebold Direct. **Listed on:** New York Stock Exchange. **Stock exchange symbol:** DBD. **Annual sales/revenues:** $2 billion. **Number of employees:** 13,100.

DIME COMMUNITY BANCSHARES, INC.
dba SAVINGS BANK OF WILLIAMSBURGH
209 Havemeyer Street, Brooklyn NY 11211. 718/782-6200 ext. 8308. **Fax:** 718/486-8793. **Contact:** Human Resources. **World Wide Web address:** http://www.dimewill.com. **Description:** Through its main subsidiary, the company operates a full-service bank with 20 branches serving the Bronx, Brooklyn, Queens, and Nassau County offering deposit options including CDs, savings, checking, NOW, and money market accounts as well as mortgages. **Subsidiaries include:** Havemeyer Investments; Dime Savings Bank of Williamsburg. **Listed on:** NASDAQ. **Stock exchange symbol:** DCOM. **Chairman/CEO:** Vincent F. Palagiano. **Annual sales/revenues:** $200 million. **Number of employees:** 365.

DINAIRE FURNITURE
145 Gruner Road, Buffalo NY 14227-1087. 716/894-1201. **Fax:** 716/894-7497. **Contact:** Karen Novo, Personnel Manager. **E-mail address:** info@dinaire.com. **World Wide Web address:** http://www.dinaire.com. **Description:** Manufactures casual dining room and kitchen furniture.

DIONICS, INC.
65 Rushmore Street, Westbury NY 11590. 516/997-7474. **Fax:** 516/997-7479. **Contact:** Human Resources. **World Wide Web address:** http://www.dionics-usa.com. **Description:** The company designs, manufactures, and sells silicon semiconductor electronic products as individual discrete components, multicomponent integrated circuits, and multicomponent hybrid circuits.

DIRECT INSITE CORPORATION
80 Orville Drive, Suite 100, Bohemia NY 11716. 631/244-1500. **Fax:** 631/563-8085. **Contact:** Human Resources. **World Wide Web address:** http://www.directinsite.com. **Description:** Direct Insite Corp. designs, markets, and supports information delivery software products including end user data access tools for personal computers and client/server environments, and systems management software products for corporate mainframe data centers. Products include dbExpress, which offers methods of searching, organizing, analyzing, and utilizing information contained in databases; systems management software products, which improve mainframe system performance, reduce hardware expenditures, and enhance the reliability and availability of the data processing environment; client/server products, which develop client/server relational database administration and programmer productivity tools. **Corporate headquarters location:** This location. **Subsidiaries include:** d.b.Express; Account Management Systems. **Listed on:** NASDAQ. **Stock exchange symbol:** DIRI. **Chairman/CEO:** James A. Cannavino. **Annual sales/revenues:** $4 million. **Number of employees:** 65.

DOMINO SUGAR
One Federal Street, Yonkers NY 10705. 914/963-2400. **Fax:** 914/963-1030. **Contact:** Human Resources Manager. **World Wide Web address:** http://www.dominosugar.com. **Description:** Refines raw sugar and distributes it to major national clients in the soft drink, confectionery, and baking industries. **Parent company:** The American Sugar Company (Moorhead MN).

DOMINO'S PIZZA, INC.
2024 West Henrietta Road, Suite 5A, Rochester NY 14623-1397. 585/427-8468. **Contact:** Director of Operations. **World Wide Web address:** http://www.dominos.com. **Description:** One location of the home-delivery pizza chain. **Positions advertised include:** General Manager; Restaurant/Food Service Manager. Founded in 1960. **Special programs:** Training. **Corporate headquarters location:** Ann Arbor MI. **Operations at this facility include:** Divisional Headquarters. **Number of employees at this location:** 200.

DONNKENNY, INC.
1411 Broadway, 10th Floor, New York NY 10018. 212/790-3900. **Contact:** Human Resources. **Description:** A sportswear manufacturer. Three distinct and expanding divisions make up Donnkenny: Donnkenny Classics, Mickey & Co., and Lewis Frimel/Flirts. **Corporate headquarters location:** This location. **Subsidiaries include:** Donnkenny Apparel, Inc. **Listed on:** Over The Counter. **Stock exchange symbol:** DKNY. **Annual sales/revenues:** $107 million. **Number of employees:** 203.

DORAL ARROWWOOD
975 Anderson Hill Road, Rye Brook NY 10573. 914/935-6651. **Fax:** 914/323-1126. **Contact:** Human Resources. **E-mail address:** sgarbo@doralarrowwood.com. **World Wide Web address:** http://www.arrowwood.com. **Description:** A hotel and conference center with 272 guest rooms and 36 meeting rooms.

DOREMUS & COMPANY, INC.
200 Varick Street, 11th Floor, New York NY 10014. 212/366-3000. **Fax:** 212/366-3060. **Contact:** Kristin Mooney, Human Resources Director. **E-mail address:** careers@doremus.com. **World Wide Web address:** http://www.doremus.com. **Description:** An agency specializing in corporate and financial advertising. Founded in 1903. **NOTE:** Entry-level positions are offered. **Special programs:** Internships. **Corporate headquarters location:** This location. **Other U.S. locations:** San Francisco CA. **International locations:** London, England; Tokyo, Japan; Frankfurt, Germany; Hong Kong, China. **Parent company:** Omnicom Group Inc. (New York NY). **Annual sales/revenues:** $43.5 million. **Number of employees:** 190

DOVER CORPORATION
280 Park Avenue, Suite 34-W, New York NY 10017-1292. 212/922-1640. **Fax:** 212/922-1656. **Contact:** Human Resources. **World Wide Web address:** http://www.dovercorporation.com. **Description:** Dover is a diversified producer of specialized industrial equipment and components for the petroleum, aerospace, construction, and electronics markets. Divisions include: Dover Technologies, which manufactures electronic circuitry assembly equipment, radio frequency filters, microwave filters, and other equipment; Dover Resources, which makes pumps, compressors, rods, valves, fittings, liquid filtration systems, and gas nozzles; Dover Industries and Dover Diversified manufacture products such as auto lifts, food preparation equipment, solid waste compaction systems, and electromechanical actuators. **Corporate headquarters location:** This location. **Subsidiaries include:** Vitronics Soltec. **Listed on:** New York Stock Exchange. **Stock exchange symbol:** DOV. **Annual sales/revenues:** $4.2 billion. **Number of employees:** 25,000.

DOW JONES & COMPANY, INC.
World Financial Center, 12th Floor, 200 Liberty Street, New York NY 10281. 212/416-2000. **Fax:** 212/416-4348. **Contact:** Human Resources. **E-mail address:** djcareers@dowjones.com. **World Wide Web address:** http://www.dowjones.com. **Description:** A highly diversified publishing and communications firm. Publishing operations include *The Wall Street Journal*, an international business daily newspaper; *The Asian Wall Street Journal*; and the weekly investor's newspaper, *Barron's*. The company offers a wide range of information services including an online library of news and financial information, an online sports information service, a real-time financial market data service, and a newswire service. Since 1882. **Positions advertised include:** Art Director; Classified Ad Sales Representative; Interactive News Assistant; Interactive News Writer; Senior Category Manager. **Corporate headquarters location:** This location. **Other U.S. locations:** Nationwide. **Subsidiaries include:** *Wall Street Journal*; Dow Jones Reuters Business Interactive LLC; Ottaway Newspapers; The Wall Street Journal Online. **Listed on:** New York Stock Exchange. **Stock exchange symbol:** DJ. **Chairman/CEO:** Peter R. Kann. **Annual sales/revenues:** $1.6 billion. **Number of employees:** 6,816.

DOWLING COLLEGE
150 Idle Hour Boulevard, Oakdale NY 11769-1999. 631/244-3020. **Fax:** 631/589-6123. **Contact:** Bridget Carroll, Human Resources. **E-mail address:** carrollb@dowling.edu. **World Wide Web address:** http://www.dowling.edu. **Description:** Dowling College is an independent, comprehensive, coeducational college. The college serves approximately 6,000 full- and part-time students, offering undergraduate programs leading to bachelor of arts, bachelor of science, and bachelor of business administration degrees. Graduate program degrees include master of science in reading and special education, master of business administration, and master of education with the following concentrations: elementary education, secondary education, special education, life-span special services, and reading. Founded in 1968. **Positions advertised include:** Adjunct Business Professor; Director of Institutional Research and Assessment; Security Officer; Clerk; Enrollment Services Associate. **Corporate headquarters location:** This location. **Number of employees at this location:** 900.

THE DRESS BARN, INC.
30 Dunnigan Drive, Suffern NY 10901. 845/369-4500. **Fax:** 845/369-4829. **Contact:** Human Resources. **E-mail address:** hrrecruit@dressbarn.com. **World Wide Web address:** http://www.dressbarn.com. **Description:** Operates a chain of 750 women's apparel stores nationwide. **Corporate headquarters location:** This location. **Listed on:** NASDAQ. **Stock exchange symbol:** DBRN. **Chairman:** Elliot S. Jaffe. **Annual sales/revenues:** $717 million. **Number of employees:** 8,900.

DRESSER-RAND COMPANY
100 Chemung Street, Painted Post NY 14870-1377. 607/937-2100. **Contact:** Human Resources. **World Wide Web address:** http://www.dresser-rand.com/steam. **Description:** Dresser-Rand's operations are divided into several industry segments: petroleum operations, energy processing and conversion equipment, and industrial specialty products. More than 80 manufacturing plants are located in the United States, Canada, and various foreign countries. **Corporate headquarters location:** Olean NY. **Other locations:** Houston TX; Olean NY; Painted Post NY; Wellsville NY. **International locations:** Norway; France; Germany; India; China. **Parent company:** Ingersoll-Rand Corporation (Woodcliff NJ) manufactures compressors, pumps, and other nonelectrical industrial equipment and machinery. Ingersoll-Rand's products include air compression systems, antifriction systems, construction equipment, air tools, bearings, locks, tools, and pumps. The company operates 93 production facilities throughout the world. **Operations at this facility include:** Manufacturing of gas compressors. **President:** Vince Volpe. **Annual sales/revenues:** $1 billion.

DRESSER-RAND COMPANY
37 Coats Street, P.O. Box 592, Wellsville NY 14895. 585/596-3100. **Fax:** 585/593-5815. **Contact:** Human Resources. **World Wide Web address:** http://www.dresser-rand.com/steam. **Description:** Dresser-Rand's operations are divided into several industry segments: petroleum operations, energy processing and conversion equipment, and industrial specialty products. More than 80 manufacturing plants are located in the United States, Canada, and various foreign countries. **Corporate headquarters location:** Olean NY. **Other locations:** Houston TX; Olean NY; Painted Post NY; Wellsville NY. **International locations:** Norway; France; Germany; India; China. **Parent company:** Ingersoll-Rand Corporation (Woodcliff NJ) manufactures compressors, pumps, and other nonelectrical industrial equipment and machinery. Ingersoll-Rand's products include air compression systems, antifriction systems, construction equipment, air tools, bearings, locks, tools, and pumps. The company operates 93 production facilities throughout the world. **Operations at this facility include:** Energy Systems Division manufacturing and sales of steam turbines. **President:** Vince Volpe. **Annual sales/revenues:** $1 billion.

DRESSER-RAND COMPANY
Paul Clark Drive, P.O. Box 560, Olean NY 14760. 716/375-3000. **Fax:** 716/375-3952. **Contact:** Human Resources. **World Wide Web address:** http://www.dresser-rand.com/steam. **Description:** Dresser-Rand's operations are divided into several industry segments: petroleum operations, energy processing and conversion equipment, and industrial specialty products. More than 80 manufacturing plants are located in the United States, Canada, and various foreign countries. **Corporate headquarters location:** This location. **Other locations:** Houston TX; Olean NY; Painted Post NY; Wellsville NY. **International locations:** Norway; France; Germany; India; China. **Parent company:** Ingersoll-Rand Corporation (Woodcliff NJ) manufactures compressors, pumps, and other nonelectrical industrial equipment and machinery. Ingersoll-Rand's products include air compression systems, antifriction systems,

construction equipment, air tools, bearings, locks, tools, and pumps. The company operates 93 production facilities throughout the world. **Operations at this facility include:** Corporate Administration; Design and Manufacture of compressors and gas turbines. **President:** Vince Volpe. **Annual sales/revenues:** $1 billion.

DREW INDUSTRIES INCORPORATED
200 Mamaroneck Avenue, Suite 301, White Plains NY 10601. 914/428-9098. **Fax:** 914/428-4581. **Contact:** Human Resources. **World Wide Web address:** http://www.drewindustries.com. **Description:** Drew Industries is the holding company of Kinro, Inc. Kinro is one of the leading producers of aluminum and vinyl windows for manufactured homes, and windows and doors for recreational vehicles. Kinro has nine domestic manufacturing plants. **Corporate headquarters location:** This location. **Subsidiaries include:** Lippert Components, Inc.; Kinro, Inc. **Listed on:** American Stock Exchange. **Stock exchange symbol:** DW. **Annual sales/revenues:** $325 million. **Number of employees:** 2,800.

THE DREYFUS CORPORATION
200 Park Avenue, 7th Floor, New York NY 10166. 212/922-6000. **Fax:** 212/922-7533. **Contact:** Human Resources. **World Wide Web address:** http://www.dreyfus.com. **Description:** A nationwide investment corporation managing over 150 mutual funds. **NOTE:** Entry-level positions are offered. **Positions advertised include:** Associate Financial Analyst; Human Resources Consultant; Regional Wholesaler; Secretary; Fund Wholesaler; Broker-Dealer Channel Wholesaler; Financial Advisor Channel Wholesaler; Portfolio Assistant; Risk Manager and Compliance Team Leader; Executive Secretary; Financial Consultant; Mellon Business Advisor. **Corporate headquarters location:** This location. **Parent company:** Mellon Financial Corporation (Pittsburgh PA).

DUART FILM AND VIDEO
245 West 55th Street, New York NY 10019. 212/757-4580. **Contact:** Supervisor. **World Wide Web address:** http://www.duart.com. **Description:** Involved in motion picture services and television broadcasting.

DUNKIRK SPECIALTY STEEL LLC
88 Howard Avenue, Dunkirk NY 14048. 716/366-1000. **Fax:** 716/366-1208. **Contact:** Human Resources. **Description:** Manufactures specialty steel bar, wire, rod, and extrusions.

DYNALEC CORPORATION
87 West Main Street, P.O. Box 188, Sodus NY 14551. 315/483-6923. **Fax:** 315/483-6656. **Contact:** Lori St. Pierre, Personnel Manager. **E-mail address:** loristp@dynalec.com. **World Wide Web address:** http://www.dynalec.com. **Description:** Manufactures communication equipment, primarily for use on naval vessels. Dynalec's products include intercoms, loudspeakers, amplifiers, and ships course instruments. Founded in 1960.

DYNAMIC INTERNATIONAL LIMITED, INC.
58 Second Avenue, Brooklyn NY 11215. 718/369-4160. **Fax:** 718/369-2210. **Contact:** Human Resources. **Description:** Dynamic Classics sells and distributes a diverse line of exercise equipment, sport bags, luggage, and gift products, which are distributed nationwide. The majority of sales are to catalog showrooms, drug chains, sporting goods chains, distributors, chain stores, discount stores, and the premium trade.

D'YOUVILLE COLLEGE
320 Porter Avenue, Buffalo NY 14201. 716/881-3200. **Contact:** Human Resources. **World Wide Web address:** http://www.dyc.edu. **Description:** A four-year liberal arts college that offers graduate and undergraduate programs. D'Youville College offers majors including business, education, and nursing. The physical therapy and occupational therapy programs both entail five years of study.

E-Z-EM INC.
717 Main Street, Westbury NY 11590. 516/333-8230. **Fax:** 516/333-1392. **Contact:** Human Resources. **E-mail address:** hr@ezem.com. **World Wide Web address:** http://www.ezem.com. **Description:** E-Z-EM is a worldwide producer of barium sulfate contrast systems for use in GI tract X-ray examinations. The company operates in two industry segments: diagnostic products and surgical products. The diagnostic products segment includes both contrast systems, consisting of barium sulfate formulations and related apparatus used in X-ray, CT-scanning, and other imaging examinations; and noncontrast systems, which include interventional radiology products, custom contract pharmaceuticals, gastrointestinal cleansing laxatives, X-ray protection equipment, and immunoassay tests. **Corporate headquarters location:** This location. **Listed on:** American Stock Exchange. **Stock exchange symbol:** EZM. **Annual sales/revenues:** $122 million. **Number of employees:** 932.

EDO CORPORATION
ELECTRONIC SYSTEMS GROUP
455 Commack Road, Deer Park NY 11729-4591. 631/595-5000. **Fax:** 631/595-6517. **Contact:** Human Resources. **E-mail address:** employment@nycedo.com. **World Wide Web address:** http://www.edocorp.com. **Description:** Engaged in the engineering and manufacturing of electronic systems including defensive avionics, ATC radar, satellite communications systems, and components. **Corporate headquarters location:** New York NY. **Subsidiaries include:** Advanced Engineering & Research Associates, Inc.; Combat Systems; Electro-Ceramic Products; Fiber Science; Marine and Aircraft Systems; Specialty Plastics; Technology Services and Analysis. **Operations at this facility include:** Administration; Manufacturing Divisions – Antenna Products & Technologies, Sensors & Force Protection, Space & Communications Products, Defense Programs and Technologies; Research and Development. **Listed on:** New York Stock Exchange. **Stock exchange symbol:** EDO. **Annual sales/revenues:** $329 million. **Number of employees:** 2,000.

E.F.L.S.
545 Eighth Avenue, Suite 401, New York NY 10018. 212/868-1126. **Fax:** 212/714-1453. **Contact:** Human Resources. **World Wide Web address:** http://www.efls.net. **Description:** Provides telephone and messaging services as well as computer consulting services for Macintosh systems.

EARTH TECH
One World Financial Center, New York NY 10281. 212/798-8500. **Fax:** 212/798-8501. **Contact:** Human Resources. **World Wide Web address:** http://www.earthtech.com. **Description:** An engineering consulting firm specializing in water, environmental, transportation, and construction. **Parent company:** Tyco International Ltd.

EASTMAN KODAK COMPANY
343 State Street, Rochester NY 14650-1139. 585/724-4000. **Fax:** 585/724-1089. **Contact:** Staffing. **E-mail address:** staffing@kodak.com. **World Wide Web address:** http://www.kodak.com. **Description:** Manufactures photographic equipment and supplies; medical products; information storage and retrieval systems; and copiers/duplicators. Consumer brand names include Kodak film, Bayer aspirin, d-Con pest control, Minwax wood finishes, and Resolve carpet cleaner. The company also produces cameras, photo CDs and players, software, printers, and batteries. **Positions advertised include:** Electronics Integration and Test Engineer; Electro-Mechanical Test Engineer; Purchasing Clerk; Lead Embedded Software Engineer; Analog/Dealer Channel WW Services Product Line Manager; Manufacturing Engineer; Electrical Manufacturing Engineer; Director of Employee Communications; Digital Radiography Product Manager; Electronics Packaging Engineer; Business/Strategy & Asset Management Services Manager; Research Scientist; Optical Systems Engineer; Mechanical Dynamics Test Engineer; Information Technology Auditor; Thermal/Mechanical Test Engineer; Audit/Corporate Auditing Manager; Corporate Auditor; Senior Optics Processing Engineer. **Special programs:** Internships. **Corporate headquarters location:** This location. **Other U.S. locations:** Nationwide. **Subsidiaries include:** Encad, Inc.; AuntMinnie.com; Kodak AG; Kodak Limited-UK. **Listed on:** New York Stock Exchange. **Stock exchange symbol:** EK. **Chairman/CEO:** Daniel A. Carp. **Annual sales/revenues:** $12.8 billion. **Number of employees:** 70,000.

ECKERD DRUG
7245 Henry Clay Boulevard, Liverpool NY 13088-3571. 315/451-8000. **Contact:** Cathleen Patterelli, Human Resources Director. **E-mail address:** cpatt3@eckerd.com. **World Wide Web address:** http://www.eckerd.com. **Description:** The company operates one of the largest chains of super drug stores in the Northeast under the name Eckerd Drugs. Eckerd Drug Store Division has over 250 drug stores located in New York, Pennsylvania, Vermont, and New Hampshire. **Parent company:** Eckerd Corporation (Largo FL). **Operations at this facility include:** One of the nine nationwide distribution centers.

ECOLOGY AND ENVIRONMENT, INC.
Buffalo Corporate Center, 368 Pleasant View Drive, Lancaster NY 14086-1397. 716/684-8060. **Fax:** 716/684-0844. **Contact:** Human Resources. **E-mail address:** resumes@ene.com. **World Wide Web address:** http://www.ene.com. **Description:** Ecology and Environment, Inc. is a leading environmental consulting firm operating 27 offices worldwide. The company offers a broad range of environmental consulting services including biological baseline and biodiversity studies; environmental audits; environmental impact assessments; terrestrial, aquatic, and marine surveys; air quality management and air pollution control; environmental engineering; noise pollution evaluations; wastewater analyses; water pollution control; industrial hygiene and occupational health studies; archaeological and cultural resource studies; and environmental infrastructure planning. Founded in 1970. **NOTE:** Word format is preferred for resumes. **Positions advertised include:** Environmental Chemist; Emergency Planner; Human Resources Recruiter; Technical Services Sales Representative. **Listed on:** American Stock Exchange. **Stock exchange symbol:** EEI. **President/Director:** Gerhard J. Neumaier. **Annual sales/revenues:** $74 million. **Number of employees:** 770.

ECONOMIC OPPORTUNITY COUNCIL OF SUFFOLK
475 East Main Street, Suite 206, Patchogue NY 11772. 631/289-2124. **Fax:** 631/289-2178. **Contact:** Songhi Scott, CFO/Human Resources. **E-mail address:** eoc@eoc-suffolk.com. **World Wide Web address:** http://www.eoc-suffolk.com. **Description:** A county agency responsible for various social programs in Suffolk County. The council provides counseling in energy conservation, outreach, summer work, health and education, housing, and employment training. **Special programs:** Internships. **Number of employees at this location:** 10. **Number of employees nationwide:** 50.

EL AL ISRAEL AIRLINES LIMITED
120 West 45th Street, 18th Floor, New York NY 10036-9998. 212/869-4164. **Contact:** Personnel Department. **World Wide Web address:** http://www.elal.co.il. **Description:** An Israeli government-owned international air carrier operating a route system that includes major United States cities, and destinations in Israel, Europe, and Africa. Founded in 1948. **Corporate headquarters location:** Ben Gurion Airport, Israel. **Annual sales/revenues:** $1.1 billion. **Number of employees:** 3,224.

ELECTROGRAPH SYSTEMS INC.
40 Marcus Boulevard, Hauppauge NY 11788. 631/436-5050. **Fax:** 631/436-5075. **Contact:** Human Resources. **World Wide Web address:** http://www.electrograph.com. **Description:** Distributes microcomputer peripherals, components, and accessories throughout the East Coast of the United States. Electrograph Systems distributes national brand names such as Mitsubishi, Sony, Hitachi, Magnavox, Toshiba, and Idex. The company's products include monitors, printers, large-screen televisions, CD-ROMs, computer video products, optical storage products, notebook computers, and personal computers. Founded in 1982. **Other U.S. locations:** Garden Grove CA; Madeira Beach FL; Woodridge IL; Olathe KS; Timonium MD; Plano TX. **Parent company:** Manchester Technologies, Inc. (also at this location).

ELLANEF MANUFACTURING CORPORATION
9711 50th Avenue, Corona NY 11368. 718/699-4000. **Fax:** 718/592-0722. **Contact:** Human Resources. **E-mail address:** henry.david@ellanef.com. **World Wide Web address:** http://www.ellanef.com. **Description:** Manufactures a wide range of aircraft components for major aerospace OEMs and airlines operating nationwide. **Parent company:** Magellan Aerospace Corporation (Mississauga, Ontario, Canada). **Operations at this facility include:** Manufacturing. **Number of employees at this location:** 500.

ELLIS HOSPITAL
1101 Nott Street, Schenectady NY 12308. 518/243-4000. **Fax:** 518/243-1402. **Contact:** Human Resources. **World Wide Web address:** http://www.ellishospital.org. **Description:** A regional referral center with 368 beds, an 82-bed nursing home, network of five primary care centers, and a Heart Center providing a variety of services including cardiovascular services, open heart surgery, oncology, neurology, critical care, day surgery, MRI, mental health, and long-term care. **NOTE:** Human Resources phone: 518/243-4004. **Positions advertised include:** Cardiology Nurse Practitioner; Physician Assistant; Cardiology Technician; Cardiovascular Technician; Patient Case Manager; Certified Nursing Assistant; Clerical Coordinator; Clinical Nurse Specialist; Clinical Resource Coordinator; Clinical Secretary; Clinical Radiology Secretary; Corporate Educator; Diet Clerk; Engineering Mechanic; Food Service Worker; Foundation Assistant; Housekeeper; Licensed Practical Nurse; Maintenance Technician; Painter; Mental Health Assistant; Mental Health Clinical Coordinator; Operating Room Technician; Patient Care Technician; Patient Registrar; Performance Improvement Specialist; Phlebotomist; Physical Therapist; Practice Manager; Project Housekeeper; Psychiatric Social Worker; Radiology Technologist; Patient Registered Nurse; Ultrasound Technologist. **NOTE:** Human Resources phone: 518/243-4004.

ELMIRA COLLEGE
One Park Place, Elmira NY 14901. 607/735-1800. **Toll-free phone:** 800/935-6472. **Contact:** Personnel Department. **World Wide Web address:** http://www.elmira.edu.

Description: A four-year, private undergraduate and graduate university. Degree programs include associate's, bachelor of arts, bachelor of science, master of business administration, and master of science. Enrollment is approximately 1,100. **Positions advertised include:** Human Services Professor; Physical Chemistry/Physics Professor; Teacher Education Professor; Psychology Professor; Graduate Assistant; Director of English as a Second Language; Executive Secretary to the President; Health Center Head Nurse; Coordinator of Performing Arts Programming and Student Activities; Director of Major Gifts.

ELMIRA PSYCHIATRIC CENTER
100 Washington Street, Elmira NY 14902-2898. 607/737-4711. **Fax:** 607/737-4722. **Contact:** Department of Human Resources. **World Wide Web address:** http://www.omh.state.ny.us/omhweb/facilities/elpc/facility.htm. **Description:** An inpatient and outpatient psychiatric care facility, the majority of whose patients suffer from chronic mental illness. **NOTE:** Human Resources phone: 607/737-4726. **Positions advertised include:** Residential Program Counselor; Psychiatric Nurse; Psychiatrist; Nurse; Dietitian.

EMIGRANT SAVINGS BANK
5 East 42nd Street, New York NY 10017. 212/850-4000. **Fax:** 212/850-4372. **Contact:** Human Resources. **E-mail address:** employment@emigrant.com. **World Wide Web address:** http://www.emigrant.com. **Description:** Offers a wide range of traditional banking services. Emigrant Savings Bank has 36 branches in Manhattan, Brooklyn, and Queens, as well as in Nassau, Suffolk, and Westchester Counties. Founded in 1850. **Positions advertised include:** Teller. **NOTE:** Human Resources phone: 212/850-4888. **Corporate headquarters location:** This location. **Other locations:** Throughout New York metropolitan area. **Subsidiaries/affiliates include:** Emigrant Mortgage Company; Emigrant Funding Corporation; American Property Financing, Inc.; Emigrant Business Credit Corporation. **Parent company:** Emigrant Bancorp (also at this location).

EMISPHERE TECHNOLOGIES, INC.
765 Old Saw Mill River Road, Tarrytown NY 10591-6751. 914/347-2220. **Fax:** 914/347-2498. **Contact:** Barbara Mohl, Human Resources Director. **E-mail address:** jobs@emisphere.com. **World Wide Web address:** http://www.emisphere.com. **Description:** Researches and develops oral drug delivery systems. **Positions advertised include:** Analytical Research Associate; Drug Delivery Research Associate; Patent Paralegal; Documentation Control Professional; Laboratory Animal Technician. **Listed on:** NASDAQ. **Stock exchange symbol:** EMIS. **Chairman/CEO:** Michael M. Goldberg. **Annual sales/revenues:** $3.4 million. **Number of employees:** 241.

EMPIRE BLUE CROSS AND BLUE SHIELD
622 3rd Avenue, New York NY 10017. 212/476-1000. **Fax:** 212/476-2343. **Contact:** Staffing Department. **World Wide Web address:** http://www.empireblue.com. **Description:** A nonprofit health insurance company offering coverage that includes comprehensive hospital, medical, prescription drug, and dental plans, as well as programs supplemental to Medicare. **Positions advertised include:** Direct Mail Operations Director; Facilities Management Director; Information Technology Auditing Director; Financial Systems Analyst; Junior Fair Hearing Officer; Lead Underwriter; Project Associate; Account Reporting Project Leader; National Accounts Project Manager; Reporting Project Manager; Secretary; Administrative Assistant; Senior Accountant; Senior Plan Sales Associate; Senior Underwriter; Staff Accountant. **Corporate headquarters location:** This location. **Parent company:** WellChoice, Inc. (also at this location).

EMPIRE BLUE CROSS AND BLUE SHIELD
P.O. Box 11800, Albany NY 12211-0800. 518/367-4737. **Physical address:** 11 Corporate Boulevard, Albany NY 12211. **Contact:** Manager of Human Resources Department. **E-mail address:** albhr@empireblue.com. **World Wide Web address:** http://www.empireblue.com. **Description:** A nonprofit health insurance company offering coverage that includes comprehensive hospital, medical, prescription drug, and dental plans, as well as programs supplemental to Medicare. **Positions advertised include:** Case Manager; Customer Service Representative; Data Entry Clerk; Claims Input Operator; Staff Assistant. **Corporate headquarters location:** New York NY. **Parent company:** WellChoice, Inc. (New York NY).

EMPIRE SCIENTIFIC CORPORATION
87 East Jefryn Boulevard, Deer Park NY 11729. 631/595-9206. **Toll-free phone:** 800/645-7220. **Fax:** 631/595-9093. **Contact:** Personnel. **World Wide Web address:** http://www.empirescientific.com. **Description:** Empire Scientific manufactures and distributes batteries, chargers, and accessories to retailers, wholesalers, and original equipment manufacturers in the cellular, video, cordless telephone and other electronics industries. **Corporate headquarters location:** This location. **Other locations:** Tampa FL; Chicago IL.

ENCOMPASS INSURANCE
P.O. Box 5000, Glens Falls NY 12801. 518/761-4000. **Fax:** 800/426-3692. **Contact:** Human Resources. **World Wide Web address:** http://www.encompassinsurance.com. **Description:** A property and casualty insurance writer offering commercial and personal policies. **Corporate headquarters location:** Chicago IL. **Parent company:** The Allstate Corporation (Northbrook IL).

ENSCO INC.
3 Holiday Hill Road, Endicott NY 13760. 607/786-9000. **Contact:** Human Resources. **World Wide Web address:** http://www.ensco.com. **Description:** The company provides engineering, science, and advanced information technologies software for the defense, security, transportation, environmental, and aerospace industries. Founded in 1969. **Positions advertised include:** Electrical Design Engineer; Technical Writer. **Corporate headquarters location:** Springfield VA. **Other locations:** Melbourne FL; Cocoa Beach FL; Beijing, China. **Number of employees:** 800.

ENVIRONMENT ONE CORPORATION (E/ONE)
2773 Balltown Road, Niskayuna NY 12309-1090. 518/346-6161. **Fax:** 518/346-6188. **Contact:** Human Resources. **E-mail address:** eone@eone.com. **World Wide Web address:** http://www.eone.com. **Description:** Environment One Corporation is an environment-oriented product and service company that operates in two business segments: sewer systems and detection systems. Detection products include Generator Overheat Monitors and The Generator Gas Analyzer. **Parent company:** Precision Castparts Corp. (Portland OR).

ENZO BIOCHEM, INC.
dba ENZO CLINICAL LABS
60 Executive Boulevard, Farmingdale NY 11735. 631/755-5500. **Fax:** 631/863-0143. **Contact:** Human Resources. **World Wide Web address:** http://www.enzo.com. **Description:** Through its subsidiaries, the company is engaged in the research, development, marketing, and manufacturing of health care products. Enzo's products and services are sold to scientists and medical personnel worldwide. The company has proprietary technologies and expertise in manipulating and modifying genetic material and other biological molecules. Founded in 1976. **Positions advertised include:** Phlebotomist; Histotechnologist; Grosser. **Subsidiaries include:** Enzo Therapeutics, Inc. is developing antisense genetic medicines to combat cancer, viral, and other diseases. Enzo Diagnostics, Inc. develops and markets proprietary DNA probe-based products to clinicians and researchers. EnzoLabs, Inc. provides diagnostic testing services to the New York medical community. **Corporate headquarters location:** This location. **Parent company:** Enzo Biochem. **Listed on:** New York Stock Exchange. **Stock exchange symbol:** ENZ. **Chairman/CEO:** Elazar Rabbani. **Annual sales/revenues:** $54 million. **Number of employees:** 231.

EON LABS, INC.
227-15 North Conduit Avenue, Laurelton NY 11413. 718/276-8600. **Toll-free phone:** 800/526-0225. **Fax:** 718/949-3120. **Contact:** Human Resources. **World Wide Web address:** http://www.eonlabs.com. **Description:** Manufactures both prescription and over-the-counter generic pharmaceuticals. **Positions advertised include:** Quality Control Chemist. **Listed on:** NASDAQ. **Stock exchange symbol:** ELAB. **Chairman:** Thomas Strüngmann. **Annual sales/revenues:** $244 million. **Number of employees:** 324.

ERIE COMMUNITY COLLEGE
121 Ellicott Street, Buffalo NY 14203. 716/842-2770. **Fax:** 716/851-1129. **Contact:** Human Resources. **World Wide Web address:** http://www.ecc.edu. **Description:** A two-year community college that offers both certificates and associate degrees. Classes are held at three campuses. **Other U.S. locations:** Williamsville NY; Orchard Park NY.

ERNST & YOUNG INTERNATIONAL
dba ERNST & YOUNG LLP
5 Times Square, New York NY 10036-6530. 212/773-3000. **Fax:** 212/773-6350. **Contact:** Human Resources. **World Wide Web address:** http://www.ey.com. **Description:** A certified public accounting partnership that also provides accounting and management consulting services. Services include data processing, financial modeling, financial feasibility studies, production planning and inventory management, management sciences, health care planning, human resources, cost accounting, and budgeting systems. **Positions advertised include:** Financial Assistant; Financial Researcher; Bilingual Japanese Administrative Assistant; risk Management Senior Manager; Technology & Security Risk Services Senior; Structured Finance Advisory Services Manager; Risk Management Services Senior; Knowledge Resources Manager; On-Call Advisory Services Senior; Credit Risk Management Advisor. **Corporate headquarters location:** This location. **Other locations:** Worldwide. **Chairman:** James (Jim) S. Turley. **Annual sales/revenues:** $10.1 billion. **Number of employees:** 110,000.

ESQUIRE DEPOSITION SERVICES
216 East 45th Street, 8th Floor, New York NY 10017. 212/687-8010. **Fax:** 212/557-2153. **Contact:** Human Resources. **World Wide Web address:** http://www.esquiredeposition.com. **Description:** A court reporting firm using state-of-the-art technology to provide printed and computerized transcripts, video recordings of testimony from depositions, and speech recognition systems to the legal profession primarily in metropolitan New York City and Southern California. The company's technologies include real-time transcription, interactive real-time transcription, full-text search and retrieval programs, compressed transcripts, and multimedia technology systems. **Parent company:** The Hobart West Group. **Annual sales/revenues:** $200 million.

ESSELTE AMERICAS
48 South Service Road, Suite 400, Melville NY 11747. 631/675-5700. **Fax:** 631/675-3456. **Contact:** Personnel. **E-mail address:** rpalen@esselte.com. **World Wide Web address:** http://www.esselteamericas.com. **Description:** Manufactures and distributes filing and marking systems, storage systems, and other office materials. Primary products are paper-based filing products, mainly suspension filing systems. The company has production and sales facilities in the United States and Canada. **Positions advertised include:** Customer Service Representative; Sales Associate; Marketing Assistant; Administrative Assistant; Finance Clerk; Information Technology Specialist. **Special programs:** Internships. **Corporate headquarters location:** This location. **Other U.S. locations:** Moonachie NJ; New York NY. **Parent company:** Esselte AB (Solna, Sweden). **Operations at this facility include:** Administration; Manufacturing; Research and Development; Sales. **Number of employees worldwide:** 6,500.

ESSEX HOUSE
160 Central Park South, New York NY 10019. 212/247-0300. **Fax:** 212/315-1839. **Contact:** Human Resources. **World Wide Web address:** http://www.essexhouse.com. **Description:** Operates a hotel with 597 guest rooms and 150 condominiums. **Parent company:** Starwood Hotels & Resorts Worldwide Inc. (White Plaines NY).

THE ESTÉE LAUDER COMPANIES INC.
767 Fifth Avenue, New York NY 10153. 212/572-4200. **Fax:** 212/572-6633. **Contact:** Human Resources. **World Wide Web address:** http://www.elcompanies.com. **Description:** Manufactures, markets, and distributes cosmetics, fragrances, and skin and hair care products. Founded in 1946. **Corporate headquarters location:** This location. **Listed on:** New York Stock Exchange. **Stock exchange symbol:** EL. **Chairman:** Leonard A. Lauder. **Annual sales/revenues:** $4.7 billion. **Number of employees:** 20,400.

EVANS NATIONAL BANK
14-16 North Main Street, P.O. Box 191, Angola NY 14006. 716/549-1000. **Contact:** Human Resources Department. **World Wide Web address:** http://www.evansnationalbank.com. **Description:** An FDIC-insured, full-service commercial bank. The bank's primary market area is located in western New York State and specifically in southern Erie County, northern Chautauqua County, and northwestern Cattaraugus County. The principal business of Evans National Bank is commercial banking and the bank offers a variety of loan products including commercial loans, commercial and residential mortgage loans, and consumer loans. In addition, the bank offers deposit products to include checking and NOW accounts, passbook and statement savings, and certificates of deposits. **Parent company:** Evans Bancorp, Inc. (also at this location).

EVERGREEN BANCORP INC.
237 Glen Street, P.O. Box 318, Glens Falls NY 12801-3507. 518/792-1151. **Contact:** Human Resources. **Description:** Evergreen Bancorp is a one-bank holding company. **Subsidiaries include:** Evergreen Bank, operates 27 banking locations in eastern New York. The bank provides its corporate, institutional, and individual customers with a wide range of deposit, lending, trust, and investment services.

EVERLAST WORLDWIDE, INC.
1350 Broadway, Suite 2300, New York NY 10018. 212/239-0990. **Fax:** 212/239-4261. **Contact:** Human Resources. **World Wide Web address:** http://www.everlast.com.

Description: Everlast Worldwide, Inc. designs, manufactures, and sells activewear and sportswear. **Corporate headquarters location:** This location. **Listed on:** NASDAQ. **Stock exchange symbol:** EVST. **Chairman/President/CEO:** George C. Horowitz. **Annual sales/revenues:** $65.5 million. **Number of employees:** 269.

EX-CELL HOME FASHIONS INC.
295 Fifth Avenue, Suite 612, New York NY 10016. 212/213-8000. **Contact:** Human Resources. **Description:** Manufactures and distributes home furnishing products including shower curtains, pillows, tablecloths, and bathroom accessories. **NOTE:** Resumes should be sent to: Human Resources, P.O. Box 1879, Goldsboro NC 27533; fax: 919/731-7209. **Corporate headquarters location:** Goldsboro NC. **Operations at this facility include:** Showroom and Sales.

FCB WORLDWIDE
100 West 33rd Street,, New York NY 10001. 212/885-3000. **Fax:** 212/885-2803. **Contact:** Director of Personnel. **E-mail address:** careersny@fcb.com. **World Wide Web address:** http://www.fcb.com. **Description:** An international advertising agency. FCB/LKP offers additional services including direct marketing, design and production of sales promotion programs; market and product research; package design; and trademark and trade name development. The company operates offices throughout Europe, Asia, and Latin America. **Corporate headquarters location:** This location. **International locations:** Worldwide. **Parent company:** Foote, Cone & Belding Communications.

FAB INDUSTRIES, INC.
200 Madison Avenue, 7th Floor, New York NY 10016. 212/592-2700. **Fax:** 212/689-6929. **Contact:** Ms. Marsha Cohen, Office Manager. **E-mail address:** fabindus@mindspring.com. **World Wide Web address:** http://www.fab-industries.com. **Description:** Fab Industries is a manufacturer of knitted textile fabrics, laces, and related finished home products, as well as polyurethane coated fabrics. The company markets its products to the apparel, home furnishings, industrial, retail, and other specialty markets. Fab operates eight manufacturing plants at five locations in North Carolina and New York with sales offices in New York and Los Angeles. **Corporate headquarters location:** This location. **Other locations:** NC; CA. **Subsidiaries include:** Gem Urethane. **Listed on:** American Stock Exchange. **Stock exchange symbol:** FIT. **Number of employees nationwide:** 1,800. **Chariman/CEO:** Samson Bitensky. **Annual sales/revenues:** $63 million. **Number of employees:** 620.

FACTS ON FILE, INC.
132 West 31st Street, 17th Floor, New York NY 10001. 212/967-8800. **Fax:** 212/896-4383. **Contact:** Human Resources. **E-mail address:** resumes@factsonfile.com. **World Wide Web address:** http://www.factsonfile.com. **Description:** A reference book publisher that specializes in books for public and school libraries. **Positions advertised include:** Copy Editor.

FAIR-RITE PRODUCTS CORPORATION
P.O. Box J, One Commercial Row, Wallkill NY 12589. 845/895-2055. **Fax:** 845/895-2629. **Contact:** Human Resources. **World Wide Web address:** http://www.fair-rite.com. **Description:** A manufacturer of ferrite components used in electronics. **Special programs:** Internships. **Corporate headquarters location:** This location. **Other U.S. locations:** Flat Rock IL; Springfield VT. **Number of employees at this location:** 200. **Number of employees nationwide:** 300.

FAIRCHILD PUBLICATIONS, INC.
7 West 34th Street, 6th Floor, New York NY 10001. 212/630-4000. **Fax:** 212/630-4295. **Contact:** Human Resources. **E-mail address:** hr@fairchildpub.com. **World Wide Web address:** http://www.fairchildpub.com. **Description:** A business and professional magazine publisher. Fairchild Publications' primary focus is on the fashion industry. Founded in 1892. **NOTE:** Human Resources phone: 212/630-4300. **Positions advertised include:** Junior Financial Reporter; Media Reporter; Senior Editor; Business Manager; Administrative Assistant; Account Executive. **Special programs:** Internships. **Corporate headquarters location:** This location. **Other U.S. locations:** Los Angeles CA; Washington DC; Chicago IL; Boston MA; Dallas TX. **Subsidiaries include:** *Children's' Business; Details; DNR; Executive Technology; Footwear News; Home Furnishings News; Jane; Salon News; Supermarket News; W; Women's Wear Daily.* **Parent company:** Advance Publications. **Operations at this facility include:** Administration; Divisional Headquarters; Sales. **Number of employees at this location:** 550. **Number of employees nationwide:** 750.

FARRAR, STRAUS AND GIROUX
19 Union Square West, New York NY 10003. 212/741-6900. **Contact:** Human Resources. **World Wide Web address:** http://www.fsgbooks.com. **Description:** A general trade book publisher known for its international list of literary fiction, nonfiction, poetry, and children's books. Founded in 1946. **Parent company:** Verlagsgruppe Georg von Holtzbrinck GmbH (Stuttgart, Germany).

FASHION INSTITUTE OF TECHNOLOGY
7th Avenue at 27th Street, New York NY 10001-5992. 212/217-7999. **Contact:** Human Resources. **World Wide Web address:** http://www.fitnyc.suny.edu. **Description:** A fashion institute offering degrees in art and design or business and technology.

FIDELITY NATIONAL TITLE INSURANCE COMPANY OF NEW YORK
2 Park Avenue, Suite 300, New York NY 10016. 212/481-5858. **Contact:** Human Resources. **World Wide Web address:** http://www.fntic.com. **Description:** Provides title insurance and escrow services nationwide. **Parent company:** Fidelity National Financial, Inc. (Santa Barbara CA).

FIDUCIARY TRUST INTERNATIONAL
600 Fifth Avenue, New York NY 10020. 212/632-3000. **Contact:** Human Resources. **World Wide Web address:** http://www.ftci.com. **Description:** Provides global investment management and custody services for institutional and individual clients with offices in 35 countries. **Positions advertised include:** Human Resources Analyst; Marketing Administrative Assistant; Credit Research Analyst; Legal Administrative Assistant; Futures Associate; Fixed Income Portfolio Analyst. **Parent company:** Franklin Templeton Investments. **Number of employees:** 6,800.

FIELDBROOK FOODS CORPORATION
One Ice Cream Drive, Dunkirk NY 14048. 716/366-5400. **Fax:** 716/366-5483. **Contact:** Human Resources Department. **E-mail address:** choward@fieldbrookfarms.com. **World Wide Web address:** http://www.fieldbrookfarms.com. **Description:** A manufacturer of ice cream and frozen desserts for customer brands and contract pack customers, for distribution through retail supermarket and food service distributors. **Positions advertised include:** Seasonal Production Worker.

FINANCIAL FEDERAL CORPORATION
733 Third Avenue, 7th Floor, New York NY 10017. 212/599-8000. **Fax:** 212/286-5885. **Contact:** Human Resources Department. **World Wide Web address:** http://www.financialfederal.com. **Description:** Provides financing of leases and capital loans on industrial, commercial, and professional equipment to middle market customers in a variety of industries. Founded in 1989. **Corporate headquarters location:** This location. **Other U.S. locations:** Irvine CA; Lisle IL; Charlotte NC; Teaneck NJ; Houston TX. **Listed on:** New York Stock Exchange. **Stock exchange symbol:** FIF. **Chairman/President/CEO:** Paul R. Sinsheimer. **Annual sales/revenues:** $139 million. **Number of employees nationwide:** 237.

FINANCIAL GUARANTY INSURANCE COMPANY
125 Park Avenue, 6th Floor, New York NY 10017. 212/312-3000. **Toll-free phone:** 800/352-0001. **Fax:** 212/312-3093. **Contact:** Human Resources. **World Wide Web address:** http://www.fgic.com. **Description:** A leading insurer of debt securities. FGIC also guarantees a variety of nonmunicipal structured obligations such as mortgage-backed securities. **Subsidiaries include:** FGIC Securities Purchase; FGIC Capital Market Services Group. **Parent company:** General Electric Capital Corporation (Fairfield CT).

FINANCIAL SECURITY ASSURANCE HOLDINGS LTD./FINANCIAL SECURITY ASSURANCE INC.
350 Park Avenue, New York NY 10022. 212/826-0100. **Fax:** 212/688-3107. **Contact:** Human Resources. **World Wide Web address:** http://www.fsa.com. **Description:** A monoline financial guaranty insurer of municipal bonds and asset-backed securities, including residential mortgage-backed securities. **Other U.S. locations:** San Francisco CA; Dallas TX. **International locations:** Sydney, Australia; Paris, France; Tokyo, Japan; Singapore; Madrid, Spain; London, United Kingdom. **Parent company:** Dexia Group (Brussels, Belgium). **Listed on:** New York Stock Exchange. **Stock exchange symbol:** FSA. **Annual sales/revenues:** $379 million. **Number of employees:** 283.

FINCH, PRUYN, & COMPANY, INC.
One Glen Street, Glens Falls NY 12801. 518/793-2541. **Toll-free phone:** 800/833-9983. **Fax:** 518/798-7433. **Contact:** Personnel. **World Wide Web address:** http://www.finchpaper.com. **Description:** Produces uncoated printing, copying, and writing papers.

FIND/SVP, INC.
625 Sixth Avenue, 2nd Floor, New York NY 10011-2020. 212/645-4500. **Fax:** 212/463-6232. **Contact:** Clodagh Whelan, Human Resources. **E-mail address:** careers@findsvp.com. **World Wide Web address:** http://www.findsvp.com. **Description:** Provides business and management consulting, research, and advisory services. The company also offers seminars, conferences, and publications. Founded in 1969. **Positions advertised include:** Industrial Products and Services Director; Corporate Sales Representative; Business Development Manager; Healthcare Team Consultant; Business Consultant; Associate Consultant. **Corporate headquarters location:** This location. **Other locations:** Nationwide. **Listed on:** Over The Counter. **Stock exchange symbol:** FSVP. **Chairman:** Martin E. Franklin. **Annual sales/revenues:** $22 million. **Number of employees:** 169.

FINLAY ENTERPRISES, INC.
529 Fifth Avenue, New York NY 10017. 212/808-2800. **Fax:** 212/557-3848. **Contact:** Personnel Manager. **E-mail address:** humanresources@fnly.com. **World Wide Web address:** http://www.finlayenterprises.com. **Description:** Operates through its subsidiary, Finlay Fine Jewelry Corporation, which sells jewelry through over 950 department store locations in the United States. **Corporate headquarters location:** This location. **Subsidiaries/affiliates include:** Thomas H. Lee; Finlay Fine Jewelry Corporation. **Listed on:** NASDAQ. **Stock exchange symbol:** FNLY. **Chairman/President/CEO:** Arthur E. Reiner. **Number of employees:** 6,500.

FIRECOM, INC.
39-27 59th Street, Woodside NY 11377. 718/899-6100. **Fax:** 718/899-1932. **Contact:** Human Resources. **E-mail address:** info@firecominc.com. **World Wide Web address:** http://www.firecominc.com. **Description:** Designs, manufactures, and distributes fire alarm and communication systems used for safety in large commercial buildings, primarily in the metropolitan New York area. Founded in 1963. **Corporate headquarters location:** This location. **Subsidiaries include:** Commercial Radio-Sound Corp. (NY); Fire Controls, Inc. (NY). **Chairman/President/CEO:** Paul Mendez. **Number of employees at this location:** 120.

FIRST ALBANY COMPANIES, INC.
30 South Pearl Street, P.O. Box 52, Albany NY 12207-0052. 518/447-8500. **Fax:** 518/447-8527. **Contact:** Human Resources. **World Wide Web address:** http://www.fac.com. **Description:** First Albany Companies offers a variety of investment and financial services through its three subsidiaries: First Albany Corporation, First Albany Asset Management Corporation, and Northeast Brokerage Services Corporation. First Albany Corporation conducts investment banking, financial advisory, and brokerage activity throughout the United States, serving private corporations, state and local governments and agencies, and individual and institutional customers. The company underwrites and distributes municipal and corporate securities and undertakes trading and market making of corporate, government, and municipal securities. First Albany Asset Management serves as investment advisor to individual and institutional clients. Northeast Brokerage provides securities brokerage services to retail customers. Founded in 1953. **Positions advertised include:** Senior LAN Administrator; Network Specialist; Research Associate. **Special programs:** Internships. **Corporate headquarters location:** This location. **Other U.S. locations:** Nationwide. **Subsidiaries include:** First Albany Corporation; First Albany Asset Management; FA Technology Ventures. **Listed on:** NASDAQ. **Stock exchange symbol:** FACT. **Chairman:** George C. McNamee. **Annual sales/revenues:** $182.5 million. **Number of employees:** 382.

FIRST ALLIED CORPORATION
270 Commerce Drive, Rochester NY 14623. 585/359-3000. **Toll-free phone:** 800/421-5327. **Fax:** 585/359-4690. **Contact:** Human Resources. **World Wide Web address:** http://www.firstalliedcorp.com. **Description:** Manages several properties including plazas, mobile homes, and nursing homes. **Corporate headquarters location:** This location. **Other locations:** CA; FL; NY. **Number of employees at this location:** 25.

FIRST INVESTORS CORPORATION
95 Wall Street, 23rd Floor, New York NY 10005. 212/858-8000. **Fax:** 212/858-8003. **Contact:** Human Resources. **E-mail address:** hr@firstinvestors.com. **World Wide Web address:** http://www.firstinvestors.com. **Description:** Specializes in the distribution and management of investment programs for individuals and corporations, as well as retirement plans. First Investors operates nationwide and through several area locations in Westchester County, New Jersey, and Long Island. Founded in 1930. **Corporate headquarters location:** This location. **Other locations:** Nationwide.

Subsidiaries include: First Investors Life Insurance Company; First Investors Federal Savings Bank; First Investors Management Company, Inc.; Administrative Data Management Corp.; SMART Tuition Management Services. **Number of employees:** 1,000.

FIRST OF LONG ISLAND CORPORATION
30 Glen Head Road, Glen Head NY 11545-1411. 516/671-4900. **Fax:** 516/671-3971. **Contact:** Debra Ryan, Human Resources. **E-mail address:** humres@optonline.net. **World Wide Web address:** http://www.fnbli.com. **Description:** First of Long Island Corporation is the holding company for First National Bank of Long Island, a full-service commercial bank that provides a broad range of financial services to individual, professional, corporate, institutional, and government customers through its 20 branches in Nassau and Suffolk counties. **Subsidiaries include:** First National Bank of Long Island; First of Long Island Agency sells insurance, primarily fixed-annuity products. Founded in 1927. **Listed on:** NASDAQ. **Stock exchange symbol:** FLIC. **Chairman/President/CEO/Director:** J. William Johnson. **Annual sales/revenues:** $42.5 million. **Number of employees:** 187.

FISHER-PRICE, INC.
636 Girard Avenue, East Aurora NY 14052. 716/687-3000. **Fax:** 716/687-3238. **Contact:** Employment Department. **E-mail address:** careers@fisher-price.com. **World Wide Web address:** http://www.fisher-price.com. **Description:** A manufacturer of toys and children's products. Among Fisher-Price's products are hair accessories, infant bedding, footwear, puzzles, bibs, bikes, sunglasses, headwear, kidswear, home safety products, children's books, and arts and crafts. **Positions advertised include:** Marketing Associate; Human Resources Information System Analyst; Computer-assisted Design Specialist; Sculptor; Staff Accountant; Bilingual Accounting Assistant; Bilingual French Consumer Affairs Representative; Bilingual Spanish Consumer Affairs Representative; Product Development Engineer. **Corporate headquarters location:** This location. **Parent company:** Mattel, Inc. (El Segundo CA). **Annual sales/revenues:** $1.2 billion. **Number of employees at this location:** 1,000.

FISHKILL HEALTH CENTER, INC.
22 Robert R. Kasin Way, Beacon NY 12508-1560. 845/831-8704. **Fax:** 845/831-1124. **Contact:** Human Resources. **World Wide Web address:** http://www.fishkillhealth.com. **Description:** The company operates a 160-bed, skilled care nursing home and the 62-bed Hudson Haven Care Center. Founded in 1973. **NOTE:** Entry-level positions and second and third shifts are offered. **Positions advertised include:** Certified Nurses Aide; Dietician/Nutritionist; Licensed Practical Nurse; Occupational Therapist; Physical Therapist; Registered Nurse; Social Worker. **Special programs:** Internships; Training; Summer Jobs. **Office hours:** Monday - Friday, 8:30 a.m. - 8:00 p.m. **Corporate headquarters location:** This location. **Other U.S. locations:** Wappingers Falls NY. **Owner:** Lynn Kasin. **Number of employees at this location:** 300. **Number of employees nationwide:** 400.

FLIGHTLINE ELECTRONICS
7625 Omni Tech Park, Victor NY 14564. 585/924-4000. **Fax:** 585/924-5732. **Contact:** Human Resources. **E-mail address:** info@ultra-fei.com. **World Wide Web address:** http://www.flightline-systems.com. **Description:** A defense contractor involved in the design, development, and manufacture of sonobuoy receivers used in military aircraft for anti-submarine warfare as well as military airborne communications equipment for use by defense departments of the U.S. and allied governments. **NOTE:** Entry-level positions are offered. **Special programs:** Co-ops. **Corporate headquarters location:** This location. **Parent company:** Ultra Electronics Holdings plc (Greenford, England). **Operations at this facility include:** Manufacturing; Research and Development. **Number of employees at this location:** 95.

FLIGHTSAFETY INTERNATIONAL, INC.
Marine Air Terminal, LaGuardia Airport, Flushing NY 11371. 718/565-4100. **Fax:** 718/565-4169. **Contact:** Personnel. **E-mail address:** jobs@flightsafety.com. **World Wide Web address:** http://www.flightsafety.com. **Description:** FlightSafety International provides high-technology training to operators of aircraft and ships from 42 training centers in North America and Europe. Total training systems are used including the company's 200 simulators and training devices, computer-based training, and professional instructors. The company's worldwide clients include corporations, airlines, the military, and government agencies. Founded in 1951. **Positions advertised include:** Pilot Simulator Instructor; Flight Engineer Instructor. **Corporate headquarters location:** This location. **Other U.S. locations:** Nationwide. **International locations:** Canada; France; United Kingdom. **Subsidiaries include:** FlightSafety Boeing Training International; MarineSafety International. **Parent company:** Berkshire Hathaway (Omaha NE). **Number of employees worldwide:** 2,000.

FLORAL GLASS
895 Motor Parkway, P.O. Box 18039, Hauppauge NY 11788. 631/234-2200. **Fax:** 631/234-8866. **Contact:** Personnel. **World Wide Web address:** http://www.floralglass.com. **Description:** Manufactures specialty glass products including beveled mirrors. Founded in 1955. **Corporate headquarters location:** This location. **Other locations:** Bohemia NY; Cheshire CT; East Rutherford NJ. **Subsidiaries include:** Shapes & Surfaces.

FLUSHING HOSPITAL MEDICAL CENTER
4500 Parsons Boulevard, Flushing NY 11355. 718/670-5000. **Recorded jobline:** 718/670-JOBS. **Contact:** Recruitment Department. **E-mail address:** yng@jhmc.org. **World Wide Web address:** http://www.flushinghospital.org. **Description:** A 428-bed hospital. Flushing Hospital Medical Center is a major teaching affiliate of The Albert Einstein School of Medicine. **NOTE:** Recruitment phone: 718/206-8670. **Number of employees at this location:** 2,400.

FOOT LOCKER, INC.
112 West 34th Street, New York NY 10120. 212/720-3700. **Fax:** 866/855-4510. **Contact:** Larry Haley, Regional HR Director. **E-mail address:** lhaley@footlocker.com. **World Wide Web address:** http://www.footlocker.com. **Description:** Formerly the Venator Group, Foot Locker, Inc. is a global retailer with stores and related support facilities in 22 countries. The company retails and distributes a broad range of footwear, apparel, and department store merchandise through more than 3,600 specialty stores and general merchandise stores. The company operates retail units under the following names: Eastbay, Kinney, Foot Locker, Champs Sports, Lady Foot Locker, Northern Reflections, Little Folks, San Francisco Music Box Company, Rx Place, and World Foot Locker as well as operating the FootLocker.com Website. Founded in 1894. **NOTE:** Entry-level positions are offered. **Positions advertised include:** Finance Associate; Human Resources Specialist; Information Systems Engineer; Legal Associate; Logistics Specialist; Real Estate Analyst. **Corporate headquarters location:** This location. **International locations:** Worldwide. **Subsidiaries include:** Champ Sports; East Bay; Foot Locker; Kids Foot Locker; Lady Foot Locker. **Listed on:** New York Stock Exchange. **Stock exchange symbol:** FL. **Chairman:** J. Carter Bacot. **Annual sales/revenues:** $4.5 billion. **Number of employees at this location:** 450. **Number of employees nationwide:** 24,000. **Number of employees worldwide:** 25,000.

FORBES INC.
60 Fifth Avenue, New York NY 10011. 212/620-2200. **Fax:** 212/206-5105. **Contact:** Human Resources. **E-mail address:** jobs@forbes.com. **World Wide Web address:** http://www.forbes.com. **Description:** Publisher of biweekly business periodical, *Forbes*, as well as other custom publications and magazines including *Forbes FYI*, *American Heritage*, and *American Legacy*. The company also operates the Forbes.com Website and produces business conferences. Founded in 1917. **Special programs:** Internships. **Corporate headquarters location:** This location. **Subsidiaries include:** American Heritage; Forbes Global; Forbes media. **Operations at this facility include:** Administration; Sales. **Chairman:** Casper W. Weinberger. **President/CEO:** Malcolm S. (Steve) Forbes Jr. **Annual sales/revenues:** $410 million. **Number of employees:** 750.

THE FORD FOUNDATION
320 East 43rd Street, New York NY 10017. 212/573-5000. **Fax:** 212/351-3677. **Contact:** Human Resources. **World Wide Web address:** http://www.fordfound.org. **Description:** One of the largest philanthropic organizations in the United States. This private, nonprofit institution donates funds for educational, developmental, research, and experimental efforts designed to produce significant advances in a wide range of social problems. The company also operates several overseas field offices in Asia, Latin America, the Middle East, and Africa. **Corporate headquarters location:** This location. **Other locations:** Worldwide.

FORD MOTOR COMPANY
3663 Lake Shore Road, Buffalo NY 14219. 800/297-0570. **Contact:** Human Resources. **E-mail address:** hireinfo@ford.com. **World Wide Web address:** http://www.ford.com. **Description:** This location manufactures fenders, bumpers, doors, hoods, and roofs. Overall, Ford Motor Company is engaged in the design, development, manufacture, and sale of cars, trucks, tractors, and related components and accessories. Ford is also one of the largest providers of financial services in the United States. Ford's two core businesses are the Automotive Group and the Financial Services Group (Ford Credit, The Associates, USL Capital, and First Nationwide). Ford is also engaged in a number of other businesses, including electronics, glass, electrical and fuel-handling products, plastics, climate-control systems, automotive service and replacement parts, vehicle leasing and rental, and land development. **Positions advertised include:** Parts, Supply, & Logistics Marketing Specialist; Manufacturing Plant Engineering Supervisor; Plant Physician; Manufacturing Quality Engineer. **Corporate headquarters location:** Dearborn MI. **Listed on:** New York Stock Exchange. **Stock exchange symbol:** F. **Annual sales/revenues:** $163.5 billion. **Number of employees at this location:** 2,500. **Number of employees worldwide:** 350,321.

FORDHAM UNIVERSITY
441 East Fordham Road, Bronx NY 10458. 718/817-1000. **Contact:** Human Resources Department. **World Wide Web address:** http://www.fordham.edu. **Description:** A private, Jesuit university offering bachelor's and master's degrees from three campuses and 11 schools. **Positions advertised include:** Public Affairs Assistant; Assistant Director of Student Financial Services; Media Relations Specialist; Custodial Services Supervisor; Security Duty Supervisor; Resident Director; Wellness Center Coordinator; Underwriting Sales Representative; Duplicating Coordinator; Financial Services Representative; Admissions Clerk; Government Documents Clerk; Serials Clerk; Executive Secretary; Secretary; On-Campus Recruitment Assistant; Enrollment Services Representative; Weekend Evening Supervisor. **Special programs:** Internships.

FOREST LABORATORIES, INC.
909 Third Avenue, 24th Floor, New York NY 10022-4731. 212/421-7850. **Fax:** 212/750-9152. **Contact:** Human Resources. **E-mail address:** staffing@frx.com. **World Wide Web address:** http://www.frx.com. **Description:** Develops, manufactures, and sells branded and generic prescription drugs for the treatment of cardiovascular, central nervous system, pulmonary, and women's health problems. In the United States, Forest Laboratories' ethical specialty products and generics are marketed directly by the company's subsidiaries Forest Pharmaceuticals and Inwood Laboratories. In the United Kingdom, Ireland, and certain export markets, Forest Laboratories products are marketed directly by the company's subsidiaries, Pharmax Ltd. and Tosara Group. **Positions advertised include:** Sales Force Automation Analyst; Forecast Analyst; Licensing Secretary; Product Manager; Senior Product Manager; Customer Planning Long Term Care/Government Manager; Customer Planning Analyst; Customer Planning Pharmacy Benefit Manager; Business Development Assistant Director; Respiratory Product Manager; Senior Respiratory Product Manager. **Special programs:** Internships; Co-ops; Summer Jobs. **Office hours:** Monday - Friday, 9:00 a.m. - 5:00 p.m. **Corporate headquarters location:** This location. **Other U.S. locations:** St. Louis MO; Jersey City NJ; Commack NY; Farmingdale NY; Inwood NY; Cincinnati OH. **International locations:** Ireland; United Kingdom. **Subsidiaries include:** Forest Pharmaceuticals, Inc.; Inwood Laboratories, Inc.; Pharmax Ltd.; Tosara Group. **Operations at this facility include:** Accounting/Auditing; Administration; Financial Offices; Marketing; Sales. **Listed on:** New York Stock Exchange. **Stock exchange symbol:** FRX. **President:** Howard Solomon. **Annual sales/revenues:** $1.6 billion. **Number of employees at this location:** 350. **Number of employees nationwide:** 3,731.

VICTOR FORSTMANN, INC.
dba THE FORSTMANN COMPANY
498 Seventh Avenue, 15th Floor, New York NY 10018-6791. 212/642-6900. **Fax:** 212/642-6870. **Contact:** Administrative Assistant. **World Wide Web address:** http://www.forstmann.com. **Description:** Designs, manufactures, and markets woolen, worsted, and other fabrics primarily used in the production of brand-name and private label apparel for men and women, as well as specialty fabrics for use in billiard and gaming tables, sports caps, and career uniforms from two manufacturing plants in Dublin, Georgia. Since 1563. **Corporate headquarters location:** Dublin GA. **Operations at this facility include:** Sales, Credit & Marketing Office. **Number of employees:** 800.

FORTUNOFF
70 Charles Lindbergh Boulevard, Uniondale NY 11553. 516/832-9000. **Fax:** 516/832-1999. **Contact:** Personnel Manager. **E-mail address:** westburyhr@fortunoff.com. **World Wide Web address:** http://www.fortunoff.com. **Description:** Fortunoff offers a wide range of merchandise including home furnishings, fine jewelry, and fine silver. **Positions advertised include:** Buyer; Administrative Assistant; Call Center Representative; Training Manager; Sales Associate; Warehouse Clerk. **Corporate headquarters location:** This location. **Other locations:** Nationwide. **Annual sales/revenues:** $425 million. **Number of employees:** 3,000.

FOSTER HOME SERVICES
JEWISH CHILD CARE ASSOCIATION
120 Wall Street, 12th Floor, New York NY 10005. 212/425-3333. **Fax:** 212/652-4731. **Contact:** Human Resources. **World Wide Web address:** http://www.jewishchildcareny.org. **Description:** Provides social services for children including the placement of abused children in foster homes, as well as training programs for future foster parents. Founded in 1822. **NOTE:** See website for a current listing of job openings with detailed application information. **Positions advertised include:** Registered Nurse; Social Worker; Residential Milieu Counselor; Recruiter/Trainer. **Corporate headquarters location:** This location. **Operations at this facility include:** Administration; Service.

FOSTER WHEELER LTD.
9431 Foster Wheeler Road, Dansville NY 14437. 716/335-3131. **Fax:** 585/335-3018. **Contact:** Human Resources. **E-mail address:** us_staffing@fwc.com. **World Wide Web address:** http://www.fwc.com. **Description:** Engaged in three business segments: process plants segment, consisting primarily of the design, engineering, and construction of process plants and fired heaters for oil refiners and chemical producers; a utility and engine segment, consisting primarily of the design and fabrication of steam generators, condensers, feedwater heaters, electrostatic precipitators, and other pollution abatement equipment; and an industrial segment that supplies pressure vessels and internals, electrical copper products, industrial insulation, welding wire, and electrodes. **Corporate headquarters location:** Clinton NJ. **Other U.S. locations:** Nationwide. **International locations:** Worldwide. **Listed on:** New York Stock Exchange. **Stock exchange symbol:** FWC. **Annual sales/revenues:** $3.5 billion. **Number of employees:** 9,000.

E. FOUGERA & COMPANY
SAVAGE LABORATORIES
60 Baylis Road, Melville NY 11747. 631/454-6996. **Contact:** Human Resources Manager. **E-mail address:** hr@altanainc.com. **World Wide Web address:** http://www.fougera.com. **Description:** Manufactures various generic pharmaceuticals including multisource topicals and ophthalmics. Products include surgical lubricants, antifungal creams, hydrocortisone ointments, and other generic treatments. **Corporate headquarters location:** This location. **Parent company:** Altana, Inc. (also at this location) also owns Savage Laboratories, which manufactures ethical pharmaceuticals. **Positions advertised include:** Microbiologist; Quality Assurance Monitor; Analytical Services Supervisor.

FOUR CORNERS ABSTRACT CORPORATION
370 East Avenue, Rochester NY 14604. 716/454-2263. **Contact:** Human Resources. **World Wide Web address:** http://www.fourcornersabstract.com. **Description:** Provides services and products including real estate title searching, preparation of abstracts of title, issuance of title insurance as an agent for certain national underwriting companies, and real estate appraisals, primarily in western and central New York state. **Other area locations:** Albany NY; Binghamton NY; Buffalo NY; Syracuse NY; Utica NY. **Subsidiaries include:** Four Corners Abstract Corporation; Proper Appraisal Specialists, Inc.

4KIDS ENTERTAINMENT, INC.
1414 Avenue of the Americas, New York NY 10019. 212/758-7666. **Fax:** 212/980-0933. **Contact:** John Gansley, Human Resources. **World Wide Web address:** http://www.4kidsentertainmentinc.com. **Description:** A vertically integrated merchandising and entertainment company. 4Kids Entertainment is involved in merchandise licensing, toy design, and TV, movie, and music production. **Positions advertised include:** Sales Clerk; Marketing Specialist; Legal Assistant; Accountant; Graphic Designer. **Corporate headquarters location:** This location. **International locations:** London, United Kingdom. **Subsidiaries include:** 4Kids Entertainment International Limited; 4Kids Entertainment Licensing, Inc.; 4Kids Entertainment Home Video, Inc.; 4Kids Productions Inc.; 4Kids Ad Sales, Inc.; Leisure Concepts UK; Leisure Concepts, Inc.; 4Kids Technology, Inc.; The Summit Media Group, Inc.; Websites 4 Kids, Inc.; 4Kids Entertainment Music, Inc. **Listed on:** New York Stock Exchange. **Stock exchange symbol:** KDE. **Chairman/CEO:** Alfred (Al) R. Kahn. **Annual sales/revenues:** $53 million. **Number of employees:** 188.

FOXCARE NETWORK
dba A.O. FOX HOSPITAL
One Norton Avenue, Oneonta NY 13820. 607/431-5900. **Fax:** 607/431-5160. **Contact:** Keith Valk, Vice President of Human Resources. **E-mail address:** djohnson@foxcarenetwork.com. **World Wide Web address:** http://www.foxcarenetwork.com. **Description:** A hospital and nursing home that provide general medical care to the surrounding community. **NOTE:** Human Resources phone: 607/431-5940. **Positions advertised include:** Anesthesiologist; Cafeteria Worker; Cold Food Worker; Cardiology Technologist; Cardiovascular Sonographer; Certified Nurse Aide; Phlebotomist; Laboratory Clerk; Coding and Reimbursement Coordinator; Cook; Crisis Counselor; Cyber Cafe Worker; Dental Assistant; Emergency Department Receptionist; File Clerk; Fitness Coach; Environmental Services Aide; Front Desk Coach; General Dentist; Hospitalist; Kitchen Aide; Licensed Practical Nurse; Family Practices Nurse; Pediatrician; Pharmacy Technician; Psychiatrist; Admission Nurse; Radiologist; Registered Nurse. **Special programs:** Internships. **Operations at this facility include:** Administration; Service. **Number of employees at this location:** 740.

FOX NEWS NETWORK, LLC
dba FOX NEWS CHANNEL
1211 Avenue of the Americas, New York NY 10036. 212/301-3000. **Fax:** 212/301-8588. **Contact:** Department of Human Resources. **E-mail address:** resume@foxnews.com. **World Wide Web address:** http://www.foxnews.com. **Description:** A cable news company operating international television news network. **Corporate headquarters location:** This location. **Parent company:** Fox Entertainment Group Inc.

SAMUEL FRENCH INC.
45 West 25th Street, 2nd Floor, New York NY 10010-2751. 212/206-8990. **Fax:** 212/206-1429. **Contact:** Personnel Director. **World Wide Web address:** http://www.samuelfrench.com. **Description:** A publishing firm engaged in the production and distribution of plays and books relating to the theater. **Other U.S. locations:** Hollywood CA. **International locations:** Toronto, Canada; London, England.

FREQUENCY ELECTRONICS, INC.
55 Charles Lindbergh Boulevard, Mitchel Field NY 11553. 516/794-4500. **Fax:** 516-794-4340. **Contact:** Human Resources Department. **E-mail address:** hr@freqelec.com. **World Wide Web address:** http://www.freqelec.com. **Description:** A manufacturer of products used to synchronize voice, data, and video transmissions in wireless communications systems for ground-based stations and commercial satellites. **Positions advertised include:** Sr. RF Design Engineer; Crystal Engineer; Sr. Technician; Material Control Planner/Administrator; Reliability Engineer. **Number of employees at this location:** 250.

FRIED, FRANK, HARRIS, SHRIVER & JACOBSON
One New York Plaza, New York NY 10004. 212/859-8621. **Fax:** 212/859-8589. **Contact:** Anwara Khanam, Human Resources Coordinator. **E-mail address:** resumes@friedfrank.com. **World Wide Web address:** http://www.ffhsj.com. **Description:** A law firm specializing in corporate law, litigation, real estate, estates, trusts, and pension. **Positions advertised include:** Attorney; Paralegal. **Corporate headquarters location:** This location. **Other U.S. locations:** Washington DC. **International locations:** London, England.

FRIENDSHIP DAIRIES, INC.
One Jericho Plaza, Jericho NY 11753-1668. 716/973-3031. **Contact:** Human Resources. **E-mail address:** myfriends@friendshipdairies.com. **World Wide Web address:** http://www.friendshipdairies.com. **Description:** Engaged in the production of dairy products such as cottage cheese, sour cream, and milk. Friendship Dairies distribute their goods nationally. **Corporate headquarters location:** Jericho NY. **Number of employees at this location:** 200.

FRONTIER CORPORATION
180 South Clinton Avenue, Rochester NY 14646. 716/777-1962. **Fax:** 716/325-7692. **Contact:** Corporate Staffing. **World Wide Web address:** http://www.frontieronline.com. **Description:** A telecommunications company. **NOTE:** Employment matters are handled through a third party representative for the parent company using the e-mail address above. **Positions advertised include:** Network Operations Specialist; Service Office Representative; Consumer Sales Executive; Communications Service Technician; Regulatory Analyst; Customer Care Supervisor; Sales and Service Consultant; Directory Assistance Operator; Senior Financial Analyst; Small Business Account Representative; Service Office Representative; Physical Security Supervisor; Regional Vice President; Marketing Vice President; Senior Systems Analyst. **Corporate headquarters location:** This location. **Other U.S. locations:** Nationwide. **Parent company:** Citizens Communications Company (Stamford CT).

FRONTIER INSURANCE GROUP
146 Rock Hill Drive, Rock Hill NY 12775-8000. 845/794-3600. **Fax:** 845/796-1925. **Contact:** Human Resources. **World Wide Web address:** http://www.frontier.com. **Description:** Frontier Insurance Group is an insurance holding company operating through its subsidiaries in all 50 states engaged as an underwriter and creator of specialty insurance products. Founded in 1934. **Special programs:** Internships. **Corporate headquarters location:** This location. **Other U.S. locations:** Nationwide. **Operations at this facility include:** Corporate Administration. **Listed on:** Over The Counter. **Stock exchange symbol:** FTER. **Annual sales/revenues:** $537 million. **Number of employees:** 600.

G-III APPAREL GROUP, LTD.
512 Seventh Avenue, New York NY 10018-4202. 212/403-0500. **Fax:** 212/403-0551. **Contact:** Human Resources. **World Wide Web address:** http://www.g-iii.com. **Description:** G-III Apparel Group, Ltd. designs, manufactures, imports, and markets an extensive range of apparel including coats, jackets, pants, skirts, and other sportswear items under its G-III, Siena, Siena Studio, Colebrook and Co., Kenneth Cole, and Nine West labels, and under private retail and licensed labels. The company also manufactures and markets a full line of women's leather apparel in junior, miss, and half sizes; and an outerwear line of men's leather apparel at a wide range of retail sales prices. The company's products also include textile outerwear, woolen coats, and sportswear. **Corporate headquarters location:** This location. **Subsidiaries include:** Cole Haan; G-III; Jones New York; Kenneth Cole; Nine West. **Listed on:** NASDAQ. **Stock exchange symbol:** GIII. **Annual sales/revenues:** $203 million. **Number of employees:** 344.

GE PLASTICS
One Noryl Avenue, Selkirk NY 12158. 518/475-5011. **Contact:** Human Resources. **World Wide Web address:** http://www.geplastics.com. **Description:** Manufactures industrial plastic pellets. **Parent company:** Through its subsidiaries, GE Plastics produces high-performance polymers used in a variety of industries including electronics, office equipment, computer, automotive, and original equipment manufacturers. **Positions advertised include:** Productivity Engineer; Inside Sales Representative. **Corporate headquarters location:** Pittsfield MA. **Other locations:** Worldwide. **Subsidiaries include:** GE Polymerland; GE Electromaterials; GE Structured Products; GE Polymershapes; GE Petrochemicals; LNP Engineering Plastics, Inc. **Parent company:** General Electric Company (Fairfield CT) is a diversified manufacturer operating in the following areas: aircraft engines (jet engines, replacement parts, and repair services for commercial, military, executive, and commuter aircraft); appliances; broadcasting (NBC); industrial (lighting products, electrical distribution and control equipment, transportation systems products, electric motors and related products, a broad range of electrical and electronic industrial automation products, and a network of electrical supply houses); materials (plastics, ABS resins, silicones, superabrasives, and laminates); power systems (products for the generation, transmission, and distribution of electricity); technical products and systems (medical systems and equipment, as well as a full range of computer-based information and data interchange services for both internal use and external commercial and industrial customers); and capital services (consumer services, financing, and specialty insurance). **President/CEO:** John Krenicki Jr. **Annual sales/revenues:** $5.2 billion. **Number of employees:** 12,000.

GE POWER SYSTEMS
One River Road, Schenectady NY 12345. 518/385-2211. **Fax:** 518/385-9051. **Contact:** Human Resources. **World Wide Web address:** http://www.gepower.com. **Description:** GE Power Systems supplies energy products to utilities and government customers worldwide including compressors, turbines, generators, and nuclear reactors as well as fuel, support services and oil and gas distribution equipment. **Positions advertised include:** Application Engineer; Equipment Management Program Engineer; Equipment Application Consulting Engineer; Performance Engineer; Application Engineer; Senior Engineer; Equipment Application Consultant; Program Engineer. **Corporate headquarters location:** This location. **Other locations:** Nationwide. **Subsidiaries include:** CONMEC, Inc. **Parent company:** General Electric Company (Fairfield CT) is a diversified manufacturer operating in the following areas: aircraft engines (jet engines, replacement parts, and repair services for commercial, military, executive, and commuter aircraft); appliances; broadcasting (NBC); industrial (lighting products, electrical distribution and control equipment, transportation systems products, electric motors and related products, a broad range of electrical and electronic industrial automation products, and a network of electrical supply houses); materials (plastics, ABS resins, silicones, superabrasives, and laminates); power systems (products for the generation, transmission, and distribution of electricity); technical products and systems (medical systems and equipment, as well as a full range of computer-based information and data interchange services for both internal use and external commercial and

industrial customers); and capital services (consumer services, financing, and specialty insurance). **Operations at this facility include:** Corporate Administration; Manufacturing equipment for the generation, transmission, and distribution of electricity. **President/CEO:** John G Rice. **Annual sales/revenues:** $23 billion. **Number of employees:** 35,000.

GE SPECIALTY MATERIALS
dba GE SILICONES
260 Hudson River Road, Building 11, Waterford NY 12188-1910. 518/237-3330. **Contact:** Human Resources. **World Wide Web address:** http://www.gesilicones.com. **Description:** GE Silicones is the unit of GE Specialty Materials that produces adhesives, resins, and sealants. The other four units of GE Specialty Materials are GE Superabrasives, GE Specialty Chemicals, GE Quartz, and GE Betz, all of which manufacture a variety of industrial compounds and chemicals. **NOTE:** Jobseekers may use http://www.gecareers.com to search and apply for open positions. **Positions advertised include:** Air/Environmental Regulatory Leader; Personal Care/Home Care Application Manager; Account Representative; Silicones Americas Controller; Environmental, Health, and Safety Manager; Senior Tax Specialist; International Finance Leader; Customer Quality Manager; Technical Development Engineer; NPI Engineer; Resins and Specialties Production Leader. **Corporate headquarters location:** Wilton CT. **Subsidiaries include:** GE Specialty Chemicals; GE Silicones; GE Superabrasives; GE Quartz; GE Betz. **Parent company:** General Electric Company operates in the following areas: aircraft engines (jet engines, replacement parts, and repair services for commercial, military, executive, and commuter aircraft); appliances; broadcasting (NBC); industrial (lighting products, electrical distribution and control equipment, transportation systems products, electric motors and related products, a broad range of electrical and electronic industrial automation products, and a network of electrical supply houses); materials (plastics, ABS resins, silicones, superabrasives, and laminates); power systems (products for the generation, transmission, and distribution of electricity); technical products and systems (medical systems and equipment, as well as a full range of computer-based information and data interchange services for both internal use and external commercial and industrial customers); and capital services (consumer services, financing, and specialty insurance). **Annual sales/revenues:** $2.4 billion.

GEICO (GOVERNMENT EMPLOYEES INSURANCE COMPANY)
750 Woodbury Road, Woodbury NY 11797. 516/496-5208. 800/645-7550 ext.5356. **Fax:** 516/496-5769. **Contact:** Human Resources Department. **E-mail address:** r2jobs@geico.com. **World Wide Web address:** http://www.geico.com. **Description:** A multiple-line property and casualty insurer offering private passenger automobile, homeowners, fire, and extended coverage; professional and comprehensive personal liability; and boat owners insurance. **Positions advertised include:** Auto Damage Adjuster; Claims Examiner; Claims Service Representative; Customer Service Insurance Counselor; Sales Counselor; Telephone Claim Representative. **Corporate headquarters location:** Chevy Chase MD. **Other U.S. locations:** Nationwide. **Parent company:** Berkshire Hathaway (Omaha NE). **Number of employees at this location:** 1,800. **Number of employees nationwide:** 20,000.

GALEY & LORD, INC.
980 Avenue of the Americas, 4th Floor, New York NY 10018-5401. 212/465-3000. **Fax:** 212/465-3024. **Contact:** Human Resources. **World Wide Web address:** http://www.gnlpromo.com. **Description:** Galey & Lord is a leading manufacturer and marketer of apparel fabric sold to clothing manufacturers. The company is a major producer of wrinkle-free cotton fabrics for uniforms and for sportswear manufacturers and printed fabrics for the home. Galey & Lord also manufactures denim. **NOTE:** Direct calls in Spanish to 212/465-3088. **Corporate headquarters location:** This location. **Other U.S. locations:** Greensboro NC. **Subsidiaries include:** G&L Service Company provides marketing services for Galey & Lord. Galey & Lord Home Fashion Fabrics manufactures and distributes fabrics used in home decorating and furnishing. Klopman International is a supplier of fabrics used in career wear. Swift Denim manufactures and distributes a wide variety of denim products. **Listed on:** Over The Counter. **Stock exchange symbol:** GYLDQ. **Chairman/President/CEO:** Arthur C. Wiener. **Annual sales/revenues:** $667 million. **Number of employees:** 5,390.

GANNETT COMPANY, INC.
535 Madison Avenue, New York NY 10022. 212/715-5300. **Contact:** Human Resources. **World Wide Web address:** http://www.gannett.com. **Description:** Gannett Company, Inc. is one of the largest news and information organizations in the United States. Gannett Company is involved in newspaper publishing, radio and television broadcasting, cable television, television entertainment programming, and outdoor advertising. The company owns and operates 15 television stations, 7 FM radio stations, and 6 AM radio stations. The company's cable division provides service to 458,000 subscribers. Gannett Outdoor Advertising operates in 19 major U.S. markets, as well as in Canada. The company has also diversified into areas such as alarm security services; commercial printing; data services; marketing; news programming; and newswire service, with operations in 44 states, as well as Washington DC, Canada, Guam, and the U.S. Virgin Islands. Average circulation of Gannett's 92 U.S. daily and nondaily newspapers and publications is approximately 6.6 million. Founded in 1906. **Corporate headquarters location:** McLean VA. **Other U.S. locations:** Nationwide. **International locations:** Canada. **Subsidiaries include:** CareerBuilder; Gannet Broadcasting on the Web; Gannett Community Newspapers; Gannett Media Technologies International; Gennett Newspapers on the Web; Gannett Television Stations; Newsquest plc. **Listed on:** New York Stock Exchange. **Stock exchange symbol:** GCI. **Annual sales/revenues:** $6.5 billion. **Number of employees at this location:** 250. **Number of employees nationwide:** 51,000.

GARAN, INCORPORATED
350 Fifth Avenue, 19th Floor, New York NY 10118. 212/563-2000. **Fax:** 212/971-2250. **Contact:** Jodi Schad, Personnel Manager. **Description:** Garan designs, manufactures, and sells apparel for children, women, and men. Products include shirts, sweatshirts, sweaters, trousers, skirts, shorts, and overalls. Trade names, trademarks, and licensed names include Garanimals, Garan by Marita, Bobbie Brooks, Garan Mountain Lion, Long Gone, Team Rated, National Football League, National Basketball Association, National Hockey League, Major League Baseball, and Disney. Founded in 1941. **Corporate headquarters location:** This location. **Subsidiaries include:** Geranimals. **Parent company:** Berkshire Hathaway (Omaha NE). **Chairman/CEO:** Seymour Lichtenstein. **Annual sales/revenues:** $257 million. **Number of employees:** 5,100.

GARLAND PUBLISHING
29 West 35th Street, 10th Floor, New York NY 10001. 917/351-7100. **Contact:** Human Resources. **World Wide Web address:** http://www.garlandscience.com. **Description:** Publishes scholarly books in the areas of science textbooks, literary manuscripts, architecture, music, and encyclopedias. **Positions advertised include:** Assistant Editor; Science Editorial Assistant; Reference Production Assistant. **Parent company:** Taylor & Francis Group (also at this location).

GARY PLASTIC PACKAGING CORPORATION
1340 Viele Avenue, Bronx NY 10474-7124. 718/893-2200. **Toll-free phone:** 800/221-8150. **Fax:** 718/378-2141. **Contact:** Personnel Director. **World Wide Web address:** http://www.plasticboxes.com. **Description:** Manufactures plastic display and storage boxes for collectibles. Founded in 1963. **Corporate headquarters location:** This location.

GATEWAY COMMUNITY INDUSTRIES, INC.
P.O. Box 5002, Kingston NY 12402-5002. 845/331-1261. **Physical address:** One Amy Kay Parkway, Kingston NY 12401. **Fax:** 845/331-2112. **Contact:** Human Resources Manager. **E-mail address:** humanresources@gatewayindustries.org. **World Wide Web address:** http://www.gatewayindustries.org. **Description:** An independent, non-profit vocational rehabilitation and training center assisting people with mental and physical disabilities to acquire, use, and maintain skills by providing comprehensive employment services including vocational evaluation, job training, job placement, vocational work center employment, supported employment, psychiatric rehabilitation, continuing day treatment, and residential rehabilitation. **Positions advertised include:** Assistant Residential Director; Backup Van Driver; Continuing Day Treatment Group Facilitator; Custom Cleaning Supervisor; Custodial Worker; Day Habilitation Assistant; Employment Specialist; Food Service Supervisor; Nurse Practitioner; Resident Counselor; Senior Counselor; Site Supervisor; Vocational Waiver Counselor.

GENERAL BEARING CORPORATION
44 High Street, West Nyack NY 10994. 845/358-6000. **Fax:** 845/348-9016. **Contact:** Ms. Fran Garner, Director of Human Resources. **E-mail address:** fran_garner@gbc.gnrl.com. **World Wide Web address:** http://www.generalbearing.com. **Description:** Manufactures bearing components and bearing products including ball bearings, tapered roller bearings, spherical roller bearings, and cylindrical roller bearings under The General and Hyatt trademarks. **Positions advertised include:** Sales Representative; Advertising Clerk; Computer Programmer; Customer Service Representative; Draftsperson; Industrial Engineer; Mechanical Engineer. **Listed on:** NASDAQ. **Stock exchange symbol:** GNRL. **Chairman:** Seymoure I. Gussack. **Annual sales/revenues:** $60 million. **Number of employees:** 1,001.

GENERAL DYNAMICS
4455 Genesee Street, Buffalo NY 14225. 716/632-7500. **Fax:** 716/631-6944. **Contact:** Lissa Carroll, Manager of Employment. **World Wide Web address:** http://www.gd-ais.com. **Description:** A major provider of high-technology services, systems, and products for the U.S. government, industry, and international customers, primarily in the areas of aerospace and electronics. Founded in 1946. **Positions advertised include:** Scientific/Software Engineer; Aerospace Engineer; Vehicle Engineer; Crash Investigator; Secretary. **Other U.S. locations:** Nationwide. **Operations at this facility include:** Divisional Headquarters.

GENERAL REINSURANCE CORPORATION
One Liberty Plaza, 22nd Floor, New York NY 10006-1433. 212/341-8000. **Fax:** 212/341-8150. **Contact:** Human Resources. **E-mail address:** jfoulds@gcr.com. **World Wide Web address:** http://www.genre.com. **Description:** A holding company for global reinsurance and risk assessment, risk transfer, and risk management operations which provides property and casualty reinsurance to primary insurers on a direct basis. The company markets reinsurance directly to these insurers through its own sales team. Reinsurance is marketed and underwritten on both a treaty and facultative basis. Treaty marketing efforts are focused on small to medium-sized regional and specialty property and casualty insurers. The company does not underwrite businesses that involve aviation, ocean marine, and professional liability. **Corporate headquarters location:** Stamford CT. **Subsidiaries include:** Gen Re Securities; General Reinsurance; General Star; Genesis; General RE New England Asset Management; Herbert Clough; USAIG; General Cologne Life Re of America; General Cologne Life RE Australia; General Cologne Life RE UK. **Parent company:** Berkshire Hathaway (Omaha NE). **Annual sales/revenues:** $8.4 billion.

GENERAL MEDIA INTERNATIONAL, INC.
11 Penn Plaza, 12th Floor, New York NY 10001. 212/702-6000. **Fax:** 212/702-6262. **Contact:** Carmela Monte, Human Resources Director. **Description:** Engaged in the publication and sale of men's and automotive magazines and produces various entertainment products. The publishing segment publishes *Penthouse* magazine and six other affiliated men's magazines. The company also publishes four domestic automotive titles, *Four Wheeler*, *Stock Car*, *Open Wheel*, and *Super Stock and Drag Illustrated*, which have a combined average monthly circulation of approximately 700,000 copies. The entertainment segment produces a number of adult-oriented entertainment products including pay-per-call telephone lines, videocassettes, pay-per-view programming, and CD-ROM interactive products. **Corporate headquarters location:** This location. **Subsidiaries include:** Penthouse Magazine. **Chairman/CEO:** Robert (Bob) C. Guccione. **Annual sales/revenues:** $65.4 million. **Number of employees:** 107.

GENERAL MILLS, INC.
54 South Michigan Avenue, Buffalo NY 14203. 716/856-6060. **Contact:** Human Resources. **World Wide Web address:** http://www.genmills.com. **Description:** Produces and markets foods including Cheerios, Wheaties, and Total cereals; Betty Crocker desserts, frostings, and mixes; Pop Secret microwave popcorn; Gorton's frozen seafood; Yoplait yogurt; Bisquick pancake mix; and Gold Medal flour. The company also operates over 1,000 Red Lobster and Olive Garden restaurants nationwide. Founded in 1928. **Corporate headquarters location:** Minneapolis MN. **Subsidiaries include:** Pillsbury; Small Planet. **Listed on:** New York Stock Exchange. **Stock exchange symbol:** GIS. **Annual sales/revenues:** $8 billion. **Number of employees nationwide:** 30,000.

GEORGIA-PACIFIC CORPORATION
327 Margaret Street, Plattsburgh NY 12901-1719. 518/561-3500. **Contact:** Human Resources. **World Wide Web address:** http://www.gp.com. **Description:** A paper and building materials manufacturing company. **Corporate headquarters location:** Atlanta GA. **Subsidiaries include:** CP&P, Inc. **Listed on:** New York Stock Exchange. **Stock exchange symbol:** GP. **Annual sales/revenues:** $23.3 billion. **Number of employees:** 61,000.

GERICARE
5 Odell Plaza, Yonkers NY 10701. 914/476-6500. **Contact:** Human Resources. **World Wide Web address:** http://www.gericaremedicalsupply.com. **Description:** A supplier of pharmaceuticals and related products to long-term care facilities, hospitals, and assisted living communities.

GETTY PETROLEUM MARKETING INC.
1500 Hampstead Turnpike, East Meadow NY 11554. 516/832-8800. **Fax:** 516/832-8272. **Contact:** Carolann Gaites, Human Resources Manager. **E-mail address:** hrdept@getty.com. **World Wide Web address:** http://www.getty.com. **Description:** A

large, independent wholesaler and retailer of gasoline and petroleum products. The company also stores and distributes petroleum and gasoline products. Service stations operate under the names Getty and Power Test. Principal products for resale include gasoline, oil, diesel fuel, and kerosene. **NOTE:** Entry-level positions are offered. **Positions advertised include:** Mechanic; Gasoline Driver. **Corporate headquarters location:** This location. **Other U.S. locations:** CT; ME; MD; NJ; PA; RI. **Parent company:** OAO LUKOIL (Moscow, Russia). **President/CEO:** Vadim Gluzman.

GIBRALTAR STEEL CORPORATION
3556 Lake Shore Road, P.O. Box 2028, Buffalo NY 14219-0228. 716/826-6500. **Fax:** 716/826-1589. **Contact:** Human Resources. **World Wide Web address:** http://www.gibraltar1.com. **Description:** Produces processed steel products, specializing in fully processed, cold-rolled strip steel. Gibraltar also produces heavy-duty steel strapping, offers computerized steel storage and distribution services, and, through its joint venture, produces steel pickling. **Corporate headquarters location:** This location. **Listed on:** NASDAQ. **Stock exchange symbol:** ROCK. **Chairman/CEO:** Brian J. Lipke. **Annual sales/revenues:** $645 million. **Number of employees:** 3,400.

GILMAN & CIOCIA INC.
1311 Mamaroneck Avenue, Suite 160, White Plains NY 10605. 914/397-4829. **Fax:** 914/997-5461. **Contact:** Victoria O'Hara, Human Resources Director. **E-mail address:** resumes@gilcio.com. **World Wide Web address:** http://www.gilcio.com. **Description:** Provides income tax and financial planning services including insurance, investments, pensions, and estate planning. **Positions advertised include:** Tax Preparer; Financial Planner; Receptionist. **Corporate headquarters location:** This location. **Listed on:** Over The Counter. **Stock exchange symbol:** GTAX. **Chairman:** James Ciocia. **Annual sales/revenues:** $ 106.5 million. **Number of employees:** 819.

GIRL SCOUTS OF THE UNITED STATES OF AMERICA
420 Fifth Avenue, New York NY 10018-2798. 212/852-8000. **Toll-free phone:** 800/GSU-SA4U. **Fax:** 212/852-6514. **Contact:** Staffing Department. **World Wide Web address:** http://www.girlscouts.org. **Description:** Girl Scouts is a non-profit national scouting organization for girls. **Positions advertised include:** Inventory Management Director; Adult Development & Instructional Design Consultant. **Corporate headquarters location:** This location. **Chairperson:** Cynthia Bramlett Thompson. **Annual sales/revenues:** 41.6 million. **Number of employees:** 480.

THE GLEASON WORKS
1000 University Avenue, P.O. Box 22970, Rochester NY 14692-2970. 585/473-1000. **Fax:** 585/461-4348. **Contact:** Human Resources. **E-mail address:** careers@gleason.com. **World Wide Web address:** http://www.gleason.com. **Description:** The Gleason Works designs, manufactures, and sells machinery and equipment for the production of gears. The company manufactures a complete line of machines and tooling for bevel gears and manufactures machines for producing parallel axis gears. The Gleason Works' major customers are in the automotive, truck, aerospace, construction, farm, and marine industries. **Corporate headquarters location:** This location.

GLENS FALLS HOSPITAL
100 Park Street, Glens Falls NY 12801. 518/926-1000. **Contact:** Human Resources. **E-mail address:** humanresources@glensfallshosp.org. **World Wide Web address:** http://www.glensfallshospital.org. **Description:** A full-service, acute care, community hospital providing inpatient and outpatient services. **NOTE:** Human Resources phone: 518/926-1801. **Positions advertised include:** Respite Care Provider; Licensed Practical Nurse; Physical Therapy Assistant; Social Worker; Mammography Technologist; Staff Registered Nurse; Psychiatric Social Worker. **Parent company:** Adirondack Health Services Corporation.

GLENS FALLS NATIONAL BANK
250 Glen Street, Glens Falls NY 12801. 518/793-4121. **Contact:** Sally Costello, Human Resources Manager. **World Wide Web address:** http://www.gfnational.com. **Description:** A full-service bank and trust company. Glens Falls National offers services including checking and savings accounts; personal and commercial loans; and trust accounts to its customers. Founded in 1851. **NOTE:** Hiring is done through the parent company's website: http://www.arrowfinancial.com/employment_opportunities. **Parent company:** Arrow Financial Corporation (also at this location).

GLOBAL GROUND
111 Great Neck Road, Great Neck NY 11021. 516/487-8610. **Fax:** 516/498-1534. **Contact:** Human Resources. **Description:** A nationwide aviation service company providing contracting services to airlines and airports including loading/unloading, cleaning planes, fueling planes, and cargo services. **Special programs:** Internships. **Corporate headquarters location:** This location. **Subsidiaries include:** Hudson Aviation Services, Inc. **Number of employees at this location:** 45.

GOLDEN BOOKS FAMILY ENTERTAINMENT, INC.
888 Seventh Avenue, 40th Floor, New York NY 10106. 212/547-6700. **Contact:** Human Resources. **World Wide Web address:** http://www.goldenbooks.com. **Description:** A publisher of children's books and family entertainment products. Titles include *The Poky Little Puppy*, *Pat the Bunny*, and *Little LuLu*. **Parent company:** Random House, Inc.

GOLDMAN SACHS & COMPANY
85 Broad Street, New York NY 10004. 212/902-1000. **Contact:** Recruiting Department. **World Wide Web address:** http://www.gs.com. **Description:** An investment banking firm. **NOTE:** Interested jobseekers should send resumes to 180 Maiden Lane, 23rd Floor, New York NY 10038. **Corporate headquarters location:** This location. **Other U.S. locations:** Nationwide. **International locations:** Worldwide.

GOODYEAR DUNLOP TIRES NORTH AMERICA LTD.
P.O. Box 1109, Buffalo NY 14240-1109. 716/879-8200. **Contact:** Employee Relations. **World Wide Web address:** http://www.dunloptire.com. **Description:** Goodyear Dunlop Tires North America is a major manufacturer of automobile and truck tires. **Operations at this facility include:** Manufacturing.

GOODYEAR TIRE & RUBBER COMPANY
5500 Goodyear Drive, Niagara Falls NY 14304. 716/236-2600. **Contact:** Human Resources. **World Wide Web address:** http://www.goodyear.com. **Description:** The Goodyear Tire & Rubber Company's principal business is the development, manufacture, distribution, and sale of tires for most applications worldwide. Goodyear also manufactures and sells a broad spectrum of rubber products and rubber-related chemicals for various industrial and consumer markets and provides auto repair services. The company operates 32 plants in the United States, 42 plants in 29 other countries, and more than 1,800 retail tire and service centers and other distribution facilities around the globe. Divisions of Goodyear Tire & Rubber include North American Tire; Kelly-Springfield, Goodyear Europe; Goodyear Latin America; Goodyear Asia; Engineered Products; Chemicals; Celeron; and Goodyear Racing. **Corporate headquarters location:** Akron OH **Operations at this facility include:** Chemical plant manufacturing of PVC resins and preservatives for the tire industry. **Listed on:** New York Stock Exchange. **Stock exchange symbol:** GT. **Annual sales/revenues:** $13.9 billion. **Number of employees worldwide:** 92,742.

GOTHAM INC.
100 Fifth Avenue, New York NY 10011. 212/414-7000. **Contact:** Patti Ransom, Director Human Resources. **E-mail address:** jobs@gothaminc.com. **World Wide Web address:** http://www.gothaminc.com. **Description:** Specializes in creating start-up brands with an emphasis on fashion and beauty advertising. Founded in 1994. **CEO:** Stone Roberts.

GOULDS PUMPS INC.
240 Fall Street, Seneca Falls NY 13148. 315/568-2811. **Contact:** Employment/EEO Specialist. **World Wide Web address:** http://www.gouldspumps.com. **Description:** A manufacturer of centrifugal pumps for industrial, commercial, and residential uses. **Positions advertised include:** Financial Analyst; Credit Analyst; Fixed Asset Analyst; Human Resource Manager; Foundry Director; Metallurgist. **Corporate headquarters location:** This location. **Other locations:** Nationwide. **Operations at this facility include:** Administration; Manufacturing; Research and Development; Sales; Service.

GRAHAM CORPORATION
20 Florence Avenue, Batavia NY 14020. 585/343-2216. **Fax:** 585/343-1097. **Contact:** Human Resources. **World Wide Web address:** http://www.grahamcorp.com. **Description:** Graham designs and manufactures vacuum and heat transfer equipment specializing in vacuum systems, pumps, compressors, and heat exchangers designed to create vacuums, condense steam, or produce heat. The principal markets for this equipment are the chemical, petrochemical, petroleum refining, and electric power generating industries. Graham equipment is sold by a combination of direct company sales engineers and independent sales representatives located in over 40 major cities. **Corporate headquarters location:** This location. **Subsidiaries include:** Graham Precision Pumps. **Parent company:** Graham Precision Pumps Limited (Congleton, Cheshire, United Kingdom). **Listed on:** American Stock Exchange. **Stock exchange symbol:** GHM. **Chairman:** Jerald D. Bidlack. **Annual sales/revenues:** $47.4 million. **Number of employees:** 288.

GRANITE BROADCASTING CORPORATION
767 Third Avenue, 34th Floor, New York NY 10017. 212/826-2530. **Fax:** 212/826-2858. **Contact:** Dolores Perez, Personnel Manager. **World Wide Web address:** http://www.granitetv.com. **Description:** Granite Broadcasting Corporation owns and operates eight network-affiliated television stations in California, Illinois, Indiana, Michigan, Minnesota, New York, and Washington. **Corporate headquarters location:** This location. **Subsidiaries include:** KBJR-TV/NBC; KBWB-TV/WB; KSEE-TV/NBC; WDWB-TV/WB; WEEK-TV/NBC; WKBW-TV/ABC; WPTA-TV/ABC; WTVH-TV/CBS. **Listed on:** NASDAQ. **Stock exchange symbol:** GBTVK. **Chairman/CEO:** W. Con Cornwall. **Annual sales/revenues:** $135 million. **Number of employees:** 732.

GRAY-SYRACUSE INC.
901 East Genesee Street, Chittenango NY 13037. 315/687-0014. **Fax:** 315/687-0023. **Contact:** Candace Orcott, Human Resources Department. **E-mail address:** gsinfo@escocorp.com. **World Wide Web address:** http://www.graysyracuse.com. **Description:** Gray-Syracuse Inc. operates a casting factory that manufactures aeronautical equipment; gas turbine engines for different vehicles; and other machinery items.

THE GREAT BRIDAL EXPO GROUP INC.
510 Montauk Highway, P.O. Box 337, West Islip NY 11795. 631/669-1200. **Fax:** 631/669-1680. **Contact:** Human Resources Department. **E-mail address:** info@greatbridalexpo.com. **World Wide Web address:** http://www.greatbridalexpo.com. **Description:** Produces and presents trade-show expositions in major cities in the United States. These expositions introduce prospective brides and grooms and their families to products and services they may need to plan their weddings, honeymoons, and homes.

GREAT NECK SAW MANUFACTURERS, INC.
165 East Second Street, Mineola NY 11501. 516/746-5352. **Contact:** Mr. Sydney Jacuff, President. **World Wide Web address:** http://www.greatnecksaw.com. **Description:** Manufactures a wide range of consumer and shop-quality hand tools. Founded in 1919. **Corporate headquarters location:** This location. **Other locations:** Nationwide. **Subsidiaries include:** Mayes Brothers.

GREENPOINT FINANCIAL CORP.
90 Park Avenue, New York NY 10016-1303. 212/834-1000. **Fax:** 212/834-1404. **Contact:** Human Resources. **World Wide Web address:** http://www.greenpoint.com. **Description:** A holding company operating 80 bank branches in the New York metropolitan area through its main subsidiary, GreenPoint Bank. The bank offers full-service banking products including consumer and insurance services in New York and services mortgages nationwide as well as offering real estate loans to low-income customers. **Positions advertised include:** Assistant Branch Manager; Branch Manager; Business Banking Specialist; Customer Service Representative; Building Services Maintenance Person; Sales Representative; Senior Business Banking Specialist; Senior Risk Analyst; Portfolio Originations Analyst. **Other area locations:** Albertson NY; Brooklyn NY; Great Neck NY; Hicksville NY; Kew Gardens NY; Ridgewood NY; Sunnyside NY. **Corporate headquarters location:** This location. **Subsidiaries include:** GreenPoint Bank; GreenPoint Mortgage Funding; GreenPoint Community Development. **Listed on:** New York Stock Exchange. **Stock exchange symbol:** GPT. **Chairman/CEO:** Thomas S. Johnson. **Annual sales/revenues:** $1.8 billion. **Number of employees:** 4,755.

GREY GLOBAL GROUP
777 Third Avenue, New York NY 10017. 212/546-2000. **Contact:** Human Resources: **E-mail address:** careers@grey.com. **World Wide Web address:** http://www.greyglobal.com. **Description:** An international advertising agency operating in 83 countries.

GRIFFIN CORPORATION
100 Jericho Quadrangle, Jericho NY 11753. 516/938-5544. **Fax:** 516/938-5644. **Contact:** Edward I. Kramer, VP of Personnel. **World Wide Web address:** http://www.griffincorp.com. **Description:** Operates through four business segments: garage doors; installation of garage doors and manufactured fireplaces; specialty plastics, diapers, medical garments, and surgical drapes; and advanced electronic communications and aerospace information systems for air-traffic control and radar systems. **Corporate headquarters location:** This location. **Subsidiaries include:** Buildex Inc.; Lightron Corporation; Telephonics Corporation. **Listed on:** New York

Stock Exchange. **Stock exchange symbol:** GFF. **Chairman/CEO:** Harvey R. Blau. **Annual sales/revenues:** $1.2 billion. **Number of employees:** 5,600.

GROUP HEALTH INCORPORATED
441 Ninth Avenue, New York NY 10001. 212/615-0000. **Fax:** 212/563-8563. **Contact:** Employment Manager. **World Wide Web address:** http://www.ghi.com. **Description:** One of the largest, nonprofit health services corporations operating throughout New York. The company provides insurance benefits and third-party administrative services. Founded in 1937. **Positions advertised include:** Oracle Database Administrator; Senior Programmer Analyst; Voice Communications Engineer; Claims Supervisor; Marketing Representative; Senior Financial Analyst; Senior Group Underwriter; Large Case Manager; Pre-Certification Nurse. **Corporate headquarters location:** This location. **Other area locations:** Albany NY; Buffalo NY; Garden City NY; Long Island NY; Rochester NY; Syracuse NY; Tarrytown NY. **Subsidiaries include:** GHI HMO. **Operations at this facility include:** Administration; Sales; Service. **Number of employees nationwide:** 2,200.

GRUBB & ELLIS COMPANY
55 East 59th Street, 10th Floor, New York NY 10022. 212/838-2000. **Contact:** Drew, O'Conner, Human Resources. **E-mail address:** jobs@grub-ellis.com. **World Wide Web address:** http://www.grubb-ellis.com. **Description:** A real estate management firm dealing primarily with commercial real estate including shopping centers, office buildings, and similar complexes. **Positions advertised include:** Real Estate Administrative Assistant; Business Analyst; Systems Analyst. **Corporate headquarters location:** Northbrook IL. **Other locations:** Worldwide. **Subsidiaries include:** The Wadley Donovan Group; Landauer Realty Group; Knight Frank. **Listed on:** Over The Counter. **Stock exchange symbol:** GBEL. **Annual sales/revenues:** $313 million. **Number of employees:** 8,300.

GUARDIAN CLEANING INDUSTRIES
170 Varick Street, 3rd Floor, New York NY 10013. 212/645-9500. **Contact:** Human Resources. **World Wide Web address:** http://www.guardian.baweb.com. **Description:** An industrial/commercial maintenance firm providing cleaning and exterminating services.

THE GUARDIAN LIFE INSURANCE COMPANY OF AMERICA
7 Hanover Square, New York NY 10004. 212/598-8000. **Fax:** 212/919-2170. **Contact:** Human Resources. **World Wide Web address:** http://www.guardianlife.com. **Description:** Guardian, a mutual company, specializes in life and disability insurance and also offers retirement programs, and provides HMO, PPO, dental, and vision health plans from 45 locations nationwide. The company offers other financial services in addition to health and live insurance. **Corporate headquarters location:** This location. **Other locations:** Nationwide. **Subsidiaries include:** First Commonwealth, Inc. **President/CEO/Director:** Dennis J. Manning. **Annual sales/revenues:** $7.2 billion. **Number of employees:** 5,500.

GUILDERLAND REINSURANCE COMPANY
52 Corporate Circle, Albany NY 12203. 518/862-7700. **Contact:** Human Resources. **Description:** Guilderland is engaged in the business of reinsuring other insurance companies.

THE GUNLOCKE COMPANY
One Gunlocke Drive, Wayland NY 14572-9515. 585/728-5111. **Fax:** 585/728-8334. **Contact:** Human Resources. **World Wide Web address:** http://www.gunlocke.com. **Description:** A manufacturer of high-end wood office furniture. **NOTE:** Human Resources phone: 800/828-8209. **Positions advertised include:** Production Manager. **Special programs:** Internships; Co-ops. **Corporate headquarters location:** This location. **Parent company:** Hon Industries (Muscatine IA). **Number of employees at this location:** 900.

GURNEY'S INN
290 Old Montauk Highway, Montauk NY 11954. 631/668-2345. **Fax:** 631/668-1881. **Contact:** Human Resources. **E-mail address:** hr@gurneys-inn.com. **World Wide Web address:** http://www.gurneys-inn.com. **Description:** Gurney's resort, spa, and convention center offers fine-dining and a full-service, 109-room hotel. **NOTE:** Entry-level positions are offered. Human Resources phone: 631/668-1770. **Positions advertised include:** Hair Stylist; Front Desk Receptionist; Message Therapist; Lifeguard; Weight Room Attendant; Spa Attendant; Porter; Fitness Instructor; Service Desk Attendant; Counter Server. **Special programs:** Internships; Apprenticeships; Summer Jobs. **Office hours:** Monday - Friday, 9:00 a.m. - 5:00 p.m. **Corporate headquarters location:** This location. **Number of employees at this location:** 250.

GUSSCO MANUFACTURING INC.
5112 Second Avenue, Brooklyn NY 11232. 718/492-7900. **Fax:** 718/492-0886. **Contact:** Arlene Thomashow, Human Resources Director. **World Wide Web address:** http://www.gussco.com. **Description:** A manufacturer of office filing supplies, cabinets, and systems. **Corporate headquarters location:** This location. **Other locations include:** Garfield NJ.

HBO (HOME BOX OFFICE)
1100 Avenue of the Americas, New York NY 10036. 212/512-1000. **Contact:** Shelley Fischel, Human Resources Director. **World Wide Web address:** http://www.hbo.com. **Description:** Operates HBO, HBO HDTV, and Cinemax, television networks dedicated to movies. Divisions of HBO include: MoreMAX, ThrillerMAX, and ActionMAX. **Positions advertised include:** Financial Operations and Reporting Assistant; Production Coordinator; Attorney; Product Development and Production Supervisor; Financial Analyst; Legal Contract Administrator; Executive Assistant; Compressionist; Writer; Producer. **Other U.S. locations:** Los Angeles CA. **Parent company:** AOL Time Warner Inc. **Chairman/CEO:** Chris Albrecht. **Annual sales/revenues:** $2.5 billion. **Number of employees:** 2,000.

HSBC BANK USA
452 Fifth Avenue, 12th Floor, New York NY 10018. 212/525-5000. **Fax:** 877/525-7575. **Recorded jobline:** 888/HRHELP4 (888/474-3574). **Contact:** HR Resourcing. **World Wide Web address:** http://www.us.hsbc.com. **Description:** A full-service bank with 400 branches in New York and operations in California, Pennsylvania, Florida, and Panama offering personal, commercial, and both residential and commercial mortgages and loans. The bank's investment products include mutual funds, wealth management services, a discount brokerage, and insurance. **Positions advertised include:** Senior Collateral Examination Officer; Senior Information Technology Audit Officer; Branch Customer Service Representative; Branch Manager; Consumer Banker; Personal Banking Officer. **Corporate headquarters location:** This location. **Other area locations:** Statewide. **locations:** CA; PA; FL. **International locations:** Panama. **Parent company:** HSBC Holdings plc. (London, United Kingdom). **Chairman:** Sir John R. H. Bond. **Annual sales/revenues:** $4.9 billion. **Number of employees:** 14,000.

HSBC BANK USA
One HSBC Center, 11th Floor, Buffalo NY 14203-2811. 716/841-2424. **Recorded jobline:** 888/HRHELP4. **Fax:** 716/841-1047. **Contact:** HR Resourcing. **World Wide Web address:** http://www.us.hsbc.com. **Description:** A full-service bank with 400 branches in New York and operations in California, Pennsylvania, Florida, and Panama offering personal, commercial, and both residential and commercial mortgages and loans. The bank's investment products include mutual funds, wealth management services, a discount brokerage, and insurance. **Positions advertised include:** Collateral Examination Officer; Commercial Real Estate Appraiser; Decision Support Analyst; Branch Customer Service Representative; Branch Manager; Consumer Banker; Personal Banking Officer; AS400 Computer Operator; Information Technology Specialist; Senior Solaris Systems Administrator; Senior Database Administrator; Senior Oracle Administrator; Residential Mortgage Processor; Proof Operator. **Corporate headquarters location:** This location. **Other area locations:** Statewide. **locations:** CA; PA; FL. **International locations:** Panama. **Parent company:** HSBC Holdings plc. (London, United Kingdom). **Chairman:** Sir John R. H. Bond. **Annual sales/revenues:** $4.9 billion. **Number of employees:** 14,000.

HABASIT BELTING INCORPORATED
1400 Clinton Street, Buffalo NY 14206-2919. 716/824-8484. **Contact:** Human Resources. **E-mail address:** hbi.habasit@us.habasit.com. **World Wide Web address:** http://www.habasitusa.com. **Description:** Manufactures conveyor belts for airports, factories, food stores, and a variety of other businesses. **NOTE:** Corporate Recruiter phone: 678/288-3508. **Corporate headquarters location:** Suwanee GA. **Other locations:** Atlanta GA; Middletown CT.

HAHN AUTOMOTIVE WAREHOUSE, INC.
415 West Main Street, Rochester NY 14608. 585/235-1595. **Fax:** 585/235-8615. **Contact:** Human Resources. **World Wide Web address:** http://www.hahnauto.com. **Description:** Hahn Automotive Warehouse is a regional distributor of automotive aftermarket parts to commercial jobbers and its own Advantage Auto Stores. The company distributes parts through 20 distribution centers. **Corporate headquarters location:** This location. **Subsidiaries include:** Advantage Auto Stores; Parts Master. **President/CEO:** Eli N. Futerman. **Annual sales/revenues:** $120 million. **Number of employees:** 1,142.

THE HAIN CELESTIAL GROUP
50 Charles Lindbergh Boulevard, Uniondale NY 11553. 516/237-6200. **Fax:** 516/237-6240. **Contact:** Maureen Paradine, Director of Human Resources. **World Wide Web address:** http://www.hain-celestial.com. **Description:** Formerly the Hain Food Group, the company markets and distributes health, organic, natural, and specialty food and beverage products. Specialty products include kosher foods, low calorie and diet foods and beverages, snack foods, and dietetic foods. **Corporate headquarters location:** This location. **Subsidiaries include:** Celestial Seasonings; Imagine Foods, Inc.; Earth's Best; Garden of Eatin'; Terra Chips; The Good Lunch; West Brae Natural; Westsoy; Yves Veggie Cuisine. **Listed on:** NASDAQ. **Stock exchange symbol:** HAIN. **Chairman/President/CEO:** Irwin D. Simon. **Annual sales/revenues:** $396 million. **Number of employees:** 1,337.

HANGER ORTHOPEDIC GROUP, INC.
151 Hempstead Turnpike, West Hempstead NY 11552. 516/481-9670. **Contact:** Human Resources. **World Wide Web address:** http://www.hanger.com. **Description:** A provider of orthotic and prosthetic rehabilitation services with 600 offices in 43 states. **NOTE:** Send resumes to: Sharon King, Recruitment Manager, P.O. Box 406, Alpharetta GA 30009; phone: 800/303-4969; fax: 800/288-5702; e-mail: sking@hanger.com. **Corporate headquarters location:** Bethesda MD. **Other U.S. locations:** Nationwide. **Operations at this facility include:** Hanger Prosthetics & Orthotics East, Inc. **Listed on:** New York Stock Exchange. **Stock exchange symbol:** HGR. **Number of employees nationwide:** 125. **Annual sales/revenues:** $525.5 million. **Number of employees:** 3,083.

HANNAFORD BROTHERS
900 Central Avenue, Albany NY 12206. 518/477-6483. **Fax:** 518/477-4095. **Contact:** Retail Employment Specialist. **E-mail address:** retail_opportunities@hannaford.com. **World Wide Web address:** http://www.hannaford.com. **Description:** A chain of grocery stores and distribution centers in the New England states and New York. Hannaford Brothers also operates as a retailer of food, general merchandise, and drug store products. **NOTE:** Apply either at local supermarket or send application materials to: Retail Employment Specialist, Hannaford Bros. Co., Mail Sort #7800, Portland ME 04104. **Corporate headquarters location:** Scarborough ME. **Other locations:** CT; RI; MA; ME; NH; NY; VT. **Parent company:** Delhaize America (Salisbury NC).

HANYS INSURANCE COMPANY
217 Great Oaks Boulevard, Albany NY 12203-5964. 518/862-0733. **Contact:** Patricia Kundel, Vice President. **Description:** Hanys Insurance specializes in medical malpractice insurance policies and claims.

HARCOURT INC.
15 East 26th Street, New York NY 10010. 212/592-1000. **Contact:** Human Resources. **World Wide Web address:** http://www.harcourt.com. **Description:** A publishing company. The operations are divided into Elementary and Secondary Education, and University and Professional Education. Elementary and Secondary Education publishes textbooks and other instructional materials, publishes and scores achievement and aptitude tests, and manufactures and markets school and office supplies and equipment. University and Professional Education publishes textbooks and other instructional materials for higher education, scientific and medical books and journals, and general fiction and nonfiction; publishes books and conducts courses and seminars for law, accounting, and business; and provides outplacement counseling services. **Corporate headquarters location:** Orlando FL.

HARDINGE INC.
One Hardinge Drive, P.O. Box 1507, Elmira NY 14902-1507. 607/734-2281. **Fax:** 607/732-4925. **Contact:** Personnel. **E-mail address:** personnel@hardinge.com. **World Wide Web address:** http://www.hardinge.com. **Description:** Manufactures machine tools and accessories. Founded in 1890. **Listed on:** NASDAQ. **Stock exchange symbol:** HDNG. **Annual sales/revenues:** $169 million. **Number of employees:** 1,150.

HARMAC MEDICAL PRODUCTS, INC.
2201 Bailey Avenue, Buffalo NY 14211. 716/897-4500. **Fax:** 716/897-0016. **Contact:** Donna Ciulis, Human Resources. **E-mail address:** info@harmac.com. **World Wide Web address:** http://www.harmac.com. **Description:** Manufactures disposable medical devices. **NOTE:** Entry-level positions and second and third shifts are offered. **Special programs:** Internships; Training. **Office hours:** Monday - Friday, 9:00 a.m. - 5:00 p.m. **International locations:** Ireland. **Number of employees at this location:** 450.

HARPERCOLLINS PUBLISHERS INC.
10 East 53rd Street, New York NY 10022. 212/207-7000. **Fax:** 212/207-7146. **Contact:** Human Resources. **E-mail address:** jobs@harpercollins.com. **World Wide Web address:** http://www.harpercollins.com. **Description:** HarperCollins Publishers is one of the largest book publishers in the world. Titles include fiction, nonfiction, and children's books. **Corporate headquarters location:** This location. **Other U.S. locations:** San Francisco CA. **Subsidiaries include:** Cliff Street Books; HarperAudio; HarperAustralia; HarperCanada; HarperCollins UK; Regan Books; Zondervan Publishing; HarperCollins Children's Books. **Parent company:** News Corporation (Sydney, Australia). **President/CEO:** Jane Friedman. **Annual sales/revenues:** $1.1 billion. **Number of employees at this location:** 600. **Number of employees worldwide:** 3,000.

HAUPPAUGE DIGITAL INC.
dba HAUPPAUGE COMPUTER WORKS INC.
91 Cabot Court, Hauppauge NY 11788. 631/434-1600. **Fax:** 631/434-3198. **Contact:** Cheryl Willins, Human Resources Manager. **World Wide Web address:** http://www.hauppauge.com. **Description:** Manufactures PC circuit boards that allow viewers to use computers to watch TV, videoconference, and watch VCRs or camcorders as well as boards that allow for radio and Internet broadcasting. **Corporate headquarters location:** This location. **Other locations:** Worldwide. **Listed on:** NASDAQ. **Stock exchange symbol:** HAUP. **Chairman/CEO:** Kenneth H. Plotkin. **Annual sales/revenues:** $43 million. **Number of employees:** 107.

HAZLOW ELECTRONICS INC.
49 Saint Bridget's Drive, Rochester NY 14605. 585/325-5323. **Fax:** 585/325-4308. **Contact:** Human Resources. **E-mail address:** info@hazlow.com. **World Wide Web address:** http://www.hazlow.com. **Description:** Manufactures cables for computers and other electronic devices. Founded in 1971.

HEALTH CARE DATA SYSTEMS INC.
6390 Fly Road, East Syracuse NY 13057. 315/437-7623. **Fax:** 315/437-8264. **Contact:** Human Resources. **World Wide Web address:** http://www.hcds.com. **Description:** Develops a variety of software products for the health care industry. **NOTE:** To inquire about opportunities contact the parent company: Jane C. Walsh, Vice President, Human Resources, Flow Management Technologies, Inc., 125 High Rock Avenue, Saratoga Springs NY 12866; phone: 518/580-9844 ext.3146; fax: 518/580-9843; email: jobs@flowmgt.com.

HEALTH MANAGEMENT SYSTEMS, INC.
401 Park Avenue South, New York NY 10016. 212/685-4545. **Fax:** 212/889-8776. **Contact:** Lewis D. Levetown, Director Human Resources. **E-mail address:** recruit@hmsy.com. **World Wide Web address:** http://www.hmsy.com. **Description:** The company works with government health agencies, Medicaid, and Medicare to recover overpaid healthcare expenses from providers by supplying information management services and software. HMS provides financial systems and consulting, retroactive insurance claims reprocessing, data processing, and third-party liability recovery services. **Corporate headquarters location:** This location. **Other U.S. locations:** Nationwide. **Affiliates include:** Accordis. **Parent company:** HMS Holdings Corp. (also at this location). **Chairman/CEO:** William (Bill) F. Miller III. **Annual sales/revenues:** $59 million. **Number of employees:** 433.

HEALTHPLEX, INC.
60 Charles Lindbergh Boulevard, Uniondale NY 11553-3608. 516/794-3000. **Fax:** 516/794-3186. **Contact:** Human Resources. **World Wide Web address:** http://www.healthplex.com. **Description:** Provides administrative services, primarily claims processing and related electronic data processing services. **Subsidiaries include:** Dentcare Delivery Systems, Inc.; International Healthcare Services, Inc.; OASYS Corporation. **Annual sales/revenues:** $21 million. **Number of employees:** 140.

THE HEARST CORPORATION
224 West 57th Street, New York NY 10019. 212/649-3660. **Fax:** 212/765-3528. **Contact:** Human Resources. **World Wide Web address:** http://www.hearstcorp.com. **Description:** A family-owned media company with operations in the publishing, broadcasting, and entertainment industries including 12 daily newspapers, 14 weekly newspapers, 15 consumer magazines, and TV and radio stations as well as interests in cable television networks and online services. The company is divided into six divisions: Newspapers, Magazines, Broadcasting, Entertainment/Syndicates, Interactive Media, and Business Media. **NOTE:** The company does not maintain a centralized listing of available job opportunities across all divisions and advises jobseekers to contact individual properties of interest directly. For the advertised Magazine positions, resumes should be mailed to: Hearst Magazines, Human Resources Department, 224 West 57th Street, 10th Floor, New York NY 10019. Jobseekers can also see http://www.hotjobs.com for employment listings. **Positions advertised include:** Good Housekeeping Institute - Assistant to the Technical Director; Esquire - Fashion & Retail Director; Good Housekeeping Institute - Chemist. **Corporate headquarters location:** This location. **Subsidiaries include:** A&E Television Networks; ESPN, Inc.; Hearst Magazines; Hearst Newspapers; Hearst-Argyle Television, Inc.; iVillage Inc.; King Features Syndicate, Inc.; Lifetime Entertainment Services. **Chairman:** George R. Hearst Jr. **Annual sales/revenues:** $3.3 billion. **Number of employees:** 17,170.

HEARST-ARGYLE TELEVISION, INC.
888 Seventh Avenue, 27th Floor, New York NY 10106. 212/887-6800. **Fax:** 212/887-6835. **Contact:** Personnel. **World Wide Web address:** http://www.hearstargyle.com. **Description:** Owns and manages 27 network affiliated television stations nationwide and manages two radio stations. The company's television stations comprise one of the largest non-network-owned television station groups. Hearst-Argyle Television, Inc.'s television stations include: 10 NBC affiliates, 12 ABC affiliated stations, two CBS affiliates, and a WB affiliate, as well as managing a UPN affiliate and an independent station. The company is involved in television production and syndication through a joint venture with NBC Enterprises and through a partnership with Internet Broadcasting Systems, Inc. is involved in convergence of local TV broadcasts and the Internet. **Corporate headquarters location:** This location. **Subsidiaries include:** Hearst-Argyle Television Productions. **Listed on:** New York Stock Exchange. **Stock exchange symbol:** HTV. **Chairman:** Victor F. Ganzi. **Annual sales/revenues:** $721 million. **Number of employees:** 3,179.

HELMSLEY ENTERPRISES, INC.
dba HELMSLEY-NOYES COMPANY INC.
230 Park Avenue, Suite 659, New York NY 10169-0399. 212/679-3600. **Fax:** 212/953-2810. **Contact:** Human Resources. **Description:** A commercial real estate agency engaged in the management of office buildings and a wide range of other institutional buildings including department stores, hotels, and corporate office buildings. **Corporate headquarters location:** This location. **Subsidiaries include:** Helmsley Hotels. **Chairperson/CEO:** Leona Helmsley. **Annual sales/revenues:** $1 billion. **Number of employees:** 3,000.

THE HELMSLEY PARK LANE HOTEL
36 Central Park South, New York NY 10019. 212/371-4000. **Fax:** 212/935-5489. **Contact:** Personnel. **World Wide Web address:** http://www.helmsleyhotels.com. **Description:** Operates a 650-room, luxury hotel with a wide range of lodging, lounge, dining, and meeting rooms. **Parent company:** Helmsley Hotels Group.

HELMSLEY-SPEAR, INC.
60 East 42nd Street, 53rd Floor, New York NY 10165. 212/687-6400. **Contact:** Human Resources Department. **World Wide Web address:** http://www. helmsleyspear.com. **Description:** One of the largest real estate service companies in the nation offering leasing (including industrial leasing, and retail and store leasing divisions); sales and brokerage; management; development; appraisals; and financing services. Founded in 1866. **Corporate headquarters location:** This location. **Parent company:** Helmsley Enterprises, Inc. (New York NY).

HENKEL LOCTITE
211 Franklin Street, Olean NY 14760-1297. 716/372-6300. **Fax:** 716/372-6864. **Contact:** Human Resources. **E-mail address:** hrclassifieds@loctite.com. **World Wide Web address:** http://www.loctite.com. **Description:** Henkel Loctite is a diverse, global manufacturing company specializing in consumer adhesives as well as cosmetics, toiletries, detergent, and home care products. The company's products include industrial and engineering adhesives and surface technologies. **Positions advertised include:** Project Engineer; Sales Representative. **Corporate headquarters location:** Rocky Hill CT. **Other U.S. locations:** Nationwide. **Parent company:** Henkel Corporation (Gulph Mills PA).

HENRY STREET SETTLEMENT
265 Henry Street, New York NY 10002. 212/766-9200. **Contact:** Human Resources. **World Wide Web address:** http://www.henrystreet.org. **Description:** Provides various social services including daycare, home care, housekeeping, Meals on Wheels, work training for 16- to 21-year-olds, after-school homework help, shelter for battered women, and care for pregnant teenagers. **Positions advertised include:** Shelter Director; Case Manager; Mental Health Care Social Worker; Information Systems Technician; Support Specialist; ESOL Instructor; Residence Assistant; Accounting Manager; Program Director; Training Coordinator; Youth Counselor; Parent Advocate Coordinator; Case Manager; Parent Advocate; Office Assistant; Case Manager; Docent Opportunity; Housekeeper; Job Developer.

HERON HOME & HEALTH CARE AGENCY
168-30 89th Avenue, Jamaica NY 11432. 718/291-8788. **Fax:** 718/291-8852. **E-mail address:** heron@heronhomecare.com. **World Wide Web address:** http://www.heronhomecare.com. **Contact:** Director. **Description:** A home health care agency providing skilled medical professionals to homebound patients and sells surgical and medical equipment. **Corporate headquarters location:** This location. **Other area locations:** Manhattan NY; Long Island NY.

HIGH FALLS BREWING COMPANY
445 Saint Paul Street, Rochester NY 14605-1726. 585/546-1030. **Fax:** 585/546-5011. **Contact:** Human Resources. **World Wide Web address:** http://www.highfalls.com. **Description:** Brews beer under the name Genesee Family of brands, Genny Light, 12 Horse Ale, Koch's Golden Anniversary, Michael Shea's, and JW Dundee. **Positions advertised include:** Liquid Packaging Machine Operator; Brewing Supervisor; Forklift Operator; Shipping Clerk.

HI-TECH PHARMACAL CO., INC.
369 Bayview Avenue, Amityville NY 11701. 631/789-8228. **Fax:** 631/789-8429. **Contact:** Carole Wood, Human Resources Manager. **World Wide Web address:** http://www.hitechpharm.com. **Description:** Develops, manufactures, and markets prescription and generic liquid and semi-solid drugs, as well as nutritional products. Hi-Tech Pharmacal manufactures more than 100 generic products marketed under the company's own brand names. **Subsidiaries include:** Health Care Products manufactures branded items marketed under the H-T, Sooth-It, and Diabetic Tussin brands. **Listed on:** NASDAQ. **Stock exchange symbol:** HITK. **Chairman:** Bernard Seltzer. **Annual sales/revenues:** $33 million. **Number of employees:** 164.

HICKEY FREEMAN COMPANY INC.
P.O. Box 30200, Rochester NY 14603-3200. 585/467-7240. **Physical address:** 1155 Clinton Avenue North, Rochester NY 14621. **Toll-free phone:** 888/603-8968. **Fax:** 585/467-1315. **Contact:** Manager of Human Resources Department. **World Wide Web address:** http://www.hickeyfreeman.com. **Description:** A manufacturer of tailored men's clothing and sportswear selling through its own retail outlets, direct marketing, and catalog sales. **Corporate headquarters location:** Chicago IL. **Parent company:** Hartmarx Corporation (Chicago IL) produces men's and women's clothing under the labels Hart Schaffner & Marx, Austin Reed, Tommy Hilfiger, Krizia, Pierre Cardin, Austin Reed, and Hickey Freeman.

HILL AND KNOWLTON INC.
466 Lexington Avenue, 3rd Floor, New York NY 10017. 212/885-0300. **Fax:** 212/885-0570. **Contact:** Human Resources Department. **World Wide Web address:** http://www.hillandknowlton.com. **Description:** One of the largest public relations/public affairs counseling firms in the world. **NOTE:** Human Resources phone: 212/885-0547. **Positions advertised include:** Senior Account Executive; Healthcare Pharmaceutical Account Representative; Bilingual Spanish/English Accountant; Controller. **Corporate headquarters location:** This location. **Other U.S. locations:** San Francisco CA; Washington DC. **International locations:** Worldwide. **Subsidiaries include:** The Wexler Group. **Parent company:** WPP Group plc (London, United Kingdom). **Chairman/CEO:** Paul Taaffe. **Annual sales/revenues:** $325 million. **Number of employees:** 1,117.

HILTONS OF WESTCHESTER
699 Westchester Avenue, Rye Brook NY 10573. 914/939-6300. **Fax:** 914/939-7374. **Contact:** Human Resources. **World Wide Web address:** http://www.hilton.com. **Description:** Hiltons of Westchester is comprised of two separate Hilton hotels: a 444-room facility in Rye Brook and a 252-room facility in Tarrytown. Founded in 1919. **NOTE:** Entry-level positions, part-time jobs, and second and third shifts are offered. **Positions advertised include:** Assistant Director of Human Resources. **Corporate headquarters location:** Beverly Hills CA. **Other U.S. locations:** Nationwide. **International locations:** Worldwide. **Parent company:** Hilton Hotels Corp. (Beverly Hills CA). **Number of employees at this location:** 500.

HIP HEALTH PLAN OF GREATER NEW YORK
7 West 34th Street, 7th Floor, New York NY 10001-8190. 212/630-5000. **Fax:** 212/630-0060. **Recorded jobline:** 212/630-8300. **Contact:** Human Resources Department – Recruitment. **E-mail address:** career_ops@hipusa.com. **World Wide Web address:** http://www.hipusa.com. **Description:** A health maintenance organization marketing a comprehensive prepaid health plan with care delivered by independent medical groups and coverage provided for hospitalization. **NOTE:** Human

Resources phone: 212/630-8510. **Positions advertised include:** Assistant Pharmacy Services Director; Pharmacy Coordinator; Account Specialist; Concurrent Reviewer; Planning Analyst; Claims Examiner; Senior Financial Analyst; Claims Data Analyst; Contract File Associate; In-House Associate; Geriatric Social Worker; Technical Support Analyst; Contractual Rebates Director; Catostrophic Case Manager; Registered Nurse; Prior Approval Nurse; Transplant Case Manager; Secretary; Marketing Associate; Contract Associate; Field Associate; Customer Service Advocate; Database Development Manager; Actuarial Student; Compliance Coordinator; Government Programs Direct Marketing Analyst; Project Manager. **Corporate headquarters location:** This location. **Number of employees at this location:** 1,000.

HIPPOCRENE BOOKS INC.
171 Madison Avenue, Suite 1602, New York NY 10016. 718/454-2366. **Fax:** 718/454-1391. **Contact:** Human Resources. **E-mail address:** contact@hippocrenebooks.com. **World Wide Web address:** http://www.hippocrenebooks.com. **Description:** Publishes foreign language dictionaries, ethnic cookbooks, Jewish and Polish interest books, and military history books. **Corporate headquarters location:** This location. **Other locations:** Jamaica NY.

HOFSTRA UNIVERSITY
205 Hofstra University, Human Resources Center, Hempstead NY 11549-1000. 516/463-6600. **Contact:** Human Resources Department. **World Wide Web address:** http://www.hofstra.edu. **Description:** A private, four-year university offering both undergraduate and graduate degree programs. The university enrolls over 12,800 students. **Positions advertised include:** Financial Aid Counselor; Assistant Cheerleading Coach; Assistant Director for the Annual Fund; Manager of Telecommunications; Director of Financial Aid; Honors College Dean; Associate Professor of Print Journalism; Education Lecturer; Assistant Sedimentology/Field Geology Professor; Associate Professor of Broadcast Journalism; Associate Dean of Library and Information Services; Assistant Business Professor; Associate Policy Studies Professor.

HONEYWELL TRANSPORTATION & POWER SYSTEMS/FRICTION MATERIALS DIVISION
3 Tibbits Avenue, Green Island NY 12183. 518/270-0200. **Fax:** 518/270-0419. **Contact:** Human Resources. **World Wide Web address:** http://www.honeywell.com. **Description:** Honeywell's Transportation & Power Systems segment is divided into three businesses (Garrett Engine Boosting Systems, Consumer Products Group, and Friction Materials) with operations in 19 countries. The Friction Materials division manufactures brake friction materials and aftermarket brake products with $718 million in sales. The division operates 13 manufacturing plants and five engineering facilities in nine countries specializing in disc brake pads, drum brake linings, and other brake products sold under the Bendix and JURID brand names. **Corporate headquarters location:** Torrance CA. **Other locations:** Worldwide. **Parent company:** Honeywell International Inc. (Morristown NJ). **Operations at this facility include:** Allied Automotive – Bendix Friction Materials Division, manufacturing brake components. **Annual sales/revenues:** $3.2 billion. **Number of employees:** 15,000.

HOTEL INTER-CONTINENTAL NEW YORK
111 East 48th Street, New York NY 10017. 212/755-5900. **Contact:** Human Resources. **World Wide Web address:** http://www.interconti.com. **Description:** A hotel with 682 rooms. **Special programs:** Internships. **Number of employees at this location:** 500.

HOWDEN BUFFALO, INC.
1775 Wehrle Drive, Williamsville, NY 14221. 716/847-5121. **Fax:** 716/817-6901. **Contact:** Human Resources Manager. **World Wide Web address:** http://www.howdenbuffalo.com. **Description:** Manufactures industrial fans including centrifugal and axial fans as well as machine tools. **Corporate headquarters location:** Camden SC. **Other locations:** Nationwide. **Parent company:** Howden Air and Gas.

THE HUDSON RIVER MUSEUM OF WESTCHESTER
ANDRUS PLANETARIUM
511 Warburton Avenue, Yonkers NY 10701. 914/963-4550. **Contact:** Human Resources. **World Wide Web address:** http://www.hrm.org. **Description:** A museum of art, history, and science. Collections include 19th-century fine and decorative arts, and 19th- and 20th-century paintings. Andrus Planetarium is the only public planetarium in Westchester County.

HUDSON TECHNOLOGIES, INC.
275 North Middletown Road, Pearl River NY 10965. 845/735-6000. **Fax:** 845/512-6070. **Contact:** Michele Chazen, Human Resources Manager. **World Wide Web address:** http://www.hudsontech.com. **Description:** Hudson provides services for the recovery and reclamation of refrigerants in response to the requirements of the United States Clean Air Act from 13 locations. The company's services consist of removing used refrigerants from air conditioning and refrigeration systems and transferring them into cylinders for collection. Hudson's reclamation services consist of cleaning used refrigerants to remove impurities and contaminants and returning them to their original purity standards. Founded in 1991. **Corporate headquarters location:** This location. **Other locations:** Nationwide. **Listed on:** NASDAQ. **Stock exchange symbol:** HDSN. **Chairman/CEO:** Kevin J. Zugibe. **Annual sales/revenues:** $20 million. **Number of employees:** 102.

HUNTER COLLEGE
THE CITY UNIVERSITY OF NEW YORK (CUNY)
695 Park Avenue, East Building, 1502, New York NY 10021. 212/772-4451. **Fax:** 212/650-3889. **Contact:** Robert McGarry, Director of Human Resources. **E-mail address:** jobs@hccs.hunter.cuny.edu. **World Wide Web address:** http://www.hunter.cuny.edu. **Description:** One of the largest coeducational colleges of CUNY. Hunter College offers undergraduate and graduate programs in arts and sciences, education, health sciences, nursing, and social work. Founded in 1870. **NOTE:** Resumes can be mailed to 71 East 94th Street, New York NY 10128. **Positions advertised include:** Associate Nursing Professor; Associate Special Education Professor; Associate Education Professor; Head Librarian; Health Professions Library Instructor; Assistant to the Chair of Biological Sciences; Director of Alumni Relations; Director of Development, Major and Planned Gifts; College Assistant; CUNY Office Assistant; CUNY Administrative Assistant; College Security Specialist; Custodial Assistant. **Other area locations:** Bronx NY; Brooklyn NY; Flushing NY; Jamaica NY; Staten Island NY.

HUNTER MOUNTAIN
P.O. Box 295, Hunter NY 12442. 518/263-3800. **Toll-free phone:** 800/486-8376. **Contact:** Human Resources. **Description:** A full feature ski resort.

RICHARD H. HUTCHINGS PSYCHIATRIC CENTER
620 Madison Street, Syracuse NY 13210. 315/473-4980. **Fax:** 315/478-4702. **Contact:** Manager of Human Resources Department. **World Wide Web address:** http://www.omh.state.ny.us/omhweb/facilities/hupc/facility.htm. **Description:** The Richard H. Hutchings Psychiatric Center is a comprehensive, community-based mental health system serving the Central New York region specializing in treating individuals with mental illness. The facility offers both inpatient and outpatient services. **Positions advertised include:** Administrative Aide; Social Worker; Recreation Therapist; Housekeeper; Psychiatrist; Food Service Worker; Mental Health Aide; Safety/Security Officer.

ALICE HYDE MEDICAL CENTER
133 Park Street, P.O. Box 729, Malone NY 12953-0729. 518/481-2268. **Fax:** 518/481-2598. **Contact:** Pat Gaglianese, Director of Human Resources. **E-mail address:** pgaglianese@alicehyde.com. **World Wide Web address:** http://www.alicehyde.com. **Description:** A full-service health facility operating a 75-bed medical center and half-a-dozen clinics and medical centers in the central New York region. **Positions advertised include:** Nurse Practitioner; Nuclear Medicine Technologist; X-Ray Technologist; CAT Scan Technician; Respiratory Therapist; Respiratory Technician; Licensed Practical Nurse; Skilled Nurse; Health Center Nurse; Medical Technologist; Concurrent Coder; Ultrasound Technologist; Radiologic Technologist; Registered Nurse.

IDS LIFE OF NEW YORK
P.O. Box 5144, Albany NY 12205-5144. 518/869-8613. **Physical address:** 20 Madison Avenue Extension, Albany NY 12203. **Toll-free phone:** 800/797-9000. **Fax:** 518/869-8753. **Contact:** Human Resources. **Description:** Administers life, disability, long-term care, and annuity products. **Parent company:** American Express Company.

IEC ELECTRONICS CORPORATION
105 Norton Street, P.O. Box 271, Newark NY 14513. 315/331-7742. **Fax:** 315/331-3547. **Contact:** Tina Devey, Human Resources Manager. **E-mail address:** tdevey@iec-electronics.com. **World Wide Web address:** http://www.iec-electronics.com. **Description:** IEC is an independent manufacturer of complex printed circuit board assemblies and electronic products and systems. IEC offers a wide range of manufacturing and management services, on either a turnkey or consignment basis, including material procurement and control, manufacturing and test engineering support, statistical quality assurance, and complete resource management. The company manufactures over 500 different assemblies that are incorporated into over 100 different products primarily for manufacturers of computers, computer peripheral equipment, office equipment, telecommunications equipment, measuring devices, and medical instruments. **Corporate headquarters location:** This location. **Subsidiaries include:** Calidad Electronics Corporation (Edinburg TX). **Listed on:** Over The Counter. **Stock exchange symbol:** IECE. **Chairman:** W. Barry Gilbert. **Annual sales/revenues:** $39.4 million. **Number of employees:** 190.

INTERNATIONAL IMAGING MATERIALS, INC. (IIMAK)
310 Commerce Drive, Amherst NY 14228. 716/691-6333. **Toll-free phone:** 888/464-4625. **Fax:** 716/691-4349. **Contact:** Susan R. Stamp, Human Resources Director. **World Wide Web address:** http://www.iimak.com. **Description:** IIMAK Produces a broad family of wax and resin bar code ribbon, three- and four-color ribbons for color printers and copiers, ribbons for plain paper facsimile machines, MICR ribbons for check encoding, and ribbons for printing airline tickets, baggage tags, and packaging films. **Positions advertised include:** International Sales Executive; Slitter Operator. **Corporate headquarters location:** This location. **International locations:** Belgium; Brazil. **Parent company:** Centre Partners. **President/CEO:** Richard Marshall. **Annual sales/revenues:** $100 million. **Number of employees:** 650.

ING AMERICAS
1325 Avenue of the Americas, New York NY 10019. 646/424-6000. **Contact:** Human Resources. **World Wide Web address:** http://www.ing.com. **Description:** A financial services company offering comprehensive financial products and services including life insurance; fixed and variable annuities; defined contribution retirement plans; and mutual funds as well as other investment and banking services. **Positions advertised include:** Internal Wholesaler. **Corporate headquarters location:** Atlanta GA. **Parent company:** ING Groep (Amsterdam, The Netherlands). **Operations at this facility:** ING U.S. Financial Services. **Number of employees:** 30,000.

IPC INFORMATION SYSTEMS
516 West 19th Street, New York NY 10011. 212/367-3600. **Contact:** Manager of Human Resources. **World Wide Web address:** http://www.ipc.com. **Description:** IPC Information Systems provides network communications solutions for the financial industry. Through its Information Transport Systems (ITS) business, the company provides its customers with voice, data, and video solutions through the design, integration, implementation, and support of local and wide area networks. ITS solutions incorporate the latest technology and are supported by a team of systems engineers. Founded in 1973. **Corporate headquarters location:** New York NY. **International locations:** Asia; Europe. **Number of employees at this location:** 70. **Number of employees nationwide:** 775.

IPC INFORMATION SYSTEMS
Wall Street Plaza, 88 Pine Street, New York NY 10005. 212/825-9060. **Fax:** 212/344-5106. **Contact:** Human Resources. **World Wide Web address:** http://www.ipc.com. **Description:** Provides network communications solutions for the financial industry. Through its Information Transport Systems (ITS) business, the company provides its customers with voice, data, and video solutions through the design, integration, implementation, and support of local and wide area networks. ITS solutions incorporate the latest technology and are supported by a team of systems engineers. Founded in 1973. **Corporate headquarters location:** This location. **International locations:** Asia; Europe. **Number of employees nationwide:** 775.

ITT-GOULDS PUMPS
240 Fall Street, Seneca Falls NY 13148. 315/568-2811. **Fax:** 315/568-2418. **Contact:** Manager of Employee Relations. **World Wide Web address:** http://www.gouldspumps.com. **Description:** Produces pumps for the chemical process industry, water and wastewater facilities, and HVAC applications. **Positions advertised include:** Credit Analyst; fixed Asset Analyst; Human Resource Manager; Foundry Metallurgist Director. **Corporate headquarters location:** This location. **Other locations:** Nationwide. **Parent company:** ITT Industries is a diversified, global enterprise engaged in three major business areas: Financial and Business Services, which includes ITT Hartford, ITT Financial Corporation, and ITT Communications and Information Services, Inc.; Manufactured Products, which includes ITT Automotive, ITT Defense and Electronics, Inc., and ITT Fluid Technology Corporation; and Sheraton Hotels (ITT Sheraton Corporation).

ITT INDUSTRIES
4 West Red Oak Lane, White Plains NY 10604. 914/641-2021. **Fax:** 914/696-2965. **Contact:** Katherine Campbell, Human Resources. **E-mail address:** Katherine.Campbell@itt.com. **World Wide Web address:** http://www.ittind.com. **Description:** A multinational company with operations divided into four business

segments: fluid technology; defense electronics; motion and flow control; and electronic components; as well as providing maintenance services for its products. **Corporate headquarters location:** This location. **Other locations:** Worldwide. **Listed on:** New York Stock Exchange. **Stock exchange symbol:** ITT. **Subsidiaries include:** ITT Defense Electronics & Services. **Chairman/President/CEO:** Louis J. Giuliano. **Annual sales/revenues:** $5 billion. **Number of employees:** 38,000.

IMCLONE SYSTEMS INC.
180 Varick Street, 6th Floor, New York NY 10014-4606. 212/645-1405. **Fax:** 212/645-2054. **Contact:** Human Resources Director. **World Wide Web address:** http://www.imclone.com. **Description:** Engaged primarily in the research and development of therapeutic products for the treatment of cancer and cancer-related diseases. **Positions advertised include:** Chemistry Research Associate; Chemistry Research Scientist; Modeling Chemistry Senior Scientist; Facilities Worker; Immunology Research Associate; Immunology Scientist; Immunology Senior Scientist; Intellectual Property Law Clerk; Molecular & Cell Biology Senior Scientist. **Corporate headquarters location:** This location. **Other locations:** Somerville NJ. **Listed on:** NASDAQ. **Stock exchange symbol:** IMCLE. **Annual sales/revenues:** $33 million. **Number of employees:** 400.

IMPATH INC.
521 West 57th Street, 5th Floor, New York NY 10019. 212/698-0300. **Fax:** 212/258-2137. **Contact:** Human Resources. **E-mail address:** hr@impath.com. **World Wide Web address:** http://www.impath.com. **Description:** Maintains a database of some one million cancer patients' profiles used to assist physicians, pharmaceutical companies, and managed care providers in the diagnosis, prognosis, and treatment of cancer. **NOTE:** Apply online. **Positions advertised include:** Lead Lab Assistant; Lab Assistant; Histology Technician; Senior A/R Manager; Sales Administration Liaison; Accounts Payable Coordinator; Clinical Research Coordinator; Accounts Payable Supervisor; Sales Representative; Regional Sales Representative; Surgical Pathologist. **Corporate headquarters location:** This location. **Other U.S. locations:** AZ; CA; MA; NJ. **Listed on:** NASDAQ. **Stock exchange symbol:** IMPH. **Chairman/CEO:** Carter H. Eckert. **Annual sales/revenues:** $188 million. **Number of employees:** 1,219.

IMPERIAL PAPER BOX CORPORATION
252 Newport Street, Brooklyn NY 11212. 718/346-6100. **Fax:** 718/346-0400. **Contact:** Personnel Director. **World Wide Web address:** http://www.imperialpaperbox.com. **Description:** A manufacturer of paper containers including boxes and packaging materials. Since 1902.

INDEPENDENCE COMMUNITY BANK CORP.
195 Montague Street, Brooklyn NY 11201. 718/722-5300. **Fax:** 718/722-5319. **Contact:** Human Resources Director. **World Wide Web address:** http://www.icbny.com. **Description:** A savings bank that offers a wide range of traditional banking services as well as specialized financial services, loans, and insurance services through 70 full-service branches serving the New York City metropolitan region. **Positions advertised include:** Assistant Branch Manager; Branch Manager; Customer Service Representative; Head Teller; Safe Deposit Attendant; Teller; Mortgage Loan Processor; Mortgage Servicer; Levy and Subpoena Representative. **Corporate headquarters location:** This location. **Other locations:** Brooklyn NY; Queens NY; Long Island NY; New Jersey. **Listed on:** NASDAQ. **Stock exchange symbol:** ICBC. **Chairman:** Charles J. Hamm. **Annual sales/revenues:** $550 million. **Number of employees:** 1,373.

INDEPENDENCE COMMUNITY BANK
7500 Fifth Avenue, Brooklyn NY 11209. 718/745-6100. **Contact:** Human Resources Director. **World Wide Web address:** http://www.icbny.com. **Description:** A savings bank that offers a wide range of traditional banking services as well as specialized financial services, loans, and insurance services through 70 full-service branches serving the New York City metropolitan region. **Positions advertised include:** Assistant Branch Manager; Customer Service Representative. **Corporate headquarters location:** Brooklyn NY. **Other locations:** Brooklyn NY; Queens NY; Long Island NY; New Jersey. **Listed on:** NASDAQ. **Stock exchange symbol:** ICBC. **Chairman:** Charles J. Hamm. **Annual sales/revenues:** $550 million. **Number of employees:** 1,373.

INDUSTRIAL ACOUSTICS COMPANY, INC.
1160 Commerce Avenue, Bronx NY 10462. 718/430-4541. **Fax:** 718/430-4766. **Contact:** Michele Pisani, Human Resources Department. **E-mail address:** hr@industrialacoustics.com. **World Wide Web address:** http://www.industrialacoustics.com. **Description:** IAC is an international company with engineering and manufacturing capabilities serving the architectural, air conditioning, industrial, medical and life sciences, power plant, and military/commercial aviation markets. The company develops and markets noise control products, turnkey systems for air conditioning and air handling units, jet engine aircraft hush-house test facilities, detention cells, acoustical ceilings for correctional institutions, and other special purpose ceilings. Founded in 1949. **Positions advertised include:** Project Engineer; Auto Cad Drafter/Designer. **Corporate headquarters location:** This location. **International locations:** Germany; United Kingdom. **President/CEO:** Robert E. Schmitt. **Annual sales/revenues:** $100 million. **Number of employees:** 300.

INFORMATION BUILDERS INC.
Two Penn Plaza, New York NY 10121-2898. 212/736-4433. **Fax:** 212/239-6674. **Contact:** Lila Goldberg, Human Resources Director. **E-mail address:** employment_opportunities@ibi.com. **World Wide Web address:** http://www.ibi.com. **Description:** A software development firm. Products include FOCUS, EDA, and SmartMart software for various platforms. **NOTE:** Jobseekers may see http://www.hotjobs.com for a listing of current openings with detailed application information. **Positions advertised include:** WebFOCUS Technical Specialist; MVS Systems Programmer; Network Operating Systems Analyst; XML Programmer; Sales Engineer; Software Engineer; Inside Sales Representative; Software Sales Representative; Direct Marketing Manager; Administrator; Senior Administratorp Business Development Analyst; Senior Implementation Manager; Project Manager; WebFOCUS Team Leader. **Corporate headquarters location:** This location. **Other U.S. locations:** Nationwide. **President:** Gerald D. Cohen. **Annual sales/revenues:** $300 million. **Number of employees:** 1,800.

INSIGNIA DOUGLAS ELLIMAN
575 Madison Avenue, New York NY 10022. 212/832-0083. **Toll-free phone:** 800/355-4626. **Fax:** 212/891-7239. **Contact:** Human Resources. **E-mail address:** inquiry@elliman.com. **Description:** A real estate firm engaged in apartment sales, rentals, and insurance. **Subsidiaries include:** Insignia/ESG, Inc.; Insignia Richard Ellis; Insignia Residential Group. **Operations at this facility include:** Administration; Sales; Service.

INTEGRAMED AMERICA, INC.
One Manhattanville Road, 3rd Floor, Purchase NY 10577-2133. 914/253-8000. **Fax:** 914/253-8008. **Contact:** Human Resources. **E-mail address:** info@integramed.com. **World Wide Web address:** http://www.integramed.com. **Description:** Manages and provides services to clinical facilities and physician practices that provide assisted reproductive technology (ART) and infertility services. ART services consist of medical, psychological, and financial consultations and administration of the appropriate ART services and techniques. Infertility services provided include diagnostic testing, fertility drug therapy, tubal surgery, and intrauterine insemination. **Corporate headquarters location:** This location. **Other locations:** Nationwide. **Listed on:** NASDAQ. **Stock exchange symbol:** INMD. **Chairman/President/CEO:** Gerarda Canet. **Annual sales/revenues:** $88 million. **Number of employees:** 660.

INTER PARFUMS, INC.
551 Fifth Avenue, Suite 1500, New York NY 10176-0198. 212/983-2640. **Fax:** 212/983-4197. **Contact:** Michelle Sharno, Corporate Controller. **E-mail address:** msharno@interparfumsinc.com. **World Wide Web address:** http://www.interparfumsinc.com. **Description:** Formerly Jean Philippe Fragrances, Inter Parfums develops manufactures and distributes a variety of perfumes and fragrances to department stores, wholesalers, and drugstores as well as personal care products and cosmetics including Aziza eye color products under license from Unilever. The company's brands include Burberry, Christian Lacroix, Celine, Diane Von Furstenberg, Molyneux, Paul Smith, S.T. Dupont and FUBU. Founded in 1983. **Subsidiaries include:** Inter Parfums, S.A. (Paris, France). **Listed on:** NASDAQ. **Stock exchange symbol:** IPAR. **Chairman/CEO:** Jean Madar. **Annual sales/revenues:** $130 million. **Number of employees:** 103.

INTERCON ASSOCIATES INCORPORATED
95 Allens Creek Road, Building 2, Suite 200, Rochester NY 14618. 585/244-1250. **Toll-free phone:** 800/422-3880. **Fax:** 585/473-4387. **Contact:** Personnel. **World Wide Web address:** http://www.interconweb.com. **Description:** Develops document assembly software and font cartridges.

INTERNATIONAL BUSINESS MACHINES CORPORATION (IBM)
1701 North Street, Endicott NY 13760-0569. 607/755-0123. **Recorded jobline:** 800/796-9876. **Contact:** IBM Staffing Services. **World Wide Web address:** http://www.ibm.com. **Description:** IBM is a developer, manufacturer, and marketer of advanced information processing products including computers and microelectronic technology, software, networking systems, and information technology-related services. The company operates in the United States, Canada, Europe/Middle East/Africa, Latin America and Asia Pacific. **Positions advertised include:** Electrical Design Engineer; Manufacturing Engineer; Production Manager; Manufacturing Technician; Physical Designer. **Corporate headquarters location:** Armonk NY. **Other locations:** Worldwide. **Subsidiaries include:** Hitachi Global Storage Technologies; IBM Canada Ltd.; IBM Credit Corporation; IBM Global Services; IBM Instruments, Inc.; IBM Software; IBM World Trade Corporation; International Business Machines – Microelectronics; Lotus Development Corporation; Tivoli Software. **Listed on:** New York Stock Exchange. **Stock exchange symbol:** IBM. **Chairman/President/CEO:** Samuel J. Palmisano. **Annual sales/revenues:** $81.2 billion. **Number of employees:** 315,889.

INTERNATIONAL BUSINESS MACHINES CORPORATION (IBM)
2455 South Road, Poughkeepsie NY 12601-5400. 845/433-1234. **Recorded jobline:** 800/796-9876. **Contact:** IBM Staffing Services Center. **World Wide Web address:** http://www.ibm.com. **Description:** IBM is a developer, manufacturer, and marketer of advanced information processing products, including computers and microelectronic technology, software, networking systems, and information technology-related services. The company operates in the United States, Canada, Europe/Middle East/Africa, Latin America, and Asia Pacific. **Positions advertised include:** Development Engineer; Human Resources Program Manager; Lotus Notes Web Developer; Programmer; Tester; Software Developer; Software Engineer; Test Technician; Web Developer. **Corporate headquarters location:** Armonk NY. **Other locations:** Worldwide. **Subsidiaries include:** Hitachi Global Storage Technologies; IBM Canada Ltd.; IBM Credit Corporation; IBM Global Services; IBM Instruments, Inc.; IBM Software; IBM World Trade Corporation; International Business Machines – Microelectronics; Lotus Development Corporation; Tivoli Software. **Listed on:** New York Stock Exchange. **Stock exchange symbol:** IBM. **Chairman/President/CEO:** Samuel J. Palmisano. **Annual sales/revenues:** $81.2 billion. **Number of employees:** 315,889.

INTERNATIONAL BUSINESS MACHINES CORPORATION (IBM)
New Orchard Road, Armonk NY 10504. 914/499-1900. **Fax:** 914/765-7382. **Recorded jobline:** 800/796-9876. **Contact:** IBM Staffing Services Center. **World Wide Web address:** http://www.ibm.com. **Description:** A developer, manufacturer, and marketer of advanced information processing products including computers and microelectronic technology, software, networking systems, and information technology-related services. **Positions advertised include:** Executive Assistant; Business Controls Advisor; EOL Administrator Analyst; Human Capital Analyst; Sales Operation Specialist; SAP Conversion Analyst; SAP Security Analyst; Senior Tax Specialist; Tax Supplemental Specialist; Treasury Operations Manager. **Corporate headquarters location:** Armonk NY. **Other locations:** Worldwide. **Subsidiaries include:** Hitachi Global Storage Technologies; IBM Canada Ltd.; IBM Credit Corporation; IBM Global Services; IBM Instruments, Inc.; IBM Software; IBM World Trade Corporation; International Business Machines – Microelectronics; Lotus Development Corporation; Tivoli Software. **Listed on:** New York Stock Exchange. **Stock exchange symbol:** IBM. **Chairman/President/CEO:** Samuel J. Palmisano. **Annual sales/revenues:** $81.2 billion. **Number of employees:** 315,889.

INTERNATIONAL FLAVORS & FRAGRANCES INC.
521 West 57th Street, New York NY 10019-2960. 212/765-5500. **Fax:** 212/708-7132. **Contact:** Human Resources. **E-mail address:** staffing.manager@iff.com. **World Wide Web address:** http://www.iff.com. **Description:** Creates and manufactures flavors and fragrances used by other manufacturers in a wide variety of consumer products. Fragrance products are sold principally to manufacturers of perfumes, cosmetics, personal care items, soaps, detergents, air fresheners, and household products. Flavor products are sold principally to manufacturers of dairy, meat, processed foods, beverages, pharmaceuticals, snacks, baked goods, confectioneries, tobacco products, oral care products, and animal foods. **Corporate headquarters location:** This location. **Other U.S. locations:** Hazlet NJ; South Brunswick NJ; Union Beach NJ. **Subsidiaries include:** Bush Booke Allen, Inc. **Operations at this facility include:** Administration; Regional Headquarters; Sales; Service. **Listed on:** New York Stock Exchange. **Stock exchange symbol:** IFF. **Chairman/CEO:** Richard A. Goldstein. **Annual sales/revenues:** $1.8 billion. **Number of employees:** 5,728.

INTERNATIONAL PAPER COMPANY
15 Pine Street, Corinth NY 12822. 518/654-9031. **Fax:** 518/654-3487. **Contact:** Human Resources. **World Wide Web address:** http://www.internationalpaper.com.

Description: A manufacturer of pulp and paper, packaging, and wood products, as well as a range of specialty products. Nine million acres of timberland are controlled by International Paper, making it one of the largest private landowners in the United States. The company is organized into five business segments including: Printing Papers, in which principal products include uncoated papers, coated papers, bristles, and pulp; Packaging, which includes industrial packaging, consumer packaging, and kraft and specialty papers; Distribution, which includes sales of printing papers, graphic arts equipment and supplies, packaging materials, industrial supplies, and office products; Specialty Products, which includes imaging products, specialty panels, nonwovens, chemicals, and minerals; and Forest Products which includes logs and wood products. **Corporate headquarters location:** Stamford CT. **Other locations:** Worldwide. **Subsidiaries include:** Arizona Chemical Company; Shorewood Packaging Corporation. **Operations at this facility include:** Production of coated publication paper used for magazine publishing. **Listed on:** New York Stock Exchange. **Stock exchange symbol:** IP. **Annual sales/revenues:** $25 billion. **Number of employees worldwide:** 91,000.

INTERNATIONAL PAPER COMPANY
1000 Shore Airport Road, Ticonderoga NY 12883. 518/585-6761. **Fax:** 518/585-5668. **Contact:** Personnel. **World Wide Web address:** http://www.internationalpaper.com. **Description:** A manufacturer of pulp and paper, packaging, and wood products, as well as a range of specialty products. Nine million acres of timberland are controlled by International Paper, making it one of the largest private landowners in the United States. The company is organized into five business segments including: Printing Papers, in which principal products include uncoated papers, coated papers, bristles, and pulp; Packaging, which includes industrial packaging, consumer packaging, and Kraft and specialty papers; Distribution, which includes sales of printing papers, graphic arts equipment and supplies, packaging materials, industrial supplies, and office products; Specialty Products, which includes imaging products, specialty panels, nonwovens, chemicals, and minerals; and Forest Products which includes logs and wood products. **Corporate headquarters location:** Stamford CT. **Other locations:** Worldwide. **Subsidiaries include:** Arizona Chemical Company; Shorewood Packaging Corporation. **Operations at this facility include:** Production of white paper for copy machines. **Listed on:** New York Stock Exchange. **Stock exchange symbol:** IP. **Annual sales/revenues:** $25 billion. **Number of employees worldwide:** 91,000.

INTERNET COMMERCE CORPORATION
805 Third Avenue, 9th Floor, New York NY 10022. 212/271-7640. **Fax:** 212/271-8580. **Contact:** Claire Schank, Human Resources Manager. **E-mail address:** hr@icc.net. **World Wide Web address:** http://www.icc.net. **Description:** Manufactures computer systems that enable protection, retrieval, and monitoring of digital information use. **Corporate headquarters location:** This location. **Other area locations:** Setauket NY. **Listed on:** NASDAQ. **Stock exchange symbol:** ICCA. **Chairman:** Charles C. Johnston. **Number of employees:** 115.

INTERPAK PLASTICS
4 Plant Street, Plattsburgh NY 12901. 518/561-2030. **Fax:** 518/561-3844. **Contact:** Cheryl Cart, Human Resources. **E-mail address:** info@cclplastic.com. **World Wide Web address:** http://www.cclind.com. **Description:** Develops, manufactures, and sells specialty closure and container products to the personal care, food and beverage, household, industrial chemical, and pharmaceutical industries. **Parent company:** CCL Industries Inc. (Toronto, Canada).

INTERPOOL, INC.
633 Third Avenue, 27th Floor, New York NY 10017. 212/916-3261. **Contact:** Human Resources. **World Wide Web address:** http://www.interpool.com. **Description:** Leases containers and chassis, primarily to container shipping lines. The company is one of the world's leading lessors of intermodal dry cargo containers and one of the largest lessors of intermodal container chassis in the United States. Founded in 1968. **Corporate headquarters location:** Princeton NJ. **International locations:** Worldwide. **Subsidiaries include:** Interpool Limited conducts the international container leasing business. **Listed on:** New York Stock Exchange. **Stock exchange symbol:** IPX. **Annual sales/revenues:** $300 million. **Number of employees:** 200.

THE INTERPUBLIC GROUP OF COMPANIES, INC.
1271 Avenue of the Americas, 44th Floor, New York NY 10020. 212/399-8000. **Fax:** 212/399-8130. **Contact:** Doris Weil, Director of Corporate Human Resources. **E-mail address:** hr@interpublic.com. **World Wide Web address:** http://www.interpublic.com. **Description:** An advertising agency doing business in 130 countries worldwide. The company plans, creates, and implements advertising campaigns in various media through either its own subsidiaries or contracts with local agencies. Other activities include publishing, market research, public relations, product development, and sales promotion. Interpublic's international business groups include McCann-Erickson WorldGroup and The Lowe Group. **Corporate headquarters location:** This location. **Subsidiaries/affiliates include:** Advanced Marketing Services; Deutsch, Inc.; DeVries Public Relations; Draft Worldwide; FutureBrand Worldwide; Hill Holliday; Jack Morton Worldwide Inc.; McCann Relationship Marketing Partners Worldwide; McCann-Erickson WorldGroup; Modem Media, Inc.; Mullen Advertising Inc.; NFO WorldGroup, Inc.; Octagon; Temerlin McClain; Weber Shandwick Worldwide. **Listed on:** New York Stock Exchange. **Stock exchange symbol:** IPG. **Chairman/President/CEO:** David A. Bell. **Annual sales/revenues:** $6.2 billion. **Number of employees:** 52,000.

INVESTEC ERNST & COMPANY
One Battery Park Plaza, 2nd Floor, New York NY 10004. 212/898-6200. **Contact:** Human Resources. **E-mail address:** info@investec.com. **World Wide Web address:** http://www.investec.com. **Description:** A securities brokerage firm. Investec Ernst & Company is one of the largest financial clearinghouses in New York City, with over 80 correspondents. **NOTE:** Human Resources phone: 212/898-6450. **Corporate headquarters location:** This location. **Other locations:** Chicago IL; New York NY; Rhinebeck NY; Stamford CT; Woodbury NY.

INVESTMENT TECHNOLOGY GROUP, INC.
380 Madison Avenue, 4th Floor, New York NY 10017. 212/588-4000. **Toll-free phone:** 800/215-4484. **Fax:** 212/444-6295. **Contact:** Human Resources. **E-mail address:** itg_hr@itginc.com. **World Wide Web address:** http://www.itginc.com. **Description:** Provides automated securities trade execution and analysis services to institutional equity investors. ITG's two main services are POSIT, one of the largest automated stock crossing systems operated during trading hours, and QuantEX, a proprietary software to enhance customers' trading efficiencies, access to market liquidity, and portfolio analysis capabilities. **NOTE:** Human resources phone number is 617/692-6700. **Corporate headquarters location:** This location. **Other U.S. locations:** Los Angeles CA; Boston MA. **International locations:** Dublin, Ireland; Toronto, Canada; Melbourne, Australia; Hong Kong, China. **Subsidiaries include:** Hoenig Group Inc. **Listed on:** New York Stock Exchange. **Stock exchange symbol:** ITG. **Chairman:** Raymond L. Killian Jr. **Annual sales/revenues:** $388 million. **Number of employees:** 635.

IONA COLLEGE
715 North Avenue, New Rochelle NY 10801. 914/633-2000. **Contact:** Rosemary Bartolomeo, Manager of Employment. **E-mail address:** rbartolomeo@iona.edu. **World Wide Web address:** http://www.iona.edu. **Description:** A four-year Catholic college offering bachelor's and master's degree programs. Founded in 1940. **NOTE:** Employment Manager phone: 914/633-2496, fax: 914/637-7732. Faculty applicants should contact the Dean's Office in the School of Arts & Sciences or the Hagan School of Business. **Positions advertised include:** Facilities Custodian; Library Document Delivery Assistant; Career Services Associate Director; Business School Academic Advisor; Director of Libraries.

IRVING TISSUE, INC.
One Eddy Street, Fort Edward NY 12828. 518/746-9431. **Fax:** 518/747-2746. **Contact:** Human Resources. **E-mail address:** resumes@irvingtissue.com. **World Wide Web address:** http://www.irvingtisue.com. **Description:** Manufactures facial tissue, toilet tissue, and napkins. **Special programs:** Summer Jobs. **Corporate headquarters location:** Moncton, Canada. **Parent company:** J.D. Irving, Ltd. **Number of employees at this location:** 250.

ITHACA COLLEGE
240 Job Hall, Ithaca NY 14850-7018. 607/274-1207. **Contact:** Martha Turnbull, Director of Human Resources. **E-mail address:** employment@ithaca.edu. **World Wide Web address:** http://www.ithaca.edu. **Description:** A four-year liberal arts college specializing in physical therapy and communications programs. Approximately 5,000 students are enrolled at Ithaca college. **NOTE:** Human Resources phone: 607/274-3245. **Positions advertised include:** Anthropology Lecturer; Art Lecturer; Art History Lecturer; Biology Lecturer; Economics Lecturer; English Lecturer; History Lecturer; Math & Computer Science Lecturer; Philosophy & Religion Lecturer; Physics Lecturer; Mail Processing Coordinator; Assistant Sociology Professor; Executive Assistant to the Dean; Psychologist; Speech Communication Instructor; Adjunct Anthropology Professor; Assistant Psychology Professor; Assistant Behavioral Neuroscience Professor; Accounts Payable and Travel Services Assistant Manager; Assistant English Professor; Assistant Biology Professor; Assistant Politics Professor; Assistant Theatre Arts Professor; Media Production Facilities and Services Director; Assistant Health Promotion and Human Movement Professor. **Number of employees:** 1,300.

ITOCHU INTERNATIONAL INC.
335 Madison Avenue, New York NY 10017. 212/818-8500. **Fax:** 212/818-8543. **Contact:** Recruiting, Human Resources. **E-mail address:** recruiting@itochu.com. **World Wide Web address:** http://www.itochu.com. **Description:** A diversified international trading company with markets that include textiles, metals, machinery, foodstuffs, general merchandise, electronics, chemicals, and energy. The company has import/export, distribution, finance, investment, transportation, and joint venture operations, all of which contribute to an annual business volume of over $12 billion. Itochu International is also engaged in direct investments and partnerships in many additional industries including high-technology manufacturing, retailing, fiber optics, satellite communications, and real estate development. **Corporate headquarters location:** This location. **Other locations:** AL; CA; CO; GA; IL; MO; WA. **Parent company:** Itochu Corporation.

JCI JONES CHEMICALS, INC.
100 Sunny Sol Boulevard, P.O. Box 115, Caledonia NY 14423. 585/538-2314. **Fax:** 585/538-2316. **Contact:** Human Resources. **World Wide Web address:** http://www.jcichem.com. **Description:** Repackages chlorine and other water purification chemicals. Formerly Jones Chemicals, the family-owned company is also engaged in the production of caustic soda, sodium bisulfite, and sodium hypochlorite for water treatment facilities and distributes to companies for repackaging as bleach as well as other industrial uses. Founded in 1930. **Positions advertised include:** Regional Sales Manager; Office Manager; Plant Operator. **Corporate headquarters location:** Sarasota FL. **Other locations:** CA; FL; IN; MI; NC; NH; NY; OH; VA; WA. **Listed on:** Privately held. **Annual sales/revenues:** $110 million. **Number of employees nationwide:** 300.

J & K HEALTHCARE SERVICES INC.
140 Huguenot Street, New Rochelle NY 10801. 914/633-7810. **Fax:** 914/633-7864. **Contact:** Manager. **Description:** A 24-hour, supplemental staffing, private nursing, and home health care agency offering nursing and personal care services to Westchester County Medicaid recipients.

JLM COUTURE, INC.
525 Seventh Avenue, Suite 1703, New York NY 10018. 212/921-7058. **Fax:** 212/921-7608. **Contact:** Human Resources. **World Wide Web address:** http://www.jlmcouture.com. **Description:** Designs, manufactures, and markets bridal gowns, bridesmaid gowns, veils, and related accessories for department stores, bridal boutiques, and sells through several Websites. **Listed on:** NASDAQ. **Stock exchange symbol:** JLMC. **Chairman:** Daniel M. Sullivan. **Annual sales/revenues:** $25 million. **Number of employees:** 70.

J.P. MORGAN CHASE & COMPANY
One Chase Square, Rochester NY 14604-1907. 585/258-5000. **Contact:** John J. Farrell Jr., VP of Human Resources. **World Wide Web address:** http://www.jpmorganchase.com. **Description:** Specializes in global financial services and retail banking. The company's consumer services include credit card; diversified consumer lending; mortgages and home finance; automobile loans; private banking; and asset management services. The bank offers commercial banking services for middle market companies and small business banking. The company is also engaged in global markets; investment banking operations; mergers and acquisition consulting, risk management; treasury and securities services and debt underwriting. **Positions advertised include:** Home Equity Retention Vice President; Business Systems Analyst; Underwriter; Customer Service Supervisor; Quality Assurance Analyst Underwriter; Subordination Specialist; Consumer Banker; File Reviewer; Direct Channel Manager; Client Associate; Teller; Senior Underwriter. **Corporate headquarters location:** New York NY. **Other locations:** Worldwide. **Subsidiaries include:** J.P. Morgan Private Bank; J.P. Morgan Fleming Asset Management; American Century; Brown & Company Securities Corp.; J.P. Morgan H&Q; J.P. Morgan Partners; Chase. **Listed on:** New York Stock Exchange. **Stock exchange symbol:** JPM. **Chairman/CEO:** William B. Harrison Jr. **Annual sales/revenues:** $43.4 billion. **Number of employees:** 94,335.

J.P. MORGAN CHASE & COMPANY
270 Park Avenue, New York NY 10017. 212/270-6000. **Fax:** 212/270-2613. **Contact:** John J. Farrell Jr., VP of Human Resources. **World Wide Web address:** http://www.jpmorganchase.com. **Description:** Specializes in global financial services and retail banking. The company's consumer services include credit card; diversified consumer lending; mortgages and home finance; automobile loans; private banking; and asset management services. The bank offers commercial banking services for

middle market companies and small business banking. The company is also engaged in global markets; investment banking operations; mergers and acquisition consulting, risk management; treasury and securities services and debt underwriting. **Positions advertised include:** Personal Financial Advisor; Client Associate; Teller; Client Service Delivery Manager; Personal Financial Services Banker; Consumer Banker; Small Business Relationship Manager; Researcher; Programmer; Group Product Manager Vice President; Home Equity Retention Vice President; Credit & Rate Markets Vice President; Credit Portfolio Group Vice President; Senior Product Manager; CFS Enterprise eCommerce Architect; Risk Manager; Junior Structure and Documentation Counsel; Client Associate Manager. **Corporate headquarters location:** This location. **Other locations:** Worldwide. **Subsidiaries include:** J.P. Morgan Private Bank; J.P. Morgan Fleming Asset Management; American Century; Brown & Company Securities Corp.; J.P. Morgan H&Q; J.P. Morgan Partners; Chase. **Listed on:** New York Stock Exchange. **Stock exchange symbol:** JPM. **Chairman/CEO:** William B. Harrison Jr. **Annual sales/revenues:** $43.4 billion. **Number of employees:** 94,335.

J.P. MORGAN CHASE & COMPANY
60 Wall Street, New York NY 10005. 212/483-2323. **Contact:** John J. Farrell Jr., VP of Human Resources. **World Wide Web address:** http://www.jpmorganchase.com. **Description:** Specializes in global financial services and retail banking. The company's consumer services include credit card; diversified consumer lending; mortgages and home finance; automobile loans; private banking; and asset management services. The bank offers commercial banking services for middle market companies and small business banking. The company is also engaged in global markets; investment banking operations; mergers and acquisition consulting, risk management; treasury and securities services and debt underwriting. **Positions advertised include:** Personal Financial Advisor; Client Associate; Teller; Client Service Delivery Manager; Personal Financial Services Banker; Consumer Banker; Small Business Relationship Manager; Researcher; Programmer; Group Product Manager Vice President; Home Equity Retention Vice President; Credit & Rate Markets Vice President; Credit Portfolio Group Vice President; Senior Product Manager; CFS Enterprise eCommerce Architect; Risk Manager; Junior Structure and Documentation Counsel; Client Associate Manager. **Corporate headquarters location:** New York NY. **Other locations:** Worldwide. **Subsidiaries include:** J.P. Morgan Private Bank; J.P. Morgan Fleming Asset Management; American Century; Brown & Company Securities Corp.; J.P. Morgan H&Q; J.P. Morgan Partners; Chase. **Listed on:** New York Stock Exchange. **Stock exchange symbol:** JPM. **Chairman/CEO:** William B. Harrison Jr. **Annual sales/revenues:** $43.4 billion. **Number of employees:** 94,335.

J.P. MORGAN CHASE & COMPANY
2 Chase Manhattan Plaza, New York NY 10081-6500. 212/270-6000. **Contact:** John J. Farrell Jr., VP of Human Resources. **World Wide Web address:** http://www.jpmorganchase.com. **Description:** Specializes in global financial services and retail banking. The company's consumer services include credit card; diversified consumer lending; mortgages and home finance; automobile loans; private banking; and asset management services. The bank offers commercial banking services for middle market companies and small business banking. The company is also engaged in global markets; investment banking operations; mergers and acquisition consulting, risk management; treasury and securities services and debt underwriting. **Positions advertised include:** Personal Financial Advisor; Client Associate; Teller; Client Service Delivery Manager; Personal Financial Services Banker; Consumer Banker; Small Business Relationship Manager; Researcher; Programmer; Group Product Manager Vice President; Home Equity Retention Vice President; Credit & Rate Markets Vice President; Credit Portfolio Group Vice President; Senior Product Manager; CFS Enterprise eCommerce Architect; Risk Manager; Junior Structure and Documentation Counsel; Client Associate Manager. **Corporate headquarters location:** New York NY. **Other locations:** Worldwide. **Subsidiaries include:** J.P. Morgan Private Bank; J.P. Morgan Fleming Asset Management; American Century; Brown & Company Securities Corp.; J.P. Morgan H&Q; J.P. Morgan Partners; Chase. **Listed on:** New York Stock Exchange. **Stock exchange symbol:** JPM. **Chairman/CEO:** William B. Harrison Jr. **Annual sales/revenues:** $43.4 billion. **Number of employees:** 94,335.

J.P. MORGAN PARTNERS
1221 6th Avenue, 39th & 40th Floors, New York City NY 10020-1080. 212/899-3400. **Fax:** 212/899-3401. **Contact:** Human Resources. **World Wide Web address:** http://www.jpmorganpartners.com. **Description:** Provides equity and other financial services.

JACO ELECTRONICS, INC.
145 Oser Avenue, Hauppauge NY 11788. 631/273-5500. **Toll-free phone:** 800/645-5112. **Fax:** 631/273-5799. **Contact:** Diane Eckhoff, Personnel Director. **E-mail address:** deckhoff@jacoelect.com. **World Wide Web address:** http://www.jacoelectronics.com. **Description:** Jaco Electronics distributes electronic components to original equipment manufacturers, which include semiconductors, transistors, diodes, capacitors, and resistors as well as offering inventory, manufacturing and computer configuration services. **NOTE:** Personnel phone extension: x3095. **Positions advertised include:** Regional Display Sales Manager. **Subsidiaries include:** Nexus Custom Electronics, Inc. a contract manufacturer of printed circuit board. **Listed on:** NASDAQ. **Stock exchange symbol:** JACO. **Chairman/President/Treasurer:** Joel H. Girsky. **Annual sales/revenues:** $194 million. **Number of employees:** 363.

JACOBI MEDICAL CENTER
1400 Pelham Parkway South, Building 2, Room 101, Bronx NY 10461. 718/918-5000. **Contact:** Barbara Juliano, Manager of Employment & Recruitment. **World Wide Web address:** http://www.ci.nyc.ny.us/html/hhc/jacobi/home.html. **Description:** A major medical center with over 700 beds operating six community-based Family Health Services Clinics and other medical centers throughout New York City. **Special programs:** Internships. **Parent company:** New York Health and Hospitals Corporation. **Operations at this facility include:** Administration; Regional Headquarters; Service. **Annual sales/revenues:** $4.3 billion. **Number of employees at this location:** 5,000. **Number of employees nationwide:** 60,000.

JEFFERIES GROUP, INC.
dba JEFFERIES & COMPANY, INC.
520 Madison Avenue, 12th Floor, New York NY 10022. 212/284-2300. **Fax:** 310/914-1066. **Contact:** See NOTE. **World Wide Web address:** http://www.jefco.com. **Description:** An investment banking firm providing banking, research, and merger consulting services to small and mid-sized business. Through the Jefferies & Company subsidiary the firm is engaged in equity, convertible debt, and taxable fixed income securities as well as brokering off-exchange trades for institutional investors and underwrites stock offerings specializing in high-yield junk bonds. **NOTE:** Fax or e-mail resumes for non-banking opportunities to Mel Locke (310/914-1066; mlocke@jefco.com), and for banking opportunities to Eastcoastrecruiting@jeffco.com. **Subsidiaries include:** Jefferies International Limited; Jefferies Pacific Limited; The Europe Company. Founded in 1962. **Corporate headquarters location:** This location. **Other U.S. locations:** Nationwide. **International locations:** Worldwide. **Listed on:** New York Stock Exchange. **Stock exchange symbol:** JEF. **Chairman/CEO:** Richard B. Handler. **Annual sales/revenues:** $755 million. **Number of employees:** 1,600.

JEFFERSON REHABILITATION CENTER
380 Gaffney Drive, P.O. Box 41, Watertown NY 13601. 315/788-2730. **Fax:** 315/788-8557. **Contact:** Human Resources. **E-mail address:** ttgagnon@jeffrehabcenter.org. **World Wide Web address:** http://www.jeffrehabcenter.org. **Description:** A health and rehabilitation center with a manufacturing facility. Jefferson Rehabilitation operates several area sites. The company is a nonprofit organization working with handicapped individuals, treating both physical impairments and mental retardation. **Positions advertised include:** Applied Behavior Specialist Assistant; Registered Nurse; Qualified Mental Retardation Professional Assistant; Maintenance Worker; Secretary; Residence Manager Aide; Cook/ Housekeeper; Direct Care Staff; Occupational Trainer; Food Services Helper/Bus Aide; therapy Aide.

JEFFERSONVILLE BANCORP
THE FIRST NATIONAL BANK OF JEFFERSONVILLE
4866 State Route 52, P.O. Box 398, Jeffersonville NY 12748. 845/482-4000. **Fax:** 845/482-3544. **Contact:** Claire A. Pecsi, VP of Human Resources. **E-mail address:** cpecsi@jeffbank.com. **World Wide Web address:** http://www.jeffbank.com. **Description:** Owns and operates 10 full-service bank branches in and around the Sullivan County region of New York. Founded in 1913. **Corporate headquarters location:** This location. **Other area locations:** Eldred NY; Liberty NY; Loch Sheldrake NY; Monticello NY; Livingston Manor NY; Narrowsburg NY; Callicoon NY; Wurtsboro NY. **Subsidiaries include:** The First National Bank of Jeffersonville (also at this location). **Listed on:** NASDAQ. **Stock exchange symbol:** JFBC. **President:** Arthur E. Keesler. **Annual sales/revenues:** $24 million. **Number of employees:** 120.

JEWISH COMMUNITY CENTER ASSOCIATION
15 East 26th Street, 10th Floor, New York NY 10010-1579. 212/532-4949. **Fax:** 212/481-4174. **Contact:** C. Carlson, Personnel Manager. **E-mail address:** info@jcca.org. **World Wide Web address:** http://www.jcca.org. **Description:** The nonprofit, national coordinating body for the Jewish Community Center movement in North America. The association has more than 50 area locations and serves as the continental coordinating body for the Jewish Community Center Movement in North America associated with over 275 JCCs, YM-YWHAs and camps operating over 500 sites in the U.S. and Canada. **Corporate headquarters location:** This location. **Other locations:** Nationwide. **International locations:** Israel.

JOHN JAY COLLEGE OF CRIMINAL JUSTICE
THE CITY UNIVERSITY OF NEW YORK (CUNY)
899 Tenth Avenue, New York NY 10019. 212/237-8000. **Contact:** Donald J. Gray, Director of Human Resources Department. **E-mail address:** dgray@jjay.cuny.edu. **World Wide Web address:** http://www.jjay.cuny.edu. **Description:** A college with undergraduate and graduate programs of study concentrating in criminal justice. **Positions advertised include:** Assistant Organic Chemistry Professor; Associate African-American Studies Professor; LSAT and GRE Preparation Instructor; Biochemist; Molecular Biologist; Forensic Chemistry Criminologist; CUNY Office Assistant.

JORDACHE ENTERPRISES
1400 Broadway, Fifth Floor, New York NY 10018. 212/944-1330. **Fax:** 212/239-0063. **Contact:** Becky Diaz, Human Resources Manager. **World Wide Web address:** http://www.jordache.com. **Description:** Manufactures and distributes designer jeans, fashion apparel products, and accessories for the youth market. Licensed products include luggage, eyeglasses, shoes, and purses and the company manufactures Gasoline and FUBU jeans. **Listed on:** Privately held. **Chairman/CEO:** Joseph (Joe) Nakash.

JUNIPER GROUP, INC.
111 Great Neck Road, Suite 604, Great Neck NY 11021. 516/829-4670. **Fax:** 516/829-4691. **Contact:** Human Resources. **E-mail address:** info@junipergroup.com. **World Wide Web address:** http://www.junipergroup.com. **Description:** Juniper Group operates in two segments: health care and entertainment. The company's principal revenues are generated from health care, which consists of management for hospitals and health care cost containment for health care payers. The entertainment segment acquires and distributes film rights to various media including home video, pay-per-view, pay television, cable television, networks, ad-hoc networks, and independent syndicated television stations. Founded in 1989. **Corporate headquarters location:** This location. **Subsidiaries include:** Juniper Internet Communications; Juniper Pictures; Nuclear Cardiac Imaging; PartnerCare. **Listed on:** NASDAQ. **Stock exchange symbol:** JUNI. **Chairman/CEO:** Vlado Paul Hreljanovic. **Annual sales/revenues:** $1.2 million. **Number of employees:** 31.

JUNO ONLINE SERVICES, INC.
1540 Broadway, 27th Floor, New York NY 10036. 212/597-9000. **Contact:** Human Resources. **World Wide Web address:** http://www.juno.com. **Description:** A leading Internet access provider offering a variety of online services. Founded in 1996. **Positions advertised include:** Corporate Systems Administrator; Project Manager, Quality Assurance Engineer. **Special programs:** Internships. **Office hours:** Monday - Friday, 9:00 a.m. - 6:00 p.m. **Parent company:** United Online, Inc. **Corporate headquarters location:** Westlake Village CA. **Listed on:** NASDAQ. **Stock exchange symbol:** UNTD.

JUST ONE BREAK, INC.
120 Wall Street, 20th Floor, New York NY 10005. 212/785-7300. **Fax:** 212/785-4513. **Contact:** Recruiter. **E-mail address:** jobs@justonebreak.com. **World Wide Web address:** http://www.justonebreak.com. **Description:** A nonprofit organization that helps people with disabilities find employment. Founded in 1947.

K&F INDUSTRIES INC.
600 Third Avenue, 27th Floor, New York NY 10016. 212/297-0900. **Fax:** 212/867-1182. **Contact:** Lisa Jones, VP for Human Resources. **Description:** A holding company for two divisions that manufacture aircraft braking systems. **Subsidiaries include:** Aircraft Braking Systems Corporation; Engineered Fabrics. **Chairman/CEO:** Bernard L. Schwartz. **Annual sales/revenues:** $355 million. **Number of employees:** 1,404

KPMG
345 Park Avenue, New York NY 10154. 212/909-5000. **Contact:** Human Resources. **World Wide Web address:** http://www.kpmgcareers.com. **Description:** KPMG delivers a wide range of value-added assurance, tax, and consulting services including legal and management services. **Positions advertised include:** Senior Associate; Recruiter; Pharmaceutical Regulatory Manager; Associate Pharmaceutical Regulator; Senior Associate Manager; Project Manager; Senior Internal Auditor; Insurance

Practice Auditor; Duplicating Operator; Tax Manager; Quantitative Analyst. **Corporate headquarters location:** Montvale NJ. **Other U.S. locations:** Nationwide. **Parent company:** KPMG International is a professional services firm with more than 85,000 employees worldwide including 6,500 partners and 60,000 professionals, serving clients in 844 cities throughout 155 countries. KPMG International is a leader among professional services firms engaged in capturing, managing, assessing, and delivering information to create knowledge that will help its clients maximize shareholder value. **Number of employees at this location:** 1300.

KSW MECHANICAL SERVICES
3716 23rd Street, Long Island City NY 11101. 718/361-6500. **Fax:** 718/784-1943. **Contact:** Human Resources. **Description:** A mechanical contracting firm engaged in the installation of heating, ventilation, and air conditioning systems in commercial buildings. **Corporate headquarters location:** This location. **Listed on:** Over The Counter. **Stock exchange symbol:** KSWW. **Chairman/CEO:** Floyd Warkol. **Annual sales/revenues:** $50 million. **Number of employees:** 45.

KADDIS MANUFACTURING CORPORATION
1100 Old Beahan, P.O. Box 92985, Rochester NY 14692-9085. 585/464-9000. **Fax:** 585/464-0008. **Contact:** Human Resources. **World Wide Web address:** http://www.kaddis.com. **Description:** Kaddis manufactures screw machine parts used in small engines or various automotive products. Other manufactured parts are used in medical supplies. Founded in 1939.

KANTEK INC.
3460 Hampton Road, Oceanside NY 11572. 516/594-4600. **Fax:** 516/594-1555. **Contact:** Human Resources Department. **E-mail address:** info@kantek.com. **World Wide Web address:** http://www.kantek.com. **Description:** Manufactures glare reduction screens for computer monitors as well as other computer and desk accessories. Founded in 1982. **NOTE:** Human Resources phone: 516/593-3212.

THE KAPLAN THALER GROUP, LTD.
World Wide Plaza, 825 Eighth Avenue, 34th Floor, New York NY 10019-7498. 212/474-5000. **Fax:** 212/474-5036. **Contact:** Human Resources. **E-mail address:** kaplanthalergroup@kaplanthaler.com. **World Wide Web address:** http://www.kaplanthaler.com. **Description:** A national advertising agency. **Corporate headquarters location:** This location. **Other U.S. locations:** Nationwide. **International locations:** Worldwide. **Parent company:** Publicis (Paris, France). **President/CEO:** Linda Kaplan Thaler. **Annual sales/revenues:** $15 million. **Number of employees:** 48.

KATHARINE GIBBS SCHOOLS INC.
50 West 40th Street, 1st Floor, New York NY 10138-1347. 212/867-9300. **Contact:** President. **World Wide Web address:** http://www.katharinegibbs.com. **Description:** One of the nation's foremost business instruction schools. **Corporate headquarters location:** Piscataway NJ. **Other U.S. locations:** MA; CT; PA; RI; VA.

KATZ MEDIA GROUP, INC.
125 West 55th Street, 21st Floor, New York NY 10019-5366. 212/424-6000. **Fax:** 212/424-6110. **Contact:** Human Resources. **World Wide Web address:** http://www.katz-media.com. **Description:** An advertising agency with 21 regional offices nationwide. **Positions advertised include:** Sales Assistant; Supervisor/Sales Manager's Assistant; Research Analyst. **Corporate headquarters location:** This location. **Parent company:** Clear Channel Communications (San Antonio TX). **Subsidiaries include:** National Cable Communications; Christal Suburban Radio. **Listed on:** New York Stock Exchange. **Stock exchange symbol:** CCU. **CEO:** Stuart (Stu) O. Olds.

KAYE SCHOLER LLP
425 Park Avenue, 12th Floor, New York NY 10022-3598. 212/836-8000. **Fax:** 212/836-8689. **Contact:** Human Resources Representative. **E-mail address:** jobs@kayescholer.com. **World Wide Web address:** http://www.kayescholer.com. **Description:** A law partnership engaged in a variety of areas including corporate, finance, real estate, and tax law specializing in anti-trust and white collar crimes from nine offices worldwide. Founded in 1917. **NOTE:** Entry-level positions, part-time jobs, and second and third shifts are offered. **Corporate headquarters location:** This location. **Other U.S. locations:** Los Angeles CA; Washington DC; West Palm Beach FL; Chicago IL. **International locations:** China; Germany; United Kingdom. **Chairman:** David Klingsberg. **Annual sales/revenues:** $272 million. **Number of employees at this location:** 600. **Number of employees nationwide:** 825.

KEANE, INC.
525 Seventh Avenue, New York NY 10018-4901. 212/677-8800. **Fax:** 212/677-9654. **Contact:** Human Resources. **E-mail address:** careers.nyc@keane.com. **World Wide Web address:** http://www.keane.com. **Description:** Keane develops, markets, and manages software for its clients and assists in project management as well as offering computer consulting services. Founded in 1965. **Company slogan:** We Get IT Done. **Positions advertised include:** Programmer Analyst; Systems Analyst; Service Delivery Manager; Application Specialist; Database Administrator; Project Manager; Business Analyst. **Corporate headquarters location:** Boston MA. **Other U.S. locations:** Nationwide. **Operations at this facility include:** Divisional Headquarters **Listed on:** American Stock Exchange. **Stock exchange symbol:** KEA. **Annual sales/revenues:** $873 million. **Number of employees:** 7,331.

KELLER TECHNOLOGY CORPORATION
P.O. Box 103, Buffalo NY 14217-0103. 716/693-3840. **Physical address:** 2320 Military Road, Tonawanda NY 14150. **Fax:** 716/693-0512. **Contact:** Doug Raham, Human Resources. **E-mail address:** hrdept@kellertechnology.com. **World Wide Web address:** http://www.kellertechnology.com. **Description:** Keller Technology designs and manufactures industrial equipment including specialty machinery used by major corporations involved in pharmaceuticals, textiles, or energy-related industries. Founded in 1918. **Corporate headquarters location:** This location. **Other locations:** Buffalo NY; Charlotte NC.

KEMPER INSURANCE COMPANIES
30 Rockefeller Plaza, 12th Floor, New York NY 10112. 646/710-7000. **Contact:** Human Resources. **World Wide Web address:** http://www.kemperinsurance.com. **Description:** Provides a wide range of commercial and personal property/casualty insurance in the United States and foreign markets. **NOTE:** See the website for more detailed application information. **Positions advertised include:** Claim Clerk; Claim Specialist; Claim Analyst; Senior Auditor; Staff Accountant. **Corporate headquarters location:** Long Grove IL. **Other U.S. locations:** Nationwide. **Annual sales/revenues:** $2.85 billion. **Number of employees:** 9,000

KENNETH COLE PRODUCTIONS
603 West 50th Street, New York NY 10019. 212/265-1500. **Fax:** 212/830-7422. **Contact:** Human Resources. **E-mail address:** nyjobs@kennethcole.com. **World Wide Web address:** http://www.kencole.com. **Description:** Manufactures men's and women's shoes, bags, scarves, watches, belts, and other accessories. **Positions advertised include:** Retail Store Manager; General Manager. **Corporate headquarters location:** This location. **Listed on:** New York Stock Exchange. **Stock exchange symbol:** KCP. **Chairman/CEO:** Kenneth D. Cole. **Annual sales/revenues:** $433 million. **Number of employees:** 1,800.

KEY FOOD STORES CO-OPERATIVE, INC.
1200 South Avenue, Staten Island NY 10314. 718/370-4200. **Fax:** 718/370-4225. **Contact:** Human Resources. **Description:** A private co-operative of 115 independently owned food stores and supermarkets throughout the New York metropolitan region. Founded in 1937. **Corporate headquarters location:** This location. **Other locations:** Bronx NY; Brooklyn NY; Queens NY; Manhattan NY; Staten Island NY; Yonkers NY. **CEO:** Richard Pallitto. **Annual sales/revenues:** $445 million. **Number of employees:** 150.

KEYSPAN ENERGY CORPORATION
dba KEYSPAN ENERGY DELIVERY
One MetroTech Center, Brooklyn NY 11201-3850. 718/403-1000. **Fax:** 718/488-1782. **Contact:** Elaine Weinstein, Human Resources VP. **E-mail address:** employment@keyspanenergy.com. **World Wide Web address:** http://www.keyspanenergy.com. **Description:** Provides natural gas service and engages in gas exploration, production, and transportation. **NOTE:** Interested applicants are requested to send resumes with the job reference code to: KeySpan, Talent Management Department , 175 East Old Country Road, Hicksville NY 11801. **Corporate headquarters location:** This location. **Subsidiaries include:** Brooklyn Union Gas Company; KeySpan Energy Delivery; KeySpan Energy Development Corporation; KeySpan Services, Inc.; The Houston Exploration Company. **Listed on:** New York Stock Exchange. **Stock exchange symbol:** KSE. **Chairman/CEO:** Robert B. Catell. **Annual sales/revenues:** $6 billion. **Number of employees:** 13,000.

KING WORLD PRODUCTIONS
1700 Broadway, 33rd Floor, New York NY 10019. 212/315-4000. **Fax:** 212/582-9255. **Contact:** Human Resources. **E-mail address:** kwjobs@kinigworld.com. **World Wide Web address:** http://www.kingworld.com. **Description:** A broadcasting company engaged in the syndication of television. **Parent company:** CBS Enterprises.

KINGSTON HOSPITAL
396 Broadway, Kingston NY 12401. 845/331-3131. **Fax:** 845/334-2850. **Contact:** Human Resources. **World Wide Web address:** http://www.kingstonhospital.org. **Description:** An 150-bed, acute care hospital. **Parent company:** Kingston Regional Health Care System. **Number of employees at this location:** 680.

KOLMAR LABORATORIES, INC.
P.O. Box 1111, Port Jervis NY 12771. 845/856-5311. **Fax:** 845/856-5507. **Contact:** Human Resources. **World Wide Web address:** http://www.kolmar.com. **Description:** Manufactures all types of color cosmetics for the face, as well as various personal care and beauty items. Kolmar's products include skin care treatments, bath care, and spa items. **Parent company:** Outsourcing Services Group.

KRAFT FOODS, INC.
7388 Utica Boulevard, Lowville NY 13367. 315/376-6575. **Contact:** Human Resources. **World Wide Web address:** http://www.kraft.com. **Description:** Kraft Foods, Inc. is one of the largest producers of packaged grocery products in North America. Major brands include Jell-O, Post, Kool-Aid, Crystal Light, Entenmann's, Miracle Whip, Stove Top, and Shake 'n Bake. Kraft markets a number of products under the Kraft brand including natural and process cheeses and dry packaged dinners. The Oscar Mayer unit markets processed meats, poultry, lunch combinations, and pickles under the Oscar Mayer, Louis Rich, Lunchables, and Claussen brand names. Kraft is also one of the largest coffee companies with principal brands including Maxwell House, Sanka, Brim, and General Foods International Coffees. Kraft Foods Ingredients Corporation manufactures private-label and industrial food products for sale to other food processing companies. **Corporate headquarters location:** Northfield IL. **Subsidiaries include:** Kraft Foods North America, Inc.; Kraft Foods International, Inc.; Nabisco. **Parent company:** Philip Morris Companies is a company whose principal wholly-owned subsidiaries are Philip Morris Inc. (Philip Morris USA), Philip Morris International Inc., Kraft Foods Inc., and Philip Morris Capital Corporation. **Operations at this facility include:** Cream Cheese Processing. **Listed on:** New York Stock Exchange. **Stock exchange symbol:** KFT. **Annual sales/revenues:** $30 billion. **Number of employees:** 109,000.

KRASDALE FOODS INC.
65 West Red Oak Lane, White Plains NY 10604. 914/694-6400. **Fax:** 914/697-5225. **Contact:** Human Resources. **World Wide Web address:** http://www.krasdalefoods.com. **Description:** Engaged in the wholesale distribution of canned goods and other processed food products throughout the tri-state area. Founded in 1908. **Corporate headquarters location:** This location. **Other locations:** Bronx NY. **President/CEO:** Charles A Krasne. **Annual sales/revenues:** $550 million. **Number of employees:** 750.

L-3 COMMUNICATIONS HOLDINGS, INC.
600 Third Avenue, New York NY 10016. 212/697-1111. **Fax:** 212/867-5249 **Contact:** Human Resources. **World Wide Web address:** http://www.l-3com.com. **Description:** Manufactures secure and specialized products for satellite, avionics, and marine communications including the black box flight recorders used on aircraft for both military and commercial industries. **Positions advertised include:** Criminal Justice Specialist; Contracting Support; Fusion System Analyst. **Corporate headquarters location:** This location. **Other locations:** Nationwide. **Listed on:** New York Stock Exchange. **Stock exchange symbol:** LLL. **Annual sales/revenues:** $4 billion. **Number of employees:** 25,000.

L-3 COMMUNICATIONS CORPORATION
265 Industrial Park Drive, P.O. Box 1237, Binghamton NY 13902-1237. 607/721-5465. **Contact:** Manager of Human Resources. **World Wide Web address:** http://www.l-3com.com. **Description:** Develops secure communication systems, training systems, avionics and ocean systems, microwave components, space and wireless products for the U.S. military and other governmental and industrial customers. **Parent company:** L-3 Communications Holdings, Inc. (New York NY).

LSI COMPUTER SYSTEMS INC.
1235 Walt Whitman Road, Melville NY 11747-3010. 631/271-0400. **Fax:** 631/271-0405. **Contact:** Human Resources. **E-mail address:** hr@lsicsi.com. **World Wide Web address:** http://www.lsicsi.com. **Description:** Manufactures integrated circuits and microchips. Founded in 1969. **Positions advertised include:** Integrated Circuit Design Engineer; Integrated Circuit Layout Designer; Test Engineer.

LAPP INSULATOR COMPANY LLC
130 Gilbert Street, LeRoy NY 14482. 585/768-6221. **Fax:** 585/768-6219. **Contact:** Renee Higgins, Human Resources Director. **World Wide Web address:** http://www.lappinsulator.com. **Description:** Lapp Insulator Corporation is a manufacturer of porcelain insulators and bushings. Products are used in the utility industry, primarily in utility poles, to insulate wires and protect electrical conductors from abrasion.

LAWYERS TITLE INSURANCE CORPORATION
10 Bank Street, Suite 1120, White Plains NY 10606. 914/682-3900. **Contact:** Human Resources. **World Wide Web address:** http://www.landam.com. **Description:** Provides title insurance and other real estate-related services on commercial and residential transactions in the United States, Canada, the Bahamas, Puerto Rico, and the U.S. Virgin Islands. Lawyers Title Insurance Corporation also provides search and examination services and closing services for a broad-based customer group that includes lenders, developers, real estate brokers, attorneys, and homebuyers. This location covers New Jersey, New York, and Pennsylvania. Founded in 1925. **Positions advertised include:** Project Manager. **Corporate headquarters location:** Richmond VA. **Other U.S. locations:** Pasadena CA; Tampa FL; Chicago IL; Boston MA; Troy MI; Westerville OH; Memphis TN; Dallas TX. **Subsidiaries include:** Datatrace Information Services Company, Inc. (Richmond VA) markets automated public record information for public and private use; Genesis Data Systems, Inc. (Englewood CO) develops and markets computer software tailored specifically to the title industry; and Lawyers Title Exchange Company functions as an intermediary for individual and corporate investors interested in pursuing tax-free property exchanges. **Parent company:** LandAmerica Financial Group, Inc.

LE MOYNE COLLEGE
1419 Salt Springs Road, Grewen Hall, room 209-E, Syracuse NY 13214. 315/445-4155. **Fax:** 315/445-6023. **Contact:** Human Resources. **E-mail address:** lemoynehr@lemoyne.edu. **World Wide Web address:** http://www.lemoyne.edu. **Description:** A four-year, co-ed, Jesuit college. Le Moyne offers bachelor of arts and bachelor of science undergraduate degrees in approximately 30 majors. Graduate programs include master's degrees in business administration and education. **Positions advertised include:** Coordinator of Housing; Residential Director; Graduate Student Residential Hall Director; Associate Professor for Special Education; Education Department Chairperson; Physician Assistant Program Director.

LEBHAR-FRIEDMAN, INC.
425 Park Avenue, 5th Floor, New York NY 10022. 212/756-5000. **Contact:** Human Resources Department. **E-mail address:** ssmith@lf.com. **World Wide Web address:** http://www.lf.com. **Description:** A publisher of retail business publications, magazines, and retail directories including *Chain Store Age*, *Drug Store News*, *National Restaurant News*. **Positions advertised include:** Associate Creative Director; Executive Editor. **Corporate headquarters location:** This location. **Other locations:** Boston MA; Chicago IL; Los Angeles CA; Tampa FL.

LEBOEUF, LAMB, GREENE & MACRAE LLP
125 West 55th Street, New York NY 10019. **Contact:** Jill A. Cameron, Manager of Legal Recruiting. **E-mail address:** jcameron@llgm.com. **World Wide Web address:** http://www.llgm.com. **Description:** One of the nation's largest law firms, focusing in a number of different practice areas. **Corporate headquarters location:** This location. **Special programs:** Summer Associates; Summer Internships.

THE LECROY CORPORATION
700 Chestnut Ridge Road, Chestnut Ridge NY 10977-6499. 845/425-2000. **Fax:** 845/578-4461. **Contact:** Corporate Staffing. **E-mail address:** hrweb@lecroy.com. **World Wide Web address:** http://www.lecroy.com. **Description:** The LeCroy Corporation is a leading manufacturer of digital oscilloscopes and related products for the electronics, computer, and communications markets. Founded in 1964. **Positions advertised include:** Corporate Accounting Manager; Sales Engineer; Field Engineer; Layout Technician; Mechanical Design Engineer; Program Manager. **Corporate headquarters location:** This location. **International locations:** Geneva, Switzerland. **Listed on:** NASDAQ. **Stock exchange symbol:** LCRY. **Annual sales/revenues:** $111.5 million. **Number of employees at this location:** 190. **Number of employees worldwide:** 407.

LEHMAN BROTHERS HOLDINGS
745 Seventh Avenue, New York NY 10019. 212/526-7000. **Contact:** Stephanie Jacobs, Recruiting. **E-mail address:** invbank.associate.us@lehman.com. **World Wide Web address:** http://www.lehman.com. **Description:** An equities trading company engaged in merchant banking and other financial services including underwriting, fixed-income products, and asset management, as well as stock trading, currency, derivatives, and commodities. **Corporate headquarters location:** This location. **Subsidiaries include:** Lehman Brothers Bank, FSB. **Chairman/CEO:** Richard (Dick) S. Fuld Jr. **Annual sales/revenues:** $17 billion. **Number of employees:** 12,343.

LEHMAN COLLEGE
THE CITY UNIVERSITY OF NEW YORK (CUNY)
250 Bedford Park Boulevard West, Shuster Hall, Room 230, Bronx NY 10468. 718/960-8181. **Contact:** Personnel Office. **World Wide Web address:** http://www.lehman.cuny.edu. **Description:** A public coeducational liberal arts college offering over 90 undergraduate and graduate programs. **NOTE:** Personnel phone: 718/960-8181.

LERNER NEW YORK, INC.
450 West 33rd Street, 5th Floor, New York NY 10001. 212/736-1222. **Fax:** 212/884-2396. **Contact:** Recruitment. **World Wide Web address:** http://www.limited.com. **Description:** A specialty women's clothing retailer specializing in city-style apparel and accessories selling name-brand and private-label clothing from over 500 mall-based stores in 43 states. **Special programs:** Internships. **Listed on:** New York Stock Exchange. **Stock exchange symbol:** LTD. **President/CEO:** Richard P. Crystal. **Annual sales/revenues:** $940 million. **Number of employees at this location:** 300. **Number of employees nationwide:** 14,000.

THE LESLIE FAY COMPANIES, INC.
1412 Broadway, 3rd Floor, New York NY 10018. 212/221-4000. **Fax:** 212/221-4245. **Contact:** Human Resources. **Description:** Engaged in the design, manufacture, and sale of a diversified line of women's dresses, sportswear, blouses, and intimate apparel and sells under several brands including Leslie Fay, Joan Leslie, David Warren, and Trio New York to specialty and department stores. **Corporate headquarters location:** This location. **Parent company:** Three Cities Research. **Chairman:** John J. Pomerantz. **Annual sales/revenues:** $170 million.

LEUCADIA NATIONAL CORPORATION
315 Park Avenue South, New York NY 10010. 212/460-1900. **Fax:** 212/598-4869. **Contact:** Laura E. Ulbrandt, Human Resources. **Description:** Leucadia National is a diversified holding company with subsidiaries with interests in over 30 companies involved in the insurance, manufacturing, banking, investments, and real estate industries. The insurance business offers property, casualty, and life insurance nationwide. **Corporate headquarters location:** This location. **Subsidiaries include:** Allcity Insurance; American Investment Bank, N.A.; American Investment Financial; Charter, CPL; Empire Insurance Group; Intramerica; MK Gold Company. **Listed on:** New York Stock Exchange. **Stock exchange symbol:** LUK. **Chairman:** Iam M. Cumming. **Annual sales/revenues:** $297 million. **Number of employees:** 1,066.

LEVITON MANUFACTURING CO. INC.
59-25 Little Neck Parkway, Little Neck NY 11362-2591. 718/229-4040. **Fax:** 800/832-9538. **Contact:** Mark Fogel, Director of Human Resources. **E-mail address:** careers@leviton.com. **World Wide Web address:** http://www.leviton.com. **Description:** A family-owned manufacturer of electronic components and electrical wiring devices. Leviton produces more than 80,000 variations of light switches, sockets, and plugs for both consumer and industrial customers. Products are used in small appliances, lamps, and similar products. Founded in 1906. **Positions advertised include:** Inside Sales Representative; Director of Business Systems; Data Entry Operator; Demand Analyst; Test Engineer; Accounts Payable Clerk; Cost Estimator; Graphic Artist; Marketing Service Coordinator; Technical Service Representative. **Corporate headquarters location:** This location. **Other U.S. locations:** Atlanta GA; Chicago IL; Coffeyville KS; Sparks NV; Pawtucket RI; Bothell WA. **International locations:** Canada; Mexico. **Subsidiaries include:** American Insulated Wire; Electricord Company; Leviton Telcom. **President/CEO:** Harold Leviton. **Annual sales/revenues:** $350 million.

LEWIS TREE SERVICE
225 Ballantyne Road, Rochester NY 14623. 585/436-3208. **Fax:** 585/235-5864. **Contact:** Human Resources. **E-mail address:** hr@lewistree.com. **World Wide Web address:** http://www.lewistree.com. **Description:** Lewis Tree Service is an employee-owned company with operations nationwide that provides complete vegetation management services specializing in working with utility companies at sites where trees obstruct the proper functioning of a particular utility. Founded in 1938. **Positions advertised include:** Climber/Operator; Crew Leader; General Foreman; Bucket Trimmer; Spray Technician; Work Coordinator. **Number of employees:** 1,350.

LEXINGTON CORPORATE PROPERTIES TRUST
355 Lexington Avenue, 14th Floor, New York NY 10017. 212/692-7260. **Toll-free phone:** 800/692-6999. **Fax:** 212/594-6600. **Contact:** Human Resources. **E-mail address:** info@lxp.com. **World Wide Web address:** http://www.lxp.com. **Description:** A real estate investment trust that owns and manages office, industrial, and retail properties located in 30 states. Founded in 1993. **Corporate headquarters location:** This location. **Subsidiaries include:** Lexington Realty Advisors. **Listed on:** New York Stock Exchange. **Stock exchange symbol:** LXP. **Chairman:** E. Robert Roskind. **Annual sales/revenues:** $102 million. **Number of employees:** 25.

LIBERTY INTERNATIONAL UNDERWRITERS INC.
55 Water Street, New York NY 10041. 212/208-4100. **Contact:** Human Resources Manager. **E-mail address:** resume@libertyinternational.com. **World Wide Web address:** http://www.libertyiu.com. **Description:** A property and casualty insurance company with some specialty lines including marine and nonstandard automotive. Founded in 1999. **Positions advertised include:** Strategic Software Architect; Professional Liability Claims Attorney; Claims Adjuster. **Parent company:** Liberty Mutual Insurance Company.

LIBERTY LINES TRANSIT INC.
475 Saw Mill River Road, P.O. Box 624, Yonkers NY 10703. 914/969-6900. **Fax:** 914/376-6440. **Contact:** Human Resources. **E-mail address:** jobs@libertylines.com. **World Wide Web address:** http://www.libertylines.com. **Description:** One of the largest and most diversified bus services in the Yonkers/Westchester area. Services include commuter and transit bus operations. Founded in 1953. **Positions advertised include:** Bus Driver. **Corporate headquarters location:** This location. **Operations at this facility include:** Administration; Service. **President:** Jerry D'Amore.

LIBERTY MUTUAL INSURANCE GROUP
1133 Avenue of the Americas, 27th Floor, New York NY 10036. 212/391-7500. **Contact:** Personnel. **World Wide Web address:** http://www.libertymutual.com. **Description:** A full-line insurance firm offering life, medical, and business insurance, as well as investment and retirement plans. **NOTE:** Jobseekers may apply online. **Positions advertised include:** Claims Manager; Legal Office Manager; Service Representative; Sales Representative; Consultant; Customer Service Coordinator; Strategic Software Architect; Professional Liability Claims Attorney; Claims Adjuster. **Special programs:** Internships. **Corporate headquarters location:** Boston MA. **Subsidiaries include:** Colorado Casualty Insurance Company; Liberty Financial. **Operations at this facility include:** Administration; Sales; Service. **Annual sales/revenues:** $14.5 billion. **Number of employees:** 35,000.

LIFETIME HOAN CORPORATION
One Merrick Avenue, Westbury NY 11590. 516/683-6000. **Fax:** 516/683-6116. **Contact:** Sally Mogavero, Director of Human Resources. **World Wide Web address:** http://www.lifetime.hoan.com. **Description:** Lifetime Hoan Corporation designs, markets, and distributes household cutlery, kitchen tools and gadgets, and other houseware products. The company manufactures a variety of carving knives under the Hoffritz, Tristar, Old Homestead, and LC Germain brand names. Lifetime Hoan Corporation also produces a deluxe line for Farberware, and operates 60 Farberware outlet stores. **Other locations:** Chicago IL; Elmsford NY; Robbinsville NJ. **International locations:** Hong Kong, China. **Listed on:** NASDAQ. **Stock exchange symbol:** LCUT. **Chairman/President/CEO:** Jeffrey (Jeff) Siegel. **Annual sales/revenues:** $131 million. **Number of employees at this location:** 300. **Number of employees worldwide:** 657.

LIGHTHOUSE INTERNATIONAL
111 East 59th Street, New York NY 10022-1202. 212/821-9200. **Toll-free phone:** 800/829-0500. **Fax:** 212/821-9708. **Recorded jobline:** 212/821-9419. **Contact:** Nicole Ruderman, Recruiting Coordinator. **E-mail address:** nruderman@lighthouse.org. **World Wide Web address:** http://www.lighthouse.org. **Description:** Enables people who are blind or partially blind to lead independent lives through education, research, information, career and social services, and vision rehabilitation. Lighthouse International serves more than 5,000 persons. **Positions advertised include:** School Nurse; Vision Rehabilitation Assistant; Administrative Coordinator; Job Coach. **Special programs:** Internships. **Other area locations:** Brooklyn NY; Poughkeepsie NY; Queens NY; White Plains NY. **Number of employees at this location:** 305. **Number of employees nationwide:** 375.

LILLIAN VERNON CORPORATION
One Theall Road, Rye NY 10580-1450. 914/925-1200. **Fax:** 914/925-1320. **Contact:** Human Resources. **E-mail address:** bgarti@lillianvernon.com. **World Wide Web**

address: http://www.lillianvernon.com. **Description:** Lillian Vernon markets gift, household, gardening, decorative, Christmas, and children's products through a variety of specialty catalogs. Catalog titles include: Lillian Vernon; Lillian Vernon Gardening; Neat Ideas; Personalized Gift; Christmas Memories; Lilly's Kids; Favorites; and Private Sale. Founded in 1951. **Office hours:** Monday - Friday, 8:30 a.m. - 5:00 p.m. **Corporate headquarters location:** This location. **Other U.S. locations:** Virginia Beach VA. **Listed on:** American Stock Exchange. **Stock exchange symbol:** LVC. **Chairperson:** Lillian Vernon. **Annual sales/revenues:** $247 million. **Number of employees at this location:** 165. **Number of employees nationwide:** 1,400.

LINCOLN CENTER FOR THE ARTS, INC.
NEW YORK CITY BALLET
70 Lincoln Center Plaza, New York NY 10023. 212/875-5255. **Fax:** 212/875-5185. **Contact:** Stacy Tonkas, Human Resources Director. **E-mail address:** humanresources@lincolncenter.org. **World Wide Web address:** http://www.lincolncenter.org. **Description:** An international center for the performing arts presenting live performances of opera, ballet, music, theater, dance, circus, and puppetry. **Positions advertised include:** Institutional Giving Director; Publicist; Human Resources Assistant; Customer Service Representative. **Executive Director:** Scott Noppe-Brandon. **Annual sales/revenues:** $25 million.

LINDBLAD SPECIAL EXPEDITIONS
720 Fifth Avenue, 6th Floor, New York NY 10019. 212/261-9000. **Contact:** Human Resources. **World Wide Web address:** http://www.specialexpeditions.com. **Description:** A cruise line operator with destinations throughout the Pacific and the Caribbean including the Galapagos Islands, Mexico's Baja Peninsula, Alaska, Antarctica, Arctic Norway, and Costa Rica, as well as up the Colorado and Snake Rivers. **Positions advertised include:** Steward; Deckhand; Physician.

LIPPINCOTT WILLIAMS & WILKINS
HEALTHCARE GROUP
345 Hudson Street, 16th Floor, New York NY 10014. 212/886-1200. **Fax:** 215/367-2140. **Contact:** Human Resources. **World Wide Web address:** http://www.lww.com. **Description:** Publishes the *American Journal of Nursing*. **Positions advertised include:** Associate Publisher; Manufacturing Coordinator; Production Editor; Senior Clinical Editor; Clerical Assistant. **Corporate headquarters location:** Philadelphia PA. **Other U.S. locations:** Baltimore MD; Hagerstown MD; Skokie IL; Springhouse PA. **International locations:** Australia; China; United Kingdom. **Operations at this facility include:** Administration; Sales; Service. **Number of employees at this location:** 75.

G.W. LISK CO., INC.
dba CLIFTRONICS INC.
2 South Street, Clifton Springs NY 14432. 315/462-2611. **Fax:** 315/462-7611. **Contact:** Personnel. **E-mail address:** marketing@gwlisk.com **World Wide Web address:** http://www.cliftronics.com. **Description:** The company manufactures solenoids, valves, and flame arresters used in aircraft, fuel lines, and fuel storage. Subsidiary Cliftronics specializes in engineering, design, and manufacture of custom solenoids, valves and flame arresters for aerospace and military applications. **Corporate headquarters location:** This location. **Other locations:** Gort, Ireland; Essex, United Kingdom.

LITTLE FLOWER CHILDREN'S SERVICES OF NEW YORK
186 Joralemon Street, Brooklyn NY 11201. 718/875-3500. **Fax:** 718/625-6102. **Contact:** Human Resources. **E-mail address:** jobs@lfchild.org. **World Wide Web address:** http://www.littleflowerny.org. **Description:** Provides foster care and adoption services, group homes, residential treatment units, shelter cottages, intermediate care facilities for mentally handicapped children, and therapeutic foster boarding homes. Little Flower Children's Services cares for approximately 2,600 children annually. **Positions advertised include:** Caseworker; Youth Counselor; Direct Care Worker; Registered Nurse; Licensed Practical Nurse; Secretary; Clerk; Maintenance Worker; Grounds Keeper; Kitchen Worker; Driver. **Corporate headquarters location:** Wading River NY. **Other locations:** Queens NY. **Number of employees:** 650.

LITTLE FLOWER CHILDREN'S SERVICES OF NEW YORK
2450 North Wading River Road, Wading River NY 11792. 631/929-6200 ext. 157. **Fax:** 631/929-6121. **Contact:** Human Resources. **E-mail address:** jobs@lfchild.org. **World Wide Web address:** http://www.littleflowerny.org. **Description:** Provides adoption and foster care services, foster homes for individuals who are mentally handicapped, intermediate care facilities, residential treatment facilities, and therapeutic foster boarding homes. Little Flower Children's Services cares for more than 2,600 children annually. **Positions advertised include:** Caseworker; Youth Counselor; Direct Care Worker; Registered Nurse; Licensed Practical Nurse; Secretary; Clerk; Maintenance Worker; Grounds Keeper; Kitchen Worker; Driver. **Special programs:** Internships. **Corporate headquarters location:** This location. **Other locations:** Brooklyn NY; Queens NY. **Number of employees:** 650.

LIZ CLAIBORNE, INC.
1441 Broadway, New York NY 10018. 212/354-4900. **Fax:** 212/626-3416. **Contact:** Human Resources. **E-mail address:** staffing@liz.com. **World Wide Web address:** http://www.lizclaiborne.com. **Description:** Liz Claiborne is comprised of 18 apparel and accessories divisions and several licenses. Products are sold under the company brand names and private labels. **Positions advertised include:** Knit Specialist Technician; Woven Designer; Associate Handbag Designer; Menswear Designer; Sigrid Olsen Handbag Designer; Senior Colorist; Junior Color Coordinator; Monet Jewelry Designer; Lucky Accessories Designer; Menswear Dress Shirt Designer; Senior Fabric Research & Development Associate; Latin America Account Executive; Senior Japan Account Executive; Sales Manager; Product Development Engineer; Merchandiser; Planner; Retail Analyst; Production Costing Specialist; Fabric Purchaser; Corporate Communications Manager; LizEdge Program Assistant. **Special programs:** Internships. **Corporate headquarters location:** This location. **Subsidiaries include:** Ellen Tracy, Inc. **Listed on:** New York Stock Exchange. **Stock exchange symbol:** LIZ. **Chairman/CEO:** Paul R. Charron. **Annual sales/revenues:** $3.7 billion. **Number of employees worldwide:** 12,000.

LOEWS CORPORATION
655 Madison Avenue, 7th Floor, New York NY 10021-8087. 212/521-2000. **Fax:** 212/521-2466. **Contact:** Margorie Kouroupos, Human Resources. **E-mail address:** hrrep@newposition.com. **World Wide Web address:** http://www.loews.com. **Description:** A holding company and one of the largest diversified financial corporations in the U.S. with interests in the financial, tobacco, hotel, drilling, and watch industries. **Positions advertised include:** Graphic Designer; Digital Image Librarian; Information Technology Security Specialist; Internal Auditor Assistant; Internal Hotel Auditor Assistant. **Corporate headquarters location:** This location. **Subsidiaries include:** CNA Financial Corporation, which provides insurance services; Carolina Group, and Lorillard, Inc., which produce tobacco products; Loews Hotels Holding Corporation, which owns and operates a nationwide chain of hotels; Diamond Offshore Drilling, Inc., an offshore drilling company; and Bulova Corporation, which distributes watches and clocks. **Listed on:** New York Stock Exchange. **Stock exchange symbol:** LTR. **Co-Chairmen:** Lawrence A. Tisch and Preston (Bob) R. Tisch. **Annual sales/revenues:** $17.5 billion. **Number of employees:** 25,800.

LONG ISLAND POWER AUTHORITY (LIPA)
333 Earle Ovington Boulevard, Suite 403, Uniondale NY 11553. 516/222-7700. **Fax:** 516/222-9137. **Contact:** Human Resources. **E-mail address:** info@lipower.org. **World Wide Web address:** http://www.lipower.org. **Description:** Supplies electric and gas service in Nassau and Suffolk Counties and the Rockaway Peninsula in Queens County. **Positions advertised include:** Rates and Pricing Manager; Marketing Assistant. **Special programs:** Internships. **Corporate headquarters location:** This location. **Other locations:** Brentwood NY; Garden City NY.

THE LONG ISLAND RAILROAD COMPANY
Sutphin Boulevard Jam, Hicksville NY 11801. 516/733-3900. **Contact:** Human Resources. **World Wide Web address:** http://www.lirr.org. **Description:** Operates one of the oldest active railroads in the United States. The company has extensive commuter passenger and freight service railroad operations, primarily between New York City and numerous points on Long Island. The Long island Railroad Company is one of the busiest passenger railroad operators in the United States. **NOTE:** Application materials should be sent to: Human Resources-SR, Mail code 1155-IT-NET, MTA Long Island Rail Road, Jamaica Station, Jamaica NY 11435. **Positions advertised include:** Assistant Conductor; Electrician. **Corporate headquarters location:** This location. **Parent company:** Metropolitan Transportation Authority. (New York NY).

LONG ISLAND UNIVERSITY
C.W. Post Campus, 720 Northern Boulevard, Brookville NY 11548-1326. 516/299-2000. **Contact:** Human Resources. **World Wide Web address:** http://www.liunet.edu. **Description:** A university offering undergraduate and graduate programs of study. The university's programs of study are offered through its six schools: College of Liberal Arts & Sciences; School of Education; College of Management; School of Health Professions; School of Visual & Performing Arts; and the Palmer School of Library & Information Sciences. **Positions advertised include:** Assistant Mathematics Professor. **Special programs:** Internships. **Corporate headquarters location:** This location. **Other area locations:** Brentwood NY; Brooklyn NY; Greenvale NY; Southampton NY. **Operations at this facility include:** Administration. **Number of employees:** 4,328.

LOOMIS FARGO & COMPANY
58 Ellicott Road, Cheektowaga NY 14277. 716/684-9600. **Fax:** 716/684-5644. **Contact:** Personnel. **World Wide Web address:** http://www.loomisfargo.com. **Description:** An armored security service specializing in transporting currency. **NOTE:** Applications will not be mailed to jobseekers. They must be picked up in person. **Other U.S. locations:** Nationwide.

LOOMIS FARGO & COMPANY
21 Railroad Avenue, Colonie NY 12205. 518/438-9074. **Fax:** 518/435-1636. **Contact:** Personnel. **World Wide Web address:** http://www.loomisfargo.com. **Description:** An armored security service specializing in transporting currency. **NOTE:** Applications will not be mailed to jobseekers. They must be picked up in person. **Other U.S. locations:** Nationwide.

LORAL SPACE & COMMUNICATIONS LTD.
600 Third Avenue, 38th Floor, New York NY 10016. 212/697-1105. **Fax:** 212/338-5662. **Contact:** Human Resources. **World Wide Web address:** http://www.loral.com. **Description:** The company is engaged in the production of satellites specializing in communications and weather satellites. Through its subsidiaries Loral offers satellite-based telephone service, broadcasting and private data communications, and delivers Internet content. **Positions advertised include:** Finance Officer; Accountant; Communications Assistant; Human Resources Associate; Legal Counselor. **Corporate headquarters location:** This location. **Other U.S. locations:** Bedminster NJ; Palo Alto CA; Washington DC. **Subsidiaries include:** Loral CyberStar, Inc.; Loral Skynet; SatMex; Globalstar; Space Systems/Loral. **Listed on:** New York Stock Exchange. **Stock exchange symbol:** LOR. **Chairman/CEO:** Bernard L. Schwartz. **Annual sales/revenues:** $1 billion. **Number of employees nationwide:** 2800.

LORD & TAYLOR
424 Fifth Avenue, New York NY 10018. 212/391-3344. **Contact:** Human Resources. **World Wide Web address:** http://www.lordandtaylor.com. **Description:** A full-line department store operating 85 stores nationwide offering clothing, accessories, home furnishings, and many other retail items. Founded in 1826. **Positions advertised include:** General Sales Associate; Commission Sales Associate; Cosmetics Beauty Advisor. **Parent company:** The May Department Stores Company (St. Louis MO).

LOWE
One Dag Hammarskjold Plaza, New York NY 10017. 212/605-8000. **Contact:** Human Resources. **E-mail address:** info@loweworldwide.com. **World Wide Web address:** http://www.loweworldwide.com. **Description:** An advertising agency.

LOWER WEST SIDE HOUSEHOLD SERVICES CORPORATION
250 West 57th Street, Suite 1511, New York NY 10107-1511. 212/307-7107. **Fax:** 212/956-2308. **Contact:** Human Resources. **E-mail address:** contact@homecareny.org. **World Wide Web address:** http://www.homecareny.org. **Description:** A nonprofit company that provides home health care services to the elderly, infants, toddlers, and adults living in the five boroughs of New York City and Westchester County. Services include nursing, custodial care, nutrition, social work, and arrangements for medical equipment. The agency also provides free custodial care for individuals and families infected with HIV/AIDS. **NOTE:** Second and thirds shifts are offered. Founded in 1969. **Positions advertised include:** Service Coordinator; Data Entry Clerk; Home Health Aide; Licensed Practical Nurse; Occupational Therapist; Physical Therapist; Social Worker; Speech-Language Pathologist. **Special programs:** Training. **Office hours:** Monday - Friday, 8:00 a.m. - 5:00 p.m. **Corporate headquarters location:** This location. **Other U.S. locations:** Scarsdale NY. **Number of employees at this location:** 250.

LUCENT TECHNOLOGIES INC.
5 Penn Plaza, 10th Floor, New York NY 10001. 212/290-5900. **Contact:** Human Resources. **World Wide Web address:** http://www.lucent.com. **Description:** Manufactures communications products including switching, transmission, fiber-optic cable, wireless systems, and operations systems, to supply the needs of telephone companies and other communications services providers. **NOTE:** Interested jobseekers should send resumes to Lucent Technologies, Inc., 600 Mountain Avenue, Murray Hill NJ 07974. **Corporate headquarters location:** Murray Hill NJ. **Subsidiaries include:** Bell Laboratories. **Listed on:** New York Stock Exchange. **Stock exchange symbol:** LU. **Annual sales/revenues:** $12.3 billion. **Number of employees:** 47,000.

LYNCH INTERACTIVE CORPORATION
401 Theodore Fremd Avenue, Rye NY 10580. 914/921-8821. **Fax:** 914/921-6410. **Contact:** Human Resources. **E-mail address:** rdolan@lynchinteractivecorp.com. **World Wide Web address:** http://www.lynchinteractivecorp.com. **Description:** A holding company with subsidiaries involved in multimedia services and manufacturing. **NOTE:** Human Resources phone: 914/921-7601. **Subsidiaries include:** Telecommunications operations consist of six exchange companies: Western New Mexico Telephone Company (NM); Inter-Community Telephone Company (ND); Cuba City Telephone Exchange Company (WI); Belmont Telephone Company (WI); Bretton Woods Telephone Company (NH); and J.B.N. Telephone Company, Inc. (KS). Services offered include local network, network access, and long distance. Lynch Entertainment Corporation and Lombardo Communications are the general partners of Coronet Communications Company, which owns a CBS-affiliated television station (WHBF-TV) serving Rock Island and Moline IL, and Davenport and Bettendorf IA. Capital Communications Corporation operates WOI-TV, an ABC affiliate broadcasting to Des Moines IA. The Morgan Group Inc. (IN), Lynch Corporation's only service subsidiary, provides services to the manufactured housing and recreational vehicle industries. Lynch Manufacturing Corporation and its subsidiary, Lynch Machinery-Miller Hydro, Inc. (GA), manufacture glass-forming machines and packaging machinery, as well as replacement parts for each. M-tron Industries, Inc. (SD) manufactures, imports, and distributes quartz crystal products and clock oscillator modules used for clocking digital circuits, precision time base references, and frequency- and time-related circuits. Safety Railway Service Corporation and its subsidiary, Entoleter, Inc. (CT), produce various capital equipment including granulators, air scrubbers, and shredders. **Corporate headquarters location:** This location. **Listed on:** American Stock Exchange. **Stock exchange symbol:** LIC. **Chairman:** Frederic V. Salerno. **Annual sales/revenues:** $86 million. **Number of employees nationwide:** 600.

LYONS LAVEY NICKEL SWIFT INC.
220 East 42nd Street, 3rd Floor, New York NY 10017. 212/771-3000. **Fax:** 212/771-3016. **Contact:** Human Resources Manager. **E-mail address:** jobs@hmcny.com. **World Wide Web address:** http://www.llns.com. **Description:** An advertising agency for pharmaceutical firms. Founded in 1972. **NOTE:** Entry-level positions are offered. **Positions advertised include:** Vice President Supervisor Aricept; Traffic Coordinator; Account Supervisor; Account Assistant; Media Coordinator; Medical Information Specialist; Medical Editor.

M&T BANK
350 Park Avenue, 5th Floor, New York NY 10022. 212/350-2000. **Contact:** Human Resources Department. **World Wide Web address:** http://www.mandtbank.com. **Description:** A full-service savings bank providing cooperative apartment loans, home improvement loans, mortgage loans, pension plans, retirement accounts, life insurance, student loans, and other traditional banking services. **Positions advertised include:** Senior Commercial Real Estate Representative; Account Representative; Branch Sales Associate; Assistant Branch Manager; Property Manager; Branch Manager. **Corporate headquarters location:** Buffalo NY. **Listed on:** New York Stock Exchange. **Stock exchange symbol:** MTB. **Chairman/President/CEO:** Robert G. Wilmers. **Annual sales/revenues:** $2.3 billion. **Number of employees:** 9,197.

M&T BANK CORPORATION
101 South Salina Street, Syracuse NY 13202. 315/424-4582. **Contact:** Human Resources Department. **World Wide Web address:** http://www.mandtbank.com. **Description:** Manufacturers and Traders Trust operates 700 branches in New York, Pennsylvania, Maryland, Virginia, West Virginia, and the District of Columbia offering retail banking services to individuals and small companies as well as insurance, real estate, and loan services. Founded in 1856. **Positions advertised include:** Teller; Select Banker; Branch Manager; Regional Security Manager; Senior Financial Consultant; Branch Sales Associate; Assistant Branch Manager; Teller Supervisor. **Corporate headquarters location:** Buffalo NY. **Other locations:** Nationwide. **Listed on:** New York Stock Exchange. **Stock exchange symbol:** MTB. **Chairman/President/CEO:** Robert G. Wilmers. **Annual sales/revenues:** $2.3 billion. **Number of employees:** 9,197.

M&T BANK CORPORATION
One M&T Plaza, Buffalo NY 14203. 716/842-5445. **Fax:** 716/842-5839. **Contact:** C. Fred Mateer, Human Resources VP. **World Wide Web address:** http://www.mandtbank.com. **Description:** The holding company for Manufacturers and Traders Trust which operates 700 branches in New York, Pennsylvania, Maryland, Virginia, West Virginia, and the District of Columbia offering retail banking services to individuals and small companies as well as insurance, real estate, and loan services. Founded in 1856. **Positions advertised include:** Accountant; Financial Analyst; Senior Compensation Analyst; Senior Employee Relations Representative; Supervisor; Strategic Sourcing Analyst; Network Planning Analyst; Retail Sales Support Manager; Senior Marketing Administrator; Branch Sales Associate. **Corporate headquarters location:** This location. **Other locations:** Nationwide. **Listed on:** New York Stock Exchange. **Stock exchange symbol:** MTB. **Chairman/President/CEO:** Robert G. Wilmers. **Annual sales/revenues:** $2.3 billion. **Number of employees:** 9,197.

MBIA INSURANCE CORPORATION
113 King Street, Armonk NY 10504. 914/273-4545. **Contact:** Human Resources. **World Wide Web address:** http://www.mbia.com. **Description:** A leading insurer of municipal bonds including new issues and bonds traded in the secondary market. The company also guarantees asset-backed transactions offered by financial institutions and provides investment management services for school districts and municipalities. **Positions advertised include:** Public Finance Managing Director; Senior Derivative Analyst. **Corporate headquarters location:** This location. **Other U.S. locations:** New York NY; San Francisco CA. **International locations:** Australia; England; France; Japan; Singapore; Spain. **Parent company:** MBIA Inc.

MGM/UNITED ARTISTS
ORION PICTURES CORPORATION
1350 Avenue of the Americas, 24th Floor, New York NY 10019. 212/708-0300. **Fax:** 212/708-0377. **Contact:** Human Resources. **World Wide Web address:** http://www.mgm.com. **Description:** Metro-Goldwyn-Mayer Inc. is one of the nation's largest film distribution companies. **Special programs:** Internships. **Corporate headquarters location:** Santa Monica CA. **Subsidiaries include:** MGM Pictures; Movielink, LLC; United Artists Corporation. **Operations at this facility include:** Administration; Sales; Service. **Listed on:** New York Stock Exchange. **Stock exchange symbol:** MGM. **Chairman/CEO:** Alex Yemenidjian. **Annual sales/revenues:** $1.65 billion. **Number of employees at this location:** 250. **Number of employees nationwide:** 1,150.

MRC BEARINGS
402 Chandler Street, Jamestown NY 14701-0280. 716/661-2600. **Contact:** Sandra Martin, Human Resources Department. **E-mail address:** resume@mrcbearings.com. **World Wide Web address:** http://www.mrcbearings.com. **Description:** Produces custom-engineered, anti-friction ball and roller bearings for use in aerospace and special industrial applications. The MRC product range includes bearings for helicopters, jet engine mainshafts and gearboxes, and bearings for all types of aircraft power transmission assemblies as well as other types of specialty applications. **Corporate headquarters location:** This location. **Other area locations:** Falconer NY. **Other U.S. locations:** Crossville TN; Kulpsville PA; Winsted CT. **Operations at this facility include:** Corporate Administration; MRC Specialty Bearings Division.

MTA BUS COMPANY
128-15 28th Avenue, Flushing NY 11354. 718/445-3100. **Contact:** Kathleen O'Shea, Director of Human Resources. **World Wide Web address:** http://www.qsbus.com. **Description:** A public transportation firm providing express and local service in Queens and Manhattan with more than 270 buses operating on nearly 20 routes. **Positions advertised include:** Bus Operator; Cleaner/Shifter; Foreman. **Special programs:** Internships. **Office hours:** Monday - Friday, 8:30 a.m. - 4:30 p.m. **Corporate headquarters location:** This location. **Operations at this facility include:** Administration. **Number of employees at this location:** 700.

MACY'S EAST
151 West 34th Street, New York NY 10001. 212/695-4400. **Fax:** 212/494-1057. **Contact:** Human Resources. **World Wide Web address:** http://www.macys.com. **Description:** Macy's East, part of the Federated Department Stores family, sells family apparel, home furnishings, and other merchandise from 115 stores in the eastern U.S. with the largest department store in the world at this location. **Positions advertised include:** Art Director; Assistant Buyer; Buyer/Merchandising Buyer; Associate Giftwrap & Extra's Buyer; Divisional Operations Director; Fire Safety Director; Macintosh Technical Support Representative; Assortment Management Planner; Publicity Coordinator; Regional Merchandise Manager; Systems Administrator. **Corporate headquarters location:** This location. **Parent company:** Federated Department Stores, Inc. (Cincinnati OH). **Chairman/CEO:** Harold (Hal) D. Kahn. **Annual sales/revenues:** $5 billion. **Number of employees:** 33,200.

MADISON SQUARE GARDEN, L.P.
2 Penn Plaza, 16th Floor, New York NY 10121. 212/465-6000. **Fax:** 212/465-6026. **Recorded jobline:** 212/465-6335. **Contact:** Human Resources. **E-mail address:** msghr@thegarden.com. **World Wide Web address:** http://www.thegarden.com. **Description:** Operates sports and entertainment events in the Arena, Rotunda, and Paramount Theatre. Professional sports teams include the NBA's New York Knicks, the WNBA's New York Liberty, and the NHL's New York Rangers. Madison Square Garden also operates the MSG Network (one of the nation's oldest regional cable television sports networks). In addition, Madison Square Garden operates its own restaurants, catering, fast food, and merchandise divisions. **NOTE:** Seasonal and part-time jobs are offered. **Positions advertised include:** Accountant; Marketing Representative; Financial Analyst; Advertising Clerk; Graphic Designer. **Special programs:** Internships. **Internship information:** Madison Square Garden has a college internship program that runs during the fall, spring, and summer semesters. For application information, call 212/465-6258. **Corporate headquarters location:** This location. **Parent company:** Regional Programming Partners. **Listed on:** Privately held. **Chairman:** James L. Dolan. **Annual sales/revenues:** $790 million.

MAINTECH
560 Lexington Avenue, 15th Floor, New York NY 10020. 212/704-2400. **Fax:** 212/944-1639. **Contact:** Jan Ferrer or Louise Ross. **E-mail address:** jferrer@voltdelta.com or lross@voltdelta.com. **World Wide Web address:** http://www.maintech.com. **Description:** Provides on-site computer maintenance services. **Corporate headquarters location:** Wallington NJ. **Other locations:** Orange CA. **Parent company:** Volt Delta Resources (also at this location).

MANCHESTER TECHNOLOGIES, INC.
160 Oser Avenue, Hauppauge NY 11788-3711. 631/435-1199. **Fax:** 631/951-7913. **Contact:** Human Resources. **E-mail address:** cdinow@mecnet.com or staffing@mecnet.com. **World Wide Web address:** http://www.mecnet.com. **Description:** A network integrator and reseller of computer systems, software, and peripherals. Manchester also services and maintains computer systems, manages networks, distributes peripherals, and offers temporary IT staffing. Founded in 1973. **NOTE:** Human Resources phone: 631/951-7065. **Positions advertised include:** Purchasing Clerk; Customer Service Representative. **Subsidiaries include:** Coastal Office Products; Electrograph Systems; ManTech Computer Services; Donovan Consulting Group; eTrack Solutions. **Listed on:** NASDAQ. **Stock exchange symbol:** MANC. **Chairman/President/CEO:** Barry R. Steinberg. **Annual sales/revenues:** $262 million. **Number of employees:** 348.

JOHN C. MANDEL SECURITY BUREAU INC.
611 Jackson Avenue, Bronx NY 10455. 718/402-5002. **Fax:** 718/402-5004. **Contact:** Personnel Department. **World Wide Web address:** http://www.johncmandel.com. **Description:** Provides security services through armed and unarmed guards on an around-the-clock basis throughout the New York City metropolitan area. Clients range from private housing developments and projects to a wide range of commercial and industrial customers. **Corporate headquarters location:** This location. **Other locations:** Amenia NY; Brooklyn NY.

MANHATTAN EYE, EAR & THROAT HOSPITAL
210 East 64th Street, New York NY 10021. 212/838-9200. **Fax:** 212/605-3765. **Contact:** Recruitment Manager. **World Wide Web address:** http://www.meeth.org. **Description:** A nonprofit hospital specializing in problems of the eye, ear, and throat. Founded in 1825. **NOTE:** Entry-level positions are offered. Recruitment phone: 212/605-3708. **Number of employees:** 450.

MAPINFO CORPORATION
One Global View, Troy NY 12180-8371. 518/285-6000. **Fax:** 518/285-6070. **Contact:** Human Resources. **E-mail address:** jobs@mapinfo.com. **World Wide Web address:** http://www.mapinfo.com. **Description:** Develops geography software and databases used in business intelligence, analysis, and forecasting by commercial and public sector clients for emergency response and planning. The company operates offices in 60 countries providing geography software in 20 languages as well as offering consulting, training, and support services. **Positions advertised include:** Channel Marketing & Events Specialist; International Quality Engineer; Quality Assurance Engineer. **Corporate headquarters location:** This location. **Other locations:** Worldwide. **Listed on:** NASDAQ. **Stock exchange symbol:** MAPS. **Chairman:** John C. Cavalier. **Annual sales/revenues:** $93 million. **Number of employees:** 681.

MARCEL DEKKER, INC.
270 Madison Avenue, New York NY 10016-0602. 212/696-9000. **Fax:** 212/685-4540. **Contact:** Human Resources Recruiter. **E-mail address:** careers@dekker.com. **World Wide Web address:** http://www.dekker.com. **Description:** A family-owned, international publisher of scientific, technological, and medical books, journals, and encyclopedias in the following fields: agriculture; biology; food science; chemistry;

engineering; environmental science and pollution control; library information science and technology; material science and physics; mathematics; statistics; medicine; social science; business and economics; packaging and converting; and technology. Marcel Dekker distributes to libraries, societies, public institutions, hospitals, colleges, universities, and professionals. **Positions advertised include:** Administrative Assistant to Acquisitions; Graphic Artist; Book Production Editor; Editorial Assistant; Journal Production Editor; Production Assistant; Marketing Assistant; Promotions Assistant. **Corporate headquarters location:** This location. **Other locations:** Monticello NY. **International locations:** Switzerland. **Founder/Chairman:** Marcel Dekker.

MARCH OF DIMES BIRTH DEFECTS FOUNDATION
1275 Mamaroneck Avenue, White Plains NY 10605. 914/428-7100. **Fax:** 914/997-4479. **Contact:** Mary Jane Scott, Human Resources. **E-mail address:** recruiter@marchofdimes.com. **World Wide Web address:** http://www.marchofdimes.org. **Description:** A private foundation operating the Campaign for Healthier Babies, which includes programs of research, community service, education, and advocacy. Birth defects are the primary focus of March of Dimes research efforts. The foundation's 55 chapters across the country work with their communities to determine and meet the needs of women, children, and families. Through specially designed programs, women are provided with access to prenatal care. Founded in 1938 by President Franklin Roosevelt to prevent polio. **Positions advertised include:** Assistant Design Director; Senior Designer; Program Quality Improvement Manager; External Program Grants Manager; Director of Program Services. **Corporate headquarters location:** This location. **Other U.S. locations:** Nationwide. **Chairman:** Gary D. Forsee. **Annual sales/revenues:** $218 million.

MARIETTA CORPORATION
37 Huntington Street, Cortland NY 13045-5250. 607/753-6746. **Fax:** 607/756-0622. **Contact:** Beth Tosh, Manager of Human Resources. **E-mail address:** jobs@mariettacorp.com. **World Wide Web address:** http://www.mariettacorp.com. **Description:** Designs, manufactures, packages, markets, and distributes guest amenity programs to the travel and lodging industries. The company's guest amenity programs feature a wide variety of nationally branded toiletries, personal care products, and accessories that travel and lodging establishments provide for the comfort and convenience of their guests. Marietta is also a provider of customized sample-size and unit-of-use packaging products and services to companies in the toiletries, cosmetics, pharmaceuticals, and household products. **NOTE:** Application materials accepted by mail, fax, online, or through the NYS Department of Labor at: Cortland Works Career Center, 99 Main St., Cortland NY 13045. Applicants for marketing positions my e-mail: marketingjobs@mariettacorp.com. **Positions advertised include:** Account Coordinator; Purchasing Agent; Group Leader; Quality Assurance Technician; Machine Operator; Equipment Mechanic. **Corporate headquarters location:** This location. **Other locations:** Olive Branch MS. **Parent company:** BMFA Holding. **Chairman:** Barry W. Florescue. **Number of employees:** 900.

MARIST COLLEGE
120 Donelly Hall, 3399 North Road, Poughkeepsie NY 12601-1387. 845/575-3349. **Fax:** 845/575-3348. **Contact:** Bruce Wagner, Assistant Vice President. **E-mail address:** human.resources@marist.edu. **World Wide Web address:** http://www.marist.edu. **Description:** A liberal arts college with an enrollment of 3,300 undergraduate and 600 graduate students. Marist College offers a variety of academic programs including business management, communication, computer science and information systems, behavioral sciences, science, and the humanities. **Positions advertised include:** Emerging Technology Adjunct Instructor; Job Corps Adjunct Instructor; Adjunct Science Instructor; Associate Criminal Justice Professor; Associate Education Professor; Associate History Professor; Assistant English Professor; Assistant Management Professor; Assistant Social Work Professor; Athletic Training Instructor; Faculty Communication Assistant; Organic Chemist; Assistant Academic Vice President of Graduate and Continuing Education; Assistant Director of Student Activities; Associate Dean of Teacher Education; School of Management Dean; Academic Technology & E-Learning Director; First Year Programs Director; Judicial Affairs Director; Organizational Leadership & Communication Program Director; Teacher Education Director; Alumni Relations Executive Director; Network Security Support Analyst; Programmer; Information Technology Analyst.

MARK IV INDUSTRIES, INC.
501 John James Audubon Parkway, Amherst NY 14226. 716/689-4972. **Fax:** 716/689-6098. **Contact:** Ms. Chris Werth, Human Resources. **E-mail address:** information@mark-iv.com. **World Wide Web address:** http://www.mark-iv.com. **Description:** Produces power transfer/fluid handling, mass transit/traffic control, and professional audio equipment and components for the automotive, industrial, transportation, and music aftermarket and original equipment manufacturers. The company operates 37 manufacturing facilities, 26 distribution outlets, and nine technical centers worldwide. **Corporate headquarters location:** This location. **Other locations:** Worldwide. **Subsidiaries include:** Mark IV Automotive. **Parent company:** BC Partners. **President:** William P. Montague. **Annual sales/revenues:** $1.2 billion. **Number of employees:** 8,000.

MARRIOTT EASTSIDE
525 Lexington Avenue, New York NY 10017. 212/755-4000. **Toll-free phone:** 800/228-9290. **Fax:** 212/751-3440. **Contact:** Director of Personnel. **World Wide Web address:** http://www.marriotthotels.com. **Description:** Operates a luxury hotel with 652 guest rooms and dining, meeting, and sales function facilities. **Parent company:** Marriott International, Inc. (Washington DC).

MARSH & McLENNAN COMPANIES, INC.
1166 Avenue of the Americas, New York NY 10036-2274. 212/345-5000. **Fax:** 212/345-4838. **Contact:** Human Resources. **World Wide Web address:** http://www.mmc.com. **Description:** Provides consulting services worldwide through an insurance brokerage and risk management firm, reinsurance intermediary facilities, and a consulting and financial services group, to clients concerned with the management of assets and risks from offices in over 100 countries. Specific services include insurance and risk management services, reinsurance, consulting and financial services, merchandising, and investment management. Founded in 1871. **Corporate headquarters location:** This location. **Other U.S. locations:** Nationwide. **International locations:** Worldwide. **Subsidiaries include:** Sedgwick Group; Guy Carpenter & Company, Inc.; Seabury & Smith; Marsh & McLennen Capital; mercer Consulting Group, Inc.; Putnam, LLC; Marsh, Inc. **Listed on:** New York Stock Exchange. **Stock exchange symbol:** MMC. **Chairman/CEO:** Jeffrey W. Greenberg. **Annual sales/revenues:** $10.4 billion. **Number of employees worldwide:** 59,900.

J.B. MARTIN COMPANY
10 East 53rd Street, Suite 3100, New York NY 10022. 212/421-2020. **Contact:** David Budd, Director of Sales. **World Wide Web address:** http://www.jbmartin.com. **Description:** Manufactures high-end velvet specializing in woven velvets for the apparel and home furnishings industries and high-spec industrial applications. Founded in 1893. **Corporate headquarters location:** This location. **Other locations:** SC. **International locations:** Mexico.

MARUBENI AMERICA CORPORATION
450 Lexington Avenue, 35th Floor, New York NY 10017-3907. 212/450-0100. **Fax:** 212/450-0715. **Contact:** Human Resources. **E-mail address:** info@marubeni-usa.com. **World Wide Web address:** http://www.marubeni-usa.com. **Description:** An international trading firm that provides importing and exporting services to and from Japan. Operations are conducted through seven groups: Metals & Minerals Group; Machinery Group; Petroleum Group; General Merchandise Group; Chemical & Plastics Group; Textile Group; and Grain, Marine, & Other Products Group. The New York and New Jersey operations involve all groups and offer a wide range of products. **Corporate headquarters location:** This location. **Other U.S. locations:** Nationwide. **Subsidiaries include:** Don Juan Sportswear Inc.; It Fabrics Inc. **Parent company:** Marubeni Corporation (Japan).

MARVEL ENTERPRISES, INC.
10 East 40th Street, 9th Floor, New York NY 10016. 212/576-4000. **Fax:** 212/576-8517. **Contact:** Mary Sprowls, Human Resources Director. **E-mail address:** msprowls@marvel.com. **World Wide Web address:** http://www.marvel.com. **Description:** Marvel Enterprises is a youth entertainment company. Operations and products include Marvel Comics, one of the largest comic book publishers in North America; Marvel character-based consumer products licensing; Fleer, a marketer of sports picture cards; Dubble Bubble confectionery products; and ToyBiz. **Corporate headquarters location:** This location. **Subsidiaries include:** Marvel Publishing. **Listed on:** New York Stock Exchange. **Stock exchange symbol:** MVL. **Chairman:** Morton E. Handel. **Annual sales/revenues:** $299 million. **Number of employees:** 369.

MARY IMMACULATE HOSPITAL
SAINT VINCENT CATHOLIC MEDICAL CENTERS
152-11 89th Avenue, Jamaica NY 11432. 718/558-2000. **Fax:** 718/558-2304. **Contact:** M. Caravel, Human Resources. **E-mail address:** mcaravello@svcmcny.org. **World Wide Web address:** http://www.svcmc.org. **Description:** One of the medical centers operated by St. Vincent Catholic Medical Centers in the New York area. **Positions advertised include:** Cat Scan Technician; Chief Physicist; Housekeeping Cleaner; Emergency Department Clerk; Radiology Clerk; Health Information Coordinator; Materials Management Coordinator; Mental Health Psychiatric Technician; Operating Room Technician; Patient Care Associate; Pharmacist; Radiological Technologist; Registered Nurse; Respiratory Therapist; Special Procedures Technician; Staff Nurse; Operating Room Nurse.

MARYKNOLL FATHERS AND BROTHERS
P.O. Box 302, Maryknoll NY 10545. 914/941-7590. **Contact:** Human Resources. **World Wide Web address:** http://www.home.maryknoll.org. **Description:** Maryknoll Fathers and Brothers is an international order of religious missionaries. Founded in 1911. **Special programs:** Summer Jobs. **Corporate headquarters location:** This location. **Other locations:** Chicago IL; Los Angeles CA; Minneapolis MN; New York NY; Ossining NY; Washington DC.

J.W. MAYS, INC.
9 Bond Street, Brooklyn NY 11201-5805. 718/624-7400. **Fax:** 718/935-0378. **Contact:** Frank Mollo, Personnel Director. **Description:** A real estate company operating seven commercial properties in Brooklyn, Jamaica, Levittown, Fishkill, and Dutchess County NY, as well as a warehouse in Circleville OH, all of which were former department store locations, which the company liquidated in 1989. Since 1924. **Corporate headquarters location:** This location. **Listed on:** NASDAQ. **Stock exchange symbol:** MAYS. **Chairman/President/CEO/COO:** Lloyd Shulman. **Annual sales/revenues:** $13.4 million. **Number of employees:** 31.

McALLISTER TOWING AND TRANSPORTATION COMPANY, INC.
17 Battery Place, Suite 1200, New York NY 10004. 212/269-3200. **Fax:** 212/509-1147. **Contact:** Nancy Errichiello, Director of Personnel. **World Wide Web address:** http://www.mcallistertowing.com. **Description:** A marine services firm providing ship docking, deep-sea and coastal towing, oil transportation, bulk transportation, special projects such as positioning tunnel and bridge segments and other services for the transportation industry. McAllister also offers full-service, in-house capabilities through a complete packaged transportation service provided to shippers. The company operates one of the largest fleets of tugs and barges on the East Coast and in the Caribbean, with ship docking services in New York NY, Philadelphia PA, Norfolk VA, Charleston SC, Jacksonville FL, Baltimore MD, and Puerto Rico. Marine towing and transportation services are operated along the East Coast, in the Caribbean, through the New York State barge canal system, and in the Great Lakes and the St. Lawrence River. Founded in 1864. **Corporate headquarters location:** This location. **Other locations:** FL; MD; PR; SC. **President:** Capt. Brian A. McAllister.

McCANN-ERICKSON WORLDWIDE
750 Third Avenue, New York NY 10017. 212/697-6000. **Contact:** Human Resources. **World Wide Web address:** http://www.mccann.com. **Description:** An advertising agency with operations in 130 countries. **Corporate headquarters location:** This location. **Other U.S. locations:** Atlanta GA; Chicago IL; Louisville KY; Houston TX; Seattle WA. **International locations:** Worldwide. **Parent company:** The Interpublic Group of Companies, Inc.

ARNOLD McGRATH WORLDWIDE
110 Fifth Avenue, New York NY 10011. 212/463-1000. **Fax:** 212/463-1628. **Contact:** Chris Martin, Director of Human Resources. **E-mail address:** cmartin@arnny.com. **World Wide Web address:** http://www.arnny.com. **Description:** An advertising agency. Founded in 1980. **Special programs:** Internships; Apprenticeships; Training. **Corporate headquarters location:** This location.

THE McGRAW-HILL COMPANIES, INC.
1221 Avenue of the Americas, New York NY 10020. 212/512-2000. **Contact:** Human Resources. **E-mail address:** career_ops@mcgraw-hill.com. **World Wide Web address:** http://www.mcgraw-hill.com. **Description:** McGraw-Hill is a publisher and a provider of information and services through books, magazines, newsletters, software, CD-ROMs, and online data, fax, and TV broadcasting services. The company operates four network-affiliated TV stations and also publishes Business Week magazine and books for the college, medical, international, legal, and professional markets. McGraw-Hill also offers financial services including Standard & Poor's, commodity items, and international and logistics management products and services. **NOTE:** Resumes may be submitted online, by email, or regular mail to: The McGraw-Hill Companies, Human Resources Service Center, 148 Princeton-Hightstown Road, Hightstown NJ 08520-1450. **Positions advertised include:** Administrative Assistant; Institutional Equity Research Services Vice President; Investor Relations Account Manager; Business Development & Strategic Marketing Vice President; Compliance Manager; Internet Director; Fulfillment Administrator; Database and Spatial Products Sales Executive; Operations Manager; Marketing Assistant; Customer Service

Representative; Financial Production Assistant; Sales Development Coordinator; Risk Solutions Group Associate Director; Taxable Pricing Product Manager; Prepub Cost Analyst; Product Management Vice President; Recruiting Specialist; Structured Finance Associate Director; Finance Manager. **Corporate headquarters location:** This location. **Subsidiaries include:** AviationNow.com; *BusinessWeek;* Construction.com; MH Education; Platts; Standard & Poor's. **Listed on:** New York Stock Exchange. **Stock exchange symbol:** MHP. **Chairman/President/CEO:** Harold (Terry) W. McGraw III. **Annual sales/revenues:** $4.8 billion. **Number of employees:** 16,500.

MEADWESTVACO
299 Park Avenue, New York NY 10171. 212/318-5000. **Contact:** Human Resources. **World Wide Web address:** http://www.meadwestvaco.com. **Description:** A producer of forestry products, paper packaging, and specialty chemicals. Worldwide, MeadWestvaco operates 50 facilities in 29 countries including paper and paperboard mills, converting plants, chemical plants, lumber mills, research and development laboratories, and real estate operations. **Corporate headquarters location:** Stamford CT. **Operations at this facility include:** Administration; Sales. **Listed on:** New York Stock Exchange. **Stock exchange symbol:** MWV. **Chairman/CEO:** John A. Luke Jr. **Annual sales/revenues:** $7.2 billion. **Number of employees:** 30,700.

MEADWESTVACO
101 O'Neil Road, Sidney NY 13838. 607/563-9411. **Fax:** 607/563-9403. **Contact:** Human Resources. **World Wide Web address:** http://www.meadwestvaco.com. **Description:** A producer of forestry products, paper packaging, and specialty chemicals. Worldwide, MeadWestvaco operates 50 facilities in 29 countries including paper and paperboard mills, converting plants, chemical plants, lumber mills, research and development laboratories, and real estate operations. **Corporate headquarters location:** Stamford CT. **Operations at this facility include:** Mead Consumer & Office Products manufacturing specializing in calendars. **Listed on:** New York Stock Exchange. **Stock exchange symbol:** MWV. **Chairman/CEO:** John A. Luke Jr. **Annual sales/revenues:** $7.2 billion. **Number of employees:** 30,700.

THE MEDICUS GROUP
1675 Broadway, New York NY 10019-5809. 212/468-3100. **Fax:** 212/468-3208. **Contact:** Emilie Schaum, Director of Human Resources. **World Wide Web address:** http://www.medicusgroup.com. **Description:** Markets a wide range of pharmaceutical and consumer health products and services to health care professionals, patients, and consumers. Services include advertising and promotions, direct-to-consumer marketing, interactive media, medical education, public relations, publication planning, and sales training. Founded in 1972. **Special programs:** Internships. **Office hours:** Monday - Friday, 9:00 a.m. - 5:00 p.m. **Corporate headquarters location:** This location. **International locations:** Worldwide. **Parent company:** Publicis. **Chairman/CEO:** Glenn DeSimone.

MENNEN MEDICAL INC.
10123 Main Street, Clarence NY 14031. 716/759-6921. **Toll-free phone:** 800/223-2201. **Fax:** 215/322-0199. **Contact:** Human Resources Director. **E-mail address:** humanresources_hr@mennenmedical.com. **World Wide Web address:** http://www.mennenmedical.com. **Description:** Mennen Medical Inc. manufactures and sells heart monitors. **Positions advertised include:** Clinical Education Specialist; Clinical Care Registered Nurse; Medical Equipment Sales Representative. **Parent company:** Charterhouse Group International.

MERCER HUMAN RESOURCE CONSULTING
1166 Avenue of the Americas, New York NY 10036. 212/345-7000. **Fax:** 212/345-7414. **Contact:** National Recruiting Coordinator. **World Wide Web address:** http://www.mercerhr.com. **Description:** An actuarial and human resources management consulting firm with 140 offices in 40 countries worldwide. The company offers advice to organizations on all aspects of employee/management relationships. Services include retirement, health and welfare, performance and rewards, communication, investment, human resources administration, risk, finance and insurance, and health care provider consulting. **Positions advertised include:** Actuarial Analyst; Actuarial Consultant; Administrative Assistant; Compensation Analyst; Consultant; Administrative Assistant Floater; Senior Consultant. **Corporate headquarters location:** This location. **Other U.S. locations:** Nationwide. **International locations:** Worldwide. **Parent company:** Marsh & McLennan Companies, Inc. **Number of employees:** 13,000.

MERCHANTS GROUP, INC.
250 Main Street, Buffalo NY 14202-4104. 716/849-3333. **Fax:** 716/849-3388. **Contact:** Christine Kanowski, Human Resources Director. **E-mail address:** krambuss@merchantsgroup.com. **World Wide Web address:** http://www.merchantsgroup.com. **Description:** Merchants Group, through its wholly-owned subsidiary, Merchants Insurance Company of New Hampshire, Inc., offers property and casualty insurance to targeted homeowners and small- to medium-size business risks throughout the Northeast. **Positions advertised include:** Loss Control Specialist; Territory Manager. **Corporate headquarters location:** This location. **Listed on:** American Stock Exchange. **Stock exchange symbol:** MGP. **Chairman:** Richard E. Garman. **Number of employees:** 347.

MERCURY INTERACTIVE CORPORATION
317 Madison Avenue, 10th Floor, New York NY 10017-5201. 212/687-4646. **Contact:** Jeff Loehr, Director of Human Resources. **World Wide Web address:** http://www.mercury.com/us. **Description:** Mercury Interactive is a provider of automated software quality tools for enterprise applications testing. The company's products are used to isolate software and system errors prior to application deployment. **Corporate headquarters location:** Sunnyvale CA. **Other U.S. locations:** Nationwide. **International locations:** Worldwide. **Subsidiaries include:** Freshwater Software, Inc. **Listed on:** NASDAQ. **Stock exchange symbol:** MERQ. **Chairman/President/CEO:** Amnon Landon. **Annual sales/revenue:** $400 million. **Number of employees:** 1,822.

MERCY COLLEGE
Verrazzano Hall, 555 Broadway, Dobbs Ferry NY 10522. 914/674-7318. **Fax:** 914/674-7578. **Contact:** Theresa Morgan, Human Resources Director. **E-mail address:** hr@mercy.edu. **World Wide Web address:** http://www.mercynet.edu. **Description:** A private commuter college offering a wide range of undergraduate, graduate, associate, and certificate programs.

MERCY HOSPITAL OF BUFFALO
565 Abbott Road, Buffalo NY 14220. 716/826-7000. **Fax:** 716/828-2700. **Contact:** Human Resources. **World Wide Web address:** http://www.chsbuffalo.org. **Description:** One of the four regional hospitals run by the Catholic Health System. Mercy is a 350-bed community hospital. Mercy's Surgical Services Department has access to multispecialty laser equipment for surgery in ophthalmology, obstetrics and gynecology, otolaryngology, gastroenterology, plastic surgery, and urology. Mercy Hospital's Radiology Department offers mammography, ultrasonography, fluoroscopy, and computed tomography. The hospital has a fully staffed, full-term nursery (Level II Nursery Intensive Care Unit). Mercy has expanded its health care network to include the Mercy Ambulatory Care Center, the Mercy Health Center, and the East Aurora Medical Center. Mercy Hospital of Buffalo also manages the ancillary services of the Mercy Diagnostic & Treatment Center-West Seneca. Founded in 1904. **Parent company:** Catholic Health System.

MERIDIAN AUTOMOTIVE SYSTEMS, INC.
203 North Street, Canandaigua NY 14424-1096. 585/394-3680. **Contact:** Personnel. **World Wide Web address:** http://www.meridianautosystems.com. **Description:** Manufactures interior trim panels for the automotive industry, as well as blowmolded and injection molded plastic components for cars and trucks. **Company slogan:** Where Solutions Take Shape. **Corporate headquarters location:** Dearborn MI. **Other U.S. locations:** Nationwide. **International locations:** Worldwide. **Annual sales/revenues:** $977. **Number of employees:** 5,900.

MERRILL LYNCH & CO., INC.
4 World Financial Center, North Tower, New York NY 10080. 212/449-1000. **Contact:** Human Resources. **World Wide Web address:** http://www.merrilllynch.com. **Description:** One of the largest securities brokerage firms in the United States, Merrill Lynch provides financial services in the following areas: securities, extensive insurance, and real estate and related services. The company also brokers commodity futures, commodity options, and corporate and municipal securities. In addition, Merrill Lynch is engaged in investment banking activities. **NOTE:** Jobseekers are asked to call or see website for specific information on where to mail resumes. **Positions advertised include:** Equity Portfolio Trader; Credit Analyst; Equity Financial Analyst; Managing Directors Administrator; Valuation and Documentation Specialist; Corporate Strategy Analyst; Market Data Project and Service Manager; Problem Management Specialist; Equity Control Group Analyst; Policies and Procedures Analyst; Senior Financial Analyst; Senior Executive Assistant; Distressed Loan Closer; Credit Policy Project Manager. **Corporate headquarters location:** This location. **Other U.S. locations:** Nationwide. **International locations:** Worldwide. **Subsidiaries include:** Merrill Lynch Investment Managers Limited. **Listed on:** New York Stock Exchange. **Stock exchange symbol:** MER. **Chairman/CEO:** Stanley (Stan) O'Neil. **Annual sales/revenues:** $28.3 billion. **Number of employees worldwide:** 50,900.

METRO CIRCUITS INC.
205 La Grange Avenue, Rochester NY 14613. 585/254-2980. **Fax:** 585/254-4614. **Contact:** Manager. **World Wide Web address:** http://www.metrocircuits.com. **Description:** A manufacturer of printed circuit boards. Founded in 1974. **Parent company:** PJC Technologies, Inc. (Huntington Beach CA).

METRO CREATIVE GRAPHICS INC.
519 Eighth Avenue, 18th Floor, New York NY 10018. 212/947-5100. **Toll-free phone:** 800/223-1600. **Fax:** 212/967-4602. **Contact:** Human Resources Department. **World Wide Web address:** http://www.metrocreativegraphics.com. **Description:** Through its subsidiaries, the company provides camera-ready graphics, editorial, and professional production services to the newspaper and graphic communication industries. **NOTE:** When submitting a resume, computer illustrators and artists should include nonreturnable samples of computer artwork. Some testing may be required. **Corporate headquarters location:** This location. **Number of employees at this location:** 60.

METLIFE, INC.
One Madison Avenue, Corporate Staffing Area 1-F, New York NY 10010-3690. 212/578-2211. **Contact:** Corporate Staffing. **World Wide Web address:** http://www.metlife.com. **Description:** The Metropolitan Life Insurance Company is a national insurance and financial services company that offers a wide range of individual and group insurance including life, annuity, disability, and mutual finds. **Positions advertised include:** Project Management Office Director; Budget Manager; Agency Services Consultant; Sales Director; Business Consultant; Senior Product Consultant; Communication Consultant; Financial Analyst; Secretary to Officer; Employee Relations Director; Procurement Compliance Consultant; National Sales Director. **Corporate headquarters location:** This location. **Other U.S. locations:** Nationwide. **Subsidiaries/affiliates include:** GenAmerica Financial Corporation; New England Financial; Reinsurance Group of America, Incorporated; State Street Research & Management Company; Texas Life Insurance Company. **Listed on:** New York Stock Exchange. **Stock exchange symbol:** MET. **Chairman/President/CEO:** Robert H. Benmosche. **Annual sales/revenues:** $33.1 billion. **Number of employees:** 48,500.

THE METROPOLITAN MUSEUM OF ART
1000 Fifth Avenue, New York NY 10028-0198. 212/535-7710. **Fax:** 212/472-2764. **Contact:** Employment Office. **E-mail address:** employoppty@metmuseum.org. **World Wide Web address:** http://www.metmuseum.org. **Description:** A museum containing one of the most extensive art collections in the world. Permanent exhibits range from ancient art to modern art. Operations include conservation and curatorial departments, education services, libraries, concerts and lectures, internships, fellowships, publications and reproductions, and exhibitions. The museum also operates The Cloisters in Fort Tryon Park.

THE METROPOLITAN OPERA ASSOCIATION, INC.
Lincoln Center, New York NY 10023. 212/362-6000. **Fax:** 212/870-7405. **Contact:** Lisa Fuld, Human Resources Associate. **E-mail address:** resumes@mail.metopera.org. **World Wide Web address:** http://www.metopera.org. **Description:** The Opera produces approximately 25 operas per year, tours internationally, and performs free outdoor concerts in New York area parks. Founded in 1883. **NOTE:** Entry-level positions, part-time jobs, and second and third shifts are offered.

METROPOLITAN TRANSPORTATION AUTHORITY (MTA)
347 Madison Avenue, New York NY 10017-3739. 212/878-7000. **Fax:** 212/878-7227. **Contact:** Human Resources Division. **E-mail address:** mtahr@mtahq.org. **World Wide Web address:** http://www.mta.nyc.ny.us. **Description:** A public benefit corporation primarily devoted to obtaining funding for mass transportation in the New York City area, as well as serving as the headquarters for the MTA's constituent agencies. **Positions advertised include:** Police Radio & Communications Specialist; Senior Executive Secretary; Summons Administrator; Business Programs Deputy Director; Financial Analyst; Facilities Manager; Facilities Operation and Support Director; Crime Analyst; Communications Operator. **Chairman/CEO:** Peter S. Kalikow. **Annual sales/revenues:** $4 billion. **Number of employees:** 64,169.

MICHAEL ANTHONY JEWELERS, INC.
115 South MacQuesten Parkway, Mount Vernon NY 10550. 914/699-0000. **Fax:** 914/699-9869. **Contact:** Human Resources. **E-mail address:** recruit@michaelanthony.com. **World Wide Web address:** http://www.michaelanthony.com. **Description:** A designer, manufacturer, and distributor of gold jewelry. The company sells its jewelry directly to retailers, wholesalers, mass merchandisers, discount stores, catalogue distributors, and television

home shopping. Michael Anthony Jewelers' largest product line is an extensive selection of gold charms and pendants that include religious symbols; popular sayings (talking charms); sport themes and team logos; animal motifs; nautical, seashore, western, musical, zodiac, and other thematic figures; initials; and abstract artistic creations. The manufacturing division manufactures gold rope chain and designs gold tubing and bangle blanks used in the production of gold bracelets. The Jardinay product line consists of gold chains, earrings, and watches. **Listed on:** American Stock Exchange. **Stock exchange symbol:** MAJ. **CEO:** Michael W. Paolercio. **Annual sales/revenues:** $119 million. **Number of employees:** 742.

MICKELBERRY COMMUNICATIONS
405 Park Avenue, Suite 1003, New York NY 10022. 212/832-0303. **Contact:** Human Resources. **World Wide Web address:** http://www.mickelberry.com. **Description:** A holding company for three marketing companies and a commercial printing group. **Parent company:** Union Capital Corporation.

MICROWAVE DISTRIBUTORS COMPANY
500 Johnson Avenue, Suite A, Bohemia NY 11716-2675. 631/589-8000. **Fax:** 631/589-8167. **Contact:** Personnel. **World Wide Web address:** http://www.microwavedistributors.com. **Description:** A distributor of microwave and RF components. **Corporate headquarters location:** This location.

MILBANK, TWEED, HADLEY & McCLOY LLP
One Chase Manhattan Plaza, 56th Floor, New York NY 10005. 212/530-5000. **Fax:** 212/530-5219. **Contact:** Personnel. **E-mail address:** info@milbank.com. **World Wide Web address:** http://www.milbank.com. **Description:** A law firm specializing in litigation, corporate law, trusts and estates, and tax law. **Corporate headquarters location:** This location. **Other U.S. locations:** Los Angeles CA; Washington DC. **Chairman:** Mel Immergut. **Annual sales/revenues:** $360 million. **Number of employees at this location:** 600.

MILLIKEN & COMPANY
1045 Sixth Avenue, New York NY 10018. 212/819-4200. **Contact:** Human Resources. **World Wide Web address:** http://www.milliken.com. **Description:** Milliken & Company is one of the world's largest privately held textile and chemical companies. Milliken ranked #16 in FORTUNE's 2004 "100 Best Companies to Work For." **Corporate headquarters location:** Spartanburg SC. **Number of employees worldwide:** 10,000.

MINERALS TECHNOLOGIES INC.
The Chrysler Building, 405 Lexington Avenue, 20th Floor, New York NY 10174-1901. 212/878-1800. **Fax:** 212/878-1801. **Contact:** Human Resources Department. **World Wide Web address:** http://www.mineralstech.com. **Description:** Minerals Technologies is a resource- and technology-based company that develops and produces performance-enhancing minerals and mineral-based and synthetic mineral products for the paper, steel, polymer, and other manufacturing industries. The company's three businesses include producing and supplying precipitated calcium carbonate to the paper industry; developing and marketing mineral-based monolithic refractory materials that are used to resist the effects of high temperatures and are usually applied as coatings to surfaces exposed to extreme heat; and mining and producing natural mineral-based products including limestone, lime, talc, calcium, and metallurgical wire products. **Corporate headquarters location:** This location. **Listed on:** New York Stock Exchange. **Stock exchange symbol:** MTX. **Chairman:** Paul R. Saueracker. **Annual sales/revenues:** $753 million. **Number of employees:** 2,400.

MITSUBISHI INTERNATIONAL CORPORATION
520 Madison Avenue, 16th Floor, New York NY 10022. 212/605-2000. **Fax:** 212/605-2597. **Contact:** Human Resources. **World Wide Web address:** http://www.mitsubishiintl.com. **Description:** Mitsubishi International operates through several trading divisions and related support divisions including Petroleum, Steel, Foods, Chemicals, Machinery, Textile, Non-Ferrous Metals, Ferrous Raw Materials, Lumber and Pulp, and General Merchandise. Regional offices are located throughout the United States. **Corporate headquarters location:** This location. **Other U.S. locations:** Nationwide. **Subsidiaries include:** Mitsubishi Trust & Banking Corporation (also at this location, 212/838-7700) is a bank with diverse activities that include real estate and foreign exchange services. **Parent company:** Mitsubishi Corporation of Japan. **Annual sales/revenues:** $119 million. **Number of employees at this location:** 400. **Number of employees nationwide:** 850.

MITSUI & CO., LTD.
200 Park Avenue, New York NY 10166. 212/878-4000. **Fax:** 212/878-4800. **Contact:** Human Resources. **World Wide Web address:** http://www.mitsui.com. **Description:** An international trading firm engaged in a wide range of import and export activities. **Corporate headquarters location:** Tokyo, Japan. **Other U.S. locations:** Nationwide. **Operations at this facility include:** Administration; Divisional Headquarters; Regional Headquarters; Sales. **Listed on:** NASDAQ. **Stock exchange symbol:** MITSY. **Annual sales/revenues:** $4.2 billion. **Number of employees:** 36,116.

MOBIUS MANAGEMENT SYSTEMS, INC.
120 Old Post Road, Rye NY 10580. 914/921-7200. **Fax:** 914/921-1360. **Contact:** Human Resources. **E-mail address:** staffing@mobius.com. **World Wide Web address:** http://www.mobius.com. **Description:** Develops and sells business-related software products including a report distribution program and an automated balance program. **Positions advertised include:** Customer Support Representative; Quality Assurance Analyst; Quality Assurance Software Developer; Software Engineer; Project Manager; Business Systems Analyst; Senior Technical Writer. **Other U.S. locations:** Nationwide. **Listed on:** NASDAQ. **Stock exchange symbol:** MOBI. **Chairman/President/CEO:** Mitchell Gross. **Annual sales/revenues:** $68 million. **Number of employees:** 408.

MOHAWK PAPER MILLS INC.
465 Saratoga Street, P.O. Box 497, Cohoes NY 12047. 518/237-1740. **Contact:** Personnel Manager. **E-mail address:** careers@mohawkpaper.com. **World Wide Web address:** http://www.mohawkpaper.com. **NOTE:** Do not include attachments to e-mails, instead cut and paste resume to the body of your e-mail. **Description:** A manufacturer of coated/uncoated text and cover paper. Mohawk Paper Mills Inc. distributes their product internationally.

MOHAWK VALLEY COMMUNITY COLLEGE
1101 Sherman Drive, Utica NY 13501-5394. 315/792-5636. **Fax:** 315/731-5858. **Contact:** Jerome Brown, Dean of Human Resources. **E-mail address:** humanresources@mvcc.edu. **World Wide Web address:** http://www.mvcc.edu. **Description:** A two-year community college with an enrollment of approximately 6,500 full- and part-time students. The college was the first of five state-operated institutes of applied arts and sciences. Mohawk Valley Community College offers developmental and remedial programming. Certificates and degrees offered include accounting, banking and insurance, chef training, chemical technology, criminal justice, drafting technology, engineering drawing, food service, graphic arts, human services, international studies, media marketing and management, photography, and respiratory care. Founded in 1946.

MONARCH LUGGAGE COMPANY INC.
475 Fifth Avenue, 3rd Floor, New York NY 10017. 212/686-6900. **Contact:** Human Resources. **Description:** Manufactures and distributes a wide range of luggage products including briefcases, tote bags, athletic bags, attaché cases, and related accessories. **Corporate headquarters location:** This location.

MONOFRAX, INC.
1870 New York Avenue, Falconer NY 14733-1797. 716/483-7200. **Fax:** 716/665-2478. **Contact:** Phillip Mobilia, Manager of Human Resources. **E-mail address:** info@monofrax.com. **World Wide Web address:** http://www.monofrax.com. **Description:** Manufactures and sells fused cast refractories for glass tank and other applications with high corrosion rates. **Positions advertised include:** Ceramics Engineer; Chemical Engineer; Computer Programmer; Customer Service Representative; Electrician; Industrial Engineer; Materials Engineer. **Corporate headquarters location:** Niagara Falls NY. **Parent company:** BP (British Petroleum). **Operations at this facility include:** Administration; Divisional Headquarters; Manufacturing; Research and Development; Sales; Service. **Listed on:** New York Stock Exchange. **Stock exchange symbol:** BP. **Number of employees at this location:** 325.

THE MONY GROUP
1740 Broadway, New York NY 10019. 212/708-2000. **Contact:** Human Resources Department. **E-mail address:** monyjobs@mony.com. **World Wide Web address:** http://www.mony.com. **Description:** A mutual life insurer. The MONY Group offers life insurance, disability income, and annuities. The company also operates investment subsidiaries engaged in the management of mutual funds and the distribution of securities. **Special programs:** Internships. **Corporate headquarters location:** This location. **Listed on:** New York Stock Exchange. **Stock exchange symbol:** MNY.

MOOG INC.
P.O. Box 18, East Aurora NY 14052-0018. 716/652-2000. **Fax:** 716/687-4457. **Contact:** Human Resources. **E-mail address:** job.inquiry@moog.com. **World Wide Web address:** http://www.moog.com. **Description:** A manufacturer of motion control components and systems. Moog actuation devices control high-performance aircraft, satellites and space vehicles; strategic and tactical missiles; and automated industrial machinery. **Positions advertised include:** Systems Analyst; Senior Programmer; Production Control Analyst; Product Line Engineering Manager; Software Design Engineering Lead. **Corporate headquarters location:** This location. **Other U.S. locations:** Torrance CA. **International locations:** Worldwide. **Listed on:** American Stock Exchange. **Number of employees at this location:** 1,650. **Number of employees nationwide:** 2,000.

MORGAN LEWIS & BOCKIUS
101 Park Avenue, New York City NY 10178-0060. 212/309-6000. **Fax:** 212/309-6001. **Contact:** Michele A. Coffey, Hiring Partner. **World Wide Web address:** http://www.morganlewis.com. **Description:** One of the nation's largest law firms, focusing in various practice areas. **Number of employees worldwide:** 1200.

MORGAN STANLEY DEAN WITTER & COMPANY
1221 Avenue of the Americas, New York NY 10020. 212/762-7100. **Contact:** Human Resources Director. **World Wide Web address:** http://www.msdw.com. **Description:** One of the largest investment banking firms in the United States. Services include financing, financial advisory services, real estate services, corporate bond services, equity services, government and money market services, merger and acquisition services, investment research services, investment management services, and individual investor services. **NOTE:** Resumes should be sent to the corporate headquarters: Human Resources, 1585 Broadway, New York NY 10036. 212/761-4000.

MORGAN STANLEY DEAN WITTER & COMPANY
1585 Broadway, New York NY 10036. 212/761-4000. **Contact:** Human Resources. **World Wide Web address:** http://www.msdw.com. **Description:** One of the largest investment banking firms in the United States. Services include financing, financial advisory services, real estate services, corporate bond services, equity services, government and money market services, merger and acquisition services, investment research services, investment management services, and individual investor services. **Corporate headquarters location:** This location.

MOSS DRAGOTI
437 Madison Avenue, New York NY 10022. 212/415-2900. **Contact:** Director of Human Resources. **World Wide Web address:** http://www.ddb.com. **Description:** An advertising agency. **Parent company:** DDB Worldwide.

MOTTS NORTH AMERICA
4363 Route 104, Williamson NY 14589-9331. 315/589-4911. **Contact:** Sally Fischer, Human Resources. **World Wide Web address:** http://www.motts.com. **Description:** Makes a broad range of juice drinks, drink mixers such as ginger ale and tonic water, Motts brand applesauce, and other food and beverage products.

MOUNT ST. MARY COLLEGE
330 Powell Avenue, Newburgh NY 12550. 845/561-0800. **Contact:** Human Resources. **World Wide Web address:** http://www.msmc.edu. **Description:** A Judeo-Christian liberal arts college. Mount St. Mary College is an independent and coeducational institution with approximately 1,800 students. Founded in 1960.

MOVIE STAR, INC.
1115 Broadway, New York NY 10010. 212/684-3400. **Contact:** Human Resources Department. **World Wide Web address:** http://www.moviestarinc.com. **Description:** A diversified apparel manufacturer. The company operates through three divisions. The largest division, Sanmark, designs, manufactures, and sells private label sleepwear, robes, loungewear, leisurewear, daywear, and undergarments to mass merchants, as well as to national and regional chains. Cinema Etoile is also an intimate apparel producer. The Irwin B. Schwabe division produces private label work and leisure shirts for chain stores and mail order catalogs as well as shirts that are sold under the Private Property brand name. The 25 Movie Star factory stores carry an assortment of merchandise, some of which is supplied by the three manufacturing divisions, as well as sportswear and accessories. **Corporate headquarters location:** This location. **Other U.S. locations:** GA; MI. **Listed on:** American Stock Exchange. **Stock exchange symbol:** MSI.

ERIC MOWER AND ASSOCIATES
500 Plum Street, Syracuse NY 13204. 315/466-1000. **Contact:** Human Resources. **E-mail address:** hrrecruiter@eric.mower.com. **World Wide Web address:** http://www.mower.com. **Description:** An advertising agency. **Other area locations:**

Buffalo NY; Rochester NY. **Annual sales/revenues:** More than $100 million. **Number of employees at this location:** 150.

MR. CHRISTMAS INC.
41 Madison Avenue, 38th Floor, New York NY 10010. 212/889-7220. **Contact:** Terry Hermanson, Office Manager. **World Wide Web address:** http://www.mrchristmas.com. **Description:** Manufactures and imports Christmas items including light sets, artificial Christmas trees, and many other Christmas novelties. **Corporate headquarters location:** This location.

MULTIMEDIA TUTORIAL SERVICES, INC.
205 Kings Highway, Brooklyn NY 11223. 718/234-0404. **Contact:** Human Resources. **Description:** Produces and markets tutorial education programs, primarily in videotape and also CD-ROM formats, for use by adults and children in homes, work, schools, libraries, and other locales. Principal products consist of a series of 92 videotapes and supplemental materials on mathematics and an interactive, audio-visual, CD-ROM based system for language instruction. The company's videotapes include colorful computer graphics and real life vignettes. **Corporate headquarters location:** This location.

MUSEUM OF MODERN ART
11 West 53rd Street, New York NY 10019. 212/708-9400. **Fax:** 212/333-1107. **Contact:** Human Resources Manager. **E-mail address:** jobs@moma.org. **World Wide Web address:** http://www.moma.org. **Description:** Houses one of the world's foremost collections of modern art. **Special programs:** Internships. **Corporate headquarters location:** This location. **Number of employees at this location:** 550.

MUTUAL OF AMERICA
320 Park Avenue, New York NY 10022. 212/224-1045. **Toll-free phone:** 800/468-3785. **Fax:** 212/224-2500. **Contact:** Human Resources. **World Wide Web address:** http://www.mutualofamerica.com. **Description:** A life insurance company that offers pension plans, tax-deferred annuities, IRAs, deferred compensation plans, individual life insurance and thrift plans, funding agreements, guaranteed interest contracts, group life insurance, and group long-term disability income insurance to nonprofit, tax-exempt employers. Mutual of America also sells 401(k) products nationally. Services include actuarial (annual valuations, cost proposals, and reports to auditors); administrative (preparation of documents, monthly billings, maintenance of employee records, benefit payment services, development of administrative manuals, calculation of benefit estimates, and annual participant benefit statements); assistance with government filings (preparation and release of ERISA Information Bulletins and distribution of employer kits for qualifying pension plans); communications (Mutual of America Report, audio/visual presentations, and annual reports); investments (17 investment funds); and field consulting. **Corporate headquarters location:** This location. **Other U.S. locations:** Nationwide. **Subsidiaries include:** Capital Management Corporation. **Operations at this facility include:** Administration; Service. **Number of employees at this location:** 650. **Number of employees nationwide:** 1,050.

MUZE INC.
304 Hudson Street, 8th Floor, New York NY 10013. 212/824-0300. **Fax:** 212/824-0422. **Contact:** Jeanne Petras, Director of Personnel. **E-mail address:** humanresource@muze.com. **World Wide Web address:** http://www.muze.com. **Description:** Muze is a multimedia company that develops software for touch-screen, point-of-sales terminals that allow users access to a musical database. **Positions advertised include:** MS Access Database Coordinator; In-house Legal Counsel; E-Commerce Developer; Java/XML Developer. **Special programs:** Internships. **Corporate headquarters location:** This location. **International locations:** United Kingdom. **Parent company:** MetroMedia. **Operations at this facility include:** Administration; Manufacturing; Research and Development; Sales; Service. **Number of employees at this location:** 120.

NBC (NATIONAL BROADCASTING COMPANY, INC.)
30 Rockefeller Plaza, New York NY 10112. 212/664-4444. **Fax:** 212/664-4426. **Contact:** Human Resources. **World Wide Web address:** http://www.nbc.com. **Description:** A national television broadcasting communications firm. Founded in 1926. **NOTE:** Interested job seekers may apply online. **Positions advertised include:** Sales Planner Supervisor. **Special programs:** Internships. **Corporate headquarters location:** This location. **Subsidiaries include:** CNBC; Bravo; Telemundo. **Parent company:** General Electric Corporation. **Listed on:** New York Stock Exchange. **Stock exchange symbol:** GE.

THE NPD GROUP, INC.
900 West Shore Road, Port Washington NY 11050. 516/625-0700. **Fax:** 516/625-4866. **Contact:** Human Resources Department. **E-mail address:** recruit99@npd.com. **World Wide Web address:** http://www.npd.com. **Description:** A market research firm offering a full line of custom and syndicated consumer research services including point-of-sale computerized audits, purchase panels, mail panels, telephone research, mathematical modeling, and consulting. Industries covered include consumer packaged goods, apparel, toys, electronics, automotive, sports, books, and food consumption. **Positions advertised include:** Account Manager; Analytic Director; Director of Retail Business Development; Director of Client Development; Manager of Financial Reporting/Analysis; Marketing Coordinator; Research Manager; Senior Account Manager; Technical Specialist; Vice President of Client Development. **Special programs:** Internships. **Corporate headquarters location:** This location. **Other area locations:** New York NY. **Other U.S. locations:** Chicago IL; Hyattsville MD; Greensboro NC; Cincinnati OH; Houston TX. **International locations:** Worldwide. **Number of employees nationwide:** 800.

NBT BANK
2950 NYS Route 11, P.O. Box 721, Whitney Point NY 13862-0721. 607/692-7200. **Contact:** Human Resources. **E-mail address:** employment@nbtbank.com. **World Wide Web address:** http://www.nbtbank.com. **Description:** A financial banking institution. **NOTE:** Resumes can be sent to 52 South Broad Street, Norwich NY 13815. 800/628-2265. **Corporate headquarters location:** Norwich NY. **Other locations:** Various counties throughout New York.

NYP HOLDINGS, INC.
1211 Avenue of the Americas, New York NY 10036. 212/930-8000. **Contact:** Human Resources. **World Wide Web address:** http://www.nypostonline.com. **Description:** Publishes the *New York Post* newspaper. **Positions advertised include:** Database Marketing /CRM Analyst. **Special programs:** Internships. **Parent company:** News America. **Operations at this facility include:** Administration; Divisional Headquarters; Research and Development; Sales. **Number of employees at this location:** 710.

NYS THEATRE INSTITUTE
37 First Street, Troy NY 12180. 518/274-3200. **Fax:** 518/274-3815. **Contact:** Arlene Leff, Intern Program Director. **World Wide Web address:** http://www.nysti.org. **Description:** A professional resident theater company that specializes in theater for family audiences with a strong arts and education approach. **Special programs:** Internships.

NALGE NUNC INTERNATIONAL
75 Panorama Creek Drive, Rochester NY 14625-2385. 716/586-8800. **Contact:** Human Resources. **World Wide Web address:** http://www.nalgenunc.com. **Description:** Manufactures ultrafiltration and centrifugal devices for use in biological and genetic research. **Positions advertised include:** New Product Manager; Product Development Project Leader. **Office hours:** Monday – Friday, 8:00 a.m. – 5:00 p.m. **Other U.S. locations:** Duluth GA; Naperville IL. **International locations:** Worldwide.

NAPCO SECURITY GROUP
333 Bayview Avenue, Amityville NY 11701. 631/842-9400. **Fax:** 631/8429137. **Contact:** Human Resources. **World Wide Web address:** http://www.napcosecurity.com. **Description:** Manufactures electronic security equipment. The company's products are used in residential, commercial, institutional, and industrial installations. **Corporate headquarters location:** This location. **International locations:** England. **Subsidiaries include:** Alarm Lock manufactures and distributes a variety of door security hardware. **Listed on:** NASDAQ. **Stock exchange symbol:** NSSC. **Chairman:** Richard Soloway. **Sales/revenue:** $54 million. **Number of employees worldwide:** 800.

NASSAU COMMUNITY COLLEGE
One Education Drive, 8th Floor, Room 820,, Garden City NY 11530. 516/572-7211. **Contact:** Beverly Harrison, Associate Vice President Human Resources. **E-mail address:** harrisb@ncc.edu. **World Wide Web address:** http://www.sunynassau.edu. **Description:** A two-year college that is part of the State University of New York educational system. **Special programs:** Internships. **Number of employees at this location:** 2,500.

NASSAU LIBRARY SYSTEM
900 Jerusalem Avenue, Uniondale NY 11553. 516/292-8920. **Fax:** 516/481-4777. **Contact:** Jan Heinlein, Personnel. **E-mail address:** heinlein@nassaulibrary.org. **World Wide Web address:** http://www.nassaulibrary.org. **Description:** An association of autonomous local public libraries and a central service center, with 54 libraries in the system. The system office supports local library service through a wide range of supplementary and complementary services, collections, specialized staff, and professional programming; provides effective and economical centralized services; initiates legislation beneficial to library service; and develops, promotes, and maintains standards of library service within Nassau County. The system also provides extensive technical services to member libraries. **Corporate headquarters location:** This location.

NATIONAL ASSOCIATION OF SECURITIES DEALERS, INC. (NASD)
One Liberty Plaza, 165 Broadway, New York NY 10006. 212/858-4000. **Contact:** Human Resources. **E-mail address:** careers.fr@nasd.com. **World Wide Web address:** http://www.nasd.com. **Description:** The self-regulatory organization of the securities industry, overseeing the over-the-counter market. Working closely with the Securities and Exchange Commission, NASD sets the standards for over the counter securities and market makers, and provides ongoing surveillance of trading activities. NASD also provides key services for its membership and companies, particularly through its cooperative efforts with governmental and other agencies on policies and legislation that affect the investment banking and securities business. **Positions advertised include:** Legal Assistant; Human Resources Manager; Regulatory Policy and Oversight Examiner. **Special programs:** Internships. **Corporate headquarters location:** Washington DC. **Other U.S. locations:** Nationwide. **President/CEO/Chairman:** Robert Glauber. **Sales/revenue:** $1.5 billion. **Number of employees at this location:** 350. **Number of employees nationwide:** 2,500.

NATIONAL BENEFIT LIFE INSURANCE COMPANY
333 West 34th Street, 10th Floor, New York NY 10001. 212/615-7500. **Toll-free phone:** 800/221-2554. **Fax:** 212/213-7321. **Contact:** Human Resources. **Description:** A nationally licensed insurance firm dealing primarily in health and life insurance. **Corporate headquarters location:** This location.

NATIONAL ENVELOPE CORPORATION
2910 Hunters Point Avenue, Long Island City NY 11101. 718/786-0300. **Contact:** Human Resources. **World Wide Web address:** http://www.nationalenvelope.com. **Description:** Manufactures a wide range of envelopes for distribution to wholesalers. Founded in 1957. **Corporate headquarters location:** This location. **Other U.S. locations:** Nationwide.

NATIONAL FUEL GAS COMPANY
10 Lafayette Square, Buffalo NY 14203. 716/857-7000. **Recorded jobline:** 716/857-7821. **Contact:** Human Resources. **E-mail address:** jobs@natfuel.com. **World Wide Web address:** http://www.natfuel.com. **Description:** A holding company with subsidiaries that explore for, produce, purchase, gather, transport, store, and distribute natural gas; market timber and coal; market compressed natural gas equipment for vehicles; conduct pipeline construction operations; operate sawmill and dry kiln; transport natural gas for customers; and invest in research and development related to the natural gas industry. **NOTE:** The company only accepts resumes in response to posted advertised positions. **Positions advertised include:** Information Technology Professional. **Corporate headquarters location:** This location. **Subsidiaries include:** National Fuel Resources; Seneca Resources Corporation; National Fuel Gas Supply Corporation; National Fuel Gas Distribution Corporation; Horizon Energy Development, Incorporated. **Listed on:** New York Stock Exchange. **Stock exchange symbol:** NFG. **CEO/Chairman:** Philip C. Ackerman.

NATIONAL HOME HEALTH CARE CORPORATION
700 White Plains Road, Suite 275, Scarsdale NY 10583. 914/722-9000. **Fax:** 914/722-9239. **Contact:** Human Resources. **World Wide Web address:** http://www.nhhc.net. **Description:** National Home Health Care, through its subsidiaries, is a national provider of a variety of health related services including home care, general care, nurses, and therapists. **Corporate headquarters location:** This location. **Subsidiaries include:** Health Acquisition Corporation provides home health care services, primarily through certified home health aides and personal care aides in the New York metropolitan area; Brevard Medical Center, Incorporated provides both primary and specialty outpatient medical services in Brevard County FL; First Health, Incorporated provides primary care outpatient medical services in Volusia County FL. **Listed on:** NASDAQ. **Stock exchange symbol:** NHHC. **President/CEO:** Steven Fialkow. **Number of employees nationwide:** 2,200.

NATIONAL REVIEW INC.
215 Lexington Avenue, 4th Floor, New York NY 10016. 212/679-7330. **Contact:** Human Resources. **World Wide Web address:** http://www.nationalreview.com.

Description: Publishes a nationally distributed conservative magazine focusing on current political issues. **Corporate headquarters location:** This location. **President:** Thomas L. Rhodes.

NATIONAL SPINNING COMPANY INC.
111 West 40th Street, 28th Floor, New York NY 10018. 212/382-6400. **Contact:** Human Resources Director. **World Wide Web address:** http://www.natspin.com. **Description:** Engaged in the manufacturing, marketing, and distribution of yarn products to knitwear manufacturers. The company also produces hand-knitting yarn and rug kits for distribution to retail chains throughout the United States. **Corporate headquarters location:** This location.

NAZARETH COLLEGE OF ROCHESTER
4245 East Avenue, Rochester NY 14618. 585/389-2065. **Fax:** 585/389-2063. **Contact:** Carol O'Neill, Director of Personnel. **E-mail address:** humanresources@naz.edu. **World Wide Web address:** http://www.naz.edu. **Description:** A four-year college that offers undergraduate and graduate programs in a wide variety of disciplines. Founded in 1924. **NOTE:** Entry-level positions and part-time jobs are offered. For faculty positions contact Dr. Dennis Silva, Vice President for Academic Affairs, or the appropriate search committee member. **Positions advertised include:** Vice President for Finance and Treasurer; Gift Processing Coordinator; Protestant Chaplain; Coordinator of Partners for Learning; Assistant Men's Lacrosse Coach; Security Officer; Security Sergeant; Art Therapy Professor; Italian/Spanish Professor; Music Theory Professor; Speech/Language Pathology Professor; Dean of the School of Health and Human Services. **Special programs:** Internships. **Office hours:** Monday – Friday, 8:30 a.m. – 4:30 p.m. **Corporate headquarters location:** This location. **Number of employees at this location:** 300.

NEW ENGLAND LAMINATE COMPANY INC.
40 Governor Drive, Newburgh NY 12550. 845/567-6200. **Fax:** 845/567-1948. **Contact:** Director of Human Resources. **E-mail address:** nycs@parknelco.com. **World Wide Web address:** http://www.parknelco.com. **Description:** Manufactures computer laminates that are integrated with circuits and then used in the manufacturing of computers and pagers. **Corporate headquarters location:** This location. **Other U.S. locations:** Nationwide. **International locations:** Worldwide. **Parent company:** Park Chemical Corporation. **Listed on:** New York Stock Exchange. **Stock exchange symbol:** PKE. **Number of employees at this location:** 400.

NEW ERA CAP COMPANY, INC.
8061 Erie Road, Derby NY 14047. 716/549-0445. **Contact:** Tim Freer, Human Resources Manager. **World Wide Web address:** http://www.neweracap.com. **Description:** Manufactures baseball caps. Founded in 1920. **Corporate headquarters location:** This location. **Other area locations:** Blasdell NY; Buffalo NY. **Number of employees at this location:** 725.

NEW HUNTINGTON TOWN HOUSE INC.
124 East Jericho Turnpike, Huntington Station NY 11746. 631/427-8485. **Contact:** Vice President. **World Wide Web address:** http://www.newhuntingtontownhouse.com. **Description:** A general service catering company specializing in weddings, organizational functions, bar mitzvahs, anniversaries, and special parties through over 25 area locations including the New York City area. **Corporate headquarters location:** This location.

NEW LINE CINEMA
888 Seventh Avenue, 19th Floor, New York NY 10106. 212/649-4900. **Contact:** Human Resources. **World Wide Web address:** http://www.newline.com. **Description:** Produces and distributes low-budget theatrical motion pictures (generally action/adventure and comedy films targeted at the younger market). The company also acquires distribution rights to films produced by others, and has agreements with distributors in ancillary markets such as home video, pay television, and free television. **Positions advertised include:** Music & Development Assistant; Contract Accounting Assistant. **Special programs:** Internships. **Parent company:** AOL Time Warner, Incorporated.

THE NEW YORK BOTANICAL GARDEN
200th Street & Southern Boulevard, Bronx NY 10458-5126. 718/817-8700. **Contact:** Human Resources. **E-mail address:** hr@nybg.org. **World Wide Web address:** http://www.nybg.org. **Description:** An internationally recognized center for botanical research offering 47 gardens and plant collections. The New York Botanical Garden is dedicated to environmental education and the conservation of plant diversity. Founded in 1891. **Positions advertised include:** Associate Vice President for Development; Director of the Plant Research Laboratory; Institutional Database Administrator; Project Manager; Manager of Public and School Programs; Director of Horticulture for Public Programs; Associate Rose Garden Curator; Gardener for Public Programs; Administrative Assistant; Assistant Gardener; Research Assistant; Herbarium Assistant; Office Assistant; Gate Attendant. **Special programs:** Internships. **Corporate headquarters location:** This location. **Operations at this facility include:** Education; Research and Development.

THE NEW YORK EYE AND EAR INFIRMARY
310 East 14th Street, Second Avenue, New York NY 10003. 212/979-4000. **Contact:** Human Resources. **World Wide Web address:** http://www.nyee.edu. **Description:** A hospital specializing in ocular and auditory care. Founded in 1820. **NOTE:** To contact Human Resources directly, call 2121/979-4275. **Positions advertised include:** Outpatient Registrar; Medical Records Clerk; Administrative Coordinator; LPN; Registered Nurse; Ancillary Technician; Nursing Assistant; Ophthalmic Technician; Physician Assistant; Social Worker; Security Guard. **Number of employees at this location:** 600.

THE NEW YORK HELMSLEY HOTEL
212 East 42nd Street, New York NY 10017. 212/490-8900. **Fax:** 212/986-4792. **Contact:** Marilyn O'Brien, Personnel Director. **E-mail address:** general_info@helmsleyhotels.com. **World Wide Web address:** http://www.helmsleyhotels.com. **Description:** Operates a 793-room luxury hotel facility with a wide range of lodging, dining, meeting, and other facilities. **Parent company:** Helmsley Hotels Group.

NEW YORK INSTITUTE OF TECHNOLOGY
P.O. Box 8000, Old Westbury NY 11568-8000. 516/686-7667. **Fax:** 516/686-7929. **Contact:** Human Resources. **E-mail address:** humanresources@nyit.edu. **World Wide Web address:** http://www.nyit.edu. **Description:** A technical university offering associate, bachelor's, and master's degree programs in health and life sciences, architecture, arts/sciences, education, technology, and management. **Positions advertised include:** Senior Technician; Assistant to the Dean; Office Assistant; Refund Coordinator; Cleaner; Assistant Fine Arts Professor; Academic Clinical Coordinator; Director of Major Gifts; Associate Director of Admissions and Operations; Associate Registrar; Dean of Students.

NEW YORK LIFE INSURANCE COMPANY
51 Madison Avenue, Room 151, New York NY 10010. 212/576-7000. **Fax:** 212/447-4292. **Contact:** Employment Department. **World Wide Web address:** http://www.newyorklife.com. **Description:** New York Life Insurance Company, its subsidiaries, and affiliates offer a wide variety of products and services. Services include life, health, and disability insurance; annuities; mutual funds; health care management services; and commercial mortgage financing. The company's Asset Management operation (including pensions, mutual funds, and NYLIFE Securities) is located in Parsippany NJ. Founded in 1845. **NOTE:** Interested job seekers may submit resumes online. **Special programs:** Internships. **Positions advertised include:** Accounting Director; Senior Marketing Services Consultant; Media Relations Consultant; Quality Control Consultant; Senior Annuity Services Consultant; Securities Operations Consultant; Accountant; Licensing Associate; Customer Service Associate; Compliance Consultant. **Corporate headquarters location:** This location. **Other U.S. locations:** Nationwide. **Operations at this facility include:** Administration; Service. **Number of employees at this location:** 3,500. **Number of employees nationwide:** 7,185.

NEW YORK MAGAZINE
444 Madison Avenue, 14th Floor, New York NY 10022. 212/508-0700. **Contact:** Sarah Jewler, Managing Editor. **World Wide Web address:** http://www.newyorkmetro.com. **Description:** Publishes a features-oriented weekly magazine, with primary emphasis on stories of interest to New York City residents. **Special programs:** Internships.

NEW YORK METHODIST HOSPITAL
506 Sixth Street, Brooklyn NY 11215. 718/768-4305. **Fax:** 718/768-4324. **Contact:** Human Resources. **World Wide Web address:** http://www.nym.org. **Description:** An acute-care teaching hospital affiliated with the Weil Medical College of Cornel University. Founded in 1881. **Positions advertised include:** Food Service Worker; Laundry Worker; Radiation Therapist; Respiratory Therapist; Stationary Engineer; Physician Assistant; Radiologic Technologist; Imaging Technologist; EEG Technician; Lab Supervisor; X-Ray Technician; Senior Accountant; LPN; Registered Nurse; Case Manager; Anesthesia Technician; Nurse Clinical Coordinator. **Operations at this facility include:** Administration; Research and Development. **Number of employees nationwide:** 2,300.

THE NEW YORK RACING ASSOCIATION
P.O. Box 90, Jamaica NY 11417. 718/641-4700. **Contact:** Human Resources. **World Wide Web address:** http://www.nyracing.com. **Description:** A state-franchised, nonprofit racing association that owns, operates, and manages three horseracing tracks: Aqueduct, Belmont Park, and Saratoga, where pari-mutuel wagering is conducted. These facilities are the site of some of America's most prestigious stakes races: The Wood Memorial, and The Belmont and Travers Stakes.

NEW YORK SHAKESPEARE FESTIVAL
425 Lafayette Street, New York NY 10003. 212/539-8500. **Contact:** General Manager. **Description:** A nonprofit organization involved in many productions: year-round on-Broadway, off-Broadway, on tour around the country, television specials of theatrical works, free Shakespearean productions in Central Park each summer, and the development of new works.

NEW YORK STATE COALITION AGAINST DOMESTIC VIOLENCE
350 New Scotland Avenue, Albany NY 12208. 518/482-5465. **Contact:** Sherry Frohman, Executive Director of Human Resources. **Description:** An organization providing support and services to battered women and their children. **Parent company:** National Coalition Against Domestic Violence is a nonprofit public education and advocacy organization and a coalition of direct service programs, currently composed of 33 member organizations offering services to battered women and their children. Activities of the coalition include public education and advocacy; technical assistance to member groups; information and technical assistance to public agencies and legislative committees; and professional training for law enforcement and human service workers. In addition, the coalition staff prepares policy statements and offers assistance and expertise in the preparation of protocols and practices for a wide variety of public and private entities.

NEW YORK STATE DEPARTMENT OF TRANSPORTATION
1220 Washington Avenue, Albany NY 12232. 518/457-6460. **Fax:** 518/457-1570. **Contact:** Human Resources. **E-mail address:** dotpersonnel@dot.state.ny.us. **World Wide Web address:** http://www.dot.state.ny.us. **Description:** Engaged in the planning, design, construction, operation, and maintenance of public transit modes, railroads, highways, airports, and ports in New York state. Eleven regional locations are involved in design, construction, right-of-way acquisition, planning, and project management. **Positions advertised include:** Highway Maintenance Worker; Intermodal Transportation Specialist; Junior Engineer; Junior Landscape Architect; Motor Equipment Mechanic; Transportation Analyst; Transportation Construction Inspector. **Corporate headquarters location:** This location. **Number of employees nationwide:** 11,500.

NEW YORK STATE ELECTRIC & GAS CORPORATION
P.O. Box 3287, Ithaca-Dryden Road, Ithaca NY 14852. 607/729-2551. **Contact:** Human Resources. **World Wide Web address:** http://www.nyseg.com. **Description:** New York State Electric & Gas is a utility company that serves 790,000 electric customers and 226,000 natural gas customers in suburban and upstate New York. The company is composed of four business units: Electric (operations and marketing), Gas (operations and marketing), Management Services (support services), and Strategic Growth (mergers and acquisitions, core-related diversifications, and research and development). The company's wholly-owned subsidiary, NGE Enterprises, Incorporated, owns XENERGY, Incorporated, an energy services and fuel management company; and EnerSoft, a Houston company that develops natural gas and pipeline capacity trading systems. **Corporate headquarters location:** This location. **Parent company:** Energy East Corporation. **Listed on:** New York Stock Exchange. **Stock exchange symbol:** EAS.

NEW YORK STOCK EXCHANGE
11 Wall Street, New York NY 10005. 212/656-2266. **Contact:** Ms. Dale Bernstein, Managing Director of Staffing and Training. **World Wide Web address:** http://www.nyse.com. **Description:** The principal securities trading marketplace in the United States, serving a broad range of industries within and outside of the securities industry. More than 2,500 corporations, accounting for approximately 40 percent of American corporate revenues, are listed on the exchange. The New York Stock Exchange is engaged in a wide range of public affairs and economic research programs. **Positions advertised include:** Confidential Secretary; Director of Listings and Client Service; Administrative Secretary. **Corporate headquarters location:** This location. **Number of employees at this location:** 1,550.

NEW YORK TIMES COMPANY
229 West 43rd Street, New York NY 10036. 212/556-1234. **Contact:** Human Resources. **World Wide Web address:** http://www.nytco.com. **Description:** Publishes *The New York Times*, one of the largest newspapers in the world (daily circulation exceeds 887,000 weekdays and 1.4 million on Sundays). In addition to *The New York Times*, this diversified, publicly owned communications firm publishes 30 dailies and weeklies in various cities; publishes three national magazines; and owns and operates three television stations, two radio stations, and a cable television system. The company also publishes syndicated news and features worldwide. The company also has interests in paper and newsprint manufacturing mills, and a partial interest in *the International Herald Tribune*. Newspaper subsidiaries are located throughout the country and have an average daily circulation of 272,000. **NOTE:** To contact the Recruiting Department directly, call 212/566-4080. **Special programs:** Summer Internships; Tuition Reimbursement Program; Training. **Corporate headquarters location:** This location. **Listed on:** New York Stock Exchange. **Stock exchange symbol:** NYT. **President/CEO/Director:** Janet L. Robinson. **Sales/revenue:** $3 billion. **Number of employees nationwide:** Over 12,000.

NEW YORK UNIVERSITY
7 East 12th Street, Main Floor, New York NY 10003-4475. 212/998-1250. **Fax:** 212/995-4229. **Contact:** Personnel Department. **World Wide Web address:** http://www.nyu.edu/hr. **Description:** A state university. **NOTE:** Interested job seekers may apply online. The University no longer accepts faxed or e-mailed resumes. **Positions advertised include:** Math Department Manager; Associate Director of Career Counseling and Placement; Administrative Aide; Administrative Assistant; Security Officer; Senior Medical Records Assistant; Senior Clinical Aide; X-Ray Technician; Director of Advisement; Administrative Secretary; Admissions Officer; Director of Theatrical Production; Junior Collector; Financial Analyst; Administrator of Alumni and Internship Services; Facilities Coordinator; Dental Hygienist; Chief Information Officer. **Office hours:** Monday – Friday, 9:00 a.m. – 4:00 p.m.

NEW YORK UNIVERSITY MEDICAL CENTER
One Park Avenue, 16th Floor, New York NY 10016. 212/263-1999. **Fax:** 212/404-3897. **Contact:** Recruitment and Staffing Department. **E-mail address:** nyumc-careers@msnyuhealth.org. **World Wide Web address:** http://www.med.nyu.edu. **Description:** A nonprofit medical center engaged in patient care, research, and education. The central component of New York University Medical Center is Tisch Hospital, a 726-bed acute care facility and a major center for specialized procedures in cardiovascular services, neurosurgery, AIDS, cancer treatment, reconstructive surgery, and transplantation. The medical center also includes the Rusk Institute of Rehabilitation Medicine, the Hospital of Joint Diseases, and several medical schools. The Rusk Institute of Rehabilitation Medicine, a 152-bed unit, is one of the world's largest university-affiliated centers for the treatment and training of physically disabled adults and children, as well as for research in rehabilitation medicine. The Hospital of Joint Diseases, with 226 beds, is dedicated solely to neuromusculoskeletal diseases. The School of Medicine, the Post-Graduate Medical School, and the Skirball Institute of Biomolecular Medicine are also part of the medical center. **Positions advertised include:** Assistant Research Scientist; Staff Physical Therapist; Divisional Assistant; Office Assistant; Departmental Assistant; Restricted Funds Manager; Executive Assistant; Assistant Laboratory Technician; Programmer; Receptionist; Network Support Specialist; Nurse Practitioner; Billing Coordinator; Library Assistant; Special Procedure Technician; MRI Specialist; CT Technologist; Business Systems Analyst; Grants Writer. **Special programs:** Internships; Summer Job; Tuition Assistance Program. **Corporate headquarters location:** This location. **Number of employees at this location:** 8,000.

NEWSDAY, INC.
235 Pinelawn Road, Melville NY 11747. 631/843-2020. **Contact:** Employment Services. **E-mail address:** jobs@newsday.com (journalist and editorial applicants) or careers@newsday.com (business applicants). **World Wide Web address:** http://www.newsday.com. **Description:** One of the largest daily newspapers in the United States with a circulation of 750,000. **Positions advertised include:** Part-time Inserter. **Special programs:** Internships. **Corporate headquarters location:** This location. **Operations at this facility include:** Administration; Divisional Headquarters; Manufacturing; Sales; Service. **President/CEO/Publisher:** Ray Jansen. **Number of employees at this location:** 600.

NEWSWEEK MAGAZINE
251 West 57th Street, New York NY 10019. 212/445-4000. **Fax:** 212/445-4575. **Contact:** Human Resources. **World Wide Web address:** http://www.newsweek.com. **Description:** One of the most comprehensive weekly news magazines in the world. The company operates a global network of more than 60 correspondents and numerous stringers, reporting on important developments in politics, national and international affairs, business, technology, science, lifestyles, society, and the arts. In addition to its English language editions, the company also publishes two foreign language editions: *Newsweek Nihon Ban* in Japanese, and *Newsweek Hanuk Pan* in Korean and operates 23 bureaus throughout the United States and abroad. Weekly circulation is more than 4 million internationally, and more than 3 million in the United States. Founded in 1933. **Corporate headquarters location:** This location. **Parent company:** The Washington Post Company. **Listed on:** New York Stock Exchange. **Stock exchange symbol:** WPO.

NEXTSOURCE
120 east 56th Street, 12th Floor, New York NY 10022. 212/736-5870. **Toll-free phone:** 800/727-6583. **Fax:** 212/736-9046. **Contact:** Human Resources. **World Wide Web address:** http://www.nextsource.com. **Description:** Develops and offers instructor-led and computer-based personal computer training programs and provides consulting services, primarily to large businesses and public sector organizations. The company's instructor-led training programs include a wide range of introductory and advanced classes in operating systems including MS/DOS, Microsoft Windows, and Macintosh systems; word processing; spreadsheets; databases; communications; executive overviews; integrated software packages; computer graphics; and desktop publishing. The company's computer-based training programs include offerings on Lotus Notes, CC Mail, Microsoft Office, and Lotus Smartsuite. The consulting division provides computer personnel on a temporary basis. **Parent company:** Formula Systems, Limited. **Listed on:** NASDAQ. **Stock exchange symbol:** FORTY. **President/CEO:** Joseph Musacchio. **Sales/revenue:** Over $700 million.

NIAGARA CORPORATION
667 Madison Avenue, 11th Floor, New York NY 10021. 212/317-1000. **Contact:** Human Resources. **Description:** Manufactures, processes, and distributes cold drawn steel bars. Niagara Corporation sells its products primarily to steel service centers in the United States and Canada. Founded in 1993. **Corporate headquarters location:** This location. **Subsidiaries include:** LaSalle Steel Company (Griffith IN; Hammond IN); Niagara LaSalle Corporation (Buffalo NY, Chattanooga TN, Midlothian TX). **Listed on:** NASDAQ. **Stock exchange symbol:** NIAG. **President/CEO:** Michael J. Scharf. **Sales/revenue:** Approximately $200 million. **Number of employees nationwide:** 1,125.

NIAGARA MOHAWK POWER CORPORATION
300 Erie Boulevard West, Syracuse NY 13202-4205. 315/474-1511. **Contact:** Human Resources. **E-mail address:** staffing@niagaramohawk.com. **World Wide Web address:** http://www.nimo.com. **Description:** Niagara Mohawk Power provides gas and electric power to the upstate New York region and parts of southern Ontario. The company owns Nine Mile Point 1 nuclear power station and part of Nine Mile Point 2. **Corporate headquarters location:** This location. **Listed on:** New York Stock Exchange. **Parent company:** National Grid Transco (UK). **Listed on:** New York Stock Exchange. **Stock exchange symbol:** NGG. **President:** William F. Edwards. **Sales/revenue:** Approximately $4 billion. **Number of employees nationwide:** 6,200.

NIAGARA MOHAWK POWER CORPORATION
1125 Broadway, Albany NY 12204. 518/449-8000. **Contact:** Human Resources. **World Wide Web address:** http://www.nimo.com. **Description:** Niagara Mohawk Power provides gas and electric power to the upstate New York region and parts of southern Ontario. The company owns Nine Mile Point 1 nuclear power station and part of Nine Mile Point 2. **Corporate headquarters location:** Syracuse NY. **Parent company:** National Grid Transco (UK). **Listed on:** New York Stock Exchange. **Stock exchange symbol:** NGG. **President:** William F. Edwards. **Sales/revenue:** Approximately $4 billion. **Number of employees nationwide:** 6,200.

NICE SYSTEMS INC.
116 John Street, Suite 1601, New York NY 10038. 646/836-6900. **Contact:** Human Resources. **World Wide Web address:** http://www.nice.com. **Description:** Develops, designs, manufactures, markets, and services digital voice recording systems. The company's products are used in a variety of telemarketing applications. **NOTE:** Jobseekers may apply for positions online. **Other U.S. locations:** Denver CO; Herndon VA. **Corporate headquarters location:** Rutherford NJ. **International locations:** Israel; England; France; Germany; Hong Kong. **Listed on:** NASDAQ. **Stock exchange symbol:** NICE. **Sales/revenue:** $127 million.

NIELSEN MEDIA RESEARCH COMPANY
7700 Broadway, New York NY 10003-9595. 646/654-8300. **Contact:** Josh Lax, Human Resources. **World Wide Web address:** http://www.nielsenmedia.com. **Description:** Nielsen Media Research measures television show audience sizes and provides this information to broadcast networks and advertising agencies. **NOTE:** Interested job seekers may apply online for specific positions or for general consideration. **Positions advertised include:** Staff Assistant; National Accounts Manager; Meeting and Event Manager; Media Field Interviewer; Executive Staff Assistant; Director of Marketing and Communications; Associate Analyst; Bilingual Technical Field Representative. **Corporate headquarters location:** This location. **Other U.S. locations:** Los Angeles CA; San Francisco CA; Dallas TX; Atlanta GA; Chicago IL; Dunedin FL. **Number of employees at this location:** 195. **Number of employees nationwide:** 3,500.

NINE WEST GROUP
Nine West Plaza, 1129 Westchester Avenue, White Plains NY 10604-3529. 914/640-6400. **Fax:** 914/640-3499. **Contact:** Melissa Tavino, Human Resources. **E-mail address:** jobs@ninewest.com. **World Wide Web address:** http://www.ninewest.com. **Description:** A manufacturer and retailer of women's shoes. **Positions advertised include:** Planner; Director of Product Development; Corporate Technical Director; Product Data Maintenance Specialist; Sample Coordinator; Merchandise Processor; Design Assistant; Allocations Manager. **Office hours:** Monday - Thursday, 9:00 a.m. - 5:00 p.m.; Friday, 8:30 a.m. - 3:00 p.m. **Corporate headquarters location:** This location. **Other U.S. locations:** Nationwide. **Parent company:** Jones Apparel Group. **Listed on:** New York Stock Exchange. **Stock exchange symbol:** JNY.

NORTH FORK BANCORPORATION, INC.
NORTH FORK BANK
275 Broad Hollow Road, Melville NY 11747. 631/844-1000. **Contact:** Human Resources. **World Wide Web address:** http://www.northforkbank.com. **Description:** A commercial bank holding company. The principal subsidiary, North Fork Bank (also at this location), is one of the largest independent commercial banks headquartered on Long Island. **Corporate headquarters location:** This location. **Listed on:** New York Stock Exchange. **Stock exchange symbol:** NFB. **President/CEO/Chairman:** John Adams Kanas.

NORTHEAST HEALTH
2212 Burdett Avenue, Troy NY 12180. 518/274-3382. **Contact:** Human Resources. **World Wide Web address:** http://www.nehealth.com. **Description:** A comprehensive network of health care and community services that operates through three hospitals: Albany Memorial Hospital, The Eddy, and Samaritan Hospital. **Positions advertised include:** Home Health Aide; Registered Nurse; LPN; Nursing Assistant; Clinical Staff Member; Ancillary Staff Member; Support Worker; Manager; Supervisor. **CEO:** Craig Duncan. **Number of employees nationwide:** Over 4,000.

NORTHERN DUTCHESS HOSPITAL
6511 Springbrook Avenue, P.O. Box 5002, Rhinebeck NY 12572-5002. 845/871-3240. **Fax:** 845/871-3252. **Contact:** Human Resources. **World Wide Web address:** http://www.ndhosp.com. **Description:** A hospital. Northern Dutchess Hospital's staff treats the physiological, psychological, social, and spiritual needs of the geriatric and physically challenged by using a multidisciplinary approach. The Thompson House, a 100-bed, skilled nursing facility, was established in 1994. Residents with Alzheimer's disease and related dementia diagnoses receive therapeutic services in The Thompson House's 20-bed Special Care Unit. Wells Manor, founded in 1987, is a senior citizen housing project that has five separate buildings with 19 efficiency apartments and 55 one-bedroom units. The Neugarten Family Birth Center, established in 1985, was the first hospital-based birthing center in New York. Since 1978, Northern Dutchess Hospital has primary health care centers in five New York communities: Beacon Community Dental (Beacon NY); Germantown Community Dental (Germantown NY); Hyde Park Medical/Dental (Hyde Park NY); Rhinebeck Community Dental (Rhinebeck NY); and Stanfordville Medical/Dental (Stanfordville NY). **NOTE:** Online applications are available. **Positions advertised include:** Food Service Supervisor; Food Service Aide; Billing Representative; Respiratory Therapist; Nurse Practitioner; Physical Therapist; Physical Therapist Aide; Nuclear Medicine Technologist; Registered Nurse Supervisor; LPN; Nurse Aide Coordinator; Surgical Technician; Staff Nurse; Registered Nurse.

NORTHROP GRUMMAN CORPORATION
1 Grumman Road West, Bethpage NY 11714. 516/575-0574. **Contact:** Human Resources. **World Wide Web address:** http://www.northgrum.com. **Description:** Manufactures military aircraft, commercial aircraft parts, and electronic systems. Northrop Grumman manufactures the B-2 Spirit Stealth Bomber, as well as parts for the F/A-18 and the 747, and radar equipment. Other operations include computer

systems development for management and scientific applications. **NOTE:** Online applications are available. **Positions advertised include:** Structural Analysis Engineer; Avionics Systems Design and Integration Engineer; Aero Design and Analysis Engineer; Engineering Liaison; Pilot; Software Engineer; Program Manager; Purchasing Price Analyst; Strategic Planner; Administrative Assistant; Business Analyst Manager; Subcontract Administrator; Web Applications Technical Leader. **Corporate headquarters location:** Los Angeles CA. **Listed on:** New York Stock Exchange. **Stock exchange symbol:** NOC. **President/CEO/Director:** Ronald D. Sugar. **Sales/revenue:** $17 billion. **Number of employees worldwide:** Over 117,000.

NOTICIAS DEL MUNDO
3842 9th Street, Long Island City NY 11101. 718/786-4343. **Contact:** Maria Perez, Human Resources Director. **Description:** Publishes a daily Spanish newspaper. **NOTE:** Entry-level positions and part-time jobs are offered. **Special programs:** Internships; Apprenticeships. **Corporate headquarters location:** This location. **Parent company:** News World Communications Inc. **Operations at this facility include:** Administration; Regional Headquarters; Sales; Service. **Number of employees at this location:** 60.

NOVO NORDISK OF NORTH AMERICA
405 Lexington Avenue, Suite 6400, New York NY 10174. 212/878-6600. **Contact:** Human Resources Department. **World Wide Web address:** http://www.novonordisk.com. **Description:** A holding company whose divisions produce insulin, industrial enzymes, and other drugs and bioindustrial items. The Health Care Group is the diabetes care division that develops and manufactures insulin and delivery systems related to the treatment of diabetes. The Biopharmaceuticals division develops, produces, and markets products for the treatment of coagulation and other blood disorders as well as growth disorders. The Bioindustrial division consists of detergents, providing enzymes to the detergent industry. **NOTE:** Human Resources is located at 100 Overlook Center, Suite 200, Princeton NJ 08540. 609/987-5800. Jobseekers may apply for positions online. **Positions advertised include:** Managed Care Account Executive; Pharmaceutical Sales Representative. **Other U.S. locations:** Davis CA; Clayton NC; Franklinton NC; Princeton NJ; Seattle WA. **Parent company:** Novo Nordisk A/S (Baysvaerd, Denmark). **Operations at this facility include:** This location is the corporate service office for North America. **Listed on:** New York Stock Exchange. **Stock exchange symbol:** NVO. **President:** Martin Soeters. **Number of employees at this location:** 25. **Number of employees nationwide:** 1,000. **Number of employees worldwide:** 13,000.

NICHOLAS H. NOYES MEMORIAL HOSPITAL
111 Clara Barton Street, Dansville NY 14437. 585/335-6001. **Fax:** 585/335-4250. **Recorded jobline:** 585/335-4233. **Contact:** Human Resources. **E-mail address:** lgriffin@noyes-hospital.org. **World Wide Web address:** http://www.noyes-health.org. **Description:** A nonprofit, 72-bed, full-service health care institution. Nicholas H. Noyes Memorial Hospital is accredited by the Joint Commission on Accreditation of Healthcare Organizations. The hospital provides medical/surgical inpatient services in most medical specialties. Patient care units include emergency room, operating room, obstetrics/gynecology, and intensive care/coronary care. Support services include a clinical laboratory, diagnostic radiology department, electrocardiology, respiratory therapy, physical therapy, and social services. **NOTE:** Resumes submitted via e-mail should be formatted in Microsoft Word or ASCII. **Company slogan:** Happiness is health care close to home. **Positions advertised include:** Certified Nursing Aide; Tradesman/Professional Finisher; Registered Nurse Coordinator. **Special programs:** Internships; Summer Jobs. **Number of employees at this location:** 430.

NUCOR STEEL AUBURN
P.O. Box 2008, 25 Quarry Road, Auburn NY 13021. 315/253-4561. **Fax:** 315/253-5377. **Contact:** Human Resources. **E-mail address:** employment@nucorauburn.com. **World Wide Web address:** http://www.nucorauburn.com. **Description:** This company manufactures and wholesales steel. Founded in 1973. **Corporate headquarters location:** Charlotte NC. **Parent company:** Nucor Corporation. **Listed on:** New York Stock Exchange. **Stock exchange symbol:** NUE.

NUTRITION 21
4 Manhattanville Road, Purchase NY 10577-2197. 914/701-4500. **Fax:** 914/696-0860. **Contact:** Human Resources Department. **E-mail address:** mail@nutrition21.com. **World Wide Web address:** http://www.nutrition21.com. **Description:** Develops and markets nutrition products. The company focuses on products with medical value for consumers concerned with cardiovascular health and diabetes. The company is composed of an Ingredients Division, a Consumer Products Division, and Therapeutic Division. Founded in 1982. **Corporate headquarters location:** This location. **Listed on:** NASDAQ. **Stock exchange symbol:** NXXI. **President/CEO/Director:** Gail Montgomery. **Sales/revenue:** $14.7 million. **Number of employees at this location:** 27.

OM TECHNOLOGIES
140 Broadway, 25th Floor, New York NY 10005. 646/428-2800. **Contact:** Human Resources. **World Wide Web address:** http://www.om.com. **Description:** OM Technologies develops software for the securities and brokerage industries. **Corporate headquarters location:** Stockholm, Sweden. **International locations:** Worldwide. **Listed on:** Stockholmsborsen. **Stock exchange symbol:** OM. **Number of employees worldwide:** Over 16,000.

OSI PHARMACEUTICALS, INC.
58 South Service Road, Suite 110, Melville NY 11747. 631/962-2000. **Fax:** 631/752-3880. **Contact:** Human Resources. **E-mail address:** employment@osip.com. **World Wide Web address:** http://www.osip.com. **Description:** A biopharmaceutical company utilizing proprietary technologies to discover and develop products for the treatment and diagnosis of human diseases. The company conducts a full range of drug discovery activities from target identification through clinical candidates for its own products and in collaborations and co-ventures with other major pharmaceutical companies. **NOTE:** Jobseekers may apply for positions online. **Positions advertised include:** Purchasing Specialist. **Corporate headquarters location:** This location. **Other area locations:** Farmingdale NY; Uniondale NY. **Other U.S. locations:** Boulder CO. **International locations:** England. **Listed on:** NASDAQ. **Stock exchange symbol:** OSIP. **President:** Dr. Colin Goddard.

OGILVY & MATHER
309 West 49th Street, New York NY 10019. 212/237-6000. **Recorded jobline:** 212/237-5627. **Contact:** Human Resources. **World Wide Web address:** http://www.ogilvy.com. **Description:** An advertising agency. **Other U.S. locations:** Nationwide. **International locations:** Worldwide. **Parent company:** WPP Group plc.

OLEAN GENERAL HOSPITAL
515 Main Street, Olean NY 14760. 716/375-6152. **Fax:** 716/375-6393. **Contact:** Larry Jeffries, Director of Human Resources. **E-mail address:** ljeffries@ogh.org. **World Wide Web address:** http://www.ogh.org. **Description:** A 217-bed, nonprofit, acute care hospital. Supported by over 100 physicians and specialists, Olean General Hospital has a wide range of services such as acute and chronic pain management, allergy immunology, anesthesiology, cardiac rehabilitation, colon and rectal surgery, dermatology, emergency services, endocrinology, family practice, gynecology, lithotripsy, nephrology, obstetrics, occupational medicine, ophthalmology, oral surgery, orthopedic surgery, otolaryngology, pathology, pediatrics, psychiatry, pulmonary medicine, radiology, and urology. Olean General Hospital offers the following state-of-the-art centers: cardiac rehabilitation, endoscopy, laparoscopic surgery, laser eye surgery, lithotripsy, mental health, pain management, and thoracic surgery. The hospital also offers free blood pressure screening clinics, support groups, 24-hour mental health crisis hotline, childbirth classes, health fairs, home lab and respiratory therapy services, public service announcements, a SeniorCare program, scholarships, organ donor awareness, basic life support classes, outpatient physical therapy, 24-hour labor epidural services, and preadmission testing. Founded in 1912. **NOTE:** To contact Human Resources directly, call 716/375-6152. Interested job seekers may apply online. **Positions advertised include:** Registered Nurse; LPN; Staff Pharmacist; Medical Technologist; Respiratory Therapist.

OLYMPUS AMERICA INC.
2 Corporate Center Drive, Melville NY 11747-3157. 631/844-5000. **Fax:** 631/844-5930. **Contact:** Human Resources. **E-mail address:** staffing@olympus.com. **World Wide Web address:** http://www.olympus.com. **Description:** Olympus America manufactures and markets cameras and imaging equipment as well as a variety of surgical and medical instruments. **Positions advertised include:** Staff Accountant; Staffing Specialist; Corporate Training Manager; Senior e-Commerce Programmer/Analyst; Staff Attorney; Digital Technology Associate Manager; Assistant Contract Specialist; Product Manager; Clinical Monitor; Software Products Technical Trainer; Loaner Retrieval Representative; Accounts Payable Administrator; Receptionist/Switchboard Operator. **Corporate headquarters location:** This location. **Other U.S. locations:** Nationwide. **International locations:** Worldwide. **Operations at this facility include:** This location houses administrative offices only. **President/CEO:** F. Mark Gumz.

ONEBEACON INSURANCE GROUP
P.O. Box 5135, Buffalo NY 14240. 716/636-9400. **Contact:** Human Resources. **E-mail address:** onebeaconjobs@onebeacon.com. **World Wide Web address:** http://www.onebeacon.com. **Description:** A carrier of property, casualty, and life insurance, licensed in all 50 states, with offices throughout the country. **NOTE:** Resumes and cover letters may be forwarded to the Human Resources Department, One Beacon Street, Boston MA 02108, or faxed to: 617/725-6262. **Special programs:** Actuarial Professional Development Program. **Corporate headquarters location:** Boston MA. **Other U.S. locations:** ME; CT; NJ; MA. **Parent company:** White Mountain Insurance Group Limited. **Listed on:** New York Stock Exchange. **Stock exchange symbol:** WTM.

ONEBEACON INSURANCE GROUP
201 North Service Road, Melville NY 11747. 631/423-4400. **Contact:** Human Resources. **E-mail address:** careers@onebeacon.com. **World Wide Web address:** http://www.onebeacon.com. **Description:** A carrier of property, casualty, and life insurance, licensed in all 50 states, with offices throughout the country. **NOTE:** Resumes and cover letters may be forwarded to the Human Resources Department, One Beacon Street, Boston MA 02108, or faxed to: 617/725-6262. **Special programs:** Actuarial Professional Development Program. **Corporate headquarters location:** Boston MA. **Other U.S. locations:** ME; CT; NJ; MA. **Parent company:** White Mountain Insurance Group Limited. **Listed on:** New York Stock Exchange. **Stock exchange symbol:** WTM.

ONEIDA DINNERWARE
500 Bailey Avenue, Buffalo NY 14210-1733. 716/824-8515. **Contact:** Human Resources. **World Wide Web address:** http://www.oneida.com. **Description:** Manufactures china products. **Special programs:** Internships. **Corporate headquarters location:** Oneida NY. **International locations:** Canada; Mexico; United Kingdom; Italy; Australia. **Parent company:** Oneida Ltd. **Listed on:** New York Stock Exchange. **Stock exchange symbol:** OCQ. **President/CEO/Chairman:** Peter J. Kallet. **Sales/revenue:** Approximately $500 million.

ONEIDA HEALTHCARE CENTER
321 Genesee Street, Oneida NY 13421. 315/361-2040. **Fax:** 315/361-2240. **Contact:** John G. Margo, Director of Personnel. **E-mail address:** jobs@oneidahealthcare.org. **World Wide Web address:** http://www.oneidahealthcare.org. **Description:** A 101-bed acute care hospital and 160-bed extended care facility adjoining three outpatient clinics serving the health care needs of Madison County in central New York. **Positions advertised include:** Registered Nurse; LPN; Child Care Assistant. **Office hours:** Monday – Friday, 9:00 a.m. – 3:00 p.m. **Corporate headquarters location:** This location. **Operations at this facility include:** Administration; Service. **Number of employees at this location:** 950.

ONEIDA LTD.
163-181 Kenwood Avenue, Oneida NY 13421. 315/361-3000. **Contact:** Personnel. **World Wide Web address:** http://www.oneida.com. **Description:** Manufactures and markets tableware and industrial wire products. Through its Consumer Operations, Oneida is one of the world's largest manufacturers of stainless steel flatware (knives, forks, and spoons). Other products include flatware in silverplate, gold electroplate, and sterling silver; silverplated hollowware (trays and coffee sets); and crystal stemware and giftware. Through its Foodservice Operations, Oneida offers the industry complete selections of dinnerware, flatware, and hollowware under the trademarks of Oneida, Buffalo, D.J., Santa Andrea, and Northland. Founded in 1880. **Corporate headquarters location:** This location. **International locations:** Canada; Mexico; United Kingdom; Italy; Australia. **Listed on:** New York Stock Exchange. **Stock exchange symbol:** OCQ. **Sales/revenue:** Approximately $500 million.

ONESOURCE FACILITY SERVICES
429 West 53rd Street, New York NY 10019. 212/408-6200. **Contact:** Human Resources. **World Wide Web address:** http://www.2onesource.com. **Description:** Provides a variety of services including janitorial, landscaping, and pest control to public institutions, retail stores, schools, industrial facilities, and commercial buildings. **Corporate headquarters location:** Atlanta GA.

ONESOURCE FACILITY SERVICES
777 Sheridan Drive, Tonawanda NY 14150. 716/874-3350. **Contact:** Human Resources. **World Wide Web address:** http://www.2onesource.com. **Description:** A janitorial service providing building cleaning and maintenance services. **Corporate headquarters location:** Atlanta GA.

OPPENHEIMER
125 Broad Street, 16th Floor, New York NY 10004. 212/668-8000. **Toll-free phone:** 800/221-5588. **Contact:** Human Resources. **E-mail address:** info@opco.com. **World**

Wide Web address: http://www.opco.com. Description: A stock brokerage firm with 89 offices nationwide serving corporate clients and individual investors. Subsidiaries include: Freedom Investments. Parent company: Fahnestock Viner Holdings Inc. (Toronto, Canada).

ORACLE CORPORATION
560 White Plains Road, Tarrytown NY 10591. 914/524-1600. **Contact:** Human Resources. **E-mail address:** resumes_us@oracle.com. **World Wide Web address:** http://www.oracle.com. **Description:** Designs and manufactures database and information management software for business and provides consulting services. **NOTE:** Resumes should be submitted online or sent to Human Resources, 500 Oracle Parkway, Redwood Shores CA 94065. **Corporate headquarters location:** Redwood Shores CA. **Other U.S. locations:** Nationwide. **International locations:** Worldwide. **Listed on:** NASDAQ. **Stock exchange symbol:** ORCL. **CEO/Chairman:** Lawrence J. Ellison. **Number of employees worldwide:** 43,000.

ORANGE AND ROCKLAND UTILITIES
71 Dolson Avenue, Middletown NY 10940. 845/342-8940. **Fax:** 845/577-2958. **Contact:** J. Renella, Human Resources. **World Wide Web address:** http://www.oru.com. **Description:** Orange and Rockland Utilities and its subsidiaries supply electric service to 254,000 customers and gas service to 108,200 customers in southeastern New York, northern New Jersey, and northeastern Pennsylvania. **NOTE:** Resumes may be mailed to Human Resources, Attention: J. Renella, Orange and Rockland Utilities, Incorporated, One Blue Hill Plaza, Pearl River NY 10965, or faxed to: 845/577-2958. **Corporate headquarters location:** Pearl River NY. **Other U.S. locations:** Spring Valley NY. **Subsidiaries include:** Rockland Electric Company (NJ); Pike County Light and Power (PA). **Parent company:** Consolidated Edison, Inc. **President:** John D. McMahon. **Number of employees nationwide:** 1,000.

ORBIT INTERNATIONAL CORPORATION
80 Cabot Court, Hauppauge NY 11788. 631/435-8300. **Contact:** Lynn Cooper, Human Resources Manager. **E-mail address:** lcooper@orbitintl.com. **World Wide Web address:** http://www.orbitintl.com. **Description:** Manufactures electronic devices for the aerospace industry. Founded in 1957. **Special programs:** Summer Jobs. **Corporate headquarters location:** This location. **Subsidiaries include:** Behlman Electronics, Inc., through its military division, designs and manufactures power conversion devices and electronic products for measurement and display. The commercial products division of Behlman produces distortion-free commercial power units and low-noise, uninterruptable power sources. **Listed on:** NASDAQ. **Stock exchange symbol:** ORBT. **Number of employees at this location:** 120.

OSMOSE WOOD PRESERVING COMPANY OF AMERICA
980 Ellicott Street, Buffalo NY 14209. 716/882-5905. Fax: 716/882-5134. **Contact:** Human Resources Department. **E-mail address:** info@osmose.com. **World Wide Web address:** http://www.osmose.com. **Description:** A wood preserving company. Osmose treats and inspects a variety of wood products including telephone poles and railroad ties. The company also sells wood treating products. **Corporate headquarters location:** This location. **Other U.S. locations:** Memphis TN; Rock Hill SC; Tangent OR. **International locations:** Worldwide. **Subsidiaries include:** Wood Protection Company; Timberland Specialties Company. **Operations at this facility include:** Administration; Research and Development.

OTIS ELEVATOR COMPANY
625 Eight Avenue, New York NY 10018. 212/947-9269. **Contact:** Human Resources. **World Wide Web address:** http://www.nao.otis.com. **Description:** Produces and distributes a line of elevators and escalators for commercial and industrial use. **Corporate headquarters location:** Farmington CT. **Other U.S. locations:** Nationwide. **International locations:** Worldwide. **Parent company:** United Technologies Corporation. **Listed on:** New York Stock Exchange. **Stock exchange symbol:** UTX. **Sales/revenue:** $6.3 billion. **Number of employees worldwide:** Approximately 61,000.

OUTOKUMPU AMERICAN BRASS
P.O. Box 981, 70 Sayre Street, Buffalo NY 14240-0981. 716/879-6700. **Contact:** Human Resources. **World Wide Web address:** http://www.outokumpu.com. **Description:** Outokumpu American Brass is a manufacturer of copper and copper alloy products primarily for the manufacture of copper strips, coils, and tubes. **International locations:** Worldwide. **Parent company:** Outokumpu Oyj (Finland). **Number of employees worldwide:** 21,000.

OWENS-ILLINOIS, INC.
7134 County House Road, Auburn NY 13021. 315/255-5201. **Contact:** Human Resources. **World Wide Web address:** http://www.o-i.com. **Description:** Owens-Brockway also has divisions nationally producing corrugated, plywood, and plastic containers, among others. Specialized glass products sold by the company include Libbey Tumblers, stemware, and decorative glassware; television bulbs for picture tubes; and Kimble scientific and laboratory ware. Overseas affiliates manufacture flat glass and related products. **Special programs:** Educational Assistance Program; Training. **Corporate headquarters location:** Toledo OH. **International locations:** Worldwide. **Operations at this facility include:** This location is primarily involved in making glass containers. **Listed on:** New York Stock Exchange. **Stock exchange symbol:** OI. **CEO/Chairman:** Joseph H. Lemieux. **Number of employees worldwide:** Over 38,000.

OWL WIRE & CABLE INC.
3127 Seneca Turnpike, P.O. Box 187, Canastota NY 13032. 315/697-2011. **Fax:** 315/697-2123. **Contact:** Human Resources. **E-mail address:** info@owlwire.com. **World Wide Web address:** http://www.owlwire.com. **Description:** Manufactures bare, uninsulated copper wire. Founded in 1954. **Number of employees at this location:** 35.

OXFORD UNIVERSITY PRESS
198 Madison Avenue, New York NY 10016-4314. 212/726-6000. **Fax:** 212/726-6458. **Contact:** Human Resources. **E-mail address:** personnel@oup-usa.org. **World Wide Web address:** http://www.oup-usa.org. **Description:** Publishes a diverse line of scholarly books. **Positions advertised include:** Reference Marketing Assistant; Editor; Online Publishing and Business Development Assistant; Development Editor. **Special programs:** Summer Internships. **Other U.S. locations:** Cary, NC; Bethesda MD. **Operations at this facility include:** This location houses the Editorial, Design, Manufacturing, Marketing, and Sales departments.

OXYGEN MEDIA, INC.
75 9th Avenue, 7th Floor, New York City NY 10011. 212/651-2000. **Contact:** Human Resources. **E-mail address:** jobs@oxygen.com. **World Wide Web address:** http://www.oxygen.com. **Description:** Produces and broadcasts television programs and Websites geared toward women viewers. **Positions advertised include:** Junior Accountant. **CEO/Chairman:** Geraldine Laybourne. **Number of employees at this location:** 450.

PDK LABS INC.
145 Ricefield Lane, Hauppauge NY 11788. 631/273-2630. **Contact:** Human Resources. **E-mail address:** info@pdklabs.com. **World Wide Web address:** http://www.pdklabs.com. **Description:** PDK Labs manufactures and distributes over-the-counter pharmaceutical products and vitamins. The company's line of products primarily consists of nonprescription caffeine products, pain relievers, decongestants, diet aids, and a broad line of vitamins, nutritional supplements, and cosmetics. The company markets its products through direct mail, regional distributors, and private label manufacturing.

P & F INDUSTRIES, INC.
dba EMBASSY INDUSTRIES, INC.
300 Smith Street, Farmingdale NY 11735-1114. 631/694-1800. **Fax:** 631/694-1836. **Contact:** Human Resources. **E-mail address:** info@pfina.com. **World Wide Web address:** http://www.pfina.com. **Description:** Through its subsidiaries, the company manufactures power tools, machine tools, hydraulic cylinders, and other construction and hardware products. The Embassy Industries subsidiary imports radiant heating systems and manufactures baseboard heating equipment, hardware, and sheet metal contracting. **Corporate headquarters location:** This location. **Other U.S. locations:** Boynton Beach FL; New Hyde Park NY. **Subsidiaries include:** Berkley Tools; Embassy Industries, Inc; Florida Pneumatic Manufacturing Company; Franklin MFG; Green Manufacturing, Inc.; Countrywide Hardware. **Listed on:** NASDAQ. **Stock exchange symbol:** PFIN. **Chairman/President/CEO:** Richard A. Horowitz. **Annual sales/revenues:** $76.5 million. **Number of employees:** 305.

PACE UNIVERSITY
One Pace Plaza, New York NY 10038-1598. 212/346-1200. **Contact:** Human Resources. **World Wide Web address:** http://www.pace.edu. **Description:** A university with three campus locations and an enrollment of nearly 14,000 students. Founded in 1906. **Positions advertised include:** Secretary; Administrative Assistant; Admissions Recruiter; Evening Program Coordinator; Assistant Vice-President of Marketing and Communications; Tutor; International Student Advisor; Coordinator of Support Services for Online Teaching and Learning; Courseware Designer; Director of Funded Research Administration; Assistant Dean of Students. **Other area locations:** Pleasantville NY; White Plains NY.

PALL CORPORATION
2200 Northern Boulevard, East Hills NY 11548-1289. 516/484-5400. **Contact:** Rita DiStefano, Human Resources. **World Wide Web address:** http://www.pall.com. **Description:** Pall Corporation is a leader in filtration technology, specializing in fluid clarification and high-end separation. The company's overall business is organized into three segments: Health Care, Aeropower, and Fluid Processing. **Corporate headquarters location:** This location. **Other area locations:** Cortland NY; Glen Cove NY; Hauppauge NY; Port Washington NY. **Other U.S. locations:** Putnam CT; Fort Myers FL; New Port Richey FL; Pinellas Park FL. **Subsidiaries include:** Pall Gelman Sciences Incorporated. **Operations at this facility include:** Administration; Manufacturing; Research and Development; Sales. **Listed on:** New York Stock Exchange. **Stock exchange symbol:** PLL. **Sales/revenue:** Approximately $1.3 billion. **Number of employees nationwide:** 6,500. **Number of employees worldwide:** 10,700.

PALL CORPORATION
25 Harbor Park Drive, Port Washington NY 11050. 516/484-3600. **Contact:** Human Resources. **World Wide Web address:** http://www.pall.com. **Description:** A world leader in filtration technology, specializing in fluid clarification and high-end separation. The company's overall business is organized into three segments: Health Care, Aeropower, and Fluid Processing. In the fluid clarification market, Pall sells disposable cartridges that fit into filter houses it has sold to clients. In the separations market, the company sells complete systems, which include both semi-permanent filters and systems that regularly consume disposable cartridges. **Corporate headquarters location:** East Hills NY. **Other area locations:** Cortland NY; Glen Cove NY; Hauppauge NY. **Other U.S. locations:** Putnam CT; Fort Myers FL; New Port Richey FL; Pinellas Park FL. **Subsidiaries include:** Pall Gelman Sciences Incorporated. **Listed on:** New York Stock Exchange. **Stock exchange symbol:** PLL. **Sales/revenue:** Approximately $1.3 billion. **Number of employees nationwide:** 6,500. **Number of employees worldwide:** 10,700.

PALL CORPORATION
225 Marcus Boulevard, Hauppauge NY 11788. 631/273-0911. **Contact:** Rita DiStephano, Human Resources Director. **World Wide Web address:** http://www.pall.com. **Description:** A world leader in filtration technology, specializing in fluid clarification and high-end separation. The company's overall business is organized into three segments: Health Care, Aeropower, and Fluid Processing. Pall Corporation products offer reliable solutions for customers, whether the client is involved in the beginning, middle, or end process of a project. In the fluid clarification market, Pall sells disposable cartridges that fit into filter houses it has sold to clients. In the separations market, the company sells complete systems, which include both semipermanent filters and systems that regularly consume disposable cartridges. **Corporate headquarters location:** East Hills NY. **Other area locations:** Cortland NY; Port Washington NY; Glen Cove NY. **Other U.S. locations:** Putnam CT; Fort Myers FL; New Port Richey FL; Pinellas Park FL. **Subsidiaries include:** Pall Gelman Sciences Incorporated. **Listed on:** New York Stock Exchange. **Sales/revenue:** Approximately $1.3 billion. **Stock exchange symbol:** PLL. **Number of employees nationwide:** 6,500. **Number of employees worldwide:** 10,700.

PALL TRINITY MICRO
P.O. Box 2030, Cortland NY 13045. 607/753-6041. **Physical address:** 3643 Route 281, Cortland NY 13045. **Fax:** 607/753-9653. **Contact:** Human Resources. **World Wide Web address:** http://www.pall.com. **Description:** Develops and manufactures filters and filtration devices and systems for global customers primarily in high-tech and industrial markets. **Company slogan:** Filtration. Separation. Solution. **Corporate headquarters location:** East Hills NY. **Other U.S. locations:** CA; FL; MA; MI; TX. **International locations:** Germany; Ireland; Japan; United Kingdom. **Parent company:** Pall Corporation is a world leader in filtration technology, specializing in fluid clarification and high-end separation. The company's overall business is organized into three segments: Health Care, Aeropower, and Fluid Processing. **Operations at this facility include:** Administration; Manufacturing; Research and Development. **Listed on:** New York Stock Exchange. **Stock exchange symbol:** PLL. **Number of employees at this location:** 750. **Number of employees worldwide:** 7,500.

PAR TECHNOLOGY CORPORATION
PAR Technology Park, 8383 Seneca Turnpike, New Hartford NY 13413. 315/738-0600. **Fax:** 315/738-0411. **Contact:** Personnel. **World Wide Web address:** http://www.partech.com. **Description:** Par Technology Corporation in involved in the manufacture of point of sale terminals and scans to detect foreign objects in glass

containers. The company also has a division that conducts research for the government. **Positions advertised include:** Facility Physical Security Specialist; Field Engineer Eastern/Western Regions; Programmer III. **Corporate headquarters location:** This location. **Listed on:** New York Stock Exchange. **Stock exchange symbol:** PTC.

PARACELSIAN
Langmuir Laboratories, 95 Brown Road, #1005, Ithaca NY 14850. 607/257-4224. **Fax:** 607/257-2734. **Contact:** Chief Financial Officer. **E-mail address:** gchabot@paracelsian.com. **World Wide Web address:** http://www.paracelsian.com. **Description:** Uses Asian herbal medicines to develop assay and molecular instruments for improved cancer diagnosis and to discover anticancer drugs. **Corporate headquarters location:** This location. **President/CEO:** NoriYoshi Inoue.

PARADE PUBLICATIONS INC.
711 Third Avenue, New York NY 10017. 212/450-7000. **Fax:** 212/450-7200. **Contact:** Carol Unger, Vice President/Director of Human Resources. **E-mail address:** carol_unger@parade.com. **World Wide Web address:** http://www.parade.com. **Description:** Publishes weekly magazines, including *Parade* and *React*. **Corporate headquarters location:** This location. **Operations at this facility include:** Administration; Manufacturing; Sales; Service. **Number of employees at this location:** 200.

PARAGON CAPITAL MARKETS
7 Hanover Square, 2nd Floor, New York NY 10004. 212/742-1500. **Contact:** Human Resources. **World Wide Web address:** http://www.paragonmarkets.com. **Description:** A full-service securities brokerage firm offering a diverse range of financial products and services. Founded in 1986. **Corporate headquarters location:** This location. **Other U.S. locations:** Boca Raton FL; Boulder CO. **Operations at this facility include:** Administration; Sales; Service. **Number of employees at this location:** 100. **Number of employees nationwide:** 150.

PARAMOUNT CENTER FOR THE ARTS
1008 Brown Street, Peekskill NY 10566. 914/739-2333. **Contact:** Human Resources. **E-mail address:** info@paramountcenter.org. **World Wide Web address:** http://www.paramountcenter.org. **Description:** A former vaudeville house revived as a performing arts facility offering programs in music, theater, film, and dance. **Office hours:** Monday – Friday, 10:00 a.m. – 6:00 p.m., Saturday, 12:00 p.m. – 4:00 p.m.

PARAMOUNT ELECTRONICS COMPANY
57 Willoughby Street, Brooklyn NY 11201. 718/237-8730. **Contact:** Human Resources. **Description:** Provides contract drafting services. **Corporate headquarters location:** This location.

PARK CENTRAL HOTEL
870 Seventh Avenue, New York NY 10019-4038. 212/247-8000. **Toll-free phone:** 800/346-1359. **Contact:** Human Resources. **World Wide Web address:** http://www.parkcentralny.com. **Description:** A 1,260-room hotel with restaurant, lounge, banquet, convention, and meeting facilities. **Corporate headquarters location:** Hampton NH. **Parent company:** Omni/Donley Hotel Group. **Operations at this facility include:** Sales; Service.

PARK EAST ANIMAL HOSPITAL
52 East 64th Street, New York NY 10021. 212/832-8417. **Fax:** 212/355-3620. **Contact:** Vicki Ungar, Office Manager. **World Wide Web address:** http://www.parkeastanimalhospital.com. **Description:** A 24-hour small animal hospital offering medical, nursing, and surgical services for pets. This location also hires seasonally. Founded in 1961. **Special programs:** Internships; Training; Summer Jobs. **Corporate headquarters location:** This location. **President:** Dr. Lewis Berman. **Number of employees at this location:** 25.

PARKER HANNIFIN CORPORATION
124 Columbia Street, Clyde NY 14433. 315/923-2311. **Contact:** Human Resources Manager. **World Wide Web address:** http://www.parker.com. **Description:** Manufactures motion control products including fluid power systems, electromechanical controls, and related components. Products are sold through direct sales employees and more than 4,900 distributors. The Motion and Control Group makes hydraulic pumps, power units, control valves, accumulators, cylinders, actuators, and automation devices to remove contaminants from air, fuel, oil, water, and other fluids. Fluid Connectors Group makes connectors, tube and hose fittings, hoses, and couplers that transmit fluid. Seal Group makes sealing devices, gaskets, and packing that insure leak-proof connections. Automotive and Refrigeration Groups make components for use in industrial and automotive air conditioning and refrigeration systems. **Special programs:** Education Reimbursement Program; Accounting Management Training Program. **Corporate headquarters location:** Cleveland OH. **Other U.S. locations:** Nationwide. **International locations:** Worldwide. **Operations at this facility include:** As part of the Gas Turbine Fuel Systems Division, this location manufactures fuel nozzles for jet engines. Principal products of the aerospace segment are hydraulic, pneumatic, and fuel systems and components. **Listed on:** New York Stock Exchange. **Stock exchange symbol:** PH. **Sales/revenue:** Over $6 billion. **Number of employees worldwide:** 48,000.

PARKER HANNIFIN CORPORATION
100 Dunn Road, Lyons NY 14489. 315/946-4891. **Contact:** Human Resources. **World Wide Web address:** http://www.parker.com. **Description:** Manufactures motion control products including fluid power systems, electromechanical controls, and related components. Products are sold through direct sales employees and more than 4,900 distributors. Repair and replacement components account for about half of the total sales. The product lines of the industrial sector cover most of the components control systems. The Motion and Control Group makes hydraulic pumps, power units, control valves, accumulators, cylinders, actuators, and automation devices to remove contaminants from air, fuel, oil, water, and other fluids. Principal products of the aerospace segment are hydraulic, pneumatic, and fuel systems and components. The Fluid Connectors Group makes connectors, tube and hose fittings, hoses, and couplers that transmit fluid. The Seal Group makes sealing devices, gaskets, and packing that insure leak-proof connections. **Special programs:** Education Reimbursement Program; Accounting Management Training Program. **Corporate headquarters location:** Cleveland OH. **Other U.S. locations:** Nationwide. **International locations:** Worldwide. **Operations at this facility include:** As part of the Automotive and Refrigeration Division, this location manufactures refrigeration and air conditioning components. **Listed on:** New York Stock Exchange. **Stock exchange symbol:** PH. **Sales/revenue:** Over $6 billion. **Number of employees worldwide:** 48,000.

PARKER HANNIFIN CORPORATION
300 Marcus Avenue, P.O. Box 9400, Smithtown NY 11787. 631/231-3737. **Contact:** Human Resources. **World Wide Web address:** http://www.parker.com. **Description:** Manufactures motion control products including fluid power systems, electromechanical controls, and related components. The Motion and Control Group makes hydraulic pumps, power units, control valves, accumulators, cylinders, actuators, and automation devices to remove contaminants from air, fuel, oil, water, and other fluids. The Fluid Connectors Group makes connectors, tube and hose fittings, hoses, and couplers that transmit fluid. The Seal Group makes sealing devices, gaskets, and packing that insure leak-proof connections. The Automotive and Refrigeration Groups make components for use in industrial and automotive air conditioning and refrigeration systems. Principal products of the aerospace segment are hydraulic, pneumatic, and fuel systems and components. **Special programs:** Education Reimbursement Program; Accounting Management Training Program. **Corporate headquarters location:** Cleveland OH. **Other U.S. locations:** Nationwide. **International locations:** Worldwide. **Operations at this facility include:** As part of the Electronic Systems Division, this location manufactures and distributes aerospace instrumentation and equipment including fuel flow instruments. **Listed on:** New York Stock Exchange. **Stock exchange symbol:** PH. **Sales/revenue:** Over $6 billion. **Number of employees worldwide:** 48,000.

PARSONS BRINCKERHOFF INC.
One Penn Plaza, New York NY 10119. 212/465-5000. **Contact:** Joe Alberti, Personnel. **E-mail address:** careeres@pbworld.com. **World Wide Web address:** http://www.pbworld.com. **Description:** Provides total engineering and construction management services, including the development of major bridges, tunnels, highways, marine facilities, buildings, industrial complexes, and railroads. Founded in 1885. **Corporate headquarters location:** This location. **International locations:** Worldwide. **Subsidiaries include:** Parsons Brinckerhoff Construction Services; Parsons Brinckerhoff Development Corporation; Parsons Brinckerhoff International; Parsons Brinckerhoff Quade & Douglas. **President/CEO:** Thomas J. O'Neill. **Sales/revenue:** Approximately $1.4 billion. **Number of employees worldwide:** Over 9,000.

PASS & SEYMOUR/LEGRAND
P.O. Box 4822, Syracuse NY 13221-4822. 315/468-6211. **Contact:** Human Resources. **E-mail address:** hrsy@pass-seymour.com. **World Wide Web address:** http://www.passandseymour.com. **Description:** Manufactures and sells wiring devices for use primarily in residential, institutional, industrial, and commercial buildings. Products include switches, electrical outlets, connectors, wallplates, weather-resistant boxes and covers, plastic outlet boxes, wire mesh cable grips, group fault interrupter receptacles, and various lighting products. **Positions advertised include:** Programmer; Regional Vice President of Sales. **Corporate headquarters location:** This location. **Other U.S. locations:** CA; NC; TX; CT. **International locations:** Worldwide. **Sales/revenue:** Approximately $6 billion. **Number of employees worldwide:** Over 27,000.

PATTERSON, BELKNAP, WEBB & TYLER LLP
1133 Avenue of the Americas, New York NY 10036. 212/336-2867. **Fax:** 212/336-2222. **Contact:** Donna M. Abramo, Director of Human Resources and Operations. **E-mail address:** dmabramo@pbwt.com. **World Wide Web address:** http://www.pbwt.com. **Description:** A law firm offering services in a variety of practice areas.

PAWLING CORPORATION
157 Charles Colman Boulevard, Pawling NY 12564. 845/855-1000. **Toll-free phone:** 800/431-0101. **Contact:** Human Resources Manager. **World Wide Web address:** http://www.pawling.com. **Description:** Manufactures rubber, plastic, and silicone products. Products range from inflatable rubber products to architectural protection products. Founded in 1945. **Corporate headquarters location:** This location. **Number of employees nationwide:** 360.

PAXAR
105 Corporate Park Drive, White Plains NY 10604. 914/697-6800. **Fax:** 914/697-6894. **Contact:** Personnel. **World Wide Web address:** http://www.paxar.com. **Description:** Manufactures various types of labels for retailers and apparel manufacturers. Alkahn offers a complete line of products including care labels, specialty weaves, and printed items. **Company slogan:** From Concept to Checkout. **Corporate headquarters location:** This location. **Other U.S. locations:** CA; IL; NC; GA. **International locations:** Hong Kong; Canada; Mexico; England.

PAYCHEX, INC.
911 Panorama Trail South, Rochester NY 14625-0397. 585/218-5100. **Fax:** 585/264-8555. **Contact:** Human Resources. **E-mail address:** jobopps@paychex.com. **World Wide Web address:** http://www.paychex.com. **Description:** Paychex, Incorporated is a national payroll processing and payroll tax preparation company for small to medium-sized businesses. While payroll is the core business, the company also provides other ancillary products and services including Taxpay, direct deposit, check signing and insertion, Section 125 cafeteria plans, insurance services, 401(k) recordkeeping, employee management services, and employee benefits pooling. Paychex has over 100 locations, serving more than 300,000 clients nationwide. Founded in 1971. **Positions advertised include:** Computer Operator; Data Center Quality Process Supervisor; Taxpayment Service Customer Support Representative; Senior Buyer/Purchasing Representative; Warehouse/Distribution Manager; Accounting Specialist; Collections Supervisor; Recovery Specialist; Risk Analysis Supervisor; National Sales Support Representative; Outside Sales Representative. **Special programs:** Internships; Training; Co-ops. **Corporate headquarters location:** This location. **Other U.S. locations:** Nationwide. **Listed on:** NASDAQ. **Stock exchange symbol:** PAYX. **CEO:** B. Thomas Golisano. **Sales/revenue:** $955 million. **Number of employees at this location:** 1,500. **Number of employees nationwide:** 5,000.

ALBERT PEARLMAN, INC.
60 East 42nd Street, Suite 1041, New York NY 10165. 212/687-5055. **Fax:** 212/687-6228. **Contact:** Human Resources. **E-mail address:** randyp@albertpearlman.com. **World Wide Web address:** http://www.albertpearlman.com. **Description:** The largest painting contractor in New York City. **Corporate headquarters location:** This location. **Other locations:** Hackensack, NJ; Long Island, NY.

PEERLESS-WINSMITH INC.
172 Eaton Street, Springville NY 14141. 716/592-9310. **Fax:** 716/592-9546. **Contact:** Human Resources. **World Wide Web address:** http://www.winsmith.com. **Description:** Manufactures speed reducers used to reduce motor speeds in order to obtain a workable RPM. Speed reducers are generally in the form of gearboxes ranging from one-eighth to 100 horsepower and can be found in the motors of elevators, conveyors, packaging equipment, overhead doors, and other electric motor-driven moving devices. Founded in 1901. **Corporate headquarters location:** This location. **Other U.S. locations:** Gainesville GA; Los Angeles CA; Chicago IL; Portland OR. **International locations:** Mississauga, Ontario, Canada.

PENCOM SYSTEMS INC.
40 Fulton Street, 18th Floor, New York NY 10038-1850. 212/513-7777. **Fax:** 212/227-1854. **Contact:** Tom Morgan, Recruiting. **E-mail address:** career@pencom.com.

World Wide Web address: http://www.pencom.com. **Description:** Provides computer consulting services including open systems management and software consulting. **NOTE:** Resumes submitted via e-mail must be formatted in HTML, Microsoft Word, or plain text. **Positions advertised include:** Research Associate; Toxicologist; Regulatory Affairs Associate; Quality Assurance Engineer; Project Manager; Pharmacist; Pharmaceutical Sales Representative; Microbiologist; Clinical Researcher; Clinical Database Designer; Biostatistician; **Corporate headquarters location:** This location. **Other U.S. locations:** Santa Clara CA; Boston MA; Ruston VA; Chicago IL; Livingston NJ.

PENGUIN PUTNAM INC.
375 Hudson Street, New York NY 10014. 212/366-2000. **Fax:** 212/366-2930. **Contact:** Human Resources. **E-mail address:** jobs@penguingroup.com. **World Wide Web address:** http://www.penguinputnam.com. **Description:** One of the nation's largest publishers of trade fiction books. Penguin Putnam is a division of Penguin Group. **NOTE:** Entry-level positions are offered. **Special programs:** Internships. **Internship information:** Internship candidates should send resumes to the attention of the Internship Coordinator in Human Resources. **Corporate headquarters location:** This location. **International locations:** Worldwide. **Parent company:** Pearson plc. is an international media group whose subsidiaries include Penguin Group. **Listed on:** New York Stock Exchange. **Stock exchange symbol:** PSO. **CEO:** David Shanks.

THE PENN TRAFFIC COMPANY
P.O. Box 4737, Syracuse NY 13221. 315/453-7284. **Physical address:** 1200 State Fair Boulevard, Syracuse NY 13221. **Fax:** 315/453-8240. **Contact:** Human Resources. **E-mail address:** resumes@penntraffic.com. **World Wide Web address:** http://www.penntraffic.com. **Description:** A food retailer and wholesaler. The company operates over 200 supermarkets in New York, Pennsylvania, Ohio, and West Virginia under the names Big Bear, Quality Markets, P&C Foods, and Bi-Lo Foods. Penn Traffic also operates wholesale food distribution businesses serving 106 licensed franchises and 90 independent operators, and the Penny Curtiss Bakery in Syracuse NY. Founded in 1942. **Positions advertised include:** Help Services Analyst. **Special programs:** Internships; Training. **Office hours:** Monday - Friday, 8:00 a.m. - 4:30 p.m. **Corporate headquarters location:** This location. **Other area locations:** Jamestown NY. **Other U.S. locations:** Columbus OH; DuBois PA. **Listed on:** NASDAQ. **Stock exchange symbol:** PNFT. **Sales/revenue:** Over $2 billion. **Number of employees at this location:** 2,000. **Number of employees nationwide:** 16,000.

PEPSI-COLA BOTTLING GROUP, INC.
One Pepsi Way, Somers NY 10589-2201. 914/767-6000. **Contact:** Human Resources. **World Wide Web address:** http://www.pbg.com. **Description:** Manufactures and distributes Pepsi-Cola beverages. **Listed on:** New York Stock Exchange. **NOTE:** Jobseekers may see http://www.pbgjobs.com for employment opportunities. **Positions advertised include:** Unix Administrator; Powerbuilder Programmer; A/R Workflow Specialist; Java Programmer; Java Developer; Tax and Financial Applications Support; Project Leader; Power PreSell Specialist; Senior Analyst; NIS Specialist. **Corporate headquarters location:** This location. **Other U.S. locations:** Nationwide. **Stock exchange symbol:** PBG. **President:** Eric J. Foss. **Sales/revenue:** Over $9 billion. **Number of employees worldwide:** 65,000.

PEPSI-COLA COMPANY
6010 Tarbell Road, Syracuse NY 13206. 315/463-8581. **Contact:** Human Resources. **World Wide Web address:** http://www.pepsico.com. **Description:** A distribution facility. **Corporate headquarters location:** Purchase NY. **Other U.S. locations:** Nationwide. **Parent company:** PepsiCo, Incorporated (Purchase NY) consists of Frito-Lay Company, Pepsi-Cola Company, The Quaker Oats Company, and Tropicana Products, Incorporated. **Listed on:** New York Stock Exchange. **Stock exchange symbol:** PEP. **CEO/Chairman:** Steve Reinemund. **Sales/revenue:** $25 billion. **Number of employees worldwide:** Over 142,000.

PEPSICO, INC.
700 Anderson Hill Road, Purchase NY 10577. 914/253-2000. **Contact:** Staffing Director. **World Wide Web address:** http://www.pepsico.com. **Description:** Operates on a worldwide basis within four companies which include Frito-Lay Company, Pepsi-Cola Company, The Quaker Oats Company, and Tropicana Products, Inc. Pepsi-Cola Company primarily markets its brands worldwide and manufactures concentrates for its brands for sale to franchised bottlers worldwide. The segment also operates bottling plants and distribution facilities located in the United States and key international markets. **NOTE:** Interested job seekers may apply online. **Positions advertised include:** Data Analyst; Corporate IT Auditor; Domestic Audit Manager; Corporate Auditor; Treasury Operations Analyst; Legal Assistant; **Corporate headquarters location:** This location. **Other U.S. locations:** Nationwide. **International locations:** Canada; Mexico; United Kingdom. **Listed on:** New York Stock Exchange; also, the Amsterdam, Chicago, Swiss, and Tokyo Stock Exchanges. **Stock exchange symbol:** PEP. **CEO/Chairman:** Steve Reinemund. **Sales/revenue:** $25 billion. **Number of employees worldwide:** Over 142,000.

PERFECT FIT INDUSTRIES, INC.
303 Fifth Avenue, New York NY 10016. 212/679-6656. **Contact:** Human Resources. **Description:** Manufactures bedding products such as mattress pads, decorative products, and related accessories.

PERFORMANCE TECHNOLOGIES
205 Indigo Creek Drive, Rochester NY 14626-5100. 585/256-0200. **Contact:** K. Mikityansky, Human Resources. **E-mail address:** km@pt.com. **World Wide Web address:** http://www.pt.com. **Description:** Develops systems, platforms, components, and software for communications infrastructure in commercial and military markets. Principal Software Engineer, Embedded Real-Time; IS Operations, Group Leader; Electronic Technician; Technical Support Engineer; Software Product Manager.

PETRY MEDIA CORPORATION
dba BLAIR TELEVISION, INC.
3 East 54th Street, New York NY 10022. 212/230-5900. **Fax:** 212/230-5843. **Contact:** Human Resources Staffing. **World Wide Web address:** http://www.petrymedia.com/blair. **Description:** Provides the media industry with national sales, marketing, and research services. The company's subsidiaries represent 250 TV stations and provides services to advertising agencies and spot TV advertisers. **Positions advertised include:** Sales Assistant; Research Analyst; Sales Associate; Account Executive. **Special programs:** Internships. **Corporate headquarters location:** This location. **Other U.S. locations:** Nationwide. **Subsidiaries include:** Blair Television, Incorporated; Petry Television Incorporated. **Operations at this facility include:** Administration; Research and Development; Sales. **Number of employees at this location:** 250. **Number of employees nationwide:** 500.

PFIZER
235 East 42nd Street, New York NY 10017. 212/573-2323. **Recorded jobline:** 212/733-4150. **Contact:** Employee Resources. **E-mail address:** resumes@pfizer.com. **World Wide Web address:** http://www.pfizer.com. **Description:** A leading pharmaceutical company that distributes products concerning cardiovascular health, central nervous system disorders, infectious diseases, and women's health worldwide. The company's brand-name products include Benadryl, Ben Gay, Cortizone, Desitin, Halls, Listerine, Sudafed, and Zantac 75. **Company slogan:** We're part of the cure. **NOTE:** Interested job seekers may apply online. **Positions advertised include:** Marketing Manager; Conventions Manager; Corporate Philanthropy Programs Manager; Administrative Assistant; Senior Human Resources Manager; Capacity and Inventory Analysis Manager; Supply Chain Manager; Corporate Counsel; Product Manager; Assistant Director of Corporate Media Relations; Regional Medical Research Specialist; Business Technology Manager. **Corporate headquarters location:** This location. **Other U.S. locations:** Nationwide. **International locations:** Worldwide. **Subsidiaries include:** Pfizer Animal Health Group; Pfizer Consumer Products Division; Pfizer Hospital Products Group; Pfizer International; Pfizer Pharmaceutical Group; Pfizer Specialty Chemicals. **Listed on:** New York Stock Exchange. **Stock exchange symbol:** PFE. **Number of employees worldwide:** 46,000.

PHILIP MORRIS INTERNATIONAL INC.
800 Westchester Avenue, Port Chester NY 10573. 914/335-5000. **Contact:** Human Resources. **World Wide Web address:** http://www.philipmorris.com. **Description:** In the tobacco industry, Philip Morris U.S.A. and Philip Morris International together form one of the largest international cigarette operations in the world. U.S. brand names include Marlboro, Parliament, Virginia Slims, Benson & Hedges, and Merit. **Corporate headquarters location:** This location. **International locations:** Worldwide. **Parent company:** Altria Group, Incorporated. **Listed on:** New York Stock Exchange. **Stock exchange symbol:** MO. **Sales/revenue:** Approximately $28 billion. **Number of employees worldwide:** 40,000.

PHILIPS ELECTRONICS NORTH AMERICA CORPORATION
1251 Avenue of the Americas, New York NY 10020. 212/536-0500. **Contact:** Denise Townsen, Supervisor of Human Resources. **World Wide Web address:** http://www.philips.com. **Description:** Philips Electronics North America is a multimarket manufacturing organization with nationwide locations and various subsidiaries, concentrating its efforts primarily in the fields of consumer electronics, consumer products, electrical and electronics components, and professional equipment. **Positions advertised include:** Quality Assurance Analyst; Quality Services Manager; Senior Customer Care Consultant; Senior Trainer. **Office hours:** Monday – Friday, 9:00 a.m. – 5:00 p.m. **Corporate headquarters location:** This location. **Operations at this facility include:** This location provides services including intellectual property, legal, tax, customs, employee benefits, communications and processing, government affairs, manufacturing technology, purchasing, travel, environmental affairs, audit, compensation, training, and development to Philips companies nationwide. **Listed on:** New York Stock Exchange. **Stock exchange symbol:** PHG. **Number of employees at this location:** 230.

PHILIPS LIGHTING COMPANY
7265 State Route 54, Bath NY 14810. 607/776-3311. **Contact:** Steve Dreiling, Human Resources Director. **World Wide Web address:** http://www.lighting.philips.com. **Description:** Manufactures specialty lighting products. Founded in 1983. **International locations:** Worldwide. **Parent company:** Philips Electronics North America Corporation. **Listed on:** New York Stock Exchange. **Stock exchange symbol:** PHG. **Number of employees at this location:** 700. **Number of employees worldwide:** 47,000.

PHILIPS RESEARCH
345 Scarborough Road, Briarcliff Manor NY 10510. 914/945-6000. **Fax:** 914/945-6375. **World Wide Web address:** http://www.research.philips.com. **Contact:** Human Resources. **Description:** This location conducts research in microelectronics, High Definition TV (HDTV), medical imaging, lighting, integrated circuit design, software engineering, materials engineering, and manufacturing automation to support Philips' international business interests. **Corporate headquarters location:** This location. **International locations:** Germany; England; the Netherlands; China. **Parent company:** Philips Electronics North America is a multimarket manufacturing organization with nationwide locations and various subsidiaries. The company concentrates its efforts primarily in the fields of consumer electronics, consumer products, electrical and electronics components, and professional equipment. **Listed on:** New York Stock Exchange. **Stock exchange symbol:** PHG. **Number of employees worldwide:** 2,500.

PHILLIPS-VAN HEUSEN CORPORATION
200 Madison Avenue, 10th Floor, New York NY 10016-3908. 212/381-3500. **Contact:** Manager of Human Resources. **E-mail address:** hr@pvh.com. **World Wide Web address:** http://www.pvh.com. **Description:** Manufactures, wholesales, and retails men's and women's apparel. **Corporate headquarters location:** This location. **Other U.S. locations:** Nationwide. **Listed on:** New York Stock Exchange. **Stock exchange symbol:** PVH. **Number of employees worldwide:** 9000.

PHOTOCIRCUITS CORPORATION
31 Sea Cliff Avenue, Glen Cove NY 11542. 516/674-1000. **Fax:** 516/609-1080. **Contact:** Human Resources. **E-mail address:** gcrecruiter@photocircuits.com. **World Wide Web address:** http://www.photocircuits.com. **Description:** A manufacturer of printed circuit boards. **Positions advertised include:** HVAC Mechanic; Maintenance Technician. **Special programs:** Internships. **Corporate headquarters location:** This location. **Other U.S. locations:** Peachtree City GA. **Operations at this facility include:** Administration; Manufacturing; Sales. **Number of employees at this location:** 1,525.

PICK QUICK FOODS INC.
83-10 Rockaway Boulevard, Ozone Park NY 11416. 718/296-9100. **Fax:** 718/296-6203. **Contact:** Human Resources. **Description:** A grocery retailer. **Corporate headquarters location:** This location.

PILLSBURY WINTHROP LLP
One Battery Park Plaza, New York NY 10004-1490. 212/858-1000. **Contact:** Human Resources. **E-mail address:** staff_ny@pillsburywinthrop.com. **World Wide Web address:** http://www.pillsburywinthrop.com. **Description:** An international law firm with a broad-based practice including corporate law, litigation, real estate, and tax law. **Positions advertised include:** Word Processing Operator; Marketing and Practice Support Manager; Paralegal; Help Desk Analyst; Technical Services Specialist; **Corporate headquarters location:** This location. **Other U.S. locations:** CA; CT; VA; DC. **International locations:** Australia; Tokyo; England; Singapore.

POLO RALPH LAUREN
650 Madison Avenue, New York NY 10022. 212/318-7000. **Fax:** 212/318-7200. **Contact:** Human Resources Department. **E-mail address:** jobs@poloralphlauren.com. **World Wide Web address:** http://www.polo.com. **Description:** Polo Ralph Lauren manufactures clothing and shoes for women and men. **Corporate headquarters**

location: This location. **Operations at this facility include:** This location is an administrative office. **Listed on:** New York Stock Exchange. **Stock exchange symbol:** RL. **CEO/Chairman:** Ralph Lauren. **Sales/revenue:** $1.7 billion. **Number of employees nationwide:** Over 10,000.

PORTA SYSTEMS CORPORATION
6851 Jericho Turnpike, Syosset NY 11791. 516/364-9300. **Fax:** 516/682-4636. **Contact:** Personnel. **E-mail address:** cu-sales@portasystems.com. **World Wide Web address:** http://www.portasystems.com. **Description:** Designs, manufactures, and markets telecommunications equipment, software, and systems to customers worldwide. Products are used for the connection, testing, management, and security of telecommunications and computer networks and systems. Porta Systems Corporation is comprised of three operating divisions: Operations Support Systems (OSS); Connection/Protection; and Signal Processing. **Corporate headquarters location:** This location. **International locations:** Mexico; Chile; England; Poland; the Philippines; China. **Operations at this facility include:** Administration; Manufacturing; Research and Development; Sales. **Listed on:** American Stock Exchange. **Stock exchange symbol:** PSI.

POSTERLOID CORPORATION
4862 36th Street, Long Island City NY 11101. 718/729-1050. **Contact:** Human Resources. **World Wide Web address:** http://www.polyvision.com. **Description:** Manufactures and markets indoor menu board display systems for the fast-food and convenience store industries and changeable magnetic display signage used primarily by banks to display interest rates and other information. These displays are custom manufactured for ceiling hanging or for window or counter displays. **Corporate headquarters location:** New York NY. **Parent company:** Alpine Group, Incorpoated is active in the defense and commercial electronics and telecommunications wire and cable industries through subsidiaries, Alpine Polyvision, Incorporated and DNE Technologies, Incorporated, both of which operate out of CT, and Superior TeleTec Incorporated in Atlanta GA. **Listed on:** New York Stock Exchange. **Stock exchange symbol:** AGI. **President:** Robert Sudack. **Number of employees at this location:** 55.

PRAXAIR MRC
542 Route 303, Orangeburg NY 10962. 845/398-8307. **Contact:** Human Resources Department. **World Wide Web address:** http://www.praxairmrc.com. **Description:** Designs and manufactures thin-film coating and etching systems used in the manufacture of integrated circuits for sale to the semiconductor, computer, and telecommunications industries. The company also processes and fabricates ultra-high-purity metals and metal alloys, principally for thin-film purposes. Praxair MRC's thin-film technology products are also used in nonelectronic applications such as protective coatings for corrosion and wear resistance in razor blades and various automotive products. The company operates in three segments: Sputtering Equipment, Associated Target Materials, and Other High-Purity Materials. **Special programs:** Internships. **Corporate headquarters location:** This location. **International locations:** France; Korea; Taiwan. **Parent company:** Praxair, Incorporated. **Listed on:** New York Stock Exchange. **Stock exchange symbol:** PX. **Number of employees at this worldwide:** Over 250.

PRECISION PHARMA
155 Duryea Road, Melville NY 11747. 631/752-7314. **Fax:** 631/845-6367. **Contact:** Human Resources. **E-mail address:** hr@precisionpharma.com. **World Wide Web address:** http://www.precisionpharma.com. **Description:** Precision Pharma is a leader in the field of pathogen inactivation of blood products. The company's technologies are designed to address the risk of viral contamination of blood products. Founded in 1995. **Positions advertised include:** Fractionation Technician; Mechanic. **Corporate headquarters location:** This location. **President/CEO:** James A. Moose.

PRECISION VALVE CORPORATION
700 Nepperhan Avenue, Yonkers NY 10703. 914/969-6500. **Fax:** 914/966-4401. **Contact:** Industrial Relations Manager. **E-mail address:** jobs@precision-valve.com. **World Wide Web address:** http://www.precision-valve.com. **Description:** An international manufacturer of aerosol valves. **NOTE:** Jobseekers may search for job opportunities on http://www.hotjobs.com. **Positions advertised include:** Warehouse Manager; Accounts Receivable Clerk; Industrial Maintenance Mechanic; Safety Manager; Facility Manager; High Speed Machine Mechanic; Machine Operator. **Corporate headquarters location:** This location. **Other U.S. locations:** Greenville SC. **International locations:** Worldwide. **Operations at this facility include:** Administration; Manufacturing; Research and Development; Sales; Service. **Number of employees at this location:** 390. **Number of employees nationwide:** 2,500.

PRICE CHOPPER SUPERMARKETS
GOLUB CORPORATION
501 Duanesburg Road, P.O. Box 1074, Schenectady NY 12306. 518/355-5000. **Recorded jobline:** 888/670-JOBS. **Contact:** Human Resources. **World Wide Web address:** http://www.pricechopper.com. **Description:** Operates a chain of grocery stores, gas stations, and convenience stores located in Connecticut, Massachusetts, New York, Pennsylvania, and Vermont. **Special programs:** Internships; Apprenticeships; Training; Co-ops; Summer Jobs. **Office hours:** Monday - Friday, 8:00 a.m. - 5:00 p.m. **Corporate headquarters location:** This location. **Parent company:** Golub Corporation (also at this location). **President/CEO:** Neil Golub. **Number of employees at this location:** 18,000.

PRICEWATERHOUSECOOPERS
1301 Avenue of the Americas, New York NY 10019. 646/471-4000. **Contact:** Human Resources. **World Wide Web address:** http://www.pwcglobal.com. **Description:** One of the largest certified public accounting firms in the world. PricewaterhouseCoopers provides public accounting, business advisory, management consulting, and taxation services. **NOTE:** Interested job seekers may apply online. **Positions advertised include:** BCS Senior Associate; Asset Advisory Associate; ISG Manager; Special Situations Associate; Insurance Manager; Senior Operational Effectiveness Associate; Executive Assistant to the Chairman; Corporate Treasury Technology Associate; Treasury and Finance Associate; OGC Secretariat Associate; Change and Learning Solutions Manager. **Corporate headquarters location:** This location. **Other U.S. locations:** Nationwide. **International locations:** Worldwide. **Chairman:** Andrew Ratcliffe. **Sales/revenue:** Over $13 billion. **Number of employees worldwide:** 125,000.

PRICEWATERHOUSECOOPERS
1177 Avenue of the Americas, New York NY 10036. 646/471-4000. **Contact:** Recruitment Department. **World Wide Web address:** http://www.pwcglobal.com. **Description:** One of the largest certified public accounting firms in the world. PricewaterhouseCoopers provides public accounting, business advisory, management consulting, and taxation services. **NOTE:** Interested job seekers may apply online. **Corporate headquarters location:** New York NY. **Other U.S. locations:** Nationwide. **International locations:** Worldwide. **Chairman:** Andrew Ratcliffe. **Sales/revenue:** Over $13 billion. **Number of employees worldwide:** 125,000.

PRICEWATERHOUSECOOPERS
80 State Street, Albany NY 12207. 518/462-2030. **Contact:** Human Resources. **World Wide Web address:** http://www.pwcglobal.com. **Description:** One of the largest certified public accounting firms in the world. PricewaterhouseCoopers provides public accounting, business advisory, management consulting, and taxation services. **NOTE:** Interested job seekers may apply online. **Positions advertised include:** Tax Middle Market Senior Associate; GRMS Senior Associate. **Corporate headquarters location:** New York NY. **Other U.S. locations:** Nationwide. **International locations:** Worldwide. **Chairman:** Andrew Ratcliffe. **Sales/revenue:** Over $13 billion. **Number of employees worldwide:** 125,000.

PRICEWATERHOUSECOOPERS
One Lincoln Center, Syracuse NY 13202. 315/474-8541. **Contact:** Human Resources. **World Wide Web address:** http://www.pwcglobal.com. **Description:** One of the largest certified public accounting firms in the world. PricewaterhouseCoopers provides public accounting, business advisory, management consulting, and taxation services. **NOTE:** Interested job seekers may apply online. **Positions advertised include:** Senior Audit Associate. **Corporate headquarters location:** New York NY. **Other U.S. locations:** Nationwide. **International locations:** Worldwide. **Chairman:** Andrew Ratcliffe. **Sales/revenue:** Over $13 billion. **Number of employees worldwide:** 125,000.

PROCTER & GAMBLE PHARMACEUTICAL INC.
P.O. Box 191, Norwich NY 13815. 607/335-2111. **Contact:** Human Resources. **World Wide Web address:** http://www.pg.com. **Description:** This location manufactures pharmaceutical prescription products including Asacol, Vrontex, Dantrium, Dantrium-IV, Didronel, Macrobid, and Macrodantin. Overall, Procter & Gamble manufactures over 300 laundry, cleaning, paper, beauty, health care, food, and beverage products in more than 140 countries. Brand-name products include Cover Girl, Max Factor, Vidal Sassoon, Clearasil, and Noxzema health and beauty products; Pepto-Bismol, Vicks, and NyQuil health care products; Bounce, Downy, Tide, Comet, and Mr. Clean cleaning products; Luvs, Pampers, Always, Tampax, Bounty, Charmin, and Puffs paper products; and Crisco, Folgers, Millstone, Sunny Delight, and Pringles food and beverage products. **Corporate headquarters location:** Cincinnati OH. **Other U.S. locations:** Nationwide. **International locations:** Worldwide. **Listed on:** New York Stock Exchange. **Stock exchange symbol:** PG. **Number of employees worldwide:** Over 100,000.

PROSKAUER ROSE
1585 Broadway New York NY 10036-8299. 212/969-3000. **Fax:** 212/969-2900. **Contact:** Diane M. Kolnik, Recruiting Manager. **E-mail address:** dkolnik@proskauer.com. **World Wide Web address:** http://www.proskauer.com. **Description:** One of the nation's largest law firms, focusing in a variety of different practice areas. **Special programs:** Summer Associate Program.

PRUDENTIAL SECURITIES INC.
199 Water Street, New York NY 10292. 212/778-1000. **Contact:** Director of Personnel. **World Wide Web address:** http://www.prudential.com. **Description:** An international securities brokerage and investment firm. The company offers clients more than 70 investment products including stocks, options, bonds, commodities, tax-favored investments, and insurance, as well as several specialized financial services. **Corporate headquarters location:** This location. **Other U.S. locations:** Nationwide. **Parent company:** Prudential Financial, Incorporated. **Listed on:** New York Stock Exchange. **Stock exchange symbol:** PRU. **President:** Michael Rice.

PUBLISHERS CLEARING HOUSE
382 Channel Drive, Port Washington NY 11050. 516/883-5432. **Contact:** Human Resources. **World Wide Web address:** http://www.pch.com. **Description:** A direct mail marketing company. Publishers Clearing House is one of the largest sources of new magazine subscribers. The company also conducts continuing research to develop effective promotions for other products and services. **Corporate headquarters location:** This location. **Subsidiaries include:** Campus Subscriptions. **CEO:** Robin B. Smith. **Sales/revenue:** Approximately $400 million. **Number of employees nationwide:** 465.

PUROLATOR PRODUCTS COMPANY
2243 Corning Road, Elmira Heights NY 14903. 607/737-8011. **Contact:** Human Resources Manager. **World Wide Web address:** http://www.facet-purolator.com. **Description:** Manufactures starter drives and fuel pumps for automobiles. Founded in 1883. **Parent company:** Mark IV.

QUAD/GRAPHICS, INC.
56 Duplainville Road, Saratoga Springs NY 12866. 518/581-4000. **Contact:** Pat Foss, Employee Services Director. **E-mail address:** quadjobs@qg.com. **World Wide Web address:** http://www.qg.com. **Description:** A commercial printer of magazines and catalogs. **Positions advertised include:** Finishing Material Handler; Over-the-Road Driver; Shipping Material Handler. **Special programs:** Corporate Internship Program; Corporate Trainee Program. **Corporate headquarters location:** Pewaukee WI. **Other U.S. locations:** Hartford WI; Lomira WI; Sussex WI; West Allis WI; Martinsburg WV; The Rock GA. **Number of employees worldwide:** Over 11,000.

QUALITY MARKETS
101 Jackson Avenue, Jamestown NY 14701. 716/664-6010. **Contact:** Human Resources. **World Wide Web address:** http://www.qualitymarkets.com. **Description:** Regional office of a chain of retail grocery stores. **Parent company:** The Penn Traffic Company (Syracuse NY) is a food retailer, wholesaler, and producer. The company operates over 230 supermarkets in New York, Ohio, Pennsylvania, and West Virginia under the names Big Bear, Insalaco's, Riverside Markets, Quality Markets, P&C Foods, and Bi-Lo Foods. Penn Traffic also wholesales to 249 stores, and operates a dairy and ice cream facility in Pennsylvania, two bakeries in New York and Ohio, and 15 discount department stores. **Operations at this facility include:** This location is an office and distribution center. **Listed on:** NASDAQ. **Stock exchange symbol:** PNFT.

QUANTRONIX
41 Research Way, East Setauket NY 11733. 631/784-6100. **Fax:** 631/784-6101. **Contact:** Human Resources. **E-mail address:** hr@quantronixlasers.com. **World Wide Web address:** http://www.quantronixlasers.com. **Description:** Manufactures laser systems for dental and medical uses. The company also manufactures lasers for industrial purposes. **NOTE:** Interested job seekers may apply online. **Positions advertised include:** High Power Industrial Laser Scientist; Diode-Pumped Laser Engineer; Ultrafast Systems Scientist; Applications Technician; Micro-Electronic Technician; Product Manager; Customer Service Representative; Marketing/Graphic Artist; CNC Operator; Optical Inspection Technician; Buyer; Senior Planner; Stockroom Clerk. **Corporate headquarters location:** This location. **International locations:** Germany; Malaysia; France; India; Japan.

QUEENS COLLEGE
THE CITY UNIVERSITY OF NEW YORK (CUNY)
65-30 Kissena Boulevard, Flushing NY 11367-1597. 718/997-4455. **Fax:** 718/997-5799. **Contact:** Human Resources Department. **World Wide Web address:** http://www.qc.edu. **Description:** A liberal arts commuter college. Founded in 1937. **Special programs:** Tuition Assistance Program.

QUEST DIAGNOSTICS INCORPORATED
575 Underhill Boulevard, Syosset NY 11791. 516/677-3800. **Fax:** 516/677-4015. **Contact:** Jamie Drumerhauser, Human Resources. **World Wide Web address:** http://www.questdiagnostics.com. **Description:** Quest Diagnostics is one of the largest clinical laboratories in North America, providing a broad range of clinical laboratory services to health care clients that include physicians, hospitals, clinics, dialysis centers, pharmaceutical companies, and corporations. The company offers and performs tests on blood, urine, and other bodily fluids and tissues to provide information for health and well-being. **NOTE:** Online applications are available. **Positions advertised include:** Laboratory Manager; District Sales Manager; Billing Supervisor; **Corporate headquarters location:** Teterboro NJ. **Other U.S. locations:** Nationwide. **International locations:** Worldwide. **Operations at this facility include:** This location is a clinical laboratory. **Listed on:** New York Stock Exchange. **Stock exchange symbol:** DGX. **Sales/revenue:** Over $4 billion. **Number of employees worldwide:** 33,400.

RADIAN REINSURANCE INC.
335 Madison Avenue, 25th Floor, New York NY 10017. 212/983-3100. **Fax:** 212/682-5377. **Contact:** Human Resources. **World Wide Web address:** http://www.radiangroupinc.com. **Description:** Radian Reinsurance Incorporated provides financial guaranty insurance and reinsurance. **Corporate headquarters location:** Philadelphia PA. **Other U.S. locations:** Dayton OH. **International locations:** London, UK. **Parent company:** Radian Group Incorporated. **Listed on:** New York Stock Exchange. **Stock exchange symbol:** RDN. **CEO/Chairman:** Frank P. Filipps. **Sales/revenue:** $1.2 billion. **Number of employees worldwide:** Over 1,400.

RADIO CITY ENTERTAINMENT
1260 Avenue of the Americas, New York NY 10020. 212/247-4777. **Contact:** Human Resources. **World Wide Web address:** http://www.radiocity.com. **Description:** A diversified entertainment production company. **NOTE:** Resumes may be mailed to the Human Resources Department, 2 Penn Plaza, New York NY 10121. **Special programs:** Internships. **Corporate headquarters location:** This location. **Parent company:** Madison Square Garden, L.P.

RAMP INDUSTRIES, INC.
One North Floral Avenue, Binghamton NY 13905-3296. 607/729-5256. **Fax:** 607/729-2977. **Contact:** Human Resources. **World Wide Web address:** http://www.rampindustries.com. **Description:** A subcontract manufacturer of printed circuit boards and cable harness assembly. Founded in 1976.

RAND INTERNATIONAL
51 Executive Boulevard, Farmingdale NY 11735. 631/249-6000. **Fax:** 631/249-6015. **Contact:** Eileen Singer, Director of Human Resources Department. **World Wide Web address:** http://www.randinternational.com. **Description:** Manufactures a complete line of bicycles, from tricycles to racing bikes, for international distribution. **Corporate headquarters location:** This location.

RANDOM HOUSE, INC.
1745 Broadway, New York NY 10019. 212/782-9000. **Fax:** 212/782-9054. **Contact:** Staffing Manager. **World Wide Web address:** http://www.randomhouse.com. **Description:** One of the largest trade publishers in the United States. Trade divisions include Villard Books, Vintage, Times Books, Pantheon/Schocken, and Knopf. Crown Publishing Group includes Crown Adult Books, Clarkson N. Potter, Fodor's Travel Guides, and Orion Books. Ballantine, Fawcett, Del Rey, and Ivy are mass-market imprints. **Positions advertised include:** Category Management Director; Publicity Director; Marketing Manager; Sub Rights Assistant Manager; Designer; Business Analyst; Subsidiary Rights Contract and Rights Administration Assistant; Art/Design Associate; **Special programs:** Summer Internship Program; Associates Program. **Corporate headquarters location:** This location. **Other U.S. locations:** Chicago IL; Westminster MD. **International locations:** Worldwide. **Parent company:** Bertelsmann, AG. **Number of employees at this location:** 900. **Number of employees nationwide:** 1,200.

THE RAYMOND CORPORATION
P.O. Box 130, South Canal Street, Greene NY 13778-0130. 607/656-2311. **Fax:** 607/656-9005. **Contact:** Mary Alice Porter, Human Resources. **E-mail address:** staffing@raymondcorp.com. **World Wide Web address:** http://www.raymondcorp.com. **Description:** Designs, manufactures, sells, and leases materials handling systems. **Positions advertised include:** Programmer/Analyst; Engineering Technical Specialist; Regional Manager; Warehouse Worker/Assembler; Digital Imaging Specialist; Engineer; Information Analyst. **Corporate headquarters location:** This location. **Subsidiaries include:** R.H.E. Ltd.; Raymond Industrial Equipment, Limited; Raymond Leasing Corporation; Raymond Sales Corporation; Raymond Transportation Corporation; The Raymond Export Corporation.

RAYMOUR & FLANIGAN FURNITURE INC.
2780 Ridge Road West, Rochester NY 14626. 716/225-9455. **Contact:** Human Resources. **World Wide Web address:** http://www.raymourflanigan.com. **Description:** A retail furniture store offering living room sets, dining room sets, bedroom sets, kitchen furniture, and desks. **Corporate headquarters location:** Liverpool NY. **Other U.S. locations:** MA; CT; PA; NJ. **Number of employees nationwide:** Over 2,300.

THE READER'S DIGEST ASSOCIATION, INC.
Reader's Digest Road, Pleasantville NY 10570. 914/238-1000. **Contact:** Human Resources. **World Wide Web address:** http://www.rd.com. **Description:** A publisher of magazines, books, music, and video products. The flagship publication, *Reader's Digest*, is a monthly general interest magazine published in 17 languages with a circulation of approximately 100 million worldwide. Special interest magazines include *American Woodworker*, *The Family Handyman*, *New Choices*, and *Walking*. **Special programs:** Internships. **Corporate headquarters location:** This location. **Other area locations:** New York NY. **Subsidiaries include:** Joshua Morris Publishing, Incorporated; QSP, Incorporated is a U.S. fundraising organization that works with schools and youth groups to raise money for educational enrichment programs. **Operations at this facility include:** Administration; Manufacturing; Regional Headquarters; Research and Development; Sales; Service. **Listed on:** New York Stock Exchange. **Stock exchange symbol:** RDA. **CEO/Chairman:** Thomas O. Ryder. **Number of employees at this location:** 1,500. **Number of employees nationwide:** 5,000.

REED BUSINESS INFORMATION
360 Park Avenue South, New York NY 10014. 646/746-6400. **Fax:** 646/746-7433. **Contact:** Director of Human Resources. **World Wide Web address:** http://www.reedbusiness.com. **Description:** Reed Business Information is a leading business-to-business magazine publisher with more than 80 specialty publications serving 16 major service and industry sectors including media, electronics, research and technology, computers, food service, and manufacturing. **Corporate headquarters location:** This location. **Other U.S. locations:** Nationwide. **International locations:** Worldwide. **Parent company:** Reed Elsevier Group plc. **Operations at this facility include:** This location publishes several magazine titles including *Broadcasting & Cable*, *Childbirth*, *Daily Variety*, *Graphic Arts Monthly*, *Library Journal*, *Modern Bride*, *Motor Boat*, and *Publishers Weekly*. **Listed on:** New York Stock Exchange. **Stock exchange symbol:** ENL; RUK. **Number of employees at this location:** 500. **Number of employees worldwide:** 12,000.

REGENERON PHARMACEUTICALS, INC.
777 Old Saw Mill River Road, Suite 10, Tarrytown NY 10591. 914/345-7400. **Fax:** 914/345-7790. **Contact:** Human Resources. **E-mail address:** jobs@regeneron.com. **World Wide Web address:** http://www.regeneron.com. **Description:** A research company that develops pharmaceuticals to treat neurological, oncological, inflammatory, allergic, and bone disorders as well as muscle atrophy. **Positions advertised include:** Senior Director; Medical Program Coordinator; Endocrinologist; Biostatistician; Assay Development Associate Director; Quality Auditor; Eye Angiogenesis; Bioreactor Development Associate Director; Cell Line and Process Development Research Associate. **Special programs:** Internships. **Corporate headquarters location:** This location. **Other area locations:** Rensselaer NY. **Listed on:** NASDAQ. **Stock exchange symbol:** REGN.

REMINGTON FIREARMS COMPANY, INC.
14 Hoefler Avenue, Ilion NY 13357. 315/895-3200. **Contact:** Employee Relations. **World Wide Web address:** http://www.remington.com. **Description:** A manufacturer of firearms. This facility also has a shooting range. Remington Firearms Company, Inc. also operates two shooting schools, one in Ilion and the other in Florida. **Corporate headquarters location:** Madison NC. **Other U.S. locations:** Elizabethtown KY; Hickory KY; Lonoke AR; Findlay OH; Ada OK. **CEO:** Tommy Millner.

RENAISSANCE WESTCHESTER HOTEL
80 West Red Oak Lane, White Plains NY 10604. 914/694-5400. **Contact:** Human Resources. **World Wide Web address:** http://www.renaissancehotels.com. **Description:** A hotel with 364 guest rooms and 18 meeting rooms. **Parent company:** Marriott International, Incorporated. **Listed on:** New York Stock Exchange. **Stock exchange symbol:** MAR.

RENSSELAER POLYTECHNIC INSTITUTE (RPI)
110 8th Street, Troy NY 12180-3590. 518/276-6302. **Fax:** 518/276-6370. **Contact:** Human Resources Department. **E-mail address:** jobs@rpi.edu. **World Wide Web address:** http://www.rpi.edu. **Description:** A private, four-year research university specializing in science and technology. **NOTE:** Interested job seekers may apply online. **Positions advertised include:** Materials Science and Engineering Assistant; Assistant Dean; Assistant Director of Research and Assessment; Assistant Director of Financial Aid, Student Records, and Financial Services; Assistant Softball Coach; Assistant Vice President for Finance; Associate Director of Planned Giving/Associate and Alumni Relations; Business Support Analyst; Cleaner; Communication Specialist; Course Developer; Federal Relations Director. **Number of employees at this location:** 1,700.

RESEARCH INSTITUTE OF AMERICA GROUP
395 Hudson Street, New York NY 10014. 212/367-6300. **Contact:** Manager of Human Resources. **World Wide Web address:** http://www.riahome.com. **Description:** Publishers of tax and other professional services publications designed for attorneys, accountants, and the business community through print, electronic, and online media. Founded in 1935. **NOTE:** Interested job seekers may apply online. **Positions advertised include:** Finance Manager; Lead Software Engineer; Associate Copy Editor; Senior Software Engineer; Senior Oracle Database Administrator; UNIX System Administrator; Software Engineer. **Corporate headquarters location:** This location. **Other area locations:** Rochester NY; Valhalla NY. **Other U.S. locations:** Washington DC; Alexandria VA; Deerfield IL; Carrollton TX. **Parent company:** Thomson Tax & Accounting. **Number of employees at this location:** 300.

RESOURCE ENERGY, INC.
6165 Plank Road, Mayville NY 14757. 716/269-7665. **Contact:** Human Resources. **Description:** Resource Energy, Incorporated has concentrated its activities in two industries: energy and real estate finance. In energy, REI produces and transports natural gas and oil from properties it owns and/or operates. In real estate, the company owns a portfolio of 12 mortgages with an aggregate face value for $30.7 million. **Corporate headquarters location:** Philadelphia PA.

RESTAURANT ASSOCIATES CORPORATION
120 West 45th Street, 16th Floor, New York NY 10036. 212/789-8201. **Fax:** 212/613-4695. **Contact:** Manager of Recruitment. **E-mail address:** careers@restaurantassociates.com. **World Wide Web address:** http://www.restaurantassociates.com. **Description:** A broad-based company that operates 60 restaurants in major cities, cultural centers, and leisure attractions along the East Coast. Private food service facilities are also offered to corporations, institutions, and clubs. **NOTE:** To contact Human Resources directly, call 212/789-8201. **Positions advertised include:** Director; Assistant Director; Restaurant Manager; Bar Manager; Beverage Manager; Sous Chef; Controller; Catering Director; Catering Sales Director. **Special programs:** Internships. **Corporate headquarters location:** This location. **Parent company:** Compass Group. **Operations at this facility include:** Divisional Headquarters.

REVLON, INC.
625 Madison Avenue, 8th Floor, New York NY 10022. 212/527-4000. **Contact:** Human Resources. **E-mail address:** jobs.mail@revlon.com. **World Wide Web address:** http://www.revlon.com. **Description:** Manufactures and distributes a line of skin care products, fragrances, and other cosmetics internationally. **Positions advertised include:** Financial Analyst; Strategic Information Analyst; Public Relations Associate; Category Management Director; Package Development Director; Assistant Product Manager; Senior Product Manager; Trade Marketing Manager; Executive Secretary; Legal Secretary. **Corporate headquarters location:** This location. **Listed on:** New York Stock Exchange. **Stock exchange symbol:** REV.

RICH PRODUCTS CORPORATION
1150 Niagara Street, Buffalo NY 14213. 716/878-8000. **Contact:** Human Resources. **World Wide Web address:** http://www.richs.com. **Description:** Rich Products is a family-owned, frozen foods manufacturer. The company operates manufacturing sites and field offices throughout North America and abroad. Rich's also operates more than

30 production facilities involved in producing a wide spectrum of premium quality products, including nondairy creamers, toppings and icings, frozen dough, baked goods, sweet goods, pastas, and specialty meats. Founded in 1945. **Positions advertised include:** Accounts Receivable and Deductions Specialist; Aseptic Technical Manager; Customer Service Representative; Human Resources Assistant; Invoicing Specialist; Organizational Development/Performance Manager; Icing and Mixes Marketing Manager; Supply Planner; Senior Compensation Analyst; Senior Credit Analyst; New Products Initiatives Senior Marketing Manager. **Special programs:** Internships. **Office hours:** Monday – Friday, 8:30 a.m. – 5:00 p.m. **Corporate headquarters location:** This location. **International locations:** Canada. **Sales/revenue:** Over $1.7 billion. **Number of employees worldwide:** 7,000.

RICHARDSON ELECTRONICS
701-1 Koehler Avenue, Ronkonkoma NY 11779. 631/468-3900. **Toll-free phone:** 800/737-6937. **Fax:** 631/468-3950. **Contact:** Sales Manager. **World Wide Web address:** http://www.rell.com. **Description:** An international distributor of electronic components including turn-key microwave generators. **Corporate headquarters location:** La Fox IL. **Other U.S. locations:** Nationwide. **International locations:** Worldwide. **Operations at this facility include:** This location supports industrial, avionics, marine, and scientific products. **Listed on:** NASDAQ. **Stock exchange symbol:** RELL.

RICHMOND CHILDREN'S CENTER
100 Corporate Drive, Yonkers NY 10701. 914/968-7170. **Contact:** Director of Human Resources. **World Wide Web address:** http://www.richmondgroup.org. **Description:** A nonprofit, intermediate care facility (residential to long-term) for individuals with severe to profound physical and developmental disabilities. Services in the main facility include medical care; recreational services; and physical, language, occupational, and speech therapies. Richmond Children's Center offers other services in the community including case management, early intervention, group homes, and respite programs (for children with special needs who are cared for at home). **Number of employees at this location:** 325.

RIDGEWOOD SAVINGS BANK
71-02 Forest Avenue, Ridgewood NY 11385. 718/240-4800. **Contact:** Human Resources Representative. **World Wide Web address:** http://www.ridgewoodbank.com. **Description:** A full-service savings bank. **Corporate headquarters location:** This location. **Other area locations:** Statewide. **Operations at this facility include:** Administration; Service. **Number of employees at this location:** 550.

RIOT MANHATTAN
545 Fifth Avenue, 5th Floor, New York NY 10017. 212/907-1200. **Fax:** 212/907-1201. **Contact:** Human Resources. **E-mail address:** info@rioting.com. **World Wide Web address:** http://www.riotmanhattan.com. **Description:** Provides post production and creative services. **Corporate headquarters location:** This location.

ROANWELL CORPORATION
2564 Park Avenue, Bronx NY 10451. 718/401-0288. **Toll-free phone:** 866/929-3301. **Fax:** 718/401-0663. **Contact:** Human Resources. **World Wide Web address:** http://www.roanwellcorp.com. **Description:** Manufactures terminal voice communication equipment. **Corporate headquarters location:** This location.

ROCHESTER GAS & ELECTRIC CORPORATION
89 East Avenue, Rochester NY 14649. 716/546-2700. **Fax:** 585/771-2895. **Contact:** Human Resources. **E-mail address:** employment_opportunities@rge.com. **World Wide Web address:** http://www.rge.com. **Description:** Produces electricity through hydro, fossil, and nuclear production, and provides electric and gas services to customers in upstate New York. **Corporate headquarters location:** This location. **Operations at this facility include:** Administration; Divisional Headquarters; Sales.

ROCHESTER INSTITUTE OF TECHNOLOGY
8 Lomb Memorial Drive, Rochester NY 14623-5604. 716/475-2424. **Fax:** 585/475-7170. **Recorded jobline:** 585/475-7095. **Contact:** Human Resources. **E-mail address:** resumes@rit.edu. **World Wide Web address:** http://www.rit.edu. **Description:** A four-year technical institute offering bachelor's and master's degrees, as well as Ph.D.s in imaging science. **Positions advertised include:** Assistant Engineering Professor; Director of North Star Center; C-Print Captionist; College of Applied Science and Technology Chairperson; Print Media Assistant Professor; Biological Sciences Assistant Professor; Science and Mathematics Instructional Faculty Member; Director of the Center for Residence Life; Post Doctoral Researcher; Electrical System Development Engineer; Child Care Teacher; Senior Custodian; Staff Nurse; Software Specialist. **Special programs:** Internships.

ROCHESTER MIDLAND CORPORATION
333 Hollenbeck Street, P.O. Box 31515, Rochester NY 14603-1515. 585/461-1333. **Toll-free phone:** 800/836-1627. **Fax:** 585/266-8919. **Contact:** Human Resources. **World Wide Web address:** http://www.rochestermidland.com. **Description:** Rochester Midland produces household and industrial cleaning products. Founded in 1888. **Positions advertised include:** Sales Representative; Food Safety Specialist. **Corporate headquarters location:** This location. **Operations at this facility include:** This location compounds chemicals for use in household and industrial cleaners, in addition to housing administrative offices.

ROME CABLE CORPORATION
421 Ridge Street, Rome NY 13440. 315/337-6369. **Fax:** 315/338-6770. **Contact:** Human Resources. **World Wide Web address:** http://www.romecable.com. **Description:** A manufacturer of wire and cable. Rome is involved primarily in the manufacturing of heavy-duty wiring. Common uses include airport lighting, underground cables, and building wires. **CEO/Chairman:** David Harvey. **Sales/revenue:** $200 million.

ROSLYN SAVINGS BANK
One Jericho North Plaza, Jericho NY 11753. 516/942-6000. **Contact:** Human Resources. **World Wide Web address:** http://www.roslyn.com. **Description:** Operates a full-service mutual savings bank. Roslyn Savings offers a full range of commercial and savings bank services through 12 offices including locations in Brooklyn, Queens, Deer Park, and Nassau County. Founded in 1895. **Corporate headquarters location:** This location. **Parent company:** Roslyn Bancorp Inc. **Listed on:** NASDAQ. **Stock exchange symbol:** RSLN.

ROUNDABOUT THEATRE COMPANY, INC.
231 West 39th Street, Suite 1200, New York NY 10018. 212/719-9393. **Fax:** 212/869-8817. **Contact:** Human Resources Department. **E-mail address:** jobs@roundabouttheatre.org. **World Wide Web address:** http://www.roundabouttheatre.org. **Description:** A theater presenting revivals of classic plays. Founded in 1965. **Positions advertised include:** Ticket Services Representative; Tele-Sales Representative. **Special programs:** Internships. **Number of employees at this location:** 50.

ROUTLEDGE INC.
29 West 35th Street, 10th Floor, New York NY 10001-2299. 212/216-7800. **Fax:** 212/244-4561. **Contact:** Human Resources. **E-mail address:** employment@taylorandfrancis.com. **World Wide Web address:** http://www.routledge-ny.com. **Description:** A progressive, international book and journal publisher focused on the humanities and social sciences. **Positions advertised include:** Acquisitions Editor; Dissertations Editor; Editorial Assistant, Humanities/Reference. **Special programs:** Internships. **Office hours:** Monday - Friday, 9:00 a.m. - 5:00 p.m. **Other U.S. locations:** Independence KY. **Parent company:** Taylor & Francis Group. **Operations at this facility include:** This location houses the editorial and marketing offices.

THE ROYAL BANK OF CANADA
165 Broadway, New York NY 10006. 212/428-6200. **Contact:** Human Resources. **World Wide Web address:** http://www.royalbank.com. **Description:** One of North America's largest banks. **Parent company:** RBC Financial Group. **Listed on:** New York Stock Exchange. **Stock exchange symbol:** RY. **President/CEO:** Gordon M. Nixon.

ROYALBLUE TECHNOLOGIES INC.
17 State Street, 42nd Floor, New York NY 10004-1501. 212/269-9000. **Contact:** Human Resources. **E-mail address:** resumes@royalblue.com. **World Wide Web address:** http://www.royalblue.com. **Description:** Develops software for the NASDAQ stock exchange. **Positions advertised include:** Technical Support Supervisor; Visual Basic Developer; Software Designer/Developer; Graduate Developer; Data Implementation Consultant; First-line Support Analyst. **International locations:** China; France; Japan; United Kingdom. **Number of employees worldwide:** Over 400.

RUDER-FINN, INC.
301 East 57th Street, New York NY 10022. 212/593-6400. **Fax:** 212/593-6397. **Contact:** Human Resources. **E-mail address:** careers@ruderfinn.com. **World Wide Web address:** http://www.ruderfinn.com. **Description:** Offers a wide range of services in the public relations field. **Special programs:** Executive Training Program. **Corporate headquarters location:** This location. **Other U.S. locations:** Los Angeles CA; San Francisco CA; Chicago IL; Washington DC. **International locations:** China; France; Israel; Singapore; United Kingdom.

RUSSER FOODS COMPANY
665 Perry Avenue, Buffalo NY 14210. 716/826-6400. **Toll-free phone:** 800/828-1885. **Contact:** Human Resources. **World Wide Web address:** http://www.russerfoods.com. **Description:** A manufacturer and packager of luncheon meats and smoked meats. **Parent company:** Tyson Foods. **Listed on:** New York Stock Exchange. **Stock exchange symbol:** TSN.

RYAN BECK & CO
650 Madison Avenue, 10th Floor, New York NY 10022. 212/407-0500. **Contact:** Staffing Specialist. **E-mail address:** jobs@ryanbeck.com. **World Wide Web address:** http://www.ryanbeck.com. **Description:** Having recently acquired Gruntal & Co. and The GMS Group, Ryan Beck now operates 35 offices in 12 states offering financial services in three distinct areas: capital markets, investment banking, and the private client group. Founded in 1946. **NOTE:** Jobseekers should contact the human resources department at the company's headquarters: Liz Maynor, Staffing Specialist, 220 South Orange Avenue, Livingston NJ 07039; phone: 973/597-5980; fax: 973-597-6408. **Positions advertised include:** Financial Consultant; Sales Associate; Client Services Representative; Operations Specialist; Investment Analyst; Senior Investment Banker. **Corporate headquarters location:** Livingston NJ. **Other U.S. locations:** Nationwide. **Parent company:** BankAtlantic Bancorp, Inc. (Fort Lauderdale FL). **Annual sales/revenues:** $44 million. **Number of employees:** 400.

SCJ ASSOCIATES INC.
60 Commerce Drive, Rochester NY 14623. 716/359-0600. **Fax:** 716/359-0856. **Contact:** Human Resources. **World Wide Web address:** http://www.scjassociates.com. **Description:** Assembles printed circuit boards. SCJ Associates also tests products and wraps cable. Founded in 1971.

SG COWEN SECURITIES CORPORATION
1221 Avenue of the Americas, 9th Floor, New York NY 10020. 212/278-6000. **Contact:** Human Resources. **World Wide Web address:** http://www.sgcowen.com. **Description:** An investment banking firm. **Special programs:** Training; Tuition Reimbursement Program; Summer Associate Program. **Corporate headquarters location:** This location. **Other area locations:** Albany NY. **Other U.S. locations:** Chicago IL; Boston MA; Cleveland OH; Dayton OH; Philadelphia PA; Dallas TX; Denver CO; San Francisco CA. **International locations:** Canada; France; Switzerland; United Kingdom. **Parent company:** Societe Generale Group (Paris, France). **Number of employees at this location:** 1,000. **Number of employees nationwide:** 2,300.

SAATCHI & SAATCHI ADVERTISING
375 Hudson Street, New York NY 10014. 212/463-2304. **Contact:** Human Resources. **World Wide Web address:** http://www.saatchi-saatchi.com. **Description:** An advertising agency. **Company slogan:** Nothing is impossible. **Office hours:** Monday - Friday, 9:00 a.m. - 5:00 p.m. **Corporate headquarters location:** This location. **Other U.S. locations:** Nationwide. **International locations:** Worldwide. **Number of employees at this location:** 500.

SAATCHI & SAATCHI ROWLAND
255 Woodcliff Drive, Suite 200, Fairport NY 14450-4219. 585/249-6100. **Contact:** Human Resources. **World Wide Web address:** http://www.saatchibiz.com. **Description:** A full-service, integrated advertising agency. **Corporate headquarters location:** New York NY. **Other area locations:** Rochester NY. **Other U.S. locations:** Wilmington DE. **International locations:** Switzerland; United Kingdom; China; France; Australia. **Parent company:** Saatchi & Saatchi plc. **President:** Christine Withers.

SACHEM ANIMAL HOSPITAL
227 Union Avenue, Holbrook NY 11741. 631/467-2121. **Contact:** Human Resources. **World Wide Web address:** http://www.sachemanimalhospital.com. **Description:** Sachem Animal Hospital provides general medical and surgical services, dental services, and boarding for domestic and exotic pets. The hospital also specializes in reproduction and infertility services.

WILLIAM H. SADLIER, INC.
9 Pine Street, New York NY 10005-1002. 212/227-2120. **Contact:** Francis Marsh, Personnel Director. **World Wide Web address:** http://www.sadlier.com. **Description:** Publishes textbooks and related workbooks, teachers' guides, and other supplementary

materials principally in the subject areas of religion, mathematics, language arts, and social studies. Founded in 1832. **Corporate headquarters location:** This location.

ST. CLARE'S HOSPITAL
600 McClellan Street, Schenectady NY 12304. 518/347-5630. **Toll-free phone:** 800/462-1713. **Fax:** 518/347-5522. **Contact:** Peter Jones, Employment Coordinator. **E-mail address:** jobs@stclares.org. **World Wide Web address:** http://www.stclares.org. **Description:** A 200-bed acute care hospital. Founded in 1949. **Positions advertised include:** Registered Nurse; LPN; Clinical Leader; Nursing Supervisor; Supervisor/Educator; Cardiology Technician; Certified Respiratory Therapy Technician; Chaplain; Diet Technician; Medical Technologist; Patient Care Dietician; Pharmacist; Physical Therapy Assistant; Security Officer; Microbiology Technical Specialist; Ultrasound Technologist; Film Librarian; Receptionist; Unit Secretary; Weekend Clerk. **Office hours:** Monday - Friday, 10:00 a.m. - 2:00 p.m. **Corporate headquarters location:** This location. **Operations at this facility include:** Administration. **President/CEO:** Paul Chodkowski. **Number of employees at this location:** 1,150.

ST. IVES INC. AVANTI
75 9th Avenue, 2nd Floor, New York NY 10011. 800/833-3807. **Contact:** Emma Medcalf, Human Resources. **World Wide Web address:** http://www.st-ives-usa.com. **Description:** the company is a commercial printing company specializing in annual reports and catalogs. **Positions advertised include:** Pressperson; Customer Service Representative. **Other U.S. locations:** Hollywood FL; Cleveland OH. **Parent company:** St. Ives Group. **Operations at this facility include:** Administration; Manufacturing; Sales. **Annual sales/revenues:** $51.4 million. **Number of employees at this location:** 276.

ST. JOHN'S UNIVERSITY
8000 Utopia Parkway, Jamaica NY 11439. 718/990-6161. **Contact:** Human Resources. **E-mail address:** employment@stjohns.edu. **World Wide Web address:** http://www.stjohns.edu. **Description:** A private, four-year university. St. John's University offers bachelor's and master's degrees. Founded in 1870.

ST. JOSEPH'S HOSPITAL
555 East Market Street, Elmira NY 14901. 607/737-1518. **Fax:** 607/737-7837. **Contact:** Kip Burlew, Human Resources. **E-mail address:** kburlew@jstjosephs.org. **World Wide Web address:** http://www.stjosephs.org. **Description:** A hospital that maintains an acute care center, an emergency care center, and a chemotherapy outpatient center. **NOTE:** Jobseekers may apply online. **Positions advertised include:** Certified Occupational Therapy Assistant; Registered Nurse; Pharmacist. **Special programs:** Internships. **CEO:** Sister Marie Castagnaro. **Number of employees at this location:** 1,100.

ST. LAWRENCE CEMENT
3 Columbia Circle, Albany NY 12203-5158. 518/452-3563. **Contact:** Human Resources. **E-mail address:** hrcorp@ciment.laurent.com. **World Wide Web address:** http://www.stlawrencecement.com. **Description:** A wholesaler and manufacturer of cement. **Corporate headquarters location:** Montreal, Quebec, Canada. **Parent company:** Holcim, Limited. **Number of employees at this location:** 350. **Number of employees worldwide:** 2,800.

ST. LUKE'S CORNWALL HOSPITAL
19 Laurel Avenue, Cornwall NY 12518. 845/534-7711. **Contact:** Human Resources. **E-mail address:** jobs@slh-tch.org. **World Wide Web address:** http://www.ststlukeshospital.org. **Description:** A 125-bed acute care, community-based, nonprofit hospital. St. Luke's Cornwall Hospital has 20 additional beds devoted to mental health care. **NOTE:** Resumes may be mailed to the Human Resources Department, 70 Dubois Street, Newburgh NY 12550. **Positions advertised include:** ASA Counselor; Nutritional Services Associate; Environmental Services Associate; Guest Services Associate; HVAC Technician; Maintenance Associate; Methadone Counselor; Registered Nurse; Occupational Therapist; Patient Accounting Associate; Physical Therapist; Programmer; Security and Safety Officer; Switchboard Operator; Valet Parking Attendant. **Office hours:** Monday – Friday, 8:00 a.m. – 5:00 p.m. **Other area locations:** Newburgh NY. **Number of employees at this location:** 500. **Number of employees statewide:** Over 1,700.

ST. LUKE'S-ROOSEVELT HOSPITAL CENTER
1111 Amsterdam Avenue, New York NY 10025. 212/523-4000. **Contact:** Recruitment. **World Wide Web address:** http://www.wehealnewyork.org. **Description:** A 1,315-bed, teaching hospital associated with Columbia University. **NOTE:** Resumes should be sent to Human Resources, 555 West 57th Street, 19th Floor, New York NY 10019 or faxed to: 212/523-7193. **Positions advertised include:** Nurse Practitioner; Neurophysiology Technician; Occupational Therapist; General Accounting Manager; Nurse Supervisor; Registered Dietician; Expeditor; Director of Safety; Patient Advocate; Medical Biller; Medical Administrative Assistant; Senior Systems Analyst; Nurse Recruiter; Medical Office Coordinator; Nurse Educator; EEG Technician; Senior Financial Analyst; Epilepsy Monitoring Technician. **Special programs:** Internships. **Parent company:** Continuum Health Partners, Inc. **Number of employees at this location:** 6,000.

ST. MARTIN'S PRESS
175 Fifth Avenue, New York NY 10010. 212/674-5151. **Contact:** Human Resources Manager. **E-mail address:** employment.opportunities@hbpub.com. **World Wide Web address:** http://www.stmartins.com. **Description:** A national trade and scholarly book publisher. Founded in 1952. **Positions advertised include:** Editorial Assistant. **Corporate headquarters location:** This location. **Parent company:** Holtzbrinck Publishers. **Number of employees nationwide:** 930.

ST. MARY'S HOSPITAL AT AMSTERDAM
427 Guy Park Avenue, Amsterdam NY 12010. 518/841-7152. **Fax:** 518/841-7158. **Recorded jobline:** 518/841-7155. **Contact:** Human Resources. **E-mail address:** hremp@smha.org. **World Wide Web address:** http://www.smha.org. **Description:** A community hospital that provides acute care as well as both inpatient and outpatient services for mental health and alcoholism treatment. **NOTE:** Interested job seekers may apply online. **Positions advertised include:** Alcoholism Counselor; Certified Nurse Aide; Clinical Systems Coordinator; Certified Coder Analyst; Financial Services Manager; LPN; Pharmacist; Psychiatric Social Worker; Psychiatric Assistant; Radiologic Technologist; Registered Nurse; Sterile Processing Technician; Third Party Payor Representative. **Special programs:** Internships. **Parent company:** Carondelet Health System. **Number of employees at this location:** 850.

ST. PETER'S HEALTHCARE SERVICES
315 South Manning Boulevard, Albany NY 12208. 518/525-1293. **Contact:** Human Resources. **E-mail address:** jobs@stpetershealthcare.org. **World Wide Web address:** http://www.stpetershealthcare.org. **Description:** Provides comprehensive health care services including hospital, primary and preventative care, educational services, addiction services, long-term care, childcare, and rehabilitation services as a member of the Eastern Mercy Health System.

ST. PETER'S HOSPITAL
315 South Manning Boulevard, Albany NY 12208. 518/525-1550. **Contact:** Human Resources. **E-mail address:** jobs@stpetershealthcare.org. **World Wide Web address:** http://www.stpetershealthcare.org. **Description:** A nonprofit general hospital. **Positions advertised include:** Accounting Assistant; Administrative Director of Laboratory Services; Audiologist; Birth Registrar; CT Technologist; Cardiovascular Technologist; Certified Home Health Aide; Clinical Care Coordinator; Clinical Nurse Specialist; Computer Operator; Dietician; Ambulatory Sites Director; Fitness Instructor; Food Service Worker; Hemodialysis Technician; Hospice Patient Care Assistant; Housekeeper; Medical Records Clerk; Laboratory Assistant. **Special programs:** Internships. **Corporate headquarters location:** This location. **Parent company:** St. Peter's Health Care Services.

SAINT-GOBAIN ABRASIVES
2600 10th Avenue, Watervliet NY 12189. 518/266-2200. **Contact:** Human Resources. **World Wide Web address:** http://www.sgabrasives.com. **Description:** This location manufactures coated abrasives. Overall, Saint-Gobain Abrasives manufactures grinding wheels and is one of the world's largest manufacturers of abrasives. The company produces three major types of abrasives: bonded abrasives, also referred to as grinding wheels; coated abrasives, commonly called sandpaper; and superabrasives. Products are sold under several names including Amplex, Carborundum Abrasives, Clipper, Norton, Penhall, and Procut. Founded in 1885. **NOTE:** Interested job seekers may submit resumes online. **Corporate headquarters location:** Worcester MA. **International locations:** Worldwide. **Parent company:** Saint-Gobain Corporation (Valley Forge PA). **Number of employees worldwide:** 16,000.

SAKS FIFTH AVENUE
611 Fifth Avenue, New York NY 10022. 212/753-4000. **Contact:** Employment Manager. **World Wide Web address:** http://www.saksincorporated.com. **Description:** Saks Fifth Avenue is a 62-store chain emphasizing soft-goods products, primarily apparel for men, women, and children. **Special programs:** Internships. **Corporate headquarters location:** Birmingham AL. **Other U.S. locations:** Nationwide. **Parent company:** Saks Incorporated is a department store holding company that operates approximately 360 stores in 36 states. The company's stores include Saks Fifth Avenue, Parisian, Proffit's, Younker's, Herberger's, Carson Pirie Scott, Boston Store, Bergner's, and Off 5th, the company's outlet store. Saks Incorporated also operates two retail catalogs and several retail Internet sites. **Operations at this facility include:** This location is a part of the nationwide specialty department store chain. **Listed on:** New York Stock Exchange. **Stock exchange symbol:** SKS. **Sales/revenue:** $5.9 billion. **Number of employees nationwide:** Approximately 55,000.

SALANT CORPORATION
1114 Avenue of the Americas, 36th Floor, New York NY 10036. 212/221-7500. **Contact:** Human Resources. **World Wide Web address:** http://www.prnewswire.com. **Description:** Designs, manufactures, imports, and markets a broad line of men's, children's, and women's apparel and accessories to retailers. Menswear is the company's largest sales category, with a focus on sportswear, dress shirts, neckwear, slacks, and jeans marketed under the Perry Ellis, J.J. Farmer, Thomson, John Henry, Gant, Manhattan, AXXA, Liberty of London, UNICEF, Peanuts, and Save the Children brand names. The company's children's brands include Joe Boxer, Dr. Denton, Power Rangers, certain Disney characters, and OshKosh B'Gosh. Women's wear includes sportswear marketed under the Made in the Shade brand name. The company's products are sold through department and specialty stores, major discounters, and mass volume retailers. Salant operates six domestic manufacturing facilities and five distribution centers. **Corporate headquarters location:** This location. **CEO/Chairman:** Michael Setola. **Listed on:** New York Stock Exchange. **Stock exchange symbol:** SLT. **Number of employees worldwide:** Over 4,000.

SALOMON SMITH BARNEY
1345 6th Avenue, New York NY 10105. 212/586-5505. **Fax:** 212/307-2879. **Contact:** Human Resources. **World Wide Web address:** http://www.salomonsmithbarney.com. **Description:** An international investment banking, market making, and research firm serving corporations, state, local, and foreign governments, central banks, and other financial institutions. **Corporate headquarters location:** This location. **Parent company:** Citigroup. **Listed on:** New York Stock Exchange. **Stock exchange symbol:** C. **Number of employees worldwide:** Over 40,000.

THE SALVATION ARMY
960 Main Street, Buffalo NY 14202. 716/883-9800. **Contact:** Director of Operations. **World Wide Web address:** http://www.salvationarmy.org. **Description:** A nonprofit organization providing several service programs including day-care centers, programs for people with disabilities, substance abuse programs and tutoring for at-risk students. The Salvation Army targets its programs to assist alcoholics, battered women, drug addicts, the elderly, the homeless, people with AIDS, prison inmates, teenagers, and the unemployed. **Corporate headquarters location:** West Nyack NY. **Other U.S. locations:** Nationwide. **International locations:** Worldwide.

SAMARITAN HOSPITAL
NORTHEAST HEALTH
2212 Burdett Avenue, Troy NY 12180. 518/274-3382. **Fax:** 518/271-3781. **Contact:** Human Resources. **World Wide Web address:** http://www.nehealth.com. **Description:** A hospital. **Positions advertised include:** Adjunct Instructor; Behavioral Health Unit Assistant; Cardiology/Neurology Technician; Clerical Associate; Clinical Dietician; Coder; Patient Accounting Liaison; Console Attendant; Courier; Environmental Services Technician; Interviewer; Laboratory Client Service Specialist; Behavioral Health Manager; Medical Receptionist; Medical Technologist.

SAMARITAN MEDICAL CENTER
830 Washington Street, Watertown NY 13601. 315/785-4000. **Toll-free phone:** 877/888-6138. **Fax:** 315/786-4939. **Contact:** Human Resources. **World Wide Web address:** http://www.samaritanhealth.com. **Description:** A 319-bed acute care hospital and referral center that offers comprehensive medical services. **Positions advertised include:** Certified Nursing Assistant; LPN; Registered Nurse; Nursing Supervisor; Environmental Service Worker; Critical Care Unit Clerk; Clinical Leader; Staff Development Educator; Food Service Worker; Laboratory Technician; Sleep Technician; Medical Technologist; Activities Aide; Data Quality Supervisor; Dosimetrist; Imaging Services Assistant. **Number of employees at this location:** 1,100.

SANBORN MAP COMPANY
629 Fifth Avenue, Pelham NY 10803. 914/738-1649. **Fax:** 914/738-1680. **Contact:** General Manager. **E-mail address:** pelham@sanborn.com. **World Wide Web address:** http://www.sanbornmap.com. **Description:** A mapping and geographical information service, Sanborn Map Company is a data source for AM/FM, GIS, and

environmental investigations. Sanborn's operations are organized through three units: Mapping, Custom Databases, and Environmental Data Services. Mapping involves building footprint maps showing street addresses and building details based on actual field inspections. Sanborn's Environmental Data Services operation uses an archive of maps dating back to 1867 to show building and land use including underground tanks and pipes, types of material stored, and owners and occupants of properties. The company's Custom Databases operation produces databases and designed digital map files based on Sanborn's existing map collection and its current field survey services. Information collected from the field survey services include land and building uses, housing unit counts, building vacancy status, building construction details, and building condition. **Corporate headquarters location:** This location. **Other area locations:** Rochester NY. **Other U.S. locations:** Chesterfield MO; San Antonio TX; Columbus OH; Colorado Springs CO; Charlotte NC. **Operations at this facility include:** Administration; Manufacturing; Research and Development; Sales. **CEO:** Pankaj Desai. **Number of employees at this location:** 35.

SANMINA-SCI CORPORATION
1200 Taylor Road, Owego NY 13827. 607/687-3425. **Fax:** 607/689-5910. **Contact:** Human Resources. **World Wide Web address:** http://www.sanmina.com. **Description:** A high-grade manufacturer of printed circuit boards and back panel assemblies. Sanmina Corporation also produces multilayer, prototypes, and volume orders. **Corporate headquarters location:** San Jose CA. **Other U.S. locations:** Nationwide. **International locations:** Worldwide. **Operations at this facility include:** Administration; Divisional Headquarters; Manufacturing; Research and Development; Sales. **Listed on:** NASDAQ. **Stock exchange symbol:** SANM. **President/COO:** Randy Furr. **Number of employees at this location:** 700. **Number of employees nationwide:** 2,200.

SARA LEE COFFEE AND TEA
500 Mamaroneck Avenue, 5th floor, Harrison NY 10528. 914/670-3300. **Contact:** Personnel. **E-mail address:** recruiting@saralee.com. **World Wide Web address:** http://www.saralee.com. **Description:** Produces a nationally distributed brand of premium coffee. The company also operates a chain of cafes and drive-thru restaurants. **Corporate headquarters location:** Chicago IL. **Other U.S. locations:** Nationwide. **Subsidiaries include:** Cain's Coffee Company; Greenwich Mills Company. **Parent company:** Sara Lee Corporation. **Operations at this facility include:** Administration; Divisional Headquarters; Sales. **Listed on:** New York Stock Exchange. **Stock exchange symbol:** SLE.

SARAH LAWRENCE COLLEGE
One Mead Way, Bronxville NY 10708. 914/395-2315. **Fax:** 914/395-2669. **Contact:** Human Resources. **E-mail address:** admin@slc.edu. **World Wide Web address:** http://www.slc.edu. **Description:** Sarah Lawrence College is a four-year, liberal arts college that emphasizes independent study through undergraduate and graduate programs. Founded in 1926. **Positions advertised include:** Assistant to the Dean of Graduate Studies; Center for Continuing Education Director; Planned Giving Officer; Cognitive Developmental Psychology Professor; Digital Imaging Faculty Member; Director of the Theatre Program; Islamic Studies Professor; Painting Instructor.

SARATOGA HOSPITAL
211 Church Street, Saratoga Springs NY 12866. 518/587-3222. **Fax:** 518/583-8428. **Contact:** Human Resources. **World Wide Web address:** http://www.saratogacare.org. **Description:** A community hospital that maintains an acute care and skilled nursing facility. Founded in 1892. **Positions advertised include:** Director of Food Services; Director of Volunteers; Emergency Room Technician; Environmental Services Associate; Medical Technologist; Mental Health Therapy Assistant; Office Assistant; Office Coordinator; Phlebotomist; Registered Nurse; Registrar; Respiratory Therapist; Secretary/Transcriptionist. **Parent company:** Saratoga Care.

SARATOGA SPRINGS WATER COMPANY
11 Geyser Road, Saratoga Springs NY 12866. 518/584-6363. **Fax:** 518/584-0380. **Contact:** Human Resources. **World Wide Web address:** http://www.saratogaspringwater.com. **Description:** Bottles, markets, and distributes natural spring water. The product line includes six water products, a sparkling water product with bicarbonates added, and noncarbonated spring water. Distributors are primarily located in New York state, the Mid-Atlantic region, and Florida. **Corporate headquarters location:** This location.

HENRY SCHEIN, INC.
135 Duryea Road, Melville NY 11747. 631/843-5500. **Fax:** 631/843-5658. **Contact:** Human Resources. **World Wide Web address:** http://www.henryschein.com. **Description:** Manufactures and distributes dental and medical instruments. Henry Schein, Incorporated serves the dental, medical, and veterinary markets. **Positions advertised include:** Associate Financial Analyst; Veterinary Division Telesales Representative; Hyperion Senior Systems Analyst; Credit and Collections Representative. **Corporate headquarters location:** This location. **Other U.S. locations:** Nationwide. **International locations:** Worldwide. **Operations at this facility include:** Sales. **Listed on:** NASDAQ. **Stock exchange symbol:** HSIC. **President/CEO/Chairman:** Stanley M. Bergman. **Sales/revenue:** $2.8 billion. **Number of employees at this location:** 1,000. **Number of employees nationwide:** 1,700.

SCHENECTADY INTERNATIONAL
2750 Balltown Road, Schenectady NY 12308. 518/370-4200. **Fax:** 518/346-3111. **Contact:** Christine Rockwell, Human Resources Specialist. **World Wide Web address:** http://www.siigroup.com. **Description:** Manufactures a variety of specialty products including resins, polymers, chemicals, and varnishes.

SCHIEFFELIN & SOMERSET COMPANY
2 Park Avenue, 17th Floor, New York NY 10016. 212/251-8200. **Fax:** 212/251-8384. **Contact:** Human Resources. **E-mail address:** hrstaffing@schieffelin-somerset.com. **World Wide Web address:** http://www.schieffelin.com. **Description:** Sells and markets premium alcoholic beverages. **NOTE:** Resumes are requested to be in Microsoft Word format. **Corporate headquarters location:** This location. **Other U.S. locations:** CA; FL; IL; NJ; TX; GA. **Parent company:** MoetHennessyLouisVuitton/Diageo. **Operations at this facility include:** Administration; Sales. **Listed on:** NASDAQ/NYSE. **Stock exchange symbol:** LVMHY/DEO. **Number of employees at this location:** 100. **Number of employees nationwide:** 200.

SCHLEGEL SYSTEMS, INC.
1555 Jefferson Road, Rochester NY 14623. 716/427-7200. **Fax:** 716/427-9993. **Contact:** Human Resources. **World Wide Web address:** http://www.schlegel.com. **Description:** Manufactures a wide range of products including plastics, textiles, polyurethane, weather stripping used around doors and windows, and components for copiers and computers. **Corporate headquarters location:** This location.

SCHLUMBERGER LTD.
153 East 53rd Street, 57th Floor, New York NY 10022. 212/350-9400. **Fax:** 212/350-9457. **Contact:** Human Resources. **World Wide Web address:** http://www.schlumberger.com. **Description:** Schlumberger provides oil field services including logging, testing, seismic, MWD, LWD, drilling, cementing, and stimulation; CAD/CAM; automatic test equipment; electricity, water, and gas metering and measurement; and fuel dispensing and monitoring systems. **Special programs:** Internships. **Corporate headquarters location:** This location. **Other U.S. locations:** TX; NJ. **Listed on:** New York Stock Exchange. **Stock exchange symbol:** SLB. **President/CEO/Chairman:** Andrew Gould. **Sales/revenue:** Over $13 billion. **Number of employees worldwide:** 78,500.

FELIX SCHOELLER TECHNICAL PAPERS INC.
179 County Route 2A, P.O. Box 250, Pulaski NY 13142-0250. 315/298-5133. **Contact:** Rodger Woods, Human Resources Manager. **E-mail address:** people@schoeller.com. **World Wide Web address:** http://www.schoeller.com. **Description:** A paper manufacturing and coating facility. The company manufactures high-quality photographic base papers, inkjet and laser papers, release and casting papers, and fine greeting card papers. Founded in 1963. **NOTE:** All inquiries about hourly positions should be directed to the New York Employment Commission. Resumes for salaried positions may be forwarded to the Industrial Relations Manager at the above address. **Corporate headquarters location:** Thus location. **International locations:** Germany; Britain; Canada. **Parent company:** The Schoeller Group (Osnabrueck, Germany) operates in four divisions: photo, digital imaging, decor, and specialty. **Number of employees at this location:** 325. **Number of employees worldwide:** 2,500.

SCHOLASTIC INC.
557 Broadway, New York NY 10012-3999. 212/343-6912. **Fax:** 212/343-6934. **Contact:** Human Resources. **E-mail address:** jobs@scholastic.com. **World Wide Web address:** http://www.scholastic.com. **Description:** Publishes and distributes children's books, classroom and professional magazines, software, CD-ROMs, and other educational materials. Products are generally distributed directly to both children and teachers in elementary and secondary schools. **Positions advertised include:** Database Marketing Analyst; Sales Support Specialist; InSchool Marketing Sales Manager. **Special programs:** Internships. **NOTE:** Resumes submitted via e-mail must be formatted in Microsoft Word or Adobe PDF. **Corporate headquarters location:** This location. **Other U.S. locations:** Nationwide. **International locations:** Australia; Canada; France; Mexico; New Zealand; United Kingdom. **Operations at this facility include:** Administration; Divisional Headquarters; Manufacturing; Research and Development. **Listed on:** NASDAQ. **Stock exchange symbol:** SCHL. **Sales/revenue:** $434 million. **Number of employees at this location:** 1,400. **Number of employees nationwide:** 5,000.

SCHONFELD SECURITIES
650 Madison Avenue, 20th Floor, New York NY 10022. 212/832-0900. **Contact:** Human Resources. **World Wide Web address:** http://www.schonfeld.com. **Description:** A securities trading firm. **Corporate headquarters location:** New York, NY. **Other area locations:** Purchase NY; Brooklyn NY. **Other U.S. locations:** Paramus NJ; Miami Beach FL; Boca Raton FL; Chicago IL; Houston TX; Los Angeles CA. **Parent company:** Schonfeld Group.

F. SCHUMACHER & COMPANY
79 Madison Avenue, New York NY 10016. 212/213-7900. **Contact:** Director of Employment. **World Wide Web address:** http://www.fschumacher.com. **Description:** A textile wholesaler specializing in rug and fabric trading. **Corporate headquarters location:** This location. **Other U.S. locations:** Nationwide. **President/CEO:** Gerald Puschel.

SCHWEIZER AIRCRAFT CORPORATION
1250 Schweizer Road, Horseheads NY 14845. 607/739-3821. **Fax:** 607/796-2488. **Contact:** Personnel. **World Wide Web address:** http://www.schweizer-aircraft.com. **Description:** A diversified aerospace company that specializes in aircraft production and subcontracting.

SCIENTIFIC AMERICAN, INC.
415 Madison Avenue, New York NY 10017. 212/754-0550. **Contact:** Human Resources. **World Wide Web address:** http://www.sciam.com. **Description:** Publishes an international monthly magazine dealing with recent scientific research. **Special programs:** Internships. **Corporate headquarters location:** This location.

SCIENTIFIC INDUSTRIES, INC.
70 Orville Drive, Bohemia NY 11716. 631/567-4700. **Toll-free phone:** 888/850-6208. **Contact:** Personnel. **World Wide Web address:** http://www.scientificindustries.com. **Description:** Manufactures and markets laboratory equipment including vortex mixers and miscellaneous laboratory apparatuses including timers, rotators, and pumps. The company develops and sells computerized control and data logging systems for sterilizers and autoclaves. Scientific Industries' products are used by hospital laboratories, clinics, research laboratories, pharmaceutical manufacturers, and medical device manufacturers. **Office hours:** Monday – Friday, 9:00 a.m. – 5:00 p.m. **Corporate headquarters location:** This location. **Listed on:** NASDAQ. **Stock exchange symbol:** SCND. **President/CEO:** Helena Santos.

SCUDDER INVESTMENTS
345 Park Avenue, New York NY 10154. 212/326-6200. **Contact:** Human Resources. **World Wide Web address:** http://www.scudder.com. **Description:** An investment firm with principal operations in securities brokerage. **Parent company:** Deutsche Asset Management.

SEARS, ROEBUCK & CO.
1425 Central Avenue, Albany NY 12205. 518/454-3000. **Contact:** Human Resources. **World Wide Web address:** http://www.sears.com. **Description:** A retailer of apparel, home, and automotive products and related services for families throughout North America. **Corporate headquarters location:** Hoffman Estates IL. **Other U.S. locations:** Nationwide. **Operations at this facility include:** One location of the nationwide retail department store chain. **Listed on:** New York Stock Exchange. **Stock exchange symbol:** S. **President/CEO/Chairman:** Alan J. Lacy. **Sales/revenue:** Over $41 billion. **Number of employees nationwide:** 289,000.

SECURITY MUTUAL LIFE INSURANCE COMPANY OF NEW YORK
P.O. Box 1625, Binghamton NY 13902. 607/723-3551. **Physical address:** 100 Court Street, Binghamton NY 13901. **Contact:** Human Resources Director. **World Wide Web address:** http://www.securitymutual-ny.com. **Description:** Provides life insurance. Founded in 1886. **Corporate headquarters location:** New York NY. **Other U.S. locations:** Cape May Point NJ.

SENECA FOODS CORPORATION
3736 South Main Street, Marion NY 14505. 315/926-8100. **Contact:** Human Resources. **World Wide Web address:** http://www.senecafoods.com. **Description:** Seneca Foods produces juice products; various vegetables; and other foods, and sells them to supermarkets and other retail businesses. Products are sold under a variety of brand names including Libby's and Blue Boy. **Corporate headquarters location:** This location. **Other U.S. locations:** ID; MN; WA; WI. **Subsidiaries include:** Seneca Flight Operations provides air charter service primarily to industries located in upstate New York. **Operations at this facility include:** This location houses the administrative offices and is also a vegetable processing plant. **Listed on:** NASDAQ. **Stock exchange symbol:** SENEB.

SENTRY GROUP
900 Linden Avenue, Rochester NY 14625-2784. 585/381-4900. **Toll-free phone:** 800/828-1438. **Fax:** 585/381-8559. **Contact:** Human Resources. **World Wide Web address:** http://www.sentrysafe.com. **Description:** A manufacturer of fireproof safes for the home and office. **Office hours:** Monday – Friday, 8:00 a.m. – 9:00 p.m. **Corporate headquarters location:** This location. **CEO/Chairman:** Douglas F. Brush.

SETON HEALTH SYSTEM
ST. MARY'S HOSPITAL OF TROY
1300 Massachusetts Avenue, Troy NY 12180. 518/268-5525. **Fax:** 518/268-5733. **Contact:** Human Resources. **World Wide Web address:** http://www.setonhealth.org. **Description:** A comprehensive health care system serving the tri-county area. St. Mary's Hospital (also at this location) is the anchor hospital in the Seton Health System. **Positions advertised include:** Nuclear Medicine Technologist; Phlebotomist; Registered Nurse; Respiratory Therapist; Multicraftsman/Construction Worker; Patient Service Representative; LPN. **Corporate headquarters location:** This location.

SEVENSON ENVIRONMENTAL SERVICES, INC.
2749 Lockport Road, Niagara Falls NY 14305-0396. 716/284-0431. **Fax:** 716/284-7645. **Contact:** Joyce Oswald, Human Resources. **World Wide Web address:** http://www.sevenson.com. **Description:** Provides a range of services for the remediation of sites and facilities contaminated by hazardous materials. **Positions advertised include:** Laboratory Technician; Heavy Truck Mechanic. **Corporate headquarters location:** This location. **Other area locations:** Buffalo NY. **Other U.S. locations:** Chadds Ford PA; Delmont PA; Merrillville IN; Long Beach CA. **Subsidiaries include:** Sevenson Environmental, Limited (also at this location); Sevenson Industrial Services, Incorporated (also at this location); Waste Stream Technology Incorporated. **Sales/revenue:** $1.2 billion.

SHEARMAN & STERLING LLP
599 Lexington Avenue, New York NY 10022-6069. 212/848-4000. **Fax:** 212/848-7179. **Contact:** Suzanne Ryan, Professional Recruiting Manager. **E-mail address:** sryann@shearman.com **World Wide Web address:** http://www.shearman.com. **Description:** One of the nation's largest law firms, focusing in a variety of different practice areas. **Corporate headquarters location:** This location.

SHERATON SYRACUSE UNIVERSITY HOTEL
801 University Avenue, Syracuse NY 13210. 315/475-3000. **Fax:** 315/475-2266. **Contact:** Human Resources. **E-mail address:** hr@sheratonsyracuse.com. **World Wide Web address:** http://www.sheratonsyracuse.com. **Description:** A 236-room hotel located on the Syracuse University campus with convenient access to the Carrier Dome and convention center.

SHERWOOD
2111 Liberty Drive, Niagara Falls NY 14304. 716/283-1010. **Contact:** Human Resources. **E-mail address:** swdinfo@harsco.com. **World Wide Web address:** http://www.sherwoodvalve.com. **Description:** Produces precision valves. **Corporate headquarters location:** Camp Hill PA. **Parent company:** Harsco Corporation provides a variety of products and services for the industrial, commercial, and construction market. The defense group provides land defense systems, primarily tracked and wheeled vehicle systems, for the U.S. and other governments. The industrial services and buildings products group includes the metal recovery and steel mill service of Heckett Mulitserv; scaffolding, shoring, and concrete forming equipment; plastic products; rental of plant equipment; roofing granules; and slay abrasives. The engineered products group includes gas control and containment products, grating products, pipe fitting, process equipment, railroad equipment, structural composites, specialty metal fabrications, decorative panels, and wear products. **Listed on:** New York Stock Exchange. **Stock exchange symbol:** HSC.

SHOWTIME NETWORKS INC.
1633 Broadway, New York NY 10019. 212/708-1600. **Contact:** Human Resources. **World Wide Web address:** http://www.mtv.com. **Description:** Operates a number of premium cable networks including SHOWTIME, SHO2, SHO3, Showtime Extreme, Showtime Beyond, The Movie Channel, The Movie Channel 2, Sundance, and FLIX. **Corporate headquarters location:** This location. **Parent company:** Viacom International Incorporated. **Listed on:** New York Stock Exchange. **Stock exchange symbol:** VIA.

SHUBERT ORGANIZATION, INC.
234 West 44th Street, 7th Floor, New York NY 10036. 212/944-3700. **Contact:** Human Resources. **World Wide Wedb address:** http://www.shubertorg.com. **Description:** Owns 16 Broadway theatres, the National Theatre in Washington DC, and the Shubert Theatre in Los Angeles CA. The Shubert Organization also produces plays. **Corporate headquarters location:** This location. **Operations at this facility include:** Administration; Sales. **President:** Phillip Smith. **Sales/revenue:** $325 million. **Number of employees nationwide:** 1,450.

SIEMENS CORPORATION
153 East 53rd Street, 56th Floor, New York NY 10022-4611. 212/258-4000. **Contact:** Human Resources. **World Wide Web address:** http://www.usa.siemens.com. **Description:** Siemens operates internationally through the following groups: power engineering and automation; electrical installations; communications; medical engineering; data systems; and components. **Corporate headquarters location:** This location. **Other U.S. locations:** Nationwide. **Parent company:** Siemens AG (Munich, Germany). **Operations at this facility include:** This location is the United States management and administrative headquarters. **Listed on:** New York Stock Exchange. **Stock exchange symbol:** SI. **President/CEO:** Klaus Kleinfeld. **Sales/revenue:** Over $20 billion. **Number of employees worldwide:** 70,000.

SIENA COLLEGE
515 Loudon Road, Loudonville NY 12211-1462. 518/783-2420. **Contact:** Human Resources. **E-mail address:** humanresources@siena.edu. **World Wide Web address:** http://www.siena.edu. **Description:** A private, co-ed, four-year, liberal arts university. Siena offers several undergraduate degrees in arts, sciences, and business, as well as an MBA in Accounting. **Positions advertised include:** Criminology Professor; Assistant Spanish Professor; Assistant Professor of Marketing and Management; Journalism Faculty Member; Assistant Director of Development; Assistant Director of the Annual Fund; Residence Director; Dispatcher; Purchase Secretary; Technical Support Specialist; Telephone Interviewer.

SIGNAL TRANSFORMER COMPANY, INC.
500 Bayview Avenue, Inwood NY 11096-1792. 516/239-5777. **Fax:** 516/239-7208. **Contact:** Human Resources. **World Wide Web address:** http://www.signaltransformer.com. **Description:** Manufactures and distributes transformers for a wide range of applications, from printed circuit board requirements to rectifiers and chokes. **Office hours:** Monday – Friday, 8:00 a.m. – 6:00 p.m. **Corporate headquarters location:** This location. **Parent company:** Insilco Technologies Group. **Operations at this facility include:** Administration; Manufacturing; Sales.

SIMMONS-BOARDMAN PUBLISHING CORP.
345 Hudson Street, 12th Floor, New York NY 10014. 212/620-7200. **Contact:** Human Resources. **Description:** Publishes trade magazines and books. **Special programs:** Internships. **Corporate headquarters location:** This location. **Operations at this facility include:** Administration; Sales.

SIMPSON THATCHER & BARTLETT LLP
425 Lexington Avenue, New York NY 10017-3954. 212/455-2000. **Fax:** 212/455-2502. **Contact:** Dee Pifer, Director Legal Employment. **E-mail address:** dpifer@stblaw.com. **World Wide Web address:** http://www.stblaw.com. **Description:** One of the nation's largest law firms, focusing in a number of different practice areas. **Corporate headquarters location:** This location. **Other U.S. locations:** Palo Alto CA; Los Angeles CA. **International locations:** England; China; Japan.

SIMON & SCHUSTER, INC.
1230 Avenue of the Americas, New York NY 10020. 212/698-7000. **Fax:** 212/698-7640. **Contact:** Human Resources Department. **E-mail address:** ssjobs1@simonandschuster.com (for positions in the Sales, IS&T, Audio/Interacitve, Online, HR/Facilities, Finance, General, and Administrative departments), ssjobs2@simonandschuster (for positions in the Children's, Production, and Supply Chain departments) and ssjobs3@simonandschuter.com (for positions in the Adult Trade and Legal departments). **World Wide Web address:** http://www.simonandschuster.com. **Description:** Publishes consumer, educational, and professional books. **Positions advertised include:** Associate Manager of Premium Sales; Editorial Assistant; National Account Manager; Online Technical Support Coordinator; Online Customer Data Coordinator; Director of Creative Services; Sales Communication Manager; Associate Producer; Senior Editor; Subsidiary Rights Assistant; Marketing Assistant. **Corporate headquarters location:** This location. **Other U.S. locations:** CA; MA; NJ; OH. **Subsidiaries include:** Macmillan; Prentice-Hall. **Parent company:** Viacom. **Operations at this facility include:** Administration; Marketing; Sales. **Listed on:** New York Stock Exchange. **Stock exchange symbol:** VIA. **Number of employees nationwide:** 4,000.

SIMPLICITY PATTERN COMPANY INC.
2 Park Avenue, 12th Floor, New York NY 10016. 212/372-0500. **Contact:** Personnel Manager. **World Wide Web address:** http://www.simplicity.com. **Description:** A manufacturer of clothing patterns. **Positions advertised include:** Illustrator; Instruction Writer. **Special programs:** Internships. **Corporate headquarters location:** This location. **Operations at this facility include:** Administration.

SITHE ENERGIES, INC.
335 Madison Avenue, 28th Floor, New York NY 10017. 212/351-0000. **Fax:** 212/351-0800. **Contact:** Human Resources. **E-mail address:** info@sithe.com. **World Wide Web address:** http://www.sithe.com. **Description:** Develops, builds, owns, and operates electricity-generating facilities throughout the United States and Canada. Revenues are derived primarily from the sale of electricity produced by natural gas-fired cogeneration plants under long-term agreements with major electric utilities. The company also sells thermal energy to the government, industries, and other users. **Corporate headquarters location:** This location. **International locations:** China; France; Philippines; Thailand. **Sales/revenue:** Approximately $1 billion. **Number of employees at this location:** 220.

SKADDEN, ARPS, SLATE, MEAGHER, & FLOM, LLP
Four Times Square, New York NY 10036. 212/735-3000. **Fax:** 212/735-2000. **Contact:** Wallace Schwartz. **World Wide Web address:** http://www.skadden.com. **Description:** One of the nation's largest law firms, focusing in many different areas of practice. **Corporate headquarters location:** This location

SKIDMORE COLLEGE
815 North Broadway, Saratoga Springs NY 12866-1632. 518/580-5800. **Fax:** 518/580-5805. **Contact:** Human Resources. **E-mail address:** jobs@skidmore.edu. **World Wide Web address:** http://www.skidmore.edu. **Description:** A private, four-year liberal arts college that offers both bachelor's and master's degrees. Founded in 1903. **Positions advertised include:** Director of Multicultural Student Affairs; Community Coordinator; Visiting Assistant Professor; Postdoctoral Fellow; Teaching Associate; Biology Instructor; History Lecturer; Trustee Visiting Scholar; Assistant Professor of Philosophy; Head Women's Soccer Coach.

SLANT/FIN CORPORATION
100 Forest Drive, Greenvale NY 11548. 516/484-2600. **Contact:** Human Resources. **E-mail address:** info@slantfin.com. **World Wide Web address:** http://www.slantfin.com. **Description:** Engaged in the manufacture and sale of heating and cooling equipment for both domestic and foreign markets. **Corporate headquarters location:** This location. **International locations:** Canada. **Number of employees worldwide:** 600.

SLATTERY SKANSKA INC.
16-16 Whitestone Expressway, Whitestone NY 11357. 718/767-2600. **Fax:** 718/767-2668. **Contact:** Larry Bolyard, Director of Human Resources Department. **E-mail address:** larry.bolyard@slattery.skanska.com. **World Wide Web address:** http://www.slatteryskanska.com. **Description:** A heavy construction firm engaged in large-scale projects such as mass transit, sewage treatment plants, highways, bridges, and tunnels. **Positions advertised include:** Estimator; Superintendent; Project Engineer. **Office hours:** Monday - Friday, 8:00 a.m. - 4:30 p.m. **Corporate headquarters location:** This location. **Parent company:** Skanska USA. **Operations at this facility include:** Administration. **Number of employees at this location:** 1,000.

SOFTWARE ETC.
1120 Avenue of the Americas, New York NY 10036. 212/921-7855. **Contact:** Store Manager. **World Wide Web address:** http://www.software-etc.com. **Description:** Retails computer software, hardware, video games, accessories, and books. **Corporate**

headquarters location: Dallas TX. **Other U.S. locations:** Nationwide. **International locations:** Worldwide. **Parent company:** Babbage's Etc.

SONY PICTURES ENTERTAINMENT
550 Madison Avenue, 7th Floor, New York NY 10022. 212/833-8500. **Fax:** 212/833-6249. **Contact:** Kathleen Alvarez, Human Resources Supervisor. **World Wide Web address:** http://www.sonypictures.com. **Description:** Sony Pictures is involved in motion pictures, television, theatrical exhibitions, and studio facilities and technology. The motion picture business distributes movies produced by Columbia TriStar Pictures. The television business, which encompasses Columbia TriStar Television, Columbia TriStar Television Distribution, and Columbia TriStar International Television, is involved with numerous cable channels and distributes and syndicates television programs such as *Days of Our Lives* and *Dawson's Creek*. Loews Cineplex Entertainment operates state-of-the-art theaters in 385 locations with 2,926 screens in 15 states. Sony Pictures Imageworks specializes in motion picture special effects and production planning through revisualization sequences. **Positions advertised include:** Administrative Assistant; Publicity Breaks Coordinator. **Special programs:** Internships. **Internship information:** Sony Pictures Entertainment offers various fall, spring, and summer internships in its Manhattan and Inwood, Long Island offices. Students must be available to work 15 to 21 hours per week. Majors in film, communications, management, and marketing are a plus, but all majors are welcome. Applicants must have basic office experience, excellent writing skills, and good interpersonal skills. Most internships are for academic credit, but some offer pay or a weekly stipend. **Office hours:** Monday – Friday, 9:00 a.m. – 5:00 p.m. **Corporate headquarters location:** Culver City CA. **Parent company:** Sony Corporation of America. **Operations at this facility include:** Administration; Sales. **Listed on:** New York Stock Exchange. **CEO/Chairman:** John Calley. **Sales/revenue:** $4.8 billion. **Stock exchange symbol:** SNE. **Number of employees at this location:** 100.

SOUTH BEACH PSYCHIATRIC CENTER
777 Seaview Avenue, Staten Island NY 10305. 718/667-2726. **Fax:** 718/667-2467. **Contact:** Human Resources. **World Wide Web address:** http://www.omh.state.ny.us. **Description:** South Beach Psychiatric Center is a New York State Office of Mental Health outpatient facility that is organized to deliver comprehensive mental health services to people in West Brooklyn, Staten Island, and New York City. **Positions advertised include:** Licensed Psychologist; Mental Health Therapy Aide; Nurse Administrator; Community Mental Health Nurse; Psychiatrist; Director of Nursing. **Corporate headquarters location:** Albany NY. **Operations at this facility include:** Administration. **Number of employees at this location:** 1,100.

SOUTH STREET SEAPORT MUSEUM
207 Front Street, New York NY 10038. 212/748-8600. **Fax:** 212/748-8610. **Contact:** Director of Human Resources Department. **World Wide Web address:** http://www.southstseaport.org. **Description:** A maritime history museum. Through educational programs, exhibitions, and the preservation of buildings and ships, the museum interprets the role of the seaport in the development of the city, state, and nation. Founded in 1967. **Special programs:** Internships.

SOUTHWORTH-MILTON
294 Ainslay Drive, Syracuse NY 13205. 315/703-7022. **Fax:** 315/476-0660**Contact:** Jill Parcels, Human Resources. **E-mail address:** jill_parcels@smilton.com. **World Wide Web address:** http://www.southworth-milton.cat.com. **Description:** Sale and lease of Caterpillar brand heavy machinery. . **Corporate headquarters location:** This location. **Number of employees at this location:** 30.

SPELLMAN HIGH VOLTAGE ELECTRONICS CORPORATION
475 Wireless Boulevard, Hauppauge New York 11788. 631/630-3000. **Fax:** 631-630-3008. **Contact:** Human Resources. **E-mail address:** hr@spellmanhv.com. **World Wide Web address:** http://www.spellmanhv.com. **Description:** A manufacturer of high voltage dc power supplies, X-ray generators, and Monoblock X-ray sources. **Positions advertised include:** Engineering Technician; Test Technician; Electro/Mechanical Inspector; Power Supply Design Engineer.

SPRINGER-VERLAG NEW YORK, INC.
175 Fifth Avenue, New York NY 10010. 212/460-1500. **Fax:** 212/473-6272. **Contact:** Human Resources. **World Wide Web address:** http://www.springeronline.com. **Description:** An international publisher of scientific, technical, and medical books, journals, magazines, and electronic media. Founded in 1842. **Special programs:** Internships; Co-ops. **Corporate headquarters location:** This location. **Parent company:** BertelsmannSpringer.

SPRINGS INDUSTRIES, INC.
104 West 40th Street, New York NY 10018. 212/556-6000. **Contact:** Human Resources. **E-mail address:** springsjobs@springs.com. **World Wide Web address:** http://www.springs.com. **Description:** Produces a wide range of finished apparel fabrics, consumer fashion fabrics, and retail and specialty fabrics. **Special programs:** Production Management Program. **Corporate headquarters location:** Fort Mills SC. **Other U.S. locations:** Nationwide. **International locations:** Canada; Mexico. **Operations at this facility include:** Divisional Headquarters; Regional Headquarters; Sales. **CEO/Chairman:** Crandall Bowles. **Number of employees worldwide:** 17,000.

SQUIRE SANDERS & DEMPSEY
350 Park Avenue, 15th Floor, New York NY 10022-6022. 212/872-9800. **Fax:** 212/872-9815. **Contact:** Nancy Christopher, Office Manager. **World Wide Web address:** http://www.ssd.com. **Description:** A law firm whose areas of practice include corporate, environmental, and tax law.

STANDARD & POOR'S CORPORATION
55 Water Street, 37th Floor, New York NY 10041. 212/438-2000. **Contact:** Human Resources. **World Wide Web address:** http://www.standardandpoors.com. **Description:** Publishes the Standard & Poor's Register and a number of other financial information products. **Parent company:** McGraw-Hill, Inc. **Listed on:** New York Stock Exchange. **Stock exchange symbol:** MHP.

STANDARD FOLDING CARTONS
85th Street & 24th Avenue, Jackson Heights NY 11370. 718/335-5500. **Fax:** 718/507-6430. **Contact:** Human Resources. **Description:** A manufacturer of folding boxes. **Corporate headquarters location:** This location.

STANDARD MANUFACTURING COMPANY INC.
750 Second Avenue, Troy NY 12182. 518/235-2200 ext. 119. **Contact:** Human Resources. **Description:** Standard Manufacturing Company manufactures men's and women's outerwear.

STANDARD MICROSYSTEMS CORPORATION
80 Arkay Drive, P.O. Box 18047, Hauppauge NY 11788. 631/435-6000. **Fax:** 631/435-0373. **Contact:** Human Resources. **E-mail address:** jobsny@smsc.com. **World Wide Web address:** http://www.smsc.com. **Description:** This location houses the VLSI circuit design and LAN hub and switch engineering centers, marketing, customer support, and wafer fabrication, as well as operations and administrative staff. The company's Component Products Division supplies MOS/VLSI circuits for personal computers and embedded control systems. These include input/output devices for disk drive control, communications interface, power management and other PC motherboard functions, Ethernet and Fast Ethernet controllers for local area network applications, and ARCNET controllers for embedded networking applications. The System Products Division provides a broad range of networking solutions for scaling, managing, and controlling LANs. Its products include network adapters, hubs, switches, and network management software. This division has an installed base of over 12 million nodes. Standard Microsystems uses internally developed integrated circuits. Founded in 1971. **Positions advertised include:** Design Engineer; Product Engineer; Design Automation Engineer. **Special programs:** Internships. **Corporate headquarters location:** This location. **Other U.S. locations:** Irvine CA; San Jose CA; Danvers MA; Austin TX. **International locations:** Worldwide. **Listed on:** NASDAQ. **Stock exchange symbol:** SMSC. **Annual sales/revenues:** More than $100 million. **Number of employees at this location:** 500. **Number of employees worldwide:** 800.

STANDARD MOTOR PRODUCTS INC.
37-18 Northern Boulevard, Long Island City NY 11101. 718/392-0200. **Contact:** Recruiting. **World Wide Web address:** http://www.smpcorp.com. **Description:** Engaged primarily in the manufacture of electrical and fuel system automotive replacement parts sold internationally under the Standard Blue Streak, Hygrade, Champ, and Four Seasons brand names. Products include ignition parts, automotive wire and cable parts, carburetor parts and kits, general service auto parts (radio antennas, gasoline cans, brooms and brushes, polishing cloths, fuses, and other auto accessories), and automotive heating and air conditioning systems. **Corporate headquarters location:** This location. **International locations:** Canada; Hong Kong; Puerto Rico. **Listed on:** New York Stock Exchange. **Stock exchange symbol:** SMP. **Number of employees worldwide:** 3,500.

STARBUCKS COFFEE
757 Third Avenue, New York NY 10017. 212/715-9884. **Contact:** Human resources. **World Wide Web address:** http://www.starbucks.com. **Description:** A worldwide retail gourmet coffee chain **NOTE:** Retail and corporate positions are available. **Corporate headquarters location:** Seattle WA **Listed on:** NASDAQ. **Stock exchange symbol:** SBUX.

STARWOOD HOTELS & RESORTS WORLDWIDE, INC.
1111 Westchester Avenue, White Plains NY 10604. 914/640-8100. **Fax:** 914/640-8310. **Contact:** Personnel. **World Wide Web address:** http://www.starwoodhotels.com. **Description:** Manages and operates hotels under the names Westin, Sheraton, Four Points, St. Regis, and others. **Corporate headquarters location:** This location. **Listed on:** New York Stock Exchange. **Stock exchange symbol:** HOT.

STATE UNIVERSITY OF NEW YORK AT ALBANY
1215 Western Avenue, UAB Room 300, Albany NY 12222. 518/437-4700. **Contact:** Human Resources. **World Wide Web address:** http://www.albany.edu. **Description:** A four-year university, offering a bachelor of arts degree, a bachelor of science degree, as well as master's and doctoral programs. Enrollment is approximately 12,000 undergraduate and 5,000 graduate students.

STATE UNIVERSITY OF NEW YORK AT BINGHAMTON
P.O. Box 6000, Binghamton NY 13902-6000. 607/777-2186. **Contact:** Human Resources. **World Wide Web address:** http://www.binghamton.edu. **Description:** A four-year undergraduate and graduate university. SUNY at Binghamton offers the following degree programs: Bachelor of Arts, Bachelor of Science, master's, MBA, and doctoral. Enrollment is approximately 9,400 undergraduate and 3,000 graduate students.

STATE UNIVERSITY OF NEW YORK AT BROCKPORT
350 New Campus Drive, Brockport NY 14420-2974. 716/395-2468. **Contact:** Human Resources. **World Wide Web address:** http://www.brockport.edu. **Description:** One of 13 four-year colleges in the State University of New York (SUNY) system.

STATE UNIVERSITY OF NEW YORK AT CORTLAND
P.O. Box 2000, Cortland NY 13045. 607/753-2302. **Contact:** Joanne Barry, Director of Human Resources. **World Wide Web address:** http://www.cortland.edu. **Description:** A four-year, undergraduate and graduate university offering the following degree programs: Bachelor of Arts, Bachelor of Science, master's, and first professional. Enrollment is approximately 6,000 undergraduate and 1,400 graduate students.

STATE UNIVERSITY OF NEW YORK AT FREDONIA
280 Central Avenue, 510 Maytum Hall, Fredonia NY 14063. 716/673-3434. **Fax:** 716/673-3210. **Contact:** Human Resources. **World Wide Web address:** http://www.fredonia.edu. **Description:** SUNY at Fredonia is a four-year, graduate and undergraduate university offering the following degree programs: Bachelor of Arts, Bachelor of Science, and master's. Enrollment is approximately 4,300 undergraduate and 300 graduate students.

STATE UNIVERSITY OF NEW YORK AT GENESEO
One College Circle, Geneseo NY 14454. 716/245-5616. **Contact:** Human Resources. **World Wide Web address:** http://www.geneseo.edu. **Description:** One of 13 four-year colleges in the SUNY system. Geneseo offers 52 degree programs ranging from comparative literature to computer science. The degrees offered by the college include Bachelor of Arts, Bachelor of Science, and Bachelor of Science in education, Master of Arts, and Master of Science in education. Founded in 1867.

STATE UNIVERSITY OF NEW YORK AT NEW PALTZ
Human Resources Department, 75 South Manheim Boulevard, Suite 9, New Paltz NY 12561-2433. 845/257-3171. **Contact:** Director, Human Resources. **World Wide Web address:** http://www.newpaltz.edu. **Description:** SUNY at New Paltz offers bachelor's, master's, and doctoral degrees. The university has over 9,000 students. Founded in 1828.

STATE UNIVERSITY OF NEW YORK AT OSWEGO
410 Culkin Hall, Oswego NY 13126. 315/312-2500. **Contact:** Marta Santiago, Personnel Department. **World Wide Web address:** http://www.oswego.edu. **Description:** SUNY at Oswego is a four-year graduate and undergraduate university offering bachelor's, master's, and first professional degrees. Enrollment is approximately 7,000 undergraduate and 700 graduate students.

STATE UNIVERSITY OF NEW YORK AT STONY BROOK
390 Administration, Stony Brook NY 11794-0751. 631/689-6151. **Fax:** 631/632-1351. **Recorded jobline:** 631/632-9222. **Contact:** Rebecca West, Human Resources. **World**

Wide Web address: http://www.sunysb.edu/hr. **Description:** A state university that offers bachelor's, master's, and doctoral degrees. The university has over 17,000 students enrolled. Founded in 1957.

STATE UNIVERSITY OF NEW YORK COLLEGE OF ENVIRONMENTAL SCIENCE AND FORESTRY
One Forestry Drive, Syracuse NY 13210. 315/470-6500. **Contact:** Elaine Irvin, Personnel Department Manager. **World Wide Web address:** http://www.esf.edu. **Description:** One of 13 four-year colleges in the SUNY system with an enrollment of approximately 1,800 students. The college offers the following areas of study: engineering, forest resources, chemistry, environmental and forest biology, environmental studies, environmental science, forest engineering, forestry, landscape architecture, and wood products engineering. Founded in 1911.

STATE UNIVERSITY OF NEW YORK DOWNSTATE MEDICAL CENTER UNIVERSITY HOSPITAL AND HEALTH SCIENCE CENTER AT BROOKLYN
151 East 34th Street, Room 103, Brooklyn NY 11203. 718/270-1000. **Physical address:** 450 Clarkson Avenue, Brooklyn NY 11203. **Fax:** 718/270-1815. **Contact:** Human Resources. **Wide Web address:** http://www.hscbklyn.edu. **Description:** An academic medical center that includes colleges of medicine, nursing, and health-related professions and a school of graduate studies as well as University Hospital of Brooklyn.

STATE UNIVERSITY OF NEW YORK EMPIRE STATE COLLEGE
One Union Avenue, Saratoga Springs NY 12866-4391. 518/587-2100. **Fax:** 518/587-5448. **Contact:** Human Resources. **E-mail address:** hr@esc.edu. **World Wide Web address:** http://www.esc.edu. **Description:** A college of arts and sciences and a leader in providing educational options for adult students. Empire State College was created to serve students who need alternatives to a fixed schedule and programming structure of campus-based education. The college offers 11 baccalaureate and associate areas of study and four graduate programs. Empire State College is a statewide institution with over 40 locations throughout New York, and is part of the State University of New York system. Empire State College enrolls over 10,000 students. Founded in 1971.

STATE UNIVERSITY OF NEW YORK INSTITUTE OF TECHNOLOGY AT UTICA/ROME
P.O. Box 3050, Utica NY 13504-3050. 315/792-7100. **Physical address:** Horatio Street, Route 12, Utica NY 13502. **Contact:** Human Resources Department. **World Wide Web address:** http://www.sunyit.edu. **Description:** Serves as an upper level extension for two-year institutions throughout New York State. SUNY Institute of Technology enrolls approximately 1,370 full-time and 845 part-time students. The college offers the following bachelor's degrees: professional studies, technology, science, arts, and business administration. Founded in 1966.

STATEN ISLAND ADVANCE
950 Fingerboard Road, Staten Island NY 10305. 718/981-1234. **Contact:** Richard Diamond, Publisher. **World Wide Web address:** http://www.silive.com/advance. **Description:** Publishes the *Staten Island Advance,* a daily local newspaper. The paper has a weekday circulation of 80,000 and a Sunday circulation of 95,000. Founded in 1886. **Corporate headquarters location:** This location. **Parent company:** Newhouse Newspapers Group. **Number of employees at this location:** 450.

STATEN ISLAND INSTITUTE OF ARTS AND SCIENCES
75 Stuyvesant Place, Staten Island NY 10301. 718/727-1135. **Fax:** 718/273-5683. **Contact:** Human Resources. **Description:** An organization that focuses on Staten Island and its people with strong collections in arts and sciences. Founded in 1881.

STEINWAY & SONS
One Steinway Place, Long Island City NY 11105. 718/721-2600. **Contact:** Michael Anesta, Director of Personnel. **World Wide Web address:** http://www.steinway.com. **Description:** A manufacturer and distributor of pianos.

STELLEX MONITOR AEROSPACE CORPORATION
1000 New Horizons Boulevard, Amityville NY 11701-1181. 631/957-2300. **Contact:** Richard Dallari, Human Resources. **E-mail address:** dallari@monair.com. **World Wide Web address:** http://www.monair.com. **Description:** Manufactures precision structural aerospace parts and assemblies for commercial and military aircraft. **Parent company:** Stellex Aerostructures, Inc.

STERIS-ISOMEDIX SERVICES
23 Elizabeth Drive, Chester NY 10918. 845/469-4087. **Contact:** Human Resources. **World Wide Web address:** http://www.steris.com/isomedix. **Description:** Provides contract sterilization services to manufacturers of prepackaged health care and consumer products.

STERLING NATIONAL BANK & TRUST COMPANY
148 West 37th Street, New York NY 10018. 212/760-9610. **Fax:** 212/490-8852. **Contact:** Human Resources. **E-mail address:** hrresumes@sterlingbancorp.com. **World Wide Web address:** http://www.sterlingbancorp.com. **Description:** A full-service commercial bank offering a complete range of corporate and individual services. **Corporate headquarters location:** This location. **Parent company:** Sterling Bancorp. **Listed on:** New York Stock Exchange. **Stock exchange symbol:** STL.

STERLING PUBLISHING COMPANY
387 Park Avenue South, New York NY 10016. 212/532-7160. **Contact:** Human Resources. **World Wide Web address:** http://www.sterlingpub.com. **Description:** Publishes a wide variety of how-to books.

STEWART'S ICE CREAM COMPANY, INC.
P.O. Box 435, Saratoga Springs NY 12866. 518/581-1000. **Physical address:** 2907 Route 9, Ballston Spa NY 12020. **Fax:** 518/581-1209. **Contact:** Human Resources. **World Wide Web address:** http://www.stewartsshops.com. **Description:** A manufacturer of ice cream and other dairy products. The company also makes soda.

L&JG STICKLEY INC.
One Stickley Drive, P.O. Box 480, Manlius NY 13104. 315/682-5500. **Fax:** 315/682-0711. **Contact:** Human Resources. **World Wide Web address:** http://www.stickley.com. **Description:** A manufacturing facility and furniture showroom. L&JG Stickley Inc. manufactures dining room, living room, and office furniture, as well as tables and desks for craftspeople. The company maintains five other locations in New York in addition to several dealerships outside of the state. Founded in 1900. **Positions advertised include:** Storeroom General Manager. **International locations:** Worldwide.

STIEFEL LABORATORIES INC.
Route 145, Building 6290, Oak Hill NY 12460. 518/239-6901. **Contact:** Human Resources. **World Wide Web address:** http://www.stiefel.com. **Description:** This location is the research and manufacturing headquarters. Overall, Stiefel Laboratories Inc. is engaged in the manufacture, research, sale, and distribution of medicated skin products. **International locations:** Worldwide.

STRIPPIT INC.
12975 Clarence Center Road, Akron NY 14001. 716/542-4511. **Fax:** 716/542-5957. **Contact:** Human Resources. **E-mail address:** info@strippit.com. **World Wide Web address:** http://www.strippit.com. **Description:** Manufactures metal fabricating machines. **Number of employees at this location:** 450.

STROBER BROTHERS, INC.
Pier 3, Furman Street, Brooklyn NY 11201. 718/875-9700. **Fax:** 718/246-3080. **Contact:** Human Resources. **World Wide Web address:** http://www.strober.com. **Description:** Strober Organization, Inc. is a supplier of building materials to professional building contractors in the residential, commercial, and renovation construction markets. The company operates 10 building centers across four states, offering a broad selection of gypsum wallboard and other drywall products, lumber, roofing, insulation and acoustical materials, plywood, siding products, metal specialties, hardware and tools, waterproofing, masonry, and steel decking products. The building centers also offer a full spectrum of millwork. Founded in 1912. **Corporate headquarters location:** This location.

STRONG MUSEUM
One Manhattan Square, Rochester NY 14607. 716/263-2700. **Fax:** 716/263-2493. **Contact:** Personnel. **World Wide Web address:** http://www.strongmuseum.com. **Description:** A public educational institution that collects, preserves, and interprets historic artifacts, manuscripts, and other materials that tell the story of everyday life in America after 1820 with a special concentration on the Northeast during the era of industrialization.

SUDLER & HENNESSEY INC.
230 Park Avenue South, New York NY 10003-1566. 212/614-4100. **Contact:** Roger Gilmore, Human Resources. **E-mail address:** roger_Gilmore@nyc.sudler.com. **World Wide Web address:** http://www.sudler.com. **Description:** An advertising agency. **NOTE:** Available positions can also be viewed at http://www.hotjobs.com. **Corporate headquarters location:** This location.

SUFFOLK BANCORP
P.O. Box 9000, 6 West Second Street, Riverhead NY 11901. 631/727-2700. **Contact:** Human Resources. **E-mail address:** info@scnb.com. **World Wide Web address:** http://www.suffolkbancorp.com. **Description:** Suffolk Bancorp is engaged in the commercial banking business through its subsidiary, Suffolk County National Bank. The bank is one of the largest independent banks headquartered on Long Island. Founded in 1890. **Subsidiaries include:** Island Computer Corporation.

SUFFOLK COOPERATIVE LIBRARY SYSTEM
627 North Sunrise Service Road, Bellport NY 11713. 631/286-1600. **Contact:** Dorothy Curto, Human Resources Specialist. **World Wide Web address:** http://www.suffolk.lib.ny.us. **Description:** A county-chartered library association that provides a variety of support services to the 52 libraries comprising the Suffolk County library system. **Corporate headquarters location:** This location.

SULZER-METCO INC.
1101 Prospect Avenue, Westbury NY 11590-0201. 516/334-1300. **Contact:** Human Resources. **E-mail address:** hr-us@sulzermetco.com. **World Wide Web address:** http://www.sulzermetco.com. **Description:** Develops a thermal spray coating process that is used on industrial surfaces to increase resistance. **Positions advertised include:** Technical Engineer. **International locations:** Germany; the Netherlands; Switzerland.

SUNBURST TECHNOLOGY
101 Castleton Street, Suite 201, Pleasantville NY 10570. 914/747-3310. **Contact:** Human Resources. **E-mail address:** hr-us@sunburst.com. **World Wide Web address:** http://www.sunburst.com. **Description:** Develops and markets educational videos and software. **Special programs:** Internships. **Office hours:** Monday - Friday, 8:00 a.m. - 5:00 p.m. **Corporate headquarters location:** This location. **Annual sales/revenues:** $21 - $50 million. **Number of employees at this location:** 150.

SUPERIOR PRINTING INK COMPANY, INC.
70 Bethune Street, New York NY 10014-1768. 212/741-3600. **Contact:** Human Resources. **World Wide Web address:** http://www.superiorink.com. **Description:** Manufactures inks and pigments used in lithographic and other printing processes.

THE SUTHERLAND GROUP, LTD.
1160 Pittsford-Victor Road, Pittsford NY 14534. 716/586-5757. **Fax:** 716/784-2212. **Contact:** Manager of Employment Development. **World Wide Web address:** http://www.suth.com. **Description:** A marketing and technology services company that develops customer management programs for *Fortune* 500 companies in information technology, telecommunications, education, and legal industries. **Positions advertised include:** Consultant; Sales and Marketing Associate; Inside Sales Representative; Customer Service Representative; Help Desk Representative. **Corporate headquarters location:** Rochester NY. **Number of employees at this location:** 500.

SWANK INC.
90 Park Avenue, 13th Floor, New York NY 10016. 212/867-2600. **Contact:** Office Manager. **World Wide Web address:** http://www.swankaccessories.com. **Description:** Swank is a manufacturer and distributor of men's and women's jewelry. **Corporate headquarters location:** This location. **Operations at this facility include:** This location houses the executive, national, and international sales offices.

SWISSPORT USA
JFK International Airport, Building 151, East Hanger Road, Jamaica NY 11430. 718/995-8405. **Fax:** 718/244-7560. **Contact:** Human Resources Department. **World Wide Web address:** http://www.swissportusa.com. **Description:** Provides a wide range of ground-handling services for airlines and airports. Services include maintenance, inspections, spare parts inventory, into-plane fueling, cargo handling, cabin cleaning, and ramp services. Swissport USA also operates reservation centers for airlines. **Parent company:** Alpha Airports Group.

SYMBOL TECHNOLOGIES INC.
One Symbol Plaza, Holtsville NY 11742-1300. 631/738-2400. **Contact:** Human Resources. **E-mail address:** jobopps@symbol.com. **World Wide Web address:** http://www.symbol.com. **Description:** Symbol Technologies designs, manufactures, and markets integrated products based on barcode laser scanning, hand-held computing, and wireless LANs. **Positions advertised include:** Senior Manager. **Corporate headquarters location:** Costa Mesa CA. **Operations at this facility include:** This location manufactures barcode and data capture equipment. **Listed on:** New York Stock Exchange. **Stock exchange symbol:** SBL.

SYRACUSE NEWSPAPER
Clinton Square, P.O. Box 4915, Syracuse NY 13221-4915. 315/470-6082. **Fax:** 315/470-6001. **Contact:** Human Resources. **World Wide Web address:** http://www.syracuse.com. **Description:** A publisher of morning, afternoon, and Sunday newspapers, including *the Syracuse Herald-Journal*, *The Post-Standard*, and *Herald American*. Founded in 1840.

SYRACUSE UNIVERSITY
Skytop Office Building, Syracuse NY 13244. 315/443-4042. **Contact:** Human Resources. **World Wide Web address:** http://www.syr.edu. **Description:** A university with an enrollment of approximately 12,000 undergraduate and 5,000 graduate students. Syracuse University offers bachelor's and master's degrees, J.D.s, and Ph.D.s.

SYSKA HENNESSY GROUP
11 West 42nd Street, New York NY 10036-2300. 212/921-2300. **Contact:** Human Resources. **E-mail address:** info@syska.com. **World Wide Web address:** http://www.syska.com. **Description:** An electrical engineering company. **Positions advertised include:** Senior Mechanical Engineer.

SYSTEMAX INC.
11 Harbor Park Drive, Port Washington NY 11050. 516/608-7000. **Fax:** 516/608-7111. **Contact:** Human Resources. **E-mail address:** recruiting@systemax.com. **World Wide Web address:** http://www.systemax.com. **Description:** A direct marketer of brand-name and private-label computer, office, and industrial products targeting mid-range and major corporate accounts, small office/home customers, and value-added resellers. Founded in 1949. **Positions advertised include:** Inside Sales Representative. **Special programs:** Internships; Summer Jobs. **Corporate headquarters location:** This location. **Other U.S. locations:** CA; FL; GA; IL; NJ; NC; OH. **Subsidiaries include:** Global Computer Supplies; Midwest Micro Corp.; Misco America, Inc.; Misco Canada Inc.; TigerDirect Inc. **Listed on:** New York Stock Exchange. **Stock exchange symbol:** SYX. **Annual sales/revenues:** More than $100 million. **Number of employees at this location:** 500. **Number of employees nationwide:** 2,000. **Number of employees worldwide:** 4,000.

T&L AUTOMATICS INC.
770 Emerson Street, Rochester NY 14613. 716/647-3717. **Fax:** 716/647-1126. **Contact:** Human Resources. **Description:** A manufacturer of aluminum shop fittings. **Corporate headquarters location:** This location. **Number of employees at this location:** 20.

TASA (TOUCHSTONE APPLIED SCIENCE ASSOCIATES, INC.)
P.O. Box 382, 4 Hardscrabble Heights, Brewster NY 10509-0382. 845/277-8100. **Fax:** 845/277-3548. **Contact:** Human Resources. **E-mail address:** tasa@tasa.com. **World Wide Web address:** http://www.tasa.com. **Description:** TASA designs, develops, publishes, and distributes educational tests, instructional materials, and microcomputer software to elementary and secondary schools, colleges, and universities. The educational tests, known as Primary, Standard, and Advanced Degrees of Reading Power tests and Degrees of Word Meaning tests, are components on the company's Degrees of Literacy Power program. **Corporate headquarters location:** This location.

TBWA/CHIAT/DAY
488 Madison Avenue, 7th Floor, New York NY 10022. 212/804-1000. **Fax:** 212/804-1200. **Contact:** Human Resources. **E-mail address:** resumes@tbwachiat.com. **World Wide Web address:** http://www.tbwachiat.com. **Description:** An advertising agency.

TD WATERHOUSE SECURITIES, INC.
100 Wall Street, New York NY 10005. 212/806-3500. **Contact:** Human Resources. **E-mail address:** careers@tdwaterhouse.com. **World Wide Web address:** http://www.tdwaterhouse.com. **Description:** TD Waterhouse Securities, Inc. provides brokerage and banking services for individuals that manage their own investments and financial affairs. **Positions advertised include:** Surveillance Manager; Institutional Sales Representative; Credit Analyst; Investment Consultant. **Corporate headquarters location:** This location. **Other U.S. locations:** Nationwide. **Parent company:** TD Waterhouse Investor Services. **Operations at this facility include:** Administration; Divisional Headquarters; Regional Headquarters; Service. **Listed on:** New York Stock Exchange. **Number of employees at this location:** 250. **Number of employees nationwide:** 800.

TIAA-CREF
730 Third Avenue, New York NY 10017-3206. 212/490-9000. **Contact:** Human Resources. **World Wide Web address:** http://www.tiaa-cref.org. **Description:** Provides insurance and investment options for current and retired teachers. **Corporate headquarters location:** This location.

TSR INC.
400 Oser Avenue, Suite 150, Hauppauge NY 11788. 631/231-0333. **Contact:** Recruiter. **World Wide Web address:** http://www.tsrconsulting.com. **Description:** Provides computer consulting services. **Positions advertised include:** Data Analyst; Senior Developer Programmer/Analyst; Senior Business Analyst; Rational Administrator; Centura/Oracle Developer. **Corporate headquarters location:** This location. **Listed on:** NASDAQ. **Stock exchange symbol:** TSRI.

TV GUIDE
1211 Avenue of the Americas, 4th Floor, New York NY 10036. 212/852-7500. **Contact:** Human Resources. **World Wide Web address:** http://www.tvguide.com. **Description:** Produces a national publication for television viewers. **Corporate headquarters location:** Radnor PA. **Parent company:** Gemstar-TV Guide International. **Listed on:** NASDAQ. **Stock exchange symbol:** GMST.

TARRYTOWN HOUSE
East Sunnyside Lane, Tarrytown NY 10591. 914/591-8200. **Contact:** Human Resources. **Description:** A historic hotel and conference center with 148 guest rooms, 30 meeting rooms, and eight private dining areas. Founded in 1981. **Special programs:** Internships; Training. **Internship information:** Internships are available year round in sales/marketing, accounting, human resources, operations, and the culinary arts. **Corporate headquarters location:** This location. **Other U.S. locations:** CT; NJ; OR; TX; WA. **International locations:** Canada; France. **Parent company:** Dolce International. **Number of employees at this location:** 235. **Number of employees worldwide:** 2,500.

TEMCO SERVICE INDUSTRIES INC.
One Park Avenue, 1st Floor, New York NY 10016. 212/889-6353. **Contact:** Human Resources. **Description:** Offers a wide variety of maintenance, security, and related services through a workforce directed by a network of experienced managers. The company operates in the following areas: Building Maintenance Services; Engineering Maintenance Services; Extermination and Security Services; and Incineration and Heat Recovery Systems. **Corporate headquarters location:** This location. **International locations:** Belgium. **Operations at this facility include:** Administration; Sales; Service.

TENDER LOVING CARE/STAFF BUILDERS
1983 Marcus Avenue, Suite 200, Lake Success NY 11042. 516/358-1000. **Fax:** 516/358-2465. **Contact:** Human Resources Department. **World Wide Web address:** http://www.tlcathome.com. **Description:** A home health care agency. **Corporate headquarters location:** This location. **Other U.S. locations:** Nationwide. **Operations at this facility include:** Administration. **Number of employees at this location:** 300. **Number of employees nationwide:** 20,000.

TENDER LOVING CARE/STAFF BUILDERS
99 Railroad Station Plaza, Suite 100, Hicksville NY 11801-2898. 516/935-3737. **Contact:** Human Resources. **World Wide Web address:** http://www.tlcathome.com. **Description:** A home health care agency. **Corporate headquarters location:** Lake Success NY. **Other U.S. locations:** Nationwide.

TERESIAN HOUSE NURSING HOME
200 Washington Avenue Extension, Albany NY 12203. 518/456-2000. **Fax:** 518/456-1142. **Contact:** Human Resources. **E-mail address:** info@teresianhouse.com. **World Wide Web address:** http://www.teresianhouse.com. **Description:** A nonprofit, 300-bed skilled and health-related nursing home. Teresian House has a dementia care and an Alzheimer's care unit, which provides private rooms for all residents. Founded in 1974. **Company slogan:** Together we are one. **Positions advertised include:** Assistant Director of Nurse; Registered Nurse; Licensed Practical Nurse; Certified Nurse Aide; Ward Clerk; Light Duty Mechanic; Food Service Worker; Activities Coordinator. **Special programs:** Internships; Summer Jobs. **Number of employees at this location:** 385.

TESTWELL LABORATORIES, INC.
47 Hudson Street, Ossining NY 10562. 914/762-9000. **Fax:** 914/762-9638. **Contact:** Personnel Director. **World Wide Web address:** http://www.testwelllabs.com. **Description:** Provides construction materials and environmental testing, inspection, and consulting services for the construction, environmental, and real estate industries. **Corporate headquarters location:** This location. **Other area locations:** Albany NY. **Other U.S. locations:** Miami FL; Mays Landing NJ. **Operations at this facility include:** Administration; Regional Headquarters; Sales; Service. **Number of employees at this location:** 90. **Number of employees nationwide:** 400.

THOMAS PUBLISHING COMPANY
5 Penn Plaza, New York NY 10001. 212/560-1887. **Contact:** Human Resources. **World Wide Web address:** http://www.thomaspublishing.com. **Description:** Publishes a directory of manufacturers, wholesalers, and distributors. **Corporate headquarters location:** This location. **Operations at this facility include:** Administration; Divisional Headquarters; Sales; Service.

THOMPSON HEALTH
350 Parrish Street, Canandaigua NY 14424. 585/396-6680. **Fax:** 585/396-6480. **Contact:** Susan Mahoney, Director of Associates. **E-mail address:** careers@thompsonhealth.com. **World Wide Web address:** http://www.thompsonhealth.com. **Description:** A locally owned, nonprofit, community-based health care facility comprised of a 113-bed hospital, a 188-bed nursing home, and a planned senior living community. Founded in 1904. **NOTE:** Entry-level positions, part-time jobs, and second and third shifts are offered. **Company slogan:** Excellence in health care. **Positions advertised include:** Asthma Educator; Clinical Secretary; EMT; Executive Assistant; Licensed Practical Nurse; Certified Nurse Aide; Nurse Practitioner; Paramedic. **Special programs:** Training; Summer Jobs. **Office hours:** Monday - Friday, 8:00 a.m. - 4:30 p.m. **CEO:** Linda Janczak. **Annual sales/revenues:** $51 - $100 million. **Number of employees at this location:** 1,100.

J. WALTER THOMPSON COMPANY
466 Lexington Avenue, New York NY 10017. 212/210-7000. **Contact:** Human Resources. **E-mail address:** nygetajob@jwt.com. **World Wide Web address:** http://www.jwt.com. **Description:** A full-service advertising agency. **Positions advertised include:** Administrative Assistant; Financial Analyst. **Corporate headquarters location:** This location. **Other U.S. locations:** Nationwide. **International locations:** Worldwide. **Parent company:** WPP Group. **Listed on:** NASDAQ. **Stock exchange symbol:** WPPGY.

THOMSON FINANCIAL
195 Broadway, New York NY 10007. 646/822-2000. **Contact:** Personnel Manager. **World Wide Web address:** http://www.thomsonfinancial.com. **Description:** Provides financial information to the investment industry through its many business units. American Banker/Bond Buyer publishes banking and financial industry information in a variety of publications. Rainmaker Information provides software products to help members of the sales and investment industries.

TIFFEN COMPANY
90 Oser Avenue, Hauppauge NY 11788-3886. 631/273-2500. **Fax:** 631/273-2557. **Contact:** Human Resources. **World Wide Web address:** http://www.tiffen.com. **Description:** Engaged in sheet metal fabrication used to manufacture photographic-related products and accessories.

TIME WARNER CABLE
One Cablevision Center, 2nd Floor, Suite 2, Ferndale NY 12734. 845/295-2650. **Fax:** 845/295-2451. **Contact:** Human Resources. **World Wide Web address:** http://www.twcnyc.com. **Description:** Time Warner Cable is one of the largest cable television operators in the United States. The company owns or manages 64 cable television systems in 18 states, serving a total of 1.3 million subscribers. The company owns and operates 50 cable television systems in 15 states, principally in New York, Pennsylvania, Massachusetts, Florida, California, North Carolina, South Carolina, and Louisiana. The company's systems offer subscribers packages of basic and cable programming services consisting of television signals available off-air; a limited number of television signals from distant cities; numerous satellite-delivered, nonbroadcast channels such as CNN, MTV, USA Network, ESPN, A&E, TNT, and Nickelodeon; displays of information such as time, news, weather and stock market reports; and public, governmental, and educational access channels. **Special programs:** Summer Jobs. **Parent company:** AOL Time Warner, Inc. **Listed on:** New York Stock Exchange. **Stock exchange symbol:** AOL. **Number of employees at this location:** 380. **Number of employees nationwide:** 27,000.

THE TIMES-HERALD RECORD
40 Mulberry Street, P.O. Box 2046, Middletown NY 10940. 845/346-3112. **Contact:** Human Resources. **World Wide Web address:** http://www.th-record.com. **Description:** Publishes a daily newspaper, with a circulation of more than 80,000.

Corporate headquarters location: Campbell NY. **Other area locations:** New Paltz NY; Newburgh NY; Port Jervis NY. **Parent company:** Ottaway Newspapers, Inc.

TIX INTERNATIONAL GROUP
201 Main Street, Nyack-On-Hudson NY 10960. 845/358-1007. **Fax:** 845/358-1266. **Contact:** Human Resources. **World Wide Web address:** http://www.tixtravel.com. **Description:** A full-service travel agency and ticket broker for concerts, sports, and theater events. **Corporate headquarters location:** This location.

TOPPS COMPANY
One Whitehall Street, New York NY 10004. 212/376-0300. **Contact:** Human Resources. **World Wide Web address:** http://www.topps.com. **Description:** Internationally manufactures and markets a variety of chewing gum, candy, and other similar products. Topps also licenses its technology and trademarks and sells its chewing gum base and flavors to other overseas manufacturers. The company is best known for its internationally registered trademark Bazooka and its perennial Topps Baseball Bubble Gum picture cards. Topps is a leading marketer, under exclusive licenses, of collectible picture cards, albums, and stickers for baseball, football, and hockey. The company is also a leading producer and distributor of cards and stickers featuring pictures of popular motion picture, television, and cartoon characters, also under exclusive licenses. **Corporate headquarters location:** This location. **Other U.S. locations:** Duryea PA. **International locations:** Ireland. **Listed on:** NASDAQ. **Stock exchange symbol:** TOPP.

TOTE ISOTONER INC.
420 Fifth Avenue, 3rd Floor, New York NY 10018. 212/944-1129. **Contact:** Human Resources. **World Wide Web address:** http://www.isotoner.com. **Description:** Produces a wide range of gloves and related accessories including nationally distributed Isotoner products.

TOWERS PERRIN
100 Summit Lake Drive, Valhalla NY 10595. 914/745-4000. **Contact:** Human Resources. **World Wide Web address:** http://www.towersperrin.com. **Description:** A management consulting firm. **Corporate headquarters location:** New York NY. **Operations at this facility include:** Administration; Regional Headquarters; Research and Development; Service.

TOWERS PERRIN
335 Madison Avenue, New York NY 10017-4605. 212/309-3400. **Contact:** Recruiting Coordinator. **World Wide Web address:** http://www.towersperrin.com. **Description:** A management consulting firm. **Corporate headquarters location:** This location.

TRACEWELL SYSTEMS
9962 Route 446, Cuba NY 14727-9797. 585/968-2400. **Toll-free phone:** 800/848-4525. **Fax:** 585/968-3948. **Contact:** Human Resources Manager. **E-mail address:** hr@tracewellsystems.com. **World Wide Web address:** http://www.tracewellsystems.com. **Description:** Provides program management to develop sophisticated electronic products. Products encompass all disciplines associated with the design and manufacture of electronics products including hardware (analog, RF, power supply, and digital interface); mechanical (structural specifications, electronic packaging, wiring, cable, and thermal); prototyping (renderings, models, and fast turnaround); and validation testing (design compliance, safety, and regulatory). Capabilities include 3-D modeling, CAD/CAE/CAM systems, HALT/HASS test equipment, and EMI. Acme Electric Corporation serves the telecommunications, computer, medical diagnostics, and industrial markets. **Positions advertised include:** Senior Digital Engineer; Backplane Design Engineer; Buyer; Mechanical Design Engineer; Electrical Engineer; Mechanical Engineer; Production Manager. **Corporate headquarters location:** Westerville OH. **Operations at this facility include:** Manufacturing; Sales; Service.

TRACK DATA
56 Pine Street, New York NY 10005. 212/943-4555. **Contact:** Human Resources. **World Wide Web address:** http://www.trackdata.com. **Description:** Electronically provides trading information, news, and third-party database services on stocks, bonds, commodities, and other securities through its Dial/Data service. The company's AIQ Systems division produces expert systems software for individual and professional investors. **Listed on:** NASDAQ. **Stock exchange symbol:** TRAC.

TRANS WORLD ENTERTAINMENT CORPORATION
38 Corporate Circle, Albany NY 12203. 518/452-1242. **Fax:** 518/862-9519. **Contact:** Human Resources. **E-mail address:** jobs@twec.com. **World Wide Web address:** http://www.twec.com. **Description:** A music and video retailer. Trans World owns approximately 1,000 stores throughout the United States and Puerto Rico including Coconuts, Record Town, Camelot Music, Music Express, Planet Music, Strawberries, and Saturday Matinee. **Positions advertised include:** Computer Operator; Customer Care Agent; Entry Level Recruiter; IT Executive; Lease Compliance Manager; Senior Accountant; Web Graphic Designer. **Corporate headquarters location:** This location. **Listed on:** NASDAQ. **Stock exchange symbol:** TWMC. **Annual sales/revenues:** More than $100 million. **Number of employees at this location:** 800.

TRANSACT TECHNOLOGIES, INC.
20 Bomax Drive, Ithaca NY 14850. 607/257-8901. **Contact:** Human Resources. **World Wide Web address:** http://www.transact-tech.com. **Description:** Manufactures and sells receipt printers. **Corporate headquarters location:** Wallingford CT. **Listed on:** NASDAQ. **Stock exchange symbol:** TACT.

TRANSATLANTIC HOLDINGS, INC.
80 Pine Street, 7th Floor, New York NY 10005. 212/770-2000. **Contact:** Human Resources. **World Wide Web address:** http://www.transre.com. **Description:** An insurance holding company providing property and casualty reinsurance through its subsidiaries. **Subsidiaries include:** Transatlantic Reinsurance Company and Putnam Reinsurance Company provide general liability, fire, inland marine, workers' compensation, automobile liability, and medical malpractice insurance. **Listed on:** New York Stock Exchange. **Stock exchange symbol:** TRH.

TRANSCAT
10 Vantage Point Drive, Suite 1, Rochester NY 14624. 716/352-9460. **Contact:** Human Resources. **World Wide Web address:** http://www.transcat.com. **Description:** Distributes a variety of test measurement and control electrical and electronic equipment.

TRAYER PRODUCTS INC.
541 East Clinton Street, Elmira NY 14901. 607/734-8124. **Fax:** 607/732-1387. **Contact:** Timothy Sullivan, Human Resources Manager. **World Wide Web address:** http://www.trayerproducts.com. **Description:** A manufacturer of auto parts for off-road vehicles and heavy-duty trucks. **Number of employees at this location:** 200.

TRIZETTO GROUP, INC.
One Columbia Circle, Albany NY 12203. 518/862-3400. **Contact:** Recruiting. **World Wide Web address:** http://www.trizetto.com. **Description:** A managed care consulting firm that works with companies to set up health maintenance organization (HMO) plans for employees. **Corporate headquarters location:** Newport Beach CA. **Listed on:** NASDAQ. **Stock exchange symbol:** TZIX.

TRIZETTO GROUP, INC.
1700 Broadway, New York NY 10019. 212/765-8500. **Contact:** Human Resources. **World Wide Web address:** http://www.trizetto.com. **Description:** Develops health management software for insurance agencies and health care providers. **NOTE:** Interested jobseekers should send resumes to 1085 Morris Avenue, Union NJ 07083. **Corporate headquarters location:** Newport Beach CA. **Listed on:** NASDAQ. **Stock exchange symbol:** TZIX.

TRUCK-LITE COMPANY INC.
310 East Elmwood Avenue, Falconer NY 14733. 716/665-6214. **Contact:** Human Resources. **World Wide Web address:** http://www.trucklite.com. **Description:** Manufactures vehicular safety lights. Truck-Lite's products are distributed worldwide. **Corporate headquarters location:** This location. **Number of employees at this location:** 250.

TURNER CORPORATION
375 Hudson Street, New York NY 10014. 212/229-6000. **Contact:** Human Resources. **World Wide Web address:** http://www.turnerconstruction.com. **Description:** A holding company involved in construction, general building, contract management, and real estate development. **Corporate headquarters location:** This location. **Subsidiaries include:** Turner Construction Company; Turner Medical Building Services.

TYCO HEALTHCARE KENDALL
453 County Route 45, Argyle NY 12809. 518/638-8222. **Contact:** Human Resources. **World Wide Web address:** http://www.tycohealthcare.com. **Description:** Engaged in the manufacture of medical tubing and catheters.

UBS PAINEWEBBER INC.
1285 Avenue of the Americas, 3rd Floor, New York NY 10019. 212/713-2000. **Contact:** Personnel. **World Wide Web address:** http://www.ubspainewebber.com. **Description:** A full-service securities firm with over 300 offices nationwide. Services include investment banking, asset management, merger and acquisition consulting, municipal securities underwriting, estate planning, retirement programs, and transaction management. Clients include corporations, governments, institutions, and individuals. Founded in 1879. **Corporate headquarters location:** This location. **Other U.S. locations:** Nationwide. **Annual sales/revenues:** More than $100 million.

UBS WARBURG LLC
299 Park Avenue, New York NY 10171-0026. 212/821-3000. **Fax:** 212/821-3285. **Contact:** Human Resources. **World Wide Web address:** http://www.ibb.ubs.com. **Description:** A national investment banking firm serving corporate clients. **Parent company:** UBS AG. **Listed on:** New York Stock Exchange. **Stock exchange symbol:** UBS.

UOP/XEROX
2344 Flatbush Avenue, Brooklyn NY 11234. 718/252-6500. **Fax:** 718/252-8585. **Contact:** Human Resources. **Description:** Sells and services copiers, fax machines, laser printers, and other types of office equipment.

U.S. DEPARTMENT OF VETERANS AFFAIRS
STRATTON VETERANS ADMINISTRATION MEDICAL CENTER
113 Holland Avenue, Albany NY 12208. 518/626-5000. **Contact:** Human Resources. **World Wide Web address:** http://www.va.gov. **Description:** A medical center operated by the U.S. Department of Veterans Affairs. From 54 hospitals in 1930, the VA health care system has grown to include 171 medical centers; more than 364 outpatient, community, and outreach clinics; 130 nursing home care units; and 37 domiciliary residences. VA operates at least one medical center in each of the 48 contiguous states, Puerto Rico, and the District of Columbia. With approximately 76,000 medical center beds, VA treats nearly 1 million patients in VA hospitals; 75,000 in nursing home care units; and 25,000 in domiciliary residences. VA's outpatient clinics register approximately 24 million visits per year. **Number of employees at this location:** 1,765.

U.S. ENVIRONMENTAL PROTECTION AGENCY (EPA)
290 Broadway, 28th Floor, New York NY 10007. 212/637-3000. **Contact:** Human Resources. **World Wide Web address:** http://www.epa.gov. **Description:** The EPA is dedicated to improving and preserving the quality of the environment, both nationally and globally, and protecting human health and the productivity of natural resources. The agency is committed to ensuring that federal environmental laws are implemented and enforced effectively; U.S. policy, both foreign and domestic, encourages the integration of economic development and environmental protection so that economic growth can be sustained over the long term; and public and private decisions affecting energy, transportation, agriculture, industry, international trade, and natural resources fully integrate considerations of environmental quality. Founded in 1970. **Special programs:** Internships. **Corporate headquarters location:** Washington DC. **Other U.S. locations:** San Francisco CA; Denver CO; Atlanta GA; Chicago IL; Kansas City KS; Boston MA; Philadelphia PA; Dallas TX; Seattle WA. **Number of employees nationwide:** 19,000.

U.S. FEDERAL RESERVE BANK OF NEW YORK
33 Liberty Street, New York NY 10045-0001. 212/720-5000. **Contact:** Human Resources. **World Wide Web address:** http://www.ny.frb.org. **Description:** One of 12 regional Federal Reserve banks that, along with the Federal Reserve Board in Washington DC and the Federal Open Market Committee, comprise the Federal Reserve System, the nation's central bank. Responsibilities include monetary policy, banking supervision and regulation, and processing payments. **Special programs:** Internships. **Other U.S. locations:** San Francisco CA; Washington DC; Atlanta GA; Chicago IL; Boston MA; Minneapolis MN; Kansas City MO; St. Louis MO; Cleveland OH; Philadelphia PA; Dallas TX; Richmond VA. **Operations at this facility include:** Administration; Regional Headquarters; Research and Development. **Number of employees at this location:** 3,200.

U.S. FUNDS FOR UNICEF
333 East 38th Street, 6th Floor, New York NY 10016. 212/686-5522. **Contact:** Employment Manager. **World Wide Web address:** http://www.unicefusa.org. **Description:** Organized for educational and charitable purposes, U.S. Funds for UNICEF aims to increase awareness of the needs of children around the world. **Special programs:** Internships. **Corporate headquarters location:** This location. **Other U.S. locations:** Los Angeles CA; Washington DC; Atlanta GA; Chicago IL; Boston MA;

Houston TX. **Operations at this facility include:** Administration; Divisional Headquarters. **Listed on:** Privately held. **Number of employees at this location:** 100.

U.S. POSTAL SERVICE
45 Hudson Avenue, Albany NY 12207. 518/462-1359. **Contact:** Human Resources. **World Wide Web address:** http://www.usps.gov. **Description:** The main office of the Albany Post Office.

U.S. SALT
P.O. Box 110, Watkins Glen NY 14891-0110. 607/535-2721. **Contact:** Human Resources. **Description:** Formerly, Akzo Nobel Salt, this location manufactures salt. **Parent company:** Cargill Corporation, its subsidiaries, and its affiliates are involved in nearly 50 individual lines of business. Overall, Cargill is a major trader of grains and oilseeds, as well as a marketer of many other agricultural and nonagricultural commodities. Cargill is also a leader in producing and marketing seed varieties and hybrids. Cargill Central Research, located at Cargill headquarters, is dedicated to developing new agricultural products to address the needs of customers around the world. The company also provides financial and technical services. Cargill's worldwide food processing businesses supply products ranging from basic ingredients used in food production to recognized name brands. Cargill also operates a number of industrial businesses, including the production of steel, industrial-grade starches, ethanol, and salt products.

USA INTERACTIVE
152 West 57th Street, New York NY 10019. 212/314-7300. **Contact:** Human Resources. **World Wide Web address:** http://www.usainteractive.com. **Description:** An e-commerce and entertainment company operating one of the nation's largest cable television networks. **Corporate headquarters location:** This location.

USA WEEKEND
535 Madison Avenue, New York NY 10022. 212/715-2100. **Contact:** Human Resources. **World Wide Web address:** http://www.usaweekend.com. **Description:** Publishes a general interest national weekly magazine, sold in syndication as a Sunday newspaper supplement. USA Weekend has approximately 31.6 million readers every weekend. Features include national affairs, sports, personal care, and other subjects. **Special programs:** Internships. **Parent company:** Gannett Company, Inc. (Arlington VA). **Operations at this facility include:** Divisional Headquarters. **Listed on:** New York Stock Exchange. **Stock exchange symbol:** GCI.

USF RED STAR EXPRESS INC.
34 Wright Avenue, Auburn NY 13021. 315/253-2721. **Contact:** Human Resources. **World Wide Web address:** http://www.old.usfc.com/usfredstar/careers.com. **Description:** A trucking company that serves as a national shipping agent for other companies. **Corporate headquarters location:** This location. **Number of employees at this location:** 150.

UNDERWRITERS LABORATORIES INC.
1285 Walt Whitman Road, Melville NY 11747-3801. 631/271-6200. **Fax:** 631/271-8259. **Contact:** Employment Coordinator. **E-mail address:** melville@us.ul.com. **World Wide Web address:** http://www.ul.com. **Description:** An independent, nonprofit organization that specializes in product safety testing and certification worldwide. **Special programs:** Summer Jobs. **Corporate headquarters location:** Northbrook IL. **Other U.S. locations:** Santa Clara CA; Research Triangle Park NC; Camas WA. **Number of employees at this location:** 800. **Number of employees worldwide:** 4,000.

UNIFLEX, INC.
383 West John Street, Hicksville NY 11802. 516/932-2000. **Contact:** Human Resources. **World Wide Web address:** http://www.uniflexinc.com. **Description:** Designs, manufactures, and markets a broad line of customized plastic packaging for sales and advertising promotions; clear bags for apparel and soft goods manufacturers; and specialized, recyclable bags and other products for use in hospitals, medical laboratories, and emergency care centers. Medical products include patented, disposable bags for the safe handling of specimens, and general purpose bags for personal belongings. Specialty advertising products include handle bags, drawstring bags, tote bags, and litter bags. The Haran Packaging Division manufactures and markets custom flexible plastic for the health care, food, financial, and other markets. Tamper-evident security bags are sold to banks, retailers, casino operations, stockbrokers, and courier firms that have security concerns for cash and other valuables. **Corporate headquarters location:** This location. **Other area locations:** Westbury NY. **Other U.S. locations:** Albuquerque NM. **Subsidiaries include:** The Cycle Plastics produces and markets jumbo flexible loop handle bags, double drawstring bags, and reclosable, resealable, Trac-Loc bags. These products are sold to retailers, cosmetics firms, food packing companies, and medical/health care supply firms.

UNILEVER CORPORATION
390 Park Avenue, New York NY 10022. 212/888-1260. **Contact:** Human Resources. **World Wide Web address:** http://www.unilever.com. **Description:** An international consumer products firm manufacturing a wide range of soaps, toiletries, and foods. **Corporate headquarters location:** This location. **Parent company:** Unilever NV (Netherlands). **Listed on:** New York Stock Exchange. **Stock exchange symbol:** UN.

UNION COLLEGE
807 Union Street, Schenectady NY 12308. 518/388-6000. **Contact:** Human Resources. **World Wide Web address:** http://www.union.edu. **Description:** An independent, four-year liberal arts college with an engineering program. Founded in 1795.

UNISON INDUSTRY
P.O. Box 310, Norwich NY 13815. 607/335-5000. **Contact:** Human Resources. **Description:** Manufactures aircraft engine electrical components, operating in the exciter, alternator, and harness divisions.

UNITED CAPITAL CORPORATION
United Capital Building, 9 Park Place, 4th Floor, Great Neck NY 11021. 516/466-6464. **Contact:** Human Resources. **Description:** United Capital Corporation invests in and manages real estate properties. **Subsidiaries include:** Metex Corporation provides antenna systems and knitted wire products to aviation and automotive markets worldwide. **Corporate headquarters location:** This location. **Listed on:** AMEX. **Stock exchange symbol:** AFP.

UNITED CEREBRAL PALSY ASSOCIATIONS OF NEW YORK STATE
330 West 34th Street, 14th Floor, New York NY 10001. 212/947-5770. **Fax:** 212/594-4538. **Contact:** Human Resources Department. **E-mail address:** info@cerebralpalsynys.org. **World Wide Web address:** http://www.cerebralpalsynys.org. **Description:** A nonprofit health care organization that provides services to persons with developmental disabilities. **Special programs:** Internships. **Corporate headquarters location:** Washington DC. **Other area locations:** Bronx NY; Brooklyn NY; Queens NY; Staten Island NY. **Operations at this facility include:** Administration; Divisional Headquarters. **Annual sales/revenues:** $51 - $100 million. **Number of employees at this location:** 1,700.

UNITED MEMORIAL MEDICAL CENTER
127 North Street, Batavia NY 14020. 585/343-6030. **Contact:** Human Resources Assistant. **Description:** An acute care hospital. St. Jerome Hospital is a member of Mercy Health System of Western New York and Eastern Mercy Health System. **Special programs:** Internships. **Corporate headquarters location:** Buffalo NY. **Operations at this facility include:** Administration; Divisional Headquarters; Service. **Number of employees at this location:** 450.

UNITED STATES TRUST COMPANY OF NEW YORK
114 West 47th Street, New York NY 10036. 212/852-1000. **Contact:** Human Resources. **World Wide Web address:** http://www.ustrust.com. **Description:** An investment management, private banking, and securities services firm. Service categories include investment management; estate and trust administration; financial planning; and corporate trust. **Corporate headquarters location:** This location.

UNITED WAY OF NEW YORK CITY
2 Park Avenue South, 2nd Floor, New York NY 10016-1601. 212/251-2500. **Contact:** Human Resources. **World Wide Web address:** http://www.uwnyc.org. **Description:** A nonprofit organization that offers referral and crisis intervention services for pregnant women and parents.

UNIVERSAL AMERICAN FINANCIAL CORP.
6 International Drive, Suite 190, Rye Brook NY 10573. 914/934-5200. **Contact:** Human Resources. **World Wide Web address:** http://www.uafc.com. **Description:** Underwrites life and accident insurance and health insurance to seniors. **Corporate headquarters location:** This location. **Listed on:** NASDAQ. **Stock exchange symbol:** UHCO. **Annual sales/revenues:** More than $100 million.

UNIVERSAL INSTRUMENTS CORPORATION
P.O. Box 825, Binghamton NY 13902-0825. 607/779-7522. **Fax:** 607/779-5125. **Contact:** Human Resources. **E-mail address:** employment@uic.com. **World Wide Web address:** http://www.uic.com. **Description:** A leader in the automation of electronic circuit assembly. Universal Instruments Corporation manufactures automated factory equipment for the electronics industry including machines that assemble PC boards used in VCRs and televisions. **Positions advertised include:** Materials Specialist. **Special programs:** Internships; Apprenticeships; Co-ops. **President:** Gerhard Meese.

UNIVERSAL MUSIC AND VIDEO DISTRIBUTION
137 East State Street, Gloversville NY 12078. 518/725-0604. **Contact:** Personnel Manager. **Description:** A record and cassette manufacturing and distribution facility.

UNIVERSAL MUSIC GROUP
825 Eighth Avenue, 28th Floor, New York NY 10019. 212/333-8000. **Contact:** Human Resources. **World Wide Web address:** http://www.universalstudios.com/music. **Description:** Produces and markets popular and classical records and is active in the areas of film development, production, and distribution, as well as event television, video theater, merchandising, touring, and music publishing. **Subsidiaries include:** MCA; Universal Concerts. **Parent company:** The Seagram Company Ltd.

UNIVERSITY OF ROCHESTER
601 Elmwood Avenue, Rochester NY 14642. 585/275-2815. **Contact:** Human Resources. **World Wide Web address:** http://www.rochester.edu. **Description:** A private, coeducational university offering bachelor's, master's, and doctoral degree programs. Founded in 1850. **NOTE:** Interested jobseekers should send resumes to Employment Center, 1325 Mount Hope Avenue, Suite 202, Rochester NY 14620.

UTICA COLLEGE OF SYRACUSE UNIVERSITY
1600 Burrstone Road, Utica NY 13502. 315/792-3111. **Contact:** Human Resources. **World Wide Web address:** http://www.utica.edu. **Description:** A four-year, undergraduate, liberal arts college. Utica College of Syracuse University offers 35 majors.

UTICA NATIONAL INSURANCE GROUP
P.O. Box 530, Utica NY 13503-0530. 315/732-0779. **Physical address:** 180 Genessee Street, New Hartford NY 13413. **Contact:** Human Resources. **World Wide Web address:** http://www.uticanational.com. **Description:** Provides property and casualty insurance. **Corporate headquarters location:** This location. **Number of employees at this location:** 800. **Number of employees nationwide:** 1,400.

VAW OF AMERICA INC.
9 Aluminum Drive, P.O. Box 667, Ellenville NY 12428. 845/647-7510. **Contact:** Lois Cronick, Human Resources Director. **World Wide Web address:** http://www.vawusa.com. **Description:** VAW manufactures aluminum extrusions such as pipes, conduits, and ladder steps. Founded in 1966.

VNU BUSINESS PUBLICATIONS, INC.
770 Broadway, New York NY 10003-9595. 646/654-5270. **Contact:** Human Resources. **E-mail address:** bmcomm@vnuinc.com. **World Wide Web address:** http://www.vnubusinessmedia.com. **Description:** Publishes a weekly trade periodical covering newspapers and an annual yearbook for the newspaper industry. **Positions advertised include:** Executive Assistant; Associate Publisher; Databases Developer. **Corporate headquarters location:** This location. **Parent company:** VNU, Inc.

VNU INC.
770 Broadway, New York NY 10003-9595. 646/654-5000. **Contact:** Human Resources. **World Wide Web address:** http://www.vnu.com. **Description:** VNU offers marketing information, media measurement information, business information and directory information. VNU publishes 67 business publications, stages 52 trade shows and conferences, and operates more than 75 business-to-business electronic media sites. **Positions advertised include:** Executive Assistant; Associate Publisher; Databases Developer. **Corporate headquarters location:** This location. **Other U.S. locations:** Nationwide. **International locations:** Worldwide.

VAIL-BALLOU PRESS INC.
P.O. Box 1005, Binghamton NY 13902. 607/723-7987. **Contact:** Human Resources. **World Wide Web address:** http://www.maple-vail.com **Description:** A book manufacturer engaged in all aspects of book production including binding and typing. Vail-Ballou prints college and medical texts, novels, car repair, and cookbooks. Founded in 1900. **Number of employees at this location:** 650.

VALUE LINE
220 East 42nd Street, 6th Floor, New York NY 10017. 212/907-1500. **Contact:** Human Resources. **World Wide Web address:** http://www.valueline.com. **Description:** An investment advisory firm. **Positions advertised include:** Junior Security Analyst. **Corporate headquarters location:** This location. **Listed on:** NASDAQ. **Stock exchange symbol:** VALU.

VASSAR COLLEGE
124 Raymond Avenue, Poughkeepsie NY 12604. 845/437-5820. **Fax:** 845/437-7729. **Contact:** Human Resources. **E-mail address:** careers@vassar.edu. **World Wide Web address:** http://www.vassar.edu. **Description:** Vassar College is a four-year undergraduate college focusing on the liberal arts. Student enrollment is approximately 2,250. Founded in 1860. **Number of employees at this location:** 1,000.

VEECO INSTRUMENTS INC.
One Terminal Drive, Plainview NY 11803. 516/349-8300. **Contact:** Human Resources. **World Wide Web address:** http://www.veeco.com. **Description:** Designs, manufactures, markets, and services a broad line of precision ion beam etching and surface measurement systems used to manufacture microelectronic products. Veeco produces and sells its ion beam etching systems under the Microtech brand name. The company also sells leak detection/vacuum equipment, which is used for the precise identification of leaks in sealed components. Leak detectors are used in a broad range of electronics, aerospace, and transportation products, ranging from air conditioning components to fiber-optic cables. Veeco's surface measurement products include surface profilers, atomic force microscopy measurement systems, and X-ray fluorescence thickness measurement systems. **Positions advertised include:** Business Analyst; Junior Accountant; Logistics Director; Quality Control Inspector; Senior Mechanical Engineer; Software Engineer; Technical Writer. **Corporate headquarters location:** This location. **Listed on:** NASDAQ. **Stock exchange symbol:** VECO.

VERAMARK TECHNOLOGIES INC.
3750 Monroe Avenue, Pittsford NY 14534. 585/381-6000. **Fax:** 585/383-6800. **Contact:** Renee Peters, Human Resources. **E-mail address:** info@veramark.com. **World Wide Web address:** http://www.veramark.com. **Description:** Designs and manufactures telecommunication management systems and voice processing products. For businesses that own a telephone system, Veramark Technologies produces call accounting systems that provide a variety of reports to help control telecommunications expenses and usage. For telephone operating companies, the company offers the INFO series of products for management of telecommunications data at the carrier's central office. **Corporate headquarters location:** This location.

VESON INC.
29 Broadway, Suite 1002, New York NY 10006. 212/422-0300. **Contact:** Michael Veson, Manager. **World Wide Web address:** http://www.veson.com. **Description:** Develops computer software for the shipping industry.

VIA HEALTH GENESEE HOSPITAL
1425 Portland Avenue, Rochester NY 14621. 585/922-4000. **Contact:** Human Resources. **World Wide Web address:** http://www.viahealth.org. **Description:** A hospital with approximately 450 beds serving the Rochester area.

VIACOM INC.
1515 Broadway, 31st Floor, New York NY 10036. 212/258-6000. **Contact:** Human Resources. **World Wide Web address:** http://www.viacom.com. **Description:** A diversified entertainment and communications company with operations in four principal segments: Networks, Entertainment, Cable Television, and Broadcasting. Viacom Networks operates three advertiser-supported basic cable television program services: MTV (Music Television including MTV Europe and MTV Latino), VH-1/Video Hits One, and Nickelodeon/Nick at Nite; and three premium subscription television services: SHOWTIME, The Movie Channel, and FLIX. Viacom Entertainment distributes television series, feature films, made-for-television movies, miniseries, and movies for prime time broadcast network television; acquires and distributes television series for initial exhibition on a first-run basis; and develops, produces, distributes, and markets interactive software for multimedia markets. Viacom Cable Television owns and operates cable television systems in California, the Pacific Northwest, and the Midwest. Viacom Broadcasting owns and operates five network-affiliated television stations and 14 radio stations. **Corporate headquarters location:** This location. **Listed on:** New York Stock Exchange. **Stock exchange symbol:** VIA.

VIACOM OUTDOOR
405 Lexington Avenue, 14th Floor, New York NY 10174. 212/297-6400. **Contact:** Human Resources. **World Wide Web address:** http://www.viacomoutdoor.com. **Description:** An advertising agency specializing in the design of billboards and posters. **Special programs:** Internships. **Other U.S. locations:** Nationwide. **Operations at this facility include:** Administration; Divisional Headquarters; Financial Offices; Marketing; Research and Development; Sales; Service.

VICTORIA & COMPANY
385 Fifth Avenue, 4th Floor, New York NY 10016. 212/725-0600. **Contact:** Office Manager. **Description:** Manufactures costume jewelry. **Corporate headquarters location:** This location.

VISHAY INTERTECHNOLOGY, INC.
10 Melville Park Road, Melville NY 11747-3113. 631/847-3000. **Contact:** Human Resources. **World Wide Web address:** http://www.vishay.com. **Description:** Manufactures transistors, transient voltage suppressors, diodes, and rectifiers. **Listed on:** New York Stock Exchange. **Stock exchange symbol:** VSH.

WSKG PUBLIC TV AND RADIO
P.O. Box 3000, Binghamton NY 13902. 607/729-0100. **Physical address:** 601 Gate Road, Vestal NY 13850. **Fax:** 607/729-7328. **Contact:** Human Resources. **World Wide Web address:** http://www.wskg.com. **Description:** A radio and television station.

WACHOVIA CORPORATION
245 Main Street, White Plains NY 10601. 914/682-7416. **Recorded jobline:** 800/FUNHIRE. **Contact:** Human Resources. **World Wide Web address:** http://www.wachovia.com. **Description:** A bank. **Parent company:** Wachovia Corporation is one of the nation's largest bank holding companies with subsidiaries operating over 1,330 full-service bank branches in the south Atlantic states. **Corporate headquarters location:** Charlotte NC. **Listed on:** New York Stock Exchange. **Stock exchange symbol:** WB.

THE WARNACO GROUP, INC.
90 Park Avenue, New York NY 10016. 212/661-1300. **Contact:** Human Resources Department. **Description:** A manufacturer, designer, and marketer of women's intimate apparel, men's wear, and men's accessories under brand names including Calvin Klein, Fruit of the Loom, Warner's, Olga, and Chaps by Ralph Lauren. Warnaco markets its products through a chain of 48 retail outlets, as well as department stores and mass merchandisers in North America and Europe. **Corporate headquarters location:** This location.

WARNER BROS. INC.
1325 Avenue of the Americas, 31st Floor, New York NY 10019. 212/636-5000. **Contact:** Department of Human Resources. **World Wide Web address:** http://www.warnerbros.com. **Description:** Offices of the diversified entertainment company. **Parent company:** AOL Time Warner. **Listed on:** New York Stock Exchange. **Stock exchange symbol:** AOL.

WASHINGTON MILLS ELECTRO MINERALS COMPANY
1801 Buffalo Avenue, P.O. Box 423, Niagara Falls NY 14302-0423. 716/278-6600. **Contact:** Human Resources. **E-mail address:** info@washingtonmills.com. **World Wide Web address:** http://www.washingtonmills.com. **Description:** Washington Mills manufactures and sells products that are used principally for abrasive, refractory, and metallurgical applications. The primary products of the company are fused aluminum oxide and silicon carbide. Other product lines include fuel specialty products that are sold to the refractory industry. **Corporate headquarters location:** This location.

WASHINGTON MUTUAL, INC.
49 East Franklin Avenue, Hempstead NY 11550. 516/489-4801. **Contact:** Human Resources. **World Wide Web address:** http://www.wamu.com. **Description:** Washington Mutual, Inc. is a financial services company that, through its subsidiaries, engages in the following lines of business: consumer banking, mortgage banking, commercial banking, financial services and consumer finance. **Positions advertised include:** Project Coordinator; Loan Coordinator; Project Analyst; Mortgage Underwriter; Mortgage Loan Coordinator. **Corporate headquarters location:** Seattle WA. **Listed on:** New York Stock Exchange. **Stock exchange symbol:** WM.

WASTE STREAM TECHNOLOGY
2749 Rockport Road, Niagara Falls NY 14305. 716/876-5290. **Contact:** Human Resources. **Description:** Provides a range of services for the remediation of sites and facilities contaminated by hazardous materials. **Corporate headquarters location:** This location.

WATER AUTHORITY OF WESTERN NASSAU COUNTY
58 South Tyson Avenue, Floral Park NY 11001. 516/327-4100. **Contact:** Janice Varley, Director of Human Resources. **Description:** The Water Authority of Western Nassau County supplies and distributes water for residential and commercial use in western Nassau County. **NOTE:** Positions are filled in accordance with Nassau County Civil Service Commission rules. **Corporate headquarters location:** This location.

WATERTOWN CITY SCHOOL DISTRICT
376 Butterfield Avenue, Watertown NY 13601. 315/785-3700. **Contact:** Director of Personnel. **Description:** Provides educational services that serve Jefferson County. Schooling ranges from elementary schools to high schools. **Number of employees at this location:** 630.

WATERVIEW NURSING CARE CENTER
119-15 27th Avenue, Flushing NY 11354. 718/461-5000. **Fax:** 718/321-1984. **Contact:** Personnel. **World Wide Web address:** http://www.healthlistings.com/waterview. **Description:** A 200-bed facility that offers specialized, long-term nursing care to chronically ill individuals of all ages. Waterview's in-house medical staff provides care in areas that include psychiatry, psychotherapy, dentistry, podiatry, otolaryngology, ophthalmology, hematology, urology, neurology, optometry, portable X-rays, and lab work. **Special programs:** Training; Summer Jobs. **Office hours:** Monday - Friday, 9:00 a.m. - 5:00 p.m. **Number of employees at this location:** 280.

WATSON LABORATORIES
33 Ralph Avenue, P.O. Box 30, Copiague NY 11726-1297. 631/842-8383. **Contact:** Personnel Director. **World Wide Web address:** http://www.watsonpharm.com. **Description:** Manufactures brand-name and generic pharmaceuticals in the areas of dermatology, women's health, neuropsychiatry, and primary care. **Positions advertised include:** Scientist; Chemist; Documentation Coordinator; Validation Engineer; Training Manager; Scheduler; Packaging Manager.

WE TRANSPORT INC.
303 Sunnyside Boulevard, Plainview NY 11803. 516/349-8200. **Contact:** Mary Prioli, Personnel Manager. **Description:** An area school bus and van transportation company. **Special programs:** Internships. **Corporate headquarters location:** This location. **Number of employees at this location:** 70.

WEGMANS FOOD MARKETS
1500 Brooks Avenue, P.O. Box 30844, Rochester NY 14603-0844. 585/328-2550. **Fax:** 585/464-4664. **Contact:** Human Resources. **E-mail address:** employment@wegmans.com. **World Wide Web Address:** http://www.wegmans.com. **Description:** Operates grocery stores in New York, Pennsylvania, New Jersey, and Virginia. **Positions advertised include:** Seafood Manager; Service Desk Associate; Producer Associate; Meat Associate; Deli Associate; Bakery Associate; Grocery Associate; Overnight Associate; Dairy Associate. **NOTE:** This location is the corporate headquarters. **Number of employees nationwide:** 32,000.

WEIGHT WATCHERS INTERNATIONAL INC.
175 Crossways Park West, Woodbury NY 11797. 516/390-1400. **Contact:** Human Resources. **World Wide Web address:** http://www.weightwatchers.com. **Description:** Conducts and supervises franchised weight-control classes in 21 countries, markets packaged products through its food licensees, and publishes the *Weight Watchers* magazine in three countries. **Corporate headquarters location:** This location. **Listed on:** New York Stock Exchange. **Stock exchange symbol:** WTW.

WEIL GOTSHAL & MANGES
767 Fifth Avenue, New York NY 10153. 212/310-8000. **Fax:** 212/310-8007. **Contact:** Pat Bowers, Human Resources Director. **World Wide Web address:** http://www.weil.com. **Description:** A law firm specializing in corporate, real estate, and tax law. **Other U.S. locations:** DC; FL; TX. **International locations:** London, England.

WELCH ALLYN MEDICAL PRODUCTS
4341 State Street Road, Skaneateles Falls NY 13153-0220. **Toll-free phone:** 800-535-6663. **Fax:** 315/685-4091. **Contact:** Human Resources. **World Wide Web address:** http://www.welchallyn.com. **Description:** A leading manufacturer of medical diagnostic and therapeutic devices, cardiac defibrillators, patient monitoring systems, and miniature precision lamps. Founded in 1915. **Positions advertised include:**

Director Global Customer Development; Document Control Manager; Engineer II/ PE Automation/Process Engineer; Engineer II/ PE; Electrical/Mfg Engineer; Process Engineer; Regulatory Affairs Engineer; Sales Trace Specialist; Senior Regulatory Affairs Engineer.

WELSBACH ELECTRIC CORPORATION
P.O. Box 560252, 111-01 14th Avenue, College Point NY 11356-0252. 718/670-7900. **Contact:** Personnel. **World Wide Web address:** http://www.welsbachelectric.com. **Description:** An electrical contractor engaged in the installation and maintenance of streetlights and traffic signals. **Corporate headquarters location:** This location. **Parent company:** EMCOR Group, Inc. **Listed on:** New York Stock Exchange. **Stock exchange symbol:** EME. **President:** Fred Goodman.

WEN TECHNOLOGY CORPORATION
999 Central Park Avenue, Yonkers NY 10704. 914/376-5435. **Fax:** 914/376-7092. **Contact:** Human Resources. **E-mail address:** info@wentech.com. **World Wide Web address:** http://www.wentech.com. **Description:** Manufactures computer monitors and displays. **Corporate headquarters location:** This location. **Annual sales/revenues:** $51 - $100 million. **Number of employees at this location:** 40.

JANE WESMAN PUBLIC RELATIONS, INC.
322 Eighth Avenue, Suite 1702, New York NY 10001. 212/620-4080. **Fax:** 212/620-0370. **Contact:** Human Resources. **E-mail address:** jane@wesmanpr.com. **World Wide Web address:** http://www.wesmanpr.com. **Description:** Provides book publicity services including press kits, author tours, radio and print publicity, and media training. **Corporate headquarters location:** This location.

WEST POINT STEVENS, INC.
1185 Avenue of the Americas, New York NY 10036. 212/930-2050. **Contact:** Human Resources. **World Wide Web address:** http://www.westpointstevens.com. **Description:** A major worldwide marketing and manufacturing organization. The company's core products are fabrics made from both natural and man-made fibers and yarns for a broad range of end uses including products for the home and apparel. **Corporate headquarters location:** This location. **Operations at this facility include:** Administration; Design; Marketing; Sales; Service. **Number of employees at this location:** 250. **Number of employees nationwide:** 19,000.

WESTCHESTER COMMUNITY OPPORTUNITY PROGRAM
2269 Saw Mill River Road, Building 3, Suite G-16, Elmsford NY 10523-3833. 914/592-5600. **Contact:** Personnel. **Description:** A county-sponsored, nonprofit social services agency operating through numerous community action programs that provides clinical services, employment training programs, energy programs, and a wide range of other community services. **Corporate headquarters location:** This location.

WESTCHESTER LIBRARY SYSTEM
410 Saw Mill River Road, Ardsley NY 10502. 914/674-3600. **Fax:** 914/674-4185. **Contact:** Personnel. **World Wide Web address:** http://www.wls.lib.ny.us. **Description:** Provides a wide range of buying, distribution, and other support services to the 38 member libraries in the Westchester County library system. **Corporate headquarters location:** This location.

WESTERN BEEF, INC.
47-05 Metropolitan Avenue, Ridgewood NY 11385. 718/456-3048. **Contact:** Human Resources. **World Wide Web address:** http://www.westernbeef.com. **Description:** A warehouse supermarket chain in the metropolitan New York area that provides a full-line of value-priced perishable and grocery products. In addition to operating 14 supermarkets, the company is also a meat and poultry distributor. **Positions advertised include:** Store Manager; Assistant Store Manager; Deli Manager.

WESTERN BEEF, INC.
4444 College Point Boulevard, Flushing NY 11355. 718/539-4900. **Contact:** Human Resources. **World Wide Web address:** http://www.westernbeef.com. **Description:** A warehouse supermarket chain in the metropolitan New York area that provides a full-line of value-priced perishable and grocery products. In addition to operating 14 supermarkets, the company is also a meat and poultry distributor. **NOTE:** Interested jobseekers should send resumes to 47-05 Metropolitan Avenue, Ridgewood NY 11385.

GEORGE WESTON BAKERIES, INC.
55 Paradise Lane, Bayshore NY 11706. 631/273-6000. **Contact:** Human Resources. **World Wide Web address:** http://www.gwbakerires.com. **Description:** Produces and distributes a variety of food products including soups, sauces, and bouillons; dressings including Hellmann's mayonnaise; starches and syrups; bread spreads including Skippy peanut butter; desserts and baking aids; and pasta. **Corporate headquarters location:** This location.

WESTSIDE VETERINARY CENTER
220 West 83rd Street, New York NY 10024. 212/580-1800. **Contact:** Human Resources. **Description:** An animal hospital offering medical, surgical, and dental services.

WHITE & CASE LLP
1155 Avenue of the Americas, New York NY 10036-2787. 212/819-8200. **Fax:** 212/354-8113. **Contact:** Human Resources Director. **World Wide Web address:** http://www.whitecase.com. **Description:** A general law firm specializing in international law, as well as 30 other practice areas.

WILDLIFE CONSERVATION SOCIETY (WCS)
BRONX ZOO
2300 Southern Boulevard, Bronx NY 10460. 718/220-5100. **Fax:** 718/220-2464. **Contact:** Mariam Benitez, Human Resources Director. **E-mail address:** hr@wcs.org. **World Wide Web address:** http://www.wcs.org/home/zoos/bronxzoo. **Description:** Operates the Aquarium for Wildlife Conservation, the Bronx Zoo, the Central Park Wildlife Center, the Prospect Park Wildlife Center, and the Queens Wildlife Center. Wildlife Conservation Society (WCS) also manages the St. Catherine Wildlife Survival Center off the coast of Georgia and nearly 300 international field projects in over 50 nations. Additionally, WCS conducts environmental education programs at local, national, and international levels. **Office hours:** Monday - Friday, 9:00 a.m. - 5:00 p.m.

JOHN WILEY & SONS, INC.
605 Third Avenue, New York NY 10158. 212/850-6000. **Fax:** 212/850-6049. **Contact:** Human Resources. **E-mail address:** info@wiley.com. **World Wide Web address:** http://www.wiley.com. **Description:** An international publishing house. Wiley publishes in four categories: Educational; Professional; Trade; and Scientific, Technical, and Medical (STM). In Educational, Wiley publishes textbooks and instructional packages for undergraduate and graduate students worldwide. Publishing programs focus on the physical and life sciences, mathematics, engineering, and accounting, with a growing business in economics, finance, business, MIS/CIS, and foreign languages. In Professional, Wiley publishes books and subscription products for lawyers, architects, accountants, engineers, and other professionals. In Trade, Wiley publishes nonfiction books in areas such as business, computers, science, and general interest. In STM, Wiley publishes approximately 260 scholarly and professional journals, as well as encyclopedias, other major reference works, and books for the research and academic communities. Major subject areas include chemistry, the life sciences, and technology. Founded in 1807. **Special programs:** Internships. **Office hours:** Monday - Friday, 8:30 a.m. - 4:30 p.m. **Corporate headquarters location:** This location. **Other U.S. locations:** Colorado Springs CO; Somerset NJ. **International locations:** Asia; Australia; Canada; Europe. **Operations at this facility include:** Administration. **Listed on:** New York Stock Exchange. **Stock exchange symbol:** JW. **Number of employees at this location:** 800. **Number of employees nationwide:** 1,200. **Number of employees worldwide:** 2,000.

WILLIAM MORRIS AGENCY, INC.
1325 6th Avenue, New York NY 10019. 212/903-1110. **Fax:** 212/903-1474. **Contact:** Human Resources. **World Wide Web address:** http://www.wma.com. **Description:** One of the largest talent and literary agencies in the world. Founded in 1898. **Positions advertised include:** Agent Trainee. **Special programs:** Training. **Corporate headquarters location:** Beverly Hills CA. **Other U.S. locations:** Nashville TN. **Operations at this facility include:** Regional Headquarters. **Number of employees at this location:** 200. **Number of employees nationwide:** 700. **Number of employees worldwide:** 750.

WILLIS OF NEW YORK, INC.
7 Hanover Square, New York NY 10004-2594. 212/344-8888. **Contact:** Human Resources. **E-mail address:** usemployment@willis.com. **World Wide Web address:** http://www.willis.com. **Description:** Provides insurance and risk management services to a broad range of commercial clients. Subsidiaries at this location include Willis Corroon Aerospace and Willis Corroon Americas. **Positions advertised include:** Senior Executive Assistant; Claims Assistant; Property Technical Broker; Senior HR Specialist; Account Manager.

THE H.W. WILSON COMPANY
950 University Avenue, Bronx NY 10452. 718/588-8400. **Toll-free phone:** 800/367-6770. **Contact:** Human Resources. **E-mail address:** eoflynn@hwwilson.com. **World Wide Web address:** http://www.hwwilson.com. **Description:** A publisher of indexes and reference works for libraries covering a broad range of the arts and sciences.

WILSON ELSER MOSKOWITZ EDELMAN & DICKER LLP
150 East 42nd Street, New York NY 10017-5639. 212/490-3000. **Fax:** 212/490-3038. **Contact:** Recruiting Manager. **World Wide Web address:** http://www.wemed.com. **Description:** One of the nation's largest law firms, focusing in a number of different practice areas. **Special programs:** Summer Internships.

THOMAS C. WILSON, INC.
21-13 44th Avenue, Long Island City NY 11101-5088. 718/729-3360. **Toll-free phone:** 800/230-2636. **Fax:** 718/361-2872. **Contact:** Personnel. **World Wide Web address:** http://www.tcwilson.com. **Description:** A manufacturer of tube cleaners and tube expanders for the boiler and condenser industry. **Corporate headquarters location:** This location. **Operations at this facility include:** Manufacturing; Sales.

WINFIELD SECURITY
35 West 35th Street, New York NY 10001. 212/947-3700. **Contact:** Human Resources. **World Wide Web address:** http://www.winfieldsecurity.com. **Description:** Provides security guard services for office buildings, schools, businesses, and manufacturers. **Corporate headquarters location:** This location. **Other area locations:** Bronx NY; Brooklyn NY; Queens NY. **Other U.S. locations:** Bloomfield NJ.

WINSTON RESOURCES, INC.
535 Fifth Avenue, Suite 701, New York NY 10017. 212/557-5000. **Contact:** Human Resources. **Description:** Winston Resources is a network of recruiting companies. Winston Resources has seven owned offices and 21 offices licensed or franchised under various names. Businesses include a wide range of industries. Founded in 1967. **Corporate headquarters location:** This location.

WOMEN'S CHRISTIAN ASSOCIATION HOSPITAL
207 Foote Avenue, Jamestown NY 14701. 716/664-8227. **Fax:** 716/664-8307. **Contact:** Gayle Lutgen, Human Resource. **E-mail address:** Gayle.Lutgen@wcahospital.org. **World Wide Web address:** http://www.wcahospital.org. **Description:** A 342-bed, nonsectarian, nonprofit, regional medical center. Founded in 1885. **Positions advertised include:** Staff Development Clinical Educator; Clinical Dietician; Nurse Manager; Registered Respiratory Therapist; Registered Nurse. **Office hours:** Monday - Friday, 7:00 a.m. - 5:00 p.m. **Number of employees at this location:** 1,300.

WORLD KITCHEN, INC.
1 Steuben Street, Corning NY 14830. 607/377-8000. **Fax:** 607/377-8946. **Contact:** Personnel. **E-mail address:** careers@worldkitchen.com. **World Wide Web address:** http://www.worldkitchen.com. **Description:** Engaged in the manufacture and marketing of cookware, cutlery, kitchen tools, commercial knives, and garden tools. **Special programs:** Internships. **Corporate headquarters location:** Reston VA.

WUNDERMAN
285 Madison Avenue, New York NY 10017. 212/941-3000. **Contact:** Careers. **World Wide Web address:** http://www.wunderman.com. **Description:** Provides communications and database technologies for the marketing industry through the company's international research and development marketing lab. **Positions advertised include:** Chief of Staff; Assistant Account Executive; Account Executive. **International locations:** Worldwide. **President/CEO:** David Sable.

WYETH
401 North Middletown Road, Pearl River NY 10965-1299. 845/732-5000. **Contact:** Personnel Director. **World Wide Web address:** http://www.wyeth.com. **Description:** Manufactures both prescription and nonprescription pharmaceutical and hospital products including pharmaceuticals for the treatment of infectious diseases, mental illness, cancer, arthritis, skin disorders, glaucoma, tuberculosis, and other diseases; adult and pediatric vaccines; vitamin, multivitamin, and mineral products; and Davis & Geck surgical sutures, wound closure devices, and other hospital products. **Listed on:** New York Stock Exchange. **Stock exchange symbol:** WYE.

WYETH RESEARCH
P.O. Box 150, Chazy NY 12921. 518/846-7123. **Contact:** Human Resources. **World Wide Web address:** http://www.wyeth.com. **Description:** Engaged in the research and manufacture of ethical and over-the-counter pharmaceuticals. **Operations at this facility include:** Manufacturing; Research and Development.

XELUS INC.
290 Woodcliff Drive, Fairport NY 14450. 716/248-9600. **Fax:** 716/248-9602. **Contact:** Human Resources Department. **E-mail address:** resumes@xelus.com. **World Wide Web address:** http://www.xelus.com. **Description:** Develops custom software for large corporations. **International locations:** United Kingdom.

XEROX CORPORATION
800 Phillips Road, Webster NY 14580-9720. 716/423-5090. **Fax:** 716/427-5400. **Contact:** Personnel. **World Wide Web address:** http://www.xerox.com. **Description:** Xerox Corporation develops, manufactures, markets, services, and finances information-processing products including copiers, scanners, electronic printing systems, word processing systems, personal computers, and computer peripherals. Xerox does business in over 120 companies. **Corporate headquarters location:** Stamford CT. **Operations at this facility include:** This location manufactures copiers and office machinery. **Listed on:** New York Stock Exchange. **Stock exchange symbol:** XRX.

YWCA
610 Lexington Avenue, New York NY 10022. 212/755-4500. **Fax:** 212/838-1279. **Contact:** Human Resources. **E-mail address:** info@ywcanyc.org. **World Wide Web address:** http://www.ywcanyc.org. **Description:** Provides counseling, physical fitness activities, a shelter, and daycare facilities for women and their children. **Corporate headquarters location:** This location. **Other U.S. locations:** Nationwide.

YONKERS RACEWAY
810 Central Park Avenue, Yonkers NY 10704. 914/968-4200. **Fax:** 914/968-1121. **Contact:** Anita Tripo, Director of Personnel. **World Wide Web address:** http://www.yonkersraceway.com. **Description:** Operates a major harness racing facility, as well as a convention and meeting facility. **Corporate headquarters location:** This location.

YOUNG & RUBICAM, INC.
285 Madison Avenue, 9th Floor, New York NY 10017. 212/210-3000. **Fax:** 212/210-5007. **Contact:** Human Resources. **World Wide Web address:** http://www.yandr.com. **Description:** An international advertising agency. The company operates through three divisions: Young & Rubicam International; Marsteller Inc., a worldwide leader in business-to-business and consumer advertising; and Young & Rubicam USA, with 14 consumer advertising agencies operating through four regional groups, and five specialized advertising and marketing agencies. **Special programs:** Internships. **Corporate headquarters location:** This location. **Other U.S. locations:** Nationwide.

ZEPTOMETRIX
872 Main Street, Buffalo NY 14202. 716/882-0920. **Toll-free phone:** 800/274-5487. **Contact:** Human Resources. **World Wide Web address:** http://www.zeptometrix.com. **Description:** A vertically integrated biotechnology company concentrating in the field of human retroviruses. The company markets and sells a line of diagnostic and research products that are used by organizations that perform biomedical research including public and private universities, hospitals, and public health labs.

ZIFF-DAVIS MEDIA INC.
28 East 28th Street, New York NY 10016. 212/503-3500. **Contact:** Human Resources. **World Wide Web address:** http://www.ziffdavis.com. **Description:** A magazine publisher whose periodicals are primarily computer related. Ziff-Davis also has minor broadcasting operations. **Corporate headquarters location:** This location.

ZOTOS INTERNATIONAL, INC.
P.O. Box 71, Geneva NY 14456. 203/656-7856. **Physical address:** 300 Forge Avenue, Geneva NY 14456. **Fax:** 315/789-7944. **Contact:** Human Resources. **World Wide Web address:** http://www.zotos.com. **Description:** A manufacturer of hair care products for professional salons. Product lines include Quantum, Naturelle, Zotos, and Lamaur. **Corporate headquarters location:** Darien CT. **Parent company:** Shiseido. **Operations at this facility include:** Administration; Divisional Headquarters; Manufacturing. **Number of employees at this location:** 320.

A.G. INDUSTRIES INC.
376 Pine Street Extension, Forest City NC 28043. 828/245-9871. **Fax:** 828/248-4848. **Contact:** Cheryl Anderson, Human Resources Manager. **World Wide Web address:** http://www.agischutz.com. **Description:** Manufactures display cabinets and display racks for wholesalers and stores.

AMT DATASOUTH
4216 Stuart Andrew Boulevard, Charlotte NC 28217. 704/523-8500. **Fax:** 704/525-6104. **Contact:** Human Resources. **E-mail address:** humanresources@amtdatasouth.com. **World Wide Web address:** http://www.amtdatasouth.com. **Description:** Designs, manufactures, and markets heavy-duty dot matrix and thermal printers used for high-volume print applications. The company's product lines include the XL series for medium-volume dot matrix printing applications and Documax, which has high-speed dot matrix printing capabilities. The company also manufactures a portable thermal printer, Freeliner, which is used primarily for printing one packing or shipping label at a time. **Corporate headquarters location:** Camarillo CA. **International locations:** Northampton, England. **Number of employees nationwide:** 125.

ACME ELECTRIC CORPORATION
4815 West Fifth Street, Lumberton NC 28358-0499. 910/738-1121. **Toll-free phone:** 800/334-5214. **Fax:** 910/739-0024. **Contact:** Human Resources. **World Wide Web address:** http://www.acmepowerdist.com. **Description:** Manufactures dry-type industrial distribution transformers and related products. **Corporate headquarters location:** This location. **International locations:** Monterrey Mexico. **Parent company:** Key Components Inc. **Operations at this facility include:** Administration; Divisional Headquarters; Management Consulting; Sales.

ACME-MCCRARY CORPORATION
P.O. Box 1287, Asheboro NC 27204. 336/625-2161. **Physical address:** 159 North Street, Asheboro NC 27203. **Fax:** 336/629-2263. **Contact:** Human Resources Manager. **E-mail address:** acmehose@acme-mccrary.com. **World Wide Web address:** http://www.acme-mccrary.com. **Description:** Manufactures women's sheer hosiery. **Corporate headquarters location:** This location.

ACTERNA
1100 Perimeter Park Drive, Suite 101, Morrisville NC 27560. 919/388-5100. **Contact:** Human Resources. **World Wide Web address:** http://www.acterna.com. **Description:** A manufacturer of data communications and telecommunications analysis products for communications test solutions. **NOTE:** Please visit website to search for jobs. **Corporate headquarters location:** Germantown MD. **Other U.S. locations:** Brandentown FL; Indianapolis IN; Salem VA; Terre Haute IN. **International locations:** Worldwide. **Listed on:** NASDAQ. **Stock exchange symbol:** ACTR. **President/CEO:** John Peeler.

ADSTREET INC.
1638 South Saunders Street, Raleigh NC 27603. 919/828-2990. **Fax:** 919/828-9889. **Contact:** Rich Styles, President. **World Wide Web address:** http://www.adstreet.com. **Description:** A full-service advertising and public relations agency. The company offers creative advertising work, sports marketing, and media buying services. **Corporate headquarters location:** This location. **Other U.S. locations:** Orlando FL. **CEO:** Rich Styles.

AGILYSYS
7500 East Independence Boulevard, Suite 100, Charlotte NC 28227. 704/567-8203. **Toll-free phone:** 888/833-2106. **Fax:** 704/567-9468. **Contact:** Human Resources. **World Wide Web address:** http://www.agilysys.net. **Description:** Writes programs, resells computer hardware and software, and offers technical support. Founded 1974. **NOTE:** Please visit website to view job listings. Send resumes to the corporate office location at 5 Artillery Road, Taylors SC 29687. **Corporate headquarters location:** Taylors SC. **Other area locations:** Arden NC. **Other U.S. locations:** Kingsport TN; Knoxville TN.

A4 HEALTH SYSTEMS
5501 Dillard Drive, Cary NC 27511. 919/851-6177. **Toll-free phone:** 888/672-3282. **Fax:** 919/851-5991. **Contact:** Human Resources. **E-mail address:** hr@A4healthsystems.com. **World Wide Web address:** http://www.a4healthsys.com. **Description:** Develops software and related hardware for hospitals. Founded 1970. **NOTE:** Please visit website to view job listings, and to find more details on applying for specific positions. **Positions advertised include:** Regional Sales Manager/Sales Representative; HealthMatics ED Project Manager; EMR Implementation Specialist; PM Ntierprise Implementation Specialist. **Corporate headquarters:** This location. **Other U.S. locations:** Novi MI; Austin TX; Nashua NH. **CEO:** John P. McConnell.

AJILON SERVICES INC.
2222 Chapel Hill, Nelson Highway, Suite 120, Durham NC 27713. 919/941-0001. **Toll-free phone:** 888/296-7575. **Fax:** 919/572-2656. **Contact:** Manager. **World Wide Web address:** http://www.ajilon.com. **Description:** Offers computer consulting services, project support, and end user services. Ajilon is also a leading Personnel and Services sources for the communications industry. **Office hours:** Monday – Friday, 8:00 a.m. – 5:00 p.m. **Corporate headquarters location:** Towson MD. **Other U.S. locations:** Nationwide. **International locations:** Worldwide. **Annual sales/revenues:** More than $100 million.

ALBA-WALDENSIAN, INC.
P.O. Box 100, Valdese NC 28690. 828/879-6500. **Physical address:** 201 St. Germain Avenue SW, Valdese NC 28690. **Toll-free phone:** 800/554-2522. **Contact:** Human Resources Manager. **E-mail address:** info@alba1.com. **World Wide Web address:** http://www.alba1.com. **Description:** A national, multifacility apparel-manufacturing company offering a variety of knit products. The company primarily produces women's knit hosiery and stretch panties. Alba-Waldensian also produces knit health care products, which are used in hospitals and nursing homes, and are distributed throughout the United States, Canada, England, Europe, and the Middle East. Founded in 1901. **Corporate headquarters location:** This location. **International locations:** Israel. **Parent company:** Tefron Limited Group. **President/CEO:** Lee N. Mortenson.

ALCATEL USA INC.
2301 Sugar Bush Road, Raleigh NC 27612. 919/850-6000. **Contact:** Human Resources Department. **E-mail address:** recruit.usa@alcatel.com. **World Wide Web address:** http://www.usa.alcatel.com. **Description:** Manufactures fiber-optic cable for the telecommunications and cable television markets. **Special programs:** Internships. **Corporate headquarters locations:** Plano TX. **Other area locations:** Concord NC; Greensboro NC; Clinton NC; Tarboro NC; Garner NC. **Other U.S. locations:** Nationwide. **International locations:** Worldwide. **Parent company:** Alcatel Alsthom (Paris, France). **Operations at this facility include:** Administration; Manufacturing; Research and Development; Service. **Listed on:** New York Stock Exchange. **Stock exchange symbol:** ALA. **Annual sales/revenues:** More than $100 million. **CEO:** Mike Quigley. **Number of employees nationwide:** 6,753.

ALLVAC
P.O. Box 5030, Monroe NC 28111-5030. 704/289-4511. **Physical address:** 2020 Ashcroft Avenue, Monroe NC 28110. **Toll-free phone:** 800/841-5491. **Fax:** 704/282-1577. **Contact:** Human Resources. **E-mail address:** hr@allvac.com. **World Wide Web address:** http://www.allvac.com. **Description:** Wholesalers of titanium and nickel alloys, as well as assorted metal and wire products. **Positions advertised include:** Inside Sales Representative; Manager – Business Process Development. **Corporate headquarters location:** This location. **Other U.S. locations:** Albany OR; Lockport NY; Richburg SC; Richland WA. **International locations:** Sheffield England. **Parent company:** Allegheny Technologies. **Operations at this facility include:** Administration; Manufacturing; Research and Development; Sales; Service. **Listed on:** New York Stock Exchange. **Stock exchange symbol:** ATI.

ALPHA OMEGA HEALTH INC.
6036 Six Forks Road, Raleigh NC 27609. 919/844-1008. **Toll-free phone:** 800/525-5293. **Fax:** 919/844-0042. **Contact:** Personnel. **E-mail address:** kray@aohealth.com. **World Wide Web address:** http://www.aohealth.com. **Description:** A home health care agency that also offers nurse-staffing services. Founded 1989. **NOTE:** Please visit website to search for jobs and to access online application form. **Positions advertised include:** Residential Habitation Technician; Qualified Professional. **Office hours:** Monday – Friday, 8:00 a.m. – 5:00 p.m. **Corporate headquarters location:** This location. **Other area locations:** Boone NC; Burnsville NC; Chapel Hill NC; Greenville NC; Lenoir NC; Smithfield NC; Wilmington NC; Winston-Salem NC.

ALTEC INDUSTRIES, INC.
1550 Aerial Avenue, Creedmoor NC 27522. 919/528-2535. **Contact:** Human Resources. **E-mail address:** webcreedmoor@altec.com. **World Wide Web address:** http://www.altec.com. **Description:** Altec Industries, Inc. manufactures a wide variety of products including utility trucks, overhead traveling cranes, hoists, and monorail systems. **NOTE:** Please visit website for online application form. **Special programs:** Internships. **Corporate headquarters location:** Birmingham AL. **Other U.S. locations:** Nationwide. **International locations:** Canada. **Operations at this facility include:** Manufacturing; Service. **Number of employees at this location:** 220. **Number of employees worldwide:** 2,500.

AMERICAN & EFIRD, INC.
22 American Street, P.O. Box 507, Mount Holly NC 28120. 704/827-4311. **Toll-free phone:** 704/82-4311. **Contact:** Human Resources. **E-mail address:** ae.careers@amefird.com. **World Wide Web address:** http://www.amefird.com. **Description:** Manufactures and distributes sewing thread internationally for industrial and consumer markets. American & Efird, Inc. has 12 manufacturing facilities in North Carolina. **NOTE:** All hiring for American & Efird, Inc. is done at this location. **Corporate headquarters location:** This location. **Other U.S. locations:** Nationwide. **International locations:** Worldwide. **Parent company:** Ruddick Corporation is a diversified holding company operating through its wholly-owned subsidiaries American & Efird, Inc.; Harris Teeter, Inc. (Charlotte NC) operates a regional supermarket chain and handles its own hiring; and Ruddick Investment Company.

AMERICAN CITY BUSINESS JOURNALS
120 West Morehead Street, Suite 200, Charlotte NC 28202. 704/973-1000. 375-7404. **Fax:** 704/973-1001. **Contact:** Human Resources. **World Wide Web address:** http://www.bizjournals.com. **Description:** Publishes 27 business newspapers, a legal newspaper, and the *Winston Cup Scene,* which is devoted to coverage of NASCAR motor sports racing. **Corporate headquarters locations:** This location. **Other U.S. locations:** Nationwide. **Subsidiaries include:** The Network of City Business Journals is a national advertising representation firm. Circulation of the business weeklies is 313,000. **CEO:** Ray Shaw.

AMERICAN GENERAL FINANCE
1724 Winkler Street, Wilkesboro NC 28697-2251. 336/838-5157. **Fax:** 336/838-7881. **Contact:** Human Resources. **World Wide Web address:** http://www.agfinance.com. **Description:** A consumer lending company with over 1,300 branches in 41 states. The company's subsidiaries are engaged in the consumer finance, credit card, and insurance businesses. Founded in 1920. **NOTE:** Please visit website to view job listings. **Positions advertised include:** Management Trainee; Customer Account Administrator; Customer Account Specialist. **Corporate headquarters location:** Evansville IN. **Other area locations:** Statewide. **Other U.S. locations:** Nationwide. **Parent company:** American General Corporation. **Number of employees nationwide:** 8,700.

AMERICAN RED CROSS
P.O. Box 36507, Charlotte NC 28236. 704/376-1661. **Physical address:** 2425 Park Road, Charlotte NC 28203. **Fax:** 704/370-0244. **Recorded jobline:** 704/347-8464. **Contact:** Chapter Manager. **E-mail address:** beasleysa@usa.redcross.org. **World Wide Web address:** http://www.redcrosshelps.org; http://www.redcross.org. **Description:** A humanitarian organization that aids disaster victims, gathers blood for crisis distribution, trains individuals to respond to emergencies, educates individuals on various diseases, and raises funds for other charitable establishments. **NOTE:** Please visit website to see job listings. **Special programs:** Internships. **Corporate headquarters location:** Washington DC. **Other U.S. locations:** Nationwide.

AMERICAN RED CROSS
601F Country Club Drive, Greenville NC 27834-0000. 252/355-3800. **Fax:** 252/355-8831. **Contact:** Ms. Charlene Lee, Executive Director. **E-mail address:** clee@pittredcross.org. **Wide Web address:** http://www.pittredcross.org. **Description:** A humanitarian organization that aids disaster victims, gathers blood for crisis distribution, trains individuals to respond to emergencies, educates individuals on various diseases, and raises funds for other charitable establishments. **Corporate headquarters location:** Washington DC. **Other U.S. locations:** Nationwide.

AMETEK, INC.
1210 North Carolina Highway 61, Whitsett NC 27377. 336/449-3400. **Contact:** Human Resources. **E-mail address:** corp.jobs@ametek.com. **World Wide Web address:** http://www.ametek.com. **Description:** AMETEK, Inc. is a global manufacturing company that serves a variety of industrial and commercial markets. The company produces and sells its products through its Electromechanical, Precision Instruments, and Industrial Materials groups. The Electromechanical Group has a leading market share in the production of electric motors for vacuum cleaners and floor care products. The company operates 32 manufacturing facilities. **NOTE:** Please mail resumes to the corporate office location at 37 North Valley Road Building 4, P.O. Box 1764, Paoli PA 19301. Phone is 610/647-2121, fax is 610/296-3412. Please visit website to link to jobsearch, or visit http://hotjobs.yahoo.com to search. **Corporate headquarters location:** Paoli PA. **International locations:** Denmark; England; Italy; Mexico. **Listed on:** New York Stock Exchange. **Stock exchange symbol:** AME.

Operations at this facility include: This location is part of Ametek's Technical Motor Division. **Number of employees worldwide:** 7,600.

ANALOG DEVICES, INC.
7910 Triad Center Drive, Greensboro NC 27409. 336/668-9511. **Contact:** Human Resources Manager. **World Wide Web address:** http://www.analog.com. **Description:** Designs, manufactures, and markets a broad line of high-performance linear, mixed-signal, and digital integrated circuits (ICs) that address a wide range of real-world signal processing applications. The company's principal products include system-level ICs and general purpose, standard linear ICs. Analog's system-level ICs are used primarily in communications and computer applications. Analog's core technologies are required for all of the emerging communications standards, providing the company numerous new product opportunities for ICs used in the wireless, fiber-optic, coaxial cable, and twisted pair applications that will be part of the new information infrastructure. Analog sells its products worldwide through a direct sales force, third-party industrial distributors, and independent sales representatives. The company has direct sales offices in 17 countries including the United States. **NOTE:** Please visit website to search for jobs. **Positions advertised include:** Senior IC Design Engineer. **Special programs:** Internships; Co-ops. **Corporate headquarters location:** Norwood MA. **Other U.S. locations:** WA; OR; CA; TX; GA; NJ; NH; MA. **International locations:** Worldwide. **Listed on:** New York Stock Exchange. **Stock exchange symbol:** ADI. **CEO:** Jerry Fishman. **Number of employees worldwide:** 8,600.

ANALYSTS INTERNATIONAL CORPORATION (AIC)
3131 RDU Center Drive, Suite 200, Morrisville NC 27560-9137. 919/460-6141. **Toll-free phone:** 800/669-2772. **Fax:** 919/460-6433. **Contact:** Recruiting Department. **World Wide Web address:** http://www.analysts.com. **Description:** An international computer consulting firm. The company assists clients in analyzing, designing, and developing systems for a variety of industries using different programming languages and software. **NOTE:** Please visit website or visit https://www.jobsatanalysts.com to register, search, and apply for jobs. **Positions advertised include:** IT&T Systems Support Analyst. **Corporate headquarters location:** Minneapolis MN. **Other U.S. locations:** Nationwide. **International locations:** Canada; Great Britain.

APAC
P.O. Box 6939, Asheville NC 28816. 828/665-1180. **Physical address:** 1188 Smokey Park Highway, Candler NC 28715. **Fax:** 828/665-9345. **Contact:** Human Resources. **World Wide Web address:** http://www.apac.com. **Description:** APAC is a leading transportation construction company, providing service and materials to customers across the country. **NOTE:** Please visit website to search for jobs and apply online. **Positions advertised include:** Marketing Representative. **Corporate headquarters location:** Alpharetta GA. **Other area locations:** Statewide. **Other U.S. locations:** Nationwide. **Operations at this facility include:** This location is engaged in the production of asphalt and asphalt paving services. **President:** Garry M. Higdem.

APAC – BARRUS CONSTRUCTION COMPANY
669 Bell Fork Road, Jacksonville NC 28541. 910/577-5659. **Contact:** Human Resources. **World Wide Web address:** http://www.apac.com. **Description:** A contracting company that handles a variety of construction projects and activities including asphalt, concrete, curbing, gutters, and the construction of highways, streets, and parking lots.

APAC – COASTAL CAROLINA DIVISION
P.O. Box 399, Kinston NC 28502. 252/527-8021. **Physical address:** 604 East New Bern Road, Kinston NC 28504. **Toll-free phone:** 800/849-1400. **Fax:** 252/527-4739. **Contact:** Marcia Potter, Human Resources Manager. **World Wide Web address:** http://www.apac.com. **Description:** A contracting company that handles a variety of construction projects and activities including asphalt, concrete, curbing, gutters, and the construction of highways, streets, and parking lots.

APPALACHIAN STATE UNIVERSITY
504 Dauph Blan Street, First Floor, Boone NC 28608. 828/262-3186. **Fax:** 828/262-6489. **Recorded jobline:** 828/262-6488. **Contact:** Human Resources. **E-mail address:** crowlnd@appstate.edu. **World Wide Web address:** http://www.appstate.edu. **Description:** A four-year state university. **NOTE:** You must complete an application form to be considered for employment. Please visit the website to search for jobs and download an application form, or visit the office to pick one up. Applications are kept on file for one year. You may also call the automated line at 828/262-6624 and leave your name and contact information. You can reach a Personnel Assistant at 828/262-6520. **Positions advertised include:** Office Assistant; Student Center Technical Director; Sales Manager; Maintenance Mechanic; Food Service Assistant; Chairperson – Various Departments; Assistant Professor – Various Departments; Dean – College of Arts and Sciences; GIS Lab Supervisor; Adjunct Faculty – Various Departments; Lecturer – Psychology; Collection Development Librarian. **Special programs:** Internships. **Operations at this facility include:** Administration; Research and Development; Service. **Number of employees at this location:** 2,034.

ASHEBORO CITY SCHOOLS
P.O. Box 1103, Asheboro NC 27204-1103. 336/625-5104. **Physical address:** 1126 South Park Street, Asheboro NC 27203. **Fax:** 336/625-9238. **Contact:** Timothy Allgood, Assistant Superintendent of Human Resources Department. **E-mail address:** tallgood@asheboro.k12.nc.us. **World Wide Web address:** http://www.asheboro.k12.nc.us. **Description:** Operates the public school system in Asheboro for students in kindergarten through grade 12. The curriculum includes both a vocational and college preparatory program. **NOTE:** Entry-level positions are offered. **Positions advertised include:** Custodian; Teacher Assistant; Bus Driver; Occupational Therapist; School Psychologist; Speech/Language Pathologist; Pre-Kindergarten Teacher; ESL Teacher; Technology Education Teacher; Elementary Teacher; Media Personnel. **Corporate headquarters location:** This location. **Number of employees at this location:** 592.

ATLANTIC VENEER CORPORATION
P.O. Box 660, Beaufort NC 28516. 252/728-3169. **Physical address:** 2457 Lennoxville Road, Beaufort NC 28516. **Fax:** 252/728-4906. **Contact:** Human Resources. **E-mail address:** atlanticveneer@coastalnet.com. **Description:** Manufactures, produccs, and sells veneer, hardwood lumber, and plywood. **Special programs:** Internships. **Corporate headquarters location:** This location. **Operations at this facility include:** Administration; Manufacturing; Research and Development; Sales; Service. **Number of employees at this location:** 700.

AW NORTH CAROLINA
4112 Old Oxford Highway, Durham NC 27712. 919/620-5500. **Fax:** 919/560-3388. **Contact:** Human Resources. **E-mail address:** resume@aw-nc.com. **World Wide Web address:** http://www.aw-nc.com. **Description:** Provides transmission components for the automotive industry. **NOTE:** Resumes may be mailed to: Employment Security Commission, 1105 S. Briggs Avenue, Durham NC 27703. **Positions advertised include:** Quality Engineers; Production Control Specialist; Manufacturing Manager; Electrical/Mechanical Maintenance Team Members; Document Control Specialist; Assistant Manager, Purchasing. **Corporate headquarters location:** This location.

B/E AEROSPACE, INC.
1455 Fairchild Road, Winston-Salem NC 27105. 336/767-2000. **Fax:** 336/744-1009. **Contact:** Human Resources. **World Wide Web address:** http://www.beaerospace.com. **Description:** B/E Aerospace, Inc. designs, manufactures, sells, and supports a wide range of commercial aircraft cabin interior product lines including seating products, passenger entertainment and service systems, and galley structures and inserts. The company supplies major airlines and airframe manufacturers. **NOTE:** Please visit website to search for jobs and apply online. **Positions advertised include:** Quality Engineer; Security Administrator; System Administrator. **Corporate headquarters location:** Wellington FL. **Other U.S. locations:** Nationwide. **International locations:** England; Singapore; Wales. **Operations at this facility include:** This location manufactures airplane seats. **Listed on:** NASDAQ. **Stock exchange symbol:** BEAV. **President/CEO:** Robert J. Khoury. **Annual sales/revenues:** More than $100 million. **Number of employees at this nationwide:** 3,300.

BASF CORPORATION
P.O. Box 13528, Research Triangle Park NC 27709-3528. 919/547-2000. **Physical address:** 26 Davis Drive, Research Triangle Park NC. **Fax:** 919/405-2244. **Contact:** Human Resources. **World Wide Web address:** http://www.basf.com. **Description:** Manufactures and markets industrial chemicals, yarns, and man-made fibers. **Corporate headquarters location:** Mount Olive NJ. **Other area locations:** Morganton NC; Enka NC; Wilmington NC; Charlotte NC. **Other U.S. locations:** Nationwide. **International locations:** Worldwide. **Listed on:** New York Stock Exchange. **Stock exchange symbol:** BASF. **Parent company:** BASF America Inc. **Number of employees worldwide:** 87,000.

BB&T CORPORATION
200 West Second Street, Winston-Salem NC 27101. 336/733-2000. **Fax:** 336/733-2009. **Contact:** Human Resources. **World Wide Web address:** http://www.bbandt.com. **Description:** BB&T Corporation is a multibank holding company. Founded in 1872. **NOTE:** Please visit website to search for jobs and apply online. Entry-level positions and part-time jobs are offered. **Positions advertised include:** Accounting Policy Manager; Compensation and Benefits Plan Administration Merger Analyst; Credit Risk Quantitative Analyst; Financial Audit Coordinator; Internal Auditor; Securities Compliance Manager; Senior Interior Designer. **Company slogan:** Respect the individual. Value the relationship. **Special programs:** Internships; Training; Summer Jobs. **Office hours:** Monday - Friday, 8:30 a.m. - 5:00 p.m. **Corporate headquarters location:** This location. **Other U.S. locations:** Eastern and Southeastern U.S. **Subsidiaries include:** BB&T of North Carolina, which offers full-service commercial and retail banking and additional financial services such as investments, leasing, factoring, and trust. **Listed on:** New York Stock Exchange. **Stock exchange symbol:** BBT. **CEO:** John Allison. **President:** Kelly King. **Purchasing Manager:** Steve Paige. **Annual sales/revenues:** More than $100 million. **Number of employees at this location:** 750. **Number of employees nationwide:** 26,300.

BB&T
500 North Chestnut Street, Lumberton NC 28359. 910/272-2131. **Fax:** 910/272-2103. **Contact:** Laurie Currie, Human Resources. **World Wide Web address:** http://www.bbandt.com. **Description:** A bank engaged in commercial banking, mortgages, discount brokerage, mutual funds, leasing, insurance, retail banking, trust services, annuities, international banking, cash management, and sales finance. **NOTE:** Please visit website to search for jobs and apply online. **Corporate headquarters location:** Winston-Salem NC. **Other U.S. locations:** Eastern and Southeastern U.S. **Parent company:** BB&T-Southern National Corporation was formed by the 1994 merger of Branch Bank & Trust Financial Corporation and Southern National Corporation. Its subsidiaries form a network of hundreds of branches in cities and communities across the Carolinas and Virginia. Other subsidiaries of BB&T-Southern National Corporation include: BB&T-Southern National Bank of South Carolina; BB&T-Southern National Savings Bank, Inc.; Branch Banking & Trust (BB&T-NC); Commerce Bank of Virginia Beach; Community Bank of South Carolina; and Lexington State Bank. **Stock exchange symbol:** BBT. **CEO:** John Allison. **Number of employees nationwide:** 26,300.

BSH HOME APPLIANCES
120 Bosch Boulevard, New Bern NC 28562-6997. 252/636-4454. **Contact:** Chuck Dale, Manager of Human Resources. **Description:** A manufacturer of electrical industrial power tools for woodworking and concrete applications. **Special programs:** Internships. **Corporate headquarters location:** Chicago IL. **Other U.S. locations:** Heber Springs AK; Walnut Ridge AR. **Operations at this facility include:** Manufacturing. **Number of employees at this location:** 350. **Number of employees nationwide:** 2,300.

BANK OF AMERICA
100 North Tryon Street, Charlotte NC 28255. 704/386-1845. **Toll-free phone:** 800/432-1000. **Fax:** 704/386-6699. **Contact:** Personnel. **World Wide Web address:** http://www.bankofamerica.com. **Description:** A full-service banking and financial institution. Bank of America operates through four business segments: Global Corporate and Investment Banking, Principal Investing and Asset Management, Commercial Banking, and Consumer Banking. **Corporate headquarters location:** This location. **Other U.S. locations:** Nationwide. **Listed on:** New York Stock Exchange. **Stock exchange symbol:** BAC. **CEO:** Kenneth D. Lewis. **Number of employees worldwide:** 133,549.

BARNHILL CONTRACTING COMPANY
P.O. Box 35376, Fayetteville NC 28303-5376. 910/488-1319. **Physical address:** 1134 Shaw Mill Road, Fayetteville NC. **Fax:** 910/488-5673. **Contact:** S. James Hughes, Jr., Vice President of Human Resources. **E-mail address:** jhughes@barnhillcontracting.com. **World Wide Web address:** http://www.barnhillcontracting.com. **Description:** Barnhill Contracting Company is a construction company operating in two divisions. The Building Division is engaged in nonresidential building construction, such as schools and public buildings. The Paved Roads Division is involved in heavy highway construction and driveway paving. **NOTE:** Please visit website to search for jobs. If there is no specific contact listed for the position you are interested in, send your resume to the above contact at P.O. Box 1529, Tarboro NC 27886. Phone is 252/823-1021, fax is 252/823-0137. **Positions advertised include:** Pipe Foreman; Asphalt Paving Machine Screed Operator; Asphalt Distributor Truck Driver; Asphalt Laborer; Scraper Operator. **Other area locations:** Elizabeth City NC; Kitty Hawk NC; Raleigh NC; Tarboro NC; Rocky Mount NC; Wilmington NC. **Other U.S. locations:** VA. **Operations at this facility include:** This location produces asphalt. **Listed on:** Privately held. **President/CEO:** Robert E. Barnhill ,Jr.

BASSETT FURNITURE INDUSTRIES, INC.
1111 East 20th Street, Newton NC 28658. 828/465-7700. **Contact:** Human Resources Department. **E-mail address:** bassett@bassettfurniture.com. **World Wide Web address:** http://www.bassettfurniture.com. **Description:** Manufactures and sells a full line of furniture for the home, such as bedroom and dining suites; accent pieces; occasional tables; wall and entertainment units; upholstered sofas, chairs, and love seats; recliners; and mattresses and box springs. **Corporate headquarters location:** Bassett VA. **Operations at this location include:** This location is part of Bassett's Upholstery Division. **Listed on:** NASDAQ. **Stock exchange symbol:** BSET. **President/CEO:** Rob Spilman. **Number of employees nationwide:** 7,800.

BAYER CROP SCIENCE
2 T.W. Alexander Drive, P.O. Box 12, Research Triangle Park NC 27709. 919/549-2000. **Toll-free phone:** 800/842-8020. **Fax:** 919/549-2641. **Contact:** Human Resources. **World Wide Web address:** http://www.bayercropscienceus.com. **Description:** Involved in the research and development of pesticides and herbicides. **NOTE:** Please visit http://www.bayerjobs.com to search for jobs. **Corporate headquarters location:** This location. **Other U.S. locations:** Kansas City MO. **International locations:** Worldwide. **Parent company:** Bayer AG. **Listed on:** New York Stock Exchange. **Stock exchange symbol:** BAY. **Number of employees at this location:** 500.

BELK STORES SERVICES INC.
P.O. Box 1099, Charlotte NC 28201-1099. 704/357-1000. **Physical address:** 2801 West Tyvola Road, Charlotte NC 28217-4500. **Toll-free phone:** 866/235-5443. **Fax:** 704/357-1876. **Contact:** Human Resources. **World Wide Web address:** http://www.belk.com. **Description:** Operates 260 department stores located in 14 southeastern states. **Special programs:** Internships. **Corporate headquarters location:** This location. **Other U.S. locations:** East and Southeast U.S. **CEO:** John M. Belk. **Number of employees nationwide:** 17,800.

BELLSOUTH ADVERTISING AND PUBLISHING CORPORATION
9144 Arrowpoint Boulevard, Suite 100, Charlotte NC 28273. 800/532-1060. **Contact:** Employment Office. **World Wide Web address:** http://www.bellsouth.com/bapco. **Description:** Publishes print telephone directories in the southeastern United States, Brazil, and Peru. **NOTE:** Please visit website to search for jobs and apply online. **Positions advertised include:** Account Executive; Network Manager; Directory Advertising; Directory Telephone Sales Representative. **Corporate headquarters location:** Atlanta GA. **Other area locations:** Statewide. **Subsidiaries include:** Stevens Graphics; The Berry Company. **Parent company:** BellSouth Corporation. **Operations at this facility include:** Administration; Regional Headquarters; Sales; Service. **Listed on:** New York Stock Exchange. **Stock exchange symbol:** BLS. **CEO:** F. Duane Ackerman.

THE BILTMORE COMPANY/BILTMORE HOUSE
1 Pack Square, Asheville NC 28801. 828/255-1333. **Toll-free phone:** 800/624-1575. **Fax:** 828/225-6744. **Contact:** Human Resources Manager. **E-mail address:** humanresouces@biltmore.com. **World Wide Web address:** http://www.biltmore.com. **Description:** The Biltmore Company is an organization dedicated to the preservation of the largest privately-owned historic house in America (Biltmore House) and its 50,000-object collection. Founded in 1986. **NOTE:** Please visit website to download application form. **Positions advertised include:** Systems Support Trainee; Parking Host; Retail Stockroom Supervisor; Sales Manager; Administrative Assistant; Education Program Coordinator; Floral Display Staff; Engineering Services Staff; Housekeeping Staff; Winery Production Staff; Call Direction Host; Food and Beverage Director; Front Desk Supervisor; Operations Specialist; Engineer; Facility Services Crew Leader; Reservation Sales Agent; Concierge; Reception and Ticket Center Host; E-commerce Customer Service and Sales Representative. **Special programs:** Internships. **Office hours:** Monday – Friday, 9:00 a.m. – 4:00 p.m. **Number of employees at this location:** 1,500.

BLAIR PUBLISHING
1406 Plaza Drive, Winston-Salem NC 27103. 336/768-1374. **Toll-free phone:** 800/222-9796. **Fax:** 336/768-9194. **Contact:** Human Resources. **E-mail address:** sakowski@blairpub.com. **World Wide Web address:** http://www.blairpub.com. **Description:** A general trade publisher of specialty regional titles including history, travel, folklore, and biographies. The company publishes 15 - 20 books per year. Founded in 1954. **Special programs:** Internships. **Corporate headquarters location:** This location. **President:** Carolyn Sakowski.

BLAST SOFTWARE
220 Chatham Business Drive, P.O. Box 818, Pittsboro NC 27312. 919/542-2535. **Toll-free phone:** 800/24B-LAST. **Fax:** 919/542-5955. **Contact:** Human Resources. **World Wide Web address:** http://www.blast.com. **Description:** Develops communications software that offers cross-platform file transfer, reliable terminal emulation, and error correction. **President:** Lyle Estill.

BLOCKADE RUNNER HOTEL
275 Waynick Boulevard, Wrightsville Beach NC 28480. 910/256-2251. **Contact:** Personnel. **E-mail address:** blockade@bellsouth.net. **World Wide Web address:** http://www.blockade-runner.com. **Description:** A full-service hotel with 150 rooms.

BLUE CROSS AND BLUE SHIELD OF NORTH CAROLINA
P.O. Box 2291, Durham NC 27702-2291. 919/489-7431. **Physical address:** 1830 US 15-501 North, Chapel Hill NC 27514. **Toll-free phone:** 800/250-3630. **Contact:** Personnel. **World Wide Web address:** http://www.bcbsnc.com. **Description:** A nonprofit health care insurance organization providing managed health care plans to both individuals and groups. Blue Cross and Blue Shield offers Point-of-Service, individual health, and HMO plans, as well as life insurance, dental insurance, accidental death and dismemberment, and short- and long-term disability. **NOTE:** Please visit website to search for jobs and apply online. **Corporate headquarters location:** This location. **Other area locations:** Winston-Salem NC; Hickory NC; Charlotte NC; Morrisville NC; Greensboro NC; Wilmington NC; Greenville NC.

BORG WARNER EMISSIONS/THERMAL SYSTEMS
P.O. Box 1509, Fletcher NC 28732. 828/684-3501. **Physical address:** 40 Cane Creek Industrial Park, Fletcher NC 23732. **Fax:** 828/687-5325. **Contact:** Human Resources. **World Wide Web address:** http://www.cs.bwauto.com. **Description:** Borg Warner is a worldwide manufacturer of hydraulic products, fluid connectors, electrical power distribution equipment, engine components, and truck drive train systems. The company serves a variety of industries including automotive, aerospace, industrial, and semiconductor. Founded 1928. **NOTE:** Please send resume to corporate office location at 3800 Automation Avenue, Suite 200, Auburn Mills MI 48326. **Special programs:** Internships. **Corporate headquarters location:** Auburn Hills MI. **International locations:** Brazil; United Kingdom; Germany; Korea; Japan; China; India. **Parent company:** BorgWarner Engine Group. **Operations at this facility include:** This location manufactures viscous fan drives. **Listed on:** New York Stock Exchange. **Stock exchange symbol:** BWA. **Number of employees at this location:** 500. **Number of employees worldwide:** 14,000.

BOSTON GEAR
701 North Interstate 85 Service Road, Charlotte NC 28216. 704/588-5610. **Contact:** Human Resources Department. **E-mail address:** hr@bostongear.com. **World Wide Web address:** http://www.bostongear.com. **Description:** Boston Gear manufactures speed-reducers used for conveyor belts including those used at retail checkout counters. **NOTE:** Please visit website to search for jobs. **Corporate headquarters location:** Quincy MA. **Parent company:** Colfax Power Transmission Group. **Operations at this facility include:** Manufacturing.

BRADY DISTRIBUTING
P.O. Box 19269, Charlotte NC 28219. 704/357-6284. **Physical address:** 2708 Yorkmont Road, Charlotte NC 28208. **Fax:** 704/357-1243. **Contact:** Sue Ballard, Human Resources Manager. **World Wide Web address:** http://www.bradydist.com. **Description:** Distributes and operates coin-operated vending machines and arcade games. **Office hours:** Monday – Friday, 8:00 a.m. – 5:00 p.m. **Corporate headquarters location:** This location. **Other U.S. locations:** Miami FL; Orlando FL; Memphis TN. **Number of employees nationwide:** 120.

BREVARD COLLEGE
400 North Broad Street, Brevard NC 28712. 828/883-8292. **Fax:** 828/884-3790. **Contact:** Employment. **World Wide Web address:** http://www.brevard.edu. **Description:** A four-year liberal arts college offering education services to more than 650 students. Founded 1853. **NOTE:** Please visit website to view job listings and for more information on applying for specific positions. **Positions advertised include:** Director – Center for Career, Service, and Learning; Director of Student Activities; Director of First Year Programs; Admissions Counselor; Director of the Academic Enrichment Center; Head Women's Soccer Coach; Assistant Professor; Athletic Director; Business and Organizational Leadership. **President:** Drew L. Van Horn.

BROOKS, PIERCE, McLENDON, HUMPHREY & LEONARD, L.L.P.
P.O. Box 26000, Greensboro NC 27420. 336/373-8850. **Physical address:** 2000 Renaissance Plaza, 230 North Elm Street, Greensboro NC 27401. **Fax:** 336/378-1001. **Contact:** Ms. Mary Beth McCausland, Recruiting Coordinator. **E-mail address:** mmccausland@brookspierce.com **World Wide Web address:** http://www.brookspierce.com. **Description:** A corporate law firm. Founded 1897. **Positions advertised include:** Attorney. **Special programs:** Summer Associate Program. **Other area locations:** Raleigh NC. **Other U.S. locations:** Washington D.C. **Number of employees at this location:** 135.

BURKE MILLS, INC.
P.O. Box 190, Valdese NC 28690. 828/874-6341. **Physical address:** 191 Sterling Street, Valdese NC. **Fax:** 828/879-7176. **Contact:** Human Resources. **World Wide Web address:** http://www.burkemills.com. **Description:** Engaged in twisting, texturing, winding, dyeing, processing, and selling filament, novelty, and spun yarns and also in the dyeing and processing of these yarns for others on a commission basis. The company's products have upholstery, apparel, and industrial uses for the knitting and weaving industry. **Corporate headquarters location:** This location. **Listed on:** Over-the-Counter. **Stock exchange symbol:** BMLS. **CEO:** Humayan N. Shaikh. **Number of employees nationwide:** 167.

CB RICHARD ELLIS
201 South College Street, Suite 1900, Charlotte NC 28244. 704/376-7979. **Fax:** 704/331-1259. **Contact:** Human Resources. **E-mail address:** cbrejobs@cbre.com. **World Wide Web address:** http://www.cbrichardellis.com. **Description:** A real estate services company offering property sales and leasing, property and facility management, mortgage banking, and investment management services. **NOTE:** Please visit website to search for jobs and apply online. Online job listings are updated every business day. **Corporate headquarters location:** Los Angeles CA. **Other area locations:** Raleigh NC. **Other U.S. locations:** Nationwide. **International locations:** Worldwide. **CEO:** Raymond Wirta. **Number of employees nationwide:** 9,600. **Number of employees worldwide:** 13,500.

CB RICHARD ELLIS
1201 Edwards Mill Road, Suite 100, Raleigh NC 27607. 919/831-8200. **Fax:** 919/856-2530. **Contact:** Human Resources. **E-mail address:** cbrejobs@cbre.com. **World Wide Web address:** http://www.cbrichardellis.com. **Description:** A real estate services company offering property sales and leasing, property and facility management, mortgage banking, and investment management services. **NOTE:** Please visit website to search for jobs and apply online. Online job listings are updated every business day. **Corporate headquarters location:** Los Angeles CA. **Other area locations:** Charlotte NC. **Other U.S. locations:** Nationwide. **International locations:** Worldwide. **CEO:** Raymond Wirta. **Number of employees nationwide:** 9,600. **Number of employees worldwide:** 13,500.

CEM CORPORATION
P.O. Box 200, Matthews NC 28106. 704/821-7015. **Physical address:** 3100 Smith Farm Road, Matthew NC 28105. **Toll-free phone:** 800/726-3331. **Fax:** 704/821-0491. **Contact:** Molly Flowers, Human Resources. **E-mail address:** human.resources@cem.com. **World Wide Web address:** http://www.cem.com. **Description:** CEM Corporation develops, manufactures, markets, and services microwave-based instrumentation for testing and analysis in the industrial and analytical laboratory markets. The company's products include microwave digestion systems, moisture/solids analyzers, fat analyzer systems, microwave extraction systems, microwave ashing systems, and SpectroPrep systems. **NOTE:** Please visit website to search for jobs. **Corporate headquarters location:** This location. **Subsidiaries include:** CEM (France); CEM GmbH (Kamp-Linfort, Germany); CEM Ltd. (Buckingham, England); CEM S.r.l. (Cologno al Serio, Italy). **CEO:** Michael Collins. **Number of employees nationwide:** 175.

CII ASSOCIATES, INC.
7200 Falls of the Neuse Road, Suite 202, Raleigh NC 27615. 919/676-8300. **Toll-free phone:** 800/832-3443. **Fax:** 919/676-8484. **Contact:** Human Resources. **E-mail address:** hr@ciinc.com. **World Wide Web address:** http://www.ciinc.com. **Description:** Offers consulting services for software developers. **NOTE:** Contact Human Resources at Ext. 159; E-mail Recruiting at Ext. 123. Contact Sue Wadkinson, Human Resources Manager at sue.wadkinson@ciinc.com. E-mail Chris Allen, Director of Technical Recruiting at chris.allen@ciinc.com. E-mail general recruiting at recruiting@ciinc.com. **President/CEO:** Ray Allen.

CSA WIRELESS
730 21st Street Drive SE, Hickory NC 28602. 828/466-0412. **Fax:** 828/327-6027. **Contact:** Human Resources. **E-mail address:** personnel@csa-wireless.com. **World Wide Web address:** http://www.csa-wireless.com. **Description:** Manufactures antenna

products and systems for the wireless and microwave markets. **International locations:** United Kingdom.

CVS
297 East 22nd Street, Kannapolis NC 28083. 704/939-6000. **Contact:** Jeannene Allen, Employee Relations Manager. **World Wide Web address:** http://www.cvs.com. **Description:** CVS operates a chain of drugstores throughout the United States. Pharmacy operations make up a large portion of the company's business, offering both brand name and generic prescription drugs. CVS stores also offer a broad range of health and beauty aids, cosmetics, greeting cards, convenience foods, photo finishing services, and other general merchandise. **Office hours:** Monday – Friday, 8:00 a.m. 5:00 p.m. **Corporate headquarters location:** Woonsocket RI. **Operations at this facility include:** This location serves as an area business office. **Listed on:** New York Stock Exchange. **Stock exchange symbol:** CVS. **Number of employees nationwide:** 110,000.

CALDWELL COUNTY SCHOOL DISTRICT
1914 Hickory Boulevard SW, Lenoir NC 28645. 828/728-8407. **Recorded jobline:** 828/728-2800. **Fax:** 828/728-0012. **Contact:** Pat Mitchell, Personnel. **E-mail address:** pmitchell@caa.k12.nc.us. **World Wide Web address:** http://www.caa.k12.nc.us. **Description:** Administrative offices of the public school district. **NOTE:** Please visit website to view job listings and apply online. You may apply online at http://schooljobs.dpi.state.nc.us. **Positions advertised include:** Wrap Around Lead Assistant; Principal; Assistant Principal; Media Coordinator; Career Development Coordinator; Rising Stars Coordinator; Exceptional Teacher Assistant – Temporary; Transportation Director.

CAROLINA FARM CREDIT
P.O. Box 1827, Statesville NC 28687. 704/873-0276. **Physical address:** 1704 Wilkesboro Highway, Statesville NC 28625. **Toll-free phone:** 800/521-9952. **Fax:** 704/873-6900. **Contact:** Human Resources. **E-mail address:** jobs@carolinafarmcredit.com. **World Wide Web address:** http://www.carolinafarmcredit.com. **Description:** Farm Credit Services provides financial services through 39 branch offices across the United States. FCS offers long-, intermediate-, and short-term financing to agricultural producers, farm-related businesses, fishermen, part-time farmers, and rural homeowners. **NOTE:** Please visit http://www.agfirst.com and click the 'Employment Opportunities' button to search for jobs. **Positions advertised include:** Appraiser; Credit Analyst. **Corporate headquarters location:** This location. **Other area locations:** Statewide.

CAROLINA INN
211 Pittsboro Street, Chapel Hill NC 27514. 919/933-2001. **Fax:** 919/918-2763. **Recorded jobline:** 919/918-2769. **Contact:** Cheryl Wendel, Human Resources. **E-mail address:** hr@carolinainn.com. **World Wide Web address:** http://www.carolinainn.com. **Description:** A 194-room hotel with conference facilities and banquet staff. The hotel has been rated with Four Diamonds on the National Register of Historic Places. **NOTE:** For management positions, please visit http://www.aramarkcareers.com to search for jobs and apply online.

CAROLINA MIRROR COMPANY
P.O. Box 1570, North Wilkesboro NC 28659-0548. 336/838-2151. **Physical address:** 201 Elkin Highway, North Wilkesboro NC. **Toll-free phone:** 800/334-7245. **Fax:** 336/838-9734. **Contact:** Human Resources. **E-mail address:** jkilby@carolinamirror.com. **World Wide Web address:** http://www.carolinamirror.com. **Description:** Manufactures mirrors. **Corporate headquarters location:** This location. **Operations at this facility include:** Administration; Manufacturing; Sales. **Listed on:** Privately held. **Number of employees at this location:** 575.

CAROLINA TURKEYS
P.O. Box 589, Mount Olive NC 28365. 919/658-6743. **Physical address:** 1628 Garner Chapel Road, Mount Olive NC. **Toll-free phone:** 800/523-4559. **Fax:** 919/658-5865. **Contact:** Human Resources. **World Wide Web address:** http://www.carolinaturkey.com. **Description:** A turkey processing company. Carolina Turkeys processes more than 22 million birds annually. The company is a fully integrated operation that includes diagnostic labs, research and breeder farms, hatcheries, and feed mills. The company's line of turkey meats is distributed across the country to restaurants, delis, hospitals, schools, and retail markets. Products include Just Perfect Turkey Breasts, Premium Turkey Breasts, Classic and Legend Turkey Breasts, Deluxe and Deli Turkey Breasts, and Cured Deli Meats & Franks. Founded in 1986. **NOTE:** Second and third shifts are offered. **Special programs:** Internships; Training. **Office hours:** Monday - Friday, 8:00 a.m. - 6:00 p.m. **Corporate headquarters location:** This location. **Parent company:** Goldsboro Milling. **CEO:** C. Daniel Blackshear. **Number of employees at this location:** 2,150.

CARSONS INC.
4200 Cheyenne Drive, P.O. Box 14186, Archdale NC 27263. 336/431-1101. **Contact:** Betty Hilton, Human Resources Manager. **World Wide Web address:** http://www.carsonsofhp.com. **Description:** Carsons Inc. manufactures upholstered furniture. The company wholesales its furniture to retail stores. **Corporate headquarters location:** This location.

CARY, TOWN OF
P.O. Box 8005, Cary NC 27512-8005. 919/469-4070. **Physical address:** 100 Charlie Gaddy Lane, Cary NC 27511. **Fax:** 919/319-4567. **Recorded jobline:** 919/319-4500x283. **Contact:** Valiria Willis, Director of Human Resources. **E-mail address:** valiria.willis@townofcary.org. **World Wide Web address:** http://www.townofcary.org. **Description:** Municipal government for one of the 10 largest cities in North Carolina. **NOTE:** Please visit website to view job listings and download an application form. You must complete an application in order to be considered for employment. Human Resources direct contact phone numbers are 919/469-4070 and 919/469-4072. Do not fax resumes. **Positions advertised include:** Police Project Manager; Operations, Construction and Fleet Management; Wastewater System Worker; Solid Waste Collector; Special Events Team Member; Utility Maintenance Worker; Engineer; Arts Director; Center Aide; Cultural Arts Teaching Assistant; Park Attendant; Recreation Program Instructor. **Office hours:** Monday – Friday, 8:00 a.m. – 5:00 p.m. **Number of employees at this location:** 750.

CASE FARMS, INC.
P.O. Box 308, Morganton NC 28680. 828/438-6900. **Physical address:** 121 Rand Street Morganton NC 28655-3925. **Fax:** 828/437-5205. **Contact:** Human Resources. **Description:** Processes chicken for sale to retailers and sells chicken parts to manufacturers of pet foods.

CASHWELL APPLIANCE PARTS, INC.
P.O. Box 2549, Fayetteville NC 28302-2549. **Physical address:** 3485 Clinton Road, Fayetteville NC 28312-6147. 910/323-1111. **Toll-free phone:** 800/277-1220. **Fax:** 910/323-5067. **Toll-free fax:** 800/277-2877. **Contact:** Human Resources. **World Wide Web address:** http://www.cashwell-appl-parts.com. **Description:** Distributes bathroom fans, ceiling fans, dryers, electrical equipment parts, and washers. **NOTE:** Please visit website to see job listings. **Positions advertised include:** Warehouse Worker. **Other area locations:** Raleigh NC; Wilmington NC; Asheville NC; Charlotte NC; Greensboro NC. **Operations at this facility include:** This location is a distribution center,

CATO CORPORATION
8100 Denmark Road, Charlotte NC 28273-5975. 704/554-8510. **Fax:** 704/551-7246. **Contact:** Lynne Morton, Recruiter. **E-mail address:** catjobs@catcorp.com. **World Wide Web address:** http://www.catocorp.com. **Description:** Owns and operates over 500 stores in 22 states. The stores operate under the names Cato, Cato Fashions, and Cato Plus, and feature women's apparel for junior, misses, and large-sized customers. The company also has an off-price division that operates 67 stores under the Its Fashion! name, featuring primarily sportswear and accessories. **Positions advertised include:** Executive Administrative Assistant; Payroll Clerk; Payroll Director; Tax Manager; Vice President – Internal Audit; Human Resources File Clerk; Programmer Analyst; Store Development Coordinator; Store Analyst; Jewelry Buyer; Technical Specialist. **Corporate headquarters location:** This location. **Other U.S. locations:** Southeast, South, East, and Middle U.S. **Number of employees nationwide:** 2,800.

CEDALION CORPORATION
401 South Sharon Amity Road, Charlotte NC 28211-2848. 704/716-1400. **Fax:** 704/716-1401. **Contact:** Bill Craemer, Human Resources. **E-mail address:** wcraemer@cedalion.net. **World Wide Web address:** http://www.cedalion.com. **Description:** Provides networking skills development training and networking expertise to companies that deploy advanced networking technologies. Founded in 1984. **NOTE:** Please visit website to download application form. **Office hours:** Monday - Friday, 8:00 a.m. - 5:00 p.m. **Listed on:** Privately held. **CEO:** Bill Thorpe.

CENTRAL PRISON
1300 Western Boulevard, Raleigh NC 27606. 919/733-0800x411. **Fax:** 919/715-2645. **Contact:** Personnel. **World Wide Web address:** http://www.doc.state.nc.us/DOP/prisons/Central.htm. **Description:** A prison hospital. **NOTE:** Please visit website to search for jobs and download application form. You must complete an application to be considered for employment. Specific contact information is available with listed jobs. **Positions advertised include:** Dentist; RN; LPN; Staff Psychologist; Correctional Officer. **Operations at this facility include:** Service. **Number of employees at this location:** 500.

CHARLOTTE, CITY OF
600 East Fourth Street, Charlotte NC 28202. 704/336-2285. **Fax:** 704/336-3236. **Recorded jobline:** 704/336-3968. **Contact:** City Human Resources Department. **E-mail address:** vacancyresumes@ci.charlotte.nc.us. **World Wide Web address:** http://www.charmeck.nc.us. **Description:** Administrative offices for the city of Charlotte and the Mecklenburg County Government. **Positions advertised include:** Administrative Officer; Animal Control Bureau Manager; Assistant Corporate Communications Director; Print Production Coordinator; Procurement Officer; Wellness Program Administrator; Assistant Project Manager; Engineering Project Manager; Planning/Design Engineer; Watershed Manager; Director of Planning; Transportation Planner; Management Analyst; Accounting Clerk; Office Assistant; Airport Law Enforcement Officer; Police Officer; Electrician; Street Maintenance Crew Member. **Corporate headquarters location:** This location. **Operations at this facility include:** Administration; Service. **Number of employees at this location:** 5,700.

CHARLOTTE MARRIOTT CITY CENTER
100 West Trade Street, Charlotte NC 28202. 704/333-9000. **Toll-free phone:** 800/4-MARRIOTT. **Fax:** 704/342-3419. **Contact:** Nancy McNeill, Director of Human Resources. **World Wide Web address:** http://www.marriottcitycenter.com. **Description:** A 421-guest room hotel featuring an indoor pool, a health club, and two restaurants. **NOTE:** Please visit website to search for jobs and apply online. **Positions advertised include:** Director of Sales; Chief Engineer. **Corporate headquarters location:** Washington D.C. **Other U.S. locations:** Nationwide. **Listed on:** New York Stock Exchange. **Stock exchange symbol:** MAR. **CEO:** J. Marriott. **Number of employees worldwide:** 128,000.

CHARLOTTE SYMPHONY ORCHESTRA
201 South College Street, Suite 110, College Street Level, Charlotte NC 28244. 704/972-2003. **Fax:** 704/972-2011. **Contact:** Celia Jelley, Orchestra Personnel Manager. **E-mail address:** celiaj@charlottesymphony.org. **World Wide Web address:** http://www.charlottesymphony.org. **Description:** Offices of the local symphony orchestra. The symphony plays 115 performances every season, to an accumulated audience of over 250,000. Founded in 1932. **Operations at this facility include:** Administration; Sales; Service. **President:** Richard L. Early.

CHARLOTTE-MECKLENBURG SCHOOL SYSTEM
P.O. Box 30035, Charlotte NC 28230-0035. 980/343-3000. **Physical address:** 701 East Second Street, Charlotte NC 28202. **Fax:** 704/343-3124. **Contact:** Human Resources. **E-mail address:** hr@cms.k12.nc.us. **World Wide Web address:** http://www.cms.k12.nc.us. **Description:** Administrative offices of the public school system. **NOTE:** Please visit website to search for jobs and apply online. Applications are kept on file for one year. **Positions advertised include:** Bus Driver; ASEP Associate; Site Coordinator; Science/Chemistry Teacher; Office Coordinator; Preschool Psychologist; Administrative Secretary; HVAC Mechanic; Grounds Worker; ISS Assistant; Early Reading First Coach; Custodian; Administrative Student Intervention Assistant; Bilingual Resource Assistant; Senior Administrative Secretary; Band Teacher; Keyboarding Teacher; Business Analyst; Technician; Talent Development Compliance Teacher. **Office hours:** Monday – Friday, 8:00 a.m. – 5:00 p.m. **Corporate headquarters location:** This location.

CHEMETALL FOOTE MINERAL COMPANY
348 Holiday Inn Drive, Kings Mountain NC 28086. 704/739-2501. **Fax:** 704/734-0208. **Contact:** Human Resources. **E-mail address:** human-resources@chemetall.com. **World Wide Web address:** http://www.chemetall.com. **Description:** One of the world's largest producers of lithium carbonide, which is used in aluminum melting, synthetic rubber, specialty glass greases, batteries, and pharmaceuticals. **Corporate headquarters location:** This location. **Other U.S. locations:** New Johnsonville TN; Silver Peak NV; Duffield VA; Berkeley Heights NJ; La Marida CA; Romulus MI. **International locations:** Worldwide. **Parent company:** Dynamit Nobel AG. **Operations at this facility include:** Administration; R&D; Sales. **Number of employees at this location:** 75. **Number of employees worldwide:** 2,514.

CHEMICAL INDUSTRY INSTITUTE OF TOXICOLOGY (CIIT)
P.O. Box 12137, 6 Davis Drive, Research Triangle Park NC 27709. 919/558-1200. **Contact:** Rusty Bramlage, Human Resources Director. **E-mail address:**

bramlage@ciit.org. **World Wide Web address:** http://www.ciit.org. **Description:** An independent, nonprofit research corporation dedicated to the training of toxicologists and the scientific, objective study of toxicological issues involved in the manufacture, handling, use, and disposal of commodity chemicals. Founded 1974. **NOTE:** Please visit website for online application form. **Positions advertised include:** Respiratory Biologist/Toxicologist; Experimental Pathologist; Postdoctoral Fellow – Biochemistry and Inhalation; Postdoctoral Fellow – Bioinformatics; Postdoctoral Fellow – Reproductive Biology; Vice President for Finance and Operations. **President:** Dr. William F. Greenlee.

CIBER INFORMATION SERVICES
201 South College Street, Suite 1450, Charlotte NC 28244. 704/548-1010. **Toll-free phone:** 800/490-9230. **Fax:** 704/548-1021. **Contact:** Administrative Assistant. **World Wide Web address:** http://www.ciber.com. **Description:** Provides strategic information technology consulting, multiline ERP/EAS consulting, and professional staff supplemental services including computer network services. Founded in 1974. **NOTE:** Part-time jobs are offered. Please visit website to search for jobs and apply online. **Special programs:** Training. **Corporate headquarters location:** Greenwood Village CO. **Other area locations:** Raleigh NC. **Other U.S. locations:** Nationwide. **International locations:** Worldwide. **Listed on:** New York Stock Exchange. **Stock exchange symbol:** CBR. **President:** Mac J. Slingerlend. **Listed on:** New York Stock Exchange. **Stock exchange symbol:** CBR. **Annual sales/revenues:** $21 - $50 million. **Number of employees at this location:** 50.

CISCO SYSTEMS, INC.
7025 Kit Creek Drive, Research Triangle Park NC 27709. 919/392-2000. **Toll-free phone:** 800/326-1941. **Fax:** 919/392-9999. **Contact:** Human Resources. **E-mail address:** apply@cisco.com. **World Wide Web address:** http://www.cisco.com. **Description:** Develops, manufactures, markets, and supports high-performance internetworking systems that enable customers to build large-scale, integrated computer networks. The company's products connect and manage communications for local and wide area networks that employ a variety of protocols, media interfaces, network topologies, and cable systems. **NOTE:** Please visit website to search for jobs and apply online. **Positions advertised include:** Solution Program Manager; Customer Support Engineer; Network Consulting Engineer; Customer Support Engineer; Design Consultant; Software/QA Engineer; AS Project Manager; IT Engineer; Manager – IT; Corporate Counsel; Human Resources Manager; Associate Inside Sales Representative. **Corporate headquarters location:** San Jose CA. **Other area locations:** Charlotte NC; Greensboro NC. **Other U.S. locations:** Nationwide. **International locations:** Worldwide. **Listed on:** NASDAQ. **Stock exchange symbol:** CSCO.

CLAYTON MARCUS
P.O. Box 100, Hickory NC 28603. 828/495-2200. **Physical address:** 166 Teague Town Road, Hickory NC 28601. **Fax:** 828/495-1378. **Contact:** Human Resources. **E-mail address:** info@claytonmarcus.com. **World Wide Web address:** http://www.claytonmarcus.com. **Description:** A furniture upholsterer. **NOTE:** Entry-level positions and second and third shifts are offered. **Special programs:** Internships; Summer Jobs. **Office hours:** Monday – Friday, 8:00 a.m. – 4:30 p.m. **Corporate headquarters location:** Greensboro NC. **Parent company:** La-Z-Boy Inc. **Operations at this facility include:** Divisional Headquarters. **President:** Michael Delgatti.

COATS NORTH AMERICA
3430 Toringdon Way, Suite 301, Charlotte NC 28277. 704/329-5800. **Toll-free phone:** 800/631-0965. **Fax:** 704/329-5829. **Contact:** Human Resources. **World Wide Web address:** http://www.coatscna.com. **Description:** A manufacturer and supplier of sewing thread and associated products for the industrial and consumer markets. The company is also engaged in manufacturing cotton and synthetic thread and yarn; metal and coil slide fasteners, tapes, trimmings, and small diecastings; wood turnings and novelties; and special machinery spools, nylon travelers, and other plastic injection moldings. **Corporate headquarters location:** This location. **Other area locations:** Gastonia NC; Marble NC; Marlon NC; Old Fort NC; Rosman NC; Stanley NC. **Other U.S. locations:** Nationwide. **Subsidiaries include:** Barbour Threads; Coats Bell; Coats Timon; Coats Caribbean and Central America. **Parent company:** Coats Viyella Group (London England). **Operations at this facility include:** Administration; Sales; Service. **CEO:** Max Perks. **Number of employees at this location:** 215. **Number of employees nationwide:** 4,225.

COCA-COLA BOTTLING COMPANY CONSOLIDATED
4100 Coca-Cola Plaza, Charlotte NC 28211-3481. 704/557-4000. **Fax:** 704/551-4646. **Contact:** Personnel. **World Wide Web address:** http://www.cokeconsolidated.com. **Description:** A bottling company packaging Coca-Cola, Barq's, and Dr. Pepper. **NOTE:** Interested jobseekers should apply online. **Positions advertised include:** Forklift Operator; Supply Chain Network Analyst; Route Supervisor; Corporate Mail Center Assistant; Sales Unit Analyst; Bulk Merchandiser; Express Checker; Diesel Mechanic; Interactive Marketing Assistant. **Corporate headquarters location:** This location. **Other area locations:** Statewide. **Other U.S. locations:** Southeast U.S. **Parent company:** The Coca-Cola Company (Atlanta GA) is one of the world's largest marketers, distributors, and producers of bottled and canned products. Coca-Cola Enterprises, part of The Coca-Cola Company, is in the liquid nonalcoholic refreshment business, which includes traditional carbonated soft drinks, still and sparkling waters, juices, isotonics, and teas. The company operates in 38 states, the District of Columbia, the U.S. Virgin Islands, the Islands of Tortola and Grand Cayman, and the Netherlands. Coca-Cola Enterprises franchise territories encompass a population of over 154 million people, representing 54 percent of the population of the United States. Coca-Cola Enterprises operates 268 facilities, approximately 24,000 vehicles, and over 860,000 vending machines, beverage dispensers, and coolers used to market, distribute, and produce the company's products. **Listed on:** NASDAQ. **Stock exchange symbol:** COKE. **CEO:** J. Frank Harrison. **Annual sales/revenues:** More than $100 million. **Number of employees nationwide:** 5,500.

COGENTRIX ENERGY, INC.
9405 Arrowpoint Boulevard, Charlotte NC 28273-8110. 704/525-3800. **Fax:** 704/529-5313. **Contact:** Personnel. **E-mail address:** hr@cogentrix.com. **World Wide Web address:** http://www.cogentrix.com. **Description:** Develops, constructs, and operates nonutility electricity generating facilities. The company has 10 operating facilities. **Corporate headquarters location:** This location. **Other U.S. locations:** Nationwide. **International locations:** Singapore. **Listed on:** Privately held. **CEO:** James E. Lewis. **Number of employees nationwide:** 500.

COLLINS & AIKMAN HOLDINGS CORPORATION
P.O. Box 580 Albemarle NC 28001. 704/983-5166. **Contact:** Human Resources Department. **E-mail address:** resume@colaik.com. **World Wide Web address:** http://www.collinsaikman.com. **Description:** Collins & Aikman Holdings Corporation and its subsidiaries manufacture home furnishings and hosiery products, as well as textile products for major automobile manufacturers. The home furnishings division produces and sells decorative upholstery fabrics through 15 manufacturing facilities and 11 showrooms across the nation. Consumer leg wear includes the brand name No-Nonsense. **NOTE:** Please send resumes to corporate office location at 250 Stephenson Highway, Troy MI 48083; fax is 248/824-1613. No phone calls regarding employment. **Special programs:** Internships. **Corporate headquarters location:** Troy MI. **Listed on:** New York Stock Exchange. **Stock exchange symbol:** CKC. **President:** Millard L. King, Jr. **Number of employees nationwide:** 23,000.

CONAGRA SPECIALTY SNACKS
4851 Jones Sausage Road, Garner NC 27529. 919/773-5011. **Fax:** 919/773-5011. **Contact:** Personnel. **World Wide Web address:** http://www.conagra.com. **Description:** A producer and marketer of meat snacks. ConAgra's principal meat snack brands include Slim Jim, Penrose, Pemmican, and Smokey Mountain. The company also produces an extruded grain snack under the Andy Capp's brand name, and produces and sells packaged meats under the Jesse Jones brand name. **NOTE:** Mail resumes to corporate office location at One ConAgra Drive, Omaha NE 68102-5001. Please visit http://www.conagrafoods.com/careers to search for jobs and apply online. **Corporate headquarters location:** Omaha NE. **Parent company:** ConAgra Foods. **Listed on:** NASDAQ. **Stock exchange symbol:** CAG. **Number of employees worldwide:** 47,000.

MOSES CONE HEALTH SYSTEM
1200 North Elm Street, Greensboro NC 27401-1020. 336/832-7400. **Toll-free phone:** 800/476-6737. **Fax:** 336/832-2999. **Contact:** Corporate Recruitment. **E-mail address:** recruitment@mosescone.com. **World Wide Web address:** http://www.mosescone.com. **Description:** A nonprofit hospital system operating the Moses H. Cone Memorial Hospital (547 beds), the Women's Hospital of Greensboro (130 beds), and Wesley Long Community Hospital. Moses Cone Memorial Hospital is a Level II trauma center as well as a teaching hospital and referral center. The hospital operates five centers specializing in neuroscience, cardiology, cancer, rehabilitation, and trauma. **NOTE:** Please visit website to search for jobs and apply online. **Positions advertised include:** Certified Medical Assistant; Clinical Nutritionist; CRNA; Development Coordinator; LPN; Physical Therapist Assistant; Physician Practice Administrator; RN. **Office hours:** Monday - Friday, 8:30 a.m. - 5:00 p.m. **Corporate headquarters location:** This location. **Operations at this facility include:** Administration. **Number of employees at this location:** 6,800.

CONE MILLS CORPORATION
804 Green Valley Road, Suite 300, Greensboro NC 27408. **Fax:** 336/379-6476. **Contact:** Director of Human Resources. **World Wide Web address:** http://www.cone.com. **Description:** Cone Mills is a major manufacturer of denim and home furnishing fabrics. The denim division produces about 400 styles and is one of the largest suppliers for Levi Strauss & Company. The division also manufactures specialty fabrics including plaids, chamois flannel, and uniform and sportswear fabrics. Founded 1891. **Corporate headquarters location:** This location. **Other area locations:** Statewide. **Other U.S. locations:** San Francisco CA; Los Angeles CA; New York NY; Dallas TX. **International locations:** Brussels, Belgium; Mexico. **Subsidiaries include:** Carlisle Finishing Company, one of the largest U.S. commission printers of home furnishing fabrics; John Wolf Decorative Fabrics, a maker of fabrics for upholstery, drapes, and bedroom products; Olympic Products Company, which manufactures foams for beds, carpets, and furniture used in the medical and consumer markets. **Listed on:** Pink Sheets. **Stock exchange symbol:** CJML. **President/CEO:** John L. Bakane. **Number of employees worldwide:** 3,000.

COOPER BUSSMANN INC.
1000 Craigmont Road, Black Mountain NC 28711. 828/669-6482. **Contact:** Human Resources Manager. **E-mail address:** blkmtn.recruit@buss.com. **World Wide Web address:** http://www.bussmann.com. **Description:** The Bussmann Division of Cooper Industries manufactures electrical protection devices, such as fuses, fuse holders, and fuse boxes. The division's major markets include secondary electrical power distribution, construction, and electronic signal transmission and control. Its products are distributed for use in general construction, plant maintenance, utilities, process and energy applications, shopping centers, parking lots, sports facilities, and data processing and telecommunications systems; through distributors and direct to manufacturers for use in electronic equipment for consumer, industrial, government, and military applications; and directly to original equipment manufacturers of appliances, tools, machinery, and electronic equipment. **NOTE:** Please visit website to search for jobs and apply online. **Corporate headquarters location:** St. Louis MO. **Other area locations:** Apex NC; Burlington NC; Charlotte NC; Goldsboro NC; LaGrange NC; Monroe NC; Raleigh NC. **Other U.S. locations:** Nationwide. **Parent company:** Cooper Industries Inc. (Houston TX) is a diversified company engaged in three primary areas of manufacturing: tools and hardware, electrical and electronic products, and automotive products. **Listed on:** New York Stock Exchange. **Stock exchange symbol:** CBE. **Number of employees at this location:** 500. **Number of employees nationwide:** 45,000.

COOPERATIVE BANKSHARES, INC.
201 Market Street, Wilmington NC 28401. 910/343-0181. **Toll-free phone:** 800/672-0443. **Contact:** Dare Rhoes, Human Resources. **E-mail address:** info@coop-bank.com. **World Wide Web address:** http://www.coop-bank.com. **Description:** A savings bank holding company. **Corporate headquarters location:** This location. **Other area locations:** Statewide. **Subsidiaries include:** Cooperative Bank For Savings, Inc., SSB is engaged in general banking activities. **Listed on:** NASDAQ. **Stock exchange symbol:** COOP.

COPELAND CORPORATION
4401 East Dixon Boulevard, Shelby NC 28152. 704/484-3011. **Contact:** Human Resources Manager. **E-mail address:** corpresume@copeland-corp.com. **World Wide Web address:** http://www.copeland-corp.com. **Description:** A manufacturer of compressors and condensing units for the commercial, industrial, and residential air conditioning and refrigeration industries. **NOTE:** Please visit website to search for jobs and apply online. **Corporate headquarters location:** Sidney OH. **International locations:** Worldwide. **Parent company:** Emerson Electric.

COX TARGET MEDIA (CTM)
6030 US Highway 301 North, Elm City NC 27822-9144. 252/236-4301. **Contact:** Human Resources. **E-mail address:** elmcity_humanresources3@coxtarget.com. **World Wide Web address:** http://www.coxtarget.com. **Description:** A direct marketing company. **NOTE:** Please visit website to view job listings and apply online. **Positions advertised include:** Inserting Supervisor. **Corporate headquarters location:** Largo FL. **Other U.S. locations:** Los Angeles CA; Tampa FL; St. Petersburg FL; Boston MA; Minneapolis MN; Houston TX. **Parent company:** CTM is a subsidiary of Cox Newspapers, which is owned by Cox Enterprises.

CRANE RESISTOFLEX COMPANY
One Quality Way, Marion NC 28752. 828/724-4000. **Fax:** 828/724-9469. **Contact:** Kevin Hall, Human Resources Manager. **World Wide Web address:** http://www.resistoflex.com. **Description:** Manufactures thermoplastic products, including thermoplastic line pipe and flexible hoses. **Corporate headquarters**

location: Stamford CT. **Other U.S. locations:** Jacksonville FL; Bay City MI. **International locations:** Germany; the Netherlands; Singapore. **Parent company:** The Crane Company manufactures and wholesales a diverse number of engineered products for a variety of industries. Its industrial production unit manufactures products and systems for the defense, aerospace, construction, and transportation markets. Products include fiberglass-reinforced panels, vending machines, water filtration and conditioning systems, pumps, valves, and coin machines. A subsidiary, Hydro-Aire, develops and manufactures brake systems, fuel pumps, and other products primarily for the aerospace industry. Crane Company's wholesaling activities are conducted through a subsidiary, Huttig Sash & Door, which operates 47 branch warehouses across the United States. This business specializes in doors, molding, trim, windows, and other construction products, and sells mostly to contractors and other larger wholesalers. **Listed on:** New York Stock Exchange. **Stock exchange symbol:** CR.

CREE INC.
4600 Silicon Drive, Durham NC 27703. 919/313-5300. **Fax:** 919/287-7569. **Contact:** Human Resources. **E-mail address:** hr@cree.com. **World Wide Web address:** http://www.cree.com. **Description:** Develops, manufactures, and markets electronic devices made from silicon carbide (SiC), a semiconductor material. The company manufactures a commercialized, super bright blue light-emitting diode based on a combination of SiC and gallium nitride. Cree Inc. markets its SiC wafers to corporate, government, and university research laboratories. Other devices developed by the company include SiC radio frequency and microwave power devices, and high-temperature semiconductors. **NOTE:** Applicants must fax or e-mail resumes. Please visit website to search for jobs. **Positions advertised include:** Cost Accountant; Credit Manager; EH&S Manager; Employee Relations Representative; Manufacturing Equipment Maintenance Technician; Manager Manufacturing Engineer; Packaging Engineer; Process Development Engineer; Process Engineer Sustaining; Program Manager; Research Scientist; SiC Power Device Scientist; Semiconductor Production Worker; SemiFab Scientist; Supply Chain Manager; Test Engineer. **Corporate headquarters location:** This location. **Listed on:** NASDAQ. **Stock exchange symbol:** CREE. **Number of employees nationwide:** 1,121.

CROSS CREEK APPAREL INC.
P.O. Drawer 1107, Mount Airy NC 27030. 336/783-3800. **Physical address:** 510 Riverside Drive, Mount Airy NC. **Fax:** 336/783-3795. **Contact:** Human Resources. **E-mail address:** jobs@crosscreek.com. **World Wide Web address:** http://www.crosscreek.com. **Description:** Produces men's apparel including knit shirts, turtlenecks, sweaters, shorts, and pants. Cross Creek Apparel also produces placket shirts for women and children. Founded in 1935. **Corporate headquarters location:** Atlanta GA. **Parent company:** Russell Corporation manufactures athletic wear and leisurewear for men, women, and children.

CURTISS-WRIGHT CORPORATION
201 Old Boiling Springs Road, Shelby NC 28152. 704/481-1150. **Fax:** 704/481-2267. **Contact:** Matthew Bulman, Senior Human Resources Manager. **World Wide Web address:** http://www.curtisswright.com. **Description:** Manufactures flight control systems. **NOTE:** Please visit website to search for jobs. **Corporate headquarters location:** Roseland NJ. **Other area locations:** Gastonia NC. **Other U.S. locations:** Nationwide. **International locations:** Denmark; Switzerland. **Parent company:** Curtiss-Wright Corporation. **Listed on:** New York Stock Exchange. **Stock exchange symbol:** CW. **Annual sales/revenues:** $51 - $100 million. **Number of employees at this location:** 250. **Number of employees worldwide:** 4,655.

DECI (DURHAM EXCHANGE CLUB INDUSTRY, INC.)
1717 Lawson Street, Durham NC 27703. 919/596-1341. **Fax:** 919/596-6380. **Recorded jobline:** 919/596-1346x501. **Contact:** Human Resources Manager. **E-mail address:** deci@deci.org. **World Wide Web address:** http://www.deci.org. **Description:** A private, nonprofit, community-based, vocational rehabilitation facility. Founded in 1966. **NOTE:** Entry-level positions are offered. **Positions advertised include:** Production Supervisor. **Special programs:** Internships; Summer Jobs. **Office hours:** Monday - Friday, 8:15 a.m. - 4:15 p.m. **Corporate headquarters location:** This location. **Listed on:** Privately held. **Number of employees at this location:** 85.

DP CONNECTIONS, INC.
348 Crompton Street, Charlotte NC 28273. 704/588-1330. **Fax:** 704/588-5420. **Contact:** Personnel. **E-mail address:** dpconnections@mindspring.com. **World Wide Web address:** http://www.dpconnections.com. **Description:** A computer reseller and acquisitions specialist. **Corporate headquarters location:** This location.

DP SOLUTIONS INC.
4905 Koger Boulevard, Suite 101, Greensboro NC 27407. 336/854-7700. **Toll-free phone:** 800/897-7233. **Fax:** 336/854-7715. **Contact:** Human Resources Department. **E-mail address:** humanresources@dpsi.com. **World Wide Web address:** http://www.dpsi.com. **Description:** Designs, develops, and supports computerized maintenance management software. Founded 1986. **NOTE:** Please visit website to view job listings, and to find more specific information on applying for positions. **Positions advertised include:** Senior Software Sales Representative. **Office hours:** Monday - Friday, 8:00 a.m. - 5:00 p.m. **Corporate headquarters location:** This location. **Other U.S. locations:** FL. **International locations:** Canada. **Listed on:** Privately held.

DANA CORPORATION
P.O. Box 1967, Gastonia NC 28053-1967. 704/864-6711. **Physical address:** One Wix Way, Gastonia NC 28054. **Fax:** 704/853-6143. **Contact:** Human Resources. **World Wide Web address:** http://www.dana.com. **Description:** Dana Corporation is a global leader in engineering, manufacturing, and marketing of products and systems for the worldwide vehicular, industrial, and mobile off-highway original equipment markets and is a major supplier to related aftermarkets. Dana is also a leading provider of lease financing services in selected markets. The company's products include drive train components, such as axles, driveshafts, clutches, and transmissions; engine parts, such as gaskets, piston rings, seals, pistons, and filters; chassis products, such as vehicular frames and cradles and heavy duty side rails; fluid power components, such as pumps, motors, and control valves; and industrial products, such as electrical and mechanical brakes and clutches, drives, and motion control devices. Dana's vehicular components and parts are used on automobiles, pickup trucks, vans, minivans, sport utility vehicles, medium and heavy trucks, and off-highway vehicles. The company's industrial products include mobile off-highway and stationary equipment applications. Founded in 1904. **NOTE:** Please visit website to search for jobs and apply online. **Special programs:** Internships; Co-ops. **Corporate headquarters location:** Toledo OH. **Other area locations:** Asheboro NC; Raleigh NC; Morganton NC; West End NC; Whitsett NC. **Other U.S. locations:** Nationwide. **International locations:** Worldwide. **Operations at this facility include:** This location manufactures air, oil, and specialty filters. **Listed on:** New York Stock Exchange. **Stock exchange symbol:** DCN. **Number of employees worldwide:** 45,000.

DAVIDSON COLLEGE
Box 7163, Davidson NC 28035-7163. 704/894-2212. **Physical address:** 431 Concord Road, #11 Jackson Court, Davidson NC. **Fax:** 704/894-2638. **Contact:** Human Resources. **E-mail address:** jobs@davidson.edu. **World Wide Web address:** http://www2.davidson.edu. **Description:** An independent liberal arts college enrolling more than 1,500 students. Founded 1837. **NOTE:** Please visit website to view job listings, register, and apply online. **Positions advertised include:** Assistant Professor – Biology; ITS Widows System Administrator; Prospect Researcher; Union Café Cook; Area Coordinator – Residence Life; Head Women's Soccer Coach; Union Café Manager; Police Officer; Communications Assistant; Research Coordinator; Research Technician; International Student Advisor; Laundry Production Assistant.

DAVIS REGIONAL MEDICAL CENTER
P.O. Box 1823, Statesville NC 28687. 704/873-0281. **Physical address:** 218 Old Marksville Road, Statesville NC 28625. **Fax:** 704/838-7114. **Recorded jobline:** 704/838-7500. **Contact:** Alison Kay, Human Resources. **E-mail address:** alison.kay@drmc.hma-corp.com. **World Wide Web address:** http://www.davisregional.com. **Description:** A 149-bed, state-of-the-art, acute care medical center. **NOTE:** Please visit website to search for jobs. Human Resources phone is 704/838-7110. Applications are kept on file for one year. **Positions advertised include:** Licensed Physical Therapy Assistant; Medical Technologist; MRI Technologist; RN – Various Departments; Telemetry Technician. **Special programs:** Internships. **Corporate headquarters location:** This location. **Parent company:** Health Trust, Inc. **Operations at this facility include:** Administration; Service. **Number of employees at this location:** 540.

DELOITTE & TOUCHE
150 Fayetteville Street Mall, Suite 1800, Raleigh NC 27601. 919/546-8000. **Fax:** 919/833-3276. **Contact:** Office Administrator. **E-mail address:** dtcareers@deloitte.com. **World Wide Web address:** http://www.us.deloitte.com. **Description:** An international firm of certified public accountants providing professional accounting, auditing, tax, and management consulting services to widely diversified clients. The company has a specialized program consisting of national industry groups and functional groups that cross industry lines. Groups are involved in various disciplines including accounting, auditing, taxation management advisory services, small and growing businesses, mergers and acquisitions, and computer applications. **NOTE:** Please visit website to search for jobs and apply online. **Corporate headquarters location:** New York NY. **Other area locations:** Charlotte NC; Hickory NC; Research Triangle Park NC. **Other U.S. locations:** Nationwide. **International locations:** Worldwide.

DOUGLAS BATTERY MANUFACTURING COMPANY
P.O. Box 12159, Winston-Salem NC 27117. 336/650-7000. **Physical address:** 500 Battery Drive, Winston-Salem NC 27107. **Toll-free phone:** 800/368-4527. **Fax:** 336/499-7832. **Contact:** Manager of Employment. **World Wide Web address:** http://www.douglasbattery.com. **Description:** A manufacturer of lead-acid batteries for industrial, automotive, lawn and garden, marine, and specialty applications. Founded 1921. **Corporate headquarters location:** This location. **Other U.S. locations:** Temple TX; Rocky Hill CT. **Operations at this facility include:** Administration; Manufacturing; Research and Development; Sales; Service. **Listed on:** Privately held. **CEO:** Wilson Douglas, Jr.

DRAKA COMTEQ
P.O. Box 39, Claremont NC 28610. 828/459-9787. **Physical address:** 2512 Penny Road, Claremont NC 28610. **Toll-free phone:** 800/729-3737. **Fax:** 828/459-9821. **Contact:** Human Resources. **E-mail address:** recruit.usa@alcatel.com. **World Wide Web address:** http://www.usa.alcatel.com. **Description:** Manufactures fiber-optic cable for the telecommunications and cable television markets. **Other U.S. locations:** Nationwide. **Parent company:** Alcatel Alsthom (Paris, France). **Operations at this facility include:** Divisional Headquarters. **Listed on:** New York Stock Exchange. **Stock exchange symbol:** ALA. **Annual sales/revenues:** More than $100 million. **CEO:** Mike Quigley. **Number of employees at this location:** 750. **Number of employees nationwide:** 6,753.

DREXEL HERITAGE FURNITURE
1925 Eastchester Drive, High Point NC 27265. 336/888-4800. **Fax:** 336/888-4815. **Contact:** Human Resources. **World Wide Web address:** http://www.drexelheritage.com. **Description:** A furniture manufacturer. **NOTE:** Job candidates are advised to contact The North Carolina Employment Security Office for available positions with the company. **Special programs:** Internships. **Corporate headquarters location:** This location. **Other area locations:** Hickory NC; Marion NC. **Other U.S. locations:** Lititz PA; Clearwater FL. **Parent company:** Masco Corporation (Taylor MI). **Operations at this facility include:** Divisional Headquarters; Manufacturing. **President/CEO:** Jeff Young. **Number of employees at this location:** 500. **Number of employees nationwide:** 1,300.

DUKE ENERGY CORPORATION
P.O. Box 1244, Charlotte NC 28201-1244. 704/594-6200. 0887. **Physical address:** 526 South Church Street, Charlotte NC 28202-1904. **Toll-free phone:** 800/873-3853. **Fax:** 704/382-3781. **Contact:** Corporate Staffing. **World Wide Web address:** http://www.duke-energy.com. **Description:** Provides electric service to approximately 2 million customers, operates pipelines that deliver 12 percent of the natural gas consumed in the United States, and is a leading producer of electricity, natural gas, and natural gas liquids. Founded in 1904. **NOTE:** Please visit website to search for jobs and submit electronic interest form. **Positions advertised include:** Accounting Assistant; Accountant; Customer Services Specialist; Hangar Attendant; Leasing Associate; Nuclear Maintenance Specialist; Technical Specialist; Web Specialist. **Special programs:** Internships; Summer Jobs. **Office hours:** Monday - Friday, 8:00 a.m. - 5:00 p.m. **Corporate headquarters location:** This location. **Subsidiaries include:** Church Street Capital Corporation; Crescent Resources, Inc.; Duke Energy Group, Inc.; Duke Engineering & Services, Inc.; Duke Merchandising; Duke Power Electric Operation; Duke Water Operations; Duke/Fluor Daniel; DukeNet Communications, Inc.; Nantahala Power and Light Company. **Listed on:** New York Stock Exchange. **Stock exchange symbol:** DUK. **CEO:** Paul M. Anderson. **Number of employees nationwide:** 17,000. **Number of employees worldwide:** 23,800.

DUKE UNIVERSITY
P.O. Box 90496 Durham NC 27708. 919/684-5600. **Physical address:** 2024 West Main Street, Durham NC. **Contact:** Human Resources Center. **Fax:** 919/668-0386. **E-mail address:** hr@mc.duke.edu. **World Wide Web address:** http://www.duke.edu. **Description:** A research university operating four campuses. Duke enrolls 5,300 undergraduates in its Trinity College of Arts and Sciences; 1,000 students in its School of Engineering; and 4,500 graduate and professional students in a variety of other programs. The university also operates the Duke University Art Museum, the Duke University Marine Laboratory, and the Duke Primate Center. Duke University Community Service Center (CSC) provides support to various groups including the Duke Cancer Patient Support Group and the Durham County Youth Home. Founded in

1892. **NOTE:** Please visit http://www.hr.duke.edu to search for jobs and apply online. **Positions advertised include:** Associate Dean of External Affairs; Musician; Administrative Secretary; Utility Worker; Research and Development Engineer; Research Technician; Program Coordinator; Steam Plant Operator; Security Officer; Public Relations Specialist; Major Gifts Officer; Senior Family/School Program Specialist; Housekeeper; Office Coordinator; Postal Clerk; Departmental Business Manager; Veterinary Technician; General Maintenance Mechanic. **President:** Nannerl O. Keohane.

DURHAM POLICE DEPARTMENT
505 West Chapel Hill Street, Durham NC 27701. 919/560-4569. **Contact:** Officer T. Hodge, Recruiting. **E-mail address:** thodge@ci.durham.nc.us. **World Wide Web address:** http://www.durhampolice.com. **Description:** Provides law enforcement services for the city of Durham. **NOTE:** For information on civilian jobs with the Durham City Police Department, please visit the Durham City employment page at http://www.ci.durham.nc.us/employment.

DURHAM PUBLIC SCHOOLS
511 Cleveland Street, P.O. Box 30002, Durham NC 27701. 919/560-2000. **Fax:** 919/560-3625. **Contact:** Human Resources. **World Wide Web address:** http://www.dpsnc.com. **Description:** Operators of the public schools in Durham. **NOTE:** Please visit website to search for jobs and to access online application form. **Positions advertised include:** Child Nutrition Assistant; School Bus Driver; Lead Translator; Painter; Elementary Literacy Specialist; Energy Management Coordinator; Group Leader – Various Schools; Assistant Manager – Before School Care; Internal Control and Risk Manager; Heavy Equipment Operator; Electrician; Computer Programmer; Preschool Facilitator; Plumber; Wellness Specialist; Coordinator of Arts Education.

DURHAM REGIONAL HOSPITAL
3643 North Roxboro Road, Durham NC 27704. 919/470-4000. **Toll-free phone:** 888/275-3853. **Fax:** 919/470-7376. **Recorded jobline:** 919/470-JOBS; 800/233-3313. **Contact:** Human Resources. **World Wide Web address:** http://www.durhamregional.org. **Description:** A full-service hospital. **Positions advertised include:** Clerk; Health Unit Coordinator; Chief Operating Officer; Clinical Speech Pathologist; Dietitian Clinician; Director of Radiology; Financial Management Analyst; Laboratory Supervisor; Manager CSR; Occupational Therapist; Physical Therapist; Senior Physicians Assistant; Security Captain; Clinical Nurse – Various Departments; Nurse Practitioner; Nursing Care Assistant; Food Services Supervisor; Patient Transporter; Computer Operator; Interventional Technologist; Pharmacy Technician; Radiologic Technician; Respiratory Care Practitioner; Surgical Technician. **Parent company:** Duke University Health System.

EDS (ELECTRONIC DATA SYSTEMS CORPORATION)
4800 Six Forks Road, Raleigh NC 27609. 919/783-8000. **Fax:** 919/783-1000. **Contact:** Marilyn Miland. **E-mail address:** careers@eds.com. **World Wide Web address:** http://www.eds.com. **Description:** Provides a variety of services for the computer and telecommunications industries including global communication solutions, Internet services, gaming software, and cable television services. **Corporate headquarters:** Plano TX. **Other area locations:** High Point NC; Cary NC; Charlotte NC. **Other U.S. locations:** Nationwide. **International locations:** Worldwide. **Listed on:** New York Stock Exchange. **Stock exchange symbol:** EDS. **CEO:** Michael H. Jordan. **Number of employees nationwide:** 64,000. **Number of employees worldwide:** 130,000.

EMC CORPORATION
62 T.W. Alexander Drive, Research Triangle Park NC 27709-3968. 919/248-5970. **Contact:** Human Resources. **World Wide Web address:** http://www.emc.com. **Description:** EMC Corporation designs, manufactures, markets, and supports high-performance storage products. The company also provides related services for selected mainframe and midrange computer systems primarily manufactured by IBM and Unisys. **NOTE:** Please visit website to search for jobs and apply online. You may submit a general application for potential future opportunities. Resumes also may be mailed to the corporate office location at P.O. Box 65, Nutting Lake MA 01865, fax is 877/621-1360. **Corporate headquarters location:** Hopkinton MA. **Other U.S. locations:** Nationwide. **International locations:** Worldwide. **Operations at this facility include:** This location performs research and development, and provides customer support. **Listed on:** New York Stock Exchange. **Stock exchange symbol:** EMC.

EPLUS TECHNOLOGY OF NORTH CAROLINA
3825 Market Street, Wilmington NC 28403. 910/763-3373. **Toll-free phone:** 888/482-1122. **Fax:** 910/762-8235. **Contact:** Human Resources. **E-mail address:** drose@eplus.com. **World Wide Web address:** http://www.eplus.com. **Description:** Leases and sells computers and other IT equipment. EPlus Technology also develops online software products that provide supply chain management solutions including electronic procurement, e-financing, and e-asset management. Founded 1990. **Corporate headquarters location:** Herndon VA. **Other area locations:** Raleigh NC; Charlotte NC. **Other U.S. locations:** Nationwide. **Listed on:** NASDAQ. **Stock exchange symbol:** PLUS. **CEO/President:** Phillip G. Norton.

EAST CAROLINA UNIVERSITY
210 East First Street, Greenville NC 27858-4353. 252/328-6352. **Fax:** 252/328-4191. **Recorded jobline:** 252/328-4851. **Contact:** Human Resources. **World Wide Web address:** http://www.ecu.edu. **Description:** A university offering undergraduate, graduate, and medical programs. **NOTE:** Please download and submit an ECU application form with your resume. **Positions advertised include:** Administrative Assistant; Office Assistant; Accounting Clerk; Clinical Pharmacist; ECU Staff Nurse; Nursing Assistant; Research Technician; Facility Architect; Enrollment Services Officer; Electronics Technician; Laboratories Mechanic; Housekeeper; Computing Consultant; Research Assistant; Assistant Professor – Various Departments; Student Employment Administrator; Faculty Position – Various Departments. **Corporate headquarters location:** This location.

EATON CORPORATION
8609 Six Forks Road, Raleigh NC 27615. 919/872-3020. **Toll-free phone:** 800/554-3448. **Fax:** 919/870-3100. **Contact:** Human Resources Manager. **World Wide Web address:** http://www.eaton.com. **Description:** Manufactures and markets uninterruptible power supplies, power control and energy storage products, and backup power management solutions. **NOTE:** Entry-level positions are offered. Please visit website to search for jobs and apply online. **Positions advertised include:** Customer Service Representative.

EATON ELECTRICAL
221 Heywood Road, Arden NC 28704. 828/684-2381. **Contact:** Human Resources. **World Wide Web address:** http://www.eatonelectrical.com. **Description:** Eaton Electrical produces industrial and commercial controls (electromechanical and electronic controls; motor starters, contractors, overloads, and electric drives; programmable controllers, counters, man/machine interface panels, and push buttons; photoelectric, proximity, temperature, and pressure sensors; circuit breakers; load centers; safety switches; panelboards; switchboards; dry type transformers; busway; meter centers; portable tool switches; commercial switches; relays; illuminated panels; annunciator panels; and electrically actuated valves and actuators); automotive and appliance controls (electromechanical and electronic controls; convenience, stalk, and concealed switches; knock sensors; climate control components; speed controls; timers; pressure switches; water valves; range controls; thermostats; gas valves; infinite switches; and temperature and humidity sensors); and specialty controls (automated material handling systems, automated guided vehicles, stacker cranes, ion implanters, engineered fasteners, golf grips, and industrial clutches and brakes). These products are sold, either directly by the company or indirectly through distributors and manufacturers' representatives, to industrial, commercial, automotive, appliance, aerospace, and government customers. **NOTE:** Resumes are only accepted when applying for specific positions. Please visit http://www.eatonjobs.com to search for jobs and apply online. **Corporate headquarters location:** Pittsburgh PA. **International locations:** Worldwide. **Parent company:** Eaton Corporation (Cleveland OH) has operations in vehicle components (truck components, passenger car components, and off-highway vehicle components, which are usually sold directly from the company's plants to original equipment manufacturers of trucks, passenger cars, and off-highway vehicles) and defense systems (strategic countermeasures, tactical jamming systems, electronic intelligence, and electronic support measures for the federal government). **Listed on:** New York Stock Exchange. **Stock exchange symbol:** ETN. **Number of employees nationwide:** 51,000.

ELECTROLUX HOME PRODUCTS
4850 West Vernon Avenue, Kinston NC 28504. 252/527-5100. **Fax:** 252/527-4848. **Contact:** Human Resources. **World Wide Web address:** http://www.frigidaire.com. **Description:** Manufactures household appliances including washing machines, ranges, dishwashers, refrigerators, freezers, air conditioners, and disposals. **NOTE:** Resumes should be sent to: 250 Bobby Jones Expressway, Martinez GA 30907. **Corporate headquarters location:** Augusta GA. **International locations:** Canada; Mexico. **Parent company:** AB Electrolux has four business areas: Household Appliances, Commercial Appliances, Outdoor Products, and Industrial Products. The main operation in Household Appliances is white goods, which account for 70 percent of sales. Other operations include floor-care products, absorption refrigerators for caravans and hotel rooms, room air-conditioners, and sewing machines, as well as kitchen and bathroom cabinets. The main operations in Commercial Appliances are food-service equipment for restaurants and institutions, and equipment for apartment-house laundry rooms and commercial laundries. Other operations include refrigeration equipment and freezers for shops and supermarkets, as well as vacuum cleaners and wet/dry cleaners for commercial use. Outdoor Products include garden equipment, chain saws, and other equipment for forestry operations. Industrial Products comprise the group's second-largest business area. Other main operations include car safety belts and other products for personal safety in cars as well as materials-handling equipment. **Number of employees worldwide:** 18,000.

EMBREX INC.
P.O. Box 13989, Research Triangle Park NC 27709-3989. 919/941-5185. **Physical address:** 1040 Swabia Court, Durham NC 27703. **Fax:** 919/314-2550. **Contact:** Personnel. **E-mail address:** employment@embrex.com. **World Wide Web address:** http://www.embrex.com. **Description:** Develops and manufactures an automated, egg-injection system, eliminating the need for manual vaccination of newly hatched broiler chicks. Its patented INOVOJECT system inoculates up to 50,000 eggs per hour. The company's research also includes viral neutralizing factors, immunomodulators, gene vaccines, and performance enhancement products that alter bird physiology for early delivery. **NOTE:** Please visit website to search for jobs and apply online. **Positions advertised include:** Facilities Technician; Inventory and Manufacturing Accountant; Research Associate; Supervisor – Shipping and Receiving; Production Manager; Lead Process Operator. **Corporate headquarters location:** This location. **International locations:** Argentina; Brazil; China; Korea; Malaysia. **Subsidiaries include:** Embrex Europe Ltd. **Listed on:** NASDAQ. **Stock exchange symbol:** EMBX. **President/CEO:** Randall L. Marcuson. **Number of employees nationwide:** 240.

EQUIFIRST
500 Forest Point Circle, Charlotte NC 28273. 704/679-4400. **Contact:** Recruiter. **E-mail address:** recruiter@equifirst.com. **World Wide Web address:** http://www.equifirst.com. **Description:** Provides products and assistance to mortgage lenders. **NOTE:** Please visit website to view job listings. Human Resources phone is 704/679-4611. **Positions advertised include:** Account Executive; Underwriter; Loan Processor. **Corporate headquarters location:** This location.

ERICSSON INC.
7001 Development Drive P.O. Box 13969, Research Triangle Park NC 27709. 919/472-7000. **Fax:** 919/472-7451. **Contact:** Human Resources. **World Wide Web address:** http://www.ericsson.com. **Description:** Provides advanced technology for wireless handset development, and sales and marketing support for North American locations. **NOTE:** Please visit http://www.ericsson.com/jobs to search for jobs and apply online. **Special programs:** Co-ops. **Corporate headquarters location:** Stockholm, Sweden. **Other U.S. locations:** CA; MD; MA; NY; TX; VA. **International locations:** Worldwide. **Parent company:** L.M. Ericsson. **Listed on:** NASDAQ. **Stock exchange symbol:** ERICY. **Annual sales/revenues:** More than $100 million. **Number of employees at this location:** 2,000. **Number of employees nationwide:** 8,000. **Number of employees worldwide:** 100,000.

ERNST & YOUNG LLP
100 North Tryon Street, Suite 380, Charlotte NC 28202. 704/372-6300. **Contact:** Human Resources. **World Wide Web address:** http://www.ey.com. **Description:** A certified public accounting firm that also provides management consulting services. Services include data processing, financial modeling, financial feasibility studies, production planning and inventory management, management sciences, health care planning, human resources, cost accounting, and budgeting systems. **NOTE:** Please visit website to search for jobs and apply online. **Positions advertised include:** Technology and Security Risk Services; Assurance Senior; Risk Management Services Manager; Business Risk Services Senior Auditor – Internal Audit Services. **Corporate headquarters location:** New York NY. **Other area locations:** Raleigh NC; Greensboro NC. **Other U.S. locations:** Nationwide.

FFWD
325 Arlington Avenue, Suite 700, Charlotte NC 28203. 704/344-7900. **Contact:** Human Resources. **E-mail address:** hr@ffwdgroup.com. **World Wide Web address:** http://www.ffwdgroup.com. **Description:** A marketing agency providing direct marketing, advertising, branding, online marketing, customer loyalty, and database marketing services. **Other U.S. locations:** New York NY; Denver CO; Chicago IL; Minneapolis MN; Dallas TX.

FM GLOBAL
14120 Ballantyne Corporate Place, Suite 460, Charlotte NC 28277. 704/752-3080. **Contact:** Human Resources. **E-mail address:** jobs@fmglobal.com. **World Wide Web address:** http://www.fmglobal.com. **Description:** A loss control service organization. FM Global's primary objective is to help owner company policyholders to protect their properties and occupancies from damage from fire, wind, flood, and explosion; from boiler, pressure vessel, and machinery accidents; and from many other insured hazards. To accomplish this objective, a wide range of engineering, research, and consulting services are provided, primarily in the field of loss control. **NOTE:** Please visit website to search for jobs and apply online. **Special programs:** Internships; Co-ops. **Corporate headquarters location:** Johnston RI. **Other U.S. locations:** Nationwide. **International locations:** Worldwide.

FMC LITHIUM
449 North Cox Road, Gastonia NC 28054. 704/868-5300. **Toll-free phone:** 888/LITHIUM. **Fax:** 704/868-5370. **Contact:** Don Taylor, Human Resources. **E-mail address:** lithium-info@fmc.com. **World Wide Web address:** http://www.fmclithium.com. **Description:** Provides solutions for companies specializing in industries including air treatment, fine chemicals, construction, glass and ceramics; and pool water treatment. **NOTE:** Contact Human Resources at 704/868-5455, fax is 704/868-0822. **Corporate headquarters location:** This location. **Other area locations:** Bessemer City NC. **Parent company:** FMC Corporation. **Listed on:** New York Stock Exchange. **Stock exchange symbol:** FMC.

FMC LITHIUM
P.O. Box 795, Highway 161, Bessemer City NC 28016. 704/868-5300. **Fax:** 704/868-5486. **Contact:** Don Taylor, Human Resources. **E-mail address:** lithium_hr@fmc.com **World Wide Web address:** http://www.fmclithium.com. **Description:** Provides solutions for companies specializing in industries including air treatment, fine chemicals, construction, glass and ceramics; and pool water treatment. **NOTE:** Contact Human Resources at 704/868-5455, fax is 704/868-0822. **Corporate headquarters location:** Gastonia NC. **Parent company:** FMC Corporation. **Operations at this facility include:** This location manufactures lithium-based compounds. **Listed on:** New York Stock Exchange. **Stock exchange symbol:** FMC.

FAMILY DOLLAR STORES, INC.
P.O. Box 1017, Charlotte NC 28201-1017. 704/847-6961. **Fax:** 704/845-0582. **Contact:** Mary D. Lauzon, Corporate Recruiter. **E-mail address:** mlauzon@familydollar.com. **World Wide Web address:** http://www.familydollar.com. **Description:** Owns and operates a chain of more than 5,000 discount stores. The company provides merchandise for family and home needs. Stores are located in 43 states, as far northwest as South Dakota, northeast to Maine, southeast to Florida, and southwest to New Mexico. Founded in 1959. **NOTE:** Entry-level positions and second and third shifts are offered. Please visit website to search for jobs and apply online. **Positions advertised include:** Corporate Attorney; Paralegal; Assistant Lease Administrator; Personnel Data Processing Clerk; Security Officer; Director of Merchandise Planning; Project Manager; Data Integrity Analyst; Accounts Payable Clerk; Human Resources Customer Services Center Representative; Store Planner; Maintenance Assistant; Division Recruiter – Store Operations; Construction Secretary; Claims Consultant; Buyer; Web Developer. **Corporate headquarters location:** This location. **Listed on:** New York Stock Exchange. **Stock exchange symbol:** FDO. **Number of employees nationwide:** 37,000.

FARMTRAC
P.O. Box 1139, Tarboro NC 27886. 252/823-4151. **Physical address:** 111 Fairview Street, Tarboro NC 27886. **Fax:** 252/823-4576. **Contact:** Human Resources Director. **World Wide Web address:** http://www.farmtrac.com. **Description:** Develops, manufactures, and markets a broad range of farm and industrial equipment including tractors, tillers, harrows, unloading equipment, elevators, backhoes, storage bins, furnaces, and wood-burning stoves. Founded 1941. **Office hours:** Monday – Friday, 8:00 a.m. – 5:00 p.m. **Corporate headquarters location:** This location. **Operations at this facility include:** Administration; Manufacturing; Research and Development; Sales; Service. **Listed on:** Privately held. **Number of employees at this location:** 325.

FARPOINT TECHNOLOGIES, INC.
808 Aviation Parkway, Suite 1300, Morrisville NC 27560. 919/460-4551. **Fax:** 919/460-7606. **Contact:** Human Resources. **E-mail address:** hr@fpoint.com. **World Wide Web address:** http://www.fpoint.com. **Description:** Develops and manufactures custom control tools for Windows programming. FarPoint Technologies' products are used by software development companies. **NOTE:** Please visit website to view job listings. **Corporate headquarters location:** This location.

FAYETTEVILLE OBSERVER TIMES
458 Whitfield Street, P.O. Box 849, Fayetteville NC 28302. 910/323-4848. **Toll-free phone:** 800/682-3476. **Fax:** 910/486-3544. **Contact:** John Holmes, Personnel Director. **E-mail address:** holmesj@fayettevillenc.com. **World Wide Web address:** http://www.fayettevillenc.com. **Description:** Publishes a daily newspaper with a circulation of approximately 70,000. **NOTE:** Contact Personnel directly at 910/486-3508.

FIRST BANCORP
FIRST BANK
P.O. Box 508, Troy NC 27371. 910/576-6171. **Physical address:** 341 North Main Street, Troy NC 27371-0508. **Toll-free phone:** 866/256-2273. **Fax:** 910/572-2884. **Contact:** Patricia McCormick, Human Resources Director. **E-mail address:** pmmcormick@firstbankcorp.com. **World Wide Web address:** http://www.firstbancorp.com. **Description:** First Bancorp is a bank holding company that owns and operates First Bank (also at this location). Founded in 1983. **Corporate headquarters location:** This location. **Other area locations:** Statewide. **Other U.S. locations:** VA; SC. **Listed on:** NASDAQ. **Stock exchange symbol:** FBNC. **President/CEO:** James H. Garner. **Number of employees nationwide:** 500.

FIRST CHARTER CORPORATION
FIRST CHARTER NATIONAL BANK
P.O. Box 37937, Charlotte NC 28237. 704/365-2880. **Fax:** 704/688-4475. **Contact:** Human Resources. **E-mail address:** careers@firstcharter.com. **World Wide Web address:** http://www.firstcharter.com. **Description:** First Charter Corporation is a holding company that operates 50 banks throughout the greater Charlotte metropolitan area. Assets total $2.7 million. **NOTE:** Applications are active for 90 days. Please apply and view job listings online. Some bank locations provide computerized-application access. **Positions advertised include:** CAM Client Advisor; Commercial Credit Analyst; Commercial Sales Assistant; Conversion Technician; Financial Center Manager; Mail Services Clerk; PAM Client Advisor; Personal Banker; Check Processor; Data Capture Operator; Data Entry Check Processor. **Corporate headquarters location:** This location. **Other area locations:** Statewide. **Subsidiaries include:** First Charter National Bank provides businesses and individuals with a broad range of financial services including banking, financial planning, funds management, investments, insurance mortgages, and employee benefits programs. **Listed on:** NASDAQ. **Stock exchange symbol:** FCTR. **President/CEO:** Lawrence M. Kimbrough.

FIRST CITIZENS BANK & TRUST
2005 Clarke Avenue, Raleigh NC 27605. 919/716-7121. **Contact:** Human Resources. **World Wide Web address:** http://www.firstcitizens.com. **Description:** A bank founded in 1898. **NOTE:** Please visit website to search for jobs and apply online. Entry-level positions and second and third shifts are offered. **Positions advertised include:** Financial Consultant; Administrative Assistant; Audit Specialist; Banker Assistant; Benefits Planning Analyst; Commercial Credit Analyst; Float Teller; Image Specialist; Investment Counselor; Market Executive; Mortgage Banker; Regional Leasing Officer; Senior Teller. **Special programs:** Training; Summer Jobs. **Office hours:** Monday - Friday, 9:00 a.m. - 5:00 p.m. Saturday, 9:00 a.m. – 12:00 p.m. **Corporate headquarters location:** This location. **Other U.S. locations:** VA; WV. **Annual sales/revenues:** $5 - $10 million. **Number of employees nationwide:** 5,000.

FLAMBEAU PRODUCTS CORPORATION
100 Grace Drive, Weldon NC 27890. 252/536-2171. **Fax:** 252/536-2201. **Contact:** Chinita Blaunt, Personnel Manager. **E-mail address:** hr@flambeau.com. **World Wide Web address:** http://www.flambeau.com. **Description:** A manufacturer of rigid plastic doublewall cases. Founded in 1947. **NOTE:** Please visit website to view job listings. **Corporate headquarters location:** Middlefield OH. **Other U.S. locations:** Redlands CA; Baraboo WI; Madison GA; Columbus IN. **International locations:** Mexico; England. **Subsidiaries include:** ArtBin; Duncan; Flambeau Contract Manufacturing; Flambeau Hardware; Flambeau Outdoors; Flambeau Packaging Solutions; Flambeau Premiums and Special Markets; Ornamates; Vichek Floral Containers. **Operations at this facility include:** Administration; Manufacturing; Sales. **Number of employees at this location:** 200. **Number of employees nationwide:** 3,000.

FLOWERS BAKING COMPANY
P.O. Box 819, Jamestown NC 27282. 336/841-8840. **Physical address:** 801 West Main Street, Jamestown NC. **Contact:** Employment. **World Wide Web address:** http://www.flowersfoods.com. **Description:** Flowers Baking operates more than 20 bakeries, which produce a wide variety of products including bread, buns, rolls, and donuts for retail sale to food stores, restaurants, and institutions. **NOTE:** This location does not accept resumes, you must apply through a temporary employment service. **Corporate headquarters location:** Thomasville GA. **Parent company:** Flowers Foods. **Operations at this facility include:** This location of Flowers Baking Company produces sandwich bread and hot dog rolls. **Listed on:** New York Stock Exchange. **Stock exchange symbol:** FLO. **President/CEO:** George E. Deese.

FLOWSERVE PUMP COMPANY
264 Wilson Park Road, Statesville NC 28625. 704/872-2468. **Fax:** 704/872-2467. **Contact:** Personnel. **World Wide Web address:** http://www.flowserve.com. **Description:** Produces multistage, submersible pumps with directly coupled water-lubricated motors for municipal, industrial, and agricultural water supply; large capacity axial flow pumps for water level control systems, flood control, dewatering applications, and power plants; maneuvering equipment for ships; and thruster equipment for dynamic positioning of ships. The company also produces submersible motors for marine technology applications. **Corporate headquarters location:** Irving TX. **Parent company:** Dresser Industries, Inc. **Operations at this facility include:** Manufacturing. **Listed on:** New York Stock Exchange. **Stock exchange symbol:** FLS. **Number of employees worldwide:** 14,000.

FOAM DESIGN, INC.
2425 South Alston Avenue, Durham NC 27713. 919/596-0668. **Fax:** 919/598-1761. **Contact:** Human Resources. **E-mail address:** rtp@foamdesign.com. **World Wide Web address:** http://www.foamdesign.com. **Description:** Manufactures cushioning products made of polyethylene, polyurethane, and polystyrene foams for the protection of products such as typewriters, printed circuit boards, medical instruments, and electronic components. Cushioning products are used for the packaging of consumer goods, the transport of aerospace and military missile components and related hardware, the handling and shipping of automotive parts, and the packaging of electronics components and assemblies. Foam Design also manufactures consumer products such as camping pads, bodyboards, and archery targets. **Corporate headquarters location:** Lexington KY.

FOOD LION, INC.
P.O. Box 1330, Salisbury NC 28145-1330. 704/633-8250. **Physical address:** 2110 Executive Drive, Salisbury NC 28147. **Fax:** 704/637-2581. **Contact:** Recruiting Manager. **World Wide Web address:** http://www.foodlion.com. **Description:** Owns a chain of discount retail food stores. Food Lion, Inc. is comprised of approximately 1,200 stores operating throughout the Eastern United States. Founded in 1957. **NOTE:** Please visit website to search for jobs and apply online. **Positions advertised include:** Produce Sales Manager; Corporate Recruiter; FT Grocery Associate; Physical Security Systems Technician; Service Associate. **Corporate headquarters location:** This location. **Other U.S. locations:** East and Southeast U.S. **Parent company:** Delhaize America Inc. **Listed on:** New York Stock Exchange. **Stock exchange symbol:** DEG. **Number of employees nationwide:** 84,000.

FORSYTH TECHNICAL COMMUNITY COLLEGE
2100 Silas Creek Parkway, Winston-Salem NC 27103-5197. 336/723-0371. **Fax:** 336/761-2309. **Contact:** Gregory M. Chase, Director of Human Resources. **World Wide Web address:** http://www.forsyth.tec.nc.us. **Description:** A community college. **NOTE:** There are five office locations in Winston-Salem, and campuses at the following locations – Kernersville NC; Danbury NC. Please visit website to view job listings and to download application form. You must submit an application to be eligible for employment. Contact Human Resources at 336/734-7246. **Positions advertised include:** Program Coordinator – Emergency Medical Science; Program Coordinator BLET & Instructor – Criminal Justice; Dean – Business Information Technologies; Coordinator – Cooperative Education; Director – Shugart Women's Center; Switchboard Operator. **Corporate headquarters location:** This location. **Operations at this facility include:** Administration; Research and Development. **Number of employees at this location:** 310.

FOUNTAIN POWERBOAT INDUSTRIES INC.
1653 Whichards Beach Road, P.O. Drawer 457, Washington NC 27889. 252/975-2000. **Fax:** 252/975-6793. **Contact:** Carol Price, Director of Human Resources. **E-mail address:** humanresources@fountainpowerboats.com. **World Wide Web address:** http://www.fountainpowerboats.com. **Description:** Designs, manufactures, and sells sport boats, sport cruisers, and sport fishing boats. **NOTE:** Contact Human Resources directly at 252/975-7017. **Positions advertised include:** Mechanic; Cabinet Builder; Carpenter; Gel Detailer; Laminator; Service Mechanic; Welder; Machinist; Painter; Screen Printer; Engine Rigger; Assembly Cabin Rigger; Assembly Cockpit Rigger; Electrical Engineering Technician; Pre-Rigger; Plexi-Glass Fabricator. **Corporate headquarters location:** This location. **Listed on:** NASDAQ. **Stock exchange symbol:**

FPWR. **President/CEO:** R.M. Fountain Jr. **Number of employees at this location:** 353.

FUJITSU TRANSACTIONS SOLUTIONS
14101 Capitol Boulevard, Youngsville NC 27596. 919/556-6721. **Fax:** 919/556-7566. **Contact:** Personnel. **E-mail address:** careers@ftxs.fujitsu.com. **World Wide Web address:** http://www.ftxs.fujitsu.com. **Description:** Designs software for the banking, food, and retail industries. **Corporate headquarters location:** Frisco TX. **Other U.S. locations:** Carrolton TX. **International locations:** Canada; Caribbean. **Parent company:** Fujitsu Limited. **President/CEO:** Austen Mulinder. **Number of employee worldwide:** 1,000.

FUTURA CREATIVE
4711 Hope Valley Road, #419, Durham NC 27707. 919/933-2150. **Fax:** 919/942-0041. **Contact:** Human Resources. **World Wide Web address:** http://www.futuracreative.com. **Description:** Offers graphic design services including corporate identity development, logos, letterhead, brochures, annual reports, and other printed media. The company also offers Website design and multimedia services. **Corporate headquarters location:** This location.

GMAC INSURANCE
P.O. Box 3199, Winston-Salem NC 27102-3199. 336/770-2000. **Physical address:** 500 West Fifth Street, Winston-Salem NC 27152. **Fax:** 336/770-2190. **Contact:** Human Resources. **World Wide Web address:** http://www.gmacinsurance.com. **Description:** An insurance company operating in 22 states through more than 11,000 independent agents. The company's East Division primarily underwrites nonstandard auto insurance in Alabama, Florida, Georgia, North Carolina, Ohio, and Virginia. The division also underwrites preferred auto, homeowners, and mobile home insurance in North Carolina. The North Division underwrites nonstandard auto insurance in Connecticut, Illinois, Indiana, Maine, Maryland, New Hampshire, New York, Pennsylvania, Rhode Island, and Vermont. The South Division underwrites nonstandard auto insurance in Kentucky, Louisiana, Mississippi, Tennessee, and Texas. The Specialty Auto division underwrites insurance for business autos and motorcycles. **NOTE:** Please visit website to search for jobs and apply online. **Positions advertised include:** Application System Analyst; Claim Service Consultant Trainee; Customer Sales Agent; Customer Service Consultant; Director of Accounting; Human Representative; Human Resources Representative; Infrastructure Project Manager; Pricing/Product Manager; Regional Marketing Manager. **Corporate headquarters location:** Southfield MI. **Number of employees worldwide:** 3,800.

GALEY & LORD, INC.
P.O. Box 35528, Greensboro NC 27425-0528. 336/665-3037. **Physical address:** 7736 McCloud Road, One Triad Center, Suite 300, Greensboro NC 27409. **Fax:** 336/665-3130. **Contact:** Personnel Manager. **Description:** Galey & Lord is a leading manufacturer and marketer of fabric sold to clothing manufacturers. The company is a major producer of wrinkle-free cotton fabrics for uniforms and printed fabrics for the home. **Corporate headquarters location:** New York NY. **Other U.S. locations:** CA; GA; SC; TX. **International locations:** Mexico. **Subsidiaries include:** Galey & Lord Industries, Inc; Klopman International; Swift Denim Group. **Operations at this facility include:** This location is a manufacturing plant. **Listed on:** Over-the-Counter. **Stock exchange symbol:** GYLDQ. **Chairman/CEO:** John J. Heldrich. **Number of employees nationwide:** 4,790.

GILBARCO
P.O. Box 22087, Greensboro NC 27420. 336/547-5000. **Physical address:** 7300 West Friendly Avenue, Greensboro NC 27410. **Fax:** 336/547-5549. **Contact:** Human Resources. **World Wide Web address:** http://www.gilbarco.com. **Description:** A manufacturer of electronic fuel dispensing equipment and peripheral devices for the petroleum industry. **NOTE:** Please visit website to search for jobs, apply online, or download application form. **Special programs:** Internships. **Corporate headquarters location:** This location. **Other U.S. locations:** Glendale CA. **International locations:** Argentina; Australia; Canada; China; Germany; Italy; New Zealand; Thailand; United Kingdom. **Parent company:** Donaher Corporation. **Listed on:** New York Stock Exchange. **Stock exchange symbol:** DHR. **Number of employees at this location:** 1,600. **Number of employees worldwide:** 4,000.

GLAXOSMITHKLINE
5 Moore Drive, Durham NC 27709-3398. 919/483-2100. **Toll-free phone:** 888/825-5249. **Fax:** 919/315-1053. **Contact:** Director or Human Resources Operations. **World Wide Web address:** http://www.gsk.com. **Description:** A pharmaceutical preparations company whose products include AZT, an AIDS treatment drug; Zantac; and Malarone, a medication for malaria. **NOTE:** Please visit website to search for jobs and apply online. **Positions advertised include:** Administrative Assistant; Advisor/Manager Respiratory Commercial Analysis; Assistant Scientist; Assistant Clinical Supplies Project Leader; Associate Program Manager; Chemical Engineer; Clinical Pharmacokineticist; Clinical Pharmacology Disease Area Manager; Director of Business Integration; Health Enhancement Manager; Epidemiologist; Manager – Various Departments; Pharmaceutical Sales Representative. **Special programs:** Internships. **Corporate headquarters location:** London, England. **Other area locations:** Zebulon NC. **Other U.S. locations:** PA; NJ; DE; MA; MI; SC. **International locations:** Worldwide. **Operations at this facility include:** Administration; Research and Development. **Listed on:** New York Stock Exchange. **Stock exchange symbol:** GSK. **Number of employees worldwide:** 100,000.

GOERLICH'S EXHAUST SYSTEMS
300 Dixie Trail, Goldsboro NC 27530. 919/580-2000. **Fax:** 919/580-1925. **Contact:** David Mozingo, Personnel Director. **E-mail address:** dmozingo@goerlichs.com. **World Wide Web address:** http://www.goerlichs.com. **Description:** Manufactures motor vehicle parts and accessories. **Positions advertised include:** Marketing Data Analyst; Product Line Coordinator; Master Scheduler/Purchasing Manager; Tubemill Manager; Senior Pricing Analyst; Engineering Technician; Machinist; Coach; Electrician; Production Scheduler. **Corporate headquarters location:** This location. **Other U.S. locations:** CT; DE; DC; MD; MA; NH; RI; VT. **President:** Vange Proimos.

GOLD KIST, INC.
484 Zimmerman Road, P.O. Box 3668, Sanford NC 27330. 919/774-7333. **Contact:** John Williams, Human Resources. **E-mail address:** nc.jobs@goldkist.com. **World Wide Web address:** http://www.goldkist.com. **Description:** A processing plant for poultry. Retail products are marketed under the Young 'n Tender label or under the customers' private labels and are sold primarily in Florida, Georgia, the Mid-Atlantic states, the Northeast, and the Midwest. The company also purchases and resells processed chicken, turkey, beef, pork, seafood, dairy, and other food products. Customers include a retail chain in the Southeast, major fast-food companies, and many other retail, institutional, and restaurant accounts. **Positions advertised include:** Division Safety Coordinator; Broiler Field Representative; Unit Manager. **Corporate headquarters location:** Atlanta GA. **Other area locations:** Bear Creek NC; Siler City NC; Staley NC. **Subsidiaries include:** AgraTrade Financing; Luker Inc. **Number of employees nationwide:** 16,000.

GOLDEN CORRAL CORPORATION
P.O. Box 29502, Raleigh NC 27626-0502. 919/781-9310. **Physical address:** 5151 Glenwood Avenue, Raleigh NC 27612. 800/284-5673. **Fax:** 919/881-4577. **Contact:** Human Resources. **World Wide Web address:** http://www.goldencorralrest.com. **Description:** Operates a chain of family steakhouses. Founded in 1973. **NOTE:** Entry-level positions are offered. Please visit website to search for jobs and apply online. If you are looking for a field position, please contact the location in your area. **Company slogan:** Making pleasurable dining affordable. **Corporate headquarters location:** This location. **Other U.S. locations:** Nationwide. **Operations at this facility include:** Administration; Research and Development; Service. **Listed on:** Privately held. **President:** Ted Fowler. **Annual sales/revenues:** More than $100 million. **Number of employees at this location:** 170. **Number of employees nationwide:** 3,700.

GOOD HOPE HOSPITAL
410 Denim Drive, Erwin NC 28339. 910/897-6151 Ext. 152. **Fax:** 910/897-4050. **Contact:** Michelle Baker, Human Resources. **E-mail address:** mbaker@goodhopehospital.org. **World Wide Web address:** http://www.goodhopehospital.org. **Description:** A 72-bed, nonprofit, acute care, community hospital. Affiliated physicians' offices are located in three surrounding communities. **NOTE:** Please visit website to search for jobs and to complete a pre-employment application. **Positions advertised include:** House Coordinator; RN – Various Departments; Radiologic Technologist; Surgical Services Manager; Pharmacist; Pharmacy Technician; Physical Therapist; MT/MLT; Echo Cardiographer Technician; Respiratory Therapist; Patient Financial Counselor. **Office hours:** Monday - Friday, 8:00 a.m. - 4:30 p.m. **Corporate headquarters location:** This location. **Parent company:** Quorum Health Resources. **Number of employees at this location:** 300.

GOODRICH CORPORATION
4 Coliseum Centre, 2730 West Tyvola Road, Charlotte NC 28217-4578. 704/423-7000. **Fax:** 704/423-7002. **Contact:** Human Resources. **World Wide Web address:** http://www.goodrich.com. **Description:** Provides components and systems for general aviation, regional, business, commercial, and military aircraft and space vehicles. The company also manufactures performance polymer systems and additives. **NOTE:** Please visit website to search for jobs and apply online. **Positions advertised include:** Executive Administrative Assistant; Manager – Global Sourcing; Legal Administrative Assistant; Supply Chain Leadership Program Worker; Financial Analyst; Senior Internal Auditor; Material Handler; Warehouse Lead. **Corporate headquarters location:** This location. **Other U.S. locations:** Nationwide. **International locations:** Worldwide. **Listed on:** New York Stock Exchange. **Stock exchange symbol:** GR. **Annual sales/revenues:** More than $100 million. **Number of employees worldwide:** 20,000.

GOODYEAR TIRE & RUBBER COMPANY
890 Pineview Road, Asheboro NC 27203. 336/495-2240. **Contact:** Warren Thacker, Human Resources Manager. **World Wide Web address:** http://www.goodyear.com. **Description:** Goodyear Tire & Rubber Company's principal business is the development, manufacture, distribution, and sale of tires. Goodyear also manufactures and sells a broad spectrum of rubber products and rubber-related chemicals for various industrial and consumer markets and provides auto repair services. The company operates 32 plants in the United States, 42 plants in 29 other countries, and more than 1,800 retail tire and service centers and other distribution facilities around the globe. Strategic business units of Goodyear Tire & Rubber include North American Tire, Kelly-Springfield, Goodyear Europe, Goodyear Latin America, Goodyear Asia, Engineered Products, Chemicals, Celeron, and Goodyear Racing. **NOTE:** Please visit website to search for jobs. **Corporate headquarters location:** Akron OH. **Other U.S. locations:** Nationwide. **International locations:** Worldwide. **Operations at this facility include:** This location manufactures steel tire cord. **Listed on:** New York Stock Exchange. **Stock exchange symbol:** GT. **Number of employees worldwide:** 92,000.

L.R. GORRELL CO.
P.O. Box 33395. Raleigh NC 27636. 919/821-1161. **Physical address:** 544 Pylon Drive, Raleigh NC 27606. **Fax:** 919/832-1542. **Contact:** Employment. **E-mail address:** raleigh@lrgorrell.com. **World Wide Web address:** http://www.lrgorrell.com. **Description:** A distributor of parts for heating and cooling equipment. Founded in 1951. **NOTE:** Entry-level positions are offered. **Corporate headquarters location:** This location. **Other area locations:** Asheville NC; Greensboro NC; Charlotte NC; Wilmington NC. **Other U.S. locations:** Greenville SC; North Charleston SC. **Listed on:** Privately held. **President:** L.R. Gorrell.

GRACE HOSPITAL
2201 South Sterling Street, Morganton NC 28655. 828/580-5000. **Fax:** 828/580-5609. **Contact:** Human Resources. **World Wide Web address:** http://www.blueridgehealth.org/our_facilities/grace_hospital.html. **Description:** A nonprofit, full-service hospital. **NOTE:** Second and third shifts are offered. Please visit website to search for jobs and download application form. **Positions advertised include:** Admitting Nurse; Aerobic/Aquatic/Pilates Instructor; Catering Supervisor; CNA; RN – Various Departments; Chief Radiologic Technologist; Coder; Director of Maternal Child Health Services; Exercise Physiologist; Food Service Assistant; Front Desk Clerk; Housekeeper; LPN; Materials Manager; Psychiatric Technician; Social Worker; Secretary. **Special programs:** Internships; Apprenticeships; Summer Jobs. **Parent company:** BlueRidge Health Care System. **Number of employees at this location:** 800.

GRAINGER
2533 North Chester Street, Gastonia NC 28052. 704/861-9239. 9235. **Fax:** 704/866-7054. **Contact:** Michael Kenney, Manager. **World Wide Web address:** http://www.grainger.com. **Description:** A national supplier of industrial equipment such as motors, pumps, and safety maintenance equipment. Grainger distributes a variety of equipment and components to the industrial, commercial, contracting, and institutional markets. Products include equipment and components for motors, air tools, hydraulic products, refrigeration items, power and hand tools, office equipment, computer supplies, replacement parts, industrial products, safety items, cold weather clothing, and storage equipment. **Positions advertised include:** Outside Sales Account Manager; Branch Manager; Warehouse Associate; Customer Service Associate. **Office hours:** Monday – Friday, 8:00 a.m. – 5:00 p.m. **Corporate headquarters location:** Chicago IL. **Other area locations:** Statewide. **Other U.S. locations:** Nationwide. **International locations:** Worldwide. **Listed on:** New York Stock Exchange. **Stock exchange symbol:** GWW. **CEO:** Richard L. Keyser.

GRANITE KNITWEAR, INC.
P.O. Box 498, Granite Quarry NC 28072-0498. 704/279-5526. **Toll-free phone:** 800/476-9944. **Fax:** 704/279-8205. **Contact:** Georgette White, Human Resources.

World Wide Web address: http://www.calcru.com. **Description:** A sportswear and fleece wear apparel manufacturer. **Corporate headquarters location:** This location. **Parent company:** Cal Cru Company Inc. **Number of employees at this location:** 170.

GREGORY POOLE EQUIPMENT COMPANY
4807 Beryl Road, Raleigh NC 27606. 919/828-0641. **Contact:** Human Resources. **E-mail address:** info@gregorypoole.com. **World Wide Web address:** http://www.gregorypoole.com. **Description:** Manufactures a range of material handling products, power system solutions, and provides construction contracting services. **Positions advertised include:** Rental Store Technician; Hydraulic Shop Tech; Construction Welder; Construction Technician; Construction Master; Technician/Field Service Technician; Construction Component Specialist.

GUILFORD MILLS, INC.
6001 West Market Street, Greensboro NC 27409. 336/316-4000. **Fax:** 336/316-4621. **Contact:** Richard Novak, Human Resources. **World Wide Web address:** http://www.guilfordmills.com. **Description:** A manufacturer, processor, and marketer of warp knit fabrics for the apparel, automotive, home furnishing, swimwear, dress, and sportswear industries. **Corporate headquarters location:** This location. **Other area locations:** Kenansville NC. **Other U.S. locations:** Madison Heights MI. **International locations:** Germany; United Kingdom. **President/CEO:** John A. Emrich. **Number of employees worldwide:** 3,600.

HACKNEY & SONS INC.
P.O. Box 880, Washington NC 27889. 252/946-6521. **Physical address:** 911 West Fifth Street, Washington NC 27889. **Toll-free phone:** 800/763-0700. **Fax:** 252/975-8344. **Contact:** Pam Pippin, Human Resources Director. **World Wide Web address:** http://www.hackneyandsons.com. **Description:** Manufactures trucks and trailers for the beverage industry. Hackney & Sons also manufactures emergency service vehicles. Founded 1946. **Corporate headquarters location:** This location. **Other U.S. locations:** KS. **International locations:** Worldwide. **Listed on:** Privately held. **Number of employees at this location:** 250. **Number of employees nationwide:** 500.

HAMILTON BEACH/PROCTOR-SILEX, INC.
261 Yadkin Road, Southern Pines NC 28387. 910/692-7676. **Toll-free phone:** 800/851-8900. **Contact:** Human Resources Administrator. **World Wide Web Address:** http://www.hamiltonbeach.com. **Description:** Manufactures small appliances including blenders, can openers, coffeemakers, food processors, irons, mixers, steamers, and toasters. **NOTE:** Please visit http://www.monster.com to search for jobs. **International locations:** Canada; Mexico. **Parent company:** NACCO Industries, Inc. **President/CEO:** Michael J. Morecroft.

HAMMARY FURNITURE COMPANY
2464 Norwood Street SW, Lenoir NC 28645. 828/728-3231. **Fax:** 828/726-3351. **Contact:** Human Resources. **World Wide Web address:** http://www.hammary.com. **Description:** Manufactures tables, wall units, couches, loveseats, and chairs. **Office hours:** Monday – Friday, 8:00 a.m. – 5:00 p.m. **Parent company:** La-Z-Boy Inc.

HANES INDUSTRIES
P.O. Box 457, Conover NC 28613-0457. 828/464-4673. **Physical address:** 500 North McLin Creek Road, Conover NC. **Toll-free phone:** 800/438-9124. **Fax:** 828/466-0723. **Contact:** Human Resources. **World Wide Web address:** http://www.hanesindustries.com. **Description:** Converts fabric and related materials for the bedding and drapery industry. **Office hours:** Monday – Friday, 8:00 a.m. – 5:00 p.m. **Corporate headquarters location:** This location. **Other U.S. locations:** Phoenix AZ; Cerritos CA; Indianapolis IN; Pontotoc MS; Carlstadt NJ; Cincinnati OH; Cleveland TN; Dallas TX; Auburn WA. **International locations:** Canada; England; Mexico. **Parent company:** Hanes Companies is a subsidiary of Leggett & Platt Inc.

HARRIS TEETER, INC.
P.O. Box 10100, Matthews NC 28106-0100. 704/844-3100. **Physical address:** 701 Crestdale Drive, Matthews NC 28105. **Toll-free phone:** 800/432-6111. **Contact:** Director of Personnel. **E-mail address:** jfranklin@harristeeter.com. **World Wide Web address:** http://www.harristeeter.com. **Description:** Operates a regional supermarket chain with over 140 stores in five southeastern states. **NOTE:** All hiring for Harris Teeter is done at this location. **Corporate headquarters location:** This location. **Other U.S. locations:** FL; GA; SC; TN; VA. **Parent company:** Ruddick Corporation (Charlotte NC) is a diversified holding company operating through wholly-owned subsidiaries American & Efird, Inc.; and Ruddick Investment Company. American & Efird (Mount Holly NC) manufactures and distributes sewing thread for worldwide industrial and consumer markets and handles its own hiring. **Listed on:** New York Stock Exchange. **Stock exchange symbol:** RDK. **Number of employees nationwide:** 13,900.

HATTERAS YACHTS
110 North Glenburnie Road, New Bern NC 28560-2799. 252/633-3101. **Contact:** Human Resources. **World Wide Web address:** http://www.hatterasyachts.com. **Description:** Hatteras Yachts builds, sells, and repairs fiberglass yachts. **NOTE:** Hatteras Yachts does not accept unsolicited faxed resumes. Please search for jobs and apply online at http://www.brunswick.com. **Positions advertised include:** Customer Service Process Representative; Director of Quality and Process Improvement; Fiberglass Application Engineer; Industrial Designer/Class A Surfacer; Interior Designer; Lean Six Sigma Black Belt. **Corporate headquarters location:** This location. **Parent company:** Brunswick Corporation. **Listed on:** New York Stock Exchange. **Stock exchange symbol:** BC. **Number of employees nationwide:** 21,000.

HENREDON FURNITURE INDUSTRIES, INC.
641 West Ward Avenue, High Point NC 27260. 336/885-9141. **Fax:** 336/888-2951. **Contact:** Human Resources Manager. **World Wide Web address:** http://www.henredon.com. **Description:** Manufactures and designs upholstered furniture and case goods. **Office hours:** Monday – Friday, 8:00 a.m. – 5:00 p.m. **Corporate headquarters location:** Morganton NC. **Other area locations:** Spruce Pine NC. **Parent company:** Furniture Brands International, Inc. **Operations at this facility include:** Administration; Divisional Headquarters; Manufacturing; Sales. **Listed on:** New York Stock Exchange. **Stock exchange symbol:** FBN. **Number of employees at this location:** 420.

HICKORY CHAIR COMPANY
P.O. Box 2147, Hickory NC 28603. 828/328-1802. **Fax:** 828/326-4223. **Contact:** Personnel Director. **World Wide Web address:** http://www.hickorychair.com. **Description:** A manufacturer of 18th-century style furniture. Founded in 1911. **NOTE:** Contact Human Resources directly at Ext. 7315. **Special programs:** Internships. **Corporate headquarters location:** Altavista VA. **Parent company:** The Lane Company Inc. **Operations at this facility include:** Administration; Divisional Headquarters; Manufacturing; Sales. **Number of employees at this location:** 1,000.

HINSHAW MUSIC, INC.
P.O. Box 470, Chapel Hill NC 27514. 919/933-1691. **Fax:** 919/967-3399. **Contact:** Manager. **E-mail address:** hinshaw@hinshawmusic.com. **World Wide Web address:** http://www.hinshawmusic.com. **Description:** A printer and publisher of choral music. Founded in 1975. **Corporate headquarters location:** This location.

HOLT HOSIERY
P.O. Box 1757, Burlington NC 27216. 336/227-1431. **Physical address:** 733 Koury Drive, Burlington NC. **Fax:** 336/227-8614. **Contact:** Tammy Dalrymple, Personnel. **Description:** A manufacturer and wholesaler of women's sheer hosiery. **Corporate headquarters location:** This location. **Operations at this facility include:** Manufacturing; Sales. **Number of employees at this location:** 200.

HOLT SUBLIMATION
P.O. Box 2017, Burlington NC 27216-2017. 336/222-3600. **Physical address:** 2208 Air Park Drive, Burlington NC 27216. **Fax:** 336/222-3560. **Contact:** Pat, Human Resources. **World Wide Web address:** http://www.holtsublimation.com. **Description:** An apparel design company whose disperse dye printing process allows the color and detail of artwork to be transferred to material. Engineered designs using the company's techniques are placed on active wear, swimwear, athletic wear, sleepwear, scarves, rugs, mats, domestics, narrow-web elastic, lace trim, labels, ribbons, shoelaces, and other products. **Special programs:** Internships. **Corporate headquarters location:** This location. **Operations at this facility include:** Administration; Manufacturing; Research and Development; Sales; Service. **Listed on:** Privately held. **President/CEO:** Frank Holt III. **Number of employees at this location:** 220.

HON INDUSTRIES
7966 NC 56 Highway West, Louisburg NC 27549. 919/496-5701. **Fax:** 919/496-2389. **Contact:** Human Resources. **World Wide Web address:** http://www.honi.com. **Description:** A diversified manufacturer and marketer of office furniture, workspace accessories, and home-building products, comprised of nine operating companies with offices, showrooms, distribution centers, and manufacturing plants nationwide. Six operating companies, marketing under various brand names (The Hon Company, Gunlocke Company, XLM, Chandler Attwood, BPI, and Holga), participate in the office furniture industry. Ring King Visibles manufactures and markets workspace accessories to improve productivity and ergonomic comfort; Heatilator, Inc. manufactures and markets factory-built fireplaces, fireplace inserts, heating stoves, and accessories; and Hon Export Limited markets the corporation's products worldwide. Founded 1944. **Corporate headquarters location:** Muscatine IA. **Listed on:** New York Stock Exchange. **Stock exchange symbol:** HNI. **President:** Stan A. Akren. **CEO:** Jack D. Michaels.

HONEYWELL
3475 North Wesleyan Boulevard North, Rocky Mount NC 27804. 252/977-2100. **Contact:** Human Resources. **World Wide Web address:** http://www.honeywell.com. **Description:** Honeywell is engaged in the research, development, manufacture, and sale of advanced technology products and services in the fields of chemicals, electronics, automation, and controls. The company's major businesses are home and building automation and control, performance polymers and chemicals, industrial automation and control, space and aviation systems, and defense and marine systems. **NOTE:** Please visit website to search for jobs and apply online. Resumes will not be accepted by mail. **Positions advertised include:** Engineer. **Special programs:** Internships. **Corporate headquarters location:** Morristown NJ. **Other area locations:** Statewide. **Other U.S. locations:** Nationwide. **International locations:** Worldwide. **Operations at this facility include:** This location manufactures aircraft parts and equipment. **Listed on:** New York Stock Exchange. **Stock exchange symbol:** HON. **Number of employees worldwide:** 100,000.

HONEYWELL NYLON INC. (HNI)
4824 Parkway Plaza Boulevard Suite 300 Charlotte NC 28817-9730. 704/423-2000. **Contact:** Human Resources. **World Wide Web address:** http://www.honeywell.com/sites/sm/nylon.htm. **Description:** Creates high-performance nylon fabrics. **Corporate headquarters location:** This location. **Other U.S. locations:** SC; VA. **International locations:** Canada; China. **Parent company:** Honeywell. **Number of employees worldwide:** 4,000.

HONEYWELL SENSOTEC, INC.
1100 Airport Road, Shelby NC 28150. 704/482-9582. **Recorded jobline:** 614/850-6000 option 3. **Contact:** Human Resources. **E-mail address:** hrdepartment2@sensotec.com. **World Wide Web address:** http://www.sensotec.com. **Description:** Supplies components to the automotive, truck, appliance, heating, and aerospace industries. **NOTE:** Please visit http://honeywell.com/careers/index.html to search for jobs and apply online. Online applications are preferred. **Corporate headquarters location:** Columbus OH. **International locations:** Worldwide. **Parent company:** Honeywell.

HOOKER FURNITURE CORPORATION
P.O. Box 617, Maiden NC 28650. 828/428-9978. **Physical address:** 2900 US Highway 321, Maiden NC 28650. **Contact:** Denise Campbell, Personnel. **World Wide Web address:** http://www.hookerfurniture.com. **Description:** Manufactures home and home office furniture. The company recently acquired Bradington-Young, and has begun developing upholstered and leather furniture. Founded 1924. **Corporate headquarters location:** Martinsville VA. **Number of employees nationwide:** 2,200.

K. HOVNANIAN HOMES
2706 North Church Street, Greensboro NC 27405. 336/375-6200. **Fax:** 336/375-6355. **Contact:** Human Resources. **World Wide Web address:** http://www.khov.com. **Description:** A real estate and construction company.

HUNTER TEXTBOOKS, INC.
701 Shallowford Street, Winston-Salem NC 27101. 336/725-0608. **Toll-free phone:** 800/367-4159. **Fax:** 336/722-0530. **Contact:** Human Resources. **E-mail address:** hunter@rbdc.com. **World Wide Web address:** http://www.huntertextbooks.com. **Description:** Specializes in the publication of college textbooks and laboratory manuals in the areas of physical education, biology, geology, and the humanities. Founded in 1976. **Corporate headquarters location:** This location.

IBM CORPORATION
8501 IBM Drive, Charlotte NC 28262-8563. 704/594-1000. **Contact:** IBM Staffing Services. **World Wide Web address:** http://www.ibm.com. **Description:** IBM manufactures, sells, and markets advanced information processing products including computers and microelectronics technology, software, networking systems, and information technology-related services. **NOTE:** Applicants should apply online. **Positions advertised include:** Helpdesk Support. **Special programs:** Internships; Co-ops. **Corporate headquarters location:** White Plains NY. **Other area locations:** Statewide. **Other U.S. locations:** Nationwide. **International locations:** Worldwide.

Subsidiaries include: IBM Credit Corporation; IBM Instruments, Inc.; IBM World Trade Corporation. **Listed on:** New York Stock Exchange. **Stock exchange symbol:** IBM. **CEO:** Sam J. Palmisano.

IBM CORPORATION
3039 Cornwallis Road, P.O. Box 12195 Research Triangle Park NC 27709. 919/543-5221. **Contact:** Staffing Services. **World Wide Web address:** http://www.ibm.com. **Description:** IBM is a developer, manufacturer, and marketer of advanced information processing products including computers and microelectronics technology, software, networking systems, and information technology-related services. **NOTE:** Applicants should apply online. **Positions advertised include:** Array Circuit Designer; Array Designer Engineer; Communications Professional; CSS Specialist; Engineer; Fulfillment Coordinator; Hardware Engineer; Licensing Technical Team Leader; Logic Design Engineer; Mechanical Engineer; Network Analyst; Network Management Professional; PeopleSoft Consultant; Physical Design Engineer; Program Manager; Scheduler; Software Engineer. **Special programs:** Internships; Co-ops. **Corporate headquarters location:** White Plains NY. **Other area locations:** Statewide. **Other U.S. locations:** Nationwide. **International locations:** Worldwide. **Subsidiaries include:** IBM Credit Corporation; IBM Instruments, Inc.; IBM World Trade Corporation. **Listed on:** New York Stock Exchange. **Stock exchange symbol:** IBM. **CEO:** Sam J. Palmisano.

IENTERTAINMENT NETWORK
124 Quade Drive, Cary NC 27513. 919/678-8301. **Fax:** 919/678-8302. **Contact:** Human Resources. **E-mail address:** hr@ient.com. **World Wide Web address:** http://www.ient.com. **Description:** Develops and produces strategy and simulation computer games and online entertainment communities. **NOTE:** Please visit website to view job listings. **Corporate headquarters location:** This location. **Listed on:** NASDAQ. **Stock exchange symbol:** IENT. **CEO:** J.W. Stealey.

INDALEX INC.
600 North Metcalf Street, Winton NC. 252/358-5811. **Toll-free phone:** 800/334-8731. **Fax:** 252/358-5683. **Contact:** Gail Miller, Human Resources. **World Wide Web address:** http://www.indalex.com. **Description:** Manufactures extruded aluminum and related products. **NOTE:** Please visit website to view job listings and post resume online. **Corporate headquarters location:** Girard OH. **Other area locations:** Burlington NC. **Other U.S. locations:** CA; CT; GA; IA; OH; PA. **International locations:** Canada. **Parent company:** Novar plc. **Number of employees at this location:** 500.

INDALEX INC.
1507 Industry Drive, Burlington NC 27216. 336/227-8826. **Toll-free phone:** 800/334-6825. **Fax:** 336/228-9813. **Contact:** Human Resources. **World Wide Web address:** http://www.indalex.com. **Description:** Manufactures extruded aluminum and related products. **NOTE:** Please visit website to view job listings and post resume online. **Corporate headquarters location:** Girard OH. **Other area locations:** Winton NC. **Other U.S. locations:** CA; CT; GA; IA; OH; PA. **International locations:** Canada. **Parent company:** Novar plc.

INGERSOLL-RAND
800 Beaty Street, Davidson NC 28036. 704/896-4000. **Contact:** Human Resources. **World Wide Web address:** http://www.irco.com. **Description:** Manufactures and sells diverse engineered products serving a range of industrial and commercial markets. **Positions advertised include:** Business development Manager; Communications Specialist; Engagement Leader; Executive Assistant to Sector President; Financial Analyst. **Corporate headquarters location:** Montvale NJ. **Other area locations:** Charlotte NC.

INGLES MARKETS, INC.
P.O. Box 6676, Asheville NC 28816. 828/669-2941. **Physical address:** 2913 US Highway 70 West, Black Mountain NC 28711. **Fax:** 828/669-3678. **Contact:** Human Resources/Recruiting. **E-mail address:** recruit@ingles-markets.com. **World Wide Web address:** http://www.ingles-markets.com. **Description:** Operates over 200 supermarkets in North Carolina, South Carolina, Georgia, Tennessee, Virginia, and Alabama. In conjunction with its supermarket activities, the company owns and operates neighborhood shopping centers. Ingles Markets also owns and operates a milk processing and packaging plant. **Positions advertised include:** Retail Pharmacist. **Corporate headquarters location:** This location. **Listed on:** NASDAQ. **Stock exchange symbol:** IMKTA. **Number of employees nationwide:** 6,512.

INSTEEL INDUSTRIES, INC.
1373 Boggs Drive, Mount Airy NC 27030. 336/719-9000. **Contact:** Human Resources. **E-mail address:** humanresources@insteel.com. **World Wide Web address:** http://www.insteel.com. **Description:** Produces industrial wire, galvanized fencing products, nails, specialty wire fabrics, concrete reinforcing products, and Insteel 3-D. **NOTE:** Human Resources phone is 336/719-9000 Ext. 3165. Please visit website to view job listings. **Corporate headquarters location:** This location. **Other U.S. locations:** DE; FL; KY; SC; TN; TX; VA. **Operations at this facility include:** Administration; Sales. **Number of employees nationwide:** 700.

INTELICOAT TECHNOLOGIES
700 Crestdale Street, Matthews NC 28105. 704/847-9171. **Toll-free phone:** 800/688-9171. **Fax:** 704/845-4307. **Contact:** Robert Thumith, Vice President of Human Resources. **E-mail address:** rthumith@intelicoat.com. **World Wide Web address:** http://www.intelicoat.com. **Description:** Specializes in custom, roll-to-roll coating and laminating of films, foils, and papers used in high-performance products. The company provides technical, pilot, and production services for companies worldwide. **NOTE:** The listed contact is in charge of employment for the entire company. **Corporate headquarters location:** South Hadley MA. **Other U.S. locations:** Portland OR. **International locations:** United Kingdom; The Netherlands. **Parent company:** Rexam plc. **Listed on:** NASDAQ. **Stock exchange symbol:** REXMY. **President:** Robert Champigny. **Number of employees worldwide:** 750.

INTERNATIONAL PAPER COMPANY
100 Gaston Road, Roanoke Rapids NC 27870. 252/533-6000. **Toll-free phone:** 800/223-1268. **Contact:** Human Resources Manager. **World Wide Web address:** http://www.internationalpaper.com. **Description:** International Paper is a manufacturer of pulp and paper, packaging, and wood products, as well as a range of specialty products. Millions of acres of timberland are controlled by International Paper, making it one of the largest private landowners in the United States. The company is organized into five business segments: Printing Papers, which includes uncoated papers, coated papers, bristles, and pulp; Packaging, which includes industrial packaging, consumer packaging, and kraft and specialty papers; Distribution, which includes printing papers, graphic arts equipment and supplies, packaging materials, industrial supplies, and office products; Specialty Products, which includes imaging products, specialty panels, nonwovens, chemicals, and minerals; and Forest Products, which includes logs and wood products. **Special programs:** Internships; Co-ops. **Office hours:** Monday – Friday, 8:00 a.m. – 4:30 p.m. **Corporate headquarters location:** Stamford CT. **U.S. locations:** Nationwide. **International locations:** Worldwide. **Listed on:** New York Stock Exchange. **Stock exchange symbol:** IP. **Number of employees worldwide:** 83,000.

INTERNATIONAL PAPER COMPANY
865 John L. Riegel Road, Riegelwood NC 28456. 910/655-3856. **Toll-free phone:** 800/672-3866. **Fax:** 800/553-1914. **Contact:** Human Resources Manager. **World Wide Web address:** http://www.internationalpaper.com. **Description:** International Paper is a manufacturer of pulp and paper, packaging, and wood products, as well as a range of specialty products. Millions of acres of timberland are controlled by International Paper, making it one of the largest private landowners in the United States. The company is organized into five business segments: Printing Papers, which includes uncoated papers, coated papers, bristles, and pulp; Packaging, which includes industrial packaging, consumer packaging, and kraft and specialty papers; Distribution, which includes printing papers, graphic arts equipment and supplies, packaging materials, industrial supplies, and office products; Specialty Products, which includes imaging products, specialty panels, nonwovens, chemicals, and minerals; and Forest Products, which includes logs and wood products. **Corporate headquarters location:** Stamford CT. **U.S. locations:** Nationwide. **International locations:** Worldwide. **Operations at this facility include:** This location is a paper mill. **Listed on:** New York Stock Exchange. **Stock exchange symbol:** IP. **Number of employees worldwide:** 83,000.

INTERNATIONAL TEXTILE GROUP
804 Green Valley Road, Suite 300, Greensboro NC 27408. 336/379-6220. **Fax:** 336/379-6476. **Contact:** Mark Collins, Human Resources. **World Wide Web address:** http://www.internationaltextilegroup.com. **Description:** A major producer of textiles including apparel and interior furnishings. Apparel products, which are designed, manufactured, and sold by five divisions within the company include yarns, wools, woven synthetics, clothes, denims, industrial uniforms, and sportswear. The interior furnishings division manufactures drapes, upholstery, bedroom ensembles, and rugs. **Special programs:** Internships.

INVERESK RESEARCH
11000 Weston Parkway, Cary NC 27513. 919/460-9005. **Fax:** 919/462-2200. 46. **Contact:** Human Resources. **E-mail address:** hr.usa@inveresk.com. **World Wide Web address:** http://www.inveresk.com. **Description:** Provides research services to pharmaceutical companies for studies that include FDA drug approval. **NOTE:** Please visit website to search for jobs and apply online. You can either apply through the website, or e-mail your resume. **Positions advertised include:** Manager – Clinical Monitoring; Project Team Assistant; Telecommunications/Facility Specialist; Financial Analyst; Associate Director Systems; Medical Director; Senior Clinical Research Associate; Clinical Research Associate; Executive Assistant; Associate Director; Clinical Project Manager; Senior Biostatistician; Director – Proposal Development. **Corporate headquarters location:** This location. **Other area locations:** Wilmington NC. **International locations:** Belgium; Canada; Czech Republic; France; Germany; Israel; Italy; Japan; Poland; Spain.

INVESTORS TITLE INSURANCE COMPANY
P.O. Drawer 2687, Chapel Hill NC 27515. 919/968-2200. **Physical address:** 121 North Columbia Street, Chapel Hill NC 27514 **Toll-free phone:** 800/326-4842. **Fax:** 919/968-2235. **Contact:** Human Resources. **E-mail address:** humanresources@invtitle.com. **World Wide Web address:** http://www.invtitle.com. **Description:** Investors Title Insurance Company, through its two title insurance subsidiaries, Investors Title Insurance Company and Northeast Investors Title Insurance Company, writes title insurance in Florida, Georgia, Illinois, Indiana, Kentucky, Maryland, Michigan, Minnesota, Mississippi, Nebraska, New York, North Carolina, Pennsylvania, South Carolina, Tennessee, and Virginia. A third subsidiary, Investors Title Exchange Corporation, serves as a qualified intermediary in tax-deferred exchanges of real property. Founded in 1972. **NOTE:** Please visit website to view job listings and apply online. **Positions advertised include:** Agency Underwriting and Operations Support Coordinator; Sales Executive; Senior Vice President of Finance; Underwriter; Vice President of Vendor Management Operations. **Corporate headquarters location:** This location. **Other area locations:** Statewide. **Other U.S. locations:** Lansing MI; Columbia SC; Pittsford NY. **Listed on:** NASDAQ. **Stock exchange symbol:** ITIC. **Annual sales/revenues:** $21 - $50 million. **Number of employees at this location:** 50. **Number of employees nationwide:** 180.

INVISTA
P.O. Box 37388, Charlotte NC 28237. 704/586-7300. **Physical address:** 4501 Charlotte Park Drive, Charlotte NC. **Fax:** 704/586-7500. **Contact:** Human Resources. **World Wide Web address:** http://www.invista.com. **Description:** One of the world's largest producers of polyester fibers, resins, and polymer products. The company has a manufacturing or marketing presence in every major market and garment region worldwide. Today it is comprised of five businesses: Apparel; Performance and Textile Fibers; Interiors; Intermediates; and Polymer and Resins. **Corporate headquarters location:** Witchita KS. **Other area locations:** Wilmington NC; Salisbury NC; Shelby NC. **Other U.S. locations:** Spartanburg SC; Winnsboro SC. **International locations:** Canada; Germany; Mexico; Netherlands. **Parent company:** Koch International Equity Investments BV. **Operations at this facility include:** Regional Headquarters. **Number of employees worldwide:** 6,500.

JC PENNEY
246 North New Hope Road, Eastridge Mall, Gastonia NC 28054. 704/867-0781. **Contact:** Store Manager. **World Wide Web address:** http://www.jcpenney.com. **Description:** A nationwide chain of retail department stores. Founded 1902. **NOTE:** Please visit website for more information on career opportunities and to apply online. **Corporate headquarters location:** Plano TX. **Other area locations:** Statewide. **Other U.S. locations:** Nationwide. **Operations at this facility include:** Sales; Customer Service. **Listed on:** New York Stock Exchange. **Stock exchange symbol:** JCP. **Number of employees nationwide:** 147,000.

JACOBSEN
3800 Arco Corporate Drive, Suite 310, Charlotte NC 28273. 704/504-6600. **Contact:** Human Resources. **E-mail address:** jobs@textron.com. **World Wide Web address:** http://www.jacobsen.com. **Description:** Manufactures equipment for lawn and turf maintenance, including the brand name products Bob-Cat, Brouwer, and Ransomes. **NOTE:** Please visit website to search for jobs. **Positions advertised include:** Lead Purchasing Analyst; Purchasing Engineer; Value Engineer; Value Group Manager; Manager – Service Parts Warehouse; Senior Financial Analyst; Senior Buyer; Service Parts Buyer; Human Resources Executive Assistant. **Parent company:** Textron, Inc. is a diversified company with manufacturing and financial services operations. The company is one of the U.S. government's largest defense contractors. Products include helicopters; gas turbine engines; combat vehicles; air cushion landing craft; missile re-entry systems; aircraft wing structures; and aerospace materials, controls, and electronics. The remainder of manufacturing primarily consists of automotive parts,

outdoor products, and specialty fasteners. Financial and other services segments include Avco Financial Services, Textron Financial Corporation, Avco Insurance Services/Balboa Life and Casualty, and Paul Revere Insurance Group. **Corporate headquarters location:** This location. **Other US. Locations:** Johnson Creek WI; Augusta GA. **International locations:** United Kingdom; Asia. **Listed on:** New York Stock Exchange. **Stock exchange symbol:** TXT. **President/CEO:** Lewis B. Campbell. **Number of employees worldwide:** 49,000.

JEFFERSON-PILOT COMMUNICATIONS
100 North Greene Street, P.O. Box 21008, Greensboro NC 27420. 704/374-3500. **Fax:** 704/374-3626. **Contact:** Human Resources. **E-mail address:** hired@jpc.com. **World Wide Web address:** http://www.jpc.com. **Description:** A television and radio broadcasting company. **NOTE:** Please visit website to view job listings. **Parent company:** Jefferson-Pilot Financial is a holding company whose subsidiaries include life annuity, accident and health, property and casualty, and title insurance operations. **Corporate headquarters:** This location. **Other area locations:** Charlotte NC. **Other U.S. locations:** San Diego CA; Denver CO; Miami FL; Atlanta GA; Charleston SC; Richmond VA. **Listed on:** New York Stock Exchange. **Stock exchange symbol:** JP.

JEFFERSON-PILOT FINANCIAL
P.O. Box 21008, Greensboro NC 27420. 336/691-3000. **Physical address:** 100 North Greene Street, Greensboro NC 27401. **Fax:** 336/691-3797. **Contact:** Human Resources. **E-mail address:** gsojobs@jpfinancial.com. **World Wide Web address:** http://www.jpfinancial.com. **Description:** A holding company whose principal insurance subsidiaries are Jefferson-Pilot Life Insurance Company, Jefferson-Pilot Fire and Casualty Company, and Jefferson-Pilot Title Insurance Company. The company also operates radio and television stations and produces televised sports programs. **Positions advertised include:** Manager – Internal Auditing; Supply Clerk; Quality Assurance Analyst; Audio-Visual Specialist; Customer Service Team Leader; Production Supervisor; Manager – Financial Reporting; Senior Accountant; Quality Assurance Analyst; JPSC Marketing Assistant; Business Analyst; Communications Specialist; Insurance Agent; Annuity Product Management; Actuarial Clerk; Manager – Annuity Product Compliance; Marketing Specialist; File Clerk. **Corporate headquarters location:** This location. **Other U.S. locations:** Concord NH; Omaha NE. **Listed on:** New York Stock Exchange. **Stock exchange symbol:** JP. **President/CEO:** Dennis R. Glass.

JORDAN LUMBER & SUPPLY, INC.
P.O. Box 98, Mount Gilead NC 27306. 910/439-6121. **Physical address:** 1939 Highway 109 South, Mount Gilead NC 27306. **Fax:** 910/439-6105. **Contact:** Personnel Director. **World Wide Web address:** http://www.jordanlumber.com. **Description:** A distributor of southern yellow pine lumber, wood chips, sawdust, bark, and related products. Founded 1939. **Corporate headquarters location:** This location. **Number of employees at this location:** 150. **President:** Bob Jordan.

JOYCE ENGINEERING
2301 West Meadowview Road, Suite 203, Greensboro NC 27407. 336/323-0092. **Fax:** 336/323-0093. **Contact:** Personnel. **E-mail address:** personnel@joyceengineering.com. **World Wide Web Address:** http://www.joyceengineering.com. **Description:** Provides waste management consulting services. Specializes in providing engineering and environmental solutions. **Positions advertised include:** Geologist/Environmental Scientist. **Corporate headquarters location:** Richmond VA.

KPMG
301 North Elm Street, Suite 700, Greensboro NC 27401. 336/275-3394. **Contact:** Pam Brown, Personnel Manager. **World Wide Web address:** http://www.us.kpmg.com. **Description:** KPMG delivers a wide range of value-added assurance, tax, and consulting services. **NOTE:** Please visit http://kpmgcareers.com/index.asp to search for jobs. **Corporate headquarters location:** Washington DC. **Parent company:** KPMG International is a leader among professional services firms engaged in capturing, managing, assessing, and delivering information to create knowledge that will help its clients maximize shareholder value. **Other U.S. locations:** Nationwide. **International locations:** Worldwide. **Number of employees at this location:** 50.

KABA ILCO CORPORATION
2941 Indiana Avenue, Winston-Salem NC 27105. 336/725-1331. **Toll-free phone:** 800/849-8324. **Fax:** 336/722-8814. **Contact:** Human Resources. **E-mail address:** cv@kaba-ilco.com. **World Wide Web address:** http://www.kaba-ilco.com. **Description:** Manufactures key blanks, key machines, and two types of locks (mechanical push-button and electronic access control). **NOTE;** Please visit website to view job listings. **Other area locations:** Rocky Mount NC. **International locations:** Montreal, Canada. **Number of employees worldwide:** 300.

KAYSER-ROTH CORPORATION
102 Corporate Center Boulevard, Greensboro NC 27408. 336/852-2030. **Contact:** Sara Newby, Human Resources. **World Wide Web address:** http://www.nononsense.com. **Description:** Distributes sheer hosiery to food and drug stores, mass merchandisers, and discount stores. Brands include No Nonsense, Renew!, Great Shapes, Almost Bare, Sheer Endurance, and Business Casuals. **Other U.S. locations:** Nationwide.

KEARFOTT GUIDANCE & NAVIGATION CORPORATION
Asheville, Route 70, Black Mountain NC 28711. 828/686-3811. **Contact:** Denise Thomas, Human Resources. **E-mail address:** humanresources@kearfott.com. **World Wide Web address:** http://www.kearfott.com. **Description:** Manufactures precision electromechanical and electronic components used to generate, sense, control, and display motion such as synchros, resolvers, cant angle sensors, and servo motors. Founded in 1917. **NOTE:** Entry-level positions and second and third shifts are offered. Please visit website to fill out Personnel application. **Special programs:** Apprenticeships; Training. **Corporate headquarters location:** Wayne NJ. **Other U.S. locations:** Little Falls NJ. **International locations:** Mexico. **Parent company:** Astronautics Corporation of America. **Listed on:** Privately held. **Annual sales/revenues:** $21 - $50 million.

KENNEDY COVINGTON LOBDELL & HICKMAN
Hearst Tower, 47th Floor, 214 North Tryon Street, Charlotte NC 28202. 704/331-7400. **Fax:** 704/331-7598. **Contact:** Human Resources. **E-mail address:** humanresources@kennedycovington.com. **World Wide Web address:** http://www.kennedycovington.com. **Description:** A law firm that specializes in employee benefits, estate litigation, real estate, taxes, and wills for corporate clients. **NOTE:** Please visit website or contact an office for more information on the application process for attorney positions. **Special programs:** Summer Associate Program. **Other area locations:** Raleigh NC; Morrisville NC. **Other U.S. locations:** Rock Hill SC; Columbia SC.

KIDDE AEROSPACE, INC.
4200 Airport Drive NW, Wilson NC 27896-8630. 252/237-7004. **Fax:** 252/246-7184. **Contact:** Human Resources. **E-mail address:** hr@kiddeaerospace.com. **World Wide Web address:** http://www.walterkidde.com. **Description:** Develops and manufactures fire detection and suppression equipment for use in aerospace and marine applications. Products are sold to aircraft manufacturers and to airlines as replacement/repair parts, and are used in defense applications. **Positions advertised include:** Lead Engineer; Senior Project Engineer; Systems Program Manager; Systems Integration Engineer. **Corporate headquarters location:** Colnbrook, England. **International locations:** Russia; Singapore; United Arab Emirates. **Parent company:** Kidde plc. **Number of employees at this location:** 240.

KIMBERLY-CLARK CORPORATION
32 Smyth Avenue, Hendersonville NC 28792-8503. 828/692-9611. **Contact:** Human Resources Director. **World Wide Web address:** http://www.kimberly-clark.com. **Description:** Kimberly-Clark Corporation manufactures and markets products for personal, business, and industrial uses throughout the world. Most of the company's products are made from natural and synthetic fibers using advanced technologies in absorbency, fibers, and nonwovens. The name brands of Kimberly-Clark Corporation include Kleenex facial and bathroom tissue, Huggies diapers and baby wipes, Pull-Ups training pants, Kotex and New Freedom feminine care products, Depend and Poise incontinence care products, Hi-Dri household towels, Kimguard sterile wrap, Kimwipes industrial wipes, and Classic business and correspondence papers. **NOTE:** Please visit website to search for job by category and apply online. Resumes are not accepted at this location. Please apply through Blue Ridge Community College. **Corporate headquarters location:** Dallas TX. **Other U.S. locations:** Nationwide. **International locations:** Worldwide. **Operations advertised include:** This location is a nonwoven fabric mill. **Listed on:** New York Stock Exchange. **Stock exchange symbol:** KMB. **CEO:** Thomas J. Falk. **Number of employees worldwide:** 62,000.

KING HICKORY FURNITURE COMPANY
P.O. Box 1179, Hickory NC 28603. 828/322-6025. **Physical address:** 1820 Main Avenue SE, Hickory NC 28603. **Toll-free phone:** 800/337-8827. **Contact:** Human Resources. **World Wide Web address:** http://www.kinghickory.com. **Description:** Manufactures sofas, sleepers, loveseats, settees, ottomans, and other furniture. All furniture has hardwood frames and hand-tied springs. Founded 1958. **Corporate headquarters location:** This location.

KING PHARMACEUTICALS, INC.
4000 Centregreen Road, Suite 300, Cary NC 27513. 919/653-7001. **Contact:** Human Resources. **World Wide Web address:** http://www.kingpharm.com. **Description:** A pharmaceutical development firm specializing in cardiovascular drugs. Founded 1994. **Corporate headquarters location:** Bristol TN. **Other area locations:** Statewide. **Other U.S. locations:** Nationwide. **Listed on:** New York Stock Exchange. **Stock exchange symbol:** KG.

KNOWLEDGE SYSTEMS CORPORATION
1143 Executive Circle, Suite G, Cary NC 27511. 919/789-8549. **Toll-free phone:** 800/348-8323. **Fax:** 919/789-8615. **Contact:** Recruiting Manager. **World Wide Web address:** http://www.ksccary.com. **Description:** Develops educational software and provides computer consulting services. Founded 1985.

LA-Z-BOY CHAIR COMPANY
1164 Burris Boulevard, Lincolnton NC 28092. 704/735-0441. **Fax:** 704/748-6559. **Contact:** Human Resources. **World Wide Web address:** http://www.la-z-boy.com. **Description:** A manufacturer of upholstered seating, and one of the nation's largest manufacturers of residential furniture. La-Z-Boy is best known for its upholstered recliners. The company also manufactures furniture for family rooms, living rooms, bedrooms, and dining rooms. The company operates in five divisions: La-Z-Boy Residential produces stationary chairs, sofas and loveseats, recliners, reclining sofas, sleeper sofas, and modular seating groups, which it sells in a national network of La-Z-Boy proprietary stores, and in department stores, furniture stores, and regional furniture chains; La-Z-Boy Canada manufactures residential seating and markets La-Z-Boy residential products in Canada; Hammary produces occasional tables, living room cabinets, wall entertainment units, and upholstered furniture sold in furniture and department stores, as well as CompaTables occasional tables, which are featured in La-Z-Boy proprietary stores; Kincaid makes solid-wood bedroom, dining room, and occasional furniture sold through in-store Kincaid Galleries, and select La-Z-Boy Furniture Galleries nationwide; La-Z-Boy Contract Furniture Group includes La-Z-Boy Business Furniture, La-Z-Boy Healthcare Furniture (hospital chairs, recliners, and special mobile recliners, marketed through contract dealers and medical sales companies), and La-Z-Boy Hospitality Furniture (specially engineered La-Z-Boy recliners that are sold directly to major hotel and motel chains and through hospitality sales companies). **Office hours:** Monday – Thursday, 7:00 a.m. – 4:30 p.m.; Friday – 7:00 a.m. 11:00 a.m. **Corporate headquarters location:** Monroe MI. **Other U.S. locations:** Nationwide. **Subsidiaries include:** Bauhaus USA Furniture; Centurion Furniture; Clayton Marcus; Hammary Furniture; Kincaid Furniture. **Listed on:** New York Stock Exchange. **Stock exchange symbol:** LZB. **Number of employees worldwide:** 17,000.

LABORATORY CORPORATION OF AMERICA (LABCORP)
309 East Davis Street, P.O. Box 2230, Burlington NC 27216. 336/229-1127. **Contact:** Human Resources. **World Wide Web address:** http://www.labcorp.com. **Description:** One of the nation's leading clinical laboratory companies, providing services primarily to physicians, hospitals, clinics, nursing homes, and other clinical labs nationwide. LabCorp performs tests on blood, urine, and other body fluids and tissue, aiding the diagnosis of disease. **NOTE:** Please visit website to search for jobs and apply online. **Positions advertised include:** Sr. Cytogenetics Technologist; Laboratory Director; national Managed Care Executive Director; Sr. Programmer/Analyst; Lead Project Analyst/Engineer. **Special programs:** Internships. **Corporate headquarters location:** This location. **Other U.S. locations:** Nationwide. **Operations at this facility include:** Administration; Regional Headquarters; Research and Development; Sales; Service. **Listed on:** New York Stock Exchange. **Stock exchange symbol:** LH. **Number of employees nationwide:** 23,000.

LABORATORY CORPORATION OF AMERICA (LABCORP)
1904 Alexander Drive, Research Triangle Park NC 27709. 919/572-6900. **Toll-free phone:** 800/800-4522. **Contact:** Human Resources. **World Wide Web address:** http://www.labcorp.com. **Description:** LabCorp is one of the nation's leading clinical laboratory companies, providing services primarily to physicians, hospitals, clinics, nursing homes, and other clinical labs nationwide. LabCorp performs tests on blood, urine, and other body fluids and tissue, aiding the diagnosis of disease. **NOTE:** Please visit website to search for jobs and apply online. **Corporate headquarters location:** Burlington NC. **Operations at this facility include:** This location is part of the Occupational Testing Division, and provides forensic drug testing services to various clients. **Listed on:** New York Stock Exchange. **Stock exchange symbol:** LH. **Number of employees nationwide:** 23,000.

LEA INDUSTRIES
P.O. Box 26777, Greensboro NC 27417. 336/294-5233. **Physical address:** 4620 Grandover Parkway, Greensboro NC 27407. **Fax:** 336/315-4380. **Contact:** Personnel. **E-mail address:** leaindustries@leaindustries.com. **World Wide Web address:** http://www.leafurniture.com. **Description:** Manufactures a variety of styles of furniture for children. Looks vary from country to 18th Century-style to contemporary pieces, and products include bunk beds, dual sleep beds, canopy beds, and desks. Some of their featured collections are the Jessica McClintock Collection, Grant Hill Collection, Dennis Connor Collection, Youth Collection, and Master Bedroom Collection. **Corporate headquarters location:** This location. **Parent company:** La-Z-Boy Inc.

LANCE, INC.
P.O. Box 32368, Charlotte NC 28232. 704/554-1421. **Physical address:** 8600 South Boulevard, Charlotte NC 28273. **Fax:** 704/556-5636. **Contact:** Ray Silinski, Human Resources. **E-mail address:** fresh@lance.com. **World Wide Web address:** http://www.lance.com. **Description:** Produces snack products under the Home-pak, Club-pak, Snack-Right, and Vista brand names. The company also operates Midwest Biscuit (Burlington IA) and Caronuts (Boykins VA). Founded in 1913. **Positions advertised include:** Records Retention Specialist. **Corporate headquarters location:** This location. **Other area locations:** Charlotte NC. **Other U.S. locations:** Burlington IA; Hyannis MA. **Listed on:** NASDAQ. **Stock exchange symbol:** LNCE.

LANDSTAR EXPRESS AMERICA, INC.
1901-A1 Associates Lane, Suite A1, Charlotte NC 28217. 704/424-9912. **Contact:** Human Resources. **E-mail address:** employment@landstar.com. **World Wide Web address:** http://www.landstar.com. **Description:** Performs expedited and emergency air and truck freight services. **Corporate headquarters location:** Jacksonville FL. **Other U.S. locations:** Rockford IL. **Listed on:** NASDAQ. **Stock exchange symbol:** LSTR. **CEO:** Jeffrey C. Crowe.

LEAD TECHNOLOGIES, INC.
1201 Greenwood Cliff, Suite 400, Charlotte NC 28204. 704/332-5532. **Toll-free phone:** 800/637-4699. **Fax:** 704/372-8161. **Contact:** Human Resources. **E-mail address:** jobs@leadtools.com. **World Wide Web address:** http://www.leadtools.com. **Description:** Develops image file format, processing, and compression tool kits. **Positions advertised include:** Technical Writer; Senior Programmer. **Corporate headquarters location:** This location.

LEE INDUSTRIES
402 West 25th Street, Newton NC 28658. 828/464-8318. **Fax:** 828/466-1479. **Contact:** Angie Doane, Human Resources. **World Wide Web address:** http://www.leeindustries.com. **Description:** An upholstery manufacturer. **Corporate headquarters location:** This location.

LEVEL 8 SYSTEMS
8000 Regency Parkway, Suite 542, Cary NC 27511. 919/380-5000. **Fax:** 919/380-5121. **Contact:** Personnel. **E-mail address:** careers@level8.com. **World Wide Web address:** http://www.level8.com. **Description:** Develops business applications software. **Corporate headquarters location:** Princeton NJ. **Other U.S. locations:** Wilmington DE, Dulles VA. **International locations:** London, England; Paris, France; Milan, Italy. **Listed on:** NASDAQ. **Stock exchange symbol:** LVEL.

LEVOLOR KAIRSCH HOME FASHIONS
4110 Premier Drive, High Point NC 27265. 336/812-8181. **Toll-free phone:** 800/538-6567. **Contact:** Human Resources Director. **E-mail address:** career.opportunities@levolor.com. **World Wide Web address:** http://www.levolor.com. **Description:** Manufactures drapery hardware, window blinds, and shades. **Corporate headquarters location:** This location.

LEXINGTON HOME BRANDS
P.O. Box 1008, Lexington NC 27293. 336/236-5300. **Toll-free phone:** 800/LEX-INFO. **Contact:** Human Resources. **World Wide Web address:** http://www.lexington.com. **Description:** A manufacturer of upholstered furniture. Lexington Upholstery is best known for its Bob Timberlake and Arnold Palmer collections. **CEO:** Bob Stec. **Number of employees at this location:** 220.

T. A. LOVING COMPANY CONSTRUCTION SERVICES
P.O. Drawer 919, Goldsboro NC 27533-0919. 919/734-8400. **Fax:** 919/580-9444. **Contact:** Paula V. Herring, Human Resources Director. **E-mail address:** pherring@taloving.com. **World Wide Web address:** http://www.taloving.com. **Description:** T.A. Loving Company provides complete construction and pre-construction services for the general building, utility and bridge/heavy trades. **Positions advertised include:** Project Manager, Superintendent, Estimator. **Number of employees nationwide:** 300.

LOWE'S COMPANIES, INC.
P.O. Box 1111, North Wilkesboro NC 28656. 336/658-4000. **Fax:** 336/658-4766. **Contact:** Human Resources. **World Wide Web address:** http://www.lowes.com. **Description:** A discount retailer of consumer durables, building supplies, and home products for the do-it-yourself and home improvement markets. The company conducts operations over 900 retail stores in 45 states, primarily in the south central and southeastern regions of the United States. Products sold include tools, lumber, building materials, heating, cooling, and water systems, and specialty goods. **NOTE:** Please visit website to search for jobs and apply online. **Positions advertised include:** Accountant; Applied Design Manager; Applied Trend Manager; Commercial Marketing Manager; Career Development Specialist; Corporate Counsel; Customer Care Associate; Designer; Director – Various Departments; Engagement Manager; Forecast Analyst; Human Resources Manager. **Company slogan:** Lowe's knows. **Special programs:** Internships. **Corporate headquarters location:** This location. **Listed on:** New York Stock Exchange. **Stock exchange symbol:** LOW. **CEO:** Robert L. Tillman. **Annual sales/revenues:** More than $100 million. **Number of employees nationwide:** 153,000.

LOWE'S FOODS
P.O. Box 20046, Greensboro NC 27420. 336/659-0180. **Fax:** 336/768-4702. **Contact:** Manager of Human Resources Department. **World Wide Web address:** http://www.lowesfood.com. **Description:** Operates a food store chain. **NOTE:** Please visit website to view job listings. **Parent company:** Alex Lee. **Corporate headquarters:** This location.

LUCENT TECHNOLOGIES INC.
P.O. Box 20046, Greensboro NC 27420. 336/279-7000. **Physical address:** 5440 Millstream, McLeansville NC 27301. **Toll-free phone:** 888/4LUCENT. **Contact:** Human Resources Department. **World Wide Web address:** http://www.lucent.com. **Description:** Lucent Technologies Inc. manufactures communications products including switches, transmitters, fiber-optic cable, and wireless systems for telephone companies and other communications services providers. **NOTE:** Please visit website to search for jobs and apply online. **Corporate headquarters location:** Murray Hill NJ. **Other U.S. locations:** Nationwide. **International locations:** Worldwide. **Operations at this facility include:** This location houses administrative offices. **Listed on:** New York Stock Exchange. **Stock exchange symbol:** LU.

MCNC - RESEARCH & DEVELOPMENT INSTITUTE
P.O. Box 13910, Research Triangle Park NC 27709-3910. 919/990/2000. **Physical address:** 3021 Cornwallis Road, Research Triangle Park NC. **Fax:** 919/248-1923. **Contact:** Personnel. **E-mail address:** bhine@mcnc.org. **World Wide Web address:** http://www.mcnc-rdi.org. **Description:** A nonprofit company that researches and develops software for electronic and information technologies. **NOTE:** Please visit website to view job listings and download application form. No phone calls regarding employment. Student positions are also available. **Positions advertised include:** Research Engineer. **Corporate headquarters location:** This location. **President/CEO:** David P. Rizzo.

MANAGEMENT INFORMATION SYSTEMS GROUP, INC.
10 Laboratory Drive, P.O. Box 13966, Research Triangle Park NC 27709-3966. 919/549-8700. **Fax:** 919/549-8733. **Contact:** Human Resources. **E-mail address:** techjobs@misg.com. **World Wide Web address:** http://www.misg.com. **Description:** Offers EDI (Electronic Data Interchange) services that help process business documents over networks. **Corporate headquarters location:** This location.

MANTECH ENVIRONMENTAL TECHNOLOGY, INC.
P.O. Box 12313, Research Triangle Park NC 27709. 919/549-0611. **Fax:** 919/549-9058. **Contact:** Human Resources. **E-mail address:** jobs@mantech.com. **World Wide Web address:** http://www.mantech.com. **Description:** An environmental engineering firm offering analytical research services and environmental information services. **NOTE:** Please visit website to search for jobs and apply online. **Positions advertised include:** Secretary/Administrative Assistant; Environmental Scientist. **Office hours:** Monday – Friday, 8:00 a.m. – 5:00 p.m. **Corporate headquarters location:** Fairfax VA. **Other area locations:** Fort Bragg NC; Havelock NC. **Other U.S. locations:** Nationwide. **International locations:** Worldwide. **Listed on:** NASDAQ. **Stock exchange symbol:** MANT. **President/CEO:** George J. Pederson. **Number of employees worldwide:** 5,000.

McGLADREY & PULLEN, LLP
P.O. Box 2470, Greensboro NC 27402-2470. 336/273-4461. **Physical address:** 230 North Elm Street, Suite 1100, Greensboro NC 27401. **Fax:** 336/274-2519. **Contact:** Jennifer Parish, Personnel. **World Wide Web address:** http://www.mcgladrey.com. **Description:** A certified public accounting firm providing audit, tax, management, data processing, and cost systems services. **Corporate headquarters location:** Bloomington MN. **Other area locations:** Statewide. **Other U.S. locations:** Nationwide.

McKESSON INFORMATION SOLUTIONS
10735 David Taylor Drive, Charlotte NC 28262. 704/549-7000. **Contact:** Tracy Schweikert, Human Resources. **World Wide Web address:** http://www.mckesson.com. **Description:** McKesson Information Solutions provides technology to health care enterprises including hospitals, integrated delivery networks, and managed care organizations. McKessonHBOC's primary products are Pathways 2000, a family of client/server-based applications that allow the integration and uniting of health care providers; STAR, Series, and HealthQuest transaction systems; and TRENDSTAR decision support system. The company also offers outsourcing services that include strategic information systems planning, data center operations, receivables management, business office administration, and major system conversions. **NOTE:** Please submit your resume at http://www.mckesson.com. **Positions advertised include:** Receptionist; Route Sales Representative; Enterprise Vice President – New Business; Regional Vice President; Account Manager. **Corporate headquarters location:** Alpharetta GA. **Other U.S. locations:** Nationwide. **International locations:** Canada; France; Netherlands; United Kingdom; Puerto Rico. **Operations at this facility include:** This location offers sales and technical support. **President:** Pamela Pure.

McKINNEY & SILVER
333 Corporate Plaza, Raleigh NC 27601. 919/828-0691. **Fax:** 919/313-0805. **Contact:** Lea Daughtridge, Human Resources. **E-mail address:** adaughtr@mckinney-silver.com. **World Wide Web address:** http://www.mckinney-silver.com. **Description:** An advertising agency offering broadcast, media, and print production services. **NOTE:** Contact Human Resources directly at 919/821-6417. **CEO:** Brad Brinegar.

MEDCATH INC.
10720 Sikes Place, Suite 300, Charlotte NC 28277. 704/708-6610. **Contact:** Human Resources. **World Wide Web address:** http://www.medcath.com. **Description:** Develops and manages cardiovascular care hospitals and catheterization laboratories. **Positions advertised include:** Senior Coding Consultant. **Corporate headquarters location:** This location. **Other area locations:** Greensboro NC; Raleigh NC; Wilmington NC. **Other U.S. locations:** Nationwide. **Listed on:** NASDAQ. **Stock exchange symbol:** MDTH.

MERCHANTS DISTRIBUTORS INC. (MDI)
P.O. Box 2148, Hickory NC 28603. 828/323-4100. **Physical address:** 5005 Alex Lee Boulevard, Hickory NC 28601. **Fax:** 828/323-4013. **Contact:** Human Resources. **World Wide Web address:** http://www.merchantsdistributors.com. **Description:** A wholesaler of groceries. **NOTE:** Please visit website to register, search for jobs, and apply online. **Special programs:** Internships. **Corporate headquarters location:** This location. **Other U.S. locations:** SC; GA; TN; VA; WV; KY. **Operations at this facility include:** Administration; Sales. **Listed on:** Privately held. **Number of employees at this location:** 1,260.

MERCK MANUFACTURING
4633 Merck Road, Wilson NC 27893. 252/243-2011. **Contact:** Human Resources. **World Wide Web address:** http://www.merck.com. **Description:** Manufactures pharmaceuticals for Merck & Company, Inc. **Corporate headquarters location:** Whitehouse Station NJ. **Other U.S. locations:** Nationwide. **International locations:** Worldwide. **Parent company:** Merck & Company, Inc. is a worldwide organization engaged primarily in the business of discovering, developing, producing, and marketing products for the maintenance of health and the environment. Products include human and animal pharmaceuticals and chemicals sold to the health care, oil exploration, food processing, textile, paper, and other industries. Merck & Company, Inc. also runs an ethical drug mail-order marketing business. **Listed on:** New York Stock Exchange. **Stock exchange symbol:** MRK.

MEREDITH COLLEGE
3800 Hillsborough Street, Raleigh NC 27607. 919/760-8600. **Fax:** 919/760-2828. **Description:** A women's college offering undergraduate and graduate programs.

NOTE: Please visit website to view job listings. **Positions advertised include:** Director of Financial Assistance; French Instructor – Part-time; Latin Instructor – Part-time; Assistant Director of the Learning Center; Director of Human Resources; Italian Instructor – Part-time; Spanish Instructor – Part-time.

METRO PRODUCTIONS
6005 Chapel Hill Road, Raleigh NC 27607. 919/851-6420. **Fax:** 919/851-6418. **Contact:** Human Resources. **World Wide Web address:** http://www.metroproductions.com. **Description:** Provides graphic design, Web offset printing, and video production services.

MILLER DESK INC.
Drawer HP-11, High Point NC 27261. 336/819-6400. **Physical address:** 1212 Lincoln Drive, High Point NC 27261. **Toll-free phone:** 800/438-4324. **Fax:** 800/756-9715. **Contact:** Human Resources. **World Wide Web address:** http://www.millerdesk.com. **Description:** A manufacturer of office furniture including both ergonomic and traditional seating.

MISSION ST. JOSEPH'S HOSPITAL
509 Biltmore Avenue, Ashville NC 28801. 828/213-1111. **Recorded jobline:** 828/213-4400. **Contact:** Human Resources. **World Wide Web address:** http://www.missionhospital.org. **Description:** A hospital licensed for over 800 beds and bassinets. The hospital has been ranked as a top 50 hospital for heart and heart surgery services, and a top 100 for breast cancer research, among other awards. **NOTE:** Contact Human Resources directly at 828/213-5600. Please visit website to search or jobs and apply online. To apply for clerical temp-to-hire positions, please go through Kelly Services. Volunteer positions are also available. Applications will remain active for 90 days. **Positions advertised include:** Nuclear Medicine Technologist; Lead Physicist; Clinical Trials Manager; Pharmacy Manager; Respiratory Therapist. **Corporate headquarters location:** This location. **Number of employees at this location:** 5,600.

MISYS, INC.
8529 Six Forks Road, Raleigh NC 27615. 919/847-8102. **Fax:** 919/848-5770. **Contact:** Human Resources. **E-mail address:** recruiter@misyshealthcare.com. **World Wide Web address:** http://www.misyshealthcare.com. **Description:** Misys develops health care management software. Products include +Medic Vision, +Medic PM, Auto Chart, AutoImage, and FasTracker. **NOTE:** Please visit website to register, search for jobs, and apply online. Online applications are preferred. **Positions advertised include:** Administrative Assistant; Application Product Specialist; Client Support Analyst; Corporate Receptionist; Director – Customer Call Center; EMR Template Care Analyst; Human Factors Engineer; Inside Sales Representative; Internal Auditor; Manager – Client Implementation Services; Product Line Director; Sales Development Executive; Sales Executive Assistant; Test Engineer. **Corporate headquarters location:** This location. **Other U.S. locations:** Nationwide. **International locations:** United Kingdom; Denmark; Ireland; Middle East. **Operations at this facility include:** This location provides sales, training, and support. **Parent company:** Misys plc. **CEO:** Tom Skelton.

MOOG COMPONENTS GROUP
POLY-SCIENTIFIC
1995 NC Highway, Murphy NC 28906-6864. 828/837-5115. **Toll-free phone:** 800/577-8685. **Fax:** 828/837-0846. **Contact:** Human Resources. **E-mail address:** staylor2@moog.com. **World Wide Web address:** http://www.polysci.com. **Description:** Moog Components Group designs and manufactures technology components. **NOTE:** Please visit website to view job listings. **Other U.S. locations:** Blacksburg VA; Springfield PA. **Operations at this facility include:** This location manufactures brush and brushless DC motors, drives and integrated motion systems.

MURATA MACHINERY USA
2120 I-85 South Charlotte NC 28208. 704/875-9280. **Toll-free phone:** 800/428-8469. **Contact:** Human Resources. **World Wide Web address:** http://www.muratec.net. **Description:** Develops, manufactures, and sells computer-controlled fabrication equipment, accessories, and systems, which provide flexibility and productivity for nonmass producers of parts made from flat materials (primarily sheet metal) in the world markets. Products include CNC Punch Press, Laser Contouring Equipment, Panel Bender, Plasma Arc, Right Angle Shears, and Twin Spindle Lathes. **NOTE:** Entry-level positions and part-time jobs are offered. **Special programs:** Internships; Co-ops; Summer Jobs. **Office hours:** Monday – Friday, 8:00 a.m. – 5:00 p.m. **Corporate headquarters location:** Kyoto, Japan. **International locations:** China; Germany; Singapore; Switzerland. **Operations at this facility include:** Administration; Manufacturing; Sales; Service. **Listed on:** Privately held. **Annual sales/revenues:** $21 - $50 million.

NATIONAL GYPSUM COMPANY
2001 Rexford Road, Charlotte NC 28211. 704/365-7300. **Fax:** 800/329-6421. **Contact:** Human Resources. **E-mail address:** ng@nationalgypsum.com. **World Wide Web address:** http://www.national-gypsum.com. **Description:** One of the largest manufacturers of gypsum wallboard in the United States, as well as a major producer of joint treatment products. National Gypsum Company operates eight mines and quarries, and its manufacturing operations include nine joint treatment, 18 gypsum wallboard, and three paper facilities. **NOTE:** Please visit website to search for jobs. **Corporate headquarters location:** This location. **Other U.S. locations:** Nationwide. **Listed on:** Privately held. **CEO:** Tom Nelson. **Number of employees at this location:** 260. **Number of employees nationwide:** 2,500.

NATIONAL INSTITUTE OF ENVIRONMENTAL HEALTH SCIENCES
111 Alexander Drive, P.O. Box 12233, Research Triangle Park NC 27709. 919/541-0218. **Recorded jobline:** 919/541-4331. **Contact:** Human Resources. **E-mail address:** hr@niehs.nih.gov. **World Wide Web address:** http://www.niehs.nih.gov. **Description:** A component of the Department of Health and Human Services, the National Institute of Environmental Health Services specializes in biomedical research programs, communication strategies, and prevention and intervention efforts. The focus of the Institute is to reduce human illness and dysfunction caused by the environment. **NOTE:** Please visit http://www.niehs.nih.gov/vacancy/niehsvac.htm or http://www.jobs.nih.gov to search for jobs. **Positions advertised include:** Health Science Administrator; Administrative Assistant; External Program Specialist; Secretary – Office Automation; Student Assistant; Program Specialist. **Special programs:** Fellowships in environmental medicine for medical students; Internships. **Corporate headquarters location:** This location. **Other U.S. locations:** Bethesda MD.

NATIONAL SPINNING COMPANY INC.
1632 Wards Bridge Road, Warsaw NC 28398. 910/293-7101. **Toll-free phone:** 800/868-7104. **Contact:** Human Resources. **World Wide Web address:** http://www.natspin.com. **Description:** Engaged in the manufacture, marketing, and distribution of yarn products for knitwear manufacturers. National Spinning Company also produces hand-knitting yarn and rug kits for distribution to retail chains throughout the United States. Founded 1921. **Corporate headquarters location:** New York NY. **Other area locations:** Beulaville NC; Glen Raven NC; Kinston NC; Washington NC; Whiteville NC. **Other U.S. locations:** LaFayette GA. **International locations:** Canada. **Operations at this facility include:** This location is a yarn plant. **President/CEO:** Jim Chesnutt.

NATIONWIDE ADVERTISING SERVICE INC.
2920 Highwoods Boulevard, Suite 110, Raleigh NC 27604-1053. 919/872-6800. **Fax:** 919/872-3926. **Contact:** Regional Manager. **E-mail address:** nas.ra@hrads.com. **World Wide Web address:** http://www.hrads.com. **Description:** With offices in 36 major U.S. and Canadian cities, Nationwide Advertising Service is one of the largest and oldest, independent, full-service advertising agencies exclusively specializing in human resource communications, promotions, and advertising. The company offers consultations, campaign planning, ad placement, research, and creative production. **NOTE:** Please visit website to search for jobs. **Corporate headquarters location:** Cleveland OH. **Other area locations:** Charlotte NC. **Other U.S. locations:** Nationwide. **International locations:** Toronto, Canada. **Parent company:** McCann-Erickson WorldGroup.

NETWORK CONTROLS INTERNATIONAL INC.
9 Woodlawn Green, Suite 120, Charlotte NC 28217-2202. 704/527-4357. **Fax:** 704/523-3502. **Contact:** Human Resources. **E-mail address:** hrdept@nci-inc.com. **World Wide Web address:** http://www.nci-inc.com. **Description:** Manufactures circuit boards to integrate computer systems in banks. **Positions advertised include:** Active Server Page Developer; Database Developer; C++ Developer; Quality Assurance Lead Programmer. **International locations:** London, England. **Parent company:** IFS International Holdings, Inc. **Listed on:** NASDAQ. **Stock exchange symbol:** IFSH.

THE NEWS & OBSERVER
P.O. Box 191, Raleigh NC 27602. 919/829-4500. **Physical address:** 215 South McDowell Street, Raleigh NC 27601. **Fax:** 919/829-8990. **Contact:** Personnel Director. **E-mail address:** hrresume@newsobserver.com. **World Wide Web address:** http://www.news-observer.com. **Description:** A daily newspaper with a Sunday circulation of 273,000 and a daily circulation of 152,000. **Corporate headquarters location:** This location.

NEWS & RECORD
P.O. Box 20848, Greensboro NC 27420-0848. 336/373-7000. **Toll-free phone:** 800/553-6880. **Fax:** 336/373-7183. **Contact:** Chevy Newton, recruiting Coordinator. **E-mail address:** employment@news-record.com. **World Wide Web address:** http://www.news-record.com. **Description:** A daily newspaper with weekday circulation of 90,000, Saturday circulation of 115,000, and Sunday circulation of 123,000. Founded in 1890. **NOTE:** Second and third shifts are offered. **Positions advertised include:** Inside Sales Representative; Interactive Account Executive; Sports Copy Editor – Part-time; Newspaper Rack Maintenance Representative – Part-time; Advertising Sales Account Executive. **Special programs:** Internships. **Corporate headquarters location:** Norfolk VA. **Parent company:** Landmark Communications, Inc. **Listed on:** Privately held. **Number of employees at this location:** 820.

NEXUS SOFTWARE, INC.
8024 Glenwood Road, Suite 305, Raleigh NC 27612. 919/788-8665. **Fax:** 919/788-8733. **Contact:** Human Resources. **World Wide Web address:** http://www.nexussoft.com. **Description:** Manufactures software for the financial industry. **Corporate headquarters location:** This location.

NORCOMP LIMITED PARTNERSHIP
P.O. Box 3867, Gastonia NC 28054-0020. 704/866-9161. **Fax:** 704/867-0577. **Contact:** Human Resources. **Description:** Engaged in the production and distribution of proprietary and custom-molded plastics for original equipment manufacturers. The company also produces and distributes interconnect devices. **Corporate headquarters location:** Minneapolis MN. **Operations at this facility include:** Administration; Manufacturing. **Listed on:** Privately held.

NORTEL NETWORKS
4001 East Chapel Hill, Nelson Highway, Research Triangle Park NC. 919/992-5000. **Contact:** Human Resources. **World Wide Web address:** http://www.nortelnetworks.com. **Description:** Designs, produces, and supports multimedia access devices for use in building corporate, public and Internet networks. The primary focus of the company's services is the consolidation of voice, fax, video, and data and multimedia traffic into a single network link. **NOTE:** Please visit website to search for jobs and apply online. Resumes are only accepted through the website. **Corporate headquarters location:** Ontario Canada. **Other area locations:** Charlotte NC; Raleigh NC. **Other U.S. locations:** Nationwide. **International locations:** Worldwide. **Listed on:** New York Stock Exchange. **Stock exchange symbol:** NT.

NORTH CAROLINA AGRICULTURAL & TECHNICAL STATE UNIVERSITY
1601 East Market Street, Greensboro NC 27411. 336/334-7500. **Fax:** 336/334-7477. **Recorded jobline:** 336/334-7292. **Contact:** Personnel. **World Wide Web address:** http://www.ncat.edu. **Description:** A state university offering graduate and undergraduate programs in agriculture, business, engineering, and other disciplines. **NOTE:** You must complete a North Carolina State Government Application for Employment. You can download one at http://www.osp.state.nc.us/jobs/gnrlinfo.htm#app. Please mail applications to 1020 East Wendover Avenue, Greensboro NC 27411. Human Resources phone is 336/334-7862. **Positions advertised include:** Residence Administrator; Processing Assistant; Police Officer; Administrative Secretary; Student Services Manager; Housekeeper; Research Technician; Director of Human Resources; Special Assistant to the Vice Chancellor for Research; Director of Research Services; Director of Development for Athletics; Professor – Various Departments; Tenure Tract Position – Various Departments; University Physician; Assistant/Associate Professor – Various Departments; Staff Psychiatrist;. **Office Hours:** Monday – Friday, 8:00 a.m. – 5:00 p.m. **Corporate headquarters location:** This location.

NORTH CAROLINA BIOTECHNOLOGY CENTER
15 T.W. Alexander Dive, Research Triangle Park NC 27709-3547. 919/541-9366. **Physical address:** 15 T.W. Alexander Drive, Research Triangle Park NC 27709. **Contact:** Personnel. **World Wide Web address:** http://www.ncbiotech.org. **Description:** A nonprofit agency dedicated to supporting biotechnology research, development, and commercialization in North Carolina. **Corporate headquarters location:** This location.

NORTH CAROLINA CENTRAL UNIVERSITY
1801 Fayetteville Street, Durham NC 27707. 919/530-6100. **Fax:** 919/530-7984. **Contact:** Director of Human Resources. **World Wide Web address:**

http://www.nccu.edu. **Description:** A university offering graduate and undergraduate programs in business, education, law, library science, and other disciplines. **NOTE:** Please visit website to view job listings and for more specific information on applying for specific jobs. **Positions advertised include:** Accounting Clerk; Accounting Technician; Administrative Secretary; Data Entry Specialist; Information Processing Technician; Mail Clerk; Office Assistant; Processing Assistant; Word Processor; Warehouse Manager; Internal Auditor; Administrative Officer; Attorney; Official Court Reporter; Reimbursement Officer.

NORTH CAROLINA DEPARTMENT OF AGRICULTURE & CONSUMER SERVICES
1001 Mail Service Center, Raleigh NC 27699-1001. 919/733-2243. **Physical address:** 2 West Edenton Street, Agriculture Building, Room 302, Raleigh NC 27601. **Fax:** 919/715-4295. **Contact:** Rosilyn McNair, Recruiting Specialist. **E-mail address:** rosilyn.mcnair@ncmail.net. **World Wide Web address:** http://www.agr.state.nc.us. **Description:** Oversees the agricultural industries of North Carolina. **Positions advertised include:** Internal Marketing Specialist; Veterinary Laboratory Director; Assistant to Farmers Market Manager; Administrative Secretary; Processing Assistant; Standards Inspector; Chemistry Technician; Processing Assistant; Chemistry Manager.

NORTH CAROLINA DEPARTMENT OF CORRECTION
4202 Mail Service Center, Raleigh NC 27699-4202. 919/716-3700. **Fax:** 919/716-3955. **World Wide Web address:** http://www.doc.state.nc.us. **Description:** Oversees the maintenance and hiring of North Carolina's prisons. **NOTE:** Please visit website for a listing of jobs statewide.

NORTH CAROLINA DEPARTMENT OF TRANSPORTATION
1517 Mail Service Center, Raleigh NC 27699-1500. 919/733-2520. **Physical address:** 1 South Wilmington Street, Raleigh NC 27611. **Toll-free phone:** 877/DOT-4YOU. **Fax:** 919/733-9150. **World Wide Web address:** http://www.ncdot.org. **Description:** Operates and maintains a transportation system that includes aviation, ferry, rail, highway, and public transportation systems. **NOTE:** Please visit website to view job listings. Contact Diane Strickland with any questions regarding employment, at 919/715-9836 Ext. 205.

NORTH CAROLINA MUTUAL LIFE INSURANCE COMPANY
411 West Chapel Hill Street, Mutual Plaza, Durham NC 27701. 919/682-9201. **Toll-free phone:** 800/626-1899. **Fax:** 919/682-1685. **Contact:** Human Resources. **E-mail address:** askhr@ncmututallife.com. **World Wide Web address:** http://www.ncmutuallife.com. **Description:** A life insurance company. The company is licensed to operate in 23 states and Washington D.C. Founded 1898. **NOTE:** Human Resources is at Ext. 318. **Corporate headquarters location:** This location. **Other area locations:** Charlotte NC; Greenville NC; Raleigh NC. **Other U.S. locations:** GA; IL; MI; PA; VA; MD. **Operations at this facility include:** Administration. **Number of employees at this location:** 145. **Number of employees nationwide:** 560. **President:** Bert Collins.

NORTH CAROLINA SCHOOL OF THE ARTS
P.O. Box 12189, Winston-Salem NC 27117-2189. 336/770-3399. **Physical address:** 1533 South Main Street, Administrative Building Room 105, Winston-Salem NC 27127-2188. **Fax:** 336/770-1462. **Contact:** Elizabeth Daum, Director of Human Resources. **E-mail address:** daumb@ncarts.edu. **World Wide Web address:** http://www.ncarts.edu. **Description:** A college offering specialized programs in the fine arts, including dance, drama, filmmaking, music, design and production, and visual arts. **NOTE:** Please visit website to view job listings. **Positions advertised include:** Program Assistant; Assistant Manager – Fitness Center; Faculty – Various Departments; Vice Chancellor of Development and Public Relations; Dean of School of Music. **Office hours:** Monday – Friday, 8:00 a.m. – 5:00 p.m.; *Summer office hours* – Monday – Thursday, 7:30 a.m. – 5:20 p.m.; Friday, 7:30 a.m. – 11:30 p.m. **Number of employees at this location:** 500.

NORTH CAROLINA STATE UNIVERSITY
2711 Sullivan Drive, Box 7210, Raleigh NC 27695-7210. 919/515-2011. **Fax:** 919/515-7543. **Contact:** Human Resources. **World Wide Web address:** http://www.ncsu.edu. **Description:** A state university offering graduate and undergraduate programs in agriculture, design, engineering, and other disciplines. **NOTE:** Please visit website to search for jobs and to download employment application. **Positions advertised include:** Associate Dean for Academic Affairs and Interdisciplinary Program; Associate General Counsel; Director – Centennial Campus Development; Executive Director of Development; Career Counselor; Costume Designer; Director – Software Systems; Grant Proposal Developer; Research Assistant; Assistant Professor – Various Departments; Lecturer – Various Departments; Housekeeper; Accountant; Groundskeeper; Laboratory Mechanic; Veterinary Technician. **Number of employees at this location:** 7,000.

NORTHERN HOSPITAL
P.O. Box 1101, Mount Airy NC 27030. 336/719-7000. **Physical address:** 830 Rockford Street, Suite 6, Mount Airy NC 27030. **Contact:** Human Resources. **World Wide Web address:** http://www.northernhospital.com. **Description:** A hospital that offers home health care services in addition to in-hospital services. **Positions advertised include:** Speech Therapist; Occupational Therapist; PRN; CRNA; RN – Home Care; RN – Various Departments; Coding Specialist; Security Officer; Spanish Interpreter; Project Manager; Patient Registration Representative; Mechanic – HVAC; Infection Control/Quality Review Practitioner. **Corporate headquarters location:** This location. **Other U.S. locations:** Cana VA. **Listed on:** Privately held. **Number of employees at this location:** 200.

NUCOR CORPORATION
2100 Rexford Road, Charlotte NC 28211. 704/366-7000. **Fax:** 704/362-4208. **Contact:** Personnel. **World Wide Web address:** http://www.nucor.com. **Description:** Manufactures steel and steel products including hot-rolled and cold-finished steel shapes, girders, joists, and beams. The company also recycles more than 14 million tons of scrap steel every year. **Corporate headquarters location:** This location. **Other U.S. locations:** Nationwide. **Subsidiaries include:** Nucor Steel produces angles, bars, light structural, sheet, and specialty steel products. **Listed on:** New York Stock Exchange. **Stock exchange symbol:** NUE.

OFFICE DEPOT
BUSINESS SERVICES DIVISION
5809 Long Creek Park Drive, Charlotte NC 28269. 704/597-8501. **Fax:** 704/598-2873. **Contact:** Human Resources. **E-mail address:** jobs@officedepot.com. **World Wide Web address:** http://www.officedepot.com. **Description:** Office Depot is a wholesale and retail dealer of office supplies. Both Wilson Office Products (a division of Office Depot) and Office Depot offer over 11,000 different business products from basic supplies such as copy and printer paper to high-tech business furniture. Product categories include furniture; desk accessories; office essentials; computers; business machines; visual communications; safety and maintenance supplies; personal organizers and dated goods; writing instruments; business cases and binders; filing and storage units; paper, envelopes and business forms; and labels and mailing supplies. **NOTE:** Please visit website to search for jobs and apply online. **Positions advertised include:** Business Development Manager; Consultant Service; Account Manager. **Corporate headquarters location:** Delray Beach FL. **Other U.S. locations:** Nationwide. **International locations:** Worldwide. **Operations at this facility include:** This location supplies office products to contract customers. **Listed on:** New York Stock Exchange. **Stock exchange symbol:** ODP. **CEO:** Bruce Nelson.

OMEGA PERFORMANCE INC.
8701 Red Oak Boulevard, Suite 450, Charlotte NC 28217-3972. 704/672-1417. **Fax:** 704/525-4852. **Contact:** Human Resources. **E-mail address:** jobs@omega-performance.com. **World Wide Web address:** http://www.omega-performance.com. **Description:** Trains personnel in financial services, telecommunications, transportation, and other industries using interactive, multimedia teaching methods along with traditional classroom instruction. **Positions advertised include:** Financial Services Training – Product Development/Instructional Designer; Executive Consultant; Regional Sales Manager; Account Manager; Relationship Manager. **Corporate headquarters location:** This location. **International locations:** Sydney, Australia; Toronto, Canada; London, England; Wellington, New Zealand; Singapore. **President/CEO:** Juan Gutierrez.

ONSLOW MEMORIAL HOSPITAL
317 Western Boulevard, Jacksonville NC 28541. 910/577-2345. **Recorded jobline:** 910/577-2250. **Contact:** Human Resources. **E-mail address:** employment@onslowmemorial.org. **World Wide Web address:** http://www.onslowmemorial.org. **Description:** A hospital equipped with 162 beds, treating more than 37,000 patients every year. **NOTE:** Jobseekers are encouraged to search and apply for jobs online. **Positions advertised include:** Occupational Therapist; Transcriptionist Coordinator; Radiologic Technician; RN – Various Departments; PC Technician; Sterile Processing and Distribution Technician; Speech/Language Pathologist; MRI Technician; Lab Assistant. **Special programs:** Internships. **Office hours:** Monday – Friday, 8:00 a.m. – 4:30 p.m. **Number of employees at this location:** 1000.

OPSWARE, INC.
11000 Regency Parkway, Suite 301, Cary NC 27511. 919/653-6000. **Contact:** Human Resources. **E-mail address:** jobs@opsware.com. **World Wide Web address:** http://www.opsware.com. **Description:** Manufactures information center automation software. **NOTE:** Please visit website to view job listings. **Special programs:** Internships. **Corporate headquarters location:** Sunnyvale CA. **Other U.S. locations:** Novi MI; New York NY; Bethesda MD. **International locations:** United Kingdom. **Listed on:** NASDAQ. **Stock exchange symbol:** OPSW. **CEO:** Ben Horowitz.

OPUS ONE GRAPHIC DESIGN
715 West Johnson Street, Suite 200, Raleigh NC 27603. 919/834-9441. **Fax:** 919/834-2275. **Contact:** Human Resources. **World Wide Web address:** http://www.opus1inc.com. **Description:** Offers graphic design services that assist clients in advertising their products.

ORACLE
2550 West Tyvola, Suite 200, Charlotte NC 28217. 704/357-3155. **Fax:** 704/423-1307. **World Wide Web address:** http://www.oracle.com. **Description:** Provides technology for managing database systems. **NOTE:** Please search for jobs and submit your resume at the company website. **Positions advertised include:** Technology Sales Representative. **Corporate headquarters location:** Redwood Shores CA. **Other area locations:** Morrisville NC. **Other U.S. locations:** Nationwide. **International locations:** Worldwide. **Number of employees worldwide:** 40,000.

ORACLE PACKAGING
2221 JR Kennedy Drive, Wilmington NC 28405. 910/763-2921. **Fax:** 910/343-9875. **Contact:** James Hummer, Plant Manager. **E-mail address:** jameshummer@oraclepkg.com. **World Wide Web address:** http://www.oraclepackaging.com. **Description:** The United States' largest supplier of private label butter packaging. The company also produces doughnut and cream cheese packaging, as well as other bakery cartoning. **Other U.S. locations:** Toledo OH; Thomaston GA. **Number of employees nationwide:** 425

ORO MANUFACTURING COMPANY
P.O. Box 5018, Monroe NC 28111-5018. 704/283-2186. **Physical address:** 5000 Stitt Street, Monroe NC 28110. **Fax:** 704/283-0269. **Contact:** Human Resources. **World Wide Web address:** http://www.oromfg.com. **Description:** Light metal fabricators operating complete facilities for fabrication and finishing operations. **Corporate headquarters location:** This location.

PCA INTERNATIONAL, INC.
P.O. Box 1393, Matthews NC 28106. 704/847-8011. **Physical address:** 815 Matthews-Mint Hill Road, Matthews NC 28105. **Toll-free phone:** 800/438-8868. **Contact:** Personnel. **E-mail address:** careers@pcaintl.com. **World Wide Web address:** http://www.pcaintl.com. **Description:** Provides family portrait photography through retailers. The exclusive operator of children's portrait photography services in over 1,400 Wal-Mart stores. Adult and family portraits are marketed through the Institutional Division, which works primarily through church promotions. **NOTE:** Please visit website to submit resume online. For employment information, dial 800/438-8868 Ext. 2410. **Corporate headquarters location:** This location. **Other U.S. locations:** Nationwide. **International locations:** Canada; Mexico; Puerto Rico; Virgin Islands. **President/CEO:** Barry J. Feld. **Annual sales/revenues:** More than $100 million. **Number of employees nationwide:** 3,300.

MARGARET R. PARDEE MEMORIAL HOSPITAL
800 North Justice Street, Hendersonville NC 28791. 828/696-1000. **Fax:** 828/696-1208. **Recorded jobline:** 828/696-4700. **Contact:** Hope Reynolds, Human Resources Director. **E-mail address:** human.resources@pardeehospital.org. **World Wide Web address:** http://www.pardeehospital.org. **Description:** A 262-bed, acute care hospital. **NOTE:** Contact Human Resources directly at 828/696-4209. Please visit website to view job listings, apply online, or download application. **Positions advertised include:** Director of Rehab Services; ER Registration Clerk; Switchboard Relief; File Room Receptionist; RN – Various Departments; CNA – Various Departments; Phlebotomist; Clinical Dietician; Certified Surgical Technician; Pharmacist; Radiation Therapist; Registered Respiratory Therapist; Trayline Supervisor; Nutrition Assistant; Supply Technician.

PARAMOUNT PAPER
953 Alma Road, Maxton NC 28364. 910/844-5293. **Contact:** Human Resources. **World Wide Web address:** http://www.paramountpaper.com. **Description:** Manufactures celluloid packaging materials for furniture companies. Founded 1958.

Office hours: Monday – Friday, 8:00 a.m. – 5:00 p.m. **Corporate headquarters location:** Quebec Canada.

PARKER POE ADAMS & BERNSTEIN
3 Wachovia Center, 401 South Tryon Street, Suite 3000, Charlotte NC 28202. 704/372-9000. **Fax:** 704/334-4706. **Contact:** Joann L. Enos, Director of Human Resources Manager. **E-mail address:** joannenos@parkerpoe.com. **World Wide Web address:** http://www.parkerpoe.com. **Description:** A law firm with 140 attorneys that primarily serves corporate clients. **NOTE:** For attorney positions or law student hiring, contact John W. Francisco (johnfrancisco@parkerpoe.com). Caryn A. Johnson (carynjohnson@parkerpoe.com) also handles law student hiring. **Corporate headquarters location:** This location. **Other area locations:** Raleigh NC. **Other U.S. locations:** Columbia SC; Spartanburg SC; Charleston SC.

PARSONS
4701 Hedgemore Drive, Charlotte NC 28209. 704/529-6246. **Fax:** 704/529-0374. **Contact:** Human Resources. **E-mail address:** employment.parsons@parsons.com. **World Wide Web address:** http://www.parsons.com. **Description:** Founded in 1944, Parsons is one of the largest 100% employee-owned engineering and construction companies in the United States. **Positions advertised include:** Project Manager, Senior Designer/Drafter, Engineering Manager, Engineer 6/ Modeler, Executive Administrative Assistant, Environmental Manager, Senior Transportation Planner, Traffic Engineer, Civil Design Engineer, Highway Engineer. **Chairman and CEO:** James F. McNulty. **Number of employees worldwide:** 9,000.

PERDUE FARMS, INC.
P.O. Box 1357, Rockingham NC 28345. 910/997-8600. **Contact:** Human Resources. **World Wide Web address:** http://www.perdue.com. **Description:** Perdue Farms is one of the largest suppliers of fresh poultry products in the United States. The company's products are sold in supermarkets, small groceries, and butcher shops from Maine to Georgia and as far west as Chicago. The company is a fully integrated operation, from breeding and hatching to delivering packaged goods to market. **NOTE:** Please visit website to search for jobs and apply online. **Corporate headquarters location:** Salisbury MD. **Other U.S. locations:** Nationwide. **Listed on:** Privately held. **Number of employees nationwide:** 20,000.

PERDUE FARMS, INC.
P.O. Box 460, Lewiston NC 27849. 252/348-4200. **Contact:** Human Resources. **World Wide Web address:** http://www.perdue.com. **Description:** Perdue Farms is one of the largest suppliers of fresh poultry products in the United States. The company's products are sold in supermarkets, small groceries, and butcher shops from Maine to Georgia and as far west as Chicago. The company is a fully integrated operation, from breeding and hatching to delivering packaged goods to market. **NOTE:** Please visit website to search for jobs and apply online. **Corporate headquarters location:** Salisbury MD. **Other U.S. locations:** Nationwide. **Listed on:** Privately held. **Number of employees nationwide:** 20,000.

PERFORMANCE FIBERS
338 Pea Ridge Road Moncure NC 27562. **Contact:** Manager of Personnel. **World Wide Web address:** http://www.performancefibers.com. **Description:** One of the world's leading suppliers of high-tenacity polyester and a global manufacturer of other man-made industrial fibers. Its products are used in a wide range of consumer and industrial applications. It was formed in December 2004,

PERRY, PERRY & PERRY
P.O. Drawer 1475, Kinston NC 28503. 252/523-5107. **Physical address:** 518 Plaza Boulevard, Kinston NC 28503. **Contact:** Office Manager. **Description:** A law firm with five attorneys who specialize in criminal, social security and disability, and real estate law. **Number of employees at this location:** 500.

PIEDMONT BEHAVIORAL HEALTH CARE
245 LePhillip Court NE, Concord NC 28025. 704/721-7000. **Fax:** 704/721-7010. **Contact:** Personnel. **World Wide Web address:** http://www.piedmontbhc.org. **Description:** Provides a variety of programs and educational services for individuals with mental health needs, substance abuse issues, and developmental disabilities. **NOTE:** Please visit website to view job listings and to download application form. **Positions advertised include:** Care Coordinator; Case Manager; Child and Youth Provider Relations Manager; Community Relations Specialist – Bilingual; DD Case Management Services Administrator; Health Care Technician. **Office hours:** Monday – Friday, 8:30 a.m. – 5:00 p.m. **Corporate headquarters location:** This location. **Other area locations:** Salisbury NC; Albemarle NC; Monroe NC. **CEO:** Dan Coughlin.

PIEDMONT BEHAVIORAL HEALTH CARE
CONSUMER PLANNING AND SUPPORT SERVICES
201 North Main Street, Monroe NC 28112. 704/289-7111. **Fax:** 704/282-4902. **Contact:** Personnel. **World Wide Web address:** http://www.piedmontbhc.org. **Description:** Provides a variety of programs and educational services for individuals with mental health needs, substance abuse issues, and developmental disabilities. **NOTE:** Please visit website to view job listings and to download application form. Mail application or resume to corporate office at 245 LePhillip Court NC, Concord NC 288025. **Positions advertised include:** Care Coordinator; Case Manager; Child and Youth Provider Relations Manager; Community Relations Specialist – Bilingual; DD Case Management Services Administrator; Health Care Technician. **Office hours:** Monday – Friday, 8:30 a.m. – 5:00 p.m. **Corporate headquarters location:** Concord NC. **Other area locations:** Salisbury NC; Albemarle NC. **CEO:** Dan Coughlin.

PIEDMONT NATURAL GAS CO., INC.
1915 Rexford Road, P.O. Box 33068, Charlotte NC 28233. 704/364-3120. **Contact:** Personnel. **E-mail address:** corporate.recruiter@piedmontng.com. **World Wide Web address:** http://www.piedmontng.com. **Description:** Sells and transports natural gas to over 625,000 commercial, industrial, and residential customers in North Carolina, South Carolina, and Tennessee. The company and its subsidiaries also sell propane. Founded in 1951. **Positions advertised include:** Rate Analyst; Senior Auditor; Customer Service Representative; Major Account Services Representative; Drafter; Environmental Engineer; Senior Service Specialist. **Special programs:** College Co-op. **Corporate headquarters location:** This location. **Other U.S. locations:** SC; TN. **Listed on:** New York Stock Exchange. **Stock exchange symbol:** PNY. **Annual sales/revenues:** More than $100 million. **President/CEO:** Thomas E. Skains. **Number of employees at this location:** 400. **Number of employees nationwide:** 2,100.

PITT COUNTY MEMORIAL HOSPITAL
UNIVERSITY HEALTH SYSTEMS OF EASTERN CAROLINA
2100 Statonsburg Road, P.O. Box 6028, Greenville NC 27835-6028. 252/816-4556. **Toll-free phone:** 800/346-4307. **Fax:** 252/847-8225. **Contact:** Manager of Employment. **World Wide Web address:** http://www.uhseast.com. **Description:** A 725-bed, Level I, regional medical center and constituent of the University Health Systems of Eastern Carolina. This location also serves as the teaching facility for the East Carolina University School of Medicine, Nursing, and Allied Health. **NOTE:** Human Resources phone is 252/847-4130. Please visit website to view job listings and apply online. **Positions advertised include:** RN – Various Departments; Accounting Clerk; Administrative Secretary; Assistant Patient Counselor; Community Resource Center Supervisor; Coordinator – Medical Staff; Credentialing Specialist; File Clerk; Medical Transcriptionist; Patient Access Representative; Vehicle Technician; Groundskeeper; Administrator – Cost Report; Manager – HIMS; Patient Care Coordinator; Central Service Technician; Electrician; Advanced Level Practitioner; Annual Fund Coordinator; Assistant Nursing Manager; Call Center Nurse Consultant; Clinical Analyst; Child Life Specialist; Contract Behavioral Health Triage; Exercise Physiologist; Home Health Nurse; Neonatal Nurse Practitioner; Pharmacist; Physical Therapist; Area Technician; Operating Room Assistant; Cytotechnologist; LPN; Paramedic. **Number of employees at this location:** 4,000.

PREMIER, INC.
2320 Cascade Pointe Boulevard, Charlotte NC 28208. 704/357-0022. **Contact:** Human Resources. **World Wide Web address:** http://www.premierinc.com. **Description:** Operates hospitals and provides healthcare. **Positions advertised include:** Clinical Analyst; Manager – Environmentally Preferred Purchasing; Senior Director – Alternate Site HealthCare; Vice President – Clinical Programs; Contract Recruiter; Application Quality Engineer; Clinical Advisor; Director – Analytics & Research; ETL Development and Applications Engineer; Perspective Analyst; Product Manager; Senior Unix Systems Administrator. **Other U.S. locations:** San Diego CA; Chicago IL; Washington D.C.

PRICEWATERHOUSECOOPERS
214 North Tryon Street, Suite 3600, Charlotte NC 28202. 704/344-7500. **Fax:** 704/344-4100. **Contact:** Personnel. **World Wide Web address:** http://www.pricewaterhousecoopers.com. **Description:** One of the largest certified public accounting firms in the world. PricewaterhouseCoopers provides public accounting, business advisory, management consulting, and taxation services. **NOTE:** Please visit website to search for jobs and apply online. **Positions advertised include:** HCP Manager; ITS Senior Associate; ISG Manager; SALT Senior Associate; Income Franchise Manager; Assurance Senior Associate; Financial Services IAS Senior Associate; Executive Assistant – Tax Services; Manager – FORCe; SPA Senior Associate; Credit Risk Management Senior Associate. **Corporate headquarters location:** New York NY. **Other U.S. locations:** Nationwide. **International locations:** Worldwide. **Number of employees worldwide:** 120,000.

PROGRESS ENERGY
P.O. Box 1551, Raleigh NC 27602-1551. 919/508-5400. **Fax:** 919/546-7784. **Contact:** Corporate Employment. **World Wide Web address:** http://www.progress-energy.com. **Description:** Provides electricity to approximately 1.2 million customers in North and South Carolina. Progress Energy owns and operates a network of 18 power plants throughout the region. The company also provides natural gas service to approximately 166,000 customers in North Carolina through its wholly-owned subsidiary, North Carolina Natural Gas. **NOTE:** Please visit website to search for jobs and apply online. **Positions advertised include:** Associate Communications Specialist; Associate Financial Specialist; Business Financial Analyst; Credit Analyst; Financial Specialist; Financial Auditor; Human Resources Representative; IT Analyst; Lead Business Financial Analyst; Operations and Strategic Planning Analyst; Senior Engineer; Supervisor – Disbursement Services. **Special programs:** Internships. **Corporate headquarters location:** This location. **Other U.S. locations:** FL; GA; SC. **Listed on:** New York Stock Exchange. **Stock exchange symbol:** PGN. **President/CEO:** Robert B. McGehee. **Number of employees nationwide:** 15,300.

PROGRESSIVE COMPUTER SYSTEMS, INC.
615 Eastowne Drive, Chapel Hill NC 27514. 919/929-3080. **Fax:** 919/929-3087. **Contact:** Lisa Mitchell, Human Resources Manager. **E-mail address:** hr@pc-net.com. **World Wide Web address:** http://www.pc-net.com. **Description:** A computer firm providing hardware assembly, sales, and service. **NOTE:** Contact Human Resources at 919/929-3087. **Corporate headquarters location:** This location.

PRUDENTIAL CAROLINAS REALTY
380 Knollwood Street, Suite 420, Winston-Salem NC 27103. 336/725-1970. **Contact:** Sales Manager. **World Wide Web address:** http://www.prudential-carolinas.com. **Description:** A real estate company specializing in residential properties. **Corporate headquarters location:** This location. **Other area locations:** Statewide. **Other U.S. locations:** Rock Hill SC. **President/CEO:** Robert E. Helms.

PUBLIC SERVICE COMPANY OF NORTH CAROLINA, INC.
P.O. Box 1398, Gastonia NC 28053-1398. 704/864-6731. **Contact:** Human Resources. **World Wide Web address:** http://www.psnc.com. **Description:** Delivers natural gas products and services to residential, commercial, industrial, transportation, and electric power generation customers, and also to other local distribution companies. Public Service Company of North Carolina's products and services include natural gas distribution; interstate and intrastate pipeline services; supply and capacity brokering; natural gas vehicle fueling; and natural gas appliance sales, installation, and service. The company serves natural gas customers in over 95 cities. **NOTE:** Please visit website to apply online. **Corporate headquarters location:** This location. **Parent company:** SCANA.

QORE PROPERTY SCIENCES
2521 Schieffelin Road, Suite 128, Apex NC 27502. 919/363-9899. **Fax:** 919/363-7916. **Contact:** David Cunningham, P.E. **E-mail address:** Raleigh@qore.net. **World Wide Web address:** http://www.qore.net. **Description:** Specializes in geotechnical engineering, environmental consulting, environmental studies and permitting. **Positions advertised include:** Engineering Field Technicians. **Corporate headquarters location:** Duluth GA.

QUALEX, INC.
3414 North Duke Street, Durham NC 27704. 919/383-8535. **Fax:** 877/268-1289. **Contact:** Human Resources. **Description:** Manufactures, markets, and services photo finishing equipment. Qualex also establishes one-hour photo labs. **Office hours:** Monday – Friday, 8:30 a.m. – 5:00 p.m. **Corporate headquarters location:** This location. **Other U.S. locations:** Tuscany CA. **Parent company:** Eastman Kodak. **Number of employees at this location:** 275. **Number of employees nationwide:** 7,500.

QUINTILES INC.
P.O. Box 13979, Research Triangle Park NC 27709-3979. 919/998-2000. **Physical address:** 4709 Creekstone Drive Durham NC 27703. **Fax:** 919/998-7579. **Contact:** Human Resources. **E-mail address:** hr.info@quintiles.com. **World Wide Web address:** http://www.quintiles.com. **Description:** A contract pharmaceutical research company. Provides professional services for pharmaceutical and biotechnology companies, as well as healthcare providers. Founded 1982. **NOTE:** Please visit website to search for jobs and apply online. **Positions advertised include:** Administrative

Assistant; Alliance Management Director; Analyst; Associate Clinical Scientist; Associate Director – Various Departments; Employee Premium Services; Global Account Executive; IT Security Architect; Pricing Analyst; Project Manager; Project Specialist; Scientific Specialist; Senior Administrative Assistant; Senior Contracts Manager; Vice President – Market Development. **Corporate headquarters location:** This location. **Other area locations:** Morrisville NC. **Other U.S. locations:** Nationwide. **International locations:** Worldwide. **Parent company:** Pharma Services Acquisition Corp.

RBC CENTURA
133 North Church Street, P.O. Box 1220, Rocky Mount NC 27804. 252/454-4400. **Fax:** 252/454-4806. **Toll-free phone:** 800/CENTURA. **Contact:** Human Resources. **World Wide Web address:** http://www.rbccentura.com. **Description:** A bank holding company that provides a full range of banking, investment, and insurance services for individuals and businesses. **NOTE:** Please visit website to search for jobs and apply online. **Positions advertised include:** Mortgage Cashiering Associate; Centura Support Specialist. **Corporate headquarters location:** This location. **Parent company:** RBC Financial Group. **Listed on:** New York Stock Exchange. **Stock exchange symbol:** RY. **CEO:** H. Kel Landis. **Number of employees nationwide:** 1,870.

RF MICRO DEVICES INC.
7628 Thorndike Road, Greensboro NC 27409-9421. 336/664-1233. **Fax:** 336/931-7454. **Contact:** Human Resources. **World Wide Web address:** http://www.rfmd.com. **Description:** Manufactures semiconductors. **NOTE:** Please visit website to view job listings and submit resume online. **Positions advertised include:** Database Administrator; E-systems Developer; MBE Equipment Technician; Reliability Engineer; SAP Basis Administrator; Staff Systems Engineer. **Corporate headquarters location:** This location. **Other area locations:** Charlotte NC. **Other U.S. locations:** Phoenix AZ; Irvine CA; Scotts Valley CA; San Jose CA; Cedar Rapids IA; Boston MA. **International locations:** Worldwide. **Listed on:** NASDAQ. **Stock exchange symbol:** RFMD. **President/CEO:** Robert A. Bruggeworth. **Annual sales/revenues:** More than $100 million. **Number of employees worldwide:** 1,800.

R.J. REYNOLDS TOBACCO HOLDINGS, INC.
401 North Main Street, Winston-Salem NC 27102. 336/741-5500. **Fax:** 336/741-4238. **Contact:** Human Resources. **World Wide Web address:** http://www.rjrt.com. **Description:** A holding company. **Office hours:** Monday – Friday, 8:00 a.m. – 4:30 p.m. **Corporate headquarters location:** This location. **Subsidiaries include:** R.J. Reynolds Tobacco Company manufactures tobacco products, including the Camel, Winston, Salem, and Doral brands. Santa Fe Natural Tobacco Company, Inc. produces American Spirit brand cigarettes. **Listed on:** New York Stock Exchange. **Stock exchange symbol:** RJR. **President/CEO:** Andrew J. Schindler.

RALEIGH, CITY OF
222 West Hargett Street, Room 101, P.O. Box 590, Raleigh NC 27602. 919/890-3315. **Fax:** 919/890-3845. **Recorded jobline:** 919/890-3305. **Contact:** Personnel Recruitment. **World Wide Web address:** http://www.raleigh-nc.org. **Description:** Provides municipal services including law enforcement, fire services, building code enforcement, water/sewer services, transportation, planning, engineering, and administration services for the city of Raleigh. **NOTE:** Entry-level positions, part-time jobs, and second and third shifts are offered. Please visit website to search for jobs and to download an application form. Please be sure to include the job number you're your application. Volunteer positions are also available. **Positions advertised include:** Police Officer; Assistant Planning Director; Systems Analyst; Administrative Assistant; Accounts Receivable Specialist; Staff Support Specialist; Code Enforcement Inspector; Site Review Specialist; Computer Operator; Traffic Signs and Marketing Technician; Senior Survey Technician; Fire Equipment Mechanic; Treatment Plant Operator; Equipment Operator; Laborer; Utility Service Field Technician; Parks and Recreation Temporary Workers. **Special programs:** Training; Summer Jobs. **Office hours:** Monday – Friday, 8:00 a.m. – 5:15 p.m. **Operations at this facility include:** Administration. **Number of employees at this location:** 2,600.

RANDOLPH HOSPITAL
P.O. Box 1048, Asheboro NC 27204-1048. 336/625-5151. **Physical address:** 364 White Oaks Street, Asheboro NC 27203. **Fax:** 336/633-7749. **Recorded jobline:** 336/629-8842. **Contact:** Employee Relations and Staffing. **E-mail address:** dvernon@randolphhospital.org. **World Wide Web address:** http://www.randolphhospital.org. **Description:** A 145-bed general hospital. **NOTE:** Please visit website to view job listings and to download an application form. **Positions advertised include:** Registered Respiratory Therapist; Senior Director – Clinical Services; Diabetic Educator; Clinical Educator; ED Patient Representative; ED Technician; Dining Commons Manager; Food Server; Home Health Aide; Occupational Therapist; Physical Therapist; Rehab Coordinator; Unit Secretary; OB Technician; RN – Various Departments. **Number of employees at this location:** 560.

RAUCH INDUSTRIES
P.O. Box 609, Gastonia NC 28053-0609. 704/867-5333. **Physical address:** 2408 Forbes Road Gastonia NC 28056. **Toll-free phone:** 800/313-1830. **Fax:** 704/810-8978. **Contact:** Personnel Manager. **E-mail address:** kdewitt@rauchindustries.com. **World Wide Web address:** http://www.rauchindustries.com. **Description:** Manufactures and imports Christmas and holiday decorations. **Corporate headquarters location:** This location.

RED HAT SOFTWARE, INC.
1801 Varsity Drive, Raleigh NC 27606. 919/754-3700. **Fax:** 919/754-3701. **Contact:** Personnel. **E-mail address:** careers@redhat.com. **World Wide Web address:** http://www.redhat.com. **Description:** Develops software for Linux systems and offers technical support. **Positions advertised include:** Lead Generation Representative; Programmer/Analyst; Database Administrator; Web Engineer; Technical Writer; Senior Corporate Communications Specialist; Legal Administrative Assistant; Product Marketing Manager; Global Account Director; Telephony Engineer; Financial Analyst; Order Entry Administrator. **Other U.S. locations:** Huntsville AL; Mountain View CA; Westford MA; Minneapolis MN; Vienna VA. **International locations:** Worldwide. **Operations at this facility include:** Regional headquarters. **Listed on:** NASDAQ. **Stock exchange symbol:** RHAT. **CEO:** Matthew Szulik. **Number of employees worldwide:** 600.

REGAL MANUFACTURING COMPANY
990 3rd Avenue SE, P.O. Box 2363, Hickory NC 28603-2363. 828/328-5381. **Fax:** 828/328-4936. **Contact:** Personnel Manager. **E-mail address:** info@regalmfgcoinc.com. **World Wide Web address:** http://www.regalmfgcoinc.com. **Description:** Develops, manufactures, and markets elastic yarn for the garment industry. Founded 1956. **Corporate headquarters location:** This location. **Subsidiaries include:** Filix-Lastex S.A.; Rubyco Inc.; Fibrexa Ltda.; Elastic Corporation of America; Elastex Inc. **Parent company:** Worldtex, Inc. **Operations at this facility include:** Administration; Manufacturing; Research and Development; Sales; Service.

REICHHOLD CHEMICALS, INC.
P.O. Box 13582, Research Triangle Park NC 27709. 919/990-7500. **Physical address:** 2400 Elis Road, Durham NC 27703. **Toll-free phone:** 800/448-3482. **Fax:** 919/990-7711. **Contact:** Human Resources. **E-mail address:** human.resources@reichhold.com. **World Wide Web address:** http://www.reichhold.com. **Description:** Researches and develops coating resins, formulated adhesives, and several other products. **Corporate headquarters location:** This location. **Other U.S. locations:** Nationwide. **International locations:** Worldwide. **Parent company:** Dainippon Ink & Chemicals (Tokyo). **Number of employees worldwide:** 2,500.

RENTAL SERVICE CORPORATION
3022 Griffith Street, Charlotte NC 28203. 704/522-8338. **Fax:** 704/522-6449. **Contact:** Ronnie Rockett, General Manager. **E-mail address:** s472mgr@rentalservice.com. **World Wide Web address:** http://www.rentalservice.com. **Description:** Engaged in equipment rental and sale to the industrial and construction markets. **Office hours:** Monday – Friday, 7:00 a.m. – 5:00 p.m. **NOTE:** Please visit website to search for jobs. **Corporate headquarters location:** Scottsdale AZ. **Other area locations:** Statewide. **Other U.S. locations:** Nationwide. **International locations:** Canada; Mexico. **Parent company:** Atlas Copco Group. **Operations at this facility include:** Sales; Service. **Listed on:** Privately held. **CEO:** Freek Nijdam. **Number of employees nationwide:** 6,000.

RESEARCH TRIANGLE INSTITUTE (RTI)
3040 Cornwallis Road, P.O. Box 12194, Research Triangle Park NC 27709-2194. 919/541-6000. **Fax:** 919/316-3791. **Contact:** Supervisor of Employment Services. **E-mail address:** jobs@rti.org. **World Wide Web address:** http://www.rti.org. **Description:** A nonprofit, independent research organization involved in many scientific fields, under contract to business; industry; federal, state, and local governments; industrial associations; and public service agencies. The institute was created as an independent entity by the joint action of North Carolina State University, Duke University, and the University of North Carolina at Chapel Hill; however, close ties are maintained with the universities' scientists, both through the active research community of the Research Triangle Park region and through collaborative research for government and industry clients. RTI responds to national priorities in health, the environment, advanced technology, and social policy with contract research for the U.S. government including applications in statistics, social sciences, chemistry, life sciences, environmental sciences, engineering, and electronics. Founded in 1958. **NOTE:** Entry-level positions are offered. Please visit website to search for jobs and apply online. **Positions advertised include:** Accountant; Accounting Manager; Acquisitions Specialist; Administrative Assistant; Analyst; Biological Lab Assistant; Biologist; Business Development Director; Call Center Services Supervisor; Chemist; Contract Billing Specialist; Economist; Engineer; Environmental Engineer; Maintenance Supervisor; Postdoctoral Chemist; Senior Research Scientist Toxicologist. **Corporate headquarters location:** This location. **Other area locations:** Durham NC; Raleigh NC; Greenville NC. **Other U.S. locations:** Washington DC; Cocoa Beach FL; Hampton VA; Rockville MD; Atlanta GA; Chicago IL; Waltham MA; Anniston AL. **International locations:** United Arab Emirates; Indonesia; England; South Africa; El Salvador. **Subsidiaries include:** RTI Polska LLC. **Listed on:** Privately held. **Annual sales/revenues:** More than $100 million. **Number of employees at this location:** 1,400.

RESIDENTIAL SERVICES
111 Providence Road, Chapel Hill NC 27514. 919/942-7391. **Fax:** 919/933-4490. **E-mail address:** mail@rsi-nc.org. **World Wide Web address:** http://www.rsi-nc.org. **Description:** A private, non-profit organization that provides living options, counseling and personal care to children and adults with developmental disabilities. **Positions advertised include:** Direct Support Professional; Supervisor of Support Services; Direct Support Coordinator.

ROCKY MOUNT CORD COMPANY
P.O. Drawer 4304, Rocky Mount NC 27803-0304. 252/977-9130. **Fax:** 252/977-9123. **Contact:** Human Resources Director. **World Wide Web address:** http://www.rmcord.com. **Description:** Manufactures braided cord and twisted rope. **Corporate headquarters location:** This location.

ROYAL & SUNALLIANCE USA
9300 Arrow Point Boulevard, Charlotte NC 28273-8135. 704/522-2000. **Contact:** Human Resources. **World Wide Web address:** http://www.royalsunalliance-usa.com. **Description:** Provides commercial property and casualty insurance as well as personal and specialty insurance. **Corporate headquarters location:** This location. **Other area locations:** Goldsboro NC. **Other U.S. locations:** Nationwide. **Parent company:** Royal & SunAlliance Insurance Group plc (London, England). **President/CEO:** John Tighe. **Number of employees nationwide:** 3,500.

ROYAL HOME FASHIONS INC.
P.O. Box 930, Durham NC 27702. 919/683-8011. **Physical address:** 2102 Fay Street, Durham NC 27704. **Fax:** 252/431-0470. **Contact:** Human Resources. **E-mail address:** jobapps@croscill.com. **World Wide Web address:** http://www.croscill.com. **Description:** Manufactures home furnishings such as window treatments, comforters, sheets, and pillows. **NOTE:** Please visit website to view job listings and apply online. Hiring for Royal Home Fashions and Croscill Home Fashions is done through the same online application, e-mail, and fax contacts. **Corporate headquarters location:** This location. **Other area locations:** Henderson NC. **Parent company:** Croscill Home Fashions. **Operations at this facility include:** Administration; Manufacturing. **Listed on:** Privately held. **Number of employees nationwide:** 1,500.

RR DONNELLEY
LITHO INDUSTRIES, A MOORE WALLACE COMPANY
P.O. Box 14106, Durham NC 27709. **Physical Address:** One Litho Way, Page Pointe Centre, Research Triangle Park, Durham NC 27703. 919/596-7000. **Contact:** JoEllen Crowfoot, Human Resources Manager. **World Wide Web address:** http://www.rrdonnelley.com. **Description:** A full-service commercial printer specializing in business forms. **Corporate headquarters location:** Chicago IL. **Other area locations:** Wilson NC. **Other U.S. locations:** Nationwide. **International locations:** Worldwide. **Operations at this facility include:** Commercial Printing. **Listed on:** New York Stock Exchange. **Stock exchange symbol:** RRD. **Number of employees worldwide:** 50,000.

RUDDICK CORPORATION
301 South Tryon Street, Suite 1800, Charlotte NC 28202. 704/372-5404. **Fax:** 704/372-6409. **Contact:** Human Resources. **World Wide Web address:** http://www.ruddickcorp.com. **Description:** A holding company. The company oversees Harris Teeter, Inc., which operates a supermarket chain; and American & Efird, Inc., a manufacturer of both industrial and consumer sewing thread. **Listed on:** New York Stock Exchange. **Stock exchange symbol:** RDK. **President/CEO:** Thomas W. Dickson.

RUTHERFORD COUNTY SCHOOLS
382 West Main Street, Forest City NC 28043-3027. 828/245-0252. **Recorded jobline:** 828/245-0252 x603. **Fax:** 828/245-4151. **Contact:** Personnel Director. **E-mail address:** rcs_eo@rutherford.k12.nc.us. **World Wide Web address:** http://www.rutherford.k12.nc.us. **Description:** Operates the Rutherford County public school system. **NOTE:** Please visit website to view job listings and access application form. **Positions advertised include:** Literacy Lead Teacher; Interim Media Coordinator; Interim Social Studies Teacher; Assistant Superintendent for Curriculum and Instruction; Business Manager; Elementary Principal; Assistant Principal.

SPX CORPORATION
13515 Ballantyne Corporate Place, Charlotte NC 28277. 704/752-4400. **Fax:** 704/752-7511. **Contact:** Human Resources. **World Wide Web address:** http://www.spx.com. **Description:** The company operates in three segments: industrial products, building products, and engineering. The industrial products segment produces sanitary pumps for the food and industrial processing industries; submersible water and petroleum pumps; petroleum leak detection equipment; compacting equipment for soil, asphalt, and refuse applications; cooling towers for power generation, industrial, and heating and cooling applications; cast-iron boilers and electrical resistance heaters for industrial and residential customers; industrial machinery and process equipment; and aerospace components. The building products segment manufactures complementary products that encompass architectural metal roofing; side-hinged and rolling steel doors; residential garage doors; pre-engineered metal buildings; loading dock systems and related equipment; and wall, roof, floor, and window systems. It also provides general and specialized contractor services. The engineering segment is comprised of the Litwin companies, which provide worldwide engineering and construction services for the refining and petrochemical, polymers, specialty chemicals, and environmental control markets. Litwin also provides advanced process control and instrumentation capabilities. **NOTE:** Please visit http://www.monster.com to search for jobs and apply online. **Corporate headquarters location:** This location. **International locations:** Worldwide. **Operations at this facility include:** This location houses the executive offices. **Listed on:** New York Stock Exchange. **Stock exchange symbol:** SPW. **Number of employees worldwide:** 22,000.

SADDLE CREEK COPAK CORPORATION
3555 Shamrock Road, Harrisburg NC 28075. 704/454-6300. **Fax:** 704/454-6301. **Contact:** Maria Russell, Human Resources. **E-mail address:** mariar@saddlecrk.com. **World Wide Web address:** http://www.saddlecrk.com. **Description:** A direct mail advertising agency with a broad range of clients. Founded 1966. **NOTE:** Please visit http://www.monster.com to search for jobs and apply online. **Positions advertised include:** Mid-Senior Manager; Warehouse Manager; Forklift Driver; Tractor/Trailer Driver; Customer Service Coordinator. **Corporate headquarters location:** Lakeland FL. **Other U.S. locations:** Southern and Southeastern U.S. **CEO:** David Lyons.

SAFT AMERICA INC.
313 Crescent Street, Valdese NC 28690. 828/874-4111. **Fax:** 828/879-5026. **Contact:** Staff Services Manager. **World Wide Web address:** http://www.saftbatteries.com. **Description:** A manufacturer of industrial aviation batteries and numerous other storage batteries for industrial use. **Corporate headquarters location:** Bagnolet, France. **Other U.S. locations:** Cockeysville MD; Valdosta GA. **International locations:** Worldwide. **Operations at this facility include:** Manufacturing. **Number of employees worldwide:** 4,000.

ST. TIMOTHY CHAIR COMPANY
P.O. Box 2427, Hickory NC 28613. 828/322-7125. **Physical address:** Highway 70-A East, Hickory NC 28601. **Fax:** 828/328-9800. **Contact:** Personnel Manager. **World Wide Web address:** http://www.sttimothychair.com. **Description:** Manufactures case goods, chairs, and other home and office furnishings. **Parent company:** Classic Leather.

SALEM COLLEGE
SALEM ACADEMY
P.O. Box 10548, Winston-Salem NC 27108-0548. 336/721-2600. **Physical address:** 601 South Church Street, Winston –Salem NC 27101. **Fax:** 336/721-2785. **Recorded jobline:** 336/917-5522. **Contact:** Human Resources. **World Wide Web address:** http://www.salem.edu. **Description:** A women's liberal arts college offering both undergraduate and graduate programs of study. Salem Academy (also at this location) is a private, college preparatory boarding and day school for girls in grades 9 through 12. **NOTE:** Please visit http://www.salem.edu/employment to view job listings and download employment application. **Positions advertised include:** Assistant Dean of Continuing Studies; Faculty – Various Departments. **Corporate headquarters location:** This location. **Operations at this facility include:** Administration; Service. **Listed on:** Privately held.

SARA LEE HOSIERY
5660 University Parkway, Winston-Salem NC 27105. 336/519-8400. **Toll-free phone:** 800/206-9196. **Fax:** 336/519-7312. **Contact:** Personnel. **World Wide Web address:** http://www.saraleehosiery.com. **Description:** Manufactures and markets a nationally distributed line of women's hosiery products. **Corporate headquarters location:** This location. **Parent company:** Sara Lee Corporation. **Listed on:** New York Stock Exchange. **Stock exchange symbol:** SLE.

SARA LEE INTIMATE APPAREL
P.O. Box 5100, Winston-Salem NC 27113-5100. 336/519-6053. **Physical address:** 3330 Healy Drive, Winston-Salem NC 27103. **Contact:** Employee Relations. **World Wide Web address:** http://www.balinet.com. **Description:** Manufactures women's intimate apparel. Brands include BALI, Wonderbra, Playtex, and Just My Size. **NOTE:** Please visit corporate website http://www.saralee.com to search for jobs and apply online. **Positions advertised include:** Manager – Financial Controls Compliance. **Corporate headquarters location:** This location. **Parent company:** Sara Lee Corporation.

SAS INSTITUTE INC.
100 SAS Campus Drive, Cary NC 27513-2414. 919/677-8000. **Toll-free phone:** 800/727-0025. **Fax:** 919/677-4444. **Contact:** Personnel. **World Wide Web address:** http://www.sas.com. **Description:** Designs a variety of software programs including those used for warehouse management, statistics, and inventory control. **NOTE:** Please visit website to search for jobs and apply online. **Positions advertised include:** Account Executive; Analytical Consultant; Applications Developer; Administrative Support Student; Data Architect; Development Tester; Food Service Associate; Human Factors Engineer; Industry Strategist; Java Development Applications Engineer; Pricing Optimization Tester; Research Statistician; Staff Assistant; Technical Writer. **Corporate headquarters location:** This location. **Other U.S. locations:** Nationwide. **International locations:** Worldwide. **President/CEO:** Jim Goodnight. **Number of employees at this location:** 3,989. **Number of employees nationwide:** 5,085. **Number of employees worldwide:** 9,227.

SCOTT & STRINGFELLOW, INC.
2626 Glenwood Avenue, Suite 430, Raleigh NC 27608. 919/571-1893. **Toll-free phone:** 800/763-1893. **Contact:** Hiring Manager. **E-mail address:** resume@scottstringfellow.com. **World Wide Web address:** http://www.scottstringfellow.com. **Description:** A full-service regional brokerage and investment banking firm. Services of Scott & Stringfellow include investment advice and brokerage for individual and institutional clients, investment banking and securities underwriting for corporations and municipalities, and a wide array of other investment-related financial services including investment advisory services through its affiliate, Scott & Stringfellow Capital Management, Inc. Founded 1893. **NOTE:** Please visit website to search for jobs. **Corporate headquarters location:** Richmond VA. **Other area locations:** Statewide. **Other U.S. locations:** SC; VA. **Parent company:** BB&T Corporation. **Listed on:** New York Stock Exchange. **Stock exchange symbol:** BBT. **Number of employees nationwide:** 600.

SCOTTY TECHNOLOGIES OF THE AMERICAS
6714 Netherlands Drive, Wilmington NC 28405. 910/395-6100. **Fax:** 910/395-6108. **Contact:** Human Resources. **E-mail address:** usrecruit@scottygroup.com. **World Wide Web address:** http://www.scottygroup.com. **Description:** A provider of video-conferencing technology. Founded 1993. **NOTE:** Please visit website to view job listings and apply online. **Corporate headquarters location:** This location. **International locations:** United Kingdom. **Number of employees worldwide:** 100.

SEALY, INC.
One Office Parkway, Trinity NC 27370. 336/861-3500. **Fax:** 336/861-3715. **Contact:** Joe Taylor, Human Resources. **World Wide Web address:** http://www.sealy.com. **Description:** One of the largest mattress and furniture manufacturers in North America. **NOTE:** Please visit website to search for jobs. **Corporate headquarters location:** This location. **Other U.S. locations:** Nationwide. **International locations:** Canada. **Operations at this facility include:** Administration. **Listed on:** Privately held. **CEO:** David McIlquham. **Number of employees nationwide:** 6,562.

SECURITAS
5108 Reagan Drive, Suite 14, Charlotte NC 28206. 704/597-0626. **Toll-free phone:** 800/232-7465. **Recorded jobline:** 888/591-4473. **Contact:** Vicki Giacomin, Human Resources. **World Wide Web address:** http://www.securitasinc.com. **Description:** Offers a wide range of protective services and contract security guard programs to businesses and government. Burns International Security Services also provides electronic security systems and security planning consultation. **Office hours:** Monday - Friday, 8:00 a.m. - 5:00 p.m. **Corporate headquarters location:** Chicago IL. **Other U.S. locations:** Nationwide. **Number of employees nationwide:** 93,000.

SHADOWLINE INC.
550 Lenoir Road, Morganton NC 28655. 828/437-3821. **Fax:** 828/437-8900. **Contact:** Personnel Manager. **World Wide Web address:** http://www.shadowline-lingerie.com. **Description:** A manufacturer of lingerie. **Special programs:** Internships. **Corporate headquarters location:** This location. **Other area locations:** Boone NC; Fallston NC; Mars Hill NC. **Other U.S. locations:** SC; TN; MO; AL; FL; OH; TX. **Operations at this facility include:** Administration; Manufacturing; Research and Development; Sales; Service. **Listed on:** Privately held.

SHAMROCK ENVIRONMENTAL SERVICES
503 Patton Avenue, P.O. Box 14987, Greensboro NC 27406. 336/375-1989. **Toll-free phone:** 800/881-1098. **Fax:** 336/375-1801. **Contact:** Human Resources. **World Wide Web address:** http://www.shamrockenviro.com. **Description:** Provides hazardous and nonhazardous material collection and disposal services. **NOTE:** Please visit website to view job listings and download employment application. **Positions advertised include:** Project Manager; Site Supervisor; Field Technician; Equipment Operator; CDL Driver. **CEO:** Gail B. McGroarty.

SIMCLAR NORTH AMERICA INC.
176 Laurie Ellis Road, P.O. Box 1369, Winterville NC 28950. 252/355-3443. **Fax:** 252/355-3144. **Contact:** Human Resources. **World Wide Web address:** http://www.simclar.com. **Description:** Manufactures parts for the large appliances industries, including makers of photocopiers, and ATMs. **NOTE:** Entry-level positions and second and third shifts are offered. **Office hours:** Monday - Friday, 8:00 a.m. - 4:30 p.m. **Corporate headquarters location:** Scotland. **Other U.S. locations:** Hialeah FL; Dayton OH; North Attleboro MA; Kenosha WI; Round Rock TX. **International locations:** Tianjin, China; Tamps, Mexico. **Parent company:** Simclar Group. **Listed on:** NASDAQ. **Stock exchange symbol:** SIMC. **Number of employees worldwide:** 2,500.

SLICKEDIT, INC.
3000 Aerial Center Parkway, Suite 120, Morrisville NC 27560. 919/473-0070. **Toll-free phone:** 800/934-EDIT. **Fax:** 919/473-0080. **Contact:** Personnel. **E-mail address:** careers@slickedit.com. **World Wide Web address:** http://www.slickedit.com. **Description:** Develops graphical programmers' editing software including Visual SlickEdit and SlickEdit text-mode version. **Positions advertised include:** Software Engineer. **Office hours:** Monday – Friday, 9:00 a.m. – 6:00 p.m. **Corporate headquarters location:** This location. **CEO:** Jill Maurer.

SMITHFIELD PACKING COMPANY, INC.
2602 West Vernon Avenue, Kinston NC 28504. 252/522-4777. **Contact:** Human Resources. **E-mail address:** humanresources@smithfieldpacking.com. **World Wide Web address:** http://www.smithfield.com. **Description:** Processes and sells ham under the brand name Smithfield Hams. The company's products are distributed nationwide. Founded 1936. **Corporate headquarters location:** Smithfield VA. **Other area locations:** Benson NC; Tarheel NC; Wilson NC. **Other U.S. locations:** VA; FL. **Parent company:** Smithfield Foods. **Listed on:** New York Stock Exchange. **Stock exchange symbol:** SFD. **Number of employees nationwide:** 9,330.

SMURFIT-STONE CONTAINER CORPORATION
2606 Wilco Boulevard, P.O. Box 3124, Wilson NC 27895-3124. 252/237-3124. **Toll-free phone:** 877/772-2999. **Contact:** Human Resources. **World Wide Web address:** http://www.smurfit-stone.com. **Description:** Smurfit-Stone Container Corporation is one of the world's leading paper-based packaging companies. The company's main products include corrugated containers, folding cartons, and multiwall industrial bags. The company is also one of the world's largest collectors and processors of recycled products that are then sold to a worldwide customer base. Smurfit-Stone Container Corporation also operates several paper tube, market pulp, and newsprint production facilities. **Corporate headquarters location:** Chicago IL. **Other area locations:** Lexington NC; Raleigh NC; Shelby NC; Statesville NC; Winston-Salem NC; Greensboro NC. **Other U.S. locations:** Nationwide. **International locations:** Canada; Mexico; China. **Operations at this facility include:** This location manufactures corrugated boxes. **Listed on:** NASDAQ. **Stock exchange symbol:** SSCC. **Number of employees worldwide:** 38,600.

M.J. SOFFE COMPANY, INC.
P.O. Box 2507, One Soffe Drive, Fayetteville NC 28312. 910/483-2500. **Fax:** 910/486-9030. **Contact:** Human Resources Director. **World Wide Web address:** http://www.mjsoffe.com. **Description:** A manufacturer of sportswear. **Corporate headquarters location:** This location. **Other area locations:** Maxton NC; Rowland NC; Bladenboro NC. **Other U.S. locations:** Lansing MI; Jacksonville FL; Springfield MA. **Listed on:** Privately held.

SONIC AUTOMOTIVE INC.
6415 Idlewild Road, Suite 109, Charlotte NC 28212. 704/566-2400. **Fax:** 704/536-4665. **Contact:** Human Resources. **E-mail address:** jobopportunities@sonicautomotive.com. **World Wide Web address:** http://www.sonicautomotive.com. **Description:** Operates a nationwide car dealership chain. Sonic Automotive also provides parts and services. **NOTE:** Please visit website to search for jobs. **Corporate headquarters location:** This location. **Listed on:** New York Stock Exchange. **Stock exchange symbol:** SAH. **CEO:** O. Bruton Smith.

SOURCE TECHNOLOGIES, INC.
2910 White Hall Park Drive, Charlotte NC 28273. 704/969-7500. **Toll-free phone:** 800/922-8501. **Contact:** Human Resources Department. **World Wide Web address:** http://www.sourcetech.com. **Description:** A reseller of computer printers and printer equipment. Source Technologies also offers a wide variety of printing solutions. **Corporate headquarters location:** This location. **Other U.S. locations:** GA; SC; MN; WA; CA; NY.

SOUTHERN FURNITURE COMPANY
1099 Second Avenue Pl SE, P.O. Box 307, Conover NC 28613. 828/464-0311. **Fax:** 828/464-0460. **Contact:** Personnel & Human Resources Director. **Description:** A manufacturer of upholstery goods and case goods. The company has plants located throughout North Carolina. **NOTE:** You may mark your resume attention to Emily, post number 8284640460. **Corporate headquarters location:** This location.

SOUTHERN INDUSTRIAL CONSTRUCTORS, INC.
6101 Triangle Drive, Raleigh NC 27617-4717. 919/782-4600. **Recorded jobline:** 888/874-2778x4202. **Fax:** 919/782-2935. **Contact:** Human Resources Department. **World Wide Web address:** http://www.southernindustrial.com. **Description:** An industrial construction firm specializing in the installation of manufacturing processes and equipment. The company operates in 33 states. **Office hours:** Monday – Friday, 8:00 a.m. – 5:00 p.m. **Corporate headquarters location:** This location. **Other area locations:** Wilmington NC; Raleigh NC. **Other U.S. locations:** Columbia SC. **Listed on:** Privately held. **President:** John G. Wilson.

SPEEDWAY MOTORSPORTS, INC.
P.O. Box 600, Concord NC 28026. 704/455-3239. **Physical address:** 5555 Concord Parkway South, Concord NC 28027. **Fax:** 704/532-3312. **Contact:** Personnel. **World Wide Web address:** http://www.speedwaymotorsports.com. **Description:** Promotes, markets, and sponsors motor sports activities including eight racing events annually sanctioned by NASCAR, five of which are associated with the Winston Cup professional stock car racing circuit and three of which are associated with the Busch Grand National circuit. The company also operates, sanctions, and promotes its Legends Cars, 5/8-scale modified cars, modeled after those driven by legendary early NASCAR racers, for use on its Legends Car Racing Circuit, which is an entry-level stock car racing series. Other Speedway Motorsports operations include two ARCA annual stock car races. **NOTE:** Please send resumes to P.O. Box 18747, Charlotte NC 28218. **Special programs:** Internships. **Office hours:** Monday - Friday, 9:00 a.m. - 5:00 p.m. **Corporate headquarters location:** This location. **Subsidiaries include:** Atlanta Motor Speedway; Bristol Motor Speedway; Infineon Raceway; Las Vegas Motor Speedway; Lowe's Motor Speedway; PRN Radio; Texas Motor Speedway. **Listed on:** New York Stock Exchange. **Stock exchange symbol:** TRK. **CEO:** O. Bruton Smith. **Number of employees at this location:** 255.

STANADYNE AUTOMOTIVE CORPORATION
230 Clarks Neck Road, P.O. Box 1105, Washington NC 27889. 252/975-2553. **Contact:** Human Resources Manager. **E-mail address:** hr@stanadyne.com. **World Wide Web address:** http://www.stanadyne.com. **Description:** Manufactures fuel injection systems for diesel engines. **Corporate headquarters location:** Windsor CT. **NOTE:** Please visit website to view job listings and apply online. **Other area locations:** Jacksonville NC. **Other U.S. locations:** Tallahassee FL. **International locations:** Brazil; Italy; France; India. **Operations at this facility include:** Manufacturing. **Number of employees at this location:** 350.

STANDARD COMMERCIAL CORPORATION
2201 Miller Road, P.O. Box 450, Wilson NC 27894-0450. 252/291-5507. **Fax:** 252/237-0018. **Contact:** Human Resources Director. **World Wide Web address:** http://www.sccgroup.com. **Description:** Buys and processes a variety of tobaccos for sale to domestic and international makers of cigarettes, cigars, and pipe tobaccos in 85 countries. Standard Commercial Corporation also purchases, processes, and markets wool to international customers. The company operates three tobacco processing plants in the United States and 17 other plants throughout the world; and eight wool manufacturing and storage plants in eight countries. The company is also involved in importing-exporting in Eastern Europe and operates a building supply company. **Corporate headquarters location:** This location. **Other area locations:** King NC. **International locations:** Worldwide. **Listed on:** New York Stock Exchange. **Stock exchange symbol:** STW. **President/CEO:** Robert E. Harrison.

STERLING HEALTHCARE
1000 Park 40 Plaza, Suite 500, Durham NC 27713. 919/383-0355. **Toll-free phone:** 800/476-4587. **Fax:** 919/382-3257. **Contact:** Carolyn Carle, Recruitment and Staff Development. **E-mail address:** carolyn.carle@phyamerica.com. **World Wide Web address:** http://www.phyamerica.com. **Description:** A national provider of physician practice management services to hospitals, government entities, managed care organizations, and other health care institutions. Under contract with its clients, the company identifies and organizes physician practices for credentialing and privileging, and coordinates the ongoing scheduling of health care professionals who provide clinical coverage in designated areas of primary care, mainly in the areas of emergency care. Sterling Healthcare also assists the client's administrative and medical staff in such areas as quality assurance, risk management, practice accreditation, and marketing, as well as in the documentation, billing, and collection of professional charges. **Positions advertised include:** Compliance Officer; Legal Assistant/Hospital Contracting Coordinator. **Corporate headquarters location:** This location. **Other U.S. locations:** Nationwide. **President/CEO:** Stephen J. Dresnick.

STRATEGIC TECHNOLOGIES
301 Gregson Drive, Cary NC 27511. 919/379-8000. **Fax:** 919/379-8100. **Contact:** Human Resources. **E-mail address:** info@stratech.com. **World Wide Web address:** http://www.stratech.com. **Description:** Provides network integration services. **NOTE:** Please visit website to view job listings and apply online. **Positions advertised include:** Oracle Technical Trainer. **Corporate headquarters location:** This location. **Other area locations:** Charlotte NC; Greensboro NC. **Other U.S. locations:** AL; CT; FL; GA; NY; SC; TN; VA. **Listed on:** Privately held. **President/CEO:** Mike Shook.

SUMITOMO ELECTRIC LIGHTWAVE CORPORATION
P.O. Box 13445, Research Triangle Park NC 27709. 919/541-8100. **Physical address:** 78 Alexander Drive, Research Triangle Park NC. **Toll-free phone:** 800/358-7378. **Fax:** 919/541-8265. **Contact:** Human Resources. **E-mail address:** humanresources@sumitomoelectric.com. **World Wide Web address:** http://www.sel-rtp.com. **Description:** Develops, manufactures, and sells fiber-optic cable products. **NOTE:** Please visit website to view job listings. **Corporate headquarters location:** This location. **Listed on:** Privately held.

SUMMUS LIMITED
434 Fayetteville Street Mall, Suite 600, Raleigh NC 27601. 919/807-5600. **Fax:** 919/807-5601. **Contact:** Human Resources. **E-mail address:** info@summus.com. **World Wide Web address:** http://www.summus.com. **Description:** Develops compression technology software for image and video data transmissions over the Internet and other networks. **Corporate headquarters location:** This location. **Other U.S. locations:** Boston MA; Kansas City KS; Chicago IL. **International locations:** Gothenburg Sweden; Split Croatia. **CEO:** Bjorn Jawerth.

SUN TRUST
111 Corcoran Street, Durham NC 27701. 919/683-7621. **Toll-free phone:** 800/422-2226. **Fax:** 919/683-7662. **Contact:** Human Resources. **World Wide Web address:** http://www.suntrust.com. **Description:** Sun Trust is a bank holding company offering a complete line of traditional banking services, as well as a full array of financial products such as investments, insurance, and trust services. This location also hires seasonally. Founded in 1903. **NOTE:** Entry-level positions and part-time jobs are offered. Please visit website to search for jobs and apply online. **Positions advertised include:** Loan Servicing Representative; Summer Teller. **Special programs:** Summer Jobs. **Corporate headquarters location:** Atlanta, GA. **Parent company:** National Commerce Financial Corporation. **Other U.S. locations:** Southeast U.S. **Listed on:** New York Stock Exchange. **Stock exchange symbol:** STI. **Chairman and CEO:** L. Phillip Humann. **Number of employees nationwide:** 28,083.

SYNGENTA BIOTECHNOLOGY, INC.
P.O. Box 12257, Research Triangle Park NC 27709-2257. 919/541-8500. **Physical address:** 3054 Cornwallis Road, Research Triangle Park NC 27709-2257. **Contact:** Human Resources. **World Wide Web address:** http://www.syngentabiotech.com. **Description:** Researches and develops products to improve crop protection and to increase crop production. **NOTE:** Please visit website to view job listings and apply online. **Corporate headquarters location:** Basel Switzerland. **Other area locations:** Greensboro NC. **Other U.S. locations:** Longmont CO; Wilmington DE; Boise ID; Des Moines IA; Downers Grove IL; Golden Valley MN; Cordova TN. **International locations:** Worldwide. **Parent company:** Syngenta. **Listed on:** New York Stock Exchange. **Stock exchange symbol:** SYT. **CEO:** Michael Pragnell. **Number of employees worldwide:** 19,000.

SYNOPSYS, INC.
1101 Slater Road, Suite 300, Durham NC 27703. 919/425-7300. **Fax:** 919/941-6700. **Contact:** Director of Human Resources. **E-mail address:** jobs@avanticorp.com. **World Wide Web address:** http://www.synopsys.com. **Description:** Develops, markets, and supports software products that assist IC design engineers in performing automated design, layout, physical verification, and analysis of advanced integrated circuits. **Corporate headquarters location:** Mountain View CA. **Other U.S. locations:** Nationwide. **International locations:** Worldwide. **Listed on:** NASDAQ. **Stock exchange symbol:** SNPS. **Number of employees at this location:** 4,362.

TARHEEL ROLLER & BRAYER
2156 Lewisville-Clemmons Road, P.O. Box 773, Clemmons NC 27012. 336/766-9823. **Fax:** 336/766-4286. **Contact:** Human Resources. **E-mail address:** hau6118@aol.com. **NOTE:** Phone number will connect you directly with the company's owner. **World Wide Web address:** http://www4.ncsu.edu/~bdhauser/tarheelroller.htm. **Description:** Manufactures composition printer rollers and paper cutter blades for paper cutting machines. **Owner:** David H. Hauser.

TEKSYSTEMS
4828 Parkway Plaza Boulevard, Suite 160, Charlotte NC 28217. 704/357-4500. **Fax:** 704/357-4490. **E-mail address:** charlotte@teksystems.com. **World Wide Web address:** http://www.teksystems.com. **Description:** Provides Information Technology services and staffing. **Positions advertised include:** Unix Systems Administrator; Information Security Manager; Desktop Support; Data Modeler; Financial Business Systems Analyst; Oracle Developer. **Other area locations:** Greensboro, Raleigh.

TESA TAPE, INC.
5825 Carnegie Boulevard, Charlotte NC 28209. 704/554-0707. **Toll-free phone:** 800/426-2181. **Fax:** 800/852-8831. **Contact:** Human Resources. **World Wide Web address:** http://www.tesatape.com. **Description:** Engaged in the production and sale of an extensive line of masking, cellophane, electrical, cloth, and other pressure-sensitive tape products for business, industrial, and household use. **Corporate headquarters location:** This location. **Other U.S. locations:** Carbondale IL; Sparta MI; Middletown NY. **International locations:** Worldwide. **Parent company:** Tesa AG (Hamburg Germany). **Operations at this facility include:** Research and Development.

THALES COMPUTERS
3100 Spring Forest Road, Raleigh NC 27616. 919/231-8000. **Toll-free phone:** 800/848-2330. **Fax:** 919/231-8001. **Contact:** Personnel. **World Wide Web address:** http://www.thalescomputers.com. **Description:** A designer and manufacturer of computer boards for use in harsh environments. **NOTE:** Please visit website to view job listings. **Corporate headquarters location:** France. **Other U.S. locations:** Jamestown RI; Moorpark CA. **International locations:** France; United Kingdom. **Operations at this facility include:** This location serves as the U.S. Headquarters.

THOMAS BUILT BUSES, INC.
1408 Courtesy Road, High Point NC 27260. . 336/889-4871. **Fax:** 336/881-6509. **Contact:** Personnel Director. **World Wide Web address:** http://www.thomasbus.com. **Description:** Manufactures motor vehicles and passenger car bodies. **NOTE:** Please contact the local NC Employment Security Commission office about employment opportunities. Mail to 919 Phillips Avenue, High Point NC 27262. **Corporate headquarters location:** This location. **Other area locations:** Jamestown NC. **International locations:** Canada. **Parent company:** Freightliner, LLC. **President/CEO:** John O'Leary. **Number of employees nationwide:** 1,600.

THOMASVILLE FURNITURE
401 East Main Street, P.O. Box 339, Thomasville NC 27361-0339. 336/472-4000. **Fax:** 336/472-4085. **Contact:** Personnel. **World Wide Web address:**

http://www.thomasville.com. **Description:** Manufactures furniture upholstery for the nationwide Thomasville furniture chain and related stores. **Corporate headquarters location:** This location. **Other area locations:** Statewide. **President/CEO:** Thomas G. Tilley.

THYSSENKRUPP PRECISION FORGE
500 Oak Tree Drive, Selma NC 27576. 919/965-5555. **Fax:** 919/202-8265. **Contact:** Human Resources. **E-mail address:** human.resources@tka-pfu.thyssenkrupp.com. **World Wide Web address:** http://www.thyssenkrupp.com. **Description:** Manufactures bevel gears, speed gears, and transmission/axle drive parts. **Positions advertised include:** CNC Operators. **Corporate headquarters location:** This location.

TOUCHPOINT SOLUTIONS
Prosperity Place, 10200 Mallard Creek Road, Charlotte NC 28262. 704/943-7242. **Contact:** Recruiting Manager. **E-mail address:** dana.stephens@fnf.com. **World Wide Web address:** http://www.touchpoint-solutions.com. **Description:** Develops software for banks and other financial institutions. **Corporate headquarters location:** Atlanta GA. **Other U.S. locations:** Little Rock AR; **Parent company:** Fidelity Information Services. **President:** Jim Szyperski.

TRANSBOTICS CORPORATION
3400 Latrobe Drive, Charlotte NC 28211. 704/362-1115. **Fax:** 704/364-4039. **Contact:** Human Resources. **E-mail address:** careers@transbotics.com. **World Wide Web address:** http://www.transbotics.com. **Description:** Supplies hardware and software that are incorporated into and used to control automatic guided vehicle systems (AGVS), which are used by customers to transport materials between various locations within a manufacturing or distribution facility. **Corporate headquarters location:** This location. **Other U.S. locations:** Fraser MI. **President/CEO:** Claude Imbleau.

TRIANGLE TRANSIT AUTHORITY
P.O. Box 13787, Research Triangle Park NC 27709. 919/549-9999. **Fax:** 919/485-7441. **Contact:** Human Resources Administrator. **E-mail address:** jobs@ridetta.org. **World Wide Web address:** http://www.ridetta.org. **Description:** Offers access to various methods of transportation including bus services, vanpooling, and carpooling to the Triangle Park area The TTA is currently planning to expand their services to include a railway system. **NOTE:** Please visit website to view job listings. **Positions advertised include:** Mechanic; Bus Operator; Dispatcher/Supervisor; Service Attendant.

TRION, INC.
101 McNeill Road, Sanford NC 27330. 919/775-2201. **Toll-free phone:** 800/884-0002. **Fax:** 919/777-6399. **Toll-free fax:** 800/458-2379. **Contact:** Director of Human Resources. **World Wide Web address:** http://www.trioninc.com. **Description:** Manufactures electronic indoor air cleaners for home, office, and industrial use. Founded in 1947. **NOTE:** Please visit website to view job listings. **Corporate headquarters location:** This location. **Parent company:** Fedders Corporation. **Operations at this facility include:** Administration; Engineering and Design; Manufacturing; Research and Development; Sales. **Listed on:** New York Stock Exchange. **Stock exchange symbol:** FJC.

TROXLER ELECTRONIC LABORATORIES, INC.
3008 Cornwallis Road, P.O. Box 12057, Research Triangle Park NC 27709. 919/549-8661. **Toll-free phone:** 877/TROXLER. **Fax:** 919/485-2257. **Contact:** Human Resources. **E-mail address:** troxlerjobs@troxlerlabs.com. **World Wide Web address:** http://www.troxlerlabs.com. **Description:** Develops electronic products for measuring characteristics in engineering materials. **NOTE:** Please visit website to view job listings and apply online. **Corporate headquarters location:** This location. **Other U.S. locations:** Rockville MD; Lakewood WA; Rancho Cordova CA; Arlington TX; Nashville TV; Downers Grove IL; Lakewood CO. **International locations:** Germany; Hong Kong; Canada. **CEO:** Billy Troxler.

TURNER CONSTRUCTION COMPANY
5955 Carnegie Boulevard, Suite 125, Charlotte NC 28209. 704/554-1001. **Fax:** 704/554-5081. **Contact:** Human Resources. **World Wide Web address:** http://www.turnerconstruction.com. **Description:** Turner is a nationwide construction company founded in 1902. **Positions advertised include:** Assistant Engineer, Assistant Estimating Engineer. **Corporate Headquarters location:** 375 Hudson Street, New York NY 10014. **Chairman and CEO:** Thomas C. Leppert.

TYCO HEALTHCARE/MALLINCKRODT
8800 Durant Road, Raleigh NC 27616. 919/878-2930. **Contact:** Human Resources. **World Wide Web address:** http://www.mallinckrodt.com. **Description:** Tyco Healthcare/Mallinckrodt, Inc. provides specialty chemicals and human and animal health products worldwide through Tyco Healthcare/Mallinckrodt and two other technology-based businesses: Mallinckrodt Chemical, Inc. and Mallinckrodt Veterinary, Inc. Mallinckrodt Chemical is a producer of pharmaceutical and specialty industrial chemicals. It is also a joint venture partner in a worldwide flavors business. The company is one of the world's largest producers of acetaminophen and a major producer of medicinal narcotics and laboratory chemicals. Mallinckrodt Veterinary is one of the world's leading animal health and nutrition companies, with approximately 1,000 products sold in more than 100 countries. Products include pharmaceuticals, livestock and pet vaccines, pesticides, surgical supplies, anesthetics, and mineral feed ingredients. **NOTE:** Please visit website to search for jobs and apply online. **Corporate headquarters location:** Hazelwood MO. **Other U.S. locations:** Nationwide. **International locations:** Worldwide. **Operations at this facility include:** This location manufactures dyes used in CT scans. Tyco Healthcare/Mallinckrodt is a provider of technologically-advanced, cost-effective products and services to five medical specialties: anesthesiology, cardiology, critical care, nuclear medicine, and radiology. **President:** Michael J. Collins.

TYSON FOODS INC.
P.O. Box 88, Wilkesboro NC 28697. 336/838-2171. **Contact:** Division Personnel Manager. **World Wide Web address:** http://www.tysonfoodsinc.com. **Description:** Tyson Foods Inc. is one of the world's largest fully-integrated producers, processors, and marketers of poultry-based food products. **NOTE:** The hiring center is located at 704 Factory Street, Wilkesboro NC 28697. **Corporate headquarters location:** Springdale AR. **International locations:** Worldwide. **Operations at this facility include:** This location is engaged in poultry processing and packaging. **Listed on:** New York Stock Exchange. **Stock exchange symbol:** TSN.

URS CORPORATION
1600 Perimeter Park Drive, Suite 400, Morrisville NC 27560. **Fax:** 919/461-1415. **Contact:** Human Resources. **World Wide Web address:** http://www.urscorp.com. **Description:** Develops solutions to technical problems for government and corporate clients. Specific technical services provided include regulatory compliance support, site investigation and remediation, air pollution controls, VOC and air toxin control, biotreatment, waste management, ambient and source monitoring, risk management, information management, project chemistry, specialty chemicals, remote sensing services, materials and machinery analysis, and electronic services. **NOTE:** Please visit website to search for jobs and apply online. **Positions advertised include:** Geologist; Project Environmental Engineer; Senior Geologist; Assistant Programmer; Civil Engineer; Environmental Scientist; Graduate Environmental Engineer; Project Civil Engineer; Structural/Facility/Foundation Engineer. **Corporate headquarters location:** San Francisco CA. **Other area locations:** Charlotte NC. **Other U.S. locations:** Nationwide. **International locations:** Worldwide. **Listed on:** New York Stock Exchange. **Stock exchange symbol:** URS.

U.S. DEPARTMENT OF AGRICULTURE FOREST SERVICE
SOUTHERN RESEARCH STATION
3041 Cornwallis Road, P.O. Box 12254, Research Triangle Park NC 27709. 919/549-4000. **Fax:** 919/549-4047. **Contact:** Human Resources. **E-mail address:** fsjobs@fs.fed.us. **World Wide Web address:** http://www.srs.fs.usda.gov. **Description:** Researches a variety of topics including forest health, global climate change, and soils. **NOTE:** All hiring is conducted through the Asheville location. Interested jobseekers should direct resumes to Human Resources, U.S. Department of Agriculture, Forest Service, Southern Research Station, 200 Weaver Boulevard, Asheville NC 28804. **Other U.S. locations:** Nationwide.

U.S. DEPARTMENT OF VETERANS AFFAIRS
DURHAM VETERANS ADMINISTRATION MEDICAL CENTER
508 Fulton Street, Durham NC 27705. 919/286-0411. **Fax:** 919/286-6825. **Contact:** Human Resources. **World Wide Web address:** http://www.va.gov. **Description:** A medical center operated by the U.S. Department of Veterans Affairs. From 54 hospitals in 1930, the VA health care system has grown to include 171 medical centers; more than 364 outpatient, community, and outreach clinics; 130 nursing home care units; and 37 domiciliary residences. The VA operates at least one medical center in each of the 48 contiguous states, Puerto Rico, and the District of Columbia. With approximately 76,000 medical center beds, the VA treats nearly one million patients in VA hospitals, 75,000 in nursing home care units, and 25,000 in domiciliary residences. The VA's outpatient clinics register approximately 24 million visits per year. **NOTE:** Please visit http://www.va.gov/jobs to search for jobs. **Corporate headquarters location:** Washington DC. **Other U.S. locations:** Nationwide.

U.S. ENVIRONMENTAL PROTECTION AGENCY (EPA)
109 T.W. Alexander Drive, Research Triangle Park NC 27711. 919/541-2201. **Fax:** 919/541-2186. **Recorded jobline:** 800/433-9633. **Contact:** Human Resources Director. **World Wide Web address:** http://www.epa.gov/easyhire. **Description:** The EPA is dedicated to improving and preserving the quality of the environment, both nationally and globally, and protecting human health and the productivity of natural resources. The agency is committed to ensuring that federal environmental laws are implemented and enforced effectively; U.S. policy, both foreign and domestic, fosters the integration of economic development and environmental protection so that economic growth can be sustained over the long term; and public and private decisions affecting energy, transportation, agriculture, industry, international trade, and natural resources fully integrate considerations of environmental quality. **NOTE:** Please visit http://www.epa.gov/ezhire to search for jobs and apply online. Resumes are not accepted when mailed to the office. **Positions advertised include:** Financial Technician; Epidemiologist. **Corporate headquarters location:** Washington DC. **Other U.S. locations:** Nationwide. **Operations at this facility include:** This location of the EPA is a research and development laboratory. **Number of employees nationwide:** 18,000.

U.S. FEDERAL RESERVE BANK OF RICHMOND
P.O. Box 30248, Charlotte NC 28230. 704/358-2100. **Physical address:** 530 East Trade Street, Charlotte NC 28202. **Contact:** Personnel Manager. **World Wide Web address:** http://www.rich.frb.org. **Description:** One of 12 regional Federal Reserve banks that, along with the Federal Reserve Board of Governors in Washington DC, and the Federal Open Market Committee (FOMC), comprise the Federal Reserve System, the nation's central bank. As the nation's central bank, the Federal Reserve is charged with three major responsibilities: monetary policy, banking supervision and regulation, and processing payments. **NOTE:** Please visit website to search for jobs and apply online. **Positions advertised include:** Supervisor; Senior Supervisor; Senior Examiner; LCBO Risk Modeling Specialist; Central Point of Contact – LCBOs. **Corporate headquarters location:** Richmond VA.

ULTIMUS
15200 Weston Parkway, Suite 106, Cary NC 27513. 919/678-0900. **Fax:** 919/678-0901. **Contact:** Office Manager. **E-mail address:** admin@ultimus.com. **World Wide Web address:** http://www.ultimus.com. **Description:** Offers workflow automation software through client/server Windows applications, allowing users to design, simulate, implement, monitor, and measure workflow for various administrative business processes. Founded in 1994. **Company slogan:** Workflow on the Web. **Positions advertised include:** Regional Sales Manager; Senior Workflow Consultant; Technical Support Specialist; Technical Trainer; Technical Training Manager; Workflow Consultant. **Office hours:** Monday - Friday, 9:00 a.m. - 5:30 p.m. **Corporate headquarters location:** This location. **International locations:** Worldwide. **Listed on:** Privately held. **CEO:** Rashid Khan.

JOHN UMSTEAD HOSPITAL
1003 12th Street, Butner NC 27509. 919/575-7943. **Fax:** 919/575-7550. **Recorded jobline:** 919/575-7680. **Contact:** Recruitment Specialist. **Description:** A psychiatric hospital providing mental health treatment and psycho-educational rehabilitation. The hospital also operates the Butner Adolescent Treatment Center, which is composed of BATC, a locked residential facility, and Oakview Residential Treatment Program, a nonsecure apartment facility. Each of these facilities can accommodate 12 male residents ages 13 to 17. **NOTE:** Please visit http://www.dhhs.state.nc.us to search for jobs and apply online. **Positions advertised include:** Health Care Technician; LPN; RN; Clinical Pharmacist; Clinical Social Worker; Cook; Food Service Assistant; Internal Escort; Housekeeper; Occupational Therapist; Painter; Physician; Quality Assurance Specialist; Substance Abuse Counselor; Teacher. **Office hours:** Monday - Friday, 8:00 a.m. - 5:00 p.m. **Number of employees at this location:** 1,400.

UNDERWRITERS LABORATORIES
12 Laboratory Drive, P.O. Box 13995, Research Triangle Park NC 27709. 919/549-1400. **Fax:** 919/547-6000. **Contact:** Human Resources Director. **E-mail address:** rtpjobs@us.ul.com. **World Wide Web address:** http://www.ul.com. **Description:** An independent, nonprofit corporation established to help reduce or prevent bodily injury, loss of life, and property damage. The organization is engaged in the scientific investigation of various materials, devices, equipment, and construction methods and systems, and in the publication of standards, classifications, specifications, and other information. The company's engineering functions are divided among six departments including electrical; burglary protection and signaling; casualty and chemical hazards; fire protection; heating, air conditioning, and refrigeration; and marine. Underwriters

Laboratories also provides a factory inspection service through offices located throughout the United States and in 54 other countries. **NOTE:** Please visit website to view job listings. **Office hours:** Monday - Friday, 7:30 a.m. - 4:30 p.m. **Other U.S. locations:** Nationwide. **International locations:** Worldwide. **Number of employees at this location:** 400. **Number of employees worldwide:** 4,000.

UNIFI, INC.
P.O. Box 19109, Greensboro NC 27419-9109. 336/294-4410. **Physical address:** 7201 West Friendly Avenue, Greensboro NC 27410. **Fax:** 336/316-5422. **Contact:** Human Resources Director. **E-mail address:** careers@unifi-inc.com. **World Wide Web address:** http://www.unifi-inc.com. **Description:** Unifi, Inc. and its subsidiaries are engaged in the processing of yarns by texturing synthetic filament polyester and nylon fibers and spinning cotton and cotton-blend fibers. The company supplies knitters and weavers for apparel, women's and men's hosiery, high-performance stretch active wear, medical products including tape and bandages that contain the company's textured nylon and covered lycra and rubber products, industrial hosiery, home furnishing, automotive upholstery, and other end use markets. **Office hours:** Monday – Friday, 8:00 a.m. – 5:00 p.m. **Corporate headquarters location:** This location. **Other area locations:** Altamahaw NC; Reidsville NC; Mayodan NC; Yadkinville NC. **International locations:** Ireland; Colombia; Brazil; China; United Kingdom; Germany; Italy. **Subsidiaries include:** Unifi Spun Yarns, Inc.; Vintage Yarns, Inc. **Listed on:** New York Stock Exchange. **Stock exchange symbol:** UFI. **Number of employees nationwide:** 4,500.

UNIFI, INC.
2920 Vance Street, P.O. Box 1437, Reidsville NC 27323. 336/342-3361. **Fax:** 336/348-6535. **Contact:** Employment Manager. **E-mail address:** careers@unifi-inc.com. **World Wide Web address:** http://www.unifi-inc.com. **Description:** The company and its subsidiaries are engaged in the processing of yarns by texturing synthetic filament polyester and nylon fiber and spinning cotton and cotton-blend fibers. The company supplies knitters and weavers for apparel, women's and men's hosiery, high-performance stretch active wear, medical products including tape and bandages that contain the company's textured nylon and covered lycra and rubber products, industrial hosiery, home furnishing, automotive upholstery, and other end use markets. **Corporate headquarters location:** Greensboro NC. **Other area locations:** Altamahaw NC; Mayodan NC; Yadkinville NC. **International locations:** Ireland; Colombia; Brazil; China; United Kingdom; Germany; Italy. **Subsidiaries include:** Unifi Spun Yarns, Inc.; Vintage Yarns, Inc. **Operations at this facility include:** This location processes and dyes yarn. **Listed on:** New York Stock Exchange. **Stock exchange symbol:** UFI. **Number of employees nationwide:** 4,500.

UNIFI, INC.
802 South Ayersville Road, Mayodan NC 27027. 336/427-1500. **Fax:** 336/427-1529. **Contact:** Employment Manager. **E-mail address:** careers@unifi-inc.com. **World Wide Web address:** http://www.unifi-inc.com. **Description:** The company and its subsidiaries are engaged in the processing of yarns by texturing synthetic filament polyester and nylon fiber and spinning cotton and cotton-blend fibers. The company supplies knitters and weavers for apparel, women's and men's hosiery, high-performance stretch active wear, medical products including tape and bandages that contain the company's textured nylon and covered lycra and rubber products, industrial hosiery, home furnishing, automotive upholstery, and other end use markets. **Corporate headquarters location:** Greensboro NC. **Other area locations:** Altamahaw NC; Yadkinville NC; Reidsville NC; Greensboro NC. **International locations:** Ireland; Colombia; Brazil; China; United Kingdom; Germany; Italy. **Subsidiaries include:** Unifi Spun Yarns, Inc.; Vintage Yarns, Inc. **Operations at this facility include:** This location produces ultra-fine to mid-denier textured nylon with various filament counts including microfibers. A portion of these products are package-dyed. **Listed on:** New York Stock Exchange. **Stock exchange symbol:** UFI. **Number of employees nationwide:** 4,500.

UNIFIRST
4700 Dwight Evans Road, Charlotte NC 28217. 704/523-9593. **Toll-free phone:** 800/888-4425. **Fax:** 704/525-9443. **Contact:** Human Resources. **World Wide Web address:** http://www.unifirst.com. **Description:** Provides laundry rental and cleaning services for hotels and restaurants. **Corporate headquarters:** Wilmington MA. **Other area locations:** Durham NC; Goldsboro NC; Kernersville NC; Rocky Mount NC; Wilmington NC. **Other U.S. locations:** Nationwide. **International locations:** Canada. **Parent company:** UniFirst Corporation. **Listed on:** New York Stock Exchange. **Stock exchange symbol:** UNF.

UNIVERSITY OF NORTH CAROLINA AT CHAPEL HILL
725 Airport Road, Campus Box 1045, Chapel Hill NC 27599-1045. 919/962-2991. **Fax:** 919/962-2658. **Contact:** Human Resources. **E-mail address:** employment@unc.edu. **World Wide Web address:** http://www.unc.edu. **Description:** A campus of the state university which offers graduate and undergraduate programs in education, dentistry, law, public health, journalism, nursing, and other disciplines. **NOTE:** Jobseekers should submit both an application and a resume. Please visit website to view job listings and for more specific information on applying for positions. **Positions advertised include:** Dean – Various Schools/Departments; Vice Chancellor of Student Affairs; University Librarian; Professor – Various Departments; Assistant Professor – Various Departments; Tenure-track Faculty – Various Departments; Clinical Instructor; Accountant; Administrative Assistant; Art Museum Registrar; Customer Network Coordinator; Computing Consultant; Grounds Worker; Housekeeper; Laboratory Research Specialist; Maintenance Mechanic; Office Assistant; Nurse Clinician; Processing Assistant; Research Analyst. **Number of employees at this location:** 8,000.

UNIVERSITY OF NORTH CAROLINA AT CHARLOTTE
9201 University City Boulevard, Charlotte NC 28223-0001. 704/687-2000. **Physical address:** King Building, Room 222, University of North Carolina, Charlotte NC 28223. **Fax:** 704/687-3239. **Contact:** Human Resources. **World Wide Web address:** http://www.uncc.edu. **Description:** A campus of the state university. The university has an enrollment of approximately 15,600 students. **NOTE:** Please visit website to view job listings. Human Resources phone is 704/687-2276. For information on staff positions, please e-mail mismith@email.uncc.edu. **Positions advertised include:** Housekeeping Assistant – Part-time; Library Clerk; Greenhouse Manager; Processing Assistant; Office Assistant; Accounting Clerk; Administrative Assistant; Residence Administrator; Computing Consultant; Faculty Engineering Specialist; Director of Purchasing; Manuscript Librarian; Senior Program Manager. **Office hours:** Monday – Friday, 8:00 a.m. – 5:00 p.m. **Number of employees at this location:** 2,500.

UNIVERSITY OF NORTH CAROLINA AT GREENSBORO
P.O. Box 26170, Greensboro NC 27402-6170. 336/334-5009. **Physical address:** 1000 Spring Garden Street, Greensboro NC 27403. **Fax:** 336/334-5585. **Recorded jobline:** 336/334-5023. **Contact:** Human Resources. **E-mail address:** staffjobs@uncg.edu. **World Wide Web address:** http://www.uncg.edu. **Description:** A campus of the state university offering a number of different academic programs ranging from accounting to women's studies. **NOTE:** Please visit website to download application form. You can also receive an application form by contacting the Greensboro Employment Security Commission. **Positions advertised include:** Director of Employee Services; Administrative Manager; Physician Extender; Processing Assistant; Administrative Secretary; Security Officer; Social Research Assistant. **Office hours:** Monday – Friday, 8:00 a.m. – 4:00 p.m. **Number of employees at this location:** 2,000.

UNIVERSITY OF NORTH CAROLINA AT WILMINGTON
University Center, 601 South College Road, Wilmington NC 28403. 910/962-3160. **Physical address:** 5051 New Centre Drive, Wilmington NC 28403-5960. **Fax:** 910/962-3840. **Recorded jobline:** 910/962-3791. **Contact:** Human Resources. **E-mail address:** hrsearch@uncw.edu. **World Wide Web address:** http://www.uncwil.edu. **Description:** A campus of the state university enrolling approximately 9,200 students. **NOTE:** Please visit website to view job listings. **Positions advertised include:** Dean – College of Arts and Sciences; Art Historian; Director of Student Life Assessment; Counselor; Director of Leadership Education Programs; Vice Chancellor – Public Service and Continuing Studies; Assistant Professor – Marine Biochemist; Director of Athletic Training; Lecturer in Athletic Training; Tenure Track Faculty – Nursing; Office Assistant; Assistant Manager – Printing Services; Assistant Director – Alumni Relations.

UNIVERSITY OF NORTH CAROLINA CENTER FOR PUBLIC TELEVISION
P.O. Box 14900, Research Triangle Park NC 27709-4900. 919/549-7000. **Contact:** Human Resources. **E-mail address:** careers@unctv.org. **World Wide Web address:** http://www.unctv.org. **Description:** This location houses administrative and fundraising offices, studios, and the technical operations center for the public television network. The station is affiliated with PBS, and was founded in 1955. **NOTE:** Please visit website to view job listings and download application form. **Special programs:** Internships.

UNIVERSITY OF NORTH CAROLINA PRESS
P.O. Box 2288, Chapel Hill NC 27515-2288. 919/966-3561. **Physical address:** 116 South Boundary Street, Chapel Hill NC 27514-3808. **Fax:** 919/966-3829. **Contact:** Human Resources. **E-mail address:** uncpress@unc.edu. **World Wide Web address:** http://uncpress.unc.edu. **Description:** Publishes nonfiction history, sociology, and related books as well as journals. Founded in 1922. **NOTE:** Please visit website to find a specific staff contact for your employment enquiries. Resumes and applications are preferred by mail. Unsolicited applications sent via e-mail and fax may not receive a response. Full-time and freelance work is generally available. **Corporate headquarters location:** This location.

VF CORPORATION
P.O. Box 21488, Greensboro NC 27420-1488. 336/424-6000. **Physical address:** 105 Corporate Center Boulevard, Greensboro NC 27408. **Fax:** 336/424-7696. **Contact:** Vice President of Human Resources. **World Wide Web address:** http://www.vfc.com. **Description:** A manufacturer of jeans wear, decorative knitwear, intimate apparel, playwear, and specialty apparel sold worldwide. VF Corporation markets its products under the brand names Vanity Fair, Barbizon, JanSport, Rustler, Girbaud, Lee, and Wrangler. Founded 1899. **NOTE:** Please visit website to search for jobs and apply online. **Positions advertised include:** AS400 Software Systems Analyst; Senior Accountant; SAP FI Systems Analyst; Senior Business Development Analyst; Senior Strategic Planning Analyst; UNIX Systems Analyst; SAP Product Costing Team Member. **Corporate headquarters location:** This location. **Other U.S. locations:** Shawnee Mission KS; Alpharetta GA; New York NY; Appleton WI; San Leandro CA; Nashville TN; Wyoming PA; Tampa FL. **International locations:** Mexico; Argentina; Spain; Belgium; Italy; China. **Subsidiaries include:** Eastpak; Jansport; Lee Sport; Red Kap Industries; Wrangler. **Listed on:** New York Stock Exchange. **Stock exchange symbol:** VFC. **Number of employees worldwide:** 52,300.

VANDERBILT MORTGAGE
P.O. Box 27081, Greensboro NC 27425-7081. 336/664-2400. **Toll-free phone:** 800/556-2080. **Fax:** 336/664-3041. **Contact:** Tina Decker, Human Resources. **World Wide Web address:** http://www.oakwoodhomes.com. **Description:** Manufactures and sells prefabricated housing under the Oakwood and Freedom brand names. Oakwood Homes also finances a portion of its installment contracts through its finance unit. **NOTE:** Please visit website to search for jobs and apply online. **Positions advertised include:** Collections Representative. **Special programs:** Internships. **Corporate headquarters location:** This location. **Other U.S. locations:** Nationwide. **Operations at this facility include:** Administration. **Listed on:** New York Stock Exchange. **Stock exchange symbol:** OH.

VARIETY WHOLESALER
218 South Garnet Street, P.O. Drawer 947, Henderson NC 27536. 252/430-2600. **Fax:** 252/430-2499. **Contact:** Francis Winslow, Director of Human Resources. **Description:** Operates a chain of retail variety stores. **Corporate headquarters location:** This location. **Other area locations:** Raleigh NC.

VERBATIM CORPORATION
1200 West W.T. Harris Boulevard, Charlotte NC 28262. 704/547-6500. **Contact:** Human Resources Manager. **World Wide Web address:** http://www.verbatimcorp.com. **Description:** Develops data storage products including computer disks and CD ROMs. **Corporate headquarters location:** This location. **Parent company:** Mitsubishi Chemical Corporation.

VERIZON COMMUNICATIONS
1058 West Club Boulevard, Durham NC 27701. 919/286-7336. **Contact:** Human Resources. **World Wide Web address:** http://www.verizon.com. **Description:** A full-service communications services provider. Verizon offers residential local and long-distance telephone services and Internet access; wireless service plans, cellular phones, and data services; a full-line of business services including Internet access, data services, and telecommunications equipment and services; and government network solutions including Internet access, data services, telecommunications equipment and services, and enhanced communications services. **NOTE:** Please visit website to search for jobs and apply online. Resumes are accepted online only. **Positions advertised include:** Building Services Technician. **Corporate headquarters location:** New York NY. **Other U.S. locations:** Nationwide. **Operations at this facility include:** This location is a retail service facility for Verizon Plus. **Listed on:** New York Stock Exchange. **Stock exchange symbol:** VZ. **Number of employees worldwide:** 260,000.

VISHAY MICRO-MEASUREMENTS
P.O. Box 27777, Raleigh NC 27611-7777. 919/365-3800. **Physical address:** 951 Wendall Boulevard, Wendall NC 27591. **Fax:** 919/365-5043. **Contact:** Deborah Barbra, Personnel. **World Wide Web address:** http://www.vishay.com. **Description:** Develops, manufactures, and markets stress analysis products for measurement of mechanical strains. **Office hours:** Monday – Friday, 8:30 a.m. – 5:30 p.m. **Corporate headquarters location:** Malvern PA. **Parent company:** Vishay is engaged in the manufacture and sale of precision stress-analysis systems and services, as well as high-

precision resistive systems. In addition to Vishay Measurements Group, Vishay also operates in two other business segments: Resistive Systems Group, which develops, manufactures, and markets resistive products; and Medical Systems Group, which develops, manufactures, and markets dental products. **Listed on:** New York Stock Exchange. **Stock exchange symbol:** VSH.

VITAFOAM INC.
4100 Pleasant Garden Road, Greensboro NC 27406. 336/378-9620. **Fax:** 336/273-0238. **Contact:** Human Resources. **World Wide Web address:** http://www.vitausa.com. **Description:** Manufactures urethane foam for the furniture, bedding, and automotive industries. **NOTE:** Please visit website to fill out employment inquiry form. **Corporate headquarters location:** High Point NC. **Other area locations:** Thomasville NC. **Other U.S. locations:** Chattanooga TN; Tupelo MS; Moonachie NJ. **International locations:** Worldwide. **Parent company:** British Vita plc. **President/CEO:** Bill Lucas. **Number of employees worldwide:** 9,000.

VITAFOAM INC.
2222 Surrett Drive, P.O. Box 2024, High Point NC 27263. 336/431-1171. **Fax:** 336/431-7747. **Contact:** Human Resources. **World Wide Web address:** http://www.vitausa.com. **Description:** Manufactures specialized polymer, fiber, and fabric components for the furnishing, transportation, apparel, packaging, and engineering industries. **NOTE:** Please visit website to fill out employment inquiry form. **Corporate headquarters location:** This location. **Other area locations:** Greensboro NC; Thomasville NC. **Other U.S. locations:** Chattanooga TN; Tupelo MS; Moonachie NJ. **International locations:** Worldwide. **Parent company:** British Vita plc. **President/CEO:** Bill Lucas. **Number of employees worldwide:** 9,000.

VULCAN MATERIALS COMPANY
P.O. Box 4239, Winston-Salem NC 27115-4239. 336/767-0911. **Physical address:** 4401 North Patterson Avenue Winston-Salem NC 27105. **Fax:** 336/744-2978. **Contact:** Human Resources. **E-mail address:** mideastresumes@vmcmail.com. **World Wide Web address:** http://www.vulcanmaterials.com. **Description:** The company primarily produces crushed stone and aggregates for the highway and construction markets. Vulcan Materials Company has 21 plant locations throughout the Southeast (14 in Georgia and seven in South Carolina). **Positions advertised include:** Staff Accountant Land and Lease. **Corporate headquarters location:** Birmingham AL. **Other area locations:** Charlotte NC. **Operations at this facility include:** Headquarters of the Mideast Division. **Listed on:** New York Stock Exchange. **Stock exchange symbol:** VMC. **CEO:** Donald M. James. **Number of employees nationwide:** 8,500.

WACHOVIA CORPORATION
301 South College Street, Suite 4000, One Wachovia Center, Charlotte NC 28288-0013. 704/374-6161. **Recorded jobline:** 800/FUN-HIRE (for customer service positions). **Contact:** Human Resources Director. **World Wide Web address:** http://www.wachovia.com. **Description:** A securities brokerage firm. **NOTE:** Please visit website to search for jobs and apply online. **Positions advertised include:** Manager – Financial Analysis and Production; Senior Credit Default Swap Trader; CIB Risk Officer; Quality Assurance Analyst; Senior Trader; Finance Senior Consultant; Junior High Yield Trader; Systems Analyst; Loan Market Research Analyst; Client Manager. **Corporate headquarters location:** This location. **Other area locations:** Statewide. **Other U.S. locations:** Nationwide. **International locations:** Worldwide. **Listed on:** New York Stock Exchange. **Stock exchange symbol:** WB. **CEO:** G. Kennedy Thompson. **Number of employees worldwide:** 87,000.

WACHOVIA CORPORATION
100 North Main Street, Winston-Salem NC 27101. 336/732-5391. **Recorded jobline:** 888/WCE-MPLO. **Contact:** Employment Manager. **World Wide Web address:** http://www.wachovia.com. **Description:** A holding company whose member companies provide a variety of banking and financial services. **NOTE:** Entry-level positions, part-time jobs, and second and third shifts are offered. Please visit website to search for jobs and apply online. **Company slogan:** We are more than a bank. **Positions advertised include:** Finance Manager; Teller; Administrative Assistant; Credit Products Manager; Issues Management and Research Manager; Learning Strategist. **Special programs:** Internships; Training; Co-ops; Summer Jobs. **Corporate headquarters location:** Charlotte NC. **Other U.S. locations:** Nationwide. **International locations:** Worldwide. **Operations at this facility include:** This office is a financial center. **Listed on:** New York Stock Exchange. **Stock exchange symbol:** WB. **CEO:** G. Kennedy Thompson. **Number of employees nationwide:** 87,000.

WAKE FOREST UNIVERSITY-BAPTIST MEDICAL CENTER
Medical Center Boulevard, Winston-Salem NC 27157. 336/716-3367. **Toll-free phone:** 800/323-9777. **Fax:** 336/716-5656. **Contact:** Human Resources. **E-mail address:** erecruit@wfubmc.edu. **World Wide Web address:** http://www.wfubmc.edu. **Description:** One of the country's leading hospitals, offering a wide variety of services. The medical center has 20 subsidiary or affiliate hospitals and 87 satellite clinics throughout the surrounding areas. **NOTE:** Please visit website to view job listings and apply online. For nursing positions, please call 336/716-3339, and email to nrsrecrt@wfubmc.edu. **Positions advertised include:** Assistant Unit Manager; Clinical Documentation Consultant; Manager – Abdominal Transplant Program; Neonatal Nurse Practitioner; OR Service Coordinator; Palliative Care Coordinator; Quality Improvement Coordinator; Staff Nurse – Various Departments; CRNA – Various Departments; Dental Assistant; Clinical Nutritionist; Histologic Technician; MRI Technologist; Physical Therapist; Respiratory Therapist; Pharmacist; Database Specialist; Community Health Program Coordinator; Assistant Manager – Best Health; Social Worker; Assistant Teacher; Dietetic Clerk; Housekeeping Technician; Carpenter; Electrician. **Corporate headquarters location:** This location. **Number of employees at this location:** 5,500.

WAKEMED
3000 New Bern Avenue, PO Box 14465, Raleigh NC 27620. 919/350-8000. **Contact:** Human Resources. **E-mail address:** recruiting@wakemed.org. **World Wide Web address:** http://www.wakemed.org. **Description:** WakeMed is a 752-bed private, not-for-profit health care system. **Positions advertised include:** Bioterrorism Disaster Planner; Client Services Analyst; Nurse Aide, Occupational Therapist. **Corporate Headquarters:** This location.

WASTE MANAGEMENT, INC.
P.O. Box 16148, Winston-Salem NC 27115. 336/723-5744. **Physical address:** 3303 North Glenn Avenue, Winston-Salem NC 27105. **Fax:** 336/725-3113. **Contact:** Human Resources. **World Wide Web address:** http://www.wm.com. **Description:** Provides garbage removal services for residential and commercial locations. **NOTE:** Please visit website to search for jobs. **Corporate headquarters location:** Houston TX. **Other U.S. locations:** Nationwide. **International locations:** Canada. **Listed on:** New York Stock Exchange. **Stock exchange symbol:** WMI. **CEO:** David P. Steiner. **Number of employees worldwide:** 51,700.

WATTS NURSING SCHOOL
3643 North Roxboro Road, Durham NC 27704. 919/470-7348. **Contact:** Human Resources. **E-mail address:** wattsson@drh.duhs.duke.edu. **World Wide Web address:** http://www.wattsschoolofnursing.org. **Description:** The oldest nursing school in North Carolina. **Parent company:** Duke University Health System.

WAVERLY MILLS INCORPORATED
23 Third Street, Laurinburg NC 28352. 910/276-1441. **Fax:** 910/276-5826. **Contact:** Personnel Director. **World Wide Web address:** http://www.waverlymills.com. **Description:** Manufactures synthetic spun yarn. **Parent company:** R.J. Kunik & Co. **President:** Robert Kunik.

WAYNE COUNTY PUBLIC SCHOOLS
P.O. Drawer 1797, Goldsboro NC 27533-1797. 919/731-5900. **Contact:** Personnel Director. **E-mail address:** kthornton@wcps.org. **World Wide Web address:** http://www.waynecountyschools.org. **Description:** Offices of the Wayne County public school district. **NOTE:** Human Resources phone is 919/705-6179. Please visit website to download application form. **Positions advertised include:** Director – Summer Focus Intervention Program; Clerical Assistant – Summer Focus Intervention Program.

WEAVEXX
51 Flex Way, Youngsville NC 27596. 919/556-7235. **Toll-free phone:** 800/932-8399. **Contact:** Human Resources. **World Wide Web address:** http://www.weavexx.com. **Description:** Manufactures forming fabrics, press felt, dryer fabrics, and wet-end drainage equipment for paper manufacturers. **NOTE:** For information about employment, call the Xerium offices at 508/616-9468. **Other U.S. locations:** Starkville MS; Greenville TN; Farmville VA; Huntington Beach CA. **International locations:** Canada; Mexico. **Parent company:** Xerium Companies.

WELCOME HOME, INC.
309 Raleigh Street, Wilmington NC 28412. 910/791-4312. **Toll-free phone:** 800/348-4088. **Fax:** 910/791-4945. **Contact:** Human Resources. **World Wide Web address:** http://www.welcomehomestores.com. **Description:** A retailer of giftware and home decor including fragrances, candles, framed art, furniture, and seasonal gifts. The company operates over 100 stores in 36 states. **Corporate headquarters location:** This location. **Other U.S. locations:** Nationwide.

WELDON CITY SCHOOL DISTRICT
301 Mulberry Street, Weldon NC 27890. 252/536-4821. **Fax:** 252/538-4247. **Contact:** Personnel Director. **World Wide Web address:** http://www.weldoncityschools.k12.nc.us. **Description:** A public school district. **Special programs:** Training. **Office hours:** Monday – Friday, 8:00 a.m. – 5:00 p.m. **Corporate headquarters location:** This location. **Number of employees at this location:** 225.

WESTERN CAROLINA UNIVERSITY
220 HFR Administration, Western Carolina University, Cullowhee NC 28723. 828/227-7218. **Fax:** 828/227-7007. **Contact:** Human Resources. **E-mail address:** allison@email.wcu.edu. **World Wide Web address:** http://www.wcu.edu. **Description:** A university offering programs in business, education, and other disciplines. **Positions advertised include:** Assistant Professor – Various Departments; Assistant Women's Basketball Coach; Director of Enrollment Support; Professor – Various Departments; Reference Librarian; Administrative Assistant; Electrician; Electric Meter Reader; Enrollment Services Officer; Floor Maintenance Assistant; Grounds Worker; Housekeeper; Library Assistant; Occupational Therapist; Speech and Language Pathologist.

WEYERHAEUSER COMPANY
NC Highway, P.O. Box 787, Plymouth NC 27962-0787. 252/793-8111. **Contact:** Human Resources Manager. **E-mail address:** careers@weyerhaeuser.com. **World Wide Web address:** http://www.weyerhaeuser.com. **Description:** Weyerhaeuser Company's principal businesses are the growing and harvesting of timber; the manufacture, distribution, and sale of forest products including logs, wood chips, and building products; real estate development and construction; and financial services. Weyerhaeuser is one of the world's largest private owners of marketable softwood timber and one of the largest producers of softwood lumber and pulp. The company is also one of North America's largest producers of forest products and recyclers of office wastepaper, newspaper, and corrugated boxes. Weyerhaeuser Company also sells electricity to utility companies generated from its 15 trash-to-energy plants and 6 small cogeneration and recycling plants. The Water Division manufactures and operates facilities and systems for water purification, water treatment, and managed by-products. The Air Division designs, manufactures, and integrates air pollution emission control and measurement systems and related equipment. **NOTE:** Please visit website to view job listings and apply online. **Special programs:** Internships. **Corporate headquarters location:** Federal Way WA. **Other area locations:** Statewide. **Other U.S. locations:** Nationwide. **International locations:** Worldwide. **Operations at this facility include:** This location manufactures pulp and paper. **Listed on:** New York Stock Exchange. **Stock exchange symbol:** WY. **President/CEO:** Steven R. Rogel. **Number of employees worldwide:** 57,000.

WEYERHAEUSER COMPANY
5419 Hovis Road, Charlotte NC 28206-1241. 704/392-4141. **Contact:** Human Resources Manager. **World Wide Web address:** http://www.weyerhaeuser.com. **Description:** Weyerhaeuser Company's principal businesses are the growing and harvesting of timber; the manufacture, distribution, and sale of forest products including logs, wood chips, and building products; real estate development and construction; and financial services. Weyerhaeuser is one of the world's largest private owners of marketable softwood timber and one of the largest producers of softwood lumber and pulp. The company is also one of North America's largest producers of forest products and recyclers of office wastepaper, newspaper, and corrugated boxes. Weyerhaeuser Company also sells electricity to utility companies generated from its 15 trash-to-energy plants and 6 small cogeneration and recycling plants. The Water Division manufactures and operates facilities and systems for water purification, water treatment, and managed by-products. The Air Division designs, manufactures, and integrates air pollution emission control and measurement systems and related equipment. **NOTE:** Please visit website to view job listings and apply online. **Special programs:** Internships. **Corporate headquarters location:** Federal Way WA. **Other area locations:** Statewide. **Other U.S. locations:** Nationwide. **International locations:** Worldwide. **Listed on:** New York Stock Exchange. **Stock exchange symbol:** WY. **President/CEO:** Steven R. Rogel. **Number of employees at this location:** 90. **Number of employees worldwide:** 57,000.

WEYERHAEUSER COMPANY
P.O. Box 408, Newton NC 28658. 828/464-3841. **Physical Address:** 1525 Mount Olive Church Road, Newton NC 28658. **Fax:** 828/465-4615. **Contact:** General Manager. **World Wide Web address:** http://www.weyerhaeuser.com. **Description:**

Weyerhaeuser Company's principal businesses are the growing and harvesting of timber; the manufacture, distribution, and sale of forest products including logs, wood chips, and building products; real estate development and construction; and financial services. Weyerhaeuser is one of the world's largest private owners of marketable softwood timber and one of the largest producers of softwood lumber and pulp. The company is also one of North America's largest producers of forest products and recyclers of office wastepaper, newspaper, and corrugated boxes. Weyerhaeuser Company also sells electricity to utility companies generated from its 15 trash-to-energy plants and 6 small cogeneration and recycling plants. The Water Division manufactures and operates facilities and systems for water purification, water treatment, and managed by-products. The Air Division designs, manufactures, and integrates air pollution emission control and measurement systems and related equipment. **NOTE:** Please visit website to view job listings and apply online. **Special programs:** Internships. **Corporate headquarters location:** Federal Way WA. **Other area locations:** Statewide. **Other U.S. locations:** Nationwide. **International locations:** Worldwide. **Listed on:** New York Stock Exchange. **Stock exchange symbol:** WY. **President/CEO:** Steven R. Rogel. **Number of employees worldwide:** 57,000.

WEYERHAEUSER COMPANY
P.O. Box 230, Moncure NC 27559. 919/542-2311. **Physical Address:** 306 Corinth Road, Moncure NC 27559. **Contact:** William Whiteman, Human Resources. **World Wide Web address:** http://www.weyerhaeuser.com. **Description:** Weyerhaeuser Company's principal businesses are the growing and harvesting of timber; the manufacture, distribution, and sale of forest products including logs, wood chips, and building products; real estate development and construction; and financial services. Weyerhaeuser is one of the world's largest private owners of marketable softwood timber and one of the largest producers of softwood lumber and pulp. The company is also one of North America's largest producers of forest products and recyclers of office wastepaper, newspaper, and corrugated boxes. Weyerhaeuser Company also sells electricity to utility companies generated from its 15 trash-to-energy plants and 6 small cogeneration and recycling plants. The Water Division manufactures and operates facilities and systems for water purification, water treatment, and managed by-products. The Air Division designs, manufactures, and integrates air pollution emission control and measurement systems and related equipment. **NOTE:** Please visit website to view job listings and apply online. **Special programs:** Internships. **Corporate headquarters location:** Federal Way WA. **Other area locations:** Statewide. **Other U.S. locations:** Nationwide. **International locations:** Worldwide. **Listed on:** New York Stock Exchange. **Stock exchange symbol:** WY. **President/CEO:** Steven R. Rogel. **Number of employees worldwide:** 57,000.

WILDON SOFTWARE
PO Box 1565, Cary NC 27512. 919/835-1514. **Contact:** Human Resources. **E-mail address:** jobs@wildon.com. **World Wide Web Address:** http://www.wildon.com. **Description:** Provides IT professionals to business and government organizations in North Carolina. **Positions advertised include:** Computer Programmer; Technical Writer. **Corporate Headquarters:** This location.

WINGFOOT COMMERCIAL TIRE SYSTEMS
3916 Highway 74 West, Monroe NC 28110. 704/238-8277. **Fax:** 704/238-8774. **Contact:** Human Resources. **World Wide Web address:** http://www.wingfootct.com. **Description:** A retail and wholesale provider of new and off-road tires. The company also provides on- and off-road truck tire retreading and repairs, as well as related on- and off-site services. **NOTE:** Please visit website to view job listings. **Corporate headquarters location:** Fort Smith AR. **Other area locations:** Candler NC; Cary NC; Charlotte NC; Greensboro NC; Salisbury NC. **Other U.S. locations:** Nationwide. **Parent company:** Goodyear.

WINSTON HOTELS, INC.
2626 Glenwood Avenue, Suite 200, Raleigh NC 27608. 919/510-6010. **Fax:** 919/510-6832. **Contact:** Patti Belle, Human Resources. **World Wide Web address:** http://www.winstonhotels.com. **Description:** Owns 16 hotels, including 11 Hampton Inns in Georgia, North Carolina, South Carolina, and Virginia; and 5 Comfort Inns in North Carolina and Virginia. **Corporate headquarters location:** This location. **Listed on:** New York Stock Exchange. **Stock exchange symbol:** WXH. **CEO:** Robert W. Winton.

WINSTON-SALEM, CITY OF
P.O. Box 2511, Winston-Salem NC 27102. **Physical Address:** 101 North Main Street, Suite 53, Winston-Salem NC 27101. 336/747-6800. **Fax:** 336/748-3053. **Recorded jobline:** 336/631-6496. **Contact:** Human Resources. **World Wide Web address:** http://www.cityofws.org. **Description:** Responsible for hiring town employees for the city of Winston-Salem. **NOTE:** Please visit website to view job listings and download application form. **Positions advertised include:** Senior Utilities Plant Mechanic; Assistant Recreation Center Supervisor; Associate Engineering Technician; Casual Laborer; Custodian; Police Officer; Recreation Center Supervisor; Senior Crew Coordinator; Trades Helper; Utilities Plant Operator; Vehicle Operator.

WINSTON-SALEM INDUSTRIES FOR THE BLIND
7730 North Point Drive, Winston-Salem NC 27106-3310. 336/759-0551. **Toll-free phone:** 800/242-7726. **Fax:** 336/759-0990. **Contact:** Jim Collier, Manager of Human Resources. **E-mail address:** jcollier@wsifb.com. **World Wide Web address:** http://www.wsifb.com. **Description:** Provides training and employment workshops for the blind. Founded 1936. **NOTE:** Please visit website to view job listings and apply online, **Positions advertised include:** Retail Store Cashier. **Corporate headquarters location:** This location. **President:** Daniel J. Boucher.

WINSTON-SALEM JOURNAL
P.O. Box 3159, Winston-Salem NC 27102. 336/727-7211. **Physical address:** 418 North Marshall Street, Winston-Salem NC 27101. **Toll-free phone:** 800/642-0925. **Fax:** 336/727-4096. **Contact:** Gina Wingfield, Human Resources. **E-mail address:** gwingfield@wsjournal.com. **World Wide Web address:** http://www.journalnow.com. **Description:** A daily newspaper. **NOTE:** In order to be considered for employment, you must submit a signed employment application. For newsroom opportunities, address your resume and application to the editor of the department you are interested in. Please visit website to view job listings. Contact Human Resources directly at 336/727-7331. **Position advertised include:** Account Executive – Retail Advertising. **Special programs:** Internships. **Corporate headquarters location:** This location. **Parent company:** Media General, Inc. **Listed on:** New York Stock Exchange. **Stock exchange symbol:** MEG. **Annual sales/revenues:** $51 - $100 million. **Number of employees at this location:** 480. **Number of employees nationwide:** 9,000.

WOMBLE CARLYLE SANDRIDGE & RICE, PLLC
P.O. Box 831, Raleigh NC 27602. 919/755-2100. **Physical address:** 150 Fayetteville Street Mall, Suite 2100, Raleigh NC 27601. **Fax:** 919/755-2150. **Contact:** Professional Development and Recruiting. **E-mail address:** jbeavers@wcsr.com. **World Wide Web address:** http://www.wcsr.com. **Description:** One of the largest law firms in the Southeastern and mid-Atlantic U.S. Founded 1876. **NOTE:** For staff positions, contact John Turlington at 919/755-2117. **Special programs:** Summer Associate Program. **Other area locations:** Charlotte NC; Greensboro NC; Research Triangle Park NC; Winston-Salem NC. **Other U.S. locations:** Washington D.C.; Tyson's Corner VA; Atlanta GA.

THE WOMEN'S HOSPITAL OF GREENSBORO
801 Green Valley Road, Greensboro NC 27408. 336/832-6500. 7000. **Contact:** Human Resources. **E-mail address:** recruitment@mosescone.com. **World Wide Web address:** http://www.mosescone.com. **Description:** A family-centered, 115-bed facility, dedicated exclusively to the care of women and newborns. The hospital offers ultrasound, mammography, surgery, and outpatient treatment. In addition, an entire floor is dedicated to a Level III neonatal intensive care unit. The hospital also specializes in the area of perinatology. **NOTE:** Resumes should be sent to: Moses Cone Health System Recruitment Department, 1200 Elm Street, Greensboro NC 27401-1020. Phone is 336/832-7400, or 800/476-6737. Fax is 336/832-2999. Please visit website to search for jobs and apply online. **Positions advertised include:** Assistant Director – Nursing Leadership; Food Service Technician; Laundry Technician; Nursing Secretary; Nursing Technician; Phlebotomist; RN – Various Departments; Scheduler; Ultrasound Technician. **Parent company:** Moses Cone Health System. **Number of employees nationwide:** 6,900.

XEROX
P.O. Box 4006 Greenville NC 27836. 252/321-7994. **Physical address:** 1706-D East Arlington Boulevard, Greenville NC 27858. **Fax:** 252/353-0690. **Contact:** Personnel. **World Wide Web address:** http://www.xerox.com. **Description:** Provides printing and publishing services as well as network printer, copiers, and fax machines. **NOTE:** Please visit website to search for jobs and apply online. **Corporate headquarters location:** Stamford CT. **Other area locations:** Winston-Salem NC; Charlotte NC; Greensboro NC; Matthews NC; Rocky Mount NC. **Other U.S. locations:** Nationwide. **International locations:** Worldwide. **Operations at this facility include:** Sales. **Listed on:** New York Stock Exchange. **Stock exchange symbol:** XRX.

ABC SEAMLESS
3001 Fiechtner Drive, Fargo ND 58103. 701/293-5952. **Toll-free phone:** 800/732-6577. **Fax:** 701-293-3107. **Contact:** Don Jennings, General Manager. **E-mail address:** theduck@abcseamless.com. **World Wide Web address:** http://www.abcseamless.com. **Description:** Manufactures and installs siding, gutters, and replacement windows. **Positions advertised include:** Siding and Gutter Installer; Sales Person; Appointment Coordinator. **Corporate headquarters location:** This location. **Other U.S. locations:** Nationwide.130

ALERUS FINANCIAL
P.O. Box 6001, Grand Forks ND 58206. 701/795-3200. **Physical address:** 401 DeMers Avenue, Grand Forks ND 58201. **Toll-free phone:** 800/279-3200. **Fax:** 701/795-3355. **Contact:** Human Resources. **World Wide Web address:** http://www.alerusfinancial.com. **Description:** A bank. **Positions advertised include:** Accounting Operations. **Special programs:** Internships. **Office Hours:** M-F, 8-5. **Corporate headquarters location:** This location. **Other area locations:** Bismarck ND; Fargo ND; Northwood ND; West Fargo ND. **Operations at this facility include:** Administration; Sales. **Number of employees at this location:** 250.

ALTRU HOSPITAL
ALTRU HEALTH INSTITUTE
1000 South Columbia Road, P.O. Box 6003, Grand Forks ND 58206-6002. 701/780-6596. **Fax:** 701/780-6641. **Contact:** Human Resources. **E-mail address:** hr@altru.org. **World Wide Web address:** http://www.altru.org. **Description:** The hospital is a 277-bed regional facility providing patient care, health-related support services, and preventive services. Altru Health Institute is a 34-bed rehabilitation hospital providing occupational and physical therapies. **NOTE:** Physicians may contact the Physicians Recruiting Department at the above address or e-mail: Jkeller@Altru.org. **Positions advertised include:** Nursing Assistant; Support Service Technician; Billing Specialist; Communication Clerk; Health Unit Coordinator; Budget/Reimbursement and Charge Master Associate; Lab Receptionist; Phlebotomist. **Special programs:** Shadowing program; staff career development programs.

AMERICAN CRYSTAL SUGAR COMPANY
P.O. Box 190, Old Highway 44 North, Drayton ND, 58225. 701/454-3326. **Contact:** Wendy Maurstead, Personnel Coordinator. **World Wide Web address:** http://www.crystalsugar.com. **Description:** Processes and markets sugar and sugar beet pulp, molasses, and seed. Customers are primarily companies in the food processing industry throughout the United States. **Corporate headquarters location:** Moorhead MN. **Other U.S. locations:** Crookston MN; East Grand Forks MN; Hillsboro ND. **Subsidiaries include:** United Sugars Corporation; Midwest Agri-Commodities; ProGold Limited Liability Company; Crystech L.L.C. **Number of employees at this location:** 260.

AMERICAN CRYSTAL SUGAR COMPANY
Rural Route 2, Box 42, Hillsboro ND 58045. 701/436-5905. **Physical address:** Highway 81 North, Hillsboro ND. **Contact:** Mary Larson, Personnel Coordinator. **World Wide Web address:** http://www.crystalsugar.com. **Description:** Processes and markets sugar and sugar beet pulp, molasses, and seed. Customers are primarily companies in the food processing industry throughout the United States. **Corporate headquarters location:** Moorhead MN. **Other area locations:** Drayton ND. **Other U.S. locations:** Crookston MN; East Grand Forks MN. **Subsidiaries include:** United Sugars Corporation; Midwest Agri-Commodities; ProGold Limited Liability Company; Crystech L.L.C. **Number of employees at this location:** 270.

ATLAS BUSINESS SOLUTIONS, INC.
P.O. Box 9013, Fargo ND 58106-9013. 701/235-5226. **Physical address:** 3330 Fiechtner Drive SW, Fargo ND 58103. **Toll-free phone:** 800/874-8801. **Fax:** 701/280-0842. **Contact:** Jay Forknell. **E-mail address:** hr@abs-usa.com. **World Wide Web address:** http://www.abs-usa.com. **Description:** Develops business software. **Positions advertised include:** Technical Support Specialist; Marketing Manager; Customer Service Associate. **Corporate headquarters location:** This location.

BANK OF NORTH DAKOTA
P.O. Box 5509, Bismarck ND 58506. 701/328-5600. **Toll-free phone:** 800/472-2166. **Fax:** 701/328-5716. **Contact:** Gayle Ciavarella, Manager Human Resources. **E-mail address:** gciavare@state.nd.us **World Wide Web address:** http://www.banknd.com. **Description:** Bank of North Dakota offers financial services to promote the development of agriculture, commerce, and industry in North Dakota, and provides loans to individuals who want to pursue postsecondary educational opportunities. **Special programs:** Internships. **Office hours:** Monday - Friday, 8:00 a.m. - 5:00 p.m. **Corporate headquarters location:** This location. **Operations at this facility include:** Service. **Sales/revenue:** $33.1 million. **President:** Eric Hardmeyer.

BASIN ELECTRIC COMPANY
1717 East Interstate Avenue, Bismarck ND 58503-0564. 701/223-0441. **Fax:** 701/224-5336. **Contact:** Sharon Klein, Employment Coordinator. **World Wide Web address:** http://www.basinelectric.com. **Description:** Operates electricity generating power plants serving 1.8 million customers. **Positions advertised include:** Service Dispatcher, Safety Representative; Electronic Technologies Demonstrator; Laborer; Mechanical Engineer III. **Corporate Headquarters:** This Location. **Subsidiaries include:** Dakota Gasification Company. **Number of employees at this location:** 1700.

BETHANY HOMES, INC.
201 South University Drive, Fargo ND 58103. 701/239-3522. **Fax:** 701/239-3237. **Contact:** Adam Broers, Employment Coordinator. **E-mail address:** abroers@bethanyhomes.org. **World Wide Web address:** http://www.bethanyhomes.org. **Description:** A 192-bed nursing home and retirement living center. Bethany Homes is a nonprofit corporation affiliated with the Evangelical Lutheran Church of America. **NOTE:** Entry-level positions and second and third shifts are offered. **Positions advertised include:** Registered Nurse; LPN; Certified Nursing Assistant; Therapeutic Recreation Personnel; Housekeeper; Cook; Cook Helper; Dietary Aide; Home Health Aide; Sitter/Companion. **Special programs:** Training. **Number of employees at this location:** 420.

BLUE CROSS AND BLUE SHIELD OF NORTH DAKOTA
4510 13th Avenue SW, Fargo ND 58121-0001. 701/282-1864. **Toll-free phone:** 800/342-4718. **Fax:** 701/277-2216. **Contact:** Human Resources Department. **World Wide Web address:** http://www.noridian.com. **Description:** A nonprofit health care insurance organization providing managed health care plans to both individuals and groups. Blue Cross and Blue Shield offers Point-of-Service, individual health, PPO, and HMO plans. **Positions advertised include:** AVP Actuarial; Intern Tech Support; Facility Security (nights). **Special Programs:** Tuition assistance program; Internships. **Office hours:** Monday – Friday, 8:00 a.m. – 4:30 p.m. **Other area locations:** Grand Forks ND; Jamestown ND. **Other U.S. Locations:** Phoenix AZ; Golden CO; Honolulu HI; Des Moines IA; Prairie City IA; Eagan MN; Portland OR; Kent WA. **Subsidiaries include:** Noridian Administrative Services; Lincoln Mutual Life & Casualty Insurance Company; The Dental Service Corporation of North Dakota; North Dakota Vision Services, Inc.; Noridian Insurance Services, Inc.; Benefit Plan Administrators; North Dakota Caring Foundation. **Number of employees nationwide:** Over 2,000.

BORDER STATES ELECTRIC SUPPLY COMPANY
105 25th Street North P.O. Box 2767, Fargo ND 58108-2767 **Phone:** 701/293-5834. **Physical address:** 105 25th Street North Fargo, ND 58108. **Fax:** 602/231-8535. **Contact:** Mark Weed. **E-mail address:** mweed@border-states.com. **World Wide Web address:** http://www.bseweb.com. **Description:** A wholesale electric power distributor that specializes in maintenance, repair, and operating systems. **Positions advertised include:** Customer Service Representative. **Corporate headquarters location:** This location. **Other area locations:** Bismarck; Grand Forks; Minot; Williston; Dickinson. **Other U.S. locations:** Nationwide. **International locations:** Juarez, Mexico.

BORDER STATES PAVING, INC.
P.O. Box 2586, Fargo ND 58108-2586. 701/237-4860. **Physical address:** 4101 32nd Street North, Fargo ND. **Fax:** 701/237-0233. **Contact:** Human Resources. **Description:** An asphalt paving company. **NOTE:** Call to request an application to be mailed. **Corporate headquarters location:** This location. **Other area locations:** Jamestown ND.

CASE CORPORATION
P.O. Box 6006, Fargo ND 58108-6006. 701/293-4545. **Physical address:** 3000 7th Avenue, Fargo ND, 58102. **Contact:** Amy Possehl, Human Resources. **World Wide Web address:** http://www.casece.com. **Description:** Designs, manufactures, markets, and distributes farming machinery and equipment as well as small and medium-sized construction equipment. **Office hours:** Monday - Thursday, 8:00 a.m. - 5:00 p.m.; Friday, 8:00 a.m. - 12:00 p.m. **Other U.S. locations:** Racine WI; Burlington IA; Burr Ridge IL; Litchfield AZ; Rocky Mount NC; Wichita KS; Lexington KY. **International locations:** Worldwide. **Number of employees at this location:** 400.

CENTURY ELECTRIC
915 South 48th Street, Grand Forks ND 58201. 701/746-8727. **Fax:** 701/775-1132. **Contact:** Greg Matson or Brian Harris, Company Owners. **E-mail address:** gregm@centuryelect.com. **World Wide Web address:** http://www.centuryelect.com. **Description:** An electrical company that provides commercial, industrial, and residential wiring services in the tri-state area. Other services include plumbing through the Century Plumbing Branch, bakery and restaurant equipment supply and repairs, and computer service. **Office hours:** Monday – Friday, 8:00 a.m. – 4:30 p.m. **Corporate headquarters:** This location. **Other U.S. locations:** Brainerd MN.

CLARICA LIFE INSURANCE COMPANY
2000 44th Street SW, Suite 200, Fargo ND 58103. 701/237-5700. **Toll-free number:** 800/283-5433. **Fax:** 701/433-8242. **Contact:** Human Resources Department. **E-mail address:** jobs.us@clarica.com. **World Wide Web address:** http://www.clarica-us.com. **Description:** A life insurance company. **Office hours:** Monday – Friday, 7:30 a.m. – 5:00 p.m. **Corporate headquarters location:** This location. Also, Brookfield WI. **Other U.S. locations:** Nationwide. **International locations:** District of Columbia. **Parent Company:** Midland National Insurance Company. **Number of employees nationwide:** Over 6,000.

CLOVERDALE FOODS
P.O. Box 667, Mandan ND 58554. 701/663-9511. **Physical address:** 3015 34th Street NW, Mandan ND 58554. **Toll-free phone:** 800/669-9511. **Fax:** 701/663-0690. **Contact:** Personnel. **World Wide Web address:** http://www.cloverdalefoods.com. **Description:** A major processor of specialty hams, bacon, and other pork products. **NOTE:** Entry-level positions are offered. **Positions advertised include:** Sanitation Worker; Meat Cutter; Warehouse Position. **Corporate headquarters location:** This location. **Other U.S. locations:** Minot ND. **Operations at this facility include:** Manufacturing. **Number of employees at this location:** 200. **Number of employees nationwide:** 285.

COMMUNITY FIRST BANKSHARES, INC.
520 Main Avenue, 7th Floor, Fargo ND 58124-0001. 800/575-6677. **Contact:** Human Resources. **World Wide Web address:** http://www.cfbx.com. **Description:** A multibank holding company offering a full-line of banking, investment, trust, and insurance services. **Positions advertised include:** Consumer Documentation Specialist; ATM and Card Specialist; Call Center Representative; Records Clerk; Quality Control Specialist; Relationships Manager; Network Communication Analyst; Lead Sales Associate; Lien Perfection Specialist; Financial Services and Trust Manager; Fraud Detection Support; File Transfer Specialist; Customer Service Agent; Funds Transfer Representative; Administrative Assistant; Online Operations Specialist; Sales Support. **Special programs:** Career development programs with tuition reimbursement. **Corporate headquarters location:** This location. **Other area locations:** Wahpeton; Lidgerwood; Dickinson; Cooperstown. **Other U.S. locations:** AZ; CA; CO; IA; MN; NE; NM; SD; UT; WI; WY. **Subsidiaries include:** Community First National Bank. **Listed on:** NASDAQ. **Stock exchange symbol:** CFBX.

CONCRETE, INC.
5000 DeMers Avenue, Grand Forks ND 58201. 701/772-6687. **Toll-free phone:** 800/732-4261. **Fax:** 701/772-4315. **Contact:** Gerlinde Olson, Human Resources Director. **World Wide Web address:** http://www.ciprecast.com. **E-mail address:** info@ciprecast.com. **Description:** Provides a wide range of concrete building services including submitting bids, designing diagrams, manufacturing concrete beams and building materials, and erecting beams. **Corporate headquarters location:** This location. **Other U.S. locations:** SD; MN. **Parent company:** Wells Concrete Products Company. **Number of employees nationwide:** 150.

DAHLGREN & COMPANY, INC.
3901 15th Avenue North, Fargo ND 58102. 701/282-4313. **Contact:** Human Resources. **World Wide Web address:** http://www.sunflowerseed.com. **Description:** Supplies raw and roasted sunflower seeds to various food-related industries. This company processes, roasts, flavors, and packages a wide range of sunflower products. **Corporate headquarters location:** Crookston MN. **Other area locations:** Grace City ND. **International locations:** Worldwide. **Parent company:** National Sun Industries, Incorporated. **Operations at this facility include:** Processing and receiving of raw field run sunflowers. **Number of employees at this location:** 30. **Number of employees nationwide:** 140.

DAKOTA CLINIC/INNOVIS HEALTH
1701 South University Drive, 58104. 701/364-3432. **Toll-free number:** 800/437-4054x3432. **Recorded jobline:** 701/364-8169. **Contact:** Human Resources Manager. **E-mail address:** humanr@dakcl.com. **World Wide Web address:** http://www.dakotaclinic.com. **Description:** A chain of approximately 15 multispecialty clinics located throughout North Dakota and Minnesota. The clinics have a network of approximately 200 physicians, 100 of which practice at this location. **NOTE:** Innovis Health employment opportunities located under separate listing. **Positions advertised**

include: Medical Receptionist; LPN/Endocrinology; LPN/Neurology; CRNA; Radiation Therapist; Medical Technologist; Bloodbank Supervisor; Nuclear Medicine Technician; Radiology Technician; Ultrasound Supervisor; Ultrasound Technician. **Other area locations:** West Fargo; Medina; Jamestown; Valley City; Lisbon; Casseltor; Wahpeton; Hankinson. **Other U.S. locations:** MN.

DAN'S SUPERMARKET
1100 Weiss Avenue, Bismarck ND 58503. 701/258-2127. **Fax:** 701/258-0064 **E-mail:** dbosch@danssupermarket.com. **World Wide Web address:** http://www.danssupermarket.com. **Description:** A retail food store. **NOTE:** Apply at individual store locations. **Positions advertised include:** Cashier/Utility Worker. **Other area locations:** Bismarck; Dickinson; Mandan; Rapid City; Gillette. **Corporate headquarters location:** This location.

DICKINSON STATE UNIVERSITY
291 Campus Drive, Dickinson ND 58601-4896. 701/483-2507. **Toll-free phone:** 800/279-4295. **Fax:** 701/483-2177. **Contact:** Gail Ebeltoft, Personnel Services. **World Wide Web address:** http://www.dsu.nodak.edu. **Description:** A public liberal arts university with approximately 1,600 students and over 80 faculty members, which offers a wide range of baccalaureate, associate, and certificate programs. The university contains the School of Arts and Sciences; the School of Education, Health, Physical Education, and Recreation; the School of Business and Administration; and the School of Applied Sciences and Technology. Preprofessional programs are also offered in a number of fields including chiropractic, dentistry, engineering, forestry, home economics, law, medicine, medical/laboratory technology, mortuary science, optometry, physics, social work, and wildlife management. **Positions advertised include:** University Bookstore Assistant; Custodian; Administrative Assistant; Accounting Faculty Member.

FARGO ASSEMBLY COMPANY
P.O. Box 2340, Fargo ND 58108-2340. 701/298-3803x140. **Contact:** Ron Bergan, Human Resources. **World Wide Web address:** http://www.facnd.com. **Description:** Manufactures electronic wire harnesses for heavy equipment including tractors and combines. **Corporate headquarters location:** This location. **Other area locations:** Michigan ND; Edgely ND; Ellendale ND; Lehr ND. **Other U.S. locations:** KS; NE; PA. **Operations at this facility include:** Administration; Manufacturing. **Listed on:** Privately held. **Number of employees at this location:** 250. **Number of employees nationwide:** 700.

FARGO GLASS & PAINT COMPANY, INC.
P.O. Box 3107, Fargo ND 58108-3107. 701/235-4441. **Physical address:** 1801 7th Avenue North, Fargo ND 58102. **Contact:** Patty Ekren, Human Resources Department. **Description:** A wholesale paint, glass, millwork, and floor covering contracting firm.

FARGO PARK DISTRICT
701 Main Avenue, Fargo ND 58103. 701/241-8160. **Fax:** 781/241-8266 **Contact:** Jim Larson, Director of Finance and Human Resources. **E-mail address:** jlarson@fargoparks.com. **World Wide Web address:** http://www.fargoparks.com. **Description:** Handles staffing for maintenance and recreational programs for public parks in the Fargo area. **NOTE:** This location hires seasonally. **Positions advertised include:** Outdoor Recreation Instructor; Little People Sports Sampler Instructor/Supervisor; Adult Volleyball Referee. **Office hours:** Monday – Friday, 7:30 a.m. – 4:30 p.m.

FARGO PUBLIC SCHOOLS
415 North 4th Street, Fargo ND 58102. 701/446-1000. **Fax:** 701/446-1200. **Recorded jobline:** 701/446-1099. **Contact:** Nancy Jordheim, Assistant Superintendent for Human Resources. **E-mail address:** prowsja@fargo.k12.nd.us. **World Wide Web address:** http://www.fargo.k12.nd.us. **Description:** Administrative offices for the Fargo public school district. The district includes two high schools, an alternative community high school, three middle schools, thirteen elementary schools, one kindergarten center, and the Trollwood Performing Arts School. **Positions advertised include:** Special Education Paraprofessional; Trollwood Program Coordinator; Substitute Teacher.

THE FORUM
P.O. Box 2020, Fargo ND 58107. 701/451-5629. **Physical address:** 101 5th Street North, Fargo ND 58102. **Contact:** Human Resources. **World Wide Web address:** http://www.in-forum.com. **Description:** Publishes an independent daily newspaper. Weekday circulation is approximately 60,000. **NOTE:** Lloyd Case should be contacted for non-editorial positions; the Managing Editor should be contacted for editorial positions. **Positions advertised include:** Circulation Dockworker/Driver. **Other U.S. locations:** Moorhead; MN.

FRASER, LTD.
2902 South University Drive, Fargo ND 58103. 701/237-5775. **Contact:** Junelle Christianson, Director of Program Operations. **World Wide Web address:** http://www.fraserltd.org. **E-mail address:** fraser@fraserltd.org. **Description:** A social service agency. In addition to counseling, residential facilities, and other services to the elderly and developmentally disabled, childcare services are available. **NOTE:** For jobs in the childcare field, ask for the Childcare Coordinator. **Operations at this facility include:** An Adult Retirement Program and Residential Facilities; Fraser Hall Group Homes for the developmentally disabled; the Independent Living Training Program which encompasses Intermediate Care Facility Training, Transitional Community Living, and Minimally Supervised Living Arrangements; Fraser Childcare Services. **Number of employees at this location:** Over 130.

GRAND FORKS, CITY OF
P.O. Box 5200, Grand Forks ND 58206-5200. 701/746-2665. **Physical address:** 255 North 4th Street, Grand Forks ND 58203. **Recorded jobline:** 701/746-2663. **Contact:** Darryl Hovland, Director of Human Resources. **E-mail address:** info@grandforksgov.com. **World Wide Web address:** http://www.grandforksgov.com. **Description:** Provides municipal services for the city of Grand Forks. **Positions advertised include:** Director of Urban Development; Senior Office Specialist; Accounting Technician; Communications Specialist; Office Specialist; Equipment Operator.

HOLSUM BAKERY
P.O. Box 2563, Fargo ND 58108. 701/235-5595. **Contact:** Personnel Department. **Description:** Manufactures wholesale baked goods. Holsum Bakery operates semi-automatic bread and bun manufacturing plants in the Midwest. **Corporate headquarters location:** Phoenix AZ. **Parent company:** Pan-O-Gold Baking Company. **Operations at this facility include:** Administration; Manufacturing; Research and Development; Sales; Service.

IR BOBCAT COMPANY
P.O. Box 5556, Bismarck ND 58506-5556. 701/222-5906. **Physical address:** 521 South 22nd Street, Bismarck ND 58506-5556. **Fax:** 701/222-5192. **Contact:** Human Resources Department. **World Wide Web address:** http://www.bobcat.com. **Description:** A manufacturer of farming machinery and equipment. **NOTE:** Applicants can view all openings and apply online at the Ingersoll-Rand Corporate Website for general consideration. **Corporate headquarters location:** West Fargo ND. **Other U.S. locations:** Gwinner ND; Grove City MN; Erskine MN; Miami FL. **International locations:** Worldwide. **Parent Company:** Ingersoll-Rand.

IR BOBCAT COMPANY
P.O. Box 128, Gwinner ND 58040-0128. 701/678-6240. **Physical address:** 210 First Avenue NE, Gwinner ND 58040-0128. **Contact:** Human Resources Department. **World Wide Web address:** http://www.bobcat.com. **Description:** A manufacturer of farming machinery and equipment. **NOTE:** Applicants can view all openings and apply online at the Ingersoll-Rand Corporate Website for general consideration. **Corporate headquarters location:** West Fargo ND. **Other U.S. locations:** Bismarck ND; Grove City MN; Erskine MN; Phoenix AZ; Miami FL. **International locations:** Worldwide. **Operations at this facility include:** Manufacturing.

IMATION CORPORATION
2100 15th Street North, Wahpeton ND 58075. 701/642-8711. **Fax:** 701/642-8206. **Contact:** Marilee Tischer, Human Resources. **E-mail address:** info@imation.com. **World Wide Web address:** http://www.imation.com. **Description:** Imation provides systems, products, and services for the handling, storage, transmission, and use of information. The company develops data storage products, medical imaging and photo products, printing and publishing systems, and customer support technologies and document imaging, and markets them under the trademark names Dry View laser imagers, Matchprint and Rainbow color proofing systems, Travan data cartridges, and LS-120 diskette technology. **NOTE:** Imation requests that jobseekers apply using its online form. Resumes that are submitted without requisition numbers may be returned. If interested in a production job opening, applications are taken at Jobservice (phone: 701/671-1500.) **Positions advertised include:** Maintenance Technician. **Special Programs:** Internships; Internal Courses. **Other U.S. locations:** Tuscon AZ; Camarillo CA; Miami FL; Oakdale MN; Weatherford OK; Nekoosa WI. **International locations:** Worldwide. **Operations at this facility include:** The manufacturing of diskettes. **Listed on:** New York Stock Exchange and Chicago Stock Exchange. **Stock exchange symbol:** IMN. **Number of employees worldwide:** 10,000.

INDUSTRIAL BUILDERS, INC.
P.O. Box 406, Fargo ND 58107. 701/282-4977. **Fax:** 701/281-1409. **Contact:** Human Resources Department. **E-mail address:** info@industrialbuilders.com. **World Wide Web address:** http://www.industrialbuilders.com. **Description:** A full-service general construction firm. **Corporate headquarters location:** This location. **President:** Paul W. Diederich.

LUTHERAN SOCIAL SERVICES OF NORTH DAKOTA
P.O. Box 389, Fargo ND 58107. 701/235-7341. **Physical address:** 1325 11th Street South, Fargo ND 58103. **Fax:** 701/471-3296. **Contact:** Kathy Thoresen, Human Resources Director. **World Wide Web address:** http://www.lssnd.org. **Description:** One of North Dakota's largest private social service agencies. Lutheran Social Services offers a wide range of programs and services including adoption assistance, pregnancy counseling, residential treatment for emotionally disturbed children, youth advocacy services, and addiction outreach. The organization also offers a variety of services to the elderly including rehabilitation, companion services, independent living, and social and educational programs for the handicapped. **NOTE:** See Website for a regularly updated list of job openings. **Positions advertised include:** Senior Companion; Attendant Care Worker; Mentor for Native Americans. **Office hours:** Monday, Wednesday, Friday, 8:00 a.m. – 5:00 p.m.; Tuesday, Thursday, 8:00 a.m. – 8:30 p.m. **Other area locations:** Bismarck ND; Grand Forks ND, Minot ND; Williston ND. **Operations at this facility include:** Center for New Americans; Independent Living Program; Youth Court Program; Great Plains Food Banks; Multicultural Children Services.

MERCY MEDICAL CENTER
1301 15th Avenue West, Williston ND 58801. 701/774-7454. **Fax:** 701/774-7670. **Contact:** Jim Hansel, Human Resources Director. **E-mail address:** JimHansel@CHI-Midwest.org. **World Wide Web address:** http://www.mercy-williston.org. **Description:** A 134-bed acute care facility. Mercy Medical Center is a member of Catholic Health Initiatives. **Positions advertised include:** Environmental Service Technician; Licensed Practical Nurse; Licensed Registered Dietician; Medical Technologist; Nurse Assistant (certified and non-certified); Occupational Therapist; Pharmacist; Physical Therapist; Registered Nurse. **Number of employees at this location:** Over 500.

MERITCARE MEDICAL CENTER
P.O. Box MC, Fargo ND 58122. 701/234-2728. **Physical address:** 720 4th Street North, Fargo ND 58122. **Toll-free number:** 800/437-4010x2728. **Fax:** 701/288-4989. **Contact:** Bonnie Green, Human Resources. **E-mail address:** bonniegreen@meritcare.com. **World Wide Web address:** http://www.meritcare.com. **Description:** A medical center that is comprised of a regional network of twenty-four primary care clinics. **Positions advertised include:** Clinical Coordinator; House Administrator; Cardiovascular Sonographer; Childcare Teacher; Child Interview Specialist; Clinical Nurse Specialist; CT Scanning Technologist; Cytotechnologist; Dosimetrist; DRG Documentation Specialist; Flight Paramedic; Hand Therapist; Industrial Hygienist; Mammography Technologist; Master Level Counselor; Medical Technologist; Nuclear Medicine Technologist; Nurse Practitioner; Nurse Practitioner – Neonatology; Occupational Therapist; Oral Surgeon/Dentist; Pharmacist; Physical Therapist; Physician; Physician Assistant; Physicist; Psychologist; Radiation Therapist; Radiologic Technologist; Recreation Therapist; Registered Nurse; Respiratory Therapist; Service Education Facilitator; Social Worker; Speech/Language Pathologist; Coding Specialist; Insurance Processing/Office Specialist; Office Assistant; Distribution Worker; Cook; Environmental Services Worker. **Special Programs:** Tuition assistance program. **Operations at this facility include:** Administration; Service. **Other area locations:** West Fargo; Hatton; Mayville; Enderlin; Wahpeton; Hillsboro; LaMoure; Edgely; Gackle; Jamestown; Wimbledon. **Other U.S. locations:** MN. **Number of employees at this location:** 2,500.

MICROSOFT GREAT PLAINS BUSINESS SOLUTIONS
One Lone Tree Road, Fargo ND 58104-3911. 701/281-6500. **Toll-free phone:** 800/456-0025. **Fax:** 701/281-3752. **Recorded job line:** 701/281-6500. **Contact:** Human Resources. **E-mail address:** careerinfo@greatplains.com. **World Wide Web address:** http://www.greatplains.com. **Description:** A leading developer of integrated and modular accounting and financial management software. The company offers solutions for customers ranging from small businesses to mid-range corporations. **NOTE:** Applicants can register online with Microsoft Careers. A feature called Job Agent then notifies you of available positions, according to your interests, via e-mail.

Positions advertised include: New Product Development Manager; Product Planner; Query Services Program Manager; Software Design Engineer; Application Framework PM; Program Manager; Application Developer; Program Manager – Financial Design; Systems Administrator; System Designer Engineer; Professional Services Program Manager; Event Production Manager; Software Test Engineer; Custom Account Manager; Outsource Partner Manager; Software Development Engineer; Test Manager; Customer Sales Consultant; Technical Writer; Administrative Assistant; Curriculum Designer; Software Test Engineer; Program Writer; Senior Financial Analyst. **Special programs:** Educational Training; Internships. **Corporate headquarters:** Redmond WA. **Other area locations:** Nationwide. **International locations:** Worldwide. **Operations at this location include:** Business software production. **Listed on:** NASDAQ. **Stock Exchange Symbol:** MSFT. **Number of employees at this location:** 550. **Number of employees worldwide:** Over 50,000.

MIDCONTINENT COMMUNICATIONS
719 Memorial Highway, Bismarck ND 58504. 701/223-4000. **Toll-free phone:** 800/888-1300. **Contact:** Lisa Peterson, Human Resources. **E-mail address:** employment@midco.net. **World Wide Web address:** http://www.midcocomm.com. **Description:** Provider of cable television, local and long-distance telephone, Internet access, paging, cable advertising, and radio software and services. MidContinent Communications is partnered with AT&T Broadband and Internet Services. **Other area locations:** Statewide. **Other U.S. locations:** SD; NE; MN. **Parent Company:** MidContinent Media, Incorporated.

MINNKOTA POWER COOPERATIVE, INC.
P.O. Box 13200, Grand Forks ND 58208-3200. 701/795-4000. **Physical address:** 1822 Mill Road, Grand Forks ND 58206-3200. **Fax:** 701/795-4214. **Contact:** Dee Rostberg, Human Resources. **E-mail address:** minnkota@minnkota.com. **World Wide Web address:** http://www.minnkota.com. **Description:** A supplier of electricity to approximately 300,000 people in northwestern Minnesota and eastern North Dakota. **Other area locations:** Statewide. **Other U.S. locations:** MN. **President/CEO:** David Loer.

MINOT STATE UNIVERSITY
500 University Avenue West, Minot ND 58707. 701/858-3361. **Toll-free phone:** 800/777-0750. **Fax:** 701/858-3396. **Contact:** Ron Rogelstad, Human Resources. **E-mail address:** msujobs@minotstateu.edu. **World Wide Web address:** http://www.minotstateu.edu. **Description:** A small university comprised of four undergraduate colleges, including a College of Arts and Sciences, of Business, of Education and Health Services, and a graduate school. Minot State offers over forty majors, fourteen master's degrees, and several pre-professional programs. **NOTE:** Resumes can be sent to MSU Career Services Office; Second Floor, Student Union. **Office Hours:** Monday – Friday, 8:00 a.m. – 4:30 p.m. **Positions advertised include:** Secretary; Small Business Development Region Director; Small Business Development Center Consultant; Scheduling Coordinator; Dean of the College of Education and Health Sciences. **President:** Dr. H. Erik Shaar. **Number of employees at this location:** 850.

MISSOURI SLOPE LUTHERAN CARE CENTER
2425 Hillview Avenue, Bismarck ND 58501. 701/223-9407. **Contact:** Patty Tangen, Director of Human Resources. **Description:** A nonprofit, residential nursing home. Founded in 1967. **NOTE:** Second and third shifts are offered. **Company slogan:** Together enriching life. **Special programs:** Internships; Training; Co-ops; Summer Jobs. **Corporate headquarters location:** This location. **Administrator:** Robert Thompson.

NAVIGATION TECHNOLOGIES CORPORATION
1715 Gold Drive, Fargo ND 58102-6400. 701/476-6104. **Fax:** 312/894-7263. **Contact:** Bill Sorenson, Human resources Manager. **E-mail address:** career@navtech.com. **World Wide Web address:** http://www.navtech.com. **Description:** Provides digital map information, software, and services for numerous applications, such as vehicle navigation, mapping and geographic information systems. Areas of specialization include Internet/wireless applications and business solutions. Founded in 1985 in Silicon Valley CA. **Corporate headquarters location:** Chicago IL. **Other U.S. locations:** Nationwide. **International locations:** The United Kingdom; France; Spain; Portugal; Italy; Czech Republic; Switzerland; Austria; Germany; Benelux; the Nordics. **Operations at this facility include:** This location is the company's worldwide production facility. **President/CEO:** Judson Green. **Number of employees worldwide:** Over 1,100.

NORTH DAKOTA STATE UNIVERSITY
P.O. Box 5345 – University Station, Old Main Room 205, Fargo ND 58105. 701/231-8525. **Toll Free Phone:** 800/366-6888. **Fax:** 710/231-9686. **Contact:** Colette Erickson, Assistant Director of Personnel. **E-mail address:** NDSU.hr@ndsu.nodak.edu. **World Wide Web address:** http://www.ndsu.nodak.edu. **Description:** A four-year state university offering undergraduate and graduate degree programs. **NOTE:** NSDU lists its open faculty positions and professional staff positions at Higher Education Jobs Online: http://www.higherjobs.com. **Positions advertised include:** Secretary/Receptionist; Custodian; Microbiologist; Research Specialist; Ruminant Nutrition Technician; Hall Director; Sign Language Interpreter; Director of Student Financial Services; Head Soccer Coach; Head Football Coach; Postdoctoral Research Fellow; Assistant/Associate Professor (position open in numerous departments); Nutrition Education Agent; Extension Agent; Part-time Lecturer; Clinical Assistant Professor; Plant Cell Biologist. **Office hours:** Monday – Friday, 8:00 a.m. – 5:00 p.m. **President:** Joseph A. Chapman. **Number of employees at this location:** 2,000.

RADISSON HOTEL FARGO
201 5th Street North, Fargo ND 58102. 701/232-7363. **Fax:** 701/298-9134. **Contact:** Human Resources. **World Wide Web address:** http://www.radisson.com. **Description:** A 151-room hotel offering seven meeting rooms. **Other U.S. locations:** Nationwide. **International locations:** Worldwide. **Executive Vice-president/Brand Leader:** Bjorn Gullaksen.

ST. ALEXIUS PRIMECARE
900 East Broadway Avenue, Bismarck ND 58501. 701/530-7175. **Recorded jobline:** 701/530-7160. **Contact:** Jackie Heil, Employment Coordinator. **E-mail address:** jheil@primecare.com. **World Wide Web address:** http://www.st.alexius.org. **Description:** A 302-bed regional Catholic hospital that provides inpatient and outpatient healthcare services. Founded in 1885 by a group of Benedictine nuns. **Positions advertised include:** General Psychiatrist; Child/Adolescent Psychiatrist; Emergency Medicine Physician; Neurosurgeon; Customer Service Representative; Account Representative; Medical Transcriptionist; Messenger Clerk; Certified Nurse Assistant; Communication Clerk; Staff Accountant; Chaplain; Social Worker; Pharmacist; Respiratory Therapist; Speech/Language Pathologist; Surgical Technician; LPN; Registered Nurse; Clinical Coordinator; Perioperative Clinical Educator; Aide; Custodian; Personal Care Attendant; Exercise Physiology Aide; Phlebotomist; Physical Therapy Aide; Psychiatry Technician; Nurse Assistant. **Office hours:** Monday – Friday, 8:00 a.m. – 4:30 p.m.

ST. JOSEPH'S HOSPITAL AND HEALTH CENTER
30 West 7th Street, Dickinson ND 58601. 701/456-4000. **Recorded Jobline:** 701/456-4554. **Contact:** Human Resources. **World Wide Web address:** http://www.stjoeshospital.org. **Description:** A 109-bed, community-based hospital with a medical staff comprised of over 30 physicians. The hospital offers an array of services, including diabetes education; obstetrics and gynecology services; a cancer center; various specialized clinics; critical care; mental health services; home care; diagnostics; medical/surgical services; children's services; Medquest Medical Equipment provision; nutrition services, restorative and rehabilitation Services; rural health clinics; a sleep diagnostics program. **Positions advertised include:** Registered Nurse; Charge Nurse; LPN; Scrub Technician; Respiratory Care Practitioner; Certified Registered Nurse Anesthetist; Nurse Practitioner; Certified Medical Assistant; Occupational Therapist; Occupational Therapy Assistant; Director of Radiology. **Subsidiaries include:** St. Joseph LifeCare Foundation coordinates fundraising, outreach education, support groups, and public relations.

SIOUX MANUFACTURING CORPORATION
P.O. Box 400, Fort Totten ND 58335. 701/766-4211x238. **Fax:** 701/766-4089. **Contact:** John Lohnes, Human Resources Supervisor. **E-mail address:** siouxman@siouxmanufacturing.com. **World Wide Web address:** http://www.siouxmanufacturing.com. **Description:** A textile manufacturer. Products include structural and ballistic composites and camouflage netting systems. **Office hours:** Monday – Friday, 7:30 a.m. – 4:00 p.m. **Corporate headquarters location:** This location. **Operations at this facility include:** Administration; Manufacturing; Research and Development.

TESORO PETROLEUM
900 Old Red Trail NE, Mandan ND 58554. 701/667-2400. **Contact:** Marcy Blotsky, Human Resources Manager. **World Wide Web address:** http://www.tesoropetroleum.com. **Description:** Engaged in the refining, transportation, and marketing of natural gas, crude oil, and related products. Other operations include exploration and oil field services such as supplying lubricants, fuels, and specialty products to the U.S. drilling industry, as well as the provision of marine logistics services. **Corporate headquarters location:** San Antonio TX. **Other U.S. locations:** AK; HI; UT; WA. **Listed on:** New York and Pacific Stock Exchanges. **Stock exchange symbol:** TSO. **Executive Vice President:** Thomas E. Rheardon. **Sales/Revenues:** Over $5 billion.

TRINITY HOSPITAL
P.O. Box 5020, Minot ND 58702-5020. 701/857-5191. **Physical address:** One West Burdick Expressway West, Minot ND 58701. **Toll-free phone:** 800/862-0005. **Fax:** 701/852-2132. **Contact:** Human Resources. **E-mail address:** jobs@trinityhealth.org. **World Wide Web address:** http://www.trinityhealth.org. **Description:** A 250-bed hospital that provides inpatient and outpatient medical care. Other services include home care, mental health services, pastoral care, and diagnostics services. **Positions advertised include:** LPN; Addiction Counselor; Licensed Counselor; Psychologist; Radiation Therapist; Office Assistant; Opthalmic Assistant; Surgical Technician; Certified Nursing Assistant; Childcare Provider; Registered Nurse; Occupational Therapist; Central Processing Unit Technician; Coder; Housekeeper; Human Resources Assistant; Maintenance Worker; Nursing Aide; Occupational Therapy Coordinator; Office Assistant; Physical Therapy Assistant; Pharmacy Technician; Respiratory Therapist; Social Worker. **Special Programs:** Internships. **President/CEO:** Terry G. Hoff.

TURTLE MOUNTAIN CORPORATION
P.O. Box 940, Dunseith ND 58329. 701/244-5242x116. **Physical address:** First Street South, Dunseith ND 58329. **Contact:** Robyn Engelstad, Human Resources. **E-mail address:** robyn.engelstad@turtlemtn.com. **World Wide Web address:** http://www.turtlemtn.com. **Description:** Develops and manufactures electronic circuit boards for IBM and other computer companies. **Other U.S. locations include:** St. Paul MN. **Parent company:** PEMSTAR, Inc. **Operations at this facility include:** Production. **Number of employees at this location:** 260.

U.S. BANK
P.O. Box 5515, Bismarck ND 58502. 701/222-6262. **Physical address:** 200 North 3rd Street, Bismarck ND 58501. **Toll-free phone:** 800/872-2657. **Fax:** 701/2272-6200. **Contact:** Human Resources. **World Wide Web address:** http://www.usbank.com. **Description:** A national banking institution. **Positions advertised include:** Financial Consultant. **Special Programs:** Tuition Reimbursement; Financial Training Courses; Adoption Assistance Reimbursement Program. **Office hours:** Monday – Friday, 9:00 a.m. – 4:00 p.m. **Other area locations:** Fargo ND; Langdon ND; Dickinson ND; Valley City ND; Williston ND; Minot ND; Jamestown ND; Grand Forks ND; Beulah ND; Grafton ND. **Other U.S. locations:** Nationwide. **Parent Company:** U.S. Bancorp. **Listed on:** New York Stock Exchange. **Stock exchange symbol:** USB.

UNIVERSITY OF MARY
7500 University Drive, Bismarck ND 58504. 701/255-7500. **Fax:** 701/255-7687. **Contact:** Sister Rosanne Zastoupil, Human Resources. **E-mail address:** mzastoup@umary.edu. **World Wide Web address:** http://www.umary.edu. **Description:** An independent, nonprofit Catholic university with approximately 165 faculty members. The University of Mary offers 22 undergraduate majors and bachelor of arts, bachelor of science, and bachelor of university studies degrees. Preprofessional programs include chiropractic, dentistry, law, medicine, pharmacy, physical therapy, optometry, and veterinary. The university also offers master's degree programs in education, nursing, and management. **Positions advertised include:** French Teacher; English Composition Teacher; Public Speaking Teacher; Music Theory Instructor; Choir Director; Adult Learner Coordinator; Physical Therapy Department Secretary/Receptionist; Registrar; Head Women's Basketball Coach; Women's Residence Hall Director; Tutor Coordinator. **University President:** Sister Thomas Welder.

UNIVERSITY OF NORTH DAKOTA (UND)
Box 8010, Grand Forks ND 58202. 701/777-4361. **Fax:** 701/777-4857. **Recorded jobline:** 701/777-6200. **Contact:** Diane Nelson, Personnel Director. **E-mail address:** human.resources@mail.und.nodak.edu. **World Wide Web address:** http://www.und.edu. **Description:** A liberal arts University offering 150 programs of graduate and undergraduate study, including special programs in humanities, integrated studies, honors, and cooperative education. It was founded in 1883, six years before North Dakota achieved statehood. **Positions advertised include:** Project Coordinator; Assistant Athletic Director; Administrative Secretary; Study Abroad Program Assistant; Marketing Coordinator; Information Technical Services Specialist; Staff Psychologist; Research Scientist/Engineer; Receptionist; Administrative Assistant; Building Services Technician. **University President:** Dr. Charles E. Kupchella.

VANITY SHOPS, INC.
P.O. Box 547, Fargo ND 58107. 701/237-3330. **Physical address:** 1001 25th Street, North, Fargo ND 58102. **Contact:** Human Resources. **World Wide Web address:** http://www.vanityshops.com. **Description:** A clothing retailer for girls and young women with over 150 stores across the country. **Corporate headquarters:** This location. **Other area locations:** Jamestown,; Grand Forks; Bismarck; Dickinson; Minot. **Other U.S. locations:** Nationwide. **Operations at this facility include:** Development of product lines and visual merchandising plans, advertising, and general support of company stores.

WBI HOLDINGS, INC.
P.O. Box 5601, Bismarck ND 58506-5650. 701/220-7900. **Physical address:** 918 East Divide Avenue, Bismarck ND 58506. **Fax:** 701/530-1099. **Contact:** Laurie Kadrmas, Vice-President of Human Resources, or Stacie Fischer, Senior Human Resources Coordinator. **World Wide Web address:** http://www.wbip.com. **Description:** Provides a broad range of natural gas services that include transportation, storage, gathering, production, and sales along with a full spectrum of energy-related administrative services. **NOTE:** Entry-level positions are offered. **Special programs:** Training. **Corporate headquarters location:** This location. **Subsidiaries include:** Innovatum, Incorporated; Prairielands Energy Marketing, Incorporated; WBI Southern, Incorporated; Williston Basin Interstate Pipeline Company; Fidelity Oil Group; Connolly-Pacific Company; Knife River Corporation. **Parent company:** MDU Resources Group, Inc. **Listed on:** New York Stock Exchange. **Stock exchange symbol:** MDU. **Annual sales/revenue:** Over $100 million. **Chairman/ President/CEO:** Martin A. White. **Number of employees at this location:** 335. **Number of employees nationwide:** 6,568.

WDAY-TV-AM
P.O. Box 2020, Fargo ND 58103. 701/237-6500. **Physical address:** 301 8th Street South, Fargo ND 58108. **Contact:** Kate Freimanis, Human Resources. **E-mail address:** djurg@forumcomm.com. **World Wide Web address:** http://www.in-forum.com /wday. **Description:** Operates an AM radio station and an ABC-affiliated television station and newspaper

WELLS FARGO BANK
2 6th Avenue North, Casselton ND 58012. 701/347-5491. **Recorded Jobline:** 888/534-5757. **Contact:** Human Resources. **World Wide Web address:** http://www.wellsfargo.com. **Description:** A diversified financial institution with over $234 billion in assets. Wells Fargo serves over 17 million customers through 5,300 independent locations worldwide. The company also maintains several stand-alone ATMs and branches within other retail outlets. Services include community banking, credit and debit cards, home equity and mortgage loans, online banking, student loans, and insurance. Wells Fargo also offers a complete line of commercial and institutional financial services. Founded in 1852. **Special programs:** Tuition reimbursement; Summer Internships; **Corporate headquarters location:** San Francisco CA. **Other U.S. locations:** Nationwide. **International locations:** Worldwide. **Listed on:** New York Stock Exchange. **Stock exchange symbol:** WFC. **Annual sales/revenues:** More than $100 million. **Number of employees nationwide:** Over 10,000. **Number of employees worldwide:** 130,000.

WELLS FARGO BANK
406 Main Avenue, Fargo ND 58103. 701/293-4219. **Recorded Jobline:** 888/534-5757. **Contact:** Human Resources. **World Wide Web address:** http://www.wellsfargo.com. **Description:** A diversified financial institution with over $234 billion in assets. Wells Fargo serves over 17 million customers through 5,300 independent locations worldwide. The company also maintains several stand-alone ATMs and branches within other retail outlets. Services include community banking, credit and debit cards, home equity and mortgage loans, online banking, student loans, and insurance. Wells Fargo also offers a complete line of commercial and institutional financial services. Founded in 1852. **Special programs:** Tuition reimbursement; Summer Internships; **Corporate headquarters location:** San Francisco CA. **Other U.S. locations:** Nationwide. **International locations:** Worldwide. **Listed on:** New York Stock Exchange. **Stock exchange symbol:** WFC. **Annual sales/revenues:** More than $100 million. **Number of employees nationwide:** Over 10,000. **Number of employees worldwide:** 130,000.

WILLISTON STATE COLLEGE
P.O. Box 1326, Williston ND 58802. 701/774-4200, extension 4240. **Physical address:** 1410 University Drive, Williston ND 58802. **Contact:** Brenda Wigness, Personnel Director. **World Wide Web address:** http://www.wsc.nodak.edu. **Description:** A two-year community college with an enrollment of 800 undergraduate students. **Positions advertised include:** Massage Therapy Instructor; Chemistry Instructor. **President:** Joe McCann. **Number of employees at this location:** Over 100.

XCEL ENERGY
P.O. Box 2747, Fargo ND 58108. **Physical Address:** 2302 Great Northern Drive, Fargo ND 58102. 701/241-8607. **Fax:** 612/330-7935. 2302 Great Northern Drive, Fargo ND 58102 **Toll free phone:** 800/481-4700. **Contact:** Personnel Department. **E-mail address:** apply@xcelenergy.com. **World Wide Web address:** http://www.xcelenergy.com. **Description:** Xcel Energy generates, transmits, and distributes electric energy. The company also transports and distributes natural gas. **NOTE:** Resumes are processed at Corporate Headquarters. Please send all resumes to: Xcel Energy Recruitment and Selection, 414 Nicollet Mall, Minneapolis MN 55401. Xcel only accepts applications for advertised positions. Entry-level positions are available. **Special programs:** Internship and Apprenticeship programs. **Corporate headquarters location:** Minneapolis MN. **Listed on:** New York, Chicago, and Pacific Stock Exchanges. **Stock exchange symbol:** XEL. **Chairman/ President/Chief Executive Officer:** Wayne Brunetti. **Sales/Revenues:** $1.6 million. **Number of employees nationwide:** Over 13,000.

AAP ST. MARYS CORPORATION
P.O. Box 419, 1100 McKinley Road, St. Marys OH 45885. 419/394-7840. **Fax:** 419/394-4776. **Contact:** Personnel Manager. **E-mail address:** aap@bright.net. **World Wide Web address:** http://www.aapstmarys.com. **Description:** Designs, manufactures, and markets wheels for the automotive industry. Founded in 1988. **Parent company:** Hitachi Metals America, Ltd. **Number of employees at this location:** 250.

ABB AUTOMATION, INC.
650 Ackerman Road, Columbus OH 43202. 614/261-2000. **Fax:** 614/261-2267. **Contact:** Human Resources. **World Wide Web address:** http://www.abb.com. **Description:** Designs and develops process control systems and related instrumentation. **Special Programs:** Internships; Global Trainee Programs. **Number of employees nationwide:** 1,650. **Listed on:** NYSE. **Stock exchange symbol:** AAB.

ABB AUTOMATION, INC.
29801 Euclid Avenue, Wickliffe OH 44092. 440/585-8500. **Fax:** 440/585-8756. **Contact:** Human Resources. **World Wide Web address:** http://www.abb.com. **Description:** Designs and develops process control systems and related instrumentation. **Number of employees nationwide:** 1,650. **Listed on:** NYSE. **Stock exchange symbol:** AAB.

ADPI
P.O. Box 499, Troy OH 45373-0499. 937/339-2241. **Physical address:** 251 South Mulberry Street, Troy OH 45373. **Toll-free phone:** 800/758-1041. **Fax:** 937/339-0070. **Contact:** Human Resources. **E-mail address:** info@adpi.com. **World Wide Web address:** http://www.adpi.com. **Description:** Designs, manufactures, and markets data acquisition and transfer products for engineers, manufacturers, plant operators, and field technicians. Founded in 1978. **President/CEO:** Jerry Davis.

AK STEEL CORPORATION
703 Curtis Street, Middletown OH 45043. 513/425-5000. **Toll-free phone:** 800/331-5050. **Fax:** 513/425-2676. **Contact:** Human Resources. **World Wide Web address:** http://www.aksteel.com. **Description:** An industrial manufacturer producing flat-rolled steels for the automotive, appliance, and construction industries. **NOTE:** Entry-level positions are offered. **Special programs:** Internships; Co-ops. **Corporate headquarters location:** This location. **Other area locations:** Mansfield OH. **Other U.S. locations:** Rockport IN; Ashland KY; Butler PA. **Operations at this facility include:** Administration; Manufacturing; Sales. **Listed on:** New York Stock Exchange. **Stock exchange symbol:** AKS. **Annual sales/revenues:** More than $100 million. **Number of employees nationwide:** 11,000.

AMS SERVICES, INC.
3737 Park East Drive, Suite 202, Beachwood OH 44122. 216/464-2180. **Toll-free phone:** 800/888-8144. **Contact:** Human Resources. **World Wide Web address:** http://www.ams-services.com. **Description:** Designs software for insurance agencies. **Corporate headquarters location:** Windsor CT.

ANH REFRACTORIES COMPANY
384 Pyro Road, Oak Hill OH 45656. 740/682-7711. **Contact:** Human Resources. **E-mail address:** humanresources@anhrefractories.com. **World Wide Web address:** http://www.hwr.com. **Description:** Develops, manufactures, and markets a complete line of refractory products for the aluminum production, chemical processing, copper, iron production, minerals processing, steel handling, and steel production industries. AP Green Refractories of Oak Hill specializes in the production of basic brick, castables, fiber, fireclay, high-alumina brick, insulating firebrick, mortars, plastics, silica, and UNACAST pre-cast shapes. **NOTE:** Resumes are accepted by mail, fax, or e-mail. Interested candidates should send a resume to the company's corporate headquarters: ANH Refractories Company, 400 Fairway Drive, Moon Township PA 15108. Fax: 412/375-6731. **Positions advertised include:** Designer. **Corporate headquarters location:** Pittsburgh PA. **Parent company:** AlliedSignal Corporation. **Operations at this facility include:** Divisional Headquarters.

AOL COLUMBUS
COMPUSERVE INC.
5000 Arlington Center Boulevard, Columbus OH 43220. 614/457-8600. **Fax:** 614/538-1780. **Contact:** Human Resources. **World Wide Web address:** http://www.compuserve.com. **Description:** An Internet access and online services provider. Founded in 1969. **Positions advertised include:** Direct Sales Associate; Installer; Technical Project Manager; Supervisor; Design Intern; Associate Space Planner; Senior Programming Manager; Senior Software Engineer; Finance and Planning Senior Manager. **Special programs:** Internships. **Corporate headquarters location:** This location. **Other area locations:** Statewide. **Other U.S. locations:** Nationwide. **Parent company:** AOL Time Warner, Inc. **Operations at this facility include:** Administration; Research and Development; Service. **Number of employees nationwide:** 2,200.

ASF-KEYSTONE INC.
1001 East Broadway Avenue, Alliance OH 44601. 330/823-6150. **Fax:** 330/823-8836. **Contact:** Personnel Director. **World Wide Web address:** http://www.asfglobal.com. **Description:** ASF-Keystone foundries supply cast steel components to the railroad freight car and locomotive industries worldwide. The company also designs and manufactures fifth wheels for the highway truck industry and hot wound coils for the agricultural and construction industries. **Corporate headquarters location:** Chicago IL. **Operations at this facility include:** This location is a manufacturing facility. **Parent company:** AMSTED Industries.

ABERCROMBIE & FITCH
P.O. Box 182168, Columbus OH 43218. 614/283-6500. **Physical address:** 6301 Fitch Path, New Albany OH 43054. **Fax:** 614/283-6710. **Contact:** Human Resources Department. **E-mail address:** awesomejobs@abercrombie.com. **World Wide Web address:** http://www.abercrombie.com. **Description:** A retailer of casual clothing for young men and women. Abercrombie & Fitch operates over 200 company-owned locations nationwide. Founded in 1892. **NOTE:** Entry-level positions are offered. **Positions advertised include:** Financial Analyst; Asset Protection Auditor; Purchasing Director; Regional Maintenance Supervisor; Merchandiser; Planner; Allocator; Sourcing Manager; Production Assistant; E-Commerce Developer; CAD Designer; Graphic Designer; Technical Designer. **Corporate headquarters location:** This location. **Other U.S. locations:** Nationwide. **Listed on:** New York Stock Exchange. **Stock exchange symbol:** ANF. **Annual sales/revenues:** More than $100 million.

ACKLIN STAMPING
d.b.a. ICE INDUSTRIES
1925 Nebraska Avenue, Toledo OH 43607-3830. 419/536-4661. **Contact:** Human Resources. **World Wide Web address:** http://www.acklin.com. **Description:** A manufacturer of stampings used in the assembly of refrigerator/freezer and air conditioning compressor units.

ADENA REGIONAL MEDICAL CENTER
272 Hospital Road, Chillicothe OH 45601. 740/779-7562. **Fax:** 740/779-7902. **Recorded jobline:** 740/779-7941. **Contact:** Human Resources. **World Wide Web address:** http://www.adena.com. **Description:** A medical center serving more than 100,000 patients annually. **Positions advertised include:** Unit Secretary; Registrar; Billing Specialist; Patient Accounts Manager; Radiologic Technologist; Occupational Therapist; System Analyst; Service Attendant; Mental Health Technician; Patient Care Associate; Surgical Technician; Staff Sonographer. **Number of employees at this location:** 800.

ADVANSTAR COMMUNICATIONS INC.
7500 Old Oak Boulevard, Cleveland OH 44130. 440/243-8100. **Fax:** 440/826-2805. **Contact:** Barbara Nieser, Human Resources. **E-mail address:** jobsclev@advanstar.com. **World Wide Web address:** http://www.advanstar.com. **Description:** A business information company that publishes magazines and journals, coordinates expositions and conferences, and provides information and communications products to professional and business markets. **Positions advertised include:** Managing Editor; Inside Advertising Account Executive; Reporter/Editor. **Corporate headquarters location:** New York NY. **Other U.S. locations:** CA; IL; MA; MN; NY; OR. **International locations:** Worldwide. **Parent company:** DLJ Merchant Banking Partners/Credit Suisse First Boston. **Operations at this facility include:** Administration. **Listed on:** Privately held. **Number of employees at this location:** 250. **Number of employees nationwide:** 1,300.

AGILYSIS, INC.
4800 East 131st Street, Cleveland OH 44105. 440/720-8500. **Fax:** 440/720-8501. **Contact:** Human Resources. **World Wide Web address:** http://www.agilysis.com. **Description:** Formerly known as Pioneer Standard Electronic, Inc., Agilysis is a leading distributor and reseller of computer hardware, software, and networking and storage products. Agilysis distributes computer equipment manufactured by IBM, Hewlett-Packard, Intel, and Oracle. **Positions advertised include:** Account Representative. **Corporate headquarters location:** Mayfield Heights OH. **Other area locations:** Solon OH. **International locations:** Canada. **Number of employees nationwide:** 1,061.

AIRBORNE EXPRESS
ABX AIR, INC.
145 Hunter Drive, Wilmington OH 45177. 937/382-1229. **Fax:** 937/383-3838. **Contact:** Recruitment. **E-mail address:** abx.recruiter@airborne.com. **World Wide Web address:** http://www.abxair.com. **Description:** A delivery service company providing overnight, next-afternoon, and second-day delivery options; same-day courier service; logistics management; and air freight, ocean transport, and customs clearance for international customers. **NOTE:** Resumes accepted for posted positions only. **Positions advertised include:** Aircraft Maintenance Instructor; Human Resources Generalist; HVAC Mechanic; Part-Time Sorter; Weekend Sorter; Teen Sorter; Seasonal Sorter. **Corporate headquarters location:** Seattle WA. **Parent Company:** Airborne Express.

AIRSTREAM INC.
419 West Pike Street, Jackson Center OH 45334. 937/596-6849. **Fax:** 937/596-6539. **Contact:** Cindy Oakley, Human Resources. **World Wide Web address:** http://www.thorindustries.com. **Description:** Develops, manufactures and markets recreational vehicles including travel trailers and motor homes. Founded in 1980. **Parent company:** Thor Industries, Inc.

AJILON SERVICES INC.
4401 Rockside Road, Suite 390, Independence OH 44131. 216/573-2370. **Toll-free phone:** 888/381-6970. **Fax:** 410/828-0106. **Contact:** Human Resources. **E-mail address:** recruit.cleveland@ajilon.com. **World Wide Web address:** http://www.ajilon.com. **Description:** Provides information technology services including functional outsourcing, IT management, systems security, systems transformation, managed maintenance, and Internet commerce enabling services to the communications, finance, manufacturing, transportation, and insurance industries. Founded in 1969. **Positions advertised include:** MVS Systems Programmer; Lotus Notes Administrator; Data Warehouse Analyst; Application Developer. **Corporate headquarters location:** Towson MD. **Other U.S. locations:** Nationwide. **Parent company:** Adecco SA.

AKRON BEACON JOURNAL
44 East Exchange Street, P.O. Box 640, Akron OH 44328. 330/996-3000. **Fax:** 330/996-3194. **Contact:** Human Resources. **World Wide Web address:** http://www.ohio.com. **Description:** A daily newspaper. **Special programs:** Internships. **Parent company:** Knight-Ridder, Inc. (San Jose CA). **Operations at this facility include:** Administration; Publishing; Research and Development; Sales; Service. **Number of employees at this location:** 650.

AKRON BRASS COMPANY
P.O. Box 86, Wooster OH 44691. 330/264-5678. **Physical address:** 343 Venture Boulevard, Wooster OH 44691. **Fax:** 330/264-2944. **Contact:** Personnel Director. **World Wide Web address:** http://www.akronbrass.com. **Description:** Develops and manufactures a variety of products including fittings, foam equipment, nozzles, turrets, valves, and related accessories for the fire-fighting industry.

AKRON, CITY OF
Personnel Department, Suite 130 CitiCenter Building, 146 South High Street, Akron OH 44308. 330/375-2723. **Recorded jobline:** 330/375/2723. **Contact:** Human Resources Department. **E-mail address:** personnel@ci.akron.oh.us. **World Wide Web address:** http://www.ci.akron.oh.us. **Description:** Houses the administrative offices of the city of Akron. **NOTE:** Please call to obtain employment information. **Positions advertised include:** Engineering Associate Co-op; School Secretary; Laborer; Semi-Skilled Laborer. **Office hours:** Monday – Friday, 8:00 a.m. – 3:30 p.m.

AKRON GENERAL MEDICAL CENTER
400 Wabash Avenue, Akron OH 44307. 330/384-6000. **Fax:** 330/344-1845. **Contact:** Division of Recruitment and Retention. **E-mail address:** careers@agmc.org. **World Wide Web address:** http://www.agmc.org. **Description:** A 537-bed, acute care teaching hospital that is affiliated with the Northeastern Ohio Colleges of Medicine. **Positions advertised include:** Clinical Nursing Manager; Coding Technician; Compensation Analyst; Licensed Practical Nurse; Medical Secretary; Nursing Assistant; Pharmacist; Research Assistant; Ultrasound Technologist. **Number of employees at this location:** 3,300.

AKRON PUBLIC SCHOOLS
70 North Broadway, Akron OH 44308. 330/761-2945. **Contact:** Jeanette Hintz. 330/761-2955. **Fax:** 330/761-3225. **E-mail address:** mdeshane@akron.k12.oh.us. **World Wide Web address:** http://www.akronschools.com. **Description:** This location

houses the administrative offices of the Akron public school system. **Positions advertised include:** Diagnostic Writing Specialist; Substitute Teacher.

AKRON ZOOLOGICAL PARK
500 Edgewood Avenue, Akron OH 44307. 330/375-2550. **Contact:** Human Resources. **World Wide Web address:** http://www.akronzoo.org. **Description:** A zoo featuring a variety of special exhibits. **Special programs:** Internships.

AKZO NOBEL CHEMICALS
P.O. Box 489, Columbus OH 43216-0489. 614/294-3361. **Physical address:** 1313 Windsor Avenue, Columbus OH 43211. **Contact:** Human Resources. **World Wide Web address:** http://www.akzonobel.com. **Description:** Akzo Nobel is a worldwide industrial organization with companies in more than 50 countries. Business activities are conducted in four units. The Chemicals Group produces polymer chemicals, rubber chemicals, catalysts, detergents, surfactants, functional chemicals, chlor-alkali, and industrial chemicals. The Coatings Group produces decorative coatings, industrial coatings, industrial wood finishes, aerospace finishes, automotive finishes, and resins. The Pharma Group produces ethical drugs, hospital supplies, nonprescription products, raw materials for the pharmaceuticals industry, generics, and veterinary products. The Fibers Group produces textile, industrial, and high-performance fibers, industrial nonwovens, and membranes for medical, technical, and industrial uses. Extensive research and development takes place in all units. **Corporate headquarters location:** Chicago IL. **Operations at this facility include:** This location manufactures paint.

ALCOA (ALUMINUM COMPANY OF AMERICA)
1600 Harvard Avenue, Cleveland OH 44105-3040. 216/641-3600. **Fax:** 216/641-4375. **Contact:** Human Resources. **World Wide Web address:** http://www.alcoa.com. **Description:** Engaged in all aspects of the aluminum industry including mining, refining, smelting, fabricating, and recycling. ALCOA also manufactures ceramic packaging for the semiconductor industry, alumina chemicals, plastic bottle closures, vinyl siding, packaging machinery, and electrical distribution systems for automobiles. **Corporate headquarters location:** Pittsburgh PA. **Annual sales/revenues:** More than $100 million.

ALLIANCE COMMUNITY HOSPITAL
264 East Rice Street, Alliance OH 44601-4341. 330/829-4000. **Fax:** 330/829-4122. **Recorded jobline:** 330/829-4101. **Contact:** Trace Pasco, Colleague Relations Specialist. **E-mail address:** jobs@achosp.org. **World Wide Web address:** http://www.achosp.org. **Description:** A full-service, acute care hospital specializing in adolescent and pediatric care, cancer care, cardio-pulmonary services, emergency care, intensive care, progressive care, rehabilitation, and surgical services. The hospital also operates a community care center and a visiting nurse's association and hospice, **Positions advertised include:** Home Health Aide; Registered Nurse; Respiratory Therapist; Physical Therapist. **Parent company:** Alliance VNA IMS. **Operations at this facility include:** Administration.

ALLIED CONSTRUCTION PRODUCTS, INC.
3900 Kelly Avenue, Cleveland OH 44114. 216/431-2600. **Fax:** 216/431-2601. **Contact:** Human Resources. **E-mail address:** recruiting@alliedcp.com. **World Wide Web address:** http://www. alliedcp.com. **Description:** Manufactures and markets a variety of construction equipment including compactors, grouser bars, impact hammers, installation kits, material and waste handling systems, mobile shears, rotary asphalt cutters, shoring systems, stationary boom systems, and underground piercing tools. **Corporate headquarters location:** This location. **Listed on:** Privately held. **Number of employees at this location:** 75.

ALLIED THERAPY ASSOCIATES, INC.
4353-D Tuller Road, Dublin OH 43017-5071. 614/764-7900. **Toll-free phone:** 800/589-8786. **Fax:** 614/764-0715. **Contact:** Mary Jane Hershey, President. **E-mail:** ata@iwaynet.net. **World Wide Web address:** http://www.alliedtherapy.com. **Description:** A service agency that provides physical, occupational, and speech therapy to facilities, agencies, and individuals throughout central Ohio. **Positions advertised include:** Part-Time Therapist; Full-Time Therapist; Occupational Therapist; Pediatric Physical Therapist; Speech Therapist.

ALLTEL COMMUNICATIONS
ALLTEL INFORMATION SERVICES
50 Executive Parkway, Hudson OH 44236. 330/650-1700. **Recorded jobline:** 888/255-3100x7311. **Contact:** Centralized Employment Services. **E-mail address:** ces@alltel.com. **World Wide Web address:** http://www.alltel.com. **Description:** ALLTEL Communications provides wireless, local telephone, long-distance, Internet, and high-speed data services to residential and business customers in 26 states. ALLTEL manages telephone systems and networks for hundreds of corporations nationwide. ALLTEL Information Services provides information-based solutions to financial, telecommunications, and mortgage clients in 54 countries and territories worldwide. ALLTEL is also a leading provider of software and data processing services to the residential lending industry. **NOTE:** Candidates must apply online. **Positions advertised include:** Marketing Services Analyst; Account Representative; Network Operations Supervisor; Engineer, Motorola Support. **Special programs:** Internships. **Corporate headquarters location:** Little Rock AR. **Other area locations:** Statewide. **Other U.S. locations:** Nationwide. **International locations:** Worldwide. **Parent company:** ALLTEL Corporation (Little Rock AR) is a *Fortune* 500 company. Other subsidiaries include ALLTEL Supply and ALLTEL Mobile. **Stock exchange symbol:** AT. **Annual sales/revenues:** More than $100 million.

ALLTEL PUBLISHING CORPORATION
100 Executive Parkway, Hudson OH 44236. 330/650-7100. **Fax:** 330/650-7411. **Recorded jobline:** 888/255-3100x7311. **Contact:** Centralized Employment Services. **E-mail address:** ces@alltel.com. **World Wide Web address:** http://www.alltel.com. **Description:** Publishes telephone directories for the company's telephone subsidiaries and other telephone companies nationwide. **NOTE:** Please send resumes to ALLTEL Communications, 50 Executive Parkway, Hudson OH 44236. **Corporate headquarters location:** Little Rock AR. **Other area locations:** Statewide. **Other U.S. locations:** Nationwide. **International locations:** Worldwide. **Parent company:** ALLTEL Corporation (Little Rock AR) is a *Fortune* 500 company whose other subsidiaries include ALLTEL Supply; and ALLTEL Mobile. **Listed on:** New York Stock Exchange. **Stock exchange symbol:** AT. **Annual sales/revenues:** More than $100 million.

ALSIDE INC.
P.O. Box 2010, Akron OH 44309. 330/929-1811. **Physical address:** 3773 State Road, Cuyahoga Falls OH 44223. **Toll-free phone:** 800/922-6009. **Fax:** 330/922-2142. **Contact:** Human Resources. **World Wide Web address:** http://www.alside.com. **Description:** Manufactures vinyl building products including windows, siding, soffit, trim, and related accessories for the construction and consumer markets. Founded in 1947. **Other U.S. locations:** Nationwide.

AMANO CINCINNATI INC.
130 Commerce Boulevard, Loveland OH 45140. 513/697-9000. **Contact:** Human Resources. **E-mail address:** dkuzsma@amano.com. **World Wide Web address:** http://www.amano.com. **Description:** Manufactures and markets automated time and attendance software solutions, parking equipment, and traditional time clocks. **Parent Company:** Amano Corporation (Japan). **Operations at this facility include:** Administration; Manufacturing; Research and Development; Sales; Service. **Other U.S. locations:** Anaheim CA; Atlanta GA; Chicago IL; Roseland NJ; Dallas TX.

AMCAST INDUSTRIAL CORPORATION
7887 Washington Village Drive, Suite 290, Dayton OH 45459. 937/291-7000. **Fax:** 937/291-7005. **Contact:** William Ilg, Director of Staffing. **E-mail address:** william.ilg@amcast.com. **World Wide Web address:** http://www.amcast.com. **Description:** A manufacturer of technology-intensive metal products, flow control products, and engineered components for OEMs. Amcast serves the aerospace, construction, automotive, and general industrial market segments. Founded in 1866. **NOTE:** E-mail inquires can also be sent to hr.dayton@amcast.com. **Positions advertised include:** Process Engineer; Tooling Engineer; Quality Engineer; Manufacturing Engineer; Metallurgical Engineer; Operations Manager. **Office hours:** Monday - Friday, 8:00 a.m. - 5:00 p.m. **Corporate headquarters location:** This location. **Other U.S. locations:** Nationwide. **Operations at this facility include:** Administration; Divisional Headquarters. **Listed on:** New York Stock Exchange. **Stock exchange symbol:** AIZ. **Annual sales/revenues:** More than $100 million.

AMERICAN CANCER SOCIETY, OHIO DIVISION
5555 Frantz Road, Dublin OH 43017. 614/718-4416. **Toll-free phone:** 800/686-4357. **Fax:** 614/718-4417. **Contact:** Tina Carper, Director of Employee Relations. **World Wide Web address:** http://www.cancer.org. **Description:** A nationwide, community-based, nonprofit, voluntary health organization dedicated to eliminating cancer as a major health problem by funding cancer research and public education. The society helps patients directly by offering services including transportation to treatment and rehabilitation services. **NOTE:** Entry-level positions and part-time jobs are offered. **Special programs:** Internships; Training; Summer Jobs. **Corporate headquarters location:** This location. **Other area locations:** Cincinnati OH; Cleveland OH; Youngstown OH. **Other U.S. locations:** Nationwide. **Annual sales/revenues:** $21 - $50 million. **Number of employees at this location:** 235. **Number of employees nationwide:** 1,000.

AMERICAN COMMERCE INSURANCE COMPANY
3590 Twin Creeks Drive, Columbus OH 43204. 614/272-6951. **Toll-free phone:** 800/848-2945. **Fax:** 614/278-3511. **Contact:** Susan Douglas, Human Resources Manager. **E-mail address:** sdouglas@acilink.com. **World Wide Web address:** http://www.acilink.com. **Description:** Provides automotive and property insurance through the AAA Auto Club. Founded in 1946. **Corporate headquarters location:** This location.

AMERICAN ELECTRIC POWER COMPANY
One Riverside Plaza, Columbus OH 43215. 614/223-1000. **Fax:** 614/716-1864. **Recorded jobline:** 800/300-1858. **Contact:** Personnel. **World Wide Web address:** http://www.aep.com. **Description:** An electric utility holding company serving approximately 4.8 million customers in 11 states. The company also performs some non-utility operations including communications, energy consulting, and power marketing. Founded in 1906. **Positions advertised include:** IT System Administrator; IT Support Specialist; Physical Security Compliance Specialist; Strategic Sourcing Specialist; Fleet Technician; Line Mechanic. **Corporate headquarters location:** This location. **Other area locations:** Statewide. **Other U.S. locations:** AR; IN; KY; LA; MI; OK; TN; TX; VA; WV. **Operations at this facility include:** Administration; Service. **Listed on:** New York Stock Exchange. **Stock exchange symbol:** AEP. **Number of employees at this location:** 2,000. **Number of employees nationwide:** 3,000.

AMERICAN FINANCIAL GROUP (AFG)
One East Fourth Street, Cincinnati OH 45202. 513/579-2121. **Contact:** Human Resources. **World Wide Web address:** http://www.amfnl.com. **Description:** Offers automobile, specialty property, and casualty insurance. AFG specializes in selling tax-deferred annuities, and life and health insurance products. **NOTE:** Hiring for American Financial Group is done through its subsidiary, Great American Insurance Company. Resumes should be sent to Great American Insurance Company, 580 Walnut Street, Cincinnati OH 45202, 513/579-6739. **Corporate headquarters location:** This location. **Listed on:** New York Stock Exchange. **Stock exchange symbol:** AFG. **Annual sales/revenues:** More than $100 million.

AMERICAN FLAT GLASS DISTRIBUTORS, INC. (AFGD)
160 North High Street, P.O. Box 220, Hebron OH 43025. 740/929-2443. **Fax:** 740/929-2440. **Toll-free phone:** 888/480-2343. **Contact:** Branch Manager. **World Wide Web address:** http://www.afgd.com. **Description:** Specializes in architectural insulated units and custom tempering. The firm manufactures a complete line of insulated units for commercial and residential applications. The product line includes clear, tint, and reflective float glass; laminated, low-emissivity, tempered, acrylic, mirror, obscure, insulated, and polished wire glass; as well as a complete line of glass handling, storage, and transportation equipment. **NOTE:** Submit resumes to the corporate office: AFGD Glass, Attention: Human Resources Generalist, 1600 Parkwood Circle Southeast, Suite 300, Atlanta GA 30339. Fax: 770/951-9100. **Corporate headquarters location:** Atlanta GA. **Other U.S. locations:** Nationwide. **Subsidiaries include:** AFGD Canada. **Parent company:** AFG Industries, Inc. **Operations at this facility include:** Manufacturing; Sales. **Listed on:** Privately held. **Number of employees at this location:** 50. **Number of employees nationwide:** 1,000.

AMERICAN GREETINGS CORPORATION
One American Road, Cleveland OH 44144. 216/252-7300. **Fax:** 216/252-6590. **Contact:** Personnel. **World Wide Web address:** http://www.americangreetings.com. **Description:** One of the world's largest publicly owned manufacturers and distributors of greeting cards and related novelty items. Products are distributed through a global network of approximately 97,000 retail outlets in 68 countries. **Positions advertised include:** Accounting Analyst; Art Director; Attorney; Corporate Engineering Director; Executive Secretary; Customer Service Manager; Production Coordinator. **Corporate headquarters location:** This location. **Subsidiaries include:** Acme Frame Products manufactures picture frames under the brand names Acme and Royal Gallery of Frames; A.G. Industries designs and manufactures custom permanent display fixtures and merchandising systems for American Greetings, its subsidiaries, consumer product companies, and retailers; CreataCard markets interactive, multimedia kiosks that allow consumers to write, personalize, and print greeting cards; Magnivision manufactures and distributes nonprescription, over-the-counter reading glasses produced primarily for mass retail distribution; Plus Mark manufactures and distributes promotional Christmas gift wrap, boxed cards, and accessories under the brand names Plus Mark and Greeneville Press; Those Characters From Cleveland develops and markets

licensed characters; Wilhold manufactures and distributes hair accessories. **Listed on:** NASDAQ. **Stock exchange symbol:** AM.

AMERICAN RED CROSS
995 East Broad Street, Columbus OH 43205. 614/253-7981. **Fax:** 614/253-4081. **Recorded jobline:** 614/251-1455. **Contact:** Human Resources. **E-mail address:** gcjobs@usa.redcross.org. **World Wide Web address:** http://columbus.redcross.org. **Description:** A humanitarian organization that aids disaster victims, gathers blood for crisis distribution, trains individuals to respond to emergencies, educates individuals on various diseases, and raises funds for other charitable establishments. **NOTE:** Resumes must be sent in regards to a specific position. **Positions advertised include:** Procurement Technician; Accounting Coordinator; Manager of Chapter Services; Special Events Coordinator. **Corporate headquarters location:** Washington DC. **Other U.S. locations:** Nationwide.

AMERICAN STANDARD COMPANIES, INC.
324 Fourth Avenue, P.O. Box 279, Tiffin OH 44883. 419/447-7515. **Fax:** 419/443-8105. **Contact:** Human Resources. **World Wide Web address:** http://www.americanstandard.com. **Description:** American Standard Companies, Inc. is a global, diversified manufacturer. The company's operations are comprised of three segments: air conditioning products, plumbing products, and automotive products. The air conditioning products segment (through subsidiary The Trane Company) develops and manufactures Trane and American Standard air conditioning equipment for use in central air conditioning systems for commercial, institutional, and residential buildings. The plumbing products segment develops and manufactures American Standard, Ideal Standard, Porcher, Armitage Shanks, Dolomite, and Standard bathroom and kitchen fixtures and fittings. The automotive products segment develops and manufactures truck, bus, and utility vehicle braking and control systems under the WABCO and Perrot brands. **Corporate headquarters location:** Piscataway NJ. **Operations at this facility include:** This location manufactures vitreous china plumbing fixtures. **Listed on:** New York Stock Exchange. **Stock exchange symbol:** ASD. **Number of employees worldwide:** 57,000.

AMERICAN TRIM
1501 Michigan Street, Sidney OH 45365. 937/492-1111. **Contact:** Personnel Director. **World Wide Web address:** http://www.amtrim.com. **Description:** Stolle Products supplies fabricated and decorative products for industrial customers, with emphasis on metal stamping and decorating. **Parent company:** American Trim LLC.

AMERILINK CORPORATION
2 Easton Oval, Suite 500, Columbus OH 43219. 614/479-2500. **Contact:** Personnel. **World Wide Web address:** http://www.amerilink.com. **Description:** Designs, constructs, installs, and maintains cable systems. The company markets its products and services to cable television suppliers, competitive access providers, direct broadcast satellite providers, DSL providers, Internet service providers, and telephone companies nationwide. Founded in 1971. **Positions advertised include:** Independent Contractor. **Corporate headquarters location:** This location.

AMERIWOOD INDUSTRIES
458 Second Avenue, Tiffin OH 44883. 419/447-7448. **Fax:** 419/447-7043. **Contact:** Rosie Arbogast, Human Resources. **World Wide Web address:** http://www.ameriwood.com. **Description:** Manufactures ready-to-assemble furniture including entertainment centers and bedroom, kitchen, office, and storage furniture. The company markets its products to major retailers nationwide including discount chains, home centers, office superstores and other major mass merchants. Founded in 1977. **Parent company:** Dorel Industries.

AMETEK ELECTROMECHANICAL GROUP
AMETEK LAMB ELECTRIC
627 Lake Street, Kent OH 44240. 330/673-3451. **Fax:** 330/677-3736. **Contact:** John Proudfit, Human Resources. **World Wide Web address:** http://www.ameteklamb.com. **Description:** Manufactures and supplies motors and motor/blower systems for commercial floor care equipment, drive motors, high-volume low-pressure sprayers, outdoor power equipment, spa blowers, vacuum cleaners, and other applications that require vacuum, pressure, or other air moving sources. The company specializes in motor design, testing, manufacturing, and customer service to a variety of businesses worldwide. **Positions advertised include:** Material Planner. **Special programs:** Internships. **Corporate headquarters location:** Paoli PA. **Other U.S. locations:** Simi Valley CA; Graham NC; Rock Creek NC; Racine WI. **International locations:** Denmark; England; Italy; Mexico. **Parent company:** AMETEK, Inc. is a global manufacturing company that serves a variety of industrial and commercial markets. The company produces and sells its products through its Electromechanical and Electronic Instruments Group. The Electromechanical Group manufactures electric motors for vacuum cleaners, floor care products and technical motor products for computer, medical, and other markets. The Electronic Instruments Group manufactures cockpit instruments, gauges, jet engine monitors, and dashboard instruments for the heavy-vehicle, process, and aerospace industries. **Operations at this facility include:** Administration; Divisional Headquarters; Manufacturing; Regional Headquarters. **Listed on:** New York Stock Exchange. **Stock exchange symbol:** AME.

AMOS PRESS INC.
P.O. Box 4129, Sidney OH 45365. 937/498-2111. **Fax:** 937/498-0888. **Contact:** Human Resources Director. **World Wide Web address:** http://www.amospress.com. **Description:** A printing and publishing company with operations in daily newspapers and a variety of periodicals including *Coin World* and *Linn's Stamp News*. **Corporate headquarters location:** This location. **Listed on:** Privately held. **Annual sales/revenues:** $21 - $50 million. **Number of employees at this location:** 200. **Number of employees nationwide:** 450.

ANALYSTS INTERNATIONAL CORPORATION (AIC)
3995 Medina Road, Suite 250, Medina OH 44256. 330/725-2553. **Toll-free phone:** 800/541-5859. **Fax:** 330/725-4133. **Contact:** Human Resources Department. **E-mail address:** jobs@analysts.com. **World Wide Web address:** http://www.analysts.com. **Description:** An international computer consulting firm. The company assists clients in analyzing, designing, and developing systems using different programming languages and software. Founded in 1966. **NOTE:** Apply online. **Corporate headquarters location:** Minneapolis MN. **Listed on:** NASDAQ. **Stock exchange symbol:** ANLY. **Annual sales/revenues:** More than $100 million. **Number of employees at this location:** 130.

ANALYSTS INTERNATIONAL CORPORATION (AIC)
8080 Beckett Center Drive, Suite 226, West Chester OH 45069. 513/874-8324. **Contact:** Human Resources Department. **E-mail address:** jobs@analysts.com. **World Wide Web address:** http://www.analysts.com. **Description:** An international computer consulting firm. The company assists clients in analyzing, designing, and developing systems using different programming languages and software. Founded in 1966. **NOTE:** Apply online. **Corporate headquarters location:** Minneapolis MN. **Listed on:** NASDAQ. **Stock exchange symbol:** ANLY. **Annual sales/revenues:** More than $100 million.

ANCHOR HOCKING COMPANY
1115 West Fifth Avenue, Lancaster OH 43130-2900. 740/687-2500. **Fax:** 740/681-6076. **Contact:** Human Resources Department. **E-mail address:** careers@anchorhocking.com. **World Wide Web address:** http://www.anchorhocking.com. **Description:** Manufactures a variety of glassware for the consumer market. The company specializes in beverageware, ovenware, servingware, and storageware. Founded in 1905. **Corporate headquarters location:** This location. **Parent company:** Newell Rubbermaid.

ANDERSON CONCRETE CORPORATION
P.O. Box 398, Columbus OH 43216. 614/443-0123. **Physical address:** 400 Frank Road, Columbus OH 43207-2423. **Fax:** 614/443-4001. **Contact:** Marty Koford, Personnel Director. **World Wide Web address:** http://www.andersonconcrete.com. **Description:** Manufactures, markets, and delivers ready-mixed concrete. The company also offers specialized concrete such as lightweight insulating concrete, heavyweight concrete, no slump concrete, and white and colored concrete.

ANHEUSER-BUSCH, INC.
700 Schrock Road, Columbus OH 43229. 614/888-6644. **Contact:** Human Resources. **World Wide Web address:** http://www.buschjobs.com. **Description:** Anheuser-Busch is a diverse company that is involved in the entertainment, brewing, baking, and manufacturing industries. The company operates breweries throughout the United States and distributes through over 900 independent wholesalers. Beer brands include Budweiser, Michelob, Busch, and King Cobra, as well as O'Doul's (non-alcoholic). Related businesses include can manufacturing, paper printing, and barley malting. Anheuser-Busch is also one of the largest operators of amusement parks in the United States, with locations in Florida, Virginia, Texas, Ohio, and California. **Positions advertised include:** Industrial Electrician. **Special programs:** Internships. **Corporate headquarters location:** St. Louis MO. **Other U.S. locations:** Nationwide. **International locations:** Worldwide. **Operations at this facility include:** This location is a brewery. **Subsidiaries include:** Campbell Taggart Inc. is one of the largest commercial baking companies in the United States, producing foods under the Colonial brand name. **Listed on:** New York Stock Exchange. **Stock exchange symbol:** BUD.

ANTIOCH COLLEGE
795 Livermore Street, Yellow Springs OH 45387. 937/769-1000. **Contact:** Lisa Lowery, Employment Specialist. **E-mail address:** llowery@antioch.edu. **World Wide Web address:** http://www.antioch-college.edu. **Description:** A private, independent liberal arts college offering baccalaureate programs in a variety of disciplines. Antioch College has an enrollment of approximately 650 students. Founded in 1852 by the Christian Church, Antioch was later reorganized as an independent, nonsectarian college. Antioch's first president was Horace Mann. **NOTE:** Mail resumes to: Antioch College, Human Resources Office, 150 E.S. College Street, Yellow Springs OH 45387. Unsolicited resumes are not accepted.

APPLETON PAPERS INC.
1030 West Alex-Bell Road, Miamisburg OH 45342. 937/859-8261. **Fax:** 937/847-7051. **Contact:** Human Resources Department. **World Wide Web address:** http://www.appletonideas.com. **Description:** Appleton Papers is a leading producer of carbonless and thermal papers as well as a broad range of coated papers used in a variety of commercial printing and specialty applications. The company markets its products under the brand names NCR PAPER, OPTIMA and UTOPIA, and Specialty Coated Products. Founded in 1907. **Corporate headquarters location:** Appleton WI. **Other U.S. locations:** Harrisburg PA; Roaring Spring PA; Combined Locks WI; Portage WI. **Operations at this facility include:** This location is a paper mill.

APPLIED INNOVATION INC.
5800 Innovation Drive, Dublin OH 43016. 614/798-2000. **Toll-free phone:** 800/247-9482. **Fax:** 614/798-8149. **Contact:** Recruiting Coordinator. **E-mail address:** hr@aiinet.com. **World Wide Web address:** http://www.aiinet.com. **Description:** Applied Innovation is a network management solutions company that simplifies and enhances the operation of complex, distributed voice and data networks. AI delivers hardware, software and service solutions that provide greater connectivity, visibility and control of network elements and the systems that support them. Founded in 1983. **NOTE:** Unsolicited resumes are not accepted. **Company slogan:** Bridging the technology gap. **Office hours:** Monday - Friday, 8:00 a.m. - 5:00 p.m. **Corporate headquarters location:** This location. **Other U.S. locations:** Denver CO; Atlanta GA; Chicago IL; Dallas TX. **Operations at this facility include:** Regional Headquarters. **Listed on:** NASDAQ. **Stock exchange symbol:** AINN. **Founder/Chairman:** Gerard Moersdorf, Jr. **President:** Robert L. Smialek. **Annual sales/revenues:** $51 - $100 million. **Number of employees at this location:** 180. **Number of employees nationwide:** 220.

ARGO-TECH CORPORATION
23555 Euclid Avenue, Euclid OH 44117. 216/692-6000. **Fax:** 216/692-5293. **Contact:** James Cunningham, Vice President of Human Resources. **E-mail address:** cunningh@argo-tech.com. **World Wide Web address:** http://www.argo-tech.com. **NOTE:** Human Resources direct line is 216/692-5830. **Description:** Develops and manufactures fuel and other precision pumps for the commercial and military aviation markets. Argo-Tech Corporation specializes in aircraft lube oil and scavenge pumps; airframe boost and transfer pumps; fuel pumps, oil pumps, and flow dividers for gas turbine power plants; main engine fuel pumps for commercial aircraft; and smaller main engine pumps for helicopters, turboprops, and business aircraft. **Special programs include:** Internships.

ARMSTRONG AIR CONDITIONING, INC.
421 Monroe Street, Bellevue OH 44811-1789. 419/483-4840. **Contact:** Human Resources Director. **World Wide Web address:** http://www.aac-inc.com. **Description:** Manufactures and markets a variety of heating and cooling products including residential gas, oil and electric furnaces; split system cooling units; and heat pumps and package units. The company markets its products under the brand names Air-Ease, Armstrong Air, Concord, and Magic-Pak. **Parent company:** Lennox International Inc.

ARVINMERITOR AUTOMOTIVE
444 Hebron Road, Heath OH 43056. 740/344-1131. **Contact:** Human Resources. **World Wide Web address:** http://www.arvinmeritor.com. **Description:** Manufactures trucks and bus equipment. **Corporate headquarters location:** Troy MI. **Other area locations:** Newark OH. **Listed on:** New York Stock Exchange. **Stock exchange symbol:** ARM.

ASHLAND DISTRIBUTION & SPECIALTY CHEMICAL COMPANY
5200 Blaser Parkway, P.O. Box 2219, Dublin OH 43017. 614/790-3333. **Contact:** Human Resources. **World Wide Web address:** http://www.ashchem.com.

Description: Develops, supplies, and distributes chemicals, plastics, and fiber reinforcements to the adhesives, automotive, boat-building, composites, foundry, merchant marine, paint, paper, plastics, and semiconductor fabrication industries. The company also specializes in products and systems for water and fuel treatment, and shipboard maintenance. Founded in 1967. **NOTE:** Entry-level positions are offered. **Positions advertised include:** Staffing Specialist; Technical Sales Representative; Laboratory Technician; Training Specialist; Import/Export Coordinator. **Internship information:** The company hires chemical engineering students to participate in a co-op program to work one rotation in Dublin OH and other rotations at different plants. Ashland Chemical prefers to hire students in their sophomore year of college. **Corporate headquarters location:** This location. **Other U.S. locations:** Nationwide. **International locations:** Worldwide. **Parent company:** Ashland, Inc. **Operations at this facility include:** Administration; Divisional Headquarters; Research and Development. **Listed on:** New York Stock Exchange. **Stock exchange symbol:** ASH. **Number of employees worldwide:** 7,100.

ASHLAND UNIVERSITY
Room 106 Founders Hall, 401 College Avenue, Ashland OH 44805-3799. 419/289-4142. **Fax:** 419/289-5993. **Contact:** Personnel Office. **World Wide Web address:** http://www.ashland.edu. **Description:** A private liberal arts and sciences institution offering undergraduate, graduate, and professional programs to approximately 6,000 students. Founded in 1878. **Positions advertised include:** Assistant Professor, Microbiology; Assistant Professor, Educational Administration; Adjunct Instructor, Art; Adjunct Instructor, Composition; Project Engineer.

ATLAS AMERICA, INC.
1026 Cookson Avenue SE, New Philadelphia OH 44663. 330/339-3155. **Contact:** Human Resources. **World Wide Web address:** http://www.atlasamerica.com. **Description:** Engaged in oil and gas production.

ATLAS INDUSTRIES, INC.
1750 East State Street, Fremont OH 43420. 419/355-1000. **Fax:** 419/355-9000. **Contact:** Director of Human Resources. **World Wide Web address:** http://www.atlas-industries.com. **Description:** Manufactures and supplies a variety of precision machined products to the air conditioning, air compression, refrigeration, small gasoline engine, and diesel engine markets. Founded in 1943. **Corporate headquarters location:** This location.

AT&T GOVERNMENT SOLUTIONS
2940 Presidential Drive, Suite 390, Fairborn OH 45324-6297. 937/429-7773. **Fax:** 937/429-7769. **Contact:** Human Resources. **World Wide Web address:** http://www.grci.com. **Description:** AT&T Government Solutions provides knowledge-based professional services and technology-based product solutions to government and commercial customers. GRC International's activities encompass telecommunications products, network systems analysis, and network software development operations for the commercial market. The company creates large-scale, decision-support systems and software engineering environments; applies operations research and mathematical modeling to business and management systems; and implements advanced database technology. AT&T Government Solutions also provides studies and analysis capabilities for policy development and planning; modeling and simulation of hardware and software used in real-time testing of sensor, weapon, and battlefield management command, control, and communication systems; and testing and evaluation. **NOTE:** Entry-level positions are offered. **Corporate headquarters location:** Vienna VA. **Other area locations:** Dayton OH. **Other U.S. locations:** Nationwide. **Operations at this facility include:** This location assists in military-based design projects and also develops some software products. **Number of employees at this location:** 50. **Number of employees worldwide:** 1,300.

ATTACHMATE CORPORATION
424 Wards Corner Road, Loveland OH 45140. 513/745-0500. **Fax:** 513/794-8108. **Contact:** Human Resources. **World Wide Web address:** http://www.attachmate.com. **Description:** Manufactures and supplies enterprise information access and management software and services to government agencies and major businesses worldwide. The company's products include authoring tools, desktop-to-host and web-to-enterprise business solutions, management software, and hardware adapters that offer secure access and management of business information. **Corporate headquarters location:** Bellevue WA. **Other U.S. locations:** Nationwide. **International locations:** Worldwide.

AULTMAN HOSPITAL
2600 Sixth Street SW, Canton OH 44710. 330/452-9911. **Contact:** Human Resources. **World Wide Web address:** http://www.aultman.com. **Description:** A full-service, acute care, 682-bed hospital specializing in diabetes, diagnostic and nuclear radiology, rehabilitation, and skilled nursing. The hospital also operates specialized departments for a variety of medical needs including cancer, coronary care, emergency/trauma medicine, maternal/child services, and surgery. Founded in 1892. **Positions advertised include:** Registered Nurse; Radiation Therapist; Neonatal Nurse Practitioner; Occupational Therapist; Clinical Pharmacist; Transcriptionist; Social Worker; Vascular Sonographer.

THE AUSTIN COMPANY
6095 Parkland Boulevard, Cleveland OH 44124. 440/544-2600. **Fax:** 440/544-2684. **Contact:** Human Resources. **E-mail address:** humanres@theaustin.com. **World Wide Web address:** http://www.theaustin.com. **Description:** An engineering, architectural design, and construction firm specializing in industrial, commercial, and government projects. The company markets its services to the air transportation, aerospace, banking, broadcasting, chemical processing, entertainment, food and beverage, general manufacturing, laboratory research and testing, metal processing, newspaper publishing, pharmaceuticals, and telecommunications industries. Founded in 1878. **Corporate headquarters location:** This location. **Other U.S. locations:** Nationwide. **International locations:** Australia; The Netherlands; United Kingdom. **Subsidiaries include:** The Austin Company of U.K. Ltd.; Ragnor Benson Inc. **Listed on:** Privately held. **President/CEO:** J. William Melsop. **Number of employees nationwide:** 610.

AUSTIN POWDER COMPANY
25800 Science Park Drive, Cleveland OH 44122. 216/464/2400. **Contact:** Personnel Director. **E-mail address:** humanresources@austinpowder.com. **World Wide Web address:** http://www.austinpowder.com. **Description:** Manufactures and markets industrial explosives and related accessories for a variety of applications. The company also provides blasting services to customers worldwide. Founded in 1833. **Corporate headquarters location:** This one. **Other area locations:** McArthur OH. **Subsidiaries include:** Austin International.

AUTOMATED PACKAGING SYSTEMS
10175 Philipp Parkway, Streetsboro OH 44241. 330/342-2000. **Toll-free phone:** 800/527-0733. **Fax:** 330/342-2485. **Contact:** Human Relations Manager. **World Wide Web address:** http://www.autopkg.com. **Description:** Designs, manufactures, and distributes packaging, machinery, and related materials. **Corporate headquarters location:** This location. **International locations:** Belgium; England. **Operations at this facility include:** Manufacturing.

AVON PRODUCTS INC.
175 Progress Place, Springdale OH 45246. 513/551-2000. **Fax:** 513/551-2510. **Contact:** Human Resources. **E-mail address:** jobs@avon.com. **World Wide Web address:** http://www.avoncareers.com. **Description:** A direct seller of beauty care products, fashion jewelry, gifts, fragrances, and decorative products. Avon, a *Fortune* 500 company, markets its products through a network of 2.8 million independent sales representatives in 135 countries worldwide. **NOTE:** Salespeople are considered independent contractors or dealers and most work part-time. If you are interested in becoming a sales representative, please call 800/FOR-AVON, or visit the company's website for more information. **Positions advertised include:** Human Resource Manager; Returns Processing Supervisor.

BP AMOCO PLC
200 Public Square, Cleveland OH 44114. 216-586-4141. **Contact:** Human Resources Department. **World Wide Web address:** http://www.bpamoco.com. **Description:** Engaged in the energy business, specializing in domestic oil and natural gas. BP Amoco is a major holder of domestic crude oil reserves and is also involved in the refining and marketing of petroleum products. **Special programs:** Internships. **Corporate headquarters location:** London, England. **Subsidiaries include:** BP Exploration. **Operations at this facility include:** Regional Headquarters. **Listed on:** New York Stock Exchange. **Stock exchange symbol:** BP.

BABCOCK & WILCOX COMPANY INC.
20 South Van Buren Avenue, P.O. Box 351, Barberton OH 44203-0351. 330/753-4511. **Fax:** 330/860-1093. **Contact:** Personnel. **E-mail address:** jobs@babcock.com. **World Wide Web address:** http://www.babcock.com. **Description:** Manufactures and markets power generation systems and related equipment to electric power, environmental, industrial, nuclear power, and pulp and paper markets worldwide. **Positions advertised include:** Scheduling Assistant; Human Resources Coordinator; Application Developer. **Corporate headquarters location:** New Orleans LA. **Parent company:** McDermott International. **Operations at this facility include:** Administration. **Listed on:** New York Stock Exchange. **Stock exchange symbol:** MDR.

BAKER & HOSTETLER LLP
65 East State Street, Suite 2100, Columbus OH 43215. 614/228-1541. **Fax:** 614/462-2616. **Contact:** Cynthia L. Wesney, Human Resources Manager. **E-mail address:** cwesney@bakerlaw.com. **World Wide Web address:** http://www.bakerlaw.com. **NOTE:** Candidates for Attorney or Summer Associate positions should contact Jeanie Fulton, Recruiting Coordinator. Phone: 614/462-4703. E-mail address: jfulton@bakerlaw.com. . **Description:** A general practice law firm. Baker & Hostetler specializes in business, employee benefits, employment and labor, intellectual property, litigation, personal planning, and tax law. Founded in 1916. **Other area locations:** Cincinnati OH; Cleveland OH. **Other U.S. locations:** Costa Mesa CA; Los Angeles CA; Denver CO; Washington DC; Orlando FL; New York NY; Houston TX.

BALDWIN-WALLACE COLLEGE
275 Eastland Road, Berea OH 44017-2088. 440/826-2900. **Contact:** Hilary B. Wilson, Human Resources Department. **E-mail address:** hwilson@bw.edu. **World Wide Web address:** http://www.bw.edu. **Description:** A private liberal arts college offering undergraduate, graduate, and pre-professional programs. Baldwin-Wallace College has an enrollment of 2,750 undergraduates, 600 graduate students, and 1,300 evening and weekend students. Founded in 1845. **Positions advertised include:** Secretary; Human Resources Director; Collection Specialist; Custodian; Lab Director; Assistant Professor, Mathematics and Computer Science; Clarinet Instructor.

BALLETMET COLUMBUS
BALLETMET DANCE ACADEMY
322 Mt. Vernon Avenue, Columbus OH 43215. 614/229-4860. **Fax:** 614/229-4858. **Contact:** Human Resources Department. **E-mail address:** dance@balletmet.org. **World Wide Web address:** http://www.balletmet.org. **Description:** A nonprofit professional dance company. The BalletMet Dance Academy (also at this location) currently ranks as one of the top five professional dance schools in the country. Founded in 1978. **Corporate headquarters location:** This location. **Annual sales/revenues:** Less than $5 million. **Number of employees at this location:** 100.

BANK ONE AKRON, N.A.
1615 South Arlington Street. Akron OH 44306. 330/972-1900. **Contact:** Human Resources Department. **E-mail address:** regionea@careersbankone.com. **World Wide Web address:** http://www.bankone.com. **Description:** Bank One is a full-service banking and financial institution serving business, commercial, and consumer markets. The company specializes in corporate finance, corporate trust, investment management, private banking, traditional lending, treasury management, and related financial services. **Corporate headquarters location:** Chicago IL. **Other U.S. locations:** AZ; CA; CO; IL; IN; KY; MI; TX; UT; WV; WI. **Parent company:** Bank One Corporation operates an affiliate network of over 75 banks in 13 states. In addition, Bank One operates corporations involved in data processing, venture capital, investment and merchant banking, trust, brokerage, investment management, leasing, mortgage banking, consumer finance, and insurance. **Listed on:** New York Stock Exchange. **Stock exchange symbol:** ONE. **Number of employees nationwide:** 50,000.

BARBERTON CITIZENS HOSPITAL
155 Fifth Street NE, Barberton OH 44203. 330/848-7771. **Fax:** 330/848-7833. **Recorded jobline:** 330/848-7777. **Contact:** Human Resources. **World Wide Web address:** http://www.barbhosp.com. **Description:** A 311-bed, full-service, acute care hospital. Barberton Citizens Hospital specializes in a number of inpatient services including coronary care, extended care, intensive care, obstetrics, pediatrics, psychiatry, and surgery. The hospital also offers outpatient services and community outreach programs. Founded in 1915. **NOTE:** Entry-level positions, part-time jobs, and second and third shifts are offered. **Positions advertised include:** Registration Specialist; Computer Operator; Hospital Aide; Porter; Phlebotomist; Medical Transcriptionist; Licensed Practical Nurse; Registered Nurse; Occupational Therapist; Operator. **Special programs:** Internships. **Parent company:** Quorum Health Group, Inc. **Listed on:** NASDAQ. **Number of employees at this location:** 1,000.

BARNES DISTRIBUTION
1301 East Ninth Street, Suite 700, Cleveland OH 44114. 216/416-7200. **Contact:** Human Resources. **E-mail address:** barnesfsjobs-midwest@bd-bgi.com. **World Wide Web address:** http://www.barnesdistribution.com. **Description:** A direct-to-user distributor of expendable parts and supplies for the industrial, transportation, and heavy-equipment maintenance markets. Founded in 1927. **Positions advertised include:** Senior Materials Planner; Purchasing Analyst. **Corporate headquarters**

location: Bristol CT. **Parent company:** Barnes Group, Inc. is a diversified manufacturer of critical parts and supplies for a wide range of industrial applications.

BARNES & NOBLE BOOKSTORES
3685 West Dublin Granville Road, Columbus OH 43235. 614/798-0077. **Fax:** 614/798-0074. **Contact:** Manager. **World Wide Web address:** http://www.bn.com. **Description:** One location of the nationwide chain of bookstores. This location also has a cafe and music department. **Corporate headquarters location:** New York NY. **Listed on:** New York Stock Exchange. **Stock exchange symbol:** BKS.

BARNES & NOBLE BOOKSTORES
4940 Monroe Street, Toledo OH 43623. 419/472-6164. **Fax:** 419/472-6176. **Contact:** Manager. **World Wide Web address:** http://www.bn.com. **Description:** One location of the nationwide chain of bookstores. This location also has a cafe and music department. **Corporate headquarters location:** New York NY. **Listed on:** New York Stock Exchange. **Stock exchange symbol:** BKS.

BARON DRAWN STEEL CORPORATION
1420 Baron Steel Avenue, Toledo OH 43607. 419/531-5525. **Fax:** 419/531-7484. **Contact:** Hank J. Goebel, Employee Relations Manager. **World Wide Web address:** http://www.baronsteel.com. **Description:** A processor of steel and wire products including cold-drawn, cut-length steel bars of various sizes, shapes, and grades; and drawn and annealed, cleaned, coated, and pickled wire coils of various sizes and grades. Founded in 1960. **NOTE:** Second and third shifts are offered. **Corporate headquarters location:** This location. **Other U.S. locations:** Canton MI. **Parent company:** The Renco Group. **Operations at this facility include:** Divisional Headquarters. **Listed on:** Privately held. **Annual sales/revenues:** $51 - $100 million. **Number of employees at this location:** 160. **Number of employees nationwide:** 201.

BASIC ELECTRIC SUPPLY
P.O. Box 12326, Columbus OH 43212. 614/481-8801. **Physical address:** 999 Kinnear Road, Columbus OH 43212. **Fax:** 614/488-0453. **Contact:** Linda Wright, Human Resources. **E-mail address:** lwright1@basicelectric.com. **World Wide Web address:** http://www.basicelectric.com. **Description:** A wholesale distributor of a wide range of electrical supplies. Founded in 1958. **Office hours:** Monday - Friday, 7:30 a.m. - 5:00 p.m., Saturday, 8:00 a.m. - 12:00 p.m. **Corporate headquarters location:** This location. **Operations at this facility include:** Sales; Service. **Listed on:** Privately held.

BATTELLE
505 King Avenue, Columbus OH 43201. 614/424-5901. **Contact:** Employment Advisor. **E-mail address:** employment@battelle.org. **World Wide Web address:** http://www.battelle.org. **Description:** An international technology organization that serves industry and government by generating, applying, and commercializing technology through research and development. With a wide range of scientific and technical capabilities, Battelle serves clients worldwide. **NOTE:** Resumes are only accepted for advertised positions and a specific job reference number must accompany every resume. Available positions are listed on the company's Website, and interested jobseekers are encouraged to apply using the online form available there. **Positions advertised include:** Research Scientist; Technician; Principal Synthesis Chemist; Pesticide Chemist; Office Assistant; Senior Internal Auditor; Payroll Tax Assistant. **Special programs:** Internships. **Corporate headquarters location:** This location. **Operations at this facility include:** Administration; Research and Development. **Number of employees at this location:** 2,000. **Number of employees nationwide:** 8,000.

BEHR DAYTON THERMAL PRODUCTS
1600 Webster Street, Dayton OH 45404. 937/369-2000. **Fax:** 937/219-2705. **Contact:** Human Resources. **E-mail address:** da.recruiting@us.behrgroup.com. **World Wide Web address:** http://www.behramerica.behrgroup.com. **Description:** Manufactures automotive air conditioning and engine cooling systems. **Positions advertised include:** Quality Engineer of Plastics. **Corporate headquarters location:** This location.

BEKAERT CORPORATION
3200 West Market Street, Suite 303, Akron OH 44333-3326. 330/876-3325. **Fax:** 330/873-3432. **Contact:** Manager of Human Resources. **E-mail address:** hr@bekaert.com. **World Wide Web address:** http://www.bekaert.com. **Description:** Bekaert Corporation develops, manufactures, and markets high-grade steel cord, steel wire, and related products. Founded in 1880. **International locations:** Belgium. **Number of employees worldwide:** 10,000.

BELCAN CORPORATION
10200 Anderson Way, Cincinnati OH 45242. 800/423-5226. **Contact:** Human Resources. **E-mail address:** tech@tech.belcan.com. **World Wide Web address:** http://www.belcan.com. **Description:** Provides IT specialists to companies in need of programming, help desk, and system administration support. **Positions advertised include:** Lab Technician; Software Engineer. **Corporate Headquarters:** This location.

BENNETT ENTERPRISES, INC.
P.O. Box 670, Perrysburg OH 43552. 419/874-1933. **Physical address:** 27476 Holiday Lane, Perrysburg OH 43552. **Fax:** 419/874-2615. **Contact:** Susan Baer, Director of Human Resources. **World Wide Web address:** http://www.bennett-enterprises.com. **Description:** Operates several restaurants and hotels including three Holiday Inns, one Hampton Inn, six Ralphie's Sports Bars, and nineteen Big Boy Family Restaurants. **NOTE:** Entry-level positions and second and third shifts are offered. **Special programs:** Internships. **Corporate headquarters location:** This location. **Operations at this facility include:** Administration; Research and Development; Sales; Service. **Listed on:** Privately held. **Annual sales/revenues:** $5 - $10 million. **Number of employees nationwide:** 1,500.

THE BERRY COMPANY
3170 Kettering Boulevard, Dayton OH 45439. 937/296-2121. **Fax:** 937/297-4542. **Contact:** Human Resources. **World Wide Web address:** http://www.lmberry.com. **Description:** This location is engaged in the sale and marketing of Yellow Pages advertising. The Berry Company also operates BerryDirect, a chain of centers providing teleservicing; Berry Network Inc., a Yellow Pages placement agency; and Berry Sales & Marketing Solutions, a worldwide chain of marketing consultants. **Corporate headquarters location:** This location. **Parent company:** BellSouth Corporation. **Operations at this facility include:** Administration; Divisional Headquarters; Regional Headquarters; Research and Development; Sales. **President/CEO:** Daniel J. Graham. **Number of employees at this location:** 750. **Number of employees nationwide:** 2,400.

BETHESDA NORTH HOSPITAL
10500 Montgomery Road, Cincinnati OH 45242-4402. 513/745-1111. **Contact:** Human Resources. **World Wide Web address:** http://www.trihealth.com. **Description:** A progressive 255-bed hospital and health care organization. Five core areas make up Bethesda North's structure: member acquisition, health status management, health services and physician services, internal services, and integrating services. Bethesda North's regional home care includes American Nursing Care, two adult DayBreak Centers, and Hospice of Cincinnati, which works with more than 30 nursing homes. Bethesda North also operates two group practices that bring primary care physicians, pharmacists, lab, and X-ray technicians together at one site. **Positions advertised include:** Fitness Technician; Receptionist; Donor Relations Officer; Physical Therapist; Rehabilitation Attendant; Lifeguard; Practice Physician; Registered Nurse; Medical Assistant.

BETLIN, INC.
1445 Marion Road, Columbus OH 43207. 614/443-0248. **Toll-free phone:** 800/932-8546. **Fax:** 614/443-4658. **Contact:** Mr. Pat Silk, Manager of Human Resources. **World Wide Web address:** http://www.betlin.com. **Description:** Manufactures customized, made-to-order athletic uniforms. The company markets its products through over 500 sporting good dealers nationwide. **Corporate headquarters location:** This location. **Operations at this facility include:** Administration; Manufacturing. **Listed on:** Privately held. **Number of employees at this location:** 100.

BICRON
12345 Kinsman Road, Newbury OH 44065. 440/564-2251. **Fax:** 440/564-9176. **Contact:** Human Resources. **World Wide Web address:** http://www.bicron.com. **Description:** Engaged in the manufacture and sale of scintillation detectors for medical, governmental, industrial, and commercial nuclear monitoring markets. The company is also involved in the manufacture and sale of optical components for infrared and ultraviolet transmittal and electronic support systems. Founded in 1969. **Other area locations:** Solon OH. **Parent company:** Saint-Gobain. **Operations at this facility include:** Administration; Divisional Headquarters; Manufacturing; Research and Development; Sales; Service. **Number of employees at this location:** 550.

BIG LOTS INC.
300 Phillipi Road, Columbus OH 43228. 614/278-6800. **Fax:** 614/278-6676. **Contact:** General Office Recruiting. **E-mail address:** careers@biglots.com. **World Wide Web address:** http://www.biglots.com. **Description:** One of the nation's largest retailers of close-out merchandise, toys and furniture. The company operates approximately 2,500 stores nationwide under the names Odd Lots, Big Lots, Mac Frugal's, Pic 'N Save, KB Toys, KB Toy Works, and KB Toy Outlet. The corporation also operates two wholesale divisions: Consolidated International and Wisconsin Toy. **Positions advertised include:** Store Help Desk Specialist; DC Routing Coordinator; Merchandise Coordinator; Allocation Analyst; Human Resources Development Specialist; Corporate Help Desk Specialist; Data Network Analyst; Payroll Coordinator. **Corporate headquarters location:** This location. **Listed on:** New York Stock Exchange. **Stock exchange symbol:** BLI.

BLACKHAWK AUTOMOTIVE PLASTICS, INC.
500 North Warpole Street, Upper Sandusky OH 43351-9051. 419/294-2317. **Contact:** Personnel Manager. **World Wide Web address:** http://www.blackhawkplastics.com. **Description:** Produces injection-molded plastics for a variety of customers. **Special programs:** Internships. **Parent company:** Worthington Industries, Inc.

BLANCHARD VALLEY REGIONAL HEALTH CENTER
145 West Wallace Street, Findlay OH 45840. 419/423-5229. **Contact:** Connie Walter, Human Resources. **E-mail address:** candidate@bvha.org. **World Wide Web address:** http://www.bvha.org. **Description:** A full-service medical center. Blanchard Valley Regional Health Center specializes in cardiac care, catheterization, cardiopulmonary care, dialysis, emergency medicine, intensive and coronary care units, laboratory services, nuclear medicine, oncology, pathology, pediatrics, pharmacy, radiology, and rehabilitation. **Positions advertised include:** Registered Nurse. **Parent company:** Blanchard Valley Health Association.

BLAUGRUND HERBERT & MARTIN
5455 Rings Road, Suite 500, Dublin OH 43017. 614/764-0681. **Fax:** 614/764-0774. **Contact:** Human Resources. **E-mail address:** bhm@bhmlaw.net. **World Wide Web address:** http://www.bhmlaw.net. **Description:** A general practice law firm representing businesses, corporations, families, government, independent agencies, individuals, and nonprofit organizations. The firm specializes in business and corporate law; domestic and family law; estate planning, succession planning, and estate administration; immigration; insolvency and creditor rights; labor law; liquor law; litigation; nonprofit and association law; public law; school and education law; and tax law. **NOTE:** Contact David Blaugrund regarding Attorney positions. All other inquiries should be directed to Human Resources. **Corporate headquarters location:** This location.

BOB EVANS FARMS, INC.
3776 South High Street, Columbus OH 43207. 614/491-2225. **Toll-free phone:** 800/272-7675. **Fax:** 614/497-4318. **Contact:** Personnel Director. **E-mail address:** employment@bobevans.com. **World Wide Web address:** http://www.bobevans.com. **Description:** Owns and operates 448 family restaurants in 21 states including Bob Evans Restaurants and Owens Family Restaurants. The company also produces sausage products and deli-style salads, which are distributed primarily through grocery stores in the Midwest, Southwest, and Southeast. **NOTE:** Part-time jobs are offered. **Positions advertised include:** Restaurant Manager; Product Development Secretary. **Special programs:** Scholarship Opportunities. **Corporate headquarters location:** This location. **Listed on:** NASDAQ. **Stock exchange symbol:** BOBE.

BOWLING GREEN STATE UNIVERSITY
100 College Park, Bowling Green OH 43403. 419/372-2227. **Fax:** 419/372-2920. **Contact:** Human Resources. **E-mail address:** ohr@bgnet.bgsu.edu. **World Wide Web address:** http://www.bgsu.edu. **Description:** A four-year university offering bachelor's, master's, and doctoral degree programs to approximately 18,500 students. **NOTE:** Classified staff jobline: 419/372-8669. Administrative staff jobline: 419/372-8522. Faculty hiring is done through Academic Affairs. **Positions advertised include:** Residence Hall Director; Assistant Football Coach; Food Service Worker; Personnel Technician.

BOYKIN LODGING COMPANY
45 West Prospect Avenue, Suite 1500, Guildhall Building, Cleveland OH 44115-1039. 216/241-6375. **Fax:** 216/241-1329. **Contact:** Human Resources. **World Wide Web address:** http://www.boykinlodging.com. **Description:** A Marriott franchisee engaged in the development and management of upscale, full-service hotels. **Special programs:** Internships. **Corporate headquarters location:** This location. **Listed on:** New York Stock Exchange. **Stock exchange symbol:** BOY.

BRIDGESTONE/FIRESTONE TECHNOLOGY COMPANY.
1200 Firestone Parkway, Akron OH 44317. 330/379-7000. **Contact:** Human Resources. **World Wide Web address:** http://www.bridgestone-firestone.com.

Description: Engaged in the development, manufacture, and sale of a broad line of tires for the original equipment and replacement markets worldwide. Bridgestone/Firestone manages its business through three primary operating groups: the World Tire Group is responsible for the design, development, testing, and manufacturing of tires throughout the world; the Sales and Marketing Group is a nationwide sales network that includes dealer outlets and automotive service centers; and the Corporate Development Group is responsible for corporate strategic planning activities. **Corporate headquarters location:** Nashville TN. **Other area locations:** Brook Park OH; Akron OH. **Other U.S. locations:** Nationwide. **International locations:** Worldwide. **Parent company:** Bridgestone/Firestone Americas Holding, Inc. **Operations at this facility include:** This is the principal research and development facility, housing Bridgestone/Firestone Research and the Bridgestone/Firestone Technology Company.

BROWN PUBLISHING COMPANY
10222 Alliance Road, Cincinnati OH 45242. 513/794-5040. **Fax:** 513/791-5480. **Contact:** Human Resources. **E-mail address:** careers@brownpublishing.com. **World Wide Web address:** http://www.brownpublishing.com. **Description:** Publishes Ohio newspapers. Founded in 1920. **Other area locations:** Urbana OH.

BRUSH WELLMAN INC.
14710 West Portage River South Road, Elmore OH 43416-9502. 419/862-2745. **Fax:** 419/862-4000. **Contact:** Human Resources Department. **World Wide Web address:** http://www.moldmax.com. **Description:** Manufactures engineered materials, supplying world markets with metallic beryllium, beryllium alloys, beryllium ceramics, specialty clad metals, and ground-engaging cutting edges. **Corporate headquarters location:** Cleveland OH. **Other U.S. locations:** AZ; PA; MA; UT; NY; RI; IL; NJ; MI. **International locations:** Singapore; England; Germany; Japan. **Operations at this facility include:** Administration; Manufacturing; Research and Development; Sales; Service.

THE BUDD COMPANY/PLASTICS DIVISION
P.O. Box 277, North Baltimore OH 45872. 419/257-2231. **Physical address:** 100 South Poe Road, North Baltimore OH 45872. **Contact:** Human Resources. **World Wide Web address:** http://www.buddcompany.com. **Description:** Manufactures and markets fiberglass-reinforced composite compounds and molded products to the automobile, engine, and trucking industries. Founded in 1912. **Corporate headquarters location:** Troy MI. **Parent company:** ThyssenKrupp Automotive AG. **Operations at this facility include:** Manufacturing. **Number of employees nationwide:** 13,000.

BUNTING BEARINGS CORPORATION
P.O. Box 729, Holland OH 43528. 419/866-7000. **Physical address:** 1001 Holland Park Boulevard, Holland OH 43528. **Toll-free phone:** 888/286-8464. **Fax:** 419/866-0653. **Contact:** Phillip Henszler, Corporate Director of Human Resources. **World Wide Web address:** http://www.buntingbearings.com. **Description:** Manufactures and markets aluminum bearings, bronze, plastic, powdered metal, and solid bars for the industrial, automotive, consumer, and construction industries. Founded in 1855. **Corporate headquarters location:** This location. **Other U.S. locations:** Cerritos CA; Kalamazoo MI; Mansfield OH; Houston TX. **Parent company:** Eagle-Picher Industries. **Operations at this facility include:** Administration; Sales; Service. **Listed on:** Privately held.

BURGESS & NIPLE, LTD.
5085 Reed Road, Columbus OH 43220. 614/459-2050. **Fax:** 614/459-9433. **Contact:** Brenda White, Human Resources. **E-mail address:** hr@burnip.com. **World Wide Web address:** http://www.burgessniple.com. **Description:** An engineering and architecture firm engaged in study, analysis, and design services. The company specializes in waterworks, wastewater, industrial services, hydropower, energy conservation, transportation, systems analysis, HVAC, and geotechnical. **Positions advertised include:** Architect; Civil Engineer; Transportation Engineer; Print Clerk; CADD Technician. **Corporate headquarters location:** This location. **Other area locations:** Akron OH; Cincinnati OH; Painesville OH. **Other U.S. locations:** Payson AZ; Phoenix AZ; Indianapolis IN; Lexington KY; Charleston WV; Parkersburg WV. **Operations at this facility include:** Administration; Divisional Headquarters. **Listed on:** Privately held. **Number of employees at this location:** 275. **Number of employees nationwide:** 480.

BURGESS & NIPLE, LTD.
50 South Main Street, Suite 600, Akron OH 44308. 330/376-5778. **Fax:** 330/376-5741. **Contact:** Human Resources. **E-mail address:** hr@burnip.com. **World Wide Web address:** http://www.burgessniple.com. **Description:** An engineering and architecture firm engaged in study, analysis, and design services. The company specializes in waterworks, wastewater, industrial services, hydropower, energy conservation, transportation, systems analysis, HVAC, and geotechnical. **NOTE:** Hiring is done through the corporate headquarters. Applicants should send a resume to Ms. Pat Forster, Director of Human Resources, 5085 Reed Road, Columbus OH 43220. **Positions advertised include:** Civil Engineer; Hydrogeologist; Travel Demand Forecaster. **Corporate headquarters location:** Columbus OH. **Other area locations:** Cincinnati OH; Painesville OH. **Other U.S. locations:** Payson AZ; Phoenix AZ; Indianapolis IN; Lexington KY; Charleston WV; Parkersburg WV. **Listed on:** Privately held. **Number of employees nationwide:** 480.

BURGESS & NIPLE, LTD.
312 Plum Street, 12th Floor, Cincinnati OH 45202-2678. 513/579-0042. **Contact:** Human Resources. **E-mail address:** hr@burnip.com. **World Wide Web address:** http://www.burgessniple.com. **Description:** An engineering and architecture firm engaged in study, analysis, and design services. The company specializes in waterworks, wastewater, industrial services, hydropower, energy conservation, transportation, systems analysis, HVAC, and geotechnical. **NOTE:** Hiring is done through the corporate headquarters. Applicants should send a resume to Ms. Pat Forster, Director of Human Resources, 5085 Reed Road, Columbus OH 43220. **Positions advertised include:** Architect; Civil Engineer; Travel Demand Forecaster. **Corporate headquarters location:** Columbus OH. **Other area locations:** Akron OH; Painesville OH. **Other U.S. locations:** Payson AZ; Phoenix AZ; Indianapolis IN; Lexington KY; Charleston WV; Parkersburg WV. **Listed on:** Privately held. **Number of employees nationwide:** 480.

BURGESS & NIPLE, LTD.
100 West Erie Street, Painesville OH 44077. 440/354-9700. **Contact:** Human Resources. **E-mail address:** hr@burnip.com. **World Wide Web address:** http://www.burgessniple.com. **Description:** An engineering and architecture firm engaged in study, analysis, and design services. The company specializes in waterworks, wastewater, industrial services, hydropower, energy conservation, transportation, systems analysis, HVAC, and geotechnical. **NOTE:** Hiring is done through the corporate headquarters. Applicants should send a resume to Ms. Pat Forster, Director of Human Resources, 5085 Reed Road, Columbus OH 43220. **Positions advertised include:** Bridge Engineer; Rod/Chain Person; Travel Demand Forecaster. **Corporate headquarters location:** Columbus OH. **Other area locations:** Akron OH; Cincinnati OH. **Other U.S. locations:** Payson AZ; Phoenix AZ; Indianapolis IN; Lexington KY; Charleston WV; Parkersburg WV. **Listed on:** Privately held. **Number of employees nationwide:** 480.

THE BURNHAM FOUNDRY
P.O. Box 3148, Zanesville OH 43702-3148. 740/452-9371. **Physical address:** 2345 Licking Road, Zanesville OH 43701. **Fax:** 740/450-8081. **Contact:** Dave Jones, Manager of Human Resources. **World Wide Web address:** http://www.burnham.com. **Description:** Engaged in the production of gray and ductile iron products. **Corporate headquarters location:** Lancaster PA. **Parent company:** The Burnham Corporation. **Operations at this facility include:** Divisional Headquarters. **Number of employees at this location:** 300.

CB RICHARD ELLIS
PNC Center, 201 East Fifth Street, Suite 1510, Cincinnati OH 45202. 513/369-1300. **Fax:** 513/241-2291. **Contact:** Human Resources. **World Wide Web address:** http://www.cbrichardellis.com. **Description:** A real estate services company offering property sales and leasing, property and facility management, mortgage banking, and investment management services. **Corporate headquarters location:** Los Angeles CA. **Other U.S. locations:** Nationwide.

CB RICHARD ELLIS
200 Public Square, Suite 2560, Cleveland OH 44114. 216/687-1800. **Fax:** 216/363-6466. **Contact:** Human Resources. **World Wide Web address:** http://www.cbrichardellis.com. **Description:** A real estate services company offering property sales and leasing, property and facility management, mortgage banking, and investment management services.

CDR PIGMENTS & DISPERSIONS
410 Glendale-Milford Road, Cincinnati OH 45215. 513/771-1900. **Toll-free phone:** 800/237-5495. **Fax:** 513/771-0332. **Contact:** Yvonne Wilson, Personnel Department. **World Wide Web address:** http://www.cdrpigments.com. **Description:** Develops, manufactures, and markets high-quality colorants and varnish for ink, paint, and plastic applications. The company also provides color technology to nonink markets including coatings for paper and nonwoven materials; dispersions for latex products; and pigments for textile printing, decorative ribbons, and paints. Founded in 1980. **Parent company:** AlliedSignal Corporation serves a broad spectrum of industries through its more than 40 strategic businesses, which are grouped into three sectors: Aerospace; Automotive; and Engineered Materials. AlliedSignal is one of the nation's largest industrial organizations. **Number of employees nationwide:** 513.

CMC ELECTRONICS CINCINNATI
BAE SYSTEMS
7500 Innovation Way, Mason OH 45040. 513/573-6100. **Toll-free phone:** 800/543-8220. **Fax:** 513/573-6741. **Contact:** Personnel Director. **E-mail address:** resumes@cmccinci.com. **World Wide Web address:** http://www.cinele.com. **Description:** A leader in the design, development, production, and field support of sophisticated high-technology military electronic equipment. The company's business areas include contract production, communications systems and equipment, electronic warfare systems, infrared systems, and space electronics. **NOTE:** Will soon be part of L-3 Communications. **Positions advertised include:** Mechanical Engineer; Electronic Engineer; Microwave Circuit Design Engineer; Component Engineer; Test Engineer; Project Engineer; Test Technician; Marketing Manager; Internal Quality Auditor. **Corporate headquarters location:** This location. **Parent company:** BAE Systems. **Operations at this facility include:** Manufacturing; Research and Development. **Listed on:** Privately held. **Number of employees at this location:** 340.

CSA INTERNATIONAL
8501 East Pleasant Valley Road, Independence OH 44131-5575. 216/524-4990. **Contact:** Human Resources Manager. **World Wide Web address:** http://www.csa-international.org. **Description:** Performs certification testing and operates research labs for gas-fired equipment. **Operations at this facility include:** Research and Development; Service.

CTC PARKER AUTOMATION
50 West TechneCenter Drive, Milford OH 45150. 513/831-2340. **Fax:** 513/831-5042. **Contact:** Human Resources. **World Wide Web address:** http://www.ctcusa.com. **Description:** Designs, develops, and manufactures computer hardware and software for industrial applications. **Corporate headquarters location:** This location. **Parent company:** Parker Hannifin Corporation.

CTRAC COMPUTER SERVICES
8300 Dow Circle #100, Cleveland OH 44136. 440/826-9000. **Fax:** 440/826-9030. **Contact:** Human Resources. **E-mail address:** ctrac@ctrac.com. **World Wide Web address:** http://www.ctrac.com. **Description:** A direct mail service bureau.

CABLES TO GO
1501 Webster Street, Dayton OH 45404. 937/224-8646. **Fax:** 937/496-2657. **Contact:** Human Resources Administrator. **E-mail address:** hr@cablestogo.com. **World Wide Web address:** http://www.cablestogo.com. **Description:** Manufactures and distributes computer connection equipment including adapters, cables, connectors, and networking equipment. **Corporate headquarters location:** This location.

CALGON CARBON
835 North Cassady Avenue, Columbus OH 43219. 614/258-9501. **Fax:** 614/258-3464. **Contact:** Diana Dee, Human Resources. **World Wide Web address:** http://www.bscarbons.com. **Description:** Develops, manufactures, and produces activated carbon for air, gas, and liquid filtration systems. The company also manufactures a wide variety of adsorbers and systems used in filtration applications including adsorption systems, bioreactors and bioscrubbers, concentrators, containment bag-in/bag-out housings, corrosive gas control systems, distillation equipment, indoor air quality systems, solvent recovery systems, and VOC/HAP emission control systems. **Other U.S. locations:** Nationwide.

THE CAMPBELL GROUP
POWERWINCH DIVISION
100 Production Drive, Harrison OH 45030-1477. 513/367-4811. **Contact:** Human Resources. **World Wide Web address:** http://www.chpower.com. **Description:** Manufactures powered equipment including power winches used for towing boats, airplanes, and anchors. **Subsidiaries include:** Campbell Hausfield; Powerwinch; PowerX; Wayne Water Systems.

CAMPBELL SOUP COMPANY
P.O. Box 311, East Maumee Avenue, Napoleon OH 43545. 419/592-1010. **Fax:** 419/599-6701. **Contact:** Human Resources Department. **World Wide Web address:**

http://www.campbellsoups.com. **Description:** Manufactures and markets a variety of food products. The company's product names include Campbell's Chunky Soups, Campbell's Condensed Soups, Campbell's Select Soups, Franco-American Gravies, Healthy Request Soups, Pace Foods, Pepperidge Farm Cookies, Pepperidge Farm Goldfish Crackers, Pepperidge Farm Puff Pastry, Prego Hearty Meat Sauces, Swanson Broth, Simply Home Soups, and V8 100% Vegetable Juice. Founded in 1869. **Positions advertised include:** Maintenance Manager. **Corporate headquarters location:** Camden NJ. **Operations at this facility include:** Administration; Manufacturing; Regional Headquarters; Research and Development; Sales. **Listed on:** New York Stock Exchange. **Stock exchange symbol:** CPB. **Number of employees at this location:** 2,700. **Number of employees nationwide:** 40,000.

CAPGEMINI
1000 Skylight Office Tower, 1660 West Second Street, Cleveland OH 44113. 216/583-3300. **Fax:** 216/583-8319. **Contact:** Recruiting Manager. **World Wide Web address:** http://www.capgemini.com. **Description:** Provides management consulting services including business strategy, operations, and people and information management. Services include systems integration; application design, development, and documentation; systems conversions and migrations; and information technology consulting. **Other U.S. locations:** Nationwide.

CAPITAL UNIVERSITY
2199 East Main Street, 136 Yochum Hall, Columbus OH 43209-2394. 614/236-6168. **Fax:** 614/236-6820. **Contact:** Theresa Feldmeier, Personnel. **E-mail address:** tfeldmei@capital.edu. **World Wide Web address:** http://www.capital.edu. **Description:** A private church affiliated university. Capital University is organized into four undergraduate units: the College of Arts and Sciences, the Conservatory of Music, the School of Nursing, and an Adult Degree Program. Two graduate colleges, the Law and Graduate Center and the Graduate School of Administration, offer degrees in law and taxation, as well as a Master of Business Administration. In addition, the School of Nursing offers a master's degree. The university offers six undergraduate degrees and more than 70 majors, as well as six graduate degrees to its approximately 3,820 students. Founded in 1830. **Positions advertised include:** Assistant Professor, Rhetoric and Composition; Director of Residence Life; Director of Student Activities; Records Management Assistant; Public Safety Officer.

CARAUSTAR
CUSTOM PACKAGING GROUP
600 Union Street, Ashland OH 44805. 419/289-2666. **Fax:** 419/281-5415. **Contact:** Personnel Manager. **World Wide Web address:** http://www.caraustar.com. **Description:** Caraustar manufactures and converts recycled paperboard and packaging products. The company's products include recycled paperboard, gypsum wallboard, and plastics; paper tubes; folding cartons; composite containers; and specialized industrial packaging. Founded in 1938. **Corporate headquarters location:** Charlotte NC. **Operations at this location include:** This location manufactures printed and unprinted folding cartons. **Listed on:** NASDAQ. **Stock exchange symbol:** CSAR.

CARAUSTAR INDUSTRIES, INC.
P.O. Box 930, St. Paris OH 43072. 937/663-4142. **Physical address:** 310 State Route 235, Saint Paris OH 43072. **Fax:** 937/663-5960. **Contact:** Lawrence J. Subler, Human Resources Manager. **World Wide Web address:** http://www.caraustar.com. **Description:** Caraustar Industries manufactures and converts recycled paperboard and packaging products. The company primarily operates through four divisions including converting operations that manufacture paper tubes, composite containers, cores, folding cartons, and specialized industrial packaging; primary manufacturing facilities for adhesives, gypsum wallboard, plastics, and recycled paperboard; recovered fiber recycling centers; and a transportation company. **Corporate headquarters location:** This location. **Operations at this facility include:** This location is engaged in the manufacture of composite cans and metal ends and is the divisional headquarters. **Listed on:** NASDAQ. **Stock exchange symbol:** CSAR.

CARDINAL HEALTH, INC.
7000 Cardinal Place, Dublin OH 43017. 614/757-5000. **Toll-free phone:** 800/234-8701. **Fax:** 614/757-8602. **Recorded jobline:** 614/757-5627. **Contact:** Human Resources Department. **World Wide Web address:** http://www.cardhealth.com. **Description:** A wholesale distributor of pharmaceuticals, medical and surgical products, and related health supplies. The company also distributes merchandise typically sold in retail drug stores, hospitals, and health care provider facilities. Cardinal Health provides specialized support services to assist clients such as order-entry and confirmation, inventory control, monitoring pricing strategies, and financial reporting. The company has developed an in-pharmacy computer system that provides prices, patient profiles, financial data, and management services. **Positions advertised include:** Senior Programmer Analyst; Graphic Designer; Compensation Analyst; Administrative Assistant; Buyer Assistant; Project Engineer; Credit Collections Specialist; Quality Assurance Analyst; Business Systems Analyst; Financial Analyst; Senior Tax Analyst; Human Resources Manager; Senior Auditor. **Special programs:** Internships. **Corporate headquarters location:** This location. **Subsidiaries include:** Medicine Shoppe International, Inc.; National PharmPak Services, Inc.; PCI Services, Inc.; ScriptLINE. **Listed on:** New York Stock Exchange. **Stock exchange symbol:** CAH. **Annual sales/revenues:** $21 - $50 million. **Number of employees at this location:** 1,300. **Number of employees nationwide:** 30,000. **Number of employees worldwide:** 36,000.

CARDINAL HEALTH
6045 Cochran Road, Cleveland OH 44139. 440/248-9300. **Contact:** Human Resources. **World Wide Web address:** http://www.nps.cardinal.com/nps/index.asp. **Description:** This location manufactures radiation measuring instruments, high-meg resistors, and medical devices. **Positions advertised include:** Assembly Worker. **Subsidiaries include:** Medicine Shoppe International, Inc.; National PharmPak Services, Inc.; PCI Services, Inc.; ScriptLINE. **Listed on:** New York Stock Exchange. **Stock exchange symbol:** CAH. **Annual sales/revenues:** $21 - $50 million. **Number of employees at this location:** 1,300. **Number of employees nationwide:** 30,000. **Number of employees worldwide:** 36,000.

CARDWARE INTERNATIONAL
432 South 22nd Street, Heath OH 43056. 740/522-2158. **Fax:** 740/345-1985. **Contact:** Human Resources. **World Wide Web Address:** http://www.13-inc.com. **Description:** Distributes credit card transaction equipment and supplies.

JOHN CARROLL UNIVERSITY
20700 North Park Boulevard, University Heights OH 44118. 216/397-4976. **Fax:** 216/397-4933. **Contact:** Lisa Mencini, Director of Human Resources. **World Wide Web address:** http://www.jcu.edu. **Description:** A university with an enrollment of approximately 4,382 undergraduate and graduate students. John Carroll University offers 58 bachelor's and master's degree programs. Founded in 1886. **Positions advertised include:** Director of Athletics and Recreation; Area Coordinator, Residential Life; Dean, College of Arts and Sciences; Hockey Coach; Technical Assistant; Gate Attendant; Bus/Van Driver. **Number of employees at this location:** 500.

CARROLS CORPORATION
1531 Boettler Road, Unit F, Uniontown OH 44685. 330/896-3838. **Fax:** 330/896-5372. **Contact:** Heather Kane, Human Resources Manager. **World Wide Web address:** http://www.carrols.com. **Description:** A franchise operator of Burger King fast food restaurants. Carrols Corporation also owns and operates restaurants under the names Pollo Tropical and Tropi Grill. **Special programs:** Internships. **Corporate headquarters location:** Syracuse NY. **Other U.S. locations:** Albany NY; Charlotte NC. **Listed on:** Privately held. **Number of employees nationwide:** 10,000.

CASCADE CORPORATION
2501 Sheridan Avenue, Springfield OH 45505. 937/327-0300. **Fax:** 937/327-0082. **Contact:** Rita Schuler, Human Resources Manager. **World Wide Web address:** http://www.cascorp.com. **Description:** Develops, designs, manufactures and markets material handling equipment and related products. Cascade Corporation specializes in the production of cylinders, forks, and lift truck equipment for the industrial markets. **Corporate headquarters location:** Portland OR.

CASS INFORMATION SYSTEMS, INC.
2675 Corporate Exchange Drive, Columbus OH 43231. 614/839-4500. **Fax:** 614/839-4299. **Contact:** Human Resources Manager. **World Wide Web address:** http://www.cassinfo.com. **Description:** A provider of logistics-related information services that include processing and payment of freight charges, preparation of transportation management reports, auditing of freight charges, and rating of freight shipments. Cass Information Systems operations are divided between its Payment Systems Group and its Software Systems Group. Founded in 1956. **NOTE:** Entry-level positions are offered. **Parent company:** Cass Commercial Corporation is also the parent company of Cass Bank & Trust, a wholly-owned bank that provides a full range of banking services to individual, corporate, and institutional customers. Cass Bank & Trust operates through its main bank in Sunset Hills MO, two downtown St. Louis facilities, and through its West Port facility in Maryland Heights MO. **Other U.S. locations:** Lowell MA; Bridgeton MO. **Listed on:** NASDAQ. **Stock exchange symbol:** CASS. **Annual sales/revenues:** $5 - $10 million. **Number of employees at this location:** 130. **Number of employees nationwide:** 650.

CAST-FAB TECHNOLOGIES INC.
3040 Forrer Street, Cincinnati OH 45209. 513/758-1000. **Fax:** 513/758-1115. **Contact:** Human Resources Manager. **E-mail address:** information@cast-fab.com. **World Wide Web address:** http://www.cast-fab.com. **Description:** Designs, develops, manufactures and markets gray and ductile iron castings, patterns, steel-welded fabrications, and precision sheet metal components to a wide range of industries.

CEDAR FAIR L.P.
One Cedar Point Drive, Sandusky OH 44870-5259. 419/627-2233. **Fax:** 419/627-2163. **Contact:** Human Resources. **E-mail address:** work@cedarpoint.com. **World Wide Web address:** http://www.cedarfair.com. **Description:** Owns and operates three seasonal amusement parks. Cedar Point, located on Lake Erie between Cleveland and Toledo, is the third-oldest amusement park still in operation in the United States. Knott's Berry Farm is located near Los Angeles, California. Valleyfair, located near Minneapolis-St. Paul, is one of the largest amusement parks in Minnesota and serves a total population of 8 million people. Worlds of Fun and Oceans of Fun are jointly located in Kansas City, Missouri. Dorney Park & Wildwater Kingdom is located near Allentown PA.

CENTURY 21
JOE WALKER & ASSOCIATES
409 West Main Street, Westerville OH 43081. 614/899-1400. **Fax:** 614/899-0955. **Contact:** Craig Barone, Recruiting and Career Development. **E-mail address:** craig.barone@aol.com. **World Wide Web address:** http://www.c21joewalker.com. **Description:** A real estate company serving nine counties in central Ohio. **Corporate headquarters location:** This location. **Other area locations:** Columbus OH; Delaware OH; Reynoldsburg OH; Sunbury OH.

CENVEO
4500 Tiedeman Road, Cleveland OH 44144. 216/430-4000. **Contact:** Personnel Manager. **World Wide Web address:** http://www.cenveo.com. **Description:** Manufactures envelopes and tags. **Other U.S. locations:** Nationwide. **International locations:** Canada; Mexico; United Kingdom.

CHAMPION COMPUTER TECHNOLOGIES
23400 Mercantile Road, Suite 7, Beachwood OH 44122. 216/831-1800. **Toll-free phone:** 800/860-7466. **Fax:** 216/831-2541. **Contact:** Personnel. **E-mail address:** hr@cctupgrades.com. **World Wide Web address:** http://www.cctupgrades.com. **Description:** Manufactures computer memory upgrades for desktops, servers, printers, and notebooks, as well as high-performance PCMCIA notebook computer adapters for communications, network connectivity, and storage. Founded in 1992.

CHARTER ONE BANK
1215 Superior Avenue, Cleveland OH 44114. 216/566-5300. **Recorded jobline:** 216/566-0253. **Contact:** Human Resources Department. **World Wide Web address:** http://www.charterone.com. **Description:** A full-service financial institution with approximately $32 billion in assets. **Positions advertised include:** Asset Recovery Account Representative; Administrative Analyst; ATM Lockbox Processor; Bill Payer Representative; Branch Sales Manager; Closing Coordinator; Credit Counselor; Customer Information Representative; Data Entry Clerk; Direct Banking Specialist; Employment Representative; Encoder; Fulfillment Specialist; Production Mail Operator; Retail Sales Associate. **Corporate headquarters location:** This location. **Parent company:** Charter One Financial. **Listed on:** NASDAQ. **Stock exchange symbol:** CHFN. **Number of employees at this location:** 1,300.

CHEMICAL ABSTRACTS SERVICE
P.O. Box 3012, Columbus OH 43210-0012. 614/447-3731. **Physical address:** 2540 Olentangy River Road, Columbus OH 43202-1505. **Toll-free phone:** 800/753-4227. **Fax:** 614/447-3713. **Contact:** Human Resources. **E-mail address:** jobs@cas.org. **World Wide Web address:** http://www.cas.org. **Description:** Collates information extracted from over 8,000 chemistry journals, conferences, and dissertations for publication in a weekly newsletter, as well as online and in CD-ROM format. **NOTE:** The company hires chemists to do research and information services personnel to maintain the database and online service. **Positions advertised include:** Editorial Assistant; Finance Assistant; Computer Operator; Technical Journal Editor; Journal Production Manager. **Corporate headquarters location:** Washington DC. **Parent company:** American Chemical Society. **Operations at this facility include:** Administration; Divisional Headquarters; Research and Development; Sales. **Listed on:** Privately held. **Number of employees at this location:** 1,200. **Number of employees nationwide:** 2,000.

CHILD & ELDER CARE INSIGHTS, INC.
19111 Detroit Road, Suite 104, Rocky River OH 44116. 440/356-2900. **Fax:** 440/356-2919. **Contact:** Elisabeth A. Bryenton, President. **E-mail address:** info@carereports.com. **World Wide Web address:** http://www.carereports.com. **Description:** A national dependent care resource and referral service that maintains two national databases: CHILDBASE and ELDERBASE. CHILDBASE provides working parents with information about child care services including family day care providers, preschools, adoption resources, in-home care, and schools. ELDERBASE provides information on nursing homes, home health agencies, nutrition services, continuing care/retirement communities, and transportation services. **Other U.S. locations:** Nationwide.

CHIQUITA BRANDS INTERNATIONAL INC.
250 East Fifth Street, Cincinnati OH 45202. 513/784-8000. **Fax:** 513/784-8030. **Contact:** Human Resources. **E-mail address:** jobs@chiquita.com. **World Wide Web address:** http://www.chiquita.com. **Description:** Produces, processes, and distributes fresh and prepared foods that are sold under the Chiquita and other brand names. Products include fresh fruits and vegetables from the United States and South and Central American countries, as well as juices, purees, salads, margarine, and shortening products. **NOTE:** Include the job number of the position you are applying for in the subject line of your e-mail or letter. **Positions advertised include:** Credit and Collections Specialist; Documentation Coordinator; Product Development Manager. **Corporate headquarters location:** This location. **Listed on:** New York Stock Exchange. **Stock exchange symbol:** CQB.

CHRIST HOSPITAL
2139 Auburn Avenue, Cincinnati OH 45219-2989. 513/585-2000. **Fax:** 513/585-3646. **Recorded jobline:** 513/585-2251. **Contact:** Human Resources. **World Wide Web address:** http://www.health-alliance.com/christ.html. **Description:** A nonprofit, 550-bed acute care hospital. The hospital specializes in advanced orthopedics, behavioral medicine, cancer care, cardiac care, geriatric medicine, internal medicine, surgical specialties, and women's health. Founded in 1889. **NOTE:** The hospital is offering a signing bonus of up to $30,000 for Registered Nurses in critical care areas who are able to make a three year commitment. **Positions advertised include:** Pharmacist; Physical Therapist; Radiologic Technologist; Clinical Supervisor; Health Unit Coordinator; Chemical Dependency Therapist; Licensed Practical Nurse; Administrative Secretary; Coder; Nurse Manager; Case Manager; Safety Security Officer; File Clerk; Ultrasound Technician; Registered Nurse.

THE CHRONICLE TELEGRAM
P.O. Box 4010, 225 East Avenue, Elyria OH 44036. 440/329-7000. **Fax:** 440/329-7177. **Contact:** Human Resources Department. **World Wide Web address:** http://www.chronicletelegram.com. **Description:** A daily newspaper. Founded in 1829.

CINCINNATI ASSOCIATION FOR THE BLIND
2045 Gilbert Avenue, Cincinnati OH 45202. 513/487-4213. **Toll-free phone:** 888/687-3935. **Fax:** 513/221-2995. **Contact:** Jennifer Glassmeyer, Human Resources Department. **E-mail address:** jennifer.glassmeyer@cincyblind.org. **World Wide Web address:** http://www.cincyblind.org. **Description:** An association that offers a variety of services for the blind including mobility instruction, rehabilitation teaching, computer training, and talking book programs. **Positions advertised include:** Accounting Clerk; Computer Access Specialist. **Special programs:** Volunteering opportunities available.

CINCINNATI BELL, INC.
201 East Fourth Street, Room M30, Cincinnati OH 45202. 513/397-9900. **Contact:** Human Resources Department. **World Wide Web address:** http://home.cincinnatibell.com. **Description:** One of the largest local telephone companies in the United States. The telephone company provides local telephone service in southwestern Ohio and parts of northern Kentucky and Indiana. The company serves 865,000 network access lines. Other businesses include a cellular mobile telephone service; Cincinnati Bell Long Distance, a reseller of long-distance communication services; and the Yellow Pages Directory services. **Special programs:** Internships. **Corporate headquarters location:** This location. **Parent company:** Broadwing.

CINCINNATI CHILDREN'S HOSPITAL MEDICAL CENTER
Professional Services Building, 2900 Vernon Place, Cincinnati OH 45229-3039. 513/636-4244. **Toll-free phone:** 800/344-2462. **Contact:** Human Resources. **E-mail address:** careers@chmcc.org. **World Wide Web address:** http://www.cincinnatichildrens.org. **Description:** A nationally recognized children's hospital serving the needs of infants, children, and adolescents. Cincinnati Children's Hospital's state-of-the-art facilities include a Heart Center, a Pediatric Liver Care Center, and a Hematology and Oncology Division. The medical center also functions as a research institution and teaching hospital for the University of Cincinnati College of Medicine. Cincinnati Children's Hospital operates several outpatient facilities located within Cincinnati and throughout Ohio. These outpatient sites offer a variety of services to supplement the treatment available at the Medical Center's main campus. **Positions advertised include:** Clinical Nurse; Nurse Practitioner; Surgical Technologist; Research Nurse; Occupational Therapist; Food Service Assistant; Respiratory Therapist; Social Worker; Health Unit Coordinator; Patient Attendant; Assistant Professor, Orthopedic Surgery. **Special programs:** Fellowships; Internships; Residency Programs. **Other area locations:** Fairfield OH; Harrison OH; Mason OH; Middletown OH; Westchester OH. **Other U.S. locations:** Crestview Hills KY. **Operations at this facility include:** Health Care. **Number of employees nationwide:** Approximately 7,200.

CINCINNATI, CITY OF
Centennial Two Plaza, Suite 200, 805 Central Avenue, Cincinnati OH 45202. 513/352-2400. **Fax:** 513/352-5223. **Recorded jobline:** 513/352-2489. **Contact:** Rodney Prince, Director of Personnel. **World Wide Web address:** http://www.cincinnati-oh.gov. **Description:** Administrative offices for the city of Cincinnati. The department's divisions include civil service, labor relations, classification and compensation, testing, training/recruitment, support staff, and EEO. **Positions advertised include:** Senior Engineer; Technical Systems Analyst; Senior Computer Programmer Analyst; Park Board Summer Counselor; Public Health Nurse; Pool Manager; Lifeguard.

CINCINNATI ENQUIRER
312 Elm Street, Cincinnati OH 45202. 513/721-2700. **Fax:** 517/768-8210. **Contact:** Personnel Director. **World Wide Web address:** http://enquirer.com. **Description:** Publishes a daily newspaper. **Positions advertised include:** Independent Sales Representative; Automotive Account Representative; Entertainment Account Representative; Circulation Sales Representative.

CINCINNATI FINANCIAL CORPORATION
P.O. Box 145496, Cincinnati OH 45250-5496. **Physical address:** 6200 South Gilmore Road, Fairfield OH 45014. 513/870-2000. **Fax:** 513/870-2911. **Contact:** Human Resources Director. **E-mail address:** personnel@cinfin.com. **World Wide Web address:** http://www.cinfin.com. **Description:** An insurance holding company that is primarily engaged in marketing and selling property and casualty coverage and life insurance. Founded in 1968. **NOTE:** If submitting a resume by e-mail, include the resume in the text of your message. **Subsidiaries include:** The Cincinnati Insurance Company is the company's leading property and casualty company; Cincinnati Casualty Company and Cincinnati Indemnity Company also offer property and casualty insurance; Cincinnati Life Insurance Company offers life, health, and accident insurance; and CFC Investment Company supports insurance subsidiaries through leasing, financing, and real estate activities. CinFin Capital Management Company offers investment management services to corporations, individuals, and institutions.

CINCINNATI HAMILTON COMMUNITY ACTION AGENCY
2904 Woodburn Avenue, Cincinnati OH 45206. 513/569-1840. **Fax:** 513/569-1251. **Contact:** Human Resources. **Description:** An agency that offers food vouchers, home energy assistance, Head Start programs, rent assistance, and utility bills assistance.

CINCINNATI OPERA
1241 Elm Street, Cincinnati OH 45210. 513/621-1919. **Fax:** 513/744-3520. **Contact:** Human Resources. **E-mail address:** info@cincinnatiopera.com. **World Wide Web address:** http://www.cincyopera.com. **Description:** The second oldest opera company in the United States. The Cincinnati Opera also offers educational and outreach programs to children, aspiring artists, and educators. Founded in 1920.

CINCINNATI PLAYHOUSE
P.O. Box 6537, Cincinnati OH 45206. 513/345-2242. **Physical address:** 962 Mount Adams Circle, Cincinnati OH 45202. **Fax:** 513/345-2254. **Contact:** Personnel. **E-mail address:** admin@cincyplay.com. **World Wide Web address:** http://www.cincyplay.com. **Description:** A professional regional theatre producing classic and contemporary comedies, dramas, musicals, and recent hits during a 10-month season. The Cincinnati Playhouse operates two theatres including The Robert S. Marx Theatre, which houses 628 seats, and the Thompson Shelterhouse, which seats 225. Founded in 1960. **Positions advertised include:** Summer Theatre Day Camp Director; Seasonal Subscription Assistant. **Special programs:** Acting Internships.

CINCINNATI PUBLIC SCHOOLS
P.O. Box 5381, Cincinnati OH 45201-5381. 513/475-7000. **Physical address:** 2651 Burnet Road, Cincinnati OH 45219. **Fax:** 513/475-4873. **Contact:** Carol Landwehr, Human Resources. **World Wide Web address:** http://www.cps-k12.org. **Description:** Administrative offices for the Cincinnati public school district. **Positions advertised include:** Instructor Assistant; Substitute Teacher; Middle School Teacher; High School English Teacher; High School Mathematics Teacher; Speech Language Pathologist; Food Services Supervisor.

CINCINNATI ZOO
3400 Vine Street, Cincinnati OH 45220. 513/559-7706. **Recorded jobline:** 513/559-7706. **Contact:** Personnel. **World Wide Web address:** http://www.cincyzoo.org. **Description:** A zoo and botanical garden housing approximately 700 different animal species and over 3,000 types of plants. The Cincinnati Zoo also operates several research and conservation programs including the Center for Research and Endangered Wildlife (CREW), Cheetah Conservation, Guam Rail Release, Mountain Gorilla Conservation, and the Zoo Conservation Fund. **NOTE:** Seasonal opportunities are available. **Number of employees at this location:** 170.

CINCOM SYSTEMS, INC.
55 Merchant Street, Cincinnati OH 45246. 513/612-2300. **Toll-free phone:** 800/224-6266. **Fax:** 513/612-2000. **Contact:** Human Resources. **World Wide Web address:** http://www.cincom.com. **Description:** Develops business software for manufacturing companies, solutions for object-oriented and fourth-generation language application development, client/server and relational object-oriented databases, workflow automation, and document solutions. Founded in 1968. **Positions advertised include:** Financial Services Consultant; Payroll Assistant; Marketing Communications Specialist. **Corporate headquarters location:** This location. **Other area locations:** Columbus OH. **Other U.S. locations:** Nationwide. **International locations:** Worldwide. **Listed on:** Privately held. **Annual sales/revenues:** More than $100 million. **Number of employees at this location:** 500. **Number of employees nationwide:** 1,000.

CINERGY CORP.
139 East Fourth Street, Cincinnati OH 45202. 513/421-9500. **Toll-free phone:** 800/544-6900. **Contact:** Human Resources. **World Wide Web address:** http://www.cinergy.com. **Description:** Primarily engaged in providing electric and gas service in the southwestern portion of Ohio and adjacent areas in Kentucky and Indiana, an area covering approximately 3,000 square miles with an estimated population of 1.7 million. **Positions advertised include:** Paralegal; Customer Project Coordinator; Gas Controller. **Special programs:** Internships; Co-ops; Leadership Development Program. **Corporate headquarters location:** This location. **Listed on:** New York Stock Exchange. **Stock exchange symbol:** CIN.

CINTAS CORPORATION
6800 Cintas Boulevard, P.O. Box 625737, Cincinnati OH 45262-5737. 513/459-1200. **Toll-free phone:** 800/786-4367. **Fax:** 513/573-4159. **Contact:** Human Resources. **World Wide Web address:** http://www.cintas-corp.com. **Description:** Designs, manufactures, and distributes uniforms and ancillary products through rental and direct sale for companies throughout the United States. Cintas Corporation has 300 locations in 39 states. **Positions advertised include:** Accountant; Customer Service Representative; Data Warehouse Analyst; Travel Consultant. **Listed on:** NASDAQ. **Stock exchange symbol:** CTAS. **Number of employees nationwide:** 23,000.

CITIZENS NATIONAL BANK
102 South Main Street, P.O. Box 88, Bluffton OH 45817-0088. 419/358-8040. **Fax:** 419/358-5227. **Contact:** Personnel Director. **E-mail address:** resume@cnbohio.com. **World Wide Web address:** http://www.cnbohio.com. **Description:** A bank.

CLEAN HARBORS, INC.
4879 Spring Grove Avenue, Cincinnati OH 45232. 513/681-6242. **Toll-free phone:** 800/805-4582. **Contact:** Human Resources Department. **World Wide Web address:** http://www.cleanharbors.com. **Description:** Clean Harbors, Inc., through its subsidiaries, provides comprehensive environmental services in 35 states in the Northeast, Midwest, Central, and Mid-Atlantic regions. Clean Harbors provides a wide range of hazardous waste management and environmental support services to a diversified customer base. The company's hazardous waste management services include treatment, storage, recycling, transportation, risk analysis, site assessment, laboratory analysis, site closure, and disposal of hazardous materials through environmentally sound methods including incineration. Environmental remediation services include emergency response, surface remediation, groundwater restoration, industrial maintenance, and facility decontamination. Customers include regional

utilities; oil, pharmaceutical, and chemical companies; small businesses; and the high-tech and biotech industries. **Positions advertised include:** Facility Technician; Field Technician; Compliance Specialist; Compliance Guard; Class A Driver. **Corporate headquarters location:** Braintree MA. **Other U.S. locations:** Nationwide. **Listed on:** NASDAQ. **Stock exchange symbol:** CLHB. **Chairman/CEO:** Alan S. McKim. **Number of employees nationwide:** 1,400.

CLEVELAND CLINIC FOUNDATION
P.O. Box 606140, Cleveland OH 44106. 216/445-1386. **Physical address:** 9500 Euclid Avenue, Cleveland OH 44195. **Fax:** 216/444-6096. **Contact:** Miriam J. Barton, Director of Human Resources. **E-mail address:** bartonm1@ccf.org. **World Wide Web address:** http://www.cchs.net. **Description:** A national referral center and international health resource center specializing in tertiary care, medical research, and medical education. Founded in 1921. **Positions advertised include:** Registered Nurse Practitioner; Registered Nurse; Licensed Nurse Practitioner. **Corporate headquarters location:** This location. **Other U.S. locations:** Fort Lauderdale FL. **Number of employees nationwide:** 10,000.

CLEVELAND INSTITUTE OF MUSIC
11021 East Boulevard, Cleveland OH 44106. 216/791-5000 ext. 219. **Fax:** 216/791-1530. **Contact:** Janice Snyder, Director of Human Resources. **E-mail address:** jms46@cwru.edu. **World Wide Web address:** http://www.cim.edu. **Description:** A leading international conservatory offering baccalaureate, graduate, and doctoral programs in Music and Musical Arts. CIM offers a joint music program with Case Western University. Founded in 1920. **Positions advertised include:** Director of the Sato Center of Suzuki Studies; Director of Opera Program.

CLEVELAND GEAR COMPANY
3249 East 80th Street, Cleveland OH 44104. 216/641-9000. **Toll-free phone:** 800/423-3169. **Fax:** 216/641-2731. **Contact:** Human Resources. **World Wide Web address:** http://www.clevelandgear.com. **Description:** Manufactures a broad range of industrial power transmission equipment. Cleveland Gear Company's products include drives, gears, modular and custom helical enclosed drives, reducers, and variators. Founded in 1912.

CLEVELAND METROPARKS ZOO
4101 Fulton Parkway, Cleveland OH 44144. 216/635-3280. **Recorded jobline:** 216/635-3211. **Fax:** 216/635-3286. **Contact:** Human Resources Department. **E-mail address:** resumes@clevelandmetroparks.com. **World Wide Web address:** http://www.clemetparks.com. **Description:** Features thousands of animals from 7 continents housed on 165 wooded acres and 2 indoor acres of tropics. The Cleveland Metroparks Zoo also offers several education programs including programs for schools and groups at the zoo, programs for schools and groups away from the zoo, distance learning programs, safaris and night tracks, and college-level courses. **NOTE:** Seasonal positions are available. **Special programs:** Internships, Part-Time and Seasonal Employment. **Internship information:** Please visit the zoo's Website for current internship information. **Office hours:** Monday - Friday, 8:00 a.m. - 5:00 p.m.

CLEVELAND MUNICIPAL SCHOOL DISTRICT
Employee Services Department, 1380 East 6th Street, Room 500N, Cleveland OH 44114. 216/574-8175. **Contact:** Human Resources. **E-mail address:** hr@cmsdnet.net. **World Wide Web address:** http://www.cmsdnet.net/jobs. **Description:** Coordinates resources and information for Cleveland area public schools. **NOTE:** Teacher recruitment information is available at: http://www.teachcleveland.com. **Positions advertised include:** Substitute Cleaner; Food Supervisor; Parent Mentor; Speech Language Pathologist.

THE CLEVELAND PLAYHOUSE
8500 Euclid Avenue, Cleveland OH 44106. 216/795-7000. **Fax:** 216/795-7005. **Contact:** Personnel. **World Wide Web address:** http://www.clevelandplayhouse.com. **Description:** A theater dedicated to the presentation of new and classical American plays. Founded in 1915. **Positions advertised include:** Telephone Sales Representative. **Internship information:** Visit the Playhouse website or call for current information.

CLEVELAND-CLIFFS INC.
1100 Superior Avenue, Cleveland OH 44114-2589. 216/694-5700. **Fax:** 216/694-5381. **Contact:** Human Resources. **E-mail address:** recruiting@cleveland-cliffs.com. **World Wide Web address:** http://www.cleveland-cliffs.com. **Description:** Engaged in the production and supply of iron ore pellets and products to the steel industry worldwide. The company is one of the nation's only full-service iron ore companies, managing mines and partnerships, selling and trading ores, and leasing reserves. **Listed on:** New York Stock Exchange. **Stock exchange symbol:** CLF.

CLOPAY CORPORATION
312 Walnut Street, Suite 1600, Cincinnati OH 45202. 513/770-4800. **Fax:** 513/770-3890. **Contact:** Troy Bartson, Human Resources Manager. **World Wide Web address:** http://www.clopay.com. **Description:** Manufactures building products and specialty plastic films. The company specializes in residential and industrial garage door systems, self-storage systems, and related products for the commercial and residential markets. Clopay's building distribution centers service both retail and dealer customers. **NOTE:** Mail resumes to: 8585 Duke Boulevard, Mason OH 45040. **Positions advertised include:** Internal Auditor; Senior Advanced Manufacturing Engineer. **Parent company:** Griffon Corporation. **Listed on:** New York Stock Exchange. **Stock exchange symbol:** GFF.

COCA-COLA ENTERPRISES INC.
5100 Duck Creek Road, Cincinnati OH 45227. 513/527-6600. **Fax:** 513/527-8328. **Recorded jobline:** 800/543-2653 ext. 8476. **Contact:** Human Resources. **E-mail address:** recruitingoh@na.cokece.com. **World Wide Web address:** http://www.cokecce.com. **Description:** One of the world's largest marketers, distributors, and producers of bottled and canned, nonalcoholic beverages. The company operates approximately 400 facilities; over 40,000 vehicles; and more than 1.5 million vending machines, beverage dispensers, and coolers. The product line includes traditional carbonated soft drinks, still and sparking waters, juices, isotonics, and teas. **Positions advertised include:** Second Shift Dispatcher; Retail Space Representative. **Corporate headquarters location:** Atlanta GA. **Other U.S. locations:** Nationwide. **Listed on:** New York Stock Exchange. **Stock exchange symbol:** CCE. **Number of employees nationwide:** 58,000.

COE MANUFACTURING COMPANY
P.O. Box 520, 609 Bank Street, Painesville OH 44077. 440/352-9381. **Fax:** 440/352-1487. **Contact:** Human Resources. **World Wide Web address:** http://www.coemfg.com. **Description:** Manufactures machinery for the production and handling of plywood, composition board, lumber, rubber and plastics, and engineered wood products. Founded in 1852.

COGNIS
5051 Estecreek Drive, Cincinnati OH 45232. 513/482-2100. **Toll-free phone:** 800/254-1029. **Fax:** 513/482-2019. **Contact:** Human Resources. **World Wide Web address:** http://www.cognis.com. **Description:** Develops, manufactures and markets specialty chemicals for the agriculture, coatings and ink, cosmetic, detergent, mining, nutrition and health, plastic, and textile industries. The company also specializes in oleochemical base materials and derivatives produced from renewable raw materials. **Internship information:** Call or check the website for current internship offerings. **Corporate headquarters location:** This location. **Other U.S. locations:** Tucson AZ; Kankakee IL; LaGrange IL; Hoboken NJ; Charlotte NC; Ambler PA; Lock Haven PA; Mauldin SC. **Number of employees worldwide:** 10,000.

COLE-LAYER-TRUMBLE COMPANY
3199 Klepinger Road, Dayton OH 45406. 937/276-5261. **Fax:** 937/278-3711. **Contact:** Christel Brooks, Human Resources Manager. **E-mail address:** cbrooks@cltco.com. **World Wide Web address:** http://www.cltco.com. **Description:** One of the nation's largest mass appraisal firms offering both manual and computer-assisted appraisals. The company also offers consulting services for appraisals, data processing, training, and systems design. Founded in 1938. **Positions advertised include:** Real Estate Appraiser. **Corporate headquarters location:** This location. **Parent company:** Tyler Technologies Inc. provides data products, software, technology, and electronic document management systems to local governments and other enterprises. **Listed on:** Privately held.

COLUMBIA GAS OF OHIO
200 Civic Center Drive, P.O. Box 117, Columbus OH 43216-0117. 614/460-2222. **Recorded jobline:** 614/460-4900. **Contact:** Human Resources. **World Wide Web address:** http://www.columbiagasohio.com. **Description:** Columbia Gas of Ohio is a utility company engaged in the sale and distribution of natural gas to customers throughout Ohio. The company also specializes in the development of natural gas technology, products, and special programs designed to reduce energy costs. **NOTE:** Interested jobseekers should call the jobline to obtain the applicable job code. Resumes without a job code may not be forwarded to the Hiring Manager. **Corporate headquarters location:** This location. **Parent company:** NiSource Inc.

THE COLUMBUS DISPATCH
34 South Third Street, Columbus OH 43215. 614/461-5000. **Fax:** 614/461-5533. **Recorded jobline:** 614/461-8822. **Contact:** Human Resources. **E-mail address:** jobs@dispatch.com. **World Wide Web address:** http://www.dispatch.com. **Description:** Publishes a morning newspaper with a daily circulation of over 250,000. **Special programs:** Internships. **Corporate headquarters location:** This location. **Operations at this facility include:** Administration; Manufacturing; Sales; Service.

COLUMBUS ZOO AND AQUARIUM
P.O. Box 400, Powell OH 43065-0400. 614/645-3550. **Physical address:** 9990 Riverside Drive, Powell OH 43065. **Contact:** Human Resources Director. **World Wide Web address:** http://www.columbuszoo.org. **Description:** A zoo featuring a wide range of exhibits including "African Forest," "Kangaroo Walk-About," a live coral reef, prairie dogs, and a migratory song bird aviary. **Special programs:** Seasonal Positions; Internships/Mentorships; Volunteer Opportunities. **Internship information:** The zoo offers annual paid mentorships for college juniors and seniors in the following departments: Human Resources, Visitor Services, and Marketing. Interested candidates should contact Jennifer Koslow for more information. E-mail: jennifer.koslow@columbuszoo.org.

COMDOC INC.
9100 South Hills Road, Broadview Heights OH 44147. 440/838-5535. **Toll-free phone:** 800/321-9448. **Contact:** Human Resources. **World Wide Web address:** http://www.comdocinc.com. **Description:** Sells and services photocopiers and other office equipment. **Corporate headquarters location:** Akron OH. **Other area locations:** Cleveland, Columbus, North Canton, Youngstown. **Other U.S. locations:** NY; PA; WV.

COMMUNITY HOSPITALS OF WILLIAMS COUNTY INC.
BRYAN HOSPITAL
433 West High Street, Bryan OH 43506. 419/636-1131. **Fax:** 419/636-3100. **Contact:** Marianne Potts, Human Resources Director. **E-mail address:** personnel@chwchospital.com. **World Wide Web address:** http://www.chwchospital.com. **Description:** An organization of three acute care hospitals offering a variety of services and treatment facilities. This location is the main campus site of Bryan Hospital. Community Hospitals of Williams County also operates Archbold Hospital and Montpelier Hospital. **NOTE:** Personnel phone extension is 1172. **Positions advertised include:** Registered Nurse; Respiratory Therapist; Licensed Occupational Therapist; Radiologic Technologist. **Corporate headquarters location:** This location. **Other area locations:** Archbold OH; Montpelier OH. **Operations at this facility include:** Administration; Service. **Number of employees at this location:** 600.

COMPAIR LEROI
P.O. Box 927, Sidney OH 45365-0927. 937/498-2580. **Physical address:** 211 East Russell Road, Sidney OH 45365-0927. **Fax:** 937/498-2270. **Contact:** Jerry Kempfer, Human Resources. **Description:** Manufactures and markets portable and stationary air compressors to construction and industrial markets worldwide. The company's products include electric industrial compressors; energy saving systems such as Econotrol capacity control systems, and natural gas compressors; diesel and portable construction compressors; field gas compressors; and related parts and accessories. Founded in 1916. **Corporate headquarters location:** This location. **Operations at this facility include:** Administration; Manufacturing; Research and Development; Sales; Service. **Listed on:** Privately held. **Parent company:** Siebe Group.

COMPREHENSIVE CANCER CENTER
OHIO STATE UNIVERSITY MEDICAL CENTER
300 West 10th Street, Columbus OH 43210. 614/293-4995. **Toll-free phone:** 800/293-5066. **Contact:** Personnel. **World Wide Web address:** http://www. jamesline.com. **Description:** A cancer research center engaged in treating patients and developing new drugs to treat the disease. **NOTE:** Please send resumes to Human Resources, 141 Means Hall, 1654 Upham Drive, Columbus OH 43210. **Positions advertised include:** Licensed Radiation Therapist; Rehabilitation Nurse; Patient Care Resource Manager.

COMPUTER ASSOCIATES INTERNATIONAL, INC.
7965 North High Street, Suite 200, Columbus OH 43235. 614/888-1775. **Contact:** Human Resources. **World Wide Web address:** http://www.ca.com. **Description:** Computer Associates International is one of the world's leading developers of client/server and distributed computing software. The company develops, markets, and supports enterprise management, database and applications development, business applications, and consumer software products for a broad range of mainframe, midrange, and desktop computers. Founded in 1976. **NOTE:** Submit resumes online.

Corporate headquarters location: Islandia NY. **Other area locations:** Beavercreek OH; Independence OH; Mason OH. **Other U.S. locations:** Nationwide. **International locations:** Worldwide. **Operations at this facility include:** This location develops software. **Listed on:** New York Stock Exchange. **Stock exchange symbol:** CA. **Annual sales/revenues:** More than $100 million. **Number of employees nationwide:** 4,000. **Number of employees worldwide:** 9,000.

COMPUTER HORIZONS CORPORATION
6450 Rockside Woods Boulevard South, Suite 270, Independence OH 44131. 216/524-8816. **Toll-free phone:** 800/321-2421. **Fax:** 216/524-9015. **Contact:** Recruiting. **E-mail address:** recruiting@computerhorizons.com. **World Wide Web address:** http://www.computerhorizons.com. **Description:** A full-service global technology services firm providing IT products and services across a full range of industries. Computer Horizons Corporation specializes in e-Business, enterprise solutions, ERP implementation, financial services, global staffing, network services, software products, and training and education. Founded in 1969. **Corporate headquarters location:** Mountain Lakes NJ. **Other area locations:** Centerville OH; Cincinnati OH. **Other U.S. locations:** Nationwide. **Operations at this facility include:** Regional Headquarters. **Listed on:** NASDAQ. **Stock exchange symbol:** CHRZ. **President/CEO:** John Cassese. **Annual sales/revenues:** More than $100 million.

COMPUTER SCIENCES CORPORATION (CSC)
5885 Landerbrook Drive, Suite 300, Cleveland OH 44124. 440/449-3600. **Fax:** 440/442-3050. **Contact:** Human Resources. **World Wide Web address:** http://www.csc.com. **Description:** Provides information technology solutions and services to commercial and government markets. CSC Consulting specializes in information systems consulting and integration; management consulting; and outsourcing and e-business solutions. Founded in 1959. **Corporate headquarters location:** El Segundo CA. **International locations:** Worldwide. **Annual sales/revenues:** More than $100 million. **Number of employees worldwide:** 52,000.

COMPUWARE CORPORATION
6480 Rockside Woods Boulevard, Suite 200, Independence OH 44131. 216/986-8500. **Fax:** 887/220-5529. **Contact:** Human Resources. **World Wide Web address:** http://www.compuware.com. **Description:** Develops, markets, and supports an integrated line of systems software products that improve the productivity of programmers and analysts in application program testing, test data preparation, error analysis, and maintenance. Compuware also provides a broad range of professional data processing services including business systems analysis, design, and programming, as well as systems planning and consulting. **Positions advertised include:** Testing Specialist; Software Sales Manager. **Corporate headquarters:** Farmington Hills MI. **Other area locations:** Cincinnati OH; Cleveland OH; Columbus OH. **Other U.S. locations:** Nationwide. **International locations:** Worldwide. **Listed on:** NASDAQ. **Stock exchange symbol:** CPWR.

CONSOLIDATED PLASTICS COMPANY, INC.
8181 Darrow Road, Twinsburg OH 44087. 330/425-3900. **Toll-free phone:** 800/362-1000. **Fax:** 330/425-3333. **Contact:** President. **World Wide Web address:** http://www.consolidatedplastics.com. **Description:** Sells commercial floor mats and matting. Products are made from various materials including polypropylene, olefin, continuous filament nylon, vinyl, and rubber. Products include economy mats and matting; plush mats; oriental mats; designer stripe and message mats; entrance matting systems; shoe scraper mats; dry mats; carpet accessories; floor care accessories; safety track tape; specialized mats and matting; sponge mats; color-coded, visual warning matting systems; safety mats; antifatigue and antislip matting; corrugated mats; antistatic mats; and scrape and dry premiere blend mats.

CONTECH CONSTRUCTION PRODUCTS INC.
1001 Grove Street, Middletown OH 45044. 513/425-5896. **Contact:** Human Resources. **E-mail address:** jobopportunities@contech-cpi.com. **World Wide Web address:** http://www.contech-cpi.com. **Description:** Contech Construction Products manufactures and markets steel, aluminum, geosynthetic, and plastic construction products for the civil construction market. The company's products are used in a variety of applications including general construction and infrastructure upgrading; airports, culverts, overpasses, railways, roads, stream enclosures, and earth retaining walls; bridge replacement and rehabilitation; and site development, storm water management, soil stabilization, and erosion control. **Corporate headquarters location:** This location. **Other area locations:** Akron OH; Cincinnati OH; Cleveland OH; Columbus OH; Port Clinton OH. **Other U.S. locations:** Nationwide. **Listed on:** Privately held.

CONTINENTAL REAL ESTATE COMPANY
150 East Broad Street, Suite 800, Columbus OH 43215. 614/221-1800. **Fax:** 614/221-6365. **Contact:** Human Resources. **E-mail address:** info@continental-realestate.com. **World Wide Web address:** http://www.continental-realestate.com. **Description:** Leases, buys, develops, and manages property.

CONVERGYS INFORMATION SYSTEMS, INC.
201 East Fourth Street, Cincinnati OH 45202. 513/723-7000. **Contact:** Human Resources. **World Wide Web address:** http://www.convergys.com. **Description:** Designs and markets information systems and provides consulting and technical services for telecommunications companies. **Positions advertised include:** Systems Analyst; Data Collection Supervisor; Senior Finance Manager; Client Support Associate; Sales Support Manager. **Parent company:** Convergys serves top companies in communications, financial services, technology, employee care and other industries in more than 30 countries. Convergys employs 44,000 people in contact centers, data centers and offices in the United States, Canada, Latin America, Israel, Europe, and Asia. **Other area locations:** Norwood OH; Toledo OH. **Other U.S. locations:** Nationwide. **International locations:** Worldwide.

COOPER POWER TOOLS
APEX OPERATION
762 West Stewart Street, Dayton OH 45408. 937/222-7871. **Contact:** Personnel Manager. **E-mail address:** dayton.recruit@coopertools.com. **World Wide Web address:** http://www.coopertools.com. **Description:** Produces a variety of hand tools and related tools for a wide range of uses. **Other area locations:** Hicksville OH; Springfield OH. **Parent company:** Cooper Industries.

COOPER STANDARD AUTOMOTIVE
2130 West 110th Street, Cleveland OH 44102. 216/281-8300. **Fax:** 216/281-4915. **Contact:** Human Resources. **World Wide Web address:** http://www.cooperstandard.com. **Description:** Produces rubber and plastic components for the automotive, construction, and marine industries, as well as tread rubber and magnetic seals used on the doors of appliances. **Corporate headquarters location:** This location. **Parent company:** Cooper Tire and Rubber Company. **Listed on:** New York Stock Exchange. **Stock exchange symbol:** CTB.

COOPER TIRE & RUBBER COMPANY
P.O. Box 550, Findlay OH 45839. 419/423-1321. **Physical address:** 701 Lima Avenue, Findlay OH 45840. **Fax:** 419/420-6070. **Contact:** Human Resources. **World Wide Web address:** http://www.coopertire.com. **Description:** Produces a wide variety rubber products for the consumer and industrial markets. Cooper Tire and Rubber Company's products include automobile, truck, and motorcycle tires; automotive sealing; hoses and hose assemblies; inner tubes; and vibration control systems. Founded in 1914. **Positions advertised include:** Senior Attorney; Materials Development Chemist; Accounting Analyst; Part-time Accountant. **Special programs:** Co-ops. **Corporate headquarters location:** This location. **Operations at this facility include:** Administration; Manufacturing; Research and Development. **Listed on:** New York Stock Exchange. **Stock exchange symbol:** CTB. **Annual sales/revenues:** More than $100 million. **Number of employees at this location:** 1,900. **Number of employees nationwide:** 10,000. **Number of employees worldwide:** 11,000.

COPELAND CORPORATION
P.O. Box 669, 1675 West Campbell Road, Sidney OH 45365-0669. 937/498-3011. **Contact:** Corporate Manager of Professional Staffing. **E-mail address:** corpresume@copeland-corp.com. **World Wide Web address:** http://www.copeland-corp.com. **Description:** A manufacturer of compressors and condensing units for the commercial, industrial, and residential air conditioning and refrigeration industries. Founded in 1921. **Positions advertised include:** Production Supervisor; Manufacturing Engineer; Maintenance Team Leader; Contractor Support Manager; District Sales Manager; Senior Project Engineer. **Special programs:** Internships. **Corporate headquarters location:** This location. **Parent company:** Emerson Electric. **President:** Thomas E. Bettcher.

CORNING INC.
1025 Martin Street, Greenville OH 45331. 937/547-8700. **Fax:** 937/547-8806. **Contact:** Human Resources. **World Wide Web address:** http://www.corning.com. **Description:** Specializes in the development, manufacture, and distribution of optical fiber, cable, and photonic products for the telecommunications industry and displays and components for television and other communications-related industries. Corning, Inc. is also engaged in the production of advanced optical materials for the semiconductor and scientific industries; ceramic substrates for the automotive industry; specialized polymer products for biotechnology applications; and other advanced materials and technologies. **Other area locations:** Cincinnati OH. **Other U.S. locations:** Nationwide. **International locations:** Worldwide.

CORPORATE EXPRESS
183 West Market Street, Akron OH 44303. 330/376-8156. **Contact:** Human Resources. **World Wide Web address:** http://www.corporateexpress.com. **Description:** Distributes a complete range of office machinery and supplies. **Other area locations:** Cincinnati OH; Cleveland OH; Columbus OH.

CRAFT HOUSE INC.
5570 Enterprise Boulevard, Toledo OH 43612. 419/536-8351. **Toll-free phone:** 800//537-0295. **Fax:** 419/536-4159. **Contact:** Personnel. **World Wide Web address:** http://www.crafthouse.net. **Description:** A mail-order catalog company and distributor of such hobby products as sun catchers, paint-by-numbers, and model cars.

CRAIN'S CLEVELAND BUSINESS
700 West St. Clair Avenue, Suite 310, Cleveland OH 44113. 216/522-1383. **Fax:** 216/694-4264. **Contact:** Human Resources. **E-mail address:** clevedit@crain.com. **World Wide Web address:** http://www.crainscleveland.com. **Description:** Publishes a weekly business newspaper. **NOTE:** Applicants should send resumes to 1400 Woodbridge Avenue, Detroit MI 48207-3187. **Corporate headquarters location:** Detroit MI. **Parent company:** Crain Communications Inc.

CRANE PERFORMACE SIDING
P.O. Box 1058, 1441 Universal Road, Columbus OH 43216. 614/443-4841. **Toll-free phone:** 800/366-8472. **Fax:** 800/733-8469. **Contact:** Human Resources. **World Wide Web address:** http://www.vinyl-siding.com. **Description:** Develops, manufactures, and distributes, exterior vinyl siding. Founded in 1947. **Parent company:** Crane Plastics.

CRANEL, INC.
8999 Gemini Parkway, Columbus OH 43240. 614/431-8000. **Fax:** 614/431-8388. **Contact:** Employment. **E-mail address:** employment@cranel.com. **World Wide Web address:** http://www.cranel.com. **Description:** Provides document imaging distribution, enterprise storage solutions, and maintenance and repair services nationwide. Cranel operates through three divisions: Document Imaging Distribution develops and distributes document imaging products; End-to-End Storage Management Solutions specializes in the design and implementation of data availability technology and data storage solutions; and the Service Division provides inventory services and maintenance service contracts for enterprise storage solutions. Cranel, Inc. is the brand parent of Adexis, Cranel Imaging, and Versitec. Founded in 1985. **Positions advertised include:** Accounts Payable Clerk; Inside Sales Consultant; Receptionist; Renewal Support Specialist; Software Engineer. **Office hours:** Monday - Friday, 8:00 a.m. - 6:00 p.m. **Corporate headquarters location:** Columbus OH. **Other area locations:** Cleveland OH. **Other U.S. locations:** Nationwide. **International locations:** Toronto Ontario. **Number of employees nationwide:** Over 200.

CROGHAN COLONIAL BANK
P.O. Box 150, Bellevue OH 44811. 419/483-2541. **Physical address:** One Union Square, Bellevue OH 44811. **Fax:** 419/483-0182. **Contact:** Human Resources. **World Wide Web address:** http://www.croghan.com. **Description:** A full-service commercial bank. Croghan Colonia Bank provides automatic teller machines; commercial, industrial, real estate, consumer installment and credit card lending; equipment and vehicle leasing; time, savings, money market, and demand deposits; and a variety of other services tailored for individual customers. The bank also offers non-FDIC insured products such as mutual funds, annuities, and other insurance products. Founded in 1888. **Other area locations:** Clyde OH; Fremont OH; Green Springs OH; Monroeville OH. **Parent company:** Croghan Bancshares, Inc.

CROWN EQUIPMENT CORPORATION
40 South Washington Street, New Bremen OH 45869. 419/629-2311. **Fax:** 419/629-2900. **Contact:** Personnel. **World Wide Web address:** http://www.crown.com. **Description:** Engaged in the manufacture and distribution of heavy-duty electric lift trucks for the commercial and industrial markets. Crown Equipment Corporations products include fork lift trucks, narrow-aisle stacking equipment, order picking equipment, and powered pallet trucks. **NOTE:** Entry-level positions are offered. **Corporate headquarters location:** This location. **Other U.S. locations:** Nationwide. **International locations:** Australia, Europe. **Listed on:** Privately held. **Number of employees nationwide:** 4,100.

CUYAHOGA COUNTY BOARD OF COMMISSIONERS
Room 417, 1219 Ontario Street, Cleveland OH 44113. 216/443-7190. **Contact:** Human Resources. **World Wide Web address:** http://www.cuyahoga.oh.us. **Description:** Oversees a budget supporting health and human service programs, a comprehensive criminal justice system, maintenance and expansion of regional infrastructure projects including roads and bridges, and ancillary governmental programs that promote the well-being and safety of all Cuyahoga County residents. **Positions advertised include:** Assessment Specialist; Program Analyst; Family Service Supervisor; Information Processor; Youth Leader.

CUYAHOGA FALLS GENERAL HOSPITAL
1900 23rd Street, Cuyahoga Falls OH 44223-1499. 330/971-7006. **Contact:** Human Resources. **E-mail address:** summajobs@summa-health.org. . **World Wide Web address:** http://www.summahealth.org. **Description:** A 257-bed, acute care hospital offering ambulatory, medical, obstetric, psychiatric, rehabilitative, and surgical services. The hospital also offers several specialized services including Easy Street Environments rehabilitation, Falls Pain Management, and the New Beginnings Maternity Center. **Positions advertised include:** Unit Clerk; Licensed Practical Nurse; Registered Nurse; Information Services Librarian; Environmental Aide. **Parent Company:** Summa Health Systems.

CYSTIC FIBROSIS FOUNDATION
2011 Madison Road, Cincinnati OH 45208. 513/533-9300. **Fax:** 513/533-9301. **Contact:** Executive Director. **World Wide Web address:** http://www.cff.org/cincinnati.htm. **Description:** A nonprofit national foundation dedicated to developing a treatment and cure for cystic fibrosis. The Cystic Fibrosis Foundation offers cystic fibrosis care centers nationwide; provides grants to scientists conducting research about cystic fibrosis; operates several cystic fibrosis research centers; supports clinical trials; and offers free brochures, fact sheets, and videos pertaining to the disease. **Corporate headquarters location:** Bethesda MD. **Other area locations:** Dayton OH; Columbus OH; Lyndhurst OH.

DAILY RECORD
P.O. Box 918, Wooster OH 44691. 330/264-1125. **Physical address:** 212 East Liberty Street, Wooster OH 44691. **Fax:** 330/264-3756. **Toll-free phone:** 800/686-2958. **Contact:** Human Resources. **World Wide Web address:** http://www.the-daily-record.com. **Description:** Publishes a daily newspaper. Founded in 1890. **Parent company:** Dix News Media.

DAIMLERCHRYSLER CORPORATION
8000 Chrysler Drive, Perrysburg OH 43551. 419/661-3440. **Contact:** Human Resources. **World Wide Web address:** http://www1.daimlerchrysler.com. **Description:** DaimlerChrysler Corporation produces cars, trucks, minivans, and sport utility vehicles for customers in more than 100 countries. **Other U.S. locations:** Nationwide. **Operations at this facility include:** This location manufactures truck converters and steering columns. **Listed on:** New York Stock Exchange. **Stock exchange symbol:** DAJ.

DAIMLERCHRYSLER CORPORATION
4400 Chrysler Drive, Toledo OH 43608. 419/727-2800. **Contact:** Human Resources. **World Wide Web address:** http://www1.daimlerchrysler.com. **Description:** DaimlerChrysler Corporation produces cars, trucks, minivans, and sport utility vehicles for customers in more than 100 countries. **Operations at this facility include:** This location manufactures Jeeps. **Listed on:** New York Stock Exchange. **Stock exchange symbol:** DAJ.

DAIMLERCHRYSLER CORPORATION
2000 East Aurora Road, Twinsburg OH 44087. 330/425-1777. **Contact:** Human Resources. **World Wide Web address:** http://www1.daimlerchrysler.com. **Description:** DaimlerChrysler Corporation manufactures cars, trucks, minivans, and sport utility vehicles for customers in more than 100 countries. **Other U.S. locations:** Nationwide. **Operations at this facility include:** This location manufactures sheet metal stampings and assemblies for the automotive industry. **Listed on:** New York Stock Exchange. **Stock exchange symbol:** DAJ.

DANA CORPORATION
P.O. Box 1000, Toledo OH 43697. 419/535-4500. **Physical address:** 4500 Dorr Street, Toledo OH 43615. **Fax:** 419/535-4758. **Contact:** Human Resources. **World Wide Web address:** http://www.dana.com. **Description:** A global leader in the engineering, manufacturing, and marketing of products and systems for the vehicular, industrial, and mobile off-highway original equipment markets and is a major supplier to the related aftermarkets. Dana is also a leading provider of lease financing services in selected markets. The company's products include drivetrain components such as axles, driveshafts, clutches, and transmissions; engine parts such as gaskets, piston rings, seals, pistons, and filters; chassis products such as vehicular frames and cradles and heavy-duty side rails; fluid power components such as pumps, motors, and control valves; and industrial products such as electrical and mechanical brakes and clutches, drives, motion control devices, and mobile off-highway and stationary equipment applications. Dana's vehicular components and parts are used on automobiles, pickup trucks, vans, minivans, sport utility vehicles, medium and heavy trucks, and off-highway vehicles. Founded in 1904. **Corporate headquarters location:** This location. **Listed on:** New York Stock Exchange. **Stock exchange symbol:** DCN. **Annual sales/revenues:** More than $100 million. **Number of employees worldwide:** 86,000.

DANIS INDUSTRIES CORPORATION
2 River Place, Suite 400, Dayton OH 45405. 937/228-1225. **Fax:** 937/228-0535. **Contact:** Marvin Goldschmidt, Human Resources. **E-mail address:** mgoldschmidt@danis.com. **World Wide Web address:** http://www.danis.com. **Description:** A building construction corporation. Danis Industries Corporation specializes solely in the development and construction of water and wastewater treatment facilities nationwide. Founded in 1916. **Corporate headquarters location:** This location. **Other U.S. locations:** Denver CO; Orlando FL; Columbia MD.

DATA-BASICS INC.
9450 Midwest Avenue, Garfield Heights OH 44125. 216/663-5600. **Toll-free phone:** 800/837-7574. **Fax:** 216/663-5454. **Contact:** Human Resources Department. **E-mail address:** hr@databasics.com. **World Wide Web address:** http://www.databasic.com. **Description:** Develops job cost accounting software and service-account management software for the construction and architecture industries.

DAVEY TREE EXPERT COMPANY
P.O. Box 5193, 1500 North Mantua Street, Kent OH 44240. 330/673-9511. **Toll-free phone:** 800/445-8733. **Fax:** 330/673-1037. **Contact:** Joseph Gregory (Field openings) jgregory@davey.com and Greg Mazur (Office) gmazur@davey.com. **World Wide Web address:** http://www.davey.com. **Description:** Provides grounds maintenance; tree, shrub, and lawn care; vegetation management; and consulting services nationwide. The Davey Tree Expert Company serves the commercial, residential, and utilities markets. Founded in 1880. **NOTE:** Applications and inquiries can be made on-line using the URL listed above. **Positions advertised include:** Landscape Entomologist; Maintenance Mechanic. **Special programs:** Internships. **Corporate headquarters location:** This location. **Other area locations:** Cleveland OH; Eastlake OH; Mansfield OH; North Royalton OH; Richfield OH; Solon OH.

DAYCO SWAN, INC.
P.O. Box 311, Bucyrus OH 44820. 419/562-1011. **Physical address:** 201 East Beal Street, Bucyrus OH 44820. **Fax:** 419/563-0112. **Contact:** Paul Higgins, Human Resources Manager. **E-mail address:** dayco_employment@markivauto.com. **World Wide Web address:** http://www.daycoproducts.com. **Description:** Engaged in the manufacture of rubber and plastic hoses for automotive, industrial, garden, hydraulic, and metal products. Founded in 1905. **Corporate headquarters location:** Tulsa OK. **Parent company:** Dayco Products, Inc. **Operations at this facility include:** Manufacturing.

DAYTON DAILY NEWS
45 South Ludlow Street, Dayton OH 45402. 937/225-2000. **Fax:** 937/225-2153. **Contact:** Personnel. **World Wide Web address:** http://www.daytondailynews.com. **Description:** A newspaper. **Parent Company:** Cox Enterprises, Inc.

DAYTON POWER AND LIGHT COMPANY
P.O. Box 8825, Dayton OH 45401. 937/224-6000. **Physical address:** 1065 Woodman Drive, Dayton OH 45432. **Fax:** 937/259-7147. **Contact:** Human Resources. **World Wide Web address:** http://www.waytogo.com. **Description:** An electric and natural gas utility company. Dayton Power and Light Company serves approximately 500,000 commercial, governmental, industrial, and residential customers in West Central Ohio. **Positions advertised include:** Part-Time Customer Account Representative; Financial Analyst. **Special programs:** Internships. **Other area locations:** Aberdeen OH; Greenville OH; Manchester OH; Miamisburg OH. **Parent company:** DPL Inc. **Number of employees nationwide:** 3,000.

DAYTON PUBLIC SCHOOLS
115 South Ludlow Street, Dayton OH 45402. 937/542-3000. **Contact:** Human Resources. **World Wide Web address:** http://www.dps.k12.oh.us. **Description:** Coordinates resources and information for the public schools of Dayton. **Positions advertised include:** Speech Language Pathologist; School Counselor; Middle School Math Teacher; High School Social Studies Teacher; High School Science Teacher; High School Music Teacher; Bus Driver.

DAYTON RELIABLE TOOL & MANUFACTURING COMPANY
P.O. Box 586, 618 Greenmount Boulevard, Dayton OH 45419. 937/298-7391. **Fax:** 937/298-7190. **Contact:** Human Resources. **World Wide Web address:** http://www.drtusa.com. **Description:** Develops, designs, and manufactures tool and die components and other manufactured products.

DAYTON RICHMOND CONCRETE ACCESSORIES
721 Richard Street, Miamisburg OH 45342. 937/866-0711. **Toll-free phone:** 800/745-3700. **Fax:** 937/866-8027. **Contact:** Human Resources. **World Wide Web address:** http://www.daytonrichmond.com. **Description:** Dayton Richmond manufactures concrete accessories including anchors and inserts, screw anchors, taper ties, form hangers, overhand brackets, and other related products. **Corporate headquarters location:** This location. **Other U.S. locations:** Nationwide. **International locations:** Canada. **Parent Company:** Dayton Superior Corporation. **Operations at this facility include:** This location houses the administrative offices, the sales and service center, and plant and technical services.

DEACONESS HOSPITAL
311 Straight Street, Cincinnati OH 45219. 513/559-2100. **Fax:** 513/475-5428. **Contact:** Human Resources. **E-mail address:** greatjobs@deaconess-cinti.com. **World Wide Web address:** http://www.deaconess-healthcare.com. **Description:** A 250-bed, nonprofit, acute care hospital. Deaconess Hospital specializes in arthritis, back treatment, cardiac care, care for the elderly, diabetes, emergency services, endoscopy, home health care, mental health, nutrition counseling, joint replacement, occupational therapy, orthopedic care, osteoporosis, physical therapy, rehabilitation, and sports medicine. Founded in 1888. **Positions advertised include:** Registered Nurse; Licensed Practical Nurse; Medical Assistant; Nurse Assistant; Occupational Therapist; Physical Therapist; Respiratory Therapist; Phlebotomist; Radiology Technician.

C.H. DEAN & ASSOCIATES, INC.
2480 Kettering Towers, Dayton OH 45423. 937/222-9531. **Toll-free phone:** 800/327-3656. **Fax:** 937/227-9304. **Contact:** Human Resources. **E-mail address:** info@chdean.com. **World Wide Web address:** http://www.chdean.com. **Description:** A private investment management company. Founded in 1972. **Corporate headquarters location:** This location. **Other area locations:** Columbus OH.

DELOITTE & TOUCHE
127 Public Square, Suite 2500, Cleveland OH 44114. 216/589-1300. **Fax:** 216/589-1369. **Contact:** Human Resources. **E-mail address:** dtcareers@deloitte.com. **World Wide Web address:** http://www.us.deloitte.com. **Description:** An international firm of certified public accountants providing professional accounting, auditing, tax, and management consulting services to widely diversified clients. The company has a specialized program consisting of national industry groups and functional groups that cross industry lines. Groups are involved in various disciplines including accounting, auditing, taxation management advisory services, small and growing businesses, mergers and acquisitions, and computer applications. **Positions advertised include:** Assurance and Advisory Manager. **Special programs:** Internships. **Corporate headquarters location:** Wilton CT. **Other area locations:** Akron OH; Cincinnati OH; Columbus OH; Dayton OH.

DELOITTE & TOUCHE
P.O. Box 5340, Cincinnati OH 45201. 513/784-7100. **Physical address:** 250 East Fifth Street, Suite 1900, Cincinnati OH 45202. **Fax:** 513/784-7204. **Contact:** Human Resources. **E-mail address:** dtcareers@deloitte.com. **World Wide Web address:** http://www.us.deloitte.com. **Description:** An international firm of certified public accountants providing professional accounting, auditing, tax, and management consulting services to widely diversified clients. The company has a specialized program consisting of national industry groups and functional groups that cross industry lines. Groups are involved in various disciplines including accounting, auditing, taxation management advisory services, small and growing businesses, mergers and acquisitions, and computer applications. **Positions advertised include:** Marketing Coordinator; Administrative Assistant; Internal Audit Partner; Senior Accountant. **Corporate headquarters location:** Wilton CT. **Other area locations:** Akron OH; Cleveland OH; Columbus OH; Dayton OH.

DENMAN TIRE CORPORATION
400 Diehl South Road, Leavittsburg OH 44430. 330/675-4242. **Contact:** Personnel. **World Wide Web address:** http://www.denmantire.com. **Description:** Develops, manufactures, and distributes tires in specialized categories for the agriculture, construction, and industrial markets. Denman Tire Corporation also operates as a private brand manufacturer for independent wholesalers and distributors. Founded in 1919.

DIEBOLD, INC.
5995 Mayfair Road, P.O. Box 3077, North Canton OH 44720-8077. 330/489-4000. **Toll-free phone:** 800/999-3600. **Fax:** 330/490-4549. **Contact:** Human Resources. **E-mail address:** hrinfo@diebold.com. **World Wide Web address:** http://www.diebold.com. **Description:** Engaged in the sale, manufacture, installation, and service of automated teller machines, physical and electronic security systems, and software for the financial and commercial industries. Other products include vaults, vault doors, lockers, safes, alarms, video surveillance systems, and data line security systems. Founded in 1859. **Positions advertised include:** Corporate Internal Auditor; Contract Administration Supervisor; Quality System Manager. **Special Programs:** Co-ops; Internships. **Corporate headquarters location:** This location. **Other U.S. locations:** Nationwide. **International locations:** Worldwide. **Operations at this facility include:** Administration; Manufacturing; Research and Development; Service. **Listed on:** New York Stock Exchange. **Stock exchange symbol:** DBD.

DIETRICH INDUSTRIES INC.
1300 Phoenix Road NE, Warren OH 44483. 330/372-3394. **Fax:** 330/372-1954. **Contact:** Human Resources. **World Wide Web address:** http://www.dietrichindustries.com. **Description:** Receives steel in coil form and then cuts it to form various products. Founded in 1959. **NOTE:** Hiring is done through the corporate office. Interested candidates can submit a resume online or mail to: Dietrich Metal Framing, Inc., Attention: Mr. Rich Burkey, 500 Grant Street, Suite 2226, Pittsburgh PA 15219. **Positions advertised include:** Marketing Manager; Project Specialist; Plant Manager; Production Superintendent; Plant Engineer. **Special programs:** Management Training Program. **Corporate headquarters location:** Pittsburgh PA. **Other area locations:** Warren OH. **Other U.S. locations:** Nationwide.

DILLARD'S DEPARTMENT STORES, INC.
3390 Westgate Mall, Fairview Park OH 44126. 440/333-3000. **Contact:** Human Resources Department. **World Wide Web address:** http://www.dillards.com. **Description:** Operates a regional group of traditional department stores offering branded fashion and private label merchandise. The stores feature fashion apparel, home furnishings, and electronics. Dillard's operates approximately 230 stores located primarily in the Southeast, Southwest, and Midwest regions of the United States. **Other area locations:** Akron OH; Canton OH; Cincinnati OH; Cleveland OH; Toledo OH; Youngstown OH.

DIVERSEYLEVER NORTH AMERICA
3630 East Kemper Road, Sharonville OH 45241. 513/554-4200. **Toll-free phone:** 800/233-1000. **Fax:** 513/326-8309. **Contact:** Director of Human Resources. **World Wide Web address:** http://www.diverseylever.com/na.nsf. **Description:** Develops, manufactures, and markets industrial chemical specialties and related products. The company primarily serves the general maintenance, lubricants, pulp and paper, surface finishing, transportation, wastewater treatment, and water management markets. **Parent Company:** JohnsonDiversey. **Number of employees at this location:** 200. **Number of employees worldwide:** 12,000.

DOCTORS HOSPITAL
5100 West Broad Street, Columbus OH 43228. 614/429-3200. **Fax:** 614/566-6953. **Contact:** Human Resources. **World Wide Web address:** http://www.ohiohealth.com. **Description:** A 256-bed, nonprofit, acute care, osteopathic hospital. Founded in 1940. **NOTE:** Entry-level positions and second and third shifts are offered. Resumes are accepted by mail or fax. Mail resumes to: Ohio Health, Attention: Human Resources, 3535 Olentangy River Road, Columbus OH 43214. **Positions advertised include:** Emergency Medical Technician; Nurse Administrator; Assistant Nurse Manager; Registered Nurse; Case Manager; Patient Escort; Materials Handler; Social Worker; Cardiac Sonographer; Radiology Technologist. **Special programs:** Medical Residencies; Internships. **Parent company:** D.H. Corporation. **Listed on:** Privately held. **Number of employees at this location:** 2,100.

DOMINION HOMES
P.O. Box 7166, 5501 Frantz Road, Dublin OH 43017-0766. 614/761-6000. **Fax:** 614/356-6010. **Contact:** Human Resources. **E-mail address:** careers@dominionhomes.com. **World Wide Web address:** http://www.dominionhomes.com. **Description:** A builder of single-family homes in central Ohio. The company offers two distinct product lines of homes and condominiums.

R.R. DONNELLEY & SONS COMPANY
1145 Conwell Avenue, Willard OH 44890. 419/935-0111. **Fax:** 419/933-5463. **Contact:** Human Resources Coordinator. **E-mail address:** rrdonnelley@trm.brassring.com. **World Wide Web address:** http://www.rrdonnelley.com. **Description:** This location specializes in the printing and binding of a wide variety of school, trade, and reference books. Also known as The Lakeside Press, R.R. Donnelley & Sons is a world leader in managing, reproducing, and distributing print and digital information for publishing, merchandising, and information technology customers. The company is one of the largest commercial printers in the world, producing catalogs, inserts, magazines, books, directories, computer documentation, and financial printing. R.R. Donnelley has more than 180 sales offices and production facilities. Principal services offered by the company are conventional and digital prepress operations, computerized printing and binding, and sophisticated pool shipping and distribution services for printed products; information repackaging into multiple formats including print, magnetic, and optical media; database management, list rental, list enhancement, and direct mail production services; turnkey computer documentation services including outsourcing, translation, printing, binding, diskette replication, kitting, licensing, republishing, and fulfillment; reprographics and facilities management; creative design and communication services; and digital and conventional map creation and related services. Founded in 1864. **NOTE:** Entry-level positions and second and third shifts are offered. **Positions advertised include:** Production Planning Coordinator; Market Support Operations Specialist. **Special programs:** Internships; Apprenticeships; Training; Co-ops. **Internship information:** The company employs several interns and co-ops each summer. Most commonly needed majors are mechanical or electrical engineering, accounting, computer engineering, and business. Applicants should send resumes to the Human Resources Coordinator with dates of availability. **Corporate headquarters location:** Chicago IL. **Other U.S. locations:** Nationwide. **International locations:** Worldwide. **Operations at this facility include:** Divisional Headquarters. **Listed on:** New York Stock Exchange. **Stock exchange symbol:** DNY. **Annual sales/revenues:** More than $100 million. **Number of employees at this location:** 1,800. **Number of employees nationwide:** 30,000. **Number of employees worldwide:** 35,000.

DRAKE CENTER, INC.
151 West Galbraith Road, Cincinnati OH 45216. 513/948-2500. **Toll-free phone:** 800/948-0003. **Fax:** 513/948-2619. **Contact:** Human Resources. **E-mail address:** info@drakecenter.com. **World Wide Web address:** http://www.drakecenter.com. **Description:** A full-service, 356-bed, rehabilitation and post-acute care facility. The Drake Center specializes in brain injury rehabilitation, cardiac rehabilitation, neurological rehabilitation, orthopedic rehabilitation, pulmonary rehabilitation, skin and wound care, stroke rehabilitation, and ventilator weaning. The Drake Center also provides on-site laboratory, pharmacy, and radiology services. **Positions advertised include:** Care Coordination Leader; Social Worker; Pharmacist; Medical Assistant; Registered Nurse; Licensed Practical Nurse; Certified Nursing Assistant; Occupational Therapist; Physical Therapist; Speech Language Pathologist; Lifeguard; Cook; Receptionist. **Operations at this facility include:** Administration. **Number of employees at this location:** 730.

R.L. DRAKE COMPANY
230 Industrial Drive, Franklin OH 45005. 937/746-4556. **Fax:** 937/743-4507. **Contact:** Steve Morgan, Vice President. **E-mail address:** morgan@rldrake.com. **World Wide Web address:** http://www.rldrake.com. **Description:** Develops, manufactures, and markets electronic communications equipment. The company specializes in products and solutions for ADA assistive listening, cable television systems, family radio service communications, shortwave radio, satellite television reception, and sound reinforcement. Founded in 1954. **Office hours:** Monday - Friday, 8:00 a.m. - 4:00 p.m. **Corporate headquarters location:** This location. **International locations:** Ontario Canada. **Listed on:** Privately held. **Number of employees at this location:** 100.

DRESSER VALVE & CONTROLS DIVISION
NIL-COR OPERATIONS
P.O. Box 2058, 12241 Rockhill Avenue NE, Alliance OH 44601. 330/823-0500. **Toll-free phone:** 800/321-9865. **Fax:** 330/821-6722. **Contact:** Personnel Director. **E-mail address:** info@nilcor.com. **World Wide Web address:** http://www.nilcor.com. **Description:** This location manufactures fiber composite ball valves. **Parent company:** Dresser Industries, Inc. is one of the leading suppliers of technology, products, and services to worldwide energy, natural resources, and industrial markets. Operations include petroleum, energy processing, and conversion; mining and construction; and general industry. The company markets its products and services in more than 100 countries.

E.I. DUPONT DE NEMOURS & COMPANY
U.S. Route 23-S, Dupont Road, Circleville OH 43113. 740/474-0111. **Fax:** 740/474-0330. **Contact:** Human Resources Manager. **World Wide Web address:** http://www.dupont.com. **Description:** E.I. DuPont de Nemours & Company's activities include the manufacturing of biomedical, industrial, and consumer products such as photographic, data-recording, and video devices; the production of man-made fiber products with applications in a variety of consumer and commercial industries; polymer products such as plastic resins, elastomers, and films; agricultural and industrial chemicals such as herbicides and insecticides, pigments, fluorochemicals, petroleum additives, and mineral acids; the exploration and production of crude oil and natural gas; the refining, marketing, and downstream transportation of petroleum; and the mining and distribution of steam and metallurgical coals. The company supplies the aerospace, agriculture, apparel, transportation, health care, and printing and publishing industries. **Corporate headquarters location:** Wilmington DE. **Other U.S. locations:** Nationwide. **Operations at this facility include** This location is a polyester/polymide manufacturing plant. **Listed on:** New York Stock Exchange. **Stock exchange symbol:** DD. **Chairman/CEO:** Charles O. Holliday, Jr. **Annual sales/revenues:** More than $100 million. **Number of employees at this location:** 1,100. **Number of employees worldwide:** 94,000.

EAST OHIO REGIONAL HOSPITAL
90 North Fourth Street, Martins Ferry OH 43935. 740/633-1100. **Contact:** Human Resources. **World Wide Web address:** http://www.eastohioregionalhospital.com. **Description:** A 249-bed hospital with two divisions: acute including cancer treatment and general surgical and medical procedures; and skilled including cardiac and other rehabilitation programs. **Positions advertised include:** Staff Nurse; Licensed Practical Nurse; Senior Staff Pharmacist; Speech Language Pathologist; Housekeeper; Dietary Aide; Medical Assistant; Phlebotomist. **Parent company:** Ohio Valley Health Services and Education Corp.

E.I.S. COMPANY
PO Box 141144, Cincinnati OH 45250. 859/384-0569. **Fax:** 859/384-7839. **Contact:** Human Resources. **E-mail address:** admin@eiscompany.com. **World Wide Web address:** http://www.eiscompany.com. **Description:** Provides sales and marketing consulting services. **Positions advertised include:** Bookkeeper/Office Manager. **Corporate headquarters location:** This location.

EATON CORPORATION
AIRFLEX DIVISION
9919 Clinton Road, Cleveland OH 44144. 216/281-2211. **Toll-free phone:** 800/247-3539. **Fax:** 216/281-3890. **Contact:** Human Resources. **World Wide Web address:** http://www.airflex.com. **Description:** A worldwide manufacturer of hydraulic products, fluid connectors, electrical power distribution equipment, engine components, and truck drivetrain systems. The company serves a variety of industries including automotive, aerospace, industrial, and semiconductor. **Positions advertised include:** Senior Attorney; Project Leader; Senior Administrative Assistant; First Officer; Internal Auditor; Financial Analyst. **Special programs:** Internships. **Operations at this facility include:** Administration; Manufacturing; Research and Development; Sales; Service. **Listed on:** New York Stock Exchange. **Stock exchange symbol:** ETN.

EFTEC
P.O. Box 13556, NR Station, Dayton OH 45413-0556. 937/890-3150. **Physical address:** 3345 Stop Eight Road, Dayton OH 45414. **Contact:** Human Resources. **World Wide Web address:** http://www.eftec.com. **Description:** Produces a broad range of adhesives, sealants, and extruded flexible plastics for the architectural and automotive industries. **Parent company:** EFTEC is a joint venture between EMS CHEMIE Holding AG and the H.B. Fuller Company.

ELDER-BEERMAN STORES CORPORATION
3155 El-Bee Road, Dayton OH 45439. 937/296-2700. **Fax:** 937/296-2948. **Contact:** Manager of Recruiting. **E-mail address:** recruiting@elder-beerman.com. **World Wide Web address:** http://www.elder-beerman.com. **Description:** Operates a chain of retail department stores. **Special programs:** Executive Training Program. **Corporate headquarters:** This location.

ELECTRA FORM, INC.
P.O. Box 5054, 852 Scholz Drive, Vandalia OH 45377. 937/898-8460. **Fax:** 937/898-1750. **Contact:** Human Resources. **Description:** Manufactures plastic injection molds. **Corporate headquarters location:** This location. **Operations at this facility include:** Administration; Manufacturing; Regional Headquarters; Research and Development; Sales; Service. **Listed on:** Privately held. **Number of employees at this location:** 225.

ELECTROLUX CORPORATION
4261 Fulton Road, Cleveland OH 44144. 216/741-8040. **Contact:** Human Resources. **World Wide Web address:** http://www.electrolux.com. **Description:** A diversified manufacturer of products for both consumer and industrial markets worldwide. Products include refrigerators, freezers, ranges, dishwashers, washers, and dryers. **Listed on:** NASDAQ. **Stock exchange symbol:** ELUX.

ELECTRONIC DATA SYSTEMS
2000 Eastman Drive, Milford OH 45150. 513/576-2400. **Fax:** 513/576-2734. **Contact:** Human Resources. **E-mail address:** careers@eds.com. **World Wide Web address:** http://www.eds.com. **Description:** An international supplier of mechanical computer-aided engineering (MCAE) software and engineering services. **Corporate headquarters location:** Plano TX. **Other U.S. locations:** Nationwide. **International locations:** Worldwide. **Operations at this facility include:** Administration; Divisional Headquarters; Regional Headquarters; Research and Development; Sales; Service. **Listed on:** New York Stock Exchange. **Stock exchange symbol:** EDS. **Number of employees at this location:** 1,000. **Number of employees worldwide:** 130,000.

ELJER PLUMBINGWARE
921 South Ellsworth Avenue, Salem OH 44460. 330/332-4691. **Fax:** 330/332-0015. **Contact:** Human Resources. **World Wide Web address:** http://www.eljer.com. **Description:** A leading manufacturer of building products for residential construction, commercial construction, and repair and remodeling markets. Eljer manufactures and markets plumbing, heating, ventilating, and air conditioning products in North America and Europe. The company markets its products through wholesale distribution channels and directly to building products retailers. **Corporate headquarters:** Dallas TX. **Parent company:** Zurn Industries, Inc.

ENTERPRISE RENT-A-CAR
24690 Sperry Drive, Westlake OH 44145. 440/885-6944. **Fax:** 440/345-7470. **Contact:** Laura Taddeo, Human Resources. **E-mail address:** laura.taddeo@erac.com. **World Wide Web address:** http://www.enterprise.com. **Description:** A car rental agency. **NOTE:** Job seekers may also apply on-line at the above URL. **Positions advertised include:** Branch Manager; Accountant; Driver; Lot Attendant. **Special programs:** Internships. **Special programs:** Management Training Program; Internships. **Corporate headquarters location:** This location. **Operations at this facility include:** Sales; Service.

ENVIRONMENTAL ENTERPRISES
10163 Cincinnati-Dayton Road, Cincinnati OH 45241. 513/772-2818. **Contact:** Human Resources. **World Wide Web address:** http://www.eeienv.com. **Description:** Operates a hazardous waste treatment and storage facility. Environmental Enterprises also offers asbestos monitoring and transportation, emergency response, household hazardous waste, laboratory, and remediation services.

ERAMET MARIETTA
P.O. Box 299, Marietta OH 45750. 740/374-1000. **Physical address:** Route 7 South, Marietta OH 45750. **Fax:** 740/374-1386. **Contact:** Human Resources. **World Wide Web address:** http://www.emspecialproducts.com. **Description:** Engaged in the production of a variety of metals products including chrome and alloys. **Corporate headquarters location:** Paris, France.

ERICO INTERNATIONAL
34600 Solon Road, Solon OH 44139-2728. 440/248-0100. **Fax:** 440/248-0723. **Contact:** Human Resources. **World Wide Web address:** http://www.erico.com. **Description:** Manufactures products for construction, welding, and electrical companies. **International locations:** Worldwide.

ERNST & YOUNG LLP
1300 Chiquita Center, 250 East Fifth Street, Cincinnati OH 45202. 513/621-6454. **Fax:** 513/621-5512. **Contact:** Personnel Department. **World Wide Web address:** http://www.ey.com. **Description:** A certified public accounting firm that also provides management consulting services. Services include data processing, financial modeling, financial feasibility studies, production planning and inventory management, management sciences, health care planning, human resources, cost accounting, and budgeting systems. **Positions advertised include:** Senior Assurance Manager; Assurance Staff Member; Business Risk Services Auditor; Tax Compliance Staff Member; IT Audit Manager. **Corporate headquarters location:** New York NY. **Other area locations:** Akron OH; Canton OH; Cleveland OH; Columbus OH; Dayton OH; Toledo OH. **Other U.S. locations:** Nationwide. **International locations:** Worldwide.

ERNST & YOUNG LLP
1300 Huntington Building, 925 Euclid Avenue, Cleveland OH 44115. 216/861-5000. **Fax:** 216/583-4966. **Contact:** Personnel Department. **World Wide Web address:** http://www.ey.com. **Description:** A certified public accounting firm that also provides management consulting services. Services include data processing, financial modeling, financial feasibility studies, production planning and inventory management, management sciences, health care planning, human resources, cost accounting, and budgeting systems. **Positions advertised include:** Executive Assistant; Health Sciences Knowledge Manager; Compliance Administrator; Webcast Developer; Area Records Manager; Assistant Administrative Coordinator; Financial Analyst. **Corporate headquarters location:** New York NY. **Other area locations:** Akron OH; Canton OH; Cincinnati OH; Columbus OH; Dayton OH; Toledo OH. **Other U.S. locations:** Nationwide. **International locations:** Worldwide.

ETHICON ENDO-SURGERY, INC.
4545 Creek Road, Cincinnati OH 45242. 513/786-7000. **Toll-free phone:** 800/USE-ENDO. **Contact:** Personnel. **World Wide Web address:** http://www.ethiconendo.com. **Description:** Develops and manufactures medical devices including instruments for endoscopic surgery. **Positions advertised include:** Medical Director; Regulatory Affairs Associate; Director, Short-Run Manufacturing. **Special programs:** Co-ops. **Parent company:** Johnson & Johnson (New Brunswick NJ).

EUCLID HITACHI HEAVY EQUIPMENT INC.
22221 St. Clair Avenue, Cleveland OH 44117. 216/383-3499. **Contact:** Human Resources. **World Wide Web address:** http://www.hcmac.com. **Description:** Manufactures earth-moving trucks and equipment for use in the mining and heavy construction industries.

EVENFLO COMPANY, INC.
1801 Commerce Drive, Piqua OH 45356. 937/773-3971. **Toll-free phone:** 800/233-5921. **Fax:** 937/415-3112. **Contact:** Human Resource Department. **E-mail address:** resume@evenflo.com. **World Wide Web address:** http://www.evenflo.com. **Description:** Develops and manufactures a wide range of products for infants and toddlers. Evenflo's products include bath accessories, bouncers, breast pumps and nursing pads, carriers, car seats, cribs, exercise and entertainment centers, gates, highchairs, humidifiers, mattresses, monitors, nursers, and strollers. **NOTE:** Submit resumes to: 707 Crossroads Court, Northwoods Business Center II, Vandalia OH 45377. **Positions advertised include:** Parent Link Consumer Resource Center Representative. **Corporate headquarters location:** This location.

EXACT MACOLA SOFTWARE
P.O. Box 1824, 333 East Center Street, Marion OH 43301. 740/382-5999. **Toll-free phone:** 800/468-0834. **Fax:** 740/382-0239. **Contact:** Human Resources. **World Wide Web address:** http://www.macola.com. **Description:** Develops client/server-based accounting, distribution, and manufacturing business software solutions. Founded in 1971. **NOTE:** Entry-level positions are offered. **Special programs:** Internships. **Office hours:** Monday - Friday, 8:30 a.m. - 5:30 p.m. **Corporate headquarters location:** This location. **Other U.S. locations:** Nationwide. **International locations:** Canada; China; Malaysia; Thailand. **Parent company:** Exact Software North America. **Listed on:** Privately held. **Number of employees at this location:** 280.

EXEL LOGISTICS
501 West Schrock Road, Westerville OH 43081-8966. 614/890-1730. **Contact:** Human Resources. **World Wide Web address:** http://www.exel-logistics.com. **Description:** One of the world's leading providers of third-party logistics systems. The company provides transportation, distribution, warehousing, and related supply chain solutions within the automotive, chemical, consumer, healthcare, retail, and technology industries. **Parent company:** NFC International Logistics and Moving Services.

F&W PUBLICATIONS INC.
4700 East Galbraith Road, Cincinnati OH 45236. 513/531-2690. **Contact:** Amy Brewer, Human Resources. **E-mail address:** careers@fwpubs.com. **World Wide Web address:** http://www.fwpublications.com. **Description:** F+W publishes over 3,000 special interest books and more than 50 magazine titles including *Writer's Digest, Popular Woodworking, The Artist's Magazine,* and *Scuba Diving*. The company offers a wide range of enthusiast and how-to publications covering a variety of topics including writing, genealogy, art, woodworking, graphic design, and other areas. F+W also owns and operates many book clubs, offers educational programs, conferences, and competitions, and maintains free and pay-based websites. Founded in 1913. **NOTE:** Entry-level positions are offered. **Company slogan:** Helping our customers realize their dreams. **Positions advertised include:** Assistant Web Developer; Associate Editor, North Light Craft Books; Book Designer; Executive Editor, *The Artist's Magazine*; Promotion Coordinator; Promotion Designer; Web Designer. **Special programs:** Internships. **Office hours:** Monday - Friday, 8:00 a.m. - 5:30 p.m. **Corporate headquarters location:** This location. **Subsidiaries include:** Adams Media Corporation; David & Charles Ltd.; *Horticulture Magazine;* Krause Publications; Memory Makers; North Light Books; *The Pastel Journal*. **Operations at this facility include:** Administration; Divisional Headquarters; Sales; Service. **Listed on:** Privately held. **President/CEO:** Stephen J. Kent. **Annual Sales/revenues:** $250 million. **Number of employees at this location:** 238. **Number of employees nationwide:** Approximately 800.

FKI LOGISTEX
THE BUSCHMAN COMPANY
10045 International Boulevard, Cincinnati OH 45246. 513/874-0788. **Toll-free phone:** 800/628-4397. **Fax:** 513/881-5251. **Contact:** Human Resources Manager. **E-mail address:** hr@fkilogistex.com. **World Wide Web address:** http://www.fkilogistex.com. **Description:** Designs, develops, manufactures, and distributes material handling systems for product distribution. The company's products include accumulation and gravity conveyors, cross docking systems, order fulfillment systems, and sortation conveyors. **Corporate headquarters location:** This location. **Parent company:** FKI plc. (United Kingdom). **Operations at this facility include:** Administration; Manufacturing; Research and Development; Sales.

FM GLOBAL
25050 Country Club Boulevard, Suite 400, North Olmsted OH 44070. 216/362-4820. **Fax:** 216/898-4651. **Contact:** Human Resources. **E-mail address:** jobs@fmglobal.com. **World Wide Web address:** http://www.fmglobal.com. **Description:** A commercial and industrial property management and risk services organization. The company helps policyholders to protect their properties and occupancies from fire, wind, flood, and explosion; boiler, pressure vessel, and machinery accidents; and many other insured hazards. **Corporate headquarters location:** Johnston RI. **Other U.S. locations:** Nationwide. **International locations:** Worldwide.

FAHLGREN
414 Walnut Street, Suite 515, Cincinnati OH 45202. 513/665-2342. **Contact:** Human Resources. **E-mail address:** jobs@fahlgren.com. **World Wide Web address:** http://www.fahlgren.com. **Description:** An advertising and marketing firm. Founded in 1962. **Other area locations:** Columbus OH.

FAIRFIELD MEDICAL CENTER
401 North Ewing Street, Lancaster OH 43130. 740/687-8017. **Fax:** 740/687-8633. **Recorded jobline:** 740/687-8450. **Contact:** Human Resources. **World Wide Web address:** http://www.fmchealth.org. **Description:** A 222-bed acute care hospital serving southeastern and central Ohio. **Positions advertised include:** Registered Nurse; Coding Supervisor; Community Services Coordinator; Home Health Aide; Infection Control Coordinator; Case Manager; Nursing Assistant; Physical Therapist. **Special programs:** Summer Jobs. **Office hours:** Monday - Friday, 6:30 a.m. - 5:00 p.m. **President:** Creighton Likes, Jr. **Number of employees at this location:** 1,400.

FALCON TRANSPORT COMPANY
650 North Meridian Road, Youngstown OH 44509. 330/793-1345. **Fax:** 330/799-2305. **E-mail address:** mjester@falcontransport.com. **Contact:** Personnel. **World Wide Web address:** http://www.falcontransport.com. **Description:** A flatbed truck and van company that transports various products including auto parts.

FECHHEIMER BROTHERS COMPANY
4545 Malsbary Road, Cincinnati OH 45242. 513/793-5400. **Toll-free phone:** 800/543-1939. **Fax:** 888/793-5400. **Contact:** Plant Manager. **E-mail address:** info@fechheimer.com. **World Wide Web address:** http://www.fechheimer.com. **Description:** Manufactures uniforms and specialty clothing products. **Parent company:** Berkshire Hathaway. **President and CEO:** Brad Kinstler.

FEDERAL-MOGUL CORPORATION
150 Fisher Avenue, Van Wert OH 45891. 419/238-0030. **Fax:** 419/238-5065. **Contact:** Personnel Department. **World Wide Web address:** http://www.federal-mogul.com. **Description:** Manufactures a variety of sealing products for industrial applications including farm implements and construction. Manufacturing processes include metal stamping, rubber molding, and light assembly. Federal-Mogul is a manufacturer of cylindrical and tapered roller bearings, oil seals, bushings, sleeve bearings, ball bearings, thrust washers, and related products for the automotive industry. The company is also a producer and distributor of precision parts to original equipment manufacturers and replacement parts such as fuel systems, suspension parts, and lighting and electrical products to worldwide markets. Brand names include Federal-Mogul, Glyco, Bruss, National, Mather, and Signal-Stat. **NOTE:** Interested candidates should submit a resume or curriculum vitae to: Corporate Human Resources Staffing, Federal-Mogul Corporation, 26555 Northwestern Highway, Southfield MI 48034. **Special programs:** Internships; Co-ops; College Recruitment Program. **Stock exchange symbol:** FMO. **Number of employees at this location:** 730. **Annual sales/revenues:** More than $100 million.

FEDERATED DEPARTMENT STORES, INC.
7 West Seventh Street, Cincinnati OH 45202. 513/579-7000. **Contact:** Human Resources. **World Wide Web address:** http://www.federated-fds.com. **Description:** Operates over 400 department stores nationwide. The retail segments include Bloomingdale's, The Bon Marche, Burdine's, Lazarus, Rich's, Goldsmith's, and Sterns. **Positions advertised include:** Staff Auditor; Claims Representative. **Special programs:** Internships. **Corporate headquarters location:** This location. **Listed on:** New York Stock Exchange. **Stock exchange symbol:** FD.

FERRO CORPORATION
1000 Lakeside Avenue, Cleveland OH 44114. 216/641-8580. **Contact:** Human Resources. **E-mail address:** resume@ferro.com. **World Wide Web address:** http://www.ferro.com. **Description:** Produces specialty materials through organic and inorganic chemical processes for the construction, furnishings, appliance, industrial, and transportation markets. Ferro Corporation specializes in coatings, colors, ceramics, electronics, plastics, and chemicals. **Corporate headquarters location:** This location. **Listed on:** New York Stock Exchange. **Stock exchange symbol:** FOE.

FERRO CORPORATION
THE DIAMONITE PLANT
453 West McConkey Street, Shreve OH 44676. 330/567-2145. **Contact:** Personnel Department. **Description:** This location manufactures alumina technical ceramic products. **Parent company:** W.R. Grace & Company is a diversified worldwide enterprise engaged in specialty and agricultural chemicals; energy production and services; retailing; restaurants; and other businesses. The firm operates over 2,500 facilities in 47 states and 42 foreign countries.

FIDELITY HEALTHCARE INC.
3832 Kettering Boulevard, Dayton OH 45439. 937/208-6400. **Toll-free phone:** 800/946-6344. **Fax:** 937/208-6539. **Contact:** Human Resources Secretary. **World Wide Web address:** http://www.fidelityhealthcare.org. **Description:** A home health care agency that provides nurses and home health aides to clients. **Positions advertised include:** Home Care Registered Nurse; Home Care Nursing Assistant; Physical Therapist; Occupational Therapist. **Office hours:** Monday - Friday, 8:00 a.m. - 5:00 p.m. **Number of employees at this location:** 325.

FIESTA SALONS, INC.
6363 Fiesta Drive, Columbus OH 43235-5200. 614/766-6363. **Contact:** Human Resources. **World Wide Web address:** http://www.fiestasalons.com. **Description:** Operates a chain of hair and tanning salons. **Positions advertised include:** Cosmetologist; Stylist; Receptionist/Intern; Associate Manager; Educator; Division Manager. **Corporate headquarters location:** This location.

FIFTH THIRD BANCORP
FIFTH THIRD BANK
38 Fountain Square Plaza, Cincinnati OH 45263. 513/579-5300. **Toll-free phone:** 800/972-3030. **Contact:** Human Resources Department. **World Wide Web address:** http://www.fifththird.com. **Description:** A regional bank holding company. **Positions advertised include:** Accountant; Customer Service Specialist; Risk Specialist; Administrative Assistant; Human Resources Director; Associate Commercial Relationship Manager; Audit Manager; Business Analyst. **Corporate headquarters location:** This location. **Other U.S. locations:** AZ; FL; IN; KY. **Subsidiaries include:** Fifth Third Bank (also at this location) is a full-service banking institution. **Listed on:** NASDAQ. **Stock exchange symbol:** FITB.

FIFTH THIRD BANK
79 South Washington Street, Tiffin OH 44883. 419/447-3213. **Toll-free phone:** 800/972-3030. **Contact:** Human Resources Department. **World Wide Web address:** http://www.fifththird.com. **Description:** A full-service bank. **Positions advertised include:** Branch Manager; Customer Service Representative; Department Manager; Human Resources Manager; Management Trainee; Purchasing Agent. **Other U.S. locations:** IN; KY. **Parent company:** Fifth Third Bancorp is a regional bank holding company. **Operations at this facility include:** Service. **Listed on:** NASDAQ. **Stock exchange symbol:** FITB.

FIFTH THIRD BANK
21 East State Street, Columbus OH 43215. 614/744-7590. **Toll-free phone:** 800/972-3030. **Contact:** Human Resources Department. **World Wide Web address:** http://www.fifththird.com. **Description:** A full-service bank. **Positions advertised include:** Administrative Assistant; Financial Specialist; Proof Operator; Vault Teller. **Other U.S. locations:** IN; KY. **Parent company:** Fifth Third Bancorp is a regional bank holding company. **Listed on:** NASDAQ. **Stock exchange symbol:** FITB.

FINDLAY INDUSTRIES INC.
4000 Fostoria Avenue, Findlay OH 45830. 419/422-1302. **Contact:** Human Resources. **E-mail address:** tjleffle@findlayindustries.com. **World Wide Web address:** http://www.findlayindustries.com. **Description:** This location manufactures automotive interior trim. **Corporate headquarters:** This location.

FIRESTONE OFFICE FEDERAL CREDIT UNION
1200 Firestone Parkway, Akron OH 44317-0001. 330/379-6400. **Toll-free phone:** 800/648-3328. **Fax:** 330/379-6657. **Contact:** Human Resources. **World Wide Web address:** http://www.fofcu.com. **Description:** A credit union that offers regular savings accounts, IRA retirement accounts, term share accounts, auto loans, personal loans, home improvement loans, first and second mortgages, home equity loans, educational loans, and financial assistance to its members. **Office hours:** Monday – Friday, 8:15 a.m. – 4:15 p.m.

FIRST COMMUNITY VILLAGE
1800 Riverside Drive, Columbus OH 43212-1814. 614/486-9511. **Toll-free phone:** 888/328-9511. **Fax:** 614/481-7190. **Contact:** Human Resources Department. **E-mail address:** career@firstcommunity.org. **World Wide Web address:** http://www.firstcommunityvillage.org. **Description:** A nonprofit, continuing care retirement community with facilities that include a nursing home, an assisted living center, and an independent living center. 175 beds. Founded in 1963. **NOTE:** Entry-level positions and second and third shifts are offered. **Positions advertised include:** Activities Coordinator; Maintenance Technician; Diet Aide; Registered Nurse; Licensed Practical Nurse; Nursing Assistant. **President/CEO:** Harry Hobson. **Number of employees at this location:** Approximately 400.

FIRSTENERGY CORPORATION
76 South Main Street, Akron OH 44308. 800/633-4766. **Fax:** 330/384-2455. **Contact:** Human Resources. **E-mail address:** professional_employment@firstenergycorp.com. **World Wide Web address:** http://www.firstenergycorp.com. **Description:** One of the largest investor-owned electric utility providers in the United States. **NOTE:** The company prefers that resumes be submitted online, however, resumes are also accepted by mail or fax. Candidates should indicate a specific job code when applying. **Positions advertised include:** Assistant Accountant; Human Resources Representative. **Special programs:** Internships; Co-ops. **Corporate headquarters location:** This location. **Other U.S. locations:** NJ; PA. **Subsidiaries include:** Illuminating Company (CEI); Toledo Edison Company; Ohio Edison; and Pennsylvania Power. **Operations at this facility include:** Administration; Sales. **Listed on:** New York Stock Exchange. **Stock exchange symbol:** FE. **Number of employees at this location:** 5,700. **Number of employees nationwide:** 15,905.

FLOWSERVE CORPORATION
P.O. Box 1145, Dayton OH 45401. 937/226-4000. **Physical location:** 2200 East Monument Avenue, Dayton OH 45402. **Contact:** Human Resources. **World Wide Web address:** http://www.flowserve.com. **Description:** Manufactures chemical processing equipment. **NOTE:** Copy and paste resume into e-mails. Attachments will not be accepted. **Corporate headquarters location:** Irving TX.

FORD MOTOR COMPANY
5401 Baumhart Road, Lorain OH 44053. 440/282-0350. **Contact:** Human Resources. **World Wide Web address:** http://www.ford.com. **Description:** Ford Motor Company is engaged in the design, development, manufacture, and sale of cars, trucks, tractors, and related components and accessories. Ford is also one of the largest providers of financial services in the United States. The company's two core businesses are the Automotive Group and the Financial Services Group (Ford Credit, The Associates, USL Capital, and First Nationwide). Ford is also engaged in a number of other businesses including electronics, glass, electrical and fuel-handling products, plastics, climate control systems, automotive service and replacement parts, vehicle leasing and rental, and land development. **Corporate headquarters location:** Dearborn MI. **Operations at this location include:** This location is an assembly plant for Thunderbirds, Cougars, and Econoline vans. **Listed on:** New York Stock Exchange. **Stock exchange symbol:** F. **Number of employees worldwide:** 300,000.

FORD MOTOR COMPANY
1155 Bible Road, Lima OH 45801. 419/226-7008. **Contact:** Human Resources. **World Wide Web address:** http://www.ford.com. **Description:** Ford Motor Company is engaged in the design, development, manufacture, and sale of cars, trucks, tractors, and related components and accessories. Ford is also one of the largest providers of financial services in the United States. The company has manufacturing, assembly, and sales affiliates in 29 countries outside the United States. The company's two core businesses are the Automotive Group and the Financial Services Group (Ford Credit, The Associates, USL Capital, and First Nationwide). Ford is also engaged in a number of other businesses including electronics, glass, electrical and fuel-handling products, plastics, climate control systems, automotive service and replacement parts, vehicle leasing and rental, and land development. **Corporate headquarters location:** Dearborn MI. **Operations at this location include:** This location manufactures engines. **Listed on:** New York Stock Exchange. **Stock exchange symbol:** F. **Number of employees worldwide:** 300,000.

FORD MOTOR COMPANY
3000 Sharon Road, Cincinnati OH 45241. 513/782-7800. **Contact:** Patricia A. Popplewell, Human Resources. **World Wide Web address:** http://www.ford.com. **Description:** Ford Motor Company is engaged in the design, development, manufacture, and sale of cars, trucks, tractors, and related components and accessories. Ford is also one of the largest providers of financial services in the United States. The company's two core businesses are the Automotive Group and the Financial Services Group (Ford Credit, The Associates, USL Capital, and First Nationwide). Ford is also engaged in a number of other businesses including electronics, glass, electrical and fuel-handling products, plastics, climate control systems, automotive service and replacement parts, vehicle leasing and rental, and land development. **Corporate headquarters location:** Dearborn MI. **Operations at this facility include:** This location manufactures automotive and transportation equipment. **Listed on:** New York Stock Exchange. **Stock exchange symbol:** F. **Number of employees worldwide:** 300,000.

FOREST CITY ENTERPRISES INC.
1100 Terminal Tower, 50 Public Square, Suite 1026, Cleveland OH 44113-2203. 216/621-6060. **Fax:** 216/263-6208. **Contact:** Human Resources. **E-mail address:** humanresources@forestcity.net. **World Wide Web address:** http://www.fceinc.com. **Description:** A real estate investment trust that acquires, develops, and operates commercial, residential, urban entertainment, and land development properties. **NOTE:** Submit resumes to: Forest City Enterprises, Inc., Human Resources Department; 50 Public Square, Suite 1026, Cleveland OH 44113. **Positions advertised include:** Administrative Assistant; East Coast Development Representative; Family Attorney; Financial Analyst; Leasing Manager; Maintenance Worker; Programmer Analyst; Project Manager; Property Analyst; Secretary; Senior Accountant; Senior Auditor; Technical Support Specialist. **Listed on:** New York Stock Exchange. **Stock exchange symbol:** FCEA.

FORUM HEALTH
NORTHSIDE MEDICAL CENTER
500 Gypsy Lane, Youngstown OH 44501. 330/884-1000. **Fax:** 330/884-0100. **Contact:** Human Resources. **E-mail address:** aondo@forumhealth.org. **World Wide Web address:** http://www.forumhealth.org. **Description:** Operates three hospitals, an outpatient surgery center, a nursing home, a laboratory, and a home health care agency. **NOTE:** See website for specific contact information regarding nursing, physician, and residency opportunities. **Positions advertised include:** Cardiovascular Care Manager; Emergency Department Coordinator; Director of Pharmacy; Culinary Operations Coordinator; Pediatric Clinical Supervisor; MRI Technologist; Charge Nurse; Gastroenterologist; Head and Neck Surgeon; Vascular Surgeon. **Special Programs:** Internships; Volunteer Opportunities.

FORT RECOVERY INDUSTRIES INC.
2440 State Route 49, Fort Recovery OH 45846. 419/375-4121. **Fax:** 419/375-4194. **Contact:** Human Resources Department. **World Wide Web address:** http://www.fortrecoveryindustries.com. **Description:** Engaged in aluminum and zinc die-casting, as well as plastic blow molding. The company specializes in plumbing hardware, RV hardware, custom-designed blow-molded products, and zinc and aluminum custom-designed die-cast products for the appliance, automotive, luggage, hardware, and industrial markets.

FOSECO INC.
20200 Sheldon Road, Cleveland OH 44142. 440/826-4548. **Contact:** Human Resources. **World Wide Web address:** http://www.foseco.com. **Description:** Manufactures products including filtration and feeding systems for steel mills and foundries.

FOX RIVER PAPER COMPANY
700 West Court Street, Urbana OH 43078. 937/653-7151. **Contact:** Human Resources Manager. **World Wide Web address:** http://www.foxriverpaper.com. **Description:** Develops, manufactures, and markets writing, text, and cover papers available in a wide range of colors, textures, finishes, and weights. Fox River Paper Company markets its products under the names Capitol Brand, Confetti, Coronado, Crushed Leaf, Evergreen, Filare, Fox River Bond, Fox River Select, Howard Linen, Quest, Starwhite, Sundance, Teton, and Valley Forge. Founded in 1883. **Corporate headquarters location:** Appleton WI.

FRANCISCAN SERVICES CORPORATION
6832 Convent Boulevard, Sylvania OH 43560. 419/882-8373. **Fax:** 419/882-7360. **Contact:** John W. O'Connell, President. **World Wide Web address:** http://www.fscsylvanian.org/fcc.htm. **Description:** This location's facilities include Providence Corporation, which offers long-term care services; Providence Hospital; Franciscan Center, a performing arts and conference center; and Franciscan Properties, which manages Convert Park Apartments, an independent living complex for senior adults. Franciscan Services Corporation is a nonprofit health care provider. Other facilities include Bethany House (Toledo OH), which serves women and children; St. John Medical Center (Steubenville OH); Trinity Medical Center (Brenham TX); Holy Cross Hospital (Detroit MI); and St. Francis Services Corporation (Bryan TX), a free clinic. **Corporate headquarters location:** This location.

FRANKLIN INTERNATIONAL
2020 Bruck Street, Columbus OH 43207. 614/443-0241. **Toll-free phone:** 800/877-4583. **Fax:** 614/443-4583. **Contact:** Human Resources. **E-mail address:** hr@franklininternational.com. **World Wide Web address:** http://www.franklini.com. **Description:** Manufactures a variety of adhesives. **Positions advertised include:** Technical Service Scientist. **Number of employees at this location:** 430.

FRANKLIN UNIVERSITY
201 South Grant Avenue, Columbus OH 43215. 614/797-4700. **Toll-free phone:** 877/341-6300. **Fax:** 614/341-6422. **Contact:** Human Resources. **E-mail address:** resume@franklin.edu. **World Wide Web address:** http://www.franklin.edu. **Description:** A four-year independent university with a focus on adult education. Franklin University has an enrollment of approximately 8,000 students. Founded in 1902. **Positions advertised include:** Adjunct Instructor, Accounting; Program Chair, Business Administration; Professor, Computer Sciences; Director, Academic Software; Administrative Assistant; Student Services Liaison; Facilities Assistant; Computer Science Lab Assistant.

FRESH MARK, INC.
P.O. Box 8440, Canton OH 44711. 330/455-5253. **Physical address:** 1600 Harmont Avenue NE, Canton OH 44705. **Contact:** Human Resources. **E-mail address:** humanresources@freshmark.com. **World Wide Web address:** http://www.freshmark.com. **Description:** Processes, packages, and distributes meats including ham, deli meats, smoked sausage, and related products. **NOTE:** Always accepting resumes, which can be sent to jobs@freshmark.com. **Positions advertised include:** Cost Accountant; Maintenance Supervisor; Production Supervisor; Quality Assurance Food Technologist; Sanitation Manager. **Corporate headquarters location:** This location. **Other area locations:** Columbus OH; Massillon OH. **Other U.S. locations:** Buffalo NY; Charleston WV; Pittsburgh PA.

FRISCH'S RESTAURANTS, INC.
2800 Gilbert Avenue, Cincinnati OH 45206. 513/961-2660. **Toll-free phone:** 888/824-4268. **Contact:** Personnel. **World Wide Web address:** http://www.frischs.com. **Description:** Operates and licenses family restaurants with drive-through service under the names Frisch's Big Boy, Kip's Big Boy, and Hardee's. The company also operates two hotels with restaurants in metropolitan Cincinnati. **NOTE:** Human Resources direct line is 888/824-4269. **Corporate headquarters location:** This location. **Other U.S. locations:** FL; IN; KY; OK; TX.

FRITO-LAY, INC.
1626 Old Mansfield Road, Wooster OH 44691. 330/262-1070. **Contact:** Human Resources. **World Wide Web address:** http://www.fritolay.com. **Description:** A worldwide manufacturer and wholesaler of snack products including Fritos Corn Chips, Lays Potato Chips, and Doritos Tortilla Chips. **Corporate headquarters location:** Plano TX. **Parent company:** PepsiCo, Inc. (Purchase NY) consists of Frito-Lay Company, Pepsi-Cola Company, and Tropicana Products, Inc.

FRONTSTEP INC.
2800 Corporate Exchange Drive, Columbus OH 43231. 614/523-7000. **Fax:** 614/895-2504. **Contact:** Personnel. **World Wide Web address:** http://www.frontstep.com. **Description:** A developer and manufacturer of open client/server software. **Positions advertised include:** Director of Customer Contacts; Collections Specialist. **Corporate headquarters location:** This location.

GBS CORPORATION
P.O. Box 2340, North Canton OH 44720. 330/494-5330. **Physical address:** 7233 Freedom Avenue NW, North Canton OH 44720. **Contact:** Laurie Quinn, Human Resources Director. **E-mail address:** hr@gbscorp.com. **World Wide Web address:** http://www.gbscorp.com. **Description:** Specializes in information management through its various business units, which print business forms, sell telephones, and offer computer services. Divisions include GBS Forms & Systems; GBS Filing Systems; GBS Computer Systems; GBS Labeling Systems; and GBS Communications. Founded in 1971. **Corporate headquarters location:** This location. **Other U.S. locations:** Tampa FL; Livonia MI; Malvern OH; Stow OH; Youngstown OH. **Operations at this facility include:** Administration; Divisional Headquarters. **Number of employees at this location:** 100. **Number of employees nationwide:** 450.

GM POWERTRAIN
P.O. Box 70, 26427 State Route 281 East, Defiance OH 43512. 419/782-7010. **Contact:** Personnel. **World Wide Web address:** http://www.gmpowertrain.com. **Description:** This location manufactures metal castings for General Motors Corporation. **Parent company:** General Motors Corporation is one of the world's largest full-line vehicle manufacturers, and also has substantial interests in information technology, electronics, and finance. GM conducts business through the following sectors: North American Automotive Operations, GM Hughes Electronics Corporation, International Operations, General Motors Acceptance Corporation (GMAC), and Electronic Data Systems Corporation (EDS). North American Automotive Operations includes Sales/Service Groups (Buick, Cadillac, Chevrolet, GMC Truck, Oldsmobile, Pontiac, and Saturn) and Vehicle Development Groups (Powertrain, Truck Group, Small Car Group, and Midsize/Luxury Car Group). GM Hughes Electronics Corporation is involved in automotive, telecommunications, and space and defense electronics. International Operations include GM Europe; Asia Pacific Operations; and Latin America, Africa, Middle East Operations. GMAC, which provides financing and insurance to GM customers and dealers, consists of North American Operations, International Operations, Motors Insurance Corporation, and GMAC Mortgage Group. EDS applies information technologies to more than 8,000 customers globally in the communications, energy/chemical, insurance, public sector, travel and transportation, financial services, manufacturing, and retail industries. **Listed on:** New York Stock Exchange. **Stock exchange symbol:** GM.

THE GARICK CORPORATION
13600 Broadway Avenue, Cleveland OH 44125. 216/581-0100. **Toll-free phone:** 800/242-7425. **Fax:** 216/475-0616. **Contact:** Don English, Vice President of Associate Relations. **E-mail address:** don.english@garick.com. **World Wide Web address:** http://www.garick.com. **Description:** Develops, manufactures, and supplies construction, landscape, and nursery materials. The Garick Corporation's products include Alabama Auburn, Animal Karpet, Dynacushion Play Mats, Equestrian Karpet, Kids Karpet, The Original Bark Bale, and Trail Karpet. **Positions advertised include:** Customer Service Manager. **Special programs:** Internships. **Corporate headquarters location:** This location. **Operations at this facility include:** Administration; Research and Development; Sales; Service. **Parent company:** Fairmount Minerals.

GEAUGA REGIONAL HOSPITAL
13207 Ravenna Road, Chardon OH 44024. 440/285-6000. **Fax:** 440/285-6483. **Contact:** Mark Jepson, Human Resources. **E-mail address:** mark.jepson@uhhs.com. **World Wide Web address:** http://www.uhhsgrh.com. **Description:** A 206-bed hospital offering acute care, oncology, physical therapy, respiratory therapy, cardiac rehabilitation, radiology, and maternity care services. **Positions advertised include:** Cook; Certified Nursing Assistant; Licensed Practical Nurse; Critical Care Nurse; Switchboard Operator. **Parent company:** University Hospitals Health System (UHHS).

GENERAL DYNAMICS ADVANCED INFORMATION SYSTEMS
5200 Springfield Pike, Suite 200, Dayton OH 45431. 937/253-4770. **Fax:** 937/476-2900. **Contact:** Human Resources. **World Wide Web address:** http://www.veridian.com. **Description:** Researches, develops, and tests many major U.S. aircraft and spacecraft. Formerly known as Veridian Engineering, the company was acquired by General Dynamics in August of 2003. Veridian's four divisions have now joined the General Dynamics Information Systems and Technology Group. Veridian's Engineering, Information Solutions, and Systems divisions will join General Dynamics Advanced Information Systems, while its Information Technology Services division will join General Dynamics Network Systems. **NOTE:** Candidates may search and apply for a position online. **Positions advertised include:** Receptionist; Financial Administrative Assistant; Lead Systems Engineer; Research Test Associate. **Corporate headquarters location:** Arlington VA. **Other U.S. locations:** Nationwide. **Parent company:** General Dynamics. **Listed on:** New York Stock Exchange. **Stock exchange symbol:** GD.

GENERAL MOTORS CORPORATION
P.O. Box 2567, 2525 West Fourth Street, Mansfield OH 44906. 419/755-5011. **Contact:** Human Resources. **World Wide Web address:** http://www.gm.com. **Description:** General Motors Corporation is one of the world's largest full-line vehicle manufacturers, and also has substantial interests in information technology, electronics, and finance. GM conducts business through the following sectors: North American Automotive Operations, International Operations, General Motors Acceptance Corporation (GMAC), Electronic Data Systems Corporation (EDS), and GM Hughes Electronics Corporation. North American Automotive Operations includes Sales/Service Groups (Buick, Cadillac, Chevrolet, GMC Truck, Oldsmobile, Pontiac, and Saturn) and Vehicle Development Groups (Powertrain, Truck Group, Small Car Group, and Midsize/Luxury Car Group). International Operations include GM Europe; Asia Pacific Operations; and Latin America, Africa, Middle East Operations. GMAC, which provides financing and insurance to GM customers and dealers, consists of North American Operations, International Operations, Motors Insurance Corporation, and GMAC Mortgage Group. EDS applies information technologies to more than 8,000 customers globally in the communications, energy/chemical, insurance, public sector, travel and transportation, financial services, manufacturing, and retail industries. GM Hughes Electronics Corporation is involved in automotive, telecommunications, and space and defense electronics. Founded in 1908. **Corporate headquarters location:** Detroit MI. **Operations at this facility include:** This location manufactures automotive stampings. **Listed on:** New York Stock Exchange. **Stock exchange symbol:** GM.

GENTIVA HEALTH SERVICES
941 Chatham Lane, Suite 207, Columbus OH 43221. 614/326-7638. **Toll-free phone:** 800/325-6696. **Fax:** 330/644-2823. **Contact:** Human Resources. **World Wide Web address:** http://www.gentiva.com. **Description:** Gentiva Health Services provides home health care services, pharmaceutical support, and supplemental staffing services. **Corporate headquarters location:** Melville NY.

GEYERS' MARKET INC.
280 East Main Street, Lexington OH 44904-1194. 419/884-1373. **Contact:** Human Resources. **E-mail address:** ej@geyers.com. **World Wide Web address:** http://www.geyers.com. **Description:** A grocery market. **Positions advertised include:** Retail Manager. **Corporate headquarters location:** This location. **Operations at this facility include:** Sales; Service. **Listed on:** Privately held. **Number of employees at this location:** 325.

GLASSTECH INC.
Ampoint Industrial Park, 995 Fourth Street, Perrysburg OH 43551. 419/661-9500. **Fax:** 419/661-9616. **Contact:** Human Resources. **World Wide Web address:** http://www.glasstech.com. **Description:** Manufactures machinery that bends and tempers glass for the automotive and architecture industries.

GLASTIC CORPORATION
4321 Glenridge Road, Cleveland OH 44121. 216/486-0100. **Fax:** 216/486-1091. **Contact:** Human Resources. **E-mail address:** sales@glastic.com. **World Wide Web address:** http://www.glastic.com. **Description:** Develops, designs, manufactures, and engineers composite materials and related products. Glastic Corporation is primarily engaged in the production of custom and stock composite materials that have excellent corrosion, dielectric, structural, and thermal properties. **Corporate headquarters location:** This location. **Other area locations:** Jefferson OH. **Other U.S. locations:** Salem MI. **International locations:** United Kingdom.

THE GLIDDEN COMPANY
300 Sprowl Road, Huron OH 44839. 419/433-0017. **Contact:** Human Resources. **World Wide Web address:** http://www.glidden.com. **Description:** Manufactures resin packaging products and decorative oil and water-based paints. **Corporate headquarters location:** Cleveland OH. **Other U.S. locations:** Nationwide. **Parent company:** ICI Inc. **Operations at this facility include:** Manufacturing. **Number of employees at this location:** 215.

GLOBE MOTORS
2275 Stanley Avenue, Dayton OH 45404. 937/228-3171. **Fax:** 937/229-8531. **Contact:** Human Resources. **World Wide Web address:** http://www.globe-motors.com. **Description:** Designs, develops, manufactures, and distributes subfractional horsepower motors and motorized devices. Globe Motors' products include AC commercial cooling fans, commercial cooling fan accessories, DC commercial cooling fans, industrial brushless DC motors and gearmotors, industrial motors and gearmotors, military/aerospace blowers, and military/aerospace motors and gearmotors. **Operations at this facility include:** Administration; Divisional Headquarters; Research and Development; Sales. **Corporate headquarters location:** This location. **Other area locations:** Dayton OH (Manufacturing). **Other U.S. locations:** Dothan AL. **International locations:** Reynosa, Mexico.

GOOD SAMARITAN HOSPITAL & HEALTH CENTER
2222 Philadelphia Drive, Dayton OH 45406. 937/278-2612 Extension 2532. **Fax:** 937/276-7618. **Recorded jobline:** 937/276-8257. **Contact:** Human Resources. **World Wide Web address:** http://www.goodsamdayton.com. **Description:** A 560-bed, nonprofit medical center specializing in cardiovascular services, mental health, emergency care, obstetrics, physical medicine, and ambulatory care. **Positions advertised include:** Registered Nurse; Nutrition Associate; Senior Data Analyst; Database Coordinator; Dentist; Senior Accountant; Pharmacist; Physical Therapist; Occupational Therapist; Respiratory Therapist; Radiation Therapist; Security Officer; Nuclear Medicine Technician; Ultrasound Technologist; Secretary; Department Assistant. **Special programs:** Internships. **Parent company:** Samaritan Health Partners. **Number of employees at this location:** 2,500.

GOODRICH AEROSPACE
AIRCRAFT WHEEL AND BRAKES
101 Waco Street, Troy OH 45373. 937/339-3811. **Contact:** Personnel. **World Wide Web address:** http://www.goodrich.com. **Description:** Designs and manufactures aircraft systems and components for aerospace, military, commercial, general aviation, commuter, and helicopter aircraft worldwide. The company's products include aircraft engine nacelles, pylons, and thrust reversers; emergency evacuation systems; flight management and control systems; ice protection systems; instruments and avionics; sensors; and wheels, brakes and landing gear. **NOTE:** All hiring for this location done through WebHire at: http://www.goodrich.com/careers.asp. **Corporate headquarters location:** Charlotte NC. **Parent company:** Goodrich provides aircraft systems, components, and services; and also manufactures a wide range of specialty chemicals. The business units comprising the aerospace division of Goodrich consist of landing systems, sensors and integrated systems, safety systems, and maintenance, repair, and overhaul. **Listed on:** New York Stock Exchange. **Stock exchange symbol:** BR. **Number of employees at this location:** 800.

GOODRICH LANDING GEAR DIVISION
8000 Marble Avenue, Cleveland OH 44105. 216/341-1700. **Contact:** Human Resources Department. **World Wide Web address:** http://www.goodrich.com. **Description:** Designs, tests, and manufactures military and commercial landing gear systems. **Positions advertised include:** Design Engineer; Principal Performance Engineer. **Corporate headquarters location:** Charlotte NC. **Parent company:** Goodrich provides aircraft systems, components, and services; and also manufactures a wide range of specialty chemicals. The business units comprising the aerospace division of Goodrich consist of landing systems, sensors and integrated systems, safety systems, and maintenance, repair, and overhaul. **Listed on:** New York Stock Exchange. **Stock exchange symbol:** BR. **Number of employees at this location:** 800.

GOODYEAR TIRE & RUBBER COMPANY
13601 Industrial Parkway, Marysville OH 43040. 937/644-8900. **Contact:** Human Resources. **World Wide Web address:** http://www.goodyear.com. **Description:** Goodyear Tire & Rubber Company's principal business is the development, manufacture, distribution, and sale of tires for applications worldwide. Goodyear also manufactures and sells a broad spectrum of rubber products and rubber-related chemicals for various industrial and consumer markets and provides auto repair services. **Corporate headquarters location:** Akron OH. **Other U.S. locations:** Nationwide. **International locations:** Worldwide. **Subsidiaries include:** Celeron; Goodyear Asia; Goodyear Europe; Goodyear Latin America; Goodyear Racing; Kelly-Springfield; North American Tire. **Operations at this facility include:** This location manufactures conveyor belts. **Listed on:** New York Stock Exchange. **Stock exchange symbol:** GT. **Annual sales/revenues:** More than $100 million. **Number of employees worldwide:** 80,000.

GOODYEAR TIRE & RUBBER COMPANY
1144 East Market Street, Akron OH 44316-0001. 330/796-2121. **Fax:** 330/796-2222. **Contact:** Human Resources. **World Wide Web address:** http://www.goodyear.com. **Description:** Goodyear Tire & Rubber Company's principal business is the development, manufacture, distribution, and sale of tires for applications worldwide. Goodyear also manufactures and sells a broad spectrum of rubber products and rubber-related chemicals for various industrial and consumer markets, and provides auto repair services. **Positions advertised include:** Paralegal; Senior Research Engineer; Corporate Security Development Intern; Earth Mover and Grader Tires Service Worker; Global Technical Buyer. **Special programs:** Internships; Co-ops. **Corporate headquarters location:** This location. **Other U.S. locations:** Nationwide. **International locations:** Worldwide. **Subsidiaries include:** Celeron; Goodyear Asia; Goodyear Europe; Goodyear Latin America; Goodyear Racing; Kelly-Springfield; North American Tire. **Operations at this facility include:** This location manufactures tires and chemicals and houses a technical center, tire proving grounds, and airship operations. **Listed on:** New York Stock Exchange. **Stock exchange symbol:** GT. **Annual sales/revenues:** More than $100 million. **Number of employees worldwide:** 80,000.

THE GORMAN-RUPP COMPANY
P.O. 1217, Mansfield OH 44901. 419/755-1011. **Physical address:** 305 Bowman Street, Mansfield OH 44903. **Fax:** 419/755-1525. **Contact:** Human Resources. **E-mail address:** hradmin@gormanrupp.com. **World Wide Web address:** http://www.gormanrupp.com. **Description:** Manufactures pumps and pump and motor controls for construction, industrial, petroleum, agricultural, water and wastewater, original equipment, and military applications. The company markets its products through wholly-owned subsidiaries and a network of independent distributors and manufacturer's representatives worldwide. Founded in 1933. **Other area locations:** Belleville OH; Sand Springs OH. **Other U.S. locations:** Toccoa GA. **Listed on:** American Stock Exchange. **Stock exchange symbol:** GRC.

GOULD ELECTRONICS INC.
34929 Curtis Boulevard, Eastlake OH 44095-4001. 440/953-5000. **Fax:** 440/953-5133. **Contact:** Human Resources. **World Wide Web address:** http://www.gould.com. **Description:** Designs and manufactures materials, components, and related technologies for the electronics marketplace and a range of original equipment manufacturers. Gould Electronics is divided into six major individual businesses: Gould Foil Division develops electro-deposited copper foil for electronic interconnection applications; Gould Copper Aluminum Copper manufactures two sheets of copper separated by aluminum; Gould Electronic Materials produces adhesiveless flexible copper laminate and other metal foils; Gould ElectroCopper Products manufactures low-cost electrolytic copper powder and extruded copper shapes; Gould Powerdex produces primary and secondary lithium batteries; and Gould Fiber Optics provides standard and customized passive coupler components and wavelength division multiplexers to the telecommunications, cable television, instrumentation, and optical sensor markets. **Corporate headquarters location:** This location. **International locations:** Asia; Europe. **Parent company:** Japan Energy Corporation. **Operations at this facility include:** Administration; Research and Development.

GRACO CHILDREN'S PRODUCTS
9600 Valley View Road, Macedonia OH 44056. 330/468-2000. **Fax:** 330/468-4489. **Contact:** Personnel Manager. **World Wide Web address:** http://www.gracochildrensproducts.com. **Description:** Graco Children's Products is one of the world's leading providers of nursery products. Graco's range of products includes car seats, strollers, travel systems, travel cots, swings and entertainment centers. **Corporate headquarters location:** Basildon, England.

GRANGE INSURANCE COMPANIES
650 South Front Street, Columbus OH 43206. 614/445-2900. **Toll-free phone:** 800/422-0550. **Fax:** 614/445-2695. **Recorded jobline:** 614/445-2468. **Contact:** Personnel. **E-mail address:** hr@grangeinsurance.com. **World Wide Web address:** http://www.grangeinsurance.com. **Description:** A holding company for a group of property, casualty, and life insurance companies. **Positions advertised include:** Operations Manager; Call Center Representative; Claims Technical Trainer; Communications and Advertising Manager; Business Lender; Commercial Lines Underwriter. **Corporate headquarters location:** This location. **Subsidiaries include:** Amerimutual; Trustgard. **Operations at this facility include:** Administration; Research and Development; Sales; Service.

GRAYDON HEAD & RITCHEY
1900 Fifth Third Center, 511 Walnut Street, Suite 1900, Cincinnati OH 45202. 513/621-6464. **Fax:** 513/651-3836. **Contact:** Alexandra Walters, Director of Professional Development. **E-mail address:** awalters@graydon.com. **World Wide Web address:** http://www.graydon.com. **Description:** A corporate law firm. Graydon Head and Ritchey specializes in business and finance, commercial litigation, commercial real estate, computer and high technology, employee benefits, human resources, international issues, and Internet commerce law. Founded in 1871. **NOTE:** People interested in Paralegal, Secretary or Staff Positions should contact Emily Cole at ecole@graydon.com. **Positions advertised include:** Employee Benefits Attorney.

GREAT AMERICAN INSURANCE COMPANY
580 Walnut Street, P.O. Box 2575, Cincinnati OH 45202. 513/369-5000. **Fax:** 513/369-5693. **Contact:** Personnel. **World Wide Web address:** http://www.greatamericaninsurance.com. **Description:** Provides a line of insurance products and services to area customers. **Positions advertised include:** Claim Technician; Staff Accountant; Product Analyst; Claims Processor.

GREAT LAKES WINDOW CORPORATION
P.O. Box 1896, 30499 Tracy Road, Toledo OH 43603. 419/666-5555. **Toll-free phone:** 800/666-0000. **Fax:** 419/661-2926. **Contact:** Human Resources Department. **World Wide Web address:** http://www.greatlakeswindow.com. **Description:** Designs, develops, manufactures, and markets vinyl windows and doors. The company's products include bay and bow windows; casement, awning, and French casement windows; double-hung windows; two- and three-section sliding windows; traditional and specialty garden windows; and sliding and hinged patio doors. **President and CEO:** Mark Watson.

GREEN MEADOWS HEALTH AND WELLNESS CENTER
7770 Columbus Road NE, Louisville OH 44641. 330/875-1456. **Fax:** 330/875-1459. **Contact:** Human Resources. **Description:** A nonprofit nursing home. **NOTE:** Entry-level positions and second and third shifts are offered. **Special programs:** Internships; Apprenticeships; Training; Summer Jobs. **Office hours:** Monday - Friday, 8:00 a.m. - 4:30 p.m. **Number of employees at this location:** 300.

GREENVILLE NATIONAL BANK
P.O. Box 190, Greenville OH 45331-0190. 937/548-1114. **Physical address:** 446 South Broadway, Greenville OH 45331. **Fax:** 937/548-0650. **Contact:** Human Resources. **World Wide Web address:** http://www.greenvillenationalbank.com. **Description:** A full-service bank. Greenville National Bank offers a wide range of commodities and services including automated teller machines, automatic transfers, bank by mail, cashier's checks, certified checks, direct deposit, credit card merchant accounts, fax services, federal tax depository, money orders, notary services, traveler's checks, safe deposit boxes, utility bill payments, and Visa check cards. Founded in 1934.

GREIF BROTHERS CORPORATION
425 Winter Road, Delaware OH 43015. 740/549-6000. **Fax:** 740/549-6100. **Contact:** Human Resources Manager. **World Wide Web address:** http://www.greif.com. **Description:** Manufactures shipping containers and materials including fibre, steel, and plastic drums, multiwall bags, and related items. The company also produces and sells containerboard and related products such as virgin and recycled containerboard, corrugated paper, and corrugated containers. **Number of employees nationwide:** 4,500.

HBD INDUSTRIES INC.
1301 West Sandusky Avenue, Bellefontaine OH 43311-1065. 937/593-5010. **Toll-free phone:** 800/543-8070. **Fax:** 937/593-4354. **Contact:** Human Resources. **E-mail address:** info@hbdthermoid.com. **World Wide Web address:** http://www.hbdthermoid.com. **Description:** Manufactures coated fabrics, conveyor belting, ducting, industrial hoses, and power transmission belts for the agricultural, automotive, aviation, construction, manufacturing, mining, and petroleum industries. HBD Industries markets its products under the Thermoid brand names including Aeroduct, Cyclone, Flex-LocTM, Flex Strength, Goldenair, Griptop, Maxecon, MaxipowerTM, Nylock, PowerplusTM, Sani-KingTM, Transporter, Ultraflex, Ultra-Chem, Valuflex, and VersiconTM.

HMI INDUSTRIES INC.
13325 Darice Parkway, Unit A, Strongsville OH 44149. 440/846-7800. **Toll-free phone:** 800/344-1840. **Contact:** Human Resources. **World Wide Web address:** http://www.filterqueen.com. **Description:** Manufactures Filter Queen vacuum cleaners and air filtration devices. **Positions advertised include:** Sales Associate; Management Trainee; Office Manager; Office Coordinator; Telemarketer; Service Technician. **Corporate headquarters location:** Seven Hills OH. **Number of employees at this location:** 140.

HALEX COMPANY
23901 Aurora Road, Bedford Heights OH 44146. 440/232-2915. **Toll-free phone:** 800/749-3261. **Fax:** 440/439-1792. **Contact:** Human Resources Director. **World Wide Web address:** http://www.halexco.com. **Description:** Halex Company manufactures electrical fittings. The company's products include fittings for electrical metallic tubing; flexible metallic conduit, armored cable, and metal clad cable; liquid-tight conduit; nonmetallic sheathed cable; rigid and intermediate metallic conduit; and service entrance cable. **Corporate headquarters location:** Westlake OH. **Operations at this facility include:** This location is the die-casting division. **Number of employees at this location:** 130.

HAMILTON FIXTURE
3550 Symmes Road, Hamilton OH 45015. 513/874-2016. **Toll-free phone:** 800/889-2165. **Fax:** 513/870-8741. **Contact:** Human Resources. **E-mail address:** hr@hamiltonfixture.com. **World Wide Web address:** http://www.hamiltonfixture.com. **Description:** A manufacturer of fixtures and displays for retail establishments. Products are made of metal, acrylic, wood, or a combination of materials. **Corporate headquarters location:** This location. **Other U.S. locations:** Nationwide. **Operations at this facility include:** Administration; Manufacturing; Sales; Service. **Listed on:** Privately held. **Annual sales/revenues:** $51 - $100 million. **Number of employees nationwide:** 800.

HARRIS INFOSOURCE
2057 East Aurora Road, Twinsburg OH 44087-1999. 330/425-9000. **Toll-free phone:** 800/888-5900. **Fax:** 330/963-3839. **Contact:** Human Resources. **E-mail address:** hr@harrisinfo.com. **World Wide Web address:** http://www.harrisinfo.com. **Description:** Publishes magazine directories and software containing lists of manufacturers nationwide. Founded in 1972. **NOTE:** Resumes are accepted on a continuous basis, and may be submitted by mail, fax, or e-mail. **Special programs:** Training. **Corporate headquarters location:** This location. **Listed on:** Privately held. **Number of employees at this location:** 100.

HEALTH CLEVELAND
FAIRVIEW HOSPITAL
18101 Lorain Avenue, Cleveland OH 44111-5612. 216/476-7000. **Fax:** 216/476-7023. **Contact:** Personnel. **World Wide Web address:** http://www.fairviewhospital.org. **Description:** A hospital. Services include a birthing center, pediatrics, a heart center, emergency services, orthopedics, a cancer center, and a hospice support system. The hospital is part of a network that includes 11 locations in 6 communities. **Positions advertised include:** Staff Pharmacist; Mammography Technologist; MRI Technician; Ultra Sound Technician; Registered Radiation Therapist; Coding Manager; Licensed Practical Nurse; Registered Nurse; Senior Operations Project Coordinator; Western Region Finance Director. **Special Programs:** Volunteering Opportunities. **Office hours:** Monday – Friday, 9:00 a.m. – 4:00 p.m. **Number of employees at this location:** 2,600.

HEINZERLING MEMORIAL FOUNDATION
Developmental Center, 1755 Heinzerling Drive, Columbus OH 43223. 614/272-8888. **Fax:** 614/272-0268. **Recorded jobline:** 614/255-3900. **Contact:** N. Christine Rafeld, Director of Human Resources Department. **E-mail address:** online_application@heinzerling.org. **World Wide Web address:** http://www.heinzerling.org. **Description:** A private, nonprofit residential treatment facility for mentally disabled individuals of all ages. The Heinzerling Memorial Foundation provides care, education, and development skills to approximately 220 residents with special needs. **Positions advertised include:** Nursing Shift Coordinator; Nurse; Dish Machine Operator; Physical Therapist; Therapy Assistant; Laundry Aide; Housekeeper; Occupational Therapist.

HIGHLIGHTS FOR CHILDREN, INC.
P.O. Box 16278, Columbus OH 43216-6278. 614/486-0631. **Physical address:** 1800 Watermark Drive, Columbus OH 43215. **Fax:** 614/487-2700. **Recorded jobline:** 614/487-2277. **Contact:** Human Resources. **E-mail address:** jobs@highlights.com. **World Wide Web address:** http://www.highlights.com. **Description:** Publishes a monthly educational children's magazine. **Positions advertised include:** Independent Sales Manager; Copy Editor; Catalog Circulation Manager. **Special programs:** Internships. **Corporate headquarters location:** This location. **Operations at this facility include:** Administration; Sales; Service. **Listed on:** Privately held. **Number of employees at this location:** 670. **Number of employees nationwide:** 700.

HILB ROGAL & HOBBS (HRH)
2245 Northbank Drive, Columbus OH 43220. 614/457-7000. **Toll-free phone:** 800/837-0503. **Fax:** 614/326-7499. **Contact:** Nancy Price, Human Resources. **World Wide Web address:** http://www.hrh.com. **Description:** A full-service insurance company specializing in association benefits, business development, commercial property and casualty, employee benefits, financial and investment services, personal home and auto, and professional liability insurance. Founded in 1973. **Other U.S. locations:** Nationwide.

HILLCREST HOSPITAL
6780 Mayfield Road, Mayfield Heights OH 44124. 440/449-4633. **Contact:** Human Resources. **World Wide Web address:** http://www.hillcresthospital.org. **Description:** Hillcrest Hospital is a 311-bed community hospital providing specialized services such as OB, NICU, critical care, oncology, ambulatory surgery, and digestive health services. **Positions advertised include:** Registered Nurse; Respiratory Therapist; Phlebotomist; Social Worker; Ultrasound Technician; Laboratory Assistant; Staff Pharmacist; Radiology Coordinator; Radiology Technician; Occupational Therapist; Patient Care Coordinator; Staffing Coordinator; Security Officer. **Corporate headquarters location:** Mayfield Village OH. **Parent company:** Cleveland Clinic Health System. **Operations at this facility include:** Service. **Number of employees nationwide:** 1,600.

HILLSHIRE FARM AND KAHN'S
3241 Spring Grove Avenue, Cincinnati OH 45225. 513/541-4000. **Fax:** 513/853-1386 (Office positions); 513/853-1197 (Plant positions). **Contact:** Human Resources. **World Wide Web address:** http://www.hillshirefarm.com. **Description:** Manufacturers of packaged meats including sausages, luncheon meats, hot dogs, and breakfast sandwiches. **Special programs:** Internships. **Corporate headquarters location:** This location. **Other U.S. locations:** Claryville KY; New London WI. **Parent company:** Sara Lee Corporation is a global manufacturer and marketer of consumer products with brand names including Hanes, Leggs, Hillshire Farms, and Playtex. **Operations at this facility include:** Administration; Manufacturing; Research and Development; Sales. **Listed on:** New York Stock Exchange. **Number of employees at this location:** 700. **Number of employees nationwide:** 2,500. **Number of employees worldwide:** 146,000.

HOLLOWAY SPORTSWEAR
607 East Pike Street, Jackson Center OH 45334. 937/596-6193. **Contact:** Human Resources. **World Wide Web address:** http://www.hollowayusa.com. **Description:** Holloway Sportswear manufactures jackets, sweatshirts, sweatsuits, golf shirts, and golf hats. **Corporate headquarters location:** This location. **Operations at this facility include:** This location houses administrative offices.

HONEYWELL
851 Jackson Street, Greenville OH 45331. 937/316-3000. **Fax:** 937/316-3376. **Contact:** Human Resources. **World Wide Web address:** http://www.honeywell.com. **Description:** Honeywell is engaged in the research, development, manufacture, and sale of advanced technology products and services in the fields of electronics, automation, and controls. The company's major businesses are home and building automation and control, industrial automation and control, space and aviation systems, and defense and marine systems. **Corporate headquarters location:** Morristown NJ. **Operations at this location include:** This location manufactures filters and spark plugs. **Listed on:** New York Stock Exchange. **Stock exchange symbol:** HON.

HONEYWELL
550 State Highway 55, P.O. Box 247, Urbana OH 43078. 937/484-2000. **Fax:** 937/484-2008. **Contact:** Human Resources. **World Wide Web address:** http://www.honeywell.com. **Description:** Honeywell is engaged in the research, development, manufacture, and sale of advanced technology products and services in the fields of chemicals, electronics, automation, and controls. The company's major businesses are home and building automation and control, performance polymers and chemicals, industrial automation and control, space and aviation systems, and defense and marine systems. **Corporate headquarters location:** Morristown NJ. **Operations at this location include:** This location designs and manufactures lighting and electronic systems for aircraft. **Listed on:** New York Stock Exchange. **Stock exchange symbol:** HON

HONEYWELL CONSUMER PRODUCTS GROUP
1600 North Union, Fostoria OH 44830. 419/435-6655. **Fax:** 419/435-5785. **Contact:** Human Resources. **World Wide Web address:** http://www.honeywell.com. **Description:** Honeywell is engaged in the research, development, manufacture, and sale of advanced technology products and services in the fields of chemicals, electronics, automation, and controls. The company's major businesses are home and building automation and control, performance polymers and chemicals, industrial automation and control, space and aviation systems, and defense and marine systems. **Corporate headquarters location:** Morristown NJ. **Operations at this location include:** This location manufactures spark plugs and oxygen sensors. **Listed on:** New York Stock Exchange. **Stock exchange symbol:** HON

HOOVER COMPANY
101 East Maple Street, North Canton OH 44720. 330/499-9200. **Contact:** Human Resources. **E-mail address:** recruiter@hoover.com. **World Wide Web address:** http://www.hoover.com. **Description:** Manufactures vacuum cleaners and related cleaning appliances. **Corporate headquarters location:** This location.

HORSBURGH & SCOTT COMPANY
5114 Hamilton Avenue, Cleveland OH 44114. 216/431-3900. **Fax:** 216/432-5850. **Contact:** Human Resources. **E-mail address:** hr-info@horsburgh-scott.com. **World Wide Web address:** http://www.horsburgh-scott.com. **Description:** Develops and manufactures industrial gears and customized mechanical gear drives. Horsburgh & Scott Company markets its products to the aluminum, coal, food processing, mining, paper, plastics, pollution control, rubber, and steel industries. Founded in 1886. **Positions advertised include:** Administrative Assistant; Customer Service Representative: Welder. **Corporate headquarters location:** This location. **Other U.S. locations:** Nationwide. **International locations:** Mexico; Philippines; South America; Taiwan.

HOWDEN BUFFALO
P.O. Box 5000, New Philadelphia OH 44663. 330/339-1111. **Physical address:** 338 South Broadway, New Philadelphia OH 44663. **Contact:** Human Resources Manager. **World Wide Web address:** http://www.howdenbuffalo.com. **Description:** Designs, develops, manufactures, tests, and markets industrial fans for commercial, mining, nuclear, and naval markets. **Corporate headquarters location:** Camden SC. **Other U.S. locations:** Springfield IL; Dearborn MI; Buffalo NY; Pittsburgh PA. **International locations:** Brazil; Canada; Mexico.

HUDSON ACCOUNTING & FINANCE
Heritage Corporate Center, 6001 East Royalton Road, Suite 150, Broadview Heights OH 44147. **Contact:** Kristen Babbin. **E-mail address:** Kristen.babbin@hhgroup.com. **World Wide Web address:** http://www.hudson.com. **Description:** Provides executive staffing solutions. **Positions advertised include:** Senior Auditor; Senior Accountant; Financial Analyst; Senior Property Accountant; Staff Accountant; Senior Tax Manager; Internal Auditor.

HUFFY CORPORATION
225 Byers Road, Miamisburg OH 45342. 937/866-6251. **Contact:** Human Resources. **World Wide Web address:** http://www.huffy.com. **Description:** Designs, manufactures, and markets recreational, leisure, and juvenile products including bicycles. The company also operates a national in-store assembly and warranty service business and provides inventory services to retailers. Founded in 1955. **Corporate headquarters location:** This location. **Number of employees nationwide:** 6,340. **Listed on:** New York Stock Exchange. **Stock exchange symbol:** HUF.

HUNTINGTON BANCSHARES INCORPORATED
41 South High Street, Columbus OH 43287. 614/480-4639. **Fax:** 614/480-4921. **Contact:** Human Resources. **World Wide Web address:** http://www.huntington.com. **Description:** A bank and financial services holding company. **Positions advertised include:** Customer Service Representative; Process Assistant; Process Specialist; Programmer Analyst; Mortgage Underwriter; Banking Office Manager; Security Specialist; Marketing Assistant; Market Research Analyst; Legal Assistant; Personal Banker. **Corporate headquarters location:** This location. **Subsidiaries include:** The Huntington National Bank (also at this location); The Huntington National Life Insurance Agency, Inc.; The Huntington Financial Services Company. **Listed on:** NASDAQ. **Stock exchange symbol:** HBAN.

HYDROCHEM INDUSTRIAL SERVICES
P.O. Box 592, 11580 Lafayette Drive, Canal Fulton OH 44614-9445. 330/854-4526. **Contact:** Human Resources. **E-mail address:** jobs@hydrochem.com. **World Wide Web address:** http://www.hydrochem.com. **Description:** An industrial cleaning company that provides heavy-duty cleaning services such as high-pressure water blasting and vacuuming for industrial plants. **NOTE:** Resumes are accepted by e-mail or fax. Fax resumes to: 713/393-5953. Please specify job code. **Corporate headquarters location:** Deer Park TX. **Other area locations:** Canton OH; Lima OH; Stratton OH; Youngstown OH. **Other U.S. locations:** Nationwide.

HYSON PRODUCTS
10367 Brecksville Road, Brecksville OH 44141. 440/526-5900. **Fax:** 440/838-7684. **Contact:** Staffing. **World Wide Web address:** http://www.hysonproducts.com. **Description:** Produces nitrogen die systems for metal stamping and pressure relief valves. **Special programs:** Internships.

ICI PAINTS
925 Euclid Avenue, Cleveland OH 44115. 216/344-8000. **Contact:** Recruiter. **World Wide Web address:** http://www.icipaints.com. **Description:** Manufactures and markets paints and industrial coatings including architectural and decorative paint; and coatings for food and drink cans worldwide. ICI Paints markets its products under the brand names Dulux, Glidden, and Hammerite. **Corporate headquarters location:** This location. **Parent company:** Imperial Chemical Industries.

IDG SCALLAN SUPPLY COMPANY
9407 Meridian Way, West Chester OH 45069. 513/942-9100. **Toll-free phone:** 800/722-5526. **Fax:** 513/942-9101. **Contact:** Human Resources. **Description:** A wholesaler of industrial supplies, cutting tools, and hand tools.

IDEAL ELECTRIC COMPANY
330 East First Street, Mansfield OH 44902. 419/522-3611. **Fax:** 419/524-4748. **Contact:** Personnel Director. **World Wide Web address:** http://www.idealelectricco.com. **Description:** Designs, manufactures, and markets custom designed generators, motors, and switchgears. Ideal Electric Company specializes in complete switchgear and control packages; synchronous and induction generators; synchronous and induction motors; and testing services. **Corporate headquarters location:** This location. **Operations at this facility include:** Administration; Manufacturing. **Listed on:** Privately held. **Number of employees at this location:** 300.

ILSCO CORPORATION
4730 Madison Road, Cincinnati OH 45227. 513/871-4000. **Contact:** Human Resources. **World Wide Web address:** http://www.ilsco.com. **Description:** A producer of electrical components and equipment including connectors.

IMPERIAL HOME DECOR GROUP
23645 Mercantile Road, Cleveland OH 44122. 216/464-3700. **Toll-free phone:** 888/608-5943. **Fax:** 800/444-7865. **Contact:** Human Resources. **World Wide Web address:** http://www.ihdg.com. **Description:** Manufactures paper and allied products. **Positions advertised include:** CAD Color Specialist. **Corporate headquarters location:** This location.

INDALEX ALUMINUM SOLUTIONS
706 South State Street, Girard OH 44420. 330/545-5415. **Toll-free phone:** 800/321-9286. **Contact:** Personnel. **World Wide Web address:** http://www.indalex.com. **Description:** A manufacturer of aluminum. **Corporate headquarters location:** Deerfield IL. **Other area locations:** Niles OH.

INDUCTIVE COMPONENTS MANUFACTURING INC. (ICMI)
1200 Ferris Road, Amelia OH 45102. 513/752-4731. **Fax:** 513/752-4738. **Contact:** Human Resources. **World Wide Web address:** http://www.icmiinc.com. **Description:** Manufactures electronic control panels, surge generators, and circuit stimulators.

INGERSOLL-RAND COMPANY
ARO FLUID PRODUCTS DIVISION
One Aro Center, P.O. Box 151, Bryan OH 43506. 419/636-4242. **Toll-free phone:** 800/276-4658. **Fax:** 800/266-7016. **Contact:** Human Resources. **World Wide Web address:** http://www.ingersoll-rand.com. **Description:** A manufacturer of industrial pumping equipment. Products include pneumatic components, fluid-handling equipment, valves and cylinders, and lubricating systems. **Corporate headquarters location:** Woodcliff Lake NJ. **Operations at this facility include:** Administration; Divisional Headquarters; Manufacturing; Research and Development; Sales. **Number of employees at this location:** 720.

INGRAM BARGE COMPANY
300 Pike Street, Cincinnati OH 45202. 513/721-4000. **Fax:** 270/444-4089. **Contact:** Human Resources. **World Wide Web address:** http://www.ingrambarge.com. **Description:** Operates a fleet of barges and towboats, principally on the Ohio and Mississippi Rivers and their tributaries, the Gulf Intra-coastal Waterway, and the Gulf of Mexico. The company also transports bulk commodities, performs repair work on marine equipment, operates two coal-dumping terminals, runs a phosphate rock and phosphate chemical fertilizer terminal, and owns a marine fuel supply facility. **Corporate headquarters location:** Nashville TN.

INNOVATIVE TECHNOLOGIES CORPORATION (ITC)
1020 Woodman Drive, Dayton OH 45432-1410. 937/252-2145. **Toll-free phone:** 800/745-8050. **Fax:** 937/254-6853. **Contact:** Judy Conn, Human Resources. **E-mail address:** connj@itc-1.com. **World Wide Web address:** http://www.itc-1.com. **Description:** A general contractor and engineering services firm. The company specializes in defense contracting. Founded in 1987. **Corporate headquarters location:** This location. **Other U.S. locations:** FL; GA; UT.

INTERNATIONAL PAPER COMPANY
101 Knightsbridge Drive, Hamilton OH 45020. 513/896-2500. **Contact:** Human Resources. **World Wide Web address:** http://www.internationalpaper.com. **Description:** International Paper Company manufactures pulp and paper, packaging, wood products, and a range of specialty products. The company is organized into five business segments: Printing Papers, with principal products that include uncoated papers, coated papers, bristles, and pulp; Packaging, which includes industrial packaging, consumer packaging, and kraft and specialty papers; Distribution, including the sale of printing papers, graphic arts equipment and supplies, packaging materials, industrial supplies, and office products; Specialty Products, which includes imaging products, specialty panels, nonwovens, chemicals, and minerals; and Forest Products, which includes logging and wood products. **Corporate headquarters location:** Stamford CT. **Other U.S. locations:** This location is a pulp and paper processor. **International locations:** Worldwide. **Operations at this facility include:** Administration. **Listed on:** New York Stock Exchange. **Stock exchange symbol:** IP.

INTERNATIONAL PAPER FOOD SERVICE
1300 South Main Street, Kenton OH 43326. 419/673-0711. **Contact:** Personnel. **World Wide Web address:** http://www.internationalpaper.com. **Description:** International Paper Company manufactures pulp and paper, packaging, wood products, and a range of specialty products. The company is organized into five business segments: Printing Papers, with principal products that include uncoated papers, coated papers, bristles, and pulp; Packaging, which includes industrial packaging, consumer packaging, and kraft and specialty papers; Distribution, including the sale of printing papers, graphic arts equipment and supplies, packaging materials, industrial supplies, and office products; Specialty Products, which includes imaging products, specialty panels, nonwovens, chemicals, and minerals; and Forest Products, which includes logging and wood products. **Corporate headquarters location:** Stamford CT. **Other U.S. locations:** Nationwide. **International locations:** Worldwide. **Parent company:** International Paper Company. **Operations at this facility include:** Manufactures paper plates and cups. **Listed on:** New York Stock Exchange. **Stock exchange symbol:** IP.

INTERSIL CORPORATION
1700 Fostoria Avenue, Findlay OH 45840. 419/423-0321. **Contact:** Human Resources. **World Wide Web address:** http://www.intersil.com. **Description:** Manufactures semiconductors. **Special programs:** Internships. **Corporate headquarters location:** Milpitas CA. **Other area locations:** Cleveland OH. **Other U.S. locations:** Nationwide. **International locations:** The Netherlands. **Listed on:** NASDAQ. **Stock exchange symbol:** ISQ.

INTERSTATE BRANDS CORPORATION
dba WONDERBREAD
178 South Forge St., Akron OH 44308. 330/376-6111. **Contact:** Personnel Director. **Description:** Interstate Brands Corporation manufactures and distributes a line of bread and cake products with brand names such as Wonderbread and Hostess. **Corporate headquarters location:** Kansas City MO. **Operations at this facility include:** This location is a bakery. **Listed on:** New York Stock Exchange. **Stock exchange symbol:** IBC.

INTUIT
20800 Harvard Road, Cleveland OH 44122. 216/464-3225. **Contact:** Human Resources. **World Wide Web address:** http://www.intuit.com. **Description:** Provides money management and tax filing software to consumers and businesses. **NOTE:** Applications many be submitted at company website. **Positions advertised include:** Business Development Representative; Consulting Product Development Manager; Strategic Solutions Specialist; Senior Software Engineer; Software Engineer; Software Quality Engineer; Strategic Sales Manager; Internal Sales Representative. **Corporate headquarters location:** Mountain View CA

INVACARE CORPORATION
P.O. Box 4028, Elyria OH 44036. 440/329-6000. **Physical address:** One Invacare Way, Elyria OH 44036. **Fax:** 440/329-6840. **Contact:** Human Resources. **E-mail address:** ivcrjobsrc@invacare.com. **World Wide Web address:** http://www.invacare.com. **Description:** Designs, manufactures, and distributes an extensive line of durable medical equipment for the home health care and extended care markets. Products include standard manual wheelchairs, motorized and lightweight prescription wheelchairs, motorized scooters, patient aids, home care beds, home respiratory products, and seating and positioning products. Invacare is one of the leading home medical equipment manufacturers in the country. **NOTE:** Entry-level positions and second and third shifts are offered. **Special programs:** Internships; Co-ops; Summer Jobs. **Corporate headquarters location:** This location. **Other U.S. locations:** CA; FL; NY; TX. **Operations at this facility include:** Administration; Divisional Headquarters; Manufacturing; Research and Development; Service. **Listed on:** New York Stock Exchange. **Stock exchange symbol:** IVC. **Annual sales/revenues:** More than $100 million. **Number of employees at this location:** 1,700. **Number of employees nationwide:** 6,000.

INVENSYS CLIMATE CONTROLS
8115 U.S. Route 42 North, Plain City OH 43064. 614/873-9000. **Contact:** Human Resources. **E-mail address:** dghr@invensys.com. **World Wide Web address:** http://www.icca.invensys.com. **Description:** A multinational producer of a widely diversified line of automated control devices used to facilitate the conservation and control of energy, the reduction and control of automobile emissions, and the maintenance of safety, physical comfort, and convenience. **Corporate headquarters location:** Carol Stream IL. **Parent company:** Invensys.

INVINCIBLE AIRFLOW SYSTEMS
P.O. Box 380, Baltic OH 43804. **Toll-free phone:** 800/282-6999. **Physical address:** 600 North Ray Street, Baltic OH 43804. **Contact:** Human Resources. **World Wide Web address:** http://www.gardnerdenver.com. **Description:** Manufactures vacuum cleaners. **NOTE:** Applications for this location processed at: Gardner Denver Inc., Blower Division Headquarters, 100 Gardner Park, Peachtree City GA 30269. 770/486-5655. **Parent company:** Gardner Denver Inc.

IOTECH, INC.
25971 Cannon Road, Cleveland OH 44146. 440/439-4091. **Toll-free phone:** 888/714-3272. **Fax:** 440/439-4093. **Contact:** Human Resources. **World Wide Web address:** http://www.iotech.com. **Description:** Develops, manufactures, and markets interfaces and data acquisition instruments. The company's hardware and software products are used primarily to support personal computers and engineering workstations. **Corporate headquarters location:** This location. **Other U.S. locations:** Nationwide. **International locations:** Worldwide. **Listed on:** Privately held. **Number of employees at this location:** 90.

JIIPROMOTIONS, INC.
454 East Main Street, Suite 1001, Columbus OH 43215. 614/255-3050. **Toll-free phone:** 800/811-2033. **Fax:** 614/224-9517. **Contact:** Human Resources. **E-mail address:** hrdept@jiipromotions.com. **World Wide Web address:** http://www.jiipromotions.com. **Description:** Engages in a variety of printing activities including calendar production, direct mail, greeting cards, and other specialty

advertising products. Sales Representative; Independent Contractor. **Special programs:** Internships. **Corporate headquarters location:** This location. **Other area location:** Coshocton OH. **Parent company:** Jordan Industries, Inc. **Operations at this facility include:** Administration; Sales; Service. **Number of employees at this location:** 600.

JACOBS ENGINEERING
P.O. Box 465600, 1880 Waycross Road, Cincinnati OH 45240. 513/595-7500. **Fax:** 513/595-7860. **Contact:** Human Resources. **World Wide Web address:** http://www.jacobs.com. **Description:** One of the largest engineering and construction companies in the United States. Jacobs provides engineering, procurement, construction, and maintenance services to selected clients and industries. These industries include chemicals and polymers, federal programs, pulp and paper, semiconductor, petroleum refining, facilities and transportation, food and consumer products, pharmaceuticals and biotechnologies, and basic resources. **Corporate headquarters location:** Pasadena CA. **Other U.S. locations:** Nationwide. **International locations:** Worldwide. **Listed on:** New York Stock Exchange. **Stock exchange symbol:** JEC.

JANESVILLE PRODUCTS
P.O. Box 349, Norwalk OH 44857. 419/668-4474. **Physical address:** 156 South Norwalk Road, Norwalk OH 44857. **Fax:** 419/668-8765. **Contact:** Human Resources. **World Wide Web address:** http://www.janesvilleproducts.com. **Description:** Manufactures insulation for automobiles. **Corporate headquarters location:** This location. **Number of employees at this location:** 40.

JCPENNEY CATALOG FULFILLMENT CENTER
5555 Scarborough Boulevard, Columbus OH 43232. 614/863-8800. **Contact:** Employment and Personnel Relations Manager. **World Wide Web address:** http://www.jcpenney.net. **Description:** A catalog fulfillment center for the major national retail merchandise sales and services corporation. **Corporate headquarters location:** Dallas TX.

JOHNS MANVILLE
600 Jackson Avenue, Defiance OH 43512. 419/784-7000. **Contact:** Human Resources Department. **World Wide Web address:** http://www.jm.com. **Description:** Develops, manufactures, and markets insulation and building products for the construction, industrial roofing, and engineered products applications. Founded in 1858. **NOTE:** Unsolicited resumes are not accepted. **Positions advertised include:** Technical Sales Engineer. **Corporate headquarters locations:** Denver CO. **Other U.S. locations:** Nationwide. **International locations:** China, Europe. **Listed on:** New York Stock Exchange. **Stock exchange symbol:** JM.

JOHNSON CONTROLS, INC.
SYSTEMS & SERVICES DIVISION/CENTRAL DIVISION
9797 Midwest Avenue, Cleveland OH 44125. 216/587-0100. **Contact:** Human Resources Manager. **World Wide Web address:** http://www.johnsoncontrols.com. **Description:** A worldwide supplier of systems and services to manage energy use, heating, ventilating and air conditioning, fire safety, and general safety for commercial buildings and industrial facilities. Johnson Controls also supplies heating and refrigeration controls for wholesalers and original equipment manufacturers. **Positions advertised include:** Sales Manager; Sales Coordinator. **Special programs:** Internships; Co-ops. **Corporate headquarters location:** Milwaukee WI. **Other U.S. locations:** IN; KY; MI. **Operations at this facility include:** Sales; Service. **Listed on:** New York Stock Exchange. **Stock exchange symbol:** JCI. **Number of employees worldwide:** 43,000.

DAVID J. JOSEPH COMPANY
300 Pike Street, Cincinnati OH 45202. 513/345-4413. **Fax:** 513/345-4423. **Contact:** Karen Hill, Human Resources. **E-mail address:** kah@djj.com. **World Wide Web address:** http://www.djj.com. **Description:** A domestic broker of ferrous and nonferrous scrap metals to steel mills and foundries. Since 1885. **Positions advertised include:** Software Engineer; Sales Representative; Assistant Controller. **Special programs:** Internships. **Corporate headquarters location:** This location. **Listed on:** Privately held. **Number of employees nationwide:** 700.

KABLE FULFILLMENT SERVICE OF OHIO
1290 Mount Vernon Avenue, Marion OH 43302. 740/725-5164. **Contact:** Nancy Headley, Human Resources Director. **E-mail address:** nheadley@kable.com. **World Wide Web address:** http://www.kable.com. **Description:** Engaged in marketing, data gathering, data processing, storing, and lettershop services for publishing and product fulfillment clients. **Positions advertised include:** Data Entry Corrections Clerk; Assistant Account Executive; Accounting Clerk. **Special programs:** Internships. **Corporate headquarters location:** Mount Morris IL. **Parent company:** Kable News Company, Inc. **Operations at this facility include:** Administration; Divisional Headquarters; Service. **Number of employees at this location:** 470. **Number of employees nationwide:** 1,500.

KARDEX SYSTEMS INC.
P.O. Box 171, Marietta OH 45750. 740/374-9300. **Physical address:** State Route 7 North, Reno OH 45773. **Toll-free phone:** 800/234-3654. **Fax:** 740/374-9953. **Contact:** Human Resources. **World Wide Web address:** http://www.kardex.com. **Description:** A producer of filing and storage equipment for office use.

THE KASSOUF COMPANY
9715 Clinton Road, Cleveland OH 44144. 216/651-3333. **Fax:** 216/651-3839. **Contact:** Edward J. Kassouf, President. **World Wide Web address:** http://www.kassouftunnel.com. **Description:** A contractor specializing in sewers, waterlines, and other underground infrastructures.

KEATING MUETHING AND KLEKAMP
1400 Provident Tower, One East Fourth Street, Cincinnati OH 45202. 513/579-6400. **Fax:** 513/579-6457. **Contact:** Lori S. Moser, Director of Human Resources. **E-mail address:** lmoser@kmklaw.com. **World Wide Web address:** http://www.kmklaw.com. **Description:** A general practice law firm. Keating Muething and Klekamp specializes in antitrust law, aviation law, bankruptcy, corporate law, domestic relations, employee benefits, environmental law, equipment leasing, estate planning, franchise law, health care, insurance law, intellectual property, international law, labor law, litigation, mergers and acquisitions, personal injury, product liability, probate, real estate, securities, taxation, and zoning. Founded in 1954. **NOTE:** Candidates for attorney positions should send resumes to: James M. Jansing, Director of the Hiring Committee. E-mail: jjansing@kmklaw.com. **Positions advertised include:** Bankruptcy Associate; Commercial Finance Associate; Corporate Associate; Employee Benefits Associate; Environmental Associate; Litigation Associate; Legal Secretary; Paralegal; Administrative Assistant; Messenger Clerk.

KELLOGG SNACK DIVISION
One Trade Street, Mariemont, Cincinnati OH 45227. 513/271-3500. **Contact:** Human Resources Manager. **E-mail address:** keebler@rpc.webhire.com. **World Wide Web address:** http://www.keebler.com. **Description:** A national manufacturer and marketer of cookies, crackers, snack foods, and other consumer food products. Keebler markets its products under the brand names Carr's, Cheez-It, Famous Amos, Murray, Plantation, and Ready Crust. Founded in 1853. **Corporate headquarters location:** Elmhurst IL. **Other U.S. locations:** Denver CO; Atlanta GA; Grand Rapids MI. **Subsidiaries include:** Little Brownie's Baker is a licensed supplier of Girl Scout Cookies.

KEITHLEY INSTRUMENTS INC.
28775 Aurora Road, Cleveland OH 44139-1891. 440/248-0400. **Toll-free phone:** 800/552-1115. **Fax:** 440/248-6168. **Contact:** Personnel. **World Wide Web address:** http://www.keithley.com. **Description:** Provides instrumentation to semiconductor manufacturers, medical equipment manufacturers, and growth segments of the electronics industry. The company's Test Instrumentation Group supplies instruments for benchtop and systems applications and automatic parametric test systems. Keithley also supplies sensitive instruments that measure a wide range of electrical properties such as voltage, resistance, current, capacitance, and charge. The products produced by the Keithley MetraByte Division include a wide range of data acquisition and analysis hardware and software products designed for use with personal computers. The Radiation Measurements Division designs, develops, manufactures, and markets products and systems that accurately measure the radiation emission levels of X-ray machines and nuclear radiation sources. **Special programs:** Internships; Co-ops. **Corporate headquarters location:** This location. **Listed on:** New York Stock Exchange. **Stock exchange symbol:** KEI.

KENNAMETAL INC.
6865 Cochran Road, Solon OH 44139. 440/349-5151. **Contact:** Human Resources. **World Wide Web address:** http://www.kennametal.com. **Description:** A manufacturer, marketer, and distributor of tools for mining, metalworking, and highway construction. Kennametal's cutting tools and wear-resistant parts are made of cemented carbides and other hard components. Metal cutting products include turning, milling, and drilling. Kennametal's mining instruments include drums, blocks, bits, and compacts. The company's construction tools include blocks, bits, grader blades, and snowplow blades. Kennametal also produces various powders for specialized industries. **Corporate headquarters location:** Latrobe PA. **Other U.S. locations:** Los Angeles CA; Windsor CT; Downers Grove IL; Moline IL; Livonia MI; Charlotte NC; Cincinnati OH; Fort Washington PA; El Paso TX; Houston TX. **International locations:** Worldwide. **Operations at this facility include:** Computer Modeling; Engineering and Design; Marketing. **Listed on:** New York Stock Exchange. **Stock exchange symbol:** KMT. **Number of employees nationwide:** 4,400.

KENNEDY MANUFACTURING COMPANY
520 East Sycamore Street, Van Wert OH 45891. 419/238-2442. **Contact:** Human Resources. **E-mail:** kmcinfo@kennedymfg.com. **World Wide Web address:** http://www.kennedymfg.com. **Description:** Kennedy Manufacturing Company designs, manufactures, and markets industrial tool storage equipment. The company's products include modular storage cabinets, roller cabinets, stationary and mobile workbenches, and steel tool chests. Founded in 1911.

KENT STATE UNIVERSITY
P.O. Box 5190, Kent OH 44242. 330/672-2901. **Physical address:** Route 59, Kent OH 44242. **Contact:** Employment Services. **E-mail address:** employment@kent.edu. **World Wide Web address:** http://www.kent.edu. **Description:** A four-year state university offering bachelor's, master's (including MBAs), and doctoral degrees. Approximately 26,000 undergraduate and 3,500 graduate students attend Kent State University. **Positions advertised include:** Spanish Instructor; Assistant Professor, Communication Studies; Instructor, College of Nursing; Payroll Manager; Research Technician; Assistant Football Coach; Assistant Wrestling Coach; Training and Development Specialist. **Other area locations:** Ashtabula OH; East Liverpool OH; Geauga OH; Salem OH; Stark OH; Trumbull OH; Tuscarawas OH.

KENWORTH TRUCK COMPANY
P.O. Box 2345, Chillicothe OH 45601. 740/774-5111. **Physical address:** 65 Kenworth Drive, Chillicothe OH 45601. **Contact:** Human Resources. **World Wide Web address:** http://www.paccar.com. **Description:** A producer of heavy-duty motor vehicles. **Parent company:** PACCAR Inc.

KENYON COLLEGE
Human Resources, The Eaton Center, Gambier OH 43022-9623. 740/427-5173. **Fax:** 740/427-5901. **Recorded jobline:** 740/427-5900. **Contact:** Jennifer Cabral, Director of Human Resources. **E-mail address:** cabral@kenyon.edu. **World Wide Web address:** http://www.kenyon.edu. **Description:** A selective private liberal arts college with an enrollment of 1,500 students. **Positions advertised include:** Director, Student Activities; Associate Director, Career Development; Visiting Assistant Professor, Russian; Visiting Assistant Professor, Classics; Assistant Professor, French and Italian; Accounts Receivable Coordinator. **Office hours:** Monday – Friday, 8:30 a.m. – 4:30 p.m. **President:** S. Georgia Nugent.

KEYBANK N.A.
34 North Main Street, Dayton OH 45402. 937/586-7280. **Recorded jobline:** 888/539-7247. **Contact:** Human Resources Manager. **World Wide Web address:** http://www.keybank.com. **Description:** KeyBank is a full-service banking institution. **Positions advertised include:** District Retail Leader; Relationship Manager. **Corporate headquarters location:** Cleveland OH. **Other U.S. locations:** Nationwide. **Parent company:** KeyCorp is a diverse financial services company offering commercial and retail banking, financial management, brokerage services, mortgage banking, and trust services. **Operations at this facility include:** This location houses the administrative offices and a branch of the bank. **Listed on:** New York Stock Exchange. **Stock exchange symbol:** KEY. **Annual sales/revenues:** More than $100 million. **Number of employees at this location:** 1,000.

KEYCORP
127 Public Square, Cleveland OH 44114. 216/689-3000. **Recorded jobline:** 888/539-7247. **Contact:** Personnel. **World Wide Web address:** http://www.keybank.com. **Description:** A diverse financial services company offering commercial and retail banking, financial management, brokerage services, mortgage banking, and trust services. **Corporate headquarters location:** This location. **Listed on:** New York Stock Exchange. **Stock exchange symbol:** KEY. **Annual sales/revenues:** More than $100 million.

KINDRED HOSPITAL
2351 East 22nd Street, Cleveland OH 44115. 216/861-1964. **Contact:** Human Resources. **World Wide Web address:** http://www.kindredhealthcare.com. **Description:** Provides health care services for acute care patients. **NOTE:** Please

apply for all positions at company website. **Positions advertised include:** Respiratory Therapist; Nurse Practitioner; Registered Nurse Night Shift; Registered Nurse.

KINETIC SOLUTIONS
515 Village Park Drive, Powell OH 43065. 614/846-9330. **Contact:** Human Resources. **E-mail address:** hr@usakinetic.com. **World Wide Web address:** http://www.usakinetic.com. **Description:** Provides targeted marketing/sales management and campaign support in the Columbus area. **Positions advertised include:** Account Executive. **Corporate Headquarters:** This location.

KIRBY COMPANY
1920 West 114th Street, Cleveland OH 44102-2322. 216/228-2400. **Contact:** Human Resources Department. **World Wide Web address:** http://www.kirby.com. **Description:** Manufactures and markets home cleaning systems and related accessories. **Parent company:** Berkshire Hathaway Inc. is the holding company of Kirby and other subsidiaries engaged in a number of diverse business activities. Berkshire Hathaway focuses on the property and casualty insurance business conducted on both a direct and reinsurance basis through a number of subsidiaries collectively referred to as the Berkshire Hathaway Insurance Group. Berkshire Hathaway Inc. also publishes the Buffalo News, a daily newspaper in upstate New York. Other business activities conducted by non-insurance subsidiaries include publication and distribution of encyclopedias and related educational and instructional material; retailing of home furnishings; and the manufacture of confectionery products, uniforms, footwear, air compressors, air tools, and painting systems.

KIRK & BLUM MANUFACTURING COMPANY
3120 Forrer Street, Cincinnati OH 45209. 513/458-2600. **Toll-free phone:** 800/333-5475. **Fax:** 513/351-5475. **Contact:** Personnel Director. **World Wide Web address:** http://www.kirkblum.com. **Description:** Manufactures ventilation equipment. **Corporate headquarters location:** This location. **Other area locations:** Defiance OH. **Other U.S. locations:** IN; KY; NC; TN.

KODAK VERSAMARK, INC.
3000 Research Boulevard, Dayton OH 45420. 937/259-3000. **Contact:** Human Resources. **World Wide Web address:** http://www.kodakversamark.com. **Description:** Formerly known as Scitex Digital Printing, the company was recently acquired by the Eastman Kodak Company. Designs, develops, and manufactures high-speed digital imaging systems. **Positions advertised include:** Curricula Developer; Printhead Integration Engineer; Quality Assurance Engineer; Service Engineer; Technical Support Engineer. **Corporate headquarters location:** This location. **Parent company:** Eastman Kodak. **Operations at this facility include:** Administration; Manufacturing; Research and Development; Sales; Service. **Listed on:** NASDAQ. **Stock exchange symbol:** SCIX. **Number of employees at this location:** 750. **Number of employees nationwide:** 800.

KOKOSING CONSTRUCTION COMPANY INC.
P.O. Box 226, Fredericktown OH 43019-9159. 740/694-6315. **Physical address:** 17531 Waterford Road, Fredericktown OH 43019-9159. **Fax:** 740/694-1481. **Contact:** Human Resources. **World Wide Web address:** http://www.kokosing-inc.com. **Description:** A general contracting firm engaged in engineering, manufacturing, and construction. **Special programs:** Internships; Co-ops. **Corporate headquarters location:** This location.

KRAFTMAID CABINETRY, INC.
P.O. Box 1055, Middlefield OH 44062. 440/632-1833. **Physical address:** 15535 South State Street, Middlefield OH 44062. **Fax:** 440/632-0032. **Contact:** Chris Allen, Human Resources. **World Wide Web address:** http://www.kraftmaid.com. **Description:** A cabinet manufacturer. Founded in 1969. **Parent company:** MASCO. **Number of employees nationwide:** 3,000.

THE KROGER COMPANY
1014 Vine Street, Cincinnati OH 45202-1100. 513/762-4000. **Contact:** Human Resources. **World Wide Web address:** http://www.kroger.com. **Description:** Operates more than 2,200 supermarkets and convenience stores. Kroger also has 37 food processing plants that supply over 4,000 private label products to its supermarkets. **Positions advertised include:** Internal Auditor; Administrative Support Personnel. **Corporate headquarters location:** This location. **Listed on:** New York Stock Exchange. **Stock exchange symbol:** KR. **Number of employees worldwide:** 300.

LSI INDUSTRIES INC.
10000 Alliance Road, Cincinnati OH 45242. 513/793-3200. **Fax:** 513/793-7890. **Contact:** Human Resources. **E-mail address:** corporatehr@lsi-industries.com. **World Wide Web address:** http://www.lsi-industries.com. **Description:** Manufactures a wide variety of indoor lighting equipment and commercial indoor lights. Products are used at many restaurants and gas stations. **NOTE:** Resumes are accepted by mail, fax, or e-mail. **President and CEO:** Robert J. Ready.

LTI POWER SYSTEMS
10800 Middle Avenue, Building B, Elyria OH 44035-7822. 440/327-5050. **Toll-free phone:** 888/327-5050. **Fax:** 440/458-8140. **Contact:** Human Resources. **World Wide Web address:** http://www.loraintechnology.com. **Description:** Engineers, develops, manufactures and markets single phase and three phase Uninterruptible Power Systems (UPS) worldwide. The company also specializes in the production of inverters.

LTV COPPERWELD
132 West Main Street, Shelby OH 44875. 419/342-2000. **Fax:** 419/342-1437. **Contact:** Larry Taylor, Human Resources Manager. **World Wide Web address:** http://www.copperweld.com. **Description:** LTV Copperweld develops, manufactures, and markets a full spectrum of pipe and tube products. The company is also a leading manufacturer of bimetallic wire products. **Corporate headquarters location:** Pittsburgh PA. **Operations at this facility include:** This location is engaged in the production of as-welded mechanical tubing for a variety of applications benefiting equipment or parts design. **Parent company:** LTV Corporation.

LAFARGE NORTH AMERICA INC.
P.O. Box 160, Paulding OH 45879. 419/399-4861. **Physical address:** 11435 Road 176, Paulding OH 45879. **Contact:** Human Resources Manager. **World Wide Web address:** http://www.lafarge.com. **Description:** Produces and sells Portland and masonry cements. **Corporate headquarters location:** Dallas TX. **Other U.S. locations:** Nationwide. **International locations:** Canada. **Parent company:** The Lafarge Group. **Listed on:** New York Stock Exchange. **Stock exchange symbol:** LAF.

LAKE ERIE SCREW CORPORATION
13001 Athens Avenue, Lakewood OH 44107. 216/521-1800. **Fax:** 216/529-7997. **Contact:** Human Resources. **World Wide Web address:** http://www.lescrew.com. **Description:** A manufacturer of screws. **Other U.S. locations:** Frankfort IN.

LAKELAND COMMUNITY COLLEGE
7700 Clocktower Drive, Kirtland OH 44094-5198. 440/953-7078. **Fax:** 440/525-7606. **Recorded jobline:** 440/975-4701. **Contact:** Barb Henderson, Manager of Recruiting. **E-mail address:** bhenderson@lakelandcc.edu. **World Wide Web address:** http://www.lakelandcc.edu. **Description:** A two-year community college. **NOTE:** Resumes are accepted for current openings only. Please consult the website for available positions. **Positions advertised include:** Psychology Professor; Environmental Biology Instructor; Early Childhood Education Instructor; Banquet Server; Summer Camp Instructor.

LAMSON & SESSIONS COMPANY
25701 Science Park Drive, Cleveland OH 44122. 216/464-3400. **Toll-free phone:** 800/321-1970. **Fax:** 216/464-1455. **Contact:** Jim Erbacher, Manager of Salaried Employment. **E-mail address:** james.erbacher@lamson-sessions.com. **World Wide Web address:** http://www.lamson-sessions.com. **Description:** Develops manufactures and markets thermoplastic enclosures, fittings, conduit and pipe, and wiring devices. Lamson and Sessions Company markets its products to the communications, construction, consumer, electrical, and power industries. The company is also engaged in the manufacture of large diameter pipe products for the waste-water market. Founded in 1866. **NOTE:** Entry-level positions are offered. **Special programs:** Co-ops. **Office hours:** Monday - Friday, 8:30 a.m. - 5:00 p.m. **Corporate headquarters location:** This location. **Other U.S. locations:** Nationwide. **Operations at this facility include:** Administration; Sales; Service. **Listed on:** American Stock Exchange. **Stock exchange symbol:** LMS. **President/CEO:** John Schulze. **Number of employees at this location:** 200. **Number of employees nationwide:** 1,000.

LANCASTER COLONY CORPORATION
37 West Broad Street, 5th Floor, Columbus OH 43215. 614/224-7141. **Contact:** Personnel. **World Wide Web address:** http://www.lancastercolony.com. **Description:** Manufactures and markets products through three divisions: the Candles Group's glassware and candles are produced and distributed through discount stores, supermarkets, mass merchandisers, gift shops, department stores, and the company's own home party plan. The Candles Group also produces and markets glass containers for the florist industry and imports table and giftware; the Specialty Foods Group includes brand names Marzetti, Pfeiffer, Gizard, Mountain Top, New York, Reames, Inn Maid, and Romanoff; the Automotive group manufactures rubber, vinyl, and carpet-on-rubber car mats. The company also manufactures pickup truck bed mats and liners, truck and trailer splashguards, and aluminum and plastic accessories for light trucks and vans. **NOTE:** Resumes may be submitted online. **Corporate headquarters location:** This location. **Other area locations:** Cincinnati OH. **Listed on:** NASDAQ. **Stock exchange symbol:** LANC.

LANCASTER COLONY CORPORATION
P.O. Box 43264, Cincinnati OH 45242. 513/563-1113. **Physical address:** 10521 Millington Court, Cincinnati OH 45242. **Contact:** Personnel. **World Wide Web address:** http://www.lancastercolony.com. **Description:** Lancaster Colony Corporation manufactures and markets products through three divisions: the Candles group's glassware and candles are produced and distributed through discount stores, supermarkets and other mass merchandisers, gift and department stores, and the company's own home party plan. The Candles group also produces and markets glass containers for the florist industry and imports table and giftware; the Specialty Foods group includes brand names Marzetti, Pfeiffer, Gizard, Mountain Top, New York, Reames, Inn Maid, and Romanoff; the Automotive group manufactures rubber, vinyl, and carpet-on-rubber car mats. The company also manufactures pickup truck bed mats and liners, truck and trailer splashguards, and aluminum and plastic accessories for light trucks and vans. **NOTE:** Resumes maybe submitted online. **Corporate headquarters location:** Columbus OH. **Operations at this facility include:** This location houses sales offices for the Candles group. **Listed on:** NASDAQ. **Stock exchange symbol:** LANC.

LANCASTER GLASS CORPORATION
P.O. Box 70, Lancaster OH 43130. 740/653-0311. **Physical address:** 240 West Main Street, Lancaster OH 43130. **Toll-free phone:** 800/264-6826. **Fax:** 740/653-9501. **Contact:** David A. Gallimore, President. **World Wide Web address:** http://www.lancasterglasscorp.htm. **Description:** Manufactures a variety of electronic and industrial glass products. **Corporate headquarters location:** This location. **Parent company:** Lancaster Colony Corporation.

LAWYERS TITLE INSURANCE CORPORATION
921 Eastwind Drive, Suite 133, Westerville OH 43081. 614/899-1700. **Contact:** Human Resources. **World Wide Web address:** http://www.ltic.com. **Description:** Lawyers Title Insurance Corporation provides title insurance and other real estate-related services for commercial and residential transactions in the United States, Canada, the Bahamas, Puerto Rico, and the U.S. Virgin Islands. Lawyers Title Insurance Corporation also provides search and examination services and closing services for a broad-based customer group that includes lenders, developers, real estate brokers, attorneys, and homebuyers. **Corporate headquarters location:** Richmond VA. **Other U.S. locations:** Pasadena CA; Tampa FL; Chicago IL; Boston MA; Troy MI; White Plains NY; Memphis TN; Dallas TX. **Operations at this facility include:** This location covers Indiana, Kentucky, and Ohio. **Subsidiaries include:** Datatrace Information Services Company, Inc. (Richmond VA) markets automated public record information for public and private use; Genesis Data Systems, Inc. (Englewood CO) develops and markets computer software tailored specifically to the title industry; and Lawyers Title Exchange Company operates out of 10 of the Lawyers Title Insurance Corporation's regional offices and functions as an intermediary for individual and corporate investors interested in pursuing tax-free property exchanges. **Parent company:** LandAmerica Financial Group. **Listed on:** New York Stock Exchange. **Stock exchange symbol:** LFG.

LEAR CORPORATION
1608 Sawmill Parkway, Huron OH 44839. 419/433-5653. **Contact:** Human Resources. **World Wide Web address:** http://www.lear.com. **Description:** Lear Corporation is a worldwide supplier of automotive seat systems, floor and acoustic systems, instrument panel systems, overhead systems, and door and interior trim systems. **Parent company:** United Technologies Corporation. **Other area locations:** Statewide. **Other U.S. locations:** Nationwide. **Operations at this facility include:** This location manufactures automotive wiring.

LEGATO SYSTEMS INC.
895 Central Avenue, 3 Centennial Plaza, Cincinnati OH 45202. 513/579-0455. **Fax:** 513/579-1064. **Contact:** Human Resources Department. **World Wide Web address:** http://www.legato.com. **Description:** Develops and markets software products for managers of open systems installations worldwide. Legato products address the needs of network management; distributed systems management including systems administration, data center management, and tape management; connectivity; and integrated office automation. The company also provides consulting and support services. **Corporate headquarters location:** Mountain View CA.

LENNOX INDUSTRIES INC.
3750 Brookham Drive, Suite A, Grove City OH 43123. 614/871-7216. **Contact:** Human Resources. **World Wide Web address:** http://www.lennox.com. **Description:** Lennox Industries is a distributor of air conditioners and heating units. **Corporate headquarters location:** Dallas TX. **Operations at this facility include:** This location is a warehouse.

LESCO INC.
15885 Sprague Road, Strongsville OH 44136. 440/783-9250. **Fax:** 440/783-3923. **Toll-free phone:** 800/321-5325. **Contact:** Human Resources. **E-mail:** jobs@lesco.com. **World Wide Web address:** http://www.lesco.com. **Description:** One of the largest national manufacturers and marketers of turf care products and equipment. LESCO brand products include Poly Plus slow-release fertilizers, turf protection products, combination fertilizer/turf protection products, and proprietary turf-grass seed. LESCO equipment includes golf course fairway and greens mowers, riding and walk-behind rotary mowers, fertilizer and seed spreaders, sprayers and dethatchers, replacement parts, power hand tools, and safety gear. **Positions advertised include:** Pest Control Technical Services Representative; Technical Services Manager. **Corporate headquarters location:** This location. **Listed on:** NASDAQ. **Stock exchange symbol:** LSCO.

LEXIS-NEXIS
P.O. Box 933, Dayton OH 45401. 937/865-6800. **Physical address:** 9443 Springboro Pike, Miamisburg OH 45342. **Toll-free phone:** 800/227-9597. **Fax:** 937/865-7476. **Contact:** Staffing Department. **E-mail address:** employment.hr@lexisnexis.com. **World Wide Web address:** http://www.lexisnexis.com. **Description:** An online, full-text database service including legal, news, business, and general information. The service enables lawyers, business professionals, and government agencies to electronically research thousands of resources from their own computers. **Positions advertised include:** Regional Sales Executive; Senior Software Engineer; Data Analyst; Web Designer; Product Manager; Systems Engineer; Employee Benefits Specialist; Telephone Sales Executive; Senior Human Resources Generalist; Market Planner; Architect; Customer Service Research Associate. **Special programs:** Internships; Co-ops. **Corporate headquarters location:** This location. **Parent company:** Reed Elsevier Group (United Kingdom).

LIBERTY CASTING COMPANY LLC
P.O. Box 220, Delaware OH 43015. 740/363-1941. **Physical address:** 550 South Liberty Road, Delaware OH 43015. **Contact:** Human Resources. **E-mail address:** hrliberty@generalcasting.com. **World wide web address:** http://www.generalcasting.com. **Description:** Formerly known as General Castings Company. Manufactures iron castings for a wide range of industrial applications. **Other area locations:** Cincinnati OH. **Other U.S. locations:** South Bend IN; Shippensburg PA.

LIEBERT CORPORATION
1050 Dearborn Drive, P.O. Box 29186, Columbus OH 43229. 614/888-0246. **Fax:** 614/841-5890. **Contact:** Human Resources. **E-mail address:** careers@liebert.com. **World Wide Web address:** http://www.liebert.com. **Description:** A leading worldwide manufacturer of computer support equipment and related applications. **NOTE:** Entry-level positions are offered. **Positions advertised included:** Service Operations Manager; Systems Analyst; Business Development Manager. **Special programs:** Internships; Training; Co-ops; Summer Jobs. **Corporate headquarters location:** This location. **Other area locations:** Westerville OH; **Other U.S. locations:** Nationwide. **Parent company:** Emerson Electric. **Number of employees at this location:** 950.

LIFEBANC
20600 Chagrin Boulevard, Suite 350, Cleveland OH 44122. 216/751-5433. **Fax:** 216/751-4204. **Contact:** Human Resources. **E-mail address:** hr@lifebanc.org. **World Wide Web address:** http://www.lifebanc.org. **Description:** Responsible for all aspects of the organ and tissue donation process in northeast Ohio. **Positions advertised include:** Advanced Practice Coordinator; Donor Referral Coordinator.

LIFECARE ALLIANCE
1699 West Mound Street, Columbus OH 43223. 614/278-3130. **Fax:** 614/278-3143. **Contact:** Personnel. **E-mail address:** hr@lifecarealliance.org. **World Wide Web address:** http://www.lifecarealliance.org. **Description:** A nonprofit home health care agency. LifeCare Alliance also provides Meals on Wheels. Founded in 1898. **NOTE:** Entry-level, part-time and seasonal positions are offered. **Positions advertised include:** Foodservice Worker; Meals on Wheels Driver; Visiting Nurse. **Special programs:** Internships. **Office hours:** Monday - Friday, 8:00 a.m. - 5:00 p.m. **Corporate headquarters location:** This location. **President and CEO:** Charles Gehring. **Number of employees at this location:** 400.

LIGGETT-STASHOWER, INC.
1228 Euclid Avenue, Suite 200, Cleveland OH 44115. 216/373-8231. **Toll-free phone:** 800/877-4573. **Fax:** 877/405-0549. **Contact:** William Niemi, Human Resources Department. **E-mail address:** bniemi@liggett.com. **World Wide Web address:** http://www.liggett.com. **Description:** An advertising agency. **Special programs:** Internships: **Internship information:** Candidates interested in the Internship Program should contact Ian Hopkins, Internship Coordinator. E-mail: ihopkins@liggett.com. **President/CEO:** Mark Nylander.

THE LIMITED STORES, INC.
3 Limited Parkway, Columbus OH 43230. 614/415-7000. **Contact:** Recruiting Office. **World Wide Web address:** http://www.limitedbrands.com. **Description:** Operates a nationwide chain of retail stores offering careerwear, sportswear, lingerie, and children's clothing. **Corporate headquarters location:** This location. **Parent company:** Limitedbrands (Also at this location). **Listed on:** New York Stock Exchange. **Stock exchange symbol:** LTD. **Annual sales/revenues:** $638 million.

THE LINCOLN ELECTRIC COMPANY
22801 St. Clair Avenue, Cleveland OH 44117-1199. 216/383-8831. **Fax:** 216/383-4765. **Contact:** Dick Conklin, Human Resources Department. **World Wide Web address:** http://www.lincolnelectric.com. **Description:** Manufactures a full line of arc welding equipment, welding products, and industrial electric motors. Founded in 1895. **NOTE:** Candidates interested in entry-level or skilled factory positions should contact George Kohn, Human Resources Department. Phone: 216/383-2081. Fax: 216/383-8385. **Positions advertised include:** Solutions Center Developer; International Logistics Manager; Systems Architect; Welding Consumable Design Engineer. **Special programs:** Internships; Co-ops; Apprenticeships. **Corporate headquarters location:** This location. **Other U.S. locations:** Miami FL; Gainesville GA; Mentor OH. **International locations:** Worldwide. **Operations at this facility include:** Administration; Manufacturing; Research and Development; Sales; Service. **Listed on:** NASDAQ. **Stock exchange symbol:** LECO. **President/CEO:** Anthony A. Massaro. **Number of employees at this location:** 2,500. **Number of employees nationwide:** 3,400. **Number of employees worldwide:** 7,000.

LINDE GAS LLC
6055 Rockside Woods Boulevard, Independence OH 44131. 216/642-6600. **Contact:** Human Resources. **World Wide Web address:** http://us.lindegas.com. **Description:** In January of 2004, Linde Gas consolidated its three existing U.S. gas companies under a single entity, Linde Gas LLC. One of the nation's leading suppliers of industrial and medical gases. The company's base market is primarily comprised of customers in the metalworking industry and the health care sector. Linde's process market is comprised mainly of customers in the metallurgy, food, chemical, and pulp and paper industries. **NOTE:** Resumes should be addressed to: Linde Gas LLC, c/o Human Resources Department, P.O. Box 94737, Cleveland OH 44101.

LIQUI-BOX CORPORATION
P.O. Box 494, Worthington OH 43085. 614/888-9280. **Physical address:** 6950 Worthington-Galena Road, Worthington OH 43085. **Fax:** 614/888-0982. **Contact:** Human Resources. **E-mail address:** liquibox@liquibox.com. **World Wide Web address:** http://www.liquibox.com. **Description:** Manufactures plastic containers used in the packaging of liquids. **Corporate headquarters location:** This location. **Other area locations:** Ashland OH; Upper Sandusky OH. **Other U.S. locations:** CA; FL; MD; MA; PA; TX. **International locations:** Romiley, England. **Listed on:** NASDAQ. **Stock exchange symbol:** LIQB.

THE LITTLE TIKES COMPANY
2180 Barlow Road, Hudson OH 44236. 330/650-3000. **Toll-free phone:** 877/6-253-8697. **Fax:** 330/650-3819. **Contact:** Human Resources Department. **E-mail address:** careers@littletikes.com. **World Wide Web address:** http://www.littletikes.com. **Description:** Manufactures a variety of plastic toys for infants and children. Founded in 1970. **Special Programs:** Internships; Co-ops. **Corporate headquarters location:** This location. **Parent company:** Newell Rubbermaid. **Listed on:** New York Stock Exchange. **Stock exchange symbol:** NWL.

LOCKHEED MARTIN TACTICAL DEFENSE SYSTEMS
1210 Massillon Road, Akron OH 44315-0001. 330/796-2800. **Contact:** Human Resources. **E-mail address:** jobs@lmco.com. **World Wide Web address:** http://www.lmco.com. **Description:** Manufacturers of simulation and training systems for flight, cockpit procedures, weapons delivery, and total air crew mission rehearsal; undersea and antisubmarine weapon systems; high-speed, parallel processing computers for airborne and undersea command and control; digital image processing systems; and tactical weapon and guidance systems. **Positions advertised include:** Hardware Engineer; Embedded S-W Engineer; Field Engineer. **Office hours:** Monday - Friday, 7:30 a.m. - 5:00 p.m. **Listed on:** New York Stock Exchange. **Stock exchange symbol:** LMT.

LOCKHEED MARTIN UTILITY SERVICES, INC.
P.O. Box 628, Mailstop 1128, Piketon OH 45661-1131. 740/897-2615. **Physical address:** 3930 U.S. Route 23 South, Piketon OH 45661. **Contact:** Employment Department. **E-mail address:** jobs@lmco.com. **World Wide Web address:** http://www.lmco.com. **Description:** Provides uranium enrichment services under contract for the United States Enrichment Corporation. **Corporate headquarters location:** Bethesda MD. **Operations at this facility include:** Administration; Manufacturing; Research and Development. **Listed on:** New York Stock Exchange. **Stock exchange symbol:** LMT.

LOGTEC
2900 Presidential Drive, Suite 130, Fairborn OH 45324. 937/429-2928. **Fax:** 937/429-3483. **Contact:** Human Resources. **E-mail address:** hr@logtec.com. **World Wide Web address:** http://www.logtec.com. **Description:** A computer services company. LOGTEC specializes in acquisition, data management, enterprise services, functional processes, logistics processes, network services, product data, and software development. Founded in 1985. **Positions advertised include:** Contracts Administrator; Acquisitions Manager; Logistician; Configuration Manager; Program Manager. **Corporate headquarters location:** This location. **Other area locations:** Columbus OH; Dayton OH. **Other U.S. locations:** Nationwide.

LOOMIS FARGO & COMPANY
36 Bissell Street, Youngstown OH 44505. 330/746-3246. **Fax:** 330/746-8939. **Contact:** Personnel. **World Wide Web address:** http://www.loomisfargo.com. **Description:** An armored security service specializing in transporting currency. **NOTE:** Applications will not be mailed to jobseekers. They must be picked up in person. **Other U.S. locations:** Nationwide.

LORAIN COUNTY COMMUNITY COLLEGE
242 College Center, 1005 North Abbe Road, Elyria OH 44035-1691. 440/366-4076. **Fax:** 440/366-4676. **Toll-free phone:** 800/995-5222. **Contact:** Personnel. **E-mail address:** careers@lorainccc.edu. **World Wide Web address:** http://www.lorainccc.edu. **Description:** A two-year community college offering associate's degrees in art, science, applied business, individualized studies, and technical studies. **Positions advertised include:** Adjunct Instructor, Real Estate; Adjunct Instructor, Practical Nursing: Principal/Administrator.

LOTT INDUSTRIES
2001 Collingwood Boulevard, Toledo OH 43620. 419/255-0064. **Toll-free phone:** 888/399-5688. **Fax:** 419/255-6432. **Contact:** Human Resources. **World Wide Web address:** http://www.lottindustries.com. **Description:** A nonprofit organization that employs mentally disabled individuals to conduct a variety of services, including packaging, document disposal, and mailing preparation

LUBRIZOL CORPORATION
29400 Lakeland Boulevard, Wickliffe OH 44092. 440/943-4200. **Contact:** Human Resources. **E-mail address:** careers@lubrizol.com. **World Wide Web address:** http://www.lubrizol.com. **Description:** A diversified specialty chemical company engaged in chemical, mechanical, and genetic research to develop products for the world markets in transportation, industry, and agriculture. **Positions advertised include:** Marketing Specialist. **Special programs:** Internships; Co-ops. **Internship information:** Summer internships are available in various areas. See website for a current listing of opportunities. **Corporate headquarters location:** This location. **Operations at this facility include:** Research and Development. **Listed on:** New York Stock Exchange. **Stock exchange symbol:** LZ.

LUCENT TECHNOLOGIES INC.
6200 East Broad Street, Columbus OH 43213-1550. 614/860-2000. **Contact:** Human Resources. **World Wide Web address:** http://www.lucent.com. **Description:** Manufactures communications products including switching, transmission, fiber-optic cable, wireless systems, and operations systems to supply the needs of telephone companies and other communications services providers. **Special programs:**

Internships. **Corporate headquarters location:** Murray Hill NJ. **Listed on:** New York Stock Exchange. **Stock exchange symbol:** LU.

LUTHERAN HOSPITAL
1730 West 25th Street, Cleveland OH 44113. 216/696-4300. **Fax:** 216/363-5199. **Recorded jobline:** 216/363-2491. **Contact:** Human Resources Department. **World Wide Web address:** http://www.lutheranhospital.org. **Description:** A 200-bed, acute care hospital. Facilities include a muscular/skeletal unit and a general psychiatric unit. **Positions advertised include:** Nuclear Medicine Technician; X-Ray Technician; Occupational Therapist; Physical Therapist; Speech Therapist; Respiratory Therapist; Licensed Practical Nurse; Registered Nurse; Nurse Practitioner; Manager, Food and Nutrition Services. **Office hours:** Monday – Friday, 8:00 a.m. – 4:30 p.m.

MBNA MARKETING SYSTEMS
25875 Science Park Drive, Beachwood OH 44122-7304. 216/595-4100. **Toll-free phone:** 888/763-0472. **Recorded jobline:** 800/637-2070. **E-mail address:** central@mbnacareers.com. **Contact:** Human Resources. **World Wide Web address:** http://www.mbnainternational.com. **Description:** Provides credit cards and cross-sells individual loan, deposit, and insurance products. **Positions advertised include:** New Account Specialist; Customer Marketing Account Manager; Customer Satisfaction Account Manager; Customer Assistance Account Manager. **Parent company:** MBNA Corporation (Newark DE) is a leading issuer of Gold MasterCards and affinity credit cards. Other operations of the company include administering home equity and personal loans, and accepting deposits. Other subsidiaries of MBNA Corporation include MBNA American Bank, N.A., a national bank. **Operations at this facility include:** Customer Service; Marketing; Regional Headquarters; Sales. **Number of employees at this location:** 600. **Corporate headquarters location:** Wilmington DE. **Other area locations:** Akron OH. **Listed on:** New York Stock Exchange. **Stock exchange symbol:** KRB.

MCSI
4750 Hempstead Station Drive, Dayton OH 45429. 937/291-8282. **Fax:** 937/291-7741. **Contact:** Marta Cash, Human Resources Department. **World Wide Web address:** http://www.mcsinet.com. **Description:** Distributes computer equipment, supplies, and accessories to corporate and government clients. MCSI also distributes office automation equipment. Founded in 1981. **Corporate headquarters location:** This location. **Listed on:** NASDAQ. **Stock exchange symbol:** MCSI. **Annual sales/revenues:** More than $100 million.

MTC TECHNOLOGIES
4032 Linden Avenue, Dayton OH 45432. 937/252-9199. **Fax:** 937/258-3863. **Contact:** Human Resources. **E-mail address:** mctjobs@mcttechnologies.com. **World Wide Web address:** http://www.modtechcorp.com. **Description:** Provides a range of sophisticated system engineering, intelligence, information technology, and program management solutions, primarily to the Department of Defense. **Positions advertised include:** Quality Controller; Group Controller; Senior Contracts Administrator. **Corporate headquarters location:** This location. **Listed on:** NASDAQ. **Stock exchanges symbol:** MTCT. **Number of employees nationwide:** 2,000.

MTL SYSTEMS, INC.
3481 Dayton-Xenia Road, Dayton OH 45432-2796. 937/426-3111. **Fax:** 937/426-8301. **Contact:** Sue App, Human Resources. **E-mail address:** sapp@mtl.com. **World Wide Web address:** http://www.mtl.com. **Description:** Engaged in electronic products systems, image exploitation, imaging technology, modeling and simulation, networking, and web-based business solutions for commercial clients and government agencies. MTL Systems specializes in computer engineering, electronic and sensor technology, and reconnaissance and intelligence activities. **Positions advertised include:** Darkroom/Production Technician; Photographic Engineer; Computer Engineer; Remote Sensing Scientist; Senior Remote Sensing Engineer. **Corporate headquarters location:** This location.

MAC TAC/MORGAN ADHESIVES INC.
4560 Darrow Road, Stow OH 44224. 330/688-1111. **Contact:** Manager of Human Resources. **E-mail:** mactacresume@mactac.com. **World Wide Web address:** http://www.mactac.com. **Description:** Produces pressure-sensitive adhesive goods and coated materials. **Other U.S. locations:** Columbus IN; North Las Vegas NV; Moosic PA. **International locations:** Worldwide. **Parent company:** Bemis Company Inc. **Listed on:** New York Stock Exchange. **Stock exchange symbol:** BMS.

MACAULAY-BROWN, INC.
4021 Executive Drive, Dayton OH 45430. 937/426-3421. **Fax:** 937/426-5364. **Contact:** Human Resources. **World Wide Web address:** http://www.macb.com. **Description:** A technical firm specializing in intelligence/threat analysis; systems engineering; digital system model development; technique development; test and evaluation of hardware in the loop; software engineering; instrumentation system design and development; computer system/LAN development; facility modification and operation; and management support. Founded in 1978. **Corporate headquarters location:** This location. **Other U.S. locations:** CA; FL; GA; IL; MD; NM; TX. **Parent company:** SYTEX Group. **Operations at this facility include:** Analysis; Computer Modeling; Management Support; Testing. **Listed on:** Privately held. **Annual Sales/Revenues:** $45 million. **Number of employees nationwide:** 460.

MALONE COLLEGE
515 25th Street NW, Canton OH 44709-3897. 330/471-8100. **Fax:** 330/454-6977. **Contact:** Human Resources. **E-mail address:** careerservices@malone.edu. **World Wide Web address:** http://www.malone.edu. **Description:** A Christian liberal arts college. Malone College is affiliated with the Evangelical Friends Church. Founded in 1957.

MANATRON SABRE
9111 Springboro Pike, Miamisburg OH 45342-4420. 937/866-6000. **Fax:** 269/567-2912. **Contact:** Personnel Manager. **E-mail address:** recruiter@manatron.com. **World Wide Web address:** http://www.manatron.com. **Description:** Provides real estate appraisal, mapping services, and data processing services for local tax jurisdictions and departments of local government. **NOTE:** Resumes are accepted by e-mail or fax. **Positions advertised include:** Sales Executive. **Corporate headquarters location:** Portage MI. **Other U.S. locations:** Nationwide. **Parent company:** Manatron, Inc. **Operations at this facility include:** Divisional Headquarters. **Listed on:** NASDAQ. **Stock exchange symbol:** MANA. **Number of employees at this location:** 50.

MANUFACTURED HOUSING ENTERPRISES, INC.
09302 U.S. Route 6, Bryan OH 43506. 419/636-4511. **Toll-free phone:** 800/821-0220. **Fax:** 419/636-6521. **Contact:** Hal Kinder, Human Resources Manager. **E-mail address:** mhe@bright.net. **World Wide Web address:** http://www.mheinc.com. **Description:** Manufactures single-wide, double-wide, and modular homes. The company also provides the chassis and components for its homes including cabinets, countertops, carpeting, and a variety of custom options. **Corporate headquarters location:** This location. **Operations at this facility include:** Administration; Manufacturing; Research and Development; Sales; Service. **President:** James Newman.

MARATHON PIPE LINE COMPANY
539 South Main Street, Findlay OH 45840-4940. 419/422-2121. **Contact:** Human Resources. **World Wide Web address:** http://www. marathon.com. **Description:** Involved in worldwide exploration, production, transportation, and marketing of crude oil and natural gas. The group is also involved in domestic refining, marketing, and transportation of petroleum products. **Special programs:** Internships. **Internship information:** Paid summer internships in a variety of fields are offered. Entry-level positions at Marathon are typically filled by candidates who have previously held internships with the company. **Corporate headquarters location:** Pittsburgh PA. **Parent company:** Marathon Oil Corporation is one of the nation's largest gatherers, processors, and transporters of natural gas. **Listed on:** New York Stock Exchange. **Stock exchange symbol:** MRO.

MARCONI
1122 F Street, Lorain OH 44052. 440/288-1122. **Toll-free phone:** 800/800-1280. **Fax:** 440/246-4171. **Contact:** Human Resources Manager. **World Wide Web address:** http://www.marconi.com. **Description:** Marconi Power provides network power systems for telecommunications, Internet, and cable television. **Corporate headquarters location:** London UK. **Other area locations:** Cleveland OH; North Ridgeville OH. **Other U.S. locations:** CA; IL; NY; PA; TX. **International locations:** Worldwide.

MARIETTA MEMORIAL HOSPITAL
401 Matthew Street, Marietta OH 45750-1635. 740/374-1400. **Fax:** 740/376-5045. **Recorded jobline:** 740/374-4997. **Contact:** James Offenberger, Employment Manager. **E-mail address:** jpoffenberger@mmhospital.org. **World Wide Web address:** http://www.mmhospital.org. **Description:** A community-based, acute care hospital. Marietta Memorial Hospital offers a variety of services including behavioral health, cardiac rehabilitation, community outreach, home nursing, mammography, radiology, outpatient surgery, and the Strecker Cancer Center. Founded in 1929. **Company slogan:** The heart of a healthy community. **Positions advertised include:** Ultrasonographer; Speech Language Pathologist; Registered Nurse; Staff Coordinator; Evening Lab Supervisor; Outpatient Services Technician; Orderly; Registration Clerk; Mechanics Assistant; Housekeeper; Food Service Worker; Laundry Aide; Social Worker; Occupational Therapist; Respiratory Therapist; Pharmacist; Home Health Aide. **Number of employees at this location:** 1,300.

MARION GENERAL HOSPITAL
1000 McKinley Park Drive, Marion OH 43302. 740/383-8690. **Fax:** 740/383-8612. **Recorded jobline:** 740/383-8695. **Contact:** Human Resources. **World Wide Web address:** http://www.mariongeneral.com. **Description:** A hospital offering a variety of specialty areas including heart care, cancer care, emergency care, women's health, mental health care, nursing services, ICU/CCU, step-down/transition, surgical/orthopedic, oncology, Center for New Beginnings (labor and delivery, mother/baby nursery, pediatrics), off-site nursing services (home care, hospice/quality of life, adult daycare, Alzheimer's), pharmacy, clinical laboratory services, nutrition, rehabilitation, work transitions, pain management, occupational therapy, physical therapy, nuclear medicine, radiology, cardiac catheter, inpatient psychiatric, recreational therapy, and social services. Founded in 1920. **NOTE:** Candidates should apply online. **Positions advertised include:** Respiratory Therapist; Social Worker; Health Unit Coordinator; Clinical Instructor; Paramedic; Licensed Practical Nurse; Registered Nurse; Nurse Assistant; Clinical Dietitian; Director of Safety; Environmental Services Technician; Pharmacist. **Special programs:** Internships. **Corporate headquarters location:** Columbus OH. **Parent company:** U.S. Health Corporation. **Number of employees at this location:** 900.

MARTIN MARIETTA MAGNESIA SPECIALTIES
755 Lime Road, Woodville OH 43469. 419/849-3111. **Contact:** Personnel Director. **World Wide Web address:** http://www.magspecialties.com. **Description:** Martin Marietta Magnesia Specialties is primarily engaged in the manufacture of monolithic refractory products and precast refractory shapes, dolomitic lime, periclase, electrical-coating materials, and water treatment chemicals. The company is also engaged in the development of chemicals for the aluminum, animal feed, ceramics, motor oil, plastics, sugar, and tile markets. **Parent company:** Martin Marietta Materials, Inc. **Number of employees nationwide:** 6,500.

MASTER BUILDERS TECHNOLOGIES
23700 Chagrin Boulevard, Cleveland OH 44122. 216/831-5500. **Fax:** 800/628-9990. **Contact:** Personnel. **World Wide Web address:** http://www.masterbuilders.com. **Description:** Master Builders Technologies develops, manufactures, and markets construction chemicals. The company's products include concrete chemical additives, grouts, adhesives, curing and joint compounds, and decorative and protective coatings and toppings Founded in 1909. **Parent company:** Sandoz Ltd.

MATRIX ESSENTIALS INC.
30601 Carter Street, Solon OH 44139. 440/248-3700. **Contact:** Human Resources. **World Wide Web address:** http://www.matrixessentials.com. **Description:** Manufactures hair care products for the professional beauty industry. Matrix Essentials, Inc. also manufactures Matrix Colors, a complete line of cosmetics. **Parent company:** Bristol-Myers Squibb Company. **Number of employees at this location:** 1,300.

MAX & ERMA'S RESTAURANTS INC.
4849 Evanswood Drive, Columbus OH 43229-6206. 614/431-5800. **Fax:** 614/431-4100. **Contact:** Human Resources. **World Wide Web address:** http://www.max-ermas.com. **Description:** Operates a chain of approximately 30 restaurants. Founded in 1972. **Positions advertised include:** Server; Cook; Host/Hostess; Carryout Person; Bus Person. **Corporate headquarters location:** This location. **Other U.S. locations:** IL; IN; KY; MI; PA.

MAX DAETWYLER CORPORATION
2133 Lyons Road, Miamisburg OH 45342. 937/439-1582. **Fax:** 937/439-1592. **Contact:** Human Resources. **World Wide Web address:** http://www.daetwyler.com. **Description:** A capital equipment manufacturer that designs and produces electronic engravers, scanners, and other prepress equipment; peripherals; and software for the gravure printing industry. Founded in 1943. **NOTE:** Entry-level positions and second and third shifts are offered. **Special programs:** Internships. **Corporate headquarters location:** Switzerland. **Other U.S. locations:** West Huntersville NC. **International locations:** Worldwide. **Listed on:** Privately held. **Annual sales/revenues:** $21 - $50 million. **Number of employees at this location:** 250.

MAYFRAN INTERNATIONAL INC.
P.O. Box 43038, Cleveland OH 44143. 440/461-4100. **Physical address:** 6650 Beta Drive, Mayfield Village OH 44143. **Contact:** Human Resources. **E-mail address:**

info@mayfran.com. **World Wide Web address:** http://www.mayfran.com. **Description:** Manufactures hinged steel belt and magnetic conveyors for the metalworking, resource recovery, municipal refuse, and automotive industries. **Corporate headquarters location:** This location. **Operations at this facility include:** Administration; Manufacturing; Research and Development; Sales; Service.

McDONALD & COMPANY INVESTMENTS, INC.
800 Superior Avenue, Cleveland OH 44114. 216/443-2300. **Contact:** Human Resources. **World Wide Web address:** http://www.mcdonaldinvest.com. **Description:** Operates a regional investment banking, brokerage, and investment advisory business. **Corporate headquarters location:** This location. **Subsidiaries include:** McDonald & Company; McDonald & Company Securities, Inc. **Parent company:** KeyCorp. **Number of employees nationwide:** 1,030.

McGOWAN & COMPANY, INC.
Old Forge Centre, 20595 Lorain Road, Fairview Park OH 44126. 440/333-6300. **Toll-free phone:** 800/545-1538. **Fax:** 440/333-3214. **Contact:** Human Resources. **E-mail address:** info@mcgowaninsurance.com. **World Wide Web address:** http://www.mcgowaninsurance.com. **Description:** Engaged in insurance underwriting. Founded in 1949. **NOTE:** Entry-level positions are offered. **Special programs:** Summer Jobs. **Office hours:** Monday - Friday, 9:00 a.m. - 5:00 p.m. **Corporate headquarters location:** This location. **Listed on:** Privately held. **President:** Thomas B. McGowan, III. **Number of employees at this location:** 40. **Number of employees nationwide:** 200.

THE McGRAW-HILL COMPANIES
8787 Orion Place, Columbus OH 43240. 614/430-4000. **Contact:** Human Resources. **World Wide Web address:** http://www.mcgraw-hill.com. **Description:** A provider of information and services through books, magazines, newsletters, software, CD-ROMs, and online data, fax, and TV broadcasting services. The company operates four network-affiliated TV stations and also publishes *Business Week* magazine and books for the college, medical, international, legal, and professional markets. McGraw-Hill also offers financial services including Standard & Poor's, commodity items, and international and logistics management products and services. **Positions advertised include:** Executive Editor; Director, Product Research; Production Editor; Director of Project Management; Content Editor; Sr. Financial Analyst; Archive Coordinator. **Special programs:** Summer Internship. **Corporate headquarters location:** New York NY. **Listed on:** New York Stock Exchange. **Stock exchange symbol:** MHP.

MEADEN & MOORE, INC.
1100 Superior Avenue, Suite 1100, Cleveland OH 44114. 216/241-3272. **Fax:** 216/771-4511. **Contact:** Human Resources. **E-mail address:** cleveland@meadenmoore.com. **World Wide Web address:** http://www.meadenmoore.com. **Description:** Engaged in certified public accounting and business consulting. **Positions advertised include:** Audit Manager; Audit Specialist; Tax Manager; Senior Manager Accountant; Staff Accountant. **Special Programs:** Internships.

MEADWESTVACO
World Headquarters, Courthouse Plaza NE, Dayton OH 45463. 937/495-6323. **Fax:** 937/495-4553. **Contact:** Personnel. **World Wide Web address:** http://www.meadwestvaco.com. **Description:** One of the world's largest manufacturers of paper. Mead produces more than 1.2 million tons annually for printing and business use and is a leader in the coated paperboard and multiple packaging markets. The company is also a distributor of paper, packaging, and business supplies made by manufacturers throughout the world. MeadWestvaco is one of the largest makers of paper-based school and home-office supplies, as well as a developer of one of the world's leading electronic information retrieval services for law, patents, accounting, finance, news, and business information. **Corporate headquarters location:** Stamford CT. **Listed on:** New York Stock Exchange. **Stock exchange symbol:** MWV.

MEDCENTRAL HEALTH SYSTEM
335 Glessner Avenue, Mansfield OH 44903. 419/526-8000. **Fax:** 419/526-8848. **Contact:** Human Resources. **E-mail address:** careers4u@medcentral.org. **World Wide Web address:** http://www.medcentral.org. **Description:** MedCentral Health System is a leading health care delivery system that operates three acute care hospitals: Crestline Hospital, Mansfield Hospital, and Shelby Hospital. The company also operates a cardiac care center, substance abuse programs, a walk-in medical center, and industrial health and safety services. **NOTE:** Apply online. **Positions advertised include:** Assistant Nurse Manager; Registered Nurse; Licensed Practical Nurse; Speech Language Pathologist; Pharmacy Manager; Respiratory Care Technician. **Other area locations:** Crestline OH; Shelby OH. **Number of employees at this location:** 2,000.

MEDEX INC.
6250 Shier Rings Road, Dublin OH 43016. 614/889-4775. **Contact:** Human Resources. **World Wide Web address:** http://www.medex.com. **Description:** An international manufacturer and supplier of critical care products and infusion systems for medical and surgical applications. These products are sold to hospitals, alternative health care facilities, home health care providers, and original equipment manufacturers. **Positions advertised include:** Internal Audit Manager; Senior Mechanical Engineer; Software Engineer; Accounts Receivable Specialist. **Special programs:** Internships. **Corporate headquarters location:** Carlsbad CA. **Other U.S. locations:** Atlanta GA. **Operations at this facility include:** Administration; Manufacturing; Sales; Service.

MEDINA GENERAL HOSPITAL
1000 East Washington Street, Medina OH 44256. 330/725-1000. **Fax:** 330/721-4925. **Contact:** Human Resources. **E-mail address:** hr@medinahospital.org. **World Wide Web address:** http://www.medinahospital.org. **Description:** An acute care facility with 118 beds. Medina General Hospital offers such services as prenatal care, an oncology unit, pediatrics, and an intensive care unit. **Positions advertised include:** Registered Nurse; Computer Operator; MRI Technologist; Phlebotomist; Physical Therapist; Radiology Technician; Security Supervisor; Housekeeping Assistant; Maintenance Worker; Nursing Assistant.

MEMORIAL HOSPITAL
715 South Taft Avenue, Fremont OH 43420. 419/332-7321. **Fax:** 419/334-6691. **Contact:** Human Resources. **World Wide Web address:** http://www.fremontmemorial.org. **Description:** A community-focused, acute care hospital. Opened in 1918. **Positions advertised include:** Licensed Practical Nurse; Medical Records Technician; Radiological Technologist; Registered Nurse; Respiratory Therapist; Surgical Technician; Account Representative; House Keeper; Cardiovascular Technician. **Operations at this facility include:** Administration; Service. **Number of employees at this location:** 570.

MERCER HUMAN RESOURCE CONSULTING
10 West Broad Street, Suite 1100, Columbus OH 43215-3475. 614/227-5500. **Fax:** 614/224-7676. **Contact:** Personnel Manager. **World Wide Web address:** http://www.mercerhr.com. **Description:** One of the world's largest actuarial and human resources management consulting firms. The company offers advice to organizations on all aspects of employee/management relationships. Services include retirement, health and welfare, performance and rewards, communication, investment, human resources administration, risk, finance and insurance, and health care provider consulting. **Special programs:** Internships; Co-ops. **Other area locations:** Cincinnati OH; Cleveland OH. **Other U.S. locations:** Nationwide.

METASYSTEMS
6 Corporation Center Drive, Broadview Heights OH 44147. 440/526-1454. **Toll-free phone:** 800/788-5253. **Fax:** 440/526-1406. **Contact:** Personnel. **E-mail address:** careers@metasystems.com. **World Wide Web address:** http://www.metasystems.com. **Description:** Develops and implements computer systems and provides network and infrastructure consulting services in partnership with Berish & Associates, which operates in the areas of client/server development, Internet/intranet development, Microsoft Office integration, LAN and WAN services, and installation and implementation. Founded in 1985. **Listed on:** Privately held. **President/Owner:** Joseph Berish. **Number of employees at this location:** 60.

METCUT RESEARCH ASSOCIATES, INC.
3980 Rosslyn Drive, Cincinnati OH 45209-1196. 513/271-5100. **Toll-free phone:** 800/966-2888. **Fax:** 513/271-9511. **Contact:** Human Resources. **E-mail address:** hr@metcut.com. **World Wide Web address:** http://www.metcut.com. **Description:** A materials engineering research and development firm engaged in specimen testing. **Corporate headquarters location:** This location. **President and CEO:** John P. Kahles.

METOKOTE CORPORATION
1340 Neubrecht Road, Lima OH 45801. 419/227-1100. **Fax:** 419/222-0946. **Contact:** Personnel. **World Wide Web address:** http://www.metokote.com. **Description:** Provides a full line of coating services including electro-coating, powder coating, and liquid paint. Metokote supplies coating solutions to the agriculture, automotive, computer, industrial equipment, and recreational markets. **Positions advertised include:** Process Engineer. **Corporate headquarters location:** This location. **Other area locations:** Cleveland OH; Dayton OH; Toledo OH. **Other U.S. locations:** IL; IA; KY; MI; SC; TN. **International locations:** Brazil; Canada; Mexico; United Kingdom. **Number of employees at this location:** 500. **Number of employees nationwide:** 1,000.

THE METROHEALTH SYSTEM
2500 MetroHealth Drive, Cleveland OH 44109. 216/778-7800. **Toll-free phone:** 800/332-4060. **Fax:** 216/778-8905. **Contact:** Human Resources. **E-mail address:** humres@metrohealth.org. **World Wide Web address:** http://www.metrohealth.org. **Description:** Provides comprehensive health care services through its member facilities and affiliation with Case Western University School of Medicine. The MetroHealth System is comprised of several facilities: MetroHealth Medical Center (also at this location) is one of the nation's most successful publicly owned hospitals. The 728-bed hospital provides a variety of medical services including dentistry, dermatology, ambulatory care, medical aircraft services, obstetrics, gynecology, psychiatry, family practice, substance abuse, and surgery; MetroHealth's Outpatient Plaza houses separate centers for rehabilitation, women and children, specialty services including cardiology and neurology, and cancer care; The Charles H. Rammelkamp, Jr., M.D. Center for Research and Education; MetroHealth Center for Rehabilitation; MetroHealth Clement Center for Family Care; and MetroHealth Center for Skilled Nursing Care. **Positions advertised include:** Occupational Therapist; Physical Therapist; Social Worker; Speech Pathologist; Communication Specialist; Laboratory Processing Clerk; Education Specialist; Coding Specialist; Communication Specialist; Grants Support Specialist; Data Entry Operator; Gift Shop Clerk; Library Aide; Clinical Dietitian; Flight Nurse Specialist; Licensed Practical Nurse; Nurse Practitioner; Registered Nurse. **Special programs:** Internships. **Office hours:** Monday - Friday, 7:30 a.m. - 5:00 p.m. **President/CEO:** John F. Sideras. **Number of employees at this location:** 6,000.

METTLER TOLEDO INC.
1900 Polaris Parkway, Columbus OH 43240. 614/438-4511. **Fax:** 614/438-4536. **Contact:** Human Resources. **E-mail address:** mtjobs@mt.com. **World Wide Web address:** http://www.mt.com. **Description:** Mettler Toledo is a leading manufacturer and marketer of weighing instruments. The company also manufactures analytic, metal detection, laboratory, and dimensioning instruments. Founded in 1902. **NOTE:** Entry-level positions and part-time jobs are offered. **Positions advertised include:** Marketing Manager; Accounting Manager; Quality Analyst. **Special programs:** Internships; Co-ops. **Office hours:** Monday - Friday, 8:00 a.m. - 6:00 p.m. **Parent company:** AEA Investors Inc. (NY). **Operations at this facility include:** This location manufactures precision instruments for global distribution. **Listed on:** New York Stock Exchange. **Stock exchange symbol:** MTD. **Annual sales/revenues:** More than $100 million. **Number of employees nationwide:** 3,000. **Number of employees worldwide:** 8,000.

MICROSOFT GREAT PLAINS BUSINESS SOLUTIONS
200 East Hardin Street, Findlay OH 45840. 419/424-0422. **Contact:** Human Resources. **World Wide Web address:** http://www.greatplains.com. **Description:** Develops accounting software. **NOTE:** Mail all resumes to: Human Resources, One Lone Tree Road, Fargo ND 58104.

MILACRON, INC.
2090 Florence Avenue, Cincinnati OH 45206. 513/487-5000. **Fax:** 513/487-5057. **Contact:** Human Resources. **E-mail address:** info@milacron.com. **World Wide Web address:** http://www.milacron.com. **Description:** A world leader in manufacturing technologies for the metalworking and plastic processing industries. Products include machine tools, numerical controls, plastic machinery, grinding wheels, coolants, coordinate measuring machines, composite processing systems, and Valenite metal-cutting tools. **Special programs:** Internships. **Corporate headquarters location:** This location. **Other U.S. locations:** MI; PA; SC; TX; VA. **International locations:** Austria; France; Germany; Great Britain; Japan; Mexico; The Netherlands. **Operations at this facility include:** Administration; Manufacturing; Research and Development. **Listed on:** New York Stock Exchange. **Stock exchange symbol:** MZ.

MILACRON, INC.
4165 Half Acre Road, Batavia OH 45103. 513/536-2000. **Contact:** Human Resources. **World Wide Web address:** http://www.milacron.com. **Description:** A world leader in manufacturing technologies for the metalworking and plastic processing industries. Products include machine tools, numerical controls, plastic machinery, grinding wheels, coolants, coordinate measuring machines, composite processing systems, and Valenite metal-cutting tools. **Corporate headquarters location:** Cincinnati OH. **Other U.S. locations:** MI; PA; SC; TX; VA. **International locations:** Austria; France; Germany; Great Britain; Japan; Mexico; The Netherlands. **Listed on:** New York Stock Exchange. **Stock exchange symbol:** MZ. **Number of employees nationwide:** 9,000.

MINSTER MACHINE COMPANY
240 West Fifth Street, P.O. Box 120, Minster OH 45865. 419/628-2331. **Fax:** 419/628-3517. **Contact:** Employee Relations Manager. **E-mail address:** hrdept@minster.com. **World Wide Web address:** http://www.minster.com. **Description:** Designs, develops, and manufactures mechanical power presses and related auxiliary equipment. Minster Machine Company markets its products to the contract stamping, OEM, electrical, lamination, and container markets. Founded in 1896. **Positions advertised include:** Security Officer. **Corporate headquarters location:** This location. **Other U.S. locations:** Beaufort SC.

MITCHELLACE INC.
P.O. Box 89, Portsmouth OH 45662-0089. 740/354-2813. **Physical address:** 830 Murray Street, Portsmouth OH 45662. **Toll-free phone:** 800/848-8696. **Fax:** 740/353-4669. **Contact:** Human Resources Manager. **World Wide Web address:** http://www.mitchellace.com. **Description:** Develops, manufactures, markets, and distributes shoelaces and other braided and woven products. **Corporate headquarters location:** This location. **Operations at this facility include:** Administration; Manufacturing; Research and Development; Sales; Service.

MODERN TECHNOLOGIES CORPORATION
4032 Linden Avenue, Dayton OH 45432. 937/252-9199. **Fax:** 937/258-3863. **Contact:** Human Resources Department. **E-mail address:** hr@modtechcorp.com. **World Wide Web address:** http://www.modtechcorp.com. **Description:** Provides engineering, system support, and management solutions and services to engineering, manufacturing, technical, and government industries. **Positions advertised include:** Lead Analyst; Associate Analyst; Financial Analyst; Accountant; Program Manager. **Corporate headquarters location:** This location. **Other area locations:** Cincinnati OH; Cleveland OH; Columbus OH. **Other U.S. locations:** Nationwide. **International locations:** Worldwide. **Subsidiaries include:** Composite Technologies Corporation. **Parent company:** MTC Technologies, Inc. **Operations at this facility include:** Administration; Divisional Headquarters; Manufacturing; Regional Headquarters; Research and Development. **Listed on:** Privately held.

MODINE MANUFACTURING COMPANY
615 Bierley Avenue, Pemberville OH 43450. 419/287-3293. **Contact:** Personnel Director. **World Wide Web address:** http://www.modine.com. **Description:** Modine Manufacturing Company is a worldwide leader in heat transfer technology serving vehicular, industrial, commercial, and building/HVAC markets. The company's major products include radiators, oil coolers, vehicular air conditioning condensers and evaporators, building/HVAC products, charge-air coolers, and radiator cores. **Corporate headquarters location:** Racine WI. **Other U.S. locations:** Nationwide. **Operations at this facility include:** This location manufactures heating machinery and components. **Subsidiaries include:** Austria Warmetauscher GmbH; Langerer & Reich. **Number of employees worldwide:** 7,500.

MOLDED FIBER GLASS COMPANY
P.O. Box 675, Ashtabula OH 44005-0675. 440/997-5851. **Physical address:** 2925 MFG Place, Ashtabula OH 44004. **Contact:** Larry Davis, Vice President of Human Resources. **E-mail address:** ldavis@moldedfiberglass.com **World Wide Web address:** http://www.moldedfiberglass.com. **Description:** Manufactures custom molded fiberglass and reinforced plastic products. **NOTE:** To contact Larry Davis directly call: 440/994-5261. **Positions advertised include:** Corporate Director of Purchasing; Sales Person. **Corporate headquarters location:** This location. **Operations at this facility include:** Manufacturing; Research and Development; Sales.

MONARCH LATHES, L.P.
P.O. Box 4609, Sidney OH 45365. 937/492-4111. **Physical address:** 615 North Oak Avenue, Sidney OH 45365. **Contact:** Human Resources. **World Wide Web address:** http://www.monarchmt.com. **Description:** A manufacturer of metal cutting lathes and manual and CNC turning machines. **Operations at this facility include:** Administration; Manufacturing; Research and Development; Sales; Service.

MONTGOMERY WATSON HARZA
1300 East Ninth Street, Suite 1100, Cleveland OH 44114. 216/621-2407. **Contact:** Human Resources. **World Wide Web address:** http://www.mwhglobal.com. **Description:** An environmental engineering, construction, and consulting firm. Montgomery Watson also specializes in applied research, construction and construction management, environmental engineering and remediation, financing, government relations, and information technology. **Positions advertised include:** Data Conversion Technician. **Special programs:** Internships. **Operations at this facility include:** Regional Headquarters.

MORSE CONTROLS
21 Clinton Street, Hudson OH 44236. 330/653-7701. **Fax:** 330/653-7799. **Contact:** Personnel. **World Wide Web address:** http://www.morsecontrols.com. **Description:** Designs, develops, manufactures, and markets mechanical and electronic controls, steering, and cable products. Morse Controls markets its products to the marine and mobile equipment markets worldwide. Founded in 1945.

MORTON SALT
151 Industrial Avenue, Rittman OH 44270. 330/925-3015. **Contact:** Employee Relations Manager. **World Wide Web address:** http://www.mortonsalt.com. **Description:** Morton Salt produces salt for the agricultural, grocery, ice control, industrial, and water softening markets. **Corporate headquarters location:** Lansing IL. **International locations:** Worldwide.

THE MOSSER GROUP
122 South Wilson Avenue, Fremont OH 43420. 419/334-3801. **Fax:** 419/332-1534. **Contact:** Human Resources. **E-mail address:** humanresources@mossergrp.com. **World Wide Web address:** http://www.mossergrp.com. **Description:** A general construction and design firm. The Mosser Group specializes in masonry, pre-engineered steel buildings, pre-cast concrete construction, renovations, and tilt-up concrete construction. Founded in 1948. **Special programs:** Internships. **Corporate headquarters location:** This location. **Other U.S. locations:** Toledo OH. **Listed on:** Privately held.

MOTORISTS INSURANCE COMPANIES
471 East Broad Street, Suite 200, Columbus OH 43215. 614/225-8211. **Fax:** 614/225-8693. **Recorded jobline:** 614/225-8313. **Contact:** Human Resources. **World Wide Web address:** http://www.youknowus.com. **Description:** Handles a wide range of property and casualty insurance lines. **Positions advertised include:** Senior Property/Casualty Accountant; Communications Specialist; Call Center Supervisor; Account Manager; Personal Lines Underwriter; Programmer; Life Marketing Representative; District Sales Manager. **Corporate headquarters location:** This location. **Operations at this facility include:** Administration; Research and Development.

MOYNO INDUSTRIAL PRODUCTS
P.O. Box 960, Springfield OH 45501-0960. 937/327-3111. **Physical address:** 1895 West Jefferson Street, Springfield OH 45506. **Toll-free phone:** 877/486-6966. **Fax:** 937/327-3177. **Contact:** Human Resources. **World Wide Web address:** http://www.moyno.com. **Description:** Manufactures fluid handling products such as progressing cavity pumps, manual and automated pinch valves and controls, and down-hold pumps for oil and gas recovery and their associated accessories. **NOTE:** Entry-level positions are offered. **Corporate headquarters location:** This location. **Parent company:** Robbins & Myers, Inc.

S.D. MYERS INC.
180 South Avenue, Tallmadge OH 44278. 330/630-7000. **Toll-free phone:** 800/444-9580. **Fax:** 330/633-4786. **Contact:** Human Resources Manager. **E-mail address:** hr@sdmeyers.com. **World Wide Web address:** http://www.sdmyers.com. **Description:** Engaged in transformer maintenance services, testing, rewinding, and maintenance seminars. Founded in 1968. **NOTE:** Entry-level positions, part-time jobs, and second and third shifts are offered. **Office hours:** Monday - Friday, 8:00 a.m. - 5:00 p.m. **Corporate headquarters location:** This location. **Other U.S. locations:** Bessemer AL; Phoenix AZ; Fremont CA; Colorado Springs CO; Bedford NH; Fort Mill SC; Seabrook TX; Seattle WA. **Operations at this facility include:** Administration; Production; Research and Development; Sales; Service. **Listed on:** Privately held.

MYERS INDUSTRIES INC.
1293 South Main Street, Akron OH 44301. 330/253-5592. **Fax:** 330/761-6115. **Contact:** Human Resources. **E-mail address:** mcareer@po.myersind.com. **World Wide Web address:** http://www.myersind.com. **Description:** Develops, manufactures, and markets plastic and rubber products for the agricultural, automotive, commercial and consumer, and industrial markets. Myers Industries markets its storage and organizations solutions, outdoor planters and accessories, plastic material handling products, plastic containers, storage systems, and tire tread and repair products under the brand names Akro-Mils, Akro-Mils Specialty, Allibert Equipement, Ameri-Kart, Buckhorn, Buckhorn Rubber, Dillon, Listo, and Patch Rubber. **NOTE:** Resumes accepted for open positions only. **Positions advertised include:** Factory Maintenance Technician. **Corporate headquarters location:** This location. **Other U.S. locations:** Nationwide. **Operations at this facility include:** Divisional Headquarters; Service. **Listed on:** New York Stock Exchange. **Stock exchange symbol:** MYE.

NCR SYSTEMEDIA GROUP
9095 Washington Church Road, Miamisburg OH 45342-4428. 937/439-8200. **Contact:** Human Resources. **World Wide Web address:** http://www.ncr.com. **Description:** Develops, produces, and markets a complete line of information technology products including transaction processing media, auto identification media, business form communication products, managing documents and media, and a full line of integrated equipment solutions. **Special programs:** Internships. **Corporate headquarters location:** Dayton OH. **Other U.S. locations:** El Segundo CA; San Diego CA; Atlanta GA; Columbia SC; Washington DC. **International locations:** Worldwide. **Parent company:** NCR Corporation. **Listed on:** New York Stock Exchange. **Stock exchange symbol:** NCR.

NACCO INDUSTRIES, INC.
5875 Landerbrook Drive, Suite 300, Mayfield Heights OH 44124. 440/449-9624. **Fax:** 440/449-9561. **Contact:** Human Resources. **E-mail address:** hr@naccoind.com. **World Wide Web address:** http://www.nacco.com. **Description:** Produces and markets a variety of products for industrial and consumer markets. The company manufactures forklift trucks and produces coal from four surface mines in North Dakota, Texas, and Louisiana. NACCO also makes household appliances including blenders, food processors, electric knives, toasters, coffeemakers, and irons under the brand names Hamilton Beach and Proctor-Silex. The company operates more than 100 Kitchen Collection factory outlets nationwide that sell kitchenware and appliances. **NOTE:** Resumes may be submitted by mail, fax, or e-mail. **Corporate headquarters location:** This location. **Listed on:** New York Stock Exchange. **Stock exchange symbol:** NC.

NASA (NATIONAL AERONAUTICS AND SPACE ADMINISTRATION)
21000 Brookpark Road, Cleveland OH 44142. 216/433-4000. **Contact:** Personnel. **World Wide Web address:** http://www.nasa.gov. **Description:** A federal aeronautical facility. **Other area locations:** Sandusky OH.

NASH FINCH COMPANY
6300 Creek Road, Cincinnati OH 45242-4107. 513/793-6300. **Fax:** 513/792-6499. **Contact:** Human Resources. **E-mail address:** careers@nashfinch.com. **World Wide Web address:** http://www.nashfinch.com. **Description:** Engaged in wholesale and retail distribution. The wholesale distribution segment supplies products to supermarkets, military bases, convenience stores, and other customers nationwide. The retail distribution segment consists of approximately 128 retail stores. Nash Finch's corporate stores operate under the names Econofoods, Sun Mart, Family Thrift Center, Food Folks, and Easter's. **Corporate headquarters location:** Edina MN. **Listed on:** NASDAQ. **Stock exchange symbol:** NAFC.

NATIONAL CITY BANK
155 East Broad Street, Columbus OH 43251. 614/463-7605. **Contact:** Recruitment Office. **World Wide Web address:** http://www.nationalcity.com. **Description:** A commercial bank. **Positions advertised include:** Senior Database Consultant; Customer Service Representative. **Other U.S. locations:** IN; KY, PA. **Parent company:** National City Corporation (Cleveland OH) is a major bank holding company. **Listed on:** New York Stock Exchange. **Stock exchange symbol:** NCC.

NATIONAL CITY BANK/NORTHWEST
P.O. Box 1688, 405 Madison Avenue, Toledo OH 43604. 419/259-7700. **Contact:** Human Resources. **World Wide Web address:** http://www.nationalcity.com. **Description:** A commercial bank. **Positions advertised:** Business Banking Representative; Private Banker; WM Senior Associate. **Other U.S. locations:** IN; KY. **Parent company:** National City Corporation (Cleveland OH) is a major bank holding company. **Listed on:** New York Stock Exchange. **Stock exchange symbol:** NCC.

NATIONAL CITY CORPORATION
1900 East Ninth Street, 4th Floor, Cleveland OH 44114-3484. 216/202-2000. **Contact:** Human Resources. **World Wide Web address:** http://www.national-city.com. **Description:** A major bank holding company. **Positions advertised include:** Analyst Programmer Consultant; Audit Manager; Bank Operator; Bank Protection Manager. **Corporate headquarters location:** This location. **Other U.S. locations:** IN; KY. **Operations at this facility include:** Administration; Regional Headquarters; Research and Development; Sales; Service. **Listed on:** New York Stock Exchange. **Stock exchange symbol:** NCC. **Number of employees at this location:** 4,300. **Number of employees nationwide:** 33,000.

NATIONAL LIME & STONE COMPANY
P.O. Box 120, 551 Lake Cascade Parkway, Findlay OH 45840. 419/422-4341. **Contact:** Hiring Manager. **World Wide Web address:** http://www.natlime.com. **Description:** Engaged in the production of crushed stone, construction aggregates, and industrial minerals. National Lime & Stone Company also produces a variety of specialty dolomite-based minerals for the glass and steel industries. The company's products are primarily used for acid neutralization and pollution control; agricultural and lawn care applications; environmental remediation; and construction and industrial applications. Founded in 1903. **Corporate headquarters location:** This location. **Other area locations:** Statewide.

NATIONWIDE ADVERTISING SERVICE INC.
411 Vine Street, Suite 4510, Cincinnati OH 45202. 513/241-3121. **Fax:** 513/241-6643. **Contact:** Personnel. **World Wide Web address:** http://www.hrads.com. **Description:** An independent, full-service advertising agency that specializes exclusively in human resource communications, promotions, and advertising. The company offers consultation, campaign planning, ad placement, research, and creative production. **Corporate headquarters location:** Cleveland OH. **Other area locations:** Cleveland OH; Columbus OH. **Other U.S. locations:** Nationwide.

NATIONWIDE INSURANCE ENTERPRISE
One Nationwide Plaza, Columbus OH 43215-2220. 614/249-7111. **Contact:** Recruiting. **World Wide Web address:** http://www.nationwide.com. **Description:** Engaged in the sale of automobile, life, group, and business insurance. **Positions advertised include:** Executive Secretary; Senior Administrative Secretary; Senior Marketing Analyst; Marketing Manager; Accounting Division Manager; Finance Officer. **Corporate headquarters location:** This location. **Operations at this facility include:** Administration; Sales; Service. **Other U.S. locations:** Nationwide.

NAVISTAR INTERNATIONAL TRANSPORTATION CORPORATION
P.O. Box 600, Springfield OH 45501. 937/390-2800. **Physical address:** 6125 Urbana Road, Springfield OH 45502. **Contact:** Employment Office. **World Wide Web address:** http://www.internationaldelivers.com. **Description:** A manufacturer of large- and medium-sized heavy-duty trucks, chassis, and mid-range diesel engines. Other operations include financing for dealers and customers, service operations, and replacement parts distribution. The company operates seven production facilities in the United States and one in Canada and sells its products throughout more than 70 countries. **Listed on:** New York Stock Exchange. **Stock exchange symbol:** NAV.

NEFF COMPANY
P.O. Box 218, 645 Pine Street, Greenville OH 45331. 937/548-3194. **Toll-free phone:** 800/232-6333. **Fax:** 937/316-3480. **Contact:** Joseph P. Andros, Vice President of Human Resources. **World Wide Web address:** http://www.neffco.com. **Description:** A manufacturer of sports awards. The company also carries a line of recognition products such as banners, plaques, jackets, T-shirts, and fleecewear. **Positions advertised include:** Sales Representative. **Corporate headquarters location:** This location. **Operations at this facility include:** Administration; Divisional Headquarters; Manufacturing; Research and Development; Sales.

NELSON STUD WELDING
P.O. Box 4019, Elyria OH 44036-2019. 440/329-0400. **Physical address:** 7900 West Ridge Road, Elyria OH 44036-2019. **Contact:** Human Resources. **World Wide Web address:** http://www.nelsonstud.com. **Description:** Produces standard and automatic stud welding systems and related stud fasteners for the construction, metal-working, and transportation industries; and cold-formed parts and specialized handling equipment.

NEOPROBE CORPORATION
425 Metro Place North, Suite 300, Dublin OH 43017. 614/793-7500. **Toll-free phone:** 800/793-0079. **Fax:** 614/793-7520. **Contact:** Human Resources. **E-mail address:** info@neoprobe.com. **World Wide Web address:** http://www.neoprobe.com. **Description:** Conducts research involving cancer diagnosis and treatment. The company is developing and commercializing products worldwide that are based on its proprietary, core RIGS technology. The RIGS system combines small radiation detectors and disease-targeting agents designed to provide surgeons with immediate information about the location of diseased tissue during surgery. **Listed on:** New York Stock Exchange. **Stock exchange symbol:** NEOP. **CEO:** David Bupp.

NESCO INC.
6140 Parkland Boulevard, Mayfield Heights OH 44124. 440/461-6000. **Fax:** 440/449-3111. **Contact:** Human Resources. **E-mail address:** hq@nescoinc.com. **World Wide Web address:** http://www.nescoinc.com. **Description:** A holding company that operates through three primary groups. The Industrial Group builds process automation and material handling systems. The Service Group specializes in engineering, design, in-house drafting, and documentation. The Real Estate Group owns and manages a variety of commercial and residential buildings. Founded in 1956. **Corporate headquarters location:** This location. **Other area locations:** Akron OH; Dayton OH; Lorain OH; Middleburg Heights; Parma OH. **Operations at this facility include:** Administration. **Number of employees at this location:** 4,000.

NESTLE USA, INC.
5750 Harper Road, Solon OH 44139. 440/248-3600. **Contact:** Plant Human Resources. **World Wide Web address:** http://www.nestleusa.com. **Description:** Nestle USA, Inc. is one of the largest food and beverage companies in the nation. Brand names include Nestle Crunch, Baby Ruth, and Butterfinger candy bars; Taster's Choice and Nescafe coffee; Contadina tomato and refrigerated pastas and sauces; Friskies and Fancy Feast cat food; and Beringer wines. **Positions advertised include:** Process Engineer; Packaging Development Engineer; Market Intelligence Analyst; Sensory Specialist; Paralegal. **Corporate headquarters location:** Glendale CA. **Other area locations:** Cleveland OH; Bainbridge OH. **Operations at this facility include:** This location produces frozen prepared foods. **Parent company:** Nestle S.A.

NEWCOME CORPORATION
9005 Antares Avenue, Columbus OH 43240. 614/848-5688. **Fax:** 614/848-9921. **Contact:** Human Resources. **World Wide Web address:** http://www.newcome.com. **Description:** Designs and installs voice and data distribution systems, primarily to support the communications needs of commercial enterprises in LAN- and WAN-based environments. Founded in 1978. **NOTE:** Entry-level positions are offered. **Positions advertised include:** Audio/Video Lead Technician. **Special programs:** Internships; Apprenticeships; Training. **Internship information:** Newcome Corporation hires interns interested in the areas of LAN/WAN environments and the design, installation, and marketing of audio/video systems. **Corporate headquarters location:** This location. **Other U.S. locations:** Somerville NJ. **Listed on:** Privately held.

NORANDEX REYNOLDS DISTRIBUTION COMPANY
8450 South Bedford Road, P.O. Box 8000, Macedonia OH 44056. 330/468-2200. **Fax:** 330/468-8116. **Contact:** Personnel Manager. **World Wide Web address:** http://www.norandex.com. **Description:** Norandex Reynolds, Inc. designs, develops, manufactures, and markets exterior building products for the construction and remodeling industries. The company's products include aluminum, steel, and vinyl siding; aluminum, wood, and vinyl window and door products; gutters and downspouts; coil stock, and related outdoor building products. **Corporate headquarters location:** This location.

NORDSON CORPORATION
100 Nordson Drive, Amherst OH 44001. 440/985-4000. **Contact:** Beth Phelan, Human Resources. **E-mail address:** bphelan@nordson.com. **World Wide Web address:** http://www.nordson.com. **Description:** Engineers, manufactures, and markets sophisticated systems that apply liquid and powder coatings, sealants, and adhesives to consumer and industrial products during manufacturing processes. **Special programs:** Internships. **Corporate headquarters location:** Westlake OH. **Other U.S. locations:** AL; CA; GA; OH; RI. **International locations:** China; Germany; The Netherlands; United Kingdom. **Operations at this facility include:** Administration; Divisional Headquarters; Manufacturing; Sales; Service. **Listed on:** NASDAQ. **Stock exchange symbol:** NDSN. **Number of employees worldwide:** 3,500.

NORMAN-SPENCER McKERNAN AGENCY, INC.
10501 Success Lane, Dayton OH 45458. 937/885-5053. **Fax:** 937/885-6102. **Contact:** Sandra Welker, Vice President. **E-mail address:** info@nsminc.com. **World Wide Web address:** http://www.nsminc.com. **Description:** An insurance brokerage house. Founded in 1929. **Corporate headquarters location:** Conshohocken PA. **Parent company:** Norman-Spencer, Inc. **Operations at this facility include:** Administration; Sales; Service.

NORTH COAST ENERGY, INC.
1993 Case Parkway, Twinsburg OH 44087-2343. 330/425-2330. **Toll-free phone:** 800/645-6427. **Fax:** 330/405-3298. **Contact:** Human Resources. **World Wide Web address:** http://www.northcoastenergy.com. **Description:** An independent company that explores and creates partnerships with natural gas and oil acquisition opportunities. It is affiliated with NUON International BV. Founded in 1981. **Corporate headquarters location:** Cleveland OH. **Listed on:** NASDAQ. **Stock exchange symbol:** NCEB.

NORTHROP GRUMMAN
TASC INC.
2555 University Boulevard, Fairborn OH 45324. 937/426-1040. **Fax:** 937/426-8888. **Contact:** Human Resources. **World Wide Web address:** http://www.tasc.com. **Description:** Offers computer consulting services to businesses and the government. **Parent company:** Northrop Grumman Corporation. **Listed on:** New York Stock Exchange. **Stock exchange symbol:** NOC.

NORWALK FURNITURE CORPORATION
100 Furniture Parkway, Norwalk OH 44857-9599. 419/744-3200. **Contact:** Human Resources Department. **World Wide Web address:** http://www.norwalkfurniture.com. **Description:** Manufactures and markets customized upholstered furniture. The company markets its products under the trade names Norwalk, J. Raymond, and Hickory Hill. Founded in 1902. **Corporate headquarters location:** This location.

NOVAR CONTROLS CORPORATION
6060 Rockside Woods Boulevard, Suite 4000, Cleveland OH 44321. 216/682-1600. **Toll-free phone:** 800/348-1235. **Contact:** Human Resources. **E-mail address:** info@novarcontrols.com. **World Wide Web address:** http://www.novarcontrols.com. **Description:** A manufacturer of building management control systems and software.

NOVEON HILTON DAVIS, INC.
2235 Langdon Farm Road, Cincinnati OH 45237-4790. 513/841-4000. **Fax:** 513/841-4900. **Contact:** Human Resources. **World Wide Web address:** http://www.noveoninc.com. **Description:** Manufactures a variety of chemical intermediates including pigments, dyes, and food colorings. **Corporate headquarters location:** Cleveland OH. **Parent company:** Noveon Inc. **Operations at this facility include:** Manufacturing; Research and Development; Sales; Service.

OATEY COMPANY
4565 Industrial Parkway, Cleveland OH 44135. 216/688-1517. **Toll-free phone:** 800/321-9532. **Fax:** 216/267-6538. **Contact:** Human Resources Department. **World Wide Web address:** http://www.oatey.com. **Description:** Manufactures plumbing and consumer hardware. Since 1916.

OBERLIN COLLEGE
173 West Lorain Street, Oberlin OH 44074. 440/775-8121. **Fax:** 440/775-8683. **Contact:** Human Resources. **World Wide Web address:** http://www.oberlin.edu. **Description:** A four-year, liberal arts college with approximately 2,800 students. **NOTE:** To contact human resources directly call: 440/775-8430. **Positions advertised include:** Programmer Analyst; Assistant Director, Housing Administration; Administrative Technician; Assistant Professor, Classics; Professor, Musicology; Professor, American Literature; Professor, Mathematics. **Special Programs:** Internships. **Office hours:** Monday – Friday, 8:30 a.m. – 4:30 p.m.

OFFICEMAX
3605 Warrensville Center Road, Shaker Heights OH 44122-5203. 216/921-6900. **Contact:** Human Resources. **World Wide Web address:** http://www.officemax.com. **Description:** A retail store specializing in the sale of office supplies and equipment. **Positions advertised include:** Shipping/Receiving Clerk; Production Analyst; Production Artist; Senior Staff Accountant; Unix Systems Administrator; Business Analyst; Loss Prevention Manager; Senior Category Manager. **Corporate headquarters location:** This location. **Listed on:** New York Stock Exchange. **Stock exchange symbol:** OMX.

OGLEBAY NORTON COMPANY
1001 Lakeside Avenue, 15th Floor, Cleveland OH 44114-2598. 216/861-3300. **Fax:** 216/861-2863. **Contact:** Human Resources. **E-mail address:** info@oglebaynorton.com. **World Wide Web address:** http://www.oglebaynorton.com. **Description:** Mines, develops, processes, and distributes industrial minerals to the environmental, construction, and lawn and garden markets. The company operates through four business segments: Industrial Sands, Lime and Limestone, Marine Services, and Specialty Minerals. Founded in 1854. **Corporate headquarters location:** This location. **Listed on:** NASDAQ. **Stock exchange symbol:** OGLE.

OHIO ART COMPANY
P.O. Box 111, Bryan OH 43506. 419/636-3141. **Physical address:** One Toy Street, Bryan OH 43506. **Fax:** 419/636-7614. **Contact:** Personnel Director. **E-mail address:** info@world-of-toys.com. **World Wide Web address:** http://www.world-of-toys.com. **Description:** Manufactures a variety of metal products including filing equipment and

children's toys. **Listed on:** American Stock Exchange. **Stock exchange symbol:** OAR. **Chairman and CEO:** William C. Killgallon. **Number of employees at this location:** 191.

THE OHIO CASUALTY GROUP
9450 Seward Road, Fairfield OH 45014. 513/867-3000. **Toll-free Phone:** 800/THE-OHIO x2034. **Fax:** 513/603-7900. **Contact:** Human Resources. **World Wide Web address:** http://www.ocas.com. **Description:** An insurance holding company. The Ohio Casualty Group is licensed to do business nationwide but is concentrated mainly in New Jersey, Pennsylvania, Ohio, and Kentucky. The Group is an underwriter of universal and personal life insurance, business life insurance, pension and profit sharing plans, and retirement annuities. **Corporate headquarters location:** This location. **Subsidiaries include:** The Ohio Casualty Insurance Company is the original operating company of the six companies that make up OCG. The remaining companies include: West American Insurance Company; American Fire and Casualty Company; Ohio Security Insurance Company; Avomark Insurance Company; and Ohio Casualty of New Jersey, Inc. **Listed on:** NASDAQ. **Stock exchange symbol:** OCAS.

OHIO DEPARTMENT OF JOBS AND FAMILY SERVICES (ODJFS)
30 East Broad Street, 31st Floor, Columbus OH 43215. 614/466-6947. **Contact:** Human Resources. **World Wide Web address:** http://jfs.ohio.gov/. **Description:** A job center run by the state government. **Corporate headquarters location:** This location.

OHIO MUTUAL INSURANCE GROUP
UNITED OHIO INSURANCE COMPANY
1725 Hopley Avenue, P.O. Box 111, Bucyrus OH 44820. 419/562-3011. **Contact:** Mike Horvath, Vice President of Human Resources. **Fax:** 877/276-5657. **E-mail address:** hr@omig.com. **World Wide Web address:** http://www.omig.com. **Description:** Specializes in providing fire and related insurance coverage to a wide variety of clients. **Corporate headquarters location:** This location.

OHIO NORTHERN UNIVERSITY
525 South Main Street, Ada OH 45810. 419/772-2000. **Fax:** 419/772-1932. **Contact:** Personnel. **E-mail address:** personnel@onu.edu. **World Wide Web address:** http://www.onu.edu. **Description:** Ohio Northern University is organized into five colleges. The Getty College of Arts and Sciences is organized into 15 different departments. The T.J. Smull College of Engineering is organized into the departments of civil, electrical, and mechanical engineering. The Raabe College of Pharmacy is organized into the departments of pharmacy practice and pharmaceutical and biomedical sciences. The College of Business Administration offers majors in accounting, international business and economics, and management. The Pettit College of Law awards the Juris Doctor degree. **NOTE:** Contact the Academic Affairs Office for faculty positions. **Positions advertised include:** Admissions Counselor.

OHIO STATE UNIVERSITY
250 Northwood/High Building, 2231 North High Street, Columbus OH 43201. 614/292-9380. **Contact:** Employment Services. **E-mail address:** employment@hr.osu.edu. **World Wide Web address:** http://www.osu.edu. **Description:** A leading teaching and researching university offering more than 170 undergraduate programs and more than 200 graduate areas of study. Ohio State University has an enrollment of 48,000 students at its main campus in Columbus. Established in 1870. **Positions advertised include:** Administrative Associate; Research Assistant; Office Associate; Food Services Manager; Dental Assistant; Academic Studies Coordinator; Librarian; Senior Lecturer, English; TV Producer; Videographer. **Other area locations:** Lima; Mansfield; Marion; Newark; Wooster. **Number of employees at this location:** 18,000.

OHIO STATE UNIVERSITY MEDICAL CENTER
THE ARTHUR G. JAMES CANCER HOSPITAL & RESEARCH INSTITUTE
164 Doan Hall, 410 West 10th Avenue, Columbus OH 43210. 614/293-4995. **Fax:** 614/293-3080. **Recorded jobline:** 614/293-4900. **Contact:** Human Resources. **E-mail address:** recruitment@medctr.osu.edu. **World Wide Web address:** http://www.jamesline.com. **Description:** An academic medical center. The Arthur G. James Cancer Hospital & Research Institute (also at this location) is a 160-bed treatment and research facility that provides care to oncology patients. **Positions advertised include:** Nurse Manager; Oncology Nurse; Licensed Radiation Therapist; Dosimetrist; Patient Care Associate; Coding Specialist; Research Associate. **Special programs:** Internships. **Number of employees at this location:** 4,500.

OHIO STATE UNIVERSITY VETERINARY HOSPITAL
601 Tharp Street, Columbus OH 43210. 614/292-6661. **Contact:** Human Resources. **World Wide Web address:** http://www.vet.ohio-state.edu. **Description:** A full-service animal hospital with services ranging from vaccinations to major surgery and cancer treatment. The hospital provides treatment for pets and small animals, as well as large farm animals, and also supports an equine center.

OHIO UNIVERSITY
169 West Union Street, Athens OH 45701-2979. 740/593-1636. **Fax:** 740/593-0386. **Recorded jobline:** 740/593-4080. **Contact:** Human Resources. **World Wide Web address:** http://www.uhr.ohiou.edu. **Description:** A four year university. 16,350 undergraduate students, with 276 majors and 775 full-time faculty. Established in 1804. **Positions advertised include:** Resident Director; Assistant Resident Director; Molecular Biology Technician; Custodial Services Manager; Assistant Manager, Dining Services; Assistant Professor, Nursing; Visiting Assistant Professor, Psychology; Assistant Professor, English; Assistant Professor, Economics; Visiting Assistant Professor, Chemistry.

OMNICARE PHARMACY OF PERRYSBURG
P.O. Box 1030, Perrysburg OH 43552-1030. 419/661-2200. **Physical address:** 7643 Ponderosa Road, Perrysburg OH 43551. **Contact:** Human Resources Department. **World Wide Web address:** http://www.omnicarewesthaven.com. **Description:** Distributes pharmaceuticals to nursing homes.

OMNOVA SOLUTIONS INC.
175 Ghent Road, Fairlawn OH 44333-3300. 330/869-4200. **Contact:** Staffing. **World Wide Web address:** http://www.omnova.com. **Description:** Omnova Solutions Inc. is a leading designer and producer of decorative and functional surfaces, coatings, and specialty chemicals. The company operates in two business segments: Decorative and Building Products, and Performance Chemicals. The Decorative and Building Products segment manufactures commercial wallcoverings, industrial films, vinyl and paper laminates, and coated fabrics that are used in office buildings, schools, hospitals, and hotels. The Performance Chemicals segment supplies emulsion polymers and specialty chemicals that are used as binders, coatings, adhesives and additives by various makers of paper, textiles, and carpet. **Corporate headquarters location:** This location. **Listed on:** New York Stock Exchange. **Stock exchange symbol:** OMN. **President and CEO:** Kevin M. McMullen.

OPEN TEXT INC.
6500 Emerald Parkway, Suite 200, Dublin OH 43016. 614/761-8083. **Toll-free phone:** 800/328-2648. **Fax:** 614/761-7290. **Contact:** Human Resources Manager. **E-mail address:** careers@opentext.com. **World Wide Web address:** http://www.opentext.com. **Description:** Develops document management and text retrieval systems. Founded in 1991. **NOTE:** Candidates should apply by completing the online application form. **Positions advertised include:** Production Specialist. **Corporate headquarters location:** Bannockburn IL. **Listed on:** NASDAQ. **Stock exchange symbol:** OTEX. **Number of employees worldwide:** 1,000.

ORMET PRIMARY ALUMINUM CORPORATION
P.O. Box 176, Hannibal OH 43931. 740/483-1381. **Physical address:** State Route 7, Hannibal OH 43931. **Fax:** 740/483-2622. **Contact:** Human Resources. **World Wide Web address:** http://www.ormet.com. **Description:** A producer of primary aluminum that is sold in the form of ingot or extrusion billet. **Corporate headquarters location:** Wheeling WV. **Operations at this facility include:** Accounting/Auditing; Management Support; Sales.

OWENS CORNING
World Headquarters, One Owens Corning Parkway, Toledo OH 43659-0001. 419/248-8000. **Contact:** Personnel. **World Wide Web address:** http://www.owenscorning.com. **Description:** Manufactures and sells thermal and acoustical insulation products including insulation for appliances, glass fiber roofing shingles, roof insulation, and industrial asphalt. Other products include windows, glass fiber textile yarns, wet process chopped strands and specialty mats, and polyester resins. **NOTE:** Candidates can search and apply for a position online. **Positions advertised include:** Market Development Manager; Project Management Leader; Division Operations Leader; Financial Process Leader; Director, Labor and Employee Relations; Asphalt Process Engineer; Treasury Analyst; Customer Service Specialist. **Special programs:** Internships. **Corporate headquarters location:** This location. **Subsidiaries include:** Barbcorp, Inc.; Dansk-Svensk Glasfiber AS; Eric Co.; European Owens-Corning Fiberglas SA; IPM Inc.; Kitsons Insulations Products Ltd.; Owens-Corning AS; Owens-Corning Building Products; Owens-Corning FSC, Inc.; and Owens-Corning Finance. **Listed on:** New York Stock Exchange. **Stock exchange symbol:** OWC. **CEO:** Glen H. Hiner.

OWENS-ILLINOIS, INC.
One SeaGate, Toledo OH 43666. 419/247-5000. **Fax:** 419/247-7107. **Contact:** Human Resources. **E-mail address:** resumes@owens-ill.com. **World Wide Web address:** http://www.o-i.com. **Description:** A worldwide manufacturer of glass and plastic packaging for industrial use. **NOTE:** Resumes may be submitted online, via e-mail, or by mail or fax. **Corporate headquarters location:** This location. **Other area locations:** Perrysburg OH. **Subsidiaries include:** Owens-Brockway Glass. **Operations at this facility include:** Administration; Research and Development; Sales; Service. **Listed on:** New York Stock Exchange. **Stock exchange symbol:** OI. **Number of employees nationwide:** 20,000.

PCC AIRFOILS, INC.
3860 Union Avenue SE, Minerva OH 44657. 330/868-6441. **Contact:** Human Resources. **E-mail address:** pcchr@pccair.com. **World Wide Web address:** http://www.pccair.com. **Description:** Produces airfoils for commercial and military engines and for land-based gas turbines. Virtually all airfoils are made of superalloys, which are produced internally via vacuum melting. PCC facilities blend ceramic material for core and shell mold systems. The company is engaged in producing preformed ceramic cores for investment casting. **Corporate headquarters location:** Beachwood OH. **Other area locations:** Crooksville OH. **Parent company:** Precision Castparts Corporation (Portland OR). **Listed on:** New York Stock Exchange. **Stock exchange symbol:** PCC. **Number of employees worldwide:** 10,000.

PCC AIRFOILS, INC.
29501 Clayton Avenue, Wickliffe OH 44092. 440/585-3100. **Fax:** 440/585-6961. **Contact:** Human Resources. **World Wide Web address:** http://www.pccsmp.com. **Description:** Produces airfoils for commercial and military engines and for land-based gas turbines. Virtually all airfoils are made of superalloys, which are produced internally via vacuum melting. PCC facilities blend ceramic material for core and shell mold systems. The company is engaged in producing preformed ceramic cores for investment casting. **Positions advertised include:** Sales Manager. **Corporate headquarters location:** Beachwood OH. **Parent company:** Precision Castparts Corporation (Portland OR). **Listed on:** New York Stock Exchange. **Stock exchange symbol:** PCP. **Number of employees at this location:** 600. **Number of employees worldwide:** 10,000.

PCC AIRFOILS, INC.
16601 Euclid Avenue, Cleveland OH 44112. 216/692-7900. **Fax:** 216/692-7931. **Contact:** Bob Stewart, Human Resources Director. **E-mail address:** rstewart@pccsri.com. **World Wide Web address:** http://www.pccsmp.com. **Description:** Produces airfoils for commercial and military engines and for land-based gas turbines. Virtually all airfoils are made of superalloys, which are produced internally via vacuum melting. PCC facilities blend ceramic material for core and shell mold systems. The company is engaged in producing preformed ceramic cores for investment casting. **Corporate headquarters location:** Beachwood OH. **Parent company:** Precision Castparts Corporation (Portland OR). **Listed on:** New York Stock Exchange. **Stock exchange symbol:** PCP. **Number of employees worldwide:** 10,000.

PNC BANK
201 East Fifth Street, 6th Floor, Cincinnati OH 45202. 513/651-8534. **Recorded jobline:** 513/651-8500. **Contact:** Human Resources. **World Wide Web address:** http://www.pncbank.com. **Description:** A full-service bank. **Positions advertised include:** Senior Portfolio Manager; Sales and Service Specialist. **Parent company:** PNC Financial Corporation (Pittsburgh PA).

PPG INDUSTRIES, INC.
COATINGS AND RESINS DIVISION
3800 West 143rd Street, Cleveland OH 44111-4901. 216/671-0050. **Contact:** Human Resources. **World Wide Web address:** http://www.ppg.com. **Description:** Supplies products for manufacturing, building, automotive, processing, and numerous other world industries. The company manufactures decorative and protective coatings, flat glass and fabricated glass products, continuous-strand fiberglass, and industrial and specialty chemicals. Founded in 1883. **NOTE:** Candidates can search and apply for jobs online. **Positions advertised include:** Sales Representative. **Corporate headquarters location:** Pittsburgh PA. **International locations:** Canada; China; France; Germany; Ireland; Italy; Mexico; The Netherlands; Portugal; Spain; Taiwan; United Kingdom. **Listed on:** New York Stock Exchange. **Stock exchange symbol:** PPG. **Number of employees worldwide:** 35,000.

PARK-OHIO INDUSTRIES, INC.
23000 Euclid Avenue, Cleveland OH 44117. 216/692-7200. **Contact:** Human Resources. **World Wide Web address:** http://www.pkoh.com. **Description:** Manufactures plastic containers, molded plastic leisure products, forged and machined products, aluminum permanent mold castings, induction heating systems, and industrial rubber products. Park-Ohio Industries' transportation segment includes forged and machined products, induction heating systems, aluminum permanent mold castings, and industrial rubber products. **Corporate headquarters location:** This location. **Other area locations:** Wellington OH. **Subsidiaries include:** Bennett Industries manufactures plastic pails for packages of food, paint, and building materials; Castle Rubber Company manufactures rubber products including roll coverings, tank linings, and pump parts; General Aluminum Manufacturing Company manufactures aluminum mold castings for the transportation industry; Kay Home Products manufactures barbecue grills, lawn spreaders, and patio tables; Tocco Inc. manufactures heating systems for heat treating, surface hardening, and forging. **Number of employees nationwide:** 1,400.

PARKER-DAYCO INDUSTRIAL
P.O. Box 1004, Dayton OH 45401-1004. 937/226-7000. **Fax:** 937/226-8698. **Contact:** Human Resources Manager. **World Wide Web address:** http://www.dayco.com. **Description:** A worldwide manufacturer and distributor of a wide range of highly-engineered rubber and plastic products, many of which are used for replacement purposes. Principal markets include the agricultural, automotive, construction, energy, printing, mining, textile, and transportation industries. **Office hours:** Monday - Friday, 8:00 a.m. - 5:00 p.m. **Corporate headquarters location:** This location. **Other U.S. locations:** Nationwide. **International locations:** Worldwide. **Parent company:** Dayco Products Inc.

PARKER HANNIFIN CORPORATION
6035 Parkland Boulevard, Cleveland OH 44124-4141. 216/896-3000. **Fax:** 216/896-4000. **Contact:** Human Resources. **World Wide Web address:** http://www.parker.com. **Description:** Parker Hannifin Corporation makes motion control products including fluid power systems, electromechanical controls, and related components. The Motion and Control Group makes hydraulic cylinders, actuators, and automation devices to remove contaminants from air, fuel, oil, water, and other fluids. The Fluid Connectors Group makes connectors, tube and hose fittings, hoses, and couplers that transmit fluid. The Seal Group makes sealing devices, gaskets, and packing that insure leak-proof connections. The Automotive and Refrigeration Groups make components for use in industrial and automotive air conditioning and refrigeration systems. The Aerospace Group makes hydraulic and pneumatic fuel systems and components. **Positions advertised include:** Buyer/Planner. **Corporate headquarters location:** This location. **International locations:** Worldwide. **Operations at this facility include:** This location manufactures hydraulic and pneumatic components and systems for the fluid industry. **Listed on:** New York Stock Exchange. **Stock exchange symbol:** PH. **Annual sales:** More than $6 billion. **Number of employees worldwide:** 46,787.

PARKER HANNIFIN CORPORATION
725 North Beech Street, Eaton OH 45320. 937/456-5571. **Contact:** Human Resources. **World Wide Web address:** http://www.parker.com. **Description:** Parker Hannifin makes motion control products including fluid power systems, electromechanical controls, and related components. The Motion and Control Group makes hydraulic pumps, power units, control valves, accumulators, cylinders, actuators, and automation devices to remove contaminants from air, fuel, oil, water, and other fluids. The Fluid Connectors Group makes connectors, tube and hose fittings, hoses, and couplers that transmit fluid. The Seal Group makes sealing devices, gaskets and packing that insure leak-proof connections. Automotive and Refrigeration Groups make components for use in industrial and automotive air conditioning and refrigeration systems. The Aerospace Group makes hydraulic, pneumatic, and fuel systems and components. **Corporate headquarters location:** Cleveland OH. **Operations at this facility include:** This location manufactures tube fittings and other components for industrial applications. **Listed on:** New York Stock Exchange. **Stock exchange symbol:** PH.

PARMA COMMUNITY GENERAL HOSPITAL
7007 Powers Boulevard, Parma OH 44129. 440/743-4900. **Fax:** 440/743-4092. **Recorded jobline:** 440/743-4005. **Contact:** Human Resources Department. **E-mail address:** employment@parmahospital.org. **World Wide Web address:** http://www.parmahospital.org. **Description:** A 339-bed, acute care hospital. **NOTE:** Resumes are accepted by mail, fax, or e-mail. **Positions advertised include:** Radiology Scheduler; Radiology Transcriptionist; Occupational Therapist; Physical Therapist; Pharmacist; Licensed Practical Nurse; Certified Physician Assistant; MRI Technologist; Operating Room Technician; Registered Nurse. **President/CEO:** Patricia A. Ruflin. **Number of employees at this location:** 2,000.

PARTS ASSOCIATES INC.
12420 Plaza Drive, Cleveland OH 44130. 216/433-7700. **Toll-free phone:** 800/321-1128. **Fax:** 216/433-9051. **Contact:** Howard Gillespie, Human Resources Department. **World Wide Web address:** http://www.pai-net.com. **Description:** A national distributor serving the automotive, fleet, industrial, maintenance, mining, and off-road equipment markets. Founded in 1948. **Positions advertised include:** Sales Representative.

PATHEON PHARMACEUTICALS
2110 East Galbraith Road, Cincinnati OH 45215. 513/948-9111. **Contact:** Human Resources Department. **E-mail address:** amy.backscheider@patheon.ca **World Wide Web address:** http://www.patheon.com. **Description:** Develops, manufactures, and markets pharmaceutical products. The company specializes in products related to allergies, arthritis, cardiology, diabetes, infectious diseases, oncology, and respiratory disorders. **Corporate headquarters location:** Mississauqua Ontario.

PATIENT FOCUS SYSTEMS (PFS)
PASCO GROUP
2096 Ravenna Street, Hudson OH 44236-4400. 330/655-2907. **Toll-free phone:** 800/787-3477. **Fax:** 330/650-0613. **Contact:** Director of Business Support. **World Wide Web address:** http://www.pasco-group.com. **Description:** PFS provides software products and services for the medical industry. **Parent company:** PASCO Group (also at this location) is a holding company with interests in a variety of information processing services: Automated Tracking Systems (also at this location) is the country's largest provider of insurance follow-up services; Quality Data Solutions (QDS) provides telemarketing, mail fulfillment, and data capture services; Customer Management Systems offers consulting products and services to automobile sales professionals; Information Management Group (also at this location) is a provider of fully-integrated information systems for the retail industry.

PAULDING COUNTY HOSPITAL
1035 West Wayne Street, Paulding OH 45879. 419/399-4080. **Fax:** 419/399-5560. **Contact:** Amy Lieb, Director of Human Resources. **E-mail address:** pchhr@saa.net. **World Wide Web address:** http://www.pauldingcountyhospital.com. **Description:** A nonprofit, county-supported hospital offering a wide range of services. **NOTE:** Entry-level positions and second and third shifts are offered. **Special programs:** Internships; Summer Jobs. **Office hours:** Monday - Friday, 8:30 a.m. - 4:30 p.m. **CEO:** Gary W. Adkins. **Number of employees at this location:** 210.

PAYCHEX, INC.
5450 Frantz Road, Suite 100, Dublin OH 43016. 614/210-0400. **Contact:** Human Resources. **World Wide Web address:** http://www.paychex.com. **Description:** A payroll processing and payroll tax preparation company for small- to medium-sized businesses. Started in 1971. **NOTE:** See website for instructions on how to submit a resume via e-mail. Resumes can also be mailed or faxed to specific office locations. **Positions advertised include:** Account Executive; Branch Manager; Client Service Representative; Computer Operator; Distribution Specialist; District Sales Assistant; Payroll Specialist; Receptionist; Sales Representative; Sales Management; Technical Support Specialist. **Corporate headquarters:** Rochester NY. **Other area locations:** Uniontown OH; Cincinnati OH; Miamisburg OH; Holland OH. **Other U.S. locations:** Nationwide. **CEO:** B. Thomas Golisano.

PECHINEY PLASTIC PACKAGING INC.
1972 Akron Peninsula Road, Akron OH 44313. 330/923-5282. **Fax:** 216/281-2340. **Contact:** Human Resources. **E-mail address:** careers@pechineyplasticpackaging.com. **World Wide Web address:** http://www.pechineyplasticpackaging.com. **Description:** Develops and manufactures plastic flexible packaging such as single and multilayer films and laminations, bags, lidstock, pouches, and thermoformed trays. The company markets its products to the food, healthcare, meat and dairy, and specialty markets. **Corporate headquarters location:** Chicago, IL. **Other area locations:** West Chester OH; Loveland OH; Bellevue OH. **International locations:** Worldwide. **Parent company:** Pechiney Group.

PENTAIR PUMP GROUP, INC.
dba HYDROMATIC PUMP
1840 South Baney Road, Ashland OH 44805. 419/289-3042. **Contact:** Human Resources. **World Wide Web address:** http://www.hydromatic.com. **Description:** Manufactures wastewater pumps. **Parent company:** Pentair Inc. **Listed on:** New York Stock Exchange. **Stock exchange symbol:** PH.

PENTAIR WATER TREATMENT
220 Park Drive, Chardon OH 44024. 440/286-4116. **Fax:** 440/285-3831. **Contact:** Personnel Manager. **World Wide Web address:** http://www.pentair.com. **Description:** Manufactures water treatment and systems equipment including products for treating, filtering, and storing water. **Parent company:** Pentair Inc. **Listed on:** New York Stock Exchange. **Stock exchange symbol:** PH.

PENTON MEDIA, INC.
Penton Media Building, 1300 East Ninth Street, Cleveland OH 44114. 216/696-7000. **Fax:** 216/696-1752. **Contact:** J.T. Neuffer, Senior Employee Relations Specialist. **E-mail address:** recruiter@penton.com. **World Wide Web address:** http://www.penton.com. **Description:** Penton Media, Inc. is a diversified business media company. Products include 35 business publications; trade shows and conferences; Internet and electronic media; and direct marketing, research, and communications services. **Positions advertised include:** Account Manager. **Special programs:** Internships. **Corporate headquarters location:** This location. **Other U.S. locations:** Chatsworth CA. **Listed on:** New York Stock Exchange. **Stock exchange symbol:** PME.

PHILIPS DISPLAY COMPONENTS COMPANY
700 North Pratt Street, Ottawa OH 45875. 419/523-4321. **Contact:** Human Resources. **Description:** A producer of cathode rays and other components used in the manufacture of television sets. **Corporate headquarters location:** Ann Arbor MI. **Operations at this facility include:** Manufacturing.

PHILIPS MEDICAL SYSTEMS
595 Miner Road, Highland Heights OH 44143. 440/473-3000. **Fax:** 440/483-6784. **Contact:** Human Resources Coordinator. **World Wide Web address:** http://www.philips.com. **Description:** Specializes in the research, design, development, and manufacture of X-ray equipment for the worldwide medical community. **Positions advertised include:** Administrator; Application Support Specialist; Clinical Scientist; Clinical Education Training Specialist; Field Service Engineer. **Special programs:** Internships.

PIERRE FOODS, LLC
9990 Princeton Road, Cincinnati OH 45246. 513/874-8741. **Contact:** Human Resources. **World Wide Web address:** http://www.pierrefoods.com. **Description:** Produces entrees including Wonderbites unbreaded, broiled finger foods; Micro-wiches microwaveable sandwiches; and Hudson Complete Meal Kits. **Parent company:** Fresh Foods, Inc.

PILKINGTON LIBBEY-OWENS-FORD COMPANY
1701 East Broadway, Toledo OH 43605. 419/247-4694. **Contact:** Bret Penrod, General Manager. **E-mail address:** bret.penrod@us.pilkington.com. **World Wide Web address:** http://www.pilkington.com. **Description:** A diversified manufacturer of fluid power and fluid systems components, automotive glass, flat and tinted glass products, and decorative laminates and molded plastics.

PINNACLE DATA SYSTEMS, INC.
6600 Port Road, Groveport OH 43125. 614/748-1150. **Fax:** 614/748-1209. **Contact:** Human Resources. **E-mail address:** jobs@pinnacle.com. **World Wide Web address:** http://www.pinnacle.com. **Description:** Builds custom computers and provides computer repair services. **Positions advertised include:** Program Manager.

THE PLAIN DEALER
Plain Dealer Plaza, 1801 Superior Avenue, Cleveland OH 44114. 216/999-5523. **Fax:** 216/999-6365. **Recorded jobline:** 216/999-4366. **Contact:** Jenny Wilson, Human Resources. **E-mail address:** jwilson@plaind.com. **World Wide Web address:** http://www.plaindealer.com. **Description:** A newspaper publisher. **NOTE:** Candidates interested in editorial positions should contact Margie Frazer, Recruitment and Development Editor. Phone: 216/999-4337. E-mail: mfrazer@plaind.com. . **Special programs:** Internships. **Corporate headquarters location:** This location. **Operations at this facility include:** Administration; Manufacturing; Sales.

PLASTECH
918 South Union Street, Bryan OH 43506. 419/636-4211. **Fax:** 419/633-1824. **Contact:** Marsha Smith, Human Resources Manager. **World Wide Web address:** http://www.plastecheng.com. **Description:** Manufactures plastic injection-molded, blow-molded parts, and metal stampings for the automotive and office furniture industries. **Special programs:** Co-ops. **Office hours:** Monday - Friday, 8:00 a.m. -

5:00 p.m. **Corporate headquarters location:** Dearborn MI. **Other U.S. locations:** IA; IN. **Operations at this facility include:** Administration; Manufacturing; Research and Development; Sales. **Listed on:** Privately held. **CEO:** Julie Brown. **Number of employees at this location:** 560. **Number of employees nationwide:** 2,200.

PLASTIC MOLDINGS CORPORATION
2181 Grand Avenue, Cincinnati OH 45214-1593. 513/921-5040. **Fax:** 513/921-5883. **Contact:** Human Resources. **E-mail address:** info@plasticmoldings.com. **World Wide Web address:** http://www.plasticmoldings.com. **Description:** Manufactures precision-molded plastic parts used in a wide variety of applications including electrical and automotive parts. Founded in 1929. **Corporate headquarters location:** This location.

POLYMER DIAGNOSTICS INC.
33587 Walker Road, Avon Lake OH 44012. 440/930-1520. **Toll-free phone:** 800/438-2335. **Fax:** 440/930-1644. **Contact:** Human Resources. **World Wide Web address:** http://www.polymerdiagnostics.com. **Description:** Manufactures and develops thermoplastic compounds, specialty resins, engineered films, color and additive systems, specialty polymers, rubber compounding, and vinyl compounds. **Corporate headquarters location:** This location.

POLYONE CORPORATION
33587 Walker Road, Avon Lake OH 44012. 440/930-1000. **Fax:** 440/930-3064. **Contact:** Human Resources Department. **World Wide Web address:** http://www.polyone.com. **Description:** Manufactures and develops thermoplastic compounds, specialty resins, engineered films, color and additive systems, specialty polymers, rubber compounding, and vinyl compounds. **NOTE:** Unsolicited resumes are not being accepted at this time. **Positions advertised include:** Senior Finance Manager; Corporate Benefits Manager; Financial Reporting Analyst. **Corporate headquarters location:** This location. **Other U.S. locations:** Nationwide. **International locations:** Worldwide. **Parent company:** M.A. Hanna Company. **Listed on:** New York Stock Exchange. **Stock exchange symbol:** POL.

POLYONE CORPORATION
800 Ken Mar Industrial Parkway, Broadview Heights OH 44147. 440/526-0230. **Toll-free phone:** 800/321-9320. **Fax:** 440/526-3183. **Contact:** Human Resources. **World Wide Web address:** http://www.polyone.com. **Description:** Manufactures and develops thermoplastic compounds, specialty resins, engineered films, color and additive systems, specialty polymers, rubber compounding, and vinyl compounds. **Corporate headquarters location:** Avon Lake OH. **Other U.S. locations:** Nationwide. **International locations:** Worldwide. **Parent company:** M.A. Hanna Company. **Listed on:** New York Stock Exchange. **Stock exchange symbol:** POL.

PORCELAIN PRODUCTS COMPANY
225 North Patterson Street, Carey OH 43316. 419/396-7621. **Fax:** 419/396-7128. **Contact:** Human Resources. **World Wide Web address:** http://www.ppcinsulators.com. **Description:** Manufactures porcelain electrical insulators for both high- and low-voltage applications. **Corporate headquarters location:** This location. **Operations at this facility include:** Administration; Divisional Headquarters; Manufacturing; Sales. **Listed on:** Privately held. **Number of employees at this location:** 110. **Number of employees nationwide:** 220.

PORT CLINTON MANUFACTURING COMPANY
P.O. Box 220, Port Clinton OH 43452-0220. 419/734-2141. **Physical address:** 328 West Perry Street, Port Clinton OH 43452. **Toll-free phone:** 800/366-7262. **Fax:** 419/734-5868. **Contact:** Human Resources. **E-mail address:** pcmc@cros.net. **World Wide Web address:** http://www.pcmfg.net. **Description:** Manufactures hardened ground precision parts, forgings, and castings. **Corporate headquarters location:** This location. **Operations at this facility include:** Administration; Manufacturing; Research and Development; Sales.

WILLIAM POWELL COMPANY
2503 Spring Grove Avenue, Cincinnati OH 45214. 513/852-2000. **Fax:** 513/852-2997. **Contact:** Sally Phelps, Human Resources Coordinator. **E-mail address:** sphelps@powellvalves.com. **World Wide Web address:** http://www.powellvalves.com. **Description:** A manufacturer of pipe fittings, valves, and related products. Established in 1846. **NOTE:** To reach Sally Phelps directly dial: 513/852-2017.

PRECISION METALSMITHS INC.
1081 East 200th Street, Euclid OH 44117. 216/481-8900. **Fax:** 216/481-8903. **Contact:** Personnel. **World Wide Web address:** http://www.precisionmetalsmiths.com. **Description:** Develops and manufactures investment cast metal products. Precision Metalsmiths, Inc. specializes in ferrous and nonferrous alloys such as aluminum, carbon, ductile iron, low alloy, and stainless steel.

PREFORMED LINE PRODUCTS COMPANY
P.O. Box 91129 Cleveland OH 41101. 440/461-5200. **Physical address:** 660 Beta Drive, Cleveland OH 44143. **Fax:** 440/461-2918. **Contact:** Human Resources. **World Wide Web address:** http://www.preformed.com. **Description:** Supplies high-quality cable anchoring and control hardware and systems, overhead and underground splice cases and related products, and fiber-optic splicing and communications systems. The company serves power utility, telecommunications, and cable television industry customers worldwide. Established in 1962 in Australia, joined the USA based company in 1978. **Corporate headquarters:** This location. **International locations:** Worldwide.

PREMIER-FARNELL
TPC WIRE & CABLE
7061 East Independence Valley, Independence OH 44131. 216/525-4300. **Contact:** Corporate Recruiting. **World Wide Web address:** http://www.tpcwire.com. **Description:** A distributor of electronic components used in the production and maintenance of equipment; a supplier of maintenance products for industrial, commercial, and institutional applications; and a manufacturer of fire fighting equipment. Formed in 1996. **Corporate headquarters location:** This location. **Listed on:** New York Stock Exchange. **Stock exchange symbol:** PFP.

PRETTY PRODUCTS INC.
437 Cambridge Road, P.O. Box 6002, Coshocton OH 43812. 740/622-3522. **Contact:** Personnel Director. **Description:** A producer of rubber products for consumers including car accessories and kitchenware. **Subsidiaries include:** Rubber Queen.

PRICEWATERHOUSECOOPERS
B.P. Tower, 27th Floor, 200 Public Square, Cleveland OH 44114-2301. 216/875-3000. **Contact:** Human Resources. **World Wide Web address:** http://www.pricewaterhousecoopers.com. **Description:** One of the largest certified public accounting firms in the world. PricewaterhouseCoopers provides public accounting, business advisory, management consulting, and taxation services. **Positions advertised include:** Senior Associate; Internal Audit Senior Associate; IT Audit Associate; Business Analyst; Tax Manager; Junior Analyst. **Corporate headquarters location:** New York NY. **Other U.S. locations:** Nationwide. **International locations:** Worldwide.

PRICEWATERHOUSECOOPERS
720 East Pete Rose Way, Suite 400, Cincinnati OH 45202. 513/723-4700. **Contact:** Human Resources. **World Wide Web address:** http://www.pricewaterhousecoopers.com. **Description:** One of the largest certified public accounting firms in the world. PricewaterhouseCoopers provides public accounting, business advisory, management consulting, and taxation services. **Corporate headquarters location:** New York NY. **Other U.S. locations:** Nationwide.

PRICEWATERHOUSECOOPERS
100 East Broad Street, Suite 2100, Columbus OH 43215. 614/225-8700. **Contact:** Human Resources. **World Wide Web address:** http://www.pricewaterhousecoopers.com. **Description:** One of the largest certified public accounting firms in the world. PricewaterhouseCoopers provides public accounting, business advisory, management consulting, and taxation services. **Corporate headquarters location:** New York NY. **Other U.S. locations:** Nationwide.

PROCTER & GAMBLE
One Procter & Gamble Plaza, Cincinnati OH 45202. 513/983-1100. **Contact:** Personnel. **World Wide Web address:** http://www.pg.com. **Description:** Procter & Gamble manufactures over 300 laundry, cleaning, paper, beauty, health care, food, and beverage products in more than 140 countries. Brand name products include Cover Girl, Max Factor, Vidal Sassoon, Clearasil, and Noxzema health and beauty products; Pepto-Bismol, Vicks, and NyQuil health care products; Bounce, Downy, Tide, Comet, and Mr. Clean cleaning products; Luvs, Pampers, Always, Tampax, Bounty, Charmin, and Puffs paper products; and Crisco, Folgers, Millstone, Sunny Delight, and Pringles food and beverage products. **Positions advertised include:** Print Production Manager: Finance and Accounting Manager; Human Resources Manager; Pharmaceuticals Attorney; Molecular Biology Researcher; Senior Internal Auditor; Occupational Health Nurse. **Special programs:** Internships. **Corporate headquarters location:** This location. **International locations:** Asia; Canada; Europe; Latin America. **Operations at this facility include:** This location houses administrative offices. **Listed on:** New York Stock Exchange. **Stock exchange symbol:** PG. **Annual sales/revenues:** More than $100 million.

PROGRESSIVE CORPORATION
6300 Wilson Mills Road, Mayfield Village OH 44143. 440/461-5000. **Contact:** Employment Center. **World Wide Web address:** http://www.progressive.com. **Description:** An insurance holding company. **Positions advertised include:** Programmer Analyst; Corporate Attorney; Quality Assurance Analyst; Interior Design Manager; Software Developer; Claims Representative Trainee; Product Manager; Brand Project Specialist; Project Leader; Customer Service Trainee; Compensation Manager. **Special programs:** Internships. **Corporate headquarters location:** This location. **Subsidiaries include:** Progressive Insurance writes auto insurance in 48 states, the District of Columbia, and Canada. **Number of employees worldwide:** 25,834.

PROVIDENT BANK
One East Fourth Street, Mail Stop 550E, Cincinnati OH 45202. 513/579-2205. **Fax:** 513/345-7190. **Recorded jobline:** 513/345-7272. **E-mail address:** humanresources@providentbank.com. **Contact:** Human Resources. **World Wide Web address:** http://www.providentbank.com. **Description:** A full-service commercial bank with 65 branches in Ohio and Kentucky. **NOTE:** Unsolicited resumes are not accepted. Please call the jobline before applying to obtain the appropriate job code to be submitted with your resume. **Positions advertised include:** Assistant Financial Center Manager; Customer Service Representative; Accountant; Business Development Representative; Personal Banker. **Special programs:** Internships. **Corporate headquarters location:** This location. **Other area locations:** Cleveland OH; Columbus OH; Dayton OH. **Other U.S. locations:** CA; FL; KY; MO. **Parent company:** Provident Financial Group, Inc. **Listed on:** NASDAQ. **Stock exchange symbol:** PFGI. **President and CEO:** Robert L. Hoverson. **Number of employees nationwide:** 3,200.

PROVIDENT BANK
PROVIDENT TECHNICAL SERVICES
1111 Superior Avenue, Cleveland OH 44114. 216/694-2332. **Recorded jobline:** 513/345-7272. **Contact:** Human Resources. **World Wide Web address:** http://www.providentbank.com. **Description:** A full-service bank. **NOTE:** All resumes should be sent to Human Resources, One East Fourth Street, Mail Stop 550-E, Cincinnati OH 45202. Resumes can also be faxed to 513/345-7190. **Positions advertised include:** Customer Service Representative. **Corporate headquarters location:** Cincinnati OH. **Other area locations:** Columbus OH; Dayton OH. **Other U.S. locations:** KY. **Parent company:** Provident Financial Group, Inc. **Listed on:** NASDAQ. **Stock exchange symbol:** PFGI. **Number of employees nationwide:** 1,700.

PUBLIC UTILITIES COMMISSION OF OHIO
180 East Broad Street, 10th Floor, Columbus OH 43215-3793. 614/466-7330. **Fax:** 614/728-7065. **Recorded jobline:** 614/644-5656. **Contact:** Human Resources. **World Wide Web address:** http://www.puc.state.oh.us. **Description:** Regulates the state utility companies, railroads, trucking, and Cedar Point Causeway. **Special programs:** Internships. **Corporate headquarters location:** This location. **Operations at this facility include:** Administration. **Number of employees at this location:** 450.

QUATECH
5675 Hudson Industrial Parkway, Hudson OH 44236. 330/655-9000. **Toll-free phone:** 800/553-1170. **Fax:** 330/655-9010. **Contact:** Human Resources. **E-mail address:** resumes@quatech.com. **World Wide Web address:** http://www.quatech.com. **Description:** A manufacturer of a line of communication, data acquisition, PCMCIA, and control products for IBM PC/XT, PC/AT, PS/2, and compatible systems. **Positions advertised include:** Customer Support Engineer; Inside Sales Engineer; Field Sales Engineer; Hardware Engineer. **Corporate headquarters location:** This location. **Other area locations:** Akron OH.

RB&W CORPORATION
2300 Euclid Avenue, Cleveland OH 44117. 216/692-7100. **Contact:** Human Resources. **World Wide Web address:** http://www.rbwmfg.com. **Description:** Manufactures a line of cold-forged nuts and specialty extruded products. **Special programs:** Internships. **Corporate headquarters location:** Cleveland OH. **Other U.S. locations:** Coraopolis PA. **Operations at this facility include:** Manufacturing. **Number of employees at this location:** 200.

RJF INTERNATIONAL CORPORATION
3875 Embassy Parkway, Fairlawn OH 44333. 330/668-7600. **Fax:** 330/668-7701. **Contact:** Human Resources. **E-mail address:** hr@rfjnet.com. **World Wide Web address:** http://www.koroseal.com. **Description:** Manufactures and markets polymer-based products under the Koroseal name. **Positions advertised include:** Sales Representative. **Special programs:** Internships. **Corporate headquarters location:** This location. **Other area locations:** Cincinnati OH; Columbus OH; Marietta OH. **Other U.S. locations:** Livonia MI.

RMI TITANIUM COMPANY
1000 Warren Avenue, Niles OH 44446. 330/652-9951. **Fax:** 330/544-7876. **Contact:** Director of Human Resources. **World Wide Web address:** http://www.rmititanium.com. **Description:** A manufacturer of titanium mill products for use in the aerospace and pipeline industries. **NOTE:** To contact the Human Resources Office directly call: 330/544-7847. **Positions advertised include:** Electrical Engineer; Mechanical Engineer; Metallurgical Engineer. **Corporate headquarters location:** This location. **Parent company:** RTI International Metals. **Listed on:** New York Stock Exchange. **Stock exchange symbol:** RTI. **Annual sales/revenues:** $200 million. **Number of employees at this location:** 685. **Number of employees nationwide:** 1,100.

RMT INC.
5890 Sawmill Road, Suite 100, Dublin OH 43017-1591. 614/793-0026. **Fax:** 614/793-0151. **Contact:** Human Resources. **E-mail address:** rmthr@rmtinc.com. **World Wide Web address:** http://www.rmtinc.com. **Description:** An environmental management firm that builds landfills and tests soil, land, and groundwater. **NOTE:** Resumes are accepted by mail, fax, or e-mail. Unsolicited resumes are not accepted. **Positions advertised include:** Senior Engineer. **Corporate headquarters location:** Madison WI. **Other U.S. locations:** Nationwide.

RPM, INC.
P.O. Box 777, Medina OH 44258. 330/273-5090. **Physical address:** 2628 Pearl Road, Medina OH 44258. **Contact:** Human Resources. **World Wide Web address:** http://www.rpminc.com. **Description:** RPM, Inc. produces protective coatings and a line of nonapparel fabrics and wall coverings. The company participates in five major markets worldwide: industrial waterproofing, industrial corrosion-control, specialty chemicals, consumer do-it-yourself, and consumer hobby and leisure. **Corporate headquarters location:** This location. **Listed on:** New York Stock Exchange. **Stock exchange symbol:** RPM. **Number of employees nationwide:** 3,500. **Number of employees worldwide:** 7,685.

RANGE KLEEN MANUFACTURING INC.
P.O. Drawer 696, Lima OH 45802. 419/331-8000. **Physical address:** 4240 East Road, Lima OH 45807. **Fax:** 419/331-4538. **Contact:** Human Resources Department. **E-mail address:** info@rangekleen.com. **World Wide Web address:** http://www.rangekleen.com. **Description:** Manufactures and markets a wide range of kitchen items and accessories. Range Kleen manufacturing's products include burner covers, broiler pans and grills, canister sets, counter mats, dust pans, hot pads, knobs and elements for ranges, and porcelain and chrome drip pans.

RELIANCE MEDICAL PRODUCTS
3535 Kings Mills Road, Mason OH 45040-2303. 513/398-3937. **Contact:** Personnel. **World Wide Web address:** http://www.reliance-medical.com. **Description:** A medical equipment manufacturer. The company primarily manufactures floor units and related equipment for optometrists.

RESOURCE AMERICA, INC. (RAI)
3500 Massillon Road, Suite 100, Uniontown OH 44685. 330/896-8510. **Contact:** Human Resources. **World Wide Web address:** http://www.resourceamerica.com. **Description:** Resource America, Inc. (RAI) has concentrated its activities in two industries: energy and real estate finance. In energy, RAI produces and transports natural gas and oil from properties it operates. Through a subsidiary, RAI provides well services to others and is the exclusive Ohio, New York, and Pennsylvania distributor of selected production equipment. In real estate, the company owns a portfolio of 12 mortgages with an aggregate face value of over $30 million. **Corporate headquarters location:** Philadelphia PA. **Other U.S. locations:** NY. **Subsidiaries include:** Resource Energy, Inc. **Operations at this facility include:** This location performs accounting functions for oil and gas well operations. **Listed on:** NASDAQ. **Stock exchange symbol:** REXI.

THE REYNOLDS & REYNOLDS COMPANY
115 South Ludlow Street, Dayton OH 45402. 937/485-2000. **Contact:** Human Resources. **World Wide Web address:** http://www.reyrey.com. **Description:** An integrated information systems company providing business services. The company has three major divisions: business forms including continuous-feed forms, lottery and entertainment tickets, and stock forms; computer products with turnkey systems; and financial services. Other products include computerized user systems for vertical marketplaces. Major clients include small businesses, financial institutions, automobile dealers, hospitals, and health care organizations. **NOTE:** Search and apply for positions online. **Positions advertised include:** Automotive Business Consultant; Business Systems Analyst; Senior Database Administrator; Sales Proposal and Process Analyst; Collection Analyst; New Markets Product Manager. **Corporate headquarters location:** This location. **Listed on:** New York Stock Exchange. **Stock exchange symbol:** REY.

RICERCA BIOSCIENCES LLC
7528 Auburn Road, P.O. Box 1000, Concord OH 44077. 440/357-3300. **Toll-free phone:** 888/763-4797. **Fax:** 440/350-7923. **Contact:** Human Resources. **World Wide Web address:** http://www.ricerca.com. **Description:** Provides research and development services on a contract basis to clients primarily in the agricultural, pharmaceutical, and specialty chemicals industries. The company also helps clients develop new products, improve existing products, and support the registration of products for regulatory compliance. **Positions advertised include:** Medical Chemist; Synthetic Chemist; Process Chemist; Chemical Process Development Engineer. **Corporate headquarters location:** This location. **Parent company:** Ishihara Sangyo Kaisha, Ltd. (Japan). **Number of employees at this location:** 300.

RICHARDS INDUSTRIES
dba JORDAN VALVE
3170 Wasson Road, Cincinnati OH 45209. 513/533-5600. **Toll-free phone:** 800/543-7311. **Fax:** 513/533-2583. **Contact:** Human Resources Administrator. **E-mail:** rihr@richardsind.com. **World Wide Web address:** http://www.jordanvalve.com. **Description:** A valve manufacturer. **Positions advertised include:** Regional Sales Manager. **Corporate headquarters location:** This location. **Other U.S. locations:** Frenchburg KY. **Subsidiaries include:** The Metalworking Group (Cincinnati OH). **Operations at this facility include:** Manufacturing. **Listed on:** Privately held. **Number of employees at this location:** 130.

RITTMAN PAPERBOARD
100 Industrial Street, Rittman OH 44270. 330/925-0222. **Contact:** Human Resources. **World Wide Web address:** http://www.caraustar.com. **Description:** A paperboard manufacturing plant. **Corporate headquarters location:** Evanston IL. **Operations at this facility include:** Management Support; Manufacturing. **Number of employees worldwide:** 9,000.

RIVERSIDE METHODIST HOSPITAL
3535 Olentangy River Road, Columbus OH 43214. 614/566-4757. **Fax:** 614/566-6953. **Contact:** Human Resources. **World Wide Web address:** http://www.grmh.org. **Description:** An acute care hospital with a medical staff of 1,200 physicians specializing in cardiac, orthopedic, and maternity services. **NOTE:** Human Resources is located at 550 Thomas Lane, Columbus OH. **Positions advertised include:** Coder; Emergency Room Chart Specialist; Ambulatory Coordinator; Administrative Assistant; Senior Medical Records Associate; Unit Coordinator; Reimbursement Specialist; Clinical Receptionist.

ROADWAY EXPRESS INC.
P.O. Box 471, Akron OH 44309-0471. 330/384-1717. **Physical address:** 1077 Gorge Boulevard, Akron OH 44310. **Contact:** Human Resources. **World Wide Web address:** http://www.roadway.com. **Description:** A leading less-than-truckload motor carrier. **Corporate headquarters location:** This location. **Other area locations:** Cincinnati OH; Copley OH; Dayton OH. **Parent company:** Roadway Corporation. **Listed on:** NASDAQ. **Stock exchange symbol:** ROAD. **Number of employees nationwide:** 24,800.

ROBIN INDUSTRIES, INC.
1265 West 65th Street, Cleveland OH 44102. 216/961-5810. **Fax:** 216.631-7002. **Contact:** Chuck Lizanich, Human Resources Director. **E-mail address:** clizanich@robin-industries.com. **World Wide Web address:** http://www.robin-industries.com. **Description:** Manufactures molded rubber products. Robin Industries produces various automotive products, as well as a full range of industrial components. **NOTE:** Company hires through staffing agency.

ROBINSON MEMORIAL HOSPITAL
6847 North Chestnut Street, Ravenna OH 44266. 330/297-0811. **Fax:** 330/297-4047. **Contact:** Director of Human Resources. **E-mail address:** humanresources@rmh2.org. **World Wide Web address:** http://www.robinsonmemorial.org. **Description:** A 280-bed hospital. **NOTE:** The Human Resources direct line is 330/297-2700. **Positions advertised include:** Director of Physician Services; Front Office Associate; Nutrition Services Aide; Medical Assistant; Telecommunications Operator; Pharmacy Technician; Surgical Technologist; Licensed Practical Nurse; Registered Nurse.

THE ROCK AND ROLL HALL OF FAME AND MUSEUM
One Key Plaza, Cleveland OH 44114. 216/781-7625. **Recorded jobline:** 216/515-1912. **Contact:** Human Resources Department. **World Wide Web address:** http://www.rockhall.com. **Description:** A non-profit institution that houses the permanent Rock and Roll Hall of Fame exhibit as well as other temporary exhibits related to Rock and Roll history. The Museum also produces programs for the public that include concerts, lectures, panel discussions, and teacher education. **NOTE:** Please reference the job number for which you are applying in your cover letter. Candidates may also complete an online application. **Positions advertised include:** Visitor Service Representative; Security Representative; Education Programs Manager. **Special programs:** Internships; Volunteer Opportunities.

ROCKWELL AUTOMATION
6935 Treeline Drive, Suite E, Brecksville OH 44141. 440/746-4792. **Contact:** Human Resources. **World Wide Web address:** http://www.rockwell.com. **Description:** Designs and manufactures automated components and systems for worldwide industrial applications. Products include electric power transmission equipment, telecommunication components, motors and related controls, generators, and transformers. The company is exploring the multimedia industry for a video-on-demand service, as well as an interactive network of video games. **Listed on:** New York Stock Exchange. **Stock exchange symbol:** ROK.

ROCKWELL AUTOMATION
ALLEN-BRADLEY
9355 Allen Road, West Chester OH 45060. 513/942-9070. **Contact:** Human Resources. **World Wide Web address:** http://www.ab.com. **Description:** Engaged in the production of industrial control equipment, software-based control equipment, magnetic materials, and electronic components. **Parent company:** Rockwell International. **Operations at this facility include:** Administration; Design; Research and Development. **Listed on:** New York Stock Exchange. **Stock exchange symbol:** ROK.

ROCKY SHOES & BOOTS INC.
39 East Canal Street, Nelsonville OH 45764. 740/753-1951. **Contact:** Human Resources. **World Wide Web address:** http://www.rockyboots.com. **Description:** Designs, develops, manufactures and markets men's and women's footwear. Rocky Shoes & Boots places an emphasis on the manufacture of waterproof footwear and is one of the largest users of Gore-Tex waterproof fabric for outdoor footwear. Founded in 1932. **Corporate headquarters location:** This location.

ROPPE CORPORATION
1602 North Union Street, P.O. Box 1158, Fostoria OH 44830. 419/435-8546. **Toll-free phone:** 800/537-9527. **Fax:** 419/435-1056. **Contact:** Personnel. **E-mail address:** hr@roppe.com. **World Wide Web address:** http://www.roppe.com. **Description:** A leading manufacturer of rubber and vinyl flooring products.

ROSEMOUNT ANALYTICAL INC.
1201 North Main Street, Orrville OH 44667. 330/682-9010. **Fax:** 330/684-4442. **Recorded jobline:** 952/828-3518. **Contact:** Leo M. Storey, Vice President of Human Resources. **E-mail address:** leo.storey@emersonprocess.com. **World Wide Web address:** http://www.rosemount.com. **Description:** A manufacturer of analog and digital combustion and process control instrumentation. **Other U.S. locations:** Nationwide. **International locations:** Worldwide. **Parent company:** Emerson Electric Company. **Operations at this facility include:** Divisional Headquarters. **Listed on:** New York Stock Exchange. **Stock exchange symbol:** EMR.

ROSS ALUMINUM FOUNDRIES
P.O. Box 609, Sidney OH 45365-0609. 937/492-4134. **Physical address:** 815 North Oak Avenue, Sidney OH 45365. **Contact:** Human Resources. **World Wide Web address:** http://www.rossal.com. **Description:** A producer of aluminum castings using green sand, permanent mold, dry sand, plaster cerm, and squeeze casting techniques. Founded in 1931. **NOTE:** Resumes accepted for posted positions only. **Corporate headquarters location:** Cincinnati OH. **Parent company:** Eagle-Picher Industries, Inc. **Operations at this facility include:** Manufacturing.

ROSS PRODUCTS
625 Cleveland Avenue, Columbus OH 43215-1724. 614/624-7677. **Contact:** Staffing Department. **World Wide Web address:** http://www.abbott.com. **Description:** Develops and markets adult and pediatric nutritionals. The company's products include Isomil and Similac infant formulas as well as Ensure adult nutritionals. Founded in 1888. **Positions advertised include:** Project Engineer; Research Scientist; Help Desk Manager; Quality Assurance Project Leader; Senior Engineer; Senior Financial Analyst; Customer Relations Coordinator; Maintenance Supervisor; Maintenance Mechanic. **Parent company:** Abbot Laboratories is a health care company that develops, manufactures and markets products and services for the prevention, diagnosis, treatment, and cure of a variety of diseases. The company specializes in developing treatments for diabetes, pain management, respiratory infections, HIV/AIDS, pediatrics and animal health. **Operations at this facility include:** Divisional Headquarters.

ROTO-ROOTER, INC.
2500 Chemed Center, 255 East Fifth Street, Cincinnati OH 45202-4725. 513/762-6900. **Fax:** 513/762-6590. **Contact:** Human Resources. **World Wide Web address:** http://www.rotorooter.com. **Description:** A provider of plumbing and drain cleaning services and one of the largest providers of residential appliance and air conditioning repair services through the sale of service contracts. The Roto-Rooter network of franchises and company-owned operations provides drain cleaning services to approximately 90 percent of the U.S. population and plumbing services to 72 percent. Founded in 1935. **Corporate headquarters location:** This location. **Subsidiaries include:** Service America; Vitas Healthcare. **Parent company:** Chemed Corporation. **Operations at this facility include:** Administration; Divisional Headquarters; Regional Headquarters; Sales. **Listed on:** NASDAQ. **Stock exchange symbol:** RRR. **Number of employees nationwide:** 3,357.

ROYAL APPLIANCE MANUFACTURING COMPANY
7005 Cochran Drive, Glenwillow OH 44139. 440/996-2000. **Contact:** Human Resources Manager. **E-mail address:** resume@royalappliance.com. **World Wide Web address:** http://www.royalappliance.com. **Description:** Manufactures and markets the Dirt Devil and Royal brand vacuum cleaners for home and commercial use. **Positions advertised include:** Industrial Designer; Quality Manager; Customer Service Coordinator. **Special programs:** Internships. **Corporate headquarters location:** This location. **Operations at this facility include:** Administration; Manufacturing; Research and Development; Sales; Service. **Listed on:** New York Stock Exchange. **Stock exchange symbol:** RAM. **Number of employees at this location:** 150. **Number of employees nationwide:** 700.

RUBBERMAID, INC.
1147 Akron Road, Wooster OH 44691-2596. 330/264-6464. **Contact:** Staffing Specialist. **World Wide Web address:** http://www.rubbermaid.com. **Description:** Manufactures and sells rubber and plastic products for the consumer and commercial markets. Products include over 2,500 items for home organization, kitchen and bath, and household repairs/do-it-yourself, as well as products for agricultural, industrial, and institutional use. **Positions advertised include:** Sales and Field Marketing Representative; Tactical Sourcing Agent. **Corporate headquarters location:** This location. **Parent company:** Newell Rubbermaid Inc. **Operations at this facility include:** Administration; Manufacturing; Research and Development; Sales; Service. **Listed on:** New York Stock Exchange. **Stock exchange symbol:** NWL. **Number of employees nationwide:** 10,000.

RUDOLPH/LIBBE, INC.
6494 Latcha Road, Walbridge OH 43465-9738. 419/241-5000. **Fax:** 419/837-9373. **Contact:** Human Resources. **World Wide Web address:** http://www.rlcos.com. **Description:** A general contractor and construction management firm. **Corporate headquarters location:** This location.

SBC CORPORATION
45 Erieview Plaza, 1st Floor, Cleveland OH 44114. 216/822-8396. **Recorded jobline:** 866/695-6271. **Contact:** Human Resources Department. **World Wide Web address:** http://www.sbc.com. **Description:** One of the largest telephone holding companies in the United States, providing telephone services to 17.9 million customers in five Midwestern states. SBC Ameritech Corporation conducts business through 15 diversified units. Services provided by these units include advertising; communications including pay phone, long-distance telephone, and cellular telephone; information services; new media; capital; and security services. **Positions advertised include:** Sales Representative; Telephone Account Representative; Competitive Account Executive; Usage Specialist. **Corporate headquarters location:** Chicago IL. **Other U.S. locations:** Nationwide. **Parent company:** SBC Communications Inc.

SAFELITE GLASS CORPORATION
2400 Farmer's Drive, Columbus OH 43235. 614/842-3000. **Contact:** Human Resources. **E-mail address:** careers@safelite.com. **World Wide Web address:** http://www.safelite.com. **Description:** Manufactures, distributes, sells, installs, and repairs automobile glass and related products. **Positions advertised include:** Warehouse Worker; Repair Technician; Installing Technician. **Corporate headquarters location:** This location. **Other U.S. locations:** Wichita KS; Enfield NC. **Operations at this facility include:** Administration. **Annual sales/revenues:** More than $100 million. **Number of employees at this location:** 450. **Number of employees nationwide:** 7,000.

SAIA-BURGESS INC.
P.O. Box 427, 801 Scholz Drive, Vandalia OH 45377. 937/898-3621. **Contact:** Human Resources. **World Wide Web address:** http://www.saia-burgess.com. **Description:** A global technology company that manufactures and provides advanced technology, systems, and services worldwide.

SALEM COMMUNITY HOSPITAL
1995 East State Street, Salem OH 44460. 330/332-7148. **Fax:** 330/332-7592. **Contact:** Human Resources. **E-mail address:** jobs@salemhosp.com. **World Wide Web address:** http://www.salemhosp.com. **Description:** A community hospital. **Positions advertised include:** Radiologic Technologist; Licensed Practical Nurse; Surgical Technologist; Pediatric Registered Nurse. **Special programs:** Internships; Co-ops. **Number of employees at this location:** 800.

THE SALVATION ARMY
P.O. Box 596, 114 East Central Parkway, Cincinnati OH 45201. 513/762-5600. **Fax:** 513/762-5679. **Contact:** Personnel. **E-mail address:** swo@salvationarmy-usaeast.org. **World Wide Web address:** http://www.salvationarmy.org. **Description:** A nonprofit organization providing several service programs including day-care centers, programs for people with disabilities, substance abuse programs and tutoring for at-risk students. The Salvation Army targets its programs to assist alcoholics, battered women, drug addicts, the elderly, the homeless, people with AIDS, prison inmates, teenagers, and the unemployed. **Corporate headquarters:** This is the divisional headquarters. **Other U.S. locations:** Nationwide.

SARCOM
8337 Green Meadows Drive North, Lewis Center OH 43035. 614/854-1300. **Contact:** Human Resources Department. **E-mail address:** hr@sarcom.com. **World Wide Web address:** http://www.sarcom.com. **Description:** A computer and software retailer. SARCOM also provides service and repairs for its commercial and residential customers. **NOTE:** To reach the Human Resources Office directly call: 614/854-1002. **Positions advertised include:** Inventory Supervisor. **Corporate headquarters location:** This location.

SARCOM COMPUTER RENTALS
4740-A Interstate Drive, Cincinnati OH 45246. 513/942-7368. **Toll-free phone:** 800/968-1247. **Contact:** Glenn Orr, Executive Vice President. **World Wide Web address:** http://www.scr-rentals.com. **Description:** A computer rental company. **Other area locations:** Columbus OH.

SAUDER WOODWORKING CO.
P.O. Box 156, Archbold OH 43502. 419/446-2711. **Physical address:** 502 Middle Street, Archbold OH 43502. **Fax:** 419/446-4957. **Contact:** Human Resources. **E-mail address:** jobs@sauder.com. **World Wide Web address:** http://www.sauder.com. **Description:** Manufactures furniture and fixtures. This location also hires seasonally. **NOTE:** Entry-level positions, part-time jobs, and second and third shifts are offered. **Positions advertised include:** Customer Service Representative; Carton Packing Team Member. **Special programs:** Internships; Apprenticeships; Training; Co-ops; Summer Jobs. **Corporate headquarters location:** This location. **Other U.S. locations:** Salt Lake City UT. **Listed on:** Privately held. **Number of employees at this location:** 3,200.

SCHNEIDER ELECTRIC
5735 College Corner Road, Oxford OH 45056-9715. 513/523-4171. **Contact:** Human Resources. **World Wide Web address:** http://www.groupeschneider.com. **Description:** A leading North American supplier of electrical distribution, automation, and industrial control products, systems, and services for the distribution, application, and control of electrical energy. The company's products are marketed to industrial customers, the construction industry, electric utilities, individual consumers, government agencies, and to other manufacturers for use in or on their products and equipment. Founded in 1903. **Corporate headquarters location:** Palatine IL. **Other U.S. locations:** AL; CA; KY; MO; NE; SC; TN; WA. **Parent company:** Groupe Schneider possesses global expertise in electrical contracting, industrial engineering, and construction. In addition to Square D, Groupe Schneider operates the following subsidiaries: Jeumont-Schneider Industries, Merlin Gerin, Spie Batignolles, and Telemecanique.

A. SCHULMAN, INC.
P.O. Box 1710, Akron OH 44309-1710. 330/666-3751. **Physical address:** 3550 West Market Street, Akron OH 44333. **Fax:** 330/668-7204. **Contact:** Director of Human Resources. **E-mail address:** info@aschulman.com. **World Wide Web address:** http://www.aschulman.com. **Description:** Supplies plastic compounds and resins to clients worldwide. The company's products include custom-engineered plastic compounds, color concentrates and additives, and rubber products for the automotive industry. The company also distributes products for other chemical manufacturers; and buys and resells plastic resins. Founded in 1928. **Corporate headquarters location:** This location. **International locations:** Canada; Europe. **Listed on:** NASDAQ. **Stock exchange symbol:** SHLM.

SCHWEBEL BAKING COMPANY
P.O. Box 6018, Youngstown OH 44501. 330/783-2860. **Physical address:** 965 East Midlothian Boulevard, Youngstown OH 44502. **Contact:** Human Resources. **World Wide Web address:** http://www.schwebels.com. **Description:** Produces bakery products and related goods. **Positions advertised include:** Salesperson; Thrift Store Clerk. **Corporate headquarters location:** This location. **Operations at this facility include:** Administration; Manufacturing; Sales.

SCOTT TECHNOLOGIES
2000 Auburn Drive, Suite 400, Beechwood OH 44122. 216/464-6153. **Contact:** Human Resources. **World Wide Web address:** http://www.scottaviation.com. **Description:** A leading designer and manufacturer of high-performance respiratory systems including air packs and drop-down oxygen masks for aerospace, aviation, defense, fire fighting, government, and industrial markets. **Corporate headquarters location:** This location. **Parent company:** Tyco International Ltd. **Listed on:** New York Stock Exchange. **Stock exchange symbol:** TYC.

THE SCOTTS COMPANY
14111 Scottslawn Road, Marysville OH 43041. 937/644-0011. **Fax:** 937/644-7244. **Contact:** Human Resources Department. **World Wide Web address:** http://www.scottscompany.com. **Description:** Manufactures and markets lawn and garden products serving do-it-yourself consumer and professional users. Brands include Scotts Turf Builder seed and spreaders; Miracle Gro lawn and garden products; and Hyponex organic products. Founded in 1870. **NOTE:** Entry-level positions and second and third shifts are offered. Openings are posted on-line. **Positions advertised include:** Process Operator; Plant Controller; Senior Analyst; Lawns Brand Finance Director; Sales Representative; Process and Formulations Specialist. **Special programs:** Internships. **Internship information:** The Scotts Company offers various internships including landscape services, human resources, and marketing. **Corporate headquarters location:** This location. **International locations:** Herleens, The Netherlands. **Subsidiaries include:** Hyponex; Miracle-Gro; Republic Tool; Sierra. **Listed on:** New York Stock Exchange. **Stock exchange symbol:** SMG. **Annual sales/revenues:** More than $100 million. **Number of employees nationwide:** 4,000.

THE E.W. SCRIPPS COMPANY
312 Walnut Street, Suite 2800, Cincinnati OH 45202. 513/977-3000. **Contact:** Human Resources. **E-mail address:** askhr@scripps.com. **World Wide Web address:** http://www.scripps.com. **Description:** The E.W. Scripps Company operates nineteen daily newspapers, nine large-market television stations, cable systems, two television production companies, a 24-hour cable channel, the Home and Garden television network, and United Media, a licenser and syndicator of news features and comics. **Positions advertised include:** Director, Controls and Compliance; Accounts Payable Supervisor. **Corporate headquarters location:** This location. **Listed on:** New York Stock Exchange. **Stock exchange symbol:** SSP. **Number of employees at this location:** 150. **Number of employees nationwide:** 8,200.

SECURITAS
1717 Brittain Road, Suite 314, Akron OH 44310. 330/633-0700. **Fax:** 330/633-1324. **Contact:** Human Resources. **World Wide Web address:** http://www.securitasusa.com. **Description:** Offers a full range of specialized protective

services including premier property and high-rise services, health care and hospital services, special event services, ATM services, and patrol services. The company serves thousands of companies worldwide with investigation, threat assessment, and executive protection services. **Corporate headquarters location:** Westlake Village CA. **Other U.S. locations:** Nationwide.

SELECT RESTAURANT COMPANY
One Chagrin Highlands, 2000 Auburn Drive, Suite 410, Beechwood OH 44122. 216/464-6606. **Fax:** 216/464-8565. **Contact:** Joan Lewis, Vice President of Human Resources Department. **E-mail address:** info@selectrestaurants.com. **World Wide Web address:** http://www.selectrestaurants.com. **Description:** A national chain of 60 full-service specialty restaurants offering everything from casual to fine dining. **NOTE:** Call or visit local restaurant for hourly positions.

SENCO PRODUCTS INC.
8485 Broadwell Road, Cincinnati OH 45244. 513/388-2000. **Fax:** 513/388-3100. **Contact:** Brenda Lowe, Human Resources. **E-mail address:** hr@senco.com. **World Wide Web address:** http://www.senco.com. **Description:** A manufacturer of air-driven tools used by construction and manufacturing companies. **President:** Rick Gerwe.

SEVERN TRENT LABORATORIES, INC.
4101 Shuffel Drive NW, North Canton OH 44720. 330/497-9396. **Fax:** 330/497-0772. **Contact:** Human Resources. **World Wide Web address:** http://www.stl-inc.com. **Description:** Provides a complete range of environmental testing services to private industry, engineering consultants, and government agencies in support of federal and state environmental regulations. The company also possesses analytical capabilities in the fields of air toxins, field analytical services, radiochemistry/mixed waste, and advanced technology. **Other U.S. locations:** CA; CO; FL; MO; TN; TX; WA.

SHAWNEE STATE UNIVERSITY
940 Second Street, Portsmouth OH 45662-4344. 740/354-3205. **Contact:** Human Resources. **World Wide Web address:** http://www.shawnee.edu. **Description:** A university offering a variety of programs through the College of Arts and Sciences, the College of Business, the College of Engineering Technologies, the College of Health Sciences, and the Center for Teacher Education. **Positions advertised include:** Adjunct Instructors, Various Disciplines; Occupational Therapy Instructor; Nursing Instructor; Chemistry Professor; Biology Professor; Accountant; Early Childhood Literacy Specialist; Outreach Summers Programs Assistant; Secretary; Account Clerk.

SHELTER ADULT WORKSHOP (SAW)
1275 Lakeside Avenue, Cleveland OH 44114. 216/861-8320. **Fax:** 216/861-0126. **Contact:** Roberta Jupin, Personnel. **World Wide Web address:** http://www.ccbmrdd.org. **Description:** A facility that employs mentally retarded and developmentally disabled individuals. Through nine locations nationwide, individuals are involved in light factory work including mailing, assembly, and packaging. SAW is affiliated with the Cuyahoga County Board of Mental Retardation. **Other area locations:** Beachwood OH; Euclid OH; Maple Heights OH; Parma OH; Rocky River OH.

THE SHERWIN-WILLIAMS COMPANY
101 Prospect Avenue NW, Cleveland OH 44115. 216/566-2000. **Contact:** Human Resources. **World Wide Web address:** http://www.sherwin.com. **Description:** Manufactures, sells, and distributes coatings and related products. Coatings are produced for original equipment manufacturers in various industries, as well as for the automotive aftermarket, the industrial maintenance market, and the traffic paint market. Sherwin-Williams labeled architectural and industrial coatings are sold through company-owned specialty paint and wallcovering stores. The Sherwin-Williams Company also manufactures paint under the Acme, Dutch Boy, Kem-Tone, Lucas, Martin-Senour, Minwax, Pratt & Lambert, Rogers, and Thompson brand names, as well as private labels, and markets its products to independent dealers, mass merchandisers, and home improvement centers. Founded in 1866. **NOTE:** Submit resume online. **Special programs:** Internships; Management Training Program. **Corporate headquarters location:** This location. **Other U.S. locations:** Nationwide. **Listed on:** New York Stock Exchange. **Stock exchange symbol:** SHW. **Annual sales/revenues:** $5 billion. **Number of employees at this location:** 1,400. **Number of employees nationwide:** 25,000.

THE SHERWIN-WILLIAMS COMPANY
CONSUMER GROUP
26300 Fargo Avenue, Bedford Heights OH 44146. 216/292-7400. **Contact:** Personnel Director. **World Wide Web address:** http://www.sherwin-williams.com. **Description:** Manufactures, sells, and distributes coatings and related products. Coatings are produced for original equipment manufacturers in various industries, as well as for the automotive aftermarket, the industrial maintenance market, and the traffic paint market. Sherwin-Williams labeled architectural and industrial coatings are sold through company-owned specialty paint and wallcovering stores. The Sherwin-Williams Company also manufactures paint under the Acme, Dutch Boy, Kem-Tone, Lucas, Martin-Senour, Minwax, Pratt & Lambert, Rogers, and Thompson brand names, as well as private labels, and markets its products to independent dealers, mass merchandisers, and home improvement centers. **NOTE:** Submit resume online. **Special programs:** Internships; Management Training Program. **Corporate headquarters location:** Cleveland OH. **Other U.S. locations:** Nationwide. **Listed on:** New York Stock Exchange. **Stock exchange symbol:** SHW. **Annual sales/revenues:** $5 billion. **Number of employees nationwide:** 25,000.

SHILOH CORPORATION
5389 West 130th Street, Cleveland OH 44130. 216/267-2600. **Contact:** Corporate Employment Manager. **E-mail address:** jobs@shiloh.com. **World Wide Web address:** http://www.shiloh.com. **Description:** A supplier of steel blanks, stampings, and processed steel to automotive, appliance, and other industrial manufacturers. Shiloh Corporation's affiliates, collectively known as Shiloh Industries, manufacture blanking and stamping components for automobiles, trucks, appliances, and lawn and garden equipment. Other steel processing operations include preparation of flat-rolled steel prior to manufacturing operations including pickling, edge trimming, slitting, roller leveling, cutting-to-length, and inspection and storage. Shiloh Industries also manufactures control devices for petroleum and natural gas pipelines and offshore drilling platforms. **Corporate headquarters location:** This location. **Subsidiaries include:** Liverpool Coil Processing, Inc. (Valley City OH); Medina Blanking, Inc. (Valley City OH); Sectional Die Company (Wellington OH); Sectional Stamping, Inc. (Wellington OH); Shafer Valve Company (Mansfield OH); Valley City Steel Company (Valley City OH). **Listed on:** NASDAQ. **Stock exchange symbol:** SHLO.

SHRINER'S HOSPITAL
3229 Burnet Avenue, Cincinnati OH 45229-3095. 513/872-6000. **Toll-free phone:** 800/875-8580. **Fax:** 513/872-6370. **Contact:** Julia Faehr, Human Resources Specialist. **E-mail address:** jfaehr@shrinenet.org. **World Wide Web address:** http://www.shrinershq.org/shc/cincinnati/index.html. **Description:** A 30-bed hospital that specializes in the treatment of child burn victims. **NOTE:** To reach Human Resources directly call: 513/872-6242. **Positions advertised include:** Human Resources Specialist; Registered Nurse; Research Specialist; Sterile Processing Technician.

R.W. SIDLEY, INC.
P.O. Box 150, Painesville OH 44077. **Physical address:** 436 Casement Avenue, Painesville OH 44077. 440/352-9343. **Toll-free phone:** 800/536-9343. **Fax:** 440/352-3822. **Contact:** Human Resources. **E-mail address:** employment@rwsidley.com. **World Wide Web address:** http://www.rwsidley.com. **Description:** Produces a variety of concrete products for a broad range of end users. **Positions advertised include:** Business Development Manager; Over-the-Road Driver. **Other area locations include:** Madison OH; Thompson OH. **Operations at this facility include:** Administration; Manufacturing.

SIEMENS ENERGY & AUTOMATION, INC.
4620 Forest Avenue, Norwood OH 45212. 513/841-3100. **Contact:** Manager of Employee Relations. **World Wide Web address:** http://www.siemens.com. **Description:** Produces generators and motors for a variety of customers. **Listed on:** New York Stock Exchange. **Positions advertised include:** Application Engineer; Consulting Business Developer; Consulting Engineer; Senior Engineer. **Special programs:** Internships. **Stock exchange symbol:** SI. **Number of employees nationwide:** 12,000.

SIFCO INDUSTRIES, INC.
970 East 64th Street, Cleveland OH 44103. 216/881-8600. **Fax:** 216/432-6281. **Contact:** Human Resources. **World Wide Web address:** http://www.sifco.com. **Description:** This location houses both the corporate offices and a factory. Overall, Sifco Industries is engaged in the forging of steel for use in the construction of airplanes. Founded in 1913. **Corporate headquarters location:** This location.

SIMONDS INDUSTRIES INC.
P.O. Box 28, 641 Heller Drive, Newcomerstown OH 43832. 740/498-8331. **Contact:** Personnel Director. **World Wide Web address:** http://www.simondsinternational.com. **Description:** Simonds Industries is a producer of tools including saws, files, rasps, and related items. **Corporate headquarters location:** Fitchburg MA. **Other U.S. locations:** Santa Fe Springs CA; Big Rapids MI; Springfield OR. **International locations:** Canada; United Kingdom. **Operations at this facility include:** This location manufactures files.

SINCLAIR COMMUNITY COLLEGE
Building 7, Room 7430, 444 West Third Street, Dayton OH 45402. 937/512-2514. **Fax:** 937/512-2777. **Contact:** Director of Human Resources. **E-mail address:** hrdept@sinclair.edu. **World Wide Web address:** http://www.sinclair.edu. **Description:** A community college. **NOTE:** No paper resumes accepted, please apply online. **Positions advertised include:** Executive Director, Project READ; Nursing Professor; Student Services Application Coordinator; Project Manager; Groundskeeper.

SKY FINANCIAL GROUP
221 South Church Street, Bowling Green OH 43402. 419/327-6300. **Contact:** Human Resources. **World Wide Web address:** http://www.skyfi.com. **Description:** A diversified financial holding providing full service banking services, as well as trust, investment and brokerage, personal and commercial insurance, and dental practice financing services. Sky Financial operates 260 financial centers in eight regions. **Positions advertised include:** Seasonal Teller; Item Processing Associate; Assistant Account Manager; Personal Banker; Project Manager; Corporate Sales Manager. **Special programs:** Internships. **Corporate headquarters location:** This location. **Other U.S. locations:** Indiana; Michigan; Pennsylvania; West Virginia.

A.O. SMITH ELECTRICAL PRODUCTS COMPANY
750 West Spring Street, Upper Sandusky OH 43351. 419/294-3824. **Contact:** Human Resources. **World Wide Web address:** http://www.aosmith.com. **Description:** A stamping plant for fractional horsepower electric motors that are used primarily in the movement of air. **Corporate headquarters location:** Milwaukee WI.

SMITHS INDUSTRIES AEROSPACE
DCS-LELAND
740 East National Road, Vandalia OH 45377. 937/898-5881. **Fax:** 937/415-0260. **Contact:** Jo Lynne Csaszar, Director of Human Resources. **World Wide Web address:** http://www.smiths-aerospace.com. **Description:** Manufactures electrical power systems for the aerospace industry. **NOTE:** Second and third shifts are offered. **Special programs:** Summer jobs. **Corporate headquarters location:** London UK. **Other U.S. locations:** Nationwide. **International locations:** Worldwide. **Number of employees worldwide:** 9,000.

SMURFIT-STONE CONTAINER CORPORATION
500 North Fourth Street, Coshocton OH 43812. 740/622-6543. **Contact:** Personnel Director. **World Wide Web address:** http://www.smurfit-stone.com. **Description:** Smurfit-Stone Container Corporation is one of the world's leading paper-based packaging companies. The company's main products include corrugated containers, folding cartons, and multiwall industrial bags. The company is also one of the world's largest collectors and processors of recycled products that are then sold to a worldwide customer base. Smurfit-Stone Container Corporation also operates several paper tube, market pulp, and newsprint production facilities. **Corporate headquarters location:** Chicago IL. **Other U.S. locations:** Nationwide. **Operations at this facility include:** This location is a pulp and paper processor. **Listed on:** NASDAQ. **Stock exchange symbol:** SSCC.

SPANGLER CANDY COMPANY
P.O. Box 71, Bryan OH 43506. 419/636-4221. **Physical address:** 400 North Portland Street, Bryan OH 43506. **Fax:** 419/636-3695. **Contact:** Personnel Director. **World Wide Web address:** http://www.spanglercandy.com. **Description:** Develops, manufactures, and markets a variety of chocolates, hard candies, and marshmallow candies. Spangler Candy Company's brand names include Astro Pops, Dum Dum Pops, Circus Peanuts, Picture Pops, Saf-T-Pops, Spangler Candy Canes and Cane Classics, Spangler Chocolates, and Spangler Circus Peanuts. Founded in 1906. **Corporate headquarters location:** This location.

SQUIRES SANDERS & DEMPSEY LLP
Administration Center, 1500 West Third Street, Suite 450, Cleveland OH 44113. 216/802-7571. **Fax:** 216/687-3401. **Contact:** Jane C. Koehl, Legal Personnel and Professional Development Manager. **World Wide Web address:** http://www.ssd.com. **Description:** A law firm. Squires Sanders & Dempsey specializes in cases pertaining to advocacy, business consulting, capital markets, industry, regulatory, taxation, and technology. Founded in 1890. **Positions advertised include:** Bankruptcy/Corporate

Transactions Associate; Labor and Employment Associate; Litigation Associate. **Special Programs:** Summer Associate Programs.

STANDARD REGISTER COMPANY
P.O. Box 1167, Dayton OH 45401-1167. 937/443-1000. **Physical address:** 600 Albany Street, Dayton OH 45408. **Contact:** Sandy Brown, Director of Human Resources. **E-mail address:** hrcorp@standardregister.com. **World Wide Web address:** http://www.stdreg.com. **Description:** Manufactures business forms, pressure sensitive products, and data systems forms for the business, health care, and other industries. The company also offers distribution, automation, management, and software products and services. **Positions advertised include:** Professional Sales Representative. **Corporate headquarters location:** This location. **Other U.S. locations:** Nationwide. **Subsidiaries include:** Stanfast. **Operations at this facility include:** Administration; Divisional Headquarters; Manufacturing; Regional Headquarters; Research and Development; Service. **Listed on:** New York Stock Exchange. **Stock exchange symbol:** SR.

STARK TRUSS COMPANY, INC.
109 Miles Avenue SW, Canton OH 44708. 330/478-2100. **Toll-free phone:** 800/933-2258. **Contact:** Human Resources. **World Wide Web address:** http://www.starktruss.com. **Description:** Manufactures wood, floor, and roof trusses that are used in the construction of buildings and houses. **Other area locations:** Washington Courthouse OH; Marysville OH; Edgerton OH; Beach City OH; Champion OH; New Philadelphia OH. **Other U.S. locations:** IN; KS; MO; KY; SC; TX.

STATE AUTO INSURANCE COMPANIES
518 East Broad Street, Columbus OH 43215. 614/464-5000. **Toll-free phone:** 800/444-9950. **Fax:** 614/464-5341. **Contact:** Human Resources. **E-mail address:** resumes@stateauto.com. **World Wide Web address:** http://www.stateauto.com. **Description:** Offers property, casualty, and life insurance. **NOTE:** Resumes are accepted by e-mail, fax, or regular mail. Consult website for contact information specific to the position for which you are applying. **Positions advertised include:** Financial Accountant; Internal Auditor; Claim Service Specialist; Database Administrator; Actuarial Analyst.

STATE INDUSTRIAL PRODUCTS
3100 Hamilton Avenue, Cleveland OH 44114. 216/861-7114. **Fax:** 888/771-9670. **Contact:** Human Resources. **E-mail address:** recruit@stateindustrial.com. **World Wide Web address:** http://www.stateindutrial.com. **Description:** Manufactures maintenance chemicals including degreasers and various institutional cleaning supplies. The company also packages and distributes industrial products. **Positions advertised include:** Inventory Manager. **Corporate headquarters location:** This location.

STATE TEACHERS RETIREMENT SYSTEM OF OHIO
275 East Broad Street, Columbus OH 43215-3771. 614/227-2908. **Fax:** 614/227-2952. **Contact:** Staffing Coordinator. **E-mail address:** resumes@strsoh.org. **World Wide Web address:** http://www.strsoh.org/jobs.htm. **Description:** One of the largest pension funds in the United States, serving Ohio's teachers and managing assets totaling $50 billion. The nonprofit fund serves over 375,000 members and retirees. Founded in 1920. **Positions advertised include:** Associate Teacher; General Counsel. **Special programs:** Internships; Co-ops. **Office hours:** Monday - Friday, 8:00 a.m. - 4:30 p.m. **Corporate headquarters location:** This location. **Number of employees at this location:** 675.

STEIN INC.
P.O. Box 5001, Sandusky OH 44870. 419/626-0304. **Physical address:** 1622 First Street, Sandusky OH 44870. **Contact:** Human Resources. **Description:** Manufactures food processing equipment such as industrial-sized ovens and fryers.

STERIS CORPORATION
5960 Heisley Road, Mentor OH 44060-1834. 440/354-2600. **Toll-free phone:** 800/548-4873. **Fax:** 440/354-7043. **Contact:** Human Resources. **World Wide Web address:** http://www.steris.com. **Description:** A leading provider of infection prevention products, contamination control, and surgical support systems and products to health care, scientific, research, and industrial customers worldwide. Founded in 1987. **NOTE:** Entry-level positions and second and third shifts are offered. Interested candidates can search and apply for positions online. **Positions advertised include:** Administrative Assistant; Internal Auditor; Financial Analyst; Applications Analyst; Chemist; Pathogenic Microbiologist; Electrical Engineer; Hardware Engineer; Project Manager. **Corporate headquarters location:** This location. **Other U.S. locations:** Nationwide. **International locations:** Worldwide. **Subsidiaries include:** Amsco International, Inc.; Iosmedix, Inc. **Listed on:** New York Stock Exchange. **Stock exchange symbol:** STE. **Number of employees worldwide:** 5,100.

STERLING COMMERCE
P.O. Box 8000, 4600 Lakehurst Court, Dublin OH 43016. 614/793-7000. **Fax:** 614/793-7092. **Contact:** Human Resources. **World Wide Web address:** http://www.sterlingcommerce.com. **Description:** Develops and markets RemoteWare, a suite of client/server systems development software tools used to automate time-sensitive information delivery processes such as order entry, inventory query, and price list and product catalog updates. RemoteWare is used to manage the exchange of information between central systems and over 465,000 remote or mobile field personnel, customers, suppliers, channels-of-distribution, or other corporate constituents. **Positions advertised include:** Attorney; Strategic Programs Manager; Software Developer; Business Development Manager; Product Marketing Manager; Tax Analyst; Sales Business Analyst; Marketing Communications Specialist; Senior Events Specialist; Administrative Assistant; Contract Negotiator. **Parent company:** SBC Communications. **Corporate headquarters location:** This location. **Number of employees worldwide:** 1,800.

STERLING JEWELERS INC.
375 Ghent Road, Akron OH 44333. 330/668-5000. **Contact:** Recruitment Manager. **World Wide Web address:** http://www.sterlingcareers.com. **Description:** Operates over 1,000 jewelry stores nationwide. **Positions advertised include:** Real Estate/Store Planning Business Analyst; Human Resources Administrator; Customer Relations Manager; Merchandise Coordinator; Report Analyst Clerk; Jewelry Supervisor; Construction Manager; Senior Programmer/Analyst; Benefits Administrator. **Corporate headquarters location:** This location. **Subsidiaries include:** Belden Jewelers; Goodman Jewelers; J.B. Robinson Jewelers; Kay Jewelers; LeRoy's Jewelers; Osterman Jewelers; Rogers Jewelers; Shaw's Jewelers; Weigfield Jewelers. **Parent company:** Signet Group plc. **Operations at this facility include:** Administration; Service. **Listed on:** NASDAQ. **Stock exchange symbol:** SIGY. **Number of employees at this location:** 1,700. **Number of employees nationwide:** 12,000.

STOCK EQUIPMENT COMPANY
16490 Chillicothe Road, Chagrin Falls OH 44023. 440/543-6000. **Fax:** 440/543-5944. **Contact:** Human Resources. **World Wide Web address:** http://www.stock.com. **Description:** Manufactures coal feeders and a variety of scales and valves for use in power and energy-related industries.

STRANG CORPORATION
8905 Lake Avenue, Cleveland OH 44102. 216/961-6767. **Contact:** Human Resources. **World Wide Web address:** http://www.strangcorp.com. **Description:** A restaurant and hotel management company. **Corporate headquarters location:** This location.

SUN NEWSPAPERS
5510 Cloverleaf Parkway, Cleveland OH 44125. 216/524-0830. **Contact:** Personnel. **E-mail address:** mhejduk@sunnews.com. **World Wide Web address:** http://www.sunnews.com. **Description:** Publishes 25 weekly local newspapers with a total circulation of more than 261,000.

SUPERIOR METAL PRODUCTS INC.
1005 West Grand Avenue, Lima OH 45801-3429. 419/228-1145. **Contact:** Human Resources. **Description:** A manufacturer of metal products for the appliance, automotive, heating, and office furniture industries.

SUPERIOR PHARMACEUTICAL COMPANY
1385 Kemper Meadow Drive, Cincinnati OH 45240. 513/851-3600. **Toll-free phone:** 800/826-5035. **Fax:** 800/255-8465. **Contact:** Personnel. **E-mail address:** info@superiorpharm.com. **World Wide Web address:** http://www.superiorpharm.com. **Description:** Distributes generic pharmaceuticals.

SYPRIS TECHNOLOGIES
1550 Marion Agosta Road, Marion OH 43301. 740/383-2111. **Fax:** 740/383-2603. **Contact:** Human Resources Department. **E-mail address:** hr@sypristechnologies.com. **World Wide Web address:** http://www.sypris.com/technology. **Description:** A provider of forged and machined components servicing the aerospace, transportation and energy industries. **Corporate headquarters location:** Louisville KY. **Parent company:** Sypris Solutions Inc. **Listed on:** NASDAQ. **Stock exchange symbol:** SYPR. **Number of employees nationwide:** 1,500.

SYSTRAN CORPORATION
4126 Linden Avenue, Dayton OH 45432. 937/252-5601. **Fax:** 937/252-1480. **Contact:** Manager of Human Resources. **E-mail address:** careers@systran.com. **World Wide Web address:** http://www.systran.com. **Description:** Manufactures I/O boards, memory systems, and network interface cards. **Positions advertised include:** Sales Manager. **Corporate headquarters location:** This location. **Listed on:** Privately held. **Number of employees at this location:** 135.

TNS NFO
2700 Oregon Road, Toledo OH 43697-0315. 419/666-8800. **Fax:** 419/661-8595. **Contact:** Human Resources. **World Wide Web address:** http://www.tns-global.com. **Description:** Provides custom and syndicated market research services primarily using a proprietary panel of pre-recruited consumer households throughout the country. Formerly known as NFO WorldGroup, TNS NFO is now part of one of the largest market research organizations in the world. **Company slogan:** The sixth sense of business. **Positions advertised include:** Senior Research Analyst; Statistical Analyst; Panel Support Specialist; Market Product Coordinator. **Corporate headquarters:** Greenwich CT. **Subsidiaries include:** Payment Systems, Inc. (FL), a leading supplier of information to the financial services industry in the United States; Advanced Marketing Solutions, Inc. (CT) provides custom computer software systems used by clients to quickly access and analyze complex business and consumer information.

TRW INC.
1900 Richmond Road, Cleveland OH 44124. 216/291-7000. **Contact:** Human Resources. **World Wide Web address:** http://www.trw.com. **Description:** Engaged in the research, development, and the engineering of materials, products, and processes; and offers metallurgical and chemical services. Other divisions of TRW produce electronics and space systems, car and truck equipment for both original equipment manufacturers and the replacement market, and a wide variety of industrial and energy components including aircraft parts, welding systems, and electromechanical assemblies. **Corporate headquarters location:** This location. **Listed on:** New York Stock Exchange. **Stock exchange:** TRW. **Annual sales/revenues:** More than $100 million.

TRW/VALVE DIVISION
1455 East 185th Street, Cleveland OH 44110. 216/692-4620. **Contact:** Human Resources. **World Wide Web address:** http://www.trw.com. **Description:** Produces engine valves, valve seat inserts, valve retainers, valve retainer locks, valve rotating mechanisms, and forged pistons. **Corporate headquarters location:** Cleveland OH. **Parent company:** TRW Inc. is a diversified technology firm with operations in electronics and space systems, car and truck equipment for both original equipment manufacturers and the replacement market, and a wide variety of industrial and energy components including aircraft parts, welding systems, and electromechanical assemblies. **Listed on:** New York Stock Exchange. **Stock exchange symbol:** TRW. **Annual sales/revenues:** More than $100 million. **Number of employees at this location:** 750.

TS TRIM INDUSTRIES INC.
10 Kenny Drive, Athens OH 45701. 740/593-5958. **Fax:** 740/593-6718. **Contact:** Human Resources Manager. **E-mail address:** hr-info@tstrim.com. **World Wide Web address:** http://www.tstrim.com. **Description:** Engaged in the cutting and sewing of fabric used in the manufacture of automotive seat covers. TS Trim is a supplier to Honda of America. **Corporate headquarters location:** Canal Winchester OH. **Parent company:** Tokyo Seat (Japan). **Operations at this facility include:** Manufacturing. **Listed on:** Privately held. **Number of employees at this location:** 400. **Number of employees nationwide:** 825.

TTC
4080 Bennett Road, Suite E, Toledo OH 43612. 419/470-8200. **Contact:** Human Resources Manager. **World Wide Web address:** http://www.ttcautomotive.com. **Description:** TTC is a global leader in the engineering, manufacturing, and marketing of products and systems for the worldwide vehicular, industrial, and mobile off-highway original equipment markets and is a major supplier to related aftermarkets. TTC is also a leading provider of lease financing services in selected markets. The company's products include drivetrain components such as axles, driveshafts, clutches, and transmissions; engine parts such as gaskets, piston rings, seals, pistons, and filters; chassis products such as vehicular frames and cradles and heavy-duty side rails; fluid power components such as pumps, motors, and control valves; and industrial products such as electrical and mechanical brakes and clutches, drives, and motion control devices. TTC's vehicular components and parts are used on automobiles, pickup trucks, vans, minivans, sport-utility vehicles, medium and heavy trucks, and off-highway vehicles. The company's industrial products include mobile off-highway and stationary equipment applications. **Operations at this facility include:** This location produces

axles, clutches, transmissions, drivetrain systems, universal joints, and driveshafts for the light- and heavy-duty truck market. Products are sold primarily to automotive original equipment manufacturers in the United States and to parts distributors.

TAYLOR'S INDUSTRIAL SERVICES
HPM DIVISION
820 Marion Road, Mount Gilead OH 43338. 419/946-0222. **Fax:** 419/946-2473. **Contact:** Personnel Director. **E-mail address:** info@taylorsind.com. **World Wide Web address:** http://www.taylorsind.com. **Description:** Produces plastic injection molding machinery, extrusion equipment, and metal die-casting equipment. **Positions advertised include:** Inside Sales Professional; Product Manager; CNC Machinist; CNC Programmer. **Corporate headquarters location:** This location. **Operations at this facility include:** Administration; Manufacturing; Research and Development; Sales; Service.

TECHNEGLAS, INC.
707 East Jenkins Avenue, Columbus OH 43207. 614/443-6551. **Fax:** 614/445-4706. **Contact:** Kathy Finnie, Personnel. **E-mail address:** kfinnie@techneglas.com. **World Wide Web address:** http://www.techneglas.com. **Description:** A producer of glass television parts including faceplates and funnels. Techneglas developed TV Solder Glass, a high-strength glass designed for sealing large color TV picture tubes. The company also produces silicon glass resins, which provide durable hard-coat protective coverings for scratch-resistant lenses and other products. **Special programs:** Internships. **Corporate headquarters location:** This location. **Other area locations:** Perrysburg OH. **Other U.S. locations:** Pittston PA. **Parent company:** Nippon Electric Glass. **Number of employees at this location:** 1,200. **Number of employees nationwide:** 2,700.

TECHNICOMP, INC.
1111 Chester Avenue, Suite 750, Cleveland OH 44114. 216/687-1122. **Toll-free phone:** 800/735-4440. **Fax:** 216/687-0637. **Contact:** Human Resources. **World Wide Web address:** http://www.technicomp.com. **Description:** A publisher of training manuals, videotapes, and workbooks for use by industrial and commercial clients. **Corporate headquarters location:** This location. **Parent company:** Excel Partnership Inc.

TELEDYNE RYAN AERONAUTICAL
TCAE TURBINE ENGINE UNIT
1330 West Laskey Road, Toledo OH 43612-0971. 419/470-3000. **Fax:** 419/470-3434. **Contact:** Professional Staffing. **Description:** Manufactures small gas turbine engines for cruise missiles and unmanned air vehicles (UAVs). **Number of employees at this location:** 130.

TENDER LOVING CARE/STAFF BUILDERS
6100 Rockside Woods Boulevard, Suite 100, Independence OH 44131. 216/642-0202. **Fax:** 216/642-3273. **Contact:** Human Resources. **World Wide Web address:** http://www.tlcathome.com. **Description:** A home health care agency. **Positions advertised include:** Home Health Aide; Licensed Practical Nurse; Registered Nurse; Physical Therapist. **Corporate headquarters location:** Lake Success NY. **Other U.S. locations:** Nationwide. **Number of employees nationwide:** 20,000.

TENNECO AUTOMOTIVE
33 Lockwood Road, Milan OH 44846. 419/499-2541. **Fax:** 419/668-5463. **Contact:** Human Resources. **World Wide Web address:** http://www.tenneco-automotive.com. **Description:** Develops and manufactures suspension systems and engine mounting systems for the control of noise, shock, and vibration for the transportation industry. **NOTE:** Interested candidates may submit a resume online. **Corporate headquarters location:** Lake Forest IL. **Other U.S. locations:** Nationwide. **International locations:** Worldwide. **Parent company:** Tenneco (Greenwich CT). **Listed on:** Privately held. **Number of employees worldwide:** 19,600.

THERM-O-DISC
1320 South Main Street, Mansfield OH 44907. 419/525-8500. **Contact:** Human Resources. **World Wide Web address:** http://www.thermodisc.com. **Description:** Develops, manufactures, and markets appliance-related temperature controls and sensors. Thermodisc also manufactures motor overload protectors, automotive controls and sensors, and electric switches for the automotive, electrical switch, and hand power tool industries. Founded in 1947. **Parent company:** Emerson Electric Company.

EJ THOMAS COMPANY
6161 Wiehe Road, Cincinnati OH 45237. 513/841-0880. **Contact:** Human Resources. **Description:** A wholesaler of chemicals and hangers for laundry and dry cleaning companies. **Other area locations:** Columbus, OH.

THOMSON CONSUMER ELECTRONICS (TCE)
24200 U.S. Route 23 South, P.O. Box 512, Circleville OH 43113. 740/474-8821. **Contact:** Manager of Employment. **Description:** Produces glass products for use in color television picture tubes. **Operations at this facility include:** Manufacturing.

THOR INDUSTRIES
P.O. Box 629, Jackson Center OH 45334-0629. 937/596-6849. **Physical address:** 419 West Pike Street, Jackson Center OH 45334. **Fax:** 937/596-6539. **Contact:** Human Resources. **World Wide Web address:** http://www.thorindustries.com. **Description:** Manufactures a wide range of recreational vehicles, and small and mid-size buses. Thor Industries is one of the largest producers of recreational vehicles in North America. Founded in 1980. **Listed on:** New York Stock Exchange. **Stock exchange symbol:** THO. **Number of employees nationwide:** 4,000.

TIME WARNER CABLE COMMUNICATIONS
11252 Cornell Park Drive, Cincinnati OH 45242. 513/489-5000. **Fax:** 513/489-5982. **Recorded jobline:** 513/489-5834. **Contact:** Human Resources. **E-mail address:** hr.applicant@twcable.com. **World Wide Web address:** http://www.twcinci.com. **Description:** A broadcasting and communications company. **NOTE:** Interested applicants may apply in person at the Blue Ash OH location: 11315 Reed Hartman Highway, Suite 108, Cincinnati OH 45241. Candidates may also search and apply for positions online, or send a resume to: TWC Processing Center, P.O. Box 549233, Suite 70, Waltham MA 02454. Unsolicited resumes are not accepted. Please reference the job code number. **Positions advertised include:** Marketing and Creative Services Specialist; Research Specialist; Call Center Associate; Inventory Analyst; Advertising Sales Account Executive; Residential Account Coordinator; Direct Sales Associate; Lobby Representative. **Parent company:** Time Warner.

TIME WARNER TELECOM
250 West Old Wilson Bridge Road, Suite 130, Worthington OH 43085-2215. 614/255-2000. **Fax:** 614/255-2665. **Contact:** Personnel. **World Wide Web address:** http://www.twtelecom.com. **Description:** A telecommunications equipment supplier specializing in fiber-optic materials. **Positions advertised include:** Account Executive. **Parent company:** Time Warner. **Operations at this facility include:** This location is a sales office.

TIMES REPORTER/MIDWEST OFFSET
P.O. Box 667, New Philadelphia OH 44663. 330/364-5577. **Physical address:** 629 Wabash Avenue NW, New Philadelphia OH 44663. **Contact:** Jack Shores, Publisher. **World Wide Web address:** http://www.timesreporter.com. **Description:** Publishes a daily newspaper. Through Midwest Offset, the company is also engaged in offset printing activities. **Corporate headquarters location:** Trenton NJ. **Parent company:** The Copley Press, Inc. **Operations at this facility include:** Service.

THE TIMKEN COMPANY
1835 Dueber Avenue SW, P.O. Box 6927, Mail Stop BIC-13, Canton OH 44706. 330/438-3000. **Fax:** 330/471-4551. **Contact:** Staffing Services Department. **E-mail address:** careers@timken.com. **World Wide Web address:** http://www.timken.com. **Description:** A leading international manufacturer of highly engineered bearings and alloy steels. **NOTE:** E-mailed resumes and cover letters must be in ASCII text file format. **Positions advertised include:** Infrastructure Services Manager; Application Engineer; Product Development Engineer; Senior Buyer; Worker's Compensation Attorney; Senior Supply Chain Analyst. **Special programs:** Internships. **Corporate headquarters location:** This location. **Subsidiaries include:** Latrobe Steel Co.; MPB Corporation; Rail Bearing Service Corp. **Listed on:** New York Stock Exchange. **Stock exchange symbol:** TKR. **Annual sales:** $2 billion. **Number of employees at this location:** 6,500. **Number of employees nationwide:** 12,000. **Number of employees worldwide:** 18,000.

TITANIUM METALS CORPORATION (TIMET)
P.O. Box 309, Toronto OH 43964. 740/537-1571. **Physical address:** 100 Titanium Way, Toronto OH 43964. **Contact:** Human Resources. **World Wide Web address:** http://www.timet.com. **Description:** One of the world's largest integrated producers of titanium metal products for aerospace and industrial applications. Titanium's unique combination of corrosion and heat-resistance, strength, and light weight make it particularly desirable for use in commercial and military aerospace applications where these qualities are prime design requirements. Products are also used in such diverse applications as power generation facilities, chemical processing equipment, medical implant devices, and sports equipment. **Corporate headquarters location:** Denver CO. **Parent company:** Tremont Corporation.

THE TOLEDO BLADE
541 North Superior Street, Toledo OH 43660. 419/245-6000. **Fax:** 419/724-6080. **Contact:** Barbara Gessel, Director of Human Resources. **E-mail address:** bgessel@toledoblade.com. **World Wide Web address:** http://www.toledoblade.com. **Description:** Publishes a morning newspaper. **Positions advertised include:** Carrier. **Listed on:** Privately held. **Number of employees at this location:** 675.

TOLEDO MOLDING & DIE INC.
1429 Coining Drive, Toledo OH 43612. 419/470-3950. **Fax:** 419/470-3977. **Contact:** Director of Corporate Human Resources. **E-mail address:** humanr@tmdinc.com. **World Wide Web address:** http://www.tmdinc.com. **Description:** Designs, engineers, and manufactures injection-molded plastic products, primarily for the automotive, appliance, and electrical industries. **Corporate headquarters location:** This location.

TOLEDO PUBLIC SCHOOLS
Office of Human Resources, Room 105, 420 East Manhattan Boulevard, Toledo OH 43608. 419/729-8231. **Recorded jobline:** 419/729-8355. **Contact:** Human Resources. **World Wide Web address:** http://www.tps.org. **Description:** Coordinates resources and information for the public schools of Toledo. **Positions advertised include:** Contract Teacher; Substitute Teacher; Substitute Bus Driver; Substitute Food Service Worker; Substitute Secretary.

TOMKINS INDUSTRIES INC.
P.O. Box 943, Dayton OH 45401-0943. 937/253-7171. **Physical address:** 4801 Springfield Street, Dayton OH 45431. **Contact:** Manager of Human Resources. **World Wide Web address:** http://www.tomkins.co.uk. **Description:** A manufacturer of a wide range of components for the manufactured housing and recreational vehicle markets, and of products for the commercial and industrial building industries. **Corporate headquarters location:** This location. **Listed on:** New York Stock Exchange. **Stock exchange symbol:** TKS.

TOTES-ISOTONER CORPORATION
9655 International Boulevard, Cincinnati OH 45246-4861. 513/682-8510. **Fax:** 513/682-8602. **E-mail address:** resume@totes.com. **Contact:** Human Resources. **World Wide Web address:** http://www.totes.com or http://www.isotoner.com. **Description:** A manufacturer of handbags, umbrellas, and related accessories for men and women.

TRANSUE & WILLIAMS STAMPING COMPANY, INC.
930 West Ely Street, Alliance OH 44601. 330/821-5777. **Fax:** 330/821-4146. **Contact:** Human Resources. **E-mail address:** info@twstamping.com. **World Wide Wed address:** http://www.twstamping.com. **Description:** A manufacturer of metal deep draw and blank stampings. The company is also engaged in welding, fabrication, annealing, and pickling services. **Corporate headquarters location:** This location.

TRAVEL CENTERS OF AMERICA, INC.
24601 Center Ridge Road, Suite 200, Westlake OH 44145-5677. 440/808-9100. **Contact:** Personnel. **World Wide Web address:** http://www.tatravelcenters.com. **Description:** Operates refueling and refreshment stops for motorists. **Corporate headquarters location:** This location. **Other U.S. locations:** Nationwide. **Annual sales/revenues:** More than $100 million. **Number of employees nationwide:** 10,500.

TRIMBLE
5475 Kellenburger Road, Dayton OH 45424-1099. 937/233-8921. **Contact:** Personnel Director. **E-mail address:** spcp191@apply.nationjob.com. **World Wide Web address:** http://www.trimble.com. **Description:** Produces control mechanisms for environmental regulating applications. **Positions advertised include:** Supplier Quality Engineer; Manufacturing Engineer; Accountant. **Special Programs:** Internships; Opportunities for Recent Graduates. **Corporate headquarters location:** Sunnyvale CA. **Number of employees worldwide:** 2,000.

TRINITY INDUSTRIES
11861 Mosteller Road, Cincinnati OH 45241. 513/771-2300. **Recorded jobline:** 214/589-8943. **Contact:** Personnel Department. **E-mail address:** resumes@trin.net. **World Wide Web address:** http://www.trin.net. **Description:** Develops, manufactures, and markets construction, industrial, and transportation products worldwide. Trinity Industries' products include container heads; flanges; highway guardrail and safety products; inland hopper and tank barges; pressure and nonpressure containers; pipefittings; ready-mix concrete and aggregate; and tank and freight railcars

and related products. **Corporate headquarters location:** Dallas TX. **Listed on:** New York Stock Exchange. **Stock exchange symbol:** TRN.

TURBINE ENGINE COMPONENTS TEXTRON
P.O. Box 17187, 23555 Euclid Avenue, Cleveland OH 44117. 216/692-5200. **Recorded jobline:** 877/483-9876. **Contact:** Human Resources. **E-mail address:** jobs@textron.com. **World Wide Web address:** http://www.textron.com. **Description:** Involved in the forging and machining of jet engine blades and related aerospace parts for military and commercial applications. **Corporate headquarters location:** Providence RI. **Parent company:** Textron. **Operations at this facility include:** Manufacturing. **Listed on:** New York Stock Exchange. **Stock exchange symbol:** TXT. **Number of employees worldwide:** 43,000.

TURNER CONSTRUCTION
1301 East Ninth Street, Suite 1400, Cleveland OH 44114. 216/522-1180. **Contact:** Human Resources. **World Wide Web address:** http://www.turnerconstruction.com. **Description:** An international general contracting and construction management firm. Founded in 1902. **Corporate headquarters location:** New York NY.

TYCO ELECTRONICS
HARTMAN DIVISION
175 North Diamond Street, Mansfield OH 44902. 419/524-1411. **Fax:** 419/521-9591. **Contact:** Kathy Castor, Personnel Director. **World Wide Web address:** http://www.tycoelectronics.com. **Description:** Develops, designs, manufactures, and markets EMI/RFI filter products, electromechanical relays, electronic relays, and solenoids for the automotive, commercial/industrial, communications, defense/ aerospace, and medical industries. **Parent Company:** Tyco International Ltd.

TYCO HEALTHCARE/MALLINCKRODT
2111 East Galbraith Road, Cincinnati OH 45237. 513/761-2700. **Contact:** Manager of Human Resources. **World Wide Web address:** http://www.mallinckrodt.com. **Description:** A producer of medical and surgical electronic equipment including X-ray equipment. **Positions advertised include:** Design Engineer. **Corporate headquarters location:** St. Louis MO. **Other U.S. locations:** Nationwide. **International locations:** Worldwide. **Parent company:** Tyco Healthcare.

URS GREINER
277 West Nationwide Boulevard, Columbus OH 43215-2566. 614/464-4500. **Contact:** Human Resources. **World Wide Web address:** http://www.urscorp.com. **Description:** An architectural, engineering, and planning consulting firm specializing in health care, corrections facilities, colleges/universities, commercial businesses, water/wastewater facilities, and surface transportation. **Positions advertised include:** Principal Architect. **Special programs:** Internships. **Corporate headquarters location:** San Francisco CA. **Other area locations:** Akron OH; Cincinnati OH; Cleveland OH. **Other U.S. locations:** Nationwide. **International locations:** Worldwide. **Parent company:** URS Corporation. **Listed on:** New York Stock Exchange. **Stock exchange symbol:** URS.

U.S. BANCORP
425 Walnut Street, Cincinnati OH 45202. 513/632-4234. **Contact:** Human Resources Department. **World Wide Web address:** http://www.usbank.com. **Description:** A full-service commercial bank. Formerly known as First Star Bank. The bank's name was changed as a result of a merger with U.S. Bancorp. **NOTE:** This firm does not accept unsolicited resumes. Candidates can apply for specific positions via the company's website. **Corporate headquarters location:** Minneapolis MN. **Listed on:** New York Stock Exchange. **Stock exchange symbol:** USB.

U.S. BANCORP
833 South State Street, Westerville OH 43081. 614/899-2001. **Contact:** Human Resources Department. **World Wide Web address:** http://www.usbank.com. **Description:** A full-service commercial bank. Formerly known as First Star Bank. The bank's name was changed as a result of a merger with U.S. Bancorp. **NOTE:** This firm does not accept unsolicited resumes. Candidates can apply for specific positions via the company's website. . **Corporate headquarters location:** Minneapolis MN. **Listed on:** New York Stock Exchange. **Stock exchange symbol:** USB.

U.S. CAN COMPANY
644 Myron Street, Hubbard OH 44425-1466. 330/534-1903. **Contact:** Human Resources. **World Wide Web address:** http://www.uscanco.com. **Description:** Manufactures a variety of metal and composite containers and specialty cans for personal care, household, automotive, paint, and industrial products. U.S. Can Company is also an international manufacturer of packaging products. **Corporate headquarters location:** Lombard IL.

U.S. COTTON
15501 Industrial Parkway, Cleveland OH 44135. 216/676-6400. **Fax:** 216/646-3681. **Contact:** Chris Pincura, Human Resources. **World Wide Web address:** http://www.uscotton.com. **Description:** Manufactures cosmetic puffs, pocket tissue packs, and cotton swabs. USC, founded in 1983, is a leading manufacturer of branded (Swisspers and Make-Offs) and store brand cotton cosmetic and health and beauty products distributed to grocery, drug, mass merchandise, and club-format retailers. **Corporate headquarters location:** Rio Rancho NM. **Other U.S. locations:** Pomfret CT; Charlotte NC; Reno NV. **International locations:** Canada; Chile; Puerto Rico. **Operations at this facility include:** Administration; Manufacturing; Regional Headquarters; Sales; Service.

U.S. DEFENSE LOGISTICS AGENCY
DEFENSE SUPPLY CENTER, COLUMBUS (DSCC)
3990 East Broad Street, Columbus OH 43216-5000. 614/692-2224. **Fax:** 614/692-4012. **Contact:** Office of Civilian Personnel. **World Wide Web address:** http://www.dscc.dla.mil. **Description:** An inventory control point for the Defense Logistics Agency engaged in weapons systems management. DSCC is primarily engaged in the supply of weapons systems spare parts and end products.

U.S. DEPARTMENT OF VETERANS AFFAIRS
CHILLICOTHE VETERANS ADMINISTRATION MEDICAL CENTER
17273 State Route 104, Chillicothe OH 45601. 740/773-1141 ext. 7560 or 7079. **Fax:** 740/ 772-7056. **Contact:** Nate Darden, Human Resources. **World Wide Web address:** http://www.chillicothe.med.va.gov. **Description:** A medical center operated by the U.S. Department of Veterans Affairs. From 54 hospitals in 1930, the VA health care system has grown to include 171 medical centers; more than 364 outpatient, community, and outreach clinics; 130 nursing home care units; and 37 domiciliary residences. VA operates at least one medical center in each of the 48 contiguous states, Puerto Rico, and the District of Columbia. With approximately 76,000 medical center beds, VA treats nearly one million patients in VA hospitals; 75,000 in nursing home care units; and 25,000 in domiciliary residences. VA's outpatient clinics register approximately 24 million visits per year. **Positions advertised include:** Registered Nurse; Licensed Practical Nurse; Occupational Therapist; Physical Therapy Assistant; Medical Technician; Physician. **Other area locations:** Athens; Lancaster; Marietta; Portsmouth.

U.S. DEPARTMENT OF VETERANS AFFAIRS
CLEVELAND VETERANS ADMINISTRATION MEDICAL CENTER
10000 Brecksville Road, Brecksville OH 44141. 440/526-3030. **Contact:** Human Resources Department. **World Wide Web address:** http://www.cleveland.med.va.gov. **Description:** A medical center operated by the U.S. Department of Veterans Affairs. From 54 hospitals in 1930, the VA health care system has grown to include 171 medical centers; more than 364 outpatient, community, and outreach clinics; 130 nursing home care units; and 37 domiciliary residences. VA operates at least one medical center in each of the 48 contiguous states, Puerto Rico, and the District of Columbia. With approximately 76,000 medical center beds, VA treats nearly 1 million patients in VA hospitals; 75,000 in nursing home care units; and 25,000 in domiciliary residences. VA's outpatient clinics register approximately 24 million visits per year. **Corporate headquarters location:** Washington DC. **Other area locations:** Akron; Canton; East Liverpool; Mansfield; McCafferty; New Philadelphia; Painesville; Ravenna; Sandusky; Wade Park; Warren; Youngstown.

U.S. DEPARTMENT OF VETERANS AFFFAIRS
DAYTON VETERANS ADMINISTRATION MEDICAL CENTER
4100 West Third Street, Dayton OH 45428. 937/268-6511. **Contact:** Human Resources. **World Wide Web address:** http://www.dayton.med.va.gov. **Description:** A medical center operated by the U.S. Department of Veterans Affairs. From 54 hospitals in 1930, the VA health care system has grown to include 171 medical centers; more than 364 outpatient, community, and outreach clinics; 130 nursing home care units; and 37 domiciliary residences. VA operates at least one medical center in each of the 48 contiguous states, Puerto Rico, and the District of Columbia. With approximately 76,000 medical center beds, VA treats nearly 1 million patients in VA hospitals; 75,000 in nursing home care units; and 25,000 in domiciliary residences. VA's outpatient clinics register approximately 24 million visits per year.

U.S. ENVIRONMENTAL PROTECTION AGENCY (EPA)
ANDREW BREIDENBACH CENTER
26 West Martin Luther King Drive, Cincinnati OH 45268. 513/569-7931. **Contact:** Human Resources. **World Wide Web address:** http://www.epa.gov. **Description:** the EPA is dedicated to improving and preserving the quality of the environment, both nationally and globally, and protecting human health and the productivity of natural resources. The agency is committed to ensuring that federal environmental laws are implemented and enforced effectively; U.S. policy, both foreign and domestic, fosters the integration of economic development and environmental protection so that economic growth can be sustained over the long term; and public and private decisions affecting energy, transportation, agriculture, industry, international trade, and natural resources fully integrate considerations of environmental quality. Founded in 1970. **NOTE:** To reach the Cincinnati Human Resources Office call: 513/569-7840. **Special programs:** Internships; Fellowships. **Corporate headquarters location:** Washington DC. **Other U.S. locations:** San Francisco CA; Denver CO; Atlanta GA; Chicago IL; Kansas City KS; Boston MA; New York NY; Philadelphia PA; Dallas TX; Seattle WA. **Operations at this facility include:** This location is a research and development laboratory. **Number of employees nationwide:** 19,000.

USG INTERIORS, INC.
1000 Crocker Road, Westlake OH 44145-1031. 440/871-1000. **Contact:** Human Resources. **World Wide Web address:** http://www.usg.com. **Description:** Manufactures interior construction products including flooring, ceiling grids, room dividers, and wall paneling. **Corporate headquarters location:** Chicago IL.

UNION METAL CORPORATION
P.O. Box 9920, Canton OH 44711. 330/456-7653. **Physical address:** 1432 Maple Avenue NE, Canton OH 44705. **Contact:** Human Resources. **E-mail address:** humanresources@unionmetal.com. **World Wide Web address:** http://www.unionmetal.com. **Description:** Manufactures metal poles for various applications including lampposts and sign structures.

UNION TOOLS COMPANY
P.O. Box 1930, Columbus OH 43216-1930. 614/222-4400. **Physical address:** 390 West Nationwide Boulevard, Columbus OH 43215. **Fax:** 614/222-4488. **Contact:** Human Resources. **E-mail address:** info@uniontools.com. **World Wide Web address:** http://www.uniontools.com. **Description:** Designs, manufactures, and markets nonpowered lawn and garden tools. The company's products include cutting tools, forks, hoes, posthole diggers, rakes, shovels, snow pushers, snow shovels, steel and aluminum scoops, striking tools, and wheelbarrows. Founded in 1890. **Corporate headquarters location:** This location.

UNITED McGILL CORPORATION
One Mission Park, Groveport OH 43125. 614/836-9981. **Fax:** 614/836-9843. **Contact:** Celeste Palanondon, Personnel Services Director. **E-mail address:** personnel@unitedmcgill.com. **World Wide Web address:** http://www.unitedmcgill.com. **Description:** An engineering, manufacturing, and construction firm. Products include spiral and rectangular ducts and fittings for HVAC, acoustical equipment, vacuum drying systems, pressure vessels, and air pollution control systems. Founded in 1951. **NOTE:** Entry-level positions are offered. **Subsidiaries include:** McGill AirClean Corporation; McGill AirFlow Corporation; McGill AirPressure Corporation; McGill AirSeal Corporation. **Special programs:** Training. **Office hours:** Monday - Friday, 8:00 a.m. - 5:00 p.m. **Corporate headquarters location:** This location. **Other area locations:** Columbus OH; Broadview Heights OH; West Chester OH; Westerville OH. **Other U.S. locations:** Nationwide. **Listed on:** Privately held. **Annual sales/revenues:** $51 - $100 million. **Number of employees nationwide:** 600.

UNIVERSITY HOSPITAL
234 Goodman Street, Cincinnati OH 45219. 513/584-2279. **Fax:** 513/584-2784. **Contact:** Human Resources. **World Wide Web address:** http://www.health-alliance.com/university.html. **Description:** A hospital specializing in acute and tertiary care. **Positions advertised include:** Radiologic Technologist; Special Procedures Technologist; Coder; Clinical Education Manager; Psychiatry Director; Patient Flow Manager; Health Unit Coordinator; Behavior Management Specialist; Administrative Secretary; Environmental Services Assistant; Paramedic; Licensed Practical Nurse; Pharmacist; Registered Nurse.

UNIVERSITY HOSPITAL BEDFORD MEDICAL CENTER
44 Blaine Avenue, Bedford OH 44146. 440/739-3900. **Recorded jobline:** 216/844-7500. **Fax:** 440/735-3552. **Contact:** Human Resources Manager. **E-mail address:** lashell.smith@uhhs.com. **World Wide Web address:** http://www.uhhsbmc.com. **Description:** A 110-bed nonprofit community hospital. **NOTE:** Second and third shifts are offered. **Positions advertised include:** Rehabilitation Aide; Licensed Practical Nurse; Nurse Practitioner; Registered Nurse; Pharmacist; Patient Registrar; Emergency

Services Technician; Laboratory Technologist; Transcriptionist. **Parent company:** University Hospitals Health System (Cleveland OH). **President:** Arlene Rak. **Number of employees at this location:** 450.

UNIVERSITY HOSPITALS OF CLEVELAND
11100 Euclid Avenue, Cleveland OH 44106. 216/844-1000. **Fax:** 216/844-4765. **Recorded jobline:** 216/844-7500. **Contact:** Manager. **World Wide Web address:** http://www.uhhs.com. **Description:** A 947-bed, tertiary medical center. University Hospitals of Cleveland includes Rainbow Babies & Children's Hospital, Ireland Cancer Center, and MacDonald Women's Hospital. **NOTE:** Entry-level positions are offered. **Positions advertised include:** Accountant; Clerical Supervisor; Clinical Lab Technician; Dietician; EEG Technologist; EKG Technician; Emergency Medical Technician; Human Resources Manager; Licensed Practical Nurse; Medical Records Technician; MIS Specialist; Nuclear Medicine Technologist; Occupational Therapist; Pharmacist; Physical Therapist; Psychologist; Registered Nurse; Social Worker; Software Engineer; Speech-Language Pathologist; Systems Analyst.

UNIVERSITY OF AKRON
Human Resources, 277 South Broadway Street, Second Floor, Akron OH 44325-4704. 330/972-5988. **Recorded jobline:** 330/972-7091. **Contact:** Employment Services. **E-mail address:** univofakron_employment@uakron.edu. **Description:** A public university serving approximately 24,000 students. The University of Akron offers 200 undergraduate majors and areas of study, as well as 100 master's degree programs, 17 doctoral degree programs, and four law degree programs. Founded in 1870 as Buchtel College. **NOTE:** Apply to posted positions only. Contact information and application procedures vary for Faculty and Professional positions. Consult website or contact Employment Services for further information regarding procedure and deadlines. **Positions advertised include:** Visiting Instructor, Mathematics; Assistant Professor, Voice; Assistant Professor, Biomedical Engineering; Spanish Instructor; Institutional Research Analyst; Residence Life Coordinator. **President:** Dr. Luis M. Proenza

UNIVERSITY OF CINCINNATI
51 Goodman Drive, P.O. Box 210117, Cincinnati OH 45221-0117. 513/556-3702. **Fax:** 513/556-9652. **Contact:** Employment Services. **E-mail address:** hrempl@ucmail.uc.edu. **World Wide Web address:** http://www.hr.uc.edu. **Description:** A university offering over 200 undergraduate and 125 graduate programs. The university is comprised of 16 colleges, a medical center, and a library with 1.8 million volumes. Founded in 1819. **NOTE:** Entry-level positions and second and third shifts are offered. **Positions advertised include:** Law Enforcement Officer; Laborer; Apprentice Stationary Engineer; Assistant Dean; Assistant Preschool Teacher; Grant Manager; Inventory Control Specialist; Training Specialist; Assistant Librarian; Adjunct Instructors, Various Disciplines; Visiting Physics Instructor; Assistant Biology Professor; Assistant Mathematics Professor . **Special programs:** Internships.

UNIVERSITY OF FINDLAY
1000 North Main Street, Findlay OH 45840-3695. 419/434-6964. **Toll-free phone:** 800/548-0932. **Fax:** 419/434-5976. **Contact:** Karen A. (Powell) Lieb, Human Resources. **E-mail address:** powell@findlay.edu. **World Wide Web address:** http://www.findlay.edu. **Description:** A private, coeducational university. Programs include Bilingual Business Education, Criminal Justice, Environmental and Hazardous Materials Management, Equestrian Studies, Japanese, Nuclear Medicine Technology, and Theatre Production. Founded in 1882. **Positions advertised include:** Professor, Art History; Assistant Professor, Accounting and Finance; Assistant Professor, Marketing; Instructor, Biology and Anatomy.

VAISALA
7450 Industrial Parkway, Plain City OH 43064. 614/873-6880. **Contact:** Peter Dunleavy, Controller. **World Wide Web address:** http://www.vaisala.com. **Description:** Designs, develops, and manufactures electronic measurement systems and related equipment for environmental sciences, industry, meteorology, and traffic safety. Vaisala markets its products primarily to air and road traffic authorities, defense forces, meteorological organizations, and research institutes. **Corporate headquarters location:** Woburn MA. **Other U.S. locations:** Sunnyvale CA; Boulder CO; Tucson AZ. **International locations:** Australia; Canada; China; France; Germany; Japan; Malaysia; Sweden; United Kingdom. **Parent Company:** Vaisala Oyj (Finland). **Number of employees worldwide:** 1,113.

VAN DYNE CROTTY, INC.
3233 Newmark Drive, Miamisburg OH 45342. 937/236-1500. **Toll-free phone:** 800/826-3963. **Fax:** 937/435-8432. **Contact:** Human Resources. **World Wide Web address:** http://www.vandynecrotty.com. **Description:** Provides uniform leasing and textile services. **Positions advertised include:** Service Representative; Sales Representative. **Corporate headquarters location:** This location. **Other area locations:** Cleveland OH; Toledo OH. **Operations at this facility include:** Administration; Sales; Service. **Listed on:** Privately held. **Number of employees at this location:** 250. **Number of employees nationwide:** 750.

VENTURE CORPORATION
P.O. Box 2002, 2109 Commerce Street, Lancaster OH 43130-9363. 740/654-6620. **Contact:** Human Resources Department. **Description:** A manufacturer of molded and painted plastic exterior components for original equipment manufacturers of cars, light trucks, sport utility vehicles, and minivans. The company's products include grille opening panels and reinforcements, bumper covers, body side moldings and claddings, fender extensions, wheel lips, spoilers, molded bumper beams, hoods, sunroofs, doors, and lift gates. Venture parts are used in vehicles manufactured by Ford, Chrysler, Honda, Mazda, Nissan, and GM. **Corporate headquarters location:** Frasier MI.

VENTURE PACKAGING, INC.
P.O. 246, 311 West Monroe Street, Monroeville OH 44847. 419/465-2539. **Contact:** Human Resources. **Description:** Manufactures plastic buckets and containers for use in the food industry. **Parent company:** Barry Plastics Corporation.

VICTORIA'S SECRET STORES
Four Limited Parkway East, Reynoldsburg OH 43068. 614/577-7000. **Fax:** 614/577-7047. **Contact:** Human Resources. **World Wide Web address:** http://www.limitedbrands.com. **Description:** Victoria's Secret operates a women's lingerie and clothing chain with over 1,000 shops nationwide. **Positions advertised include:** Senior Financial Analyst; Visual Merchandising Manager; Senior Marketing Analyst; Merchandise Planner; Inventory Control Accountant; Accounting Processor; Director, Human Resources; Divisional Planning Manager; Insurance Analyst. **Parent company:** Limited Brands. **Operations at this facility include:** This location houses divisional headquarters administrative offices. **Listed on:** New York Stock Exchange. **Stock exchange symbol:** LTD. **Number of employees at this location:** 800.

VOLT SERVICES GROUP
4027 Colonel Glenn Highway, Suite 100, Beavercreek OH 45431. 937/431-5239. **Fax:** 937/431-5280. **Contact:** Human Resources. **E-mail address:** dayton@volt.com. **World Wide Web address:** http://www.volt.com. **Description:** Provides staffing solutions in telecommunications and Information Technology. **Positions advertised include:** Forklift Operator; Electronic Assembler.

WBNS-TV
DISPATCH BROADCAST GROUP
P.O. Box 1010, Columbus OH 43216. 614/460-3700. **Physical address:** 770 Twin Rivers Drive, Columbus OH 43215. **Fax:** 614/460-3927. **Contact:** Lori Lewellen, Director of Human Resources. **World Wide Web address:** http://www.wbns10tv.com. **Description:** A local television station. **NOTE:** Part-time jobs are offered. **Positions advertised include:** Executive Producer of Special Projects; Internet Sales Manager; Business Manager; Assignment Editor; Producer; Reporter. **Special programs:** Internships. **Corporate headquarters location:** This location. **Other U.S. locations:** Indianapolis IN. **Parent company:** Dispatch Broadcast Group (also at this location) has several operations in addition to WBNS-TV: Dispatch Interactive Television offers wireless interfaces using the television remote control; Dispatch Productions provides programming services; Ohio News Network provides up-to-the-minute news, sports, and weather across the state; Radio Sound Network is a satellite delivery system; Radiohio is comprised of WBNS-AM, an all-sports radio station, and WBNS-FM, an oldies station; WALV-TV offers a variety of television programming; and WTHR-TV is an all-news television station. **Operations at this facility include:** Administration; Sales. **Listed on:** Privately held. **President/CEO:** Michael J. Fiorile. **Information Systems Manager:** Dan Black. **Number of employees at this location:** 325. **Number of employees nationwide:** 600.

WCI STEEL COMPANY
999 Pine Avenue SE, Warren OH 44483-6528. 330/841-8218. **Toll-free phone:** 800/535-0103. **Contact:** Human Resources. **World Wide Web address:** http://www.wcisteel.com. **Description:** Produces flat-rolled steel products for the automotive, construction, electrical equipment manufacturing, and strip converter industries. WCI Steel Company specializes in alloy, custom carbon, and electrical steel products. **NOTE:** As of January 2004, the company has been working to cut costs in an effort to emerge from bankruptcy. **Corporate headquarters location:** This location. **Operations at this facility include:** Administration; Manufacturing; Sales; Service. **Number of employees at this location:** 1,800.

WLWT-CHANNEL 5
1700 Young Street, Cincinnati OH 45210. 513/412-5000. **Contact:** Human Resources. **World Wide Web address:** http://www.wlwt.com. **Description:** A television station. **Positions advertised include:** Assistant Editor; TV Engineer; Part-Time Production Assistant. **Special Programs:** Internships.

WACHOVIA SECURITIES
2300 Kettering Towers, Dayton OH 45423. 937/228-2828. **Toll-free phone:** 800/543-9083. **Fax:** 937/226-6767. **Contact:** Human Resources. **World Wide Web address:** http://www.wachovia.com. **Description:** An international securities brokerage and investment firm. The company offers clients more than 70 different investment products including stocks, options, bonds, commodities, tax-favored investments, and insurance, as well as several specialized financial services. **Other U.S. locations:** Nationwide.

WARREN FABRICATING AND MACHINING CORPORATION
P.O. Box 1032, Warren OH 44482. 330/847-0596. **Physical address:** 3240 Mahoning Avenue, Warren OH 44483. **Contact:** Human Resources. **E-mail address:** info@warfab.com. **World Wide Web address:** http://www.warfab.com. **Description:** Engaged in the fabrication of large steel fabrications and heavy machining for the large press, power generation, surface mining, and steel industries. Warren Fabricating and Machining Corporation specializes in large fabrications, heavy machining, steel mill repair, and surface mining replacement parts.

WASHINGTON GROUP INTERNATIONAL
1500 West Third Street, Cleveland OH 44113. 216/523-5600. **Fax:** 216/523-5922. **Contact:** Human Resources. **World Wide Web address:** http://www.wgint.com. **Description:** An engineering and construction firm operating through five major divisions: Government, Industrial/Process, Infrastructure & Mining, Petroleum & Chemicals, and Power. Washington Group International offers construction, engineering, and program-management services to the environmental, industrial, mining, nuclear-services, power, transportation, and water resources industries. **Corporate headquarters location:** Boise ID. **Other U.S. locations:** Nationwide. **International locations:** Worldwide. **Number of employees worldwide:** 26,000.

WASTEQUIP
25800 Science Park Drive, Suite 140, Cleveland OH 44122. 216/292-2554. **Contact:** Personnel. **World Wide Web address:** http://www.wastequip.com. **Description:** Develops, manufactures, and markets mobile and stationary solid waste handling equipment. Products include dump bodies and conversion hoists. **Corporate headquarters location:** Sterling Heights MI. **Parent company:** McClain Industries. **Listed on:** New York Stock Exchange. **Stock exchange symbol:** MCCL.

WASTE MANAGEMENT, INC.
1006 Walnut Street, Canal Winchester OH 43110. 614/833-9155. **Fax:** 614/833-5280. **Contact:** Tim Turner, Personnel. **E-mail address:** tturner@wm.com. **World Wide Web address:** http://www.wm.com. **Description:** A non-hazardous solid waste management business. **Positions advertised include:** Commercial Driver; Customer Service Representative; Laborer; Mechanic. **Corporate headquarters location:** Houston TX. **Other U.S. locations:** Nationwide. **Listed on:** New York Stock Exchange. **Stock exchange symbol:** WMI. **Number of employees nationwide:** 51,700.

WAXMAN INDUSTRIES, INC.
24460 Aurora Road, Bedford Heights OH 44146. 440/439-1830. **Fax:** 440/439-8678. **Contact:** Personnel. **World Wide Web address:** http://www.waxmanind.com. **Description:** A holding company that supplies plumbing hardware, and floor and surface protection products to the repair and remodeling markets. Waxman Industries, Inc. operates through six divisions: Medal of Pennsylvania, Inc. distributes construction hardware products to independent retailers; WAMI Sales distributes pipe nipples, fittings, valves and related plumbing products to industrial distributors; Waxman Consumer Products Group, Inc. distributes floor, plumbing, and surface protection products to retailers; and CWI, The Orient Group, and TWI are the company's foreign operating divisions that manufacture and package products for distribution. Founded in 1934. **Corporate headquarters location:** This location.

WEBSTER INDUSTRIES, INC.
325 Hall Street, Tiffin OH 44883. 419/447-8232. **Toll-free phone:** 800/243-9327. **Fax:** 419/448-1618. **Contact:** Personnel Department. **World Wide Web address:** http://www.websterchain.com. **Description:** Manufactures and markets castings, conveyors, and welded steel chains. Webster Industries, Inc. specializes in apron

conveyors; cast and steel sprockets and traction wheels; drive chains; engineered steel chains, hardened steel bushed roller-less chains; malleable cast and combination chains; malleable iron castings; steel bushed roller chains; vibrating conveyors; and welded steel chains. Founded in 1876. **Corporate headquarters location:** This location. **Other U.S. locations:** Meridian MS; Tualatan OR. **Parent company:** Chelsea Industries, Inc. (Peabody MA). **Listed on:** Privately held. **Number of employees at this location:** 270. **Number of employees nationwide:** 325.

WELDED CONSTRUCTION COMPANY
P.O. Box 470, Perrysburg OH 43552-0470. 419/874-3548. **Physical address:** 26933 Eckel Road, Perrysburg OH 43551. **Fax:** 419/874-4883. **Contact:** Alexandra Shroyer. **E-mail address:** ashroyer@welded.com. **World Wide Web address:** http://www.welded-construction.com. **Description:** A construction company that specializes in the manufacture and installation of pipeline for the natural gas, oil and product pipeline markets. In addition to mainline construction, Welded Construction Company also provides compressor station installation, emergency repair, meter station installation, testing and rehabilitation, and valve replacement.

WENDY'S INTERNATIONAL, INC.
4288 West Dublin Granville Road, Dublin OH 43017. 614/764-3100. **Contact:** Human Resources. **World Wide Web address:** http://www.wendysintl.com. **Description:** One of the world's largest restaurant franchising companies. Wendy's International is comprised of Wendy's, a fast-food restaurant chain, and Tim Horton's, a coffee and baked goods restaurant chain. **Positions advertised include:** Marketing Research Manager; Administrative Assistant; Advertising Production Supervisor; Director, Investor Communications; Director, Construction Planning; Equipment Specialist; Treasury Analyst. **Corporate headquarters location:** This location. **Other U.S. locations:** Nationwide. **Listed on:** New York Stock Exchange. **Stock exchange symbol:** WEN.

WESTERN AND SOUTHERN LIFE INSURANCE COMPANY
400 Broadway, Cincinnati OH 45202. 513/629-1800. **Contact:** Human Resources. **E-mail address:** human.resources@westernsouthernlife.com. **World Wide Web address:** http://www.westernsouthernlife.com. **Description:** Provides life insurance services. **Positions advertised include:** Accounting Analyst; Annuity Service Representative; Application Specialist; Computer Operator; Direct Marketing Manager; Technical Sales Manager; Sales Representative. **Subsidiaries include:** Western-Southern Life Assurance Company (also at this location) offers life and annuity products. **Parent company:** The Western-Southern Enterprise is a diversified financial service company operating through Western and Southern Life Insurance Company and its subsidiary. Subsidiaries of the parent company include: Capital Analysis Inc.; Columbus Life Insurance Company; Eagle Realty Group; Fort Washington Investment Advisors; IFS Financial Services; Touchstone Funds.

WESTFIELD GROUP
One Park Circle, P.O. Box 5001, Westfield Center OH 44251. 330/887-0101. **Toll-free phone:** 800/243-0210. **Contact:** Human Resources Department. **E-mail address:** hrshare@westfield-cos.com. **World Wide Web address:** http://www.westfieldgrp.com. **Description:** In business for over 150 years, Westfield Group conducts property and casualty insurance through approximately 2,000 independent insurance agents in 16 states. Westfield Group also provides banking services through Westfield Bank and insurance industry support and outsourcing solutions through Westfield Services Inc. Westfield Group has approximately $2 billion in assets and holds an A (Excellent) rating from A.M. Best, a leading insurance financial rating agency. The company has approximately 2,300 employees working in 60 offices servicing 16 states. Though headquartered at this location, claims and agency marketing activities are handled in local offices. Westfield Group is ranked in the top 40 among P & C insurers in the United States. They are the ninth largest farm writer in the nation, ranked number one in Ohio for Fidelity and Surety, and have $1 billion in direct written premiums. **Corporate headquarters location:** This location.

WHIRLPOOL CORPORATION
P.O. Box 1808, Marion OH 43301-1808. 740/383-7122. **Physical address:** 1300 Marion Agosta Road, Marion OH 43302. **Contact:** Personnel. **E-mail address:** careers@email.whirlpool.com. **World Wide Web address:** http://www.whirlpool.com. **Description:** Whirlpool Corporation manufactures and markets home appliances. The company markets its products worldwide under brand names such as Whirlpool, KitchenAid, Roper, Estate, Bauknecht, Ignis, Laden, and Inglis. Whirlpool also manufactures and supplies major home appliances to Sears, Roebuck and Company under the Kenmore brand name. **NOTE:** Interested candidates can search and apply for positions online. **Corporate headquarters location:** Benton Harbor MI. **Operations at this facility include:** This location manufactures clothes dryers. **Listed on:** New York Stock Exchange. **Stock exchange symbol:** WHR. **Number of employees worldwide:** 68,000.

WHIRLPOOL CORPORATION
4901 North Main Street, Findlay OH 45840. 419/423-8123. **Contact:** Ed Moore, Human Resources Manager. **E-mail address:** careers@email.whirlpool.com. **World Wide Web address:** http://www.whirlpool.com. **Description:** Whirlpool Corporation manufactures and markets home appliances. The company markets its products worldwide under brand names such as Whirlpool, KitchenAid, Roper, Estate, Bauknecht, Ignis, Laden, and Inglis. Whirlpool also manufactures and supplies major home appliances to Sears, Roebuck and Company under the Kenmore brand name. **NOTE:** Search and apply for positions online. **Corporate headquarters location:** Benton Harbor MI. **Operations at this facility include:** This location manufactures both industrial and commercial machinery. **Listed on:** New York Stock Exchange. **Stock exchange symbol:** WHR. **Number of employees at this location:** 2,000. **Number of employees worldwide:** 68,000.

WHIRLPOOL CORPORATION
119 Birdseye Street, Clyde OH 43410. 419/547-7711. **Contact:** Human Resources. **E-mail address:** careers@email.whirlpool.com. **World Wide Web address:** http://www.whirlpool.com. **Description:** Whirlpool Corporation manufactures and markets home appliances. The company markets its products worldwide under brand names such as Whirlpool, KitchenAid, Roper, Estate, Bauknecht, Ignis, Laden, and Inglis. Whirlpool also manufactures and supplies major home appliances to Sears, Roebuck and Company under the Kenmore brand name. **NOTE:** Search and apply for positions online. **Corporate headquarters location:** Benton Harbor MI. **Operations at this facility include:** This location manufactures washing machines. **Listed on:** New York Stock Exchange. **Stock exchange symbol:** WHR. **Number of employees worldwide:** 68,000.

WHITE CASTLE SYSTEM INC.
555 West Goodale Street, Columbus OH 43215. 614/228-5781. **Contact:** Human Resources Manager. **World Wide Web address:** http://www.whitecastle.com. **Description:** White Castle owns and operates 380 hamburger restaurants, primarily in the Midwest. **Positions advertised include:** Accountant. **Corporate headquarters location:** This location. **Number of employees nationwide:** 13,000.

WIL RESEARCH LABORATORIES
1407 George Road, Ashland OH 44805. 419/289-8700. **Contact:** Human Resources. **E-mail address:** info@wilresearch.com. **World Wide Web address:** http://www.wilresearch.com. **Description:** A contract pharmaceutical and chemical laboratory. **NOTE:** Entry-level positions are offered. Interested candidates should submit a completed employment application (which may be downloaded from the website), along with a resume for review. **Positions advertised include:** Reproductive Toxicologist; Juvenile Toxicologist; Biologist; Staff Pathologist; Research Assistant; Formulations Specialist; Chemist; Report Writer; Auditor; Histologist. **Number of employees at this location:** 175.

WILL-BURT COMPANY
P.O. Box 900, Orrville OH 44667-0900. 330/682-7015. **Physical address:** 169 South Main Street, Orrville OH 44667. **Fax:** 330/684-5261. **Contact:** Human Resources. **E-mail address:** employment@willburt.com. **World Wide Web address:** http://www.willburt.com/channels. **Description:** Manufactures fabricated and machined original equipment including lights and antennae. Founded in 1918. **NOTE:** Second and third shifts are offered. **Positions advertised include:** Mechanical Engineer; Engineering Systems Administrator. **Corporate headquarters location:** This location. **Operations at this facility include:** Administration; Manufacturing; Sales; Service. **Listed on:** Privately held. **CEO:** Jeffrey Evans. **Annual sales/revenues:** $21 - $50 million. **Number of employees at this location:** 370.

WILLIS OF OHIO, INC.
655 Metro Place South, Suite 900, Dublin OH 43017. 614/766-8900. **Contact:** Human Resources. **World Wide Web address:** http://www.willis.com. **Description:** Provides insurance sales and service. **Corporate headquarters location:** Nashville TN. **Parent company:** Willis Group Holdings. **Operations at this facility include:** Sales. **Listed on:** New York Stock Exchange. **Stock exchange symbol:** WSH.

WINEGARDNER AND HAMMONS INC.
4243 Hunt Road, Cincinnati OH 45242. 513/891-1066. **Fax:** 513/794-2595. **Contact:** Dave Gordon, Human Resources. **E-mail address:** dave.gordon@whihotels.com. **World Wide Web address:** http://www.whihotels.com. **Description:** A hotel managing agency. **Positions advertised include:** Business Development Account Manager.

WIZARD COMPUTER SERVICES, INC.
6908 Engle Road, Suite J, Middleburg Heights OH 44130. 440/891-0060. **Fax:** 440/891-0066. **Contact:** Human Resources Department. **E-mail address:** info@wizardcomputer.com. **World Wide Web address:** http://www.wizardcomputer.com. **Description:** Wizard Computer Services provides a variety of computer services including planning networks, providing hardware, integrating operating systems, and continual service and support.

WOOSTER BRUSH COMPANY
604 Madison Avenue, P.O. Box 6010, Wooster OH 44691-6010. 330/264-4440. **Contact:** Personnel. **World Wide Web address:** http://www.woosterbrush.com. **Description:** Wooster Brush Company develops, manufactures, and markets paint application products and related equipment. The company's products include buckets and surface prep tools; paintbrushes and roller covers; and roller frames and extension poles. **Corporate headquarters location:** This location. **Other U.S. locations:** Reno NV. **Number of employees nationwide:** 600.

WORLD KITCHEN INC.
359 State Avenue NW, Massillon OH 44647. 330/832-5026. **Fax:** 607/377-8962. **Contact:** Human Resources. **E-mail address:** careers@worldkitchen.com. **World Wide Web address:** http://www.worldkitchen.com. **Description:** Manufactures baking equipment for household use. **NOTE:** Mail resumes to: Human Resources Department, World Kitchen Inc., 11911 Freedom Drive, Suite 600, Reston VA 20190-5629. **Corporate headquarters location:** Reston VA. **Number of employees worldwide:** 3,000.

WORTHINGTON INDUSTRIES, INC.
1205 Dearborn Drive, Columbus OH 43085. 614/438-3210. **Contact:** Director of Personnel. **E-mail address:** jobs@worthingtonindustries.com. **World Wide Web address:** http://www.worthingtonindustries.com. **Description:** Worthington Industries, Inc. is a value-added steel processor. The company specializes in manufactured metal products including automotive aftermarket stampings, laser welded blanks, metal ceiling grid systems, and pressure cylinders. **Positions advertised include:** Credit Union Manager; Part-time Medical Receptionist. **Special programs:** Internships. **Corporate headquarters location:** This location. **Listed on:** New York Stock Exchange. **Stock exchange symbol:** WOR.

WRIGHT STATE UNIVERSITY
3640 Colonel Glenn Highway, 280 University Hall, Dayton OH 45435. 937/775-2120. **Fax:** 937/775-3040. **Recorded jobline:** 937/775-4562. **Contact:** Human Resources. **E-mail address:** human_resources@wright.edu. **World Wide Web address:** http://www.wright.edu. **Description:** A university engaged in teaching, research, and service. **NOTE:** Resumes only accepted for posted positions. **Positions advertised include:** Research Assistant; University Engineer; Adjunct Mathematics Instructor, Assistant Professor, Obstetrics and Gynecology; Faculty Associate, Modern Languages. **Operations at this facility include:** Education. **Number of employees at this location:** 2,300.

WYSE ADVERTISING, INC.
25 Prospect Avenue West, Suite 1700, Cleveland OH 44115. 216/696-2424. **Contact:** Human Resources. **E-mail address:** info@wyseadv.com. **World Wide Web address:** http://www.wyseadv.com. **Description:** An advertising agency. Wyse Advertising, Inc. specializes in account service, broadcast production, information systems, media, print production, and strategic planning. **CEO:** Marc Wyse.

XAVIER UNIVERSITY
3800 Victory Parkway, Cincinnati OH 45207-4641. 513/745-3638. **Fax:** 513/745-3644. **Contact:** Kathleen Riga, Assistant Vice President of Human Resources. **E-mail address:** hr@xu.edu. **World Wide Web address:** http://www.xu.edu. **Description:** A private, coeducational, liberal arts, Jesuit university. **NOTE:** Candidates interested in Adjunct Faculty positions should forward a resume to the Chair of the appropriate department. **Positions advertised include:** Assistant Professor, Psychology; Visiting Assistant Professor, Economics and Human Resources.

XETRON CORPORATION
460 West Crescentville Road, Cincinnati OH 45246. 513/881-3254. **Fax:** 513/881-3275. **Contact:** Art Bush, Human Resources. **E-mail address:** resumes@xetron.com.

World Wide Web address: http://www.xetron.com. **Description:** Engaged in the research and development of electronic communication systems. Founded in 1973. **Positions advertised include:** Digital Signal Processing Engineer; Software Design Engineer; Embedded Software Engineer; Senior Project/Systems Engineer. **Special programs:** Internships. **Corporate headquarters location:** This location. **Parent company:** Northrop Grumman. **Operations at this facility include:** Administration; Manufacturing; Research and Development; Sales; Service. **Annual sales/revenues:** $21 - $50 million. **Number of employees at this location:** 150.

XOMOX CORPORATION
4444 Cooper Road, Cincinnati OH 45242. 513/745-6000. **Fax:** 513/745-6972. **Contact:** Nick Powell, Vice President of Human Resources. **E-mail address:** careers@xomox.com. **World Wide Web address:** http://www.xomox.com. **Description:** Designs, develops, and manufactures quarter turn on-off process valves in alloy and fluorocarbon lined materials. Xomox Corporation markets its products under the Tufline brand name to the chemical, hydrocarbon processing, petrochemical and pulp and paper industries. **Positions advertised include:** Supply Chain Development Engineer. **Corporate headquarters location:** This location. **International locations:** Canada; England; France; Germany; India; Mexico.

XTEK INC.
11451 Reading Road, Cincinnati OH 45241. 513/733-7800. **Fax:** 513/733-7939. **Contact:** Jennifer King, Director of Human Resources. **World Wide Web address:** http://www.xtek.com. **Description:** A manufacturer of engineered products for heavy industry including gearing, crane wheels, couplings, and cold rolling rolls. **Corporate headquarters location:** This location. **Operations at this facility include:** Administration; Manufacturing; Research and Development; Sales; Service.

YMCA OF CENTRAL OHIO
40 West Long Street, Columbus OH 43215. 614/224-1142. **Fax:** 614/224-0639. **Contact:** Lori Leist, Human Resources Director. **E-mail address:** lleist@ymca-columbus.com. **World Wide Web address:** http://www.ymca-columbus.com. **Description:** One of the nation's largest and most comprehensive nonprofit service organizations. The YMCA provides health and fitness; social and personal development; sports and recreation; education and career development; and camps and conferences to children, youths, adults, the elderly, families, disabled individuals, refugees and foreign nationals, YMCA residents, and community residents through a broad range of specific programs. This location also hires seasonally. **NOTE:** Entry-level positions and part-time jobs are offered. **Positions advertised include:** Supportive Housing Program Case Manager; Swimming/Water Fitness Lifeguard; Custodian; Childcare Teacher; Camp Counselor. **Special programs:** Summer Jobs. **Other U.S. locations:** Nationwide. **International locations:** Worldwide. **President/CEO:** John Bickley. **Number of employees at this location:** 800.

YORK INTERNATIONAL CORPORATION
9000 Bank Street, Cleveland OH 44125. 216/447-0696. **Contact:** Human Resources. **World Wide Web address:** http://www.york.com. **Description:** Manufactures air conditioners and furnaces for both commercial and residential applications. **Corporate headquarters location:** York PA. **Listed on:** New York Stock Exchange. **Stock exchange symbol:** YRK. **Number of employees worldwide:** 23,000.

YOUNGSTOWN STATE UNIVERSITY
One University Plaza, Youngstown OH 44555. 330/941-3122. **Fax:** 330/941-3716. **Contact:** Human Resources Department. **World Wide Web address:** http://www.ysu.edu. **Description:** A state university offering a wide range of associate, baccalaureate, and graduate degrees and certificate programs. **Positions advertised include:** Assistant Professor, Geography; Assistant Professor, Center for Working Class Studies; Assistant Professor, Psychology; Assistant Professor, Social Work; Electronic Services Librarian; Bursar. **Office hours:** Monday – Friday, 8:00 a.m. – 5:00 p.m. **President:** David C. Sweet.

ZF BATAVIA
1981 Front Wheel Drive, Batavia OH 45103. 513/732-4000. **Fax:** 513/732-4072. **Contact:** Personnel. **World Wide Web address:** http://www.zf.com. **Description:** This location manufactures front-wheel drive transmissions. **Parent company:** ZF Friedrichshafen AG.

ZUMBIEL PACKAGING
2339 Harris Avenue, Cincinnati OH 45212. 513/531-3600. **Fax:** 513/531-0072. **Contact:** Personnel Director. **World Wide Web address:** http://www.zumbiel.com. **Description:** A producer of paper and related packaging goods including Rewrite folding cartons, set-up boxes, and acetate beverage carriers including beer and soft drink 12- and 24-packs. **Corporate headquarters location:** This location. **Operations at this facility include:** Administration; Manufacturing; Sales.

AAON INC.
2425 South Yukon Avenue, Tulsa OK 74107. 918/583-2266. **Fax:** 918/583-6094. **Contact:** Human Resources. **E-mail address:** aaonhr@aaon.com. **World Wide Web address:** http://www.aaon.com. **Description:** Engineers, manufactures, and markets air conditioning and heating equipment. **Corporate headquarters location:** This location. **Other U.S. locations:** Longview TX. **Listed on:** NASDAQ. **Stock exchange symbol:** AAON. **CEO/President:** Norman Asbjornson. **Sales/Revenues:** Approximately $41.7 million.

AMCAT (AMERICAN COMPUTER & TELEPHONE, INC.)
1603 SE 19th Street, Suite 112, Edmond OK 73013. 405/216-8080. **Toll-free phone:** 800/364-5518. **Contact:** Nicole Hutchinson, Human Resources Director. **World Wide Web address:** http://www.amcat.com. **Description:** Specializes in the manufacture and distribution of telemarketing automation products and predictive dialers. **Corporate headquarters location:** This location. **International locations:** London, England. **President:** Rich Tehrani.

AMERICAN ELECTRIC POWER PSO
P.O. Box 201, Tulsa OK 74102-0201. 918/599-2000. **Physical address:** 212 East 6th Street, Tulsa OK 74119. **Contact:** Human Resources. **World Wide Web address:** http://www.aep.com. **Description:** An electric utility company that provides power to eastern and southwestern Oklahoma. **NOTE:** Applications available online for specific positions or general consideration. Applicants for this location can also inquire through the Oklahoma Employment Agency. **Special Programs:** Co-ops; Internships. **Corporate headquarters location:** Columbus OH. **Other area locations:** Lawton OK. **Other U.S. locations:** AR; IN; KY; LA; MI; OH; TN; TX; VA; WV. **International locations:** Australia; Brazil; China; Mexico; Norway; Sweden; United Kingdom; continental Europe. **Subsidiaries include:** AEP Energy Services; AEP Coal, Incorporated; AEP North American Energy Delivery; AEP Retail Energy; AEP ProServ, Incorporated; Houston Pipeline Company; Louisiana Intrastate Gas Company; MEMCO Barge Line; Numanco; United Sciences Testing, Incorporated. **Listed on:** New York Stock Exchange. **Stock exchange symbol:** AEP. **President/CEO/Executive Officer:** E. Linn Draper Junior. **Sales/Revenue:** Approximately $61.3 billion. **Number of employees nationwide:** Over 22,000.

AMETEK PRESTOLITE MOTORS
1211 East Cherokee, Wagoner OK 74467. 918/485-5572. **Contact:** Human Resources. **World Wide Web address:** http://www.prestolite.com. **Description:** Produces breaker points, rotors, coils, condensers, electronic engine controls, and related products, marketed under the Prestolite Electric, Indiel, and Leece-Neville brand names. **NOTE:** Ametek Prestolite Motors utilizes the Cherokee Temp Agency in Muskogee OK for hiring purposes. **Office hours:** Monday – Friday, 7 a.m. – 4 p.m. **Corporate headquarters location:** Ann Arbor MI. **Other U.S. locations:** Arcade NY; Florence KY. **International locations:** United Kingdom; South Africa; South America. **Parent Company:** Presolite Electric, Incorporated. **Sales/Revenue:** $167.1 million.

ARINC INCORPORATED
6400 SE 59th Street, Oklahoma City OK 73135. 405/601-6000. **Fax:** 405/ 601-6041. **Contact:** Sophia Jones, Recruiter. **World Wide Web address:** http://www.arinc.com. **Description:** An engineering and management consulting firm that provides technical studies, analyses, and evaluations of aircraft and ship systems, as well as communication and information systems. Customers of ARINC include the Department of Defense, the Department of Energy, the Department of Transportation, and the Federal Aviation Administration. **NOTE:** ARINC prefers that applications be submitted on their Website. **Positions advertised include:** Aircraft Sensor Operator; Senior Tool Designer; Principal Engineer; Senior Financial Analyst; Logistics Analyst; Aircraft Mission Specialist; Staff Analyst; Avionics Technician; Helicopter Mechanic; Aircraft Technician; Aircraft Mission Specialist; Aviation Advisor; Senior Technical Reviewer; Technical Manager. **Special programs:** Educational Assistance Program; Training; Internships; Co-ops. **Office hours:** Monday - Friday, 8:00 a.m. - 5:00 p.m. **Corporate headquarters location:** Annapolis MD. **Other U.S. locations:** Nationwide. **International locations:** Worldwide. **Chairman/CEO:** James Pierce. **Sales/Revenue:** $608 million. **Number of employees at this location:** 85. **Number of employees worldwide:** 3,000.

ARVEST BANK
P.O. Box 999, Bartlesville OK 74005. 918/337-3442. **Physical address:** 121 SW 4th Street, Bartlesville OK 74005. **Recorded jobline:** 918/337-3442. **Fax:** 918/337-3530. **Contact:** Paula Lowe, Human Resources. **World Wide Web address:** http://www.arvest.com. **Description:** Provides banking and other financial services to residents of Bartlesville and the surrounding towns. **NOTE:** Part-time positions available. The bank only accepts applications for current openings. **Office hours:** Monday – Friday, 8:00 a.m. – 4:00 p.m. **Corporate headquarters location:** Prairie Grove AR. **Other area locations:** Statewide. **Other U.S. locations:** AR; MO. **Parent company:** WestStar Bank. **Sales/Revenues:** $4 billion. **Number of employees nationwide:** Over 2,700.

BALDOR ELECTRIC COMPANY
P.O. Box 305, Westville OK 74965. 918/723-5424. **Fax:** 918/723-4554. **Physical address:** 305 Ballman Road, Westville OK 74965. **Contact:** Bob Kiefer, Personnel Coordinator. **World Wide Web address:** http://www.baldor.com. **Description:** Designs, manufactures, and markets industrial electrical components such as drives, generators, and motors. **NOTE:** Baldor Electric typically hires through two temp agencies. Job seekers can contact Personnel Consultants in Stilwell OK or Staff Marks in Siloam Springs OK. **Corporate headquarters location:** Fort Smith AR. **Other U.S. locations:** Nationwide. **International locations:** Worldwide. **Listed on:** New York Stock Exchange. **Stock exchange symbol:** BEZ. **President/Chief Executive Officer:** John A. McFarland.

BAR-S FOODS COMPANY
P.O. Box 339, Clinton OK 73601. 580/323-2468. **Fax:** 580/331-1686. **Physical address:** 200 Locust Avenue, Clinton OK 73601. **Contact:** Paul Adams, Personnel Director. **World Wide Web address:** http://www.bar-s.com. **Description:** Produces and distributes smoked meat products, including ham, bacon, franks, sausage, luncheon meat, and cheese. Founded in 1981. **Corporate headquarters location:** Phoenix AZ. **Other area locations:** Altus OK; Elk City OK; Lawton OK. **Operations at this facility include:** This location is a meat-processing plant. **Number of employees nationwide:** 1,600.

THE BEARD COMPANY
Enterprise Plaza, 5600 North May Avenue, Suite 320, Oklahoma City OK 73112. 405/842-2333. **Fax:** 405/842-9901. **Contact:** Linda Shrum or Rebecca Witcher, Human Resources. **E-mail address:** info@beardco.com. **World Wide Web address:** http://www.beardco.com. **Description:** Primary operations include carbon dioxide production, coal reclamation projects, and chemical compound fertilizer initiatives in China through their subsidiary, Beard Sino-American Resources, as well as the pursuit of e-commerce activities related to Starpay. **Subsidiaries include:** Beard Sino-American Resources Co., Inc. (Beijing, China); Beard Technologies (Pittsburgh PA); starpay.com (Oklahoma City OK). **Listed on:** OTC. **Stock exchange symbol:** BRCO. **President:** Herb Mee, Junior.

BIOS
309 East Dewey Avenue, Sapulpa OK 74066. 918/227-3734x196. **Fax:** 918/227-8378. **Contact:** Michael Shaw, Employee Relations. **E-mail address:** mshaw@bioscorpok.com. **World Wide Web address:** http://www.bioscorpok.com. **Description:** Provides residential services to people with developmental disabilities by teaching life, community, social, and vocational skills. **NOTE:** Online applications are available, to be faxed, e-mailed, or printed and sent to the Human Resources Department at given address. **Special programs:** College Reimbursement Plan. **Positions advertised include:** Vocational Habilitation Training Specialist; Habilitation Training Specialist. **Corporate headquarters location:** This location. **Other area locations:** Sapulpa OK; Bartlesville OK; Muskogee OK; Oklahoma City OK; Enid OK. **CEO:** Eddie Miller.

BLUE CROSS BLUE SHIELD OF OKLAHOMA
P.O. Box 1581, Tulsa OK 74102. 918/560-3500. **Physical address:** 1215 South Boulder Avenue, Tulsa OK 74119. **Fax:** 918/560-3060. **Recorded jobline:** 918/560-7888. **Contact:** Harry Wolohon, Employment Manager. **E-mail address:** hwolohon@bcbsok.com. **World Wide Web address:** http://www.bcbsok.com. **Description:** A nonprofit health care insurance organization providing managed health care plans to both individuals and groups. Blue Cross Blue Shield offers Point-of-Service, individual health, PPO, and HMO plans, as well as dental insurance. **Positions advertised include:** Internal Audit Clerk; Accounting Clerk; Auditor; Managed Care Registered Nurse; ABC/CFO Accountant; Manager. **Subsidiaries include:** GHS Property and Casualty. **Chairman/CEO/ President:** Ron King.

BOEING COMMERCIAL AIRPLANES
P.O. Box 582808, Tulsa OK 74158. 918/832-3384. **Physical address:** 3330 North Mingo Road, Tulsa OK 74158. **Fax:** 918/832-3288. **Contact:** Human Resources. **E-mail address:** EmploymentOperations@boeing.com. **World Wide Web address:** http://www.boeing.com. **Description:** Develops, fabricates, and assembles aerospace structures including sheet metal assemblies and machine parts. **NOTE:** Boeing no longer accepts resumes via mail, e-mail, or fax. For consideration, applicants must fill out a personal profile or resume on the company Website. **Special Programs:** Education Assistance Program; On-job and Off-hour Training; Commuting Assistance Program; Internships. **Corporate headquarters location:** Chicago IL. **Other U.S. locations:** Nationwide. **International locations:** Worldwide. **Listed on:** New York Stock Exchange; also, the Amsterdam, Brussels, London, Swiss, and Tokyo stock exchanges. **Stock exchange symbol:** BA. **Sales/revenues:** Over $2.8 billion. **Number of employees worldwide:** 186,900.

CMI TEREX CORPORATION
P.O. Box 1985, Oklahoma City OK 73101. 405/491-2969. **Physical address:** I-40 and Morgan Road, Oklahoma City OK 73128. **Fax:** 405/ 491-2457. **Contact:** Laurie Hess, Recruiter. **World Wide Web address:** http://www.cmicorp.com. **Description:** A manufacturer and supplier of equipment across a broad range of industries, including construction, quarrying, recycling, mining, utility, infrastructure, and maintenance. **Positions advertised include:** Inter-level clerk. **Special Programs:** Employee Stock Purchase Program. **Corporate headquarters location:** Westport CT. **Other U.S. locations:** Nationwide. **International locations:** Worldwide. **Operations at this facility include:** This location specializes in paving machinery production and supply. **Listed on:** New York Stock Exchange. **Stock exchange symbol:** TEX. **Annual sales/revenues:** Over $1.8 billion. **Number of employees at this location:** 1,000. **Number of employees nationwide:** 1,200.

CABLE ONE
303 North Fourth Street, Ponca City OK 74601. 580/762-6684. **Contact:** Customer Service Manager. **World Wide Web address:** http://www.cableone.net. **Description:** A cable and satellite television and Internet access provider. **Positions advertised include:** Cable Technician. **Special Programs:** Training. **Corporate headquarters location:** Phoenix AZ. **Other U.S. locations:** Nationwide. **President/CEO:** Thomas O. Might. **Number of employees nationwide:** 1,600.

CHEROKEE NATION INDUSTRIES, INC.
P.O. Box 860, Stilwell OK 74960. 918/696-3151. **Physical address:** Highway 51 West, Stilwell OK 74960. **Toll-free phone:** 800/259-7772. **Fax:** 918/696-5510. **Contact:** Nancy Collins, Human Resources Director. **World Wide Web address:** http://www.cnicnd.com. **Description:** Manufactures products such as cable assemblies, wire harnesses, electrical control units, and printed circuit assemblies for customers in the telecommunications, defense, and aerospace industries. The company also provides distribution, inventory management, and professional services for its customers. **Special programs:** Internships. **Corporate headquarters location:** This location. **Operations at this facility include:** Administration; Manufacturing. **Listed on:** Privately held. **President:** Jim Majewski. **Number of employees worldwide:** 350.

CONOCOPHILLIPS
180 Plaza Office Building, 411 South Keeler, Bartlesville OK 74004. 918/661-6600. **Contact:** Human Resources. **E-mail address:** www.conocophillips.com/careers. **World Wide Web address:** http://www.phillips66.com. **Description:** An energy company whose major operations include the gathering, processing, and marketing of natural gas, the exploration and production of petroleum, and the refining, marketing, and distribution of chemicals and plastics. **NOTE:** Recruiting is conducted through the corporate headquarters in Houston TX. **Positions advertised include:** Fuels Analyst. **Special programs:** Internships. **Corporate headquarters location:** Houston TX. **Other U.S. locations:** Nationwide. **International locations:** Worldwide. **Subsidiaries include:** ARCO Alaska, Incorporated; Tosco Corporation. **Operations at this facility include:** Research and development. **Listed on:** New York Stock Exchange. **Stock exchange symbol:** COP. **President/CEO:** James Mulva. **Sales/revenues:** Approximately $26.9 billion. **Number of employees at this location:** 3,000. **Number of employees worldwide:** Over 50,000.

COWETA, CITY OF
Box 850, 108 North Broadway, Coweta OK 74429. 918/486-2189. **Fax:** 918/486-3773. **Contact:** Tom Tillotson, Human Resources Manager. **E-mail address:** ttillotson@coweta.lib.ok.us. **World Wide Web address:** http://www.coweta.lib.ok.us. **Description:** This location oversees major government offices for the town of Coweta and includes the city hall, the library, the municipal court, the utilities office, the police and fire departments, public works, and maintenance offices. **NOTE:** The City of Coweta does not accept unsolicited resumes or applications. **Positions advertised include:** Communications Officer.

DECISIONONE
2488 East 81st Street, Suite 1100, Tulsa OK 74137-4275. 918/384-3300. **Contact:** Human Resources. **World Wide Web address:** http://www.decisionone.com.

Description: Worldwide technology support provider whose operations include planning and consulting, call center services, technical deployment and support, network services, and logistics. **Positions advertised include:** Field Service Engineer. **Office hours:** Monday – Friday, 8:00 a.m. – 5:00 p.m. **Corporate headquarters location:** Frazer PA. **Other U.S. locations:** Nationwide. **International locations:** Canada. **Sales/revenue:** Approximately $450 million. **Number of employees worldwide:** Over 4,000.

DELPHI
1301 Main Parkway, Catoosa OK 74015. 918/266-4838. **Contact:** Annie Hazzard, Human Resources. **E-mail address:** apply@hrservicesinc.com. **World Wide Web address:** http://www.delphi.com. **Description:** Delphi is primarily a chemical coating company, and focuses on developing innovative technology to be used in the manufacture of emission control catalysts. **NOTE:** Entry-level positions and second and third shifts are offered. **Special programs:** Co-ops; Internships. **Office hours:** Monday – Friday, 8:00 a.m. – 5:00 p.m. **Corporate headquarters location:** Troy MI. **Other U.S. locations:** Nationwide. **International locations:** Worldwide. **Listed on:** New York Stock Exchange. **Stock exchange symbol:** DPH. **Chairman/CEO/President:** J.T. Battenberg III. **Annual sales/revenues:** $5 - $10 million. **Number of employees nationwide:** 61,000.

ESKER SOFTWARE
100 East 7th Avenue, Stillwater OK 74074. 405/624-2254. **Fax:** 405/624-3010. **Contact:** Cathy Buzzard, Personnel. **E-mail address:** recruiting@esker.com. **World Wide Web address:** http://www.esker.com. **Description:** Develops and delivers communications software such as Delivery Ware, Fax Server, and Host Access solutions for use by large corporations. **Other U.S. locations:** Madison WI; Lake Forest CA. **International locations:** United Kingdom; Germany; Spain; Italy; Australia. **Subsidiaries include:** Teubner and Associates; Persoft; V-Systems, Incorporated. **CEO:** Jean Michel Berard. **Number of employees worldwide:** Over 300.

FLEMING COMPANIES, INC.
P.O. Box 26647, Oklahoma City OK 73126-0647. 405/840-7200. **Physical address:** 5701 North Shartel Avenue, Oklahoma City OK 73118. **Fax:** 972/906-1562. **Recorded jobline:** 972/906-1240. **Contact:** Personnel Services. **E-mail address:** success@fleming.com. **World Wide Web address:** http://www.fleming.com. **Description:** Distributes a wide variety of meats, dairy and delicatessen products, frozen foods, fresh produce, and other food-related merchandise, and in addition offers retail services, to supermarkets nationwide. Fleming Companies also operates 240 company-owned stores. **NOTE:** Entry-level positions are offered. Job seekers can apply online at the company Website. **Positions advertised include:** Senior Staff Consultant. **Corporate headquarters:** Lewisville TX. **Other U.S. locations:** Nationwide. **Listed on:** New York Stock Exchange. **Stock exchange symbol:** FLM. **Chairman/CEO:** Mark Hansen. **Annual sales/revenues:** Approximately $15.5 billion.

FLINT ENERGY CONSTRUCTION COMPANY
P.O. Box 3044, Tulsa OK 74101-3044. 918/294-3030x223. **Physical address:** 7633 East 63rd Place, Suite 500, Tulsa OK 74133. **Fax:** 918/307-8956. **Contact:** Marilyn Graham, Personnel Department. **E-mail address:** hr@ flint-energy.com. **World Wide Web address:** http://www.flintenergy.com. **Description:** An oil and gas company that specializes in construction and maintenance, specifically offering fabrication and module services, oil and gas transportation, electrical services, infrastructure services, and project consultation. Founded in 1924. **NOTE:** Entry-level positions and part-time jobs are offered. **Special programs:** Internships; Training; Co-ops; Summer Jobs. **Corporate headquarters location:** This location. **Other area locations:** Wilburton OK. **Other U.S. locations:** Tuscaloosa AL; Fort Smith AR; Fort Lupton CO; Ulysses KS; Farmington NM; Liberty TX; Odessa TX; Sundown TX. **International locations:** Calgary, Alberta, Canada. **Parent Company:** Flint Energy Services. **Listed on:** Privately held. **CEO/President:** Brian F. Butlin. **Annual sales/revenues:** $51 - $100 million. **Number of employees worldwide:** 4,500.

FOODBRANDS AMERICA, INC.
P.O. Box 26724, Oklahoma City OK 73126-0724. 405/879-4100. **Physical address:** 1601 NW Expressway, Suite 1700, Oklahoma City OK 73118. **Fax:** 405/879-5430. **Contact:** Beth Smith, Tyson Foods Recruiter. **E-mail address:** beth.g.smith@tyson.com. **World Wide Web address:** http://www.tysonfoodsinc.com. **Description:** Manufactures and markets brand name and private label processed perishable foods. The company specializes in processed meat products including ham, sausage, bacon, pepperoni, delicatessen meats, sauces, and meat toppings for the supermarket, warehouse, food service, restaurant, institutional, and fast food industries. **NOTE:** For positions at this location, resumes and inquiries should be directed to Beth Smith at Tyson Foods, Incorporated. Mailing address: P.O. Box 2020, Springdale AR 72765. Telephone: 479/290-7360. Fax: 479/290-6794. Resumes may also be submitted online. **Corporate Headquarters:** This location. **Other U.S. locations:** Nationwide. **Parent company:** IBP, Incorporated, which is part of the Tyson Foods family. **Listed on:** New York Stock Exchange. **Stock exchange symbol:** IBP. **CEO:** R. Randolph Devening. **Sales/Revenues:** Approximately $15 billion. **Number of employees nationwide:** 15,000.

FRONTIER ELECTRONIC SYSTEMS CORPORATION
P.O. Box 1023, Stillwater OK 74075. 405/624-1769. **Physical address:** 4500 West 6th Avenue, Stillwater OK 74075. **Fax:** 405/624-7719. **Contact:** Terinda Schroder, Human Resources. **E-mail address:** human resources@fescorp.com. **World Wide Web address:** http://www.fescorp.com. **Description:** An electronic systems, product, and support company that provides services for government, naval, and avionics applications. Founded in 1981. **Positions advertised include:** Accountant; Hardware Engineer. **Corporate headquarters location:** This location. **Other area locations:** Midwest City OK. **CEO:** Peggy Shreve. **Number of employees nationwide:** 110.

GEMSTAR-TV GUIDE INTERNATIONAL
7140 South Lewis Avenue, Tulsa OK 74136-5422. 918/488-4000. **Fax:** 918/488-4979. **Contact:** Human Resources. **E-mail address:** mediajobs@gemstar.com. **World Wide Web address:** http://www.gemstartvguide.com. **Description:** A satellite communications company providing video, audio, data, and program promotion services to a worldwide network of cable companies, satellite dish owners, and radio stations. Founded in 1965. **NOTE:** Applications are only accepted for currently available positions. **Positions advertised include:** Credit Collector; Senior Network Administrator; Senior Quality Assurance Engineer; Director of Production; Network Administrator; Sales Assistant. **Corporate headquarters location:** Pasadena CA. **Other U.S. locations:** Radner PA; New York City NY; Bedford MA. **Subsidiaries include:** Prevue Networks; SpaceCom Systems; SSDS; Superstar Satellite Entertainment; UVTV. **Listed on:** NASDAQ. **Stock exchange symbol:** GMST. **CEO:** Jeff Shell. **Annual sales/revenues:** Approximately $300 million.

HEALTHSOUTH SPORTS MEDICINE&REHABILITATION CENTER
1601 West 9th Street, Stillwater OK 74074. 405/624-7600. **Fax:** 405/624-7557. **Contact:** Joe Ogle, Administrator. **World Wide Web address:** http://www.healthsouth.com. **Description:** A healthcare service provider with over 1,900 facilities in the U.S., as well as locations abroad, and operating divisions in outpatient and inpatient care, occupational health, diagnostics, and surgery. Founded in 1984. **Positions advertised include:** Physical Therapist. **Special programs:** Continuing Education Program; Tuition Reimbursement Program. **Corporate headquarters location:** Birmingham AL. **Other area locations:** Muskogee OK; Ada OK; Owasso OK; El Reno OK; Norman OK; Tulsa OK; Oklahoma City OK; Bethany OK; Midwest City OK; Edmond OK. **Other U.S. locations:** Nationwide. **International locations:** United Kingdom; Puerto Rico; Australia; Saudi Arabia. **Subsidiaries include:** ASC Network Corporation; Health Images, Incorporated. **Listed on:** New York Stock Exchange. **Stock exchange symbol:** HRC. **President/CEO/Founder:** Richard M. Scrushy. **Number of employees worldwide:** Over 32,000.

HELMERICH & PAYNE, INC.
1579 East 21st Street, Tulsa OK 74114. 918/742-5531. **Fax:** 918/748-5485. **Contact:** Tina York, Senior Employment Administrator. **E-mail address:** okcjobs@hpidc.com. **World Wide Web address:** http://www.hpinc.com. **Description:** A diversified company whose primary focus is oil and gas well drilling, production, and exploration in the United States and South America. The company also manufactures chemicals and develops real estate. **NOTE:** Helmerich & Payne, Incorporated does not accept unsolicited resumes. For current job openings, refer to the *Tulsa World* classifieds. **Special programs:** Educational Assistance Program. **Corporate headquarters location:** This location. **Other U.S. locations:** Alice TX; Jackson MS; Ventura CA. **Operations at this facility include:** Administration; Divisional Headquarters. **Listed on:** New York Stock Exchange. **Stock exchange symbol:** HP. **President/CEO:** Hans Helmerich. **Sales/revenues:** Over $100 million. **Number of employees at this location:** 1,600. **Employees worldwide:** 3,675.

HERTZ RENTAL CORPORATION
10401 North Pennsylvania Avenue, Oklahoma City OK 73120. 405/749-3655. **Contact:** Chris Baugh, Human Resources Manager. **World Wide Web address:** http://www.hertz.com. **Description:** A car rental company with approximately 6,500 locations operating in 143 countries. **NOTE:** Do not mail resumes. Call the company directly to set up an appointment. **Positions advertised include:** Developer; Enterprise Application Architect; Information Security Analyst; Programmer Analyst; RDS Administrator; Telecommunications LAN Analyst; Management Trainee. **Office hours:** Monday – Friday, 8:30 a.m. – 5:00 p.m. **Corporate headquarters location:** Park Ridge NJ. **Other U.S. locations:** Nationwide. **International locations:** Worldwide. **Operations at this facility include:** Administration; Sales; Service. **Subsidiaries include:** Hertz Equipment Rental Corporation; Hertz Claim Management Corporation; Hertz Local Edition. **Parent company:** Ford Motor Company. **Listed on:** New York Stock Exchange. **Stock exchange symbol:** F. **President/CEO:** Craig R. Noch. **Number of employees at this location:** Over 1,000.

HIGH POINTE
6501 NE 50th Street, Oklahoma City OK 73141-9613. 405/424-3383. **Fax:** 405/424-0729. **Contact:** Human Resources. **Description:** A 65-bed inpatient psychiatric hospital that provides services for children and adolescents. **Positions advertised include:** Registered Nurse; LPN; Certified Nursing Assistant; Certified Coder; Mental Health Technician.

HILLCREST MEDICAL CENTER
1120 South Utica, Tulsa OK 74104. 918/579-1000. **Fax:** 918/579-7808. **Contact:** Lindsay Annette, Recruiter. **E-mail address:** lannett@hillcrest.com. **World Wide Web address:** http://www.hillcrest.com. **Description:** A 495-bed tertiary hospital that is part of the Hillcrest Healthcare System network and provides a full range of diagnostic and therapeutic services to eastern Oklahoma. Established in 1916. **NOTE:** Online applications are available. For nursing positions, contact the Nurse Recruiter at 918/579-7645 or e-mail skeith@hillcrest.com. **Positions advertised include:** Registered Nurse; Staff Pharmacist; Pharmacy Technician; Nursing Support Staff; Certified Nursing Assistant; Administrative Director; Emergency Department Manager; ECC/Rehabilitation Clinical Specialist; LPN; Charge Nurse; Clinical Dietician; Radiology Technician; MRI Technician; Surgical Technician; Speech Therapist; Occupational Therapist; Physical Therapy Assistant; Respiratory Therapist; Sterile Processing Technician; Ultrasound Technician; Physical Therapist; Therapeutic Recreation Specialist. **President/CEO:** Donald A. Lorack, Jr.

HITACHI COMPUTER PRODUCTS
P.O. Box 1203, Norman OK 73070-1203. 405/360-5500. **Physical address:** 1800 East Imhoff Road, Norman OK 73071. **Contact:** Human Resources. **World Wide Web address:** http://www.hicam.hitachi.com. **Description:** A provider of electronic manufacturing services, whose products include application software, personal computers, workstations, servers, mainframe and high performance computers, and network and storage products. **NOTE:** This location typically hires through Kelly Employment Services. **Corporate headquarters location:** Tokyo, Japan. **Other U.S. locations:** Nationwide. **International locations:** Worldwide. **Parent Company:** Hitachi, Ltd. **Operations at this facility include:** Manufacturing. **Listed on:** New York Stock Exchange. **Stock exchange symbol:** HIT. **President:** Etsuniko Shoyama. **Sales/revenues:** $60.1 billion. **Number of employees nationwide:** Approximately 5,400.

KERR-McGEE CORPORATION
P.O. Box 25861, Oklahoma City OK 73125-0861. 405/270-1313. **Physical address:** 123 Robert S. Kerr Avenue, Oklahoma City OK 73102. **Fax:** 405/270-3109. **Contact:** Human Resources. **E-mail address:** jobs@kmg.com. **World Wide Web address:** http://www.kerr-mcgee.com. **Description:** An energy and inorganic chemicals company whose central focus is petroleum and natural gas exploration, as well as the production and marketing of titanium dioxide pigment. The company is also involved in the marketing and processing of petrochemicals, the mining of coal, and the refinement of crude oil. Exploration and production of oil and natural gas is conducted off-shore in the North Sea, the Gulf of Mexico, and the South China Sea, and on-shore in Ecuador, Indonesia, Kazakhistan, and the United States. Founded in 1929. **NOTE:** Job positions are listed in *The Oklahoman* or online at www.newsok.com. **Positions advertised include:** Legal Secretary. **Corporate headquarters location:** This location. **Other U.S. locations:** Hamilton MS; Savannah GA; Atlanta GA; Mobile AL; Irving TX; Brea CA. **International locations:** Australia; Germany; Belgium; Netherlands; Switzerland; Singapore. **Subsidiaries include:** Kerr-McGee Chemical LLC; Kerr-McGee North Sea (U.K.) Limited; Kerr-McGee Oil & Gas Corporation; Kerr-McGee Onshore L.P.; Kerr-McGee Oil (U.K.) ITD; Kerr-McGee Pigments GmbH & Co. KG; Kerr-McGee Resources (U.K.) Limited; Kerr-McGee Rocky Mountain Corporation. **Listed on:** New York Stock Exchange. **Stock exchange symbol:** KMG. **Chairman/CEO:** Luke Corbett.

KIMBERLY-CLARK CORPORATION
P.O. Box 3000, Jenks OK 74037-3000. 918/366-5000. **Physical address:** 13252 South Yale Place, Jenks OK 74037. **Recorded jobline:** 918/366-5120. **Contact:** Human Resources Team Leader. **World Wide Web address:** http://www.kimberly-clark.com. **Description:** Kimberly-Clark Corporation manufactures and markets paper supplies and cleaning products for personal, business, and industrial uses throughout the world. Most of the company's products are made from natural and synthetic fibers using advanced technologies and are dispersed under such brand names as Scott, Wypall, Kleenguard, Cottonelle, Huggies, Kleenex, and Kimtech. The company also produces disposable medical goods. **NOTE:** For general consideration contact the Oklahoma Employment Securities Commission at 918/437-4473. **Special programs:** Co-ops; Internships; Mentoring Programs. **Other U.S. locations:** Nationwide. **International locations:** Worldwide. **Listed on:** New York Stock Exchange. **Stock exchange symbol:** KMB. **CEO:** Thomas J. Falk. **Sales/revenue:** $13.6 billion. **Number of employees worldwide:** Over 64,000.

LANGSTON UNIVERSITY
P.O. Box 1205, Langston OK 73050-1205. 405/466-3203. **Physical address:** Highway 33 East, Langston OK 73050. **Fax:** 405/466-6002. **Contact:** Beverly H. Smith, Personnel Director. **World Wide Web address:** http://www.lunet.edu. **Description:** A four-year, liberal arts university that offers both undergraduate and graduate studies and consists of a school of arts and sciences, of business, of education and behavioral sciences, of agriculture and applied sciences, of nursing and health professions, and a school of physical therapy. **Positions advertised include:** Chemical Dependency Counselor. **President:** Ernest L. Holloway. **Number of employees at this location:** 450.

LAUREATE PSYCHIATRIC CLINIC AND HOSPITAL
6655 South Yale Avenue, Tulsa OK 74136. 918/491-3742. **Fax:** 918/481-4080. **Recorded jobline:** 918/491-5662. **Contact:** Human Resources. **World Wide Web address:** http://www.laureate.com. **Description:** Provides psychiatric treatment and substance abuse care for children, adolescents, and adults, as well as furnishing clinical research and education. **NOTE:** Online applications are available. **Positions advertised include:** Intake Counselor; Psychiatric Technician; Secretary; Licensed Practical Nurse; Registered Nurse; Nurse Assistant; Unit Manager; Registered Dietician; Research Systems Analyst; Patient Services Supervisor. **Special programs:** Tuition Assistance Plan. **Office hours:** Monday – Friday, 8:00 a.m. – 4:30 p.m.

LOVE'S COUNTRY STORES
P.O. Box 26210, Oklahoma City OK 73126. 405/749-1744. **Physical address:** 10601 North Pennsylvania Avenue, Oklahoma City OK 73120. **Toll-free phone:** 800/388-0983. **Fax:** 405/749-9143. **Contact:** Carl Martincich, Human Resources. **E-mail address:** hr@loves.com. **World Wide Web address:** http://www.loves.com. **Description:** Operates more than 140 retail convenience stores, travel stops, and restaurants in the Midwest. **NOTE:** Online applications are available. **Positions advertised include:** Fuel Delivery Driver; Travel Stop Manager; Travel Stop Assistant Manager; Restaurant Manager; Assistant Restaurant Manager; Convenience Store Manager. **Special programs:** Internships. **Corporate headquarters location:** This location. **Other U.S. locations:** CO; KS; NM; TX. **Listed on:** Privately held. **CEO:** Tom Love. **Sales/revenues:** Over $1 billion. **Number of employees nationwide:** 2,000.

LOWRANCE ELECTRONICS INC.
12000 East Skelly Drive, Tulsa OK 74128. 918/437-6881. **Fax:** 918/234-1705. **Contact:** Human Resources Department. **E-mail address:** jobs@lowrance.com. **World Wide Web address:** http://www.lowrance.com. **Description:** Designs and markets SONAR, GPS mapping instruments, and navigation plotters for a wide range of outdoor applications, including sport fishing, recreational boating, hiking, and hunting. **Positions advertised include:** Senior Buyer. **Other U.S. locations:** Nationwide. **International locations:** Worldwide. **Listed on:** NASDAQ. **Stock exchange symbol:** LEIX. **President/CEO:** Darrel Lowrance. **Number of employees worldwide:** 1,000.

MPSI SYSTEMS, INC.
4343 South 118th East Avenue, Tulsa OK 74146. 918/877-6774. **Toll-free phone:** 800/727-6774. **Contact:** Bill Webb, Director of Human Resources. **E-mail address:** hr@mpsisys.com. **World Wide Web address:** http://www.mpsisys.com. **Description:** An information services firm that provides market research solutions and develops and markets decision support systems for retail petroleum and convenience food marketers. **Corporate headquarters location:** This location. **International locations:** Brazil; China; England; Japan; Singapore; South Africa; South Korea. **Listed on:** OTC. **Stock exchange symbol:** MPSI. **President/ CEO/Chairman:** Ronald Harper. **Sales/revenues:** Approximately $8.8 million. **Number of employees nationwide:** 120. **Number of employees worldwide:** 300.

MARK IV AUTOMOTIVE
6120 South Yale Avenue, Suite 900, Tulsa OK 74136. 918/481-2500. **Fax:** 918/481-2488. **Contact:** Heather Paris, Human Resources. **World Wide Web address:** http://www.markivauto.com. **Description:** As part of the aftermarket division of Mark IV Industries, this company produces and supplies automotive filters, fuel systems, and power transmission systems, as well as automotive belts and hoses under the brand name Dayco. **Special programs:** Internships. **Corporate headquarters location:** This location. **International locations:** Canada; France; Germany; Spain; Sweden; Italy; United Kingdom; Argentina; Mexico; Singapore; Australia. **Parent company:** Mark IV Industries, Incorporated. **Subsidiaries include:** Dayco Products, Incorporated. **Operations at this facility include:** Administration; Divisional Headquarters. **President:** William P. Montague. **Sales/revenue:** $812 million. **Number of employees worldwide:** 5,300.

MATRIX SERVICE COMPANY
10701 East Ute Street, Tulsa OK 74116. 918/838-8822. **Contact:** Melissa Harvey, Recruiter. **World Wide Web address:** http://www.matrixservice.com. **Description:** Provides specialized on-site maintenance and construction services for petroleum refineries, pipelines, chemical plants, and storage facilities. **NOTE:** Matrix Service Company only accepts applications and resumes for advertised openings. **Special programs:** Training; Tuition Reimbursement; Professional Development Program. **Corporate headquarters location:** This location. **Other U.S. locations:** Bellingham WA; Orange CA; Baypoint CA; Houston TX; Temperance MI; Newark DE; Bristol PA; Bethlehem PA. **International locations:** Sarnia, Ontario, Canada. **Listed on:** NASDAQ. **Stock exchange symbol:** MTRX. **President/CEO:** Bradley Vetal. **Sales/revenue:** $112.6 million. **Number of employees at this location:** 830. **Number of employees worldwide:** 1,374.

MICRO FIRMWARE, INC.
330 West Gray Street, Suite 120, Norman OK 73069-7111. 405/321-8333. **Fax:** 405/573-5539. **Contact:** Human Resources. **World Wide Web address:** http://www.firmware.com. **Description:** Develops and distributes Phoenix ROM BIOS upgrade software. **Office hours:** Monday – Friday, 9:00 a.m. – 5:00 p.m. **Corporate headquarters location:** This location.

NDCHEALTH CORPORATION
One Warren Place, 6100 South Yale Avenue, Suite 1900, Tulsa OK 74136. 918/496-2451. **Contact:** Christina Ferguson, Human Resources. **E-mail address:** careers@ndchealth.com. **World Wide Web address:** http://www.ndchealth.com. **Description:** Develops software and Web-base applications used by hospitals and other health care providers for electronic billing and other EDI transactions. **NOTE:** Job seekers can apply online for specific positions and for general consideration. **Positions advertised include:** Director of Customer Support. **Other U.S. locations:** AZ; GA; IL; IN; NJ; OH; PA; SC; TX; VA. **International locations:** Canada; Germany; United Kingdom. **Listed on:** New York Stock Exchange. **Stock exchange symbol:** NDC. **CEO:** Walter Hoff. **Sales/revenue:** $105.3 million. **Number of employees worldwide:** 1,790.

THE NORDAM GROUP
P.O. Box 3365, Tulsa OK 74101-3365. 918/587-4105. **Physical address:** 510 South Lansing, Tulsa OK 74120. **Contact:** Human Resources. **World Wide Web address:** http://www.nordam.com. **Description:** Provides a wide range of services for various divisions of the aerospace and aviations industries. Founded in 1869, the NORDAM Group specializes in aircraft component manufacturing, overhaul, and repair. **NOTE:** The Nordham Group prefers to receive resume submissions online. **Positions advertised include:** Telecommunications Technician; Director of Contracts and Legal Affairs. **Corporate headquarters location:** This location. **Other U.S. locations:** Fort Worth TX; Wichita KS. **International locations:** Mexico; Brazil; Peru; England; Germany; Netherlands; United Kingdom; France; United Arab Emirates; Singapore; China; Australia. **Operations at this facility include:** Administration; Divisional Headquarters; Manufacturing; Research and Development; Sales; Service. **Chairman/CEO:** Ray H. Siegfried II. **Sales/revenues:** Over $100 million. **Number of employees at this location:** 1,500. **Number of employees nationwide:** Over 2,500.

OKLAHOMA PUBLISHING COMPANY
P.O. Box 25125, Oklahoma City OK 73125. 405/475-3280. **Physical address:** 9000 Broadway Exit, Oklahoma City OK 73114. **Fax:** 405/475-3970. **Recorded jobline:** 405/475-3993. **Contact:** Wanda Matula, Human Resources Director. **E-mail address:** humanresources@oklahoman.com. **World Wide Web address:** http://www.newsok.com. **Description:** Publishes *The Daily Oklahoman*, a conservative newspaper founded in 1804. **NOTE:** The Oklahoma Publishing Company does not accept unsolicited resumes or applications. **Positions advertised include:** Support Services Representative; Counter Clerk; Classifieds Advertisement Representative; District Assistant; Metro Circulation Clerk; Telemarketer; Distribution Center Assistant; Customer Service Representative; Packaging Department Inserter. **Office hours:** Monday – Friday, 8:30 a.m. – 11:30 a.m., 1:30 p.m. – 4:30 p.m. **Publisher:** Edward L. Gaylord.

OKLAHOMA STATE UNIVERSITY
106 Whitehurst Hall, Stillwater OK 74078-1037. 405/744-5646. **Fax:** 405/744-8345. **Contact:** Personnel Services. **E-mail address:** osups@okstate.edu. **World Wide Web address:** http://www.okstate.edu. **Description:** A four-campus state university with an enrollment of approximately 26,000 students that offers bachelor's, master's, and doctor's degrees in a wide range of fields. **NOTE:** Vacancies are also posted with the Oklahoma State Employment Agency and online at www.okstate.edu/osuper. For faculty positions, contact individual departments. **Positions advertised include:** Financial Assistant; Library Technician Assistant; Office Assistant; Senior Account Clerk; Senior Office Assistant; Senior Secretary; Senior Unit Assistant; Staff Assistant; Unit Assistant; Accountant; Administrative Assistant; Analyst; Assistant Coordinator; Assistant Director; Assistant Chief Flight Instructor; Coordinator; Graduate Program Director; Local Government Specialist; Conference Services Manager; University Food Services Manager; Marketing Manager; Research Engineer; Research Specialist; Residence Hall Coordinator; Talent Search Director; University Registrar; Baker; Building Superintendent; Custodian; Food Service Aide; Housekeeper; Laundry Worker; Maintenance Mechanic; Assistant Park Ranger; Lab Technologist; University Police Officer; Licensed Practical Nurse. **Special programs:** Staff development programs. **Office hours:** Monday – Friday, 8:00 a.m. – 5:00 p.m. **Operations at this facility include:** Administration; Research and Development; Service. **President/CEO:** Dr. David J. Schmidly. **Number of employees at this location:** 6,000. **Number of employees nationwide:** 10,000.

ORCHIDS PAPER PRODUCTS COMPANY
Route 3, Box 69-8, Pryor OK 74361. 918/825-0616. **Toll-free phone:** 800/832-4908. **Fax:** 918/825-0060. **Contact:** Laura Fox, Personnel Director. **World Wide Web address:** http://www.orchidspaper.com. **Description:** A manufacturer of consumer paper products such as paper towels, bath tissue, and napkins.

PARK VIEW HOSPITAL
P.O. Box 129, El Reno OK 73036-0129. 405/262-2640x3023. **Physical address:** 2115 Park View Drive, El Reno OK 73036. **Fax:** 405/422-2521. **Contact:** Human Resources. **E-mail address:** parkviewhospital@yahoo.com. **World Wide Web address:** http://www.parkview-hospital.com. **Description:** A nonprofit hospital that provides inpatient care, inpatient/outpatient surgical care, and outpatient services. **NOTE:** Entry-level positions, part-time jobs, and second and third shifts are offered. **Positions advertised include:** Registered Nurse; Physician; Insurance Clerk. **Company slogan:** Quality care in a family environment. **Administrator:** Lex Smith. **Number of employees at this location:** 350.

PARKER DRILLING COMPANY
2021 South Lewis, Suite 600, Tulsa OK 74104. 918/281-2700. **Contact:** George Gentry, Director of Human Resources. **E-mail address:** humanresources@parkerdrilling.com. **World Wide Web address:** http://www.parkerdrilling.com. **Description:** A leading land drilling contractor for the oil and gas industry that specializes in deep drilling and remote location drilling worldwide. Parker Drilling provides contract drilling to major oil companies, independent oil and gas producers, governments, and industrial end users. **NOTE:** The Human Resources Department is located in the Houston TX office. You may fax resumes to George Gentry at 281/406-2001. **Special programs:** Training. **Corporate headquarters location:** Houston TX. **Other U.S. locations:** New Iberia LA; Odessa TX; Victoria TX. **International locations:** Worldwide. **Subsidiaries include:** Quail Tools. **Listed on:** New York Stock Exchange. **Stock exchange symbol:** PKD. **President/CEO:** Robert L. Parker, Junior. **Sales/revenue:** Approximately $300 million. **Number of employees worldwide:** 3,654.

PEGASUS IMAGING
P.O. Box 1358, Stillwater OK 74076. 405/377-0880. **Physical address:** 206 West 6th Avenue, Stillwater OK 74074. **Toll-free phone:** 800/944-7654. **Fax:** 405/742-1710. **Contact:** Wendy Cruz, Personnel Manager. **E-mail address:** jobs@tmsinc.com. **World Wide Web address:** http://www.pegasusimaging.com. **Description:** Develops

a wide range of business management software products. Founded in 1981. **Positions advertised include:** Technical Business Development Professional. **Special programs:** Tuition Reimbursement Program; Engineering Employee Equipment Purchase Program. **Corporate headquarters location:** Tampa FL. **Listed on:** OTC. **Stock exchange symbol:** TMSS.OB. **President:** Debbie Klarfeld. **Sales/revenue:** Over $1 million.

PLAZA MEDICAL GROUP
3433 NW 56th Street, Suite 400, Oklahoma City OK 73112. 405/951-4325. **Fax:** 405/951-4359. **Contact:** Loretta Tran, Recruiter. **E-mail address:** hr@ plazamed.com. **Description:** Multispecialty physicians' offices. **Positions advertised include:** Registered Nurse; LPN; Scheduling Coordinator; Message Clerk. **Corporate headquarters location:** This location. **Listed on:** Privately held. **Number of employees at this location:** 140.

RENAISSANCE HOTEL
10 North Broadway, Oklahoma City OK 73102. 405/228-8000. **Fax:** 405/228-2574. **Contact:** Human Resources. **World Wide Web address:** http://www.jqhhotels.com. **Description:** A hotel and convention center. John Q. Hammonds Hotels also owns and operates resorts and hotels under such trade names as Embassy Suites, Holiday Inn, Sheraton, and the Marriott. **Positions advertised include:** Assistant Executive Housekeeper; Banquet Manager; Sous Chef; Pastry Chef; Line Cook; Hostess; Cashier; Coffee Server; Bar Tender; Assistant Manager; Utility Worker; Room Attendee. **Special programs:** Training. **Corporate Headquarters location:** Springfield MO. **Other U.S. locations:** Nationwide. **Parent Company:** John Q. Hammons Hotels, Incorporated. **Listed on:** American Stock Exchange. **Stock exchange symbol:** JQH. **CEO/Chairman:** John Q. Hammons.

SAMEDAN OIL CORPORATION
P.O. Box 909, Ardmore OK 73402. 580/223-4110. **Physical address:** 110 West Broadway, Ardmore OK 73401. **Contact:** Gail Donica, Human Resources. **World Wide Web address:** http://www.nobleaff.com. **Description:** An oil and gas exploration and production company with domestic and international operations on and offshore. **NOTE:** Job openings are advertised in the *Daily Ardmoreite* or online at www.Armoreite.com. **Corporate headquarters location:** Houston TX. **Parent company:** Noble Energy, Incorporated. **Subsidiaries include:** EDC Ecuador, Ltd.; EDC China, Incorporated; EDC (Europe) Limited. **Operations at this facility include:** Administration. **Listed on:** New York Stock Exchange. **Stock exchange symbol:** NBL. **President/CEO/ Chairman:** Charles D. Davidson. **Sales/revenues:** Over $100 million. **Number of employees at this location:** 190. **Number of employees nationwide:** 600.

SARA LEE BAKERY GROUP
P.O. Box 1638, Oklahoma City OK 73101. 405/524-8454. **Physical address:** 1916 North Broadway, Oklahoma City OK 73103. **Contact:** Human Resources. **Description:** Produces a wide range of bakery products including bread and rolls. **NOTE:** Positions are advertised and applications made available through the Workforce Oklahoma Employment Agency. **Corporate headquarters location:** St. Louis MO.

SCHLUMBERGER
P.O. Box 1181, Bartlesville OK 74005. 918/661-2434. **Physical address:** 509 West Henslay Boulevard, Bartlesville OK 74003. **Contact:** Human Resources. **World Wide Web address:** http://www.slb.com. **Description:** A global technology services company that consists of two business divisions, one specializing in oil and gas exploration, production, and product supply, and another that offers support systems and business solutions for customers across a broad range of industries. **NOTE:** See the Oklahoma Employment Security Commission for job openings. **Special programs:** Internships; Training; Continuing Education Programs. **Other U.S. locations:** Nationwide. **International locations:** Worldwide. **Operations at this location include:** The manufacturing of oil field equipment and industrial supplies. **Listed on:** New York Stock Exchange; the Euronext Paris, London, and Amsterdam Stock Exchanges; BES Swiss Stock Exchange. **Stock exchange symbol:** SLB. **CEO/Chairman:** Euan Baird. **Number of employees worldwide:** Over 80,000.

SEAGATE TECHNOLOGY
10321 West Reno, Oklahoma City OK 73127. 405/324-3379. **Fax:** 405/ 324-3002. **Contact:** Earl Welsh, Staffing Recruiter. **World Wide Web address:** http://www.seagate.com. **Description:** A designer and manufacturer of data storage devices and related products including hard disk drives, tape drives, software, and systems for many different computer-related applications and operating systems. Customers include computer equipment manufacturers such as Dell, IBM, EMC, Hewlett-Packard, and Sun Microsystems. **NOTE:** Online applications are available. **Positions advertised include:** Assistant Engineer Intern; General Engineering Intern; Control Engineering Intern; Integration Engineering Intern; Help Desk Technician; Software Engineer; Engineering Support Technical Intern; General Technical Intern; Development Technical Intern. **Special programs:** Internships; Co-ops. **Corporate headquarters location:** Scotts Valley CA. **International locations:** Worldwide. **Subsidiaries include:** Arcada Holdings, Incorporated, an information protection and storage management software company serving several operating systems; Conners Storage Systems; Crystal Decisions. **Operations at this facility include:** Production. **Listed on:** New York Stock Exchange. **Stock exchange symbol:** STX. **CEO/Chairman:** Stephen J. Luczo. **Sales/revenues:** Over $3.31 billion. **Number of employees worldwide:** 45,000.

SOFTOUCH SYSTEMS, INC.
5601 NW 72nd, Suite 347 Oklahoma City OK 73132. 405/703-8080. **Toll-free phone:** 800/944-3036. **Fax:** 405/703-8094. **Contact:** Chad Akers, Vice President of Operations. **World Wide Web address:** http://www. softouch.com. **Description:** Develops custom software for the OS/2 operating system and IBM mainframes. The company also offers mainframe-related consulting and engineering services to their customers. Founded in 1980. **Positions advertised include:** Remote Software Sales Agent; Software Salesperson. **CEO/President:** Richard Jones.

SONIC INDUSTRIES
101 Park Avenue, Suite 1400, Oklahoma City OK 73102. 405/280-7654. **Contact:** Molly Scalf, Personnel Director. **E-mail address:** SonicCorpHR@sonicdrivein.com. **World Wide Web address:** http://www.sonicdrivein.com. **Description:** Operates and franchises more than 1,200 drive-in restaurants, which specialize in made-to-order fast food. There are also 149 company-owned Sonic restaurants, which are located principally in the south central region of the United States. **NOTE:** See current job openings at www.jobsok.com. **Company slogan:** Sonic, America's Drive-In. **Special programs:** Tuition Assistance Program; Internships. **Corporate headquarters location:** This location. **Other U.S. locations:** Sonic Drive-Ins exist nationwide. **Listed on:** NASDAQ. **Subsidiaries include:** Sonic Industries, Incorporated; Sonic Restaurants, Incorporated. **Stock exchange symbol:** SONC. **Sales/revenue:** Approximately $2.2 billion. **CEO/Chairman:** Cliff Hudson. **Number of employees at this location:** 282.

SOUTHERN NAZARENE UNIVERSITY
6729 NW 39th Expressway, Bethany OK 73008. 405/491-6333. **Fax:** 405/491-6381. **Contact:** Rick Powell, Human Resources Director. **E-mail address:** rpowell@snu.edu. **World Wide Web address:** http://www. snu.edu. **Description:** A private liberal arts university affiliated with the Church of the Nazarene that has an enrollment of approximately 2,120 and offers undergraduate, graduate, and adult studies programs. Founded in 1899. **NOTE:** For faculty positions, submit resumes to Don W. Dunnington, Vice-President of Academic Affairs, or e-mail ddunning@snu.edu. **Company slogan:** Character, Culture, Christ. **Positions advertised include:** Computing and Information Science Professor; Business Marketing Professor; Biology Professor; Nursing Department Faculty Member. **Other area locations include:** Tulsa OK. **President:** Lorn P. Gresham. **Number of employees at this location:** 120.

SOUTHWESTERN MEDICAL CENTER
5602 SW Lee Boulevard, Lawton OK 73505. 580/531-4700. **Fax:** 580/510-2816. **Recorded jobline:** 580/510-2817. **Contact:** Human Resources. **E-mail address:** Hrdept@swmconline.com. **World Wide Web address:** http://www.swmconline.com. **Description:** A civilian hospital offering inpatient and outpatient services, as well as specialized services through its behavioral health, cancer, rehabilitation, and women's centers. Founded in 1907. **Positions advertised include:** Ultrasonographer; Physical Therapist; Staff Pharmacist; Registered Nurse. **Special programs:** Internships. **Parent company:** The Healthcare Company. **Number of employees at this location:** 570.

STAR BUILDING SYSTEMS
P.O. Box 94910, Oklahoma City OK 73143-4910. 405/636-2240. **Physical address:** 8600 South Interstate 35, Oklahoma City OK 73149. **Toll-free phone:** 800/654-3921. **Fax:** 405/636-2238. **Contact:** Dawna Mitchell, Personnel. **Email address:** dawna.mitchell@rccorp.net. **World Wide Web address:** http://www.starbuildings.com. **Description:** A construction company that manufactures pre-engineered metal buildings for institutional, commercial, industrial, recreational, and agricultural applications. Founded in 1927. **Positions advertised include:** Computer-based Structural Drafter. **Corporate headquarters location:** This location. **Other U.S. locations:** Lockeford CA; Monticello IA; Elizabethton TN. **International locations:** Ontario, Canada. **Parent company:** Robertson-Ceco Corporation. **Number of employees nationwide:** 580.

STARBUCKS COFFEE COMPANY
2116 West Memorial Road, Oklahoma City OK 73134. 405/748-4443. **Contact:** Store Manager. **World Wide Web address:** http://www.starbucks.com. **Description:** A retailer and roaster of specialty coffee beverages that also markets a variety of pastries, confections and coffee-related merchandise. **NOTE:** Job seekers can download an application from the company Website or obtain an application from their local retail store. Each Starbucks retail store independently hires and manages its own team. **Positions advertised include:** Store Manager. **Special programs:** Training. **Corporate headquarters location:** Seattle WA. **Other area locations:** There are a total of eight Starbucks retail stores in the Tulsa area. **Other U.S. locations:** Nationwide. **International locations:** Worldwide. **Listed on:** NASDAQ. **Stock exchange symbol:** SBUX. **President/CEO:** Orin C. Smith.

STATSOFT, INC.
2300 East 14th Street, Tulsa OK 74104. 918/749-1119. **Fax:** 918/749-2217. **Contact:** Human Resources. **E-mail address:** jobs@statsoft.com. **World Wide Web address:** http://www.statsoft.com. **Description:** A manufacturer of data analysis software utilized at research centers, universities, corporations, and manufacturing facilities. Statsoft's major product line is *STATISTICA*. **NOTE:** Entry-level positions are offered. **Positions advertised include:** Statistical Support/Data Mining Analyst; Operations Administrator; Sales Associate/Account Manager; Localization Engineer; Quality Control Consultant; Configuration Engineer; Software Test Engineer; Technical Writer; Application Developer; Advanced System Programmer; Senior Statistical Developer; Statistical Support Specialist; Consultant. **Special programs:** Training. **Corporate headquarters location:** This location. **Operations at this facility include:** Sales; Training; Consulting Services. **International locations:** Worldwide. **Listed on:** Privately held.

THRIFTY RENT-A-CAR SYSTEM INC.
5310 East 31st Street, 5th floor, Dollar Thrifty Plaza Complex, Tulsa OK 74135. 918/665-3930. **Physical address:** 5310 East 31st Street, Tulsa OK 74135. **Contact:** Human Resources. **E-mail address:** great_jobs@thrifty.com. **World Wide Web address:** http://www.thrifty.com. **Description:** A franchised car rental company that serves both the airport and local car rental markets, with a fleet of over 82,000 cars and more than 1,200 rental locations spanning the globe. **NOTE:** Unsolicited resumes and applications are not accepted. **Special programs:** Education Assistance Plan; Health Club Membership. **Office hours:** Monday – Friday, 9:00 a.m. – 4:00 p.m. **Corporate headquarters location:** This location. **Other U.S. locations:** Nationwide. **International locations:** Worldwide. **Parent Company:** Dollar Thrifty Automotive Group, Incorporated. **Subsidiaries include:** Thrifty Car rental; Thrifty Car Sales. **Listed on:** New York Stock Exchange. **Stock exchange symbol:** DTG. **President/CEO:** Don Himelfarb. **Sales/revenue:** $56.8 million. **Number of employees worldwide:** Over 7,500.

TYSON FOODS, INC.
P.O. Box 220, Highway 259-70 South, Broken Bow OK 74728. 580/584-9191. **Contact:** Dana Whisenhunt, Human Resources. **World Wide Web address:** http://www.tyson.com. **Description:** A fully-integrated producer, processor, and marketer of chicken, pork, and beef products that services supermarket and restaurant chains, foodservice distributors, and wholesale clubs worldwide. **Corporate headquarters location:** Springdale AR. **Other U.S. locations:** Nationwide. **International locations:** Worldwide. **Subsidiaries include:** Holly Farms; Hudson Foods; IBP. **Operations at this location include:** This location is a chicken processing plant. **Listed on:** New York Stock Exchange. **Stock exchange symbol:** TSN. **CEO/Chairman:** John H. Tyson. **Sales/revenue:** Approximately $5.8 billion. **Number of employees worldwide:** 120,000.

TYSON FOODS, INC.
Route 2, Box 94-1, Stilwell OK 74960. 918/696-7666. **Contact:** Tina Luethje, Director of Personnel. **World Wide Web address:** http://www.tyson.com. **Description:** A fully-integrated producer, processor, and marketer of chicken, pork, and beef products that services supermarket and restaurant chains, foodservice distributors, and wholesale clubs worldwide. **Corporate headquarters location:** Springdale AR. **Other U.S. locations:** Nationwide. **International locations:** Worldwide. **Subsidiaries include:** Holly Farms; Hudson Foods; IBP. **Operations at this location include:** This location is a chicken processing plant. **Listed on:** New York Stock Exchange. **Stock exchange symbol:** TSN. **CEO/Chairman:** John H. Tyson. **Sales/revenue:** Approximately $5.8 billion. **Number of employees worldwide:** 120,000.

U.S. DEPARTMENT OF VETERANS AFFAIRS VETERANS ADMINISTRATION MEDICAL CENTER
921 NE 13th Street, Oklahoma City OK 73104. 405/270-0501. **Contact:** Shea Bandy, Human Resources and Development. **E-mail address:** shea.bandy@med.va.gov. **Description:** A 169-bed facility that serves as a primary, secondary, and tertiary care center for veterans. Founded in 1930, the VA Healthcare System has grown to include 171 medical centers, more than 364 outpatient, community, and outreach clinics, 130 nursing home care units, and 37 domiciliary residences. **NOTE:** Available positions are posted on www.usajobs.opm.gov. Applications must be submitted either via mail or in person. **Positions advertised include:** Nursing Assistant; Nuclear Medicine Technologist; Personnel Clerk; Counseling Psychologist; Clinical Psychologist; Chaplain; Clinical Pastoral Education Supervisor. **Office hours:** Monday – Friday, 8:00 a.m. – 4:30 p.m. **Other area locations:** Lawton OK; Ponca City OK; Ardmore OK; Clinton OK; Konawa OK. **Other U.S. locations:** AR; LA; TX; MS. **Operations at this facility include:** Health care; referral; research; education. This location is classified under tertiary care as a Clinical Referral Level II Facility. **Number of employees nationwide:** Over 1,400.

UNIT PARTS COMPANY
P.O. Box 26021, Oklahoma City OK 73126. 405/677-3361. **Physical address:** 4600 SE 63rd Street, Oklahoma City OK 73135. **Fax:** 405/672-9979. **Contact:** Human Resources. **World Wide Web address:** http://www.upc.com. **Description:** Produces a variety of replacement parts and accessories for a broad range of vehicles.

UNIVERSITY OF CENTRAL OKLAHOMA
Lilliard Administration Building, Room 204, 100 North University Drive, Edmond OK 73034. 405/974-2366. **Recorded jobline:** 405/974-3089. **Contact:** Fran Petties, Employment Services Manager. **E-mail:** fpetties@ucok.edu. **World Wide Web address:** http://www.ucok.edu. **Description:** A state university accredited by the North Central Association of Colleges and Schools as a bachelor's and master's degree granting institution. **NOTE:** For academic positions, contact appropriate department. **Positions advertised include:** Nurse Practitioner; INS Assistant; Building Operations Manager; Financial Aid Counselor; Human Resources Specialist; Physics and Engineering Laboratory Associate; Library Technician; Electrician; Plumber. **President:** W. Robert Webb.

UNIVERSITY OF OKLAHOMA
905 Asp Avenue, Room 205, Norman OK 73019-6043. 405/325-1826. **Fax:** 405/325-7627. **Recorded jobline:** 405/325-1826. **Contact:** Personnel Services. **E-mail address:** ohr@ou.edu. **World Wide Web address:** http://www.ou.edu/persvcs. **Description:** A doctoral-degree granting state university that is composed of nineteen colleges and offers 154 majors. **Positions advertised include:** Development Associate; Program Administrator; Public Management Staff Assistant; Program Specialist; Marketing/Public Relations Specialist; Equipment Operations Maintenance Person; Library Staff Assistant; Shipping and Receiving Technician; Transportation Person; Information Technology Technician; Food Service Worker; Temporary Employee; University Student Services Assistant; Account and Budget Representative; Information Technology Analyst; Managerial Associate; Flight Instructor; Grants Specialist; FAA Employee; Public Safety Officer; Communications Paraprofessional; USPS Training Instructor; USPS Educational Specialist. **Special programs:** PEAK Temporary Employment Program; Training. **President:** David L. Boren. **Number of employees at this location:** 8,872.

UROCOR LABS
840 Research Parkway, Oklahoma City OK 73104. 405/290-4000. **Fax:** 405/290-4413. **Contact:** Diana Blakney, Human Resources Director. **World Wide Web address:** http://www.urocor.com. **Description:** Provides urological diagnostic testing services. **Positions advertised include:** Data Entry. **Corporate headquarters location:** This location. **Other U.S. locations:** Nationwide.

VETERINARY TEACHING HOSPITAL
One Boren Veterinary Medicine Teaching Hospital, Stillwater OK 74078. 405/744-7000. **Contact:** Human Resources. **World Wide Web address:** http://www.cvm.okstate.edu. **Description:** A full-service veterinary teaching hospital for both small and large animals. The hospital is affiliated with Oklahoma State University. **NOTE:** Job seekers must contact the Oklahoma State University Human Resources Department for available positions. **Positions advertised include:** Equine Emergency Clinician/Surgeon. **Special programs:** Internships.

WABASH COMPUTER PRODUCTS
4720 West 90th Street, Suite 104, Tulsa OK 74132. 918/447-8977. **Toll-free phone:** 800/323-9868. **Contact:** Human Resources. **World Wide Web address:** http://www.wabashcomp.com. **Description:** Manufactures magnetic tapes, cartridges, and flexible diskettes. **Corporate headquarters location:** This location.

WELLS FARGO BANK
1276 North Interstate Drive, Norman OK 73072. 405/447-6772. **Contact:** Human Resources. **World Wide Web address:** http://www.wellsfargo. com. **Description:** A diversified financial institution with over $234 billion in assets. Wells Fargo serves over 17 million customers through 5,300 independent locations worldwide. The company also maintains several stand-alone ATMs and branches within other retail outlets. Services include community banking, credit and debit cards, home equity and mortgage loans, on-line banking, student loans, and insurance. Wells Fargo also offers a complete line of commercial and institutional financial services. Founded in 1852. **Corporate headquarters location:** San Francisco CA. **Other U.S. locations:** Nationwide. **International locations:** Worldwide. **Listed on:** New York Stock Exchange. **Stock exchange symbol:** WFC. **Annual sales/revenues:** More than $100 million. **Number of employees worldwide:** 120,000.

WEYERHAEUSER COMPANY
HC74 Box 100, Wright City OK 74766. 580/981-1220. **Contact:** Cheryl Hughes, Personnel. **World Wide Web address:** http://www. weyerhaeuser.com. **Description:** A forest-products company whose primary businesses are growing and harvesting timber, the manufacture, distribution, and marketing of forest products including logs, wood chips, pulp, paper, packaging and building products, and real estate construction, development, and financial service. **Special programs:** Tuition Reimbursement; Training. **Corporate headquarters location:** Tacoma WA. **Other U.S. locations:** AL; AR; MS; GA; NC; OR; WA. **Operations at this facility include:** The manufacturing of pine plywood and lumber. **Listed on:** New York Stock Exchange. **Stock exchange symbol:** WY. **President:** Stephen R. Rogel. **Sales/revenue:** $4.7 billion. **Number of employees nationwide:** 37,000. **Number of employees worldwide:** Approximately 60,000.

WEYERHAEUSER COMPANY
P.O. Box 890, Valliant OK 74764. 580/933-1494. **Physical address:** Highway 70 West, Valliant OK 74764. **Contact:** Wanda Graham, Human Resources Director. **World Wide Web address:** http://www.weyer haeuser.com. **Description:** A forest-products company whose primary businesses are growing and harvesting timber, the manufacture, distribution, and marketing of forest products including logs, wood chips, pulp, paper, packaging and building products, and real estate construction, development, and financial service. **Special programs:** Tuition Reimbursement; Training. **Corporate headquarters location:** Tacoma WA. **Other U.S. locations:** AL; AR; MS; GA; NC; OR; WA. **Operations at this facility include:** The manufacturing of cardboard packaging. **Listed on:** New York Stock Exchange. **Stock exchange symbol:** WY. **President:** Stephen R. Rogel. **Sales/revenue:** $4.7 billion. **Number of employees nationwide:** 37,000. **Number of employees worldwide:** Approximately 60,000.

WILLIAMS COMPANIES, INC.
P.O. Box 22087, Tulsa OK 74121. 918/573-2000. **Physical address:** One Williams Center, 50th Floor, Tulsa OK 74172. **Fax:** 918/573-0503. **Contact:** Employee Relations. **E-mail address:** e-resumes@williams.com. **World Wide Web address:** http://www.williams.com. **Description:** An energy company whose central activities include the transportation, management, and marketing of natural gas, liquid hydrocarbons, petroleum, and other energy-related products. Williams Companies, Incorporated is organized into three primary divisions: interstate natural gas pipelines, natural gas exploration and production, and onshore and offshore natural gas gathering and processing. **NOTE:** Job seekers can register online with Job Finder to be notified via e-mail of open positions that suit their profile. **Positions advertised include:** Environmental Engineer; Operator; Real Estate Representative; Welder. **Special programs:** Internships; Training; Educational Reimbursement Program. **Corporate headquarters location:** This location. **Subsidiaries include:** Northwest Pipeline Corporation; Williams Information Services Corp; Williams Natural Gas Company; Williams Pipe Line Company; Wiltel; Barrett Resources. **Listed on:** The New York Stock Exchange. **Stock exchange symbol:** WMB. **President/CEO/Chairman:** Steven J. Malcolm. **Sales/revenue:** $6.52 billion. **Number of employees worldwide:** 12,433.

WORLD PUBLISHING COMPANY
P.O. Box 1770, Tulsa OK 74102. 918/583-2161. **Physical address:** 315 South Boulder Avenue, Tulsa OK 74103. **Fax:** 918/584-8966. **Contact:** Human Resources. **E-mail address:** hr@tulsaworld.com. **World Wide Web address:** http://www.tulsaworld.com. **Description:** Publishes *The Tulsa World* newspaper. **Positions advertised include:** Marketing Manager. **Operations at this facility include:** Administration; Manufacturing; Sales. **Number of employees at this location:** 700.

XETA TECHNOLOGIES
1814 West Tacoma, Broken Arrow OK 74012. 918/664-8200. **Fax:** 918/664-6876. **Contact:** Cindy Earnest, Human Resources. **E-mail address:** human.resources@xeta.com. **World Wide Web address:** http://www.xeta.com. **Description:** A data and technologies company that provides a wide array of communications services and business solutions. XETA provides voice and data networking, consulting, engineering and systems design, as well as equipment installation and maintenance. Founded in 1981. **Corporate headquarters location:** This location. **Other U.S. locations:** Nationwide. **Listed on:** NASDAQ. **Stock exchange symbol:** XETA.

ABC BUILDING PRODUCTS
3610 SE 29th Avenue, Portland OR 97202. 503/239-6543. **Fax:** 239-0131. **Contact:** Human Resources. **World Wide Web address:** http://www.abcsupply.com. **Description:** A leading distributor of building products including insulation, industrial metals, roofing materials, vinyl siding, and millwork. Founded in 1991.

ACS, INC.
1220 SW Morrison, Suite 700, Portland OR 97205. 503/228-2567. **Contact:** Human Resources. **E-mail address:** info@acs-inc.com. **World Wide Web address:** http://www.acs-inc.com. **Description:** Provides diversified business processing and information technology and outsources solutions to commercial and governmental clients worldwide. ACS is a Fortune 500 company and was founded in 1988. **Company slogan:** People Making Technology Work. **NOTE:** Applications and resumes are accepted through the corporate headquarters location at 2828 N Haskell, Building 1, Dallas TX 75204. 214/841-6111. **Positions advertised include:** Computer Operator; Customer Service Representative; Workforce Supervisor; Project Manager; Business Systems Analyst. **Listed on:** New York Stock Exchange. **Stock exchange symbol:** ACS. President/CEO/Owner: Jeffrey A. Rich. **Number of employees worldwide:** 40,000.

A-DEC, INC.
P.O. Box 111, Newberg OR 97132. 503/538-9471. **Physical address:** 2601 Crestview Drive, Newberg OR 97132. **Fax:** 503/538-0210. **Recorded jobline:** 503/537-2765. **Contact:** Leslie Dotson, Senior Employment Recruiter. **E-mail address:** hr@a-dec.com. **World Wide Web address:** http://www.a-dec.com. **Description:** Manufactures dental equipment and furniture including hand pieces, chairs, stools, and cabinets. **Positions advertised include:** Territory Manager; Machine Operator; Regional Sales Manager; Financial Analyst; Clerk. **Special programs:** Internships. **Corporate headquarters location:** This location. **Other U.S. locations:** Nationwide. **Operations at this facility include:** Administration; Manufacturing; Research and Development; Sales; Service.

ADP DEALER SERVICES
2525 SW First Avenue, Suite 450, Portland OR 97201. 503/294-4200. **Toll-free phone:** 800/225-5237. **Fax:** 503/294-4262. **Contact:** Senior Technical Recruiter. **World Wide Web address:** http://www.adp.com. **Description:** One of the largest companies in the world dedicated to providing computerized transaction processing, data communications, and information services. **Positions advertised include:** Tech Support Specialist; Administrative Coordinator; Hardware Client Technical Analyst; Materials Handler; Software Engineer; Columbia Repair Manager; Client Trainer. **Corporate headquarters location:** Roseland NJ. **Other U.S. locations:** Nationwide. **Operations at this facility include:** Research and Development; Sales; Service. **Listed on:** New York Stock Exchange. **Stock exchange symbol:** ADP.

AT&T BROADBAND
3075 NE Sandy Boulevard, Portland OR 97232. 503/230-2099. **Contact:** Human Resources. **World Wide Web address:** http://www.cable.att.com. **Description:** One of the nation's largest cable television and broadband services companies. **Positions advertised include:** Broadband Technician; Lead Customer Service Representative.

ACRES GAMING INC.
815 NW Ninth Street, Corvallis OR 97330. 541/753-7648. **Contact:** Human Resources. **E-mail address:** resume@acresgaming.com. **World Wide Web address:** http://www.acresgaming.com. **Description:** Develops, manufactures, and markets electronic equipment for casino slot machines. Acres' Concept III technology enables gaming machines to automatically pay double jackpots and provide free plays and extra jackpot combinations. Founded in 1991. **Other U.S. locations:** Las Vegas NV.

ADIDAS AMERICA
5055 North Greeley Avenue, Portland OR 97217. 971/234-2300. **Fax:** 971/234-2450. **Contact:** Human Resources. **World Wide Web address:** http://usa.adidas.com. **Description:** Adidas America is a diversified apparel manufacturer specializing in athletic wear. **Corporate headquarters location:** This location. **Parent company:** Adidas-Salomon (Germany). **Operations at this facility include:** This location houses administrative offices.

ADVENTIST MEDICAL CENTER
10123 SE Market Street, Portland OR 97216. 503/257-2500. **Recorded jobline:** 503/251-6195. **Contact:** Human Resources. **E-mail address:** hrdept@ah.org. **World Wide Web address:** http://www.adventisthealthnw.com. **Description:** A 300-bed hospital. **NOTE:** The jobline number is for nursing postings only. For all other listings, please call 503/251-6295. **Positions advertised include:** Staff RN; Therapist; Surgical Technologist; Visiting RN; Account Representative; Department Secretary; Receptionist; Imaging Assistant; Cleaning Technician; Patient Service Representative; Plant Services Engineer; Staff Technologist; Security Officer. **Corporate headquarters location:** Rosedale CA. **Parent company:** Advent Health System.

AG-BAG INTERNATIONAL LIMITED
2320 SE Ag-Bag Lane, Warrenton OR 97146. 503/861-1644. **Toll-free phone:** 800/334-7432. **Fax:** 503/861-2527. **Contact:** Human Resources. **World Wide Web address:** http://www.ag-bag.com. **Description:** Ag-Bag International Limited has developed an alternate method of storing feed for livestock in plastic bags. The company sells ancillary products that complement its main line of products. The grain bagging division assembles and sells grain-bagging machines that enable farmers to store whole grains and other products in the company's recyclable plastic bags. In addition, the company has adapted its bagging machines to permit the bagging of compostable organic matter and developed plastic bag bailers that enable the company to bail and pick up the recyclable plastic bags from its customers. **Corporate headquarters location:** This location.

AGGREGATE MACHINERY INC. (AMI)
3575 Blossom Drive NE, Salem OR 97305. 503/390-6284. **Fax:** 503/390-6342. **Contact:** Personnel. **World Wide Web address:** http://www.thunderbird2.com. **Description:** Manufactures crushing and recycling equipment and machinery for the construction and mining industries.

ALBANY DEMOCRAT-HERALD
P.O. Box 130, 600 Lyon Street SW, Albany OR 97321-0041. 541/926-2211. **Fax:** 541/926-5298. **Contact:** Human Resources. **World Wide Web address:** http://www.dhonline.com. **Description:** A general interest information provider that publishes a daily newspaper (excluding Sundays), with a circulation of 22,000. The company also operates a commercial printing and distribution center. Founded in 1865. **Corporate headquarters location:** This location. **Parent company:** ABC, Inc.

ALBERTSON'S INC.
17505 NE San Rafael Street, Portland OR 97230. 503/251-9200. **Contact:** Human Resources. **World Wide Web address:** http://www.albertsons.com. **Description:** Albertson's operates retail grocery stores. **Corporate headquarters location:** Boise ID. **Operations at this facility include:** This location is a warehouse.

AMALGAMATED SUGAR COMPANY LLC
P.O. Box 1766, 105 E Main Street, Nyssa OR 97913-0266. 541/372-2277. **Fax:** 541/372-1057. **Contact:** Human Resources Manager. **Description:** One of the nation's largest producers of sugar, accounting for approximately 10 percent of the annual sugar production in the United States. The company's White Satin brand is sold primarily to industrial users in the Pacific, Intermountain, and Midwest states. **Corporate headquarters location:** Ogden UT.

AMERICA'S TIRE COMPANY
8380 SE Sunnyside Road, Clackamas OR 97015. 503/652-4353. **Fax:** 503/652-2591. **Contact:** Office Manager. **E-mail address:** jobs@discounttire.com. **World Wide Web address:** http://www.discounttire.com. **Description:** Engaged in the retail sale of tires and wheels. **Other U.S. locations:** Nationwide.

AMERICAN AIRLINES, INC.
7000 NE Airport Way, Portland OR 97218. 503/249-4450. **Contact:** Human Resources. **World Wide Web address:** http://www.aa.com. **Description:** Provides scheduled jet service to more than 170 destinations, primarily throughout North America, Latin America, Europe, and the Pacific. American Airlines, Inc.'s Passenger Division is one of the largest passenger airlines in the world. Founded in 1934. **NOTE:** Jobseekers are encouraged to apply via the Website: http://www.aacareers.com. **Parent company:** AMR Corporation's operations fall within three major lines of business: the Air Transportation Group, the SABRE Group, and the AMR Management Services Group. The Air Transportation Group consists primarily of American Airlines, Inc.'s Passenger and Cargo Division and AMR Eagle, Inc., a subsidiary of AMR Corporation.

AMERICAN EXPRESS TRAVEL SERVICES
1100 SW Sixth Avenue, Portland OR 97204. 206/441-8622. **Toll-free phone:** 800/227-5868. **Contact:** Team Leader. **World Wide Web address:** http://www.americanexpress.com. **Description:** A travel agency. **Positions advertised include:** Corporate Travel Counselor; Leisure Travel Counselor; Outside Sales Representative. **International locations:** Worldwide.

AMERICAN RED CROSS
3131 North Vancouver Avenue, Portland OR 97227. 503/284-1234. **Recorded jobline:** 503/280-1474. **Contact:** Human Resources Department. **World Wide Web address:** http://www.redcross.org. **Description:** A humanitarian organization that aids disaster victims, gathers blood for crisis distribution, trains individuals to respond to emergencies, educates individuals on various diseases, and raises funds for other charitable establishments.

AMERICAN STEEL L.L.C.
P.O. Box 10086, Portland OR 97296. 503/226-1511. **Physical address:** 4033 NW Yeon Avenue, Portland OR 97210. **Contact:** Sheri Lynch, Human Resources Director. **World Wide Web address:** http://www.american-steel.com. **Description:** A steel service center engaged in the distribution of carbon steel products.

AMERICONTINENTAL COLLECT COMPANY
P.O. Box 3514, Portland OR 97208. 503/241-1118. **Physical address:** 101 SW Market Street, Portland OR 97201. **Contact:** Human Resources. **World Wide Web address:** http://www.accountsreceivable.com. **Description:** A collection agency. **Corporate headquarters location:** This location.

ANALOG DEVICES, INC.
1100 NW Compton Drive, Suite 301, Beaverton OR 97006-1994. 503/690-1333. **Fax:** 503/690-1347. **Contact:** Human Resources Department. **World Wide Web address:** http://www.analog.com. **Description:** Designs, manufactures, and markets a broad line of high-performance linear, mixed-signal, and digital integrated circuits (ICs) that address a wide range of real-world signal processing applications. The company's principal products include system-level, general purpose, and standard linear ICs. Other products include devices manufactured using assembled product technology, such as hybrids, which combine unpackaged IC chips and other chip-level components in a single package. Analog's system-level ICs are used primarily in communications and computer applications. **Corporate headquarters location:** Norwood MA.

ANKMAR
1744 Main Street, Sweet Home OR 97386. 541/367-6157. **Contact:** Human Resources. **World Wide Web address:** http://www.linmar.com. **Description:** Recycles newspaper and manufactures particle board. **Corporate headquarters location:** Norcross GA.

ANKMAR
P.O. Box 1620, Corvallis OR 97339. 541/929-5262. **Contact:** Human Resources. **World Wide Web address:** http://www.linmar.com. **Description:** Recycles newspaper and manufactures particle board. **Corporate headquarters location:** Norcross GA.

ANKMAR
P.O. Box 70, Newberg OR 97132-0070. 503/538-2151. **Contact:** Human Resources. **World Wide Web address:** http://www.linmar.com. **Description:** Recycles newspaper and manufactures particle board. **Corporate headquarters location:** Norcross GA.

APCON, INC.
17938 SW Upper Boones Ferry Road, Portland OR 97224. 503/639-6700. **Toll-free phone:** 800/624-6808. **Fax:** 503/639-6740. **Contact:** Human Resources. **E-mail address:** hire@apcon.com. **World Wide Web address:** http://www.apcon.com. **Description:** Manufactures and markets a line of products for SCSI computer systems. APCON, Inc. manufactures PowerSwitch/NT, a clustering solution for Windows NT, which protects network servers from downtime. The company also offers PowerLink, which provides disaster recovery for RAIDS's and tape backup devices. Founded in 1986. **Positions advertised include:** Hardware Design Engineer; International Sales Representative; Product Marketing Manager. **Office hours:** Monday - Friday, 7:30 a.m. - 5:00 p.m. **Corporate headquarters location:** This location.

APPLIED INFORMATION SERVICES (AIS)
4000 Kruseway Place, Building 1, Suite 300, Lake Oswego OR 97035. 503/636-7696. **Fax:** 503/697-0234. **Contact:** Human Resources. **World Wide Web address:** http://www.applied-info.com. **Description:** Offers a variety of network integration and computer systems services. Applied Information Services specializes in the development and installation of computer systems for businesses. Founded in 1970. **Positions advertised include:** Field Service Representative. **Parent company:** Savin Corp.

AQUA GLASS WEST
5855 Washburn Way, Klamath Falls OR 97603-9364. 541/882-7711. **Contact:** Human Resources. **World Wide Web address:** http://www.aquaglass.com. **Description:** Glass

Corporation is a manufacturer of showers, bathtubs, whirlpools, steam showers, and specialty care products. **Parent company:** Masco Corporation. **Operations at this facility include:** This location manufactures fiberglass bathtubs. **Corporate headquarters location:** Adamsville TN. **Parent company:** Masco Corporation.

ARTISAN DENTAL LABORATORY
2532 SE Hawthorne Boulevard, Portland OR 97214. 503/238-6006. **Toll-free phone:** 800/222-6721. **Fax:** 503/231-3684. **Contact:** Human Resources. **World Wide Web address:** http://www.addl.com. **Description:** A dental laboratory that manufactures dentures, implants, crowns, bridges, and other ceramic dental products.

ASCENTRON
994 Antelope Road, White City OR 97503. 541/826-2405. **Fax:** 541/826-1205. **Contact:** Human Resources. **E-mail address:** employment@ascentron.com. **World Wide Web address:** http://www.ascentron.com. **Description:** Assembles electro-mechanical products on a contract basis. Founded in 1982. **Positions advertised include:** Controller. **Office hours:** Monday - Friday, 8:00 a.m. - 5:00 p.m. **Corporate headquarters location:** This location.

ASH GROVE CEMENT COMPANY
P.O. Box 240, Portland OR 97207. 503/293-2333. **Physical address:** 6720 SW Macadam Avenue, Suite 300, Portland OR 97219. **Contact:** Human Resources. **World Wide Web address:** http://www.ashgrove.com. **Description:** Ash Grove Cement Company manufactures lime and operates a cement manufacturing plant. **Positions advertised include:** Plant Manager; Production Manager; Maintenance Manager; Process Engineer; Plant Engineer; Chief Chemist; Environmental and Safety Manager; Quarry Superintendent; Human Resources Manager. **Corporate headquarters location:** This location. **Other area locations:** Durkee OR. **Operations at this facility include:** This location houses administrative offices.

ASH GROVE CEMENT COMPANY
P.O. Box 287, Durkee OR 97905. 541/877-2411. **Physical address:** 330 Cement Plant Road, Durkee OR 97905. **Contact:** Maxine Murray, Office Manager. **World Wide Web address:** http://www.ashgrove.com. **Description:** A cement manufacturing plant. **Positions advertised include:** Plant Manager; Production Manager; Maintenance Manager; Process Engineer; Plant Engineer; Chief Chemist; Environmental and Safety Manager; Quarry Superintendent; Human Resources Manager. **Corporate headquarters location:** Portland OR.

ASSISTED LIVING CONCEPTS, INC.
2825 Neff Road, Bend OR 97701. 541/317-8464. **Fax:** 541/317-4147. **Contact:** Personnel. **E-mail address:** hr@alcco.com. **World Wide Web address:** http://www.alcco.com. **Description:** Owns, operates, and develops assisted living facilities for elderly persons. The company also provides personal care and support services. **Positions advertised include:** Regional Nurse Consultant; Assisted Living Administrator; Regional Director of Operations; Community Sales Coordinator; Lead Cook; Cook; Nurse Consultant; Activity Services Coordinator; Lead Personal Services Assistant; Maintenance Technician; Personal Service Assistant. **Corporate headquarters location:** Dallas TX. **Other U.S. locations:** Nationwide. **Operations at this facility include:** Administration; Service. **Listed on:** American Stock Exchange. **Stock exchange symbol:** ALF.

ASTORIA RED LION INN
400 Industry Street, Astoria OR 97103. 503/325-7373. **Fax:** 503/325-8727. **Contact:** Human Resources. **World Wide Web address:** http://www.redlion.com. **Description:** A full-service, 124-room hotel offering a variety of business services and tourist information. **Positions advertised include:** Night Auditor; Room Attendant.

ATER WYNNE LLP
222 SW Columbia Street, Suite 1800, Portland OR 97201. 503/226-1191. **Contact:** Randy Johnson for attorney employment matters. **E-mail address:** raj@aterwynne.com. **World Wide Web address:** http://www.aterwynne.com. **Description:** A general practice law firm providing a variety of legal services to regional, national, and international businesses and clients. **NOTE:** Contact Traci Quiroz for staff employment matters, taq@aterwynne.com. **Other area locations:** Seattle WA.

AZUMANO CARLSON WAGONLIT TRAVEL
320 SW Stark Street, Suite 600, Portland OR 97204. 503/223-6245. **Toll-free phone:** 800/777-2018. **Fax:** 503/294-6474. **Contact:** Human Resources. **E-mail address:** jobs@azumano.com. **World Wide Web address:** http://www.azumano.com. **Description:** A travel agency. Founded in 1949. **Positions advertised include:** Cruise Agent. **Other U.S. locations:** Denver CO; Vancouver WA.

BANK OF AMERICA
1001 SW Fifth Avenue, 3rd Floor, Portland OR 97204. 503/279-3445. **Contact:** Human Resources. **World Wide Web address:** http://www.bankofamerica.com. **Description:** Bank of America is a full-service banking and financial institution. The company operates through four business segments: Global Corporate and Investment Banking, Principal Investing and Asset Management, Commercial Banking, and Consumer Banking. **Positions advertised include:** Proof Operator; Recruiting Coordinator; Associate Operations Representative; Cash Vault Representative; Sales Assistant. **Corporate headquarters location:** Charlotte NC. **Other U.S. locations:** Nationwide. **Operations at this facility include:** This location is a bank branch.

BANK OF TOKYO-MITSUBISHI, LTD.
2300 Pacwest Center, 1211 SW Fifth Avenue, Portland OR 97204. 503/222-3661. **Contact:** Human Resources. **World Wide Web address:** http://www.btmny.com. **Description:** A full-service bank.

BARCOVIEW INC.
1600 NW Compton Drive, Beaverton OR 97006. 503/690-1550. **Fax:** 503/690-1525. **Contact:** Personnel. **World Wide Web address:** http://www.barcomedical.com. **Description:** Designs, manufactures, and markets high-resolution graphics equipment for medical imaging systems. **Positions advertised include:** Mechanical Design Engineer; Business Applications Analyst; Lead Assembler. **International locations:** Worldwide.

BARRETT BUSINESS SERVICES, INC.
4724 SW Macadam Avenue, Portland OR 97201. 503/220-0988. **Toll-free phone:** 800/494-5669. **Fax:** 503/220-0987. **Contact:** Human Resources. **World Wide Web address:** http://www.barrettbusiness.com. **Description:** Provides employees for a diverse set of customers including forest products and agriculture-based companies, electronics manufacturers, transportation and shipping enterprises, professional firms, and general contractors. In a professional employer arrangement, Barrett becomes a co-employer of the client-company's workforce and assumes responsibility for handling some or all of the personnel-related matters, including payroll and payroll taxes, employee benefits, health insurance and workers' compensation coverage, risk management, and related administrative responsibilities. **Positions advertised include:** Marketing Manager; Bookkeeper; Truck Driver; Landscaper; Welder. **Corporate headquarters location:** This location. **Subsidiaries include:** D&L Personnel Department Specialists, Inc.; JRL Services, Inc.

J.H. BAXTER AND COMPANY
P.O. Box 10797, Eugene OR 97440-2797. 541/689-3020. **Toll-free phone:** 800/776-9321. **Fax:** 541/689-8319. **Contact:** Joe Harbert, District Manager. **World Wide Web address:** http://www.jhbaxter.com. **Description:** J.H. Baxter and Company operates through three areas of business: chemical licensing, timberland management, and wood treatment. **NOTE:** As the sales office and the manufacturing plant share a post office box, jobseekers should indicate to which location they are applying. Jobseekers interested in working in sales should direct resumes to the above contact name. Jobseekers interested in working at the plant should direct resumes to Jim Burkert, Plant Manager. **Corporate headquarters location:** San Mateo CA. **Operations at this facility include:** This location houses sales offices.

BEAR CREEK CORPORATION
HARRY & DAVID
P.O. Box 712, Medford OR 97501. 541/864-2121. **Physical address:** 2500 South Pacific Highway, Medford OR 97501. **Recorded jobline:** 541/864-2232. **Contact:** Human Resources. **E-mail address:** jobs@bco.com. **World Wide Web address:** http://www.bco.com. **Description:** Produces and markets fruit, gourmet food, and specialty gifts. Bear Creek Corporation is most famous for the Fruit of the Month Club, Royal Riviera Pears, Oregold Peaches, and roses. Mail order catalogs include Harry & David, Jackson & Perkins, and Northwest Express. **Positions advertised include:** Vice President; Executive Art Director; Director of Internal Audit; Product Designer; Assistant Buyer; Stores Sales. **Corporate headquarters location:** This location. **Operations at this facility include:** Administration; Advertising; Design; Manufacturing; Research and Development; Sales; Service.

BEAUTIFUL AMERICA PUBLISHING COMPANY
2600 Progress Way, P.O. Box 244, Woodburn OR 97071. 503/982-4616. **Contact:** Beverly Paul, President. **World Wide Web address:** http://www.beautifulamericapub.com. **Description:** A publisher of scenic photography books, calendars, and related products. **Corporate headquarters location:** This location.

BEAVER MOTOR COACHES
P.O. Box 5639, Bend OR 97708. 541/389-1144. **Physical address:** 20545 Murray Road, Bend OR 97701. **Contact:** Human Resources. **World Wide Web address:** http://www.beavermotorcoaches.com. **Description:** Designs, manufactures, and markets Class A motor coaches, which incorporate living, dining, sleeping, and bathing facilities on a specially designed motor vehicle chassis. Beaver models include the Patriot and the Marquis, the Contessa, the Monterey, and the Solitaire. **Parent company:** Monaco Coach Corporation.

BEAVERTON COURTYARD INN
8500 SW Nimbus Drive, Beaverton OR 97008. 503/641-3200. **Contact:** Manager. **World Wide Web address:** http://www.courtyard.com. **Description:** A 149-room hotel that offers a restaurant, meeting facilities, recreational facilities, and business services. **Corporate headquarters location:** Washington DC. **Parent company:** Marriott International Inc. has nearly 4,200 units with operations and franchises in 50 states and 25 countries. The company operates lodging facilities and is the franchiser under four separate brand names, each serving a part of the lodging market: Marriott Hotels, Resorts, and Suites (full-service), Courtyard Inn (moderate price), Residence Inn (extended stay), and Fairfield Inn (economy). The company also develops and operates Marriott Ownership Resorts (vacation timesharing).

BEAVERTON SCHOOL DISTRICT
16550 SW Merlo Road, Beaverton OR 97006. 503/591-8000. **Recorded jobline:** 503/591-4397. **Contact:** Human Resources. **World Wide Web address:** http://www.beavton.k12.or.us. **Description:** A state school district comprised of 29 elementary schools, seven middle schools, four high schools, and two alternative high schools (with programs such as continuing education for young parents and an evening academy). **Positions advertised include:** Custodian; Satellite Leader; Cafeteria Manager.

BENNETT, HARTMAN & REYNOLDS
111 SW Fifth Avenue, Suite 1650, Portland OR 97204. 503/227-4600. **Contact:** Human Resources. **Description:** Practices labor, domestic relations, and personal injury law.

THE BENSON HOTEL
309 Southwest Broadway, Portland OR 97205. 503/228-2000. **Fax:** 503/471-3920. **Contact:** Human Resources. **World Wide Web address:** http://www.bensonhotel.com. **Description:** A luxury hotel and conference facility. Founded in 1912. **Parent company:** WestCoast Hotels.

BENTON, COUNTY OF
408 SW Monroe Avenue, Suite 103, Corvallis OR 97333. 541/766-6081. **Fax:** 541/766-6752. **Recorded jobline:** 541/766-6755. **Contact:** Human Resources. **World Wide Web address:** http://www.co.benton.or.us. **Description:** Administrative offices of Benton County. Founded in 1847. **Positions advertised include:** Corrections Deputy; Park Maintenance Worker; Property Appraiser. **Special programs:** Internships. **Operations at this facility include:** Administration.

BENTWOOD FURNITURE INC.
310 NW Morgan Lane, Grants Pass OR 97526. 541/474-0996. **Toll-free phone:** 800/545-4625. **Contact:** Human Resources. **World Wide Web address:** http://www.bentwoodfurn.com. **Description:** Manufactures wooden household furniture.

BFI
6161 NW 61st Avenue, Portland OR 97210. 503/226-6161. **Contact:** Human Resources. **World Wide Web address:** http://www.awin.com. **Description:** Engaged primarily in the collection, disposal, and recycling of solid wastes for commercial, industrial, and residential customers. Services include landfill services, waste-to-energy programs, hazardous waste removal, and liquid waste removal. **Corporate headquarters location:** Scottsdale AZ. **Parent company:** Allied Waste Industries, Inc. **Listed on:** New York Stock Exchange. **Stock exchange symbol:** AW.

BIOSTIM
4150 North Suttle Road, Portland OR 97217. 503/286-2713. **Contact:** Manager. **Description:** Recycles oil, fuels, car fluids, and oil clean-up materials. **World Wide**

Web address: http://www.biostim.com. **Corporate headquarters location:** San Antonio TX.

BLACK & VEATCH
4800 Meadows Road, Suite 200, Lake Oswego OR 97035. 503/699-7556. **Fax:** 503/697-3699. **Contact:** Human Resources. **World Wide Web address:** http://www.bv.com. **Description:** Black & Veatch is an environmental/civil engineering and construction firm serving utilities, commerce, and government agencies in more than 40 countries worldwide. Black & Veatch provides a broad range of study, design, construction management, and turnkey capabilities to clients in the water and wastewater fields. The firm is one of the leading authorities on drinking water treatment through the use of activated carbon, ozone, and other state-of-the-art processes. Black & Veatch is also engaged in wastewater treatment work including reclamation and reuse projects and the beneficial use of wastewater residuals. Other services are provided for solid waste recycling and disposal, transportation, and storm water management. In the energy field, Black & Veatch is a leader in providing engineering procurement and construction for electric power plants. The firm's areas of expertise include coal-fueled plants, simple and combined-cycle combustion turbines, fluidized bed combustion, waste-to-energy facilities, hydroelectric plants, and cogeneration facilities. Black & Veatch's capabilities also include nuclear power projects, advanced technology, air quality control, performance monitoring, plant life management, and facilities modification. In addition, Black & Veatch operates in the transmission and distribution field. In the industrial sector, Black & Veatch focuses on projects involving cleanrooms, industrial processes and planning, utility systems, and cogeneration. In addition to engineering, procurement, and construction, Black & Veatch offers a variety of management and financial services including institutional strengthening, privatization, strategic financial planning, and information management. **Corporate headquarters location:** Overland Park KS. **Operations at this facility include:** This location operates a division engaged in electrical engineering and a division engaged in environmental engineering and wastewater treatment.

BLACKWELL'S BOOK SERVICES
6024 SW Jean Road, Building G, Lake Oswego OR 97035-8598. 503/684-1140. **Contact:** Human Resources. **World Wide Web address:** http://www.blackwell.com. **Description:** Distributes and sells books to libraries.

BOEING COMMERCIAL AIRPLANE GROUP
P.O. Box 20487, Mail Stop 5P-11, Portland OR 97294. 503/667-8000. **Physical address:** 19000 NE Sandy Boulevard, Portland OR 97230. **Contact:** Human Resources. **World Wide Web address:** http://www.boeing.com. **Description:** Applies advanced aerospace technology to a wide range of space, defense, electronic, and computing programs. The Boeing Company is divided into four business segments: Commercial Airplanes, Missile Aircraft and Missile Systems, Space and Communications, and Phantom Works, the company's advanced research and development segment. The Commercial Airplane Group is the company's largest operating unit. **Corporate headquarters location:** Renton WA. **Parent company:** The Boeing Company is one of the largest aerospace firms in the United States, one of the nation's top exporters, and one of the world's leading manufacturers of commercial jet transports. The company is a major U.S. government contractor, with capabilities in missiles and space, electronic systems, military aircraft, helicopters, and information systems management. **Operations at this facility include:** This location manufactures a wide variety of commercial aircraft parts.

BOISE CASCADE CORPORATION
1917 Jackson Avenue, La Grande OR 97850. 541/962-2037. **Contact:** Human Resources. **World Wide Web address:** http://www.bc.com. **Description:** Boise Cascade Corporation is a producer and distributor of pulp and paper, a direct distributor of office products, and a manufacturer and distributor of building products. The company has more than 90 manufacturing and distribution locations in 27 states. Boise Cascade Corporation's paper is used for commercial printing and publishing, forms, envelopes, reprographics, tablets, and packaging. Boise Cascade Corporation provides customers with direct delivery of office and computer supplies. Boise Cascade Corporation also produces engineered wood products such as laminated veneer lumber and wood I-joists. Founded in 1957. **NOTE:** Does not accept unsolicited resumes. Apply for open positions at the employment center at the above location. **Corporate headquarters location:** Boise ID. **Operations at this facility include:** This location is the northeast regional office for four area mills that produce lumber, chipboard, plywood, and particle board. **Listed on:** New York Stock Exchange. **Stock exchange symbol:** BCC.

BOISE CASCADE CORPORATION
450 Pacific Avenue North, Monmouth OR 97361. 503/838-1610. **Contact:** Human Resources. **World Wide Web address:** http://www.bc.com. **Description:** Boise Cascade Corporation is a producer and distributor of pulp and paper, a direct distributor of office products, and a manufacturer and distributor of building products. The company has more than 90 manufacturing and distribution locations in 27 states. Boise Cascade Corporation's paper is used for commercial printing and publishing, forms, envelopes, reprographics, tablets, and packaging. Boise Cascade Corporation provides customers with direct delivery of office and computer supplies. Boise Cascade Corporation also produces engineered wood products such as laminated veneer lumber and wood I-joists. Founded in 1957. **NOTE:** Does not accept unsolicited resumes. Apply for open positions at the Boise Cascade Mill located at 900 Walnut Street in Independence, OR. **Corporate headquarters location:** Boise ID. **Operations at this facility include:** This location is a regional office for the company's area mills, which produce lumber, chipboard, plywood, and particle board. **Listed on:** New York Stock Exchange. **Stock exchange symbol:** BCC.

BOISE CASCADE CORPORATION
P.O. Box 128, Willamina OR 97396-0128. 503/876-2221. **Contact:** Human Resources. **World Wide Web address:** http://www.bc.com. **Description:** Boise Cascade Corporation is a producer and distributor of pulp and paper, a direct distributor of office products, and a manufacturer and distributor of building products. The company has more than 90 manufacturing and distribution locations in 27 states. Boise Cascade Corporation's paper is used for commercial printing and publishing, forms, envelopes, reprographics, tablets, and packaging. Boise Cascade Corporation provides customers with direct delivery of office and computer supplies. Boise Cascade Corporation also produces engineered wood products such as laminated veneer lumber and wood I-joists. Founded in 1957. **NOTE:** Does not accept unsolicited resumes. **Corporate headquarters location:** Boise ID. **Operations at this facility include:** This location is a green veneer mill. **Listed on:** New York Stock Exchange. **Stock exchange symbol:** BCC.

BOISE CASCADE CORPORATION
90 South 21st Street, Elgin OR 97827. 541/437-2611. **Contact:** Human Resources. **World Wide Web address:** http://www.bc.com. **Description:** Boise Cascade Corporation is a producer and distributor of pulp and paper, a direct distributor of office products, and a manufacturer and distributor of building products. The company has more than 90 manufacturing and distribution locations in 27 states. Boise Cascade Corporation's paper is used for commercial printing and publishing, forms, envelopes, reprographics, tablets, and packaging. Boise Cascade Corporation provides customers with direct delivery of office and computer supplies. Boise Cascade Corporation also produces engineered wood products such as laminated veneer lumber and wood I-joists. Founded in 1957. **NOTE:** Does not accept unsolicited resumes. **Corporate headquarters location:** Boise ID. **Operations at this facility include:** This location is a sawmill and plywood plant. **Listed on:** New York Stock Exchange. **Stock exchange symbol:** BCC.

BOISE CASCADE CORPORATION
P.O. Box 100, Medford OR 97501. 541/776-6666. **Contact:** Human Resources. **World Wide Web address:** http://www.bc.com. **Description:** Boise Cascade Corporation is a producer and distributor of pulp and paper, a direct distributor of office products, and a manufacturer and distributor of building products. The company has more than 90 manufacturing and distribution locations in 27 states. Boise Cascade Corporation's paper is used for commercial printing and publishing, forms, envelopes, reprographics, tablets, and packaging. Boise Cascade Corporation provides customers with direct delivery of office and computer supplies. Boise Cascade Corporation also produces engineered wood products such as laminated veneer lumber and wood I-joists. Founded in 1957. **NOTE:** Does not accept unsolicited resumes. **Corporate headquarters location:** Boise ID. **Operations at this facility include:** This location manufactures plywood and veneer. **Listed on:** New York Stock Exchange. **Stock exchange symbol:** BCC.

BONNEVILLE POWER ADMINISTRATION
P.O. Box 3621, Portland OR 97208. 503/230-3055. **Fax:** 360/418-2063. **Recorded jobline:** 503/230-5784. **Contact:** Human Resources. **World Wide Web address:** http://www.bpa.gov. **Description:** A federally run electric power marketing and transmission agency for the Pacific Northwest. Founded in 1932. **NOTE:** Jobseekers can apply via the Website: http://www.bpa.gov/ebr/personnelservices/employment. **Positions advertised include:** Secretary; Program Analyst; Substation Operator. **Special programs:** Internships; Apprenticeships; Co-ops; Summer Jobs. **Other U.S. locations:** ID; MT; WA.

BONNEVILLE POWER ADMINISTRATION
3920 Columbia View Drive East, The Dalles OR 97058. 541/296-4684. **Contact:** Human Resources. **World Wide Web address:** http://www.bpa.gov. **Description:** A federally run electric power marketing and transmission agency for the Pacific Northwest. Founded in 1932. **NOTE:** Jobseekers can apply via the Website: http://www.bpa.gov/ebr/personnelservices/employment. **Positions advertised include:** Secretary; Program Analyst; Substation Operator. **Special programs:** Internships; Apprenticeships; Co-ops; Summer Jobs. **Other U.S. locations:** ID; MT; WA.

BOOK NEWS, INC.
5739 NE Sumner Street, Portland OR 97218. 503/281-9230. **Fax:** 503/287-4485. **Contact:** Jane Erskine, Managing Editor. **E-mail address:** booknews@booknews.com. **World Wide Web address:** http://www.booknews.com. **Description:** Reviews newly published books. *Book News* reviews are carried by Barnes & Noble, Amazon.com, and BookScope, a library reference CD-ROM. **Corporate headquarters location:** This location.

BOYDS COFFEE COMPANY
19730 NE Sandy Boulevard, Portland OR 97230. 503/666-4545. **Toll-free phone:** 800/545-4077. **Fax:** 503-669-2223. **Contact:** Human Resources Manager. **E-mail address:** info@boyds.com. **World Wide Web address:** http://www.boyds.com. **Description:** Roasts, packages, and distributes coffee, tea, and food products. **Positions advertised include:** Sales; Corporate; Manufacturing; Retail. **Corporate headquarters location:** This location.

BRIGHT WOOD CORPORATION
P.O. Drawer 828, Madras OR 97741-0828. 541/475-2234. **Fax:** 541/475-7758. **Physical address:** 335 NW Hess Street, Madras OR 97741. **Contact:** Human Resources. **E-mail address:** resume@brightwood.com. **World Wide Web address:** http://www.brightwood.com. **Description:** Bright Wood is one of the largest millwork manufacturers in the world. Fourteen production plants work together to process over 150 million feet of board lumber annually. Bright Wood is a multiple species manufacturer using firs and pines from New Zealand, Chile, Canada, and other countries. **Corporate headquarters location:** This location.

BROWN & CALDWELL
1025 Willamette Street, Suite 300, Eugene OR 97401. 541/686-9915. **Contact:** Human Resources Manager. **World Wide Web address:** http://www.brownandcaldwell.com. **Description:** An employee-owned environmental engineering and consulting firm. Brown & Caldwell specializes in the planning, engineering, and design of waste management systems. The company is also engaged in construction management and environmental analytical testing. **Positions advertised include:** Principal Engineer; Business Development; Geologist/Hydrologist. **Corporate headquarters location:** Pleasant Hill CA. **Operations at this facility include:** Regional Headquarters.

BROWNSTEIN, RASK, ARENZ, SWEENY, KERR & GRIM
1200 SW Main, Portland OR 97205-2039. 503/221-1772. **Fax:** 503/221-1074. **Contact:** Human Resources. **World Wide Web address:** http://www.brownrask.com. **Description:** A general practice law firm.

THE BULLETIN
P.O. Box 6020, Bend OR 97708. 541/382-1811. **Fax:** 541/383-2373. **Physical address:** 1777 SW Chandler Avenue, Bend OR 97702. **Contact:** Sharlene Crabtree, Director of Human Resources. **E-mail address:** sharlene@bendbulletin.com. **World Wide Web address:** http://www.bendbulletin.com. **Description:** Publishes a daily newspaper with a circulation of approximately 28,000. **Positions advertised include:** Distribution Employee; Advertising Sales Professional. **Internship information:** One reporting intern is hired each summer to work general assignment and vacation relief. The company requires a cover letter, resume, 10 to 12 clips, and three to four references with phone numbers by March 15. Pay is $1,500 per month. **Corporate headquarters location:** This location. **Other area locations:** Baker OR; Brookings OR; Burns OR; Hermiston OR; La Grande OR; Redmond OR. **Other U.S. locations:** Crescent City CA. **Operations at this facility include:** Administration; Manufacturing; Sales; Service.

BURNS BROTHERS INC.
4800 SW Meadows Road, Suite 475, Lake Oswego OR 97035. 503/697-0666. **Contact:** Human Resources. **Description:** A diversified manufacturer, wholesaler, and retailer of auto parts, accessories, and fuel. Other activities include real estate development and the wholesaling of battery-powered lighting products. **Corporate headquarters location:** This location.

CH2M HILL, INC.
P.O. Box 428, Corvallis OR 97339. 541/752-4271. **Physical address:** 2300 NW Walnut Boulevard, Corvallis OR 97330. **Contact:** Human Resources. **World Wide Web address:** http://www.ch2m.com. **Description:** Provides planning, engineering design, and operation and construction management services to help clients apply technology, safeguard the environment, and develop infrastructure. The professional staff includes specialists in environmental engineering and waste management, water management, transportation, industrial facilities, and a broad spectrum of infrastructure systems. The company operates through three business groups: Energy, Environment, and Systems; Transportation; and Water. Founded in 1946. **Positions advertised include:** Facilities Operations Manager; Project Delivery Leader; Risk Assessor. **Corporate headquarters location:** Greenwood Village CO.

CADENCE DESIGN SYSTEM
13221 SW 68th Parkway, Suite 200, Portland OR 97223. 503/968-5400. **Toll-free phone:** 800/671-9511. **Fax:** 503/968-7888. **Contact:** Human Resources. **World Wide Web address:** http://www.cadence.com. **Description:** Develops desktop electronic design automation (EDA) software. Cadence Design System's Windows-based software aids in the design of field-programmable gate arrays, complex programmable logic devices, and printed circuit boards. **Positions advertised include:** Design Engineer; Applications Engineer; Executive Administrator; Marketing Director. **Corporate headquarters location:** San Jose CA.

CALBAG METALS COMPANY
P.O. Box 10067, Portland OR 97296. 503/226-3441. **Toll-free phone:** 800/398-3441. **Fax:** 503/228-0184. **Physical address:** 2495 NW Nicolai Street, Portland OR 97210. **Contact:** Human Resources. **World Wide Web address:** http://www.calbag.com. **Description:** Recycles scrap metal.

CAP GEMINI AMERICA
1500 SW First Avenue, Suite 890, Portland OR 97201. 503/295-1909. **Contact:** Human Resources Manager. **World Wide Web address:** http://www.usa.capgemini.com. **Description:** A leading provider of information technology consulting services. The company provides its clients with the solutions needed to achieve business and operational goals. CGA's principal focus is on three major activities: consultancy, implementation, and systems integration. **Other U.S. locations:** Nationwide. **Parent company:** The Cap Gemini Sogeti Group is a top-ranked provider of information technology services throughout Europe and its major markets.

CARLTON COMPANY
P.O. Box 68309, Milwaukie OR 97268-0309. 503/659-8911. **Toll-free phone:** 800/524-0685. **Fax:** 503/659-8616. **Contact:** Human Resources. **E-mail address:** carlton_co@sawchain.com. **World Wide Web address:** http://www.sawchain.com. **Description:** Manufactures saw chains, guide bars, and related accessories. **International locations:** Worldwide.

CASCADE CORPORATION
P.O. Box 20187, Fairview OR 97294. 503/669-6300. **Fax:** 503/669-6716. **Physical address:** 2201 NE 201st Avenue, Fairview OR 97024. **Contact:** Human Resources. **World Wide Web address:** http://www.cascorp.com. **Description:** Manufactures industrial equipment and materials handling machinery including hydraulic lift equipment. **Corporate headquarters location:** This location. **Listed on:** New York Stock Exchange. **Stock exchange symbol:** CAE. **Number of employees worldwide:** 1,400.

CASCADE FRUIT COMPANY
OREGON CHERRY GROWERS
P.O. Box 7359, 1520 Woodrow Street NE, Salem OR 97303. 541/296-5487. **Contact:** Human Resources Manager. **Description:** Grows, processes, and sells cherries. Oregon Cherry Growers (also at this location) is a cooperative that also grows, processes, and sells cherries.

CASCADE STEEL ROLLING MILLS
3200 North Highway 99W, P.O. Box 687, McMinnville OR 97128. 503/472-4181. **Contact:** Mike Hereford, Human Resources. **E-mail address:** careers@metalsuppliersonlime.com. **World Wide Web address:** http://www.suppliersonline.com. **Description:** Manufactures steel reinforcement products for agricultural and industrial use. **Corporate headquarters location:** This location. **Parent company:** Schnitzer Steel. **Operations at this facility include:** Administration; Manufacturing; Sales.

CHAMPION HOMES, INC.
1204 Mill Street, Silverton OR 97381. 503/873-6381. **Contact:** Human Resources Department. **World Wide Web address:** http://www.championoregon.com. **Description:** The Northwest division of one of the largest advanced-design home builders in the world. Founded in 1937. **Listed on:** New York Stock Exchange. **Stock exchange symbol:** CHB.

CHEMEKETA COMMUNITY COLLEGE
4000 Lancaster Drive NE, P.O. Box 14007, Salem OR 97309. 503/589-7691. **Recorded jobline:** 503/399-5228. **Contact:** Human Resources. **E-mail address:** humanresources@chemeketa.edu. **World Wide Web address:** http://www.chemeketa.edu. **Description:** A community college with an enrollment of approximately 44,000 students including full-time, part-time, and noncredit students.

CHINOOK WINDS CASINO
1777 NW 44th Street, Lincoln City OR 97367-5094. 541/996-5800. **Fax:** 541/996-5857. **Recorded Jobline:** 888/CHINOOK ext. 8097. **Contact:** Human Resources. **World Wide Web address:** http://www.chinookwindscasino.com. **Description:** A full-service casino. In addition to gaming tables and slot machines, Chinook Winds Casino offers a supervised child care facility, a video arcade, a gift shop, dining facilities, and complementary valet and shuttle services. **Positions advertised include:** Utility Worker; Food and Beverage Worker; Dining Room Busser; Beverage Server; Buffet Server; Banquet Server; Valet Attendant; Blackjack Dealer.

CHRISTENSON VELAGIO
1631 NW Thurman Street, Suite 200, Portland OR 97209. 503/419-3600. **Toll-free phone:** 800/234-4115. **Fax:** 503/419-3636. **Contact:** Human Resources. **E-mail address:** info@christenson.com. **World Wide Web address:** http://www.christenson.com. **Description:** An electrical and technology contractor that works in various locations including high-rise buildings and industrial businesses. Christenson Velagio leverages core competencies in electrical services and information technology in the areas of voice, data, video and life-safety into enterprise energy management solutions. Christenson Velagio has the ability to deliver turnkey solutions from energy management solutions to technology infrastructure implementation, including: Enterprise Energy Management Solutions, Electrical and Lighting Services, Electrical Design and Implementation, Digital Video CCTV Systems and Infrastructure, Telecommunications Systems and Infrastructure, Wireless Networking Solutions, IT Network (Voice and Data) Design and Implementation, Enterprise Security and Life–Safety Systems. **Corporate headquarters location:** This location.

CLACKAMAS COMMUNITY COLLEGE
19600 South Molalla Avenue, Oregon City OR 97045-7998. 503/657-6958 ext. 2318. **Fax:** 503/650-7348. **Recorded jobline:** 503/650-6655. **Contact:** Human Resources. **E-mail address:** debbiej@clackamas.edu. **World Wide Web address:** http://www.clackamas.edu. **Description:** A community college offering associate's degrees to approximately 27,000 students. **Positions advertised include:** Project Management Instructor; Skills Development Department Instructor; Faculty.

CLACKAMAS, COUNTY OF
2051 Kaen Road, Oregon City OR 97045. 503/655-8459. **Fax:** 503/635-8946. **Recorded jobline:** 503/655-8894. **Contact:** Department of Employee Services. **World Wide Web address:** http://www.co.clackamas.or.us. **Description:** Houses administrative offices for the county of Clackamas. **Positions advertised include:** Community Development Project Coordinator; Community Health Nurse; Senior Cook; Information Services Assistant Director; Office Specialist; Records and Electronics Technician; Sheriff's Office Administrative Services Manager; Wastewater Maintenance Services Manager. **Office hours:** Monday - Friday, 8:30 a.m. - 5:00 p.m.

CLARK'S QUALITY ROOFING
521 N Janzen, #448 Portland OR 97219. 503/209-5079. **Fax:** 360/260-3005. **Contact:** Human Resources. **E-mail address:** info@cqrinc.com. **World Wide Web address:** http://www.cqrinc.com. **Description:** Clark's Quality Roofing specializes in commercial membrane roofing installations. Their professional services include waterproofing, maintenance and repairs, metal roofing installations and sheet metal specialty fabrication. They are certified by leading roof manufacturers to install a wide variety of systems. **Positions advertised include:** Roofer; Foreman; Repair Technician. **Corporate headquarters location:** Salt Lake City UT.

CLEAR PINE MOULDING
1155 N Main, P.O. Box 309, Prineville OR 97754. 541/447-4195. **Fax:** 541/447-6479. **Contact:** Human Resources Manager. **Description:** A sawmill and laminating company. **NOTE:** Second and third shifts are offered. **Special programs:** Summer Jobs. **Corporate headquarters location:** Portland OR. **Parent company:** Contact Lumber. **CEO:** Bob Donnelly.

COCA-COLA BOTTLING COMPANY OF OREGON
9750 SW Barber Street, Wilsonville OR 97070-9233. 503/682-2800. **Contact:** Human Resources. **World Wide Web address:** http://www.cokecce.com. **Description:** A bottling company packaging Coca-Cola, Barq's and Dr. Pepper. **Positions advertised include:** Merchandiser; Loader. **Parent company:** Coca-Cola Company is one of the world's largest marketers, distributors, and producers of bottle and can products. Coca-Cola Enterprises, part of the Coca-Cola Company, is in the liquid nonalcoholic refreshment business, which includes traditional carbonated soft drinks, still and sparkling waters, juices, isotonics, and teas. The company operates in 38 states, the District of Columbia, the U.S. Virgin Islands, the Islands of Tortola and Grand Cayman, and the Netherlands. **Listed on:** New York Stock Exchange. **Stock exchange symbol:** CCE.

COE MANUFACTURING COMPANY
7930 Hunziker Road, P.O. Box 23366, Tigard OR 97223. 503/639-3121. **Fax:** 503/684-7570. **Contact:** Human Resources. **World Wide Web address:** http://www.coemfg.com. **Description:** Manufactures machinery for the production and handling of plywood, composition board, lumber, rubber and plastics, and engineered wood products. Founded in 1952. **Corporate headquarters location:** Painesville OH. **Number of employees at this location:** 300.

COLDWELL BANKER
BARBARA SUE SEAL PROPERTIES, INC.
7420 SW Bridgeport Road, Portland OR 97224. 503/241-5505. **Toll-free phone:** 800/342-7767. **Contact:** Personnel. **E-mail address:** recruiting@cbseal.com. **World Wide Web address:** http://www.cbportland.com. **Description:** A residential real estate company with 15 sales offices. Founded in 1983.

COLLINS PRODUCTS, LLC
6410 Hwy 66, P.O. Box 16, Klamath Falls OR 97601. 541/885-4836. **Toll-free phone:** 800/329-1219. **Fax:** 541/882-8870. **Contact:** Murf Karns, Human Resources. **World Wide Web address:** http://www.collinswood.com. **Description:** A lumber company that produces certified hardwood, softwood, and engineered wood products. Collins Pine Company also owns, operates, and preserves three certified forests, maintaining environmental and wildlife protection and safety. **Positions advertised include:** Process Control Engineer. **Parent company:** The Collins Companies. **Corporate headquarters location:** Portland OR.

COLUMBIA CASCADE
1975 SW Fifth Avenue, Portland OR 97201-5293. 503/223-1157. **Fax:** 503/223-4530. **Contact:** Human Resources. **World Wide Web address:** http://www.timberform.com. **Description:** A manufacturer of playground slides, climbing structures, and related equipment. Columbia Cascade manufactures outdoor furniture and bicycle management structures.

COLUMBIA HELICOPTERS, INC.
P.O. Box 3500, Portland OR 97208. 503/678-1222. **Fax:** 503/678-5841. **Physical address:** Aurora State Airport, 14452 Arndt Road NE, Aurora OR 97002. **Contact:** Personnel Department. **E-mail address:** rosep@colheli.com. **World Wide Web address:** http://www.colheli.com. **Description:** Offers external-load, heavy-lift helicopter services. Founded in 1957. **Positions advertised include:** Aviation Field Mechanic; Ground Service Attendant; Helicopter Log Hooker; Knot Bumper; 2-Person Watch Team; Copilot; Timber Cutter; Aviation Field Electrician/Mechanic.

COLUMBIA MANAGEMENT GROUP
121 SW Morrison, Suite 1400, Portland OR 97204. 503/222-3600. **Contact:** Human Resources. **World Wide Web address:** http://www.columbiamanagement.com. **Description:** An investment management firm. **Parent company:** Bank of America.

COLUMBIA PLYWOOD CORPORATION
P.O. Box 1780, Klamath Falls OR 97601-0241. 541/882-7281. **Contact:** Carolyn Becchi, Manager of Human Resources Department. **World Wide Web address:** http://www.columbiaforestproducts.com. **Description:** Manufactures hardwood plywood. **Parent company:** Columbia Forest Products.

COLUMBIA SPORTSWEAR COMPANY
14375 NW Science Park Drive, Portland OR 97203. 503/985-4000. **Contact:** Human Resources. **World Wide Web address:** http://www.columbia.com. **Description:** A manufacturer of sportswear, footwear, and accessories for men and women. Founded in 1938. **Positions advertised include:** Designer; Programmer; Footwear Production Specialist; Corporate Trainer; Sales Associate; Apparel Visual Field Merchandiser.

COLUMBIA STEEL CASTING COMPANY INC.
P.O. Box 83095, Portland OR 97283-0095. 503/286-0685. **Toll-free phone:** 800/547-9471. **Fax:** 503/286-1743. **Physical address:** 10425 N. Bloss Avenue, Portland OR 97203-6143. **Contact:** David Randall, Human Resources Manager. **E-mail address:** service@columbiasteel.com. **World Wide Web address:** http://www.columbiasteel.com. **Description:** Manufactures wear-resistant, steel replacement parts for industrial applications. Founded in 1901.

COMPAQ COMPUTER CORPORATION
15115 SW Sequoia Parkway, Suite 100, Portland OR 97224. 503/598-8000. **Contact:** Human Resources. **World Wide Web address:** http://www.hp.com. **Description:** Compaq Computer Corporation designs, manufactures, sells, and services computers and associated peripheral equipment, and related software and supplies. Applications and programs include scientific research, computation, communications, education, data analysis, industrial control, time sharing, commercial data processing, graphic arts, word processing, health care, instrumentation, engineering, and simulation. **Corporate headquarters location:** Houston TX. **Operations at this facility include:** This location is an administrative and service office. **Listed on:** New York Stock Exchange. **Stock exchange symbol:** HPQ.

COMPVIEW
10035 SW Arctic Drive, Beaverton OR 97005. 503/641-8439. **Fax:** 503/626-8439. **World Wide Web address:** http://www.compview.com. **Description:** CompView is a premier provider of presentation technology and group communication solutions. **Corporate Headquarters:** This location.

CONAGRA FOODS
P.O. Box 705, Hermiston OR 97838. 541/567-2211. **Contact:** Human Resources Manager. **E-mail address:** resume@conagrafoods.com. **World Wide Web address:** http://www.conagrafoods.com. **Description:** A processor of a broad line of nationally-distributed frozen potato products including french fries. **Corporate headquarters location:** Kennewick WA. **Other U.S. locations:** Nationwide. **Parent company:** ConAgra, Inc. is a diversified, international food company. Products range from convenient prepared foods to supplies farmers need to grow their crops. ConAgra has major businesses in branded grocery products -- shelf-stable and frozen foods, processed meats, chicken and turkey products, and cheeses -- as well as major businesses in potato products, private label grocery products, beef, pork, seafood, grain and pulse (edible beans) merchandising, grain processing, specialty trailing, crop protection chemicals, fertilizers, and animal feed. **Operations at this facility include:** Administration; Manufacturing.

CONSOLIDATED METCO INC.
P.O. Box 83201, Portland OR 97283-0201. 503/286-5741. **Toll-free phone:** 800/547-9473. **Fax:** 503/240-5488. **Contact:** Human Resources. **E-mail address:** info@conmet.com. **World Wide Web address:** http://www.conmet.com. **Description:** Manufactures aluminum hubs and related products for the automotive industry. The company also markets aluminum castings, die castings, and structural products. Founded in 1964. **Corporate headquarters location:** This location.

COORSTEK
555 NE 53rd Avenue, Hillsboro OR 97124. 303/271-7000. **Toll-free phone:** 800/821-6110. **Fax:** 303/271-7009. **Contact:** Human Resources Department. **E-mail address:** careers@coorstek.com. **World Wide Web address:** http://www.coorstek.com. **Description:** Manufactures a variety of advanced materials including technical ceramics, precision-machined metals, and engineered plastics for the electronics, industrial, automotive, and telecommunications markets. **Corporate headquarters location:** Golden CO. **Listed on:** NASDAQ. **Stock exchange symbol:** CRTK.

CORVALLIS MICROTECHNOLOGY INC.
413 SW Jefferson Avenue, Corvallis OR 97333. 541/752-5456. **Fax:** 541/752-4117. **Contact:** Human Resources Department. **World Wide Web address:** http://www.cmtinc.com. **Description:** Develops, manufactures, and markets handheld computers for the forestry, environmental, wildlife, and utility markets.

COUNTRY COACH INC.
135 E 1st Avenue, P.O. Box 400, Junction City OR 97448. 541/998-3720. **Toll-free phone:** 800/547-8015. **Contact:** Human Resources Department. **E-mail address:** dbedore@counrtycoach.com. **World Wide Web address:** http://www.countrycoach.com. **Description:** Manufactures recreational vehicles and coaches. The company's motorcoach lines include Affinity, Allure, Concept, Intrigue, Magna, Prevost H3-45 Conversion, and Prevost XL Conversion.

COUNTRYWIDE HOME LOANS INC.
9738 SE Washington Street, Suite S, Portland OR 97216. 503/255-7584. **Fax:** 503/255-8093. **Contact:** Human Resources. **World Wide Web address:** http://www.countrywide.com. **Description:** Offers consumer home loans. **Positions advertised include:** Home Loans Consultant. **Corporate headquarters location:** Calabasas CA. **Parent company:** Countrywide Financial Corporation.

COURIER PUBLISHING COMPANY
P.O. Box 1468, Grants Pass OR 97526. 541/474-3700. **Toll-free phone:** 800/228-0457. **Physical location:** 409 SE 7th Street, Grants Pass OR 97526. **Contact:** Human Resources. **E-mail address:** comments@thedailycourier.com. **World Wide Web address:** http://www.thedailycourier.com. **Description:** Publisher of *Grants Pass Daily Courier*, a daily newspaper that is printed Monday through Saturday.

COURTYARD INN-PORTLAND AIRPORT
11550 NE Airport Way, Portland OR 97220. 503/252-3200. **Contact:** Manager. **World Wide Web address:** http://www.courtyard.com. **Description:** A full-service hotel offering a restaurant, exercise facilities, conference rooms, and business services. **Corporate headquarters location:** Washington DC. **Parent company:** Marriott International has nearly 4,200 units, with operations and franchises in 50 states and 22 countries. The company operates lodging facilities and is the franchiser under four separate brand names, each serving a part of the lodging market: Marriott Hotels, Resorts, and Suites (full-service), Courtyard Inn (moderate price), Residence Inn (extended stay), and Fairfield Inn (economy). The company also develops and operates Marriott Ownership Resorts (vacation timesharing).

DAHLIN/FERNANDEZ/FRITZ DENTAL LABORATORY
6421 North Cutter Circle, P.O. Box 4755, Portland OR 97217. 503/240-1910. **Toll-free phone:** 800/422-5779. **Fax:** 503/240-1905. **Contact:** Human Resources Department. **E-mail address:** leonetti@dff-dentallab.com. **World Wide Web address:** http://www.dff-dentallab.com. **Description:** Manufactures crowns, prosthetics, and partials.

THE DAILY ASTORIAN
949 Exchange St., P.O. Box 210, Astoria OR 97103. 503/325-3211. **Toll-free phone:** 800/781-3210. **Fax:** 503/325-6573. **Contact:** Debbie Schendel, Personnel Administrator. **E-mail address:** astorian@dailyastorian.com. **World Wide Web address:** http://www.dailyastorian.info. **Description:** Publishes a daily local newspaper. **Special programs:** Internships. **Corporate headquarters location:** Pendleton OR. **Other U.S. locations:** Salem OR; Long Beach WA. **Parent company:** East Oregonian Publishing Company. **Operations at this facility include:** Administration; Sales; Service.

DANNER SHOE MANUFACTURING COMPANY
18550 NE Riverside Parkway, Portland OR 97230-1027. 503/251-1100. **Toll-free phone:** 800/345-0430. **Fax:** 503/382-2550. **E-mail address:** hr@danner.com. **Contact:** Human Resources. **World Wide Web address:** http://www.danner.com. **Description:** Manufactures boots and shoes. Founded in 1932. **Positions advertised include:** Business Development Manager; Product Development Manager; Staff Accountant; Shoemaker.

DARIGOLD INC.
1300 Court Street, Medford OR 97501. 541/772-2965. **Toll-free phone:** 800/333-6455. **Fax:** 541/772-5639. **Contact:** Human Resources. **World Wide Web address:** http://www.darigold.com. **Description:** Manufactures, markets, and sells dairy products. Founded in 1918. **Corporate headquarters location:** Seattle WA.

DARK HORSE COMICS
10956 SE Main Street, Milwaukie OR 97222. 503/652-8815. **Contact:** Human Resources. **E-mail address:** jobs@darkhorse.com. **World Wide Web address:** http://www.darkhorse.com. **Description:** Publishes comic books. **NOTE:** Submission of resume in plain text or PDF preferred. **Positions advertised include:** Macintosh Help Desk Technician.

DELOITTE & TOUCHE
111 SW Fifth Avenue, Suite 3900, Portland OR 97204. 503/222-1341. **Contact:** Human Resources. **World Wide Web address:** http://www.us.deloitte.com. **Description:** An international firm of certified public accountants providing professional accounting, auditing, tax, and management consulting services to widely diversified clients. The company has a specialized program consisting of national industry groups and functional groups that cross industry lines. Groups are involved in various disciplines including accounting, auditing, taxation management advisory services, small and growing businesses, mergers and acquisitions, and computer applications. **Positions advertised include:** Senior Consultant; Internal Audit Supervisor; Accountant; Consultant. **Other U.S. locations:** Nationwide.

DENNIS UNIFORM MANUFACTURING COMPANY
714 NE Hancock Street, Portland OR 97212. 503/238-7123. **Toll-free phone:** 800/854-6951. **Fax:** 877/291-5480. **Contact:** Joe Shearman, Foreman. **World Wide Web address:** http://www.dennisuniform.com. **Description:** A manufacturer of school uniforms and accessories. Founded in 1920. **NOTE:** For office positions, contact Greg Donaca.

DEPARTMENT OF ENVIRONMENTAL QUALITY
811 SW Sixth Avenue, Portland OR 97204-1390. 503/229-5696. **Toll-free phone:** 800/452-4011. **Fax:** 503/229-6124. **Recorded jobline:** 503/229-5785. **Contact:** Human Resources. **E-mail address:** deq.info@deq.state.or.us. **World Wide Web address:** http://www.deq.state.or.us. **Description:** A governmental agency responsible for overseeing and enforcing environmental laws. Founded in 1969. **Positions advertised include:** Natural Resource Specialist; Principal Contributor; Vehicle Emissions Technician.

DESCHUTES NATIONAL FOREST
CRESCENT RANGER DISTRICT
P.O. Box 208, Crescent OR 97733. 541/433-3200. **Contact:** Human Resources. **World Wide Web address:** http://www.fs.fed.us/r6/deschutes. **Description:** Manages public forestlands. **NOTE:** Online application process preferred. **Special programs:** Summer Jobs.

DIAMOND FRUIT GROWERS INC.
P.O. Box 185, Odell OR 97044. 541/354-5300. **Fax:** 541/354-2123. **Contact:** Dave Simons, Human Resources. **World Wide Web address:** http://www.diamondfruit.com. **Description:** Processes fruits to be distributed both in the United States and internationally. **Corporate headquarters location:** This location. **Number of employees nationwide:** 1,000.

R.R. DONNELLEY NORWEST INC.
17401 NE Halsey Street, Portland OR 97230-6027. 503/255-2455. **Recorded jobline:** 503/251-3505. **Contact:** Janet Bryant, Human Resources Coordinator. **World Wide Web address:** http://www.rrdonnelley.com. **Description:** R.R. Donnelley Norwest is a worldwide telephone directory printer. **Positions advertised include:** Regional Sourcing Leader; Progress Manager. **Parent company:** R.R. Donnelley & Sons (Chicago IL) is a world leader in managing, reproducing, and distributing print and digital information for publishing, merchandising, and information technology customers. The company is one of the largest commercial printers in the world, producing catalogs, inserts, magazines, books, directories, computer documentation, and financial printing. R.R. Donnelley has more than 180 sales offices and production facilities worldwide. Principal services offered by the company are conventional and digital prepress operations; computerized printing, binding, and sophisticated pool shipping and distribution services for printed products; information repackaging into multiple formats (print, magnetic, and optical media); database management, list rental, list enhancement, and direct mail production services; turnkey computer documentation services (outsourcing, translation, printing, binding, diskette replication, kitting, licensing, republishing, and fulfillment); reprographics and facilities management; creative design and communication services; and digital and conventional map creation and related services.

DOUBLETREE HOTEL
310 SW Lincoln, Portland OR 97201. 503/221-0450. **Toll-free phone:** 800/541-1111. **Contact:** Personnel. **World Wide Web address:** http://www.doubletreehotels.com. **Description:** A full-service hotel that offers a restaurant, club, conference facilities, airport transportation, and exercise facilities. **Parent company:** Hilton Hotels.

DOUBLETREE HOTEL PORTLAND LLOYD CENTER
1000 NE Multnomah, Portland OR 97232. 503/281-6111. **Recorded jobline:** 503/296-3384. **Contact:** Personnel. **World Wide Web address:** http://www.doubletree.com. **Description:** A full-service 493-room hotel offering three restaurants, meeting facilities, exercise facilities, and business services. **Positions advertised include:** Assistant Restaurant Manager; Kitchen Supervisor. **Parent company:** Hilton Hotels Corporation is a hospitality, gaming, and lodging company. With its Hilton and Conrad brands, the company develops, owns, manages, and franchises hotel-casinos, resorts, vacation ownership, and hotel properties throughout the world. Other subsidiaries of Hilton Hotel Corporation include Conrad International, Hilton Equipment Corporation, Hilton Grand Vacation Company, and Hilton Inns, Inc.

EASTMORELAND HOSPITAL
2900 SE Steele Street, Portland OR 97202. 503/230-2508. **Contact:** Manager of Human Resources. **World Wide Web address:** http://www.eastmorelandhospital.com. **Description:** A for-profit, acute-care hospital with 100 beds. **Positions advertised include:** District Nurse; Registered Nurse; Certified Nurse Assistant; Nuclear Medical Technician; Case Manager; Respiratory Therapist. **Corporate headquarters location:** Nashville TN. **Parent company:** ORNDA Healthcorp.

ELECTRO SCIENTIFIC INDUSTRIES, INC. (ESI)
13900 NW Science Park Drive, Portland OR 97229. 503/641-4141. **Fax:** 503/671-5571. **Contact:** Human Resources. **World Wide Web address:** http://www.esi.com. **Description:** Electro Scientific Industries, Inc. designs and builds advanced production equipment used throughout the world in electronics manufacturing. The principal end markets for products made using ESI equipment include the computer, telecommunications, and automotive industries. ESI's principal product lines include precision, high-speed test equipment for ceramic capacitor manufacturing; laser manufacturing systems for semiconductor yield improvement; precision laser and mechanical drilling systems for electronic interconnection; machine vision systems; and advanced laser trimming systems for the precise tuning of electronic circuits. Founded in 1949. **Positions advertised include:** Electro Mechanical Integrator; Laser/Optics Manufacturing Supervisor; Operations Specialist; Checkout Technician. **Corporate headquarters location:** This location. **Operations at this facility include:** Administration; Manufacturing; Research and Development; Sales; Service.

ELMER'S RESTAURANTS, INC.
P.O. Box 16938, Portland OR 97292. 503/252-1485. **Fax:** 503/257-7448. **Contact:** President. **E-mail address:** employment@elmers-restaurants.com. **World Wide Web address:** http://www.elmers-restaurants.com. **Description:** Owns and operates 11 Elmer's Pancake & Steak House restaurants and sells franchises. Franchises and company-owned stores are located throughout the western United States. **Positions advertised include:** General Manager; Kitchen Manager; Assistant Manager; Supervisor; Server; Cashier; Host; Dishwasher; Cook. **Corporate headquarters location:** This location. **Listed on:** NASDAQ. **Stock exchange symbol:** ELMS.

EPSON PORTLAND INC.
3950 NW Aloclek Place, Hillsboro OR 97124-7199. 503/645-1118. **Contact:** Human Resources. **World Wide Web address:** http://www.epson.com. **Description:** Epson develops and manufactures computers, electronic and crystal devices, factory automation systems, liquid crystal displays (LCDs), printers, and watches. **Corporate headquarters location:** Torrance CA. **Parent company:** Seiko Epson Corporation. **Operations at this facility include:** This location is a manufacturing facility.

ESCO CORPORATION
2141 NW 25th Avenue, Portland OR 97210-2578. 503/228-2141. **Fax:** 503/242-9037. **Contact:** Human Resources. **E-mail address:** epinfo@esco.com. **World Wide Web address:** http://www.escocorp.com. **Description:** Manufactures steel products including brackets, dredge cutters, tractor and dozer equipment, chain conveying systems, and custom castings for the mining, food processing, construction, and logging industries. Founded in 1913. **Positions advertised include:** Senior Tax Accountant. **Corporate headquarters location:** This location. **Operations at this facility include:** Manufacturing; Sales; Service.

EUGENE SCHOOL DISTRICT 4J
200 North Monroe Street, Eugene OR 97402. 541/687-3123. **Recorded jobline:** 541/687-3344. **Contact:** Human Resources Department. **World Wide Web address:** http://www.4j.lane.edu. **Description:** A state school district comprised of 23 elementary schools, 11 middle schools, and 4 high schools. **Positions advertised include:** Teacher; School Nurse; Occupational/Physical Therapist; Driver.

EUGENE WATER AND ELECTRIC BOARD
P.O. Box 10148, Eugene OR 97440. 541/484-2411. **Fax:** 541/334-4608. **Physical address:** 500 East Fourth Avenue, Eugene OR 97401. **Recorded jobline:** 541/484-3769. **Contact:** Human Resources. **World Wide Web address:** http://www.eweb.org./jobs. **Description:** A local government department responsible for water and electric utilities. **NOTE:** Applicants must use the required job application form and can return it by mail or fax. **Positions advertised include:** Utility Arborist; CAD/GIS Technician; Energy Management Program Services.

EVANITE FIBER CORPORATION
1115 SE Crystal Lake Drive, P.O. Box E, Corvallis OR 97339-0598. 541/753-1211. **Fax:** 541/753-0388. **Contact:** Human Resources. **World Wide Web address:** http://www.evanite.com. **Description:** Manufactures and markets hardwood products for cabinets, furniture, and shelves.

EVERGREEN INTERNATIONAL AVIATION, INC.
3850 Three Mile Lane, McMinnville OR 97128. 503/472-9361. **Fax:** 503/434-4225. **Contact:** Steve Cilenti, Recruiting Manager. **E-mail address:** recruit@evergreenaviation.com. **World Wide Web address:** http://www.evergreenaviation.com. **Description:** A global aviation services company that leases, sells, and repairs aircraft; transports cargo; supplies aircraft parts; and provides ground handling and logistics for other carriers. Founded in 1960. **Positions advertised include:** Air Cargo Sales Representative; Airline Sales and Marketing Administrator; Maintenance Trainer. **Corporate headquarters location:** This location. **Other U.S. locations:** Marana AZ; Los Angeles CA; New York NY.

EVERGREEN TECHNOLOGIES, INC.
808 NW Buchanan Avenue, P.O. Box 1930 Corvallis OR 97339-1930. 541/745-5562. **Fax:** 541/757-7350. **Contact:** Human Resources Manager. **E-mail address:** employ@evertech.com. **World Wide Web address:** http://www.evertech.com. **Description:** Designs, develops, manufactures, and markets upgrades for computer processors.

FEI COMPANY
7451 NW Evergreen Parkway, Hillsboro OR 97124-5830. 503/640-7500. **Contact:** Human Resources. **World Wide Web address:** http://www.feic.com. **Description:** FEI Company is a leader in the design, manufacture, and sale of focused ion beam workstations and components based on field emission technology. Founded in 1971. **Listed on:** NASDAQ. **Stock exchange symbol:** FEIC.

FASTENAL COMPANY
4882 Industry Drive, Central Point OR 97502. 541/770-5411. **Contact:** Human Resources. **World Wide Web address:** http://www.fastenal.com. **Description:** A wholesaler and distributor of industrial fasteners. Founded in 1967. **Corporate headquarters location:** Winona MN. **Listed on:** NASDAQ. **Stock exchange symbol:** FAST.

FEDEX FREIGHT INC.
9010 NE 13th Avenue, Portland OR 97220. 503/285-5810. **Fax:** 503/285-9106. **Contact:** George Childs, Manager. **World Wide Web address:** http://www.fedexfreight.fedex.com. **Description:** A worldwide freight company. **Operations at this facility:** This is a northwest distribution center.

FLEETWOOD HOMES OF OREGON
P.O. Box 628, Woodburn OR 97071-0628. 503/981-3136. **Contact:** Personnel. **World Wide Web address:** http://www.fleetwoodhomes.com. **Description:** Manufactures factory-crafted residential homes.

FLIGHTCRAFT, INC.
P.O. Box 547, Eugene OR 97440. **Physical Address:** 90454 Boeing Drive, Eugene OR 97402. 541/683-5073. **Contact:** Human Resources. **E-mail address:** jobs@pape.com. **World Wide Web address:** http://www.flightcraft.com. **Description:** Provides aircraft maintenance services, charter services, and fulfills fuel orders. **NOTE:** Address applications to the parent company at P.O. Box 407, Portland OR 97440. **Parent company:** The Pape Group.

FLIR SYSTEMS, INC.
16505 SW 72nd Avenue, Portland OR 97224. 503/684-3731. **Fax:** 503/372-6199. **Contact:** Human Resources. **World Wide Web address:** http://www.flir.com. **Description:** Designs, manufactures, and markets thermal imaging systems for law enforcement and drug interdiction agencies, search and rescue units, border and maritime patrols, and environmental protection. **Positions advertised include:** Engineer; Controller. **Corporate headquarters location:** This location.

FOSTER FARMS
33464 West Lane, P.O. Box 8, Creswell OR 97426-0008. 541/895-2161. **Contact:** Human Resources. **World Wide Web address:** http://www.fosterfarms.com. **Description:** Operates feed mills, hatcheries, ranches, processing plants, and delivery systems. Founded in 1939. **Positions advertised include:** Delivery Driver; Marketing Information Systems Analyst; Senior Microbiologist; Workers Compensation Manager.

FRED MEYER, INC.
GO West 1/Cus, Portland OR 97242. 503/232-8844. **Contact:** Human Resources. **E-mail address:** fredmeyer@webhire.com. **World Wide Web address:** http://www.fredmeyer.com. **Description:** Operates a chain of approximately 400 retail stores offering a wide range of food, products for the home, apparel, fine jewelry, and home improvement items. **Corporate headquarters location:** This location. **Other U.S. locations:** AK; CA; ID; MT; UT; WA. **Parent company:** The Kroger Company.

FREIGHTLINER, LLC
4747 North Channel Avenue, Portland OR 97217-7699. 503/745-8000. **Toll-free phone:** 800/385-4357. **Fax:** 503/745-8921. **Contact:** Human Resources Department. **World Wide Web address:** http://www.freightliner.com. **Description:** Manufactures and markets heavy-duty trucks and chassis. **Positions advertised include:** Customs Manager; Project Planning Engineer; Senior Design Engineer; Senior Manufacturing Release Analyst. **Corporate headquarters location:** This location.

FRITO-LAY, INC./WESTERN DIVISION
6220 SW 112th Avenue, Beaverton OR 97008. 503/643-4711. **Contact:** Human Resources. **World Wide Web address:** http://www.fritolay.com. **Description:** Frito-Lay is a worldwide manufacturer and wholesaler of snack products including the brand names Fritos Corn Chips, Doritos Tortilla Chips, Lays Potato Chips, and Smartfood Popcorn. **Parent company:** PepsiCo, Inc. (Purchase NY) consists of Frito-Lay Company, Pepsi-Cola Company, Quaker Oats Company, and Tropicana Products, Inc. **Operations at this facility include:** This location produces pretzels and cookies.

FUJIMI CORPORATION
11200 SW Leveton Drive, Tualatin OR 97062. 503/682-7822. **Fax:** 503/612-9721. **Contact:** Human Resources. **E-mail address:** info@fujimico.com. **World Wide Web address:** http://www.fujimico.com. **Description:** Manufactures polishing products.

FUJITSU COMPUTER PRODUCTS OF AMERICA INC.
7245 NW Evergreen Parkway, Suite 150, Hillsboro OR 97124-5827. 503/681-7300. **Fax:** 503/693-2020. **Contact:** Human Resources. **World Wide Web address:** http://www.fcpa.com. **Description:** Manufactures computer components including hard drives, laptop computers, and notebook computers. **Corporate headquarters location:** San Jose CA. **Parent company:** Fujitsu Corporation.

GEFFEN MESHER & COMPANY
888 SW Fifth Avenue, Suite 800, Portland OR 97204. 503/221-0141. **Contact:** Human Resources Department. **E-mail address:** hr@gmco.com. **World Wide Web address:** http://www.gmco.com. **Description:** A diversified accounting and business consulting firm. **Positions advertised include:** Audit Manager.

GEORGIA-PACIFIC CORPORATION
505 NE Third Street, Canby OR 97013. 503/266-1933. **Contact:** Human Resources. **World Wide Web address:** http://www.gp.com. **Description:** Georgia-Pacific Corporation is a manufacturer, wholesaler, and distributor of building products, industrial wood products, pulp, paper, packaging, and related chemicals. The company is one of the world's largest manufacturers of forest products, with facilities in 48 states and overseas. **NOTE:** Jobseekers are encouraged to submit their resume via the Website: http://gp.equest.com. **Corporate headquarters location:** Atlanta GA. **Operations at this facility include:** This location is a paper and wood manufacturing plant. **Listed on:** New York Stock Exchange. **Stock exchange symbol:** GPW.

GEORGIA-PACIFIC CORPORATION
93783 Newport Lane, P.O. Box 1268, Coos Bay OR 97420. 541/269-1171. **Contact:** Human Resources. **World Wide Web address:** http://www.gp.com. **Description:** Georgia-Pacific Corporation is a manufacturer, wholesaler, and distributor of building products, industrial wood products, pulp, paper, packaging, and related chemicals. The company is one of the world's largest manufacturers of forest products, with facilities in 48 states and overseas. **NOTE:** Jobseekers are encouraged to submit their resume via the Website: http://gp.equest.com. **Corporate headquarters location:** Atlanta GA.

Operations at this facility include: This location is a sawmill. **Listed on:** New York Stock Exchange. **Stock exchange symbol:** GPW.

GEORGIA-PACIFIC CORPORATION
92326 Taylorville Road, Clatskanie OR 97016. 503/455-2221. **Contact:** Human Resources. **World Wide Web address:** http://www.gp.com. **Description:** Georgia-Pacific Corporation is a manufacturer, wholesaler, and distributor of building products, industrial wood products, pulp, paper, packaging, and related chemicals. The company is one of the world's largest manufacturers of forest products, with facilities in 48 states and overseas. **NOTE:** Jobseekers are encouraged to submit their resume via the Website: http://gp.equest.com. **Positions advertised include:** Manager-Analysis. **Corporate headquarters location:** Atlanta GA. **Operations at this facility include:** This location is a manufacturer of paper products, plastic tableware, and retail packaging products such as cartons, bags, and wraps. **Listed on:** New York Stock Exchange. **Stock exchange symbol:** GPW.

GEORGIA-PACIFIC CORPORATION
P.O. Box 1618, Eugene OR 97440. 541/689-1221. **Physical address:** 2350 Prairie Road, Eugene OR 97402. **Contact:** Human Resources. **World Wide Web address:** http://www.gp.com. **Description:** Georgia-Pacific Corporation is a manufacturer, wholesaler, and distributor of building products, industrial wood products, pulp, paper, packaging, and related chemicals. The company is one of the world's largest manufacturers of forest products, with facilities in 48 states and overseas. **NOTE:** Jobseekers are encouraged to submit their resume via the Website: http://gp.equest.com. **Corporate headquarters location:** Atlanta GA. **Operations at this facility include:** This location manufactures specialty hardwood plywood. **Listed on:** New York Stock Exchange. **Stock exchange symbol:** GPW.

GEORGIA-PACIFIC CORPORATION
P.O. Box 215, Halsey OR 97348. 541/369-2293. **Contact:** Human Resources. **World Wide Web address:** http://www.gp.com. **Description:** Georgia-Pacific Corporation is a manufacturer, wholesaler, and distributor of building products, industrial wood products, pulp, paper, packaging, and related chemicals. The company is one of the world's largest manufacturers of forest products, with facilities in 48 states and overseas. **NOTE:** Jobseekers are encouraged to submit their resume via the Website: http://gp.equest.com. **Corporate headquarters location:** Atlanta GA. **Operations at this facility include:** This location is a manufacturer of paper products, plastic tableware, and retail packaging products such as cartons, bags, and wraps. **Listed on:** New York Stock Exchange. **Stock exchange symbol:** GPW.

GEORGIA-PACIFIC CORPORATION
199 Foothills Road, Lake Oswego OR 97034. 503/636-3910. **Contact:** Human Resources. **World Wide Web address:** http://www.gp.com. **Description:** Georgia-Pacific Corporation is a manufacturer, wholesaler, and distributor of building products, industrial wood products, pulp, paper, packaging, and related chemicals. The company is one of the world's largest manufacturers of forest products, with facilities in 48 states and overseas. **NOTE:** Jobseekers are encouraged to submit their resume via the Website: http://gp.equest.com. **Corporate headquarters location:** Atlanta GA. **Operations at this facility include:** This location is a manufacturer of paper products, plastic tableware, and retail packaging products such as cartons, bags, and wraps. **Listed on:** New York Stock Exchange. **Stock exchange symbol:** GPW.

GEORGIA-PACIFIC CORPORATION
900 SW Fifth Avenue, Portland OR 97204-1255. 503/294-8510. **Contact:** Human Resources. **World Wide Web address:** http://www.gp.com. **Description:** Georgia-Pacific Corporation is a manufacturer, wholesaler, and distributor of building products, industrial wood products, pulp, paper, packaging, and related chemicals. The company is one of the world's largest manufacturers of forest products, with facilities in 48 states and overseas. **NOTE:** Jobseekers are encouraged to submit their resume via the Website: http://gp.equest.com. **Corporate headquarters location:** Atlanta GA. **Operations at this facility include:** This location houses regional administrative offices. **Listed on:** New York Stock Exchange. **Stock exchange symbol:** GPW.

GEORGIA-PACIFIC CORPORATION
3838 NW Front Avenue, Portland OR 97210. 503/226-6901. **Contact:** Human Resources. **World Wide Web address:** http://www.gp.com. **Description:** the company manufactures paper products, plastic tableware, and retail packaging products such as cartons, bags, and wraps. Paper products include tissues, towels, business and correspondence paper, coated papers for catalogs, and premium printing papers. Brand names include Brawny, Quilted Northern, Vanity Fair, Nice 'n Soft, and Dixie. **NOTE:** Jobseekers are encouraged to submit their resume via the Website: http://gp.equest.com. **Office hours:** Monday - Friday, 8:00 a.m. - 4:30 p.m. **Corporate headquarters location:** Atlanta GA. **Operations at this facility include:** This location is a distribution center for Georgia-Pacific paper products. **Listed on:** New York Stock Exchange. **Stock exchange symbol:** GPW.

GEORGIA-PACIFIC CORPORATION
P.O. Box 580, Toledo OR 97391. 541/336-2211. **Contact:** Human Resources. **World Wide Web address:** http://www.gp.com. **Description:** Georgia-Pacific Corporation is a manufacturer, wholesaler, and distributor of building products, industrial wood products, pulp, paper, packaging, and related chemicals. The company is one of the world's largest manufacturers of forest products, with facilities in 48 states and overseas. **NOTE:** Jobseekers are encouraged to submit their resume via the Website: http://gp.equest.com. **Corporate headquarters location:** Atlanta GA. **Operations at this facility include:** This location is a pulpmill. **Listed on:** New York Stock Exchange. **Stock exchange symbol:** GPW.

GLACIER NORTHWEST
1050 North River Street, Portland OR 97227. 503/335-2600. **Contact:** Human Resources. **E-mail address:** humanresources@glacierw.com. **World Wide Web address:** http://www.glaciernw.com. **Description:** A supplier of ready mixed concrete, sand, rock, gravel, rock, and building materials.

GLADSTONE SCHOOL DISTRICT
17789 Webster Road, Gladstone OR 97027. 503/655-2777. **Recorded jobline:** 503/650-2573. **Contact:** Human Resources Department. **World Wide Web address:** http://www.gladstone.k12.or.us. **Description:** A state school district comprised of one elementary school, one middle school, and one high school. **Positions advertised include:** Part-Time Cook; ESL Assistant Teacher; Teacher.

GOLD'S GYM
3589 Fairview Industrial Drive SE, Salem OR 97302. 503/581-4766. **Fax:** 503/391-1267. **Contact:** Hiring Manager. **World Wide Web address:** http://www.goldsgym.com. **Description:** A full-service health and fitness club. Each club is complete with weights and cardiovascular equipment, fitness and aerobic classes, tanning, personal training, and childcare facilities. **NOTE:** Part-time jobs and entry-level positions are offered. **Corporate headquarters location:** Palm Springs CA.

GOOD SAMARITAN HOSPITAL CORVALLIS
3600 NW Samaritan Drive, Corvallis OR 97330. 541/757-5072. **Fax:** 541/768-6400. **Contact:** Human Resources Recruiter. **E-mail address:** hrgsrm@goodsam.org. **World Wide Web address:** http://www.samhealth.org. **Description:** A for-profit hospital offering general medical care and 180 beds. **Positions advertised include:** Account Analyst; Cash Specialist; Assistant Department Manager; Engineer; Supervisor; Housekeeper; Blood Bank Assistant; Laboratory Assistant Manager; Certified Nurses Assistant. **Parent company:** Legacy Health System also operates area hospitals Emanuel, Mount Hood, and Meridian Park Medical Center.

GOODWILL INDUSTRIES
1943 SE Sixth Avenue, Portland OR 97214-3579. 503/238-6100. **Contact:** Human Resources. **E-mail address:** hr@goodwill.org. **World Wide Web address:** http://www.goodwill.org. **Description:** A nonprofit provider of employment training for the disabled and the poor. Goodwill Industries also operates approximately 1,400 thrift stores nationwide. **Positions advertised include:** Business Partnerships Manager; Government Relations Manager; Technical Trainer; Resource Development Director; Communications Specialist; User Support Specialist.

GOODYEAR TIRE & RUBBER COMPANY
1825 NE Argyle Street, Portland OR 97211. 503/285-5211. **Contact:** Human Resources. **World Wide Web address:** http://www.goodyear.com. **Description:** Goodyear Tire & Rubber Company's principal business is the development, manufacture, distribution, and sale of tires for most applications worldwide. Goodyear also manufactures and sells a broad spectrum of rubber products and rubber-related chemicals for various industrial and consumer markets and provides auto repair services. The company operates 32 plants in the United States, 42 plants in 29 other countries, and more than 1,800 retail tire and service centers and other distribution facilities around the globe. Strategic business units of Goodyear Tire & Rubber include North American Tire; Kelly-Springfield; Goodyear Europe; Goodyear Latin America; Goodyear Asia; Engineered Products; Chemicals; Celeron; and Goodyear Racing. **Operations at this facility include:** This location remanufactures retreads.

W.W. GRAINGER
6335 North Basin Avenue, Portland OR 97217. 503/283-0366. **Fax:** 503/285-8624. **Contact:** Human Resources. **World Wide Web address:** http://www.grainger.com. **Description:** Distributes a variety of equipment and components to the industrial, commercial, contracting, and institutional markets nationwide. Products include equipment and components for motors, air tools, hydraulic products, refrigeration items, power and hand tools, office equipment, computer supplies, replacement parts, industrial products, safety items, cold weather clothing, and storage equipment. Founded in 1927. **Corporate headquarters location:** Lake Forest IL. **Other U.S. locations:** Nationwide. **Listed on:** New York Stock Exchange. **Stock exchange symbol:** GWW.

GRANDE RONDE HOSPITAL
900 Sunset Drive, La Grande OR 97850-1396. 541/963-8421. **Contact:** Personnel. **World Wide Web address:** http://www.grh.org. **Description:** A hospital with 49 acute care beds, a 14-bed transitional care unit, and a family birthing center. Grande Ronde Hospital also offers home health, hospice, and outpatient services. **Positions advertised include:** Registered Nurse; Respiratory Therapist.

GRAPHIC ARTS CENTER INC.
2000 NW Wilson Street, Portland OR 97209-1817. 503/224-7777. **Fax:** 503/248-7206. **Contact:** Director of Human Resources. **World Wide Web address:** http://www.gacnw.com. **Description:** A printing company that produces annual reports and catalogs.

THE GREENBRIER COMPANIES, INC.
One Centerpointe Drive, Suite 200, Lake Oswego OR 97035. 503/684-7000. **Fax:** 503/684-7553. **Contact:** Jeanne Onchi, Human Resources. **World Wide Web address:** http://www.gbrx.com. **Description:** Operates in two primary business segments: manufacturing and refurbishing railcars and marine vessels; and leasing and managing surface transportation equipment and providing related services. **Corporate headquarters location:** This location. **International locations:** Canada; Germany; Mexico; Poland. **Subsidiaries include:** Gunderson Inc. manufactures and refurbishes railroad freight cars and marine barges.

GREEN MOUNTAIN ENERGY
550 Capitol Street NE #215, P.O. Box 2148, Salem OR 97308-2404. **Toll-free phone:** 866/468-6633. **Contact:** Human Resources. **World Wide Web address:** http://www.greenmountain.com. **Description:** The largest retailer of less-polluting electricity in the U.S. All of the electricity comes from sources like wind, water, solar, biomass, geothermal, and natural gas. **Positions advertised include:** Energy Sales Associate; Direct Sales Representative; Help Center Technician. **Corporate headquarters location:** Austin TX.

GRIFFITH RUBBER MILLS
2631 West Fifth Avenue, Eugene OR 97402. 541/344-6227. **Contact:** Human Resources. **Description:** Manufactures molded rubber truck parts for the automotive industry.

GUARD PUBLISHING COMPANY
P.O. Box 10188, Eugene OR 97440-2188. 541/485-1234. **Contact:** Human Resources. **World Wide Web address:** http://www.registerguard.com. **Description:** Publishes the daily newspaper *Register Guard*. Weekly circulation averages 75,400 and weekend circulation is approximately 163,000.

GUNDERSON INC.
4350 NW Front Avenue, Portland OR 97210. 503/972-5700. **Toll-free phone:** 800/253-4350. **Fax:** 972/598-7503. **Recorded jobline:** 503/972-5901. **Contact:** Recruiting Coordinator. **E-mail address:** hr@gundersoninc.com. **World Wide Web address:** http://www.gundersoninc.com. **Description:** Manufactures and refurbishes railroad freight cars and marine barges. **NOTE:** Entry-level positions and second and third shifts are offered. **Positions advertised include:** Fitter/Welder; Plate Shop Helper; Maintenance Dispatcher; Marine Planner/Estimator; Maintenance Helper; Rolling Stock Mechanic. **Special programs:** Training. **Corporate headquarters location:** Lake Oswego OR. **Other area locations:** Springfield OR. **Other U.S. locations:** Pine Bluff AR; Cleburne TX. **International locations:** Poland. **Parent company:** The Greenbrier Companies, Inc. **Operations at this facility include:** Administration; Manufacturing.

HACH ULTRA ANALYTICS
481 California Avenue, Grants Pass OR 97526. **Toll-free phone:** 800/866-7889. **Fax:** 541/472-6566. **Contact:** Roxanne McClure, Human Resources Department. **World Wide Web address:** http://www.hachultra.com. **Description:** Manufactures particle-monitoring instruments used to size and count particles in air, liquids, and gases.

Primary markets (both domestic and international) are the pharmaceutical, semiconductor, fluid power, and aerospace industries. **Positions advertised include:** Support Engineer. **Corporate headquarters location:** Newport CA.

HAMPTON LUMBER SALES COMPANY
9600 SW Barnes Road, Suite 200, Portland OR 97225-6660. 503/297-7691. **Toll-free phone:** 888/310-1464. **Contact:** Harriet Curtis, Office Administration Manager. **World Wide Web address:** http://www.hamptonlumber.com. **Description:** Manufactures and sells lumber. The company owns and operates timberlands, mills, and distribution facilities.

HANSON PIPE & PRODUCTS INC.
755 NE Columbia Boulevard, P.O. Box 11305, Portland OR 97211-0305. 503/285-8391. **Toll-free phone:** 800/509-7473. **Fax:** 503/286-0603. **Contact:** Human Resources. **Description:** A manufacturer of precast concrete products such as pipe, manholes, and utility vaults. **Corporate headquarters location:** Ontario, Canada. **Other U.S. locations:** Bend OR; Salem OR; Tacoma WA.

HARLAND FINANCIAL SOLUTIONS
400 SW Sixth Avenue, Suite 200, Portland OR 97204. 503/274-7280. **Toll-free phone:** 800/274-7280. **Fax:** 503/274-7284. **Contact:** Anne Centis, Employment Manager. **World Wide Web address:** http://www.harlandfinancialsolutions.com. **Description:** A leading provider of integrated, financial software. Founded in 1978. **NOTE:** Unsolicited resumes are not accepted. **Positions advertised include:** Database Administrator; G/L Accountant; Senior Programmer; Network Administrator. **Special programs:** Internships. **Corporate headquarters location:** This location. **Other U.S. locations:** Nationwide. **Parent company:** John H. Harland Company. **Listed on:** New York Stock Exchange. **Stock exchange symbol:** JH.

HARRANG LONG GARY RUDNICK P.C.
360 E 10th Avenue, Suite 300, Eugene OR 97401-3248. 541/485-0220. **Toll-free phone:** 800/315-4172. **Fax:** 541/686-6564. **Contact:** Joanne Austin. **World Wide Web address:** http://www.harrang.com. **Description:** A regional law firm that offers experience in a variety of practice areas. **Other area locations:** Portland OR, Salem OR.

THE HASSON COMPANY REALTORS
15400 SW Boones Ferry Road, Lake Oswego OR 97035. 503/635-9801. **Contact:** Human Resources. **World Wide Web address:** http://www.hasson.com. **Description:** Specializes in the buying and selling of residential property. **NOTE:** Human Resources mailing address is 4500 Cruz Way, Suite 170, Lake Oswego OR 97035. **Corporate headquarters location:** This location. **Other U.S. locations:** Portland OR.

THE HASSON COMPANY REALTORS
12809 93rd Avenue, Clackamus OR 97015. 503/652-9801. **Contact:** Office Manager. **World Wide Web address:** http://www.hasson.com. **Description:** A realty company specializing in residential properties. **Corporate headquarters location:** Lake Oswego OR.

THE HASSON COMPANY REALTORS
25 NW 23rd Place, Portland OR 97210. 503/228-9801. **Contact:** Human Resources. **World Wide Web address:** http://www.hasson.com. **Description:** A realty company specializing in residential properties. **Corporate headquarters location:** Lake Oswego OR.

HATFIELD MARINE SCIENCE CENTER
2030 SE Marine Science Drive, Newport OR 97365. 541/867-0100. **Fax:** 541/867-0138. **Contact:** Human Resources. **E-mail address:** hmsc@oregonstate.edu. **World Wide Web address:** http://www.hmsc.orst.edu. **Description:** A research and teaching facility operated by Oregon State University. The Hatfield Marine Science center offers estuarine and marine education and research, a base for oceanographic studies, and a variety of laboratory capabilities.

HEALTH NET OREGON
13221 SW 68th Parkway, Suite 200, Tigard OR 97223. **Toll-free phone:** 888/802-7001. **Contact:** Human Resources. **E-mail address:** service@health.net. **World Wide Web address:** http://www.healthnetoregon.com. **Description:** A health maintenance organization serving Oregon and Southwest Washington. **NOTE:** Online applications preferred.

HEALTHSOUTH
2330 Flanders Street, Portland OR 97258. 503/228-8575. **Contact:** Human Resources. **World Wide Web address:** http://www.healthsouth.com. **Description:** Provides comprehensive outpatient rehabilitation services to patients suffering from work-, sports-, and accident-related injuries. **Corporate headquarters location:** Birmingham AL.

HEINZ FROZEN FOODS
175 NE 6th Avenue, P.O. Box 10, Ontario OR 97914. 541/889-8611. **Contact:** Human Resources. **World Wide Web address:** http://www.heinz.com. **Description:** One of the nation's largest diversified frozen food companies. **Listed on:** New York Stock Exchange. **Stock exchange symbol:** HNZ.

HERALD AND NEWS
1301 Esplanade Avenue, P.O. Box 788, Klamath Falls OR 97601. 541/885-4410. **Contact:** Human Resources. **World Wide Web address:** http://www.heraldandnews.com. **Description:** Publishes a daily newspaper with a circulation of over 19,000. **NOTE:** Herald and News only accepts resumes for positions that are currently being advertised. Before submitting a resume, check for open positions on its parent company's Website. **Parent company:** Pioneer Newspapers, Inc. (Seattle WA).

HERTZ EQUIPMENT RENTAL CORPORATION
4939 NE Columbia Boulevard, Portland OR 97218. 503/287-4326. **Fax:** 503/287-4326. **Contact:** Human Resources. **E-mail address:** jgodaert@hertz.com. **World Wide Web address:** http://www.hertzequip.com. **Description:** A construction equipment rental company. **Positions advertised include:** Mechanic; Driver; Sales Coordinator.

HEWLETT-PACKARD COMPANY
15115 SW Sequoia Parkway, Suite 100, Portland OR 97224. 503/598-8000. **Contact:** Human Resources. **World Wide Web address:** http://www.hp.com. **Description:** Hewlett-Packard is engaged in the design and manufacturing of measurement and computation products and systems used in business, industry, engineering, science, health care, and education. Principal products are integrated instrument and computer systems (including hardware and software), peripheral products, and medical electronic equipment and systems. **NOTE:** Jobseekers are encouraged to apply via the Website: http://www.jobs.hp.com. **Special programs:** Internships. **Corporate headquarters location:** Palo Alto CA. **Other U.S. locations:** Nationwide. **Operations at this facility include:** This location is a sales office. **Listed on:** New York Stock Exchange. **Stock exchange symbol:** HPQ.

HICKORY SPRINGS MANUFACTURING COMPANY
3900 NE 158th Avenue, Portland OR 97230-5002. 503/255-4650. **Fax:** 503/253-9216. **Contact:** Human Resources. **World Wide Web address:** http://www.hickorysprings.com. **Description:** Manufactures carpet padding, polyurethane foams, carbon steel wire, and polyester fibers for the furniture and bedding industries. Founded in 1944. **Corporate headquarters location:** Hickory NC.

HILTON EUGENE & CONFERENCE CENTER
66 East Sixth Avenue, Eugene OR 97401. 541/342-2000. **Fax:** 541/349-8610. **Contact:** Human Resources Manager. **World Wide Web address:** http://www.hilton.com. **Description:** A 270-room hotel that offers extensive conference, convention and banquet facilities, two restaurants, exercise facilities, and business services. **Corporate headquarters location:** Beverly Hills CA. **Parent company:** Hilton Hotels Corporation is a hospitality, gaming, and lodging company. With its Hilton and Conrad brands, the company develops, owns, manages, and franchises hotel-casinos, resorts, vacation ownership, and hotel properties throughout the world. Other subsidiaries of Hilton Hotel Corporation include Conrad International, Hilton Equipment Corporation, Hilton Grand Vacation Company, and Hilton Inns, Inc.

HILTON PORTLAND HOTEL
921 SW Sixth Avenue, Portland OR 97204. 503/226-1611. **Recorded jobline:** 503/220-2560. **Contact:** Human Resources. **World Wide Web address:** http://www.hilton.com. **Description:** A 455-room hotel. **Positions advertised include:** Assistant Financial Director; Room Service Server; Valet; Cafeteria Cook; Host. **Corporate headquarters location:** Beverly Hills CA. **Parent company:** Hilton Hotels Corporation is a hospitality, gaming, and lodging company. With its Hilton and Conrad brands, the company develops, owns, manages, and franchises hotel-casinos, resorts, vacation ownership, and hotel properties throughout the world. Other subsidiaries of Hilton Hotel Corporation include Conrad International, Hilton Equipment Corporation, Hilton Grand Vacation Company, and Hilton Inns, Inc.

HOFFMAN CORPORATION
805 SW Broadway, Suite 2100, Portland OR 97205. 503/221-8811. **Contact:** Sheri Sundstrom, Personnel. **E-mail address:** sheri-sundstrom@hoffmancorp.com. **World Wide Web address:** http://www.hoffmancorp.com. **Description:** A full-service commercial and industrial construction company. Founded in 1922. **Positions advertised include:** Electrical Cost Engineer/Estimator, Mechanical Cost Control/Estimator, Project Accountant, Project Scheduler. **Corporate headquarters location:** This location.

HOLLYWOOD ENTERTAINMENT CORPORATION
9275 SW Peyton Lane, Wilsonville OR 97070. 503/570-1600. **Contact:** Human Resources. **World Wide Web address:** http://www.hollywoodvideo.com. **Description:** Owns and operates more than 1,600 video retail superstores. Each of the company's stores rents videocassettes, DVDs, video games, and video game systems and sells videocassettes, accessories, and confectionery items. **Positions advertised include:** Materials Specialist; Category Manager; Allocation Manager; Lease Compliance Specialist; Security Specialist; Payroll Manager; Operations Supervisor. **Office hours:** Monday - Friday, 8:00 a.m. - 5:00 p.m. **Corporate headquarters location:** This location. **Other U.S. locations:** Nationwide.

HOLY ROSARY MEDICAL CENTER
351 SW Ninth Street, Ontario OR 97914. 541/889-5331. **Toll-free phone:** 877/225-4762. **Contact:** Karen Kosowan, Human Resources Director. **E-mail address:** info@holyrosary-ontario.org. **World Wide Web address:** http://www.holyrosary-ontario.org. **Description:** An 80-bed hospital providing general medical services. **Positions advertised include:** Registered Nurse; Radiology Technician; Registrar; Physical Therapist; Certified Occupational Therapist; Respiratory Care Sleep Technician.

HOUSING AUTHORITY OF PORTLAND
135 SW Ash Street, Portland OR 97204. 503/802-8300. **Fax:** 503/802-8573. **Contact:** Personnel. **World Wide Web address:** http://www.hapdx.org. **Description:** The Portland governmental agency for housing. Provides lodging solutions to individuals and families with financial or special needs. **Positions advertised include:** Assistant Site Manager; Desk Clerk. **Number of employees at this location:** 200.

IKON OFFICE SOLUTIONS
12100 SW Garden Place, Portland OR 97223. 503/620-2800. **Fax:** 503/620-3500. **Contact:** Human Resources. **World Wide Web address:** http://www.ikon.com. **Description:** A wholesaler and distributor of copy machines, fax machines, and related office supplies. **Positions advertised include:** Document Specialist; Account Executive; Associate Sales Representative; Major Account Executive; Account Manager; Customer Service Representative; Copy/Mail Operator. **Corporate headquarters location:** Malvern PA. **International locations:** Worldwide. **Listed on:** New York Stock Exchange. **Stock exchange symbol:** IKN.

INFINITY INTERNET
511 SW 10th Avenue, Suite 300, Portland OR 97205. 503/223-4277. **Toll-free phone:** 800/469-1424. **Contact:** Human Resources. **World Wide Web address:** http://www.iinet.com. **Description:** An Internet service provider for residential and commercial applications. **NOTE:** Hiring is done through the headquarters location in 1101 SE Tech Center Drive, Suite 150, Vancouver WA 98683. 360/735-3700. 800/469-1424. **Operations at this facility include:** Server co-location,

INFOCUS SYSTEMS, INC.
27700B SW Parkway Avenue, Wilsonville OR 97070-9215. 503/685-8888. **Toll-free phone:** 800/294-6400. **Fax:** 503/685-8887. **Contact:** Human Resources Department. **World Wide Web address:** http://www.infocus.com. **Description:** A leader in developing, manufacturing, and marketing projection products and services to present video, audio, and data from personal computers and other electronic devices. The company's products include projection panels and portable projection systems with integrated full-motion video, data, and audio. Panels are used with overhead projectors to display data and video from personal computers, or from LiteShow presentation software onto a screen for meetings and presentations. **Corporate headquarters location:** This location.

INITIAL SECURITY
3720 SW 141st Avenue, Suite 100, Beaverton OR 97005. 503/626-6444. **Fax:** 503/626-4044. **Contact:** Human Resources Department. **E-mail address:** initial@initialsecurity.com. **World Wide Web address:** http://www.initialsecurity.com. **Description:** Provides a variety of security services

including consulting, guards, investigations, patrols, strike coverage, and special events. Founded in 1928.

INSPIRATION SOFTWARE, INC.
7412 SW Beaverton Hillsdale Highway, Suite 102, Portland OR 97225-2167. 503/297-3004. **Toll-free phone:** 800/877-4292. **Fax:** 503/297-4676. **Contact:** Personnel. **E-mail address:** jobs@inspiration.com. **World Wide Web address:** http://www.inspiration.com. **Description:** Develops visual creative learning tools for the education market. **Positions advertised include:** Palm OS Programmer. **Corporate headquarters location:** This location.

INTEGRA TELECOM
1201 NE Lloyd Blvd., Suite 500, Portland OR 97232. 503/453-8000. **Fax:** 503/453-8221. **Recorded jobline:** 866/223-1230. **Contact:** Human Resources. **World Wide Web address:** http://www.integratelecom.com. **Description:** Integra Telecom is a facilities-based, integrated communications provider (ICP), primarily focused on serving small and midsize companies located in the business centers of Minnesota, North Dakota, Oregon, Utah, and Washington. **Positions advertised include:** Account Executive; Field Services Technician; Central Office Technician; Systems Administrator, Collections Coordinator; Carrier Services Auditor; Customer Care Representative; Associate Account Executive. **Corporate headquarters location:** This location.

INTEGRATED SERVICES
12242 SW Garden Place, Portland OR 97223. 503/968-8100. **Toll-free phone:** 800/922-3099. **Fax:** 503/968-9100. **Contact:** Human Resources Department. **World Wide Web address:** http://www.ints.com. **Description:** Develops management software for automobile lube shops and car washes.

INTEL CORPORATION
5200 NE Elam Young Parkway, Hillsboro OR 97124. 503/696-8080. **Toll-free phone:** 800/238-0486. **Contact:** Personnel. **World Wide Web address:** http://www.intel.com. **Description:** Intel is one of the largest semiconductor manufacturers in the world. Other operations include supercomputers; embedded control chips and flash memories; video technology software; multimedia hardware; personal computer enhancement products; and designing, making, and marketing microcomputer components, modules, and systems. **NOTE:** Jobseekers are encouraged to apply via the Website: http://www.intel.com/jobs. **Positions advertised include:** Administrative Assistant; Administrative Audit Specialist; Cellular Hardware Design Engineer; CAD Specialist; Electronics Engineer; Patent Attorney; Software Engineer; Technical Project Manager. **Operations at this facility include:** This location manufactures computer microprocessors and computer related parts. **Corporate headquarters location:** Santa Clara CA.

INTERSTATE DISTRIBUTOR COMPANY
10110 SW Ridder Road, Wilsonville OR 97070. 503/682-1097. **Fax:** 800/795-1034. **Contact:** Human Resources. **E-mail address:** resumes2@intd.com. **World Wide Web address:** http://www.intd.com. **Description:** A transportation/trucking company operating in the Western United States, the Midwest, and the East Coast. **Positions advertised include:** Shop Service Writer; Front Desk Receptionist; Corporate Accountant; Driver Recruiter/Orientation Facilitator; Customer Service Representative; Road Call Coordinator; Shop Foreman; Mechanic. **Corporate headquarters location:** Tacoma WA.

JANTZEN, INC.
P.O. Box 3001, Portland OR 97208-3001. 503/238-5000. **Toll-free phone:** 800/238-7946. **Fax:** 503/238-5020. **Contact:** Connie Wicks, Human Resources. **World Wide Web address:** http://www.jantzensport.com. **Description:** Manufactures and markets a line of swimsuits and women's sportswear. Founded in 1910.

LUHR JENSEN & SONS INC.
400 Portway Avenue, P.O. Box 297, Hood River OR 97031. 541/386-3811. **Contact:** Human Resources. **World Wide Web address:** http://www.luhr-jensen.com. **Description:** A manufacturer of sporting goods including fishing lures and the Little Chief Electric Smokehouse, an appliance that smoke-cures meat.

JEWETT-CAMERON TRADING COMPANY LTD.
32275 NW Hillcrest, P.O. Box 1010, North Plains OR 97133. 503/647-0110. **Fax:** 503/647-2272. **Contact:** Don Boone, CEO. **World Wide Web address:** http://www.msipro.com. **Description:** A supplier to the building supply and home improvement trades located throughout the western United States and the islands of the South Pacific. The company operates in the following business segments: warehouse distribution and direct sales of building materials to home improvement centers; export of finished building materials to overseas customers; and specialty wood products for government and industrial sales, primarily on a contract-bid basis. **Corporate headquarters location:** Tigard OR. **Subsidiaries include:** Jewett-Cameron Lumber Corporation; Jewett-Cameron South Pacific Ltd.; Material Supply International.

JOHNSON ACOUSTICAL & SUPPLY COMPANY (JASCO)
2001 NW 19th Avenue, Portland OR 97209. 503/226-2100. **Toll-free phone:** 800/935-2726. **Fax:** 503/226-2104. **Contact:** Human Resources. **World Wide Web address:** http://www.jasco-usa.com. **Description:** A contractor of specialized acoustic building interiors. The company is also engaged in the distribution of related industrial supplies.

JONES SPORTS COMPANY
17230 NE Sacramento Street, Portland OR 97230. 503/255-1410. **Contact:** Human Resources. **E-mail address:** info@jones-golf.com. **World Wide Web address:** http://www.jonessports.com. **Description:** Manufactures golf bags and related accessories.

KPMG
1300 SW Fifth Avenue, Suite 3800, Portland OR 97201. 503/221-6500. **Contact:** Recruiting Coordinator. **World Wide Web address:** http://www.kpmg.com. **Description:** KPMG delivers a wide range of value-added assurance, tax, and consulting services. Founded in 1897. **Corporate headquarters location:** Montvale NJ. **Other U.S. locations:** Nationwide. **International locations:** Worldwide. **Parent company:** The company is a leader among professional services firms engaged in capturing, managing, assessing, and delivering information to create knowledge that will help its clients maximize shareholder value. **Operations at this facility include:** This location houses the offices of the company's legal department as well as the top management staff.

KPTV 12
14975 NW Greenbrier Parkway, Portland OR 97006. 503/906-1249. **Contact:** Human Resources. **World Wide Web address:** http://www.kptv.com. **Description:** A television station affiliated with the United Paramount Network (UPN).

KAISER PERMANENTE CENTER FOR HEALTH RESEARCH
3800 North Interstate Avenue, Portland OR 97227. 503/335-2400. **Contact:** Human Resources. **E-mail address:** information@kpchr.org. **World Wide Web address:** http://www.kpchr.org. **Description:** Conducts health care research including clinical trials, intervention studies, and social economic studies. **Corporate headquarters location:** Oakland CA.

KEATING, JONES, STEIN, AND HUGHES, PC
One SW Columbia, Suite 800, Portland OR 97258. 503/222-9955. **Fax:** 503/796-0699. **Contact:** Human Resources. **World Wide Web address:** http://www.keatingjones.com. **Description:** A law firm.

KENTROX LLC
20010 NW Tanasbourne Drive, Portland OR 97124. 503/643-1681. **Contact:** Human Resources Department. **World Wide Web address:** http://www.kentrox.com. **Description:** Manufactures standards-based, high-speed digital network access and service internetworking products for connectivity of local area networks (LANs) and customer premises equipment over wide area networks (WANs).

KEYBANK N.A.
1211 SW Fifth Avenue, Suite 500, Portland OR 97204. 503/790-7600. **Contact:** Human Resources Department. **World Wide Web address:** http://www.keybank.com. **Description:** A commercial bank with approximately $85 billion in assets. **Corporate headquarters location:** Cleveland OH. **Parent company:** KeyCorp.

KINZUA RESOURCES
P.O. Drawer AA, Pilot Rock OR 97868. 541/443-2261. **Fax:** 541/443-3432. **Contact:** Peggie Tolman, Human Resources. **World Wide Web address:** http://www.kinzuaresources.com. **Description:** Harvests timber and converts it into a wide range of wood products including lumber, panel products, and doors.

KNOWLEDGE LEARNING CORPORATION
650 NE Holladay Street, Portland OR 97232. 503/872-1300. **Toll-free phone:** 800/633-1488. **Contact:** Human Resources. **World Wide Web address:** http://www.kindercare.com. **Description:** A leading provider of early childhood care and educational services to children ages six weeks to five years old. KinderCare operates approximately 1,130 facilities.

LANE COMMUNITY COLLEGE
4000 East 30th Avenue, Eugene OR 97405. 541/463-5211. **Fax:** 541/463-3970. **Contact:** Human Resources Director. **World Wide Web address:** http://www.lanecc.edu. **Description:** A community college with an enrollment of approximately 40,000 students per year. Founded in 1964. **Positions advertised include:** Executive Chef. **Number of employees at this location:** 1,000.

LANE, COUNTY OF
125 East Eighth Avenue, Eugene OR 97401. 541/682-3665. **Contact:** Human Resources. **World Wide Web address:** http://www.co.lane.or.us. **Description:** This location houses the administrative offices of Lane County.

LATTICE SEMICONDUCTOR CORPORATION
5555 NE Moore Court, Hillsboro OR 97124. 503/681-0118. **Fax:** 503/268-8174. **Contact:** Human Resources. **World Wide Web address:** http://www.latticesemi.com. **Description:** A leader in the design, development, and marketing of high-speed Programmable Logic Devices (PLDs) in both low-density and high-density ranges. Lattice products are sold primarily to original equipment manufacturers of microcomputers, graphic systems, workstations, peripherals, telecommunications, military, and industrial controls. CMOS PLDs are assembled in 20 to 207 PIN standard packages and offered with various speed, power, and packaging options in commercial, industrial, and military temperature versions. **Corporate headquarters location:** This location.

LEGACY EMANUEL CHILDREN'S HOSPITAL
1120 NW 20th Street, Suite 111, Portland OR 97209. 503/415-5405. **Toll-free phone:** 866/888-4428. **E-mail address:** employment@lhs.org. **Contact:** Personnel Department. **World Wide Web address:** http://www.legacyhealth.org. **Description:** A for-profit hospital offering children's and general medical services. **NOTE:** Applications are required with resumes. **Positions advertised include:** Benefits Specialist; Clinical Nursing Coordinator; Office Assistant; Registered Nurse. **Parent company:** Legacy Health System also operates the following area hospitals: Good Samaritan, Meridian Park, and Mount Hood Medical Center.

LEGACY HEALTH SYSTEM
1919 NW Lovejoy Street, Portland OR 97209. 503/225-8600. **Fax:** 503/415-5788. **Contact:** Human Resources. **World Wide Web address:** http://www.legacyhealth.org. **Description:** Operates four Portland area hospitals and offers visiting nurse services. **Corporate headquarters location:** This location.

LEGACY LABORATORY SERVICES
1225 NE Second Avenue, Portland OR 97232. 503/413-5000. **Toll-free phone:** 877/270-5566. **Fax:** 503/413-5048. **Contact:** Manager. **Description:** A clinical laboratory that provides a variety of services for area hospitals.

LEGACY MERIDIAN PARK HOSPITAL
19300 SW 65th Avenue, Tualatin OR 97062-9741. 503/692-1212. **Contact:** Human Resources. **World Wide Web address:** http://www.legacyhealth.org. **Description:** A 100-bed hospital providing general medical care. **Parent company:** Legacy Health System (Portland OR).

LEGACY MOUNT HOOD HOSPITAL
24800 SE Stark Street, Gresham OR 97030. 503/667-1122. **Contact:** Human Resources. **World Wide Web address:** http://www.legacyhealth.org. **Description:** A 120-bed for-profit hospital. **Corporate headquarters location:** Portland OR. **Parent company:** Legacy Health System also operates area hospitals Good Samaritan, Meridian Park, and Emanuel.

LEUPOLD & STEVENS INC.
P.O. Box 688, Beaverton OR 97075-0688. 503/526-5186. **Contact:** Human Resources. **E-Mail Address:** hrdept@leupold.com. **World Wide Web address:** http://www.leupold.com. **Description:** A manufacturer of sports optical equipment such as riflescopes and binoculars. **Positions advertised include:** Sales Forecast Analyst; Sales Service Representative; Tactical Market Specialist. **Corporate headquarters location:** This location.

LINN-BENTON COMMUNITY COLLEGE
6500 SW Pacific Boulevard, Albany OR 97321. 541/917-4421. **Fax:** 541/917-4435. **Recorded jobline:** 541/917-4434. **Contact:** Manger of Human Resources Department.

E-mail address: employ@linnbenton.edu. **World Wide Web address:** http://www.linnbenton.edu/employment. **Description:** A two-year community college. **Positions advertised include:** Nurse; Child Care Provider. **Number of employees at this location:** 1,000.

MACHEEZMO MOUSE RESTAURANTS INC.
1020 SW Taylor Street, Suite 685, Portland OR 97205. 503/221-4900. **Fax:** 503/274-4369. **Contact:** Human Resources. **Description:** Operates a chain of 15 quick-service restaurants that offer Mexican-style food. Macheezmo Mouse restaurants offer dine-in and take-out lunch and dinner service in the Portland OR and Seattle WA metropolitan areas. **Corporate headquarters location:** This location.

MACKENZIE WILLAMETTE HOSPITAL
1460 G Street, Springfield OR 97477. 541/744-8547. **Contact:** Human Resources Department. **World Wide Web address:** http://www.mckweb.com. **Description:** A hospital with 114 beds. **Positions advertised include:** Special Procedures Technologist; Patient Access Clerk; Home Care Physical Therapist.

MAIL TRIBUNE
111 N Fir Street, P.O. Box 1108, Medford OR 97501. 541/776-4411. **Fax:** 541/776-4439. **Contact:** Human Resources. **E-mail address:** gmenzie@mailtribune.com. **World Wide Web address:** http://www.mailtribune.com. **Description:** Publishes the local newspaper, *Mail Tribune*, with a circulation of over 30,000. **Parent company:** Ottaway Newspapers Group.

MAIL-WELL ENVELOPES
12990 SE Highway 212, Clackamus OR 97015. 503/654-3141. **Contact:** Human Resources. **World Wide Web address:** http://www.mail-well.com. **Description:** One of the largest stock and custom envelope manufacturers worldwide. The company has 50 sales offices and 29 manufacturing plants. Mail-Well Envelopes produces 115 million envelopes a day. **Corporate headquarters location:** Englewood CO. **Other area locations:** Portland OR; Eugene OR. **Other U.S. locations:** Nationwide.

MALARKEY ROOFING COMPANY
3131 N Columbia Boulevard, P.O. Box 17217, Portland OR 97217. 503/283-1191. **Contact:** Human Resources. **World Wide Web address:** http://www.malarkey-rfg.com. **Description:** Manufactures roofing products for both residential and commercial use.

MARLETTE HOMES, INC.
400 W Elm Avenue, P.O. Box 910, Hermiston OR 97838. 541/567-5546. **Toll-free phone:** 800/547-2444. **Fax:** 541/567-7851. **Contact:** General Manager. **World Wide Web address:** http://www.marlettehomes.com. **Description:** A manufacturer of homes. Founded in 1953. **NOTE:** This office only accepts resumes for office workers and sales representatives. All production and factory workers are hired through the Oregon State Employment Office. **Other U.S. locations:** Middlebury IN. **Parent company:** Schult Homes Corporation.

McCORMICK & SCHMICK MANAGEMENT GROUP
720 SW Washington Street, Suite 550, Portland OR 97205. 503/226-3440. **Fax:** 503/228-7729. **Contact:** Senior Personnel Coordinator. **World Wide Web address:** http://www.mccormickandschmicks.com. **Description:** A management company that operates a chain of upscale seafood restaurants. The restaurants operate as Jake's Grill, Jake's Famous Crawfish, McCormick & Schmicks Seafood Restaurant, Spenger's Fresh Fish Grotto, M & S Grill, and McCormick's Fish House & Bar. **Corporate headquarters location:** This location. **Other U.S. locations:** Nationwide.

McDONALD WHOLESALE
2350 W. Broadway, Eugene OR 97402-2704. 541/345-8421. **Fax:** 541/345-7146. **Contact:** Human Resources. **Description:** A food and alcohol wholesaler and distributor. **Corporate headquarters location:** This location. **Number of employees at this location:** 330.

MEGGITT SILICONE PRODUCTS
2010 Lafayette Avenue, McMinnville OR 97128. 503/472-0045. **Fax:** 503/434-6454. **Contact:** Yazmin Funes, Human Relations Manager. **E-mail address:** yfunes@mspaerospace.com. **World Wide Web address:** http://www.meggittsilicone.com. **Description:** A maker of silicone aircraft parts. **Parent company:** Meggitt Polymers and Composites.

MEIER AND FRANK
621 SW Fifth Avenue, Portland OR 97204. 503/223-0512. **Contact:** Human Resources. **World Wide Web address:** http://www.meierandfrank.com. **Description:** Meier and Frank operates a department store chain consisting of eight stores in Oregon. **Corporate headquarters location:** This location. **Parent company:** The May Department Stores Company. **Operations at this facility include:** This location houses administrative offices and the downtown store.

MEIER AND FRANK
1100 Lloyd Center, Portland OR 97232. 503/281-4797. **Contact:** Human Resources. **World Wide Web address:** http://www.meierandfrank.com. **Description:** One location of the department store chain. The company operates eight stores in Oregon. **Positions advertised include:** General Sales Associate; Commission Sales Associate; Cosmetics Beauty Advisor. **Parent company:** The May Department Stores Company.

MEIER AND FRANK
9300 SW Washington Square Road, Tigard OR 97223. 503/620-3311. **Contact:** Human Resources. **World Wide Web address:** http://www.meierandfrank.com. **Description:** One location of the department store chain. The company operates eight stores in Oregon. **Positions advertised include:** General Sales Associate; Commission Sales Associate; Cosmetics Beauty Advisor. **Parent company:** The May Department Stores Company.

MEIER AND FRANK
12100 SE 82nd Avenue, Portland OR 97226. 503/653-8811. **Contact:** Human Resources. **World Wide Web address:** http://www.meierandfrank.com. **Description:** One location of the department store chain. The company operates eight stores in Oregon. **Positions advertised include:** General Sales Associate; Commission Sales Associate; Cosmetics Beauty Advisor. **Parent company:** The May Department Stores Company.

MEIER AND FRANK
400 High Street NE, Salem OR 97301. 503/363-2211. **Contact:** Human Resources. **World Wide Web address:** http://www.meierandfrank.com. **Description:** One location of the department store chain. The company operates eight stores in Oregon. **Positions advertised include:** General Sales Associate; Commission Sales Associate; Cosmetics Beauty Advisor. **Parent company:** The May Department Stores Company.

MEIER AND FRANK
1800 North Riverside Drive, Medford OR 97501. 541/772-3700. **Contact:** Human Resources. **World Wide Web address:** http://www.meierandfrank.com. **Description:** One location of the department store chain. The company operates eight stores in Oregon. **Positions advertised include:** General Sales Associate; Commission Sales Associate; Cosmetics Beauty Advisor. **Parent company:** The May Department Stores Company.

MEIER AND FRANK
100 Valley River Center, Eugene OR 97401. 541/342-6611. **Contact:** Human Resources. **World Wide Web address:** http://www.meierandfrank.com. **Description:** One location of the department store chain. The company operates eight stores in Oregon. **Positions advertised include:** General Sales Associate; Commission Sales Associate; Cosmetics Beauty Advisor. **Parent company:** The May Department Stores Company.

MENTOR GRAPHICS CORPORATION
8005 SW Boeckman Road, Wilsonville OR 97070-7777. 503/685-7000. **Toll-free phone:** 800/592-2210. **Recorded jobline:** 800/554-5259. **Contact:** Manager of Human Resources Department. **World Wide Web address:** http://www.mentor.com/jobs. **Description:** Develops electronic design automation (EDA) software used to automate the design, analysis, and documentation of electronic components and systems. The company is one of the world's leading suppliers of EDA software and professional services, and markets its products primarily to companies in the aerospace, computer, consumer electronics, semiconductor, and telecommunications industries. Founded in 1981. **Positions advertised include:** Database Administrator; QA Engineer; Systems Administrator; Assistant Treasurer; Substitute Early Childhood Teacher; Software Engineer; Technical Marketing Engineer. **Special programs:** Internships. **Corporate headquarters location:** This location. **Other U.S. locations:** San Jose CA; Warren NJ; Dallas TX. **Operations at this facility include:** Administration; Research and Development.

MERANT INC.
3445 NW 211th Terrace, Hillsboro OR 97124. 503/645-1150. **Fax:** 503/645-4576. **Contact:** Human Resources. **World Wide Web address:** http://www.merant.com. **Description:** Provides computer programming and software services. **Positions advertised include:** Answerline Manager; Customer Marketing Manager; Paralegal; Product Marketing Manager; Senior Technical Writer; Staff Software Developer. **International locations:** Worldwide.

MERCY MEDICAL CENTER
2700 Stewart Parkway, Roseburg OR 97470. 541/673-0611. **Toll-free phone:** 800/962-2406. **Fax:** 541/677-2176. **Contact:** Human Resources & Learning Center. **E-mail address:** carriethompson@chiwest.com. **World Wide Web address:** http://www.mercyrose.org. **Description:** A 200-bed hospital providing general medical care. **Number of employees at this location:** 1,400.

MERIX CORPORATION
1521 Poplar Lane, P.O. Box 3000, Forest Grove OR 97116. 503/359-9300. **Fax:** 503/357-1504. **Contact:** Vice President of Human Resources. **E-mail address:** hr@merix.com. **World Wide Web address:** http://www.merix.com. **Description:** Merix Corporation is a leading manufacturer of electronic interconnect solutions including printed circuit boards, backpanels, flexible circuits, and subassemblies for use in sophisticated electronics equipment. The company provides these complex electronic interconnect products to a diversified base of manufacturers in the industrial and medical instrumentation, computer, and communications segments of the electronics industry. The company's broad range of interconnect products employs a variety of technologies including rigid and high-performance substrates and flexible circuitry. **Positions advertised include:** CAD Designer; Engineering Manager; Director of Human Resources; Production Expeditor; Delivery Focal. **Corporate headquarters location:** This location.

MERLE WEST MEDICAL CENTER
2865 Daggett Avenue, Klamath Falls OR 97601. 541/882-6311. **Recorded jobline:** 541/883-6020. **Contact:** Human Resources Department. **World Wide Web address:** http://www.mwmc.org. **Description:** A 176-bed hospital. **Positions advertised include:** Nursing Supervisor; Patient Care Coordinator; RN; Case manager; Radiologic Technologist. **Number of employees at this location:** 1,100.

METRO ONE TELECOMMUNICATIONS
11200 Murray Scholls Place, Beaverton OR 97007. 503/643-9500. **Contact:** Human Resources. **E-mail address:** corp.jobs@metro1.com. **E-mail address:** mpoe@mwmc.org. **World Wide Web address:** http://www.metro1.com. **Description:** Provides directory assistance for cellular customers. **Positions advertised include:** Quality Assurance Engineer; Call Center Operator; Call Center Lead Operator; Call Center Trainer; Call Center Janitor/Maintenance Worker. **Corporate headquarters location:** This location. **Listed on:** NASDAQ. **Stock exchange symbol:** MTON.

MICROSOFT CORPORATION
10260 SW Greenburg Road, Suite 600, Portland OR 97223. 503/452-6400. **Contact:** Lori Colby, Human Resources. **World Wide Web address:** http://www.microsoft.com. **Description:** Microsoft designs, sells, and supports a product line of systems and applications microcomputer software for business, home, and professional use. Microsoft also produces related books and hardware products. Software products include spreadsheet, desktop publishing, project management, graphics, word processing, and database applications as well as operating systems and programming languages. **NOTE:** Resumes can be sent by mail to: Microsoft Corporation, One Microsoft Way, Suite 303, Redmond WA 98052-8303 or sent along with an online application via the Internet **Operations at this facility include:** The primary function of this location is sales and consulting.

MILGARD MANUFACTURING INC.
20789 SW 1115th Avenue. Tualatin OR 97070. 503/682-3270. **Fax:** 503/685-9134. **Contact:** John Underwood, Personnel Manager. **World Wide Web address:** http://www.milgard.com. **Description:** A manufacturer of doors, skylights, and windows. **Corporate headquarters location:** Tacoma WA.

MILLER & NASH
3400 U.S. Bancorp Tower, 111 SW Fifth Avenue, Portland OR 97204-3699. 503/224-5858. **Toll-free phone:** 877-220-5858. **Fax:** 503/224-0155. **Contact:** Katie McCoy, Director of Legal Recruitment. **E-mail address:** katie.mccoy@millernash.com. **World Wide Web address:** http://www.millernash.com. **Description:** A law firm specializing in corporate law.

MOLECULAR PROBES, INC.
29851 Willow Creek Road, Eugene OR 97402. 541/335-0338. **Toll-free phone:** 800/438-2209. **Fax:** 541/335-0305. **Contact:** Human Resources. **World Wide Web**

address: http://www.probes.com. **Description:** A biotechnology company that develops fluorescent technology for biochemistry, cell biology, diagnostics, immunology, microbiology, molecular biology, and neuroscience research and studies. **Positions advertised include:** Biosciences Associate Scientist; Biosciences Quality Control Manager; Cell Biologist; Paralegal; Patent Attorney; Senior Manager; Staff Scientist; Technical Editor; Technical Writer.

MONACO COACH CORPORATION
91320 Coburg Industrial Way, Coburg OR 97408. 541/686-8011. **Toll-free phone:** 800/634-0855. **Fax:** 541/681-8899. **Contact:** Human Resources. **World Wide Web address:** http://www.monaco-online.com. **Description:** Monaco Coach Corporation is one of the nation's leading manufacturers of high-line motor coaches. The company has five distinct lines: the Windsor, the Dynasty, the Executive, the Crowne Royale Signature Series, and Royale Coach bus conversions. **Corporate headquarters location:** This location.

MORSE BROS. INC.
23505 Peoria Road, Harrisburg OR 97446. 541/995-6327. **Contact:** Scott Trent, Human Resources. **World Wide Web address:** http://www.morsebros.com. **Description:** Manufactures concrete and other aggregates. **Positions advertised include:** Pipe Foreman; Grade Crew Operator; Pipe/Grade Crew Member; Quality Control Technician; Mechanic; Crusher Operator; Groundman. **Other area locations:** Albany; Coffee Lake; Deer Island; Lebanon; Salem; Stayton; and Tangent OR.

MOSS ADAMS LLP
Fox Tower, 805 SW Broadway, Suite 1200, Portland OR 97205. 503/242-1447. **Fax:** 503/274-2789. **Contact:** Human Resources. **E-mail address:** portlandor@mossadams.com. **World Wide Web address:** http://www.mossadams.com. **Description:** One of the nation's largest accounting firms offering assurance, consulting, and tax and audit services.

MOUNT HOOD COMMUNITY COLLEGE
26000 SE Stark Street, Gresham OR 97030. 503/491-6422. **Fax:** 503/491-7257. **Recorded jobline:** 503/491-7645. **Contact:** Human Resources. **E-mail address:** hr@mhcc.edu. **World Wide Web address:** http://www.mhcc.cc.or.us. **Description:** A community college offering associate's degrees in applied science and arts to approximately 26,000 students. Founded in 1966. **Positions advertised include:** Instructor of Respiratory Care; Instructor of Mathematics; Instructor-Automotive Program; Director of Library Resources; Financial Aid Coordinator; KMHD Development Coordinator; Center Assistant/Driver; Teacher/Home Visitor.

MULTNOMAH EDUCATIONAL SERVICE DISTRICT
11611 NE Ainsworth Circle, P.O. Box 301039, Portland OR 97220. 503/255-1841. **Fax:** 503/257-1519. **Recorded jobline:** 503/257-1510. **Contact:** Human Resources Department. **World Wide Web address:** http://w3.mesd.k12.or.us. **Description:** Provides services and programs for the Multnomah School District including early intervention, environmental education, job training, functional living skills, and substitute teacher call-in systems. **Positions advertised include:** Autism Specialist; Supervisor of Special Education; Teacher of Special Education; Occupational Therapist; Physical Therapist; Communications Assistant; Office Assistant; Translator. **Office hours:** Monday - Friday, 8:00 a.m. - 5:00 p.m.

MURRAYHILL VETERINARY HOSPITAL
14831 SW Teal Boulevard, Beaverton OR 97007. 503/579-3300. **Fax:** 503/579-4645. **Contact:** Human Resources. **E-mail address:** staff@murrayhillvethospital.com. **World Wide Web address:** http://www.murrayhillvethospital.com. **Description:** Murrayhill Veterinary Hospital offers complete animal care including surgery, dentistry, and neuropathic care.

MYERS CONTAINER CORPORATION
8435 NE Killingsworth Street, Portland OR 97220-4660. 503/255-0553. **Contact:** Human Resources. **World Wide Web address:** http://www.myerscontainer.com. **Description:** A manufacturer and reconditioner of steel drum containers. Founded in 1984. **Parent company:** IMACC Corporation.

NABISCO BRANDS INC.
10001 North Kerby Avenue, Portland OR 97217. 503/289-1535. **Contact:** Human Resources. **World Wide Web address:** http://www.nabisco.com. **Description:** Nabisco is one of the largest consumer foods operations in the nation. The company markets a broad line of cookie and cracker products including brand names such as Oreo, Ritz, Premium, Teddy Grahams, Chips Ahoy!, and Wheat Thins. The company operates 13 cake and cookie bakeries, a flourmill, and a cheese plant. The bakeries produce over 1 billion pounds of finished products each year. **Corporate headquarters location:** East Hanover NY. **Operations at this facility include:** This location is a bakery.

NACCO MATERIALS HANDLING GROUP, INC.
4000 NE Blue Lake Road, Fairview OR 97024. 503/721-6205. **Fax:** 503/721-6002. **Contact:** Human Resources. **Description:** Manufactures forklifts, agricultural components, and winches. **Corporate headquarters location:** Mayfield Heights OH.

NATIONAL FROZEN FOODS CORPORATION
745 30th Avenue SW, Albany OR 97321. 541/928-3306. **Contact:** Human Resources. **E-mail address:** bwallace@nationalfrozenfoods.com. **World Wide Web address:** http://www.nationalfrozenfoods.com. **Description:** Processes, packages, and distributes frozen fruits and vegetables. Founded in 1912. **Company slogan:** The Best of the Great Northwest. **Corporate headquarters location:** Seattle WA.

NATIONWIDE DIRECT
P.O. Box 4114, Portland OR 97228. **Toll-free phone:** 888/634-7328. **Fax:** 503/230-7249. **Contact:** Human Resources. **E-mail address:** hr@ndirect.com. **World Wide Web address:** http://www.nationwide.com. **Description:** Sells automobile, life, group, and business insurance. **Positions advertised include:** Processing Technician; Programmer Analyst; Technical Clerk. **Corporate headquarters location:** Columbus OH.

nCUBE
1825 NW 167th Place, Beaverton OR 97006. 503/629-5088. **Toll-free phone:** 800/654-2823. **Fax:** 503/645-1737. **Contact:** Human Resources. **E-mail address:** hr@ncube.com. **World Wide Web address:** http://www.ncube.com. **Description:** Develops and manufactures media servers that process audio and video data through networks. **Positions advertised include:** ODA Java Developer; Senior Technical Writer.

NEUROCOM INTERNATIONAL INC.
9570 SE Lawnfield Road, Clackamas OR 97015-9611. 503/653-2144. **Contact:** Human Resources. **World Wide Web address:** http://www.onbalance.com. **Description:** Specializes in balance and mobility and manufactures medical equipment for the treatment of chronic dizziness and mobility disorders.

THE NEWS REVIEW
345 NE Winchester Street, P.O. Box 1248, Roseburg OR 97470. 541/672-3321. **Contact:** Catharina Burgess, Business Manager. **World Wide Web address:** http://www.oregonnews.com. **Description:** Publishes a six-day newspaper with a daily circulation of more than 20,000. **Corporate headquarters location:** Reno NV. **Parent company:** Swift Newspapers, Inc.

NIKE, INC.
One SW Bowerman Drive, Beaverton OR 97005-6453. 503/671-6453. **Toll-free phone:** 800/344-6453. **Fax:** 503/671-6300. **Contact:** Recruiter. **World Wide Web address:** http://www.nike.com. **Description:** Develops, manufactures, and markets a line of athletic shoes, casual shoes, accessories, and athletic apparel. The company markets its products in over 110 countries, and operates over 60 retail outlets. Founded in 1964. **Special programs:** Internships. **Corporate headquarters location:** This location. **International locations:** Brazil; China; Mexico; the Netherlands. **Listed on:** New York Stock Exchange. **Stock exchange symbol:** NKE. **Number of employees worldwide:** 23,000.

NIKE, INC.
Howard Vollum Park, Building 16, 13630 SW Perman Road, Beaverton OR 97076. 503/671-1500. **Contact:** Recruiter. **World Wide Web address:** http://www.nike.com. **Description:** Nike, Inc. develops, manufactures, and markets a line of athletic shoes, casual shoes, accessories, and athletic apparel. The company markets its products in over 110 countries, and operates over 60 retail outlets. **NOTE:** Send resumes to: Nike, Inc. Human Resources, One Bowerman Drive, Beaverton OR 97005. **International locations:** Brazil; China; Mexico; the Netherlands. **Operations at this facility include:** As part of the airsole division, this location manufactures airbags for Nike shoes. **Listed on:** New York Stock Exchange. **Stock exchange symbol:** NKE.

NIKE, INC./WESTERN REGIONAL CUSTOMER SERVICE
27255 SW 95th Avenue, Wilsonville OR 97070-9248. 503/682-6453. **Contact:** Human Resources. **World Wide Web address:** http://www.nike.com. **Description:** Nike, Inc. develops, manufactures, and markets a line of athletic shoes, casual shoes, accessories, and athletic apparel. The company markets its products in over 110 countries, and operates over 60 retail outlets. **NOTE:** Send resumes to: Nike, Inc. Human Resources, One Bowerman Drive, Beaverton OR 97005. **Corporate headquarters location:** Beaverton OR. **International locations:** Brazil; China; Mexico; the Netherlands. **Operations at this facility include:** This location is a distribution and customer service center for retail operations. **Listed on:** New York Stock Exchange. **Stock exchange symbol:** NKE.

NORPAC FOODS, INC.
930 West Washington Street, P.O. Box 458, Stayton OR 97383-0458. 503/769-2101. **Contact:** Ron Fritz, Human Resources Director. **World Wide Web address:** http://www.norpac.com. **Description:** Processes and packages fruits and vegetables for retail stores and restaurants.

NORPAC FOODS, INC.
4755 Brooklake Road NE, Salem OR 97305. 503/393-4221. **Contact:** Human Resources. **World Wide Web address:** http://www.norpac.com. **Description:** Processes and packages fruits and vegetables for retail stores and restaurants. **NOTE:** Resumes should be sent to: Ron Fritz, 930 West Washington Street, P.O. Box 458, Stayton OR 97383.

NORPAC FOODS, INC.
2325 Madrona Avenue SE, Salem OR 97302. 503/581-1426. **Contact:** Human Resources. **World Wide Web address:** http://www.norpac.com. **Description:** Processes and packages fruits and vegetables for retail stores and restaurants. **NOTE:** Resumes should be sent to: Ron Fritz, 930 West Washington Street, P.O. Box 458, Stayton OR 97383.

NORRIS, BEGGS & SIMPSON REALTORS
121 SW Morrison Street, Suite 200, Portland OR 97204. 503/223-7181. **Fax:** 503/273-0256. **Contact:** Human Resources. **World Wide Web address:** http://www.nbsrealtors.com. **Description:** A realty company specializing in consulting, sales, leasing, investments, asset management, property management, and real estate finance. Founded in 1932. **Other U.S. locations:** WA.

NORTH PACIFIC LUMBER COMPANY
P.O. Box 3915, Portland OR 97208-3915. 503/231-1166. **Physical Address:** 815 NE Davis Street, Portland OR 97232. **Toll-free phone:** 800/547-8440. **Fax:** 503/238-2646. **Contact:** Human Resources Manager. **World Wide Web address:** http://www.north-pacific.com. **Description:** A domestic and international wholesale distributor of forest products and other commodities. **Positions advertised include:** Trader; Domestic Hardwood Trader; Sales Support Specialist; Export Trader; Graphic Designer. **Corporate headquarters location:** This location. **Operations at this facility include:** Administration; Sales; Service.

NORTHWEST ALUMINUM COMPANY
3313 West Second Street, The Dalles OR 97058-4169. 541/296-6161. **Contact:** Human Resources. **World Wide Web address:** http://www.nwaluminum.com. **Description:** Produces aluminum alloy billets. **Corporate headquarters location:** This location.

NORTHWEST NATURAL GAS COMPANY
220 NW Second Avenue, Portland OR 97209-3911. 503/226-4211. **Recorded jobline:** 503/226-4211 ext. 2434. **Contact:** Human Resources. **World Wide Web address:** http://www.nwnatural.com. **Description:** An area distributor of natural gas. **NOTE:** NW Natural Gas does not accept unsolicited resumes or applications. **Positions advertised include:** Utility Crew Helper; Engineer; Distributor.

NORTHWEST PIPE & CASING COMPANY
200 SW Market Street, Suite1800, Portland OR 97201. 503/946-1200. **Fax:** 503/240-6615. **Contact:** Human Resources Manager. **World Wide Web address:** http://www.nwpipe.com. **Description:** A manufacturer of steel pipes for use in agricultural, energy, industrial, and construction applications. **Positions advertised include:** General Laborer; Electrician; Welder; Maintenance Mechanic. **Corporate headquarters location:** This location.

NORTHWEST POWER PLANNING COUNCIL
851 SW Sixth Avenue, Suite 1100, Portland OR 97204. 503/222-5161. **Toll-free phone:** 800/452-5161. **Fax:** 503/820-2370. **Contact:** Human Resources. **E-mail address:** info@nwcouncil.org. **World Wide Web address:** http://www.nwppc.org. **Description:** A council established by Congress for the states (Idaho, Montana, Oregon, and Washington) that use electricity generated from the Columbia River. The

council has three main purposes, which are to establish a power plan that ensures low-cost electricity, to develop a program to rebuild the fish population, and to involve the public in any decision-making processes. Founded in 1980.

NOSLER INC.
107 SW Columbia Street, Bend OR 97702. 541/382-3921. **Contact:** Human Resources. **World Wide Web address:** http://www.nosler.com. **Description:** Manufactures bullets and bullet casings. **NOTE:** Contact corporate office for a list of available positions.

NUTECH SOFTWARE SOLUTIONS, INC.
11575 SW Pacific Highway, Suite 109, Tigard OR 97223-8671. 503/443-2000. **Fax:** 503/968-1877. **Contact:** Human Resources. **E-mail address:** resume@nutech.com. **World Wide Web address:** http://www.nutech.com. **Description:** Develops SQL database, Web connectivity software, and Web-based video servers.

ODS HEALTH PLANS
P.O. Box 40384. Portland OR 97240-0384. 503/228-6554. **Fax:** 503/243-3895. **Physical address:** 601 SW Second Avenue, Portland OR 97204. **Contact:** Human Resources. **World Wide Web address:** http://www.odshp.com. **Description:** A dental and medical insurance organization. **Positions advertised include:** Medical Claims Processor; Medical and Dental Customer Service Representative; Care Coordinator RN. **Corporate headquarters location:** This location. **Subsidiaries include:** Best Choice Administrators; Dentist Benefit Insurance Corporation; Dentist Management Corporation. **Operations at this facility include:** Administration; Sales; Service.

OECO CORPORATION
4607 SE International Way, Milwaukie OR 97222-4619. 503/659-5999. **Fax:** 503/659-3447. **Contact:** Kimberley Posey, Human Resources. **E-mail address:** kimp@oeco.com. **World Wide Web address:** http://www.oeco.com. **Description:** A manufacturer of power supplies, dimmers, and circuit boards. **Positions advertised include:** Electrical Engineer; Mechanical Engineer; Manufacturing Engineer. **Corporate headquarters location:** This location.

OREGON CATHOLIC PRESS
P.O. Box 18030, Portland OR 97218. 503/281-1191. **Toll-free phone:** 800/548-8749. **Fax:** 800/462-7329. **Contact:** Personnel Manager. **E-mail address:** hr@ocp.org. **World Wide Web address:** http://www.ocp.org. **Description:** Publishes, prints, and distributes various Catholic publications. **Positions advertised include:** Bindery Assistant.

OREGON CITY SCHOOL DISTRICT
1417 12th Street, P.O. Box 2110, Oregon City OR 97045. 503/785-8427. **Recorded jobline:** 503/785-8449. **Contact:** Linda Matsies, Human Resources Director. **E-mail address:** matsiesl@orecity.k12.or.us. **World Wide Web address:** http://www.orecity.k12.or.us. **Description:** A state school district comprised of ten elementary schools, two middle schools, and one high school. **Positions advertised include:** Assistant Transportation Supervisor.

OREGON COAST AQUARIUM
2820 SE Ferry Slip Road, Newport OR 97365. 541/867-3474. **Fax:** 541/867-6846. **Contact:** Human Resources. **World Wide Web address:** http://www.aquarium.org. **Description:** A nonprofit aquarium offering a variety of special events including an annual music festival, whale watching cruises, artist workshops, bay cruises, and "Breakfast with the Animals." The aquarium focuses on education and features fish and animal species found off the Oregon coast. **NOTE:** Entry-level positions are offered. **Positions advertised include:** Security Officer. **Special programs:** Internships; Summer Jobs. **Office hours:** Monday - Friday, 9:00 a.m. - 6:00 p.m. **Corporate headquarters location:** This location.

OREGON CUTTING SYSTEMS
P.O. Box 22127, Portland OR 97269-2127. 503/653-8881. **Fax:** 503/653-6406. **Recorded jobline:** 503/653-4441. **Contact:** Chelsea Fursp, Human Resources. **E-mail address:** work@oregonchain.com. **World Wide Web address:** http://www.oregonchain.com. **Description:** Manufactures saw chains and related power saw accessories. **Positions advertised include:** Maintenance Machinist; Production; Manufacturing Specialist; Line Administrator. **Corporate headquarters location:** This location. **International locations:** Worldwide. **Parent company:** Blount Inc.

OREGON FARM BUREAU FEDERATION
3415 Commercial Street SE, Salem OR 97302. 503/399-1701. **Contact:** Human Resources. **World Wide Web address:** http://www.oregonfb.org. **Description:** A nonprofit organization concerned with farming and agricultural issues.

OREGON FREEZE DRY INC.
P.O. Box 1048, Albany OR 97321-0407. 541/926-6001. **Fax:** 541/967-6527. **Contact:** Delene Powell, Human Resources Manager. **World Wide Web address:** http://www.ofd.com. **Description:** Develops, manufactures, and markets freeze-dried food ingredients for military, food, and consumer markets. **Positions advertised include:** Quality Assurance Specialist. **Corporate headquarters location:** This location.

OREGON GRADUATE INSTITUTE OF SCIENCE & TECHNOLOGY
20000 NW Walker Road, Beaverton OR 97006. 503/748-1121. **Contact:** Director of Personnel. **World Wide Web address:** http://www.ohsu.edu/hr/sum.htm. **Description:** A private graduate institute offering master's and Ph.D. programs in five areas: computer science and engineering; management in science and technology; biochemistry and molecular biology; environmental science and engineering; and electrical and computer engineering. Founded in 1963. **Positions advertised include:** Financial Analyst; Administrative Assistant; Management Analyst; Program Technician; Emergency Department Technician; Photographer; Medical Laboratory Technician.

OREGON HEALTH SCIENCES UNIVERSITY
2525 SW 3rd Avenue, Suite 110, Portland OR 97239-3098. 503/494-8060. **Recorded jobline:** 503/494-6478. **Fax:** 503/494-6469. **Contact:** Human Resources. **World Wide Web address:** http://www.ohsu.edu. **Description:** A university comprised of the Schools of Dentistry, Medicine, and Nursing; Biomedical Information Communication Center; Center for Research on Occupational and Environmental Toxicology; University Hospital; Doernbecher Children's Hospital; and the Oregon Regional Primate Research Center. The Oregon Health Sciences University also includes the Vollum Institute, a neurological research center at this location, Mail Code L474, and can be reached at 503/494-5042. **NOTE:** The nursing jobline may be reached by dialing 503/494-6546. **Positions advertised include:** Assistant Hospital Director of Information; Laboratory Animal Technician; MRI Technician; Pharmacist; Physical Therapist.

OREGON INSTITUTE OF TECHNOLOGY
3201 Campus Drive, Klamath Falls OR 97601. 541/885-1120. **Recorded jobline:** 541/885-1500. **Contact:** Human Resources. **E-mail address:** oithr@oit.edu. **World Wide Web address:** http://www.oit.edu. **Description:** A college that offers associate's and bachelor's degrees in a variety of engineering fields and a master's program in engineering technology to approximately 2,800 students. **Positions advertised include:** Assistant Professor of Physics; Communication Faculty Member; Manufacturing Consultant; Computer Systems Laboratory Manager.

OREGON INTERNATIONAL PORT OF COOS BAY
125 Central Avenue, Suite 300, P.O. Box 1215, Coos Bay OR 97420-0311. 541/267-7678. **Fax:** 541/269-1475. **Contact:** Human Resources. **E-mail address:** portcoos@portofcoosbay.com. **World Wide Web address:** http://www.portofcoosbay.com. **Description:** Oregon International Port of Coos Bay is the port authority for Oregon's bay area, which encompasses the cities of Coos Bay and North Bend, and the fishing village of Charleston. The port owns marine terminals and industrial property in the bay area, serves as a marketing and economic development agency for the region, owns and operates a commercial/recreational marina, owns a recreational vehicle park, and operates a small vessel boatyard in the Charleston area. Founded in 1909. **Office hours:** Monday - Friday, 8:00 a.m. - 5:00 p.m. **Corporate headquarters location:** This location.

OREGON MEDICAL LABORATORIES
722 East 11th Avenue, Eugene OR 97401. 541/349-8464. **Toll-free phone:** 800/826-3616. **Fax:** 541/984-8255. **Contact:** Human Resources. **E-mail address:** jobs@omlabs.com. **World Wide Web address:** http://www.omlabs.com. **Description:** A clinical laboratory that provides testing and consultation services to area hospitals and physicians. Oregon Medical Laboratory is also a certified drug-testing facility. **Positions advertised include:** IS Help Desk Specialist; Technical Specialist, Blood Bank; Chief Financial Officer; Medical Technologist. **Corporate headquarters location:** This location.

OREGON MUSEUM OF SCIENCE AND INDUSTRY (OMSI)
1945 SE Water Avenue, Portland OR 97214. 503/797-4000. **Recorded jobline:** 503/797-4665. **Contact:** Personnel. **E-mail address:** employment@omsi.edu. **World Wide Web address:** http://www.omsi.edu. **Description:** A science museum featuring an Omnimax theater, the Murdoch Sky Theatre Planetarium, and submarine tours on the U.S.S. Blueback. **NOTE:** OMSI accepts resumes for current open positions only. **Positions advertised include:** Special Projects Educator; Administrative Assistant; Museum Educator; Sales Associate; Summer Camp Counselor.

OREGON PUBLIC BROADCASTING (OPB)
7140 SW Macadam Avenue, Portland OR 97219. 503/244-9900. **Recorded jobline:** 503/293-1972. **Contact:** Human Resources Department. **World Wide Web address:** http://www.opb.org. **Description:** A television station affiliated with the nonprofit Public Broadcasting System (PBS) offering educational, arts, news, and other noncommercial programming. **Positions advertised include:** VP Marketing and Planning; Corporate Support Representative; Grant Analyst/Accountant; Operations Executive Assistant.

OREGON SCIENTIFIC
19861 SW 95th Place, Tualatin OR 97062. 949/608-2848. **Fax:** 503/691-6208. **E-mail address:** jobs@oscientific.com. **Contact:** Human Resources. **World Wide Web address:** http://www.oregonscientific.com. **Description:** Oregon Scientific is a leading designer and marketer of award-winning, upscale personal electronic products in the consumer electronics industry.

OREGON SPICE COMPANY
13320 NE Jarrett Street, Portland OR 97230. 503/238-0664. **Toll-free phone:** 800/565-1599. **Fax:** 503/238-3872. **Contact:** Human Resources. **World Wide Web address:** http://www.oregonspice.com. **Description:** Supplies food processors, manufacturers, gourmet specialists, and health food stores throughout North America with the freshest, highest quality herbs and spices from around the world. Certified organic spices offered.

OREGON STATE HOSPITAL
1121 NE 2nd Avenue, Portland OR 97232. 503/731-8620. **Contact:** Human Resources Department. **World Wide Web address:** http://www.dhs.state.or.us/jobs/. **Description:** A 68-bed satellite hospital of Oregon State Hospital in Portland.

OREGON STATE UNIVERSITY
122 & 204 Kerr Administration, Corvallis OR 97331-2132. 541/737-3103. **Contact:** Stephanie Taylor, Employment Services Supervisor. **Toll-free phone:** 800/735-2900. **Fax:** 541/737-0553. **World Wide Web address:** http://www.oregonstate.edu/jobs. **Description:** A state university offering bachelor's, master's, and doctoral degrees to approximately 15,100 students.

THE OREGONIAN
1320 SW Broadway Street, Portland OR 97201. 503/221-8327. **Contact:** Tom Whitehouse, Director of Human Resources. **World Wide Web address:** http://www.oregonian.com. **Description:** A daily newspaper with a circulation of 350,000 on weekdays and 445,000 on Sundays. The newspaper maintains several bureaus in the Portland area and throughout Oregon, as well as a national bureau in Washington DC. **Corporate headquarters location:** This location.

ORGANIC WINE PRESS
175 2nd Street, Bandon OR 97411 (at Pacific Blues). 541/347-3326. **Contact:** Human Resources. **World Wide Web address:** http://www.organicwinepress.com. **Description:** Provides organic, no sulfite, and no spray wines from around the world.

ORION AUTO
P.O. Box 7138, Salem OR 97303. 503/585-5313. **Toll-free phone:** 800/547-7830. **Contact:** Human Resources. **World Wide Web address:** http://www.orionauto.com. **Description:** A writer of nonstandard personal automobile insurance sold through independent agents nationwide. Founded in 1955. **Parent company:** Royal & Sun Alliance USA.

OROWHEAT
10750 SW Fifth Street, Beaverton OR 97005-3441. 503/643-5541. **Contact:** Personnel. **World Wide Web address:** http://www.oroweat.com. **Description:** A producer of breads and other baked goods. **NOTE:** Jobseekers should inquire about employment through the Beaverton Employment Office, 12901 SW Jenkins Road, Suite C, Beaverton OR 97005. **Parent company:** Bimbo Bakeries USA, the company's brand names include Arnold and Freihoffer's breads, Thomas' English muffins, Sahara pita breads, and Boboli pizza crusts. **Corporate headquarters location:** Fort Worth TX.

OWENS-BROCKWAY
9710 NE Glass Plant Road, Portland OR 97220. 503/254-7331. **Contact:** Human Resources. **Description:** Owens-Brockway manufactures a vast assortment of packaging items including glass containers, plastic containers, and corrugated packaging. Other products include Lily paper and plastic disposable products, Kimble laboratory ware, and Libbey glassware. **Corporate headquarters location:** Toledo OH. **International locations:** Worldwide. **Operations at this facility include:** This location manufactures glass bottles and jars.

PCC STRUCTURALS, INC.
4600 SE Harney Drive, Portland OR 97206. 503/777-3881. **Contact:** Personnel. **World Wide Web address:** http://www.pcc-structurals.com. **Description:** A manufacturer of critical tolerance investment casting for aerospace and medical applications. **Corporate headquarters location:** This location. **International locations:** France. **Operations at this facility include:** Manufacturing; Research and Development; Sales.

PSC, INC.
959 Terry Street, Eugene OR 97402-9150. 541/683-5700. **Toll-free phone**: 800/695-5700. **Fax:** 541/345-7140. **Contact:** Human Resources. **World Wide Web address:** http://www.pscnet.com. **Description:** Develops, manufactures, and markets bar code reading products including fixed-station decoders and portable data terminals, for the automatic identification and data collection market. The company also markets bar code input devices manufactured by others for use with the company's fixed-station decoders and portable data terminals. The company's products are used principally in point-of-sale and point-of-service applications in a wide variety of industries including retail, education, manufacturing, health care, and package delivery. **Positions advertised include:** Customer Account Specialist; Electric Engineer; Mechanical Engineer.

PW EAGLE
1550 Valley River Drive, Eugene OR 97440. 541/343-0200. **Fax:** 541/686-9248. **Contact:** Neil Chinn, Manager of Human Resources. **World Wide Web address:** http://www.pwpipe.com. **Description:** Manufactures PVC pipes.

PW POLY
800 David Eccles Road, Baker City OR 97814. 541/523-5445. **Contact:** Tim Lethlean, Supervisor. **World Wide Web address:** http://www.pwpoly.com. **Description:** This location is a manufacturer of polyethylene pipe products. **Parent company:** PW Eagle.

PACIFIC SHRIMP COMPANY
P.O. Box 1230, Newport OR 97365. 541/265-4215. **Contact:** Human Resources. **World Wide Web address:** http://www.pacseafood.com. **Description:** A crab and shrimp fishing and processing company. **NOTE:** Jobs are largely seasonal and available only through the Oregon State Employment Office. **Positions advertised include:** Fleet Manager; Seafood Buyer; Local Driver; Long Haul Driver; Sales Representative. **Corporate headquarters location:** This location.

PACIFIC SOFTWARE ASSOCIATES
5605 NE Elam Young Parkway, Hillsboro OR 97124. 800/764-8326. **Contact:** Human Resources. **World Wide Web address:** http://www.psateam.com. **Description:** A provider of business solutions including, hardware systems, disaster recovery options, application software, e-commerce business-to-business solutions.

PACIFIC UNIVERSITY
2043 College Way, Forest Grove OR 97116-1797. 503/357-6151. **Contact:** Human Resources. **World Wide Web address:** http://www.pacificu.edu. **Description:** A university offering graduate and undergraduate programs to approximately 2,000 students. Areas of study include liberal arts, education, and health care. Founded in 1849. **NOTE:** The faculty is hired through the Dean's Office, while administration is hired through Human Resources. **Positions advertised include:** Faculty Position-School of Occupational Therapy; Campus Public Safety Officer; Certified Medical Assistant; Resident Director-Student Life.

PACIFICARE
SECURE HORIZONS
20510 NW Evergreen Parkway, P.O. Box 3007, Hillsboro OR 97123-3007. 503/533-6300. **Fax:** 503/533-6666. **Recorded jobline:** 503/603-7133. **Contact:** Human Resources. **World Wide Web address:** http://www.pacificare.com. **Description:** PacifiCare is a regionally focused health care company with six HMOs operating in California, Oklahoma, Oregon, Texas, Florida, and Washington. Services include PPOs, life and health insurance, Medicare risk management program, dental care services, and pharmacy services. The company has a contract to provide health services to military personnel and their dependents in 19 states. **Operations at this facility include:** This location is a customer service center. Departments include membership services, claims, customer service, and information systems.

PACIFICORP
825 NE Multnomah Street, Mail Stop LCT 1800, Portland OR 97232. 503/813-5000. **Contact:** Human Resources. **E-mail address:** hrquestions@pacificorp.com. **World Wide Web address:** http://www.pacificorp.com. **Description:** PacificCorp is an electric utility company. **NOTE:** Pacificorp does not accept unsolicited resumes. **Positions advertised include:** Design Specialist; Plant Supervisor; Generation Clerk; Engineer; Financial Analyst; Intern. **Corporate headquarters location:** This location. **Operations at this facility include:** This location houses administrative offices.

PACTRUST
15350 SW Sequoia Parkway, Suite 300, Portland OR 97224. 503/624-6300. **Fax:** 503/624-7755. **Contact:** Human Resources Department. **World Wide Web address:** http://www.pactrust.com. **Description:** A real estate investment trust, founded in 1972, with both developed and un-developed properties in its portfolio.

PALO ALTO SOFTWARE, INC.
144 East 14th Avenue, Eugene OR 97401. 541/683-6162. **Fax:** 541/683-6250. **Contact:** Human Resources. **E-mail address:** info@palo-alto.com. **World Wide Web address:** http://www.pasware.com. **Description:** Develops business plan and marketing software including Business Plan Pro, Marketing Plus, and DecisionMaker. **International locations:** London UK, Ireland, Canada.

PAULSON INVESTMENT COMPANY
811 SW Naito Parkway, Suite 200, Portland OR 97204. 503/243-6000. **Fax:** 503/243-6018. **Contact:** Human Resources. **World Wide Web address:** http://www.paulsoninvestment.com. **Description:** Paulson Investment Company is a full-service brokerage firm engaged in the purchase and sale of securities, trading, market-making, and other investment banking activities. The company has independent branch offices in cities throughout the West, Midwest, and on the East Coast. **Corporate headquarters location:** This location. **Parent company:** Paulson Capital Corporation.

PECO MANUFACTURING INC.
SUNNE CONTROLS
P.O. Box 82189, Portland OR 97282-0189. 503/233-6401. **Fax:** 503/233-6407. **Physical address:** 4707 SE 17th Avenue, Portland OR 97202. **Contact:** Human Resources Manager. **World Wide Web address:** http://www.peco-sunne.com. **Description:** Manufactures thermostats and provides diecasting, injection molding, screw machining, finishing, and electromechanical assembly services.

PENDLETON WOOLEN MILLS INC.
220 NW Broadway, P.O. Box 3030, Portland OR 97208-3030. 503/226-4801. **Toll-free phone:** 800/522-9665. **Contact:** Gary Benson, Personnel Director. **World Wide Web address:** http://www.pendleton-usa.com. **Description:** Pendleton manufactures a variety of woolen products including blankets, scarves, and jackets. **Operations at this facility include:** This location is a fabric mill and the headquarters.

PENDLETON WOOLEN MILLS INC.
1307 SE Court Place, Pendleton OR 97801-3219. 541/276-6911.**Contact:** Personnel Department. **World Wide Web address:** http://www.pendleton-usa.com. **Description:** Pendleton manufactures a variety of woolen products including blankets, scarves, and jackets. **Operations at this facility include:** This location is a mill where wool is woven, carded, and spun.

PEPSI-COLA BOTTLING COMPANY
P.O. Box 10729, Eugene OR 97440. 541/687-0251. **Physical address:** 86776 McBay Highway, Eugene OR 97405. **Contact:** Human Resources. **World Wide Web address:** http://www.pepsico.com. **Description:** A bottling facility and a division of Pepsi-Cola Company. **Positions advertised include:** Human Resources Coordinator; Operations Resource. **Parent company:** PepsiCo, Inc. (Purchase NY) consists of Frito-Lay Company, Pepsi-Cola Company, Quaker Oats Company, and Tropicana Products, Inc.

PHILIPS PRODUCTS INC.
1620 Wilco Road, Stayton OR 97383. 503/769-6321. **Contact:** Human Resources. **World Wide Web address:** http://www.philipsproducts.com. **Description:** Manufactures vinyl and aluminum doors and windows for homes, manufactured homes, and recreational vehicles. **Corporate headquarters location:** Elkhart IN. **Parent company:** Tomkins Industries.

PHILLIPS & COMPANY SECURITIES, INC.
220 NW Second Avenue, Suite 950, Portland OR 97209. 503/224-0858. **Toll-free phone:** 888/667-4114. **Fax:** 503/224-8207. **Contact:** Executive Recruiter. **World Wide Web address:** http://www.phillipsandco.com. **Description:** A brokerage firm specializing in corporate and private client accounts. Founded in 1992. **NOTE:** Entry-level positions are offered. **Special programs:** Training. **Corporate headquarters location:** This location.

PHOENIX GOLD INTERNATIONAL, INC.
9300 North Decatur, Portland OR 97203. 503/286-9300. **Toll-free phone:** 800/950-1449. **Fax:** 503/978-3380. **Contact:** Human Resources. **World Wide Web address:** http://www.phoenixgold.com. **Description:** Designs, manufactures, and markets consumer electronics, accessories, and speakers for the car audio aftermarket, and for professional sound and custom audio/video home theater applications. The company also manufactures commercial/professional sound amplifiers. **NOTE:** Entry-level positions are offered. **Corporate headquarters location:** This location. **Subsidiaries include:** Carver Professional (also at this location) manufactures stereo amplifiers. **Listed on:** NASDAQ. **Stock exchange symbol:** PGLD.

PINKERTON'S INC.
15075 SW Koll Parkway, Portland OR 97204. 503/226-1233. **Contact:** Human Resources. **E-mail address:** hr@ci-pinkerton.com. **World Wide Web address:** http://www.pinkertons.com. **Description:** Operating for more than 130 years, Pinkerton's Inc. is one of the oldest and one of the largest nongovernmental security services organizations in the world today. The company's principal business is providing high-quality security, investigative, and consulting services to a multitude of commercial, industrial, institutional, governmental, and residential clients. Pinkerton's operates from 129 offices in the United States, Canada, and Great Britain. Major services include industrial and nuclear plant security, institutional security, commercial and residential building security, retail security, construction security, patrol and inspection services, community security, sports and special events services, K-9 patrol services, courier services, inventory services, investigation services, security consultation, and equipment evaluation. **Parent company:** Securitas.

PLANAR SYSTEMS, INC.
1195 NW Compton Drive, Beaverton OR 97006-1992. 503/748-1100. **Fax:** 503/748-1493. **Contact:** Director of Human Resources Department. **World Wide Web address:** http://www.planar.com. **Description:** A manufacturer of both high-performance flat-panel and CRT-based display products including electroluminescent and taut shadow mask CRT displays. Founded in 1983. **Special programs:** Internships. **Positions advertised include:** Supplier Quality Engineer; Process Engineer; Supply Chain Operations Manager; Process Technician; Regulatory Compliance Engineer. **Subsidiaries include:** Planar Advance, Inc.; Planar International. **Parent company:** Planar Systems, Inc. **Operations at this facility include:** Administration; Divisional Headquarters; Manufacturing; Research and Development; Sales; Service.

PLATT ELECTRIC SUPPLY INC.
10605 SW Allen Boulevard, Beaverton OR 97005. 503/641-6121. **Toll-free phone:** 800/2575288. **Contact:** Human Resources. **World Wide Web address:** http://www.platt.com. **Description:** Platt Electric Supply distributes electrical products for remodeling and construction projects. **Operations at this facility include:** This location houses administrative offices and a distribution center.

POORMAN-DOUGLAS CORPORATION
10300 SW Allen Boulevard, Beaverton OR 97005. 503/350-5800. **Contact:** Human Resources Department. **World Wide Web address:** http://www.poorman-douglas.com. **Description:** Provides data processing services for other businesses.

POPE & TALBOT INC.
1500 SW First Street, Suite 200, Portland OR 97201. 503/228-9161. **Recorded jobline:** 503/220-5530. **Contact:** Beth Hardman, Director of Personnel. **World Wide Web address:** http://www.poptal.com. **Description:** A diversified manufacturer of wood and related products. Wood products include lumber, wood chips, and pulp sold to paper producers, international trading firms, forest product firms, and lumber wholesalers. Paper products include tissue products, newsprint, and disposable diapers, which are marketed to supermarkets and related stores and distribution companies. Pope & Talbot also acts as a pulp chip broker. **NOTE:** Pope & Talbot lists positions through the Oregon State Department of Employment, and the *Oregonian*. **Positions**

advertised include: Traffic/Customs/Documents Manager. **Other area locations:** Halsey OR. **Other U.S. locations:** Eau Claire WI; Ladysmith WI.

PORTLAND COMMUNITY COLLEGE
705 N Killingsworth, Student Services Building, 3rd Floor,, Portland OR 97280-0990. 503/978-5857. **Fax:** 503/286-0410. **Recorded jobline:** 503/978-5858. **Contact:** Human Resources. **E-mail address:** pccjobs@pcc.edu. **World Wide Web address:** http://www.pcc.edu. **Description:** A community college with an enrollment of approximately 8,000 full-time students. **Positions advertised include:** Accounting Clerk; Division Assistant, English and Modern Languages; Division Dean, Business and Humanities; Instructor/Clinic Dentist, Dental Hygiene; Manager, Campus Computer and Facilities Resources; Project Assistant; Senior Accountant.

PORTLAND GENERAL ELECTRIC COMPANY
121 SW Salmon Street, Portland OR 97204. 503/464-8000. **Fax:** 503/464-2676. **Recorded jobline:** 888/346-3291. **Contact:** Human Resources. **World Wide Web address:** http://www.portlandgeneral.com. **Description:** Provides electric power services to area customers. **NOTE:** Entry-level positions are offered. **Positions advertised include:** Human Resources Consultant. **Special programs:** Training; Summer Jobs. **Corporate headquarters location:** This location. **Parent company:** Enron Corporation. **Operations at this facility include:** Administration; Divisional Headquarters; Research and Development; Sales; Service. **Listed on:** New York Stock Exchange. **Stock exchange symbol:** ENE.

THE PORTLAND GROUP, INC. (PGI)
9150 SW Pioneer Court, Wilsonville OR 97070. 503/682-2806. **Fax:** 503/682-2637. **Contact:** Personnel. **World Wide Web address:** http://www.pgroup.com. **Description:** Develops compilers and software development tools for parallel computing. **Corporate headquarters location:** This location. **Parent company:** ST Microelectronics.

PORTLAND MARRIOTT HOTEL DOWNTOWN
1401 SW Naito Parkway, Portland OR 97201. 503/226-7600. **Recorded jobline:** 503/499-6334. **Contact:** Jim Coull, Director of Human Resources. **World Wide Web address:** http://www.marriott.com. **Description:** A 503-room, full-service hotel that offers a restaurant and lounge, a fitness club, 18 meeting rooms, and business services. **Positions advertised include:** Guest Service Agent; Host/Cashier. **Corporate headquarters location:** Washington DC.

PORTLAND TEACHERS CREDIT UNION
P.O. Box 3750, Portland OR 97208-3750. 503/228-7077. **Toll-free phone:** 800/527-3932. **Contact:** Human Resources. **World Wide Web address:** http://www.ptcu.com. **Description:** A credit union for the employees of schools and nonprofit educational organizations in the Clackamas, Columbia, Multnomah, Washington, and Yamhill counties. This is a nonprofit company. Founded in 1932.

PORTLAND TRAILBLAZERS BASKETBALL CLUB
One Center Court, Suite 200, Portland OR 97227. 503/234-9291. **Contact:** Human Resources. **E-mail address:** jobs@rosequarter.com. **World Wide Web address:** http://www.rosequarter.com. **Description:** The administrative offices of the Portland Trailblazers, a professional basketball team playing in the National Basketball Association (NBA). **Positions advertised include:** Finance; Internships.

POZZI WINDOW COMPANY
62845 Boyd Acres Road, Bend OR 97701. 541/382-4411. **Contact:** Human Resources. **World Wide Web address:** http://www.jeld-wen.com. **Description:** Manufactures wooden window frames. Founded in 1968. **Corporate headquarters location:** Klamath Falls OR. **Parent company:** Jeld-Wen.

PRECISION INTERCONNECT
10025 SW Freeman Court, Wilsonville OR 97070. 503/620-9400. **Fax:** 503/685-9300. **Contact:** Human Resources. **World Wide Web address:** http://www.precisionint.com. **Description:** Manufactures cables and cable assemblies for medical, test, and measurement equipment. Founded in 1972. **Positions advertised include:** Sales Engineer; Safety and Environmental Coordinator. **Parent company:** Tyco.

PRICEWATERHOUSECOOPERS
1300 SW Fifth Avenue, Suite 3100, Portland OR 97201. 971/544-4000. **Fax:** 971/544-4100. **Contact:** Personnel. **World Wide Web address:** http://www.pricewaterhousecoopers.com. **Description:** One of the largest certified public accounting firms in the world. PricewaterhouseCoopers provides public accounting, business advisory, management consulting, and taxation services. **Positions advertised include:** Senior Manager; State Tax Income Franchise Generalist; Middle Market Senior Associate; Consumer Products Tax Senior Associate; Middle Market Associate; Senior Associate; Systems Assurance Senior. **Corporate headquarters location:** New York NY. **Other U.S. locations:** Nationwide. **International locations:** Worldwide.

PROVIDENCE MEDFORD MEDICAL CENTER
1111 Crater Lake Avenue, Medford OR 97504. 541/732-5078. **Contact:** Director of Human Resources. **World Wide Web address:** http://www.providence.org/medford. **Description:** A 168-bed general hospital. **NOTE:** See website for monthly recruiting events. **Positions advertised include:** Accounting Clerk; Central Service Supply Technician; Emergency Room Technician; Central Point Medical Assistant; Medical Lab Technologist. **Corporate headquarters location:** Seattle WA. **Other U.S. locations:** AL; CA. **Parent company:** Sisters of Providence Health System.

PROVIDENCE MILWAUKIE HOSPITAL
10150 SE 32nd Avenue, Milwaukie OR 97222. 503/652-8300. **Recorded jobline:** 503/513-8488. **Contact:** Human Resources Director. **World Wide Web address:** http://www.providence.org. **Description:** A 56-bed hospital. **NOTE:** It is recommended that employment matters are handled through the website, or the central location at 1235 NE 47th Street, 503/215-5770. **Corporate headquarters location:** Seattle WA. **Parent company:** Providence Health System.

PROVIDENCE PORTLAND MEDICAL CENTER
4805 NE Glisan Street, Portland OR 97213. 503/215-1111. **Recorded jobline:** 503/215-6292. **Contact:** Human Resources. **World Wide Web address:** http://www.providence.org. **Description:** A 483-bed medical center. **Positions advertised include:** Acute Care Manager; Purchasing Agent; Business Analyst; Bilingual Medical Assistant; Care Manager; Cashier; Cleaning Attendant; Certified Nurses Aide; Collections Representative; Culinary Assistant. **Corporate headquarters location:** Seattle WA. **Parent company:** Providence Health System.

THE PRUDENTIAL NORTHWEST PROPERTIES
14945 SW Sequoia Parkway, Suite 150, Portland OR 97224. 503/646-7826. **Contact:** Human Resources. **E-mail address:** careers@pru-nw.com. **World Wide Web address:** http://www.pru-nw.com. **Description:** Provides a wide range of real estate services to corporate and residential clients. **Corporate headquarters location:** This location.

PURDY CORPORATION
13201 North Lumbard Street, Portland OR 97203-6410. 503/286-8217. **Fax:** 503/286-5336. **Contact:** Human Resources. **E-mail address:** info@purdycorp.com. **World Wide Web address:** http://www.purdycorp.com. **Description:** Manufactures handcrafted painting tools, brushes, rollers, and accessories. **Corporate headquarters location:** This location. **International locations:** United Kingdom, Canada, Australia.

QUEST DIAGNOSTICS INCORPORATED
6600 SW Hampton Street, Portland OR 97223. 503/306-1010. **Toll-free phone:** 800/222-7941. **Fax:** 503/306-1540. **Contact:** Janet Napoleon, Director Human Resources. **World Wide Web address:** http://www.questdiagnostics.com. **Description:** Quest Diagnostics is one of the largest clinical laboratories in North America, providing a broad range of clinical laboratory services to health care clients that include physicians, hospitals, clinics, dialysis centers, pharmaceutical companies, and corporations. The company offers and performs tests on blood, urine, and other bodily fluids and tissues to provide information for health and well-being. **Positions advertised include:** Medical Transcriptionist; Phlebotomy Services Representative. **Corporate headquarters location:** Teterboro NJ. **Other U.S. locations:** Nationwide. **Operations at this facility include:** This location is a diagnostic laboratory performing clinical testing for clients throughout the Pacific Northwest.

QWEST COMMUNICATIONS
2201 Lloyd Center, Portland OR 97232. 503/281-3362. **Toll-free phone:** 800/603-6000. **Contact:** Personnel. **E-mail address:** staffing@qwest.com. **World Wide Web address:** http://www.qwest.com. **Description:** A long-distance telecommunications carrier that provides a broad array of domestic and international voice, data, and Internet services to commercial and residential customers. Qwest Communications provides service to customers through its network of digital fiber-optic facilities. **Corporate headquarters location:** Denver CO. **NOTE:** See the website for upcoming recruiting events. **Listed on:** New York Stock Exchange. **Stock exchange symbol:** Q.

RSG FOREST PRODUCTS INC.
28890 S Highway 213, P.O. Box 169, Molalla OR 97038. 503/829-7200. **Fax:** 503/829-7320. **Contact:** Human Resources. **Description:** RSG Forest Products produces paper and wood products. **Operations at this facility include:** This location is a sawmill.

RADISYS CORPORATION
5445 NE Dawson Creek Drive, Hillsboro OR 97124. 503/615-1100. **Toll-free phone:** 800/950-0044. **Fax:** 503/615-1115. **Contact:** Personnel. **E-mail address:** info@radisys.com. **World Wide Web address:** http://www.radisys.com. **Description:** Designs and manufactures embedded computer technology used by OEMs in the manufacturing automation, telecommunications, medical devices, transportation, test and measurement, and retail automation industries. RadiSys offers a broad range of embedded computer subsystems, board-level modules, and chip-level products at varying levels of customization from standard products to full custom solutions. **Positions advertised include:** PC Board Designer; Mechanical Engineer; Senior Financial Reporting Analyst. **Corporate headquarters location:** This location. **Listed on:** NASDAQ. **Stock exchange symbol:** RSYS.

REED COLLEGE
3203 SE Woodstock Boulevard, Portland OR 97202-8199. 503/771-1112. **Fax:** 503/777-7769. **Recorded jobline:** 503/777-7706. **Contact:** Human Resources. **E-mail address:** mary.sullivan@reed.edu. **World Wide Web address:** http://www.reed.edu. **Description:** A liberal arts college with an enrollment of approximately 1,350 students. **Positions advertised include:** Assistant Director of the Annual Fund; Research Associate, Chemistry.

RENTRAK CORPORATION
P.O. Box 18888, Portland OR 97218. 503/284-7581. **Physical address:** One Airport Center, 7700 NE Ambassador Place, 3rd Floor, Portland OR 97220. **Fax:** 503/282-9017. **Contact:** Human Resources Department. **E-mail address:** gti@rentrak.com. **World Wide Web address:** http://www.rentrak.com. **Description:** A video distributor. **NOTE:** Online applications preferred in Adobe Acrobat format, phone calls are discouraged. **Positions advertised include:** Programmer Analyst. **Corporate headquarters location:** This location.

RESERS FINE FOODS, INC.
P.O. Box 8, Beaverton OR 97075-0008. 503/643-6431. **Physical address:** 15570 SW Jenkins Road, Beaverton OR 97006. **Toll-free:** 800/333-6431. **Fax:** 503/646-9233. **Recorded jobline:** 503/526-8399. **Contact:** Director of Human Resources. **World Wide Web address:** http://www.resers.com. **Description:** A food processor specializing in salads, desserts, dips, meat, and Mexican foods. **Positions advertised include:** Quality Assurance Lab Technician, Director of Purchasing. **Special programs:** Internships. **Corporate headquarters location:** This location. **Other U.S. locations:** Nationwide. **Operations at this facility include:** Administration; Manufacturing; Sales; Service.

RESIDENCE INN PORTLAND SOUTH
15200 SW Bangy Road, Lake Oswego OR 97035. 503/684-2603. **Contact:** General Manager. **World Wide Web address:** http://www.residenceinn.com. **Description:** A 112-room hotel that offers two conference rooms, dinner delivery services, and business services. **Corporate headquarters location:** Washington DC. **Parent company:** Marriott International has nearly 4,200 units, with operations and franchises in 50 states and 25 countries. The company operates lodging facilities and is a franchiser under four separate brand names, each serving a part of the lodging market: Marriott Hotels, Resorts, and Suites (full-service), Courtyard Inn (moderate price), Residence Inn (extended stay), and Fairfield Inn (economy). The company also develops and operates Marriott Ownership Resorts (vacation timesharing).

RESIDENCE INN PORTLAND WEST
18855 NW Tanasbourne Drive, Hillsboro OR 97124. 503/531-3200. **Contact:** General Manager. **World Wide Web address:** http://www.residenceinn.com. **Description:** A 122-room hotel that offers two conference rooms, exercise facilities, and business services. **Corporate headquarters location:** Washington DC. **Parent company:** Marriott International has nearly 4,200 units, with operations and franchises in 50 states and 25 countries. The company operates lodging facilities and is the franchiser under four separate brand names, each serving a part of the lodging market: Marriott Hotels, Resorts, and Suites (full-service), Courtyard Inn (moderate price), Residence Inn (extended stay), and Fairfield Inn (economy). The company also develops and operates Marriott Ownership Resorts (vacation timesharing).

THE RIVERPLACE HOTEL
1510 SW Harbor Way, Portland OR 97201. 503/228-3233. **Fax:** 503/295-6190. **Contact:** Personnel. **World Wide Web address:** http://www.riverplacehotel.com. **Description:** A European-style hotel and waterfront resort offering 84 rooms, banquet and conference facilities, a fitness center, and several dining areas. **Parent company:** WestCoast Hotels.

THE KEN ROBERTS COMPANY
333 SW Fifth Street, Grants Pass OR 97526. 541/955-2700. **Fax:** 541/955-2730. **Contact:** Human Resources. **World Wide Web address:** http://www.kenroberts.net. **Description:** Distributes materials to educate individuals about the commodities/stock markets. **NOTE:** Entry-level positions are offered. **Office hours:** Monday - Friday, 8:30 a.m. - 5:00 p.m.

ROCKEY HILL & KNOWLTON
700 NE Multnomah, Suite 975, Portland OR 97232. 503/248-9468. **Fax:** 503/274-7689. **Contact:** Human Resources. **World Wide Web address:** http://www.rockey-seattle.com **Description:** A full-service public relations agency. **Special programs:** Internships. **Corporate headquarters location:** Seattle WA.

RODGERS INSTRUMENTS LLC
1300 NE 25th Avenue, Hillsboro OR 97124. 503/648-4181. **Fax:** 503/681-6508. **Contact:** Personnel. **E-mail address:** recruiting@rodgers.rain.com. **World Wide Web address:** http://www.rodgersinstruments.com. **Description:** Manufactures pipe and digital organs. **Positions advertised include:** Finishing Technician; Sales Agent; Dealer Salesperson.

ROGUE WAVE SOFTWARE
815 NW Ninth Street, Suite L145, Corvallis OR 97330. 541/754-4096. **Fax:** 541/753-1912. **Contact:** Human Resources. **E-mail address:** hr@roguewave.com. **World Wide Web address:** http://www.roguewave.com. **Description:** Develops C++ and Java reusable cross-platform software and tools. **NOTE:** Entry-level positions and part-time jobs are offered. **Corporate headquarters location:** Boulder CO. **Other U.S. locations:** Nationwide. **International locations:** Worldwide.

ROSBORO LUMBER COMPANY
P.O. Box 20, Springfield OR 97477. 541/746-8411. **Fax:** 541/726-8919. **Contact:** Personnel Director. **E-mail address:** info@rosboro.com. **World Wide Web address:** http://www.rosboro.com. **Description:** An integrated lumber company that operates a dimension mill, plywood plant, and stud mill.

ROSEBURG FOREST PRODUCTS COMPANY
P.O. Box 1088, Roseburg OR 97470. 541/679-3311. **Toll-free phone:** 800/245-1115. **Fax:** 541/679-9543. **Contact:** Personnel Manager. **World Wide Web address:** http://www.rfpco.com. **Description:** Manufactures softwood, plywood, particleboard, vinyl laminates, shelving, and hardwood plywood using Douglas fir, pine, and hemlock wood. **Corporate headquarters location:** This location.

ROSEN AVIATION DISPLAYS
1020 Owen Loop South, Eugene OR 97402. 541/434-4510. **Fax:** 541/342-4912. **Contact:** Personnel. **E-mail:** sales@rosenaviation.com. **World Wide Web address:** http://www.rosenaviation.com. **Description:** Manufactures and markets flat-panel display (FPD) products for the automotive, hospitality, rail, and consumer markets. Founded in 1980. **Corporate headquarters location:** This location.

ROSS ISLAND SAND & GRAVEL COMPANY
P.O. Box 82249, Portland OR 97282-0249. 503/239-5504. **Fax:** 503/235-1350. **Contact:** Human Resources. **Description:** A producer of premixed concrete and related building and construction products including mortar, sand, and crushed rock.

ROTH I.G.A. FOODLINERS
1130 Wallace Road NW, Salem OR 97304. 503/393-9427. **Contact:** Kathy Moreland, Human Resources. **World Wide Web address:** http://www.iga.com. **Description:** Operates an area retail grocery chain with a number of local outlets. **Corporate headquarters location:** Salem OR. **Other U.S. locations:** Nationwide.

SABROSO COMPANY
P.O. Box 4310, Medford OR 97501. 541/772-5653. **Fax:** 541/779-3572. **Contact:** Human Resources. **World Wide Web address:** http://www.sabroso.com. **Description:** Sabroso is a world leader in sourcing, producing and distributing quality fruit products for the food manufacturing and foodservice industries. **Positions advertised include:** Food Technologist; Product Developer; Maintenance Lead; Administrative Assistant. **Corporate headquarters location:** This location.

SMC CORPORATION
SAFARI MOTOR COACHES
P.O. Box 5639, Bend OR 97708. 541/317-3638. **Physical address:** 20545 Murray Road, Bend OR 97701. **Fax:** 541/317-3677. **Contact:** Candy Barnett, Human Resources Department. **World Wide Web address:** http://www.smccorporation.com. **Description:** One of the largest designers, manufacturers, and marketers of high-line, Class A motor coaches, which incorporate living, dining, sleeping, and bathing facilities on a specially designed motor vehicle chassis. **Corporate headquarters location:** This location. **International locations:** Barbados. **Subsidiaries include:** Beaver Motor Coaches, Inc. (Bend OR) manufactures luxury motor coaches; Composite Technologies, Inc. (Hines OR) manufactures fiberglass; Electronic Design & Assembly, Inc. (Bend OR) manufactures electronic systems for motor coaches; Harney County Operations, Inc. (Hines OR) manufactures Class C motor coaches; Magnum Manufacturing, Inc. (Harrisburg OR) manufactures RV chassis; SMC Midwest, Inc. (Minneapolis KS) manufactures Honorbuilt motor homes; Safari Motor Coaches (also at this location, http://www.safarimotorcoaches.com) manufactures luxury motor coaches. **Listed on:** NASDAQ. **Stock exchange symbol:** SMCC.

SACRED HEART MEDICAL CENTER
1255 Hilyard Street, Eugene OR 97401. 541/686-7300. **Recorded jobline:** 541/686-6960. **Contact:** Human Resources. **World Wide Web address:** http://www.peacehealth.org. **Description:** A hospital with approximately 432 beds. **NOTE:** Jobseekers are encouraged to apply via the Website. **Positions advertised include:** Charge Nurse; Data Analyst; Diagnostic Technician; Database Systems Analyst; Emergency Room Technician; Licensed Practical Nurse; Patient Access Specialist; Pharmacist; Physical Therapist; Registered Nurse; Surgical Technician. **Parent company:** Peace Health.

SAFETY-KLEEN CORPORATION
16540 SE 130th Avenue, Clackamas OR 97015. 503/655-5798. **Fax:** 503/655-3952. **Contact:** Human Resources. **E-mail address:** info@safety-kleen. **World Wide Web address:** http://www.safety-kleen.com. **Description:** An environmental services company providing the collection, recycling, and disposal of both hazardous and nonhazardous waste. **Corporate headquarters location:** Plano TX.

SAFETY-KLEEN CORPORATION
550 Shelley Street, Suite A, Springfield OR 97477. 541/747-5804. **Fax:** 541/747-5293. **Contact:** Branch Manager. **World Wide Web address:** http://www.safety-kleen.com. **Description:** Safety-Kleen Corporation is an environmental services company providing the collection, recycling, and disposal of both hazardous and nonhazardous waste. **Operations at this facility include:** This location is a transfer station that collects hazardous waste and packages it for its final destination. **Corporate headquarters location:** Plano TX.

SAFEWAY STORES, INC.
P.O. Box 523, Clackamas OR 97015. 503/656-1461. **Recorded jobline:** 503/657-6400. **Contact:** Human Resources. **World Wide Web address:** http://www.safeway.com. **Description:** Safeway Stores, Inc. is one of the world's largest food retailers. The company operates approximately 1,665 stores in the western, Rocky Mountain, southwestern, and mid-Atlantic regions of the United States and in western Canada. In support of its stores, the company has an extensive network of distribution, manufacturing, and food processing facilities. Safeway also holds a 49 percent interest in Casa Ley, S.A. de C.V., which operates food/variety, clothing, and wholesale outlet stores in western Mexico. **Corporate headquarters location:** Pleasanton CA. **Operations at this facility include:** One location of the retail chain that also produces baked goods and dairy products.

ST. CHARLES MEDICAL CENTER
2500 NE Neff Road, Bend OR 97701. 541/388-7770. **Contact:** Human Resources. **E-mail address:** scmc@scmc.org. **World Wide Web address:** http://www.scmc.org. **Description:** A 181-bed community hospital offering general medical care. **Positions advertised include:** RN; Assistant Unit Manager; Care Associate; Dietician; Registered Medical Technologist; Pharmacist; Occupational Therapist; Physical Therapist; Accounting Clerk; Admitting Representative; PC Support Specialist; Patient Account Representative; Refund Analyst; Behavioral Health Clerk; Central Processing Technician; Preparation Cook; Team Leader; Application Analyst; Laboratory Manager; Purchasing Coordinator. **Number of employees at this location:** 1,200.

ST. VINCENT DEPAUL REHABILITATION SERVICE
4660 Portland Road NE, Suite 108, NE, Salem OR 97305. 503/856-9563. **Toll-free phone:** 800/755-5880. **Fax:** 503/856-9848. **Contact:** Human Resources Department. **World Wide Web address:** http://www.stvincentdepaul.org. **Description:** Provides vocational training to disabled individuals. The nonprofit agency also offers job placement services. **Positions advertised include:** Custodian; Certified Flagger. **Corporate headquarters location:** Portland OR. **Other area locations:** Corvallis OR; Hillsboro OR; Springfield OR.

SALEM HOSPITAL
P.O. Box 14001, Salem OR 97309. 503/561-5200. **Toll-free phone:** 800/825-5199. **Physical address:** 665 Winter Street SE, Salem OR 97301. **Contact:** Employment Office. **E-mail address:** human.resources@salemhospital.org. **World Wide Web address:** http://www.salemhospital.org. **Description:** A nonprofit hospital with approximately 454 beds. **Positions advertised include:** RN; Cancer Registrar; Director of Maternal Child Health; Licensed Physical Therapy Assistant; Nuclear Medical Technician; Occupational Therapist; Radiology Technician; Clerk; Security Officer; Transcriptionist; Maintenance Helper.

SALEM-KEIZER SCHOOL DISTRICT
2450 Lancaster Drive NE, Suite 100, Salem OR 97305. 503/399-3061. **Contact:** Human Resources. **World Wide Web address:** http://www.salkeiz.k12.or.us. **Description:** A public school district comprised of 38 elementary schools, 9 middle schools, and 5 high schools. **Positions advertised include:** Clerical Specialist; Accounting Clerk; Special Programs Instructional Assistant; Head Structural Worker; Employee Relations Director.

SALISHAN LODGE INC.
7760 Highway 101, Gleneden Beach OR 97388. 541/764-2371. **Contact:** Human Resources. **World Wide Web address:** http://www.salishan.com. **Description:** A resort hotel offering three restaurants, a wine cellar, an 18-hole golf course, a driving range, guest activities, exercise facilities, banquet and conference rooms, and business services. **NOTE:** Staffing is reduced during the off-season to approximately 280. **Corporate headquarters location:** Portland OR. **Parent company:** Westin.

THE SALVATION ARMY
1785 NE Sandy Boulevard, Portland OR 97232. 503/234-0825. **Contact:** Human Resources. **World Wide Web address:** http://www.salvationarmy.org. **Description:** A nonprofit organization providing several service programs including day-care centers, programs for people with disabilities, substance abuse programs and tutoring for at-risk students. The Salvation Army targets its programs to assist alcoholics, battered women, drug addicts, the elderly, the homeless, people with AIDS, prison inmates, teenagers, and the unemployed.

SAPA INC.
7933 NE 21st Avenue, Portland OR 97211. 503/972-1404. **Fax:** 503/972-1459. **Contact:** Pam Muehleck, Human Resources Manager. **E-mail address:** pam.muehleck@sapagroup.com. **World Wide Web address:** http://www.sapagroup.com. **Description:** Manufactures anodized and extruded aluminum products. Founded in 1964. **Parent company:** Sapa Group. **International locations:** Worldwide.

SANIPAC
P.O. Box 10928, Eugene OR 97440. 541/736-3600. **Physical Address:** 1650 Glenwood Boulevard, Eugene OR 97403. **Fax:** 541/736-3650. **Contact:** Human Resources. **E-mail address:** info@sanipac.com. **World Wide Web address:** http://www.sanipac.com. **Description:** Collects and recycles garbage.

SCA PACKAGING
3550 NW 215th Avenue, Hillsboro OR 97124. 503/439-6060. **Contact:** Human Resources. **E-mail address:** recruitment@sca.com. **World Wide Web address:** http://www.sca.com. **Description:** A manufacturer of packaging materials such as corrugated cardboard and Styrofoam. **Corporate headquarters location:** New Brighton PA.

SCENIC FRUIT COMPANY
7510 SE Altman Road, Gresham OR 97080. 503/663-3434. **Toll-free phone:** 800/554-5578. **Fax:** 503/663-7095. **Contact:** Human Resources. **World Wide Web address:** http://www.scenicfruit.com. **Description:** A berry processing and packing plant. **NOTE:** Work is largely seasonal with staffing reduced to approximately 15 during the winter. **Corporate headquarters location:** This location.

SCHWABE, WILLIAMSON & WYATT, PC
1211 SW Fifth Avenue, Parkwest Center, Suite 1600-1900, Portland OR 97204. 503/222-9981. **Contact:** Karen Kervin, Director of Legal Recruiting. **E-mail address:** kkervin@schwabe.com. **World Wide Web address:** http://www.schwabe.com. **Description:** A law firm operating through two departments: Transactions and Litigation. The Transactions Department provides a wide range of legal services to area businesses, specializing in general business, corporate tax, energy, environment, natural resources, and real estate. The Litigation Department specializes in admiralty, commercial litigation, intellectual property, product liability, workers' compensation, and insurance. Founded in 1892. **Positions advertised include:** Patent Attorney; Litigation Associate; Business/Corporate Paralegal. **Corporate headquarters location:** This location. **Other U.S. locations:** Seattle WA; Vancouver WA.

SENTROL, INC.
12345 SW Leveton Drive, Tualatin OR 97062. 503/692-4052. **Fax:** 503/691-7569. **Contact:** Human Resources. **World Wide Web address:** http://www.sentrol.com. **Description:** Manufactures security devices including control panels, glassbreak sensors, magnetic contacts, and space detection. **Special programs:** Internships. **Corporate headquarters location:** This location. **Other U.S. locations:** Hickory NC. **Parent company:** GE Corporation.

SHRINER'S HOSPITAL
3101 SW Sam Jackson Park Road, Portland OR 97201. 503/241-5090. **Fax:** 503/221-3475. **Recorded jobline:** 503/221-3459. **Contact:** Human Resources. **World Wide Web address:** http://www.shrinershq.org/shc/portland/. **Description:** A children's and general care hospital with approximately 40 beds. **Positions advertised include:** Maintenance Technician; Registered Nurse; House Supervisor; Care Coordinator. **Corporate headquarters location:** Tampa FL.

SIEMENS ENERGY & AUTOMATION, INC.
6427 NE 59th Place, Portland OR 97218. 503/288-0101. **Contact:** Human Resources. **World Wide Web address:** http://www.sea.siemens.com. **Description:** Manufactures and markets a broad range of primarily large-scale electrical products including a variety of circuit protection devices that are sold to electronics OEMs throughout the country. The company also produces circuit-breaker load centers, metering panels, and related accessories. These products are sold primarily to electric utilities and industrial manufacturers. **Positions advertised include:** Licensed Field Service Technician; Maintenance Mechanic; Planner Scheduler. **Corporate headquarters location:** Alpharetta GA. **Parent company:** Siemens Corporation. **Listed on:** New York Stock Exchange. **Stock exchange symbol:** SI.

SILVERCREST WESTERN HOMES CORPORATION
P.O. Box 565, Woodburn OR 97071. 503/981-8808. **Contact:** Human Resources. **World Wide Web address:** http://www.silvercrest.com. **Description:** A manufacturer of mobile homes. **Corporate headquarters location:** Corona CA. **Other U.S. locations:** TX. **Parent company:** Champion Enterprises, Inc. **Listed on:** New York Stock Exchange. **Stock exchange symbol:** CHB.

SIMPLEXGRINNELL
6305 SW Rosewood Street, Lake Oswego OR 97035. 503/683-9000. **Contact:** Human Resources. **World Wide Web address:** http://www.simplexgrinnell.com. **Description:** Manufactures and installs fire alarm, sprinkler, and detection systems. Founded in 1850. **Positions advertised include:** Administrative; Hard Analysis; Manufacturing; Sales; System Programming; Corporate Departments. **Corporate headquarters location:** Exeter NH. **Other U.S. locations:** Nationwide. **International locations:** Worldwide. **Parent company:** Tyco International Ltd.

J.R. SIMPLOT
P.O. Box 850, Hermiston OR 97838. 541/567-9733. **Contact:** Linda Stenovich, Personnel Director. **World Wide Web address:** http://www.simplot.com. **Description:** Processes and markets a variety of frozen foods including potatoes, fruits, and vegetables. The company specializes in potato products and french fries with brand names including Spudsters, Classic Potatoes, Quick N Easy, and Conquest. **Positions advertised include:** Process Specialist; Process Specialist; Boiler/Refrigeration Supervisor; Quality Assurance Supervisor. **International locations:** Worldwide.

SKYLINE HOMES
550 Booth Bend Road, McMinnville OR 971280388. 503/472-3181. **Fax:** 503/472-6463. **Contact:** Human Resources. **E-mail address:** hresources@skylinecorp.com. **World Wide Web address:** http://www.skylinecorp.com. **Description:** Manufactures prefabricated homes. **NOTE:** Human Resources address: P.O. Box 743, Elkhart IN 46515-0743. **Positions advertised include:** Production Worker. **Corporate headquarters location:** Elkhart IN. **Parent company:** Skyline. **Number of employees at this location:** 200.

SOW ORGANIC SEED
P.O. Box 527, Williams OR 97544. **Toll-free phone:** 888/709-7333. **Contact:** Human Resources. **E-mail address:** organic@organicseed.com. **World Wide Web address:** http://www.organicseed.com. **Description:** Provides certified organic, open-pollinated, non-hybrid, non-GMO garden seeds along with credible scientific growing information.

SMITH FROZEN FOODS INC.
P.O. Box 68, Weston OR 97886. 541/566-3515. **Contact:** Personnel Manager. **World Wide Web address:** http://www.smithfrozenfoods.com. **Description:** A processor of corn, peas, and carrots. **NOTE:** Work here is largely seasonal and staffing is cut to 300 in the winter. **Corporate headquarters location:** Pendleton OR. **Number of employees at this location:** 1,500.

SOLOFLEX INC.
570 NE 53rd Avenue, Hillsboro OR 97124. 503/640-8891. **Fax:** 503/648-0864. **Contact:** Donna Compton, Human Resources Department. **World Wide Web address:** http://www.soloflex.com. **Description:** Manufactures home exercise equipment. **Corporate headquarters location:** This location.

SOUTH COAST LUMBER COMPANY
17345 Carpenterville Road, P.O. Box 670, Brookings OR 97415. 541/469-2136. **Contact:** Human Resources **Description:** Manufactures and markets wood products to domestic and export wholesalers. The company's products include chips, lumber, and veneer. **NOTE:** This company hires through the Oregon State Employment Office. **Corporate headquarters location:** This location.

SPARTECH CORPORATION
4150 Riverside Drive, McMinnville OR 97128. 503/472-6191. **Contact:** Human Resources. **World Wide Web address:** http://www.spartech.com. **Description:** Manufactures various types of plastic sheets. **Corporate headquarters location:** Clayton MO.

SPIRIT MOUNTAIN CASINO
P.O. Box 39, Grand Ronde OR 97347. 503/879-2350. **Toll-free phone:** 800/760-7977. **Fax:** 503/879-2486. **Physical address:** 27100 SW Salmon River Highway, Grand Ronde OR 97396. **Contact:** Human Resources. **World Wide Web address:** http://www.spirit-mountain.com. **Description:** A gaming facility that offers a 100-room lodge, casino gambling, live entertainment, and four restaurants. **Positions advertised include:** Cage Cashier; Lead Main Kitchen Cook; Executive Chef; Administrative Assistant; Bus Person; Wait Staff Member; Hostess; Cashier; Shift Lead; Inventory Systems Administrator; Prep Cook; Valet Attendant; Dealer. **Parent company:** Spirit Mountain Gaming Inc.

SPRINGFIELD SCHOOL DISTRICT
525 Mill Street, Springfield OR 97477. 541/747-3331. **Contact:** Human Resources. **World Wide Web address:** http://www.sps.lane.edu. **Description:** A state school district comprised of 16 elementary schools, 5 middle schools, 2 high schools, and an alternative education program. **Positions advertised include:** High School Principal; School Psychologist; Accountant; Head Men's Basketball Coach; Head Women's Basketball Coach; Head Wrestling Coach. **Number of employees at this location:** 1,500.

SPRINGFIELD UTILITY BOARD
223 A Street, Suite H, Springfield OR 97477. 541/726-2398. **Contact:** Human Resources. **World Wide Web address:** http://www.subutil.com. **Description:** Provides electric and water services to area customers.

THE STANDARD
1100 SW Sixth Avenue, Portland OR 97204-1093. 503/321-7000. **Fax:** 503/321-6776. **Recorded jobline:** 503/321-OPEN. **Contact:** Human Resources. **World Wide Web address:** http://www.standard.com. **Description:** Provides individual and group insurance and retirement plan services nationwide. **Positions advertised include:** Data Architect; Director of IT Training; Electronic Commerce Administrator; Project Manager; Vice President of Sales and Marketing; Actuarial Assistant; Community Relations Specialist; Nurse Case Manager; Staff Assistant. **Corporate headquarters location:** This location.

STANLEY HYDRAULIC TOOLS
3810 SE Naef Road, Milwaukie OR 97267-5623. 503/659-5660. **Fax:** 503/652-1780. **Contact:** Human Resources Manager. **World Wide Web address:** http://www.stanleyworks.com. **Description:** Manufactures industrial, hydraulic tools used for underwater drilling, posthole digging, and tree trimming. **Corporate headquarters location:** New Britain CT.

STARBUCKS COFFEE
7737 SW Capitol Highway, Portland OR 97219. 503/245-1961. **Contact:** Manager. **World Wide Web address:** http://www.starbucks.com. **Description:** Starbucks Coffee sells whole-bean coffees, along with hot coffees and Italian-style espresso beverages through more than 2,500 retail stores worldwide. The company purchases green coffee beans for its coffee varieties from coffee-producing regions throughout the world and custom roasts them In addition to coffee beans and beverages, the company's stores offer a selection of coffee-making equipment, accessories, pastries, and confections. Also, the company sells whole-bean coffees through a specialty sales group and a national mail-order operation. **Corporate headquarters location:** Seattle WA. **Operations at this facility include:** This location is one location of a national chain of cafes.

STARBUCKS COFFEE
4735 SW 77th Avenue, Portland OR 97225. 503/291-7191. **Contact:** Manager. **World Wide Web address:** http://www.starbucks.com. **Description:** Starbucks Coffee sells whole-bean coffees, along with hot coffees and Italian-style espresso beverages through more than 2,500 retail stores worldwide. The company purchases green coffee beans for its coffee varieties from coffee-producing regions throughout the world and custom roasts them In addition to coffee beans and beverages, the company's stores offer a selection of coffee-making equipment, accessories, pastries, and confections. Also, the company sells whole-bean coffees through a specialty sales group and a national mail-order operation. **Corporate headquarters location:** Seattle WA. **Operations at this facility include:** This location is one location of a national chain of cafes.

STARPLEX CROWD MANAGEMENT
714 SW 20th Place, Portland OR 97205. 503/222-5957. **Contact:** Human Resources. **E-mail address:** custserv@starplexcms.com. **World Wide Web address:** http://www.starplexcms.com. **Description:** Provides crowd management services for special events.

THE STASH TEA COMPANY
P.O. Box 910, Portland OR 97207. 503/684-4482. **Physical address:** 7204 SW Durham Road, Suite 200, Tigard OR 97224. **Contact:** Human Resources. **World Wide Web address:** http://www.stashtea.com. **Description:** A catalog retailer of specialty teas, cookies, breads, and related gift items. Founded in 1972. **Corporate headquarters location:** This location.

STATES INDUSTRIES INC.
P.O. Box 7037, Eugene OR 97401. 541/688-7871. **Toll-free phone:** 800/626-1981. **Fax:** 541/689-8051. **Contact:** Human Resources Manager. **E-mail address:** kmegown@statesind.com. **World Wide Web address:** http://www.statesind.com. **Description:** Manufactures and markets hardwood panel products to industrial and consumer markets. **Positions advertised include:** CNC Operator. **Corporate headquarters location:** This location. **Other U.S. locations:** Mocksville NC. **Number of employees at this location:** 300.

STATESMAN JOURNAL COMPANY
P.O. Box 13009, Salem OR 97309-1015. 503/399-6899. **Physical address:** 280 Church Street NE, Salem OR 97301. **Contact:** Kelly Acevedo, Human Resources Director. **World Wide Web address:** http://www.statesmanjournal.com. **Description:** Publishes a daily newspaper with a circulation of 59,000. **Parent company:** Gannet Company Inc.

STIMSON LUMBER COMPANY
520 SW Yamhill Street, Suite 700, Portland OR 97204-1326. 503/222-1676. **Contact:** Human Resources. **World Wide Web address:** http://www.stimsonlumber.com. **Description:** A lumber mill. **NOTE:** Interested jobseekers should send resumes to Human Resources, P.O. Box 68, Forest Grove OR 97116. **Other area locations:** Clatskanie OR; Forest Grove OR.

STIMSON LUMBER COMPANY
P.O. Box 346, 865 Stimson Mill Road, Clatskanie OR 97016-0346. 503/728-2166. **Contact:** Foreman. **World Wide Web address:** http://www.stimsonlumber.com. **Description:** A sawmill. Stimson also operates mills in Portland and Forest Grove.

Corporate headquarters location: Portland OR. **Other area locations:** Forest Grove OR; Portland OR.

STOEL RIVES LLP
900 SW Fifth Avenue, Suite 2600, Portland OR 97204-1268. 503/224-3380. **Fax:** 503/220-2480. **Contact:** Human Resources. **World Wide Web address:** http://www.stoel.com. **Description:** A law firm specializing in corporate law. **NOTE:** Recruiting is done separately for attorneys and staff. **Corporate headquarters:** This location.

SULZER BINGHAM PUMPS INC.
2800 NW Front Avenue, P.O. Box 10247, Portland OR 97210. 503/226-5203. **Fax:** 503/226-5598. **Contact:** Human Resources Manager. **World Wide Web address:** http://www.sulzer.com. **Description:** A manufacturer of water, chemical, and petroleum pumps and parts. **Parent company:** Sulzer Switzerland.

SWAN ISLAND DAIRY, INC.
4950 North Basin Avenue, Portland OR 97217-3547. 503/240-5150. **Fax:** 503/797-5030. **Contact:** Human Resources. **Description:** This location is a plant involved in dairy production. **Corporate headquarters location:** Portland OR. **Other U.S. locations:** AK; CA; ID; MT; UT; WA. **Parent company:** The Kroger Company operates a chain of over 131 retail stores offering a wide range of food, home products, apparel, fine jewelry, and home improvement items.

SWANSON GROUP
2635 Old Highway 99 South, Roseburg OR 97470. 541/492-1103. **Contact:** Human Resources. **E-mail address:** john@sunstuds.com. **World Wide Web address:** http://www.swansongroupinc.com. **Description:** A sawmill specializing in studs and related products for the construction industry.

SYNTHETECH, INC.
1290 Industrial Way, Albany OR 97322. 541/967-6575. **Fax:** 541/967-9424. **Contact:** Human Resources Department. **E-mail address:** brett@synthetech.com. **World Wide Web address:** http://www.synthetech.com. **Description:** A manufacturer of fine chemicals. The company's primary products are specialty amino acids used by drug companies as raw materials to make peptide-based drugs. **Positions advertised include:** Associate Analytical Scientist. **Corporate headquarters location:** This location. **Operations at this facility include:** Administration; Manufacturing; Research and Development; Sales. **Listed on:** NASDAQ. **Stock exchange symbol:** NZYM.

TMT PATHWAY
1675 Commercial Street NE, Salem OR 97303. 503/364-2277. **Toll-free phone:** 800/835-3357. **Fax:** 503/364-1029. **Contact:** Linda Bergerson, Manager of Human Resources Department. **World Wide Web address:** http://www.tmtpathway.com. **Description:** Manufactures traffic marking paint for use on highways and other roads.

TRM COPY CENTERS CORPORATION
5208 NE 122nd Avenue, Portland OR 97230. 503/257-8766. **Toll-free phone:** 800/877-8762. **Fax:** 800/998-3721. **Contact:** Angela Childers, Human Resources. **E-mail address:** angelachilders@trm.com. **World Wide Web address:** http://www.trm.com. **Description:** A leading provider of self-service photocopying centers. The company owns, maintains, and monitors over 34,000 ATMs and photocopiers located in independent retail establishments such as pharmacies, stationery stores, hardware stores, convenience stores, and gift shops. **Corporate headquarters location:** This location. **International locations:** Belgium; Canada; France; United Kingdom.

TEAM BRIGHT WOOD
630 SE First Street, Railroad Boulevard, Redmond OR 97756. 541/548-4513. **Fax:** 541/548-3272. **Contact:** Human Resources. **E-mail address:** resume@brightwood.com. **World Wide Web address:** http://www.brightwood.com. **Description:** Bright Wood Corporation is one of the largest millwork manufacturers in the world. Thirteen production plants work together to process over 150 million feet of board lumber annually. Bright Wood is a multiple species manufacturer using firs and pines from New Zealand, Chile, Canada, and other countries. **Corporate headquarters location:** Madras OR. **Other U.S. locations:** ID; MT; OR; WA. **Operations at this facility include:** This location manufactures pine lumber, fir lumber, plywood, and door-window molding parts.

TEKTRONIX, INC.
P.O. Box 500, Mail Stop 55-545, Beaverton OR 97077-0001. 503/627-7111. **Contact:** Professional Staffing. **World Wide Web address:** http://www.tek.com. **Description:** Tektronix, Inc. produces electronic test and measurement, computer graphics, and communications equipment. Test and measurement products include oscilloscopes, logic analyzers, digitizers, and curve tracers. Computer graphics products include printers and terminals primarily for scientific and engineering uses. Communications equipment includes vectorscopes, waveform monitors, signal generators, cable and fiber-optic testers, demodulators, and television routing and switching items. **Positions advertised include:** Engineering Director; Product Engineer; Security Support Associate; Senior Package Design Engineer; Wireless Regional Marketing Manager; Principal ASIC Engineer; Americas Field Marcom Manager. **Special programs:** Internships. **Corporate headquarters location:** This location. **Other area locations:** Wilsonville OR. **Other U.S. locations:** Nationwide. **Operations at this facility include:** This location manufactures oscilloscopes.

TEUFEL NURSERIES INC.
12345 NW Barnes Road, Portland OR 97229. 503/646-1111. **Toll-free phone:** 800/483-8335. **Fax:** 503/646-1112. **Recorded jobline:** 503/643-8706. **Contact:** Human Resources Representative. **E-mail address:** personnel@teufel.com. **World Wide Web address:** http://www.teufel.com. **Description:** Engaged in nursery production, wholesale horticultural supplies, wholesale plant sales, and landscape construction. Founded in 1890. **NOTE:** Entry-level positions are offered. **Positions advertised include:** Landscape Irrigator. **Special programs:** Internships; Training. **Corporate headquarters location:** This location. **Other U.S. locations:** Seattle WA.

THERMO FLUIDS INC.
6400 SE 101st Avenue, Portland OR 97266-5130. 503/788-4612. **Toll-free phone:** 800/350-7565. **Contact:** Human Resources. **World Wide Web address:** http;//www.thermofluids.com. **Description:** Recycles antifreeze, oil and oil filters and provides some oil clean-up services. The company also offers environmental consulting services. Founded in 1978. **Parent company:** HIG Capital.

THIN PATH SYSTEMS
26200 SW 95th Avenue, Suite 301, Wilsonville OR 97070. 971/404-3285. **Fax:** 971/404-3245. **Contact:** Human Resources. **E-mail address:** info@tp-sys.com. **World Wide Web address:** http://www.thinpathsystems.com. **Description:** Provides desktop information access solutions for network computing environments. Thin Path Systems is a worldwide supplier of X Window System terminals and PC-X server software products, which integrate Microsoft Windows- and DOS-based PCs into X/UNIX networks. The company also supplies the Z-Mail family of cross-platform electronic mail and messaging software for open systems environments, as well as Mariner, an Internet access and navigation software tool that provides a unified interface to all Internet resources. **Corporate headquarters location:** This location. **Operations at this facility include:** This location develops and manufactures hardware and software that enables computers to be networked.

THUNDERBIRD HOTEL
1401 North Hayden Island Drive, Portland OR 97217. 503/283-2111. **Contact:** Human Resources. **Description:** A 320-room luxury hotel that offers several restaurants, conference centers, exercise facilities, and business services. **Positions advertised include:** Assistant Restaurant Manager; Kitchen Supervisor. **Corporate headquarters location:** This location.

TIGARD COURTYARD INN
15686 SW Sequoia Parkway, Tigard OR 97224. 503/684-7900. **Contact:** Manager. **World Wide Web address:** http://www.courtyard.com. **Description:** A moderately priced, 110-room hotel offering a restaurant, meeting center, exercise facilities, and business services. **Parent company:** Marriott International has nearly 4,200 units, with operations and franchises in 50 states and 25 countries. The company operates lodging facilities and is the franchiser under four separate brand names, each serving a part of the lodging market: Marriott Hotels, Resorts, and Suites (full-service), Courtyard Inn (moderate price), Residence Inn (extended stay), and Fairfield Inn (economy). The company also develops and operates Marriott Ownership Resorts (vacation timesharing).

TILLAMOOK COUNTY CREAMERY ASSOCIATION
4175 Highway 101 N, P.O. Box 313, Tilamook OR 97141. 503/842-4481. **Fax:** 503/815-1380. **Contact:** Human Resources Manager. **E-mail address:** jobs@tillamook.com. **World Wide Web address:** http://www.tillamookcheese.com. **Description:** An area processor of a wide range of dairy and creamery products including butter, cheese, and milk. Founded in 1909. **Positions advertised include:** Package Line Attendant; Food Processing Maintenance; Site Maintenance; Seasonal Retail Cashier; Ice Cream Shift Leader. **Corporate headquarters location:** This location. **Listed on:** Privately held.

TIMBER PRODUCTS COMPANY
P.O. Box 269, Springfield OR 97477-0055. 541/747-4577. **Toll-free phone:** 800/547-9520. **Fax:** 541/744-4296. **Physical address:** 305 South Fourth Street, Springfield OR 97477. **Contact:** Gary Kroetta, Human Resources Manager. **World Wide Web address:** http://www.timberproducts.com. **Description:** Timber Products Company is a fully integrated wood products company. **NOTE:** Employment matters are handled through this location. **Corporate headquarters location:** This location. **Operations at this facility include:** This location manufactures a wide variety of wood products.

TIMBER PRODUCTS COMPANY
125 NE Mill Street, Grants Pass OR 97526. 541/479-6822. **Contact:** Human Resources. **World Wide Web address:** http://www.timberproducts.com. **Description:** Timber Products Company is a fully integrated wood products company. **NOTE:** Employment matters are handled through the main office. **Corporate headquarters location:** Springfield OR. **Other area locations:** Medford OR; Springfield OR. **Subsidiaries include:** Seply Inc. (White City OR). **Operations at this facility include:** This location is a sawmill.

TIMBER PRODUCTS COMPANY
25 East McAndrews Road, P.O. Box 1669, Medford OR 97501. 541/773-6681. **Contact:** Human Resources. **World Wide Web address:** http://www.timberproducts.com. **Description:** Timber Products Company is a fully integrated wood products company. **NOTE:** Employment matters are handled through the main office. **Corporate headquarters location:** Springfield OR. **Other area locations:** Grants Pass OR; Medford OR. **Subsidiaries include:** Seply Inc. (White City OR). **Operations at this facility include:** This location is a sawmill.

TIMBERLINE SOFTWARE CORPORATION
15195 NW Greenbrier Parkway, Beaverton OR 97006-5701. 503/690-6775. **Fax:** 503/439-5819. **Contact:** Personnel. **E-mail address:** jobs@timberline.com. **World Wide Web address:** http://www.timberline.com. **Description:** Timberline Software Corporation develops and markets computer software programs, primarily for the construction and property management industries. **Positions advertised include:** Lead Install Engineer; Payroll Administrator; Senior Accounting Clerk; Technical Support Specialist; Technical Writer; QA Manager; Vice President of Information Technology. **Corporate headquarters location:** This location.

TOSOH QUARTZ INC.
14380 NW Science Park Drive, Portland OR 97229. 503/605-5600. **Fax:** 503/605-5696. **Contact:** Kathy Copeland, Human Resources Manager. **E-mail address:** jobs@tosohquartz.com. **World Wide Web address:** http://www. tosohquartz.com. **Description:** Manufactures quartz semiconductors. Founded in 1957. **Positions advertised include:** Manufacturing Tech; Inspector. **Number of employees worldwide:** 200.

TURNER CONSTRUCTION COMPANY
5200 SW Macadam Avenue, Suite 370, Portland OR 97239. 503/226-9825. **Fax:** 503/226-9836. **Contact:** Human Resources. **World Wide Web address:** http://www.turnerconstruction.com. **Description:** Turner is a nationwide construction company founded in 1902. **Positions advertised include:** Assistant Engineer; Assistant Estimating Engineer. **Corporate Headquarters location:** 375 Hudson Street, New York NY 10014. **Chairman and CEO:** Thomas C. Leppert.

TREESOURCE INDUSTRIES, INC.
P.O. Box 370, Glide OR 97443-0370. 541/496-3571. **Contact:** Randy Eatherton Mill Manager. **World Wide Web address:** http://www.treesource.com. **Description:** One of the 10 largest volume producers of lumber products in the United States. Its 12 mills in Oregon, Washington, and Vermont manufacture softwood stud and dimension lumber, as well as hardwood lumber. These products are marketed throughout the United States, Canada, and a number of other foreign markets under the TreeSource brand name. **Corporate headquarters location:** Tumwater WA.

TRIMET
4012 SE 17th Street, Portland OR 97202. 503/962-7635. **Fax:** 503/962-7440. **Recorded jobline:** 503/962-3000. **Contact:** Human Resources. **E-mail address:** jobs@trimet.org. **World Wide Web address:** http://www.tri-met.org. **Description:** Operates area bus and rail service. **Positions advertised include:** Bus Driver; Manager Fare Equipment Systems.

TRIQUINT SEMICONDUCTOR, INC.
2300 NE Brookwood Parkway, Hillsboro OR 97124. 503/615-9000. **Fax:** 503/615-8900. **Contact:** Corporate Staffing. **E-mail address:** info_hr@tqs.com. **World Wide Web address:** http://www.tqs.com. **Description:** TriQuint Semiconductor designs, develops, manufactures, and markets a broad range of high-performance analog and mixed-signal integrated circuits for the wireless communications, telecommunications, and computing markets. **Positions advertised include:** Receptionist; Payroll Specialist; Design Engineer. **Corporate headquarters location:** This location. **Operations at this facility include:** This location houses administrative offices.

TRUSERV CORPORATION
2150 Olympic Street, Springfield OR 97477. 541/726-8243. **Contact:** Human Resources. **Description:** This location is a distribution facility for the hardware store company. **NOTE:** Corporate employment matters are handled through the corporate headquarters location, while distribution center employment is handled locally. **Corporate headquarters location:** Chicago IL.

24 HOUR FITNESS
1210 NW Johnson Street, Portland OR 97209. 503/222-1210. **Contact:** Human Resources. **World Wide Web address:** http://www.24hourfitness.com. **Description:** A 24-hour fitness club that offers rock climbing, group cycling, personal training, tanning, and child care in addition to cardio and weight training equipment. **Positions advertised include:** Front Desk; Fuel Station Attendant; Kid's Club; Personal Trainer; Sales Counselor. **Corporate headquarters location:** San Ramon CA.

TYCO PRINTED CIRCUIT GROUP
1270 SE Monmouth Cutoff Road, Dallas OR 97338. 503/623-9273. **Fax:** 503/623-7410. **Contact:** Deborah McCurry, Personnel. **World Wide Web address:** http://www.printedcircuits.tycoelectronics.com. **Description:** Tyco Corporation manufactures electrical and electronic components, medical products, flow control products, and security systems. **Other area locations:** White City OR. **Operations at this facility include:** This location manufactures multilayer, fine-line printed circuit boards.

UBS PAINEWEBBER INC.
805 SW Broadway, Suite 2600, Portland OR 97205. 503/221-5800. **Contact:** Kerry McHale, Personnel Director. **World Wide Web address:** http://www.financialservicesinc.ubs.com. **Description:** A full-service securities firm with over 300 offices nationwide. Services include investment banking, asset management, merger and acquisition consulting, municipal securities underwriting, estate planning, retirement programs, and transaction management. UBS PaineWebber offers its services to corporations, governments, institutions, and individuals. Founded in 1879. **Corporate headquarters location:** New York NY. **Other U.S. locations:** Nationwide.

UPS AVIATION TECHNOLOGIES
2345 Turner Road SE, Salem OR 97302. 503/581-8101. **Toll-free phone:** 800/525-6726. **Fax:** 503/364-2138. **Contact:** Human Resources Manager. **World Wide Web address:** http://www.upsat.com. **Description:** A manufacturer of avionics and navigational equipment. **Corporate headquarters location:** Atlanta GA. **Parent company:** United Parcel Service (UPS).

U.S. BANK
299 NE 181st Avenue, Portland OR 97230. **Toll-free phone:** 800/872-2657. **Fax:** 503-257-1833. **Contact:** Human Resources. **Description:** A commercial bank with over 2,370 branch locations in 24 states nationwide. **Positions advertised include:** Financial Analyst; Sales Officer; Client Service Specialist; Treasury Management Product Development Manager; Private Banking Relationship Manager; Branch Manager; Network Analyst; Mortgage Loan Processor; Administrative Assistant. **Corporate headquarters:** Minneapolis MN. **Listed on:** New York Stock Exchange. **Stock exchange symbol:** USB.

U.S. BUREAU OF LAND MANAGEMENT/PRINEVILLE DISTRICT DESCHUTES RESOURCES AREA
3050 North East 3rd Street, Prineville OR 97754. 541/416-6707. **Fax:** 541/416-6798. **Contact:** Cynthia Buehner, Personnel Manager. **World Wide Web address:** http://www.or.blm.gov. **Description:** Manages public land and resources in the Prineville District.

U.S. DEPARTMENT OF VETERANS AFFAIRS PORTLAND VETERANS ADMINISTRATION MEDICAL CENTER
3710 SW U.S. Veterans Hospital Road, Portland OR 97239. 503/220-8262. **Fax:** 503/402-2838. **Contact:** Human Resources. **World Wide Web address:** http://www1.va.gov. **Description:** A medical center operated by the U.S. Department of Veterans Affairs. From 54 hospitals in 1930, the VA health care system has grown to include 171 medical centers; more than 364 outpatient, community, and outreach clinics; 130 nursing home care units; and 37 domiciliarr residences. VA operates at least one medical center in each of the 50 states, Puerto Rico, and the District of Columbia. With approximately 76,000 medical center beds, VA treats nearly 1 million patients in VA hospitals; 75,000 in nursing home care units; and 25,000 in domiciliary residences. VA's outpatient clinics register approximately 24 million visits per year. **NOTE:** Resumes must be mailed or dropped off in person. Faxed resumes not accepted. **Positions advertised include:** Accounting Technician; Accounts Receivable Assistant; Administrative Support Clerk; Biological Science Lab Technician; Certified Respiratory Therapy Technician; Clinical Nurse Specialist; Fiscal Accounts Technician.

U.S. DEPARTMENT OF VETERANS AFFAIRS ROSEBURG VETERANS ADMINISTRATION MEDICAL CENTER
913 NW Garden Valley Boulevard, Roseburg OR 97470-6513. 541/440-1000. **Fax:** 541/440-1225. **Contact:** Human Resources. **World Wide Web address:** http://www1.va.gov. **Description:** A medical center operated by the U.S. Department of Veterans Affairs. From 54 hospitals in 1930, the VA health care system has grown to include 171 medical centers; more than 364 outpatient, community, and outreach clinics; 130 nursing home care units; and 37 domiciliary residences. VA operates at least one medical center in each of the 50 states, Puerto Rico, and the District of Columbia. With approximately 76,000 medical center beds, VA treats nearly 1 million patients in VA hospitals; 75,000 in nursing home care units; and 25,000 in domiciliary residences. VA's outpatient clinics register approximately 24 million visits per year. **Positions advertised include:** Biomedical Engineering Technician; Clinical Pharmacist.

U.S. FEDERAL RESERVE BANK OF SAN FRANCISCO
P.O. Box 3436, Portland OR 97208-3436. 503/221-5900. **Physical address:** 915 SW Stark Street, Portland OR 97205. **Contact:** Human Resources. **World Wide Web address:** http://www.sf.frb.org. **Description:** A branch bank of the Federal Reserve System, which consists of 12 regional Federal Reserve banks that, along with the Federal Reserve Board of Governors in Washington DC, and the Federal Open Market Committee, comprise the Federal Reserve System, the nation's central bank. **Positions advertised include:** Project Analyst.

UMPQUA BANK
200 SW Market Street, Suite 1900, Portland OR 97201. 503/973-5556. **Fax:** 503/228-2167. **Contact:** Human Resources. **E-mail address:** jobs@umpquabank.com. **World Wide Web address:** http://www.umpquabank.com. **Description:** An Oregon-chartered bank that is recognized for its entrepreneurial approach, innovative use of technology, and distinctive banking solutions. Umpqua has 66 locations throughout Oregon and Southern Washington. Umpqua tailors financial services and products to individual customers, and provides a consumer friendly atmosphere, which includes serving gourmet coffee. **Positions advertised include:** Operations Manager; Loan Officer; Account Executive; Universal Associate. **Parent company:** Umpqua Holdings Corporation. **Listed on:** NASDAQ. **Stock exchange symbol:** UMPQ.

UNITED STATES BAKERY
P.O. Box 14769, Portland OR 97293. 503/232-2191. **Contact:** Human Resources. **World Wide Web address:** http://www.usbakery.com. **Description:** A producer of baked goods including fresh and frozen bread. **NOTE:** This company hires through the State of Oregon Employment Department, 30 North Webster, Suite E, Portland OR 97217. 503/280-6046. Do not e-mail resumes. Resumes received without an application will not be considered. **Positions advertised include:** Bakers; Sanitarians; Office Personnel. **Corporate headquarters location:** This location.

UNITED WAY
619 SW 11th Avenue, Suite 300, Portland OR 97205-2646. 503/228-9131. **Fax:** 503/226-9385. **Contact:** Human Resources. **World Wide Web address:** http://www.unitedway-pdx.org. **Description:** Through a network of volunteers and local charities, United Way organizations throughout America help meet the health and human care needs of millions of people. **Positions advertised include:** Development Officer. **Corporate headquarters location:** Alexandria VA. **Other U.S. locations:** Nationwide.

UNIVERSAL FOREST PRODUCTS
2895 Progress Way, P.O. Box 296, Woodburn OR 97071-0296. 503/226-6240. **Fax:** 503/981-9509. **Contact:** Human Resources. **World Wide Web address:** http://www.ufpi.com. **Description:** The company manufactures and engineers: wood and wood-alternative products for do-it-yourself retail home centers; engineered wood components for the site-built construction market; specialty wood packaging for the industrial and other markets; and structural lumber products for the manufactured housing industry. **Corporate headquarters location:** Grand Rapids MI. **Listed on:** National Association of Securities Dealers Automated Quotations. **Stock exchange symbol:** UFPI. **Number of employees worldwide:** 9000.

UNIVERSITY OF OREGON
5210 University of Oregon, Eugene OR 97403-5210. 541/346-3159. **Fax:** 5641/346-2548. **Contact:** Linda King, Director of Personnel. **World Wide Web address:** http://www.uoregon.edu. **Description:** A state university offering graduate and undergraduate programs to approximately 16,700 students. **NOTE:** Unsolicited resumes are not accepted. **Positions advertised include:** Office Specialist; Education Project Assistant; Custodian; Food Service Worker; Analyst Programmer; Complex Director; Program Coordinator; Director of Development; Head Scientific Instrument Researcher; Visiting Instructor of Norwegian; Assistant Professor; Tenure Track Faculty Member.

UNIVERSITY OF PORTLAND
5000 North Willamette Boulevard, Portland OR 97203. 503/943-7331. **Fax:** 503/943-7399. **Recorded jobline:** 503/943-7536. **Contact:** James Kuffner, Human Resources Director. **E-mail address:** kuffner@up.edu. **World Wide Web address:** http://www.up.edu. **Description:** A Catholic university offering graduate and undergraduate programs in sciences, engineering, education, business, arts, humanities, and nursing. The University of Portland has an enrollment of approximately 2,600 students. Founded in 1901. **NOTE:** The university also hires through the Oregon State Employment Office. **Positions advertised include:** Assistant Director of Student Media and Adult Programs Coordinator. **Employees at this location:** 700.

VALLEY RIVER INN
1000 Valley River Way, Eugene OR 97401. 541/681-5077. **Fax:** 541/681-5064. **Recorded jobline:** 541/686-2803. **Contact:** Sandra de Jonge, Human Resources Director. **E-mail address:** sandrad@valleyriverinn.com. **World Wide Web address:** http://www.valleyriverinn.com. **Description:** A 257-room hotel offering meeting facilities, the Sweetwaters restaurant, airport transportation, exercise facilities, and business services. **Positions advertised include:** Assistant Baker; Banquet Server; Front Desk Agent; Restaurant Supervisor. **Corporate headquarters location:** Seattle WA. **Parent company:** Westcoast Hotels.

VESTA CORPORATION
309 SW Sixth Avenue, Fourth Floor, Portland OR 97204. 503/790-2500. **Fax:** 503/790-2525. **Contact:** Human Resources. **E-mail address:** jobs@trustvesta.com. **World Wide Web address:** http://www.trustvesta.com. **Description:** Vesta Corporation is a provider of stored value commerce solutions such as account recharge, payment processing, risk management, customer service, and program management. **Positions advertised include:** IVR Call Flow Programmer; Chief Operations Officer; Senior NET Engineer; Channel Marketing Manager; Security Specialist; Customer Service Representative.

THE WACKENHUT CORPORATION
5319 SW Westgate Drive, Suite 125, Portland OR 97221-2411. 503/291-1005. **Fax:** 503/291-1073. **Contact:** Human Resources. **World Wide Web address:** http://www.wackenhut.com. **Description:** The Wackenhut Corporation is a diversified provider of services to government, industrial, commercial, and professional organizations and agencies worldwide. The Wackenhut Corporation specializes in security-related services including physical security, investigations, the management of correctional and detention facilities, rehabilitative programs, and information security. The company also provides educational services and training, facility management, food service to jails and prisons, design, financial services and construction management for correctional facilities, and fire prevention and emergency services. The Wackenhut Corporation is a leader in the privatization of public services to municipal, state, and federal governments worldwide. Founded in 1954. **Other U.S. locations:** Nationwide. **International locations:** Worldwide. **CEO:** George R. Wackenhut.

WACKER SILTRONIC CORPORATION
13105 SE 197th Street, P.O. Box 83180, Boring OR 97009. 503/658-3347. **Fax:** 503/658-6369. **Recorded jobline:** 503/241-7547. **Contact:** Senior Corporate Recruiter. **E-mail address:** employment@siltronic.com. **World Wide Web address:** http://www.siltronic.com. **Description:** Manufactures polish and epitaxially coated

silicon wafers for the semiconductor industry. **Positions advertised include:** Operators; Material Handler. **Corporate headquarters location:** Munich, Germany. **Parent company:** Wacker Siltronic A.G.

R.M. WADE & COMPANY
10025 SW Allen Boulevard, Beaverton OR 97005. 503/641-1865. **Fax:** 503/626-8298. **Contact:** Human Resources. **World Wide Web address:** http://www.waderain.com. **Description:** Manufactures a full line of micro irrigation products and farm machinery including tractors, sprinklers, and conventional irrigation systems.

WAH CHANG
1600 Old Salem Road NE, P.O. Box 460, Albany OR 97321. 541/926-4211. **Fax:** 541/967-6990. **Contact:** Manager of Human Resources Department. **World Wide Web address:** http://www.wahchang.com. **Description:** A leading producer of specialty metals. Products include titanium sponge, engineered products, ingot, mill products, and castings. **Positions advertised include:** Senior Systems Developer. **Special programs:** Internships. **Corporate headquarters location:** This location. **Parent company:** Allegheny Technologies Incorporated.

WARN INDUSTRIES, INC.
12900 SE Capps Road, Clackamas OR 97015. 503/722-1200. **Fax:** 503/722-1411. **Contact:** Human Resources. **E-mail address:** te689@warn.com. **World Wide Web address:** http://www.warn.com. **Description:** A manufacturer of winches and four-wheel drive accessories. **NOTE:** Send applications to 12900 SE Capps Road, Clackamas OR 97015, or by e-mail to the above address. **Positions advertised include:** Manufacturing Manager; Product Designer; Design Engineer; Senior Regional Sales Manager.

WARN INDUSTRIES INC.
13270 SE Pleasant Court, Milwaukie OR 97222. 503/659-8750. **Fax:** 503/722-1411. **Recorded jobline:** 503/786-4449. **Contact:** Human Resources Department. **E-mail address:** te689@warn.com. **World Wide Web address:** http://www.warn.com. **Description:** A manufacturer of winches and four-wheel drive accessories. **NOTE;** Send applications to 12900 SE Capps Road, Clackamas OR 97015, or by e-mail to the above address. **Positions advertised include:** Machinist; Finance Controller; Quality Technician; Engineer; Copy Writer/Public Relations.

WASHINGTON, COUNTY OF
155 North First Avenue, Suite 320, Hillsboro OR 97124-3072. 503/846-8606. **Fax:** 503/846-3777. **Recorded jobline:** 503/846-8607. **Contact:** Human Resources Department. **E-mail address:** hr@co.washington.or.us. **World Wide Web address:** http://www.co.washington.or.us. **Description:** This location houses the administrative offices of Washington County. **Positions advertised include:** Residential Services Monitor; Community Health Nurse; Accounting Assistant; Engineering Technician; Traffic Analyst; Facilities Maintenance Technician; GIS Coordinator. **Number of employees at this location:** 1,200.

WASHINGTON FEDERAL SAVINGS BANK
611 Main Street, Dallas OR 97338. 503/623-2361. **Fax:** 503/623-6741. **Contact:** Human Resources. **World Wide Web address:** http://www.washingtonfederal.com. **Description:** A federal savings bank with more than 100 branch locations in the western United States. **Positions advertised include:** Customer Service Representative; Loan Coordinator.

WASTE MANAGEMENT OF PORTLAND
7227 NE 55th Avenue, Portland OR 97218. 503/249-8078. **Contact:** Human Resources. **Description:** A waste disposal company specializing in the hauling of waste materials. **Parent company:** WMX Technologies is an international provider of comprehensive waste management services, as well as engineering and construction, industrial, and related services, with operations in 19 countries.

WEBTRENDS CORPORATION
851 SW 6th Avenue, Suite 700, Portland OR 97204. 503/294-7025. **Toll-free phone:** 888/932-8736. **Fax:** 503/294-7130. **Contact:** Personnel. **World Wide Web address:** http://www.webtrends.com. **Description:** Develops and markets e-business solutions to help businesses manage their Internet infrastructure, e-commerce strategies, and e-marketing. **Corporate headquarters location:** San Jose CA. **Parent company:** NetIQ.

WELCH ALLYN PROTOCOL, INC.
8500 SW Creekside Place, Beaverton OR 97008. 503/530-7500. **Fax:** 503/526-4200. **Contact:** Manager of Human Resources Department. **World Wide Web address:** http://www.protocol.com. **Description:** A manufacturer of portable systems for monitoring patients' vital signs. **Positions advertised include:** Assembler; Buyer; Marketing Director; QA Director; Engineering Technician. **Corporate headquarters location:** This location. **Operations at this facility include:** Administration; Manufacturing; Research and Development; Sales; Service.

WEST COAST BANK
P.O. Box 428, Salem OR 97308. 503/315-2836. **Fax:** 503/391-6383. **Physical address:** 550 Center NE, Salem OR 97301. **Contact:** Beth Bonnet, Recruiting. **World Wide Web address:** http://www.westcoastbancorp.com. **Description:** An association of community banks and closely related businesses. In total, West Coast Bank operates 41 branch locations. **Positions advertised include:** Project Officer; Teller; Personal Banker; Call Center Agent; Network Services Manager. **Corporate headquarters location:** This location. **Parent company:** West Coast Bancorp.

WESTERN ELECTRONICS CORPORATION
19400 SW Teton Avenue, Tualatin OR 97602. 503/612-2100. **Fax:** 360/566-8088. **Contact:** Human Resources Manager. **E-mail address:** recruiting@westernelectronics.com. **World Wide Web address:** http://www.westernelectronics.com. **Description:** This location supplies finishing to products: vacuum shielding, screen printing, and painting. Western Electronics is a manufacturer of wire cable.

WESTERN OREGON UNIVERSITY
345 North Monmouth Avenue, Monmouth OR 97361. 503/838-8490. **Toll-free phone:** 877/877-1593. **Fax:** 503/838-8144. **Contact:** Personnel. **World Wide Web address:** http://www.wou.edu. **Description:** A state university with an enrollment of approximately 4,500 students. **NOTE:** All jobs other than faculty positions are filled through the Oregon State Employment Office. **Positions advertised include:** Director of Public Safety; Registrar; Administrative Assistant to the Dean; Visiting Art Gallery Director; Assistant Professor of Special Education; Assistant Professor of Criminal Justice; Adjunct Faculty of Spanish.

WEYERHAEUSER
P.O. Box 428, Albany OR 97321. 541/928-3341. **Physical address:** 2550 Old Salem Road, Albany OR 97321. **Contact:** Human Resources. **World Wide Web address:** http://www.weyerhaeuser.com. **Description:** Weyerhaeuser Company's principal businesses are the growing and harvesting of timber; the manufacture, distribution, and sale of forest products including logs, wood chips, and building products; real estate development and construction; and financial services. Weyerhaeuser Company is one of the world's largest private owners of marketable softwood timber and also one of the largest producers of softwood lumber and pulp. The company is also one of North America's largest producers of forest products and recyclers of office wastepaper, newspaper, and corrugated boxes. Weyerhaeuser Company also sells electricity to utility companies generated from its 15 trash-to-energy plants and 6 small cogeneration or recycling plants. The Water Division manufactures and operates facilities and systems for water purification, water treatment, and managed by-products. The Air Division designs, manufactures, and integrates air pollution emission control and measurement systems and related equipment. **Corporate headquarters location:** Tacoma WA. **Operations at this facility include:** This location manufactures engineered wood products. **Listed on:** New York Stock Exchange. **Stock exchange symbol:** WY.

WEYERHAEUSER COMPANY
P.O. Box 339, Albany OR 97321. 541/926-2281. **Contact:** Human Resources. **World Wide Web address:** http://www.weyerhaeuser.com. **Description:** Weyerhaeuser Company's principal businesses are the growing and harvesting of timber; the manufacture, distribution, and sale of forest products including logs, wood chips, and building products; real estate development and construction; and financial services. Weyerhaeuser Company is one of the world's largest private owners of marketable softwood timber and also one of the largest producers of softwood lumber and pulp. The company is also one of North America's largest producers of forest products and recyclers of office wastepaper, newspaper, and corrugated boxes. Weyerhaeuser Company also sells electricity to utility companies generated from its 15 trash-to-energy plants and 6 small cogeneration or recycling plants. The Water Division manufactures and operates facilities and systems for water purification, water treatment, and managed by-products. The Air Division designs, manufactures, and integrates air pollution emission control and measurement systems and related equipment. **Corporate headquarters location:** Tacoma WA. **Operations at this facility include:** This location is a paper mill. **Listed on:** New York Stock Exchange. **Stock exchange symbol:** WY.

WEYERHAEUSER COMPANY
P.O. Box 907, Albany OR 97321. 541/926-7771. **Contact:** Michelle Payne, Personnel Manager. **World Wide Web address:** http://www.weyerhaeuser.com. **Description:** Weyerhaeuser Company's principal businesses are the growing and harvesting of timber; the manufacture, distribution, and sale of forest products including logs, wood chips, and building products; real estate development and construction; and financial services. Weyerhaeuser Company is one of the world's largest private owners of marketable softwood timber and also one of the largest producers of softwood lumber and pulp. The company is also one of North America's largest producers of forest products and recyclers of office wastepaper, newspaper, and corrugated boxes. Weyerhaeuser Company also sells electricity to utility companies generated from its 15 trash-to-energy plants and 6 small cogeneration or recycling plants. The Water Division manufactures and operates facilities and systems for water purification, water treatment, and managed by-products. The Air Division designs, manufactures, and integrates air pollution emission control and measurement systems and related equipment. **Corporate headquarters location:** Tacoma WA. **Operations at this facility include:** This location is the head sales office for the lumber and plywood producing company. **Listed on:** New York Stock Exchange. **Stock exchange symbol:** WY.

WEYERHAEUSER COMPANY
P.O. Box 1245, Bend OR 97709. 541/382-6001. **Contact:** Human Resources. **World Wide Web address:** http://www.weyerhaeuser.com. **Description:** Weyerhaeuser Company's principal businesses are the growing and harvesting of timber; the manufacture, distribution, and sale of forest products including logs, wood chips, and building products; real estate development and construction; and financial services. Weyerhaeuser Company is one of the world's largest private owners of marketable softwood timber and also one of the largest producers of softwood lumber and pulp. The company is also one of North America's largest producers of forest products and recyclers of office wastepaper, newspaper, and corrugated boxes. Weyerhaeuser Company also sells electricity to utility companies generated from its 15 trash-to-energy plants and 6 small cogeneration or recycling plants. The Water Division manufactures and operates facilities and systems for water purification, water treatment, and managed by-products. The Air Division designs, manufactures, and integrates air pollution emission control and measurement systems and related equipment. **Corporate headquarters location:** Tacoma WA. **Operations at this facility include:** This location manufactures Korpine particleboard. **Listed on:** New York Stock Exchange. **Stock exchange symbol:** WY.

WEYERHAEUSER COMPANY
77629 South Pacific Highway, Cottage Grove OR 97424. 541/942-6208. **Contact:** Human Resources. **World Wide Web address:** http://www.weyerhaeuser.com. **Description:** Weyerhaeuser Company's principal businesses are the growing and harvesting of timber; the manufacture, distribution, and sale of forest products including logs, wood chips, and building products; real estate development and construction; and financial services. Weyerhaeuser Company is one of the world's largest private owners of marketable softwood timber and also one of the largest producers of softwood lumber and pulp. The company is also one of North America's largest producers of forest products and recyclers of office wastepaper, newspaper, and corrugated boxes. Weyerhaeuser Company also sells electricity to utility companies generated from its 15 trash-to-energy plants and 6 small cogeneration or recycling plants. The Water Division manufactures and operates facilities and systems for water purification, water treatment, and managed by-products. The Air Division designs, manufactures, and integrates air pollution emission control and measurement systems and related equipment. **Corporate headquarters location:** Tacoma WA. **Operations at this facility include:** This location is a paper products manufacturer. **Listed on:** New York Stock Exchange. **Stock exchange symbol:** WY.

WEYERHAEUSER COMPANY
1300 SW Fifth Avenue, Suite 3800, Portland OR 97201. 503/227-5581. **Contact:** Human Resources. **World Wide Web address:** http://www.weyerhaeuser.com. **Description:** Weyerhaeuser Company's principal businesses are the growing and harvesting of timber; the manufacture, distribution, and sale of forest products including logs, wood chips, and building products; real estate development and construction; and financial services. Weyerhaeuser Company is one of the world's largest private owners of marketable softwood timber and also one of the largest producers of softwood lumber and pulp. The company is also one of North America's largest producers of forest products and recyclers of office wastepaper, newspaper, and corrugated boxes. Weyerhaeuser Company also sells electricity to utility companies generated from its 15 trash-to-energy plants and 6 small cogeneration or recycling plants. The Water Division manufactures and operates facilities and systems for water

purification, water treatment, and managed by-products. The Air Division designs, manufactures, and integrates air pollution emission control and measurement systems and related equipment. **Corporate headquarters location:** Tacoma WA. **Listed on:** New York Stock Exchange. **Stock exchange symbol:** WY.

WEYERHAEUSER COMPANY
375 Dillard Gardens Road, Winston OR 97496. 541/679-9589. **Contact:** Human Resources. **World Wide Web address:** http://www.weyerhaeuser.com. **Description:** Weyerhaeuser Company's principal businesses are the growing and harvesting of timber; the manufacture, distribution, and sale of forest products including logs, wood chips, and building products; real estate development and construction; and financial services. Weyerhaeuser Company is one of the world's largest private owners of marketable softwood timber and also one of the largest producers of softwood lumber and pulp. The company is also one of North America's largest producers of forest products and recyclers of office wastepaper, newspaper, and corrugated boxes. Weyerhaeuser Company also sells electricity to utility companies generated from its 15 trash-to-energy plants and 6 small cogeneration or recycling plants. The Water Division manufactures and operates facilities and systems for water purification, water treatment, and managed by-products. **Corporate headquarters location:** Tacoma WA. **Operations at this facility include:** This location is a laminating and veneer sawmill. **Listed on:** New York Stock Exchange. **Stock exchange symbol:** WY.

DON WHITAKER LOGGING AND HAULING INC.
5706 North Umpqua Highway, Roseburg OR 97470. 541/673-6116. **Contact:** Human Resources. **Description:** This facility is involved in logging and heavy equipment hauling.

WHITE'S ELECTRONICS
1011 Pleasant Valley Road, Sweet Home OR 97386. 541/367-6121. **Toll-free phone:** 800/547-6911. **Contact:** Human Resources Manager. **E-mail address:** asmith@whiteselectronics.com. **World Wide Web address:** http://www.treasurenet.com/whites. **Description:** Manufactures, develops, and markets portable metal detectors for recreational use. **Corporate headquarters location:** This location.

WHITTIER WOOD PRODUCTS
P.O. Box 2827, Eugene OR 97402. 541/687-0213. **Fax:** 541/485-4359. **Contact:** Human Resources. **Description:** A manufacturer of ready-to-assemble wood furniture. **Corporate headquarters location:** This location.

WIEDEN AND KENNEDY
224 NW 13th Avenue, Portland OR 97209. 503/937-7530. **Fax:** 503/937-7209. **Contact:** Human Resources Manager. **E-mail address:** jobs@wk.com. **World Wide Web address:** http://www.wk.com. **Description:** An advertising firm involved in television, radio, magazines, billboards, and other media.

WILD HORSE GAMING RESORT
72777 Highway 331, Pendleton OR 97801-3379. 541/278-2274. **Fax:** 541/966-1990. **Contact:** Human Resources. **E-mail address:** jobs@wildhorseresort.com. **World Wide Web address:** http://www.wildhorseresort.com. **Description:** A casino/hotel that also has an RV park and a championship golf course. **Positions advertised include:** Director of Slot Operations; Director of Information Systems; Administrative Assistant; Tablegames Supervisor.

WILLAMETTE DENTAL GROUP, P.C.
OREGON DENTAL SPECIALISTS, P.C.
14025 SW Farmington Road, Beaverton OR 97005. 503/644-6444. **Recorded jobline:** 503/671-9486. **Contact:** Human Resources. **World Wide Web address:** http://www.denkor.com. **Description:** Willamette Dental Group operates dentist's offices in Oregon and Washington and provides dental insurance plans. **Corporate headquarters location:** This location. **Parent company:** Denkor Dental Management Corporation. **Operations at this facility include:** This location houses administrative offices.

WILLAMETTE VALLEY MEDICAL CENTER
2700 Three Mile Lane, McMinnville OR 97128. 503/472-6131. **Fax:** 503/435-6374. **Recorded jobline:** 503/435-6372. **Contact:** Human Resources Director. **World Wide Web address:** http://www.wvmcweb.com. **Description:** An acute-care inpatient and outpatient medical center. Founded in 1904. **NOTE:** Part-time jobs and second and third shifts are offered. **Positions advertised include:** Charge Nurse; RN Critical Care; Radiology Technologist; RN Emergency; RN Medical/Surgery. **Office hours:** Monday - Friday, 8:00 a.m. - 5:00 p.m. **Corporate headquarters location:** Dallas TX. **Other U.S. locations:** Nationwide. **Parent company:** Triad Hospital, Inc. **Listed on:** NASDAQ. **Stock exchange symbol:** TRIH.

WILLAMETTE VALLEY VINEYARDS
8800 Enchanted Way SE, Turner OR 97392. 503/588-9463. **Toll-free phone:** 800/344-9463. **Fax:** 503/588-8894. **Contact:** Human Resources. **World Wide Web address:** http://www.wvv.com. **Description:** Produces and sells premium, super-premium and ultra-premium varietal table wines. The company's wines are made from grapes grown at its vineyard and fermented and made into wine at the company's winery. The wines are sold under the company's Willamette Valley Vineyard and Oregon Trail labels. **Listed on:** NASDAQ. **Stock exchange symbol:** WVV.

WILLIAMS CONTROLS, INC.
14100 SW 72nd Avenue, Portland OR 97224. 503/684-8600. **Fax:** 503/624-3812. **Contact:** Human Resources. **E-mail address:** hr@wmco.com. **World Wide Web address:** http://www.wmco.com. **Description:** Through its subsidiaries, Williams Controls manufactures and markets a wide range of products for the automotive, aerospace, agricultural, industrial, forestry, trucking, and transportation industries. Founded in 1937. **Positions advertised include:** Design Engineer; CAD Designer; Environmental Health and Safety Officer. **Corporate headquarters location:** This location. **Subsidiaries include:** Aptek Williams, Inc. develops and manufactures sensors and circuits for the communications and automotive industries. GeoFocus, Inc. develops GIS/GPS information-based products including data collection, mapping, and tracking systems, for agricultural, governmental, and transportation markets. Hardee Williams, Inc. manufactures and markets equipment for the agricultural industry. NESC Williams, Inc. develops gasoline conversion kits, designed to reduce pollution, for the automotive industry. ProActive Pedals, Inc. designs, manufactures, and assembles adjustable pedal systems for the automotive industry. Premier Plastic Technologies, Inc. develops injection-molded products for the automotive, industrial, aerospace, and transportation industries. Williams Controls Industries, Inc. designs and manufactures electronic throttle, hydraulic, and pneumatic controls for the heavy-duty truck market. Williams World Trade markets consumer and industrial goods to and from Asian markets.

WOODGRAIN MILLWORK
P.O. Box 687, Prineville OR 97754-0685. 541/447-4177. **Physical address:** 1948 North Main Street, Prineville OR 97554. **Contact:** Human Resources. **World Wide Web address:** http://www.apinepro.com. **Description:** Manufactures moldings, doorframes, window frames, and specialty millwork. **Corporate headquarters location:** Chesterfield MO. **Positions advertised include:** Graders; Cutters; Operators; Technical Positions. **Parent company:** Huttig Building Products.

THE WORLD
350 Commercial Avenue, P.O. Box 1840, Coos Bay OR 97420. 541/269-1222. **Contact:** Human Resources Manager. **World Wide Web address:** http://www.theworldlink.com. **Description:** Publishes *World News*, a daily newspaper with a circulation of over 17,000, and a weekly newspaper, *South Coast Weekly*. **Special programs:** Internships. **Corporate headquarters location:** Herndon VA. **Other U.S. locations:** Nationwide. **Parent company:** SLNI, Inc. **Operations at this facility include:** Administration; Manufacturing.

XEROX CORPORATION
121 SW Morrison Street, Suite 500, Portland OR 97204. 503/221-1850. **Contact:** Human Resources. **World Wide Web address:** http://www.xerox.com. **Description:** Manufactures business machines, copiers, computer systems, and word processors. The company also publishes educational materials through various subsidiaries and manufactures aerospace systems and components, electrostatic printers, microfiche printers, and many other related products. In addition, Xerox provides international communications services and systems. **NOTE:** Jobseekers are encouraged to apply via the Website. **Positions advertised include:** Accounting and Internal Controls Specialist; Accounting Manager; Accounts Payable Specialist; Color Imaging Scientist; Sales Executive; Supplier Quality Engineer. **Corporate headquarters location:** Stamford CT.

YMCA OF GRANTS PASS
1000 Redwood Avenue, P.O. Box 5439, Grants Pass OR 97527-0439. 541/474-0001. **Contact:** Human Resources. **World Wide Web address:** http://www.ymca.com. **Description:** One of the nation's largest and most comprehensive service organizations. The YMCA provides health and fitness, social and personal development, sports and recreation, education and career development, and camps and conferences to children, youths, adults, the elderly, families, the disabled, refugees and foreign nationals, YMCA residents, and community residents, through a broad range of specific programs.

YOCREAM INTERNATIONAL
5858 NE 87th Avenue, Portland OR 97220. 503/256-3754. **Fax:** 503/256-3976. **Contact:** Human Resources. **E-mail address:** info@yocream.com. **World Wide Web address:** http://www.yocream.com. **Description:** Develops, manufactures, and markets frozen desserts, snacks, and beverages. The company specializes in frozen yogurt, ice cream, smoothies, and sorbet. Founded in 1976.

AAA MID-ATLANTIC
2040 Market Street, Suite 200, Philadelphia PA 19103. 215/864-5050. **Fax:** 215/864-5438. **Contact:** Ron Gray, Manager of Human Resources. **World Wide Web address:** http://www.aaamidatlantic.com. **Description:** Provides insurance, travel, and a wide variety of services to motorists through a network of over 50 branch offices. **Positions advertised include:** Business Systems Analyst; Insurance Counselor; Retail Agent; Office Supervisor; Travel Agent. **Corporate headquarters location:** Heathrow FL. **Other U.S. locations:** Nationwide.

AAA MID-ATLANTIC
9475 Roosevelt Boulevard, Philadelphia PA 19114. 215/289-6100. **Contact:** Michelle Vandoran, Personnel. **World Wide Web address:** http://www.aaamidatlantic.com. **Description:** Provides insurance, travel, and a wide variety of services to motorists through a network of more than 50 branch offices. **Positions advertised include:** Business Systems Analyst; Insurance Counselor; Retail Agent; Office Supervisor; Travel Agent. **Corporate headquarters location:** Heathrow FL. **Other U.S. locations:** Nationwide.

ABB INSTRUMENTATION CO.
125 East County Line Road, Warminster PA 18974. 215/674-6000. **Contact:** Ms. Aimee Watson, Manager of Employee Relations. **World Wide Web address:** http://www.abb.com. **Description:** Engaged in the design, manufacture, sale, and service of electronic and pneumatic instruments, specific process analyzers, and analog and digital systems that measure and control flow temperatures, pressure, and level. **Positions advertised include:** Field Service Engineer; Marketing Engineer; Human Resources; Applications Engineer; Assistant Controller. **Corporate headquarters location:** Zurich Switzerland. **Listed on:** New York Stock Exchange. **Stock exchange symbol:** ABB.

ADT SECURITY SERVICES, INC.
2858 Banksville Road, Pittsburgh PA 15216. 412/572-8000. **Contact:** Human Resources. **World Wide Web address:** http://www.adt.com. **Description:** ADT designs, programs, markets, and installs protective systems to safeguard life and property from hazards such as burglary, robbery, and fire. **NOTE:** See http;//www.monster.com for a listing of available jobs at ADT. **Corporate headquarters location:** Boca Raton FL. **Operations at this facility include:** This location is a sales and service office.

AK STEEL BUTLER WORKS
One ARMCO Drive, P.O. Box 832, Butler PA 16003-0832. 724/284-2000. **Fax:** 724/284-2198. **Contact:** Leslie Bergbigler, Human Resources. **E-mail address:** career.oppt@aksteel.com. **World Wide Web address:** http://www.aksteel.com. **Description:** Manufactures specialty and electrical flat-rolled steel products. **Corporate headquarters location:** Middletown OH. **Listed on:** New York Stock Exchange. **Stock exchange symbol:** AKS.

AM COMMUNICATIONS
1900 AM Drive, Quakertown PA 18951-2107. 215/536-1354. **Fax:** 215/538-8779. **Contact:** Patricia Eynon, Human Resources. **E-mail address:** careers@ amcomm.com. **World Wide Web address:** http://www.amcomm.com. **Description:** One of the world's leading suppliers of network status and performance monitoring systems for hybrid fiber/coaxial telecommunications networks. Products are sold directly to cable system operators and through original equipment manufacturers. Founded in 1974. **NOTE:** E-mail human resources through the web site to learn about employment opportunities. **Corporate headquarters location:** This location.

AMI DODUCO
Murray Corporate Park, 1003 Corporate Lane, Export PA 15632. 724/733-8332. **Fax:** 724/733-2880. **Contact:** Human Resources. **E-mail address:** anoble@amidoduco.com. **World Wide Web address:** http://www.amidoduco.com. **Description:** Producers of electrical current carrying wiring devices. **Corporate headquarters location:** This location.

AT&T WIRELESS SERVICES
2400 Penn Avenue, Pittsburgh PA 15222. 412/803-3600. **Contact:** Human Resources. **World Wide Web address:** http://www.attwireless.com. **Description:** Provides mobile phone services. **Positions advertised include:** Billing Analyst; Manager-Cross Sell; Legal Compliance Analyst; Application Solution Consultant. **Parent company:** AT&T Company is a major long-distance telephone company providing domestic and international voice and data communications and management services, telecommunications products, and leasing and financial services. The company manufactures data communications products, computer products, switching and transmission equipment, and components. Its subsidiary, AT&T Capital Corporation, offers financing and leases and provides consumer credit through its AT&T Universal credit card.

ACCO CHAIN & LIFTING PRODUCTS
P.O. Box 792, York PA 17405. 717/741-4863. **Toll-free phone:** 800/967-7222. **Fax:** 800/881-7955. **Physical address:** 76 ACCO Drive, York PA 17402. **Contact:** Mr. Terry Staley, Human Resources Manager. **World Wide Web address:** http://www.accochain.com. **Description:** Manufactures welded and weldless chains, hooks, slings, tire chains, load binders, hoists, and other lifting equipment. **Corporate headquarters location:** Fairfield CT. **Operations at this facility include:** Administration; Design; Divisional Headquarters; Manufacturing; Sales; Service.

ACCU-SORT SYSTEMS, INC.
511 School House Road, Telford PA 18969. 215/723-0981. **Toll-free phone:** 800/BAR-CODE. **Fax:** 215/996-8249. **Contact:** Roxanne Detweiler, Human Resources. **E-mail address:** jobs@accusort.com. **World Wide Web address:** http://www.accusort.com. **Description:** A leading manufacturer of bar code scanners and other material handling systems. **NOTE:** Entry-level positions and part-time jobs are offered. **Company slogan:** Solutions with vision. **Special programs:** Internships; Training; Co-ops; Summer Jobs. **Office hours:** Monday - Friday, 8:00 a.m. - 5:30 p.m. **Corporate headquarters location:** This location. **Other U.S. locations:** Nationwide. **International locations:** Worldwide. **Number of employees nationwide:** 500.

ACCUWEATHER, INC.
385 Science Park Road, State College PA 16803. 814/237-0309. **Fax:** 814/235-8599. **Contact:** John Graham, Human Resources Manager. **E-mail address:** resume@accuwx.com. **World Wide Web address:** http://www.accuweather.com. **Description:** One of the world's leading commercial weather services providing information and products to customers nationwide. Founded in 1962. **NOTE:** Entry-level positions and second and third shifts are offered. **Positions advertised include:** Forecaster; Production Manager; Marketing Manager Multimedia; Purchasing Assistant; Administrative Assistant; Account Executive; Meteorological Programmer. **Special programs:** Internships. **Corporate headquarters location:** This location. **Subsidiaries include:** Perfect Date. **Number of employees at this location:** 320.

ACME CORRUGATED BOX
2700 Turnpike Drive, Hatboro PA 19040. 215/444-8000. **Fax:** 215/956-0675. **Contact:** Human Resources. **World Wide Web address:** http://www.acmebox.com. **Description:** Acme Corrugated Box company is a supplier and manufacturer of corrugated boxes. **NOTE:** Please apply for positions through company website or fax resume to 215/956-0675. **Positions advertised include:** Customer Service Representative; Forklift Operator; Plant Supervisor.

ACME MANUFACTURING COMPANY
7601 State Road, Philadelphia PA 19136. 215/338-2850. **Contact:** General Manager. **E-mail address:** merrimanc@acmemfg.com. **World Wide Web address:** http://www.acmemfg.com. **Description:** Manufactures sheet metal products including heating and air conditioning equipment. **Corporate headquarters location:** Auburn Hills MI.

ACTION MANUFACTURING COMPANY
100 East Erie Avenue, Philadelphia PA 19134. 215/739-6400. **Contact:** Mr. Toni Capella, Personnel. **World Wide Web address:** http://www.action-mfg.com. **Description:** A manufacturer of precision electromechanical instruments and ordnance products. **Corporate headquarters location:** This location. **Operations at this facility include:** Administration; Manufacturing; Regional Headquarters.

ADALTIS U.S. INC.
754 Roble Road, Suite 70, Allentown PA 18109. 610/264-0885. **Fax:** 610/264-8102. **Contact:** Linda Kurtz, Manager of Human Resources. **E-mail address:** generalinfo.usa@adaltis.com. **World Wide Web address:** http://www.adaltis.com. **Description:** A manufacturer and distributor of diagnostic medical instrument systems. **Special programs:** Internships. **Corporate headquarters location:** Boston MA. **Operations at this facility include:** Manufacturing; Sales.

ADELPHIA COMMUNICATIONS CORPORATION
One North Main Street, Coudersport PA 16915. 814/274-9830. **Fax:** 814/274-6692. **Contact:** Human Resources. **World Wide Web address:** http://www.adelphia.com. **Description:** Provides digital cable television, long-distance telephone, paging, and high-speed Internet connection services. **NOTE:** Entry-level positions are offered. **Special programs:** Internships; Training. **Corporate headquarters location:** This location. **Other U.S. locations:** FL; MA; MI; NH; NJ; NY; NC; OH; SC; VA. **Operations at this facility include:** Administration; Divisional Headquarters; Regional Headquarters; Research and Development; Sales; Service. **Listed on:** NASDAQ. **Stock exchange symbol:** ADLAE. **Annual sales/revenues:** $21 - $50 million. **Number of employees at this location:** 300. **Number of employees nationwide:** 3,000.

ADONIX TRANSCOMM, INC.
2200 Georgetowne Drive, Sewickley PA 15143. 724/933-1377. **Fax:** 724/933-1379. **Contact:** Human Resources. **E-mail address:** careers@adonix.com. **World Wide Web address:** http://www.adonix.com. **Description:** A leading provider of business software and consulting services. The company's software products include TOLAS and Baan, which are used for sales, customer service, product distribution, logistics, warehouse management, inventory, and financial control. **Positions advertised include:** ERP Consultant; Financial Consultant; Manufacturing Consultant. **Other U.S. locations:** Huntington Beach CA; Tarrytown NY. **Listed on:** Privately held. **President:** Ronald Book. **Number of employees nationwide:** 200.

ADVANCED CAST PRODUCTS
18700 Mill Street, P.O. Box 417, Meadville PA 16335-3644. 814/724-2600. **Fax:** 814/333-1118. **Contact:** Donna Fletcher, Personnel. **E-mail address:** hr@advancedcast.com. **World Wide Web address:** http://www.advancedcast.com. **Description:** Manufactures duct wire and castings.

ADVANTA CORPORATION
Welsh & McKean Roads, P.O. Box 844, Spring House PA 19477-0844. 215/657-4000. **Contact:** Human Resources. **World Wide Web address:** http://www.advanta.com. **Description:** Advanta Corporation is a consumer financial services holding company. The company provides origination and management services for credit cards and mortgages; markets deposit products; and engages in credit insurance, life insurance, disability insurance, and unemployment insurance services. **Corporate headquarters location:** This location. **Other U.S. locations:** CA; MD; NJ; NY. **Operations at this facility include:** This location is the principal operating office. **Subsidiaries include:** Advanta Leasing Corporation specializes in small-ticket equipment leasing; Colonial National Bank offers traditional financial services. **Listed on:** NASDAQ. **Stock exchange symbol:** ADVNA; ADVNB. **Number of employees nationwide:** 1,750.

AETNA U.S. HEALTHCARE
980 Jolly Road, Blue Bell PA 19422-1904. 215/775-4800. **Contact:** Human Resources. **World Wide Web address:** http://www.aetna.com. **Description:** Operates health maintenance organizations. **NOTE:** All resumes should be sent to Aetna U.S. Healthcare, National Scanning Center, 151 Farmington Avenue, Hartford CT 06156. **Corporate headquarters location:** Hartford CT. **Operations at this facility include:** Administration; Sales; Service.

AETNA U.S. HEALTHCARE
5313 Campbells Run Road, Pittsburgh PA 15205. 412/788-0500. **Contact:** Human Resources. **World Wide Web address:** http://www.aetna.com. **Description:** Operates health maintenance organizations. **NOTE:** All resumes should be sent to Aetna U.S. Healthcare, National Scanning Center, 151 Farmington Avenue, Hartford CT 06156.

AGERE SYSTEMS
2525 North 12th Street, Reading PA 19605. 610/939-7011. **Toll-free phone:** 800/372-2447. **Contact:** Mike Deloretta, Director of Human Resources. **World Wide Web address:** http://www.agere.com. **Description:** Manufactures communications products including switching, transmission, fiber-optic cable, wireless systems, and operations systems, to supply the needs of telephone companies and other communications service providers. **Positions advertised include:** Applications Manager; Product Engineer; Technical Manager; Analog Designer; Marketing Manager; Employee Communications Manager. **Listed on:** New York Stock Exchange. **Stock exchange symbol:** AGR.

AIR PRODUCTS AND CHEMICALS, INC.
7201 Hamilton Boulevard, Allentown PA 18195-1501. 610/481-4911. **Toll-free phone:** 800/272-5442. **Contact:** Human Resources. **World Wide Web address:** http://www.airproducts.com. **Description:** Manufactures industrial gases, process equipment, and chemicals. The company's products include cryogenic equipment, air separation systems, hydrogen purification devices, and nitrogen rejection equipment. In addition, the company provides engineering services, and is involved in landfill gas recovery, waste management, waste-to-energy ventures, flue gas desulfurization, and cogeneration operations. **Special programs:** Internships. **Corporate headquarters**

location: This location. **Other U.S. locations:** Nationwide. **International locations:** Worldwide. **Listed on:** New York Stock Exchange. **Stock exchange symbol:** APD. **Annual sales/revenues:** More than $100 million.

AIR PRODUCTS AND CHEMICALS, INC.
Freeport Road Route 28, Creighton PA 15030. 724/226-1513. **Toll-free phone:** 800/272-5442. **Contact:** Human Resources. **World Wide Web address:** http://www.airproducts.com. **Description:** Air Products and Chemicals is a manufacturer of industrial gases, process equipment, and chemicals. Products include cryogenic equipment, air separation systems, hydrogen purification devices, and nitrogen rejection equipment. In addition, the company is a provider of engineering services, and is involved in landfill gas recovery, waste management, waste-to-energy ventures, flue gas desulfurization, and cogeneration operations. **NOTE:** Resumes should be addressed to Career Development, Air Products & Chemicals, Inc., 7201 Hamilton Boulevard, Allentown PA 18195. **Corporate headquarters location:** Allentown PA. **Other U.S. locations:** Nationwide. **International locations:** Worldwide. **Operations at this facility include:** This location produces industrial gases including oxygen and nitrogen. **Listed on:** New York Stock Exchange. **Stock exchange symbol:** APD. **Annual sales/revenues:** More than $100 million.

AIRGAS, INC.
259 North Radnor-Chester Road, Suite 100, Radnor PA 19087. 610/687-5253. **Fax:** 610/687-5611. **Contact:** Personnel. **E-mail address:** jobs@airgas.com. **World Wide Web address:** http://www.airgas.com. **Description:** Airgas, Inc. distributes industrial, medical, and specialty gases; protective equipment; and welding accessories. **Positions advertised include:** Medical Manager; Staff Accountant; Distribution Center Manager; Inside Sales; Cryogenic Technician. **Listed on:** New York Stock Exchange. **Stock exchange symbol:** ARG. **Number of employees nationwide:** 2,800.

AJILON SERVICES INC.
5 Tower Bridge, Suite 550, 300 Bar Harbor Drive, Conshohocken PA 19428. 610/834-8290. **Toll-free phone:** 800/627-8082. **Contact:** Recruiting. **World Wide Web address:** http://www.ajilon.com. **Description:** Provides computer consulting services, project support, and end user services. **Other U.S. locations:** Nationwide.

ALBERT EINSTEIN MEDICAL CENTER
5501 Old York Road, Philadelphia PA 19141. 215/456-7890. **Contact:** Human Resources. **World Wide Web address:** http://www.einstein.edu. **Description:** A teaching hospital specializing in behavioral health; coronary care; geriatrics; liver, kidney, and pancreas transplants; orthopedics; and women's and children's health. **NOTE:** For additional job information contact: Albert Einstein Healthcare Network Recruiting and Placement Center, One Penn Boulevard, 1st Floor Main Building, Philadelphia PA 19144. **Positions advertised include:** File Clerk; Billing Analyst; Rehabilitation Coordinator; Physical Therapist; Secretary; Research Assistant; Account Executive; Clerk Service Representative; Occupational Therapist; Clinical Trial Coordinator; Social Worker.

ALBRIGHT CARE SERVICES
1700 Normandie Drive, York PA 17404. 717/764-6262. **Toll-free phone:** 888/970-6565. **Contact:** Human Resources. **E-mail address:** normandie@albrightcare.org. **World Wide Web address:** http://www.albrightcare.org. **Description:** Albright Care Services owns and operates senior living communities that offer a range of housing and healthcare options. **Positions advertised include:** CAN; LPN; RN; Director of Environmental Services.

ALBRIGHT CARE SERVICES
3201 River Road, Lewisburg PA 17837. 570/524-2271. **Toll-free phone:** 888/791-0096. **Contact:** Human Resources. **E-mail address:** riverwoodsemployment@albrightcare.org. **World Wide Web address:** http://www.albrightcare.org. **Description:** Albright Care Services owns and operates senior living communities that offer a range of housing and healthcare options. **Positions advertised include:** Nurse; Nursing Assistant; Nurse Supervisor.

ALCOA (ALUMINUM COMPANY OF AMERICA)
201 Isabella Street, Pittsburgh PA 15212-5858. 412/553-4545. **Fax:** 412/553-4498. **Contact:** Human Resources Manager. **World Wide Web address:** http://www.alcoa.com. **Description:** Engaged in all aspects of the aluminum industry including mining, refining, smelting, fabricating, and recycling. ALCOA also manufactures ceramic packaging for the semiconductor industry, alumina chemicals, plastic bottle closures, vinyl siding, packaging machinery, and electrical distribution systems for automobiles. **Corporate headquarters location:** This location. **Other U.S. locations:** Nationwide. **International locations:** Worldwide. **Listed on:** New York Stock Exchange. **Stock exchange symbol:** AA. **Annual sales/revenues:** More than $100 million. **Number of employees worldwide:** 120,000.

ALCOA TECHNICAL CENTER
100 Technical Drive, ALCOA Center PA 15069. 724/339-6651. **Fax:** 724/337-4186. **Contact:** Human Resources. **World Wide Web address:** http://www.alcoa.com. **Description:** Engaged in all aspects of the aluminum industry including mining, refining, smelting, fabricating, and recycling. ALCOA also manufactures ceramic packaging for the semiconductor industry, alumina chemicals, plastic bottle closures, vinyl siding, packaging machinery, and electrical distribution systems for automobiles. **Corporate headquarters location:** Pittsburgh PA. **Listed on:** New York Stock Exchange. **Stock exchange symbol:** AA. **Annual sales/revenues:** More than $100 million. **Number of employees worldwide:** 120,000.

ALFA LAVAL SEPARATION INC.
955 Mearns Road, Warminster PA 18974. 215/443-4000. **Fax:** 215/443-4253. **Contact:** Human Resources. **E-mail address:** humanresources.usa@alfalaval.com. **World Wide Web address:** http://www.alfalaval.com. **Description:** Alfa Laval Separation is divided into five market sectors: Industrial Separation supplies separation equipment for the chemical, pharmaceutical, and other process industries; Marine and Power specializes in cleaning and conditioning systems for fuel oils and lubricant oils in marine and power station diesel engines, as well as fuel cleaning and forwarding systems for gas-turbine power stations; Desalination supplies desalination plants for producing freshwater for ships, power stations, and offshore platforms; Pulp and Paper's products include equipment for pulp cleaning, filters and presses for dewatering, and new technology for processing recycled fibers; and Oil Field products include high-capacity separation systems for use in onshore and offshore oil and gas production, and in the storage and refining of crude oil. **Special programs:** Internships. **Corporate headquarters location:** This location. **Parent company:** Alfa Laval, one of Sweden's oldest companies, was formed in 1883 to market the continuous separator. Operations include environmental protection, optimal utilization of energy, and food supply. The group develops and markets products such as separators, heat exchangers, flow equipment, and computerized control systems. Alfa Laval has production facilities, marketing companies, and representatives throughout the world. **Operations at this facility include:** Administration; Manufacturing; Research and Development; Sales; Service. **Listed on:** Privately held. **Number of employees at this location:** 450. **Number of employees nationwide:** 600.

ALL-LUMINUM PRODUCTS, INC.
10981 Decatur Road, Philadelphia PA 19154-3297. 215/632-2800. **Fax:** 215/824-1172. **Contact:** Human Resources Manager. **World Wide Web address:** http://www.all-luminum.com. **Description:** A manufacturer of casual outdoor and indoor furniture. **Corporate headquarters location:** This location. **Operations at this facility include:** Administration; Manufacturing; Research and Development; Sales; Service.

ALL SEASONS SERVICES
4060 Blanche Road, Bensalem PA 19020. 215/638-8800. **Contact:** Human Resources. **E-mail address:** jobs@allseasonsservices.com. **World Wide Web address:** http://www.allseasonsservices.com. **Description:** Provides a wide variety coffee, snacks, and vending machines to businesses. **Positions advertised include:** Sales Executive; Area Manager; Dining Center Manager; Cook; Operations Manager; Route Supervisor; Warehouse Personnel.

ALLEGHENY COLLEGE
520 North Main Street, Meadville PA 16335. 814/332-2312. **Contact:** Human Resources. **E-mail address:** info@allegheny.edu. **World Wide Web address:** http://www.alleg.edu. **Description:** A four-year college awarding B.A. and B.S. degrees. Allegheny College has an undergraduate enrollment of approximately 1,950 students.

ALLEGHENY ENERGY, INC.
800 Cabin Hill Drive, Greensburg PA 15601. 724/838-6617. **Fax:** 724/830-5801. **Recorded jobline:** 877/276-7364. **Contact:** Manager of Human Resources. **E-mail address:** resumes@alleghenyenergy.com. **World Wide Web address:** http://www.alleghenyenergy.com. **Description:** A utility holding company comprised of three businesses: Allegheny Energy Supply, an electricity generation business; Allegheny Power, a utility transmission/distribution/customer service company; and Allegheny Ventures, which comprises unregulated business ventures such as telecommunications. **NOTE:** Entry-level positions, part-time jobs, and second and third shifts offered. **Company slogan:** America's Best Energy Value. **Positions advertised include:** Accountant; Senior Accountant; Planning Engineer; Substation Support Engineer. **Special programs:** Internships; Apprenticeships; Summer Jobs. **Corporate headquarters location:** Hagerstown MD. **Listed on:** New York Stock Exchange. **Stock exchange symbol:** AYE. **Annual sales/revenues:** $5 - $10 million. **Number of employees nationwide:** 5,000.

ALLEGHENY LUDLUM CORPORATION
100 River Road, Brackenridge PA 15014. 724/224-1000. **Contact:** Human Resources. **World Wide Web address:** http://www.alleghenyludlum.com. **Description:** Produces and markets specialty materials including stainless steels, tolls steels, and advanced alloys to a customer base in more than 30 countries. **NOTE:** Vacant positions are listed on Monster.com. **Positions advertised include:** Metallurgist; Safety Professional; Inside Sales Representative; Electrical Engineer. **Parent company:** Allegheny Technologies.

ALLEGHENY TECHNOLOGIES INCORPORATED
1000 Six PPG Place, Pittsburgh PA 15222. 412/394-2800. **Contact:** Human Resources. **World Wide Web address:** http://www.alleghenytechnologies.com. **Description:** Manufactures specialty materials including stainless steel, nickel-based alloys and superalloys, titanium alloys, zirconium alloys, and tungsten powder. **NOTE:** Vacant positions are listed on http://www.monster.com. **Corporate headquarters location:** This location.

ALLEGHENY VALLEY SCHOOL
1996 Ewings Mill Road, Coraopolis PA 15108. 412/299-7777. **Fax:** 412/299-6701. **Contact:** Richard R. Rizzutto, Director of Human Resources. **World Wide Web address:** http://www.alleghenyvalleyschool.com. **Description:** A nonprofit company that operates residential facilities for individuals with mental disabilities. Founded in 1960. **NOTE:** Entry-level positions, part-time jobs, and second and third shifts are offered. **Positions advertised include:** Program Development Assistant; Assistant House Manager; Direct Care Worker; House Manager Aide; Registered Nurse; Licensed Practical Nurse; Program Instructor. **Corporate headquarters location:** This location. **Executive Director:** Regis G. Champ. **Annual sales/revenues:** $51 - $100 million. **Number of employees at this location:** 1,000.

ALLEGRO MICROSYSTEMS
3900 Welsh Road, Willow Grove PA 19090-2995. 215/657-8400. **Contact:** Human Resources. **E-mail address:** allegro@rpc.webhire.com. **World Wide Web address:** http://www.allegromicro.com. **Description:** Manufactures semiconductors and mixed-signal integrated circuits. **Corporate headquarters location:** Worcester MA. **Parent company:** Sanken Electric Company Ltd.

ALLEN ORGAN COMPANY
150 Locust Street, P.O. Box 36, Macungie PA 18062-0036. 610/966-2202. **Fax:** 610/965-3098. **Contact:** T. O'Malley, Personnel Department. **E-mail address:** tomalley@allenorgan.com. **World Wide Web address:** http://www.allenorgan.com. **Description:** A manufacturer of electronic keyboard musical instruments including digital computer organs and related accessories. **Corporate headquarters location:** This location.

ALLEN-SHERMAN-HOFF
P.O. Box 3006, 185 Great Valley Parkway, Malvern PA 19355-1321. 610/647-9900. **Fax:** 610/648-8724. **Contact:** Human Resources. **World Wide Web address:** http://www.ebizdiamondpower.com. **Description:** Engaged in the design engineering of material handling systems for power plants and industrial applications.

ALLIANCE IMAGING, INC.
20 Stanwix Street, 11th Floor, Pittsburgh PA 15222. 412/281-5660. **Toll-free phone:** 800/453-8135. **Fax:** 412/281-1767. **Contact:** Human Resources Manager. **E-mail address:** info@allianceimaging.com. **World Wide Web address:** http://www.allianceimaging.com. **Description:** Provides medical diagnostic imaging services to hospitals, physicians, and patients. Services include MRI, Open MRI, computer tomography (CT), ultrasound, and position emission tomography (PET). **Positions advertised include:** MRI/CT Technologist; Driver; **Corporate headquarters location:** Anaheim CA. **Listed on:** New York Stock Exchange. **Stock exchange symbol:** AIQ.

ALLIED SECURITY INC.
3606 Horizon Drive, King of Prussia PA 19406. 610/239-1100. **Toll-free phone:** 800/437-8803. **Fax:** 610/239-1107. **Contact:** Human Resources. **World Wide Web address:** http://www.alliedsecurity.com. **Description:** One of the largest national contract security officer companies in the United States. Allied Security provides loss

prevention services to private businesses and government agencies. **Positions advertised include:** Security Guard. **Special programs:** Internships. **Office hours:** Monday - Friday, 8:00 a.m. - 5:00 p.m. **Corporate headquarters location:** This location. **Subsidiaries include:** Allsafe Security Inc. **Operations at this facility include:** Administration; Sales; Service. **Listed on:** Privately held. **Annual sales/revenues:** More than $100 million. **Number of employees at this location:** 45. **Number of employees nationwide:** 8,000.

ALLSTATE INSURANCE COMPANY
701 Lee Road, Wayne PA 19087. 610/240-3000. **Contact:** Human Resources. **World Wide Web address:** http://www.allstate.com/careers. **Description:** One of the nation's largest insurance companies, Allstate provides a full spectrum of property, liability, life, reinsurance, and commercial lines of insurance. **Positions advertised include:** Claim Adjuster; Claim Trainee; Financial Analyst; Staff Associate. **Corporate headquarters location:** Northbrook IL. **Listed on:** New York Stock Exchange. **Stock exchange symbol:** ALL.

ALLTECH APPLIED SCIENCE LABORATORIES
2701 Carolean Industrial Drive, State College PA 16801. 814/238-2406. **Toll-free phone:** 800/255-8324. **Fax:** 814/234-3594. **Contact:** Sharon McKinley, Manager of Operations Department. **World Wide Web address:** http://www.alltechweb.com. **Description:** A chemical manufacturer and chromatography laboratory.

ALLVAC
Route 981 North, Latrobe PA 15650-0151. 724/537-5551. **Contact:** Human Resources. **E-mail address:** hr@allvac.com. **World Wide Web address:** http://www.allvac.com. **Description:** Manufactures and sells an assortment of metal and wire products for use in critical environments such as aerospace, oil and gas, chemical, nuclear, and biomedical industries. **NOTE:** Employment matters are best handled through the website. **Parent company:** Allegheny Ludlum.

ALMO CORPORATION
2709 Commerce Way, Philadelphia PA 19154. 215/698-4000. **Fax:** 215/698-4080. **Contact:** Ms. Terry Vittorelli, Human Resources Director. **E-mail address:** employment@almo.com. **World Wide Web address:** http://www.almo.com. **Description:** A multiregional distributor of computer products, consumer electronics, major appliances, and specialty wire and cable. **NOTE:** Entry-level positions are offered. **Corporate headquarters location:** This location. **Other U.S. locations:** MA; MD; MO; WI. **Operations at this facility include:** Administration; Divisional Headquarters; Sales. **Number of employees at this location:** 90.

ALTEC INDUSTRIES, INC.
250 Laird Street, Plains PA 18705. 570/822-3104. **Fax:** 570/822-7437. **Contact:** Human Resources. **World Wide Web address:** http://www.altec.com. **Description:** Manufactures utility trucks and equipment. **Corporate headquarters location:** Birmingham AL. **Other U.S. locations:** Nationwide. **Operations at this facility include:** Administration; Manufacturing; Sales; Service. **Listed on:** Privately held. **Number of employees at this location:** 170. **Number of employees nationwide:** 1,400.

ALTEC LANSING TECHNOLOGIES, INC.
Route 6 & 209, P.O. Box 277, Milford PA 18337-0277. 570/296-4434. **Toll-free phone:** 866/570-5702. **Fax:** 570/296-6887. **Contact:** Personnel. **E-mail address:** resumes@alteclansing.com. **World Wide Web address:** http://www.altecmm.com. **Description:** Manufactures speakers and surround sound systems for computers. **NOTE:** Entry-level positions are offered. **Special programs:** Internships; Co-ops. **Office hours:** Monday - Friday, 8:30 a.m. - 5:00 p.m. **Corporate headquarters location:** This location. **Other U.S. locations:** Nationwide. **International locations:** Worldwide. **Listed on:** Privately held. **Number of employees at this location:** 130.

ALTOONA, CITY OF
1301 12th Street, Suite 301, Altoona PA 16601-3458. 814/949-2428. **Fax:** 814/949-2437. **Contact:** Human Resources. **E-mail address:** personnel@altonnapa.gov. **World Wide Web address:** http://www.altoonapa.gov. **Description:** The administrative offices of the city of Altoona, responsible for staffing of all municipal departments. **Positions advertised include:** Building Inspector. **City Manager:** Joseph F. Weakland. **Number of employees at this location:** 300.

AMERICAN BANK NOTE COMPANY
2520 Metropolitan Drive, Trevose PA 19053. 215/396-8707. **Fax:** 215/396-9049. **Contact:** Human Resources. **E-mail address:** recruiter@abncompany.com. **World Wide Web address:** http://www.abncompany.com. **Description:** A printer of counterfeit-resistant documents and one of the largest security printers in the world. American Bank Note creates secure documents of value for governments and corporations worldwide. Products include currencies; passports; stock and bond certificates; bank, corporate, government, and traveler's checks; food coupons; gift vouchers and certificates; driver's licenses; product authentication labels; and vital documents. **Corporate headquarters location:** New York NY. **Other U.S. locations:** Burbank CA; Long Beach CA; San Francisco CA; Washington DC; Atlanta GA; Bedford Park IL; Needham MA; St. Louis MO; Huntington Valley PA; Philadelphia PA; Pittsburgh PA; Dallas TX. **Parent company:** American Bank Note Corporation also operates two other subsidiaries. American Bank Note Holographics, Inc. is one of the world's largest producers of the laser-generated, three-dimensional images that appear on credit cards and products requiring proof of authenticity; and American Bank Note Company Brazil is one of Brazil's largest private security printers and a provider of personalized checks, financial transaction cards, and prepaid telephone cards.

AMERICAN BANK NOTE HOLOGRAPHICS, INC.
1448 County Line Road, Huntington Valley PA 19006. 215/357-5300. **Fax:** 215/357-5331. **Contact:** Human Resources. **E-mail address:** recruiter@abnh.com. **World Wide Web address:** http://www.abnh.com. **Description:** American Bank Note Holographics is one of the world's largest producers of the laser-generated, three-dimensional images that appear on credit cards and products requiring proof of authenticity. **Corporate headquarters location:** New York NY. **Other U.S. locations:** Burbank CA; Long Beach CA; San Francisco CA; Washington DC; Atlanta GA; Bedford Park IL; Needham MA; St. Louis MO; Horsham PA; Philadelphia PA; Pittsburgh PA; Dallas TX. **Operation at this facility include:** This location is a holographic printing facility. **Parent company:** American Bank Note Corporation operates two other subsidiaries. American Bank Note Company is a printer of counterfeit-resistant documents and one of the largest security printers in the world. American Bank Note Company creates secure documents of value for governments and corporations worldwide. Products include currencies; passports; stock and bond certificates; bank, corporate, government, and traveler's checks; food coupons; gift vouchers and certificates: driver's licenses; product authentication labels; and vital documents. American Bank Note Company Brazil is one of Brazil's largest private security printers and a provider of personalized checks, financial transaction cards, and prepaid telephone cards.

AMERICAN EAGLE OUTFITTERS
150 Thorn Hill Drive, Warrendale PA 15086. 724/776-4857. **Fax:** 724/779-5568. **Contact:** Jeff Skogelind, Vice-President of Human Resources. **E-mail address:** cooljobs@ae.com. **World Wide Web address:** http://www.ae.com. **Description:** A specialty retailer selling casual clothing and accessories for men and women. American Eagle Outfitters operates over 300 stores throughout the United States. **NOTE:** Employment matters are best handled through the website. **Positions advertised include:** Web Designer; Creative Manager; Merchandise Planner; Assistant Buyer. **Corporate headquarters location:** This location. **Operations at this facility include:** Sales; Service. **Listed on:** NASDAQ. **Stock exchange symbol:** AEOS. **Number of employees nationwide:** 6,000.

AMERICAN EXPRESS TRAVEL RELATED SERVICES
2 PPG Place, Market Square, Pittsburgh PA 15222. 412/577-6911. **Contact:** Human Resources. **Description:** Provides travel services including trip planning, reservations, and ticketing for corporate clients. **Parent company:** American Express Company is a diversified travel and financial services company operating in 160 countries around the world. American Express Travel Related Services offers consumers the Personal, Gold, and Platinum Cards, as well as revolving credit products such as Optima Cards, which allow customers to extend payments. Other products include the American Express Corporate Card, which helps businesses manage their travel and entertainment expenditures; and the Corporate Purchasing Card, which helps businesses manage their expenditures on supplies, equipment, and services.

AMERICAN METER COMPANY
300 Welsh Road, Building One, Horsham PA 19044-2224. 215/830-1800. **Contact:** Department WE&E. **E-mail address:** hra@americanmeter.com. **World Wide Web address:** http://www.americanmeter.com. **Description:** Manufactures vapor gas measurement products. **Positions advertised include:** Senior Design Engineer. **Corporate headquarters location:** This location. **Parent company:** Elster-amco.

AMERICAN WIRE WORKS
3380 Tulip Street, Philadelphia PA 19134. 215/744-6600. **Contact:** Personnel Department. **Description:** A wire manufacturer and processor. **Number of employees at this location:** 15.

AMERISOURCEBERGEN CORPORATION
1300 Morris Drive, Suite 100, Chesterbrook PA 19087-5594. 610/727-7000. **Toll-free phone:** 800/829-3132. **Fax:** 610/727-3611. **Contact:** Lisa Hickman, Human Resources Manager. **World Wide Web address:** http://www.amerisourcebergen.com. **Description:** A large pharmaceutical distribution company serving hospitals, nursing homes, clinics, and pharmacy chains. The company also provides health and beauty aids, general merchandise, inventory control, emergency delivery, and marketing and promotional services. **Corporate headquarters location:** This location. **Other U.S. locations:** Orange CA. **Listed on:** New York Stock Exchange. **Stock exchange symbol:** ABC. **Annual sales/revenues:** More than $100 million.

AMETEK DREXELBROOK
205 Keith Valley Road, Horsham PA 19044. 215/674-1234. **Contact:** Personnel Department. **World Wide Web address:** http://www.drexelbrook.com. **Description:** A manufacturer of level control and level measurement instrumentation for the process control industry. **Corporate headquarters location:** This location.

AMETEK, INC.
900 Clymer Avenue, Sellersville PA 18960. 215/257-6531. **Fax:** 215/257-8652. **Contact:** Human Resources. **World Wide Web address:** http://www.ametek.com. **Description:** AMETEK is a global manufacturing company that serves a variety of industrial and commercial markets through its Electromechanical, Precision Instruments, and Industrial Materials Groups. The Electromechanical Group has a leading market share in the production of electric motors for vacuum cleaners and floor care products, with a growing business in technical motor products for computer, medical, and other markets. The company operates more than 30 manufacturing facilities in 12 states. **Corporate headquarters location:** Paoli PA. **International locations:** Denmark; England; Italy; Mexico. **Operations at this facility include:** This location manufactures various types of gauges. **Listed on:** New York Stock Exchange. **Stock exchange symbol:** AME. **Number of employees worldwide:** 6,200.

AMETEK, INC.
37 North Valley Road, Building 4, P.O. Box 1764, Paoli PA 19301. 610/647-2121. **Toll-free phone:** 800/473-1286. **Fax:** 610/296-3412. **Contact:** Human Resources Department. **E-mail address:** corp.jobs@ametek.com. **World Wide Web address:** http://www.ametek.com. **Description:** A global manufacturing company that serves a variety of industrial and commercial markets through its Electromechanical, Precision Instruments, and Industrial Materials Groups. **NOTE:** To view current career opportunities, visit http://www.hotjobs.com. **Corporate headquarters location:** This location. **Other U.S. locations:** Nationwide. **International locations:** Denmark; England; Italy; Mexico. **Listed on:** New York Stock Exchange. **Stock exchange symbol:** AME. **Number of employees at this location:** 90. **Number of employees worldwide:** 6,200.

AMKOR TECHNOLOGIES
1345 Enterprise Drive, West Chester PA 19380-5964. 610/431-9600. **Fax:** 610/431-5881. **Contact:** Mr. Chris Roberts, Recruiting. **World Wide Web address:** http://www.amkor.com. **Description:** Provides semiconductor packaging and test service. Founded in 1968. **Positions advertised include:** Senior Administrative Assistant. **Corporate headquarters location:** This location. **Other U.S. locations:** Chandler AZ.

AMPCO PITTSBURGH CORPORATION
600 Grant Street, Suite 4600, Pittsburgh PA 15219-2702. 412/456-4400. **Contact:** Human Resources. **World Wide Web address:** http://www.ampcopgh.com. **Description:** Manufactures a variety of industrial products for the construction, utilities, chemical processing, marine, and defense industries including fans, heat exchange coils, and pumps. The company also manufactures machine parts for the plastics industry and forged hardened steel rolls for the metals processing industry. **Listed on:** New York Stock Exchange. **Stock exchange symbol:** AP.

AMTRAK
30th Street Station, 2nd Floor South, Box 43, Philadelphia PA 19104. 215/349-1108. **Recorded jobline:** 215/349-1069. **Contact:** Patricia Kerins, Human Resources Manager. **E-mail address:** necjobs@amtrak.com. **World Wide Web address:** http://www.teamrewards.net/amtrak. **Description:** Manages and operates an interstate passenger rail service with connections throughout the United States. **NOTE:** This office is responsible for hiring in Philadelphia PA and Wilmington DE. **Special programs:** Internships. **Operations at this facility include:** Administration; Divisional Headquarters; Regional Headquarters; Sales; Service.

ANDRITZ, INC.
35 Sherman Street, Muncy PA 17756. 570/546-8211. **Fax:** 570/546-1306. **Contact:** Pekka Ignatius, Director of Human Resources. **E-mail address:** pekka.Ignatius@andritz.com. **World Wide Web address:** http://www.andritz.com. **Description:** Engineers and manufactures capital equipment for the pulp, paper, feed, and grain industries. Founded in 1866. **NOTE:** For positions in the U.S.A. send your resume/application to the above contact at: 10745 Westside Parkway, Alpharetta GA 30004. 770/640-2500. Fax: 770/640-2521. **Special programs:** Co-ops. **Office hours:** Monday - Friday, 8:00 a.m. - 5:00 p.m. **Corporate headquarters location:** Graz, Austria. **Other U.S. locations:** GA; NY; LA; OR; AL; CA. **Parent company:** Andritz Group. **Operations at this facility include:** Pulp and paper mill facility. **Annual sales/revenues:** More than $100 million. **Number of employees at this location:** 450. **Number of employees nationwide:** 500. **Number of employees worldwide:** 4,771.

ALFRED ANGELO, INC.
1301 Virginia Drive, Suite 110, Fort Washington PA 19034. 215/659-5300. **Contact:** John Fogliano, Human Resources. **E-mail address:** jfogliano@alfredangelo.com. **World Wide Web address:** http://www.alfredangelo.com. **Description:** Designs, manufactures, and wholesales bridal gowns, special occasion dresses, and a wide range of related accessories. **Corporate headquarters location:** Delray Beach FL. **Operations at this facility include:** Administration; Design; Manufacturing; Sales; Service.

ANSYS, INC.
Southpointe, 275 Technology Drive, Canonsburg PA 15317. 724/746-3304. **Fax:** 724/514-9494. **Contact:** Human Resources. **E-mail address:** jobs@ansys.com. **World Wide Web address:** http://www.ansys.com. **Description:** Develops finite element analysis software for engineering firms. **Positions advertised include:** Field Program Manager; Technical Sales Representative; Assistant Controller; Documentation Manager. **Corporate headquarters location:** This location. **Number of employees at this location:** 600. **Listed on:** NASDAQ. **Stock exchange symbol:** ANSS.

AON RISK SERVICES
One Liberty Place, 1650 Market Street, Suite 1000, Philadelphia PA 19103. 215/255-2000. **Fax:** 215/255-1893. **Contact:** Personnel. **World Wide Web address:** http://www.aon.com. **Description:** An insurance brokerage firm. Overall, Aon Risk Services is primarily involved with property and casualty, marine, and public entities specialties. **Corporate headquarters location:** Chicago IL. **Other U.S. locations:** Nationwide. **International locations:** Worldwide. **Operations at this facility include:** Administration/sales pertaining to hospitality and lodging. **Listed on:** New York Stock Exchange. **Stock exchange symbol:** AOC.

APPLETON PAPERS INC.
100 Paper Mill Road, Roaring Spring PA 16673. 814/224-2131. **Contact:** Brad Reist, Human Resources. **World Wide Web address:** http://www.appletonideas.com. **Description:** Appleton Papers Inc. manufactures NCR brand carbonless paper, as well as other coated papers including those used in the graphic arts industry. **Positions advertised include:** Human Resources Representative; Process Engineer; **Corporate headquarters location:** Appleton WI. **Operations at this facility include:** This location is a paper mill.

APPLIED INDUSTRIAL TECHNOLOGIES
4350 H Street, Philadelphia PA 19124. 215/744-6330. **Contact:** Personnel. **E-mail address:** career@applied.com. **World Wide Web address:** http://www.applied.com. **Description:** Distributes bearings and power transmission equipment. **NOTE:** Please visit http://www.monster.com for current employment opportunities. **Corporate headquarters location:** Cleveland OH. **Other area locations:** Statewide. **Other U.S. locations:** Nationwide. **Listed on:** New York Stock Exchange. **Stock exchange symbol:** AIT.

APRIA HEALTHCARE GROUP INC.
16 Creek Parkway, Boothwyn PA 19061. 610/364-2100. **Fax:** 610/364-2270. **Contact:** Regional Human Resources. **World Wide Web address:** http://www.apria.com. **Description:** One of the largest national providers of home health care products and services, providing a broad range of respiratory therapy services, home medical equipment, and infusion therapy services. Apria has over 400 branches throughout the United States and two respiratory therapy branches in the United Kingdom. Apria's home health care services are provided to patients who have been discharged from hospitals, skilled nursing facilities, or convalescent homes and are being treated at home. In conjunction with medical professionals, Apria personnel deliver, install, and service medical equipment, as well as provide appropriate therapies and coordinate plans of care for their patients. Apria personnel also instruct patients and caregivers in the correct use of equipment and monitor the equipment's effectiveness. Patients and their families receive training from registered nurses and respiratory therapy professionals concerning the therapy administered, including instruction in proper infusion technique and the care and use of equipment and supplies. **Corporate headquarters location:** Costa Mesa CA.

AQUA AMERICA, INC.
762 West Lancaster Avenue, Bryn Mawr PA 19010-3489. 610/525-1400. **Contact:** Human Resources. **World Wide Web address:** http://www.suburbanwater.com. **Description:** A water utility company serving nearly 2.5 million residents. **Listed on:** New York Stock Exchange. **Stock exchange symbol:** WTR.

ARAMARK BUSINESS SERVICES GROUP
ARAMARK Tower, 1101 Market Street, Philadelphia PA 19107. 215/238-3591. **Fax:** 215/238-8195. **Contact:** Human Resources. **E-mail address:** resumes@aramark.com. **World Wide Web address:** http://www.aramark.com. **Description:** ARAMARK Business Services consists of Business Dining Services and Conference Center Management. Business Dining Services serves over 3 million people every business day at over 7,000 locations and offers a wide range of operations, marketing, and merchandising programs for executive dining rooms, plant cafeterias, and fully catered functions. Business Dining Services offers Cafe Connection service that brings food management to small and mid-sized facilities with limited production capabilities. ARAMARK's Conference Center Management provides comprehensive specialized services, ranging from food and beverage to total hospitality and property management. Services are provided in both residential and nonresidential centers such as executive retreats, corporate training complexes, resorts, and continuing education centers. **Parent company:** ARAMARK is one of the world's leading providers of managed services. The company operates in all 50 states and 10 foreign countries, offering a broad range of services to businesses of all sizes including many *Fortune* 500 companies and thousands of universities; hospitals; and municipal, state, and federal government facilities. ARAMARK is employee-owned. The company is among the market leaders in all of its businesses, which are: Food, Leisure and Support Services, including Campus Dining Services, School Nutrition Services, Leisure Services, Business Dining Services, International Services, Healthcare Support Services, Conference Center Management, and Refreshment Services; Facility Services; Correctional Services; Industrial Services; Uniform Services, which includes Wearguard, a direct marketer of work clothing; Health and Education Services including Spectrum Healthcare Services and Children's World Learning Centers; and Book and Magazine Services. **Listed on:** New York Stock Exchange. **Stock exchange symbol:** RMK. **Annual sales/revenues:** More than $100 million. **Number of employees nationwide:** 150,000.

ARAMARK CAMPUS DINING SERVICES
ARAMARK Tower, 1101 Market Street, Philadelphia PA 19106. 215/238-3085. **Contact:** Human Resources. **World Wide Web address:** http://www.aramark.com. **Description:** ARAMARK's Campus Dining Services serve more than 200 million meals a year at over 300 college and university campuses. Campus Dining Services provides an integrated program of national brand franchises as well as ARAMARK's own signature brands such as Itza Pizza and Deli Corner. **Parent company:** ARAMARK is one of the world's leading providers of managed services. The company operates in all 50 states and 10 foreign countries, offering a broad range of services to businesses of all sizes including many *Fortune* 500 companies and thousands of universities; hospitals; and municipal, state, and federal government facilities. ARAMARK is employee-owned. The company is among the market leaders in all of its businesses, which are: Food, Leisure and Support Services including Campus Dining Services, School Nutrition Services, Leisure Services, Business Dining Services, International Services, Healthcare Support Services, Conference Center Management, and Refreshment Services; Facility Services; Correctional Services; Industrial Services; Uniform Services, which includes Wearguard, a direct marketer of work clothing; Health and Education Services including Spectrum Healthcare Services and Children's World Learning Centers; and Book and Magazine Services. **Listed on:** New York Stock Exchange. **Stock exchange symbol:** RMK. **Annual sales/revenues:** More than $100 million. **Number of employees nationwide:** 150,000.

ARAMARK CORPORATION
ARAMARK LEISURE SERVICES GROUP
ARAMARK Tower, 1101 Market Street, Philadelphia PA 19107. 215/238-3000. **Contact:** Personnel. **World Wide Web address:** http://www.aramark.com. **Description:** One of the world's leading providers of managed services. The company operates in all 50 states and 10 foreign countries, offering a broad range of services to businesses of all sizes including most *Fortune* 500 companies and thousands of universities; hospitals; and municipal, state, and federal government facilities. ARAMARK Corporation is employee-owned. The company is among the market leaders in all of its businesses, which are: Food, Leisure and Support Services, including Campus Dining Services, School Nutrition Services, Leisure Services, Business Dining Services, International Services, Healthcare Support Services, Conference Center Management, and Refreshment Services; Facility Services; Correctional Services; Industrial Services; Uniform Services, which includes Wearguard, a direct marketer of work clothing; Health and Education Services, including Spectrum Healthcare Services and Children's World Learning Centers; and Book and Magazine Services. **Listed on:** New York Stock Exchange. **Stock exchange symbol:** RMK. **Corporate headquarters location:** This location. **Annual sales/revenues:** More than $100 million. **Number of employees nationwide:** 150,000.

ARAMARK FACILITY SERVICES
ARAMARK Tower, 1101 Market Street, Philadelphia PA 19107. 215/238-2000. **Contact:** Human Resources. **World Wide Web address:** http://www.aramark.com. **Description:** Provides housekeeping and maintenance services. **Corporate headquarters location:** This location. **Parent company:** ARAMARK Corporation is one of the world's leading providers of managed services. The company operates in all 50 states and 10 foreign countries, offering a broad range of services to businesses of all sizes, including most *Fortune* 500 companies and thousands of universities; hospitals; and municipal, state, and federal government facilities. ARAMARK is employee-owned. The company is among the market leaders in all of its businesses, which are: Food, Leisure and Support Services, including Campus Dining Services, School Nutrition Services, Leisure Services, Business Dining Services, International Services, Healthcare Support Services, Conference Center Management, and Refreshment Services; Facility Services; Correctional Services; Industrial Services; Uniform Services, which includes Wearguard, a direct marketer of work clothing; Health and Education Services including Spectrum Healthcare Services and Children's World Learning Centers; and Book and Magazine Services. **Listed on:** New York Stock Exchange. **Stock exchange symbol:** RMK. **Annual sales/revenues:** More than $100 million. **Number of employees nationwide:** 150,000.

ARAMARK HEALTHCARE SUPPORT SERVICES
ARAMARK Tower, 1101 Market Street, Philadelphia PA 19107. 215/238-3541. **Contact:** Human Resources. **World Wide Web address:** http://www.aramark.com. **Description:** ARAMARK Healthcare Support Services serves 115 million meals annually for over 300 health care customers nationwide and also provides food service, clinical nutrition management, facility services, and engineering support to assist health care administrators. ARAMARK Healthcare Support provides value-added services related to resource management, revenue generation, and business planning. **Parent company:** ARAMARK is one of the world's leading providers of managed services. The company operates in all 50 states and 10 foreign countries, offering a broad range of services to businesses of all sizes including many *Fortune* 500 companies and thousands of universities; hospitals; and municipal, state, and federal government facilities. ARAMARK is employee-owned. The company is among the market leaders in all of its businesses, which are: Food, Leisure and Support Services including Campus Dining Services, School Nutrition Services, Leisure Services, Business Dining Services, International Services, Healthcare Support Services, Conference Center Management, and Refreshment Services; Facility Services; Correctional Services; Industrial Services; Uniform Services, which includes Wearguard, a direct marketer of work clothing; Health and Education Services including Spectrum Healthcare Services and Children's World Learning Centers; and Book and Magazine Services. **Listed on:** New York Stock Exchange. **Stock exchange symbol:** RMK. **Annual sales/revenues:** More than $100 million. **Number of employees nationwide:** 150,000.

ARAMARK INTERNATIONAL SERVICES
ARAMARK Tower, 1101 Market Street, Philadelphia PA 19107. 215/238-3077. **Contact:** Human Resources. **World Wide Web address:** http://www.aramark.com. **Description:** ARAMARK International Services provides a broad range of food and related services for customers worldwide. **Parent company:** ARAMARK is one of the world's leading providers of managed services. The company operates in all 50 states and 10 foreign countries, offering a broad range of services to businesses of all sizes including many *Fortune* 500 companies and thousands of universities; hospitals; and municipal, state, and federal government facilities. ARAMARK is employee-owned. The company is among the market leaders in all of its businesses, which are: Food, Leisure and Support Services including Campus Dining Services, School Nutrition Services, Leisure Services, Business Dining Services, International Services, Healthcare Support Services, Conference Center Management, and Refreshment Services; Facility Services; Correctional Services; Industrial Services; Uniform Services, which includes Wearguard, a direct marketer of work clothing; Health and

Education Services including Spectrum Healthcare Services and Children's World Learning Centers; and Book and Magazine Services. **Listed on:** New York Stock Exchange. **Stock exchange symbol:** RMK. **Annual sales/revenues:** More than $100 million. **Number of employees nationwide:** 150,000.

ARAMARK REFRESHMENT SERVICES
ARAMARK Tower, 1101 Market Street, Philadelphia PA 19107. 215/238-3525. **Contact:** Human Resources. **World Wide Web address:** http://www.aramark.com. **Description:** ARAMARK Refreshment Services serves more than 1 billion cups of coffee, 400 million cans and cups of soda, and 200 million snacks annually. Over 70 market centers across the country provide service to customers. ARAMARK Refreshment Services operates more than 900 joint accounts with other ARAMARK lines of business including health care, education, leisure, and business dining. **Parent company:** ARAMARK is one of the world's leading providers of managed services. The company operates in all 50 states and 10 foreign countries, offering a broad range of services to businesses of all sizes including many *Fortune* 500 companies and thousands of universities; hospitals; and municipal, state, and federal government facilities. ARAMARK is employee-owned. The company is among the market leaders in all of its businesses, which are: Food, Leisure and Support Services including Campus Dining Services, School Nutrition Services, Leisure Services, Business Dining Services, International Services, Healthcare Support Services, Conference Center Management, and Refreshment Services; Facility Services; Correctional Services; Industrial Services; Uniform Services, which includes Wearguard, a direct marketer of work clothing; Health and Education Services including Spectrum Healthcare Services and Children's World Learning Centers; and Book and Magazine Services. **Listed on:** New York Stock Exchange. **Stock exchange symbol:** RMK. **Annual sales/revenues:** More than $100 million. **Number of employees nationwide:** 150,000.

ARAMARK SCHOOL SUPPORT SERVICES
ARAMARK Tower, 1101 Market Street, Philadelphia PA 19107. 215/238-3526. **Contact:** Human Resources. **World Wide Web address:** http://www.aramark.com. **Description:** ARAMARK School Support Services provides professional food service management for more than 1 million students in over 280 school districts. The company offers comprehensive services including menu management to food-handling safety, marketing, merchandising, nutrition education, and recycling programs. **Parent company:** ARAMARK is one of the world's leading providers of managed services. The company operates in all 50 states and 10 foreign countries, offering a broad range of services to businesses of all sizes including many *Fortune* 500 companies and thousands of universities; hospitals; and municipal, state, and federal government facilities. ARAMARK is employee-owned. The company is among the market leaders in all of its businesses, which are: Food, Leisure and Support Services including Campus Dining Services, School Nutrition Services, Leisure Services, Business Dining Services, International Services, Healthcare Support Services, Conference Center Management, and Refreshment Services; Facility Services; Correctional Services; Industrial Services; Uniform Services, which includes Wearguard, a direct marketer of work clothing; Health and Education Services including Spectrum Healthcare Services and Children's World Learning Centers; and Book and Magazine Services. **Listed on:** New York Stock Exchange. **Stock exchange symbol:** RMK. **Annual sales/revenues:** More than $100 million. **Number of employees nationwide:** 150,000.

ARMSTRONG WORLD INDUSTRIES, INC.
P.O. Box 3001, Lancaster PA 17604-3001. 717/397-0611. **Physical address:** 2500 Columbia Avenue, Lancaster PA 17603. **Contact:** Human Resources Department. **World Wide Web address:** http://www.armstrong.com. **Description:** Manufactures flooring, ceiling systems, furniture, and industrial specialty products through approximately 85 plants worldwide. **Positions advertised include:** Administrative Assistant; Builder Sales Specialist; Cost Accountant; Transportation Analyst; Process Engineer; Credit Supervisor; Financial Analyst. **Corporate headquarters location:** This location. **Parent company:** Armstrong Holdings, Inc. **Operations at this facility include:** Administration; Manufacturing; Research and Development; Sales; Service. **Listed on:** New York Stock Exchange. **Stock exchange symbol:** ACK. **Number of employees nationwide:** 20,000.

ARMSTRONG WORLD INDUSTRIES, INC.
1018 11th Street, Beaver Falls PA 15010. 724/843-5700. **Contact:** Rick Phillips, Human Resources Manager. **World Wide Web address:** http://www.armstrong.com. **Description:** Manufactures flooring, ceiling systems, furniture, and industrial specialty products through 85 plants worldwide. **Corporate headquarters location:** Lancaster PA. **Parent company:** Armstrong Holdings, Inc. **Listed on:** New York Stock Exchange. **Stock exchange symbol:** ACK. **Number of employees nationwide:** 20,000.

ARROW INTERNATIONAL INC.
P.O. Box 12888, Reading PA 19612-2888. 610/378-0131. **Fax:** 610/478-3194. **Physical address:** 2400 Bernville Road, Reading PA 19605. **Contact:** Staffing Manager. **E-mail address:** staffing.manager@arrowintl.com. **World Wide Web address:** http://www.arrowintl.com. **Description:** Develops, manufactures, and markets central vascular access catheterization products. Arrow's products are also used for patient monitoring, diagnosis, pain management, and treating patients with heart and vascular disease. **Corporate headquarters location:** This location. **Other U.S. locations:** NJ; NC. **Operations at this facility include:** Administration; Manufacturing; Research and Development. **Listed on:** NASDAQ. **Stock exchange symbol:** ARRO. **Number of employees nationwide:** 1,540.

ART INSTITUTE OF PITTSBURGH
420 Boulevard of the Allies, Pittsburgh PA 15219. 412/263-6600. **Toll-free phone:** 800/275-2470. **Contact:** Melinda Hallett, Personnel Director. **World Wide Web address:** http://www.aip.aii.edu. **Description:** A two-year art school with an enrollment of approximately 2,500. The Art Institute of Pittsburgh also offers four-year Bachelor of Science degree programs in computer animation, interior design, industrial design, and graphic design.

ARTHRITIS FOUNDATION
219 North Broad Street, 2nd Floor, Philadelphia PA 19107. 215/564-9800. **Contact:** Branch Director. **World Wide Web address:** http://www.arthritis.org. **Description:** The Arthritis Foundation is a nonprofit organization that is engaged in research to find a cure for arthritis and to educate those who have the disease. Founded in 1948. **NOTE:** The foundation encourages applicants for volunteer positions. **Positions advertised include:** Chapter President; Chief Scientific Officer; Public Health Officer. **Office hours:** Monday - Friday, 8:30 a.m. - 4:30 p.m. **Corporate headquarters location:** Atlanta GA. **Number of employees nationwide:** 650.

ASHLAND CHEMICAL COMPANY
400 Island Park Road, Easton PA 18042-6899. 610/258-9135. **Toll-free phone:** 877/560-4084. **Contact:** Personnel. **World Wide Web address:** http://www.ashland.com. **Description:** Manufactures, markets, and distributes a wide variety of chemical products through facilities worldwide. **NOTE:** Electronic copies of resumes unaccompanied by the standard online application will not be accepted. **Positions advertised include:** Technical Sales Representative; Alliance Manager. **Corporate headquarters location:** Dublin OH. **Parent company:** Ashland Oil, Inc. **Listed on:** New York Stock Exchange. **Stock exchange symbol:** ASH.

ASPIRE MARKETING TECHNOLOGIES
P.O. BOX 18444, Pittsburgh PA 15236. 412/884-2212. **Fax:** 412/884-2212. **Contact:** Personnel. **E-mail address:** aspire@sgi.ast. **World Wide Web address:** http://www.aspireweb.com. **Description:** A marketing communications firm that focuses on web design, corporate identity, printing and media to advance brand awareness and create the results that the client desires.

ASSOCIATED CREDIT BUREAU SERVICES INC.
5910 Hamilton Boulevard, Allentown PA 18106. 610/398-7300. **Toll-free phone:** 866/530-2227. **Contact:** Human Resources. **E-mail address:** careers@acbsi.com. **World Wide Web address:** http://www.acbsi.com. **Description:** A full-service business information company providing consumer credit information and employment reports to a variety of businesses, state and local governments, retailers, and schools. Founded in 1916. **Corporate headquarters location:** This location.

ASTEA INTERNATIONAL INC.
240 Gibraltar Road, Horsham PA 19044-2306. 215/682-2500. **Toll-free phone:** 800/347-7334. **Fax:** 215/682-2515. **Contact:** Lisa Nagle, Director of Human Resources. **E-mail address:** hr@astea.com. **World Wide Web address:** http://www.astea.com. **Description:** Develops, markets, and supports a variety of applications for client/server and host-based environments that permit organizations of various sizes across a wide range of industries to automate and integrate field service and customer support functions. Astea also offers a full range of consulting, training, and customer support services. **NOTE:** Entry-level positions are offered. **Corporate headquarters location:** This location. **Other U.S. locations:** San Mateo CA; Denver CO; Bedford MA. **Listed on:** NASDAQ. **Stock exchange symbol:** ATEA. **Annual sales/revenues:** $21 - $50 million. **Number of employees at this location:** 200. **Number of employees nationwide:** 450.

ATOFINA CHEMICALS, INC.
2000 Market Street, Philadelphia PA 19103-3222. 215/419-7000. **Contact:** Human Resources Department. **World Wide Web address:** http://www.atofinachemicals.com. **Description:** A chemical manufacturer with products that include polymers, fluorochemicals, carbons, and specialty chemicals. The company also produces petroleum products. **Corporate headquarters location:** This location. **Other U.S. locations:** Nationwide. **International locations:** Worldwide. **Parent company:** Elf Atochem S.A. **Listed on:** New York Stock Exchange. **Stock exchange symbol:** TOT. **Annual sales/revenues:** More than $100 million. **Number of employees worldwide:** 6,000.

ATOTECH USA
500 Science Park Road, State College PA 16803-2299. 814/238-0514. **Contact:** Human Resources Manager. **E-mail address:** personal.de@atotech.de. **World Wide Web address:** http://www.atotech.com. **Description:** Manufactures parts and equipment for the fabrication of circuit boards. **Positions advertised include:** Chemical Engineers; Surface Technology Engineer; Plating Technicians; Metallurgists; Ph.D.'s Chemistry/Physics; Development Engineers.

AUTOMATIC DATA PROCESSING (ADP)
1125 Virginia Drive, Fort Washington PA 19034. 215/283-4113. **Contact:** Human Resources. **World Wide Web address:** http://www.adp.com. **Description:** Provides computerized transaction processing, record keeping, data communications, and information services. ADP helps more than 300,000 clients improve their business performance by providing services such as payroll, payroll tax, and human resource information management; brokerage industry market data, back office, and proxy services; industry-specific services to auto and truck dealers; and computerized auto repair and replacement estimating for auto insurance companies and body repair shops. Employer Services, Brokerage Services, Dealer Services, and Claims Services are the company's four largest businesses. **Corporate headquarters location:** Roseland NJ. **Listed on:** New York Stock Exchange. **Stock exchange symbol:** ADP. **Number of employees at this location:** 250.

AUTOMATIC DATA PROCESSING (ADP)
P.O. Box 700, Pittsburgh PA 15230. 412/788-1530. **Physical address:** 100 Commerce Drive, Pittsburgh PA 15275. **Contact:** Human Resources. **World Wide Web address:** http://www.adp.com. **Description:** Provides computerized transaction processing, record keeping, data communications, and information services. ADP helps more than 300,000 clients improve their business performance by providing services such as payroll, payroll tax, and human resource information management; brokerage industry market data, back office, and proxy services; industry-specific services to auto and truck dealers; and computerized auto repair and replacement estimating for auto insurance companies and body repair shops. **Corporate headquarters location:** Roseland NJ. **Listed on:** New York Stock Exchange. **Stock exchange symbol:** ADP.

AVENTIS PASTEUR
Discovery Drive, Box 187, Swiftwater PA 18370-0187. 570/839-7187. **Fax:** 570/839-0561. **Contact:** Human Resources Department. **World Wide Web address:** http://www.us.aventispasteur.com. **Description:** A pharmaceutical manufacturing firm with an emphasis on developing vaccines to prevent diseases such as Lyme disease, AIDS, and malaria. **Positions advertised include:** Business Information Systems Analyst; Senior Auditor; Laboratory Coordinator; Filing & Packaging Technician.

AVERSTAR INC.
65 West Street, Warminster PA 18974-2863. 215/674-2913. **Contact:** Personnel Department. **World Wide Web address:** http://www.titan.com. **Description:** AverStar provides software systems, services, and products to a broad base of customers around the world. The company's expertise includes language design and programmer productivity tools; digital signal processing tools and applications; hardware and system simulation; computer and network security products; guidance, navigation, and control products; and information systems integration. The products and services are used by major corporations and government agencies for applications in such fields as transportation, financial management and decision support, automotive, communications, manned space flight, air traffic control, antisubmarine warfare, and command and control. Along with building programming tools and environments, the company responds directly to customer needs by developing software system solutions; analyzing system requirements; performing rapid prototyping; performing integration, verification, and validation testing; re-engineering systems; maintaining operational software; and providing training and support. **Corporate Operations at this facility include:** This location engineers software. **Parent company:** Titan Corporation. **Number of employees at this location:** 600.

AVERY DENNISON CORPORATION
7722 Dungan Road, Philadelphia PA 19111. 215/725-4700. **Contact:** Human Resources. **World Wide Web address:** http://www.averydennison.com. **Description:** Avery Dennison Corporation is a worldwide manufacturer of self-adhesive products, pressure sensitive base materials, label components, labeling systems, office products, and related products. **NOTE:** Online applications are preferred. **Positions advertised include:** Technical Service Chemist. **Corporate headquarters location:** Pasadena CA. **Other U.S. locations:** Nationwide. **International locations:** Worldwide. **Operations at this facility include:** This location manufactures industrial marking machines, tickets, tags, tapes, and related products. **Listed on:** New York Stock Exchange. **Stock exchange symbol:** AVY.

B-FAST CORPORATION
660 Newtown-Yardley Road, Newtown PA 18940. 215/860-5600. **Contact:** James Affleck, Director of Human Resources. **Description:** Provides ground support services for general aviation aircraft including demand line services such as fueling, ground handling, and storage of aircraft.

BAE SYSTEMS
305 Richardson Road, Lansdale PA 19446. 215/996-2000. **Fax:** 215/996-2081. **Contact:** Kim Lundy, Human Resources Representative. **World Wide Web address:** http://www.na.baesystems.com/careers. **Description:** A leading supplier of electronic countermeasure systems and developer of electronic warfare systems that provide protection for aircraft, ships, and tanks from various missile threats. **Positions advertised include:** Electronics Technician; Project Manager/Licensed Surveyor; Test Technician Electronics; Electronic Assembler.

BACOU-DALLOZ
1150 First Avenue, Park View Tower, Suite 400, King of Prussia 19406. 610/728-1900. **Contact:** Rodney M. Fogelman, Director of Human Resources. **E-mail address:** resumes@dallozsafety.com. **World Wide Web address:** http://www.bacou-dalloz.com. **Description:** Manufactures respiratory protection and personal safety protection products for the head, ears, and eyes. **Corporate headquarters location:** This location. **Parent company:** Christian Dalloz (also at this location).

MICHAEL BAKER CORPORATION
P.O. 12259, Pittsburgh PA 15231. 412/269-6300. **Toll-free phone:** 800/MIBAKER. **Fax:** 412/375-3977. **Physical address:** Airside Business Park, 100 Airside Drive, Moon Township PA 15108. **Contact:** Human Resources. **World Wide Web address:** http://www.mbakercorp.com. **Description:** An architectural and engineering firm that provides engineering, management, and operations services to the construction, energy, environmental, and transportation markets. **Corporate headquarters location:** This location. **Other area locations:** Coraopolis; Philadelphia; Pittsburgh; Beaver; Harrisburg; Horsham; & Gibsonia. **Other U.S. locations:** Nationwide.

MICHAEL BAKER CORPORATION
4301 Dutch Ridge Road, Beaver PA 15009. 724/495-7711. **Contact:** Human Resources. **World Wide Web address:** http://www.mbakercorp.com. **Description:** Michael Baker Corporation is an engineering and architectural consulting company providing civil, water resources, facility design, environmental, geological, transportation, construction management, surveying, and mapping services to industrial, institutional, and government clients. **Corporate headquarters location:** Coraopolis PA. **Other area locations:** Coraopolis; Philadelphia; Pittsburgh; Beaver; Harrisburg; Horsham; & Gibsonia. **Other U.S. locations:** Nationwide. **Operations at this facility include:** This location houses the civil, airport, accounting, and billing departments.

BALDWIN HARDWARE CORPORATION
841 East Wyomissing Boulevard, P.O. Box 15048, Reading PA 19612-5048. 610/777-7811. **Fax:** 610/796-4434. **Contact:** Mr. Carl Salmon, Vice President of Human Resources. **E-mail address:** hr@baldwinhq.com. **World Wide Web address:** http://www.baldwinhardware.com. **Description:** Manufacturer of decorative hardware including handle sets, doorknobs, and hinges. The company also manufactures a variety of home decor products including bath accessories, candlesticks, sconces, and both interior and exterior lighting products. **Positions advertised include:** Commodity Specialist; Quality Engineer. **Special programs:** Training; Summer Jobs. **Corporate headquarters location:** This location. **Parent company:** MASCO Corporation. **Operations at this facility include:** Administration; Divisional Headquarters; Manufacturing; Research and Development; Service.

BARBIERI & ASSOCIATES
1542 McDaniel Drive, West Chester PA 19380. 610/431-4102. **Fax:** 215/546-4848. **Contact:** Pietro Barbieri. **E-mail address:** peterlaw@icdc.com. **Description:** A law firm that offers a range of services in a number of practice areas.

BARLEY SNYDER SENFT & COHEN LLC.
126 East King Street, Lancaster PA 17602-2893. 717/299-5201. **Fax:** 717/291-4660. **Contact:** Mr. David Keller. **E-mail address:** dkeller@barley.com. **World Wide Web address:** http://www.barley.com. **Description:** A Pennsylvania law firm that offers a range of civil law services in a number practice areas. **Other area locations:** Berwyn; Chambersburg; Hanover; Harrisburg; Lancaster; Reading: & York.

BARNES & NOBLE BOOKSTORES
5909 Peach Street, Erie PA 16509. 814/864-6300. **Contact:** Human Resources. **World Wide Web address:** http://www.bn.com. **Description:** A discount bookstore chain with locations nationwide. In addition to its book departments, this location also has a cafe and music department. **Positions advertised include:** Retail; Corporate. **Other U.S. locations:** Nationwide.

BARNES-KASSON COUNTY HOSPITAL S.N.F.
400 Turnpike Street, Susquehanna PA 18847. 570/853-3135. **Toll-free phone:** 800/323-2051. **Fax:** 570/853-3223. **Contact:** Human Resources. **World Wide Web address:** http://www.barnes-kasson.org. **Description:** A 50-bed community hospital with an attached 58-bed skilled nursing facility. The hospital also offers home health services and outpatient therapy. **NOTE:** Second and third shifts are offered. **Positions advertised include:** Physician; Physical Therapist; RN; LPN; CPN. **Special programs:** Internships; Summer Jobs. **CEO:** Sara Iveson. **Annual sales/revenues:** $11 - $20 million. **Number of employees at this location:** 350.

BAYER CLOTHING GROUP, INC.
Rural Delivery #4, Box 91-B, Clearfield PA 16830. 814/765-7521. **Contact:** Edith Levin, Human Resources Manager. **Description:** Manufactures men's clothing, including suits and sportswear.

BAYER CORPORATION
100 Bayer Road, Pittsburgh PA 15205. 412/777-2000. **Contact:** Human Resources. **World Wide Web address:** http://www.bayerus.com. **Description:** Produces polyurethane raw materials, polymer thermoplastic resins and blends, coatings, industrial chemicals, and other related products.

BELMONT CENTER FOR COMPREHENSIVE TREATMENT
4200 Monument Road, Philadelphia PA 19131. 215/877-2000. **Contact:** Human Resources Department. **World Wide Web address:** http://www.einstein.edu. **Description:** Offers inpatient and outpatient treatment to adolescents, adults, and families for a range of problems including addictions and eating disorders. **Parent company:** Albert Einstein Healthcare Network.

BEMIS COMPANY INC.
Valmont Industrial Park, 20 Jaycee Drive, West Hazleton PA 18202-1142. 570/455-7741. **Contact:** John Meier, Human Resources Manager. **World Wide Web address:** http://www.bemis.com. **Description:** Bemis is a diversified producer of consumer and industrial packaging materials, film products, and business products. Packaging products include tapes, paper bags, and packaging for pharmaceuticals, candy, toilet paper, and detergents. The company also produces roll labels, laminates, and adhesive products. **Corporate headquarters location:** Minneapolis MN. **Listed on:** New York Stock Exchange. **Stock exchange symbol:** BMS.

BENCO DENTAL COMPANY
370 North Penn Avenue, Wilkes-Barre PA 18702. 570/825-7781. **Toll-free phone:** 800/GO-BENCO. **Contact:** Human Resources. **World Wide Web address:** http://www.benco.com. **Description:** Distributes and rents dental equipment to hospitals, schools, and governmental agencies. **Positions advertised include:** Territory Representatives; Service Technicians.

BENEFICIAL SAVINGS BANK
530 Walnut, Philadelphia PA 19106. 215/864-6730. **Contact:** Joseph Vetter, Personnel Manager. **E-mail address:** info@beneficialsavingsbank.com. **World Wide Web address:** http://www.beneficialsavings.com. **Description:** A full-service savings bank that also offers home mortgaging. **Positions advertised include:** Teller; Branch Manager; Commercial Lender; Warehouse Clerk.

BENTLEY SYSTEMS INC.
685 Stockton Drive, Exton PA 19341. 610/458-5000. **Contact:** Human Resources. **World Wide Web address:** http://www.bentley.com. **Description:** Develops CAD software for universities, students, and engineers.

BERGER BROTHERS
805 Pennsylvania Boulevard, Feasterville PA 19053. 215/355-1200. **Toll-free phone:** 800/523-8852. **Fax:** 215/355-0913. **Contact:** Personnel. **E-mail address:** info@bergerbros.com. **World Wide Web address:** http://www.bergerbros.com. **Description:** Manufactures roofing and drainage systems. Founded in 1874.

THE BETHLEHEM CORPORATION
25th & Lennox Streets, Easton PA 18045. 610/258-7111. **Contact:** Human Resources. **E-mail address:** info@bethcorp.com. **World Wide Web address:** http://www.bethcorp.com. **Description:** Engaged in the development, manufacture, and sale of equipment for environmental, energy, and continuous processing applications. The Bethlehem Corporation also provides subcontracting services for industrial products made to customers' specifications. Typical products include multiple-hearth furnaces, filter presses, industrial dryers, flow tubes, and transfer cars. **Operations at this facility include:** Administration; Manufacturing; Research and Development; Sales.

BIG BROTHERS/BIG SISTERS OF AMERICA
230 North 13th Street, Philadelphia PA 19107. 215/567-7000. **Fax:** 215/567-0394. **Contact:** Human Resources. **E-mail address:** nationalcareers@bbbsa.org. **World Wide Web address:** http://www.bbbsa.org. **Description:** The National Office of Big Brothers/Big Sisters of America. Provides volunteer and professional services to assist children and youth in achieving their highest potential as they grow. There are over 505 Big Brothers/Big Sisters agencies nationwide where more than 75,000 children are matched with adult volunteers. The agency also provides counseling, referral, and family support services to parents and children in more 110,000 families each year. Additional programs focus on children with special needs including physical or learning disabilities, as well as those who are abused, neglected, or have dropped out of school. Special prevention and intervention programs at many agencies address the problems of drug abuse, teen pregnancy, foster care, and juvenile delinquency. Founded in 1904. **Positions advertised include:** Administrative Assistant; Customer Service Representative; Database Manager; Director of Child Safety; Instructional Designer. Performance Management Analyst; VP of Philanthropy. **Corporate headquarters location:** This location. **Other U.S. locations:** Nationwide.

BINNEY & SMITH, INC.
P.O. Box 431, Easton PA 18044-0431. 610/253-6272 ext. 4394 (corporate). 610/253-6272 ext. 4550 (plant). **Physical address:** 1100 Church Lane, Easton PA 18040. **Contact:** Nancy Mazzarese for corporate employment, Karen Smith for plant employment. **World Wide Web address:** http://www.binney-smith.com. **Description:** Produces a line of crayons, markers, writing instruments, chalk, clay, artist kits, oils, acrylics, watercolors, and brushes. Brand names include Crayola, Magic Marker, Liquitex, and Artista. **Special programs:** Internships. **Corporate headquarters location:** This location. **Other U.S. locations:** Winfield KS. **Parent company:** Hallmark Corporation. **Operations at this facility include:** Administration; Divisional Headquarters; Manufacturing; Marketing; Regional Headquarters; Research and Development; Sales; Service. **Number of employees at this location:** 900. **Number of employees nationwide:** 1,200.

BINSWANGER
2 Logan Square, 4th Floor, Philadelphia PA 19103. 215/448-6000. **Contact:** Frank G. Binswanger III. **E-mail address:** fgbiii@binswanger.com. **World Wide Web address:** http://www.cbbi.com. **Description:** Sells commercial and industrial real estate. **Corporate headquarters location:** This location. **Other U.S. locations:** Nationwide. **International locations:** Worldwide.

BIO-IMAGING TECHNOLOGIES, INC.
826 Newtown-Yardley Road, Newtown PA 18940-1721. 267/757-3000. **Fax:** 267/757-3007. **Contact:** Maria Kraus, Controller. **E-mail address:** careers@bioimaging.com. **World Wide Web address:** http://www.bioimaging.com. **Description:** Processes and analyzes data for clinics and labs. The company receives lab data from clinical tests, including MRIs and ultrasounds, and then digitizes the information.

BIOSIS
3501 Market Street, Philadelphia PA 19104. 215/386-0100. **Toll-free phone:** 800/336-4474. **Fax:** 215/243-2208. **Contact:** Dana Felt, Senior Human Resources Generalist. **E-mail address:** info@biosis.org. **World Wide Web address:** http://www.biosis.org. **Description:** A nonprofit educational organization. Its mission is to foster the growth,

communication, and use of biological knowledge. BIOSIS offers one of the world's largest collections of abstracts and bibliographical references of biological and medical literature available for public use. Founded in 1926. **NOTE:** Entry-level positions are offered. **Corporate headquarters location:** This location. **International locations:** Worldwide. **Subsidiaries include:** BIOSIS (UK). **Operations at this facility include:** Administration; Marketing; Production; Sales. **President:** John E. Anderson. **Annual sales/revenues:** $21-$50 million. **Number of employees at this location:** 250.

BLACK BOX CORPORATION
1000 Park Drive, Lawrence PA 15055. 724/873-6506. **Fax:** 724/873-6502. **Contact:** Human Development. **E-mail address:** bbcareers@blackbox.com. **World Wide Web address:** http://www.blackbox.com. **Description:** Manufactures modems and switches. Founded in 1976. **Positions advertised include:** Accounting Representative; Cash Management Analyst; Financial Analyst; Master Planner; Technical Account Manager.

BLANK ROME LLP
One Logan Square, Philadelphia PA 19103-6998. 215/569-5500. **Fax:** 215/569-5555. **Contact:** Marilyn Mason, Personnel Director. **World Wide Web address:** http://www.blankrome.com. **Description:** A law firm, specializing in bankruptcy law.

BLILEY ELECTRIC COMPANY
P.O. Box 3428, 2545 West Grandview Boulevard, Erie PA 16508-0428. 814/456-9191. **Fax:** 814/833-2712. **Contact:** Human Resources. **E-mail address:** info@bliley.com. **World Wide Web address:** http://www.bliley.com. **Description:** A manufacturer of quartz oscillators and electronic components.

BLOCKBUSTER VIDEO
1101 North Atherton Street, State College PA 16803-2927. 814/238-6379. **Contact:** Store Manager. **World Wide Web address:** http://www.blockbuster.com. **Description:** A video rental store and part of the nationwide chain. Blockbuster operates approximately 2,000 outlets across the country. **Positions advertised include:** Field Operations; Local Retail Store.

BOEKEL SCIENTIFIC
855 Pennsylvania Boulevard, Feasterville PA 19053. 215/396-8200. **Toll-free phone:** 800/336-6929. **Contact:** Human Resources Manager. **World Wide Web address:** http://www.boekelsci.com. **Description:** Provides abstracting and indexing services for biological and medical research. The company also provides access to life sciences literature worldwide, offering more than 90 products and services including several online databases.

BOLLMAN HAT COMPANY
P.O. Box 517, Adamstown PA 19501. 717/484-4361. **Fax:** 717/484-2139. **Physical address:** 110 East Main Street, Adamstown PA 19501. **Contact:** Angie Bushong, Human Resources Manager. **World Wide Web address:** http://www.bollmanhats.com. **Description:** A manufacturer of wool, fur, cloth, and straw hats. Bollman Hat Company also cleans and processes wool. **Positions advertised include:** Vice President of Sales and Marketing; Block Designer. **Corporate headquarters location:** This location. **Operations at this facility include:** Administration; Manufacturing; Research and Development; Sales.

BOMBARDIER TRANSPORTATION
1501 Lebanon Church Road, Pittsburgh PA 15236. 412/655-5700. **Contact:** Human Resources. **World Wide Web address:** http://www.bombardier.com. **Description:** A manufacturer of rapid transit systems including rail systems such as the Bay Area Rapid Transit (BART) in San Francisco CA, and people movers conveyors found in airports and other public facilities. **Positions advertised include:** Field Service Representative; Programmer Analyst; Feasibility Planner. **Number of employees nationwide:** 800.

THE BON-TON
2801 East Market Street, York PA 17402. 717/757-7660. **Contact:** Sue Hulme, Manager of Executive Employment. **E-mail address:** cshorts@bonton.com. **World Wide Web address:** http://www.bonton.com. **Description:** One of the largest department stores in America with over 70 locations. The Bon-Ton offers brand-name merchandise for men, women, children, and the home. **NOTE:** Entry-level positions are offered, and online application is preferred. **Positions advertised include:** BSR Analyst; Administrative Assistant; Instant Credit Telephone Representative. **Special programs:** Training; Summer Jobs. **Corporate headquarters location:** This location. **Other U.S. locations:** MD; MA; NJ; NY; WV. **Operations at this facility include:** Administration. **Listed on:** NASDAQ. **Stock exchange symbol:** BONT. **President/CEO:** Heywood Wilansky. **Number of employees at this location:** 500. **Number of employees nationwide:** 12,000.

BOYD'S MILL PRESS
803 Church Street, Honesdale PA 18431. 570/253-1164. **Contact:** Human Resources. **E-mail address:** admin@boydsmillpress.com. **World Wide Web address:** http://www.boydsmillpress.com. **Description:** A publisher of children's literature and the trade division for "Highlights for Children". Founded in 1990.

BRADFORD WHITE CORPORATION
725 Talamore Drive, Ambler PA 19002-2755. 215/641-9400. **Fax:** 215/641-1612. **Contact:** Michael Marcellino, Manager of Human Resources. **World Wide Web address:** http://www.bradfordwhite.com. **Description:** Manufactures and markets water heaters. **Operations at this facility include:** Regional Headquarters.

BRASHEAR LP
615 Epsilon Drive, Pittsburgh PA 15238. 412/967-7700. **Fax:** 412/967-7973. **Contact:** Recruiter. **E-mail address:** recruiter@brashearlp.com. **World Wide Web address:** http://www.brashearlp.com. **Description:** Designs and produces precision instrumentation for the electro-optical, electromechanical, and simulation and test fields for defense and commercial applications. **Positions advertised include:** Materials Engineer; Marketing Engineer; Sr. Systems Engineer; Electrical Engineer; Mechanical Engineer; Program Cost Analyst; Program Manager.

B. BRAUN MEDICAL, INC.
901 Marcon Boulevard, Allentown PA 18109. 610/266-0500. **Fax:** 610/266-5702. **Contact:** Carolyn Johnson. Human Resources. **E-mail address:** hr.allentown@bbraunusa.com. **World Wide Web address:** http://www.bbraunusa.com. **Description:** Manufactures intravenous systems and solutions. The company also offers IV accessories, critical care products, epidural anesthesia, and pharmaceutical devices. **Other area locations:** Bethlehem, PA. **Parent company:** B. Braun of America.

B. BRAUN MEDICAL, INC.
824 12th Avenue, Bethlehem PA 18018. 610/226-1522. **Fax:** 610/861-5991. **Contact:** Human Resources. **E-mail address:** hr.bethlehem@bbraunusa.com. **World Wide Web address:** http://www.bbraunusa.com. **Description:** Administration and sales related to the manufacture of intravenous systems and solutions. The company also offers IV accessories, critical care products, epidural anesthesia, and pharmaceutical devices. **Corporate headquarters location:** This location. **Other area locations:** Allentown PA. **Parent company:** B. Braun Worldwide.

BREEZE INDUSTRIAL PRODUCTS
3582 Tunnelton Road, Saltsburg PA 15681-9594. 724/639-3571. **Fax:** 724/639-3020. **Contact:** Mark Gaia, Human Resources Manager. **E-mail address:** breeze@breezeclamps.com. **World Wide Web address:** http://www.breezeclamps.com. **Description:** Manufactures a complete line of standard and specialty gear-driven band fasteners in high-grade stainless steel for use in highly engineered applications. **Corporate headquarters location:** Union NJ. **Parent company:** TransTechnology Corporation designs, manufactures, sells, and distributes specialty fasteners through several subsidiaries. The Palnut Company (Mountainside NJ) manufactures light- and heavy-duty single and multithread specialty fasteners. Industrial Retaining Ring (Irvington NJ) manufactures a variety of retaining rings made of carbon steel, stainless steel, and beryllium copper. The Seeger Group (Somerville NJ) manufactures retaining clips, circlips, spring pins, and similar components. Breeze-Eastern (Union NJ) designs, develops, manufactures, and services sophisticated lifting and restraining products, principally helicopter rescue hoist and cargo hooks systems; winches and hoists for aircraft and weapon systems; and aircraft cargo tie-down systems.

BRIDGESTONE/FIRESTONE, INC.
180 Sheree Boulevard, Suite 2000, Exton PA 19341. 610/594-6181. **Contact:** Bob Pierce, Personnel Manager. **World Wide Web address:** http://www.bridgestone-firestone.com. **Description:** This location is a zone office responsible for supporting and directing more than 250 retail stores throughout the Northeast. **Corporate headquarters location:** Nashville TN. **Other U.S. locations:** Nationwide. **Parent company:** Bridgestone Corporation. **Operations at this facility include:** Administration; Service.

BRITE STAR MANUFACTURING COMPANY
2900 South 20th Street, Philadelphia PA 19145. 215/271-7600. **Contact:** Mr. Sandy Kinderman, Vice President. **E-mail address:** dje@britestar.com. **World Wide Web address:** http://www.britestar.com. **Description:** Manufactures and imports a wide variety of Christmas decorations, trees, and other holiday items. **Corporate headquarters location:** This location. **Operations at this facility include:** Manufacturing.

BROCK AND COMPANY, INC.
257 Great Valley Parkway, Malvern PA 19355. 610/647-5656. **Fax:** 610/647-0867. **Contact:** Mark Snyder, Human Resources Manager. **E-mail address:** hr@brockco.com. **World Wide Web address:** http://www.brockco.com. **Description:** A contract food service company offering corporate dining, vending, and office coffee services. **Positions advertised include:** General Manager; Executive Chef; Chef Manager; Director of Food Service; Assistant Director; Catering Manager; Culinary Manager in Training. **Special programs:** Apprenticeships; Co-ops. **Corporate headquarters location:** This location. **Annual sales/revenues:** $11 - $20 million. **Number of employees at this location:** 300.

BRODART AUTOMATION
500 Arch Street, Williamsport PA 17701. **Toll-free phone:** 800/474-9802 ext. 6772. **Fax:** 800/999-6799. **Contact:** Human Resources. **E-mail address:** salesmkt@brodart.com. **World Wide Web address:** http://www.brodart.com. **Description:** A leading provider of automated library services including computer-based bibliographic maintenance. Founded in 1975. **Parent company:** Brodart Company.

M.A. BRUDER & SONS INC.
600 Reed Road, Broomall PA 19008. 610/353-5100. **Toll-free phone:** 800/MAB-1899. **Fax:** 610/325-2718. **Contact:** Randy McCullough, Director of Human Resources. **E-mail address:** careers@mabpaints.com. **World Wide Web address:** http://www.mabpaints.com. **Description:** A national manufacturer and marketer of paint, operating over 250 retail and wholesale locations. Founded in 1899. **Corporate headquarters location:** This location.

BRYN MAWR BANK CORPORATION
801 Lancaster Avenue, Bryn Mawr PA 19010-3396. 610/581-4864. **Fax:** 610/520-7278 **Contact:** Human Resources. **E-mail address:** mdeantoniis@bmtc.com. **World Wide Web address:** http://www.bmtc.com. **Description:** A holding company. **NOTE:** You may also send resumes to creese@bmtc.com. **Corporate headquarters location:** This location. **Subsidiaries include:** Bryn Mawr Trust operates 14 banks throughout Eastern Pennsylvania. **Listed on:** NASDAQ. **Stock exchange symbol:** BMTC.

BRYN MAWR COLLEGE
101 North Merion Avenue, Bryn Mawr PA 19010-2899. 610/526-5000. **Fax:** 610/526-7478. **Contact:** Human Resources. **E-mail address:** jobs@brynmawr.edu. **World Wide Web address:** http://www.brynmawr.edu. **Description:** A women's liberal arts college with an enrollment of 1,700 offering undergraduate, master's and Ph.D. programs.

BRYN MAWR HOSPITAL
130 South Bryn Mawr Avenue, Bryn Mawr PA 19010. 610/526-3026. **Fax:** 610/526-3068. **Contact:** Human Resources Department. **World Wide Web address:** http://www.mainlinehealth.org/bmh. **Description:** A teaching hospital that provides medical, psychiatric, and surgical services, and offers the surrounding community the following specialized programs: Primary Care Services, the Arthritis and Orthopaedic Center, Comprehensive Cancer Care Center, Cardiovascular Center, and Women and Children's Health Resources. In addition, the hospital provides a wide array of other community programs including support groups, educational programs, physician referral services, health screenings, and a speakers bureau. **NOTE:** Please see http://www.employment.jefferson.edu/bmh for application details. **Positions advertised include:** Clinical Coordinator; Physician Assistant; Social Worker; Case Manager; Certified Nurse Assistant; Clinical Nurse Educator; Patient Care Manager; Mental Health Assistant; Patient Resource Representative. **Corporate headquarters location:** Radnor PA. **Parent company:** Mainline Health System.

BUCHANAN INGERSOLL, P.C.
One Oxford Centre, 301 Grant Street, 20th Floor, Pittsburgh PA 15219-1410. 412/562-8800. **Fax:** 412/562-1041. **Contact:** Steven Ferber, Director of Human Resources. **E-mail address:** info@bipc.com. **World Wide Web address:** http://www.bipc.com. **Description:** A law firm specializing in commercial litigation. Clients include individuals, start-up companies, privately and publicly held institutions, and multinational conglomerates. Founded in 1850. **Special programs:** Summer Associate Program.

BUCK COMPANY, INC.
897 Lancaster Pike, Quarryville PA 17566-9738. 717/284-4114. **Fax:** 717/284-3737.**Contact:** Mark Broich, Employee Services Manager. **E-mail address:** bsafe@buckcompany.com. **World Wide Web address:** http://www.buckcompany.com. **Description:** Manufactures malleable aluminum and related products, and brass alloy and gray iron castings.

BUCKEYE PIPE LINE COMPANY, LP
5002 Buckeye Road, Emmaus PA 18049. 484/232-4000. **Fax:** 484/232-4541. **Contact:** Administrator, Human Resources. **E-mail address:** resumes@buckeye.com. **World Wide Web address:** http://www.buckeye.com. **Description:** One of the largest independent pipeline common carriers of refined petroleum products in the United States, with over 3,000 miles of pipeline serving 10 states. **NOTE:** Resumes can also be mailed to OP.O. Box 368, Emmaus PA 18049. **Positions advertised include:** Apprentice Pipeliner; Dispatcher; Drafter; Electrical Technician; Field Operations Assistant. **Special programs:** Internships. **Corporate headquarters location:** This location. **Parent company:** Buckeye Partners, L.P.'s other subsidiaries include Buckeye Tank Terminals Company, L.P.; Everglades Pipe Line Company; Laurel Pipe Line Company. **Listed on:** New York Stock Exchange. **Stock exchange symbol:** BPL. **Number of employees at this location:** 200. **Number of employees nationwide:** 525.

BUCKLEY & COMPANY, INC.
3401 Moore Street, Philadelphia PA 19145. 215/334-7500. **Contact:** Joseph Martosella, Vice President. **Description:** A heavy construction firm specializing in highways, bridges, tunnels, and other large-scale construction projects.

BUCKS COUNTY COMMUNITY COLLEGE
Tyler Hall, Room 130, 275 Swamp Road, Newtown PA 18940. 215/968-8000. **Fax:** 215/504-8506. **Contact:** Human Resources Office. **World Wide Web address:** http://www.bucks.edu. **Description:** A public, two-year community college offering certificates and associate's degrees in more than 50 academic disciplines.

BURLINGTON COAT FACTORY
339 Sixth Avenue, Pittsburgh PA 15222-2515. 412/765-1499. **Contact:** Ron Giannandrea, Store Manager. **World Wide Web address:** http://www.coat.com. **Description:** An all name-brand apparel discounter for men, women, and children. **NOTE:** Employment opportunities are available at the corporate, distribution, and retail levels. Please send your application/resume correspondingly: corporate.employment@coat.com, warehouse.opportunities@coat.com, or employment.opportunities@coat.com. Resumes can also be mailed to human resources at 1830 Route 130, Burlington NJ 08016. **Corporate headquarters location:** Burlington NJ.

BURNHAM CORPORATION
1135 Dillerville Road, P.O. Box 3079, Lancaster PA 17604. 717/397-4701. **Fax:** 717/390-7808. **Contact:** Robert Beecher, Human Resources Director. **World Wide Web address:** http://www.burnham.com. **Description:** Manufactures boilers and related heating equipment for residential, commercial, and industrial applications. The company operates through two groups: The Distributor Products Group offers a broad range of residential boilers, radiators, and light commercial boilers to plumbing and heating wholesale distributors through America's Boiler Company, New Yorker Boiler, and Governale, Inc. The Commercial Group provides boilers, burners, and boiler room accessories for large commercial and industrial applications through Burnham Commercial Boilers and Kewanee Boiler. The company's operations are supported by the Burnham Foundry Division, which produces castings for commercial sales. **NOTE:** Submit your application online or by visiting the facility. **Positions advertised include:** Financial Analyst; Test Technician. **Corporate headquarters location:** This location. **Number of employees at this location:** 460. **Number of employees nationwide:** 1,000.

W. ATLEE BURPEE & COMPANY
300 Park Avenue, Warminster PA 18974. 215/674-4900. **Contact:** Stuart Hopkins, Director of Human Resources. **World Wide Web address:** http://www.burpee.com. **Description:** A major distributor of seeds nationwide. **Corporate headquarters location:** This location.

BURSON-MARSTELLER
One Gateway Center, 20th Floor, Pittsburgh PA 15222. 412/471-9600. **Contact:** Human Resources. **World Wide Web address:** http://www.bm.com. **Description:** A global public relations and public affairs firm. **Subsidiaries include:** Cohn & Wolfe, Public Relations.

BUSY BEAVER BUILDING CENTERS INC.
3130 William Pitt Way, Building A6, Pittsburgh PA 15238. 412/655-1230. **Contact:** Personnel. **World Wide Web address:** http://www.busybeaver.com. **Description:** Busy Beaver is a chain of building supply stores. **Positions advertised include:** General Manager; Store Manager; Administrative Manager; Sales Manager; Full/Part Time Sales; Front End Department; Stock & Warehouse. **Corporate headquarters location:** This location. **Operations at this facility include:** This location houses purchasing offices.

C-COR ELECTRONICS
60 Decibel Road, State College PA 16801. 814/238-2461. **Toll-free phone:** 800/233-2267. **Contact:** Mary Beahm, Vice President of Human Resources. **E-mail address:** jobs@c-cor.net. **World Wide Web address:** http://www.c-cor.net. **Description:** Manufactures electronic equipment used in cable TV products. **Positions advertised include:** Senior Buyer; Corporate Accountant. **Listed on:** NASDAQ. **Stock exchange symbol:** CCBL. **Number of employees at this location:** 460.

C&D TECHNOLOGIES
1400 Union Meeting Road, P.O. Box 3053, Blue Bell PA 19422. 215/619-2700. **Fax:** 215/619-7840. **Contact:** Human Resources. **E-mail address:** cdjobs@cdtechno.com. **World Wide Web address:** http://www.cdtechno.com. **Description:** Manufactures and supplies industrial and reserve power systems and batteries for the telecommunications and utility switchgear markets. **Positions advertised include:** Collections Representative; Director of Publishing; Divisional Controller; Network Administrator; Payroll Supervisor; Senior Sales Representative. **Corporate headquarters location:** This location. **Listed on:** New York Stock Exchange. **Stock exchange symbol:** CHP.

CB RICHARD ELLIS
1800 JFK Boulevard, Philadelphia PA 19103-3272. 215/561-8900. **Fax:** 215/557-6719. **Contact:** Human Resources Manager. **World Wide Web address:** http://www.cbrichardellis.com. **Description:** A real estate services company offering property sales and leasing, property management, corporate facilities management, mortgage banking, and market research. **NOTE:** Please see the website for current job openings in each division. Online applications are welcome. **Corporate headquarters location:** Los Angeles CA. **Other U.S. locations:** Nationwide. **Number of employees worldwide:** 13,500.

CB RICHARD ELLIS
1200 Liberty Ridge Drive, Suite 320, Wayne PA 19087. 610/251-0820. **Fax:** 610/889-9168. **Contact:** Human Resources Manager. **World Wide Web address:** http://www.cbrichardellis.com. **Description:** A real estate service company offering property sales and leasing, property and facility management, mortgage banking, and investment management services. **NOTE:** Please see the website for current job openings in each division. Online applications are welcome. **Corporate headquarters location:** Los Angeles CA. **Other U.S. locations:** Nationwide. **Number of employees worldwide:** 13,500.

CB RICHARD ELLIS/PITTSBURGH
600 Grant Street, Suite 1400, Pittsburgh PA 15219. 412/471-9500. **Fax:** 412/471-0995. **Contact:** Human Resources Manager. **World Wide Web address:** http://www.cbrichardellis.com. **Description:** A real estate service company. **NOTE:** Please see the website for current job openings in each division. Online applications are welcome. **Corporate headquarters location:** Los Angeles CA. **Other U.S. locations:** Nationwide. **Number of employees worldwide:** 13,500.

CCL CONTAINER AEROSOL DIVISION
One Llodio Drive, Hermitage PA 16148-9015. 412/981-4420. **Contact:** Personnel Director. **World Wide Web address:** http://www.cclind.com. **Description:** Manufactures toothpaste tubes, aluminum aerosol cans, aluminum and tin squeeze tubes, barrier systems, laminate tubes, closures, and related products. **International locations:** Canada; Costa Rica; Mexico.

CJ SYSTEMS AVIATION GROUP
57 Allegheny County Airport, West Mifflin PA 15122. 412/466-2500. **Toll-free phone:** 800/245-0230. **Fax:** 412/469-1556. **Contact:** Dawn Chambers, Director of Human Resources. **E-mail address:** resumes@cjsystemsaviation.com. **World Wide Web address:** http://www.corpjet.com. **Description:** Corporate Jets, Inc. is a general aviation company, primarily engaged in providing both charter and air medical services including patient and organ transport. Founded in 1969. **Corporate headquarters location:** This location. **Other U.S. locations:** Scottsdale AZ. **International locations:** Naples; Singapore. **Operations at this facility include:** This location houses the company's aircraft maintenance facility. **Parent company:** FSS Airholdings Inc. **Number of employees at this location:** 320. **Number of employees nationwide:** 520.

CRC INDUSTRIES, INC.
885 Louis Drive, Warminster PA 18974. 215/674-4300. **Fax:** 215/674-2196. **Contact:** Human Resources. **World Wide Web address:** http://www.crcindustries.com. **Description:** Produces a variety of cleaners, greases, lubricators, and other specialty chemicals for the automotive, marine, electrical, industrial, and aviation markets. Founded in 1958. **Positions advertised include:** Machine Operator; Mixer; Senior Mechanic. **Corporate headquarters location:** This location.

CSS INDUSTRIES, INC.
1845 Walnut Street, Suite 800, Philadelphia PA 19103-4755. 215/569-9900. **Contact:** Jacqueline Tully, Manager of Administration. **World Wide Web address:** http://www.cssindustries.com. **Description:** Manufactures and distributes business forms and supplies, and specialty metal containers. **Positions advertised include:** Benefits Compensation Clerk; Customer Service Specialist. **Parent company:** Philadelphia Industries, Inc. **Number of employees nationwide:** 11,650.

CTI DATA SOLUTIONS INC.
2550 Eisenhower Avenue, Norristown PA 19403. 610/666-1700. **Fax:** 610/666-7707. **Contact:** Human Resources. **E-mail address:** hrdirector@ctigroup.com. **World Wide Web address:** http://www.ctigroup.com. **Description:** Through its subsidiaries, CTI Group Holdings designs, develops, and markets software and systems for the telecommunications industry. Founded in 1968. **Positions advertised include:** Technical Architect. **Corporate headquarters location:** Indianapolis IN. **Parent company:** CTI Group.

C.W. INDUSTRIES, INC.
130 James Way, Southampton PA 18966-3838. 215/355-7080. **Fax:** 215/355-1088. **Contact:** Human Resources. **E-mail address:** info@cwind.com. **World Wide Web address:** http://www.cwind.com. **Description:** Produces a wide range of electrical switches and connectors.

CABLE DESIGN TECHNOLOGIES (CDT)/ WEST PENN WIRE
2833 West Chestnut Street, P.O. Box 762, Washington PA 15301. 724/222-7060. **Contact:** Personnel. **World Wide Web address:** http://www.westpenn-cdtc.com. **Description:** Manufactures electronic data transmission cables for a variety of industrial applications including voice and data wiring and fiber-optic connective solutions. **Corporate headquarters location:** Schaumburg IL. **Other U.S. locations:** Chino CA; Irvine CA; Los Angeles CA; Northbridge CA; Manchester CT; Miami FL; Atlanta GA; Chicago IL; Wheeling IL; Auburn MA; Leominster MA; Westborough MA; Icard NC; Las Vegas NV; Whitestone NY; Wadsworth OH; Sharon Hill PA; Washington PA; Dallas TX; Houston TX; Seattle WA. **International locations:** Australia; Canada; China; Denmark; Germany; Italy; Malaysia; Mexico; Poland; Spain; Sweden; United Kingdom. **Subsidiaries include:** Admiral/CDT; Anglo/CDT; Barcel/CDT; Cekan/CDT; Dearborn/CDT; HEW/CDT; ITC/CDT; Manhattan/CDT; Mohawk/CDT; Montrose/CDT; NEK/CDT; Norcom/CDT; NORDX/CDT; Orebro/CDT; Phalo/CDT; Raydex/CDT; Red Halk/CDT; Stronglink/CDT; Thermax/CDT; West Penn Wire/CDT; X-Mark/CDT. **Listed on:** New York Stock Exchange. **Stock exchange symbol:** CDT. **President/CEO:** Paul M. Olson. **Annual sales/revenues:** More than $100 million.

CABOT SUPERMETALS
County Line Road, P.O. Box 1608, Boyertown PA 19512-1608. 610/367-1500. **Fax:** 610/367-6383. **Contact:** Debby Eschbach, Human Resources. **World Wide Web address:** http://www.cabot-corp.com. **Description:** Manufactures aluminum master alloys and tantalum metal products. **Corporate headquarters location:** This location. **Parent company:** Cabot Corporation.

CADMUS SPECIALTY PUBLICATIONS
1991 Northampton Street, Easton PA 18041-3199. 610/258-9111. **Toll-free phone:** 800/677-6225. **Fax:** 610/250-7285. **Contact:** Richard Cory, Corporate Industrial Relations Manager. **World Wide Web address:** http://www.cadmus.com. **Description:** Provides a wide range of printing and publications services including publication and catalog printing, photocomposition, and binding.

CALGON CARBON CORPORATION
P.O. Box 717, Pittsburgh PA 15203-0717. 412/787-6700. **Fax:** 412/787-6737. **Contact:** Invest in People Department. **E-mail address:** jobs@calgoncarbon.com.

World Wide Web address: http://www.calgoncarbon.com. **Description:** Provides purification, separation, and concentration products and services to consumers worldwide. **Corporate headquarters location:** This location. **Other U.S. locations:** Blue Lake CA; Catlettsburg KY; Pearlington MS; Neville Island PA. **Listed on:** New York Stock Exchange. **Stock exchange symbol:** CCC. **Number of employees at this location:** 300. **Number of employees worldwide:** 1250.

CALIFORNIA UNIVERSITY OF PENNSYLVANIA
Dixon Hall, Room 408, 250 University Avenue, California PA 15419. 724/938-4427. **Contact:** Office of Human Resources. **E-mail address:** cupjobs@cup.edu. **World Wide Web address:** http://www.cup.edu. **Description:** A university offering two-year, four-year, and graduate programs leading to associate's, bachelor's, and master's degrees. Enrollment includes approximately 6,000 undergraduates and 700 graduate students. **Positions advertised include:** Digital Preservationist; Psychologist/Counselor; Assistant Professor/Head Athletic Trainer.

CALKINS NEWSPAPERS INC.
THE INTELLIGENCER-RECORD
P.O. Box 858, Doylestown PA 18901. 215/345-3000. **Physical address:** 333 North Broad Street, Doylestown PA 18901. **Contact:** Human Resources. **World Wide Web address:** http://www.phillyburbs.com. **Description:** Publishes the *Intelligencer*, a newspaper with a daily circulation of 44,100 and a Sunday circulation of 62,000. Calkins Newspapers also publishes the *Record*, *Burlington County Times*, and *Bucks County Courier Times*.

CAM CO ENTERPRISES, INC.
125 South College Street, Washington PA 15301. 724/222-2315. **Contact:** Human Resources. **World Wide Web address:** http://www.camconet.com. **Description:** Manufactures and sells computer systems and provides networking and Website design services.

CAMELBACK SKI AREA
Exit 299 I-80, P.O. Box 168, Tannersville PA 18372. 570/629-1661. **Toll-free phone:** 800/233-8100. **Fax:** 570/620-0942. **E-mail address:** cooljobs@skicamelback.com. **World Wide Web address:** http://www.skicamelback.com. **Description:** A ski resort in the Pocono Mountains. **Positions advertised include:** Life Guards; Ambassadors; Customer Service; Janitorial; Water Park/ Lift Attendants; Ticket Sales. **NOTE:** See website for dates on seasonal hiring sessions.

CAMP DRESSER & McKEE, INC. (CDM)
205 Granite Run Drive, Suite 350, Lancaster PA 17601. 717/560-7500. **Fax:** 717/560-7525. **Contact:** Human Resources. **World Wide Web address:** http://www.cdm.com. **Description:** Camp Dresser & McKee is a worldwide provider of environmental engineering, scientific, planning, and management services. The company focuses on professional activities for the management of water resources, hazardous and solid wastes, wastewater, infrastructure, and environmental systems for industry and government. **Positions advertised include:** Environmental Engineer. **Corporate headquarters location:** Cambridge MA.

CANNON SLINE
213 Jones Boulevard, Suite 106, Pottstown PA 19464. 610/495-1444. **Fax:** 610/495-1440. **Contact:** Human Resources. **World Wide Web address:** http://www.cannonsline.com. **Description:** Provides painting, coating, and related services to industrial and commercial clients.

CANNONDALE CORPORATION
172 Friendship Village Road, Bedford PA 15522. 814/623-9073. **Fax:** 814/623-6604. **Contact:** Human Resources. **E-mail address:** usajobs@cannondale.com. **World Wide Web address:** http://www.cannondale.com. **Description:** This location houses the company's senior corporate management, accounting, sales, marketing, customer service, payroll, and research and development departments. Overall, Cannondale is a leading manufacturer of high-performance mountain, racing, hybrid, touring, and specialty bicycles. Products are sold through specialty bicycle retailers in the United States and in more than 60 foreign countries. Cannondale also manufactures and sells bicycle accessories including clothing, packs and bags, bike trailers, and components. **Corporate headquarters location:** Bethel CT. **Other area locations:** Philipsburg PA. **Listed on:** NASDAQ. **Stock exchange symbol:** BIKE. **Number of employees nationwide:** 720.

CAPSULE COMMUNICATIONS
2 Greenwood Square, 3331 Street Road, Suite 275, Bensalem PA 19020-2052. 215/633-9400. **Toll-free phone:** 800/872-3369. **Fax:** 888/970-7700. **Contact:** Human Resources Department. **World Wide Web address:** http://www.capsulecom.com. **Description:** A switch-based interexchange carrier providing long-distance telephone communications primarily to small and medium-sized businesses. The company also provides inbound 800 long-distance services, as well as other telecommunications services, such as calling cards, cellular, paging, dedicated access, data services, and debit cards. The company uses its own switching facilities to originate, transport, and terminate calls for customers generally located between Boston MA, Norfolk VA, and Pittsburgh PA. For calls originating or terminating outside the company's own network, the company uses services provided by other long-distance companies. **Parent company:** Covista. **Listed on:** NASDAQ. **Stock exchange symbol:** CVST.

CAR MATE TRAILERS
P.O. Box 155, Route 66, Leeper PA 16233. 814/744-8855. **Toll-free phone:** 800/733-8856. **Contact:** Human Resources. **World Wide Web address:** http://www.carmate-trailers.com. **Description:** A manufacturer of car, cargo, and utility trailers; bunkhouses; and concession stands.

CARBIDE GRAPHITE GROUP, INC.
One Gateway Center, 19th Floor, Pittsburgh PA 15222. 412/562-3700. **Contact:** Human Resources. **World Wide Web address:** http://www.cggi.com. **Description:** Makers of graphite products including electrodes used in electric arc steel manufacturing and machined graphite specialty products used by the semiconductor, metal processing, and other industries. The company also manufactures calcium carbide.

CARBONE OF AMERICA
215 Stackpole Street, St. Marys PA 15857-1488. 814/781-1234. **Fax:** 814/781-8434. **Contact:** Sylvia Feldbaur, Director of Human Resources Department. **World Wide Web address:** http://www.carbonelorraine.com. **Description:** Manufactures carbon and graphite products for automotive parts such as starters, alternators, and fan belts.

CARDONE INDUSTRIES
5501 Whitaker Avenue, Philadelphia PA 19124-1799. 215/912-3000. **Fax:** 215/912-3700. **Contact:** Human Resources. **World Wide Web address:** http://www.cardone.com. **Description:** Engaged in automotive reconditioning and rebuilding.

CARLISLE SYNTEC INCORPORATED
1285 Ritner Highway, P.O. Box 7000, Carlisle PA 17013. 717/245-7000. **Toll-free phone:** 800/4-SYNTEC. **Fax:** 717/245-7285. **Contact:** Human Resources Manager. **World Wide Web address:** http://www.carlislesyntec.com. **Description:** Manufactures elastomeric roofing membrane and related building products for the commercial roofing market. **Positions advertised include:** Accountant/Auditor; Chemical Engineer. **Corporate headquarters location:** Syracuse NY. **Parent company:** Carlisle Companies Inc. **Operations at this facility include:** Divisional Headquarters; Manufacturing; Research and Development; Sales. **Listed on:** New York Stock Exchange. **Stock exchange symbol:** CSL. **Number of employees at this location:** 400. **Number of employees nationwide:** 1,040.

CARLOW COLLEGE
FWH 2nd Floor, 3333 Fifth Avenue, Pittsburgh PA 15213. 412/578-8897. **Recorded jobline:** 412/578-6054. **Fax:** 412/578-6265. **Contact:** Andra Tokarsky, Human Resources. **E-mail address:** atokarsky@carlow.edu. **World Wide Web address:** http://www.carlow.edu. **Description:** Carlow College is a four-year college offering certificate, B.A., B.S., and master's degree programs. Undergraduate enrollment is approximately 1,600 students.

G.O. CARLSON, INC.
350 Marshallton-Thorndale Road, Downington PA 19335-2063. 610/384-2800. **Toll-free phone:** 800/338-5622. **Fax:** 610/383-6032. **Contact:** Kristin DiFonzo, Human Resources Manager. **E-mail address:** kdifonzo@gocarlson.com. **World Wide Web address:** http://www.gocarlson.com. **Description:** Manufactures stainless steel, nickel alloys, and titanium plate and plate products. **Corporate headquarters location:** This location. **Operations at this facility include:** Administration. **Number of employees at this location:** 150.

CARMEUSE NA
11 Stanwix Street, 11th Floor, Pittsburgh PA 15222-2682. 412/995-5500. **Contact:** Human Resources. **E-mail address:** resumes@carmeusena.com. **World Wide Web address:** http://www.carmeuse.be. **Description:** Produces lime products for a variety of commercial and industrial uses. **Corporate headquarters location:** This location.

CARNEGIE MELLON UNIVERSITY
143 North Craig Street, Whitfield Hall, Pittsburgh PA 15213-3890. 412/268-4747. **Recorded jobline:** 412/268-8545. **Contact:** Human Resources. **E-mail address:** hrhelp@andrew.cmu.edu. **World Wide Web address:** http://hr.cmu.edu. **Description:** A university offering certificate, associate's, B.A., B.S., master's, M.B.A., and doctoral programs. Enrollment is approximately 4,300 undergraduates and 2,600 graduate students. **NOTE:** Please see website for online application details. **Positions advertised include:** Administrative/Executive; Information Technologies; Research; Technical.

CARNEGIE MUSEUMS OF PITTSBURGH
4400 Forbes Avenue, Pittsburgh PA 15213. 412/622-3310. **Fax:** 412/622-5582. **Contact:** Human Resources. **E-mail address:** employment@carnegiemuseums.org. **World Wide Web address:** http://www.carnegiemuseums.org. **Description:** Association of the Andy Warhol Museum, Carnegie Museum of Art, Carnegie Museum of Natural History, and the Carnegie Science Center. **Jobs advertised include:** maintenance, program presenter, host, and projectionist.

CATHOLIC HEALTH EAST
14 Campus Boulevard, Suite 300, Newtown Square PA 19073. 610/355-2106. **Fax:** 610/355-2107. **Contact:** Human Resources. **E-mail address:** info@che.org. **World Wide Web address:** http://www.che.org. **Description:** Catholic Health East is a health care system operation 28 regional systems in 10 Eastern states. The health care system includes three behavioral health facilities, 32 hospitals, and 28 skilled nursing centers. **Operations at this facility include:** This location houses administrative offices. Number of employees nationwide: 43,000.

CELLOMICS, INC.
100 Technology Drive, Pittsburgh PA 15219. 412/770-2200. **Fax:** 412/770-2440. **Contact:** Human Resources. **E-mail address:** humanresources@cellomics.com. **World Wide Web address:** http://www.cellomics.com. **Description:** Develops research components for pharmaceutical and biotechnology companies to aid in faster, more efficient drug discovery processes. Cellomics, Inc. delivers genomic- and cell-based solutions. Founded in 1996. **Positions advertised include:** Executive Assistant; Lead Customer Support Specialist; Key Account Manager; Application Software Specialist. **Corporate headquarters location:** This location. **Listed on:** Privately held.

CENTOCOR, INC.
200 Great Valley Parkway, Malvern PA 19355. 610/651-6000. **Fax:** 610/651-6100. **Contact:** Frances Littlewood, Human Resources. **World Wide Web address:** http://www.centocor.com. **Description:** Develops biopharmaceutical therapeutics and diagnostic products for cardiovascular, inflammatory, and infectious diseases, and cancer. Centocor concentrates on research, development, and manufacturing with a technological focus on monoclonal antibodies, peptides, and nucleic acids. **NOTE:** On-line applications can be made via the Johnson and Johnson Careers Website. **Positions advertised include:** Packaging Engineer; Principal Engineer; Staff Engineer; DSP Supervisor; Associate Scientist. **Corporate headquarters location:** This location. **Subsidiaries include:** Centocor B.V. (the Netherlands); Centocor U.K. Limited (England); and Nippon Centocor K.K. (Japan). **Parent company:** Johnson & Johnson. **Listed on:** New York Stock Exchange. **Stock exchange symbol:** JNJ.

CENTRE DAILY TIMES
3400 East College Avenue, P.O. Box 89, State College PA 16804. 814/238-5000. **Toll-free phone:** 800/327-5500. **Contact:** Human Resources. **World Wide Web address:** http://www.centredaily.com. **Description:** Publishes the *Centre Daily Times* newspaper.

CEPHALON, INC.
145 Brandywine Parkway, West Chester PA 19380. 610/344-0200. **Fax:** 610/738-6312. **Contact:** Ms. Pat Vandenberg, Recruiting. **World Wide Web address:** http://www.cephalon.com. **Description:** Develops, manufactures, and markets pharmaceutical products for the treatment of neurological disorders, sleep disorders, and cancer. **Positions advertised include:** Analytical Chemistry; Biostatistics; Business Development; Clinical Research; Commercial Operations; Corporate Communications; Development Manufacturing; Drug Disposition; Medical Affairs; Quality Assurance; Regulatory Affairs. **Corporate headquarters location:** This location. **Subsidiaries include:** Cephalon Development Corporation; Cephalon International Holdings, Inc.; Cephalon Investments, Inc.; Cephalon Property

Management, Inc.; Cephalon Technology, Inc. **Listed on:** NASDAQ. **Stock exchange symbol:** CEPH.

CERRO METAL PRODUCTS COMPANY
P.O. Box 388, Bellefonte PA 16823. 814/355-6330. **Fax:** 814/355-6227. **Contact:** Larry Yont, Human Resources Director. **World Wide Web address:** http://www.cerrometal.com. **Description:** Manufactures brass rods.

CERTAINTEED CORPORATION
P.O. Box 860, 750 East Swedesford Road, Valley Forge PA 19482. 610/341-7000. **Toll-free phone:** 800/233-8990. **Fax:** 610/341-7784. **Contact:** Ms. Kathyrn Ferrante, Human Resources Director. **E-mail address:** ctrecruitment@saint-gobain.com. **World Wide Web address:** http://www.certainteed.com. **Description:** Certainteed Corporation manufactures and distributes building materials, fiberglass products, and piping products. Principal products are used in residential, commercial, and industrial construction; repair and remodeling; fiberglass reinforcement applications; water and sewer systems; and other underground utility systems. Other products include roofing, acoustical insulation, fiberglass thermal insulation, air handling products, glass fiber, vinyl siding, and PVC piping. **Corporate headquarters location:** This location. **Other U.S. locations:** Nationwide. **Parent company:** Compagnie de Saint-Gobain. The U.S. and Canadian operations of four of the company's worldwide branches are Abrasives, Construction Materials, Industrial Ceramics, and Insulation and Reinforcements. The Saint-Gobain companies based in North America are organized under the umbrella of the Saint-Gobain Corporation, which includes the Certainteed Corporation, Norton Company, and all of their subsidiaries. **Operations at this facility include:** Administration. **Number of employees at this location:** 450. **Number of employees nationwide:** 8,000.

CHARMING SHOPPES, INC.
450 Winks Lane, Bensalem PA 19020. 215/245-9100. **Recorded jobline:** 800/543-2562. **Contact:** Phil Brunone, Director of Human Resources. **E-mail address:** hr@charming.com. **World Wide Web address:** http://www.charmingshoppes.com. **Description:** A retail holding company. **Special programs:** Internships. **Corporate headquarters location:** This location. **Subsidiaries include:** Fashion Bug and Fashion Bug Plus specialize in the sale of junior, miss, and plus size merchandise. **Listed on:** NASDAQ. **Stock exchange symbol:** CHRS. **Number of employees worldwide:** 24,000.

CHARTER COMMUNICATIONS
313 1/2 East Cherry Street, Clearfield PA 16830. 814/765-5313. **Contact:** Human Resources. **World Wide Web address:** http://www.chartercom.com. **Description:** A broadcasting and communications company. **NOTE:** Online application preferred.

CHATHAM COLLEGE
Woodland Road, Pittsburgh PA 15232. 412/365-1847. **Contact:** Personnel. **E-mail address:** chathr@chatham.edu. **World Wide Web address:** http://www.chatham.edu. **Description:** A four-year college offering certificate, bachelor's, and master's degree programs. At the undergraduate level, the school has an all-women enrollment. Graduate programs are coed. The combined undergraduate and graduate enrollment is approximately 1,000 students. **Positions advertised include:** Program Director Landscape Architecture; Director of Environmental Initiatives; Director of Business Programs; Database Coordinator; Registered Nurse; Head Soccer Coach.

CHESTER COUNTY HOSPITAL
701 East Marshall Street, West Chester PA 19380. 610/431-5000. **Recorded jobline:** 610/430-2903. **Fax:** 610/430-2956. **Contact:** Human Resources. **World Wide Web address:** http://www.cchosp.com. **Description:** A hospital. **Positions advertised include:** Case Manager; Social Worker; Registered Nurse; Payroll Clerk; Catering Associate; Lab Assistant; Admissions Registrar; Customer Relations Manager. **Number of employees at this location:** 1,400.

CHILDREN'S HOSPITAL OF PITTSBURGH
3705 Fifth Avenue, Pittsburgh PA 15213-2524. 412/692-7500. **Recorded jobline:** 412/692-8000 (non-clinical positions); 412/692-5366 (clinical positions). **Contact:** Human Resources. **E-mail address:** jobs@chp.edu. **World Wide Web address:** http://www.chp.edu. **Description:** A pediatric hospital serving children up to the age of 18.

CHILDREN'S INSTITUTE
6301 Northumberland Street, Pittsburgh PA 15217. 412/420-2400. **Contact:** Human Resources. **World Wide Web address:** http://www.amazingkids.org. **Description:** A rehabilitation hospital. **NOTE:** Interested jobseekers should address their resume to the department in which their interest lies. **Positions advertised include:** Behavioral Specialist; Feeding Specialist; Payroll Specialist.

CHROMALOX
103 Gamma Drive Extension, Pittsburgh PA 15238. 412/967-3940. **Fax:** 412/967-3938. **Contact:** Barbara Richmond, Human Resources. **E-mail address:** employment@chrmaloxheating.com. **World Wide Web address:** http://www.mychromalox.com. **Description:** Engaged in the manufacture of electrical heating elements, systems, and controls, in addition to administration and sales. **Office hours:** Monday - Friday, 8:30 a.m. - 5:15 p.m. **Corporate headquarters location:** This location. **Other U.S. locations:** Nationwide. **Parent company:** Emerson Electric Company. **Listed on:** New York Stock Exchange. **Stock exchange symbol:** EMR. **Annual sales/revenues:** More than $100 million. **Number of employees at this location:** 65. **Number of employees worldwide:** 1,150.

CHROMALOX HEATUBE COMPANY
103 Gamma Drive Extension, Pittsburgh PA 15238. 412/967-3940. **Fax:** 412/967-3938. **Contact:** Barbara Richmond, Human Resources. **World Wide Web address:** http://www.mychromalox.com. **Description:** This facility is engaged in the manufacture of electrical heating elements. **Corporate headquarters location:** This location. **Other U.S. locations:** Nationwide. **Parent company:** Emerson Electric Company. **Listed on:** New York Stock Exchange. **Stock exchange symbol:** EMR. **Annual sales/revenues:** More than $100 million.

CHUBB GROUP OF INSURANCE COMPANIES
4 Penn Center, 1600 JFK Boulevard, Philadelphia PA 19103. 215/569-9660. **Fax:** 215/569-9418. **Contact:** Ms. Latrell Johnson, Human Resources Manager. **World Wide Web address:** http://www.chubb.com. **Description:** A property and casualty insurer with more than 115 offices in 30 countries worldwide. The Chubb Group of Insurance Companies offers a broad range of specialty insurance products and services designed for individuals and businesses including high technology, financial institutions, and general manufacturers. **Corporate headquarters location:** Warren NJ. **Listed on:** New York Stock Exchange. **Stock exchange symbol:** CB. **Number of employees nationwide:** 8,500.

CITIZENS BANK
122 West College Avenue, State College PA 16801. 814/234-6311. **Contact:** Human Resources. **World Wide Web address:** http://www.citizensbank.com. **Description:** A bank. **NOTE:** Employment matters are handled through the corporate headquarters location at: One Citizens Plaza, Providence RI 02903, 401/456-7000. **Corporate headquarters location:** Providence RI. **Other U.S. locations:** DE; MD; MA; RI; NJ; CT; ME; VT. **Corporate headquarters location:** Providence RI. **Other U.S. locations:** Northeast. **Listed on:** NASDAQ. **Stock exchange symbol:** CBCF. **Number of employees nationwide:** 20,000.

CITIZENS BANK
8-18 West Market Street, Wilkes-Barre PA 18711. 570/826-2901. **Contact:** Human Resources. **World Wide Web address:** http://www.citizensbank.com. **Description:** A bank. As part of the Northeastern Region, this location serves consumer and small to mid-sized commercial markets in northeastern Pennsylvania. **NOTE:** Employment matters are handled through the corporate headquarters location at: One Citizens Plaza, Providence RI 02903, 401/456-7000. **Corporate headquarters location:** Providence RI. **Other U.S. locations:** DE; MD; MA; RI; NJ; CT; ME; VT. **Listed on:** NASDAQ. **Stock exchange symbol:** CBCF. **Number of employees nationwide:** 20,000.

CITIZENS NATIONAL BANK OF SOUTHERN PENNSYLVANIA
35 North Carlisle Street, Greencastle PA 17225. 717/597-2191. **Contact:** Human Resources. **World Wide Web address:** http://www.citizensbsp.com. **Description:** A full-service bank. **NOTE:** Employment matters are handled through the corporate headquarters location at: One Citizens Plaza, Providence RI 02903, 401/456-7000. **Parent company:** Susquehanna Bancshares, Inc. is a multifinancial institution. Since 1982, Susquehanna has grown from one bank serving one county with 14 offices to six banks serving eight counties with 83 offices. The company also operates a leasing company whose market encompasses Pennsylvania, Maryland, New Jersey, Virginia, West Virginia, and Delaware. **Other U.S. locations:** DE; MD; MA; RI; NJ; CT; ME; VT.

CITY SHIRT COMPANY
242 Industrial Park Road, Frackville PA 17931. 570/874-4251. **Contact:** Human Resources. **Description:** City Shirt Company is a manufacturer and retailer of uniform shirts and slacks.

CLARION UNIVERSITY OF PENNSYLVANIA
B29, Carrier Administration Building, Clarion PA 16214. 814/393-2000. **Toll-free phone:** 800/672-7171. **Contact:** Human Resources. **E-mail address:** info@clarion.edu. **World Wide Web address:** http://www.clarion.edu. **Description:** A university offering two-year, four-year, and graduate degree programs. Degrees awarded include associate's, bachelor's, master's, and MBAs. Enrollment includes approximately 5,700 undergraduates and 450 graduate students. **NOTE:** Faculty and staff openings are posted on www.higheredjobs.com.

CLEAN HARBORS, INC.
401 Mt. Nebo Road, Pittsburgh PA 15237. 412/358-8790. **Contact:** Human Resources. **World Wide Web address:** http://www.cleanharbors.com. **Description:** Clean Harbors, Inc., through its subsidiaries, provides comprehensive environmental services in 35 states in the Northeast, Midwest, Central, and Mid-Atlantic regions. Clean Harbors provides a wide range of hazardous waste management and environmental support services to a diversified customer base from over 40 locations. The company's hazardous waste management services include treatment, storage, recycling, transportation, risk analysis, site assessment, laboratory analysis, site closure, and disposal of hazardous materials through environmentally sound methods. Environmental remediation services include emergency response, surface remediation, groundwater restoration, industrial maintenance, and facility decontamination. Customers include nearly 300 of the *Fortune* 500 companies; regional utilities; oil, pharmaceutical, and chemical companies; small businesses; and the high-tech and biotech industries. **NOTE:** Please send resumes to the appropriate party as shown on the website. **Corporate headquarters location:** Braintree MA. **Other U.S. locations:** Nationwide. **Operations at this facility include:** This location is a sales office. **Listed on:** NASDAQ. **Stock exchange symbol:** CLHB. **Number of employees nationwide:** 1,400.

COLLEGE CREDIT CARD CORPORATION
1500 JFK Boulevard, Suite 800, Philadelphia PA 19102. 215/568-1700. **Fax:** 215/568-1701. **Contact:** Edward Soloman, President. **Description:** Markets credit cards and other financial services to college students on-campus and to the general public at special events and venues. **Special programs:** Internships. **Corporate headquarters location:** This location. **Other U.S. locations:** Monroeville PA. **Parent company:** Campus Dimensions Inc. **Listed on:** Privately held. **Number of employees at this location:** 60. **Number of employees nationwide:** 115.

COLONIAL METALS COMPANY
217 Linden Street, Columbia PA 17512. 717/684-2311. **Contact:** Robert Shaffer, Personnel Manager. **Description:** Manufactures bronze, brass, and aluminum ingots. **Corporate headquarters location:** This location.

COLONIAL PENN
399 Market Street, Philadelphia PA 19181. 215/928-8000. **Contact:** Gay Woltemate, Personnel Manager. **World Wide Web address:** http://www.colonialpenn.com. **Description:** Provides life insurance, specializing in graded-benefit policies. Founded in 1957.

COMCAST
1155 Benner Pike, State College PA 16801. 814/238-3096. **Contact:** Employment. **World Wide Web address:** http://www.comcast.com. **Description:** One of the nation's largest cable television and broadband services companies.

COMCAST CORPORATION
1500 Market Street, Philadelphia PA 19102. 215/665-1700. **Contact:** Human Resources Department. **World Wide Web address:** http://www.comcast.com. **Description:** A cable television system operator that also distributes Muzak and provides cellular phone services. **Corporate headquarters location:** This location. **Listed on:** NASDAQ. **Stock exchange symbol:** CMCSA and CMCSK. **Annual sales/revenues:** More than $100 million. **Number of employees nationwide:** 68,000.

COMCAST-SPECTACOR, LP
3601 South Broad Street, Philadelphia PA 19148. 215/336-3600. **Recorded jobline:** 215/952-4180. **Contact:** Human Resources Manager. **World Wide Web address:** http://www.comcast-spectacor.com. **Description:** A sports/entertainment firm managing the Philadelphia Flyers, 76ers, Wings, Kixx, and Phantoms; Comcast SportsNet; the First Union Spectrum; and the First Union Center. The First Union Spectrum and Center are host to Flyers and Phantoms hockey, 76ers basketball, Kixx soccer and over 500 other sporting, musical, and entertainment events each year.

Comcast SportsNet is a 24-hour sports network dedicated to the Philadelphia-area sports world. **NOTE:** Online application is encouraged. **Special programs:** Internships. **Internship information:** A variety of internship opportunities are available to college students during the fall, spring, and summer terms. **Corporate headquarters location:** This location. **Parent company:** Comcast Corporation. **Operations at this facility include:** Administration; Sales; Service. **Listed on:** New York Stock Exchange. **Stock exchange symbol:** CCZ. **Number of employees at this location:** 800.

COMMONWEALTH BANK
P.O. Box 2100, Valley Forge PA 19482-2100. 610/313-1600. **Toll-free phone:** 800/327-9885. **Fax:** 610/313-1509. **Contact:** Human Resources Department. **E-mail address:** hrrecruit@commonwealthbank.com. **World Wide Web address:** http://www.commonwealthbank.com. **Description:** A full-service community bank serving retail and small business customers in northeast Pennsylvania. Founded in 1924. **NOTE:** Part-time jobs are offered. **Special programs:** Training; Summer Jobs. **Corporate headquarters location:** This location. **Listed on:** NASDAQ. **Stock exchange symbol:** CMSB.

COMMUNITY COLLEGE OF ALLEGHENY COUNTY
808 Ridge Avenue Pittsburgh PA 15212. 412/371-8651. **Contact:** Mr. Patrick Leonard, Executive Dean. **World Wide Web address:** http://www.ccac.edu. **Description:** A two-year community college with an enrollment of approximately 4,500. **Positions advertised include:** Administrative Assistant IT; Custodian/Laborer; Distance Learning Educational Technician; Grants Support Technician; Nursing Faculty; Senior Clerk.

COMMUNITY COLLEGE OF BEAVER COUNTY
One Campus Drive, Monaca PA 15061. 724/775-8561. **Contact:** Human Resources. **World Wide Web address:** http://www.ccbc.edu. **Description:** A two-year community college, with an enrollment of approximately 3,000.

COMMUNITY COLLEGE OF PHILADELPHIA
1700 Spring Garden Street, Room M2-3, Philadelphia PA 19130. 215/751-8035. **Fax:** 215/972-6307. **Contact:** Human Resources. **World Wide Web address:** http://www.ccp.cc.pa.us. **Description:** A two-year community college offering certificates and associate's degrees. Approximately 40,000 students attend Community College of Philadelphia. **NOTE:** Please see the website for a complete listing of current openings. Online application is preferred.

COMPUNETICS, INC.
2420 Mosside Boulevard, Monroeville PA 15146. 412/373-8110. **Contact:** Aimee Miller, Human Resources Director. **E-mail address:** hr@compunetics.com. **World Wide Web address:** http://www.compunetics.com. **Description:** Produces printed circuit boards. **Positions advertised include:** Printed Circuit Boards R&D Engineer.

COMPUTER ASSOCIATES INTERNATIONAL
220 West Germantown Pike, Plymouth Meeting PA 19462. 610/940-9900. **Contact:** Human Resources. **World Wide Web address:** http://www.cai.com. **Description:** One of the world's leading developers of client/server and distributed computing software. The company develops, markets, and supports enterprise management, database and applications development, business applications, and consumer software products for a broad range of mainframe, midrange, and desktop computers. Computer Associates International serves major business, government, research, and educational organizations. Founded in 1976. **NOTE:** Resumes/applications if mailed, should be submitted to One Computer Associates Plaza, Islandia NY 11749, 800/454-3788. Online applications are preferred. **Corporate headquarters location:** Islandia NY. **Other U.S. locations:** Nationwide. **Listed on:** New York Stock Exchange. **Stock exchange symbol:** CA.

COMPUTER HARDWARE SERVICE COMPANY (CHSC)
11 Vincent Circle, Ivyland PA 18974. 215/443-9220. **Fax:** 215/443-9024. **Contact:** Human Resources. **E-mail address:** jobs@chscinc.com. **World Wide Web address:** http://www.chscinc.com. **Description:** Provides computer network maintenance and repair services.

CONAGRA FOODS, INC.
30 Marr Street, Milton PA 17847. 570/742-7621. **Contact:** Human Resources. **World Wide Web address:** http://www.conagra.com. **Description:** Manufactures and markets branded, food service, and store-branded food products. Product names include Bumble Bee, Chef Boyardee, Clover Leaf, Crunch 'n Munch, Louis Kemp, Gulden's, and PAM. **NOTE:** Mail employment correspondence to: ConAgra Foods, Inc., Attn: Resume Processing Center, One ConAgra Drive, Omaha NE 68102-5001. **Listed on:** New York Stock Exchange. **Stock exchange symbol:** CAG.

THE CONAIR GROUP INC.
455 Allegheny Boulevard, P.O. Box 790, Franklin PA 16323. 814/437-6861. **Fax:** 814/432-6227. **Contact:** Ms. Libby Stover, Human Resources. **E-mail address:** peopleservices@conairgroup.com. **World Wide Web address:** http://www.conairnet.com. **Description:** Manufactures equipment for use in plastics processing including dryers, loaders, blenders, granulators, robotics, pelletizers, and temperature control equipment. **NOTE:** Second and third shifts are offered. **Special programs:** Internships. **Corporate headquarters location:** Pittsburgh PA.

CONESTOGA WOOD SPECIALTIES, INC.
P.O. Box 158, East Earl PA 17519. 717/445-6701. **Physical address:** 245 Reading Road, East Earl PA 17519. **Fax:** 717/445-3428. **Contact:** Recruiter. **World Wide Web address:** http://www.conestogawood.com. **Description:** Manufactures and supplies wood products including panel doors, components, and moldings to the construction industry. **NOTE:** Current openings are listed on http://www.headhunter.net. **Special programs:** Internships. **Corporate headquarters location:** This location. **Other U.S. locations:** Jacksonville AR; Darlington MD; Kenlet NC; Kramer PA. **Operations at this facility include:** Administration; Divisional Headquarters; Manufacturing; Sales; Service. **Listed on:** Privately held. **Number of employees at this location:** 675. **Number of employees nationwide:** 1,500.

CONGOLEUM CORPORATION
4401 Ridge Road, Marcus Hook PA 19061. 610/485-8890. **Contact:** Human Resources. **World Wide Web address:** http://www.congoleum.com. **Description:** Congoleum Corporation is a diversified manufacturer and distributor operating in the areas of home furnishings, shipbuilding, and automotive and industrial distribution. **Special programs:** Internships. **Corporate headquarters location:** Mercerville NJ. **Other U.S. locations:** Cedarhurst MD; Trenton NJ. **Operations at this facility include:** This location manufactures sheet vinyl and floor tile. **Listed on:** American Stock Exchange. **Stock exchange symbol:** CGM. **Number of employees at this location:** 1,400.

CONSOL ENERGY INC.
CONSOL Plaza, 1800 Washington Road, Pittsburgh PA 15241-1421. 412/831-4000. **Contact:** Kent Eden, Human Resources Consultant. **World Wide Web address:** http://www.consolenergy.com. **Description:** A coal mining holding company. **Special programs:** Summer Jobs. **Corporate headquarters location:** This location. **Other U.S. locations:** Nationwide. **Subsidiaries include:** Consolidation Coal Company performs the coal mining operations for CONSOL Inc. **Listed on:** Privately held. **Annual sales/revenues:** More than $100 million. **Number of employees at this location:** 440. **Number of employees nationwide:** 7,700.

CONSOLIDATED CONTAINER COMPANY
6831 Ruppsville Road, Allentown PA 18106. 610/481-0655. **Fax:** 610/481-0658. **Contact:** Human Resources. **E-mail address:** resumes@ccllc.com. **World Wide Web address:** http://www.ccllc.com. **Description:** A manufacturer of blow-molded custom and stock plastic containers.

CONSOLIDATED RAIL CORPORATION (CONRAIL)
2001 Market Street, 16th Floor, Philadelphia PA 19101-1600. 215/209-5099. **Recorded jobline:** 215/209-5006. **Contact:** Human Resources. **World Wide Web address:** http://www.conrail.com. **Description:** A railroad company. **NOTE:** Electronic resumes and faxed resumes are not accepted. **Corporate headquarters location:** This location.

CONTAINER RESEARCH CORPORATION
P.O. Box 159, Glen Riddle PA 19037. 610/459-2160. **Toll-free phone:** 877/610-7773. **Fax:** 610/358-9297. **Contact:** Hank Kalinowsky, Personnel Manager. **World Wide Web address:** http://www.crc-flex.com. **Description:** Engaged in the fabrication and service of a wide variety of shipping container products.

CONTINENTAL AIRLINES CARGO FREIGHT FACILITY
Cargo City, West PAC Building C-2, Door 9, Philadelphia PA 19153. 215/492-4301. **Contact:** Human Resources Manager. **World Wide Web address:** http://www.con.com. **Description:** Provides air transportation services. **NOTE:** Resumes should be sent to Continental Airlines main cargo facility at Terminal D, Philadelphia PA 19153.

CONTINENTAL BOX COMPANY
1147 North Fourth Street, Philadelphia PA 19123. 215/627-4700. **Contact:** Human Resources. **Description:** Manufactures paper containers including boxes and packaging materials.

COPPERWELD CORPORATION
2200 4 Gateway Center, Pittsburgh PA 15222-1211. 412/263-3200. **Fax:** 412/263-6975. **Contact:** Human Resources. **E-mail address:** info@copperweld.com. **World Wide Web address:** http://www.copperweld.com. **Description:** Produces fabricated metal pipe fittings and related pipe products. **Corporate headquarters location:** This location. **Number of employees worldwide:** 2500.

COVE SHOE COMPANY
107 Highland Street, Martinsburg PA 16662. 814/793-3786. **Contact:** Human Resources. **World Wide Web address:** http://www.coveshoe.com. **Description:** Manufactures boots and shoes. Cove Shoe Company's principal buyers are retailers and the military.

COURIER CORPORATION
11311 Roosevelt Boulevard, Philadelphia PA 19154. 888/333-1863. **Fax:** 215/856-9930. **Contact:** Human Resources. **World Wide Web address:** http://www.courier.com. **Description:** Prints and binds books, religious products, reference texts, software manuals, and technical documentation. The company also provides electronic prepress and fulfillment services. **Corporate headquarters location:** North Chelmsford MA. **Other U.S. locations:** Kendallville IN; Lowell MA; Stoughton MA; Westford MA. **Parent company:** Courier Corporation.

CRAFTEX MILLS, INC.
450 Sentry Parkway East, Blue Bell PA 19422. 610/941-1212. **Fax:** 610/941-7171. **Contact:** Human Resources. **World Wide Web address:** http://www.craftex.com. **Description:** Produces upholstery fabrics for furniture manufacturers. **Corporate headquarters location:** This location.

CRANE NUCLEAR, INC.
2600 Eisenhower Avenue, Trooper PA 19403. 713/671-4614. **Fax:** 770/429-4754. **Contact:** Dorma Rohrman, Human Resources. **E-mail address:** drohrman@cranevs.com. **World Wide Web address:** http://www.cranenuclear.com. **Description:** Provides diagnostic, condition monitoring, and nondestructive testing systems and services to customers in the power and process industries worldwide. **NOTE:** Mail employment correspondence to: 1202 Hahlo Street, Houston TX 77020.

CROWN CORK & SEAL COMPANY, INC.
One Crown Way, Philadelphia PA 19154. 215/698-5100. **Fax:** 215/676-7245. **Contact:** Personnel. **World Wide Web address:** http://www.crowncork.com. **Description:** Founded in 1892. Crown Cork & Seal manufactures cans, plastic bottles, and metal and plastic closures, as well as machinery for the packaging industry and disposable medical devices and closures. **NOTE:** Entry-level positions are offered. **Positions advertised include:** Lead Implementation Manager; Senior Accountant. **Special programs:** Internships; Co-ops; Summer Jobs. **Corporate headquarters location:** This location. **International locations:** Worldwide. **Operations at this facility include:** Administration; Divisional Headquarters; Manufacturing. **Listed on:** New York Stock Exchange. **Stock exchange symbol:** CCK. **Annual sales/revenues:** More than $100 million. **Number of employees at this location:** 600. **Number of employees nationwide:** 22,000. **Number of employees worldwide:** 50,000.

CROWN CORK & SEAL COMPANY, INC.
1840 Baldridge Street, Connellsville PA 15425. 724/626-0120. **Contact:** Human Resources Manager. **World Wide Web address:** http://www.crowncork.com. **Description:** Crown Cork & Seal manufactures cans, plastic bottles, and metal and plastic closures, as well as machinery for the packaging industry and disposable medical devices and closures. **Corporate headquarters location:** Philadelphia PA. **International locations:** Worldwide. **Operations at this facility include:** This location manufactures packaging materials. **Listed on:** New York Stock Exchange. **Stock exchange symbol:** CCK. **Annual sales/revenues:** More than $100 million. **Number of employees nationwide:** 22,000. **Number of employees worldwide:** 50,000.

CROZER-CHESTER MEDICAL CENTER
One Medical Center Boulevard, Upland PA 19013-3995. 610/447-2262. **Contact:** Human Resources Department. **World Wide Web address:** http://www.crozer.org. **Description:** This location is a 675-bed teaching hospital. The medical center also offers the Antepartum Assessment Center, Comprehensive Breast Health Program,

Crozer Home, Crozer Regional Cancer Center, Heart Surgery/Cardiac Center, John E. DuPont Trauma Center, Maternity Center, and Nathan Speare Burn Center. **Positions advertised include:** CAT Scan Technician; Cardiac Echo Technician; Carpenter; Child Resource Coordinator; Clinical Instructor; Data Quality Supervisor; Director of Purchasing Services; Intensive Case Manager; Lab Services Representative; Paramedic; Registered Nurse; Licensed Practical Nurse. **Parent company:** Crozer-Keystone Health System.

CUSTOM ENGINEERING COMPANY
2800 McClelland Avenue, P.O. Box 10008, Erie PA 16510-0008. 814/898-2800. **Fax:** 814/898-2825. **Contact:** James Borelli, Human Resource Manager. **E-mail address:** jborelli@customeng.com. **World Wide Web address:** http://www.customeng.com. **Description:** Manufactures press platens for the paper, rubber, and wood industries. **NOTE:** Entry-level positions and second and third shifts are offered. **Annual sales/revenues:** $11 - $20 million. **Number of employees at this location:** 150.

CUTLER DAIRY PRODUCTS, INC.
612-30 West Sedgley Avenue, Philadelphia PA 19140. 215/229-5400. **Toll-free phone:** 800/468-1443. **Fax:** 215/229-5637. **Contact:** Human Resources Manager. **World Wide Web address:** http://www.cutleregg.com. **Description:** Processes and supplies eggs to the food industry. **Corporate headquarters location:** This location. **Other U.S. locations:** Abbeyville AL. **Operations at this facility include:** Administration; Manufacturing; Sales; Service. **Number of employees at this location:** 100. **Number of employees nationwide:** 250.

CYBERTECH INC.
935 Horsham Road, Suite I, Horsham PA 19044. 215/957-6220. **Fax:** 215/674-8515. **Contact:** Human Resources. **World Wide Web address:** http://www.cbrtech.com. **Description:** Manufactures specialty printers for corporate customers.

DMD DRESSER
41 Fisher Avenue, Bradford PA 16701. 814/368-3131. **Contact:** Personnel. **World Wide Web address:** http://www.halliburton.com. **Description:** Manufactures pipe couplings. **Parent company:** Halliburton Company.

DAISY DATA INC.
2850 Lewisberry Road, York Haven PA 17370. 717/932-9999. **Fax:** 717/932-8000. **Contact:** Human Resources. **E-mail address:** shefetv@daisydata.com. **World Wide Web address:** http://www.daisydata.com. **Description:** Manufactures rugged computers for industrial environments.

DALLCO INDUSTRIES INC.
1155 Elm Street, P.O. Box 2727, York PA 17403-2727. 717/854-7875. **Fax:** 717/845-5283. **Contact:** Human Resources. **World Wide Web address:** http://www.dallco.com. **Description:** Manufactures sleepwear and loungewear for women and children. **Corporate headquarters location:** This location. **Number of employees at this location:** 300.

DANA CORPORATION
125 South Keim Street, Pottstown PA 19464. 610/323-4200. **Contact:** Linda Matz, Personnel Manager. **World Wide Web address:** http://www.dana.com. **Description:** Dana Corporation is a global leader in the engineering, manufacturing, and marketing of products and systems for the worldwide vehicular, industrial, and mobile off-highway original equipment markets and is a major supplier to the related aftermarkets. Dana Corporation is also a provider of lease financing services in selected markets. The company's products include drivetrain components such as axles, driveshafts, clutches, and transmissions; engine parts such as gaskets, piston rings, seals, pistons, and filters; chassis products such as vehicular frames and cradles and heavy-duty side rails; fluid power components such as pumps, motors, and control valves; and industrial products such as electrical and mechanical brakes and clutches, drives, and motion control devices. Dana's vehicular components and parts are used on automobiles, pickup trucks, vans, minivans, sport utility vehicles, medium and heavy trucks, and off-highway vehicles. The company's industrial products include mobile off-highway and stationary equipment. Founded in 1905. **NOTE:** Application process must include the TORI Profile System found on the website. **Corporate headquarters location:** Toledo OH. **Operations at this facility include:** This location builds driveshafts. **Listed on:** New York Stock Exchange. **Stock exchange symbol:** DCN. **Number of employees worldwide:** 45,000.

DANA CORPORATION
PARISH DIVISION
Robeson and Weiser Street, Reading PA 19601. 610/371-7000. **Contact:** Dan Hartung, Human Resources Manager. **World Wide Web address:** http://www.dana.com. **Description:** Dana Corporation is a global leader in the engineering, manufacturing, and marketing of products and systems for the worldwide vehicular, industrial, and mobile off-highway original equipment markets and is a major supplier to the related aftermarkets. Dana Corporation is also a provider of lease financing services in selected markets. The company's products include drivetrain components such as axles, driveshafts, clutches, and transmissions; engine parts such as gaskets, piston rings, seals, pistons, and filters; chassis products such as vehicular frames and cradles and heavy-duty side rails; fluid power components such as pumps, motors, and control valves; and industrial products such as electrical and mechanical brakes and clutches, drives, and motion control devices. Dana's vehicular components and parts are used on automobiles, pickup trucks, vans, minivans, sport utility vehicles, medium and heavy trucks, and off-highway vehicles. The company's industrial products include mobile off-highway and stationary equipment. Founded in 1905. **NOTE:** Application process must include the TORI Profile System found on the website. **Positions advertised include:** Lead Project Engineer; Project/Process Engineer; Senior Project Engineer. **Corporate headquarters location:** Toledo OH. **Operations at this facility include:** This location stamps, forms, and bends metal parts used in the assembly of vehicular frames for OEM customers. **Listed on:** New York Stock Exchange. **Stock exchange symbol:** DCN. **Number of employees worldwide:** 45,000.

DANAHER MOTION INC.
110 Westtown Road, West Chester PA 19382. 610/692-2700. **Fax:** 610/696-4598. **Contact:** Personnel. **E-mail address:** info@danahermcg.com. **World Wide Web address:** http://www.danahermotion.com. **Description:** Manufactures resolvers, brushless DC motors, and geared assemblies. **Corporate headquarters location:** Washington DC. **Parent company:** Danaher Corporation. **Listed on:** New York Stock Exchange. **Stock exchange symbol:** DHR. **President:** Patrick J. Dulin. **Number of employees at this location:** 105. **Number of employees nationwide:** 1,500.

DATA-CORE SYSTEMS INC.
3700 Market Street, Philadelphia PA 19104. 215/243-1990. **Fax:** 215/243-1978. **Contact:** Human Resources. **World Wide Web address:** http://www.datacoresystems.com. **Description:** Develops database applications software. **Parent company:** DC Kuljian Group is a diversified holding company engaged in engineering, construction management, software, communications, chemicals, and health care.

DATACAP SYSTEMS, INC.
100 New Britain Boulevard, Chalfont PA 18914. 215/997-8989. **Contact:** Human Resources. **World Wide Web address:** http://www.dcap.com. **Description:** Develops software and point-of-sale systems.

DAVID'S BRIDAL
1001 Washington Street, Conshohocken PA 19428. 610/943-5000. **Contact:** Fred Postelle, Vice President of Human Resources. **World Wide Web address:** http://www.davidsbridal.com. **Description:** Sells a full line of bridal merchandise including apparel and accessories. **Special programs:** Internships. **Corporate headquarters location:** This location. **Number of employees at this location:** 215.

DAVIS ADVERTISING INC.
1700 Market Street, Suite 2626, Philadelphia PA 19103. 215/282-2500. **Toll-free phone:** 800/777-3284. **Fax:** 215/282-2600. **Contact:** Human Resources Manager. **E-mail address:** ejohnston@davisadv.com. **World Wide Web address:** http://www.davisadv.com. **Description:** An advertising company specializing in recruitment advertising. **Positions advertised include:** Copywriter.

DAVITA, INC.
1180 West Swedesford Road, Suite 300, Berwyn PA 19312. 610/644-4796. **Toll-free phone:** 800/633-9757. **Contact:** Recruiting. **World Wide Web address:** http://www.davita.com. **Description:** One of the largest providers of dialysis services to patients suffering from End Stage Renal Disease (ESRD). Davita's services have come to include clinical laboratory and pharmacy services, and both pre- and postsurgery management. Founded in 1988. **Positions advertised include:** Account Receivables Collections Assistant; Administrative Assistant; Clinical Quality and Education Manager; Collections Representative; Compliance Specialist; Help Desk Analyst. **Special programs:** Internships. **Office hours:** Monday - Friday, 9:00 a.m. - 5:00 p.m. **Corporate headquarters location:** El Segundo CA. **Other U.S. locations:** Nationwide. **International locations:** Argentina. **Subsidiaries include:** Renal Diagnostic Laboratory (Las Vegas NV). **Operations at this facility include:** Divisional Headquarters. **Listed on:** New York Stock Exchange. **Stock exchange symbol:** RXT. **CEO:** Robert Mayer. **Annual sales/revenues:** More than $100 million. **Number of employees at this location:** 250. **Number of employees nationwide:** 3,400.

DAY & ZIMMERMANN, INC.
1818 Market Street, Philadelphia PA 19103. 215/299-8000. **Contact:** Human Resources. **World Wide Web address:** http://www.dayzim.com. **Description:** Provides a wide range of professional services including engineering design, construction, and procurement; clean room design and validation; construction management; technical services; automation and data processing consulting; mass real estate appraisal; security guard services; munitions manufacturing services; naval ship alterations; and logistical support. **NOTE:** See website for current openings and application details. **Positions advertised include:** Director of Strategic Compensation and Benefits; Director of Tax Planning and Compliance; ERP Support Specialist; Project Accountant; Project Director; Validation Specialist. **Corporate headquarters location:** This location. **Operations at this facility include:** Administration; Sales; Service. **Number of employees at this location:** 200. **Number of employees nationwide:** 20,000.

DAY-TIMER, INC.
One Willow Lane, East Texas PA 18046. 610/398-1151. **Toll-free phone:** 800/225-5005. **Contact:** Human Resources Manager. **World Wide Web address:** http://www.daytimer.com. **Description:** Designs and manufactures personal and organizational calendars, accessories, and software. **NOTE:** Online application is encouraged at http://www.jobs.acco.icims.com. **Corporate headquarters location:** This location.

DEB SHOPS, INC.
9401 Bluegrass Road, Philadelphia PA 19114. 215/676-6000. **Contact:** Ms. Pat Okun, Office Manager. **World Wide Web address:** http://www.debshops.com. **Description:** A chain of specialty apparel stores offering moderately priced, coordinated sportswear, dresses, coats, and accessories for juniors. The company operates 285 stores in 40 states. **NOTE:** Search current openings at http://www.hotjobs.com. Online application encouraged. **Corporate headquarters location:** This location. **Other U.S. locations:** Nationwide. **Listed on:** NASDAQ. **Stock exchange symbol:** DEBS. **Number of employees at this location:** 200. **Number of employees nationwide:** 2,500.

DECISIONONE
50 East Swedesford Road, Frazer PA 19355. 610/296-6000. **Toll-free phone:** 800/767-2876. **Fax:** 610/296-2910. **Contact:** Human Resources Department. **World Wide Web address:** http://www.decisionone.com. **Description:** An international supplier of plug-compatible computer equipment and accessories. Products include disk and tape storage devices, terminals, intelligent workstations and systems, controllers, printers, airline reservation systems, and a comprehensive range of computer supplies. **Corporate headquarters location:** This location. **International locations:** Nationwide.

DELAWARE INVESTMENTS
2005 Market Street, Philadelphia PA 19103. 215/255-1200. **Fax:** 215/255-1002. **Contact:** Personnel. **World Wide Web address:** http://www.delawarefunds.com. **Description:** Specializes in mutual funds and investment management.

DELOITTE & TOUCHE
2500 One PPG Place, Pittsburgh PA 15222. 412/338-7200. **Contact:** Kristin Lazzari, Recruiting Director. **World Wide Web address:** http://www.us.deloitte.com. **Description:** An international firm of certified public accountants providing professional accounting, auditing, tax, and management consulting services to widely diversified clients. The company has a specialized program consisting of national industry groups and functional groups that cross industry lines. Groups are involved in various disciplines including accounting, auditing, taxation management advisory services, small and growing businesses, mergers and acquisitions, and computer applications.

DELTA WUNDIES
1501 West Third Street, Williamsport PA 17701-7814. 570/326-2451. **Contact:** Human Resources. **Description:** Manufactures and wholesales women's and children's underwear and children's sleepwear.

DELUXE CHECK PRINTERS, INC.
P.O. Box 2852, Pittsburgh PA 15230. 412/788-2105. **Physical address:** 615 McMichael Road, Pittsburgh PA 15205. **Contact:** Marcie Dickson, Human Resources.

World Wide Web address: http://www.deluxe.com. **Description:** Engaged in the printing and selling of a variety of checks, deposit tickets, and related forms to banks and other financial institutions. The company also manufactures documents imprinted on magnetic ink. Printing operations are carried out at more than 50 plants throughout the United States. **Corporate headquarters location:** Shoreview MN. **Parent company:** Deluxe Corporation, an international *Fortune* 500 company, provides check printing, electronic funds transfer processing services, and related services to the financial industry; check authorization and collection services to retailers; and electronic benefit transfer services to state governments. Deluxe also produces forms, specialty papers, and other products for small businesses, professional practices, and medical/dental offices; and provides tax forms and electronic tax filing services to tax preparers. Through the direct mail channel, Deluxe sells greeting cards, giftwrap, and related products to households. **Listed on:** New York Stock Exchange. **Stock exchange symbol:** DLX.

DENDRITE
701 Main Street, Stroudsburg PA 18360. 570/420-0800. **Fax:** 570/420-0818. **Contact:** Human Resources. **World Wide Web address:** http://www.dendrite.com. **Description:** Develops sales force automation software. Founded in 1986. **Special programs:** Internships. **Corporate headquarters location:** Morristown NJ. **Listed on:** NASDAQ. **Stock exchange symbol:** DRTE. **Annual sales/revenues:** $11 - $20 million. **Number of employees at this location:** 190.

DENTSPLY INTERNATIONAL INC.
Susquehanna Commerce Center, 221 West Philadelphia Street, P.O. Box 872, York PA 17405-0872. 717/845-7511. **Toll-free phone:** 800/877-0020. **Fax:** 717/849-4762. **Contact:** Human Resources. **E-mail address:** corpjobs@dentsply.com. **World Wide Web address:** http://www.dentsply.com. **Description:** A leading manufacturer of X-ray equipment and other products for the dental field including artificial teeth, prophylaxis paste, ultrasonic sealers, and bone substitute/grafting materials. **Corporate headquarters location:** This location. **Other U.S. locations:** Carlsbad CA; Encino CA; Los Angeles CA; Lakewood CO; Milford DE; Des Plaines IL; Elgin IL; Burlington NJ; Maumee OH; Tulsa OK; Johnson City TN. **International locations:** Argentina; Australia; Brazil; Canada; China; England; France; Germany; Hong Kong; India; Italy; Japan; Mexico; Philippines; Puerto Rico; Russia; Switzerland; Thailand; Vietnam. **Listed on:** NASDAQ. **Stock exchange symbol:** XRAY.

DENVER & EPHRATA TELEPHONE AND TELEGRAPH COMPANY (D&E)
124 East Main Street, P.O. Box 458, Ephrata PA 17522-0458. 717/738-8603. **Fax:** 717/859-4803. **Contact:** Recruiter. **E-mail address:** hr@decommunications.com. **World Wide Web address:** http://www.decommunications.com. **Description:** Furnishes telephone service to an estimated population of 100,000 in parts of Berks, Lancaster, and Lebanon Counties in Pennsylvania. Two host switching centers are owned and operated in the boroughs of Ephrata and Lititz. The company also owns and operates 25 remote digital dial tone facilities throughout its service area. Local, national, and international telephone services are furnished through these facilities and interconnections with the facilities of other companies. The company also provides videoconferencing services and one-way tone, display, and wide-area paging services. **Positions advertised include:** Programmer; Sales Engineer; Temporary Storekeeper; Account Executive; Sales Engineer. **Listed on:** NASDAQ. **Stock exchange symbol:** DECC. **Subsidiaries include:** Red Rose Systems, Inc. sells, installs, and maintains telecommunications equipment, and provides long-distance telephone services; D&E Marketing Corporation provides residential and business telecommunications services in Hungary.

DESALES UNIVERSITY
2755 Station Avenue, Center Valley PA 18034. 610/282-1100. **Fax:** 610/282-3206. **Contact:** Judi Shaughnessy, Employment and Benefits Manager. **World Wide Web address:** http://www.desales.edu. **Description:** A small, Catholic liberal arts college. **NOTE:** Formerly known as Allentown College.

DEZURIK/COPES-VULCAN
9843 Martin Avenue, P.O. Box 577, Lake City PA 16423. 814/774-1500. **Contact:** Yvette Hindman, Human Resources Representative. **World Wide Web address:** http://www.dezurik.com. **Description:** A manufacturer of control valves for commercial and industrial use. **Parent company:** SPX Corporation.

DICK CORPORATION
P.O. Box 10896, Pittsburgh PA 15236. 412/384-1000. **Fax:** 412/384-1424. **Contact:** Vicki Senko, Human Resources Administrator. **E-mail address:** jobs@dickcorp.com. **World Wide Web address:** http://www.dickcorp.com. **Description:** A general construction and construction management corporation.

DIEBOLD, INC.
260 Executive Drive, Suite 100, Cranberry Township PA 16066. 724/779-1500. **Contact:** Human Resources. **World Wide Web address:** http://www.diebold.com. **Description:** Diebold is engaged in the manufacture, installation, sale, and service of automated teller machines, physical and electronic security systems, and software for the financial and commercial industries. Other products include vaults, vault doors, lockers, safes, alarms, video surveillance systems, and data line security systems. Founded in 1859. **International locations:** Worldwide. **Operations at this facility include:** This location manufactures an automated medication and supply dispensing system for health care facilities. **Listed on:** New York Stock Exchange. **Stock exchange symbol:** DBD. **Number of employees worldwide:** 18000.

DIGITAL SOLUTIONS, INC. (DSI)
4200 Industrial Park Drive, Altoona PA 16602. 814/944-0405. **Contact:** Human Resources. **World Wide Web address:** http://www.dsicdi.com. **Description:** A worldwide criminal justice and public safety automation industry leader.

DOLLAR BANK
3 Gateway Center, Pittsburgh PA 15222. 412/261-4900. **Contact:** Human Resources. **World Wide Web address:** http://www.dollarbank.com. **Description:** A general services bank with branches throughout metropolitan Pittsburgh.

DOMINION PITTSBURGH POWER
625 Liberty Avenue, Pittsburgh PA 15222. 412/471-5100. **Contact:** Human Resources. **E-mail address:** human_resources@dom.com. **World Wide Web address:** http://www.dom.com. **Description:** A public utility engaged in natural gas distribution. **Positions advertised include:** Lead Accountant. **Corporate headquarters location:** Richmond VA. **Parent company:** Dominion. **Listed on:** New York Stock Exchange. **Stock exchange symbol:** D. **Number of employees at this location:** 1,250.

R. H. DONNELLEY
19 Bert Collins Drive, 11 Keystone Industrial Park, Scranton PA 18503. 570/348-6900. **Contact:** Personnel. **World Wide Web address:** http://www.rhdonnelley.com. **Description:** Engaged in selling advertising space in the Yellow Pages. Founded in 1886. **Corporate headquarters location:** Purchase NY. **Other U.S. locations:** Los Angeles CA; Miami FL; Chicago IL; New York NY. **Parent company:** Dun & Bradstreet Corporation. **Listed on:** New York Stock Exchange. **Stock exchange symbol:** RHD.

DORRANCE PUBLISHING COMPANY INC.
701 Smithfield Street, Third Floor, Pittsburgh PA 15222. 412/288-4543. **Fax:** 412/288-1786. **Contact:** Human Resources. **World Wide Web address:** http://www.dorrancepublishing.com. **Description:** A publishing company offering books of all types from a variety of authors. Founded in 1920.

DOUBLE-H BOOT COMPANY
30 North 3rd Street, Womelsdorf PA 19567. 610/589-4586. **Contact:** Human Resources. **World Wide Web address:** http://www.doublehboots.com. **Description:** Manufactures boots including the Harley-Davidson line, western, steel toe, biker, and pull-on work boots. Founded in 1955.

DOYLESTOWN HOSPITAL
595 West State Street, Doylestown PA 18901. 215/345-2200. **Fax:** 215/345-2827. **Recorded jobline:** 215/345-2538. **Contact:** Human Resources. **E-mail address:** info@dhjobs.org. **World Wide Web address:** http://www.dh.org. **Description:** A hospital. **Positions advertised include:** Assistant Teacher; Cardiac Therapist; CAT Scan Technician; Chief Information Officer; Food Service Worker; Housekeeper; Occupational Therapist; Registered Nurse; Licensed Practical Nurse. **Number of employees at this location:** 1,400.

DREXEL UNIVERSITY
3141 Chestnut Street, Philadelphia PA 19104. 215/895-2850. **Physical address:** 3201 Arch Street, 4th Floor, Suite 430, Philadelphia PA 19104. **Recorded jobline:** 215/895-2562. **Fax:** 215/895-5813. **Contact:** Human Resources. **E-mail address:** hrdept@drexel.edu. **World Wide Web address:** http://www.drexel.edu. **Description:** A four-year university offering bachelor's and master's degrees including MBAs. Approximately 8,000 undergraduate and 3,700 graduate students attend Drexel University.

DRINKER BIDDLE AND REATH LLP
One Logan Square, 18th & Cherry Streets, Philadelphia PA 19103-6996. 215/988-2700. **Fax:** 215/988-2757. **Contact:** Personnel Recruiter. **World Wide Web address:** http://www.dbr.com. **Description:** A full service law firm founded in 1849.

DUANE, MORRIS & HECKSCHER LLP
One Liberty Place, 42nd Floor, 1650 Market Street, Philadelphia PA 19103-7396. 215/979-1000. **Fax:** 215/979-1020. **Contact:** Patricia Stacey, Director, Legal Hiring. **E-mail address:** recruiting@duanemorris.com. **World Wide Web address:** http://www.duanemorris.com. **Description:** A law firm practicing in over 50 disciplines including administrative and regulatory law, employment, energy, medical malpractice, real estate, and taxation. Founded in 1904. **Positions advertised include:** Attorney; Paralegal. **Special programs include:** Summer Program. **Operations at this facility include:** Service.

DUN & BRADSTREET INFORMATIONAL RESOURCES
899 Eaton Avenue, Bethlehem PA 18025. 610/882-7000. **Contact:** Human Resources. **E-mail address:** perezd@dnb.com. **World Wide Web address:** http://www.dnb.com. **Description:** Provides business-to-business credit, marketing, and investment management services. **Positions advertised include:** Customer Relationship Manager; Inside Sales. **Corporate headquarters location:** Short Hills NJ.

DUQUESNE LIGHT COMPANY
411 Seventh Avenue, P.O. Box 1930, Pittsburgh PA 15219. 412/393-6000. **Contact:** Human Resources. **World Wide Web address:** http://www.duquesnelight.com. **Description:** An electric utility. Duquesne Light Company produces, transmits, distributes and sells electric energy. **Parent company:** DQE, Inc.

DUQUESNE UNIVERSITY
200 Fisher Hall, 600 Forbes Avenue, Pittsburgh PA 15282. 412/396-6575. **Contact:** Carol Moessinger, Assistant to Department Heads. **E-mail address:** hr.office@duq.edu. **World Wide Web address:** http://www.duq.edu. **Description:** A private university offering programs up to the doctoral level. Approximately 9,000 students attend Duquesne University. **NOTE:** See the website for a listing of staff and faculty positions and online application information.

DURALOY TECHNOLOGIES, INC.
120 Bridge Street, Scottdale PA 15683. 724/887-5100. **Fax:** 724/887-5224. **Contact:** Personnel. **World Wide Web address:** http://www.duraloy.com. **Description:** Manufactures high alloy cast components and fabrications used by petrochemical companies and steel mills for heat-resistant, corrosion-resistant, and wear-resistant applications. Founded in 1931. **NOTE:** Second and third shifts are offered. **Company slogan:** The tradition of new ideas continues. **Special programs:** Co-ops. **Corporate headquarters location:** This location. **Parent company:** WHEMCO Corp. **Listed on:** Privately held. **President:** Vince Schiavoni. **Annual sales/revenues:** $21 - $50 million. **Number of employees at this location:** 135.

DURON PAINTS AND WALLCOVERINGS
711 First Avenue, King of Prussia PA 19406. 610/962-9927. **Fax:** 610/962-9859. **Contact:** Human Resources. **E-mail address:** employment@duron.com. **World Wide Web address:** http://www.duron.com. **Description:** A retailer and wholesaler of paints, wallcoverings, window treatments, and related items. **NOTE:** Mail employment correspondence to: Duron Human Resources, 10406 Tucker Street, Beltsville MD 20705-2297. **Positions advertised include:** Inside Counter Sales Representative; Material Handler; Order Processing Purchasing Clerk; Technician. **Operations at this facility include:** Administration; Regional Headquarters; Sales.

EMI COMPANY
603 West 12th Street, Erie PA 16501. 814/452-6431. **Contact:** Personnel Manager. **Description:** A manufacturer of automotive parts and engine parts for tractor-trailers.

EAST PENN MANUFACTURING COMPANY INC.
P.O. Box 147, Deka Road, Lyon Station PA 19536. 610/682-6361. **Fax:** 610/682-4781. **Contact:** Personnel. **E-mail address:** eastpenn@eastpenn-Deka.com. **World Wide Web address:** http://www.eastpenn-deka.com. **Description:** Produces automotive and industrial batteries. Founded in 1946. **Corporate headquarters location:** This location. **Operations at this facility include:** Administration; Manufacturing; Research and Development; Sales; Service.

EASTERN INDUSTRIES, INC.
4401 Camp Meeting Road, Suite 200, Center Valley PA 18034. 610/866-0932. **Fax:** 610/867-1886. **Contact:** Steve Sandbrook, Safety Manager. **World Wide Web**

address: http://www.eastern-ind.com. **Description:** Engaged in the extraction of stone from quarries for the production of concrete, blacktop, and other building block supplies. **NOTE:** You may download an employment application on the website. **Positions advertised include:** Paving Foreman; Small Engine Repair Mechanic; Diesel Mechanic; Loader Operator; Laborer. **Parent company:** Stabler Companies Inc.

EASTON HOSPITAL
250 South 21st Street, Easton PA 18042. 610/250-4120. **Fax:** 610/250-4876. **Contact:** Human Resources. **World Wide Web address:** http://www.easton-hospital.com. **Description:** A hospital. **Positions advertised include:** Imaging Services Associate; Patient Care Attendant.

EBIX.COM, INC.
2 Parkway Center, Suite 100, Pittsburgh PA 15200. 412/920-7025. **Fax:** 412/937-3688. **Contact:** Human Resources. **E-mail address:** jobs@ebix.com. **World Wide Web address:** http://www.ebix.com. **Description:** Ebix.com develops management applications software for insurance agencies. **Corporate headquarters location:** Atlanta GA. **Operations at this facility include:** This location develops software and offers technical support.

EDINBORO UNIVERSITY OF PENNSYLVANIA
Reeder Hall, 2nd Floor, Edinboro PA 16444. 814/732-2703. **Fax:** 814/732-2885. **Contact:** Ms. Janet Dean, Associate Vice President of Human Resources. **World Wide Web address:** http://www.edinboro.edu. **Description:** A four-year state university offering graduate and doctoral programs. Approximately 7,000 students attend Edinboro University. **NOTE:** See website for a list of current openings, however online applications are discouraged unless otherwise stated. **Number of employees at this location:** 840.

EGAMES, INC.
2000 Cabot Boulevard West, Suite 110, Langhorne PA 19047-1811. 215/750-6606. **Fax:** 215/750-3722. **Contact:** Human Resources. **E-mail address:** jobs@egames.com. **World Wide Web address:** http://www.egames.com. **Description:** Publishes and distributes CD-ROM software containing a variety of games. Founded in 1992.

ELJER MANUFACTURING
1301 Eljer Way, Ford City PA 16226. 724/763-1621. **Contact:** Lee Harnish, Director Human Resources. **World Wide Web address:** http://www.eljer.com. **Description:** Manufactures china products such as toilets and sinks for the home. **Parent company:** Eljer Industries Inc. is a leading manufacturer of building products for the residential construction, commercial construction, and repair and remodeling markets. Eljer Industries Inc. manufactures and markets plumbing, heating, ventilating, and air conditioning products in North America and Europe. The company markets its products through wholesale distribution channels and, in North America, directly to building products retailers. In North America, Eljer Industries Inc. is one of only a few full-line suppliers of bath and kitchen fixtures and faucets and is a leading supplier of registers, grilles, and venting systems. In Europe, the company is a leading manufacturer of prefabricated chimneys and venting systems. **Corporate headquarters location:** Dallas TX.

ELLIOTT COMPANY
901 North Fourth Street, Jeannette PA 15644. 724/527-2811. **Fax:** 724/600-8442. **Contact:** Human Resources Manager. **E-mail address:** info@elliot-turbo.com. **World Wide Web address:** http://www.elliott-turbo.com. **Description:** A manufacturer of heavy turbomachinery. **Corporate headquarters location:** This location. **Other U.S. locations:** Nationwide. **International locations:** Worldwide. **Annual sales/revenues:** More than $100 million. **Number of employees at this location:** 1,350.

ELMWOOD PARK ZOO
1661 Harding Boulevard, Norristown PA 19401. 610/277-3825. **Fax:** 610/292-0332. **Contact:** Personnel. **World Wide Web address:** http://www.elmwoodparkzoo.org. **Description:** A zoo featuring over 150 wild animals of North America. **Positions advertised include:** Zookeeper; Food Service; Face Painter; Guest Services; Summer Camp Counselor.

ELSEVIER SCIENCE
170 South Independence Mall West, 300 East, Philadelphia PA 19106-3399. 215/238-7800. **Contact:** Human Resources. **World Wide Web address:** http://www.elsevier.com. **Description:** The company publishes textbooks, clinical reference books, and periodicals for the medical, nursing, and health-related professions. Founded in 1888. **Other U.S. locations:** St. Louis MO. **Parent company:** Harcourt General, Inc. (Chestnut Hill MA). **Operations at this facility include:** Publishing. **Number of employees at this location:** 400. **Number of employees nationwide:** 5,000.

ELWYN INC.
111 Elwyn Road, Elwyn PA 19063. 610/891-2414. **Fax:** 610/891-7395. **Contact:** Susan Ladd, Human Resources. **E-mail address:** susan_ladd@elwyn.org. **World Wide Web address:** http://www.elwyn.org. **Description:** A long-term care rehabilitation center for people with physical and mental disabilities.

EMPORIUM SPECIALTIES COMPANY, INC.
P.O. Box 65, 10 Foster Avenue, Austin PA 16720. 814/647-8661. **Fax:** 814/647-5536. **Contact:** Human Resources. **E-mail address:** info@empspec.com. **World Wide Web address:** http://www.empspec.com. **Description:** Manufactures wire forms and stampings, hand tools, and industrial burners.

EMPOWER FIDELITY
50 South Water Avenue, Sharon PA 16146. 724/981-5087. **Fax:** 724/981-4323. **Contact:** Melissa Thomas, Human Resources. **E-mail address:** carolpe@eastsoft.com. **World Wide Web address:** http://www.empower.fnis.com. **Description:** Develops software for consumer mortgage lending and commercial loans.

ENVIRONMENTAL TECTONICS COMPANY (ETC)
125 James Way, Southampton PA 18966. 215/355-9100. **Fax:** 215/357-4000. **Contact:** Personnel Department. **E-mail address:** personnel@etcusa.com. **World Wide Web address:** http://www.etcusa.com. **Description:** Designs and manufactures sterilization systems, hyperbaric systems, air crew training systems, and environmental testing equipment. **Positions advertised include:** Test Technician; Electrician; HVAC Mechanic. **Corporate headquarters location:** This location. **Other U.S. locations:** Orlando FL.

ENVIROSOURCE
1155 Business Center Drive, Horsham PA 19044. 215/956-5500. **Fax:** 215/956-5588. **Contact:** Michael R. Rochester, Human Resources Director. **E-mail address:** m.rochester@enso.net. **World Wide Web address:** http://www.enso.net. **Description:** A steel slag recovery company. **Corporate headquarters location:** This location. **Parent company:** IMS.

EPLUS, INC.
130 Futura Drive, P.O. Box 479, Pottstown PA 19464. 610/495-7800. **Fax:** 610/495-2800. **Contact:** Darren Raiguel, Human Resources. **E-mail address:** draiguel@eplus.com. **World Wide Web address:** http://www.eplus.com. **Description:** Leases and sells computers and other IT equipment. ePlus also develops online software products that provide supply chain management solutions including electronic procurement, e-financing, and e-asset management. **Corporate headquarters location:** Herndon VA. **Other U.S. locations:** Scottsdale AZ; Sacramento CA; San Diego CA; Lenexa KS; Columbia MD; Minneapolis MN; Greenville NC; Raleigh NC; Waxhaw NC; Wilmington NC; West Chester PA; Harrisburg PA; Dallas TX; Austin TX. **Listed on:** NASDAQ. **Stock exchange symbol:** PLUS.

EQUITABLE RESOURCES, INC. (ERI)
One Oxford Centre, Suite 3300, Pittsburgh PA 15219. 412/553-5700. **Contact:** Human Resources Manager. **E-mail address:** resume@eqt.com. **World Wide Web address:** http://www.eqt.com. **Description:** Equitable Resources is divided into two groups: utilities services and energy sources. The utility segment serves more than 264,000 customers in southwestern Pennsylvania, northern West Virginia, and eastern Kentucky. The energy sources segment consists of the exploration, development, and production of natural gas and oil in the Appalachian region, and to a lesser extent in the Southwest, Gulf Coast (offshore), Rocky Mountains, and in areas of Colombia, South America. **Listed on:** New York Stock Exchange. **Positions advertised include:** Income Tax Specialist; Director Corporate Communications; Project Engineer; Senior Pipeline Engineer; Senior Financial Analyst. **Stock exchange symbol:** EQT. **Number of employees nationwide:** 2,300.

ERIE, CITY OF
626 State Street, Room 300, Erie PA 16501-1128. 814/870-1241. **Fax:** 814/870-1386. **Contact:** Andrea Hoffman, Human Resources Manager. **E-mail address:** ahoffman@ci.eerie.pa.us. **World Wide Web address:** http://www.ci.erie.pa.us. **Description:** The administrative offices for the city of Erie, responsible for staffing of all municipal departments, except for the Erie Water Authority. **Number of employees at this location:** 700.

ERIE PLASTICS
844 Route 6, Corry PA 16407-0903. 814/664-4661. **Fax:** 814/663-0410. **Contact:** Membership Department. **World Wide Web address:** http://www.erieplastics.com. **Description:** A custom, plastic injection molding company specializing in packaging and closures. Founded in 1960. **NOTE:** Entry-level positions and second and third shifts are offered. **Positions advertised include:** Production Team Leader. **Special programs:** Internships; Training; Co-ops; Summer Jobs. **Other U.S. locations:** Westborough MA; Cincinnati OH. **Listed on:** Privately held. **Annual sales/revenues:** $51 - $100 million. **Number of employees at this location:** 350. **Number of employees nationwide:** 400.

ERIE SCHOOL DISTRICT
148th West 21st, Erie PA 16502. 814/874-6001. **Fax:** 814/874-6010. **Contact:** Mary Blucas, Personnel Director. **E-mail address:** mblucas@eriesd.iu5.org. **World Wide Web address:** http://esd.iu5.org. **Description:** Administrative offices for the Erie school district. The office is responsible for staffing 19 area schools including three high schools, three middle schools, and 13 elementary schools.

ERNST & YOUNG LLP
2 Commerce Square, 2001 Market Street, Suite 4000, Philadelphia PA 19103-7096. 215/448-5000. **Fax:** 215/448-4069. **Contact:** Thomas G. Elicker, Director of Human Resources. **World Wide Web address:** http://www.ey.com. **Description:** A certified public accounting firm that also provides management consulting services. Services include data processing, financial modeling, financial feasibility studies, production planning and inventory management, management sciences, health care planning, human resources, cost accounting, and budgeting systems. **Corporate headquarters location:** New York NY.

ERNST & YOUNG LLP
2100 One PPG Place, Pittsburgh PA 15222. 412/644-7800. **Fax:** 412/644-0477. **Contact:** Dawn Wallace, Human Resources. **World Wide Web address:** http://www.ey.com. **Description:** A certified public accounting firm that also provides management consulting services. Services include data processing, financial modeling, financial feasibility studies, production planning and inventory management, management sciences, health care planning, human resources, cost accounting, and budgeting systems. **Corporate headquarters location:** New York NY.

ESSROC MATERIALS INC.
3251 Bath Pike, Nazareth PA 18064. 610/837-6725. **Contact:** Human Resources. **World Wide Web address:** http://www.essroc.com. **Description:** Administration and sales pertaining to the manufacture of cement. **Positions advertised include:** BASIS Analyst; Director of Quality Control; Financial Analyst; Maintenance Supervisor. **Corporate headquarters location:** This location. **Parent company:** Italcementi Group.

ESSROC MATERIALS INC.
P.O. Box 779, Bessemer PA 16112. 724/667-7702. **Fax:** 724/667-1067. **Physical address:** Second Street, Bessemer PA 16112. **Contact:** Human Resources. **World Wide Web address:** http://www.essroc.com. **Description:** Manufactures cement and related products. **Corporate headquarters location:** Nazareth PA. **Parent company:** Italcementi Group.

ETHAN ALLEN INC.
Route 446, Eldred PA 16731. 814/225-4744. **Contact:** Manager of Employment. **World Wide Web address:** http://www.ethanallen.com. **Description:** An international retailer of home furnishings, operating approximately 350 stores. **NOTE:** For employment opportunities at one of their corporately owned stores send applications to Ethan Allen Drive, P.O. Box 1966, Danbury CT 06813-1966, fax: 203/743-8609. For employment opportunities at one of the independently owned stores see the detailed contact information for each location at the website. **Corporate headquarters location:** Danbury CT. **Listed on:** New York Stock Exchange. **Stock exchange symbol:** ETH.

EXPEDIENT
Crane Building, 40 24th Street, Suite 300, Pittsburgh PA 15222. **Toll-free phone:** 877/570-7827. **Contact:** Human Resources. **E-mail address:** resumes@expedient.com. **World Wide Web address:** http://www.expedient.com. **Description:** A national telecommunications company offering innovative services in more than 20 cities. **Positions advertised include:** Software Developer; Inside Sales Representative.

EXPONENT, INC.
3401 Market Street, Suite 300, Philadelphia PA 19104. 215/446-3325. **Fax:** 215/446-3380. **Contact:** Human Resources. **E-mail address:** hr@exponent.com. **World Wide Web address:** http://www.exponent.com. **Description:** A technical consulting firm dedicated to the investigation, analysis, and prevention of accidents and failures of an engineering or scientific nature. The company provides a multidisciplinary approach to analyze how failures occur. The company specializes in accident reconstruction, biomechanics, construction/structural engineering, aviation and marine investigations, environmental assessment, materials and product testing, warning and labeling issues, accident statistical data analysis, and risk prevention/mitigation. Founded in 1967. **NOTE:** All hiring is conducted through corporate headquarters. Please send resumes to Exponent, Inc., Human Resources, 149 Commonwealth Drive, Menlo Park CA 94025. 888/656-EXPO. **Positions advertised include:** Thermal Engineer; Engineer; Radiologist; Biometrics Engineer. **Corporate headquarters location:** Menlo Park CA. **Listed on:** NASDAQ. **Stock exchange symbol:** EXPO.

THE EXPRESS TIMES
30 North Fourth Street, P.O. Box 391, Easton PA 18044-0391. 610/258-7171. **Contact:** Human Resources. **World Wide Web address:** http://www.penn.nj.com/expresstimes **Description:** A newspaper publisher.

FCI/BERG ELECTRONICS
511 Spruce Street, Clearfield PA 16830-1942. 814/765-2431. **Contact:** Human Resources. **World Wide Web address:** http://www.fciconnect.com. **Description:** Manufactures electronic connectors. FCI is a multinational corporation serving virtually every segment of industry through the design, manufacture, and sale of a broad line of electrical and electronic connectors and related products. **Parent company:** Areva. **Number of employees worldwide:** 12,000.

F.L. SMIDTH
2040 Avenue C, Bethlehem PA 18017-2188. 610/264-6011. **Toll-free phone:** 800/523-9482. **Fax:** 610/264-6170. **Contact:** Human Resources. **E-mail address:** info-us@flsmidth.com. **World Wide Web address:** http://www.flsmidth.com. **Description:** An international producer of equipment for the cement and minerals processing industry. F.L. Smidth designs, engineers, manufactures, and installs these products for customers worldwide. **NOTE:** To search for current openings online, go to http://www.flscareeronline.com. **Corporate headquarters location:** This location. **Parent company:** FLS Industries. **Operations at this facility include:** Administration; Sales; Service. **Number of employees at this location:** 800. **Number of employees nationwide:** 1,200.

FM GLOBAL
101 Lindenwood Drive, Suite 200, Malvern PA 19301. 610/296-3100. **Fax:** 610/993-0892. **Contact:** Human Resources. **World Wide Web address:** http://www.fmglobal.com. **Description:** A loss control services organization. The primary objective of FM Global is to help owner company policyholders to protect their properties and occupancies from damage due to fire, wind, flood, and explosion; boiler, pressure vessel, and machinery accidents; and many other insured hazards. **NOTE:** Resumes for unsolicited positions are not considered. **Corporate headquarters location:** Johnston RI. **Other U.S. locations:** Nationwide. **International locations:** Worldwide.

FMC CORPORATION
1735 Market Street, Philadelphia PA 19103. 215/299-6000. **Fax:** 215/299-6618. **Contact:** Human Resources. **World Wide Web address:** http://www.fmc.com. **Description:** A diversified manufacturer of specialty, industrial, and agricultural chemicals; defense-related systems; and industrial machinery. The company is also engaged in the processing of gold, silver, and petroleum. **NOTE:** Part-time jobs are offered. **Special programs:** Co-ops. **Office hours:** Monday - Friday, 8:30 a.m. - 5:00 p.m. **Corporate headquarters location:** Chicago IL. **International locations:** Worldwide. **Listed on:** New York Stock Exchange. **Stock exchange symbol:** FMC. **Annual sales/revenues:** More than $100 million. **Number of employees at this location:** 500. **Number of employees worldwide:** 20,000.

FAIRCHILD SEMICONDUCTOR
125 Crestwood Road, Mountain Top PA 18707. 570/474-6761. **Fax:** 207/775-8045. **Contact:** Human Resources. **E-mail address:** corporate.resume@fairchildsemi.com. **World Wide Web address:** http://www.fairchildsemi.com. **Description:** Manufactures semiconductors. **NOTE:** Mail resumes to: Mail Stop 35-1D, 82 Running Hill Road, South Portland ME 04106. You may also submit your resume online. **Positions advertised include:** Product Engineer; Integration Engineer; Reliability/Failure Analysis Engineer; Photolithography Process Development Engineer. **Listed on:** New York Stock Exchange. **Stock exchange symbol:** FCS.

FAIRMONT SUPPLY COMPANY
401 Technology Drive, Canonsburg PA 15317. 724/514-3900. **Fax:** 724/514-3889. **Contact:** Human Resources. **E-mail address:** humanresources@fairmontsupply.com. **World Wide Web address:** http://www.fairmontsupply.com. **Description:** An industrial supply, wholesaling company. **Operations at this facility include:** Customer service.

FASTENAL COMPANY
5416 Sixth Avenue, Altoona PA 16602. 814/941-8703. **Fax:** 814/941-8705. **Contact:** Human Resources. **World Wide Web address:** http://www.fastenal.com. **Description:** A full-line, industrial distributor with products including fasteners, construction accessories, strut and pipe hangers, and power tools. Fastenal Company is one of the largest fastener distributors in the United States. Founded in 1967.

FEDERAL-MOGUL CORPORATION
400 East Second Street, Boyertown PA 19512. 610/367-2604. **Fax:** 610/369-2141. **Contact:** David Weik, Plant Manager. **World Wide Web address:** http://www.federal-mogul.com. **Description:** Federal-Mogul designs, develops, manufactures, and markets automotive products that are sold to OEMs and auto parts distributors, as well as retailers of replacement parts and equipment. **Corporate headquarters location:** Southfield MI. **Operations at this facility include:** This location manufactures sealed beam headlamps. **Listed on:** New York Stock Exchange. **Stock Number of employees at this location:** 300. **exchange symbol:** FMO. **Annual sales/revenues:** More than $100 million.

FEDERAL-MOGUL SYSTEMS PROTECTION GROUP
241 Welsh Pool Road, Exton PA 19341. 610/363-2600. **Fax:** 610/524-8348. **Contact:** Joanne Eachus, Site Manager. **World Wide Web address:** http://www.federal-mogul.com. **Description:** A manufacturer of protective sleeving, heat shields, oven-seal gaskets, and advanced composites. **Special programs:** Internships. **Parent company:** T&N, plc. **Operations at this facility include:** Manufacturing of sleeving products that house and protect wire harnesses, etc. **Listed on:** New York Stock Exchange. **Stock exchange symbol:** FMO. **Annual sales/revenues:** More than $100 million. **Number of employees at this location:** 260.

FEDERATED INVESTORS
Federated Investors Tower, 1001 Liberty Avenue, Pittsburgh PA 15222-3779. 412/288-1900. **Contact:** Human Resources Department. **E-mail address:** resume@federatedinv.com. **World Wide Web address:** http://www.federatedinvestors.com. **Description:** Sells and manages mutual funds. **NOTE:** Online application is encouraged.

FIBRE METAL PRODUCTS COMPANY
P.O. Box 248, Concordville PA 19331. 610/459-5300. **Fax:** 610/358-2120. **Physical address:** Route 1, Brinton Lake Road, Concordville PA 19331. **Contact:** Personnel Director. **E-mail address:** rwoodard@fibre-metal.com. **World Wide Web address:** http://www.fibre-metal.com. **Description:** Produces welding and head safety products.

FIDELITY MUTUAL LIFE INSURANCE COMPANY
250 King of Prussia Road, Radnor PA 19087. 610/964-7000. **Contact:** Mary Culbreath, Human Resources. **Description:** A life insurance company. **Corporate headquarters location:** This location.

FINCOR ELECTRONICS
IMO INDUSTRIES, INC.
3750 East Market Street, York PA 17402. 717/751-4200. **Toll-free phone:** 800/334-3040. **Fax:** 717/751-4263. **Contact:** Human Resources. **World Wide Web address:** http://www.fincor.net. **Description:** Produces electronic controls for industrial and graphic arts uses. **Corporate headquarters location:** Lawrenceville NJ. **Operations at this facility include:** Manufacturing. **Listed on:** New York Stock Exchange. **Number of employees at this location:** 250. **Number of employees nationwide:** 6,200.

THE FINISH LINE, INC.
196 West Moreland Mall, Route 30 East, #114, Greensburg PA 15601-3593. 724/832-8025. **Contact:** Manager. **E-mail address:** hr@finishline.com. **World Wide Web address:** http://www.thefinishline.com. **Description:** Operates a chain of retail stores offering a broad selection of men's, women's, and children's brand-name athletic and leisure footwear, activewear, and accessories. **NOTE:** Apply online for current retail and corporate openings. **Corporate headquarters location:** Indianapolis IN.

FIRST CLEARFIELD FUNDS INC.
1801 JFK Boulevard, Suite 1109, Philadelphia PA 19103. 215/557-8620. **Contact:** Human Resources. **Description:** Provides homeowner loans.

FIRST COMMONWEALTH FINANCIAL CORPORATION
Southwest Corner, 600 Philadelphia Street, Indiana PA 15701. 724/463-8555. **Contact:** Human Resources. **World Wide Web address:** http://www.fcfbank.com. **Description:** A bank holding company. **Positions advertised include:** Application Specialist; Retail Loans Specialist; Financial Services Representative; Section Coordinator. **Subsidiaries include:** Central Bank; Cenwest Bank; Deposit Bank; First Bank of Leechburg; NBOC Bank; First Commonwealth Trust Company; Peoples Bank; Peoples Bank of Western Pennsylvania; Reliable Bank; Southwest Bank, Unitas Bank. **Listed on:** New York Stock Exchange. **Stock exchange symbol:** FCF.

FIRST COMMONWEALTH FINANCIAL CORPORATION
SOUTHWEST BANK
111 South Main Street, P.O. Box 760, Greensburg PA 15601-0760. 724/834-2310. **Fax:** 724/836-6732. **Contact:** Human Resources. **E-mail address:** hr@fcfbank.com. **World Wide Web address:** http://www.swbank.com. **Description:** A commercial bank holding company. **Corporate headquarters location:** This location. **Listed on:** New York Stock Exchange. **Stock exchange symbol:** FCF.

FIRST COMMONWEALTH TRUST COMPANY
P.O. Box 400, 614 Philadelphia Street, Indiana PA 15701. 724/465-3282. **Fax:** 724/463-5719. **Contact:** Rose Cogley, Personnel Manager. **World Wide Web address:** http://www.fcfbank.com. **Description:** A state-chartered trust company specializing in estate planning, living trusts, pension plans, and investment management. **Corporate headquarters location:** This location. **Other U.S. locations:** Bridgeville PA; Chambersburg PA; DuBois PA; Hollidaysburg PA; Huntingdon PA; Johnstown PA; New Castle PA. **Parent company:** First Commonwealth Financial Corporation. **Operations at this facility include:** Administration; Divisional Headquarters; Regional Headquarters; Sales; Service. **Listed on:** New York Stock Exchange. **Stock exchange symbol:** FCF. **Number of employees at this location:** 20. **Number of employees nationwide:** 35.

FIRST NATIONAL BANK OF CHESTER COUNTY
P.O. Box 523, West Chester PA 19381-0523. 610/692-3000. **Contact:** Human Resources. **World Wide Web address:** http://www.1st-national.com. **Description:** A full-service bank. **Positions advertised include:** Tellers; Financial Consultant; Retail Financial Specialist; Call Center Specialist.

FIRST NATIONAL BANK OF PENNSYLVANIA
One FNB Boulevard, Hermitage PA 16148. 724/983-3449. **Toll-free phone:** 800/555-5455. **Fax:** 724/983-3509. **Contact:** Mary Loomis, Employment Officer. **World Wide Web address:** http://www.fnb-pa.com. **Description:** A banking corporation with 31 branches located throughout Pennsylvania. **NOTE:** Entry-level positions are offered. **Positions advertised include:** Teller. **Office hours:** Monday - Friday, 8:30 a.m. - 5:00 p.m. **Corporate headquarters location:** This location. **Parent company:** FNB Corporation is a holding company that, in addition to performing savings bank operations, also provides mortgage banking and leasing services, real estate activities, insurance services, and other financial activities. **Annual sales/revenues:** More than $100 million. **Number of employees at this location:** 510. **Number of employees nationwide:** 1,300.

FIRST NATIONAL BANK OF PENNSYLVANIA
532-34 Main Street, Johnstown PA 15901. 814/532-3801. **Contact:** Human Resources. **World Wide Web address:** http://www.fnb-pa.com. **Description:** A banking corporation with 31 branches located throughout Pennsylvania. **NOTE:** Entry-level positions are offered. **Corporate headquarters location:** Hermitage PA. **Parent company:** FNB Corporation is a holding company that, in addition to performing savings bank operations, also provides mortgage banking and leasing services, real estate activities, insurance services, and other financial activities.

FIRSTENERGY CORPORATION
2800 Pottsville Pike, Reading PA 19605. 610/929-3601. **Contact:** Human Resources. **World Wide Web address:** http://www.firstenergycorp.com. **Description:** Engaged in the generation, transmission, distribution, and sale of electricity. The company provides service to a population of approximately 830,000. **Positions advertised include:**

Claims Representative; Business Analyst; Human Resources Representative; Lineman/woman; Accountant. **Corporate headquarters location:** Akron OH.

FISCHBACH AND MOORE ELECTRIC, INC.
761 Fifth Avenue, King of Prussia PA 19406. 610/992-9442. **Fax:** 908/508-2624. **Contact:** Human Resources. **E-mail address:** cgraham@fmeinc.com. **World Wide Web address:** http://www.fischbachandmoore.com. **Description:** An electrical contracting firm. The company specializes in infrastructure electrical construction for traffic and transit management systems. Founded in 1924. **NOTE:** For employment opportunities contact: Ms. Cyndie Graham, Human Resources Manager, 675 Central Avenue, New Providence NJ 07974. 908/508-2612. **Special programs:** Internships. **Internship information:** Internships are offered in field installation work. **Office hours:** Monday - Friday, 8:00 a.m. - 5:00 p.m. **Corporate headquarters location:** New Providence NJ. **Other U.S. locations:** Nationwide. **Parent company:** Exelon Infrastructure Services. **Operations at this facility include:** Regional Headquarters. **President:** James Kimsey. **Annual sales/revenues:** $21 - $50 million.

FISERV
2005 Market Street, Philadelphia PA 19103-3212. 215/636-3000. **Contact:** Anna DiDio, Vice President of Human Resources. **World Wide Web address:** http://www.fiserv.com. **Description:** Provides integrated processing and support services to securities brokerage affiliates of its owner institutions. **Positions advertised include:** Financial Services Associate. **Corporate headquarters location:** Brookfield WI. **Listed on:** NASDAQ. **Stock exchange symbol:** FISV.

FISHER SCIENTIFIC
2000 Park Lane, Pittsburgh PA 15275. 412/490-8300. **Contact:** Human Resources. **World Wide Web address:** http://www.fishersci.com. **Description:** Offers a selection of more than 150,000 products and services to research centers and industrial customers worldwide. Fisher Scientific serves scientists engaged in biomedical, biotechnology, pharmaceutical, chemical, and other fields of research and development in companies, educational and research institutions, and government agencies. The company also supplies clinical laboratories, hospitals, environmental testing centers, remediation companies, quality-control laboratories, and other industrial facilities. In addition, Fisher Scientific represents its customers as a third-party purchaser of maintenance materials and other basic supplies.

FLEET BANK
1503 Linden Street, Bethlehem PA 18017. 610/865-8467. **Contact:** Human Resources. **World Wide Web address:** http://www.fleet.com. **Description:** A full-service financial institution that serves corporate, retail, and private markets. **Parent company:** Bank of America.

FLEXSTEEL INDUSTRIES, INC.
107 Pitney Road, P.O. Box 10908, Lancaster PA 17605. 717/392-4161. **Fax:** 717/291-1748. **Contact:** Deborah Frey, Human Resources Representative. **World Wide Web address:** http://www.flexsteel.com. **Description:** Flexsteel Industries manufactures and markets upholstered furniture for the retail furniture market and the recreational vehicle field. Products of Flexsteel Industries include a variety of wood and upholstered chairs, rockers, sofas, sofabeds, loveseats, bucket seats, and convertible bedding units for use in offices, homes, vans, and recreational vehicles. **Office hours:** Monday - Friday, 8:00 a.m. - 5:00 p.m. **Corporate headquarters location:** Dubuque IA. **Operations at this facility include:** This location manufactures upholstered living room furniture.

FLOWERS MILL VETERINARY HOSPITAL P.C.
10 South Flowers Mill Road, Langhorne PA 19047. 215/752-1010. **Contact:** Human Resources. **Description:** Offers boarding services and general medical and surgical care to small and exotic animals.

FOAMEX INC.
466 South Shady Avenue, Corry PA 16407. 814/664-7771. **Contact:** Andrew Johnson, Human Resources. **E-mail address:** recruiting@foamex.com. **World Wide Web address:** http://www.foamex.com. **Description:** A manufacturer and fabricator of flexible polyurethane foam, used primarily in bedding. **Parent company:** Foamex International, Inc. **Corporate headquarters location:** Linwood PA. **Other U.S. locations:** Nationwide. **Listed on:** NASDAQ. **Stock exchange symbol:** FMXI. **Annual sales/revenues:** More than $100 million. **Number of employees worldwide:** 3,600.

FOAMEX INTERNATIONAL, INC.
1000 Columbia Avenue, Linwood PA 19061-3997. 610/859-3000. **Contact:** Human Resources. **E-mail address:** recruiting@foamex.com. **World Wide Web address:** http://www.foamex.com. **Description:** One of the nation's largest manufacturers of flexible polyurethane foam products. Foamex products are classified into four groups: Cushion Foams are used for mattresses, quilting and borders, home and office furniture, computer and electronics packaging, and padding foams for health care; Carpet Cushions include prime, bonded, sponge rubber, felt carpet cushion, synthetic grass turf, and a variety of textured carpeting and wall coverings; Automotive Foams include foams for cushioning and seating, acoustical foams, headliner foams, trim foams, and foams for door panel parts; Technical Foams include those for filtration, reservoiring, sound absorption and transmission, carburetors, high-speed inkjet printers, speaker grilles, oxygenators, and EKG pads, as well as cosmetic applicators, mop heads, paint brushes, and diapers. **Positions advertised include:** Staff Accountant; National Sales Manager. **Corporate headquarters location:** This location. **Other U.S. locations:** Nationwide. **Listed on:** NASDAQ. **Stock exchange symbol:** FMXI. **Annual sales/revenues:** More than $100 million. **Number of employees worldwide:** 3,600.

L.B. FOSTER COMPANY
415 Holiday Drive, Pittsburgh PA 15220. 412/928-3400. **Contact:** Human Resources. **World Wide Web address:** http://www.lbfoster.com. **Description:** Manufactures, fabricates, and distributes tubular products including line, standard, and structural grade pipe; rail and trackwork; piling; pile driving equipment; and highway products including bridge decking and aluminum bridge rail. **Corporate headquarters location:** This location.

FOX CHASE CANCER CENTER
333 Cottman Avenue, Philadelphia PA 19111-2497. 215/728-6900. **Contact:** Human Resources. **World Wide Web address:** http://www.fccc.edu. **Description:** A comprehensive cancer center that serves as a national resource for converting research findings into medical applications. Applications are designed to improve cancer detection, treatment, and prevention. **Corporate headquarters location:** This location. **Number of employees at this location:** 1,700.

FOX POOL CORPORATION
P.O. Box 549, York PA 17405. 717/764-8581. **Physical address:** 3490 Board Road, York PA 17402. **Contact:** Human Resources. **World Wide Web address:** http://www.foxpool.com. **Description:** Manufactures and sells in and aboveground swimming pools.

FRANCE COMPRESSOR PRODUCTS
104 Pheasant Run, Newtown PA 18940. 215/968-5959. **Contact:** Human Resources. **World Wide Web address:** http://www.francecomp.com. **Description:** Manufactures compressor rings and other sealing components. **NOTE:** Resumes that are mailed or delivered by hand are preferred.

FRANCIS, CAUFFMAN, FOLEY, AND HOFFMAN
2120 Arch Street, Philadelphia PA 19103. 215/568-8250. **Fax:** 215/568-2639. **Contact:** Tom Gavin, Human Resources. **World Wide Web address:** http://www.fcfh-did.com. **Description:** A full-service architectural firm serving the communications, health care, pharmaceutical, and corporate markets. Founded in 1954. **Positions advertised include:** Communications Director; Business development; Healthcare Planner; Project Manager; Project Architect; R&D Architect; Staff Architect. **Other U.S. locations:** Syracuse NY; Hunt Valley MD.

FRANKFORD HOSPITAL
Knights and Red Lion Roads, Philadelphia PA 19114. 215/612-4000. **Fax:** 215/612-4073. **Contact:** Human Resources Department. **World Wide Web address:** http://www.frankfordhospitals.org. **Description:** A full-service hospital providing a cancer center, inpatient medicine, a Level II neonatal care, a Level II trauma center, obstetrics, and surgery. **NOTE:** See website for a listing of current openings with application details. **Positions advertised include:** Certified Nurse Assistant; ER Physician; Home Care Registered Nurse; Medical Technician; Physical Therapist; Speech Pathologist; Emergency Record Coder; Registrar.

FRANKLIN AND MARSHALL COLLEGE
P.O. Box 3003, Lancaster PA 17604-3003. 717/291-3911. **Fax:** 717/291-3969. **Contact:** Human Resources. **World Wide Web address:** http://www.fandm.edu. **Description:** A small, private, four-year college. **NOTE:** Job opportunities are posted on the above Website. No phone calls or walk-ins. **Positions advertised include:** Athletics and Recreation Director; Facilities Painter; Warehouse Delivery Specialist; Assistant Dean; Public Safety Officers; Program Coordinator.

THE FRANKLIN INSTITUTE SCIENCE MUSEUM
222 North 20th Street, Philadelphia PA 19103. 215/448-1200. **Fax:** 215/448-1121. **Contact:** Human Resources. **World Wide Web address:** http://sln.fi.edu. **Description:** A nonprofit scientific and educational corporation. The Franklin Institute Science Museum consists of The Science Center, The Mandel Futures Center, The Fels Planetarium, and The Tuttleman Omniverse Theater, with a wide range of interactive and educational exhibits in many different scientific areas. Founded in 1824. **Positions advertised include:** Sponsorship Program Coordinator; Community Outreach Manager; Educator; Director of Development; Greeter; Admission/Retail Sales and Service Representative; Camp Counselor.

FRANKLIN MINT
M/D 405 M, Franklin Centre PA 19091. 610/459-6000. **Fax:** 610/459-6750. **Contact:** Human Resources. **E-mail address:** jobs@web.franklinmint.com. **World Wide Web address:** http://www.franklinmint.com. **Description:** Manufactures jewelry, precious metals, and collectibles.

FRICK HOSPITAL
508 South Church Street, Mount Pleasant PA 15666-1790. 724/547-1500. **Contact:** Human Resources. **Description:** A 175-bed general hospital with a variety of specialists on staff. **Parent company:** University of Pittsburgh Medical Center (UPMC).

FRISKIES PET CARE COMPANY
2050 Pope Road, Allentown PA 18104-9308. 610/395-3301. **Contact:** Human Resources. **World Wide Web address:** http://www.friskies.com. **Description:** Produces and sells the Alpo brand of premium canned dog foods and the Friskies brand of premium canned cat foods. Friskies Pet Care Company is one of the largest dog and cat food manufacturers and distributors in the United States. **NOTE:** Applications can be made online at http://www.purina.com/company/careers. **Corporate headquarters location:** St. Louis MO. **Parent company:** Nestle Purina Pet Care Company.

FRITO-LAY
380 Arch Street, Williamsport PA 17701. 570/321-9038. **Contact:** Human Resources. **World Wide Web address:** www.fritolayjobs.com. **Description:** Frito—Lay is the fun foods division of Pepsico and supplies brands such as Frito-Lay, Doritos, and Fritos. **NOTE:** No mail or phone calls. Please use company website to apply for open positions. **Positions advertised include:** Operations Safety Manager; Human Resources Manager; Maintenance Resource. **Parent company:** Pepsico.

FRY COMMUNICATIONS INC.
800 West Church Road, Mechanicsburg PA 17055. 717/766-0211. **Toll-free phone:** 800/334-1429 ext. 1404. **Contact:** Frank Hopkins, Director of Human Resources. **E-mail address:** info@frycomm.com. **World Wide Web address:** http://www.frycomm.com. **Description:** Fry Communications is one of the top 15 printing companies in the nation. This company prints and publishes magazines, catalogs, directories, cable listings and other periodicals including *The Guide*. **NOTE:** Second and third shifts are offered. **Annual sales/revenues:** More than $100 million. **Number of employees at this location:** 1,700.

FUELLGRAF ELECTRIC COMPANY
600 South Washington Street, Butler PA 16001. 724/282-4800. **Fax:** 724/282-1926. **Contact:** Human Resources. **E-mail address:** feco@fuellgraf.com. **World Wide Web address:** http://www.fuellgraf.com. **Description:** An electrical construction and engineering firm. Founded in 1946. **NOTE:** Entry-level positions are offered. **Office hours:** Monday - Friday, 7:00 a.m. - 5:00 p.m. **Corporate headquarters location:** This location. **Other U.S. locations:** Williamsport PA. **Operations at this facility include:** Regional Headquarters. **Annual sales/revenues:** $11 - $20 million. **Number of employees at this location:** 100.

FULTON FINANCIAL CORPORATION
FULTON BANK
One Penn Square, P.O. Box 4887, Lancaster PA 17604. 717/291-2467. **Toll-free phone:** 800/752-9580. **Fax:** 717/295-4783. **Contact:** Human Resources. **World Wide Web address:** http://www.fult.com. **Description:** A bank holding company. **Corporate headquarters location:** This location. **Subsidiaries include:** Fulton Bank (also at this location); Dearden, MacGuire, Weaver, and Barrett LLC; Fulton Insurance Services Group, Inc.; Fulton Mortgage Company.

GE INFRASTRUCTURE WATER & PROCESS TECHNOLOGIES
4636 Somerton Road, Trevose PA 19053-6783. 215/355-3300. **Fax:** 215/942-3383. **Contact:** Human Resources. **World Wide Web address:** http://www.gewater.com. **Description:** Manufactures and markets a variety of specialty chemical products used in the chemical treatment of water, wastewater, and process systems. GE Water & Process Technologies operates in a variety of industrial and commercial applications, with particular emphasis on the chemical, petroleum refining, paper, automotive, electrical utility, and steel industries. The company's chemical treatment programs are used in boilers, cooling towers, heat exchangers, paper and petroleum process streams, and both influent and effluent systems. **NOTE:** Search and apply for positions online. **Corporate headquarters location:** This location. **Subsidiaries include:** GE Betz, GE Osmonics, and GE Glegg. **Parent company:** General Electric Company. **Number of employees worldwide:** 3,000.

GE ENERGY SERVICES
2849 Sterling Drive, Hatfield PA 19440. 215/996-9200. **Fax:** 215/996-9201. **Contact:** Human Resources. **World Wide Web address:** http://www.enertec.com. **Description:** Formerly KVB-Enertec Inc., now a division of GE Power Systems. A manufacturer of SNIFFER computerized CEM (continuous emissions monitoring) systems used to test for state and EPA compliance for pollutant-emitting sources such as incinerators, boilers, turbines, and cogeneration plants. **Corporate headquarters location:** Atlanta GA. **Parent company:** General Electric Company. **Listed on:** New York Stock Exchange. **Stock exchange symbol:** GE. **Number of employees worldwide:** 35,000.

GMAC MORTGAGE CORPORATION
100 Witmer Road, P.O. Box 963, Horsham PA 19044-0963. 215/682-1000. **Contact:** Human Resources. **E-mail address:** staffing@gmacm.com. **World Wide Web address:** http://www.gmacmortgage.com. **Description:** Provides a wide range of mortgage banking and related financial services. Founded in 1908. **Special programs:** Internships. **Office hours:** Monday - Friday, 8:30 a.m. - 5:00 p.m. **Corporate headquarters location:** Bloomington MN. **Other U.S. locations:** Nationwide. **Subsidiaries include:** Residential Funding Corporation. **Parent company:** General Motors Corporation is one of the world's largest full-line vehicle manufacturers with substantial interests in information technology, electronics, and finance. GM conducts business through the following sectors: North American Automotive Operations includes Sales/Service Groups (Buick, Cadillac, Chevrolet, GMC Truck, Oldsmobile, Pontiac, and Saturn) and Vehicle Development Groups (Powertrain, Truck Group, Small Car Group, and Midsize/Luxury Car Group). Delphi Automotive Systems consists of Delphi Chassis Systems, Delphi Packard Electric Systems, Delphi Energy & Engine Management Systems, Delphi Saginaw Steering Systems, Delphi Harrison Thermal Systems, Delphi Interior & Lighting Systems, Delphi Automotive Systems European Region, Delphi Automotive Systems Asia/Pacific Region, and Delphi Automotive Systems South America. International Operations include GM Europe; Asia Pacific Operations; and Latin America, Africa, Middle East Operations. EDS applies information technologies to more than 8,000 customers globally in the communications, energy/chemical, insurance, public sector, travel and transportation, financial services, manufacturing, and retail industries. GM Hughes Electronics Corporation is involved in automotive electronics, telecommunications and space electronics, and defense electronics. **Operations at this facility include:** Administration; Research and Development; Sales; Service. **Number of employees at this location:** 800. **Number of employees nationwide:** 3,300.

GANNON UNIVERSITY
109 University Square, Erie PA 16541-0001. 814/871-7351. **Physical address:** Student Services Building, S101-109, Gannon University, Erie PA 16541. **Fax:** 814/871-7514. **Contact:** Robert J. Cline, Human Resources Director. **E-mail address:** hrdept@gannon.edu. **World Wide Web address:** http://www.gannon.edu. **Description:** A four-year university offering certificate, associate's, bachelor's, master's, and M.B.A. degrees. Total enrollment is approximately 3,300 undergraduate and 550 graduate students.

GARLAND U.S. RANGE
185 South Street, Freeland PA 18224-1916. 570/636-1000. **Toll-free phone:** 800/424-2411. **Contact:** Human Resources. **World Wide Web address:** http://www.garland-group.com. **Description:** A manufacturer of commercial cooking equipment. The company's products include ovens, ranges, pizza ovens, and deep fryers. **Parent company:** Enodis.

GASBOY INTERNATIONAL, INC.
P.O. Box 309, Lansdale PA 19446-0309. 215/855-4631. **Physical address:** 707 North Valley Forge Road, Lansdale PA 19446. **Fax:** 215/361-5404. **Contact:** Human Resources. **E-mail address:** hr@gasboy.com. **World Wide Web address:** http://www.gasboy.com. **Description:** Develops, manufactures, and markets petroleum dispensing pumps, computer-controlled management systems, and related components. Founded in 1819. **NOTE:** Entry-level positions and part-time jobs are offered. **Special programs:** Training; Co-ops; Summer Jobs. **Corporate headquarters location:** Greensboro NC. **Parent company:** Danaher Corporation **Listed on:** New York Stock Exchange. **Stock exchange symbol:** DHR.

GEISINGER MEDICAL CENTER
100 North Academy Avenue, Danville PA 17822. 570/271-6211. **Toll-free phone:** 877/564-6447. **Fax:** 570/271-5060. **Contact:** Human Resources Department. **E-mail address:** careers@geisinger.edu. **World Wide Web address:** http://www.geisinger.org. **Description:** A tertiary care teaching hospital with 45 regional clinics in central and northeastern Pennsylvania. Geisinger Medical Center is a Level I trauma center. **Positions advertised include:** Cardiologist; Gastroenterologist; Radiologist; Dermatologist; Hematologist; Neurologist. **Operations at this facility include:** Administration; Divisional Headquarters; Research and Development. **Number of employees at this location:** 3,500.

GENAERA CORPORATION
5110 Campus Drive, Plymouth Meeting PA 19462. 610/941-4020. **Fax:** 610/941-5399. **Contact:** Human Resources Department. **E-mail address:** resumes@genaera.com. **World Wide Web address:** http://www.genaera.com. **Description:** A biopharmaceutical company engaged in the development of medicine for infectious and genetic diseases. The company's clinical development efforts are focused on oncology with ongoing research efforts in respiratory and infectious diseases. **Listed on:** NASDAQ. **Stock exchange symbol:** GENR. **Number of employees at this location:** 40.

GENERAL ELECTRIC COMPANY
2901 East Lake Road, Erie PA 16531. 814/875-2234. **Contact:** Human Resources. **World Wide Web address:** http://www.ge.com. **Description:** General Electric operates in the following areas: aircraft engines including jet engines, replacement parts, and repair services for commercial, military, executive, and commuter aircraft; appliances; broadcasting through NBC; industrial including lighting products, electrical distribution and control equipment, transportation systems products, electric motors and related products, a broad range of electrical and electronic industrial automation products, and a network of electrical supply houses; materials including plastics, ABS resins, silicones, superabrasives, and laminates; power systems including products for the generation, transmission, and distribution of electricity; technical products and systems including medical systems and equipment, as well as a full range of computer-based information and data interchange services for both internal use and external commercial and industrial customers; and capital services including consumer services, financing, and specialty insurance. **NOTE:** See website for detailed employment application process. **Operations at this facility include:** This location manufactures locomotives. **Listed on:** New York Stock Exchange. **Stock exchange symbol:** GE. **Annual sales/revenues:** $134.2 Billion. **Number of employees worldwide:** 315,000.

GENERAL ELECTRIC COMPANY
6901 Elmwood Avenue, Philadelphia PA 19142. 215/726-2626. **Contact:** Joanne McGroarty, Human Resources. **World Wide Web address:** http://www.ge.com. **Description:** General Electric operates in the following areas: aircraft engines including jet engines, replacement parts, and repair services for commercial, military, executive, and commuter aircraft; appliances; broadcasting through NBC; industrial including lighting products, electrical distribution and control equipment, transportation systems products, electric motors and related products, a broad range of electrical and electronic industrial automation products, and a network of electrical supply houses; materials including plastics, ABS resins, silicones, superabrasives, and laminates; power systems including products for the generation, transmission, and distribution of electricity; technical products and systems including medical systems and equipment, as well as a full range of computer-based information and data interchange services for both internal use and external commercial and industrial customers; and capital services including consumer services, financing, and specialty insurance. **NOTE:** See website for detailed employment application process. **Operations at this facility include:** This location is the switchgear division, manufacturing components and parts. **Listed on:** New York Stock Exchange. **Stock exchange symbol:** GE. **Annual sales/revenues:** $134.2 Billion. **Number of employees worldwide:** 315,000.

GENERAL KINETICS INC.
110 Sunray Drive, Johnstown PA 15905. 814/255-6891. **Fax:** 814/255-4106. **Contact:** Human Resources. **E-mail address:** info@gi.com. **World Wide Web address:** http://www.gki.com. **Description:** A leading designer, producer, and marketer of secure digital facsimile equipment and secure local area networks, principally for domestic and foreign governments, through its Secure Communications Division. Secure facsimile equipment utilizes technological safeguards to prevent interception of sensitive communications by unauthorized parties. Through its Electronic Enclosure Division, General Kinetics also designs and manufactures precision enclosures for electronic systems, principally for sale to the U.S. Department of Defense and the U.S. Navy. Founded in 1954. **Corporate headquarters location:** Manassas VA. **Number of employees nationwide:** 120.

GENERAL MOTORS CORPORATION
1451 Lebanon School Road, West Mifflin PA 15122. 412/469-6500. **Contact:** Human Resources. **World Wide Web address:** http://www.gm.com. **Description:** General Motors Corporation is one of the world's largest full-line vehicle manufacturers, and also has substantial interests in information technology, electronics, and finance. GM conducts business through the following sectors: North American Automotive Operations, International Operations, General Motors Acceptance Corporation (GMAC), and Electronic Data Systems Corporation (EDS). North American Automotive Operations includes Sales/Service Groups (Buick, Cadillac, Chevrolet, GMC Truck, Oldsmobile, Pontiac, and Saturn) and Vehicle Development Groups (Powertrain, Truck Group, Small Car Group, and Midsize/Luxury Car Group). International Operations include GM Europe; Asia Pacific Operations; and Latin America, Africa, Middle East Operations. GMAC, which provides financing and insurance to GM customers and dealers, consists of North American Operations, International Operations, Motors Insurance Corporation, and GMAC Mortgage Group. EDS applies information technologies to more than 8,000 customers globally in the communications, energy/chemical, insurance, public sector, travel and transportation, financial services, manufacturing, and retail industries. Founded in 1908. **Corporate headquarters location:** Detroit MI. **Operations at this facility include:** This location manufactures automotive body parts. **Listed on:** New York Stock Exchange. **Stock exchange symbol:** GM.

GENERAL NUTRITION COMPANIES, INC.
GENERAL NUTRITION CENTERS (GNC)
300 Sixth Avenue, Pittsburgh PA 15222. 412/288-4600. **Fax:** 412/288-2074. **Contact:** Corporate Recruiter. **E-mail address:** corporaterecruiter@gnc-hq.com. **World Wide Web address:** http://www.gnc.com. **Description:** One of the largest specialty retailers of nutritional supplements and other health and self-care products in the United States. General Nutrition's products are sold through a network of more than 3,000 company and franchised locations in all 50 states and 16 foreign countries. The company also operates one of the largest vitamin supplement manufacturing facilities in the United States. Founded in 1935. **NOTE:** Entry-level positions are offered. **Positions advertised include:** Corporate; Retail Sales/Management; Distribution; Transportation; Manufacturing. **Special programs:** Summer Jobs. **Corporate headquarters location:** This location. **Other U.S. locations:** Nationwide. **Number of employees at this location:** 600. **Number of employees nationwide:** 10,000.

GENESIS HEALTH VENTURES, INC.
101 East State Street, Kennett Square PA 19348. 610/444-6350. **Fax:** 610/925-4352. **Contact:** Recruitment Manager. **World Wide Web address:** http://www.ghv.com. **Description:** Provides services, centers, and programs for the elderly. Genesis Health Ventures operates its skilled nursing and assisted living centers under the Genesis ElderCare name. Founded in 1985. **Positions advertised include:** Billing Representative; Billing Specialist; Certified Nurse Aide; Clinical Specialist; Delinquent Account Specialist; Infusion Nurse Consultant; Medical Records Technician; Occupational Therapist; Pharmacy Therapist. **Corporate headquarters location:** This location. **Listed on:** New York Stock Exchange. **Stock exchange symbol:** GHVI. **Number of employees at this location:** 270. **Number of employees nationwide:** 30,000.

GENESIS OF PITTSBURGH, INC.
P.O. Box 41017, Pittsburgh PA 15202-2905. 412/766-2693. **Contact:** Human Resources. **World Wide Web address:** http://trfn.clpgh.org/genesis. **Description:** A fully licensed maternity care center. Genesis is a social service agency providing options to women facing an unplanned pregnancy. Genesis provides its clients with housing, education, counseling, clothing, food, baby needs, pregnancy testing, and adoption services. Founded in 1983.

GENEVA COLLEGE
3200 College Avenue, Beaver Falls PA 15010. 724/847-6560. **Contact:** Donald McBurney, Human Resources Director. **World Wide Web address:** http://www.geneva.edu. **Description:** A four-year college offering associate's,

bachelor's, and master's degree programs. Enrollment includes 1,200 undergraduates and 250 graduate students. **Positions advertised include:** Counseling Center Director; Assistant/Associate Professor of Education; Communication Disorders Faculty Position; Reference/Instruction Librarian; Political Science Faculty Position.

GILES & RANSOME, INC.
2975 Galloway Road, Bensalem PA 19020. 215/639-4300. **Fax:** 215/245-2831. **Contact:** Richard Smith, Manager of Personnel. **E-mail address:** rsmith@ransome.com. **World Wide Web address:** http://www.ransome.cat.com. **Description:** A regional distributor of Caterpillar heavy construction and industrial equipment including diesel engines and generators, construction vehicles, and material-handling equipment. **Positions advertised include:** Technical Trainer. **Corporate headquarters location:** This location.

GLASGOW, INC.
Willow Grove Avenue and Limekiln Pike, P.O. Box 1089, Glenside PA 19038-1089. 215/884-8800. **Fax:** 215/886-2043. **Contact:** Human Resources. **World Wide Web address:** http://www.glasgowinc.com. **Description:** A heavy construction and highway contracting firm. **Corporate headquarters location:** This location. **Operations at this facility include:** Administration. **President:** Bruce Rambo.

GLASS PRODUCTS INC.
P.O. Box 313, Carbondale PA 18407. 570/282-6711. **Fax:** 570/282-1382. **Contact:** Tom Zaccone, Branch Manager. **World Wide Web address:** http://www.afgd.com. **Description:** Manufactures laminated safety glass used in windows and doors. **NOTE:** See the website for current openings at the nearest location. Applications are made through the headquarters location or via the website. **Corporate headquarters location:** Atlanta GA. **Other U.S. locations:** Nationwide. **Subsidiaries include:** AFGD Canada. **Parent company:** American Flat Glass Distributors (AFGD) specializes in architectural insulated units and custom tempering. The firm manufactures a complete line of insulated units for commercial and residential applications. The product line includes clear, tinted and reflective float glass; laminated, low-emissivity, tempered, acrylic, mirror, obscure, insulated, and polished wire glass; and a complete line of glass-handling, storage, and transportation equipment. **Operations at this facility include:** Manufacturing; Sales. **Number of employees at this location:** 75. **Number of employees nationwide:** 1,000.

P.H. GLATFELTER COMPANY
228 South Main Street, Spring Grove PA 17362. 717/225-4711. **Fax:** 717/225-2850. **Contact:** Mark Oberdick, Employee Services Manager. **E-mail address:** sg-hr@glatfelter.com. **World Wide Web address:** http://www.glatfelter.com. **Description:** Manufactures fine quality papers for the printing, book publishing, business forms, and technical specialties markets. **NOTE:** Entry-level positions and second and third shifts are offered. **Special programs:** Internships; Apprenticeships; Training; Co-ops; Summer Jobs. **Corporate headquarters location:** York PA. **Operations at this facility include:** Administration; Divisional Headquarters; Manufacturing; Regional Headquarters; Research and Development; Sales; Service. **Listed on:** New York Stock Exchange. **Stock exchange symbol:** GLT. **Annual sales/revenues:** More than $100 million. **Number of employees at this location:** 1,100. **Number of employees nationwide:** 2,500. **Number of employees worldwide:** 3,700.

GLAXOSMITHKLINE CORPORATION
One Franklin Plaza, P.O. Box 7929, Philadelphia PA 19101-7929. 215/751-4000. **Contact:** Personnel Department. **World Wide Web address:** http://www.gsk.com. **Description:** GlaxoSmithKline Corporation is a health care company engaged in the research, development, manufacture, and marketing of ethical pharmaceuticals, animal health products, ethical and proprietary medicines, and eye care products. The company's principal divisions include GlaxoSmithKline Pharmaceuticals, GlaxoSmithKline Animal Health, and GlaxoSmithKline Consumer Healthcare. The company is also engaged in many other aspects of the health care field including the production of medical and electronic instruments. Through its subsidiary, Menley & James Laboratories, the company also manufactures proprietary medicines including Contac Cold Capsules, Sine-Off sinus medicine, Love cosmetics, and Sea & Ski outdoor products. **NOTE:** Online application is encouraged. **Corporate headquarters location:** This location. **Operations at this facility include:** This location is the U.S. headquarters. **Listed on:** New York Stock Exchange. **Stock exchange symbol:** GSK. **Number of employees nationwide:** 20,000.

GLAXOSMITHKLINE CORPORATION
1000 GSK Drive, Carnegie PA 15108. 412/200-4000. **Contact:** Human Resources. **World Wide Web address:** http://www.gsk.com. **Description:** A health care company engaged in the research, development, manufacture, and marketing of ethical pharmaceuticals, animal health products, ethical and proprietary medicines, and eye care products. The company's principal divisions include GlaxoSmithKline Pharmaceuticals, GlaxoSmithKline Animal Health, and GlaxoSmithKline Consumer Healthcare. The company is also engaged in many other aspects of the health care field including the production of medical and electronic instruments. Through its subsidiary, Menley & James Laboratories, the company also manufactures proprietary medicines including Contac Cold Capsules, Sine-Off sinus medicine, Love cosmetics, and Sea & Ski outdoor products. **Listed on:** New York Stock Exchange. **Stock exchange symbol:** GSK.

GLOBAL SPORTS, INC.
GLOBAL SPORTS INTERACTIVE
935 First Avenue, King of Prussia PA 19406. 610/491-7000. **Fax:** 610/265-0736. **Contact:** Melissa Reinish, Human Resources Director. **E-mail address:** jobs@globalsports.com. **World Wide Web address:** http://www.globalsports.com. **Description:** Provides e-commerce outsourcing solutions for retailers, manufacturers, media companies, and professional sports organizations. Founded in 1991. **Positions advertised include:** Business Operations Manager; Financial Analyst; Senior Cost Analyst; Production Support Analyst. **Special programs:** Internships. **Office hours:** Monday - Friday, 8:30 a.m. - 5:30 p.m. **Corporate headquarters location:** This location. **Listed on:** NASDAQ. **Stock exchange symbol:** GSPT. **Annual sales/revenues:** More than $100 million. **Number of employees at this location:** 85. **Number of employees nationwide:** 95. **Number of employees worldwide:** 140.

HERMAN GOLDNER COMPANY
7777 Brewster Avenue, Philadelphia PA 19153. 215/365-5400. **Contact:** Human Resources. **World Wide Web address:** http://www.goldner.com. **Description:** A mechanical construction company. The company also supplies pipes, valves, fittings, and building control systems to the construction industry. **NOTE:** Applications must be mailed or hand delivered to the above address.

GOOD LAD APPAREL
431 East Tioga Street, Philadelphia PA 19134. 215/739-0200. **Contact:** Personnel Department. **Description:** A manufacturer of outerwear and children's clothing.

GOODALL RUBBER COMPANY
790 Birney Highway, Aston PA 19014. 610/361-0800. **Fax:** 610/361-0813. **Contact:** Personnel. **E-mail address:** jobs.goodall@trelleborg.com. **World Wide Web address:** http://www.goodallonline.com. **Description:** Manufactures, distributes, and sells rubber through 45 U.S. and Canadian sales and service centers. Products include hoses, belting products, lined pipes, and fittings. **NOTE:** See http://www.monster.com for a current listing of open positions. **Corporate headquarters location:** This location.

GRADUATE HOSPITAL
1800 Lombard Street, Philadelphia PA 19146. 215/893-2000. **Recorded jobline:** 215/893-4111. **Fax:** 215/892-7506. **Contact:** Sharita Barnett, Human Resources. **E-mail address:** sharita.barnett@tenethealth.com. **World Wide Web address:** http://www.graduatehospital.com. **Description:** A full-service hospital consisting of 303 inpatient beds, four intensive care units, an emergency department, and a variety of inpatient and outpatient diagnostic and treatment facilities. **Positions advertised include:** Phlebotomist; Registered Nurse; Licensed Practical Nurse; Nurse Manager; Financial Counselor; Pharmacist; Case Manager. **Parent company:** Tenet Healthcare.

GREATER PHILADELPHIA RADIO GROUP
One Bala Plaza, Suite 424, Bala-Cynwyd PA 19004. 610/667-8500. **Fax:** 610/771-9610. **Contact:** Human Resources. **E-mail address:** jobs@greaterphila.com. **World Wide Web address:** http://www.greaterphila.com. **Description:** Operates four radio stations in the Philadelphia area: MAX 95.7; WMGK-FM; WMMR-FM; and WPEN-AM. **Parent company:** Greater Media Inc.

GREEN COUNTY MEMORIAL HOSPITAL
350 Bonar Avenue, Waynesburg PA 15370. 724/627-3101. **Contact:** Human Resources. **Description:** A general medical and surgical hospital. The hospital's skilled nursing unit has 20 beds; specialty care has five beds; and medical/surgical has 35 beds.

GROVE CITY COLLEGE
100 Campus Drive, Grove City PA 16127-2104. 724/458-2200. **Contact:** Human Resources. **World Wide Web address:** http://www.gcc.edu. **Description:** A four-year Christian-based college offering B.A. and B.S. degrees. Enrollment is approximately 2,200 students.

GROVE WORLDWIDE
P.O. Box 21, Shady Grove PA 17256. 717/597-8121. **Fax:** 717/597-4062. **Physical address:** 1565 Buchanan Trail East, Shady Grove PA 17256. **Contact:** Human Resources. **E-mail address:** careers@groveworldwide.com. **World Wide Web address:** http://www.groveworldwide.com. **Description:** A manufacturer of mobile lifting and access equipment. **Corporate headquarters location:** This location. **Parent company:** Hanson Industries. **Operations at this facility include:** Administration; Manufacturing; Research and Development; Sales. **Number of employees at this location:** 2,000.

GRUBB & ELLIS COMPANY
600 Six PPG Place, Pittsburgh PA 15222. 412/281-0100. **Contact:** Property Management Department. **E-mail address:** jobs@grubb-ellis.com. **World Wide Web address:** http://www.grubb-ellis.com. **Description:** A commercial and industrial real estate brokerage house. Grubb & Ellis also specializes in property management, and institutional and individual investment. **Other U.S. locations:** Nationwide. **Listed on:** New York Stock Exchange. **Stock exchange symbol:** GBE.

HCR MANORCARE HEALTH SERVICES
600 West Valley Forge Road, King of Prussia PA 19406. 610/337-1775. **Contact:** Human Resources. **E-mail address:** jobline@hcr-manorcare.com. **World Wide Web address:** http://www.hcr-manorcare.com. **Description:** An inpatient and outpatient rehabilitation center providing physical, occupational, and speech therapies. **Positions advertised include:** Admissions Clerk; Business Development Specialist; General Clerk; Activity Assistant; Receptionist; Cook. **Corporate headquarters location:** Toledo OH. **Listed on:** New York Stock Exchange. **Stock exchange symbol:** HCR.

HCR MANORCARE HEALTH SERVICES
200 Second Avenue, Kingston PA 18704. 570/288-9315. **Contact:** Human Resources. **E-mail address:** jobline@hcr-manorcare.com. **World Wide Web address:** http://www.hcr-manorcare.com. **Description:** An inpatient and outpatient rehabilitation center providing physical, occupational, and speech therapies. **Positions advertised include:** Admissions Clerk; Business Development Specialist; General Clerk; Activity Assistant; Receptionist; Cook. **Corporate headquarters location:** Toledo OH. **Listed on:** New York Stock Exchange. **Stock exchange symbol:** HCR.

HCR MANORCARE HEALTH SERVICES
940 Walnut Bottom Road, Carlisle PA 17013. 717/249-0085. **Contact:** Human Resources. **E-mail address:** jobline@hcr-manorcare.com. **World Wide Web address:** http://www.hcr-manorcare.com. **Description:** An inpatient and outpatient rehabilitation center providing physical, occupational, and speech therapies. **Positions advertised include:** Certified Nurses Aide; Human Resources Manager; Licensed Practical Nurse; Occupational Therapist; Physical Therapist; Registered Nurse; Speech-Language Pathologist. **Corporate headquarters location:** Toledo OH. **Listed on:** New York Stock Exchange. **Stock exchange symbol:** HCR.

HCR MANORCARE HEALTH SERVICES
800 Court Street, Sunbury PA 17801. 570/286-7121. **Contact:** Human Resources. **World E-mail address:** jobline@hcr-manorcare.com. **Wide Web address:** http://www.hcr-manorcare.com. **Description:** An inpatient and outpatient rehabilitation center providing physical, occupational, and speech therapies. **NOTE:** Part-time jobs and second and third shifts are offered. **Positions advertised include:** Certified Nurses Aide; Human Resources Manager; Licensed Practical Nurse; Medical Records Technician; Occupational Therapist; Physical Therapist; Physical Therapy Assistant; Registered Nurse; Social Worker; Speech-Language Pathologist. **Office hours:** Monday - Friday, 7:30 a.m. - 5:30 p.m. **Corporate headquarters location:** Toledo OH. **Operations at this facility include:** Administration; Sales; Service. **Listed on:** New York Stock Exchange. **Stock exchange symbol:** HCR. **Number of employees at this location:** 130.

HCR MANORCARE HEALTH SERVICES
2600 Northampton Street, Easton PA 18045. 610/250-0150. **Contact:** Human Resources. **E-mail address:** jobline@hcr-manorcare.com. **World Wide Web address:** http://www.hcr-manorcare.com. **Description:** An inpatient and outpatient rehabilitation center providing physical, occupational, and speech therapies. **NOTE:** Second and third shifts are offered. **Positions advertised include:** Certified Nurses Aide; Human Resources Manager; Licensed Practical Nurse; Occupational Therapist; Physical Therapist; Registered Nurse; Speech-Language Pathologist. **Special programs:** Training. **Corporate headquarters location:** Toledo OH. **Listed on:** New York Stock Exchange. **Stock exchange symbol:** HCR.

HCR MANORCARE HEALTH SERVICES
300 Leader Drive, Williamsport PA 17701. 570/323-3600. **Contact:** Human Resources Director. **E-mail address:** jobline@hcr-manorcare.com. **World Wide Web address:** http://www.hcr-manorcare.com. **Description:** An inpatient and outpatient rehabilitation center providing physical, occupational, and speech therapies. **Positions advertised include:** Licensed Practical Nurse; Occupational Therapist; Physical Therapist; Recreational Therapist; Registered Nurse; Social Worker. **Corporate headquarters location:** Toledo OH. **Operations at this facility include:** Administration. **Listed on:** New York Stock Exchange. **Stock exchange symbol:** HCR.

HCR MANORCARE HEALTH SERVICES
1265 South Cedar Crest Boulevard, Allentown PA 18103. 610/776-7522. **Contact:** Human Resources. **E-mail address:** jobline@hcr-manorcare.com. **World Wide Web address:** http://www.hcr-manorcare.com. **Description:** An inpatient and outpatient rehabilitation center providing physical, occupational, and speech therapies. **Positions advertised include:** Certified Nurses Aide; Human Resources Manager; Licensed Practical Nurse; Occupational Therapist; Physical Therapist; Registered Nurse; Speech-Language Pathologist. **Corporate headquarters location:** Toledo OH. **Listed on:** New York Stock Exchange. **Stock exchange symbol:** HCR.

HCR MANORCARE HEALTH SERVICES
640 Bethlehem Pike, Montgomeryville PA 18936. 215/368-4350. **Contact:** Human Resources. **E-mail address:** jobline@hcr-manorcare.com. **World Wide Web address:** http://www.hcr-manorcare.com. **Description:** An inpatient and outpatient rehabilitation center providing physical, occupational, and speech therapies. **NOTE:** Part-time jobs and second and third shifts are offered. **Positions advertised include:** Certified Nurses Aide; Human Resources Manager; Licensed Practical Nurse; Occupational Therapist; Physical Therapist; Registered Nurse; Speech-Language Pathologist. **Special programs:** Training. **Corporate headquarters location:** Toledo OH. **Listed on:** New York Stock Exchange. **Stock exchange symbol:** HCR.

HDR ENGINEERING, INC.
3 Gateway Center, 3rd Floor, Pittsburgh PA 15222-1074. 412/497-6000. **Fax:** 412/497-6080. **Contact:** Susan Philipp, Human Resources Manager. **E-mail address:** careers@hdrinc.com. **World Wide Web address:** http://www.hdrinc.com. **Description:** Provides water, transportation, and waste and energy services including studies, design, and implementation for complex projects. **Parent company:** HDR, Inc. is a holding company for both HDR Engineering, Inc. and Henningson, Durham & Richardson, Inc., which specializes in the design of health care facilities including hospitals and integrated health care networks, ambulatory care centers, oncology and cardiology centers, diagnostic and treatment centers, and strategic facilities assessment; justice facilities including courthouse and administrative facilities, adult and juvenile detention facilities, and state correctional facilities; and science and industry facilities including research facilities, advanced technology facilities, telecommunications, university science facilities, and manufacturing facilities. **Corporate headquarters location:** Omaha NE.

HMG INTERMARK WORLDWIDE MANUFACTURING, INC.
234 South Eighth Street, P.O. Box 1217, Reading PA 19602. 610/376-5701. **Contact:** Human Resources. **Description:** Produces a wide range of plastic displays, safety lenses, precision glasswork, and industrial products. **Parent company:** HMG Worldwide Inc. (New York NY). **Operations at this facility include:** Divisional Headquarters; Manufacturing. **Annual sales/revenues:** $51 - $100 million. **Number of employees at this location:** 70. **Number of employees nationwide:** 250.

HMW ENTERPRISES INC.
207 North Franklin Street, P.O. Box 309, Waynesboro PA 17268. 717/765-4690. **Fax:** 717/765-4660. **Contact:** Human Resources. **World Wide Web address:** http://www.hmwent.com. **Description:** Manufactures industrial computers.

HNTB
8 Penn Center, 7th Floor, 1628 John F Kennedy Boulevard, Philadelphia PA 19103. **Contact:** Human Resources. **World Wide Web address:** http://www.hntb.com. **Description:** HNTB is engineering, architectural, and planning company involved in public infrastructure projects. **NOTE:** Search and apply for positions or complete profile online. **Positions advertised include:** Highway Engineer; Bridge Engineer; Receptionist.

HRI INC.
1750 West College Avenue, State College PA 16801. 814/238-5071. **Contact:** Dan Cornali, Human Resources. **Description:** A road construction company.

HANOVER HOSPITAL
300 Highland Avenue, Hanover PA 17331. 717/633-2143. **Toll-free phone:** 800/673-2426. **Fax:** 717/633-2217. **Contact:** Jen Walton, Human Resources. **World Wide Web address:** http://www.hanoverhospital.org. **Description:** A 174-bed, acute care hospital. **Positions advertised include:** Licensed Practical Nurse; Nuclear Medicine Technologist; Occupational Therapist; Pharmacist; Physical Therapist; Radiological Technologist; Registered Nurse; Respiratory Therapist; Speech-Language Pathologist; Surgical Technician. **Special programs:** Internships. **Parent company:** Hanover HealthCare Plus Network. **Number of employees at this location:** 800.

HARLEY-DAVIDSON MOTOR COMPANY, INC.
1425 Eden Road, York PA 17402. 717/848-1177. **Contact:** Human Resources. **World Wide Web address:** http://www.harley-davidson.com. **Description:** Designs, manufactures, and distributes a world-recognized line of motorcycles. **Positions advertised include:** Continuous Improvement Engineer; Operations Planner; Supply Chain Analyst. **Corporate headquarters location:** Milwaukee WI. **Operations at this facility include:** Machining fabrication, paint and final assembly, manufacture of current and non-current replacement parts, and factory-custom motorcycles. **Listed on:** New York Stock Exchange. **Stock exchange symbol:** HDI.

HARLEYSVILLE INSURANCE COMPANIES
355 Maple Avenue, Harleysville PA 19438-2297. 215/256-3300. **Toll-free phone:** 800/523-6344. **Fax:** 215/256-5602. **Contact:** Human Resources Department. **E-mail address:** resumes@harleysvillegroup.com. **World Wide Web address:** http://www.harleysvillegroup.com. **Description:** A multiline property/casualty and life insurance carrier with offices located throughout the Mid-Atlantic states. Products are marketed through an independent agency system. **Positions advertised include:** Actuarial Analyst; Customer Service Representative; Claims Auditor; Underwriter; Information Systems Technician; Associate Coder; Process Analyst. **Corporate headquarters location:** This location. **Other U.S. locations:** East, Midwest, Southeast.

HARSCO CORPORATION
P.O. Box 8888, Camp Hill PA 17001-8888. 717/763-7064. **Physical address:** 350 Poplar Church Road, Camp Hill PA 17001. **Fax:** 717/612-5619. **Contact:** Human Resources. **E-mail address:** employment@harsco.com. **World Wide Web address:** http://www.harsco.com. **Description:** Harsco Corporation is a diversified industrial manufacturing and service company that conducts business through 10 divisions and has 16 classes of products and services. Operations fall into three groups: Metal Reclamation and Mill Services includes scrap management, slab management systems, iron making, materials handling, equipment rental, recycling technology, aggregate marketing, and nonferrous metallurgical industry services; Infrastructure and Construction includes railway maintenance equipment, industrial grating products, and scaffolding, shoring, and concrete forming equipment; and Process Industry Products includes industrial pipe fittings, process equipment, and gas control and containment equipment. **Positions advertised include:** Staff Auditor; PC Support Analyst; Accounting Manager; Security Manager; Director Engineering and Production. **Special programs:** Internships. **Corporate headquarters location:** This location. **Other U.S. locations:** Nationwide. **Listed on:** New York Stock Exchange. **Stock exchange symbol:** HSC. **Number of employees at this location:** 90. **Number of employees worldwide:** 13,000.

HARTE-HANKS, INC.
2080 Cabot Boulevard West, Langhorne PA 19047. 215/970-3500. **Contact:** Brian Jacobs, Human Resources Director. **World Wide Web address:** http://www7.harte-hanks.com. **Description:** Provides direct marketing services for various companies and publishes a weekly shopping guide. **Positions advertised include:** Account Coordinator; Account Executive; Account Manager; Administrative Assistant; Business Systems Manager; Database Programmer; Healthcare Copywriter; Print Media Coordinator. **Corporate headquarters location:** San Antonio TX.

THE HARTFORD
ITT HARTFORD
20 Stanwix Street, 3rd Floor, Pittsburgh PA 15222-4800. 412/281-8833. **Contact:** Human Resources. **World Wide Web address:** http://www.thehartford.com. **Description:** A *Fortune* 100 company and one of the largest insurance organizations in the United States. The company offers a full line of business, farm, home, automobile, life, and health insurance coverage, as well as marine insurance, fidelity and surety bonds, and reinsurance. **Positions advertised include:** Director Regional Service; Account Manager; Service Manager; Rookie Sales Representative. **Corporate headquarters location:** Hartford CT.

HASKELL SENATOR INTERNATIONAL
231 Haskel Lane, Verona PA 15147. 412/828-6000. **Fax:** 412/828-6262. **Contact:** Belinda Saix, Manager of Human Resources. **Description:** Manufactures steel office furniture. This location also hires seasonally. **NOTE:** Entry-level positions are offered. **Corporate headquarters location:** This location. **Annual sales/revenues:** $21 - $50 million. **Number of employees at this location:** 350.

HATCH
Gateway View Plaza, 1600 West Carson Street, Pittsburgh PA 15219-1031. 412/497-2000. **Fax:** 412/497-2212. **Contact:** Ms. Geri Rupert, Human Resources Director. **E-mail address:** hr@hatch.ca. **World Wide Web address:** http://www.hatch.ca. **Description:** One of the nation's largest engineering, construction, and consulting services companies. Hatch provides fully-integrated capabilities to clients worldwide in four related market areas: environment, infrastructure, industry, and energy. The majority of Hatch professionals study and resolve environmental problems. Projects address issues such as hazardous and radioactive waste clean-up, waste minimization and disposal, risk assessment, permitting, environmental compliance, global climate change, clean air, alternative fuels, groundwater contamination, and pollution of harbors and waterways. Hatch also has extensive experience in the infrastructure and industrial fields. Projects include the design, construction, and management of rapid transit systems, highways, hydroelectric plants, and mining and manufacturing facilities. **Corporate headquarters location:** Irving TX. **International locations:** Worldwide. **Number of employees worldwide:** 5,700.

HATFIELD QUALITY MEATS INC.
2700 Funks Road, P.O. Box 902, Hatfield PA 19440-0902. 215/368-2500. **Toll-free phone:** 800/523-5291. **Fax:** 215/368-3018. **Contact:** Recruiter. **World Wide Web address:** http://www.hqm.com. **Description:** Manufactures meat products.

HAVEN CONVALESCENT HOME
725 Paul Street, New Castle PA 16101. 724/654-8833. **Contact:** Personnel. **World Wide Web address:** http://www.havenconvalescenthome.com. **Description:** Haven Convalescent Home is a 91-bed long-term, acute care facility for the elderly.

GLENN O. HAWBAKER, INC.
P.O. Box 135, State College PA 16804-0135. 814/237-1444. **Toll-free phone:** 800/350-5078. **Fax:** 814/235-3654. **Contact:** Mr. Page L. Gaddis, Personnel Manager. **E-mail address:** plg@goh-inc.com. **World Wide Web address:** http://www.goh-inc.com. **Description:** Engaged in heavy construction services including paving, road construction, bridge construction, and other related services. Founded in 1952. **Positions advertised include:** Aggregate Lab Technician; Asphalt Lab Technician; Laborer; Heavy Equipment Operator; Parts Runner; Welder. **Special programs:** Internships; Summer Jobs. **Office hours:** Monday - Friday, 8:00 a.m. - 5:00 p.m. **Corporate headquarters location:** This location. **Other area locations:** DuBois PA; Montoursville PA; Turtlepoint PA. **Operations at this facility include:** Administration; Sales. **Listed on:** Privately held. **Annual sales/revenues:** $21 - $50 million. **Number of employees at this location:** 600.

HAY GROUP INC.
The Wanamaker Building, 100 Penn Square East, Philadelphia PA 19107-3388. 215/861-2000. **Fax:** 215/861-2111. **Contact:** Personnel. **World Wide Web address:** http://www.haygroup.com. **Description:** An international human resources and management consulting firm that provides a variety of services including total compensation planning, strategic management, business culture, employee surveys, and outplacement. **Positions advertised include:** Accounting Specialist; Temporary Analyst. **Corporate headquarters location:** This location. **Number of employees worldwide:** 2200.

HAZLETON PUMPS, INC.
225 North Cedar Street, Hazleton PA 18201. 570/455-7711. **Contact:** Ernest Stauffer, Personnel Manager. **World Wide Web address:** http://www.hazletonpumps.com. **Description:** Manufactures a wide range of centrifugal pumps. **Corporate headquarters location:** This location. **Parent company:** Warman International Group (Australia). **Operations at this facility include:** Administration; Manufacturing; Research and Development; Sales; Service. **Number of employees at this location:** 200.

HEALTHCARE SERVICES GROUP
3220 Tillman Drive, Suite 300, Bensalem PA 19020. 215/639-8191. **Toll-free phone:** 800/363-4274. **Fax:** 215/639-2152. **Contact:** Human Resources. **E-mail address:**

jobs@hcsgcorp.com. **World Wide Web address:** http://www.hcsgcorp.com. **Description:** Provides cleaning and laundering services for nursing homes and hospitals. **Other area locations:** Doylestown PA. **Corporate headquarters location:** This location.

HEALTHSOUTH REHABILITATION HOSPITAL OF GREATER PITTSBURGH
2380 McGinley Road, Monroeville PA 15146. 412/856-2400. **Contact:** Human Resources. **Description:** A rehabilitation hospital licensed for 89 beds. **Special programs:** Internships. **Corporate headquarters location:** Birmingham AL. **Listed on:** New York Stock Exchange. **Stock exchange symbol:** HRC. **Number of employees nationwide:** 18,000.

H.J. HEINZ
600 Grant Street, Pittsburgh PA 15219. 412/237-5757. **Contact:** Human Resources. **World Wide Web address:** http://www.heinz.com. **Description:** A worldwide producer of food products including ketchup, sauces, condiments, baby food, seafood, pet food, frozen potato products, frozen meats, beverages, and a wide selection of other processed consumables. These foods are marketed under brand names including Heinz, Steak-Umm, and Ore-Ida. The company also operates and sells franchise licenses for Weight Watchers International weight-control classes and related programs. **Corporate headquarters location:** This location. **Subsidiaries include:** Starkist Foods; Weight Watchers. **Listed on:** New York Stock Exchange. **Stock exchange symbol:** HNZ. **Annual sales/revenues:** More than $100 million.

HENKELS & McCOY, INC.
985 Jolly Road, Blue Bell PA 19422-0900. 215/283-7688. **Fax:** 215/283-7659. **Contact:** Vincent Benedict, Director of Personnel. **World Wide Web address:** http://www.henkelsandmccoy.com. **Description:** An engineering and construction firm that specializes in designing, building, and maintaining infrastructure. Founded in 1923. **Positions advertised include:** Electrical Transmission Engineer; Mechanical Engineer; Senior Telecom Engineer. **Corporate headquarters location:** This location. **Other U.S. locations:** Nationwide. **Listed on:** Privately held. **Number of employees nationwide:** 5,000.

HERALD PRESS
MENNONITE PUBLISHING HOUSE
616 Walnut Avenue, Scottdale PA 15683. 724/887-8500. **Contact:** Wanda Pritts, Human Resources. **World Wide Web address:** http://www.mph.org. **Description:** A publisher of religious materials including books, periodicals, and church programs.

HEXCEL CORPORATION
P.O. Box 179, Pottsville PA 17901. 570/429-1741. **Contact:** Human Resources Department. **World Wide Web address:** http://www.hexcel.com. **Description:** Hexcel Corporation is a manufacturing firm engaged in two primary business segments. The structural materials segment includes aerospace products, nonaerospace honeycomb resins, resin-impregnated industrial fabrics, and nonimpregnated fabrics. The specialty chemicals segment includes bulk pharmaceuticals, custom and special purpose chemicals, specialty resins, and industrial maintenance chemicals. **Operations at this facility include:** This location manufactures structural honeycomb products for the aerospace industry. **Listed on:** New York Stock Exchange. **Stock exchange symbol:** HXL.

HIGH CONCRETE STRUCTURES
125 Denver Road, Denver PA 17517. 717/336-9300. **Contact:** Personnel. **World E-mail address:** lford@high.net. **Wide Web address:** http://www.highconcrete.com. **Description:** Manufactures precast concrete for use by the construction industry. **Positions advertised include:** Cafeteria Attendant; Room Attendant; Head of Hotel Maintenance; Job Superintendent; Estimator/Buyer; Assistant General Manager. **Parent company:** High Industries, Inc.

HIGH INDUSTRIES, INC.
P.O. Box 10008, 1853 William Penn Way, Lancaster PA 17605-0008. 717/293-4486. **Contact:** Vincent Mizeras, Director of Human Resources. **World Wide Web address:** http://www.high.net. **Description:** Operates through several areas of business including design and construction, food services, hotel management, prestress/precast concrete products, real estate development and management, and steel fabrication. **Corporate headquarters location:** This location. **Operations at this facility include:** Administration; Manufacturing.

HOFMANN INDUSTRIES, INC.
3145 Shillington Road, P.O. Box 2147, Sinking Spring PA 19608. 610/678-8051. **Fax:** 610/670-2221. **Contact:** Human Resources. **World Wide Web address:** http://www.hofmann.com. **Description:** Manufactures and markets fabricated, powder-coated, zinc-plated, and electric-welded steel tubing to the houseware, hardware, furniture, lawn and garden, automotive, and recreational markets. **Corporate headquarters location:** This location. **Other U.S. locations:** Eau Claire MI. **Annual sales/revenues:** $21 - $50 million. **Number of employees at this location:** 300. **Number of employees nationwide:** 375.

HOLY REDEEMER HOSPITAL
1648 Huntingdon Pike, Meadowbrook PA 19046. 215/947-3000. **Recorded jobline:** 877/499-4473. **Fax:** 215/214-0678. **Contact:** Human Resources. **E-mail address:** recruiter@holyredeemer.com. **World Wide Web address:** http://www.holyredeemer.com. **Description:** A 299-bed community hospital offering a variety of inpatient, outpatient, and emergency services. **Positions advertised include:** Medical Messenger Operator; Operating Room Staff Nurse; Registered Nurse; Hospital Librarian; Occupational Therapist; Physical Therapist; Speech Language Pathologist; Housekeeper; Certified Nurse Assistant; Food Service Worker; Clinical Engineering Technician.

HOLY SPIRIT HEALTH SYSTEM
503 North 21st Street, Camp Hill PA 17011. 717/763-2100. **Fax:** 717/763-2351. **Recorded jobline:** 717/972-4121. **Contact:** Employment Manager. **E-mail address:** resume@hsh.org. **World Wide Web address:** http://www.hsh.org. **Description:** A nonprofit health system that operates a 349-bed hospital as well as several home health, hospice, and family care centers. Holy Spirit Health System also provides ambulance and emergency care services. Founded in 1963. **NOTE:** Entry-level positions, part-time jobs, and second and third shifts are offered. **Positions advertised include:** Administrative Assistant; Certified Nurses Aide; Claim Representative; EEG Technologist; EKG Technician; Emergency Medical Technician; Help-Desk Technician; Home Health Aide; Licensed Practical Nurse; Medical Assistant; Medical Records Technician; Medical Secretary; Network/Systems Administrator; Nuclear Medicine Technologist; Occupational Therapist; Pharmacist; Physical Therapist; Radiological Technologist; Registered Nurse; Respiratory Therapist; Secretary; Social Worker; Speech-Language Pathologist; Surgical Technician. **Special programs:** Internships. **Office hours:** Monday - Friday, 7:30 a.m. - 4:00 p.m. **Corporate headquarters location:** This location. **Parent company:** Holy Spirit Health System. **Number of employees at this location:** 2,000.

HONEYWELL INC.
1100 Virginia Drive, Fort Washington PA 19034. **Toll-free phone:** 800/525-7439. **Contact:** Human Resources. **World Wide Web address:** http://www.honeywell.com. **Description:** Honeywell is engaged in the research, development, manufacture, and sale of advanced technology products and services in the fields of chemicals, electronics, automation, and controls. The company's major businesses are home and building automation and control, performance polymers and chemicals, industrial automation and control, space and aviation systems, and defense and marine systems. **Corporate headquarters location:** Morristown NJ. **Operations at this facility include:** This location manufactures industrial and programmable controls for a wide range of manufacturers. **Listed on:** New York Stock Exchange. **Stock exchange symbol:** HON.

HONEYWELL INC.
1005 South Bee Street, Pittsburgh PA 15220. 412/928-4200. **Contact:** Human Resources. **World Wide Web address:** http://www.honeywell.com. **Description:** Honeywell is engaged in the research, development, manufacture, and sale of advanced technology products and services in the fields of chemicals, electronics, automation, and controls. The company's major businesses are home and building automation and control, performance polymers and chemicals, industrial automation and control, space and aviation systems, and defense and marine systems. **Corporate headquarters location:** Morristown NJ. **Operations at this facility include:** This location manufactures, sells, and services HVAC equipment. **Listed on:** New York Stock Exchange. **Stock exchange symbol:** HON.

HONEYWELL INC.
RD 3, Box 56A, Smethport PA 16749. 814/887-5501. **Contact:** Human Resources. **World Wide Web address:** http://www.honeywell.com. **Description:** Honeywell is engaged in the research, development, manufacture, and sale of advanced technology products and services in the fields of chemicals, electronics, automation, and controls. The company's major businesses are home and building automation and control, performance polymers and chemicals, industrial automation and control, space and aviation systems, and defense and marine systems. **Corporate headquarters location:** Morristown NJ. **Operations at this facility include:** This location is a petroleum refinery and producer of petroleum wax and also has research and development facilities. **Listed on:** New York Stock Exchange. **Stock exchange symbol:** HON.

HONEYWELL INC.
P.O. Box 934, York PA 17405. 717/771-8100. **Contact:** Human Resources. **World Wide Web address:** http://www.honeywell.com. **Description:** Honeywell is engaged in the research, development, manufacture, and sale of advanced technology products and services in the fields of chemicals, electronics, automation, and controls. The company's major businesses are home and building automation and control, performance polymers and chemicals, industrial automation and control, space and aviation systems, and defense and marine systems. **Corporate headquarters location:** Morristown NJ. **Operations at this facility include:** This location manufactures industrial and programmable controls for a wide range of manufacturers. **Listed on:** New York Stock Exchange. **Stock exchange symbol:** HON.

HOPE ENTERPRISES INC.
136 Catawissa Avenue, P.O. Box 1837, Williamsport PA 17703-1837. 570/326-3745. **Fax:** 570/326-1258. **Contact:** Human Resources Department. **E-mail address:** info@heionline.org. **World Wide Web address:** http://www.heionline.org. **Description:** Offers workshop training for individuals with mental disabilities. Hope Enterprises also operates over 20 group homes, a preschool, and an adult training facility that teaches domestic skills and personal hygiene. **Positions advertised include:** Accounting Clerk; Active Treatment Aide; ATF Trainer; Behavior Specialist; Custodian; Job Coach; Teacher; Van Driver. **Number of employees worldwide:** 450.

HOSPITAL CENTRAL SERVICES INC.
2171 28th Street SW, Allentown PA 18103. 610/791-2222. **Fax:** 610/791-2919. **Contact:** Human Resources. **E-mail address:** hr@hcsc.org. **World Wide Web address:** http://www.hcsc.org. **Description:** Provides management services for hospitals including laundry services, physician billing, and the operation of blood centers.

HOUGHTON INTERNATIONAL INC.
Madison and Van Buren Avenues, P.O. Box 930, Valley Forge PA 19482-0930. 610/666-4000. **Fax:** 610/666-1376. **Contact:** Human Resources. **World Wide Web address:** http://www.houghtonintl.com. **Description:** Engaged in the manufacture of lubricating oil and grease products for metalworking and manufacturing processes. Founded in 1865. **Positions advertised include:** Contract Technician. **Corporate headquarters location:** This location.

HPCII
2nd Street and Blueball Avenue, P.O. Box 429, Marcus Hook PA 19061. 215/295-9319. **Contact:** Human Resources. **E-mail address:** Rhodia@rpc.webhire.com. **World Wide Web address:** http://www.us.rhodia.com. **Description:** Supplies specialty and intermediate chemicals for consumer and industrial applications. **Special programs:** Internships; Rotational Engineering Development Program. **Corporate headquarters location:** Cranbury NJ. **Other U.S. locations:** Nationwide. **Parent company:** Rhodia Inc. **Number of employees nationwide:** 2,700.

HUNT CORPORATION
One Commerce Square, 2005 Market Street, 7th Floor, Philadelphia PA 19103. 215/656-0300. **Fax:** 215/656-3700. **Contact:** Human Resources. **World Wide Web address:** http://www.hunt-corp.com. **Description:** Manufactures art supplies, office supplies, and office furniture. **Corporate headquarters location:** This location. **Other U.S. locations:** AL; CT; KY; NC; TX; WI. **Listed on:** New York Stock Exchange. **Stock exchange symbol:** HUN. **Number of employees at this location:** 1,000.

HUTSPAH SHIRTS
185 West Wyoming Avenue, Philadelphia PA 19140-1691. 215/329-7700. **Fax:** 215/329-4650. **Contact:** Ken Williams, Personnel Director. **Description:** Manufactures shirts and nightwear. **Corporate headquarters location:** This location.

HYDRO SERVICE AND SUPPLIES, INC.
1426 Manning Boulevard, Levittown PA 19057. 215/547-0332. **Fax:** 215/547-5734. **Contact:** Human Resources. **E-mail address:** jobs@hydroservice.com. **World Wide Web address:** http://www.hydroservice.com. **Description:** Sells and services water ultrapurification laboratory equipment. **NOTE:** Mail employment correspondence to: Human Resources, P.O. Box 12197, Research Triangle Park NC 27709. **Corporate headquarters location:** Research Triangle Park NC.

IBM TRANSARC CORPORATION
11 Stanwix Street, Pittsburgh PA 15222. 412/667-4400. **Contact:** Staffing Manager. **World Wide Web address:** http://www.transarc.com. **Description:** Develops AFS and DCE software. **Parent company:** IBM Corporation.

ICI PAINTS
301 Bern Street, Reading PA 19601. 610/373-4111. **Contact:** Gary Noll, Human Resources Manager. **World Wide Web address:** http://www.ici.com. **Description:** Manufactures and distributes a complete range of paints, varnishes, lacquers, rust inhibitors, and other protective coatings. **Corporate headquarters location:** United Kingdom. **International locations:** Worldwide.

ICT GROUP, INC.
100 Brandywine Boulevard, Newtown PA 18940. 215/478-2011. **Toll-free phone:** 800/799-6880. **Contact:** Human Resources Department. **World Wide Web address:** http://www.ictgroup.com. **Description:** A direct marketing agency engaged in telemarketing, customer service, and market research. The company serves the energy, financial services, health care, insurance, media, and telecommunications industries. Founded in 1983. **Positions advertised include:** Tele-services Division; Management Service Division; Marketing Services Division. **Corporate headquarters location:** This location. **Listed on:** NASDAQ. **Stock exchange symbol:** ICTG. **Number of employees at this location:** 270. **Number of employees nationwide:** 2,100.

IMC GROUP
165 Township Line Road, One Pitcairn Place, Suite 1200, Jenkintown PA 19046-3531. **Fax:** 215/517-6090. **Contact:** Human Resources. **E-mail address:** hr@imc-group.com. **World Wide Web address:** http://www.imc-group.com. **Description:** A metals refinery that is also engaged in the distribution of metals and chemicals. **Positions advertised include:** Sales Representative; Customer Service Representative. **Corporate headquarters location:** This location. **Other U.S. locations:** Shelbyville NC. **Operations at this facility include:** Administration; Manufacturing; Regional Headquarters; Sales; Service.

ITT INDUSTRIES ENGINEERED VALVES
33 Centerville Road, P.O. Box 6164, Lancaster PA 17603-2064. 717/291-1901. **Fax:** 717/509-2214. **Contact:** Jane A. Keller, Human Resources Administrator. **E-mail address:** engvalves_hr@fluids.ittind.com. **World Wide Web address:** http://www.engvalves.com. **Description:** Manufactures industrial valves. **Positions advertised include:** Manager Sales & Marketing; Director of Biopharm Process System Engineering. **Corporate headquarters location:** New York NY. **Parent company:** ITT Corporation.

IGATE CORPORATION
1000 Commerce Drive, Suite 500, Pittsburgh PA 15275. 412/787-2100. **Contact:** Human Resources. **E-mail address:** careers@igate.com. **World Wide Web address:** http://www.igatecorp.com. **Description:** Provides high value information technology services including e-business solutions, enterprise solutions implementation, network services, and supply chain management solutions and applications design. Founded in 1986. **NOTE:** See website for detailed application information. **Corporate headquarters location:** This location. **International locations:** Worldwide. **Subsidiaries include:** iGate Global Solutions Ltd.; iGate Professional Services; iGate Virtual University; iGate Clinical Research. **Listed on:** NASDAQ. **Stock exchange symbol:** IGTE. **Number of employees worldwide:** 5,500.

IKON OFFICE SOLUTIONS
70 Valley Stream Parkway, Malvern PA 19355. 610/296-8000. **Fax:** 478/471-2417. **Contact:** Kathy Brodhag, Director of Human Resources. **World Wide Web address:** http://www.ikon.com. **Description:** Markets and distributes office equipment and paper products. IKON Office Solutions is one of the largest independent copier distribution networks in North America. **Positions advertised include:** Enterprise Test Manager; Senior IT Manager; Senior Supply Chain Analyst; Online Marketing Manager; Senior Help Desk Technician; Paralegal. **Special programs:** Internships. **Corporate headquarters location:** This location. **Operations at this facility include:** Administration. **Number of employees at this location:** 225.

INDEPENDENCE BLUE CROSS OF GREATER PHILADELPHIA
1901 Market Street, 25th Floor, Philadelphia PA 19103. 215/241-2400. **Fax:** 215/241-3237. **Contact:** Human Resources. **E-mail address:** recruiter@ibx.com. **World Wide Web address:** http://www.ibx.com. **Description:** Provides individual and group subscribers with health benefits that complement their lifestyle and their medical and financial needs.

INDEPENDENCE FINANCIAL GROUP
150 Monument Road, Suite 310, Bala-Cynwyd PA 19004. 610/771-0800. **Contact:** Human Resources. **Description:** Offers a variety of financial products including individual and group life and health insurance, individual and group pension policies, annuities, individual stocks and bonds, and professionally managed investment funds. **Special programs:** Internships. **Corporate headquarters location:** Horsham PA. **Parent company:** Penn Mutual Life Insurance Company. **Operations at this facility include:** Sales.

INDIANA UNIVERSITY OF PENNSYLVANIA (IUP)
Sutton Hall, 1011 South Drive, Indiana PA 15705. 724/357-2431. **Fax:** 724/357-2685. **Recorded jobline:** 724/357-7536. **Contact:** Human Resources Representative. **World Wide Web address:** http://www.iup.edu/humanresources. **Description:** One of the largest schools of the Pennsylvania State System of Higher Education, IUP is approximately 50 miles northeast of Pittsburgh. **Positions advertised include:** Assistant Physics Professor; Assistant Chemistry Professor; Assistant Poetry Professor; Residence Director; Custodian. **Special programs:** Internships.

INDSPEC CHEMICAL CORPORATION
411 Seventh Avenue, Suite 300, Pittsburgh PA 15219-1905. 412/765-1200. **Fax:** 412/765-0439. **Contact:** Human Resources. **World Wide Web address:** http://www.indspec-chem.com. **Description:** Develops, produces and markets resorcinol, resorcinol-based resins and adhesives, and other derivatives, and produces sodium sulfate and salt-cake as by-products of resorcinol production.

INGERSOLL-RAND COMPANY
312 Ingersoll Drive, Shippensburg PA 17257-9125. 717/532-9181. **Contact:** Human Resources. **World Wide Web address:** http://www.irco.com. **Description:** Ingersoll-Rand Company is a manufacturer of road machinery and forklifts. **Corporate headquarters location:** Woodcliff Lake NJ.

INOLEX CHEMICAL COMPANY
Jackson & Swanson Streets, Philadelphia PA 19148-3497. 215/271-0800. **Toll-free phone:** 800/246-6539. **Fax:** 215/271-2621. **Contact:** Human Resources. **World Wide Web address:** http://www.inolex.com. **Description:** Manufactures specialty chemicals for the cosmetics, lubricants, and polyurethane industries. **Corporate headquarters location:** This location. **Operations at this facility include:** Administration; Manufacturing; Research and Development; Sales; Service. **Listed on:** Privately held.

INSTITUTE FOR SCIENTIFIC INFORMATION
3501 Market Street, Philadelphia PA 19104. 215/386-0100. **Toll-free phone:** 800/336-4474. **Fax:** 215/386-2911. **Contact:** Brian Richards, Employment/Employee Relations Manager. **World Wide Web address:** http://www.isinet.com. **Description:** Supplies researchers and scientists with needed information in electronic formats. Institute for Scientific Information produces indexes and databases that provide information from journals, books, and other significant materials published in the sciences, social sciences, and arts and humanities. The company also offers online services and technical support. **Positions advertised include:** Client Manager; Customer Training Executive; Senior Chemist; Senior Financial Analyst; Computer Operator; Data Capture Analyst; Software Engineer. **Corporate headquarters location:** This location. **Other area locations:** Cherry Hill NJ; Mount Laurel NJ. **Parent company:** Thomson Company. **Number of employees at this location:** 450. **Number of employees nationwide:** 750.

INTEGRATED CIRCUIT SYSTEMS, INC.
2435 Boulevard of the Generals, Norristown PA 19403. 610/630-5300. **Fax:** 610/630-5399. **Contact:** Human Resources. **E-mail address:** hr@icst.com. **World Wide Web address:** http://www.icst.com. **Description:** Integrated Circuit Systems, Inc. designs, develops, and markets innovative, very large-scale integrated (VSLI) circuits including standard and custom application-specific integrated circuit (ASIC) products, using mixed analog/digital technology. Products are marketed to original equipment manufacturers for use in video graphics display products, CPU (central processing unit) systems, PC multimedia, and portable device battery charging applications. **Corporate headquarters location:** This location. **Listed on:** NASDAQ. **Stock exchange symbol:** ICST.

INTEGRATED HEALTH SERVICES/BROOMALL
50 North Malin Road, Business Office, Broomall PA 19008. 610/356-0800. **Fax:** 610/325-9499. **Contact:** Human Resources. **Description:** A sub-acute care nursing facility with an oncology specialty unit. **NOTE:** For information on employment throughout Pennsylvania, contact the Division Recruitment office: 866/212-0510. **Corporate headquarters location:** Owings Mills MD. **Other U.S. locations:** Nationwide. **Operations at this facility include:** Administration; Service. **Number of employees at this location:** 310.

INTEGRATED HEALTH SERVICES/WHITEMARSH
9209 Ridge Pike, Whitemarsh PA 19128. 610/825-6560. **Fax:** 610/825-9478. **Contact:** Employment. **Description:** A subacute care nursing home. **NOTE:** For information on employment throughout Pennsylvania, contact the Division Recruitment office: 866/212-0510. **Corporate headquarters location:** Owings Mills MD. **Other U.S. locations:** Nationwide.

INTER-MEDIA MARKETING SOLUTIONS
204 Carter Drive, West Chester PA 19382. 610/429-1822. **Toll-free phone:** 800/835-3466. **Fax:** 610/429-5137. **Contact:** R. Dougherty, Human Resources. **E-mail address:** jobs@imminc.com. **World Wide Web address:** http://www.intermediamarketing.com. **Description:** A direct marketing and research firm focusing on e-commerce, sales, and customer service management solutions. Founded in 1983. **Positions advertised include:** Management Trainee; Inbound Customer Service Representative; Outbound Sales Representative.

INTERACTIVE MEDIA CORPORATION
245 Pittsburgh Road, Suite 200, Butler PA 16001. 724/284-7300. **Fax:** 724/285-8884. **Contact:** Human Resources. **World Wide Web address:** http://www.interactive-media.com. **Description:** Offers computer and multimedia training programs. **NOTE:** Resume may be submitted online.

INTERFORM SOLUTIONS
1901 Mayview Road, P.O. Box A, Bridgeville PA 15017. 412/221-3300. **Contact:** Human Resources. **World Wide Web address:** http://www.interformsolutions.com. **Description:** Produces business forms and direct mail printing. **Parent company:** Champion Industries, Inc.

INTERNAL REVENUE SERVICE
P.O. Box 21145, Philadelphia PA 19114. 215/516-JOBS. **Contact:** Delegated Examining Unit. **World Wide Web address:** http://www.irs.gov. **Description:** The IRS provides American taxpayers service by helping them to understand and meet their tax responsibilities and by applying tax laws. **Operations at this facility include:** This location is a submission processing and customer service center. **Number of employees nationwide:** 85,000.

INTERNATIONAL PAPER COMPANY
1540 East Lake Road, Erie PA 16533. 814/870-5000. **Contact:** Human Resources. **World Wide Web address:** http://www.internationalpaper.com. **Description:** International Paper manufactures pulp and paper, packaging, and wood products as well as a range of specialty products. Millions of acres of timberland are controlled by International Paper, making it one of the largest private landowners in the United States. The company is organized into five business segments: Printing Papers includes uncoated papers, coated papers, bristles, and pulp; Packaging includes industrial packaging, consumer packaging, and kraft and specialty papers; Distribution includes sales of printing papers, graphic arts equipment and supplies, packaging materials, industrial supplies, and office products; Specialty Products includes imaging products, specialty panels, nonwovens, chemicals, and minerals; and Forest Products includes logs and wood products. **Corporate headquarters location:** Purchase NY. **Other area locations:** Philadelphia PA. **Operations at this facility include:** This location is a paper mill. **Listed on:** New York Stock Exchange. **Stock exchange symbol:** IP.

INTERNATIONAL STEEL GROUP
ARC Building, 139 Modena Road, Box 3001, Coatesville PA 19320. 610/383-2412. **Contact:** Human Resources Administrator. **World Wide Web address:** http://www.intlsteel.com. **Description:** Manufactures carbon, alloy, clad plate steel, stainless sheet, and strip plate. Customers include steel service centers, OEMs, and fabricators. **Corporate headquarters location:** Richfield OH. **Other U.S. locations:** NY; IN; IL; OH; PA. **Listed on:** New York Stock Exchange. **Stock exchange symbol:** ISG.

INTERSTATE CONTAINER CORPORATION
P.O. Box 317, Reading PA 19603. 610/376-7124. **Toll-free phone:** 800/822-2002. **Fax:** 610/376-0350. **Physical address:** Grace and Meade Streets, Reading PA 19611. **Contact:** Human Resources. **E-mail address:** careers@iripaper.com. **World Wide Web address:** http://www.interstatecontainer.com. **Description:** Manufactures corrugated shipping containers and operates a paper mill that produces corrugating

medium. **Corporate headquarters location:** Rosslyn VA. **Operations at this facility include:** Manufacturing.

INVENSYS APPLIANCE CONTROLS
1046 Corporate Lane, Export PA 15632. 724/387-3112. **Contact:** Human Resources. **E-mail address:** staffing@invensys.com. **World Wide Web address:** http://www.invensys.com. **Description:** An electronics and engineering company for the automation and controls industry. Invensys operates through four segments, Intelligent Automation, Industrial Drive Systems, Power Systems, and Controls. **Corporate headquarters location:** London, England. **Number of employees worldwide:** 100,000.

INVENSYS METERING SYSTEMS
450 North Gallatin Avenue, Uniontown PA 15401. 724/439-7700. **Contact:** Human Resources. **World Wide Web address:** http://www.invensys.com. **Description:** Manufactures fluid meters and other industrial measurement devices.

IRWIN & LEIGHTON, INC.
1030 Continental Avenue, King of Prussia PA 19406. 610/989-0100. **Fax:** 610/989-0200. **Contact:** Personnel. **E-mail address:** info@irwinleighton.com. **World Wide Web address:** http://www.irwinleighton.com. **Description:** A full-service construction services firm. Founded in 1909. **Corporate headquarters location:** This location.

J&L SPECIALTY STEEL, INC.
Westpointe Corporate Center One, P.O. Box 1425, Coraopolis PA 15108-6934. 412/375-1731. **Fax:** 412/375-1746. **Contact:** Human Resources. **E-mail address:** hum.res@jlspecialty.com. **World Wide Web address:** http://www.jlspecialty.com. **Description:** Produces stainless and strip steel for commercial, industrial, and consumer uses. Products include pipes, storage tanks, processing equipment, restaurant equipment, automotive trim, catalytic converters, kitchen sinks, and flatware. **Corporate headquarters location:** This location. **Other U.S. locations:** MI; OH.

J&L SPECIALTY STEEL, INC.
1200 Midland Avenue, Midland PA 15059-1696. 724/773-2700. **Contact:** Human Resources. **E-mail address:** hum.res@jlspecialty.com. **World Wide Web address:** http://www.jlspecialty.com. **Description:** Produces stainless and strip steel for commercial, industrial, and consumer uses. The company operates facilities in Pennsylvania, Ohio, and Michigan. Products include pipes, storage tanks, processing equipment, restaurant equipment, automotive trim, catalytic converters, kitchen sinks, and flatware. **NOTE:** Mail employment correspondence to: Westpointe Corporate Center One, P.O. Box 1425, Coraopolis PA 15108-6934.

JLG INDUSTRIES, INC.
One JLG Drive, McConnellsburg PA 17233. 717/485-5161. **Fax:** 717/485-6466. **Recorded jobline:** 717/485-6684. **Contact:** Corporate Employment Manager. **World Wide Web address:** http://www.jlg.com. **Description:** A leading manufacturer, distributor, and international marketer of mobile work platforms. Founded in 1969. **NOTE:** Entry-level positions are offered. **Positions advertised include:** Application Analyst; Design Engineer. **Special programs:** Internships; Apprenticeships; Co-ops. **Office hours:** Monday - Friday, 8:00 a.m. - 4:45 p.m. **Corporate headquarters location:** This location. **Other U.S. locations:** Bedford PA. **International locations:** Australia; Scotland. **Listed on:** New York Stock Exchange. **Stock exchange symbol:** JLG. **Number of employees at this location:** 1,840. **Number of employees worldwide:** 2,760.

JANNEY MONTGOMERY SCOTT INC. (JMS)
1801 Market Street, 9th Floor, Philadelphia PA 19103. 215/665-6000. **Toll-free phone:** 800/JAN-NEYS. **Fax:** 215/587-9623. **Contact:** Human Resources. **E-mail address:** careers@jmsonline.com. **World Wide Web address:** http://www.janneys.com. **Description:** A full-service brokerage firm with over 60 branch offices. **Positions advertised include:** Receptionist; Mutual Funds Clerk; New Accounts Clerk; Sales Assistant. **Corporate headquarters location:** This location. **Parent company:** Penn Mutual Life Insurance Company. **Operations at this facility include:** Sales.

JCPENNEY INC.
Oxford Valley Mall, 2300 East Lincoln Highway, Langhorne PA 19047. 215/752-5300. **Contact:** Corporate Human Resources. **E-mail address:** apply@jcpenney.com. **World Wide Web address:** http://www.jcpenney.net. **Description:** J.C. Penney operates over 1,250 stores. Most stores carry extensive lines of women's, men's, and children's apparel, as well as cosmetics, jewelry, and home furnishings. Founded in 1913. **NOTE:** Mail resumes to: J.C. Penney Inc., Human Resources Department, BA/SF, P.O. Box 10001, Dallas TX 75301-8115. **Corporate headquarters location:** Dallas TX. **Other U.S. locations:** Nationwide. **International locations:** Chile; Mexico; Puerto Rico. **Operations at this facility include:** This location is the district office. **Listed on:** New York Stock Exchange. **Stock exchange symbol:** JCP. **Annual sales/revenues:** More than $100 million.

JEFFERSON HOSPITAL
565 Coal Valley Road, P.O. Box 18199, Pittsburgh PA 15236-0119. 412/469-5000. **Fax:** 412/469-5918. **Contact:** Personnel. **E-mail address:** resumes@jeffersonregional.com. **World Wide Web address:** http://www.shhspgh.org. **Description:** A 360-bed hospital. **Parent company:** South Hills Health System. **Positions advertised include:** Anesthesia Technician; Clinical Technician; Corporate Communications Specialist; Department Assistant; Dispatcher; File Associate; Food Service Worker; Laundry Associate; Medic; OR Technician.

THOMAS JEFFERSON UNIVERSITY
201 South 11th Street, The Martin Building, Philadelphia PA 19107. 215/955-6000. **Fax:** 215/503-2183. **Contact:** Office of Employee Selection & Placement. **Recorded jobline:** 215/503-8313. **World Wide Web address:** http://www.tju.edu. **Description:** An academic medical university. Thomas Jefferson University includes one of the largest private medical schools in the United States, a hospital, and graduate programs in the biomedical sciences. **Positions advertised include:** Administrator; Associate Registrar; Continuing Medical Education Specialist; Grants Administrator; Grants and Contracts Specialist; Insurance Administrator; Merchandise Buyer/Coordinator; Technology Licensing Specialist.

JENNERSVILLE REGIONAL HOSPITAL
1015 West Baltimore Pike, West Grove PA 19390. 610/869-1121. **Fax:** 610/869-1246. **Recorded jobline:** 610/869-1200. **Contact:** Employment Coordinator. **World Wide Web address:** http://www.jennersville.com. **Description:** A 75-bed, nonprofit acute care medical center that offers a surgery/ER center, an intensive care unit, and maternity and outpatient services. The hospital also operates Jenner's Pond, an independent and assisted living retirement community. Founded in 1920. **NOTE:** Entry-level positions, part-time jobs, and second and third shifts are offered. **Special programs:** Summer Jobs. **Number of employees at this location:** 600.

JOHNSON MATTHEY INC.
456 Devon Park Drive, Suite 600, Wayne PA 19087. 610/971-3000. **Fax:** 610/971-3022. **Contact:** Human Resources. **World Wide Web address:** http://www.matthey.com. **Description:** Manufactures automotive catalytic systems. **NOTE:** Entry-level positions and second and third shifts are offered. **Special programs:** Summer Jobs. **Corporate headquarters location:** London UK.

EDWARD JONES
2550 Mosside Boulevard, Suite 104, Monroeville PA 15146. 412/372-3511. **Contact:** Human Resources. **World Wide Web address:** http://www.edwardjones.com. **Description:** A securities brokerage firm.

JONES APPAREL GROUP, INC.
180 Rittenhouse Circle, Bristol PA 19007. 215/785-4000. **Fax:** 215/826-8902. **Contact:** Human Resources Director. **E-mail address:** jobs@jiny.com. **World Wide Web address:** http://www.jny.com. **Description:** Designs, manufactures, and markets a broad range of women's sportswear, suits, and dresses. Jones Apparel Group markets its products under the brand names Jones New York, Jones*Wear, Saville, Rena Rowan for Saville, Evan-Picone, Ellen Kaye, and under the licensed name Christian Dior. The company also has licenses for the Jones New York brand name and for the Evan-Picone brand name with selected manufacturers of related apparel and accessories such as women's rainwear, coats, footwear, intimate apparel, hosiery, handbags, belts, men's tailored clothing, and eyewear. **NOTE:** See the website for a current listing of open positions with detailed application information. **Positions advertised include:** Programmer/Analyst; Customs Compliance Manager; PC/LAN Support Specialist; Senior Accountant; Corporate Customs Relations Manager; Network Technician; Systems Engineer; Quality Technician; Retail Lease Analyst; Accounting Assistant. **Corporate headquarters location:** This location. **Other U.S. locations:** Los Angeles CA; Atlanta GA; Chicago IL; New York NY; Lawrenceburg TN; Dallas TX; Seattle WA. **International locations:** Ciudad Juarez, Mexico; Kowloon, Hong Kong; Toronto, Canada. **Operations at this facility include:** Administration; Research and Development; Service. **Listed on:** New York Stock Exchange. **Stock exchange symbol:** JNY. **Number of employees at this location:** 1,000. **Number of employees nationwide:** 2,000.

JONES DAY REAVIS & POGUE
One Mellon Center, 31st Floor, 500 Grant Street, Pittsburgh PA 15219. 412/391-3939. **Fax:** 412/394-7959. **Contact:** Human Resources. **World Wide Web address:** http://www.jonesday.com. **Description:** Jones Day Reavis & Pogue is an international law firm with specialists in all areas. **Corporate headquarters location:** Cleveland OH. **International locations:** China; France; Germany; India; Japan; Switzerland. **Operations at this facility include:** This location specializes in almost all types of law except personal injury and divorce.

JOSTENS PRINTING & PUBLISHING
401 Science Park Road, State College PA 16803. 814/237-5771. **Contact:** Human Resources. **World Wide Web address:** http://www.jostens.com. **Description:** Jostens produces recognition products and educational software through the following business segments: School Products, Recognition, and Jostens Learning. The School Products segment is comprised of five businesses: Printing and Publishing, Jewelry, Graduation Products, U.S. Photography, and Jostens Canada. School Products include yearbooks, commercial printing, desktop publishing curriculum kits, class rings, graduation accessories, diplomas, trophies, plaques and other awards, school pictures, group photographs for youth camps and organizations, and senior graduation portraits. This segment serves schools, colleges, and alumni associations in the United States and Canada through 1,100 independent sales representatives. Jostens Learning serves more than 4 million students in 10,000 schools nationwide. Jostens Learning's 100-person sales force focuses on the K-12 market. **Corporate headquarters location:** Minneapolis MN.

JOY MINING MACHINERY
120 Liberty Street, Franklin PA 16323. 814/437-5731. **Fax:** 814/432-1628. **Contact:** Human Resources. **World Wide Web address:** http://www.joy.com. **Description:** Manufactures capital equipment for coal mining, oil and gas wells, air pollution control, air compression, ore processing, minerals and metals mining, and various other industries. Products are manufactured in more than 30 plants and are distributed worldwide.

JUNIATA COLLEGE
1700 Moore Street, Huntingdon PA 16652. 814/641-3195. **Fax:** 814/641-3199. **Contact:** Gail Ulrich, Director of Human Resources. **E-mail address:** ulrichg@juniata.edu. **World Wide Web address:** http://www.juniata.edu. **Description:** A four-year college offering B.A. and B.S. degrees. Juniata's enrollment is approximately 1,100 students.

KBA-MOTTER CORPORATION
P.O. Box 12015, York PA 17402-0615. 717/755-1071. **Contact:** Gerrit Zwergel, Personnel Administrator. **Description:** Produces high-speed, web-fed rotogravure presses and related equipment. **Corporate headquarters location:** This location. **Parent company:** Koening & Bauer-Albert. **Number of employees at this location:** 135.

KDKA CHANNEL 2
One Gateway Center, Pittsburgh PA 15222. 412/575-2200. **Contact:** Human Resources. **World Wide Web address:** http://www.kdka.com. **Description:** A CBS-affiliated television station.

KLB MANAGEMENT
dba McDONALD'S
P.O. Box 859, Erie PA 16512-0859. 814/454-3933. **Physical address:** 401 Peach Street, Erie PA 16507. **Contact:** Human Resources. **World Wide Web address:** http://www.mcdonalds.com. **Description:** A management company for several area McDonald's fast food franchises.

KPMG
1600 Market Street, 12th Floor, Philadelphia PA 19103. 215/299-3100. **Contact:** Human Resources. **World Wide Web address:** http://www.kpmg.com. **Description:** KPMG delivers a wide range of value-added assurance, tax, and consulting services. **Corporate headquarters location:** Montvale NJ. **Other U.S. locations:** Nationwide. **International locations:** Worldwide. **Parent company:** KPMG International is a leader among professional services firms engaged in capturing, managing, assessing, and delivering information to create knowledge that will help its clients maximize shareholder value. **Listed on:** NASDAQ. **Stock exchange symbol:** KCIN. **Number of employees worldwide:** 85,000.

KPMG
One Mellon Center, 25th Floor, Pittsburgh PA 15219. 412/391-9710. **Contact:** Personnel. **World Wide Web address:** http://www.kpmg.com. **Description:** Delivers a wide range of value-added assurance, tax, and consulting services. **Corporate headquarters location:** Montvale NJ. **Parent company:** KPMG International has more than 85,000 employees worldwide including 6,500 partners and 60,000 professional staff, serving clients in 844 cities in 155 countries. KPMG International is a leader among professional services firms engaged in capturing, managing, assessing, and delivering information to create knowledge that will help its clients maximize shareholder value. **Operations at this facility include:** Accounting services for KPMG. **Listed on:** NASDAQ. **Stock exchange symbol:** KCIN.

KANE COMMUNITY HOSPITAL
4372 Route 6, Kane PA 16735. 814/837-4725. **Fax:** 814/837-8139. **Contact:** Director of Employee Services. **E-mail address:** lcole@kanehospital.org. **World Wide Web address:** http://www.kanehosp.com. **Description:** A 53-bed hospital. **Positions advertised include:** Medical Technologist; Physical Therapist; Radiologic Technician; Registered Nurse.

KAWNEER COMPANY, INC.
500 East 12th Street, Bloomsburg PA 17815. 570/784-8000. **Toll-free phone:** 877/505-3756. **Fax:** 570/389-6238. **Contact:** Human Resources. **World Wide Web address:** http://www.kawneer.com. **Description:** Kawneer Company manufactures and markets fabricated products including nonresidential architectural building products such as storefronts, building entrances, facings, window framing, and curtain wall systems. **Other U.S. locations:** Springdale AR; Visalia CA; Jonesboro GA; Franklin IN. **Operations at this facility include:** This location manufactures aluminum doors and windows. **Parent company:** ALCOA. **Operations at this facility include:** Manufacturing. **Listed on:** New York Stock Exchange. **Stock exchange symbol:** AA. **Number of employees at this location:** 485. **Number of employees worldwide:** 14,000.

KEANE, INC.
460 Norristown Road, Suite 200, Blue Bell PA 19422. 610/260-0640. **Contact:** Human Resources. **E-mail address:** careers@keane.com. **World Wide Web address:** http://www.keane.com. **Description:** Offers businesses a variety of computer consulting services. Keane also develops, markets, and manages software for its clients and assists in project management. **Positions advertised include:** Systems Administrator; Technical Support Analysis; Management Consultant; Project Manager. **Corporate headquarters location:** Boston MA. **Listed on:** American Stock Exchange. **Stock exchange symbol:** KEA.

KEATING BUILDING CORPORATION
The Phoenix, Suite 300, 1600 Arch Street, Philadelphia PA 19103-2028. 610/668-4100. **Fax:** 610/660-4950. **Contact:** Career Coordinator. **E-mail address:** careers@keatingnet.com. **World Wide Web address:** http://www.keatingweb.com. **Description:** A general construction firm that specializes in development, emissions, construction, and housing programs. **NOTE:** Entry-level positions are offered. **Special programs:** Internships. **Corporate headquarters location:** This location. **Other U.S. locations:** CT; FL; NJ; OH. **Operations at this facility include:** Administration. **Annual sales/revenues:** More than $100 million. **Number of employees at this location:** 100. **Number of employees nationwide:** 175.

KENNAMETAL INC.
P.O. Box 231, 1600 Technology Way, Latrobe PA 15650-0231. 724/539-5000. **Fax:** 724/539-6657. **Contact:** Human Resources. **World Wide Web address:** http://www.kennametal.com. **Description:** As part of the Mining and Construction Division, this location manufactures wear-resistant parts through a metallurgical powder technology. Overall, Kennametal manufactures, purchases, and distributes a broad range of tools, tooling systems, supplies, and services for the metalworking, mining, and highway construction industries. The company's metal-cutting tools are made of cemented carbides, ceramics, and other hard materials. Kennametal manufactures a complete line of tool holders and tool holding systems by machining and fabricating steel bars and other metal alloys. The company's mining and construction cutting tools are tipped with cemented carbide and are used for underground coal mining and highway construction, repair, and maintenance. Metallurgical products consist of powders made from ore concentrates, compounds, and secondary materials. **Positions advertised include:** Manufacturing Associate; Analyst; Buyer; Mechanical Technician; Insides Sales Representative. **Corporate headquarters location:** This location. **Other U.S. locations:** Troy MI; Henderson NC; Roanoke Rapids NC; Fallon NV; Orwell OH; Solon OH; Bedford PA; Johnson City TN; New Market VA. **International locations:** Canada; China; England; Germany; the Netherlands. **Subsidiaries include:** Greenfield Industries, Inc.; JLK Direct Distribution Inc.; Kennametal Asia Pacific; Kennametal Hertel AG; Metalworking North America. **Listed on:** New York Stock Exchange. **Stock exchange symbol:** KMT. **President/CEO:** Robert McGeehan. **Number of employees worldwide:** 13,500.

KENNAMETAL INC.
442 Chalybeate Road, Bedford PA 15522-0161. 814/623-2711. **Contact:** Barry Novotny, Human Resources. **World Wide Web address:** http://www.kennametal.com. **Description:** Kennametal manufactures, purchases, and distributes a broad range of tools, tooling systems, supplies, and services for the metalworking, mining, and highway construction industries. Kennametal specializes in developing and manufacturing metal-cutting tools and wear-resistant parts using a specialized type of powder metallurgy. The company's metal-cutting tools are made of cemented carbides, ceramics, and other hard materials. Kennametal manufactures a complete line of tool holders and tool holding systems by machining and fabricating steel bars and other metal alloys. The company's mining and construction cutting tools are tipped with cemented carbide and are used for underground coal mining and highway construction, repair, and maintenance. Metallurgical products consist of powders made from ore concentrates, compounds, and secondary materials. **Corporate headquarters location:** Latrobe PA. **Other U.S. locations:** Troy MI; Henderson NC; Roanoke Rapids NC; Fallon NV; Orwell OH; Solon OH; Johnson City TN; New Market VA. **International locations:** Canada; China; England; Germany; the Netherlands. **Operations at this facility include:** This location manufactures cutting teeth. **Listed on:** New York Stock Exchange. **Stock exchange symbol:** KMT. **Number of employees worldwide:** 13,500.

KENNYWOOD PARK
4800 Kennywood Boulevard, West Mifflin PA 15122. 412/461-0500. **Fax:** 412/464-0719. **Contact:** Personnel. **World Wide Web address:** http://www.kennywood.com. **Description:** A family amusement park, consisting of rides, games, food, and other entertainment and concessions. **NOTE:** See website for seasonal employment schedule.

KERR GROUP, INC.
500 New Holland Avenue, Lancaster PA 17602. 717/299-6511. **Contact:** Human Resources. **World Wide Web address:** http://www.kerrgroup.com. **Description:** Manufactures plastic containers, closures, and vials for the pharmaceutical and food and beverage industries.

KETCHUM
6 PPG Place, Pittsburgh PA 15222. 412/456-3500. **Contact:** Mary Lou Finn, Human Resources Relationship Manager. **E-mail address:** pit.resume@ketchum.com. **World Wide Web address:** http://www.ketchum.com. **Description:** A public relations and advertising agency that specializes in directory advertising. **Positions advertised include:** Intern, Brand Marketing; Account Coordinator; Account Executive. **Other U.S. locations:** Nationwide. **International locations:** Worldwide.

KEYSTONE AREA COUNCIL OF THE BOY SCOUTS OF AMERICA
One Baden-Powell Lane, P.O. Box 389, Mechanicsburg PA 17055. 717/766-1591. **Fax:** 717/795-8721. **Contact:** Human Resources. **World Wide Web address:** http://www.keystonebsa.org. **Description:** The national scouting organization for young adults. The Boy Scouts of America has 340 local councils nationwide. **Corporate headquarters location:** Irving TX.

KEYSTONE COMPUTER ASSOCIATES
1055 Virginia Drive, Fort Washington PA 19034. 215/643-3800. **Fax:** 215/643-0115. **Contact:** Human Resources. **World Wide Web address:** http://www.keystoneca.com. **Description:** A computer consulting firm. **Positions advertised include:** IT Management; Project Management.

KEYSTONE NAZARETH BANK AND TRUST
P.O. Box 25012, Lehigh Valley PA18002-5012. 610/861-5000. **Physical address:** 90 Highland Avenue, Bethlehem PA 18017. **Contact:** Human Resources. **E-mail address:** hr@knbt.com. **World Wide Web address:** http://www.knbt.com. **Description:** A community bank providing full financial services through 41 local branches. **Positions advertised include:** AS400 Systems Administrator; Builder Relationship Manager; Online Assistant Manager; Sales Associate; Senior Auditor; Service Associates. **Corporate headquarters location:** This location. **Parent company:** KNBT Bancorp, Inc.

KEYSTONE REHABILITATION SYSTEMS
665 Philadelphia Street, Indiana PA 15701. 724/465-3213. **Contact:** Human Resources. **World Wide Web address:** http://www.keystonerehab.com. **Description:** A leading provider of rehabilitation therapy in western Pennsylvania, offering services at outpatient rehabilitation clinics to patients with physical disabilities. **NOTE:** See http://www.benchmarkmed.com for employment information. **Positions advertised include:** Physical Therapist. **Parent company:** Benchmark Medical. **Operations at this facility include:** Administration.

L. ROBERT KIMBALL & ASSOCIATES, INC.
615 West Highland Avenue, P.O. Box 1000, Ebensburg PA 15931. 814/472-7700 ext. 409. **Fax:** 814/472-7712. **Contact:** Deborah Locke, Corporate Recruiter. **E-mail address:** hmnres@lrkimball.com. **World Wide Web address:** http://www.lrkimball.com. **Description:** A national, full-service consulting firm specializing in engineering, architecture, mapping sciences, and environmental services. **NOTE:** Entry-level positions are offered. **Positions advertised include:** Structural Engineer; Mechanical Engineer; Business Development Specialist; Secretary; Assistant Manager of Construction Services; Transportation Project Manager. **Special programs:** Training. **Corporate headquarters location:** This location. **Other area locations:** Harrisburg PA; Philadelphia PA; Pittsburgh PA; State College PA. **Other U.S. locations:** Raleigh NC; Cranford NJ; Syracuse NY; Richmond VA. **Operations at this facility include:** Administration; Sales. **Annual sales/revenues:** $21 - $50 million. **Number of employees at this location:** 350. **Number of employees nationwide:** 500.

KING FIFTH WHEEL COMPANY
701 Crestwood Drive, P.O. Box 68, Mountaintop PA 18707. 570/474-6371. **Fax:** 570/474-9901. **Contact:** Human Resources Manager. **E-mail address:** info@sateckfw.com. **World Wide Web address:** http://www.k5w.com. **Description:** Manufactures flash welded rings and machined components for aerospace engines. **Other area locations:** Wilkes-Barre PA. **Other U.S. locations:** Agawam MA; Asheville NC; Laconia NH. **International locations:** Birmingham, England; Ontario, Canada.

KLEINERT'S INC.
120 West Germantown Pike, Suite 100, Plymouth Meeting PA 19462. 610/828-7261. **Fax:** 610/828-4589. **Contact:** Denise Hale, Vice President of Human Resources. **Description:** Manufactures children's sportswear and sleepwear. The company is also engaged in knitting polyester, cotton/polyester blends, and acrylic fabrics for a variety of uses. Founded in 1869. **Corporate headquarters location:** This location. **Other U.S. locations:** Elba AL; Wilmington DE; Gastonia NC; New York NY. **International locations:** San Pedro Sula, Honduras. **Operations at this facility include:** Administration. **President/CEO:** Jack Brier. **Number of employees at this location:** 10. **Number of employees worldwide:** 1,000.

KLING LINDQUIST
2301 Chestnut Street, Philadelphia PA 19103. 215/569-2900. **Fax:** 215/569-5963. **Contact:** Sydney Koerner, Human Resources Director. **E-mail address:** employment@tklp.com. **World Wide Web address:** http://www.tklp.com. **Description:** Provides architectural, engineering, and interior design services. Founded in 1946. **NOTE:** Entry-level positions are offered. **Positions advertised include:** Senior Projects Control Engineer; Junior Projects Control Engineer. **Special programs:** Internships; Training; Co-ops; Summer Jobs. **Office hours:** Monday - Friday, 8:30 a.m. - 5:30 p.m. **Corporate headquarters location:** This location. **Other U.S. locations:** Washington DC; Fort Meade MD. **CEO:** Mel Sotnick. **Annual sales/revenues:** $21 - $50 million. **Number of employees at this location:** 350. **Number of employees nationwide:** 400.

KNOX McLAUGHLIN GORNALL & SENNETT
120 West 10th Street, Erie PA 16501-1461. 814/459-2800. **Fax:** 814/453-4530. **Contact:** Tammy Hagerty, Director of Administration. **E-mail address:** thagerty@kmgslaw.com. **World Wide Web address:** http://www.kmgslaw.com. **Description:** A law firm specializing in business and corporate law. **NOTE:** Attorneys and Summer clerks are recruited by Mark Wassell, mwassell@kmgslaw.com.

KOA SPEER ELECTRONICS INC.
Bolivar Drive, P.O. Box 547, Bradford PA 16701. 814/362-5536. **Fax:** 814/362-8883. **Contact:** Human Resources. **World Wide Web address:** http://www.koaspeer.com. **Description:** Manufactures electronic resistors. **NOTE:** Koa Speer Electronics hires through the Pennsylvania State Employment Office. **Operations at this facility include:** Administration; Warehouse/Distribution.

KOEHLER-BRIGHT STAR, INC.
380 Stewart Road, Wilkes-Barre PA 18706. 570/825-1900. **Fax:** 570/825-1984. **Contact:** Patti Leonard, Human Resources Manager. **World Wide Web address:** http://www.flashlight.com. **Description:** Manufactures and distributes industrial batteries, dry cell batteries, and other related lighting products. **Corporate headquarters location:** This location. **Other U.S. locations:** Passaic NJ; Paterson NJ.

KRAEMER TEXTILES, INC.
240 South Main Street, P.O. Box 72, Nazareth PA 18064. 610/759-4030. **Contact:** Employment. **Description:** Manufactures spun yarns for the apparel, home furnishings, and crafts markets. **Corporate headquarters location:** This location.

KREISHER & GREGOROWICZ
401 Market Street, Bloomsburg PA 17815. 570/784-5211. **Fax:** 570/387-1477. **Contact:** Human Resources. **E-mail address:** info@columbiacountylaw.com. **World Wide Web address:** http://www.columbiacountylaw.com. **Description:** A small, local law firm that provides services in a wide range of practice areas.

KULICKE & SOFFA INDUSTRIES, INC. (K&S)
2101 Blair Mill Road, Willow Grove PA 19090. 215/784-6000. **Toll-free phone:** 800/523-1321. **Fax:** 215/659-7588. **Contact:** Human Resources. **E-mail address:** hr@kns.com. **World Wide Web address:** http://www.kns.com. **Description:** A leader in semiconductor assembly systems and services. The company designs, manufactures, markets, and supports equipment for IC and MCM/hybrid semiconductor manufacturers worldwide. Kulicke & Soffa Industries, Inc.'s product lines include wafer and hard materials dicing, die bonding and wire bonding equipment, service and spare parts, and the Micro-Swiss line of bonding and dicing tools and production accessories. With sales and service operations in 15 countries, K&S is one of the largest suppliers of semiconductor assembly equipment in the world, as well as one of the world's largest suppliers of automatic wire bonders. Founded in 1951. **Positions advertised include:** Technical Staff; Senior Process Engineer; Advanced Mechanical Engineer; Technical Support Systems Specialist. **Corporate headquarters location:** This location. **Other U.S. locations:** Santa Clara CA. **International locations:** Worldwide. **Operations at this facility include:** Administration; Manufacturing; Research and Development; Sales; Service. **Listed on:** NASDAQ. **Stock exchange symbol:** KLIC. **Annual sales/revenues:** More than $100 million. **Number of employees at this location:** 900. **Number of employees worldwide:** 2,400.

KURTZ BROTHERS INC.
400 Reed Street, P.O. Box 392, Clearfield PA 16830-0392. **Toll-free phone:** 800/252-3811. **Fax:** 814/765-8690. **Contact:** Human Resources. **World Wide Web address:** http://www.kurtzbros.com. **Description:** A paper converter and school supply distributor.

KUTZTOWN UNIVERSITY
P.O. Box 730, Kutztown PA 19530-0730. 610/683-1353. **Physical address:** Personnel Office, Stratton Administration Center, Room 109, Kutztown PA 19530. **Fax:** 610/683-4641. **Contact:** Personnel Department. **World Wide Web address:** http://www.kutztown.edu. **Description:** A four-year university offering bachelor's and master's degrees including MBAs. Approximately 9,000 undergraduate and 800 graduate students attend Kutztown University.

LWB REFRACTORIES
P.O. Box 1189, York PA 17405. 717/848-1501. **Contact:** Human Resources Manager. **World Wide Web address:** http://www.bakerref.com. **Description:** Produces refractory products consisting of such substances as dolomite and agricultural limestone. **Corporate headquarters location:** This location.

LA ROCHE COLLEGE
9000 Babcock Boulevard, Pittsburgh PA 15237. 412/536-1115. **Fax:** 412/536-1048. **Contact:** George Zaffuto, Human Resources Department. **E-mail address:** zaffutg1@laroche.edu. **World Wide Web address:** http://www.laroche.edu. **Description:** A four-year college offering B.A., B.S., and master's degree programs. La Roche College has an enrollment of approximately 1,500 undergraduates and 340 graduate students.

LA SALLE UNIVERSITY
1900 West Olney Avenue, Philadelphia PA 19141. 215/951-1013. **Contact:** Human Resources. **World Wide Web address:** http://www.lasalle.edu. **Description:** A four-year university offering bachelor's and master's degrees including MBAs. Approximately 3,600 undergraduate and 900 graduate students attend La Salle University.

LACKAWANNA COLLEGE
501 Vine Street, Scranton PA 18509. 570/961-7841. **Contact:** Personnel Office. **World Wide Web address:** http://www.lackawanna.edu. **Description:** A college offering associate degrees.

LAFRANCE CORPORATION
One LaFrance Way, Concordville PA 19331. 610/361-4300. **Fax:** 610/361-4301. **Contact:** Personnel. **World Wide Web address:** http://www.lafrancecorp.com. **Description:** A manufacturer of three-dimensional nameplates for product identification.

LANCASTER AERO REFINISHERS
311 Airport Drive, Smoketown PA 17576. 877/574-5422. **Fax:** 877/574-5422. **Contact:** Human Resources. **E-mail address:** lanaero@aol.com. **World Wide Web address:** http://www.lancasteraero.com. **Description:** Engaged in the repair and service of aircraft parts and engines.

LANCASTER NEWSPAPERS, INC.
P.O. Box 1328, Lancaster PA 17608-1328. 717/291-8681. **Physical address:** 8 West King Street, Lancaster PA 17608. **Fax:** 717/293-4311. **Contact:** Human Resources. **E-mail address:** humanresources@lnpnews.com. **World Wide Web address:** http://www.lancnews.com. **Description:** Publishes the morning *Intelligencer Journal*, the evening *Lancaster New Era*, and the *Sunday News*, with a combined daily circulation of over 100,000. Founded in 1794. **NOTE:** Entry-level positions and second and third shifts are offered. **Special programs:** Internships. **Internship information:** Lancaster Newspapers offers internships in journalism and marketing/advertising. Please apply by March 1 for a 13-week summer internship. **Corporate headquarters location:** This location. **Listed on:** Privately held. **Annual sales/revenues:** $51 - $100 million. **Number of employees at this location:** 1,000.

LANKENAU HOSPITAL
100 Lancaster Avenue, Wynnewood PA 19096. 610/645-2000. **Fax:** 610/645-8492. **Contact:** Personnel. **World Wide Web address:** http://www.mainlinehealth.org/lh. **Description:** A hospital. **Parent company:** Mainline Health. **Positions advertised include:** Administrative Coordinator; Charge Pharmacist; Clinical Dietician; Clinical Leader; Site Manager; Social Worker; Pharmacy Supervisor; Certified Registered Nurse; Licensed Practical Nurse; Coding Specialist; Information Clerk.

LASKO PRODUCTS, INC.
820 Lincoln Avenue, West Chester PA 19380. 610/692-7400. **Contact:** Human Resources. **E-mail address:** hr@laskoproducts.com. **World Wide Web address:** http://www.laskoproducts.com. **Description:** Manufactures consumer and industrial fans as well as other home comfort appliances. **Positions advertised include:** Data Processing Clerk; Credit/Collections Manager; Accounts Receivable Specialist.

LAW OFFICES OF HERBERT S. WOLFSON
Lewis Tower, Suite 701, 225 South Fifteenth Street, Philadelphia PA 19102. 215/545-5428. **Fax:** 215/545-5429. **Contact:** Recruiting. **World Wide Web address:** http://www.abudhabilaw.com. **Description:** A law firm offering a wide range of services to clients doing business in the Middle East. The firm is operated in association with a network of lawyers in a variety of other Middle Eastern countries. **International locations:** Dubai.

LAW OFFICE OF T.M. PEELER
350 South River Road, Suite D4, New Hope PA 18938. 215/575-1108. **Fax:** 215/862-1274. **Contact:** Ms. Theresa Parker. **E-mail address:** tmpjd@home.com. **Description:** A law firm that provides service in a range of practice areas.

LEAR CORPORATION
50 Spring Road, P.O. Box 40, Carlisle PA 17013. 717/249-1866. **Contact:** Rich Zeff, Vice President of Human Resources. **World Wide Web address:** http://www.lear.com. **Description:** A leading designer and manufacturer of automotive interior systems and components including floor systems, acoustic systems, soft-surface interior and luggage compartment trim components, and dash insulators for the global automotive market. **NOTE:** Online application is encouraged. Unsolicited resumes are not accepted, and resumes cannot be submitted via fax. **Special programs:** Co-op Internship program. **Corporate headquarters location:** Southfield MI. **Other U.S. locations:** Nationwide. **International locations:** Worldwide. **Number of employees at this location:** 3,250.

LEBANON VALLEY FARMERS BANK
555 Willow Street, P.O. Box 1285, Lebanon PA 17042-1285. 717/274-6871. **Fax:** 717/274-6838. **Contact:** Human Resources. **World Wide Web address:** http://www.lvfb.com. **Description:** A full-service bank. **NOTE:** Hand delivery or mailing of resume is encouraged. **Special programs:** Internships. **Corporate headquarters location:** This location. **Parent company:** Fulton Financial Corporation. **Operations at this facility include:** Administration; Sales; Service. **Number of employees at this location:** 325.

LEE INDUSTRIES
P.O. Box 688, Philipsburg PA 16866. 814/342-0461. **Fax:** 814/342-5660. **Physical address:** 514 West Pine Street, Philipsburg PA. **Contact:** Sue Montler, Human Resources. **E-mail address:** lee@leeind.com. **World Wide Web address:** http://www.leeind.com. **Description:** A designer and fabricator of stainless steel processing equipment.

AL PAUL LEFTON COMPANY, INC.
100 Independence Mall West, Philadelphia PA 19106. 215/923-9600. **Fax:** 215/351-4297. **Contact:** Human Resources. **World Wide Web address:** http://www.lefton.com. **Description:** A full-service advertising and public relations firm. Founded in 1928. **Corporate headquarters location:** This location.

LEHIGH UNIVERSITY
428 Brodhead Avenue, Bethlehem PA 18015-1687. 610/758-3900. **Fax:** 610/758-6226. **Contact:** Human Resources. **E-mail address:** inhro@lehigh.edu. **World Wide Web address:** http://www.lehigh.edu. **Description:** A four-year university offering bachelor's, master's (including MBAs), and doctoral degrees. Approximately 4,400 undergraduate and 2,000 graduate students attend Lehigh University. **Corporate headquarters location:** This location. **Operations at this facility include:** Service.

LEHIGH VALLEY DAIRIES, L.P.
880 Allentown Road, Lansdale PA 19446. 215/855-8205. **Toll-free phone:** 800/937-3233. **Fax:** 215/393-3363. **Contact:** Diane Kett, Human Resources Manager. **Description:** A dairy products company. **Corporate headquarters location:** This location. **Other U.S. locations:** Schuylkill Haven PA. **Operations at this facility include:** Administration; Manufacturing; Sales. **President/CEO:** Robert Allen. **Number of employees at this location:** 350. **Number of employees nationwide:** 560.

LENOX COLLECTION
900 Wheeler Way, Langhorne PA 19047. 215/741-7670. **Fax:** 609/844-1554. **Contact:** Human Resources. **E-mail address:** hr@lenox.com. **World Wide Web address:** http://www.lenox.com. **Description:** Manufactures crystal goblets, wine glasses, and dinnerware.

KURT J. LESKER COMPANY
1515 Worthington Avenue, Clairton PA 15025. 412/233-4200. **Fax:** 412/233-4275. **Contact:** Human Resources. **World Wide Web address:** http://www.lesker.com. **Description:** A manufacturer of vacuum systems and components.

LEVLANE ADVERTISING/PR/INTERACTIVE
One Belmont Avenue, Bala-Cynwyd PA 19004. 610/667-7313. **Fax:** 610/667-3176. **Contact:** Human Resources. **World Wide Web address:** http://www.levlane.com. **Description:** An advertising agency and public relations firm. Founded in 1984. **NOTE:** Entry-level positions are offered. **Special programs:** Internships; Apprenticeships. **Office hours:** Monday - Friday, 9:00 a.m. - 5:30 p.m. **Corporate headquarters location:** This location. **Other U.S. locations:** Tampa FL. **Annual sales/revenues:** $21 - $50 million. **Number of employees at this location:** 40.

LEYBOLD VACUUM PRODUCTS, INC.
5700 Mellon Road, Export PA 15632-8900. 724/327-5700. **Fax:** 724/325-4585. **Contact:** Personnel. **E-mail address:** humanresources@leyboldvacuum.com. **World Wide Web address:** http://www.leyboldvacuum.com. **Description:** A manufacturer of vacuum pumps and pumping equipment. **NOTE:** Entry-level positions and second and third shifts are offered. **Special programs:** Internships; Training; Summer Jobs. **Office hours:** Monday - Friday, 8:00 a.m. - 4:45 p.m. **International locations:** Worldwide. **Listed on:** Privately held. **Annual sales/revenues:** $51 - $100 million. **Number of employees at this location:** 170. **Number of employees nationwide:** 230.

LIBERTY MUTUAL INSURANCE GROUP
15 Kings Grant Drive, Bala-Cynwyd PA 19004. 610/664-6380. **Toll-free phone:** 800/300-4472. **Fax:** 603/664-2134. **Contact:** Personnel. **World Wide Web address:** http://www.libertymutual.com. **Description:** A diversified financial services company

with $8.9 billion in consolidated revenue and more than $37 billion in consolidated assets. Liberty Mutual Insurance Group has been a leading provider of workers' compensation insurance, programs, and services for 60 years, and is one of the largest multi-line insurers in the property/casualty field. The company provides a wide array of products and services including commercial insurance, personal insurance, international services, individual life products, and group products. **NOTE:** Jobseekers should send resumes to: Liberty Mutual Insurance Group, Employment 01-D, 175 Berkeley Street, Boston MA 02116. **Positions advertised include:** Office Assistant; Senior Account Executive; Workers' Compensation Insurance Assistant; Service Director. **Corporate headquarters location:** Boston MA. **Operations at this facility include:** Divisional Headquarters.

LIBERTY MUTUAL INSURANCE GROUP
One North Shore Center, 12 Federal Street, Suite 310, Pittsburgh PA 15212. 412/231-1331. **Fax:** 603/422-9670. **Contact:** Human Resources. **World Wide Web address:** http://www.libertymutual.com. **Description:** A diversified financial services company with $8.9 billion in consolidated revenue and more than $37 billion in consolidated assets. Liberty Mutual Insurance Group has been a leading provider of workers' compensation insurance, programs, and services for 60 years, and is one of the largest multiline insurers in the property/casualty field. The company provides a wide array of products and services including commercial insurance, personal insurance, international services, individual life products, and group products. **NOTE:** Jobseekers should send resumes to: Liberty Mutual Insurance Group, Employment 01-D, 175 Berkeley Street, Boston MA 02116. **Positions advertised include:** Legal Secretary; Associate Underwriter; Senior Property Loss Specialist. **Corporate headquarters location:** Boston MA. **Operations at this facility include:** National Sales Office.

LIBERTY TRAVEL
1737 Chestnut Street, Philadelphia PA 19103. 215/972-0200. **Contact:** Human Resources. **World Wide Web address:** http://www.libertytravel.com. **Description:** A travel agency. **Other U.S. locations:** Nationwide.

LIMBACH COMPANY
4 Northshore Center, Pittsburgh PA 15212. 412/359-2100. **Fax:** 412/359-2389. **Contact:** Human Resources. **World Wide Web address:** http://www.smcco.org/limbach.htm. **Description:** Construction contractors specializing in plumbing, heating, and air conditioning. **Corporate headquarters location:** Columbus OH. **Parent company:** SMCCO.

LINCOLN NATIONAL CORPORATION (LNC)
dba LINCOLN FINANCIAL GROUP
Center Square, West Tower, 1500 Market Street, Suite 3900, Philadelphia PA 19102. 215/448-1400. **Contact:** Human Resources. **World Wide Web address:** http://www.lfg.com. **Description:** An insurance holding company with businesses that sell insurance and investment products. **Corporate headquarters location:** This location. **Subsidiaries include:** Delaware Investments (investment management services); First Penn-Pacific Life Insurance Company (life insurance); Lincoln National Life Insurance Company (individual life, annuities, and pensions); Lincoln Re (life and health reinsurance); Vantage Investment Advisors (investment management services).

LINK COMPUTER CORPORATION
Stadium Drive, Bellwood PA 16617. 814/742-7700. **Fax:** 814/742-7900. **Contact:** Karen Barr, Human Resources. **E-mail address:** kbarr@linkcorp.com. **World Wide Web address:** http://www.linkcorp.com. **Description:** Provides a wide range of information technology solutions including networking services, consulting, programming, Internet development, and systems analysis. Founded in 1980. **NOTE:** Entry-level positions are offered. **Positions advertised include:** Account Manager. **Special programs:** Internships; Co-ops; Summer Jobs. **Corporate headquarters location:** This location. **Other U.S. locations:** Pittsburgh PA. **Listed on:** Privately held. **Annual sales/revenues:** $21 - $50 million. **Number of employees at this location:** 80. **Number of employees nationwide:** 110.

LIPPINCOTT WILLIAMS & WILKINS
530 Walnut Street, Philadelphia PA 19106-3621. 215/521-8300. **Fax:** 215/521-8902. **Contact:** Human Resources. **World Wide Web address:** http://www.lww.com. **Description:** A global publisher of medical, nursing, and allied health information resources in book, journal, newsletter, loose-leaf, and electronic media formats. **NOTE:** Entry-level positions and part-time jobs are offered. **Special programs:** Internships; Co-ops; Summer Jobs. **Other U.S. locations:** Baltimore MD; Hagerstown MD; New York NY. **International locations:** Worldwide. **Parent company:** Wolters Kluwer. **Annual sales/revenues:** More than $100 million. **Number of employees at this location:** 400. **Number of employees nationwide:** 1,200. **Number of employees worldwide:** 6,000.

ARTHUR D. LITTLE, INC.
Noble Plaza, Suite 210, 801 Old York Road, Jenkintown PA 19046-1611. 215/576-8700. **Contact:** Human Resources. **E-mail address:** careers.mc@adlittle.com. **World Wide Web address:** http://www.arthurdlittle.com. **Description:** An employee-owned, international management and technology consulting firm. The company offers services in three areas: management consulting; technology and product development; and environmental, health, and safety consulting. Services include cost reduction, total quality management consulting, market assessments, logistics management, telecommunications management, auditing, safety programs, software development, and toxicology. Clients operate in a variety of industries including aerospace, automotive, telecommunications, electronics, and consumer products. Founded in 1886. **NOTE:** Mail resumes to: Human Resources, Acorn Park, Cambridge MA 02140-2390. 617/498-5000. **Positions advertised include:** Business Analyst; Consultant. **International locations:** Asia; Europe; Latin America; Middle East. **Number of employees worldwide:** 16,000.

LOCKHEED MARTIN AEROPARTS, INC.
221 Industrial Park Road, Johnstown PA 15904. 814/262-3000. **Fax:** 814/266-2957. **Contact:** Nikki Simpson, Human Resources. **E-mail address:** jobs.lmco@lmco.com. **World Wide Web address:** http://www.lmco.com. **Description:** This location manufactures machined aircraft parts. **Corporate headquarters location:** Bethesda MD. **Other U.S. locations:** Nationwide. **International locations:** Worldwide. **Parent company:** Lockheed Martin Corporation is a diversified defense contractor with interests in engineering contracting, civil space programs, government services, commercial electronics, aeronautical systems, avionics, aerodynamics, and materials. **Listed on:** New York Stock Exchange. **Stock exchange symbol:** LMT. **Number of employees at this location:** 100. **Number of employees nationwide:** 62,000.

LOCKHEED MARTIN NAVAL ELECTONICS & SURVEILLANCE SYSTEMS
459 Kennedy Drive, Archbald PA 18403. 570/803-2300. **Contact:** Human Resources Representative. **E-mail address:** jobs.lmco@lmco.com. **World Wide Web address:** http://www.lmco.com. **Description:** Manufactures instrumentation and controls for the U.S. Nuclear Reactor Program; fusing and sensor systems; expendable jammers; live-fire training missiles and rounds; and a complete line of thickness gages for the production of steel and aluminum worldwide. Overall, Lockheed Martin is an aerospace and technology company engaged in the design, manufacture, and management of systems and products in the fields of space, defense, electronics, communications, information management, energy, and materials. **Listed on:** New York Stock Exchange. **Stock exchange symbol:** LMT.

LOGI-TECH INC.
P.O Box 603, Monroeville PA 15146. 724/337-0407. **Contact:** Joe Perhac, Human Resources. **Description:** Provides sales, service, and repairs of mining and related equipment.

LONGWOOD GARDENS INC.
Route 1, P.O. Box 501, Kennett Square PA 19348-0501. 610/388-1000. **Fax:** 610/388-2079. **Contact:** Administrative Services. **E-mail address:** jobs@longwoodgardens.org. **World Wide Web address:** http://www.longwoodgardens.org. **Description:** A horticultural display garden. Longwood Gardens also offers a restaurant and meeting facilities. **Positions advertised include:** CAD/GIS Systems Coordinator; Librarian; Outdoor Display Gardener; Performing Arts Coordinator; Research and Production Division Leader; Continuing Education Secretary.

LORD CORPORATION
1635 West 12th Street, P.O. Box 10039, Erie PA 16514-0039. 814/456-8511. **Fax:** 814/454-7445. **Contact:** Personnel. **World Wide Web address:** http://www.lordcorp.com. **Description:** Lord Corporation is a worldwide designer, manufacturer, and marketer of products that control mechanical motion and noise. Products directed at the aerospace industry include APU, engine, and electronic equipment mountings; torque struts; lead lay dampers; spindle bearings; and aircraft quieting systems. **NOTE:** Interested jobseekers should direct resumes to their specific division of interest. Call this location for specific manager names. **Corporate headquarters location:** Cary NC. **Other U.S. locations:** Nationwide. **International locations:** Brazil; England; Japan; Korea; Mexico. **Operations at this facility include:** This location houses its own Chemical and Mechanical Products Divisions. The Chemical Division is engaged in producing adhesives and coatings. The Mechanical Division is engaged in shock and vibration research, and has an aerospace subdivision. **Number of employees at this location:** 500. **Number of employees nationwide:** 2,500.

LOWE'S HOME CENTERS, INC.
249 Lowes Boulevard, State College PA 16803. 814/237-2100. **Contact:** Human Resources. **World Wide Web address:** http://www.lowes.com. **Description:** A discount retail store selling consumer durables, building supplies, and home products for the do-it-yourself and home improvement markets. Overall, the company conducts operations through 311 retail stores in 20 states, mostly in south central and southeastern United States. Products sold include tools; lumber; building materials; heating, cooling, and water systems; and specialty goods. **NOTE:** See website for a list of current openings with detailed application information.

LUGARU SOFTWARE, LTD.
1645 Shady Avenue, Pittsburgh PA 15217. 412/421-5911. **Fax:** 412/421-6371. **Contact:** Human Resources. **World Wide Web address:** http://www.lugaru.com. **Description:** Manufactures an EMACS-style programmer's text editor for Windows, DOS, and OS/2 called Epsilon Programmer's Editor. **Corporate headquarters location:** This location.

LUZERNE OPTICAL LABORATORIES, INC.
180 North Wilkes-Barre Boulevard, P.O. Box 998, Wilkes-Barre PA 18703-0998. 570/822-3183. **Toll-free phone:** 800/233-9637. **Fax:** 800/525-5597. **Contact:** Lorraine Dougherty, Human Resources Representative. **E-mail address:** vision@luzerneoptical.com. **World Wide Web address:** http://www.luzerneoptical.com. **Description:** Manufactures optical products including eyeglasses and contact lenses. Founded in 1973. **NOTE:** Entry-level positions and second and third shifts are offered. **Company slogan:** With an eye on service and quality. **Office hours:** Monday - Friday, 7:00 a.m. - 6:30 p.m. **Corporate headquarters location:** This location. **President:** John Dougherty. **Annual sales/revenues:** $11 - $20 million. **Number of employees at this location:** 110.

LYON METAL PRODUCTS
524 B Imperial Court, Bensalem PA 19020. 215/244-7930. **Fax:** 630/264-4548. **Contact:** Human Resources. **World Wide Web address:** http://www.lyonmetal.com. **Description:** Manufactures and sells steel products for industrial, commercial, office, and institutional use. Products include shelving, lockers, desktops, workbenches, office furniture, and custom products. Products are distributed nationally through dealers and direct sales. **NOTE:** Applications can be done online, or sent to the corporate headquarters location at P.O. Box 671, Aurora IL 60507-0671. 630/892-8941.

LYONDELL CHEMICAL
3801 West Chester Pike, Newtown Square PA 19073. 610/359-2000. **Contact:** Human Resources Department. **World Wide Web address:** http://www.lyondell.com. **Description:** A chemical manufacturer and marketer specializing in plastics, foams, fuel additives, and other intermediate chemicals. **Positions advertised include:** Auditor; Credit Assistant; Disbursements Clerk; Engineer; Internal Controls Manager; Public Relations Manager. **Corporate headquarters:** Houston TX. **Listed on:** New York Stock Exchange. **Stock exchange symbol:** LYO.

M&K POWERTOOLS, INC.
364 Wilmington-West Chester Pike, Glen Mills PA 19342. 610/459-4122. **Contact:** Human Resources. **Description:** A power tool retailer and repair shop, specializing in Makita power tools.

M&T BANK
One South Centre Street, Pottsville PA 17901-7150. 215/956-7001. **Toll-free phone:** 800/724-2440. **Fax:** 570/628-9212. **Contact:** Christine Pfeiffenberger, Personnel. **World Wide Web address:** http://www.mandtbank.com. **Description:** A full-service banking institution. **Corporate headquarters location:** Horsham PA.

M&T BANK
15 South Franklin Street, Wilkes-Barre PA 18711. 570/821-7168. **Fax:** 570/831-8810. **Contact:** Rita Bartol, Director of Human Resources. **World Wide Web address:** http://www.mandtbank.com. **Description:** A bank.

M&T BANK
601 Dresher Road, Horsham PA 19044. **Toll-free phone:** 800/724-2440. **Fax:** 215/956-7122. **Contact:** Personnel. **World Wide Web address:** http://www.mandtbank.com. **Description:** A full-service banking institution. **Corporate headquarters location:** This location.

M&T COMPANY
2186 East High Street, Sanatoga Village Center, Pottstown PA 19464. 610/495-9320. **Toll-free phone:** 800/724-2440. **Fax:** 610/970-5088. **Contact:** Personnel Department. **World Wide Web address:** http://www.mandtbank.com. **Description:** Provides a wide range of technical services including engineering, designing, drafting, and graphic arts services.

MB RESEARCH LABORATORIES
PO Box 178, Spinnerstown PA, 18968. 215/536-4110. **Fax:** 215/536-1816. **Contact:** Human Resources. **E-mail address:** mbweb@mbresearch.com. **World Wide Web address:** http://www.mbresearch.com. **Description:** Research laboratory that conducts acute, chronic, and chronic toxicology and pharmacology studies since 1972. **Positions advertised include:** Senior Quality Assurance Auditor; Marketing Manager/Director of Client Services; Research Assistant; Laboratory Technician; Biological Technician; Maintenance/Cleaning Staff.

MI HOME PRODUCTS INC.
650 West Market Street, Gratz PA 17030. 717/365-3300. **Contact:** Human Resources. **World Wide Web address:** http://www.mihomeproducts.com. **Description:** Manufactures metal doors and frames.

MACINTOSH LINEN AND UNIFORM RENTAL
1202 West Allen Street, Allentown PA 18102. 610/437-5435. **Contact:** Human Resources. **Description:** Rents linen and uniforms to a variety of industries including restaurants, hospitals, and nursing homes.

MACK TRUCKS INC.
P.O. Box M, Allentown PA 18105-5000. 610/709-3011. **Fax:** 610/709-3656. **Contact:** Bonnie Miller, Employment Manager. **E-mail address:** job.opportunities@macktrucks.com. **World Wide Web address:** http://www.macktrucks.com. **Description:** Manufactures and sells heavy-duty trucks, truck tractors, and truck replacement parts. The company also provides repair and maintenance services for these products. Mack Trucks is one of the largest producers of oversized trucks in the United States. **Positions advertised include:** Coordinator Order & Distribution; Associate Engineer; District Parts Manager; Service Training Instructor; Quality Engineer; Senior Buyer; Reliability Engineer. **Corporate headquarters location:** This location. **Operations at this facility include:** Administration. **Number of employees at this location:** 5,400.

MACTEC
5205 Militia Hill Road, Plymouth Meeting PA 19462. 610/941-9700. **Contact:** Personnel Director. **World Wide Web address:** http://www.mactec.com. **Description:** Offers a full range of services in environmental and engineering consulting, laboratory analysis, asbestos management, industrial hygiene, engineering, and architecture for governmental, industrial, and commercial clients. **NOTE:** Applications for positions at other branch locations may be sent to the main human resources office at 1627 Cole Boulevard, Golden CO 84101. **Positions advertised include:** Principal Engineer; Project Engineer. **Corporate headquarters location:** Alpharetta GA. **Other U.S. locations:** Nationwide.

MADISON BANK
Madison Bank Building, 1767 Sentry Parkway West, Blue Bell PA 19422. 215/641-1111. **Contact:** Personnel. **World Wide Web address:** http://www.madisonbank.com. **Description:** A retail and commercial bank. The bank offers a broad range of consumer and commercial deposit banking services including both commercial and consumer deposit accounts. The bank places an emphasis on serving the needs of individuals, small and medium-sized businesses, executives, professionals, and professional organizations. **Corporate headquarters location:** This location. **Other area locations:** Conshohocken PA.

MAIL-WELL ENVELOPE
P.O. Box 21050, Lehigh Valley PA 18009. 610/264-0530. **Physical address:** One Cascade Drive, Allentown PA 18109. **Contact:** Personnel Manager. **World Wide Web address:** http://www.mail-well.com. **Description:** Produces envelopes for the direct mail market. **NOTE:** Mail-Well is undergoing a name change to "Cenveo". **Corporate headquarters location:** Englewood CO. **Operations at this facility include:** Administration; Manufacturing; Sales; Service. **Listed on:** New York Stock Exchange. **Stock exchange symbol:** MWL.

MAIL-WELL GRAPHICS
7625 Suffolk Avenue, Philadelphia PA 19153. 215/492-0200. **Toll-free phone:** 800/338-1280. **Fax:** 215/492-8241. **Contact:** Kathleen Schaefer, Personnel Director. **World Wide Web address:** http://www.mail-well.com. **Description:** A printer of catalogs, handbooks, directories, journals, and related items. **NOTE:** Mail-Well is undergoing a name change to "Cenveo". **Corporate headquarters location:** Englewood CO. **Listed on:** New York Stock Exchange. **Stock exchange symbol:** MWL.

MANAGEMENT SCIENCE ASSOCIATES, INC.
6565 Penn Avenue, Pittsburgh PA 15206-4490. 412/362-2000. **Toll-free phone:** 800/MSA-INFO. **Fax:** 412/363-8878. **Contact:** Human Resources Director. **E-mail address:** careers@msa.com. **World Wide Web address:** http://www.msa.com. **Description:** Develops analytical software and related systems. **NOTE:** Part-time jobs are offered. **Positions advertised include:** Receptionist; Senior Secretary; Application Manager; Database Administrator; Senior Applications Engineer; Senior Software Engineer; Senior Technical Writer; Database Administrator Manager. **Special programs:** Summer Jobs.

THE MAPLE-VAIL BOOK MANUFACTURING GROUP
THE MAPLE PRESS COMPANY
P.O. Box 2695, York PA 17405. 717/764-5911. **Fax:** 717/764-2538. **Physical address:** 480 Willow Springs Lane, York PA 17402. **Contact:** Shirley Baker, Personnel Manager. **World Wide Web address:** http://www.maple-vail.com. **Description:** Provides bookbinding services including printing and photo composition. The Maple Press Company (also at this location) is a manufacturing facility. **Corporate headquarters location:** This location.

MARCONI
1000 Marconi Drive, Warrendale PA 15086-7502. 866/627-2664. **Fax:** 724/742-6464. **Contact:** Human Resources. **World Wide Web address:** http://www.marconi.com. **Description:** Manufactures LAN and WAN switches. Marconi also develops internetworking software and network management software. **Positions advertised include:** Software Engineer; Lead Software Engineer; Vice President Marketing. **Corporate headquarters location:** London UK. **Other U.S. locations:** Nationwide. **International locations:** Worldwide. **Listed on:** NASDAQ. **Stock exchange symbol:** MONI.

MARITRANS INC.
EASTERN OPERATIONS GROUP
2 International Plaza, Suite 335, Philadelphia PA 19113. 610/595-8000. **Contact:** Human Resources. **World Wide Web address:** http://www.maritrans.com. **Description:** Operates storage terminals. **Parent company:** Maritrans Inc. provides marine transportation for the petroleum distribution process, delivering about 10.6 billion gallons a year, and owns oil storage terminals. Maritrans offers a full line of distribution services including product exchanges, marine transportation, scheduling, terminal storage, and automated truck rack delivery systems. Marispond Inc. serves the growing international need for oil spill contingency planning and spill management in U.S. waters. This business capitalizes on Maritrans' spill response capabilities and is growing into the related areas of safety training and dry cargo contingency planning. **NOTE:** See website for a complete listing of shoreside and seagoing positions with detailed application information. **Corporate headquarters location:** Tampa FL.

MARKEL CORPORATION
435 School Lane, P.O. Box 752, Plymouth Meeting PA 19462. 610/272-8960. **Contact:** Human Resources. **World Wide Web address:** http://www.markelcorporation.com. **Description:** Produces sleevings and wire and cable products.

MARS ELECTRONICS INTERNATIONAL
1301 Wilson Drive, West Chester PA 19380. 610/430-2500. **Fax:** 610/430-2694. **Contact:** Human Resources. **World Wide Web address:** http://www.meiglobal.com. **Description:** Manufactures card-based cashless payment systems, electronic audit, and electronic coin/bill acceptors and change-giving machines for the amusement, gaming, retail, telecommunications, and transport industries. **Parent company:** Mars, Inc.

MARSH USA, INC.
6 PPG Place, Suite 300, Pittsburgh PA 15222. 412/552-5000. **Fax:** 412/552-5999. **Contact:** Human Resources. **World Wide Web address:** http://www.marshweb.com. **Description:** A professional firm that provides advice and services worldwide through an insurance brokerage and risk management firm, reinsurance intermediary facilities, and a consulting and financial services group, to clients concerned with the management of assets and risks. Specific services include insurance and risk management services, reinsurance, consulting and financial services, merchandising, and investment management. The company has subsidiaries and affiliates in 57 countries, with correspondents in 20 other countries. Founded in 1871. **Office hours:** Monday - Friday, 8:30 a.m. - 4:45 p.m. **Corporate headquarters location:** New York NY. **Other U.S. locations:** Nationwide. **International locations:** Worldwide. **Parent company:** Marsh & McLennan Companies, Inc. **Annual sales/revenues:** More than $100 million. **Listed on:** New York Stock Exchange. **Stock exchange symbol:** MMC. **Number of employees worldwide:** 39,000.

MARSULEX ENVIRONMENTAL TECHNOLOGIES
200 North Seventh Street, Lebanon PA 17046-5000. 717/274-7000. **Contact:** Human Resources. **World Wide Web address:** http://www.marsulex.com. **Description:** Manufactures industrial air pollution control equipment for the utilities industry. **Corporate headquarters location:** Toronto, Canada.

C.F. MARTIN & COMPANY, INC.
510 Sycamore Street, P.O. Box 329, Nazareth PA 18064-0329. 610/759-2837. **Fax:** 610/759-5757. **Contact:** Debbie Karlowitch, Personnel Manager. **E-mail address:** info@martinguitar.com. **World Wide Web address:** http://www.mguitar.com. **Description:** Produces a line of acoustic guitars and guitar strings and is engaged in the processing of selected hardwoods.

MATTHEWS INTERNATIONAL CORPORATION
2 North Shore Center, Pittsburgh PA 15212-5851. 412/442-8200. **Contact:** Human Resources. **E-mail address:** mpdjobs@matw.com. **World Wide Web address:** http://www.matthewsinternational.com. **Description:** Through its subsidiaries, Matthews International is a provider of creative surface graphics design, printing plates, cutting dies, and final press-side assistance in package printing operations. The company also designs and manufactures equipment and supplies used by industry to mark components, finished products, packaging, and packaging containers, and produces and distributes cast bronze memorial plaques, cremation urns, fabricated niche units, cemetery features, granite block and granite foundations for bronze memorials, and related products. Founded in 1850. **NOTE:** mpdjobs@matthewsinternational.com is an additional e-mail address that could be used for employment matters. **Positions advertised include:** Staff Accountant; Programmer/Analyst; Tax Specialist; Wide Area Network Specialist. **Corporate headquarters location:** This location. **Other U.S. locations:** Nationwide.

MATTHEWS INTERNATIONAL CORPORATION
1315 West Liberty Avenue, Pittsburgh PA 15226. 412/571-5500. **Contact:** Human Resources. **E-mail address:** mpdjobs@matw.com. **World Wide Web address:** http://www.matthewsinternational.com. **Description:** Matthews International is a provider of initial creative surface graphics design, printing plates, cutting dies, and final press-side assistance in package printing operations. Through its subsidiaries, the company also designs and manufactures equipment and supplies used by industry to mark components, finished products, packaging, and packaging containers, and produces and distributes cast bronze memorial plaques, cremation urns, fabricated niche units, cemetery features, granite block and granite foundations for bronze memorials, and related products. **NOTE:** mpdjobs@matthewsinternational.com is an additional e-mail address that could be used for employment matters. **Positions advertised include:** Staff Accountant; Programmer/Analyst; Tax Specialist; Wide Area Network Specialist. **Corporate headquarters location:** Pittsburgh PA. **Other U.S. locations:** Nationwide. **Operations at this facility include:** This location manufactures plaques.

MAXWELL SYSTEMS, INC.
2500 DeKalb Pike, Norristown PA 19401. 610/277-3515. **Contact:** Human Resources. **World Wide Web address:** http://www.maxwellsystems.com. **Description:** Maxwell Systems sells business management software to construction, service, and related industries. **NOTE:** An online request can be done to get employment information sent to your e-mail address. **Corporate headquarters location:** This location. **Operations at this facility include:** This location is a computer training facility.

McCOURT LABEL COMPANY
20 Egbert Lane, Lewis Run PA 16731. 814/362-3851. **Contact:** Jane Luzzi, Human Resources. **E-mail address:** szampogna@mccourtlabel.com. **World Wide Web address:** http://www.mccourtlabel.com. **Description:** Prints paper labels. **Positions advertised include:** Customer Service Representative; Account Manager; Goal Oriented Salesperson.

McKESSON CORPORATION
5 Country View Road, Malvern PA 19355-1421. 610/407-0736. **Contact:** Human Resources. **World Wide Web address:** http://www.mckesson.com. **Description:** Provides information systems and technology to health care enterprises including hospitals, integrated delivery networks, and managed care organizations. McKesson's primary products are Pathways 2000, a family of client/server-based applications that allow the integration and uniting of health care providers; STAR, Series, and HealthQuest transaction systems; TRENDSTAR decision support system; and QUANTUM enterprise information system. The company also offers outsourcing services that include strategic information systems planning, data center operations, receivables management, business office administration, and major system conversions. **Positions advertised include:** Software Support Engineer. **Corporate headquarters location:** San Francisco CA. **Other U.S. locations:** Boston MA. **Operations at this facility include:** Administration; Divisional Headquarters; Research and Development; Sales; Service. **Number of employees at this location:** 155. **Number of employees nationwide:** 175.

McKESSON CORPORATION
One Penn Center West, Suite 120, Carnegie PA 15276. 412/787-7780. **Contact:** Human Resources. **World Wide Web address:** http://www.mckesson.com. **Description:** This location is involved in technical support and sales. Overall, McKesson is an information solutions company that provides information systems and technology to health care enterprises including hospitals, integrated delivery networks, and managed care organizations. McKesson 's primary products are Pathways 2000, a family of client/server-based applications that allow the integration and uniting of health care providers; STAR, Series, and HealthQuest transaction systems; TRENDSTAR decision support system; and QUANTUM enterprise information system. The company also offers outsourcing services that include strategic information systems planning, data center operations, receivables management, business office administration, and major system conversions. **Positions advertised include:** Software Upgrade Specialist; Automation Consultant Trainee; Software Development Engineer; General Ledger Accountant; Technical Product Support Specialist; Assistant Product Manager; Account Manager; Physician Sales Representative. **Corporate headquarters location:** San Francisco CA. **Subsidiaries include:** HBO & Company Canada Ltd.; HBO & Company Limited.

McNEIL CONSUMER HEALTH CARE
JOHNSON & JOHNSON MERCK CONSUMER PHARMACEUTICALS CO.
7050 Camp Hill Road, Fort Washington PA 19034-2292. 215/273-7000. **Contact:** Human Resources. **World Wide Web address:** http://www.tylenol.com. **Description:** Manufactures and markets a wide range of consumer pharmaceutical products, including Tylenol. Johnson & Johnson Merck Consumer Pharmaceuticals Company (also at this location) develops and markets a variety of over-the-counter items. **NOTE:** All hiring is done through the corporate office. Interested jobseekers should direct resumes to Johnson & Johnson Headquarters, Shared Services Recruiting, Johnson Hall JH-215, New Brunswick NJ 08901. **Parent company:** Johnson & Johnson (New Brunswick NJ).

W.C. McQUAIDE, INC.
153 Mac Ridge Avenue, Johnstown PA 15904. 814/269-6000. **Fax:** 814/269-6189. **Contact:** Human Resources. **World Wide Web address:** http://www.mcquaide.com. **Description:** A freight carrier. **Corporate headquarters location:** This location. **Other U.S. locations:** NJ; NY; OH; WV. **Operations at this facility include:** Administration; Sales; Service. **Number of employees at this location:** 200. **Number of employees nationwide:** 415.

MEADVILLE MEDICAL CENTER
751 Liberty Street, Meadville PA 16335. 814/333-5000. **Fax:** 814/333-5471. **Contact:** John Andrews, Assistant Director of Human Resources. **E-mail address:** careers@mmchs.org. **World Wide Web address:** http://www.mmchs.org. **Description:** A medical center. **Positions advertised include:** Certified Nurse Aide; Food Service Worker; Housekeeper; Invasive Cardiologist; Licensed Practical Nurse; Medical Technologist; Registered Nurse; Respiratory Therapist. **Special programs:** Internships. **Operations at this facility include:** Service. **Number of employees at this location:** 980.

MEADWESTVACO
P.O. Box 317, Main Street & Barrie Road, Alexandria PA 16611. 814/669-4446. **Contact:** Edna Querry, Human Resources Department. **World Wide Web address:** http://www.meadwestvaco.com. **Description:** Manufactures school supplies. **Parent company:** MeadWestvaco is one of the world's largest manufacturers of paper, producing more than 1.2 million tons annually for printing and business use. Mead is a leader in coated paperboard and multiple packaging. The company is also a $1.6 billion distributor of paper, packaging, and business supplies made by manufacturers throughout the world. Mead is one of the largest makers of paper-based school and home-office supplies, as well as a developer of one of the world's leading electronic information retrieval services for law, patents, accounting, finance, news, and business information. **Corporate headquarters location:** Stamford CT. **Listed on:** New York Stock Exchange. **Stock exchange symbol:** MWV.

MEDIC COMPUTER SYSTEMS
Foster Plaza #6, 681 Andersen Drive, Pittsburgh PA 15220. 412/937-0690. **Contact:** Human Resources. **World Wide Web address:** http://www.misyshealthcare.com. **Description:** Develops health care management software. Products include +Medic Vision, +Medic PM, Auto Chart, AutoImage, and FasTracker. **Operations at this facility include:** This location provides sales, training, and support.

MEDRAD, INC.
One Medrad Drive, Indianola PA 15051-0780. 412/767-2400. **Fax:** 412/767-4128. **Contact:** Corporate Recruiting Manager. **E-mail address:** jobs@medrad.com. **World Wide Web address:** http://www.medrad.com. **Description:** Designs, manufactures, and markets high-tech equipment and disposable products such as CT and angiography injectors, syringes, magnetic resonance coils, and other imaging equipment. **Positions advertised include:** Customer Support Specialist; Senior Reliability Engineer; Senior Manufacturing Engineer; Project Engineer; New Products Mechanical Engineer; Resource Leader; Receiving Clerk. **Corporate headquarters location:** This location. **International locations:** Brazil; Canada; France; Germany; Italy; Japan; Singapore; the Netherlands; United Kingdom. **Parent company:** Schering AG (Berlin, Germany). **Operations at this facility include:** Administration; Manufacturing; Research and Development; Sales; Service. **Annual sales/revenues:** More than $100 million. **Number of employees at this location:** 670. **Number of employees nationwide:** 780. **Number of employees worldwide:** 870.

MELLON FINANCIAL CORPORATION
500 Grant Street, One Mellon Bank Center, Room 705, Pittsburgh PA 15258-0001. 412/234-5000. **Contact:** Human Resources. **E-mail address:** recruiting@mellon.com. **World Wide Web address:** http://www.mellon.com. **Description:** Mellon Financial Corporation is a holding company for national commercial banks with assets of $30 billion. Through its subsidiaries, the company offers consumer investment services (private asset management services and retail mutual funds); consumer banking services (consumer lending, branch banking, credit cards, mortgage loan origination and servicing, and jumbo residential mortgage lending); corporate/institutional investment services (institutional trust and custody, institutional asset and institutional mutual fund management and administration, securities lending, foreign exchange, cash management, and stock transfer); corporate/institutional banking services (large corporate and middle market lending, asset-based lending, certain capital market and leasing activities, commercial real estate lending, and insurance premium financing); and real estate workout (commercial real estate and mortgage banking recovery operations). **Positions advertised include:** Buyer; Distributed Application Developer; Operations Specialist; Project Manager; Senior Buyer; Trust Operations Specialist. **Corporate headquarters location:** This location. **Subsidiaries include:** Mellon Mortgage Company. **Listed on:** New York Stock Exchange. **Stock exchange symbol:** MEL. **Annual sales/revenues:** More than $100 million.

MEMORIAL HOSPITAL
325 South Belmont Street, P.O. Box 15118, York PA 17405. 717/849-5479. **Fax:** 717/849-5495. **Contact:** Human Resources Department. **E-mail address:** hrinfo@mhyork.org. **World Wide Web address:** http://www.mhyork.org. **Description:** An acute care, community-based, teaching hospital serving York County. **Positions advertised include:** Administrative Assistant; Cardiovascular Specialist; Care Management Coordinator; Certified Registered Nurse; Child & Adolescent Therapist; Clinical Staff Pharmacist; Community Relations Manager; Critical Care Technician; Customer Service/Billing Representative; Dietary Aide; Registered Nurse; Licensed Practical Nurse. **Parent company:** Memorial Healthcare System. **Operations at this facility include:** Administration; Service. **Annual sales/revenues:** $21 - $50 million. **Number of employees at this location:** 900.

MERCK & COMPANY, INC.
P.O. Box 4, West Point PA 19486. 215/652-5000. **Physical address:** 770 Sumneytown Pike, West Point PA 19486. **Contact:** Human Resources. **World Wide Web address:** http://www.merck.com. **Description:** Merck & Company is a worldwide organization engaged primarily in the business of discovering, developing, producing, and marketing products for the maintenance of health and the environment. Products include human and animal pharmaceuticals and chemicals sold to the health care, oil exploration, food processing, textile, and paper industries. Merck also runs an ethical drug, mail-order marketing business. **Corporate headquarters location:** Whitehouse Station NJ. **Operations at this facility include:** This location researches and manufactures prescription drugs, and performs administrative and human resources functions.

MERCY FITZGERALD HOSPITAL
1500 Lansdowne Avenue, Darby PA 19023. 610/237-4000. **Fax:** 610/853-7030. **Contact:** Central Employment Office. **E-mail address:** mercyjobs@mercyhealth.org. **World Wide Web address:** http://www.mercyhealth.org. **Description:** A 441-bed, acute-care, community hospital that serves southwest Pennsylvania. **NOTE:** For employment opportunities contact: Central Employment Office, 2000 Old West Chester Pike, Havertown PA 19083. 610/853-7333. **Positions advertised include:** Accounts Payable Specialist; Activities Therapist; Cafeteria Supervisor; Chief Executive Officer; Collection Representative; Data Facilitator; Diet Technician; Emergency Department Nurse; Licensed Practical Nurse; Medical Technologist; Nurse Practitioner; Nursing Assistant; Paramedic. **Parent company:** Mercy Health System.

MERCY HOSPITAL OF PHILADELPHIA
501 South 54th Street, Philadelphia PA 19143. 215/748-9000. **Fax:** 610/853-7030. **Contact:** Central Employment Office. **E-mail address:** mercyjobs@mercyhealth.org. **World Wide Web address:** http://www.mercyhealth.org. **Description:** A 200-bed medical center. **NOTE:** For employment opportunities contact: Central Employment Office, 2000 Old West Chester Pike, Havertown PA 19083. 610/853-7333. **Positions advertised include:** Accounts Payable Specialist; Activities Therapist; Cafeteria Supervisor; Chief Executive Officer; Collection Representative; Data Facilitator; Diet Technician; Emergency Department Nurse; Licensed Practical Nurse; Medical Technologist; Nurse Practitioner; Nursing Assistant; Paramedic.

MERCYHURST COLLEGE
501 East 38th Street, Erie PA 16546-0001. 814/824-2000. **Toll-free phone:** 800/825-1926. **Contact:** Human Resources. **World Wide Web address:** http://www.mercyhurst.edu. **Description:** A college offering four-year, two-year, and graduate programs. Degrees awarded include certificate, associate's, bachelor's, and master's degrees. Enrollment is approximately 2,000 undergraduates and 100 graduate students.

MERRILL LYNCH
120 Regent Court, Suite 200, State College PA 16801. 814/238-0100. **Contact:** Cynthia Karchar, Office Manager. **World Wide Web address:** http://www.ml.com. **Description:** Provides financial services in the areas of securities, extensive insurance, and real estate and related services. Merrill Lynch, which is one of the largest securities brokerage firms in the United States, also brokers commodity futures and options, and corporate and municipal securities, and is engaged in investment banking activities.

MET-PRO CORPORATION
160 Cassell Road, P.O. Box 144, Harleysville PA 18964. 215/723-6751. **Fax:** 215/723-6758. **Contact:** Human Resources. **E-mail address:** mpr@met-pro.com. **World Wide Web address:** http://www.met-pro.com. **Description:** Through its divisions and subsidiaries, Met-Pro manufactures a wide range of products for industrial, commercial, and residential markets. These products include pollution control systems and allied equipment for purification of air and liquids, and fluid handling equipment for corrosive, abrasive, and high-temperature liquids. **Listed on:** New York Stock Exchange. **Stock exchange symbol:** MPR.

METALS USA PLATES AND SHAPES - PITTSBURGH
2025 Greentree Road, Pittsburgh PA 15220. 412/572-3400. **Contact:** Human Resources. **World Wide Web address:** http://www.metalsusa.com. **Description:** Operates a metal service center. **Corporate headquarters location:** Houston TX. **Operations at this facility include:** Accounts Payable and Human Resources. **Parent company:** Metals USA.

METHODIST HOSPITAL
Thomas Jefferson University Hospital, 2301 South Broad Street, Philadelphia PA 19148. 215/952-9000. **Fax:** 215/952-9588. **Contact:** Human Resources. **World Wide Web address:** http://www.jeffersonhospital.org/methodist. **Description:** A hospital licensed for 165 beds. Methodist Hospital is affiliated with Thomas Jefferson University Hospital. **Positions advertised include:** Clinical Dietician; Clinical Pharmacist; Clinical Supervisor; Insurance and Benefit Counselor; Trauma Registrar; Case Manager; Emergency Department Clerk; Endoscopy Nurse; Nurse Manager; Physician Assistant; Security Analyst; Nursing Assistant.

MICHAEL BEST & FRIEDRICH LLP (LEHIGH VALLEY OFFICE)
Stabler Corporate Center, 3773 Corporate Parkway, Center Valley PA 18034. 610/798-2170. **Fax:** 610/798-2180. **Contact:** Human Resources. **E-mail address:** info@mbf-law.com. **World Wide Web address:** http://www.mbf-law.com. **Description:** A broad based business law firm with clients ranging from small businesses to Fortune 500 companies. **NOTE:** Attorneys are also licensed to practice in most other states. **Other U.S. locations:** WI; PA; IL. **Number of employees worldwide:** 346.

HENRY F. MICHELL COMPANY
P.O. Box 60160, King of Prussia PA 19406. **Fax:** 610/337-7726. **Contact:** D. Valenteen. **World Wide Web address:** http://www.michells.com. **Description:** Henry F. Michell Company is a horticultural wholesaler. **Positions advertised include:** Assistant to Production Manager.

MILLERSVILLE UNIVERSITY OF PENNSYLVANIA
Dilworth Building, P.O. Box 1002, Millersville PA 17551-0302. 717/872-3011. **Contact:** Human Resources. **World Wide Web address:** http://muweb.millersv.edu. **Description:** A four-year university offering associate's, bachelor's, and master's degrees to approximately 7,500 students. **NOTE:** Unsolicited resumes are not accepted. Applications/resumes must be mailed or hand delivered to the above address.

MINE SAFETY APPLIANCES COMPANY (MSA)
P.O. Box 426, Pittsburgh PA 15230. **Physical address:** 121 Gamma Drive, RIDC Industrial Park, O'Hara Township, Pittsburgh PA 15238. 412/967-3000. **Toll-free phone:** 800/MSA-2222. **Contact:** Mr. Benedict DeMaria, Human Resources Director. **World Wide Web address:** http://www.msanet.com. **Description:** Manufactures a variety of gas masks and respiratory protection products, protective headgear, and gas and vapor sensors. The company's products are generally supplied to the fire service, mining, construction, and industrial subcontracting industries. The company is divided into two major operating groups. MSA's Safety Products Division designs and manufactures full face pieces for self-contained breathing apparatuses, respirators, communication equipment for breathing apparatuses, cooling vests designed to combat heat stress, and a hand-held infrared heat detector. The company's Instrument Division makes a variety of monitors and sensors. MSA's international affiliates manufacture a wide array of equipment, ranging from thermal imaging cameras to air supply units. The company's products are sold worldwide. **NOTE:** See http://www.monster.com for a current list of open positions. **Corporate headquarters location:** This location.

MINE SAFETY APPLIANCES COMPANY (MSA)
3880 Meadowbrook Road, Murrysville PA 15668-1753. 724/733-9100. **Contact:** Human Resources. **World Wide Web address:** http://www.msanet.com. **Description:** Manufactures a variety of gas masks and respiratory protection products, protective headgear, and gas and vapor sensors. The company's products are generally supplied to the fire service, mining, construction, and industrial subcontracting industries. The company is divided into two major operating groups. MSA's Safety Products Division designs and manufactures full face pieces for self-contained breathing apparatus, respirators, communication equipment for breathing apparatus, cooling vests designed to combat heat stress, and a hand-held infrared heat detector. The company's Instrument Division makes a variety of monitors and sensors. MSA's international affiliates manufacture a wide array of equipment, ranging from thermal imaging cameras to air supply units. The company's products are sold worldwide. **NOTE:** See http://www.monster.com for a current list of open positions. **Corporate headquarters location:** Pittsburgh PA.

MOLDED FIBER GLASS COMPANIES
55 Fourth Avenue, Union City PA 16438. 814/458-4831. **Toll-free phone:** 800/458-0863. **Contact:** Larry Davis, Vice President of Human Resources. **E-mail address:** ldavis@moldedfiberglass.com. **World Wide Web address:** http://www.moldedfiberglass.com. **Description:** A manufacturer of custom molded fiberglass and reinforced plastic products. **NOTE:** Resumes should be mailed to: P.O. Box 675, 2925 MFG Place, Ashtabula OH 44005-0675. 440/994-5261. **Positions advertised include:** Manufacturing Manager; Plant Manager; Information Technology Director.

MOLDED FIBER GLASS TRAY COMPANY
6175 U.S. Highway 6, Linesville PA 16424. 814/683-4500. **Toll-free phone:** 800/458-6090. **Fax:** 814/683-4504. **Contact:** Personnel. **E-mail address:** info@mfgtray.com. **World Wide Web address:** http://www.mfgtray.com. **Description:** Manufactures molded fiberglass trays for industrial and food service use.

MONTGOMERY NEWSPAPERS COMPANY
290 Commerce Street, Fort Washington PA 19034. 215/542-0200. **Contact:** Diane Dumke, Personnel. **World Wide Web address:** http://www.montgomerynews.com. **Description:** Publishes *Today's Spirit*, a daily newspaper for the Hatboro/Warminster area and weekly newspapers in Ambler, Glenside, Huntingdon Valley, Jenkintown, King of Prussia, Springfield, and Willow Grove. **Corporate headquarters location:** This location. **Operations at this facility include:** Manufacturing. **Annual sales/revenues:** $5 - $10 million. **Number of employees at this location:** 200. **Number of employees nationwide:** 300.

MOORE WALLACE
218 North Braddock Avenue, Pittsburgh PA 15208. 215/536-8200 ext. 336. **Contact:** Human Resources. **World Wide Web address:** http://www.moorewallace.com. **Description:** Manufactures business systems, forms, and equipment. The company has more than 280 sales offices and branches in 39 countries. **Parent company:** RR Donnelley.

MORAVIAN COLLEGE
MORAVIAN THEOLOGICAL SEMINARY
1200 Main Street, Bethlehem PA 18018. 610/861-1527. **Physical address:** Colonial Hall, 3rd Floor, Main Street and Elizabeth Avenue, Bethlehem PA 18018. **Fax:** 610/625-7883. **Contact:** Human Resources. **E-mail address:** employment@moravian.edu. **World Wide Web address:** http://www.moravian.edu. **Description:** A four-year college offering bachelor's degrees and MBAs to approximately 1,200 students. Moravian Theological Seminary (also at this location) is a graduate-professional school of theology. **Positions advertised include:** Director of Continuing and Graduate Studies; Director of International Studies; Groundskeeper; Associate Professor of Music; Visiting Assistant Professor of Sociology. **Operations at this facility include:** Administration; Service. **Number of employees at this location:** 400.

MORNING CALL
101 North Sixth Street, P.O. Box 1260, Allentown PA 18105. 610/820-6500. **Contact:** Human Resources. **World Wide Web address:** http://www.mcall.com. **Description:** Publishes a newspaper with a daily circulation of 150,000 and a Sunday circulation of 180,000.

JAMES D. MORRISSEY, INC.
9119 Frankford Avenue, Philadelphia PA 19114. 215/333-8000. **Fax:** 215/624-3308. **Contact:** Bruce Angst, Human Resources. **E-mail address:** jobs@jdm-inc.com. **World Wide Web address:** http://www.jdm-inc.com. **Description:** A heavy construction firm that specializes in large-scale projects such as highways and commercial buildings. **Positions advertised include:** Superintendent; Foreman; Estimator's Assistant; Highway Estimator; Bituminous Paving Foreman; Field Office Manager. **Corporate headquarters location:** This location.

MOTION CONTROL INDUSTRIES INC.
One Gillis Avenue, Ridgway PA 15853-1603. 814/773-3185. **Fax:** 814/776-5464. **Contact:** John Orsulak, Human Resources Manager. **World Wide Web address:** http://www.carlislemotion.com. **Description:** This location manufactures heavy-duty brake systems for industrial vehicles. **Corporate headquarters location:** Charlottesville VA. **Parent company:** Carlisle Companies has diversified operations in several fields. Operating in the construction materials field, Carlisle SynTec Inc. manufactures elastomeric membranes (EPDM), adhesives, and related items for roofing systems and water barrier applications. Transportation products include brake linings for heavy-duty trucks, trailers, and off-road vehicles; dry disc brakes and actuation systems for construction equipment; custom rubber and plastic components for use in passenger cars, appliances, and other purposes; specialty industrial friction products; and insulated wire products. General industry products include plastic food service products and melamine dinnerware, small pneumatic tires and stamped and roll-formed wheels used by most major lawn and garden equipment manufacturers, and insulated wire and cable products.

MOTOR COILS MANUFACTURING COMPANY
100 Talbot Avenue, Braddock PA 15104. 412/201-6462. **Contact:** Human Resources. **Description:** A gray and ductile iron foundry. **Parent company:** Motive Power Industries.

MOTOROLA, INC.
BROADBAND COMMUNICATIONS SECTOR
101 Tournament Drive, Horsham PA 19044. 215/323-1000. **Contact:** Human Resources. **World Wide Web address:** http://www.motorola.com. **Description:** Motorola provides applied research, development, manufacturing, and marketing of high-tech systems and components for industry and government in the fields of electronics, communications, automotive, controls, semiconductor, information systems, and office information. Motorola manufactures communications equipment and electronic products including car radios, cellular phones, semiconductors, computer systems, cellular infrastructure equipment, pagers, cordless phones, and LANs. **Positions advertised include:** Account Representative. **Operations at this facility include:** This location houses the administrative offices of the Broadband Communications Sector.

MOUNT ALOYSIUS COLLEGE
7373 Admiral Peary Highway, Cresson PA 16630-1999. 814/886-6930. **Toll-free phone:** 888/823-2220. **Fax:** 814/886-6441. **Contact:** Nick Mignon, Director of Human Resources. **E-mail address:** nmignon@mtaloy.edu. **World Wide Web address:** http://www.mtaloy.edu. **Description:** A college offering four-year programs. Degrees offered include B.A. and B.S. degrees.

MUHLENBERG COLLEGE
2400 Chew Street, Allentown PA 18104-5586. 484/664-3166. **Fax:** 484/664-3107. **Contact:** Anne W. Hochella, Vice President Human Resources. **E-mail address:** hocella@muhlenberg.edu. **World Wide Web address:** http://www.muhlenberg.edu. **Description:** A four-year, undergraduate, liberal arts college. Founded in 1848. **Positions advertised include:** Athletics Director; Adjunct Communications Professor; Network Administrator; Visiting Psychology Professor; Residence Coordinator. **President:** Arthur R. Taylor. **Number of employees at this location:** 500.

MULTISERV
612 North Main Street, Box 1071, Butler PA 16001. 724/283-5741. **Contact:** John Cupps, Vice President of Administration. **E-mail address:** info@multiservgroup.com. **World Wide Web address:** http://www.multiservgroup.com. **Description:** Provides steel mill services. **Corporate headquarters location:** Surrey, United Kingdom. **Parent company:** Harsco Corporation.

MURATA ELECTRONICS
1900 West College Avenue, State College PA 16801. 814/237-1431. **Contact:** Mr. Charles McClellan, Employment Manager. **World Wide Web address:** http://www.murata-northamerica.com. **Description:** An electronics company that manufactures capacitors, oscillators, and gigafilters.

MYLAN LABORATORIES INC.
1500 Corporate Drive, Suite 400, Canonsburg PA 15321. 724/514-1800. **Contact:** Human Resources. **E-mail address:** resume@myanlabs.com. **World Wide Web address:** http://www.mylan.com. **Description:** One of the nation's largest manufacturers of generic pharmaceutical products in finished tablet, capsule, and powder dosage forms for resale by others under their own labels. Mylan Laboratories, through its subsidiaries, also develops and manufactures wound care products. **Positions advertised include:** Quality Control Specialist; Formulation Specialist; Legal Secretary; Senior Regulatory Affairs Associate. **Corporate headquarters location:** This location. **Listed on:** New York Stock Exchange. **Stock exchange symbol:** MYL. **Number of employees nationwide:** 1,240.

NBC 10-WCAU
10 Monument Road, Bala-Cynwyd PA 19004-1771. 610/668-5510. **Contact:** Human Resources Department. **World Wide Web address:** http://www.nbc10.com. **Description:** An NBC-affiliated television station. This location is also home to WOGL-FM Oldies 98 and WGMD-AM 'The Game.'

NCO GROUP, INC.
507 Prudential Road, Horsham PA 19044. 215/441-3000. **Toll-free phone:** 800/220-2274. **Contact:** Human Resources. **World Wide Web address:** http://www.ncogroup.com. **Description:** Provides accounts-receivable and delinquency management, collection services, billing, market research, and telemarketing services to a variety of businesses. Founded in 1926. **Corporate headquarters location:** This location. **Listed on:** NASDAQ. **Stock exchange symbol:** NCOG.

NCR CORPORATION
600 Old Pond Road, Suite 507, Bridgeville PA 15017-1273. 412/504-1600. **Toll-free phone:** 800/225-5627. **Contact:** Human Resources. **World Wide Web address:** http://www.ncr.com. **Description:** NCR Corporation is a worldwide provider of computer products and services. The company provides computer solutions to three targeted industries: retail, financial, and communications. NCR Computer Systems Group develops, manufactures, and markets computer systems. NCR Financial Systems

Group is an industry leader in three target areas: financial delivery systems, relationship banking data warehousing solutions, and payment systems/item processing. NCR Retail Systems Group is a world leader in end-to-end retail solutions serving the food, general merchandise, and hospitality industries. NCR Worldwide Services provides data warehousing services solutions and end-to-end networking services, and designs, implements, and supports complex open systems environments. NCR Systemedia Group develops, produces, and markets a complete line of information products to satisfy customers' information technology needs including transaction processing media, auto identification media, business form communication products, managing documents and media, and a full line of integrated equipment solutions. **Corporate headquarters location:** Dayton OH. **Operations at this facility include:** This location offers sales, service, and customer support. **Listed on:** New York Stock Exchange. **Stock exchange symbol:** NCR. **Number of employees nationwide:** 19,000. **Number of employees worldwide:** 38,000.

NVR MORTGAGE FINANCE INC.
111 Ryan Court, Pittsburgh PA 15205. 412/276-4225. **Fax:** 412/429-4542. **Contact:** Human Resources. **E-mail address:** kkimberl@nvrinc.com. **World Wide Web address:** http://www.nvrinc.com. **Description:** Provides financial and mortgage services. **NOTE:** Mail resumes to: NVR Inc., Human Resources Department, 7601 Lewinsville Road, Suite 300, McLean VA 22102. 703/761-2000. **Positions advertised include:** Financial Analyst; Management Trainee; Sales and Marketing Associate. **Corporate headquarters location:** McLean VA. **Other U.S. locations:** Nationwide. **Parent company:** NVR. **Number of employees at this location:** 140. **Number of employees nationwide:** 500.

NABISCO BISCUIT COMPANY
12000 East Roosevelt Boulevard, Philadelphia PA 19116. 215/673-4800. **Contact:** Human Resources. **World Wide Web address:** http://www.nabisco.com. **Description:** Nabisco is one of the largest consumer food operations in the country. The company markets a broad line of cookie and cracker products including brand names such as Oreo, Ritz, Premium, Teddy Grahams, Chips Ahoy!, and Wheat Thins. **Special programs:** Internships. **Corporate headquarters location:** East Hanover NJ. **International locations:** Asia; Canada; Europe. **Operations at this facility include:** This location is a bakery and distribution center. **Parent company:** Kraft Foods, Inc. **Operations at this facility include:** Manufacturing. **Listed on:** New York Stock Exchange. **Stock exchange symbol:** KFT.

NARCO AVIONICS
270 Commerce Drive, Suite 200, Fort Washington PA 19034. 215/643-2905. **Toll-free phone:** 800/234-7551. **Fax:** 215/643-0197. **Contact:** Kevin Davis, Controller. **World Wide Web address:** http://www.narco-avionics.com. **Description:** Produces a wide range of instruments and systems for general aviation uses.

NATIONAL CITY BANK OF PENNSYLVANIA
20 Stanwix Street, Pittsburgh PA 15222. 412/644-7922. **Contact:** Human Resources. **World Wide Web address:** http://www.national-city.com. **Description:** A bank. **Corporate headquarters location:** Cleveland OH.

NATIONAL FULFILLMENT SERVICES
100 Pine Avenue, Building 4, Holmes PA 19043. 610/532-4700. **Toll-free phone:** 800/NFS-1306. **Fax:** 610/586-3232. **Contact:** Human Resources. **World Wide Web address:** http://www.nfsrv.com. **Description:** Provides direct marketing services. **Positions advertised include:** Bilingual Spanish/English Professor. **Corporate headquarters location:** This location. **Operations at this facility include:** Administration; Sales; Service. Listed on: Privately held. **Number of employees at this location:** 110.

NATIONAL PENN BANK
P.O. Box 547, Boyertown PA 19512. 610/367-6001. **Toll-free phone:** 800/822-3321. **Fax:** 610/369-6429. **Contact:** Earl Houseknecht, Senior Vice-President of Human Resources. **World Wide Web address:** http://www.natpennbank.com. **Description:** A bank. **Parent company:** National Penn Bancshares, Inc. is a $2.1 billion bank holding company. Other subsidiaries of National Penn Bancshares include Investors Trust Company.

NAVIGANT CONSULTING, INC.
Bell Atlantic Tower, 1717 Arch Street, Suite 3610, Philadelphia PA 19103. 215/832-4400. **Fax:** 215/832-4401. **Contact:** Human Resources. **World Wide Web address:** http://www.navigantconsulting.com. **Description:** Navigant is an independent consulting firm providing litigation, financial, healthcare, energy, and operational consulting services to government agencies, legal counsel, and large companies. **NOTE:** Applicants may apply through online application at company website.

NAZARETH HOSPITAL
2601 Holme Avenue, Philadelphia PA 19152. 215/335-6260. **Fax:** 610/335-6258. **Contact:** Human Resources. **E-mail address:** mercyjobs@mercyhealth.org. **World Wide Web address:** http://www.nazarethhospital.org. **Description:** An acute care hospital serving the northeast Philadelphia community. **NOTE:** Mail resumes to: Central Employment Office, 2000 Old West Chester Pike, Havertown PA 19083. 610/853-7333. **Positions advertised include:** Accounts Payable Specialist; Activities Therapist; Administrative Nursing Supervisor; Collection Representative; Development Records Coordinator; Dietary Aide; ER Technician; Home Health Aide; Licensed Practical Nurse; Registered Nurse; Medical Technologist; Nursing Assistant; Occupational Therapist; Paramedic. **Special programs:** Internships. **Parent company:** Mercy Health System. **Number of employees at this location:** 1,400.

NEAPCO, INC.
740 Queen Street, Pottstown PA 19464. 610/323-6000. **Contact:** Mary A. Csapo, Human Resources Manager. **World Wide Web address:** http://www.neapco.com. **Description:** Manufactures power driveline components, u-joints, and front-wheel drive products. NEAPCO operates in the OEM and aftermarket areas with customers in the automotive, heavy-duty, and agricultural lines. **Corporate headquarters location:** This location. **Other U.S. locations:** CA; MO; NE. **Parent company:** UIS, Inc. (New York NY). **Operations at this facility include:** Manufacturing; Research and Development; Sales.

NEIGHBORCARE
9 Creek Parkway, Boothwyn PA 19061. 610/364-2789. **Fax:** 610/364-2799. **Contact:** Human Resources. **World Wide Web address:** http://www.neighborcare.com. **Description:** Distributes home medical equipment including wheelchairs, diabetic equipment, and home medical supplies. **Positions advertised include:** Billing Account Manager; Billing Representative; Business Office Manager; Collections Representative; Infusion Nurse Consultant; Infusion Nurse Manager; Medical Records Technician. **Corporate headquarters location:** Baltimore MD.

NEOWARE SYSTEMS, INC.
400 Feheley Drive, King of Prussia PA 19406. 610/277-8300. **Fax:** 610/275-5739. **Contact:** Human Resources. **E-mail address:** iresume@neoware.com. **World Wide Web address:** http://www.neoware.com. **Description:** Designs, manufactures, and markets a family of desktop computing devices including multimedia capable X Window stations.

NEW CASTLE YOUTH DEVELOPMENT CENTER
Rural Route 6, Box 21-A, Frew Mill Road, New Castle PA 16101. 724/656-7300. **Fax:** 724/656-7414. **Contact:** Personnel. **Description:** A residential correction facility for juvenile offenders. **Office hours:** Monday - Friday, 8:00 a.m. - 5:00 p.m. **Parent company:** Philadelphia Department of Public Welfare. **Executive Director:** Robert Liggett. **Number of employees at this location:** 470.

NEW HOLLAND, INC.
P.O. Box 1895, New Holland PA 17557-0903. 717/355-1121. **Fax:** 717/363-6556. **Contact:** Linda Tajnai, Human Resources. **World Wide Web address:** http://www.newholland.com. **Description:** A manufacturer of agricultural equipment including tractors and balers. **Special programs:** Internships. **Corporate headquarters location:** London, England. **Parent company:** Fiat. **Operations at this facility include:** Administration; Divisional Headquarters; Manufacturing; Research and Development; Sales; Service. **Number of employees at this location:** 2,000. **Number of employees nationwide:** 4,000.

NEW WORLD PASTA
P.O. Box 126457, Harrisburg PA 17112-6457. 717/526-2200. **Contact:** Human Resources. **World Wide Web address:** http://www.nwpasta.com. **Description:** Produces a variety of pasta products including macaroni, spaghetti, and egg noodles. **Parent company:** Hershey Foods Corporation (Hershey PA). **Operations at this facility include:** Manufacturing; Service. **Listed on:** New York Stock Exchange. **Stock exchange symbol:** HSY.

NEW YORK & COMPANY
9th and Market Streets, Gallery Market East, Philadelphia PA 19107. 215/627-2550. **Contact:** Manager. **E-mail address:** recruiting@nyandcompany.com. **World Wide Web address:** http://www.nyandcompany.com. **Description:** A store location of the national women's moderately priced specialty apparel store chain. **NOTE:** Resumes should be sent to 450 West 33rd Street, 5th Floor, New York NY 10001. **Corporate headquarters location:** New York NY. **Parent company:** Limited, Inc. owns over 2,300 stores nationwide operating under such names as The Limited, Express, Victoria's Secret, Lane Bryant, and Size Unlimited, and also operates a mail order catalog business. **Operations at this facility include:** Sales; Service. **Listed on:** New York Stock Exchange. **Stock exchange symbol:** LTD.

NEWS AMERICA PUBLICATIONS, INC.
TV GUIDE
4 Radnor Corporate Center, 100 Matsonford Road, Radnor PA 19088. 610/293-8500. **Fax:** 610/293-6204. **Contact:** Human Resources. **World Wide Web address:** http://www.tvguide.com. **Description:** Publishes *TV Guide* magazine. **Special programs:** Internships. **Corporate headquarters location:** This location. **Operations at this facility include:** Administration; Sales; Service. **Number of employees at this location:** 1,300.

NOBEL LEARNING COMMUNITIES
1615 West Chester Pike, West Chester PA 19382. 484/947-2000. **Contact:** Human Resources. **World Wide Web address:** http://www.nobellearning.com. **Description:** Provides for the care and education of children from infancy through eighth grade. The daycare and early developmental programs are provided by the Rocking Horse Child Care division, which consists of 40 centers, while the preschool through eighth grade educational programs are provided through Merryhill Country Schools in California; and Chesterbrook Academy in Pennsylvania, New Jersey, North Carolina, and Illinois. Founded in 1982. **NOTE:** Teachers interested in employment opportunities may send their resumes to nobelteacher@nlcinc.com. The job postings for administrative/executive positions are listed on http://www.monster.com. **Positions advertised include:** Executive Director; Principal.

NORTH AMERICAN COMMUNICATIONS
Route 220 & 22, Y-Switches, Duncansville PA 16635. 814/696-3553. **Fax:** 814/696-2535. **Contact:** Ms. Tera Herman, Human Resources. **World Wide Web address:** http://www.nacmail.com. **Description:** A vertically integrated direct mail company. North American Communications performs all phases of production, from printing to mailing. Clients include *Fortune* 500 companies, primarily financial institutions. **Positions advertised include:** Account Executive; Machine Operator; Mechanic; Quality Assurance; Sheetfeed Operator. **Special programs:** Internships. **Internship information:** Internships are offered year-round. Positions are available in engineering, customer service, and accounting, and some positions are paid. Contact Human Resources for more information. **Other U.S. locations:** San Diego CA. **Operations at this facility include:** Administration; Manufacturing; Research and Development. **Annual sales/revenues:** $51 - $100 million. **Number of employees at this location:** 555. **Number of employees nationwide:** 800.

NORTH AMERICAN PUBLISHING COMPANY
401 North Broad Street, Philadelphia PA 19108. 215/238-5300. **Contact:** Human Resources. **World Wide Web address:** http://www.napco.com. **Description:** A publisher of trade and business magazines. **NOTE:** Entry-level positions are offered. **Positions advertised include:** Advertising Sales Representative; Editorial; Production. **Special programs:** Internships. **Office hours:** Monday - Friday 8:30 a.m. - 5:00 p.m. **Corporate headquarters location:** This location. **President:** Ned S. Borowsky.

NORTH PITTSBURGH TELEPHONE COMPANY
4008 Gibsonia Road, Gibsonia PA 15044. 724/443-9600. **Contact:** Human Resources. **World Wide Web address:** http://www.nptc.com. **Description:** A communications holding company. **Parent company:** North Pittsburgh Systems, Inc.

NOVA CHEMICALS
400 Frankfurt Road, Monaca PA 15061. 724/774-1000. **Recorded jobline:** 888/371-0161. **Contact:** John Thayer, Manager of Personnel. **World Wide Web address:** http://www.novachem.com. **Description:** Manufactures and markets chemicals specializing in plastics, foams, fuel additives, and other intermediate chemicals. **Listed on:** New York Stock Exchange. **Stock exchange symbol:** NCX.

NOVACARE REHABILITATION
680 American Avenue, Suite 200, King of Prussia PA 19406. 610/992-7200. **Toll-free phone:** 800/331-8840. **Contact:** Human Resources. **World Wide Web address:** http://www.novacare.com. **Description:** Provides comprehensive medical rehabilitation services to patients with physical disabilities. NovaCare's services include speech-language pathology, occupational therapy, and physical therapy. Services are provided

on a contract basis primarily to long-term health care institutions, through inpatient rehabilitation hospitals and community-integrated programs, and through a national network of patient care centers providing orthotic and prosthetic rehabilitation services. **Positions advertised include:** Cash Applications Representative; Medical Collections Representative; Customer Service Representative; Customer Service Supervisor; Athletic Trainer. **Corporate headquarters location:** This location. **Other U.S. locations:** Nationwide. **Parent company:** Select Medical. **Listed on:** New York Stock Exchange. **Stock exchange symbol:** NOV.

NUTRISYSTEM L.P.
202 Welsh Road, Horsham PA 19044. 215/706-5300. **Fax:** 215/706-5388. **Contact:** Human Resources. **World Wide Web address:** http://www.nutrisystem.com. **Description:** A chain of weight loss/weight maintenance centers providing professionally supervised services through a network of 700 company-owned and franchised centers. **Corporate headquarters location:** This location. **Other U.S. locations:** Nationwide. **International locations:** Canada; Saudi Arabia. **Listed on:** NASDAQ. **Stock exchange symbol:** THIN. **Number of employees at this location:** 75. **Number of employees nationwide:** 600.

NUTRITION MANAGEMENT SERVICES COMPANY
2071 Kimberton Road, P.O. Box 725, Kimberton PA 19442. 610/935-2050. **Fax:** 610/935-8287. **Contact:** Personnel Department. **World Wide Web address:** http://www.nmsc.com. **Description:** A food service management company specializing in food service programs for health care, retirement, and acute care facilities. **Positions advertised include:** District Manager; Food Service Director; Assistant Food Service Director. **Corporate headquarters location:** This location.

OCCIDENTAL CHEMICAL CORPORATION
375 Arm and Hammer Boulevard, P.O. Box 699, Pottstown PA 19464. 610/327-6400. **Contact:** Human Resources. **World Wide Web address:** http://www.oxychem.com. **Description:** Manufactures a wide range of PVC resins, compounds, and fabricated products. **NOTE:** Unsolicited applications are not accepted. **Corporate headquarters location:** Dallas TX. **Parent company:** Occidental Petroleum Corporation is a natural resources company engaged in the exploration for and the development of oil and natural gas in the United States.

OGDEN MANUFACTURING COMPANY
423 West Plum Street, Edinboro PA 16412. 814/734-5625. **Contact:** Cathi Mitchell, Personnel. **World Wide Web address:** http://www.ogdenmfg.com. **Description:** A manufacturer of heating elements for a wide variety of products including consumer products and commercial and industrial heaters. **Corporate headquarters location:** Arlington Heights IL.

OHIO VALLEY GENERAL HOSPITAL
Heckel Road, Kennedy Township, McKees Rocks PA 15136-1694. 412/777-6218. **Fax:** 412/777-6804. **Recorded jobline:** 412/777-6397. **Contact:** Human Resources Department. **World Wide Web address:** http://www.ohiovalleyhospital.org. **Description:** A 118-bed, nonprofit community hospital serving Pittsburgh's western suburbs and the Pittsburgh International Airport area. **NOTE:** Resumes are accepted in person in the Human Resources office Monday through Friday, from 9:00 a.m. - 4:00 p.m. Entry-level positions, part-time jobs, and second and third shifts are offered. **Positions advertised include:** Registered Nurse; Nursing Supervisor; Cardiology Technician; Physical Therapy Assistant. **Operations at this facility include:** Administration; Health Care; Service. **Number of employees at this location:** 600.

OLIVE GARDEN RESTAURANT
6000 Oxford Drive, Bethel Park PA 15102-1826. 412/835-6353. **Fax:** 412/835-6047. **Contact:** Human Resources. **World Wide Web address:** http://www.olivegarden.com. **Description:** One location in a chain of family-style Italian restaurants. **Positions advertised include:** Service Manager; Sales Manager; Culinary Manager; Server. **Parent Company:** Darden Restaurants.

OMNOVA SOLUTIONS INC.
1001 Chambers Avenue, Jeannette PA 15644. 724/523-5441. **Contact:** Human Resources. **World Wide Web address:** http://www.omnova.com. **Description:** Produces specialty chemicals, coatings, and coverings for use in a variety of industries. Omnova operates through two divisions, Decorative & Building Products and Performance Chemicals.

ONEBEACON INSURANCE
100 Corporate Center Drive, Camp Hill PA 17001-8851. 717/763-7331. **Contact:** Deb Singer, Human Resources. **E-mail address:** onebeaconjobs@onebeacon.com. **World Wide Web address:** http://www.onebeacon.com. **Description:** A carrier of property, casualty, and life insurance. **NOTE:** Resumes should be directed to: 46 Walnut Street, Philadelphia PA 191016. Fax: 215/625-1046. **Positions advertised include:** Claims Adjuster; Claims Supervisor. **Corporate headquarters location:** Boston MA. **Other U.S. locations:** Nationwide.

ORASURE TECHNOLOGIES, INC.
150 Webster Street, Bethlehem PA 18015. 610/882-1820. **Fax:** 610/882-1830. **Contact:** Jill Manning. **World Wide Web address:** http://www.orasure.com. **Description:** Produces biomedical diagnostic products. **Positions advertised include:** Senior Accountant; Purchasing Manager; Inventory Quality Specialist; Quality Assurance Specialist; Engineering Co-Op Student; Creative Services Specialist. **Corporate headquarters location:** Beaverton OR.

ORTHO-McNEIL PHARMACEUTICAL
Welsh Road at McKean Road, Spring House PA 19477-0776. 215/628-5000. **Contact:** Employment Manager. **World Wide Web address:** http://www.ortho-mcneil.com. **Description:** Develops and sells pharmaceutical products including women's health, infectious disease, and wound healing products. **NOTE:** Jobs are posted on the Johnson & Johnson corporate Website: http://www.jnj.com. **Corporate headquarters location:** This location. **Parent company:** Johnson & Johnson (New Brunswick NJ). **Operations at this facility include:** Administration; Manufacturing; Research and Development.

OSRAM SYLVANIA, INC.
1128 Roosevelt Avenue, York PA 17404. 717/848-8080. **Fax:** 717/852-0875. **Contact:** Deb Barshinger, Human Resources. **E-mail address:** deb.barshinger@sylvania.com. **World Wide Web address:** http://www.sylvania.com. **Description:** Operates in four divisions: Coated Coil Operation produces tungsten filaments coated with high-performance insulator aluminum oxide for use in television electron guns; Special Refractory Products manufactures products made from refractory metals that are used as furnace hardware; The Ceramics Department produces various types of steatite ceramic electrical insulators used in bases of light bulbs; The Quartz Department produces and finishes quartz crucibles for use by the semiconductor industry. Founded in 1953. **NOTE:** Second and third shifts are offered. **Positions advertised include:** General Foreman; Foreman. **Special programs:** Apprenticeships; Co-ops. **Office hours:** Monday - Friday, 7:30 a.m. - 4:30 p.m. **Corporate headquarters location:** Danvers MA. **Operations at this facility include:** This location manufactures automotive connectors, deep-drawn metal stampings, lighting components, metal base and stampings, wire drawing and lead wires, formed metal components for the lighting industry, custom metal stampings, and connector products. **Parent company:** OSRAM. **Annual sales/revenues:** $51 - $100 million. **Number of employees at this location:** 310. **Number of employees nationwide:** 16,000.

OSRAM SYLVANIA, INC.
816 Lexington Avenue, Warren PA 16365. 814/726-6500. **Contact:** Craig Rieder, Human Resources Manager. **World Wide Web address:** http://www.sylvania.com. **Description:** Operates in four divisions: Coated Coil Operation produces tungsten filaments coated with high-performance insulator aluminum oxide for use in television electron guns; Special Refractory Products manufactures products made from refractory metals that are used as furnace hardware; The Ceramics Department produces various types of steatite ceramic electrical insulators used in bases of light bulbs; The Quartz Department produces and finishes quartz crucibles for use by the semiconductor industry. **Corporate headquarters location:** Danvers MA. **Operations at this facility include:** This location manufactures electronic and plastic parts for cars, as well as specialty wire for a variety of end uses. **Parent company:** OSRAM. **Number of employees nationwide:** 16,000.

OVERHEAD DOOR CORPORATION
23 Industrial Park Road, Lewistown PA 17044-0110. 717/248-0131. **Contact:** Human Resources. **E-mail address:** jobs@overheaddoor.com. **World Wide Web address:** http://www.overheaddoor.com. **Description:** Designs, manufactures, and installs upward-lifting doors including commercial and industrial systems and residential garage doors and openers. Founded in 1923. **Positions advertised include:** Customer Service Representative; Occupational Safety and Health Administrator. **Corporate headquarters location:** Dallas TX.

OWENS-BROCKWAY CORPORATION
151 Grand Avenue, Clarion PA 16214-1708. 814/226-0536. **Contact:** Employment Manager. **E-mail address:** resumes@us.o-i.com. **World Wide Web address:** http://www.o-i.com. **Description:** Owens-Brockway primarily produces glass containers. The company also produces and sells containerboard, corrugated containers, printing plates and ink, plywood and dimension lumber, blown plastic containers, plastic beverage bottles, plastic drums, metal and plastic closures, tamper-resistant closures, plastic and glass prescription containers, pharmaceutical items, labels, and multipack plastic carriers for containers. Specialized glass products made and sold by the company include Libbey tumblers, stemware, decorative glassware, television bulbs for picture tubes, and Kimble scientific and laboratory ware. Some overseas affiliates also manufacture flat glass and related products. **NOTE:** Mailed resumes should be sent to One SeaGate, Toledo OH 43666. **Parent company:** Owens Illinois. **Operations at this facility include:** This location manufactures glass bottles.

OWENS-BROCKWAY CORPORATION
P.O. Box B, Plant 19, Brockway PA 15824-9802. 814/261-5306. **Contact:** Jackie Anderson, Human Resources. **World Wide Web address:** http://www.o-i.com. **Description:** Owens-Brockway primarily produces glass containers. The company also produces and sells containerboard, corrugated containers, printing plates and ink, plywood and dimension lumber, blown plastic containers, plastic beverage bottles, plastic drums, metal and plastic closures, tamper-resistant closures, plastic and glass prescription containers, pharmaceutical items, labels, and multipack plastic carriers for containers. Specialized glass products made and sold by the company include Libbey tumblers, stemware, decorative glassware, television bulbs for picture tubes, and Kimble scientific and laboratory ware. Some overseas affiliates also manufacture flat glass and related products. **Operations at this facility include:** This plant produces glass containers.

PDG ENVIRONMENTAL, INC.
1386 Beulah Road, Building 801, Pittsburgh 15235. 412/856-2200. **Toll-free phone:** 800/972-7341. **Fax:** 412/243-4900. **Contact:** Human Resources. **World Wide Web address:** http://www.pdge.com. **Description:** Provides asbestos and lead abatement services, environmental hazard clean-up services, and building demolition.

PDS INC. (PERSONNEL DATA SYSTEMS)
650 Sentry Parkway, Blue Bell PA 19422. 610/238-4600. **Fax:** 610/238-4550. **Contact:** Human Resources. **E-mail address:** jobs@pdssoftware.com. **World Wide Web address:** http://www.pdssoftware.com. **Description:** PDS designs and develops human resources and payroll systems software for PC networks, IBM mainframes, and operating environments with strong emphasis on client/server technology. **Positions advertised include:** Application Product Support Specialist; HRMS Software Implementation Consultant.

PEI-GENESIS
2180 Hornig Road, Philadelphia PA 19116-4289. 215/673-0400. **Toll-free phone:** 800/675-1214. **Fax:** 215/552-8022. **Contact:** Human Resources Director. **World Wide Web address:** http://www.pei-genesis.com. **Description:** A distributor of a variety of electronic parts. Founded in 1946.

PG ENERGY
One PEI Center, Wilkes-Barre PA 18711-0601. 570/829-8600. **Contact:** Human Resources. **E-mail address:** info@pgenergy.com. **World Wide Web address:** http://www.pgenergy.com. **Description:** A gas utility company that serves over 154,000 customers in northeastern and central Pennsylvania. PG Energy maintains a distribution system of 2,300 miles of pipelines. **Parent company:** Southern Union Company. **Number of employees nationwide:** 450.

THE PMA INSURANCE GROUP
380 Sentry Parkway, P.O. Box 3031, Blue Bell PA 19422-0754. 610/397-5000. **Toll-free phone:** 800/222-2719. **Contact:** Human Resources. **E-mail address:** employment@pmagroup.com. **World Wide Web address:** http://www.pmagroup.com. **Description:** Provides workers' compensation insurance. **Positions advertised include:** Actuarial Student; Senior Account Claims Representative; Financial Analyst; Corporate Medical Specialist; Business Analyst; Claims Service Adjuster; Disability Management Coordinator; Integrated Disability Underwriter. **Special programs:** Internships. **Corporate headquarters location:** This location. **Other area locations:** Allentown PA; Harrisburg PA; Pittsburgh PA; Ridgeway PA; Valley Forge PA; Williamsport PA. **Other U.S. locations:** Hunt Valley MD; Charlotte NC; Raleigh NC; Mount Laurel NJ; Richmond VA; Roanoke VA. **Number of employees at this location:** 1,050.

PNC BANK
11 West Market Street, Wilkes-Barre PA 18768. 570/826-4614. **Recorded jobline:** 800/PNC-JOBS. **Fax:** 800/267-3755. **Contact:** Human Resources. **E-mail address:** resumes@pncbank.com. **World Wide Web address:** http://www.pncbank.com.

Description: A bank. **Positions advertised include:** Risk Analyst; Teller; Manager; Statistician. **Parent company:** PNC Bank Corporation is one of the nation's largest financial services companies. The company's major divisions include Corporate Banking, Consumer Banking, PNC Mortgage, and PNC Asset Management Group. With nearly 500 offices across Delaware, Indiana, Kentucky, Ohio, and Pennsylvania, PNC is one of the largest banking franchises in the Midwest and Mid-Atlantic. **Listed on:** New York Stock Exchange. **Stock exchange symbol:** PNC.

PNC BANK
18 South Bryn Mawr Avenue, Bryn Mawr PA 19010. 610/520-5151. **Recorded jobline:** 800/PNC-JOBS. **Fax:** 800/267-3755. **Contact:** Human Resources Department. **E-mail address:** resumes@pncbank.com. **World Wide Web address:** http://www.pncbank.com. **Description:** A bank. **Positions advertised include:** Financial Consultant; Branch Manager; Bank Teller; Business Banker. **Parent company:** PNC Bank Corporation is one of the nation's largest financial services companies. The company's major divisions include Corporate Banking, Consumer Banking, PNC Mortgage, and PNC Asset Management Group. With nearly 500 offices across Delaware, Indiana, Kentucky, Ohio, and Pennsylvania, PNC is one of the largest banking franchises in the Midwest and Mid-Atlantic. **Listed on:** New York Stock Exchange. **Stock exchange symbol:** PNC.

PNC BANK
901 State Street, Erie PA 16501. 814/871-9316. **Recorded jobline:** 800/PNC-JOBS. **Fax:** 800/267-3755. **Contact:** Human Resources Department. **E-mail address:** resumes@pncbank.com. **World Wide Web address:** http://www.pncbank.com. **Description:** A bank. **Positions advertised include:** Finance Project Manager; Client Service Representative; Administrative Assistant; Sales Associate; Teller; Risk Analyst; Senior Accountant. **Parent company:** PNC Bank Corporation is one of the nation's largest financial services companies. The company's major divisions include Corporate Banking, Consumer Banking, PNC Mortgage, and PNC Asset Management Group. With nearly 500 offices across Delaware, Indiana, Kentucky, Ohio, and Pennsylvania, PNC is one of the largest banking franchises in the Midwest and Mid-Atlantic. **Listed on:** New York Stock Exchange. **Stock exchange symbol:** PNC.

PNC FINANCIAL SERVICES GROUP
2 PNC Plaza, 620 Liberty Avenue, 2nd Floor, Pittsburgh PA 15222-2719. **Fax:** 800/267-3755. **Recorded jobline:** 800/PNC-JOBS. **Contact:** Human Resources Department. **E-mail address:** resumes@pncbank.com. **World Wide Web address:** http://www.pnc.com. **Description:** Offers a complete range of financial services and products to individuals and corporations. Major businesses include corporate banking, consumer banking, PNC Mortgage, and PNC Asset Management Group. **NOTE:** Entry-level positions, part-time jobs, and second and third shifts are offered. Mailed in resumes should be sent in a scannable format, check the Website for further details. **Positions advertised include:** Branch Financial Sale Consultant; Branch Services Manager; Customer Service Associate; Senior Financial Consultant; Teller; Financial Processor. **Special programs:** Training; Co-ops; Summer Jobs. **Corporate headquarters location:** This location. **Other area locations:** Philadelphia PA. **Other U.S. locations:** Nationwide. **Subsidiaries include:** Blackrock Financial Management; PNC Mortgage. **Operations at this facility include:** Administration; Sales. **Listed on:** New York Stock Exchange. **Stock exchange symbol:** PNC. **Annual sales/revenues:** More than $100 million. **Number of employees at this location:** 5,000.

PPG INDUSTRIES, INC.
One PPG Place, Suite 700, Pittsburgh PA 15272. 412/434-3131. **Contact:** Human Resources. **World Wide Web address:** http://www.ppg.com. **Description:** A diversified global manufacturer, PPG Industries is a supplier of products for manufacturing, building, automotive, processing, and numerous other industries. The company makes decorative and protective coatings, flat glass and fabricated glass products, continuous-strand fiberglass, and industrial and specialty chemicals. Founded in 1883. **Positions advertised include:** Accounting Coordinator; Legal Secretary; Human Resources Intern; Environmental Engineer Intern; IT Auditor/Analyst. **Corporate headquarters location:** This location. **International locations:** Worldwide. **Listed on:** New York Stock Exchange. **Stock exchange symbol:** PPG. **Annual sales/revenues:** More than $100 million.

PPG INDUSTRIES, INC.
400 Park Drive, Carlisle PA 17013. 717/486-3366. **Contact:** Human Resources. **World Wide Web address:** http://www.ppg.com. **Description:** PPG Industries is a diversified global manufacturer supplying products for manufacturing, building, automotive, processing, and numerous other world industries. The company makes decorative and protective coatings, flat glass and fabricated glass products, continuous-strand fiberglass, and industrial and specialty chemicals. Founded in 1883. **Corporate headquarters location:** Pittsburgh PA. **International locations:** Worldwide. **Operations at this facility include:** This location manufactures flat glass. **Listed on:** New York Stock Exchange. **Stock exchange symbol:** PPG. **Annual sales/revenues:** More than $100 million.

PPG INDUSTRIES, INC.
150 Ferry Street, Creighton PA 15030. 724/224-6500. **Contact:** Human Resources. **World Wide Web address:** http://www.ppg.com. **Description:** PPG Industries is a diversified global manufacturer supplying products for manufacturing, building, automotive, processing, and numerous other world industries. The company makes decorative and protective coatings, flat glass and fabricated glass products, continuous-strand fiberglass, and industrial and specialty chemicals. Founded in 1883. **Corporate headquarters location:** Pittsburgh PA. **International locations:** Worldwide. **Operations at this facility include:** This location manufactures windshields. **Listed on:** New York Stock Exchange. **Stock exchange symbol:** PPG. **Annual sales/revenues:** More than $100 million.

PPG INDUSTRIES, INC.
125 Colfax Street, Springdale PA 15144-1506. 724/274-7900. **Contact:** Human Resources. **World Wide Web address:** http://www.ppg.com. **Description:** PPG Industries is a diversified global manufacturer supplying products for manufacturing, building, automotive, processing, and numerous other industries. The company makes decorative and protective coatings, flat glass and fabricated glass products, continuous-strand fiberglass, and industrial and specialty chemicals. Founded in 1883. **Corporate headquarters location:** Pittsburgh PA. **International locations:** Worldwide. **Operations at this facility include:** This location manufactures coatings and resins. **Listed on:** New York Stock Exchange. **Stock exchange symbol:** PPG. **Annual sales/revenues:** More than $100 million.

PPG INDUSTRIES, INC.
5123 Victory Boulevard, P.O. Box 800, Meadville PA 16335. 814/336-4411. **Contact:** Human Resources. **World Wide Web address:** http://www.ppg.com. **Description:** PPG Industries is a diversified global manufacturer supplying products for manufacturing, building, automotive, processing, and numerous other industries. The company makes decorative and protective coatings, flat glass and fabricated glass products, continuous-strand fiberglass, and industrial and specialty chemicals. Founded in 1883. **Positions advertised include:** Systems Administrator; Office Space Coordinator; Audit Team Leader; Manager Cash Operations; Telecommunications Engineer; Simulator Instructor; Regional Sales Manager. **Corporate headquarters location:** Pittsburgh PA. **International locations:** Worldwide. **Operations at this facility include:** This location manufactures glass. **Listed on:** New York Stock Exchange. **Stock exchange symbol:** PPG. **Annual sales/revenues:** More than $100 million.

PPL CORPORATION
2 North Ninth Street, Allentown PA 18101. 610/774-5151. **Fax:** 610/774-4245. **Contact:** Jan Thomas, HR Consultant. **World Wide Web address:** http://www.pplweb.com. **Description:** An electric utility company serving 1.2 million customers in the Pennsylvania area. **Positions advertised include:** Paralegal; Call Center Representative; Origination Manager; Regulatory Research Analyst; Transmission Specialist; Quantitative Business Analyst; Senior Engineer; Foreman; Operator Helper; Marketing Communications Manager. **Corporate headquarters location:** This location. **Listed on:** New York Stock Exchange. **Stock exchange symbol:** PPL. **Number of employees at this location:** 6,400.

PPL GAS UTILITIES CORPORATION
P.O. Box 189, 76-80 Mill Street, Port Allegany PA 16743. **Toll-free phone:** 800/652-0550. **Fax:** 814/642-2510. **Contact:** Personnel. **World Wide Web address:** http://www.pplweb.com. **Description:** A gas utility. **Positions advertised include:** Systems Administrator; Corporate Communications Specialist; Business Analyst; Tax Planning Analyst. **Office hours:** Monday - Friday, 8:00 a.m. - 5:00 p.m. **Corporate headquarters location:** Oxford PA. **Parent company:** Penn Fuel Gas Inc. **Number of employees worldwide:** 12,500.

PQ CORPORATION
P.O. Box 840, Valley Forge PA 19482-0840. 610/651-4200. **Physical address:** 1200 West Swedesford Road, Berwyn PA 19312-1077. **Fax:** 610/651-4435. **Contact:** Human Resources. **E-mail address:** HR@pqcorp.com. **World Wide Web address:** http://www.pqcorp.com. **Description:** Manufactures a wide range of glass products including reflective glass for automotive and highway safety use, decorative glass, and industrial glass products. **NOTE:** An alternative e-mail address is staffing@pqcorp.com. **Positions advertised include:** Payroll/HRIS Coordinator; Business Group Manager; Administrative Associate. **Corporate headquarters location:** This location.

PTC ALLIANCE
Copperleaf Corporate Centre, 6051 Wallace Road Ext., Suite 200, Wexford PA 15090. 412/299-7900. **Fax:** 412/299-2619. **Contact:** Human Resources Manager. **World Wide Web address:** http://www.ptcalliance.com. **Description:** A steel-rolling mill. **Corporate headquarters location:** This location. **Listed on:** NASDAQ. **Stock exchange symbol:** PMTC.

PACE RESOURCES INC.
P.O. Box 15040, York PA 17405-7040. **Physical address:** 40 South Richland, York PA 17404. 717/852-1300. **Contact:** Frank Weaver, Human Resources Director. **Description:** A holding company for architectural and engineering firms, as well as a testing laboratory, a computer service center, and a printing company. Founded in 1970.

R.M. PALMER COMPANY
P.O. Box 1723, Reading PA 19603. 610/372-8971. **Contact:** Human Resources Manager. **World Wide Web address:** http://www.rmpalmer.com. **Description:** Manufactures chocolates and other confections for Halloween, Christmas, Easter, and Valentine's Day. **Operations at this facility include:** Administration; Manufacturing; Sales.

PARADISE DATACOM LLC
1012 East Boal Avenue, Boalsburg PA 16827. 814/466-6275. **Contact:** Human Resources. **World Wide Web address:** http://www.paradisedata.com. **Description:** Develops and manufactures satellite communication equipment. Products include satellite modems, low noise amplifiers, solid-state power amplifiers, and clock reference and sync distribution equipment. **International locations:** United Kingdom.

PARENTE RANDOLPH, PC
46 Public Square, Suite 400, Wilkes-Barre PA 18701. 570/820-0166. **Fax:** 570/820-0166. **Contact:** Vicky Micheletti, Human Resources Manager. **E-mail address:** hr@parentenet.com. **World Wide Web address:** http://www.parentenet.com. **Description:** Parente Randolph is one of the mid-Atlantic's leading independent accounting and consulting firms. The firm's 400 employees provide accounting, audit, tax, and general business consulting services to corporations and closely held businesses from 10 offices in Pennsylvania, New Jersey, and Delaware. Industry expertise includes healthcare, senior living services, financial services, education, government/nonprofit, manufacturing, construction, real estate, retail, wholesale, and distribution. Specialty services include corporate finance, business reorganization, forensic accounting, and litigation support. Parente Randolph affiliates provide technology consulting, energy consulting, HR consulting, leadership development and training, and executive search services. Founded in 1970. **Positions advertised include:** Staff Assistant; Staff Accountant; Supervisor; Manager; Principal. **Special programs:** Internship.

PARKVIEW HOSPITAL
1333 East Wyoming Avenue, Philadelphia PA 19124. 215/537-7601. **Contact:** Employment Manager. **E-mail address:** parkviewjobs@tenethealth.com. **World Wide Web address:** http://www.parkviewhosp.com. **Description:** A hospital. **Positions advertised include:** Registered Nurse; Pharmacist; Coder; Therapist; Physical Therapist. **Special programs:** Internships. **Other U.S. locations:** Reading PA. **Parent company:** Tenet Health Care Group. **Annual sales/revenues:** $21 - $50 million. **Number of employees at this location:** 800.

PARSONS POWER GROUP INC.
2675 Morgantown Road, Reading PA 19607. 610/855-2560. **Fax:** 610/855-2186. **Contact:** Human Resources. **World Wide Web address:** http://www.parsons.com. **Description:** Provides a wide range of engineering and consulting services including electrical, mechanical, structural, and nuclear engineering; construction management; procurement; and consulting services. The company's major services are the design, engineering, and supervision of the construction of electrical power generating stations, and electrical transmission and distribution systems, as well as the upgrading and retrofitting of existing power plants. Parsons Power Group also renders services to industrial clients and various government agencies. **Parent company:** The Parsons Corporation.

PAYCHEX, INC.
7450 Tilghman Street, Suite 107, Allentown PA 18106. 610/398-7518. **Fax:** 610/398-8632. **Contact:** Human Resources. **World Wide Web address:** http://www.paychex.com. **Description:** A payroll processing and payroll tax preparation company for small to medium-sized businesses. **Positions advertised include:** Account Executive; Branch Manager; Client Services Representative; Computer Operator; Distribution Specialist; District Sales Assistant; Payroll Specialist; Receptionist. **Corporate headquarters location:** Rochester NY. **Other U.S. locations:** Nationwide. **Number of employees nationwide:** 3,300.

PECO ENERGY
2301 Market Street, Philadelphia PA 19101. 215/841-4000. **Fax:** 215/841-5473. **Contact:** Human Resources Staffing. **E-mail address:** careers@exeloncorp. **World Wide Web address:** http://www.peco.com. **Description:** An operating utility that provides electric and gas service in southeastern Pennsylvania. Two subsidiaries own and a third subsidiary operates the Conowingo Hydroelectric Project, and one distribution subsidiary provides electric service in two counties in northeastern Maryland. **Special programs:** Internships. **Corporate headquarters location:** This location. **Parent company:** Exelon. **Annual sales/revenues:** More than $100 million. **Number of employees at this location:** 9,300.

PEERLESS HEATER COMPANY
231 North Walnut Street, Boyertown PA 19512-0121. 610/367-2153. **Contact:** Human Resources. **World Wide Web address:** http://www.peerlessheater.com. **Description:** Manufactures cast iron boilers for commercial and residential customers.

PEIRCE-PHELPS, INC.
2000 North 59th Street, Philadelphia PA 19131. 215/879-7000. **Contact:** Human Resources. **World Wide Web address:** http://www.peirce.com. **Description:** Distributes a variety of electrical appliances including washers, dryers, and air conditioners.

PENCO PRODUCTS, INC.
P.O. Box 378, 99 Brower Avenue, Oaks PA 19456. 610/666-0500. **Fax;** 610/666-7561. **Contact:** Human Resources. **World Wide Web address:** http://www.pencoproducts.com. **Description:** Manufactures steel storage products including lockers, shelves, and cabinets.

PENN ENGINEERING & MANUFACTURING CORPORATION
P.O. Box 1000, Danboro PA 18916. 215/766-8853. **Physical address:** 5190 Old Easton Road, Danboro PA 18916. **Contact:** Human Resources. **World Wide Web address:** http://www.pemnet.com. **Description:** Manufactures stainless steel and aluminum fasteners and fastening equipment.

PENN LINE SERVICES
300 Scottdale Avenue, P.O. Box 462, Scottdale PA 15683. 724/887-9110. **Contact:** Human Resources. **World Wide Web address:** http://www.pennline.com. **Description:** A contracting firm that offers a range of specialties including electrical, guardrail, landscaping, and tree trimming services.

PENN MUTUAL LIFE INSURANCE COMPANY
600 Dresher Road, Horsham PA 19044. 215/956-8000. **Contact:** Human Resources. **E-mail address:** careers@pennmutual.com. **World Wide Web address:** http://www.pennmutual.com. **Description:** Offers life insurance and annuities. **Positions advertised include:** Extract, Transform, and Load Specialist; Extract, Transform, and Load Team Leader. **Corporate headquarters location:** This location. **Subsidiaries include:** Independence Financial Group.

PENN NATIONAL RACE COURSE
P.O. Box 32, Grantville PA 17028. 717/469-2211. **Contact:** Human Resources. **World Wide Web address:** http://www.pnrc.com. **Description:** A thoroughbred racetrack. **Parent company:** Penn National Gaming, Inc.

PENN POWER
P.O. Box 891, New Castle PA 16103-0891. 724/652-5531. **Contact:** Human Resources. **World Wide Web address:** http://www.firstenergycorp.com. **Description:** An electric utility company. **NOTE:** Jobseekers should contact First Energy Corporate Headquarters: 76 South Main Street, Akron OH 44308. **Parent company:** First Energy Corporation.

PENN TRAFFIC COMPANY
RIVERSIDE BI-LO FOODS
P.O. Box 607, DuBois PA 15801. 814/375-3663. **Physical address:** Shaffer Road, Route 255, Dubois PA 15801. **Contact:** Cathy Huey, Human Resources. **Description:** A food retailer, wholesaler, and producer. The company operates more than 230 supermarkets in New York, Ohio, Pennsylvania, and West Virginia under the names Big Bear, Insalaco's, Riverside Markets, Quality Markets, and P&C Foods. Penn Traffic Company also wholesales to 249 stores and operates a dairy and ice cream manufacturing facility in Pennsylvania, two bakeries in New York and Ohio, and 15 discount department stores. **Corporate headquarters location:** Syracuse NY.

PENN TREATY AMERICAN CORPORATION
3440 Lehigh Street, Allentown PA 18103. 610/965-2222. **Toll-free phone:** 800/222-3469. **Fax:** 877/LTC-FAXX. **Contact:** Human Resources. **E-mail address:** jobs@penntreaty.com. **World Wide Web address:** http://www.penntreaty.com. **Description:** A long-term care insurance company. Through its wholly owned subsidiaries, the company underwrites, markets, and sells individual supplemental accident and health insurance policies designed to cover the costs of long-term care. The company also offers life insurance policies, supplemental accident and health insurance policies, and policies providing benefits to supplement Medicare payments. **Positions advertised include:** Care Management Nurse; Claims Examiner.

PENN-UNION CORPORATION
229 Waterford Street, Edinboro PA 16412. 814/734-1631. **Contact:** Human Resources. **World Wide Web address:** http://www.penn-union.com. **Description:** Manufactures electronic connectors.

PENNSYLVANIA ASSOCIATION FOR SUSTAINABLE AGRICULTURE
114 West Main Street, P.O. Box 419, Millheim PA 16854. 814/349-9856. **Fax:** 814/349-9840. **Contact:** Human Resources. **E-mail address:** info@pasafarming.org. **World Wide Web address:** http://www.pasafarming.org. **Description:** A statewide, member based, non-profit for the benefit of the economic and social growth of food and agriculture in Pennsylvania. PASA addresses the sustainability of the entire food system, and is involved with all participating parties.

PENNSYLVANIA CERTIFIED ORGANIC
406 South Pennsylvania Avenue, Centre Hall PA 16828. 814/364-1344. **Fax:** 814/364-4431. **Contact:** Human Resources. **E-mail address:** info@paorganic.org. **World Wide Web address:** http://www.paorganic.org. **Description:** Pennsylvania's branch of the USDA's National Organic Program, with the goal to assure the integrity of organic products through education, inspection, and the certification of growers, producers and handlers.

PENNSYLVANIA HOSPITAL
800 Spruce Street, Philadelphia PA 19107. 215/829-3000. **Contact:** Human Resources/Employment. **World Wide Web address:** http://www.pahosp.com. **Description:** A 513-bed hospital. Founded in 1751. **Positions advertised include:** Night Shift Pharmacist; Radiation Therapist; Clinical Pharmacist; Administrative Assistant; Nurse Practitioner; Registered Nurse; Staff Nurse; Medical Technologist; Clinical Information Specialist.

PENNSYLVANIA HOUSE
137 North 10th Street, Lewisburg PA 17837. 570/523-1285. **Contact:** Human Resources. **World Wide Web address:** http://www.pennsylvaniahouse.com. **Description:** Manufactures upholstered furniture.

PENNSYLVANIA NEWSPAPER ASSOCIATION
3899 North Front Street, Harrisburg PA 17110. 717/703-3000. **Fax:** 717/703-3001. **Contact:** Human Resources. **World Wide Web address:** http://www.pnpa.com **Description:** The official trade organization for all Pennsylvania newspapers. Provides representation in the legislature and educational services, and acts as an information clearinghouse. **Subsidiaries include:** Mid-Atlantic Newspaper Services, Inc. & Pennsylvania Newspaper Association Foundation.

PENNSYLVANIA REAL ESTATE INVESTMENT TRUST
200 South Broad Street, 3rd Floor, Philadelphia PA 19102-3803. 215/875-0700. **Fax:** 215/546-7311. **Contact:** Human Resources. **World Wide Web address:** http://www.preit.com. **Description:** An equity real estate investment trust engaged in the business of managing, acquiring, and holding for investment real estate and interests in real estate. The trust's principal real estate assets consist of 48 properties, 20 of which are wholly-owned and 28 of which are owned by partnerships or joint ventures. **Positions advertised include:** Director of Corporate Communications; Information Management Analyst; Specialist Leasing Coordinator; Office Manager. **Listed on:** New York Stock Exchange. **Stock exchange symbol:** PEI.

PENNSYLVANIA STATE CIVIL SERVICE COMMISSION
Strawberry Square Complex, 2nd Floor, P.O. Box 569, Harrisburg PA 17108-0569. 717/783-3085. **Fax:** 717/772-2685. **Contact:** Recruitment Specialist. **World Wide Web address:** http://www.scsc.state.pa.us. **Description:** Engaged in government administration and management at the state level. **Positions advertised include:** Accountant; Actuarial Associate; Auditor; Budget Analyst; Business Enterprise Analyst; Field Human Resources Officer; Insurance Investigator; Management Analyst; Statistical Assistant; Statistician; Corrections Records Specialist. **Corporate headquarters location:** This location. **Number of employees at this location:** 60,000.

PENNSYLVANIA STATE UNIVERSITY
120 South Burrowes Street, University Park PA 16801-3857. 814/865-1387. **Fax:** 814/865-3750. **Recorded jobline:** 814/865-JOBS. **Contact:** Employment Division. **World Wide Web address:** http://www.hbg.psu.edu. **Description:** A state university offering undergraduate and graduate programs. Approximately 3,500 students attend Penn State Harrisburg. **Special programs:** Internships. **Corporate headquarters location:** University Park PA. **Number of employees at this location:** 350. **Number of employees nationwide:** 16,000.

PENNSYLVANIA STATE UNIVERSITY
Penn State New Kensington, 3550 Seventh Street, Route 780, Upper Burrell PA 15068. 724/334-6025. **Contact:** Human Resources. **World Wide Web address:** http://www.nk.psu.edu. **Description:** The New Kensington location of the state university system. This campus offers a four-year program and awards associate degrees. Enrollment is 1,100 undergraduates.

PENNSYLVANIA STATE UNIVERSITY
THE BEHREND COLLEGE
5091 Station Road, Erie PA 16563-0103. 814/865-1387. **Fax:** 814/865-3750. **Recorded jobline:** 814/865-JOBS. **Contact:** Employment Division. **World Wide Web address:** http://www.ohr.psu.edu. **Description:** A location of the Penn State University system. The Behrend College, with an enrollment of 2,800 undergraduates and 200 graduate students, offers four-year undergraduate as well as graduate programs. Penn State awards associate, bachelor's, and master's degrees including MBAs. **NOTE:** For employment information contact: Penn State Employment Division, 120 South Burrowes Street, University Park PA 16801-3857. 814/865-1387.

PENNTECQ INC.
106 Kuder Drive, Greenville PA 16125. 724/646-4250. **Contact:** Human Resources. **World Wide Web address:** http://www.penntecq.com. **Description:** Manufactures automotive parts including window moldings and door trim.

PENTAMATION ENTERPRISE INC.
225 Marketplace, Bethlehem PA 18018. 610/691-3616. **Fax:** 610/691-1031. **Contact:** Human Resources. **World Wide Web address:** http://www.pentamation.com. **Description:** Develops software and computer systems for school districts and government facilities. **Positions advertised include:** Programmer. **Parent company:** Sungard.

PEP BOYS
3111 West Allegheny Avenue, Philadelphia PA 19132. 215/227-9000. **Contact:** Human Resources. **World Wide Web address:** http://www.pepboys.com. **Description:** Primarily engaged in the retail sale of a wide range of automotive parts and accessories, and the installation of automobile components and merchandise. Pep Boys operates over 660 stores in 37 states. **Corporate headquarters location:** This location. **Operations at this facility include:** Administration. **Listed on:** New York Stock Exchange. **Stock exchange symbol:** PBY. **Number of employees at this location:** 600. **Number of employees worldwide:** 22,000.

PEPPER HAMILTON LLP
3000 Two Logan Square, 18th & Arch Streets, Philadelphia PA 19103-2799. 215/981-4000. **Fax:** 215/981-4750. **Contact:** Ms. Meg Urbanski, Director of Recruitment. **E-mail address:** urbanskim@pepperlaw.com. **World Wide Web address:** http://www.pepperlaw.com. **Description:** An international law firm. **NOTE:** Part-time jobs are offered. **Positions advertised include:** Health Affects Litigation Associate; Insurance/Reinsurance Associate; Commercial Litigation Associate. **Corporate headquarters location:** This location. **Operations at this facility include:**

Administration. **Number of employees at this location:** 560. **Number of employees nationwide:** 910.

PEPPERIDGE FARM, INC.
421 Boot Road, Downingtown PA 19335. 610/873-4400. **Contact:** Human Resources Department. **World Wide Web address:** http://www.pepperidgefarm.com. **Description:** Pepperidge Farm, Inc. manufactures and distributes a range of fresh and frozen baked goods and confections including bread, cookies, cakes, pastries, and Goldfish brand crackers. **Operations at this facility include:** This location is a frozen food plant. **NOTE:** Employment opportunities are listed at http://www.monster.com and at the Campbell Career Center. **Corporate headquarters location:** Norwalk CT. **Parent company:** Campbell Soup Company.

PEPSI-COLA BOTTLING COMPANY
5701 Perry Highway, Erie PA 16509. 814/868-5234. **Contact:** Human Resources. **World Wide Web address:** http://www.pepsico.com. **Description:** A regional warehouse for Pepsi-Cola Company. **Parent company:** PepsiCo, Inc. (Purchase NY) consists of Frito-Lay Company, Pepsi-Cola Company, and Tropicana Products, Inc.

PEPSI-COLA COMPANY
11701 Roosevelt Boulevard, Philadelphia PA 19154. 215/676-6400. **Contact:** Personnel. **World Wide Web address:** http://www.pepsico.com. **Description:** Pepsi-Cola Company produces and distributes a wide variety of beverages including the brand names Pepsi-Cola, Mountain Dew, Mug Root Beer, and Slice. **Parent company:** PepsiCo, Inc. (Purchase NY) consists of Frito-Lay Company, Pepsi-Cola Company, and Tropicana Products, Inc. **Operations at this facility include:** This location is a sales office and a warehousing facility.

PERFECSEAL
9800 Bustleton Avenue, Philadelphia PA 19115. 215/673-4500. **Fax:** 215/676-1311. **Contact:** Mr. Reno Bianco, Human Resources Manager. **World Wide Web address:** http://www.perfecseal.com. **Description:** Manufactures sterilizable medical packaging for the medical device industry. The company is a world leader in thermoplastic flexible packaging, heat-sealed coated Tyvek, and paper. Products include Perfecseal adhesive coating on Tyvek and paper, film and foil lamination; Breather Bag and linear tear packaging; easy-open and chevron peel pouches; oriented films; custom thermoformed trays and die-cut lids; pharmaceutical labels, cold seal technology, extrusion and saran coating, flexographic and rotogravure printing; and vacuum metallizing. Founded in 1905. **NOTE:** Entry-level positions and second and third shifts are offered. **Special programs:** Internships. **Corporate headquarters location:** This location. **Other U.S. locations:** Mankato MN; New London WI; Oshkosh WI. **International locations:** Carolina, Puerto Rico; Londonderry, Northern Ireland. **Parent company:** Bemis, Inc. **Operations at this facility include:** Administration; Manufacturing; Research and Development; Sales; Service. **Annual sales/revenues:** More than $100 million. **Number of employees at this location:** 200. **Number of employees worldwide:** 700.

PERIPHERAL DYNAMICS INC. (PDI)
5150 Campus Drive, Plymouth Meeting PA 19462-1197. 610/825-7090. **Contact:** Human Resources. **World Wide Web address:** http://www.pdiscan.com. **Description:** Manufactures scanners, optical readers, and other peripherals used in computer data entry.

THE PFALTZGRAFF COMPANY
140 East Market Street, York PA 17401. 717/848-5500. **Contact:** Mr. William Scott, Vice President of Corporate Human Resources. **World Wide Web address:** http://www.pfaltzgraff.com. **Description:** A stoneware and dinnerware manufacturer. The Pfaltzgraff Company also produces a line of tabletop accessories. **Corporate headquarters location:** This location.

PFIZER
400 West Lincoln Avenue, Lititz PA 17543. 717/626-2011. **Fax:** 717/627-9548. **Contact:** Human Resources. **World Wide Web address:** http://www.pfizer.com. **Description:** Pfizer is a leading pharmaceutical company that distributes products concerning cardiovascular health, central nervous system disorders, infectious diseases, and women's health worldwide. The company's brand-name products include Benadryl, Ben Gay, Cortizone, Desitin, Halls, Listerine, Sudafed, and Zantac 75. **Corporate headquarters location:** New York NY. **Operations at this facility include:** This location is a manufacturing and distribution facility.

PHILADELPHIA BUSINESS JOURNAL
400 Market Street, Suite 300, Philadelphia PA 19106. 215/238-1450. **Contact:** Personnel. **World Wide Web address:** http://www.bizjournals.com/philadelphia. **Description:** A weekly business journal. **Number of employees at this location:** 40.

PHILADELPHIA CENTER FOR AQUATIC REHABILITATION
3600 Grant Avenue, Philadelphia PA 19114. 215/677-0400. **Contact:** Human Resources. **World Wide Web address:** http://www.aquahab.com. **Description:** Provides aquatic physical therapy, land therapy, and work conditioning for people recovering from back and neck injuries, industrial injuries, sports-related orthopedic injuries, post-operative arthroscopic surgeries, joint replacement, postfracture recovery and postoperative knee/shoulder recovery.

PHILADELPHIA FEDERAL CREDIT UNION
12800 Townsend Road, Philadelphia PA 19154-1003. 215/934-3500. **Fax:** 215/934-3574. **Contact:** Human Resources. **E-mail address:** hr@pfcu.com. **World Wide Web address:** http://www.pfcu.com. **Description:** Philadelphia Credit Union offers a variety of financial services including checking and savings accounts, share certificates, bill payment services, loans, and a Visa credit card. **Positions advertised include:** Teller; Member Services Representative. **Operations at this facility include:** This location is a service center.

PHILADELPHIA GEAR CORPORATION
One Montgomery Plaza, Suite 700, Norristown PA 19401. 610/265-3000. **Toll-free phone:** 800/766-5120. **Fax:** 610/337-5637. **Contact:** Kurt Keseric, Human Resources. **World Wide Web address:** http://www.philagear.com. **Description:** Produces a wide variety of gears and gear drives for various industrial uses. Founded in 1892. **Corporate headquarters location:** This location. **Other U.S. locations:** Lynwood CA; Houston TX. **Parent company:** American Manufacturing Group. **Operations at this facility include:** Administration; Manufacturing; Research and Development; Sales; Service. **Annual sales/revenues:** $51 - $100 million. **Number of employees at this location:** 390. **Number of employees nationwide:** 550.

PHILADELPHIA INQUIRER
PHILADELPHIA DAILY NEWS
P.O. Box 8263, P.O. Box 7788, Philadelphia PA 19101. 215/854-2000. **Physical address:** 400 North Broad Street, Philadelphia PA 19130. **Contact:** Personnel. **World Wide Web address:** http://www.phillynews.com. **Description:** *Philadelphia Inquirer* is one of America's largest daily newspapers, with a weekday circulation of more than 700,000. Sunday circulation is more than 1 million. *Philadelphia Daily News* is a daily newspaper. **Parent company:** Knight-Ridder Newspaper Group.

PHILADELPHIA MUSEUM OF ART
Benjamin Franklin Parkway & 26th Street, P.O. Box 7646, Philadelphia PA 19101-7646. 215/763-8100. **Fax:** 215/684-7977. **Contact:** Human Resources. **E-mail address:** jobs@philamuseum.org. **World Wide Web address:** http://www.philamuseum.org. **Description:** An art museum housing a collection of European and American paintings and decorative arts, as well as Indian and East Asian art. Founded in 1876. **NOTE:** The museum also has many volunteer opportunities. **Positions advertised include:** Deputy Director of Development; Executive Assistant; Receptionist; Retail Accountant; Telemarketer; Office Manager. **Special programs:** Internships. **Number of employees at this location:** 350.

PHILADELPHIA PARK RACETRACK
3001 Street Road, Bensalem PA 19020. 215/639-9000. **Contact:** Personnel. **World Wide Web address:** http://www.philadelphiapark.com. **Description:** A thoroughbred racetrack. The company also operates several off-track betting facilities located throughout the greater Philadelphia area.

PHILADELPHIA STOCK EXCHANGE INC.
1900 Market Street, Philadelphia PA 19103. 215/496-5000. **Fax:** 215/496-1196. **Contact:** Human Resources. **World Wide Web address:** http://www.phlx.com. **Description:** A stock exchange. **Positions advertised include:** Senior Network Administrator; Equities Trading System Project Manager; Senior Stratus Application Developer; Senior Unix Application Developer.

PHILADELPHIA UNIVERSITY
School House & Henry Avenue, Philadelphia PA 19144. 215/951-2965. **Contact:** Kathryn Flannery, Director Human Resources. **E-mail address:** humanresources@philau.edu. **World Wide Web address:** http://www.philau.edu. **Description:** A four-year college offering bachelor's and master's degrees including MBAs. Approximately 3,100 undergraduate and graduate students attend Philadelphia University.

PHILADELPHIA ZOO
3400 West Girard Avenue, Philadelphia PA 19104. 215/243-1100. **Fax:** 215/243-5219. **Contact:** Human Resources. **E-mail address:** hr@phillyzoo.org. **World Wide Web address:** http://www.phillyzoo.org. **Description:** One of America's first zoos featuring over 2,000 animals and the Peco Primate Reserve exhibit. Founded in 1874.

PHILHAVEN BEHAVIORAL HEALTH SERVICES
283 South Butler Road, P.O. Box 550, Mount Gretna PA 17064. 717/270-2451. **Fax:** 717/270-2455. **Contact:** Human Resources. **E-mail address:** hr@philhaven.com. **World Wide Web address:** http://www.philhaven.com. **Description:** A psychiatric treatment center offering inpatient, outpatient, residential, and community-based services. **NOTE:** Entry-level positions and second and third shifts are offered. **Positions advertised include:** Clinical Director; Coordinator of Family Based Mental Health Services; Mobile Therapist; Psychiatrist; Licensed Practical Nurse; Registered Nurse. **Corporate headquarters location:** This location. **Operations at this facility include:** Administration; Service. **CEO:** LaVern J. Yutzy. **Annual sales/revenues:** $21 - $50 million. **Number of employees at this location:** 600.

PILOT AIR FREIGHT CORPORATION
701 B Ashland Avenue, Building 23, Suite 14, Folcroft PA 19032. 610/583-6200. **Fax:** 610/583-6266. **Contact:** Human Resources. **E-mail address:** phl@pilotair.com. **World Wide Web address:** http://www.pilotair.com. **Description:** A freight forwarding company. **Corporate headquarters location:** Lima PA. **Other area locations:** Allentown PA.

PILOT AIR FREIGHT CORPORATION
744 Roble Road, Suite 110, Allentown PA 18103. 610/264-8777. **Fax:** 610/264-8550. **Contact:** Human Resources. **E-mail address:** abe@pilotair.com. **World Wide Web address:** http://www.pilotair.com. **Description:** A freight forwarding company. **Corporate headquarters location:** Lima PA. **Other area locations:** Folcroft PA.

PILOT AIR FREIGHT CORPORATION
314 North Middletown Road, P.O. Box 97, Lima PA 19037. 610/891-8100. **Fax:** 610/264-8550. **Contact:** Bill Morgan, Human Resources Director. **E-mail address:** hipilot@pilotair.com. **World Wide Web address:** http://www.pilotair.com. **Description:** A freight forwarding company. **Corporate headquarters location:** This location. **Other area locations:** Allentown PA; Folcroft PA. **Operations at this facility include:** Administration. **Number of employees at this location:** 85.

PINCUS BROTHERS, INC.
Independence Mall East, Fifth and Race Street, Philadelphia PA 19106. 215/922-4900. **Contact:** Personnel. **Description:** Manufactures men's suits and coats.

PIPER RUDNICK LLP
Two Logan Square, 1650 Market Street, Suite 3400, Philadelphia PA 19103. 215/656-3300. **Fax:** 215/656-3301. **Contact:** William F. Kiniry Jr., Managing Partner. **World Wide Web address:** http://www.piperrudnick.com. **Description:** A business law firm, focusing on litigation, real estate, business & technology, government affairs, and international law. Founded 1999. **Corporate headquarters:** Baltimore MD. **Other U.S. locations:** MD; MA; IL; TX; NV; CA; NY; FL; WA. **Number of employees nationwide:** 975

PITTSBURGH BREWING COMPANY
3340 Liberty Avenue, Pittsburgh PA 15201. 412/682-7400. **Contact:** Valerie Stoltz, Personnel Director. **World Wide Web address:** http://www.pittsburghbrewingco.com. **Description:** Produces premium beers and other malt beverages. **NOTE:** Applications should be hand delivered or mailed to the above address.

PITTSBURGH BUSINESS TIMES
2313 East Carson Street, Suite 200, Pittsburgh PA 15203. 412/481-6397. **Contact:** Personnel. **World Wide Web address:** http://www.amcity.com/pittsburgh. **Description:** A weekly business periodical.

PITTSBURGH CORNING CORPORATION
800 Presque Isle Drive, Pittsburgh PA 15239. 724/327-6100. **Fax:** 724/325-9704. **Contact:** Human Resources. **World Wide Web address:** http://www.pittsburghcorning.com. **Description:** Producers of flat glass.

PITTSBURGH CORNING CORPORATION
P.O. Box 37, Port Allegany PA 16743. 814/642-2552. **Physical address:** 723 North Main Street, Port Allegany PA 16743. **Contact:** Personnel. **World Wide Web address:** http://www.pittsburghcorning.com. **Description:** A producer of glass blocks.

PITTSBURGH MERCY HEALTH SYSTEM
1400 Locust Street, Pittsburgh PA 15219. 412/232-7970. **Recorded jobline:** 412/232-7225. **Fax:** 412/232-7408. **Contact:** Central Employment Office. **E-mail address:** employment@mercy.pmhs.com. **World Wide Web address:** http://www.mercylink.org. **Description:** A nonprofit health care system operating several hospitals in the Pittsburgh area. **Positions advertised include:** Admission Representative; Medical Records Coder; Medical Transcriptionist; Patient Account Representative; Unit Secretary; Clinical Nurse; Licensed Practical Nurse; Relief Clinical Supervisor; Case Manager; Occupational Therapist. **Corporate headquarters location:** This location. **Subsidiaries include:** Mercy Hospital of Pittsburgh; Mercy Providence Hospital; Mercy Psychiatric Institute; St. Joseph Nursing and Health Care Center. **Operations at this facility include:** Administration; Health Care; Research and Development; Service. **Number of employees at this location:** 2,500. **Number of employees nationwide:** 5,000.

PITTSBURGH PIRATES
P.O. Box 7000, Pittsburgh PA 15212. 412/323-5000. **Contact:** Human Resources. **World Wide Web address:** http://www.pirateball.com. **Description:** Offices of the Pittsburgh Pirates Major League Baseball team.

PITTSBURGH PRESS
PITTSBURGH POST-GAZETTE
34 Boulevard of the Allies, Pittsburgh PA 15222. 412/263-1100. **Contact:** Human Resources. **World Wide Web address:** http://www.post-gazette.com. **Description:** Publishes *Pittsburgh Post-Gazette*, a daily morning newspaper. Founded in 1786.

PITTSBURGH STEELERS
3400 South Water Street, Pittsburgh PA 15203-2349. 412/432-7800. **Fax:** 412/432-7878. **Contact:** Human Resources Department. **World Wide Web address:** http://www.steelers.com. **Description:** Administrative offices of the National Football League's Pittsburgh Steelers.

PITTSBURGH ZOO & AQUARIUM
One Wild Place, Pittsburgh PA 15206-1178. 412/665-3640. **Toll-free phone:** 800/474-4966. **Contact:** Human Resources. **E-mail address:** krysc@zoo.pgh.pa.us. **World Wide Web address:** http://zoo.pgh.pa.us. **Description:** A zoo featuring the Kids Kingdom, an interactive attraction in which children are encouraged to act like animals.

POLY-PLANAR, INC.
P.O. Box 2578, Warminster PA 18974. 215/675-7805. **Fax:** 215/675-7920. **Physical address:** 1095 Mearns Road, Warminster PA 18974. **Contact:** Barbara Lange, Personnel Director. **World Wide Web address:** http://www.polyplanar.com. **Description:** Produces and distributes portable electronics products including all-weather loudspeakers for communications systems. Poly-Planar also manufactures consumer audio products, primarily speakers. **Corporate headquarters location:** This location.

PORT ERIE PLASTICS INC.
909 Troupe Road, Harborcreek PA 16421. 814/899-7602. **Contact:** Personnel. **E-mail address:** info@porterie.com. **World Wide Web address:** http://www.skidmarx.com. **Description:** A plastic injection molding company. Products are marketed under the Skidmarx brand name.

PORTOLA PACKAGING, INC.
P.O. Box 7259, 1902 New Butler Road, New Castle PA 16107. 724/658-9019. **Toll-free phone:** 800/294-0843. **Fax:** 724/658-5720. **Contact:** Human Resources. **World Wide Web address:** http://www.portpack.com. **Description:** Manufactures plastic caps for a variety of containers including milk jugs, soda bottles, and water bottles.

POTTSTOWN MEMORIAL MEDICAL CENTER
1600 East High Street, Pottstown PA 19464. 610/327-7057. **Fax:** 610/327-7690. **Contact:** Human Resources Department. **E-mail address:** hr@pmmctr.com. **World Wide Web address:** http://www.pmmctr.org. **Description:** A full-service hospital. **NOTE:** Entry-level positions and second and third shifts are offered. **Positions advertised include:** CT Technologist; Respiratory Therapist; X-Ray Technician; Registered Nurse; Licensed Practical Nurse; Nursing Assistant. **Corporate headquarters location:** This location. **Number of employees at this location:** 1,100.

THE POTTSVILLE HOSPITAL AND WARNE CLINIC
420 South Jackson Street, Pottsville PA 17901. 570/621-5097. **Contact:** Human Resources. **World Wide Web address:** http://www.pottsville.com/hospital. **Description:** An acute care facility providing a full range of medical services including the Inpatient Rehabilitation Unit, the Institute for Behavioral Health (an inpatient psychiatric unit), and the Schuylkill Rehabilitation Center (a comprehensive outpatient rehabilitation facility). **Positions advertised include:** Mental Health Technician; Certified Therapeutic Recreational Therapist; Licensed Practical Nurse; Registered Nurse; Pharmacist; Respiratory Care Practitioner; Speech/Language Pathologist. **Operations at this facility include:** Administration; Service. **Number of employees at this location:** 800.

POWEREX, INC.
200 East Hillis Street, Youngwood PA 15697. 724/925-7272. **Contact:** Andy Varga, Human Resources Director. **World Wide Web address:** http://www.pwrx.com. **Description:** Manufactures semiconductors. **Corporate headquarters location:** This location. **President/CEO:** Stan Hunt. **Number of employees at this location:** 325.

PRECISE TECHNOLOGY, INC.
501 Mosside Boulevard, North Versailles PA 15137. 412/823-2100. **Toll-free phone:** 800/949-2101. **Fax:** 412/823-4110. **Contact:** Human Resources. **World Wide Web address:** http://www.precisetech.com. **Description:** Manufactures a variety of plastic injection molds.

PREMIER MEDICAL PRODUCTS
1710 Romano Street, Plymouth Meeting PA 19462. 610/239-6000. **Toll-free phone:** 888/670-6100. **Contact:** Karen Giannone, Director Human Resources. **World Wide Web address:** http://www.premusa.com. **Description:** Manufactures and distributes tracheal and laryngectomy tubes, as well as medical instruments used in gynecology and podiatry.

PRESBYTERIAN MEDICAL CENTER
39th & Market Streets, Philadelphia PA 19104. 215/662-8000. **Fax:** 215/662-8936. **Recorded jobline:** 215/662-8222. **Contact:** Human Resources. **Description:** A teaching hospital specializing in oncology, cardiology, general medicine, and surgery. **Special programs:** Internships. **Operations at this facility include:** Administration; Research and Development; Service. **Number of employees at this location:** 1,500.

PRESCIENT SYSTEMS, INC.
1247 Ward Avenue, Suite 200, West Chester PA 19380. 610/719-1600. **Toll-free phone:** 888/610-1800. **Fax:** 610/719-8575. **Contact:** Human Resources. **E-mail address:** hr@prescientsystems.com. **World Wide Web address:** http://www.prescientsystems.com. **Description:** A developer and supplier of forecasting and logistics software solutions. The company's supply chain management software provides a solution for demand forecasting, inventory planning, and continuous replenishment. This software is used by manufacturers, distributors, and retailers worldwide. **Corporate headquarters location:** This location. **Operations at this facility include:** Administration; Research and Development; Sales; Service. **Annual sales/revenues:** Less than $5 million. **Number of employees at this location:** 30. **Number of employees nationwide:** 45.

PRICEWATERHOUSECOOPERS
2 Commerce Square, Suite 1700, 2001 Market Street, Philadelphia PA 19103. 215/575-5000. **Contact:** Human Resources Department. **World Wide Web address:** http://www.pwcglobal.com. **Description:** One of the largest certified public accounting firms in the world. PricewaterhouseCoopers provides public accounting, business advisory, management consulting, and taxation services. **Corporate headquarters location:** New York NY. **Other U.S. locations:** Nationwide.

PRICEWATERHOUSECOOPERS
600 Grant Street, 52nd Floor, Pittsburgh PA 15219-2777. 412/355-6000. **Contact:** Personnel. **World Wide Web address:** http://www.pwcglobal.com. **Description:** One of the largest certified public accounting firms in the world. PricewaterhouseCoopers provides public accounting, business advisory, management consulting, and taxation services. **Corporate headquarters location:** New York NY. **Other U.S. locations:** Nationwide.

PRIMAVERA SYSTEMS INC.
3 Bala Plaza West, Suite 700, Bala-Cynwyd PA 19004. 610/667-8600. **Fax:** 610/949-6761. **Contact:** Joanne McCool, Vice President of Human Resources. **E-mail address:** careers@primavera.com. **World Wide Web address:** http://www.primavera.com. **Description:** Develops and supports an array of project management software for assisting clients in risk analysis, large-scale projects, contract management, team communication, and remote real-time updating. Founded in 1983. **NOTE:** Entry-level positions are offered. **Positions advertised include:** Senior Software Engineer; Public Relations Specialist; Solutions Architect; Proposal Coordinator; Corporate Account Executive. **Special programs:** Internships; Co-ops. **Office hours:** Monday - Friday, 8:00 a.m. - 5:00 p.m. **Corporate headquarters location:** This location. **Other U.S. locations:** Nationwide. **International locations:** Worldwide. **Annual sales/revenues:** $21 - $50 million. **Number of employees at this location:** 180. **Number of employees nationwide:** 230. **Number of employees worldwide:** 260.

PROGRESS BANK
P.O. Box 3036, 4 Sentry Parkway, Blue Bell PA 19422-2311. 610/825-8800. **Physical address:** 4 Sentry Parkway, Suite 200, Blue Bell PA 19422. **Contact:** Human Resources. **World Wide Web address:** http://www.progressbank.com. **Description:** A federally chartered stock savings bank that conducts community banking throughout Eastern Pennsylvania. **Corporate headquarters location:** This location. **Other area locations:** Conshohocken PA; Jeffersonville PA; King of Prussia PA; Norristown PA; Philadelphia PA; Plymouth Meeting PA; Rosemont PA. **Listed on:** NASDAQ. **Stock exchange symbol:** PFNC.

PROPHET 21 INC.
19 West College Avenue, Yardley PA 19067. 215/493-8900. **Fax:** 215/321-8008. **Contact:** Human Resources. **E-mail address:** hr@p21.com. **World Wide Web address:** http://www.p21.com. **Description:** Supplies software solutions to the distribution industry. Founded in 1967. **Positions advertised include:** Database Administrator; Functional Analyst; Senior PowerBuilder Developer. **Listed on:** NASDAQ. **Stock exchange symbol:** PXXI.

PRUDENTIAL INSURANCE COMPANY OF AMERICA
1100 Horizon Circle, Chalfont PA 18914. 215/996-0803. **Contact:** Human Resources Department. **World Wide Web address:** http://www.prudential.com. **Description:** One of the largest diversified financial services organizations in the world and one of the largest insurance companies in North America. The company's primary business is to offer a full range of products and services in three areas: insurance, investment, and home ownership for individuals and families; health care management and other benefit programs for employees of companies and members of groups; and asset management for institutional clients and their associates. The company insures or provides other financial services to more than 50 million people worldwide. **Corporate headquarters location:** Newark NJ. **Number of employees worldwide:** 100,000.

PUBLIC FINANCIAL MANAGEMENT, INC.
2 Logan Square, Suite 1600, Philadelphia PA 19103. 215/567-6100. **Fax:** 215/567-4180. **Contact:** Marie Biggans, Human Resources Associate. **E-mail address:** recruit@publicfm.com. **World Wide Web address:** http://www.pfm.com. **Description:** A leading financial advisory firm serving the public sector. Public Financial Management oversees $7.5 billion in public sector funds. **Corporate headquarters location:** This location. **Other area locations:** Harrisburg PA. **Other U.S. locations:** Newport Beach CA; San Francisco CA; Washington DC; Miami FL; Fort Myers FL; Orlando FL; Sarasota FL; Atlanta GA; Des Moines IA; Boston MA; Trenton NJ; New York NY; Harrisburg PA; Pittsburgh PA; Memphis TN; Dallas TX; Austin TX; Houston TX. **Parent company:** Marine Midland Bank. **CEO:** F. John White. **Number of employees at this location:** 50.

PULSE SPECIALTY COMPONENTS
2 Pearl Buck Court, Bristol PA 19007-6812. 215/781-6400. **Contact:** Donna Ricciuti, Human Resources Manager. **World Wide Web address:** http://www.pulseeng.com. **Description:** One of the world's leading suppliers of magnetic components. Overall, Pulse Engineering designs, manufactures, and markets a variety of electronic components and modules for original equipment manufacturers in the data processing, telecommunications networking, and power supply market. **Corporate headquarters location:** San Diego CA. **Parent company:** Technitrol.

QVC NETWORK, INC.
1365 Enterprise Drive, West Chester PA 19380. 610/431-8463. **Contact:** Human Resources Manager. **World Wide Web address:** http://www.qvc.com. **Description:** A leader in electronic retailing with shopping available via television 24 hours per day. The retail programming is transmitted to over 55 million U.S. households. Founded in 1986. **Positions advertised include:** Staff Planning and Scheduling Manager. **Special programs:** Internships. **Internship information:** The company has internships in a

variety of areas including broadcasting, merchandising, customer service, distribution, guest relations, information systems and technology, finance, and creative services. Please send a resume and cover letter to the College Relations Department. Applications are accepted on a rolling basis. **Corporate headquarters location:** This location. **Other U.S. locations:** DE; TX; VA. **International locations:** Germany; United Kingdom. **Parent company:** Comcast Corporation. **Annual sales/revenues:** More than $100 million. **Number of employees at this location:** 2,500. **Number of employees nationwide:** 8,000. **Number of employees worldwide:** 8,500.

QUAD SYSTEMS CORP
2405 Maryland Road, Willow Grove PA 19090. 215/657-6202. **Fax:** 215/784-4514. **Contact:** Rick Whitehurst, Human Resources Director. **World Wide Web address:** http://www.tycoelectronics.com. **Description:** Distributes, markets, designs, manufactures and supports surface mount technology (SMT) equipment used in the assembly of printed circuit wiring boards. **Parent company:** Tyco. **Number of employees at this location:** 280.

QUADRANT
2120 Fairmount Avenue, P.O. Box 14235, Reading PA 19612-4235. 610/320-6600. **Fax:** 610/320-6868. **Contact:** Frank Luff, Personnel Department. **World Wide Web address:** http://www.quadrantepp.com. **Description:** Manufactures and markets engineering plastics. Founded in 1946. **Corporate headquarters location:** This location. **International locations:** Worldwide.

QUAKER CHEMICAL CORPORATION
One Quaker Park, 901 Hector Street, Conshohocken PA 19428. 610/832-4000. **Fax:** 610/832-4282. **Contact:** James Geiere, Vice President of Human Resources. **World Wide Web address:** http://www.quakerchem.com. **Description:** Manufactures rolling lubricants for steel and nonferrous metals; corrosion preventives; machining, grinding, and drawing compounds; hydraulic fluids; metal finishing compounds; and other products. Quaker Chemical Corporation also provides chemical management services to industrial customers. **Positions advertised include:** Accountant III; Development Chemist. **Corporate headquarters location:** This location. **Other U.S. locations:** Savannah GA; Detroit MI. **Listed on:** New York Stock Exchange. **Listed on:** KWR. **Annual sales/revenues:** More than $100 million. **Number of employees at this location:** 230. **Number of employees worldwide:** 925.

QUEBECOR PRINTING ATGLEN INC.
4581 Lower Valley Road, Route 372, P.O. Box 465, Atglen PA 19310-0465. 610/593-5173. **Fax:** 610/593-5717. **Contact:** Human Resources Department. **World Wide Web address:** http://www.quebecorworldinc.com. **Description:** One of the world's largest commercial printers with 84 printing and related services facilities in Canada, the United States, France, the United Kingdom, Mexico, and India. The company's major product categories include inserts and circulars, magazines, books, catalogs, directories, checks, bonds and banknotes, specialty printing, and newspapers. Quebecor Printing also offers web offset, gravure, and sheet-fed printing capacity, plus related services that include advanced electronic prepress and imaging, database and list management, shipping and distribution, and CD-ROM mastering and replicating. **Corporate headquarters location:** Montreal, Canada. **Parent company:** Quebecor Printing Montreal.

QUEST DIAGNOSTICS INCORPORATED
400 Egypt Road, Norristown PA 19403. 610/631-4200. **Contact:** Human Resources Department. **World Wide Web address:** http://www.questdiagnostics.com. **Description:** One of the largest clinical laboratories in North America, providing a broad range of clinical laboratory services to health care clients that include physicians, hospitals, clinics, dialysis centers, pharmaceutical companies, and corporations. The company offers and performs tests on blood, urine, and other bodily fluids and tissues to provide information for health and well-being. **Positions advertised include:** Billing Coordinator; Specimen Technician; Customer Service Representative; Payroll Management Team Leader. **Other U.S. locations:** Nationwide.

QUEST DIAGNOSTICS INCORPORATED
875 Greentree Road, 4 Parkway Center, Pittsburgh PA 15220. 412/920-7600. **Contact:** Human Resources. **World Wide Web address:** http://www.questdiagnostics.com. **Description:** Quest Diagnostics is one of the largest clinical laboratories in North America, providing a broad range of clinical laboratory services to health care clients that include physicians, hospitals, clinics, dialysis centers, pharmaceutical companies, and corporations. The company offers and performs tests on blood, urine, and other bodily fluids and tissues to provide information for health and well-being. **Positions advertised include:** Phlebotomy Services Representative; Specimen Technician; Billing Coordinator; Data Entry Operator; Phlebotomy Service Floater; Field Operations Representative. **Other U.S. locations:** Nationwide. **Operations at this facility include:** This location is a specimen testing facility.

RADIAN GUARANTY INC.
1601 Market Street, Philadelphia PA 19103. 215/564-6600. **Contact:** Human Resources. **World Wide Web address:** http://www.radianmi.com. **Description:** A national insurance company providing private mortgage insurance and risk management services to mortgage lending institutions. **Positions advertised include:** Default Analyst; Default Associate Supervisor; Data Modeler; Financial Analyst; Project Manager; Customer Account Representative; Customer Service Supervisor. **Corporate headquarters location:** This location. **Other U.S. locations:** Nationwide. **Parent company:** Radian Group Inc. (also at this location).

RADISSON HOTEL GREENTREE
101 Radisson Drive, Pittsburgh PA 15205. 412/922-8400. **Contact:** Human Resources. **Description:** A 500-room hotel, featuring a swimming pool, a putting green, a whirlpool bath, a sauna, and an exercise room.

RADISSON VALLEY FORGE HOTEL & CONVENTION CENTER
1160 First Avenue, King of Prussia PA 19406. 610/337-2000. **Fax:** 610/354-8214. **Contact:** Human Resources. **World Wide Web address:** http://www.Radisson.com/kingofprussia. **Description:** A 488-room hotel and tri-level convention center featuring three full-service restaurants, and Lily Langtry's, a Las Vegas-style dinner theater facility. **NOTE:** Entry-level positions are offered. **Special programs:** Internships. **Parent company:** GF Management. **Number of employees at this location:** 600.

RAINMAKER SOFTWARE, INC.
475 Sentry Parkway, Suite 4000, Blue Bell PA 19422. 610/567-3400. **Contact:** Kim Robinson, Human Resources. **E-mail address:** krobinson@rainmakerlegal.com. **World Wide Web address:** http://www.rainmakerlegal.com. **Description:** Develops computer applications for the legal industry. **Corporate headquarters location:** Framingham MA. **Parent company:** ASA International Ltd. designs and develops proprietary vertical market software and installs software on a variety of computers and networks.

RAYTHEON COMPANY
P.O. Box 60, 300 Science Park Road, State College PA 16804. 814/238-4311. **Contact:** Nancy Boozer, Human Resources Manager. **World Wide Web address:** http://www.raytheon.com. **Description:** Raytheon Systems designs, manufactures, and installs state-of-the-art communications and integrated command-and-control systems for military and industrial customers worldwide. The company markets its products to the commercial and defense electronics industry. **Positions advertised include:** Configuration Analyst; System Architect; Technical Support Associate; Principal Systems Engineer; UNIX Systems Administrator; Software Engineer II; Management Assistant. **Corporate headquarters location:** Waltham MA. **Operations at this facility include:** This location develops software.

READCO MANUFACTURING INC.
P.O. 1552, 460 Grim lane, York PA 17402. 717/848-2801. **Toll-free phone:** 800/395-4959. **Fax:** 717/848-1401. **Contact:** Human Resources. **World Wide Web address:** http://www.readco.com. **Description:** Designs and manufactures a line of solids-processing equipment for the mixing and blending industries, ranging in size from pilot to full-scale production.

REDSIREN TECHNOLOGIES, INC.
650 Smithfield Street, Suite 910,, Pittsburgh PA 15222. 412/281-4427. **Toll-free phone:** 877/360-7602. **Fax:** 412/434-1264. **Contact:** Jim Leindecker, Director of Human Resources. **E-mail address:** careers@redsiren.com. **World Wide Web address:** http://www.redsiren.com. **Description:** Provides systems management solutions and data processing services. Founded in 1996. **Office hours:** Monday - Friday, 8:30 a.m. - 5:00 p.m. **Corporate headquarters location:** This location. **Annual sales/revenues:** Less than $5 million. **Number of employees at this location:** 35.

REED BUSINESS INFORMATION
3 Gateway Center, Suite 1651, 401 Liberty Avenue, Pittsburgh PA 15222. 412/281-4400. **Fax:** 412/471-7203. **Contact:** Human Resources. **World Wide Web address:** http://www.reedbusiness.com. **Description:** A diversified business press publisher of magazines and books. **Special programs:** Internships. **Corporate headquarters location:** New York NY. **Parent company:** Reed Elsevier PLC. **Number of employees at this location:** 800.

REED SMITH SHAW & McCLAY LLP
2500 One Liberty Place, 1650 Market Street, Philadelphia PA 19103. 215/851-8100. **Fax:** 215/851-1420. **Contact:** Denise Papanier, Human Resources Manager. **World Wide Web address:** http://www.rssm.com. **Description:** A business-oriented law firm specializing in financial and corporate law. **Positions advertised include:** Litigation Associate; Trust and Estates Associate; Intellectual Property Legal Secretary; Library Technical Services Assistant; Litigation Clerk; Litigation Support Analyst; Litigation Support Manager; Serials Assistant. **Other U.S. locations:** Washington DC; Princeton NJ; Harrisburg PA; Pittsburgh PA; McLean VA.

REGINA NURSING CENTER
230 North 65th Street, Philadelphia PA 19139. 215/472-0541. **Contact:** Human Resources. **E-mail address:** mc@reginanursingcenter.org. **World Wide Web address:** http://www.reginanursingcenter.org. **Description:** A 44-bed nursing care center.

REGINA NURSING CENTER
550 East Fornance Street, Norristown PA 19401-3561. 610/272-5600. **Fax:** 610/279-0529. **Contact:** Bonnie A. Dudley, RN, Director of Nursing. **E-mail address:** mc@reginanursingcenter.org. **World Wide Web address:** http://www.reginanursingcenter.org. **Description:** A 121-bed nursing care center.

REICHHOLD CHEMICALS, INC.
1000 Presto-Sygan Road, Bridgeville PA 15017. 412/257-5700. **Contact:** Human Resources. **World Wide Web address:** http://www.reichhold.com. **Description:** A chemical plant manufacturing coating resins, epoxy, epoxy hardeners, acrylic, and co-polymer resins. **Positions advertised include:** Technician. **Corporate headquarters location:** Durham NC. **International locations:** Worldwide.

THE RELIZON COMPANY
P.O. Box 128, Emigsville PA 17318. 717/764-5902. **Contact:** Human Resources. **World Wide Web address:** http://www.relizon.com. **Description:** Provides business communications and customer relationship management solutions. **Corporate headquarters location:** Dayton OH. **Other U.S. locations:** Nationwide.

RENT-WAY, INC.
One Rent-Way Place, Erie PA 16505. 814/455-5378. **Fax:** 814/461-5483. **Contact:** Beth Reske, Recruiting Coordinator. **E-mail address:** recruiting@rentway.com. **World Wide Web address:** http://www.rentway.com. **Description:** Offers rental-purchase programs to customers on a short-term basis. **Positions advertised include:** Assistant Store Manager; Store Manager; Customer Service Associate. **Corporate headquarters location:** This location. **Other U.S. locations:** Nationwide. **Listed on:** New York Stock Exchange. **Stock exchange symbol:** RWY. **Annual sales/revenues:** More than $100 million.

REPRODUCTIVE SCIENCE INSTITUTE
950 West Valley Road, Suite 2401, Wayne PA 19087. 610/964-9663. **Fax:** 610/964-0536. **Contact:** Personnel. **World Wide Web address:** http://www.ihr.com/rsi. **Description:** A medical laboratory specializing in hormonal studies and endocrinology research.

RESPIRONICS INC.
1001 Murry Ridge Lane, Murrysville PA 15668-8550. 724/733-0200. **Fax:** 724/387-4299. **Contact:** Personnel. **World Wide Web address:** http://www.respironics.com. **Description:** Manufactures respiratory medical products. **NOTE:** Entry-level positions are offered. **Positions advertised include** Manufacturing Specialist; Product Assurance Engineer; Accounts Payable Associate; International Customer Service Associate; Electrical Engineer; Senior Sales Trainer; Director of Business Development. **Special programs:** Internships. **Corporate headquarters location:** This location. **Operations at this facility include:** Administration; Divisional Headquarters; Manufacturing; Research and Development; Sales; Service. **Listed on:** NASDAQ. **Stock exchange symbol:** RESP. **Annual sales/revenues:** More than $100 million. **Number of employees at this location:** 480. **Number of employees nationwide:** 515. **Number of employees worldwide:** 1,100.

RIDDLE MEMORIAL HOSPITAL
1068 West Baltimore Pike, Media PA 19063. 610/566-9400. **Fax:** 610/891-3644. **Contact:** Human Resources. **E-mail address:** wzaloga@riddlehospital.org. **World Wide Web address:** http://www.riddlehospital.org. **Description:** A short-term, acute care, community hospital and outpatient medical facility. **Number of employees at this location:** 1,300.

RIGHT MANAGEMENT CONSULTANTS
1818 Market Street, 33rd Floor, Philadelphia PA 19103. 215/988-1588. **Toll-free phone:** 800/237-4448. **Contact:** Human Resources. **E-mail address:** careers@right.com. **World Wide Web address:** http://www.right.com. **Description:** Provides management and human resources consulting services. Founded in 1980. **Corporate headquarters location:** This location. **Listed on:** NASDAQ. **Stock exchange symbol:** RMCI.

RITE AID CORPORATION
30 Hunter Lane, Camp Hill PA 17011. 717/761-2633. **Fax:** 717/972-3971. **Contact:** Gina Grundusky, Corporate Recruiter. **E-mail address:** recruiter@riteaid.com. **World Wide Web address:** http://www.riteaid.com. **Description:** Operates 550 retail drug stores in 12 states. Founded in 1939. **Positions advertised include:** Coordinator; Assistant Store Manager; Systems Engineer; Shift Supervisor; Payment Coordinator; Customer Service Representative; Insurance Coordinator; Senior Auditor; Pharmacist. **Special programs:** Internships. **Corporate headquarters location:** This location. **Other U.S. locations:** Nationwide. **Subsidiaries include:** Payless Drug Stores. **Listed on:** New York Stock Exchange. **Stock exchange symbol:** RAD. **Annual sales/revenues:** More than $100 million. **Number of employees nationwide:** 83,000.

RITE AID PHARMACY
200 Chamber Plaza, Charleroi PA 15022-1605. 724/489-0870. **Contact:** Manager. **World Wide Web address:** http://www.riteaid.com. **Description:** A retail drugstore. **Corporate headquarters location:** Harrisburg PA. **Parent company:** Rite Aid Corporation operates 550 retail drug stores in 12 states. Subsidiary Payless Drug Stores offers over 45,000 different items. **Listed on:** New York Stock Exchange. **Stock exchange symbol:** RAD. **Number of employees nationwide:** 40,000.

RITE AID PHARMACY
900 Mount Royal Boulevard, Pittsburgh PA 15223. 412/487-5706. **Contact:** Manager. **World Wide Web address:** http://www.riteaid.com. **Description:** A retail drugstore. **Corporate headquarters location:** Harrisburg PA. **Parent company:** Rite Aid Corporation operates 550 retail drug stores in 12 states. **Listed on:** New York Stock Exchange. **Stock exchange symbol:** RAD. **Number of employees nationwide:** 40,000.

RITTENHOUSE FINANCIAL SERVICES
100 Matsonford Road, 5 Radnor Corporate Center, Suite 300, Radnor PA 19087-4541. **Toll-free phone:** 800/847-6369. **Contact:** Barbara Fox, Human Resources Department. **E-mail address:** barbara.fox@nuveen.com. **World Wide Web address:** http://www.rittenhousefinancial.com. **Description:** A money management firm. **Parent company:** Nuveen.

ROBICON CORPORATION
500 Hunt Valley Drive, New Kensington PA 15068. 724/339-9500. **Fax:** 724/339-9562. **Contact:** Human Resources. **E-mail address:** resume@us.asirobicon.com. **World Wide Web address:** http://www.robicon.com. **Description:** Manufactures relays and industrial controls. **NOTE:** Phone calls are not accepted. **Positions advertised include:** Quality Engineer; Network Administrator; Electrical Engineering Intern.

RODALE PRESS & COMPANY
33 East Minor Street, Emmaus PA 18098-0099. 610/967-5171. **Contact:** Human Resources. **E-mail address:** hr@rodale.com. **World Wide Web address:** http://www.rodalepress.com. **Description:** Publishes a wide variety of general interest trade books and magazines. **Positions advertised include:** Alternative Media Sales Assistant; Associate Consumer Marketing Assistant; Associate Database Marketing Associate; Classified Advertising Representative; Copywriter; Help Desk Analyst.

ROHM & HAAS COMPANY
P.O. Box 904, Spring House PA 19477-0904. 215/641-7000. **Physical address:** 727 Norristown Road, Spring House PA. **Contact:** Human Resources Department. **World Wide Web address:** http://www.rohmhaas.com. **Description:** Rohm & Haas is a specialty chemicals company operating in four industry segments: Polymers, Resins, and Monomers; Plastics; Industrial Chemicals; and Agricultural Chemicals. The company is also engaged in non-chemical industries such as forestry products, carpet production, and biomedical testing. **Corporate headquarters location:** Philadelphia PA. **Operations at this facility include:** This location is a research facility. **Listed on:** New York Stock Exchange. **Stock exchange symbol:** ROH. **Annual sales/revenues:** More than $100 million.

ROHM & HAAS COMPANY
100 Independence Mall West, Philadelphia PA 19106-2399. 215/592-3000. **Contact:** Corporate Staffing. **World Wide Web address:** http://www.rohmhaas.com. **Description:** A specialty chemicals company that produces polymers, resins, and monomers; plastics; industrial chemicals; and agricultural chemicals. Rohm & Haas Company is also engaged in nonchemical industries such as forestry products, carpet production, and biomedical testing. **Corporate headquarters location:** This location. **Listed on:** New York Stock Exchange. **Stock exchange symbol:** ROH. **Annual sales/revenues:** More than $100 million.

ROHM & HAAS COMPANY
P.O. Box 584, Bristol PA 19007. 215/785-8000. **Physical address:** Route 413 and State Road, Bristol PA 19007. **Contact:** Human Resources. **World Wide Web address:** http://www.rohmhaas.com. **Description:** Rohm & Haas is a specialty chemicals company operating in four business segments: Polymers, Resins, and Monomers; Plastics; Industrial Chemicals; and Agricultural Chemicals. Rohm & Haas is also engaged in nonchemical industries such as forestry products, carpet production, and biomedical testing. **Corporate headquarters location:** Philadelphia PA. **Operations at this facility include:** This location manufactures acrylic plastics used by the automotive industry to make taillights. **Listed on:** New York Stock Exchange. **Stock exchange symbol:** ROH. **Annual sales/revenues:** More than $100 million.

ROYAL BANK OF PENNSYLVANIA
732 Montgomery Avenue, Narberth PA 19072. 610/668-4700. **Fax:** 610/668-3670. **Contact:** Human Resources. **E-mail address:** careers@royalbankpa.com. **World Wide Web address:** http://www.royalbankpa.com. **Description:** A community bank operating through 14 branches in the Philadelphia area. **Positions advertised include:** Mortgage Closer; Floating Teller; Office Manager/Executive Assistant; Loan Accounting Associate.

RUNNING PRESS
125 South 22nd Street, Philadelphia PA 19103-4399. 215/567-5080. **Fax:** 215/568-2919. **Contact:** Mr. Mike Bonanno, Human Resources Representative. **E-mail address:** mbonanno@runningpress.com. **World Wide Web address:** http://www.runningpress.com. **Description:** Publishes nonfiction, children's, and art books. **Positions advertised include:** Editor; Intern.

RUTGERS ORGANICS CORPORATION
201 Struble Road, State College PA 16801. 814/238-2424. **Fax:** 814/235-1567. **Contact:** Human Resources Department. **E-mail address:** humanres@ruetgers-organics-corp.com. **World Wide Web address:** http://www.ruetgers-organics-corp.com. **Description:** A chemical manufacturer specializing in custom and intermediate chemicals such as hydrotapes, surfactants, and specialty sulfuric acids. Founded in 1951. **Positions advertised include:** New Business Development Manager; Production Supervisor; Purchasing Manager. **Corporate headquarters location:** This location. **Other U.S. locations:** Augusta GA; Cincinnati OH. **Parent company:** RUTGERS AG. **Annual sales/revenues:** $51 - $100 million. **Number of employees at this location:** 150. **Number of employees nationwide:** 250.

SAP AMERICA, INC.
3999 West Chester Pike, Newtown Square PA 19073. 610/355-2500. **Contact:** Human Resources. **World Wide Web address:** http://www.sap.com. **Description:** Develops a variety of client/server computer software packages including programs for finance, human resources, and materials management applications. **Corporate headquarters location:** This location. **Other U.S. locations:** Nationwide. **International locations:** Germany. **Parent company:** SAP AG. **Number of employees nationwide:** 3,000. **Number of employees worldwide:** 13,000.

SCT CORPORATION
4 Country View Road, Malvern PA 19355. 610/647-5930. **Toll-free phone:** 800/223-7036. **Fax:** 610/578-5102. **Contact:** Human Resources. **World Wide Web address:** http://www.sctcorp.com. **Description:** Develops software and offers computer-related services to the higher education, local government, utility, and manufacturing communities. The company operates through the following divisions: Information Resource Management (IRM); Software & Technology Services (STS); SCT Public Sector, Inc.; and SCT Utility Systems, Inc. **NOTE:** Entry-level positions are offered. **Positions advertised include:** Senior Vice President of Sales; Product Marketing Manager; Technical Specialist. **Corporate headquarters location:** This location. **Annual sales/revenues:** More than $100 million.

SEI INVESTMENTS COMPANY
One Freedom Valley Drive, Oaks PA 19456. 610/676-1000. **Contact:** Human Resources. **E-mail address:** careers@seic.com. **World Wide Web address:** http://www.seic.com. **Description:** SEI Investments operates primarily in two business markets: Trust and Banking and Fund Sponsor/Investment Advisory. The company invests for clients worldwide in both public and private markets. SEI Investments also provides investment and business solutions to those who serve their own investor clients. SEI Investments provides direct investment solutions for $100 billion of investable capital and delivers systems and business solutions to organizations investing nearly $1 trillion. SEI Investments is one of the largest providers of trust systems in the world. **NOTE:** Jobseekers should indicate area of interest when applying. **Positions advertised include:** Private Equity Accountant; Hedge Fund Accountant; Fund Accounting Supervisor; Investor Services Representative. **Operations at this facility include:** Administration; Research and Development; Sales; Service. **Listed on:** NASDAQ. **Stock exchange symbol:** SEIC. **CEO:** Alfred West. **Annual sales/revenues:** More than $100 million. **Number of employees nationwide:** 1,300. **Number of employees worldwide:** 1,400.

SEI INVESTMENTS COMPANY
One Freedom Valley Drive, Oaks PA 19456. 610/676-1000. **Toll-free phone:** 800/610-1114. **Fax:** 484/676-1490. **Contact:** Human Resources. **E-mail address:** jcrompton@seic.com. **World Wide Web address:** http://www.seic.com. **Description:** SEI operates primarily in two business markets: Trust and Banking, and Fund Sponsor/Investment Advisory. The company invests for clients worldwide in both public and private markets, and also provides investment and business solutions to those in the investment business that in turn serve their own investor clients. SEI provides direct investment solutions for $50 billion of investable capital and delivers systems and business solutions to organizations investing nearly $1 trillion. SEI is one of the largest providers of trust systems in the world. Founded in 1968. **NOTE:** Entry-level positions are offered. **Company slogan:** The art of the people. The science of results. **Positions advertised include:** Private Equity Accountant; Hedge Fund Accountant; Fund Accounting Supervisor; Investor Services Representative. **Office hours:** Monday - Friday, 8:30 a.m. - 5:30 p.m. **Corporate headquarters location:** This location. **Listed on:** NASDAQ. **Stock exchange symbol:** SEIC. **CEO:** Alfred West. **Annual sales/revenues:** More than $100 million. **Number of employees at this location:** 1,200. **Number of employees nationwide:** 1,300. **Number of employees worldwide:** 1,400.

SI HANDLING SYSTEMS INC.
PARAGON TECHNOLOGIES COMPANY
600 Kubler Road, Easton PA 18040. 610/252-7321. **Fax:** 610/252-3102. **Contact:** Human Resources. **World Wide Web address:** http://www.sihs.com. **Description:** Designs, manufactures, sells, and installs computer-directed, automated material handling and automated order selection systems and equipment worldwide. **Corporate headquarters location:** This location. **Parent company:** Paragon Technologies Company (also at this location). **Operations at this facility include:** Administration; Manufacturing; Research and Development; Sales; Service. **Number of employees at this location:** 175. **Number of employees nationwide:** 225.

SKF USA INDUSTRIES
1111 Adams Avenue, Norristown PA 19403-2403. 610/630-2800. **Fax:** 610/630-2727. **Contact:** Human Resources. **World Wide Web address:** http://www.skfusa.com. **Description:** Produces tapered roller bearings. **Positions advertised include:** Customer Channel Planner; Quality Engineer. **Number of employees worldwide:** 42,000.

SPD TECHNOLOGIES
13500 Roosevelt Boulevard, Philadelphia PA 19116. 215/677-4900. **Fax:** 215/677-1504. **Contact:** Jackie Taylor, Employee Relations Generalist. **World Wide Web address:** http://www.spdtech.com. **Description:** A world leader in the design, development, and manufacture of circuit breakers, switchgear, and related electrical protection systems for shipboard applications worldwide. **Positions advertised include:** Product Engineer. **Corporate headquarters location:** This location. **Subsidiaries include:** Henschel, Newburyport MA; Pac Ord, San Diego CA; SPD Switchgear, Montgomeryville PA. **Operations at this facility include:** Administration; Divisional Headquarters; Manufacturing; Research and Development; Sales. **Number of employees at this location:** 450. **Number of employees worldwide:** 800.

SPS TECHNOLOGIES
301 Highland Avenue, Jenkintown PA 19046. 215/572-3000. **Fax:** 215/572-3790. **Contact:** Human Resources. **World Wide Web address:** http://www.spstech.com. **Description:** Engaged in the design, manufacture, and marketing of high-tech fastener products, including precision components and computer-controlled tightening equipment and special materials. SPS Technologies maintains more than 15

manufacturing plants and sales offices located worldwide. **Corporate headquarters location:** Newtown PA. **Subsidiaries include:** Henschel (Newburyport MA); Pac Ord (San Diego CA); SPD Switchgear (Montgomeryville PA). **Operations at this facility include:** Administration; Divisional Headquarters; Manufacturing; Research and Development; Sales; Service. **Listed on:** New York Stock Exchange.

STV INCORPORATED
205 West Welsh Drive, Douglassville PA 19518. 610/385-8213. **Fax:** 610/385-8515. **Contact:** Patrick Austin, Human Resources Director. **World Wide Web address:** http://www.stvinc.com. **Description:** Provides engineering and architectural consulting and design services for a variety of projects, as well as construction inspection services for numerous industries, institutions, and sectors. The company operates four business segments including civil engineering, which provides services for the construction of highways, bridges, airports, and marine ports; defense systems engineering, which serves the U.S. Department of Defense in the development of equipment and special hardware; industrial process engineering, which consists of services for the development of manufacturing equipment and process systems; and transportation engineering, which involves consulting, design, and construction supervision services for transportation facilities. Founded in 1945. **Positions advertised include:** Civil Engineering Intern; Civil Engineer. **Special programs:** Co-ops; Summer Jobs. **Corporate headquarters location:** This location. **Other U.S. locations:** Nationwide. **Parent company:** STV Group Inc. **Operations at this facility include:** Regional Headquarters. **Listed on:** NASDAQ. **Stock exchange symbol:** STVI. **Annual sales/revenues:** $51 - $100 million. **Number of employees at this location:** 275. **Number of employees nationwide:** 1,000.

SAEGERTOWN MANUFACTURING CORPORATION
One Crawford Street, P.O. Box 828, Saegertown PA 16433. 814/763-2655. **Fax:** 814/763-2069. **Contact:** Eileen Miller, Personnel. **World Wide Web address:** http://www.smc-coldform.com. **Description:** Manufactures cold-formed steel products.

SAFEGUARD SCIENTIFICS, INC.
800 Safeguard Building, 435 Devon Park Drive, Wayne PA 19087. 610/293-0600. **Toll-free phone:** 877/506-7371. **Fax:** 610/293-0601. **Contact:** Personnel Department. **World Wide Web address:** http://www.safeguard.com. **Description:** A strategic information systems holding company. **Corporate headquarters location:** This location. **Subsidiaries include:** Cambridge Technology Partners; ChromaVision Medical Systems; CompuCom Systems, Inc.; Diamond Technology Partners; DocuCorp International; OAD Technology Solutions; Sanchez Computer Association; Tangram Enterprise Solutions; and USDATA Corporation. **Listed on:** New York Stock Exchange. **Stock exchange symbol:** SFE.

ST. IVES BURRUPS
1617 JFK Boulevard, Suite 430, Philadelphia PA 19103. 215/563-9000. **Fax:** 215/563-3810. **Contact:** Human Resources. **World Wide Web address:** http://www.st-ives.com. **Description:** A publisher and printer of a wide range of books and magazines concerning the securities, legal, and general finance industries.

SAINT LUKE'S MINERS MEMORIAL MEDICAL CENTER
360 West Ruddle Street, Coaldale PA 18218-0067. 570/645-8113. **Fax:** 570/645-8149. **Contact:** Human Resources. **World Wide Web address:** http://www.slhn-lehighvalley.org. **Description:** A 108-bed, acute care facility with a 48-bed geriatric center. **NOTE:** Entry-level positions and second and third shifts are offered. **Positions advertised include:** Certified Occupational Therapist; Manager of Pharmacy; Pharmacist; Registered Nurse; Vascular Technologist. **Special programs:** Internships. **Operations at this facility include:** Administration; Service. **Number of employees at this location:** 400.

SAINT-GOBAIN CONTAINERS
One Glass Place, Port Allegany PA 16743. 814/642-2521. **Contact:** Barry Healy, Human Resources Director. **World Wide Web address:** http://www.sgcontainers.com. **Description:** A manufacturer of glass containers including glass canning jars, food containers, and glass containers for a variety of industrial and commercial uses.

THE SALVATION ARMY
P.O. Box 6176, Erie PA 16512. 814/456-4237. **Physical address:** 1209 Sassafras Street, Philadelphia PA 16501. **Contact:** Human Resources. **World Wide Web address:** http://www.salvationarmy.org. **Description:** A nonprofit organization providing several service programs including day-care centers, programs for people with disabilities, substance abuse programs and tutoring for at-risk students. The Salvation Army targets its programs to assist alcoholics, battered women, drug addicts, the elderly, the homeless, people with AIDS, prison inmates, teenagers, and the unemployed.

SARGENT ELECTRIC COMPANY
2801 Liberty Avenue, P.O. Box 30, Pittsburgh PA 15230. 412/391-0588. **Fax:** 412/394-7535. **Contact:** Human Resources. **World Wide Web address:** http://www.sargent.com. **Description:** An electrical contractor.

SARTORIUS BBI SYSTEMS
999 Postal Road, Allentown PA 18109. 610/266-6262. **Toll-free phone:** 800/258-9000. **Fax:** 610/266-9319. **Contact:** Human Resources. **E-mail address:** info@sartorius-bbi-systems.com. **World Wide Web address:** http://www.bbraunbiotech.com. **Description:** Manufactures custom-built fermentation/cell culture bioreactor systems. B. Braun Biotech also produces a line of accessory products for laboratories including shakers, homogenizers, freeze-dryers, and heating/cooling circulator baths.

SCHNADER HARRISON SEGAL & LEWIS LLP
1600 Market Street, Suite 3600, Philadelphia PA 19103. 215/751-2000. **Contact:** Wanda Whitted, Human Resources Manager. **World Wide Web address:** http://www.shsl.com. **Description:** A law firm.

SCHNEIDER, DOWNS & COMPANY
1133 Penn Avenue, Pittsburgh PA 15222-4205. 412/261-3644. **Fax:** 412/261-4876. **Contact:** Amy Parkinson, Human Resources. **E-mail address:** aparknson@sdcpa.com. **World Wide Web address:** http://www.schneiderdowns.com. **Description:** A professional accounting, tax, and business consulting firm.

SCHRAMM, INC.
800 East Virginia Avenue, West Chester PA 19380. 610/696-2500. **Contact:** Personnel Department. **World Wide Web address:** http://www.schramminc.com **Description:** Manufactures truck- and crawler-mounted drilling rigs and self-propelled air compressors. Products are marketed to mining, water well, and general contractors.

SCHUTTE & KOERTING, INC.
2233 State Road, Bensalem PA 19020. 215/639-0900. **Fax:** 215/639-1533. **Contact:** Director of Human Resources. **World Wide Web address:** http://www.s-k.com. **Description:** Manufactures power and process vacuum equipment and turbine meter instrumentation. Founded in 1876. **Corporate headquarters location:** This location. **Annual sales/revenues:** $11 - $20 million. **Number of employees at this location:** 100.

SELAS CORPORATION OF AMERICA
2034 South Limekiln Pike, Dresher PA 19025. 215/646-6600. **Fax:** 215/646-3536. **Contact:** Robert W. Mason, Director of Human Resources and Administration. **World Wide Web address:** http://www.selas.com. **Description:** A diversified firm that engages in the design, development, engineering, and manufacturing of a wide range of specialized industrial heat processing systems and equipment for steel, glass, and other manufacturers. **Corporate headquarters location:** This location. **Subsidiaries include:** Deuer Manufacturing, Inc. manufactures spare tire holders, lifts, and related products, primarily based on cable winch designs, for use as original equipment by the pick-up truck and minivan segment of the automotive industry; Resistance Technology, Inc. designs and manufactures microminiature components and molded plastic parts primarily for the hearing instrument manufacturing industry worldwide. **Operations at this facility include:** Administration; Manufacturing; Research and Development; Sales; Service. **Listed on:** American Stock Exchange. **Stock exchange symbol:** SLS. **Annual sales/revenues:** $51 - $100 million. **Number of employees at this location:** 75. **Number of employees nationwide:** 500. **Number of employees worldwide:** 600.

SERVICE BY AIR INC.
850 Calcoon Hook Road, Sharon Hill PA 19079. 610/586-5050. **Toll-free phone:** 800/719-0001. **Fax:** 610/586-5511. **Contact:** Human Resources. **World Wide Web address:** http://www.servicebyair.com. **Description:** An air transportation company. **NOTE:** All resumes must indicate location of interest and be sent to: Service By Air Inc., Human Resources, 55 East Ames Court, Plainview NY 11803.

SETON COMPANY
Horton Drive, P.O. Box 190, Saxton PA 16678. 814/635-2937. **Fax:** 248/689-0991. **Contact:** Human Resources. **E-mail address:** hr@setonco.com. **World Wide Web address:** http://www.setonleather.com. **Description:** Seton's operations are conducted primarily through two business segments: Leather is involved in tanning, finishing, and distributing of whole-hide cattle leathers for the automotive and furniture upholstery industries; cattle hide side leathers for the footwear, handbag, and other markets; and cattle hide products for collagen, rawhide pet items, and other applications; and Chemicals and Coated Products is engaged in the manufacture and distribution of epoxy and urethane chemicals, specialty leather finishes, industrial and medical tapes, foams, films, and laminates. **Other U.S. locations:** Wilmington DE; Toledo OH; Malvern PA; Norristown PA. **Operations at this facility include:** This location cuts finished leathers.

SETON COMPANY
1000 Madison Avenue, Norristown PA 19403. 610/666-9600. **Contact:** Human Resources Manager. **E-mail address:** hr@setonco.com. **World Wide Web address:** http://www.setonleather.com. **Description:** Seton's operations are conducted primarily through two business segments: Leather is involved in tanning, finishing, and distributing of whole-hide cattle leathers for the automotive and furniture upholstery industries; cattle hide side leathers for the footwear, handbag, and other markets; and cattle hide products for collagen, rawhide pet items, and other applications; and Chemicals and Coated Products is engaged in the manufacture and distribution of epoxy and urethane chemicals, specialty leather finishes, industrial and medical tapes, foams, films, and laminates. **Operations at this facility include:** This location manufactures leather car seats.

7-ELEVEN, INC.
2711 Easton Road, Willow Grove PA 19090. 215/672-5711. **Contact:** Human Resources. **World Wide Web address:** http://www.7-eleven.com. **Description:** 7-Eleven is one of the world's largest retailers, with approximately 7,000 7-Eleven convenience units in the United States and Canada. **Corporate headquarters location:** Dallas TX. **Operations at this facility include:** This location houses administrative offices.

SHAMOKIN AREA COMMUNITY HOSPITAL
4200 Hospital Road, Coal Township PA 17866. 570/644-4200. **Fax:** 570/644-4356. **Contact:** Human Resources Representative. **E-mail address:** l.schoch@shamokinhospital.org. **World Wide Web address:** http://www.shamokinhospital.org. **Description:** A 61-bed nonprofit, community hospital offering acute care, general surgery, subacute and outpatient rehabilitation, inpatient and partial hospitalization care for geriatric-psychiatric patients, 24-hour emergency services, occupational health, specialty clinics and community health programs. Founded in 1912. **NOTE:** Entry-level positions, part-time jobs, and second and third shifts are offered. **Company slogan:** Quality care close to home. **Positions advertised include:** Registered Nurse; Psychiatry Technician; Department Secretary. **Special programs:** Summer Jobs. **Office hours:** Monday - Friday, 8:00 a.m. - 5:00 p.m. **Corporate headquarters location:** This location. **Other U.S. locations:** Elysburg PA. **Subsidiaries include:** Northumberland Health Services. **President/CEO:** John P. Wiercinski. **Annual sales/revenues:** $21 - $50 million. **Number of employees at this location:** 285.

SHARON REGIONAL HEALTH SYSTEM
740 East State Street, Sharon PA 16146. 724/983-3831. **Contact:** Human Resources. **E-mail address:** jobs@srhs-pa.org. **World Wide Web address:** http://www.sharonregional.com. **Description:** A comprehensive health care system that offers a variety of clinical programs and services. **Positions advertised include:** Charge Nurse; Paramedic; Nurse Aide; Licensed Practical Nurse; Registered Nurse; Psychiatrist.

SHARON TUBE COMPANY
134 Mill Street, P.O. Box 492, Sharon PA 16146. **Toll-free phone:** 800/242-1221. **Fax:** 724/953-1031. **Contact:** Personnel. **World Wide Web address:** http://www.sharontube.com. **Description:** A wholesaler of plumbing and heating supplies. Founded in 1929.

SHAW ENVIRONMENTAL & INFRASTRUCTURE CORPORATION
2790 Mosside Boulevard, Monroeville PA 15146. 412/372-7701. **Toll-free phone:** 877/869-9269. **Contact:** Ann Harris, Vice President of Human Resources. **E-mail address:** jobnorth@theitgroup.com. **World Wide Web address:** http://www.theitgroup.com. **Description:** Delivers a full range of environmental management services through an integrated approach for total turnkey solutions. The company applies engineering, analytical, remediation, and pollution control expertise to meet the environmental needs of its clients, from site assessment to remediation. **Positions advertised include:** Assistant Engineer; Project Manager; Payroll Clerk; Estimator; Accountant; Scientist; Project Business Administrator; Consultant. **Corporate headquarters location:** Baton Rouge LA. **Parent company:** Shaw Group

Inc. **Listed on:** New York Stock Exchange. **Stock exchange symbol:** SGR. **Number of employees worldwide:** 4,000.

SHERWOOD
2200 North Main Street, Washington PA 15301. 724/225-8000. **Contact:** Director of Human Resources. **World Wide Web address:** http://www.sherwoodvalve.com. **Description:** Produces a variety of flow control devices for the compressed gas, air conditioning, and refrigeration industry. **Corporate headquarters location:** Harrisburg PA. **Parent company:** Harsco Corporation. **Operations at this facility include:** Divisional Headquarters; Manufacturing; Sales. **Listed on:** New York Stock Exchange. **Stock exchange symbol:** HSC. **Number of employees at this location:** 285.

SHIELD'S RUBBER COMPANY
2130 Colonial Avenue, Erie PA 16506. 814/838-6561. **Contact:** Pat McCullough, Operations Manager. **Description:** Manufactures rubber products including O-rings and gaskets.

SHIPPENSBURG UNIVERSITY
1871 Old Main Drive, Shippensburg PA 17257-2299. 717/477-1124. **Fax:** 717/477-4037. **Contact:** Office of Human Resources. **E-mail address:** hr@ship.edu. **World Wide Web address:** http://www.ship.edu. **Description:** A four-year university offering bachelor's and master's degrees. Approximately 5,200 undergraduates and 1,200 graduate students attend Shippensburg University. **Positions advertised include:** Adjunct Geography Instructor; Assistant Spanish Professor; Assistant Woman's Basketball Coach; Custodial Worker.

R.M. SHOEMAKER COMPANY
One Tower Bridge, 100 Front Street, Suite 1300, P.O. Box 888, West Conshohocken PA 19428. 610/941-5500. **Fax:** 610/941-4203. **Contact:** Human Resources. **E-mail address:** hr@rmsco.com. **World Wide Web address:** http://www.rmshoemaker.com. **Description:** An industrial and commercial construction company. **Positions advertised include:** Project Manager; Project Superintendent; Project Engineer; Project Accountant; Estimator.

SHOP VAC CORPORATION
2323 Reach Road, P.O. Box 3307, Williamsport PA 17701. 570/326-0502. **Fax:** 570/321-7089. **Contact:** Employment Coordinator. **E-mail address:** hr@shopvac.com. **World Wide Web address:** http://www.shopvac.com. **Description:** Manufactures and wholesales vacuum cleaners. **Positions advertised include:** Vacuum Assembly Associate; Injection Molding Associate; Injection Molding Process Technician; Production Set-up Worker; Detail Drafter. **Corporate headquarters location:** This location.

SIEMENS ENERGY AND AUTOMATION, INC.
1201 Sumneytown Pike, MS 530, Spring House PA 19477-0900. 215/646-7400. **Fax:** 215/283-6341. **Contact:** Human Resources. **World Wide Web address:** http://www.smpa.siemens.com. **Description:** A manufacturer and seller of process control systems and industrial instruments. **Positions advertised include:** Field Service Engineer; Senior Systems Engineer; Senior Technical Instructor. **Corporate headquarters location:** This location. **Operations at this facility include:** Administration; Manufacturing; Research and Development; Sales; Service. **Listed on:** New York Stock Exchange. **Stock exchange symbol:** SI.

SIEMENS MEDICAL SOLUTIONS HEALTH SERVICES CORPORATION
51 Valley Stream Parkway, Malvern PA 19355. 610/219-6300. **Fax:** 610/219-3124. **Contact:** Human Resources. **World Wide Web address:** http://www.smed.com. **Description:** A leading provider of health information and service solutions to hospitals, multi-entity health care corporations, integrated health networks, physician groups, and other health care providers in North America and Europe. The company also provides a full complement of solutions for the newly emerging community health information networks, which include payers and employers as well as providers. Shared Medical Systems offers a comprehensive line of health care information systems including clinical, financial, administrative, ambulatory, and decision support systems for both the public and private health care sectors. These systems are offered on computers operating at the customer site, at the SMS Information Services Center, or as part of a distributed network. Shared Medical Systems also provides a portfolio of professional services including systems installation, support, and education. In addition, the company provides specialized consulting services for the design and integration of software and networks, facilities management, information systems planning, and systems-related process reengineering. Founded in 1969. **NOTE:** Entry-level positions are offered. **Special programs:** Internships. **Corporate headquarters location:** This location. **Other U.S. locations:** Nationwide. **Operations at this facility include:** Administration; Research and Development; Sales; Service. **Listed on:** New York Stock Exchange. **Stock exchange symbol:** SMS. **Annual sales/revenues:** More than $100 million. **Number of employees at this location:** 3,200. **Number of employees worldwide:** 5,000.

SILVER OAKS NURSING CENTER
715 Harbor Street, New Castle PA 16101. 724/652-3863. **Fax:** 724/652-1756. **Contact:** Human Resources. **Description:** A nursing home specializing in the care of patients with Alzheimer's disease.

SIMKAR CORPORATION
700 Ramona Avenue, Philadelphia PA 19120-4691. 215/831-7700. **Fax:** 215/831-7752. **Contact:** Human Resources. **E-mail address:** resume@simkar.com. **World Wide Web address:** http://www.simkar.com. **Description:** Manufactures and markets H.I.D., fluorescent, and vandal-proof lighting fixtures for the industrial and consumer markets. **Corporate headquarters location:** This location.

SKILLS OF CENTRAL PENNSYLVANIA, INC.
341 Science Park Road, Suite 6, State College PA 16803. 814/238-3245. **Fax:** 814/238-5117. **Contact:** John Fox, Human Resources Director. **E-mail address:** jfox@skillsgroup.org. **World Wide Web address:** http://www.skillsofcentralpa.org. **Description:** A nonprofit company offering services for individuals with mental or physical disabilities. **Positions advertised include:** Residential Services Assistant; Vocational Training Services Assistant; Community Support Specialist.

SLIPPERY ROCK UNIVERSITY
205 Old Main Building, Slippery Rock PA 16057. 724/738-2070. **Fax:** 724/738-4475. **Contact:** Human Resources. **World Wide Web address:** http://www.sru.edu. **Description:** A four-year university offering several undergraduate, graduate, and doctoral programs. Enrollment at Slippery Rock University is approximately 7,500.

L.E. SMITH GLASS COMPANY
1900 Liberty Street, Mount Pleasant PA 15666. 724/547-3544. **Fax:** 724/547-2077. **Contact:** Bonnie Telsord, Personnel. **World Wide Web address:** http://www.lesmithglass.com. **Description:** Produces glass goods such as tabletop and lighting accessories and giftware items.

SMITHS INDUSTRIES
101 Lindenwood Drive, Suite 125, Malvern PA 19355. 610/578-9600. **Contact:** Vice President of Human Resources. **World Wide Web address:** http://www.smithsind-aerospace.com. **Description:** Engaged in a variety of businesses through three business groups: Smiths Industries Aerospace Group manufactures instrumentation and systems for civil and military aircraft; Smiths Industries Medical Systems Group (SIMS) manufactures surgical, dental, veterinary, and home health care supplies; Smiths Industries Industrial Group operates in four divisions. Flex-Tek produces flexible ducting and conduits. Vent-Axia produces ventilation fans. Engineering produces specialized engineering products. Hypertac Interconnect manufactures electrical connectors. **Corporate headquarters location:** London, England. **Other U.S. locations:** Irvine CA; Sunnyvale CA; Clearwater FL; Fort Myers FL; Hudson MA; Rockland MA; Grand Rapids MI; St. Paul MN; Keene NH; Florham Park NJ; Abbeville SC; Cookeville TN. **Parent company:** Smiths Industries plc. **Annual sales/revenues:** More than $100 million. **Number of employees nationwide:** 6,000. **Number of employees worldwide:** 13,000.

SMITHS INDUSTRIES AEROSPACE
255 Great Valley Parkway, Malvern PA 19355. 610/296-5000. **Fax:** 610/296-0912. **Contact:** Human Resources. **World Wide Web address:** http://www.smithsind-aerospace.com. **Description:** Develops and manufactures instrumentation and systems for civil and military aircraft. Founded in 1920. **Special programs:** Internships; Co-ops. **Internship information:** Internships are available in Engineering/Manufacturing, Engineering, and Marketing. **Corporate headquarters location:** London, England. **Other U.S. locations:** Nationwide. **International locations:** France; Germany; South America. **Parent company:** Smiths Industries. **Listed on:** European Bourse. **CEO:** Keith Butler-Wheelhouse. **Number of employees at this location:** 165. **Number of employees nationwide:** 2,500. **Number of employees worldwide:** 15,000.

SMURFIT-STONE CONTAINER CORPORATION
5000 Flat Rock Road, Philadelphia PA 19127. 215/984-7000. **Fax:** 215/984-7170. **Contact:** Human Resources. **World Wide Web address:** http://www.smurfit-stone.com. **Description:** Smurfit-Stone Container Corporation is the world's leading paper-based packaging company. The company's main products include corrugated containers, folding cartons, and multiwall industrial bags. The company is also the world's largest collector and processor of recycled products that are then sold to a worldwide customer base. Smurfit-Stone Container Corporation also operates several paper tube, market pulp, and newsprint production facilities. **Special programs:** Training. **Corporate headquarters location:** Chicago IL. **Other U.S. locations:** Nationwide. **International locations:** Worldwide. **Operations at this facility include:** This location manufactures clay-coated boxboard made from recycled paper. **Listed on:** NASDAQ. **Stock exchange symbol:** SSCC. **General Manager:** Rusty Miller. **Annual sales/revenues:** More than $100 million. **Number of employees at this location:** 300. **Number of employees nationwide:** 20,000.

SMURFIT-STONE CONTAINER CORPORATION
Tulip & Decatur Streets, Philadelphia PA 19136. 877/772-2932. **Contact:** Beverly Kantner, Personnel Director. **World Wide Web address:** http://www.smurfit-stone.com. **Description:** Smurfit-Stone Container Corporation is one of the world's leading paper-based packaging companies. The company's main products include corrugated containers, folding cartons, and multiwall industrial bags. The company is also one of the world's largest collectors and processors of recycled products that are then sold to a worldwide customer base. Smurfit-Stone Container Corporation also operates several paper tube, market pulp, and newsprint production facilities. **Corporate headquarters location:** Chicago IL. **Other U.S. locations:** Nationwide. **Operations at this facility include:** This location manufactures corrugated boxes. **Listed on:** NASDAQ. **Stock exchange symbol:** SSCC. **Annual sales/revenues:** More than $100 million.

SNAP-TITE INC.
8325 Hessinger Drive, Erie PA 16509-4679. 814/838-5700. **Fax:** 814/833-0145. **Contact:** Human Resources. **E-mail address:** snaptite@snap-tite.com. **World Wide Web address:** http://www.snap-tite.com. **Description:** Designs, develops, manufactures, markets, and services equipment and systems capable of withstanding extreme pressure and temperature. Originally developed for use in high-pressure chemical research, the company's products have been applied over the years to create equipment for use in industrial research and production, petrochemical and chemical processing, materials forming, semiconductor microchip production, and defense applications. **Corporate headquarters location:** This location.

SNAP-TITE INC.
6420 West Ridge Road, Erie PA 16506. 814/838-3190. **Fax:** 814/833-5439. **Contact:** Mike Taylor, Assembly Supervisor. **E-mail address:** sv_sales@snap-tite.com. **World Wide Web address:** http://www.snap-tite.com. **Description:** Snap-Tite, Inc. designs, develops, manufactures, markets, and services equipment and systems capable of withstanding extreme pressure and temperature. Originally developed for use in high-pressure chemical research, the company's products have been applied over the years to create equipment for use in industrial research and production, petrochemical and chemical processing, materials forming, semiconductor microchip production, and defense applications. **Operations at this facility include:** This location manufactures solenoid valves, electric valves, and fire hose.

SODEXHO MARRIOTT
1000 Liberty Avenue, 2nd Floor, Pittsburgh PA 15222. 412/261-3660. **Contact:** Human Resources. **World Wide Web address:** http://www.Marriott.com. **Description:** Manages the food service facility at a Pittsburgh federal office building. **Parent company:** Marriott International owns and manages retail restaurants, hotels, and institutional food services. Marriott International also operates food and beverage concessions in airports; merchandise gift and specialty shops in airports, hotels, and resorts; brand food and retail concessions on turnpikes; and food and beverage concessions in stadiums and arenas.

SOFTMART, INC.
450 Acorn Lane, Downingtown PA 19335. 610/518-4058. **Fax:** 610/518-3014. **Contact:** Recruiting Manager. **E-mail address:** hresource@softmart.com. **World Wide Web address:** http://www.softmart.com. **Description:** Resells computer software and hardware to government and commercial clients. Founded in 1983. **NOTE:** Entry-level positions and second and third shifts are offered. **Special programs:** Internships; Training; Summer Jobs. **Office hours:** Monday - Friday, 8:30 a.m. - 5:30 p.m. **Corporate headquarters location:** This location. **President:** Elliot Levine. **Annual sales/revenues:** More than $100 million. **Number of employees at this location:** 490.

SOLUTIONS CONSULTING LLC
370 Southpointe Boulevard, Canonsburg PA 15317. 724/514-5000. **Fax:** 724/514-5050. **Contact:** Human Resources. **World Wide Web address:** http://www.scglobal.com. **Description:** A computer consulting firm. Solutions Consulting provides mid- to large-sized corporations services in the following areas: business-to-business and business-to-customer e-commerce solutions; supply chain management; customer relationship management; and enterprise resource planning (ERP) applications. **Other U.S. locations:** Phoenix AZ; Chicago IL; Cincinnati OH.

SOUTHERN HOME SERVICES
3149 Germantown Avenue, Philadelphia PA 19133. 215/221-1700. **Contact:** Personnel. **Description:** Operates a child and family treatment center. Southern Home Services provides children's services including after-school programs, foster care, and residential care. **NOTE:** Entry-level positions and second and third shifts are offered. **Annual sales/revenues:** $5 - $10 million. **Number of employees at this location:** 160.

SOUTHWOOD PSYCHIATRIC HOSPITAL
2575 Boyce Plaza Road, Pittsburgh PA 15241. 412/257-2290. **Toll-free phone:** 888/907-5437. **Fax:** 412/257-0374. **Contact:** Jill Yesko, Personnel Manager. **World Wide Web address:** http://www.southwoodhospital.com. **Description:** A psychiatric hospital that offers inpatient and outpatient care to adolescents. **NOTE:** Entry-level positions are offered. **Corporate headquarters location:** This location. **Parent company:** Youth & Family Centered Services. **Number of employees at this location:** 250.

SOVEREIGN BANK
449 Eisenhower Boulevard, Harrisburg PA 17111. 866/929-7646. **Fax:** 717/909-7457. **Contact:** Personnel. **World Wide Web address:** http://www.sovereignbank.com. **Description:** A savings and loan association. **Other U.S. locations:** DE; NJ; CT; MA; RI. **Listed on:** New York Stock Exchange. **Stock exchange symbol:** SOV. **Number of employees nationwide:** 10,000.

SOVEREIGN BANK
1130 Berkshire Boulevard, P.O. Box 12646, Reading PA 19612. 610/320-8400. **Physical address:** 1130 Berkshire Boulevard, Wyomissing PA 19610. **Fax:** 610/376-8379. **Contact:** Recruiting. **World Wide Web address:** http://www.sovereignbank.com. **Description:** A full-service banking institution serving the Mid-Atlantic and Northeast regions. **Positions advertised include:** Administrator; Community Banking Assistant Manager; Customer Service Manager; Teller; Loan Processor. **Special programs:** Internships; Training; Summer Jobs. **Corporate headquarters location:** This location. **Other U.S. locations:** DE; NJ; CT; MA; RI. **Listed on:** New York Stock Exchange. **Stock exchange symbol:** SOV. **Number of employees nationwide:** 10,000.

SPECIALTY BAR PRODUCTS COMPANY
200 Martha Street, P.O. 127, Blairsville PA 15717. 724/459-7500. **Fax:** 724/459-0630. **Contact:** Human Resources. **Description:** Manufactures specialty fasteners and custom machining work for the power generation industry, military and commercial aircraft, land based track vehicles, naval applications, and the oil industry.

SPECTRUM CONTROL, INC.
8061 Avonia Road, Fairview PA 16415. 814/474-1571. **Contact:** Human Resources. **World Wide Web address:** http://www.spectrumcontrol.com. **Description:** Spectrum Control, Inc. designs, manufactures, and markets a broad line of electromagnetic compatibility (EMC) products designed to protect electronic equipment against interference from random electromagnetic waves. The company's product offerings include discrete electromagnetic interference (EMI) and radio frequency interference (RFI) filters, filtered connectors, multiline EMI and RFI filters, and specialty ceramic capacitors. Spectrum Control also offers customer consulting, diagnostic testing, and manufacturing services. These services include testing for EMC problems, analyzing test results, proposing design solutions, producing required components, and supplying these components on a continuing basis. The company sells its EMC testing services and components to a broad base of customers for use in communications systems, data processing, telecommunications, and process control. **Positions advertised include:** Materials Manager; Senior Ceramics Project Manager. **Corporate headquarters location:** This location. **Operations at this facility include:** This location manufactures filtered connectors. **Listed on:** NASDAQ. **Stock exchange symbol:** SPEC. **Number of employees worldwide:** 670.

SPINDLE PUBLISHING COMPANY, INC.
4136 Library Road. Pittsburgh PA 15234. 412/531-9742. **Fax:** 412/531-2004. **Contact:** Human Resources. **E-mail address:** info@spindlepub.com. **World Wide Web address:** http://www.spindlepub.com. **Description:** A publishing company specializing in local, national, & international resource publications for readers in a variety of sectors. Founded in 1976.

SPRINGS WINDOW FASHIONS
8601, Route 405 Highway South, Montgomery PA 17752. 570/547-6671. **Contact:** Human Resources. **World Wide Web address:** http://www.springs.com. **Description:** A manufacturer of window dressings. The company specializes in horizontal, vertical, and pleated blinds as well as vinyl shades.

STATE COLLEGE AREA SCHOOL DISTRICT
131 West Nittany Avenue, State College PA 16801. 814/231-1051. **Contact:** Dennis Guthe, Personnel Director. **World Wide Web address:** http://www.scasd.k12.pa.us. **Description:** Administrative offices of the State College public school district. The district is comprised of 11 elementary schools, two middle schools, and one high school.

STATE OF THE ART INC.
2470 Fox Hill Road, State College PA 16803. 814/355-8004. **Contact:** Dianne Kerly, Human Resources. **World Wide Web address:** http://www.resistor.com. **Description:** Manufactures chip resistors.

STERIS CORPORATION
2424 West 23rd Street, Erie PA 16506. 814/452-3100. **Contact:** Laurene Bucci, Human Resources. **World Wide Web address:** http://www.steris.com. **Description:** Develops, manufactures, and distributes infection/contamination-preventing devices and surgical supplies, services, and technologies to the health care, scientific, agricultural, and industrial markets. **Positions advertised include:** Lab Technician; Administrative Assistant; Director Environmental Health and Safety; Contract Specialist; Senior Designer. **Corporate headquarters location:** Mentor OH. **Other U.S. locations:** Montgomery AL; Wilson NY; Apex NC. **Listed on:** New York Stock Exchange. **Stock exchange symbol:** STE.

STERLING PAPER COMPANY
2155 East Castor Avenue, Philadelphia PA 19134. 215/744-5350. **Contact:** Human Resources. **Description:** Manufactures a wide variety of paper plates, cups, and related products. **Corporate headquarters location:** This location.

STIVERS STAFFING
1 Penn Center Plaza, 1617 JFK Boulevard, Suite 825, Philadelphia PA 19103. 215/561-1355. **Fax:** 215/567-2876. **E-mail address:** philly@stivers.com. **World Wide Web address:** http://www.stivers.com. **Description:** Places applicants into a wide range of careers and companies. **Positions advertised include:** Mailroom Staff; Receptionist; Administrative Assistant.

STORAGE TECHNOLOGY CORPORATION
6 Tower Bridge, Suite 400, 181 Washington Street, Conshohocken PA 19428. 484/530-4100. **Contact:** Personnel. **E-mail address:** stkjobs@storagetek.com. **World Wide Web address:** http://www.storagetek.com. **Description:** Manufactures, sells, and services data storage devices. Overall, Storage Technology Corporation manufactures high-performance computer information storage and retrieval systems for mainframe and mid-frame computers and networks. Products include automated cartridge systems, random access subsystems, and fault-tolerant disk arrays. The company also distributes equipment; sells new peripherals, software, and hardware; and offers support services. **Positions advertised include:** Financial Analyst/Accountant; Intern-Finance/Accounting. **Corporate headquarters location:** Louisville CO.

STRAWBRIDGE'S
801 Market Street, Philadelphia PA 19107. 215/829-0346. **Contact:** Personnel. **World Wide Web address:** http://www.mayco.com. **Description:** Operates a chain of department stores in Pennsylvania, Delaware, and New Jersey. **NOTE:** Strawbridge's 150-hour buyers training program begins in September of each year. **Special programs:** Internships. **Corporate headquarters location:** This location. **Parent company:** The May Department Stores Company. **Number of employees nationwide:** 12,000.

STRICK CORPORATION
225 Lincoln Highway, Fairless Hills PA 19030. 215/949-3600. **Contact:** Human Resources. **World Wide Web address:** http://www.stricktrlr.com. **Description:** A manufacturer of trailers, flatbeds, and chassis. **Corporate headquarters location:** Monroe IN. **Other U.S. locations:** IN. **Operations at this facility include:** Administration; Research and Development; Sales; Service. **Number of employees at this location:** 65. **Number of employees nationwide:** 1,000.

A. STUCKI COMPANY
2600 Neville Road, Pittsburgh PA 15225. 412/771-7300. **Fax:** 412/771-7308. **Contact:** John Faryniak, President. **World Wide Web address:** http://www.stucki.com. **Description:** A manufacturer of load stabilizers and related equipment for the railroad industry.

SUN CHEMICAL/GENERAL PRINTING INC.
3348 West Clearfield Street, Philadelphia PA 19129. 215/223-8220. **Fax:** 215/223-2155. **Contact:** Mr. Louis A. Schiliro, Director of Human Resources. **World Wide Web address:** http://www.sunchemical.com. **Description:** Manufactures printing ink and graphic arts coatings.

SUNCOM INDUSTRIES INC.
128 Water Street, P.O. Box 46, Northumberland PA 17857. 570/473-8352. **Physical address:** 128 Water Street, Northumberland PA 17857. **Fax:** 570/473-0159. **Contact:** Peggy Vitale, Chief Executive Officer. **World Wide Web address:** http://www.suncom.org. **Description:** Operates a workshop for people with physical and mental disabilities. **Facilities Manager:** Roger Dietz.

SUNGARD ASSET MANAGEMENT SYSTEMS, INC.
333 Technology Drive, Malvern PA 19355. 610/251-6500. **Fax:** 610/251-6585. **Contact:** Teresa Urban, Human Resources Coordinator. **World Wide Web address:** http://www.sungard.com. **Description:** Develops, markets, and supports software for the financial industry. **NOTE:** Entry-level positions are offered. **Positions advertised include:** Data Communications Engineer; Resource Analyst; Recovery Specialist; Customer Service Representative. **Special programs:** Internships; Training. **Corporate headquarters location:** This location. **Other U.S. locations:** Nationwide. **Operations at this facility include:** Administration; Sales; Service. **Listed on:** Privately held. **Annual sales/revenues:** $21 - $50 million.

SUNGARD DATA SYSTEMS INC./SUNGARD RECOVERY SERVICES
680 East Swedesford Road, Wayne PA 19087. 484/582-2000. **Contact:** Anne Beeson, Vice President of Human Resources. **World Wide Web address:** http://www.sungard.com. **Description:** Provides specialized computer services including proprietary investment support systems for the financial services industry and computer disaster planning/recovery services. SunGard Data Systems Inc.'s investment accounting and portfolio systems maintain the books and records of large investment portfolios including those managed by banks and mutual funds. The company's disaster recovery services include alternate-site backup, testing, and recovery services for IBM, Prime, Stratus, Tandem, and Unisys computer installations. The company's computer service unit provides remote-access IBM computer processing, direct marketing, and automated mailing services. SunGard Data Systems Inc. also provides computer software, data processing, programming, and repair services. SunGard Recovery Systems (also at this location) provides business recovery services for both mainframe and mid-range computer platforms. **Corporate headquarters location:** This location. **Number of employees at this location:** 2,100.

SUNOCO, INC.
3144 West Passyunk Avenue, Philadelphia PA 19145. 215/339-2286. **Contact:** Human Resources Department. **World Wide Web address:** http://www.sunocoinc.com. **Description:** Sunoco is one of the country's largest independent petroleum refiner-marketers. With 3,500 stations operating under the Sunoco brand name, the company claims a presence in 17 states. Sunoco's lubricant and petrochemical products are marketed worldwide. **Positions advertised include:** Transportation Analyst; Pilot; Instrument Engineer; Process Control Engineer. **Corporate headquarters location:** Philadelphia PA. **Operations at this facility include:** This location is a refinery. **Listed on:** New York Stock Exchange. **Stock exchange symbol:** SUN. **Number of employees worldwide:** 11,000.

SUNOCO, INC.
100 Green Street, P.O. Box 426, Marcus Hook PA 19061. 610/859-1300. **Contact:** Human Resources Department. **World Wide Web address:** http://www.sunocoinc.com. **Description:** One of the country's largest independent petroleum refiner-marketers. With 3,500 stations operating under the Sunoco brand name, the company claims a presence in 17 states. Sunoco's lubricant and petrochemical products are marketed worldwide. **Corporate headquarters location:**

Philadelphia PA. **Listed on:** New York Stock Exchange. **Stock exchange symbol:** SUN. **Number of employees worldwide:** 11,000.

SUNOCO, INC.
10 Penn Center, 1801 Market Street, Philadelphia PA 19103-1699. 215/977-3000. **Fax:** 215/977-3409. **Contact:** Human Resources. **World Wide Web address:** http://www.sunocoinc.com. **Description:** One of the country's largest independent petroleum refiner-marketers. With 3,500 stations operating under the Sunoco brand name, the company claims a presence in 17 states. Sunoco's lubricant and petrochemical products are marketed worldwide. **Corporate headquarters location:** This location. **Listed on:** New York Stock Exchange. **Stock exchange symbol:** SUN. **Number of employees worldwide:** 11,000.

SUNOCO CHEMICALS
200 Neville Road, Neville Island 15225. 412/778-3322. **Contact:** Rick Woolbert, Human Resources. **World Wide Web address:** http://www.sunocochem.com. **Description:** A diversified worldwide chemicals and polymers manufacturer, marketing a broad range of products that are converted into consumer items. Markets served include automotive, construction, marine, and recreational. Products include phenol, bisphenol-A, polypropylene, acrylic sheet, coal chemicals, dibasic acids, 2-ethylhexanol, cumene, plasticizers, and unsaturated polyester resins. **Corporate headquarters location:** Philadelphia PA. **Parent company:** Sunoco Inc. **Listed on:** New York Stock Exchange. **Stock exchange symbol:** SUN.

SUNOCO CHEMICALS
Margaret & Bermuda Streets, Philadelphia PA 19137. 215/533-3000.**Contact:** Human Resources. **World Wide Web address:** http://www.sunocochem.com. **Description:** Produces a variety of chemical products including synthetic phenol, acetone, alpha methyl styrene, and cumene hydroperoxide. **Special programs:** Internships. **Corporate headquarters location:** Philadelphia PA. **Parent company:** Sunoco Inc. **Listed on:** New York Stock Exchange. **Stock exchange symbol:** SUN.

SUPELCO, INC.
595 North Harrison Road, Bellefonte PA 16823. 814/359-3441. **Contact:** Diane Lidgett, Human Resources Director. **World Wide Web address:** http://www.sigma-aldrich.com. **Description:** Manufactures chromatography supplies used for chemical separations. **Corporate headquarters location:** St. Louis MO. **Parent company:** Sigma-Aldrich. **Number of employees at this location:** 300.

SUPERVALUE EASTERN REGION
3900 Industrial Road, P.O. Box 2261, Harrisburg PA 17105. 717/232-6821. **Contact:** Human Resources. **Description:** Supervalue is a full-service grocery wholesaler and retailer. As one of the largest grocery wholesalers in the Mid-Atlantic region, the company supplies more than 13,000 regional brand and 1,000 private label products. The grocery division also operates several Basics supermarkets in the metropolitan Baltimore and Washington DC areas. **Other U.S. locations:** DE; NJ; VA; WV. **Operations at this facility include:** This location houses administrative offices.

SURE FIT INC.
939 Marcon Boulevard, Allentown PA 18109. 610/264-7300. **Fax:** 610/336-8995. **Contact:** Kenneth J. Guerin, Director of Human Resources. **E-mail address:** hr@surefit.net. **World Wide Web address:** http://www.surefit.net. **Description:** Manufactures decorative home textiles including furniture covers and throw pillows. **Positions advertised include:** Cloth Spreader; Cutting Room Worker; Sewing Machine Operator. **Corporate headquarters location:** New York NY. **Operations at this facility include:** Administration; Manufacturing.

SURGICAL LASER TECHNOLOGIES, INC.
147 Keystone Drive, Montgomeryville PA 18936. 215/619-3600. **Toll-free phone:** 800/366-4758. **Fax:** 215/619-3208. **Contact:** Colleen Hamilton, Personnel Director. **World Wide Web address:** http://www.slti.com. **Description:** Develops, manufactures, and sells proprietary laser systems for contact surgery. The company's Contact Laser System allows the surgeon to use a laser in direct contact with the tissue being treated, thereby making laser surgery both more precise and easier to perform. Surgical Laser Technologies also provides free-beam, noncontact laser delivery systems. Its product line includes six portable Contact Laser units of various power levels; a family of disposable optical fibers and handpieces; and more than 80 probes, scalpels, fibers, and hand pieces that provide different wavelength conversion effect properties, power densities, and configurations appropriate for cutting, coagulation, or vaporization. As a result of the system's design, a single contact laser system can be used within most surgical specialties to perform a broad range of minimally invasive and open surgical procedures. **Corporate headquarters location:** This location. **Number of employees at this location:** 160.

SUSQUEHANNA BANCSHARES, INC.
401 City Avenue, Suite 220, Bala Cynwyd PA 19004. 610/617-2600. **Fax:** 610/617-2689. **Contact:** Human Resources. **E-mail address:** recruiting@sig.com. **World Wide Web address:** http://www.susq.com. **Description:** A multifinancial institution that operates six banks serving eight counties with 83 offices. The company also operates a leasing company. Its market encompasses Pennsylvania, Maryland, New Jersey, Virginia, West Virginia, and Delaware. Founded in 1982. **Positions advertised include:** Assistant Trader Recruiting Sourcer; Brokerage Desk Billing Clerk; Configuration Manager. **Subsidiaries include:** Citizens National Bank of Southern Pennsylvania, Greencastle PA; Farmers and Merchants Bank & Trust, Hagerstown MD; Farmers First Bank, Lititz PA; First National Trust Bank, Sunbury PA; Spring Grove National Bank, Spring Grove PA; Williamsport National Bank, Williamsport PA. **Listed on:** NASDAQ. **Stock exchange symbol:** SUSQ.

SWARTHMORE COLLEGE
500 College Avenue, Swarthmore PA 19081. 610/328-7797. **Fax:** 610/690-2040. **Recorded jobline:** 610/328-8494. **Contact:** Human Resources. **E-mail address:** jobapps@swarthmore.edu. **World Wide Web address:** http://www.swarthmore.edu. **Description:** Swarthmore College is a small, private, liberal arts college.

SYNYGY, INC.
555 North Lane, Suite 6000, Conshohocken PA 19428. 610/664-7433 ext. 7715. **Fax:** 610/664-7343. **Contact:** Stephanie Salamon, Technical Recruiter. **E-mail address:** salamon@synygy.com. **World Wide Web address:** http://www.synygy.com. **Description:** A management consulting and information technology company. Founded in 1991. **NOTE:** Entry-level positions are offered, you may apply online. **Company slogan:** Turning information into action. **Positions advertised include:** System Architect; Associate Business Analyst; Software Documentation Specialist; Software Training Specialist; Assistant General Counsel. **Special programs:** Summer Jobs. **Office hours:** Monday - Friday, 9:00 a.m. - 6:00 p.m. **Corporate headquarters location:** This location. **CEO:** Mark Stiffler. **Annual sales/revenues:** $5 - $10 million. **Number of employees at this location:** 50.

TAMA MANUFACTURING COMPANY INC.
100A Cascade Drive, Allentown PA 18103. 610/231-3100. **Contact:** Human Resources. **Description:** A contract manufacturer of women's clothing. **NOTE:** Interested jobseekers should apply in person to the Human Resources office between the hours of 8:00 a.m. and 4:30 p.m.

TASTY BAKING COMPANY
2801 Hunting Park Avenue, Philadelphia PA 19129. 215/221-8500. **Contact:** Debbie Clarke, Manager of Human Resources. **World Wide Web address:** http://www.tastykake.com. **Description:** Engaged in the manufacture and sale of a variety of small, single-portion cakes, pies, and cookies under the brand name Tastykake. The company offers approximately 45 different products. **Corporate headquarters location:** This location. **Listed on:** American Stock Exchange. **Stock exchange symbol:** TBC.

TAYLOR PACKING COMPANY INC.
P.O. Box 188, Wyalusing PA 18853. 570/746-3000. **Fax:** 570/746-3888. **Contact:** Human Resources. **E-mail address:** info_wylusing@cargill.com. **World Wide Web address:** http://www.taylorpacking.com. **Description:** Taylor Packing Company is a multimillion-dollar operation capable of processing 1,800 cattle daily. Taylor Packing produces a complete line of vacuum-packaged, boxed beef cuts; custom-blended coarse ground beef; and fresh, vacuum-packed, and frozen variety meats for sale to supermarket chains, wholesalers, food-service distributors, institutions, and processed beef manufacturers. **NOTE:** For employment information see http://www.pacareerlink.state.pa.us. **Special programs:** Internships; Apprenticeships; Training; Summer Jobs. **Corporate headquarters location:** This location. **Operations at this facility include:** This location is a beef processing plant. **Subsidiaries include:** Taylor By-Products, Inc. (also at this location) operates a modern rendering plant that produces tallow and protein meals for sale to feed companies, pet food manufacturers, and chemical processors. This location also hires seasonally. **Number of employees at this location:** 1,050.

TECHINT TECHNOLOGIES, INC.
Cherrington Corporation Center, 100 Corporate Center Drive, Coraopolis PA 15108-3185. 412/262-2240. **Contact:** Sue Love, Human Resources Director. **World Wide Web address:** http://www.techint-technologies.com. **Description:** Designs, manufactures, and installs heavy industrial equipment, primarily for the metals and coal industries including industrial furnaces, metal-processing equipment, and coal-processing equipment.

TELEFLEX INC.
SERMATECH
155 South Limerick Road, Limerick PA 19468. 610/948-5100. **Contact:** Human Resources. **World Wide Web address:** http://www.tfxsermatech.com. **Description:** Operates in two industry segments: The Technical Products and Services segment includes the manufacturing of precision mechanical and electromechanical control equipment and other products for the aerospace, chemical processing, and medical industries. The Commercial Products segment is engaged in the design and manufacture of commercial controls, control systems, hydraulics, instruments, and other products with applications in the automotive, marine, and other industries. **NOTE:** Please send all resumes to Ronald Boldt, Vice President of Human Resources, Teleflex Inc., 630 West Germantown Pike, Suite 450, Plymouth Meeting PA 19462. **Corporate headquarters location:** This location.

TEMPLE CONTINUING CARE CENTER
5301 Old York Road, Philadelphia PA 19141. 215/456-2900. **Fax:** 215/456-2048. **Recorded jobline:** 215/456-2929. **Contact:** Human Resources. **World Wide Web address:** http://www.health.temple.edu. **Description:** A nonprofit nursing home. **NOTE:** Entry-level positions and second and third shifts are offered. **Special programs:** Internships. **Number of employees at this location:** 1,000.

TEMPLE UNIVERSITY
University Services Building, 1601 North Broad Street, USB Room 202, Philadelphia PA 19122. 215/204-7174. **Contact:** Personnel Department. **World Wide Web address:** http://www.temple.edu. **Description:** A four-year university offering bachelor's, master's (including MBAs), first professional, and doctoral degrees. Approximately 22,000 undergraduate and 9,400 graduate students attend Temple University. **Positions advertised include:** Accounts Payable Clerk; Administrative Assistant; Assistant Area Manager; Assistant Director of Residential Life; Bibliographic Assistant; Carpenter; Claims Manager; Coding Specialist; Director of Development; General Mechanic; Laboratory Technician. **Corporate headquarters location:** This location. **Number of employees at this location:** 9,000.

TEMPLE UNIVERSITY HOSPITAL
3401 North Broad Street, GSB Room 107, Philadelphia PA 19140. 215/707-3145. **Contact:** Human Resources Department. **World Wide Web address:** http://www.temple.edu/tuhs. **Description:** A hospital that also operates a physicians' information bureau. **Positions advertised include:** Administrative Assistant; Assistant Director of Corporate Accounting; Clinical Pharmacist.

TEN UNITED
444 Liberty Avenue, Pittsburgh PA 15233. 412/471-5300. **Contact:** Human Resources. **E-mail address:** pghjobs@tenunited.com. **World Wide Web address:** http://www.tenunited.com. **Description:** An advertising and public relations agency.

TENDER LOVING CARE/STAFF BUILDERS
25 Bala Avenue, Suite 100, Bala-Cynwyd PA 19004. 610/668-2800. **Fax:** 610/668-9990. **Contact:** Human Resources. **World Wide Web address:** http://www.tlcathome.com. **Description:** A home health care agency. **Positions advertised include:** Account Executive; General Manager. **Corporate headquarters location:** Lake Success NY. **Other U.S. locations:** Nationwide. **Number of employees nationwide:** 20,000.

TENEX SYSTEMS INC.
201 Stanwix Street, Pittsburgh PA 15222. 610/239-9988. **Fax:** 610/239-9995. **Contact:** Minh Hien Le Pham, Human Resources. **E-mail address:** jobs@tenexsys.com. **World Wide Web address:** http://www.tenexsys.com. **Description:** Provides administrative software development and support services for school districts. **Office hours:** Monday - Friday, 7:30 a.m. - 4:30 p.m. **President:** Ron Cranford.

THE PACKAGING GROUP
441 County Line Road, Gilbertsville PA 19525. 610/367-2991. **Contact:** Human Resources. **Description:** The Packaging Group is a manufacturer of flexible packaging materials primarily used in the food service and the medical industries. **Corporate headquarters location:** Ontario Canada. **Other Area locations:** BC Canada, U.S. **Operations at this facility include:** This location manufactures packing materials.

THERAKOS, INC.
437 Creamery Way, Exton PA 19341. 610/280-1000. **Contact:** Human Resources. **World Wide Web address:** http://www.jnj.com. **Description:** Develops and manufactures the UVAR Photopheresis System. The system is used in phototherapy treatment for certain types of cancers. **Parent company:** Johnson & Johnson (New Brunswick NJ).

THRESHOLD REHABILITATION SERVICES
1000 Lancaster Avenue, Reading PA 19607. 610/777-7691. **Fax:** 610/777-1295. **Contact:** Human Resources. **E-mail address:** hr@trsinc.org. **World Wide Web address:** http://www.trsinc.org. **Description:** Provides rehabilitation services to individuals with emotional, physical, or mental disabilities.

TIERNEY & PARTNERS
200 South Broad Street, Philadelphia PA 19102. 215/732-4100. **Contact:** Bernadette Nolan, Personnel. **World Wide Web address:** http://www.tierney.com. **Description:** A full-service advertising and public relations firm. **Special programs:** Internships. **Corporate headquarters location:** Frisco TX. **Other U.S. locations:** Los Angeles CA; San Francisco CA; New York NY. **Parent company:** Foote, Cone & Belding, Inc.

TIPPINS INC.
435 Butler Street, Pittsburgh PA 15223-2126. 412/781-7600. **Contact:** Human Resources. **World Wide Web address:** http://www.tippins.com. **Description:** Manufactures rolling mill machinery and equipment.

TOLL BROTHERS, INC.
3103 Philmont Avenue, Huntingdon Valley PA 19006. 215/938-8000. **Fax:** 215/938-8291. **Contact:** Personnel. **World Wide Web address:** http://www.tollbrothers.com. **Description:** Designs and builds luxury homes. Founded in 1967. **Positions advertised include:** Administrative Assistant; Assistant Branch Manager; Floating Secretary; Mortgage Loan Processor; Network Administrator. **Corporate headquarters location:** This location. **Other U.S. locations:** Nationwide. **Subsidiaries include:** Coleman Homes; Geoffrey Edmonds & Associates. **Listed on:** New York Stock Exchange. **Stock exchange symbol:** TOL. **Annual sales/revenues:** More than $100 million. **Number of employees at this location:** 200. **Number of employees nationwide:** 2,000.

TOPFLIGHT CORPORATION
277 Commerce Drive, Glen Rock PA 17327. 717/227-5400. **Fax:** 717/227-1415. **Contact:** Human Resource Manager. **E-mail address:** smeashey@topflight.com. **World Wide Web address:** http://www.topflight.com. **Description:** Manufactures pressure-sensitive labels. **Positions advertised include:** Flexographic Printer. **Corporate headquarters location:** This location. **Subsidiaries include:** Adhesives Research. **Number of employees at this location:** 220. **Number of employees nationwide:** 420.

TOTAL CONTAINMENT, INC.
P.O. Box 939, Oaks PA 19456. 610/666-7777. **Physical address:** 422 Business Center, A130 North Drive, Oaks PA 19456. **Contact:** Human Resources. **World Wide Web address:** http://www.totalcontainment.com. **Description:** Designs, engineers, and sells underground systems and products for the conveyance and containment of petroleum- and alcohol-based motor vehicle fuels including gasoline and gasohol, from underground storage tanks to above-ground fuel dispensers. Total Containment's systems and products are used in connection with the installation of new and the retrofitting of existing underground fuel containment and distribution systems worldwide. The principal end users of the company's products are major oil companies and convenience stores, as well as government bodies, utilities, and other fleet vehicle operators. **Corporate headquarters location:** This location. **Number of employees nationwide:** 85.

TRACO INC.
71 Progress Avenue, Cranberry Township PA 16066. 724/776-7000. **Fax:** 724/776-7000. **Contact:** Human Resources. **World Wide Web address:** http://www.traco.com. **Description:** Manufactures, installs, and sells commercial and residential windows. **Positions advertised include:** Assistant Director of Metal Extrusion; Credit Risk Manager; Corporate Purchasing Manager.

TRANE COMPANY
2501 Smallman Street, Pittsburgh PA 15222. 412/394-9021. **Contact:** Human Resources. **World Wide Web address:** http://www.trane.com. **Description:** Trane Company develops, manufactures, and sells air conditioning equipment designed for use in central air conditioning systems for commercial, institutional, industrial, and residential buildings. The company's products are designed to cool water, and to cool, heat, humidify, dehumidify, move, and filter air. Other products include similar systems for buses and rapid transit vehicles, refrigeration equipment for trucks, and pollution control equipment. **Positions advertised include:** Account Manager; HVAC Technician. **Corporate headquarters location:** Tyler TX. **Operations at this facility include:** This location is a sales office.

TRANSCONTINENTAL DIRECT U.S.A. INC.
75 Hawk Road, Ivyland PA 18974. 215/672-6900. **Fax:** 215/957-4366. **Contact:** Human Resources. **E-mail address:** info@transcontinentaldirect.com. **World Wide Web address:** http://www.transcontinentaldirect.com. **Description:** A direct mail marketing company. Founded in 1972. **NOTE:** Search and apply for positions online. **Positions advertised include:** MIS Manager; Systems Administrator; Project Manager; Account Executive; Account Manager. **Other U.S. locations:** Downey CA; Fort Worth TX; Bohemia NY. **Number of employees nationwide:** 1,500.

TRI-COUNTY MOUNT TREXLER MANOR
5021 St. Joseph's Road, P.O. Box 1001, Limeport PA 18060. 610/965-9021. **Contact:** William Mains, Administrator. **Description:** A residential psychiatric treatment facility. Tri-County Mount Trexler Manor also runs a nonresident day program for people with mental illnesses. **Special programs:** Internships. **Corporate headquarters location:** Doylestown PA. **Other U.S. locations:** Quakertown PA. **Parent company:** Tri-County Respite operates another subsidiary, Quakertown House. **Operations at this facility include:** Administration; Divisional Headquarters; Service. **Number of employees nationwide:** 60.

TRIBUNE-REVIEW PUBLISHING COMPANY
622 Cabin Hill Drive, Greensburg PA 15601. 724/834-1151. **Contact:** Human Resources. **World Wide Web address:** http://triblive.com. **Description:** Publishes seven daily newspapers in the Pittsburgh area including the *Greensburg Daily Tribune*, *Pittsburgh Tribune-Review*, *Daily Courier*, and *Leader Times*. The company also operates the PittsburghLIVE Website, offering all seven newspapers in an electronic format.

TRITON ETD
3100 Charlotte Avenue, Easton PA 18044-0100. 610/252-7331. **Fax:** 610/258-6279. **Contact:** Human Resources. **World Wide Web address:** http://www.tritonetd.com. **Description:** Manufactures and markets special-purpose electron tubes and integrated microwave subsystems for use in communications, defense, industrial, scientific, and medical applications. **Corporate headquarters location:** New York NY.

TRIVERSITY INC.
311 Sinclair Street, Bristol PA 19007. 215/785-4321. **Toll-free phone:** 888/989-7274. **Fax:** 215/785-5329. **Contact:** Human Resources Manager. **E-mail address:** triversity@rpc.webhire.com. **World Wide Web address:** http://www.triversity.com. **Description:** Provides transaction processing and customer relationship management solutions for physical, catalog, and online retailers. **Positions advertised include:** Senior Project Manager; Office Administrator. **Corporate headquarters location:** Toronto, Canada.

TUSCARORA INC.
800 Fifth Avenue, New Brighton PA 15066. 724/843-8200. **Toll-free phone:** 800/887-2276. **Fax:** 724/843-4402. **Contact:** Human Resources. **E-mail address:** humanresources@tuscarora.com. **World Wide Web address:** http://www.tuscarora.com. **Description:** Designs and manufactures interior protective packaging and material handling solutions for a broad range of manufactured products. Tuscarora also supplies customers with molded plastic thermoformed components for a number of industrial and consumer product applications. The company uses a variety of materials to develop customized internal protective packaging products, material handling solutions, and components, and integrates multiple materials such as corrugated paperboard, molded and/or die-cut foam plastics, thermoformed plastics, wood, and aluminum to meet customers' specific end use requirements. **Corporate headquarters location:** This location.

II-VI INC.
375 Saxonburg Boulevard, Saxonburg PA 16056. 724/352-1504. **Fax:** 724/352-4980. **Contact:** Human Resources. **E-mail address:** info@ii-vi.com. **World Wide Web address:** http://www.ii-vi.com. **Description:** Designs, manufactures, and markets optical and electro-optical components, devices and materials for precision use in infrared, near-infrared, visible light, and X-ray/gamma-ray instruments and applications. II-VI Inc.'s infrared products are used in high-power carbon dioxide lasers for industrial processing and for commercial and military sensing systems. The company's near-infrared and visible products (VLOC) are used in industrial, scientific, and medical instruments, and in solid-state yttrium aluminum garnet lasers. II-VI Inc. also develops and markets X-ray and gamma-ray products (eV PRODUCTS) for the nuclear radiation detection industry. **Positions advertised include:** Administrative Assistant; Shipping Clerk; Semiconductor Engineer; Mechanical Design Engineer; Cost Accountant; Fabrication Technician; AMDC Technician; Marketing Coordinator. **Corporate headquarters location:** This location. **Listed on:** NASDAQ. **Stock exchange symbol:** IIVI.

TYCO VALVES & CONTROLS
83 General Warren Boulevard, Malvern PA 19355. 610/296-2000. **Fax:** 610/296-8038. **Contact:** Janine DePallo, Personnel. **World Wide Web address:** http://www.tycovalves-na.com. **Description:** Manufactures gauges, valves, steam traps, and flow control equipment and indicators. **Corporate headquarters location:** This location.

TYLER PIPE INDUSTRIES, INC.
101 North Church Street, Macungie PA 18062. 610/966-3491. **Contact:** Joe Maziarz, Personnel Manager. **World Wide Web address:** http://www.tylerpipe.com. **Description:** Manufactures and distributes soil pipe and pipe fittings. Tyler Pipe Industries, Inc. is also a national producer of both plastic and iron piping for large-volume users. **Corporate headquarters location:** Tyler TX.

UBS FINANCIAL SERVICES
2 Logan Square, Suite 2400, Philadelphia PA 19103. 215/972-6800. **Contact:** Human Resources. **World Wide Web address:** http://www.financialservicesinc.ubs.com. **Description:** A full-service securities firm with over 300 offices nationwide. Services include investment banking, asset management, merger and acquisition consulting, municipal securities underwriting, estate planning, retirement programs, and transaction management. Services are offered to corporations, governments, institutions, and individuals. Founded in 1879. **Corporate headquarters location:** New York NY. **Other U.S. locations:** Nationwide. **Annual sales/revenues:** More than $100 million.

UGI CORPORATION
460 North Gulph Road, P.O. Box 858, Valley Forge PA 19482. 610/337-1000. **Contact:** Personnel Director. **World Wide Web address:** http://www.ugicorp.com. **Description:** A holding company. UGI's utilities segment is divided into two segments: the Gas Division is a medium-sized, local natural gas distributor serving 238,000 customers in 14 eastern and southeastern Pennsylvania counties; the Electric Division is a small electric utility serving 60,000 customers in the Wilkes-Barre area. UGI's propane segment is divided into two segments: AmeriGas and Petrolane, also a national propane marketer, of which UGI owns 35 percent. **Corporate headquarters location:** This location. **Subsidiaries include:** UGI Utilities, Inc. is a gas and electric utility located in eastern Pennsylvania. AmeriGas, Inc. is a national marketer of propane. **Listed on:** New York Stock Exchange; Philadelphia Exchange. **Stock exchange symbol:** UGI. **Number of employees nationwide:** 5,230.

UPMC BEAVER VALLEY
2500 Hospital Drive, Aliquippa PA 15001-2191. 724/857-1212. **Fax:** 724/857-1298. **Contact:** Human Resources. **World Wide Web address:** http://www.upmc.com. **Description:** A nonprofit hospital. **NOTE:** Entry-level positions, part-time jobs, and second and third shifts are offered. See employment information on the website, http://www.jobs.upmc.com. **Positions advertised include:** Clinical Associate; Business Analyst; Clinical Pharmacy Specialist; Customer Service Generalist; Business Analyst; Social Worker; Outreach Representative; Provider Relations Representative; Systems Analyst; Product Manager.

UPMC BRADDOCK
400 Holland Avenue, Braddock PA 15104-1599. 412/636-5000. **Contact:** Employment Coordinator. **World Wide Web address:** http://www.upmc.com/braddock. **Description:** A general medical hospital with 250 beds. **NOTE:** Entry-level positions, part-time jobs, and second and third shifts are offered. See employment information on the website, http://www.jobs.upmc.com. **Positions advertised include:** Registered Nurse; Respiratory Therapist; Licensed Practical Nurse; Patient Care Technician; Admissions Coordinator; Chemical Addiction Coordinator. **Number of employees at this location:** 725.

UPMC HORIZON
110 North Main Street, Greenville PA 16125. 724/588-2100. **Contact:** Monica Rischel, Employment Coordinator. **World Wide Web address:** http://www.upmc.com/horizon. **Description:** A 350-bed, acute care hospital. **NOTE:** Entry-level positions, part-time jobs, and second and third shifts are offered. See employment information on the website, http://www.jobs.upmc.com. **Positions advertised include:** Clinical Assistant; Registered Nurse; Licensed Practical Nurse; Patient Accounting Clerk; Environmental Services Assistant; Registered Respiratory Therapist; Case Manager; Pharmacist. **Special programs:** Internships. **Parent company:** Horizon/CMS Healthcare Corporation acquires and operates long-term care facilities throughout the United States; provides health care services such as nursing care and rehabilitation; provides institutional pharmacy services; provides specialty care to Alzheimer's patients; and offers subacute care services.

UPMC PASSAVANT HOSPITAL
9100 Babcock Boulevard, Pittsburgh PA 15237-5842. 412/367-6700. **Recorded jobline:** 412/367-5290. **Contact:** Karen Habenstein, Human Resources Administrator. **World Wide Web address:** http://www.upmc.com/passavant. **Description:** A hospital. **NOTE:** Entry-level positions, part-time jobs, and second and third shifts are offered. See employment information on the website, http://www.jobs.upmc.com. **Positions advertised include:** General Maintenance Mechanic; Medical Assistant; Registered Nurse; Data Entry Clerk; Food Service Attendant; Case Manager; Environmental Services Technician; MRI Technologist; Social Worker; Nursing Assistant; Unit Director.

UPMC PRESBYTERIAN
200 Lothrop Street, Pittsburgh PA 15213-2582. 412/647-5555. **Contact:** Human Resources. **World Wide Web address:** http://www.upmc.com/presbyterian. **Description:** A general medical and surgical hospital. **NOTE:** Entry-level positions, part-time jobs, and second and third shifts are offered. See employment information on the website, http://www.jobs.upmc.com. **Positions advertised include:** Transporter; Floor & Project Technician; HIM Technician; Clinical Transplant Coordinator; Pharmacy Technician; Nursing Assistant; Housekeeper; Medical Assistant; Clinical Research Coordinator; Admissions Scheduling Representative; Microbiology Technician.

UPMC SHADYSIDE HOSPITAL
5230 Centre Avenue, Pittsburgh PA 15232-1381. 412/623-2414. **Contact:** Personnel. **World Wide Web address:** http://www.upmc.com/shadyside. **Description:** A hospital. **NOTE:** Entry-level positions, part-time jobs, and second and third shifts are offered. See employment information on the website, http://www.jobs.upmc.com. **Positions advertised include:** Physical Therapy Assistant; Clinical Director; Pharmacy Technician; Nursing Assistant; Respiratory Care Technician.

UPMC SOUTH SIDE
2000 Mary Street, Pittsburgh PA 15203. 412/488-5550. **Contact:** Human Resources. **World Wide Web address:** http://www.upmc.com/southside. **Description:** A nonprofit hospital. **NOTE:** Entry-level positions, part-time jobs, and second and third shifts are offered. See employment information on the website, http://www.jobs.upmc.com. **Positions advertised include:** Lead Medical Technologist; Environmental Services Aide; Pharmacist; Professional Staff Nurse; Primary Resource Nurse; Coding Liaison; Surgical Aide; Dietary Aide; Unit Secretary.

US AIRWAYS
1000 Commerce Drive, Building One, 4th Floor, Pittsburgh PA 15275. 412/472-2400. **Contact:** Human Resources Recruiting Department. **World Wide Web address:** http://www.usairways.com. **Description:** A leading air carrier at Pittsburgh International, US Airways has 53 gates and over 500 flights per day. US Airways has regional, national, and international scheduled air services and express cargo operations. The company's primary hubs are in Philadelphia PA, Pittsburgh PA, Charlotte NC, and Baltimore MD/Washington DC. **NOTE:** You may call the main human resources office in Washington D.C for additional information: 800/872-4782. **Positions advertised include:** Flight Training & Standards Analyst; MAA Passenger Service Coordinator. **Corporate headquarters location:** Arlington VA. **Parent company:** United Airlines, Inc. **Listed on:** New York Stock Exchange. **Stock exchange symbol:** U.

U.S. DEPARTMENT OF DEFENSE
DEFENSE SUPPLY CENTER PHILADELPHIA
700 Robbins Avenue, Philadelphia PA 19111-5092. 215/737-2332. **Fax:** 215/692-0266. **Contact:** Elizabeth Warden, Human Resources. **E-mail address:** cso-phil@hr.dla.mil. **World Wide Web address:** http://www.dscp.dla.mil. **Description:** Provides federal logistical services and distributes food, clothing, and medical supplies to members of the U.S. armed forces and their families.

U.S. DEPARTMENT OF HEALTH AND HUMAN SERVICES
150 South Independence Mall West, Public Ledger Building, Suite 436, Philadelphia PA 19106. 215/861-4633. **Toll-free phone:** 800/368-1019. **Contact:** Office of Human Resources. **World Wide Web address:** http://www.hhs.gov. **Description:** Protects and provides necessary health care and human services, especially to those who cannot provide for themselves.

U.S. DEPARTMENT OF THE AIR FORCE
913TH SPTG/DPC
1051 Fairchild Street, Willow Grove ARS PA 19090-5203. 215/443-1034. **Contact:** Personnel. **World Wide Web address:** http://www.usajobs.opm.gov. **Description:** Trains Air Force reservists to perform aerial resupply missions including the task of delivering people, equipment, and supplies to the battlefield. **NOTE:** Jobseekers must have an active reserve membership.

U.S. DEPARTMENT OF VETERANS AFFAIRS
BUTLER VETERANS ADMINISTRATION MEDICAL CENTER
325 New Castle Road, Butler PA 16001-2480. 724/287-4781. **Contact:** Human Resources. **World Wide Web address:** http://www.va.gov. **Description:** A medical center operated by the U.S. Department of Veterans Affairs. From 54 hospitals in 1930, the VA health care system has grown to include 171 medical centers; more than 364 outpatient, community, and outreach clinics; 130 nursing home care units; and 37 domiciliary residences. VA operates at least one medical center in each of the 48 contiguous states, Puerto Rico, and the District of Columbia. With approximately 76,000 medical center beds, VA treats nearly 1 million patients in VA hospitals; 75,000 in nursing home care units; and 25,000 in domiciliary residences. VA's outpatient clinics register approximately 24 million visits per year.

U.S. DEPARTMENT OF VETERANS AFFAIRS
PITTSBURGH VETERANS ADMINISTRATION HEALTHCARE SYSTEM
7180 Highland Drive, Pittsburgh PA 15206. 412/365-4900. **Contact:** Human Resources. **Description:** A medical center operated by the U.S. Department of Veterans Affairs. From 54 hospitals in 1930, the VA health care system has grown to include 171 medical centers; more than 364 outpatient, community, and outreach clinics; 130 nursing home care units; and 37 domiciliary residences. The VA operates at least one medical center in each of the 48 contiguous states, Puerto Rico, and the District of Columbia. With approximately 76,000 medical center beds, the VA treats nearly 1 million patients in VA hospitals; 75,000 in nursing home care units; and 25,000 in domiciliary residences. The VA's outpatient clinics register approximately 24 million visits per year. **Corporate headquarters location:** Washington DC.

U.S. DEPARTMENT OF VETERANS AFFAIRS
VETERANS ADMINISTRATION MEDICAL CENTER
1111 East End Boulevard, Wilkes-Barre PA 18711. 570/824-3521 ext. 7209. **Contact:** Reese Thomas III, Chief of Human Resources Management Service. **Description:** A medical center operated by the U.S. Department of Veterans Affairs. From 54 hospitals in 1930, the VA health care system has grown to include 171 medical centers; more than 364 outpatient, community, and outreach clinics; 130 nursing home care units; and 37 domiciliary residences. The VA operates at least one medical center in each of the 48 contiguous states, Puerto Rico, and the District of Columbia. With approximately 76,000 medical center beds, the VA treats nearly 1 million patients in VA hospitals, 75,000 in nursing home care units, and 25,000 in domiciliary residences. The VA's outpatient clinics register approximately 24 million visits per year. **Special programs:** Internships. **Corporate headquarters location:** Washington DC. **Other U.S. locations:** Nationwide. **Operations at this facility include:** Administration. **Number of employees at this location:** 1,300.

U.S. DEPARTMENT OF VETERANS AFFAIRS
VETERANS ADMINISTRATION PITTSBURGH HEALTHCARE SYSTEM
University Drive C, Pittsburgh PA 15240. 412/688-6000. **Contact:** Human Resources. **Description:** A medical center operated by the U.S. Department of Veterans Affairs. From 54 hospitals in 1930, the VA health care system has grown to include 171 medical centers; more than 364 outpatient, community, and outreach clinics; 130 nursing home care units; and 37 domiciliaries. The VA operates at least one medical center in each of the 48 contiguous states, Puerto Rico, and the District of Columbia. With approximately 76,000 medical center beds, the VA treats nearly 1 million patients in VA hospitals; 75,000 in nursing home care units; and 25,000 in domiciliaries. The VA's outpatient clinics register approximately 24 million visits per year.

U.S. ENVIRONMENTAL PROTECTION AGENCY (EPA)
1650 Arch Street, Philadelphia PA 19103-2029. 215/814-5240. **Contact:** Human Resources-3PM40. **World Wide Web address:** http://www.epa.gov. **Description:** The EPA is dedicated to improving and preserving the quality of the environment, both nationally and globally, and protecting human health and the productivity of natural resources. The agency is committed to ensuring that federal environmental laws are implemented and enforced effectively; U.S. policy, both foreign and domestic, encourages the integration of economic development and environmental protection so that economic growth can be sustained over the long term; and public and private decisions affecting energy, transportation, agriculture, industry, international trade, and natural resources fully integrate considerations of environmental quality. **Special programs:** Internships. **Corporate headquarters location:** Washington DC. **Other U.S. locations:** San Francisco CA; Denver CO; Atlanta GA; Chicago IL; Kansas City KS; Boston MA; New York NY; Dallas TX; Seattle WA. **Number of employees nationwide:** 19,000.

U.S. FEDERAL BUREAU OF INVESTIGATION (FBI)
8th Floor, William J. Green Jr. FOB, 600 Arch Street, Pittsburgh PA 19106. 215/418-4000. **Contact:** Personnel. **World Wide Web address:** http://www.fbi.gov. **Description:** The Federal Bureau of Investigation (FBI) is a federal law enforcement agency. The agents carry out the responsibilities of the FBI by enforcing more than 260 federal statutes. This involves conducting investigations in organized crime, white-collar crime, civil rights violations, bank robbery, kidnapping, terrorism, foreign counterintelligence, fugitive and drug trafficking matters, and many other violations against federal statutes. **Special programs:** Internships. **Corporate headquarters location:** Washington DC.

U.S. FOODSERVICE
1200 Hoover Avenue, Allentown PA 18109. 610/821-9000. **Toll-free phone:** 800/441-0998. **Fax:** 610/776-2179. **Contact:** Human Resources. **World Wide Web address:** http://www.usfoodservice.com. **Description:** An institutional food production and distribution company with clients in the restaurant and health care industries. **Corporate headquarters location:** Columbia MD. **Number of employees nationwide:** 12,000. **Number of employees worldwide:** 14,000.

U.S. FOODSERVICE
P.O. Box 632, Altoona PA 16603-0632. 814/946-1201. **Toll-free phone:** 800/252-3831. **Fax:** 814/949-8398. **Contact:** Human Resources. **World Wide Web address:** http://www.usfoodservice.com. **Description:** An institutional food production and distribution company with clients in the restaurant and health care industries. **Corporate headquarters location:** Columbia MD. **Number of employees nationwide:** 12,000. **Number of employees worldwide:** 14,000.

U.S. FOODSERVICE
13 Rutledge Drive, Pittston PA 18640. 570/654-3374. **Fax:** 570/654-2510. **Contact:** Human Resources. **World Wide Web address:** http://www.usfoodservice.com. **Description:** An institutional food production and distribution company with clients in the restaurant and health care industries. **Corporate headquarters location:** Columbia MD. **Number of employees nationwide:** 12,000. **Number of employees worldwide:** 14,000.

U.S. GENERAL SERVICES ADMINISTRATION
20 North 8th Street, Philadelphia PA 19107-3396. 202/501-1805. **Contact:** Regional Personnel Officer. **E-mail address:** gsajobs@gsa.gov. **World Wide Web address:** http://www.gsa.gov. **Description:** A diversified, government-wide operation engaged in building management, supply, real and personal property sales, telecommunication services, data processing, and motor vehicle operations. It is the job of the GSA to ensure that governmental entities are receiving the highest quality products and services at the best prices. **NOTE:** employment matters are handled through the main office in Washington D.C. **Special programs:** Internships. **Corporate headquarters location:** Washington DC. **Other U.S. locations:** San Francisco CA; Denver CO; Atlanta GA; Auburn GA; Chicago IL; Boston MA; Kansas City MO; New York NY; Fort Worth TX. **Operations at this facility include:** Regional Headquarters. **Number of employees at this location:** 1,500. **Number of employees nationwide:** 14,000.

U.S. STEEL CORPORATION
600 Grant Street, Pittsburgh PA 15219. 412/433-1121. **Contact:** Personnel Department. **World Wide Web address:** http://www.ussteel.com. **Description:** U.S. Steel Corporation is a diversified conglomerate, with operations in petroleum and natural gas, chemicals, and steel. US Steel Group (also at this location) operates a steel

mill. **Parent company:** Marathon Oil Corporation is a diversified conglomerate, with operations in petroleum and natural gas, chemicals, and steel. **Corporate headquarters location:** This location. **Operations at this facility include:** This location houses administrative offices.

USS CORPORATION/CLAIRTON WORKS
400 State Street, Clairton PA 15025. 412/233-1035. **Contact:** Human Resources. **World Wide Web address:** http://www.ussteel.com. **Description:** A steel mill. **Parent company:** Marathon Oil Corporation is a diversified conglomerate, with operations in petroleum and natural gas, chemicals, and steel.

UNI-MARTS, INC.
477 East Beaver Avenue, State College PA 16801-5690. 814/234-6000. **Contact:** Human Resources. **World Wide Web address:** http://www.uni-mart.com. **Description:** An independent regional operator of over 400 convenience stores located in the Mid-Atlantic region. **Positions advertised include:** Store Sales Clerk; Store Manager; Assistant Store Manager; Store Supervisor; Clerical. **Corporate headquarters location:** This location. **Other U.S. locations:** DE; MD; NJ; NY; OH; PA; VA; WV.

UNICAST COMPANY
241 North Washington Street, Boyertown PA 19512. 610/367-0155. **Contact:** James Mooney, Human Resources. **World Wide Web address:** http://www.unicastco.com. **Description:** A manufacturer of gray iron and aluminum castings. **Corporate headquarters location:** This location. **Operations at this facility include:** Administration; Manufacturing; Sales. **Number of employees at this location:** 120.

UNION FIDELITY LIFE INSURANCE COMPANY
500 Virginia Drive, Fort Washington PA 19034. 267/468-3000. **Contact:** Personnel. **World Wide Web address:** http://www.gefn.com. **Description:** An insurance company specializing in accident policies and life insurance. **Parent company:** GE Financial Network.

UNION SWITCH & SIGNAL INC.
1000 Technology Drive, Pittsburgh PA 15219. 412/688-2400. **Toll-free phone:** 800/351-1520. **Contact:** Human Resources. **E-mail address:** jobs@switch.com. **World Wide Web address:** http://www.switch.com. **Description:** Designs, engineers, produces, distributes, and services integrated railway signaling and automation and control systems. The company provides after-sale service of integrated railway signaling, automation and control systems, and related component products that provide a variety of train control and rail operations management capabilities. The company's customers include all Class 1 freight railroads and virtually all major rail-based transit systems in the United States, as well as rail transportation in select foreign countries. Advanced railway operations control systems designed and produced by the company currently control over 50 percent of the miles of road operated by the Class 1 freight railroads in the United States. The company's systems and products are also used by major metropolitan mass transit systems in the United States including systems in New York, Boston, Chicago, Washington DC, and Los Angeles, where the company is providing fully automated, driverless urban transit control systems. **Parent company:** Ansaldo Signal. **President/CEO:** James Sanders.

THE UNIONTOWN HOSPITAL
500 West Berkeley Street, Uniontown PA 15401. 724/430-5000. **Fax:** 724/430-5646. **Recorded jobline:** 724/430-5290. **Contact:** Employment Manager. **World Wide Web address:** http://www.unionhospital.com. **Description:** An acute care hospital. **Positions advertised include:** Registered Nurse; Certified Occupational Therapist Assistant; Medical Technologist; Physical Therapist; MRI Technician; Credit Analyst. **Special programs:** Internships. **Corporate headquarters location:** This location. **Parent company:** UHRI. **Operations at this facility include:** Service. **Number of employees at this location:** 1,000.

UNISOURCE
One East Uwchlan Avenue, Exton PA 19341-0649. 610/280-5700. **Fax:** 610/280-5405. **Contact:** Human Resources. **World Wide Web address:** http://www.unisourcelink.com. **Description:** Markets and distributes printing and imaging papers, packaging systems, and maintenance supplies. **Corporate headquarters location:** Norcross GA. **Annual sales/revenues:** More than $100 million.

UNISYS CORPORATION
Township Line & Union Meeting Roads A, Unisys Way, Blue Bell PA 19424. 215/986-4011. **Fax:** 215/986-6732. **Contact:** Recruiting and Staffing. **E-mail address:** jobs@unisys.com. **World Wide Web address:** http://www.unisys.com. **Description:** Provides information services, technology, and software. Unisys specializes in developing critical business solutions based on open information networks. The company's Enabling Software Team creates a variety of software projects that facilitate the building of user applications and the management of distributed systems. The company's Platforms Group is responsible for UNIX Operating Systems running across a wide range of multiple processor server platforms including all peripheral and communication drivers. The Unisys Commercial Parallel Processing Team develops microkernel-based operating systems, I/O device drivers, ATM hardware, diagnostics, and system architectures. The System Management Group is in charge of the overall management of development programs for UNIX desktop and entry-server products. **NOTE:** Entry-level positions and part-time jobs are offered. **Positions advertised include:** Knowledge Management Expert; Communications Intern; Architecture Specialist; Computer Operator; Senior Recruiter; Program Manager. **Special programs:** Internships; Training; Co-ops; Summer Jobs. **Corporate headquarters location:** This location. **Other U.S. locations:** Nationwide. **International locations:** Worldwide. **Listed on:** New York Stock Exchange. **Stock exchange symbol:** UIS. **CEO:** Larry Weinbach. **Annual sales/revenues:** More than $100 million. **Number of employees at this location:** 2,500. **Number of employees nationwide:** 37,000. **Number of employees worldwide:** 49,000.

UNISYS CORPORATION
2476 Swedesford Road, Malvern PA 19355. 610/648-4000. **Fax:** 610/648-4545. **Contact:** Human Resources. **World Wide Web address:** http://www.unisys.com. **Description:** Unisys Corporation provides information services, technology, and software. Unisys specializes in developing critical business solutions based on open information networks. The company's Enabling Software Team creates a variety of software projects that facilitate the building of user applications and the management of distributed systems. The company's Platforms Group is responsible for UNIX Operating Systems running across a wide range of multiple processor server platforms including all peripheral and communication drivers. The Unisys Commercial Parallel Processing Team develops microkernel-based operating systems, I/O device drivers, ATM hardware, diagnostics, and system architectures. The System Management Group is in charge of the overall management of development programs for UNIX desktop and entry-server products. **Corporate headquarters location:** Blue Bell PA. **Other U.S. locations:** Nationwide. **International locations:** Worldwide. **Operations at this facility include:** This location is a software engineering facility. **Listed on:** New York Stock Exchange. **Stock exchange symbol:** UIS. **CEO:** Larry Weinbach. **Annual sales/revenues:** More than $100 million. **Number of employees nationwide:** 37,000. **Number of employees worldwide:** 49,000.

UNITED DEFENSE
1100 Bairs Road, P.O. Box 15512, York PA 17405-1512. 717/225-8000. **Contact:** Human Resources. **World Wide Web address:** http://www.uniteddefense.com. **Description:** Manufactures military tracked vehicles and personnel carriers. **Positions advertised include:** Engineering Intern. **Corporate headquarters location:** Arlington VA. **Operations at this facility include:** Manufacturing. **Listed on:** New York Stock Exchange. **Stock exchange symbol:** UDI. **Number of employees nationwide:** 2,000.

UNITED REFRIGERATION INC.
11401 Roosevelt Boulevard, Philadelphia PA 19154. 215/698-9100. **Contact:** Human Resources. **World Wide Web address:** http://www.uri.com. **Description:** A worldwide distributor of refrigerators, air conditioners, and heating equipment. Founded in 1947. **Corporate headquarters location:** Philadelphia PA. **Other U.S. locations:** Nationwide. **International locations:** Canada; France; United Kingdom.

UNIVERSAL HEALTH SERVICES, INC.
367 South Gulph Road, P.O. Box 61558, King of Prussia PA 19406. 610/768-3300. **Toll-free phone:** 800/347-7750. **Fax:** 610/768-3466. **Contact:** Coleen Johns, Personnel. **E-mail address:** cjohns@uhsinc.com. **World Wide Web address:** http://www.uhsinc.com. **Description:** Owns and operates acute care hospitals, behavioral health centers, ambulatory surgery centers, and radiation/oncology centers. The company operates 29 hospitals with approximately 3,600 licensed beds. Of these facilities, 15 are general acute care hospitals and 14 are psychiatric care facilities (two of which are substance abuse facilities). The company, as a part of its Ambulatory Treatment Centers Division, owns, operates, or manages surgery and radiation therapy centers located in various states. Universal Health Services has also entered into other specialized medical service arrangements including laboratory services, mobile computerized tomography and magnetic imaging services, preferred provider organization agreements, health maintenance organization contracts, medical office building leasing, construction management services, and real estate management and administrative services. **Corporate headquarters location:** This location. **Operations at this facility include:** Administration. **Listed on:** New York Stock Exchange. **Stock exchange symbol:** UHS. **Number of employees at this location:** 145. **Number of employees nationwide:** 81,000.

UNIVERSITY OF PENNSYLVANIA
3401 Walnut Street, Suite 527A, Philadelphia PA 19104-6228. 215/898-7284. **Contact:** Human Resources. **World Wide Web address:** http://www.hr.upenn.edu/jobs. **Description:** An Ivy League university offering undergraduate and graduate degrees. **NOTE:** Resumes must be submitted online. Please check the Website for more information. Current Penn staff can forward resumes to recruitment@hr.upenn.edu. **Positions advertised include:** Accountant; Administrative Assistant; Assistant Director of Operations; Business Manager; Caseworker; Clinic Clerk; Data Entry Clerk; Driver/Escort; Electrician. **Special programs:** Internships; Training.

UNIVERSITY OF PENNSYLVANIA HEALTH SYSTEM
3930 Chestnut Street, Philadelphia PA 19104. 215/615-2606. **Recorded jobline:** 215/615-2688. **Fax:** 215/662-7835. **Contact:** Staffing Department. **World Wide Web address:** http://pennhealth.com/jobs. **Description:** A 722-bed, academic, teaching hospital involved in patient care, education, and research. **Positions advertised include:** Clinical Nurse Specialist; Check Request Processor; Dental Assistant; Clerk; Speech Pathologist; Refund Coordinator; Program Manager; Patient Registration Supervisor; Clinical Pharmacist; Director of Staffing; Customer Service Representative. **Number of employees at this location:** 5,000.

UNIVERSITY OF PENNSYLVANIA VETERINARY HOSPITAL
3800 Spruce Street, Philadelphia PA 19104. 215/746-0398. **Contact:** Amy Shields, Recruiting. **World Wide Web address:** http://www.vet.upenn.edu. **Description:** A full-service animal hospital whose many departments include oncology, radiology, dermatology, internal medicine, and emergency.

UNIVERSITY OF PITTSBURGH
200 South Craig Street, 100 Craig Hall, Pittsburgh PA 15260. 412/624-8150. **Fax:** 412/624-8720. **Contact:** Human Resources. **World Wide Web address:** http://www.pitt.edu. **Description:** A university. **Corporate headquarters location:** This location. **Operations at this facility include:** Administration; Research and Development; Service.

UNIVERSITY OF PITTSBURGH AT BRADFORD
7 Dickinson House, 300 Campus Drive, Bradford PA 16701. 814/362-7531. **Fax:** 814/362-5079. **Contact:** Laurel E. Butler, Human Resources Manager. **E-mail address:** leb2@pitt.edu. **World Wide Web address:** http://www.upb.pitt.edu. **Description:** As part of the University of Pittsburgh system, the University of Pittsburgh at Bradford offers 39 baccalaureate and professional programs. **NOTE:** Teaching positions are filled through the Academic Affairs Department. **Number of employees at this location:** 200.

UNIVERSITY OF PITTSBURGH AT GREENSBURG
1150 Mount Pleasant Road, Greensburg PA 15601. 724/837-7040. **Contact:** Human Resources. **World Wide Web address:** http://www.pitt.edu/~upg. **Description:** The Greensburg location of the University of Pittsburgh. **NOTE:** Hiring is conducted through the Pittsburgh campus Human Resources Office.

UNIVERSITY OF SCRANTON
St. Thomas Hall, Room 104, Scranton PA 18510. 570/941-7452. **Fax:** 570/941-5937. **Contact:** Darrell Frederick, Director Human Resources. **World Wide Web address:** http://www.uofs.edu. **Description:** A four-year university offering certificates, associate's, bachelor's, and master's degrees (including MBAs). Approximately 3,950 undergraduate and 700 graduate students attend the University of Scranton.

UNIVEST CORPORATION OF PENNSYLVANIA
10 West Broad Street, Souderton PA 18964. 215/721-2400. **Fax:** 215/721-2427. **Contact:** Human Resources. **E-mail address:** univest@rpc.webhire.com. **World Wide Web address:** http://www.univest-corp.com. **Description:** A holding company. **Subsidiaries include:** Fin-Plan Group is a financial services group offering asset management, financial planning, insurance, and investments. George Becker Associates is a full-service insurance company. Pennview Savings Bank is a full-service bank. Union National Bank is a full-service bank. **Special programs:** Summer Jobs. **Number of employees at this location:** 455.

URBAN OUTFITTERS
1627 Walnut Street, 5th Floor, Philadelphia PA 19103. 215/569-3131. **Fax:** 800/959-8795. **Contact:** Human Resources. **World Wide Web address:** http://www.urbn.com. **Description:** A clothing and housewares retail chain. **Corporate headquarters location:** This location. **Listed on:** NASDAQ. **Stock exchange symbol:** URBN.

VWR SCIENTIFIC PRODUCTS
1310 Goshen Parkway, West Chester PA 19380. 610/431-1700. **Fax:** 610/436-1763. **Contact:** Human Resources. **E-mail address:** hrwc@vwr.com. **World Wide Web address:** http://www.vwrsp.com. **Description:** Provides laboratory equipment, chemicals, and supplies to the scientific marketplace worldwide. VWR Scientific is organized into five operating units that are aligned to serve specific market niche opportunities both in North America and overseas. VWR Scientific, the company's main domestic operating unit, is a full-line distributor of scientific supplies, laboratory chemicals and apparatus, and research equipment. VWR Scientific Products serves customers in a wide variety of markets including pharmaceuticals, biotechnology, chemicals, environmental testing, food, electronics, and education. VWR Canada provides the Canadian marketplace with a single coast-to-coast supplier. VWR International exports scientific equipment and supplies to more than 54 countries worldwide. Bender & Hobein is a joint venture with E. Merck of Germany and is one of the largest scientific distributors in the German marketplace. Sargent-Welch Scientific sells scientific instruments to the education market for the teaching of science in public and private schools throughout the United States. **Positions advertised include:** Buyer. **Corporate headquarters location:** Pompano Beach FL. **Number of employees nationwide:** 1,635.

VALLEY FORGE FLAG COMPANY, INC.
1700 Conrad Weiser Parkway, Womelsdorf PA 19567. 610/589-5888. **Fax:** 610/589-1145. **Contact:** Cindy O'Roark, Personnel. **E-mail address:** info@valleyforge.com. **World Wide Web address:** http://www.valleyforge.com. **Description:** Manufactures banners and flags. **Corporate headquarters location:** Great Neck NY. **Operations at this facility include:** Manufacturing; Sales. **Number of employees at this location:** 310.

VALSPAR CORPORATION
2000 Westhall Street, Pittsburgh PA 15233. 412/766-9300. **Contact:** Human Resources. **World Wide Web address:** http://www.valspar.com. **Description:** Valspar is engaged in the manufacture and distribution of paint and coatings through its Consumer Coatings, Industrial Coatings, and Special Products divisions. The Consumer Coatings division manufactures and distributes a full line of latex and oil-based paints, stains, and varnishes for consumer and industrial use. The Industrial Coatings division manufactures and distributes decorative and protective finishes for OEMs, as well as other specialized industrial coatings. The Special Products division produces and markets resins, emulsions, colorants, and paint specialty colors. **Positions advertised include:** Chemist; Sales Representative; Engineer; Corporate/Field Services Representative. **Operations at this facility include:** This facility manufactures chemical coatings that are used to line the insides of food and beverage cans. **Listed on:** New York Stock Exchange. **Stock exchange symbol:** VAL.

THE VANGUARD GROUP, INC.
100 Vanguard Valley, Malvern PA 19355. 610/669-1000. **Contact:** Human Resources. **World Wide Web address:** http://www.vanguard.com. **Description:** A mutual funds company that also offers assistance in educational financing, retirement planning, and trust services. **Corporate headquarters location:** This location.

VECTOR SECURITY INC.
3400 McKnight East Drive, Pittsburgh PA 15237-6425. 724/981-1933. **Toll-free phone:** 888/832-8671. **Contact:** Corporate Services Offices. **World Wide Web address:** http://www.vectorsecurity.com. **Description:** Manufactures search and detection systems. **NOTE:** See website for a current listing of employment opportunities with detailed application information. **Positions advertised include:** Security Officer; National Accounts Project Coordinator; Alarm Installer/Technician; Dispatch Operator.

VERIZON COMMUNICATIONS
1717 Arch Street, 17th Floor, Philadelphia PA 19103. 215/963-6000. **Contact:** Human Resources. **World Wide Web address:** http://www.verizon.com. **Description:** A full-service communications services provider. Residential customers are offered local and long-distance phone services; dial-up and high-speed Internet access; wireless service plans and equipment; and additional phone services and accessories. Commercial customers are offered data services; local and long-distance phone services; dial-up and high-speed Internet access; payphones; and additional telecommunications equipment and services. Verizon Communications also offers a full range of services and equipment for government clients, and sells its products and services wholesale to other long-distance and wireless service providers. **Corporate headquarters location:** New York NY. **Listed on:** New York Stock Exchange. **Stock exchange symbol:** VZ.

VERTEX SYSTEMS INC.
1041 Old Cassatt Road, Berwyn PA 19312. 610/640-4200. **Contact:** Human Resources. **E-mail address:** jobs@vertexinc.com. **World Wide Web address:** http://www.vertexinc.com. **Description:** Provides corporate clients with tax manuals and tax reference products and software. **Positions advertised include:** Senior Software Developer; Software Developer; Enterprise Architect.

VERTIS
181 Rittenhouse Circle, Bristol PA 19007. 215/785-0101. **Contact:** Human Resources. **World Wide Web address:** http://www.vertisinc.com. **Description:** Develops a variety of direct marketing services including inline printing and finishing, promotional printing, and personalization technologies.

VICTAULIC COMPANY OF AMERICA
P.O. Box 31, Easton PA 18044-0031. 610/252-6400. **Fax:** 610/250-8817. **Physical address:** 4901 Kesslerville Road, Easton PA 18040-6714. **Contact:** Personnel Department. **World Wide Web address:** http://www.victaulic.com. **Description:** An international marketer, manufacturer, and designer of industrial and commercial piping systems products that include pipe couplings, fittings, valves, piping accessories, specialty piping products, and pre-assembled packages. **Positions advertised include:** Sales Representative; Project Engineer; Fire Protection Sales Representative; Customer Service Representative; Security Guard.

VILLA TERESA
1051 Avila Road, Harrisburg PA 17109. 717/652-5900. **Fax:** 717/652-5941. **Contact:** Personnel Director. **Description:** Provides skilled nursing care for the elderly. Founded in 1973. **Office hours:** Monday - Friday, 8:00 a.m. - 4:00 p.m. **Corporate headquarters location:** This location. **Number of employees at this location:** 230.

VILLANOVA UNIVERSITY
800 Lancaster Avenue, Villanova PA 19085-1699. 610/519-7900. **Fax:** 610/519-6667. **Contact:** Barbara Kearns, Employment Coordinator. **E-mail address:** hr@villanova.edu. **World Wide Web address:** http://www.villanova.edu. **Description:** A Catholic university serving approximately 6,000 full-time undergraduates and 4,000 graduate and part-time students in the Colleges of Arts & Sciences, Engineering, Commerce & Finance, Nursing, and Law, as well as an MBA program. Founded in 1842. **Corporate headquarters location:** This location. **President:** Reverend Edmund J. Dobbin. **Annual sales/revenues:** More than $100 million. **Number of employees at this location:** 1,500.

VISHAY INTERTECHNOLOGY INC.
63 Lincoln Highway, Malvern PA 19355-2120. 610/644-1300. **Fax:** 610/296-8775. **Contact:** Judy Eyerdom, Senior Manager of Human Resources. **World Wide Web address:** http://www.vishay.com. **Description:** Operates in three business segments: Measurement Group develops, manufactures, and markets precision stress analysis products; Resistive Systems Group (also at this location) develops, manufactures, and markets high-precision resistive products; Medical Systems Group develops, manufactures, and markets dental products. **Corporate headquarters location:** This location.

VOCOLLECT INC.
701 Rodi Road, Suite 200, Pittsburgh PA 15235. 412/829-8145. **Fax:** 412/829-0972. **Contact:** Human Resources. **E-mail address:** jobs@vocollect.com. **World Wide Web address:** http://www.vocollect.com. **Description:** Manufactures voice-activated computing systems. **Positions advertised include:** Director of Industry Marketing; Software Engineer; Services Manager; Warehouse Supervisor.

WBEB-FM
10 Presidential Boulevard, Bala-Cynwyd PA 19004. 610/667-8400. **Fax:** 610/667-6795. **Contact:** Personnel. **World Wide Web address:** http://www.b101radio.com. **Description:** WBEB-FM is a radio station featuring adult contemporary music.

WEA MANUFACTURING INC.
1400 East Lackawanna Avenue, Olyphant PA 18448. 570/383-2471. **Contact:** Human Resources. **Description:** Produces and retails prerecorded music in the form of compact discs, records, cassettes, and CD-ROMs. **Parent company:** AOL Time Warner.

WPXI CHANNEL 11
11 Television Hill, Pittsburgh PA 15214. 412/237-1100. **Recorded jobline:** 412/622-1368. **Contact:** Jeff Tate, Human Resources. **World Wide Web address:** http://www.wpxi.com. **Description:** An NBC-affiliated television station.

WQED CHANNEL 13
4802 Fifth Avenue, Pittsburgh PA 15213. 412/622-1300. **Fax:** 412/622-1368. **Contact:** Rachel Zola, Human Resources Coordinator. **E-mail address:** jobs@wqed.org. **World Wide Web address:** http://www.wqed.org. **Description:** A public television station.

WTAE CHANNEL 4
400 Ardmore Boulevard, Pittsburgh PA 15221. 412/242-4300. **Contact:** Human Resources. **World Wide Web address:** http://www.thepittsburghchannel.com. **Description:** An ABC-affiliated television station.

WABTEC CORPORATION
1001 Air Brake Avenue, Wilmerding PA 15148. 412/825-1000. **Fax:** 412/825-1091. **Contact:** Patricia Pagnanelli, Human Resources Manager. **World Wide Web address:** http://www.wabco-rail.com. **Description:** A manufacturer of locomotive air brakes. **Listed on:** New York Stock Exchange. **Stock exchange symbol:** WAB.

WACHOVIA BANK
50 Huntington Pike, Rockledge PA 19111. 215/379-8777. **Fax:** 215/379-5204. **Contact:** Human Resources. **World Wide Web address:** http://www.wachovia.com. **Description:** A financial services institution. **Corporate headquarters location:** Charlotte NC. **Listed on:** New York Stock Exchange. **Stock exchange symbol:** WB. **Number of employees worldwide:** 85,000.

WACHOVIA BANK
2560 Huntingdon Pike, Huntingdon Valley PA 19006. 215/947-3700. **Fax:** 215/938-7974. **Contact:** Human Resources. **World Wide Web address:** http://www.wachovia.com. **Description:** A financial services institution. **Corporate headquarters location:** Charlotte NC. **Listed on:** New York Stock Exchange. **Stock exchange symbol:** WB. **Number of employees worldwide:** 85,000.

WACHOVIA BANK
1500 Market Street, Philadelphia PA 19102. 215/786-5980. **Fax:** 215/786-5979. **Contact:** Human Resources. **World Wide Web address:** http://www.wachovia.com. **Description:** A financial services institution. **Corporate headquarters location:** Charlotte NC. **Listed on:** New York Stock Exchange. **Stock exchange symbol:** WB. **Number of employees worldwide:** 85,000.

THE WACKENHUT CORPORATION
4156 Library Road, Building 3, Suite 4, Pittsburgh PA 15234. 412/341-7311. **Contact:** Personnel. **World Wide Web address:** http://www.wackenhut.com. **Description:** Provides physical security services, correction services, and products to businesses, governments, and individuals through more than 150 domestic and foreign offices. Specific services include security and corrections staffing; security guard and fire and crash rescue personnel training; fire protection and emergency ambulance service; and security consulting. Wackenhut has 90 offices located in most major United States cities. **Positions advertised include:** Security Officer; Sales Representative; Armed Custom Protection Officer. **Subsidiaries include:** Wackenhut Corrections, Inc.; Wackenhut International.

WADDELL & REED
2 Meridian Boulevard, Wyomissing PA 19610. 610/374-6249. **Fax:** 610/374-6293. **Contact:** Human Resources. **World Wide Web address:** http://www.waddell.com. **Description:** Waddell and Reed is a mutual fund and financial planning company that also offers a multitude of insurance plans. **Positions advertised include:** Financial Planners.

WARD MANUFACTURING INC.
115 Gulick Street, Blossburg PA 16912. 570/638-2131. **Fax:** 570/638-3410. **Contact:** Human Resources Manager. **E-mail address:** hr@wardmfg.com. **World Wide Web address:** http://www.wardmfg.com. **Description:** Manufactures cast iron and malleable iron pipe fittings.

WARNACO
P.O. Box 247, Duncansville PA 16635. 814/696-2011. **Contact:** Human Resources. **Description:** Warnaco is a large manufacturer, designer, and marketer of women's intimate apparel, men's wear, and men's accessories under brand names including Fruit of the Loom, Warner's, Olga, Chaps by Ralph Lauren, and Calvin Klein. **Operations at this facility include:** This location is a distribution center.

WASHINGTON GROUP INTERNATIONAL, INC.
301 Chelsea Parkway, Boothwyn PA 19061. 610/497-8000. **Fax:** 610/497-8005. **Contact:** Human Resources. **World Wide Web address:** http://www.wgint.com. **Description:** A diversified corporation engaged in the design, engineering, and construction of industrial plants; architectural and community services; heavy machinery design and construction; industrial facilities; and mining and metallurgy. **Corporate headquarters location:** Boise ID.

WAWA INC.
260 West Baltimore Pike, Wawa PA 19063. 610/358-8000. **Contact:** Personnel Director. **World Wide Web address:** http://www.wawa.com. **Description:** Wawa is a convenience store chain with operations throughout Pennsylvania. **Corporate headquarters location:** This location. **Operations at this facility include:** This location houses administrative offices.

WEIS MARKETS, INC.
1000 South Second Street, Sunbury PA 17801. 570/286-4571. **Fax:** 570/286-3286. **Contact:** Jim Kessler, Director of Management and Development. **World Wide Web address:** http://www.weis.com. **Description:** Operates over 165 supermarkets. **Positions advertised include:** POS Maintenance Technician; Fleet Maintenance Body Mechanic; Cashier; Store Manager; Clerk; Manager Trainee. **Special programs:** Internships. **Corporate headquarters location:** This location. **Other U.S. locations:** MD; NJ; NY; VA; WV. **Listed on:** New York Stock Exchange. **Stock exchange symbol:** WMK.

WERNER COMPANY
93 Werner Road, Greenville PA 16125-9499. 724/588-8600. **Fax:** 724/588-0315. **Contact:** Human Resources. **World Wide Web address:** http://www.wernerco.com. **Description:** A fabricated metals company specializing in architectural and ornamental metal work.

WERZALIT INC.
40 Holley Avenue, Bradford PA 16701. 814/362-3881. **Toll-free phone:** 800/999-3730. **Fax:** 814/362-4257. **Contact:** Personnel. **World Wide Web address:** http://www.werzalit-usa.com. **Description:** Manufactures wood siding, tabletops, and casket lids.

WESCO DISTRIBUTION, INC.
Commerce Court, Suite 700, 4 Station Square, Pittsburgh PA 15219. 412/454-2254. **Contact:** Human Resources. **World Wide Web address:** http://www.wescodist.com. **Description:** Distributors of electrical supplies, data communications products, industrial automation equipment, and industrial supplies. **Corporate headquarters location:** This location. **Listed on:** New York Stock Exchange. **Stock exchange symbol:** WCC. **Annual sales/revenues:** More than $100 million.

WEST CHESTER UNIVERSITY
201 Carter Drive, West Chester PA 19383. 610/436-2800. **Fax:** 610/436-3464. **Recorded jobline:** 610/436-3464. **Contact:** Office of Human Resources. **World Wide Web address:** http://www.wcupa.edu. **Description:** A four-year university offering certificates, associate's, bachelor's, and master's degrees. Approximately 9,300 undergraduate and 1,800 graduate students attend West Chester University.

WEST PENN PLASTIC INC.
Route 422 West, Rural Route 2, Box 2801, New Castle PA 16101. 724/654-2081. **Fax:** 724/654-5126. **Contact:** Personnel. **World Wide Web address:** http://www.westpennplastic.com. **Description:** Manufactures injection-molding for bottle caps.

WEST PHARMACEUTICAL SERVICES
101 Gordon Drive, P.O. 645, Lionville PA 19341-0645. 610/594-2900. **Fax:** 610/594-3011. **Contact:** Employment Supervisor. **World Wide Web address:** http://www.westpharma.com. **Description:** Researches and develops drug molecule delivery systems; designs and manufactures packaging components, systems, and devices that deliver and differentiate drugs and health care products; provides contract laboratory services; and performs commercialization processes for the manufacturing, filling, and packaging of drug and health care products. **Corporate headquarters location:** This location. **International locations:** Worldwide. **Listed on:** New York Stock Exchange. **Stock exchange symbol:** WST. **Number of employees at this location:** 300.

WESTINGHOUSE LIGHTING CORPORATION
12401 McNulty Road, Philadelphia PA 19154. 215/671-2000. **Fax:** 215/767-3720. **Contact:** Gloria Mangini, Personnel Director. **World Wide Web address:** http://www.westinghouselighting.com. **Description:** A wholesaler of light bulbs, lighting fixtures, replacement glassware, wall plates, lighting hardware, and other products. **Corporate headquarters location:** This location. **International locations:** Mexico; Germany; United Kingdom; China; Hong Kong; Taiwan. **Operations at this facility include:** Sales. **Number of employees at this location:** 125. **Number of employees nationwide:** 2,500.

WESTINGHOUSE SPECIALTY METALS
Rural Delivery 4, Box 333, Blairsville PA 15717. 412/256-3015. **Contact:** Human Resources. **World Wide Web address:** http://www.westinghouse.com. **Description:** Manufactures nuclear tubing. **Parent company:** Westinghouse Electric Corporation is a diversified manufacturing company with interests in defense electronics, environmental services, broadcasting, mobile refrigeration units, office furniture, energy systems, and power generation. Other subsidiaries include Thermo King, The Knoll Group, and Westinghouse Broadcasting. The company conducts operations through 791 locations in the United States and over 30 other countries. **Parent company:** BNFL Group.

WIDENER UNIVERSITY
One University Place, Chester PA 19013-5792. 610/499-4278. **Contact:** Personnel. **World Wide Web address:** http://www.widener.edu. **Description:** A four-year university offering bachelor's, master's (including MBAs), and doctoral degrees. Approximately 4,900 undergraduate and 3,000 graduate students attend Widener.

WILKES UNIVERSITY
256 South Franklin Street, Wilkes-Barre PA 18766. 570/408-4630. **Fax:** 570/408-7863. **Contact:** Mary Lorusso, Manager Human Resources. **World Wide Web address:** http://www.wilkes.edu. **Description:** A four-year university offering bachelor's and master's degrees. Approximately 1,900 undergraduate and 800 graduate students attend Wilkes University.

WILLIARD INC.
375 Highland Avenue, Jenkintown PA 19046. 215/885-5000. **Contact:** Human Resources Manager. **World Wide Web address:** http://www.williard.com. **Description:** A mechanical/electrical contracting firm specializing in HVAC, electrical, plumbing, and water treatment construction and services. **Corporate headquarters location:** This location.

WILLIG WILLIAMS & DAVIDSON
1845 Walnut Street, 24th Floor, Philadelphia PA 19103-4708. 215/656-3600. **Fax:** 215/561-5135. **Contact:** Personnel. **World Wide Web address:** http://www.willigwilliamsdavidson.com. **Description:** A law firm.

WILTON ARMETALE
Plumb & Square Streets, P.O. Box 600, Mount Joy PA 17552. 717/653-4444. **Contact:** Kathleen Adams, Human Resources Director. **World Wide Web address:** http://www.armetale.com. **Description:** Produces Armetale (10-metal composite) giftware products. **Corporate headquarters location:** This location. **Number of employees at this location:** 180.

WISTAR INSTITUTE OF ANATOMY AND BIOLOGY
3601 Spruce Street, Philadelphia PA 19104. 215/898-3700. **Fax:** 215/898-2204. **Contact:** Jo-Ann Mendel, Human Resources Director. **World Wide Web address:** http://www.wistar.upenn.edu. **Description:** A nonprofit, biomedical research facility. As a federally designated Basic Cancer Research Center, the institute emphasizes cancer studies in addition to searching for ways to prevent and cure other devastating diseases. Wistar Institute develops model systems and tools for biomedical research, such as cell lines, monoclonal antibodies, viral vectors, and other products of genetic engineering. **Positions advertised include:** Associate Professor; Lab Assistant; Postdoctoral Researcher; Research Assistant.

WOLF BLOCK SCHORR AND SOLIS-COHEN
325 Swede Street, Norristown PA 19401. 610/272-5555. **Fax:** 610/272-6976. **Contact:** Ms. Lynne Gold-Bikin. **E-mail address:** lgoldbikin@wolfblock.com. **World Wide Web address:** http://www.wolfblock.com. **Description:** A regional law firm offering a variety of services in business transactions, legal matters and litigation in the Mid-Atlantic area. **Other U.S. locations:** PA; NY; NJ; DE; Washington D.C. **Number of employees nationwide:** 300.

WOOLRICH, INC.
2 Mill Street, Woolrich PA 17779. 570/769-6464. **Contact:** Roger Sheets, Director of Human Resources. **World Wide Web address:** http://www.woolrich.com. **Description:** Manufactures a wide variety of outerwear and sweaters for men and women. **Corporate headquarters location:** This location.

WORD ASSOCIATION PUBLISHERS
205 Fifth Avenue. Tarentum PA 15084. 800/827-7903. **Contact:** Human Resources. **E-mail address:** publish@wordassociation.com **World Wide Web address:** http://www.wordassociation.com. **Description:** A publishing company offering a wide scope of the services involved in the publishing process including services from editing and proofreading to distribution and fulfillment.

WORLD KITCHEN, INC.
100 Eighth Street, Charleroi PA 15022. 724/483-6531. **Contact:** Personnel Department. **World Wide Web address:** http://www.worldkitchen.com. **Description:** Manufactures Pyrex glassware as well as Corning plates, saucers, and other flatware. **Parent company:** Corning Inc. is a diverse manufacturer of specialty glass and glass ceramic products such as specialty materials, consumer products, and fiber-optic cable.

WYETH-AYERST PHARMACEUTICALS
611 East Nield Street, West Chester PA 19382. 610/696-3100. **Contact:** Personnel Director. **World Wide Web address:** http://www.ahp.com/ahp/wyeth.htm. **Description:** Produces a wide range of pharmaceutical products and proprietary medicines. **NOTE:** Entry-level positions are offered. **Special programs:** Summer Jobs. **Corporate headquarters location:** Radnor PA. **Listed on:** New York Stock Exchange. **Stock exchange symbol:** WYE.

XEROX CONNECT, INC.
411 Eagleview Boulevard, Exton PA 19341. 610/458-5500. **Toll-free phone:** 800/884-4736. **Contact:** Sherri Haines, Human Resources Administrator. **World Wide Web address:** http://www.xeroxconnect.com. **Description:** Offers systems integration services. The company operates in three service groups: Consulting and Design Services, Systems Integration, and Operations and Support Services. **Parent company:** Xerox Corporation. **COO:** Tim Wallace.

XEROX CORPORATION
100 Tournament Drive, Suite 300, Horsham PA 19044. 215/956-0200. **Toll-free phone:** 800/222-9283. **Contact:** Human Resources. **World Wide Web address:** http://www.xerox.com. **Description:** Xerox Corporation is a global company in the document processing market. The company's document processing activities encompass the designing, developing, manufacturing, marketing, and servicing of a complete range of document processing products and systems that make office work more efficient. **Corporate headquarters location:** Stamford CT. **Operations at this facility include:** This location is a sales office.

XEROX CORPORATION
8 Penn Center West, Pittsburgh PA 15276. 412/506-4000. **Contact:** Rocco Manzo, Employee Development Manager. **World Wide Web address:** http://www.xerox.com. **Description:** Xerox is a global company in the document processing market. The company's document processing activities encompass the designing, developing, manufacturing, marketing, and servicing of a complete range of document processing products and systems. **Positions advertised include:** Account Executive; Sales Executive. **Corporate headquarters location:** Stamford CT. **Operations at this facility include:** This location is a sales office.

YORK COLLEGE OF PENNSYLVANIA
Country Club Road, York PA 17405-7199. 717/846-7788. **Contact:** Human Resources. **E-mail address:** kgood@ycp.edu. **World Wide Web address:** http://www.ycp.edu. **Description:** A four-year college offering associate's, bachelor's, and master's degrees including MBAs. Approximately 4,900 undergraduate and 50 graduate students attend York College. **NOTE:** Unsolicited resumes not accepted. **Positions advertised include:** Assistant Dean of Athletics and Recreation; Adjunct Instructor; Academic Advisor; Laboratory Coordinator; Administrative Support.

YORK INTERNATIONAL CORPORATION
P.O. Box 1592, York PA 17405-1592. 717/771-7890. **Physical address:** 631 South Richland Avenue, York PA 17403. **Contact:** Amanda King, Corporate Employment Recruiter. **World Wide Web address:** http://www.york.com. **Description:** Manufactures and markets a full line of residential, commercial, and industrial air conditioning and refrigeration equipment and systems, heating systems, and food refrigeration systems. **Positions advertised include:** Airside Lab Support Specialist. **Special programs:** Internships. **Corporate headquarters location:** This location. **International locations:** Worldwide. **Subsidiaries include:** York Engineered Systems; York Refrigeration; York Unitary Products. **Listed on:** New York Stock Exchange. **Stock exchange symbol:** YRK. **Number of employees worldwide:** 25,000.

YORK TAPE AND LABEL, INC.
P.O. Box 1309, York PA 17405. 717/266-9675. **Physical address:** 405 Willow Springs Lane, York PA 17402. **Contact:** Deidra A. Foore, Human Resources Manager. **World Wide Web address:** http://www.yorklabel.com. **Description:** Prints and converts pressure-sensitive labels used for product identification. **Corporate headquarters location:** This location. **Other U.S. locations:** Columbia SC. **Parent company:** Uarco, Inc. **Listed on:** Privately held. **Number of employees at this location:** 200. **Number of employees nationwide:** 275.

YORKTOWNE, INC.
P.O. Box 231, Red Lion PA 17356. 717/244-4011. **Toll-free phone:** 800/777-0065. **Physical address:** 100 Redcoe Avenue, Red Lion PA 17356. **Contact:** James Burtnett, Vice President/Human Resources. **E-mail address:** cabinets@yorktwn.com. **World Wide Web address:** http://www.yorktowneinc.com. **Description:** Manufactures and markets kitchen cabinets and bathroom vanities for the residential construction industry. **Parent company:** Wickes Corporation (San Diego CA).

YOUTH ADVOCATE PROGRAM
127 West Market Street, Suite 200, York PA 17401. 717/845-8731. **Contact:** Human Resources. **World Wide Web address:** http://www.yapi.org. **Description:** Dedicated to promoting the rights and well-being of youths on a worldwide basis. The organization pays particular attention to needy youths.

ZANY BRAINY, INC.
2520 Renaissance Boulevard, King of Prussia PA 19406. 610/278-7800. **Contact:** Human Resources. **World Wide Web address:** http://www.zanybrainy.com. **Description:** A location of the retail store chain offering a broad range of educationally oriented children's toys and other products such as books, videotapes, audiotapes, computer software, and crafts. **Corporate headquarters location:** This location.

ZIPPO MANUFACTURING COMPANY
33 Barbour Street, Bradford PA 16701. 814/368-2700. **Contact:** Personnel. **World Wide Web address:** http://www.zippomfg.com. **Description:** Manufactures lighters.

ZURN INDUSTRIES, INC.
1801 Pittsburgh Avenue, Erie PA 16514. 814/455-0921. **Fax:** 814/875-1402. **Contact:** Robert Phillips, Director of Human Resources. **World Wide Web address:** http://www.zurn.com. **Description:** Zurn Industries operates in two other industry segments as well. The Power Systems segment designs, constructs, and operates small to medium-sized alternate energy and combined-cycle power plants; designs steam generators and waste heat energy recovery and incineration systems; and produces equipment and fans to control emissions of solid particulate and gaseous pollutants. The last segment, Lynx Golf, manufactures golf clubs in Nevada, which are finished and assembled in California, Mexico, and Scotland for distribution worldwide. **Operations at this facility include:** This location manufactures flexible gear and diaphragm couplings, flexible spindle couplings, torque and overload release clutches, and universal joints as part of the Mechanical Power Transmission segment and manufactures plumbing products including drains, flush valves, backwater valves, interceptors, hydrants, traps, and supports as part of the Water Control segment.

A & H MANUFACTURING
1 Carding Lane, Johnston RI 02919. 401/943-5040. **Fax:** 401/942-1160. **Contact:** Human Resources. **E-mail address:** Scarr@aandhusa.com. **World Wide Web address:** http://www.aandhusa.com. **Description:** Manufactures products for the fashion accessories industry. **Positions advertised include:** Production Supervisor; Customer Service Representative. **Corporate headquarters location:** This location.

AAA SOUTHERN NEW ENGLAND
110 Royal Little Drive, Providence RI 02904. 401/868-2040. **Fax:** 401/868-2085 **Contact:** Human Resources. **E-mail address:** humanresources@aaasne.com. **World Wide Web address:** http://www.aaasne.com. **Description:** Provides insurance, travel, and related services through a network of branch offices nationwide. **NOTE:** Entry-level positions and second and third shift available. **Positions advertised include:** Tow/Flatbed Driver; Light Service Driver; Member Service Counselor; Auto Travel Specialist; Assistant Branch Manager; Dispatcher; Call Counselor; Mortgage Loan Originator; Insurance Agent; Travel Agent; Security Guard. **Other area locations:** Barrington RI; Cranston RI; Greenville RI; Middletown RI; Providence RI; Woonsocket RI. **Other U.S. locations:** Nationwide.

ABC CHANNEL 6
WLNE - TV
10 Orms Street, Providence RI 02904. 401/453-8000. **Fax:** 401/331-4039. **Contact:** Human Resources. **World Wide Web address:** http://www.abc6.com. **Description:** A television news station covering the Providence RI and New Bedford MA areas. **NOTE:** Entry-level positions and second and third shifts are offered. **Positions advertised include:** Part-Time Production Technician; Producer; Account Executive; Photojournalist; News Reporter. **Special programs:** Internships. **Corporate headquarters location:** Irvine CA. **Other U.S. locations:** Nationwide. **Parent company:** Freedom Broadcasting of New Southern New England, Inc. **Listed on:** Privately held. **Number of employees at this location:** 135.

ACS INDUSTRIES
P.O. Box 1010, Woonsocket RI 02895-4835. 401/769-4700. **Physical address:** 191 Social Street, Woonsocket RI 02895. **E-mail address:** acsind@acsind.com. **Toll-free phone:** 800/343-2257. **Fax:** 401/762-3984. **Contact:** Human Resources Manager. **World Wide Web address:** http://www.acsindustries.com. **Description:** Manufactures stainless steel wire, telephone cords, exhaust seal gaskets, and specialized filters. Founded in 1939. **Other area locations:** Middletown RI; Newport RI. **Other U.S. locations:** Eastern United States. **Parent company:** GBB Merger Corporation. **President:** Steven Buckler.

ABAQUS, INC.
166 Valley Street, Providence RI 02909. 401/276-4400. **Fax:** 401/276-4408. **Contact:** Catherine Kelleher, Human Resources. **E-mail address:** info@abaqus.com. **World Wide Web address:** http://www.hks.com. **Description:** Develops and sells Abaqus software. **Positions advertised include:** Development Group Manager; Engineering Specialist; Project Manager; Senior Financial Analyst; Software License Specialist; Senior Development Engineer. **Corporate headquarters location:** This location. **Other area locations:** Warwick RI. **Other U.S. locations:** Cleveland OH; West Lafayette IN; Lewisville TX; Fremont CA. **President and CEO:** Mark Goldstein.

ADVANCED INTERCONNECTIONS CORPORATION
5 Energy Way, P.O. Box 1019, West Warwick RI 02893. 401/823-5200. **Toll-free phone:** 800/424-9850. **Fax:** 401/823-8723. **Contact:** Dana DaCosta, Personnel. **E-mail address:** ddacosta@advintcorp.com. **World Wide Web address:** http://www.advintcorp.com. **Description:** Designs, develops, and manufactures interconnect products for the electronics industry. Founded in 1982. **NOTE:** Entry-level positions are offered. **Positions advertised include:** Engineering Manager. **Corporate headquarters location:** This location. **Listed on:** Privately held. **Annual sales/revenues:** $5 - $10 million. **Number of employees at this location:** 140.

AMERICAN CANADIAN CARIBBEAN LINE, INC.
461 Water Street, P.O. Box 368, Warren RI 02885. 401/247-0955. **Toll-free phone:** 800/556-7450. **Fax:** 401/247-2350. **Contact:** Human Resources. **E-mail address:** info@accl-smallships.com. **World Wide Web address:** http://www.accl-smallships.com. **Description:** A small-ship cruise line sailing to domestic and foreign ports. **Positions advertised include:** Captain; First Mate; Engineer; Cruise Director; Chef; Assistant Chef; Steward/Stewardess; Deckhand; Destination Specialist. **Corporate headquarters location:** This location. **Listed on:** Privately held. **President:** Nancy E. Blount.

AMERICAN INSULATED WIRE CORPORATION
95 Grand Avenue, Pawtucket RI 02862. 401/726-0700. **Toll-free phone:** 800/366-2492. **Fax:** 401/642-2480. **Contact:** Human Resources. **World Wide Web address:** http://www.aiwc.com. **Description:** Produces insulated wire and cable. **Parent Company:** Leviton.

AMERICAN POWER CONVERSION (APC)
132 Fairgrounds Road, West Kingston RI 02892. 401/789-5735. **Toll-free phone:** 888/289-2722. **Fax:** 401/788-2710. **Contact:** Human Resources. **E-mail address:** apcresumes@apcc.com. **World Wide Web address:** http://www.apcc.com. **Description:** Designs, develops, manufactures, and markets surge suppressers, uninterruptible power supplies (UPS), power conditioning equipment, and related software for computer and computer-related equipment including local area networks (LANs), midrange computers, and engineering workstations. American Power Conversion also publishes a newsletter called APC Currents that provides news about the company and the company's products. **Positions advertised include:** Accountant; Collections Representative; Assistant Corporate Controller; Safety Engineer; Safety Specialist; Test Engineer; Business Systems Analyst; Programmer Analyst; Marcom Project Leader; Senior Product Manager; Configuration Center Representative; Director of Worldwide Sales Operations; Inside Sales Representative; Technical Support Engineer; Training Director; Software Engineer; General Operative; Senior Service Assistant; Quality Assurance Technician; Electrical Engineer. **Corporate headquarters location:** This location. **Other area locations:** East Providence RI; West Warwick RI. **Other U.S. locations:** Billerica MA; St. Louis MO. **International locations:** Worldwide. **Operations at this facility include:** Administration; Divisional Headquarters; Manufacturing; Sales; Service. **Listed on:** NASDAQ. **Stock exchange symbol:** APCC. **Number of employees at this location:** 1,400.

AMGEN INC.
40 Technology Way, West Greenwich RI 02817. 401/392-1200. **Toll-free phone:** 800/842-6436. **Contact:** Human Resources. **World Wide Web address:** http://www.amgen.com. **Description:** The world's largest biotechnology company. Founded in 1980. **NOTE:** Apply online. All resumes are processed centrally. It is not necessary to address a cover letter to a specific individual. **Positions advertised include:** Area Human Resources Manager; Associate Director of Process Development; Associate Scientist; Business Analyst; Construction Engineer. **Corporate headquarters location:** Thousand Oaks CA. **Other U.S. Locations:** CO; KY; MA; D.C.; WA. **Operations at this facility include:** Manufacturing. **Listed on:** NASDAQ. **Stock exchange symbol:** AMGN. **Chairman/President/CEO:** Kevin W. Sharer. **Number of employees worldwide:** 10,100.

AMICA MUTUAL INSURANCE COMPANY
100 Amica Way, Lincoln RI 02865. 401/334-6000. **Toll-free phone:** 800/242-6422. **Fax:** 401/334-1491. **Contact:** Human Resources. **E-mail address:** careers@amica.com. **World Wide Web address:** http://www.amica.com. **Description:** A personal lines, property, and casualty insurance company. **NOTE:** Please paste cover letter and resume directly into e-mail. Attachments will not be opened. Mail resumes to: P.O. Box 529, East Taunton MA 02718. **Positions advertised include:** Associate Adjuster; Associate Account Manager. **Corporate headquarters location:** This location. **Operations at this facility include:** Actuarial Services; Administration; Divisional Headquarters. **Other U.S. locations:** Nationwide. **CEO:** Thomas A. Taylor. **Number of employees nationwide:** 3,300.

AMTROL, INC.
1400 Division Road, West Warwick RI 02893. 401/884-6300. **Fax:** 401/885-7470. **Contact:** Human Resources. **E-mail address:** jobs@amtrol.com. **World Wide Web address:** http://www.amtrol.com. **Description:** A leading North American producer and marketer of flow and expansion control technology used in water systems and HVAC products. Founded in 1946. **Positions advertised include:** Manufacturing Engineer. **Special programs:** Internships. **Corporate headquarters location:** This location. **Other U.S. locations:** KY; MD. **International locations:** Germany; Portugal. **Subsidiaries include:** American Granby; Clayton Mark; Water Soft. **Operations at this facility include:** Administration; Divisional Headquarters; Manufacturing; Research and Development; Sales; Service. **Listed on:** NASDAQ. **Stock exchange symbol:** AMTL. **Number of employees at this location:** 500. **Number of employees worldwide:** 1,700.

ANTEON CORPORATION
One Corporate Place, Middletown RI 02842. 401/849-5952. **Fax:** 401/846-7811. **Contact:** Human Resources. **E-mail address:** careers@anteon.com. **World Wide Web address:** http://www.anteon.com. **Description:** A leading provider of technology-based solutions in the areas of engineering services, information technologies, and interactive multimedia services. **Positions advertised include:** Project Manager; Staff Network Engineer; Military Systems Engineer; Human Resources Administrator; Contracts Administrator. **Special programs:** Internships; Co-ops. **Office hours:** Monday - Friday, 8:00 a.m. - 5:00 p.m. **Corporate headquarters location:** Fairfax VA. **Other area locations:** Newport RI. **Other U.S. locations:** Nationwide. **International locations:** Germany; Italy; Canada; United Kingdom; Australia. **Listed on:** New York Stock Exchange. **Stock exchange symbol:** ANT. **President and CEO:** Joseph M. Kampf. **Number of employees worldwide:** 7,600.

ARKWRIGHT INC.
538 Main Street, Fiskeville RI 02823-0139. 401/821-1000. **Toll-free phone:** 800/942-5900. **Fax:** 401/822-1559. **Contact:** Kim Butts, Human Resources. **E-mail address:** info-na@arkwright.com. **World Wide Web address:** http://www.arkwright.com. **Description:** Manufactures imaging films for presentation graphics and design engineering applications. **Corporate headquarters location:** This location. **Other U.S. locations:** Nationwide. **Parent company:** Oce Van Der Grinten. **Listed on:** Privately held. **Number of employees at this location:** 240.

ARTIFICIAL KIDNEY CENTER
318 Waterman Avenue, East Providence RI 02914. 401/438-5930. **Fax:** 401/438-5090. **Contact:** Human Resources. **E-mail address:** clinic1170@fmc-na.com. **Description:** Provides dialysis services, C.A.P.D. training, and dietary instruction. **Other area locations:** Providence RI; North Providence RI; Pawtucket RI; Wakefield RI; Westerly RI; Warwick RI. **Other U.S. locations:** Nationwide. **International locations:** Worldwide.

ASTRO-MED, INC.
600 East Greenwich Avenue, West Warwick RI 02893. 401/828-4000. **Fax:** 401/822-0139. **Contact:** Human Resources. **E-mail address:** humanresources@astro-med.com. **World Wide Web address:** http://www.astro-med.com. **Description:** Manufactures and supplies specialty printers that display, monitor, analyze, and print data for aerospace, industrial, and medical applications. Products are sold under the Grass-Telefactor, QuickLabel Systems, and Astro-Med brand names. Customers include leading aircraft manufacturers, automotive product manufacturers, telecommunications companies, electrical utility companies, steel companies, and paper manufacturers. Founded in 1969. **Positions advertised include:** Technical Support Engineer; Inside Sales Specialist; Manufacturing Manager. **Corporate headquarters location:** This location. **International locations:** Worldwide. **Listed on:** NASDAQ. **Stock exchange symbol:** ALOT. **Number of employees at this location:** 250.

BARNES & NOBLE BOOKSTORES
1350-B Bald Hill Road, Warwick RI 02886. 401/826-8885. **Contact:** Manager. **World Wide Web address:** http://www.bn.com. **Description:** A discount bookstore chain operating nationwide. This location has a cafe in addition to its book departments.

BLUESTREAK
155 South Main Street, Suite 100, Providence RI 02903. 401/341-3300. **Contact:** Neil Johnson. **Physical address:** 76 Hammarlund Drive, Middletown RI 02482. **E-mail address:** resumes@bluestreak.com. **World Wide Web address:** http://www.bluestreak.com. **Description:** Executes online and e-mail marketing campaigns. **Positions advertised include:** Account Executive; Software Engineer; MS SQL Administrator and Developer. **CEO:** Peter A. Corrao.

EMMA PENDLETON BRADLEY HOSPITAL
1011 Veterans Memorial Parkway, East Providence RI 02915. 401/432-1141. **Fax:** 401/432-1511. **Contact:** Human Resources. **E-mail address:** coliveira@lifespan.org. **World Wide Web address:** http://www.lifespan.org/partners/bh/. **Description:** Offers a full spectrum of mental health services for children ranging from outpatient counseling and therapy to hospitalization. The hospital's 60-bed, inpatient services are for children ages 2 to 18 who are suffering from more serious problems and are in need of short-term stabilization, assessment, and treatment. Inpatient services provide many levels of care including a highly secure unit for children who require around-the-clock attention, less intensive 24-hour crisis intervention for those who do not need a secure inpatient unit, a partial hospitalization option for those who require hospital-level treatment during the day and can go home at night, and brief in-home care as a transition from the hospital to home and as an alternative to hospitalization. The facility is associated with Brown University's Medical School. Founded in 1931. **NOTE:** Part-Time and Per-Diem shift are available. **Positions advertised include:** Senior Clinical Research Assistant; Milieu Therapist; Emergency Services Clinician; Residential Care Counselor; Classroom Behavior Specialist; Social Worker; Administrative Secretary; Clinical Staff Nurse; Speech Pathologist.

BROOKS/MAXI DRUG, INC.
50 Service Avenue, Warwick RI 02886. 401/825-3900. **Fax:** 401/825-3707. **Contact:** Roy Greene, Director of Human Resources. **E-mail address:** hr@brooks-rx.com. **World Wide Web address:** http://www.brooks-rx.com. **Description:** Operates over 230 retail drugstores located throughout New England. **NOTE:** See job listings on website for contact information regarding specific positions. Applicants for corporate positions send resume and salary requirements to the above address. **Positions advertised include:** Pharmacy Technician; Manager; Assistant Manager; Sales Associate. **Corporate headquarters location:** This location. **Other U.S. locations:** CT; MA; ME; NH; VT. **Parent company:** The Jean Coutu Group. **Listed on:** Privately held. **President and CEO:** Michel Coutu. **Number of employees nationwide:** 8,900.

BROWN & SHARPE MANUFACTURING
Precision Park, 200 Frenchtown Road, North Kingstown RI 02852-1700. 401/886-2000. **Contact:** Human Resources. **E-mail address:** resume@us.bnsmc.com **World Wide Web address:** http://www.brownandsharpe.com. **Description:** Manufactures machine tool accessories. **Corporate headquarters location:** This location.

BROWN UNIVERSITY
P.O. Box 1879, 164 Angell Street, Providence RI 02912. 401/863-3175. **Fax:** 401/863-1833. **Contact:** Human Resources. **E-mail address:** hrweb@brown.edu. **World Wide Web address:** http://www.brown.edu. **Description:** An Ivy League university with 7,700 students. **Corporate headquarters location:** This location. **Positions advertised include:** Gift Administration Manager; Research Assistant; Lead Database Administrator; Programmer Analyst; Assistant Supervisor, Catering Operations; Senior Science Writer; Security Officer; Box Office Manager; Library Clerk.

BUTLER HOSPITAL
345 Blackstone Boulevard, Providence RI 02906. 401/455-6245. **Fax:** 401/455-6301. **Contact:** Human Resources. **E-mail address:** jobs@butler.org. **World Wide Web address:** http://www.butler.org. **Description:** Rhode Island's only private, non-profit psychiatric and substance abuse treatment hospital. It provides assessment and treatment for children, adolescents, and adults for all major psychiatric illnesses and substance abuse problems. Butler is affiliated with Brown Medical School. **NOTE:** Applications are accepted by mail, fax, or online. **Positions advertised include:** Research Secretary; Research Assistant; Registered Nurse; Staff Nurse; Nurse Supervisor; Director of Nursing Education; Intake Coordinator; Mental Health Worker.

CVS
One CVS Drive, Woonsocket RI 02895. 401/765-1500. **Contact:** Human Resources. **World Wide Web address:** http://www.cvs.com. **Description:** CVS operates a chain of drugstores throughout the United States. Pharmacy operations make up a large portion of the company's business, offering both brand name and generic prescription drugs. CVS stores also offer a broad range of health and beauty aids, cosmetics, greeting cards, convenience foods, photo finishing services, and other general merchandise. Founded in 1963. **Positions listed include:** Accountant; Administrative Assistant; Asset Associate; Associate Print Media Buyer; Bank Accounting Associate; Senior Budget Analyst; Care Management Nurse; Corporate Legal Assistant; Customer Service Representative; Database Administrator; Divisional Merchandise Manager; In Stock Team Member; Inventory Shrink Analyst; Lead Instructional Design Technologist. **Special programs:** Internships available. **Corporate headquarters location:** This location. **Other U.S. locations:** Nationwide. **Parent company:** Mark Steven Service Merchandisers. **Listed on:** New York Stock Exchange. **Stock exchange symbol:** CVS. **Annual sales/revenues:** More than $100 million.

CITIZENS BANK
One Citizens Plaza, Providence RI 02903. 401/456-7000. **Contact:** Human Resources. **E-mail address:** rijobs@citizensbank.com. **World Wide Web address:** http://www.citizensbank.com. **Description:** A savings bank. **NOTE:** For teller positions call 887/TELLER-1, for branch manager positions call 887/INAISLE. **Positions advertised include:** Underwriter; Senior Database Administrator; Lead Developer, Architecture; Payments Product Manager; Senior Storage Engineer; Internet Business Development Manager; In-Store Banker; Senior Staff Accountant; Teller. **Other area locations:** Statewide. **Other U.S. locations:** MA; CT; NH; PA; DE. **Parent company:** Citizens Financial Group, Inc.

CLARIANT
500 Washington Street, Coventry RI 02816. 401/823-2000. **Fax:** 401/823-2555. **Contact:** Human Resources. **E-mail address:** hr.coventry@clariant.com. **World Wide Web address:** http://www.clariant-northamerica.com. **Description:** Manufactures dyes, pigments, and pharmaceutical ingredients. **NOTE:** Fax resume and salary requirements to the number listed above.

CLEAN HARBORS, INC.
8 Dexter Road, East Providence RI 02914. 401/431-1847. **Toll-free phone:** 800/645-8265. **Contact:** Human Resources. **World Wide Web address:** http://www.cleanharbors.com. **Description:** Clean Harbors, Inc., through its subsidiaries, provides comprehensive environmental services in 35 states in the Northeast, Midwest, Central, and Mid-Atlantic regions. Clean Harbors provides a wide range of hazardous waste management and environmental support services to a diversified customer base from over 40 locations. The company's hazardous waste management services include treatment, storage, recycling, transportation, risk analysis, site assessment, laboratory analysis, site closure, and disposal of hazardous materials through environmentally sound methods, including incineration. Environmental remediation services include emergency response, surface remediation, groundwater restoration, industrial maintenance, and facility decontamination. Customers include nearly 300 of the *Fortune* 500 companies; regional utilities; oil, pharmaceutical, and chemical companies; small businesses; and the high-tech and biotech industries. **NOTE:** Please send resumes to: Human Resources, 1501 Washington Street, Braintree MA 02185. **Corporate headquarters location:** Braintree MA. **Other U.S. locations:** Nationwide. **Number of employees nationwide:** 1,400.

COMMUNITY COLLEGE OF RHODE ISLAND (CCRI)
400 East Avenue, Warwick RI 02886-1807. 401/825-2311. **Fax:** 401/825-2345. **Contact:** Human Resources. **World Wide Web address:** http://www.ccri.cc.ri.us. **Description:** One of the largest public, two-year, degree-granting colleges in New England. Community College of Rhode Island (CCRI) provides a variety of career, technical, and academic programs. CCRI enrolls more than 16,000 students in credit courses each semester. There are approximately 300 full-time faculty members. The college offers associate degrees in arts, science, applied science, applied science in technical studies, and fine arts degrees. One-year certificates are also awarded. **Positions advertised include:** Adjunct Faculty, Nursing; Help Desk Technical Support Specialist. **Other area locations:** Newport RI.

COMMUNITY COLLEGE OF RHODE ISLAND (CCRI)
1762 Louisquisset Pike, Lincoln RI 02865-4585. 401/333-7000. **Contact:** Human Resources. **World Wide Web address:** http://www.ccri.cc.ri.us. **Description:** One of the largest public, two-year, degree-granting colleges in New England. Community College of Rhode Island (CCRI) provides a variety of career, technical, and academic programs. CCRI enrolls more than 16,000 students in credit courses each semester. There are approximately 300 full-time faculty members. The college offers associate degrees in arts, science, applied science, applied science in technical studies, and fine arts degrees. One-year certificates are also awarded.

COMMUNITY COLLEGE OF RHODE ISLAND (CCRI)
One Hilton Street, Providence RI 02905-2304. 401/455-6000. **Contact:** Human Resources. **World Wide Web address:** http://www.ccri.cc.ri.us. **Description:** One of the largest public, two-year, degree granting colleges in New England. Community College of Rhode Island (CCRI) provides a variety of career, technical, and academic programs. CCRI enrolls more than 16,000 students in credit courses each semester. There are approximately 300 full-time faculty members, of which nearly 20 percent hold doctoral degrees. The college offers associate degrees in arts, science, applied science, applied science in technical studies, and fine arts. One-year certificates are also awarded.

CRANSTON PRINT WORKS COMPANY
1381 Cranston Street, Cranston RI 02920. 401/943-4800. **Fax:** 401/943-3971. **Contact:** Marilyn Ceprano, Human Resources. **E-mail address:** Corporate@cpw.com. **World Wide Web address:** http://www.cpw.com. **Description:** A finisher, converter, and printer of textiles. **Corporate headquarters location:** This location. **Other U.S. locations:** New York NY; Webster MA. **Number of employees at this location:** 1,550.

CREDIT UNION CENTRAL FALLS
693 Broad Street, Central Falls RI 02863. 401/725-1535. **Fax:** 401/727-7927. **Contact:** Human Resources. **World Wide Web address:** http://www.cucf.org. **Description:** Rhode Island's leading credit union. Founded in 1915. **NOTE:** Mail resume to: James Carney, Credit Union Central Falls, P.O. Box 206, Central Falls RI 02863. **Corporate headquarters:** This location. **Other area locations:** Cumberland RI; Lincoln RI; Pawtucket RI; Woonsocket RI.

A.T. CROSS COMPANY
One Albion Road, Lincoln RI 02865-3700. 401/333-1200. **Fax:** 401/333-9854. **Contact:** Kathy Gaidimas, Human Resources Generalist. **World Wide Web address:** http://www.cross.com. **Description:** An international manufacturer of fine writing instruments. These products are sold to the consumer gift market through selected jewelry, department, stationery, gift, and bookstores, and sold to the business gift market via a network of companies specializing in recognition programs. Founded in 1846. **NOTE:** Phone inquiries not accepted. **Corporate headquarters location:** This location. **Listed on:** American Stock Exchange. **Stock Exchange Symbol:** ATX. **President:** David Whalen.

DAVOL INC.
100 Sockanossett Crossroad, Box 8500, Cranston RI 02920. 401/463-7000. **Fax:** 401/464-9446. **Contact:** Human Resources. **E-mail address:** info@davol.com. **World Wide Web address:** http://www.davol.com. **Description:** Develops, manufactures, and markets specialty medical products for use in surgical and nonsurgical procedures. Davol specializes in products relating to hernia repair, laparascopy, and orthopedics. Founded in 1874. **Corporate headquarters location:** This location. **Parent company:** C.R. Bard, Inc. **Listed on:** New York Stock Exchange. **Stock exchange symbol:** BCR.

DEUTSCHE NICKEL AMERICA, INC.
100 Higginson Avenue, Lincoln RI 02865. 401/721-2158. **Toll-free phone:** 800/258-7766. **Contact:** Human Resources. **World Wide Web address:** http://www.dn-america.com. **Description:** Sells and distributes nickel alloys, stainless steel, brass/copper alloys, and wire-rope products to industrial clients worldwide. **Other U.S. locations:** Jacksonville FL; Charles IL; Houston TX; Ventura CA.

DIPRETE
2 Stafford Court, Cranston RI 02920. 401/943-1000. **Fax:** 401/464-6006. **Contact:** Karen King. **E-mail address:** Karen@diprete-eng.com. **World Wide Web address:** http://www.diprete-eng.com. **Description:** Civil Engineering and land surveying firm performing work throughout New England. **Positions advertised include:** Receptionist. **Corporate headquarters location:** This Location.

DONNELLY'S SCHOOL APPAREL
333 Niantic Avenue, Providence RI 02907. 401/942-5202. **Fax:** 401/942-2425. **Contact:** Peter C. Donnelly. **E-mail address:** pcd@donnellysclothing.com. **World Wide Web address:** http://www.donnellysclothing.com. **Description:** Designs and manufactures school and corporate uniforms. **Positions advertised include:** Monogram Specialist; Associate Customer Service Representative; Embroidery Machine Operator. **Corporate headquarters location:** This location.

EASTERN COLOR & CHEMICAL COMPANY
35 Livingston Street, PO Box 6161, Providence RI 02940. 401/331-9000. **Fax:** 401/331-2155. **Contact:** Human Resources. **World Wide Web address:** http://www.easterncolor.net. **Description:** Manufactures specialty chemicals and pigments for textile, paper, and leather. **NOTE:** Does not take employment phone calls, please apply through web site. **Positions advertised include:** Maintenance Engineer; Chemist. **Corporate headquarters location:** This location.

ELECTRO STANDARDS LAB INC.
36 Western Industrial Drive, Cranston RI 02921. 401/943-1164. **Toll-free phone:** 887/943-1164. **Fax:** 401/946-5790. **Contact:** Human Resources. **E-mail address:** eslab@electrostandards.com. **World Wide Web address:** http://www.electrostandards.com. **Description:** A manufacturer of computer cables. **Special Programs:** Engineering Internships. **Positions advertised include:** Electrical Engineer; Computer Engineer; Test and Implementation Agent/Representative.

EMISSIVE ENERGY CORPORATION
135 Circuit Drive, North Kingston RI 02852. 401/294-2030. **Fax:** 401/294-2050. **Contact:** Human Resources. **World Wide Web address:** http://www.inovalight.com. **Description:** Manufactures Consumer Electronics. **Positions advertised include:** Sales Administrator.

ESS GROUP, INC.
401 Wampanoag Trail, Suite 400, East Providence RI 02915. 401/434-5560. **Fax:** 401/434-8158. **Contact:** Human Resources. **E-mail address:** adurrell@essgroup.com. **World Wide Web address:** http://www.essgroup.com. **Description:** Environmental Science Services is an environmental consulting engineering firm offering a variety of services including soil sampling, water sampling, and hazardous materials services. Established in 1979. **Positions advertised include:** Environmental Engineer/Scientist; Environmental Field Engineer/Geologist; Civil Engineer. **Other U.S. locations:**

Sandwich MA; Wellesley MA. **Operations at this facility include:** Air quality sampling.

FM GLOBAL
1301 Atwood Avenue, Johnston RI 02919. 401/275-3000. **Toll-free phone:** 800/343-7722. **Fax:** 401/275-3029. **Contact:** Elena Gargana. **E-mail address:** jobs@fmglobal.com. **World Wide Web address:** http://www.fmglobal.com. **Description:** A loss-control services organization. FM Global's primary objective is to help owner/company policyholders protect their properties and occupancies from damage from fire, wind, flood, and explosion; boiler, pressure vessel, and machinery accidents; and from many other insured hazards. Founded in 1835. **Positions advertised include:** Information Services Senior Specialist; Methods Analyst; Production Designer; Lead Specialist, Document Management; Lead Business Analyst. **Special programs:** Internships; Co-ops. **Corporate headquarters location:** This location. **Other U.S. locations:** Nationwide. **International locations:** Worldwide. **Number of employees at this location:** 700. **Number of employees worldwide:** 4,000.

GILBANE BUILDING COMPANY
7 Jackson Walkway, Providence RI 02903. 401/456-5800. **Fax:** 401/456-5936. **Toll-free phone:** 800/GILBANE. **Contact:** Human Resources. **World Wide Web address:** http://www.gilbaneco.com. **Description:** A full-service construction and real estate development company offering services in site selection, financing, programming, and construction. The company is involved in all major construction markets including industrial, corporate, health care, education, airports, convention centers, and correctional facilities. Founded in 1873. **Office hours:** Monday - Friday, 8:00 a.m. - 5:00 p.m. **NOTE:** See website for a listing of disciplines in which Gilbane seeks candidates on an ongoing basis. Credentials can be submitted online. **Corporate headquarters location:** This location. **Other U.S. locations:** Nationwide. **Listed on:** Privately held. **Annual sales/revenues:** More than $100 million. **CEO:** Paul Choquette, Jr. **Number of employees at this location:** 200. **Number of employees nationwide:** 1,000.

THE GRODEN CENTER
610 Manton Avenue, Providence RI 02909. 401/274-6310. **Fax:** 401/421-1161. **Contact:** Human Resources. **E-mail address:** hiring@grodencenter.org. **World Wide Web address:** http://www.grodencenter.org. **Description:** Provides support to children and adults with autism and other developmental disabilities and behavioral challenges. **Positions advertised include:** Treatment Teacher; Bookkeeper; Research Assistant; Quality Assurance Coordinator; Assistant to Director; Human Resource Recruiter; Administrator of Rehabilitative Services. **Other area locations:** Warwick RI.

GTECH CORPORATION
55 Technology Way, West Greenwich RI 02817. 401/392-1000. **Fax:** 401/392-4950. **Contact:** Human Resources. **E-mail address:** info@gtech.com. **World Wide Web address:** http://www.gtech.com. **Description:** Supplies computerized systems and services for government-authorized lotteries. Subsidiaries operate online lottery networks; sell, deliver, and install turn-key online lottery systems under contract agreements; and design, manufacture, and provide point-of-sale terminals used in its online lottery networks. **NOTE:** Resumes must be submitted online. **Positions advertised include:** Business Analyst; Director of Marketing; Director of Finance; Senior Financial Analyst; Front End Technologist; Information Systems Auditor; Integration Engineer; IT Asset Manager; Marketing Analyst; Procurement Specialist; Senior Proposal Writer; Senior Technical Writer. **Special programs:** Internships; Apprenticeships. **Corporate headquarters location:** This location. **Other area locations:** Coventry RI. **Other U.S. locations:** Nationwide. **Listed on:** New York Stock Exchange. **Stock exchange symbol:** GTK. **Annual sales/revenues:** More than $100 million. **Number of employees at this location:** 1,500. **Number of employees nationwide:** 4,300.

HANDY AND HARMAN ELECTRONIC MATERIALS CORPORATION
231 Ferris Avenue, East Providence RI 02916. 401/434-6543. **Fax:** 401/432-9936. **Contact:** Personnel Manager. **World Wide Web address:** http://www.handyharman.com. **Description:** A manufacturer of plated and stamped parts for connectors, interconnectors, conductors, and other parts. Primary customers are computer manufacturers and companies using integrated circuits and connectors. **Parent Company:** WHX Corporation. **Operations at this facility include:** Administration; Manufacturing; Research and Development; Sales. **Listed on:** New York Stock Exchange. **Stock exchange symbol:** WHX.

HASBRO, INC.
P.O. Box 1059, Pawtucket RI 02862-1059. 401/431-8697. **Physical address:** 1027 Newport Avenue, Pawtucket RI 02861-2500. **Contact:** Human Resources. **World Wide Web address:** http://www.hasbro.com. **Description:** A major producer and marketer of toys including brand names GI Joe, My Little Pony, Tonka Trucks, Cabbage Patch Kids, Play-Doh, and Nerf. The company also has a large stake in the board game market. The Hasbro Playskool affiliate manufactures preschool toys, child-care products, play sets, and children's apparel. **Positions advertised include:** Consumer Affairs Representative; Retail Merchandiser; Reliability Engineer; Part-Time Human Resources Coordinator; Temporary Senior Executive Assistant; Digital Product Photographer; Package Engineer. **Corporate headquarters location:** This location. **Other U.S. locations:** Chicago IL; East Longmeadow MA; Seattle WA. **Listed on:** New York Stock Exchange. **Stock exchange symbol:** HAS. **Annual sales/revenues:** More than $100 million.

HOLLAND & KNIGHT
One Financial Plaza, Suite 1800, Providence RI 02903. 401/751-8500. **Fax:** 401/553-6850. **Contact:** Human Resources. **World Wide Web address:** http://www.hklaw.com. **Description:** A law firm with a broad variety of specialties including corporate, environmental, and litigation. **Special programs:** Summer opportunities for law students.

THE HOLSON BURNES COMPANY
582 Great Road, North Smithfield RI 02896. 401/762-5617. **Contact:** Human Resources. **Description:** Manufactures, assembles, markets, and distributes picture frames, photo albums, and other photo storage devices. The current product line includes the brand names Holson, Terragrafics, Showbox, and Burnes. **Corporate headquarters location:** This location. **Parent company:** Newell Rubbermaid. **Listed on:** NASDAQ. **Stock exchange symbol:** NWL. **Number of employees nationwide:** 500.

IGUS
50 North Broadway, East Providence RI 02916.401/438-2200. **Fax:** 401/435-0102. **Contact:** Anne Hardee. **E-mail address:** ahardee@igus.com. **World Wide Web address:** http://www.igus.com. **Description:** Develops and manufactures cable carriers, continuous-flex cables, plastic plain bearings, and linear guide systems. **Positions advertised include:** Inside Technical Sales. **Corporate headquarters location:** This location.

INTERIM HEALTHCARE
245 Waterman Street, Providence RI 02906. 401/272-3520. **Toll-free phone:** 888/560-3520. **Fax:** 401/331-0081. **Contact:** Janice Gustafson, Human Resources Manager. **E-mail address:** janicegustafson@interimhealthcarene.com. **World Wide Web address:** http://www.interimhealthcare.com. **Description:** A home health care agency. Founded in 1966. **Positions advertised include:** Medical Assistant; Registered Nurse; Pediatric Nurse. **Corporate headquarters location:** Sunrise FL. **Other U.S. locations:** Nationwide.

JAY PACKAGING GROUP INC.
100 Warwick Industrial Drive, Warwick RI 02886. 401/739-7200. **Fax:** 401/739-2807. **Contact:** Human Resources. **E-mail address:** humres@jaypack.com. **World Wide Web address**: http://www.jaypack.com. **Description:** A leading manufacturer of blister card packaging. The company produces the plastic blister as well as the printed cards and boxes. **Positions advertised include:** Receptionist. **Other U.S. locations:** Scottsburg IN. **Parent company:** Exeter Corporation. **Operations at this facility include:** Administration; Manufacturing; Sales. **Number of employees at this location:** 200. **Number of employees nationwide:** 250.

JEWEL CASE EXPRESS
300 Niantic Avenue, Providence RI 02907. 401/943-1400. **Toll-free phone:** 800/441/4447. **Fax:** 401/943-1426. **Contact:** Human Resources. **E-mail address:** Contact@JewelCase.com. **World Wide Web address:** http://www.jewelcase.com. **Description:** Manufactures high-quality gift, jewelry, watch, and coin packaging in both covered metal and wrapped paperboard boxes. The company has been engaged in the gift packaging industry for more than 40 years. The company manufactures all of its products' components, including the small 'C' springs used in the hinges of their boxes. In addition to manufacturing, Jewel Case also operates a packaging design and development department.

JOHNSON & WALES UNIVERSITY
8 Abbott Park Place, Providence RI 02903. 401/598-1000. **Contact:** Human Resources. **E-mail address:** work@jwu.edu. **World Wide Web address:** http://work.jwu.edu. **Description:** A university concentrating in the culinary arts and hotel management. **NOTE:** Applications are only accepted online. **Positions advertised include:** IT Security Engineer; Registered Nurse; Career Management Educator; Bus Driver. **Other U.S. locations:** SC; VA; FL; CO. **International locations:** Sweden.

KPMG CONSULTING
600 Fleet Center, 50 Kennedy Plaza, Providence RI 02903. 401/421-6600. **Contact:** Human Resources. **World Wide Web address:** http://www.kpmg.com. **Description:** KPMG delivers a wide range of value-added assurance, tax, and consulting services. **NOTE:** Entry-level positions available. **Special programs:** Internships offered in Audit, Tax, and Risk Advisory Services. **Corporate headquarters location:** Montvale NJ. **Other U.S. locations:** Nationwide. **Parent company:** KPMG International is a leader among professional services firms engaged in capturing, managing, assessing, and delivering information to create knowledge that will help its clients maximize shareholder value. KPMG International has more than 85,000 employees worldwide including 6,500 partners and 60,000 professional staff, serving clients in 844 cities in 155 countries.

KENNEY MANUFACTURING COMPANY
1000 Jefferson Boulevard, Warwick RI 02886. 401/739-2200. **Toll-free phone:** 800/753-6639. **Fax:** 401/736-1822. **Contact:** Human Resources. **E-mail address:** info@kenney.com. **World Wide Web address:** http://www.kenney.com. **Description:** Manufactures window dressings and accessories including venetian blinds and a variety of drapery items. **Positions advertised include:** Quality Assurance Engineer; Product Manager. **Corporate headquarters location:** This location.

KENT HOSPITAL
455 Tollgate Road, Warwick RI 02886. 401/736-4290. **Fax:** 401/736-1030. **Contact:** Human Resources. **World Wide Web address:** http://www.kenthospital.org. **Description:** A 395-bed, nonprofit, acute care hospital offering a comprehensive range of inpatient and outpatient services. The second largest single-site hospital in the state. **NOTE:** Applications are accepted by mail, fax, or online. **Position advertised include:** Administrative Assistant; Certified Nursing Assistant; Clinical Pharmacist; Dietary Aide; File Clerk; Hospitality Associate; Mammography Technician; Physical Therapist; Primary Care Physician; Receptionist; Security Officer; Unit Secretary.

KVH INDUSTRIES, INC
50 Enterprise Drive, Middletown RI 02842. 401/847-3327. **Fax:** 401/849-0045. **Contact:** Human Resources. **E-mail address:** resumes@kvh.com. **World Wide Web address:** http://www.kvh.com. **Description:** Develops and manufactures mobile and high bandwith satellite communications systems, tactical navigation products and fiber optic products. **Positions advertised include:** Embedded Software Engineer; Customer Service Technician; Antenna Design Engineer; Contracts Administrator. **CEO:** Martin A. Kits van Heyningen.

LANDMARK MEDICAL CENTER
115 Cass Avenue, P.O. Box L, Woonsocket RI 02895. 401/769-4100. **Recorded jobline:** 877/733-8383. **Contact:** Human Resources. **World Wide Web address:** http://www.landmarkmedical.org. **Description:** A 214-bed acute care hospital with 24-hour emergency services, as well as diagnostic, surgical, psychiatric, pediatric, and obstetric care. **NOTE:** Human Resources phone extension is 2041. **Positions advertised include:** Buyer; Director of Radiology Services; Medical Record Coder; Pharmacist; Registered Nurse. **Special programs:** Internships, Volunteering Opportunities. **Other area locations:** North Smithfield RI. **Operations at this facility include:** Administration; Emergency Care. **President:** Gary J. Gaube. **Number of employees at this location:** 1,100.

LEVITON MANUFACTURING COMPANY
745 Jefferson Boulevard, Warwick RI 02886. 401/737-4500. **Fax:** 401/736-1457. **Contact:** Manuel Resendes, Director of Human Resources. **E-mail address:** careers@leviton.com. **World Wide Web address:** http://www.leviton.com. **Description:** Manufactures electrical wiring devices. **Corporate headquarters location:** Little Neck NY. **Operations at this facility include:** Manufacturing. **President and CEO:** Harold Leviton. **Number of employees at this location:** 1,030.

LIN TELEVISION CORPORATION
Four Richmond Square, Providence RI 02906. 401/454-2880. **Fax:** 401/454-2817**Contact:** Human Resources. **World Wide Web address:** http://www.lintv.com. **Description:** Owns and operates seven network-affiliated television stations, two low-power television networks, and two-low power television stations. The company also provides programming and advertising services to four television stations through local

marketing agreements. The seven affiliated stations include WISH-TV (Indianapolis IN); WANE-TV (Fort Wayne IN); WAVY-TV (Portsmouth/Norfolk VA); WTNH-TV (New Haven/Hartford CT); KXAN-TV (Austin TX); KXAS-TV (Dallas/Fort Worth TX); and WAND-TV (Decatur/Champaign IL). **Other U.S. locations:** Washington DC.

M&F CASE INTERNATIONAL, INC.
717 School Street, Pawtucket RI 02860. 401/722-4830. **Fax:** 401/725-8652. **Contact:** Human Resources. **Description:** Manufactures custom loose-leaf binders and indexes. The company also provides screen process printing and decals. **Corporate headquarters location:** This location. **Listed on:** American Stock Exchange; New York Stock Exchange.

MAHR FEDERAL INC.
1144 Eddy Street, Providence RI 02905. **Toll-free phone:** 800/FED-GAGE (in U.S. only). **Fax:** 401/784-3414. **Contact:** Kim Kimball, Human Resource Specialist. **E-mail address:** kkimball@fedprod.com. **World Wide Web address:** http://www.mahrfederal.com. **Description:** Produces spinning pumps used in the production of textile threads, rotary stroke bearings, and measurement instruments. Products are used by machine tool builders; precision mechanical equipment manufacturers; and the automotive, plastics, and textile industries. **Corporate headquarters location**: This location. **Other U.S. locations:** Cincinnati OH; Cypress CA.

MEMORIAL HOSPITAL
111 Brewster Street, Pawtucket RI 02860. 401/729-2000. **Fax:** 401/729-3054. **Recorded jobline:** 401/729-2562. **Contact:** Human Resources. **World Wide Web address:** http://www.mhri.org. **Description:** A nonprofit hospital that offers a variety of services including adult day care, a birthing center, cardiology, home care, pediatric, primary care, neurology, radiology, and rehabilitation. **NOTE:** Entry-level positions, part-time jobs, and second and third shifts are offered. **Positions advertised include:** Receptionist; Nursing Assistant; Unit Secretary; Registered Nurse; Echocardiogram Technician; Physical Therapist; Registered Technologist; Respiratory Care Practitioner; Administrative Coordinator; Biller; Lab Assistant; Account Representative. **Special programs:** Internships; Training. **Office hours:** Monday – Friday, 8:30 a.m. – 5:00 p.m. **Corporate headquarters location:** This location. **President:** Francis R. Dietz.

MERCURY PRINT & MAIL
1110 Central Avenue, Pawtucket RI 02861. 401/724-7600. **Fax:** 401/724-9920. **Contact:** Human Resources. **E-mail address:** info@mpmri.com. **World Wide Web address:** http://www.mpmri.com. **Description:** Provides printing and direct mail advertising services. Founded in 1953. **Facilities Manager:** Dennis Dress. **Information Systems Manager:** Scott Machado. **Purchasing Manager:** Charlie Harrington. **Sales Manager:** Al Ervey.

METRO EAST
One Metro Park Drive, Cranston RI 02910. 401/461-2200. **Contact:** Human Resources. **World Wide Web address:** http://www.metroglobal.com. **Description:** A leader in the adult entertainment industry, with operations in four primary business segments: adult film video production and distribution, including pay-per-view and other cable programming; magazine publishing and distribution; retail store operation and franchising by its Airborne for Men, Ltd. subsidiary; and, through its Arcus Media Group, adult-oriented digital multimedia products such as Virtual Valerie 2 and CD-ROM versions of the company's film and video titles. The company owns distribution rights to more than 1,300 adult film titles, one of the largest libraries of its kind in the United States, and operates a regional distributorship for its own products as well as those of other adult entertainment companies. **Positions advertised include:** Receptionist; Construction Project Coordinator; Carpenter; Construction Assistant; Store Manager; Visual Merchandiser; Interim Store Manager. **Corporate headquarters location:** Chatsworth CA. **Subsidiaries include:** Metro International Distributors, Inc. **Parent company:** Metro Inc. **President:** Gregory N. Alves.

THE MIRIAM HOSPITAL
164 Summit Avenue, Providence RI 02906. 401/793-2500. **Recorded jobline:** 866/626-JOBS. **Contact:** Human Resources. **World Wide Web address:** http://www.lifespan.org/partners/tmh. **Description:** A private, non-profit, 247-bed acute care hospital founded in 1926 by Rhode Island's Jewish community. **NOTE:** Affiliated with Brown Medical School. **Positions advertised include:** Security Officer; Phlebotomist; Cardiac Physician Assistant; Cardiac Rehabilitation Program Manager; Teen Weight Loss Project Director; Intervention Coordinator; Research Nurse; Patient Registration Representative; Respiratory Therapist; Staff Nurse; Operating Room Assistant; Director of Surgical Business Affairs; Cook.

MORGAN STANLEY DEAN WITTER & COMPANY
1900 Financial Plaza, 19th Floor, Providence RI 02903. 401/863-8400. **Contact:** Human Resources. **World Wide Web address:** http://www.msdw.com. **Description:** Offers diversified financial services including equities, fixed income securities, commodities, money market instruments, and investment banking services.

NARRAGANSETT ELECTRIC COMPANY, INC.
P.O. Box 1438, 280 Melrose Street, Providence RI 02901. 401/784-7000. **Contact:** Human Resources. **World Wide Web address:** http://www.narragansett.com. **Description:** An electric utility company. **NOTE:** Resumes are only accepted for advertised openings and should be sent to Human Resources, 25 Research Drive, Westborough MA 01582. **Parent company:** National Grid.

NARRAGANSETT IMAGING
P.O. Box 278, Slatersville RI 02876. 401/762-3800. **Fax:** 401/747-4405. **Contact:** Claire Mundy, Human Resources. **E-mail address:** Claire.mundy@nimaging.com. **World Wide Web address:** http://www.nimaging.com. **Description:** This facility offers custom services for precision glass and metal technologies. The typical services available are glass fabrication, precision assembly of metal parts, metal evaporation, cleaning and packaging, and encapsulation. Manufacturing, assembly, and engineering operations are performed in 25,000 square feet of Class 100 and Class 10,000 clean room areas. In addition to the manufacturing and assembly areas, the support areas include a chemical processing area, chemical laboratory, glass grinding area, electronics laboratory, incoming quality control, factory quality control, applications laboratory, and a full machine shop for manufacturing and testing. Overall, Narragansett Imaging manufactures electronic components for industrial, telecommunications, and computer companies.

NEPTCO, INC.
30 Hamlet Street, P.O. Box 2323, Pawtucket RI 02861. 401/722-5500. **Toll-free phone:** 800/354-5445. **Fax:** 401/722-6378. **Contact:** Human Resources. **World Wide Web address:** http://www.neptco.com. **Description:** Designs, manufactures, and supplies laminated flexible products, composite materials, and outside plant products for use in a variety of applications. These materials include advanced polymeric coatings and laminates for films, foils, fibers, composites, papers, nonwovens, and custom-formulated adhesives. Founded in 1953. **Corporate headquarters location:** This location.

NEW ENGLAND GAS COMPANY
100 Weybosset Street, Providence RI 02903. 401/272-5040. **Contact:** Human Resources. **World Wide Web address:** http://www.negasco.com. **Description:** A utilities holding company. **NOTE:** Resumes accepted for advertised positions only, check local classifieds. **Other area locations:** P.O. Box 7900, Cumberland RI 02864. 401/334-1188. **Corporate headquarters location:** This location. **Parent company:** Southern Union Company. **Listed on:** New York Stock Exchange. **Stock exchange symbol:** SUG.

NEW ENGLAND INSTITUTE OF TECHNOLOGY (NEW ENGLAND TECH)
2500 Post Road, Warwick RI 02886. 401/467-7744. **Toll-free phone:** 800/736-7744. **Contact:** Human Resources. **World Wide Web address:** http://www.neit.edu. **Description:** A technical school offering associate's degrees (18 months or more) and bachelor's degrees (three years or more) in a wide variety of fields including applied technical studies, architectural/building engineering, architectural drafting, auto body technology, automotive/marine technology, building construction, business management, CAD, computer information systems, computer/network servicing, computerized business management, electronics, heating, interior design, Internet communications, manufacturing engineering, marine technology, mechanical design, medical administration, multimedia, occupational therapy, plumbing, refrigeration/air conditioning, surgical technology, telecommunications, and video/radio production. New England Institute of Technology's career services office is available to graduates for the duration of their careers.

NEWPORT HOSPITAL
11 Friendship Street, Newport RI 02840. 401/845-1302. **Contact:** Victoria Williams, Human Resources Representative. **World Wide Web address:** http://www.newporthospital.org. **Description:** A private, nonprofit, general hospital with 200 beds. The hospital is licensed by the state Department of Health, and accredited by the Joint Commission on Accreditation of Healthcare Organizations and the Commission on Accreditation of Rehabilitation Facilities. Newport Hospital participates in cooperative programs with colleges and universities for the education of nurses, X-ray technicians, physical therapists, and other allied health care personnel. Founded in 1873. **NOTE:** Second and third shifts are offered. **Positions advertised include:** Medical Assistant; Clinical Nurse; Nursing Assistant; Mental Health Aide; Dietary Aide; Medical Legal Coordinator; Pharmacist; Surgical Technologist; Cardiac Sonographer; Plant Manager; Case Manager; Speech Pathologist; Switchboard Receptionist. **Special programs:** Internships. **Corporate headquarters location:** This location. **Parent company:** Newport Healthcare Corporation (NHCC). **Listed on:** Privately held. **Number of employees at this location:** 850.

NORTEK, INC.
50 Kennedy Plaza, Providence RI 02903. 401/751-1600. **Fax:** 401/751-4724. **Contact:** Jane White, Director of Human Resources. **World Wide Web address:** http://www.nortek-inc.com. **Description:** A diversified manufacturer of residential and commercial building products operating within three principal product groups: Residential Building Products; Air Conditioning and Heating Products; and Plumbing Products. Through these groups, the company manufactures and sells products for the residential and commercial construction, manufactured housing, and the do-it-yourself and professional remodeling and renovation markets primarily in the United States and Canada. Products include furnaces, ventilation systems, cabinets, security products, garage door openers, heat pumps, and energy management systems under the brand names Braun, Nautilus, and Air Care. Plumbing products include faucets, fixtures, vanities, spas, whirlpools, shower components, tubs, and other accessories. Established in 1967. **Corporate headquarters location:** This location. **Listed on:** New York Stock Exchange. **Stock exchange symbol:** NTK. **CEO:** Richard Bready.

NORTHROP GRUMMAN.
Metro Center Boulevard, Suite 104, Warwick RI 02886. 401/732-9000. **Fax:** 401/732-9009. **Contact:** Human Resources. **World Wide Web address:** http://www.northropgrumman.com. **Description:** Engaged in the research, development, and engineering of materials, products, and processes and offers metallurgical and chemical services. Other divisions of TRW produce electronics and space systems, car and truck equipment for both original equipment manufacturers and the replacement market, and a wide variety of industrial and energy components including aircraft parts, welding systems, and electromechanical assemblies. **NOTE:** Send resumes to 12011 Sunset Hills Road, Reston VA 20190. **Positions advertised include:** Systems Programmer; Systems Administrator; Software Engineer.

NORTH SAFETY PRODUCTS
2000 Plainfield Pike, Cranston RI 02921. 401/943-4400. **Fax:** 401/943-7974. **Contact:** Human Resources. **E-mail address:** humanresources@northsafety.com. **World Wide Web address:** http://www.northsafety.com. **Description:** Manufactures a variety of safety equipment pieces including protective eyewear, ear plugs and hearing protectors, hard hats, and respiratory equipment. The company also operates a hand protection division, which manufactures a wide array of gloves, and a health care division, which produces emergency burn kits and first aid supplies. **Other U.S. locations:** Charleston SC; Stokie IL; Tallmadge IL; Clover SC; Maiden NC. **Parent Company:** Norcross Safety Products.

ON SEMICONDUCTOR CORPORATION
2000 South County Trail, East Greenwich RI 02818. 401/885-3600. **Fax:** 401/886-3954. **Contact:** Karen Gales, Staffing Manager. **E-mail address:** karen.gales@onsemi.com. **World Wide Web address:** http://www.onsemi.com. **Description:** Manufactures linear integrated circuits for use in automotive, computer, and industrial control equipment. **Positions advertised include:** Design Engineer; Device Engineer; Maintenance Technician; Process Engineer. **Corporate headquarters location:** Phoenix, AZ. **Listed on:** NASDAQ. **Stock exchange symbol:** ONNN.

PERKINELMER
15 Pioneer Avenue, Warwick RI 02888. 401/781-4700. **Contact:** Human Resources Manager. **E-mail address:** hrwarwick@perkinelmer.com. **World Wide Web address:** http://www.perkinelmer.com. **Description:** Manufactures mechanical seals and welded metal bellows for aerospace, defense, and commercial applications. PerkinElmer operates through four separate business units. The Instruments Unit designs and manufactures products for detecting, measuring, and testing purposes, and markets them to the pharmaceuticals, food, chemical, plastics, and environmental industries. The Life Sciences Unit designs and manufactures bioanalytic and diagnostic instrument systems and markets them to medical research facilities, hospitals, and clinics. The Fluid Sciences Unit manufactures sealing systems, advanced pneumatic components, and static and dynamic valves for use by OEMs and end users. The Optoelectronics Unit produces silicon-based sensor products, imaging technology, and a range of light

sources. **Positions advertised include:** Design Engineer; Process Development Engineer. **Corporate headquarters location:** Boston MA.

PROVIDENCE COLLEGE
549 River Avenue, Providence RI 02918. 401/865-1000. **Contact:** Kathleen Alvino, Director of Human Resources. **E-mail address:** hr@providence.edu. **World Wide Web address:** http://www.providence.edu. **Description:** The only college in the United States under the stewardship of the Dominican Friars. The college offers bachelor's, master's, and doctoral degrees in arts and sciences. The curriculum includes 36 academic majors and 23 minors and has strong pre-law and pre-med advisement. Host to 3,600 undergraduates, the college is located on a 105-acre campus. The college faculty is comprised of 312 members, offering a student/faculty ratio of 14 to 1. The school has more than 80 student clubs and is accredited by the New England Association of Schools and Colleges. Founded in 1917. **Positions advertised include:** Director of Major Gifts; Assistant Director, Office of Institutional Advancement; Part-Time Staff Counselor; Security Officer.

PROVIDENCE FINANCIAL NETWORK
1 Richmond Square, 1st Floor Suite 330-D, Providence RI 02906. 888/359-8260. **Fax:** 206/495-6504. **Contact:** Vicki Moore. **E-mail address:** vmoore@pnfdirect.com. **World Wide Web address:** http://www.pfndirect.com. **Description:** Provides financial services in the residential and business sectors. **Positions advertised include:** Executive Assistant; Writer/Assistant Editor; Liquidation Services executive/consultant; Sales Associate; Multimedia Specialist. **Corporate headquarters location:** This location.

THE PROVIDENCE JOURNAL COMPANY
75 Fountain Street, Providence RI 02902-9985. 401/277-7000. **Contact:** Human Resources. **World Wide Web address:** http://www.projo.com. **Description:** Publishes *The Providence Journal* with a daily circulation of 175,000 and *The Sunday Providence Journal* with a circulation of 250,000. **Special programs:** Internships. **Subsidiaries include:** *Rhode Island Monthly*. **Parent company:** Belo Corporation. **Number of employees at this location:** 1,500.

REHABILITATION HOSPITAL OF RHODE ISLAND
116 Eddie Dowling Highway, North Smithfield RI 02896. 401/766-0800. **Fax:** 401/766-5037. **Contact:** Michelle Vaillancourt, Human Resources. **E-mail address:** humanresources@rhri.net. **World Wide Web address:** http://www.rhri.net. **Description:** A joint venture between Braintree Hospital Rehabilitation Network and Landmark Medical Center, the hospital is an 82-bed, fully-accredited rehabilitation facility. Rehabilitation Hospital of Rhode Island's programs include behavioral neurology, amputee, spinal cord injury, burn recovery, oncology, pulmonary, arthritis, orthopedic, and multisystem failure rehabilitation. **Positions advertised include:** Nursing Coordinator; Inpatient Physical Therapist; Registered Nurse; CNA; LPN; Occupational Therapist.

RHODE ISLAND COALITION AGAINST DOMESTIC VIOLENCE
422 Post Road, Suite 202, Warwick RI 02888-1524. 401/467-9940. **Fax:** 401/467-9943. **Contact:** Deborah DeBare, Executive Director. **E-mail address:** ricadv@ricadv.org. **World Wide Web address:** http://www.ricadv.org. **Description:** A nonprofit public education and advocacy organization and a coalition of direct service programs, offering services to battered women and their children. Activities of the coalition include public education and advocacy; technical assistance to member groups, information and technical assistance to public agencies and legislative committees, and professional training for law enforcement and human service workers. In addition, the coalition staff prepares policy statements and offers assistance and expertise in the preparation of protocols and practices for a wide variety of public and private companies. Incorporated in 1979. **Corporate headquarters location:** Denver CO. **Parent company:** National Coalition Against Domestic Violence.

RHODE ISLAND COLLEGE
600 Mount Pleasant Avenue, Providence RI 02908. 401/456-8216. **Fax:** 401/456-8217. **Contact:** Robert G. Tetreault, Office of Human Resources. **E-mail address:** rtetreault@ric.edu. **World Wide Web address:** http://www.ric.edu. **Description:** A four-year college. **Positions advertised include:** Associate Professor, School of Social Work; Senior Programmer Consultant; Supervising Word Processing Typist; Substitute Teacher.

RHODE ISLAND DEPARTMENT OF MENTAL HEALTH, RETARDATION & HOSPITALS
Office of Operations, 14 Harrington Road, Cranston RI 02920. 401/462-3405. **Contact:** Gail Krikorian, Human Resources. **E-mail address:** gkrikorian@mhrh.state.ri.us. **World Wide Web address:** http://www.mhrh.state.ri.us. **Description:** Provides services for more than 26,000 state residents who have a disability that limits independence. The individuals who receive services from this state agency may need short-term treatment for episodes of depression, anxiety, substance abuse, stress related problems, or treatment for more serious and persistent mental illness. Other clients and consumers of the department's service delivery system have developmental disabilities associated with cognitive functions or disabling conditions including autism, epilepsy, or cerebral palsy. In addition, the department's hospital-level services provide special expertise in caring for persons with long-term mental illness, coma, cancer, AIDS, neurological disorders, as well as debilitating conditions due to aging.

RHODE ISLAND HOSPITAL
593 Eddy Street, Providence RI 02903. 401/444-4000. **Recorded jobline:** 866/626-JOBS. **Contact:** Human Resources. **World Wide Web address:** http://www.lifespan.org/partners/rih. **Description:** Rhode Island's largest private, non-profit, acute-care hospital, providing comprehensive inpatient and outpatient services. Rhode Island Hospital also serves as Southeastern New England's only Level One Trauma Center. Rhode Island Hospital's pediatric division, Hasbro Children's Hospital, is world renowned for its level of care and family-friendly environment. Built in 1994, Hasbro Children's Hospital is a seven-story building that is adjacent to Rhode Island Hospital. Hasbro houses the states only pediatric intensive care unit, as well as separate surgical and emergency units for pediatric patients. **NOTE:** Per-Diem and Part-Time positions, as well as second and third shifts are available. **Positions advertised include:** Assistant Clinical Manager; Child Life Assistant; Clinical Research Assistant; CT Scan Technologist; Emergency Department Billing Clerk; Interpreter; MRI Technologist; Nurse Practitioner; Outpatient Services Representative; Pathology Technologist; Pharmacist; Professional Nurse; Radiation Therapist; Radiologic Technologist; Research Fellow; Social Worker; Secretary; Speech Pathologist; Washroom Attendant; Cafeteria Assistant. **President:** Joseph Amaral, MD.

RHODE ISLAND MEDICAL IMAGING
20 Catamore Boulevard, East Providence RI 02914. 401/432-2520. **Fax:** 401/432-2412. **Contact:** Susan Logan. **E-mail address:** slogan@rimirad.com. **World Wide Web address:** http://www.rimirad.com. **Description:** Provides diagnostic imagery health care services. **Positions advertised include:** Radiologic Technologist Assistant; Property Superintendent; Patient Scheduler; X-ray/mammography Technologist. **Other area locations:** Pawtucket RI.

RHODE ISLAND SCHOOL OF DESIGN
2 College Street, Providence RI 02903-2784. 401/454-6100. **Recorded jobline:** 888/816-7473. **Fax:** 401/454-6565. **Contact:** Human Resources. **World Wide Web address:** http://www.risd.edu. **Description:** One of the preeminent art and design colleges in the United States. Rhode Island School of Design enrolls 1,840 undergraduates and 140 graduate students from the United States and more than 50 other countries. Courses of study include: apparel design, architecture, art education, ceramics, film/video, furniture design, glass, graphic design, illustration, industrial design, interior architecture, painting, photography, printmaking, sculpture, and textiles. **Positions advertised include:** Readers Services Librarian; Facilities Custodian; Technical Assistant; Museum Security Guard.

ROGER WILLIAMS MEDICAL CENTER
825 Chalkstone Avenue, Providence RI 02908-4735. 401/456-2000. **Recorded jobline:** 401/456-2689. **Contact:** Human Resources. **World Wide Web address:** http://www.rwmc.com. **Description:** Roger Williams Medical Center is a major medical complex that provides advanced diagnostic, treatment, education, and support services. The hospital provides treatment for a wide range of medical and surgical conditions as well as advanced cancer care, including the state's only bone marrow transplant unit. The facility also offers diagnostic and imaging services and houses an alcohol and substance abuse treatment center. The center's Elmhurst Extended Care offers rehabilitative, respite, and long-term nursing care, and the Home Care Department serves hundreds of patients across the state each day. Roger Williams Medical Center is also a major teaching and research facility affiliated with Boston University School of Medicine. **Positions advertised include:** Benefits Analyst; Clinical Leader, Emergency; Clinical Manager, Behavioral Medicine; Emergency Medical Technician; Clinical Nurse Specialist; Nuclear Medicine Technologist; Research Assistant; Speech Pathologist; Occupational Therapist; Stress Test Physiologist; Foodservice Worker; Senior Animal Care Technician; Transcriptionist; Registered Nurse.

ROGER WILLIAMS PARK ZOO
1000 Elmwood Avenue, Providence RI 02907. 401/785-3510. **Fax:** 401/941-3988. **Contact:** Rob Upham, Human Resources. **World Wide Web address:** http://www.rogerwilliamsparkzoo.org. **Description:** Features exhibits and educational programs designed to promote a better understanding of how different types of animals function in their individual habitats. The park also has a working carousel and hosts a number of musical and recreational events throughout the year. **Positions advertised include:** Data Entry Clerk.

ROGER WILLIAMS UNIVERSITY
One Old Ferry Road, Bristol RI 02809. 401/254-3028. **Fax:** 401/254-3370. **Contact:** Human Resources. **E-mail address:** human_resources@rwu.edu. **World Wide Web address:** http://www.rwu.edu. **Description:** An independent, coeducational university of liberal arts and selected professional programs accredited by the New England Association of Schools and Colleges. It enrolls approximately 3,800 students in 31 majors, instructed by 300 full-time and adjunct faculty in a primarily residential campus setting. The academic programs of the university are structured within two colleges and four schools, which combine traditional liberal arts education with professional training. The Schools of Architecture, Business, and Engineering comprise the three undergraduate professional schools. The undergraduate liberal arts component of the university is offered through the College of Arts and Sciences, which includes the areas of fine and performing arts, humanities, science and math, and social sciences. The university also has a school of law. **Positions advertised include:** Public Services Librarian; Web and Electronic Communication Coordinator; Student Services Systems Coordinator; Government Documents Assistant; Assistant Director, Multicultural Center; Employment and Training Coordinator; Human Resources Generalist; Coordinator of Residence Education; Development Officer; Financial Aid Counselor; Vice President of University Advancement.

SAIC ENTERPRISE SOLUTIONS
28 Jacome Way, Middleton RI 02840. 401/849-8900. **Fax:** 401/848-0638. **Contact:** Human Resources. **World Wide Web address:** http://www.saic.com. **Description:** Develops software for local and state governments. Products are used to automate court systems. **Positions advertised include:** Software Engineer, Business Process Consultant, Financial Analyst. **Corporate headquarters location:** San Diego CA. **Other area locations:** Newport RI. **Other U.S. locations:** Nationwide. **International locations:** Worldwide

ST. JOSEPH HOSPITAL
21 Peace Street, Providence RI 02907. 401/456-3200. **Fax:** 401/456-4167. **Contact:** Human Resources. **World Wide Web address:** http://www.saintjosephri.com. **Description:** A specialty hospital focusing on rehabilitation, psychiatric services, and clinic/urgent care services. Founded in 1892. **Positions advertised include:** Bilingual Receptionist; Clinical Coordinator, Psychiatry; Concurrent Review Analyst; Cooks Helper; Environmental Services Aide; Laboratory Assistant; Massage Therapist; Patient Transporter; Phlebotomist; Registered Nurse, Psychiatry; Secretary.

SALVE REGINA UNIVERSITY
100 Ochre Point Avenue, Newport RI 02840-4192. 401/847-6650. **Fax:** 401/341-2921. **Contact:** Diane Blanchette, Director of Human Resources. **E-mail address:** resumes@salve.edu. **World Wide Web address:** http://www.salve.edu. **Description:** A coeducational university of arts and sciences founded by the Sisters of Mercy with an enrollment of more than 2,200. The university offers more than 40 concentrations leading to associate's and bachelor's degrees and offers master's degrees in 15 majors. Six fields of study are also available for the university's five-year plan, which allows students to graduate in five academic years with both a bachelor's and master's degree. **Positions advertised include:** Training and Special Events Manager; Executive Director, Pell Center for International Relations and Public Policy; Information Security Advisor.

SAMSONITE/AMERICAN TOURISTER
91 Main Street, Warren RI 02885. 401/245-2100. **Contact:** David Pacheco, Director of Human Resources. **World Wide Web address:** http://www.samsonite.com. **Description:** Manufactures luggage. **Operations at this location include:** Retail.

T. SARDELLI & SONS, INC.
195 Dupont Drive, Providence RI 02907-3105. 401/944-8510. **Toll free phone:** 800/347-4641. **Contact:** Human Resources. **World Wide Web address:** http://www.sarde.com. **Description:** One of the largest manufacturers of precious metal earrings in the United States. Product materials include gold, semiprecious, and precious stones. **Special programs:** Internships. **Corporate headquarters location:** This location. **Listed on:** Privately held. **Number of employees at this location:** 250.

SEA CORP
62 Johnny Cake Hill, Middletown RI 02842. 401/847-2260. **Fax:** 401/841-5860. **E-mail address:** hr@seacorp.com. **Contact:** Human Resources. **World Wide Web address:** http://www.seacorp.com. **Description:** Provides systems integration and networking services under government contract. Founded in 1981. **Positions advertised include:** Ship Alteration Support Engineer; Programmer; Electrical Engineer; Computer Engineer.

STANLEY-BOSTITCH, INC.
Route 2, Briggs Drive, East Greenwich RI 02818. 401/884-2500. **Toll-free phone:** 800/556-6696. **Contact:** Human Resources Department. **World Wide Web address:** http://www.stanleyworks.com. **Description:** Manufactures fastening products for industrial and construction users. Established in 1896. **Positions advertised include:** Employment Manager. **Parent Company:** The Stanley Works. **CEO:** John M. Trani.

STERALOIDS, INC.
P.O. Box 689, Newport RI 02840-0689. 401/848-5422. **Fax:** 401/848-5638. **Contact:** Human Resources. **World Wide Web address:** http://www.steraloids.com. **Description:** Engaged in the supply of hormones and steroids to scientists and researchers.

TEKNOR APEX COMPANY
505 Central Avenue, Pawtucket RI 02861. 401/725-8000. **Toll-free phone:** 800/556-3864. **Fax:** 401/726-0341. **Contact:** Human Resources. **World Wide Web address:** http://www.teknorapex.com. **Description:** Manufactures custom-compounded PVC (thermoplastic), color concentrates, pre-cured tread rubber, custom rubber compounds, garden hoses, and rubber mats. Founded in 1924. **Positions advertised include:** Export Analyst; Development Chemist. **Corporate headquarters location:** This location. **Other area locations:** Cumberland RI. **Other U.S. locations:** CA; MA; SC; TN; TX; KY; OH; VT. **Operations at this facility include:** Headquarters and Manufacturing. **Listed on:** Privately held. **Number of employees at this location:** 650. **Number of employees nationwide:** 2,400.

TEXTRON INC.
40 Westminster Street, Providence RI 02903-2596. 401/421-2800. **Fax:** 401/457-3599. **Recorded jobline:** 877/483-9876. **Contact:** Human Resources. **E-mail address:** jobs@textron.com. **World Wide Web address:** http://www.textron.com. **Description:** A diversified conglomerate with over 30 separate companies in four primary areas: Aerospace and Defense Technology; Financial Services; Industrial; and Automotive. Founded in 1923. **NOTE:** The recruitment function is decentralized. Send resume to department of interest within company. Entry-level positions are offered. **Positions advertised include:** Federal Tax Accountant; Senior Corporate Financial Analyst; Staff Accountant. **Special programs:** Internships; Training; Co-ops; Summer Jobs. **Office hours:** Monday - Friday, 8:30 a.m. - 5:00 p.m. **Corporate headquarters location:** This location. **Other U.S. locations:** Nationwide. **International locations:** Worldwide. **Subsidiaries include:** Bell Helicopter; Cessna Aircraft Company. **Listed on:** New York Stock Exchange. **Stock exchange symbol:** TXT. **Chairman/CEO:** Lewis Campbell. **Annual sales/revenues:** More than $100 million. **Number of employees at this location:** 400. **Number of employees worldwide:** 68,000.

TORAY PLASTICS AMERICA
50 Belver Avenue, North Kingstown RI 02852. 401/294-4511. **Fax:** 401/294-2154. **Contact:** Kristin Wilson, Human Resources. **World Wide Web address:** http://www.toray.com. **Description:** A leading developer of oriented polypropylene and polyester film products and technology. Products are used in food packaging and magnetic tape manufacturing. An affiliate of Toray Industries, Inc., Toray Plastics is part of a corporate structure that encompasses textiles, biotechnology, medicine, specialty fibers, and office equipment, in addition to plastics and chemicals. More than 15 percent of Toray Industries' total work force is dedicated exclusively to research and development. **Corporate headquarters location:** New York, New York. **Other U.S. locations:** Nationwide.

UNCAS MANUFACTURING COMPANY
150 Niantic Avenue, Providence RI 02907. 401/944-4700. **Contact:** Human Resources. **Description:** Manufactures costume jewelry, primarily rings made from semi-precious metals. The company also designs pendants, chains, and other pieces of jewelry.

UNIVERSITY OF RHODE ISLAND
80 Lower College Road, Kingston RI 02881. 401/874-2416. **Fax:** 401/874-5530. **Recorded jobline:** 401/874-7117. **Contact:** Human Resources. **E-mail address:** humanres@etal.uri.edu. **World Wide Web address:** http://www.uri.edu. **Description:** A public university with an enrollment of over 10,000 undergraduates and over 3,000 graduate students. URI offers undergraduate and graduate programs in the Liberal Arts and Sciences as well as focus programs in areas such as: marine and environmental studies; health; children, families, and communities; and enterprise and advanced technology. **NOTE:** Applicants for academic and professional positions should consult website for individual contacts and requirements. **Positions advertised include:** Assistant Professor, Psychology; Research Fellow, various disciplines; Research Associate; Information Security Architect; Budget Specialist; Sports Information Coordinator; Campus Police Officer; Housekeeper; Principal Cook; Cook's Helper. **Special programs:** Tuition Waivers for employees, their spouses and dependents. **Office hours:** Monday – Friday, 8:30 a.m. – 4:30 p.m. **Other area locations:** Providence RI; West Greenwich RI. **President:** Robert L. Carothers.

WASHINGTON TRUST BANCORP, INC.
23 Broad Street, Westerly RI 02891. 401/348-1200. **Toll-free phone:** 800/475-2275. **Contact:** Betsy Flanagan, Assistant Vice-President. **E-mail address:** recruiter@washtrust.com. **World Wide Web address:** http://www.washtrust.com. **Description:** The holding company of The Washington Trust Company. **Positions advertised include:** Head Teller; Assistant Head Teller; Mortgage Originator; Senior Accountant; Merchant Sales Representative. **Subsidiaries include:** The Washington Trust Company. Founded in 1800. **Listed on:** NASDAQ. **Stock exchange symbol:** WASH. **Other U.S. locations:** CT.

WOLVERINE JOINING TECHNOLOGIES
235 Kilvert Street, Warwick RI 02886. 401/739-9550x103. **Toll-free phone:** 800/225-2130. **Fax:** 401/739-9555. **Contact:** Human Resources. **E-mail address:** brazeinfo@wlv.com. **World Wide Web address:** http://www.silvaloy.com. **Description:** Manufactures all forms of silver and copper phosphorous brazing alloys and solders, as well as the supplementary fluxes and a complete line of automated brazing and soldering equipment.

WOMEN & INFANTS HOSPITAL
45 Willard Street, Providence RI 02905. 401/274-1100. **Fax:** 401/453-7683. **Contact:** Human Resources Department. **E-mail address:** wihjobs@careen.org. **World Wide Web address:** http://www.womenandinfants.com. **Description:** One of southeastern New England's premier hospitals for the care of women and newborns. Founded in 1884. **NOTE:** Entry-level positions and second and third shifts are offered. Applications are accepted online, by fax, or by mail. **Positions advertised include:** Administrative Nursing Supervisor; Assistant Director of Engineering; Audiology Coordinator; Bilingual Certified Nurses Aide; Bilingual Financial Counselor; Business Office Representative; Phlebotomist; Clinical Nutrition Specialist; Clinical Social Worker; Core Laboratory Manager; Grant Accountant; Graphics Processor; Registered Nurse; Senior Secretary; Ultrasound Manager; Ultra-Sound Technologist; Watch Engineer.

X-RAY ASSOCIATES
6725 Post Road, North Kingstown RI 02852. 401/886-4830. **Fax:** 401/886-4533. **Contact:** Human Resources. **E-mail address:** hr@xrayassociates.com. **World Wide Web address:** http://www.xrayassociates.com. **Description:** Outpatient imaging center. **Positions advertised include:** Ultrasound Technologist; X-ray/mammography Technologist.

ABB POWER T&D COMPANY, INC.
P.O. Box 100524, Florence SC 29501-0524. 843/665-4144. **Physical address:** 2300 Mechanicsville Road, Florence SC 29501. **Contact:** Human Resources. **World Wide Web address:** http://www.abb.com/us. **Description:** Manufactures medium- and low-voltage circuit breakers and kirk lock (interlock) systems. **Corporate headquarters location:** Norwalk CT. **Other U.S. locations:** Nationwide. **Parent company:** ABB Group (Zurich, Switzerland). **Operations at this facility include:** Manufacturing; Research and Development; Sales. **Number of employees nationwide:** 10,000.

AVX CORPORATION
801 17th Avenue South, P.O. Box 867, Myrtle Beach SC 29578-0867. 843/448-9411. **Fax:** 843/448-7662. **Contact:** Dennis Overfield, Human Resources. **E-mail address:** doverfield@avxus.com. **World Wide Web address:** http://www.avxcorp.com. **Description:** A worldwide manufacturer and supplier of a broad line of passive electronic components and related products, operating 12 manufacturing facilities in 12 countries. Passive electronic components include ceramic and tantalum capacitors, both in leaded and surface-mount versions. AVX Corporation's customers include original equipment manufacturers in industries such as telecommunications, computers, automotive electronics, medical devices and instrumentation, industrial instrumentation, military and aerospace electronic systems, and consumer electronics. The company also manufactures and sells electronic connectors and distributes and sells certain components and connectors manufactured by its parent company. **Positions advertised include:** Internal Auditor; Compliance Manager. **Corporate headquarters location:** This location. **Other U.S. locations:** Nationwide. **International locations:** Northern Ireland; England; France; Israel. **Parent company:** Kyocera Corporation (Kyoto, Japan). **Listed on:** New York Stock Exchange. **Stock exchange symbol:** AVX. **Chairman:** Benedict P. (Dick) Rosen. **Annual sales/revenues:** $1.25 billion. **Number of employees:** 12,900.

ACTARIS METERING SYSTEMS
dba ACTARIS NEPTUNE DIVISION
1310 Emerald Road, Greenwood SC 29646. 864/223-1212. **Fax:** 864/942-2204. **Contact:** Joseph Askew, Human Resources. **E-mail address:** jaskew@greenwood.actaris.com. **World Wide Web address:** http://www.actaris.com. **Description:** Manufactures measurement equipment and systems for various energy applications, including petroleum meters, with 60 facilities in 30 countries. Founded in 1892. **NOTE:** Human Resources phone: 864/942-2274. **Positions advertised include:** Project Manager; Electrical Engineer; Mechanical Engineer. **Special programs:** Internships. **Annual sales/revenues:** $750 million. **Number of employees worldwide:** 7,000.

ACUMEN DESIGN AND CONSULTING
3620 Pelham Road, PMB 9, Greenville SC 29615. 864/331-2400. **Fax:** 864/271-9000. **Contact:** Human Resources. **E-mail address:** employment@acumendesign.net. **World Wide Web address:** http://www.acumendesign.net. **Description:** Provides IT solutions for medium and small businesses. **Positions advertised include:** Help Desk; Programmer. **Corporate headquarters location:** This location.

ADC ENGINEERING
1226 Yeamans Hall Road, Hanahan SC 29406. 843/566-0161. **Fax:** 843/566-0162. **Contact:** Rich Cook, Human Resources. **E-mail address:** email@adcengineering.com. **World Wide Web address:** http://www.adcengineering.com. **Description:** Full service structural engineering roofing, water proofing, consulting and landscaping company. **Positions advertised include:** Auto Cad Technician.

AGFIRST FARM CREDIT BANK
P.O. Box 1499, Columbia SC 29202. 803/799-5000. **Physical address:** 1401 Hampton Street, Columbia SC 29201. **Fax:** 803/771-0752. **Contact:** Recruiter. **E-mail address:** cmccroskey@agfirst.com. **World Wide Web address:** http://www.agfirst.com. **Description:** A cooperative set up by Congress in 1916 which acts as an agricultural lender to 80,000 farmers, ranchers, rural homeowners, and agribusinesses in 15 United States and Puerto Rico as well as offering crop, life, and timber insurance; equipment leasing; tax services; and record keeping. The company provides more than $10 billion in loans and originates real estate, operating, and home mortgages. Instead of accepting deposits, it funds activities by selling bonds and notes on capital markets. **NOTE:** Entry-level positions are offered. **Positions advertised include:** Lead Network Analyst; Customer Support Analyst; Special Events Assistant; Loan Officer; Accountant; Administrative Assistant; Systems Analyst. **Corporate headquarters location:** This location. **Other locations:** Nationwide. **Chairman:** F.A. (Andy) Lowrey. **Annual sales/revenues:** $754 million.

AIKEN STANDARD
P.O. Box 456, Aiken SC 29802. 803/648-2311. **Fax:** 803/648-6052. **Contact:** Judy Randall, Executive Secretary. **E-mail address:** editorial@duesouth.net. **World Wide Web address:** http://www.aikenstandard.com. **Description:** Publishes *Aiken Standard*, a daily newspaper with a circulation of 15,000. **Positions advertised include:** Lead Pressman; Press Operator; Circulation District Manager; Route Carrier; Route Driver. **Office hours:** Monday – Friday, 8:30 a.m. – 5:30 p.m. **Parent company:** Aiken Communications, Inc.

ALABAMA THEATRE
4750 Highway 17 South, North Myrtle Beach SC 29582. 843/272-5758. **Fax:** 843/272-1111. **Contact:** Talent Department. **E-mail address:** bradshaw@alabama-theatre. com. (for audition information). **World Wide Web address:** http://www.alabama-theatre.com. **Description:** A performing arts showcase featuring dance, comedy and country music performances. **Positions advertised include:** Singer; Dancer; Musician.

ALCOA (ALUMINUM COMPANY OF AMERICA)
3575 US Highway 52, P.O. Box 1000, Goose Creek SC 29445. 843/572-3700. **Fax:** 843/572-5297. **Contact:** Human Resources. **World Wide Web address:** http://www.alcoa.com. **Description:** Engaged in all aspects of the aluminum industry including mining, refining, smelting, fabricating, and recycling. ALCOA also manufactures ceramic packaging for the semiconductor industry, alumina chemicals, plastic bottle closures, vinyl siding, packaging machinery, and electrical distribution systems for automobiles. **NOTE:** Applications may be submitted at company website. **Positions advertised include:** Maintenance; Brick Mason; Mechanic; Machinist. **Corporate headquarters location:** Pittsburgh PA. **Other area locations:** Gaffney SC (Home Exteriors/Building Products); McBee SC (Southern Graphic Systems/Digital Services); Spartanburg SC (Alcoa Fujikura, Ltd/Telecommunications). **Other U.S. locations:** Nationwide. **International Locations:** Worldwide. **Subsidiaries include:** Alcoa Fujikura Ltd.; Howmet Castings; Integris Metals, Inc.; Ivex Packaging Corp. **Operations at this facility include:** The Mt. Holly Works in Goose Creek is a primary aluminum production facility and foundry producing billet, rolling slab, tee-pure/foundry, standard ingot-pure/foundry. **Listed on:** New York Stock Exchange. **Stock exchange symbol:** AA. **Chairman/President/CEO:** Alain J. P. Belda. **Annual sales/revenues:** $20.3 billion. **Number of employees worldwide:** 129,000.

AMERICAN FIBER & FINISHING
P.O. Box 379, Newberry SC 29108. 803/276-2843. **Physical address:** 2802 Fair Avenue, Newbury SC 29108. **Toll-free number:** 800/949-8203. **Fax:** 803/276-2324. **Contact:** Human Resources Manager. **E-mail address:** sales@affinc.com. **World Wide Web address:** http://www.affinc.com. **Description:** Manufactures cloth from cotton. The company wholesales this material to other companies that make finished apparel and textile products. Founded in 1986. **Corporate headquarters location:** Albemarle NC. **Operations at this facility include:** Greiger Cloth production.

AMERICAN GENERAL FINANCE
412 Bells Highway, Walterboro SC 29488. 843/549-5536. **Fax:** 843/549-6543. **Contact:** Human Resources. **World Wide Web address:** http://www.agfinance.com. **Description:** A large consumer lending company with over 1,300 branches nationwide. The company's subsidiaries are engaged in the consumer finance, credit card, and insurance businesses. Founded in 1920. **NOTE:** Jobseekers should send resumes to the corporate headquarters location at: 601 NorthWest Second Street, Evansville IN 47701. **Positions advertised include:** Management Trainee; Customer Account Administrator; Customer Account Specialist. **Corporate headquarters location:** Evansville IN. **Parent company:** American International Group, Inc. (New York NY).

AMERICAN INVESTMENT AND MANAGEMENT COMPANY (AIMCO)
P.O. Box 1089, Greenville SC 29602. 864/239-1000. **Physical address:** 55 Beattie Place, Third Floor, Greenville SC 29601. **Fax:** 864/239-5819. **Contact:** Martin Haider, Human Resources. **E-mail address:** martin.haider@aimco.com. **World Wide Web address:** http://www.aimco.com. **Description:** A real estate investment trust, management and mortgage banking company managing over 300,000 apartments nationwide. **NOTE:** Human Resources phone for corporate opportunities: 864/239-2678. For site opportunities fax Sherry Riddle: 864/239-0710 or e-mail: sherry.riddle@aimco.com. **Positions advertised include:** Reporting Accountant Associate; Real Estate Accountant; Payroll Processing Representative. **Corporate headquarters location:** Denver CO. **Other area locations:** Statewide. **Other U.S. locations:** Nationwide. **Subsidiaries include:** Amreal Corporation; Coventry Properties, Inc.; Dalcap Management, Inc.; First Piedmont Mortgage Company, Inc.; IFGP Corporation; Insignia Commercial Group, Inc.; Insignia Management Corporation; Shelter Realty Corporation. **Listed on:** New York Stock Exchange. **Stock exchange symbol:** AIV. **Annual sales/revenues:** $1.6 billion. **Number of employees nationwide:** 7,800.

THE AMERICAN RED CROSS BLOOD SERVICES
CAROLINAS BLOOD SERVICES REGION
2751 Bull Street, Columbia SC 29201 803/251-6000. **Fax:** 803/251-6191. **Recorded jobline:** 803/251-6035. **Contact:** Human Resources Manager. **World Wide Web address:** http://www.redcrossblood.org. **Description:** A nonprofit, blood collection and distribution organization serving over 100 hospitals and medical centers in an 82-county area covering North Carolina, parts of South Carolina, Georgia, and Tennessee distributing 1,500 blood products daily. **NOTE:** Entry-level positions, part-time jobs, and second and third shifts are offered. **Company slogan:** Together, We Can Save a Life. **Positions advertised include:** Collections Technicians Specialist; Lab Technician: Tele Recruiter. **Special programs:** Training. **Corporate headquarters location:** Charlotte NC. **Other U.S. locations:** Nationwide. **Parent company:** American Red Cross (Washington DC). **Operations at this facility include:** Central South Carolina Chapter. **Number of employees:** 1,050.

ANCHOR SIGN
P.O. Box 6009, Charleston SC 29405. 843/747-5901. **Toll-free phone:** 800/213-3331. **Fax:** 843/747-5807. **Contact:** Darrell Edwards, Human Resources. **E-mail address:** dedwards@anchorsign.com. **World Wide Web address:** http://www.anchorsign.com. **Description:** A sign making company specializing in business-to-business solutions. **Positions advertised include:** Accounts Payable Clerk.

ANDERSON AREA MEDICAL CENTER
800 North Fant Street, Anderson SC 29621. 864/261-1000. **Fax:** 864/261-1952. **Recorded jobline:** 800/423-2172. **Contact:** Human Resources. **E-mail address:** sblakene@anmed.com. **World Wide Web address:** http://www.anmed.com. **Description:** A 567-bed, acute care, regional medical center. **Positions advertised include:** Compliance Auditor; Counselor; Certified Registered Nursing Assistant; Nursing Director; Food Service Worker; Histotechnologist; Licensed Practical Nurse; Nurse Assistant; Office Clerk.

ANDERSON COUNTY SCHOOL DISTRICT 1
P.O. Box 99, Williamston SC 29697. 864/847-7344. **Fax:** 864/847-3543. **Contact:** Personnel. **E-mail address:** jobopportunities@.anderson1.k12.sc.us. **World Wide Web address:** http://www.anderson1.k12.sc.us. **Description:** Administrative offices for the public school district. **NOTE:** As of February 2003 there is a temporary hiring freeze due to state budget cuts and most positions are on hold. **Positions advertised include:** Elementary Education Director; Bus Driver Assistant; Custodian; School Nurse.

APAC-CAROLINA INC.
P.O. Box 521, Darlington SC 29540. 843/393-2837. **Contact:** Human Resources. **World Wide Web address:** http://www.apac.com. **E-mail address:** apac@Ashland.com. **Description:** The Apac group of construction companies operates in 14 Southern and Midwestern states providing highway construction, road paving, and bridge construction services. The companies operate 36 quarries, 61 production facilities, 67 ready-mix concrete plants, and 242 asphalt plants. **NOTE:** Human Resources extension: x3029. **Positions advertised include:** Dozer Operator; Grader Operator; Concrete Mixer Truck Driver. **Corporate headquarters location:** Kinston NC. **Other area locations:** Statewide. **Other U.S. locations:** AL; AR; FL; GA; KS; MS; NC; OK; TN; TX; VA; WV. **Parent company:** Ashland Inc. (Covington KY). **Operations at this facility include:** Coastal Carolina Division. **President:** Charles F. Potts. **Number of employees nationwide:** 11,000.

ARCADIA PUBLISHING
420 Wando Park Boulevard, Mount Pleasant SC 29464. 843/853-2070. **Fax:** 843/853-8044. **Contact:** Jane Elliot, Human Resources. **E-mail address:** jelliot@arcadiapublishing.com. **World Wide Web address:** http://www.arcadiapublishing.com. **Description:** The largest local and regional history publisher in the U.S. **Note:** Intern applications are always accepted. **Positions advertised include:** Marketing Manager. **Corporate headquarters location:** This location. **Other U.S. locations:** San Francisco CA; Chicago IL; Portsmouth NH.

BASF CORPORATION
440 Masters Boulevard, Anderson SC 29624. 864/332-1000 **Contact:** Human Resources. **World Wide Web address:** http://www.basf.com. **Description:** The company, the North American arm of the German chemical company BASF, manufactures and markets industrial chemicals, yarns, and man-made fibers through seven groups: Fine Chemicals/Pharmaceuticals; Agricultural Chemicals;

Biotechnology; Automotive and Coil Coatings; Chemicals; Plastics; and Fibers, and is the parent company's NAFTA region representative. Founded in 1968. **Corporate headquarters location:** Mount Olive NJ. **Other area locations:** Clemson SC; Whitestone SC. **Other U.S. locations:** Nationwide. **International locations:** Canada; Mexico. **Parent company:** BASF AG (Ludwigshafen, Germany). **Operations at this facility include:** Anderson Plant Production; Fiber Products Division Manufacturing. **Chairman:** Peter Oakley. **Number of employees at this location:** 1,200. **Number of employees in North America:** 14,600.

BECTON DICKINSON AND COMPANY (BD)
P.O. Box 2128, Sumter SC 29151-2128. 803/469-8010. **Contact:** Human Resources Department. **World Wide Web address:** http://www.bd.com. **Description:** A medical and pharmaceutical company engaged in the manufacture of health care products, medical instrumentation, a line of diagnostic products, and industrial safety equipment. Becton Dickinson's major product lines for medical equipment include hypodermics, intravenous equipment, operating room products, thermometers, gloves, and specialty needles. The company also offers contract packaging services. **NOTE:** Human Resources extension: x1610. **Positions advertised include:** Project Engineer; Product Development Engineer; Manufacturing Process Engineer; Equipment Technician; Electrical Engineer; Industrial Engineer; Mechanical Engineer; Operations Manager. **Special programs:** Internships; Coops. **Company Slogan:** Helping all people live healthy lives. **Corporate headquarters location:** Franklin Lakes NJ. **Other area locations:** Seneca SC. **Other U.S. locations:** Nationwide. **International locations:** Worldwide. **Operations at this facility include:** Manufacturing of blood collection supplies. **Listed on:** New York Stock Exchange. **Stock exchange symbol:** BDX. **Chairman/President/CEO:** Edward J. Ludwig. **Annual sales/revenues:** $4 billion. **Number of employees:** 25,250.

BMW MANUFACTURING CORPORATION
P.O. Box 11000, Spartanburg SC 29304. 864/968-6000. **Contact:** Human Resources. **World Wide Web address:** http://www.bmwusa.com. **Description:** As the only production facility in the U.S., BMW Manufacturing is responsible for production of all BMW roadsters, coupes, and X5 Sports Activity Vehicles. The company also operates a Visitor's Center with the BMW Zentrum Museum of BMW's engineering and manufacturing. Since 1993. **NOTE:** Resumes, along with salary history and a job reference code, may be sent to the parent company's address: BMW of North America, LLC, P.O. Box 964, Hewitt NJ 07461. E-mail address (with the word 'resume' in the subject field): bmwna@hreasy.com. **Positions advertised include:** Inventory Accuracy Analyst; Operations Manager; Mechanical Engineer; Field Service Manager. **Other area locations:** Greer SC. **U.S. locations:** Houston TX. **Parent company:** BMW of North America, LLC (Woodcliff Lake NJ); Bayerische Motoren Werke AG (Munich, Germany). **Operations at this facility include:** Spartanburg Factory (X5 and Z3 model production; Zentrum Museum. **Number of employees at this location:** 4,300.

BABIES 'R US
605 Haywood Road, Greenville SC 29607. 864/297-9444. **Contact:** Human Resources. **E-mail address:** bruregion3@toysrus.com. **World Wide Web address:** http://www5.toysrus.com/our/bru. **Description:** A retailer of baby and young children's products including infant and toddler apparel, furniture, and feeding supplies at over 165 stores nationwide. Founded in 1996. **NOTE:** Resumes are requested to be sent by e-mail. **Positions advertised include:** Assistant Manager; Cashier; Management; Sales Executive; Services Sales Representative; Stock Clerk. **Other area locations:** Augusta SC; Columbia SC; Greenville SC; North Charleston SC. **Other U.S. locations:** Nationwide. **Parent company:** Toys "R" Us, Inc. (Paramus NJ).

BAUSCH & LOMB INCORPORATED
8507 Pelham Road, Greenville SC 29615. 864/297-5500. **Contact:** Human Resources Manager. **World Wide Web address:** http://www.bausch.com. **Description:** Manufactures eye care products, pharmaceuticals, and surgical equipment including contact lenses; lens care solutions; premium sunglasses (sold under Ray-Ban and Revo brands) prescription and over-the-counter ophthalmic drugs; and equipment used for cataract and ophthalmic surgery. **NOTE:** Apply online through the company Website. **Positions advertised include:** Transportation Specialist; Chemistry Technician III. **Special programs:** Summer Internships. **Corporate headquarters location:** Rochester NY. **Other area locations:** Columbia SC. **Other U.S. locations:** Nationwide. **Operations at this facility include:** Manufacturing. **Listed on:** New York Stock Exchange. **Stock exchange symbol:** BOL. **Chairman/CEO:** Ronald L. Zarrella. **Annual sales/revenues:** $1.8 billion. **Number of employees:** 11,600.

BERKELEY CITIZENS
1301 Old Highway 52 South, P.O. Drawer 429, Moncks Corner SC 29461. 843/761-0300. **Fax:** 843/761-0303. **Contact:** Human Resources. **E-mail address:** admin@berkeleycitizens.org **World Wide Web address:** http://www.berkeleycitizens.org. **Description:** Provides support services for people with mental retardation, head and spinal cord injuries, autism, and related disabilities. **Positions advertised include:** Conifer Associate; House Manager.

BI-LO, INC.
P.O. Drawer 99, Mauldin SC 29662. 864/234-1600. **Physical address:** 208 Industrial Boulevard, Greenville SC 29607. **Fax:** 864/234-6999. **Contact:** Scott Santos, Employment Office. **E-mail address:** BILOHR@aholdusa.com. **World Wide Web address:** http://www.bi-lo.com. **Description:** Operates a supermarket chain with stores in South Carolina, North Carolina, Georgia, and Tennessee. **NOTE:** Second shifts offered. Resumes should be submitted online via the company Website. **Positions advertised include:** Perishable Management Auditor. **Corporate headquarters location:** This location. **Parent company:** Ahold USA. **President/CEO:** Dean Cohagan. **Annual sales/revenues:** $3.6 billion. **Number of employees:** 26,000.

BLACKBAUD, INC.
2000 Daniel Island Drive, Charleston SC 29492-7541. 800/468-8996. **Fax:** 843/216-6100. **Contact:** Laura Kennedy, Personnel Coordinator. **E-mail address:** recruiting@blackbaud.com. **World Wide Web address:** http://www.blackbaud.com. **Description:** Provides computer programming services for nonprofit companies and designs software that helps companies with a wide variety of activities including fundraising, administration, and organization. Founded in 1981. **NOTE:** Submit resumes online through the company Website. **Positions advertised include:** Customer Service Representative; Staff Accountant; Division Controlling Associate; Blackbaud Director; Prospect Researcher; Consulting Representative; Corporate Revenue Analyst; Customer Support Analyst; Application Developer; Software Instructor; High Tech Recruiters; Corporate Para legal; Product Marketing Manager; Sales Manager; System Administrator. **Special programs:** Internships. **Corporate headquarters location:** This location. **Other locations:** Glasgow, Scotland; Sydney, Australia. **Listed on:** Privately held. **CEO:** Robert (Bob) J. Sywolski. **Annual sales/revenues:** $105.2 million. **Number of employees:** 700.

BOWATER INC.
P.O. Box 7, Catawba SC 29704. 803/981-8000. **Fax:** 803/981-8031. **Contact:** Barry Baker, Personnel Manager. **World Wide Web address:** http://www.bowater.com. **Description:** Produces three million tons of newsprint annually manufacturing coated and uncoated groundwood papers, bleached kraft pulp, and lumber products at 12 pulp and paper mills and 12 sawmills supported by 1.5 million acres of timberland in the U.S. and Canada with timber-cutting rights of 33 million acres in Canada. The company is one of the largest users of recycled newspapers and magazines. **NOTE:** Personnel Office phone: 803/981-8110. **Positions advertised include:** Chemical Engineer; Chemist; Production Engineer; Forester/Conservation Scientist; Mechanical Engineer. **Corporate headquarters location:** Greenville SC. **Other U.S. locations:** AL; MI; MS; SC; TN. **International locations:** throughout Canada; South Korea. **Operations at this facility include:** Coated & Specialty Papers Division manufacturing coated paper, market pulp, newsprint, and uncoated groundwood paper. **Listed on:** New York Stock Exchange; London Stock Exchange; Toronto Stock Exchange. **Stock exchange symbol:** BOW; BDX. **Chairman/President/CEO:** Arnold M. Nemorow. **Annual sales/revenues:** $2.6 billion. **Number of employees worldwide:** 8,600.

BOWATER INC.
P.O. Box 1028, Greenville SC 29602. 864/271-7733. **Physical address:** 55 East Camperdown Way, Greenville SC 29602-1028. **Fax:** 864/282-9482. **Contact:** James T. Wright, Human Resources. **World Wide Web address:** http://www.bowater.com. **Description:** Produces three million tons of newsprint annually manufacturing coated and uncoated groundwood papers, bleached kraft pulp, and lumber products at 12 pulp and paper mills and 12 sawmills supported by 1.5 million acres of timberland in the U.S. and Canada with timber-cutting rights of 33 million acres in Canada. The company is one of the largest users of recycled newspapers and magazines. **Positions advertised include:** Accountant/Auditor; Financial Analyst; Human Resources Manager; Marketing Specialist; Mechanical Engineer; Sales Representative. **Corporate headquarters location:** This location. **Other U.S. locations:** AL; MI; MS; SC; TN. **International locations:** throughout Canada; South Korea. **Operations at this facility include:** Corporate Administration. **Listed on:** New York Stock Exchange; London Stock Exchange; Toronto Stock Exchange. **Stock exchange symbol:** BOW; BDX. **Chairman/President/CEO:** Arnold M. Nemorow. **Annual sales/revenues:** $2.6 billion. **Number of employees worldwide:** 8,600.

CALE YARBOROUGH HONDA/MAZDA
2723 West Palmetto Street, Florence SC 29501. 843/669-5556. **Fax:** 843/667-0964. **Contact:** William Howell, Services Manager. **Description:** An automobile dealership that sells new and used Hondas and Mazdas as well as other vehicles. Cale Yarborough Honda/Mazda also offers automobile repair services. **Positions advertised include:** Automotive Mechanic.

CAMBAR SOFTWARE, INC.
2387 Clements Ferry Road, Charleston SC 29492. 843/856-2822. **Toll-free phone:** 800/756-4402. **Fax:** 842/881-4893. **Contact:** Human Resources. **E-mail address:** recruiting@cambarsoft.com. **World Wide Web address:** http://www.cambarsoftware.com. **Description:** Develops order and warehouse system software used by large distributors and manufacturers. **Corporate headquarters location:** This location. **Other locations:** Bohemia NY. **Parent company:** Supply Chain Holdings, LLC (Charleston SC).

CANAL INSURANCE COMPANY
P.O. Box 7, Greenville SC 29602. 864/242-5365. **Physical address:** 400 East Stone Avenue, Greenville SC 29601. **Contact:** Office/Personnel Manager. **E-mail address:** hr@canal-ins.com. **World Wide Web address:** http://www.canal-ins.com. **Description:** An insurance company that specializes in commercial vehicle insurance. Founded in 1933.

CARAVELLE RESORT INC.
6900 North Ocean Boulevard, Myrtle Beach SC 29572. 843/918-8000. **Toll-free phone:** 800/785-4460. **Fax:** 843/918-7036. **Contact:** Grace Andrews, Personnel. **World Wide Web address:** http://www.thecaravelle.com. **Description:** A resort with 590 rooms and villas. **Parent company:** Caravelle Properties Ltd Partnership (also at this location). **Affiliates include:** Santa Maria Restaurant; Saint Johns.

CERAMTEC NORTH AMERICA
P.O. Box 89, Highway 14, Laurens SC 29360-0089. 864/682-3215. **Physical address:** One Technology Place, Laurens SC 29360-1669. **Fax:** 864/682-1140. **Contact:** Employment Manager. **E-mail address:** hr@ceramtec.com. **World Wide Web address:** http://www.ceramtech.com. **Description:** Manufactures ceramic products made out of alumina, zirconia, and titania. **Positions advertised include:** Field Sales Representative; Ceramics Engineer; Mechanical Engineer; Marketing Representative. **Corporate headquarters location:** This location. **Other locations:** New Lebanon NY. **Parent company:** CeramTec AG (Germany). **Operations at this facility include:** Laurens Operations – Ceramic Products; Corporate Offices.

CHARLESTON COUNTY GOVERNMENT
Lonnie Hamilton III Public Services Building, 4045 Bridge View Drive, North Charleston SC 29405-7464. 843/958-4700. **Fax:** 843/958-4720. **Recorded jobline:** 843/958-4719. **Contact:** Joyce Moseley, Charleston County Human Resources. **E-mail address:** job@charlestoncounty.org. **World Wide Web address:** http://www.charlestoncounty.org. **Description:** Provides a broad range of services including public safety (law enforcement, emergency medical services, emergency preparedness, detention facilities, and fire protection); engineering services; economic development; street and drainage maintenance; waste disposal; recycling; planning and zoning administration; grants administration; criminal prosecution services; criminal, civil, probate, and family court administration; document recording services; tax assessment; collection and dispersal; alcohol and other drug abuse services; library services; veteran's assistance; and voter registration. **Positions advertised include:** Paramedic (pool); Human Resources Generalist; County Service Representative; Civil Structural Engineer; Equipment Operator; Emergency Service Dispatcher. **Number of employees:** 2,000.

CHARLESTON MUSEUM
360 Meeting Street, Charleston SC 29403. 843/722-2996. **Contact:** Human Resources. **E-mail address:** info@charlestownmuseum.org. **World Wide Web address:** http://www.charlestonmuseum.org. **Description:** One of the oldest municipal museums, the Charleston Museum features collections of arts, crafts, textiles, and furniture with an emphasis on the history of South Carolina.

THE CLUB GROUP, LTD.
71 Lighthouse Road, Suite 300, Hilton Head SC 29938. 843/363-5699. **Contact:** Christiana G. Martin, Controller. **Description:** Operates a resort. **Positions advertised include:** Cook; Hotel Manager; Food Service Manager. **Subsidiaries include:** Harbour Town Resorts; National Liability & Fire Insurance Company.

COASTAL CAROLINA UNIVERSITY
P.O. Box 261954, Conway SC 29528-6054. 843/347-3161. **Contact:** Human Resources. **World Wide Web address:** http://www.coastal.edu. **Description:** A private four-year university offering both Graduate and Undergraduate programs that currently enrolls 6,780 students. **Positions advertised include:** Athletic Training Instructors; Director of Counseling Services; Security Officer. **Office Hours:** Monday – Friday, 8:30 a.m. – 4:30 p.m.

THE COLEMAN COMPANY, INC.
P.O. Box 1119, Lake City SC 29560. 843/394-8893. **Contact:** Personnel Director. **E-mail address:** careers@coleman.com. **World Wide Web address:** http://www.colemancareers.com. **Description:** The Coleman Company manufactures, markets, and distributes outdoor recreation gear such as sleeping bags, lanterns, flashlights, coolers, backpacks, camp stoves, canoes and fishing boats, water ski boats, sleeping bags, fuel, and hot tubs. Nationally, the company manufactures the following brands: Coleman, Campingaz, Peak 1, Outing Sports Products; Hobie Cat and O'Brien Marine Products; Coleman Camping Trailers; Home Heating and Air Conditioning Products; and Recreational Vehicle Products. Its Coleman Powermate division produces portable generators, fuel cell generators, and compressors. The company operates internationally through Coleman Canadian Sales and Coleman Foreign Sales. **NOTE:** Resumes accepted through the company Website. **Positions advertised include:** Project Analyst; Design Engineer. **Corporate headquarters location:** Wichita KS. **Other area locations:** Statewide. **Other U.S. locations:** AR; FL; KS; OK; TX. **International locations:** Worldwide. **Subsidiaries include:** Coleman Powermate, Inc. **Parent company:** American Household (formerly Sunbeam). **Chairman:** Jerry W. Levin. **Annual sales/revenues:** $1 billion. **Number of employees at this location:** 100. **Number of employees nationwide:** 2,000.

COLLINS & AIKMAN CORPORATION
199 Blackhawk Road, Greenville SC 29611. 864/295-5000. **Contact:** Director of Human Resources. **World Wide Web address:** http://www.colaik.com. **Description:** Manufactures automotive products including carpet and trunk liners for automobiles. **NOTE:** Resumes should be sent to the company headquarters address: Human Resources, 250 Stephenson Highway, Troy MI 48083. Fax: 248/824-1613. **Special programs:** Internships. **Corporate headquarters location:** Troy MI. **Other locations:** Nationwide. **International locations:** Worldwide. **Operations at this facility include:** Manufacturing. **Listed on:** New York Stock Exchange. **Stock exchange symbol:** CKC. **Annual sales/revenues:** $3.9 billion. **Number of employees worldwide:** 26,000.

COLONIAL LIFE & ACCIDENT INSURANCE COMPANY
P.O. Box 1365, Columbia SC 29202. 803/798-7000. **Fax:** 803/731-2618. **Recorded jobline:** 803/750-0088. **Contact:** Don Montgomery, Human Resources. **World Wide Web address:** http://www.coloniallife.com. **Description:** An accident and health insurance company specializing in supplemental insurance offered to employees at their worksite, as well as underwriting lines such as accident, disability, life, and cancer insurance. Founded in 1939. **Positions advertised include:** Sales Director; Atraus Consultant; Account Service Representative; Independent Contractor. **Corporate headquarters location:** This location. **Parent company:** UNUMProvident Corporation (Portland ME). **Number of employees:** 900.

COMCAST CABLEVISION
4400 Belle Oaks Drive, North Charleston SC 29405. 843/554-4100. **Contact:** Human Resources Manager. **World Wide Web address:** http://www.comcast.com. **Description:** A cable television company. Founded in 1963. **NOTE:** Applicants may only apply for positions via the company website at http://www.careers.comcast.net. **Positions advertised include:** Customer Service Sales Supervisor; Traffic Assistant; Communications Technician. **Other area locations:** Walterboro SC. **Other U.S. locations:** Nationwide. **Parent company:** Comcast Corporation (Philadelphia PA). **Number of employees worldwide:** 20,000.

COMPOSITES ONE LLC
467 Lakeshore Parkway, Rock Hill SC 29732-8212. 803/328-3862. **Fax:** 803/327-8089. **Contact:** Ann Ward, Distribution Manager. **World Wide Web address:** http://www.compositesone.com. **E-mail address:** info@CompositeOne.com. **Description:** A wholesale distributor of fiberglass, chemicals and related composite materials including additives, adhesives, gel coats, pigments, putties, polyester, and vinyl ester resins. **Positions advertised include:** Software Engineer; Production Manager; Chemicals Scientist. **Corporate headquarters location:** Arlington Heights IL. **Other U.S. locations:** Nationwide.

COOPER INDUSTRIES INC.
COOPER TOOLS DIVISION
670 Industrial Drive, Lexington SC 29072. 803/359-1200. **Contact:** Human Resources. **E-mail address:** lexington.recruit@coopertools.com. **World Wide Web address:** http://www.cooperindustries.com. **Description:** Manufactures pneumatic hand tools, air motors, air feed drills, and hoists. Overall, Cooper Industries Inc. is engaged in three primary areas of manufacturing: tools and hardware, electrical and electronic products, and automotive products. **Positions advertised include:** Draftsperson; Industrial Designer; Production Engineer; Mechanical Engineer; Quality Control Supervisor. **Corporate headquarters location:** Houston TX. **Other area locations:** Cherow SC; Georgetown SC; Greenwood SC; Sumter SC. **Other U.S. locations:** Nationwide. **Listed on:** New York Stock Exchange. **Stock exchange symbol:** CBE. **Chairman/President/CEO:** H. John Riley Jr. **Annual sales/revenues:** $4 billion. **Number of employees nationwide:** 28,500.

CROWN HOLDINGS, INC.
100 Evans Row, P.O. Box 759, Cheraw SC 29020. 843/537-9794. **Fax:** 843/537-4382. **Contact:** Personnel Manager. **World Wide Web address:** http://www.crowncork.com. **Description:** A worldwide manufacturer and distributor of a wide range of crowns, seals, and aluminum/steel cans including aerosol and beverage cans. The company also manufactures bottling equipment. **NOTE:** The company requests resumes to be submitted online. **Positions advertised include:** Corporate Trainer; Production Engineer; Manufacturing Supervisor; Production Foreman. **Corporate headquarters location:** Philadelphia PA. **Other area locations:** Spartanburg SC. **Other U.S. locations:** Nationwide. **International locations:** Worldwide. **Subsidiaries include:** Crown Cork & Seal Company. **Operations at this location include:** Beverage Division. **Listed on:** New York Stock Exchange. **Stock exchange symbol:** CCK. **Chairman/President/CEO:** John W. Conway. **Annual sales/revenues:** $7.2 billion. **Number of employees:** 33,050.

CROWNE PLAZA RESORT
130 Shipyard Drive, Hilton Head Island SC 29928. 843/842-2400. **Fax:** 843/785-4879. **Contact:** Melissa Love, Assistant Director of Human Resources. **World Wide Web address:** http://www.crowneplazaresort.com. **Description:** A 340-room hotel located in Shipyard Plantation. This location also hires seasonally. **NOTE:** Entry-level positions, part-time jobs, and second and third shifts are offered. **Positions advertised include:** Part Time PM Line Cook; Loss Preventing Associate; Part Time Night Auditor; Mini Bar Attendant; Bartender; Restaurant Servers; Restaurant Supervisor. **Special programs:** Internships; Training; Summer Jobs. **International locations:** Worldwide. **Parent company:** Six Continents PLC (London, United Kingdom).

CUMMINGS OIL COMPANY, INC.
P.O. Box 186, Hampton SC 29924. 803/943-3921. **Contact:** Human Resources. **E-mail Address:** cummingsoil@earthlink.net. **Description:** Sells gas, diesel fuel, and propane primarily to residential customers. **Corporate headquarters location:** This location. **Other area locations:** Walterboro SC. **Other U.S. locations:** Nationwide.

CUTLER-HAMMER, INC.
P.O. Box 1406, Greenwood SC 29648. 864/229-3006. **Contact:** Rick McLain, Human Resources Manager. **World Wide Web address:** http://www.cutler-hammer.com. **Description:** Part of the electrical and electronic controls segment of Eaton Corporation that produces industrial and commercial controls (electromechanical and electronic controls; motor starters, contractors, overloads, and electric drives; programmable controllers, counter, man-to-machine interface panels, and push buttons; photoelectric, proximity, temperature, and pressure sensors; circuit breakers; load centers; safety switches; panelboards; switchboards; dry tape transformers; busway; meter centers; portable tool switches; commercial switches; relays; illuminated panels; annunciator panels; and electrically-actuated valves and actuators); automotive and appliance controls (electromechanical and electronic controls; convenience, stalk, and concealed switches; knock sensors; climate control components; speed controls; timers; pressure switches; water valves; range controls; thermostats; gas valves; infinite switches; and temperature and humidity sensors); and specialty controls (automated material handling systems, automated guided vehicles, stacker cranes, ion implanters, engineered fasteners, golf grips, and industrial clutches and brakes). These products are sold directly by the company or indirectly through distributors and manufacturers' representatives to industrial, commercial, automotive, appliance, aerospace, and government customers. **Positions advertised include:** Lean Coordinator; Mechanical Drafting Engineer; Manufacturing Engineer; Network Administrator. **Corporate headquarters location:** Pittsburgh PA. **Parent company:** Eaton Corporation (Cleveland OH).

DATASTREAM SYSTEMS, INC.
50 Datastream Plaza, Greenville SC 29605. 864/422-5001. **Fax:** 800/905-8980. **Contact:** Gary Craft, Human Resources. **E-mail address:** datastream@rpc.webhire.com. **World Wide Web address:** http://www.dstm.com. **Description:** Develops maintenance management software. Datastream serves many major industries including government, health care, hospitality, manufacturing, and transportation. Founded in 1996. **NOTE:** Human Resources phone: 864/422-5305. **Positions advertised include:** Corporate Accounting Manager; Tax Compliance Manager; Systems Administrator; Account Manager; Technical Writer; Product Engineer; Project Manager; Billable Consultant; Senior Consultant; Software Developer. **Special programs:** Internships. **Corporate headquarters location:** This location. **Other locations:** GA; IL; NJ; PA; TX. **International locations:** Canada; China; Japan; Singapore. **Listed on:** NASDAQ. **Stock exchange symbol:** DSTM. **Chairman/President/CEO:** Larry G. Blackwell. **Annual sales/revenues:** $90 million. **Number of employees:** 713.

DAVIS ELECTRICAL CONSTRUCTORS, INC.
429 North Main Street, P.O. Box 1907, Greenville SC 29602. 864/250-2500. **Fax:** 864/250-2555. **Contact:** Bill Dyar, Human Resources. **World Wide Web address:** http://www.daviselectrical.com. **Description:** An electrical and instrumentation contractor for power plants, textile manufacturers, and chemical producers. Founded in 1965. **NOTE:** Human Resources phone: 864/250-2471. **Positions advertised include:** Electrical Engineer; Project Coordinator. **Corporate headquarters location:** This location. **Other U.S. locations:** Baton Rouge LA; Debary FL; Shelby NC; Gulfport MS.

DAYCO PRODUCTS INC.
108 West Street, P.O. Box 500, Williston SC 29853. 803/266-7046. **Contact:** David Hayes, Personnel Manager. **E-mail address:** Dayco_Employment@markivanto.com. **World Wide Web address:** http://www.dayco.com. **Description:** A worldwide manufacturer and distributor of a wide range of highly engineered rubber and plastic products, many of which are used for replacement purposes. Principal markets include the agricultural, automotive, construction, energy, printing, mining, textile, and transportation industries. **Corporate headquarters location:** Dayton OH. **Parent company:** Mark IV Industries.

DEFENDER SERVICES
P.O. Box 1775, Columbia SC 29202-1775. 803/776-4220. **Physical address:** 9031 Garner's Ferry Road, Columbia SC 29209. **Fax:** 803/776-1580. **Contact:** Personnel Department. **E-mail address:** johns@defenderservices.com or humanresources@defenderservices.com. **World Wide Web address:** http://www.defenderservices.com. **Description:** Defender Services offers cleaning, painting, floor sanding, maintenance, yard work, grounds work, housekeeping, trash removal, and security. **Corporate headquarters location:** This location. **Other area locations:** Anderson SC; Charleston SC; Greenwood SC; Lancaster SC. **Other U.S. locations:** Nationwide. **Number of employees nationwide:** 7,000.

DELTA WOODSIDE INDUSTRIES, INC.
100 Augusta Street, P.O. Box 6126, Greenville SC 29606. 864/255-4100. **Fax:** 864/255-4165. **Contact:** Jerry Tucker, Personnel. **World Wide Web address:** http://www.deltawoodside.com. **Description:** Manufactures and sells textiles and finished apparel fabrics operating six manufacturing plants in North and South Carolina. **Corporate headquarters:** This location. **Other area locations:** Edgefield SC; Wallace SC. **Subsidiaries include:** Delta Mills, Inc. **Listed on:** New York Stock Exchange. **Stock exchange symbol:** DLW. **Director/President/CEO:** William F. Garrett. **Annual sales/revenues:** $175 million. **Number of employees:** 1,750.

DISABILITIES BOARD OF CHARLESTON COUNTY
995 Morrison Drive, P.O. Box 22708, Charleston SC 29413-2708. 843/805-5800. **Fax:** 843/805-5805. **Contact:** Human Resources. **World Wide Web address:** http://www.dsncc.com. **Description:** Provides a variety of services for people with disabilities including early intervention, residential living assistance, and supportive employment programs. **Positions advertised include:** Early Interventionist; Community Training Home Coordinator; Rehabilitative Support Specialist; Job Coach. **Executive Director:** Karolyn Elliot.

DIVERSCO INC.
105 Diversco Drive, P.O. Box 5527, Spartanburg SC 29304. 864/579-3420. **Toll-free phone:** 800/277-3420. **Fax:** 864/579-9578. **Contact:** Raina Tuten, Human Resources Manager. **World Wide Web address:** http://www.diversco.com. **Description:** Provides outsourcing services including janitorial and building maintenance, security, temporary staffing, food processing equipment, sanitation, and contract services to industrial clients. **Corporate headquarters location:** This location. **Other locations:**

Nationwide. **Parent company:** Diversco Holdings, Inc. (also at this location). **Subsidiaries include:** Personnel Management, Inc.; Spartan Security.

R.R. DONNELLEY & SONS COMPANY
300 Jones Road, Spartanburg SC 29307. 864/579-6000. **Contact:** Doug Winslow, Human Resources Manager. **E-mail address:** rrdonnelley@hiresystems.com. **World Wide Web address:** http://www. rrdonnelley.com. **Description:** The company is engaged in managing, reproducing, and distributing print and digital information for publishing, merchandising, and information technology customers. The company is one of the largest commercial printers in the world, producing catalogs, inserts, magazines, books, directories, computer documentation, and financial printing. R.R. Donnelley & Sons Company has more than 180 sales offices and production facilities. Principal services offered by the company are conventional and digital prepress operations, computerized printing and binding, and sophisticated pool shipping and distribution services for printed products; information repackaging into multiple formats (print, magnetic, and optical media); database management, list rental, list enhancement, and direct mail production services; turnkey computer documentation services (outsourcing, translation, printing, binding, diskette replication, kitting, licensing, republishing, and fulfillment); reprographics and facilities management; creative design and communication services; and digital and conventional map creation and related services. Founded in 1864. **Positions advertised include:** Safety Technician; Process Engineer. **Corporate headquarters location:** Chicago IL. **Other U.S. locations:** Nationwide. **International locations:** Worldwide. **Subsidiaries include:** Lakeside Press. **Operations at this facility include:** Commercial printing of catalogues and newspaper inserts. **Listed on:** New York Stock Exchange. **Stock exchange symbol:** RRD. **Chairman/President/CEO:** William L. Davis. **Annual sales/revenues:** $4.75 billion. **Number of employees:** 33,000.

DUNES PROPERTIES OF CHARLESTON, INC.
1400 Palm Boulevard, P.O. Box 524, Isle of Palms SC 29451. 843/886-5600. **Toll-free phone:** 800/476-8444. **Fax:** 843/886-4953. **Contact:** Human Resources. **World Wide Web address:** http://www.dunesproperties.com. **Description:** Rental agent for resort and vacation properties. **Positions advertised include:** Administrative Assistant; Front Desk Sales Agent; Property and Real Estate Manager. **Corporate headquarters location:** This location. **Other locations:** Folley Beach SC; Johns Island SC. **Listed on:** Privately held

EAST COOPER MEDICAL CENTER
1200 Johnnie Dodds Boulevard, Mount Pleasant SC 29464. 843/881-0100. **Fax:** 843/881-4396. **Contact:** Human Resources Department. **World Wide Web address:** http://www.eastcoopermedctr.com. **Description:** Offering a comprehensive range of services with the patient in mind first. **Positions advertised include:** Registered Nurse; Physical Therapist; Admit Communications Representative; Imaging Assistant; Assistant Nurse.

ELECTROLUX HOME PRODUCTS OF NORTH AMERICA
2500 Saint Matthews Road, North, SC. 803/534-1685. **Physical address:** 172 Old Elloree Road, Orangeburg SC 29115. **Contact:** Betty Johnson-Pringle, Human Resources. **World Wide Web address:** http://na.electrolux.com. **Description:** Formerly Frigidaire Home Products, Electrolux manufactures household appliances including washing machines, ranges, dishwashers, refrigerators, freezers, air conditioners, and disposals at 14 manufacturing locations in North America. **NOTE:** Resumes may be sent to the company's headquarters address: 250 Bobby Jones Expressway, Martinez GA 30907. **Positions advertised include:** Process Owner Customer Service; Electrical Control Engineer; Electrical Engineer; Quality Engineer; Project Manager; Information Technology Support Analyst; Mechanical Engineer. **Corporate headquarters location:** Martinez GA. **Other area locations:** Anderson SC. **Other U.S. locations:** Nationwide. **International locations:** Canada; Mexico. **Subsidiaries/affiliates include:** Frigidaire; White Westinghouse; Tappan; Gibson. **Parent company:** AB Electrolux (Stockholm, Sweden). **Operations at this facility include:** Manufacturing/Engineering. **Annual sales/revenues:** $4 billion. **Number of employees:** 19,000.

ELLETT BROTHERS, INC.
267 Columbia Avenue, P.O. Box 128, Chapin SC 29036. 803/345-3751. **Contact:** Human Resources. **World Wide Web address:** http://www.ellettbrothers.com. **Description:** Manufacturers leisure products focusing on outdoor recreational sports such as hunting and shooting, marine activities, camping, and archery. Founded in 1933. **Positions advertised include:** Sales Representative; Business Unit Manager. **Corporate headquarters location:** This location. **Other locations:** Newbury SC; Taylorsville NC; Houston MO; Monroe MI. **Subsidiaries include:** Evans Sports, Inc.; Vintage Editions, Inc.; Archery Center International. **Parent company:** Tuscarora Incorporated (New Brighton PA). **Operations at this facility include:** Distribution; Product Sourcing; Teleservicing Operations. **Listed on:** Privately held. **President/CEO:** Bob McBeth. **Annual sales/revenues:** $150 million. **Number of employees nationwide:** 411.

ELLIOT DAVIS & COMPANY LLP
P.O. Box 6286, Greenville SC 29606. 864/242-3370. **Physical address:** 200 East Broad Street, Greenville SC 29601. **Fax:** 864/232-7161. **Contact:** Nancy Browder, Office Manager. **E-mail address:** hr@elliottdavis.com. **World Wide Web address:** http://www.elliottdavis.com. **Description:** The company ranks in the top 40 corporate accounting firms in the U.S. offering comprehensive tax, audit, and consulting services and is affiliated with the international firm Moore Stephens Elliot Davis, LLC. Founded in 1925. **NOTE:** Apply online. **Positions advertised include:** Senior Tax Accountant; Senior Auditor. **Corporate headquarters location:** This location. **Other locations:** Statewide.

ENGELHARD CORPORATION
554 Engelhard Drive, Seneca SC 29678. 864/882-9841. **Fax:** 864/882-4651. **Contact:** Andy Tunstall, Human Resources. **World Wide Web address:** http://www.engelhard.com. **Description:** Manufactures precious metal catalysts for the petrochemicals and fine chemicals industries; base metal catalysts for specialty chemical producers; catalysts for the hydrogenation of fats and oils; and separation products encompassing a wide variety of treated natural minerals for the enhancement, purification, and bleaching of chemical products. **Company slogan:** Change the Nature of Things. **Corporate headquarters location:** Iselin NJ. **Other area locations:** Duncan SC; North Charleston SC. **Other U.S. locations:** Nationwide. **Operations at this facility include:** Manufacturing of Process Catalysts; PM Salts and Solutions; Precious Metal Refining. **Listed on:** New York Stock Exchange. **Stock exchange symbol:** EC. **Chairman/President/CEO:** Barry W. Perry. **Annual sales/revenues:** $3.75 billion. **Number of employees:** 6,550.

ERNST & YOUNG LLP
P.O. Box 10647, Greenville SC 29603. 864/242-5740. **Contact:** Phil Snipes, Partner. **World Wide Web address:** http://www.ey.com. **Description:** A certified public accounting firm that also provides management consulting services. Services include data processing, financial modeling, financial feasibility studies, production planning and inventory management, management sciences, health care planning, human resources, cost accounting, and budgeting systems. **NOTE:** The company requests resumes to be submitted online. **Positions advertised include:** Technology Support Specialist. **Corporate headquarters location:** New York NY. **Other locations:** Worldwide. **Chairman/CEO:** James (Jim) S. Turley. **Annual sales/revenues:** $10.1 billion. **Number of employees:** 110,000.

EVENING POST PUBLISHING COMPANY
134 Columbus Street, Charleston SC 29403-4800. 843/577-7111. **Contact:** Paul Sharry, Personnel Department. **E-mail address:** jobs@postandcourier.com. **World Wide Web address:** http://www.evepost.net. **Description:** An umbrella corporation for several newspaper publishing companies throughout South Carolina. The Evening Post Publishing Company owns *The Post Courier*, which has a daily circulation of 115,000 and a Sunday circulation of 125,000. Evening Post Publishing Company's business holdings include: several television stations in Arizona, Colorado, Kentucky, Louisiana, Montana, and Texas; daily and weekly newspapers in South Carolina, North Carolina, and Texas; an English-language daily newspaper in Buenos Aires, Argentina; a Florida-based feature article subsidiary; and a Southern pine timberlands management company. Founded in 1803. **NOTE:** The company prefers resumes sent by mail; or by e-mail with job title in the subject line; but does not accept faxed resumes. **Positions advertised include:** Press Operator; Packaging and Distribution Helper; Classified Advertising Clerk; Graphic Designer; Marketing Associate; Data Entry Operator; Advertising Production Graphic Designer. **Subsidiaries include:** *Moultrie News*; *The Salisbury Post*; *The Georgetown Times*; *The* (Kingstree) *News*; *Aiken Standard*; *Buenos Aires Herald*; Editors Press Service, Inc.; KRIS-TV Channel 6; KVOA-TV Channel 4; KOAA-TV Channels 5/30; KPAX-TV Channel 8; KTVQ-TV Channel 2; KXLF-TV Channel 4; KRTV-TV Channel 3; KBZK-TV Channel 7; WLEX-TV Channel 13; KATC-TV Channel 3; *Summerville Journal-Scene*; *Davie County Enterprise*; *The Clemmons Courier*. **Other locations:** Black Eagle MT; Corpus Christi TX; Tucson AZ; Pueblo/Colorado Springs CO; Missoula MT; Billings MT; Butte MT; Great Falls MT; Bozeman MT; Lexington KY; Lafayette LA. **Chairman:** Peter Manigault.

FIRST CITIZENS BANCORPORATION OF SOUTH CAROLINA, INC.
dba FIRST CITIZENS BANK
Drawer I, P.O. Box 29, Columbia SC 29202. 803/771-8700. **Physical address:** 1230 Main Street, Columbia SC 29201. **Fax:** 803/733-3480. **Recorded jobline:** 866/733-3482. **Contact:** Annette Rollins, Human Resources Department. **E-mail address:** jobs@fcbsc.com. **World Wide Web address:** http://www.fcbsc.com. **Description:** A bank holding company with statewide subsidiaries engaged in commercial banking, credit card services, and mortgage banking. Founded in 1913. **NOTE:** Human Resources address: 1213 Lady Street, Columbia SC 29201. Human Resources phone: 803/733-3482. **Positions advertised include:** Personal Banker; Teller. **Office Hours:** Monday – Friday, 9:00 a.m. – 4:00 p.m. **Corporate headquarters location:** This location. **Other locations:** Statewide. **Subsidiaries/Affiliates include:** First Citizens Bank & Trust Company of South Carolina; The Exchange Bank of South Carolina; First Citizens BancShares. **Listed on:** Over The Counter. **Stock exchange symbol:** FBCN. **Chairman/CEO:** Jim B. Apple. **Annual sales/revenues:** $282.7 million. **Number of employees:** 1,550.

FIRST FINANCIAL HOLDINGS, INC.
P.O. Box 118068, Charleston SC 29423-8068. 843/529-5933. **Physical address:** 34 Broad Street, Charleston SC 29401. **Fax:** 843/529-5929. **Contact:** Jerry P. Gazes, Human Resources. **World Wide Web address:** http://www. firstfinancialholdings.com. **Description:** A multiple thrift holding company serving retail banking markets. **Corporate headquarters location:** This location. **Subsidiaries include:** First Federal Savings and Loan Association of Charleston; First Southeast Fiduciary & Trust Services, Inc.; First Southeast Insurance Services, Inc.; First Southeast Investor Services, Inc. **Listed on:** NASDAQ. **Stock exchange symbol:** FFCH. **Chairman:** A.L. Hutchinson Jr. **Annual sales/revenues:** $185 million. **Number of employees:** 763.

FIRST NATIONAL CORPORATION
dba SOUTH CAROLINA BANK & TRUST, N.A.
P.O. Box 1287, Orangeburg SC 29116-1287. 803/531-0511. **Physical address:** 950 John C. Calhoun Drive South East, Orangeburg SC 29115. **Fax:** 803/531-8757. **Recorded jobline:** 866/722-8562. **Contact:** Human Resources. **E-mail address:** jobs@scbandt.com. **World Wide Web address:** http://www.bankfcnb.com. **Description:** A bank holding company whose subsidiaries perform commercial banking operations and provide other financial services. **Positions advertised include:** Client Server Engineer I; Account Service Representative; Financial Sales Representative; Teller. **Corporate headquarters location:** This location. **Other locations:** Statewide. **Subsidiaries include:** South Carolina Bank & Trust, N.A.; South Carolina Bank & Trust of Piedmont; South Carolina Bank & Trust of Pee Dee; CreditSouth Financial Services. **Listed on:** American Stock Exchange. **Stock exchange symbol:** FNC. **Chairman:** Robert R. Horger. **Annual sales/revenues:** $88.2 million. **Number of employees:** 442.

FLUOR CORPORATION
100 Fluor Daniel Drive, Greenville SC 29607-2762. 864/281-4400. **Fax:** 864/281-6913. **Contact:** Human Resources. **E-mail address:** careers@fluor.com. **World Wide Web address:** http://www.fluor.com. **Description:** Operates within the fields of engineering, global services, coal production, and procurement and construction through four operation groups. Fluor Daniel provides engineering, procurement, and construction services. Fluor Global Services provides a wide range of products and related services including consulting services; equipment rental sales and service; operations; and maintenance services. Fluor Signature Services provides business support services to Fluor Corporation. A.T. Massey Coal Group produces coal for the steel industry. **NOTE:** Human Resources phone: 864/281-8600. **Positions advertised include:** Safety Technician; Senior Maintenance Engineering Manager; Senior Estimator; Senior Auditor; Audit Manager; Business Project Analyst; Sales Director; Principal Estimator; Project Manager; Senior Mechanical Estimator; Operations Director. **Corporate headquarters location:** Aliso Viejo CA. **Other U.S. locations:** Nationwide. **International locations:** Worldwide. **Subsidiaries include:** Duke/Fluor Daniel; ICA Fluor Daniel; Del-Jen, Inc.; Plant Performance Services, LLC; Fluor and Aspentech Integrated Process Solutions; ICI & ETB/Fluor Daniel Chlor-Alkali Technology. **Operations at this facility include:** Fluor Enterprises, Inc.; Fluor Constructors International, Inc. (250 Executive Center Drive, Greenville SC 29615). **Listed on:** New York Stock Exchange. **Stock exchange symbol:** FLR. **Chairman/CEO:** Alan L. Boeckmann. **Annual sales/revenues:** $10 billion. **Number of employees worldwide:** 51,300.

FREY MEDIA
2 Park Lane, Suite H, Hilton Head Island SC 29928. 843/842-7878. **Fax:** 843/842-5743. **Contact:** Personnel. **E-mail address:** fminfo@hargray.com. **World Wide Web address:** http://www.freymedia.com. **Positions advertised include:** Regional Publisher Associate. **Description:** Publishes regional magazines including *Golfer's*

Guide and *Home Resource Book*. **NOTE:** Contact regional publishers for open positions. **Other locations:** Kennesaw GA.

GE MEDICAL SYSTEMS
3001 West Radio Drive, Florence SC 29501. 843/667-9799. **Contact:** Personnel. **World Wide Web address:** http://www.gemedicalsystems.com. **Description:** Manufactures superconducting magnets for magnetic resonance imaging. **Positions advertised include:** Field Service Engineer; Process Engineer; X-ray Engineer; Regional Manager; Field Solutions Engineer; Program Coordinator; Electrical Engineer; Mechanical Engineer; Physicist. **Other area locations:** Anderson SC; Charleston SC. **Other U.S. locations:** Nationwide. **Parent company:** General Electric Company (Fairfield CT) is a diversified manufacturer operating in the following areas: aircraft engines (jet engines, replacement parts, and repair services for commercial, military, executive, and commuter aircraft); appliances; broadcasting (NBC); industrial (lighting products, electrical distribution and control equipment, transportation systems products, electric motors and related products, a broad range of electrical and electronic industrial automation products, and a network of electrical supply houses); materials (plastics, ABS resins, silicones, superabrasives, and laminates); power systems (products for the generation, transmission, and distribution of electricity); technical products and systems (medical systems and equipment, as well as a full range of computer-based information and data interchange services for both internal use and external commercial and industrial customers); and capital services (consumer services, financing, and specialty insurance). **Operations at this facility include:** Manufacturing; Research and Development.

GENERAL ENGINEERING LABORATORIES, LLC
P.O. Box 30712, Charleston SC 29417. 843/556-8171. **Physical address:** 2040 Savage Road, Charleston SC 29407. **Fax:** 843/769-1176. **Recorded jobline:** 843/769-7376 ext4798. **Contact:** Rosemary Keikow, Human Resources Director. **E-mail address:** hr@gel.com. **World Wide Web address:** http://www.gel.net. **Description:** Provides environmental testing on soil, air, water, and sludge for private industry and the government. This location also hires seasonally. Founded in 1981. **NOTE:** Entry-level positions, part-time jobs, and second and third shifts are offered. **Positions advertised include:** Laboratory Technician; Senior Civil Engineer; Chemical Engineer; Computer Support Technician; Draftsperson; Environmental Engineer; Industrial Engineer; Project Manager. **Special programs:** Internships. **Affiliates include:** General Engineering & Environmental, LLC; General Engineering Geophysics, LLC. **Parent company:** The GEL Group, Inc.

GENERAL PHYSICS CORPORATION
2391 Centennial Avenue, Suite 100, Aiken SC 29803. 803/649-0515. **Fax:** 803/649-3017. **Contact:** Human Resources. **World Wide Web address:** http://www.genphysics.com. **Description:** Provides training, engineering, and technical services to clients in the aerospace, automotive, defense, government, manufacturing, utility, independent power, pharmaceutical, and process industries. **Corporate headquarters location:** Elkridge MD. **Subsidiaries include:** GP Environmental; GP Technologies.

GLAXOSMITHKLINE PLC
65 Windham Boulevard, Aiken SC 29805. 803/649-3471. **Contact:** Human Resources Manager. **World Wide Web address:** http://www.gsk.com. **Description:** GlaxoSmithKline Corporation is a health care company engaged in the research, development, manufacture, and marketing of ethical pharmaceuticals, animal health products, ethical and proprietary medicines, and eye care products. **Positions advertised include:** Sales Representative. **Corporate headquarters location:** Middlesex, United Kingdom. **Operations at this facility include:** Production of Aquafresh toothpaste and Vivarin sleep inhibitors. **Listed on:** New York Stock Exchange. **Stock exchange symbol:** GSK. **Chairman:** Sir Christopher A. Hogg. **Annual sales/revenues:** $32 billion. **Number of employees worldwide:** 107,900.

GOLD KIST, INC.
2050 Highway 15 South, Sumter SC 29150-8799. 803/481-8555. **Contact:** Human Resources. **E-mail address:** jobs@goldkist.com. **World Wide Web address:** http://www.goldkist.com. **Description:** Processes and markets whole and cut chicken throughout the Northeast and the Midwest operating nine integrated poultry divisions in Alabama, Georgia, Florida, North Carolina and South Carolina. Founded in 1933. **NOTE:** Resumes should be sent to the company's headquarters address: Gold Kist Inc., Corporate Employment, P.O. Box 2210, Atlanta GA 30301. **Positions advertised include:** Breeder Field Representative; Yield Processing Supervisor. **Number of employees nationwide:** 18,000.

W.W. GRAINGER
730 Congaree Road, Greenville SC 29607. 864/288-0110. **Fax:** 864/297-1799. **Contact:** Human Resources. **World Wide Web address:** http://www.grainger.com. **Description:** A national supplier of industrial and commercial products to the industrial, commercial, contracting, and institutional markets. Products include equipment and components for motors, air tools, hydraulic products, refrigeration items, power and hand tools, office equipment, computer supplies, replacement parts, industrial products, safety items, cold weather clothing, and storage equipment. Founded in 1927. **Office hours:** 8:00 a.m. - 5:00 p.m. **Positions advertised include:** Customer Service Associate; Outside Sales Territory Manager; Account Manager; Warehouse Associate; Distribution Associate; Project Manager. **Annual sales/revenues:** $5 billion.

GREENVILLE HOSPITAL SYSTEM
701 Grove Road, Greenville SC 29605. 864/455-8976. **Fax:** 864/455-1799. **Recorded jobline:** 864/455-8799. **Contact:** Human Resources. **World Wide Web address:** http://www.ghs.org. **Description:** A multihospital system that provides health care services to several communities and major tertiary referral services for the upstate area. **NOTE:** Applicants are required to submit a completed "Authorization for Release of Information for Employment Purposes" form to be considered for any position. Forms are available on the company Website and should be sent to: Greenville Hospital System, 701 Grove Road, Greenville SC 29605; or faxed to GHS: 864/455-6218. **Office hours:** Monday – Friday, 8:00 a.m. – 5:00 p.m. **Positions advertised include:** Nurse Supervisor; Registered Nurse; Pediatrician; Chief Technician; Radiology; Physical Therapy. **Number of employees at this location:** 6,500.

THE GREENVILLE NEWS
305 South Main Street, P.O. Box 1688, Greenville SC 29602-1688. 864/298-4006. **Fax:** 864/298-4063. **Contact:** Ms. Elgin, Human Resources Specialist. **E-mail address:** resumehr@greenvillenews.com. **World Wide Web address:** http://www.greenvilleonline.com. **Description:** Publishes *The Greenville News*, a daily newspaper with a circulation of over 100,000 on weekends and slightly less on weekdays. The company also operates an online service. Founded in 1874. **NOTE:** Entry-level positions and second and third shifts are offered. Human Resources phone: 864/298-4452. **Positions advertised include:** Advertising Sales Representative; Automotive Sales Representative; Senior Advertising Sales Representative; Consumer Marketing Manager; Computer Programmer; Customer Service Representative; Graphic Artist; Reporter. **Special programs:** Internships. **Parent company:** Gannett, Inc. (Arlington VA).

GREENWOOD MILLS, INC.
P.O. Box 1017, Greenwood SC 29648-1017. 864/229-2571. **Physical address:** 300 Morgan Avenue, Greenwood SC 29646. **Fax:** 864/229-1111. **Contact:** Warren Moore, Vice President of Human Resources. **Description:** A family-owned textile manufacturer specializing in finished fabrics for clothing, bed linens, garments, jeans and denim products as well as operating golf courses, resorts, and real estate developments. Founded in 1888. **Other locations:** Orangeburg SC; Mexico. **Affiliates include:** SingleSource Apparel. **Listed on:** Privately held. **Chairman:** William Self. **Annual sales/revenues:** $400 million. **Number of employees:** 4,000.

GUARDIAN INDUSTRIES CORPORATION
610 LNC Railway Distribution Park, State Highway 9, Richburg SC 29729. 803/789-6100. **Fax:** 803/789-6859. **Contact:** Tom Monzitta, Human Resources Representative. **E-mail address:** tom_monzitta@guardian.com. **World Wide Web address:** http://www.guardian.com. **Description:** Guardian Industries Corporation is an international manufacturer of glass including tempered glass, reflective coatings, and insulated glass. **Positions advertised include:** Production Manager; Ceramics Engineer; Materials Engineer; Mechanical Engineer; Metallurgical Engineer. **Corporate headquarters location:** Auburn Hills MI. **Other U.S. locations:** Nationwide. **Operations at this facility include:** Float Glass Plant/Manufacturing. **Number of employees nationwide:** 19,000.

HABITAT FOR HUMANITY
CENTRAL SOUTH CAROLINA HABITAT FOR HUMANITY
P.O. Box 11502, Columbia SC 29211. 803/252-3570. **Physical address:** 209 South Sumter Street, Columbia SC 29201-4558. **Fax:** 803/252-7525. **Contact:** Director. **World Wide Web address:** http://www.habitat.org. **Office hours:** Monday – Friday, 8:00 a.m. – 5:00 p.m. **Description:** A social services organization that builds homes for the homeless. **NOTE:** The majority of this organization's staff consists of volunteers. **Special programs:** Internships. **Corporate headquarters location:** Americus GA. **Other U.S. locations:** Nationwide.

HAMPSHIRE DESIGNERS, INC.
215 Commerce Boulevard, Anderson SC 29625. 864/225-6232. **Fax:** 864/225-4421. **Contact:** Martha Camberrell, Human Resources. **E-mail address:** hr@ hamp.com. **World Wide Web address:** http://www.hamp.com. **Description:** One of the largest manufacturers of full-fashion sweaters in the United States. The company designs, manufactures, and markets sweaters under the brand name Designers Originals. **Positions advertised include:** Customer Service Representative; Designer; Financial Specialist; Accountant; Information Technology Associate; Merchandiser; Production Manager; Sales Representative; Sourcing Specialist. **Corporate headquarters location:** This location. **Other locations:** Hauppauge NY; New York NY. **Affiliates include:** Hampshire Investments, Limited; Item-Eyes, Inc. **Parent company:** Hampshire Group, Limited (also at this location). **Listed on**: Nasdaq. **Stock exchange symbol:** HAMP.

HAMRICK'S, INC.
742 Peachoid Road, Gaffney SC 29341. 864/489-6095. **Fax:** 864/489-8734. **E-mail address:** jobs@hamricks.com. **Contact:** Greg Burnett, Director of Personnel. **World Wide Web address:** http://www.hamricks.com. **Description:** Operates a chain of men's clothing stores. These stores are located in the southeastern United States at 20 different locations. **Positions advertised include:** Assistant Store Manager; District Manager; Retail Management Trainee. **Corporate headquarters location:** This location. **Other U.S. locations:** GA; NC; TN.

HAWTHORNE CORPORATION
P.O. Box 61000, Charleston SC 29419. 843/797-8484. **Fax:** 843/797-5258. **Physical address:** 6543 Fair Street, Charleston SC 29419. **E-mail address:** Info@hawthornecorp.com. **Contact:** Human Resources. **World Wide Web address:** http://www.hawthornecorp.com. **Description:** A holding company whose subsidiaries are engaged in a wide variety of industries including aviation (operating airports); real estate operations that develop land for fixed base operations; and financial services (investor services). **Corporate headquarters location:** This location.

HAYNSWORTH SINKLER BOYD, P.A.
P.O. Box 2048, Greenville SC 29602. 864/240-3200. **Fax:** 864/240-3300. **Physical address:** 75 Beattie Place, Two Liberty Square, 11th Floor, Greenville SC 29601. **E-mail address:** cgantt@hsblawfirm.com. **Contact:** Office Manager. **World Wide Web address:** http://www.hsblawfirm.com **Description:** A law firm with approximately 50 attorneys that specializes in different areas of the law including bond, corporate, insurance, and real estate. **Special programs:** Summer employment program.

HONEYWELL
4401 St. Andrews Road, Columbia SC 29210. 803/772-2700. **Contact:** Personnel Manager. **World Wide Web address:** http://www.honeywell.com. **Description:** Honeywell is engaged in the research, development, manufacture, and sale of advanced technology products and services in the fields of chemicals, electronics, automation, and controls. The company's major businesses are home and building automation and control, performance polymers and chemicals, industrial automation and control, space and aviation systems, and defense and marine systems. **Operations at this facility include:** Production of nylon textile yarns and related products. **Listed on:** New York Stock Exchange. **Stock exchange symbol:** HON.

HYDRO ALUMINUM
117 Blake Dairy Road, P.O. Box 627, Belton SC 29627. 864/338-8000. **Contact:** Human Resources. **World Wide Web address:** http://www.hydroaluminuma.com. **Description:** Engaged in aluminum extrusion operations. **Positions advertised include:** Manufacturing Manager; Draftsperson; Mechanical Engineer; Operations Manager. **Parent company:** Hydro Aluminum North America (Linthicum MD). **Operations at this facility include:** Belton Operations, advanced extrusion, fabrication, and finishing services using three extrusion presses. **Number of employees at this location:** 200.

IKON OFFICE SOLUTIONS
7 Technology Circle, Columbia SC 29203. 803/758-5555. **Contact:** Human Resources. **World Wide Web address:** http://www.ikon.com. **Description:** Distributes, sells, and repairs office equipment including photocopiers, fax machines, and printers. **Positions advertised include:** Account Executive. **Corporate headquarters location:** Malvern PA. **Other U.S. locations:** Nationwide. **International locations:** Worldwide. **Annual sales/revenues:** $5.3 billion. **Number of employees statewide:** 300. **Number of employees worldwide:** 37,000.

INTERNATIONAL EMPLOYMENT GAZETTE
423 Townes Street, Greenville SC 29601. 864/235-4444. **Toll-free phone:** 800/882.9138. **Fax:** 864/235-3369. **Contact:** Del Hymen, General Manager. **E-mail address:** info@intemployment.com. **World Wide Web address:** http://www.intemployment.com. **Description:** Publishes *International Employment Gazette*, a bi-monthly magazine with over 400 international job listings per issue. Job listings are primarily in the areas of science/technology, public/social services, computer science, construction and trades, and education. Founded in 1990.

INTERNATIONAL PAPER COMPANY
700 South Kaminski Street, Georgetown SC 29440. 843/546-6111. **Fax:** 843/545-2695. **Contact:** Personnel. **World Wide Web address:** http://www.internationalpaper.com. **Description:** International Paper Company manufactures pulp and paper, packaging, wood products, and a range of specialty products. The company is organized into five business segments: Printing Papers, with principal products that include uncoated papers, coated papers, bristles, and pulp; Packaging, which includes industrial packaging, consumer packaging, and kraft and specialty papers; Distribution, including the sale of printing papers, graphic arts equipment and supplies, packaging materials, industrial supplies, and office products; Specialty Products, which includes imaging products, specialty panels, nonwovens, chemicals, and minerals; and Forest Products which includes logging and wood products. **Positions advertised include:** Mill Communications Manager. **Note:** Applicants may apply for jobs at the company website under people category. **Corporate headquarters location:** Stamford CT. **Other locations:** Worldwide. **Listed on:** New York Stock Exchange. **Stock exchange symbol:** IP. **Chairman/CEO:** John Dillon. **Annual sales/revenues:** $25 billion. **Number of employees worldwide:** 91,000.

INTERTAPE POLYMER GROUP
2000 South Beltline Boulevard, Columbia SC 29201-5110. 803/799-8800. **Contact:** Sandra Rivers, Human Resources Manager. **E-mail address:** info@tape.com. **World Wide Web address:** http://www.intertapepolymer.com. **Description:** Manufactures a variety of pressure-sensitive tape products and polyolefin plastic products. The company's products include duct tape and masking tape. **Positions advertised include:** Accountant; Chemist; Controls Engineer; Electrical Engineer; Electrician; Industrial Engineer; Mechanical Engineer; Production Manager; Process Engineer. **Corporate headquarters location:** Montreal, Canada. **Other U.S. locations:** Nationwide. **Operations at this facility include:** Administration; Manufacturing; Research and Development; Sales; Service. **Listed on:** New York Stock Exchange. **Stock exchange symbol:** ITP. **Chairman/CEO:** Melbourne F. Yull. **Annual sales/revenues:** $595 million. **Number of employees nationwide:** 2,900.

JPS INDUSTRIES
555 North Pleasantburg Drive, Suite 202, Greenville SC 29607. 864/239-3900. **Fax:** 864/271-9939. **Contact:** Monnie L. Broome, Human Resources Manager. **Description:** A holding company with companies that are engaged in the following areas of business: manufacturing industrial roofing; automotive products; home furnishings; and residential and commercial carpets. Founded in 1964. **Corporate headquarters location:** This location. **Other locations:** Nationwide. **Subsidiaries include:** JPS Elastomerics; JPS Glass; AstroQuartz. **Listed on:** NASDAQ. **Stock exchange symbol:** JPST. **Chairman/President/CEO:** Michael L. Fulbright. **Annual sales/revenues:** $127 million. **Number of employees:** 620.

JACOBS APPLIED TECHNOLOGY
2040 Bushy Park Road, Goose Creek SC 29445. 843/824-1100. **Fax:** 843/824-1103. **Contact:** Human Resources Manager. **World Wide Web address:** http://www.jacobs.com. **Description:** Designs, fabricates, and constructs propane-air gas plants and process plants for the chemical, petrochemical, fine chemical, specialty chemical, food and beverage, pharmaceutical, and consumer industries. Founded in 1947. **Positions advertised include:** Project Manager. **Parent company:** Jacobs Engineering Group, Inc. (Pasadena CA) provides engineering, procurement, construction, and maintenance services to the chemicals and polymers, federal programs, pulp and paper, semiconductor, petroleum refining, facilities and transportation, food and consumer products, pharmaceutical and biotechnology, and basic resources industries. Through Jacobs College and other site-specific programs, the company trains more than 5,000 employees per year. **Operations at this facility include:** Administration; Manufacturing; Sales.

JACOBS SIRRINE ENGINEERS, INC.
1041 East Butler Road, P.O. Box 5456, Greenville SC 29607. 864/676-6000. **Fax:** 864/676-5096. **Contact:** Mary Johnson, Human Resources Representative. **World Wide Web address:** http://www.jacobs.com. **Description:** Provides architectural, engineering, and construction management consulting services. **Positions advertised include:** Civil Inspector; Customer Service Representative; Sales Manager; Civil Engineer; Electrical Engineer; Mechanical Engineer.

KPMG
55 Beattie Place, Suite 900, Greenville SC 29601. 864/250-2600. **Contact:** Human Resources. **World Wide Web address:** http://www.kpmg.com. **Description:** Delivers a wide range of value-added auditing, accounting, taxation, and consulting services. **Other area locations:** Greensboro SC. **Other locations:** Worldwide. **Parent company:** KPMG International (Amstelveen, Netherlands). **Number of employees at this location:** 75.

KANAWHA INSURANCE COMPANY, INC.
South White Street, P.O. Box 610, Lancaster SC 29721. 803/283-5300. **Fax:** 803/283-5676. **Contact:** Human Resources. **E-mail address:** lbranham@kanawha.com. **World Wide Web address:** http://www.kanawha.com. **Description:** An insurance company specializing in health, life, supplemental, and long-term care insurance. **Positions advertised include** Account Manager; Assistant Counsel Associate; Claims Examiner; Medical Claims Review Registered Nurse. **Corporate headquarters location:** This location. **Other area locations:** Statewide. **Other U.S. locations:** IA; NC.

KENNAMETAL INC.
P.O. Box 872, Clemson SC 29633-0872. 864/654-4922. **Contact:** Human Resources. **World Wide Web address:** http://www.kennametal.com. **Description:** Manufactures and markets tools, services, related supplies, and specially engineered products for metalworking, mining, construction, and other industrial applications with operations in over 60 countries and specializes in cemented tungsten carbide, high-speed steel tools, and wear-resistant carbide components. **Positions advertised include:** Human Resources Generalist; Administrative Support Associate; Administrator; Industrial Engineer; Information Technology Administrator; Inside Sales; Outside Sales; Project Manager; Attorney; General Counsel. **Corporate headquarters location:** Latrobe PA. **Other locations:** Worldwide. **Subsidiaries include:** Greenfield Industries Inc.; JLK Direct Distribution Inc.; Widia Group. **Listed on:** New York Stock Exchange. **Stock exchange symbol:** KMT. **Chairman/President/CEO:** Markos I. Tanbakeras. **Annual sales/revenues:** $1.6 billion. **Number of employees worldwide:** 14,000.

KERSHAW COUNTY MEDICAL CENTER
1315 Roberts Street, P.O. Box 7003, Camden SC 29020. 803/432-4311. **Fax:** 803/425-6369. **Contact:** Human Resources. **E-mail address:** info@kcmc.org. **World Wide Web address:** http://www.kcmc.org. **Description:** A 121-bed acute care facility and 88-bed long term care facility operating facilities in Camden and Lugoff South Carolina. **NOTE:** Apply online. **Positions advertised include:** Licensed Practical Nurse; Registered Nurse; Community Health Educator; Physical Therapist; Recruiter; Speech Therapist; CT Scan Diagnostic Technologist; Polysonographer; Respiratory Therapist.

KIAWAH ISLAND REAL ESTATE
P.O. Box 12001, Charleston SC 29422. 843/768-3400. **Toll-free phone:** 888/559-9024. **Contact:** Patrick McKinney, Broker-in-Charge. **E-mail address:** karla_story@kiawahisland.com. **World Wide Web address:** http://www.kiawahisland.com. **Description:** A real estate company specializing in residential properties. **NOTE:** Those interested in support staff positions (including secretarial) should direct resumes to Michelle Canaday, Office Manager. **Office Hours:** Monday – Friday, 9:00 a.m. – 5:30 p.m.

KINGS ELECTRONICS COMPANY INC.
1685 Overview Drive, Rock Hill SC 29730. 803/909-5000. **Fax:** 803/909-5029. **Contact:** Charles Robinson, Director of Human Resources. **E-mail address:** hrinfo@kingselectronics.com. **World Wide Web address:** http://www.kingselectronics.com. **Description:** Manufactures, sells, and distributes a large line of specialized RF coaxial connectors for various electronics and aerospace industry applications. **NOTE:** Human Resources phone: 803/909-5042.

KOSA
1551 Sha Lane, Spartanburg SC 29304. 864/579-5750. **Fax:** 864/579-5678. **Contact:** Human Resources. **World Wide Web address:** http://www.kosa.com. **Description:** One of the world's largest producers of polyester fibers, resins, and polymer products. KoSa is a joint venture between Koch Industries Inc. (Wichita KS) and IMASAB S.A. de C.V. (Mexico). **Corporate headquarters location:** Houston TX. **Other U.S. locations:** NC. **International locations:** Canada; Germany; Mexico; Netherlands. **Site Manager:** Bill Every. **Number of employees:** 8,000.

LABORATORY CORPORATION OF AMERICA (LABCORP)
25 Woods Lake Road, Suite 602, Greenville SC 29607. 864/232-0636. **Contact:** Human Resources. **World Wide Web address:** http://www.labcorp.com. **Description:** One of the nation's leading clinical laboratory companies, providing services primarily to physicians, hospitals, clinics, nursing homes, and other clinical labs nationwide. LabCorp performs tests of blood, urine, and other body fluids and tissue, as well as aiding the diagnosis of disease. Founded in 1971. **Positions advertised include:** Technical Specialist; Service Representative. **NOTE:** Resumes should be sent to the company's headquarters address: LabCorp, Human Resources, 309 East Davis Street, Burlington NC 27215. **Corporate headquarters location:** Burlington NC. **Listed on:** New York Stock Exchange. **Stock exchange symbol:** LH. **Annual sales/revenues:** $2.5 billion. **Number of employees:** 20,000.

LEATHERWOOD WALKER TODD & MANN P.C.
P.O. Box 87, Greenville SC 29602. 864/242-6440. **Contact:** Margaret Watson, Human Resources Manager. **E-mail address:** mwatson@lwtm.com. **World Wide Web address:** http://www.lwtmlaw.com. **Description:** A law firm with over 50 lawyers that has a variety of specialties including tax and bankruptcy litigation.

LEXINGTON MEDICAL CENTER
2720 Sunset Boulevard, West Columbia SC 29169. 803/791-2000. **Fax:** 803/359-2267. **Recorded jobline:** 803/739-3562. **Contact:** Betsy Brooks, Employment Coordinator. **E-mail address:** bsbrooks@lexhealth.org. **World Wide Web address:** http://www.lexmed.com. **Description:** A 292-bed metropolitan medical complex, which includes six community medical centers serving Lexington County, an occupational health center and 16 affiliated physician practices. **NOTE:** For physician opportunities contact: Crystal Smith, 2720 Sunset Boulevard, West Columbia SC 29169; Phone: 803/791-2958; E-mail address: csmith@lexhealth.org. For all other opportunities contact: LMC Extended Care, Human Resources, 815 Old Cherokee Road, Lexington SC 29072. Employment Coordinator phone: 803/996-6240. **Positions advertised include:** Nursing Supervisor; Registered Nurse; Licensed Practical Nurse; Certified Nurses Aide; Ward Clerk; Occupational Manager; Social Worker. **Office hours:** Monday – Friday, 9:00 a.m. – 4:00 p.m.

THE LIBERTY CORPORATION
135 South Main Street, P.O. Box 502, Greenville SC 29602. 864/241-5427. **Fax:** 864/241-5492. **Contact:** Mary Anne Bunton, Human Resources. **World Wide Web address:** http://www.libertycorp.com. **E-mail address:** info@libertycorp.com. **Description:** The company's Cosmos Broadcasting subsidiary owns and operates 15 network-affiliated television stations throughout the South and Midwest. It also operates and owns Take Ten, a video production company; CableVantage, a cable advertising sales company; and Broadcast Merchandising Corp, a broadcast equipment dealer. **Corporate headquarters location:** this location. **Listed on:** New York Stock Exchange. **Stock exchange symbol:** LC. **Chairman/CEO:** W. Hayne Hipp. **Annual sales/revenues:** $296 million. **Number of employees at this location:** 34. **Number of employees nationwide:** 1,300.

LIBERTY INSURANCE SERVICES CORPORATION
2000 Wade Hampton Boulevard, Greenville SC 29615. 864/609-8334. **Fax:** 864/609-3120. **Contact:** Human Resources. **E-mail address:** recruiters@lisinfo.com. **World Wide Web address:** http://www.rbclibertyinsurance.com. **Description:** Provides a broad range of insurance services. **NOTE:** Jobseekers are encouraged to apply via the Website. **Positions advertised include:** Accountant; Customer Service Representative; Department Manager; Insurance Agent; Broker; Marketing Specialist; Underwriter; Assistant Underwriter. **Corporate headquarters location:** This location. **Parent company:** RBC Insurance (Canada). **Subsidiaries/affiliates include:** Genelco Software. New York Stock Exchange. **Stock exchange symbol:** RY.

LOCKHEED MARTIN AIRCRAFT AND LOGISTICS CENTER
244 Terminal Road, Greenville SC 29605. 864/422-6262. **Fax:** 864/422-6397. **Contact:** Human Resources Department. **World Wide Web address:** http://lmalc.external.lmco.com. **Description:** Manufactures aircraft parts and equipment at over 90 facilities worldwide supporting defense departments of the U.S. government, other federal agencies, other Lockheed Martin companies, international and national customers. **Positions advertised include:** Aircraft Mechanic; Aeronautical Engineer; Aircraft Maintenance; Electronics Technician; Business Operations Manager; Production Control Clerk; Program Manager; Proposal Analyst; Sales Representative. **Parent company:** Lockheed Martin Corporation (Bethesda MD), a diversified defense contractor has businesses in engineering contracting, civil space programs, government services, commercial electronics, aeronautical systems, avionics, aerodynamics, and materials. Subsidiaries of Lockheed Martin include a missiles and

space systems group, an aeronautical systems group, a technology services group, an electronic systems group, and Lockheed Financial Corporation.

LOCKWOOD GREENE ENGINEERS, INC.
P.O. Box 491, Spartanburg SC 29304. 864/578-2000. **Toll-free phone:** 888/(LOCKWOOD) 5625-9663. **Fax:** 864/599-6400. **E-mail address:** careers@lg.com. **Contact:** Trudy Wofford, Personnel Manager. **World Wide Web address:** http://www.lg.com. **Description:** A consulting firm providing engineering and architectural design for industrial and commercial clients. Specifically, the company is involved in the planning and project management of industrial plants and production facilities. **Positions advertised include:** Electrical Design Engineer; Marketing Coordinator; Project Manager; Architectural Engineer; Chemical Engineer; Civil Engineer; Computer Programmer; Draftsperson; Electrical Engineer; Industrial Engineer; Mechanical Engineer; Systems Analyst. **Corporate headquarters location:** This location. **Parent company:** J.A. Jones, Inc. (Charlotte NC). **Operations at this facility include:** Computer-aided design, process, and environmental engineering, control systems engineering, computer systems integration and testing, and construction. **Annual sales/revenues:** $1 billion. **Number of employees:** 3,000.

LORIS HEALTHCARE SYSTEM
LORIS COMMUNITY HOSPITAL
3655 Mitchell Street, Loris SC 29569. 843/716-7000. **Fax:** 843/716-7254. **Recorded jobline:** 843/716-7000, ext5320. **Contact:** Theresa Pougnaud, Director of Human Resources, or Wendy Harrelson. **E-mail address:** wharrels@sccoast.net. **World Wide Web address:** http://www.lorishealthcaresystem.com. **Description:** A general, acute care hospital. **NOTE:** Application materials should be sent to: Employment Coordinator, Loris Healthcare System, 3655 Mitchell System Box 690001, Loris SC 29569-9601. Human Resources phone: 843/716-7196. **Positions advertised include:** Carpenter; Cashier; Executive Physiologist; Licensed Practical Nurse; Nuclear Medical Technician; Pharmacist; Physical Therapist; Radiological Technician; Receptionist; Registered Nurse; Transcriptionist; Utility Aide.

LOUIS RICH COMPANY
3704 Louis Rich Drive, Newberry SC 29108. 803/276-5015. **Fax:** 803/321-7254. **Contact:** Natalie Marzan, Human Resources Manager. **World Wide Web address:** http://www.louisrich.com. **Description:** A poultry processor. **Positions advertised include:** Production Supervisor; Maintenance Technician; Sanitation Technician; Production Manager; Support Mechanic; Project Engineer. **Parent company:** Kraft Foods North America (Northfield IL).

MACK TRUCKS INC.
One Bulldog Boulevard, Winnsboro SC 29180. 803/635-8000. **Contact:** Dave Frueauf, Director of Personnel. **E-mail address:** job_opportunities@macktrucks.com. **World Wide Web address:** http://www.macktrucks.com. **Description:** Manufactures and sells heavy-duty trucks, truck tractors, and truck replacement parts; and provides repair and maintenance service for these products. **NOTE:** Resumes should be sent to the company's headquarters address: P.O. Box M, Allentown PA 18105, or fax to: 610/709-3699. **Positions advertised include:** Truck Technician; Sales Administrator; Leasing Agent; Recovery Specialist; Production Advisor. **Other area locations:** Greenville SC. **Parent company:** Volvo Group (Gothenburg, Sweden).

MARCH OF DIMES BIRTH DEFECTS FOUNDATION
240 Stoneridge Drive, One Graystone Building, Suite 206, Columbia SC 29210. 803/252-5200. **Fax:** 803/799-4549. **Contact:** Carryl Krohne, Human Resources. **E-mail address:** ckrohne@marchofdimes.com. **World Wide Web address:** http://www.modimes.org. **Description:** Operates the Campaign for Healthier Babies, which includes programs of research, community services, education, and advocacy. March of Dimes chapters across the country work with their communities to determine and meet the needs of women, babies, and families. Through specially designed programs, women are provided access to prenatal care and empowered to improve their futures and those of their children. **Positions advertised include:** Senior Community Director.

MARTIN COLOR-FI, INC.
320 Neeley Street, Sumter SC 29150. 803/436-4200. **Fax:** 803/436-4220. **Contact:** Human Resources. **World Wide Web address:** http://www.colorfi.com. **Description:** Produces polyester fiber and pellets from recycled plastic materials such as soft drink bottles, polyester fiber waste, and film waste. The company uses low-cost waste materials to produce polyester fibers for a wide range of markets including automotive fabrics, carpet, home furnishings, industrial materials, construction reinforcement materials, and pelletized plastics for injection molding and thermoforming processes. The company also produces carpet and rug yarns and specialty carpets for the recreational vehicle and manufactured housing markets. **Positions advertised include:** Draftsperson; Electrician; Production Manager; Purchasing Agent; Systems Analyst; Traffic Specialist; Accountant. **Corporate headquarters location:** Edgefield SC.

MCANGUS, GOUDELOCK & COURIE
PO Box 12519, Columbia SC 29211. 803/779-2300. **Physical address:** 700 Gervais Street, Suite 300, Columbia SC 29201. **Fax:** 803/748-0526. **Contact:** Sterling Davies, Recruitment Committee Chairman. **E-mail address:** sdavies@mgclaw.com. **World Wide Web address:** http://www.mgclaw.com. **Description:** Law firm that specializes in the areas of: Administrative Law and Governmental Relations, Arson/Fraud, Captive Insurance, Commercial Litigation and Bankruptcy, Employment Law, Estate Planning, Probate, and Business Law Practice, General Liability, and Workers' Compensation. **Positions advertised Include:** Human Resources Manager, Associates, Summer Associates. **Other area Locations:** Charleston SC; Greenville SC.

McLEOD & ASSOCIATES INCORPORATED
P.O. Box 3518, West Columbia SC 29171. 803/739-6900. **Toll-free number:** 800/951-3977. **Fax:** 803/739-6901. **Contact:** Office Manager. **E-mail address:** marketing@realestate-guides.com. **World Wide Web address:** http://www.realestate-guides.com. **Description:** A publishing and public relations firm serving over 400 cities offering several publications for the real estate industry and providing advertising through three publications for realtors which welcome new residents to the area. **Corporate headquarters location:** This location. **Other locations:** Camden SC; Cayce SC.

McNAIR LAW FIRM
P.O. Box 11390, Columbia SC 29211. 803/799-9800. **Physical address:** Bank of America Tower, 1301 Gervais Street, Columbia SC 29201. **Fax:** 803/799-9804. **Contact:** Risa Hudson, Personnel Manager. **World Wide Web address:** http://www.mcnair.net. **Description:** A law firm with approximately 55 attorneys who have broad ranges of specializations in the fields of corporate and civil law. Founded in 1971. **NOTE:** For summer associate program contact Bonnie Nelson, Recruiting Coordinator by e-mail: bnelson@mcnair.net. **Positions advertised include:** Associate Lawyer; Law Clerk; Summer Associate. **Special programs:** Summer Associate program. **Corporate headquarters location:** This location. **Other locations:** Anderson SC; Charleston SC; Charlotte NC; Georgetown SC; Greenville SC; Hilton Head Island SC; Myrtle Beach SC; Raleigh NC.

MERRILL LYNCH & CO., INC.
One Chamber of Commerce Drive, P.O. Box 5607, Hilton Head SC 29938. 843/785-9620. **Contact:** Human Resources. **World Wide Web address:** http://www.ml.com. **Description:** One of the largest securities brokerage firms in the world, Merrill Lynch provides financial services in securities, financial planning, insurance, estate planning, mortgages, and related areas. The company also brokers commodity futures and options, is a major underwriter of new securities issues, and is a dealer in corporate and municipal securities. **Positions advertised include:** Financial Advisor; Underwriter; Investment Officer; Auditor; Cash Flow Director; Real Estate Team Leader; Account Executive; Credit Officer. **Corporate headquarters location:** New York NY. **Other locations:** Worldwide. **Listed on:** New York Stock Exchange. **Stock exchange symbol:** MER. **Chairman/CEO:** E. Stanley (Stan) O'Neil. **Annual sales/revenues:** $28.3 billion. **Number of employees worldwide:** 50,900.

MICHELIN NORTH AMERICA, INC.
P.O. Box 19001, Greenville SC 29602-9001. 864/458-5000. **Physical address:** One Parkway South, Greenville SC 29615. **Contact:** Human Resources. **World Wide Web address:** http://www.michelin.com. **Description:** Manufactures passenger, light truck, and high-performance tires. **Positions advertised include:** Quality Pipeline Engineer; Supply Chain Specialist; Purchasing Specialist; Senior Information Technology Auditor; Public Relations Manager; General Ledger System Administrator. **Corporate headquarters location:** This location. **Other locations:** Nationwide. **International locations:** Algeria; Brazil; Canada; Mexico.

MINERAL MINING CORPORATION
2526 Mineral Mining Road, P.O. Box 458, Kershaw SC 29067. 803/285-3965. **Contact:** Human Resources. **Description:** Formerly Mineral Mining Company, the company specializes in the mining of gold and mineralite mica. **Affiliates include:** Piedmont Gold Company, Inc.; Haile Mine Properties. **Parent company:** Piedmont Mining Co. (Charlotte NC).

MODIS IT RESOURCE MANAGEMENT
1122 Lady Street, Suite 640, Columbia SC 29201. 803/227-3010. **Fax:** 803/227-3020. **Contact:** Human Resources. **E-mail address:** columbia@modisit.com. **World Wide Web address:** http://www.modisit.com. **Description:** A provider of information technology resource management services and solutions. **Positions advertised include:** Web Tester; Business Objects Server Administrator. **Corporate headquarters location:** Jacksonville FL. **Other area locations:** Greenville SC. **Other U.S. locations:** Nationwide. **Parent company:** MPS Group.

MUSCULAR DYSTROPHY ASSOCIATION
2700 Middleburgh, Suite 240, Columbia SC 29204. 803/799-7435. **Contact:** Susan Beach, District Director. **World Wide Web address:** http://www.mdausa.org. **Description:** A social services organization that provides funding for research to cure neuromuscular diseases. The group also offers support groups, summer camps, and educational programs. **Corporate headquarters location:** Tucson AZ. **Other area locations:** Charleston SC; Greenville SC. **Other U.S. locations:** Nationwide.

NAN YA PLASTICS CORPORATION, AMERICA
P.O. Box 939, Lake City SC 29560-0939. 843/389-7800. **Fax:** 843/389-6993. **Contact:** Human Resources. **World Wide Web address:** http://www.npcusa.com. **Description:** The company's products include PVC rigid film; PET sheet; PVC panel and pipe; electronic-related products (printed circuit boards, copper-clad laminates, copper foil, epoxy, BPA, and glass fiber and cloth); PP synthetic paper (a product similar in quality to wood pulp paper); and polyester fiber. Founded in 1990. **NOTE:** Entry-level positions are offered. **Positions advertised include:** Account Manager; Chemical Engineer; Civil Engineer; Electrical Engineer; Industrial Engineer; Manufacturing Engineer; Mechanical Engineer; Operations Manager; Production Manager; Project Manager; Quality Control Supervisor; Sales Representative; Systems Analyst. **Office hours:** Monday - Friday, 8:00 a.m. - 5:00 p.m. **Corporate headquarters location:** Livingston NJ. **Other locations:** Wharton TX. **Parent company:** NAPCOR (Charlotte NC). **Operations at this facility include:** Manufacturing of polyester, chip, and filament fibers.

NESTLE USA
P.O. Box 1419, Gaffney SC 29342. 864/487-7111. **Physical address:** 2132 Old Georgia Highway, Gaffney SC 29340. **Contact:** Human Resources. **World Wide Web address:** http://www.nestleusa.com. **Description:** Manufactures prepared frozen food products. **Positions advertised include:** Retail Sales Representative; Pediatric Nutrition Representative. **Parent company:** Nestle S.A. (Vevey, Switzerland). **Chairman/CEO:** Joe Weller. **Annual sales/revenues:** $8.1 billion. **Number of employees worldwide:** 16,000.

NEWARK ELECTRONICS
217 Wilcox Avenue, Gaffney SC 29340-8650. 864/487-1900. **Contact:** Human Resources. **World Wide Web address:** http://www.newark.com. **Description:** Distributes electronic parts and products through sales offices in North America and Europe. **Positions advertised include:** Order Processor; Export Specialist; Operations Supervisor; Sales Associate; Customer Service Representative. **Other U.S. locations:** Nationwide. **Parent company:** Premier Farnell PLC is a broad line distributor of electronic components used in the production and maintenance of equipment; a supplier of maintenance products for industrial, commercial, and institutional applications; and a manufacturer of fire-fighting equipment.

NEXSEN PRUET JACOBS & POLLARD, LLC
P.O. Drawer 2426, Columbia SC 29202-2426. 803/771-8900. **Physical address:** 1441 Main Street, Suite 1500, Columbia SC 29201. **Fax:** 803/253-8277. **Contact:** Human Resources. **World Wide Web address:** http://www.npjp.com. **Description:** A law firm with a wide variety of specialties including real estate, corporate law, banking and finance, securities, tax and estate planning, health care, employee benefits, construction, labor and employment, environmental law, communications, patents and intellectual property, international, regulatory, administrative and legislative law. **Positions advertised include:** Attorney; Litigation Software Support Specialist; File Clerk; Paralegal; Litigation Paralegal; Legal Secretary; Records Clerk. **Corporate headquarters location:** This location. **Other locations:** Charleston SC; Greenville SC; Hilton Head SC; Myrtle Beach SC; Charlotte NC.

NUCOR STEEL
300 Steel Mill Road, P.O. Box 525, Darlington SC 29540. 843/393-5841. **Fax:** 843/895-8708. **Contact:** Human Resources. **World Wide Web address:** http://www.nucor.com. **Description:** Nucor Steel manufactures carbon and alloy steel in bar, sheet, and structural forms, steel joist and joist girders, steel deck, cold finished steel, steel grinding balls, steel fasteners, metal building systems, and steel bearing products. **Corporate headquarters location:** Charlotte NC. **Other area locations:**

Florence SC; Swanson SC. **Other U.S. locations:** AZ; NE; TX; UT. **Parent company:** Nucor Corporation is a manufacturer of steel products, with other divisions that include Vulcraft, one of the nation's largest producers of steel joists and joist girders; Nucor Cold Finish, which produces cold-finished steel bars used extensively for shafting and machined precision parts; Nucor Grinding Balls, which produces steel grinding balls for the mining industry; Nucor Fastener, a steel bolt-making facility; Nucor Bearing Products, Inc., which produces steel bearings and machined steel parts; and Nucor Building Systems, which produces metal buildings and components. **Operations at this facility include:** Production of carbon steel angles, bars, light structural, sheet, and special steel products.

ORANGEBURG CONSOLIDATED SCHOOL DISTRICT 5
578 Ellis Avenue, Orangeburg SC 29115. 803/534-7936. **Contact:** Dr Charles G. Spell. Assistant Superintendent of Human Resources/Support Services. **E-mail address:** cgs45@orangeburg5.k12.sc.us. **World Wide Web address:** http://www.orangeburg5.k12.sc.us. **Description:** A public school district comprised of eight elementary schools, five middle schools, and three high schools. **Positions advertised include:** Elementary School Principal; Educable Mentally Disabled Learning Teacher; Emotionally Disabled Teacher; Social Studies Teacher; Occupational Therapist; Registered Nurse; Adult Bus Driver; Building Fund Management Specialist; Guidance Counselor; Mechanic.

ORDERS DISTRIBUTING COMPANY, INC.
P.O. Box 17189, Greenville SC 29606. 864/288-4220. **Physical address:** 1 Whitlee Court, Greenville SC 29607. **Fax:** 864/458-7348. **Contact:** Mr. Wiley Johnson, Vice President of Human Resources. **World Wide Web address:** http://www.ordersdistributing.com. **Description:** A supplier of a broad range of floor coverings including hardwood, vinyl, carpet, and ceramic. Founded in 1955. **Corporate headquarters location:** This location. **Other locations:** Greensboro NC; Johnson City TN; Roanoke VA.

OWEN STEEL COMPANY
727 Mauney Drive, Columbia SC 29201. 803/251-7680. **Fax:** 803/251-7613. **Contact:** Deloris Walters, Human Resources. **E-mail address:** information@owensteel.com or deloris.walters@ownsteel.com. **World Wide Web address:** http://www.owensteel.com. **Description:** Manufactures structural and reinforcing steel used in large-scale construction. Founded in 1936. **Positions advertised include:** Structural Steel Detailer; Draftsperson; Electrician; Structural Engineer. **Operations at this facility include:** Administration; Manufacturing; Sales. **Parent company:** ADF Group Inc. (Terrebonne, Quebec, Canada).

OWENS CORNING
P.O. Box 1367, Anderson SC 29622. 864/296-4000. **Contact:** Human Resources Manager. **World Wide Web address:** http://www.owenscorning.com. **Description:** Manufactures and sells thermal and acoustical insulation products including insulation for appliances, glass-fiber roofing shingles, and roof insulation and industrial asphalt. Other products of the company include windows, glass-fiber textile yarns, wet process chopped strands and specialty mats, and polyester resins. Founded in 1938. **NOTE:** Second and third shifts offered, as well as on-call/24-hour positions. Human Resources phone: 864/296-4055. **Positions advertised include:** Concrete Process Engineer; Health Specialist; Operations Leader; Plant Leader. **Corporate headquarters location:** Toledo OH. **Other area locations:** Aiken SC; Chester SC; Duncan SC. **Other locations:** Worldwide. **Subsidiaries include:** Advanced Glassfiber Yarns LLC. **Operations at this facility include:** Composite materials manufacturing. **Listed on:** Over The Counter. **Stock exchange symbol:** OWENQ. **Chairman/CEO:** Michael H. Thaman. **Annual sales/revenues:** $4.8 billion. **Number of employees nationwide:** 19,000.

PALMETTO HEALTH
P.O. Box 2266, Columbia SC 29202. 803/434-7000. **Physical address:** 5 Richland Medical Park Drive, Columbia SC 29203. **Fax:** 803/296-5928. **Contact:** Human Resources. **World Wide Web address:** http://www.palmettohealth.org. **Description:** A locally-owned, non-profit healthcare system operating several hospitals and medical centers with a total of 1,247 beds. **NOTE:** Human Resources phone: 803/296-2100. **Positions advertised include:** Administrative Associate; Business Analyst; Communications Coordinator; Communications Advocate; Information Technology Business Analyst; Network Engineer; Manager; Nurse Practitioner; Planning Analyst; Project Manager; Workers Compensation Manager. **Office hours:** Monday – Friday, 9:00 a.m. – 4:00 p.m. **Corporate headquarters location:** Columbia SC. **Subsidiaries include:** Palmetto Health Baptist; Palmetto Health Richland; Palmetto Health South Carolina Cancer Center; Palmetto Health South Carolina Comprehensive Breast Center; Gamma Knife Center of the Carolinas; CareForce; Palmetto Health Hospice. **Number of employees:** 7,000.

PARKER HANNIFIN CORPORATION
3025 West Croft Circle, P.O. Box 15009, Spartanburg SC 29302-0201. 864/573-7332. **Fax:** 864/515-6086. **Contact:** Human Resources. **E-mail address:** tsdjobs@parker.com. **World Wide Web address:** http://www.parker.com. **Description:** Designs and manufactures flight, missile, and engine controls for both commercial and military programs. The company's product lines consist of electronics, hydraulics, and electrohydraulic components. **Positions advertised include:** Administrative Sales Manager; Inside Sales Representative; Accounting Manager; Network Applications Manager. **Corporate headquarters location:** Cleveland OH. **Operations at this facility include:** TechSeal Division manufacturing. **Annual sales/revenues:** $6 billion. **Number of employees worldwide:** 48,000.

PERRIGO COMPANY
P.O. Box 1968, Greenville SC 29602. 864/288-5521. **Physical address:** 4615 Dairy Drive, Greenville SC 29607. **Contact:** Ms. Jimmie Fannell, Personnel Manager. **World Wide Web address:** http://www.perrigo.com. **Description:** Manufactures and sells generic pharmaceuticals, vitamins, and personal care products for the store brand market, nationally and internationally. **Positions advertised include:** Research & Development Formulator. **Corporate headquarters location:** Allegan MI. **Other locations:** CA; MI; NJ. **International locations:** England; Mexico. **Operations at this facility include:** Vitamin manufacturing; Warehouse and Distribution Center also in Greenville SC. **Listed on:** NASDAQ. **Stock exchange symbol:** PRGO. **Annual sales/revenues:** $826. **Number of employees nationwide:** 4,250.

PIRELLI CABLE CORPORATION
700 Industrial Drive, Lexington SC 29072. 803/951-4800. **Contact:** Human Resources. **World Wide Web address:** http://www.pirelli.com. **Description:** A manufacturer of a broad range of energy cables, fiber-optic telecommunications cables, optical-electronic devices, systems for the telecommunications market, and associated accessories and services. **Positions advertised include:** Chemical Engineer; Computer Programmer; Electrical Engineer; Production Manager; Materials Engineer; Mechanical Engineer; Operations Manager; Purchasing Agent; Quality Control Supervisor; Systems Analyst. **Corporate headquarters location:** This location. **Other area locations:** Abbeville SC. **Other U.S. locations:** Colusa CA. **Operations at this facility include:** Administration; Manufacturing; Research and Development; Sales; Service.

PRESIDION SOLUTIONS, INC.
One Harbison Way, Suite 114, Columbia SC 29212. 803/781-7810. **Toll-free phone:** 800/948-8524. **Contact:** Human Resources Manager. **World Wide Web address:** http://www.presidionsolutions.com. **Description:** Performs general accounting functions, as well as human resources, payroll, and workers' compensation for other companies. **Corporate headquarters location:** Troy MI. **Other locations:** Ten sales offices throughout the state of Florida. **Parent company:** Presidion Corporation (Troy MI). **President/CEO:** Craig Vanderburg.

PROGRESS LIGHTING, INC.
P.O. Box 989, Cowpens SC 29330. 864/463-3274. **Fax:** 864/599-6153. **Contact:** Vice President for Human Resources. **E-mail address:** jobs@progresslighting.com. **World Wide Web address:** http://www.progresslighting.com. **Description:** A manufacturer of home and commercial lighting systems and fixtures. **Positions advertised include:** Sales Representative.

PROPEX
320 Shiloh Road, Seneca SC 29678. 864/882-5660. **Fax:** 864/882-4981. **Contact:** Human Resources. **World Wide Web address:** http://www.fabricsandfibers.com. **E-mail address:** fabrics.info@usa.com. **Description:** BP Fabrics and Fibers Company is part of BP's conversion and specialty chemicals division, converting polypropylene into woven carpet-backing and fabrics and yarns for home, automotive, industrial, and medical applications. The company's products include non-woven fabrics, multifilament yarns, and fibers. Since 1965. **Positions advertised include:** Transport Driver; Chemical Engineer. **Corporate headquarters location:** Austell GA. **Other U.S. locations:** AL CA; GA. **International locations:** Australia; Brazil; China; Mexico. **Operations at this facility include:** The Seneca Mills manufactures furniture, bedding, and automotive non-woven fabrics and civil engineering non-woven fabrics. **Number of employees worldwide:** 3,500.

PROVIDENCE HOSPITALS
2709 Laurel Street, Columbia SC 29204. 803/256-5410. **Fax:** 803/256-5838. **Recorded jobline:** 803/256-5627. **Contact:** Human Resources. **E-mail address:** hr@providencehospitals.com. **World Wide Web address:** http://www.provhosp.com. **Description:** The Sisters of Charity Providence Hospitals is a non-profit organization operating three facilities with a total of 311 beds: Providence Hospital, Providence Heart Institute, and Providence Hospital Northeast serving the Midlands region of South Carolina. **Positions advertised include:** Office Coordinator; Executive Secretary; Collections Specialist; Environmental Services Technician; Assembly Analyst; Phlebotomist; Registered Nurse; Sleep Lab Technician; Affairs Vice President; Medical Lab Student; Pharmacy Specialist. **Parent company:** Sisters of Charity of Saint Augustine Health System. **Number of employees statewide:** 1,500.

RICHLAND MEMORIAL HOSPITAL
5 Richland Medical Park, Columbia SC 29203. 803/434-7733. **Contact:** Employment Services Department. **World Wide Web address:** http://www.rmh.edu. **Description:** A 626-bed, regional, community teaching hospital. Richland Memorial Hospital's facilities include a Children's Hospital; the Center for Cancer Treatment and Research; the Heart Center; the Midlands Trauma Center; and Richland Springs, a free-standing psychiatric hospital. Specialty services include a partially matched bone marrow transplantation program, high-risk obstetrics, orthopedics, psychiatry, cardiology, oncology, nephrology, neonatology, neurology, neurosurgery, and medical and surgical services. The hospital is affiliated with the University of South Carolina and other universities. **Positions advertised include:** Physician Office Manager; Assistant Nurse Manager; Clinical Nurse Specialist; Licensed Practical Nurse; Neonatal Nurse Practitioner; Nurse Manager; Registered Nurse; Certified Occupational Therapist; Clinical Engineering Manager; Dietician; Magnetic Resonance Imaging Technician; Pharmacist; Physical Therapist; Radiology Technician; Research Assistant; Respiratory Therapist; Health Information Assistant Accounting Specialist; Collector; Data Processor; Dental Assistant; Laboratory Assistant; Linen Technician; Mechanical Engineer; Mental Health Assistant; Emergency Department Nurse; Phlebotomist; Cardiac Care Technician. **Special programs:** Internships. **Parent company:** Palmetto Health.

RIVERBANKS ZOO & GARDEN
P.O. Box 1060, Columbia SC 29202-1060. 803/779-8717. **Fax:** 803/253-6381. **Contact:** Human Resources Director. **E-mail address:** jobs@riverbanks.org. **World Wide Web address:** http://www.riverbanks.org. **Description:** A zoo featuring over 2,000 animals and a 70-acre botanical garden. **NOTE:** For positions with the zoo's food service, catering and merchandiser, Aramark Sports and Entertainment Services, phone: 803/779-8717 ext1303. **Positions advertised include:** Horticulturist; Mammal Keeper; Herpetological Keeper; Night Watch Person; Pony Ride Attendant; Development Director; Hospital Keeper; Guest Services Representative; Curator; Lorikeet Aviary Attendant.

ROCK HILL TELEPHONE COMPANY
1969 Canterbury Glen Lane, Manchester Village, P.O. Box 470, Rock Hill SC 29731. 803/326-6025. **Fax:** 803/326-7225. **Recorded jobline:** 803/323-6565. **Contact:** Personnel Office. **E-mail address:** employment@comporium.com. **World Wide Web address:** http://www.rhtelco.com. **Description:** A local telephone company. **Office hours include:** 8:00 a.m. – 4:00 p.m. **Positions advertised include:** Call Center Attendant; Graphics Coordinator; Staff Accountant; Programmer; Systems Analyst; Computer Engineer; Technician; Construction Lineman; Engineering Associate. **Parent company:** Comporium Group (also at this location).

RYAN'S FAMILY STEAK HOUSES, INC.
P.O. Box 100, Greer SC 29652. 864/879-1011. **Fax:** 864/894-0256. **Contact:** Kim Lynch, Human Resources. **World Wide Web address:** http://www.ryansinc.com. **Description:** Owns and franchises over 250 restaurants in 21 states. **NOTE:** Contact the company's recruiter in South Carolina, Kim Lynch at: 864/879-1011 ext3572. Fax: 828/894-0256. For restaurant positions, contact local restaurants directly. **Positions advertised include:** Manager Trainee; Cook; Server; Cashier; Host/Hostess; Utility Worker; Restaurant/Food Service Manager. **Corporate headquarters location:** This location. **Listed on:** NASDAQ. **Stock exchange symbol:** RYAN. **Annual sales/revenues:** $774 million. **Number of employees nationwide:** 21,300.

SACO LOWELL, INC.
P.O. Box 2327, Greenville SC 29602. 864/850-4400. **Fax:** 864/859-2908. **Contact:** Gene Dunlap, Human Resources. **World Wide Web address:** http://www.sacolowell.com. **E-mail address:** bkhaleghi@sacolowell.com. **Description:** Saco Lowell, Inc. designs and manufactures textile machinery including parts, attachments, and accessories. The company's primary customers are textile mills. **Positions advertised include:** Computer-assisted Design Operator; Draftsperson;

Electrical Engineer; Industrial Engineer; Production Manager; Machinist; Mechanical Engineer; Sheet-Metal Worker; Tool and Die Maker.

SAFETY-KLEEN CORPORATION
1301 Gervais Street, Columbia SC 29201. 803/933-4200. **Contact:** Human Resources. **World Wide Web address:** http://www.safety-kleen.com. **E-mail address:** info@safety-kleen.com. **Description:** A landfill company that accepts mainly nonhazardous waste from companies. **Corporate headquarters location:** Plano TX. **Other locations:** Nationwide.

SALOMON SMITH BARNEY
P.O. Box 2628, Spartanburg SC 29304. 864/585-7761. **Contact:** Fran Godshall, Human Resources. **World Wide Web address:** http://www.salomonsmithbarney.com. **Description:** An investment banking and securities broker. Salomon Smith Barney also provides related financial services including stocks, bonds, and money market accounts. **Parent company:** Citigroup.

THE SALVATION ARMY
P.O. Drawer 2786, Columbia SC 29202-1374. 803/765-0260. **Physical address:** 2025 Main Street, Columbia SC 29201. **Fax:** 803/254-6465. **Contact:** June Bergman, Head Secretary. **World Wide Web address:** http://www.salvationarmy.org. **Description:** A nonprofit organization providing several service programs including day-care centers, programs for people with disabilities, substance abuse programs and tutoring for at-risk students. The Salvation Army targets its programs to assist alcoholics, battered women, drug addicts, the elderly, the homeless, people with AIDS, prison inmates, teenagers, and the unemployed. **Other U.S. locations:** Nationwide.

SANDS RESORTS
201 74th North Avenue, Myrtle Beach SC 25978. 843/445-9406. **Fax:** 843/445-2737. **Contact:** Ms. Sandi Madorno, Director of Human Resources. **World Wide Web address:** http://www.sandsresorts.com. **Description:** Owns and manages several resorts in Myrtle Beach and one resort in North Carolina. **Positions advertised include:** Customer Service Representative; Human Resources Manager. **Corporate headquarters location:** This location. **Listed on:** Privately held.

SCANSOURCE, INC.
6 Logue Court, Greenville SC 29615. 864/288-2432. **Fax:** 864/288-1165. **Contact:** Human Resources. **E-mail address:** jobs@scansource.com. **World Wide Web address:** http://www.scansource.com. **Description:** A reseller and distributor of barcode, automatic data capture, and point-of-sale equipment as well as voice, data, and telephony products through its subsidiary, Catalyst Telecom. Since 1992. **Positions advertised include:** Product Asset Manager; Product Manager; Marketing Manager; Business Development Specialist; Financial Analyst; Credit Vice President. **Corporate headquarters location:** This location. **Other locations:** Worldwide. **Subsidiaries include:** Catalyst Telecom; Paracon. **Listed on:** NASDAQ. **Stock exchange symbol:** SCSC. **Chairman:** Steven H. Owings. **Annual sales/revenues:** $842 million. **Number of employees:** 700.

SCHLUMBERGER RESOURCE MANAGEMENT SERVICES
313 North Highway 11, West Union SC 29696. 864/638-8300. **Contact:** Sue Gray, Personnel Supervisor. **World Wide Web address:** http://www.slb.com. **Description:** A global technology services company with operations in 100 countries divided into two business segments: Schlumberger Oilfield Services and SchlumbergerSema. The company provides services for utilities, energy service providers, and industry worldwide through consulting, meter deployment and management, data collection and processing, and information analysis in all utility sectors including water, gas, electricity, and heat. **Positions advertised include:** Field Engineer; Field Specialist; Account Manager; Assistant Accountant; Web Developer; Data Architect; Chemical Product Developer; Chemical Engineer; Compensation & Compliance Specialist; Electrical Development Engineer; Electrical Engineer; Oilfield Services Electronic Technician; Field Marketing Manager; GeoScientist; Applications Engineer; Design Engineer; Sales Engineer; Software Engineer. **Corporate headquarters location:** New York NY. **Other locations:** Worldwide. **Parent company:** Schlumberger Ltd. manufactures measurement, electronics, and testing products and provides well site exploration and computer aided design.

SCOTSMAN ICE SYSTEMS
Industrial Park, P.O. Box 890, Fairfax SC 29857. 803/632-2511. **Contact:** Human Resources. **World Wide Web address:** http://www.scotsman-ice.com. **Description:** A manufacturer of commercial ice machines. **Office hours:** Monday – Friday, 7:00 a.m. – 4:00 p.m. **Positions advertised include:** Industrial Engineer; Management Trainee; Production Manager; Quality Control Supervisor. **Corporate headquarters location:** Vernon Hills IL. **Parent company:** Enodis.

SEA PINES ASSOCIATES, INC.
32 Greenwood Drive, Hilton Head Island SC 29928. 843/785-3333. **Fax:** 843/842-1412. **Contact:** Monica Nash, Director of Human Resources. **World Wide Web address:** http://www.seapines.com. **Description:** A holding company. **NOTE:** Human Resources phone: 843/842-1882. **Special programs:** Internships. **Corporate headquarters location:** This location. **Subsidiaries include:** Sea Pines Company, Inc. (also at this location) operates resort assets including three golf courses, a 28-court racquet club, a home and villa rental management business, retail sales outlets, food services operations, and other resort recreational facilities. Sea Pines Real Estate Company, Inc. is an independent real estate brokerage firm with 18 offices. Sea Pines Country Club, Inc. owns and operates a full-service private country club providing golf, tennis, and clubhouse facilities for approximately 1,500 club members.

SECURITY FINANCE CORPORATION
P.O. Box 811, Spartanburg SC 29304. 864/582-8193. **Contact:** Human Resources. **E-mail address:** careers@security-finance.com. **World Wide Web address:** http://www.securityfinancecorp.com. **Description:** A credit institution providing commercial and personal loans.

THE SEIBELS BRUCE GROUP, INC.
P.O. Box One, Columbia SC 29202-0001. 803/748-2000. **Physical address:** 1501 Lady Street, Columbia SC 29201. **Fax:** 803/748-8394. **Contact:** Recruiter. **E-mail address:** recruiter@seibels.com. **World Wide Web address:** http://www.seibels.com. **Description:** An automobile, flood, property and casualty insurance company. Founded in 1869. **Positions advertised include:** Associate Underwriter; Commercial Lines Rater. **Corporate headquarters location:** This location. **Other locations:** Winston-Salem NC. **Subsidiaries include:** Agency Specialty of Kentucky, Inc.; Agency Specialty, Inc.; Catawba Insurance Company; Consolidated American Insurance Company; FLT Plus, Inc.; Forest Lake Travel Service, Inc.; Investors National Life Insurance Company of South Carolina; Kentucky Insurance Company; Policy Finance Company; Seibels Bruce Service Corporation; Seibels, Bruce & Company; South Carolina Insurance Company. **Number of employees at this location:** 329.

THE SHAW GROUP, INC.
dba B.F. SHAW, INC.
366 Old Airport Road, Laurens SC 29360. 864/682-4000. **Fax:** 864/683-4771. **Contact:** Human Resources. **World Wide Web address:** http://www.alloypipingproducts.com. **Description:** A union shop fabricator of piping components for both new construction and the maintenance of existing systems. **Positions advertised include:** Project Administrator; Draftsperson; Pipe Fitter; Welder. **Corporate headquarters location:** Baton Rouge LA. **Other area locations:** Greenville SC. **Other locations:** Worldwide. **Operations at this facility include:** Manufacturing. **Number of employees worldwide:** 20,000.

SMURFIT-STONE CONTAINER CORPORATION
Paper Mill Road, P.O. Box 100544, Florence SC 29501-0544. 843/662-0313. 843/772-2932. **Contact:** Bill Flynn, Director of Human Resources. **World Wide Web address:** http://www.smurfit-stone.com. **Description:** A paper-based packaging company specializing in corrugated containers, folding cartons, and multiwall industrial bags. The company is also one of the world's largest collectors and processors of recycled products that are then sold to a worldwide customer base. Smurfit-Stone Container Corporation also operates several paper tube, market pulp, and newsprint production facilities. **NOTE:** Accepts applications through the South Carolina Unemployment Office. **Corporate headquarters location:** Chicago IL. **Other area locations:** Columbia SC; Latta SC; Spartanburg SC. **Other U.S. locations:** CO; FL; MO; OH; PA; TN. **Operations at this facility include:** The Florence Mill manufactures containerboard, paperboard and linerboard for cardboard boxes. **Listed on:** NASDAQ. **Stock exchange symbol:** SSCC. **Annual sales/revenues:** $7.5 billion. **Number of employees worldwide:** 38,600.

SOLUTIENCE.
25 East Court Street, Suite 203, Greenville SC 29601. 864/242-6302. **Fax:** 864/242-6303. **Contact:** Human Resources. **World Wide Web address:** http://www.soultience.com. **E-mail address:** jobs@solutience.com. **Description:** Develops, markets, and supports software for banks and insurance companies. Founded in 1971. **Positions advertised include:** Warehouse Manager; Console Consultant; Quality Management Consultant; Functional Consultant. **Corporate headquarters location:** This location. **Other U.S. locations:** Alpharetta GA; Birmingham AL; Jersey City NJ; Orangeburg SC; Southfield MI. **Parent company:** The BMW Group Munich, Germany).

SONOCO PRODUCTS
One North Second Street, Hartsville SC 29550. 843/383-7000. **Fax:** 843/383-3334. **Contact:** Lisa Spears, Human Resources. **E-mail address:** Lisa.Spears@sonoco.com. **World Wide Web address:** http://www.sonoco.com. **Description:** Manufactures paper and plastic cones, tubes, cores and spools; composite cans and containers; plastic bottles; plastic meter boxes and underground enclosures; specialties; partitions and pads; paperboard; aluminum and steel textile beams; machinery products; hardwood lumber; plastic grocery bags; metal, plastic, and wood reels; adhesives; fiber and plastic drums; and dual oven trays operating over 300 facilities in 32 countries. **Positions advertised include:** Auditor; Commercial Analyst; Corporate Accountant; Corporate Fleet Manager; Financial Analyst; IPD Quality Manager; Operations Manager; Senior Sourcing Specialist; Timber Procurement Forester; Segment Services Quality Manager. **Corporate headquarters location:** This location. **Other area locations:** Union SC. **Other U.S. locations:** Nationwide. **International locations:** Worldwide. **Listed on:** New York Stock Exchange. **Stock exchange symbol:** SON. **Number of employees worldwide:** 18,000

SOUTH CAROLINA DEPARTMENT OF AGRICULTURE
Wade Hampton Building, Fifth Floor, P.O. Box 11280, Columbia SC 29211-1280. 803/734-2199. **Contact:** Clarissa Adams, Administrative and Human Resources Manager. **World Wide Web address:** http://www.state.sc.us/scda. **Description:** This location of the Department of Agriculture provides services that include working with farmers to market their produce and testing products (produce and gasoline) in a laboratory. **NOTE:** Human Resources phone: 803/734-2196.

SOUTH CAROLINA ELECTRIC AND GAS COMPANY
1115 East Main Street, Lake City SC 29560. 843/394-8043. **Contact:** Human Resources. **World Wide Web address:** http://www.sceg.com. **Description:** A public service organization that produces and distributes electricity and natural gas. **NOTE:** Send resumes to Human Resources, South Carolina Electric and Gas, Columbia SC 29218. Each department is responsible for its own hiring. Jobseekers should address inquiries to a particular area of interest. **Positions advertised include:** Maintenance Mechanic; Right of Way Agent; Apprentice Mechanic; Customer Service Support Associate; Technical Assistant; Safe Guard; Contract Analyst; Remittance Processor; Copy Writer; Line Man. **Corporate headquarters location:** Columbia SC. **Parent company:** SCANA Corporation.

SOUTH CAROLINA STATE MUSEUM
P.O. Box 100107, Columbia SC 29202-3107. 803/898-4921. **Physical address:** 301 Gervais Street, Columbia SC 29201. **E-mail address:** PublicRelations@museum.state.sc.us. **Contact:** Charles Lee, Director of Human Resources. **World Wide Web address:** http://www.museum.state.sc.us. **Description:** A museum featuring art, history, natural history, and science and technology. **Corporate headquarters location:** This location.

SOUTH COAST COMMUNITY BANK
P.O. Box 1561, Mount Pleasant SC 29465. 843/884-0504. **Fax:** 843/216-3071. **Physical address:** 530 Johnnie Dodds Boulevard, Mount Pleasant SC 29464. **Contact:** Human Resources. **E-mail address:** lcalhoun@southcoastbank.com. **World Wide Web address:** http://www.southcoastbank.com. **Description:** A state chartered commercial bank. **Positions advertised include:** Branch Manager.

SOUTH TRUST
145 King Suite 302, Charleston SC 29401. 843/460-1310. **Contact:** Human Resources. **E-mail address:** careers@southtrust.com. **World Wide Web address:** http://www.southtrust.com. **Description:** A full service bank offering financial and banking services for personal and business accounts. **Positions advertised include:** Teller; Teller Supervisor. **Corporate headquarters:** Birmingham, Alabama. **Listed on:** NASDAQ. **Stock exchange symbol:** SOTR. **Annual Sales / Revenue:** 51.9 billion.

SOUTHEASTERN COMMERCIAL SERVICES
P.O. Box 6958, Hilton Head Island SC 29938. 843/686-6660. **Office Hours:** Monday – Friday, 9:00 a.m. – 5:00 p.m. **Fax:** 843/342-3428. **Contact:** Susan Underwood, Office Manager. **Description:** A commercial property real estate company.

SPAN-AMERICA MEDICAL SYSTEMS, INC.
P.O. Box 5231, Greenville SC 29606. 864/288-8877. **Toll-free phone:** 800/888-6752. **Fax:** 864/288-8692. **Contact:** Human Resources. **E-mail address:**

employment@spanamerica.com. **World Wide Web address:** http://www.spanamerica.com. **Description:** Manufactures and distributes a variety of polyurethane foam products for the health care, consumer, and industrial markets. The company's principal health care products consist of polyurethane foam mattress overlays including its Geo-Matt overlay, therapeutic replacement mattresses, patient positioners, and single-use flexible packaging products. These products are marketed primarily to hospitals but are also marketed to long-term care facilities in the United States. Span-America's specialty products are sold under the trademark Span-Aids, which consists of over 300 different foam items that relieve the basic patient positioning problems of elevation, immobilization, muscle contraction, foot drop, and foot or leg rotation. Founded in 1970. **Corporate headquarters location:** This location. **Other locations:** Norwalk CA. **Listed on:** NASDAQ. **Stock exchange symbol:** SPAN. **Number of employees:** 225.

SPARTANBURG STEEL PRODUCTS INC.
1290 New Cut Road, P.O. Box 6428, Spartanburg SC 29304. 864/585-5211. **Fax:** 864/583-5641. **Contact:** Human Resources. **World Wide Web address:** http://www.ssprod.com. **E-mail address:** info@ssprod.com. **Description:** Manufactures a variety of steel products including automotive stampings, beverage containers, and beer kegs. **Positions advertised include:** Draftsperson; Electrical Engineer; Industrial Designer; Industrial Engineer; Mechanical Engineer. **Corporate headquarters location:** This location. **Parent company:** The Reserve Group (Akron OH). **Operations at this facility include:** Manufacturing; Research and Development; Sales.

SPIRAX SARCO INC.
1150 Northpoint Boulevard, Blythewood SC 29016. 803/714-2000. **Fax:** 803/714-2222. **Contact:** Human Resources. **World Wide Web address:** http://www.spiraxsarco-usa.com. **Description:** A leading supplier of steam system solutions. The company manufactures regulators, controls, steam traps, strainers, pumps, and other steam specialty products operating 39 facilities in 28 countries including 12 manufacturing locations. **Positions advertised include:** Draftsperson; Electrician; Environmental Engineer; Materials Engineer; Mechanical Engineer; Operations/Production Manager. **Corporate headquarters location:** This location. **Parent company:** Spirax Sarco Engineering PLC. **Operations at this facility include:** Administration; Manufacturing; Research and Development; Sales; Service. **Number of employees worldwide:** 3,900.

SPRINGS INDUSTRIES, INC.
P.O. Box 70, Fort Mill SC 29716. 803/547-1500. **Physical address:** 205 North White Street, Fort Mill SC 29715. **Contact:** Human Resources. **World Wide Web address:** http://www.springs.com. **Description:** A producer of home furnishings, finished fabrics, and other fabrics for industrial uses. Products include bedroom accessories, bath products, novelties, window treatments, and specialty fabrics for the apparel, home furnishing, home sewing, and sporting good industries. Brand names include Wamsutta, Springmaid, Nanik, Graber, Bali, Springs Baby, Daisy Kingdom, and Regal Rugs operating 40 facilities in North America. Founded in 1887. **Positions advertised include:** Process Engineer; Field Sales Representative. **Corporate headquarters location:** This location. **Other locations:** Nationwide. **International locations:** Canada; Mexico. **Listed on:** Privately held. **Chairman:** Crandall Bowles. **Annual sales/revenues:** $2.1 billion. **Number of employees:** 12,000.

SQUARE D COMPANY
1990 Sandifer Boulevard, Seneca SC 29678. 864/882-2414. **Contact:** Russ Karpick, Human Resources Director. **E-mail address:** uwb@schneiderelectricjobs.com. **World Wide Web address:** http://www.squared.com. **Description:** A manufacturer of electrical distribution products for the construction industry. The company's products are used in commercial and residential construction, industrial facilities, and machinery and original equipment manufacturers products. Residential building products feature circuit breakers with an exclusive quick-open mechanism that isolates potential dangers quickly, and a complete home wiring system connecting multiple telephone lines, audio signals, VCR, cable, or closed circuit television. Square D also manufactures a Home Power System that reduces installation times and cuts labor costs. In office developments, hotels and restaurants, retail shops, and other businesses, Square D Company provides products ranging from parking lot gate controls and uninterrupted power systems for personal computers to space-saving remote-controlled lighting and custom circuit breaker panel boards. Square D Company also equips public buildings such as schools, stadiums, museums, hospitals, prisons, military bases, and wastewater treatment plants with electrical distribution systems. **Positions advertised include:** Application Engineer. **Corporate headquarters location:** Palatine IL. **Other U.S. locations:** AZ; CA; KY; MO; NE; OH; TN. **Parent company:** Schneider Electric.

THE STATE NEWSPAPER
P.O. Box 1333, Columbia SC 29202. 803/771-8350. **Recorded jobline:** 803/771-8562. **Contact:** Holly Rogers, Human Resources Director. **World Wide Web address:** http://www.thestate.com. **Description:** Publishes *The State*, a daily newspaper with a weekday circulation exceeding 145,000. **NOTE:** Human Resources phone: 803/771-8350. **Positions advertised include:** Retail Account Executive; Lake Murray Sales Representative; Field Service Assistant. **Corporate headquarters location:** This location. **Parent company:** Knight-Ridder, Inc., a major newspaper publishing company, owns 28 dailies in 15 states, and three nondailies. The company also publishes larger papers including the *Miami Herald*, *Philadelphia Inquirer*, *Philadelphia Daily News*, *Detroit Free Press*, and *San Jose Mercury News*. Knight-Ridder also has interests in the information distribution market through Business Information Services, with subsidiaries Knight-Ridder Information, Inc., Knight-Ridder Financial, and Technimetrics. Knight Ridder's online information retrieval serves the business, scientific, technology, medical and education communities in more than 100 countries. Knight-Ridder Financial provides real-time financial news and pricing information through primary products MoneyCenter, Digital Datafeed, ProfitCenter, and TradeCenter. Knight-Ridder also has interests in cable television and other businesses. Other interests include partial ownership of the Seattle Times Company, two paper mills, a newspaper advertising sales company, and SCI Holdings.

STEINBERG LAW FIRM
61 Broad Street, Charleston SC 29402. 843/720-2800. **Fax:** 843/722-1190. **Contact:** Human Resources Director. **E-mail address:** tprior@steinberglawfirm.com. **World Wide Web address:** http://www.steinberglawfirm.com. **Description:** A law firm. **Positions advertised include:** Runners.

SUITT CONSTRUCTION COMPANY INC.
P.O. Box 8858, Greenville SC 29604. 864/250-5000. **Physical address:** 201 East McBee Avenue, Suite 300, Greenville SC 29601. **Fax:** 864/250-5230. **Contact:** Human Resources. **E-mail address:** careers@suitt.com. **World Wide Web address:** http://www.suitt.com. **Description:** A diversified, single-source provider of construction and design-build services engaged in new construction, renovation and expansion. Founded in 1968. **Positions advertised include:** Project Engineer; Project Manager. **Corporate headquarters location:** This location. **Other U.S. locations:** Atlanta GA; Orlando FL; Providence RI; Raleigh NC; Richmond VA. **International locations:** Mexico. **Parent company:** BE&K Inc. (Birmingham AL). **Number of employees:** 1,500.

SUPERIOR ESSEX
P.O. Box 640, Chester SC 29706. 803/581-9200. **Physical address:** 995 Old York Road, Chester SC 29706. **Contact:** Human Resources. **World Wide Web address:** http://www.superioressex.com. **E-mail address:** career_ops@superior.essex.com. **Description:** A manufacturer and distributor of electrical wire and cable and electrical insulation products including magnetic wire, building wire, telephone cable, and other related products operating 30 facilities nationwide. **NOTE:** Accepts resumes for open positions only. **Positions advertised include:** District Operator; Customer Service Representative; Accounting Associate; Manufacturing Supervisor; Distribution Administrator; Manufacturing Engineer. **Corporate headquarters location:** Fort Wayne IN. **Parent company:** Superior TeleCom Inc. (East Rutherford NJ). **Listed on:** Privately held. **Number of employees:** 4,000.

SYNNEX INFORMATION TECHNOLOGIES, INC.
39 Pelham Ridge Drive, Greenville SC 29615. 864/289-4000. **Toll-free phone:** 800/756-9888. **Fax:** 864/289-4284. **E-mail address:** hr@synnex.com. **Contact:** Human Resources. **World Wide Web address:** http://www.synnex.com. **Description:** Formerly Gates Arrow Distributors, Synnex distributes microcomputers, networking software, and computer peripheral equipment including monitors, hard-disk drives, and modems. The company also packages computer systems, offers systems integration services, and provides technical support services. **NOTE:** Resumes for openings at this facility may be sent to the above fax or e-mail, or to: Human Resources, SYNNEX Information Technologies, Inc., 1041 East Butler Road, Suite 1200, Greenville SC 29607. Applicants may fill out applications online. **Positions advertised include:** Computer Operator; Computer Programmer; Customer Service Representative; Services Sales Representative. **Corporate headquarters location:** Fremont CA. **Operations at this facility include:** Administration; Sales.

3M COMPANY
1400 Perimeter Road, Greenville SC 29605. 864/277-8270. **Contact:** Human Resources. **World Wide Web address:** http://www.3m.com. **Description:** The company manufactures products in three sectors: industrial and consumer; information, imaging, and electronic; and life sciences. The industrial and consumer sector includes a variety of products under brand names including 3M, Scotch, Post-it, Scotch-Brite, and Scotchgard. The information, imaging, and electronic sector is a leader in several high-growth global industries including telecommunications, electronics, electrical, imaging, and memory media. The life sciences sector serves two broad market categories: health care, and traffic and personal safety. In the health care market, 3M is a leading provider of medical and surgical supplies, drug delivery systems, and dental products. In traffic and personal safety, 3M is a leader in products for transportation safety, worker protection, vehicle and sign graphics, and out-of-home advertising. Founded in 1929. **Corporate headquarters location:** St. Paul MN. **Operations at this facility include:** Tape manufacturing. **Listed on:** New York Stock Exchange. **Stock exchange symbol:** MMM. **Number of employees nationwide:** 71,600.

TIETEX INTERNATIONAL
P.O. Box 6218, Spartanburg SC 29304. 864/574-0500. **Physical address:** 3010 North Blackstock Road, Spartanburg SC 29301. **Toll-free phone:** 800/843-8390. **Fax:** 864/574-9476. **Contact:** Mr. Jackie Johnson, Director of Human Resources. **E-mail address:** info@tietex.com. **World Wide Web address:** http://www.tietex.com. **Description:** One of the world's largest manufacturers of stitch-bonded fabrics. Other services provided by the company include warp knitting and textile finishing. Finishing processes include flexographic printing, dyeing, acrylic foam coating, heat transfer printing, napping, hot melt adhesive laminating, and embossing. Tietex products include mattress ticking (printed tickings, box spring filler cloth, and commercial tickings with flame retardants); vertical blinds (custom and ready-made vertical and pleated shade fabrics); bedding (prints and solids for comforters, bedspreads, pillow shams, and dust ruffles); upholstery (prints, faux leathers, and suedes); outdoor furniture (cushion and umbrella prints); drapery and curtains (prints and solids that can be napped, latex foam-backed, or flame-retarded); industrial fabrics; vacuum cleaner bags (foam-backed filter media for outside of the bags on residential and commercial uprights and stick brooms); roofing (reinforcement for cold process roofing and modified bitumen membranes); shoes (shoe lining and innersole fabrics); medical (fabrics for orthopedic soft goods, arm slings, and restraint vests); sleeping bags (shells and linings for sleeping bags); and home furnishings (Tietex's largest area of business). Founded in 1972. **Corporate headquarters location:** This location. **Other locations:** Chonburi, Thailand. **Listed on:** Privately held.

THE TIMKEN COMPANY
P.O. Box 565, Honea Path SC 29654. 864/369-7395. **Contact:** Human Resources Manager. **E-mail address:** careers@timken.com. **World Wide Web address:** http://www.torrington.com. **Description:** Formerly the Torrington Company, Timken develops, manufactures, and markets antifriction bearings and produces universal joints and precision metal components and assemblies for the automotive industry with operations in 24 countries. **NOTE:** Due to the February 2003 acquisition of Torrington, resumes should be sent to the parent company headquarters address: 1835 Dueber Avenue SW, P.O. Box 6932, Canton OH 44706-0932. Fax: 330/471-4551. **Positions advertised include:** Draftsperson; Electrical Engineer; Mechanical Engineer. **Corporate headquarters location:** Canton OH. **Operations at this facility include:** Manufacturing. **Listed on:** New York Stock Exchange. **Stock exchange symbol:** TKR. **Annual sales/revenues:** $2.4 billion. **Number of employees:** 18,200.

TRICO ENGINEERING
4425 Belle Oaks Drive, North Charleston SC 29405. 843/740-7700. **Contact:** Human Resources. **E-mail address:** jobs@tricoengineering.com. **World Wide Web address:** http://www.tricoengineering.com. **Description:** An engineering company that does surveying projects. **Positions advertised include:** Survey Instrument Person. **Corporate headquarters location:** This location.

TUOMEY HEALTHCARE SYSTEM
129 North Washington Street, Sumter SC 29150. 803/778-9000. **Fax:** 803/778-9494. **Contact:** Employment Supervisor. **E-mail address:** ptruluck@tuomey.com. **World Wide Web address:** http://www.tuomey.com. **Description:** A non-profit medical system, which includes the 266-bed Tuomey Regional Medical Center and a staff of over 150 physicians. Facilities include a 36-bed nursery, expanded ICU, 10 operating suites and a satellite medical park as well as diagnostic and treatment capabilities with a Cancer Treatment Center, cardiac catheterization and updated HiSpeed Computed Tomography. Transitional care is provided via Home Services and a Subacute Skilled Care program. **NOTE:** Human Resources phone: 803/778-8760 or 800/648-1195. For Nursing/Allied Health Recruiter: 803/778-8762. **Positions advertised include:** Echo Vascular Technologist; Licensed Practical Nurse; Mammography Technician; Medical Lab Assistant; Medical Technician; Nurse Technician Extern; Occupational Therapist; Physical Therapist; Registered Nurse; Surgical Technician.

TURNER PADGET GRAHAM & LANEY
P.O. Box 1473, Columbia SC 29202. 803/254-2200. **Physical address:** Bank of America Plaza, 17th Floor, 1901 Main Street, Columbia SC 29201. **Fax:** 803/799-3957. **Contact:** Mimi Love, Human Resources Manager. **E-mail address:** mwl@tpgl.com. **World Wide Web address:** http://www.tpgl.com. **Description:** A law firm specializing in a variety of legal areas including corporate, insurance defense, medical malpractice, and tax. **NOTE:** Human Resources phone: 803/227-4211. For summer internships contact Recruitment Committee Chairman, Drew Williams by e-mail: daw@tpgl.com. **Positions advertised include:** Attorney; Law Clerk; Paralegal; Secretary; Administrative Assistant. **Corporate headquarters location:** This location. **Other locations:** Charleston SC; Florence SC.

TYCO HEALTHCARE
dba KENDALL HEALTHCARE COMPANY
525 North Emerald Road, Greenwood SC 29646. 864/223-4281. **Contact:** Human Resources. **World Wide Web address:** http://www.tycohealthcare.com. **Description:** Manufactures and distributes disposable incontinence products. **NOTE:** Entry-level positions and second and third shifts are offered. **Positions advertised include:** Production Superintendent. **Special programs:** Internships. **Corporate headquarters location:** Mansfield MA. **Other area locations:** Camden SC; Seneca SC. **Other U.S. locations:** Nationwide. **International locations:** Worldwide. **Parent company:** Tyco International (Portsmouth NH). **Operations at this facility include:** Administration; Divisional Headquarters; Manufacturing; Sales.

U.S. FOODSERVICE
P.O. Box 1328, Greenville SC 29602. 864/676-8600. **Contact:** Personnel. **World Wide Web address:** http://www.usfoodservice.com. **Description:** A leading foodservice distributor with over 100 distribution centers nationwide. **NOTE:** Employment applications and resumes should be directed to the Human Resources office at the company's headquarters to the attention of: Jodie Manning. Fax: 410/910-2225. E-mail: jmanning@usfood.com. **Positions advertised include:** Dispatcher; Dispatcher Trainee. **Corporate headquarters location:** Columbia MD. **Other locations:** Nationwide.

U.S. POSTAL SERVICE
1900B North Main Street, Anderson SC 29621. 864/226-1595. **Contact:** Human Resources. **World Wide Web address:** http://www.usps.com. **Description:** One of the 38,000 locations of the U.S. postal service. **NOTE:** For all positions at the post office, applicants must apply in person to South Carolina Employment Security Commission, 309 West Whitner Street, Anderson SC 29621. 864/226-6273. **Number of employees nationwide:** 800,000.

UNITED DEFENSE
15 Windham Boulevard, Aiken SC 29805. 803/643-2500. **Contact:** Human Resources. **World Wide Web address:** http://www.uniteddefense.com. **Description:** Fabricates, machines, and welds aluminum, steel, and titanium component parts for medium and heavy armored combat vehicles. **Positions advertised include:** Project Engineer; Systems Engineer; Internal Auditor; Program Manager; Electrical Engineer. **Operations at this facility includes:** Ground System Division. **Corporate headquarters location:** Arlington VA. **Other U.S. locations:** Nationwide. **International locations:** Japan; Turkey; Korea.

UNIVERSITY OF SOUTH CAROLINA
508 Assembly Street, Columbia SC 29208. 803/777-3821. **Physical address:** USC Employment Office 1600 Hampton Street, Columbia SC 29208. **Fax:** 803/777-0302. **Contact:** Loretta Poston, Employment Office. **E-mail address:** loretta@gwm.sc.edu. **Note:** Do not e-mail applications. **World Wide Web address:** http://www.sc.edu. **Description:** A four-year, state university. The university awards bachelors, masters, and doctoral degrees and enrolls over 25,000 students per year. The University of South Carolina also has campuses in Spartanburg and Aiken. Founded in 1801. **Positions advertised include:** Administrative Coordinator; Lab Technician; Technical Medical Associate; Administrative Specialist; Research Technician; Public Information Coordinator; Data Entry & Control Clerk. **Corporate headquarters location:** This location. **Operations at this facility include:** Administration; Research and Development; Service.

WACHOVIA CORPORATION
FIRST UNION/WACHOVIA
P.O. Box 1329, Greenville SC 29602. 864/467-2500. **Physical address:** 15 South Main Street, Greenville SC 29601. **Contact:** Paul G. George, Human Resources. **World Wide Web address:** http://www.wachovia.com. **Description:** Formerly First Union National Bank of South Carolina, Wachovia is a full-service commercial bank providing corporate and consumer services with 2,700 locations in East Coast states and some 65 branches in South Carolina. Founded in 1879. **Positions advertised include:** Profit Family Analyst; Teller; Small Business Banker; Conservative Lending Specialist; Teller Management; Community Bank Market. **NOTE:** Contact Corporate Human Resources at: 800386HIRE (800/386-4473). **Corporate headquarters location:** Charlotte NC. **Subsidiaries include:** OFFITBANK; Wachovia Securities, Inc. **Listed on:** New York Stock Exchange. **Stock exchange symbol:** WB. **Chairman/President/CEO:** G. Kennedy (Ken) Thompson. **Number of employees nationwide:** 84,000.

WASHINGTON MUTUAL HOME LOANS
1333 Main Street, Columbia SC 29201. 803/929-7900. **Contact:** Human Resources. **World Wide Web address:** http://www.wamuhomeloans.com. **Description:** A servicer of single-family residential mortgages and one of the nation's largest originators of home loans. **Positions advertised include:** Loan Specialist; Home Loan Manager; Support Specialist; Mortgage Underwriter. **Office hours:** Monday – Friday, 8:00 a.m. – 5:00 p.m. **Other area locations:** Florence SC; Greenville SC. **Parent company:** Washington Mutual, Inc.

WESTINGHOUSE ELECTRIC CORPORATION
P.O. Drawer R, Columbia SC 29205. 803/776-2610. **Physical address:** 5801 Bluff Road, Columbia SC 29250. **Contact:** Human Resources. **World Wide Web address:** http://www.westinghouse.com. **Description:** Westinghouse Electric Corporation is a diversified manufacturing company with interests in defense electronics, environmental services, broadcasting, mobile refrigeration units, office furniture, energy systems, and power generation. The company conducts operations through 791 locations in the United States and over 30 other countries. **NOTE:** Send resumes to: Westinghouse Electric Corporation, University Relations, P.O. Box 355, Energy Center Complex, Pittsburgh PA 15230-0355. **Corporate headquarters location:** Pittsburgh PA. **Operations at this facility include:** Chemical manufacturing, international headquarters for fuel marketing and contract administration, U.S. manufacturing operations, mechanical fabrication facilities, product engineering and testing laboratories. **Parent company:** British Nuclear Fuels.

WEYERHAEUSER COMPANY
300 Northpark Drive, Rock Hill SC 29730. 803/328-3800. **Fax:** 803/328-3085. **Contact:** Human Resources. **World Wide Web address:** http://www.weyerhaeuser.com. **Description:** An integrated forest products company with offices and operations in 18 countries, Weyerhaeuser is principally engaged in the growing and harvesting of timber; the manufacture, distribution, and sale of forest products; and real estate construction, development and related activities. Founded in 1900. **NOTE:** Applications materials and resumes should be sent to the company's headquarters address: Recruiting, Staffing & Diversity, P.O. Box 9777, Federal Way WA 98063-9777; or by fax: 206/374-2210. The company prefers resumes posted to the company Website. **Positions advertised include:** Operations Manager; Mill Supply Representative; Finance and Planning Manager. **Corporate headquarters location:** Federal Way WA. **Other locations:** Worldwide. **Operations at this facility include:** Manufacturing of continuous stock computer forms. **Listed on:** New York Stock Exchange. **Stock exchange symbol:** WY. **Chairman/President/CEO:** Steven R Rogel. **Annual sales/revenues:** $18.5 billion. **Number of employees worldwide:** 58,000.

WEYERHAEUSER COMPANY
1445 Lancaster Highway, P.O. Box 1110, Chester SC 29706. 803/581-7164. **Fax:** 803/581-4036. **Contact:** Regional Manager. **World Wide Web address:** http://www.weyerhaeuser.com. **Description:** An integrated forest products company with offices and operations in 18 countries, Weyerhaeuser is principally engaged in the growing and harvesting of timber; the manufacture, distribution, and sale of forest products; and real estate construction, development and related activities. Founded in 1900. **NOTE:** Applications materials and resumes should be sent to the company's headquarters address: Recruiting, Staffing & Diversity, P.O. Box 9777, Federal Way WA 98063-9777; or by fax: 206/374-2210. The company prefers resumes posted to the company Website. **Positions advertised include:** Technical Service Representative; Green End Night Shift Coordinator; Instrumentation Journeyman; Account Manager; Retail Marketing Manager; Electrician; Sales Representative; Outside Sales Representative; Products Supervisor; Mill Supply Representative. **Corporate headquarters location:** Federal Way WA. **Other locations:** Worldwide. **Operations at this facility include:** Plywood manufacturing. **Listed on:** New York Stock Exchange. **Stock exchange symbol:** WY. **Chairman/President/CEO:** Steven R Rogel. **Annual sales/revenues:** $18.5 billion. **Number of employees worldwide:** 58,000.

WEYERHAEUSER COMPANY
191 West Main Street, P.O. Box 219, Tatum SC 29594. 843/523-5058. **Contact:** Donnie Culbertson, Plant Manager. **World Wide Web address:** http://www.weyerhaeuser.com. **Description:** An integrated forest products company with offices and operations in 18 countries, Weyerhaeuser is principally engaged in the growing and harvesting of timber; the manufacture, distribution, and sale of forest products; and real estate construction, development and related activities. Founded in 1900. **NOTE:** Application materials and resumes should be sent to the company's headquarters address: Recruiting, Staffing & Diversity, P.O. Box 9777, Federal Way WA 98063-9777; or by fax: 206/374-2210. The company prefers resumes posted to the company Website. **Positions advertised include:** Technical Service Representative; Green End Night Shift Coordinator; Instrumentation Journeyman; Account Manager; Retail Marketing Manager; Electrician; Sales Representative; Outside Sales Representative; Products Supervisor; Mill Supply Representative. **Corporate headquarters location:** Federal Way WA. **Other locations:** Worldwide. **Operations at this facility include:** A paper conversion plant. **Listed on:** New York Stock Exchange. **Stock exchange symbol:** WY. **Chairman/President/CEO:** Steven R Rogel. **Annual sales/revenues:** $18.5 billion. **Number of employees worldwide:** 58,000.

WEYERHAEUSER COMPANY
P.O. Box 636, Bennettsville SC 29512. 843/479-3002. **Fax:** 842/479-2711. **Contact:** Cynthia Carruth, Human Resource Manager. **World Wide Web address:** http://www.weyerhaeuser.com. **Description:** An integrated forest products company with offices and operations in 18 countries, Weyerhaeuser is principally engaged in the growing and harvesting of timber; the manufacture, distribution, and sale of forest products; and real estate construction, development and related activities. Founded in 1900. **NOTE:** Application materials and resumes should be sent to the company's headquarters address: Recruiting, Staffing & Diversity, P.O. Box 9777, Federal Way WA 98063-9777; or by fax: 206/374-2210. The company prefers resumes posted to the company Website. **Positions advertised include:** Technical Service Representative; Green End Night Shift Coordinator; Instrumentation Journeyman; Account Manager; Retail Marketing Manager; Electrician; Sales Representative; Outside Sales Representative; Products Supervisor; Mill Supply Representative. **Corporate headquarters location:** Federal Way WA. **Other locations:** Worldwide. **Operations at this facility include:** Fiberboard manufacturing. **Listed on:** New York Stock Exchange. **Stock exchange symbol:** WY. **Chairman/President/CEO:** Steven R Rogel. **Annual sales/revenues:** $18.5 billion. **Number of employees worldwide:** 58,000.

WEYERHAEUSER COMPANY
581 Willamette Highway, P.O. Box 678, Bennettsville SC 29512-0678. 843/479-0200. **Fax:** 843/479-2985. **Contact:** Donald Newton, Director of Human Resources. **E-mail address:** resume@weyerhaeuser.com. **World Wide Web address:** http://www.weyerhaeuser.com. **Description:** An integrated forest products company with offices and operations in 18 countries, Weyerhaeuser is principally engaged in the growing and harvesting of timber; the manufacture, distribution, and sale of forest products; and real estate construction, development and related activities. Founded in 1900. **NOTE:** Application materials and resumes should be sent to the company's headquarters address: Recruiting, Staffing & Diversity, P.O. Box 9777, Federal Way WA 98063-9777; or by fax: 206/374-2210. The company prefers resumes posted to the company Website. **Positions advertised include:** Technical Service Representative; Green End Night Shift Coordinator; Instrumentation Journeyman; Account Manager; Retail Marketing Manager; Electrician; Sales Representative; Outside Sales Representative; Products Supervisor; Mill Supply Representative. **Corporate headquarters location:** Federal Way WA. **Other locations:** Worldwide. **Operations at this facility include:** Marlboro Facility, produces papergrade pulps, market pulp, uncoated papers, and copy machine paper. **Listed on:** New York Stock Exchange. **Stock exchange symbol:** WY. **Chairman/President/CEO:** Steven R Rogel. **Annual sales/revenues:** $18.5 billion. **Number of employees worldwide:** 58,000.

WILLIAMSBURG COUNTY SCHOOL DISTRICT
423 School Street, P.O. Box 1067, Kingstree SC 29556. 843/355-5571. **Fax:** 843/355-0804. **Contact:** Mr. Francis Burrows, Director of Human Resources. **E-mail address:** wcsd@hotmail.com. **World Wide Web address:** http://www. wcsd.k12.sc.us. **Description:** Early Childhood Education Teacher; Family Consulting Services; Heating and Air Mechanic; Music Teacher; Language Arts Teacher; Mathematics Teacher; Physical Education Teacher; Science Teacher; Special Education Teacher. **Number of employees:** 450.

WILSON SPORTING GOODS COMPANY
206 Georgia Street, Fountain Inn SC 29644. 864/862-4416. **Fax:** 864/862-6150. **Contact:** Personnel. **World Wide Web address:** http://www.wilson.com. **Description:** The company manufactures sports-related products for golf, tennis, and team sports operating eight domestic manufacturing plants and 11 other facilities located outside the United States. Wilson Sporting Goods Company has been affiliated with the National Football League since 1941, has produced the official baseball of the National Collegiate Athletic Association championships since 1986 and the official ball of many of professional baseball's minor league teams. The company also manufactures and supplies uniforms to the National Football League, Major League Baseball, and the National Basketball Association, as well as many colleges, universities, and high schools throughout the United States. **NOTE:** Application materials and resumes may be sent to the attention of Corporate Human Resources at: Wilson Sporting Goods Co., 8700 West Bryn Mawr Avenue, Chicago IL 60631. **Positions advertised include:** Chemical Engineer; Chemist; Draftsperson; Electrical Engineer; Electrician; Industrial Engineer; Mechanical Engineer; Operations Manager. **Corporate headquarters location:** Chicago IL. **Other U.S. locations:** Nationwide. **Parent company:** Amer Group, Ltd. (Helsinki, Finland) is an international, highly diversified conglomerate also involved in the marketing of motor vehicles, paper, communications, and tobacco. **Operations at this facility include:** Tennis ball and racquetball manufacturing. **Listed on:** Privately held. **Number of employees worldwide:** 3,062.

WOODLANDS RESORT & INN
125 Parsons Road, Summerville SC 29483. 843/875-2600. **Toll-free phone:** 800/774-9999. **Fax:** 843/875-2603. **Contact:** Human Resources. **E-mail address:** dlester@woodlands.com. **World Wide Web address:** http://www. woodlandinn.com. **Description:** One of Charleston's most luxurious hotels AAA Five Diamond. **Positions advertised include:** Pastry Chef; Maintenance Help; Dishwasher; Server.

WOVEN ELECTRONICS CORPORATION
P.O. Box 189, Mauldin SC 29662. 864/963-5131. **Physical address:** Old Stage Road, Simpsonville SC 29680. **Contact:** Human Resources. **World Wide Web address:** http://www.wovenelectronics.com. **Description:** Manufactures cable harness systems and electrical wiring. The company also offers electrical engineering services. Founded in 1924. **Corporate headquarters location:** Greenville SC. **Other locations:** Charleston SC; China; Great Britain; Merrimack NH. **Subsidiaries include:** Woven Electronics, Ltd. **Parent company:** Southern Weaving Corporation. **Number of employees:** 400.

ZIFF PROPERTIES
701 East Bay Street, Charleston SC 29403. 843/724-3500. **Contact:** Human Resources. **E-mail address:** email@spi.net. **World Wide Web address:** http://www.zpi.net. **Description:** Specializing in acquisition of shopping centers, office buildings and light industrial properties in the South East. **Positions advertised include:** Accountant; Accounts Payable Supervisor. **Number of employees:** 30.

THE ABERDEEN AMERICAN NEWS & FARM FORUM
P.O. Box 4430, Aberdeen SD 57401-4430. 605/225-4100. **Physical address:** 124 South Second Street, Aberdeen SD 57402. **Toll-free phone:** 800/925-4100. **Fax:** 605/229-7532. **Contact:** Susan Bostian, Human Resources Director. **E-mail address:** sbostian@aberdeennews.com. **World Wide Web address:** http://www.aberdeennews.com. **Description:** Publisher of one of the largest daily newspapers in South Dakota. **NOTE:** Contact phone number is 605/622-2224 or 800/409-2277 Ext.224.Part-time jobs are offered. **Corporate headquarters location:** San Jose CA. **Parent company:** Knight-Ridder, Inc. (San Jose CA.) **Listed on:** New York Stock Exchange. **Stock exchange symbol:** KRI.

ADAMS THERMAL SYSTEMS, INC.
47920 Fifth Street, Canton SD 57013-5802. 605/764-2347. **Contact:** Human Resources Manager. **World Wide Web address:** http://www.adamsthermalsystems.com. **Description:** Manufactures heat transfer products for military and off-road equipment. **Number of Employees at this location:** 200.

ALAMO GROUP (SMC) INC.
300 East 60th Street North, Sioux Falls SD 57104. 605/336-3628. **Contact:** Lori Meyer, Personnel Manager. **E-mail address:** careers@alamo-group.com. **World Wide Web address:** http://www.alamo-group.com. **Description:** Manufactures bunk feeders, loaders for 10 to 100 HP, lo-boy semi-trailers, mixer-feeders, and tractors. **NOTE:** Please see website for online application form. **Office business hours:** Monday – Friday 7:00 a.m. – 5:00 p.m. **Listed on:** New York Stock Exchange. **Stock exchange symbol:** ALG.

ALCOA (ALUMINUM COMPANY OF AMERICA)
2500 Alumax Road, Yankton SD 57078. 605/665-6063. **Fax:** 605/665-5505. **Contact:** Human Resources. **World Wide Web address:** http://www.alcoa.com. **Description:** Engaged in all aspects of the aluminum industry including mining, refining, smelting, fabricating, and recycling. ALCOA also manufactures ceramic packaging for the semiconductor industry, alumina chemicals, plastic bottle closures, vinyl siding, packaging machinery, and electrical distribution systems for automobiles. **NOTE:** Please see website for online application form. **Corporate headquarters location:** Pittsburgh PA. **Other U.S. locations:** Nationwide. **International locations:** Worldwide. **Listed on:** New York Stock Exchange. **Stock exchange symbol:** AA. **Annual sales/revenues:** More than $100 million. **Number of employees worldwide:** 120,000.

ALTAIRE ENTERPRISES, INC.
144 East Grant, Spearfish SD 57783. 605/642-1400. **Contact:** Human Resources. **E-mail address:** info@mato.com. **World Wide Web address:** http://www.mato.com. **Description:** Operates a Website that provides Internet access and e-mail accounts to customers in the northern Black Hills of South Dakota. **Corporate headquarters location:** This location.

ANZA, INC.
P.O. Box 1445, Watertown SD 57201. 605/886-3889. **Physical address:** 121 Airport Drive, Watertown SD 57201. **Fax:** 605/886-0112. **E-mail address:** anza@anza.com. **Contact:** Corporate Recruiter. **World Wide Web address:** http://www.anza.com. **Description:** A holding company. **Special programs:** Internships. **Corporate headquarters location:** This location. **Subsidiaries include:** PERSONA, Inc. is one of the nation's largest sign manufacturers, shipping signs to all 50 states, Canada, and Mexico. MIDCOM, Inc. is the largest of the ANZA group, serving its customers by designing and manufacturing analog, digital, and switchboard power transformers for the telecommunications industry. OEM Worldwide, Inc. is a full-service electronics manufacturing company providing design/development, consulting, and state-of-the-art manufacturing services to its customers in an environmentally controlled facility. ICONtrol, Inc. develops business management software. **Operations at this facility include:** Manufacturing; Research and Development; Sales; Service. **Listed on:** Privately held. **Number of employees at this location:** 1,500. **Number of employees nationwide:** 2,000.

ARGUS LEADER
P.O. Box 5034, Sioux Falls SD 57117-5034. 605/331-2200. **Physical address:** 200 South Minnesota Avenue, Sioux Falls SD 57104. **Fax:** 605/331-2279. **Contact:** Jean Healy, Human Resources Director. **E-mail address:** jhealy@argusleader.com. **World Wide Web address:** http://www.argusleader.com. **Description:** Publishes a daily newspaper with a weekday circulation of more than 53,000 and a Sunday circulation of 75,000. The company is also involved in general and commercial printing including the printing of direct mail publications and newspaper inserts. Founded in 1881. **NOTE:** Human Resources phone is 605/331-2369. Walk-in hours are Monday – Friday 8:00am – 5:00pm. **Positions advertised include:** Online/Special Publications Manager; Part-time Circulation Sales Associate; Kiosk Sales; Outside Sales Leader; Circulation Sales – Temporary; Carrier. **Special programs:** Internships. **Corporate headquarters location:** McLean VA. **Parent company:** Gannett Company, Inc. (Arlington VA). **Operations at this facility include:** Administration; Sales; Service. **Listed on:** New York Stock Exchange. **Stock exchange symbol:** GCI. **Number of employees at this location:** 300.

AUGUSTANA COLLEGE
2001 South Summit Avenue, Sioux Falls SD 57197. 605/274-0770. **Toll-free phone:** 800/727-2844. **Fax:** 605/274-5547. **Contact:** Human Resources. **E-mail address:** humanresources@augie.edu. **World Wide Web address:** http://www.augie.edu. **Description:** A liberal arts college of the Evangelical Lutheran Church in America that offers associate's, bachelor's, and master's degrees. Augustana's Division of Graduate Studies provides advanced training and research at the master's level and offers master of arts degrees in teaching, secondary and special education, and selected studies. **NOTE:** Human Resources phone is 605/274-4110. Applications are kept on file for six months. **Parent company:** Augustana College Association.

AUSTAD'S
2801 E 10th Street, Sioux Falls SD 57103. 605/331-4653. **Toll-free phone:** 800/759-4653. **Contact:** Human Resources. **World Wide Web address:** http://www.austads.com. **Description:** A mail order company specializing in golf equipment. **Corporate headquarters location:** This location. **Other U.S. locations:** Blaine MN; Maplewood MN; Lincoln NE; Omaha NE; Fargo ND.

AVERA McKENNAN HOSPITAL & UNIVERSITY HEALTH CENTER
P.O. Box 5045, Sioux Falls SD 57117-5045. 605/322-8000. **Physical address:** 800 East 21st Street, Sioux Falls SD 57117. **Contact:** Human Resources. **E-mail address:** teresa_frederick@mckennan.org. **World Wide Web address:** http://www.mckennan.org. **Description:** A member of Avera Health, with over 400 beds and a 42-acre campus. The McKennan campus includes McKennan Hospital, the Dakota Midwest Cancer Institute, McGreevy Clinic, Sioux Falls Surgical Center, Central Plains Clinic, Midwest Cardiovascular Center, Physician's Office Building, Wee Care, and Center Inn. Programs include state-of-the-art cardiac care; advanced burn treatment; a 24-hour neonatal intensive care; diagnostic, research, treatment, and consultative services and resources for pediatric and adult cancer; kidney transplantation services; orthopedic treatment for adults and pediatrics (congenital conditions and injury); poison prevention, treatment, and statewide hotline; a 44-bed, complete rehabilitation facility including the innovative Easy Street environment and specialized staff; sports medicine clinic with comprehensive wellness programs, exercise, nutrition, massage, health screenings, workshops, and courses; air ambulance system for regional emergency transport with specially trained emergency medical flight personnel; and emergency services. **NOTE:** Human Resources phone is 605/322-7850 or toll-free at 888/677-3222. Walk-in interviews are available the second Tuesday of every month from 3 – 6pm in the Physician's Office Building, Suite 101. Please visit website to register and apply online. **Positions advertised include:** Architect; Business Office Assistant; Business Office Representative; Certified Nurse Practitioner; Certified Nursing Assistant; Certified Pharmacy Technician; Clinic Nurse; Director of Foundation; Housekeeper; Nuclear Medicine Technologist; Occupational Therapist; Pharmacist; Physical Therapist. **Number of employees at this location:** 2,000.

AVERA QUEEN OF PEACE HOSPITAL
525 North Foster, Mitchell SD 57301. 605/995-2000. **Contact:** Human Resources. **World Wide Web address:** http://www.averaqueenofpeace.org. **Description:** An acute care and long-term care hospital. Founded in 1906. **NOTE:** Human Resources phone is 605/995-2496. Please visit website to register and apply online. **Positions advertised include:** Certified Massage Therapist; Food Service Worker; MRI Tech; Nursing Assistant; Physical Therapist; Radiation Therapist; Registered Nurse. **Corporate headquarters location:** Sioux Falls SD. **Parent company:** Avera Health. **Operations at this facility include:** Service. **Number of employees at this location:** 700.

AVERA ST. LUKE'S MIDLAND REGIONAL MEDICAL CENTER
305 South State Street, P/O/ Box 4450, Aberdeen SD 57402-4450. 605/622-5000. **Toll-free phone:** 800/22-LUKES. **Contact:** Human Resources. **World Wide Web address:** http://www.averastlukes.org. **Description:** A 225-bed medical center. St. Luke's Midland was the pioneer facility of the Presentation Health System, an organization now operating 10 hospitals and other health care facilities in four northern plains states. **NOTE:** Please visit website to register and apply online. **Positions advertised include:** Data Specialist; Food Service Associate; Nurse Assistant; Nursing Coordinator; Registered Nurse; Supply Tech. **Parent company:** Avera Health. **Number of employees at this location:** 1,100.

BADLANDS NATIONAL PARK
P.O. Box 6, Interior SD 57750. 605/433-5361. **Contact:** Human Resources. **E-mail address:** badl_information@nps.gov. **World Wide Web address:** http://www.badlands.national-park.com. **Description:** An organization that works to protect national resources within the park. **NOTE:** Jobs usually filled through the Federal Register and the National Park Service. Links and information are available on the Badlands website, or call or write for more information. **Special programs:** Internships, Volunteer positions.

BLACK HILLS NATIONAL FOREST
25041 North Highway 16, Custer SD 57730. 605/673-9200. **Contact:** Personnel Department. **E-mail address:** r2blackhillswebinfo@fs.fed.us. **World Wide Web address:** http://www.fs.fed.us/outernet/bhnf. **Description:** Organization protecting Black Hills National Forest. **NOTE:** Employees are recruited through various methods, some of which require you to contact another organization. Contact information for each of these groups is available on the Black Hills website under "Jobs." **Special programs:** Summer Jobs; Volunteer positions.

BLACK HILLS SPECIAL SERVICES COOPERATIVE
P.O. Box 218, Sturgis SD 57785. 605/347-4467. **Fax:** 605/347-5223. **Contact:** Human Resources. **World Wide Web address:** http://www.bhssc.org. **Description:** A direct extension of 12 South Dakota public school districts (Belle Fourche, Custer, Douglas, Edgemont, Haakon County, Hill City, Hot Springs, Lead-Deadwood, Meade 46-1, Oelrichs, Rapid City, and Spearfish). It provides a wide range of services, many statewide, which schools cannot establish independently. Major services are day and residential programs for students with developmental disabilities, at-risk youth, and youth from disadvantaged backgrounds (programs are based in Belle Fourche, Deadwood, Rapid City, Spearfish, and Sturgis); vocational assessment and training for youth and adult clients with special needs, moving them from supported employment to competitive employment; a vocational equity program helping girls and women broaden their career views; the Center for Restructuring, providing school modernization training, coordination, and evaluation statewide; a diagnostic center, determining the needs of children and adults with disabilities; Project 2000, a dropout prevention program; Technology in Education, a program that helps educators statewide use the latest instructional technology; Northern Hills Career Learning Center, placing unemployed adults into the workforce; Prairie Winds Writers Project for improving student and teacher writing statewide; Northern Hills Community Development, Inc., a school-community partnership strengthening the Black Hills business climate to ensure jobs for local graduates; asbestos, lead, and radon management; in-service, curriculum publication; and educational video production. **NOTE:** Human Resources phone is 605/423-4444. **Positions advertised include:** Residential Assistant. **Number of employees at this location:** 450.

BLACK HILLS STATE UNIVERSITY
1200 University Street, Unit 9502, Spearfish SD 57799. 605/642-6545. **Fax:** 605/642-6254. **Contact:** Anita Haeder, Human Resource Officer. **E-mail address:** anitahaeder@bhsu.edu. **World Wide Web address:** http://www.bhsu.edu. **Description:** A university offering associate's, bachelor's, and master's degrees. The university is composed of the College of Arts and Sciences; the College of Business and Technology; and the College of Education. Black Hills State also offers the following special programs and specialized educational divisions: the Center for Business and Tourism; the Center for American Indian Studies; the Division of Military Science; the Junior College; and extension/summer session services. Founded in 1885. **NOTE:** Entry-level positions and internships are offered. Please visit website for online application form. **Positions advertised include:** Assistant Professor – Various Departments; Career Counselor; Library Associate; Custodial Worker. **Special programs:** Internships; Volunteer positions. **Corporate headquarters location:** This location. **Parent company:** South Dakota Board of Regents. **Number of employees at this location:** 305.

CHS NUTRITION
P.O. Box 5047, Sioux Falls SD 57117. 605/339-1050. **Physical address:** 1211 North Ellis Road Sioux Falls SD 57107. **Fax:** 605/339-1483. **Contact:** Human Resources. **World Wide Web address:** http://www.harveststatesfeed.com. **Description:** Manufactures livestock feeds, minerals and premixes, and pet foods. **Special programs:** Internships. **Corporate headquarters location:** St. Paul MN. **Parent company:** CHS Inc. **Operations at this facility include:** Administration; Divisional Headquarters; Manufacturing; Research and Development; Sales.

CNA SURETY CORPORATION
P.O. Box 5077, Sioux Falls SD 57117-5077. 605/336-0850. **Toll-free phone:** 888/736-9704. **Physical address:** 101 South Phillips Avenue, Sioux Falls SD 57104-6703. **Contact:** Human Resources. **E-mail address:** employment@cnasurety.com. **World Wide Web address:** http://www.cnasurety.com. **Description:** Writes fidelity and surety bonds. **Positions advertised include:** Human Resources Generalist; Junior Accountant; Senior Financial Analyst; Underwriting Services Associate. **Special programs:** Internships. **Other U.S. locations:** Nationwide. **Listed on:** New York Stock Exchange. **Stock exchange symbol:** SUR.

CORRAL WEST RANCHWEAR
1615 North Harrison, Pierre SD 57501. 605/224-8802. **Toll-free phone:** 800/688-9888. **Contact:** Human Resources. **E-mail address:** personnel@corralewest.com. **World Wide Web address:** http://www.corralwest.com. **Description:** The largest western-wear apparel chain in the world. Company has retail stores and a website "eCatalog Business." **NOTE:** To apply for positions, contact corporate headquarters – Corral West Ranchwear Human Resources Department, 4519 Frontier Mall Drive, Cheyenne WY 82009. Fax at 800/974-0219. **Corporate headquarters location:** Cheyenne WY. **Other U.S. locations:** Nationwide.

DAKOTA STATE UNIVERSITY
820 North Washington Avenue, Madison SD 57042. 605/256-5127. **Toll-free phone:** 800/877-1113. **Fax:** 605/256-5316. **Contact:** Nancy Grassel, Director of Human Resources. **E-mail address:** Nancy.Grassel@dsu.edu. **World Wide Web address:** http://www.dsu.edu. **Description:** A four-year, nonprofit university consisting of the College of Liberal Arts, the College of Natural Sciences, the College of Business and Information Systems, and the College of Education. **Positions advertised include:** Information Assurance Faculty. **President:** Jerald Tunheim. **Number of employees at this location:** 220.

DACOTAH BANKS, INC.
P.O. Box 1210, Aberdeen SD 57402-1210. 605/225-5611. **Physical address:** 308 South Main Street, Aberdeen SD 57401. **Fax:** 605/229-5409. **Contact:** Human Resources. **World Wide Web address:** http://www.dacotahbank.com. **Description:** A multibank holding company that also owns insurance firms. One of the Dakota area's largest independent banks. Dacotah Banks, Inc. has locations throughout North Dakota and South Dakota.

DAKTRONICS, INC.
P.O. Box 5128, Brookings SD 57006-5128. 605/697-4000. **Physical address:** 331 32nd Avenue, Brookings SD 57006. **Fax:** 605/697-4700. **Contact:** Nancy Bohlen, Human Resources Manager. **E-mail address:** recruiter@daktronics.com. **World Wide Web address:** http://www.daktronics.com. **Description:** Designs, manufactures, sells, and services computer-programmable display systems such as stadium and arena scoring systems. Founded in 1968. **NOTE:** Entry-level positions and second and third shifts are offered. **Special programs:** Internships; Summer Jobs. **Corporate headquarters location:** This location. **Other U.S. locations:** Nationwide. **Operations at this facility include:** Administration; Engineering and Design; Manufacturing; Sales; Service. **Listed on:** NASDAQ. **Stock exchange symbol:** DAKT. **Number of employees at this location:** 870.

DISH NETWORK
1832 West Main Street, Rapid City SD 57701. 605/343-3610. **Contact:** Human Resources. **World Wide Web address:** http://www.dishnetwork.com. **Description:** A direct broadcast satellite cable provider. Founded in 1980. **Corporate headquarters location:** Littleton Co. **Other U.S. locations:** Nationwide. **Listed on:** NASDAQ. **Stock exchange symbol:** DISH. **Number of employees nationwide:** More than 10,000.

EDWARD JONES
3001 South Phillips Avenue, Sioux Falls SD 57105. 605/330-0090. **Toll-free phone:** 800/999-5650. **Contact:** Human Resources. **World Wide Web address:** http://www.edwardjones.com. **Description:** An investment firm. **NOTE:** Please see website to search for jobs and apply online. **Corporate headquarters:** St. Louis MO. **Other U.S. locations:** Nationwide. **International locations:** Worldwide.

FIRST WESTERN BANK (RAPID CITY WEST)
P.O. Box 2530, Rapid City SD 57709-2530. 605/348-3322. **Physical address:** 632 Main Street, Rapid City SD 57701. **Toll-free phone:** 800/363-7698. **Fax:** 605/754-6425. **Contact:** Human Resources. **E-mail address:** rcinfo@firstwesternbank.com. **World Wide Web address:** http://www.firstwesternbank.com. **Description:** A bank serving communities in Western South Dakota, through the Black Hills and the Badlands. **NOTE:** Lobby hours are Monday – Friday 9:00 a.m. – 5:00 p.m. **Other area locations:** Belle Fourche SD; Custer SD; Deadwood SD; Edgemont SD; Hill City SD; Hot Springs SD; New Underwood SD; Black Hawk SD; Spearfish SD; Sturgis SD; Wall SD.

GAGE BROTHERS CONCRETE PRODUCTS INC.
P.O. Box 1526, Sioux Falls SD 57101. 605/336-1180. **Physical address:** 4301 West 12th Street, Sioux Falls SD 57106. **Toll-free phone:** 800/348-4243. **Fax:** 605/330-0560. **Contact:** Personnel Director. **World Wide Web address:** http://www.gagebrothers.com. **Description:** Manufactures concrete blocks, precast concrete, ready mix, precast panels, prestressed floors, roofs, feed bunks, and hog stats. **Corporate headquarters location:** This location. **Other area locations:** Harrisburg SD. **Other U.S. locations:** MN.

GATEWAY, INC.
P.O. Box 2000, 610 Gateway Drive, North Sioux City SD 57049. 800/846-2000. **Recorded jobline:** 605/232-2222. **Contact:** Human Resources. **World Wide Web address:** http://www.gateway.com.. **Description:** A computer manufacturer with business that is generated primarily through mail order. Founded in 1985. **Positions advertised include:** General Manager; Retail Sales Leader; Retail Operations Advisor. **Other area locations:** Sioux Falls. **Other U.S. locations:** Nationwide. **Listed on:** New York Stock Exchange. **Stock exchange symbol:** GTW.

GRANITE CITY FOOD & BREWERY
2620 South Louise Avenue, Sioux Falls SD 57104. 605/362-0000. **Contact:** Tim Cary, Chief Operating Officer. **E-mail address:** tcary@gcfb.net. **World Wide Web address:** http://www.gcfb.net. **Description:** A casual dining restaurant. Founded in 1999. **Positions advertised include:** Management; Hourly Positions.

GREAT WESTERN BANK
P.O. Box 2290, Rapid City SD 57709-2290. 605/343-9230. **Physical address:** 14 Saint Joseph Street, Rapid City SD 57701. **Toll-free phone:** 800/809-9230. **Fax:** 605/343-8418. **Contact:** Human Resources Department. **World Wide Web address:** http://www.greatwesternbanksd.com. **Description:** A bank. **NOTE:** Part-time jobs are offered. **Special programs:** Summer Jobs.

HILLS MATERIALS COMPANY
P.O. Box 2320, Rapid City SD 57709-2320. 605/394-3300. **Physical location:** 3975 Sturgis Road, Rapid City SD 57702. **Fax:** 605/341-3446. **Contact:** Human Resources. **E-mail address:** jobs@hillsmaterials.com. **World Wide Web address:** http://hillsmaterials.com. **NOTE:** Please visit website to download application form. **Description:** A heavy highway construction company that also operates several concrete plants.

HOMESTAKE MINING COMPANY
630 East Summit Street, Lead SD 57754. 605/584-4653 Ext.4671. **Contact:** Rodger Andrews, Human Resources Director. **Description:** A gold mining company. **Corporate headquarters location:** Toronto, Ontario, (Canada). **Parent company:** Barrick Gold Corporation. **Listed on:** New York Stock Exchange. **Stock exchange symbol:** ABX. **Number of employees at this location:** 1,000.

HUB CITY, INC.
P.O. Box 1089, Aberdeen SD 57402. 605/225-0360. **Physical address:** 2914 Industrial Avenue, Aberdeen SD 57401. **Fax:** 605/225-0567. **Contact:** Director of Human Resources. **E-mail address:** hubcityhr@hubcityinc.com. **World Wide Web address:** http://www.hubcityinc.com. **Description:** Designs, manufactures, and markets a broad range of specialized drive systems that enable industries to use mechanical, electrical, and hydraulic power systems more efficiently. **Corporate headquarters location:** Beloit WI. **Parent company:** Regal-Beloit Corporation.

HUTCHINSON TECHNOLOGY INC.
2301 East 60th Street North, Sioux Falls SD 57104-0569. 605/978-2200. **Fax:** 605/978-2210. **Contact:** Human Resources. **World Wide Web address**: http://www.htch.com. **Description:** Manufactures suspension assemblies for disk drives. **NOTE:** Hutchinson Technology Inc. does not accept unsolicited resumes. Please specify the job you are applying for when sending your resume. **Corporate headquarters location:** Hutchinson MN. **Other U.S. locations:** Plymouth MI; Eau Claire WI. International locations: Tokyo, Japan; Dongguan, China; Bangkok, Thailand; Singapore. **Listed on:** NASDAQ. **Stock exchange symbol:** HTCH. **Number of employees at this location:** 1,500. **Number of employees nationwide:** 4,000.

INTERBAKE FOODS, INC.
One Devilsfood Drive, North Sioux City SD 57049-5134. 605/232-4900. **Contact:** John Kreber, Human Resources. **World Wide Web address:** http://www.interbake.com. **Description:** Produces cookies and crackers sold nationwide under the Interbake brand name. Founded in 1899. **Office hours:** Monday – Friday 8:00 a.m. – 4:30 p.m. **Corporate headquarters location:** Richmond VA. **Other U.S. locations:** Elizabeth NJ; Somerset PA; Columbus OH; Green Bay WI; Los Angeles CA.

KOLBERG-PIONEER, INC.
P.O. Box 20, Yankton SD 57078. 605/665-9311. **Physical address:** 700 West 21st Street, Yankton SD 57078. **Toll-free phone:** 800/542-9311. **Fax:** 605/665-8858. **E-mail address:** personnel@kolbergpioneer.com. **World Wide Web address:** http://www.kolbergpioneer.com. **Description:** Manufactures a variety of heavy industrial machinery used for screening, remediation, sludge processing, and material handling. **Parent company:** Astec Industries, Inc. **Listed on:** NASDAQ. **Stock exchange symbol:** ASTE.

LARSON MANUFACTURING COMPANY
2333 Eastbrook Drive, Brookings SD 57006. 605/692-6115. **Contact:** Human Resources. **World Wide Web address**: http://www.larsondoors.com. **Description:** Manufactures storm doors and storm windows. **Corporate headquarters location:** This location.

MEDIAONE ADVERTISING/MARKETING
3918 South Western Avenue, Sioux Falls SD 57105. 605/339-0000. **Contact:** Human Resources. **E-mail address:** info@m-1.com. **World Wide Web address:** http://www.m-1.com. **Description:** A full-service advertising agency and production house providing integrated marketing resources and in-house production services to national, regional, and local clients. The firm helps clients draft long-range marketing plans by offering full in-house production services including airbrushing, photography, graphic design, and video production.

MIDCOM, INC.
P.O. Box 1330, Watertown SD 57201-6330. 605/886-4385. **Physical address:** 121 Airport Drive, Watertown SD 57201. **Toll-free phone:** 800/643-2661. **Fax:** 605/886-4486. **Contact:** Human Resources Manager. **E-mail address:** hrrecruit@midcom-inc.com. **World Wide Web address:** http://www.midcom-inc.com. **Description:** Manufactures telecommunications transformers, which are used around the world in analog and digital telephone systems, modems, circuit management, networking, multiplexing, D4 channel banks, signaling, automatic call distribution, public data transmission, e-mail, bulletin board services, mobile communications, security systems, and a wide variety of amplifiers and recorders for the sound system market. The company offers a full range of design engineering services and manufactures, tests, and supplies samples and prototypes according to customers' specifications. **Positions advertised include:** Production Manager; Supply Chain Manager. **Corporate headquarters location:** This location. **Parent company:** ANZA, Inc.

MINNESOTA RUBBER
600 Quadee Drive, Watertown SD 57201. 605/886-8000. **Contact:** Human Resources. **World Wide Web address:** http://www.mnrubber.com. **NOTE:** Please visit website for job listings and information on applying. **Description:** Engaged in the custom molding of rubber and plastic parts for a variety of applications. **Corporate headquarters location:** Minneapolis MN. **Parent company:** Quadion Corporation. **Operations at this facility include:** Manufacturing; Vertical injection molding; Compression and transfer molding; Insert molding; Secondary operations; Mixing rubber/stock/silicone.

JOHN MORRELL & COMPANY
1400 North Weber Avenue, Sioux Falls SD 57104. 605/330-3333. **Fax:** 605/330-3154. **Contact:** Aggie Carlson, Corporate Manager, Human Resources. **World Wide Web address:** http://www.johnmorrell.com. **Description:** A full-line meat-packing and processing plant. The company sells approximately one billion pounds of meat per year. Founded in England in 1857. **Positions advertised include:** Mechanical Engineer; Structural Engineer; Design Engineer; Project Engineer; Quality Control Specialist; Food Technologist/Chemist; Programmer; Business Analyst; Database Administrator; Project Leader; Applications Development Systems Manager; Industrial Maintenance Mechanic; Industrial Maintenance Electrician; Stationary Engineer; Sales Representative. **Special programs:** Internships. **Corporate headquarters location:** Cincinnati OH. **Subsidiaries include:** Curly Foods, Iowa Quality Meats, Mohawk Packing Company; Saratoga Specialties. **Parent company:** Smithfield Foods, Inc. **Number of employees at this location:** 3,000.

NASH FINCH COMPANY
1313 East Patrick Street, Rapid City SD 57701. 605/343-0175. **Contact:** Human Resources. **E-mail address:** careers@nashfinch.com. **World Wide Web address:** http://www.nashfinch.com. **Description:** A distribution center for the nationwide distributor of food and related products and services. Nash Finch is engaged in wholesale distribution, retail distribution, and produce marketing. The wholesale distribution segment supplies products to approximately 5,700 affiliated and independent supermarkets, military bases, convenience stores, and other customers in 31 states. The retail distribution segment consists of approximately 120 retail stores the company owns in 16 states. Nash Finch's corporate stores operate under the names Econofoods, Sun Mart, Family Thrift Center, Food Folks, and Easter's. **Corporate headquarters location:** Edina MN. **Other area locations:** Sioux Falls. **Other U.S. locations:** Nationwide. **Listed on:** NASDAQ. **Stock exchange symbol:** NAFC. **Number of employees nationwide:** 10,000.

NATIONAL PARK SERVICE
WINDCAVE NATIONAL PARK
Rural Route 1, Box 190, Hot Springs SD 57747-9430. 605/745-4600. **Fax:** 605/745-4207. **Contact:** Human Resources. **World Wide Web address:** http://www.nps.gov/wica. **Description:** Protects and preserves caves in the national park and maintains the park's natural resources. **NOTE:** Search for jobs through the USAJOBS website - http://www.usajobs.opm.gov/.

NEXTEL PARTNERS
5000 South Minnesota Avenue, Suite 102, Sioux Falls SD 57108. 605/977-1090. **Contact:** Human Resources. **World Wide Web address:** http://www.nextelpartners.com. **Description:** A wireless communications provider. Founded in 1998. **NOTE:** Please visit website for online application form. **Positions advertised include:** Account Executive; Market Manager; Market Sales Manager; Retail Wireless Consultant. **Corporate headquarters:** Kirkland WA. **Other U.S. locations:** Nationwide. **Listed on:** NASDAQ. **Stock exchange symbol:** NXTP.

NORTHERN STATE UNIVERSITY
1200 South Jay Street, Aberdeen SD 57401-7198. 605/626-3011. **Fax:** 605/626-3022. **Contact:** Human Resources. **E-mail address:** lehrme@northern.edu. **World Wide Web address:** http://www.northern.edu. **Description:** Offers bachelor's degree programs in the arts and sciences, fine arts, business, technology, and education; associate's degree programs in business, commercial art, criminal justice studies, general studies, industrial technology, office administration, and social services; preprofessional programs (one- and two-year) in pre-architecture, prechiropractic, pre-engineering, prejournalism, and premortuary; and master's degree programs in education. **NOTE:** Direct Human Resources phone is 605/626-2520. **Number of employees at this location:** 300.

NORTHWESTERN PUBLIC SERVICE COMPANY
125 S. Dakota Avenue, Sioux Falls SD 57104-6403. 605/978-2908. **Fax:** 605/978-2840. **Contact:** Human Resources. **E-mail address:** careers@northwestern.com. **World Wide Web address:** http://www.northwestern.com. **Description:** Provides electricity and natural gas to customers in eastern South Dakota. **Positions advertised include:** Apprentice Lineman; Director of Risk Management; Customer Service Representative; Customer Associate. **Corporate headquarters location:** This location. **Other area locations:** Huron; Armour; Scotland. **Other U.S. locations:** Nationwide.

PAM COMPANIES
P.O. Box 5200, Sioux Falls SD 57117-5200. 605/336-1788. **Physical address:** 200 South Petro Avenue, Sioux Falls SD 57107. **Fax:** 605/367-6511. **Contact:** Human Resources. **E-mail address:** cflanaga@pamoil.com. **World Wide Web address:** http://www.pam-companies.com. **Description:** An oil company. **Corporate headquarters location:** This location. **Other U.S. locations:** Denver CO; Boise ID; Minneapolis MN; Omaha NE; Fargo ND; Salt Lake City UT. **Operations at this facility include:** This location is a distribution center and an automotive oil wholesaler. **Listed on:** Privately held. **Number of employees at this location:** 195. **Number of employees nationwide:** 325.

PEERLESS TYRE COMPANY
1221 East Saint Joseph, Rapid City SD 57701. 605/348-5525. **Toll-free phone:** 800/999-7810. **Contact:** Human Resources. **World Wide Web address:** http://www.peerlesstyreco.com. **Description:** Provider of tires and other car parts. Founded in 1949. **Positions advertised include:** Manager Trainee; Alignment/Brake Technician; Manager Trainee; Alignment/Brake Technician; Warehouse Worker. **Other area locations:** NE; KS; TX; WY; CO; NM. **Number of employees nationwide:** 250.

PERSONA
700 21st Street SW, Watertown SD 57201. 605/882-2244. **Fax:** 605/882-3521. **Contact:** Brad Jones, Human Resources Manager. **World Wide Web address:** http://www.persona-inc.com. **Description:** A multifaceted sign manufacturing operation with production facilities designed to handle the full range of sign and sign program needs, from standard to highly customized applications. PERSONA offers fabrication consultation during the design phase; interfacing with clients' design firms; complete materials evaluation; prototype fabrication; in-house design capability; and extensive, in-house computer support. The company's products and product features include aluminum frames and cabinets, steel frames and cabinets, flexible faces, rigid faces (both flat and formed plastic, and routed and nonrouted aluminum), vinyl decoration, heat transfer decoration, awnings, channel letters, neon, and custom signs. The company's Corporate Identity Division, established for the sole purpose of project management on a national or regional basis, offers services such as image control sales coordinators, surveys and survey analysis, site analysis, obtaining permits and variances, elevation drawings, photo-scan and imaging services, sign installation and location coordination, detailed construction prints, complete customized location status reports, and indoor storage of inventory. **Corporate headquarters location:** This location. **Other U.S. locations:** Madison SD. **Parent company:** ANZA, Inc.

PETE LIEN & SONS, LTD.
P.O. Box 440, Rapid City SD 57709-0440. 605/342-7224. **Physical address:** 3401 Universal Drive, Rapid City SD 57709. **Fax:** 605/342-6979. **Contact:** Human Resources. **E-mail address:** pbirrenkott@petelien.com. **World Wide Web address:** http://petelien.com. **Description:** A mining corporation. Founded in 1944. **Positions advertised include:** Ready Mix Driver; Fabricator. Maintenance Manager. **President:** Pete Lien. **Number of employees nationwide:** 450.

PRAIRIE LAKES HOSPITAL AND CARE CENTER
401 9th Avenue NW, Watertown SD 57201. 605/882-7000. **E-mail address:** info@prairielakes.com. **World Wide Web address:** http://www.prairielakes.com. **Description:** A regional health care facility that houses an 83-bed licensed hospital and a 51-bed nursing home. **NOTE:** Please visit website for online application form. **Positions advertised include:** Lab Assistant; Medical Physicist; Nutritional Services Aide; Occupational Therapist; Pharmacist; Radiology Technologist; Registered Nurse.

PRECISION COMPUTER SYSTEMS
4501 South Technology Drive, Sioux Falls SD 57106. 605/362-1260. **Fax:** 605/362-9442. **Contact:** Human Resources. **E-mail address:** hr@pcsbanking.com. **World Wide Web address:** http://www.pcs-sd.com. **Description:** Develops, markets, and supports software applications for community banking and city governments. **NOTE:** To apply for positions, please send a letter, resume, and a completed application form. Application forms are available on the company's website. **Positions advertised include:** Conversion Programmer/Analyst; Customer Services Representative, Bank Software Support; Installation Services Representative, Bank Software Support; Quality Assurance Representative; Software Quality Assurance. **Number of employees at this location:** 200.

RAVEN INDUSTRIES
P.O. Box 5107, Sioux Falls SD 57117-5107. 605/336-2750. **Fax:** 605/335-0165. **Physical address:** 205 East Sixth Street, Sioux Falls SD 57104. **Contact:** Human Resources Manager. **E-mail address:** hrdept@ravenind.com. **World Wide Web address:** http://ravenind.com. **Description:** A diversified manufacturer of a variety of consumer and industrial products including snow and ski clothing, electronic systems, balloons, and parachutes. **NOTE:** Human Resources phone is 605/336-2750. **Positions advertised include:** Quality Assurance Engineer; Credit Manager; Corporate Facilities Manager; Manufacturing Engineer; Flexible Films Operator; Electronics Assembler; Process Clerk. **Listed on:** NASDAQ. **Stock exchange symbol:** RAVN.

SKF SEALING SOLUTIONS
P.O. Box 567, Springfield SD 57062. 605/369-2222. **Contact:** Personnel Director. **World Wide Web address:** http://www.skf.com. **Description:** Fabricates rubber-to-metal bonded shaft seals for an international market. Founded in 1878. **Corporate headquarters location:** Elgin IL. **International locations:** Worldwide. **Parent company:** SKF, Inc.

SANMINA-SCI CORPORATION
222 Disk Drive, Rapid City SD 57701. 605/394-6200. **Fax:** 605/394-6287. **Contact:** Personnel Manager. **E-mail address:** 4jobs@sanmina-sci.com. **World Wide Web address:** http://www.sanmina.com. **Description:** Sanmina-SCI designs, develops, manufactures, markets, distributes, and services electronic products for the computer, aerospace, defense, telecommunications, medical, and consumer industries, as well as for the U.S. government. SCI is one of the world's largest electronics contract manufacturers and operates one of the largest surface mount technology (SMT) production facilities in the merchant market. Operations are conducted through a Commercial Division and a Government Division. The Commercial Division operates in six geographically-organized business units: Eastern, Central, and Western Regions of North America; and European and Asian Regions. Each unit operates multiple plants that manufacture components, subassemblies, and finished products for original equipment manufacturers. Design, engineering, purchasing, manufacturing, distribution, and support services are also offered. The Government Division provides data management, instrumentation, and communications services, and computer subsystems to the U.S. government and its prime contractors, as well as to several foreign governments. **NOTE:** Please visit website for online application form. **Positions advertised include:** Plant Controller. **Special programs:** Internships; Jobs for recent graduates. **Corporate headquarters location:** San Jose CA. **Operations at this facility include:** This location manufactures printed circuit boards. **Listed on:** NASDAQ. **Stock exchange symbol:** SANM.

SARA LEE BAKERY GROUP
221 North Chapel Hill Road, Sioux Falls SD 57103. 605/336-2035. **Contact:** Human Resources Manager. **Description:** Produces bread and a variety of other wholesale bakery products. **World Wide Web address:** http://www.saraleebakery.com. **Corporate headquarters location:** St. Louis MO.

SENCORE ELECTRONICS INC.
3200 West Sencore Drive, Sioux Falls SD 57107. 605/339-0100. **Toll-free phone:** 800/SEN-CORE. **Fax:** 605/335-6379. **Contact:** Human Resources. **E-mail address:** hr@sencore.com. **World Wide Web address:** http://www.sencore.com. **Description:** Designs, manufactures, and markets electronic test equipment. **Positions advertised include:** CATV Account Manager; CATV Application Engineer; DTV Account Manager; DTV Application Engineer; Technical Sales Engineer; Mechanical Engineer. **Corporate headquarters location:** This location. **Operations at this facility include:** Manufacturing; Sales; Service.

SHOPKO STORES INCORPORATED
1845 Haines Avenue, Rapid City SD 57701. 605/342-1551. **Contact:** Human Resources. **E-mail address:** careers@shopko.com. **World Wide Web address:** http://www.shopko.com. **Description:** A department store. Founded in 1962. **Positions advertised include:** Business Analyst; Third Party Financial Health Analyst; Optician; Optical Manager; Optometrist; Pharmacist; Senior Benefit Analyst; Payroll Supervisor; System Architect; Manager of Licensing; Photo Stylist; Loss Prevention Investigator; Real Estate Coordinator; Store Manager; Assistant Store Manager; Human Resource Manager; Merchandise Presentation Analyst; Seasonal/Holiday Help. **Corporate headquarters location:** Green Bay WI. **Other area locations:** Aberdeen; Mitchell; Sioux Falls, Watertown. **Other U.S. locations:** Nationwide. **Subsidiaries include:** Payless Shoe Source; Pamida Stores. **Listed on:** New York Stock Exchange. **Stock exchange symbol:** SKO.

SIOUX VALLEY HOSPITAL
P.O. Box 5039, Sioux Falls SD 57117-5039. 605/333-1000. **Physical address:** 1305 West 18th Street, Sioux Falls SD 57117. **Fax:** 605/333-1967. **Contact:** Human Resources. **E-mail address:** hremploy@siouxvalley.org. **World Wide Web address:** http://www.siouxvalley.org. **Description:** A hospital providing home health services, a hospice cottage, pharmaceutical services, a Sleep Disorders Center, and the South Dakota Asthma Institute. **Positions advertised include:** Cardiologist; Dermatologist; Gastroenterologist; Hermatologist; Hospitalist; Perinatologist; Neurologist; OB/GYN; Pediatric Critical Care Position; Pediatric Neurologist; Research Associate; Oncology Clinical Research Leader; Payroll and Office Assistant. **Special programs:** Summer of Excellence – Summer jobs.

SOUTH DAKOTA SCHOOL OF MINES & TECHNOLOGY
501 East St. Joseph Street, Rapid City SD 57701. 605/394-2400. **Toll-free phone:** 800/544-8162. **Fax:** 605/394-6131. **Contact:** Deborah Sloat, Director of Human Resources. **E-mail address:** deborah.sloat@sdsmt.edu. **World Wide Web address:** http://www.sdsmt.edu. **Description:** A university of engineering and science offering bachelor's, master's, and doctoral degrees. The school has approximately 2,500 undergraduate and graduate students from 38 different states and more than 30 foreign countries. The school is divided into four colleges: the College of Earth Systems; the College of Interdisciplinary Studies; the College of Chemical, Physical, and Material

Science and Engineering; and the College of Systems Engineering. Founded in 1885. **NOTE:** Human Resources phone is 605/394-1203. Please visit website to download application form and view application details. **Positions advertised include:** Director of Mining Engineering and Management; Special Projects Manager; Chemical Equipment and Instrumentation Specialist; Golf Coach; Assistant or Associate Professor – Various Departments; Secretary.

SOUTH DAKOTA STATE UNIVERSITY
P.O. Box 2201, Brookings SD 57007. 605/688-4128. **Toll-free phone:** 800/952-3541. **Fax:** 605/688-5822. **Contact:** Mary Larson, Human Resources Generalist. **World Wide Web address:** http://www.sdstate.edu. **Description:** A state university offering bachelor's, master's, and doctoral degrees in agriculture and biological sciences; arts and sciences; education and counseling; engineering; family and consumer sciences; general registration; nursing; pharmacy; and graduate school studies. Founded in 1881. **NOTE:** Human Resources phone is 605/688-4128. **Positions advertised include:** Temporary Senior Secretary; Engineering Technician/Mechanist; Custodial Services Supervisor; Senior Claims Clerk; Laboratory Technician; Microbiologist; Secretary; Staff Nurse; Financial Aid Counselor; Assistant or Associate Professor – Various Departments; Assistant Football Coach; Research Associate; Residence Hall Director; Nursing Faculty. **Corporate headquarters location:** This location. **President:** Dr. Peggy Gordon Miller. **Number of employees at this location:** 1,700.

STARMARK
700 East 48th Street North, Sioux Falls SD 57104. 605/335-8600. **Toll-free phone:** 800/594-9444. **Contact:** Human Resources Manager. **World Wide Web address:** http://www.starmarkcabinetry.com. **Description:** A wood cabinet manufacturer that offers a full-line of stock, semicustom, and custom cabinetry for kitchens, baths, and other rooms.

SUPER 8 MOTELS, INC.
P.O. Box 4090, Aberdeen SD 57402-4090. 605/229-8981. **Fax:** 605/229-8910. **Physical address:** 1800 Eighth Avenue NE, Aberdeen SD 57401. **Toll-free phone:** 800/800-8000. **Contact:** Human Resources. **World Wide Web address:** http://www.super8.com. **Description:** Provides office support for the Super 8 Motels lodging chain. **Special programs:** Internships. **Corporate headquarters location:** This location.

TEREX TELELECT
P.O. Box 1150, Watertown SD 57201. 605/882-4000. **Physical address:** 600 Oakwood Road, Watertown SD 57201. **Contact:** Terry Mueller, Manager of Human Resources. **E-mail address:** terrym@teletect.com. **World Wide Web address:** http://www.telelect.com. **Description:** Manufactures derricks, truck bodies, and hydraulic cylinders. **NOTE:** Human Resources phone is 605/882-5507. Fax is 605/882-5505. **Positions advertised include:** Cost Accountant; Drafter; Boom Bonder Finisher; Paint Prep; Maintenance Technician; Welder; Health Safety and Environment Specialist. **Corporate headquarters location:** Westport CT. **Listed on:** New York Stock Exchange. **Stock exchange symbol:** TEX.

3M
P.O. Box 5227, Brookings SD 57006-5227. 605/692-9433. **Physical address:** 601 22nd Avenue South, Brookings SD 57006. **Contact:** Personnel. **World Wide Web address:** http://www.3m.com. **Description:** 3M manufactures products in three sectors: Industrial and Consumer; Information, Imaging, and Electronic; and Life Sciences. The Industrial and Consumer Sector includes a variety of products under the brand names 3M, Scotch, Post-it, Scotch-Brite, and Scotchgard. The Information, Imaging, and Electronic Sector is a leader in several high-growth global industries including telecommunications, electronics, electrical, imaging, and memory media. The Life Sciences Sector serves two broad market categories: health care, and traffic and personal safety. In the health care market, 3M is a leading provider of medical and surgical supplies, drug delivery systems, and dental products. In traffic and personal safety, 3M is a leader in products for transportation safety, worker protection, vehicle and sign graphics, and out-of-home advertising. **NOTE:** Please visit website to search for local jobs and to apply online. **Corporate headquarters location:** St. Paul MN. **Other U.S. locations:** Nationwide. **International locations:** Worldwide. **Operations at this facility include:** This location manufactures surgical drapes. **Listed on:** New York Stock Exchange. **Stock exchange symbol:** MMM.

3M
610 North County Road 19, Aberdeen SD 57401. 605/229-5002. **Contact:** Personnel. **World Wide Web address:** http://www.3m.com. **Description:** 3M manufactures products in three sectors: Industrial and Consumer; Information, Imaging, and Electronic; and Life Sciences. The Industrial and Consumer Sector includes a variety of products under the brand names 3M, Scotch, Post-it, Scotch-Brite, and Scotchgard. The Information, Imaging, and Electronic Sector is a leader in several high-growth global industries including telecommunications, electronics, electrical, imaging, and memory media. The Life Sciences Sector serves two broad market categories: health care, and traffic and personal safety. In the health care market, 3M is a leading provider of medical and surgical supplies, drug-delivery systems, and dental products. In traffic and personal safety, 3M is a leader in products for transportation safety, worker protection, vehicle and sign graphics, and out-of-home advertising. **NOTE:** Please visit website to search for local jobs and to apply online. **Corporate headquarters location:** St. Paul MN. **Other U.S. locations:** Nationwide. **International locations:** Worldwide. **Operations at this facility include:** This location slits tape (cutting down one large roll of tape into many smaller rolls) and makes respirators. **Listed on:** New York Stock Exchange. **Stock exchange symbol:** MMM.

TOSHIBA AMERICA BUSINESS SOLUTIONS
901 North Foster, Mitchell SD 57301. 605/996-7731. **Fax:** 605/995-2056. **Contact:** Human Resources. **E-mail address:** TPDEmployment@tabs.toshiba.com. **World Wide Web address:** http://www.toshiba.com. **Description:** Toshiba America Business Solutions, Inc., (TABS) is an independent operating company of Toshiba Corp., a large electronics/electrical equipment company, and is a manufacturer and distributor of office product solutions for businesses in the United States, Latin America and Caribbean. Toshiba Corp. TABS specializes in the digital copier and color markets. **Positions advertised include:** Account Executive, Field Service Engineer, Field Service Technician, Operations Billing Analyst, Sales Professionals, Senior Process Engineer, Staff Network Engineer, Telemarketing Representative. **Corporate headquarters location:** New York NY.

TRAIL KING INDUSTRIES, INC.
300 East Norway, Mitchell SD 57301. 605/996-6482. **Toll-free phone:** 800/843-3324. **Contact:** Human Resources. **E-mail address:** careers@trailking.com. **World Wide Web address:** http://www.trailking.com. **Description:** Manufactures specialized trailers for construction and commercial purposes. **Positions advertised include:** Production Welder. **Corporate headquarters location:** Syracuse NY. **Parent company:** Carlisle Companies, Inc. **Listed on:** Privately held.

TWIN CITY FAN & BLOWER COMPANY
101 Sunrise Ridge Road South, Brookings SD 57006. 605/692-7333. **Contact:** Human Resources. **E-mail address:** hr@tcf.com. **World Wide Web address:** http://www.tcf.com. **Description:** Designs and manufactures air-moving equipment. The company has a complete line of fans and blowers from 1/6 HP to over 1,000 HP for every commercial and industrial air-moving need. Products include airfoil design ventilating fans, packaged ventilating sets, material-handling fans, high pressure and induced draft fans, axial fans, propeller fans, and custom designs and accessories. Customization of wheel type, size, fan arrangement, construction design, special materials and finishes, and accessories ensure that every product will meet the performance and mechanical needs of each installation. **Positions advertised include:** Safety Manager; Wirefeed Welder; Machine Operator; Production Worker; Assembler. **Corporate headquarters location:** Minneapolis MN. **Number of employees at this location:** 263.

TYCO PLASTICS, INC.
1800 North M Avenue, Sioux Falls SD 57104. 605/334-0334. **Contact:** Human Resources. **World Wide Web address:** http://www.tycoplastics.com. **Description:** Tyco Plastics manufactures and markets plastic products such as Film-Gard brand plastic sheeting; a full-line of sheeting products available in more than 250 sizes and thickness including construction film for building and remodeling; do-it-yourself products such as drop cloths and landscape films; and agricultural products for farm applications. Tyco also manufactures Ruffies value brand trash bags including Sure Strength high-density plastic trash bags; Color Scents color-scented trash bags; Shop Sak heavy-duty clean-up, business, and specialty bags; Christmas tree disposable bags; Eco-Choice concentrated high-density plastic trash bags with 33.3 percent recycled plastic content; and Ultra-Flex proprietary formula of high-density plastic trash bags. In addition, Tyco also makes private label products such as garbage, waste, and tall kitchen household bags; lawn and leaf bags; sandwich bags; and resealable bags. **Corporate headquarters location:** Minneapolis MN. **Parent company:** Tyco International, Ltd. **Operations at this facility include:** This location manufactures printed circuit boards. **Listed on:** New York Stock Exchange. **Stock exchange symbol:** TYC. **Number of employees nationwide:** 2,100.

TYSON FOODS, INC.
1800 Stevens Port Drive, Dakota Dunes SD 57049. 605/235-2061. **Contact:** Personnel. **World Wide Web address:** http://www.tysonfoodsinc.com. **Description:** Tyson is one of the world's largest providers of meat such as chicken, beef, and pork. The company also produces corn and flour tortilla items, as well as pre-prepared foods. **NOTE:** Entry-level positions are offered. Send resumes for all jobs to Tyson Foods, Inc., ATTN: Personnel/Careers@tyson.com, P.O. Box 2020, Springdale AR 72765. **Special programs:** Internships; Training. **Corporate headquarters location:** Springdale, AR. **Listed on:** New York Stock Exchange. **Stock exchange symbol:** TSN. **Number of employees nationwide:** 52,000.

U.S. DEPARTMENT OF VETERANS AFFAIRS
FORT MEADE VETERANS ADMINISTRATION MEDICAL CENTER
113 Comanche Road, Fort Meade SD 57741. 605/347-2511. **Fax:** 605/720-7171. **Contact:** Human Resources. **World Wide Web address:** http://www.va.gov. **Description:** A medical center operated by the U.S. Department of Veterans Affairs. From 54 hospitals in 1930, the VA health care system has grown to include 171 medical centers; more than 364 outpatient, community, and outreach clinics; 130 nursing home care units; and 37 domiciliary residences. VA operates at least one medical center in each of the 48 contiguous states, Puerto Rico, and the District of Columbia. With approximately 76,000 medical center beds, VA treats nearly a million patients in VA hospitals, 75,000 in nursing home care units and 25,000 in domiciliary residences. VA's outpatient clinics register approximately 24 million visits a year. **NOTE:** Please see website for information on how to search for and apply to jobs.

U.S. DEPARTMENT OF VETERANS AFFAIRS
ROYAL C. JOHNSON VETERANS MEMORIAL HOSPITAL
P.O. Box 5046, Sioux Falls SD 57117-5046. 605/336-3230. **Physical address:** 2501 West 22nd Street, Sioux Falls SD 57105. **Fax:** 605/333-6878. **Contact:** Human Resources. **World Wide Web address:** http://www.va.gov. **Description:** One of eight combined VA Medical and Regional Office Centers throughout the country. A 194-bed teaching facility providing acute medical, surgical, and psychiatric services; intermediate medical inpatient services; and ambulatory care services. In addition, it has a 75-bed extended care unit. The medical center provides medical care to the veteran population in eastern South Dakota, northwestern Iowa, and southwestern Minnesota. It also functions as a referral center for the Fort Meade and Hot Springs VA Medical Centers, which are located in western South Dakota. The center treats approximately 3,800 acute care inpatients per year, and ambulatory care volume is over 56,000 visits annually. The medical center provides patients with services in a wide variety of specialized diagnostic and treatment areas including laser surgery, advanced cardiology, geriatric evaluation and management, podiatry, optometry, audiology, and outpatient substance abuse treatment. Other specialized services at the center include a pulmonary function laboratory, electrophysiology capabilities, a stress testing laboratory, an acute hemodialysis unit, an oncology unit, a women's health clinic, and a mental hygiene clinic. The medical center also serves as the primary teaching hospital for the University of South Dakota School of Medicine and also supports 22 additional affiliated training programs from 13 institutions in six states. The center also has a research building. The regional office works with veterans in processing benefit claims related to compensation and pension, insurance, education, and medical care. It also provides assistance to veterans in understanding and obtaining their benefits. **NOTE:** Please see website for information on how to search for and apply to jobs. **Number of employees at this location:** 780.

U.S. DEPARTMENT OF VETERANS AFFAIRS
VETERANS ADMINISTRATION MEDICAL CENTER/HOT SPRINGS
500 North Fifth Street, Hot Springs SD 57747-1497. 605/745-2000. **Fax:** 605/745-2091. **Contact:** Herb Doering, Chief of Human Resources. **World Wide Web address:** http://www.va.gov. **Description:** A medical center operated by the U.S. Department of Veterans Affairs. From 54 hospitals in 1930, the VA health care system has grown to include 171 medical centers; more than 364 outpatient, community, and outreach clinics; 130 nursing home care units; and 37 domiciliary residences. VA operates at least one medical center in each of the 48 contiguous states, Puerto Rico, and the District of Columbia. With approximately 76,000 medical center beds, VA treats nearly 1 million patients in VA hospitals, 75,000 in nursing home care units and 25,000 in domiciliary residences. VA's outpatient clinics register approximately 24 million visits a year. **NOTE:** Please see website for information on how to search for and apply to jobs.

UNIVERSITY OF SOUTH DAKOTA
414 East Clark Street, Vermillion SD 57069. 605/677-5671. **Fax:** 605/677-6630. **Contact:** Diane Zak, Personnel Director. **E-mail address:** dzak@usd.edu. **World Wide Web address:** http://www.usd.edu. **Description:** A university composed of the following colleges and schools: the College of Arts and Sciences, the School of Law,

the School of Medicine, the School of Education, the School of Business, the Graduate School, and the College of Fine Arts. Degrees offered range from two-year associate degrees to the Doctor of Philosophy, Juris Doctor, and M.D. degrees. **Positions advertised include:** Assistant or Associate Professor – Various Departments; Chairperson – Various Departments; Clinical Research Nurse; Computer Scientist; Dean – College of Fine Arts; Executive Director – Alumni; Head Women's Tennis Coach; Lab Animal Technician; Patrol Officer; Research Associate; Senior Secretary; Sign Language Interpreter.

VISHAY DALE ELECTRONICS, INC.
P.O. Box 180, Yankton SD 57078. 605/665-9301. **Physical address:** 1505 East Highway 50, Yankton SD 57078. **Contact:** Human Resources. **World Wide Web address:** http://www.vishay.com. **Description:** Vishay Dale Electronics is one of the largest manufacturers of fixed resistors and inductors in the United States and a producer of other passive electronic components including transformers, specialty connectors, and plasma displays. **Corporate headquarters location:** Malvern PA. **Other U.S. locations:** Norfolk NE. **Parent company:** Vishay Intertechnology was founded in 1962 and is a leader in passive electronic component manufacturing. Other Vishay subsidiaries include Draloric Electronic GmbH, one of the largest manufacturers of resistors in Germany and also a producer of specialty ceramic capacitors; Sfernice, S.A., one of the largest manufacturers of fixed and variable resistors (potentiometers) and printed circuit boards in France; Sprague, a leading supplier of tantalum capacitors to the commercial, industrial, military, and aerospace electronics markets, and also a manufacturer of thick film resistor networks; and Roederstein, a leading European and U.S. film capacitor manufacturer and also a producer of tantalum, aluminum, and ceramic disk capacitors, hybrids, and other passive electronic components. **Operations at this facility include:** This location manufactures connectors, transformers, and arrestors.

WELLS FARGO BANK
P.O. Box 1040, Rapid City SD 57709-1040. 605/394-3800. **Physical address:** 825 Saint Joseph Street, Rapid City SD 57701. **Contact:** Human Resources. **World Wide Web address:** http://www.wellsfargo.com. **Description:** A diversified financial institution with over $234 billion in assets serving over 17 million customers through 5,300 independent locations worldwide. Services include community banking, credit and debit cards, home equity and mortgage loans, online banking, student loans, and insurance. **Positions advertised include:** Teller; Lead Teller. **Other U.S. locations:** Nationwide. **International locations:** Worldwide. **Listed on:** New York Stock Exchange. **Stock exchange symbol:** WFC. **Annual sales/revenues:** More than $100 million. **Number of employees worldwide:** 104,000.

AFG INDUSTRIES, INC.
P.O. Box 929, Kingsport TN 37662. 423/229-7200. **Physical address:** 1400 Lincoln Street, Kingsport TN 37660. **Fax:** 423/229-7459. **Contact:** Director of Human Resources. **World Wide Web address:** http://www.afglass.com. **Description:** Manufactures, distributes, and packages flat glass. **Corporate headquarters location:** This location. **Subsidiaries include:** American Flat Glass Distributors, Inc. (AFGD).

AFL AUTOMOTIVE
830 Crescent Centre Drive, Suite 600, Franklin TN 37067. 800/627-7854. **Contact:** Human Resources. **World Wide Web address:** http://www.alcoa.com. **Description:** Supplies electrical/electronic distribution systems solutions to major vehicle manufacturers and their sub-suppliers. **NOTE:** Search and apply for positions online. **Parent company:** Alcoa, Inc.

AFL TELECOMMUNICATIONS
830 Crescent Centre Drive, Suite 600, Franklin TN 37067. 615/778-6000. **Fax:** 615/778-5927. **Contact:** Human Resources: **World Wide Web address:** http://www.alcoa.com. **Description:** Produces telecommunications products including cable, interconnects, and closures. **NOTE:** Search and apply for positions online. **Parent company:** Alcoa, Inc.

ACE PRODUCTS INC.
613 West Broadway, Newport TN 37821. 423/623-2876. **Fax:** 423/623-8860. **Contact:** Personnel Manager. **World Wide Web address:** http://www.aceproductsinc.com. **Description:** A manufacturer of off-road semi-pneumatic rubber tires, solid rubber tires, and plastic wheel assemblies. **Corporate headquarters location:** Los Angeles CA.

ADAMS, CRAFT, HERZ, WALKER
800 Oak Ridge Turnpike, Suite A400, Oak Ridge TN 37830-6988. 865/482-4451. **Fax:** 865/482-4454. **Contact:** Human Resources Department. **World Wide Web address:** http://www.achw.com. **Description:** Provides architectural, engineering, planning, and surveying services.

THE ADVERTISING CHECKING BUREAU INC.
1610 Century Center Parkway, Suite 104, Memphis TN 38134. 901/346-9941. **Fax:** 901/345-8812. **Contact:** Human Resources. **World Wide Web address:** http://www.acbcoop.com. **Description:** An advertising agency that provides co-op and trade promotion program management, advertising tracking services and other marketing services.

ADVO INC.
4481 Distriplex Cove, Memphis TN 38118. 901/794-0804. **Fax:** 901/794-0889. **Contact:** Human Resources. **E-mail address:** resumeme@advo.com. **World Wide Web address:** http://www.advo.com. **Description:** A direct mail advertising firm. **NOTE:** Search and apply for positions online. **Corporate headquarters location:** Windsor CT. **Number of employees nationwide:** 3,600.

ADVOCAT INC.
277 Mallory Station Road, Suite 130, Franklin TN 37067. 615/771-7575. **Contact:** Director of Employee and Client Relations. **World Wide Web address:** http://www.irinfo.com/avc. **Description:** A nursing and social services provider. The company operates assisted living facilities and skilled nursing facilities in 10 states and three Canadian provinces. **Other U.S. locations:** AL; AR; FL; KY; OH; TX; WV. **International locations:** Canada.

AIRCON CORPORATION
2873 Chelsea Avenue, P.O. Box 80446, Memphis TN 38108-0446. 901/452-0230. **Toll-free phone:** 800/238-9140. **Fax:** 901/452-0264. **Contact:** Human Resources Manager. **Description:** A wholesaler of air pollution and dust control systems and equipment.

ALADDIN MANTLE LAMP COMPANY
681 International Boulevard, Clarksville TN 37040. 931-647-4949. Toll-free phone: 800/457-5267 Fax: 931-647-4517. Contact: Human Resources. World Wide Web address: http://www.aladdinlamps.com. **Description:** Manufactures non-electric Aladdin lamps.

ALBAHEALTH
425 North Gateway Boulevard, Rockwood TN 37854. 865/354-0410. **Contact:** Human Resources. **World Wide Web address:** http://www.alba1.com. **Description:** A hosiery manufacturer. AlbaHealth also produces knitted health care products including dressings, gloves, and other related products. **Corporate headquarters location:** Greensboro NC. **Parent company:** Alba Waldensian Inc.

ALCOA (ALUMINUM COMPANY OF AMERICA)
2300 North Wright Road, Alcoa TN 37701. 865/977-2011. **Contact:** Human Resources. **World Wide Web address:** http://www.alcoa.com. **Description:** ALCOA is engaged in all aspects of the aluminum industry including mining, refining, smelting, fabricating, and recycling. The company also manufactures ceramic packaging for the semiconductor industry, alumina chemicals, plastic bottle closures, vinyl siding, packaging machinery, and electrical distribution systems for automobiles. **NOTE:** Search and apply for positions online. **Positions advertised include:** CCM Maintenance Supervisor; Power System Operator; Facility Maintenance Supervisor; Manager, Human Resources. **Operations at this facility include:** This location provides aluminum and ingot fabricating, and can-recycling services. **Annual sales/revenues:** More than $100 million. **Number of employees worldwide:** 120,000.

ALCOA ENGINEERED PRODUCTS
1999 State Line Road, Elizabethton TN 37643. 423/543-3561. **Contact:** Human Resources. **World Wide Web address:** http://www.alcoa.com. **Description:** ALCOA is engaged in all aspects of the aluminum industry including mining, refining, smelting, fabricating, and recycling. The company also manufactures ceramic packaging for the semiconductor industry, alumina chemicals, plastic bottle closures, vinyl siding, packaging machinery, and electrical distribution systems for automobiles. **Operations at this facility include:** This location is engaged in the extrusion of aluminum. **Number of employees worldwide:** 120,000.

ALLTRISTA ZINC PRODUCTS, L.P.
2500 Old State Road, P.O. Box 1890, Greeneville TN 37744-1890. 423/639-8111. **Fax:** 423/798-0841. **Contact:** Bill Musick, Director of Human Resources. **World Wide Web address:** http://www.allzinc.com. **Description:** Manufactures solid zinc strip in a variety of alloys, which are rolled into master coils weighing up to 13,000 pounds each. Founded in 1993. **NOTE:** Entry-level positions and second and third shifts are offered. **Office hours:** Monday - Friday, 8:00 a.m. - 5:00 p.m. **Corporate headquarters location:** Indianapolis IN. **Parent company:** Jarden Corporation. **Operations at this facility include:** Manufacturing. **Listed on:** New York Stock Exchange. **Stock exchange symbol:** JAH.

ALTAMA DELTA CORPORATION
340 Natchez Trace Drive, P.O. Box 368, Lexington TN 38351. 731/967-9600. **Fax:** 731/967-9200. **Contact:** Human Resources Department. **E-mail address:** recruiting@altama.com. **World Wide Web address:** http://www.altama.com. **Description:** Manufactures footwear for the military. **Corporate headquarters location:** Atlanta GA.

AMERICA SERVICE GROUP
PRISON HEALTH SERVICES INC.
105 Westpark Drive, Suite 200, Brentwood TN 37027. 615/373-3100. **Contact:** Human Resources. **E-mail address:** jobs@asgr.com. **World Wide Web address:** http://www.asgr.com. **Description:** America Service Group Inc., through its subsidiaries, provides a wide range of healthcare and pharmacy programs to correctional agencies for the medical care of inmates. **Corporate headquarters location:** This location. **Subsidiaries include:** UniSource Inc. provides mail-order pharmaceuticals, medical supplies, and institutional pharmacy services to its contract sites and private sector customers. **Listed on:** NASDAQ. **Stock exchange symbol:** ASGR. **Number of employees nationwide:** 7,000.

AMERICAN COLOR GRAPHICS
100 Winners Circle, Brentwood TN 37027-5012. 615/377-7500. **Toll-free phone:** 800/621-7746. **Fax:** 615/377-0370. **Contact:** Human Resources. **E-mail address:** info@americancolor.com. **World Wide Web address:** http://www.americancolor.com. **Description:** Provides commercial offset and flexo printing services. American Color Graphics also prints color comic sections and newspaper inserts for periodicals nationwide. Founded in 1926. **Corporate headquarters location:** This location. **Other U.S. locations:** Al; CA; IA; MD; MN; OH; PA; TX.

AMERICAN GENERAL LIFE AND ACCIDENT INSURANCE COMPANY
American General Center-MC 338N, Nashville TN 37250. 877/891-2535. **Toll-free phone:** 800/888-2452. **Fax:** 615/255-2685. **Contact:** Human Services. **World Wide Web address:** http://www.agla.com. **Description:** Engaged in individual life and health insurance sales and service. **Special programs:** Internships. **Parent company:** American General Corporation. **Operations at this facility include:** Administration; Sales; Service. **Number of employees nationwide:** 4,200.

AMERICAN GREETINGS CORPORATION
1236 American Way, Ripley TN 38063. 731/635-3000. **Contact:** Human Resources. **World Wide Web address:** http://www.americangreetings.com. **Description:** One of the world's largest publicly owned manufacturers and distributors of greeting cards and related novelty items. The company's core products are everyday, seasonal, and personalized greeting cards, which together account for 65 percent of the company's net sales. **Corporate headquarters location:** Cleveland OH. **International locations:** Canada; France; Mexico; United Kingdom. **Subsidiaries include:** Carlton Cards; Balloon Zone; Magnivision; GuildHouse Candles; DesignWare; Plus Mark; Learning Horizons; AG Industries; John Sands.

AMERICAN HEALTHWAYS
3841 Green Hills Village Drive, Nashville TN 37215. 800/327-3822. **Fax:** 615/263-1707. **Recorded jobline:** 800/292-5004 ext. 7575. **Contact:** Human Resources. **E-mail address:** hr@amhealthways.com. **World Wide Web address:** http://www.americanhealthways.com. **Description:** American Healthways provides chronic disease management services to hospitals, physicians, and other health care providers. The company specializes in providing treatment and services relating to diabetes, cardiac care, and respiratory disease. Founded in 1981. **NOTE:** Search and apply for positions online. **Positions advertised include:** Manager, Physician Support Services; Accreditation Director; Corporate Recruiter; Director of Transition Management; Director of CEC Education; Director of Procurement and Facility; Data Analyst; Database Analyst; OLAP Developer; Programmer Analyst. **Corporate headquarters location:** This location. **Listed on:** NASDAQ. **Stock exchange symbol:** AMHC. **CEO:** Tom Cigarran. **Number of employees at this location:** 80. **Number of employees nationwide:** 650.

AMERICAN HOMEPATIENT, INC.
5200 Maryland Way, Suite 400, Brentwood TN 37027. 615/221-8884. **Fax:** 615/373-9932. **Contact:** Human Resources Department. **E-mail address:** hr@ahom.com. **World Wide Web address:** http://www.ahom.com. **Description:** Provides home health care products and services through 80 locations in 13 states in the southwestern and southeastern United States. The company's main services include respiratory and infusion therapy, enteral and parenteral nutrition, and the rental and sale of medical equipment and related supplies for the home. **Corporate headquarters location:** This location. **Number of employees nationwide:** 3,500.

AMERICAN PAPER & TWINE COMPANY
7400 Cockrill Bend Boulevard, Nashville TN 37209. 615/350-9000. **Toll-free phone:** 800/251-2437. **Fax:** 615/350-8999. **Contact:** Human Resources Department. **E-mail address:** d.james@aptcommerce.com. **World Wide Web address:** http://www.aptcommerce.com. **Description:** A wholesale distributor of industrial packaging material, office supplies, and maintenance supplies. **Other area locations:** Chattanooga TN; Memphis TN. **Other U.S. locations:** Little Rock AR.

AMERICAN RED CROSS
836 Commercial Court, Murfreesboro TN 37130-3667. 615/893-4272. **Contact:** Human Resources. **World Wide Web address:** http://www.redcross.org. **Description:** A humanitarian organization that aids disaster victims, gathers blood for crisis distribution, trains individuals to respond to emergencies, educates individuals on various diseases, and raises funds for other charitable establishments.

AMERICAN WATER HEATER COMPANY
500 Princeton Road, Johnson City TN 37601. 423/283-8000. **Contact:** Human Resources Director. **World Wide Web address:** http://www.americanwaterheater.com. **Description:** Manufactures water heaters for commercial and residential applications. **NOTE:** Search for positions online. **Corporate headquarters location:** This location. **Parent company:** GSW Inc.

AMETEK
ADVANCED MEASUREMENT TECHNOLOGY INC.
801 South Illinois Avenue, Oak Ridge TN 37831-0895. 865/482-4411. **Contact:** Human Resources. **World Wide Web address:** http://www.ametek-online.com. **Description:** Manufactures solid-state image sensors for electronics applications. **Subsidiaries:** Ortec; Princeton Applied Research; Signal Recovery.

AMSOUTH BANK
315 Deaderick Street, Nashville TN 37201. 615/748-2091. **Contact:** Human Resources. **World Wide Web address:** http://www.amsouth.com. **Description:** A regional bank holding company with 660 branch locations. **Corporate headquarters location:** Birmingham AL. **Other U.S. locations:** AL; FL; MS; LA; GA. **Parent company:** AmSouth Bancorporation. **Listed on:** New York Stock Exchange. **Stock exchange symbol:** ASO.

APAC
1210 Harbor Avenue, Memphis TN 38113. 901/947-5600. **Fax:** 901/947-5699. **World Wide Web address:** http://www.ashland.com. **Description:** APAC is the largest transportation construction contractor in the U.S. **Positions advertised include:** Quality Control Specialist. **Corporate headquarters location:** Atlanta GA. **Parent company:** Ashland Inc.

AQUA GLASS CORPORATION
320 Industrial Park Drive, Adamsville TN 38310. 731/632-0911. **Contact:** Human Resources. **World Wide Web address:** http://www.aquaglass.com. **Description:** Manufactures bathroom products and appliances including showers, bathtubs, steam showers, whirlpools, and related cleaning products. **Parent company:** Masco Inc.

AQUA-CHEM, INC.
3001 East John Sevier Highway, Knoxville TN 37914. 865/544-2065. **Fax:** 865/546-4330. **Contact:** Angie Bearden, Human Resources Manager. **World Wide Web address:** http://www.aqua-chem.com. **Description:** Manufactures water purification and desalination systems. The company also manufactures evaporators for the chemical process industry. **Corporate headquarters location:** Milwaukee WI. **Number of employees nationwide:** 1,200.

ASTEC INDUSTRIES, INC.
4101 Jerome Avenue, Chattanooga TN 37407. 423/867-4210. **Fax:** 423/867-4127. **Contact:** Personnel Manager. **World Wide Web address:** http://www.astecindustries.com. **Description:** A holding company for a group of companies that manufacture a variety of equipment for aggregate processing, asphalt road building, and pipeline and utility trenching. **NOTE:** Search for positions online. Resumes accepted only for open positions. **Subsidiaries include:** American Augers, Inc. manufactures boring machines, directional drills, and fluid/mud systems for the underground construction market. Astec Financial Services, Inc. provides financing for the lease or purchase of Astec products. Astec, Inc. manufactures hot-mix asphalt plants, environmental remediation, and soil purification equipment. Breaker Technology, Inc. manufactures breaker systems, hydraulic rock breakers, and mobile mining equipment. CEI Enterprises manufactures heaters, mixing tanks, and storage tanks used at hot-mix asphalt plants. Heatec, Inc. manufactures heaters, mixing tanks, and storage tanks for asphalt cement. Johnson Crushers International, Inc. specializes in horizontal screens, portable plants, and roller bearing cone crushers. Kolberg-Pioneer, Inc. manufactures aggregate processing equipment. Pavement Technology, Inc. manufactures analyzers, mobile laboratories, and testing equipment. Production Engineered Products, Inc. manufactures portable screening plants and vibrating screens. Superior Industries manufactures portable and stationary conveyor systems. Telsmith, Inc. manufactures aggregate processing and handling equipment. Trencor, Inc. manufactures excavating and trenching equipment. **Listed on:** NASDAQ. **Stock exchange symbol:** ASTE.

ASURION
648 Grassmere Park Drive, Suite 300, Nashville TN 37211. 615/837-3000. **Fax:** 615/837-3001. **Contact:** Human Resources. **World Wide Web address:** http://www.asurion.com. **Description:** Asurion provides enhanced services to wireless subscribers. Products include handset and data dev ice insurance programs, roadside assistance services, warranty management plans, and equipment management solutions. Founded in 1994. **NOTE:** Search and apply for positions online. **Positions advertised include:** Call Center Director; Contract Project Manager; Inventory Control Manager; Material Manager; Sr. Manager, Strategic Performance management; Training Manager. **Corporate headquarters location:** This location. **Other area locations:** Smyrna TN. **Other U.S. locations:** Houston TX; Dallas TX; San Mateo CA. **Number of employees worldwide:** 1,700.

ATLANTIC PACIFIC AUTOMOTIVE
1900 Exeter Road, Suite 200, Germantown TN 38138. **Toll-free phone:** 800/238-5153. **Fax:** 800/562-2370. **Contact:** Human Resources. **World Wide Web address:** http://www.apauto.com. **Description:** An independent wholesale distributor of automotive parts and chemicals. **Listed on:** Privately held.

AUTOZONE
P.O. Box 2198, Department 8130, Memphis TN 38101-2198. 901/495-6500. **Physical address:** 123 South Front Street, Memphis TN 38103. **Fax:** 901/722-4674. **Contact:** Recruiting. **E-mail address:** az.jobs@autozone.com. **World Wide Web address:** http://www.autozone.com. **Description:** Operates a 3,300 unit chain of do-it-yourself, retail auto parts stores located in 42 states and Mexico. Founded in 1920. **NOTE:** Search and apply for positions online. Internet access is available at local branch stores. **Positions advertised include:** Sr. Financial Analyst; Merchandising Analyst; Commercial Process Analyst; Project Manager; Sr. Supply Chain Analyst; HR Generalist; Marketing Manager; Programmer Analyst; Real Estate Development Manager; Sr. System Analyst. **Corporate headquarters location:** This location. **Listed on:** New York Stock Exchange. **Stock exchange symbol:** AZO. **Number of employees at this location:** 850. **Number of employees nationwide:** 17,400.

AVERY DENNISON CORPORATION
3461 East Raines Road, Memphis TN 38118. 901/365-3100. **Fax:** 901/365-3130. **Contact:** Human Resources. **World Wide Web address:** http://www.averydennison.com. **Description:** Avery Dennison is a world leader in pressure-sensitive adhesives, office products, labels, tags, retail systems, and specialty chemicals. The company specializes in producing a wide variety of labels, primarily clear labels, for use in packaging products including apparel, motor oil, liquid soap, and automobiles. Labels are marketed under the Avery and Fasson brand names. **NOTE:** Search for positions online. **Corporate headquarters location:** Pasadena CA. **Operations at this facility include:** This location is a distribution center.

AZO INC.
4445 Malone Road, Memphis TN 38118. 901/794-9480. **Fax:** 901/794-9934. **Contact:** Human Resources. **E-mail address:** humanresources@azo.com. **World Wide Web address:** http://www.azo-inc.com. **Description:** Produces enclosed materials handling systems. AZO's systems identify ingredients and manage inventory, formulas, material flow lines, and production orders. **NOTE:** Positions usually available for engineers and designers with experience in mechanical engineer, electrical engineering, or PLC programming.

BBA FIBERWEB REEMAY, INC.
70 Old Hickory Boulevard, Old Hickory TN 37138-3651. 615/847-7000. **Fax:** 615/847-7068. **Contact:** Human Resources Director. **World Wide Web address:** http://www.reemay.com. **Description:** Manufactures polyester and polypropylene fabrics for a variety of industrial and consumer applications.

BBA MATERIALS TECHNOLOGY GROUP
One Lakeview Place, Suite 204 25 Century Boulevard, Nashville TN. 615/847-7503. **Contact:** Human Resources. **World Wide Web address:** http://www.bbafiberweb.com. **Description:** One of the world's largest international groups in the nonwovens industry to the hygiene, medical, technical, and industrial markets.

BDO SEIDMAN, LLP
5100 Poplar Avenue, Suite 2600, Memphis TN 38137. 901/680-7600. **Fax:** 901/680-7601. **Contact:** Human Resources. **World Wide Web address:** http://www.bdo.com. **Description:** A national professional services firm providing assurance, tax, financial advisory and consulting services to private and publicly traded businesses. **NOTE:** Search and apply for positions online. **Positions advertised include:** Assurance Associate; Assurance Manager.

BFI
700 Murfreesboro Road, Nashville TN 37210. 615/244-6250. **Fax:** 615/256-5219. **Contact:** Human Resources. **World Wide Web address:** http://www.disposal.com. **Description:** Engaged primarily in the collection and disposal of solid wastes for commercial, industrial, and residential customers. Services provided include landfills, waste-to-energy programs, hazardous waste removal, and liquid waste removal. **Other U.S. locations:** Nationwide. **International locations:** Worldwide. **Parent Company:** Allied Waste Industries, Inc. **Annual sales/revenues:** More than $100 million.

BFI
3840 Homewood Avenue, Memphis TN 38118. 901/794-3800. **Fax:** 901/362-4334. **Contact:** Human Resources. **World Wide Web address:** http://www.bfi.com. **Description:** Engaged primarily in the collection and disposal of solid waste for commercial, industrial, and residential customers. Services provided include landfills, waste-to-energy programs, hazardous waste removal, and liquid waste removal. **Other U.S. locations:** Nationwide. **International locations:** Worldwide. **Parent Company:** Allied Waste Industries, Inc. **Annual sales/revenues:** More than $100 million.

BACK YARD BURGERS, INC.
1657 North Shelby Oaks Drive, Suite 105, Memphis TN 38134. 901/367-0888. **Fax:** 901/367-0999. **Contact:** Ms. Coy Cella, Human Resources Department. **E-mail address:** ccella@backyardburgers.com. **World Wide Web address:** http://www.backyardburgers.com. **Description:** Operates and franchises a 132-unit chain of fast-food restaurants in 17 states. **Corporate headquarters location:** This location. **Listed on:** NASDAQ. **Stock exchange symbol:** BYBI. **Chairman/CEO:** Lattimore M. Michael.

BAKER, DONELSON, BEARMAN AND CALDWELL
211 Commerce Street, Suite 1000, Nashville TN 37201. 615/726-5600. **Fax:** 615/774-5563. **Contact:** Human Resources. **World Wide Web address:** http://www.bdbc.com. **Description:** A corporate law firm representing local, national, and international clients in a number of industries including aerospace, banking, construction, defense, energy, engineering, insurance, pharmaceuticals, restaurant chains, securities, technology, and telecommunications. **Other area locations:** Memphis TN; Knoxville TN; Chattanooga TN; Johnson City TN. **Other U.S. locations:** Jackson MS; Washington DC; Atlanta GA; Birmingham AL; New Orleans; LA.

BAKER, DONELSON, BEARMAN AND CALDWELL
165 Madison Avenue, Suite 2000, Memphis TN 38103. 901/526-2000. **Fax:** 901/577-2303. **Contact:** Hiring Partner. **World Wide Web address:** http://www.bdbc.com. **Description:** A corporate law firm representing local, national, and international clients in a number of industries including aerospace, banking, construction, defense, energy, engineering, insurance, pharmaceuticals, restaurant chains, securities, technology, and telecommunications. **Other area locations:** Nashville TN; Knoxville TN; Chattanooga TN; Johnson City TN. **Other U.S. locations:** Jackson MS; Washington DC; Atlanta GA; Birmingham AL; New Orleans; LA.

BANCORPSOUTH INC.
310 East Main Street, Jackson TN 38301. 731/422-9200. **Contact:** Fran Turner, Personnel Officer. **E-mail address:** fran.turner@bxx.com. **World Wide Web address:** http://www.bancorpsouth.com. **Description:** A bank holding company with operations in commercial and consumer banking, investment services, insurance, and other financial services. **Corporate headquarters location:** Tupelo MS. **Parent company:** BancorpSouth, Inc. **Listed on:** New York Stock Exchange. **Stock exchange symbol:** BXS.

BAPTIST HEALTH SYSTEM
P.O. Box 1788, Knoxville TN 37901-1788 865/632-5936. **Physical address:** 137 Blount Avenue, Knoxville TN 37920. **Fax:** 865/632-5223. **Recorded jobline:** 865/632-5977. **Contact:** Human Resources. **E-mail address:** hrbaptist@bhset.org. **World Wide Web address:** http://www.bhset.org. **Description:** Operates Baptist Hospital of East Tennessee, Baptist Hospital of Cocke County, Baptist hospital West and Baptist hospital for Women, and eight senior health centers. Founded in 1948. **NOTE:** Search and apply for positions online. **Corporate headquarters location:** This location. **Subsidiaries include:** Home Care East. **Annual sales/revenues:** $5 - $10 million.

BAPTIST HOSPITAL
2000 Church Street, Nashville TN 37236. 615/284-5455. **Fax:** 615/284-5205. **Contact:** Staffing Manager. **World Wide Web address:** http://www.baptisthospital.com. **Description:** A 683-bed, acute care hospital offering services in a variety of specialties including cardiac care, eye care, cancer care, neurosciences, and medical/surgical. Baptist Hospital provides a comprehensive cardiac program that includes angioplasty, open-heart surgery, and cardiac rehabilitation. **NOTE:** Search for positions and download employment application online. **Parent company:** Saint Thomas Health Services. **Number of employees at this location:** 3,300.

BAPTIST MEMORIAL HEALTH CARE SYSTEM
350 North Humphreys Boulevard, Memphis TN 38120. **Toll-free phone:** 800/422-7847. **Fax:** 901/227-5699. **Recorded jobline: 901/227-4515.** **Contact:** Employment Services. **E-mail address:** employment@bmhcc.org. **World Wide Web address:** http://www.baptistonline.org. **Description:** A health care system that operates 17 hospitals an array of home care and hospice agencies, minor medical clinics, behavioral health programs and a network of surgery, rehabilitation and other outpatient centers. **NOTE:** Physicians may send a CV and cover letter to Lynn Buff, Director of Recruitment at above address or e-mail to: PracticeOpps@bmhcc.org. Resumes for nursing positions may be sent to 6141 Walnut Grove Road, Memphis TN 38120, faxed

to 901/226-4501, or e-mailed to: NursingJobs@bmhcc.org. **Positions advertised include:** Contract manager; Director, Baptist Clinical Research Center; Marketing Coordinator; Marketing Specialist; Clinical Resource Nurse; Registered Respiratory Therapist; Staff Development Instructor Specialist; RN's.

BARGE, WAGGONER, SUMNER & CANNON
820 Broad Street, Suite 200, Chattanooga TN 37402. 423/756-3025. **Fax:** 423/756-8477. **Contact:** Human Resources. **World Wide Web address:** http://www.bargewaggoner.com. **Description:** An employee-owned design firm offering services in engineering, architecture, planning, landscape architecture, and surveying. **NOTE:** Please apply online. **Positions advertised include:** Civil Engineer. **Corporate headquarters location:** Nashville TN. **Other U.S. locations:** Dothan AL; Huntsville AL; Montgomery AL; Indianapolis IN; Lexington KY; Jackson MS; Miamisburg OH; Blountville TN; Knoxville TN; Memphis TN; Oak Ridge TN.

BARGE, WAGGONER, SUMNER & CANNON
1009 Commerce Park Drive, Suite 500, Oak Ridge TN 37830. 865/481-0496. **Fax:** 865/481-3895. **Contact:** Dick Parker, Office Manager. **World Wide Web address:** http://www.bargewaggoner.com. **Description:** An employee-owned design firm offering services in engineering, architecture, planning, landscape architecture, and surveying. **NOTE:** Please apply online. **Corporate headquarters location:** Nashville TN. **Other U.S. locations:** Dothan AL; Huntsville AL; Montgomery AL; Indianapolis IN; Lexington KY; Jackson MS; Miamisburg OH; Morristown TN; Blountville TN; Knoxville TN; Memphis TN.

BARGE, WAGGONER, SUMNER & CANNON
The Forum 1, Suite 720, 6750 Poplar Avenue, Memphis TN 38138. 901/755-7166. **Contact:** Personnel. **World Wide Web address:** http://www.bargewaggoner.com. **Description:** An employee-owned design firm offering services in engineering, architecture, planning, landscape architecture, and surveying. **NOTE:** Please apply online. **Corporate headquarters location:** Nashville TN. **Other U.S. locations:** Dothan AL; Huntsville AL; Montgomery AL; Indianapolis IN; Lexington KY; Jackson MS; Miamisburg OH; Morristown TN; Blountville TN; Knoxville TN; Oak Ridge TN.

BARGE, WAGGONER, SUMNER & CANNON
211 Commerce Street, Suite 600, Nashville TN 37201. 615/254-1500. **Contact:** Human Resources. **World Wide Web address:** http://www.bargewaggoner.com. **Description:** An employee-owned design firm offering services in engineering, architecture, planning, landscape architecture, and surveying. **NOTE:** Please apply online. **Positions advertised include:** Civil/Environmental Designer. **Corporate headquarters location:** This location. **Other U.S. locations:** Jasper AL; Dothan AL; Huntsville AL; Montgomery AL; Birmingham AL; Lexington KY; Dayton OH; Morristown TN; Blountville TN; Knoxville TN; Memphis TN; Oak Ridge TN.

BATESVILLE CASKET COMPANY
175 Monogard Drive, Manchester TN 37355. 931/728-2231. **Contact:** Human Resources. **E-mail address:** employment@batesvillecasket.net **World Wide Web address:** http://www.batesville.com. **Description:** Manufactures a line of cremation urns and caskets. **Corporate headquarters location:** Batesville IN. **Parent company:** Hillenbrand Industries. **Number of employees nationwide:** 3,500.

BAXTER HEALTHCARE CORPORATION
4835 South Mendenhall Road, Memphis TN 38141. 901/795-7970. **Contact:** Human Resources. **World Wide Web address:** http://www.baxter.com. **Description:** Baxter Healthcare is a global medical products and services company that is a leader in technologies related to blood and the circulatory system. The company has market-leading positions in four global businesses: biotechnology, which develops therapies and products in transfusion medicine; cardiovascular medicine, which develops products and provides services to treat late-stage cardiovascular disease; renal therapy, which develops products and services to improve therapies to fight kidney disease; and intravenous systems/medical products, which develops technologies and systems to improve intravenous medication delivery and distributes disposable medical products. **NOTE:** Search and apply for positions online. **Positions advertised include:** Quality Associate. **Corporate headquarters location:** Deerfield IL. **Operations at this facility include:** This location is a distribution and service center for the medical equipment manufacturer. **Number of employees worldwide:** 35,000.

BEARINGPOINT, INC.
3200 West End Avenue, Suite 500, HQ West End Center, Nashville TN 37203. 615/783-1620. **Fax:** 615/783-1619. **Contact:** Human Resources. **World Wide Web address:** http://www.bearingpoint.com. **Description:** A business consulting, systems integration, and managed services firm providing business and technology strategy, systems design, architecture, applications implementation, and network infrastructure services to business, government agencies, and other organizations. **NOTE:** Search and apply for positions online. **Positions advertised include:** Financial Solutions Development Lead; Hyperion Reporting Analysis Consultant. **Corporate headquarters location:** McLean VA. **Listed on:** New York Stock Exchange. **Stock exchange symbol:** BE. **Number of employees worldwide:** 16,000.

BECHTEL JACOBS COMPANY LLC,
P. O. Box 4699, Oak Ridge, Tennessee 37831-7020. 865/576-4006. **Toll-free phone:** 800/382-6938. **Fax:** 865-241-1379. **E-mail address:** bcf@bechteljacobs.com. **World Wide Web address:** http://www.bechteljacobs.com. **Description:** Bechtel Jacobs is the environmental management contractor for the U. S. Department of Energy's Oak Ridge Operations Office, located in Oak Ridge, Tennessee. **NOTE:** Resumes accepted only for posted positions. **Positions advertised include:** Engineering Supervisor; Sr. Engineering Specialist; Purchasing Specialist; Project QA Manager; Health Physicist.

BELMONT UNIVERSITY
1900 Belmont Boulevard, Nashville TN 37212-3757. 615/460-6456. **Fax:** 615/460-5454. **Contact:** Human Resources. **E-mail address:** humanresources@mail.belmont.edu. **World Wide Web address:** http://www.belmont.edu. **Description:** A co-ed Christian university with an enrollment of approximately 3,300. Belmont University's six schools offer undergraduate degrees in 57 major areas of study.

BELZ ENTERPRISES
100 Peabody Place, Suite 1400, Memphis TN 38103. 901/260-7348. **Fax:** 901/260-7378. **Contact:** Irvin Scopp, Director of Human Resources. **E-mail address:** info@belz.com. **World Wide Web address:** http://www.belz.com. **Description:** A real estate development and property management company. Belz Enterprises specializes in hotel, industrial, office, residential, retail, warehouse, and underdeveloped land properties. **Corporate headquarters location:** This location.

BETTERBILT SMYRNA
704 12th Avenue, Smyrna TN 37167. 615/459-4161. **Fax:** 615/223-2272. **Contact:** Human Resources. **World Wide Web address:** http://www.miwd.com. **Description:** Manufactures aluminum doors and windows. **Corporate headquarters location:** This location. **Other U.S. locations:** Prescott Valley AZ. **Parent company:** Caradon PLC. **Number of employees at this location:** 700. **Number of employees nationwide:** 1,000.

BISHOP BAKING COMPANY
P.O. Box 370, Cleveland TN 37320-0370. 423/472-1561. **Physical address:** 1355 South Ocoee Street, Cleveland TN 37311. **Fax:** 423/478-3320. **Contact:** Human Resources. **Description:** Bakes snack cakes that are sold individually and in family packs. **Corporate headquarters location:** Atlanta GA. **Parent company:** Flowers Foods. **Number of employees at this location:** 300.

BLAINE CONSTRUCTION CORPORATION
6510 Deane Hill Drive, Knoxville TN 37919. 865/693-8900. **Fax:** 865/691-7606. **Contact:** Sherri Housely, Personnel. **E-mail address:** jobs@blaineconstrcution.com. **World Wide Web address:** http://www.blaineconstruction.com. **Description:** A full-service general contractor serving commercial, industrial, institutional, and specialty construction markets. Founded in 1969. **Other U.S. locations:** Nationwide.

BLOUNT MEMORIAL HOSPITAL
907 East Lamar Alexander Parkway, Maryville TN 37804-5016. 865/977-5659. **Contact:** Patricia Knight, Director of Human Resources. **World Wide Web address:** http://www.blountmemorial.org. **Description:** A fully accredited, 334-bed, acute care facility. The hospital provides care and education in hospital, outpatient, worksite, and community settings. Blount Memorial Hospital offers a 24-hour physician-staffed emergency department (a designated Level III Trauma Center); comprehensive therapeutic and diagnostic facilities; a state-of-the-art surgery center, same-day surgery, and an intensive care unit; industrial medicine, occupational health, and employee assistance programs for business and industry; a primary care and occupational health clinic network; a family birthing center; and alcohol, drug, and eating disorders treatment. **NOTE:** Entry-level positions are offered. Search and apply for positions online. **Positions advertised include:** Administrative supervisor; CNA's; CT Technologist; Dietitian; Director MSO; HIM Imaging Technician; LPN's; Physical Therapist; Speech Pathologist; Surgical Technician. **Special programs:** Training. **Operations at this facility include:** Administration; Service. **Annual sales/revenues:** $51 - $100 million. **Number of employees at this location:** 1,300.

BLUE CROSS AND BLUE SHIELD OF TENNESSEE
801 Pine Street, Chattanooga TN 37402-2555. 423/755-5600. **Recorded jobline:** 423/755-5616. **Contact:** Employment. **E-mail address:** jobs@bcbst.com. **World Wide Web address:** http://www.bcbst.com. **Description:** A nonprofit health care insurance organization providing managed health care plans to both individuals and groups. Blue Cross and Blue Shield offers Point-of-Service, individual health, PPO, and HMO plans. Founded in 1945. **NOTE:** Search and apply for positions online. **Positions advertised include:** Analyst Programmer; Assistant Reinsurance Analyst; Clinical Research Analyst; Coordinator Financial Monitoring and Support; Counsel; Disease Management Specialist; IM Developer/Analyst.

BOEING DEFENSE & SPACE GROUP
767 Boeing Road, Oak Ridge TN 37831. 865/481-7100. **Contact:** Human Resources. **E-mail address:** EmploymentOperations@boeing.com. **World Wide Web address:** http://www.boeing.com. **Description:** Operates a manufacturing plant that primarily works on subassemblies for commercial jetliners built by the Boeing Commercial Airplane Group. The company primarily works on defense projects including building components and supplying the turret for the U.S. Army's Pedestal Mounted Stinger/Avenger air defense system. **Corporate headquarters location:** Chicago IL. **Parent company:** Boeing Company is one of the largest aerospace firms in the United States, one of the nation's top exporters, and one of the world's leading manufacturers of commercial jet transports. The company is a major U.S. government contractor with capabilities in missile and space, electronic systems, military aircraft, helicopters, and information systems management. The Boeing Company is divided into four business segments: Commercial Aircraft, Space & Communications, Military Aircraft and Missiles, and Shared Services. The Commercial Aircraft Group is the company's largest operating unit. **Number of employees at this location:** 780.

BOULT, CUMMINGS, CONNERS & BERRY
414 Union Street, Suite 1600, Nashville TN 37219-1744. 615/244-2582. **Fax:** 615/252-3035. **Contact:** Ms. Tara Boosey, Recruiting Manager. **E-mail address:** tboosey@boultcummings.com. **World Wide Web address:** http://www.bccb.com. **Description:** A law firm specializing in real estate, commercial finance, taxation, litigation, corporate, and health care law.

BOWATER NEWSPRINT/CALHOUN OPERATION
5020 Highway 11 South, Calhoun TN 37309. 423/336-2211. **Contact:** Human Resources. **World Wide Web address:** http://www.bowater.com. **Description:** Bowater Newsprint is a producer of world-traded wood fiber products including virgin and recycled-content newsprint and directory papers, coated publication and book papers, groundwood specialties, market pulp, and lumber. Bowater is also a leading converter of communication paper for use with computers and other business applications. Bowater also operates eight continuous-feed paper plants where communication papers are converted and dimension lumber is produced at three sawmills. Computer and other business papers are marketed through 30 distribution centers. **Corporate headquarters location:** Greenville SC. **Other U.S. locations:** MI; SC; AL; MS; WA. **International locations:** Nova Scotia, Canada; Korea. **Operations at this facility include:** This location manufactures and recycles newsprint, and produces bleached kraft market pulps. **Parent company:** Bowater, Inc. **Number of employees at this location:** 900.

BRACH'S CONFECTIONS, INC.
P.O. Box 22427, Chattanooga TN 37422. 423/899-1100. **Physical Address:** 4120 Jersey Pike, Chattanooga TN 37421. **Toll-free phone:** 800/999-0204. **Contact:** Human Resources. **World Wide Web address:** http://www.brachs.com. **Description:** A candy and snack food manufacturer and marketer. **Positions advertised include:** Assistant Buyer. **Corporate headquarters location:** This location. **Operations at this facility include:** Administration; Manufacturing; Research and Development; Sales; Service. **Listed on:** Privately held. **Number of employees at this location:** 1,000. **Number of employees nationwide:** 3,500.

BROTHER INDUSTRIES (U.S.A.), INC.
7819N Brother Boulevard, Bartlett TN 38133. 901/377-7777. **Fax:** 901/372-1325. **Contact:** Human Resources. **World Wide Web address:** http://www.brother.com. **Description:** Manufactures and markets a variety of office equipment including computer keyboards, fax machines, printers, and typewriters. The company also manufactures electronic stationery products, sewing machines, and knitting machines. Founded in 1908. **International locations:** Worldwide.

BRUCE HARDWOOD FLOOR COMPANY
160 Rosedale Street, Jackson TN 38302-1334. 731/422-7727. **Contact:** Personnel. **World Wide Web address:** http://www.brucehardwoodfloors.com. **Description:** Manufactures hardwood flooring. Founded in 1884. **NOTE:** Search and apply for positions online. Unsolicited resumes not accepted. Only electronically submitted applications will be considered. **Positions advertised include:** Continuous Improvement Engineer; Production Supervisor; Quality Manager. **Parent company:** Armstrong World Industries. **Listed on:** New York Stock Exchange. **Stock exchange symbol:** ACK.

BRUCE HARDWOOD FLOOR COMPANY
5400 Centennial Boulevard, Nashville TN 90726. 615/350-8060. **Contact:** Human Resources. **World Wide Web address:** http://www.brucehardwoodfloors.com. **Description:** Manufactures hardwood flooring. Founded in 1884. **NOTE:** Search and apply for positions online. Unsolicited resumes not accepted. Only electronically submitted applications will be considered. **Positions advertised include:** Black Belt. **Parent company:** Armstrong World Industries. **Listed on:** New York Stock Exchange. **Stock exchange symbol:** ACK.

BRYCE CORPORATION
4505 Old Lamar Avenue, Memphis TN 38118. 901/369-4400. **Toll-free phone:** 800/238-7277. **Contact:** Human Resources. **World Wide Web address:** http://www.brycecorp.com. **Description:** Manufactures flexible packaging for the bakery, candy, document protection, and snack food industries.

BUNTIN GROUP
1001 Hawkins Street, Nashville TN 37203. 615/244-5720. **Contact:** Debbie Goodwyn, Human Resources. **E-mail address:** dgoodwyn@buntingroup.com. **World Wide Web address:** http://www.buntingroup.com. **Description:** An advertising agency. Founded in 1972. **Number of employees at this location:** 80.

BUSH BROTHERS & COMPANY
3304 Chestnut Hill Road, Dandridge TN 37725. 865/509-2361. **Contact:** Human Resources. **World Wide Web address:** http://www.bushbeans.com. **Description:** Bush Brothers & Company specializes in canned vegetables, focusing primarily on baked beans. **NOTE:** Unsolicited resumes not accepted. **Corporate headquarters location:** Knoxville TN. **Operations at this facility include:** This location is a food processing plant.

BUSHLINE INC.
P.O. Box 527, New Castle TN 37824. **Physical Address:** 707 Industrial Park Drive, New Tazewell TN 37824. 423/626-5246. **Fax:** 423/626-7237. **Contact:** Human Resources. **Description:** A furniture manufacturer. Products include living room sets, chairs, tables, and dinette sets.

C-E MINERALS
P.O. Box 1540, Greenville TN 37744. 423/639-6891. **Physical Address:** 1625 Snapps Ferry Road, Greeneville TN 37745-5828. **Contact:** Human Resources. **World Wide Web address:** http://www.ceminerals.com. **Description:** Manufactures industrial minerals including alumina-silica calcines, and a variety of fused minerals. **Corporate headquarters location:** King of Prussia PA. **Other U.S. locations:** Andersonville GA; Newell WV. **International locations:** China; Venezuela. **Parent company:** Imerys (France).

CCL CUSTOM MANUFACTURING INC.
1725 South Third Street, Memphis TN 38109-7711. 901/947-5400. **Fax:** 901/947-5484. **Contact:** Human Resources. **E-mail address:** jarseneault@cclind.com. **World Wide Web address:** http://www.cclcustom.com. **Description:** Manufactures aerosols, fragrances, cosmetics, and toiletries. **Corporate headquarters location:** Rosemont IL.

CHD MERIDIAN HEALTHCARE
40 Burton Hills Boulevard, Suite 200, Nashville TN 37215. 615/665-9500. **Fax:** 615/234-9026. **Contact:** Human Resources. **E-mail address:** HumanResources@CHDMeridian.com. **World Wide Web address:** http://www.chdmeridian.com. **Description:** Provides employer-sponsored healthcare services to large and mid-sized employers. **NOTE:** Search and apply for positions online. **Positions advertised include:** IS Analyst. **Corporate headquarters location:** This location. **Other U.S. locations:** Nationwide.

CH2M HILL
151 Lafayette Drive, Suite 110, Oak Ridge TN 37830. 865/483-9032. **Fax:** 865/481-3541. **Contact:** Human Resources. **World Wide Web address:** http://www.ch2m.com. **Description:** CH2M Hill is a group of employee-owned companies operating under the names CH2M Hill, Inc.; Industrial Design Corporation; Operations Management International; CH2M Hill International; and CH2M Hill Engineering. The company provides planning, engineering design, and operation and construction management services to help clients apply technology, safeguard the environment, and develop infrastructure. The professional staff includes specialists in environmental engineering and waste management, water management, transportation, industrial facilities, and a broad spectrum of infrastructure systems. **NOTE:** Search and apply for positions or submit resume online. **Positions advertised included:** Staff Engineer; Security Escort. **Corporate headquarters location:** Denver CO. **Operations at this facility include:** This location provides environmental consulting services and subcontracts to Bechtel National, Inc. **Number of employees nationwide:** 5,000.

CTI MOLECULAR IMAGING, INC.
810 Innovation Drive, Knoxville TN 379322571. 865/218-2000. **Fax:** 865/218-3003. **Contact:** Human Resources Manager. **E-mail address:** hr@ctimi.com. **World Wide Web address:** http://www.ctimi.com. **Description:** Develops and manufactures equipment used in Positron Emission Tomography (PET), a noninvasive medical imaging technique that is able to detect abnormal functions of the body in the early stages by imaging biochemical and metabolic changes. **NOTE:** Search and apply for positions online. **Positions advertised included:** Computer Service Engineer; Customer Solutions Specialist; Internal Audit Sr. Manager; Oracle Applications Specialist; Oracle Developer; PET/CT Specialist. **Corporate headquarters location:** This location. **Listed on:** NASDAQ. **Stock exchange symbol:** CTMI. **Number of employees at this location:** 150.

CAMPBELLRHEA
1865 North Market Street, Paris TN 38242. 731/642-4251. **Fax:** 731/642-4262. **Contact:** Human Resources. **World Wide Web address:** http://www.campbellrhea.com. **Description:** A manufacturer of laboratory furniture. The company's primary markets are elementary, middle, and high schools, and universities and research facilities. Founded in 1951. **Parent company:** Sagus International.

CAPITOL NASHVILLE
3322 West End Avenue, 11th Floor, Nashville TN 37203. 615/269-2000. **Contact:** Director of Office Services. **World Wide Web address:** http://www.capitol-nashville.com. **Description:** Offices of the record company.

CARHARTT INC.
1 Carhartt Drive, P.O. Box 280, Dover TN 37058-0280. 931/232-5341. **Contact:** Rita Collins, Plant Manager. **World Wide Web address:** http://www.carhartt.com. **Description:** Manufactures men's work clothes. Founded in 1889. **Corporate headquarters location:** Dearborn MI. **Number of employees nationwide:** 2,500.

CARRIER CORPORATION
P.O. Box 104, McMinnville TN 37111. 931/668-2811. **Physical Address:** 284 Carrier Drive, McMinnville TN 37111. **Fax:** 931/668-6204. **Contact:** Human Resources. **World Wide Web address:** http://www.carrier.com. **Description:** A commercial manufacturer of heating, ventilation, and air conditioning equipment. **Positions advertised include:** HVAC Parts Sales Associate. **Corporate headquarters location:** Farmington CT. **International locations:** Worldwide. **Parent company:** United Technologies Corporation.

CARRIER CORPORATION
97 South Byhalia Road, Collierville TN 38017. 901/854-3000. **Contact:** Human Resources. **World Wide Web address:** http://www.carrier.com. **Description:** A commercial manufacturer of heating, ventilation, and air conditioning equipment. **Corporate headquarters location:** Farmington CT. **International locations:** Worldwide. **Parent company:** United Technologies.

CASTILLION INC.
P.O. Box 1108, Shelbyville TN 37162-1108. 931/685-9057. **Physical address:** 220 Calsonic Way, Shelbyville TN 37160. **Fax:** 931/685-9059. **Contact:** T.J. Judge, General Manager. **World Wide Web address:** http://www.castillion.com. **Description:** Manufactures aerospace products including engine supports, floor beams for fuselages, frames for jet stream windows in the cockpit, and wing ribs. Founded in 1989.

CATERPILLAR FINANCIAL SERVICES CORPORATION
2120 West End Avenue, Nashville TN 37203-0001. 615/341-1000. **Contact:** Human Resources. **World Wide Web address:** http://www.cat.com. **Description:** Provides financing for Caterpillar brand equipment. **NOTE:** Search and apply for positions or submit resume online. **Positions advertised included:** Credit Manager; Associate Tax Accountant; Accountant. **Corporate headquarters location:** This location. **Other U.S. locations:** Nationwide. **International locations:** Worldwide.

CATHERINES STORES CORPORATION
3742 Lamar Avenue, Memphis TN 38118. 901/363-3900. **Contact:** Human Resources. **E-mail address:** great.jobs@catherines.com. **World Wide Web address:** http://www.catherines.com. **Description:** Catherine's Stores Corporation is a specialty retailer of women's plus-size clothing and accessories, operating 400 stores nationwide. **NOTE:** Search for positions through Monster.com. **Corporate headquarters location:** This location. **Other U.S. locations:** Nationwide. **Operations at this facility include:** This location houses administrative offices. **Subsidiaries include:** Added Dimensions; PS Plus Sizes; and The Answer. **Operations at this facility include:** Administration. **Number of employees at this location:** 450. **Number of employees nationwide:** 3,800.

CEBAL AMERICA
P.O. Box 747, Shelbyville TN 37162. **Physical Address:** 1209 New Tullahoma Highway, Shelbyville TN 37160. **Toll-free phone:** 800/251-4228. **Fax:** 931/684-0722. **Contact:** Human Resources Manager. **World Wide Web address:** http://www.cebalamerica.com. **Description:** Manufactures a variety of container products as a unit of the packaging firm. **Corporate headquarters location:** Norwalk CT. **Other U.S. locations:** CA; NJ; TX; IL; NC. **International locations:** Canada; Mexico; Brazil. **Parent company:** Cebal SA France).

CELERITY SYSTEMS, INC.
122 Perimeter Park Drive, Knoxville TN 37922. 865/539-3561. **Fax:** 865/539-3502. **Contact:** Human Resources. **World Wide Web address:** http://www.celerity.com. **Description:** Designs, develops and markets advanced digital set-top-boxes and video servers for interactive television and high-speed Internet. Founded in 1993. **Corporate headquarters location:** This location. **Listed on:** OTC Bulletin Board. **Stock exchange symbol:** CESY. **Number of employees at this location:** 80.

CENTEX RODGERS, INC.
2636 Elm Hill Pike, Suite 200, Nashville TN 37214. 615/889-4400. **Fax:** 615/872-1107. **World Wide Web address:** http://www.centex-construction.com. **Description:** Provides healthcare construction management services. Part of the Centex Construction Group. **Parent company:** Centex Corporation.

CENTRAL PARKING CORPORATION
2401 21st Avenue South, Nashville TN 37212. 615/297-4255. **Contact:** Human Resources. **World Wide Web address:** http://www.parking.com. **Description:** A leading provider of parking services in the United States. The company operates over 3,700 parking facilities in 38 states, and the District of Columbia. The company provides management services to multilevel parking facilities and surface lots. Central Parking Corporation also provides parking consulting services, shuttle services, valet services, parking meter enforcement services, and billing and collection services. Clients include building owners and developers of mixed-use projects, major office building complexes, sports stadiums, hotels, and municipalities. **NOTE:** Search and apply for positions online. **Positions advertised included:** Chief Internal Auditor. **Corporate headquarters location:** This location. **Other U.S. locations:** Nationwide. **International locations:** Chile; Germany; Ireland; Malaysia; Mexico; Puerto Rico; Spain; the Netherlands; United Kingdom. **Listed on:** New York Stock Exchange. **Stock exchange symbol:** CPC. **Chairman/CEO:** Monroe J. Carell, Jr.

CHARLES SCHWAB
320 North Cedar Bluff Road, The Stokely Building, Suite 101, Knoxville TN 37923. 800/435-4000. **Contact:** Human Resources. **World Wide Web address:** http://www.schwab.com. **Description:** Provides investment services. **NOTE:** Submitting your resume online is the fastest and most efficient way to express interest in job opportunities at Charles Schwab. **Positions advertised include:** Investment Specialist. **Corporate headquarters location:** San Francisco CA. **Other area locations:** Memphis TN; Brentwood TN.

CHARLESTON HOSIERY INC.
P.O. Box 2190, Cleveland TN 37320-2190. 423/472-5095. **Fax:** 423/479-5522. **Contact:** Human Resources. **World Wide Web address:** http://www.charlestonhosiery.com. **Description:** A manufacturer of men's, women's,

and children's socks. Founded in 1939. **Other U.S. locations:** Fort Payne AL; Biscoe NC.

CHASE SCIENTIFIC GLASS, INC.
234 Cardiff Valley Road, Rockwood TN 37854. 865/354-1212. **Toll-free phone:** 800/451-4351. **Fax:** 865/354-3853. **Contact:** Human Resources. **E-mail address:** sroy@chasescientific.com. **World Wide Web address:** http://www.chasescientific.com. **Description:** Manufactures laboratory, hospital, and scientific glassware including test tubes and slides.

CHICAGO METALLIC PRODUCTS, INC.
1502 North Central Avenue, Humboldt TN 38343. 731/784-7140. **Contact:** Glenda Johnson, Human Resources Manager. **World Wide Web address:** http://www.bakingpans.com. **Description:** Manufactures commercial bakeware.

CHRISTIAN BROTHERS UNIVERSITY
650 East Parkway South, Memphis TN 38104. 901/321-3000. **Contact:** Human Resources. **World Wide Web address:** http://www.cbu.edu. **Description:** A Catholic university with an enrollment of 1,900 students offering bachelor of arts, bachelor of science, master's, and M.B.A. degrees. Founded in 1871.

CIBER, INC.
3800 Forest Hill Irene Road, Suite 100, Memphis TN 38125. 901/754-6577. **Fax:** 901/754-8463. **Contact:** Recruiting. **World Wide Web address:** http://www.ciber.com. **Description:** A system integration consultancy for private and government clients. **NOTE:** Search and apply for positions or submit resume online. **Positions advertised included:** Business/Technical Architect. **Corporate headquarters location:** Greenwood Village CO. **Number of employees worldwide:** 6,000.

CLARKSVILLE, CITY OF
350 Pageant Lane, Clarksville TN 37040. 931/648-5530. **Contact:** Wilbur Hill, Director of Personnel. **World Wide Web address:** http://www.cityofclarksville.com. **Description:** This location houses the administrative offices of the city of Clarksville. **NOTE:** Application required for all vacancies.

CLAYTON HOMES AND VANDERBILT MORTGAGE, INC.
P.O. Box 9790, Maryville TN 37802. 865/380-3000. **Fax:** 865/380-3789. **Contact:** Human Resources. **World Wide Web address:** http://www.clayton.net. **Description:** A vertically-integrated builder and seller of low- to medium-priced manufactured homes operating in 49 states. The company provides financing and insurance services to its retail customers and owns and operates 88 manufactured housing communities in 12 states. Founded in 1966. **Corporate headquarters location:** This location. **Parent company:** Berkshire Hathaway. **Operations at this facility include:** Administration. **Number of employees nationwide:** 5,000.

CLIENTLOGIC
Two American Center, 3102 West End Avenue, Suite 900, Nashville TN 37203. 615/301-7100. **Contact:** Human Resources. **E-mail address:** nashvillejobs@clientlogic.com. **World Wide Web address:** http://www.clientlogic.com. **Description:** ClientLogic is an international provider of integrated customer management solutions including integrated customer acquisition, list management and brokerage, database design and development, multi-channel customer and technical support, eCommerce services, and warehousing/fulfillment. The company operates in 52 locations in 12 countries throughout North America, Europe and Asia. **NOTE:** Search for positions at: Monster.com. **Positions advertised include:** Market Research Specialist; Paralegal/Compliance Specialist. **Corporate headquarters location:** This location. **Parent company:** Onex Corporation (Canada). **Number of employees worldwide:** 16,500.

COLE VISION CORPORATION
5780 Shelby Drive East, Memphis TN 38141. 901/375-0015. **Toll-free phone:** 800/336-4535. **Fax:** 901/375-0668. **Contact:** Human Resources. **World Wide Web address:** http://www.colenational.com. **Description:** Manufactures prescription eyewear including contact lenses, eyeglasses, frames, lenses, and sunglasses. **NOTE:** Entry-level positions and second and third shifts are offered. **Special programs:** Summer Jobs. **Office hours:** Monday - Friday, 8:00 a.m. - 5:00 p.m. **Corporate headquarters location:** Twinsburg OH. **Other U.S. locations:** Salt Lake City UT; Richmond VA. **Parent company:** Cole National Corporation. **Annual sales/revenues:** $5 - $10 million.

COLLINS & AIKMAN
660 Massman Drive, Nashville TN 37210. 615/883-0058. **Fax:** 615/872-9216. **Contact:** Human Resources. **World Wide Web address:** http://www.collinsaikman.com. **Description:** Engaged in injection molding of parts for the automotive industry.

COMDATA HOLDINGS CORPORATION
5301 Maryland Way, Brentwood TN 37027. 615/370-7000. **Fax:** 615/370-7828. **Contact:** Human Resources. **E-mail address:** resumes@comdata.com. **World Wide Web address:** http://www.comdata.com. **Description:** Comdata provides credit and debit processing and reporting for commercial fleets and merchants, electronic cash, gift and smart/chip card programs for retailers and governmental agencies, payroll services for food, retail and other service industries, and point-of-sale equipment, software and auxiliary services for merchants and convenience stores. **Positions advertised include:** Applications Specialist; Credit Implementation Representative; Retention Account Executive; Sr. Manager, Corporate Communications; Technical Representative; Wintel Systems Administrator. **Corporate headquarters location:** This location. **Other U.S. locations:** Los Angeles CA; Denver CO; Atlanta GA; Cincinnati OH; Dallas TX. **International locations:** Toronto, Canada. **Parent company:** Ceridian Corporation. **Operations at this facility include:** Administration; Sales; Service. **Number of employees nationwide:** 1,800.

COMMODORE ADVANCED SCIENCES
800 Oak Ridge Turnpike, Suite C-260, Oak Ridge TN 37830. 865/483-1274. **Contact:** Human Resources. **World Wide Web address:** http://www.commodore.com. **Description:** A technical services consulting firm that provides innovative, multidisciplinary solutions to a wide range of environmental challenges. A staff of environmental professionals provides services in waste management, environmental sciences, advanced technologies, and bioremediation. **Corporate headquarters location:** New York NY. **Parent company:** Commodore.

COMMUNITY HEALTH SYSTEMS, INC.
155 Franklin Road, Suite 400, Brentwood TN 37027-4000. 615/373-9600. **Contact:** Human Resources. **World Wide Web address:** http://www.chs.net. **Description:** Owns and manages 72 hospitals in 22 states. **NOTE:** Search and apply for positions or submit resume online. **Listed on:** New York Stock Exchange. **Stock exchange symbol:** CYH.

CONAGRA GROCERY PRODUCTS
540 East Broadway, Newport TN 37821. 423/623-2333. **Fax:** 423/625-9369. **Contact:** Personnel. **World Wide Web address:** http://www.cgpci.com. **Description:** A food processing company. Products processed at this location include Van Camps canned pork and beans, Beanee Weenee canned beans and wieners, Hunt's spaghetti and tomato sauce, and Manwich sauces. **Corporate headquarters location:** Chicago IL. **Other U.S. locations:** Jackson TN. **Parent company:** ConAgra International.

CONCORD EFS, INC.
2525 Horizon Lake Drive, Suite 120, Memphis TN 38133. **Toll-free phone:** 800/238-7675. **Contact:** Human Resources Department. **World Wide Web address:** http://www.concordefs.com. **Description:** Engaged in debit and credit card authorization and processing, check authorization, ATM transaction processing, Internet transaction processing, and the development of new payment methods. **Parent company:** First Data. **Listed on:** New York Stock Exchange. **Stock exchange symbol:** FDC. **Annual sales/revenues:** More than $100 million. **Number of employees worldwide:** 30,000.

CONLEY FROG SWITCH & FORGE COMPANY
387 East Bodley Avenue, Memphis TN 38109. 901/948-4591. **Contact:** Human Resources. **Description:** Manufactures railroad track crossings and switches, accessories, and commercial forgings.

CONTROL TECHNOLOGY, INC.
5734 Middlebrook Pike, Knoxville TN 37921. 865/584-0440. **Fax:** 865/584-5720. **Contact:** Personnel. **World Wide Web address:** http://www.controltechnology.com. **Description:** Manufactures communications hardware, software, and input/output modules for industrial customers worldwide.

COOKEVILLE REGIONAL MEDICAL CENTER
142 West Fifth Street, Cookeville TN 38501. 931/528-2541. **Fax:** 931/646-2635. **Contact:** Human Resources. **E-mail address:** kbailey@crmchealth.org. **World Wide Web address:** http://www.crmchealth.org. **Description:** A nonprofit, acute care medical center with 247 beds. Services offered include general medical and surgical care, a heart catheterization lab, critical care unit, obstetrics, and medical oncology. Founded in 1950. **NOTE:** Entry-level positions and second and third shifts are offered. **Positions advertised include:** Certified Nurses Aide; Pharmacy Technician; Licensed Practical Nurse; Pharmacist; CT Technologist; Registered Nurse; Respiratory Therapist; Secretary; Surgical Technician. **Special programs:** Internships. **President/CEO:** Mike Mayes.

COOPER COMPANIES
1407 Union Avenue, Suite 400, Memphis TN 38104. 901/725-9631. **Contact:** Pace Cooper, President. **World Wide Web address:** http://www.cooperhotels.com. **Description:** Provides property management and real estate services and operates several hotels.

COORS BREWING COMPANY
5151 East Raines Road, Memphis TN 38118. 901/375-2000. **Contact:** Director of Human Resources. **World Wide Web address:** http://www.coors.com. **Description:** A brewery. Coors Brewing is one of the world's largest brewing companies and the largest subsidiary of Adolph Coors Company. **NOTE:** Search and apply for positions or submit resume online. **Positions advertised include:** HR Group Manager; Operations Coordinator; Business Unit Manager; Utilities Operating Engineer. **Parent company:** Adolph Coors Company is a holding company with subsidiaries that produce and distribute malt beverages such as beer. Through its ACX Technologies subsidiary, Adolph Coors also operates Golden Aluminum Company; Graphic Packaging Corporation; Coors BioTech Inc.; Coors Energy Company; Golden Technologies Company, Inc.; and Coors Ceramics.

CORRECTIONS CORPORATION OF AMERICA
10 Burton Hills Boulevard, Nashville TN 37215. 615/263-3000. **Toll-free phone:** 800/624-2931. **Fax:** 615/263-3140. **Contact:** Personnel. **E-mail address:** humanresources@correctionscorp.com. **World Wide Web address:** http://www.correctionscorp.com. **Description:** A leading private-sector provider of detention and correctional services to federal, state, and local governments. The company designs, finances, constructs, renovates, and manages jails and prisons, and provides escort and court services and long-distance transportation of inmates. Its expertise covers adult and juvenile offenders, at all levels of security classification. **Corporate headquarters location:** This location. **Subsidiaries include:** CAA International furnishes similar services abroad in Puerto Rico, Australia, and the United Kingdom. **Listed on:** New York Stock Exchange. **Stock exchange symbol:** CXW. **Number of employees nationwide:** 15,000.

COVANCE INC.
150 4th Avenue North, Suite 600, Nashville TN 37219. 615/313-6700. **Contact:** Human Resources. **World Wide Web address:** http://www.covance.com/careers. **Description:** A drug development services company. **NOTE:** Search and apply for positions or submit resume online. **Positions advertised include:** Clinical Research Associate; Trial Logistics Associate. **Corporate headquarters location:** Princeton NJ. **Listed on:** New York Stock Exchange. **Stock exchange symbol:** CVD. **Number of employees worldwide:** 6,500.

COVENANT HEALTH
Knoxville TN 37902. 865/531-5040. **Contact:** Human Resources. **E-mail address:** eservice@covhlth.com. **World Wide Web address:** http://www.covenanthealth.com. **Description:** A healthcare system operating five acute-care facilities, two outpatient cancer centers, a rehabilitation center, and an inpatient behavioral health hospital. **NOTE:** Search and apply for positions or submit resume online. **Positions advertised include:** Application Support Analyst; Development Manager; Computer Operator.

CRACKER BARREL OLD COUNTRY STORE, INC.
P.O. Box 787, Lebanon TN 37088-0787. 615/444-5533. **Fax:** 615/443-9476. **Contact:** Judy Brodhead, Employment Coordinator. **World Wide Web address:** http://www.crackerbarrelocs.com. **Description:** Operates a restaurant/retail chain with over 430 locations. Founded in 1969. NOTE: Search and apply for positions online. **Positions advertised include:** Accounting Manager; Manager of Financial Planning and Analysis; Construction Project Manager; Sr. Restaurant Analyst; Sr. Tax Research Analyst. **Corporate headquarters location:** This location. **Parent company:** CBRL Group, Inc. **Listed on:** NASDAQ. **Stock exchange symbol:** CBRL. **Annual sales/revenues:** More than $100 million. **Number of employees at this location:** 700.

CRESCENT HOSIERY MILLS
P.O. Box 669, Niota TN 37826-0669. 423/568-2101. **Contact:** Human Resources. **World Wide Web address:** http://www.hosierymills.com. **Description:** A manufacturer of men's, women's, and children's socks.

CROCKETT HOSPITAL
1607 South Locust Avenue, Highway 43, P.O. Box 847, Lawrenceburg TN 38464. 931/762-6571. **Fax:** 931/766-3248. **Contact:** Bob Augustin, Director of Human Resources. **E-mail address:** robert.augustin@lifepointhospitals.com. **World Wide Web address:** http://www.crocketthospital.com. **Description:** A 107-bed acute-care hospital. Crockett Hospital offers a variety of inpatient and outpatient services including 24-hour emergency care, women's health services, a full range of surgical capabilities, critical care, rehabilitation, diabetes management, and nutrition and dietary counseling. **Positions advertised include:** Respiratory Therapist; Physical Therapist; Registered Nurse.

CROWE CHIZEK AND COMPANY LLC
105 Continental Place, Suite 200, Brentwood TN 37024. 615/370-9852. **Fax:** 615/399-3663. **Contact:** Recruiting. **World Wide Web address:** http://www.crowechizek.com. **Description:** A provider of assurance, consulting, risk management, tax and technology services to large and middle market public companies and large privately-held businesses. **NOTE:** For entry-level positions, e-mail resumes to: campus_recruiting@crowechizek.com. Search and apply online for experienced positions. **Positions advertised include:** Litigation Practice Executive; Information Security Audit Manager; Internal audit Manager; Senior Manager. **Other area locations:** Knoxville TN. **Other U.S. locations:** IN; IL; KY; OH; MI; FL. **Parent company:** Horwath International. **Number of employees worldwide:** 1,600.

CRYE-LEIKE REALTORS
5111 Maryland Way, Brentwood TN 37027. 615/373-2044. **Contact:** Human Resources. **World Wide Web address:** http://www.crye-leike.com. **Description:** A full-service real estate firm with 10 offices across the state. **Positions advertised include:** Relocation Consultant.

CUMMINS ORIGINAL EQUIPMENT REMANUFACTURING
4155 Quest Way Drive, Memphis TN 38115. 901/546-5306. **Toll-free phone:** 800/777-3266. **Fax:** 901/546-5317. **Contact:** Human Resources Manager. **World Wide Web address:** http://www.cummins-oer.com. **Description:** Develops, manufactures, and markets remanufactured gasoline engines and components for the automotive and industrial machinery markets. **Corporate headquarters location:** This location. **Parent company:** Cummins Engine Company.

DANKA OFFICE IMAGING COMPANY, INC.
1638 Sycamore View Road, Memphis TN 38134. 901/387-5600. **Contact:** Personnel. **World Wide Web address:** http://www.danka.com. **Description:** A wholesaler of photocopiers, printers, and fax machines. Founded in 1977. **NOTE:** Search and apply for positions online. **Corporate headquarters location:** St. Petersburg FL.

DATA RESEARCH AND APPLICATIONS INC.
10425 Cogdill Road, Suite 450, Knoxville TN 37932. 865/671-4474. **Fax:** 865/671-3533. **Contact:** Human Resources. **E-mail address:** jobs@dra-hq.com. **World Wide Web address:** http://www.dra-international.com. **Description:** Develops software for data recovery and provides computer hardware.

DEKALB COUNTY BOARD OF EDUCATION
110 South Public Square, Smithville TN 37166. 615/597-4084. **Contact:** Director of Schools Office. **World Wide Web address:** http://www.dekalbschools.com. **Description:** This location houses the administrative offices of the DeKalb County Board of Education.

DELOITTE & TOUCHE LLP
424 Church Street, Suite 2400, Nashville TN 37219. 615/259-1800. **Fax:** 615/259-1862. **Contact:** Human Resources Department. **World Wide Web address:** http://www.us.deloitte.com. **Description:** An international firm of certified public accountants providing professional accounting, auditing, tax, and management consulting services to widely diversified clients. The company has a specialized program consisting of national industry groups and functional groups that cross industry lines. Groups are involved in various disciplines including accounting, auditing, taxation management advisory services, small and growing businesses, mergers and acquisitions, and computer applications. **Corporate headquarters location:** Wilton CT. **Other U.S. locations:** Nationwide. **International locations:** Worldwide. **Number of employees nationwide:** 30,000. **Number of employees worldwide:** 120,000.

DELTA MEDICAL CENTER
3000 Getwell Road, Memphis TN 38118. 901/369-8100. **Toll-free phone:** 800/285-9502. **Recorded jobline:** 901/369-4747. **Fax:** 901/369-8527. **Contact:** Human Resources. **World Wide Web address:** http://www.deltamedcenter.com. **Description:** A 243-bed medical/surgical hospital. The center offers a complete range of services including a 24-hour physician-staffed emergency center, inpatient and outpatient health care, mental health services, and treatment for chemical dependency. The hospital's Health Resource Center offers free monthly health seminars and health screenings. **Positions advertised include:** Registered Nurse; House Supervisor; UR Nurse; Speech Therapist; LPN; Nursing Assistant. **Parent company:** Regent Health Group, Inc.

DENARK CONSTRUCTION
1635 Western Avenue, Knoxville, TN 37921. 865/637-1925. **Fax:** 865/637-2837. **Contact:** Human Resources. **E-mail address:** hr@denark.com. **World Wide Web address:** http://www.denark.com. **Description:** Denark Construction is a full-service general contractor/design-builder/construction manager. Denark Construction's services include: design-build teams, construction management, general contracting, light commercial work, and high-end residential. **Positions advertised include:** Project Managers; Project Estimators, Project Engineers, Project Accountants, Entry Level/College Graduates. **Corporate Headquarters:** This location.

DENSO MANUFACTURING TENNESSEE, INC.
1720 Robert C. Jackson Drive, Maryville TN 37801. 865/982-7000. **Fax:** 865/981-5262. **Contact:** Human Resources. **E-mail address:** densojobs@dmtn.com. **World Wide Web address:** http://www.densocorp-na.com. **Description:** Manufactures automobile starters, alternators, and speedometers. **NOTE:** Search and apply for positions online. **Positions advertised include:** Production Associate; Supplier Quality Engineer; Quality Assurance Engineer; **Parent company:** Denso Company, Ltd. is one of the world's largest suppliers of automotive components. The company supplies components and systems to nearly all the world's automakers, including the Big Three U.S. automakers, as well as most of the Japanese and European automakers. Products are manufactured in 31 nations. Denso is a leader in automotive electronics, as well as in systems for electronic fuel injection, braking control, and navigation. The company is one of the world's largest manufacturers of automobile heaters and air conditioners. Other products include hand-held bar code readers, factory automation systems, and portable telephones. **Number of employees nationwide:** 14,000. **Number of employees worldwide:** 89,000.

DIXIEWIRE
5901 California Avenue, P. O. Box 90208, Nashville TN 37209. 615/383-6803. **Contact:** Human Resources. **World Wide Web address:** http://www.alcoa.com. **Description:** DixieWire is a leading supplier of insulated and non-insulated wire, multi-conductor cables, battery cables, convolute tubing, and other logistical services to the automotive, appliance, electronic, power, control and signal, and building markets. **NOTE:** Search and apply for positions online. **Parent company:** Alcoa, Inc.

DODGE ROCKWELL AUTOMATION
100 Rockwell Drive, Rogersville TN 37857. 423/272-2686. **Contact:** Human Resources. **World Wide Web address:** http://www.dodge-pt.com. **Description:** Manufactures industrial bearings. **Parent company:** Rockwell International provides products for the printing, military, automotive, and aerospace industries through its electronics, automotive, and graphics divisions. Products include military and commercial communication equipment, guidance systems, electronics, components for automobiles, and printing presses. A major client of Rockwell is the U.S. government. Rockwell provides the government with parts and services for bombers, as well as power systems for the space station, and is a major contractor for the Space Shuttle Orbiter program.

DOLLAR GENERAL CORPORATION
100 Mission Ridge Drive, Goodlettsville TN 37072. 615/855-4000. **Recorded jobline:** 800/909-5627. **Contact:** Human Resources Department. **World Wide Web address:** http://www.dollargeneral.com. **Description:** Operates 6,700 general merchandise stores in 29 states. Founded in 1939. **NOTE:** Entry-level positions and second and third shifts are offered. Search and apply for positions online. **Positions advertised include:** AS 400 Systems Administrator; Sr. Claims Representative; Commercial Construction Project Manager; Director of External Relations; Employee Relations Report Coordinator; Financial Analyst; Fleet Operations Supervisor; Programmer; Sr. Staff Accountant. **Corporate headquarters location:** This location. **Operations at this facility include:** Divisional Headquarters; Regional Headquarters. **Listed on:** New York Stock Exchange. **Stock exchange symbol:** DG. **Annual sales/revenues:** More than $100 million. **Number of employees at this location:** 1,000. **Number of employees nationwide:** 57,000.

DUNAVANT ENTERPRISES
3797 New Getwell Road, Memphis TN 38118. 901/369-1500. **Fax:** 901/369-1608. **Contact:** Human Resources. **E-mail address:** jobs@dunavant.com. **World Wide Web address:** http://www.dunavant.com. **Description:** One of the world's largest cotton dealers. Activities include the merchandising, warehousing, and ginning of cotton. **Listed on:** Privately held.

DURA AUTOMOTIVE SYSTEMS
132 Ferro Road, P.O. Box 669, Pikeville TN 37367-0669. 423/447-6861. **Fax:** 423/447-2736. **Contact:** Phil Rasnick, Human Resources Manager. **World Wide Web address:** http://www.duraauto.com. **Description:** Manufactures automotive window lift systems and seat back recliners. **Corporate headquarters location:** Rochester Hills MI. **Operations at this facility include:** Manufacturing. **Listed on:** NASDAQ. **Stock exchange symbol:** DRRA. **Annual sales/revenues:** More than $100 million. **Number of employees at this location:** 500. **Number of employees nationwide:** 8,000.

DURAKON
1330 Carden Farm Drive, Clinton TN 37716. 865/457-8244. **Contact:** Kathy Richards, Human Resources Director. **World Wide Web address:** http://www.durakon.com. **Description:** Manufactures truck bed protection products. **Operations at this facility include:** Manufacturing.

DURACELL INTERNATIONAL, INC.
P.O. Box 3390, Cleveland TN 37320-3390. 423/478-6000. **Physical address:** 501 Mouse Creek Road NW, Cleveland TN 37312. **Contact:** Human Resources Manager. **World Wide Web address:** http://www.duracell.com. **Description:** Manufactures a line of batteries sold worldwide under the Duracell trademark. The company also manufactures batteries used in hearing aids, and photographic and communications equipment. A subsidiary conducts marketing operations for a line of lighting products under the Durabeam brand name. **Number of employees worldwide:** 7,900.

DYE, VAN MOL, & LAWRENCE
209 Seventh Avenue North, Nashville TN 37219. 615/244-1818. **Fax:** 615/780-3302. **Contact:** Ronald Roberts, Personnel. **E-mail address:** ronald.roberts@dvl.com. **World Wide Web address:** http://www.dvl.com. **Description:** An advertising and public relations firm. Founded in 1980. **Number of employees at this location:** 40.

EAGLE SYSTEMS TECHNOLOGY, INC.
1300 Wolf Park Drive, Germantown TN 38138. 901/737-3990. **Toll-free phone:** 800/845-6471. **Fax:** 901/685-3706. **Contact:** Human Resources. **E-mail address:** eaglem@eaglemphs.com. **World Wide Web address:** http://www.eaglemphs.com. **Description:** Engaged in systems integration and contract programming services. Founded in 1986.

EARTHGRAINS BAKERY
2407 Franklin Road, Nashville TN 37204. 615/297-5393. **Fax:** 615/386-1494. **Contact:** Human Resources. **E-mail address:** hr@slbg.com. **World Wide Web address:** http://www.earthgrains.com. **Description:** A national producer of a wide range of bakery products including bread and rolls. **NOTE:** Search and apply for positions online. **Corporate headquarters location:** St. Louis MO. **Parent company:** Sara Lee.

EAST TENNESSEE CHILDREN'S HOSPITAL
2018 Clinch Avenue, P.O. Box 15010, Knoxville TN 37901-5010. 865/541-8000. **Fax:** 865/541-8340. **Recorded jobline:** 865/541-8565. **Contact:** Human Resources. **E-mail address:** jobs@etch.com. **World Wide Web address:** http://www.etch.com. **Description:** Provides care to 60,000 children from east Tennessee, southeast Kentucky, southwest Virginia, and western North Carolina. Annually, East Tennessee Children's Hospital is one of the region's leading pediatric referral centers. Services include the hospital's Pediatric Intensive Care Unit; the Neonatal Intensive Care Unit; the Pediatric Critical Care Transport Team and the Neonatal Transport Team; the Pediatric Emergency Department and Trauma Center; pediatric medical floors; outpatient clinics; pediatric surgical services; home health; rehabilitation center; hospital intensive psychiatric services; the child life department; pastoral care; nutrition services; and social work. **Positions advertised include:** Registered Nurse; Nursing Director of Critical Care Services; Licensed Practical Nurse; Nursing Supervisor;

Pharmacist; Development Phlebotomist; Sonongrapher; CT Technologist; Director of Health Information Management.

EAST TENNESSEE STATE UNIVERSITY
ETSU Box 70564, Johnson City TN 37614-1707. 423/439-4457. **Fax:** 423/439-8354. **Contact:** Human Resources. **World Wide Web address:** http://www.etsu.edu. **Description:** A state university with an enrollment of approximately 11,000 students. The university offers over 100 academic programs including two-year, four-year, and graduate degrees. **NOTE:** E-mailed applications and resumes are not accepted. Search for positions and download application form online. Positions advertised include: Instructor, Various Departments; Assistant/Associate Professor, Various Departments; Research Analyst; Assistant Athletic Director; Associate Vice President for University Advancement Capital Campaign.

EASTMAN CHEMICAL COMPANY
P.O. Box 1975, Kingsport TN 37662-5075. 423/229-2000. **Contact:** Employment. **World Wide Web address:** http://www.eastman.com. **Description:** An international chemical company offering more than 1,200 plastic, chemical, and fiber products. Eastman Chemical is the world's largest supplier of polyester plastics for packaging; a leading supplier of coatings raw materials, specialty chemicals and plastics; and a major supplier of cellulose acetate fibers and basic chemicals. Eastman is a top global supplier of custom-manufactured fine chemicals for pharmaceuticals, agricultural chemicals and other markets. **NOTE:** Search and apply for positions or submit resume online. **Positions advertised include:** Technical Service Representative; Occupational Health Nurse; Electrical Engineer; Market Development Representative. **Special programs:** Internships. **Corporate headquarters location:** This location. **Other U.S. locations:** AK; IL; IA; SC; GA; IN; TX; CA; AL; NJ; PA; OR; NY. **International locations:** Worldwide. **Operations at this facility include:** Administration; Manufacturing; Research and Development; Sales; Service. **Listed on:** New York Stock Exchange. **Stock exchange symbol:** EMN. **Number of employees worldwide:** 15,000.

EATON AEROQUIP
609 Swan Avenue, Hohenwald TN 38462. 931/796-3272. **Contact:** Human Resources. **World Wide Web address:** http://www.eaton.com. **Description:** Eaton Corporation is a diversified, integrated operating company with four business segments: fluid power, industrial and commercial controls, automotive, and truck components. **Corporate headquarters location:** Cleveland OH. **Operations at this facility include:** This location produces rubber hoses for a variety of industrial purposes. **Number of employees worldwide:** 51,000.

EATON GLOBAL HOSE
860 Blankenship Street, Newbern TN 38059. 731/627-2531. **Contact:** Human Resources. **World Wide Web address:** http://hydraulics.eaton.com/boston. **Description:** Eaton Corporation is a diversified, integrated operating company with four business segments: fluid power, industrial and commercial controls, automotive, and truck components. **NOTE:** Search and apply for positions or submit resume online. **Positions advertised include:** Lean Coordinator; Manufacturing Manager. **Corporate headquarters location:** Cleveland OH. **Operations at this facility include:** This location produces rubber hoses for a variety of industrial purposes. **Number of employees worldwide:** 51,000.

ECONOCOM USA
6750 Poplar Avenue, Suite 202, Memphis TN 38138. 901/685-0021. **Fax:** 901/685-1105. **Contact:** Human Resources. **World Wide Web address:** http://www.econocomusa.com. **Description:** Leases computer hardware to commercial customers. **NOTE:** Search and apply for positions or submit resume online. **Positions advertised include:** Account Executive/Storage Solutions. **Parent company:** Econocom Group. **Number of employees worldwide:** 2,400.

EDISON AUTOMATION, INC.
3712 Ringgold Road, Suite133, Chattanooga TN 37412. 423/304-7789. **Fax:** 706/866-7415. **Contact:** Human Resources. **World Wide Web address:** http://www.edisonautomation.com. **Description:** Edison Automation is an independent automation and controls company serving primarily the Middle Tennessee industrial market. Edison distributes a broad selection of industrial motion and control products and supports these products with wide ranging technical services. **Positions advertised include:** Electrical Panel Fabricator; Field Service Representative; Technician.

ELDON
1427 William Blount Drive, Maryville TN 37801. 865/977-5477. **Fax:** 865/380-2545. **Contact:** Personnel. **World Wide Web address:** http://www.eldon.com. **Description:** Manufactures office accessories, office furnishings, and filing systems. Brand names include Rubbermaid, Households, Rogers, Rolodex, and Spacemaker. **Special programs:** Internships. **Parent company:** Newell Rubbermaid. **Operations at this facility include:** Administration; Distribution; Divisional Headquarters; Manufacturing; Research and Development; Sales.

THE ELECTRIC POWER BOARD OF CHATTANOOGA
P.O. Box 182255, Chattanooga TN 37422-7255. 423/756-2706. **Fax:** 423/648-3576. **Contact:** Human Resources. **E-mail address:** jobs@epb.net. **World Wide Web address:** http://www.epb.net. **Description:** A nonprofit agency that provides electrical service to residents and businesses in the Chattanooga area. All electricity is purchased from the Tennessee Valley Authority under terms of a wholesale power contract. Founded in 1935. **NOTE:** Search and apply for positions or submit resume online. **Positions advertised include:** Finance Manager; Substation Technician; Telecom Administrator; Application Developer; System Analyst.

EMBASSY SUITES-MEMPHIS
1022 South Shady Grove Road, Memphis TN 38120. 901/684-1777. **Contact:** General Manager. **World Wide Web address:** http://www.embassy-suites.com. **Description:** A 200-suite hotel. Features include Frank Grisanti's Restaurant and six conference suites. **NOTE:** Search for positions online.

EMERSON MACHINERY HEALTH MANAGMENT
835 Innovation Drive, Knoxville TN 37932. 865/675-2110. **Fax:** 865/218-1401. **Contact:** Personnel. **World Wide Web address:** http://www.compsys.com. **Description:** One of the world's largest manufacturers of Reliability-Based Maintenance (RBM) products and allied services. CSI is a technical leader in vibration analysis, with products in four major categories: batteries, adapters, vibration software modules, and advanced machinery analyzer minilabs. CSI's tribology products and services include the Tribology, the Tribology Total Solution system, and its Fluid Analysis Lab. CSI's infrared thermography systems include a focal-plane array camera and Infranalysis data/image management system, which provide a systematic route-based approach to IR that saves time and simplifies diagnoses. CSI's alignment and balancing services include both electromechanical and laser alignment systems. **Positions advertised include:** Accounts Payable Supervisor. **Corporate headquarters location:** This location. **Other U.S. locations:** San Diego CA; Detroit MI; Eddystone PA; Houston TX. **International locations:** Belgium; Germany; Italy; United Kingdom. **Parent company:** Emerson Electric Company. **Operations at this facility include:** Administration; Manufacturing; Research and Development; Sales; Service. **Listed on:** Privately held. **Number of employees nationwide:** 400.

ENVIRONMENTAL SYSTEMS CORPORATION
200 Tech Center Drive, Knoxville TN 37912. 865/688-7900. **Fax:** 865/219-0992. **Contact:** Human Resources. **E-mail address:** hr@envirosys.com. **World Wide Web address:** http://www.envirosys.com. **Description:** Manufactures custom-designed environmental and engineering systems and provides services for air quality monitoring, hazardous waste management, and ground water management for the coal and nuclear energy industry. **NOTE:** Search and apply for positions online. **Positions advertised include:** Customer Service Supervisor; Engineer; Software Support; Project Engineer; Regulations Specialist; Director, Manufacturing; Sr. Engineer; Technical Manager; Calibration Technologist; Configuration Manager; Programmer Analyst; Database Administrator.

ERLANGER MEDICAL CENTER
975 East Third Street, Chattanooga TN 37403-9975. 423/778-7000. **Contact:** Human Resources. **World Wide Web address:** http://www.erlanger.org. **Description:** An 818-bed hospital and teaching facility. Erlanger Medical Center is one of the largest public hospitals in the state. Facilities include a Level I trauma center, the Erlanger Cancer Center, the Miller Eye Center, and T.C. Thompson Children's Hospital. **NOTE:** Search and apply for positions online. **Positions advertised include:** RN's; LPN's; Cytogenetic Lab Director; Surgical Technologist; Phlebotomy Specialist; Medical Technologist; Radiation Therapist; Nuclear Medicine Technologist; Diagnostic Ultrasonographer.

ERNST & YOUNG LLP
424 Church Street, Suite 1100, Nashville TN 37219-1779. 615/252-2000. **Fax:** 615/242-9128. **Contact:** Human Resources. **World Wide Web address:** http://www.ey.com. **Description:** A certified public accounting firm that also provides management consulting services. Services include data processing, financial modeling, financial feasibility studies, production planning and inventory management, management sciences, health care planning, human resources, cost accounting, and budgeting systems. **NOTE:** Search and apply for positions online. **Corporate headquarters location:** New York NY. **Other U.S. locations:** Nationwide. **Number of employees worldwide:** 103,000.

EXEL TRANSPORTATION SERVICES INC.
965 Ridge Lake Boulevard, Suite 103, Memphis TN 38120. 901/767-4455. **Fax:** 901/767-1929. **Contact:** Human Resources. **World Wide Web address:** http://www.exel.com. **Description:** One of the country's leading providers of single-source transportation services to some of the largest shippers in the world. The company provides a full complement of logistics management services such as dedicated fleet, warehousing, and risk management, as well as the component services involved in these activities. The company's areas of operation include Intermodal Trucking Services; Carload, International, and Dimensional Traffic; Consolidation and Distribution Services; and Air Freight services. Services offered include double stack, trailers, and containers on rail cars; trucks; and ocean-going transportation. Commodities transported include paper, food, empty containers, retail products, and household goods. **Corporate headquarters location:** England. **Other U.S. locations:** Nationwide.

FAMILY INNS OF AMERICA
P.O. Box 10, Pigeon Forge TN 37868-0010. 865/453-4988. **Contact:** Dian Robertson, Human Resources. **World Wide Web address:** http://www.familyinnsofamerica.com. **Description:** Operates a nationwide motel chain. **Special programs:** Internships. **Corporate headquarters location:** This location. **Parent company:** KMS Enterprises, Inc.

FEDERAL-MOGUL CORPORATION
167 Bentley Harris Way, Gordonsville TN 38563. 615/683-8000. **Fax:** 615/683-6122. **Contact:** Human Resources. **World Wide Web address:** http://www.federal-mogul.com. **Description:** Manufactures automotive components. Founded in 1899. **NOTE:** Send resume to: Corporate Human Resources Staffing, Federal-Mogul Corporation, 26555 Northwestern Highway, Southfield MI 48034. **Special programs:** Internships and co-op opportunities offered. **Listed on:** New York Stock Exchange. **Stock exchange symbol:** FMO. **Annual sales/revenues:** More than $100 million.

FIDELITY INTEGRATED FINANCIAL SOLUTIONS
202 East Broadway Avenue, Maryville TN 37804-5782. 865/982-0116. **Fax:** 678/982-1879. **Contact:** Human Resources. **World Wide Web address:** http://www.fidelity.com. **Description:** Provides technology products and services to the financial industry, including core processing, check imaging and item processing, electronic funds transfer, debit card processing, communications management and related products and services. Operates 30 processing centers nationwide. **NOTE:** Search and apply for positions online. **Positions advertised include:** Product Specialist. **Other area locations:** Cookeville TN; Nashville TN.

FIRST HORIZON NATIONAL CORPORATION
165 Madison Avenue, Memphis TN 38103. 901/523-4444. **Contact:** Human Resources. **World Wide Web address:** http://www.firsttennessee.com. **Description:** a bank holding company serving 1 million consumers and 90,000 business customers through 1,000 offices in 42 states. **Subsidiaries include:** First Tennessee; First Horizon Home Loans; FTN Financial. **NOTE:** Search and apply for positions or submit resume online at http://www.ftncareers.com. **Positions advertised include:** Commercial Loan Relationship Manager, Customer Relations Specialist; Engineer; Enterprise Technologist; Financial Analyst; Loan Originator; Manager, Quality Assurance; Marketing Database Analyst. **Listed on:** New York Stock Exchange. **Stock exchange symbol:** FHN. **Number of employees nationwide:** 12,000.

FISHER & COMPANY
766 Squirrel Hollow Drive, Linden TN 37096. 931/589-2195. **Fax:** 931/589-5311. **Contact:** Human Resources. **World Wide Web address:** http://www.fisherco.com. **Description:** Manufacture of interior car parts such as seat recliners, headrests, armrests, and floor latches. **Positions advertised include:** Material Manager; Continuous Improvement Manager; Buyer; Controller. **Corporate headquarters location:** St. Clair Shores MI.

FLEETGUARD INC.
2931 Elm Hill Road, Nashville TN 37214. 615/367-0040. **Contact:** Human Resources Manager. **E-mail address:** fgd.nel.resumes@fleetguard.com. **World Wide Web address:** http://www.fleetguard.com. **Description:** Manufactures more than 12,000 filtration and exhaust system products. **NOTE:** Resumes may be e-mailed in plain text format to address above or mailed to: Cummins Inc., 500 Jackson Street, MC 60808,

Columbus IN 47201. Include reference code per instructions on website. **Number of employees worldwide:** 6,000.

FLINTCO, INC.
2179 Hillshire Circle, Memphis TN 38133-6074. 901/372-9600. **Contact:** Human Resources. **World Wide Web address:** http://www.flintco.com. **Description:** A general construction contractor. **Corporate headquarters location:** Tulsa OK.

FLOWERS BAKING COMPANY
330 Livingston Road, Crossville TN 38555. 931/456-5345. **Contact:** Human Resources Department. **World Wide Web address:** http://www.flowersfoods.com. **Description:** A bakery that produces breads and rolls. **Parent company:** Flowers Foods is one of the largest producers of baked goods in the United States. The company operates through two businesses: Flowers Bakeries, Inc. and Mrs. Smith's Bakeries, Inc.

FLOWERS BAKING COMPANY
P.O. Box 1774, Morristown TN 37816. 423/586-2471. **Contact:** Human Resources. **E-mail address:** resume@flocorp.com. **World Wide Web address:** http://www.flowersfoods.com. **Description:** A bakery that produces breads and rolls. **Parent company:** Flowers Foods is one of the largest producers of baked goods in the United States. The company operates through two businesses: Flowers Bakeries, Inc. and Mrs. Smith's Bakeries, Inc.

FLOWSERVE CORPORATION
5599 East Holmes Road, Memphis TN 38118. 901/546-9226. **Contact:** Human Resources. **World Wide Web address:** http://www.flowserve.com. **Description:** Manufactures flow management products for the industrial and process industries. The company also manufactures automated and manual quarter-twin valves, control valves and actuators, engineered pumps, and precision mechanical seals. **Corporate headquarters location:** Irving TX.

FOAMEX INTERNATIONAL, INC.
328 Hamblen Avenue, Morristown TN 37813. 423/581-8350. **Contact:** Director of Staffing and Development. **E-mail address:** recruiting@foamex.com. **World Wide Web address:** http://www.foamex.com. **Description:** Foamex produces comfort cushioning for bedding, furniture, carpet cushion and automotive markets as well as technical foams for applications in industrial, consumer, electronics, and transportation industries. **Corporate headquarters location:** Linwood PA. **Other U.S. locations:** Nationwide. **International locations:** Canada; Mexico; Thailand. **Listed on:** NASDAQ. **Stock exchange symbol:** FMXI. **Annual sales/revenues:** More than $100 million. **Number of employees worldwide:** 3,600.

FORT SANDERS PARKWEST MEDICAL CENTER
9352 Park West Boulevard, Knoxville TN 37923. 865/373-1000. **Contact:** Human Resources. **World Wide Web address:** http://www.fsparkwest.com. **Description:** A full-service, acute care hospital. Fort Sanders Parkwest Medical Center specializes in cardiology, critical care, diagnostics, emergency care, gastroenterology, joint replacement, maternity services, oncology, neurosurgery, physical therapy, radiology, and respiratory therapy. **NOTE:** Search and apply for positions online. **Positions advertised include:** RN's; PCA/CNA's; Director, Patient Care Services; LPN's. **Parent company:** Covenant Health.

FORT SANDERS REGIONAL MEDICAL CENTER
1901 Clinch Avenue, Knoxville TN 37916. 865/541-1111. **Contact:** Human Resources. **World Wide Web address:** http://www.fsregional.com. **Description:** A 539-bed, acute care hospital. Fort Sanders Regional Medical Center specializes in cardiology, emergency care, gynecology, pulmonary care, neurology, oncology, orthopedics, and rehabilitation. The medical center also operates The Teddy Bear Hospital, The Hope Center, and The Patricia Neal Rehabilitation Center. Other hospitals and facilities of Covenant Health include Fort Sanders Louden Medical Center, Fort Sanders Parkwest Medical Center, Fort Sanders Sevier Medical Center, Fort Sanders West, Maternity Center of East Tennessee, and Thompson Cancer Survival Center. **NOTE:** Search and apply for positions online. **Positions advertised include:** RN's; Periop Tech; PCA/CNA; Occupational Therapist; Manager of Critical Care; Director, Health Information Management; Physical Therapist; PACS Administrator; Surgical Tech. **Parent company:** Covenant Health.

FORT SANDERS SEVIER MEDICAL CENTER
709 Middle Creek Road, Sevierville TN 37864. 865/429-6100. **Contact:** Human Resources. **World Wide Web address:** http://www.fssevier.com. **Description:** A 79-bed acute care hospital and a 54-bed nursing home. **NOTE:** Search and apply for positions online. **Positions advertised include:** ER Tech; PCA/CNA; RN's; Surgical Tech; Nurse Manager; LPN. **Parent company:** Covenant Health.

FRED'S INC.
4300 New Getwell Road, Memphis TN 38118. 901/365-8880. **Fax:** 901/328-0354. **Contact:** Human Resources. **E-mail address:** H2@fredsinc.com. **World Wide Web address:** http://www.fredsinc.com. **Description:** Operates 530 discount general merchandise stores and 245 pharmacies in 14 southeastern states. The company also markets goods and services to 37 franchised stores. Founded in 1947. **Listed on:** NASDAQ. **Stock exchange symbol:** FRED. **Number of employees nationwide:** 9,000.

FRIGIDAIRE HOME PRODUCTS
1100 Industrial Drive, Springfield TN 37172. 615/384-2431. **Contact:** Human Resources. **World Wide Web address:** http://www.frigidaire.com. **Description:** Frigidaire Home Products manufactures a variety of household appliances including dehumidifiers, dishwashers, dryers, freezers, ranges, refrigerators, and room air conditioners. Part of Electrolux Home Products, which includes Frigidaire, Gibson, Tappan, White-Westinghouse, Weed Eater, and Poulan. **NOTE:** Send resumes to: Electrolux Home Products, 250 Bobby Jones Expressway, Martinez GA 30907. **Corporate headquarters location:** Martinez GA. **Other U.S. locations:** Nationwide. **Operations at this facility include:** This location manufactures oven ranges.

FRITO-LAY, INC.
101 Eagle Drive, Fayetteville TN 37334. 931/433-3800. **Contact:** Employee Relations Manager. **World Wide Web address:** http://www.fritolay.com. **Description:** A worldwide manufacturer and wholesaler of snack products including the brand names Fritos Corn Chips, Doritos Tortilla Chips, Lays Potato Chips, and Smartfood Popcorn. **NOTE:** Search and apply for positions online. **Positions advertised include:** Sanitation Resource. **Corporate headquarters location:** Plano TX. **Parent company:** PepsiCo, Inc. (Purchase NY) consists of Frito-Lay Company, Pepsi-Cola Company, Quaker Oats Company, and Tropicana Products, Inc.

FULTON BELLOWS COMPONENTS, INC.
2318 Kingston Pike, Knoxville TN 37919. 865/546-0550. **Toll-free phone:** 800/643-2110. **Fax:** 865/544-5191. **Contact:** Human Resources. **World Wide Web address:** http://www.fultonbellows.com. **Description:** A producer of bellows, devices to help measure and control changes in pressure, temperature, motion, vibration and other environmental effects, for automotive, medical, aerospace and industrial applications.

GTS DURATEK
1009 Commerce Park Drive, Suite 100, Oak Ridge TN 37830. 865/425-4600. **Fax:** 865/481-2087. **Contact:** Human Resources. **E-mail address:** oakrec@duratekinc.com. **World Wide Web address:** http://www.duratekinc.com. **Description:** Processes low-level radioactive waste. **NOTE:** Search and apply for positions online. **Positions advertised include:** Senior Radiological Engineer; Waste Engineer; Waste Handler/Project Technician. **Corporate headquarters location:** Columbia MD. **Other area locations:** Memphis TN. Other U.S. locations: Lakewood CO; Barnwell SC. **Listed on:** NASDAQ. **Stock exchange symbol:** DRTK.

GALBRAITH LABORATORIES, INC.
P.O. Box 51610, Knoxville TN 37950-1610. 865/546-1335. **Physical address:** 2323 Sycamore Drive, Knoxville TN 37921-1700. **Toll-free phone:** 877/449-8797. **Fax:** 865/546-7209. **Contact:** Jim Cummings, Manager of Human Resources. **E-mail address:** labinfo@galbraith.com. **World Wide Web address:** http://www.galbraith.com. **Description:** One of the world's largest microanalytical laboratories. Galbraith provides laboratory services to all segments of industry, government, and the academic world. These services include analysis for all elements, trace analyses, physical property testing, environmental testing, compendium methods, and assays. Industry-specific expertise covers pharmaceuticals, pulp and paper, plastics, environmental testing, agriculture, chemicals, petroleum, textiles, and mining. Founded in 1950.

GAYLORD ENTERTAINMENT COMPANY
One Gaylord Drive, Nashville TN 37214. 615/316-6000. **Contact:** Human Resources. **World Wide Web address:** http://www.gaylordentertainment.com. **Description:** Operates convention resorts as well as a number of specialty entertainment and media companies including the Grand Ole Opry, Gaylord Opryland Resort & Convention Center in Nashville, Tennessee, Gaylord Palms Resort & Convention Center, near Orlando, Florida and Gaylord Texan Resort & Convention Center, on Lake Grapevine, near Dallas. **NOTE:** Search and apply for positions online. **Positions advertised include:** Manager, Construction Accounting; Director of Staffing; Director of Compensation and HRIS; Database Administrator. **Listed on:** New York Stock Exchange. **Stock exchange symbol:** GET.

GEMTRON CORPORATION
615 Highway 68, Sweetwater TN 37874. 423/337-3522. **Fax:** 423/337-7979. **Contact:** Human Resources. **E-mail address:** hrinfo@gemtron.com. **World Wide Web address:** http://www.gemtron.com. **Description:** Manufactures bent and flat glass and glass products, molded products, and fabricated metal products for appliances, furniture, and bath enclosures as well as fitness, vending, medical, industrial automation, and food service markets. Founded in 1973. **Corporate headquarters location:** This location. **Other U.S. locations:** Vincennes IN; Holland MI; Wheaton IL; Madisonville KY. **International locations:** Canada; Mexico.

GENERAL ELECTRIC COMPANY
2150 NW Broad Street, Murfreesboro TN 37129. 615/893-2900. **Contact:** Human Resources. **World Wide Web address:** http://www.ge.com. **Description:** General Electric operates in the following areas: aircraft engines; appliances; capital services; industrial products; technical and medical products and services; broadcasting; materials; and power systems. **Corporate headquarters location:** Fairfield CT. **Other U.S. locations:** Nationwide. **Operations at this facility include:** This location manufactures electric motors. **Listed on:** New York Stock Exchange. **Stock exchange symbol:** GE. **Number of employees worldwide:** 313,000.

GENERAL ELECTRIC COMPANY
P.O. Box 389, Selmer TN 38375. 731/645-6121. **Contact:** Becky Johnson, Human Resources Director. **World Wide Web address:** http://www.ge.com. **Description:** General Electric operates in the following areas: aircraft engines; appliances; capital services; industrial products; technical and medical products and services; broadcasting; materials; and power systems. **Corporate headquarters location:** Fairfield CT. **Other U.S. locations:** Nationwide. **Operations at this facility include:** This location manufactures busways for industrial electrical uses. **Listed on:** New York Stock Exchange. **Stock exchange symbol:** GE. **Number of employees worldwide:** 313,000.

GENERAL SHALE PRODUCTS CORPORATION
P.O. Box 3547, Johnson City TN 37602. 423/282-4661. **Toll-free phone:** 800/414-4661. **Fax:** 423/952-4104. **Contact:** Human Resources Department. **World Wide Web address:** http://www.generalshale.com. **Description:** Manufactures blocks, bricks, ready-mix concrete, sand, and related products. In addition to manufacturing, the company is engaged in engineering, architectural, and construction consulting services. Founded in 1928. **Positions advertised include:** AS/400 Programmer/Analyst. **Corporate headquarters location:** This location. **Other area locations:** Elizabethton TN; Kingsport TN; Knoxville TN. **Other U.S. locations:** Huntsville AL; Atlanta GA; Mooresville IN; Corbin KY; Louisville KY. **Parent company:** Wienerberger Group (Austria). **Number of employees nationwide:** 2,000.

GENESCO, INC.
1415 Murfreesboro Road, P.O. Box 731, Nashville TN 37202-0731. 615/367-8222. **Fax:** 615/367-8579. **Contact:** Human Resources. **E-mail address:** employment@genesco.com. **World Wide Web address:** http://www.genesco.com. **Description:** Markets, distributes, and manufactures men's footwear. The company owns and licenses footwear brands, sold through both wholesale and retail channels, including Johnston & Murphy, Dockers, Nautica, and Jarman. Genesco products are sold at wholesale to a number of leading department, specialty, and discount stores. Products are also sold at retail through the company's own network of retail shoe stores. Founded in 1924. **Corporate headquarters location:** This location. **Listed on:** New York Stock Exchange. **Stock exchange symbol:** GCO.

GEORGIA BOOT INC.
235 Noah Drive, Franklin TN 37064. 615/794-1556. **Fax:** 615/794-8319. **Contact:** Human Resources. **E-mail address:** jobsopps@georgiaboot.com. **World Wide Web address:** http://www.georgiaboot.com. **Description:** Manufactures men's, women's, and children's boots. **Parent company:** EJ Footwear LLC.

GERDAU AMERISTEEL CORPORATION
4323 Outland Road, Memphis TN 38133-7010. 901/794-9910. **Toll-free phone:** 800/221-9453. **Fax:** 901/363-1398. **Contact:** Human Resources. **World Wide Web address:** http://www.ameristeel.com. **Description:** Manufactures steel and wire. **NOTE:** Search and apply for positions online. **Positions advertised include:** Industrial Sales Trainee. **Corporate headquarters location:** Tampa FL.

GERDAU AMERISTEEL CORPORATION
801 Gerdau Ameristeel Road, Jackson TN 38305. 731/424-5600. **Fax:** 731/422-4247. **Contact:** Bill Kipp, Human Resources Manager. **E-mail address:** bkipp@gerdauameristeel.com. **World Wide Web address:** http://www.ameristeel.com. **Description:** Manufactures steel industrial products such as rebar. **NOTE:** Search and apply for positions online. **Positions advertised include:** General Supervisor, Facilities & Engineering. **Corporate headquarters location:** Tampa FL.

GIBSON AND GREGORY
201 Fourth Avenue North, Suite 1900, Nashville TN 37219. 615/242-7700. **Contact:** Office Manager. **Description:** A law firm specializing in general law, excluding divorce and criminal defense.

GIBSON USA
309 Plus Park Boulevard, Nashville TN 37217. 615/871-4500. **Toll-free phone:** 800/444-2766. **Fax:** 615/889-5509. **Contact:** Human Resources. **World Wide Web address:** http://www.gibson.com. **Description:** Manufactures and distributes electric and acoustic guitars, as well as other musical instruments and related accessories. **NOTE:** Search for positions online. **Corporate headquarters location:** This location. **Other U.S. locations:** Huntington Beach CA; Oakland CA; Elgin IL; Bozeman MT. **Listed on:** Privately held.

GLASTONBURY SOUTHERN GAGE
46 Industrial Park Road, P.O. Box 509, Erin TN 37061. 931/289-4242. **Contact:** Human Resources. **World Wide Web address:** http://www.gsgage.com. **Description:** Manufactures gauges for use in aeronautical, automotive, and oil field applications.

GLAXOSMITHKLINE
201 Industrial Drive, Bristol TN 37620-5413. 423/652-3100. **Contact:** Human Resources. **World Wide Web address:** http://www.gsk.com. **Description:** Manufactures penicillin, vitamins, vaccines, cancer treatments, and other pharmaceutical products. **NOTE:** Search and apply for positions online. **Positions advertised include:** Manager, Environmental Affairs. **Corporate headquarters location:** Philadelphia PA. **Other area locations:** Memphis TN. **Parent company:** GlaxoSmithKline Corporation is a health care company engaged in the research, development, manufacture, and marketing of prescription medicines, vaccines, and consumer healthcare products. **Number of employees worldwide:** 100,000.

GOODY'S FAMILY CLOTHING, INC.
P.O. Box 22000, Knoxville TN 37933-2000. 865/966-2000. **Fax:** 865/777-4220. **Contact:** Personnel. **World Wide Web address:** http://www.goodysonline.com. **Description:** An apparel retailer for women, men, and children. The company operates more than 335 stores in 18 states. **NOTE:** For corporate positions, fax resume to number above. Search and apply online for store positions. **Corporate headquarters location:** This location. **Other U.S. locations:** AL; AR; FL; GA; IL; IN; KY; LA; MO; MS; NC; OH; OK; SC; TN; TX; VA; WV. **Listed on:** NASDAQ. **Stock exchange symbol:** GDYS. **Chairman/CEO:** Robert M. Goodfriend. **Number of employees nationwide:** 4,335.

GOODMAN COMPANY
1810 Wilson Parkway, Fayetteville TN 37334-3559. 931/433-6101. **Fax:** 931/433-1312. **Contact:** Manager of Human Resources. **World Wide Web address:** http://www.amana-hac.com. **Description:** Designs, develops, manufactures, and sells heating, ventilation, and air conditioning products. **Corporate headquarters location:** Amana IA. **Other U.S. locations:** Nationwide. **Parent company:** Raytheon Corporation. **Operations at this facility include:** Administration; Divisional Headquarters; Manufacturing; Research and Development; Sales; Service. **Number of employees at this location:** 1,000.

GOODYEAR TIRE & RUBBER COMPANY
3260 Goodyear Boulevard, Union City TN 38261. 731/885-1558. **Contact:** Personnel. **World Wide Web address:** http://www.goodyear.com. **Description:** Goodyear Tire & Rubber Company's principal business is the development, manufacture, distribution, and sale of tires for most applications worldwide. Goodyear also manufactures and sells a broad spectrum of rubber products and rubber-related chemicals for various industrial and consumer markets and provides auto repair services. Business units of Goodyear Tire & Rubber include: North American Tire; Kelly-Springfield; Goodyear Europe; Goodyear Latin America; Goodyear Asia; Engineered Products; Chemicals; Celeron; and Goodyear Racing. **Corporate headquarters location:** Akron OH. **Other U.S. locations:** Nationwide. **International locations:** Worldwide. **Operations at this facility include:** This location is a manufacturing plant for car and truck tires. **Number of employees worldwide:** 92,000.

W.R. GRACE & COMPANY
REMEDIAN GROUP
6401 Poplar Avenue, Suite 301, Memphis TN 38119-4840. 901/820-2020. **Contact:** Human Resources. **E-mail address:** careers@grace.com. **World Wide Web address:** http://www.grace.com. **Description:** W.R. Grace & Company is a diversified worldwide enterprise consisting of energy production and services, retailing, restaurants, and other businesses. The firm operates over 2,500 facilities worldwide. **NOTE:** E-mail resumes to the address above or mail to: W.R. Grace & Co., Human Resources, 7500 Grace Drive, Columbia MD 21044. **Corporate headquarters location:** Columbia MD. **Operations at this facility include:** This location produces anhydrous ammonia. **Number of employees worldwide:** 80,000.

GUARDSMARK, INC.
22 South Second Street, Memphis TN 38103-2695. 901/522-7800. **Contact:** Recruitment Manager. **World Wide Web address:** http://www.guardsmark.com. **Description:** Provides security, life safety, and fire and protective services, as well as background screening, investigative services, and consulting. Founded in 1963. **Corporate headquarters location:** New York NY. **Other U.S. locations:** Nationwide. **Listed on:** Privately held. **Annual sales/revenues:** More than $100 million. **Number of employees at this location:** 125. **Number of employees nationwide:** 14,000.

HCA
One Park Plaza, Nashville TN 37203. 615/344-9551. **Contact:** Human Resources. **E-mail address:** executive.recruitment@hcahealthcare.com. **World Wide Web address:** http://www.hcahealthcare.com. **Description:** A full-service health care system operating approximately 200 hospitals and medical centers in 23 states, England and Switzerland. **NOTE:** Search and apply for positions online. **Corporate headquarters location:** This location. **Annual sales/revenues:** More than $100 million. **Listed on:** New York Stock Exchange. **Stock exchange symbol:** HCA. **Number of employees at this location:** 2,000.

HSB PROFESSIONAL LOSS CONTROL, INC.
P.O. Box 585, Kingston TN 37763-0585. 865/376-1131. **Fax:** 865/376-5078. **Contact:** Human Resources. **World Wide Web address:** http://www.hsbplc.com. **Description:** Provides engineering services in the areas of fire protection, safety, and environmental protection. **Parent company:** HSB Global Standards

W.L. HAILEY AND COMPANY
2971 Kraft Drive, P.O. Box 40646, Nashville TN 37204-0646. 615/255-3161. **Fax:** 615/256-1316. **Contact:** Human Resources. **E-mail address:** humanresources@wlhailey.com. **World Wide Web address:** http://www.wlhailey.com. **Description:** Engaged in heavy construction including pipelines, bridges, tunnels, marine structures, and treatment plants. **Other U.S. locations:** Atlanta GA; Birmingham AL.

HARDAWAY GROUP, INC.
615 Main Street, Nashville TN 37206. 615/254-5461. **Fax:** 615/254-4518. **Contact:** Randy Swinehart, Personnel Director. **E-mail address:** rswinehart@hardaway.net. **World Wide Web address:** http://www.hardaway.net. **Description:** A full-service construction firm. Founded in 1924. **NOTE:** Entry-level positions are offered. **Corporate headquarters location:** This location. **Operations at this facility include:** Administration. **Listed on:** Privately held. **Annual sales/revenues:** More than $100 million. **Number of employees at this location:** 400. **Number of employees nationwide:** 500.

HARDIN'S SYSCO FOOD SERVICES, LLC
4359 B.F. Goodrich Boulevard, Memphis TN 38118-7306. 901/795-2300. **Fax:** 901/367-0445. **Contact:** Human Resources. **World Wide Web address:** http://www.sysco.com. **Description:** Markets and distributes a wide variety of foods and food-related items to restaurants and businesses. In addition to foods, the company also sells kitchen equipment, paper supplies, utensils, and furniture for dining rooms. Founded in 1859. **Corporate headquarters location:** Houston TX. **Parent company:** SYSCO Corporation.

HARLEYSVILLE INSURANCE
One Lakeview Place, 25 Century Boulevard, Suite 400, Nashville TN 37214-3686. 615/391-3202. **Toll-free phone:** 800/391-1199. **Fax:** 888/492-7524. **Contact:** Human Resources. **E-mail address:** seresumes@harleysvillegroup.com. **World Wide Web address:** http://www.harleysvillegroup.com. **Description:** A small business insurer offering a range of property and casualty insurance products in 32 Eastern and Midwestern States. **NOTE:** Search and apply for positions or submit resume online. **Positions advertised include:** Sr. Claims Specialist. **Corporate headquarters location:** Harleysville PA.

HARRAH'S ENTERTAINMENT
1023 Cherry Road, Memphis TN 38117. 901/762-8600. **Contact:** Human Resources. **World Wide Web address:** http://www.harrahs.com. **Description:** Owns and operates 26 casinos in 13 states under the Harrah's, Harveys, Rio, and Showboat names. **NOTE:** Search and apply for positions online. **Positions advertised include:** Associate Contract Manager; Programmer Analyst; Director Strategic Sourcing; Associate Systems Analyst; Computer Operations specialist; Unix Engineer; Network Engineer; Network Architect; Systems Analyst, CMS; Property marketing Advisor. **Corporate headquarters location:** Las Vegas NV. **Operations at this facility:** Corporate services. **Number of employees nationwide:** 26,000.

HART'S FURNITURE
141 Eastley Street, Collierville TN 38017. 901/853-8595. **Fax:** 901/854-0614. **Contact:** Personnel. **World Wide Web address:** http://www.hartfurniture.com. **Description:** Manufactures home furniture including beds and home entertainment centers.

HARTCO FLOORING COMPANY
P.O. Box 4009, Oneida TN 37841-4009. 423/569-8526. **Physical address:** 565 Hartco Drive, Oneida TN 37841. **Fax:** 423/569-0780. **Contact:** Human Resources. **World Wide Web address:** http://www.hartcoflooring.com. **Description:** Manufactures hardwood flooring. **NOTE:** Search and apply for positions online. Unsolicited resumes not accepted. Only electronically submitted applications will be considered. **Positions advertised include:** Maintenance Engineering Manager; Warehouse Manager. **Corporate headquarters location:** This location. **Other U.S. locations:** Somerset KY. **Parent company:** Armstrong. **Operations at this facility include:** Administration; Divisional Headquarters; Manufacturing; Sales. **Number of employees at this location:** 800.

HARTMANN LUGGAGE COMPANY
1301 West Baddour Parkway, Lebanon TN 37087. 615/444-5000. **Contact:** Ed Henderson, Director of Human Resources Department. **World Wide Web address:** http://www.hartmann.com. **Description:** A luggage manufacturer, founded in 1877.

HAULERS INSURANCE COMPANY, INC.
1101 Santa Fe Pike, P.O. Box 270, Columbia TN 38402-0270. 931/381-5406. **Toll-free phone:** 800/346-6071. **Fax:** 65/256-7481. **Contact:** Human Resources. **Description:** Writes policies covering both personal auto and professional auto insurance.

HECKETHORN MANUFACTURING COMPANY
2005 Forrest Street, Dyersburg TN 38024. 731/285-3310. **Fax:** 731/286-2739. **Contact:** Personnel. **E-mail address:** info@hecomfg.com. **World Wide Web address:** http://www.hecomfg.com. **Description:** Manufactures precision products, components, and assemblies for the automotive and trucking industries and aftermarkets. Products include exhaust clamps, hangers, and tubing. **Other U.S. locations:** MI; IN.

HENNESSY INDUSTRIES INC.
1601 J.P. Hennessy Drive, La Vergne TN 37086. 615/641-7533. **Contact:** Teena Welch, Human Resources Manager. **World Wide Web address:** http://www.hennessy-ind.com. **Description:** Manufactures a variety of automotive equipment. Products include AMMCO brake lathes and lifts; BADA wheel balancing weights; and COATS tire changers and wheel balancers. **Parent company:** Danaher Corporation.

HENRY COUNTY MEDICAL CENTER
P.O. Box 1030, Paris TN 38242-1030. 731/644-8472. **Physical address:** 301 Tyson Avenue, Paris TN 38242. **Fax:** 731/644-8474. **Recorded jobline:** 731/644-8470. **Contact:** Human Resources. **World Wide Web address:** http://www.hcmc-tn.org. **Description:** A general, acute care hospital and nursing home. Founded in 1952. **NOTE:** Search for positions and download application online. **Positions advertised include:** RN's; CNA's; LPN's; Occupational Therapist; Physical Therapist. **Operations at this facility include:** Administration. **Number of employees at this location:** 600.

HERSHEY FOODS
975 Kansas Street, Memphis TN 38106. 901/775-2960. **Contact:** Human Resources. **World Wide Web address:** http://www.hersheys.com. **Description:** This location manufactures a variety of hard candies. **Parent company:** Hershey Foods Corporation is the nation's leading domestic producer of chocolate and non-chocolate confectionery products, and has a variety of international operations. **Corporate headquarters location:** Hershey PA.

HI-TECH MOLD AND ENGINEERING SOUTHEAST
466 Baxter Lane, Winchester TN 37398. 931/962-3332. **Fax:** 931/962-4401. **Contact:** Personnel. **E-mail address:** jobs@hitechmold.com. **World Wide Web address:** http://www.hitechmold.com. **Description:** Manufactures plastic injection molds. **Corporate headquarters location:** Rochester Hills MI.

THE HILTON HOTEL CORPORATION
755 Crossover Lane, Memphis TN 38117. 901/374-5000. **Contact:** Human Resources. **World Wide Web address:** http://www.hilton.com. **Description:** Owns, operates, and franchises several hotel chains including Hilton, Hampton Inn, Doubletree, Embassy Suites, Homewood Suites by Hilton, Conrad International. **NOTE:** Search for positions online. **Positions advertised include:** Sr. Customer Support Specialist; Accounting Specialist; Financial Analyst; Manager, Loss Prevention; Manager, Brand Distribution; Product Manager; Programmer, Corporate Systems; Sr. Regional Revenue Manager. **Operations at this facility include:** Corporate regional office.

HOLIDAY INN CHATTANOOGA CHOO CHOO
1400 Market Street, Chattanooga TN 37402. 423/266-5000. **Fax:** 423/267-5261. **Contact:** Human Resources. **World Wide Web address:** http://www.choochoo.com. **Description:** A hotel and tourist attraction. **Special programs:** Internships. **Corporate headquarters location:** Atlanta GA. **Operations at this facility include:** Sales; Service. **Number of employees at this location:** 400.

HONEYWELL INTERNATIONAL INC.
3000 20th Street NE, Cleveland TN 37323. 423/478-0700. **Contact:** Human Resources. **World Wide Web address:** http://www.honeywell.com. **Description:** Honeywell is engaged in the research, development, manufacture, and sale of aerospace products and services; control technologies for buildings, homes and industry; automotive products; turbochargers; specialty chemicals; fibers; and electronic and advanced materials. **NOTE:** Search and apply for positions online. **Corporate headquarters location:** Morristown NJ. **Operations at this facility include:** This location manufactures brake linings, nonasbestos disc brakes, block brakes, and segments for both original and used cars.

HOWMET CORPORATION
5650 Commerce Boulevard, Morristown TN 37814. 423/587-4910. **Fax:** 423/581-1828. **Contact:** Human Resources. **World Wide Web address:** http://www.howmet.com. **Description:** Engaged in the casting of superalloys and titanium for aircraft and industrial gas turbine engines. The company also supplies ceramic products, superalloy metals, and titanium ingots to a variety of industries. **Corporate headquarters location:** Greenwich CT. **Parent company:** ALCOA.

HUNTER FAN COMPANY
2500 Frisco Avenue, Memphis TN 38114. 901/743-1360. **Contact:** Human Resources. **World Wide Web address:** http://www.hunterfan.com. **Description:** Manufactures ceiling fans, portable fans, thermostats, vaporizers, humidifiers, and air purifiers.

HURD CORPORATION
P.O. Box 1450, Greeneville TN 37744-1450. 423/787-8800. **Physical address:** 503 Bohannon Avenue, Greeneville TN 37745. **Fax:** 423/787-8839. **Contact:** Human Resources Manager. **Description:** Manufactures lock sets for industrial and automotive customers including Steelcase, Tri-Mark, and Ford Motor Company. Founded in 1919. **Corporate headquarters location:** Upland IN. **Parent company:** Avis Industrial Corporation. **Operations at this facility include:** Administration; Manufacturing; Sales. **Listed on:** Privately held. **Number of employees at this location:** 1,075.

ICG HOLLISTON
P.O. Box 478, Kingsport TN 37662. 423/357-6141. **Physical address:** Highway 11 West, Holliston Mills Road, Church Hill TN 37642. **Toll-free phone:** 800/251-0451. **Fax:** 423/357-8840. **Contact:** Nancy Smith, Human Resources Manager. **World Wide Web address:** http://www.icgholliston.com. **Description:** Manufactures book cloth used for edition binding, library binding, loose-leaf binders, schoolbooks, and textbooks.

INNLINK, LLC
130 Maple Drive North, Hendersonville TN 37075. **Toll-free phone:** 800/525-4658. Fax: 615/264-1898. **Contact:** Human Resources. **E-mail address:** info@innlink.com. **World Wide Web address:** http://www.innlink.com. **Description:** Provides reservation products and services for hotels and hotel companies. **Parent company:** ShoLodge, Inc.

INTERNATIONAL COMFORT PRODUCTS
650 Heil Quaker Avenue, P.O. Box 128, Lewisburg TN 37091. 931/359-3511. **Fax:** 931/270-3312. **Contact:** Employment Manager. **E-mail address:** recruiting@icpusa.com. **World Wide Web address:** http://www.icpusa.com. **Description:** Manufactures and markets central heating and air conditioning units. **NOTE:** Current openings posted online. **Parent company:** United Technologies Corporation.

INTERNATIONAL PAPER COMPANY
6400 Poplar Avenue, Memphis TN 38197. 901/419-7000. **Contact:** Supervisor of Staffing. **World Wide Web address:** http://www.internationalpaper.com. **Description:** International Paper Company has operations in 40 countries for the manufacture of paper and paper distribution, packaging, and forest products, including building materials. **NOTE:** Search and apply for positions online. **Positions advertised include:** IT Business Analyst; Counsel EHS; Counsel, Industrial Packaging; Information Technology Attorney; Enterprise Systems Analyst. **Corporate headquarters location:** Stamford CT. **Other U.S. locations:** Nationwide. **Operations at this facility include:** Administration. **Number of employees worldwide:** 83,000.

INTERNATIONAL SPECIALTY SUPPLY
820 East 20th Street, Cookeville TN 38501. 931/526-1106. **Fax:** 931/526-8338. **Contact:** Diane Boatman, Personnel. **Description:** A designer and manufacturer of hydroponic farm equipment. The company also manufactures water reclamation equipment. **Number of employees at this location:** 75.

INVISTA
4501 North Access Road, Chattanooga TN 37415. **Contact:** Human Resources. **World Wide Web address:** http://www.invista.com. **Description:** Yarn manufacturing plant. **NOTE:** Apply and search for positions at http://www.careers.invista.com. **Corporate headquarters location:** Wichita KS. **Chairman and CEO:** Jeff Walker.

JABIL CIRCUIT, INC.
5238 Lamar Avenue, Memphis TN 38118. 901/202-7500. **Fax:** 901/202-7460. **Contact:** Human Resources. **World Wide Web address:** http://www.jabil.com. **Description:** A leader in the electronic manufacturing services industry, offering services such as circuit design, product research and development, assembly, fulfillment, and repair services to electronics companies in the aerospace, automotive, computing, consumer, defense, instrumentation, medical, networking, peripherals, storage, and telecommunications markets. **NOTE:** Search and apply for positions online. **Positions advertised include:** Planner; Team Lead; Inventory Control Analyst; Quality Engineer. **Listed on:** New York Stock Exchange. **Corporate headquarters location:** St. Petersburg FL. **Stock exchange symbol:** JBL. **Number of employees worldwide:** 35,000.

JACKSON OIL
110 Needmore Road, Clarksville TN 37040. 931/648-4771. **Contact:** Personnel. **Description:** A fuel and oil distributor. Founded in 1970.

JACOBS ENGINEERING GROUP INC.
600 William Northern Boulevard, Tullahoma TN 37388. 931/455-6400. **Fax:** 931/393-6210. **Contact:** Employment. **World Wide Web address:** http://www.jacobs.com. **Description:** A professional and engineering services firm supporting NASA, U.S. Department of Defense entities, and private companies. **NOTE:** Search and apply for positions or submit resume online. **Positions advertised include:** IT Help Desk Coordinator. **Corporate headquarters location:** Pasadena CA. **Listed on:** New York Stock Exchange. **Stock exchange symbol:** JEC. **Number of employees at this location:** 200. **Number of employees worldwide:** 4,000.

JEFFREY CHAIN CORPORATION
2307 Maden Drive, Morristown TN 37813. 423/586-1951. **Toll-free phone:** 800/251-9012. **Fax:** 423/581-2399. **Contact:** Human Resources. **World Wide Web address:** http://www.jeffrey **Description:** Manufactures engineered chain products used in a variety of industrial equipment. Founded in 1887. **Corporate headquarters location:** This location. **Parent company:** Renold plc (England). **Operations at this facility include:** Administration; Manufacturing; Research and Development; Sales; Service.

JIMMY DEAN FOODS
2000 Biffle Road, Newburn TN 38018. 901/753-1600. **Contact:** Human Resources. **World Wide Web address:** http://www.jimmydean.com. **Description:** Produces and markets breakfast sausages, dinner entrees, bacon, and prepared sandwiches. Founded in 1969. **Corporate headquarters location:** Chicago IL. **Parent company:** Sara Lee Foods.

JOHN DEERE HEALTH CARE
2578 East Stone Drive, Suite A, Kingsport TN 37660. 423/378-5122. **Contact:** Human Resources. **World Wide Web address:** http://www.JohnDeere.com. **Description:** John Deere has four main divisions: agricultural equipment, commercial and consumer equipment, construction and forestry equipment, and John Deere Power Systems. The health care subsidiary provides health-care-management services. **Positions advertised include:** Quality Improvement Coordinator. **Number of employees worldwide:** 43,000.

JOHNSON CITY MEDICAL CENTER
400 North State of Franklin Road, Johnson City TN 37604-6094. 423/431-6111. **Fax:** 423/431-6189. **Contact:** Recruiter/Employment Specialist. **E-mail address:** careers@msha.com. **World Wide Web address:** http://www.msha.com. **Description:** A 410-bed, nonprofit, acute-care teaching hospital, affiliated with the East Tennessee State University College of Medicine. Johnson City Medical Center Hospital is also a major medical referral center serving Tennessee, Virginia, North Carolina, and Kentucky, and includes Level I Trauma Care and the region's only dedicated emergency medical air transport service. **NOTE:** Entry-level positions and second and third shifts are offered. Search and apply for positions online. **Positions advertised include:** Registered Nurses; Licensed Practical Nurses; Corporate Purchasing Manager; CT Tech; Diagnostic Imaging Tech; Director, Marketing; Director, Medical Records; Director, Organizational Development; EEG Technologist; HR Analyst; Phlebotomist; Physical Therapist; Radiation Therapist; Surgical Tech. **Special programs:** Internships; Training. **Parent company:** Mountain States Health Alliance. **Number of employees at this location:** 2,200.

JOHNSON CONTROLS, INC.
1890 Mines Road, Pulaski TN 38478. 931/363-5666. **Contact:** Human Resources. **World Wide Web address:** http://www.johnsoncontrols.com. **Description:** Johnson Controls is a global market leader in automotive systems, facility management, and control systems. In the automotive market, it is a major supplier of integrated seating and interior systems, and batteries. For nonresidential facilities, Johnson Controls provides control systems and services including comfort, energy and security management. Founded in 1885. **NOTE:** Search and apply for positions or submit resume online. **Corporate headquarters location:** Milwaukee WI. **Operations at this facility include:** This facility produces foam used in the manufacture of automotive seating. **Number of employees worldwide:** 119,000.

JOSTENS INC.
1312 Dickson Highway, Clarksville TN 37040. **Toll-free phone:** 800/248-9725. **Fax:** 931/905-1894. **Contact:** Human Resources. **World Wide Web address:** http://www.jostens.com. **Description:** The company's products include yearbooks, class rings and affiliation jewelry, graduation products, school photography, and products for athletic organizations and their fans. **Corporate headquarters location:** Minneapolis MN. **Operations at this facility include:** This location prints books, magazines, flyers, catalogs, and calendars.

KPMG
Suite 900, Morgan Keegan Tower, 50 North Front Street, Memphis TN 38103-1194. 901/523-3131. **Fax:** 901/523-8877. **Contact:** Human Resources. **World Wide Web address:** http://www.us.kpmg.com. **Description:** A provider of assurance, tax and legal, and financial advisory services. **NOTE:** Search and apply for positions online. **Positions advertised include:** Manager, Internal Audit Services; Sr. Manager, Internal Audit Services; Sr. Associate.

KELLOGG COMPANY
KELLOGG USA CONVENIENCE FOODS DIVISION
585 Morrison Road, Rossville TN 38066. 901/853-6458. **Contact:** Human Resources. **World Wide Web address:** http://www.kellogg.com. **Description:** Kellogg is a diversified international company specializing in the manufacturing and marketing of ready-to-eat cereals, as well as frozen waffles, toaster pastries, cereal bars, frozen pies,

and other convenience foods. Kellogg products are manufactured in 18 countries in North America, Europe, Asia-Pacific, and Latin America, and are distributed in more than 150 countries. Founded in 1906. **NOTE:** Search and apply for positions online. **Positions advertised include:** Business Unit Manager; Human Resources Representative; Maintenance Supervisor; Production Supervisor. **Corporate headquarters location:** Battle Creek MI. **Other U.S. locations:** Nationwide. **International locations:** Ontario, Canada. **Operations at this facility include:** This location manufactures products such as Kellogg's Pop-Tarts toaster pastries, Eggo waffles, Kellogg's Nutri-Grain bars, Kellogg's Low Fat Granola bars, Kellogg's Croutettes stuffing mix, and Kellogg's Corn Flake Crumbs.

KEMMONS WILSON, INC.
8700 Trail lake Drive West, Suite 300, Memphis TN 38125. 901/346-8800. **Fax:** 901/396-3570. **Contact:** Human Resources. **World Wide Web address:** http://www.kwilson.com. **Description:** Involved in the development and management of hotels, real estate, banking, and manufacturing. **Listed on:** Privately held. **Number of employees at this location:** 600. **Number of employees nationwide:** 2,700.

KENNAMETAL INC.
128 Roweland Drive, Johnson City TN 37601. 423/928-7251. **Contact:** Angela Wolford, Human Resources Director. **World Wide Web address:** http://www.kennametal.com. **Description:** Manufactures, purchases, and distributes a broad range of tools, tooling systems, supplies, and services for the metalworking, mining, and highway construction industries. **NOTE:** Search and apply for positions or submit resume online. **Corporate headquarters location:** Latrobe PA. **Other U.S. locations:** Nationwide. **International locations:** Canada; China; England; Germany; the Netherlands; Mexico; Poland; Spain. **Operations at this facility include:** This location manufactures carbide cutting tools. **Listed on:** New York Stock Exchange. **Stock exchange symbol:** KMT. **Number of employees nationwide:** 4,400.

KEY SAFETY SYSTEMS, INC.
1601 Midpark Road, Suite 100, Knoxville TN 37921. 865/584-9141. **Fax:** 865/558-4737. **Contact:** Human Resources. **E-mail address:** knoxcareer@keysafetyinc.com. **World Wide Web address:** http://www.keysafetyinc.com. **Description:** Manufactures airbags, seatbelts, steering wheels, and safety systems. **NOTE:** Second and third shifts are offered. **Corporate headquarters location:** Sterling Heights MI. **Number of employees at this location:** 580.

KEYSTONE AUTOMOTIVE
85B Cleveland Street, Nashville TN 37207. 615/373-2050. **Contact:** Alison Howell, Director of Human Resources. **World Wide Web address:** http://www.keystone-auto.com. **Description:** Distributes a line of automobile replacement parts. The company also distributes a number of replacement parts for heavy-duty trucks, snowmobiles, motorcycles, farm and marine equipment, and other types of machinery through its automotive distribution centers and stores; and new replacement parts to repair vehicles damaged in collisions. Distribution centers located in Nashville and Atlanta sell products to automotive collision repair shops and smaller parts distributors. **Corporate headquarters location:** Pomona CA.

KING PHARMACEUTICALS, INC.
501 Fifth Street, Bristol TN 37620. 423/989-8000. **Toll-free phone:** 800/776-3637. **World Wide Web address:** http://www.kingpharm.com. **Description:** A vertically integrated branded pharmaceutical company. **NOTE:** Search and apply for positions online. **Positions advertised include:** Supervisor, Medicaid; Contract Coordinator; Financial Analyst; Senior Project Manager; Manager, Contract Quality Assurance. **Corporate headquarters location:** This location. **Listed on:** New York Stock Exchange. **Stock exchange symbol:** KG.

KINGSTON COMPANY
P.O. Box 687, Miller Road, Smithville TN 37166-0170. 615/597-4096. **Fax:** 615/597-7863. **Contact:** Marie Johnson, Human Resources Director. **World Wide Web address:** http://www.kingstonproducts.com. **Description:** Manufactures motors, generators, and electrical-mechanical products for the appliance, commercial, HVAC, and sign industries.

KIRBY BUILDING SYSTEMS INC.
dba ASSOCIATED BUILDING SYSTEMS
124 Kirby Drive, Portland TN 37148. 615/325-4165. **Fax:** 800/348-7799. **Contact:** Charles Wilcox, Personnel Director. **World Wide Web address:** http://www.kirbybuildingsystems.com. **Description:** Manufactures prefabricated metal buildings and components. **Parent company:** Magnatrax Corporation.

KNOXVILLE NEWS-SENTINEL COMPANY
2332 News Sentinel Drive, Knoxville TN 37921-5761. 865/523-3131. **Fax:** 865/342-6995. **Contact:** Human Resources Department. **World Wide Web address:** http://www.knoxnews.com. **Description:** A daily newspaper. Founded in 1921. **Special programs:** Internships. **Corporate headquarters location:** Cincinnati OH. **Parent company:** E.W. Scripps Company. **Number of employees at this location:** 570.

KNOXVILLE UTILITIES BOARD
P.O. Box 59017, Knoxville TN 37950-9017. 865/524-2911. **Fax:** 865/558-2168. **Recorded jobline:** 865/558-2420. **Contact:** Human Resources Department. **E-mail address:** jobs@kub.org. **World Wide Web address:** http://www.kub.org. **Description:** A utility company providing wastewater/sewage removal, electricity, gas, and water services to customers in Knoxville and seven surrounding counties. Founded in 1939. **NOTE:** Search and apply for positions online. **Positions advertised include:** Business Management Analyst.

KOHLER COMPANY
2000 North Fifth Street, Union City TN 38281-0769. 731/885-1200. **Fax:** 731/885-0286. **Contact:** Personnel. **World Wide Web address:** http://www.sterlingplumbing.com. **Description:** Manufactures kitchen and bathroom appliance including faucets, sinks, tubs, showers, tub and shower enclosures, and toilets.

KOMATSU AMERICA
P.O. Box 168, Chattanooga TN 37401-0168. 423/267-1066. **Physical address:** 409 Signal Mountain Road, Chattanooga TN 37405. **Fax:** 423/267-1131. **Contact:** Personnel Manager. **World Wide Web address:** http://www.komatsuamerica.com. **Description:** Manufactures construction equipment including hydraulic excavators and wheel loaders. **NOTE:** Search and apply for positions online. **Corporate headquarters location:** Vernon Hills IL. **Other U.S. locations:** Hayward CA; Norcross GA; Libertyville IL; Peoria IL; Galion OH. **Parent company:** Komatsu Ltd. (Tokyo, Japan) manufactures and sells construction equipment, industrial machinery, components, and other products, while diversifying into other manufacturing markets, electronics, civil engineering and architectural construction, computer software, real estate, and trading. Other U.S. subsidiaries and affiliated companies include: Komatsu America Corporation (Miami FL); Cummins Komatsu Engine Company (Seymour IN); Komatsu America Industries Corporation (Wood Dale IL); Danly-Komatsu L.P. (Chicago IL); and Komatsu Cutting Technologies, Inc. (Medford MA). Komatsu Ltd. also has subsidiaries and affiliates in Mexico, Brazil, Belgium, United Kingdom, Germany, France, Indonesia, Singapore, India, Thailand, Malaysia, Philippines, Australia, Hong Kong, China, Canada, Italy, Russia, Turkey, Iran, Saudi Arabia, Pakistan, Vietnam, and South Africa.

THE KRYSTAL COMPANY
The Krystal Building, One Union Square, Chattanooga TN 37402. **Toll-free phone:** 800/458-5841. **Fax:** 423/757-5610. **Contact:** Human Resources. **World Wide Web address:** http://www.krystalco.com. **Description:** Develops, owns and operates, or franchises 428 full-size Krystal and drive-through Krystal Kwik fast-food hamburger restaurants in 12 states. Founded in 1932. **NOTE:** Apply online for corporate positions. For restaurant management positions, forward resume to: Marlene Cole, Regional Recruiter, mcole@crystalco.com or via fax: 800/835-0429. **Parent company:** Port Royal Holdings, Inc.

KYZEN CORPORATION
430 Harding Industrial Drive, Nashville TN 37211. 615/831-0888. **Fax:** 615/831-0889. **Contact:** Human Resources. **World Wide Web address:** http://www.kyzen.com. **Description:** Manufactures and markets chemical solutions and processes for use in high-technology cleaning applications including electronic assemblies and precision metal and plastic components. The company also manufactures and markets process water reuse machines used in these chemical cleaning applications, and offers integrated process support services. These products can be sold as a package, as a cleaning process, or as separate items that can be integrated into the customer's cleaning process. Because industrial cleaning is one of the largest single applications of ozone depleting chemicals, Kyzen was organized to develop chemical solutions and processes to replace ozone depleting chemicals used in the cleaning of electronic assemblies and precision metal components.

LAKESIDE BEHAVIORAL HEALTH SYSTEM
2911 Brunswick Road, Memphis TN 38133. 901/377-4700. **Fax:** 901/373-0912. **Recorded jobline:** 901/373-0949. **Contact:** Human Resources. **World Wide Web address:** http://www.lakesidebhs.com. **Description:** Lakeside Behavioral Health System offers health services to children, adolescents, and adults for a variety of behavioral and emotional problems. Services provided include treatments for eating disorders, phobias, substance abuse, stress, suicidal tendencies, and adolescent emotional problems. **NOTE:** Entry-level positions and second and third shifts are offered. **Number of employees at this location:** 400.

LASKO PRODUCTS, INC.
P.O. Box 130, Franklin TN 37065-0130. 615/794-2531. **Physical address:** 300 Confederate Drive, Franklin TN 37064. **Fax:** 615/794-2612. **Contact:** Human Resources Manager. **E-mail address:** fdoins@laskoproducts.com. **World Wide Web address:** http://www.laskoproducts.com. **Description:** Manufactures household electric fans. **NOTE:** Entry-level positions and second and third shifts are offered. **Positions advertised include:** Production Manager. **Special programs:** Training. **Office hours:** Monday - Friday, 7:00 a.m. - 4:00 p.m. **Corporate headquarters location:** West Chester PA. **Listed on:** Privately held. **Annual sales/revenues:** $21 - $50 million.

LAUGHLIN MEMORIAL HOSPITAL
1420 Tusculum Boulevard, Greeneville TN 37745. 423/787-5000. **Fax:** 423/787-5083. **Contact:** Human Resources. **E-mail address:** hr@laughlinmemorial.org. **World Wide Web address:** http://www.laughlinmemorial.org. **Description:** A 140-bed hospital specializing in echo-cardiology, intensive/coronary care, intensive neonatal care, neurology, nuclear medicine, obstetrics, occupational medicine, oncology, outpatient surgery, pediatrics, radiation oncology, and a women's health center. **NOTE:** Search and apply for positions online. **Positions advertised include:** Certified Nursing Assistant; Licensed Practical Nurse; Registered Nurse; Staff Pharmacist.

LAUREN ENGINEERS AND CONSTRUCTORS
139 Fox Road, Suite 204, Knoxville TN 37922. 865/690-8610. **Fax:** 865/691-0321. **Contact:** Human Resources. **E-mail address:** hr@laurenec.com. **World Wide Web address:** http://www.laurenec.com. **Description:** Provides engineering and design services for the chemical process, steel and metals, and nuclear and fossil power generation industries. **Corporate headquarters location:** Abilene TX. **Number of employees nationwide:** 200.

LAWYERS TITLE INSURANCE CORPORATION
6363 Poplar Avenue, Centrum Building Suite 208, Memphis TN 38119-4898. 901/685-2500. **Fax:** 901/682-3003. **Contact:** Personnel. **World Wide Web address:** http://www.lawyerstitle.com. **Description:** Provides title insurance and other real estate-related services on commercial and residential transactions in the United States, Canada, the Bahamas, Puerto Rico, and the U.S. Virgin Islands. Lawyers Title Insurance Corporation also provides search and examination services and closing services for a broad-based customer group that includes lenders, developers, real estate brokers, attorneys, and homebuyers. **Corporate headquarters location:** Richmond VA. **Other U.S. locations:** Pasadena CA; Tampa FL; Chicago IL; Boston MA; Troy MI; White Plains NY; Westerville OH; Dallas TX. **Parent company:** LandAmerica Financial Group Inc.

LE BONHEUR CHILDREN'S MEDICAL CENTER
50 North Dunlap Street, Memphis TN 38103. 901/572-3315. **Recorded jobline:** 901/726-8395. **Fax:** 901/516-0777. **Contact:** Staffing Services. **E-mail address:** employment@methodisthealth.org. **World Wide Web address:** http://www.lebonheur.org. **Description:** A fully accredited, 225-bed medical center. Le Bonheur Children's Medical Center is a pediatric specialty and subspecialty referral center. The center serves more than 105,000 children and adolescents each year through inpatient care, specialty clinics, and a fully staffed emergency department. Facilities include the Crippled Children's Foundation Research Center, a same-day surgery unit, an emergency department, an 18-bed intensive care unit, and a 12-bed transitional care unit. Le Bonheur also serves as the pediatric teaching facility of the University of Tennessee, Memphis. **NOTE:** Search for positions and download application form online. **Positions advertised include:** HIM Supervisor; HR Manager; Medical Technologist; Marketing Strategist; Lead Certified Anesthesia Tech; Pharmacist; Radiology Tech; CT Tech; Ultrasound Tech; Physical Therapist; Occupational Therapist; Speech Therapist; RN's. **Parent company:** Methodist Health.

LEGGETT & PLATT, INC.
400 Davidson Street, Nashville TN 37213. 615/734-1600. **Fax:** 615/734-6489. **Contact:** Mike Abraham, Human Resources Manager. **E-mail address:** resumes@leggett.com. **World Wide Web address:** http://www.leggett.com. **Description:** Manufactures products made from recycled materials including bedding and furniture fiber components, textile commodities, industrial wiping cloths, and

synthetic fiber carpet cushion. This division participates in trading and marketing products with a national and international customer base. **NOTE:** Direct resumes to: Employment Manager, P.O. Box 757, Carthage MO 64836, or telephone: 417/358-8131. **Corporate headquarters location:** Carthage MO. **Other U.S. locations:** Villa Rica GA; Pineville NC; Cincinnati OH; Mexico TX. **Operations at this facility include:** Divisional Headquarters. **Number of employees worldwide:** 32.000.

LENOIR EMPIRE FURNITURE
1625 Cherokee Road, Johnson City TN 37604. 423/929-7283. **Fax:** 423/929-7040. **Contact:** Human Resources Department. **World Wide Web address:** http://www.hfnet.com/lenoirempirefurniture. **Description:** A discount distributor of home furnishing including bedroom, living room, and dining room furniture.

LEVI STRAUSS & COMPANY
2307 Beaver Creek Drive, Powell TN 37849. 865/938-5384. **Contact:** Human Resources. **World Wide Web address:** http://www.levi.com. **Description:** Levi Strauss & Company designs, manufactures, and markets worldwide a diversified line of apparel, primarily jeans and jeans-related products under the brand names Levi's and Brittania. **Corporate headquarters location:** San Francisco CA. **Operations at this facility include:** This location manufactures the Dockers line of clothing for distribution in the United States. **Number of employees worldwide:** 11,000.

LIPSCOMB UNIVERSITY
3901 Granny White Pike, Nashville TN 37204-3951. 615/279-7007. **Toll-free phone:** 800/333-4358. **Recorded jobline:** 615/279-6191. **Contact:** Human Resources. **World Wide Web address:** http://www.lipscomb.edu. **Description:** A private university offering more than 100 bachelor's and master's degree programs. Lipscomb University is affiliated with the churches of Christ. **Company slogan:** Lighting the way.

LOGAN'S ROADHOUSE, INC.
3011 Armory Drive, Suite 300, Nashville TN 37204. 615/885-9056. **Toll-free phone:** 800/815-9056. **Fax:** 615/884-5490. **Contact:** Recruiting Department. **World Wide Web address:** http://www.logansroadhouse.com. **Description:** Operates 106 company-owned and 18 franchised Logan's Roadhouse restaurants in 17 states. Founded in 1991. **Positions advertised include:** Assistant Manager; Management Trainee. **Corporate headquarters location:** This location. **Other U.S. locations:** Nationwide. **Parent company:** CBRL Group, Inc. **Listed on:** NASDAQ. **Stock exchange symbol:** RDHS. **Annual sales/revenues:** $51 - $100 million. **Number of employees nationwide:** 1,600.

MTV NETWORKS NASHVILLE
COUNTRY MUSIC TELEVISION (CMT)
330 Commerce Street, Nashville TN 37201. 615/335-8340. **Fax:** 615/335-8614. **Contact:** Human Resources. **E-mail address:** employment@cmt.com. **World Wide Web address:** http://www.cmt.com. **Description:** A cable network serving 95 percent of national cable viewers with country music and country lifestyle programming. Country Music Television (also at this location) is a 24-hour country music video channel featuring top country hits. **Parent company:** Viacom.

MAHLE INC.
One Mahle Drive, P.O. Box 748, Morristown TN 37815-0748. 423/581-6603. **Fax:** 423/587-5170. **Contact:** Ron Peyton, Recruiting Manager. **E-mail address:** ron_peyton@mahleinc.com. **World Wide Web address:** http://www.mahleinc.com. **Description:** Manufactures pistons and engine components. **NOTE:** Search and apply for positions online. **Positions advertised include:** Industrial Engineer; Mechanical Engineer; Warranty Engineer.

MARK IV AUTOMOTIVE
1921 North Broad Street, Lexington TN 38351. 731/968-4281. **Contact:** Human Resources. **World Wide Web address:** http://www.markivauto.com. **Description:** Produces automotive filters, fuel systems, and power transmission systems. Mark IV Automotive also manufactures automotive belts and hoses under the brand name Dayco.

MARSH, INC.
P.O. Box 171377, Memphis TN 38187-1377. 901/761-1550. **Physical address:** 1000 Ridgeway Loop Road, Memphis TN 38120. **Fax:** 901/761-0408. **Contact:** Human Resources. **World Wide Web address:** http://www.marshweb.com. **Description:** An international insurance broker engaged in insurance booking, risk management, and benefits consulting. **NOTE:** Search and apply for positions online. **Positions advertised include:** Client Representative. **Special programs:** Internships. **Corporate headquarters location:** New York NY. **Parent company:** Marsh & McLennan Companies, Inc. (MMC). **Operations at this facility include:** Administration; Sales; Service.

MARVIN WINDOWS & DOORS
101 Marvin Road, Ripley TN 38063. 731/635-5190. **Contact:** Director of Human Resources. **World Wide Web address:** http://www.marvin.com. **Description:** Manufactures wood windows and doors. **NOTE:** Search and apply for positions online. **Positions advertised include:** Manufacturing/Process Engineer. **Corporate headquarters location:** Warroad MN. Other U.S. locations: OR; ND. **Listed on:** Privately held. **Number of employees at this location:** 800. **Number of employees nationwide:** 4,500.

MAURY REGIONAL HOSPITAL
1224 Trotwood Avenue, Columbia TN 38401. 931/380-4017. **Fax:** 931/540-4306. **Recorded jobline:** 931/380-4111. **Contact:** Employment Coordinator. **E-mail address:** employmentcoordinator@mrhs.com. **World Wide Web address:** http://www.mauryregional.com. **Description:** A 255-bed, nonprofit community hospital that provides specialized services to an eight-county area. Maury provides educational and training services on a regional basis for students through clinical affiliation with Columbia State Community College in the areas of X-ray, respiratory care, and registered nursing. **NOTE:** Search for positions online. **Positions advertised include:** Registered Nurse; Nurse Practitioner; Director, Decision Support – Finance; Pharmacy Manager; Occupational Therapist; Respiratory Therapist; Physical Therapist; Radiation Therapist. **Number of employees at this location:** 2,000.

McKEE FOODS CORPORATION
P.O. Box 750, Collegedale TN 37315. 423/238-7111. **Physical Address:** 10260 McKee Road, Collegedale TN 37315. **Fax:** 423/238-7163. **Contact:** Human Resources. **World Wide Web address:** http://www.mckeefoods.com. **Description:** Produces and markets snacks, snack cakes, and granola cereals. McKee Foods Corporation markets its products under the names Little Debbie and Sunbelt. Founded in 1934. **NOTE:** Search and apply for positions online. **Positions advertised include:** Risk Management Analyst. **Corporate headquarters location:** This location. **Other U.S. locations:** Gentry AR; Stuarts Draft VA.

MECO CORPORATION
1500 Industrial Road, Greeneville TN 37745. 423/639-1171. **Toll-free phone:** 800/251-7558. **Fax:** 423/639-2570. **Contact:** Human Resources. **World Wide Web address:** http://www.meco.net. **Description:** Manufactures folding tubular steel furniture such as chairs, card tables, and banquet tables. Meco Corporation also manufactures electric and charcoal grills. Founded in 1959. **Corporate headquarters location:** This location.

MEDTRONIC SOFAMOR DANEK
1800 Pyramid Place, Memphis TN 38132. 901/396-2695. **Contact:** Director of Human Resources. **World Wide Web address:** http://www.medtronic.com. **Description:** Develops, manufactures, and markets spinal implant devices and instruments used in the surgical treatment of spinal degenerative diseases and deformities. **NOTE:** Search and apply for positions online. **Positions advertised include:** Associate Product Development Engineer; Clinical Submissions Writer; Financial Analyst; Manager, Mechanical Testing Lab; Quality Engineer; Regulatory Affairs Associate; Sr. Product Manager; Sr. IT Developer. **Other U.S. locations:** KY; CO; IN. **Number of employees nationwide:** 300.

MEMORIAL NORTH PARK HOSPITAL
2051 Hammill Road, Hixson TN 37343. 423/495-7100. **Contact:** Director of Human Resources. **World Wide Web address:** http://www.memorial.org. **Description:** A fully accredited, 83-bed, acute care facility. Memorial North Park Hospital offers a full range of patient services including cardiopulmonary care, cosmetic surgery, diet counseling, 24-hour emergency treatment, outpatient and home heath care, laser surgery, gastrointestinal/pulmonary care, nuclear medicine, ophthalmology, physical therapy, physician referral, and radiology. As an affiliate of the hospital, Home Health Care provides nursing, physical therapy, speech therapy, and medical social services. **NOTE:** Search and apply for positions online. **Positions advertised include:** Registered Vascular Tech; Medical Technologist; Polysomnographic Tech; Coordinator, Media Relations; Pharmacist; Vascular Tech; Physical Therapist; Registered Nurses; Licensed Practical Nurses. **Number of employees at this location:** 650.

MEMPHIS HARDWOOD FLOORING
1551 North Thomas Street, Memphis TN 38107. 901/526-7306. **Fax:** 901/525-0059. **Contact:** Human Resources, Plant. **World Wide Web address:** http://www.chickasawflooring.com. **Description:** Manufactures hardwood flooring.

MEMPHIS INTERNATIONAL AIRPORT
491 Winchester Road, Suite 113, Memphis TN 38116-3856. 901/922-8000. **Contact:** Human Resources. **World Wide Web address:** http://www.memphisairport.org. **Description:** An international airport. **Parent Company:** Memphis-Shelby County Airport Authority. **Chairman:** Arnold E. Perl.

MEMPHIS ZOO
2000 Prentiss Place, Memphis TN 38112. 901/276-9453. **Recorded jobline:** 901/333-6736. **Contact:** Human Resources. **World Wide Web address:** http://www.memphiszoo.org. **Description:** A zoo. **NOTE:** Search for positions and download application online. Phone calls and e-mails are not accepted. Seasonal positions available. **Positions advertised include:** Accounting Manager;

MERRILL LYNCH
101 South Highland Avenue, Jackson TN 38301. 731/422-6600. **Contact:** Personnel. **World Wide Web address:** http://www.ml.com. **Description:** One of the largest securities brokerage firms in the United States. Merrill Lynch provides financial services in securities, insurance, real estate, and related services. The company also brokers commodity futures, commodity options, and corporate and municipal securities. In addition, Merrill Lynch is engaged in investment banking activities. **NOTE:** Search and apply for positions online. **Corporate headquarters location:** New York NY. **Other area locations:** Memphis TN; Chattanooga TN; Nashville TN. **Other U.S. locations:** Nationwide.

METAL ROOFING WHOLESALERS
1178 Topside Road, Louisville TN 37777. 865/379-7777. **Toll-free phone:** 877/646-6382. **Fax:** 865/982-4222. **Contact:** Human Resources. **World Wide Web address:** http://www.metalroofingwholesalers.com. **Description:** A wholesaler and distributor of metal roofing products.

METHODIST HEALTHCARE, INC.
1211 Union Avenue, Memphis TN 38104. 901/516-7000. **Recorded jobline:** 901/726-8394. **Contact:** Personnel. **E-mail address:** employment@methodisthealth.org. **World Wide Web address:** http://www.methodisthealth.org. **Description:** Operates a regional network of health care facilities serving eastern Arkansas, western Tennessee, and northern Mississippi. Methodist Healthcare operates eight hospitals, several rural health clinics, and a home health agency. **Special programs:** Summer Jobs. **Corporate headquarters location:** Memphis TN. **Number of employees nationwide:** 10,250.

METHODIST UNIVERSITY HOSPITAL
1265 Union Avenue, Memphis TN 38104. 901/516-7000. **Contact:** Human Resources. **World Wide Web address:** http://www.methodisthealth.org. **Description:** A 696-bed teaching hospital for the University of Tennessee. **Positions advertised include:** Histology Tech; Surgical Pathology Tech; Sr. Histotechnologist; Nuclear Medicine Technologist; Surgical Tech; Lead Invasive Cardio Tech; Pharmacist; MRI Tech; Radiology Tech; Radiology Systems Coordinator; Mammography Tech; Manager, Special Imaging; Director, Clinical Support Services; RN's PRN's; LPN's.

MIDDLE TENNESSEE MEDICAL CENTER (MTMC)
400 North Highland Avenue, Murfreesboro TN 37130. 615/849-4100. **Contact:** Human Resources. **World Wide Web address:** http://www.mtmc.net. **Description:** A 286-bed private, not-for-profit hospital. MTMC is a member of Saint Thomas Health Services and Ascension Health. Established in 1927, MTMC serves the health care needs of Middle Tennesseans. **NOTE:** Search and apply for positions or submit resume online. **Positions advertised include:** RN's; Chief Radiation Therapist; Director of Compliance; Mammographer; Medical Technologist; Pharmacist; Physical Therapist; Radiation Therapist; Respiratory Therapist; Anesthesia Tech.

MIDDLE TENNESSEE STATE UNIVERSITY
Cope Administration Building, Room 215, Murfreesboro TN 37132. 615/898-2928. **Fax:** 615/898-5444. **Recorded jobline:** 615/898-5353. **Contact:** Human Resource Services. **E-mail address:** hrs@mtsu.edu. **World Wide Web address:** http://www.mtsu.edu. **Description:** A state university with a total student enrollment of approximately 21,000 students. Founded in 1911. **Positions advertised include:** Director of Alumni Relations; Director of Records; Assistant Dean for Judicial Affairs and Mediation Services; Psychologist; Coordinator of Field Placements; Coordinator, College of Liberal Arts; Academic Advisor; Faculty Positions. **Number of employees at this location:** 1,400.

MILAN SEATING SYSTEMS
3000 Kefauver Drive, Milan TN 38358. 731/686-0805. **Fax:** 731/686-0819. **Contact:** Daphne Johnson, Human Resources Manager. **Description:** Manufactures seating components and complete seating systems for major automakers. Operations include cutting, sewing, mechanical assembly, and urethane foam production. **Special programs:** Co-ops. **Corporate headquarters location:** Farmington Hills MI. **Parent company:** Magna International. **Number of employees at this location:** 330.

MILLER & MARTIN
Volunteer Building Suite 1000, 832 Georgia Avenue, Chattanooga TN 37402-2289. 423/756-6600. **Fax:** 423/785-8480. **Contact:** Allison Lee, Recruiting Director for Tennessee. **E-mail address:** alee@millermartin.com. **World Wide Web address:** http://www.millermartin.com. **Description:** A full-service law firm specializing in bankruptcy, corporate securities, environmental law, estate planning, e-commerce and technology, financial institutions, immigration, international law, labor and employment, litigation, and mergers and acquisitions. Founded in 1867. **Other area locations:** Nashville TN. **Other U.S. locations:** Atlanta GA.

MODINE MANUFACTURING COMPANY
2009 Remke Avenue, Lawrenceburg TN 38464-2243. 931/762-1675. **Fax:** 931/766-2047. **Contact:** Personnel. **World Wide Web address:** http://www.modine.com. **Description:** An independent, worldwide leader in heat transfer technology, serving vehicular (passenger car, van, truck, off-highway equipment, earth moving equipment, construction equipment, and agricultural equipment); industrial (a mixed category of OEM customers, including the makers of engines, air compressors, refrigeration equipment, and hydraulic-pneumatic devices); commercial; and building/HVAC (heating, ventilating, and air conditioning) markets. Products include heat exchangers, radiators, oil coolers, vehicular air conditioning condensers and evaporators, building/HVAC products, charge-air coolers, and radiator cores. **NOTE:** Search and apply for positions through careerbuilder.com. **Positions advertised include:** Plant Accountant. **Corporate headquarters location:** Racine WI. **Other U.S. locations:** Nationwide. **Number of employees worldwide:** 7,500.

MOHAWK YARN, INC.
P.O. Box 348, South Pittsburg TN 37380-0348. 423/837-7192. **Contact:** Human Resources Department. **World Wide Web address:** http://www.mohawkyarn.com. **Description:** Manufactures yarn for use in carpet production. **Parent company:** Mohawk Industries.

MONTGOMERY BELL ACADEMY
4001 Harding Road, Nashville TN 37205. 615/298-5514. **Fax:** 615/297-0271. **Contact:** Headmaster. **World Wide Web address:** http://www.montgomerybell.com. **Description:** An all-male, private high school with a total enrollment of 660. Founded in 1867.

MORGAN KEEGAN & COMPANY
Morgan Keegan Tower, 50 North Front Street, Memphis TN 38103. 901/524-4100. **Fax:** 901/579-4833. **Contact:** Personnel. **E-mail address:** jobs@morgankeegan.com. **World Wide Web address:** http://www.morgankeegan.com. **Description:** A regional investment firm serving individual investors throughout the southeastern United States. Morgan Keegan & Company also serves institutional clients nationwide and abroad. **NOTE:** Search and apply for positions online. **Positions advertised include:** Associate Analyst; Editor, Equity Research; Annuity Processor; Technical Analyst. **Listed on:** New York Stock Exchange. **Stock exchange symbol:** MOR. **Corporate headquarters location:** This location. **Other U.S. locations:** Nationwide. **Parent company:** Regions Financial Corporation.

MORRILL MOTORS INC.
229 South Main Avenue, Erwin TN 37650. 423/743-7000. **Fax:** 423/735-0117. **Contact:** Human Resources Department. **World Wide Web address:** http://www.morrillmotors.com. **Description:** Manufactures small electric motors.

MUELLER COMPANY
1401 Mueller Avenue, Chattanooga TN 37406. 423/698-8811. **Contact:** Steve Jones, Director of Personnel. **World Wide Web address:** http://www.muellerflo.com. **Description:** Manufactures water and gas valve products. **Corporate headquarters location:** Decatur IL.

MUELLER GAS PRODUCTS
Highway 64 East, P.O. Box 748, Waynesboro TN 38485-0748. 931/722-5422. **Fax:** 931/722-5427. **Contact:** Dona Edwards, Human Resources Manager. **World Wide Web address:** http://www.muellerindustries.com. **Description:** Manufactures brass valves and other related items. **Parent company:** Mueller Industries.

MURRAY GUARD, INC.
58 Murray Guard Drive, Jackson TN 38302. 731/668-3400. **Toll-free phone:** 800/238-3830. **Contact:** Danny Underwood, Vice President of Human Resources. **World Wide Web address:** http://www.murrayguard.com. **Description:** A security services firm. Founded in 1967. **NOTE:** Complete application online. **Corporate headquarters location:** This location.

MURRAY, INC.
100 Hannon Drive, Lawrenceburg TN 38464. 931/762-0100. **Fax:** 931/766-3827. **Contact:** Human Resources Manager. **World Wide Web address:** http://www.murrayinc.com. **Description:** Manufactures lawnmowers, bicycles, snowblowers, and edgers. Customers include major discounters such as Wal-Mart, Kmart, and Home Depot. **Operations at this facility include:** Manufacturing. **Annual sales/revenues:** More than $100 million. **Number of employees at this location:** 3,600. **Number of employees nationwide:** 5,600.

NASHVILLE STATE COMMUNITY COLLEGE
120 White Bridge Road, Nashville TN 37209. 615/353-3511. **Contact:** Human Resources. **E-mail address:** hr@nscc.edu. **World Wide Web address:** http://www.nscc.edu. **Description:** A two-year college offering associate's degree programs in science, applied science, and arts, as well as one-year certificates. The Tennessee Technology Center, which offers vocational programs, is also at this location. **NOTE:** Search and apply for positions online.

NATIONAL BANK OF COMMERCE
One Commerce Square, Memphis TN 38150. 901/523-3434. **Contact:** Human Resources. **World Wide Web address:** http://www.nbcbank.com. **Description:** A full-service bank. **NOTE:** Search and apply for positions online. **Positions advertised include:** Area Representative, Appraisal Operations; Regional Manager, Operations; Division Manager, Operations. **Parent company:** National Commerce Financial. **Listed on:** New York Stock Exchange. **Stock exchange symbol:** NCF.

NATIONAL HEALTH INVESTORS, INC. (NHI)
100 Vine Street, Murfreesboro TN 37130. 615/890-9100. **Fax:** 615/890-0123. **Contact:** Human Resources. **World Wide Web address:** http://www.nhinvestors.com. **Description:** A real estate investment trust that specializes in the purchase and leaseback of health care real estate, as well as the creation of mortgage loans for health care operators. NHI owns or mortgages 167 properties in 20 states. **Listed on:** New York Stock Exchange. **Stock exchange symbol:** NHI.

NATIONAL HEALTHCARE CORPORATION (NHC)
P.O. Box 1398, Murfreesboro TN 37133-1398. 615/890-2020. **Physical address:** 100 East Vine Street, Murfreesboro TN 37130. **Contact:** Vice President of Personnel. **Description:** Operates 76 long-term health care centers with approximately 9,300 beds, 32 home health care programs, six independent living centers, and 19 assisted living centers. Founded in 1971.

NATIONAL MULTIPLE SCLEROSIS SOCIETY
4219 Hillsboro Road, Suite 306, Nashville TN 37215. 615/269-9055. **Toll-free phone:** 800/269-9055. **E-mail address:** tns@nmss.org. **Contact:** Human Resources Department. **World Wide Web address:** http://www.msmidsouth.org. **Description:** A national nonprofit organization providing services such as health care equipment and financial aid. **Other U.S. locations:** Nationwide.

THOMAS NELSON INC.
P.O. Box 141000, Nashville TN 37214-1000. 615/889-9000. **Recorded jobline:** 615/902-1430. **Contact:** Director of Human Resources. **World Wide Web address:** http://www.thomasnelson.com. **Description:** One of the world's leading publishers of Bibles and Christian and inspirational books. The company also sells gift and stationery products and develops and markets Christmas and Christian music and video products. Founded in 1798. **NOTE:** Search and apply for positions online. **Positions advertised include:** Associate Editor; Customer Service Rep; Data Entry Operator; Editor, Backlist; Editor, Curriculum; Production Manager; Project Manager; Sales Director; Sr. Editor

NISSAN NORTH AMERICA - SMYRNA
983 Nissan Drive, Smyrna TN 37167. 615/459-1400. **Fax:** 615/459-1575. **Contact:** Employment Department. **E-mail address:** smyrna.careers@nmm.nissan-usa.com. **World Wide Web address:** http://www.nissanusa.com. **Description:** Manufactures the Nissan Frontier, Xterra, and Altima. **NOTE:** Search and apply for positions online. **Positions advertised include:** Manufacturing Engineer. **Number of employees at this location:** 5,800.

NU-KOTE INTERNATIONAL
200 Beasley Drive, Franklin TN 37064. 615/794-9000. **Fax:** 615/794-4425. **Contact:** Human Resources. **World Wide Web address:** http://www.nukote.com. **Description:** A manufacturer and distributor of office imaging supplies including typewriter and computer ribbons, carbon paper, inkjet/laser cartridges, and toner. Nu-Kote International markets its products under the brand names LCD, ICMI, Nu-Kote, and Pelikan. **NOTE:** Entry-level positions are offered. **Corporate headquarters location:** Dallas TX. **Other U.S. locations:** CA; KY; PA. **International locations:** Columbia; Germany; Mexico; Scotland; Switzerland. **Subsidiaries include:** Future Graphics; ICMI. **Operations at this facility include:** Administration; Divisional Headquarters; Manufacturing; Regional Headquarters; Research and Development; Sales; Service. **Annual sales/revenues:** More than $100 million. **Number of employees at this location:** 450. **Number of employees nationwide:** 1,000.

NUCLEAR FUEL SERVICE
1205 Banner Hill Road, Erwin TN 37650. 423/743-1755. **Fax:** 423/743-9025. **Contact:** Personnel Resources Specialist. **E-mail address:** rvbishop@nuclearfuelservices.com. **World Wide Web address:** http://www.nuclearfuelservices.com. **Description:** Provides advanced nuclear technology, manufacturing, and management services to both government and commercial clients. Founded in 1957. **Office hours:** Monday - Friday, 8:00 a.m. - 5:00 p.m. **Listed on:** Privately held. **Number of employees at this location:** 500.

OAK RIDGE ASSOCIATED UNIVERSITIES
P.O. Box 117, Mail-Stop 31, Oak Ridge TN 37831-0117. 865/576-3000. **Contact:** Employment Department. **E-mail address:** empdept@orau.gov. **World Wide Web address:** http://www.orau.org. **Description:** A nonprofit association of more than 50 colleges and universities acting as prime contractor for research, training, education, and information activities. **NOTE:** Search and apply for positions online. **Positions advertised include:** Health Physicist; Operations Planner; Proposal Analyst; Contracts Specialist; Engineering Technician; System Support Specialist.

O'CHARLEY'S INC.
3038 Sidco Drive, Nashville TN 37204. 615/256-8500. **Fax:** 615/782-5043. **Contact:** Human Resources. **E-mail address:** resumes@ocharleys.com. **World Wide Web address:** http://www.ocharleys.com. **Description:** Operates and franchises over 214 full-service restaurants in the southern and midwestern United States. **Corporate headquarters location:** This location. **Listed on:** NASDAQ. **Number of employees at this location:** 175.

OPRYLAND HOTEL CONVENTION CENTER
2800 Opryland Drive, Nashville TN 37214. 615/889-1000. **Fax:** 615/871-7740. **Recorded jobline:** 800/899-6779. **Contact:** Employment Manager. **World Wide Web address:** http://www.gaylordhotels.com/gaylordopryland. **Description:** Operates entertainment attractions including Opryland Hotel, a 3,000-room convention center; General Jackson Showboat; Springhouse Golf Club; Opryland River Taxis; Grand Ole Opry Tours; and the Opryland USA/KOA Campground. **NOTE:** Search and apply for positions online. Online applications preferred. **Corporate headquarters location:** This location. **Parent company:** Gaylord Entertainment Company is a diversified entertainment and communications company operating principally in three industry divisions: entertainment, cable networks, and broadcasting. The broadcasting division owns two television stations in Texas and one in Seattle WA, as well as two radio stations in Tennessee and one in Oklahoma City OK. **Operations at this facility include:** Administration. **Annual sales/revenues:** More than $100 million.

ORGILL BROTHERS & COMPANY
3742 Tyndale Drive, Memphis TN 38125. 901/754-8850. **Fax:** 901/752-8989. **Contact:** Human Resources. **World Wide Web address:** http://www.orgill.com. **Description:** A hardware distributor. Founded in 1847. **Parent company:** West Union Corporation. **Listed on:** Privately held.

ORMET ALUMINUM MILL PRODUCTS CORPORATION
P.O. Box 129, Jackson TN 38302. 731/424-2000. **Fax:** 731/422-7805. **Contact:** Human Resources. **World Wide Web address:** http://www.ormet.com. **Description:** Manufactures aluminum in a variety of forms for industrial use. **Corporate headquarters location:** Wheeling WV.

ROBERT ORR/SYSCO FOOD SERVICES COMPANY
P.O. Box 305137, Nashville TN 37230-0140. 615/350-7100. **Fax:** 615/350-2133. **Contact:** Human Resources. **World Wide Web address:** http://www.sysco.com. **Description:** Markets and distributes a wide variety of foods and food-related items to restaurants and businesses. In addition to foods, the company also sells kitchen equipment, paper supplies, utensils, and furniture for dining rooms. Founded in 1859. **Corporate headquarters location:** Houston TX. **Parent company:** SYSCO Corporation.

ORTALE, KELLEY, HERBERT AND CRAWFORD
P.O. Box 198985, Nashville TN 37219-8985. 615/256-9999. **Physical address:** Noel Place, 200 Fourth Avenue North, 3rd Floor, Nashville TN 37219. **Fax:** 615/726-1494. **Contact:** Office Manager. **World Wide Web address:** http://www.ortalekelley.com. **Description:** A full-service law firm specializing in bankruptcy, civil rights, corporate law, domestic law, estate planning, litigation, real estate, and taxation. Founded in 1971. **Other area locations:** Franklin TN.

OSHKOSH B'GOSH INC.
330 Birch Street, Gainesboro TN 38562. 931/268-0224. **Contact:** Human Resources. **World Wide Web address:** http://www.oshkoshbgosh.com. **Description:** Manufactures children's wear, as well as casual apparel and related products for adults. OshKosh B'Gosh and Baby B'Gosh products are sold worldwide through catalogs and in department and specialty stores. OshKosh B'Gosh operates more than 159 retail outlets throughout the United States. Founded in 1895. **Corporate headquarters location:** Oshkosh WI. **Other area locations:** Celina TN; White House TN. **Other U.S. locations:** Columbia KY; Liberty KY. **Operations at this facility include:** This location distributes apparel. **Listed on:** NASDAQ. **Stock exchange symbol:** GOSHA.

PAI CORPORATION
116 Milan Way, Oak Ridge TN 37830-6913. 865/483-0666. **Fax:** 865/481-0003. **Contact:** Office Manager. **E-mail address:** hr.dept@paicorp.com. **World Wide Web address:** http://www.paicorp.com. **Description:** PAI Corporation provides services to commercial and government programs that require expertise in science, technology, and regulations. **Corporate headquarters location:** This location. **Other U.S. locations:** Moffet Field CA; Las Vegas NV. **Operations at this facility include:** This location provides technical and environmental support services to the Department of Energy; engineering, environmental, research, and development services to Lockheed Martin Energy Systems, Inc.; and environmental restoration and management support to DOE/OR through Jacobs Engineering Group.

PACKAGING CORPORATION OF AMERICA
P.O. Box 33, Counce TN 38326-0033. 731/689-3111. **Fax:** 731/689-1471. **Contact:** Human Resources. **World Wide Web address:** http://www.packagingcorp.com. **Description:** Packaging Corporation of America manufactures and distributes containerboard and corrugated packaging. The company also offers multicolor graphics for customized packaging. **Corporate headquarters location:** Lake Forest IL. **Operations at this facility include:** This location is a containerboard mill. **Listed on:** New York Stock Exchange. **Stock exchange symbol:** PKG.

PARKER SEALS
104 Hartmann Drive, Lebanon TN 37087. 615/444-0191. **Contact:** Human Resources. **Description:** Manufactures and distributes elastomeric and thermoplastic seals to the automotive, construction, and diesel engine industries worldwide.

PARTHENON PAVILION
2401 Parman Place, Nashville TN 37203. 615/342-1450. **Contact:** Personnel. **World Wide Web address:** http://parthenonpavilion.com. **Description:** A 158-bed psychiatric hospital that offers a comprehensive program of mental health services for adolescents, adults, and the elderly. Founded in 1971. **Parent company:** Centennial Medical Center.

PASMINCO
1800 Zinc Plant Road, P.O. Box 1104, Clarkesville TN 37041-1104. 931/552-4200. **Fax:** 931/552-0471. **Contact:** Human Resources. **World Wide Web address:** http://www.pasminco.com.au. **Description:** The U.S. operation of Pasminco consists of a zinc mine and a smelter. **Corporate headquarters location:** Melbourne, Australia. **International locations:** China; the Netherlands. **Operations at this facility include:** This location is a refinery.

PDS CONSULTING
25 Maple Grove Drive, Suite 101, Crossville TN 38555. 931/456-2999. **Fax:** 931/456-6182. **Contact:** Human Resources. **E-mail address:** crossville@pdsconsulting.com. **World Wide Web address:** http://www.pdsconsulting.com. **Description:** A Hewlett-Packard PC and peripherals reseller. PDS Consulting also custom builds its own line of computers, and is engaged in computer repair, networking, and upgrading. Founded in 1995. **Other area locations:** Knoxville TN; Morristown TN.

PEPSIAMERICAS
2221 Democrat Road, Memphis TN 38132. 901/344-7100. **Contact:** Human Resources. **World Wide Web address:** http://www.pepsiamericas.com. **Description:** A Pepsi-Cola and 7-Up bottling and sales company with operations in 18 U.S. locations as well as eight international locations. **NOTE:** Search and apply for positions online. **Positions advertised include:** Product Availability Manager. **Corporate headquarters location:** Rolling Meadows IL. **Other U.S. locations:** AK; LA; MI. **Operations at this facility include:** Manufacturing; Sales. **Listed on:** New York Stock Exchange. **Stock exchange symbol:** PAS. **Number of employees at this location:** 1,500.

PEPSI BOTTLING GROUP
715 Thompson Lane, Nashville TN 37204-0968. 615/383-7000. **Contact:** Human Resources Manager. **World Wide Web address:** http://www.pepsico.com. **Description:** Produces and distributes a variety of beverages including the brand names Pepsi-Cola, Mountain Dew, Mug Root Beer, and Slice. **NOTE:** Search and apply for positions online. **Positions advertised include:** Product Availability Supervisor. **Parent company:** PepsiCo, Inc. (Purchase NY) consists of Frito-Lay Company, Pepsi-Cola Company, Quaker Oats Company, and Tropicana Products, Inc. **Operations at this facility include:** Administration; Manufacturing; Regional Headquarters; Sales. **Listed on:** New York Stock Exchange. **Stock exchange symbol:** PEP. **Number of employees at this location:** 580. **Number of employees worldwide:** 143,000.

PERCEPTICS CORPORATION
Pellissippi Office Center, Suite 200 North, 9737 Cogdill Road, Knoxville TN 37932-3350. 865/966-9200. **Fax:** 865/966-9330. **Contact:** Human Resources. **World Wide Web address:** http://www.perceptics.com. **Description:** Provides development, design, manufacture, integration, and support of specialized information and imaging systems for applications in machine vision, intelligent character recognition, and document managing systems. **NOTE:** Search and apply for positions online. **Positions advertised include:** Sales Executive. **Parent company:** Northrop Grumman Corporation.

PERFORMANCE DEVELOPMENT CORPORATION
109 Jefferson Avenue, Oak Ridge TN 37830. 865/482-9004. **Contact:** Personnel Administrator. **World Wide Web address:** http://www.pdcnet.com. **Description:** An environmental management and information systems consulting firm. Performance Development Corporation (PDC) also offers training programs to corporate clients. Founded in 1987.

PERKINS FAMILY RESTAURANTS, L.P.
6075 Poplar Avenue, Suite 800, Memphis TN 38119. 901/766-6400. **Toll-free phone:** 800/877-7375. **Fax:** 901/766-6482. **Contact:** Human Resources. **E-mail address:** jobs@perkinsrestaurants.com. **World Wide Web address:** http://www.perkinsrestaurants.com. **Description:** Operates a restaurant chain with approximately 500 locations in 35 states and Canada. Most of the restaurant locations also include a retail bakery. **NOTE:** Search and apply for positions online. **Positions advertised include:** Financial Planning Manager. **Corporate headquarters location:** This location. **Number of employees worldwide:** 25,000.

PERMANENT GENERAL AND TENNESSEE INSURANCE COMPANY
2636 Elm Hill Pike, Suite 510, Nashville TN 37214. **Toll-free phone:** 800/280-1466. **Fax:** 615/744-1970. **Contact:** Susan Marshall, Human Resources Department. **E-mail address:** smarshall@pgac.com. **World Wide Web address:** http://www.pgac.com. **Description:** A nonstandard automobile insurance company. Founded in 1963. **NOTE:** Entry-level positions are offered. Search and apply for positions online. **Positions advertised include:** WebSphere Applications Developer; Sr. AS400 Applications Developer; Sales Agent; Underwriter. **Office hours:** Monday - Friday, 8:00 a.m. - 5:00 p.m. **Corporate headquarters location:** This location. **Other area locations:** Knoxville TN; Memphis TN. **Other U.S. locations:** Mission Viejo CA; Marietta GA; New Orleans LA; Valley View OH. **Parent company:** Ingram Industries, Inc. **Listed on:** Privately held.

PERSHING YOAKLEY & ASSOCIATES
One Perkins Place, 525 Portland Street, Knoxville TN 37919. 865/673-0844. **Fax:** 865/673-0173. **Contact:** Deanna Sexton, Director of Human Resources. **E-mail address:** recruiter@pyapc.com. **World Wide Web address:** http://www.pyapc.com. **Description:** An accounting firm offering tax services, business consulting, strategic planning, health care management, audit services, real estate and strategic facilities planning, and other professional and health care consulting services. Founded in 1983. **NOTE:** Search and apply for positions online. **Positions advertised include:** Audit Manager; Managed Care Executive; Sr. Coding & Compliance Consulting Staff; Physician Services Coding Consultant. **Other U.S. locations:** Atlanta GA; Tampa FL; Charlotte NC.

PETERBILT MOTORS/PACCAR INC.
P.O. Box 487, Madison TN 37116-0487. 615/868-0197. **Physical address:** 430 Myatt Drive, Madison TN 37115. **Contact:** Human Resources. **E-mail address:** corp_jobs@PACCAR.com. **World Wide Web address:** http://www.paccar.com. **Description:** A commercial truck manufacturer. **NOTE:** Search for positions online. E-mail resumes to address above or mail to: Corporate Human Resources, P.O. Box 1518, Bellevue WA 98009, or fax to: 425/468-8216. **Positions advertised include:** Black Belt/Master Black Belt; Supplier Quality Manager. **Corporate headquarters location:** Bellevue WA.

PHILIPS CONSUMER ELECTRONICS CORPORATION
One Philips Drive, P.O. Box 14810, Knoxville TN 37914-1810. 865/521-4316. **Contact:** Human Resources Manager. **World Wide Web address:** http://www.philipsusa.com. **Description:** An audio, video, and television equipment manufacturer specializing in engineering, design, and development for Magnavox, Philips, and audio-video products. **Parent company:** Philips Electronics North America. **Operations at this facility include:** Administration; Divisional Headquarters. **Number of employees at this location:** 800. **Number of employees nationwide:** 5,000.

PHILIPS SERVICES CORPORATION
P.O. Box 1182, Nashville TN 37202-1182. 615/271-3300. **Physical address:** 710 South First Street, Nashville TN 37213. **Contact:** Mr. Tracy Rhodes, Director of Human Resources. **World Wide Web address:** http://www.contactpsc.com. **Description:** Buys and recycles scrap metal. **Corporate headquarters location:** Rosemont IL. **Other U.S. locations:** Nationwide. **Number of employees nationwide:** 12,000.

PHILLIPS & JORDAN INC.
6621 Wilbanks Road, Knoxville TN 37912. 865/688-8342. **Fax:** 865/688-8369. **Contact:** Susan Williams, Human Resources. **E-mail address:** swilliams@pandj.com. **World Wide Web address:** http://www.pandj.com. **Description:** A general contractor specializing in land clearing, earthwork, site development, project management, and disaster recovery services. Founded in 1953.

PIONEER AIR SYSTEMS, INC.
210 Flatfork Road, Wartburg TN 37887. 423/346-6693. **Fax:** 423/346-3865. **Contact:** Patricia Abbott, Human Resources Director. **World Wide Web address:** http://www.pioneerair.com. **Description:** A manufacturer of refrigerators and regenerative dryers. **Positions advertised include:** Project/Design Engineer.

PLANT MAINTENANCE SERVICE CORPORATION
P.O. Box 280883, Memphis TN 38168. 901/353-9880. **Fax:** 901/353-0882. **Contact:** Human Resources Manager. **World Wide Web** address: http://www.pmscmphs.com. **Description:** Engaged in metal plate fabrication for pressure vessels, heat exchangers, process vessels, boiler repairs, and tanks. **Corporate headquarters location:** This location. **Subsidiaries include:** PMSC-IRBY Steel, Gulfport MS. **Operations at this facility include:** Administration; Manufacturing; Sales; Service. **Listed on:** Privately held. **Annual sales/revenues:** $21 - $50 million. **Number of employees at this location:** 350. **Number of employees nationwide:** 450.

POLYONE CORPORATION
P.O. Box 807, Dyersburg TN 38025-0807. 731/285-4353. **Physical address:** 150 South Connell Avenue, Dyersburg TN 38024. **Contact:** Gaylon Rasberry, Manager of Human Resources. **World Wide Web address:** http://www.polyone.com. **Description:** Manufactures rubber compounds and sponge rubber moldings for gaskets and seals, as well as some plastic products. **Corporate headquarters location:** Avon Lake OH. **Other U.S. locations:** Nationwide. **International locations:** Worldwide. **Listed on:** New York Stock Exchange. **Stock exchange symbol:** POL. **Annual sales/revenues:** More than $100 million.

PORTER CABLE CORPORATION
4825 Highway 45 North, P.O. Box 2468, Jackson TN 38302-2468. 731/668-8600. **Fax:** 731/660-9535. **Contact:** Human Resources. **World Wide Web address:** http://www.porter-cable.com. **Description:** Manufactures portable power tools. Founded in 1906. **NOTE:** Search and apply for positions online. **Positions advertised include:** PC Support Supervisor; Product Line Manager.

PRECIPITATOR SERVICES GROUP
P.O. Box 339, Elizabethton TN 37644-0339. 423/543-7331. **Toll-free phone:** 800/345-0484. **Fax:** 423/543-8737. **Contact:** Human Resources. **World Wide Web address:** http://www.psgtn.net. **Description:** A manufacturer of air pollution control equipment, replacement parts, and upgrade components. Replacement components and services include discharge electrodes, bottle weights, collecting plates, plate repair, rappers, and rapper accessories. Accessory components include high-voltage components and bus ducts, high-voltage frames and hanger assemblies, rapper trains, collecting plate support beams, spacer bars and assemblies, access doors, and antisway assemblies.

PREMIER TRANSPORTATION SERVICES
581 South 2nd Street, Memphis TN 38126. 901/577-7777. **Fax:** 901/577-7765. **Contact:** Human Resources. **E-mail address:** info@premierofmemphis.com. **World Wide Web address:** http://www.premierofmemphis.com. **Description:** Provides a variety of passenger ground transportation services: Chauffeured Limousine & Sedan, School Service, Convention and Ground Transportation, Contract Transportation Management, Casino Transportation, Taxicab Services.

PROTHERICS
5214 Maryland Way, Suite 405, Brentwood TN 37027. 615/327-1027. **Fax:** 615/320-1212. **Contact:** Human Resources Department. **World Wide Web address:** http://www.protherics.com. **Description:** An international biopharmaceutical company, engaged in the development, production and commercialization of immunopharmaceuticals and cancer therapies. **Corporate headquarters location:** London.

QUALITY COMPANIES, INC.
P.O. Box 18428, Memphis TN 38181-0428. 901/367-8200. **Physical address:** 4690 Hungerford Road, Memphis TN 38118. **Contact:** Human Resources. **Description:** Engaged in the marketing of incentive programs for other companies, as well as individual and group travel programs.

QUEST DIAGNOSTICS INCORPORATED
525 Mainstream Drive, Nashville TN 37228. 615/687-2000. **Contact:** Human Resources. **World Wide Web address:** http://www.questdiagnostics.com. **Description:** One of the largest clinical laboratories in North America, providing a broad range of clinical laboratory services to health care clients, which include physicians, hospitals, clinics, dialysis centers, pharmaceutical companies, and corporations. The company offers and performs tests on blood, urine, and other bodily fluids and tissues to provide information for health and well-being. **NOTE:** Search and apply for positions online. **Corporate headquarters location:** Teterboro NJ. **Operations at this facility include:** This is a major laboratory facility.

QUORUM HEALTH RESOURCES, INC.
105 Continental Place, Brentwood TN 37027-5014. 615/371-7979. **Fax:** 615/221-3206. **Contact:** Recruitment. **E-mail address:** recruitment@qhr.com. **World Wide Web address:** http://www.qhr.com. **Description:** Provides management advisory services, implementation support, education and training programs, consulting and related services to independent hospitals and health systems. QHR manages more than 200 acute care hospitals. **NOTE:** QHR recruits CEO's and CFO's for health care facilities in the Northeast, Southeast, Midwest, and West. **Corporate headquarters location:** Plano TX. **Other U.S. locations:** Dothan AL; Enterprise AL; Gadsen AL; Jacksonville AL; Macon GA; Fort Wayne IN; Frankfort IN; Hattiesburg MS; Vicksburg MS; Las Vegas NV; Barberton OH; Massillon OH; Florence SC; Kingstree SC; Lake City SC; Spartanburg SC; Abilene TX. **Operations at this facility include:** This is a marketing and service center. **Number of employees nationwide:** 8,500.

RADIAN INTERNATIONAL
1093 Commerce Park Drive, Suite 100, Oak Ridge TN 37830-8029. 865/483-9870. **Fax:** 865/483-9061. **Contact:** Human Resource Manager. **World Wide Web address:** http://www.urscorp.com. **Description:** Offers professional planning and design, systems engineering and technical assistance, program and construction management, and operations and maintenance services for surface transportation, air transportation, rail transportation, industrial process, facilities and logistics support, water/wastewater treatment, hazardous waste management and military platforms support. **NOTE:** Search and apply for positions online. **Positions advertised include:** IS Manager; Inspector; Project Manager; Sr. Environmental Engineer; Staff Programmer. **Corporate headquarters location:** San Francisco CA. **Other U.S. locations:** Nationwide. **International locations:** Worldwide. **Listed on:** New York Stock Exchange. **Stock exchange symbol:** URS. **Number of employees worldwide:** 26,000.

C.B. RAGLAND COMPANY, INC.
2720 Eugenia Avenue, Nashville TN 37204. 615/259-4622. **Contact:** Jim Ragland, Director of Personnel. **Description:** A wholesale grocery products distributor. **Corporate headquarters location:** This location.

RED KAP INDUSTRIES
325 Iris Drive, Sparta TN 38583. 931/738-4300. **Contact:** Human Resources Department. **World Wide Web address:** http://www.redkap.com. **Description:** Manufactures occupational apparel. Specialties include safety and flame-resistant products including high-visibility and reflective-trim garments, as well as fluid-resistant and other protective apparel. The company also produces durable press, easy-care, 100 percent cotton products. Brand names of work utility wear include Big Ben and WorkWear. **Parent company:** VF Corporation.

REGAL CINEMAS, INC.
7132 Regal Lane, Knoxville TN 37918. 865/922-1123. **Fax:** 865/925-0561. **Contact:** Human Resources. **E-mail address:** jobs@regalcinemas.com. **World Wide Web address:** http://www.regalcinemas.com. **Description:** A leading motion picture exhibitor in the eastern United States. The company primarily shows first-run movies at its 562 multiscreen theaters in 39 states. Founded in 1989. **Corporate headquarters location:** This location. **Number of employees nationwide:** 18,300.

REGIONAL MEDICAL CENTER AT MEMPHIS
Adams Pavilion Building, 842 Jefferson Avenue, Suite 200, Memphis TN 38103. 901/545-7569. **Fax:** 901/545-8315. **Recorded jobline:** 866/687-8432. **Contact:** Human Resources. **World Wide Web address:** http://www.the-med.org. **Description:** A health care center serving the Mid-South region, with inpatient and outpatient facilities, a trauma center, a burn/wound center, and a neonatal center. **NOTE:** Search and apply for positions online. **Positions advertised include:** Diagnostic Medical Sonographer; Director, Emergency Services; LPN's; Lead Rehab Therapist; Manager, Diagnostic Cardiology Services; Nuclear Medicine Technologist; Nurse Coordinator; Physical Therapist; Radiologic Technologist; RN's. **Operations at this facility include:** Administration; Service.

RENAL CARE GROUP
2525 West End Avenue, Suite 600, Nashville TN 37203. 615/345-5500. **Fax:** 615/345-5505. **Contact:** Human Resources Department. **World Wide Web address:** http://www.renalcaregroup.com. **Description:** Provides care to patients with kidney disease through 390 kidney dialysis centers. Renal Care Group also provides acute dialysis services through approximately 190 hospitals throughout the United States. **NOTE:** Search and apply for positions online. **Positions advertised include:** Director of Contracting; System Developer; Systems Analyst; Network Analyst; Security Analyst. **Corporate headquarters location:** This location. **Listed on:** New York Stock Exchange. **Stock exchange symbol:** RCI. **Annual sales/revenues:** More than $100 million. **Number of employees nationwide:** 8,000.

REXNORD CORPORATION
250 Yarnell Industrial Parkway, Clinton TN 37716. 865/220-7700. **Fax:** 423/457-4187. **Contact:** Human Resources. **World Wide Web address:** http://www.rexnord.com. **Description:** A manufacturer of power transmission and conveying components. **Corporate headquarters location:** Milwaukee WI.

RHEA & IVY, PLC
6000 Poplar Avenue, Suite 250, Memphis TN 38119. 901/761-3000. **Toll-free phone:** 888/RHE-AIVY. **Fax:** 901/761-9667. **Contact:** Human Resources. **World Wide Web address:** http://www.rheaivy.com. **Description:** A certified public accounting firm specializing in tax, audit, and business consulting services.

RHODES COLLEGE
2000 North Parkway, Memphis TN 38112-1690. 901/843-3750. **Recorded jobline:** 901/843-3759. **Contact:** Human Resources. **E-mail address:** hr@rhodes.edu. **World Wide Web address:** http://www.rhodes.edu. **Description:** A four-year liberal arts college with an enrollment of 1,500. Founded in 1848.

RICH PRODUCTS CORPORATION
5885 Jetway Drive, Arlington TN 38002. 901/867-2903. **Contact:** Human Resources. **World Wide Web address:** http://www.rich.com. **Description:** Rich Products Corporation is a family-owned, frozen foods producer. Rich Products Corporation operates manufacturing sites and field offices throughout North America and abroad. The company also operates more than 30 production facilities involved in producing nondairy creamers, toppings and icings, frozen dough, baked goods, sweet goods, pastas, and specialty meats. **Corporate headquarters location:** Buffalo NY.

RICH PRODUCTS CORPORATION
625 Butler Drive, Murfreesboro TN 37127. 615/890-4211. **Contact:** Mike Gallo, Human Resources Director. **World Wide Web address:** http://www.rich.com. **Description:** A family-owned, frozen foods producer. Rich Products Corporation operates manufacturing sites and field offices throughout North America and abroad. The company also operates more than 30 production facilities involved in producing nondairy creamers, toppings and icings, frozen dough, baked goods, sweet goods, pastas, and specialty meats. **Corporate headquarters location:** Buffalo NY.

ROCKFORD MANUFACTURING COMPANY
3901 Little River Road, Rockford TN 37853-3305. 865/970-3131. **Fax:** 865/970-7056. **Contact:** Personnel. **Description:** A textile manufacturer specializing in rough yarns.

ROGERS GROUP, INC.
P.O. Box 25250, Nashville TN 37202-5250. 615/780-5668. **Fax:** 615/780-7958. **Contact:** Human Resources. **World Wide Web address:** http://www.rogersgroup.com. **Description:** Rogers Group manufactures and distributes asphalt, crushed stone, sand and gravel, and other construction materials. The company is also engaged in highway construction and concrete masonry. **Special programs:** Internships. **Corporate headquarters location:** This location. **Other U.S. locations:** IN; KY; OH. **Operations at this facility include:** This location houses administrative offices only. **Listed on:** Privately held. **Number of employees at this location:** 100. **Number of employees nationwide:** 1,500.

RUBY TUESDAY INC.
150 West Church Avenue, Maryville TN 37801. 865/379-5737. **Fax:** 865/379-6826. **Contact:** Human Resources. **World Wide Web address:** http://www.rubytuesday.com. **Description:** The Ruby Tuesday Group operates low-priced, casual restaurants under the name Ruby Tuesday. There are more than 700 company-owned and franchised restaurants worldwide. **NOTE:** Download application online. **Special programs:** Internships. **Corporate headquarters location:** This location. **Listed on:** New York Stock Exchange. **Stock exchanges symbol:** RI. **Number of employees at this location:** 300. **Number of employees nationwide:** 15,000.

RUSSELL STOVER CANDIES
1976 Chocolate Drive, Cookeville TN 38501. 931/528-6434. **Fax:** 931/528-1759. **Contact:** Human Resources. **World Wide Web address:** http://www.russellstover.com. **Description:** Candy manufacturing plant. **Positions advertised include:** Production Supervisor, Sales Representative.

SW MANUFACTURING, INC.
1111 West Broad Street, Smithville TN 37166. 615/597-8870. **Fax:** 615/597-8876. **Contact:** Personnel Manager. **Description:** Manufactures automobile window regulators and seat adjusters. **Corporate headquarters location:** This location. **Parent company:** Shiroki Corporation (Japan). **Listed on:** Privately held. **Number of employees at this location:** 450.

ST. FRANCIS HOSPITAL
5959 Park Avenue, Memphis TN 38119. 901/765-1000. **Contact:** Human Resources Department. **World Wide Web address:** http://www.saintfrancishosp.com. **Description:** A 611-bed hospital offering a wide range of inpatient, outpatient, and home health services. Founded in 1974. **NOTE:** Search and apply for positions online. **Positions advertised include:** RN's; Nuclear Medicine Tech; Pharmacist; MRI Tech; LPN's; Respiratory Therapist; Clinical Lab Scientist. **Parent company:** Tenet Healthcare Corporation.

ST. JUDE CHILDREN'S RESEARCH HOSPITAL
332 North Lauderdale Street, Memphis TN 38105. 901/495-2339. **Toll-free phone:** 888/419-5833. **Fax:** 901/495-3123. **Contact:** Human Resources. **World Wide Web address:** http://www.stjude.org. **Description:** A nonprofit, nonsectarian institution that provides care for children with chronic illnesses. The hospital performs laboratory research on the molecular, genetic, and biochemical bases of childhood cancer and

other diseases. St. Jude Children's Research Hospital also maintains outreach/consultation programs with other health care providers. **NOTE:** Search and apply for positions online. **Positions advertised include:** Pharmacist; Biostatistician; Research Technologist; Ultrasound Technologist; Sr. Training Analyst; Cytogenetic Technologist; Medical Technologist; Proteomics Analyst; Molecular Interaction Analyst; Sr. Database Architect; Sr. Research Technologist; Manager, Diagnostic Imaging; Pediatric Oncology Nurse; Sr. Internal Auditor.

THE SALVATION ARMY
631 Dickerson Road, Nashville TN 37207. 615/242-0411. **Fax:** 615/242-0016. **Contact:** Human Resources. **World Wide Web address:** http://www.salvationarmy.org. **Description:** A nonprofit organization providing several service programs including day-care centers, programs for people with disabilities, substance abuse programs and tutoring for at-risk students. The Salvation Army targets its programs to assist alcoholics, battered women, drug addicts, the elderly, the homeless, people with AIDS, prison inmates, teenagers, and the unemployed.

SATURN CORPORATION
100 Saturn Parkway, P.O. Box 1500, Spring Hill TN 37174. 931/486-5000. **Recorded jobline:** 931/489-4313. **Contact:** Human Resources. **World Wide Web address:** http://www.saturn.com. **Description:** Manufactures automobiles. **Corporate headquarters location:** Troy MI. **Parent company:** General Motors Corporation.

W.J. SAVAGE COMPANY
P.O. Box 157, Knoxville TN 37901. 865/637-9441. **Contact:** Robert Klingerman, President. **World Wide Web address:** http://www.savagesaws.com. **Description:** Manufactures a variety of industrial spindle saws. The company markets its products under the brand names Campbell, Continental, Robert Stone, Savage, and Tysaman.

SCHATTEN PROPERTIES MANAGEMENT COMPANY, INC.
1514 South Street, Nashville TN 37212. 615/329-3011. **Contact:** Controller. **World Wide Web address:** http://www.schattenproperties.com. **Description:** A property management firm. Founded in 1940. **Positions advertised include:** Maintenance Technician; Leasing Agent. **Corporate headquarters location:** This location.

SCHERING-PLOUGH CORPORATION
3030 Jackson Avenue, Memphis TN 38151. 901/320-2011. **Contact:** Human Resources Department. **World Wide Web address:** http://www.schering-plough.com. **Description:** Engaged in the discovery, development, manufacture, and marketing of pharmaceutical and consumer products. Pharmaceutical products include prescription drugs, over-the-counter medicines, eye care products, and animal health products promoted to the medical and allied health professions. The consumer products group consists of proprietary medicines, toiletries, cosmetics, and foot care products marketed directly to the public. Products include Coricidin cough and cold medicines, Dr. Scholl's foot care products, and Coppertone skincare products. **NOTE:** Search and apply for positions online. **Positions advertised include:** Customer Logistics Manager; Sr. Scientist; Financial Operations analyst; Sr. Systems Analyst; Scientist; Deductions Resolution Specialist; Sr. Customer Support Specialist. **Corporate headquarters location:** Kenilworth NJ. Other **U.S. locations:** Nationwide. **International locations:** Worldwide. **Operations at this facility include:** This location houses administrative offices for HealthCare Products. **Number of employees nationwide:** 2,000. **Number of employees worldwide:** 30,500.

SCIENCE APPLICATIONS INTERNATIONAL CORPORATION (SAIC)
P.O. Box 2501, Oak Ridge TN 37831-2501. 865/482-9031. **Physical Address:** 151 Lafayette Drive, Oak Ridge TN 37831-2501. **Contact:** Kathy Phillips, Human Resources Manager. **World Wide Web address:** http://www.saic.com. **Description:** Offers engineering services, nuclear fuel cycle and waste storage analysis, technical information services, information systems, environmental analysis and modeling, program management, and document preparation. **NOTE:** Search and apply for positions online. **Positions advertised include:** Project Control Analyst; Sr. Financial Controller; Project Controls Analyst; Sr. Programmer/Analyst; WNP Fallout Specialist; Subcontract Administrator. **Corporate headquarters locations:** San Diego. **Number of employees worldwide:** 43,000.

SEA RAY BOATS, INC.
2600 Sea Ray Boulevard, Knoxville TN 37914. 865/522-4181. **Contact:** Human Resources. **World Wide Web address:** http://www.searay.com. **Description:** One of the nation's leading manufacturers of recreational pleasure boats. Sea Ray offers a line of nearly 60 models in seven product families including sport boats, sport cruisers, sport yachts, and yachts. **NOTE:** Search and apply for positions online. **Positions advertised include:** Manufacturing Engineer; Production Supervisor. **Parent company:** Brunswick Corporation.

SENIOR FLEXONICS CORPORATION
115 Franklin Road, Oak Ridge TN 37830. 865/483-7444. **Fax:** 865/482-5600. **Contact:** Human Resources. **E-mail address:** careers@myej.net. **World Wide Web address:** http://www.pathwayb.com. **Description:** A designer and manufacturer of metal and fabric expansion joints. The company also performs on-site expansion joint analysis, repair, and original installation.

SERV-A-COMP INC.
1813 South Market Street, Chattanooga TN 37408. 423/265-8010. **Contact:** Personnel. **Description:** Provides repair service for computers, printers, and monitors. Serv-A-Comp Inc. also sells refurbished hardware.

SEVERN TRENT LABORATORIES, INC.
5815 Middlebrook Pike, Knoxville TN 37921. 865/291-3000. **Fax:** 865/584-4315. **Contact:** Human Resources. **World Wide Web address:** http://www.stl-inc.com. **Description:** Provides a complete range of environmental testing services to private industry, engineering consultants, and government agencies in support of federal and state environmental regulations. The company also possesses analytical capabilities in the fields of air toxins, field analytical services, radiochemistry/mixed waste, and advanced technology. **NOTE:** Search and apply for positions online. **Other U.S. locations:** Nationwide. **Parent company:** Severn Trent Plc (London). **Number of employees nationwide:** 2,100.

SHARP MANUFACTURING COMPANY OF AMERICA
Sharp Plaza Boulevard, Memphis TN 38193. 901/795-6510. **Fax:** 901/367-5493. **Contact:** Mr. T.C. Jones, Vice President of Human Resources. **E-mail address:** resume@sharpsec.com. **World Wide Web address:** http://www.sharp-usa.com. **Description:** Manufactures microwave ovens and copier toner.

SHAW INDUSTRIES INC.
210 East 11th Street, South Pittsburg TN 37380. 423/837-8651. **Contact:** Human Resources. **World Wide Web address:** http://www.shawinc.com. **Description:** Manufactures tufted floor coverings and related products. The company manufactures and sells tufted carpet for both residential and commercial use. All products are marketed through retailers, distributors, and other end-users and are exported worldwide. Brand names include Philadelphia Carpet Company, Fashion Statements, Expressive Designs, Sutton, Shaw Commercial Carpets, ShawRugs, Stratton Commercial Carpets, and Salemcarpets. **Corporate headquarters location:** Dalton GA. **Operations at this facility include:** This location prepares and twists yarn for carpets that are manufactured at other locations. **Parent company:** Berkshire Hathaway. **Number of employees nationwide:** 24,000.

SHOLODGE, INC.
130 Maple Drive North, Hendersonville TN 37075. 615/264-8000. **Contact:** Jim Grout, Executive Vice President of Human Resources. **World Wide Web address:** http://www.sholodge.com. **Description:** ShoLodge is the exclusive franchiser of Shoney's Inns, a chain of motels located throughout the Southeast, and GuestHouse International Inns and Suites. **Corporate headquarters location:** This location. **Other U.S. locations:** Nationwide. **Listed on:** NASDAQ. **Stock exchange symbol:** LODG.

SHONEY'S
1727 Elm Hill Pike, Nashville TN 37210. 615/391-5395. **Contact:** Human Resources. **World Wide Web address:** http://www.shoneys.com. **Description:** A full-service, family-style restaurant with 318 locations in 21 states.

SIGNATURE FLIGHT SUPPORT
2488 Winchester Road, Memphis TN 38116. 901/345-4700. **Fax:** 901/345-4733. **Contact:** Personnel. **World Wide Web address:** http://www.signatureflight.com. **Description:** Engaged in flight support operations including fueling, ground handling, passenger services, maintenance, and fuel purchasing. **NOTE:** Contact local HR Representative for employment information. **Corporate headquarters location:** Orlando FL. **Other U.S. locations:** Nationwide. **Parent company:** BBA Aviation. **Number of employees nationwide:** 1,300.

SILVERDALE PENAL FARM
7609 Standifer Gap Road, Chattanooga TN 37421. 423/892-0921. **Fax:** 423/209-6881. **Recorded jobline:** 423/209-6006. **Contact:** Hamilton County Personnel Department. **World Wide Web address:** http://www.hamiltontn.gov/corrections. **Description:** A county correctional facility providing incarceration for misdemeanants and short-term felons. **NOTE:** Download employment application online. Application must accompany resume. Search for Hamilton County, Tennessee positions online. **Positions advertised include:** Adult Probation Officer (Female); Food Service Technician.

SIMPLEXGRINNELL
644 Eastern Star Road, Kingsport TN 37663. 423/349-6109. **Fax:** 423/349-6309. **Contact:** Ron Jacobs, Branch Manager. **E-mail address:** ronjacobs@tycoint.com. **World Wide Web address:** http://www.tyco.com. **Description:** SimplexGrinnell designs, manufactures, installs, and services electronic security systems, fire protection, detection and suppression systems, sprinklers, and fire extinguishers. **Positions advertised include:** Sprinkler Designer. **Parent company:** Tyco. **Corporate headquarters location:** Princeton NJ. **Number of employees worldwide:** 90,000.

SKYLINE MEDICAL CENTER
3441 Dickerson Pike, Nashville TN 37207. 615/769-2000. **Contact:** Nurse Manager. **World Wide Web address:** http://www.skylinemedicalcenter.com. **Description:** A 203-bed, full-service medical center serving the middle Tennessee and southern Kentucky areas. Skyline Medical Center specializes in emergency care, neurology, neurosurgery, oncology, orthopedics, and outpatient care. Founded in 1952. **NOTE:** Search and apply for positions online. **Positions advertised include:** RN's; LPN's; Cath Lab Technologist; Internal Relations Coordinator; Medical Technologist; MRI Technologist; Pharmacist; Phlebotomist; Polysomnographic Technologist; Radiation Therapist; **Parent company:** Tri Star Health System.

SMITH & NEPHEW
1450 Brooks Road, Memphis TN 38116. 901/396-2121. **Toll-free phone:** 800/821-5700. **Contact:** Human Resources. **World Wide Web address:** http://www.smith-nephew.com. **Description:** Manufactures and markets medical products used in endoscopy, orthopedics, and wound management. **NOTE:** Search and apply for positions online. **Positions advertised include:** Sr. Product Manager; Team Unit Manager; Sr. Legal Assistant; Sr. Product Development Engineer; Education and Training Administrative Coordinator; Packaging Development Engineer. **Corporate headquarters location:** London. **Listed on:** New York Stock Exchange. **Stock exchange symbol:** SNN. **Number of employees worldwide:** 7,000.

A.O. SMITH WATER PRODUCTS COMPANY
500 Lindahl Parkway, Ashland City TN 37015. 615/792-4371. **Contact:** Human Resources. **E-mail address:** jobpost@hotwater.com. **World Wide Web address:** http://www.hotwater.com. **Description:** Manufactures and markets commercial and residential water heaters, expansion tanks, and pump tanks to professional contractors. Founded in 1946. **Corporate headquarters location:** This location. **Parent company:** A.O. Smith Corporation. **Listed on:** New York Stock Exchange. **Stock exchange symbol:** AOS.

SMURFIT-STONE CONTAINER CORPORATION
700 Cawan Street, Nashville TN 37207. 615/256-8965. **Contact:** Lance Greenwalt, Controller. **World Wide Web address:** http://www.smurfit-stone.com. **Description:** One of the world's leading paper-based packaging companies. The company's main products include corrugated containers, folding cartons, and multiwall industrial bags. The company is also one of the world's largest collectors and processors of recycled products that are then sold to a worldwide customer base. Smurfit-Stone Container Corporation also operates several paper tube, market pulp, and newsprint production facilities. **Corporate headquarters location:** Chicago IL. **Other U.S. locations:** Nationwide. **International locations:** Dublin, Ireland. **Listed on:** NASDAQ. **Stock exchange symbol:** SSCC. **Annual sales/revenues:** More than $100 million. **Number of employees worldwide:** 35,000.

SMURFIT-STONE CONTAINER CORPORATION
P.O. Box 307, Humboldt TN 38343-0307. 731/784-1500. **Physical address:** 1720 Ninth Avenue, Humboldt TN 38343. **Contact:** Human Resources. **World Wide Web address:** http://www.smurfit-stone.com. **Description:** Smurfit-Stone Container Corporation is one of the world's leading paper-based packaging companies. The company's main products include corrugated containers, folding cartons, and multiwall industrial bags. The company is also one of the world's largest collectors and processors of recycled products that are then sold to a worldwide customer base. Smurfit-Stone Container Corporation also operates several paper tube, market pulp, and newsprint production facilities. **Corporate headquarters location:** Chicago IL. **Other U.S. locations:** Nationwide. **International locations:** Dublin, Ireland. **Operations at this facility include:** This location manufactures corrugated shipping containers. **Listed on:**

NASDAQ. **Stock exchange symbol:** SSCC. **Annual sales/revenues:** More than $100 million.

SMURFIT-STONE CONTAINER CORPORATION
1125 Haley road, Murfreesboro TN 37129. 615/893-2254. **Contact:** Human resources. **World Wide Web address:** http://www.smurfit-stone.com. **Description:** Smurfit-Stone Container Corporation is one of the world's leading paper-based packaging companies. The company's main products include corrugated containers, folding cartons, and multiwall industrial bags. The company is also one of the world's largest collectors and processors of recycled products that are then sold to a worldwide customer base. Smurfit-Stone Container Corporation also operates several paper tube, market pulp, and newsprint production facilities. **Parent company:** Smurfit-Stone Container Corporation. **Operations at this facility include:** This location manufactures corrugated shipping containers. **Listed on:** NASDAQ. **Stock exchange symbol:** SSCC.

SNAP-ON TOOLS COMPANY
2195 State Line Road, Elizabethton TN 37643. 423/543-5771. **Fax:** 423/543-8677. **Contact:** Plant Manager. **World Wide Web address:** http://www.snapon.com. **Description:** Manufactures and distributes tools, storage units, and diagnostic equipment for professional repair, maintenance, and industrial use. Snap-On's product line includes over 14,000 tools, tool chests, custom tools, and diagnostic equipment. **NOTE:** Search and apply for positions online. **Positions advertised include:** Industrial Engineer. **Corporate headquarters location:** Kenosha WI. **Number of employees worldwide:** 14,000.

SONY BMG - RCA RECORDS
1400 18th Avenue South, Nashville TN 37212. 615/858-1200. **Contact:** Human Resources. **World Wide Web address:** http://www.bmg.com. **Description:** Offices of the national record company. **Corporate headquarters location:** New York NY. **Parent company:** Bertelsmann AG and Sony Corporation.

SOUTHDOWN CORPORATION
500 Wilson Pike Circle, Suite 100, Brentwood TN 37027. 615/371-8150. **Fax:** 615/371-8383. **Contact:** Human Resources. **Description:** One of the largest franchisee companies in the Southeast, operating 40 Burger King restaurants.

SOUTHERN HOSPITALITY CORPORATION
1101 Kermit Road, Suite 310, Nashville TN 37217. 615/399-9700. **Fax:** 615/399-3373. **Contact:** Human Resources. **Description:** Operates Wendy's fast-food franchises. **Other U.S. locations:** Nationwide. **Parent company:** Davco Restaurants Inc. **Number of employees at this location:** 1,000.

SOUTHWEST TENNESSEE COMMUNITY COLLEGE
5983 Macon Cove, Memphis TN 38134-7693. 901/333-4226. **Fax:** 901/333-5264. **Contact:** Human Resources Department. **World Wide Web address:** http://www.southwest.tn.edu. **Description:** A two-year technical institute offering associate's degrees with an enrollment of 12,000. **NOTE:** Search and apply for positions online. **Positions advertised include:** Instructor, Radiologic Technology; Program Coordinator; Instructor, Biology; Instructor, Mathematics.

SPRING ARBOR DISTRIBUTORS
One Ingram Boulevard, La Vergne TN 37086. 615/793-5000. **Toll-free phone:** 800/395-4340. **Fax:** 615/213-5192. **Contact:** Human Resources. **World Wide Web address:** http://www.springarbor.com. **Description:** A distributor of Christian books, music, and gift items. **Corporate headquarters location:** This location. **Other U.S. locations:** Harrison AR; Bakersfield CA; Portland OR; Newport TN; Dallas TX. **Parent company:** Ingram Book Company. **Listed on:** Privately held. **Number of employees at this location:** 250. **Number of employees nationwide:** 610.

SPRINGS INDUSTRIES, INC.
P.O. Box 516, Nashville TN 37202-0516. 615/350-7400. **Physical address:** 7201 Cockrill Bend Road, Nashville TN 37209. **Fax:** 615/350-7428. **Contact:** Human Resources. **E-mail address:** springsjobs@springs.com. **World Wide Web address:** http://www.springs.com. **Description:** Springs Industries supplies retailers with a line of sheets, towels, comforters, blankets, rugs, window treatments and other home furnishings. The Company's major brands are Wamsutta®, Springmaid®, Regal®, Graber®, Bali®, Nanik®, and Dundee®. Springs also markets bed and bath products for institutional and hospitality customers, home sewing fabrics, and baby products. The company operates facilities in 13 U.S. states, Mexico and Canada. **Corporate headquarters location:** Fort Mill SC. **Number of employees at this location:** 700.

SPRINT PUBLISHING & ADVERTISING
1615 Bluff City Highway, Bristol TN 37620. 423/844-1400. **Contact:** Human Resources. **World Wide Web address:** http://www.sprintyp.com. **Description:** Publishes ads for the Yellow Pages. **Parent company:** R.H. Donnelley.

SQUARE D COMPANY
330 Weakley Lane, Smyrna TN 37167. 615/459-5026. **Contact:** Human Resources. **E-mail address:** UWB@SchneiderElectricJobs.com. **World Wide Web address:** http://www.squared.com. **Description:** Square D manufactures electrical distribution products for the construction industry. Square D's industrial control and electrical distribution products, systems, and services are used worldwide in industrial facilities and equipment, commercial and residential construction, and original equipment manufacturers' products. **NOTE:** Search and apply for positions online. **Positions advertised include:** Application Engineer; Designer; Materials Analyst; Mechanical Engineer; Quality Engineer; Sr. Manufacturing Engineer; Sr. Materials Analyst. **Corporate headquarters location:** Palatine IL. **Other U.S. locations:** Nationwide. **Operations at this facility include:** This location manufactures electrical switchgear. **Parent company:** Schneider Electric (France).

A.E. STALEY MANUFACTURING
198 Blair Bend Drive, Loudon TN 37774. 865/458-5681. **Contact:** Human Resources. **World Wide Web address:** http://www.tateandlyle.com. **Description:** A corn refinery that produces animal feeds, citric acid, ethanol, starches, and sweeteners. **Corporate headquarters location:** Decatur IL. **Parent company:** Tate & Lyle Plc (England).

STATE FARM INSURANCE AGENCY
2500 Memorial Boulevard, Murfreesboro TN 37131. 615/898-6000. **Fax:** 615/692-6143. **Contact:** Human Resources. **E-mail address:** jobopps.scentral@statefarm.com. **World Wide Web address:** http://www.statefarm.com. **Description:** Sells and services auto, home owner's, life, long-term care, and renter's insurance to individuals and small businesses. **NOTE:** Search and apply for positions online. **Corporate headquarters location:** Bloomington IL. **Number of employees nationwide:** 79,000.

STEWARD INC.
1200 East 36th Street, P.O. Box 510, Chattanooga TN 37401-0510. 423/308-1690. **Toll-free phone:** 800/634-2673. **Fax:** 423/308-1622. **Contact:** Personnel. **World Wide Web address:** http://www.steward.com. **Description:** Produces ferrite and related materials used in the copier, electronics, automotive, and military industries. The company manufactures EMI shielding components, wide-band transformer and filter toroids, copier developer materials, and iron silicide powders. Steward's nickel ferrite parts are used in the suppression of electromagnetic interference known as EMI. Products are used in pulse transformers and data line and power filters. Steward manufactures carrier bead ferrite materials used to formulate developers for both mono- and dual-component xerographic applications.

J. STRICKLAND & COMPANY
1400 Ragan Street, P.O. Box 840, Memphis TN 38101. 901/774-9023. **Contact:** Human Resources. **Description:** Manufactures hair and skin care products specifically designed for African-Americans.

SUBURBAN MANUFACTURING COMPANY
676 Broadway Street, P.O. Box 399, Dayton TN 37321-0399. 423/775-2131. **Fax:** 423/775-7015. **Contact:** Personnel. **E-mail address:** info@suburbanmanufacturing.com. **World Wide Web address:** http://www.suburbanmanufacturing.com. **Description:** Manufactures heating equipment for the commercial and industrial markets as well as the recreational vehicle industry. **Parent company:** Airxcel, Inc.

SUN COKE COMPANY
1111 Northshore Drive, Suite N600, Knoxville TN 37919. 865/558-0300. **Fax:** 865/558-3281. **Contact:** Human Resources. **World Wide Web address:** http://www.suncoke.com. **Description:** A blast furnace coke manufacturer serving the steel industry. **Other U.S. locations:** Vansant VA; East Chicago IN; Haverhill OH.

SUNBEAM-OSTER HOUSEHOLD PRODUCTS
150 Cadillac Lane, McMinnville TN 37110. 931/668-4121. **Fax:** 931/668-4125. **Contact:** Human Resources. **World Wide Web address:** http://www.sunbeam.com. **Description:** This location manufactures, engineers, and markets clippers and blades for the professional, personal, and animal grooming markets worldwide. **Positions advertised include:** Business Logistics Manager; Customer Support Manager; Financial Controller; Product Manager; Senior Forecasting Manager. **Corporate headquarters location:** Boca Raton FL. **International locations:** Worldwide. **Parent company:** Sunbeam **Operations at this facility include:** Administration; Divisional Headquarters; Manufacturing.

SUNTRUST BANKS, INC.
700 East Hill Avenue, Knoxville TN 37915. 865/544-2250. **Contact:** Human Resources. **World Wide Web address:** http://www.suntrust.com. **Description:** A full-service commercial bank. **Parent company:** SunTrust Banks, Inc. (Atlanta GA) is a commercial banking organizations with operations in Florida, Georgia, Tennessee, Maryland, Virginia, and the District of Columbia with other selected markets nationally. **NOTE:** Search and apply for positions online. **Listed on:** New York Stock Exchange. **Stock exchange symbol:** STI.

SWIFT TRANSPORTATION
P.O. Box 30788, Memphis TN 38130-0788. 901/332-2500. **Contact:** Recruiting. **World Wide Web address:** http://www.swifttrans.com. **Description:** An irregular-route truckload carrier transporting a wide range of commodities in the United States, Canada, and Mexico. The principal types of freight transported are packages, retail goods, nonperishable foodstuffs, paper and paper products, household appliances, furniture, and packaged petroleum products. **Positions advertised include:** Corporate Driver. **Corporate headquarters location:** Phoenix AZ. **Operations at this facility include:** Administration; Customer Service; Marketing; Purchasing; Sales; Service. **Number of employees at this location:** 450. **Number of employees nationwide:** 20,000.

TBA ENTERTAINMENT CORPORATION
300 10th Avenue South, Nashville TN 37203. 615/742-9000. **Fax:** 615/742-9199. **Contact:** Human Resources. **E-mail address:** personnel@tbaent.com. **World Wide Web address:** http://www.tbaent.com. **Description:** A strategic communications and entertainment company. **Other U.S. locations:** Nationwide.

TBC CORPORATION
4770 Hickory Hill Road, Memphis TN 38141. 901/363-8030. **Contact:** Human Resources. **World Wide Web address:** http://www.tbccorp.com. **Description:** A marketer and distributor of private-brand tires. TBC sells tires to a network of distribution centers in the U.S., Canada, and Mexico including Big O Tires stores, Tire Kingdom/Merchants stores, and NTB stores. **Listed on:** NASDAQ. **Stock exchange symbol:** TBCC.

TDS TELECOM
P.O. Box 22995, Knoxville TN 37933-0995. 865/966-4700. **Physical address:** 9737 Cogdill Road, Suite 230, Knoxville TN 37932-3374. **Contact:** Human Resources. **World Wide Web address:** http://www.tdstelecom.com. **Description:** Provides telecommunications, telephone, cable television, radio paging, and cellular services.

TPI CORPORATION
P.O. Box 4973, Johnson City TN 37602-4973. 423/477-0086. **Fax:** 423/477-8289. **Contact:** Human Resources. **World Wide Web address:** http://www.tpicorp.com. **Description:** Manufactures electric heating, air ventilation, lighting, and control products. **Corporate headquarters location:** This location. **Other U.S. locations:** Nationwide. **Subsidiaries include:** Columbus Electric; Fostoria Industries. **Operations at this facility include:** Administration; Manufacturing; Research and Development; Sales; Service. **Listed on:** Privately held. **Number of employees at this location:** 425.

TAKOMA ADVENTIST HOSPITAL
401 Takoma Avenue, Greeneville TN 37743. 423/639-3151. **Fax:** 423/636-0338. **Contact:** Human Resources. **World Wide Web address:** http://www.takoma.org. **Description:** A hospital with services that include patient and family care; a physical therapy unit; a home health agency; specialized care, such as obstetrics/gynecology, urology, orthopedics, ophthalmology, and oral and general surgery; diagnostic care, such as radiology and ultrasound mammography services; emergency care including a 7-bed, 24-hour unit; psychiatric care including an 18-bed inpatient unit; maternal and child health care including two birthing rooms and a nursery; and community care including Takoma's IndustriCare occupational medicine program. **NOTE:** Search and apply for positions online. **Positions advertised include:** Certified Respiratory Technician; RN's; Director of ICU; Physical Therapist; Speech Pathologist.

TAP PUBLISHING COMPANY
174 Fourth Street, Crossville TN 38555. 931/484-5137. **Fax:** 931/484-2532. **Contact:** Human Resources. **World Wide Web address:** http://www.trade-a-plane.com. **Description:** Publishes trade journals in the areas of aviation, construction equipment, oil/gas, and amateur radio operation.

TECHMER PM, LLC
One Quality Circle, Clinton TN 37716. 865/457-6700. **Fax:** 865/457-3012. **Contact:** Human Resources. **World Wide Web address:** http://www.techmerpm.com. **Description:** A manufacturer of custom colorants and additives for plastics and fibers. **Corporate headquarters location:** Rancho Dominguez CA. **Other U.S. locations:**; Gainesville GA; Wichita KS; Dalton GA. **Listed on:** Privately held. **Annual sales/revenues:** $51 - $100 million. **Number of employees at this location:** 230. **Number of employees nationwide:** 340.

TECHNOLOGY FOR ENERGY CORPORATION
10737 Lexington Drive, Knoxville TN 37932-3294. 865/966-5856. **Fax:** 865/675-1241. **Contact:** Jane Hall, Human Resources. **E-mail address:** jane.hall@tec-usa.com. **World Wide Web address:** http://www.tec-usa.com. **Description:** Supplies diagnostic instruments for the nuclear power production industry, materials testing, aviation maintenance, and electric power industry.

TELEDYNE ELECTRONIC TECHNOLOGIES
P.O. Box 326, Lewisburg TN 37091-0326. 931/359-4531. **Physical address:** 1425 Higgs Road, Lewisburg TN 37901. **Contact:** John Boultwell, Director of Human Resources. **World Wide Web address:** http://www.teledyne.com. **Description:** A commercial and government contracted manufacturer of printed circuit boards. **NOTE:** Search and apply for positions online. **Corporate headquarters:** Los Angeles CA. **Listed on:** New York Stock Exchange. **Stock exchange symbol:** TDY.

TENDER LOVING CARE/STAFF BUILDERS
6126 Macon Road, Memphis TN 38134. 901/388-4663. **Fax:** 901/371-8454. **Contact:** Human Resources. **E-mail address:** ktoma@tlchhc.com. **World Wide Web address:** http://www.tlcathome.com. **Description:** A home health care agency. **Positions advertised include:** Registered Nurse; Licensed Practical Nurse. **Corporate headquarters location:** Lake Success NY. **Other U.S. locations:** Nationwide. **Number of employees nationwide:** 20,000.

THE TENNESSEAN
1100 Broadway, Nashville TN 37203. 615/259-8300. **Fax:** 615/726-5920. **Recorded jobline:** 615/259-8888. **Contact:** Human Resources. **World Wide Web address:** http://www.tennessean.com. **Description:** Publishes a newspaper with a daily circulation of 180,000 and a Sunday circulation of 250,000. **NOTE:** Search and apply for positions online. **Positions advertised include:** Accounting Manager; District Manager; Online Specialist. **Parent company:** The Gannett Co., Inc.

TENNESSEE AMERICAN WATER COMPANY
P.O. Box 6338, Chattanooga TN 37401-6338. 423/755-7616. **Physical address:** 1101 Broad Street, Chattanooga TN 37402. **Contact:** Human Resources. **World Wide Web address:** http://www.tawc.com. **Description:** An independent water services company. Tennessee-American Water Company collects and purifies water from the Tennessee River and supplies it to customers in the Chattanooga area. **Corporate headquarters location:** Voorhees NJ. **Parent company:** RWE Thames Water. **Listed on:** New York Stock Exchange. **Stock exchange symbol:** AWK.

TENNESSEE CHRISTIAN MEDICAL CENTER
500 Hospital Drive, Madison TN 37115. 615/865-2373. **Fax:** 615/860-6352. **Contact:** Human Resources Director. **E-mail address:** TCMCHR@ahss.org. **World Wide Web address:** http://www.tcmconline.com. **Description:** A 309-bed hospital. The facility serves roughly 35,000 patient visits per year, providing outpatient and inpatient acute care, as well as behavioral and rehabilitation programs. Tennessee Christian Medical Center is a nonprofit institution and a member of the Adventist Health System, a network of 500 health care facilities around the world. **NOTE:** Search and apply for positions online. **Positions advertised include:** Acute Care Nurse Practitioner; clinical Dietitian; Physical Therapist; Radiology Technologist; RN's; Speech Language Pathologist. **Parent company:** Adventist Health System. **Number of employees at this location:** 220.

TENNESSEE DEPARTMENT OF TRANSPORTATION
505 Deaderick Street, Suite 700, James K. Polk Building, Nashville TN 37243. 615/741-3461. **Fax:** 615/253-1477. **Contact:** Ken Becker, Director of Personnel. **World Wide Web address:** http://www.tdot.state.tn.us. **Description:** This location houses the administrative offices for the Tennessee Department of Transportation.

TENNESSEE MAT COMPANY, INC.
1414 Fourth Avenue South, Nashville TN 37210. 615/254-8381. **Fax:** 615/255-4428. **Contact:** Human Resources. **World Wide Web address:** http://www.wearwell.com. **Description:** Manufactures and distributes matting for industrial and commercial applications. Tennessee Mat Company specializes in safety, ergonomic, and anti-fatigue mats designed to enhance the comfort and productivity of standing workers. **President:** Elliot Greenberg. **Number of employees nationwide:** 145.

TENNESSEE REHABILITATION CENTER
460 Ninth Avenue, Smyrna TN 37167. 615/459-6811. **Fax:** 615/355-1373. **Contact:** Human Resources. **Description:** A state-operated comprehensive rehabilitation center offering vocational training and physical rehabilitation services to disabled individuals. Founded in 1977. **NOTE:** Second and third shifts are offered. **Company slogan:** Caring for the present. Preparing for the future. **Special programs:** Internships. **Corporate headquarters location:** Nashville TN. **Number of employees at this location:** 125.

TENNESSEE RIVERBOAT COMPANY
300 Neyland Drive, Knoxville TN 37902. 865/525-7827. **Toll-free phone:** 800/509-2628. **Contact:** Human Resources. **World Wide Web address:** http://tnriverboat.com. **Description:** The Tennessee Riverboat Company operates the Star of Knoxville riverboat. The Star of Knoxville is an authentic paddlewheeler with a capacity of 325 passengers. It's main deck seats 144 passengers and is fully enclosed, air conditioned, and heated for year-round operation. The vessel is equipped with two bars, a dance floor, and band stage.

TENNESSEE STATE UNIVERSITY
3500 John A. Merritt Boulevard, Campus Box 9628, Nashville TN 37209. 615/963-5281. **Contact:** Human Resources Office. **World Wide Web address:** http://www.tnstate.edu. **Description:** A state university with an enrollment of approximately 8,750 students. Founded in 1912. **NOTE:** Search for positions online. **Positions advertised include:** Director, School of Nursing; Assistant/Associate Professor, Health Sciences; Assistant/Associate Professor, Criminal Justice.

TENNESSEE TECHNOLOGICAL UNIVERSITY
Derryberry Hall, One William Jones Drive, Room 146, P.O. Box 5132, Cookeville TN 38505. 931/372-3713. **Fax:** 931/372-3898. **Recorded jobline:** 931/372-3048. **Contact:** Tammy Reynolds, Employment Manager. **E-mail address:** treynolds@ tntech.edu. **World Wide Web address:** http://www.tntech.edu. **Description:** A technical university with a total enrollment of approximately 9,100 graduate and undergraduate students. The school offers 44 bachelor's degree and 20 graduate programs. **NOTE:** Search for positions online. **Positions advertised include:** Network Support Specialist; Assistant Professor (several disciplines); Chairperson, civil and Environmental Engineering; Chairperson, English Department; Chairperson, Mechanical Engineering Department.

TENNESSEE VALLEY AUTHORITY (TVA)
400 West Summit Hill Drive, Knoxville TN 37902-1499. 865/632-2101. **Fax:** 865/632-4452. **Recorded jobline:** 888/975-4882. **Contact:** Staffing and Recruiting. **E-mail address:** Resumix@tva.com. **World Wide Web address:** http://www.tva.gov. **Description:** A federal corporation and one of the nation's largest electricity producers. Tennessee Valley Authority is a regional economic development agency and a steward of the Tennessee River basin, established by the U.S. Congress in 1933 to provide flood control, navigation, and electric power in the Tennessee Valley region. **NOTE:** Search and apply for positions online. **Corporate headquarters location:** This location. **Other area locations:** Chattanooga TN; Nashville TN; Muscle Shoals AL. **Number of employees nationwide:** 13,000.

TENNESSEE WILDLIFE RESOURCES AGENCY
Ellington Agricultural Center, P.O. Box 40747, Nashville TN 37204. 615/781-6622. **Personnel phone:** 615/781-6594. **Contact:** Personnel. **World Wide Web address:** http://www.state.tn.us/twra. **Description:** Dedicated to the preservation and conservation on native wildlife. The Tennessee Wildlife Resources Agency also issues fishing and hunting licenses statewide. Founded in 1949. **Office hours:** Monday - Friday, 8:00 a.m. - 4:30 p.m. **Corporate headquarters location:** This location. **Other U.S. locations:** Crossville TN; Morristown TN; Jackson TN.

TENNESSEE WIRE TECHNOLOGIES
1350 Highway 149 East, Cumberland City TN 37050. 931/827-4000. **Fax:** 931/827-2270. **Contact:** Ms. Freda Lewis, Personnel. **E-mail address:** twt.personnel@tennesseewire.com. **World Wide Web address:** http://www.tennesseewire.com. **Description:** Manufactures wire harnesses and control panels. **Other U.S. locations:** Hopkinsville KY.

TEPRO INC.
590 Baxter Lane, Winchester TN 37398. 931/967-5189. **Fax:** 931/962-0246. **Contact:** Human Resources. **Description:** Produces moldings and automotive parts and supplies them to Nissan and other car companies.

TETRA TECH NUS
800 Oak Ridge Turnpike, Suite A600, Oak Ridge TN 37830. 865/483-9900. **Fax:** 865/483-2014. **Contact:** Norma Gillespie, Human Resources Representative. **World Wide Web address:** http://www.tetratech.com. **Description:** Provides environmental services, water/wastewater management, infrastructure services, communications support, and outsourcing services. **NOTE:** Search and apply for positions online. **Corporate headquarters location:** Pasadena CA. **Number of employees worldwide:** 9,000.

TEXAS BOOT, INC.
P.O. Box 460, Lebanon TN 37088-0460. 615/695-2000. **Physical address:** 127 East Forest Avenue, Lebanon TN 37087. **Toll-free phone:** 800/628-2668. **Fax:** 615/449-2037. **Contact:** Human Resources Representative. **World Wide Web address:** http://www.texasboot.com. **Description:** Texas Boot manufactures western-style boots. **Operations at this facility include:** This location is the main administrative office.

TEXAS BOOT, INC.
231 Western Avenue, Hartsville TN 37074. 615/374-2211. **Contact:** Human Resources. **World Wide Web address:** http://www.texasboot.com. **Description:** Manufactures western-style boots.

THETA ENGINEERING
101 East Tennessee Avenue, Oak Ridge TN 37830. 865/482-0056. **Fax:** 865/482-7583. **Contact:** Human Resources. **E-mail address:** humanresources@theta-hq.com. **World Wide Web address:** http://www.theta-hq.com. **Description:** Offers engineering subcontracting and project management support.

THOMAS & BETTS CORPORATION
8155 T&B Boulevard, Memphis TN 38125. 901/252-5000. **Toll-free phone:** 800/888-0211. **Contact:** Human Resources Manager. **World Wide Web address:** http://www.tnb.com. **Description:** Thomas & Betts Corporation is engaged in the design, manufacture, and marketing of electrical and electronic components and systems for connecting, fastening, protecting, and identifying wires, components, and conduits. The company's products include fittings and accessories for electrical raceways; solderless terminals for small wires and heavy power cables; wire fastening devices and markers; insulation products, flat cable, connectors, and IC sockets for electronic applications; ceramic chip capacitors for electronic circuitry; fiber-optic connectors and accessories; wire management systems; and customer specific products for major original equipment manufacturers. **Corporate headquarters location:** This location. **Operations at this facility include:** This location manufactures street lighting equipment. **Listed on:** New York Stock Exchange. **Stock exchange symbol:** TNB. **Number of employees nationwide:** 50,000.

J. WALTER THOMPSON COMPANY
5050 Poplar Avenue, Suite 1000, Memphis TN 38157. 901/682-9656. **Contact:** Human Resources. **World Wide Web address:** http://www.jwt.com. **Description:** An advertising and public relations firm. **NOTE:** Search and apply for positions or submit resume online. **Other U.S. locations:** Nationwide. **International locations:** Worldwide. **Parent company:** WPP.

THYSSEN KRUPP ELEVATOR SYSTEMS INC.
100 Dover Street, Middleton TN 38052-0370. 731/376-3000. **Contact:** Don McDonhil, Personnel Manager. **Description:** Manufactures and markets elevators, elevator equipment, and offers repair services.

THYSSEN KRUPP ELEVATOR SYSTEMS INC.
1650 Shelby Oaks Drive North, Suite 6, Memphis TN 38134. 901/377-1993. **Contact:** Donna Ryan, Human Resources Director. **Description:** Manufactures and markets elevators, elevator equipment, and offers repair services.

TIME WARNER TELECOM
65 Germantown Court, Suite 400, Cordova TN 38018. 901/260-5000. **Fax:** 901/260-5050. **Contact:** Human Resources. **World Wide Web address:** http://www.twtelecom.com. **Description:** Provides local and regional optical networks and broadband services to business customers. Time Warner Telecom delivers data, voice, and dedicated Internet access to businesses in 22 states and 44 metropolitan

areas. **NOTE:** Search and apply for positions or submit resume online. **Corporate headquarters location:** Littleton CO.

THE TIMKEN COMPANY
P.O. Box 597, Kathleen Drive, Pulaski TN 38478-0597. 931/363-7661. **Contact:** Human Resources. **World Wide Web address:** http://www.torrington.com. **Description:** Designs, develops, manufactures, and markets antifriction bearings. The Torrington Company also produces universal joints and precision components and assemblies. **Corporate headquarters location:** Torrington CT. **Other U.S. locations:** Nationwide. **International locations:** Australia; Brazil; Canada; England; Germany; Japan. **Parent company:** The Timken Company. **Number of employees nationwide:** 10,500.

TOSHIBA AMERICA CONSUMER PRODUCTS
1420 Toshiba Drive, Lebanon TN 37087. 615/444-8501. **Fax:** 615/4444-5160. **Contact:** Human Resources. **E-mail address:** employment@tacp.com. **World Wide Web address:** http://www.tacp.toshiba.com. **Description:** Toshiba America Consumer Products is a diversified consumer electronics manufacturer. **NOTE:** Search and apply for positions online. **Parent company:** Toshiba America, Inc. is a holding company that operates through six companies including Toshiba America Business Solutions, Inc.; Toshiba America Consumer Products, Inc.; Toshiba America Electronic Components, Inc.; Toshiba America Information Systems, Inc.; Toshiba America Medical Systems, Inc.; and Toshiba International Corporation. **Operations at this facility include:** This location manufactures televisions.

TOXCO
109 Flint Road, Oak Ridge TN 37830. 865/482-5532. **Contact:** Human Resources. **World Wide Web address:** http://www.toxco.com. **Description:** A battery recycling company. **Corporate headquarters location:** Anaheim CA. **Operations at this facility include:** Administration; Service. **President:** Terry Adams.

TRACTOR SUPPLY COMPANY (TSC)
200 Powell Place, Brentwood TN 37027. 615/366-4600. **Contact:** Human Resources. **World Wide Web address:** http://www.mytscstore.com. **Description:** With 430 stores in 30 states, TSC is one of the largest operators of retail farm stores throughout the United States. The company supplies the daily farming and maintenance needs of hobby, part-time, and full-time farmers, as well as suburban customers, contractors, and tradesmen. The company sells farm maintenance products (fencing, tractor parts and accessories, agricultural spraying equipment, and tillage parts); animal products (specialty feeds, supplements, medicines, veterinary supplies, and livestock feeders); general maintenance products (air compressors, welders, generators, pumps, plumbing, and tools); lawn and garden products (riding mowers, tillers, and fertilizers); light truck equipment; and work clothing. **Positions advertised include:** Database Administrator; EDI Coordinator; Manager, Merchandise Control Team; Telecommunications Engineer. **Corporate headquarters location:** This location. **Listed on:** NASDAQ. **Stock exchange symbol:** TSCO. **Number of employees nationwide:** 2,200.

TREVECCA NAZARENE UNIVERSITY
333 Murfreesboro Road, Nashville TN 37210-2877. 615/248-1200. **Fax:** 615/248-1432. **Contact:** Human Resources. **World Wide Web address:** http://www.trevecca.edu. **Description:** A fully accredited, four-year, liberal arts college. The school emphasizes the authority of the Bible and the doctrine, experience, and ethic of Christian holiness as interpreted by the Wesleyan tradition. Founded in 1901.

TRICO PRODUCTS
101 Evergreen Drive, Springfield TN37172. 615/384-0089. **Fax:** 615/384-1922. **Contact:** Human Resources. **World Wide Web address:** http://www.tricoproducts.com. **Description:** An electronics manufacturing and assembly plant.

TRIDON INC.
8100 Tridon Drive, Smyrna TN 37167. 615/459-5800. **Contact:** Human Resources. **World Wide Web address:** http://www.tricoproducts.com. **Description:** Manufactures a variety of products for automotive manufacturers including wiper blades and systems, signal flashers, and seat belt control modules. **Parent company:** Trico.

TUTCO INC.
500 Gould Drive, Cookeville TN 38506. 931/432-4141. **Contact:** Human Resources. **World Wide Web address:** http://www.tutco.com. **Description:** Designs, develops, and manufactures electric heater assemblies for the air conditioning, heating, and home appliance industry. Founded in 1938.

TYSON FOODS INC.
P.O. Box 8, Shelbyville TN 37162-0008. 931/684-8180. **Fax:** 931/684-6396. **Contact:** Human Resources. **World Wide Web address:** http://www.tysonfoodsinc.com. **Description:** Tyson Foods is engaged in chicken slaughtering, dressing, cutting, packaging, and deboning. The company is one of the world's largest fully integrated producers, processors, and marketers of poultry-based food products. **NOTE:** Search and apply for positions online. **Corporate headquarters location:** Springdale AR. **Operations at this facility include:** Chicken processing.

UBS FINANCIAL SERVICES.
3102 West End Avenue, Suite 500, Nashville TN 37203. 615/750-8000. **Contact:** Human Resources. **World Wide Web address:** http://www.ubs.com. **Description:** A full-service securities firm with over 300 offices nationwide. Services include investment banking, asset management, merger and acquisition consulting, municipal securities underwriting, estate planning, retirement programs, and transaction management. UBS PaineWebber offers its services to corporations, governments, institutions, and individuals. Founded in 1879. **Corporate headquarters location:** New York NY. **Other area locations:** Chattanooga TN; Cookeville TN; Jackson TN; Kingsport TN; Knoxville TN; Memphis TN; Oak Ridge TN. **Other U.S. locations:** Nationwide. **Annual sales/revenues:** More than $100 million.

U.S.A. MOBILITY
2416 Hillsboro Road, Nashville TN 37212. 615/385-4500. **Fax:** 615/292-9752. **Contact:** Personnel Department. **World Wide Web address:** http://www.usamobility.com. **Description:** A regional provider of paging, mobile communications, and telemessaging services through 100 offices nationwide. **NOTE:** Search and apply for positions online. **Positions advertised include:** Account Executive; B2B Wireless Account Executive. **Corporate headquarters location:** Alexandria VA. **Other U.S. locations:** Nationwide.

U.S. BANK
150 Fourth Avenue North, Nashville TN 37219. 615/251-9200. **Contact:** Human Resources. **World Wide Web address:** http://www.usbank.com. **Description:** A full-service commercial bank providing corporate and consumer services. **NOTE:** Search and apply for positions online. **Parent company:** U.S. Bancorp is one of the nation's largest bank holding companies operating over 2,200 bank offices in 24 states. The company provides banking, brokerage, insurance, investment, mortgage, trust, and payment services products to consumers, businesses, and institutions. **Number of employees nationwide:** 32,000.

U.S. DEPARTMENT OF VETERANS AFFAIRS
NASHVILLE VETERANS ADMINISTRATION MEDICAL CENTER
1310 24th Avenue South, Nashville TN 37212-2637. 615/327-4751. **Fax:** 615/321-6350. **Contact:** Human Resources. **World Wide Web address:** http://www.va.gov. **Description:** The Mid South Veterans Healthcare Network, operated by the U.S. Department of Veterans Affairs, serves one million veterans with seven anchor medical centers located in Lexington and Louisville KY; Memphis, Mountain Home, Murfreesboro, and Nashville TN; and Huntington WV. The Network also maintains five nursing home care units, and two long-term psychiatric care programs. **NOTE:** Search and apply for positions at: http://www.vacareers.com. **Corporate headquarters location:** Washington DC.

U.S. PIPE AND FOUNDRY COMPANY
2501 Chestnut Street, Chattanooga TN 37408. 423/752-3858. **Contact:** Personnel. **World Wide Web address:** http://www.uspipe.com. **Description:** Manufactures ductile iron fittings and valves. **Corporate headquarters location:** Birmingham AL. **Parent company:** Walter Industries, Inc.

UNDERWOOD AIR SYSTEMS, INC.
2969 Armory Drive, Suite 400A, P.O. Box 40567, Nashville TN 37204. 615/251-4555. **Fax:** 615/254-1152. **Contact:** Personnel. **World Wide Web address:** http://www.underwoodair.com. **Description:** Develops, manufactures, and markets equipment and systems designed to cool, clean, distribute, heat, and move air for material handling and ventilation applications in commercial and industrial environments. **Corporate headquarters location:** Atlanta GA. **Parent company:** John L. Underwood Company, Inc. is a holding company for five operating subsidiaries including Lockwood Marine, Inc., Lockwood Products, Inc., Underwood Administrative Services, Inc., Underwood Air Systems, Inc., and Underwood HVAC, Inc.

UNION PLANTERS BANK
7130 Goodlett Farms Parkway, Cordova TN 38018. 901/580-6000. **Contact:** Human Resources. **World Wide Web address:** http://www.upb.com. **Description:** A bank with 866 offices in Tennessee, Florida, Illinois, Indiana, Iowa, Louisiana, Missouri, Texas, Arkansas, Mississippi, Kentucky, and Alabama. Union Planters Bank also offers real estate mortgage, construction, consumer, and lease financing services. **NOTE:** Search and apply for positions online. **Parent company:** Union Planters Corporation (Memphis TN).

UNION UNIVERSITY
1050 Union University Drive, Box 1805, Jackson TN 38305-3697. 731/668-1818. **Fax:** 731/661-5177. **Contact:** Director of Human Resources. **World Wide Web address:** http://www.uu.edu. **Description:** A private, four-year, coeducational, liberal arts college that is fully accredited and affiliated with the Tennessee Baptist Convention. Union University offers a complete liberal arts curriculum in more than 40 fields of study in the arts, sciences, humanities, and social sciences. More than 2,800 undergraduate and graduate students are enrolled. Founded in 1823.

UNIPRES USA INC.
P.O. Box 799, 201 Kirby Drive, Portland TN 37148. 615/325-7311. **Fax:** 615/325-4956. **Contact:** Human Resources. **World Wide Web address:** http://www.unipres.com. **Description:** Manufactures automotive stampings.

UNISYS CORPORATION
3150 Lenox Park Boulevard, Suite 200, Memphis TN 381154396. 901/368-7600. **Contact:** Human Resources. **World Wide Web address:** http://www.unisys.com. **Description:** Provides information services, technology, and software. Unisys specializes in developing critical business solutions based on open information networks. The company's Enabling Software Team creates a variety of software projects that facilitate the building of user applications and the management of distributed systems. The company's Platforms Group is responsible for UNIX Operating Systems running across a wide range of multiple processor server platforms including all peripheral and communication drivers. The Unisys Commercial Parallel Processing Team develops microkernel-based operating systems, I/O device drivers, ATM hardware, diagnostics, and system architectures. The System Management Group is in charge of the overall management of development programs for UNIX desktop and entry-server products. **NOTE:** Search and apply for positions online. **Other area locations:** Knoxville TN; Dyersburg TN; Chattanooga TN; Alcoa TN; Blountville TN. **Other U.S. locations:** Nationwide. **Number of employees worldwide:** 37,000.

UNITED KNITTING
310 Industrial Drive, Cleveland TN 37311. 423/476-9163. **Contact:** Human Resources Manager. **Description:** A manufacturer of knit fabrics. **Number of employees at this location:** 300.

THE UNITED METHODIST PUBLISHING HOUSE
201 Eighth Avenue South, P.O. Box 801, Nashville TN 37202. 615/749-6535. **Contact:** Employment Office. **World Wide Web address:** http://www.umph.org. **Description:** As The United Methodist Church's official publisher, the publishing house develops, produces, and distributes books for home, church, and official denominational church school curriculum. Overall, the company is one of the oldest and largest general agencies of The United Methodist Church. Founded in 1789. **NOTE:** Request application from Employment Office. Search for positions online. **Positions advertised include:** Accounts Payable Specialist; Business Systems Analyst; Customer Service Representative; Children's Resource Consultants; Production Editor; Senior Editor. **Special programs:** Internships. **Corporate headquarters location:** This location.

UNIVERSAL LIGHTING TECHNOLOGIES
26 Century Boulevard, Suite 500, Nashville TN 37214. 615/316-5100. **Toll-free phone:** 800/225-5278. **Fax:** 615/316-5100. **Contact:** Human Resources. **E-mail address:** hr@universalballast.com. **World Wide Web address:** http://www.universalballast.com. **Description:** Manufactures electronic and magnetic ballasts. **Corporate headquarters location:** Los Angeles CA. **Listed on:** New York Stock Exchange. **Stock exchange symbol:** MAG.

UNIVERSITY OF TENNESSEE, CHATTANOOGA
Department 3603, 615 McCallie Avenue, Chattanooga TN 37403-2598. 423/755-4221. **Contact:** Personnel Services Department. **E-mail address:** personnel@utc.edu. **World Wide Web address:** http://www.utc.edu. **Description:** A campus of the state

university. **NOTE:** Search and apply for positions or download employment application (for non-faculty positions) online. **Positions advertised include:** Assistant Professor, Various Disciplines;

UNIVERSITY OF TENNESSEE, KNOXVILLE
221 Conference Center Building, Knoxville TN 37996-4125. 865/974-6642. **Fax:** 865/974-0659. **Recorded jobline:** 865/974-6644. **Contact:** Office of Human Resources. **E-mail address:** rgresshoff@utk.edu. **World Wide Web address:** http://www.utk.edu. **Description:** A university and research institution with a total enrollment of 27,300 students. **NOTE:** Search for positions online. **Positions advertised include:** Accounting Specialist; Financial Systems Analyst; IT Specialist; Research Assistant; Assistant/Associate Professor, Various Disciplines; Dean, Education, Health and Human Sciences. **Special programs:** Training. **Operations at this facility include:** Administration. **Number of employees at this location:** 4,500.

UNUMPROVIDENT CORPORATION
P.O. Box 180109, Chattanooga TN 37401-7109. 423/755-1011. **Fax:** 423/642-4023. **Recorded jobline:** 423/755-8507. **Contact:** Recruiter. **E-mail address:** jobs@unumprovident.com. **World Wide Web address:** http://www.unum.com. **Description:** An insurance company providing income protection to small and medium-sized employers through a broad range of life, health, disability, and retirement products. **NOTE:** Search and apply for positions online. **Positions advertised include:** Sr. Compensation Analyst; Marketing Consultant; RACF Security Administrator; Communications Consultant. **Special programs:** Internships; Training; Co-ops; Summer Jobs. **International locations:** Worldwide. **Listed on:** New York Stock Exchange. **Stock exchange symbol:** UNM. **Number of employees at this location:** 2,400. **Number of employees nationwide:** 14,000. **Number of employees worldwide:** 20,000.

USTER TECHNOLOGIES, INC.
P.O. Box 51270, Knoxville TN 37950-1270. 865/588-9716. **Fax:** 865/588-0914. **Contact:** Human Resources. **World Wide Web address:** http://www.uster.com. **Description:** Manufactures fiber-testing equipment for the textile industry.

VP BUILDINGS
P.O. Box 17967, Memphis TN 38187. 901/748-8000. **Physical address:** 3200 Players Club Circle, Memphis TN 38125. **Toll-free phone:** 800/238-3246. **Fax:** 901/748-9321. **Contact:** Human Resources Department. **E-mail address:** humanresources@vp.com. **World Wide Web address:** http://www.vp.com. **Description:** Designs and manufactures pre-engineered metal building systems for the low-rise, nonresidential market. **Positions advertised include:** Entry Level Engineer; Experienced Structural Engineer; Project Technician. **Corporate headquarters location:** This location. **Other U.S. locations:** Pine Bluff AR; Rainsville AL; Turlock CA; Van Wert OH; St. Joseph MO; Kernersville NC; Evansville WI. **Parent company:** Grupo IMSA (Mexico).

VANDERBILT UNIVERSITY MEDICAL CENTER
2525 West End Avenue, Station B, Box 357700, Nashville TN 37235. 615/322-8300. **Toll-free phone:** 800/288-6622. **Fax:** 615/343-7143. **Recorded jobline:** 615/322-JOBS. **Contact:** Recruitment and Staffing. **World Wide Web address:** http://www.mc.vanderbilt.edu. **Description:** A comprehensive health care facility that combines the education of health professionals, patient care, and biomedical research. Through its programs, Vanderbilt University Medical Center has become a major referral center for the Southeast and the nation. The medical center consists of The School of Medicine, The School of Nursing, The Vanderbilt Clinic, Children's Hospital, Vanderbilt Psychiatric Hospital, and Vanderbilt Stallworth Rehabilitation Hospital. **Positions advertised include:** Account Reimbursement Specialist; Administrative Assistant; Architect; Assistant Manager Patient Care Services; Audiologist; Care Partner; Case Manager; Coding Specialist; Computer Systems Administrator; Data Coordinator; Echocardiography Technologist; Histotechnologist; LAN Manager; LPN's; MRI Technologist. **Number of employees at this location:** 9,000.

VESTAL MANUFACTURING
P.O. Box 420, Sweetwater TN 37874-0420. 423/337-6125. **Physical address:** 176 Industrial Park Road, Sweetwater TN 37874. **Toll-free phone:** 800/456-9562. **Contact:** Human Resources. **World Wide Web address:** http://www.vestalmfg.com. **Description:** Manufactures a wide variety of cast iron and steel building materials. Vestal Manufacturing operates both a steel fabricating plant and a foundry.

VINYLEX CORPORATION
P.O. Box 7187, Knoxville TN 37921. 865/690-2211. **Physical Address:** 2636 Byington-Solway Road, Knoxville TN 37931. **Toll-free phone:** 800/624-4435. **Fax:** 865/691-6273. **Contact:** Human Resources. **E-mail address:** admin@vinylex.com. **World Wide Web address:** http://www.vinylex.com. **Description:** Engaged in custom plastic extrusion. **Other U.S. locations:** Dallas TX.

VOLUNTEER ELECTRIC COOPERATIVE
P.O. Box 277, 18359 State Highway 58 North, Decatur TN 37322. 423/334-1020. **Toll-free phone:** 800/362-9684. **Contact:** Human Resources. **World Wide Web address:** http://www.vec.org. **Description:** An electric utility that distributes electricity to 17 counties in eastern and middle Tennessee. **Office hours:** Monday - Friday, 8:00 a.m. - 5:00 p.m. **Corporate headquarters location:** This location.

VOLVO PENTA MARINE PRODUCTS
200 Robert Wallace Drive, Lexington TN 38351. 731/968-0151. **Contact:** Human Resources. **World Wide Web address:** http://www.volvo.com/volvopenta. **Description:** Manufactures outboard motors and engines. The company also manufactures replacement parts and accessories, offers boat rentals, and provides related financial services.

VOUGHT AIRCRAFT INDUSTRIES, INC.
1431 Vultee Boulevard, Nashville TN 37217-2007. 615/361-2206. **Contact:** Human Resources. **E-mail address:** vought_resume@voughtaircraft.com. **World Wide Web address:** http://www.vought.com. **Description:** Produces wing and tail sections for a variety of prime contractors, and manufactures advanced composites and metal bonded structures. **NOTE:** Vought Aircraft accepts resumes only for currently posted positions. Search for positions online. **Other U.S. locations:** Brea CA; Everett WA. **Parent company:** Vought Aircraft Industries, Inc. **Number of employees at this location: 1,000.**

VULCAN MATERIALS COMPANY
5310 Councilor Lane, Knoxville TN 37914. 865/546-8000. **Fax:** 865/673-5185. **Contact:** Human Resources. **World Wide Web address:** http://www.vulcanmaterials.com. **Description:** Manufactures aggregates, including crushed stone, sand, and gravel. **NOTE:** Search for positions online. Apply to: Human Resources, P.O. Box 7, Knoxville TN 37901. **Positions advertised include:** Accountant. **Corporate headquarters location:** Birmingham AL. **Other U.S. locations:** Nationwide. **Number of employees nationwide:** 9,000.

WACHOVIA SECURITIES
10 Cadillac Drive, Suite 300, Brentwood TN 37027. 931/552-1300. **Toll-free phone:** 800/736-1300. **Fax:** 931/551-8031. **Contact:** Human Resources. **World Wide Web address:** http://www.wachoviasec.com. **Description:** Provides a broad range of financial services including asset management, lending, trust services, and investment banking. **Corporate headquarters location:** Richmond VA.

WALLER LANSDEN DORTCH & DAVIS
P.O. Box 198966, Nashville TN 37219-8966. 615/244-6380. **Physical address:** 511 Union Street, Suite 2700, Nashville TN 37219. **Fax:** 615/244-6804. **Contact:** Melissa McKinney, Director of Professional Recruiting and Practice Support Services. **E-mail address:** mmckinney@wallerlaw.com. **World Wide Web address:** http://www.wallerlaw.com. **Description:** A general practice law firm covering a variety of disciplines including bankruptcy, real estate, and tax law. **Positions advertised include:** Corporate Attorney; Healthcare Attorney. **Other area locations:** Columbia TN; Brentwood TN. **Other U.S. locations:** Los Angeles CA.

WARNER REPRISE NASHVILLE
20 Music Square East, Nashville TN 37203-4326. 615/748-8000. **Contact:** Human Resources. **World Wide Web address:** http://www.wbrnashville.com. **Description:** A record production company.

WELLMONT BRISTOL REGIONAL MEDICAL CENTER
One Medical Park Boulevard, P.O. Box 8964, Bristol TN 37620. 423/844-3700. **Fax:** 423/844-3720. **Contact:** Employment. **E-mail address:** employment@wellmont.org. **World Wide Web address:** http://www.wellmont.org. **Description:** A 348-bed, nonprofit, regional referral center that provides medical services and resources for patients in northeast Tennessee, southwest Virginia, Kentucky, West Virginia, and North Carolina. The center specializes in acute care, cancer care, diabetes treatment, emergency care, neurosciences, outpatient services, psychiatric care, and women's health. **Positions advertised include:** Assistant Director, Radiology; Diagnostic Technologist; Director, Health Information Services; Physical Therapist; LPN; Radiation Therapist; Registered Nurse. **Parent company:** Wellmont Health System. **Number of employees at this location:** 1,500.

WELLMONT HOLSTON VALLEY MEDICAL CENTER
130 Ravine Road, P.O. Box 238, Kingsport TN 37662-0238. 423/224-6450. **Physical address:** 130 West Ravine Road, Kingsport TN 37662. **Fax:** 423/224-6419. **Contact:** Human Resources Director. **E-mail address:** employment@wellmont.org. **World Wide Web address:** http://www.wellmont.org. **Description:** A full-service, 540-bed, acute-care medical center. The Holsten Valley Medical Center operates specialty clinics including The Christine LaGuardia Phillips Cancer Center, James H. Quillen Regional Heart Center, and the Regional Children's Center. **NOTE:** Search and apply for positions online. **Positions advertised include:** Cardiac Sonographer; Clinical Manager; Director of Surgical Services; Physical Therapist; Registered Nurses; Licensed Practical Nurses Staff Pharmacist; Surgical Tech. **Parent company:** Wellmont Health System. **Number of employees at this location:** 2,100.

WERTHAN PACKAGING INC.
1515 Fifth Avenue North, Nashville TN 37208-1310. 615/259-9331. **Contact:** Human Resources. **World Wide Web address:** http://www.werthan.com. **Description:** Manufactures multiwall paper shipping sacks. **Number of employees at this location:** 400.

WEYERHAEUSER COMPANY
1621 Welch Road, Brownsville TN 38012. 731/779-0200. **Contact:** Human Resources. **World Wide Web address:** http://www.weyerhaeuser.com. **Description:** Willamette Industries is a diversified, integrated forest products company with 90 plants and mills manufacturing containerboard, bag paper, fine paper, bleached hardwood market pulp, specialty printing papers, corrugated containers, business forms, cut sheet paper, paper bags, inks, lumber, plywood, particleboard, medium-density fiberboard, laminated beams, and value-added wood products. **NOTE:** Search and apply for positions or submit resume online. **Corporate headquarters location:** Federal Way WA. **Operations at this facility include:** This location cuts paper into 8 1/2 x 11 inch sheets and packages them into reams for customers. **Listed on:** New York Stock Exchange. **Stock exchange symbol:** WY. **Number of employees worldwide:** 57,000.

SHELBY WILLIAMS INDUSTRIES, INC.
150 Shelby Williams Drive, Morristown TN 37813. 423/586-7000. **Fax:** 423/586-2260. **Contact:** Personnel. **World Wide Web address:** http://www.shelbywilliams.com. **Description:** Manufactures lounge, lobby, and casino seating; stacking chairs; folding tables; bar stools; service carts; booths; and related office furniture for the hospitality and food service industries. **Corporate headquarters location:** This location. **Other U.S. locations:** Los Angeles CA; Aurora CO; Plantation FL; Honolulu HI; Chicago IL; New York NY; Houston TX. **Parent company:** Falcon Products, Inc.

WILLIAMS-SONOMA, INC.
4300 Concorde Road, Memphis TN 38118. 901/795-2625. **Contact:** Human Resources Director. **World Wide Web address:** http://www.williams-sonoma.com. **Description:** Williams-Sonoma is a retailer of cookware, serving equipment, and other specialty items. Products are sold both through retail stores and mail-order catalogs under the brand names Williams-Sonoma, Hold Everything, Gardener's Eden, Pottery Barn, and Chambers. **NOTE:** Search and apply for positions online. **Positions advertised include:** General Operations Manager; Maintenance Manager. **Operations at this facility include:** This location is the company's distribution center.

WILLIAMSON MEDICAL CENTER
2021 Carothers Road, Franklin TN 37067. 615/435-5151. **Recorded jobline:** 615/435-5114. **Contact:** Melodie Reed, Human Resources Director. **E-mail address:** humanresources@williamsonmedicalcenter.org. **World Wide Web address:** http://www.williamsonmedicalcenter.org. **Description:** A hospital offering comprehensive inpatient and outpatient services. **NOTE:** Search or positions and download application form online. **Positions advertised include:** Administrator, Ambulatory Surgery Center; Registered Nurses; CT Technologist.

WRIGHT INDUSTRIES LLC
707 Spence Lane, Nashville TN 37217-1143. 615/361-6600. **Fax:** 615/366-1864. **Contact:** Human Resources. **World Wide Web address:** http://www.wrightind.com. **Description:** Supplies custom-designed automation and manufacturing systems, and integrates robotics, machine vision, and other advanced automation technologies. **Parent company:** Doerfer Companies.

WILLIS CORPORATION
P.O. Box 305191, Nashville TN 37230. 615/872-3000. **Physical address:** 26 Century Boulevard, Nashville TN 37214. **Fax:** 615/872-3813. **Recorded jobline:** 615/872-6343. **Contact:** Employment Services. **E-mail address:** usemployment@willis.com. **World Wide Web address:** http://www.willis.com. **Description:** An insurance company that provides program design, risk assessment, risk control services, risk strategy, and risk transfer transactions. Founded in 1905. **Positions advertised include:** Actuary; Sr. Support coordinator; Project Manager; Principal Operational Auditor; Infrastructure Technical Specialist; Certificate Processor. **International locations:** Worldwide. **Listed on:** New York Stock Exchange. **Stock exchange symbol:** WSH. **Number of employees at this location:** 900. **Number of employees worldwide:** 10,000.

WILSON SPORTING GOODS
4600 Roberts Matthews Highway, Sparta TN 38583. 931/738-7500. **Contact:** Human Resources. **World Wide Web address:** http://www.wilsonsports.com. **Description:** Wilson Sporting Goods manufactures sporting goods for golf, tennis, and team sports. Wilson has been affiliated with the NFL since 1941, has produced the official baseball of the NCAA championships since 1986, and has produced the official ball of many of professional baseball's minor league teams. Wilson also manufactures and supplies uniforms to the NFL, MLB, NBA, and many colleges, universities, and high schools throughout the United States. **NOTE:** Submit resumes to: Wilson Sporting Goods Co., Attn: Corporate Human Resources, 8700 West Bryn Mawr Avenue, Chicago IL 60631. **Corporate headquarters location:** Chicago IL. **Parent company:** Amer Group, Plc (Finland). **Operations at this facility include:** This location manufactures uniforms. **Number of employees nationwide:** 2,500. **Number of employees worldwide:** 3,100.

WORTH, INC.
P.O. Box 88104, Tullahoma TN 37388-8104. 931/455-0691. **Physical address:** 2100 North Jackson Street, Tullahoma 37388. **Contact:** Sherri Willis, Human Resources Director. **World Wide Web address:** http://www.worthsports.com. **Description:** A manufacturer of sporting goods equipment. Primary products include batting gloves, baseball bats, baseball gloves, sporting bags, baseballs, softballs, and other sports accessories.

24HOUR FITNESS
4600 West Park Boulevard, Plano TX 75093. 972/612-6960. **Fax:** 962/612-6497. **Contact:** Human Resources. **World Wide Web address:** http://www.24hourfitness.com. **Description:** The world's largest sports and fitness center chain. **NOTE:** Please visit website to search for job and apply online. **Positions advertised include:** Front Desk Personnel; Kid's Club Worker; Personal Trainer; Sales Counselor. **Corporate headquarters location:** Carlsbad CA. **Other area locations:** Statewide. **Other U.S. locations:** Western, Southern, and Midwestern U.S. **Operations at this facility include:** This location is a Super Sport Club. **CEO:** Mark S. Mastrov.

AAVID THERMALLOY INC.
2700 Research Drive, Suite 200, Plano TX 55074. 972/633-9371. **Fax:** 972/633-5291. **Contact:** Human Resources. **World Wide Web address:** http://www.aavidthermalloy.com. **Description:** Produces a variety of electronics components and systems, plastics, and machined products including ceramic electrical products, electronic semiconductor equipment, semiconductor insulating covers, screw machine products, plastic injected molding products for electronics use, and printed circuit board guides. **Parent company:** Aavid Thermalloy (Concord NH.)

ABB LUMMUS GLOBAL
3010 Briar Park Drive, Houston TX 77042. 713/821-5000. **Fax:** 713/821-3589. **Contact:** Personnel Director. **World Wide Web address:** http://www.abb.com/us. **Description:** An engineering firm serving power plants, chemical plants, and petrochemical and oil refineries, as well as other industries such as aviation and storage. **NOTE:** Please visit website to search for jobs and apply online. **Corporate headquarters location:** Zurich Switzerland. **Other U.S. locations:** Nationwide. **International locations:** Worldwide. **Parent company:** ABB Group. **Listed on:** New York Stock Exchange. **Stock exchange symbol:** ABB. **CEO:** Samir Brikho. **Number of employees nationwide:** 9,500. **Number of employees worldwide:** 115,000.

ACR GROUP, INC.
3200 Wilcrest Drive, Suite 440, Houston TX 77042-6039. 713/780-8532. **Fax:** 713/780-4067. **Contact:** Human Resources. **E-mail address:** humanresources@acrgroup.com. **World Wide Web address:** http://www.acrgroup.com. **Description:** A wholesale distributor of heating, ventilation, air conditioning, and refrigeration equipment, parts, and supplies. ACR Group's products include motors, fiberglass air handling products, sheet metal products, copper tubing, flexible duct, controls, grilles, registers, and pipe vents. The company has 18 distribution outlets in the United States. Founded in 1990. **Corporate headquarters location:** This location. **Other U.S. locations:** Western and Southern U.S. **Subsidiaries include:** ACH Supply (CA); ACR Supply, Inc. (TX and LA); Contractors Heating & Supply, Inc. (CO, TX, and NM); Florida Cooling Supply, Inc. (FL); Heating and Cooling Supply, Inc. (NV); Total Supply, Inc. (GA, TN).

ACS, INC.
2828 North Haskell, Building 1, Dallas TX 75204. 214/841-6111. **Contact:** Human Resources. **World Wide Web address:** http://www.acs-inc.com. **Description:** A full-service provider of data processing services, computer outsourcing, facilities management, electronic transaction processing, and telecommunications services. The firm owns several data centers across the United States and a telecommunications network that encompasses leading-edge technologies. The company uses many different computer platforms including IBM, Amdahl, Hewlett-Packard, Tandem, and UNIX-based systems. **Positions advertised include:** Software Support Analyst; Vice President – Network Services; Real Estate Associate; Global Licensing Analyst; Payroll Tax Specialist; HR Specialist; Executive Administrative Assistant; HRIS Analyst; Network Solutions Technical Architect; Network Security Analyst; e-learning Instructional Designer; Export Compliance Officer; Development Specialist; Senior Project Manager; Senior Accountant; Call Center Team Manager; Accounting Manager. **Corporate headquarters location:** This location. **Other U.S. locations:** Nationwide. **Listed on:** New York Stock Exchange. **Stock exchange symbol:** ACS. **Number of employees worldwide:** 40,000.

ADS ENVIRONMENTAL SERVICES INC.
10450 Stancliff Road, Suite 115, Houston 77099. 281/933-0951. **Contact:** Human Resources Department. **E-mail address:** careers@adsenv.com. **World Wide Web address:** http://www.adsenv.com. **Description:** Provides diagnostic testing services of water and wastewater, flow monitoring, and sewer system evaluation. Founded in 1974. **NOTE:** Send resumes to: ADS Corporation, 5030 Bradford Drive, Building One, Suite 210, Huntsville AL 35805; phone is 256/430-3366. **Corporate headquarters location:** Huntsville AL. **Parent company:** ADS Corporation. **President/CEO:** Karl Boone.

ADT SECURITY SERVICES
1817 West Breaker Lane, Suite 400, Austin TX 78758-3605. 512/832-0122. **Fax:** 512/832-2988. **Contact:** Paul Ebersol, Human Resources. **World Wide Web address:** http://www.adtsecurityservices.com. **Description:** Designs, installs, sells, and monitors fire and burglar alarm systems for commercial and industrial retail customers. ADT Security also offers armed and unarmed security guards. **Corporate headquarters location:** Boca Raton FL. **Parent company:** Tyco International, Ltd. **Listed on:** New York Stock Exchange. **Stock exchange symbol:** TYC. **Number of employees nationwide:** 15,000.

ADT SECURITY SERVICES
140 Heimer Road, Suite 100, San Antonio TX 78232. 210/491-0300. **Fax:** 210/491-3259. **Contact:** Sandy McDonald, Human Resources. **World Wide Web address:** http://www.adtsecurityservices.com. **Description:** Designs, installs, sells, and monitors fire and burglar alarm systems for commercial and industrial retail customers. ADT Security also offers armed and unarmed security guards. **NOTE:** Contact Human Resources directly at 310/491-3231. **Corporate headquarters location:** Boca Raton FL. **Parent company:** Tyco International, Ltd. **Listed on:** New York Stock Exchange. **Stock exchange symbol:** TYC. **Number of employees nationwide:** 15,000.

AMC INDUSTRIES
P.O. Box 171290 San Antonio TX, 78217. 210/545-2566. **Physical address:** 3535 Metro Parkway, San Antonio TX 78247. **Fax:** 210/545-2977. **Contact:** Human Resources. **Description:** A wholesale distributor of water well parts. **Corporate headquarters location:** This location. **Other U.S. locations:** Austin TX; Houston TX; Pharr TX; Buda TX.

AMC INDUSTRIES
5112 Steadmont Drive, Houston TX 77040. 713/462-0007. **Contact:** Human Resources. **Description:** A wholesale distributor of water well parts. **Corporate headquarters location:** San Antonio TX. **Other U.S. locations:** Austin TX; Pharr TX; Buda TX.

APW WYOTT FOOD SERVICE EQUIPMENT
729 Third Avenue, Dallas TX 75226. 214/421-7366. **Toll-free phone:** 800/527-2100. **Fax:** 214/565-0976. **Contact:** Human Resources. **E-mail address:** info@apwwyott.com. **World Wide Web address:** http://www.apwwyott.com. **Description:** Manufactures counter top equipment, equipment used in fabrication plans for restaurants or concessions, heavy-duty ovens, cooking equipment, and deck ovens.

ABATIX CORPORATION
8201 Eastpoint Drive, Suite 500, Dallas TX 75227. 214/381-0322. **Toll-free phone:** 888/222-8499. **Fax:** 214/381-9513. **Contact:** Human Resources. **E-mail address:** hr@abatix.com. **World Wide Web address:** http://www.abatix.com. **Description:** A supplier of industrial safety supplies, construction tools, general safety products such as protective clothing and eyewear, and clean-up equipment. Abatix Corporation has eight distribution centers serving customers throughout the Southwest, Midwest, and the Pacific Coast. **NOTE:** Please visit website to view job listings. **Corporate headquarters location:** This location. **Other area locations:** Houston TX. **Other U.S. locations:** AZ; CA; NV; WA. **President/CEO:** Terry W. Shaver. **Listed on:** NASDAQ. **Stock exchange symbol:** ABIX.

ABATIX CORPORATION
1430 North Post Oak Road, Houston TX 77055. 713/956-2062. **Toll-free phone:** 800/542-6296. **Fax:** 713/956-1350. **Contact:** Human Resources. **E-mail address:** hr@abatix.com. **World Wide Web address:** http://www.abatix.com. **Description:** Provides the asbestos and lead abatement, hazardous material remediation, and construction industries with a full-line of durable and nondurable supplies. Products include industrial safety supplies, construction tools, general safety products such as protective clothing and eyewear, and clean-up equipment. Abatix Environmental Corporation has eight distribution centers serving customers throughout the Southwest, Midwest, and the Pacific Coast. **NOTE:** Please visit website to view job listings. **Corporate headquarters location:** Dallas TX. **Other U.S. locations:** AZ; CA; NV; WA. **President/CEO:** Terry W. Shaver. **Listed on:** NASDAQ. **Stock exchange symbol:** ABIX.

ABBOTT DIAGNOSTICS
1921 Hurd Street, Irving TX 75038. 972/518-6000. **Contact:** Human Resources. **World Wide Web address:** http://www.abbott.com. **Description:** Designs, develops, and manufactures automated laboratory instruments, primarily used in the fields of clinical chemistry, microbiology, and therapeutic drug monitoring. **NOTE:** Please visit website to search for jobs and apply online. **Positions advertised include:** Technical Support Personnel; Information Technology Specialist. **Special programs:** Internships; Co-ops; Summer programs. **Corporate headquarters location:** Abbott Park IL. **Other U.S. locations:** Nationwide. **International locations:** Worldwide. **Parent company:** Abbott Laboratories is an international manufacturer of a wide range of health care products including pharmaceuticals, hospital products, diagnostic products, chemical products, and nutritional products. **Listed on:** New York Stock Exchange. **Stock exchange symbol:** ABT. **Number of employees worldwide:** 70,000.

ABBOTT LABORATORIES
3900 Howard Lane, Austin TX 78728. 512/255-2000. **Contact:** Human Resources. **World Wide Web address:** http://www.abbott.com. **Description:** This location manufactures intravenous bags for the medical industry. Overall, Abbott Laboratories manufactures a wide range of health care products including pharmaceuticals, hospital products, diagnostic products, chemical products, and nutritional products. **NOTE:** Please visit website to search for jobs and apply online. **Positions advertised include:** Quality Assurance and Regulatory Affairs Specialist; Sales and Marketing Specialist. **Special programs:** Internships; Co-ops; Summer programs. **Corporate headquarters location:** Abbott Park IL. **Other U.S. locations:** Nationwide. **International locations:** Worldwide. **Parent company:** Abbott Laboratories is an international manufacturer of a wide range of health care products including pharmaceuticals, hospital products, diagnostic products, chemical products, and nutritional products. **Listed on:** New York Stock Exchange. **Stock exchange symbol:** ABT. **Number of employees worldwide:** 70,000.

ABILENE AERO INC.
2850 Airport Boulevard, Abilene TX 79602. 325/677-2601. **Fax:** 325/671-8018. **Contact:** Mr. Joe Crawford, General Manager. **E-mail address:** jcrawford@abileneaero.com. **World Wide Web address:** http://www.abileneaero.com. **Description:** Operates a small airport offering flight instruction, charter and pilot service, aircraft fueling, parts, and maintenance. Founded in 1968. **Corporate headquarters location:** This location.

ABILENE CHRISTIAN UNIVERSITY
ACU Station, Box 29106, Abilene TX 79699-9106. 915/674-2000. **Physical address:** Abilene Christian University, Hardin Administration Building, Room 213, Abilene TX. **Fax:** 915/674-6899. **Contact:** Human Resources. **Recorded jobline:** 325/674-5621. **World Wide Web address:** http://www.acu.edu. **Description:** A Church of Christ-affiliated university with 117 undergraduate programs, 39 graduate fields of study, and one doctoral program in theology. Approximately 4,700 students are enrolled in the university. **NOTE:** Please visit website to view job listings and download application form. **Positions advertised include:** Landscaping Coordinator; Assistant Registrar and Record Technology Coordinator; Residence Director; Program Coordinator; Library Technician and Assistant Cataloger; Career Services Specialist; Administrative Associate; Faculty – Various Departments.

J.D. ABRAMS LP
111 Congress Avenue, Suite 2400, Austin TX 78701-4083. 512/322-4000. **Fax:** 512/322-4018. **Contact:** Mr. Dean Bernal, Vice President of Human Resources. **E-mail address:** dbernal@jdabrams.com. **World Wide Web address:** http://www.jdabrams.com. **Description:** A heavy, civil construction company specializing in public works infrastructure projects. Founded 1966. **Positions advertised include:** Estimator; Project Manager; Project Engineer; Field Engineer; Scheduler; Accountant; Human Resources Representative; Clerk. **Corporate headquarters location:** This location. **Other area locations:** Dallas TX; El Paso TX; Houston TX. **President:** Jon Abrams.

ABRAXAS PETROLEUM CORPORATION
P.O. Box 701007, San Antonio TX 78270-1007. 210/490-4788. **Physical address:** 500 North Loop 1604 East, Suite 100, San Antonio TX 78232. **Fax:** 210/490-8816. **Contact:** Carol O'Brien, Human Resources. **E-mail address:** cobrienabraxaspetroleum.com. **World Wide Web address:** http://www.abraxaspetroleum.com. **Description:** An independent crude oil and natural gas exploration and production company with operations concentrated in western Canada, Texas, and Wyoming. The company has participated in the drilling of over 500 wells in 17 states. Abraxas Petroleum Corporation owns interests in over 450 oil wells, 120 gas wells, and 170 service wells. The company operates the following three centralized production facilities in Texas: Abraxas Production Corporation (Midland TX), Abraxas Production Corporation (Ira TX), and Portilla Gas Plant (Sinton TX). Founded in 1977. **Corporate headquarters location:** This location. **International locations:** Calgary, Alberta Canada. **Listed on:** American Stock Exchange. **Stock exchange symbol:** ABP. **President/CEO:** Robert L.G. Watson.

ACAP CORPORATION
P.O. Box 42814, Houston TX 77242-2814. 713/974-2242. **Physical address:** 10555 Richmond Avenue, 2nd Floor, Houston TX 77042. **Toll-free phone:** 800/527-2567. **Fax:** 713/953-7920. **Contact:** Personnel Director. **Description:** A holding company for life insurance subsidiaries. **NOTE:** Entry-level positions are offered. **Corporate headquarters location:** This location. **Subsidiaries include:** American Capitol Insurance Company; Imperial Plan; Statesman National Life Insurance Company; Texas Imperial Life Insurance Company.

ACCENTURE
2929 Allen Parkway, Suite 2000, Houston TX 77019-7107. 713/837-1500. **Fax:** 713/837-1593. **Contact:** Human Resources. **World Wide Web address:** http://www.accenture.com. **Description:** A management and technology consulting firm. Accenture offers a wide range of services including business re-engineering, customer service system consulting, data system design and implementation, Internet sales systems research and design, and strategic planning. **NOTE:** Please visit website to search for jobs and apply online. **Other area locations:** Austin TX; Dallas TX. **Other U.S. locations:** Nationwide. **International locations:** Worldwide. **Listed on:** New York Stock Exchange. **Stock exchange symbol:** ACN. **CEO:** Joe W. Forehand. **Number of employees worldwide:** 90,000.

ACCENTURE
1501 South MoPac Expressway, Suite 300, Austin TX 78746. 512/732-5300. **Fax:** 512/476-7765. **Contact:** Human Resources. **World Wide Web address:** http://www.accenture.com. **Description:** A management and technology consulting firm. Accenture offers a wide range of services including business re-engineering, customer service system consulting, data system design and implementation, Internet sales systems research and design; and strategic planning. **NOTE:** Please visit website to search for jobs and apply online. **Corporate headquarters location:** Hamilton, Bermuda. **Other area locations:** Houston TX; Dallas TX. **Other U.S. locations:** Nationwide. **International locations:** Worldwide. **Listed on:** New York Stock Exchange. **Stock exchange symbol:** ACN. **Number of employees worldwide:** 90,000.

ACCOR HOTELS
4001 International Parkway, Carrollton TX 75007. 972/360-9000. **Fax:** 972/360-5996.**Contact:** Human Resources. **E-mail address:** careers@accor-na.com. **World Wide Web address:** http://www.accor.com. **Description:** Accor Hotels operates over 4,000 hotels, including Motel 6 and Red Roof Inn, in 90 countries. **NOTE:** Please visit website to search for jobs and apply online. **Special programs:** Internships. **International locations:** Worldwide. **Operations at this facility include:** This location houses the administrative offices for the U.S. **Number of employees nationwide:** 18,800. **Number of employees worldwide:** 158,000.

ACE AMERICA'S CASH EXPRESS INC.
1231 Greenway Drive, Suite 800, Irving TX 75038. 972/550-5000. **Fax:** 972/582-1410. **Contact:** Human Resources. **E-mail address:** employment@acecashexpress.com. **World Wide Web address:** http://www.acecashexpress.com. **Description:** One of the largest check cashing companies in the United States, offering check cashing services for government and payroll checks. **NOTE:** Contact Human Resources directly at 972/550-5106. Please visit website for a listing of store positions. **Corporate headquarters location:** This location. **Other U.S. locations:** Nationwide. **Listed on:** NASDAQ. **Stock exchange symbol:** AACE.

ACKELS & ACKELS LLP
2777 Stemmons Freeway, Suite 879, Dallas TX 75207. 214/267-8600. **Fax:** 214/267-8605. **Contact:** Office Manager. **Description:** A law firm that specializes in civil, criminal, and commercial litigation, and also practices personal injury, juvenile, and entertainment law.

ACKERMAN McQUEEN, INC.
600 Commerce Tower, 545 East John Carpenter Freeway, Suite 600, Dallas TX 75062. 972/444-9000. **Fax:** 972/869-4363. **Contact:** Human Resources. **World Wide Web address:** http://www.am.com. **Description:** A full-service advertising agency. Founded in 1939. **NOTE:** Entry-level positions are offered. **Special programs:** Internships. **Internship information:** Unpaid internships are offered each fall, spring, and summer semester for college credit. **Corporate headquarters location:** Oklahoma City OK. **Other U.S. locations:** Colorado Springs CO; Tulsa OK; San Francisco CA. **International locations:** London England. **Subsidiaries include:** Mercury Group; OK Events. **CEO:** Angus McQueen.

ADAMS RESOURCES AND ENERGY
P.O. Box 844, Houston TX 77001. 713/881-3600. **Physical address:** 4400 Post Oak Parkway, Houston TX 77027. **Fax:** 713/881-3491. **Contact:** Human Resources. **Description:** A petroleum exploration and production company. **Corporate headquarters location:** This location.

ADLETA & POSTON, REALTORS
300 Crescent Court, Dallas TX 75201. 214/696-0900. **Fax:** 214/369-6996. **Contact:** Personnel. **World Wide Web address:** http://www.adletaposton.com. **Description:** A residential real estate brokerage specializing in the luxury housing and corporate relocation markets. **Positions advertised include:** Real Estate Agent; Receptionist; Secretary. **Special programs:** Internships. **Corporate headquarters location:** This location. **Operations at this facility include:** Administration; Sales. **Number of employees at this location:** 10.

ADVANCE PCS
750 West John Carpenter Freeway, Suite 1200, Irving TX 75039. 469/524-4700. **Toll-free phone:** 800/749-6199. **Fax:** 469/524-4702. **Contact:** Human Resources. **World Wide Web address:** http://www.advancepcs.com. **Description:** A mail-order prescription and healthcare supply company. **NOTE:** Apply online. **Parent company:** Caremark Company (Nashville TN.)

ADVANCED MICRO DEVICES, INC. (AMD)
5204 East Ben White Boulevard, Mail Stop 556, Austin TX 78741. 512/602-1000. **Contact:** Employment. **World Wide Web address:** http://www.amd.com. **Description:** Designs, develops, manufactures, and markets complex, monolithic integrated circuits for use by electronic equipment and systems manufacturers, primarily in instrument applications and products for computation and communication. **NOTE:** Please mail resumes to corporate office at 1 AMD Place, P.O. Box 3453, MS 935, Sunnyvale CA 947088. **Positions advertised include:** Administrative Assistant; Applications Manager; Advanced Process Control Engineer; Business Controller; Business Development Manager; Business Operations Manager; Compiler Optimization Engineer; Corporate Manufacturing Competitive Intelligence Project Manager; Design Engineer; Executive Assistant; Global Advertising Manager; Inside Sales Representative; Marketing Manager; Senior Design Engineer. **Corporate headquarters location:** Sunnyvale CA. **Other area locations:** Dallas TX; Houston TX. **Other U.S. locations:** Nationwide. **International locations:** Worldwide. **Operations at this facility include:** This location manufactures semiconductors. **Listed on:** New York Stock Exchange. **Stock exchange symbol:** AMD. **President/CEO:** Hector de J. Ruiz. **Number of employees nationwide:** 14,000.

ADVO INC.
8950 Railwood Drive, Houston TX 77078. 713/636-7200. **Fax:** 713/633-0839. **Contact:** Human Resources. **World Wide Web address:** http://www.advo.com. **Description:** A direct mail advertising agency. Specialties include Missing Child cards and the ShopWise program. **NOTE:** Please visit website to search for jobs and apply online. **Corporate headquarters location:** Windsor CT. **Other area locations:** El Paso TX; Dallas TX; San Antonio TX. **Other U.S. locations:** Nationwide. **Listed on:** New York Stock Exchange. **Stock exchange symbol:** AD. **Number of employees nationwide:** 3,600.

AEGIS COMMUNICATIONS GROUP
7880 Bent Branch Road, Suite 150, Irving TX 75063. 972/830-1800. **Toll-free phone:** 800/332-0266. **Fax:** 972/836-1804. **Contact:** Human Resources Department. **E-mail address:** info@aegiscomgroup.com. **World Wide Web address:** http://www.aegiscomgroup.com. **Description:** A teleservices provider that offers integrated marketing services to large corporations. Services include customer acquisition, customer care, and marketing research. **NOTE:** Please visit website to view job listings. **Positions advertised include:** Vice President – Business Development; Executive Assistant to CEO; Payroll Administrator; Senior IT Support Technician. **Corporate headquarters location:** This location. **Other U.S. locations:** GA; FL; IN; NC; WV; AZ; CA; MO. **Listed on:** NASDAQ. **Stock exchange symbol:** AGIS.

AERIFORM CORPORATION
4201 FM 1960, Suite 590, Houston TX 77068. 281/631-0667. **Fax:** 281/631-9849. **Contact:** Human Resources. **E-mail address:** humanresources@aeriform.com. **World Wide Web address:** http://www.aeriform.com. **Description:** Aeriform ranks among the nation's largest independent suppliers of specialty gases, medical gases, welding equipment, and cryogenic products. **Positions advertised include:** Driver; Inside/Counter Sales Representative; Branch Manager; Customer Service Manager. **Corporate headquarters location:** This location. **Other area locations:** Statewide. **Other U.S. locations:** KS; OK; AK; LA.

AERIFORM CORPORATION
3813 County Road West, Odessa TX 79764. 432/362-0384. **Fax:** 432/362-3512. **Contact:** Human Resources. **E-mail address:** humanresources@aeriform.com. **World Wide Web address:** http://www.aeriform.com. **Description:** Aeriform ranks among the nation's largest independent suppliers of specialty gases, medical gases, welding equipment, and cryogenic products. **Positions advertised include:** Driver; Inside/Counter Sales Representative; Branch Manager; Customer Service Manager. **Corporate headquarters location:** Houston TX. **Other area locations:** Statewide. **Other U.S. locations:** KS; OK; AK; LA.

AIDS SERVICES OF AUSTIN
P.O. Box 4874, Austin TX 78765. 512/458-2437. **Fax:** 512/452-3299. **Contact:** Personnel. **E-mail address:** asa.mail@asaustin.org. **World Wide Web address:** http://www.asaustin.org. **Description:** This organization has 600 volunteers that work together to assist the community and individuals who are HIV-positive. AIDS Services of Austin is involved in philanthropy, wellness educational programs, safe sex seminars, counseling, and financial aid for HIV-positive individuals. **NOTE:** Volunteer positions are also available. **Special programs:** Internship. **Office hours:** Monday – Friday, 8:30 a.m. – 5:30 p.m.

AIM MANAGEMENT GROUP INC.
P.O. Box 4739, Houston TX 77210-4739. 713/626-1919. **Physical address:** 11 Greenway Plaza, Suite 100, Houston TX 77046. **Contact:** Human Resources. **World Wide Web address:** http://www.aiminvestments.com. **Description:** Manages mutual funds. **Positions advertised include:** Analyst/Automation Specialist; Financial Reporting Accountant; Administrative Assistant; Senior Financial Writer; Project Event Coordinator; Internal Wholesaler; Accounting Clerk; Fund Accountant; HR Business Partner; Quantitative Research Associate; Compliance Specialist; Multimedia Specialist; Manager – Competitive Research. **Corporate headquarters location:** This location. **Other U.S. locations:** Denver CO; San Francisco CA. **Listed on:** Privately held. **President/CEO:** Mark Williamson. **Number of employees nationwide:** 2,368.

AIR PRODUCTS & CHEMICALS, INC.
1423 Highway 225, Pasadena TX 77501. 713/477-6841. **Contact:** Human Resources. **World Wide Web address:** http://www.airproducts.com. **Description:** Manufactures specialty chemicals, industrial gases, and related equipment. **NOTE:** Please visit website to search for jobs and apply online. **Special programs:** Internships; Co-ops. **Corporate headquarters location:** Allentown PA. **Other area locations:** Statewide. **Other U.S. locations:** Nationwide. **International locations:** Worldwide. **Operations at this facility include:** This location manufactures polyurethane intermediates. **Listed on:** New York Stock Exchange. **Stock Exchange Symbol:** APD. **Number of employees worldwide:** 18,500.

AKZO NOBEL CATALYSTS
13000 Bay Park Road, Pasadena TX 77058. 281/474-2864. **Fax:** 281/474-0351. **Contact:** Carlea Thurman, Human Resources. **World Wide Web address:** http://www.akzonobel-catalysts.com. **Description:** Akzo Nobel is a worldwide manufacturer of chemicals, coatings, health care products, and fibers. Business activities are conducted in four units: The Chemicals Group produces polymer chemicals, rubber chemicals, catalysts, detergents, surfactants, functional chemicals, chlor-alkali, and industrial chemicals. The Coatings Group produces decorative coatings, car refinishes, industrial coatings, industrial wood finishes, aerospace finishes, automotive finishes, and resins. The Pharma Group includes ethical drugs, hospital supplies, nonprescription products, raw materials for the pharmaceuticals industry, generics, and veterinary products. The Fibers Group produces textile, industrial, and high-performance fibers, industrial nonwovens, and membranes for medical, technical, and industrial uses. **International locations:** Worldwide. **Operations at this facility include:** This location manufactures catalysts.

ALAMO CAFE
P.O. BOX 790721, San Antonio TX 78279-0721. 210/341-1336. **Fax:** 210/341-3036. **Contact:** Human Resources. **World Wide Web address:** http://www.alamocafe.com. **Description:** A family-style restaurant that serves both American and Mexican foods. **Corporate headquarters location:** This location. **Parent company:** Alamo Restaurants Inc.

ALAMO GROUP, INC.
P.O. Box 549, Seguin TX 78156-0549. 830/379-1480. **Physical address:** 1502 East Walnut, Seguin TX 78155. **Toll-free phone:** 800/882-5762. **Fax:** 830/379-4363. **Contact:** Gabrielle Garcia, Personnel Manager. **E-mail address:** info@alamo-

group.com. **World Wide Web address:** http://www.alamo-group.com. **Description:** A manufacturer of agricultural and industrial machinery. Founded 1969. **NOTE:** Please visit website to search for jobs and apply online. Online applications are preferred. Positions advertised include: Manufacturing Engineer. **Corporate headquarters location:** This location. **Other U.S. locations:** Sioux Falls SD; Holton KS; Indianola IA; Gibson City IL; Huntsville AL. **International locations:** England; France; the Netherlands; Canada; Australia. **Listed on:** New York Stock Exchange. **Stock exchange symbol:** ALG. **President/CEO:** Ronald A. Robinson.

ALAMO IRON WORKS, INC.
P.O. Box 231, San Antonio TX 78291. 210/223-6161. **Physical address:** 943 Coliseum Road, San Antonio TX 78219. **Toll-free phone:** 800/292-7817. **Fax:** 210/704-8409. **Contact:** Vice President of Human Resources. **Recorded jobline:** 210/704-8491. **E-mail address:** aiw@aiwnet.com. **World Wide Web address:** http://www.aiwnet.com. **Description:** Distributes industrial supplies and operates a foundry and a steel service center. **Positions advertised include:** Welder; Rebar Laborer; Driver; Fleet Mechanic. **Office hours:** Monday, Wednesday, Friday, 8:30 a.m. – 11:00 a.m.; 1:30 p.m. – 4:00 p.m. **Corporate headquarters location:** This location. **Other area locations:** Corpus Christi TX; Brownsville TX; San Angelo TX; El Paso TX; Houston TX. **Other U.S. locations:** Albuquerque NM. **Operations at this facility include:** Administration; Manufacturing; Sales. **Listed on:** Privately held.

ALBEMARLE CORPORATION
P.O. Box 2500, Pasadena TX 77501-2500. 713/740-1000. **Physical address:** 2500 North South Street, Pasadena TX 77503. **Fax:** 713/740-1600. **Contact:** Human Resources. **World Wide Web address:** http://www.albemarle.com. **Description:** Albemarle Corporation is a global supplier of specialty and performance chemicals that enhance consumer products. The company serves markets for petroleum and agricultural chemicals, detergents, polymers, electronics, and pharmaceuticals and is one of the world's leading producers of alpha olefins, bromine chemicals, and ibuprofen. **NOTE:** The company does not accept unsolicited resumes. **Corporate headquarters location:** Richmond VA. **Other U.S. locations:** Orangeburg SC Magnolia AR; Baton Rouge LA; Tyrone PA; Dayton OH. **International locations:** China; Singapore; Japan; France; Belgium; United Kingdom; Germany; Austria. **Operations at this facility include:** This location manufactures specialty chemicals for plastics manufacturing.

ALCATEL USA INC.
3400 West Plano Parkway, Suite 210, Plano TX 75075-5813. 972/519-3000. **Toll-free phone:** 800/252-2835. **Fax:** 800/561-4847. **Contact:** Human Resources. **World Wide Web address:** http://www.usa.alcatel.com. **Description:** Manufactures telecommunications equipment including fiber-optic transmission systems and optical networks. **NOTE:** Please visit website to search for jobs and apply online. **Positions advertised include:** Consulting Engineer; Systems Developing Engineer; Contracts Manager; Marketing Manager; Product Systems Engineer; Software Developer Engineer; Program/Project Management Technician; Vice President of Business Development; Auditor. **Corporate headquarters location:** This location. **Other U.S. locations:** Petaluma CA; Calabasas CA; Milpitas CA; Nogales AZ; Claremont NC; Raleigh NC; Reston VA. **Listed on:** New York Stock Exchange. **Stock exchange symbol:** ALA. **CEO:** Serge Tchuruk.

ALCOA (ALUMINUM COMPANY OF AMERICA)
P.O. Box 101, Point Comfort TX 77978. 361/987-2631. **Physical address:** State Highway 35, Point Comfort TX 77978. **Fax:** 361/987-6431. **Contact:** Human Resources. **World Wide Web address:** http://www.alcoa.com. **Description:** Engaged in all aspects of the aluminum industry including mining, refining, smelting, fabricating, and recycling. ALCOA also manufactures ceramic packaging for the semiconductor industry, alumina chemicals, plastic bottle closures, vinyl siding, packaging machinery, and electrical distribution systems for automobiles. **NOTE:** Please visit website to search for jobs and apply online. **Special programs:** Internships; Co-ops. **Corporate headquarters location:** Pittsburgh PA. **Other area locations:** Statewide. **Other U.S. locations:** Nationwide. **International locations:** Worldwide. **Operations at this facility include:** Manufacturing. **Listed on:** New York Stock Exchange. **Stock exchange symbol:** AA. **CEO:** Alain Belda. **Annual sales/revenues:** More than $22 billion. **Number of employees worldwide:** 120,000.

ALLERGAN, INC.
P.O. Box 2675, Waco TX 76702-2675. 254/666-3331. **Physical address:** 8301 Mars Drive, Waco TX 76712. **Fax:** 254/666-3011. **Contact:** Human Resources. **World Wide Web address:** http://www.allergan.com. **Description:** Develops, manufactures, and distributes prescription and nonprescription pharmaceutical products in the specialty fields of ophthalmology and dermatology. **NOTE:** Please visit website to search for jobs and apply online. **Positions advertised include:** Controller; Compliance Officer. **Special programs:** Internships. **Corporate headquarters location:** Irvine CA. **Listed on:** New York Stock Exchange. **Stock exchange symbol:** AGN. **President/CEO:** David E.I. Pyott. **Number of employees worldwide:** 5,200.

ALLIED SECURITY INC.
9027 North Gate Boulevard, Suite 110, Austin TX 78758. 512/836-8599. **Fax:** 512/836-8579. **Contact:** Human Resources. **World Wide Web address:** http://www.alliedsecurity.com. **Description:** One of the largest contract security officer companies in the nation. Allied Security provides loss prevention services to private businesses and government agencies. **NOTE:** Please visit website to fill out online application form. **Corporate headquarters location:** King of Prussia PA. **Other area locations:** Dallas TX; Houston TX; San Antonio TX. **Other U.S. locations:** Nationwide.

ALLIED SECURITY INC.
1635 NE Loop 410, Suite 206, San Antonio TX 78209. 210/829-1711. **Fax:** 210/829-1731. **Contact:** Human Resources. **World Wide Web address:** http://www.alliedsecurity.com. **Description:** One of the largest contract security officer companies in the nation. Allied Security provides loss prevention services to private businesses and government agencies. **NOTE:** Please visit website to fill out online application form. **Corporate headquarters location:** King of Prussia PA. **Other area locations:** Dallas TX; Houston TX; San Antonio TX. **Other U.S. locations:** Nationwide.

ALLIED VAUGHN
3694 Westchase Drive, Houston TX 77042. 713/266-4269. **Toll-free phone:** 800/394-4546. **Fax:** 713/266-9538. **Contact:** Human Resources. **E-mail address:** human.resources@alliedvaughn.com. **World Wide Web address:** http://www.alliedvaughn.com. **Description:** One of the nation's leading independent, multimedia manufacturing companies, offering CD-audio and CD-ROM mastering and replication; videocassette and audiocassette duplication; laser video disc recording; off-line and online video editing; motion picture film processing; film-to-tape and tape-to-film transfers; and complete finishing, packaging, warehousing, and fulfillment services. **NOTE:** Please visit website to view job listings. **Other area locations:** Irving TX. **Listed on:** Privately held.

ALLIED VAUGHN
6305 North O'Connor Road, Suite 111, Building 4, Irving TX 75039. 972/869-0100. **Toll-free phone:** 800/486-1539. **Fax:** 972/869-2117. **Contact:** Human Resources. **E-mail address:** human.resources@alliedvaughn.com. **World Wide Web address:** http://www.allied-digital.com. **Description:** One of the nation's leading independent multimedia manufacturing companies, offering CD-audio and CD-ROM mastering and replication; videocassette and audiocassette duplication; laser video disc recording; off-line and online video editing; motion picture film processing; film-to-tape and tape-to-film transfers; and complete finishing, packaging, warehousing, and fulfillment services. **NOTE:** Please visit website to view job listings. **Other area locations:** Houston TX. **Listed on:** Privately held.

AMARILLO COLLEGE
P.O. Box 447, Amarillo TX 79178-0001. 806/371-5040. **Contact:** Human Resources. **World Wide Web address:** http://www.actx.edu/hr. **Description:** A two-year community college. Approximately 7,300 students are enrolled at this location. Amarillo College has three other campuses in Amarillo. **NOTE:** Please visit website to view job listings and to download application forms. Resumes are not accepted online; you must mail your resume. The Human Resources office is located at the Washington Street Campus, on the second floor of the Student Service Center, Suite 280. **Positions advertised include:** Instructor – Various Departments; Director of Human Resources; Director of Broadcasting Operations; Associate Director – Center for Continuing Healthcare Education; Dean of Student Services; Police Officer; Staff Assistant; Student Services and Outreach Representative; Senior Programmer/Analyst; Maintenance Mechanic.

AMARILLO GLOBE-NEWS
P.O. Box 2091, Amarillo TX 79166. 806/376-4488. **Fax:** 806/345-3370. **Contact:** Human Resources. **World Wide Web address:** http://www.amarillonet.com. **Description:** Publishes morning and afternoon daily papers. The Sunday edition has a circulation of approximately 74,000. **NOTE:** Human Resources phone is 806/345-3333.

AMARILLO NATIONAL BANK
P.O. Box 1, Amarillo TX 79105. 806/378-8000. **Physical address:** 410 South Taylor, Amarillo TX 79101. **Fax:** 806/378-8066. **Contact:** Personnel. **World Wide Web address:** http://www.anb.com. **Description:** A full-service bank with 12 locations. Services include intra-bank funds transfers, mortgages, and online banking. **Corporate headquarters location:** This location. **Other area locations:** Statewide.

AMERADA HESS CORPORATION
P.O. Box 2040 Houston TX 77252. 713/609-5000. **Physical address:** One Allen Center, 500 Dallas Street, Houston TX 77002. **Contact:** Barbara Dickey. **World Wide Web address:** http://www.hess.com. **Description:** An international oil and gas exploration company. **Corporate headquarters location:** New York NY. **International locations:** Worldwide. **Operations at this facility include:** Administration. **Listed on:** New York Stock Exchange. **Stock exchange symbol:** AHC.

AMERICAN AIRLINES PUBLISHING
4255 Amon Carter Boulevard, MD 4255, Fort Worth TX 76155. 817/967-1804. **Fax:** 817/967-1571. **Contact:** Halli Adams. **World Wide Web address:** http://www.americanwaymag.com. **Description:** Publishes the in-flight magazine American Way. **Office hours:** Monday – Friday, 9:00 a.m. – 4:45 p.m.

AMERICAN BANK
P.O. Box 6469, Corpus Christi TX 78466-6469. 361/992-9901. **Recorded jobline:** 361/653-5391. **Contact:** Human Resources. **E-mail address:** internetbanking@americanbank.com. **World Wide Web address:** http://www.americanbank.com. **Description:** A full-service bank with 10 locations. This location is its corporate office and main branch. Founded in 1971. **Positions advertised include:** E-Branch Officer; Teller Supervisor; Teller. **Other area locations include:** Port Aransas TX; Austin TX.

AMERICAN ELECTRIC POWER (AEP)
P.O. Box 660164, Dallas TX 75266-0164. 214/777-1000. **Physical address:** 1616 Woodall Rogers Freeway, Dallas TX 75202. **Contact:** Human Resources. **World Wide Web address:** http://www.aep.com. **Description:** An electric utility company serving approximately 4.8 million customers in the United States and over 4 million customers outside the United States. **NOTE:** Please visit website to search for jobs and apply online. Send resumes to corporate office at American Electric Power, 1 Riverside Plaza, Columbus OH 43215; fax is 614/716-1864. **Special programs:** Internships. **Corporate headquarters location:** Columbus OH. **Other U.S. locations:** Southern U.S. **Listed on:** New York Stock Exchange. **Stock exchange symbol:** AEP. **Number of employees nationwide:** 21,000.

AMERICAN EXCELSIOR COMPANY
850 Avenue H East, Arlington TX 76011. 817/385-3500. **Toll-free phone:** 800/777-7645. **Fax:** 817/649-7816. **Contact:** Marci Webb, Director of Human Resources. **E-mail address:** mwebb@americanexcelsior.com. **World Wide Web address:** http://www.amerexcel.com. **Description:** A packaging company engaged in the production of environmentally sound, water-soluble packaging materials, foam protective shipping pads, fabricated polyurethane foam, shaped packaging, and other related packaging products. **Corporate headquarters location:** This location. **Other U.S. locations:** WI; AL; WA; MN; TN; IL; OH; NC; GA. **President/CEO:** Terry Sadowski. **Number of employees nationwide:** 650.

AMERICAN EXPRESS FINANCIAL ADVISORS
9442 Capital of Texas Highway North, Plaza One Suite 800, Austin TX 78759. 512/346-5400. **Fax:** 512/338-1705. **Contact:** Katie Froelich. **E-mail address:** advisor.resumes@aexp.com. **World Wide Web address:** http://www.americanexpress.com/advisors. **Description:** Offers financial planning, annuities, mutual funds, insurance, investment certificates, and institutional investment advisory trust, tax preparation, and retail securities brokerage services. **NOTE:** Reach listed contact at Ext. 320. Learn more about financial advisor careers at http://americanexpress.com/advisorcareers, **Corporate headquarters location:** Minneapolis MN. **Other U.S. locations:** Nationwide. **Parent company:** American Express Company (New York NY).

AMERICAN FLAT GLASS DISTRIBUTORS, INC. (AFGD)
1201 Highway 67 East, Alvarado TX 76009. 817/477-1144. **Toll-free phone:** 800/777-5171. **Fax:** 817/783-7123. **Contact:** Doris Williams, Human Resources. **World Wide Web address:** http://www.afgd.com. **Description:** Specializes in architectural insulated glass units and custom tempering. AFGD manufactures a complete line of

insulated glass units for commercial and residential applications. The product line includes clear, tint, and reflective glass; wire glass; and equipment for the handling, storage, and transportation of glass. There are 50 AFGD locations throughout North America. **Corporate headquarters location:** Atlanta GA. **Other area locations:** Austin TX; Houston TX; San Antonio TX. **Other U.S. locations:** Nationwide. **International locations:** Canada. **Subsidiaries include:** AFGD Canada. **Parent company:** AFG Industries, Inc. **Operations at this facility include:** Manufacturing; Sales. **Listed on:** Privately held. **President:** John Stilwell.

AMERICAN FLAT GLASS DISTRIBUTORS, INC. (AFGD)
3822 Airport Boulevard, Austin TX 78722. 512/474-2375. **Fax:** 512/474-5821. **Contact:** Human Resources. **World Wide Web address:** http://www.afgd.com. **Description:** Specializes in architectural insulated glass units and custom tempering. AFGD manufactures a complete line of insulated glass units for commercial and residential applications. The product line includes clear, tint, and reflective glass; wire glass; and equipment for the handling, storage, and transportation of glass. There are 50 AFGD locations throughout North America. **Corporate headquarters location:** Atlanta GA. **Other area locations:** Austin TX; Houston TX; San Antonio TX. **Other U.S. locations:** Nationwide. **International locations:** Canada. **Subsidiaries include:** AFGD Canada. **Parent company:** AFG Industries, Inc. **Operations at this facility include:** Manufacturing; Sales. **Listed on:** Privately held. **President:** John Stilwell.

AMERICAN FLAT GLASS DISTRIBUTORS, INC. (AFGD)
10750 Sentinel Drive, San Antonio TX 78217. 210/653-7790. **Toll-free phone:** 800/727-7790. **Fax:** 210/655-3945. **Contact:** Human Resources. **World Wide Web address:** http://www.afgd.com. **Description:** Specializes in architectural insulated glass units and custom tempering. AFGD manufactures a complete line of insulated glass units for commercial and residential applications. The product line includes clear, tint, and reflective glass; wire glass; and equipment for the handling, storage, and transportation of glass. There are 50 AFGD locations throughout North America. **Corporate headquarters location:** Atlanta GA. **Other area locations:** Austin TX; Houston TX; San Antonio TX. **Other U.S. locations:** Nationwide. **International locations:** Canada. **Subsidiaries include:** AFGD Canada. **Parent company:** AFG Industries, Inc. **Operations at this facility include:** Manufacturing; Sales. **Listed on:** Privately held. **President:** John Stilwell.

AMERICAN FLAT GLASS DISTRIBUTORS, INC. (AFGD)
5901 Milwee Street, Houston TX 77292-4767. 713/686-2509. **Toll-free phone:** 800/695-2343. **Fax:** 713/686-7650. **Contact:** Human Resources. **World Wide Web address:** http://www.afgd.com. **Description:** Specializes in architectural insulated glass units and custom tempering. AFGD manufactures a complete line of insulated glass units for commercial and residential applications. The product line includes clear, tint, and reflective glass; wire glass; and equipment for the handling, storage, and transportation of glass. There are 50 AFGD locations throughout North America. **Corporate headquarters location:** Atlanta GA. **Other area locations:** Austin TX; Houston TX; San Antonio TX. **Other U.S. locations:** Nationwide. **International locations:** Canada. **Subsidiaries include:** AFGD Canada. **Parent company:** AFG Industries, Inc. **Operations at this facility include:** Manufacturing; Sales. **Listed on:** Privately held. **President:** John Stilwell.

AMERICAN GENERAL CORPORATION
P.O. Box 3247, Houston TX 77253. 713/522-1111. **Physical address:** 2929 Allen Parkway, Houston TX 77019-2155. **Contact:** Human Resources. **World Wide Web address:** http://www.agc.com. **Description:** One of the largest public insurance companies in the United States. Other services include mortgage loans, real estate investment and development, investment counseling, and management and distribution of mutual funds. **NOTE:** Please visit website to search for jobs and apply online. **Positions advertised include:** Administrative Assistant; Technical Analyst – Data Security; Lotus Notes Systems Administrator; Processing Technician; Fund Accountant; Sarbanes-Oxley Accountant; Fitness Specialist; Consulting Business Analyst; AWD System Administrator; Project Manager; Customer Service Representative. **Corporate headquarters location:** This location. **Subsidiaries include:** American General Annuities; American General Life Company. **Parent company:** AIG. **Listed on:** New York Stock Exchange. **Stock exchange symbol:** AIG.

AMERICAN HEART ASSOCIATION (AHA)
7272 Greenville Avenue, Dallas TX 75231. 214/373-6300. **Fax:** 214/706-1191. **Contact:** Human Resources Department. **E-mail address:** aharesume@heart.org. **World Wide Web address:** http://www.americanheart.org. **Description:** One of the oldest and largest national, nonprofit, voluntary health associations dedicated to reducing disability and death from cardiovascular diseases and stroke. AHA-funded research has yielded such discoveries as CPR, bypass surgery, pacemakers, artificial heart valves, microsurgery, life-extending drugs, and new surgical techniques to repair heart defects. The AHA's interactive public education programs emphasize quitting smoking; controlling high blood pressure; eating a low-fat; low-cholesterol diet; and being physically active. The AHA also teaches the warning signs of heart attack and stroke and what to do if they occur. The association trains about 5 million Americans per year in emergency care procedures. Founded in 1924. **NOTE:** Please visit website to view job listings. **Positions advertised include:** National Senior Account Manager – Healthcare; Senior Bilingual Editor/Writer; Manager – Food Certification Communications; Accounts Payable Supervisor; Staff Accountant; Senior Financial Systems Analyst; Director – ECC Healthcare Markets; Project Coordinator – Emergency Cardiovascular Care Programs; Director – Foundation Giving; Developer – Java, Web, VB; E-Business Architect; Marketing Information Consultant; Director of Healthcare Strategy; Virtual Customer Manager. **Special programs:** Internships. **Corporate headquarters location:** This location. **Other U.S. locations:** Nationwide. **CEO:** M. Cass Wheeler.

AMERICAN HOMESTAR CORPORATION
2450 South Shore Boulevard, Suite 300, League City TX 77573. 281/334-9700. **Fax:** 281/334-9737. **Contact:** Personnel. **E-mail address:** marketing@hstr.com. **World Wide Web address:** http://www.americanhomestar.com. **Description:** Designs, manufactures, and sells houses throughout the southwestern United States. Founded 1971. **Corporate headquarters location:** This location. **Other U.S. locations:** OK; LA; NM; CO.

AMERICAN NATIONAL INSURANCE COMPANY
One Moody Plaza, Galveston TX 77550. 409/763-4661. **Fax:** 409/766-6417. **Contact:** Human Resources. **World Wide Web address:** http://www.american-national.com. **Description:** A leading insurance company that, directly and through its subsidiaries, offers a broad line of insurance coverage including individual life, health, and annuities; group life and health; and credit insurance. **NOTE:** Please visit website to view job listings. Human Resources phone is 409/766-6090. **Positions advertised include:** Lead Data Security Analyst; Senior Programmer Analyst; VUL Field Wholesaler; Senior Plan Administrator; Information Systems Auditor; Internal Auditor. **Corporate headquarters location:** This location. **Subsidiaries include:** American National Property and Casualty Insurance Company; Standard Life and Accident Insurance Company. **Listed on:** NASDAQ. **Stock exchange symbol:** ANAT.

AMERICAN PHYSICIANS SERVICE GROUP, INC. (APS)
1301 South Capital of Texas Highway, Suite C-300, Austin TX 78746. 512/328-0888. **Fax:** 512/314-4398. **Contact:** Human Resources. **World Wide Web address:** http://www.amph.com. **Description:** A management and financial services firm with subsidiaries and affiliates that provide medical malpractice insurance services for doctors, brokerage and investment services to institutions and individuals, lithotripsy services in 34 states, refractive vision surgery, and dedicated care facilities for Alzheimer's patients. **Corporate headquarters location:** This location. **Subsidiaries include:** APS Financial Corporation; AMPC Insurance Services; American Physicians Insurance Exchange. **Listed on:** NASDAQ. **Stock exchange symbol:** AMPH.

AMERICAN RED CROSS
3642 East Houston Street, San Antonio TX 78219. 210/224-5151. **Toll-free phone:** 800/775-6803. Fax: 210/226-9973. **Contact:** Human Resources. **E-mail address:** infosatx@usa.redcross.org. **World Wide Web address:** http://www.saredcross.org. **Description:** A humanitarian organization that aids disaster victims, gathers blood for crisis distribution, trains individuals to respond to emergencies, educates individuals on various diseases, and raises funds for other charitable establishments. **NOTE:** Please visit website to view job listings and to fill out online job application. **Positions advertised include:** Instructor; Associate Director of Financial Development. **Corporate headquarters location:** Washington D.C.

AMERICAN RED CROSS
908 West Pine Avenue, Orange TX 77630. 409/883-2322. **Fax:** 409/883-8316. **Contact:** Human Resources Department. **E-mail address:** martinb@usa.redcross.org. **World Wide Web address:** http://orangecountytx.redcross.org. **Description:** A humanitarian organization that aids disaster victims, gathers blood for crisis distribution, trains individuals to respond to emergencies, educates individuals on various diseases, and raises funds for other charitable establishments.

AMERICAN RICE, INC. (ARI)
P.O. Box 2587, Houston TX 77252-2587. 281/272-8800. **Physical address:** 10700 North Freeway, Suite 800, Houston TX 77037. **Contact:** Human Resources. **World Wide Web address:** http://www.amrice.com. **Description:** An international agribusiness company active in all phases of rice milling, processing, and marketing. ARI markets parboiled rice, white rice, instant rice, brown rice, and rice mixes, primarily under proprietary, trademarked brand names throughout the world. ARI operates rice-processing facilities in the United States, Jamaica, and Haiti. Founded in 1987. **Office hours:** Monday – Friday, 8:00 a.m. – 5:00 p.m. **Corporate headquarters location:** This location.

AMERICREDIT CORPORATION
801 Cherry Street, Suite 3900, Fort Worth TX 76102. 817/302-7000. **Toll-free phone:** 866/411-HR4U. **Fax:** 817/302-7878. **Contact:** Personnel. **World Wide Web address:** http://www.americredit.com. **Description:** A national consumer finance company specializing in the purchasing, securitizing, and servicing of automobile loans. **Position advertised include:** Centralized Funding Analyst; Credit Risk Analyst. **Corporate headquarters location:** This location. **Other U.S. locations:** Nationwide. **Listed on:** New York Stock Exchange. **Stock exchange symbol:** ACF.

AMERIMAX BUILDING PRODUCTS, INC.
5208 Tennyson Parkway, Suite 100, Plano TX 75024. 469/366-3200. **Toll-free phone:** 800/258-6295. **Fax:** 469/366-3260. **Contact:** Human Resources Manager. **World Wide Web address:** http://www.amerimaxbp.com. **Description:** Fabricates building products of aluminum, steel, and vinyl. The company sells its products to manufacturers of recreational vehicles and prefabricated housing, retail building products suppliers, construction firms, and others. Amerimax's facilities include 15 fabrication plants located throughout the United States. Founded in 1954. **Corporate headquarters location:** This location. **Other area locations:** Mansfield TX. **Other U.S. locations:** CA; PA; IN; AR; CO; NV; OR; GA. **Operations at this facility include:** Administration; Manufacturing; Research and Development; Sales.

AMERIPATH NORTH TEXAS.
4300 Alpha Road, Dallas TX 75244. 972/341-5800. **Contact:** Human Resources. **World Wide Web address:** http://www.ameripath.com. **Description:** An outsourcing firm providing diagnostic and medical testing. **NOTE:** Resumes may also be mailed to Ms. Sutton at 7289 Garden Road, Suite 200, Rivera Beach, FL 33404. **Positions advertised include:** Pathologist; Quality Assurance Software Analyst; Dermapathologist; Cytotechnologist; Histotechnologist; Territory Sales Manager. **Corporate headquarters location:** FL. **Other area locations:** San Antonio TX; Lubbock TX. **Other U.S. locations:** FL; WI; CA; NY, OH, AL. **Listed on:** Privately held.

AMFELS, INC.
P.O. Box 3107, Brownsville TX 78523-3107. 956/831-8220. **Physical address:** 20000 South Highway 48, Brownsville TX 75821. **Fax:** 956/831-6220. **Contact:** Human Resources. **World Wide Web address:** http://www.keppelfelsamfels.com. **Description:** A shipyard that fabricates steel. **Other area locations:** Houston TX. **Other U.S. locations:** New Providence NJ. **International locations:** Singapore; Brazil; Azerbaijan; Norway; Bulgaria; India; Vietnam; China; Australia; the Netherlands. **Parent company:** KeppelFELS.

AMR CORPORATION
4333 Amon Carter Boulevard, Fort Worth TX 76155. 817/963-1234. **Fax:** 817/967-9641. **Contact:** Human Resources. **World Wide Web address:** http://www.amrcorp.com. **Description:** Operates American Airlines, one of the largest airline carriers in the world. With its sister companies American Eagle and American Connection, American Airlines transports approximately 88 million passengers annually. It also has a partnership with British Airways. **NOTE:** In addition to its corporate headquarters, American Airlines has positions throughout airports and other offices in Texas. See website for listings and apply online. **Positions advertised include:** Application Development Manager; Financial Auditors; Commodity Managers; Editor – Spirit Magazine; Lead Call Center Engineer; Operations Research Consultant. **Listed on:** New York Stock Exchange. **Stock exchange symbol:** AMR. **Number of employees worldwide:** 90,000.

ANADARKO PETROLEUM CORPORATION
P.O. Box 1330, Houston TX 77251. 832/636-1000. **Physical address:** 1201 Lake Robbins Drive, The Woodlands TX 77380. **Contact:** Human Resources Department. **E-mail address:** employment@anadarko.com. **World Wide Web address:** http://www.anadarko.com. **Description:** Involved in the exploration and recovery of petroleum. **Corporate headquarters location:** This location. **Other U.S. locations:** Anchorage AK. **International locations:** Canada; United Kingdom; Tunisia; Algeria;

Oman; Qatar; Republic of Gabon. **Listed on:** New York Stock Exchange. **Stock exchange symbol:** APC. **CEO:** Jim Hackett.

ANALYSTS INTERNATIONAL CORPORATION (AIC)
7000 North Mopac Expressway, Suite 220, Austin TX 78731. 512/206-2700. **Toll-free phone:** 800/654-8194. **Fax:** 512/206-2720. **Contact:** Human Resources. **World Wide Web address:** http://www.analysts.com. **Description:** An international computer consulting firm. The company assists clients in developing systems in a variety of industries using diverse programming languages and software. Founded in 1966. **NOTE:** Please visit website to register, search for jobs, and apply online. **Positions advertised include:** Cisco Consultant. **Corporate headquarters location:** Minneapolis MN. **Other U.S. locations:** Nationwide. **International locations:** Canada; England. **Listed on:** NASDAQ. **Stock exchange symbol:** ANLY. **President/CEO:** Mike LaVelle.

ANALYSTS INTERNATIONAL CORPORATION (AIC)
3030 LBJ Freeway, Suite 820 LB52, Dallas TX 75234-7703. 972/243-2001. **Toll-free phone:** 800/800-8699. **Fax:** 972/243-7468. **Contact:** Human Resources. **World Wide Web address:** http://www.analysts.com. **Description:** An international computer consulting firm. The company assists clients in developing systems in a variety of industries using different programming languages and software. Founded in 1966. **NOTE:** Please visit website to register, search for jobs, and apply online. **Corporate headquarters location:** Minneapolis MN. **Other U.S. locations:** Nationwide. **International locations:** Canada; England. **Listed on:** NASDAQ. **Stock exchange symbol:** ANLY. **President/CEO:** Mike LaVelle.

ANALYSTS INTERNATIONAL CORPORATION (AIC)
2550 North Loop West, Suite 200, Houston TX 77092. 713/869-3420. **Toll-free phone:** 800/487-1881. **Fax:** 713/861-7933. **Contact:** Human Resources Department. **World Wide Web address:** http://www.analysts.com/houston. **Description:** An international computer consulting firm. The company assists clients in analyzing, designing, and developing systems using different programming languages and software. Founded in 1966. **NOTE:** Please visit website to register, search for jobs, and apply online. **Positions advertised include:** Access/Excel Developer. **Corporate headquarters location:** Minneapolis MN. **Other U.S. locations:** Nationwide. **International locations:** Canada; England. **Listed on:** NASDAQ. **Stock exchange symbol:** ANLY. **President/CEO:** Mike LaVelle.

ANCIRA ENTERPRISES INC.
6111 Bandera Road, San Antonio TX 78238-1643. 210/681-4900. **Contact:** Human Resources. **World Wide Web address:** http://www.ancira.com. **Description:** Sells new and used automobiles including Chevrolet, Subaru, and Volkswagen. This location also has a service, parts, and body shop. **Corporate headquarters location:** This location.

M.D. ANDERSON CANCER CENTER
P.O. Box 301402, Unit 629. Houston TX 77230-1402. **Physical address:** 1515 Holcombe Boulevard, Houston TX 77030. 713/792-6161. **Toll-free phone:** 800/392-1611. **Recorded jobline:** 713/792-8010. **Contact:** Human Resources. **World Wide Web address:** http://www.mdanderson.org. **Description:** Works to eliminate cancer and allied diseases by developing and maintaining integrated quality programs in patient care, research, education, and prevention. **NOTE:** Entry-level positions are offered. The Human Resources office is located at 2450 Holcombe Boulevard, Suite TMC 1.2176. Please visit website to search for jobs and apply online. **Positions advertised include:** Director – Information Security; Director – Chaplaincy & Pastoral Education; Clinical Investigation Technician; Pharmacy Technician; Pathology Assistant; Dispatcher; Bone Marrow Aspiration Technician; Editorial Assistant; Research Administrator; Legal Assistant; Electrician; Animal Technician. **Special programs:** Training. **Corporate headquarters location:** This location. **Parent company:** The University of Texas System. **Operations at this facility include:** Administration; Research and Development; Service. **Number of employees at this location:** 12,000.

ANDREW CORPORATION
2601 Telecom Parkway, Richardson TX 75082. 972/952-9700. **Fax:** 972/952-0000. **Contact:** Personnel Manager. **World Wide Web address:** http://www.andrew.com. **Description:** A manufacturer of telecommunications equipment including Earth station satellite, cellular, and microwave antennas, towers, shelters, cables, and associated equipment. **NOTE:** Please visit website to view job listings and apply online. **Special programs:** Internships. **Corporate headquarters location:** Orland Park IL. **Other area locations:** Irving TX; Carrollton TX; Dallas TX; McAllen TX; Euless TX; Richardson TX; Round Rock TX. **Other U.S. locations:** Nationwide. **International locations:** Worldwide. **Operations at this facility include:** Administration; Divisional Headquarters; Manufacturing; Regional Headquarters; Research and Development; Sales; Service. **Listed on:** NASDAQ. **Stock exchange symbol:** ANDW. **Number of employees nationwide:** 5,000.

ANDREWS & KURTH L.L.P.
600 Travis Street, Suite 4200, Houston TX 77002. 713/220-4200. **Fax:** 713/220-4285. **Contact:** Deborah Ganjavi, Human Resources Director. **E-mail address:** debbieganjavi@akllp.com. **World Wide Web address:** http://www.andrews-kurth.com. **Description:** A law firm. **NOTE:** Please visit website to search for jobs by category and apply online. Contact Human Resources at this location at 713/220-4174. **Positions advertised include:** Litigation Legal Secretary. **Special programs:** Summer Clerkship Programs. **Corporate headquarters location:** This location. **Other area locations:** Austin TX; Dallas TX; The Woodlands TX. **Other U.S. locations:** Los Angeles CA; Washington DC; New York NY. **International locations:** London England. **Operations at this facility include:** Administration.

ANGELO STATE UNIVERSITY
P.O. Box 11009, ASU Station, San Angelo TX 76909. 325/942-2168. **Physical address:** 2601 West Avenue North, San Angelo TX 76909. **Contact:** Office of Human Resources. **E-mail address:** laura.billings@angelo.edu. **World Wide Web address:** http://www.angelo.edu. **Description:** A state university offering 45 bachelor's degree and 21 master's degree programs. Angelo State University has an enrollment of approximately 6,300 students. Founded in 1976. **NOTE:** Please visit website to view job listings and access application forms. **Positions advertised include:** Assistant Professor – Various Departments; Head – Department of Computer Science; Head – Department of Physical Therapy; Physical Therapy Faculty; Professional Specialist; Director of Institutional Effectiveness; Assistant Director – Recreation and Intramurals; Assistant Manager of Infrastructure Services; Area Coordinator.

ANHEUSER-BUSCH, INC.
1800 West Loop South, Suite 1100, Houston TX 77027. 713/622-2400. **Fax:** 713/964-2180. **Contact:** Human Resources. **World Wide Web address:** http://www.anheuser-busch.com. **Description:** A brewer with a high-tech brewing process and high-speed packaging lines. Brand names include Budweiser, Michelob, and Busch beers. **NOTE:** Please visit website to search for jobs and apply online. **Positions advertised include:** Maintenance Supervisor; Quality Assurance Manager. **Corporate headquarters location:** St. Louis MO. **Parent company:** Anheuser-Busch Companies is a diverse company involved in the entertainment, brewing, baking, and manufacturing industries. Anheuser-Busch Companies is one of the largest domestic brewers, operating 13 breweries throughout the United States and distributing through over 900 independent wholesalers. Beer brands include Budweiser, Michelob, Busch, King Cobra, and O'Doul's nonalcoholic beverages. Related businesses include can manufacturing, paper printing, and barley malting. Anheuser-Busch Companies is also one of the largest operators of theme parks in the United States, with locations in Florida, Virginia, Texas, Ohio, and California. Through subsidiary Campbell Taggart Inc., Anheuser-Busch is one of the largest commercial baking companies in the United States, producing foods under the Colonial brand name, among others. Anheuser-Busch Companies also has various real estate interests.

ANHEUSER-BUSCH, INC.
775 Gellhorn Drive, Houston TX 77029. 713/675-2311. **Fax:** 713/678-3802. **Contact:** Human Resources. **World Wide Web address:** http://www.anheuser-buschbudweiser.com. **Description:** A brewer with a high-tech brewing process and high-speed packaging lines. Brand names include Budweiser, Michelob, and Busch beers. **NOTE:** Please visit website to search for jobs and apply online. **Positions advertised include:** Maintenance Supervisor; Quality Assurance Manager. **Corporate headquarters location:** St. Louis MO. **Parent company:** Anheuser-Busch Companies is a diverse company involved in the entertainment, brewing, baking, and manufacturing industries. Anheuser-Busch Companies is one of the largest domestic brewers, operating 13 breweries throughout the United States and distributing through over 900 independent wholesalers. Beer brands include Budweiser, Michelob, Busch, King Cobra, and O'Doul's nonalcoholic beverages. Related businesses include can manufacturing, paper printing, and barley malting. Anheuser-Busch Companies is also one of the largest operators of theme parks in the United States, with locations in Florida, Virginia, Texas, Ohio, and California. Through subsidiary Campbell Taggart Inc., Anheuser-Busch is one of the largest commercial baking companies in the United States, producing foods under the Colonial brand name, among others. Anheuser-Busch Companies also has various real estate interests.

ANTHONY NAK FINE JEWELRY
800 Brazos Street, Suite 300, Austin TX 78701. 512/454-7029. Fax: 512/454-7031. **Contact:** Human Resources. **E-mail address:** retail@anthonynak.com. **World Wide Web address:** http://www.anthonynak.com. **Description:** A specialty art jewelry store known for its appeal to movie stars and other high-profile people. **NOTE:** Apply during store hours or mail resume. **Office hours:** Tuesday, Thursday, Saturday, 10:00 a.m. to 6:00 p.m.

APAC TEXAS, INC.
TEXAS BITULITHIC DIVISION
P.O. Box 224048, Dallas TX 75222-4048. 214/741-3531. **Physical address:** 2121 Irving Boulevard, Dallas TX 75207. **Fax:** 214/742-3540. **Contact:** Human Resources. **World Wide Web address:** http://www.apac.com. **Description:** A general contracting company specializing in concrete and asphalt paving work. **NOTE:** The president at this location is Stephen B. Robertson. Please visit website to search for jobs and apply online. **Positions advertised include:** Office Assistant. **Corporate headquarters location:** Alpharetta GA. **Other area locations:** Beaumont TX. **Other U.S. locations:** Southern and Southeastern U.S. **Parent company:** Ashland. **Listed on:** New York Stock Exchange. **Stock exchange symbol:** ASH.

APAC TEXAS, INC.
TROTTI AND THOMSON DIVISION
P.O. Box 20779, Beaumont TX 77720-0779. 409/866-1444. **Physical address:** 12907 U.S. Highway 90, Beaumont TX 77713. **Contact:** Human Resources. **World Wide Web address:** http://www.apac.com. **Description:** A general contracting company specializing in concrete and asphalt paving work. **NOTE:** The president at this location is Stephen R. Koonce. Please visit website to search for jobs and apply online. **Corporate headquarters location:** Alpharetta GA. **Other area locations:** Dallas TX. **Other U.S. locations:** Southern and Southeastern U.S. **Parent company:** Ashland. **Listed on:** New York Stock Exchange. **Stock exchange symbol:** ASH.

APACHE CORPORATION
2000 Post Oak Boulevard, Suite 100, Houston TX 77056-4400. 713/296-6000. **Contact:** Human Resources. **World Wide Web address:** http://www.apachecorp.com. **Description:** An independent oil and gas exploration and production company that owns large reserves of oil and natural gas. Apache Corporation's domestic operations are located primarily in the Gulf of Mexico; the Gulf Coast of Texas and Louisiana; the Permian Basin of West Texas and New Mexico (almost half of the company's daily crude oil production comes from this region); the Anadarko Basin of Oklahoma; and in the Green River Basin of the Rocky Mountains. Founded in 1954. **Positions advertised include:** Senior Treasury Assistant; Production Services Supervisor; Desktop Support Analyst; Community Affairs Coordinator. **Corporate headquarters location:** This location. **Other U.S. locations:** Tulsa OK. **International locations:** Buenos Aires Argentina; West Perth Australia; Alberta Canada; Beijing China; Cairo Egypt; Warsaw Poland; Aberdeen United Kingdom. **Listed on:** New York Stock Exchange. **Stock exchange symbol:** APA. **President/CEO:** Raymond Plank.

APPLE COMPUTER, INC.
2420 Ridgepoint Drive, Austin TX 78754. 512/674-2000. **Contact:** Employment. **World Wide Web address:** http://www.apple.com. **Description:** Apple Computer manufactures personal computers and computer-related products for home, business, scientific, industrial, professional, and educational use. **NOTE:** Please visit https://jobs.apple.com to search for jobs and apply online. **Positions advertised include:** Inside Software Sales Account Executive; K12 Education Inside Account Executive; Product Administration Specialist; Professional Video Technical Support Representative; Senior Tax Accountant. **Special programs:** Internships. **Corporate headquarters location:** Cupertino CA. **Operations at this facility include:** This location offers sales and technical support to companies and educational institutions. **Listed on:** NASDAQ. **Stock exchange symbol:** AAPL.

APPLIED BIOSYSTEMS
13215 North Promenade Boulevard, Stafford TX 77477. 281/340-6200. **Fax:** 281/340-6210. **Contact:** Human Resources. **World Wide Web address:** http://www.appliedbiosystems.com. **Description:** Manufactures products for genetic analysis, molecular agriculture, and human and microbial identification. **NOTE:** Please visit website to search for jobs. **Corporate headquarters location:** Foster City CA. **Listed on:** New York Stock Exchange. **Stock exchange symbol:** ABI.

AQUENT
8140 North Mopac, Building I Suite 150, Austin TX 78759. 512/442-0992. **Fax:** 512/442-2462. **Contact:** Human Resources. **World Wide Web address:** http://www.aquent.com. **Description:** Engaged in software consulting, training, and

staffing. Founded 1986. **Corporate headquarters location:** Boston MA. **Other area locations:** Dallas TX; Houston TX. **Other U.S. locations:** Nationwide. **International locations:** Worldwide. **Operations at this facility include:** This office is part of the Marketing and Creative Services division.

ARAMCO SERVICES COMPANY
P.O. Box 4530, Houston TX 77210-4530. 713/432-4000. **Physical address:** 9009 West Loop South, Houston TX 77002. **Fax:** 713/432-4600. **Contact:** Personnel. **World Wide Web address:** http://www.aramcoservices.com. **Description:** Provides support services to its parent company, Saudi Aramco, one of the world's leading producers and exporters of oil and gas. **NOTE:** Please visit website to view job listings, submit resume online, and download application form. **Positions advertised include:** Information Technology Implementation Specialists. **Corporate headquarters location:** This location. **Other U.S. locations:** Washington D.C. **Subsidiaries include:** Saudi Petroleum International, Inc; Aramco Associated Company; Saudi Refining, Inc; Aramco Training Services Company; Aramco Financial Services Company; Motiva Enterprises LLC. **Parent company:** Saudi Aramco. **Operations at this facility include:** Service. **Listed on:** Privately held. **Number of employees nationwide:** 450.

ARLINGTON MEMORIAL HOSPITAL
800 West Randol Mill Road, Arlington TX 76012. 817/548-6100. **Contact:** Human Resources. **World Wide Web address:** http://www.texashealth.org. **Description:** A 357-bed acute care hospital with more than 2,500 physician, staff and volunteers. **NOTE:** Apply online at the website. **Parent company:** Texas Health Resources.

ARMBRUST & BROWN L.L.P.
100 Congress Avenue, Suite 1300, Austin TX 78701-2744. 512/435-2300. **Fax:** 512/435-2360. **Contact:** Human Resources Department. **World Wide Web address:** http://www.abaustin.com. **Description:** A law firm specializing in real estate and product liability law.

ARROW ELECTRONICS, INC.
6340 International Parkway, Plano TX 75093. 972/380-6464. **Toll-free phone:** 800/777-2776. **Contact:** Human Resources. **World Wide Web address:** http://www.arrow.com. **Description:** A distributor of electronic components, systems, and related items through a network in North America, Europe, and Asia. The company operates 150 marketing facilities, 10 primary distribution centers, and over 4,000 remote computer terminals that supply components to about 125,000 original equipment manufacturers and commercial customers. Semiconductors account for more than half of Arrow Schweber's sales. **NOTE:** Please visit website to search for jobs and apply online. Submit resumes to the corporate office at 50 Marcus Drive, Melville NY 11747; phone is 631/847-2000. **Corporate headquarters location:** Melville NY. **Subsidiaries include:** Arrow Electronics Components Group; Arrow/Zeus Electronics; Marubun/Arrow USA, LLC. **Listed on:** New York Stock Exchange. **Stock exchange symbol:** ARW.

ARMSTRONG WOOD PRODUCTS
16803 Dallas Parkway, Addison TX 75001. 214/887-2000. **Contact:** Human Resources. **World Wide Web address:** http://www.armstrong.com **Description:** Manufactures hardwood dimension and flooring. Brand names include Bruce, Hartco, and Robbins flooring and cabinets. **NOTE:** This company has several locations throughout Texas. See its website for locations, job listings and application information. **Corporate headquarters location:** Lancaster PA. **Listed on:** NASDAQ. **Stock exchange symbol:** ACKH. **Number of employee worldwide:** 15,200.

THE ART INSTITUTE OF DALLAS
2 North Park East, 8080 Park Lane, Suite 100, Dallas TX 75231. 214/692-8080. **Toll-free phone:** 800/275-4243. **Fax:** 214/361-0178. **Contact:** Human Resources. **E-mail address:** aidjobs@aii.edu. **World Wide Web address:** http://www.aid.aii.edu. **Description:** A two-year accredited institute with associate degree programs in art, fashion, photography, interior design, and music and video production. **NOTE:** View job listings and apply online. **Positions advertised include:** Animation Instructor; Assistant Director of Admissions; Digital Audio Instructor; Director of Residential Life and Housing. **Parent company:** Art Institutes International.

ASARCO INC.
P.O. Box 1111, El Paso TX 79999-1111. 915/541-1800. **Physical address:** 2301 West Paisano Drive, El Paso TX 79922. **Fax:** 915/541-1866. **Contact:** Human Resources. **World Wide Web address:** http://www.asarco.com. **Description:** Asarco is one of the world's leading producers of nonferrous metals, primarily copper, lead, zinc, and silver, from its own mines and through its interest in Southern Peru Copper Corporation. Asarco also produces specialty chemicals and construction aggregates and provides environmental services. Asarco's copper operations consist of its Mission and Ray mines in Arizona, smelters in Hayden AZ and El Paso TX, and a refinery in Amarillo TX. In Missouri, the company operates an integrated lead circuit consisting of West Fork and Sweetwater mines, which provide over 90 percent of the feed for the nearby Glover smelter and refinery. The Tennessee mines division accounts for 57 percent of the total zinc concentrates produced by the company. The remaining 43 percent is produced as a coproduct at the West Fork and Sweetwater lead mines in Missouri and at the Leadville mine in Colorado. **Corporate headquarters location:** Phoenix AZ. **International locations:** Australia; Mexico; Peru. **Operations at this facility include:** This location smelts copper. **Parent Company:** Grupo Mexico S.A. de C.V.

ASHBROOK CORPORATION
11600 East Hardy Road, Houston TX 77093. 281/449-0322. **Toll-free phone:** 800/362-9041. **Fax:** 281/449-1324. **Contact:** Human Resources. **World Wide Web address:** http://www.ashbrookcorp.com. **Description:** Manufactures wastewater treatment equipment and dewatering devices for sanitation plants.

ASPEN TECHNOLOGY, INC.
1293 Eldridge Parkway, Houston TX 77077. 281/584-1000. **Fax:** 281/584-4329. **Contact:** Human Resources. **World Wide Web address:** http://www.aspentech.com. **Description:** Aspen Technology, Inc. supplies computer-aided chemical engineering software to the chemical, petroleum, pharmaceutical, metal, mineral, food product, consumer product, and utility industries. **NOTE:** Please visit website to search for jobs and apply online. **Positions advertised include:** Director of Oil and Gas Solutions; Human Resources Generalist; Human Resource Manager; Business Operations Manager; Industry Consultant – Petroleum; Marketing Coordinator; Strategic Account Manager; Territory Account Manager. **Corporate headquarters location:** Cambridge MA. **Other U.S. locations:** CA; NJ; OHL CO; DE; MD; WA. **International locations:** Worldwide. **Operations at this facility include:** This location develops software. **Listed on:** NASDAQ. **Stock exchange symbol:** AZPN. **President/CEO:** David L. McQuillin. **Number of employees worldwide:** 1,850.

ASSOCIATED AIRCRAFT SUPPLY CO., INC.
6020 Cedar Springs Road, P.O. Box 35788, Dallas TX 75235-5788. 214/331-4381. **Toll-free phone:** 800/369-3212. **Fax:** 214/339-9840. **Contact:** Tommy DeRossett, Human Resources. **World Wide Web address:** http://www.associated-aircraft.com. **Description:** A distributor of aircraft parts and machinery. Products include switches, relays, and circuit breakers. **Corporate headquarters location:** This location.

ASSOCIATED BUILDING SERVICES COMPANY
1910 Napoleon Street, Houston TX 77003. 713/844-7800. **Fax:** 713/621-1429. **Contact:** Human Resources. **E-mail address:** resumes@abslink.com. **World Wide Web address:** http://www.abslink.com. **Description:** One of the largest facility maintenance contractors in the nation. Founded 1945. **NOTE:** Contact the hiring office at 713/844-7884. **Positions advertised include:** Janitor; Supervisor; Administrative Personnel; Sales Personnel; Project Manager; Branch Manager; District Manager; Operations Manager. **Corporate headquarters location:** This location. **Other area locations:** Dallas TX; The Woodlands TX; Austin TX; San Antonio TX. **Other U.S. locations:** WA; OR; CO; TN; AZ; VA.

ATLAS MATCH LLC
P.O. Box 1227, Euless TX 76039. 817/354-7474. **Physical address:** 1801 South Airport Circle, Euless TX 76040. **Toll-free phone:** 800/628-2426. **Fax:** 817/354-7478. **Contact:** Human Resources. **World Wide Web address:** http://www.atlasmatch.com. **Description:** Manufactures a wide variety of matchbooks with advertisements. Founded 1960.

ATMOS ENERGY CORPORATION
P.O. Box 650205, Dallas TX 75265-0205. 972/934-9227. **Fax:** 972/855-4039. **Contact:** Manager of Compensation and Employment. **E-mail address:** employment@atmosenergy.com. **World Wide Web address:** http://www.atmosenergy.com. **Description:** Distributes natural gas and propane. **Corporate headquarters location:** This location. **Other U.S. locations:** CO; KY; LA; KS. **Subsidiaries include:** Energas; Greeley Gas; Trans Louisiana Gas; Western Kentucky Gas. **Operations at this facility include:** Administration. **Listed on:** New York Stock Exchange. **Stock exchange symbol:** ATO. President/CEO: Robert W. Best. **Number of employees nationwide:** 2,900.

ATOFINA CHEMICAL
2231 Haden Road, Houston TX 77015. 713/455-1211. **Fax:** 713/450-6773. **Contact:** Resources Manager. **World Wide Web address:** http://www.atofinachemicals.com. **Description:** A chemical manufacturer with products that include polymers, fluorochemicals, carbons, and specialty chemicals. **Corporate headquarters location:** Philadelphia PA. **Other area locations:** Beaumont TX; Crosby TX. **Other U.S. locations:** AL; KY; MN; CT; TN; MI; WA. **International locations:** Canada. **Parent company:** Atofina. President/CEO: Jean-Pierre Seeuws. **Number of employees nationwide:** 2,600.

ATOFINA PETROCHEMICALS, INC.
P.O. Box 849, Port Arthur TX 77641-0849. 409/962-4421. **Physical address:** Highway 366 32nd Street Port Arthur TX 77642. **Contact:** Human Resources. **World Wide Web address:** http://www.petrochemicals.atofina.com. **Description:** Explores for crude oil and natural gas; markets natural gas; refines, supplies, transports, and markets petroleum products; manufactures and markets specialty chemicals, primarily petrochemicals and plastics including polypropylene, polystyrene, styrene monomer, high-density polyethylene, and aromatics; licenses certain chemical processes; and manufactures and markets paints and coatings.

AT&T BUSINESS SOLUTIONS
6100 Bandera Road, Suite 505, San Antonio TX 78238. 210/520-7878. **Fax:** 210/520-7881. **Contact:** Human Resources. **World Wide Web address:** http://www.att.com/hr/gvtsol.html. **Description:** AT&T Business Solutions (formerly GRC International) creates large-scale, decision-support systems and software engineering environments; applies operations research and mathematical modeling to business and management systems; and implements advanced database technology. GRC International also provides studies and analysis capabilities for policy development and planning; modeling and simulation of hardware and software used in real-time testing of sensor, weapon, and battlefield management command, control, and communication systems; and testing and evaluation. GRC International's services are offered primarily to government and commercial customers. **NOTE:** Job listings by location can be found at http://www.att.hire.com. **Corporate headquarters location:** Vienna VA. **Other U.S. locations:** Nationwide. **Operations at this facility include:** This location is involved in technical research. **Parent company:** AT&T Corporation. **Listed on:** New York Stock Exchange. **Stock exchange symbol:** T.

JOHN ATWOOD LAW OFFICE
3500 Oak Lawn Avenue Suite 400, Dallas TX 75219. 214/523-9520. **Contact:** Personnel Department. **Description:** A law firm that specializes in corporate, real estate, administrative, and taxation law.

AUSTIN AMERICAN-STATESMAN
P.O. Box 670, Austin TX 78767. 512/445-3709. **Physical address:** 305 South Congress Avenue, Austin TX 78704. **Fax:** 512/445-3883. **Recorded jobline:** 512/416-5700 Ext. 5621. **Contact:** Personnel Director. **E-mail address:** aa-sjobs@statesman.com. **World Wide Web address:** http://www.statesman.com. **Description:** Publishes the *Austin American-Statesman*, a daily newspaper. **NOTE:** Call Human Resources at 512/445-3709. Please visit http://jobs.statesman.com to search for jobs and apply online. You may also visit the office to fill out an application in person. **Positions advertised include:** Telemarketing Representative; Research Analyst; New Business Development Sales Representative; National Advertising Sales Representative. **Office hours:** Monday – Friday, 8:30 a.m. – 5:00 p.m.

AUSTIN, CITY OF
EMPLOYMENT SERVICES DIVISION
P.O. Box 1088, Austin TX 78767. 512/974-3210. **Toll-free phone:** 800/526-9159. **Fax:** 512/974-3321. **Contact:** Human Resources. **E-mail address:** employment.services@ci.austin.tx.us. **World Wide Web address:** http://www.ci.austin.tx.us/cityjobs. **Description:** Administrative offices for the City of Austin. **NOTE:** Interested jobseekers may send their resumes, apply online or in person at the Employment Services Division office during business hours. The City of Austin has another location for employment located at 2209 Rosewood Avenue, Suite 205, Austin TX 78702. See website for the location's office hours. **Positions advertised include:** Assistant Police Monitor; Chief Financial Officer; Dental Assistant; Electrical Systems Controller; Energy Marketer; Polygraph Examiner; Police Dispatcher; Production Specialist. **Office hours:** Monday – Thursday, 7:30 a.m. – 6:30 p.m.; Friday, 8:00 a.m. – 5:00 p.m.; Saturday, 9:00 a.m. – 1:00 p.m.

AUSTIN COMMERCIAL INC.
P.O. Box 2879, Dallas TX 75221. 214/443-5700. **Physical address:** 3535 Travis Street, Suite 300, Dallas TX 75204. **Contact:** Human Resources Department. **E-mail address:** aclpjobs@austin-ind.com. **World Wide Web address:** http://www.austin-ind.com. **Description:** A commercial construction company providing general

contracting, construction management, and preconstruction services including cost estimating and scheduling. **Positions advertised include:** Safety Manager; Senior MEP Superintendent; Assistant FOM; Superintendent. **Other area location:** Austin TX. **Other U.S. locations:** Phoenix AZ. **Parent company:** Austin Industries. **President:** David Walls.

AUSTIN COMMUNITY COLLEGE
5930 Middle Fiskville Road, Austin TX 78752. 512/223-7000. Recorded jobline: 512/223-5621. **Contact:** Human Resources. **World Wide Web address:** http://www.austin.cc.tx.us. **Description:** A two-year community college. **NOTE:** Call the enrollment office at 512/223-7534 or -7573. Please visit website to search for jobs and download employment application. **Positions advertised include:** Coordinator – Internal Audit; Coordinator – Texas Success Initiative Program; Clerk; Associate Vice President for Institutional Effectiveness; Web Development Specialist; Safety Officer; Internal Programs Manager; Technical Office Assistant; Construction Buyer; Evening Supervisor; Specialist – Student Recruitment; Counselor – Part-time; Child Care Assistant; Senior Computer Support Technician; Online Application Software Administrator; Account Executive; Instructor – Various Departments; Faculty – Various Departments. Office hours: Monday – Friday, 8:00 a.m. – 5:00 p.m.

THE AUSTIN DIAGNOSTIC CENTER
12221 North Mopac Expressway, Austin TX 78758. 512/901-1111. **Toll-free phone:** 800/925-8899. **Recorded jobline:** 512/901-4050. **Contact:** Human Resources. **E-mail address:** jobs@adclinic.com. **World Wide Web address:** http://www.adclinic.com. **Description:** A physician-owned clinic with approximately 120 doctors in various specialties., such audiology, cosmetic laser surgery, diabetes management, menopause management, and optometry. Founded in 1995. **NOTE:** The center has several health facilities throughout Texas. The website lists jobs for all locations. All resumes must accompany an application which can be downloaded at the website or picked up at this location. **Positions advertised include**: LVN; Orthopedic Cast Technician; Business Associate Coordinator; IMX Data Entry; Cardiologist; Adult and Child Psychiatrist; Endocrinologist; Internal Medicine Physician.

AUSTIN INDEPENDENT SCHOOL DISTRICT
1111 West Sixth Street, Austin TX 78703. 512/414-1700. **Contact:** Human Resources. **World Wide Web address:** http://www.austin.isd.tenet.edu. **Description:** This location serves as the administrative offices for the entire Austin K-12 school system. **NOTE:** This website has job listings for all of the schools in the Austin district. See website and apply online. **Positions advertised include:** Accounting Clerk; Art Teacher; Assistant Band Director; Bilingual Behavior Specialist; Biology/Athletics Teacher; Elementary Special Education Teacher; Geography Teacher; French Teacher; High School Librarian; History Teacher; Housekeeping Services Specialist.

AUSTIN MUSEUM OF ART
823 Congress Avenue, Austin TX 78701. 512/495-9224. **Fax:** 512/496-9159. **Contact:** Human Resources. **E-mail address:** jobs@aoma.org. **World Wide Web address:** http://www.amoa.org. **Description:** This museum's collection includes outdoor sculptures. Paintings, photos, and drawings are also on display. The property for this location was donated in 1970s. It also houses an art school.

AUSTIN NATURE CENTER
301 Nature Center Drive, Austin TX 78746. 512/327-8181. **Fax:** 512/306-8470. **Contact:** Personnel. **World Wide Web address:** http://www.ci.austin.tx.us/ansc/ http://www.ci.austin.tx.us/ansc. **Description:** An indoor/outdoor nature center housing exhibits, live animals, interactive games, and discovery labs. Austin Nature Center is situated on an 80-acre preserve, with more than two miles of hiking trails. **NOTE:** Volunteer positions are also available.

AUSTIN REGIONAL CLINIC
6633 Highway 290 East, Suite 300, Austin TX, Austin TX 78723. 512/407-4636. **Fax:** 512/407-6464. **Contact:** Human Resources. **E-mail address:** jobs@covenantmso.com. **World Wide Web address:** http://www.austinregionalclinic.com. **Description:** An acute care, outpatient, multispecialty facility that offers primary care for adults and children, OB/GYN, occupational medicine, mental health services, dermatology, surgery, optometry, allergy treatment, and immunology. **Positions advertised include:** Accounts Payable Technician; Coding Specialist; Patient Registration Representative; Accounts Receivable Clerk; Medical Lab Technician; LVN; Medical Assistant; Patient Services Representative; HIM Technician; Patient Services Representative; RN Team Leader.

AUSTIN STATE HOSPITAL
4110 Guadalupe Street, Austin TX 78751. 512/452-0381. **Fax:** 512/419-2306. **Contact:** Human Resources. **World Wide Web address:** http://www.mhmr.state.tx.us/hospitals/austinsh/austinsh.html. **Description:** A 350-bed, acute psychiatric hospital. Austin State Hospital has many services to offer including a Deaf Unit, Children's Unit, and the Trinity Treatment Center, which aids people with mental retardation. **NOTE:** Please visit website to search for jobs and to download application forms. You may subscribe to have job postings e-mailed to you: Send an e-mail to hiring.services@mhmr.state.tx.us with the word "Subscribe" in the subject; do not send resumes or applications to this e-mail address. **Positions advertised include:** Psychiatrist; Clerk; MHMR Services Assistant; Custodian; Clinical Social Worker; Interpreter; Nurse; Nurse RN; LVN.

AUTOMATIC DATA PROCESSING (ADP)
2735 North Stemmons Freeway, Dallas TX 75207. 214/630-9311. **Toll-free phone:** 800/829-2237. **Contact:** Human Resources. **World Wide Web address:** http://www.adp.com. **Description:** Provides computerized transaction processing, record keeping, data communications, and information services. ADP helps more than 500,000 clients improve their business performance by providing services such as payroll, payroll tax, and human resource information management; brokerage industry market data, back office, and proxy services; industry-specific services to auto and truck dealers; and computerized auto repair and replacement estimating for auto insurance companies and body repair shops. The company's four largest businesses are Employer Services, Brokerage Services, Dealer Services, and Claims Services. **NOTE:** Please visit website to search for jobs and apply online. Online applications are preferred. **Positions advertised include:** New Account Coordinator; Corporate Sales Manager; Supervisor – Quality Control; Client Service Representative; Implementation Specialist; MADM; SBS Outside Sales Associate; Program Manager; Project Leader Implementation; Banking Representative; Overflow Operator; Client Technical Analyst; Account Executive; Manager – Financial Services; Network Technical Support Specialist; Customer Support Executive; Tax Service Representative; human Resources Director. **Special programs:** Co-ops; Internships. **Corporate headquarters location:** Roseland NJ. **Other U.S. locations:** Nationwide. **International locations:** Worldwide. **Listed on:** New York Stock Exchange. **Stock exchange symbol:** ADP.

AVANCE
2816 Swiss Avenue Dallas TX. 214/887-9907. **Contact:** Human Resources. **E-mail address:** avance-dallas@avance.org. **World Wide Web address:** http://www.avance-dallas.org. **Description:** A non-profit company that provides educational programs aimed at Hispanic at-risk children and their families. **Other area locations:** Austin TX; Corpus Christi TX; El Paso TX; Houston TX; Laredo TX; San Antonio TX; Waco TX; Texas Rio Grand Valley area; Texas Middle Rio Grande Valley. **Other U.S. locations:** Los Angeles, CA.

AVNET ELECTRONICS MARKETING
1400 Gillingham Lane, Sugarland TX 77478. 281/243-7330. **Toll-free phone:** 800/408-8353. **Contact:** Human Resources. **World Wide Web address:** http://www.em.avnet.com. **Description:** Distributes electronic parts and equipment including connectors, printers, and semiconductors. **Corporate headquarters location:** Phoenix AZ. **Other area locations:** El Paso TX; Dallas TX; Austin TX; McAllen TX. **Other U.S. locations:** Nationwide. **International locations:** Brazil; Canada; Mexico; Puerto Rico. **Parent company:** Avnet Inc. **President:** Andy Bryant.

AVNET, INC.
1130 Rutherford Lane, Building 2 Suite 208, Austin TX 78753. 512/835-1152. **Recorded jobline:** 800/459-1225. **Contact:** Human Resources. **E-mail address:** avnet.staffing@avnet.com. **World Wide Web address:** http://www.avnet.com. **Description:** Avnet is the world's largest distributor of semiconductors, interconnect, passive, and electromechanical components, computer products, and embedded systems from leading manufacturers. **NOTE:** Contact the corporate information line, at 800/882-8638 option 4, for more information on applying for jobs. Please visit website to view job listings and apply online. Online applications are preferred. **Positions advertised include:** Field Application Engineer. **Corporate headquarters location:** Phoenix AZ. **Other U.S. locations:** Nationwide. **International locations:** Worldwide. **Listed on:** New York Stock Exchange. **Stock exchange symbol:** AVT. **Number of employees worldwide:** 10,000.

AVNET, INC.
11333 Pagemill Road, Dallas TX 75243. 214/343-5000. **Recorded jobline:** 800/459-1225. **Contact:** Human Resources. **E-mail address:** avnet.staffing@avnet.com. **World Wide Web address:** http://www.avnet.com. **Description:** Avnet, Inc. is one of the nation's largest distributors of electronic components and computer products for industrial and military customers. The company also produces and distributes electronic, electrical, and video communications products. **NOTE:** Contact the corporate information line, at 800/882-8638 option 4, for more information on applying for jobs. Please visit website to view job listings and apply online. Online applications are preferred. **Positions advertised include:** Account Manager; Engineer; Supply Chain Analyst. **Corporate headquarters location:** Chandler AZ. **Other U.S. locations:** Nationwide. **International locations:** Worldwide. **Operations at this facility include:** This location is engaged in the distribution of company-manufactured electronics products. **Listed on:** New York Stock Exchange. **Stock exchange symbol:** AVT. **Number of employees worldwide:** 10,000.

BAE SYSTEMS
6500 Tracor Lane, Austin TX 78725-2070. 512/926-2800. **Contact:** Human Resources. **World Wide Web address:** http://www.na.baesystems.com. **Description:** Provides a full spectrum of systems engineering and technical services in the areas of systems development, operation, and maintenance. Technical services include system design, integration, and testing; software development, engineering, and maintenance; and integrated logistics support including safety, reliability, and quality assurance engineering. **NOTE:** Please visit website to search for jobs. Unsolicited resumes are not accepted; you must submit a resume for a particular listed job. **Positions advertised include:** Accounting Supervisor; Quality Engineer; Reliability Engineer; SW Test Engineer; Systems Engineer; Business Unit Analyst; Contract Administrator. Special programs: Internships. **Corporate headquarters location:** Rockville MD. **Other U.S. locations:** Nationwide. **International locations:** Worldwide. **Number of employees worldwide:** 90,000.

BASF CORPORATION
602 Copper Road, Freeport TX 77541. 979/238-6100. **Fax:** 979/415-6319. **Contact:** Human Resources. **World Wide Web address:** http://www.basf.com. **Description:** An international manufacturer and distributor of chemical products, doing business in five operating groups: Agricultural Chemicals; Chemicals; Colors and Auxiliaries; Pigments and Organic Specialties; and Polymers. **NOTE:** Please visit website to search for jobs and apply online. **Corporate headquarters location:** Mount Olive NJ. **Other area locations:** Pasadena TX; Carrolton TX; Beaumont TX. **Listed on:** New York Stock Exchange. **Stock exchange symbol:** BASF. **Number of employees worldwide:** 87,000.

BFI – BROWNING FERRIS INDUSTRIES
11757 Katy Freeway, Houston TX 77079. 281/848-3700. **Contact:** Human Resources. **World Wide Web address:** http://www.alliedwaste.com. **Description:** Engaged primarily in the collection and disposal of solid waste for commercial, industrial, and residential customers. Services provided include landfill services, waste-to-energy programs, hazardous waste removal, and liquid waste removal. The company has worldwide operations at more than 500 facilities. **Corporate headquarters location:** Scottsdale AZ. **Other U.S. locations:** Nationwide. **Parent company:** Allied Waste Industries. **Listed on:** New York Stock Exchange. **Stock exchange symbol:** AW. **CEO:** Thomas H. Van Weelden.

BFI – BROWNING FERRIS INDUSTRIES
757 North Eldridge, Houston TX 77079. 281/870-8100. **Contact:** Human Resources. **World Wide Web address:** http://www.alliedwaste.com. **Description:** Engaged in the collection and disposal of solid waste for commercial, industrial, and residential customers. Services provided include landfill services, waste-to-energy programs, hazardous waste removal, and liquid waste removal. **Corporate headquarters location:** Scottsdale AZ. **Other U.S. locations:** Nationwide. **Parent company:** Allied Waste Industries. **Listed on:** New York Stock Exchange. **Stock exchange symbol:** AW. **CEO:** Thomas H. Van Weelden.

BFI – BROWNING FERRIS INDUSTRIES
13630 Fondren Road, Houston TX 77085. 713/937-9955. **Fax:** 713/937-0108. **Contact:** Human Resources. **World Wide Web address:** http://www.alliedwaste.com. **Description:** Engaged in the collection and disposal of solid waste for commercial, industrial, and residential customers. Services provided include landfill services, waste-to-energy programs, hazardous waste removal, and liquid waste removal. **Corporate headquarters location:** Scottsdale AZ. **Other U.S. locations:** Nationwide. **Parent company:** Allied Waste Industries. **Listed on:** New York Stock Exchange. **Stock exchange symbol:** AW. **CEO:** Thomas H. Van Weelden.

BHP BILLITON
1360 Post Oak Boulevard, Suite 150, Houston TX 77056-3020. 713/961-8500. **Fax:** 713/961-8400. **Contact:** Personnel Supervisor. **World Wide Web address:** http://www.bhp.com. **Description:** Mines coal and other minerals. **NOTE:** Please visit website to search for jobs and apply online. **Positions advertised include:** Senior Reservoir Engineer; HR Consultant; Contracts Coordinator; Stewardship Specialist; Counsel; Chief Geoscientist; Accounts Payable Work Lead; Finance Controller; Senior Financial Analyst; Payroll Accountant; Project Procurement Manager; Operations Coordinator; Maintenance Systems Coordinator; Appraisal Geologist; Asset Protection Emergency Response and Business Continuity Coordinator; Senior Strategic Planner; Geotechnical Assistant; Commercial Manager; Team Leader; Geophysicist; Lead Engineering Economist. **International locations:** Worldwide. **Listed on:** New York Stock Exchange. **Stock exchange symbol:** BHP. **CEO:** Charles Goodyear. **Number of employees worldwide:** 35,000.

B.J. SERVICES COMPANY
5500 NW Central Drive, Houston TX 77092. 713/462-4239. **Fax:** 713/895-5851. **Contact:** Human Resources. **World Wide Web address:** http://www.bjservices.com. **Description:** An energy consulting firm offering technical services such as cementing, stimulation (including acidizing), and nitrogen services. B.J. Services Company is a division of Hughes Tool Company (Houston TX) and Dresser Industries (Dallas TX). **NOTE:** Please visit website to search for jobs. **Corporate headquarters location:** This location. **Listed on:** New York Stock Exchange. **Stock exchange symbol:** BJS. CEO: Bill Stewart.

BMC SOFTWARE, INC.
2101 City West Boulevard, Houston TX 77042-2827. 713/918-8800. **Toll-free phone:** 800/841-2031. **Fax:** 713/918-8000. **Contact:** Human Resources. **E-mail address:** careers@bmc.com. **World Wide Web address:** http://www.bmc.com. **Description:** Develops, markets, and supports standard systems software products to enhance and increase the performance of large-scale (mainframe) computer database management systems and data communications software systems. Founded in 1980. **NOTE:** Please visit website to search for jobs and apply online. **Positions advertised include:** les Representative; Advisory Software Consultant; Disaster Recovery Analyst; Systems Programmer; Accountant; Inside Sales Associate; Recruiting Advisor; Senior Executive Secretary; Administrative Support Assistant. **Corporate headquarters location:** This location. **Listed on:** New York Stock Exchange. **Stock exchange symbol:** BMC. **Annual sales/revenues:** More than $1.5 billion. **President/CEO:** Robert E. Beauchamp. **Number of employees nationwide:** 6,200.

BP AMOCO PLC
501 Westlake Park Boulevard, Houston TX 77079. 281/366-2000. **Contact:** Employment Office. **World Wide Web address:** http://www.bp.com. **Description:** Engaged in exploratory and developmental drilling and in advanced recovery techniques. **NOTE:** Please visit http://www.bpfutures.com/us to search for jobs and apply online. **Positions advertised include:** Compliance Advisor; Project Leader. **Other area locations:** Statewide. **Other U.S. locations:** Anchorage AK; Warrenville IL; Los Angeles CA; New York NY; Linthicum MD. **International locations:** Worldwide. **Operations at this facility include:** Administration; Service. **Listed on:** New York Stock Exchange. **Stock exchange symbol:** BP. **Number of employees nationwide:** 42,000.

BRSG (BLACK ROGERS SULLIVAN GOODNIGHT)
701 Brazos, Suite, 1010 Austin TX 78701. 512/320-8511. **Fax:** 512/320-8990. **Fax:** 713/783-1592. **World Wide Web address:** http://www.brsg.com. **Contact:** Employment. **Description:** A marketing communications firm. **Special programs:** Internships. **Office hours:** Monday - Friday, 8:00 a.m. - 5:00 p.m. **Corporate headquarters location:** This location. **Operations at this facility include:** Administration; Research and Development.

BAKER BOTTS LLP
2001 Ross Avenue, Suite 600, Dallas TX 75201-2980. 214/953-6500. **Fax:** 214/953-6503. **Contact:** Recruiting. **World Wide Web address:** http://www.bakerbotts.com. **Description:** A law firm providing services in almost all areas of civil law. Baker Botts LLP is one of the nation's oldest and largest law firms. **NOTE:** Please visit website for more specific contact information for individual areas of interest and locations. **Corporate headquarters location:** Houston TX. **Other area locations:** Austin TX. **Other U.S. locations:** Washington DC; New York NY. **International locations:** Azerbaijan; England; Russia; Saudi Arabia.

BAKER BOTTS LLP
One Shell Plaza, 910 Louisiana Street, Houston TX 77002. 713/229-1234. **Fax:** 713/229-1522. **Contact:** Recruiting. **World Wide Web address:** http://www.bakerbotts.com. **Description:** A law firm providing services in almost all areas of civil law. Baker Botts, LLP is one of the nation's oldest and largest law firms. **NOTE:** Please visit website for more specific contact information for individual areas of interest and locations. **Positions advertised include:** Real Estate Associate; Legal Assistant. **Special programs:** Summer Associate Program. **Corporate headquarters location:** This location. **Other area locations:** Austin TX; Dallas TX. **Other U.S. locations:** Washington DC; New York NY. **International locations:** Azerbaijan; England; Russia; Saudi Arabia. **Operations at this facility include:** Service.

BAKER ENERGY
16340 Park Ten Place, Suite 320, Houston TX 77084. 281/579-7850. **Fax:** 281/579-4545. **Contact:** Human Resources. **World Wide Web address:** http://www.mbakercorp.com. **Description:** Maintains and operates oilrig platforms. **NOTE:** Please visit website to search for jobs and apply online. **Positions advertised include:** Civil Associate; Environmental Specialist; GIS Specialist; Offshore Oil and Gas Platform Operation; Operations Manager; Project Manager; Support Technician; Technical Specialist; Training Specialist. **Corporate headquarter location:** Moon Township PA. **Other area locations:** Austin TX; Borger TX. **Other U.S. locations:** Nationwide. **International locations:** Nigeria; Thailand; Venezuela; United Kingdom; Mexico; Trinidad. **Parent company:** Michael Baker Corporation. **Listed on:** American Stock Exchange. **Stock Exchange symbol:** BKR.

BAKER HUGHES INC.
P.O. Box 4740, Houston TX 77210-4740. 713/439-8600. **Physical address:** 3900 Essex Lane, Suite 1200, Houston TX 77027. **Fax:** 713/439-8699. **Contact:** Human Resources. **World Wide Web address:** http://www.bakerhughes.com. **Description:** Provides vital information to many segments of the energy industry through high-technology data acquisition operations. **NOTE:** Please visit website to search for job and apply online. **Positions advertised include:** HS&E Specialist; Formation Evaluation Analyst; Parts Finisher; Legal Secretary; Facilities Specialist; Senior Financial Benefits Specialist; Manufacturing Engineer; Electro-Mechanical Technician; HR Administrator; Ethics Director; Accounting Clerk; International Tax Specialist; Technical Support Engineer; Directional Driller. **Corporate headquarters location:** This location. **Other U.S. locations:** Western and Southern U.S. **International locations:** Worldwide. **Operations at this facility include:** Administration; Divisional Headquarters; Manufacturing; Regional Headquarters; Research and Development; Sales. **Listed on:** New York Stock Exchange. **Stock exchange symbol:** BHI. **President/CEO:** Mike Wiley. **Number of employees worldwide:** 24,500.

BAKER PETROLITE
12645 West Airport Boulevard, P.O. Box 5050, Sugar Land TX 77487. 281/276-5400. **Fax:** 281/275-7392. **Contact:** Human Resources. **World Wide Web address:** http://www.bakerhughes.com/bakerpetrolite. **Description:** Engaged in the manufacture and sale of chemicals. **NOTE:** Please visit website to search for jobs and apply online. **Positions advertised include:** Programs Support Administrator; Department Administrator; Applications Research Chemist; Senior Financial Analyst; Strategic Product Manager; Marketing Communications Specialist. **Corporate headquarters location:** This location. **Parent company:** Baker Hughes Inc. **Listed on:** New York Stock Exchange. **Stock exchange symbol:** BHI.

BALDWIN DISTRIBUTION SERVICES
P.O. Box 51618, Amarillo TX 79159. 806/383-7650. **Physical address:** 7702 Broadway, Amarillo TX 79108. 806/383-7650. **Toll-free phone:** 800/692-1333. **Contact:** Recruiting. **World Wide Web address:** http://www.baldwin-dist.com. **Description:** Provides long-haul trucking services. Baldwin Distribution Services operates in 48 states, Canada, and Mexico. **NOTE:** Contact Recruiting office at 866/4-BALDWIN. Recruiting office is located at I 40 & Loop 335, Amarillo TX. **Positions advertised include:** Long Haul Driver; Lease Purchase Operator. **Corporate headquarters location:** This location. **President/CEO:** Dudley Baldwin.

BANCTEC, INC.
P.O. Box 660204, Dallas TX 75266-0204. 972/579-6000. **Physical address:** 2701 East Grauwyler Road, Irving TX 75061. **Toll-free phone:** 800/226-2832. **Fax:** 972/579-5812. **Contact:** Human Resources Manager. **World Wide Web address:** http://www.banctec.com. **Description:** Engaged in systems integration and specializes in document management solutions. The company also provides network support services and develops image management software. **NOTE:** Please visit website to search for jobs and apply online. **Corporate headquarters location:** This location. **Other U.S. locations:** Nationwide. **Listed on:** Privately held. **Number of employees worldwide:** 3,000.

BANK OF AMERICA
9660 Hillcroft Street, Houston TX 77096. 713/551-7400. **Contact:** Human Resources. **World Wide Web address:** http://www.bankofamerica.com. **Description:** Bank of America is a full-service banking and financial institution. The company operates through four business segments: Global Corporate and Investment Banking, Principal Investing and Asset Management, Commercial Banking, and Consumer Banking. **NOTE:** Please visit website to search for jobs and apply online. **Positions advertised include:** Teller; Personal Banker; Proof Operator; BCC Market Training Leader; Trust Specialist; Full Service Financial Advisor. **Corporate headquarters location:** Charlotte NC. **Other area locations:** Statewide. **Operations at this facility include:** This location is a bank. **Listed on:** New York Stock Exchange. **Stock exchange symbol:** BAC.

BANK OF AMERICA
2200 NASA Road One, Houston TX 77058. 281/333-8600. **Contact:** Human Resources. **World Wide Web address:** http://www.bankofamerica.com. **Description:** Bank of America is a full-service banking and financial institution. The company operates through four business segments: Global Corporate and Investment Banking, Principal Investing and Asset Management, Commercial Banking, and Consumer Banking. **NOTE:** Please visit website to search for jobs and apply online. **Positions advertise include: Positions advertised include:** Teller; Personal Banker; Proof Operator; BCC Market Training Leader; Trust Specialist; Full Service Financial Advisor. **Corporate headquarters location:** Charlotte NC. **Other area locations:** Statewide. **Operations at this facility include:** This location is a bank. **Listed on:** New York Stock Exchange. **Stock exchange symbol:** BAC.

BANK OF AMERICA
303 West Wall Street, Midland TX 79701. 432/685-2000. **Contact:** Human Resources. **World Wide Web address:** http://www.bankofamerica.com. **Description:** Bank of America is a full-service banking and financial institution. The company operates through four business segments: Global Corporate and Investment Banking, Principal Investing and Asset Management, Commercial Banking, and Consumer Banking. **NOTE:** Please visit website to search for jobs and apply online. **Positions advertised include:** Teller. **Corporate headquarters location:** Charlotte NC. **Other area locations:** Statewide. **Operations at this facility include:** This location is a bank. **Listed on:** New York Stock Exchange. **Stock exchange symbol:** BAC.

BANK ONE SECURITIES
1600 Redbud Boulevard, McKinney TX 75069. 214/290-2000. **Toll-free phone:** 877/226-5663. **Contact:** Human Resources. **World Wide Web address:** http://www.bankone.com. **Description:** Provides financial services in the areas of stocks, bonds, and mutual funds. **NOTE:** Please visit website to search for jobs and apply online. **Corporate headquarters location:** Chicago IL. **Other area locations:** Statewide. **Other U.S. locations:** Nationwide. **International locations:** Worldwide. **Parent company:** Bank One Corporation. **Listed on:** New York Stock Exchange. **Stock exchange symbol:** ONE.

BANK ONE TEXAS
420 Throckmorton Street, Fort Worth TX 76102. 817/884-4000. **Contact:** Human Resources. **World Wide Web address:** http://www.bankone.com. **Description:** A full-service, commercial bank. **NOTE:** Please visit website to search for jobs and apply online. **Corporate headquarters location:** Chicago IL. **Other area locations:** Statewide. **Other U.S. locations:** Nationwide. **International locations:** Worldwide. **Parent company:** Bank One Corporation. **Listed on:** New York Stock Exchange **Stock exchange symbol:** ONE.

BANTA GLOBAL TURNKEY
6315 West By Northwest Boulevard, Houston TX 77046. 713/354-1300. **Contact:** Human Resources. **World Wide Web address:** http:/www.banta.com. **Description:** Printing and digital imaging company. Publishes and distributes catalogs, books, directories, and direct mail. This location is a fulfillment center. **NOTE:** Apply online. **Positions advertised include:** Director of Finance and Administration; Group Commodity Manager; Inventory Analyst; IS Project manager; Production Supervisor; Production and Shipping Coordinator; Warehouse Manager. **Corporate headquarters location:** Menasha WI. **Parent company:** Banta Inc. **Listed on:** New York Stock Exchange. **Stock exchange symbol:** BN.

BANKERS DIGEST
9550 Forest Lane, Suite 125, Dallas TX 75243-5928. 214/221-4544. **Fax:** 214/221-4546. **Contact:** Editor. **E-mail address:** bankersd@airmail.net. **World Wide Web**

address: http://www.bankersdigest.com. **Description:** A trade magazine that provides Texas banking news. *Bankers Digest* has a circulation of 4,800. **Corporate headquarters location:** This location.

W.O. BANKSTON LINCOLN MERCURY
4747 LBJ Freeway, Dallas TX 75380. 972/233-1441. **Fax:** 972/386-8292. **Contact:** Human Resources. **World Wide Web address:** http://www.bankstonlincoln.com. **Description:** A car dealer offering both new and used vehicles. **Other area locations:** Frisco TX; Lewisville TX; Dallas TX; Irving TX; Grand Prairie TX.

BAPTIST MEDICAL CENTER
111 Dallas Street, San Antonio TX 78205-1230. 210/297-7000. **Fax:** 210/297-0951. **Contact:** Annette Dunlap, Recruiter. **E-mail address:** amdunlap@baptisthealthsystem.com. **World Wide Web address:** http://www.baptisthealthsystem.org/bmc.asp. **Description:** A 689-bed, nonprofit, acute care hospital offering complete medical facilities for cardiac care, intensive care, emergency services, maternity, surgery, and other specialized services. **NOTE:** Please visit website to view job listings, apply online, or download application form. You may submit your resume or application directly to the hospital, or you can contact the Human Resources Center at 417 Camden, San Antonio TX 78215, fax is 210/297-0093. Volunteer positions are also available. **Positions advertised include:** Certified Occupational Therapy Assistant; LVN; Physical Therapist; RN. . **Parent company:** Baptist Memorial Hospital System is a health care system that is comprised of five acute care, nonprofit hospitals: Baptist Medical Center, Northeast Baptist Hospital, Southeast Baptist Hospital, North Center Baptist Hospital, and St. Luke's Baptist Hospital. In total, these hospitals contain 1,700 beds.

BAPTIST ST. ANTHONY HEALTH SYSTEM
1600 Wallace Boulevard, Amarillo TX 79106. 806/212-2000. **Contact:** Human Resources Manager. **World Wide Web address:** http://www.bsahs.com. **Description:** A 255-bed general hospital. Baptist St. Anthony Health System also offers home health services, a hospice program, a rehabilitation/skilled nursing facility, a senior health center and a sports and occupational health center. **NOTE:** Please visit website to search for jobs and apply online. **Positions advertised include:** Area Technician; Administrative Assistant; Facility Technician; Billing Clerk; Cook; Office Clerk; RN; Nursing Technician; CNA; Paramedic; Biomedical Technician; Radiology Equipment Specialist; Nurse Practitioner; Physical Therapist; Respiratory Therapist; Speech Therapist.

BARNES & NOBLE BOOKSTORES
2545 Town Center Boulevard, Sugar Land TX 77479. 281/265-4620. **Contact:** Manager. **World Wide Web address:** http://www.barnesandnoble.com. **Description:** A bookstore chain operating nationwide. **NOTE:** please visit http://www.barnesandnobleinc.com for more information on the company, and for a listing of newly established stores in your area. **Corporate headquarters location:** New York NY. **Operations at this facility include:** This location is a retail store. **Number of employees nationwide:** 40,000.

BARNES & NOBLE BOOKSTORES
7626 Westheimer, Houston TX 77063. 713/783-6016. **Contact:** Manager. **World Wide Web address:** http://www.barnesandnoble.com. **Description:** A bookstore chain operating nationwide. **NOTE:** please visit http://www.barnesandnobleinc.com for more information on the company, and for a listing of newly established stores in your area. **Corporate headquarters location:** New York NY. **Operations at this facility include:** This location is a retail store. **Number of employees nationwide:** 40,000.

BARNES & NOBLE BOOKSTORES
7700 West Northwest Highway, Suite 300, Dallas TX 75225. 214/739-1124. **Contact:** Manager. **World Wide Web address:** http://www.barnesandnoble.com. **Description:** A bookstore chain operating nationwide. **NOTE:** please visit http://www.barnesandnobleinc.com for more information on the company, and for a listing of newly established stores in your area. **Corporate headquarters location:** New York NY. **Operations at this facility include:** This location is a retail store. **Number of employees nationwide:** 40,000.

BARNES & NOBLE BOOKSTORES
3634 Irving Mall, Irving TX 75062. 972/257-8320. **Contact:** Manager. **World Wide Web address:** http://www.barnesandnoble.com. **Description:** A bookstore chain operating nationwide. **NOTE:** please visit http://www.barnesandnobleinc.com for more information on the company, and for a listing of newly established stores in your area. **Corporate headquarters location:** New York NY. **Operations at this facility include:** This location is a retail store. **Number of employees nationwide:** 40,000.

BARON & BUDD, P.C.
3102 Oak Lawn Avenue, Suite 1100, Dallas TX 75219-4281. 214/521-3605. **Toll-free phone:** 800/946-9646. **Fax:** 888/822-2766. **E-mail address:** work@baronbudd.com. **Contact:** Recruiting. **World Wide Web address:** http://www.baronbudd.com. **Description:** A plaintiffs' law firm specializing in environmental and toxic tort litigation. Founded 1977. NOTE: Please visit website to specific contact details. **Special programs:** Summer Associate Program. **Corporate headquarters location:** This location. **Other U.S. locations:** Glen Carbon IL; Cleveland OH; Baton Rouge LA; Canton NY.

BASELL POLYOLEFINS
12001 Bay Area Boulevard, Pasadena TX 77507. 281/474-4481. **Fax:** 281/474-7921. **Contact:** Human Resources. **World Wide Web address:** http://www.basell.com. **Description:** Produces polypropylene resins and advanced materials supplied to manufacturers in the plastics, synthetic fibers, automobiles, and household products industries. **International locations:** Worldwide. **Operations at this facility include:** Administration; Manufacturing. **President:** Werner Breuers.

BAY LTD.
P.O. Box 9908 Corpus Christi TX 78469. 361/693-2100. **Physical address:** 401 Corn Products Road, Corpus Christi TX 78409. **Fax:** 361/289-5005. **Contact:** Porfilio Silva, Personnel. **E-mail address:** silvap@bayltd.com. **World Wide Web address:** http://www.bayltd.com. **Description:** Provides construction and fabrication services to the petroleum industry. **NOTE:** Contact Personnel directly at 361/289-2400. **Corporate headquarters location:** This location. **Other area locations:** Friendswood TX. **Other U.S. locations:** Amerlia LA. **International location:** Mexico. **Parent company:** Berry Contracting Inc.

BAYLOR MEDICAL CENTER AT GARLAND
2300 Marie Curie Boulevard, Garland TX 75042. 972/487-5000. **Contact:** Human Resources. **World Wide Web address:** http://www.baylorhealth.com. **Description:** A 206-bed acute care medical and surgical center. **NOTE:** Please visit website to search for jobs and apply online. **Positions advertised include:** RN; Radiologic Technologist; Physical Therapist; PRN; Medical Assistant; OR Technician; Medical Technologist; Director of Radiology; Ultrasound Technologist; Patient Care Assistant; Coding Auditor; Administrative Assistant. **Parent company:** Baylor Health Care System. **Number of employees nationwide:** 14,000.

BAYLOR MEDICAL CENTER AT IRVING
1901 North MacArthur Boulevard, Irving TX 75061. 972/579-8100. **Contact:** Human Resources Department. **World Wide Web address:** http://www.baylorhealth.com. **Description:** A 288-bed, full-service hospital. The hospital employs specialists in the areas of oncology, neurosurgery, neurology, cardiology, and gastroenterology. **NOTE:** Please visit website to search for jobs and apply online. **Positions advertised include:** RN – Various Departments; Physical Therapist; OR Technician; Oncology Care Coordinator; Unite Secretary; Sterile Processing Technician; Senior Anesthesia Technician; Patient Care Assistant; LVN; Nurse Extern; Scheduling Clerk; HIM Associate; Laboratory Director. **Parent company:** Baylor Health Care System. **Number of employees nationwide:** 14,000.

BAYLOR SENIOR HEALTH CENTER
820 West Arapaho Road, Suite 200, Richardson TX 75080. 972/498-4500. **Contact:** Human Resources. **World Wide Web address:** http://www.baylorhealth.com. **Description:** An outpatient facility that offers comprehensive primary care services to senior citizens. Founded in 1995. **Parent company:** Baylor Health Care System.

BAYLOR UNIVERSITY
700 University Parks Drive, Clifton Robinson Tower, 2nd Floor, Waco TX 76798. 254/710-2219. **Fax:** 254/710-3819. **Contact:** Human Resources. **World Wide Web address:** http://www.baylor.edu. **Description:** One of the largest Baptist universities in the nation. Baylor University has over 13,000 students enrolled in a wide range of undergraduate and graduate programs. Founded in 1845. **NOTE:** Please visit website to search for jobs and to find more specific contact information. Applications are only accepted for open positions. Applications are kept on file for six months. Contact a Human Resources Specialist at 254/710-8539. **Office hours:** Monday – Friday, 8:00 a.m. – 12:00 p.m.; 1:00 a.m. – 5:00 p.m. **Corporate headquarters location:** This location.

BAYLOR UNIVERSITY MEDICAL CENTER
3500 Gaston Avenue, Dallas TX 75246. 214/820-2525. **Contact:** Human Resources. **World Wide Web address:** http://www.baylorhealth.com. **Description:** A full-service, tertiary, teaching hospital. As the flagship hospital of the Baylor Health Care System, Baylor University Medical Center is comprised of five connecting hospitals. Hospital departments include family medicine, neurosurgery, obstetrics, gynecology, oncology, ophthalmology, orthopedic surgery, pathology, pediatrics, physical rehabilitation, plastic and reconstructive surgery, psychiatry, radiology, urology, and anesthesiology. **Positions advertised include:** Medical Technologist; Physical Therapist; Medical Physicist; GN/RN; RN – Various Departments; Nutrition Educator; Utility Aide; Nutrition Services Retail Supervisor; Nutrition Attendant; Certified Respiratory Therapist; Clinical Dietitian; Licensed Vocational Nurse; Clinical Pharmacist; Medical Assistant; Director – Core Laboratory; Health Care Representative; BMET; Social Worker; Ultrasound Supervisor; Access Services Coordinator; Phone Scheduler; Trauma Registrar; Font Desk Registration Representative. **Operations at this facility include:** Administration; Research and Development.

BAYLOR/RICHARDSON MEDICAL CENTER
401 West Campbell Road, Richardson TX 75080. 972/498-4000. **Fax:** 972/498-4978. **Contact:** Human Resources. **World Wide Web address:** http://www.baylorhealth.com. **Description:** A 174-bed, nonprofit medical, surgical, and psychiatric hospital. Hospital specialties include family medicine, pediatrics, women's services, oncology, emergency medicine, cardiology, radiology and imaging, chemical dependency, skilled nursing, respiratory therapy, and home health.

THE BAYTOWN SUN
P.O. Box 90, Baytown TX 77522. 281/422-8302. **Physical address:** 1301 Memorial Drive, Baytown TX 75520. **Contact:** Human Resources. **World Wide Web address:** http://www.baytownsun.com. **Description:** A daily newspaper. **NOTE:** Please visit website to view job listings.

BAYTOWN YMCA
201 YMCA Drive, Baytown TX 77521-4121. 281/427-1797. **Contact:** Employment. **Wide Web address:** http://www.ymcahouston.org. **Description:** One of the nation's largest and most comprehensive service organizations. The YMCA provides health and fitness services, social and personal development, sports and recreation, education and career development, and camps and conferences to children, youths, adults, the elderly, families, the disabled, refugees and foreign nationals, YMCA residents, and community residents, through a broad range of programs. **NOTE:** Please visit website to download and view job listings. **Positions advertised include:** Membership/Marketing Director; Director of Center Operations; Program Director; Membership Coordinator; Group Executive; Director of Communications; Pre-School Care Giver; Day Camp Counselor; Gymnastics Instructor; Swim Instructor; Lifeguard; Aerobics Instructor; Tai Chi Instructor; After School Child Care Giver; Group Fitness Instructor. **Corporate headquarters location:** Chicago IL.

BEAR, STEARNS & COMPANY, INC.
300 Crescent Court, Suite 200, Dallas TX 75201. 214/979-7900. **Fax:** 214/979-7911. **Contact:** Human Resources. **World Wide Web address:** http://www.bearstearns.com. **Description:** A leading worldwide investment banking, securities trading, and brokerage firm. The firm's business includes corporate finance, mergers and acquisitions, public finance, institutional equities, fixed income sales and trading, private client services, foreign exchange, future sales and trading, derivatives, and asset management. **Corporate headquarters location:** New York NY. **Other U.S. locations:** Nationwide. **Parent company:** The Bear Stearns Companies Inc. also operates Bear, Stearns Securities Corporation, providing professional and correspondent clearing services including securities lending; and Custodial Trust Company, providing master trust, custody, and government securities services. **Listed on:** New York Stock Exchange. **Stock exchange symbol:** BSC. **Number of employees nationwide:** 10,500.

BECHTEL CORPORATION
P.O. Box 2166, Houston TX 77056. 713/235-2000. **Physical address:** 3000 Post Oak Boulevard, Houston TX 77056. **Fax:** 713/960-9031. **Contact:** Human Resources. **E-mail address:** staffpx@bechtel.com. **World Wide Web address:** http://www.bechtel.com. **Description:** Operates in the following areas: engineering, construction, financing operations, electricity, nuclear fuels, metals, minerals, procurement management, transportation, and pollution control. Founded 1898. **NOTE:** Please visit http://www.bechtel.com/careers to search for jobs. **Positions advertised include:** Senior Engineer' Engineering Supervisor; IS&T Manager; Senior Technical Support Specialist; Senior Designer. **Corporate headquarters location:** San Francisco CA. **Other U.S. locations:** Washington D.C.; San Diego CA; Richland WA;

Oak Ridge TN; New York NY; McLean VA; Louisville KY; North Las Vegas NV; Glendale AZ; Frederick MD. **International locations:** Worldwide. **Number of employees worldwide:** 42,000.

BEELER PROPERTIES, INC.
7500 San Felipe, Suite 750, Houston TX 77063. 713/785-8200. **Fax:** 713/785-4143. **Contact:** Human Resources. **E-mail address:** apachall@beelerproperties.com. **World Wide Web address:** http://www.reliabilitymall.com/members/beeler_properties.htm. **Description:** Specializes in the development, construction, and management of apartment buildings. **Office hours:** Monday – Friday, 8:00 a.m. – 5:00 p.m. **Corporate headquarters location:** This location. **Parent company:** Beeler-Sanders, Inc.

BELDON ROOFING COMPANY
P.O. Box 13380, San Antonio TX 78213. 210/341-3100. **Physical address:** 5039 West Avenue, San Antonio TX 78213. **Toll-free phone:** 800/688-7663. **Fax:** 210/341-2959. **Contact:** Human Resources. **E-mail address:** greatjob@beldon.com. **World Wide Web address:** http://www.beldon.com. **Description:** A construction company that specializes in roofing and sheet metal work for all types of buildings. Founded in 1946. **NOTE:** Please visit website to view job listings and access online application. Please note whether your desired position requires an online application. Resumes are not kept on file. **Positions advertised include:** Roofer; Sheet Metal Installer. **Office hours:** Monday - Friday, 8:00 a.m. - 5:00 p.m.

BELL HELICOPTER TEXTRON
P.O. Box 482, Fort Worth TX 76101. 817/280-2011. **Physical address:** 600 East Hurst Boulevard, Fort Worth TX 76053. **Fax:** 817/280-2321. **Contact:** Employment Department. **World Wide Web address:** http://www.bellhelicopter.textron.com. **Description:** Bell Helicopter Textron manufactures a variety of commercial and civilian helicopters and also conducts extensive research and development activities. **NOTE:** Please visit website to search for jobs and apply online. **Positions advertised include:** Business Development Specialist; Marketing Specialist; Senior Licensing and Compliance Specialist; Cost/Schedule Analyst; Senior Program Administrator; Associate Engineering Technical Administrator; Chief Configuration Management; Chief Rotor Systems Analyst; Engineer; Senior Electronic Design Engineer; Human Resources Personnel; Customer Support Specialist; Data Administrator; Senior CPR Administrator; Regional Account Coordinator. **Corporate headquarters location:** This location. **Other U.S. locations:** Nationwide. **International locations:** Worldwide. **Parent company:** Textron Inc. **Listed on:** New York Stock Exchange. **Stock exchange symbol:** TXT.

BELLAIRE MEDICAL CENTER
5314 Dashwood Drive, Houston TX 77081-4689. 713/512-1200. **Fax:** 713/512-1577. **Recorded jobline:** 713/512-1580. **Contact:** Director of Human Resources. **World Wide Web address:** http://www.bellairemedicalcenter.com. **Description:** A 350-bed medical center offering a range of inpatient and outpatient care including a diabetes center, an intensive care psychiatric unit, and a women's services center. Bellaire Medical Center also provides geriatric day programs and support groups for chemical dependency. **NOTE:** Applications are only accepted for advertised positions. **Positions advertised include:** RN; Therapist; Distribution/Supply Specialist; LVN; EVS Technician; Recreation Therapist; LPTA. **Operations at this facility include:** Administration; Divisional Headquarters; Regional Headquarters; Service.

BELLVILLE GENERAL HOSPITAL
P.O. Box 977, Bellville TX 77418. 979/865-3141. **Physical address:** 44 North Cummings, Bellville TX. **Fax:** 979/865-9631. **Contact:** Jackie McEuen, Human Resources. **World Wide Web address:** http://www.bellvillehospital.com. **Description:** A nonprofit, rural hospital with 32 beds. Services at Bellville General Hospital include emergency room care, a nursery, obstetrics, outpatient care, and surgical procedures. Bellville General Hospital is accredited by the Joint Commission on Accreditation of Healthcare Organizations (JCAHO). **NOTE:** Contact Human Resources at Ext. 135. Second and third shifts are offered. **Positions advertised include:** Registered Nurse. **CEO:** Michael Morris.

BELO CORPORATION
THE DALLAS MORNING NEWS
P.O. Box 655237, Dallas TX 75265. 214/977-6606. **Physical address:** 508 Young Street, Dallas TX 75202. **Contact:** Employment Manager. **E-mail address:** jobs@belo.com. **World Wide Web address:** http://www.belo.com. **Description:** A.H. Belo Corporation owns and operates newspapers and network-affiliated television stations in seven U.S. metropolitan areas. *The Dallas Morning News* (also at this location) has a circulation of 550,000 during the week and 800,000 on Sunday. A.H. Belo traces its roots to *The Galveston Daily News*, which was first published in 1842. **NOTE:** Please visit website to search for jobs. This physical location is home to both The Dallas Morning News, and the Belo Corporation's headquarters. **Positions advertised include:** Financial Applications Programmer; Network Engineer; Staffing Specialist; System Analyst/Corporate Applications. **Other U.S. locations:** WA; OR; ID; CA; AZ; LA; MO; KY; NC; VA; RI. **Subsidiaries include:** DFW Printing Company, Inc.; DFW Suburban Newspapers, Inc. **Listed on:** New York Stock Exchange. **Stock exchange symbol:** BLC. **President/CEO:** Robert W. Dechard. **Number of employees nationwide:** 7,800.

THE BENCHMARK COMPANY
907 South Congress Avenue, Suite 7, Austin TX 78704. 512/707-7500. **Fax:** 512/707-7757. **Contact:** Human Resources Department. **E-mail address:** thebenc@earthlink.net. **World Wide Web address:** http://www.thebenchmarkcompany.net. **Description:** Gathers data and research about radio listeners. Benchmark is also involved in researching broadcasting companies. **President/CEO:** Dr. Robert E. Balon.

BENCHMARK ELECTRONICS, INC.
3000 Technology Drive, Angleton TX 77515. 979/849-6550. **Contact:** Human Resources. **World Wide Web address:** http://www.bench.com. **Description:** Assembles printed circuit boards for original equipment manufacturers. **NOTE:** Please visit website to view job listings. **Corporate headquarters location:** This location. **Other area locations:** Angleton TX. **Other U.S. locations:** Beaverton OR; Loveland CO; Hudson NH; Huntsville AL; Manassas VA; Winona MN. **International locations:** Brazil; Mexico; Ireland. England; Thailand; Singapore; China. **Listed on:** New York Stock Exchange. **Stock exchange symbol:** BHE. **President:** Cary Fu. **CEO:** Donald Nigbor.

THE BERGAILA COMPANIES
11200 Westheimer Road, Suite 500, Houston TX 77042. 713/780-4227. **Fax:** 281/496-4705. **Contact:** Human Resources. **World Wide Web address:** http://www.bergaila.com. **Description:** An engineering and drafting service contractor. **NOTE:** Please visit individual subsidiaries websites (available through corporate website) for more information about employment. **Subsidiaries include:** Bergaila & Associates, Inc.; BES Engineering.

BERNARD JOHNSON YOUNG, INC.
9050 North Capital of Texas Highway, Building 3, Suite 170, Austin TX 78759. 512/231-8900. **Fax:** 512/231-9052. **Contact:** Human Resources. **World Wide Web address:** http://www.bjy.com/phoenix. **Description:** An architectural engineering firm. The company also provides technical services, using the Internet to provide a full-time video link to customers. **Special programs:** Internships. **Corporate headquarters location:** This location. **Other area locations:** Dallas TX; Houston TX. **Other U.S. locations:** Rockville MD; Washington D.C.; Peoria IL; Phoenix AZ; American Fork UT; Pleasanton CA. **Operations at this facility include:** Administration; Regional Headquarters; Research and Development; Sales. **Listed on:** Privately held.

BEST MAID
P.O. Box 1809, Fort Worth TX 76104. 817/335-5494. **Physical address:** 1401 South Riverside Drive, Fort Worth TX 76104. **Contact:** Personnel Manager. **World Wide Web address:** http://www.bestmaidproducts.com. **Description:** Manufactures and distributes pickled fruits and vegetables. Founded 1926. **Corporate headquarters location:** This location.

BEST VALUE INN & SUITES
6911 North Interstate Highway 35, Austin TX 78752. 512/459-9274. **Contact:** Human Resources. **World Wide Web address:** http://www.bestvalueinn.com. **Description:** One location of the nationwide hotel chain. **Other area locations:** Buda TX.

BEST VALUE INN & SUITES
2525 North 11th Street, Beaumont TX 77703. 409/924-7300. **Contact:** Human Resources. **World Wide Web address:** http://www.bestvalueinn.com. **Description:** One location of the nationwide hotel chain. **Other area locations:** Buda TX.

BETTY HARDWICK CENTER
2616 South Clack, Abilene TX 79606. 325/690-5100. **Fax:** 325/690-5136. **Contact:** Human Resources. **World Wide Web address:** http://bhcmhmr.org. **Description:** An outpatient counseling facility for mentally challenged people. **NOTE:** Please visit website to view jobs listings and apply online. **Positions advertised include:** Contract Foster Care Provider; HCS Trainer; Skills Trainer.

BICKEL & BREWER
4800 Bank One Center, 1717 Main Street, Dallas TX 75201. 214/653-4000. **Fax:** 214/653-1015. **Contact:** Human Resources. **E-mail address:** counsel@bickelbrewer.com. **World Wide Web address:** http://www.bickelbrewer.com. **Description:** A law firm specializing in corporate litigation including bankruptcy. **Other U.S. locations:** New York NY.

BIG SPRING STATE HOSPITAL
1901 North Highway 87, Big Spring TX 79720. 432/267-8216. **Fax:** 432/268-7263. **Contact:** Dennis Warrington, Director of Human Resources. **E-mail address:** dennis.warrington@mhmr.state.tx.us. **World Wide Web address:** http://www.dshs.state.tx.us. **Description:** A nonprofit, state-governed facility that specializes in the treatment of patients with mental illness. **NOTE:** Entry-level positions and second and third shifts are offered. **Special programs:** Internships. **Corporate headquarters location:** Austin TX. **Parent company:** Department of State Health Services. **Operations at this facility include:** Administration. **Number of employees at this location:** 650.

BIMBO BAKERIES USA
P.O. Box 937, Fort Worth TX 76101. 817/293-6230. **Physical address:** 7301 South Freeway, Fort Worth TX. **Contact:** Human Resources. **World Wide Web address:** http://www.bimbobakeriesusa.com. **Description:** Manufactures, distributes, and markets bread, cakes and cookies. **Corporate headquarters location:** This location. **Other U.S. locations:** CA; OH. **Parent company:** Grupo Bimbo. **Number of employees nationwide:** 5,300.

BIRDS EYE FOODS
P.O. Box 1223, Frankston TX 75763. 903/876-4030. **Contact:** Office Manager. **World Wide Web address:** http://www.birdseyefoods.com. **Description:** Packages frozen vegetables. Brands include Birds Eye, Comstock, Freshlike, and McKenzie's. **Corporate headquarters location:** Rochester NY. **President/CEO:** Dennis M. Mullen.

BLACKMON MOORING STEAMATIC
308 Arthur Street, Fort Worth TX 76107. 817/810-9200. **Toll-free phone:** 877/730-1948. **Fax:** 817/810-5639. **Contact:** Human Resources. **World Wide Web address:** https://www.blackmonmooring.com. **Description:** A high-tech restoration and cleaning firm with affiliate companies involved in providing environmental services. BMS Enterprises Inc. has specific technical expertise with electronics and wet document recovery. The company provides disaster restoration services following fire and water catastrophes. BMS Enterprises Inc. is also involved in providing HVAC services to improve indoor air quality. **Corporate headquarters location:** This location. **Operations at this facility include:** Administration; Research and Development; Sales; Service. **Listed on:** Privately held.

BLOCKBUSTER ENTERTAINMENT GROUP
1201 Elm Street, Suite 2100, Dallas TX 75270. 214/854-3000. **Fax:** 214/854-3241. **Contact:** Personnel Director. **World Wide Web address:** http://www.blockbuster.com. **Description:** Operates a chain of video rental and music retail stores. There are approximately 7,100 Blockbuster locations worldwide. **NOTE:** Please visit website to search for jobs and apply online. Entry-level positions are offered. **Positions advertised include:** Accounting Analyst; Application Software Analyst; Application Software Engineer; Business Process Engineer; Communications Support Supervisor; Database Analyst; Development Manager; Director – Investor Relations; DVD Trading Specialist; Financial Analyst; Human Resources Manager; IT Executive; Loss Prevention Representative; Sales Representative. **Office hours:** Monday - Friday, 8:30 a.m. - 5:30 p.m. **Corporate headquarters location:** This location. **Other U.S. locations:** Nationwide. **International locations:** Worldwide. **Parent company:** Viacom. **Listed on:** New York Stock Exchange. **Stock exchange symbol:** BBI. **Number of employees worldwide:** 89,000.

BLUE CROSS BLUE SHIELD OF TEXAS
P.O. Box 655730, Dallas TX 75265-5730. 972/766-6900. **Physical address:** 901 South Central Expressway, Richardson TX 75080. **Fax:** 972/766-6102. **Recorded jobline:** 972/766-5364. **Contact:** Director of Employment. **E-mail address:** staffing@bcbstx.com. **World Wide Web address:** http://www.bcbstx.com. **Description:** A nonprofit health care insurance organization providing managed health care plans to both individuals and groups. Blue Cross and Blue Shield offers Point-of-Service, individual health, indemnity, PPO, and HMO plans. **NOTE:** Please visit website to search for jobs and for more details on applying for specific positions. **Positions advertised include:** Junior Staff Accountant; Senior Manager of Remote Facilities; Graphic Designer; Senior Diversity Analyst; Audit Coordinator; Hospital

Contract Representative; Performance Based Reimbursement Director; Marketing Communication Consultant; Regional Sales Executive; Director of Pharmacy Programs; Medical Reviewer; Data Warehouse Architect; Senior Network Operations; Senior Claims Examiner. **Corporate headquarters location:** This location. **Other area locations:** Statewide. **Number of employees nationwide:** 5,500.

BLUE DOLPHIN ENERGY COMPANY
801 Travis Street, Suite 2100, Houston TX 77002. 713/227-7660. **Fax:** 713/227-7626. **Contact:** Human Resources. **World Wide Web address:** http://www.blue-dolphin.com. **Description:** Engaged in the acquisition, exploration, and development of oil and gas properties. **Listed on:** NASDAQ. **Stock exchange symbol:** BDCO. **President:** Mike Jacobson.

BLOOD AND TISSUE CENTER OF CENTRAL TEXAS
P.O. Box 4679, Austin TX 78765-4679. 512/206-1266. **Physical address:** 4300 North Lamar Boulevard, Austin TX 78756. **Fax:** 512/206-1261. **Recorded jobline:** 512/467-53416. **Contact:** Human Resources. **E-mail address:** resumes@tcms.com. **World Wide Web address:** http://www.bloodandtissue.org. **Description:** The blood bank for 100 Central Texas-area hospitals. It also provides human tissue and organs for 66 area hospitals. **NOTE:** Part-time positions offered. Resumes may be faxed, e-mailed or mailed. Interested jobseekers may also apply in person at the Human Resources office. **Positions advertised include:** Apheresis Technician; Technical Services Director; Donor Coordinator; Medical History Interviewer; Mobile Staff Training Coordinator. **Office hours:** Monday – Friday, 9:00 a.m. – 4:00 p.m.

BLUE WHALE MOVING COMPANY
8291 Springdale Road, Suite 100, Austin TX 78724. 512/328-6688. **Fax:** 512/454-1463. **Contact:** Human Resources. **E-mail address:** bluewhale@bluewhale.com. **World Wide Web address:** http://www.bluewhale.com. **Description:** Provides both furniture storage and moving services throughout Texas. Founded in 1985.

BOBBIT, HALTER & WATSON
8700 Crownhill Boulevard, Suite 300, San Antonio TX 78209. 210/824-1555. **Fax:** 210/820-3441. **Contact:** Richard Halter, Managing Partner. **Description:** A law firm involved in many different areas including real estate, litigation, wills, and probates.

THE BOEING COMPANY
13100 Space Center Boulevard, Houston TX 77059. 281/244-4000. **Contact:** Human Resources. **World Wide Web address:** http://www.boeing.com. **Description:** The Boeing Company is one of the largest aerospace firms in the United States, one of the nation's top exporters, and one of the world's leading manufacturers of commercial jet transports. The company is a major U.S. government contractor, with capabilities in missile and space, electronic systems, military aircraft, helicopters, and information systems management. **NOTE:** Please visit website to search for jobs and apply online. Resumes are only accepted online. **Positions advertised include:** Compiler Engineer; ISS Tool Evaluator; Technical Services Specialists; Software Engineer; Engineer/Scientist – Systems Engineering; Technical Services Specialist; Staff Analyst; Quality Engineer; Contract and Pricing Administrator; Embedded Software Engineer; Business and Planning Analyst. **Special programs:** Internships. **Corporate headquarters location:** Chicago IL. **Other U.S. locations:** Nationwide. **Operations at this facility include:** This location provides engineering services and other consulting services as a division of the major aerospace and electronics manufacturer. **Listed on:** New York Stock Exchange. **Stock Exchange symbol:** BA.

THE BOEING COMPANY
9566 Railroad Drive, El Paso TX 79924. 915/834-1000. **Contact:** Human Resources. **World Wide Web address:** http://www.boeing.com. **Description:** The Boeing Company is one of the largest aerospace firms in the United States, one of the nation's top exporters, and one of the world's leading manufacturers of commercial jet transports. The company is a major U.S. government contractor, with capabilities in missile and space, electronic systems, military aircraft, helicopters, and information systems management. **NOTE:** Please visit website to search for jobs and apply online. Resumes are only accepted online. **Corporate headquarters location:** Chicago IL. **Other U.S. locations:** Nationwide. Navy. **Listed on:** New York Stock Exchange. **Stock Exchange symbol:** BA.

BOEING-IRVING
P.O. Box 152707, Irving TX 75015. 972/659-2600. **Physical address:** 3131 West Story, Irving TX. **Contact:** Human Resources Department. **World Wide Web address:** http://www.boeing.com. **Description:** Manufactures electrical components for aircraft. **NOTE:** Please visit website to search for jobs and apply online. Resumes are only accepted online. **Corporate headquarters location:** Chicago IL. **Other U.S. locations:** Nationwide. **Parent company:** The Boeing Company. **Listed on:** New York Stock Exchange. **Stock Exchange symbol:** BA.

BOISE CASCADE CORPORATION
10550 Bekay, Dallas TX 75238. 214/341-9000. **Contact:** Personnel Director. **World Wide Web address:** http://www.bc.com. **Description:** An integrated paper and forest products company with operations located nationwide. The company manufactures and distributes paper and paper products, office products, and building products; and owns and manages timberland to support these operations. Boise Cascade is one of the largest pulp and paper producers in the United States. The company has the capacity to produce 3.2 million tons of uncoated and coated papers, newsprint, containerboard, and pulp each year. Founded in 1957. **NOTE:** Please visit website to search for jobs and apply online. **Corporate headquarters location:** Boise ID. **Listed on:** New York Stock Exchange. **Stock Exchange symbol:** BCC.

THE BOMBAY COMPANY, INC.
550 Bailey Avenue, Suite 700, Fort Worth TX 76107-2111. 817/870-1847. **Fax:** 817/348-7090. **Recorded jobline:** 817/339-3799. **Contact:** Human Resources. **E-mail address:** hr@us.bombayco.com. **World Wide Web address:** http://www.bombayco.com. **Description:** A specialty retailer of ready-to-assemble home furnishings, prints, and accessories. Products are sold through over 400 Bombay Company and Alex & Ivy Stores. **NOTE:** Please visit http://www.monster.com or http://www.hotjobs.com to search for jobs and apply online. No phone calls regarding employment. **Positions advertised include:** Talent Acquisition Manager; Staff Accountant; Staff Auditor; Internet Marketing Business Development Manager; On-Line Store Manager; Human Resources Generalist; Buyer – Lighting and Candles. **Special programs:** Internships. **Corporate headquarters location:** This location. **Other U.S. locations:** Nationwide. **International locations:** Canada. **Operations at this facility include:** Administration; Sales. **Listed on:** New York Stock Exchange. **Stock exchange symbol:** BBA. **Number of employees nationwide:** 4,000.

BOOTH, INC.
P.O. Box 111754, Carrolton TX 75006-1754. 214/369-9085. **Physical address:** 1205 North Main, Carrolton TX. **Fax:** 972/245-6949. **Contact:** Human Resources Department. **World Wide Web address:** http://www.boothair.com. **Description:** An industrial manufacturing company specializing in the production of air conditioning and heating systems. **Parent company:** Trane. **Owner:** Tony Booth,

BORDER APPAREL LAUNDRY LTD.
6969-B Industrial Avenue, El Paso TX 79915. 915/772-7170. **Fax:** 915/772-4527. **Contact:** Employment. **E-mail address:** mflores@tramexdelnorte.com. **World Wide Web address:** http://www.blaundry.com. **Description:** Manufactures jeans for Levi and CK. **NOTE:** There are three facilities located in El Paso. **Corporate headquarters location:** This location. **International locations:** Toreon Mexico.

BOUDREAUX & LEONARD, P.C.
Two Houston Center, 9090 Sannin, Suite 2350, Houston TX 77010. 713/757-0000. **Fax:** 713/757-0178. **Contact:** Human Resources Manager. **World Wide Web address:** http://www.boudreauxleonard.com. **Description:** A law office. Founded in 1981. **NOTE:** Entry-level positions are offered. **Special programs:** Summer Jobs. **Corporate headquarters location:** This location. **Listed on:** Privately held.

BOWDEN TRAVEL SERVICE
CLEBURNE TRAVEL
1643 West Henderson Street, Suite A, Cleburne TX 76033-4174. 817/641-3477. **Toll-free phone:** 800/426-9336. **Fax:** 817/641-4477. **Contact:** Human Resources. **World Wide Web address:** http://www.bowdentravel.com. **Description:** A travel agency. **Company slogan:** Let us take the ravel out of your travel. **Annual sales/revenues:** Less than $5 million.

BOY SCOUTS OF AMERICA
P.O. Box 152079, Irving TX 75015-2079. **Physical address:** 1325 West Walnut Hill Lane, Irving TX 75015-2079. 972/580-2000. **Contact:** Professional Selection and Placement. **World Wide Web address:** http://www.scouting.org. **Description:** The national scouting organization for young men. Boy Scouts of America has more than 300 local councils nationwide. **Special programs:** Internships. **Corporate headquarters location:** This location. **Other U.S. locations:** Nationwide. **Listed on:** Privately held.

BRACEWELL AND PATTERSON LLP
711 Louisiana Street, Suite 2900, Houston TX 77002-2781. 713/223-2900. **Fax:** 713/221-1212. **Contact:** Jean Lenzner, Director of Attorney Employment. **E-mail address:** jlenzner@bracepatt.com. **World Wide Web address:** http://www.bracepatt.com. **Description:** A law firm divided into a litigation group and a business group. The litigation group specialties include trial, bankruptcy, and appellate law. The business group specialties include corporate, energy, and real estate law. **Other area locations:** Austin TX; Dallas TX; Corpus Christi TX; Fort Worth TX. **Other U.S. locations:** Reston VA; Washington D.C. **International locations:** Kazakhstan; London England.

BRADFIELD PROPERTIES INC.
11306 Sir Winston, San Antonio TX 78216. 210/340-6500. **Fax:** 210/340-7130. **Contact:** Boyd Bradfield, Human Resources. **World Wide Web address:** http://www.bradfieldproperties.com. **Description:** A real estate company specializing in residential, commercial, and multifamily property management. Founded 1982. **NOTE:** There are seven locations in San Antonio in addition to the corporate office. **Corporate headquarters location:** This location. **Other area locations:** Boerne TX; Bulverde TX; New Braunfels TX.

BRAZOSPORT FACTS
P.O. Box 549, Clute TX 77531. 979/265-7411. **Physical address:** 720 South Main Street, Clute TX. **Fax:** 979/265-0870. **Contact:** Dena Matthews. **World Wide Web address:** http://www.thefacts.com. **Description:** A daily newspaper.

BREDERO SHAW PRICE COMPANY
2350 North Sam Houston Parkway East, Suite 500, Houston TX 77032-3130. 281/886-2350. **Fax:** 281/886-2353. **Contact:** Human Resources. **World Wide Web address:** http://www.brederoshaw.com. **Description:** Produces corrosion coatings, weight coatings, and insulation coatings for pipelines. **Office hours:** Monday - Friday, 8:00 a.m. - 5:00 p.m. **Other area locations:** Pearland TX. **Other U.S. locations:** Orem UT; Mobile AL; Fontana CA; Etiwanda CA. **International locations:** Worldwide. **Parent company:** ShawCor Ltd. (Toronto Canada).

BRIDGESTONE AMERICAS HOLDING, INC. /FIRESTONE, INC.
6050 South Padre Island A, Corpus Christi TX 78412. 361/993-1375. **Contact:** Sandy Scarbro, Human Resources. **World Wide Web address:** http://www.bridgestone-firestone.com. **Description:** An automotive services and manufacturing company. **Corporate headquarters location:** Nashville TN. **Operations at this facility include:** This location is a district office for south Texas.

BRINKER INTERNATIONAL INC.
6820 LBJ Freeway, Dallas TX 75240. 972/980-9917. **Contact:** Corporate Recruiting. **World Wide Web address:** http://www.brinker.com. **Description:** Operates full-service, casual dining restaurants including Chili's Grill & Bar, Corner Bakery Café, Maggiano's Little Italy, On the Border, Romano's Macaroni Grill, Big Bowl Asian Kitchen, Rockfish Seafood Grill, and Spageddie's Italian Foods. **NOTE:** Please visit website to search for jobs and apply online. **Positions advertised include:** Concept Planner; Construction Project Administrator; Database Analyst; Director of Concept Development; Director of Training; Disbursement Exception Specialist; G&A Accountant; Human Resources Manager; Marketing Brand Manager; Nutritionist; Payroll Associate; Payroll Accountant; Project Coordinator; Project Manager; Quality Assurance; Real Estate Manager; Regional Training Specialist; Restaurant Accountant; Senior Concept Compensation Analyst; Vice President – Investor Relations. **Corporate headquarters location:** This location. **Other U.S. locations:** Nationwide. **Listed on:** New York Stock Exchange. **Stock exchange symbol:** EAT. **President/CEO:** Douglas H. Brooks. **Number of employees nationwide:** 90,000.

THE BRINKMANN CORPORATION
4215 McEwen Road, Dallas TX 75244. 972/387-4939. **Fax:** 972/770-8577. **Contact:** Human Resources Department. **World Wide Web address:** http://www.thebrinkmanncorp.com. **Description:** A diversified manufacturer producing items such as meat smokers, spotlights, and metal detectors. **Corporate headquarters location:** This location. **Operations at this facility include:** Manufacturing; Sales.

BROOKHAVEN COLLEGE
3939 Valley View Lane, Farmers Branch TX 75244. 972/860-4813. **Fax:** 972/860-4897. **Recorded jobline:** 214/860-243.8. **Contact:** Human Resources Department. **E-mail address:** bhcresume@dcccd.edu. **World Wide Web address:** http://www.dcccd.edu/bhc. **Description:** A two-year community college offering a full range of transferable, freshman- and sophomore-level college courses. The college serves the northern portion of Dallas County, including North Dallas, Carrollton,

Farmers Branch, Addison, Lewisville, Flower Mound, and The Colony. Brookhaven College serves 2,400 international students representing more than 100 countries and 65 languages. Founded in 1978. **NOTE:** Please visit website to view job listings. **Positions advertised include:** Instructional Dean; Dispatcher; **Corporate headquarters location:** This location. **Parent company:** Dallas County Community College District.

BROOKSHIRE BROTHERS INC.
P.O. Box 1688, Lufkin TX 75902. 936/634-8155. **Physical address:** 1201 Ellen Trout Drive, Lufkin TX 75904. **Contact:** Human Resources. **World Wide Web address:** http://www.brookshirebrothers.com. **Description:** Operates a retail grocery chain. **NOTE:** Please visit website to submit your resume online. **Office hours:** Monday – Friday, 8:00 a.m. – 5:00 p.m. **Corporate headquarters location:** This location.

BROUILLARD COMMUNICATIONS INC
1845 Woodhall Rogers Highway, Dallas TX 75201. 214/855-5155. **Fax:** 214/871-7028. **Contact:** Human Resources. **World Wide Web address:** http://www.brouillard.com. **Description:** An advertising agency. **Corporate headquarters location:** New York NY. **Other area locations:** Dallas TX. **Other U.S. locations:** Chicago IL; San Francisco CA. **International locations:** London England. **Operations at this facility include:** Administration; Divisional Headquarters. **President/CEO:** Bill Lyddan.

THE BROWN SCHOOLS
DALLAS COUNTY JUVENILE JUSTICE CHARTER SCHOOLS
1825 Market Center Boulevard, Suite 600, Dallas TX 75207. 214/752-5976. **Contact:** Human Resources. **E-mail address:** educationcareers@cedu.com. **World Wide Web address:** http://www.brownschools.com. **Description:** Provides specialty services including psychiatric and behavioral services, rehabilitation services, educational services, home health services, outpatient services, residential treatment, and adoption and foster care. The Brown Schools operate more than 25 facilities in ten states. **Corporate headquarters location:** North Palm Beach FL. **Operations at this facility include:** This school provides a Juvenile Justice Education program in a day school setting for children from age 10 – 17. The school also provides services for those placed with the Dallas County Juvenile Probation Department.

THE BROWN SCHOOLS
EXCEL ACADEMY
2525 Murworth Street, Suite 100, Houston TX 77054. 713/669-0799. **Contact:** Human Resources. **E-mail address:** educationcareers@cedu.com. **World Wide Web address:** http://www.brownschools.com/excelacademy.html. **Description:** Provides specialty services including psychiatric and behavioral services, rehabilitation services, educational services, home health services, outpatient services, residential treatment, and adoption and foster care. The Brown Schools operate more than 25 facilities in ten states. **Corporate headquarters location:** North Palm Beach FL. **Operations at this facility include:** This school provides a public education program in a day school setting for children from age 10 – 17. The school also provides transitioning services for youth leaving the Harris County Juvenile Justice Charter School.

THE BROWN SCHOOLS
HARRIS COUNTY JUVENILE JUSTICE CHARTER SCHOOLS
2525 Murworth Street, Suite 100, Houston TX 77054. 713/669-0799. **Contact:** Human Resources. **E-mail address:** educationcareers@cedu.com. **World Wide Web address:** http://www.brownschools.com/harriscounty.html. **Description:** Provides specialty services including psychiatric and behavioral services, rehabilitation services, educational services, home health services, outpatient services, residential treatment, and adoption and foster care. The Brown Schools operate more than 25 facilities in ten states. **Corporate headquarters location:** North Palm Beach FL. **Operations at this facility include:** This school provides a Juvenile Justice Education program in a day school setting for children from age 10 – 17. The school also provides services for those placed with the Harris County Juvenile Probation Department.

BROWN SIMS, P.C.
1177 West Loop South, 10th Floor, Houston TX 77027. 713/629-1580. **Fax:** 713/629-5027. **Contact:** Pat Bynum. **E-mail address:** pbynum@brownsims.com. **World Wide Web address:** http://www.brownsims.com. **Description:** A law firm specializing in shipping law. **Positions advertised include:** Legal Secretary. **Corporate headquarters location:** This location.

BROWNING-FERRIS INDUSTRIES
P.O. Box 3151, 757 North Eldridge, Houston TX 77079. **Toll-free phone:** 800/840-5409. **Contact:** Human Resources. **World Wide Web address:** http://www.investor.awin.com. **Description:** The second-largest waste management company in the United States, serving 37 states. **Parent company:** Allied Waste. **Operations at this facility include:** This location is the company's National Account Sales and Service Center. **Listed on:** New York Stock Exchange. **Stock exchange symbol:** AW.

BRUCE FOODS CORPORATION
8000 Ashley Road, El Paso TX 79934. 915/821-2500. **Fax:** 915/821-1744. **Contact:** Human Resources. **World Wide Web address:** http://www.brucefoods.com. **Description:** Processes a wide range of foods. Products include Bruce's Yams, Cajun King, Casa Fiesta, Louisiana Gold, Louisiana Hot Sauce, and Mexene Chili Products. **NOTE:** For information about employment, please call 915/821-1323. **Corporate headquarters location:** New Iberia LA. **Number of employees nationwide:** 1,200.

BUDGET RENT A CAR CORPORATION
13536 Preston Road, Suite 104, Dallas TX 75240. 972/720-0420. **Contact:** Human Resources. **World Wide Web address:** http://www.budgetrentacar.com. **Description:** A car and truck rental service. **Positions advertised include:** Agency Operator. **Other area locations:** Statewide. **Other U.S. locations:** Nationwide. **Parent company:** Cendant Corporation. **Listed on:** New York Stock Exchange. **Stock exchange symbol:** CD.

BUELL DOOR COMPANY
5200 East Grand Avenue, Dallas TX 75223. 214/827-9260. **Toll-free phone:** 800/556-0155. **Fax:** 214/826-9163. **Contact:** Human Resources. **World Wide Web address:** http://www.buelldoor.com. **Description:** A manufacturer of architectural doors and hardware.

BUNGE FOODS GROUP
P.O. Box 163289, Fort Worth TX 76161-3289. 817/625-2331. **Physical address:** 400 Exchange Avenue, Fort Worth TX 76106. **Fax:** 817/625-0057. **Contact:** Human Resources. **World Wide Web address:** http://www.bungenorthamerica.com. **Description:** Produces shortening and margarine. **NOTE:** Please visit website to submit your resume online. **Corporate headquarters location:** St. Louis MO. **Parent company:** Bunge North America. **Operations at this facility include:** Administration; Manufacturing; Sales.

BURK ADVERTISING & MARKETING, INC.
2906 McKinney Avenue, Suite 100, Dallas TX 75204. 214/953-0494. **Fax:** 214/953-6236. **Contact:** Human Resources. **World Wide Web address:** http://www.wambam.com. **Description:** An advertising and marketing agency offering a variety of print and multimedia services.

BURLINGTON NORTHERN AND SANTA FE RAILWAY COMPANY
P.O. Box 961057, Fort Worth TX 76161-0057. 817/352-1000. **Physical address:** 2650 Lou Menk Drive, Second Floor, Fort Worth TX 76131. **Toll-free phone:** 800/795-2673. **Contact:** Human Resources. **World Wide Web address:** http://www.bnsf.com. **Description:** A railroad transportation company operating on 24,500 miles of track in 25 western states and 2 Canadian provinces. The company is one of the largest haulers of low-sulfur coal and grain in North America. **NOTE:** No phone calls regarding employment. Faxed resumes are not accepted. Please visit website to search for jobs and apply online. **Positions advertised include:** Auditor; Maintenance of Way Truck Driver; Management Trainee – Various Departments; Manager of Marketing Budgets; Manager of Organization Effectiveness; Manager of Technology Services; Senior Analyst; Senior Operations Research Specialist; Track Measurement Technician. **Special programs:** Internships. **Corporate headquarters location:** This location. **Listed on:** New York Stock Exchange. **Stock exchange symbol:** BNI. **Number of employees worldwide:** 38,000.

BURLINGTON RESOURCES
5051 Westheimer Road, Suite 1400, Houston TX 77056. 713/624-9000. **Contact:** Human Resources. **World Wide Web address:** http://www.br-inc.com. **Description:** Explores for, develops, and manufactures petroleum and natural gas products. **NOTE:** Please visit website to search for jobs and apply online. Online applications are preferred. **Positions advertised include:** Geophysicist; Support Analyst. **Corporate headquarters location:** This location. **Subsidiaries include:** Meridian Oil Holdings operates pipelines and sells natural gas liquids. **Listed on:** New York Stock Exchange. **Stock exchange symbol:** BR. **President/CEO:** Bobby S. Shackouls. **Number of employees worldwide:** 2,100.

BUZZI UNICEM
1801 Lone Star Drive, Dallas TX 75212. 972/386-0400. **Contact:** Human Resources. **Description:** Manufactures and distributes cement, ready-mix concrete, and construction products. **Corporate headquarters location:** Italy.

C C CREATIONS
112 Hollerman Drive, College Station TX 77840. 979/693-9664. **Toll-free phone:** 800/324-1268. **Contact:** Human Resources. **World Wide Web address:** http://www.cccreationsonline.com. **Description:** A custom manufacturer of screen-printed and embroidered apparel and accessories.

CEC ENTERTAINMENT INC.
dba CHUCK E. CHEESE
P.O. Box 152077, Irving TX 75015. 972/258-8507. **Physical address:** 4441 West Airport Freeway, Irving TX 75062. **Fax:** 972/258-4237. **Contact:** Human Resources. **E-mail address:** careers@cecentertainment.com. **World Wide Web address:** http://www.chuckecheese.com. **Description:** Operates over 400 Chuck E. Cheese's pizza and amusement franchises throughout the United States and Canada. **NOTE:** No phone calls regarding employment. Please visit website to search for jobs and apply online. **Positions advertised include:** Manager of Loss Prevention. **Corporate headquarters location:** This location. **Listed on:** New York Stock Exchange. **Stock exchange symbol:** CEC.

CFAN COMPANY
1000 Technology Way, San Marcos TX 78666. 512/353-2832. **Fax:** 512/353-2838. **Contact:** Human Resources. **World Wide Web address:** http://www.c-fan.com. **Description:** CFAN Company manufactures composite fan blades for G.E. Aircraft Engines.

CGI
300 Burnett Street, Fort Worth TX 76113. 817/348-3681. **Contact:** Human Resources. **World Wide Web address:** http://www.cgi.com. **Description:** CGI provides technical, outsourcing and consulting services to a wide variety of companies worldwide. **NOTE:** This company offers entry-level positions. Jobseekers must create an employment profile at the company's website. **Corporate headquarters location:** Montreal CA. **Listed on:** New York Stock Exchange. **Stock exchange symbol:** GIB. **Number of employees worldwide:** 20,000.

CGI
1225 North Loop West, Suite 825, Houston TX 77008. 713/868-5537. **Fax:** 713/868-4014. **Contact:** Human Resources. **World Wide Web address:** http://www.cgi.com. **Description:** CGI provides technical, outsourcing and consulting services to a wide variety of companies worldwide. **NOTE:** This company offers entry-level positions. Jobseekers must create an employment profile at the company's website. **Corporate headquarters location:** Montreal CA. **Listed on:** New York Stock Exchange. **Stock exchange symbol:** GIB. **Number of employees worldwide:** 20,000.

CNA COMMERCIAL INSURANCE
P.O. Box 219011, Dallas TX 75221-9011. 214/220-1300. **Physical address:** 600 North Pearl Street, Plaza of the Americas, Dallas TX 75201. **Fax:** 214/220-1690. **Contact:** Human Resources. **World Wide Web address:** http://www.cna.com. **Description:** A property and casualty insurance writer offering commercial and personal policies. **NOTE:** Please visit website to register, search for jobs, and apply online. **Positions advertised include:** Claims Specialist; Risk Control Specialist Underwriting Consultant; Underwriting Director; Underwriting Specialist. **Corporate headquarters location:** Chicago IL. **Other area locations:** Addison TX; Austin TX; Houston TX; San Antonio TX. **Other U.S. locations:** Nationwide. **Operations at this facility include:** This location specializes in commercial insurance policies including worker's compensation. **Listed on:** New York Stock Exchange. **Stock exchange symbol:** CNA.

CSI INTERNATIONAL
P.O. Box 266307, Houston TX 77207. 713/845-1500. **Physical address:** 6614 Dixie Drive, Houston TX 77087. **Fax:** 713/845-1515. **Contact:** Human Resources. **E-mail address:** hr@csiionline.com. **World Wide Web address:** http://www.csiionline.com. **Description:** Manufactures control valves. **Corporate headquarters location:** This location.

CSC
400 West Cesar Chavez Street, Austin TX 78701. 512/345-5700. **Contact:** Sherry Reese, Recruiter. **World Wide Web address:** http://www.csc.com. **Description:** Develops software and provides related services for the financial services industry.

NOTE: Please visit http://careers.csc.com to search for jobs and apply online. **Positions advertised include:** Programmer Analyst; HR Generalist. **Corporate headquarters location:** El Segundo CA. **Other area locations:** Dallas TX; El Paso TX; Fort Hood TX; Fort Worth TX; Houston TX; Irving TX; McKinney TX. **Other U.S. locations:** Nationwide. **International locations:** Worldwide. **Listed on:** New York Stock Exchange. **Stock exchange symbol:** CSC. **Number of employees worldwide:** 90,000.

CABOT OIL & GAS CORPORATION
P.O. Box 4544, Houston TX 77210-4544. 281/589-4600. **Physical address:** 1200 Enclave Parkway, Houston TX 77077-1607. **Recorded jobline:** 281/589-5700. **Contact:** Human Resources Department. **E-mail address:** hr@cabotog.com. **World Wide Web address:** http://www.cabotog.com. **Description:** Involved in all facets of oil and gas, from production and drilling to the selling of refined products. **Positions advertised include:** Paralegal/Lease Analyst; Reservoir Engineer. **Corporate headquarters location:** This location. **Other U.S. locations:** Denver CO; Charleston WV. **Listed on:** New York Stock Exchange. **Stock exchange symbol:** COG. **President/CEO:** Dan O. Dinges.

CACTUS FEEDERS INC.
P.O. Box 3050, Amarillo TX 79116. 806/373-2333. **Physical address:** 22309 West 7th Avenue, Amarillo TX 79106. **Contact:** Kevin Hazelwood, Director of Employment. **E-mail address:** jobs@cactusfeeders.com. **World Wide Web address:** http://www.cactusfeeders.com. **Description:** Feeds and prepares cattle for delivery to meat packing plants and slaughterhouses. **NOTE:** Contact Employment directly at 806/371-4751. **Corporate headquarters location:** This location. **Other area locations:** Cactus TX; Spearman TX; Hereford TX; Hale Center TX; Stratford TX; Perryton TX; Tulia TX. **Other U.S. locations:** KS. **Number of employees nationwide:** 500.

CACTUS PIPE & SUPPLY COMPANY
One Greenway Plaza, Suite 450, Houston TX 77046. 713/877-1948. **Fax:** 713/877-8204. **Contact:** Controller. **Description:** A distributor of oil field pipes. **Corporate headquarters location:** This location.

CALYX SOFTWARE
3535 Travis Street, Dallas TX 75204. 214/320-8601. **Contact:** Personnel. **World Wide Web address:** http://www.calyxsoftware.com. **Description:** Designs and markets POINT for Windows, a processing application for mortgage professionals, and POINTMan, a processing application for loan agents. **Corporate headquarters location:** San Jose CA.

CAMDEN PROPERTY TRUST
3 Greenway Plaza, Suite 1300, Houston TX 77046. 713/354-2500. **Recorded jobline:** 866/524-3592. **Toll-free phone:** 800/9-CAMDEN. **Contact:** Recruiting Manager. **E-mail address:** jobs@camdenliving.com. **World Wide Web address:** http://www.camdenliving.com. **Description:** A real estate investment trust that buys, sells, builds, and manages apartment communities throughout the Southwest. **NOTE:** Entry-level positions are offered. Please visit website to search for jobs. **Positions advertised include:** Director of Internal Audit; Financial Analyst. **Corporate headquarters location:** This location. **Other area locations:** Austin TX; Corpus Christi TX; Dallas TX; El Paso TX; Fort Worth TX; San Antonio TX. **Other U.S. locations:** AZ; CA; CO; FL; KY; MO; NC; NV. **Operations at this facility include:** Administration. **Listed on:** New York Stock Exchange. **Stock exchange symbol:** CPT. **Number of employees nationwide:** 1,750.

CAMPBELL SOUP COMPANY
500 Northwest Loop 286, P.O. Box 9016, Paris TX 75460. 903/784-3341. **Contact:** Human Resources. **World Wide Web address:** http://www.campbellsoup.com. **Description:** Campbell Soup Company produces commercial soups, juices, pickles, frozen foods, canned beans, canned pasta products, spaghetti sauces, and baked goods. The company's products are distributed worldwide. U.S. brand names include Campbell's, Vlasic, V8, Chunky, Home Cookin', Prego, Pepperidge Farm, LeMenu, and Swanson. European foods are sold under brand names such as Pleybin, Biscuits Delacre, Freshbake, Groko, Godiva, and Betis. **NOTE:** Please visit website to search for jobs and apply online. **Positions advertised include:** Electrical Engineer. **Corporate headquarters location:** Camden NJ. **Other area locations:** Houston TX. **Other U.S. locations:** Sacramento CA; Maxton NC; Napoleon OH; La Grange KY; Manassas VA. **Operations at this facility include:** This location produces and cans soup. **Subsidiaries include:** Prego; Pace; V8; Pepperidge Farm; Godiva; Arnotts Biscuits of Australia. **Listed on:** New York Stock Exchange. **Stock exchange symbol:** CPB. **President/CEO:** Douglas R. Conant. **Number of employees nationwide:** 25,000.

CANTEY & HANGER, LLP
801 Cherry Street, Suite 2100, Burnett Plaza, Fort Worth TX 76102-6881. 817/877-2800. **Fax:** 817/877-2807. **Contact:** Personnel. **World Wide Web address:** http://www.canteyhanger.com. **Description:** A law firm specializing in corporate law. Founded 1882. **NOTE:** Please visit website under "Recruitment" for more information on employment. **Special programs:** Summer Associate Program. **Other area locations:** Dallas TX; Austin TX. **Other U.S. locations:** Washington D.C.

CAPITAL CITY CONTAINER CORP.
P.O. Box 870, Buda TX 78610-0870. 512/312-1222. **Physical address:** 150 Precision Drive, Buda TX. **Fax:** 512/295-4375. **Contact:** Human Resources. **World Wide Web address:** http://www.capitalcitycontainer.com. **Description:** Manufactures corrugated containers and provides die cut, direct print, and four-color process services.

CAPITAL METRO
2910 East Fifth Street, Austin TX 78702. 512/389-7400. **Fax:** 512/369-6010. **Recorded jobline:** 512/389-7450. **Contact:** Human Resources. **E-mail address:** application@capmetro.org. **World Wide Web address:** http://www.capmetro.austin.tx.us. **Description:** Operates the public bus system for the metropolitan Austin area. **NOTE:** Contact Human Resources directly at 512/389-7445. Please visit website for a listing of jobs and download application form. Resumes are accepted for additional information, but you must complete an application. **Positions advertised include:** Fleet Mechanic; Marketing Coordinator; Data Analyst; Budget Analyst. **Office hours:** Monday – Friday, 8:00 a.m. – 5:00 p.m. **Corporate headquarters location:** This location.

CAPROCK MANUFACTURING, INC.
2303 120th Street, Lubbock TX 79423. 806/745-6454. **Fax:** 806/745-9441. **Contact:** Human Resources. **E-mail address:** caprock@caprock-mfg.com. **World Wide Web address:** http://www.caprock-mfg.com. **Description:** A plastic injection molding company that manufactures plastic parts for cellular phones including phone windows and battery cases. Founded 1983. **NOTE:** Second and third shifts are offered. **Corporate headquarters location:** This location. **Listed on:** Privately held. **President:** Ryan Provenzano. **Number of employees at this location:** 160.

CAPSTONE REAL ESTATE SERVICES
210 Baron Springs Road, Suite 300, Austin TX 78704. 512/646-6700. **Fax:** 512/646-6798. **Contact:** Human Resources. **E-mail address:** info@capstonemanagement.com. **World Wide Web address:** http://www.capstonerealestate.com. **Description:** Sells, rents, and leases apartments and commercial properties. **Corporate headquarters location:** This location. **Other area locations:** Houston TX; Dallas/Fort Worth TX; San Antonio TX. **Other U.S. locations:** FL. **President:** James W. Berkey. **Number of employees nationwide:** 550.

CARDINAL HEALTH
One Butterfield Trail, El Paso TX 79906. 915/779-3681. **Fax:** 915/775-9125. **Contact:** Human Resources. **World Wide Web address:** http://www.cardinal.net. **Description:** Cardinal Health is a producer, developer, and distributor of medical products and technologies for use in hospitals and other health care settings. **NOTE:** Please visit website to register, search for jobs, and apply online. **Positions advertised include:** Distribution Expeditor; Inventory Cycle Counter; Technical Associate; Maintenance Supervisor; Sterilization Superintendent; Human Resources Manager; Raw Material Wholesale Supervisor; Group Plant Controller; Drafter; Production Supervisor; Programmer Analyst. **Corporate headquarters location:** Dublin OH. **Operations at this facility include:** This location manufactures disposable hospital gowns and drapes. **Listed on:** New York Stock Exchange. **Stock exchange symbol:** CAH. **Number of employees worldwide:** 55,000.

CARBOMEDICS, INC.
1300 East Anderson Lane, Austin TX 78752-1799. 512/435-3200. **Fax:** 512/435-3350. **Recorded jobline:** 512/435-3413. **Contact:** Human Resources. **E-mail address:** employment@carbomedics.com. **World Wide Web address:** http://www.carbomedics.com. **Description:** A manufacturer of heart valve replacement products. **Parent company:** Sorin Group.

CARGILL STEEL & WIRE
220 Avenue A, Beaumont TX 77701-2610. 409/835-3712. **Toll-free phone:** 800/365-6374. **Fax:** 409/832-7663. **Contact:** Human Resources Department. **World Wide Web address:** http://www.cargillsteel.com. **Description:** Manufactures patented concrete-reinforcing wire mesh for road and building construction customers. **NOTE:** Please visit http://www.cargill.com/hr to search for jobs and apply online. **Corporate headquarters location:** Edina MN. **Other area locations:** Carrollton TX. **Other U.S. locations:** Memphis TN. **Parent company:** Cargill Inc., with its subsidiaries and its affiliates, is involved in nearly 50 individual lines of business. The company deals in commodity trading, handling, transporting, processing, and risk management. Cargill is a major trader of grains and oilseeds, as well as a marketer of other agricultural and nonagricultural commodities. As a transporter, the company moves bulk commodities using a network of rail and road systems, inland waterways, and ocean-going routes combining its own fleet and transportation services purchased from outside sources. Agricultural products include a wide variety of feed, seed, fertilizers, and other goods and services for producers worldwide. Cargill is also a leader in producing and marketing seed varieties and hybrids. Cargill Central Research aims to develop new agricultural products to address the needs of customers around the world. The company also provides financial and technical services. Cargill's Financial Markets Division supports Cargill and its subsidiaries with financial products and services, including financial instrument trading, emerging markets instrument trading, value investing, and money management. Cargill's worldwide food processing businesses supply products ranging from basic ingredients used in food production to name brands. The company also operates a number of industrial businesses including the production of steel, industrial-grade starches, ethanol, and salt products. **Listed on:** Privately held. **President:** Jim Thompson.

CARGILL TURKEY
P.O. Box 20788, Waco TX 76702. 254/799-6211. **Contact:** Human Resources. **World Wide Web address:** http://www.cargill.com. **Description:** A turkey processor. **NOTE:** This company has many locations throughout Texas. See its corporate website for job listings. **Special Programs:** Paralegals. **Corporate headquarters location:** Minneapolis MN. **Other U.S. locations:** Nationwide. **International locations:** Worldwide.

CARLSON RESTAURANTS WORLDWIDE INC.
4201 Marsh Lane, Carrollton TX 75007. 972/662-5400. **Fax:** 972/776-5468. **Contact:** Employee Relations. **World Wide Web address:** http://www.tgifridays.com. **Description:** Operates the TGI Friday's chain of casual-dining restaurants, which has 825 restaurants that can be found in55 countries. **NOTE:** Please visit http://www.carlson.com to search for jobs. **Corporate headquarters location:** This location. **Subsidiaries include:** T.G.I. Friday's U.S.A.; T.G.I. Friday's International; Pick Up Stix. **Parent company:** Carlson Companies, Inc. (Minneapolis MN). **President/CEO:** Richard Snead.

CARRINGTON LABORATORIES
2001 Walnut Hill Lane, Irving TX 75038. 972/518-1300. **Fax:** 972/550-7556. **Contact:** Human Resources. **E-mail address:** info@carringtonlabs.com. **World Wide Web address:** http://www.carringtonlabs.com. **Description:** Develops, manufactures, and markets a number of wound care products, pharmaceutical products, and veterinary products, all of which are based on complex carbohydrates derived from aloe vera. Products include Carrasyn Hydrogel Wound Dressing; CarraSorb H Calcium Alginate Wound Dressing; CarraFilm Transparent Film Dressing; CarraSorb M Freeze-Dried Gel; DiaB, a line of wound care products for diabetics; and RadiaCare, a line of products to treat radiation dermatitis. **Corporate headquarters location:** This location. **Subsidiaries include:** DelSite; Finca Sabila; Sabila Industrial; Caraloe, Inc. manufactures and markets nutritional aloe drinks. **Parent company:** AVACARE, Inc. **Listed on:** NASDAQ. **Stock exchange symbol:** CARN. **President/CEO:** Dr. Carlton E. Turner.

CARROLL COMPANY
2900 West Kingsley Road, Garland TX 75041. 972/278-1304. **Toll-free phone:** 800/527-5722. **Fax:** 214/556-0064. **Recorded jobline:** 972/278-1304 Ext. 600. **Contact:** Human Resources Manager. **E-mail address:** info@carrollco.com. **World Wide Web address:** http://www.carrollco.com. **Description:** A manufacturer of institutional cleaning products. Founded in 1921. **NOTE:** Entry-level positions and second and third shifts are offered. **Positions advertised include:** Compounder; Warehouse Personnel; Utility Worker; Machine Operator; General Maintenance Worker. **Corporate headquarters location:** This location. **Other U.S. locations:** Santa De Springs CA; Walbridge OH. **Operations at this facility include:** Administration; Manufacturing; Regional Headquarters; Research and Development; Sales. **Listed on:** Privately held.

CARTER BURGESS INC.
777 Main Street, Fort Worth TX 76102-5304. 817/735-7161. **Fax:** 817/735-6148. **Contact:** Human Resources. **World Wide Web address:** http://www.c-b.com. **Description:** An architectural, engineering and construction firm specializing in large buildings, such as skyscrapers and public facilities, such as museums. Founded in 1939. **NOTE:** Apply online. **Positions advertised include:** Civil Designer; Mechanical CADD Technician; Mechanical Engineer; Rod Operator; Senior Marketing Coordinator; Instrument Operator; Business Development; Regional Finance Manager. **Special programs:** Internships. **Corporate headquarters location:** This location. **Other area locations:** Austin TX; Dallas TX; Houston TX; Arlington TX; San Antonio TX. **Other U.S. locations:** Nationwide. **Number of employees nationwide:** 2,300.

CAVALIER HOMES, INC.
P.O. Box 5003, Wichita Falls TX 76307. 940/723-5523. **Physical address:** 719 Scott Avenue, Suite 600, Wichita Falls TX 76301. **Contact:** Human Resources. **World Wide Web address:** http://www.cavhomebuilders.com. **Description:** Overall, Cavalier Homes, Inc. designs and manufactures a wide range of homes and markets them through approximately 500 independent dealers nationwide. **Corporate headquarters location:** Addison AL. **Operations at this facility include:** This location houses administrative offices. **Subsidiaries include:** Cavalier Acceptance Corporation provides installment sale financing to qualifying retail customers of these exclusive dealers. **Listed on:** New York Stock Exchange. **Stock Exchange symbol:** CAV.

CELANESE AG
P.O. Box 509, FM 3057, Bay City TX 77404. 979/241-4000. **Fax:** 979/241-4239. **Contact:** Human Resources. **World Wide Web address:** http://www.celanese.com. **Description:** Manufactures industrial inorganic chemicals. Celanese AG is an industrial chemical company operating in five business segments: Acetyl Products; Chemical Intermediates; Celanese Acetate Textiles; Ticona Technical Polymers; and Nurtovina Performance Products. **Other area locations:** Bishop TX; Corpus Christi TX; Dallas TX; Pampa TX; Pasadena TX. **Listed on:** New York Stock Exchange. **Stock exchange symbol:** CZ. **Number of employees worldwide:** 9,500.

CELANESE AG
Highway 77 South, P.O. Box 428, Bishop TX 78343. 361/584-6000. **Fax:** 361/584-6606. **Contact:** Human Resources. **World Wide Web address:** http://www.celanese.com. **Description:** A manufacturing plant producing chemicals and plastics. Celanese AG is an industrial chemical company operating in five business segments: Acetyl Products; Chemical Intermediates; Celanese Acetate Textiles; Ticona Technical Polymers; and Nutrovina Performance Products. **Special programs:** Internships; Co-ops. **Other area locations:** Bay City TX; Corpus Christi TX; Dallas TX; Pampa TX; Pasadena TX. **Other U.S. locations:** Nationwide. **Listed on:** New York Stock Exchange. **Stock exchange symbol:** CZ. **Number of employees worldwide:** 9,500.

CELEBRITY, INC.
P.O. Box 6666, Tyler TX 75710. 903/561-3981. **Physical address:** 4520 Old Troup Highway, Tyler TX 75707. **Contact:** Human Resources. **World Wide Web address:** http://www.celebrity-inc.com. **Description:** A supplier of artificial flowers, foliage, flowering bushes, and other decorative accessories to craft stores and other specialty retailers and to wholesale florists throughout North America and Europe. Celebrity imports over 7,000 home accent, decorative accessory, and giftware items including artificial floral arrangements; floor planters and trees; a wide range of decorative brass and textile products; and a broad line of seasonal items such as Christmas trees, wreaths, garlands and other ornamental products. **Corporate headquarters location:** This location.

CENTERPOINT ENERGY
P.O. Box 1700, Houston TX 77251-1700. 713/207-1111. **Recorded jobline:** 713/207-7373. **Contact:** Human Resources. **World Wide Web address:** http://www.centerpointenergy.com. **Description:** Formerly part of Reliant Energy Resources, CenterPoint delivers natural gas to approximately 3 million customers across six states. Also operates energy plants and transmission facilities. **NOTE:** Apply online at this company's website for open positions. **Positions advertised include:** Compensation Analyst; Gas Distribution Leader; Crewman. **Corporate headquarters location:** This location. **Listed on:** New York Stock Exchange. **Stock exchange symbol:** CNP. **Number of employees at this nationwide:** 11,000.

CENTEX CONSTRUCTION COMPANY, INC.
3100 McKinnon, 7th Floor, Dallas TX 75201. 214/468-4700. **Fax:** 214/468-4505. **Contact:** Human Resources. **E-mail address:** human.resources@checmail.com. **World Wide Web address:** http://www.centex-construction.com. **Description:** A commercial general contractor that provides preconstruction, construction, management, and general contracting services. **NOTE:** Please visit http://www.centex-careers.com to search for jobs and apply online. **Positions advertised include:** Marketing Coordinator. **Corporate headquarters location:** This location. **Other area locations:** San Antonio TX. **Other U.S. locations:** Pasadena CA; Rochester MN; Indianapolis IN; Livonia MI; Fairfax VA; Charlotte NC; Nashville TN; Marietta GA; FL (Multiple locations). **Subsidiaries include:** Centex Rogers; Centex Rooney; Centex Southeast; Centex Southwest; Centex Mid Atlantic. **Parent company:** Centex Corporation. **Listed on:** New York Stock Exchange. **Stock exchange symbol:** CTX. **CEO:** Robert C. Van Cleave.

CENTEX CORPORATION
P.O. Box 199000, Dallas TX 75219. 214/981-5000. **Physical address:** 2728 North Harwood Street, Dallas TX 75201. **Contact:** Human Resources. **E-mail address:** human.resources@checmail.com. **World Wide Web address:** http://www.centex.com. **Description:** Provides home building, mortgage banking, contracting, and construction products and services. **Positions advertised include:** Loan Officer. **Corporate headquarters location:** This location. **Other U.S. locations:** Nationwide. **International locations:** United Kingdom. **Subsidiaries include:** Centex Homes is one of America's largest homebuilders. CTX Mortgage Company is among the top retail originators of single-family home mortgages. Centex Construction Company, Inc. is one of the largest general building contractors in the United States, as well as one of the largest constructors of health care facilities. Centex Construction Products, Inc., which manufactures and distributes cement, ready-mix concrete, aggregates, and gypsum wallboard, is one of the largest U.S.-owned cement producers. Centex Development Company, LP conducts real estate development activities. **Listed on:** New York Stock Exchange. **Stock exchange symbol:** CTX. **Number of employees worldwide:** 18,000.

CENTRAL FREIGHT LINES, INC.
6315 Highway 347, Beaumont TX 77705. 409/722-8371. **Contact:** Human Resources. **E-mail address:** recruitingoffice@centralfreight.com. **World Wide Web address:** http://www.centralfreight.com. **Description:** One of the largest regional motor carriers in the United States operating through 77 terminals. Founded in 1925. **NOTE:** Please send resumes to corporate office at P.O. Box 2638, Waco TX 76702; fax is 254/741-5251. **Corporate headquarters location:** Waco TX. **Other area locations:** Statewide. **Other U.S. locations:** Nationwide.

CENTRAL FREIGHT LINES, INC.
2615 Spur 482, Irving TX 75062-4949. 972/579-4111. **Contact:** Human Resources. **E-mail address:** recruitingoffice@centralfreight.com. **World Wide Web address:** http://www.centralfreight.com. **Description:** One of the largest regional motor carriers in the United States operating through 77 terminals. Founded in 1925. **NOTE:** Please send resumes to corporate office at P.O. Box 2638, Waco TX 76702; fax is 254/741-5251. **Corporate headquarters location:** Waco TX. **Other area locations:** Statewide. **Other U.S. locations:** Nationwide.

CENTRAL FREIGHT LINES, INC.
P.O. Box 2638, Waco TX 76702. 254/772-2120. **Toll-free phone:** 800/782-5036. **Physical address:** 5601 West Waco Drive, Waco TX 76710. **Fax:** 254/741-5251. **Contact:** Human Resources. **E-mail address:** recruitingoffice@centralfreight.com. **World Wide Web address:** http://www.centralfreight.com. **Description:** One of the largest regional motor carriers in the United States operating through 77 terminals. Founded in 1925. **Corporate headquarters location:** This location. **Other area locations:** Statewide. **Other U.S. locations:** Nationwide.

CERNER RADIOLOGY INFORMATION SYSTEMS
5 Greenway Plaza, Suite 2000, Houston TX 77046. 832/325-1500. **Contact:** Human Resources. **World Wide Web address:** http://www.cerner.com. **Description:** Engaged in the design, development, and support of hospital information systems for both clinical and business applications. **NOTE:** Please visit website to search for jobs and apply online. **Corporate headquarters location:** Kansas City MO. **Other U.S. locations:** Detroit MI; St Louis MO; Denver CO; Lake Mary FL; Waltham MA; Washington D.C. **International locations:** Worldwide. **Parent company:** Cerner Corporation. **Listed on:** NASDAQ. **Stock exchange symbol:** CERN. **Number of employees worldwide:** 5,105.

CERUTTI PRODUCTIONS
3410 Saddle Point, San Antonio TX 78259-3625. 210/403-0800. **Contact:** Mark Cerutti, President. **E-mail address:** Marc@Cerutti.org. **World Wide Web address:** http://www.filcro.com/cerutti.html. **Description:** A video production studio offering talent, engineering, and technical services. **NOTE:** See website for instructions about how to submit resumes and portfolio items. **Positions advertised include:** Production Assistants; Writers; Post Production Assistants; Marketing Assistants; Sales Representatives; Voice-over talent. **Listed on:** Privately held.

CHANNEL 2 KPRC-TV
P.O. Box 2222, Houston TX 77252-2222. 713/222-2222. **Physical address:** 8181 Southwest Freeway, Houston TX 77074. **Contact:** Human Resources. **World Wide Web address:** http://www.click2houston.com. **Description:** A television broadcasting company and NBC affiliate. **NOTE:** Please visit website to view job listings. **Positions advertised include:** News Producer Trainee; Sports Anchor; News Managing Editor; Producer; National Sales Manager; Junior Sales Account Executive; News Associate Producer; Graphic Designer; Technical Director; News Producer; Public File Report. **Special programs:** Internships.

CHARLES SCHWAB
100 Congress Street, Austin TX 78701. 512/370-3880. **Toll-free phone:** 877/729-2379. **Contact:** Human Resources. **World Wide Web address:** http://www.schwab.com. **Description:** Founded in 1974, this company is a large financial firm marketing its services to individuals, institutions, and financial professionals. This location manages the operations for its online trading subsidiary, Cybertrader. **NOTE:** To read more about Cybertrader, visit its website at http://www.cybertrader.com. Apply online. **Positions advertised include:** Technology Solutions Staff; Staff Software Developer; Reporter Developer; Associate Web Application Developer. **Listed on:** New York Stock Exchange. **Stock exchange symbol:** SCH. **Number of employees worldwide:** 19,000.

CHASE BANK OF TEXAS
2200 Ross Avenue, Suite 720, Dallas TX 75201. 214/965-2925. **Contact:** Human Resources. **World Wide Web address:** http://www.chase.com. **Description:** Operates through a network of 40 member banks in Texas. Operations include energy, commercial, real estate, and international banking. **NOTE:** Please visit http://careers.jpmorganchase.com to search for jobs and apply online. **Other U.S. locations:** Nationwide. **International locations:** Worldwide. **Parent company:** J.P. Morgan.

CHASE BANK OF TEXAS
712 Main Street, Houston TX 77002. 713/216-4952. **Contact:** Human Resources. **World Wide Web address:** http://www.chase.com. **Description:** A banking organization, operating through a network of 40 member banks in Texas. Operations include energy, commercial, real estate, and international banking. **NOTE:** Please visit http://careers.jpmorganchase.com to search for jobs and apply online. **Other U.S. locations:** Nationwide. **International locations:** Worldwide. **Parent company:** J.P. Morgan.

CHEMICAL LIME COMPANY
P.O. Box 985004, Fort Worth TX 76185-5004. **Physical address:** 3700 Hulen Street, Fort Worth TX 76107. 817/732-8164. **Fax:** 817/732-8564. **Contact:** Debbie Childress, Human Resources. **World Wide Web address:** http://www.chemicallime.com. **Description:** A manufacturer and distributor of chemical lime products. The company's principal products are high calcium limestone, dolomite limestone, dolomite glass flux, high-calcium quicklime, dolomitic quicklime, calcium-hydrated lime, and dolomitic-hydrated lime under the trade name Type S Hydrated Lime for use in the construction industry. **Corporate headquarters location:** This location. **Other area locations:** Statewide. **Other U.S. locations:** Nationwide.

CHESHIER AND FULLER, L.L.P.
14175 Proton Road, Dallas TX 75244-3604. 972/387-4300. **Toll-free phone:** 800/834-8586. **Fax:** 972/960-2810. **Contact:** John Gallagher, Human Resources. **World Wide Web address:** http://www.cheshier-fuller.com. **Description:** Offers accounting, tax, audit, management advisory, business valuation, and litigation support services. Founded in 1956. **Special programs:** Training; Summer Jobs. **Office hours:** Monday - Friday, 8:30 a.m. - 5:30 p.m. **Corporate headquarters location:** This location. **Listed on:** Privately held.

CHEVRON PHILLIPS CHEMICAL COMPANY.
P.O. Box 4910, The Woodlands TX 77387-4910. 832/813-4100. **Physical address:** 10001 Six Pine Drive, The Woodlands TX 77380. **Toll-free phone:** 800/231-1212. **Contact:** Human Resources. **World Wide Web address:** http://www.chpchem.com. **Description:** Manufactures specialty chemicals for the oil, mining and related industrial markets. Founded in 2000. **NOTE:** Apply online. **Positions advertised**

include: Mechanical Reliability Engineer. **Parent company:** ChevronTexaco Corporation and ConocoPhillips. **Listed on:** Privately held. **Number of employees worldwide:** 5,000.

CHEVRONTEXACO CORPORATION
1111 Bagby Street, Houston TX 77002. 713/752-6000. **Contact:** Employment Office. **World Wide Web address:** http://www.chevrontexaco.com. **Description:** A global energy company engaged in all aspects of the oil and gas industry, including exploration and production; refining, marketing and transportation; chemicals manufacturing and sales; and power generation. **NOTE:** Please visit website to search for jobs and apply online. **Positions advertised include:** Guide Curve Attorney; Trading Representative; Senior Information Specialist; Trading Analyst; Information Analyst; Technical Analyst; Contract Administrator; Global Compliance Specialist; Lease Trading Analyst. **Special programs:** Internships. **Corporate headquarters location:** San Ramon CA. **International locations:** Worldwide. **Listed on:** New York Stock Exchange. **Stock exchange symbol:** CVX. **Number of employees worldwide:** 53,000.

CHEVRONTEXACO CORPORATION
1301 McKinney, Houston TX 77010. 713/754-2000. **Contact:** Human Resources Department. **World Wide Web address:** http://www.chevrontexaco.com. **Description:** Produces petrochemicals. Chevron Texaco is a global energy company engaged in all aspects of the oil and gas industry, including exploration and production; refining, marketing and transportation; chemicals manufacturing and sales; and power generation. **NOTE:** Please visit website to search for jobs and apply online. **Positions advertised include:** Guide Curve Attorney; Trading Representative; Senior Information Specialist; Trading Analyst; Information Analyst; Technical Analyst; Contract Administrator; Global Compliance Specialist; Lease Trading Analyst. **Special programs:** Internships. **Corporate headquarters location:** San Francisco CA. **International locations:** Worldwide. **Operations at this facility include:** Administration; Divisional Headquarters; Sales. **Listed on:** New York Stock Exchange. **Stock exchange symbol:** CVX. **Number of employees worldwide:** 53,000.

CHICAGO TITLE INSURANCE COMPANY
909 Fannon, Suite 200, Houston TX 77010. 713/659-1411. **Fax:** 713/286-6298. **Contact:** Mary Wisnoski, Employee Services Officer. **E-mail address:** wisnoskim@ctt.com. **World Wide Web address:** http://www.houston.ctic.com. **Description:** Provides title insurance. **Corporate headquarters location:** Chicago IL. **Other area locations:** Statewide. **Other U.S. locations:** Nationwide. **Subsidiaries include:** Ticor Title Security Union. **Parent company:** Fidelity National Financial. **Operations at this facility include:** Administration; Divisional Headquarters; Sales; Service. **Listed on:** New York Stock Exchange. **Stock exchange symbol:** FNF.

CHILD CARE ASSOCIATES
P.O. Box 7935, Fort Worth TX 76111. 817/838-0055. **Physical address:** 3000 East Belknap, 3rd Floor, Fort Worth TX 76111. **Contact:** Human Resources. **World Wide Web address:** http://www.childcareassociates.org. **Description:** A nonprofit daycare association. The organization's primary function is assisting low-income families in finding affordable daycare. **NOTE:** Please visit website to view job listings. There area several offices located in Fort Worth. **Positions advertised include:** Assistant Center Director; Center Director; Cook; Early Head Start Teacher; Housekeeper; Teacher; Teacher Assistant; Disabilities Services Assistant; Mentor Teacher; Secretary/Clerk. **Corporate headquarters location:** This location. **Other area locations:** Denton TX; Plano TX; Abilene TX.

CHILDREN'S MEDICAL CENTER OF DALLAS
1935 Motor Street, Dallas TX 75235. 214/456-7000. **Contact:** Human Resources. **World Wide Web address:** http://www.childrens.com. **Description:** A private, 322-bed children's medical center operating through 50 specialty clinics. **NOTE:** Please visit website to view job listings and apply online. Contact Human Resources directly at 214/456-2895. **Positions advertised include:** Advanced Practice Nurse; Licensed Vocational Nurse; Management; Nursing Support; RN; Associate Diagnostic Imaging Technician; Cancer Registrar; Child Life Assistant; Clinical Pharmacist; Clinical Research Associate; Dental Hygienist; Lab Support Specialist; Nutrition Technician; Pharmacist; Speech Pathologist; Manager – Clinical Research; Respiratory Care Practitioner; Financial Counselor; Events Specialist; Guest Relations Representative; Payroll Specialist; Volunteer Coordinator; Office Support – Various Departments.

CHILDREN'S NUTRITION RESOURCE CENTER (CNRC)
1100 Bates Street, Houston TX 77030. 713/798-7000. **Contact:** Human Resources. **E-mail address:** cnrc@bcm.tmc.edu **World Wide Web address:** http://www.bcm.tmc.edu/cnrc. **Description:** Researches the nutrition needs of children, pregnant women, and nursing mothers. **NOTE:** Please visit website to view job listings, apply online, or download application form. **Positions advertised include:** Senior Research Assistant. **Parent company:** Baylor College of Medicine and the U.S. Department of Agriculture.

CHRISTUS ST. JOSEPH HOSPITAL
1401 Saint Joseph's Parkway, Houston TX 77002. 713/756-5604. **Contact:** Human Resources. **E-mail address:** careers.stjoseph@christushealth.org. **World Wide Web address:** http://www.christusstjoseph.org. **Description:** A 834-bed, nonprofit medical center. Founded in 1887. **NOTE:** Entry-level positions and second and third shifts are offered. Please visit https://jobs.christushealth.org to search for jobs and apply online. **Positions advertised include:** Buyer; Case Manager; Certified Respiratory Therapist; Clinical Nurse – Various Departments; Coder; Coding Coordinator; Cook; Customer Service Representative; Director of Emergency Department; ER Room Lab Supervisor; Financial Counselor; House Supervisor; Lab Assistant; Maintenance Mechanic; Medical Technologist; Mental Health Technician; Patient Care Technician; Physical Therapist; Reimbursement Specialist; Security Officer; Staff Accountant; Sterile Processing Technician. **Special programs:** Internships; Training; Co-ops. **Parent company:** CHRISTUS Health. **Operations at this facility include:** Service. **Listed on:** Privately held.

CHRISTUS SANTA ROSA HOSPITAL
333 North Santa Rosa Street, San Antonio TX 78207. 210/704-2011. **Contact:** Human Resources. **World Wide Web address:** http://www.christussantarosa.org. **Description:** Santa Rosa Hospital is an acute care hospital with 500 beds. **NOTE:** Contact Human Resources at 210/704-2067. Visit http://heavenlycareers.com to search for jobs. **Positions advertised include:** Registered Nurse; Pre Access Nurse; Licensed Vocational Nurse; Nurse Liaison; Respiratory Therapist; Medical Technologist; Physical Therapist; Registered Nuclear Medicine Technologist; Histology Technician; Medical Lab Technician; Radiology Technician; Laboratory Section Supervisor; OR Technician; Physical Therapy Assistant; Pharmacist; Case Manager; Social Worker; Enterstomal Therapy Nurse; PAL Supervisor; Speech Pathologist; Recreation Therapist; Occupational Therapist; Radiology Director; Senior Financial Analyst; Clerk Phlebotomist. **Parent company:** CHRISTUS Health.

CHRISTUS SPOHN HOSPITAL SHORELINE
600 Elizabeth Street, Corpus Christi TX 78404. 361/881-3000. **Contact:** Human Resources. **World Wide Web address:** http://www.christusspohn.org. **Description:** A 432-bed acute care medical facility. **NOTE:** Please visit website to search for jobs and apply online. **Positions advertised include:** Vice President of Strategic Planning and Business Development; Clinical Dietitian; CRT; LVN; OR Technician; Radiology Technologist; RN – Various Departments; Registered Respiratory Therapist; Ultrasound Technician. **Corporate headquarters location:** San Antonio TX. **Parent company:** CHRISTUS Health. **Operations at this facility include:** Service.

CHS FOODS
899 North Houston Street, Fort Worth TX 76106. 817/624-2123. **Contact:** Human Resources. **World Wide Web address:** http://www.chsinc.com. **Description:** A national association of food and grains cooperatives. **NOTE:** For Corporate job listings available on website. Job listings for cooperatives can be found on http://www.mbrservices.com/Employment. **Corporate headquarters location:** Inver Grove Heights MN. **Other U.S. locations:** Nationwide. **Operations at this facility include:** Manufacturing of frozen Mexican foods. **Listed on:** NASDAQ. **Stock exchange symbol:** CHSCP.

CHUBB GROUP OF INSURANCE COMPANIES
2001 Brian Street, Suite 3400, Dallas TX 75201-3068. 214/754-0777. **Fax:** 214/754-8129. **Contact:** Personnel Manager. **E-mail address:** dallasresumes@chubb.com. **World Wide Web address:** http://www.chubb.com. **Description:** A property and casualty insurer with more than 130 offices in 32 countries worldwide. Chubb Group of Insurance Companies offers a broad range of specialty insurance services designed for individuals and businesses, serving industries including high-technology, financial institutions, and general manufacturers. Founded in 1882. **NOTE:** Please visit website to search for jobs. **Positions advertised include:** Multi-Line Commercial Underwriter; Senior Examiner; Underwriting Associate. **Corporate headquarters location:** Warren NJ. **Other area locations:** Austin TX; Houston TX; San Antonio TX. **Other U.S. locations:** Nationwide. **International locations:** Worldwide. **Number of employees worldwide:** 12,000.

CHUNG'S GOURMET FOOD
3907 Dennis Street, Houston TX 77004. 713/741-2118. **Toll-free phone:** 800/8-CHUNGS. **Fax:** 713/741-2330. **Contact:** Human Resources. **E-mail address:** work@chungsfoods.com. **World Wide Web address:** http://chungsfoods.com. **Description:** Manufactures food products including egg rolls and other Chinese entrees. **CEO:** Bridgette Heller.

CINEMARK USA, INC.
3900 Dallas Parkway, Suite 500, Plano TX 75093-7865. 972/665-1000. **Fax:** 972/665-1004. **Contact:** Human Resources. **World Wide Web address:** http://www.cinemark.com. **Description:** Operates approximately 300 theatres with 3,000 screens nationwide and internationally. Also manages the IMAX theatres. **NOTE:** To apply for corporate, sales, mechanical or management positions, mail resume with specific salary requirements to the Dallas office. For theatre attendant positions, visit the nearest location. See website for locations.

CIRRUS LOGIC, INC.
2901 Via Fortuna, Austin TX 78746. 512/851-4000. **Contact:** Human Resources. **World Wide Web address:** http://www.cirrus.com. **Description:** Designs, markets, and tests computer chips for audio, digital, multimedia, and telecommunication products. Cirrus Logic also supplies high-performance analog circuits. **Positions advertised include:** Operations Production Control Planner Product Marketing Manager; Senior Digital Design Engineer; Analog Design Engineer; Applications Engineer; Senior Internal Auditor; Digital Design Engineer; Staff Design Engineer. **Special programs:** Internships. **Corporate headquarters location:** This location. **International locations:** Hong Kong China; Tokyo Japan; Henley-on-Thames United Kingdom.

CISCO-EAGLE
2120 Valley View Lane, Dallas TX 75234. 972/406-9330. **Toll-free phone:** 800/877-3861. **Fax:** 972/406-9577. **Contact:** Human Resources. **E-mail address:** personnel@cisco-eagle.com. **World Wide Web address:** http://www.cisco-eagle.com. **Description:** Cisco-Eagle's expertise in is warehouse management, including warehouse space and design, process flow, material handling, labor needs and technology. They also sell warehouse furnishings, such as benches, ladders, pallets; containers; carts and trucks. **Corporate headquarters location:** This location. **Other U.S. locations:** OK; AK. **Operations at this facility include:** This location serves as the company's main engineering office and warehouse.

CISCO JUNIOR COLLEGE
717 East Industrial, Abilene TX 79602. 915/673-4567. **Contact:** Personnel. **World Wide Web address:** http://www.cisco.cc.tx.us. **Description:** A junior college. **NOTE:** Please visit website to view job listings and download application form. **Positions advertised include:** Custodian; Plant/Operations Supervisor. **Other area locations:** Cisco TX.

CISCO JUNIOR COLLEGE
101 College Heights, Cisco TX 76437. 254/442-2567. **Contact:** Personnel. **World Wide Web address:** http://www.cisco.cc.tx.us. **Description:** A junior college. **NOTE:** Please visit website to view job listings and download application form. Contact Personnel directly at 254/442-5121. **Positions advertised include:** Assistant Director of Financial Aid. **Other area locations:** Abilene TX.

CITICORP US SERVICE CENTER
100 Citibank Drive, San Antonio TX 78245-3214. 210/677-6500. **Fax:** 210/677-7047. **Contact:** Human Resources. **World Wide Web address:** http://careers.citibank.com/sanantonio. **Description:** A data and customer service center for the nationwide banking company.

CITGO
CORPUS CHRISTI REFINERY
1802 Nueces Bay Boulevard Corpus Christi TX 78408. 361/844-4000. **Contact:** Human Resources. **World Wide Web address:** http://www.citigroup.com. **Description:** One of the world's largest oil producers. It produces about 1 million gallons a day. It has 13,000 gas stations nationwide. **Positions advertised include:** Environmental Advisor; Manager Machinery Maintenance & Reliability, Project Engineers; Project Manager. **NOTE:** Apply online. Other U.S. locations include: LA; IL.

CITIGROUP
6400 Las Colinas Boulevard, Irving TX 75039. 972/653-3436. **Fax:** 972/653-8154. **Contact:** Jim Price, Human Resources. **World Wide Web address:** http://www.citigroup.com. **Description:** Citigroup offers financial solutions with home

mortgages, credit cards, personal loans, insurance, business financing, banking and investments. **NOTE:** Please visit website to search for jobs and apply online. **Positions advertised include:** Citified Loan Processor, Marketing Administrator; Credit Specialist; Senior Underwriter; Mortgage Processor; Senior Lead Analyst; QC Analyst; Associate Finance Director; Vice President of Financial Planning. Corporate headquarters location: New York NY. **Other U.S. locations:** Nationwide. **Listed on:** New York Stock Exchange. **Stock exchange symbol:** C.

CITIZENS, INC.
P.O. Box 149151, Austin TX 78714. 512/837-7100. 400 East Anderson Lane, Austin TX 78752. **Fax:** 512/836-9785. **Contact:** Human Resources. **World Wide Web address:** http://www.citizensinc.com. **Description:** A life insurance holding company. **NOTE:** Please visit website to view job listings and apply online. **Positions advertised include:** Executive Assistant; Accounting Manager; Commissions Technician; Actuarial Manager; Operations Manager; Claims Processor; Customer Relations Manager; Assistant Counselor; Training Director. **Corporate headquarters location:** This location. **Listed on:** New York Stock Exchange. **Stock exchange symbol:** CIA.

CITIZENS MEDICAL CENTER
P.O. Box 2024, Victoria TX 77902. 361/573-9181. **Physical address:** 2701 Hospital Drive, Victoria TX 77901. **Fax:** 361/573-0611. **Contact:** Human Resources. **E-mail address:** sfrank@cmcvtx.org. **World Wide Web address:** http://www.citizensmedicalcenter.com. **Description:** A 368-bed acute care medical center. Citizens Medical Center provides many services including a Women's Pavilion and a cancer treatment floor. Founded in 1956. **NOTE:** Contact Employment directly at 361/572-5066. **Positions advertised include:** Fitness Specialist; Physical Therapist; Physical Therapy Assistant; RN – Various Departments. **Number of employees at this location:** 1,300.

CITY MACHINE & WELDING, INC.
P.O. Box 51018, Amarillo TX 79159-1018. 806/358-7293. **Physical address:** 9701 Interchange 552, Amarillo TX 79124. **Fax:** 806/358-7906. **Contact:** Human Resources. **World Wide Web address:** http://www.cmwelding.com. **Description:** Manufactures transport trailers and performs welding services. **President:** L.A. Oeschger.

CLARK, THOMAS & WINTERS
P.O. Box 1148, Austin TX 78767. 512/472-8800. **Physical address:** 300 West 6th Street, 15th Floor, Austin TX 78701. **Fax:** 512/474-1129. **Contact:** Jean Atkisslin, Assistant to the President. **World Wide Web address:** http://www.ctw.com. **Description:** A law firm specializing in a variety of areas including antitrust, environmental, and product liability law. **NOTE:** Please visit website to view job listings. **Corporate headquarters location:** This location. **Other area locations:** San Antonio TX.

CLARKE AMERICAN CHECKS, INC.
10931 Laureate Drive, San Antonio TX 78249. 210/697-8888. **Recorded jobline:** 210/690-6500. **Contact:** Human Resources. **World Wide Web address:** http://www.clarkeamerican.com. **Description:** A leading printer of checks and share drafts for the financial industry. Founded in 1874. **NOTE:** Please visit http://www.monster.com to search for jobs and apply online. **Positions advertised include:** Director of e-Commerce; Vice President of Information Technology Service Delivery; Human Resources Generalist. **Special programs:** Internships. **Corporate headquarters location:** This location. **Other U.S. locations:** Nationwide. **Parent company:** Novar plc. **Operations at this facility include:** Regional Headquarters. **Listed on:** Privately held. **Number of employees nationwide:** 3,500.

CLAYTON WILLIAMS ENERGY
6 Desta Drive, Suite 3000, Midland TX 79705. 432/682-6324. **Contact:** Patty Hollums, Personnel Manager. **World Wide Web address:** http://www.claytonwilliams.com. **Description:** Engaged in oil exploration and development. This company also manages Cyberbasin, an Internet service provider (Midland TX). **Corporate headquarters location:** This location. **Other U.S. locations:** NM. **Listed on:** NASDAQ. **Stock exchange symbol:** CWEI.

CLEAR CHANNEL COMMUNICATIONS
200 Basse Road, San Antonio TX 78209. 210/822-2828. **Fax:** 210/822-2299. **Contact:** Personnel. **World Wide Web address:** http://www.clearchannel.com. **Description:** A nationwide television and radio broadcasting company. Clear Channel Communications operates approximately 1,225 radio and 37 television stations in the United States. **NOTE:** Please visit http://www.clearcareers.com to search for jobs and apply online. Clear Channel also has a location in Corpus Christi TX. To apply or for more information, e-mail the company at corpuschristijobs@clearchannel.com. **Positions advertised include:** Treasury Analyst; Photographer – Part-time; Production Assistant; Traffic Anchor; Traffic Department; Payroll Tax Specialist. **Corporate headquarters location:** This location. **Listed on:** New York Stock Exchange. **Stock exchange symbol:** CCU.

CLINICAL LABS USA
4747 Irving Boulevard, Suite 245, Dallas TX 75247. 214/630-5227. **Contact:** Human Resources. **Description:** A full-service medical laboratory that provides comprehensive clinical laboratory services, such as tests and blood work, for long-term care facilities and for people in home health care.

COACH USA, INC.
One Riverway, Suite 500, Houston TX 77056. 713/888-0104. **Toll-free phone:** 888/262-2487. **Fax:** 713/888-0257. **Contact:** Human Resources. **World Wide Web address:** http://www.coachusa.com. **Description:** One of the largest bus transportation companies. Among its services are sightseeing tours in major metropolitan cities. **Other U.S. locations include:** CA; CT; GA; MN; MD; NJ; NY; NC. **International locations:** Canada. **Parent company:** Stagecoach International (United Kingdom). **Listed on:** New York Stock Exchange. **Stock exchange symbol:** CUI.

COCA-COLA BOTTLING COMPANY
2400 West Expressway 83, McAllen TX 78501. 956/632-3700. **Fax:** 956/632-3719. **Contact:** Employee Relations Manager. **World Wide Web address:** http://www.coca-cola.com. **Description:** This location is packages Coca-Cola, Barq's, and Dr. Pepper. **Corporate headquarters location:** Atlanta GA. **Other U.S. locations:** Nationwide. **Parent company:** Coca-Cola Company is one of the world's largest marketers, distributors, and producers of bottle and can products. Coca-Cola Enterprises, part of the Coca-Cola Company, is in the liquid nonalcoholic refreshment business, which includes traditional carbonated soft drinks, still and sparkling waters, juices, isotonics, and teas. The company operates in 38 states, the District of Columbia, the U.S. Virgin Islands, the Islands of Tortola and Grand Cayman, and the Netherlands. Including recent acquisitions, Coca-Cola Enterprises franchise territories encompass a population of over 154 million people, representing 54 percent of the population of the United States. Coca-Cola Enterprises operates 268 facilities, approximately 24,000 vehicles, and over 860,000 vending machines, beverage dispensers, and coolers used to market, distribute, and produce the company's products. **Listed on:** New York Stock Exchange. **Stock exchange symbol:** KO. **Number of employees worldwide:** 49,000.

COCA-COLA BOTTLING COMPANY
2311 Denton Drive, Austin TX 78758. 512/836-9051. **Contact:** Human Resources. **World Wide Web address:** http://www.coca-cola.com. **Description:** A distribution plant that bottles and ships Coca-Cola products to the surrounding area. **Corporate headquarters location:** Atlanta GA. **Other U.S. locations:** Nationwide. **Parent company:** Coca-Cola Company is one of the world's largest marketers, distributors, and producers of bottle and can products. Coca-Cola Enterprises, part of the Coca-Cola Company, is in the liquid nonalcoholic refreshment business, which includes traditional carbonated soft drinks, still and sparkling waters, juices, isotonics, and teas. The company operates in 38 states, the District of Columbia, the U.S. Virgin Islands, the Islands of Tortola and Grand Cayman, and the Netherlands. Including recent acquisitions, Coca-Cola Enterprises franchise territories encompass a population of over 154 million people, representing 54 percent of the population of the United States. Coca-Cola Enterprises operates 268 facilities, approximately 24,000 vehicles, and over 860,000 vending machines, beverage dispensers, and coolers used to market, distribute, and produce the company's products. **Listed on:** New York Stock Exchange. **Stock exchange symbol:** KO. **Number of employees worldwide:** 49,000.

COCA-COLA BOTTLING COMPANY OF NORTH TEXAS
P.O. Box 132008, Dallas TX 75313-9773. 214/357-1781. **Physical address:** 6011 Lemmon Avenue, Dallas TX 75209. **Recorded jobline:** 214/902-2634. **Contact:** Human Resources. **World Wide Web address:** http://www.coca-cola.com. **Description:** Coca-Cola Bottling Company of North Texas is a regional subsidiary of Coca-Cola Enterprises. **Special programs:** Internships. **Corporate headquarters location:** Atlanta GA. **Other U.S. locations:** Nationwide. **Parent company:** Coca-Cola Enterprises Inc. is in the liquid, nonalcoholic refreshment business, which includes traditional carbonated soft drinks, still and sparkling waters, juices, isotonics, and teas. The company operates in 38 states, the District of Columbia, the U.S. Virgin Islands, the Islands of Tortola and Grand Cayman, and the Netherlands. **Operations at this facility include:** This location houses executive offices. **Listed on:** New York Stock Exchange. **Stock exchange symbol:** KO. **Number of employees worldwide:** 49,000.

COCA-COLA BOTTLING COMPANY OF THE SOUTHWEST
P.O. Box 58, San Antonio TX 78291. 210/225-2601. **Recorded jobline:** 210/229-0485. **Contact:** Human Resources. **World Wide Web address:** http://www.cokecce.com. **Description:** A bottling company packaging Coca-Cola, Barq's, and Dr. Pepper. **Parent company:** Coca-Cola Enterprises, Inc. is a public and independent company from Coca-Cola, Inc. Coca-Cola Enterprises markets, bottles and distributes Coke and other non-alcoholic beverages, such as still and sparkling waters, juices, isotonics, and teas. This company has facilities in most of the major metropolitan Texas cities. **NOTE:** See website for Coca-Cola Bottling Company of the Southwest job listings and application information. **Listed on:** New York Stock Exchange. **Stock exchange symbol:** CCE.

COLDWELL BANKER
7447 North MacArthur Boulevard, Suite 190, Irving TX 75063. 469/420-3900. **Fax:** 972/373-0853. **Contact:** Personnel. **World Wide Web address:** http://www.coldwellbanker.com. **Description:** One of the largest residential real estate companies in the United States and Canada in terms of total home sales transactions. Coldwell Banker is also a leader in corporate relocation services. **NOTE:** This office hires agents only. Please visit website to search for jobs. **Corporate headquarters location:** Parsippany NJ. **Other U.S. locations:** Nationwide. **Parent company:** Cendant Corporation. **Listed on:** New York Stock Exchange. **Stock exchange symbol:** CD. **Number of employees worldwide:** 112,000.

COLDWELL BANKER
2801 Gateway Drive, Suite 180, Irving TX 75063. 972/582-9202. **Contact:** Personnel. **World Wide Web address:** http://www.coldwellbanker.com. **Description:** One of the largest residential real estate companies in the United States and Canada in terms of total home sales transactions. Coldwell Banker is also a leader in corporate relocation services. **NOTE:** Please visit website to search for jobs. **Corporate headquarters location:** Parsippany NJ. **Other U.S. locations:** Nationwide. **Parent company:** Cendant Corporation. **Listed on:** New York Stock Exchange. **Stock exchange symbol:** CD. **Number of employees worldwide:** 112,000.

COLDWELL BANKER
4920 A Seawall Boulevard, Galveston TX 77554. 409/740-4040. **Toll-free phone:** 800/701-1016. **Fax:** 409/740-3586. **Contact:** Personnel. **E-mail address:** galveston@coldwellbankerunited.com. **World Wide Web address:** http://www.coldwellbanker.com. **Description:** One of the largest residential real estate companies in the United States and Canada in terms of total home sales transactions. Coldwell Banker is also a leader in corporate relocation services. **NOTE:** Please visit website to search for jobs. **Corporate headquarters location:** Parsippany NJ. **Other U.S. locations:** Nationwide. **Parent company:** Cendant Corporation. **Listed on:** New York Stock Exchange. **Stock exchange symbol:** CD. **Number of employees worldwide:** 112,000.

COLDWELL BANKER
3100 Padre Boulevard, South Padre Island TX 78597-3469. 956/761-7802. **Fax:** 956/761-4855. **Contact:** Personnel. **World Wide Web address:** http://www.coldwellbanker.com. **Description:** Coldwell Banker is one of the largest residential real estate companies in the United States and Canada in terms of total home sales transactions. Coldwell Banker is also a leader in corporate relocation services. **NOTE:** Please visit website to search for jobs. **Corporate headquarters location:** Parsippany NJ. **Other U.S. locations:** Nationwide. **Parent company:** Cendant Corporation. **Listed on:** New York Stock Exchange. **Stock exchange symbol:** CD. **Number of employees worldwide:** 112,000.

COLLIN COUNTY COMMUNITY COLLEGE DISTRICT
P.O. Box 869055, Plano TX 87506. 972/985-3783. **Physical address:** 4800 Preston Park Boulevard, Suite B303, Plano TX 75093. . **Fax:** 972/985-3778. **Recorded jobline:** 972/881-5627. **Contact:** Vicki York, Human Resources. **E-mail address:** vyork@ccccd.edu. **World Wide Web address:** http://www.ccccd.edu. **Description:** A community college offering courses in computer science, humanities, international studies, fine arts, mathematics/natural science, health sciences, education, and engineering. **NOTE:** Please visit website to search for jobs and apply online., Phone for listed contact is 972/985-3781. **Positions advertised include:** Lifeguard; Associate Professor – Various Departments; Classroom Assistant; Grounds Supervisor; Natatorium Facilities Operator; Classroom Assistant; Professor – Various Departments; Lab Assistant; Reference Librarian; Program Coordinator for Student Life and Student Organizations; Counselor Instructional Associate; Corporate Trainer; Head Lifeguard; Division Secretary; Operator Maintenance Technician; Fitness Center Assistant;

Financial Aid/Veterans Affairs Advisor; Periodicals Assistant; Circulation Assistant. Safety and Security Officer; Accounts Payable Supervisor; Classroom Assistant; Corporate Trainer; Grant Coordinator. **Special programs:** Internships. **Corporate headquarters location:** This location. **Other area locations:** Allen TX; McKinney TX; Frisco TX; Rockwall TX.

COLUMBIA GULF TRANSMISSION
2603 Augusta, Suite 300, Houston TX 770057-5687. 713/267-4100. **Contact:** Personnel. **E-mail address:** kmerritt@nisource.com. **World Wide Web address:** http://www.columbiagastrans.com/cgt.html. **NOTE:** All hiring is done through the West Virginia office. Please mail resumes to 1700 MacCorkale Avenue Southeast, Charleston WV 25314; phone is 304/357-2000. **Description:** Engaged in the transmission and distribution of natural gas. Founded 1954. **Office hours:** Monday – Friday, 7:30 a.m. – 4:30 p.m. **Parent company:** NiSource. **President:** Glen Kettering.

COMDATA CORPORATION
6000 Western Place, Suite 900, Fort Worth TX 76107. 817/731-8721. **Contact:** Human Resources. **E-mail address:** resumes@comdata.com. **World Wide Web address:** http://www.comdata.com. **Description:** Provides transaction processing and information services to the transportation, gaming, and retail industries. Comdata links more than 20,000 telecommunication ports of entry, processing over 100 million transactions per year. Services for the transportation industry increase productivity and control for trucking companies and truck stops. Products encompass fuel purchase, cash advance, driver settlement, money transfer, load matching, route planning, legalization permitting, fuel tax reporting, and management reporting. Comdata's consumer services include money transfer for emergencies or leisure activities. The company helps gaming organizations adapt to new technologies such as smart cards, linked progressive slot machines, and player tracking systems. Retail services include a check acceptance network to shorten customer checkout time and reduce losses from returned checks. **NOTE:** Please visit website to view job listings. Send resumes to the corporate office at Attention Human Resources, Comdata Corporation, 5301 Maryland Way, Brentwood TN 37027. Fax to 615/370-7828. **Parent company:** Ceridian Corporation. **Listed on:** New York Stock Exchange. **Stock exchange symbol:** CEN.

COMMEMORATIVE BRANDS
P.O. Box 149107, Austin TX 78714-9207. 512/444-0571. **Physical address:** 7211 Circle S. Road, Austin TX 78745. **Contact:** Human Resources. **World Wide Web address:** http://www.artcarved.com. **Description:** Manufactures custom jewelry for schools, sports, and businesses. Other areas of activity include service award programs and the printing of announcements. **Corporate headquarters location:** This location. **Operations at this facility include:** Administration; Divisional Headquarters; Manufacturing; Sales; Service.

COMMUNITIES IN SCHOOL
2150 West 18th Street, Suite 100, Houston TX 77008. 713/654-1515. **Fax:** 713/655-1302. **Contact:** Human Resources Department. **World Wide Web address:** http://www.cishouston.org. **Description:** A social service agency offering school programs to prevent dropouts. **NOTE:** Volunteer positions are also available. **Other area locations:** Statewide. **Other U.S. locations:** Nationwide.

COMPUCOM SYSTEMS, INC.
7171 Forest Lane, Dallas TX 75230. 972/865-3600. **Toll-free phone:** 800/225-1475. **Contact:** Human Resources. **E-mail address:** easyhr@compucom.com. **World Wide Web address:** http://www.compucom.com. **Description:** A leading PC integration services company providing product procurement, advanced configuration, network integration, and support services. Founded 1987. **Positions advertised include:** Call Center Team Leader; EDI Developer/Programmer. **Corporate headquarters location:** This location. **Other U.S. locations:** Nationwide. **Listed on:** NASDAQ. **Stock exchange symbol:** CMPC. **President/CEO:** J. Edward Coleman. **Number of employees nationwide:** 3,300.

COMPUSA INC.
14951 North Dallas Parkway, Dallas TX 75254. 972/982-4000. **Fax:** 972/982-4942 **Contact:** Human Resources. **World Wide Web address:** http://www.compusa.com. **Description:** CompUSA Inc. operates over 218 high-volume computer superstores in 54 metropolitan areas throughout the United States. Each computer superstore offers more than 5,000 computer products including hardware, software, accessories, and related products, at discount prices to retail, business, government, and institutional customers. The computer superstores also offer full-service technical departments and classroom facilities. **NOTE:** Please visit http://compusa.newjobs.com to search for jobs and apply online. **Positions advertised include:** Communications Specialist; Staff Accountant; Technology Training Customer Service Representative; E-Commerce Product Cross-Sell Supervisor; Commercial Sales Representative; Planogram Coordinator; Corporate Human Resources Manager; Multivendor Support; Problem and Change Management Analyst; In-Store Media Coordinator; Accounting/Finance Specialist; Media Buyer; Senior CRM Programmer; Front End Manager; Tax Accountant; Staff Accountant; DC Warehouse Manager; Lease Analyst; Sales Manager in Training. **Corporate headquarters location:** This location. **Other U.S. locations:** Nationwide. **Parent company:** Grupo Sanborns. **Operations at this facility include:** This location houses administrative offices. **Listed on:** Privately held.

COMPUTALOG DRILLING SERVICES
500 Winscott Road, Fort Worth TX 76126. 817/249-7000. **Contact:** Human Resources. **E-mail address:** jobs-usa@computalog.com. **World Wide Web address:** http://www.precisiondrilling.com. **Description:** Manufactures, sells, and services oil well equipment for the oil field service industry. **NOTE:** Please visit website to view job listings and apply online. Resumes are not usually accepted at this location. Contact the office for more information. . **Office hours:** Monday - Friday, 8:00 a.m. - 5:00 p.m. **Parent company:** Precision Drilling.

COMPUTER ASSOCIATES INTERNATIONAL, INC.
5465 Legacy Drive, Plano TX 75024-3109. 214/473-1000. **Contact:** Human Resources Manager. **World Wide Web address:** http://www.cai.com. **Description:** Computer Associates International is one of the world's leading developers of client/server and distributed computing software. The company develops, markets, and supports enterprise management, database and applications development, business applications, and consumer software products for a broad range of mainframe, midrange, and desktop computers. Computer Associates International serves major business, government, research, and educational organizations. Founded in 1976. **Positions advertised include:** Assistant Teacher; Services Specialist; Senior Alliance Program Manager. **Special programs:** Internships; Co-ops. **Corporate headquarters location:** Islandia NY. **Other area locations:** Austin TX; Houston TX. **Other U.S. locations:** Nationwide. **International locations:** Worldwide. **Operations at this facility include:** This location develops and sells software, and offers support services. **Listed on:** New York Stock Exchange. **Stock exchange symbol:** CA. **Number of employees worldwide:** 16,000.

COMPUTER HORIZONS CORPORATION
2900 North Loop West, Suite 1230, Houston TX 77092. 713/688-8005. **Toll-free phone:** 800/880-2246. **Fax:**713/688-8002. **Contact:** Human Resources. **World Wide Web address:** http://www.computerhorizons.com. **Description:** A full-service technology solutions company offering contract staffing, outsourcing, re-engineering, and network management. **Corporate headquarters location:** Mountain Lakes NJ. **Other U.S. locations:** Nationwide. **International locations:** Canada; India. **Listed on:** NASDAQ. **Stock exchange symbol:** CHRZ. **President/CEO:** William J. Murphy. **Number of employees worldwide:** 3,000.

COMPUTER SCIENCES CORPORATION (CSC)
8616 Freeport Parkway Irving TX 75063. 972/386-0020. **Fax:** 469/499-8180. **Contact:** Human Resources. **World Wide Web address:** http://www.csc.com. **Description:** Computer Sciences Corporation helps clients in industry and government use information technology to achieve strategic and operational objectives. The company tailors solutions from a broad suite of integrated service and technology offerings including e-business strategies and technologies, management and IT consulting, systems development and integration, application software, and IT and business process outsourcing. Founded in 1959. **NOTE:** Please visit http://careers.csc.com to search for jobs and apply online. **Positions advertised include:** Administrative Assistant/Functional Coordinator; Technology Architect; Business Developer; Data Architect; Enterprise Package Solutions Specialist. **Corporate headquarters location:** El Segundo CA. **International locations:** Worldwide. **Operations at this facility include:** This location develops and markets software for financial institutions. **Listed on:** New York Stock Exchange. **Stock exchange symbol:** CSC. **Number of employees worldwide:** 90,000.

COMPUTER SCIENCES CORPORATION (CSC)
4606 Centerview, Suite 170, San Antonio TX 78228.210/737-0721. **Fax:** 210/737-3273. **Contact:** Human Resources. **World Wide Web address:** http://www.csc.com. **Description:** CSC is in the Information Technology services industry, offering a broad array of professional services to clients in the global commercial and government markets. **Positions advertised include:** Third Party Administrator; Life Claims Examiner; Data Entry Clerk; Data Imaging Processor; Business Developer. **Corporate headquarters location:** El Segundo CA. **International locations:** Worldwide. **Operations at this facility include:** This location is a sales office. **Listed on:** New York Stock Exchange. **Stock exchange symbol:** CSC. **Number of employees worldwide:** 68,000.

COMPUTIZE
1008 Wirt Road, Suite 140, Houston TX 77055. 713/957-0057. **Fax:** 713/613-4814. 66. **Contact:** Human Resources. **E-mail address:** johnson@computize.com. **World Wide Web address:** http://www.computizeinc.com. **Description:** A computer reseller. Computize also offers e-commerce development, networking, and IS project support through its technical division, DomiNet. Founded in 1983. **Positions advertised include:** Sales Representative. **Corporate headquarters location:** This location. **Other area locations:** Richardson TX; Austin TX. **Other U.S. locations:** Waukesha WI; Los Gatos CA. **Annual sales/revenues:** More than $100 million.

CONOCOPHILLIPS
P.O. Box 2197, Houston TX 77252-2197. 281/293-1000. **Physical address:** 600 North Dairy Ashford, Houston TX 77079-1175. **Contact:** Human Resources. **World Wide Web address:** http://www.conocophillips.com. **Description:** Engaged in the development and production of crude oil, natural gas, and natural gas liquids. Exploration and production operations currently include exploration activity in 15 countries on six continents. Conoco produces more than 453,000 barrels of petroleum liquids and 1.2 billion cubic feet of gas each day. Downstream operations comprise refining crude oil and other feedstock into petroleum products, trading crude oil and products, distributing, and marketing petroleum products. Marketing activities include selling gasoline, diesel, and motor oils mainly under the Conoco, Jet, and Seca brand names through more than 7,900 retail outlets in the United States, Europe, and the Asia Pacific region. The company also manufactures and markets a wide range of industrial lubricants and specialty products. It is one of the world's leading suppliers of graphite coke, a premium product used to make electrodes for the steel manufacturing industry. **NOTE:** Please visit http://www.conocophillips.com/careers to view job listings and apply online. **Positions advertised include:** Power Settlements Analyst; Facility Engineer; West Texas District Engineer. **Corporate headquarters location:** This location. **International locations:** Worldwide. **Listed on:** New York Stock Exchange. **Stock exchange symbol:** COP. **Number of employees worldwide:** 39,000.

CONSELIUM
14221 Dallas Parkway, Suite 1500, Dallas TX 75254. 214/540-8428. **Contact:** Maurice Gilbert, Managing Director. **E-mail address:** maurice@conselium.com. **World Wide Web address:** http://www.conselium.com. **Description:** Provides auditing services. Specialty areas are high-tech, financial and operations services for Fortune 500 companies. **Positions advertised include:** IT Auditors; Auditor Senior. **Other area locations include:** Houston TX. **Other U.S. locations:** NY; CA. **Listed on:** Privately held.

CONSOLIDATED GRAPHICS, INC.
5858 Westheimer Road, Suite 200, Houston TX 77057. 713/787-0977. **Fax:** 713/787-5013. **Contact:** Rachel S. Koenig, Ed.D., National Manager of Recruiting and Development. **World Wide Web address:** http://www.consolidatedgraphics.com. **Description:** Operates commercial printing companies nationwide. **Corporate headquarters location:** This location. **Other U.S. locations:** Nationwide. **Subsidiaries include:** Apple Graphics, Inc. (Los Angeles CA); Automated Graphics Systems (Washington DC and Cleveland OH); Bridgetown Printing Company (Portland OR); Byrum Lithographing Company (Columbus OH); CMI (Chicago IL); Emerald City Graphics (Seattle WA) produces technical and training manuals; Everett Graphics, Inc. (Oakland CA); Graphtec, Inc. (Washington DC); McKay Press, Inc. (Midland MI); Maryland Comp.com (Baltimore MD); Metropolitan Printing Service, Inc. (Bloomington IN); Mount Vernon Printing Company (Washington DC); Multiple Images Printing, Inc. (Chicago IL); Piccari Press, Inc. (Philadelphia PA); Precision Litho (Vista CA); Superior Colour Graphics (Kalamazoo MI); Wentworth Printing Corp. (Columbia SC). **Listed on:** New York Stock Exchange. **Stock exchange symbol:** CGX.

CONSTRUCTION DATA CORPORATION
11940 Jollyville Road, Suite 305-S, Austin TX 78759. 512/219-5150. **Toll-free phone:** 800/872-7878. **Fax:** 772/299-0818. **Contact:** Human Resources. **E-mail address:** jobs@cdcnews.com. **World Wide Web address:** http://www.cdcnews.com. **Description:** A construction trade publication that provides planning news and bidding opportunities. CDC produces 29 editions from Maine to California. Founded in 1977. **NOTE:** Entry-level positions and part-time jobs are offered. **Positions advertised include:** Reporter/Editor; Inside Sales Representative. **Special programs:** Internships. **Corporate headquarters location:** Vero Beach FL. **Listed on:** Privately held.

CONTEMPORARY ARTS MUSEUM OF HOUSTON
5216 Montrose Boulevard, Houston TX 77006-6598. 713/284-8250. **Fax:** 713/284-8275. **Contact:** Human Resources. **World Wide Web address:** http://www.camh.org. **Description:** A non-profit museum that showcases modern art from Texas, the United States and abroad. The museum is free to the public. **Special programs:** Internships. **Internship information:** Send resume, cover letter and references to this location's Department of Education and Public Programs.

CONTI WINDOW FASHIONS
408 Arlington Street, Houston TX 77007-2696. 713/863-7761. **Contact:** Human Resources. **Description:** A manufacturer and wholesaler of window coverings for retailers.

CONTINENTAL AIRLINES
1600 Smith Street, Houston TX 77002-4330. 713/324-4700. **Fax:** 713/324-5940. **Contact:** Human Resources. **World Wide Web address:** http://www.continental.com. **Description:** One of the largest airlines in the United States, offering flights to 149 domestic and 117 international locations daily. Operating through its major hubs in Newark, Houston, Cleveland, and Guam. Continental offers extensive service to Latin America and Europe. Founded in 1934. **NOTE:** Entry-level positions and second and third shifts are offered. Apply online. **Corporate headquarters location:** This location. **Subsidiaries include:** Continental Express. **Listed on:** New York Stock Exchange. **Stock exchange symbol:** CAL. **Number of employees nationwide:** 42,900.

CONTINENTAL CARBON COMPANY
333 Cypress Run, Suite 100, Houston TX 77094. 281/647-3700. **Fax:** 281/647-3863. **Contact:** Human Resources. **E-mail address:** jobs@continentalcarbon.com. **World Wide Web address:** http://www.continentalcarbon.com. **Description:** Manufactures carbon black for the tire and rubber industries. **Corporate headquarters location:** This location.

CONTINENTAL MANUFACTURING COMPANY
9797 Old Galveston Road, Houston TX 77034. 713/947-2600. **Contact:** Human Resources. **World Wide Web address:** http://www.cbmwmixers.com. **Description:** Distributes cement mixer trucks, parts and related services.

CONTINENTAL PLASTIC CONTAINERS, INC.
6831 Silsbee Road, Houston TX 77033. 713/643-2638. **Contact:** Human Resources Administrator. **Description:** Manufactures and distributes plastic packaging products such as bottles for the chemical and food industries.

CONVERGYS
12031 North Freeway, Houston TX 77060. 281/765-3400. **Contact:** Human Resources. **World Wide Web address:** http://www.convergys.com. **Description:** This company provides billing, customer and service support to large businesses, especially utilities. **NOTE:** This company provides a complete list of job openings at each of its Texas locations. See website and apply online. **Corporate headquarters location:** Cincinnati OH. **Other area locations:** Austin TX; Dallas TX; Irving TX; Lubbock TX; Brownsville TX; Killeen TX; Pharr TX. **Other U.S. locations:** Nationwide. **International locations:** Worldwide. **Number of employees worldwide:** 50,000.

CONVEYORS, INC.
P.O. Box 50817, Ft. Worth TX 76105. 817/473-4645. **Physical address:** 620 South Fourth Avenue, Mansfield TX 76063. **Contact:** Human Resources. **World Wide Web address:** http://www.conveyorsinc.net. **Description:** A manufacturer and retailer of conveyors and conveyor-related equipment.

COOK CHILDREN'S MEDICAL CENTER
801 Seventh Avenue, Fort Worth TX 76104-2733. 682/885-4000. **Fax:** 817/885-3947. **Recorded jobline:** 682/885-4414. **Contact:** Human Resources. **World Wide Web address:** http://www.cookchildrens.org. **Description:** A pediatric health care center. Founded in 1985. **NOTE:** Entry-level positions and second and third shifts are offered. Apply online or in person at 617 Seventh St., Fort Worth TX. **Positions advertised include:** Surgery Center Director; Diet Aide; Controller; Radiographer; Medical Records Technician; Nurse Manager; Patient Access Specialist; Physical Therapist; Medical Receptionist; Director of Pharmacy Services.

COOPER CAMERON VALVES
16500 South Main Street, Missouri City TX 77489-1300. 281/499-8511. **Contact:** Human Resources. **World Wide Web address:** http://www.ccvalve.com. **Description:** Manufactures valves, well heads, actuators, and safety systems for oil field markets worldwide, as well as valves for use in chemical, plastics, food-processing, and paper-making plants, and conventional and geothermal steam power-producing facilities. **Corporate headquarters location:** This location. **Parent company:** Cooper Cameron Corporation. **Operations at this facility include:** Administration; Manufacturing; Research and Development; Sales; Service.

COOPER INDUSTRIES INC.
P.O. Box 4446, Houston TX 77210. 713/209-8400. **Physical address:** 600 Travis, Suite 5800, Houston TX 77002. **Contact:** Human Resources. **E-mail address:** recruit@cooperindustries.com. **World Wide Web address:** http://www.cooperindustries.com. **Description:** Cooper Industries is a *Fortune* 500 company engaged in tools and hardware manufacturing and electrical and electronic products manufacturing. **Corporate headquarters location:** This location. **Listed on:** New York Stock Exchange. **Stock exchange symbol:** CBE. **Number of employees nationwide:** 28,000.

CORAL ENERGY, LLC
909 Fannin Street, Suite 700, Houston TX 77010. 713/767-5400. **Contact:** Human Resources **E-mail address:** recruitment@shell.com. **World Wide Web address:** http://www.coral-energy.com. **Description:** Operates a natural gas pipeline and purchases, gathers, processes, treats, transports, and markets natural gas. Gathering and transportation operations are situated mainly in the gas-producing areas of southern Texas, eastern Texas, and the Texas-Louisiana Gulf Coast regions. **NOTE:** Visit http://www.shell.com/careers to search and apply for open positions. **Other U.S. locations:** OK; WV. **Parent company:** Shell Trading. **Listed on:** Privately held.

COREL, INC.
8144 Walnut Hill Lane, Suite 1050, Dallas TX 75231. 469/232-1000. **Fax:** 469/232-1194. **Contact:** Human Resources. **World Wide Web address:** http://www.corel.com. **Description:** Develops, markets, and supports a line of graphic application software products for IBM PCs and compatibles running under the Microsoft Windows operating environment. Products are designed for both business and professional use and include professional illustration, basic drawing and charting products, data-driven graphics, image editing, and reusable clip-art libraries. Corel, Inc. also offers systems software products designed to enhance the Windows and OS/2 operating environments. **Positions advertised include:** Marketing Manager and Sales Manager. **Corporate headquarters location:** Ottawa, Canada. **Listed on:** NASDAQ. **Stock exchange symbol:** CORL. **Number of employees worldwide:** 889.

CORNING CABLE SYSTEMS
9275 Denton Highway, Keller TX 76248. 817/431-1521. **Contact:** Human Resources. **World Wide Web address:** http://www.corningcablesystems.com. **Description:** Manufactures fiber-optic telecommunications equipment. **Listed on:** New York Stock Exchange. **Stock exchange symbol:** GLW. **Number of employees worldwide:** 20,000.

CORPUS CHRISTI CALLER-TIMES
P.O. Box 9136, Corpus Christi TX 78469-9136. 361/884-2011. **Physical address:** 820 North Lower Broadway, Corpus Christi TX 78401. **Toll-free phone:** 800/827-2011. **Fax:** 361/884-5357. **Contact:** Veronica Rodriguez, Human Resources. **World Wide Web address:** http://www.caller.com. **Description:** A daily newspaper delivered throughout southwestern Texas. Founded in 1883. **Parent company:** Scripps Howard.

CORPUS CHRISTI, CITY OF
1201 Leopard, Corpus Christi TX 78401. 361/880-3300. **Toll-free phone:** 800/735-2989. **Recorded jobline:** 361/886-4848. **Contact:** Human Resources. **E-mail address:** personnel@cctexas.com. **World Wide Web address:** http://www.cctexasjobs.com. **Description:** The main offices for the city's government and administrative activities. **NOTE:** A completed application is required for any position. The application can be downloaded at the website or interested jobseekers may apply online.

CORRECTIONS PRODUCTS COMPANY
10700 Sentinel Street, San Antonio TX 78217. 210/829-7951. **Fax:** 210/824-3119. **Contact:** Personnel. **Description:** Manufactures locks and sliding devices for security within prison and jail systems.

CORSICANA DAILY SUN
P.O. Box 622, Corsicana TX 75151. 903/872-3931. **Contact:** Human Resources. **World Wide Web address:** http://www.corsicanadailysun.com. **Description:** Publishes a daily newspaper with a circulation of 7,100 during the week and 8,100 on Sunday.

COX MEDIA
401 Cantu Road, Suite D, Del Rio TX 78840. 830/774-5538. **Fax:** 830/774-5438. **Contact:** Human Resources. **World Wide Web address:** http://www.coxmedia.com. **Description:** Provides advertising services for businesses through major cable networks such as CNN. **NOTE:** Please visit website to search for jobs and apply online. **Corporate headquarters location:** Macon GA. **Other area locations:** Statewide. **Other U.S. locations:** Nationwide. **Parent company:** Cox Communications. **Number of employees nationwide:** 1,400.

CROWN CENTRAL PETROLEUM CORPORATION
111 Red Bluff Road, Pasadena TX 77506. 713/473-5381. **Fax:** 713-660-4538. **Contact:** Human Resources. **E-mail address:** recruiter@crowncentral.com. **World Wide Web address:** http://www.crowncentral.com. **Description:** An independent refiner and marketer of petroleum products. Crown Central Petroleum and its La Gloria Oil and Gas Company subsidiary operate two refineries in Texas with a combined capacity of 152,000 barrels per day. Crown Central Petroleum markets its refined products at 376 retail gasoline stations and convenience stores in seven Mid-Atlantic and Southeastern states. The company's wholesale operations extend from its Texas refineries into the Southeastern, Mid-Atlantic, and Midwestern regions of the United States. **Operations at this facility include:** Wholesale Marketing, Retail and Refinery. **Corporate headquarters location:** Baltimore MD.

CRUM & FORSTER INSURANCE
6404 International Parkway, Suite 1000, Plano TX 75093. 972/380-3000. **Toll-free phone:** 800-232-7380. **Fax:** 972-380-3185. **Contact:** Human Resources. **World Wide Web address:** http://www.cfins.com. **Description:** Offers property and casualty insurance to commercial customers. **Corporate headquarters location:** Toronto, Ontario, Canada. **Parent company:** Fairfax Financial Holdings Limited. **Listed on:** the Toronto and New York Stock Exchanges. **Stock exchange symbol:** FFH.

CULINAIRE INTERNATIONAL, INC.
2121 San Jacinto Street, Suite 3100, Dallas TX 75201. 214/754-1880. **Fax:** 214/754-1894. **Contact:** Human Resources. **E-mail address:** recruit@culinaireintl.com. **World Wide Web address:** http://www.culinaireintl.com. **Description:** Provides the food and beverage services for a wide range of corporate clients. **Positions advertised include:** Chef/Catering. **Corporate headquarters location:** This location.

CUSTOM DRAPERY, BLINDS, & CARPET
1312 Live Oak Street, Houston TX 77003. 713/225-9211. **Contact:** Human Resources. **Description:** Manufactures and installs custom-designed window treatments and hardware as well as carpeting.

CYBERBASIN INTERNET SERVICES
407 North Big Spring Street, Midland TX 79701. 432/620-0051. **Contact:** Human Resources. **E-mail address:** info@cyberbasin.com. **World Wide Web address:** http://www.cyberbasin.com. **Description:** This company is an Internet Service Provider. Provides Network and hosting services. **NOTE:** E-mail resumes to this company. **Parent company:** Southwest Royalties, Inc. **Listed on:** Privately held.

CYPRESS FAIRBANKS MEDICAL CENTER HOSPITAL
10655 Steepletop Drive, Houston TX 77065-4222. 281/897-3500. **Fax:** 281/890-0236. **Recorded jobline:** 281/897-3530. **Contact:** Human Resources. **World Wide Web address:** http://www.cyfairhospital.com. **Description:** A 146-bed acute care hospital offering diagnostic services on both outpatient and inpatient bases. Founded in 1983. **NOTE:** Entry-level positions, part-time jobs, and second and third shifts are offered. **Positions advertised include:** Therapist; Secretary; Registered Nurse; Nurse Manager; Coder; Case Manager; CT Scanner Technician. **Parent company:** Tenet Houston Health System.

CYPRESS SEMICONDUCTOR TEXAS INCORPORATED
17 Cypress Boulevard, Round Rock TX 78664. 512/244-7789. **Contact:** Human Resources. **World Wide Web address:** http://www.cypress.com. **Description:** Manufactures semiconductors. **NOTE:** Apply on-line. Positions advertised include: Equipment Maintenance Technician and Test Engineer. **Corporate headquarters location:** San Jose CA. **Listed on:** New York Stock Exchange. **Stock exchange symbol:** CY.

CYRO INDUSTRIES
101 East Park Boulevard, Suite 1039, Plano TX 75074. 972/424-6830. **Contact:** Human Resources Supervisor. **E-mail address:** human_resources@cyro.com. **World**

Wide Web address: http://www.cyro.com. **Description:** Cyro Industries is a manufacturer of acrylite plastic sheets. **NOTE:** Mail resumes to Cyro Industries, HR Supervisor, 100 Enterprise Dr., Rockaway NJ 07866. Fax: 973/442-6114. **Corporate headquarters location:** Rockaway NJ. **Operations at this facility include:** This location is a sales office. **Number of employees nationwide:** 600.

CYTEC FIBERITE INC.
4300 Jackson Street, Greenville TX 75402. 903/454-2004. **Contact:** Human Resources. **World Wide Web address:** http://www.cytec.com. **Description:** Cytec Fiberite manufactures advanced composite and adhesives for aerospace, industrial, recreational, and other applications. **Corporate headquarters location:** West Paterson NJ. **Operations at this facility include:** This location manufactures graphite composite materials. **Listed on:** New York Stock Exchange. **Stock exchange symbol:** CYT.

DDB NEEDHAM
1999 Bryan Street, Suite 2300, Dallas TX 75201. 214/259-4200. **Contact:** Human Resources Department. **World Wide Web address:** http://www.ddbdallas.com. **Description:** A full-service, international advertising agency. **NOTE:** Job listings can be found on ddbjobs.com. **Internship information:** E-mail resume to Staci Williams at hr@omsdal.com. **Corporate headquarters location:** New York NY.

DMC MANAGEMENT
6363 Woodway, Suite 1000, Houston TX 77057. 713/977-4806. **Contact:** Human Resources. **Description:** A real estate management firm specializing in multifamily properties.

DPT LABORATORIES INC.
307 East Josephine Street, San Antonio TX 78215. 210/223-3281. **Fax:** 210/476-0794. **Contact:** Human Resources. **E-mail address:** hr.sa@dptlabs.com. **World Wide Web address:** http://www.dptlabs.com. **Description:** Provides pharmaceutical manufacturing and development services from prototype development to worldwide distribution. **NOTE:** Entry-level positions and second and third shifts are offered. Corporate headquarters location: 318 McCullough Street, San Antonio TX. **Positions advertised include:** Packaging Engineer; Industrial Engineer; Account Coordinator; Administrative Assistant.

DRS BROADCAST TECHNOLOGY
4212 South Buckner Boulevard, Dallas TX 75227-0879. 214/381-7161. **Contact:** Human Resources. **E-mail address:** hradmin@contelec.com. **World Wide Web address:** http://www.contelec.com. **Description:** A manufacturer and distributor of radio and television transmitters and machinery. **Corporate headquarters location:** This location. **Parent company:** Tech-Sym Corporation. **Operations at this facility include:** Administration; Divisional Headquarters; Manufacturing; Research and Development.

DX SERVICE COMPANY
P.O. Box 130410, Houston TX 77219. 713/863-1947. 713/863-8316. **Contact:** Human Resources. **E-mail address:** hr@dixiechemical.com. **World Wide Web address:** http://www.dixiechemical.com. **Description:** A holding company with subsidiaries that manufacture and distribute chemicals.

DAIMLERCHRYSLER CORPORATION
P.O. Box 110370, Carrollton TX 75011. 972/418-4600. **Contact:** Human Resources. **World Wide Web address:** http://www.daimlerchrysler.com. **Description:** Manufactures cars, trucks, minivans, and sport-utility vehicles for customers in more than 100 countries. **NOTE:** Apply online for jobs at www.careers.chrysler-group.com. **Special programs**: Interns and new graduates. **Corporate headquarters location:** Auburn Hills MI **Listed on:** New York Stock Exchange. **Stock exchange symbol:** DCX.

DAL-TILE CORPORATION
7834 C.F. Hawn Freeway. Dallas TX 75217. 214/398/1411. **Contact:** Human Resources. **World Wide Web address:** http://www.daltile.com. **Description:** Manufactures and distributes ceramic tiles. **Positions advertised include:** Staff Accountant. **Parent company:** Mohawk Industries. **Listed on:** New York Stock Exchange. **Stock exchange symbol:** MHK.

DALLAS, CITY OF
City Hall, 1500 Marilla St., Room 1C/South. Dallas TX, 75201. 214/670-3120. **Fax:** 214/670-5855. **Recorded jobline:** 214/670-5908. **Contact:** Civil Service Department. **Email address:** daldvsrv@ci.dallas.tx.us. **World Wide Web address:** http://www.dallascityhall.com. **Description:** Nonprofit, local government agency. This location also hires seasonally. **NOTE:** Open positions for the Dallas Police Department and for the Dallas Public Works and Transportation Department can be found also on the website. **Positions advertised include:** Call Taker; Police Dispatcher; Network Analyst; Recreation Program Specialist; Field Maintenance. **Corporate headquarters location:** This location.

DALLAS AREA RAPID TRANSIT (DART)
P.O. Box 660163, Dallas TX 75266-7240. 214/749-3259. **Fax:** 214/749-3636. **Recorded jobline:** 214/749-3690. **Contact:** Human Resources. **World Wide Web address:** http://www.dart.org. **Description:** A nonprofit, rapid transit system serving the Dallas metropolitan area. **Positions advertised include:** Contract Specialist; Maintenance Specialist; Fare Inspector; Bus Operator; Rail Operator; Train Operator; Mechanic; DART Police Officer; Bus Mechanic. **Number of employees at this location:** 2,925.

DALLAS BAPTIST UNIVERSITY
3000 Mountain Creek Parkway, Dallas TX 75211-9299. 214-333-5334. **Toll-free phone:** 800/460-1DBU. **Fax:** 214/333-5536. **Contact:** Human Resources. **World Wide Web address:** http://www.dbu.edu. **Description:** An accredited university offering 34 undergraduate majors and eight master's programs.

DALLAS BUSINESS JOURNAL
12801 North Central Expressway, Suite 800, Dallas TX 75231-2111. 214/696-5959. **Fax:** 214/696-1486. **Contact:** Human Resources. **World Wide Web address:** http://www.bizjournals.com/dallas. **Description:** A weekly business periodical with a circulation of 18,000. **Parent company:** American City Business Journals Inc. (Charlotte NC) publishes 41 business journals in cities nationwide.

DALLAS CHRISTIAN COLLEGE
2700 Christian Parkway, Dallas TX 75234. 972/241-3371. **Toll-free phone:** 800/688-1029. **Contact:** Ray Kelley, Academic Dean. **World Wide Web address:** http://www.dallas.edu. **Description:** Offers undergraduate programs in religious studies. Degree programs include pastoral ministry, youth ministry, education, music, and counseling.

DALLAS COUNTY COMMUNITY COLLEGE DISTRICT
12800 Abrams Road, Dallas TX 75243. 214/860-2431. **Recorded job line:** 214/860-2438. **Contact:** Human Resources. **World Wide Web address:** http://www.dcccd.edu. **Description:** A consortium of seven community colleges. **NOTE:** Online job listings for each of the community colleges in the district. **Positions advertised include:** Administrative, Full-time and part-time faculty, Information and Technology; Professional Support Staff. **Corporate headquarters location:** This location.

DALLAS COWBOYS
One Cowboys Parkway, Irving TX 75063. 972/556-9900. **Contact:** Human Resources. **World Wide Web address:** www.dallascowboys.com. **Description:** Administrative offices for the National Football League team. **Corporate headquarters location:** This location.

DALLAS INDEPENDENT SCHOOL DISTRICT
3700 Ross Avenue, Dallas TX 750204. 972/925-3700. **Contact:** Human Resources. **World Wide Web address:** http://www.dallasisd.org. **Description:** The administrative offices for the Dallas school district. **NOTE:** This website provides job listings for all the schools in the Dallas area. An application is required for any position. Apply online. **Positions advertised include:** Band/Orchestra Teacher; ESL Elementary Teacher; Bilingual Elementary Teacher; Food and Child Nutrition Division Manager.

DALLAS MUSEUM OF ART
1717 North Harwood Street, Dallas TX 75201. 214/922-1215. **Contact:** Scott Gensemer, Director of Human Resources **E-mail address:** sgensemer@dm-art.org. **World Wide Web address:** http://www.dm-art.org. **Description:** Offers a wide range of exhibits in all art media. **Positions advertised include:** Curator of American Art; Carpenter; Exhibitions Assistant; Associate/Assistant Registrar.

DALLAS MUSEUM OF NATURAL HISTORY
P.O. Box 150349, Dallas TX 75315-0349. 214/421-3466. **Fax:** 214-428-4356. **E-mail address:** employment@dmnhnet.org. **Contact:** Employment Manager. **E-mail address:** employment@dmnhnet.org. **World Wide Web address:** http://www.dallasdino.org. **Description:** Operates a natural history museum offering a full range of exhibits and presentations. **Positions advertised include:** Chief Operating Officer; Vice President-Advancement; Director of Education.

DALLAS SEMICONDUCTOR
4401 South Beltwood Parkway, Dallas TX 75244-3292. 972/371-4000. **Fax:** 972-778-6335. **Contact:** Recruiting Department. **World Wide Web address:** http://www.maxim-ic.com. **Description:** Manufactures semiconductors. **NOTE:** Entry-level positions are offered. **Positions advertised include:** Analog/Mixed Signal Design Engineer; Applications Engineer; Customer Service Representative; Layout Designer; Inside Sales Associate; Network Administrator. **Listed on:** NASDAQ. **Stock exchange symbol:** MXIM.

DALLAS COUNTY SHERIFF'S DEPARTMENT
521 N. Industrial Boulevard, Dallas TX 75207. 214/741-1094. **Recorded jobline:** 214/653-3400. **Contact:** W.F. Aldrich, Human Resources Manager. **Description:** Enforces justice, public order, and safety for the city of Dallas. **Positions advertised include:** Detention Service Officer and Sheriff.

DALLAS-FORT WORTH INTERNATIONAL AIRPORT
P.O. Drawer 619428, DFW Airport TX 75261-9428. 972/574-8888. **Fax:** 972/574-5732. **Physical address:** 3200 East Airfield Drive, DFW Airport TX 75261. **Recorded jobline:** 972/574-8024. **Contact:** Human Resources. **World Wide Web address:** http://www.dfwairport.com. **Description:** An international airport with flights worldwide on 25 commercial airlines and several charter airlines. **NOTE:** Security screening positions for the airport can be found on the National Transportation Security Administration's website (http://www.tsa.gov.) All other positions can be found on the DFW Airport's website. **Positions advertised include:** AVP Airport Real Estate; Budget Analyst; Energy Plant Operations/Maintenance Technician; Organizational Development Manager.

DANIEL INDUSTRIES, INC.
9720 Oldkaty Road, Houston TX 77055. 713/467-6000. **Fax:** 713/827-4326. **E-mail address:** Human.Resources@emersonprocess.com. **Contact:** Human Resources. **World Wide Web address:** http://emersonprocess.com. **Description:** A manufacturer of fluid measurement products, primarily for the oil and natural gas industries. **Corporate headquarters location:** This location. **Parent company:** Emerson Electric. **Listed on:** New York Stock Exchange. **Stock exchange symbol:** EMR.

DANKWORTH PACKAGING
1609 Eubank Street, Ballinger TX 76821. 325-/365-3553. **Fax:** 325/365-2367. **Contact:** Plant Manager. **Description:** A meat packaging plant. **Corporate headquarters location:** This location.

DARLING INTERNATIONAL INC.
251 O'Connor Ridge Boulevard, Suite 300, Irving TX 75038. 972/717-0300. **Fax:** 972/717-1588. **Contact:** Julie Brewster, Human Resources. **World Wide Web address:** http://www.darlingii.com. **Description:** Recycles animal by-products including fats and proteins into tallow, protein meals, and yellow grease. **Listed on:** American Stock Exchange. **Stock exchange symbol:** DAR.

DART CONTAINER CORPORATION
850 Solon Road, Waxahachie TX 75165. 972/937-7270. **Toll-free phone:** 877/562-3278 **Contact:** Human Resources. **E-mail address:** hrcoordinator@dart.biz. **World Wide Web address:** http://www.dartcontainer.com. **Description:** Manufactures and wholesales Styrofoam cups, plates, and beverage coolers. **Corporate headquarters location:** Mason MI.

DATAMATIC, LTD.
3600 K Street, Plano TX 75074. 972/234-5000. **Toll-free phone:** 800/880-2878. **Fax:** 972/234-1134. **Contact:** Human Resources. **Description:** Supplies test and measurement systems to investor-owned utilities and municipalities. Founded in 1977. **Office hours:** Monday - Friday, 8:00 a.m. - 5:00 p.m. **Positions advertised include:** Sales Director; Training/System Installation; Project Manager.

DAVE & BUSTER'S, INC.
2481 Manana Drive, Dallas TX 75220. 214/357-9588. **Fax:** 214/904-2532. **Contact:** Recruiting Department. **World Wide Web address:** http://www.daveandbusters.com. **Description:** An operator of 20 restaurant/entertainment complexes. Each location houses eating venues and amusement facilities including billiards, video games, and virtual reality games. Founded in 1982. **Corporate headquarters location:** This location. **Internship information:** College junior majoring in hospitality, culinary or related field. Two-year minimum field experience. **NOTE:** Management, hourly, and worldwide positions available. Hourly positions must apply at respective local location

between 1 p.m. and 5 p.m. All other positions can apply on-line at website; via fax; or by mail. **Other U.S. locations:** Nationwide. **International locations:** Canada; Taiwan. **Listed on:** New York Stock Exchange. **Stock exchange symbol:** DAB.

DAVIS MUNCK
13155 Noel Road, Suite 900, Dallas TX 75240. 972/628-3600. Fax: 972/628-3616. **Email address:** hr@davismunck.com. **Contact:** Recruiting. **World Wide Web address:** http://www.davismunck.com. **Description:** A law firm specializing in corporate, IPO, estate, and real estate law.

DAVIS FOOD CITY INC.
P.O. Box 8748, Houston TX 77249-8748. 713/695-2826. **Fax:** 713/695-4057. **Contact:** Human Resources. **E-mail address:** employment@davisfoodcity.com. **World Wide Web address:** http://www.davisfoodcity.com. **Description:** Operates a grocery store chain. **NOTE:** Full-time and part-time positions. Can apply by visiting store location or via fax, mail, e-mail or online. **Positions advertised include:** Sackers, Cashiers, Grocery Stockers; Meat Department Personnel; Produce Department Personnel; Front-End Managers; Store Management. **Corporate headquarters location:** This location.

DE SOTO ANIMAL HOSPITAL
200 North Hampton, De Soto TX 75115. 972/223-4840. **Contact:** Human Resources. **Description:** Provides general medical and surgical services to domestic animals. Other services include radiology, dentistry, behavior counseling, allergy testing, and boarding.

DEAN FOODS
2515 McKinney Avenue, Suite 1200, Dallas TX 75201. 214/303-3400. **Toll-free phone:** 800/4231-9214. **Fax:** 214/303-3499. **Contact:** Human Resources. **World Wide Web address:** http://www.deanfoods.com. **Description:** Manufactures and distributes fresh milk and related dairy products, shelf-stable and refrigerated food and beverage products, frozen food products, coffee, and plastic containers. This company has 120 manufacturing facilities nationwide. **NOTE:** Apply online at the company's website. **Positions advertised include:** Auditor; Executive Assistant. **Corporate headquarters location:** This location. **Listed on:** New York Stock Exchange. **Stock exchange symbol:** DF.

DECIBEL PRODUCTS INC.
P.O. Box 569610, Dallas TX 75356. 214/634-8502. **Fax:** 214/819-4262. **Contact:** Human Resources. **World Wide Web address:** http://www.decibelproducts.com. **Description:** A manufacturer and distributor of telecommunications products including cables, connectors, and sway brace kits. **Corporate headquarters location:** Beachwood OH. **Parent company:** Allen Telecom Systems.

DECISION ANALYST, INC.
604 Avenue H East, Arlington TX 76011. 817/640-6166. **Toll-free number:** 800/262-5974. **Fax:** 817/640-6567. **Contact:** Human Resources. **E-mail address:** jobs@decisionanalyst.com. **World Wide Web address:** http://www.decisionanalyst.com. **Description:** A market research and consulting firm offering product testing, tracking research, and Internet surveys. **Corporate headquarters location:** This location.

DEGUSSA ENGINEERED CARBONS, INC.
9300 Needlepoint Road, Baytown TX 77521. 281/421-2500. **Contact:** Human Resources. **Description:** Produces carbon black for conductive and nonconductive electrical cables, superthin rubber membranes, plastic applications, printing ink, and other specialty products. **Corporate headquarters location:** Parsippany NJ.

DEL MONTE FOODS
2205 Old Uvalde Highway, Crystal City TX 78839. 830/374-3451. **Contact:** Human Resources. **World Wide Web address:** http://www.delmonte.com. **Description:** Del Monte Foods is an international processor and distributor of foods, operating in the following business segments: Processed Foods, Fresh Fruit, Transportation, and Institutional Services. The Processed Foods Division processes canned, frozen, dried, and chilled foods. Del Monte's operations include can manufacturing, label printing, seed production, and agricultural and scientific research. The company's products are distributed in more than 60 countries under the brand names Del Monte, Granny Goose, and Award. **Corporate headquarters location:** San Francisco CA. **Operations at this facility include:** This location cans a variety of vegetables such as spinach, carrots, peas, tomatoes, and tomato paste. **Listed on**: New York Stock Exchange. **Stock exchange symbol:** DLM. **Number of employees worldwide:** 17,600.

DELL INC.
One Dell Way, Round Rock TX 78682. 512/338-4400. **Fax:** 800/816-4643. **Contact:** Human Resources. **World Wide Web address:** http://www.dell.com. **Description:** Designs, develops, manufactures, markets, services, and supports personal computer systems and related equipment including servers, workstations, notebooks, and desktop systems. The company also offers over 4,000 software packages and peripherals. **Special programs:** Dell for MBA's; Dell for Undergrad/Masters; Internships. **Corporate headquarters location:** This location. **International locations:** Ireland; United Kingdom. **Listed on:** NASDAQ. **Stock exchange symbol:** DELL. **Number of employees worldwide:** 46,000.

DELOITTE & TOUCHE
5550 LBJ Freeway, Suite 700, Dallas TX 75240. 972/776-6000. **Contact:** Steve Gass, Human Resources Director. **World Wide Web address:** http://www.us.deloitte.com. **Description:** An international firm that provides accounting, auditing, tax, and management consulting services. **NOTE:** This international company has locations also in Austin, Fort Worth, Houston, and San Antonio TX. See website for Texas locations' mailing addresses and phone numbers. **Positions advertised include:** Auditing; Financial Advising; Taxes; Consulting, Administrative. **Special programs:** Internships. **Corporate headquarters location:** New York City. **Operations at this facility include:** Regional Headquarters. **Number of employees worldwide:** 120,000.

DELTA AIR LINES, INC.
6763 Hillcrest Avenue, Dallas TX 75261-0348. 800/221-1212. **Contact:** Human Resources. **E-mail address:** delta.careers@delta.com. **World Wide Web address:** http://www.delta.com. **Description:** One of the largest airlines in the United States. The company provides scheduled air transportation for passengers, freight, and mail on an extensive route that covers most of the country and extends to 32 foreign nations. The route covers 205 domestic cities in 46 states, the District of Columbia, Puerto Rico, the U.S. Virgin Islands, and 47 cities abroad. Major domestic hubs of Delta include Atlanta, Dallas-Fort Worth, Salt Lake City, and Cincinnati with minor hubs in Los Angeles and Orlando. Delta has over 550 aircraft in its fleet. Founded in 1929. **NOTE:** All hiring is done through Delta Air Lines, Inc., Recruitment and Employment Office, P.O. Box 20530, Atlanta GA 30320. 404/715-2600. **Corporate headquarters location:** Atlanta GA. **Listed on:** New York Stock Exchange. **Stock exchange symbol:** DAL. **Number of employees worldwide:** 60,000.

DENTON, COUNTY OF
1450 East McKinney Street, Denton TX 76209-4524. 940/348-2600. **Fax:** 940-349-2601. **Contact:** Human Resources. **World Wide Web address:** http://www.co.denton.tx.us. **Description:** Headquarters for the Denton County government and its services, including jail system, law enforcement, construction, and tax. **NOTE:** See website for a complete listing of jobs in the county and contact information. **Positions advertised include:** Attorney, Investigator; Detention Officer; Heavy Equipment Operator; Correction Facilities Technician; Juvenile Probation Officer; Foreman; Data Processing Coordinator; Nutrition Technician.

DERCO AEROSPACE, INC.
22 Ocean Drive, Corpus Christi TX 78419. 361/937-8334. **Contact:** Human Resources. **E-mail address:** resumes@dercoaerospace.com. **World Wide Web address:** http://www.dercoaerospace.com. **Description:** Military aircraft parts distributor and repair company. **NOTE:** To apply, write to Derco Aerospace, Inc., Human Resources, P.O. Box 250970, Milwaukee, WI 53225; or fax a resume to 414/214-2040. Resumes may also be e-mailed. **Positions advertised include:** Warehouse Professionals.

DESIGN SOURCE
P.O. Box 420406, Dallas TX 75342-1068. 214/742-8234. **Contact:** Kenny Pane, General Manager. **Description:** A manufacturer of wooden and upholstered furniture for the home.

DEVON ENERGY CORPORATION
2001 Timberloch, The Woodlands TX 77380. 713/377-5500. **Fax:** 713/377-5680. **Contact:** Human Resources. **World Wide Web address:** http://www.devonenergy.com. **Description:** Engaged in oil and gas exploration, production, and property acquisitions. **Corporate headquarters:** Oklahoma City OK. **International locations:** Canada. **Listed on:** American Stock Exchange. **Stock exchange symbol:** DVN. **Number of employees worldwide:** 4,000.

DEVRY INSTITUTE OF TECHNOLOGY
4800 Regent Boulevard, Irving TX 75063. 972/929-9392.: **Contact:** Ms. Amy Rhodes, Human Resources Manager. **E-mail address:** gwilliams@dal.devry.edu. **World Wide Web address:** http://www.dal.devry.edu. **Description:** Devry Institute of Technology is a fully accredited college offering baccalaureate degrees in business and technology. **Office hours:** Monday – Friday, 8:00 a.m. – 5:00 p.m. **Corporate headquarters location:** Oakbrook Terrace IL. **Listed on:** New York Stock Exchange. **Stock exchange symbol:** DV.

DIAMOND OFFSHORE DRILLING, INC.
P.O. Box 4558, Houston TX 77210-4558. 281/492-5300. **Fax:** 281/647-2295. **Contact:** Employment. **World Wide Web address:** http://www.diamondoffshore.com. **Description:** A drilling contractor for oil and gas companies. **Corporate headquarters location:** This location. **Other U.S. locations:** Louisiana. **International locations:** Brazil; Scotland, West Africa; Singapore; Indonesia; Australia. **Listed on:** New York Stock Exchange. **Stock exchange symbol:** DO.

DILLY UNIFORM COMPANY
235 Berry Road, Houston TX 77022. 713/692-7142. **Contact:** Human Resources. **Description:** Manufactures hospital apparel such as doctors' and nurses' uniforms.

DIVERSE WORKS
1117 East Freeway, Houston TX 77002. 713/223-8346. **Fax:** 713-223-4608. **Contact:** Hiring Manager. **World Wide Web address:** http://www.diverseworks.org. **Internship program:** E-mail resume to info@diverseworks.org. **Description:** A nonprofit art gallery and theater for the performing and visual arts. Diverse Works is affiliated with the Cultural Arts Council. **Office hours:** Monday – Friday, 10:00 a.m. – 6 p.m.

DR PEPPER/7-UP COMPANY
P.O. Box 869077, Plano TX 75086-9077. 972/673-7000. **Physical address:** 5301 Legacy Drive, Plano TX 75024. **Fax:** 972/673-7980. **Contact:** Human Resources. **World Wide Web address:** http://www.dpsu.com. **Description:** Dr Pepper/7-Up Company manufactures, markets, and distributes soft drink syrups, concentrates, and extracts to bottlers. A food service segment distributes products to restaurants and convenience stores. **Other U.S. locations:** Nationwide. **Parent company:** Cadbury Schweppes PLC. **Operations at this facility include:** This location houses the company's U.S. headquarters. **Listed on:** New York Stock Exchange. **Stock exchange symbol:** CSG.

DOCTORS HOSPITAL
9440 Poppy Drive #205 West, Dallas TX 75218. 214/324-6297. **Fax:** 214/324-6547. **Recorded jobline:** 214/324-6700. **Contact:** Human Resources. **World Wide Web address:** http://www.doctorshospitaldallas.com. **Description:** A hospital specializing in coronary, wound and hospice care. Founded in 1959. **Positions advertised include:** Registered Nurse; LPN; Controller; Pharmacist; Technician. **Other U.S. locations:** Nationwide. **Parent company:** Tenet Healthcare Corporation owns and operates a network of hospitals and related businesses nationwide. **Operations at this facility include:** Administration. **Listed on:** New York Stock Exchange. **Stock exchange symbol:** THC.

DOUBLETREE GUEST SUITES HOTEL
303 West 15th Street, Austin TX 78701. 512/478-7000. **Fax:** 512/478-3562. **Contact:** Monica D'Richards, Human Resources Director. **NOTE:** Applications only on Mondays and Tuesdays from 9:00 a.m.-noon. **World Wide Web address:** http://www.doubletree.com. **Description:** A 189-room hotel. **Parent company:** Hilton.

DOW CHEMICAL COMPANY
P.O. Box 685, La Porte TX 77572-0685. 713/246-0369. **Physical address:** 550 Battleground Road, La Porte TX 77572-0685. **Contact:** Human Resources Department. **World Wide Web address:** http://www.dow.com. **Description:** Manufactures petrochemicals. **Operations at this facility include:** Manufacturing; Research and Development.

DOW CHEMICAL COMPANY
400 West Sam Houston Parkway South, Houston TX 77042. 713/978-2971. **Contact:** Human Resources Department. **World Wide Web address:** http://www.dow.com. **Description**: Manufactures chemicals, plastics, and agricultural products for the consumer market. **Corporate headquarters location:** Midland MI. **Other area locations:** Deer Park; Freeland; Garland; La Porte; Seadrift; Texas City. **Operations at this facility include:** Drafting, construction, and other services for Dow U.S.A.

THE DOZIER COMPANY
2547 Farrington, Dallas TX 75207. 214/744-2800. **Fax:** 214/744-1240. **Contact:** Human Resources. **World Wide Web address:** http://www.thedoziercompany.com. **Description:** A full-service advertising and public relations agency. Founded in 1987. **Special programs:** Internships. **Corporate headquarters location:** This location.

DRESSER-RAND COMPANY
1200 West Sam Houston Parkway North, Houston TX 77043. 713/467-2221. **Contact:** Human Resources. **E-mail address:** USA_Resumes@dresser-rand.com. **World Wide Web address:** http://www.dresser-rand.com. **Description:** Offers high-technology repair services for turbines, compressors, pumps, engines, and blowers. **Positions advertised include:** Field Service Representative. **Corporate headquarters location:** Corning NY. **Parent company:** Ingersoll-Rand Company.

DRIL-QUIL INC.
13550 Hempstead Parkway, Houston TX 77040. 713/939-7711. **Fax:** 713/939-8063. **Contact:** Human Resources. **E-mail address:** hr@dril-quip.com. **World Wide Web address:** http://www.drilquip.com. **Description:** Manufacturer of offshore drilling and production products, such as pipes and connectors. Its customers include large companies in the United States and abroad. **NOTE:** Mail or e-mail resumes. **Positions advertised include:** Senior Engineer; Gate Valve Design Engineer; Drilling or Production Riser Design Engineer; Subsea Christmas Tree Design Engineer; Subsea Manifold Design Engineer. **Corporate headquarters location:** This location. **Other area locations:** New Orleans LA. **International locations:** Worldwide. **Subsidiaries include:** Dril-Quip Europe; Dril-Quip Asia Pacific; DQ Holdings PTY, and Dril-Quip Brasil. (Scotland); **Operations at this facility include:** Manufacturing; Sales; Service. **Listed on:** New York Stock Exchange. **Stock exchange symbol:** DRQ.

DUKE ENERGY CORPORATION
P.O. Box 1642, Houston TX 77251-1642. 713/627-5400. **Physical address:** 5400 Westheimer Court, Houston TX 77056-5310. **Contact:** Human Resources. **World Wide Web address:** http://www.duke-energy.com. **Description:** Involved in natural gas pipeline operations. The company owns and operates an interstate natural gas transmission system that consists of more than 4,300 miles of pipeline. **Positions advertised include:** Accounting Analyst; Administrative Assistant; Metallurgical Engineer; Manager. Special programs: Internships. **Corporate headquarters location:** Charlotte, N.C. **Listed on**: New York Stock Exchange. **Stock exchange symbol:** DUK.

DUNLAP COMPANY
200 Bailey Avenue, Suite 100, Fort Worth TX 76107. 817/336-4985. **Contact:** Human Resources. **World Wide Web address:** http://www.dunlaps.com. **Description:** Operates a chain of department stores with over 50 locations. The stores operate under the following names: Dunlaps, McClurkans, Kerr's; M.M. Cohn, Heironimus, Stripling & Cox, Porteus, and The White House. Founded in 1892. **NOTE:** Applicants interested in retail sales should apply at the closest store location. **Corporate headquarters location:** This location. **Other U.S. locations:** Nationwide. **Operations at this facility include:** Administration. **Listed on:** Privately held. **President:** Edward Martin.

E.I. DUPONT DE NEMOURS & COMPANY
P.O. Box 347, La Porte TX 77572-0347. 281/471-2771. **Physical address:** 12501 Strang Road, La Porte TX 77571. **Contact:** Human Resources. **World Wide Web address:** http://www.dupont.com. **Description:** E.I. DuPont de Nemours & Company's activities include the manufacturing of biomedical, industrial, and consumer products (such as photographic, data-recording, and video devices); the production of man-made fiber products (with applications in a variety of consumer and commercial industries), polymer products (such as plastic resins, elastomers, and films), and agricultural and industrial chemicals (such as herbicides and insecticides, pigments, fluorochemicals, petroleum additives, and mineral acids); the exploration and production of crude oil and natural gas; the refining, marketing, and downstream transportation of petroleum; and the mining and distribution of steam and metallurgical coals. The company supplies the aerospace, agriculture, apparel, transportation, health care, and printing and publishing industries. **NOTE:** Job openings and online application can be found at http://www.careers.DuPont.com. **Corporate headquarters location:** Wilmington DE. **Operations at this facility include:** This location manufactures specialty chemicals used in coatings, paper, plastic, textile, and other industries; manufactures specialty fibers for textile, apparel, and other markets; produces polymers for packaging, construction, electrical, paper, and other industries; explores for, produces, refines, markets, supplies, and transports crude oil; produces and transports natural gas and related products; produces agricultural chemicals; and owns and operates refineries. **Listed on:** New York Stock Exchange. **Stock exchange symbol:** DD.

E.I. DUPONT DE NEMOURS & COMPANY
P.O. Box 2626, Victoria TX 77902-2626. 361/572-1111. **Physical address:** 2695 Old Bloomington Road North, Victoria TX 77905. **Contact:** Human Resources. **World Wide Web address:** http://www.dupont.com. **Description:** E.I. DuPont de Nemours & Company's activities include the manufacturing of biomedical, industrial, and consumer products (such as photographic, data-recording, and video devices); the production of man-made fiber products (with applications in a variety of consumer and commercial industries); polymer products (such as plastic resins, elastomers, and films); agricultural and industrial chemicals (such as herbicides and insecticides, pigments, fluorochemicals, petroleum additives, and mineral acids); the exploration and production of crude oil and natural gas; the refining, marketing, and downstream transportation of petroleum; and the mining and distribution of steam and metallurgical coals. The company supplies the aerospace, agricultural, apparel, transportation, health care, and printing and publishing industries. **NOTE:** Job openings and online application can be found at http://www.careers.DuPont.com. **Corporate headquarters location:** Wilmington DE. **Operations at this facility include:** This location is a chemical processing plant. **Listed on:** New York Stock Exchange. **Listed on:** New York Stock Exchange. **Stock exchange symbol:** DD. **Number of employees worldwide:** 77,000.

THE DWYER GROUP
P.O. Box 3146, 1010 North University Parks Drive, Waco TX 76707. 254/745-2400. **Fax:** 254/745-2590. **Contact:** Human Resources. **World Wide Web address:** http://www.dwyergroup.com. **Description:** An international provider of specialty services through a group of service-based franchisers. **Subsidiaries include:** Rainbow International Carpet Dyeing & Cleaning Company has more than 300 franchises in the United States, 30 franchises in Canada, and more than 140 franchise operations in 16 other foreign countries. Rainbow specializes in indoor restoration and cleaning services including upholstery and drapery cleaning, carpet dyeing and cleaning, ceiling cleaning, deodorization, and comprehensive fire and water damage restoration and cleanup. Mr. Rooter Corporation is a complete residential and commercial plumbing service company, with a total of 300 franchises in the United States. Aire Serv Heating & Air Conditioning, Inc. is a franchiser of heating, ventilation, and air conditioning maintenance and repair services. The primary client base for its franchisees includes residential and light commercial applications. Aire Serv has nearly 40 U.S. franchises. Mr. Electrician electrical contracting service franchise. Glass Doctor is a residential, business and auto glass franchisor. DreamMaker Bath & Kitchen by Worldwide offers kitchen and bath remodeling franchise opportunities.

DYNAMEX INC.
1870 Crown Drive, Dallas TX 75234. 214/561-7500. **Fax:** 214/561-7499. **Contact:** Human Resources. **World Wide Web address:** http://www.dynamex.com. **Description:** Offers customized warehousing and local outsourcing delivery services for companies without private trucks or delivery vehicles. Founded in 1985. **Listed on:** American Stock Exchange. **Stock exchange symbol:** DDN.

DYNEGY, INC.
P.O. Box 4777, Houston TX 77210. 713/507-6400. **Physical address:** 1000 Louisiana, Suite 5800, Houston TX 77002. **Contact:** Human Resources. **World Wide Web address:** http://www.dynegy.com. **Description:** Produces gas, oil, and electric power. **NOTE:** Resumes and applications accepted via website only. **Corporate headquarters location:** This location. **Other U.S. locations:** Nationwide. **Operations at this facility include:** Administration. **Listed on:** New York Stock Exchange. **Stock exchange symbol:** DYN. **Number of employees nationwide:** 4,000.

EDS (ELECTRONIC DATA SYSTEMS CORPORATION)
5400 Legacy Drive, Plano TX 75024-3199. 972/605-2700. **Fax:** 800/562-6241. **Contact:** Human Resources. **E-mail address:** careers@eds.com. **World Wide Web address:** http://www.eds.com. **Description:** Provides consulting, systems development, systems integration, and systems management services for large-scale and industry-specific applications. Founded in 1962. **NOTE:** Entry-level positions are offered. **Positions advertised include:** Systems Engineering; Technical Delivery; Customer Business Service; Operations; Communications; Marketing; Contractors. **Special programs:** Internships; Training. **Corporate headquarters location:** This location. **Listed on:** New York Stock Exchange. **Stock exchange symbol:** EDS. **Annual revenues:** $21.5 billion.

ENSR INC.
4888 Loop Central Drive, Loop Central One, Suite 600, Houston TX 77081-2214. 713/520-9900. **Contact:** Human Resources. **E-mail address:** hrcentral@ensr.com. **World Wide Web address:** http://www.ensr.com. **Description:** Offers comprehensive environmental services including consulting, engineering, and remediation. **NOTE:** Entry-level opportunities available. **Other area locations include:** Plano; Austin. **Positions advertised include:** Staff Specialist; Project Manager. **Corporate headquarters location:** Westford MA.

E.O.A.C.
500 Franklin Avenue, Waco TX 76701. 254/753-0331. **Contact:** Employment. **Description:** Offers Head Start programs for three- and four-year-olds; charter school for children ages five years through third grade; Youth in Action, an alcohol and drug prevention program for teenagers; assistance with rent and utilities payments; and a variety of services for the homeless. **Operations at this facility include:** This is the central office of E.O.A.C.

EOG RESOURCES
P.O. Box 4362, Houston TX 77210. 713/651-7000. **Toll-free phone:** 877/363-3647. **Fax:** 713/651-6995. **Contact:** Human Resources. **World Wide Web address:** http://www.eogresources.com. **Description:** Engaged in the exploration, development, and production of natural gas and crude oil. **Position advertised include:** Senior Petroleum Engineer; Senior Exploration Geologist; Lead Geologic Tech/Geoscience Association. **Corporate headquarters location:** This location. **Other area locations:** Corpus Christi; Tyler; Midland. **Listed on:** New York Stock Exchange. **Stock exchange symbol:** EOG.

ETS LINDGREN
1301 Arrow Point Drive, Cedar Park TX 78613. 512/531-6400. **Fax:** 512/531-6578. **Contact:** Human Resources. **E-mail address:** resumes@ets-lindgren.com. **World Wide Web address:** http://www.ets-lindgren.com. **Description:** Designs, manufactures, and maintains products that measure, contain, and suppress electromagnetic, RF, and microwave energy. The company markets its products under the names Rantec, EMCO, Rayproof, and Enroshield. Founded in 1995. **Other U.S. locations:** Illinois. **International locations:** United Kingdom; Finland; Singapore; France; Japan; China. **Parent company:** ESCO Technologies Corporation is a diversified producer of commercial products. ESCO's products include electronic equipment, valves and filters, filtration and fluid flow components, automatic test equipment, utility load management equipment, and anechoic/shielding systems. ESCO's other operating subsidiaries include PTI Technologies, Inc.; VACCO Industries; Distribution Control Systems, Inc.; Rantec Microwave & Electronics; Lindgren RF Enclosures; Comtrak Technologies, Inc.; and Filtertek Inc. **Listed on:** New York Stock Exchange. **Stock exchange symbol:** ESE.

EAST TEXAS MEDICAL CENTER
1000 South Beckham, Tyler TX 75701. 903/597-0351. **Recorded jobline:** 903/531-8016. **Contact:** Human Resources. **World Wide Web address:** http://www.etmc.org. **Description:** A 454-bed general hospital. Services include acute care rehabilitation, cardiovascular care, neurological services, obstetrical services, and a level-one trauma center. **NOTE:** Full-time and part-time, weekdays and weekend positions available. **Positions advertised include:** Department Secretary; File Clerk; LPN; Physical Therapist; Speech Pathologist; Housekeeper; Phlebotomist; Technician; Dietary Aide. **Parent company:** East Texas Medical Center Regional Healthcare System.

EASTFIELD COLLEGE
3737 Motley Drive, Mesquite TX 75150. 972/860-7630. **Contact:** Kate Kelley, College Director, Human Resources. **World Wide Web address:** http://www.efc.dcccd.edu. **Description:** A community college.

ECKERT, INGRUM, TINKLER, OLIPHANT, & FEATHERSTON, L.L.P.
P.O. Box 5821, San Angelo TX 76902-5821. 915/944-3571. **Fax:** 915/942-1093. **Contact:** Hiring Partner. **Description:** An accounting firm involved in bookkeeping, taxes, and auditing of various institutions including schools, governments, and banks. **NOTE:** Entry-level positions are offered. **Corporate headquarters location:** This location.

ECOM ELITE COMPUTER CONSULTANTS
10333 NW Freeway, Suite 414, Houston TX 77092. 713/686-9740. **Toll-free phone:** 800/929-3266. **Fax:** 713/686-1661. **Contact:** Human Resources. **E-mail address:** Ecom@ecom-inc.com. **Corporate headquarters location:** This location. **Other area locations:** Dallas; San Antonio. **Other U.S. locations:** Kansas City; St. Louis. **World Wide Web address:** http://www.ecom-inc.com. **Description:** A computer consulting firm. **NOTE:** Contract and permanent positions offered. **Positions advertised include:** Support; Team Leader; Programmer/Analyst; Software Engineer; Developer; Technology Specialist; PC Coordinator; Global Windows & Messaging Manager.

EDINBURG REGIONAL MEDICAL CENTER
1102 West Trenton Road, P.O. Box 2000, Edinburg TX 78539. 956/388-6000. **Contact:** Human Resources. **World Wide Web address:** http://www.edinburgregional.com. **Description:** A 130-bed medical center offering a wide variety of medical and diagnostic services. **NOTE:** Job listings found on UHS website: uhsinc.com. **Corporate headquarters location:** King of Prussia PA. **Parent company:** Universal Health Services, Inc. **Listed on:** New York Stock Exchange. **Stock exchange symbol:** UHS.

A.G. EDWARDS & SONS
2305 Cedars Spring Road, Suite 300, Dallas TX 75201. 214/954-1999. **Contact:** Human Resources. **E-mail address:** employment@agedwards.com. **World Wide Web address:** http://www.agedwards.com. **Description:** An investment firm offering bonds, money market accounts, mutual funds, IRAs, annuities, estate planning, and related services. Founded in 1887. **NOTE:** Mail resume to A.G. Edwards Employment Department; One North Jefferson; St. Louis MO 63103; or, complete online resume. **Corporate headquarters location:** St. Louis MO.

EL CENTRO COLLEGE
801 Main Street, Dallas TX 75212. 214/860-2064. **Contact:** Human Resources. **World Wide Web address:** http://www.dcccd.edu. **Description:** A two-year community college. El Centro College operates as part of the Dallas County Community College District, which is comprised of seven area colleges.

EL CHICO RESTAURANTS, INC.
12200 Stemmons Freeway, Suite 100, Dallas TX 75234. 972/888-8146. **Contact:** Human Resources. **E-mail address:** recruiting@croinc.com. **World Wide Web address:** http://www.elchico.com. **Description:** Operates a chain of full-service restaurants. **NOTE:** Management candidates must have two or more years of experience in casual dining or related experience; good leadership and communication skills. **Corporate headquarters location:** This location. **Parent company:** Consolidated Restaurants Inc. (also at this location). **Operations at this facility include:** Administration; Manufacturing; Research and Development.

EL PASO ASSOCIATION FOR THE PERFORMING ARTS
P.O. Box 31340, El Paso TX 79931. 915/565-6900. **Contact:** Human Resources. **World Wide Web address:** http://www.viva-ep.org. **Description:** Hosts various Shakespeare productions in conjunction with the McKelligon Canyon Amphitheater (also at this location).

EL PASO, CITY OF
2 Civic Center Plaza, El Paso TX 79901-1196. 915/541-4504. **Fax:** 915/541-4220. **Recorded jobline:** 915/541-4094. **Contact:** Human Resources. **World Wide Web address:** http: www.elpasotexas.gov. **Description:** Administrative offices for the city of El Paso. **NOTE:** Applications must be received by Human Resources no later than 5:00 p.m. on the last day of the job's filing period. **Positions advertised include:** Geographic Information Systems Technician; Police Chief; Assistant Director of Facilities Management; Legal File Clerk; Water Conservation Technician; Library Branch Manager. **Office hours:** Monday – Friday; 8:00 a.m. – 5:00 p.m.

EL PASO CORPORATION
Coastal Tower, 9 Greenway Plaza, Houston, TX 77046-0995. 713/420-2600. **Contact:** Human Resources. **World Wide Web address:** http://www.elpaso.com. **Description:** Engaged in oil extraction, marketing, and transmission, with over 20,000 miles of pipeline. El Paso Corporation also refines, markets, and distributes petroleum and related products; conducts oil and gas exploration; mines for coal; manufactures chemicals; and operates trucking facilities. **NOTE:** This company only accepts resumes for open positions. Check website for current list of openings. **Internship information:** For information, e-mail this company at internships@elpaso.com. **Positions advertised include:** Accountant; Network Operations Center Technician. **Parent company:** El Paso Energy Corporation.

EL PASO ELECTRIC COMPANY
P.O. Box 982, Location – 245, El Paso TX 79960. 915/543-2027. Fax: 915/521-4787. Recorded jobline: 915/543-2233. **Contact:** Human Resources. **E-mail address:** Human_Resources@epelectric.com. **World Wide Web address:** http://www.epelectric.com. **Description:** El Paso Electric generates and distributes electricity through an interconnected system to approximately 314,000 customers in El Paso and an area of the Rio Grande Valley in west Texas and southern New Mexico. The company's service area extends about 110 miles northwest from El Paso to the Caballo Dam in New Mexico and about 120 miles southeast from El Paso to Van Horn TX. Founded in 1901. **Listed on:** New York Stock Exchange. **Stock exchange symbol:** EE.

EL PASO ENERGY CORPORATION
1001 Louisiana Street, Suite W1419B, Houston TX 77002. 713/420-2131. **Contact:** Human Resources. **World Wide Web address:** http://www.epenergy.com. **Description:** A holding company with subsidiaries engaged in transporting and selling natural gas, mining and selling minerals, and manufacturing industrial products. **NOTE:** This company only accepts resumes for open positions. Check website for current list of openings. **Internship information:** For information, e-mail this company at internships@elpaso.com. **Positions advertised include:** Accountant; Analyst; Field Operations. **Corporate headquarters location:** This location. **Operations at this facility include:** Administration; Research and Development. **Listed on:** New York Stock Exchange. **Stock exchange symbol:** EP.

EL PASO NATURAL GAS COMPANY
100 North Stanton, El Paso TX 79901. 915/496-2600. **Contact:** Human Resources. **World Wide Web address:** http://www.epenergy.com. **Description:** Owns and operates one of the nation's largest field and mainline natural gas transmission systems. The company has over 17,000 miles of pipeline connecting natural gas supply regions in New Mexico, Texas, Oklahoma, and Colorado to markets in California, Nevada, Arizona, New Mexico, Texas, and Mexico. **NOTE:** This company only accepts resumes for open positions. Check website for current list of openings. **Internship information:** For information, e-mail this company at internships@elpaso.com. **Parent company:** El Paso Energy Corporation.

EL PASO TIMES INC.
P.O. Box 20, El Paso TX 79999. 915/546-6100. **Contact:** Malena Field, Human Resources Director. **World Wide Web address:** http://www.elpasotimes.com. **Description:** Writes, publishes, prints, and distributes a daily newspaper throughout Texas and New Mexico. The newspaper reaches250,000 people daily. The company also publishes and distributes the *El Paso Herald Post*.

EL PASO WATER UTILITIES
P.O. Box 511, El Paso TX 79961. 915/594-5519. **Physical address:** 1154 Hawkins Boulevard, El Paso TX 79925. **Fax:** 915/594-5679. **Contact:** Fred Lawrence, Human Resources. **NOTE:** Job listings and resumes are accepted for this company by the City of El Paso on its website, http://www.elpasotexas.gov. **World Wide Web address:** http://www.epwu.org. **Description:** A nonprofit provider of water and wastewater services for the city of El Paso and the surrounding region.

ELCOR CORPORATION
14911 Quorum Drive, Suite 600, Dallas TX 752-54-1491. 972/851-0500. **Contact:** Human Resources. **World Wide Web address:** http://www.elcor.com. **Description:** Manufactures roofing products including fiberglass asphalt shingles. **Corporate headquarters location:** This location. **Subsidiaries include:** Elk Corporation of Texas. **Listed on:** New York Stock Exchange. **Stock exchange symbol:** ELK.

ELK CORPORATION
202 Cedar Road, Ennis TX 75119. 972/875-9611. **Toll-free phone:** 800/288-6789. **Fax:** 972/872-2392. **Contact:** Human Resources. **World Wide Web address:** http://www.elkcorp.com. **Description:** Manufactures residential roofing products and fiberglass mats. Founded in 1955. **Corporate headquarters location:** Dallas TX. **Other U.S. locations:** Tuscaloosa AL; Shafter CA; Myerstown, PA. **Parent company:** Elcor Corporation. **Operations at this facility include:** Administration; Manufacturing; Sales. **Listed on:** New York Stock Exchange. **Stock exchange symbol:** ELK.

EMBASSY SUITES HOTEL
300 South Congress Avenue, Austin TX 78704. 512/469-9000. **Contact:** Human Resources Department. **World Wide Web address:** http://www.embassy-suites.com. **Description:** A 262-room hotel.

EMBASSY SUITES HOTEL
4250 Ridgemont Drive, Abilene TX 79606. 915/698-1234. **Contact:** Human Resources Department. **World Wide Web address:** http://www.embassy-suites.com. **Description:** A 176-room hotel.

EMERSON PROCESS MANAGEMENT
8301 Cameron Road, Austin TX 78754-3895. 512/835-2190. **Contact:** Human Resources. **World Wide Web address:** http://www.emersonprocess.com. **Description:** Offers a wide variety of process control and assess management solutions. **Parent company:** Emerson Electric. **Listed on:** New York Stock Exchange. **Stock exchange symbol:** EMR.

ENERGY TRANSFER
800 East Sonterra Boulevard, Suite 400, San Antonio TX 78258. 210/403-7300. **Fax:** 210/403-7500. **Contact:** Human Resources. **World Wide Web address:** http://www.energytransfer.com. **Description:** Purchases, gathers, transports, processes, and markets natural gas and natural gas liquids. **Other area locations:** Dallas TX. **Other U.S. locations:** Tulsa OK. **Listed on:** New York Stock Exchange. **Stock exchange symbol:** ETP.

ENCYSIVE PHARMACEUTICALS
7000 Fannin, Floor 20, Houston TX 77030. 713/796-8822. **Fax:** 713/578-6720. **Contact:** Human Resources. **World Wide Web address:** http://www.tbc.com. **Description:** A pharmaceutical research and development firm that specializes in pharmaceuticals for the treatment of acute cardiovascular conditions. **Positions advertised include:** Senior Research Technician. **Corporate headquarters location:** Bellaire TX. **Listed on:** NASDAQ. **Stock exchange symbol:** ENCY.

ENGINE COMPONENTS INC.
9503 Middlex Drive, San Antonio TX 78217. 210/820-8100. **Contact:** Human Resources. **World Wide Web address:** http://www.eci2fly.com. **Description:** Manufactures and repairs engine components for aircraft. **Corporate headquarters location:** This location. **Other U.S. locations:** Bradenton FL; Aurora OR.

ENNIS BUSINESS FORMS
1510 North Hampton, Suite 300, DeSoto TX 75115. 972/228-7801. **Contact:** Human Resources. **World Wide Web address:** http://www.ennis.com. **Description:** Produces business forms, checks, and other printed forms. **Listed on:** New York Stock Exchange. **Stock exchange symbol:** EBF.

ENSCO INTERNATIONAL INCORPORATED
1445 Ross Avenue, Suite 2700, Dallas TX 75202. 214/922-1500. **Toll-free phone:** 800/423-8006. **Contact:** Human Resources. **E-mail address:** employment@enscous.com. **World Wide Web address:** http://www.enscous.com. **Description:** One of the world's largest offshore oil and gas drilling companies. **Corporate headquarters location:** This location. **Listed on:** New York Stock Exchange. **Stock exchange symbol:** ESV.

EPSIIA CORPORATION
1101 Capital of Texas Highway South, Building K, Suite 200, Austin TX 78746. 512/329-0081. **Toll-free phone:** 800/401-4774. Fax: 512/329-0086. **Contact:** Human Resources. **E-mail address:** jobs@EPSIIA.com. **World Wide Web address:** http://www.epsiia.com. **Description:** Develops retrieval and conversion software. **Positions advertised include:** Sales Account Executive. **Corporate headquarters location:** This location. **International locations:** United Kingdom; Brazil. **Parent company:** Fiserv Resources.

ERICSSON INC.
6300 Legacy Drive, Plano TX 75024. 972/583-0000. **Contact:** Human Resources. **World Wide Web address:** http://www.ericsson.com. **Description:** Designs and manufactures advanced telecommunications equipment for wired and mobile communications in public and private networks. **Special programs:** Internships. **Corporate headquarters location:** Sweden. **Other U.S. locations:** New York NY; Lynchburg VA; Washington, D.C.; Research Park Triangle NC; Richardson TX; Reston VA; San Diego CA; Hauppauge NY; Rockville MD **Operations at this facility include:** Research and Development. **Listed on:** NASDAQ. **Stock exchange symbol:** ERICY.

ERNST & YOUNG LLP
2121 San Jacinto, Suite 1500, Dallas TX 75201. 214/969-8000. **Fax:** 214/969-8587. **Contact:** Director of Human Resources. **World Wide Web address:** http://www.ey.com. **Description:** A certified public accounting firm that also provides management consulting services. Services include data processing, financial modeling, financial feasibility studies, production planning and inventory management, management sciences, health care planning, human resources, cost accounting, and budgeting systems. **Corporate headquarters location:** New York NY. **Other area locations:** Austin, Fort Worth, Houston, San Antonio TX. **Other U.S. locations:** Nationwide. **Listed on:** Privately held.

ESSILOR GROUP
13515 North Stemmons Freeway, Dallas TX 75234. 972/241-4141. **Contact:** Human Resources. **World Wide Web address:** http://www.essilor.com. **Description:** A manufacturer of prescription optical lenses and ophthalmic products. **Corporate headquarters location:** France.

ETHICON, INC.
3348 Pulliam Street, San Angelo TX 76905-4430. 915/482-5200. **Contact:** Human Resources. **World Wide Web address:** http://www.ethicon.com. **Description:** Manufactures products for precise wound closure including sutures, ligatures, mechanical wound closure instruments, and related products. The company makes its own surgical needles and provides thousands of needle-suture combinations to surgeons. Ethicon also provides women's health products under the trade name Gynecare. **Parent company:** Johnson & Johnson (New Brunswick NJ). **Listed on:** New York Stock Exchange. **Stock exchange symbol:** JNJ.

ETHYL CORPORATION
P.O. Box 472, Pasadena TX 77501. **Physical address:** 1000 N. South Ave., Pasadena TX 77503. 713/740-8300. **Fax:** 713-740-8311. **Contact:** Human Resources. **World Wide Web address:** http://www.ethyl.com. **Description:** Manufactures fuel and lubricant additives including products for gas and diesel fuels, engine oils, automatic transmission fluids, gear oils, hydraulic fluids, and industrial oils.

J.C. EVANS CONSTRUCTION COMPANY
P.O. Box 9647, Leander TX 78641. **Physical address:** 301 County Road 271, Leander TX 78646, 512/244-1400. **Fax:** 512/244-1900. **Contact:** Human Resources. **World Wide Web address:** http://www.jcevans.com. **Description:** A general contracting company. **Positions advertised include:** Concrete Finisher. **Corporate headquarters location:** This location.

EXECUTRAIN OF TEXAS
12201 Merit Drive, Suite 300, Two Forest Plaza, Dallas TX 75251. 972/387-1212. Fax: 972/387-0000. **Contact:** Human Resources. **World Wide Web address:** http://www.executrain.com/. **Description:** Trains businesses in the use of computer software and offers IT certification. **Corporate headquarters location:** Alpharetta GA. **Other U.S. locations:** Nationwide. **International locations:** Worldwide.

THE EXPLORATION COMPANY
500 North Loop 1604 East, Suite 250, San Antonio TX 78232. 210/496-5300. **Fax:** 210/496-3232. **Contact:** Human Resources. **World Wide Web address:** http://www.txco.com. **Description:** Acquires, explores, and develops oil and gas properties. The Exploration Company operates through three divisions: Oil and Gas Operations, ExproFuels Operations, and Mineral Properties. The company also converts vehicle engines that use gasoline for combustion to propane or natural gas, supplies alternative fuels to customers, and constructs alternative fuels refueling facilities. **Listed on:** NASDAQ. **Stock exchange symbol:** TXCO.

EXPLORATION CONSULTANTS LTD. INC.
9801 Westheimer Road, Suite 1060, Houston TX 77042. 713/784-5800. **Fax:** 713/974-3687. **Contact:** Human Resources. **World Wide Web address:** http://www.ecqc.com. **Description:** Provides consulting services for exploration in the oil and gas industries.

EXPONENT, INC.
10899 Kinghurst Drive, Suite 245, Houston TX 77099. 281/879-6161. **Fax:** 281/879-0687. **Contact:** Personnel. **World Wide Web address:** http://www.exponent.com. **Description:** A technical consulting firm dedicated to the investigation, analysis, and prevention of accidents and failures of an engineering or scientific nature. The company provides a multidisciplinary approach to analyze how failures occur. The company specializes in accident reconstruction, biomechanics, construction/structural engineering, aviation and marine investigations, environmental assessment, materials and product testing, warning and labeling issues, accident statistical data analysis, and risk prevention/mitigation. Founded in 1967. **NOTE:** Applications and resumes accepted online or via e-mail. See website. **Corporate headquarters location:** Menlo Park CA. **Parent company:** Exponent. **Listed on:** NASDAQ. **Stock exchange symbol:** EXPO.

EXXONMOBIL CORPORATION
5959 Las Colinas Boulevard, Irving TX 75039-2298. 972/444-1000. **Fax:** 972/444-1348. **Contact:** Human Resources. **World Wide Web address:** http://www.exxonmobil.com. **Description:** An integrated oil company engaged in the worldwide marketing, refining, manufacturing, exploration, production, transportation, and research and development of petroleum and chemical products. The company also has subsidiaries involved in the aviation and marine markets and in mining operations. Note: Resumes only accepted online at website. **Corporate headquarters location:** This location. **Other U.S. locations:** Houston TX; Fairfax VA. **International locations:** United Kingdom. **Listed on:** New York Stock Exchange. **Stock exchange symbol:** XOM.

FAS TECHNOLOGIES
P.O. Box 550128, Dallas TX 75355-0128. **Physical address:** 10480 Markison Road, Dallas TX 75238. 214/343-5300. **Fax:** 214/343-5350. **Contact:** Human Resources. **World Wide Web address:** http://www.fas.com. **Description:** Manufactures semiconductor processing equipment. Founded in 1988. **Corporate headquarters location:** This location. **International locations:** Japan. **Subsidiaries include:** FAS-Asia, Ltd. **Listed on:** Privately held. **Operations at this location:** Research and development.

FFE TRANSPORTATION SERVICES, INC.
P.O. Box 655888, Dallas TX 75265-5888. **Physical address:** 1145 Empire Central Place, Dallas TX 75247-4309. 214/630-8090. **Contact:** Human Resources. **NOTE:** For additional information, driver applicants can call 800/569-9233; owner/operator applicants can call 800/569-9298; administrative and maintenance applicants can call 800/569-9200. All applicants can also apply online via the website. **World Wide Web address:** http://www.ffeinc.com. **Description:** Provides trucking and transportation services nationwide.

F.F.P./NU-WAY OIL COMPANY, INC.
2801 Glenda Avenue, Fort Worth TX 76117. 817/838-4700. **Contact:** Human Resources. **E-mail address:** info@ffpmarketing.com. **NOTE:** Application form available at website. **World Wide Web address:** http://www.ffpmarketing.com. **Description:** Operates a chain of convenience stores that also offer drive-up gasoline pumps.

FIC INSURANCE GROUP
6500 River Place Boulevard, Building 1, Austin, TX 78730. 512/404-5000. **Contact:** Human Resources. **World Wide Web address:** http://www.ficgroup.com. **Description:** An insurance company that specializes in life insurance. **NOTE:** Resumes can be sent via company's website. **Corporate headquarters location:** This location. **Other U.S. locations:** Seattle WA.

FM GLOBAL
5800 Granite Parkway, Suite 600, Plano TX 75024. 972/377-4808. **Fax:** 972/731-1800. **Contact:** Human Resources. **World Wide Web address:** http://www.fmglobal.com. **Description:** A loss control services organization. FM Global helps owner company policyholders to protect their properties and occupancies from damage caused by fire, wind, flood, and explosion; boiler, pressure vessel, and machinery accidents; and many other insured hazards. **Corporate headquarters location:** Johnston RI. **Other U.S. locations:** Nationwide. **International locations:** Worldwide.

FM INDUSTRIES, INC.
8600 Will Rogers Boulevard, Fort Worth TX 76140. 817/293-4220. **Fax:** 817/551-5801. **Contact:** Human Resources. **World Wide Web address:** http://www.fmionline.net. **Description:** Produces hydraulic cushioning systems for railroad freight cars.

FARM CREDIT BANK OF TEXAS
4801 Plaza on Lake Drive, Austin TX 78746. 512/465-0400. **Contact:** Human Resources. **World Wide Web address:** http://www.farmcreditbank.com. **Corporate headquarters location:** This location. **Other area locations:** McKinney, Bowie, Mulesoe, Kenedy, Weatherford, Lubbock, and Robstown TX. **Description:** A bank that provides loans to the agricultural industry. **Positions advertised include:** Junior Loan Processor; Office/Clerical Assistant; Debt and Investment Accounting Analyst; Relationship Manager Trainee.

FARMERS INSURANCE GROUP
P.O. Box 149044, Austin TX 78714-9044. 512/238-4400. **Contact:** Human Resources. **World Wide Web address:** http://www.farmersinsurance.com. **Description:** Operates as the center for applications and payments for processing auto, home, boat, and life insurance.

FAMILY CHRISTIAN STORES
5303 Walzem Road, San Antonio TX 78218. 210/656-3403. **Contact:** Human Resources. **World Wide Web address:** http://www.familychristian.com. **Description:** A location of the national chain of retail stores selling inspirational books, videos, and other items. Family Christian stores has three locations in San Antonio and more than 300 locations nationwide. **NOTE:** Apply online or at the nearest store location. **Positions advertised include:** Store Manager. **Corporate headquarters location:** Grand Rapids, MI. **Listed on:** Privately held.

FAROUK SYSTEMS
250 Pennbright Drive, Houston TX 77090. 281/876-2000. **Fax:** 281/876-1700. **Contact:** Human Resources. **World Wide Web address:** http://www.farouk.com. **Description:** Manufactures a wide variety of consumer spa, personal and hair care products. Owned and operated by professional hairstylists.

FARSIGHT COMPUTER
1219 West University Boulevard, Odessa TX 79764-7119. 915/335-0879. **Fax:** 915/335-8411. **Contact:** Human Resources. **World Wide Web address:** http://www.farsweb.com. **Description:** A computer wholesaler, specializing in custom-built PCs.

FEDERAL EXPRESS CORPORATION (FEDEX)
1220 Riverbend, Dallas TX 75247. 800/GOF-EDEX. **Contact:** Recruiting. **World Wide Web address:** http://www.fedex.com. **Description:** One of the world's largest express transportation companies serving 215 countries worldwide. FedEx ships approximately 3.2 million packages daily. FedEx operates more than 45,000 drop-off locations, and has a fleet that consists of more than 640 aircraft and 44,5000 vehicles. **Corporate headquarters location:** Memphis TN. **Other U.S. locations:** Nationwide. **International locations:** Worldwide. **Listed on:** New York Stock Exchange. **Stock exchange symbol:** FDS.

FERGUSON ENTERPRISES, INC.
19 Burwood Lane, San Antonio TX 78216. 210/344-4950. **Fax:** 210/344-1253. **Contact: Human Resources. E-mail address:** resumes@ferguson.com. **World Wide Web address:** http://www.ferguson.com. **Description:** A retail and wholesale distributor of plumbing supplies. **Positions advertised include:** Sales/Management Trainee; Controller Trainee. **Corporate headquarters location:** This location. **Other U.S. locations:** Nationwide.

FERGUSON MANUFACTURING AND EQUIPMENT CO. INC.
4900 Harry Hines Boulevard, Dallas TX 75235. 214/631-3000. **Fax:** 214/637-1530. **Contact:** Human Resources. **World Wide Web address:** http://www.fergusonrollers.com. **Description:** Manufactures and distributes construction machines and equipment.

FIDELITY INVESTMENTS
400 East Las Colinas Boulevard, Mail Zone CP7I, Irving TX 75039. 972/584-7000. **Fax:** 972/584-7275. **Contact:** Human Resources. **World Wide Web address:** http://www.fidelity.com. **Description:** One of the nation's leading investment counseling and mutual fund/discount brokerage firms. **NOTE:** Entry-level positions and second and third shifts are offered. **Positions advertised include:** Principal Operating Systems Consultant. **Special programs:** Internships. **Internship information:** The company has an MIS internship program. Applications must be submitted by March 1st via e-mail or in writing. **Corporate headquarters location:** Boston MA. **Other U.S. locations:** Nationwide. **Listed on:** Privately held.

FIESTA MART INC.
5235 Katy Freeway, Houston TX 77007. 713/869-5060. **Fax:** 713/869-6197. **Contact:** Human Resources. **World Wide Web address:** http://www.fiestamart.com. **Description:** Operates a chain of grocery stores throughout Texas. **Corporate headquarters location:** This location. **Other area locations:** Dallas/Ft. Worth; Austin; Waco TX.

THE FINANCE COMPANY
2201 South W.S. Young Drive, Suite 106C, Killeen TX 76543. 254/526-8390. **Contact:** Human Resources. **Description:** Engaged primarily in buying and servicing installment contracts originated by used car dealers. Most of The Finance Company's income comes from interest charged on contracts and from the discounts at which it purchases contracts. The company also receives revenue from the commissions received on ancillary products, such as credit insurance, limited physical damage insurance, and product warranties offered by the company and underwritten by third-party vendors. **NOTE:** Send resumes to: The Finance Company, Human Resources, P.O. Box 10306, Norfolk VA 23513.

FINSA INDUSTRIAL PARKS
973 South Minnesota, Brownsville TX 78521. 956/550-9017. **Contact:** Human Resources. **World Wide Web address:** http://www.finsa.net. **Description:** A company that constructs, owns, sells, and leases industrial park property.

FIRST AMERICAN FLOOD DATA SERVICES
11902 Burnet Road, Suite 400, Austin TX 78758. 512/834-9595. **Toll-free number:** 800/447-1772. **Fax:** 800/447-2258. **Contact:** Judy Ellison, Human Resources Director. **World Wide Web address:** http://floodcert.com. **Description:** Determines whether properties are in a flood zone for mortgage companies and banks.

FIRST CASH, INC.
690 East Lamar Boulevard, Suite 400, Arlington TX 76011. 817/460-3947. **Contact:** Human Resources. **World Wide Web address:** http://www.firstcash.com. **Description:** Acquires, establishes, and operates pawn and short-term loan stores. First Cash also operates more than 25 check-cashing stores. **Corporate headquarters location:** This location. **Other U.S. locations:** CA; OR; VA: DC; IL; MD; MO; OK; SC. **International locations:** Mexico.

FIRST CHOICE POWER
4100 International Plaza, Fort Worth TX 76109. 817/731-0099. **Fax:** 817/735-5731. **Contact:** Human Resources. **World Wide Web address:** http://www.firstchoicepower.com. **Description:** This company sells electricity to approximately 200,000 residences throughout Texas. It sister company, Texas-New Mexico Power, transmits and distributes electricity. **NOTE:** See this company's website for job listings and e-mail resumes. **Positions advertised include:** Senior Pricing Analyst; Power Trader/Analyst; Director of Portfolio Management; Customer Accounts Manager; Supervisor of Quality Assurance. **Corporation headquarters location:** This location. **Parent company:** TNP Enterprises. **Listed on:** Privately held.

FIRST NATIONAL BANK OF ABILENE
P.O. Box 701, Abilene TX 79604. 915/627-7000. **Recorded jobline:** 325/627-7356. **Contact:** Human Resources. **World Wide Web address:** http://www.fnbabilene.com. **Description:** A full-service bank that offers online banking, loan, and investment services. **NOTE:** Applicants should apply in person at the company's Human Resources offices at 400 Pine Street, Abilene TX. Online application can be found on the company's website. **Positions advertised include:** Teller; Cashier; Infrastructure Support Technician.

FIRST SOUTHWEST COMPANY
1700 Pacific Avenue, Suite 500, Dallas TX 75201-4652. 214/953-4000. **Fax:** 214/953-8790. **Contact:** Human Resources. **World Wide Web address:** http://www.firstsw.com. **Description:** Offers a full line of investment services including public, private, and corporate banking; funds management; trading of debt and equity securities; institutional sales; and clearing. **Corporate headquarters location:** This location. **Other area locations:** Abilene TX; Austin TX; Fort Worth TX; Houston TX; Lubbock TX; San Antonio TX. **Other U.S. locations:** AR; FL; CA; NY; AL.

FISERV, INC.
595 Orleans Street, Beaumont TX 77701. 409/839-0600. **Contact:** Human Resources. **World Wide Web address:** http://www.fiserv.com. **Description:** An independent provider of data processing outsourcing capabilities and related products and services for financial institutions. FiServ's system applications are designed to increase the operating efficiency, customer service, and marketing capability of banks, credit unions, mortgage banks, savings institutions, and other financial intermediaries. **Corporate headquarters location:** Brookfield WI. **Other area locations:** Statewide. **Other U.S. locations:** Nationwide. **Listed on:** NASDAQ. **Stock exchange symbol:** FISV.

FISHER SCIENTIFIC COMPANY
9999 Veterans Memorial Drive, Houston TX 77038. 281/878-3500. **Contact:** Human Resources. **World Wide Web address:** http://www.fisherscientific.com. **Description:** One of the oldest and largest providers of instruments, equipment, and other products to the scientific community. The company offers a selection of more than 150,000 products and services to research centers and industrial customers worldwide. Fisher serves scientists engaged in biomedical, biotechnology, pharmaceutical, chemical, and other fields of research and development; and scientists in companies, educational and research institutions, and government agencies. The company also supplies clinical laboratories, hospitals, environmental testing centers, remediation companies, quality control laboratories, and other industrial facilities. In addition, Fisher represents its customers as a third-party purchaser of maintenance materials and other basic supplies. **NOTE:** Submit resume online at the company's website.

FLAGSHIP HOTEL OVER THE WATER
2501 Seawall Boulevard, Galveston TX 77550. 409/762-9000. **Toll-free phone:** 800/392-6542. **Fax:** 409/762-1619. **Contact:** Human Resources. **World Wide Web address:** http://www.galveston.com/ flagship. **Description:** A hotel and resort.

FLEXITALLIC GASKET COMPANY
6915 Highway 225, Deer Park TX 77536. 281/604-2400. **Toll-free phone:** 800/527-1935. **Contact:** Human Resources. **E-mail address:** hr@flexitallic.com. **World Wide Web address:** http://www.flexitallic.com. **Description:** Manufactures spiral gaskets. **Corporate headquarters location:** Houston TX. **Other U.S. locations:** NJ.

FLIGHTSAFETY INTERNATIONAL, INC.
8900 Trinity Boulevard, Hurst TX 76053. 817/276-7500. **Fax:** 817/276-7501. **Contact:** Phyllis Lovelace, Manager of Human Resources. **World Wide Web address:** http://www.flightsafety.com. **Description:** Provides high-technology training to operators of aircraft and ships. Total training systems are used including sophisticated simulators and training devices, computer-based training, and professional instructors. **Corporate headquarters location:** Flushing NY. **Other U.S. locations:** Nationwide. **Listed on:** New York Stock Exchange. **Number of employees nationwide:** 2,000.

FLINT HILLS RESOURCES LP
P.O. Box 2608, Corpus Christi TX 78403-2608. 361/241-4811. **Physical address:** 2825 Suntide Road, Corpus Christi TX 78410. **Contact:** Human Resources. **World Wide Web address:** http://www.fhr.com. **Description:** A manufacturer of chemicals. **Positions advertised include:** Product Specialist; Senior Process Engineer. **Corporate headquarters location:** Wichita KS. **Other area locations:** Austin TX; Ft. Worth TX. **Parent company:** Koch Industries.

FLOW PRODUCTS INCORPORATED
800 Koomey Road, Brookshire TX 77423. 281/934-6014. **Toll-free phone:** 800/955-5847. **Fax:** 800/945-4777. **Contact:** Human Resources. **World Wide Web address:** http://www.paco-pumps.com. **Description:** Manufactures industrial pumps and valves through its subsidiaries. **Positions advertised include:** Cell Machinist; Storekeeper; Senior Systems Administrator. **Corporate headquarters location:** This location. **Other U.S. locations:** AL; CA; OR; TN; UT; VA; WA. **Subsidiaries include:** Johnston Pump; PACO Pumps; General Valve. All three companies are also at this location.

FLOWSERVE CORPORATION
5215 N. O'Connor Boulevard, Suite 2300, Irving TX 75039. 972/443-6500. **Fax:** 972/443-6800. **Contact:** Human Resources. **World Wide Web address:** http://www.flowserve.com. **Description:** Manufactures valves, pumps and seals for the chemical and petroleum industries. **Corporate headquarters location:** This location. **Listed on:** New York Stock Exchange. **Stock exchange symbol:** FLS.

FOGARTYKLEINMONROE
7155 Old Katy Road, Suite 100, Houston TX 77024. 713/862-5100. **Contact:** Debbie Ray-Walder, Human Resources Director. **E-mail address:** drwalder@fkmagency.com. **World Wide Web address:** http://www.fkmagency.com. **Description:** A full-service advertising and public relations agency.

FOLEY'S
1110 Main Street, Houston TX 77002. 713/405-7035. **Contact:** Human Resources. **World Wide Web address:** http://www2.shopmay.com. **Description:** One location of the department store chain operating through over 50 stores. **NOTE:** Apply online at the company's website or at the nearest Foley's store location. **Positions advertised include:** General Sales Associate; Commission Sales Associate; Cosmetics Beauty Advisor; Fine Jewelry Associate. **Parent company:** The May Department Stores Company.

FOOD BASKET IGA
4202 South Bryant Boulevard, San Angelo TX 76903. 325/658-5602. **Contact:** Human Resources. **Description:** A grocery store chain with locations throughout Texas. **Corporate headquarters location:** This location.

FORDYCE COMPANY
P.O. Box 1417, Victoria TX 77902. 361/573-4309. **Physical address:** 120 South Main Place, Suite 500, Victoria TX 77901. **Contact:** Human Resources. **Description:** Produces sand and gravel. **Corporate headquarters location:** This location. **Number of employees at this location:** 120.

FORESTERS
10333 Richmond Avenue, Suite 700, Houston TX 77042. 713/266-3463. **Contact:** Human Resources. **E-mail address:** recruitsoft@foresters.biz. **World Wide Web address:** http://www.forester.com. **Description:** A financial services company specializing in life insurance and annuities. **NOTE:** This company has several sales offices throughout Texas and the U.S. See website for job listings and locations. Apply online. **Positions advertised include:** Financial Representative. **Corporate headquarters location:** Toronto Canada. **Other area locations:** Amarillo TX; Austin TX; Bedford TX; San Antonio TX. **International locations:** United Kingdom.

FORETRAVEL, INC.
1221 NW Stallings Drive, Nacogdoches TX 75964. 936/569-7906. **Contact:** Human Resources. **World Wide Web address:** http://www.foretravel.com. **Description:** Manufactures motor homes. **Corporate headquarters location:** This location.

FORT WORTH, CITY OF
1000 Throckmorton Street, Fort Worth TX 76102. 817/392-2255. **Recorded jobline:** 817/392-7760. **Contact:** Human Resources. **World Wide Web address:** http://www.fortworthgov.org. **Description:** This location houses the city's administrative offices and departments, including police and fire. **NOTE:** Part-time and temporary positions available. The city's website provides job listings and contact information for all its departments and related agencies, including its Police and Fire Departments. A completed application is required for any position. See website for listings, contact information and application process. **Positions advertised include:** Assistant Development Director; Assistant Water Director; Street Services Manager; Senior Planner; Eligibility Specialist.

FORNEY CORPORATION
3405 Wiley Post Road, Carrollton TX 75006. 972/458-6100. **Toll-free phone:** 972/458-6195. **Fax:** 972/458-6650. **Contact:** Ellen Bath, Human Resources Director. **E-mail address:** ellen.bath@forneycorp.com. **World Wide Web address:** http://www.forneycorp.com. **Description:** Manufactures industrial boiler burners, and burner and process control equipment and systems. **Positions advertised include:** Aftermarket Sales; Project Engineering; Project Management; Product Development -- Mechanical; Product Development -- Electrical; BMS Design Engineer. **Parent company:** Kidde PLC.

FOSSIL, INC.
2280 North Greenville Avenue, Richardson TX 75082-4412. 972/234-2525. **Contact:** Human Resources. **E-mail address:** jobs@fossil.com. **World Wide Web address:** http://www.fossil.com. **Description:** Manufactures watches, leather accessories, T-shirts, and sunglasses. **NOTE:** Job listings available online at company's website. **Corporate headquarters location:** This location. **Other U.S. locations:** Nationwide. **Listed on:** NASDAQ. **Stock exchange symbol:** FOSL.

FOUR SEASONS HOTEL HOUSTON
1300 Lamar Street, Houston TX 77010. 713/650-1300. **Fax:** 713/650-0434. **Recorded jobline:** 713/652-6240. **E-mail address:** jobs.Houston@fourseasons.com. **Contact:** Human Resources. **World Wide Web address:** http://www.fourseasons.com/employment.com. **Description:** A 399-room hotel that also houses the DeVille Restaurant. Four Seasons Hotels & Resorts operates approximately 55 luxury hotels and resorts in 25 countries. Founded in 1960. **Corporate headquarters location:** Toronto, Canada. **Other area locations:** Austin TX. **Other U.S. locations:** Nationwide. **International locations:** Worldwide.

FOUR SEASONS RESORT AND CLUB
4150 North MacArthur Boulevard, Irving TX 75038. 972/717-0700. **Fax:** 972-717-2578. **Recorded jobline:** 972/717-2544. **Contact:** Human Resources. **E-mail address:** jobs.dalls@fourseasons.com. **World Wide Web address:** http://www.fourseasons.com. **Description:** A 357-room resort offering two championship golf courses, 12 tennis courts, a spa, and a conference center. The 18-hole TPC championship golf course is the site of the annual Byron Nelson Classic on the PGA Tour. The 176,000-square-foot sports club and spa has a racquet sports center, indoor and outdoor pools and tracks, and complete personal training facilities. The 20,000-square-foot conference center includes 26 multipurpose meeting and function rooms. Overall, Four Seasons Hotels & Resorts operates approximately 50 luxury hotels and resorts in 22 countries. Founded in 1960. **NOTE:** Entry-level positions, part-time jobs, and second and third shifts are offered. **Special programs:** Training;

Summer Jobs. **Corporate headquarters location:** Toronto, Canada. **Other U.S. locations:** Nationwide. **International locations:** Worldwide.

FOXTRONICS INC.
3448 West Mockingbird Lane, Dallas TX 75235. 214/358-4425. **Fax:** 214/358-1519. **Contact:** Human Resources. **World Wide Web address:** http://www.foxtronics.com. **Description:** Engaged in the sale and service of aircraft batteries.

FOXWORTH-GALBRAITH
P.O. Box 799002, 1711 Waterview Park, Dallas TX 75379-9002. 972/437-6100. **Fax:** 972-454-4251. **Contact:** Human Resources. **World Wide Web address:** http://www.foxgal.com. **Description:** A building materials retailer. **Office hours:** Monday – Friday, 7:30 a.m. -- 4:30 p.m. **Corporate headquarters locations:** This location. **Other area locations:** Statewide. **Other U.S. locations:** AZ; CO; NM. **Listed on:** Privately held.

FREEDMAN DISTRIBUTORS
2901 Polk, Houston TX 77003. 713/229-8000. **Toll-free phone:** 800/299-3371. **Fax:** 713/223-5001. **Contact:** Human Resources. **World Wide Web address:** http://www.freedmanfoods.com. **Description:** Distributes boxed meat products to retail outlets. **Corporate headquarters location:** This location. **Other area locations:** Statewide.

THE FREEMAN COMPANIES
1421 W. Mockingbird Lane, Dallas TX 75247. 713/433-2400. **Toll-free phone:** 888/670-3060. **Contact:** Human Resources. **World Wide Web address:** http://www.totalshowcase.com. **Description:** Offers set-up and display services for theater productions; trade shows and conventions.

FRIEDMAN INDUSTRIES, INC.
4001 Homestead Road, Houston TX 77028. 713/672-9433. **Contact:** Human Resources Manager. **World Wide Web address:** http://www.friedmanindustries.com. **Description:** Engaged in the steel processing and distribution business. The company has two product classifications: hot-rolled steel sheet and plate, and tubular products. At its facilities in Lone Star TX, Houston TX, and Hickman AK, the company processes semifinished, hot-rolled steel coils into flat, finished sheet and plate, and sells these products on a wholesale, rapid-delivery basis in competition with steel mills, importers, and steel service centers. The company also processes customer-owned coils on a fee basis. Products and services are sold principally to steel distributors and to customers fabricating steel products such as storage tanks, steel buildings, farm machinery and equipment, construction equipment, transportation equipment, conveyors, and other similar products. The company, through its Texas Tubular Products operation (Lone Star TX), also markets and processes pipe.

FRIENDLY CHEVROLET COMPANY, INC.
P.O. Box 7066, Dallas TX 75209. 214/920-1905. **Physical address:** 2754 North Stemmons Freeway, Dallas TX 75207. **Contact:** Trisha Casey, Human Resources Manager. **World Wide Web address:** http://www.friendlychevy.com. **Description:** A dealership of both new and used automobiles.

FRITO-LAY, INC.
P.O. Box 660634, Dallas TX 75266-0634. 972/334-7000. **Physical address:** 7701 Legacy Drive, Plano TX 75024-4099. **Toll-free number:** 800/352-4477. **Fax:** 972/334-2019. **Contact:** Staffing. **World Wide Web address:** http://www.fritolayjobs.com. **Description:** A worldwide manufacturer and wholesaler of a wide range of snack products including Fritos Corn Chips, Doritos Tortilla Chips, Lays Potato Chips, Ruffles Potato Chips, Cracker Jack caramel popcorn, Chee-tos, and Smartfood Popcorn. **NOTE:** Local, Texas and national job listings available on the company's website. Resumes accepted online only. **Positions advertised include:** Category Manager; S&D Project Engineer; Principal Research Chemist; Sales Manager. **Special programs:** Internships. **Corporate headquarters location:** This location. **Other area locations:** Lubbock TX; Irving TX; Houston TX; Rosenberg TX. **Other U.S. locations:** Nationwide. **Parent company:** PepsiCo, Inc. (Purchase NY) consists of Frito-Lay Company, Pepsi-Cola Company, Quaker Oats, and Tropicana Products, Inc. **Listed on:** New York Stock Exchange. **Stock exchange symbol:** PEP.

FRONTIER ENTERPRISES
8520 Crownhill Boulevard, San Antonio TX 78209-1199. 210/828-1493. **Contact:** Wendi Scarborough, Human Resources. **World Wide Web address:** http://www.jimsrestaurants.com. **Description:** Owns and operates Jim's Family Restaurants, Magic Time Machine Restaurants, and Towers of America Restaurants. Magic Time Machine Restaurants are seafood and steak dining establishments and the Towers of America Restaurants are family-style restaurants set approximately 6,000 feet in the air. **NOTE:** Online applications available at company's website for all Texas locations. **Positions advertised include:** Manager; Assistant Manager; Waitstaff; Cook; Busperson; Cashier. **Corporate headquarters location:** This location. **Other area locations:** Austin TX; San Antonio TX; Waco TX.

FRONTIER OIL CORPORATION
10000 Memorial, Suite 600, Houston TX 77024-3341. 713/688-9600. **Fax:** 713/688-0616. **Contact:** Human Resources. **E-mail address:** HR@frontieroil-den.com. **World Wide Web address:** http://www.frontieroil.com. **Description:** Engaged in oil and gas exploration and production. **Other U.S. locations:** WY; KS; CO. **Listed on:** New York Stock Exchange. **Stock exchange symbol:** FTO.

FROST NATIONAL BANK
CULLEN/FROST BANKERS, INC.
P.O. Box 1600, San Antonio TX 78296-1400. 210/220-4011. **Recorded jobline:** 210/220-5627. **Contact:** Human Resources. **World Wide Web address:** http://www.frostbank.com. **Description:** A bank that offers online banking, financial management, and loan services. There are 81 locations in major Texas cities. **NOTE:** Human Resources office hours vary from bank location. Check company's website for office hours and scheduling pre-employment tests. **Corporate headquarters location:** This location. **Other area locations:** Statewide. **Parent company:** Cullen/Frost Bankers, Inc. **Listed on:** New York Stock Exchange. **Stock exchange symbol:** CFR.

FUGRO GEOSCIENCES
6105 Rookin, Houston TX 77074. 713/778-5580. **Contact:** Human Resources. **World Wide Web address:** http://www. fugro.com. **Description:** A conglomerate of international engineering and geoscience consulting firms serving the offshore, industrial, public works, and commercial industries. The firms offer geosciences, earth sciences, and waste management services. **NOTE:** There are 12 different divisions located at this Houston location with separate Human Resource offices. See website for divisions and contact information. **Corporate headquarters location:** The Netherlands.

FUJI SEMICONDUCTOR, INC.
P.O. Box 702708, Dallas TX 75370. 972/733-1700. **Physical address:** 2532 Highlander Way, Carrollton TX 75006. **Contact:** Human Resources. **World Wide Web address:** http://www.fujisemiconductor.com. **Description:** Manufactures and distributes semiconductors. **Corporate headquarters location:** Tokyo. **Parent company:** Fuji Electric Co.

FUJITSU
900 One Galleria Tower, 13355 Noel Road, Suite 800, Dallas TX 75240. 972/239-8611. **Contact:** Human Resources. **World Wide Web address:** http://www.us.fujitsu.com. **Description:** Provides computer consulting, including outsourcing and systems integration. **Corporate headquarters location:** Edison NJ.

FUJITSU NETWORK COMMUNICATIONS
2801 Telecom Parkway, Richardson TX 75082. 972/690-6000. **Toll-free phone:** 800/777-3278. **Contact:** Human Resources. **World Wide Web address:** http://www.us.fujitsu.com/telecom. **Description:** Fujitsu Network Communications develops and manufactures broadband transmission and switching technologies to deliver voice, video, and data capabilities. **Operations at this facility include:** This location is engaged in the repair of cellular telephones.

FULBRIGHT AND JAWORSKI LLP
1301 McKinney Street, Suite 5100, Houston TX 77010-3095. 713/651-5151. **Contact:** Human Resources. **World Wide Web address:** http://www.fulbright.com. **Description:** An international legal firm specializing in all areas of law. **Positions advertised include:** Project Manager; Legal Assistant; Project Assistant; Contract Technical Writer. **Special programs:** Internships. **Corporate headquarters location:** This location. **Other area locations:** Austin TX; San Antonio TX. **Other U.S. locations:** Los Angeles CA; Minneapolis MN; New York NY; Washington DC. Nationwide. International locations: United Kingdom; Germany. **Operations at this facility include:** Administration.

FUTRON CORPORATION
1120 NASA Road One, Suite 310, Houston TX 77058-3302. 281/333-0190. **Contact:** Human Resources. **E-mail address:** resume@futron.com. **World Wide Web address:** http://www.futron.com. **Description:** Provides management and technical consulting services for aerospace and defense companies. Founded in 1986.

GAF MATERIALS CORPORATION
2600 Singleton Boulevard, Dallas TX 75212. 214/637-1060. **Contact:** Human Resources. **World Wide Web address:** http://www.gaf.com. **Description:** A multiproduct manufacturer with sales in both consumer and industrial construction markets. The company's product line includes building, roofing, and insulation materials for the construction trades; specialty chemicals and plastics; and reprographic products. **Corporate headquarters location:** Wayne NJ. **Other U.S. locations:** Nationwide. **Operations at this facility include:** Manufacturing; Sales. **Listed on:** Privately held.

GB TECH INC.
2200 Space Park Drive, Suite 400, Houston TX 77058. 281/333-3703. **Fax:** 281/333-3745. **Contact:** Human Resources. **E-mail address:** hr@gbtech.net. **World Wide Web address:** http://www.gbtech.net. **Description:** Performs aerospace and computer engineering services. GB Tech contracts with several organizations including NASA. **NOTE:** Job listings may be also obtained by calling the company. **Positions advertised include:** Mechanical Engineer; Fracture Mechanics Engineer; Safety Engineer; Communication Systems Engineer; Chemical Engineer. **Corporate headquarters location:** This location.

GC SERVICES
6330 Gulfton Street, Houston TX 77081. 713/777-4441. **Fax:** 713/776-6619. **Contact:** Human Resources. **World Wide Web address:** http://www.gcserv.com. **Description:** A collection agency. **Positions advertised include:** Account Reconciliation Clerk; Accounting Manager; Accounts Payable Analyst; Inventory Reconciliation Clerk; Remittance Processing Supervisor. **Corporate headquarters location:** This location: **Other U.S. locations:** Nationwide.

GSD&M ADVERTISING
828 West Sixth Street, Austin TX 78703. 512/427-4736. **Contact:** Marci Rogers, Recruiting Coordinator; at 512/242-5932. **E-mail address:** marci_rogers@gsdm.com. **World Wide Web address:** http://www.gsdm.com. **Description:** An advertising agency. **Positions advertised include:** Media Supervisor; Broadcast Supervisor; Media Research Analyst; Administrative Assistant. **Corporate headquarters location:** This location.

GSE LINING TECHNOLOGY, INC.
19103 Gundle Road, Houston TX 77073-3598. 281/443-8564. **Toll-free phone:** 800/435-2008. **Fax:** 281/230-2504. **Contact:** Human Resources. **World Wide Web address:** http://www.gseworld.com. **Description:** Manufactures and installs plastic environmental liners for ponds and landfills. **Special programs:** Internships. **Corporate headquarters location:** This location. **International locations:** Worldwide. **Parent company:** Gundle/SLT Environmental, Inc. **Listed on:** New York Stock Exchange. **Stock exchange symbol:** GSE. **President/CEO:** Samir Badawi.

GALACTIC TECHNOLOGIES, INC.
400 North Loop 1604 East, Suite 210, San Antonio TX 78232. 210/496-7250. **Fax:** 210/490-6790. **Contact:** Human Resources. **World Wide Web address:** http://www.galactictech.com. **Description:** Provides computer hardware and software engineering, PC support, and networking services. Galactic Technologies also operates as a value-added reseller. **Positions advertised include:** Software Engineer; PC Technician. **Office hours:** Monday - Friday, 7:30 a.m. - 5:00 p.m. **Corporate headquarters location:** This location.

GALVESTON COLLEGE
4015 Avenue Q, Galveston TX 77550-7496. 409/763-6551. **Fax:** 409/762-0973. **Contact:** Human Resources. **E-mail address:** hrmail@gc.edu. **World Wide Web address:** http://www.gc.edu. **Description:** A community college with an enrollment of 2,500. **NOTE:** Some positions require an application and proof of credentials. See website for specific requirements. **Positions advertised include:** Full-time faculty; Adjunct Faculty; Administrative; Classified; Part-Time.

GALVESTON COUNTY DAILY NEWS
P.O. Box 628, Galveston TX 77553. 409/744-3611. **Fax:** 409/744-6268. **Contact:** Rosetta Bonnin, Business Office Manager (newsroom positions); Deane Gordon, Classified Ads Supervisor (advertising positions). **World Wide Web address:** http://www.galvnews.com. **Description:** A daily newspaper with a circulation of 24,000. **Parent company:** Southern Newspapers Inc. **Listed on:** Privately held.

GALVESTON POLICE DEPARTMENT
5303 Avenue S, Galveston TX 77550. 409/741-0068. **Contact:** Human Resources. **World Wide Web address:** http://www.galpd.org/emp.html. **Description:** Provides law enforcement services to the Galveston area.

GAMESTOP
2250 William D. Tate Avenue, Grapevine TX 76051. 817/424-2000. **Fax:** 817/424-2800. **Contact:** Human Resources. **World Wide Web address:** http://www.gamestop.com. **Description:** A national retailer of interactive games and accessories. Babbage's Etc. operates more than 475 stores in the United States and Puerto Rico under the names Babbage's, Software Etc., Gamestop, SuperSoftware, and Planet X. **NOTE:** Address correspondence to the attention of Michelle. **Corporate headquarters location:** This location. **Listed on:** New York Stock Exchange. **Stock exchange symbol:** GME. **CEO:** R. Richard Fontaine.

GANDY'S DAIRIES INC.
201 University Avenue, Lubbock TX, 79415. 806/765-8833.**Contact:** Judy Gooch, Human Resources Director. **Description:** A milk distribution company. **Parent company:** Dean Foods.

GAS EQUIPMENT COMPANY
11616 Harry Hines Boulevard, P.O. Box 29242, Dallas TX 75229. 972/241-2333. **Toll-free phone:** 800/821-1829. **Fax:** 800/875-8553. **Contact:** Human Resources. **World Wide Web address:** http://www.gasequipment.com. **Description:** A wholesale distributor of liquefied petroleum products. **Corporate headquarters location:** This location. **Listed on:** Privately held.

GEER TANK TRUCKS INC.
P.O. Drawer J, Jacksboro TX 76458. 940/567-2677. **Toll-free phone:** 800/349-4337. **Contact:** Human Resources. **World Wide Web address:** http://www.geertanktrucks.com. **Description:** A crude oil purchaser. The company also hauls various substances including oil and saltwater.

GENERAL ALUMINUM CORPORATION
P.O. Box 819022, Dallas TX 75381. 972/242-5271. **Contact:** Human Resources. **Description:** Manufactures aluminum doors and windows, partition screens, sliding glass doors, and related products.

GENERAL CABLE COMPANY
800 East Second Street, Bonham TX 75418. 903/583-2181. **Contact:** Human Resources. **World Wide Web address:** http://www.generalcable.com/North_America. **Description:** The company's business units include the Electrical Group, the Telecommunications and Electronics Group, the Consumer Products Group, and the Manufacturing Group. The Electrical Group operates under the business units General Cable/Guardian, which manufactures and distributes a full line of copper building wire, tray cable, power cable, and other cable products; Carol Cable Electrical, which manufactures industrial, power, mining, and control cable, THHN building wire, entertainment cable, rubber portable cord, and cordsets insulated with plastic and thermosetting compounds; and Capital Wire and Cable, which manufactures insulated wire and cable using both aluminum and copper conductors. The Telecommunications and Electronics Group operates under the business units Outside Products, which markets wire and cable designed for use in the outside plant network; Premise Products, which manufactures wire products that support the central office and commercial premise markets; and Electronics, which manufactures computer and control cables, IBM cabling products, Ethernet, coaxial, twin axial, and fire alarm cables. The Consumer Products Group operates under the business units Carol Cable, which manufactures extension cords, portable lights, and home office power supplies; General/Capital Wire Retail, which sells building wire to the retail market; and the OEM Engineered Cordsets Division, which manufactures cord and cordsets for data processing equipment, tools, floor care products, and other appliances. **Corporate headquarters location:** Highland Heights KY. **Operations at this facility include:** This location produces commercial cable for telephone companies. **Listed on:** New York Stock Exchange. **Stock exchange symbol:** BGC.

GENERAL REINSURANCE CORPORATION
8144 Walnut Hill Lane, Suite 1250, Dallas TX 75231-3309. 214/691-3000. **Contact:** J. Foulds. **E-mail address:** jfoulds@genre.com. **World Wide Web address:** http://www.genre.com. **Description:** Provides property and casualty reinsurance to primary insurers on a direct basis.

GEO-MARINE, INC.
550 East 15th Street, Plano TX 75074. 972/423-5480. **Contact:** Human Resources. **Fax:** 972/422-2736. **World Wide Web address:** http://www.geo-marine.com. **Description:** An environmental, engineering, consulting firm that provides services to government, business, and industry. Geo-Marine specializes in hazardous materials/waste management, natural resources management, energy management, and utility privatization, and NEPA Consulting. **Positions advertised include:** Senior Project Manager; Wetlands Specialist; Architectural Historian. **Corporate headquarters location:** This location. **Other area locations:** El Paso TX; San Antonio TX. **Other U.S. locations:** CA; FL; NV; OK; TX; VA.

GEOTECH INSTRUMENTS, LLC
10755 Sanden Drive, Dallas TX 75238. 214/221-0000. **Contact:** Human Resources. **World Wide Web address:** http://www.geoinstr.com. **Description:** Manufactures earthquake-monitoring equipment. **Positions advertised include:** Seismologist.

GIDDINGS STATE SCHOOL
P.O. Box 600, Giddings TX 78942. 979/542-3686x214. **Fax:** 979/542-0177. **Contact:** Human Resources. **World Wide Web address:** http://www.tyc.state.tx.us. **Description:** A government-run school and home for juvenile offenders. **NOTE:** Jobseekers must obtain an application from the state employment agency and submit it along with a resume. **Parent company:** Texas Youth Commission.

GILLMAN COMPANIES
10595 West Sam Houston Parkway South, Houston TX 77099. 713/776-7005. **Toll-free phone:** 800/933-7809. **Fax:** 713/776-4849. **Contact:** Human Resources. **World Wide Web address:** http://www.gillmanauto.com. **Description:** An automobile dealership group. Gillman operates dealerships selling Acura, Honda, Hyundai, Lincoln, Mazda, Mercury, Mitsubishi, Nissan, Subaru, and Suzuki automobiles. Founded in 1938. **NOTE:** See corporate website for list of Human Resources contact by dealer.

THE GLADNEY CENTER
6300 John Ryan Drive, Fort Worth TX 76132-4122. 817/922/6088. **Toll-free number:** 800/452-3639. **Contact:** Human Resources. **World Wide Web address:** http://www.gladney.org. **Description:** A nonprofit adoption agency providing services to young women who seek adoptive parents for their infants; individuals seeking to build their families through adoptions; and adoptees. Founded in 1887.

GLOBAL INDUSTRIES, LTD.
11490 Westheimer, Suite 400, Houston TX 77077. 281/529-7979. **Fax:** 281/529-7980. **Contact:** Human Resources. **World Wide Web address:** http://www.globalind.com. **Description:** Provides construction and diving services to the offshore oil and gas industry. **Corporate headquarters location:** Lafayette LA. **Subsidiaries include:** Global Pipeline PLUS's fleet of seven multipurpose barges is one of the largest in the Gulf. The barges have various combinations of pipelay, pipebury, and derrick capabilities, which offer a range of services including deepwater installation, pipelay by the reel method, and pipeline maintenance and repair. Global Movable Offshore's three derrick barges provide offshore lifting services, including installation and removal of platforms and associated components, drilling and workover rigs, and other equipment. Global Divers' fleet of four dive support vessels (DSV) provides diving services for virtually every phase of offshore oil and gas development and production. Global Divers has one of the largest DSVs with a dedicated saturation system in the Gulf and is a leader in deepwater diving, underwater welding technology, subsea completions, and nuclear power plant diving services. A full service trucking company, Pelican transports general commodities as well as oil field equipment, pipe, and supplies. The Red Adair Company is a worldwide leader in wild well control. In addition to fire fighting, the company offers contingency planning and training, engineering, well plug and abandonment, and rig inspection services. **Listed on:** NASDAQ. **Stock exchange symbol:** GLBL.

GLOBAL SANTA FE CORPORATION
P.O. Box 4577, Houston TX 77210-4577. **Physical address:** 15375 Memorial Drive, Houston TX 77079-4101. 281/925-6000. **Toll-free phone:** 800/231-5754. **Fax:** 281/925-6010. **Contact:** Human Resources. **World Wide Web address:** http://www.gsfdrill.com. **Description:** An oil and gas offshore drilling contractor. **Listed on:** New York Stock Exchange. **Stock exchange symbol:** GSF.

GLOBAL SHOP SOLUTIONS
975 Evergreen Circle, The Woodlands TX 77380-3637. 281/681-1959. **Fax:** 281/681-2663. **Contact:** Dick Alexander, President. **World Wide Web address:** http://www.globalshopsolutions.com. **Description:** Designs and sells manufacturing software systems. Founded in 1976.

GOLDEN CORRAL
4610 Garth Road, Baytown TX 77522. 281/422-3455. **Contact:** Human Resources. **World Wide Web address:** http://www.goldencorralrest.com. **Description:** One location of a chain of family steakhouses. **Corporate headquarters location:** Raleigh NC. **Other U.S. locations:** Nationwide.

GOLFSMITH INTERNATIONAL INC.
11000 North Interstate Highway 35, Austin TX 78753. 512/837-8810. **Fax:** 512/821-4191. **Contact:** Human Resources. **E-mail address:** hr@golfsmith.com. **World Wide Web address:** http://www.golfsmith.com. **Description:** Designs, assembles, and distributes golf equipment. **Positions advertised include:** Floor Supervisor; Sales Associate; Retail Advertising Coordinator; Accounts Receivable Clerk. **Operations at this facility include:** Administration; Manufacturing; Sales; Service.

GOODRICH AEROSPACE AEROSTRUCTURES GROUP
2005 Technology Way, San Marcos TX 78666. 512/754-3600. **Contact:** Human Resources. **World Wide Web address:** http://www.goodrich.com. **Description:** Designs, integrates, manufactures, sells, and supports aircraft engine nacelle systems and components for large commercial and military aircraft. **Positions advertised include:** Quality Inspector; Tooler; Manufacturing Engineer; Administrative Assistant; Aerospace Assembler. **Corporate headquarters location:** Charlotte NC. **Parent company:** Goodrich Company provides aircraft systems, components, and services and manufactures a wide range of specialty chemicals. The business units comprising the aerospace division of Goodrich consist of landing systems; sensors and integrated systems; safety systems; and maintenance, repair, and overhaul. Specialty chemical business units include specialty plastics; specialty additives; sealants, coatings, and adhesives; and water systems and services. **Listed on:** New York Stock Exchange. **Stock Exchange Symbol:** GR. **Number of employees nationwide:** 23,000.

GOODRICH PETROLEUM COMPANY
808 Travis, Suite 1320, Houston TX 77002. 713/780-9494. **Fax:** 713/780-9254. **Contact:** Human Resources. **World Wide Web address:** http://www.goodrichpetroleum.com. **Description:** A petroleum and natural gas exploration and production company. **NOTE:** Human Resources department is located in the Shreveport LA office, 318/429-1375. **Listed on:** New York Stock Exchange. **Stock exchange symbol:** GDP.

GOODWILL INDUSTRIES
460 Wall, Beaumont TX 77701. 409/838-9911. **Fax:** 409/832-1822. **Contact:** Human Resources. **World Wide Web address:** http://www.goodwillbmt.org. **Description:** A nonprofit provider of employment training for the disabled and the poor, operating 1,800 thrift stores nationwide. **Other U.S. locations:** Nationwide. **Parent company:** Goodwill Industries International, Inc.

GOODWILL INDUSTRIES
3020 N. Westmoreland Road, Dallas TX 75212. 214/638-2800. **Contact:** Human Resources. **World Wide Web address:** http://www.goodwilldallas.org. **Description:** A nonprofit provider of employment training for the disabled and the poor, operating 1,800 thrift stores nationwide. **Other U.S. locations:** Nationwide. **Parent company:** Goodwill Industries International, Inc.

GOODYEAR CHEMICAL
P.O. Box 26003, Beaumont TX 77720-6003. 409/794-5230. **Contact:** Employment. **World Wide Web address:** http://www.goodyearchemical.com. **Description:** Goodyear Tire & Rubber Company manufactures and sells thousands of products including metal, rubber, and plastic products for the transportation industry, and various industrial and consumer markets; synthetic rubber; and numerous high-technology products for aerospace, defense, and nuclear energy applications. The company's principal business is the development, manufacture, distribution, and sale of tires of every type. **NOTE:** Job listings provided on the corporate website at http://www.goodyear.com/careers. **Corporate headquarters location:** Akron OH. **Operations at this facility include:** This location manufactures synthetic rubber and hydrocarbon resins. **Parent company:** Goodyear Tire & Rubber Company. **Listed on:** New York Stock Exchange. **Stock exchange symbol:** GT.

W.W. GRAINGER
430 Sun Belt Drive, Corpus Christi TX 78408. 361/289-9201. **Fax:** 361/289-7943. **Contact:** Human Resources. **World Wide Web address:** http://www.grainger.com. **Description:** W.W. Grainger is a national supplier of industrial equipment such as

motors, pumps, and safety maintenance equipment. The company distributes a variety of equipment and components to the industrial, commercial, contracting, and institutional markets. Products are sold through local branches and include equipment and components for motors, air tools, hydraulic products, refrigeration items, power and hand tools, office equipment, computer supplies, replacement parts, industrial products, safety items, cold weather clothing, and storage equipment. Founded in 1927. **Operations at this facility include:** This location sells industrial supplies. **Other area locations:** Statewide. **Other U.S. locations:** Nationwide.

THE GRAND 1894 OPERA HOUSE
2020 Post Office Street, Galveston TX 77550. 409/763-7173. **Toll-free phone:** 800/821-1894. **Fax:** 409/763-1068. **Contact:** Maureen Patton, Executive Director. **World Wide Web address:** http://www.thegrand.com. **Description:** A 1040-seat opera house offering ballet, symphony, opera, and other musical and theatrical performances.

GRANT GEOPHYSICAL, INC.
P.O. Box 219950, Houston TX 77218-9950. 281/398-9503. **Physical address:** 16850 Park Row, Houston TX, 77218-9950. **Fax:** 281/647-9464. **Contact:** Human Resources. **E-mail address:** hr@grantgeo.com. **World Wide Web address:** http://www.grantgeo.com. **Description:** Plans and conducts 3-D and 2-D land and transition zone seismic data acquisition surveys for oil companies worldwide. **Special programs:** Internships. **Corporate headquarters location:** This location. **Other U.S. locations:** LA; OK. **International locations:** Indonesia; South America. **Operations at this facility include:** Administration; Research and Development; Sales.

GRANT THORNTON LLP
Bank One Center, Suite 500, 1717 Main Street, Dallas TX 75201. 214/561-2300. **Fax:** 214/561-2370. **Contact:** Personnel. **World Wide Web address:** http://www.grantthornton.com. **Description:** An international certified public accounting organization offering consulting and accounting services as well as strategic and tactical planning assistance to a diverse clientele. **NOTE:** Entry-level positions are offered. **Special programs:** Internships; Training. **Corporate headquarters location:** Chicago IL. **Other U.S. locations:** Nationwide. **Operations at this facility include:** Administration; Regional Headquarters; Sales; Service. **Listed on:** Privately held. **Annual sales/revenues:** More than $485 million. **Number of employees nationwide:** 2,900. **Number of employees worldwide:** 21,500.

GREAT WESTERN DIRECTORIES
2400 Lakeview Drive, Suite 109, Amarillo TX 79109. 806/353-5155. **Contact:** Human Resources. **World Wide Web address:** http://www.worldpages.com. **Description:** A publisher of telephone directories. **NOTE:** Job listings for all locations available on the company's website. **Parent company:** Transwestern Publishing Company. **Corporate headquarters location:** San Diego CA.

GREATER TUNA CORPORATION
3660 Stone Ridge Road, Suite C101, Austin TX 78746. 512/328-8862. **Fax:** 512/347-8975. **Contact:** Human Resources. **World Wide Web address:** http://www.greatertuna.com. **Description:** Produces a variety of comedic theater performances including *Greater Tuna,* a political satire shown in theaters nationwide. Other shows have included *A Tuna Christmas* and *Red, White and Tuna.*

GREENSHEET
2601 Main Street, Houston TX 77251. 713/655-3100. **Fax:** 713/371-3541. **Recorded jobline:** 713/371-3542. **Contact:** Recruiter. **World Wide Web address:** http://www.thegreensheet.com. **Description:** *Greensheet* is a free tabloid for business and personal advertising. The company publishes 16 weekly editions, with a readership of over 1 million. **Office hours:** Monday – Friday, 9:00 a.m. – 3:00 p.m.

GREYHOUND LINES INC.
P.O. Box 660606, Dallas TX 75266-0606. 972/789-7000. **Contact:** Human Resources. **World Wide Web address:** http://www.greyhound.com. **Description:** One of the country's largest private transportation networks. Greyhound conducts regular route, package express, charter, and food service operations. The fleet consists of over 1,650 buses that travel to more than 2,600 destinations.

GREYWOLF DRILLING
10370 Richmond Avenue, Suite 600, Houston TX 77042-4136. 713/435-6100. **Fax:** 713/435-6170. **Contact:** Human Resources Manager. **E-mail address:** jobs@gwdrilling.com. **World Wide Web address:** http://www.gwdrilling.com. **Description:** Engaged in gas and oil drilling. The company's primary drilling sites are located throughout southern Texas. **Listed on:** American Stock Exchange. **Stock exchange symbol:** GW.

GRISSOM, RICHARDS, AND FEATHERSTON
2211 Norfolk Street, Houston TX 77098. 713/526-4773. **Contact:** Human Resources. **Description:** A law firm specializing in personal injury and worker's compensation.

GROCERS SUPPLY COMPANY, INC.
3131 East Holcombe Boulevard, Houston TX 77021. 713/747-5000. **Contact:** Human Resources. **World Wide Web address:** http://www.grocerybiz.com. **Description:** A wholesaler of a variety of goods including hardware and groceries. **NOTE:** Job listings and application available at the company's website. **Corporate headquarters location:** This location. **Operations at this facility include:** Administration; Manufacturing; Sales; Service. **Listed on:** Privately held.

GROTH CORPORATION
1202 Halo Street, Houston TX 77020. 713/675-6151. **Toll-free phone:** 800/354-7684. **Fax:** 281/295-6999. **Contact:** Human Resources Manager. **E-mail address:** hr@grothcorp.com. **World Wide Web address:** http://www.grothcorp.com. **Description:** Engaged in the manufacture, sale, and service of valves and related instrumentation products. The company's customer base includes petrochemical and paper/pulp plants, and municipalities. **Corporate headquarters location:** This location. **Operations at this facility include:** Manufacturing; Sales; Service.

GRUBB & ELLIS
1000 Signature Place II, 14785 Preston Road, Suite 1000, Dallas TX 75240. 972/450-3300. **Contact:** Human Resources. **World Wide Web address:** http://www.grubbellis.com. **Description:** A real estate services firm dealing primarily with commercial properties including shopping centers, office buildings, and similar complexes. Founded in 1958. **Corporate headquarters location:** Northbrook IL.

GRUBB & ELLIS
1330 Post Oak Boulevard, Suite 1400, Houston TX 77056-3017. 713/626-8888. Fax: 713/626-2288. **Contact:** Human Resources. **World Wide Web address:** http://www.grubbellis.com. **Description:** A real estate services firm dealing primarily with commercial properties including shopping centers, office buildings, and similar complexes. Founded in 1958. **Corporate headquarters location:** Northbrook IL.

GUARDIAN INDUSTRIES CORPORATION
3801 South Highway 287, Corsicana TX 75109. 903/872-4871. **Fax:** 903/874-8647. **Contact:** Human Resources. **World Wide Web address:** http://www.guardian.com. **Description:** Manufactures fabricated and float glass primarily for the construction and automotive industries. **Corporate headquarters location:** Auburn Hills MI. **Other U.S. locations:** Nationwide. **International locations:** Worldwide.

C.H. GUENTHER & SON, INC.
128 E. Guenther Street, San Antonio TX 78291. 210/227-1401. **Fax:** 210/227-1409. **Contact:** Human Resources. **World Wide Web address:** http://www.chguenther.com. **Description:** A mill that produces baked goods, mixes and tortillas. It has also food services and frozen baked good divisions. **Corporate headquarters location:** This location.

GULF MARINE FABRICATORS
P.O. Box 3000, Aransas Pass TX 78335. 361/776-7551. **Fax:** 361/776-8102. **Contact:** Human Resources. **World Wide Web address:** http://technip.com. **Description:** Manufactures offshore rigs. **Corporate headquarters location:** Paris. **Other area locations:** Houston TX. **Other U.S. locations:** AL; LA; CA; NJ; FL. **International locations:** Worldwide. **Parent company:** Technip. **Listed on:** New York Stock Exchange. **Stock exchange symbol:** TKP.

GULF PUBLISHING COMPANY
2 Greenway Plaza, Suite 1020, Houston TX 77046. 713/529-4301. **Fax:** 713/520-4433. **Contact:** Human Resources. **World Wide Web address:** http://www.gulfpub.com. **Description:** A publishing company that covers news and events in the crude oil pipeline transportation, refined petroleum, natural gas, and gas distribution markets.

GULF STATES ASPHALT COMPANY
P.O. Box 508, South Houston TX 77587-0508. 713/941-4410. **Physical address:** 300 Christy Place, South Houston TX 77587-0508. **Contact:** Human Resources. **World Wide Web address:** http://www.gsac.net. **Description:** An asphalt manufacturing plant.

GULFMARK OFFSHORE
5 Post Oak Park, Suite 1170, 4400 Post Oak Parkway Building, Houston TX 77027. 713/963-9522. **Contact:** Human Resources. **World Wide Web address:** http://www.gulfmark.com. **Description:** Provides offshore marine transportation and erosion control services. **International locations:** Worldwide. **Listed on:** NASDAQ. **Stock exchange symbol:** GMRK.

GULFSTREAM AEROSPACE CORPORATION
P.O. Box 7145, Dallas TX 75209. **Physical address:** 7440 Aviation Place, Dallas TX 75235. 214/902-7500. **Fax:** 214/902-4964. **Contact:** Human Resources. **World Wide Web address:** http://www.gulfstream.com. **Description:** Refurbishes and performs completion work on corporate aircraft. **Special programs:** Co-ops. **Parent company:** General Dynamics.

H&R BLOCK
Village At Bachman Lake, 3701 West Northwest Highway, #169C, Dallas TX 75220. 214/358-4560. **Contact:** Human Resources. **World Wide Web address:** http://www.hrblock.com. **Description:** Primarily engaged in consumer tax preparation, operating more than 9,500 U.S. offices and preparing more than 10 million tax returns each year. H&R Block has established offices in over 750 Sears stores in both the United States and Canada. The company is also engaged in a number of other tax-related activities including group tax programs, executive tax service, tax training schools, and real estate tax awareness seminars. **Corporate headquarters location:** Kansas City MO. **Other U.S. locations:** Nationwide. **Listed on:** New York Stock Exchange. **Stock exchange symbol:** HRB. **Number of employees nationwide:** 80,000.

HCA - THE HEALTHCARE COMPANY
7400 Fannin, Suite 650, Houston TX 77054. 713/852-1500. **Contact:** Human Resources. **World Wide Web address:** http://www.hcahouston.com. **Description:** HCA owns several hundred surgical centers and hospitals. Founded in 1992. **NOTE:** This location recruits for 10 hospitals in the Houston area. See company's website for more information. **Other U.S. locations:** Nationwide. **Operations at this facility include:** This location is a regional administrative office.

HCA LONESTAR
10030 North MacArthur Boulevard, Suite 100, Irving TX 75039. 469/420-4928. **Contact:** Human Resources. **World Wide Web address:** http://www.lonestarhealth.com. **Description:** HCA owns more than 200 surgical centers and hospitals. Local HCA medical facilities are located throughout northern Texas. **NOTE:** Applicants can also contact the All About Staffing Group at 972/556-6470. List of affiliated hospitals, job listings and volunteer opportunities available on company's website. **Corporate headquarters location:** Nashville TN. **Other area locations:** Statewide. **Other U.S. locations:** Nationwide. **Operations at this facility include:** This location is a regional administrative office for northern Texas. **Number of employees at this location:** 5,000.

HDR, INC.
17111 Preston Road, Suite 300, Dallas TX 75248. 972/960-4000. **Fax:** 972/960-4185. **Contact:** Human Resources. **World Wide Web address:** http://www.hdrinc.com. **Description:** Offers architectural and engineering design services, in addition to construction consulting and interior design services. The company's three main business sectors are health care, justice, and science and industry. Founded in 1917. **Corporate headquarters location:** Omaha NE. **Other U.S. locations:** Alexandria VA. **Operations at this facility include:** Administration; Marketing; Regional Headquarters; Service. **Listed on:** Privately held.

HEB GROCERY COMPANY
P.O. Box 839999, San Antonio TX 78283. 210/938-8000. **Recorded jobline:** 210/938-5222. **Contact:** Human Resources. **E-mail address:** careers@heb.com. **World Wide Web address:** http://www.heb.com. **Description:** Operates a chain of retail grocery stores. Founded in 1905. **NOTE:** Interested jobseekers should contact the jobline before sending a resume. **Office hours:** Monday - Friday, 8:00 a.m. - 5:00 p.m. **Corporate headquarters location:** This location. **Listed on:** Privately held. **President:** Charles Butt.

HNTB CORPORATION
5910 West Plano Parkway, Suite 200, Plano TX 75093. 972/661-5626. **Fax:** 972/661-5614. **Contact:** Human Resources. **World Wide Web address:** http://www.hntb.com. **Description:** Offers architectural, engineering, and planning services to public agencies

and private industry. **NOTE:** Applicants should apply online at the company's website. **Positions advertised include:** Municipal Department Manager; Aviation Project Manager; Municipal Project Manager; Aviation Engineer; Public Involvement Manager. **Corporate headquarters location:** Kansas City MO. **Other area locations:** Austin TX; San Antonio TX. **Other U.S. locations:** Nationwide. **Subsidiaries include:** HNTB Design/Build, Inc.; HNTB International Corporation; HNTB Architecture, Inc. **Operations at this facility include:** Sales. **Listed on:** Privately held.

HP
20555 SH 249, Houston TX 77070. 281/370-0670. **Fax:** 281/514-1740. **Contact:** Human Resources. **World Wide Web address:** http://www.hp.com. **Description:** Designs, manufactures, sells, and services computers, peripheral equipment, and related software and supplies. Applications and programs include scientific research, computation, communications, education, data analysis, industrial control, time-sharing, commercial data processing, graphic arts, word processing, health care, instrumentation, engineering, and simulation. **NOTE:** Please visit website to search for jobs and apply online. **Positions advertised include:** Mechanical Engineer; Manager – Service Delivery; Manager – Service Business Management; Senior Operations Research Analyst; Product Manager; IT Application Designer; Manager – Industrial Design Engineer; Business Planning Analyst; Credit Analyst; Product Manager; Business Strategy Manager; Plan of Record Manager. **Special programs:** Internships. **Corporate headquarters location:** Palo Alto CA. **Other U.S. locations:** Nationwide. **International locations:** Worldwide. **Number of employees worldwide:** 140,000.

HVJ ASSOCIATES
6120 South Dairy Ashford Road, Houston TX 77072. 281/933-7388. **Contact:** Human Resources. **World Wide Web address:** http://www.hvj.com. **Description:** An engineering consulting firm specializing in geotechnology, construction materials; pavement; and facilities and environmental management. Founded in 1985. **Other area locations:** Austin TX; San Antonio TX.

HAGGAR CLOTHING COMPANY
Two Colinas Crossing, 15111 Luna Road, Dallas TX 75234. 214/352-8481. 214/956-4235. **Fax:** 214/956-4419. **Contact:** Human Resources. **E-mail address:** recruiter2@haggar.com. **World Wide Web address:** http://www.haggar.com. **Description:** A designer, manufacturer, importer, and marketer of men's dress and casual clothing. **NOTE:** Job listings available online at the company's website. When applying by email, send resume as ACSII text. **Corporate headquarters location:** This location. **Parent company:** Haggar Corporation. **Operations at this facility include:** Administration; Research and Development; Service. **Listed on:** NASDAQ. **Stock exchange symbol:** HGGR.

MAC HAIK CHEVROLET INC.
11711 Katy Freeway, Houston TX 77079. 281/497-6600. **Contact:** Human Resources. **World Wide Web address:** http://www.machaikchevy.com. **Description:** An automobile dealership.

HALFF ASSOCIATES
8616 Northwest Plaza Drive, Dallas TX 75225. 214/346-6251. **Fax:** 214/217-6451. **Contact:** Susie Nevitt. **E-mail address:** careers@halff.com. **World Wide Web address:** http://www.halff.com. **Description:** Provides architecture and engineering consulting services. **Positions advertised include:** Utility Locators; Structural CADD Technician; Environmental Scientist; Landscape Architect; Land Surveyors; Mechanical/Electrical Engineers. **Other area locations:** Forth Worth TX; Houston TX; McAllen TX; Austin TX; Frisco TX; San Antonio TX.

HALLIBURTON COMPANY
3600 Lincoln Plaza, 500 N. Akard, Dallas TX 75201. 214/978-2600. **Fax:** 214/978-2611. **Contact:** Human Resources. **World Wide Web address:** http://www.halliburton.com. **Description:** A leading diversified energy services, engineering, construction, maintenance, and energy equipment company. **NOTE:** Job listings and application process information is available at the company's website. **Operations at this facility include:** Administration; Training. **Special programs:** Internships; Apprenticeships; Graduate. **Corporate headquarters location:** This location. **Other U.S. locations:** Nationwide. **Listed on:** New York Stock Exchange. **Stock exchange symbol:** HAL.

HAMILTON AND ASSOCIATES
4415 Spring Cypress Road, Spring TX 77388. 281/353-6691. **Fax:** 281/288-8570. **Contact:** Bill Hamilton, Owner. **World Wide Web address:** http://www.tola.com. **Description:** A re-seller of high-technology products in the areas of OEM, Connectivity, data communications and retail. In addition to sales, the company markets the products and provides technical support. **Positions advertised:** Sales. **Other U.S. locations:** OK; LA; AK.

HANSON PIPE & PRODUCTS, INC.
3500 Maple Avenue, Suite 1500, Dallas TX, 75219. 214/525-5500. **Fax:** 214/525-5817. **Contact:** Human Resources. **World Wide Web address:** http://www.hansonconcreteproducts.com. **Description:** Produces concrete pressure pipe and pipefittings. **Other U.S. locations:** Nationwide. **International locations:** Canada.

HARBISON-FISCHER MANUFACTURING COMPANY
P.O. Box 2477, Fort Worth TX 76113-2477. 817/297-2211. **Physical address:** 901 North Crowley Road, Crowley TX 76036-3798. **Fax:** 817/297-4248. **Contact:** Leon Gregory, Human Resources Director. **World Wide Web address:** http://www.hfpumps.com. **Description:** Manufactures subsurface oil well pumping equipment. **Corporate headquarters location:** This location. **Other U.S. locations:** Worldwide. **Operations at this facility include:** Administration; Manufacturing; Research and Development; Sales; Service.

HARBOR VIEW CARE CENTER
1314 Third Street, Corpus Christi TX 78404. 361/888-5511. **Contact:** Jill Doire, Divisional Recruiter. **World Wide Web address:** http://www.tricare.com. **Description:** A 116-bed hospital. Founded in 1993. **Parent company:** Trans Healthcare.

HARDIN-SIMMONS UNIVERSITY
HSU Box 16030, Abilene TX 79698. 915/670-1507. **Physical address:** 2200 South Hickory Street, Abilene TX 79601. **Fax:** 915/670-5874. **Contact:** Earl T. Garrett, Human Resources. **World Wide Web address:** http://www.hsutx.edu. **Description:** A Southern Baptist university offering both graduate and undergraduate degrees. This university also offers a nursing program. **NOTE:** Job listings for faculty and staff are listed on the company's website. Applicants interested in faculty positions should send resumes to the contact names provided in the listings. **Positions advertised include:** Faculty Positions; University Communications Director; Financial Aid Director. Recruiting Director; Campus Recreation Director; Visitor Coordinator. **Corporate headquarters location:** This location. **Operations at this facility include:** Administration. **Number of employees at this location:** 300.

HARMONY FAMILY SERVICES
1111 Industrial Boulevard, Abilene TX 79602. 915/691-2800. **Contact:** Human Resources. **Description:** A social services agency that offers many programs including a residential treatment center for runaway and homeless youths.

HARRINGTON CANCER CENTER
1500 Wallace Boulevard, Amarillo TX 79106. 806/359-4673. **Toll-free phone:** 800/274-HOPE. **Fax:** 806/354-5881. **Contact:** Lynda McCarty, Human Resources Manager. **World Wide Web address:** http://www.harringtoncc.org. **Description:** Provides various services to cancer patients who formerly had to travel hundreds of miles for treatment. Medical specialties include radiation services, medical oncology, blood diseases and hematology, supportive care, a women's center, and cancer prevention and education. Volunteer opportunities are available. **NOTE:** All interested jobseekers must fill out a job application to be considered for employment. Applications can be picked up in the Human Resources Department or obtained online.

HARRIS CORPORATION
5727 Farinon Drive, San Antonio TX 78249. 210/561-7300. **Fax:** 210/561-7499. **Contact:** Human Resources. **World Wide Web address:** http://www.harris.com. **Description:** Harris Corporation is a communications equipment company that provides broadcast, network, government, and wireless support products and systems. Founded in 1895. **Corporate headquarters location:** Melbourne FL. **Operations at this facility include:** This location develops and manufactures wireless microwave radios. **Listed on:** New York Stock Exchange. **Stock exchange symbol:** HRS. **Number of employees nationwide:** 10,000.

HARRIS METHODIST FORT WORTH HOSPITAL
1301 Pennsylvania Avenue, Fort Worth TX 76104. 817/882-2882. **Fax:** 817/882-2865. **Contact:** Human Resources. **World Wide Web address:** http://www.texashealth.org. **Description:** A member of the Texas Health Resources, a consortium of 13 hospitals. **NOTE:** Entry-level positions, part-time jobs, and second and third shifts are offered. Interested jobseekers can apply in person at the hospital or on the corporate website at http://www.texashealth.org. **Special programs:** Internships; Administrative Fellowship Program **Office hours:** Monday - Friday, 8:00 a.m. - 5:00 p.m. **Parent company:** Texas Health Resources.

HART & COOLEY
12504 Weaver Road, El Paso TX 79928. 915/852-9111. **Fax:** 915/852-1309. **Contact:** Human Resources. **World Wide Web address:** http://www.hartandcooley.com. **Description:** Manufactures registers and grills for heating and cooling systems. **Parent company:** Tomkins PLC.

HARCOURT ASSESSMENT, INC.
19500 Bulverde, San Antonio TX 78259. 800/872-1726. **Contact:** Human Resources. **World Wide Web address:** http://www.marketplace.psychcorp.com. **Description:** One of the oldest and largest commercial test publishers in the nation. The company provides tests (e.g. the Stanford Achievement Test Series, the Metropolitan Achievement Tests, and Wechsler Intelligence Scales for Children and Adults) and related services to schools and colleges, clinicians and professional organizations, businesses, and public entities. The company's services include test research and development, printing, marketing, distribution, administration, and scoring. **NOTE:** This company also seeks people test administrators and test writers. See website for contact information. **Positions advertised include:** Requirements Analyst; Production Coordinator-Planning; Senior Associate, Sampling; Psychometrician; Test Development Manager; Senior Programmer Analyst. **Corporate headquarters location:** This location.

HARTE-HANKS, INC.
P.O. Box 269, San Antonio TX. **Physical address:** 200 Concord Plaza Drive, San Antonio TX 78216. 210/829-9000. **Contact:** Human Resources. **World Wide Web address:** http://www.harte-hanks.com. **Description:** Provides direct marketing services for various companies and publishes a weekly shopping guide. **NOTE:** Interested jobseekers should apply online at the corporate website. **Corporate headquarters location:** This location. **Other U.S. locations:** Nationwide.

THE C.D. HARTNETT COMPANY
P.O. Box 1989, Weatherford TX 76086. 817/594-3813. **Physical address:** 302 North Main Street, Weatherford TX, 76086. **Contact:** Human Resources. **E-mail address:** resume@cd-hartnett.com. **World Wide Web address:** http://www.cd-hartnett.com. **Description:** Distributes groceries to convenience stores and food service companies. Products include produce, dairy items, frozen food, and candy. Founded in 1904.

HARVEY HOTEL/DFW AIRPORT
4545 West John Carpenter Freeway, Irving TX 75063. 972/929-4500**Contact:**Human Resources. **World Wide Web address:** http://www.harveyhotelscom. **Description:** A traditional hotel with 500-rooms. Features guest services and amenities such as typing, copying, fax, car rental information, travel agency information, and word processing services. **NOTE:** Entry-level positions and second and third shifts are offered. The Harvey Hotel has a sister all-suites hotel next door, Harvey All-Suites Hotel/DFW Airport. **Corporate headquarters location:** Addison TX. **Parent company:** Felcor.

HARVEY ALL-SUITES HOTEL/DFW AIRPORT
4550 West John Carpenter Freeway, Irving TX 75063. 972/929-4499. **Contact:** Human Resources. **World Wide Web address:** http://www.harveyhotelscom. **Description:** A hotel featuring 163 luxury suites. Harvey All-Suites offers typing, copying, fax, car rental information, travel agency information, and word processing services. **NOTE:** Jobseekers should go to the Harvey Hotel, its sister company, at 4545 West John Carpenter Freeway, to apply for position. Entry-level positions and second and third shifts are offered. **Corporate headquarters location:** Addison TX. **Parent company:** Felcor.

HATCO
601 Marion Drive, Garland TX 75042. 972/494-0511. **Contact:** Human Resources. **World Wide Web address:** http://www.resistolhat.com. **Description:** Manufactures a variety of men's weather-resistant hats and headgear, specializing in cowboy hats. **Corporate headquarters location:** This location. **Parent company:** Arena Brands.

HEALTHLINK, INC.
3800 Buffalo Speedway, Suite 550, Houston TX 77030. 713/790-0800. **Fax:** 713/852-2151. **Contact:** Human Resources. **World Wide Web address:** http://www.healthlink.com. **Description:** Offers management consulting services for the health care industry. Healthlink services are organized into three main program areas: re-engineering; strategic information systems and project planning; and implementation. IMG also designs computer-based patient records systems for

hospitals and medical centers. **Corporate headquarters location:** St. Louis MO. **Other U.S. locations:** AR; IL; IN; IA; KY.

HEALTHSOUTH
3340 Plaza 10 Boulevard, Beaumont TX 77707. 409/835-0835. **Fax:** 409/835-1401. **Contact:** Ellen Zimmerman, Human Resources Director. **World Wide Web address:** http://www.healthsouth.com. **Description:** A physical rehabilitation hospital that also offers outpatient and home care services. **NOTE:** Part-time jobs and second and third shifts are offered. **Other U.S. locations:** Nationwide. **International locations:** Worldwide. **Listed on:** New York Stock Exchange. **Stock exchange symbol:** HRC. **Number of employees worldwide:** 33,700.

HEALTHSOUTH
2124 Research Row, Dallas TX 75235. 214/904-6100. **Contact:** Human Resources. **World Wide Web address:** http://www.healthsouth.com. **Description:** A comprehensive medical rehabilitation hospital specializing in orthopedic surgery. HealthSouth also operates an outpatient facility. **Positions advertised include:** Physical Therapist; Radiology Technician; Site Coordinator. **Corporate headquarters location:** Birmingham AL. **Other U.S. locations:** Nationwide. **Listed on:** New York Stock Exchange. **Stock exchange symbol:** HRC. **Number of employees worldwide:** 33,700.

HELEN OF TROY LTD.
One Helen of Troy Plaza, El Paso TX 79912. 915/225-8000. **Fax:** 915/225-8010. **Contact:** Human Resources. **World Wide Web address:** http://www.hotus.com. **Description:** Helen of Troy markets hair care appliances through major retail outlets worldwide. The company manufactures products under brand names including Vidal Sassoon, Revlon, Sable, and Helen of Troy. The company also services the professional retail market with an extensive collection of professional hair care appliances for salon use. **Corporate headquarters location:** This location. **Operations at this facility include:** This division serves as one of the primary development arenas for all corporate product lines. **Listed on:** NASDAQ. **Stock exchange symbol:** HELE.

HELI-DYNE SYSTEMS, INC.
9000 Trinity Boulevard, Hurst TX 76053. 817/282-9804. **Contact:** Human Resources. **World Wide Web address:** http://www.helidyne.net. **Description:** A helicopter completion company with a specialty in special mission, air medical, executive transport, and multimission aircraft. The company is an affiliate of CJ Systems Aviation Group and Corporate Jets, Inc.

HENDERSON MEMORIAL HOSPITAL
300 Wilson Street, Henderson TX 75652. 903/657-7541. **Toll-free phone:** 800/329-7541. **Fax:** 903/655-3661. **Recorded jobline:** 903/655-3773. **Contact:** Human Resources. **World Wide Web address:** http://www.hmhnet.org. **Description:** A private, nonprofit, acute care hospital. **NOTE:** Applications are required for all positions and can be found on the company's website. Entry-level positions and second and third shifts are offered. **Positions advertised include:** Physical Therapist; Transcriptionist; Executive Director of HMH Foundation; Relief Cook/Food Service Worker. **Office hours:** Monday – Friday, 8:00 a.m. – 5:00 p.m. **Corporate headquarters location:** This location. **Operations at this facility include:** Administration; Service. **Listed on:** Privately held.

HENDRICK HEALTH SYSTEM
1242 North 19th Street, Abilene TX 79601-2316. 915/670-2000. **Fax:** 325/670-4417. **Recorded jobline:** 325/670-3300. **Contact:** Human Resources. **E-mail address:** hrdept@ehendrick.org. **World Wide Web address:** http://www.hendrickhealth.org. **Description:** Operates a 525-bed, general hospital. Founded in 1924. **Positions advertised include:** Admitting Representative; Attendant; Audiologist; Cafeteria Aide; Certified Surgical Technician; Clinical Coordinator/Educator; Construction Technician; Cook; Customer Service Representative; Environmental Services Technician; File Technician; Financial Analyst; General Supervisor; Home Health Aide; LVN; Medical Office Specialist; Medical Technologist; Nurse Aide; Nurse Practitioner; Physical Therapist; Registered Nurse; Security Officer; Specialty Technician; Storage/Retrieval Technician; Trayline Aide. **Parent company:** Baptist General Convention of Texas.

G.H. HENSLEY INDUSTRIES, INC.
2108 Joe Field Road, Dallas TX 75229. 972/241-2321. **Contact:** Tom McCormack, Human Resources Director. **World Wide Web address:** http://www.hensleyind.com. **Description:** Operates a steel foundry producing steel castings and construction equipment parts. **Corporate headquarters location:** This location. **Other area locations:** Mansfield TX. **Parent company:** Komatsu Ltd.

HERNANDEZ ENGINEERING
16055 Space Center Boulevard, Suite 725, Houston TX 77062. 281/280-5159. **Contact:** Human Resources. **World Wide Web address:** http://www.hernandezengineering.com. **Description:** Provides technical and engineering services for NASA, the Johnson Space Center, and various high-tech organizations. Founded in 1983. **Positions advertised include:** Data Resource Administrator; Engineer; Word Processing Operation Specialist; Editor. **Other U.S. locations:** OH; CO; CA; VA; FL; AL; MS; Washington DC.

HEWLETT-PACKARD COMPANY
3000 Waterview Parkway, Richardson TX 75080. 972/497-4000. **Contact:** Human Resources. **World Wide Web address:** http://www.hp.com. **Description:** Hewlett-Packard is engaged in the design and manufacture of measurement and computation products and systems used in business, industry, engineering, science, health care, and education. Principal products are integrated instrument and computer systems (including hardware and software), peripheral products, and electronic medical equipment and systems. This company also manufacturers computer hardware and related equipment for the consumer market. **NOTE:** Jobseekers are encouraged to apply via the Website: http://www.jobs.hp.com. **Positions advertised include:** Financial Specialist; Commodity Manager; Strategic Program Manager; Remote Application Engineer; Client Manager; Pre-sale Consultant. **Special programs:** Internships. **Corporate headquarters location:** Palo Alto CA. **Other U.S. locations:** Nationwide. **International locations:** Worldwide. **Operations at this facility include:** This location builds computer servers. **Listed on:** New York Stock Exchange. **Stock exchange symbol:** HPQ.

HI-LINE
2121 Valley View Lane, Dallas TX 75234. 972/247-6200. **Toll-free number:** 800/944-5463. **Fax:** 800/860-8254. **Contact:** Human Resources. **E-mail address:** careers@hi-line.com. **World Wide Web address:** http://www.hi-line.com. **Description:** A distributor of fasteners including nuts, bolts, screws, and rivets; terminals including solder splice connectors, mechanical lugs, and ferrules; cable lugs; battery terminals; insulating materials including shrink tubing, grommets, and specialty tape; wiring accessories; drill bits; and various other industrial products. Founded in 1959. **NOTE:** To be considered for a Territory Sales Manager position, complete an online application at the company's website. **Corporate headquarters location:** This location. **Operations at this facility include:** Administration; Sales. **Number of employees at this location:** 160.

HICKAM INDUSTRIES, INC.
11518 Old La Porte Road, La Porte TX 77571. 713/567-2700. **Toll-free phone:** 800/324-6540. **Contact:** Human Resources. **World Wide Web address:** http://www.hickam.com. **Description:** Provides turbine repair services.

HILITE INDUSTRIES, INC.
1671 South Broadway, Carrollton TX 75006. 972/242-2116. **Contact:** Human Resources. **World Wide Web address:** http://www.hilite-ind.com. **Description:** Designs, manufactures, and sells automotive components including brake proportioning valves, electromagnetic clutches and machined components, springs, stampings, and assemblies. **Corporate headquarters location:** Cleveland OH. **Other U.S. locations:** Auburn Hills MI.

HILL COUNTRY MEMORIAL HOSPITAL
P.O. Box 835, Fredericksburg TX 78624-0835. 830/997-4353. **Physical address:** 1020 South State Highway 16, Fredericksburg TX 78624. **Contact:** Human Resources. **World Wide Web address:** http://www.hillcountrymemorial.com. **E-mail address:** hr@hillcountrymemorial.com. **Description:** A 77-bed, acute care hospital. Hill County Memorial Hospital offers a skilled nursing unit, medical surgery, OB/GYN, urology, and orthopedics. The hospital also has a Wellness Center that offers preventative care. Founded in 1971. **NOTE:** Applications for positions can be found at the company's website. **Positions advertised include:** RN; LVN; Physical Therapist; Nurse Aide; Thrift Shop Helper; Computer Technician; Staffing Clerk; Staffing Clerk.

HINES PROPERTIES INC.
Williams Tower, 2800 Post Oak Boulevard, 48th Floor, Houston TX 77056. 713/966-2629. **Fax:** 713/621-8000. **Contact:** Human Resources. **E-mail address:** Hines_HR@hines.com. **World Wide Web address:** http://www.hines.com. **Description:** Engaged in commercial real estate development and property management. The company has properties in 39 U.S. cities. **NOTE:** Resumes must be submitted online via the company's website or via e-mail. **Corporate headquarters location:** This location. **Other U.S. locations:** Nationwide. **International locations:** Worldwide. **Operations at this facility include:** Administration.

HISCO, INC.
6650 Concord Park Drive, Houston TX 77040. 713/934-1700. **Fax:** 713/934-1764. **Contact:** Priscilla Everett, Human Resources. **E-mail address:** hr@hisonic.com. **World Wide Web address:** http://www.hiscoinc.com. **Description:** A distributor for the electronics industry. Hisco's clients include IBM, Motorola, and Compaq. Founded in 1970. **NOTE:** See company's website for job listings. All resumes must be faxed. **Other area locations:** Austin TX; El Paso TX; San Antonio TX; Harlingen TX; Dallas TX. **Other U.S. locations:** Nationwide. **Listed on:** Privately held.

HOBART CORPORATION
8120 Jetstar Drive, Suite 100, Irving TX 75063. 972/915-3822. **Toll-free phone:** 800/356-3942. **Contact:** Human Resources. **World Wide Web address:** http://www.hobartcorp.com. **Description:** Manufactures food equipment for restaurants and supermarkets. Products include slicers, mixers, scales, fryers, food cutters, and toasters. **Corporate headquarters location:** Troy OH. **Parent company:** Food Equipment Group. **Operations at this facility include:** Sales; Service.

BERNARD HODES ADVERTISING
7502 Greenville Avenue, Suite 630, Dallas TX 75231. 214/361-9986. **Contact:** Jill Hawkins, Branch Manager. **World Wide Web address:** http://www.hodes.com. **Description:** An advertising agency specializing in recruitment and employee communications. **Corporate headquarters location:** New York NY. **Other U.S. locations:** Nationwide.

HOFFBRAU STEAKS
5075 Garth Road, Baytown TX 77520. 281/421-1998. **Contact:** Human Resources. **World Wide Web address:** http://www.hoffbrausteaks.com. **Description:** A casual-dining steak house and beer garden. Hoffbrau Steaks operates through 26 locations. Founded in 1939. **Corporate headquarters location:** Austin TX.

HOFFBRAU STEAKS
2310 North 11th Street, Beaumont TX 77703. 409/892-6911. **Contact:** Human Resources. **World Wide Web address:** http://www.hoffbrausteaks.com. **Description:** A casual-dining steak house and beer garden. Hoffbrau Steaks operates through 26 locations. Founded in 1939. **Corporate headquarters location:** Austin TX.

HOLIDAY INN BEAUMONT PLAZA
3950 Interstate 10 South, Beaumont TX 77705. 409/842-5995. **Fax:** 409/842-0315. **Contact:** Human Resources Department. **World Wide Web address:** http://www.ichotelsgroup.com. **Description:** This is a franchise location of the national hotel chain. Holiday Inn Beaumont Plaza offers 235 guest rooms and has one of the largest hotel conference centers in Texas. **NOTE:** Holiday Inn has another location in Beaumont and throughout Texas. See its website for additional locations. **Other U.S. locations:** Nationwide. **Parent company:** Six Continents Hotels.

HOLIDAY INN EXPRESS
5222 Interstate 10 East, Baytown TX 77521. 281/421-7200. **Fax:** 281/421-7209. **Contact:** Human Resources Department. **World Wide Web address:** http://www.ichotelsgroup.com. **Description:** One location of the national hotel chain. **NOTE:** Holiday Inn has several locations throughout Texas. See its website for additional locations. **Other U.S. locations:** Nationwide. **Parent company:** Six Continents Hotels.

HOLLAND PHOTO IMAGING
1221 South Lamar Boulevard, Austin TX 78704. 512/442-4274. **Toll-free phone:** 800/477-4024. **Fax:** 512/442-5898. **Contact:** Human Resources. **World Wide Web address:** http://www.hollandphoto.com. **Description:** A film and digital photo processing company. This company offers scanning, restoration, shipping, duplicating and mounting services. Founded in 1982.

HOLLY CORPORATION
100 Crescent Court, Suite 1600, Dallas TX 75201-6927. 214/871-3555. **Contact:** Human Resources. **E-mail address:** hr@hollycorp.com. **World Wide Web address:** http://www.hollycorp.com. **Description:** A holding company that refines and markets petroleum products through its subsidiaries. The company also operates a jet fuel terminal in Idaho for the U.S. government. **NOTE:** This company does not accept unsolicited resumes and all resumes must be submitted with completed applications. An application can be found on the company's website. **Subsidiaries include:** Montana Refining Company (Great Falls MT); Navajo Refining Company (Artesia NM). **Listed**

on: New York Stock Exchange. **Stock exchange symbol:** HOC. **Number of employees nationwide:** 521.

HOLLY SUGAR CORPORATION
P.O. Drawer 1778, Hereford TX 79045. 806/364-2590. **Contact:** Human Resources Manager. **World Wide Web address:** http://www.dixiecrystals.com. **Description:** Grows, harvests, and processes sugar beets into granulated sugar. Sugar is packaged at this location year round. **NOTE:** See the corporate website for job listing information. **Parent company:** Imperial Holly Corporation (Sugar Land TX). **Subsidiaries include:** Dixie Crystals.

HOMETOWN BANK OF GALVESTON
1801 45th Street, Galveston TX, 77751. 409/763-1271. **Contact:** Human Resources. **World Wide Web address:** http://www.bankofgalveston.com. **Description:** A full-service bank. **NOTE:** This bank has two locations. The other branch is located at 4424 Seawall Boulevard, Galveston TX, 77551. 409/763-5252.

HONEYWELL
8440 Westglen Drive, Houston TX 77063. 713/780-6500. **Contact:** Human Resources. **World Wide Web address:** http://www.honeywell.com. **Description:** Engaged in the research, development, manufacture, and sale of advanced technology products and services for the satellite technology field. Overall, Honeywell is engaged in the research, development, manufacture, and sale of advanced technology products and services in the fields of aerospace, fibers, plastics, chemicals, electronics, automation, and controls. The company's major businesses are home and building automation and control, performance polymers and chemicals, industrial automation and control, space and aviation systems, and defense and marine systems. **NOTE:** See company website for additional Texas locations. Job listings for all locations are available on this company's website. Resumes must be submitted online. **Corporate headquarters location:** Morristown NJ. **Other U.S. locations:** Nationwide. **International locations:** Worldwide. **Operations at this facility include:** Sales. **Listed on:** New York Stock Exchange. **Stock exchange symbol:** HON. **Number of employees worldwide:** 100,000.

HOOVER'S, INC.
5800 Airport Boulevard, Austin TX 78752. 512/374-4500. **Fax:** 512/374-4501. **World Wide Web address:** http://www.hoovers.com. **Description:** A leading provider of business information for sales, marketing, business development, and other professionals who need intelligence on U.S. and global companies, industries, and people. This information is available through an online service, corporate intranets and distribution agreements with licensees, as well as via print and CD-ROM products. **NOTE:** Search and apply for positions online. **Positions advertised include:** Applications Manager; Direct Marketing Program Coordinator; Director of Retention Marketing; Editorial Operations Analyst; Industry Editor; Product Marketing Specialist - Large Accounts; Product Training Manager; Sales Manager; Sales Operations Analyst; Saleslogix Programmer; VP Acquisition Marketing; VP Managing Editor. **Parent company:** Dun & Bradstreet.

HORIZON MILLING LLC
1100 South Main Street, Galena Park TX 77547. 713/676-1100. **Contact:** Human Resources. **World Wide Web address:** http://www.horizonmilling.com. **Description:** This facility provides a full line of flours for baking, manufacturing, and private-label applications. **Parent company:** Cargill Flour Milling & Harvest States Milling. **Other U.S. locations:** Nationwide. **Listed on:** Privately held. **Number of employees worldwide:** 90,000.

HORMEL FOODS CORPORATION
700 Highlander Boulevard, Suite 200, Arlington TX 76015. 817/465-4772. **Contact:** Human Resources. **E-mail address:** careers@hormel.com. **World Wide Web address:** http://www.hormel.com. **Description:** One of the leading processors and marketers of branded, value-added meat and food products. Principal products of the company are branded, processed meat and food entrees, which are sold fresh, frozen, cured, smoked, cooked, and canned. These include sausages, hams, franks, bacon, canned luncheon meats, shelf-stable microwaveable entrees, stews, chili, hash, meat spreads, and frozen processed products. The majority of the company's products are sold under the Hormel brand name. Other trademarks of the company include Farm Fresh, Little Sizzlers, Quick Meal, Kid's Kitchen, Chi-Chi's, House of Tsang, Mary Kitchen, Dinty Moore, Light & Lean, Chicken by George, Black Label, and SPAM. **Positions advertised include:** Staff Accountant; Engineer; Computer Analyst; Production Manager. **Special programs:** Internships. **Corporate headquarters location:** Austin MN. **Other U.S. locations:** CA; GA; IA; KS; NE; OK; WI. **International locations:** Australia; England; Japan; Korea; Panama; Philippines. **Subsidiaries include:** Dan's Prize, Inc.; Dubuque Foods; Farm Fresh Catfish Company; Jennie-O Foods. **Listed on:** New York Stock Exchange. **Stock exchange symbol:** HRL. **Number of employees nationwide:** 14,700.

D.R. HORTON, INC.
1901 Ascension Boulevard, Suite 210, Arlington TX 76006. 817/856-8200. **Fax:** 817/856-8238. **Contact:** Human Resources. **World Wide Web address:** http://www.drhorton.com. **Description:** D.R. Horton, Inc. and its operating subsidiaries are engaged primarily in the construction and sale of single-family homes designed principally for the entry-level and move-up market segments. **NOTE:** Interested jobseekers should see the company's website for contact information. **Operations at this facility include:** Regional office. **Listed on:** New York Stock Exchange. **Stock exchange symbol:** DHI. **Number of employees nationwide:** 4,300.

HOTELS.COM
8140 Walnut Hill Lane, Dallas TX 75231. 214/361-7311. **Toll-free phone:** 800/964-6835. **Fax:** 214/361-7299. **Contact:** Human Resources. **E-mail address:** careers@hotels.com. **World Wide Web address:** http://www.hotels.com. **Description:** An Internet hotel booking service that offers travelers discounts. Hotels.com has partnerships with large, global hotel chains. **Positions advertised include:** Senior Financial Planning Analyst; Java Programmer Analyst. Senior Staff Accountant; Senior Java Programmer/Analyst; Group Sales Account Manager; Strategic Corporate Account Manager; Senior Director of Brand Marketing; HRIS Analyst. **NOTE:** Apply online. **Other U.S. locations:** FL; VA. **Parent company:** InterActiveCorp (New York NY). **Listed on:** NASDAQ. **Stock exchange symbol:** IACI.

THE HOUSE COMPANY
2615 Broadway, Galveston TX 77550. 409/763-8030. **Contact:** Human Resources. **World Wide Web address:** http://www.thehousecompany.com. **Description:** A real estate agency dealing with residential properties and specializing in relocation services.

HOUSTON AREA URBAN LEAGUE
1301 Texas Avenue, Houston TX 77002. 713/393-8700. **Contact:** James Lacy, Manager of Operations. **World Wide Web address:** http://www.haul.org. **Description:** A social service agency that also provides employment services.

THE HOUSTON BUSINESS JOURNAL
1001 West Loop South, Suite 650, Houston TX 77027. 713/688-8811. **Fax:** 713/963-0482. **Contact:** Human Resources. **World Wide Web address:** http://www.bizjournals.com/houston. **Description:** A daily business journal. **Corporate headquarters location:** This location. **Parent company:** American City Business Journal.

HOUSTON CHRONICLE
801 Texas Avenue, Houston TX 77002. 713/220-7171. **Contact:** Ann Turnbach, Personnel Director. **World Wide Web address:** http://www.houstonchronicle.com. **Description:** A daily newspaper. **Corporate headquarters location:** This location.

HOUSTON, CITY OF
611 Walker Street, Houston TX 77002. 713/837-9302. **Recorded jobline:** 713/837-9498 (general employment); 713/837-9499 (professional employment). **Contact:** Human Resources. **E-mail address:** hrresume@cityofhouston.net. **World Wide Web address:** http://www.cityofhouston.gov **Description:** As the government offices for the city of Houston, this location houses the mayor's office as well as city council offices. **NOTE:** Application are required for all positions, which can be found on the city's website or by going to the city's HR office on Walker Street. **Office hours:** Monday – Friday, 9:00 a.m.-- 4:30 p.m.

HOUSTON COCA-COLA BOTTLING COMPANY
2800 Bissonnett, Houston TX 77005. 713/664-3451. **Recorded jobline:** 713/669-3260. **Contact:** Human Resources. **World Wide Web address:** http://www.cokecce.com. **Description:** A regional subsidiary of Coca-Cola Enterprises Inc., one of the world's largest marketers, distributors, and producers of the bottled and canned products of The Coca-Cola Company. The company also serves as a significant bottler of several other national and regional beverage brands such as Barq's and Dr. Pepper. **NOTE:** This location accepts applications for bottling and distribution positions in the surrounding Texas communities. Call the recorded Jobline or see the company's website for additional information. Resumes are not accepted for any positions; only applications. **Office hours:** Monday – Thursday; 8:00 a.m. – 3:00 p.m.; Friday – 8:00 a.m. – 1:00 p.m. **Parent company:** Coca-Cola Enterprises Inc. is in the liquid nonalcoholic refreshment business, which extends the company's product line beyond traditional carbonated soft drink categories to beverages such as still and sparkling waters, juices, isotonics, and teas. The company operates in 38 states, the District of Columbia, the U.S. Virgin Islands, the Islands of Tortola and Grand Cayman, and the Netherlands. **Operations at this facility include:** Administration; Manufacturing; Sales. **Listed on:** New York Stock Exchange. **Stock exchange symbol:** CCE. **Number of employees worldwide:** 72,000.

HOUSTON INDEPENDENT SCHOOL DISTRICT
3310 Cummins Lane, Houston TX 77027-5810. 713/892-7338. **Toll-free phone:** 800/446-2821. **Contact:** Human Resources. **E-mail address:** jobs@houstonisd.org. **World Wide Web address:** http://www.houstonisd.org. **Description:** The administrative offices for Houston's schools. **NOTE:** The job listings for all the schools in the district are available on this website. Apply online. **Positions advertised include:** Instructional Coordinator; Early Childhood Specialist; Evaluation Specialist; Itinerant Teacher; Librarian; Counselor.

HOUSTON MUSEUM OF NATURAL SCIENCE
One Hermann Circle Drive, Houston TX 77030. 713/639-4600. **Contact:** Human Resources. **World Wide Web address:** http://www.hmns.org. **Description:** Offers numerous educational exhibits in many different areas of natural sciences.

HOUSTON SYMPHONY
615 Louisiana Street, Suite 102, Houston TX 77002. 713/224-4240. **Fax:** 713/222-7024. **Contact:** Human Resources. **E-mail address:** office@houstonsymphony.org. **World Wide Web address:** http://www.houstonsymphony.org. **Description:** A symphony orchestra.

HOUSTON WIPER & MILL SUPPLY COMPANY
P.O. Box 24962, 9800 Market Street, Houston TX 77229-4962. 713/672-0571. **Toll-free phone:** 800/633-5968. **Fax:** 713/673-7637. **Contact:** Human Resources. **World Wide Web address:** http://www.houstonwiper.com. **Description:** A secondary textile recycler. Founded in 1954. **Office hours:** Monday - Friday, 8:00 a.m. - 5:00 p.m. **Corporate headquarters location:** This location. **Operations at this facility include:** Manufacturing. **Listed on:** Privately held. **President:** Michael J. Brown.

HOUSTON WIRE AND CABLE COMPANY
10201 North Loop East, Houston TX, 77029. 713/609-2100. **Contact:** Human Resources. **World Wide Web address:** http://www.houwire.com. **Description:** Engaged in the distribution of specialty wire and cable. The company also offers cable management and asset management programs. **NOTE:** Job listings are available on this company's website. **Other U.S. locations:** Nationwide.

HOWE-BAKER ENGINEERS, INC.
P.O. Box 956, Tyler TX 75710. 903/597-0311. **Physical address:** 3102 East Fifth Street, Tyler TX 75701. **Contact:** Michael Osborn, Human Resources. **E-mail address:** mosborn@Cblepc.com. **World Wide Web address:** http://www.howebaker.com. **Description:** Provides mechanical, civil, and electrical engineering services. **Positions advertised include:** Process Engineer; Project Engineer; Mechanical Engineer; Civil Engineer; Electrical Engineer.

HOWELL INSTRUMENTS, INC.
P.O. Box 985001, Fort Worth TX 76185-5001. 817/336-7411x223. **Physical address:** 3479 West Vickery Boulevard, Fort Worth TX 76107. **Fax:** 817/336-7874. **Contact:** Nell Whaylen, Human Resources Manager. **E-mail address:** nmwhaylen@howellinst.com. **World Wide Web address:** http://www.howellinst.com. **Description:** Manufacturer of turbine engine instrumentation and test equipment for military, commercial, and private aviation applications. **NOTE:** Entry-level positions are offered. **Positions advertised include:** Field Engineer. **Corporate headquarters location:** This location.

HOWREY, SIMON, ARNOLD & WHITE
750 Bering Drive, Houston TX 77057. 713/787-1400. **Contact:** Human Resources. **World Wide Web address:** http://www.howrey.com. **Description:** A law firm specializing in antitrust matters. **NOTE:** Jobseekers interested in applying for open attorney positions should refer to the company's website for contact names. **Positions advertised include:** Legal; Consultant; Staff. **Other U.S. locations:** Nationwide. **International locations:** Worldwide.

HUGHES CHRISTENSEN COMPANY
P.O. Box 2539, Houston TX 77252. 281/363-6000. **Physical address:** 9110 Grogans Mill Road, The Woodlands TX 77380. **Fax:** 281/363-6025. **Contact:** Human Resources. **World Wide Web address:** http://www.bakerhughes.com. **Description:** A

manufacturer of rock bits and diamond bits for the oil and gas industries. **NOTE:** Interested jobseekers must apply online for open positions. **Positions advertised include:** Financial Analyst; Drafter; Process Specialist; Electrical Engineer; Legal Assistant; Inspector; Formulation Evaluation Analyst; Test Lab Mechanic. **Corporate headquarters location:** This location. **Parent company:** Baker Hughes, Inc. **Listed on:** New York Stock Exchange. **Stock exchange symbol:** BHI.

HUGULEY MEMORIAL MEDICAL CENTER
11801 South Freeway, P.O. Box 6337, South Fort Worth TX 76115-0337. 817/293-9110. **Fax:** 817/568-1296. **Contact:** Human Resources. **E-mail address:** huguleyresumes@ahss.org. **World Wide Web address:** http://www.huguley.org. **Description:** A 213-bed acute care facility. Huguley Memorial Medical Center also owns Willow Creek (Arlington TX), a mental health facility. **NOTE:** Send resumes to P.O. Box only. **Positions advertised include:** Nurse Practitioner; Educator; RN: LVN: Central Services Technician; Kids Klub Attendant; Swim Instructor; Respiratory Therapist; Exercise Physiologist. **Special programs:** Internships. **Operations at this facility include:** Administration; Service.

HUMBLE INDEPENDENT SCHOOL DISTRICT
P.O. Box 2000, Humble TX 77346. 281/641-5000. **Contact:** Human Resources. **World Wide Web address:** http://www.humble.k12.tx.us. **Description:** Offices for the Humble school district, which comprises fifteen elementary schools, six middle schools, and five high schools. **NOTE:** Applications are available online for all positions. **Positions advertised include:** Attendance Specialist; Library Aide; Special Education Aide.

HUITT-ZOLLARS
3131 Mckinney Avenue, Suite 600, Dallas TX 75204. 214/871-3311. **Fax:** 214/871-0757. **Contact:** Human Resources. **World Wide Web address:** http://www.huitt-zollars.com. **Description:** Provides consulting services in engineering, architecture, planning, landscape architecture, surveying, and construction management. **Positions advertised include:** Land Development Technician; Land Development EIT; Land Development PE.

HUNT CONSOLIDATED/HUNT OIL COMPANY
1445 Ross Avenue, Suite 1400, Dallas TX 75202. 214/978-8000. **Contact:** Human Resources. **E-mail address:** recruiter@huntoil.com. **World Wide Web address:** http://www.huntoil.com. **Description:** Refines and distributes petroleum and natural gas. **Corporate headquarters location:** This location. **Operations at this facility include:** Administration. **Listed on:** Privately held.

HUNT PETROLEUM
1601 Elm Street, Suite 4700 Dallas TX 75201. 214/880-8800. **Contact:** Human Resources. **E-mail address:** recruitment@huntpetroleum.com. **World Wide Web address:** http://www.huntpetroleum.com. **Description:** Conducts onshore and offshore exploration and development activities in the Gulf Coast and Rocky Mountain areas and supplies its parent company with natural gas via exploration, production, and acquisition activities. **Positions advertised include:** Engineering Technician; Production Engineer; Oil & Gas Lease Analyst; Receptionist. **Other area locations:** Houston TX. **Other U.S. locations:** Shreveport LA.

J.B. HUNT TRANSPORT SERVICES, INC.
5701 West Kiest Boulevard, Dallas TX 75236. 214/333-9768. **Contact:** Human Resources. **World Wide Web address:** http://www.jbhunt.com. **Description:** A major freight transportation company. **Corporate headquarters location:** Lowell AR. **Listed on:** NASDAQ. **Stock exchange symbol:** JBHT.

HUNTSMAN POLYMERS CORPORATION
3040 Post Oak Boulevard, Houston TX 778056. 915/640-7200. **Toll-free phone:** 800/333-7210. **Fax:** 915/640-8400. **Contact:** Human Resources. **World Wide Web address:** http://www.huntsman.com. **Description:** Manufactures plastic materials (including plastic films), thermoplastic resins, and other synthetic resins, polyethylene, and polypropylene. The company's products are used to make a wide variety of products ranging from dashboards to diapers and medical supplies. **Corporate headquarters location:** Salt Lake City UT. **Number of employees worldwide:** 15,000.

HUNTSVILLE MEMORIAL HOSPITAL
P.O. Box 4001, Huntsville TX 77342-4001. 936/291-4521. **Recorded jobline:** 936/291-4522. **Fax:** 936/291-4241. **Contact:** Dick Hoolahan, Human Resources Director. **E-mail address:** dickh@huntsvillememorial.com. **World Wide Web address:** http://www.huntsvillememorial.com. **Description:** A full-service hospital offering specialized outpatient facilities. **Positions advertised include:** Ultrasonographer; RN; Physician Assistant; Transcriptionist; Histotechnician. **Office hours:** Monday – Friday, 8:00 a.m. – 4:30 p.m.

HYATT REGENCY DALLAS AT REUNION
300 Reunion Boulevard, Dallas TX 75207. 214/651-1234. **Contact:** Human Resources. **World Wide Web address:** http://www.hyatt.com. **Description:** A luxury hotel offering an 18-story atrium that houses dining and entertainment facilities including a pool, a fully equipped fitness center, tennis and basketball courts, three restaurants, and a revolving rooftop lounge. **Positions advertised include:** Assistant Restaurant Manager; Cocktail Server; Front Office Agent; On-Call Bartender; On-call Banquet Server; Restaurant Server. **Corporate headquarters location:** Chicago IL. **Other U.S. locations:** Nationwide. **Parent company:** Hyatt Hotel Corporation.

HYATT REGENCY HILL COUNTRY RESORT AND SPA
9800 Hyatt Resort Drive, San Antonio TX 78251. 210/647-1234. **Contact:** Penny Nichols Bowden, Human Resources Director. **World Wide Web address:** http://www.hyatt.com. **Description:** Operates as a unit of the nationwide chain of hotels. Hyatt Regency Hill Country Resort has six locations throughout Texas. **Positions advertised include:** Banquet Server; Bartender; Bell Attendant; Cocktail Server; Food Runner; Deli Attendant; Massage Therapist; Nail Technician; Spa Attendant; Retail Clerk; Sales Manager; Room Service Server; Valet Attendant; Yoga Instructor. **Parent company:** Hyatt Hotels Corporation.

HYATT REGENCY HOUSTON
1200 Louisiana Street, Houston TX 77002. 713/654-1234. **Contact:** Human Resources. **World Wide Web address:** http://houstonregency.hyatt.com. **Description:** A 963-room hotel with meeting and banquet facilities. **Positions advertised include:** Cocktail Server; Culinary Lead; Food Server Assistant; Housekeeper. **Corporate headquarters location:** Chicago IL. **Other U.S. locations:** Nationwide. **International locations:** Worldwide. **Parent company:** Hyatt Hotels Corporation.

HYDRIL COMPANY
3300 North Sam Houston Parkway East, Houston TX 77032. 281/449-2000. **Fax:** 281/985-3480. **Contact:** Human Resources. **World Wide Web address:** http://www.hydril.com. **Description:** Manufactures oil field machinery and petroleum equipment. Founded in 1933. **Corporate headquarters location:** This location. **Listed on:** NASDAQ. **Stock exchange symbol:** HYDL. **Number of employees worldwide:** 1,500.

HYDROCHEM INDUSTRIAL SERVICES
P.O. Box 478, Baytown TX 77522-0478. 281/834-7767. **Fax:** 713/393-5953. **Contact:** Human Resources. **E-mail address:** jobs@hydrochem.com. **World Wide Web address:** http://www.hydrochem.com. **Description:** An industrial cleaning company that provides heavy-duty cleaning services such as high-pressure water blasting and vacuuming for industrial plants. **Positions advertised include:** Equipment Trainee. **Corporate headquarters location:** Canal Fulton OH.

I-SECTOR CORPORATION
6401 Southwest Freeway, Houston TX 77074. 713/795-2000. **Fax:** 713/795-2001. **Contact:** Human Resources. **E-mail address:** careers@I-sector.com. **World Wide Web address:** http://www.i-sector.com. **Description:** Owns and operates subsidiary companies that are engaged in various aspects of the information and technology industries. **Corporate headquarters location:** This location. **Listed on:** American Stock Exchange. **Stock exchange symbol:** ISR. **Number of employees nationwide:** 211.

IBM CORPORATION
1605 LBJ Freeway, Dallas TX 75234. 972/280-1000. **Toll-free phone:** 800/426-4968. **Contact:** IBM Staffing Services. **World Wide Web address:** http://www.ibm.com. **Description:** IBM is a developer, manufacturer, and marketer of advanced information processing products including computers and microelectronic technology, software, networking systems, and information technology-related services. **NOTE:** Jobseekers should apply online via the company's website. **Special programs:** Internships; Co-ops. **Corporate headquarters location:** Armonk NY. **International locations:** Worldwide. **Operations at this facility include:** This location is a regional development and training office. **Subsidiaries include:** IBM Global; IBM Financing; IBM Technology; IBM Personal Servers; IBM Research; IBM Servers; IBM Software. **Listed on:** New York Stock Exchange. **Stock exchange symbol:** IBM.

IBM CORPORATION
11400 Burnett Road, Austin TX 78758. 512/823-0000. **Toll-free phone:** 800/796-7876. **Contact:** Human Resources. **World Wide Web address:** http://www.ibm.com. **Description:** IBM Corporation is a developer, manufacturer, and marketer of advanced information processing products including computers and microelectronic technology, software, networking systems, and information technology-related services. **NOTE:** Jobseekers should apply online via the company's website. **Corporate headquarters location:** Armonk NY. **International locations:** Worldwide. **Operations at this facility include:** This location is a sales office. **Subsidiaries include:** IBM Global; IBM Financing; IBM Technology; IBM Personal Servers; IBM Research; IBM Servers; IBM Software. **Listed on:** New York Stock Exchange. **Stock exchange symbol:** IBM.

ICO POLYMERS, INC.
5333 Westheimer, Suite 600, Houston TX 77056. 713/351-4100. **Fax:** 713/335-2201. **Contact:** Human Resources. **World Wide Web address:** http://www.icopolymers.com. **Description:** A manufacturer of plastic and film products for the industrial market. **Corporate headquarters location:** This location. **Operations at this facility include:** Service. **Listed on:** NASDAQ. **Stock exchange symbol:** ICOC.

IQ PRODUCTS COMPANY
16212 State Highway 249, Houston TX 77269. 281/444-6454. **Fax:** 281/444-0185. **Contact:** Human Resources. **World Wide Web address:** http://www.iqproducts.com. **Description:** Manufactures and packages personal care products, insecticides, and automotive products. **Positions advertised include:** Sales Project Coordinator; Project Specialist; Industrial Engineer; Chemistry Product Coordinator; QA Coordinator.

I.T. PARTNERS, INC.
2735 Villa Creek Drive, Suite 175, Dallas TX 75234. 972/484-5300. **Fax:** 972/484-5605. **Contact:** Human Resources. **E-mail address:** employment@itpartners.com. **World Wide Web address:** http://www.itpartners.net. **Description:** Offers computer consulting services, software training, network implementation, and Web services (Web hosting and development).

I2 TECHNOLOGIES
One i2 Place, 11701 Luna Road, Dallas TX 75234. 469/357-1000. **Toll-free phone:** 800/800-3288. **Fax:** 214/860-6060. **Contact:** Human Resources. **World Wide Web address:** http://www.i2.com. **Description:** Develops and provides e-commerce, business-to-business, and open marketplace solutions. Founded in 1988. **Positions advertised include:** Director of Internal Audit; Information Systems Engineer; Senior Training Analyst. **Corporate headquarters location:** This location. **Other U.S. locations:** Nationwide. **International locations:** Worldwide. **Listed on:** NASDAQ. **Stock exchange symbol:** ITWO.

IGLOO PRODUCTS CORPORATION
1001 West Sam Houston Parkway North, Houston TX 77013. 713/465-2571. **Contact:** Human Resources. **World Wide Web address:** http://www.igloocoolers.com. **Description:** Manufactures beverage coolers, ice chests, and similar products. Igloo Products Corporation is a division of Coca-Cola Company.

IKON OFFICE SOLUTIONS
7401 East Ben White Boulevard, Building 2, Austin TX 78741-7418. 512/385-5100. **Contact:** Human Resources. **E-mail address:** resumes@ikon.com. **World Wide Web address:** http://www.ikon.com. **Description:** IKON Office Solutions is one of the largest independent copier distribution networks in North America. **Positions advertised include:** Recruiter/Trainer; Strategic Account Sales Analyst; Major Account Executive. **Operations at this facility include:** This location is a sales and service center.

IMMUDYNE, INC.
11200 Wilcrest Green Drive, Houston TX 77042. 713/783-7034. **Contact:** Human Resources. **World Wide Web address:** http://www.immudyne.com. **Description:** Develops, manufactures, and markets dietary supplements and skin care products. **Corporate headquarters location:** This location.

IMPERIAL SUGAR COMPANY
P.O. Box 9, Sugar Land TX 77487. 281/491-9181. **Contact:** Ron Sims, Personnel. **World Wide Web address:** http://www.imperialsugar.com. **Description:** A producer and seller of refined cane and beet sugar. Imperial Sugar Company operates four processing plants in California, two in Wyoming, two in Texas, and one in Montana. Other operations include the production and refinement of molasses, beet pulp, beet seed, and other by-products. **NOTE:** This company only accepts resumes for open

positions, which can be found on its website. **Subsidiaries include:** Holly Sugar and Dixie Crystals.

INDUSTRIAL MOLDING CORPORATION
616 East Slaton Road, Lubbock TX 79404. 806/474-1000. **Contact:** Keri Mathews, Human Resources Manager. **World Wide Web address:** http://www.indmolding.com. **Description:** Manufactures injection molded plastics. **Corporate headquarters location:** This location.

INDUSTRIAL PROFILE SYSTEMS
6703 Theall Road, Houston TX 77066. 281/893-0100. **Contact:** Human Resources. **World Wide Web address:** http://www.parker.com. **Description:** Manufactures aluminum work centers for industrial automation and machine building. **Positions advertised include**: Territory Sales Manager. **Other U.S. locations:** Nationwide. **International locations:** Worldwide. **Parent company:** Parker-Hannifin. **Listed on:** New York Stock Exchange. **Stock exchange symbol:** PH.

INGERSOLL-RAND COMPANY
P.O. Box 462288, Garland TX 75040. 972/495-8181. **Contact:** Human Resources. **World Wide Web address:** http://www.ingersoll-rand.com. **Description:** Manufactures compressors, pumps, and other non-electrical industrial equipment and machinery. Ingersoll-Rand Company's products include air compression systems, antifriction systems, construction equipment, air tools, bearings, locks, tools, and pumps. The company operates 93 production facilities throughout the world. **Corporate headquarters location:** Woodcliff Lake NJ. **Listed on:** New York Stock Exchange. **Stock exchange symbol:** IR.

INITIAL SECURITY
3355 Cherry Ridge, Suite 200, San Antonio TX 78230. 210/349-6321. **Toll-free phone:** 800/683-7771. **Fax:** 210/349-0213. **Contact:** Human Resources. **E-mail address:** initial@initialsecurity.com. **World Wide Web address:** http://www.initialsecurity.com. **Description:** Offers security guard services throughout the greater San Antonio area. **NOTE:** This company offers entry-level positions and training.

INPUT/OUTPUT, INC.
12300 Parc Crest Drive, Stafford TX 77477. 281/933-3339. **Contact:** Human Resources. **E-mail address:** careers@I-o-.com. **World Wide Web address:** http://www.i-o.com. **Description:** Designs, manufactures, and markets seismic data acquisition systems and related equipment. **Positions advertised include:** DSP Software Development Engineer; Product Marketing Director; Engineering Project Coordinator; Senior Embedded Software Engineer; Senior High Speed Computing Engineer; Senior Software Engineer; Senior Test Engineer. **Corporate headquarters location:** This location. **Other area locations:** Richardson TX. **Subsidiaries include:** Output Exploration Company conducts geophysical operations and acquires oil and gas leases. Founded in 1968. **Listed on:** New York Stock Exchange. **Stock exchange symbol:** IO.

INSITUFORM TECHNOLOGIES, INC.
16619 Aldine Westfield Road, Houston TX 77032. 281/821-7070. **Contact:** Human Resources. **E-mail address:** careers@insituform.com. **World Wide Web address:** http://www.insituform.com. **Description:** Insituform Technologies, Inc. uses various trenchless technologies for rehabilitation, new construction, and improvements of pipeline systems including sewers; gas lines; industrial waste lines; water lines; and oil field, mining, and industrial process pipelines. **NOTE:** Resumes can also be mailed to 702 Spirit 40 Park Drive, Chesterfield MO 63005, Attention: Human Resources. **Parent company:** Insituform Technologies, Inc. provides a wide variety of technologies including Insituform, PALTEM, Tite Liner, and tunneling. **Operations at this facility include:** This location conducts pipeline rehabilitation. **Listed on:** NASDAQ. **Stock exchange symbol:** INSU.

INSTITUTIONAL SALES ASSOCIATES
3827 Promontory Point Drive, Austin TX 78744. 512/447-1245. **Contact:** Sue McArdle, Human Resources. **E-mail address:** smcardle@isaonline.net. **World Web address:** http://www.isaonline.net. **Description:** Provides institutional food distribution services. **Note:** Resumes should be mailed to P.O. Box 8938, Houston Texas 77249. **Corporate headquarters location:** Houston.

INTEGRATED DEVICE TECHNOLOGY, INC.
15851 Dallas Parkway, Suite 335, Addison TX 75001-6064. 972/490-6167. **Contact:** Human Resources. **World Wide Web address:** http://www.idt.com. **Description:** Integrated Device Technology, Inc. designs, manufactures, and markets high-speed CMOS VLSI integrated circuits. The company focuses its efforts on four product areas: SRAM cache, specialty memory products, logic, and RISC microprocessors that are used in the desktop/server, data communications, and office automation markets. **NOTE:** Jobseekers must send resumes to Human Resources, 2975 Stender Way, M/S C9-015, Santa Clara CA 95954. Fax: 888/722-5627. **Positions advertised include:** Product Marketing Engineers; Design Engineers; Product Engineers; Test Engineers; Application Engineers; Software Engineers; Process Engineers; Database Administrators. **Corporate headquarters location:** Santa Clara CA.

INTEGRATED ELECTRICAL SERVICES INC.
1800 West Loop South, Suite 500, Houston TX 77027-9408. 713/860-1500. **Toll-free phone:** 800/696-1044. **Fax:** 713/860-1599. **Contact:** Bob Callahan, Human Resources Representative. **World Wide Web address:** http://www.ielectric.com. **Description:** An electrical contractor providing construction and maintenance services to a variety of business segments. The company's services include design and installation work for new and renovation projects, preventative maintenance, and emergency repair work. **Corporate headquarters location:** This location. **Other U.S. locations:** Nationwide. **Listed on:** New York Stock Exchange. **Stock exchange symbol:** IES. **Number of employees nationwide:** 13,000.

INTERCRAFT-BURNES COMPANY
One Intercraft Plaza, Taylor TX 76574. 888/963-7263. **Contact:** Human Resources. **E-mail address:** human.resources@burnesgroup.com. **World Wide Web address:** http://www.intercraft.com. **Description:** A manufacturer of picture frames sold to volume purchasers. **Positions advertised include:** Category Management Analyst; Master Scheduler; Sales Manager. **Corporate headquarters location**: This location. **Other U.S. locations:** NC; NH; RI; TN. **International locations:** Canada; France; Mexico. **Parent company:** Newell Rubbermaid Company. **Operations at this facility include:** Administration; Manufacturing; Sales. **Listed on:** New York Stock Exchange. **Stock exchange symbol:** NWL. **Number of employees worldwide:** 3,600.

INTERNATIONAL AVIATION COMPOSITES (IAC)
P.O. Box 376, Haslet TX 76052-0376. 817/491-6755. **Contact:** Human Resources. **World Wide Web address:** http://www.iac-ltd.com. **Description:** Repairs main and tail rotor blades on helicopters. **Corporate headquarters location:** This location. **Operations at this facility include:** Administration; Manufacturing; Research and Development; Sales; Service. **Listed on:** Privately held.

INTERNATIONAL BANK OF COMMERCE
P.O. Box 1359, Laredo TX 78042-1359. 956/722-7611. **Physical address:** 1200 San Bernardo Avenue, Laredo TX 78042-1359. **Contact:** Human Resources. **World Wide Web address:** http://www.iboc.com. **Description:** A full-service bank with locations throughout Texas that offers checking and savings accounts, CDs, wire transfers, mortgage loans, ATMs, and Right Checking Accounts. **Corporate headquarters location:** This location.

INTERNATIONAL BIOMEDICAL, INC.
8508 Cross Park Drive, Austin TX 78754. 512/873-0033. **Contact:** Human Resources. **World Wide Web address:** http://www.int-bio.com. **Description:** A manufacturer of high-technology medical instruments including infant incubators and radiation gloves. International Biomedical also manufactures electronic equipment used in research, testing, and teaching. **Corporate headquarters location:** Cleburne TX. **Operations at this facility include:** Manufacturing.

INTERNATIONAL MAINTENANCE CORPORATION
P.O. Box 1029, Beaumont TX 77704. 409/722-8031. **Contact:** Human Resources. **Description:** Provides plant maintenance, including shut-downs and turn-arounds; pipe fabrication; tank cleaning; hauling; and rigging services. **Other area locations:** Texas City TX. **Other U.S. locations:** Nationwide. **Parent company:** Turner Industries.

INTERNATIONAL PAPER COMPANY
P.O. Box 870, Texarkana TX 75504-0870. 903/796-7101. **Contact:** Human Resources. **World Wide Web address:** http://www.internationalpaper.com. . **Description:** International Paper is a manufacturer of pulp and paper, packaging, and wood products, as well as a range of specialty products. The company is organized into five business segments: Printing Papers, in which principal products include uncoated papers, coated papers, bristles, and pulp; Packaging, which includes industrial packaging, consumer packaging, and kraft and specialty papers; Distribution, which includes sales of printing papers, graphic arts equipment and supplies, packaging materials, industrial supplies, and office products; Specialty Products, which includes imaging products, specialty panels, nonwovens, chemicals, and minerals; and Forest Products, which includes logs and wood products. **Special programs:** Internships; Co-ops; Training Programs. See http://www.careers-ipaper.com for specific information. **Other area locations:** El Paso TX. **Corporate headquarters location:** Stamford CT. **Operations at this facility includes:** This location manufactures folding cartons. **Listed on:** New York Stock Exchange. **Stock exchange symbol:** IP. **Number of employees worldwide:** 100,000.

INTERNATIONAL SEMATECH
2706 Montopolis Drive, Austin TX 78741. 512/356-3588. **Fax:** 512/356-3086. **Contact:** Human Resources. **E-mail address:** staffing@sematech.com. **World Wide Web address:** http://www.sematech.org. **Description:** International SEMATECH is a consortium of U.S. semiconductor manufacturers, working with government and academia, to sponsor and conduct research in semiconductor manufacturing technology for the United States. Results are transferred to consortium members including the Department of Defense for both military and commercial applications. **NOTE:** See website for job listings and contact information. **Operations at this facility include:** This location develops advanced semiconductor manufacturing methods, materials, and equipment.

INTERPHASE CORPORATION
2901 North Dallas Parkway, Dallas TX 75093. 214/654-5000. **Toll-free phone:** 800/777-3722. **Fax:** 214/654-5500. **Contact:** Human Resources. **E-mail address:** iphase.resumes@iphase.com. **World Wide Web address:** http://www.interphase.com. **Description:** A developer, manufacturer, and marketer of networking and mass storage controllers, as well as stand-alone networking devices for computer systems. Networking products are primarily sold to OEMs, value-added resellers, systems integrators, and large end users. **Corporate headquarters location:** This location. **Operations at this facility include:** Administration; Manufacturing; Research and Development; Sales. **Listed on:** NASDAQ. **Stock exchange symbol:** INPH.

INTERVOICE-BRITE, INC.
17811 Waterview Parkway, Dallas TX 75252. 972/454-8000. **Fax:** 972/454-8408. **Contact:** Human Resources. **World Wide Web address:** http://www.intervoice-brite.com. **Description:** Develops, sells, and services interactive voice response systems that allow individuals to access a computer database using a telephone keypad, computer keyboard, or human voice. Applications are functioning in industries including insurance, banking, higher education, government, utilities, health care, retail distribution, transportation, and operator services. **Special programs:** Co-ops. **Positions advertised include:** Help Desk Coordinator; Senior Engineer; Engineer; Project Manager; Business Development Manager. **Listed on:** NASDAQ. **Stock exchange symbol:** INTV. **Corporate headquarters location:** This location.

ITAC SYSTEMS, INC.
3113 Benton Street, Garland TX 75042. 972/494-3073. **Toll-free phone:** 800/533-4822. **Fax:** 972/494-4159. **Contact:** Human Resources. **World Wide Web address:** http://www.itacsystems. com. **Description:** Manufactures the mouse-trak trackball, a computer peripheral product. Founded in 1993. **NOTE:** Entry-level positions are offered. **Corporate headquarters location:** This location. **Listed on:** Privately held.

INVESTOOLS INC.
5959 Corporate Drive, Suite LL250, Houston TX 77036. 281/588-9700. **Fax:** 281/588-9797. **Contact:** Human Resources. **World Wide Web address:** http://www.investools.com. **Description:** Develops and provides proprietary analytics and content to investors. **Corporate headquarters location:** This location. **Listed on:** American Stock Exchange. **Stock exchange symbol:** IED.

J.P. MORGAN CHASE & COMPANY
P.O. Box 250, Arlington TX 76004-0250. 817/856-3277. **Contact:** Human Resources. **World Wide Web address:** http://www.jpmorganchase.com. **Description:** Specializes in global financial services and retail banking. J.P. Morgan Chase and Company's services include asset management, card member services, community development, commercial banking for middle market companies, diversified consumer lending, global markets, home finance, investment banking, private banking, private equity, regional consumer and small business banking, and treasury and securities services. **NOTE:** Job seekers are encouraged to apply via the company's website: http://careers.jpmorganchase.com. **Other U.S. locations:** Nationwide. **International locations:** Worldwide. **Listed on:** New York Stock Exchange. **Stock exchange symbol:** JPM.

JRC HALLIBURTON ENERGY SERVICES, INC.
3120 County Road 401, Alvarado TX 76009. 817/790-2038. **Contact:** Human Resources Manager. **World Wide Web address:** http://www.halliburton.com.

Description: Provides evaluation services in connection with the drilling and completion of gas and oil wells. The company also manufactures and sells the equipment and supplies required to perform these services. **Positions advertised include:** Account Representative; Field Service Engineer. **Other U.S. locations:** Nationwide. **Parent company:** Halliburton Company. **Listed on:** New York Stock Exchange. **Stock exchange symbol:** HAL.

JACK IN THE BOX
1111 North Loop West, Suite 600, Houston TX 77008. 713/293-6200. **Contact:** Human Resources. **E-mail address:** careers@jackinthebox.com. **World Wide Web address:** http://www.jackinthebox.com. **Description:** Operates and franchises more than 1,600 Jack in the Box restaurants, which are primarily in the western and southwestern United States. International operations currently include restaurants in Hong Kong and Mexico. **Positions advertised include:** Assistant Manager. **Listed on:** New York Stock Exchange. **Stock exchange symbol:** JBX.

JACKSON WALKER L.L.P.
1401 McKinney Street, Suite 1900, Houston TX 77010. 713/752-4347. **Fax:** 713/752-4435. **Contact:** Bette Avante, Administrator. **E-mail address:** bavante@jw.com. **World Wide Web address:** http://www.jw.com. **Description:** A full-service law firm with a worldwide client base. Jackson Walker specializes in corporate, trust, and estate law. **Special programs:** Internships. **Other area locations:** Dallas TX; Fort Worth TX; Richardson TX; San Antonio TX. **Corporate headquarters location:** Dallas TX.

JALCO, INC.
P.O. Box 27368, Houston TX 77227. 713/728-8480. **Fax:** 713/729-6553. **Contact:** Nilo S. Cruz, Administrative Officer. **E-mail address:** jalcohou@aol.com. **Description:** A heavy-construction company.

JAMAK FABRICATION, INC.
1401 North Bowie Drive, Weatherford TX 76086. 817/594-8771. **Fax:** 817/594-8324. **Contact:** Human Resources. **World Wide Web address:** http://www.jamak.com. **Description:** Manufacturers of synthetic silicone rubber products. Founded in 1971. **Parent company:** JMK International. **Number of employees at this location:** 300. **Number of employees worldwide:** 700.

JC PENNEY COMPANY, INC.
6501 Legacy Drive, Plano TX 75024. Dallas TX 75301. 972/431-1000. **Contact:** Human Resources. **World Wide Web address:** http://www.jcpenney.net. **Description:** JC Penney Company is a national retail merchandise sales and service corporation with department stores nationwide. JC Penney sells apparel, home furnishings, and leisure lines in catalogs and 1,111 stores. **NOTE:** Jobseekers should apply online or at a nearby store location. This store also has positions in its Hair and Nail Salons, Portrait Galleries and Optical Departments. **Positions advertised include:** Intimate Apparel Technical Designer; Bindery Equipment Operator; Department Manager Trainee; Claims Specialist; Fit Model; Administrative Support. **Special programs:** Internships. **Corporate headquarters location:** This location. **Other U.S. locations:** Nationwide. **Operations at this facility include:** This location houses administrative offices. **Listed on:** New York Stock Exchange. **Stock exchange symbol:** JCP. **Number of employees worldwide:** 267,000.

JEFFERIES & COMPANY, INC.
13355 Noel Road, Suite 1400, Dallas TX 75240. 972/701-3000. **Contact:** Human Resources. **World Wide Web address:** http://www.jefco.com. **Description:** Engaged in equity, convertible debt and taxable fixed income securities brokerage and trading, and corporate finance. Jefferies & Company is one of the leading national firms engaged in the distribution and trading of blocks of equity securities primarily in the third market. Founded in 1962. **NOTE:** This company has positions in investment banking and in office support. For investment banking, jobseekers should e-mail their resumes to Westcoastrecruiting@jefco.com. Office support inquires should be faxed to Mel Locke, Director of People Services, at 310/914-1066 or via e-mail at mlocke@jefco.com. **Corporate headquarters location:** New York NY. **Other area locations:** Houston TX. **Parent company:** Jefferies Group, Inc. is a holding company which, through its primary subsidiaries Jefferies & Company; Investment Technology Group; Inc., Jefferies International Limited; and Jefferies Pacific Limited, is engaged in securities brokerage and trading, corporate finance, and other financial services.

JEFFERSON, COUNTY OF
Jefferson County Courthouse, 1225 Pearl Street, Beaumont TX 77701. 409/839-2391. **Recorded jobline:** 409/839-2384. **Contact:** Human Resources. **E-mail address:** hrdept@co.jefferson.tx.us. **World Wide Web address:** http://www.co.jefferson.tx.us. **Description:** Location for the county's government offices, including the Sheriff's Department. **NOTE:** Part-time positions are offered. A completed application is required for any position. The application can be downloaded online at the website. Do not e-mail applications. **Positions advertised include:** Detention Control Center Operator; Substance Abuse Assessment Specialist; Pharmacist; Data Processing Specialist; Residential Supervisor.

THE JEWISH HERALD-VOICE
P.O. Box 153, Houston TX 77001. 713/630-0391. **Contact:** Mrs. Jeanne Samuels, Editor. **World Wide Web address:** http://jhvonline.com. **Description:** A weekly newspaper for the Jewish community.

JIFFY LUBE INTERNATIONAL, INC.
P.O. Box 2967, Houston TX 77252-2967. 713/546-4100. **Contact:** Human Resources. **World Wide Web address:** http://www.jiffylube.com. **Description:** Provides automobile maintenance services including oil changes, tire rotations, and wheel balancing. **NOTE:** Interested jobseekers should apply to the nearest Jiffy Lube location. **Positions advertised include:** Service Center Manager; Service Center Technician. **Corporate headquarters location:** This location. **Parent company:** Pennzoil Products.

JOBE CONCRETE PRODUCTS INC.
One McKelligon Canyon Road, El Paso TX 79930. 915/565-4681. **Fax:** 915/562-6218. **Contact:** Linda Armendariz, Human Resources Manager. **World Wide Web address:** http://www.jobeconcrete.com. **Description:** Manufactures concrete and related products. Jobe Concrete Products also provides landscaping services. **Other area locations:** El Paso TX. **Other U.S. locations:** NM.

JOHN DEERE COMPANY
4040 McEwen, Suite 200, Dallas TX 75244-5032. 972/385-1701. **Contact:** Human Resources. **World Wide Web address:** http://www.deere.com. **Description:** John Deere manufactures, distributes, and finances the sale of heavy equipment and machinery for use in the agricultural equipment and industrial equipment industries. The agricultural equipment sector manufactures tractors, soil, seeding, and harvesting equipment. The industrial equipment segment manufactures a variety of earth moving equipment, tractors, loaders, and excavators; the consumer products division manufactures a variety of tractors and products for the homeowner. Financial services, including personal and commercial lines of insurance, retail, and managed health care services, are also offered. **Corporate headquarters location:** Moline IL. **Other U.S. locations:** Nationwide. **International locations:** Worldwide. **Operations at this facility include;** This location is the regional marketing office. **Listed on:** New York Stock Exchange. **Stock exchange symbol:** DE.

JOHNSON & JOHNSON MEDICAL, INC.
2500 East Arbrook Boulevard, Arlington TX 76014. 817/262-3900. **Contact:** Human Resources. **World Wide Web address:** http://www.jnj.com/careers. **Description:** Manufactures and markets an extensive line of disposable packs and gowns, surgical products, decontamination and disposal systems, latex gloves, and surgical antiseptics. **NOTE:** Jobseekers should apply online at the website for open positions. **Positions advertised include:** Sales Representative. **Special programs:** Internships. **Corporate headquarters location:** This location. **Other U.S. locations:** CA; CT; FL. **Parent company:** Johnson & Johnson (New Brunswick NJ). **Operations at this facility include:** Administration; Manufacturing; Research and Development; Sales. **Listed on:** New York Stock Exchange. **Stock exchange symbol:** JNJ. **Number of employees worldwide:** 109,500.

JOHNSON CONTROLS, INC.
3021 West Bend Drive, Irving TX 75063. 972/869-4494. **Contact:** Human Resources. **World Wide Web address:** http://www.johnsoncontrols.com. **Description:** Manufactures and markets automobile, marine, and commercial storage batteries for sale to private labels. **NOTE:** Interested jobseekers should see the company's website for specific procedures for resume and applications submissions. **Special programs:** Co-ops; Internships. **Corporate headquarters location:** Milwaukee WI. **Operations at this facility include:** Manufacturing; Sales; Service. **Listed on:** New York Stock Exchange. **Stock exchange symbol:** JCI. **Number of employees worldwide:** 119,000.

JOHNSON SUPPLY AND EQUIPMENT
10151 Stella Link, Houston TX 77025. 713/661-6666. **Toll-free number:** 800/833-5455. **Contact:** Human Resources. **World Wide Web address:** http://www.johnsonsupply.com. **Description:** A supplier of air conditioning systems and equipment. **NOTE:** This company has several locations throughout Texas. Each location manages its applicant screening and hiring. See the company's website for additional locations.

JONES BLAIR COMPANY
P.O. Box 35286, Dallas TX 75235. 214/353-1661. **Toll-free phone:** 800/492-9400. **Fax:** 800/325-6321. **Contact:** Human Resources. **World Wide Web address:** http://www.jones-blair.com. **Description:** A manufacturer of paints, resins, elastomers, and powder coatings. **Corporate headquarters location:** This location. **Other area locations:** Austin TX; Houston TX. **Other U.S. locations:** North Little Rock AR; Chattanooga TN. **Operations at this facility include:** Administration; Manufacturing; Research and Development; Sales; Service. **Listed on:** Privately held.

JORDAN HEALTH SERVICES
P.O. Box 840, Mount Vernon TX 75457. 903/537-7612x311. **Toll-free:** 800/665-0639. **Fax:** 903/537-4565. **Contact:** John McAuley, Human Resources Manager. **E-mail address:** jmcauley@jhsi.com. **World Wide Web address:** http://www.jhsi.com. **Description:** A diversified home health care agency. **Positions advertised include:** Accounts Payable Specialist; Administrator; PC Technician; Assistant Administrator; Assistant Controller; Benefits Specialist; Billing Specialist; Case Manager; Clerical Specialist; Data Entry Specialist; Director of Nursing; Intake Coordinator; Licensed Vocational Nurse; Registered Nurse; Information System Manager; Payroll Specialist. **Operations at this facility include:** Administration. **Listed on:** Privately held.

JOSTENS, INC.
P.O. Box AC, Denton TX 76202-1836. 940/891-0434. **Contact:** Human Resources. **World Wide Web address:** http://www.jostens.com. **Description:** Jostens, Inc.'s primary business segments are School Products, Recognition, and Jostens Learning. The School Products segment is comprised of five businesses: Printing and Publishing, Jewelry, Graduation Products, U.S. Photography, and Jostens Canada. Products include yearbooks, commercial printing, desktop publishing curriculum kits, class rings, graduation accessories, diplomas, trophies, plaques and other awards, school pictures, group photographs for youth camps and organizations, and senior graduation portraits. This segment serves schools, colleges, and alumni associations in the United States and Canada through independent sales representatives. Jostens also maintains an international sales force for American schools and military installations. The Recognition segment provides products and services that reflect achievements in service, sales, quality, productivity, attendance, safety, and retirements. It also produces awards for championship team accomplishments and affinity products for associations. This segment serves companies, professional and amateur sports teams, and special interest associations through an independent sales force. Jostens Learning produces educational software for children in kindergarten through grade 12, offering software-based curriculum in reading, mathematics, language arts, science programs, and early childhood instruction, as well as programs for at-risk learning and home learning. **Positions advertised include:** Quality Systems Manager. **NOTE:** Interested jobseekers should apply online. **Corporate headquarters location:** Minneapolis MN. **Operations at this facility include:** This location manufactures jewelry, which is sold to consumers through independent contract salespeople.

JUMPKING INC.
1371 South Town East Boulevard, Mesquite TX 75149. 972/290-7300. **Contact:** Personnel. **World Wide Web address:** http://www.jumpking.com. **Description:** Manufactures trampolines and related accessories. **Parent company:** Icon Fitness (Logan UT).

JUSTIN BOOT COMPANY
610 West Dagget Street, Fort Worth TX 76104. 817/332-4385. **Toll-free phone:** 800/358-7846. **Fax:** 817/348-2037. **Contact:** Human Resources. **World Wide Web address:** http://www.justinboots.com. **Description:** Manufactures cowboy boots, leather belts, handbags, and billfolds. **Parent company:** Berkshire Hathaway.

KCI (KINECTIC CONCEPTS, INC.)
14th Floor, KCI Tower, 8023 Vantage Drive, San Antonio TX 78265-9508. 210/524-9000. **Toll-free phone:** 210/275-4524. **Fax:** 210/255-6998. **Contact:** Human Resources. **World Wide Web address:** http://www.kci1.com. **Description:** Manufactures, sells, services, and rents hospital beds for the critically ill. **NOTE:** This company provides job listings and specific contact information on its website. **Corporate headquarters location:** This location. **Listed on:** New York Stock Exchange. **Stock exchange symbol:** KCI.

KFDA-TV
NEWS CHANNEL 10
P.O. Box 10, Amarillo TX 79105. 806/383-1010. **Contact:** Human Resources. **World Wide Web address:** http://www.newschannel10.com. **Description:** A CBS-affiliated television broadcasting station.

KLBK-TV
7403 South University Avenue, Lubbock TX 79423. 806/745-2345. **Contact:** Human Resources. **World Wide Web address:** http://www.klbk.com. **Description:** A CBS-affiliated television broadcasting station.

KPMG
717 North Harwood Street, Suite 3100, Dallas TX 75201. 214/840-2000. **Contact:** Human Resources. **World Wide Web address:** http://www.kpmg.com. **Description:** Delivers a wide range of value-added assurance, tax, and consulting services. **NOTE:** Interested jobseekers should see the company's website for job listings and other Texas locations. **Corporate headquarters location:** Montvale NJ. **Other U.S. locations:** Nationwide. **International locations:** Worldwide. **Parent company:** KPMG International provides professional consulting services that capture, manage, assess, and deliver information. **Number of employees worldwide:** 98,000.

KRLD/TEXAS STATE NETWORKS
1080 Ballpark Way, Arlington TX 76011. 817/543-5400. **Contact:** Human Resources. **World Wide Web address:** http://www.krld.com. **Description:** An AM, all news format radio station. **Positions advertised include:** Account Executive.

KVII-TV
One Broadcast Center, Amarillo TX 79101. 806/373-1787. **Contact:** Human Resources. **World Wide Web address:** http://www.kvii.com. **Description:** An ABC-affiliated television broadcasting station.

KVIL-AM/FM 103.7
4131 North Central Expressway, Suite 1200, Dallas TX 75204. 214/526-9870. **Fax:** 214/891-7966. **Contact:** Human Resources. **World Wide Web address:** http://www.kvil.com. **Description:** An adult contemporary radio station broadcasting on AM and FM. **Positions advertised include:** Fill-in On-Air Talent; Promotions Assistant; Commissioned Sales; Retail Account Executive. **Parent company:** Infinity Broadcasting Corporation of Texas.

KXXV-TV
P.O. Box 2522, 1909 South New Road, Waco TX 76702. 254/754-2525. **Contact:** Human Resources. **World Wide Web address:** http://www.kxxv.com. **Description:** An ABC-affiliated television station. **Positions advertised include:** Production Switcher; Producer; Video Editor; Executive Producer; News Anchor/Reporter. **Office hours:** Monday – Friday, 8:30 a.m. – 5:00 p.m.

KANEB SERVICES, INC.
2435 North Central Expressway, Suite 700, Richardson TX 75080. 972/699-4023. **Fax:** 972/699-4025. **Contact:** Personnel. **E-mail address:** employment@kaneb.com. **World Wide Web address:** http://www.kaneb.com. **Description:** A holding company with subsidiaries that are engaged in the technical application and refinement of petroleum products. **Corporate headquarters location:** This location. **Listed on:** New York Stock Exchange. **Stock exchange symbol:** KSL. **Annual sales/revenues:** More than $100 million.

KASPER WIRE WORKS INC.
P.O. Box 667, Shiner TX 77984-0667. 361/594-3327. **Toll-free phone:** 800/337-0610. **Fax:** 361/594-3311. **Contact:** Human Resources. **World Wide Web address:** http://www.kasperwireworks.com. **Description:** Manufactures wire and metal products used in restaurants, hospitals, and other industries.

KAST FABRICS
540 Preston, Pasadena TX 77501. 713/473-4848. **Toll-free phone:** 800/733-5278. **Fax:** 888/217-5278. **Contact:** Human Resources. **World Wide Web address:** http://www.kastfabrics.com. **Description:** A wholesale distributor of decorative fabrics for drapes and upholstery. The company also manufactures bedding such as quilts, bedspreads, and dust ruffles. Founded in 1952. **Corporate headquarters location:** This location.

KAUFMAN AND BROAD
9990 Richmond Avenue, Suite 400, Houston TX 77042. 713/977-6633. **Contact:** Human Resources. **World Wide Web address:** http://www.kaufmanandbroad.com. **Description:** A single-family residential homebuilder. **NOTE:** Interested jobseekers must apply online for all positions. This company has locations throughout Texas. **Positions advertised include:** Director of Land Acquisition; Senior Land Development Manager; Land Development Superintendent; Closing Coordinator; Sales Representative; Field Loan Counselor; Studio Assistant; Receptionist; File Clerk; Office Assistant. **Corporate headquarters location:** Los Angeles CA.

KELLER WILLIAMS REALTORS (LAKE CITIES)
405 Mayfield Avenue, Garland TX 75041. 972/240-4416. **Contact:** Human Resources. **World Wide Web address:** http://www.mc.kw.com. **Description:** A realty company offering both residential and commercial properties. **NOTE:** This is one location of this company. See the corporate website at http://www.kw.com for additional locations throughout Texas and the United States. All interested jobseekers must apply online. **Positions advertised include:** Team Leader; Market Center Administrator; Administrative Assistant; Listing Specialist/Coordinator; Buyer Specialist.

KELLOGG, BROWN & ROOT
601 Jefferson Street, Houston TX 77002. 713/753-2000. **Contact:** Human Resources. **World Wide Web address:** http://www.halliburton.com. **Description:** A full-service design, engineering, procurement, construction, and contract management firm. The company serves the process and energy industries worldwide and is primarily involved in hydrocarbon-processing plants including oil-refining units, petrochemical manufacturing plants, ammonia and fertilizer plants, and gas-processing units. **NOTE:** Job listings and applications are available at the company's website. **Special programs:** Internships; Apprenticeships; Graduate. **Corporate headquarters location:** Dallas TX. **Other U.S. locations:** Nationwide. **Operations at this facility include:** Engineering. **Listed on:** New York Stock Exchange. **Stock exchange symbol:** HAL.

KELLY-SPRINGFIELD TIRE COMPANY
P.O. Box 4670, Tyler TX 75712-4670. 903/535-1500. **Contact:** Human Resources. **World Wide Web address:** http://www.kelly-springfield.com. **Description:** Manufactures tires and inner tubes. **Corporate headquarters location:** Cumberland MD. **Other U.S. locations:** Freeport IL; Fayetteville NC. **Parent company:** Goodyear Tire & Rubber Company. **Listed on:** New York Stock Exchange. **Stock exchange symbol:** GT.

KERR McGEE CORPORATION
5625 North MacArthur Boulevard, Irving TX 75038. 972/751-1571. **Contact:** Human Resources. **World Wide Web address:** http://www.kerr-mcgee.com. **Description:** Explores for, acquires, develops, produces, and sells oil and natural gas worldwide. **Corporate headquarters location:** Oklahoma City OK. **Listed on:** New York Stock Exchange. **Stock exchange symbol:** KMG.

KERRVILLE STATE HOSPITAL
721 Thompson Drive, Kerrville TX 78028. 830/896-2211. **Contact:** Human Resources. **Description:** A psychiatric hospital with 200 inpatient beds and 33 medical unit beds. Founded in 1951. **World Wide Web address:** http://www.mhmr.state.tx.us/hospitals/kerrvillesh. **NOTE:** A completed application must be submitted with each resume. The application can be found on the website. **Positions advertised include:** RN; LVN. **Corporate headquarters location:** Austin TX.

KEWAUNEE SCIENTIFIC CORPORATION
1300 SM 20 East, Lockhart TX 78644. 512/398-5292. **Contact:** Human Resources. **E-mail address:** humanresources@kewaunee.com. **World Wide Web address:** http://www.kewaunee.com. **Description:** Manufactures laboratory and technical workstations, furniture, and related accessories for industrial and commercial markets. **NOTE:** Interested jobseekers may mail their resumes to Human Resources Department, Kewaunee Scientific Corporation; P.O. Box 182, Statesville NC 28687-1842. **Corporate headquarters location:** Statesville NC. **Listed on:** NASDAQ. **Stock exchange symbol:** KEQU.

KIMBELL ART MUSEUM
3333 Camp Bowie Boulevard Fort Worth TX 76107-2792. 817/332-8451. **Fax:** 817/877-1264. **Contact:** Robert Newcombe, Photography Department. **E-mail address:** rnewcombe@kimbellmuseum.org. **World Wide Web address:** http://www.kimbellart.org. **Description:** An art gallery known for its large collection of Asian arts, international art and period pieces. **NOTE:** Mail or e-mail cover letter, resume and references. **Special programs:** Internships.

KIMBERLY-CLARK CORPORATION
P.O. Box 619100, Dallas TX 75261. 972/281-1200. **Contact:** Human Resources. **E-mail address:** opportunities@kc-careers.com. **World Wide Web address:** http://www.kimberly-clark.com. **Description:** Manufactures and markets products for personal, business, and industrial uses throughout the world. The name brands of Kimberly-Clark Corporation include Kleenex facial and bathroom tissue, Huggies diapers and baby wipes, Pull-Ups training pants, Kotex and New Freedom feminine care products, Depend and Poise incontinence care products, Hi-Dri household towels, Kimguard sterile wrap, Kimwipes industrial wipers, and Classic business and correspondence papers. Most of the company's products are made using advanced technologies in absorbency, fibers, and nonwovens. Kimberly-Clark Corporation has extensive overseas operations in Europe and Asia. **Corporate headquarters location:** This location. **Listed on:** New York Stock Exchange. **Stock exchange symbol:** KMB.

KIMBERLY-CLARK TECNOL INC.
14 Finnegan Drive, Del Rio TX 78840. 830/774-7482. **Contact:** Human Resources. **World Wide Web address:** http://www.kchealthcare.com. **Description:** A warehouse that distributes medical products. **Parent company:** Kimberly-Clark Corporation. **Listed on:** New York Stock Exchange. **Stock exchange symbol:** KMB.

KINDER MORGAN
500 Dallas Street, Suite 1000, Houston TX 77002. 713/369-9000. **Toll-free phone:** 800/324-2900. **Fax:** 713/369-9100. **Contact:** Human Resources. **World Wide Web address:** http://www.kindermorgan.com. **Description:** Distributes natural gas. **NOTE:** This company has other Texas locations. See its corporate website for job listings for other locations and contact information. **Corporate headquarters location:** This location. **Listed on:** New York Stock Exchange. **Stock exchange symbol:** KMI.

KING RANCH, INC.
3 Riverway, Suite 1600, Houston TX 77056. 832/681-5700. **Contact:** Human Resources. **World Wide Web address:** http://www.king-ranch.com. **Description:** One of the largest private agribusinesses in the world. The company also operates ranches and farms in Arizona, Kentucky, Florida, and Brazil. Founded in 1850. **Special programs:** Co-ops. **Office hours:** Monday - Friday, 8:00 a.m. - 5:00 p.m. **Listed on:** Privately held.

KITTY HAWK CARGO
1535 West 20th Street, P.O. Box 612787, DFW Airport TX 75261. 972/456-2200. **Contact:** Human Resources. **E-mail address:** jobs@kha.com. **World Wide Web address:** http://www.khcargo.com. **Description:** Provides charter management and cargo services.

KNOWLEDGEBASE MARKETING
701 North Plano Road, Richardson TX 75081. 972/690-4493. . **Contact:** Bill Jackson, Human Resources. **E-mail address:** recruiter@kbm1.com. **Description:** A list brokerage providing a variety of data mining services for direct marketers, including marketing database development, segmentation analysis, merge/purge, list enhancement, and list rental fulfillment. **NOTE:** Resumes may be faxed also to 713/995-2201. **Positions advertised include:** Processing Specialist.

KOCH INDUSTRIES, INC.
P.O. Box 1478, Houston TX 77251-1478. 713/544-4123. **Contact:** Selection Supervisor. **World Wide Web address:** http://www.kochcareers. com. **Description:** Koch Industries, Inc. is involved in virtually all phases of the oil and gas industry, as well as in chemicals, chemical technology products, agriculture, hard minerals, trading, and financial investments. **NOTE:** This company requires that all resumes be submitted online at their website. **Special programs:** Internships. **Positions advertised include:** Accounting Consultant; Business and Process Analyst; Financial Reporting; Trading Operations and Risk Analyst; Financial Trading Operations. **Corporate headquarters location:** Wichita KS. **Other U.S. locations:** Nationwide. **Operations at this facility include:** This location operates Koch Capital Markets, a financial trading consulting group. **Listed on:** Privately held.

KOHLER COMPANY
P.O. Box 1709, Brownwood TX 76804. 915/643-2661. **Contact:** Human Resources. **World Wide Web address:** http://www.kohler.com. **Description:** A large manufacturer of vitreous china. Kohler also has a plastics division that produces showers and baths. **Special programs:** Internships. **Corporate headquarters location:** Kohler WI. **Operations at this facility:** Manufactures plumbing parts and accessories.

KONE & CRANE
7300 Chippewa Boulevard, Houston TX 77086. 281/445-2225. **Contact:** Human Resources. **World Wide Web address:** http://www.konecranes.com. **Description:** Manufactures and services industrial cranes and hoists. **Corporate headquarters location:** Finland. **Other U.S. locations:** Nationwide. **Operations at this facility include:** Administration; Divisional Headquarters; Manufacturing; Research and Development; Sales; Service.

KRAFT FOODS, INC.
2340 Forest Lane, Garland TX 75042. 972/272-7511. **Contact:** Human Resources Supervisor. **World Wide Web address:** http://www.kraftfoods.com. **Description:** Kraft Foods, Inc. is one of the largest producers of packaged grocery products in North America. Major brands include Jell-O, Post, Kool-Aid, Crystal Light, Entenmann's, Miracle Whip, Stove Top, and Shake 'n Bake. Kraft markets a number of products under the Kraft brand name including natural and processed cheeses, and dry packaged dinners. The company's products are supplied to more than 100 countries worldwide. **Parent company:** Philip Morris Companies is a holding company with principal wholly-owned subsidiaries Philip Morris Inc. (Philip Morris U.S.A.), Philip Morris International Inc., Kraft Foods, Inc., Miller Brewing Company, and Philip Morris Capital Corporation. The Oscar Mayer unit markets processed meats, poultry, lunch combinations, and pickles under the Oscar Mayer, Louis Rich, Lunchables, and Claussen brand names. Kraft Foods Ingredients Corporation manufactures private-label and industrial food products for sale to other food processing companies. In the tobacco industry, Philip Morris U.S.A. and Philip Morris International together form one of the largest international cigarette operations in the world. U.S. brand names include Marlboro, Parliament, Virginia Slims, Benson & Hedges, and Merit. Miller Brewing Company brews beer under brand names including Molson Ice, Miller Genuine Draft, Miller High Life, Sharp's, Red Dog, Miller Lite, Icehouse, Foster's Lager, and Lowenbrau. Philip Morris Capital Corporation is engaged in financial services and real estate. **NOTE:** Kraft Foods only accepts resumes via its website. **Operations at this facility include:** This location produces a variety of food products including barbecue sauce, mayonnaise, tartar sauce, Miracle Whip, Catalina dressing, and salad products. **Listed on:** New York Stock Exchange. **Stock exchange symbol:** KFT. **Number of employees nationwide:** 114,000.

KRAFT FOODS, INC./MAXWELL HOUSE DIVISION
P.O. Box 248, Houston TX 77001-0248. 713/221-8785. **Contact:** Human Resources. **World Wide Web address:** http://www.kraftfoods.com. **Description:** Maxwell House is a Kraft Foods brand. This location processes and markets Maxwell House coffee, which is supplied to more than 100 countries worldwide. **NOTE:** Interested jobseekers should apply online at Kraft Foods website. **Parent company:** Philip Morris.

KROGER'S
3612 North Beltline Road, Irving TX 75062. 972/252-7413. **Contact:** Human Resources. **World Wide Web address:** http://www.kroger.com. **Description:** A location of this national supermarket chain. **NOTE:** Kroger's has locations throughout Texas and the United States. See the company's website for additional locations and hiring information. **Parent company:** The Kroger Company (Cincinnati OH) is a major supermarket and convenience store operator and food processor. The company operates over 1,250 supermarkets, 789 convenience stores, and 398 jewelry stores. The Kroger Company also has 37 food processing plants. which supply over 4,000 private label products to its supermarkets. **Listed on:** New York Stock Exchange. **Stock exchange symbol:** KR.

KROGER'S
3300 Montrose Boulevard, Houston TX 77006. 713/526-7865. **Contact:** Human Resources. **World Wide Web address:** http://www.kroger.com. **Description:** A location of this national supermarket chain. **NOTE:** Kroger's has locations throughout Texas and the United States. See the company's website for additional locations and hiring information. **Parent company:** The Kroger Company (Cincinnati OH) is a major supermarket and convenience store operator and food processor. The company operates over 1,250 supermarkets, 789 convenience stores, and 398 jewelry stores. The Kroger Company also has 37 food processing plants. which supply over 4,000 private label products to its supermarkets. **Listed on:** New York Stock Exchange. **Stock exchange symbol:** KR.

KUPER REALTY CORPORATION
6606 North New Braunfels Avenue, San Antonio TX 78209. 210/822-8602. **Toll-free phone:** 800/584-5400. **Fax:** 210/822-6646. **Contact:** Human Resources. **World Wide Web address:** http://www.kuperrealty.com. **Description:** A real estate agency engaged in the sale of residential and commercial properties as well as ranches and land. Kuper Realty has additional locations throughout San Antonio.

KVAERNER PROCESS SYSTEMS
7909 Parkwood Circle Drive, 6th Floor, Houston TX 77036. 713/271-7086. **Contact:** Human Resources. **World Wide Web address:** http://www.kvaerner.com. **Description:** Engaged in the engineering and manufacturing of hydraulic and electrohydraulic control systems for subsea oil production and drilling operations, as well as system engineering, integration, and analysis for subsea production completion. **NOTE:** This company is restructuring it business units. Interested jobseekers should consult Kvaerner's website for additional information.

KWIK KOPY CORPORATION
12715 Telge Road, Cypress TX 77429. 281/256-4100. **Toll-free phone:** 888/280-2053. **Fax:** 281/373-4450. **Contact**: Human Resources. **World Wide Web address:** http://www.kwikkopy.com. **Description:** A retail center for printing, copying, and mailing services and items. Founded in 1967. **NOTE:** See website for nearest store locations and apply in person. **Corporate location:** This location. **Operations at this facility include:** Administration. **Listed on:** Privately held.

LDB CORPORATION
444 Sidney Baker Street South, Kerrville TX 78028. 830/257-2000. **Contact:** Barbara Fisher, Human Resources Manager. **Description:** Operates the Mr. Gatti's national pizza chain. **Corporate headquarters location:** This location.

LSI SPECIALTY ELECTRICAL PRODUCTS
1231 Shadowdale, Houston TX 77043. 713/464-1393. **Fax:** 713/464-7731. **Contact:** Human Resources. **World Wide Web address:** http://www.lsispecialty.com. **Description:** Distributes electrical products used in hazardous areas and harsh environments. **Corporate headquarters location:** This location. **Other U.S. locations:** Lafayette LA; Oklahoma City OK. **Operations at this facility include:** Administration; Sales.

LA QUINTA INNS, INC.
909 Hidden Ridge, Suite 600, Irving TX 75038. 210/302-6000. **Contact:** Human Resources. **World Wide Web address:** http://www.lq.com. **Description:** Develops, owns, and operates a nationwide chain of lodging inns. La Quinta Inns has more than 330 locations in 32 states. Founded in 1964. **NOTE:** To apply for hotel positions, see company's website for job listings. **Positions advertised include:** PeopleSoft Administrator. **Corporate headquarters location:** This location. **Parent company:** Meditrust. **Listed on:** New York Stock Exchange. **Stock exchange symbol:** LQI. **Number of employees nationwide:** More than 7,000.

LABATT FOOD SERVICE
P.O. Box 2140, San Antonio TX 78297-2140. 210/661-4216. **Physical address:** 4500 Industry Park, San Antonio TX 78218. **Fax:** 210/661-0973. **Contact:** Human Resources Department. **World Wide Web address:** http://www.labattfood.com. **Description:** A food distributor for restaurants, hospitals, military bases, schools, and other institutions. **NOTE:** Jobseekers interested in positions at this location can fax or mail their resumes. See website for other locations, positions and mailing addresses. **Other area locations:** Corpus Christi TX; Austin TX; Harlingen TX; Houston TX. **Operations at this facility include:** Office; Warehouse.

LABORATORY CORPORATION OF AMERICA (LABCORP)
4207 James Casey Street, Suite 101, Austin TX 78745. 512/443-0538. **Fax:** 210/735-0512. **Contact:** Human Resources. **World Wide Web address:** http://www.labcorp.com. **Description:** One of the nation's leading clinical laboratory companies, providing services primarily to physicians, hospitals, clinics, nursing homes, and other clinical labs nationwide. LabCorp performs tests on blood, urine, and other body fluids and tissue, aiding the diagnosis of disease. **NOTE:** This company has locations in Houston and Dallas. For a complete list of jobs and locations, see the company's website. **Corporate headquarters location:** Burlington NC. **Other U.S. locations:** Nationwide. **Operations at this facility include:** This location is a blood-drawing facility. **Listed on:** New York Stock Exchange. **Stock exchange symbol:** LH. **Number of employees nationwide:** 19,600.

LADY BIRD JOHNSON WILDFLOWER CENTER
4801 La Crosse Avenue, Austin TX 78739. 512/292-4200. **Contact:** Human Resources. **World Wide Web address:** http://www.wildflower.org. **Description:** A nonprofit organization that serves to educate people on the value and beauty of native plants. Lady Bird Johnson Wildflower Center also houses Wild Ideas: The Store, a retail store offering books, art, and clothing dedicated to generating an interest in plant life; and The Wildflower Cafe, a coffee shop and eatery. **Special programs:** Internships. **Corporate headquarters location:** This location.

TONY LAMA COMPANY
1137 Tony Lama Street, El Paso TX 79915. 915/778-8311. **Fax:** 915/778-5237. **Contact:** Human Resources. **World Wide Web address:** http://www.tonylama.com. **Description:** A manufacturer of men's and women's cowboy boots. **Corporate headquarters location:** Fort Worth TX. **Parent company:** Berkshire Hathaway. **Operations at this facility:** Manufacturing.

LAMAR UNIVERSITY
P.O. Box 11127, Beaumont TX 77710. 409/880-8375. **Recorded jobline:** 409/880-8371. **Contact:** Human Resources. **World Wide Web address:** http://www.dept.lamar.edu/humanresources. **Description:** A university offering associate's, bachelor's, master's, and doctoral degrees. Both two- and four-year programs are available. Approximately 7,300 undergraduate and 700 graduate students attend Lamar University. **NOTE:** An application must be submitted with a resume. The application can be found at the company's website. Applications and resumes may be submitted online or hand-delivered to the Human Resources Office located at 1030 E. Florida, Beaumont TX. **Positions advertised include:** Faculty; Staff. **Corporate headquarters location:** This location.

ROBERT LAMONS AND ASSOCIATES
P.O. Box 5278, Granbury TX 76049. 713/828-7000. **Contact:** Human Resources. **World Wide Web address:** http://www.ads2biz.com. **Description:** A business-to-business marketing communications specialist.

LANCER CORPORATION
6655 Lancer Boulevard, San Antonio TX 78219. 210/310-7000. **Contact:** Human Resources. **World Wide Web address:** http://www.lancercorp.com. **Description:** A manufacturer of soft drink and related food service equipment. **Positions advertised include:** Project Cost Analyst; Tester; Mechanical Assembler; Manufacturing Engineer. **Corporate headquarters location:** This location. **International locations:** Mexico; Australia; Belgium; New Zealand; Russia; Brazil. **Listed on:** American Stock Exchange. **Stock exchange symbol:** LAN. **Number of employees nationwide:** 1,500.

LANDMARK EQUIPMENT
5000 Airport Freeway, Fort Worth TX 76117. 817/834-8131. **Fax:** 817/831-8775. **Contact:** General Manager. **World Wide Web address:** www.landmarkeq.com. **Description:** A wholesale dealer of tractors, lawn mowers, and related equipment. **NOTE:** Please visit website to view job listings and for more information on how to apply for specific positions. **Other area locations:** Irving TX; McKinney TX.

LANDMARK GRAPHICS
P.O. Box 42806, Houston TX 77242. 713/839-2000. **Fax:** 713/839-2691. **Contact:** Human Resources. **World Wide Web address:** http://www.lgc.com. **Description:** Software developer whose primary market is the oil industry. Products include data management, geophysical technology, and integrated interpretation applications. Other services include reservoir management and drilling and well consulting. **NOTE:** Landmark Graphics has a nearby shipping and receiving location at 2101 City West Boulevard, Building 1, Suite 200, Houston TX 77042; 713/839-2000. Job listings for all locations are available on the company's website. Apply online. **Other area locations:** Austin TX. **Other U.S. locations:** Anchorage, AK; Denver CO. **International locations:** Canada. Parent company: Halliburton (Dallas TX). **Operations at this facility include:** Administration; Sales; Service.

LANDRY'S RESTAURANTS, INC.
1510 West Loop South, Houston TX 77027. 713/850-1010. **Contact:** Human Resources. **World Wide Web address:** http://www.landrysseafood.com. **Description:** Operates a chain of seafood restaurants. **Positions advertised include:** Front Manager; Accounts Payable Manager; Administrative Assistant; Assistant Building Engineer' Benefits Administrator; Brand Marketing Manager; Cash Analyst; Director of Training; Inventory Control; Loss Prevention Analyst; Marketing Assistant. **Corporate headquarters location:** This location. **Operations at this facility include:** Administration; Sales.

LAREDO COMMUNITY COLLEGE
West End Washington Street, Laredo TX 78040. 956/721-5138. **Fax:** 956/721-5367. **Contact:** Human Resources. **World Wide Web address:** http://www.laredo.cc.tx.us. **Description:** Offers a variety of Associate's degrees in programs including business, computers, electronics, and nursing. Approximately 6,900 students attend the college. Founded in 1947. **NOTE:** An application must be submitted via mail for any position.

The application can be downloaded on the college's website. **Positions advertised include:** Catalog Librarian; Chemistry Instructor; ENSL Spanish Instructor; Government Instructor; Mathematics Instructor; Music/Strings; Speech/Theater; Assistant Plumber.

LAREDO NATIONAL BANK
700 San Bernardo Avenue, Laredo TX 78040. 956/723-1151. **Contact:** Human Resources. **E-mail address:** lnbhr@lnb.com. **World Wide Web address:** http://www.lnb.com. **Description:** A full-service bank that markets its services to the Hispanic community. The bank offers checking and savings accounts, CDs, mortgages, and wire transfers. **NOTE:** This company requires its employees to speak English and Spanish. **Positions advertised include:** Teller. **Other area locations:** Austin TX; Brownsville TX; Corpus Christi TX; Houston TX: Dallas TX: McAllen TX.

LAUREN ENGINEERS & CONSTRUCTORS
901 South First Street, Abilene TX 79602. 325/670-9660. **Fax:** 325/670-9663. **Contact:** Human Resources. **E-mail address:** hr@laurenec.com. **World Wide Web address:** http://www.laurenec.com. **Description:** Designs and builds power plants, refineries, and related large-scale projects. **Positions advertised include:** Process Engineering Manager; Senior Mechanical Engineer. **Corporate headquarters location:** This location. **Other U.S. locations**: Knoxville TN; Duluth GA.

LAWYERS TITLE INSURANCE CORPORATION
7557 Rambler Road, Suite 1200, L.B 31, Dallas TX 75231. 214/346-7200. **Toll-free phone:** 800/442-7067. **Fax:** 877/803-4304. **Contact:** Human Resources. **World Wide Web address:** http://www.lawyerstitle.com. **Description:** Provides title insurance and other real estate-related services on commercial and residential transactions in the United States, Canada, the Bahamas, Puerto Rico, and the U.S. Virgin Islands. Lawyers Title Insurance Corporation also provides search and examination services and closing services for a broad-based customer group that includes lenders, developers, real estate brokers, attorneys, and homebuyers. This location covers Kansas, New Mexico, Oklahoma, and Texas. **Corporate headquarters location:** Richmond VA. **Other U.S. locations:** Nationwide. **Parent company:** Land America Financial Group. **Listed on:** New York Stock Exchange. **Stock exchange symbol:** LFG.

LEAD DOGS
2433 Rutland Drive, Suite 210, Austin TX 78758. 512/990-2000. **Toll-free phone:** 800/336-2616. **Fax:** 512/990-8999. **Contact:** Tina Tripoli, Human Resources Director, ext. 106. **E-mail address:** Ttripoli@leaddogs.com. **World Wide Web address:** http://www.leaddogs.com. **Description:** Provides direct marketing services for high-tech companies including event management and database development. **Positions advertised include:** Marketing Pre-Sales Representative; Account Manager; Call Center Manager.

LEGAL DIRECTORIES PUBLISHING COMPANY, INC.
P.O. Box 189000, 9111 Garland Road, Dallas TX 75218-9000. 214/321-3238. **Contact:** Human Resources. **World Wide Web address:** http://www.legaldirectories.com. **Description:** One of the nation's largest publishers of state legal directories.

LELAND MEDICAL PLAZA
2696 West Walnut Street, Garland TX 75042. 972/276-7116. **Contact:** Human Resources. **World Wide Web address:** http://www.lelandmedical.com. **Description:** A 113-bed hospital specializing in industrial, behavioral, orthopedic, plastic surgery, and surgical weight loss programs. **Parent company:** Leland Medical Centers.

LENNOX INTERNATIONAL, INC.
P.O. Box 799900, Dallas TX 75379-9900. 972/497-5000. **Physical address:** 2140 Lake Park Boulevard, Richardson TX 75080. **Fax:** 972/497-5476. **Contact:** Human Resources. **World Wide Web address:** http://www.lennoxinternational.com. **Description:** Manufactures and services refrigeration, heating and air-conditioning equipment. **Positions advertised include:** Customer Financial Services Coordinator; Product Manager; Accounting Analyst; Customer Financial Services Administrator; Accounting Support; Pricing Services Analyst. **Special programs:** Internships. **Corporate headquarters location:** This location. **Subsidiaries include:** Armstrong Air Conditioning Inc.; Heatcraft Inc.; Lennox Global Ltd.; Lennox Industries, Inc. **Operations at this facility include:** Administration. **Listed on:** New York Stock Exchange. **Stock exchange symbol:** LII. **Number of employees worldwide:** 21,000.

LEON'S TEXAS CUISINE
P.O. Box 1850, McKinney TX 75070-1850. 972/529-5050. **Fax:** 972/529-2244. **Contact:** Cindy Stephens, Vice President of Human Resources and Administration. **E-mail address:** cindy@texascuisine.com. **World Wide Web address:** http://www.texascuisine.com. **Description:** Produces corn dogs and other southwestern-style items that are sold and distributed to retail grocery stores nationwide. **NOTE:** Entry-level positions are offered. **Corporate headquarters location:** This location.

LEPCO
5204 North Expressway, Brownsville TX 78597. 956/350-5650. **Contact:** Human Resources. **World Wide Web address:** http://www.ies.net/lepco. **Description:** A manufacturer of transformers and conductors. **Corporate headquarters location:** This location.

LEWIS & LAMBERT METAL
5963 Eden Drive, Haltom City TX 76117. 817/834-7146. **Contact:** Human Resources. **Description:** A leader in sheet metal installation and fabrication.

LIANT SOFTWARE CORPORATION
8911 North Capital of Texas Highway, Austin TX 78759. 512/343-1010. **Toll-free phone:** 800/349-9222. **Fax:** 512/371-7609. **Contact:** Human Resources. **World Wide Web address:** http://www.liant.com. **Description:** Develops software including Relativity, an SQL relational access through ODBC to COBOL managed data for client/server Windows applications, and Open PL/I, which offers transitions of PL/I mainframe and minicomputer applications from legacy systems to open, client/server environments. **Corporate headquarters location:** Framingham MA. **Operations at this facility include:** This location is engaged in software packaging and distribution. **Listed on:** Privately held.

LIGHTHOUSE OF HOUSTON
P.O. Box 130345, Houston TX 77219-0435. 713/527-9561. **Contact:** Human Resources. **World Wide Web address:** http://www.thelighthouseofhouston.org. **Description:** A nonprofit organization for the blind offering adult day care, recreational activities, and social services.

LINCO-ELECTROMATIC, INC.
4580 West Wall Street, Midland TX 79703. 432/694-9644. **Fax:** 432/694-0921. **Contact:** Human Resources. **World Wide Web address:** http://www.lemc.comm. **Description:** Founded in 1967, this company manufactures and distributes calibration and measurement equipment. Primary markets are the oil and related industries. **NOTE:** Mail resumes to: P.O. Box 4096, Midland TX 797704; Attention: Fabrication West. Jobseekers may e-mail resumes to dbaumbach@lemc.com. **Positions advertised include:** Service/Meter Technician. **Other area locations:** Kilgore TX; Houston TX; Corpus Christi TX; Wichita Falls TX. **Other U.S. locations:** OK.

LINCO-ELECTROMATIC, INC.
330 Houston Street, Kilgore TX 75662. 903/984-6246. Fax: 903/984-4870. **Contact:** Human Resources. **World Wide Web address:** http://www.lemc.comm. **Description:** Founded in 1967, this company manufactures and distributes calibration and measurement equipment. Primary markets are the oil and related industries. **NOTE:** Search for positions online. **Corporate headquarters location:** Midland TX. **Other area locations:** Houston TX; Corpus Christi TX; Wichita Falls TX. **Other U.S. locations:** OK.

LINCO-ELECTROMATIC, INC.
1674 W. Sam Houston Parkway North, Houston TX 77043. 713/464-1642. Fax: 713/464-9425. **Contact:** Human Resources. **World Wide Web address:** http://www.lemc.comm. **Description:** Founded in 1967, this company manufactures and distributes calibration and measurement equipment. Primary markets are the oil and related industries. **NOTE:** Search for positions online. **Corporate headquarters location:** Midland TX. **Other area locations:** Kilgore TX; Corpus Christi TX; Wichita Falls TX. **Other U.S. locations:** OK.

LINCOLN PROPERTY COMPANY
3300 Lincoln Plaza, 500 North Akard Street, Dallas TX 75201. 214/740-3300. **Contact:** Human Resources. **World Wide Web address:** http://www.lincolnproperty.com. **Description:** A property management company with commercial, residential, and industrial properties. **Positions advertised include:** Tenant Service Coordinator.

LINX DATA TERMINALS, INC.
625 Digital Drive, Suite 100, Plano TX 75075. 972/964-7090. **Contact:** Human Resources. **World Wide Web address:** http://www.linxdata.com. **Description:** A manufacturer of networked data collection terminals and host connectivity software.

ARTHUR D. LITTLE, INC.
2525 South Shore Boulevard, Suite 202, League City TX 77573. 281/334-6970. **Contact:** Human Resources. **World Wide Web address:** http://www.adlittle-us.com. **Description:** Offers services in three areas: management consulting; technology and product development; and environmental, health, and safety consulting. The company's clients include a wide range of firms in manufacturing industries including aerospace, automotive, consumer products, industrial electronics, information and telecommunications, medical products, and pharmaceuticals; process industries including chemicals, energy, food, and metals; and service industries, including financial services, health care, information and communications services, transportation, travel and tourism, and utilities. **Positions advertised include:** Business Analyst; Consultant; Intern.

LOCKE LIDDELL & SAPP LLP
3400 J.P. Morgan Chase Tower, 600 Travis, Houston TX 77002. 713/226-1200. **Contact:** Brooke Patton, Human Resources. **E-mail address:** bpatton@lockeliddell.com. **World Wide Web address:** http://www.lockeliddell.com. **Description:** A firm practicing in all segments of corporate law. **Special programs:** Internships. **Other area locations:** Austin TX; Dallas TX. **Other U.S locations:** New Orleans LA.

LOCKHEED MARTIN CORPORATION
2400 NASA Road One, Mail Stop B03, Houston TX 77058. 281/333-5411. **Fax:** 281/333-6100. **Contact:** Human Resources Representative. **World Wide Web address:** http://www.lockheadmartin.com. **Description:** Lockheed Martin Corporation operates in five major areas: Aeronautics, Electronic Systems, Information and Technology Services; Integrated Systems and Solutions, and Space Systems. Its chief client is the United States Department of Defense, including Homeland Security. It also provides services to international governments. The Aeronautics Division researches and develops combat aircrafts. In its Electrical Systems Division, the company designs maritime systems and sensors, and missiles and fire control. Lockheed Martin's Space Systems provides engineering and scientific support to NASA/Johnson Space Center. In its Integrated Systems and Solutions division, Lockheed Martin develops intelligence devices. The Information and Technology Services designs defense and space systems. **NOTE:** Lockheed Martin has locations throughout Texas, including Houston (Space Operations), Forth Worth (Aeronautics) and Dallas (Aeronautics). The website provides job listings for all its divisions and jobseekers must submit their resumes online. **Parent company: Corporate headquarters location:** Bethesda MD. **Other U.S. locations:** Nationwide. **International locations:** Worldwide. **Listed on:** New York Stock Exchange. **Stock exchange symbol:** LM. **Number of employees nationwide:** 130,000.

LOCKWOOD, ANDREWS & NEWNAM, INC.
2925 Briarpark Drive, Houston TX 77042. 713/266-6900. **Toll-free phone:** 800/688-7590. **Contact:** Human Resources. **E-mail address:** hr@lan-inc.com. **World Wide Web address:** http://www.lan-inc.com. **Description:** Provides complete architectural, construction management, engineering, planning, and project management. The company also operates within the fields of infrastructure, thermal energy, and transportation. **NOTE:** A completed application must accompany a resume. The application can be downloaded on the company's website. Part-time jobs are offered. **Positions advertised include:** Bridge Design Engineer; Drafter; Electrical Engineer; Facilities Group Manager; Project Manager; Land Development Project Manager; Transportation Planner. **Special programs:** Internships; Summer Jobs. **Corporate headquarters location:** This location. **Other area locations:** Austin TX; Dallas TX; Fort Worth TX; San Antonio TX; Waco TX: San Marcos TX. **Other U.S. locations:** Phoenix AZ, **Parent company:** Leo A. Daly Company. **Listed on:** Privately held.

THE LOFLAND COMPANY
P.O. Box 35466, Dallas TX 75235. 214/631-5250. **Toll-free phone:** 800/288-5250. **Fax:** 213/631-2044. **Contact:** Susan Lane, Human Resources. **E-mail address:** slane@loftlandco.com. **World Wide Web address:** http://www.loflandcompany.com. **Description:** A steel fabricator and distributor of construction materials. **Corporate headquarters location:** This location. **Other area locations:** Fort Worth TX. **Other U.S. locations:** OK; MS; AR; LA. **Operations at this facility include:** Administration; Manufacturing; Sales; Service.

LONE STAR STEEL COMPANY
P.O. Box 803546, Dallas TX 75380-3546. 972/386-3981. **Toll-free phone:** 800/527-4615. **Fax:** 972/770-6409. **Contact:** Human Resources. **World Wide Web address:** http://www.lonestarsteel.com. **Description:** Manufactures steel tubular goods used for oil and gas drilling. **Corporate headquarters location:** This location.

LONG REACH MANUFACTURING COMPANY
P.O. Box 450069, Houston TX 77245-0069. 713/365-1000. **Physical address:** 12300 Amelia Drive, Houston TX 77045. **Toll-free phone:** 800/285-7000. Human Resources. **E-mail address:** hr@alliedsystems.com. **World Wide Web address:** http://www.long-reach.com. **Description:** Engaged in the manufacture of hydraulic forklift attachments. **Positions advertised include:** Electronic Maintenance Technician; Technical Illustrator; Manufacturing Engineer. **Corporate headquarters location:** This location. **Parent company:** Allied Systems Company. **Operations at this facility include:** Administration; Manufacturing; Research and Development; Service; Wholesaling.

LONGVIEW REGIONAL MEDICAL CENTER
P.O. Box 14000, Longview TX 75607. 903/232-3725. **Fax:** 903/232-3888. **Recorded jobline:** 903/232-3726. **Contact:** Human Resources. **World Wide Web address:** http://www.longviewregional.com. **Description:** A 164-bed, acute care, medical center providing cardiovascular, pediatric, dialysis, intensive care, intermediate care, outpatient care, and laboratory services. Founded in 1980. **NOTE:** Entry-level positions, part-time jobs, and second and third shifts are offered. An application is required for any position. An application can be completed or downloaded at the company's website. **Positions advertised include:** Registered Nurse; LPN; Nursing Assistant; Mid-level Provider; Clinical Nutrition Manager; Respiratory Therapist; Emergency Room Technician; Certified Diabetes Educator; Accounting Clerk; Housekeeper; Speech Therapist. **Office hours:** Monday – Thursday, 8:30 a.m. – 4:00 p.m. **Corporate headquarters location:** Dallas TX. **Other U.S. locations:** Nationwide.

LONZA INC.
9700 Bayport Boulevard, Pasadena TX 77507. 281/291-2300. **Contact:** Human Resources. **World Wide Web address:** http://www.lonza.com. **Description:** Manufactures organic intermediates that are used to produce paints, dyes, and pharmaceuticals.

LOOMIS, FARGO & COMPANY
611 South Presa Street, San Antonio TX 78210. 210/226-0195. **Contact:** Human Resources. **World Wide Web address:** http://www.loomisfargo.com. **Description:** Provides armored transportation, cash vault, and ATM services. **NOTE:** This company has locations throughout Texas and the United States. See the company's website for job listings by location and for mailing addresses. **Corporate headquarters location:** Houston TX. **Other U.S. locations:** Nationwide.

LORD & TAYLOR
450 Northpark Center, Dallas TX 75225. 214/691-6600. **Contact:** Human Resources. **World Wide Web address:** http://www.lordandtaylor.com. **Description:** A location of a department store chain carrying clothing, accessories, home furnishings, and a wide range of other items. Founded in 1826. **NOTE:** Part-time jobs are offered. Interested jobseekers may set up interviews online at the company's website. **Positions advertised include:** Sales Associate; Commissioned Sales Associate; Cosmetics Beauty Advisor; Fine Jewelry Associate. **Office hours:** Monday - Friday, 10:00 a.m. - 9:00 p.m. **Corporate headquarters location:** New York NY.

LOUISIANA-PACIFIC CORPORATION
P.O. Box 268, New Waverly TX 77358. 936/295-5471. **Contact:** Human Resources. **World Wide Web address:** http://www.lpcorp.com. **Description:** Louisiana-Pacific Corporation is a building products firm that harvests timber and converts it into a wide range of wood products including lumber, panel products, and doors. The company also manufactures vinyl siding and mouldings. Louisiana-Pacific Corporation operates more than 40 manufacturing facilities in North America. **NOTE:** Jobseekers interested in salaried or management positions must apply online at the company's website. Hourly positions are available by completing an application at the nearest company location. **Other area locations:** Carthage TX; Conroe TX. **Corporate headquarters location:** Portland OR. **Other U.S. locations:** Nationwide. **International locations:** Canada; Chile. **Operations at this facility include:** This location is a sales office. **Listed on:** New York Stock Exchange. **Stock exchange symbol:** LPX. **Number of employees worldwide:** 7,000.

BRUCE LOWRIE CHEVROLET
711 Southwest Loop 820, Fort Worth TX 76134. 817/293-5811. **Toll-free phone:** 800/256-9743. **Contact:** Human Resources. **World Wide Web address:** http://www.brucelowrie.com. **Description:** A new and used car dealership. **NOTE:** A jobseeker may submit a general application online. See company's website for job titles. **Positions advertised include:** New Car and Truck Salesman.

LOWER COLORADO RIVER AUTHORITY CORPORATE HEADQUARTERS
3700 Lake Austin Boulevard, Austin TX 78703. 512/473-3200. **Recorded jobline:** 800/776-5272x3333. **Contact:** Human Resources. **E-mail address:** jobline@lcra.org. **World Wide Web address:** http://www.lcra.org. **Description:** A low-cost electricity supplier to rural customers in the Central Texas region. Manages water utilities and public recreation locations. **NOTE:** Full-time and part-time positions available. Resumes and applications may be mailed, e-mailed or hand-delivered. An application can be downloaded online at the website. **Positions advertised include:** Administrative Associate; Construction Worker/Helper; Senior Accountant; System Reliability Analyst. **Special programs:** Internships; Volunteer.

LUBBOCK AVALANCHE-JOURNAL
P.O. Box 491, Lubbock TX 79408. 806/762-8844. **Contact:** Shelby Caballero, Human Resources Manager. **E-mail address:** Shelby.caballero@lubbockonline.com. **World Wide Web address:** http://www.lubbockonline.com. **Description:** A daily newspaper. The *Lubbock Avalanche-Journal* has a circulation of approximately 67,000 daily and 74,000 on Sundays.

LUBBOCK CHRISTIAN UNIVERSITY
5601 Nineteenth Street, Lubbock TX 79407. 806/720-7215. **Contact:** Human Resources. **E-mail address:** careers@lcu.edu. **World Wide Web address:** http://www.lcu.edu. **Description:** A private institution offering courses in divinity, kinesiology and environmental science. **NOTE:** To apply, mail resume or visit the Human Resources in person in Room 112 of the Administration Building. **Positions advertised include:** Human Resources Director; Continuing Education Specialist.

LUBRICATION ENGINEERS INC.
P.O. Box 7128, Fort Worth TX 76111. 817/834-6321. **Physical address:** 3851 Airport Freeway, Fort Worth TX 76111. Human Resources. **World Wide Web address:** http://www.le-inc.com. **Description:** Produces a variety of industrial lubricants including lubrication oils, greases, transmission fluids, synthetic fuels, and oil supplements. **Positions advertised include:** Sales Representative. **Corporate headquarters location:** This location.

LUBRIZOL CORPORATION
P.O. Box 158, Deer Park TX 77536-0158. 281/479-2851. **Contact:** Human Resources. **World Wide Web address:** http://www.lubrizol.com. **Description:** A diversified specialty chemical company engaged in chemical, mechanical, and genetic research to develop products for transportation, industry, and agriculture. **Corporate headquarters location:** Wickliffe OH. **Operations at this facility include:** Manufacturing plant. **Listed on:** New York Stock Exchange. **Stock exchange symbol:** LZ.

LUBY'S CAFETERIAS
P.O. Box 33069, San Antonio TX 78265. 210/654-9000. **Fax:** 210/225-5750. **Physical address:** 2211 NE Loop 410, San Antonio TX 78217. **Contact:** Human Resources. **E-mail address:** careers@lubys.com. **World Wide Web address:** http://www.lubys.com. **Description:** A national chain restaurant that serves cafeteria-style food. **NOTE:** Hourly positions available. **Positions advertised include:** Restaurant Manager. **Special programs:** Management Training. **Corporate headquarters location:** This location. **Listed on:** New York Stock Exchange. **Stock exchange symbol:** LUB. **Number of employees nationwide:** 11,000.

LUCCHESE BOOT COMPANY
40 Walter Jones Boulevard, El Paso TX 79906. 915/778-3066. **Contact:** Human Resources. **World Wide Web address:** http://www.lucchese.com. **Description:** A manufacturer, retailer, and marketer of men's and women's cowboy boots. **NOTE:** This company also has an outlet store in El Paso TX.

LUCENT TECHNOLOGIES INC.
3000 Skyline Drive, Mesquite TX 75149. 972/284-2000. **Contact:** Human Resources Department. **World Wide Web address:** http://www.lucent.com. **Description:** Lucent Technologies Inc. manufactures communications products including switching, transmission, fiber-optic cable, wireless systems, and operations systems, to supply the needs of telephone companies and other communications services providers. **NOTE:** All interested jobseekers should apply online at the company's website. **Special programs:** Internships; Minority and Women's Recruitment; Early Career Identification. **Corporate headquarters location:** Murray Hill NJ. **Other U.S. locations:** Nationwide. **Operations at this facility include:** This location manufactures electronic power components for the communications industry. **Listed on:** New York Stock Exchange. **Stock exchange symbol:** LU.

LUFKIN INDUSTRIES, INC.
P.O. Box 849, Lufkin TX 75902. 936/634-2211. **Contact:** Viron Barbay. **E-mail address:** vbarbay@Lufkin.com. **World Wide Web address:** http://www.lufkin.com. **Description:** Designs and fabricates gears for power transmission products; iron castings; oil field pumps; and platforms and dump trailers for the over-the-road transportation industry. **Positions advertised include:** Accountant; CNC Machine Operator; Electrician; Electronics Technician; Maintenance Mechanic; Manufacturing Engineer; Welder. **Corporate headquarters location:** This location. **Other area locations:** Houston TX; San Antonio TX. **Other U.S. locations:** LA; AR; TN. **Listed on:** NASDAQ. **Stock exchange symbol:** LUFK.

LUMINEX CORPORATION
12212 Technology Boulevard, Austin TX. 78727-6115. 512/219-8020. **Toll-free phone:** 888/219-8020. **Fax:** 512/219-5195. **Contact:** Human Resources. **World Wide Web address:** http://www.luminexcorp.com. **Description:** Manufacturer of sensor and measurement equipment for biotechnology companies. **NOTE:** Apply online. **Positions advertised include:** Software Quality Assurance Engineer. **Listed on:** NASDAQ. **Stock exchange symbol:** LMNX.

LUMINATOR
1200 East Plano Parkway, Plano TX 75074. 972/424-6511. **Fax:** 972/423-0255. **Contact:** Greg Evans, Human Resources. **World Wide Web address:** http://www.luminatorusa.com. **Description:** Manufactures aircraft parts, bus products, and rail products. Luminator aircraft products include batteries, lamps, searchlights, interiors, and crew stations. Bus products include flip-out signs and voice systems. Rail products include various types of lighting, flip dot sign systems, electronic maps, voice systems, and air diffusers. **Positions advertised include:** Credit Manager; Cost Accountant; Program Manager. **Corporate headquarters location:** This location. **Parent company:** Mark IV Industries.

LUTCHER THEATER FOR THE PERFORMING ARTS
P.O. Box 2310, Orange TX 77631. 409/745-5535. **Toll-free phone:** 800/828-5535. **Contact:** Human Resources. **World Wide Web address:** http://www.lutcher.org. **Description:** A performing arts theater.

LYDA COMPANY
P.O. Box 680907, San Antonio TX 78268. 210/684-1770. **Contact:** Human Resources. **Description:** One of the largest general commercial contractors in Texas. Past projects included the Alamo Dome.

LYNNTECH INC.
3900 State Highway 6, South, College Station TX 77840. 979/694-5255. **Fax:** 979/694-5271. **Contact:** Human Resources. **E-mail address:** hrlynntech@lynntech.com. **World Wide Web address:** http://www.lynntech.com. **Description:** Offers a broad range of research services including environmental and genetic research. Lynntech receives most of its business from government contracts. **Corporate headquarters location:** This location.

LYONDELL CHEMICAL COMPANY
10801 Choate Road, Pasadena TX 77507. 281/474-4191. **Contact:** Human Resources. **World Wide Web address:** http://www.lyondell.com. **Description:** Specializes in the production of propylene derivatives, olefins, and refining chemicals. **NOTE:** This company provides job listings for all its U.S. locations on its website. Interested jobseekers should apply online. **Corporate headquarters location:** Houston TX. **Other area locations:** Beaumont TX; Chocolate Bayou TX; Corpus Christi TX; La Porte TX; Matagorda TX; Victoria TX; Channelview TX; Dallas TX. **Operations at this facility include:** This location is one of the world's leading producers of propylene oxide, propylene glycol, and isobutylene. **Subsidiaries include:** Equistar Chemicals, LP; Lyondell Methanol Company, LP; Lyondell-Citgo Refining Company, Ltd. **Listed on:** New York Stock Exchange. **Stock exchange symbol:** LYO.

M7 AEROSPACE
P.O. Box 790490, San Antonio TX 78279-0490. 210/824-9421. **Fax:** 210/824-9476. **Contact:** Human Resources. **E-mail address:** employment@m7aerospace. **World**

Wide Web address: http://www.m7aerospace.com. **Description:** Manufactures aircraft and provides a wide range of aviation services. **Corporate headquarters location:** This location.

M-I L.L.C.
P.O. Box 42842, Houston TX 77242-2842. 713/739-0222. **Contact:** Human Resources. **World Wide Web address:** http://www.midf.com. **Description:** Manufactures drilling fluid systems and oil field production chemicals.

MKS INSTRUMENTS
3019 Alvin Debane Boulevard, Suite 210, Austin TX 78714. 512/385-1800. **Contact:** Human Resources. **World Wide Web address:** http://www.mksinst.com. **Description:** Manufactures, sells, and services RS generators used in the semiconductor industry. **NOTE:** Interested jobseekers should apply online at the company's website. **Operations at this facility:** Sales; Customer Service. **Listed on:** New York Stock Exchange. **Stock exchange symbol:** MKSI.

MACFARLAN REAL ESTATE
10100 North Central Expressway, Suite 200, Dallas TX 75231. 214/932-3100. **Fax:** 214/932-3199. **Contact:** Human Resources. **E-mail address:** careers@macfarlan.com. **World Wide Web address:** http://www.macfarlan.com. **Description:** A commercial real estate agency. **Corporate headquarters location:** This location.

MADIX INC.
P.O. Box 729, Terrell TX 75160-0729. 972/524-5744. **Contact:** Human Resources. **World Wide Web address:** http://www.madixinc.com. **Description:** A manufacturer of store fixtures such as grocery store shelving.

MAINTENANCE ENGINEERING CORPORATION
3711 Clinton Drive, Houston TX 77020. 713/222-2351. **Toll-free phone:** 800/969-5775. **Contact:** Human Resources. **World Wide Web address:** http://www.mecoonline.com. **Description:** Manufactures and distributes water conditioning chemicals and related products. **Other U.S. locations:** Baton Rouge LA.

MANN & MANN MEDIA SERVICES, INC.
84 NE Loop 410, Suite 126, San Antonio TX 78216. 210/525-8148. **Fax:** 210/525-8246. **Contact:** Wanda Mann, President. **Description:** A media buying firm. Mann & Mann Media Services serves as a negotiator between advertisers and radio and television stations, newspapers, and magazines. Founded in 1986. **Corporate headquarters location:** This location. **Listed on:** Privately held.

MARATHON NORCO AEROSPACE, INC.
P.O. Box 8233, Waco TX 76714-8233. 254/776-0650. **Fax:** 254/776-6558. **Contact:** Human Resources. **World Wide Web address:** http://www.mptc.com. **Description:** Manufactures nickel-cadmium aircraft batteries and electronic assemblies. **Corporate headquarters location:** This location.

THE M/A/R/C GROUP
7700 Bent Branch Drive, Suite 100, Irving TX 75063. 972/506-3901. **Fax:** 972/506-3612. **Contact:** Human Resources. **World Wide Web address:** http://www.marcgroup.com. **Description:** The M/A/R/C Group is a holding company for M/A/R/C Research and Targetbase. M/A/R/C Research (also at this location) specializes in providing strategic customer research for marketing purposes. Targetbase (also at this location) is a customer relationship management firm. **Positions advertised include:** Telephone Interviewer; Senior Strategic Business Analyst. **Other U.S. locations:** Los Angeles CA; Greensboro NC.

MAREK BROTHERS
3539 Oak Forest Drive, Houston TX 77018. 713/681-2626. **Fax:** 713/681-6540. **Contact:** Human Resources. **E-mail address:** info@marekbros.com. **World Wide Web address:** http://www.marekbros.com. **Description:** A construction contractor. Marek Brothers specializes in drywall and insulation installation for residential and office buildings. **Subsidiaries include:** Oak Forest Lumber & Supply; Markek Interior Systems, Inc.; MEMCO.

MARRIOTT SOUTH CENTRAL REGIONAL OFFICE
5151 Beltline Road, Suite 500, Dallas TX 75254. 972/385-1600. **Contact:** Regional Director. **World Wide Web address:** http://www.marriott.com. **Description:** Marriott Corporation is a nationwide, diversified food service, retail merchandising, and hospitality company, doing business in more than 25 U.S. airports, as well as operating restaurants under various names nationwide. **NOTE:** This company's website has job listings for all its Texas locations. Interested jobseekers should apply online. **Special programs:** Internships. **Corporate headquarters location:** Washington DC. **Operations at this facility include:** This location houses the regional office for the hotel chain. **Listed on:** New York Stock Exchange. **Stock exchange symbol:** MAR.

MARSH USA, INC.
1000 Louisiana Street, Suite 4000, Houston TX 77002. 713/654-0400. **Contact:** Human Resources. **World Wide Web address:** http://www.marsh.com. **Description:** Provides advice and services worldwide to clients concerned with the management of assets and risks. Specific services include insurance and risk management services, reinsurance, consulting and financial services, merchandising, and investment management. The company has subsidiaries and affiliates in 57 countries, with correspondents in 20 other countries. **NOTE:** This company has offices throughout Texas and the United States. See its website for a complete list. Resumes must be submitted online. **Corporate headquarters location:** New York NY. **Parent company:** Marsh & McLennan Companies (MMC). **Listed on:** New York Stock Exchange. **Stock exchange symbol:** MMC.

MARTIN LUTHER HOMES OF TEXAS INC.
332 South Loop 123 Business, Suite 400, Seguin TX 78155. 830/372-3075. **Contact:** Human Resources. **World Wide Web address:** http://www.mosiacinfo.org. **Description:** An agency that provides housing and support services for individuals with mental retardation. This company is now part of Mosaic, an organization created by the Lutheran Church.

MARTIN MARIETTA MATERIALS
4243 North FM 1604 West, San Antonio TX 78257. 210/696-8500. **Contact:** Human Resources. **World Wide Web address:** http://www.martinmarietta.com. **Description:** Martin Marietta Materials produces a wide variety of construction aggregates and related materials. **Corporate headquarters location:** Raleigh NC. **Operations at this facility include:** This location is a surface mining company that manufactures products including limestone, base materials, and asphalt. **Listed on:** New York Stock Exchange. **Stock exchange symbol:** MLM.

MARTIN SPROCKET & GEAR INC.
3100 Sprocket Drive, Arlington TX 76015. 817/467-5181. **Contact:** Human Resources. **E-mail:** mail@martinsprocket.com. **World Wide Web address:** http://www.martinsprocket.com. **Description:** Manufactures metal and plastic moldings and products for power transmissions and conveyor belts. **NOTE:** Interested jobseekers may apply by mailing or emailing a resume to the corporate office or by visiting the nearest location. For a list of Texas locations and office hours, see the company's website. **Corporate headquarters location:** This location. **Other U.S. locations:** Nationwide. **Listed on:** Privately held.

MARTINAIRE INC.
4745 Frank Luke Drive, Addison TX 75001. 972/349-5700. **Fax:** 972/349-5750. **Contact:** Tony Holcomb, Maintenance Director. **E-mail address:** tholcomb@martinaire.com. **World Wide Web address:** http://www.martinaire.com. **Description:** An air cargo carrier operating a fleet of 20 aircraft. **Positions advertised include:** Pilot.

MARY KAY, INC.
P.O. Box 799045, Dallas TX 75379. 972/687-5266. **Contact:** Human Resources. **World Wide Web address:** http://www.marykay.com. **Description:** Manufactures and distributes cosmetics and other health and beauty aids. In addition to its corporate headquarters in Dallas, this company produces and develops its products in Texas. Mary Kay distributes its cosmetics through its 300,000 direct sales consultants across worldwide. **NOTE:** Jobseekers interested in sales positions should call 800/627-9529. **Positions advertised include:** Brand Development Director; Project Manager Internal Audit; Senior Print Producer; Senior Analyst Programmer; Market Research Manager.

MASSEY CADILLAC
11675 LBJ Freeway, Garland TX 75047. 214/348-2211. **Contact:** Human Resources. **World Wide Web address:** http://www.masseycadillacdallas.com. **Description:** A new and used auto dealership. Massey Cadillac also offers maintenance and repair services.

MATAGORDA GENERAL HOSPITAL
1115 Avenue G, Bay City TX 77414. 979/241-6690. **Recorded jobline:** 979/241-6695. **Contact:** Human Resources. **Description:** A full-service hospital offering outpatient diagnostic service facilities. This hospital is part of Matagorda County Hospital District, which includes an assisted living facility; an independent living facility; a women's health center, a public clinic and a clinic for low-income mothers and babies. **Positions advertised include:** RN; Certified Respiratory Therapy Technician; Radiologist Technologist; Medical Staff Coordinator.

MAURITZ AND COUEY
102 South Mechanic Street, El Paso TX 77437. 979/543-3922. **Fax:** 979/244-5070. **Contact:** Human Resources. **Description:** A marketer of petroleum products to commercial locations and convenience stores. **Other area locations:** El Campo, TX; Edna TX; Ganado TX; Port Lavaca TX.

MATTRESS GIANT
14655 Midway Road, Addison TX. 75001. 972/393-2202. **Toll-free phone:** 800/442-6823. **Contact:** Human Resources. **World Wide Web address:** http://www.mattressgiant.com. **Description:** With more than 250 stores nationwide, Mattress Giant is a leading retailer of bedding. **NOTE:** Part-time positions offered. Apply online. **Positions advertised include:** Sales Professionals; Store Porter.

MAYFLOWER TRANSIT, LLC
1735 West Crosby Road, Carrolton TX 75006. 972/466-1111. **Toll-free phone:** 800/648-7825. **Fax:** 972/233-3921. **Contact:** Human Resources. **World Wide Web address:** http://www.mayflower.com. **Description:** Offers a full range of moving and storage services to both commercial and individual customers. **Positions advertised include:** Driver. **Parent company:** Unigroup Inc.

MCALLEN MEDICAL CENTER
301 West Expressway 83, McAllen TX 78503. 956/632-4000. **Contact:** Human Resources. **World Wide Web address:** http://www.mcallenmedicalcenter.com. **Description:** Part of the South Texas Health System, a full-service acute care hospital. The medical center has a well-known heart hospital, too. **NOTE:** Apply online for open positions. **Parent company:** Universal Health Network.

MCDONALD FINANCIAL CORPORATION
1616 South Voss Road, Suite 870, Houston TX 77207. 713/977-2113. **Fax:** 713/977-4055. **Contact:** Human Resources. **World Wide Web address:** http://www.mcdonaldfinancial.com. **Description:** MFC Finance Company provides financing for construction.

McGRAW-HILL COMPANIES
220 East Danieldale Road, De Soto TX 75115. 972/224-1111. **Contact:** Human Resources. **World Wide Web address:** http://www.mcgraw-hill.com. **Description:** McGraw-Hill is a provider of information and services through books, magazines, newsletters, software, CD-ROMs, online data, fax, and TV broadcasting services. The company operates four network-affiliated TV stations and also publishes *Business Week* magazine and books for college, medical, international, legal, and professional markets. McGraw-Hill also offers financial services including Standard & Poor's, commodity items, and international and logistics management products and services. **Positions advertised includes:** Field Marketing Services Director; Order Entry Operator; Field Marketing Manager. **Other area locations:** Houston TX; Dallas TX; Fort Worth TX; San Antonio TX. **Other U.S. locations:** Nationwide. **International locations:** Worldwide. **Operations at this facility include:** This location publishes textbooks. **Listed on:** New York Stock Exchange. **Stock exchange symbol:** MHP.

McGRAW-HILL COMPANIES
333 Clay Street, Suite 3800, Houston TX 77002-4000. 713/658-9261. **Contact:** Human Resources. **World Wide Web address:** http://www.mcgraw-hill.com. **Description:** McGraw-Hill is a provider of information and services through books, magazines, newsletters, software, CD-ROMs, online data, fax, and TV broadcasting services. The company operates four network-affiliated TV stations and also publishes *Business Week* magazine and books for college, medical, international, legal, and professional markets. McGraw-Hill also offers financial services including Standard & Poor's, commodity items, and international and logistics management products and services. **Positions advertised includes:** Sales Representative. **Other area locations:** De Soto TX; Dallas TX; Fort Worth TX; San Antonio TX. **Other U.S. locations:** Nationwide. **International locations:** Worldwide. **Operations at this facility include:** This location publishes energy information and services. **Listed on:** New York Stock Exchange. **Stock exchange symbol:** MHP.

MCLANE COMPANY, INC.
4747 McLane Parkway, Temple TX 76504. 254/771-7500. **Toll-free phone:** 800/299-1401. **Fax:** 254/771-7244. **Contact:** Human Resources. **World Wide Web address:** http://www.mclaneco.com. **Description:** Major distributor of wholesale foods and non-perishable items. Also produces its own food products for distribution. **NOTE:** This company and its subsidiaries have several locations throughout Texas. See website for job listings and locations and apply online. **Positions advertised include:** Compensation Analyst; Dispatcher; Executive Secretary; Industrial Engineer; Internal Auditor; Logistics Analyst; National Account Sales Secretary. Subsidiaries include: McLane Grocery Distribution; McLane Foodservice Distribution; McLane Information Systems; Professional Datasolutions, Inc, Vantix Logistics.

McKENNA MEMORIAL HOSPITAL
600 North Union Avenue, New Braunfels TX 78130. 830/606-9111. **Recorded jobline:** 830/606-2151. **Contact:** Human Resources Coordinator. **E-mail address:** hr@mckenna.org. **World Wide Web address:** http://www.mckenna.org. **Description:** A 116-bed, short-term care hospital. McKenna Memorial Hospital also offers an occupational health department. **NOTE:** An application must submitted for any position. The application can be obtained at the company's website. **Positions advertised include:** Coder; Care Coordinator; Parenting Instructor; Medical Technologist; Clinical Recruiter; Occupational Therapist; Monitor Technician; RN; LVN; Ultrasound Technician; Radiology Technician; Respiratory Therapist.

McMURRY UNIVERSITY
McMurry Station, P.O. Box 308, Abilene TX 79697. 915/793-3800. **Contact:** Human Resources. **World Wide Web address:** http://www.mcm.edu. **Description:** A four-year university offering undergraduate degrees. Approximately 1,425 students attend McMurry University **NOTE:** This company lists all job listings and specific contact information on its website. **Positions advertised include:** Instructor; Night Custodian; Assistant Professor.

McNEIL CONSUMER & SPECIALTY PHARMACEUTICALS
4001 North Interstate Highway 35, Round Rock TX 78664. 512/255-4111. **Contact:** Human Resources. **Description:** A scientific research and development company that is also involved in the manufacturing of pharmaceutical products. McNeil is a subsidiary of Johnson and Johnson. **NOTE:** Interested jobseekers should apply online at Johnson and Johnson's corporate website: http://www.jnj.com/careers.

MEADWESTVACO
5215 North O'Connor Boulevard, Suite 200, Irving TX 75039. 972/868-9060. **Contact:** Human Resources. **World Wide Web address:** http://www.meadwestvaco.com. **Description:** MeadWestvaco manufactures, sells, and markets pulp, paper, paperboard, shipping containers, packaging, lumber, school supplies, office supplies, stationery products, and electronic publishing and information retrieval systems. **Operations at this facility include:** This location is a sales office. **Listed on:** New York Stock Exchange. **Stock exchange symbol:** MWV.

MEDICAL CENTER HOSPITAL/ODESSA
500 West Fourth Street, Odessa TX 79761. 915/640-4000. **Fax:** 915/640-1245. **Contact:** Candy Powell RN, Recruitment/Retention Coordinator. **E-mail address:** lmelson@echd.org. **World Wide Web address:** http://www.odessamch.org. **Description:** A 396-bed, acute care hospital. Medical Center Hospital provides various services including a neonatal care nursery, skilled nursing facility, Intensive Care Unit, Critical Care Unit, and 24-hour emergency care. **NOTE:** An application must be submitted for any position. See company's website for application **Positions advertised include:** Charge RN; Unit Clerk; Divisional Director; Paramedic.

THE MEDICAL CENTER OF MESQUITE
1011 North Galloway Street, Mesquite TX 75149. 214/320-7000. **Fax:** 324/889-7970. **Contact:** Human Resources. **World Wide Web address:** http://www.hma-corp.com/tx1.html. **Description:** Full-service acute care 176-bed hospital operated by Health Management Associates, Inc. **NOTE:** Search for positions online.

MEDICAL CENTER OF PLANO
3901 West 15th Street, Plano TX 75075. 972/596-6800. **Contact:** Human Resources. **World Wide Web address:** http://www.medicalcenterofplano.com. **Description:** A 400-bed medical center providing acute and residential care. **NOTE:** Interested jobseekers must apply online at the company's website.

MEDICAL CITY DALLAS HOSPITAL
7777 Forest Lane, Building B, Suite D-250, Dallas TX 75230. 972/566-7070. **Toll-free phone:** 800/224-4733. **Contact:** Human Resources. **World Wide Web address:** http://www.medicalcityhospital.com. **Description:** A full-service hospital. **NOTE:** Interested jobseekers must apply online at the company's website.

MEGGER
4271 Bronze Way, Dallas TX 75237. 214/333-3201. **Fax:** 214/331-7399. **Contact:** Human Resources. **World Wide Web address:** http://www.megger.com/us.com. **Description:** Manufactures test equipment and measurement instruments for electric power applications. **Positions advertised include:** Electrical Safety Engineer; Bilingual International Sales Specialist. **Corporate headquarters location:** This location. **Other U.S. locations:** Norristown PA. **International locations:** Worldwide.

MEMORIAL HERMANN/MEMORIAL CITY HOSPITAL
920 Frostwood, Houston TX 77024. 713/932-3000. **Fax:** 713/932-3627. **Contact:** Human Resources. **World Wide Web address:** http://www.mhhs.org. **Description:** An acute care general hospital. This hospital is part of a group of 11 medical facilities in the Houston area. **Positions advertised include:** Coding Manager; Dietician; Medical Technologist; OR Attendant; Pharmacist; Radiology Technologist.

MEN'S WEARHOUSE
5803 Glenmont Drive, Houston TX 77081. 713/664-3692. **Contact:** Human Resources Department. **World Wide Web address:** http://www.menswearhouse.com. **Description:** One of the largest off-price retailers of men's tailored business attire in the United States. The stores offer designer brand-name and private-label suits, sports jackets, slacks, dress shirts, and accessories at discount prices. This company has retail locations throughout Texas. **Positions advertised include:** Operations Manager; Customer Service Assistant; Wardrobe Consultant; Tailor, Store Manager; Professional Truck Driver. **Corporate headquarters location:** This location. **Other U.S. locations:** Nationwide. **International locations:** Canada. **Listed on:** New York Stock Exchange. **Stock exchange symbol:** MW.

MENSOR CORPORATION
201 Barnes Drive, San Marcos TX 78666-5917. 512/396-4200. **Fax:** 512/396-1820. **Contact:** Human Resources. **World Wide Web address:** http://www.mensor.com. **Description:** Manufactures precision instruments and pressure systems.

MERCER MANAGEMENT CONSULTING
3500 Chase Tower, 2200 Ross Avenue, Dallas TX 75201. 214/758-1880. **Contact:** Human Resources. **E-mail address:** careers@mercermc.com. **World Wide Web address:** http://www.mercermc.com. **Description:** Provides strategy and management consulting services. **NOTE:** Interested jobseekers may apply online at the company's website or by mailing their resumes to the company's Boston office at John Hancock Tower, 200 Clarendon Street, 12th Floor, Boston MA 02116. **Positions advertised include:** Principal; Senior Associate; Associate; Consultant; Analyst.

MERCHANTS METALS
3838 North Sam Houston Parkway E., Suite 600, Houston TX 77032-3418. 281/372-3800. **Toll-free phone:** 866/888-5611. **Contact:** Human Resources. **World Wide Web address:** http://www.merchantsmetals.com. **Description:** A manufacturer and distributor of wire and fabricated steel. **NOTE:** This company has several locations in Texas and across the United States. See the company's website for locations and mailing addresses.

MERISOL
11821 East Freeway, Houston TX 77029. 713/428-5400. **Contact:** Human Resources. **World Wide Web address:** http://www.merisol.com. **Description:** Manufactures water conditioning chemicals used in cooling towers and boiler treatments. **Operations at this facility include:** Sales.

MERIT MEDICAL
1111 South Velasco Street, Angleton TX 77515. 979/848-5000. **Contact:** Human Resources. **E-mail address:** recruiting@merit.com. **World Wide Web address:** http://www.merit.com. **Description:** Provides technologically advanced, cost-effective products and services to five medical specialties: anesthesiology, cardiology, critical care, nuclear medicine, and radiology. **Positions advertised include:** Engineer; Senior Process Engineer; Senior Manufacturing Engineer. **Listed on:** NASDAQ. **Stock exchange symbol:** MMSI.

MERRILL LYNCH
701 South Taylor Street, Suite 100, Amarillo TX 79101. 806/376-4861. **Contact:** Human Resources. **World Wide Web address:** http://www.ml.com. **Description:** Brokers in securities, option contracts, commodities, financial futures contracts, and insurance. **NOTE:** Interested jobseekers must apply online at the corporate website. **Positions advertised include:** Commercial Banking Professionals; Financial Advisor. **Other U.S. locations:** Nationwide. **Listed on:** New York Stock Exchange. **Stock exchange symbol:** MER.

MESA HILLS SPECIALTY HOSPITAL
2311 North Oregon Street, Fifth Floor, El Paso TX 79902. 915/545-1823. **Contact:** Jill Doire, Divisional Recruiter. **World Wide Web address:** http://www.tricare.com. **Description:** A 181-bed long-term, acute care hospital. Parent company: Trans Healthcare.

MESQUITE COMMUNITY HOSPITAL
3500 Interstate 30, Mesquite TX 75150. 972/698-3300. **Fax:** 972/698-2580. **Recorded jobline:** 972/698-2463. **Contact:** Human Resources. **World Wide Web address:** http://www.mchtx.com. **Description:** A hospital with 172 beds. Founded in 1978. **Positions advertised include:** RN; Buyer; Radiologist; Respiratory Therapist; Risk Manager.

MESQUITE SOFTWARE, INC.
8500 North Mopac, Suite 825, Austin TX 78759. 512/338-9153. **Contact:** Human Resources. **World Wide Web address:** http://www.mesquite.com. **Description:** Develops software and provides support services for the system simulation market. The company's product line includes CSIM18-The Simulation Engine. **Corporate headquarters location:** This location.

METALS USA , INC.
One Riverway, Suite 1100, Houston TX 77056. 713/965-0990. **Toll-free phone:** 888/871-8701. **Fax:** 713/965-0067. **Contact:** Human Resources. **World Wide Web address:** http://www.metalsusa.com. **Description:** Manufactures aluminum. Founded in 1954. **Corporate headquarters location:** This location. **Listed on:** NASDQ. **Stock exchange symbol:** MUSA.

THE METHODIST HOSPITAL
6600 Fannin, Suite 903, Houston TX 77030. 713/394-6614. **Fax:** 713/793-7128. **Contact:** Human Resources. **World Wide Web address:** http://www.methodisthealth.com. **Description:** A full-service hospital. It is part of a group of three other hospitals in the Houston area. The Methodist Hospital is also the primary teaching hospital for the Baylor College of Medicine. **NOTE:** All resumes must be submitted with a completed application which can be found online at the hospital's website. **Positions advertised include:** Unit Secretary; Program Development Specialist; Orthopedic Technician; Patient Care Assistant; Physical Therapist; Blood Donor; RN; Service Line Marketing Director. **Corporate headquarters location:** This location. **Parent company:** Methodist Health Care System.

METHODIST DALLAS MEDICAL CENTER
1441 North Beckley Avenue, Dallas TX 75203. 214/947-6510. **Contact:** Human Resources. **World Wide Web address:** http://www.methodisthealthsystem.com. **Description:** An acute care medical center licensed for 478 beds. This medical center has units for organ transplants and trauma. **Positions advertised include:** Assistant Director; Audit Specialist; Capital Project Coordinator; Community-Based Case Manager; Director; Echo Technician; Nurse Manager; Pharmacy Technician, Quality Coordinator, RN.

METHODIST SPECIALTY AND TRANSPLANT HOSPITAL
8026 Floyd Curl Drive, San Antonio TX 78229. 210/575-8110. **Recorded jobline:** 210/575-4562. **Contact:** Human Resources. **World Wide Web address:** http://www.mhshealth.com. **Description:** A 382-bed, licensed medical facility specializing in organ and tissue transplants, impotency treatments, incontinence treatments, gastroenteric procedures, and laparoscopic surgery. **NOTE:** Interested jobseekers may apply online at the company's website. **Positions advertised include:** Activity Therapist; Ancillary Support Technician; Diet Clerk; Echo Technician; LVN; RN: Physical Therapist.

METROMEDIA RESTAURANT GROUP
6500 International Parkway, Suite 1000, Plano TX 75093. 972/588-5000. **Fax:** 972/588-5467. **Contact:** Human Resources Manager. **World Wide Web address:** http://www.metromediarestaurants.com. **Description:** One of the largest, full-service, restaurant chain operators in the nation. The company operates nearly 1,000 restaurants in 45 states and two countries including Bennigan's, Bonanza, Ponderosa, And Steak and Ale. **NOTE:** Jobseekers interested in management or hourly positions at specific

restaurants should contact the locations or see the chains' separate websites. **Corporate headquarters location:** This location. **Operations at this facility include:** Accounting; Sales; Guest Relations; Public Relations. **Listed on:** Privately held.

METROPOLITAN METHODIST HOSPITAL
1310 McCullough Avenue, San Antonio TX 78212. 210/208-2200. **Fax:** 210/208-2924. **Recorded jobline:** 210/575-4562. **Contact:** Human Resources. **World Wide Web address:** http://www.metro.sahealth.com. **Description:** A 263-bed hospital that offers both long-term and short-term care. This hospital is part of the Methodist Healthcare System. **NOTE:** Interested jobseekers must complete an application which can be found on the company's website. **Positions advertised include:** Coding/Compliance Manager; Data Entry Clerk; Decentralized Pediatric Pharmacist; Histology Technician; Radiologist.

METROWERKS INC.
7700 West Parmer Lane, Austin TX 78729. 512/996-5300. **Fax:** 512/996-4910. **Contact:** Human Resources. **World Wide Web address:** http://www.metrowerks.com. **Description:** Develops and markets software development and programming tools for computers, Internet, and wireless applications as well as games. Founded in 1985. **Corporate headquarters location:** This location. **Other U.S. locations:** CA; MA; WA: UT; TX. **International locations:** Worldwide.

MICHAEL'S STORES, INC.
P.O. Box 619566, Dallas TX 75261-9566. 972/409-1300. **Physical address:** 8000 Bent Branch Drive, Irving TX 75063. **Contact:** Human Resources. **World Wide Web address:** http://www.michaels.com. **Description:** A nationwide specialty retailer of art, crafts, and decorative items and supplies, offering over 40,000 items, from picture framing materials to seasonal and holiday merchandise. Michael's Stores operates 628 stores in 48 states, Canada, and Puerto Rico. **NOTE:** Jobseekers interested in hourly positions should apply at the nearest store. **Positions advertised include:** Training Designer; Construction Coordinator; Associate Buyer; Human Resources Generalist; Field Recruitment Manager; Administrative Assistant; Set-up Coordinator; Senior Program Analyst. **Corporate headquarters location:** This location. **Listed on:** New York Stock Exchange. **Stock exchange symbol:** MIK.

MICRO COMPUTER SYSTEMS INC.
6335 North State Highway 161, Irving TX 75039-2402. 214/262-3530. **Fax:** 214/262-3531. **Contact:** Human Resources. **World Wide Web address:** http://www.mcsdallas.com. **Description:** Develops software including Local Area Network (LAN) communication systems and configuration utilities for EISA computers. This company also designs websites. **Parent company:** NEC America.

MID-JEFFERSON HOSPITAL
2630 Highway 365, Nederland TX 77627. 409//721-3183. **Contact:** Human Resources. **World Wide Web address:** http://www.midjeffersonhospital.com. **Description:** A full-service hospital with specialized outpatient facilities. **NOTE:** Park Place Medical Center is a sister hospital of Mid-Jefferson and is nearby. For job listings, visit its website at http://www.parkplacemediccalcenter.com. **Positions advertised include:** RN: LVN; Pharmacist. **Corporate headquarters location:** Franklin TN. **Parent company:** Iasis Healthcare. **Listed on:** Privately held.

MIDLAND MEMORIAL HOSPITAL
2200 West Illinois Avenue, Midland TX 79701. 432/685-1111. **Contact:** Maria McAllister, Human Resources Director. **World Wide Web address:** http://www.midland-memorial.com. **Description:** A full-service, 300-bed health facility. Midland Memorial is part of a group of three hospitals serving the Midland area. The other hospitals are Memorial West and Memorial Rehabilitation **NOTE:** Interested jobseekers must complete an application for all positions. The application can be found on the company's website. **Positions advertised include:** RN; Respiratory Care Technician; Human Resources Assistant; Paramedic; Nuclear Medicine Technician; Physical Therapist.

MIDWESTERN STATE UNIVERSITY
3410 Taft Boulevard, Wichita Falls TX 76308. 940/397-4221. **Fax:** 940/397-4780. **Contact:** Jane Wolf, Human Resources. **E-mail address:** jane.wolf@mwsu.edu. **World Wide Web address:** http://www.mwsu.edu. **Description:** A state university with approximately 6,000 students enrolled in its undergraduate and graduate degree programs. **NOTE:** Interested jobseekers should see the university's website for listings and specific contact information. **Positions advertised include:** Admissions Assistant II; Custodian I; Intensive English Language Institute. **Corporate headquarters location:** This location.

MIILLE APPLIED RESEARCH COMPANY
1730 South Richey, Pasadena TX 77502. 713/472-6272. **Fax:** 713/472-0318. **Contact:** Human Resources. **World Wide Web address:** http://www.miille.com. **Description:** Manufactures and distributes modems and protocol converters for computers.

MILLER BREWING COMPANY
7001 South Freeway, Fort Worth TX 76134. 817/551-3200. **Contact:** Human Resources. **World Wide Web address:** http://www.millerbrewing.com. **Description:** Miller Brewing Company produces and distributes beer and other malt beverages. Principal beer brands include Miller Lite, Lite Ice, Miller Genuine Draft, Miller Genuine Draft Light, Miller High Life, Miller Reserve, Lowenbrau, Milwaukee's Best, Meister Brau, Red Dog, and Icehouse. Miller also produces Sharp's, a nonalcoholic beer. **NOTE:** Interested jobseekers may apply in person at this location or online at the company's website. **Corporate headquarters location:** Milwaukee WI. **Operations at this facility include:** This location brews a variety of beer brands. **Subsidiaries include:** Jacob Leinenkugel Brewing Company (Chippewa Falls WI) brews Leinenkugel's Original Premium, Leinenkugel's Light, Leinie's Ice, Leinenkugel's Limited, Leinenkugel's Red Lager, and four seasonal beers: Leinenkugel's Genuine Bock, Leinenkugel's Honey Weiss, Leinenkugel's Autumn Gold, and Leinenkugel's Winter Lager. Molson Breweries U.S.A., Inc. (Reston VA) imports Molson beers from Canada, as well as Australia's Foster's Lager and many other brands. Miller is also majority owner of Celis Brewery Inc. (Austin TX). **Parent company:** Philip Morris Companies Inc. (New York). **Listed on:** New York Stock Exchange. **Stock exchange symbol:** MO.

MINYARD FOOD STORES, INC.
777 Freeport Parkway, Coppell TX 75019. 972/393-8333. **Fax:** 972/304-3828. **Contact:** Human Resources. **E-mail address:** jobs@minyards.com. **World Wide Web address:** http://www.minyards.com. **Description:** A retail grocery chain with more than 70 stores. Stores include Minyard Food Stores, Sack 'n Save, and Carnival Food Stores. **NOTE:** Jobseekers interested in management or corporate positions should submit their resumes to the home office in Coppell. For store positions, jobseekers should visit the nearest location to complete an application. **Office hours:** Monday – Friday; 9:00 a.m. – 4:30 p.m. **Corporate headquarters location:** This location. **Listed on:** Privately held.

FRED MISKO, JR., P.C.
3811 Turtle Creek Boulevard, Suite 1000, Dallas TX 75219. 214/443-8000. **Toll-free phone:** 800/443-8088. **Contact:** Human Resources. **World Wide Web address:** http://www.misko.com. **Description:** A trial practice specializing in class action and personal injury law.

MISSION HOSPITAL, INC.
900 South Bryan Road, Mission TX 78572. 956/580-9188. **Contact:** Marissa Aldrete, Hospital Recruiter at 956/584-4683. . **E-mail address:** maldrete@missionhospital.org. **World Wide Web address:** http://www.missionhospital.org. **Description:** A 138-bed acute care facility. **Positions advertised include:** Respiratory Therapist; Registered Nurse; Radiology Technician; Registration Representative. **Operations at this facility include:** Health Care; Service.

MISSION RESOURCES
1331 Lamar, Suite 1455, Houston TX 77010. 713/495-3000. **Contact:** Leslee Ranly, Human Resources Director. **E-mail address:** humanresources@mrcorp.com. **World Wide Web address:** http://www.mrcorp.com. **Description:** Engaged in the development, exploration, and production of oil and gas properties in the Gulf Coast region. **Listed on:** NASDAQ. **Stock exchange symbol:** MSSN.

MISYS HEALTHCARE SYSTEMS
2020 North Loop West, Suite 140, Houston TX 77018. 713/688-3181. **Contact:** Human Resources. **World Wide Web address:** http://www.misyshealthcare.com. **Description:** Develops health care management software. Products include +Medic Vision, +Medic PM, Auto Chart, AutoImage, and FasTracker. **NOTE:** Please send resumes to: MISYS Healthcare Systems, Human Resources, 8529 Six Forks Road, Raleigh NC 27615. **Operations at this facility include:** This location is a sales and engineering facility.

MODIS, INC.
1235 North Loop West, Suite 1100, Houston TX 77008. 713/880-0232. **Contact:** Human Resources. **World Wide Web address:** http://www.modisit.com. **Description:** Provides a wide range of computer consulting services. **Corporate headquarters location:** Jacksonville FL. **Parent company:** MPS Group. **Listed on:** New York Stock Exchange. **Stock exchange symbol:** MPS.

MOHAWK LABORATORIES
2727 Chemsearch Boulevard, Irving TX 75062. 972/438-0226. **Contact:** Human Resources. **World Wide Web address:** http://www.nch.com. **Description:** Operates laboratories that manufacture specialty cleaning and polishing chemicals. **NOTE:** Resumes should be sent to NCH Corporation, Human Resources Department, 2727 Chemsearch Boulevard, Irving TX 75062. **Parent company:** NCH.

MONARCH PAINT COMPANY
4220 Lock Field, Houston TX 77092. 713/680-2799. **Contact:** Human Resources. **World Wide Web address:** http://www.monarchpaint.com. **Description:** Manufactures and distributes paints, resins, and spray equipment.

MOORE SUPPLY COMPANY
P.O. Box 448, 200 West Loop 336 North, Conroe TX 77305. 936/756-4445. **Fax:** 936/441-8468. **Contact:** Human Resources. **World Wide Web address:** http://www.mooresupply.com. **Description:** Engaged in the retail and wholesale of plumbing supplies, lavatory supplies, tubs, and toilets. **NOTE:** This company has retail and warehouse locations throughout Texas. For warehouse positions, contact Ross Ryon at 214/351-6411. For management positions, contact Karen Landry at kvlandry@lcr-m.com or at 800/888-9915x4214. **Operations at this facility include:** Administration.

MORGAN
P.O. Box 660280, Dallas TX 75266-0280. 972/864-7300. **Physical address:** 2780 McCree Road, Garland TX 75041. **Fax:** 972/864-7316. **Contact:** Human Resources. **World Wide Web address:** http://www.morganusa.com. **Description:** Manufactures, transports, and retails re-locatable buildings, spas, recreational vehicles, swimming pools, and decks to consumers, businesses, government buyers, and institutional buyers. **NOTE:** This company has retail locations throughout Texas. Interested jobseekers should consult its website for listings. For sales and office positions, contact Leslie McLeod, at lmcleod@morganusa.com. For all other positions, e-mail resumes to S. Morgan at smorgan@morganusa.com. **Positions advertised include:** Traveling Operational Inventory Auditor; Administrative Assistant (Customer Service); Inside Sales; Spa Technicians; Dispatchers; Yard Foremen; Clerical; Receptionists. **Corporate headquarters location:** This location. **Other U.S. locations:** AL; AR; CO; GA; LA; MO; MS; NM; OK; TN. **Operations at this facility include:** Administration. **Listed on:** Privately held.

MORRISON SUPPLY COMPANY
311 East Vickery Boulevard, Fort Worth TX 76104. 817/336-0451. **Contact:** Charles Allen, Human Resources Manager. **World Wide Web address:** http://www.morsco.com. **Description:** A wholesaler of plumbing and heating equipment, tools, and supplies. **Corporate headquarters location:** This location.

MOTHERAL PRINTING COMPANY
510 South Main Street, Fort Worth TX 76104. 817/335-1481. **Contact:** Human Resources. **World Wide Web address:** http://www.motheral.com. **Description:** A commercial lithography and printing company. **Special programs:** Internships. **Corporate headquarters location:** This location. **Operations at this facility include:** Administration; Manufacturing; Sales.

MOTIVA ENTERPRISES
1100 Louisiana, P.O. Box 4453, Houston TX 77002. 713/277-8000. **Contact:** Human Resources. **World Wide Web address:** http://www.motivaenterprises.com. **Description:** Engaged in the offshore drilling of oil off the Gulf and East Coasts of the United States. **NOTE:** Graduates must submit applications and provide other documentation with resumes. For a complete list of job requirements, visit http://www.shell.com. Professionals must submit resumes online at the same website. **Parent company:** Shell Company and Saudi Refining, Inc.

MOTOROLA, INC.
5555 North Beach Street, Fort Worth TX 76137. 817/245-6000. **Contact:** Human Resources. **World Wide Web address:** http://www.mot.com. **Description:** Motorola manufactures communications equipment and electronic products including car radios, cellular phones, semiconductors, computer systems, cellular infrastructure equipment, pagers, cordless phones, and LAN systems. **NOTE:** Motorola has offices throughout Texas and all job listings are available on its website. **Special programs:** Internships. **Corporate headquarters location:** Schaumburg IL. **Other area locations:** Austin TX; Brownsville, TX; Richardson TX; Seguin TX. **Other U.S. locations:** Nationwide. **International locations:** Worldwide. **Operations at this facility include:** This

location manufactures pagers. **Listed on:** New York Stock Exchange. **Stock exchange symbol:** MOT. **Number of employees worldwide:** 111,000.

MRS. BAIRD'S BAKERIES
P.O. Box 937, Fort Worth TX 76101. 214/526-7201. **Contact:** Human Resources. **World Wide Web address:** http://www.mrsbairds.com. **Description:** Bakes bread and other goods. The company operates facilities located throughout Texas. **Parent company:** Bimbo Bakeries USA.

MUR-TEX FIBERGLASS
P.O. Box 31240, Amarillo TX 79120. 806/373-7418. **Toll-free phone:** 800/299-7418. **Fax:** 806/373-9448. **Contact:** Human Resources. **World Wide Web address:** http://www.mur-tex. com. **Description:** Manufactures fiberglass tanks for industrial usage. **Corporate headquarters location:** This location.

THE MUSEUM OF FINE ARTS - HOUSTON
1001 Bissonnet, Houston TX 77005. 713/639-7560. **Fax:** 713/639-7597. **Recorded jobline:** 713/639-7888. **Contact:** Human Resources. **World Wide Web address:** http://www.mfah.org. **Description:** An art museum with exhibits including The Glassell Collection of African Gold, Art of Asia, and Modern and Contemporary Art. **NOTE:** Interested jobseekers must complete an employment profile online at the museum's website. **Positions advertised include:** Administrative Assistant; Assistant Archivist; Cataloger; Library Director; Program Coordinator; Education Manager; Assistant Register; Security Officer. **Special programs:** Internships. **Corporate headquarters location:** This location. **Number of employees at this location:** 600.

MUSTANG ENGINEERING
16001 Park 10 Place, Houston TX 77084. 713/215-8000. **Fax:** 713/215-8506. **Contact:** Human Resources. **E-mail address:** human.resources@mustangeng.com. **World Wide Web address:** http://www.mustangeng.com. **Description:** An engineering firm that specializes in offshore structures, pipeline systems and services, process plant facilities, environmental services, and process automation and control for the energy industry. Founded in 1987. **NOTE:** Entry-level positions are offered. **Special programs:** Summer Jobs. **Office hours:** Monday - Friday, 7:30 a.m. - 4:30 p.m. **Corporate headquarters location:** This location. **Other U.S. locations:** Monroe LA. **Operations at this facility include:** Administration; Sales. **Listed on:** Privately held. **Number of employees nationwide:** 1,600.

MUSTANG TRACTOR & EQUIPMENT COMPANY
P.O. Box 1373, Houston TX 77252. 713/460-7232. **Fax:** 713/690-2287. **Recorded jobline:** 713/460-7267. **Contact:** Human Resources. **World Wide Web address:** http://www.mustangcat.com. **Description:** Sells and services Caterpillar heavy equipment and engines. **Special programs:** Development Sales/Management Training. **NOTE:** This company has locations throughout Texas. See its website for locations and job listings. **Corporate headquarters location:** This location. **Operations at this facility include:** Administration; Manufacturing; Sales; Service.

MYKROLIS CORPORATION
915 Enterprise Boulevard, Allen TX 75013-8003. 972/359-4000. **Contact:** Human Resources. **World Wide Web address:** http://www.mykrolis.com. **Description:** Manufactures pressure gauges used by pharmaceutical, agricultural, and oil and gas companies. **Positions advertised include:** Customer Service Representative; Quality Engineer; Material Manager; Product Engineer; Manufacturing Engineer. **Corporate headquarters location:** Bedford MA. **Other area locations:** Austin TX. **Other U.S. locations:** CA. **Listed on:** New York Stock Exchange. **Stock exchange symbol:** MYK

MYLAN BERTEK DOW HICKAM PHARMACEUTICALS INC.
12720 Dairy Ashford, Sugar Land TX 77478. 281/240-1000. **Fax:** 281/240-0002. **Contact:** Human Resources. **World Wide Web address:** http://www.mylan.com. **Description:** Develops drugs for viral, autoimmune, inflammatory, and neurodegenerative diseases as well as developing oral active pharmaceuticals for drug-resistant cancer and hemoglobin disorders.

NCH CORPORATION
P.O Box 152170, Irving TX 75015. **Toll-free phone:** 800/527-9919. **Fax:** 972/438-0707. **Recorded jobline:** 972/721-6116. **Contact:** Human Resources. **World Wide Web address:** http://www.nch.com. **Description:** Manufactures and supplies specialty chemicals, water treatment products, fasteners, welding supplies, plumbing and electronic parts, and safety supplies to a worldwide customer base. Founded in 1919. **NOTE:** Resumes should be sent to NCH Corporation, Human Resources Department, 2727 Chemsearch Boulevard, Irving TX 75062. Entry-level positions and part-time jobs are offered. **Company slogan:** World class products and services. **Special programs:** Internships; Training. **Corporate headquarters location:** This location. **Other U.S. locations:** El Segundo CA; Atlanta GA; Chicago IL; Paramus NJ; Seattle WA. **International locations:** Asia; Australia; Europe; South America.

NCI BUILDING SYSTEMS
10943 North Sam Houston Parkway West, Houston TX 77064. . 281/897-7788. **Contact:** Human Resources. **World Wide Web address:** http://www.ncilp.com. **Description:** Designs, manufactures, and markets metal building systems and components for commercial, industrial, agricultural, and community service uses. This company has 11 divisional groups with offices throughout the Texas and the United States. **NOTE:** NCI's lists employment opportunities for its corporate and division offices at its website. See website for specific contact information. **Other area locations:** Houston TX; Lubbock TX; Ennis TX; San Antonio TX; Dallas TX; La Grange TX: Fort Worth TX; Hempstead TX. **Operations at this facility include:** Administration.

NCR CORPORATION
450 East John Carpenter Freeway, Irving TX 75062. 972/650-9081. **Contact:** Human Resources Consultant. **World Wide Web address:** http://www.ncr.com. **Description:** NCR Corporation is a worldwide provider of computer products and services. The company provides computer solutions to three targeted industries: retail, financial, and communication. NCR Computer Systems Group develops, manufactures, and markets computer systems. NCR Financial Systems Group is an industry leader in financial delivery systems, relationship banking data warehousing solutions, and payments systems/item processing. NCR Retail Systems Group is a world leader in end-to-end retail solutions serving the food, general merchandise, and hospitality industries. NCR Worldwide Services provides data warehousing services solutions; end-to-end networking services; and designs, implements, and supports complex open systems environments. NCR Systemedia Group develops, produces, and markets a complete line of information products to satisfy customers' information technology needs including transaction processing media, auto identification media, business form communication products, managing documents and media, and a full line of integrated equipment solutions. **Special programs:** Internships. **Corporate headquarters location:** Dayton OH. **Other U.S. locations:** Nationwide. **Operations at this facility include:** This location is a sales and service office. **Listed on:** New York Stock Exchange. **Stock exchange symbol:** NCR. **Number of employees worldwide:** 29,000.

NEC AMERICA INC.
6535 North Street, Highway 161, Irving TX 75039. 214/262-2000. **Contact:** Human Resources Department. **World Wide Web address:** http://www.nec.com. **Description:** Manufactures communications systems and equipment, computers, industrial electronics systems, electronics devices, and home electronics products. NEC America consists of six subsidiaries: NEC Electronics America, NEC Mitsubishi Electronics Display, NEC Laboratories America, NEC Solutions America, NEC USA. **NOTE:** Each NEC America subsidiary has its own website with job listings. The links for the websites can be found at http://www.nec.com/global/job. **Other U.S. locations:** Nationwide. **International locations:** Worldwide. **Parent company:** NEC of Japan. **Listed on:** NASDAQ. **Stock exchange symbol:** NIPNY.

NL INDUSTRIES, INC.
16825 Northchase, Suite 1200, Houston TX 77060. 281/423-3300. **Contact:** Human Resources. **World Wide Web address:** http://www.nl-ind.com. **Description:** Manufactures and markets titanium dioxide pigments and other specialty chemicals used in a wide variety of products including paints, plastics, inks, and paper. **Corporate headquarters location:** This location. **International locations:** Worldwide. **Subsidiaries include:** Kronos, Inc.; Rheox, Inc. **Listed on:** New York Stock Exchange. **Stock exchange symbol:** NL.

NABORS INDUSTRIES
515 West Greens Road, Suite 1200, Houston TX 77067. 281/874-0035. **Contact:** Human Resources. **World Wide Web address:** http://www.nabors.com. **Description:** Provides contract drilling and oil field services worldwide. Services include comprehensive oilfield management, logistics, and engineering. Nabors Industries is active in the United States, Canada, Gulf of Mexico, United Kingdom, North Sea, Middle East, and other locations around the globe. **Operations at this facility include:** Administration; Sales. **Listed on:** American Stock Exchange. **Stock exchange symbol:** NBR.

NACE INTERNATIONAL
1440 South Creek Drive, Houston TX 77084. 281/228-6200. **Fax:** 281/228-6356. **Contact:** Human Resources. **World Wide Web address:** http://www.nace.org. **Description:** NACE (National Association of Corrosion Engineers) International disseminates information about protection/performance in corrosive environments through its two monthly journals, one bimonthly magazine, and a variety of technical reports and journals. **Corporate headquarters location:** This location.

NALCO ENERGY SERVICES.
P.O. Box 87, Sugar Land TX 77487-0087. 281/263-7000. **Contact:** Personnel. **World Wide Web address:** http://www.nalco.com. **Description:** Engaged in the manufacture and sale of highly specialized service chemicals used in water treatment, pollution control, energy conservation, oil production, oil refining, steelmaking, papermaking, mining, and other industrial processes. **NOTE:** This company has office locations throughout Texas. See its website for a complete list of locations, job listings and contact information. **Positions advertised include:** Application Engineer; **Corporate headquarters location:** Naperville IL.

NASA JOHNSON SPACE CENTER
2101 NASA Road One, Mail Code AHE, Houston TX 77058. 281/483-2135. **Contact:** Employment Specialist. **World Wide Web address:** http://www.j.nasa.gov. **Description:** A federal government agency responsible for developing and operating the space shuttle and a space station. **NOTE:** NASA posts its job listings on its website at http://www.nasajobs.nasa.gov/. Interested jobseekers must create profiles to access listings and to apply for positions. **Special programs:** Co-ops; Internships; Faculty Fellowships. **Corporate headquarters location:** Washington DC.

NASH SPORTS
315 West Ripy Street, Fort Worth TX 76110. 817/926-5225. **Contact:** Human Resources. **World Wide Web address:** http://www.nashmfg.com. **Description:** Manufactures sports and athletic equipment including skateboards and water skis.

NATHAN, SOMMERS, LIPPMAN, JACOBS & GORMAN
2800 Post Oak Boulevard, 61st Floor, Houston TX 77056. 713/960-0303. **Contact:** Kristie Ratliff, Financial Administrator. **Description:** A corporate law firm specializing in bankruptcy law, litigation, and real estate law. **Special programs:** Internships. **Corporate headquarters location:** This location.

THE NATIONAL ALLIANCE FOR INSURANCE EDUCATION & RESEARCH
P.O. Box 27027, Austin TX 78755-1027. 512/345-7932. **Fax:** 512/343-2167. **Contact:** Amy Schott, Human Resources Director. **World Wide Web address:** http://www.scic.com. **Description:** A nonprofit insurance education organization offering the Certified Insurance Counselors (CIC) designation, the Certified Insurance Service Representatives (CISR) designation, and the Certified Risk Manager (CRM) designation. The Academy of Producers Insurance Studies is the research arm of The National Alliance.

NATIONAL BANNER COMPANY
11938 Harry Hines Boulevard, Dallas TX 75234. 972/241-2131. **Contact:** Human Resources. **World Wide Web address:** http://www.nationalbanner.com. **Description:** Manufactures and wholesales flags, banners, and pennants.

NATIONAL ELECTRIC COIL
3330 East 14th Street, Brownsville TX 78521. 956/541-1759. **Fax:** 956/982-7525. **Contact:** Edward K. Rice, Human Resources Manager. **World Wide Web address:** http://www.national-electric-coil.com. **Description:** Manufactures and installs high-voltage generator windings. **Corporate headquarters location:** Nashville TN. **Operations at this facility include:** Administration; Manufacturing; Sales; Service. **Number of employees nationwide:** 850.

NATIONAL FOUNDATION LIFE INSURANCE COMPANY
777 Main Street, Fort Worth TX 76102. 817/878-3300 **Toll-free phone:** 800/221-9039. **Contact:** Human Resources. **World Wide Web address:** http://www.nationalfoundation.net. **Description:** A life insurance company. **Corporate headquarters location:** This location. **Operations at this facility include:** Administration.

NATIONAL INSTITUTIONAL PHARMACY SERVICES, INC. (NIPSI)
8977 Interchange Drive, Houston TX 77054. 713/668-7596. **Contact:** Human Resources. **Description:** Provides a full range of prescription drugs, enteral and perenteral nutritional therapy products, and infusion therapy products. The company offers antibiotic therapy, pain management, and chemotherapy services to over 520 facilities. NIPSI operates a network of 22 pharmacies in nine states.

NATIONAL INSTRUMENT CORPORATION
11500 North Mopac Expressway, Austin TX 78759-3504. 512/794-0100. **Fax:** 512/683-8745. **Contact:** Human Resources. **World Wide Web address:** http://www.ni.com. **Description:** Manufactures interface boards for the test measurement industry. **Corporate headquarters location:** This location. **International locations:** Worldwide. **Listed on:** NASDAQ. **Stock exchange symbol:** NATI.

NATIONAL LINEN SERVICE
620 Yorktown Road, Dallas TX 75208. 214/741-1751. **Contact:** Human Resources Manager. **World Wide Web address:** http://www.national-linen.com. **Description:** A service that launders and delivers various kinds of linens including tablecloths and napkins to hotels and restaurants. **Positions advertised include:** Sales Representative. **Other area locations:** Lubbock TX; Wichita Falls TX. **Other U.S. locations:** Nationwide.

NATIONAL MARINE FISHERIES SERVICE
4700 Avenue U, Galveston TX 77551. 409/766-3500. **Contact:** Human Resources. **World Wide Web address:** http://galveston.ssp.nmfs.gov/galv/. **Description:** A laboratory that researches the management processes of commercial and recreational shellfish and works to protect coastal habitats. **NOTE:** Applicants are asked to forward resumes, college transcripts, and a list of references. **Positions advertised include:** Biological Science Technician. **Special programs:** Internships.

NATIONAL OILWELL
10000 Richmond Avenue, Houston TX 77042. 713/346-7500. **Toll-free phone:** 888/262-8645. **Contact:** Human Resources. **World Wide Web address:** http://www.natoil.com. **Description:** Designs and develops electronic control systems for industrial applications. The company is a world leader in the field of power conversion equipment. It is one of the largest suppliers of variable speed drives to the oil industry and one of the world's largest users of large thyristor devices. **NOTE:** This company has 43 sales, service and distribution centers throughout Texas. See its website for locations and contact information. **Corporate headquarters location:** This location. **Listed on:** New York Stock Exchange. **Stock exchange symbol:** NOI. **Number of employees at nationwide:** 6,200.

NATIONAL SEMICONDUCTOR CORPORATION
1111 West Bardin Road, Arlington TX 76017. 817/468-6300. **Contact:** Human Resources. **World Wide Web address:** http://www.national.com. **Description:** Designs, develops, and manufactures microprocessors, consumer products, integrated circuits, memory systems, computer products, telecommunication systems, and high-speed bipolar circuits. **Positions advertised include:** Engineering Technician; Field Applications Engineer; Circuit Design Engineer; Senior Sales Engineer. **Corporate headquarters location:** Santa Clara CA. **International locations:** Scotland. **Operations at this facility include:** Design. **Listed on:** New York Stock Exchange. **Stock exchange symbol:** NSM.

NATIONWIDE ADVERTISING SERVICE INC.
7500 San Felipe, Suite 340, Houston TX 77063. 713/780-0770. **Contact:** Regional Manager. **World Wide Web address:** http://www.hrads.com. **Description:** One of the largest independent, full-service advertising agencies specializing exclusively in human resource communications and promotions. The company offers consultations, campaign planning, ad placement, research, and creative production. **Corporate headquarters location:** Cleveland OH. **Other area locations:** Dallas TX: San Antonio TX. **Other U.S. locations:** Nationwide. **International locations:** Canada. **Parent company:** McCann-Erickson World Group.

NEIGHBORHOOD CENTERS INC.
P.O. Box 271389, Houston TX 77277-1389. 713/669-5256. **Fax:** 713/669-5349. **Recorded jobline:** 713/669-5389. **Contact:** Diana Salazar, Human Resources. **E-mail address:** diana.salazar@neighborhood-centers.org. **World Wide Web address:** http://www.neighborhood-centers.org. **Description:** A human services organization offering a variety of programs to assist low-income families. Some of the programs offered include Healthy Start, which provides prenatal services and Early Head Start, which promotes the emotional and physical growth of children. Founded in 1907. **Positions advertised include:** Process Analyst; Family Service Worker; Assistant Children's Activity Leader; Athletic Specialist; Parent Educator; Program Support Coordinator; Driver; Maintenance Engineer; Receptionist; Bus Driver; Building Service Worker. **Parent company:** United Way.

THE NEIMAN MARCUS GROUP, INC.
1618 Main Street, Dallas TX 75201. 214/573-5688. **Contact:** Human Resources. **World Wide Web address:** http://www.neimanmarcus.com. **Description:** Operates two specialty retailing businesses: Neiman Marcus and Bergdorf Goodman. Combined, these two chains offer men's and women's apparel, fashion accessories, jewelry, fine china, and moderately priced crystal and silver. Neiman Marcus has an Information Technology facility in Irving TX and a National Service Center in Longview TX. **NOTE:** Neiman Marcus has all corporate and retail job openings listed on its corporate website. **Corporate headquarters location:** This location. **Subsidiaries include:** NM Direct is a direct marketing company, which advertises primarily through the use of such specialty catalogs as Neiman Marcus and Horchow.

NESTFAMILY.COM, INC.
1461 South Beltline Road, Suite 500, Coppell TX 75019. 972/402-7100. **Contact:** Human Resources. **World Wide Web address:** http://www.nestfamily.com. **Description:** Develops educational games, CD-ROMs, music, and videotapes for children. Founded in 1988. **Positions advertised include:** Business-to-Business Telesales Representative; Marketing Manager.

NETIQ
1233 West Loop South, Suite 1800, Houston TX 77027. 713/548-1700. **Toll-free phone:** 888/323-6768. **Fax:** 713/548-1771. **Contact:** Human Resources. **World Wide Web address:** http://www.netiq.com. **Description:** Developer of software that protects servers and databases, website and e-mail applications. NetIQ has partnerships with many of the world's leading computer hardware and software developers. **NOTE:** Apply online. **Positions advertised include:** Business Unit Director of Finance; Facilities Coordinator; Senior Usability Engineer; Senior Software Engineer; Senior Technical Writer; Channel Marketing Manager; Corporate Sales Representative; Project Manager; Services Billing Administrator; Customer Care Representative; Technical Support Engineer. **Corporate headquarters location:** San Jose CA. **Other U.S. locations:** WA; NC; OR. **International locations:** Worldwide. **Listed on:** NASDAQ. **Stock exchange symbol:** NTIQ.

NETQOS
6504 Bridge Point Parkway, Suite 501, Austin TX 78730. **Toll-free phone:** 877/835-9575. **Fax:** 512/407-8629. **Contact:** Human Resources. **E-mail address:** careers@netqos.com. **World Wide Web address:** http://www.netqos.com. **Description:** Develops software and consulting services to manage the performance of enterprise computer networks of Fortune 1000 companies. **NOTE:** Send resume and cover letter to the company. **Positions advertised include:** Software Engineer; Account Manager; WAN Network Engineer; Sales Executive (New York City area).

NETWORK ASSOCIATES, INC.
13465 Midway Road, Dallas TX 75244. 972/308-9960. **Contact:** Human Resources. **World Wide Web address:** http://www.nai.com. **Description:** Designs, manufactures, markets, and supports software-based analysis and monitoring tools primarily for managing enterprisewide computer networks. Products include McAfee antivirus, Gauntlet firewall, PGP encryption, Sniffer network analyzers, and Magic Help Desk applications. Founded in 1989. **Corporate headquarters location:** Santa Clara CA. **Other area locations:** Plano TX. **Other U.S. locations:** Nationwide. **International locations:** Worldwide. **Listed on:** New York Stock Exchange. **Stock exchange symbol:** NET.

NEW SYSTEMS
1201 North Industrial Boulevard, Round Rock TX 78681. 512/388-4806. **Contact:** Human Resources.: Engineers and manufactures kits used for installing navigational equipment in commercial aircraft.

NEWDATA STRATEGIES
5339 Alpha Road, Suite 200, Dallas TX 75240. 972/735-0001. **Fax:** 972/735-8008. **Contact:** Human Resources. **E-mail address:** resumes@newdata.com. **World Wide Web address:** http://www.newdata.com. **Description:** Provides customized data technologies to clients. **Positions advertised include:** CIS Programmer/Analyst; CIS Project Manager; C# Architect; Cisco Engineer; Bilingual Enterprise Exchange 2003 Engineer; .NET Developer.

NEWFIELD EXPLORATION
363 North Sam Houston Parkway East, Suite 2020, Houston TX 77060. 281/847-6000. **Contact:** Human Resources. **World Wide Web address:** http://www.newfld.com. **Description:** Engaged in oil and gas exploration. **Listed on:** New York Stock Exchange. **Stock exchange symbol:** NFX.

NEWPARK SHIPBUILDING & REPAIR INC.
2102 Broadway, Houston TX 77012. 713/847-4600. **Toll-free phone:** 888/399-9283. **Fax:** 713/847-4601. **Contact:** Human Resources. **World Wide Web address:** http://www.fwav.com. **Description:** Manufactures barges, towboats, and riverboats for a wide range of customers. **Corporate headquarters location:** Houston TX. **Other area locations:** Galveston TX; Pasadena TX. **Operations at this facility include:** Administration. **Parent company:** Firstwave Marine. **Operations at this facility include:** Service.

NEWTEK INC.
5131 Beckwith Boulevard, San Antonio TX 78249. 210/370-8000. **Contact:** Human Resources. **World Wide Web address:** http://www.newtek.com. **Description:** Designs and develops software used for animation and graphics. **Positions advertised include:** Video Software Engineer. **Corporate headquarters location:** This location.

NICHOLS FORD
2401 East Interstate 20 at Campus Drive, Fort Worth TX 76119. 817/429-7750. **Contact:** Human Resources. **World Wide Web address:** http://www.nicholsford.com. **Description:** A new and used car dealership.

NIX HEALTH CARE SYSTEM
414 Navarro Street, San Antonio TX 78205. 210/271-1800. **Fax:** 210/271-2167. **Contact:** Human Resources. **World Wide Web address:** http://www.nixhealth.com. **Description:** Operates a 150-bed hospital. Nix Health Care offers such services as prenatal care, a geriatric psychiatry unit, and a skilled nursing unit. **Positions advertised include:** Financial Analyst; Needs Assessment Clinician; Community Education Coordinator; Commercial/Managed Care Collector; Medicare Collector; Patient Access Specialist; RN; LVN; Food Service Aide; Food Service Supervisor.

NOBLE CONSTRUCTION EQUIPMENT, INC.
1802 East 50th Street, Lubbock TX 79404. 806/747-4663. **Contact:** Human Resources. **World Wide Web address:** http://www.noblecei.com. **Description:** Manufactures and distributes industrial machinery and other industrial equipment. **International locations:** Mexico.

NOBLE DRILLING CORPORATION
13135 South Dairy Ashford, Suite 800, Sugar Land TX 77478. 281/276-6100. **Fax:** 281/276-6464. **Contact:** Human Resources. **E-mail address:** jobs@noblecorp.com. **World Wide Web address:** http://www.noblecorp.com. **Description:** Provides offshore drilling services. **Positions advertised include:** Telecommunications Administrator; Financial Controller; Service Technician; Alliance Coordinator; Crane Operator; Driller; Electrician; Electronics Technician; Subsea Engineer. **Corporate headquarters location:** This location. **Listed on:** New York Stock Exchange. **Stock exchange symbol:** NE.

NOKIA USA
6000 Connection Drive, Irving TX 75039. 972/894-5000. **Contact:** Human Resources. **Toll-free phone:** 800/547-9810. **World Wide Web address:** http://www.nokia.com. **Description:** A leading manufacturer and supplier of mobile phones as well as a supplier of mobile, broadband, and IP networks. This company also has a location in Fort Worth TX. **NOTE:** Resumes must be submitted via this company's website. **Positions advertised include:** Benefits Consultant; Legal Department Assistant; Project Manager; Research Engineer. **Listed on:** New York Stock Exchange. **Stock exchange symbol:** NOK. **Number of employees worldwide:** 52,700.

NORTH LAKE COLLEGE
5001 North MacArthur Boulevard, Irving TX 75038. 972/273-3000. **Contact:** Human Resources. **World Wide Web address:** http://www.northlakecollege.edu. **Description:** A two-year community college offering technical occupational courses as well as general studies. Approximately 6,200 students are enrolled. North Lake College operates as part of the Dallas County Community College District. **NOTE:** Interested jobseekers may apply at the college's Human Resources Office, Third Floor of the Administration Building Monday – Friday, 8:00 a.m. – 5:00 p.m.; Friday, 8:00 a.m. – 4:30 p.m. Job listings and applications are located also on the Dallas County Community College District's website: http://www.dcccd.edu.

NORTHEAST BAPTIST MRI CENTER
8815 Village Drive, San Antonio TX 78217. 210/297-2870. **Contact:** Human Resources. **World Wide Web address:** http://www.baptisthealth.org. **Description:** A medical center that performs MRIs. The center is part of Baptist Hospital.

NORTHROP GRUMMAN ELECTRO-OPTICAL SYSTEMS
3414 Herrmann Drive, Garland TX 75041. 972/840-5600. **Contact:** Human Resources. **World Wide Web address:** http://www.littoneos.com. **Description:** Manufactures a diverse line of military equipment and electro-optical systems including guided-missile launchers, optical sighting and fire control equipment, laser range finders, night-vision sights, and systems for weapons and high-intensity searchlights. **NOTE:** Entry-level positions and second and third shifts are offered. **Positions advertised include:** Electromechanical Engineer; Purchasing Planning and Coordinator; Business Development Manager; Computer Operator. **Other U.S. locations:** Tempe AZ. **Parent company:** Northrop Grumman. **Operations at this facility include:** Administration; Manufacturing; Research and Development; Sales. **Listed on:** New York Stock Exchange. **Stock exchange symbol:** NOC.

NORTHWEST TEXAS HEALTHCARE SYSTEM
1506 Coulter Street, Amarillo TX 79106. 806/354-1000. **Recorded jobline:** 806/354-1905. **Contact:** Human Resources. **World Wide Web address:** http://www.nwtexashealthcare.com. **Description:** Operates Northwest Texas Hospital and The Pavilion. Northwest Texas Hospital offers more than 35 medical specialties and subspecialties. The Pavilion is a full-service mental health facility that provides a comprehensive range of services to people of all ages. **NOTE:** Applications are only accepted in the office for current positions. Application is available online. **Positions advertised include:** RN; LVN. **Parent company:** Universal Health Services. **Office hours:** Monday – Friday, 7:00 a.m. – 5:00 p.m.

NORWOOD PROMOTIONAL PRODUCTS, INC.
106 East Sixth Street, Suite 300, Austin TX 78701. 512/476-7100. **Contact:** Human Resources. **World Wide Web address:** http://www.norwood.com. **Description:** Through its subsidiaries and divisions, Norwood Promotional Products imprints and distributes over 1,000 promotional items to over 6,500 distributors nationwide. Product lines include badges, business gifts, buttons, headwear, Koozie insulator products, mugs and glassware, paper products, packet specialties, recognition and award items, and writing instruments. The company markets its products under trade names including The Action Line, Barlow, Econ-O-Line, Koozie, RCC, and Salam. **Positions advertised include:** Credit Analyst; Manufacturing Engineer; Paralegal; Territory Sales Representative. **Subsidiaries include:** ArtMold; Barlow; Key; RCC. **International locations:** Canada; Hong Kong. **Number of employees worldwide:** 3,500.

NOVA CHEMICAL CORPORATION
12222 Port Road, Pasadena TX 77507. 281/474-1000. **Contact:** Human Resources. **World Wide Web address:** http://www.novachem.com. **Description:** Manufactures plastics materials including films, thermoplastic resins, and other synthetic resins; polyethylene; and polypropylene. The company's products are used to make a wide variety of products ranging from dashboards to diapers and medical supplies. **NOTE:** This company does not accept unsolicited resumes. For job openings, call: 888/371-0161. **Corporate headquarters location:** Canada. **International locations:** France, The Netherlands; United Kingdom. **Operations at this facility include:** Manufacturing.

NUEVO ENERGY COMPANY
1021 Main Street, Suite 2100, Houston TX 77002. 713/652-0706. **Contact:** Human Resources. **World Wide Web address:** http://www.nuevoenergy.com. **Description:** Engaged in the exploration, development, and acquisition of crude oil and natural gas. **Corporate headquarters location:** This location. **Listed on:** New York Stock Exchange. **Stock exchange symbol:** NEV.

NURSEFINDERS
1341 W. Mockingbird, Suite 245 W, Dallas TX 75247. 214/520-8770. **Toll-free phone:** 888/338-0572. **Fax:** 214/520-8675. **Contact:** Human Resources. **World Wide Web address:** http://www.nursefinders.com. **Description:** A home health care agency. Nursefinders has staffing offices throughout Texas. **NOTE:** This company offers per diem, contract, home care, permanent, managed care and travel positions. Interested jobseekers can apply online for positions or visit the nearest staffing location. **Positions advertised include:** Registered Nurse; Home Health Care Nurse; Case Manager. **Corporate headquarters location:** Arlington TX. **Other U.S. locations:** Nationwide.

NURSES TODAY INCORPORATED
4230 LBJ Freeway, Suite 110, Dallas TX 75244. 972/233-9966. **Toll-free phone:** 800/830-7616. **Fax:** 972/233-5354. **Contact:** Anita Porco, Human Resources Manager. **World Wide Web address:** http://www.nursestoday.com. **Description:** Provides home health care and case management services. Founded in 1982. **NOTE:** Permanent, contract, temporary and part-time jobs are offered. **Positions advertised include:** Licensed Vocational Nurse; Registered Nurse; Certified Nurse Assistant; Medical Transcriptionist. **Corporate headquarters location:** This location.

O&M SALES, INC.
8705 Shoal Creek Boulevard, Suite 103, Austin TX 78757-6839. 512/453-0275. **Contact:** Human Resources. **World Wide Web address:** http://www.o-m-sales.com. **Description:** A wholesaler of semiconductors and other electronic components.

OAKS TREATMENT CENTER
1407 West Stassney Lane, Austin TX 78745. 512/464-0200. **Toll-free phone:** 800/843-6257. **Fax:** 512/464-0439. **Contact:** Human Resources. **World Wide Web address:** http://www.psysolutions.com/facilities/oaks. **Description:** A residential and treatment center for children and young adults with behavioral, emotional, or developmental disabilities. **NOTE:** See website for job listings. **Positions advertised include:** Speech/Language Pathologist; Occupational Therapist; RN. **Corporate headquarters location:** This location. **Parent company:** Psychiatric Solutions Inc. (PSI).

OCCIDENTAL CHEMICAL CORPORATION
P.O. Box 809050, Dallas TX 75380. **Physical address:** Occidental Tower, 5005 LBJ Freeway, Dallas TX 75244. 972/404-3800. **Fax:** 972/404-3669. **Contact:** Human Resources. **World Wide Web address:** http://www.oxychem.com. **Description:** Occidental Chemical Corporation manufactures commodity and specialty chemicals. The company has manufacturing facilities nationwide and internationally. . This company has a location in Deer Park TX that manufactures plastic materials and synthetic resins. **NOTE:** This company only accepts resumes for current openings. See website for job listings. **Corporate headquarters location:** This location. **Other U.S. locations:** Nationwide. **Positions advertised include:** Oracle Financials Supply Chain Application Consultant. **Parent company:** Occidental Petroleum Corporation. **Listed on:** New York Stock Exchange. **Stock exchange symbol:** OXY. **Number of employees nationwide:** 8,200.

OCEANEERING INTERNATIONAL, INC.
11911 FM 529, Houston TX 77041. 713/329-4500. **Fax:** 713/329-4869. **Contact:** Human Resources. **World Wide Web address:** http://www.oceaneering.com. **Description:** Offers underwater diving, equipment, and related services to marine and space companies. Oceaneering sells also under the trade name of Solus Schall. Founded in 1964. This company has offices throughout Texas. **NOTE:** See the company's website for job listings by location and for specific contact information. **Corporate headquarters location:** This location. **Other U.S. locations:** Nationwide. **International locations:** Worldwide. **Listed on:** New York Stock Exchange. **Stock exchange symbol:** OII. **Number of employees worldwide:** 3,500.

ODESSA REGIONAL HOSPITAL
520 East Sixth Street, Odessa TX 79760. 915/334-8397. **Contact:** Human Resources. **World Wide Web address:** http://www.odessaregionalhospital.com. **Description:** A hospital offering specialized labor/delivery services, pediatrics, family care, and surgical services. **NOTE:** An application is required for any position. The application can be found online at the hospital's website. **Positions advertised include:** RN; Respiratory Therapist; Medical Auditor. **Parent company:** IASIS Healthcare. **Listed on:** Privately held.

ODYSSEY HEALTHCARE
14205 Burnet Road, Suite 400, Austin TX 78728. 512/310-0214. **Contact:** Human Resources. **E-mail address:** resume@odyshealth.com. **World Wide Web address:** http://www.odyshealth.com. **Description:** Hospice provider for end of life care patients. **Positions advertised include:** Certified Nurse, Patient Secretary.

ODYSSEY HEALTHCARE
717 North Harwood Street, suite 1500, Dalls TX 75201. 214/922-9711. **Contact:** human resources. **E-mail address:** resume@odyshealth.com. **World Wide Web address:** http://www.odyshealth.com. **Description:** Hospice provider for end of life patients. **Positions advertised include:** general manager, analyst for accounts receivable, executive assistant, director of inpatient development.

OFFICE DEPOT, INC.
2209 Rutland Drive, Suite A100, Austin TX 78758. 512/837-8999. **Fax:** 512/837-1221. **Contact:** Human Resources. **World Wide Web address:** http://www.officedepot.com. **Description:** One of the nation's leading office products dealers. The company offers over 11,000 business products including furniture; desk accessories; office essentials; computer products; business machines; visual communications; safety and maintenance supplies; personalized organizers and dated goods; writing instruments; business cases and binders; filing and storage; paper, envelopes, and business forms; and labels and mailing supplies. This company has locations throughout Texas and the United States. **NOTE:** This location is part of Office Depot's Business Services division, which focuses primarily on sales and service to the business market. There is another location in Houston. Job listings for the Business Services Division, as well other divisions, including retail, can be found on the company's website. **Corporate headquarters location:** Delray Beach FL. **Subsidiaries include:** Viking Office Products is a direct mail marketer. **Listed on:** New York Stock Exchange. **Stock exchange symbol:** ODP.

OFFICE DEPOT, INC.
10525 Gulf Freeway, Houston TX 77034-1805. 713/947-7590. **Contact:** Human Resources. **World Wide Web address:** http://www.officedepot.com. **Description:** One of the nation's leading office products dealers. The company offers over 11,000 business products including furniture; desk accessories; office essentials; computer products; business machines; visual communications; safety and maintenance supplies; personalized organizers and dated goods; writing instruments; business cases and binders; filing and storage; paper, envelopes, and business forms; and labels and mailing supplies. This company has locations throughout Texas and the United States. **NOTE:** This location is part of Office Depot's Business Services division, which focuses primarily on sales and service to the business market. Job listings for the Business Services Division, as well other divisions, including retail, can be found on the company's website. **Corporate headquarters location:** Delray Beach FL. **Subsidiaries include:** Viking Office Products is a direct mail marketer. **Listed on:** New York Stock Exchange. **Stock exchange symbol:** ODP.

OFFICE OF THE SECRETARY OF THE STATE OF TEXAS
1019 Brazo, Room 405, P.O. Box 12887, Austin TX 78711-2887. 512/463-5701. **Contact:** Human Resources. **World Wide Web address:** http://www.sos.state.tx.us. **Description:** A constitutional officer of the executive branch appointed by the governor with the consent of the senate. This agency is organized into five functional divisions: Executive, Elections, Information Services, Statutory Filings, and Administrative Services. **NOTE:** An application must be submitted with a resume. The application can be downloaded at the website.

O'HAIR SHUTTERS
P.O. Box 2764, Lubbock TX 79408. 806/765-5791. **Toll-free phone:** 800/582-2625. **Fax:** 888/765-7140. **Contact:** Human Resources. **World Wide Web address:** http://www.ohair.com. **Description:** Manufactures outdoor shutters for homes. **Corporate headquarters location:** This location.

OLDCASTLE GLASS GROUP
2805 Dallas Parkway, Suite 450, Plano TX 75093. 972/747-3800. **Fax:** 972/747-3838. **Contact:** Human Resources. **World Wide Web address:** http://www.oldcastleglass.com. **Description:** A leading manufacturer of glass products. The company's product line includes laminated glass, insulating glass units, heat-treated glass, silk-screened and decorative glass, and structural glass wall systems. **Corporate headquarters location:** This location. **Parent company:** CRH plc.

OMNI HOTELS
420 Decker Drive, Suite 200, Irving TX 75062-3952. 972/730-6664. **Fax:** 972/871-5669. **Contact:** Bethany Senger, Corporate Recruiting Manager. **World Wide Web address:** http://www.omnihotels.com. **Description:** Operates an international chain of hotels, motels, and resorts. **NOTE:** Entry-level positions are offered. The corporate website lists all open positions throughout the chain's operations, including the corporate office. **Special programs:** Internships; Training. **Corporate headquarters location:** This location. **Other U.S. locations:** Nationwide. **Parent company:** TRT. **Operations at this facility include:** Administration. **Listed on:** Privately held. **Number of employees worldwide:** 8, 000.

183 ANIMAL HOSPITAL
1010 West Airport Freeway, Irving TX 75062. 972/579-0115. **Contact:** Human Resources. **Description:** Provides general medical and surgical services along with diagnostic testing, radiography, and dentistry for small animals.

ONYX ENVIRONMENTAL
1800 South Highway 146, Baytown TX 77520. 281/427-4099. **Contact:** Human Resources. **World Wide Web address:** http://www.onyxes.com. **Description:** A provider of comprehensive waste management services, as well as engineering and construction, industrial, and related services, with operations in 19 countries. **NOTE:** Resumes should be faxed to: 626/334-4563. **Positions advertised include:** National

Accounts Manager; Project Manager. **Other U.S. locations:** Nationwide. **Operations at this facility include:** Sales.

OPENCONNECT SYSTEMS, INC.
2711 LBJ Freeway, Suite 700, Dallas TX 75234. 972/484-5200. **Fax:** 972/888-0458. **Contact:** Human Resources. **E-mail address:** hr@oc.com. **World Wide Web address:** http://www.oc.com. **Description:** A leading provider of software for computer servers, desktops and mainframes. Founded in 1981. **NOTE:** Interested jobseekers should NOT include a cover letter with their resumes when applying via e-mail. **Corporate headquarters location:** This location. **Listed on:** Privately held.

OPTEK TECHNOLOGY INC.
1645 Wallace Drive, Carrollton TX 75006. 972/323-2200. **Toll-free phone:** 800/341-4747. **Fax:** 972/323-2396, **Contact:** Human Resources. **E-mail address:** hr@optekinc.com. **World Wide Web address:** http://www.optekinc.com. **Description:** Produces fiber-optic, log-wavelength, light-emitting diodes; hybrid components; gallium arsenide and gallium aluminum arsenide circuits; and related products.

OPTIMIZED PROCESS DESIGNS (OPD)
P.O. Box 810, Katy TX 77493. 281/371-7500. **Physical address:** 25610 Clay Road, Katy TX 77493. **Fax:** 281/371-0132. **Contact:** Human Resources. **World Wide Web address:** http://www.opd-inc.com. **Description:** Designs, engineers, and constructs natural gas treatment facilities. **Parent company:** Koch Industries, Inc. **Listed on:** Privately held.

ORACLE CORPORATION
111 Congress Street, Austin TX 78701. 512/703-6200. **Fax:** 512/703-6250. **Contact:** Human Resources. **World Wide Web address:** http://www.oracle.com. **Description:** Designs and manufactures database and information management software for businesses. The company also provides consulting services. **Positions advertised include:** Staff Sales Consultant; Contracts Administrator; Product Manager; Telesales Representative; Contracts Manager; Field Support Sales; Applications Developer; Technical Writer; Quality Assurance Engineer; Manager Business Development. **Corporate headquarters location:** Redwood Shores CA. **Other U.S. locations:** Nationwide. **Listed on:** NASDAQ. **Stock exchange symbol:** ORCL.

ORTHOFIX INC.
1720 Bray Central Drive, McKinney TX 75069. 469/742-2500. **Contact:** Human Resources. **World Wide Web address:** http://www.orthofix.com. **Description:** Orthofix Inc. develops, manufactures, markets, and distributes medical devices to promote bone healing. Products are primarily used by orthopedic surgeons. **Positions advertised include:** Accountant; Marketing Coordinator; Mechanical Engineer; Associate Territory Manager; Customer Service Representative. **Operations at this facility include:** Administration; Divisional Headquarters; Manufacturing; Research and Development; Sales; Service.

OSHMAN'S SPORTING GOODS INC.
2320 Maxwell Lane, Houston TX 77023. 713/928-3171. **Contact:** Human Resources. **World Wide Web address:** http://www.oshmans.com. **Description:** Offers a broad line of sporting goods and equipment as well as active sports apparel. Most stores operate under the name SuperSports USA. **Corporate headquarters location:** This location.

OVERHEAD DOOR CORPORATION
1900 Crown Drive, Farmer's Branch TX 75234. 972/233-6611. **Contact:** Human Resources. **E-mail address:** jobs@overheaddoor.com. **World Wide Web address:** http://www.overheaddoor.com. **Description:** Manufactures aluminum, steel, fiberglass, and wooden overhead doors, rolling steel fire doors, grilles, and metal insulated entrance doors. Products are distributed through a network of more than 400 authorized distributors in the United States and Canada. The company also manufactures truck and trailer doors. **Corporate headquarters location:** This location. **Other area locations:** Carrollton TX; Corpus Christi TX; Fort Worth TX; Houston TX; Mount Pleasant TX; Richardson TX. **Parent company:** Sanwa Shutter Corporation.

OWENS COUNTRY SAUSAGE INC.
1403 East Lookout Drive, Richardson TX 75082. 972/235-7181 **Toll-free phone:** 800/966-9367.**Contact:** Human Resources. **World Wide Web address:** http://www.owensinc.com. **Description:** Produces sausage and other pork products. The company also operates Spring Creek Farm and several Owen Restaurants throughout the United States. **Corporate headquarters location:** This location. **Parent company:** Bob Evans.

OWENS-CORNING FIBERGLAS CORPORATION
8360 Market Street, Houston TX 77029-2498. 713/672-8338. **Contact:** Human Resources Director. **World Wide Web address:** http://www.owenscorning.com. **Description:** Owens-Corning Fiberglas Corporation manufactures and sells thermal and acoustical insulation products including insulation for appliances, glass fiber roofing shingles, roof insulation and industrial asphalt. Other products include windows, glass fiber textile yarns, wet process chopped strands and specialty mats, and polyester resins. **NOTE:** Interested jobseekers should apply online at the company's website. **Special programs:** Internships. **Other area locations:** Dallas TX (Parts Manufacturing); Amarillo TX (Fiberglas Manufacturing). **Subsidiaries include:** Barbcorp, Inc.; Dansk-Svensk Glasfiber AS; Eric Co.; European Owens-Corning Fiberglas SA; IPM Inc.; Kitsons Insulations Products Ltd.; Owens-Corning AS; Owens-Corning Building Products; Owens-Corning Finance; Owens-Corning FSC, Inc. **Corporate headquarters location:** Toledo OH. **Operations at this facility include:** This location manufactures roofing and asphalt shingles. **Listed on:** NASDQ. **Stock exchange symbol:** OWENQ.

PPD DEVELOPMENT
4009 Banister Lane, Austin TX 78704. 512/447-2663. **Contact:** Human Resources. **World Wide Web address:** http://www.ppdi.com. **Description:** Provides research and development services for companies in the biotechnology and pharmaceutical industries. **Positions advertised include:** Clinical Data Associate; Project Manager; Clinical Research Associate; Project Manager; Medical Writer; Senior Scientist. **Parent company:** PPD, Inc. **Listed on:** NASDAQ. **Stock exchange symbol:** PPDI.

PABST BREWING COMPANY
P.O. Box 1661, San Antonio TX 78296. 210/226-0231. **Contact:** Human Resources. **E-mail address:** hr@pabst.com. **World Wide Web address:** http://www.pabst.com. **Description:** Produces a line of widely distributed beers and malt beverages including Pabst Blue Ribbon, Pabst Light, and Pabst Extra Light.

PADGETT PRINTING CORPORATION
1313 North Industrial Boulevard, Dallas TX 75207. 214/742-4261. **Contact:** Human Resources. **World Wide Web address:** http://www.padgett.com. **Description:** A printing company. **Other area locations:** Austin TX; Houston TX; San Antonio TX. **Corporate headquarters location:** This location. **Operations at this facility include:** Administration; Manufacturing; Sales. **Listed on:** Privately held.

PAK-MOR LTD.
2191 Rudeloff Road, Seguin TX 781055. 830/303-7256. **Contact:** Human Resources. **Description:** A manufacturer of refuse trucking equipment. **Corporate headquarters location:** This location.

PALM HARBOR HOMES INC.
15303 Dallas Parkway, Suite 800, Addison TX, 75001. 972/991-2422. **Fax:** 512/385-2910. **Contact:** Human Resources. **World Wide Web address:** http://www.palmharbor.com. **Description:** Produces manufactured houses. Founded in 1978. **NOTE:** This company has retail and sales positions located throughout Texas. In addition, it has job openings in Manufacturing and Service. Interested jobseekers should apply online at the company's website. **Special programs:** Sale Training; Quality Training. **Corporate headquarters location:** Addison TX. **Other U.S. locations:** AL; AZ; FL; GA; NC; OH; OR. **Listed on:** NASDAQ. **Stock exchange symbol:** PHHM. **Number of employees nationwide:** 4,100.

PALO PINTO GENERAL HOSPITAL
400 SW 25th Avenue, Mineral Wells TX 76067. 940/328-6229. **Fax:** 940/328-6230. **Recorded jobline:** 940/328-6298. **Contact:** Human Resources. **World Wide Web address:** http://www.ppgh.com. **Description:** A 99-bed, nonprofit, acute care hospital. **NOTE:** Entry-level positions, part-time jobs, and second and third shifts are offered. **Positions advertised include:** Client Care Coordinator; RN; LVN.

PANCHO'S MEXICAN BUFFET, INC.
P.O. Box 7407, Fort Worth TX 76111-0407. 817/831-0081. **Physical address:** 3500 Noble Street, Fort Worth TX 76111. **Contact:** Human Resources. **World Wide Web address:** http://www.panchosmexicanbuffet.com. **Description:** Pancho's Mexican Buffet operates a chain of Mexican restaurants with a buffet-style format. Pancho's Mexican Buffet operates 40 restaurants in Texas, Arizona, Louisiana, New Mexico, and Oklahoma. Founded in 1966. **NOTE:** This chain offers management and hourly positions. Jobseekers interested in management positions should request an application packet online at the company's website. Jobseekers interested in hourly positions should apply at the nearest location. **Corporate headquarters location:** This location. **Operations at this facility include:** This location houses administrative offices.

PANHANDLE COMMUNITY SERVICES
P.O. Box 763, Clarendon TX 79226. 806/874-2573. **Contact:** Human Resources. **Description:** Offers housing, energy, transportation, and food banks for homeless and low-income families.

PANHANDLE ENERGY
5444 Westheimer, Houston TX 77056. 713/989-7000. **Contact:** Human Resources. **World Wide Web address:** http://www.panhandleenergy.com. **Description:** Operates more than 10,000 miles of interstate pipeline transporting natural gas from the Gulf of Mexico to major U.S. markets. **Parent company:** Southern Union. **Number of employees nationwide:** 1,100.

PARIS REGIONAL MEDICAL CENTER
820 Clarksville Street, Paris TX 75460. 903/785-4521. **Fax:** 903/737-3887. **Contact:** Human Resources. **World Wide Web address:** http://www.stjosephs.com. **Description:** A nonprofit, 216-bed, acute care hospital that provides comprehensive heart programs, inpatient and outpatient dialysis, rehabilitation services, oncology, radiation therapy, and nuclear medicine services. **NOTE:** Contact Human Resources at 903/737-3943. Please visit website to search for jobs or to download application form. **Positions advertised include:** Director of Cardiology; Registrar; Phlebotomist; Certified Scrub Technologist; Licensed Vocational Nurse; Nurse's Aide; RN; Director of Surgical Services; House Supervisor; Pulmonary Rehab Coordinator; Director of Radiology; Mammography Coordinator; Radiographer; Registered Ultra Sonographer; Kids Klub Attendant.

PARK PLACE MEDICAL CENTER
3050 Thirty-Ninth Street, Port Arthur TX 77642. 409/985-0303. **Contact:** Human Resources. **World Wide Web address:** http://www.parkplacemedicalcenter.com. **Description:** A full-service hospital with 244 beds. Its medical specialties are: cardiology, orthopedics, women's health, infant intensive care, and long-term acute care. Founded in 1958. **NOTE:** Apply online at this hospital's website. Park Place Medical Center has a nearby sister facility called Mid-Jefferson Hospital. To apply for positions at Mid-Jefferson, visit its website at http://www.midjeffersonhospital.com. **Positions advertised include:** RN; Scheduler; Physical Therapist; Pharmacy Technician. **Corporate headquarters location:** Franklin TN. **Parent company:** IASIS Healthcare. **Listed on:** Privately held.

PARK PLACE MOTORCARS
4023 Oak Lawn Avenue, Dallas TX 75219. 214/526-8701. **Toll-free phone:** 888-354-7176. **Fax:** 214/443-8270. **Contact:** Human Resources. **World Wide Web address:** http://www.parkplacetexas.com. **Description:** A new and pre-owned car dealership for Mercedes-Benz, Porsche, Lexus, and Audi automobiles. Motocars, its parent company, has several dealerships throughout Dallas and Texas. **NOTE:** This company's website lists job openings for its corporate office and its dealerships. Entry-level positions are offered. **Corporate headquarters location:** This location. **Other area locations:** Houston TX; Plano TX.

PARK PLAZA HOSPITAL
1313 Hermann Drive, Houston TX 77004. 713/527-5090. **Recorded jobline:** 713/527-5091. **Contact:** Human Resources. **World Wide Web address:** http://www.parkplazahospital.com. **Description:** A full-service hospital with 446 beds. **NOTE:** A completed application is required for any position. Apply online. **Positions advertised include:** Case Manager; Occupational Therapist; Surgical Technician; RN (Various), Dialysis Technician; Radiology Technician; Physical Therapy Assistant. **Parent company:** Tenet Healthcare.

PARKER HANNIFIN CORPORATION
STRATOFLEX DIVISION
220 Roberts Cuts-off Road, Fort Worth TX 76114. 817/738-6543. **Fax:** 817/738-9920. **Contact:** Human Resources. **World Wide Web address:** http://www.parker.com. **Description:** The company makes motion and control products for many industries, including aerospace. It has seven groups with separate subsidiaries. The groups are Automation, Climate and Industrial Controls, Filtration, Fluid Connections, Hydraulics, Instrumentation, and Sales. Parker Hannifin has facilities worldwide. **Positions advertised include:** Territory Sales Manager. **Corporate headquarters location:** Cleveland OH. **Operations at this facility include:** This location is a subsidiary and it manufactures hose fittings and hose assemblies for the aerospace, military, and marine

markets. **Listed on:** New York Stock Exchange. **Stock exchange symbol:** PH. **Number of employees worldwide:** 45,000.

PARKLAND HEALTH AND HOSPITAL SYSTEM
5201 Harry Hines Boulevard, Dallas TX 75235. 214/590-8000. **Contact:** Employment Services. **World Wide Web address:** http://www.pmh.org. **Description:** A Level I trauma center, and a 900-bed teaching hospital. The system operates also neighborhood health centers throughout the Dallas area. Parkland manages also the Parkland Foundation and a North Texas Poison Center. **NOTE:** The system has three types of employment positions: Nursing, Physicians and Employment Service, which includes clerical and support. All job postings and contact information is provided on the website and applicants are encouraged to apply electronically. Nursing resumes may be faxed to 214/590-8991. Employment Service resumes may be faxed to 214/590-2767. Physician resumes may be faxed to 214/590-0024. The Human Resources Office accepts walk-in resumes during certain time periods. See the website for specific days and times. **Number of employees nationwide:** 6,500.

PARKVIEW METAL PRODUCTS INC.
400 Barnes Drive, San Marcos TX 78666. 512/754-0200. **Contact:** Human Resources. **E-mail address:** hrsanmarcos@parkv.com. **World Wide Web address:** http://www.parkviewmetal.com. **Description:** A manufacturer of metal stamping and metal parts for computers, radios, and VCRs. **Other U.S. locations:** IL; NM. **International locations:** Mexico.

PASSAGE SUPPLY COMPANY
P.O. Box 971395, El Paso TX 79997-1395. 915/778-9377. **Fax:** 915/772-9602. **Contact:** Ron Passage, General Manager. **Description:** A heating and cooling systems distributor. **Corporate headquarters location:** This location.

PATTERSON-UTI ENERGY, INC.
P.O. Drawer 1416, Snyder TX 79550. 915/573-1831. **Physical address:** 4510 Lamesa Highway, Snyder TX 79549. **Contact:** Human Resources. **World Wide Web address:** http://www.patenergy.com. **Description:** Engaged in onshore drilling for oil and gas; and the exploration, development, and production of oil and gas. The company's operations are conducted in Texas, New Mexico, Oklahoma, Louisiana, Mississippi, Colorado, Utah, and Wyoming. **Corporate headquarters location:** This location. **Other area locations:** Midland TX. **Listed on:** NASDQ. **Stock exchange symbol:** PTEN.

PAYCHEX, INC.
4242 Woodcock Drive, Suite 100, San Antonio TX 78228. 512/469-0550. **Contact:** Human Resources. **World Wide Web address:** http://www.paychex.com. **Description:** A payroll accounting firm. It also offers services to help employers track attendance. **NOTE:** Jobseekers should apply at the corporate website which lists openings and contact e-mail addresses. **Other area locations:** Houston TX; Dallas TX; Fort Worth TX; Austin TX. **Corporate headquarters location:** Rochester NY. **Listed on:** NASDAQ. **Stock exchange symbol:** PAYX.

PEARLE VISION, INC.
2534 Royal Lane, Dallas TX 75229. 972/277-5000. **Fax:** 972/277-6415. **Contact:** Human Resources. **World Wide Web address:** http://www.pearlevision.com. **Description:** Manufactures and retails prescription eyewear. **Corporate headquarters location:** Twinsburg OH. **Other U.S. locations:** Nationwide. **Parent company:** Cole National Corporation. **Operations at this facility include:** Administration; Manufacturing. **Listed on:** New York Stock Exchange. **Stock exchange symbol:** CNJ.

PEP BOYS AUTOMOTIVE SUPERCENTER
1950 North Belt Line Road, Irving TX 75061. 972/986-2200. **Contact:** Human Resources. **World Wide Web address:** http://www.pepboys.com. **Description:** An automotive retail store and service center. There are more approximately 600 Pep Boy locations in the United States. Founded in 1921. **NOTE:** Part-time positions are offered. Apply online for all positions. **Positions advertised include:** Store Manager; Sales Associates; Automotive Service Manager; Service Advisors; Automotive Lube Technicians. **Corporate headquarters location:** Philadelphia PA. **Other area locations:** Statewide. **Other U.S. locations:** Nationwide. **Listed on:** New York Stock Exchange. **Stock exchange symbol:** PBY.

PENNZOIL COMPANY
P.O. Box 2967, Houston TX 77252-2967. 713/546-4000. **Contact:** Human Resources. **World Wide Web address:** http://www.pennzoil.com. **Description:** Engaged in oil and gas exploration and production; processing, refining, and marketing oil, gas, and refined petroleum products; and mining and marketing sulfur. Pennzoil's products are manufactured by SOPUS (former parent company Pennzoil-Quaker State Company and Shell Oil). **Corporate headquarters location:** This location. **Parent company:** Shell.

PEPSI BOTTLING GROUP
4532 Highway 67, Mesquite TX 75150. 214/324-8500. **Contact:** Human Resources. **World Wide Web address:** http://www.pepsico.com. **Description:** Bottles and distributes Pepsi-Cola beverages including the brand names Pepsi-Cola, Mountain Dew, Mug Root Beer, and Slice. Pepsi Bottling Group has 30 beverage manufacturing sites throughout Texas. **NOTE:** See the website http://www.pepsiplace.com for a complete list of Texas plants and contact information. **Parent company:** PepsiCo, Inc. (Purchase NY) consists of Frito-Lay Company, Gatorade/Tropicana North America, Pepsi-Cola Company, and Quaker Oats Company. **Listed on:** New York Stock Exchange. **Stock exchange symbol:** PEP.

PEROT SYSTEMS CORPORATION
2300 West Plano Parkway, Plano TX 75057-8427. 972/577-0000. **Toll-free phone:** 888/407-3768. **Fax:** 972/340-6100. **Contact:** Human Resources. **World Wide Web address:** http://www.perotsystems.com. **Description:** Operated by the former presidential candidate Ross Perot, this company provides technology consulting and outsourcing for global companies primarily in the engineering, financial, government and healthcare markets. Founded in 1988, it is on the Fortune 1000 list of companies. **NOTE:** Apply online. **Positions advertised include:** Senior Recruiter; Human Resources Analyst; Senior Developer/Team Lead; Technical Writer; Project Manager; Infrastructure Strategist. **Corporate headquarters location:** This location. **Other area locations:** Lubbock TX; Dallas TX. **Other U.S. location:** Nationwide. **Listed on:** New York Stock Exchange. **Stock exchange symbol:** PER.

PER-SE TECHNOLOGIES, INC.
9441 LBJ Freeway, Suite 400, Dallas TX 75243. 972/664-6900. **Contact:** Human Resources. **World Wide Web address:** http://www.per-se.com. **Description:** A leading provider of comprehensive business management services, financial and clinical software, and Internet solutions to physicians and other healthcare professionals. This company has offices throughout Texas and the United States. **NOTE:** Per-Se Technologies only accepts resumes for open positions. Interested jobseekers should check the company's website for positions and contact information. **Corporate headquarters location:** Atlanta GA. **Listed on:** NASDAQ. **Stock exchange symbol:** PSTI.

PERRY EQUIPMENT CORPORATION
P.O. Box 640, Mineral Wells TX 76068-0640. 940/325-2575. **Fax:** 940/325-3935. **Contact:** Recruiting Manager. **E-mail address:** hr@perryequipment.com. **World Wide Web address:** http://www.pecousa.com. **Description:** Manufactures filtration separation cartridges, flow-measurement systems, and systems for the oil, gas, and chemical processing industries. **Positions advertised include:** Field Engineer. **Corporate headquarters location:** This location. **Other area locations:** Amarillo TX; Houston TX. Forrest Hill MD. **International locations:** Mexico; Italy; France; Canada; United Kingdom; Malaysia; Bahrain. **Listed on:** Privately held.

PERVASIVE SOFTWARE INC.
12365 Riata Trace Parkway, Building Two, Austin TX 78727. 512/231-6000. **Toll-free phone:** 800/287-4383. **Fax:** 512/231-6010. **Contact:** Human Resources. **E-mail address:** greatjobs@pervasive.com. **World Wide Web address:** http://www.pervasive.com. **Description:** Develops embedded database software. **Positions advertised include:** Quality Technician; Engineering Consultant; Senior Marketing Programs Specialist; Senior Developer. **Corporate headquarters location:** This location. **International locations:** Belgium; Canada; England; France; Germany; Hong Kong; Ireland; Japan. **Listed on:** NASDAQ. **Stock exchange symbol:** PVSW.

PETERBILT MOTORS COMPANY
P.O. Box 550, Denton TX 76202. 940/566-7100. **Contact:** Human Resources. **World Wide Web address:** http://www.peterbilt.com. **Description:** Designs and markets custom heavy-duty trucks. Founded in 1939. **NOTE:** The website lists job postings for its corporate offices and dealerships. **Positions advertised include:** Mechanical Design Engineer. **Corporate headquarters location:** This location. **Parent company:** PACCAR, Inc. **Operations at this facility include:** Administration; Manufacturing. **Other U.S. locations:** Nationwide. **International locations:** Canada.

SID PETERSON MEMORIAL HOSPITAL
710 Water Street, Kerrville TX 78028. 830/258-7440. **Recorded jobline:** 830/258-7562. **Contact:** Human Resources. **E-mail address:** jobs@spmh.com. **World Wide Web address:** http://www.spmh.com. **Description:** A long-term care general hospital offering centers for cardiac rehabilitation, osteoporosis, and cancer treatment. **NOTE:** This hospital requires interested jobseekers to complete an application. Applications can be downloaded at the website. Full-time and part-time positions are available. **Positions advertised include:** Floor Technician; Housekeeper; Clinical Coordinator; LVN; RN; Administrative Assistant; Speech Language Pathologist; Rehabilitation Aide; Case Manager; Coder; Communications Operator.

PHARMERICA
3019 Interstate Drive, San Antonio TX 78219. 210/227-5262. **Contact:** Human Resources. **World Wide Web address:** http://www.pharmerica.com. **Description:** A supplier of pharmaceuticals and related products to long-term care facilities, hospitals, and assisted living communities. PharMerica also provides nurse consultant services, infusion therapy and training, medical records consulting, and educational programs. This company has locations throughout Texas and the United States. **NOTE:** PharMerica lists its Texas locations on its website and job listings for each location. Interested jobseekers are encouraged to visit the website and apply online. **Corporate headquarters location:** Tampa FL.

PHILIP SERVICES CORPORATION
5151 San Felipe, Suite 1600, Houston TX 77056. 713/623-8777. **Contact:** Human Resources. **World Wide Web address:** http://www.contactpsc.com. **Description:** Provides specialized turn-around maintenance and environmental, electrical, and instrumentation contracting services. Principal markets include petroleum refiners, natural gas processors, petrochemical firms, oil producers, and paper and pulp companies throughout the United States and Europe. Services include turnkey heat exchanger maintenance, tower and vessel maintenance, petroleum and petrochemical storage tank cleaning, and sludge control. In addition, Philip Services Corporation offers turnaround management services, supervising all aspects of periodic maintenance projects. The company also installs electrical and instrumentation systems for offshore production platforms and petrochemical facilities.

PIER 1 IMPORTS
P.O. Box 961020, Fort Worth TX 76161-0020. 817/878-8000. **Contact:** Staffing Manager. **World Wide Web address:** http://www.pier1.com. **Description:** Pier 1 Imports is engaged in the specialty retailing of handcrafted decorative home furnishings and accessories imported from approximately 50 countries around the world. Pier 1 Imports has a distribution center in Fort Worth and many retail locations. The company also owns CargoKids, a children's furniture and accessories store. **NOTE:** The company's website lists all management positions for its corporate office, distribution centers and retail stores. Interested jobseekers should apply online at the website. Jobseekers interested in hourly retail positions can also visit the nearest store. **Positions advertised include:** Merchandise Planner; Check Collector; Payroll Tax Specialist; Allocations Analyst; Assistant Manager; Distribution Center Associates; Divisional Visual Manager; Retail Sales Associate. **Corporate headquarters location:** This location. **Other U.S. locations:** Nationwide. **Operations at this facility include:** This location houses administrative offices. **Listed on:** New York Stock Exchange. **Stock exchange symbol:** PIR. **Number of employees worldwide:** 18,000.

PILGRIM'S PRIDE CORPORATION
P.O. Box 93, Pittsburg TX 75686-0093. 903/855-1000. **Toll-free phone:** 800/824-1159. **Contact:** Human Resources. **World Wide Web address:** http://www.pilgrimspride.com. **Description:** Produces chicken products and eggs for the restaurant, institutional, food service, grocery, and wholesale markets. The company's operations include breeding, hatching, growing, processing, packaging, and preparing poultry. Pilgrim's Pride Corporation also produces animal feeds and ingredients. The company is one of the largest producers of chicken products in the United States and Mexico. The company's primary domestic distribution is handled through restaurants and retailers in central, southwestern, and western United States, and through the food service industry throughout the country. **NOTE:** Pilgrim's Pride lists all positions and contact information on its website. Entry-level positions are available as well as day and evening shifts. **Positions advertised include:** Shipping Supervisor; Accounting Manager; Cost Accountant; Refrigeration Shift Supervisor; Breeder Service Technician; Continuous Improvement Advisor. Special programs: **Corporate headquarters location:** This location. **Other area locations:** Arlington TX; Dallas TX; Center TX; Nacogdoches TX; Mount Pleasant TX; Lufkin TX; Rockwell TX; San Antonio TX; Waco TX. **Other U.S. locations:** AR; AZ; OK. **Listed on:** New York Stock Exchange. **Stock exchange symbol:** CHX. **Number of employees worldwide:** 40,000.

PINDLER & PINDLER INC.
1617 Hi Line Drive, Suite 250, Dallas TX 75207. 214/939-9116. **Contact:** Human Resources. **World Wide Web address:** http://www.pindler.com. **Description:** Designs and distributes upholstery and drapery fabrics. **Corporate headquarters:** Moorpark CA.

PIONEER NATURAL RESOURCES
5205 North O'Connor Boulevard, Suite 900, Irving TX 75039-3747. 972/444-9001. **Fax:** 972/969-3591. **Recorded jobline:** 972/696-3832. **Contact:** Human Resources. **E-mail address:** recruiter@ pioneernrc.com. **World Wide Web address:** http://www.pioneernrc.com. **Description:** Engaged in the exploration and production of petroleum oil and natural gas. **Special programs:** Internships; Summer Jobs. **Internship information:** Internships are offered in accounting, engineering, and geology. **Corporate headquarters location:** This location. **International locations:** Buenos Aires, Argentina; Calgary, Canada. **Listed on:** New York Stock Exchange. **Stock exchange symbol:** PXD. **CEO:** Scott Sheffield.

PIZZA HUT, INC.
14841 Dallas Parkway, Dallas TX 75254. 972/338-7700. **Contact:** Human Resources. **World Wide Web address:** http://www.pizzahut.com. **Description:** An international chain of pizza restaurants. **Positions offered include:** Administrative Assistant; Network Analyst; Director Design and Standards; Sourcing Specialist; Business Financial Analyst; Paralegal; Senior Manager Equipment Engineering; Director of Aviation. **Corporate headquarters location:** This location. **Parent company:** Yum Brands. **Listed on:** New York Stock Exchange. **Stock exchange symbol:** YUM.

PIZZA INN INC.
3551 Plano Parkway, The Colony TX 75056. 469/384-5000. **Fax:** 469/384-5058. **Contact:** Human Resources. **E-mail address:** jobs@pizzainn.com. **World Wide Web address:** http://www.pizzainn.com. **Description:** Engaged primarily in operating and franchising restaurants serving pizza and complimentary foods and beverages. Pizza Inn operates more than 430 restaurants in 20 states. **NOTE:** Jobseekers interested in Assistant Manager and Delivery Driver positions should apply at the nearest location. All other positions should be e-mailed or faxed. **Positions advertised include:** Training Systems Manager; Corporate Restaurant General Manager; Over the Road Truck Driver; Field Training Specialist. **Operations at this facility include:** Administration; Sales. **Listed on:** NASDAQ. **Stock exchange symbol:** PZZI.

PLAINS RESOURCES, INC.
799 Milam Street, Suite 3100, Houston TX 77002. 832/239-6000. **Fax:** 832/239-6500.**Contact:** Human Resources. **E-mail address:** careers@plainsresources.com. **World Wide Web address:** http://www.plainsresources.com. **Description:** A *Fortune* 500 energy company that is involved in the acquisition, development, exploitation, exploration, and production of crude oil. **NOTE:** Jobseekers are encouraged to submit their resumes by fax or e-mail. **Corporate headquarters location:** This location. **Listed on:** New York Stock Exchange. **Stock exchange symbol:** PLX.

PLAZA SPECIALTY HOSPITAL
1300 Binz Street, Houston TX 77004. 713/285-1000. **Contact:** Human Resources. **World Wide Web address:** http://www.plazaspecialtyhospital.com. **Description:** This hospital provides acute care, including special services for patients with infectious diseases, kidney ailments, cancer, and chronic pain. The hospital is noted for its physical and pulmonary rehabilitation and wound care services. **NOTE:** A completed application is required for any position. Apply online. **Positions advertised include:** Pharmacy Clinical Coordinator; Occupational Therapist; Wound Care Coordinator; RN (Various); LVN (Various); Physical Therapy Assistant. **Parent company:** Tenet Healthcare.

PLANO, CITY OF
P.O. Box 860358, Plano TX 75086-0358. 972/941-7115. **Physical address:** 1520 Avenue K, Suite 130, Plano TX 75074. **Recorded jobline:** 972/941-7116 (General employment). 972/941-7299 (Police positions); 972/941-7402 (Fire positions). **Contact:** Human Resources. **World Wide Web address:** http://www.ci.plano.tx.us. **Description:** Administrative offices for the city of Plano. **NOTE**: The City of Plano has consolidated its Human Resources functions. The website contains job listings for all Plano government positions, including for the Police and Fire departments. The Human Resources office only accepts applications for open positions. A complete list of positions and an application can be downloaded at the website. Interested jobseekers can visit also the office. Some positions may require a Skill Assessment test as part of the application. The tests are administered Monday – Thursday, 8:00 a.m. – 4:00 p.m., Friday, 8:00 a.m. – 1:00 p.m. **Positions advertised include:** Public Services Librarian; Commercial Services Coordinator; Police Statistician; Warrant Clerk; Senior Administrative Assistant; Labor Maintenance Worker; Animal Services Officer; Food Service Attendant; Recreation Aide; Life Guard; Fire Emergency Management.

PLUNKETT & GIBSON, INC.
70 Northeast Loop 410, Suite 1100, San Antonio TX 782161. 210/734-7092. **Fax:** 210/734-0379. **Contact:** Human Resources. **World Wide Web address:** http://www.plunkett-gibson.com. **Description:** A defense law firm specializing in a variety of areas including insurance, medical malpractice, bankruptcy, and litigation.

POGO PRODUCING COMPANY
P.O. Box 2504, Houston TX 77252-2504. 713/297-5000. **Physical address:** 5 Greenway Plaza, Suite 2700, Houston TX 77252-2504. **Contact:** Human Resources. **E-mail address:** humanresources@pogoproducing.com. **World Wide Web address:** http://www.pogoproducing.com. **Description:** Engaged in the exploration, development, and production of oil and natural gas. **Corporate headquarters location:** This location. **Other area locations:** Midland TX. **International locations:** Thailand; Hungary. **Listed on:** New York Stock Exchange. **Stock exchange symbol:** PPP.

POLITICAL RESEARCH, INC.
Tegoland at Bent Tree, 16850 Dallas Parkway, Dallas TX 75248. 972/931-8827. **Toll-free phone:** 800/782-9002. **Fax:** 972/248-7159. **Contact:** Human Resources. **World Wide Web address:** http://www.politicalresearch.com. **Description:** A publisher of reference services on current state, federal, and international governments. Primary customers include educational institutions, libraries, government offices, and businesses. **Corporate headquarters location:** This location. **Operations at this facility include:** Administration; Research and Development; Sales; Service.

POLY-AMERICA INC.
2000 West Marshall Drive, Grand Prairie TX 75051. 972/647-4374. **Fax:** 972/337-7410. **Recorded jobline:** 972/337-7107. **Contact:** Human Resources Department. **E-mail address:** jobs@poly-america.com. **World Wide Web address:** http://www.poly-america.com. **Description:** A leading producer of polyethylene construction film and trash bags and a leading supplier of geomembrane liners. **Positions advertised include:** Administrative Assistant; Sales Representative; Receptionist; Sales Assistant; Machine Operator; Warehouse Staff. **Corporate headquarters location:** This location. **Other U.S. locations:** Cottage Grove MN; Las Vegas NV; Columbia SC; Mt. Belvieu TX.

POLY-FLEX, INC.
2000 West Marshall Drive, Grand Prairie TX 75051. 972/337-7113. **Toll-free phone:** 888/765-9359. **Fax:** 972/337-7233. **Contact:** Human Resources. **World Wide Web address:** http://www.ployflex.com. **Description:** Manufactures synthetic liners to protect ground and water from contaminants. Primary markets are waste and industrial treatment management plants and agricultural industries. The company also provides construction services for its liners.

POLYONE CORPORATION
635 Tower Drive, Kennedale TX 76060. 817/483-9797. **Fax:** 817/483-1978. **Contact:** Human Resources. **World Wide Web address:** http://www.polyone.com. **Description:** Manufactures and develops thermoplastic compounds, specialty resins, engineered films, color and additive systems, specialty polymers, rubber compounding, and vinyl compounds. **Corporate headquarters location:** Cleveland OH. **Other area locations:** Pasadena TX. **Other U.S. locations:** Nationwide. **International locations:** Worldwide. **Operations at this facility include:** Manufacturing. **Listed on:** New York Stock Exchange. **Stock exchange symbol:** POL.

POOL COMPANY
P.O. Box 1117, Crane TX 79731. 915/558-2561. **Fax:** 915/558-2402. **Contact:** Human Resources. **Description:** Engaged in pulling wells and hauling water. **Corporate headquarters location:** This location.

PORT OF HOUSTON AUTHORITY
P.O. Box 2562, Houston TX 77252-2562. 713/670-2400. **Physical address:** 111 East Loop North, Houston TX 77029. **Fax:** 713/670-2400. **Contact:** Human Resources. **E-mail address:** PHA-Resumes@poha.com. **World Wide Web address:** http://www.portofhouston.com. **Description:** Administers and regulates the Port of Houston Authority. Responsibilities include fire and safety protection along the 50-mile Houston Ship Channel. The Port Authority owns 43 general cargo wharves, two liquid-cargo wharves, and many other facilities. **NOTE:** Interested jobseekers must submit completed applications along with their resumes. A list of positions and the application can be found on the website. **Positions advertised include:** Sergeant; Vessel Services Superintendent; Mechanic. **Special programs:** Internships. **Internship information:** The Port of Houston Authority runs programs throughout the year. For more information, see the website or call Deborah Garner at 731/670-216. **Office hours:** Monday – Friday, 8:00 a.m. – 5:00 p.m.

PORTA-KAMP MANUFACTURING COMPANY INC.
P.O. Box 7064, Houston TX 77248-7064. 713/674-3163. **Physical address:** 555 Gelhorn Drive, Houston TX 77029. **Fax:** 713/674-4844. **Contact:** Human Resources. **World Wide Web address:** http://www.portakamp.com. **Description:** Manufactures offshore drilling equipment and metal portable buildings. **Corporate headquarters location:** This location.

POWELL INDUSTRIES, INC.
P.O. Box 12818, Houston TX 77217-2818. 713/944-6900. **Contact:** Human Resources. **World Wide Web address:** http://www.powellind.com. **Description:** Manufactures a wide variety of power distribution equipment including switchgear and power breakers, switchboards, instrument panels, and portable control houses. **Corporate headquarters location:** This location. **Operations at this facility include:** Administration; Manufacturing; Research and Development; Sales; Service. **Listed on:** NASDAQ. **Stock exchange symbol:** POWL.

PRATT & WHITNEY
1177 North Great Southwest Parkway, Grand Prairie TX 75050. 972/343-1300. **Contact:** Human Resources. **World Wide Web address:** http://www.pratt-whitney.com. **Description:** Repairs aircraft engine components, blades, vanes, and casings. **NOTE:** Entry-level positions and second and third shifts are offered. Pratt & Whitney has several facilities throughout Texas. See the company's website for a complete list. **Special programs:** Internships; Co-ops. **Corporate headquarters information:** Hartford CT. **Parent company:** United Technologies Corporation. **Listed on:** New York Stock Exchange. **Stock exchange symbol:** UTX. **Number of employees worldwide:** 30,000.

PRECISION AVIATION
5240 South Collins Street, Suite 100, Arlington TX 76018. 817/465-0908. **Contact:** Human Resources. **World Wide Web address:** http://www.bobflies.com. **Description:** An aircraft maintenance company that works primarily on small passenger planes.

PRICE'S CREAMERIES
600 North Piedras Street, El Paso TX 79923. 915/565-2711. **Fax:** 915/724-3605. **Contact:** Bernice Estrada, Human Resources Manager. **World Wide Web address:** http://www.pricesmilk.com. **Description:** A creamery that manufactures and distributes ice cream, milk, and fruit juices.

PRICEWATERHOUSECOOPERS
1201 Louisiana, Suite 2900, Houston TX 77002. 713/356-4000. **Contact:** Human Resources. **World Wide Web address:** http://www.pwc.com. **Description:** One of the largest certified public accounting firms in the world. PricewaterhouseCoopers provides public accounting, business advisory, management consulting, and taxation services. **NOTE:** PriceWaterHouseCoopers is a global company. See website for job openings at specific locations in Texas. **Corporate headquarters location:** New York NY. **Other area locations:** Dallas TX; Austin TX; Fort Worth TX. **Other U.S. locations:** Nationwide. **Annual sales/revenue:** $14.5 billion. **Number of employees worldwide:** 120,000.

PRIME MEDICAL SERVICES, INC.
1301 Capital of Texas Highway South, Suite C-300, Austin TX 78746. 512/328-2892. **Contact:** Human Resources. **World Wide Web address:** http://www.primemedical.com. **Description:** Through its subsidiaries, Prime Medical Services provides non-medical management services to lithotripsy and cardiac rehabilitation centers. Prime Medical Services operates 67 lithotripters. **Listed on:** NASDAQ. **Stock exchange symbol:** PMSI.

PRIMEDIA WORKPLACE LEARNING
4101 International Parkway, Carrollton TX 75007. 972/309-4000. **Fax:** 972/309-4986. **Contact:** Human Resources. **E-mail address:** jobs@pwpl.com. **World Wide Web address:** http://www.pwpl.com. **Description:** Produces and distributes educational videos to academic, corporate, and industrial clients.

PRINCIPAL FINANCIAL GROUP
7330 San Pedro Street, Suite 700, San Antonio TX 78216. 210/349-5454. **Contact:** Human Resources. **World Wide Web address:** http://www.principal.com. **Description:** Provides financial services including real estate, annuities, home mortgages, mutual funds, and retirement plans. The Principal Financial Group also offers dental, disability, health, life, and vision insurance policies. **NOTE:** This company has offices throughout Texas. See the website for job listings and contact information. **Other U.S. locations:** Nationwide. **Corporate headquarters location:** Des Moines IA.

PRINT MAILERS
707 West Road, Houston TX 77038. 832/201-2000. **Fax:** 832/201-2001. **Contact:** Human Resources. **World Wide Web address:** http://www.pminet.com. **Description:** Provides turnkey direct marketing, printing, and mailing services.

PRO-LINE CORPORATION
2121 Panoramic Circle, Dallas TX 75212. 214/631-4247. **Contact:** Human Resources. **E-mail address:** jobs@proline-intl.com. **World Wide Web address:** http://www.prolinecorp.com. **Description:** Manufactures hair care products including relaxers, botanicals, and perm repair products. **NOTE:** See http://www.alberto.com for job listings and how to apply. **Positions advertised include:** Production Supervisor. **Corporate headquarters location:** This location. **Parent company:** Alberto Culver.

PROGRESSIVE COUNTY MUTUAL INSURANCE COMPANY
1124 South IH 35, Austin TX 78704. 512/441-2000. **Fax:** 512/464-1136. **Recorded jobline:** 512/464-1164. **Contact:** Human Resources. **World Wide Web address:** http://www.progressive.com. **Description:** An automobile insurance company. **NOTE:** Progressive has many locations throughout Texas. See website for additional locations. **Positions advertised include:** Direct Sales Representative; Customer Service Trainee; Claims Representative Trainee; National Claims Processor. **Other U.S. locations:** Nationwide. **Listed on:** New York Stock Exchange. **Stock exchange symbol:** PGR.

PROVIDENCE HEALTH CENTER
6901 Medical Parkway, Waco TX 76712. 254/751-4000. **Fax:** 254/751-4909. **Recorded jobline:** 254/751-4477. **Contact:** Human Resources. **World Wide Web address:** http://www.providence.net. **Description:** A 170-bed, acute care hospital. Founded in 1905. **NOTE:** An application is required for any position. It is available online at the website. Jobseekers may mail or fax their resumes. When applying for RN, LVN, CAN, PT, OT or Speech Therapy positions, send resume and cover letter to: rgoforth@phn-waco.org. For all other positions, send e-mail to: kwest@phn-waco.org. Jobseekers may also complete an application at the Human Resources Office. **Office hours:** Monday -- Friday, 8:00 a.m. – 4:30 p.m. **Corporate headquarters location:** This location. **Parent company:** Providence Healthcare Network (also at this location). **Positions advertised include:** RN; Patient Care Coordinator; Dietician; Receptionist/File Clerk; Environmental Service Technician; Revenue Integrity Value Analyst.

PRUDENTIAL TEXAS PROPERTIES
3637 Highway 80, Mesquite TX 75150. 972/698-9700. **Contact:** Human Resources. **World Wide Web address:** http://www.prudentialtexas.com. **Description:** A local branch of the national realty company specializing in residential and commercial properties. **Positions advertised include:** Experienced Realtor. **Parent company:** Cendant.

PUBLICIS USA
14185 North Dallas Parkway, Dallas TX 75254. 972/628-7500. **Contact:** Carey Myers, Human Resources. **E-mail address:** resume@publicis-usa.com. **World Wide Web address:** http://www.publicis-usa.com. **Description:** An advertising agency with four locations nationwide. Founded in 1952. **Parent company:** Publicis Group (Paris.)

QVC INC.
9855 West Stover Hills Boulevard, San Antonio TX 78251. 210/522-4300. **Recorded jobline:** 866/782-4473. **Contact:** Human Resources. **World Wide Web address:** http://www.qvc.com. **Description:** A nationwide home shopping television network. **NOTE:** QVC has offices throughout the U.S. See website for job listings. **Operations at this location:** Service center.

THE QUAKER OATS COMPANY
2822 Glenfield Avenue, Dallas TX 75233. 214/340-0370. **Contact:** Human Resources. **World Wide Web address:** http://www.quakeroats.com. **Description:** The Quaker Oats Company is best known for Old Fashioned Quaker Oats. Other products include Aunt Jemima syrups and pancake mixes, and Rice-A-Roni instant rice. The Quaker Oats Company is a unit of PepsiCo Beverages and Food. **NOTE:** See website for Quaker Oats job listings and application information as well as other Pepsico companies in Texas. **Positions advertised include:** Materials & Supply Supervisor; Mechanical Technician. **Corporate headquarters location:** Chicago IL. **Other area locations:** Arlington, TX. **Operations at this facility include:** This location is a distribution center. **Parent company:** PepsiCo. **Listed on:** New York Stock Exchange. **Stock exchange symbol:** PEP.

QUALITY CABINETS
515 Big Stone Gap Road, Duncanville TX 75137. 972/298-6101. **Contact:** Human Resources. **World Wide Web address:** http://www.qualitycabinets.com. **Description:** Manufactures cabinets. **Corporate headquarters location:** This location. **Parent company:** Texwood Industries.

QUALITY INN BAYTOWN
300 South Highway 146 Business Road, Baytown TX 77520. 281/427-7481. **Contact:** Human Resources. **World Wide Web address:** http://www.qualityinn.com. **Description:** A full-service hotel, operating as part of the national chain. **Other U.S. locations:** Nationwide. **Parent company:** Choice Hotels International. **Listed on:** NYSE. **Stock exchange symbol:** CHH.

QUANEX CORPORATION
1900 West Loop South, Suite 1500, Houston TX 77027. 713/961-4600. **Contact:** Human Resources. **World Wide Web address:** http://www.quanex.com. **Description:** Engaged in the manufacture of carbon-alloy steel pipes, bars, and tubing. Quanex also manufactures aluminum products for the home improvement, commercial construction, and lawn and garden industries. **Listed on:** New York Stock Exchange. **Stock exchange symbol:** NX.

QUANTUM RESEARCH INTERNATIONAL
7505B Lockheed Drive, El Paso TX 79925. 915/772-2700. **Fax:** 915/772-2250. **Contact:** Human Resources. **World Wide Web address:** http://www.quantum-intl.com. **Description:** Engaged in weapons research and general engineering for the army. **NOTE:** Mail resumes to 991 Discovery Drive, Huntsville, AL 35806; or fax them to 256/971-1802; or e-mail them to personnel@quantum-intl.com. **Corporate headquarters location:** Huntsville AL.

QUEBECOR DALLAS
4800 Spring Valley Road, Dallas TX 75244. 972/233-3400. **Contact:** Human Resources. **World Wide Web address:** http://www.quebecorworld.com. **Description:** A commercial printing company. Quebecor Dallas handles large print runs for commercial magazines including *Time* and *Sports Illustrated* for the regional market. The company also prints retail inserts and catalogs. **NOTE:** This company only accepts resumes for open positions. See website for job listings. **Listed on:** New York Stock Exchange. **Stock exchange symbol:** IQW.

QUEST DIAGNOSTICS INCORPORATED
8933 Interchange Drive, Houston TX 77054. 713/667-5829. **Contact:** Human Resources. **World Wide Web address:** http://www.questdiagnostics.com. **Description:** One of the largest clinical laboratories in North America, providing a broad range of clinical laboratory services to health care clients that include physicians, hospitals, clinics, dialysis centers, pharmaceutical companies, and corporations. The company offers and performs tests on blood, urine, and other bodily fluids and tissues to provide information for health and well-being. **NOTE:** This company has second and third shift positions. **Positions advertised include:** Phlebotomist Services Representative; Medical Technologist; Route Service Representative. **Other area locations:** Irving TX: Fort Worth TX; Beaumont TX; San Antonio TX; Austin, TX; Dallas TX. **Listed on:** New York Stock Exchange. **Stock exchange symbol:** DGX.

QUEST MEDICAL, INC./ATRION CORPORATION
One Allentown Parkway, Allen TX 75002-4211. 972/390-9800. **Toll-free phone:** 800/627-0226. **Fax:** 972/390-2881. **Contact:** Human Resources. **E-mail address:** hrstaffing@atrioncorp.com. **World Wide Web address:** http://www.questmedical.com. **Description:** Develops, manufactures, markets, sells, and distributes proprietary products to the healthcare industry. **NOTE:** Jobseekers should send resumes to the parent company, Atrion, at the same address. **Corporate headquarters location:** This location. **Parent company:** Atrion Corporation (also at this location) is a holding company that designs, develops, manufactures, markets, sells, and distributes proprietary products and components for the healthcare industry. Other subsidiaries of Atrion Corporation include Atrion Medical Products and Halkey-Roberts. **Listed on:** NASDAQ. **Stock exchange symbol:** ATRI.

RBC DAIN RAUSCHER
2711 North Haskell Avenue, Suite 2400, Dallas TX 75204. 214/989-1000. **Contact:** Jamie Tiland, Office Administrator. **World Wide Web address:** http://www.rbcdain.com. **Description:** A financial consulting and securities firm. The company also provides real estate syndication and property investment services, as well as data processing services. **Corporate headquarters location:** Minneapolis MN. **Parent company:** Royal Bank of Canada. **Operations at this location:** This office specializes in personal investing. **Listed on:** New York Stock Exchange. **Stock exchange symbol:** RY. **Number of employees worldwide:** 6,000.

RF MONOLITHICS, INC.
4347 Sigma Road, Dallas TX 75244. 972/233-2903. **Fax:** 972/233-2051. **Contact:** Human Resources. **E-mail address:** resume@rfm.com. **World Wide Web address:** http://www.rfm.com. **Description:** Designs, develops, manufactures, and sells a broad range of radio frequency components and modules for the low-power wireless, high-frequency timing, and telecommunications markets. The company's products are based on surface acoustic wave reduced power consumption. The company markets its line of resonators, filters, delay lines, and related modules to original equipment manufacturers worldwide. **Corporate headquarters location:** This location. **Listed on:** NASDAQ. **Stock exchange symbol:** RFMI. **Number of employees:** 223.

RHD MEMORIAL MEDICAL CENTER
7 Medical Parkway, Dallas TX 75234. 972/888-7259. **Recorded jobline:** 972/888-7159. **Contact:** Human Resources. **E-mail address:** RHDRecruiting@tenethealth.com. **World Wide Web address:** http://www.rhdmemorial.com. **Description:** A 160-bed, acute care community hospital. **NOTE:** A completed application must be completed for any position. See website for application. **Parent company:** Tenet Health System. **Positions advertised include:** RN; Nurse Manager; Laboratory Medical Technician; Medical Staff Services Director; Pharmacy Technician.

RIA
2395 Midway Road, Carrollton TX 75006. 972/250-7000. **Fax:** 972/250-7763. **Contact:** Human Resources. **World Wide Web address:** http://www.riahome.com. **Description:** One of the world's largest providers of solutions for tax research, compliance, and information. **NOTE:** This company prefers that jobseekers apply online at its corporate website: http://www.thomsoncareers.com. **Parent company:** Thomson Tax and Accounting.

R2 TECHNOLOGIES
15455 North Dallas Parkway, Suite 475, Addison TX 75001. 469/621-2421. **Fax:** 214/853-5736. **Contact:** Human Resources. **E-mail address:** r2recruiter@r2now.com. **World Wide Web address:** http://www.r2now.com. **Description:** Provides professional consulting and technical services that support clients' information technology business needs. **Positions advertised include:** Business Intelligence Analyst; Consultant, Enterprise Planner; Customer Support Analyst; Data Modeler Data Warehouse; Data Warehouse Data Architect.

RVSI ACUITY CIMATRIX
6311 North O'Connor Road, Suite N50, Irving TX 75039. 972/869-7684. **Contact:** Human Resources. **E-mail address:** hr@rvsi.net. **World Wide Web address:** http://www.rvsi.com. **Description:** RVSI Acuity CiMatrix provides data collection integrators with complete solutions including scanning components, networking, software tools, and support services. Products and related services fall into four major categories: omnidirectional scanning systems, intelligent fixed position line scanners, data collection terminals, and networking products. RVSI's foreign subsidiaries are located in Canada, Belgium, England, France, and Germany. **NOTE:** Send resumes to Human Resources, 486 Amherst Street, Nashua NH 03063. **Corporate headquarters location:** Canton MA. **Other U.S. locations:** CA; GA; IL; MI; OH. **Operations at this facility include:** This location is a sales office. **Listed on:** NASDAQ. **Stock exchange symbol:** RVSI.

RADIOSHACK
300 West Third Street, Suite 200, Fort Worth TX 76102. 817/415-3700. **Fax:** 817/415-3243. **Recorded jobline:** 817/415-2949. **Contact:** Employment Opportunities. **World Wide Web address:** http://www.radioshack.com. **Description:** Sells a wide variety of consumer electronic parts and equipment through more than 7,000 stores nationwide. **Corporate headquarters location:** This location. **Operations at this facility include:** Administration; Advertising; Customer Service. **Listed on:** New York Stock Exchange. **Stock exchange symbol:** RSH.

RAILAMERICA, INC
4040 Broadway, Suite 200, San Antonio TX 78209. 210/841-7600. **Fax:** 561/226-1627. **Contact:** Human Resources. **E-mail address:** employment@railamerica.com. **World Wide Web address:** http://www.railamerica.com. **Description:** A leading operator of short line railroads nationwide. **Positions advertised include:** Electrician. **NOTE:** Send resumes to: RailAmerica, Inc., Employment, 5300 Broken Sound Boulevard Northwest, Boca Raton FL 33487.

RAILWORKS
P.O. Box 15217, Houston TX 77220. 713/673-6208. **Contact:** Human Resources. **E-mail address:** careers@railworks.com. **Description:** A railroad construction contractor. **Corporate headquarters location:** White Plains NY. **Operations at this facility include:** This location is the administrative office for the South-Central Division of Railworks. **Listed on:** Privately held. **Number of employees worldwide:** 3,000.

RALSTON DRUG AND DISCOUNT LIQUOR
3147 Southmore Boulevard, Houston TX 77004. 713/524-3045. **Contact:** Human Resources. **Description:** Operates discount liquor and drug stores with 18 local outlets.

RANDALLS FOOD MARKETS
3663 Briar Park, Houston TX 77042.**Fax:** 713/435-2499. **Recorded jobline:** 713/268-3404. **Contact:** Recruiter. **E-mail address:** employment@randalls.com. **World Wide Web address:** http://www.randalls.com. **Description:** Operates 138 retail grocery stores in Texas. It is a subsidiary of Safeway Inc., a chain with stores throughout the United States and Canada. **Corporate headquarters location:** This location. **Listed on:** New York Stock Exchange. **Stock exchange symbol:** SWY.

RANGER INSURANCE COMPANY
P.O. Box 2807, Houston TX 77252-2807. 713/954-8100. **Toll-free phone:** 800/392-1970. **Contact:** Human Resources. **World Wide Web address:** http://www.rangerinsurance.com. **Description:** Markets specialty lines of commercial property and casualty insurance as well as nonstandard automobile insurance. **Corporate headquarters location:** This location.

RAYMOND JAMES & ASSOCIATES
6034 West Courtyard Drive, Suite 305, Austin TX 78730. 512/418-1700. **Contact:** Human Resources. **World Wide Web address:** http://www.raymondjames.com. **Description:** An investment brokerage firm offering financial planning, investment banking, asset management, and trust services. Founded in 1962. **NOTE:** This company has 10 other locations in the Austin area. See website for additional addresses and contact information.

RAYTHEON
P.O. Box 6056, Greenville TX 75403-6056. 903/455-3450. **Contact:** Human Resources. **World Wide Web address:** http://www.raytheon.com. **Description:** Raytheon Systems designs, manufactures, and installs state-of-the-art communications and integrated command-and-control systems for military and industrial customers worldwide. **NOTE:** See website for job listings and application information. **Other area locations:** Dallas TX (High-technology software). **Parent company:** Raytheon Company is a diversified, international, multi-industry technology-based company ranked among the 100 largest U.S. industrial corporations. Raytheon has 110 facilities in 28 states and the District of Columbia. Overseas facilities and representative offices are located in 26 countries, principally in Europe, the Middle East, and the Pacific Rim. The company's four business segments include Electronics, Major Appliances, Aircraft Products, and Energy and Environmental. **Operations at this facility include:** This location manufactures electronic equipment for the military and commercial electronics industries. Military products include reconnaissance and surveillance equipment; command, control, and communications equipment; navigation and control systems; and aircraft maintenance and navigation systems. Nonmilitary products include mass media storage equipment, medical imaging devices, and data handling products. **Listed on:** New York Stock Exchange. **Stock exchange symbol:** RTN. **Number of employees worldwide:** 78,000.

READER'S WHOLESALE DISTRIBUTORS INC.
1201 Naylor, Houston TX 77002. 713/224-8300. **Contact:** Human Resources. **World Wide Web address:** http://www.readerswholesale.net. **Description:** A wholesaler of flooring materials such as carpet, tile, and wood.

REDSALSA TECHNOLOGIES
13800 Montfort Drive, Suite 230, Dallas TX 75240. 972/503-4200. **Fax:** 972/503-7900. **Contact:** Human Resources. **E-mail address:** jobs@redsalsa.com. **World Wide Web address:** http://www.redsalsa.com. **Description:** Provides application development and testing, business process outsourcing, enterprise content and document management, and IT staffing services. **Positions advertised include:** Software Engineer; Programming Analyst.

REED-HYCALOG COMPANY
6501 Navigation, Houston TX 77011. 713/924-5200. **Contact:** Human Resources. **World Wide Web address:** http://www.grantsprideco.com. **Description:** Manufactures rock bits and other machinery for use in offshore drilling. **Parent company:** Grant Pride Co. **Listed on:** New York Stock Exchange. **Stock exchange symbol:** GRP.

RELIABILITY INC.
P.O. Box 218370, Houston TX 77218. 281/492-0550. **Fax:** 281/492-0615. **Contact:** Human Resources. **World Wide Web address:** http://www.relinc.com. **Description:** Engaged in the testing of electronic components. **Office hours:** Monday - Thursday, 7:00 a.m. - 5:00 p.m.; Friday, 7:00 a.m. - 11:00 a.m. **Corporate headquarters location:** This location. **International locations:** Singapore. **Operations at this facility include:** Manufacturing; Research and Development; Sales; Service. **Listed on:** NASDAQ. **Stock exchange symbol:** REAL.

RELIANT ENERGY, INC.
1000 Main Street, Houston TX 77002. 713/497-3000. **Contact:** Human Resources. **World Wide Web address:** http://www.reliant.com. **Description:** Generates and distributes energy to wholesale and retail re-sellers. **NOTE:** Apply online at the company's website. **Positions advertised include:** Load Forecasting Analyst; Energy Sales Representative; Environmental Air Compliance Analyst; Sales Manager; Mechanic. **Corporate headquarters location:** This location. **Other U.S. locations:** NJ; MD; NY; PA; FL; NV; CA. **Listed on:** New York Stock Exchange. **Stock exchange symbol:** RRI. **Number of employees nationwide:** 16,500.

RENT-A-CENTER
5700 Tennyson Parkway, 3rd Floor, Plano TX 75024. 972/801-1100. **Toll-free phone:** 800/275-2696. **Fax:** 972/943-0119. **Contact:** Staffing. **World Wide Web address:** http://www.rentacenter.com. **Description:** Rents furniture, appliances, stereos, and other furnishings and equipment. **Special programs:** Internships. **Corporate headquarters location:** This location. **Other U.S. locations:** Nationwide. **Listed on:** NASDAQ. **Stock exchange symbol:** RCII. **Number of employees nationwide:** 15,400.

RENTAL SERVICE CORPORATION (RSC)
16225 Park Ten Place, Suite 200, Houston TX 77084. 281/578-5600. **Contact:** Human Resources. **World Wide Web address:** http://www.rentalservice.com. **Description:** A wholesale and rental that provides a wide variety of construction and industrial equipment for industrial users and homeowners. RSC has two sister companies, Prime Energy and Prime Industrial. **NOTE:** This company's website lists Texas-area job openings. Check website for contact information. **Corporate headquarters location:** This location. **Parent company:** Atlas Copco Group. **Operations at this facility:** Regional Office.

REPUBLIC BEVERAGE
1010 Isuzu Parkway, Grand Prairie TX 75050. 972/595-6100. **Contact:** Human Resources. **E-mail address:** resumes@republicbeverage.com. **World Wide Web address:** http://www.republicbeverage.com. **Description:** A wine and alcohol wholesale distributor. **Positions advertised include:** Administrative Assistant; Area Manager-On Premise Spirits; Customer Service Representative; Fine Wine Division Manager; Key Account Specialist—Costco; Sales Vice President. **Special programs:** Internships. **Other area locations:** Houston TX; Longview TX; Beamont, TX; Abilene TX; Amarillo TX; El Paso TX.

REPUBLIC SUPPLY COMPANY
5646 Milton Street, Suite 800, Dallas TX 75206. 214/987-9868. **Contact:** Human Resources. **Description:** Distributes oil field supplies and industrial machine equipment. **Corporate headquarters location:** This location. **Operations at this facility include:** Administration. **Listed on:** Privately held.

REXEL INC.
P.O. Box 9085, Addison TX 75001-9085. 972/387-3600. **Physical address:** 6700 Lyndon B Johnson Freeway, Suite 3200, Dallas TX 75240-6503. **Fax:** 972/934-2056. **Contact:** Human Resources. **World Wide Web address:** http://www.rexelusa.com. **Description:** One of the world's largest distributors of electronic parts and supplies. **NOTE:** Resumes should be sent to Human Resources, 6700 LBJ Freeway, Suite 3700, Dallas TX 75240. **Corporate headquarters location:** This location. **Parent company:** Pinault-Printemps-Redoute. **Operations at this facility include:** Administration.

REYNOLDS INTERNATIONAL INC.
P.O. Box 550, McAllen TX 78505-0550. 956/687-7500. **Contact:** Human Resources. **World Wide Web address:** http://www.reynoldsinternational.com. **Description:** Manufactures tractor equipment. **Corporate headquarters location:** This location.

RIBELIN SALES INC.
12720 Hillcrest Road, Suite 820, Dallas TX 7230. 972/272-1594. **Fax:** 972/404-9683. **Contact:** Human Resources. **World Wide Web address:** http://www.ribelin.com. **Description:** Ribelin Sales Inc. is a wholesale distributor of raw materials for the paint and coating industry. Founded in 1936. **Other area locations:** Garland TX; Houston TX. **Other U.S. locations:** AZ; GA; FL.

RICE EPICUREAN MARKETS INC.
5333 Gulfton, Houston TX 77081. 713/662-7700. **Fax:** 713/662-7757. **Contact:** Human Resources. **E-mail address:** employment@riceepicurean.com. **World Wide Web address:** http://www.riceepicurean.com. **Description:** Operates and manages a chain of five food stores in the Houston area. **NOTE:** All positions require an application which can found on the company's website. Jobseekers may fax, e-mail, mail or deliver their applications and resumes. **Positions advertised include:** Cashier; Sacker; Meat Cutters; Maid; Bakery Attendants. **Office hours:** Monday - Friday, 8:00 a.m. - 5:00 p.m. **Corporate headquarters location:** This location. **Operations at this facility include:** Administration.

RICE UNIVERSITY
Employment Office -- MS-56, P.O. Box 1892, Houston TX 77251-1892. 713/348-4074. **Fax:** 713/348-5496. **Recorded jobline:** 713/348-6080. **Contact:** Human Resources. **E-mail address:** careers@rice.edu. **World Wide Web address:** http://employment.rice.edu. **Description:** An independent, co-educational, private university for undergraduate and graduate studies, research, and professional training in selected disciplines. Rice University has an undergraduate student enrollment of approximately 2,700; a graduate and professional student enrollment of approximately 1,400. **NOTE:** An application is required for any position. It can be located on the website. Jobseekers may apply in person at the Human Resources Office at 6100 Main Street, Allen Center, Room 111, Houston TX. **Positions advertised include:** Assistant Director; Research Analyst; Police Officer; Internal Auditor; Bookkeeper; Office Assistant; Program Coordinator; Staff Assistant; Custodian; Groundskeeper; Laundry Manager; Painter. **Office hours:** Monday - Friday, 8:00 a.m. - 5:00 p.m.

THE RICHARDS GROUP
8750 North Central Expressway, Suite 1200, Dallas TX 75231-6437. 214/891-5700. **Contact:** Human Resources. **World Wide Web address:** http://www.richards.com. **Description:** A full-service advertising agency offering public relations, media, direct marketing, promotional marketing, naming, graphic design, and interactive communications services. **Listed on:** Privately held.

THE RICHARDSON HOTEL
701 East Campbell Road, Richardson TX 75081. 972/231-9600. **Contact:** Human Resources. **World Wide Web address:** http://www.therichardshotel.com. **Description:** A 342-room hotel with two restaurants, meeting facilities, and a fitness center. **Listed on:** Privately held.

RICHLAND COLLEGE
12800 Abrams Road, Dallas TX 75243-2199. 972/238-6240. Recorded jobline: 214/860-2438. **Contact:** Human Resources Director. **World Wide Web address:** http://www.rlc.dcccd.edu. **Description:** A junior college offering one- and two-year associate's degrees and certificates to approximately 12,500 students. Richland College operates as part of the Dallas County Community College District. **NOTE:** See the Dallas County's Community College District's website for job listings: http://www.dccd.edu. An application is required for any open position. It can be found on the District's website. **Positions advertised include:** Program Administrator; Dance Instructor; English Instructor; Department Assistant; Instructional Associate.

RIO VISTA REHABILITATION HOSPITAL
1740 Curie Drive, El Paso TX 79902. 915/544-3399. **Contact:** Human Resources. **World Wide Web address:** http://www.sphn.com. **Description:** An inpatient and outpatient rehabilitation facility that assists patients experiencing orthopedic problems, joint replacement, trauma, arthritis, or amputation. **NOTE:** Apply online at this

hospital's website. **Positions advertised include:** RN; LVN; Endoscopy Technician; Case Manager; Surgery Coordinator; Laboratory Assistant; Administrative Director. **Parent company:** Tenet Health System.

RIVIANA FOODS INC.
P.O. Box 2636, Houston TX 77252. 713/529-3251. **Fax:** 713/529-1661. **Contact:** Human Resources. **E-mail address:** lpagel@riviana.com. **World Wide Web address:** http://www.riviana.com. **Description:** Produces and distributes rice under the Mahatma, Carolina, and River brand names. **Listed on:** NASDAQ. **Stock exchange symbol:** RVFD.

JACK ROACH FORD
6445 Southwest Freeway, Houston TX 77074. 281/588-5000. **Contact:** Human Resources. **World Wide Web address:** http://www.jackroach.com. **Description:** A new and used vehicle dealership.

ROCHESTER GAUGES, INC.
11616 Harry Hines Boulevard, Dallas TX 75229. 972/241-2161. **Fax:** 972/620-1403. **Contact:** Human Resources. **World Wide Web address:** http://www.rochestergauges.com. **Description:** A manufacturer of gauges, thermometers, and measuring devices. **NOTE:** Entry-level positions are offered. **Corporate headquarters location:** This location. **Operations at this facility include:** Manufacturing. **Listed on:** Privately held.

ROCK-TENN COMPANY
1385 Northwestern Drive, El Paso TX 79912. 915/581-5492. **Contact:** Human Resources. **World Wide Web address:** http://www.rocktenn.com. **Description:** Manufactures recycled paperboard and paperboard products. Over two-thirds of paperboard production is used by the company's own converting plants to produce folding cartons, book and notebook covers, components for the furniture industry, and solid fiber partitions used in shipping glass and plastic containers. **Positions advertised include:** Mill Superintendent. **Corporate headquarters location:** Norcross GA. **Other U.S. locations:** Nationwide. **Listed on:** New York Stock Exchange. **Stock exchange symbol:** RKT.

ROHM & HAAS TEXAS, INC.
1900 Tidal Road, Deer Park TX 77536. 281/228-8100. **Contact:** Human Resources. **World Wide Web address:** http://www.rohmhaas.com. **Description:** Rohm & Haas Company is a specialty chemicals company operating in four industry segments: Polymers, Resins, and Monomers; Plastics; Industrial Chemicals; and Agricultural Chemicals. Rohm & Haas Company is also engaged in non-chemical industries such as forestry products, carpet production, and biomedical testing. **Special programs:** Internships; MBA Training. **Corporate headquarters location:** Philadelphia PA. **Operations at this facility include:** This location manufactures a variety of chemicals including ammonia and cyanide. **Listed on:** New York Stock Exchange. **Stock exchange symbol:** ROH.

THE RONALD McDONALD HOUSE OF GALVESTON
P.O. Box 1045, Galveston TX 77553. 409/762-0609. **Fax:** 409/762-5338. **Contact:** Human Resources. **E-mail address:** ronmcd@galveston.com. **World Wide Web address:** http://www.rmgalveston.org. **Description:** A nonprofit organization providing support services for families of children afflicted with serious illnesses.

ROUND ROCK MEDICAL CENTER
2400 Round Rock Avenue, Round Rock TX 78681. 512/341-5156. **Contact:** Human Resources. **World Wide Web address:** http://www.roundrockhospital.com. **Description:** A 109-bed general hospital. Services include a 24-hour emergency room, Family Birthing Center, medical/surgical unit, six-bed intensive care unit, and a nine-bed skilled nursing unit. Founded in 1983. This hospital is part of the HealthCare Partnership with three other hospitals in Austin TX. **NOTE:** Submit resume online for open positions. **Positions advertised include:** Clinical Dietitian; RN; Supervisor; Pharmacy Technician; Food Services Associate; Security Guard; Mammographer; Speech Language Pathologist.

RUBBERMAID, INC.
7121 Shelby Avenue, Greenville TX 75402. 903/455-0011. **Contact:** Human Resources. **World Wide Web address:** http://www.rubbermaid.com. **Description:** Rubbermaid manufactures and sells rubber and plastic products for the consumer and commercial markets. Products include over 2,500 items for home organization, kitchen and bath, household repairs/do-it-yourself, and agricultural, industrial, and institutional use. **Corporate headquarters location:** Wooster OH. **Operations at this facility include:** This location manufactures household products such as plastic food storage containers.

POLLY RYON MEMORIAL HOSPITAL
1705 Jackson Street, Richmond TX 77469. 281/341-4831. **Fax:** 281/341-2883. **Recorded jobline:** 281/341-2852. **Contact:** Human Resources. **E-mail address:** jobs@pollyryon.org. **World Wide Web address:** http://www.pollyryon.org. **Description:** A nonprofit, acute care medical facility with 185 beds. In addition to general medical and surgical procedures, Polly Ryon offers a wide range of services including active health education in the community; PROMISE, the birthing center; imaging services such as CT scanning, mammography, and MRIs; hospice care; and STAR, the Sports Therapy and Rehabilitation service. Founded in 1949. **NOTE:** Second and third shifts are offered as well as on-call positions. **Positions advertised include:** Microbiologist; Clinical Educator; Radiology Technologist; Ultrasound Technologist; Executive Secretary; Cook; Account Representative; RN; LVN. **Office hours:** Monday – Friday, 7:30 a.m. – 4:30 p.m. **Corporate headquarters location:** This location. **Operations at this facility include:** Administration; Service.

S&B ENGINEERS AND CONSTRUCTORS
7825 Park Place Boulevard, Houston TX 77087. 713/645-4141. **Recorded jobline:** 713/845-7950. **Contact:** Human Resources. **World Wide Web address:** http://www.sbec.com. **Description:** A construction company. **NOTE:** For engineering positions, contact Ken Miller via e-mail at employment@sbec.com or fax at 713/645-4347. For all other positions, mail resumes to Human Resources. **Positions advertised include:** Project Engineer; Electrical Engineer; Metallurgist/Welding Engineer; Pressure Vessel Engineer; Heat Transfer Engineer; Field Heater Engineer; Civil/Structural Engineer; Project Manager; Senior Estimator; Project Controls Manager. **Office hours:** Monday – Friday, 7:30 a.m. – 4:30 p.m. **Other area locations:** McAllen TX; Austin TX. **Other U.S. locations:** LA; SC; Washington D.C. **International locations:** United Kingdom; India; Saudi Arabia; Singapore. **Listed on:** Privately held.

SABRE HOLDINGS COMPANY
3150 Sabre Drive, Southlake TX 76092. 682/605-1000. **Fax:** 682/605-8267. **Contact:** Human Resources. **World Wide Web address:** http://www.sabre-holdings.com. **Description:** A giant in the travel reservation industry. This company owns and manages the popular website Travelocity. It also manages the reservations system used by travel agents to book airline seats, hotel rooms, rental cars and cruises. **NOTE:** Apply online. **Positions advertised include:** Senior Business Systems Analyst; Sales Analyst; IT Project Management Senior; Marketing Communications Manager; Senior Data Warehouse Developer; Insides Sales Representative. **Special programs:** Internships. **Other U.S. locations:** CA; FL; NV; NY; WA; Washington DC. **Listed on:** New York Stock Exchange. **Stock exchange symbol:** TSG.

SBC COMMUNICATIONS INC.
SOUTHWESTERN BELL
175 East Houston Street, San Antonio TX 78205. 210/821-4105. **Recorded jobline:** 210/820-6832. **Contact:** Human Resources. **World Wide Web address:** http://www.sbc.com. **Description:** Provides telecommunications products and services throughout the United States and internationally. **NOTE:** SBC's website provides job listings for all its Texas locations. See website for listings and application information. **Corporate headquarters location:** This location. **Subsidiaries include:** Ameritech, CellularOne, Nevada Bell, Pacific Bell, SBC Telecom, SNET, and Southwestern Bell (also at this location) provides local telephone and cellular services. **Listed on:** New York Stock Exchange. **Stock exchange symbol:** SBC. **Number of employees worldwide:** 168,000.

SCS/FRIGETTE CORPORATION
P.O. Box 40557, Fort Worth TX 76140. **Physical address:** 1200 West Risinger Road, Fort Worth TX 76134. 817/293-5313. **Contact:** Human Resources. **World Wide Web address:** http://www.scsfrigette.com. **Description:** A manufacturer of automobile air conditioning and heating systems, cruise controls, security systems, and accessories. **Corporate headquarters location:** This location. **Operations at this facility include:** Administration; Manufacturing; Research and Development; Sales; Service. **Listed on:** Privately held.

ST MICROELECTRONICS
1310 Electronics Drive, Carrollton TX 75006. 972/466-6000. **Contact:** Human Resources. **World Wide Web address:** http://www.us.st.com. **Description:** ST Microelectronics designs, develops, manufactures, and markets a broad range of semiconductor integrated circuits and discrete devices used in a variety of microelectronic applications. These applications include telecommunications systems, computer systems, consumer products, automotive products, and industrial automation and control systems. Founded in 1987. **NOTE:** Apply online at this company's website. **Positions advertised include:** Market Development Manager; Facilities Engineer; Manufacturing Quality Engineer; EES Technician. **Corporate headquarters location:** Montgomeryville PA. **Operations at this facility include:** This location manufactures microchips. **Listed on:** New York Stock Exchange. **Stock exchange symbol:** STM.

SACHNOWITZ & COMPANY
3410 West Dallas, Houston TX 77019. 713/521-1010. **Contact:** Human Resources. **E-mail address:** Dave@sachnowitz.com. **World Wide Web address:** http://www.sachnowitz.com. **Description:** A marketing and advertising agency specializing in radio, television, and magazine ads.

SAFETY STEEL SERVICE INC.
P.O. Box 2298, Victoria TX 77902. 361/575-4561. **Contact:** Human Resources. **Description:** Provides a variety of services for the steel industry including manufacturing rebar and structural pipes.

SAFETY-KLEEN CORPORATION
1722 Cooper Creek Road, Denton TX 76208. 940/483-5200. **Contact:** Human Resources. **World Wide Web address:** http://www.safety-kleen.com. **Description:** The company offers treatment, recycling, and disposal services. **NOTE:** This company has administrative and sales offices throughout Texas. See the company's website for job listings and application information. **Corporate headquarters location:** Plano TX. **Other U.S. locations:** Nationwide. **Operations at this facility include:** This location is a recycling center for hazardous waste.

SAI PEOPLE SOLUTIONS, INC.
2313 Timber Shadows Drive, Suite 200, Kingwood TX 77339. 281/358-1858. **Fax:** 281/358-8952. **Contact:** Human Resources. **World Wide Web address:** http://www.saisoft.com. **Description:** A computer consulting company. Sai People Solutions offers IT staffing expertise and off-site automated software testing services to *Fortune* 500 firms in a wide range of industries including telecommunications, banking, medical, manufacturing, and transportation. **Corporate headquarters location:** This location. **Other U.S. locations:** CA; AZ; CO: MI; IL; OH; PA; NY; GA; NC; SC; Washington D.C.

ST. DAVID'S MEDICAL CENTER
98 San Jacinto Boulevard, Suite 1800, Austin TX, 78701. 512/708-9700. **Contact:** Human Resources. **World Wide Web address:** http://www.stdavids.com. **Description:** A 400-bed hospital specializing in all types of adult medical care. **Positions advertised include:** Patient Care Technician; Phlebotomist; Pharmacy Technician; RN; Physical Therapist; Radiology Technician; Physical Therapist; Diet Clerk.

ST. EDWARD'S UNIVERSITY
Campus Mailbox 1042, 3001 South Congress Avenue, Austin TX 78748. 512/448-8587. **Fax:** 512/464-8813. **Recorded jobline:** 512/448-8541. **Contact:** Human Resources. **World Wide Web address:** http://www.stedwards.edu/humr/jobs.htm. **Description:** A private university affiliated with the Catholic Church. St. Edward's University offers a liberal arts program to undergraduate and graduate students interested in business or human services. **NOTE:** See website for job listings and contact information. **Positions advertised include:** Dean, School of Business; Assistant Professor, Finance; Assistant Professor, Bioinformatics; Library Instruction Coordinator; Adjunct Faculty; Residence Hall Director; Senior Secretary; Public Relations Assistant; Groundskeeper; Graduate Internship; Office Specialist. **Corporate headquarters location:** This location. **Operations at this facility include:** Administration. **Listed on:** Privately held.

ST. LUKE'S EPISCOPAL HOSPITAL
P.O. Box 20269, Houston TX 77225-0269. 713/785-8537. **Physical address:** 6720 Bertner Street, Houston TX 77030. **Recorded jobline:** 800/231-1000. **Contact:** Human Resources. **World Wide Web address:** http://www.sleh.com. **Description:** A full-service hospital specializing in pulmonary care in its Texas Heart Institute. This hospital is the flagship for the St. Luke's Health System, which includes three additional healthcare facilities: Kelsey-Seybold, Community Medical Center (The Woodlands) and the Episcopal Health Charities. **NOTE:** Jobseekers may apply online at the hospital's website; apply in person at the Human Resources Department, or mail their resumes. **Positions advertised include:** RN; Home Health Aides; Patient Care Assistant; Unit Secretary; Physical Therapist; Staff Pharmacist; Surgical Technicians;

Provider Relations Coordinator; Infection Control Practitioner; Senior Information Protection Analyst; Administrative Secretary; Employment Representative; Senior Admitting Interviewer. **Special programs:** Residencies. **Office hours:** Monday – Friday, 8:00 a.m. – 4:00 p.m.

ST. MARY'S UNIVERSITY
One Camino Santa Maria, San Antonio TX 78228-8565. 210/436-3725. **Fax:** 210/431-2223. **Recorded jobline:** 210/436-3343. **Contact:** Human Resources Director. **World Wide Web address:** http://www.stmarytx.edu. **Description:** A liberal arts university affiliated with the Catholic Church. St. Mary's University has three undergraduate programs and two graduate programs including a law school. The school is one of the oldest and largest Catholic universities in the Southwest. Founded in 1852. **NOTE:** An application is required for certain positions. See the university's website for additional information. **Special programs:** Internships. **Positions advertised include:** Systems Manager; Counselor/Assistant Director; Physician Assistant. **Corporate headquarters location:** This location. **Operations at this facility include:** Administration; Research and Development; Service. **Listed on:** Privately held.

ST. PAUL TRAVELERS
P.O. Box 660456, Dallas TX 75266. 972/866-4748. **Physical address:** 7920 Beltline Road, Dallas TX 75240. **Contact:** Human Resources. **World Wide Web address:** http://www.stpaultravelers.com. **Description:** Offers a wide range of insurance products to commercial customers including workers' compensation, property, liability, and surety bonds. The company also provides homeowners and auto insurance to consumers. **NOTE:** Apply online at the company's website. **Positions advertised include:** Agency Portfolio Consultant; Medical Case Manager; Unit Manager. **Corporate headquarters location:** Saint Paul, MN **Listed on:** New York Stock Exchange. **Stock exchange symbol:** STA.

SAKS FIFTH AVENUE
13550 North Dallas Parkway, Dallas TX 75240. 972/458-7000. **Contact:** Human Resources Manager. **World Wide Web address:** http://www.saksincorporated.com. **Description:** Saks Fifth Avenue is a retail chain emphasizing soft-goods products, primarily apparel for men, women, and children. **NOTE:** Jobseekers interested in management positions should apply online at the company's website. Jobseekers interested in sales positions can apply online at the website or visit the nearest store location. **Corporate headquarters location:** Birmingham AL. **Parent company:** Saks Incorporated is a department store holding company that operates approximately 380 stores in 396 states. The company's stores include Saks Fifth Avenue, Parisian, Proffit's, Younker's, Herberger's, Carson Pirie Scott, Boston Store, Bergner's, and Off 5th, the company's outlet store. Saks Incorporated also operates two retail catalogs and several retail Internet sites. **Listed on:** New York Stock Exchange. **Stock exchange symbol:** SKS. **Number of employees nationwide:** 55,000.

SALVATION ARMY
TEXAS DIVISION
6500 Harry Hines Boulevard, Dallas TX 75235. 214/956-6000. **Contact:** Human Resources. **World Wide Web address:** http: www.salvationarmytexas.org. **Description:** A world-renown Christian volunteer organization that helps distribute money, food, clothing and other items to those in need, whether due to economic or social hardship, natural disaster or war. Also operates thrift stores. **NOTE:** In addition to the Texas division's office, the Salvation Army has several thrift stores throughout the state. See the website for locations.

SAM HOUSTON STATE UNIVERSITY
P.O. Box 2356, Huntsville TX 77341. 936/294-1069. **Physical address:** 1903 University Avenue, Estill Building #334, Huntsville TX 77341. **Fax:** 936/294-3611. **Recorded jobline:** 936/294-1067. **Contact:** Human Resources. **World Wide Web address:** http://www.shsu.edu. **Description:** A four-year state university offering programs through its four colleges: Arts & Sciences, Business Administration, Criminal Justice, and Educational and Applied Sciences. **NOTE:** Application forms must be submitted for any position. See website for forms, job listings and contact information. **Positions advertised include:** Assistant Professor; Lecturer; Full Professor; Staff Assistant; Computer Systems Technician; Staff Associate.

SAMSILL CORPORATION
5740 Hartman Road, P.O. Box 15066, Fort Worth TX 76119. 817/536-1906. **Fax:** 817/535-6900. **Contact:** Human Resources. **E-mail address:** resumes@samsill.com. **World Wide Web address:** http://www.samsill.com. **Description:** Manufactures office products such as plastic binders and sheet protectors.

SAMSUNG AUSTIN SEMICONDUCTOR
12100 Samsung Boulevard, Austin TX 78754. 512/672-1000. **Contact:** Human Resources. **World Wide Web address:** http://www.samsungusa.com. **Description:** Manufactures semiconductors. This is Samsung's only production plant located outside of Korea. **NOTE:** For job listings and contact information, apply online at the corporate website, http://www.samsungusa.com. **Positions advertised include:** Environmental Engineer; Facilities Electrical Engineer; Human Resources Specialist; Manufacturing Supervisor; Procurement Assistant; Senior Administrative Assistant. **Corporate headquarters location:** Seoul, Korea. **Other U.S. locations:** Nationwide. **International locations:** Worldwide. **Parent company:** Samsung USA, a subsidiary of Samsung Electronics Co. Ltd. **Subsidiaries include:** Samsung Information Technology; Samsung Consumer Electronics Division; **Operations at this facility include:** Sales; Marketing.

SAN ANTONIO AEROSPACE, L.P.
9800 John Saunders Road, San Antonio TX 78216. 210/293-3200. **Contact:** Steve Klein, SAA Recruiting Department. **Description:** Repairs, modifies, and designs aircraft.

SAN ANTONIO, CITY OF
111 Plaza De Armas, San Antonio TX 78207. 210/207-8108 **Recorded jobline:** 210/207-7280. **Contact:** Human Resources. **World Wide Web address:** http://www.sanantonio.gov. **Description:** Administrative offices for the City of San Antonio, including its Fire and Police Departments. **NOTE:** Part-time and temporary jobs available. See website for job listings and application information. **Positions advertised include:** Parking Supervisor; Events Attendant; Management Analyst; Senior Engineer; Contracts Services Manager; Assistant Marketing Manager; Special Projects Coordinator; Community Center Coordinator; Equipment Operator; Enrichment Specialist.

SAN ANTONIO INDEPENDENT SCHOOL DISTRICT
141 Lavaca Street, San Antonio TX 78210. 210/299-5606. **Contact:** Human Resources. **World Wide Web address:** http://www.saisd.net. **Description:** Administrative offices for the K-12 school system in San Antonio. **NOTE:** See the district's website for job listings for all schools in San Antonio and apply online. **Positions advertised include:** Librarian; Food Service Accounting Director; Assistant Principal; Special Education/Educational Diagnostician; Curriculum Lead Teacher; Technology Grant Specialist; Campus Social Worker; Data Clerk; Head Golf Coach; Head Soccer Coach; General Assistant Coach; Scheduler; Bus Driver; Head Custodian; Electrician; Police Officer.

SAN ANTONIO EXPRESS NEWS
P.O. Box 2171, San Antonio TX 78297-2171. **Physical address:** 309 North Alamo, San Antonio TX 78297-2171. 210/225-7411. **Contact:** Human Resources. **E-mail address:** employment@express-news.net. **World Wide Web address:** http://www.mysanantonio.com. **Description:** A newspaper with a circulation of approximately 250,000 daily and 365,000 on Sundays. **Positions advertised include:** Classified Account Executive; Sales Assistant; New Business Development Sales Representative; Quality Service Representative; Customer Service Representative.

SAN JACINTO COLLEGE DISTRICT
4624 Fairmont Parkway, Suite 106, Pasadena TX 77504. 281/998-6115. **Toll-free phone:** 800/825-5069. **Recorded jobline:** 281/998-6399. **Contact:** Human Resources. **World Wide Web address:** http://www.sjcd.cc.tx.us. **Description:** This location houses the administrative offices for the community college. Campuses are located in Pasadena and Houston. **NOTE:** See website for job listings and application requirements. **Positions advertised include:** Administrative Assistant; Accounting Assistant; Biology Professor; Graphic Artist Instructor; Adjunct Professor; Part-time Professor.

SAN MARCOS TREATMENT CENTER
120 Bert Brown Road, San Marcos TX 78666. 512/396-8500. **Fax:** 512/754-3883. **Contact:** Human Resources. **World Wide Web address:** http://www.psysolutions.com. **Description:** A 186-bed neuropsychiatric hospital that specializes in treating adolescents and young adults who have not had success in other settings. The center's patients are primarily those who experience emotional disturbances, severe impulses, aggressive behavior patterns, unprovoked mood swings, known neurological or organic disorders, seizure disorders, language problems, or severe learning complications due to substance abuse and sexual trauma. Founded in 1940. **NOTE:** Jobseekers should visit the center to complete an application. **Office hours:** Monday – Friday, 7:00 a.m. – 11:00 p.m. **Parent company:** Psychiatric Solutions, Inc.

SANZ
11104 West Airport Boulevard, Suite 156, Stafford TX 77477-3035. 214/674-0001. **Contact:** Human Resources. **World Wide Web address:** http://www.stornet.com. **Description:** The largest vendor-independent data-storage service company in the United States. This company provides technical support to its customers. **NOTE:** See the company's website for job listings and contact information. **Corporate headquarters location:** Castle Rock CO. **Other area locations:** Dallas TX (Sales); Richardson TX (Technical Support). **Operations at this facility include:** This location is a Regional Office. **Listed on:** NASDAQ. **Stock exchange symbol:** SANZ.

SARA LEE BAKERY GROUP
3500 Manor Way, Dallas TX 75235. 214/357-1754. **Fax:** 214/353-1408. **Contact:** Human Resources. **World Wide Web address:** http://www.saraleebakerygroup.com. **Description:** Bakes and distributes breads and other baked goods. **NOTE:** This company has several plants throughout Texas. See the company's website for job listings and apply online. **Positions advertised include:** Maintenance Mechanic; General Laborer. **Corporate headquarters location:** St. Louis MO. **Other U.S. locations:** Nationwide. **Operations at this facility include:** Administration; Manufacturing; Sales. **Listed on:** New York Stock Exchange. **Stock exchange symbol:** SLE. **Number of employees nationwide:** 22,300.

SARA LEE COFFEE & TEA
235 North Norwood, Houston TX 77011. 713/928-6281. **Contact:** Human Resources. **World Wide Web address:** http://www.saralee.com. **Description:** This division of Sara Lee Corporation produces dry-roasted coffee for consumers under such brand names as Chock Full O' Nuts and Hill Brothers, and it produces products for food service. **NOTE:** Apply online at this company's website. **Listed on:** New York Stock Exchange. **Stock exchange symbol:** SLE. **Number of employees nationwide:** 22,300.

SASOL NORTH AMERICA, INC.
900 Threadneedle Street, Suite 100, Houston TX 77079. 281/588-3000. **Fax:** 281/588-3144. **Contact:** Human Resources. **World Wide Web address:** http://www.sasolnorthamerica.com. **Description:** Manufactures specialty and commodity chemicals for domestic and international markets. **Corporate headquarters location:** This location. **Other area locations:** Austin TX (Research Center). **Other U.S. locations:** LA; MD; AZ. **International locations:** Mexico. **Operations at this facility include:** Administration; Sales.

SAVANE INTERNATIONAL CORPORATION
P.O. Box 13800, 4171 North Mesa Building D, El Paso TX 79902. 915/496-7000. **Contact:** Human Resources. **World Wide Web address:** http://www.savane.com. **Description:** A manufacturer of men's wear for department stores. **Corporate headquarters location:** Tampa FL. **Parent company:** Tropical Sportswear International Corporation. **Listed on:** NASDAQ. **Stock exchange symbol:** TSIC.

SCHLUMBERGER INFORMATION SOLUTIONS
5599 San Felipe, Suite 1700, Houston TX 77056. 713/513-2000. **Contact:** Human Resources. **World Wide Web address:** http://www.slb.com. **Description:** Develops and sells advanced scientific and engineering software to major oil companies and governments. The company helps find and produce oil and gas, manage environmental concerns, and plan regional and urban development. **NOTE:** This company does not accept unsolicited resumes. Apply online at the company's website for open positions. **Parent company:** Schlumberger Limited. **Operations at this facility include:** This facility provides consulting services for information technologies. **Listed on:** New York Stock Exchange. **Stock exchange symbol:** SLB.

SCHLUMBERGER OILFIELD SERVICES
7030 Ardmore, Houston TX 77054. 713/747-4000. **Contact:** Human Resources. **World Wide Web address:** http://www.slb.com. **Description:** Engaged in manufacturing, selling, and servicing a broad range of oil tool equipment. Principal products are gas lift equipment, well completion and safety equipment, wireline units and tools, and energy measurement and control equipment. The company also supplies solid and conductor wireline services and maintains a wireline fleet comprised of hydraulically operated reels mounted on barges, trucks, and skid units. **NOTE:** This company does not accept unsolicited resumes. Apply online at the company's website for open positions. **Parent company:** Schlumberger Limited. **Operations at this facility include:** This facility provides oil well productivity consulting services. **Listed on:** New York Stock Exchange. **Stock exchange symbol:** SLB.

SCOPE IMPORTS INC.
8020 Blankenship Drive, Houston TX 77055. 713/688-0077. **Contact:** Human Resources. **Description:** An importer of men's apparel, primarily activewear and T-shirts.

SEA WORLD OF TEXAS
10500 Sea World Drive, San Antonio TX 78251-3002. 210/523-3198. **Contact:** Human Resources. **World Wide Web address:** http://www.seaworld.com. **Description:** Sea World is home to all types of marine life, and includes such entertainment as shows, exhibits, and a water park. **NOTE:** Seasonal, professional and hourly positions offered. Apply at the nearest Sea World location. **Special programs:** Student and Senior Employment.

SECURITAS
9441 LBJ Freeway, Suite 25, Dallas TX 75243. 972/238-5994. **Contact:** Human Resources. **World Wide Web address:** http://www.pinkertons.com. **Description:** Offers a full range of specialized protective services including property and high-rise services, health care and hospital services, special event services, ATM services, and patrol services. The company serves thousands of companies worldwide with investigation, threat assessment, and executive protection services. **NOTE:** Securitas has more than 50 locations throughout Texas. The company offers security, management and support positions. Jobseekers interested in security positions must apply at the nearest Securitas office. A list of offices can be found on the website as well as information about job qualifications. Management and support positions are listed on the corporate website along with contact information. **Positions advertised include:** Business Development Manager; Office Assistant; Branch Manager; Area Manager; Account Manager; Human Resources Manager; Recruiter; Scheduling Manager. **Corporate headquarters location:** Westlake Village CA. **Other U.S. locations:** Nationwide. **International locations:** Worldwide. **Operations at this facility include:** This location is engaged in industrial and private security, investigation, and security consulting. **Number of employees:** 200,000.

SECURITAS
5825 Callaghan, Suite 107, San Antonio TX 78228. 210/647-9770. **Fax:** 210/543-1102. **Contact:** Melissa Perze, Human Resources. **World Wide Web address:** http://www.securitasinc.com. **Description:** A security service that sends guards to secure various locations and functions. **Corporate headquarters location:** Chicago IL. **Parent company:** Securitas AB (Sweden). **Number of employees nationwide:** 93,000.

SEED RESOURCE, INC.
P.O. Box 326, Tulia TX 79088. 806/995-3882. **Contact:** Weldon Mote, Manager. **World Wide Web address:** http://www.seedresource.com. **Description:** Distributes forage seed including Sorghum Sudans, which it produces, alfalfa, turf grass seed, and wheat seed. The company also produces wheat. **Parent company:** AgriBioTech, Inc. (ABT) is a specialized distributor of forage (hay crops) and turf grass seed. The forage and turf grass seed industry supplies seed to the forage and turf cash crop sectors. The company also distributes non-seed products including Bloatenz Plus, a liquid bloat preventative administered to the drinking water of cattle, permitting them to graze on alfalfa safely; and PDS-1000, marketed in conjunction with Bloatenz Plus, is a microprocessor-controlled precision dispensing system designed to dispense solutions into the drinking water of livestock at a preset dosage rate. Other subsidiaries of ABT include Scott Seed Company; Hobart Seed Company; Halsey Seed Company; and Sphar & Company. Combined, these companies cover the following distribution territories: IN; KY; NM; NY; OK; OR; PA; TX; WA.

NATHAN SEGAL AND COMPANY INC.
24 East Greenway Plaza, Suite 910, Houston TX 77046. 713/621-2000. **Contact:** Human Resources. **World Wide Web address:** http://www.nathansegal.com. **Description:** A merchandiser of feed ingredients for livestock companies. **President:** Jack Goldfield.

SEMCO DOT METAL PRODUCTS
18757 Bracken Drive, San Antonio TX 78266. 210/651-6331. **Toll-free phone:** 800/331-9966. **Fax:** 210/651-5825. **Contact:** Human Resources. **World Wide Web address:** http://www.gibraltar1.com. **Description:** Manufactures a variety of metal products including metal edging. **Corporate headquarters location:** Buffalo NY. **Other area locations:** Houston TX. **Parent company:** Gibraltar. **Listed on:** NASDAQ. **Stock exchange symbol:** ROCK.

SERCEL INC.
17200 Park Row, Houston TX 77084. 281/492-6688. **Fax:** 281/579-7505. **Recorded jobline:** 281/647-7166. **Contact:** Human Resources. **World Wide Web address:** http://www.sercel.com. **Description:** Manufactures and markets a wide range of geophysical data acquisition equipment and specialized cable for the energy industry. Sercel is a leading international supplier of geophones, cable, and connectors to the oil and gas exploration industry. **International locations:** Worldwide. **Operations at this facility include:** Administration; Sales; Manufacturing.

SERVICE CORPORATION INTERNATIONAL (SCI)
1929 Allen Parkway, Houston TX 77219. 713/522-5141. **Contact:** Human Resources. **World Wide Web address:** http://www.sci-corp.com. **Description:** Engaged in the operation of cemeteries and also provides cremation services and grief counseling. **NOTE:** Apply online at this company's website. **Positions advertised include:** Attorney; Senior Web Developer; Location Manager; Assistant Sales Manager. **Corporate headquarters location:** This location. **Other U.S. locations:** Nationwide. **International locations:** Worldwide. **Listed on:** New York Stock Exchange. **Stock exchange symbol:** SRV.

SETON HEALTHCARE NETWORK
1201 West 38th Street, Austin TX 78705. 512/324-4000. **Toll-free phone:** 800/880-0038. **Fax:** 512/324-1672. **Recorded jobline:** 512/324-1679. **Contact:** Human Resources Recruiters. **World Wide Web address:** http://www.seton.net. **Description:** A nonprofit, multi-facility health care network. Facilities include four acute care hospitals, community clinics, home care providers, outreach programs, and physicians' offices. **NOTE:** Entry-level positions and second and third shifts are offered. See the company's website for application information and job listings or visit the Human Resources office. **Company slogan:** Health.Care.Made Simpler. **Office hours:** Monday – Friday, 8:00 a.m. – 4:30 p.m. **Corporate headquarters location:** St. Louis MO. **Parent company:** Daughters of Charity.

SEVERN TRENT LABORATORIES, INC.
14046 Summit Drive, Suite 111, Austin TX 78728. 512/244-0855. **Fax:** 512/244-0160. **Contact:** Human Resources. **World Wide Web address:** http://www.stl-inc.com. **Description:** Provides a complete range of environmental testing services to private industry, engineering consultants, and government agencies in support of federal and state environmental regulations. The company also possesses analytical capabilities in the fields of air toxins, field analytical services, radiochemistry/mixed waste, and advanced technology. **Corporate headquarters location:** United Kingdom. **Other area locations:** Corpus Christi TX; Houston TX; Baytown TX. **Other U.S. locations:** Nationwide. **Number of employees worldwide:** 2,800.

SEVERN TRENT LABORATORIES, INC.
6310 Rothway Drive, Suite 130, Houston TX 77040. 713/690-4444. **Fax:** 713/690-5646. **Contact:** Human Resources. **World Wide Web address:** http://www.stl-inc.com. **Description:** Provides a complete range of environmental testing services to private industry, engineering consultants, and government agencies in support of federal and state environmental regulations. The company also possesses analytical capabilities in the fields of air toxins, field analytical services, radiochemistry/mixed waste, and advanced technology. **Corporate headquarters location:** United Kingdom. **Other area locations:** Corpus Christi TX; Austin TX; Baytown TX. **Other U.S. locations:** Nationwide. **Number of employees worldwide:** 2,800.

SHANNON CLINIC
120 East Beauregard, San Angelo TX 76903. 325/658-1511x3159. **Fax:** 325/481-2181. **Contact:** Human Resources. **World Wide Web address:** http://www.shannonhealth.com. **Description:** Part Of The Shannon Health System, this clinic is composed of specialty physicians in Cardiology, Vision, OB/GYN, and Pediatrics. **NOTE:** See website for job listings and applications. **Other area locations:** Del Angelo TX; Big Lake TX.

SHELBY REGIONAL MEDICAL CENTER
602 Hurst Street, Center TX 75935. 936/598-2781. **Contact:** Human Resources. **World Wide Web address:** http://www.shelbyregional.com. **Description:** A 54-bed community hospital. Specialty areas include centers for the treatment of allergies, asthma, and diabetes. Also provides cardiopulmonary and emergency care. **Positions advertised include:** Radiology Technician; RN; Plant Operations Supervisor. **Corporate headquarters location: Parent company:** Tenet Healthcare. **Listed on:** New York Stock Exchange. **Stock exchange symbol:** THC.

SHANNON MEDICAL CENTER
120 East Harris, San Angelo TX 76903. 325/657-5243. **Fax:** 325/481-8521. **Recorded jobline:** 325/657-5298. **Contact:** Human Resources. **E-mail address:** jobs@shannonhealthorg. **World Wide Web address:** http://www.shannonhealth.com. **Description:** A 400-bed, non-profit hospital offering surgery, intensive care, orthopedic, oncology, telemetry, skilled nursing, and cardiac services. Shannon Medical Center also operates a Level III trauma and sleep disorder center. Founded in 1932. This medical center is affiliated with three other healthcare facilities. **NOTE:** Entry-level positions and second and third shifts are offered. **Positions advertised include:** Cashier; Surgery Assistant; Registration Assistant; Dietitian; Medical Technologist; Occupational Therapist; Recreational Therapist; RN; Food Service Worker; Monitor Technician. **Special programs:** Training. **Office hours:** Monday - Friday, 8:00 a.m. - 5:00 p.m. **Corporate headquarters location:** This location.

SHEPLER'S
9103 East Almeda Road, Houston TX 77054. 713/799-1150. **Toll-free phone:** 800/729-1150. **Fax:** 713/799-8431. **Contact:** Anna Olizares, Human Resources Manager. **E-mail address:** human.resources@shelpers.com. **World Wide Web address:** http://www.cmcsheplers.com. **Description:** A supplier of concrete accessories, highway products, and form systems. **NOTE:** Entry-level positions are offered. This company has locations throughout Texas. See website for additional locations. **Special programs:** Internships; Training. **Corporate headquarters location:** This location. **Parent company:** CMC Steel Group. **Operations at this facility include:** Administration; Sales.

THE SHERWIN-WILLIAMS COMPANY
P.O. Box 38469, Dallas TX 75238-0469. 214/553-2950. **Physical address:** 10440 East NW Highway, Dallas TX 75238. **Fax:** 214/553-3903. **Contact:** Human Resources. **World Wide Web address:** http://www.sherwin.com. **Description:** Manufactures, sells, and distributes coatings and related products. Coatings are produced for original equipment manufacturers in various industries, as well as for the automotive aftermarket, the industrial maintenance market, and the traffic paint market. Sherwin-Williams labeled architectural and industrial coatings are sold through company-owned specialty paint and wallcovering stores. The Sherwin-Williams Company also manufactures paint under the Acme, Dutch Boy, Kem-Tone, Lucas, Martin-Senour, Minwax, Pratt & Lambert, Rogers, and Thompson brand names, as well as private labels, and markets its products to independent dealers, mass merchandisers, and home improvement centers. The company has 2,600 stores in North America. **NOTE:** Apply online at the company's website. **Special programs:** Internships; Management Training. **Positions advertised include:** Computer Help Desk Attendant; IT Specialist; MIS Specialist. **Corporate headquarters location:** Cleveland OH. **Other U.S. locations:** Nationwide. **Listed on:** New York Stock Exchange. **Stock exchange symbol:** SHW. **Number of employees nationwide:** 25,000.

SHOPPER'S GUIDE
1209 West North Carrier Parkway, Suite 300, Grand Prairie TX 75050. 972/641-7690. **Contact:** Human Resources. **Description:** A weekly shopper's newspaper with a circulation of approximately 430,000. **NOTE:** Apply online at this company's website. **Corporate headquarters:** San Antonio TX. **Other area locations:** Austin TX; Dallas TX; Fort Worth TX. **Other U.S. locations:** Nationwide.

SHOWCASE CHEVROLET
5327 LBJ Freeway, Dallas TX 75240. 972/233-3500. **Contact:** Human Resources. **World Wide Web address:** http://www.showcasechev.com. **Description:** A new and used car dealership. **NOTE:** Salespeople should apply in person and be prepared to fill out an application. See website for showroom hours.

SHRINER'S HOSPITAL BURN INSTITUTE
815 Market Street, Galveston TX 77550. 409/770-6600. **Contact:** Human Resources. **World Wide Web address:** http://www.shrinershq.org/shc/galveston. **Description:** A 31-bed, children's burn treatment facility and research center. **NOTE:** There is another Shriner's Hospital in Houston TX. **Positions advertised include:** Medical Technologist.

SIEMENS BUSINESS SERVICES, INC.
2400 Dallas Parkway, Plano TX. 972/535-2100. **Contact:** Human Resources. **World Wide Web address:** http://www.sbs-usa.siemens.com. **Description:** Provides systems integration, help desk, and PC repair services to *Fortune* 1000 companies and federal clients. The company also resells hardware and software products. **NOTE:** Apply online at this company's website. **Corporate headquarters location:** Norwalk CT. **Other area locations:** Austin TX; Houston TX. **Other U.S. locations:** Nationwide. **International locations:** Worldwide. **Parent company:** Siemens Corporation. **Listed on:** New York Stock Exchange. SI.

SIEMENS DEMATIC POSTAL AUTOMATION
2910 Avenue F, 76011 P.O. Box 95080, Arlington TX 76005-1080. 972/947-7200. **Contact:** Human Resources. **World Wide Web address:** http://www.pa.siemens-dematic.com. **Description:** Designs, manufactures, integrates, and services high-speed automated document-processing, materials-handling, mobile data, and voice communications systems. Primary customers are the U.S. Postal Service and other government agencies. **NOTE:** Apply online at the company's website. **Corporate headquarters location:** This location. **Parent company:** Siemens Corporation. **Operations at this facility include:** Administration; Manufacturing. **Number of employees worldwide:** 3,000.

SIEMENS INTELLIGENT TRANSPORTATION SYSTEMS
8004 Cameron Road, Austin TX 78754. 512/837-8310. **Fax:** 512/837-0196. **Contact:** Human Resources. **World Wide Web address:** http://www.eagletcs.com. **Description:** Manufactures traffic control systems and lights. **Parent company:** Siemens Energy & Automation, Inc.

SIERRA PROVIDENCE HEALTH NETWORK
1625 Medical Center Drive, El Paso, TX 79902. 915/577-6000. **Contact:** Human Resources. **World Wide Web address:** http://www.sphn.com. **Description:** The network consists of three hospitals in the area: The Sierra Medical Center, Providence Memorial Hospital, and Rio Vista, a rehab hospital. Combined the network has nearly 900 beds and provides comprehensive acute care medical services. Rio Vista provides services to those patients with brain injuries. **NOTE:** A completed application is required for any position at any of the three hospitals. The website provides job listings for all three facilities. Apply online. **Positions advertised include:** EKG Technician; ECHO Technician; Assistant Security Director; Medical Transcriptionist; RN (Various); LVN (Various); Plant Maintenance; Insurance Verifier; Secretary; Admitting Representative; Speech Therapist; Ultrasound Technician; Pharmacist; Medical Records Coder. **Parent company:** Tenet Healthcare.

SILGAN PLASTICS CORPORATION
6814 Kirbyville, Houston TX 77033. 713/644-5201. **Fax:** 713/641-1824. **Contact:** Human Resources. **World Wide Web address:** http://www.silganplastics.com. **Description:** Produces a wide range of plastic closures, bottles, dispensers, and packaging. **Corporate headquarters location:** Triadelphia WV. **Operations at this facility include:** This location manufactures plastic sanitary containers.

SILICON HILLS DESIGN, INC.
8504 Cross Park Drive, Austin TX 78754. 512/836-1088. **Fax:** 512/835-0404. **Contact:** Human Resources. **E-mail address:** Humanresources@siliconhills.com. **World Wide Web address:** http://www.siliconhills.com. **Description:** Designs printed circuit boards for computers as well as for the space and satellite markets.

SIX FLAGS FIESTA TEXAS
17000 Interstate Highway 10 West, San Antonio TX 78257. 210/697-5000. **Contact:** Human Resources. **World Wide Web address:** http://www.sixflags.com. **Description:** A theme park offering attractions, shows, and a water park. **NOTE:** Full-time, part-time and seasonal positions offered. Apply in person or online at the company's website. **Positions advertised include:** Admissions Attendant; Food Services Assistant; Merchandise Host Assistant; Technician. **Office hours:** Monday – Sunday, 9:00 a.m. – 5:00 p.m. **Parent company:** Premier Parks (OK) owns and operates 35 theme parks nationwide.

SIX FLAGS HOUSTON
SIX FLAGS ASTROWORLD, WATERWORLD, & SPLASHTOWN
9001 Kirby Drive, Houston TX 77054. 713/794-3217. **Fax:** 713/799-1030. **Contact:** Human Resources. **World Wide Web address:** http://www.sixflagsjobs.com. **Description:** An amusement and theme park. Six Flags AstroWorld offers seven theme lands based on the nations of the world, past and present. Six Flags AstroWorld has 11 roller coasters and also offers Wonderland, filled with rides and activities for younger children. The park also offers entertainment including shows and concerts. Six Flags WaterWorld offers water slides, waterfalls, a fantasy water playground for kids, a game room, specialty shops, a restaurant, and food stands. Six Flags SplashTown is a family-oriented water park. **NOTE:** Jobseekers can apply online at the company's website or in person, if possible. Six Flags Houston hires over 3,000 employees each season. Entry-level positions, part-time jobs, and second and third shifts are offered. **Positions advertised include:** Ride Worker; Warehouse Worker; Games Host; Food Services Attendant; Admission Attendant. **Special programs:** Internships; Training; Summer Jobs; Senior Jobs. **Internship information:** Some paid summer internships are offered and housing is available. For more information, e-mail or write to the Human Resources Department. **Office hours:** Monday - Friday, 9:00 a.m. - 12:00 p.m., 1:00 p.m. - 6:00 p.m. **Parent company:** Premier Parks (OK) owns and operates 35 theme parks nationwide.

SIX FLAGS OVER TEXAS
HURRICANE HARBOR
2201 Road To Six Flags, Arlington TX 76010. 817/640-8900x4216. **Contact:** Human Resources. **World Wide Web address:** http://www.sixflags.com. **Description:** Dallas-area location of the popular amusement park. Rollercoasters, rides, and events are the attraction, including a new SpongeBob SquarePants ride. Hurricane Harbor is a nearby waterpark. **NOTE:** Seasonal, full-time, part-time positions available. Apply online or in person at the park. Hurricane Harbor has its own Human Resources. For job information, call: 817/265-3356 or e-mail sfhhhr@sftp.com. **Positions advertised include:** Host/Hostess; Plumber; Cash Control. **Office hours:** Monday – Friday, 12:00 p.m. – 6:30 p.m.; Saturday, 12:00 p.m. – 5:00 p.m.

SKEETER PRODUCTS INC.
P.O. Box 230, Kilgore TX 75662. 903/984-0541. **Contact:** Human Resources. **World Wide Web address:** http://www.skeeterboats.com. **Description:** Manufactures fishing boats.

SKY HELICOPTERS
2559 South Jupiter Road, Garland TX 75041-6011. 214/349-7000. **Contact:** Human Resources. **World Wide Web address:** http://www.skyhelicopters.com. **Description:** Engaged in helicopter transportation for both public and private use.

SKYLINE INDUSTRIES, INC.
P.O. Box 821, Fort Worth TX 76101. 817/551-1967. **Contact:** Human Resources. **World Wide Web address:** http://www.skyline-usa.com. **Description:** A manufacturer of aircraft parts including armored pilot seats, floor armor, seat covers, ground handling equipment, and aerospace fasteners. **Corporate headquarters location:** This location.

SMITH INTERNATIONAL, INC.
16740 East Hardy Road, Houston TX 77032. 281/443-3370. **Toll-free phone:** 800/877-6484. **Fax:** 281/233-5199. **Contact:** Human Resources. **World Wide Web address:** http://www.smith.com. **Description:** Smith International, Inc. is a worldwide supplier of products and services to the oil and gas drilling, completion and production, and mining industries. **NOTE:** This company has several locations throughout Texas. See website for additional locations and addresses. **Corporate headquarters location:** This location. **Other U.S. locations:** Nationwide. **International locations:** Worldwide. **Operations at this facility include:** Administration; Divisional Headquarters; Manufacturing; Regional Headquarters; Research and Development; Sales; Service. **Listed on:** New York Stock Exchange. **Stock exchange symbol:** SII.

SMURFIT-STONE CONTAINER CORPORATION
6701 South Freeway, Fort Worth TX 76134. 817/568-3400. **Contact:** Human Resources. **World Wide Web address:** http://www.smurfit-stone.com. **Description:** Smurfit-Stone Container Corporation is one of the world's leading paper-based packaging companies. The company's main products include corrugated containers, folding cartons, and multiwall industrial bags. The company is also one of the world's largest collectors and processors of recycled products that are then sold to a worldwide customer base. Smurfit-Stone Container Corporation also operates several paper tube, market pulp, and newsprint production facilities. **NOTE:** This company has several Texas manufacturing plants. See website for additional locations and addresses. **Corporate headquarters location:** Chicago IL. **Other U.S. locations:** Nationwide. **International locations:** Worldwide. **Operations at this facility include:** This location manufactures corrugated fiberboard boxes. **Listed on:** NASDAQ. **Stock exchange symbol:** SSCC.

SOFTWARE SPECTRUM INC.
2140 Merritt Drive, Garland TX 75041. 972/840-6600. **Fax:** 972/864-3219. **Contact:** Human Resources. **World Wide Web address:** http://www.softwarespectrum.com. **Description:** Resells microcomputer software and services to businesses and government agencies. Software Spectrum also offers technical support and volume software license services. **NOTE:** Apply online for open positions at this company's website. **Corporate headquarters location:** This location. **Other U.S. locations:** Nationwide. **International locations:** Worldwide. **Subsidiaries include:** Spectrum Integrated Services. **Operations at this facility include:** Administration; Sales; Service. **Listed on:** NASDAQ. **Stock exchange symbol:** LVLT.

SOLO CUP COMPANY
4444 West Ledbetter Drive, Dallas TX 75236. 214/339-3131. **Contact:** Human Resources. **World Wide Web address:** http://www.solocup.com. **Description:** Manufactures and distributes a variety of food serviceware including plates, cups, bowls, drinking straws, and ice cream cones, as well as containers for use in packaging food and dairy products. **NOTE:** See the company's website for job listings and contact information.

SOLVAY AMERICA, INC.
P.O. Box 27328, Houston TX 77227-7328. 713/525-6000. **Physical address:** 3333 Richmond Avenue, Houston TX 77098. **Toll-free phone:** 800/443-2785. **Contact:** Human Resources. **World Wide Web address:** http://www.solvayamerica.com. **Description:** A manufacturer of sodium-based products through the mining and processing of trona. Solvay Minerals produces soda ash, caustic soda, sodium sulfite, and trona products. The company offers mechanically refined sodium sesquicarbonate to the merchant market. Coarse product is exclusively marketed and sold to the animal feed market by an outside company. Other products are marketed directly by Solvay Minerals for acid gas and acid neutralization applications. **NOTE:** This company has several manufacturing locations throughout Texas. See website for additional locations and addresses. **Other U.S. locations:** Nationwide. **International locations:** Mexico. **Parent company:** Solvay America. **Number of employees:** 970.

SOURCESUITE LLC
5601 Executive Drive, Suite 200, Irving TX 75038. 469/524-0116. **Contact:** Human Resources. **E-mail address:** employment@sourcesite.com. **World Wide Web address:** http://www.srcm.com. **Description:** A leader in interactive content and navigation for interactive television. **Corporate headquarters location:** This location. **Parent company:** Insight Communications Company, Inc.

SOUTH AUSTIN HOSPITAL
901 West Ben White Boulevard, Austin TX 78704. 512/448-7110. **Toll-free phone:** 800/568-3297. **Contact:** Human Resources. **World Wide Web address:** http://www.southaustinhospital.com. **Description:** An acute care, 162-bed hospital that provides basic care for the region. **NOTE:** Apply online at this hospital's website. **Positions advertised include:** Health Information Management Director; Food Service Supervisor; Pharmacy Technician; Medical Technician; Patient Care Technician; Anesthesia Technician; RN; Food Services Associate.

SOUTH PLAINS COLLEGE
1401 South College Avenue, Levelland TX 79336. 806/894-9611. **Fax:** 806/894-6880. **Contact:** Human Resources. **World Wide Web address:** http://www.spc.cc.tx.us. **Description:** A two-year, state-funded college. South Plains College offers majors in education, arts and sciences, nursing, and continuing education. The college has an enrollment of approximately 5,400 students. **NOTE:** An application is required for any position. See website for job listings and application information.

SOUTH TEXAS COLLEGE OF LAW
1303 San Jacinto Street, Houston TX 77002-7000. 713/646-1812. **Fax:** 713/646-1833. **Contact:** Human Resources. **World Wide Web address:** http://www.stcl.edu. **Description:** A private law school with an enrollment of approximately 1,250 students. Founded in 1923. **NOTE:** An application is required for any position. See website for job listings and application information. **Corporate headquarters location:** This location. **Operations at this facility include:** Administration. **Listed on:** Privately held.

SOUTHERN CLAY PRODUCTS INC.
1212 Church Street, Gonzales TX 78629. 830/672-2891. **Fax:** 830/672-1908. **Contact:** Human Resources. **World Wide Web address:** http://www.scprod.com. **Description:** Mines and processes clay minerals for use in a variety of products including paint. **Corporate headquarters location:** This location.

SOUTHERN INVESTORS SERVICE COMPANY
2727 North Loop West, Suite 200, Houston TX 77008. 713/869-7800. **Contact:** Human Resources. **Description:** Offers commercial construction, real estate development, distribution and installation of construction products, and savings and loan services. **Corporate headquarters location:** This location.

SOUTHERN METHODIST UNIVERSITY
P.O. Box 750232, Dallas TX 75275-0232. 214/768-2000. **Contact:** Employment Office. **World Wide Web address:** http://www.smu.edu. **Description:** A private university offering bachelor's, master's, professional, and doctoral degrees to approximately 9,700 students. **NOTE:** Apply online at this company's website. Cover

letters and resumes are required for all positions. Full-time and part-time shifts are offered for professional, service, clerical and trade positions. Temporary positions are periodically available. **Special programs:** Internships. **Corporate headquarters location:** This location

SOUTHERN UNION COMPANY
221 West Sixth Street, Austin TX 78701. 512/370-8321. **Fax:** 512/370-8380. **Contact:** Human Resources. **World Wide Web address:** http://www.southernunionco.com. **Description:** A natural gas distribution and utility company with subsidiaries serving several U.S. states. This website has job listings for corporate jobs and utility jobs in Wilkes Barre PA. Each subsidiary features its job listings on its own websites. See the corporate site for links. **Special programs:** Internships. **Corporate headquarters location:** Wilkes Barre PA. **Other U.S. locations:** FL; MA; MO; PA; OK; RI. **Subsidiaries include:** Panhandle Energy (Houston TX) operates major pipelines to distribute natural gas throughout the country. Missouri Gas Energy, (Kansas City MO) serves approximately500,000 customers in central and western Missouri. PG Energy (Wilkes Barre PA) serves nearly 160,000 customers in central PA. New England Gas Co. (Providence RI) provides natural gas to about 290,000 customers in Rhode Island and Massachusetts. **Operations at this facility include:** Administration; Sales. **Listed on:** New York Stock Exchange. **Stock exchange symbol:** SUG.

SOUTHLAND CORPORATION
P.O. Box 711, Dallas TX 75221. 214/828-7011. **Physical address:** 2711 North Haskell Avenue, Dallas TX 75204-2906. **Fax:** 214/841-6688. **Recorded jobline:** 866/471-1562. **Contact:** Human Resources. **World Wide Web address:** http://www.7eleven.com. **Description:** Owns and operates 7-Eleven convenience stores. **NOTE:** Jobseekers interested in hourly retail positions should call the recorded jobline between 7 a.m. and 11 p.m. CST to speak with a recruiter. Jobseekers interested in corporate and divisional positions should apply online at the company's website. **Corporate headquarters location:** This location. **Listed on:** New York Stock Exchange. **Stock exchange symbol:** SE. **Number of employees nationwide:** 33,000.

SOUTHWEST AIRLINES COMPANY
P.O. Box 36644, Dallas TX 75235-1644. 214/792-4213. **Physical address:** 2702 Love Field Drive, Dallas TX 75235. **Fax:** 214/792-7015. **Recorded jobline:** 214/792-4803 (Dallas TX); 602/389-3738 (Phoenix AZ). **Contact:** SWA People Department. **World Wide Web address:** http://www.southwest.com. **Description:** A major short-haul, low-fare, point-to-point carrier in the United States. Southwest Airlines, a *Fortune* 500 company, flies to 59 cities in 30 states and offering 2,900 flights daily. **NOTE:** On its website, this airline provides job listings; job requirements, and resume and application procedures. See website before applying for any position. **Positions advertised include:** Aircraft Appearance Technician; Mechanic; Flight Attendant; Pilot, Provisioning Agent; Reservation Sales Agent; System Administrator; Accountant; Attorney. **Special programs:** Internships. **Corporate headquarters location:** This location. **Other U.S. locations:** Nationwide. **Listed on:** New York Stock Exchange. **Stock exchange symbol:** LUV. **Number of employees worldwide:** 32,000.

SOUTHWEST COLLEGIATE INSTITUTE FOR THE DEAF
3200 Avenue C, Big Spring TX 79720-9960. 915/264-3700. **Fax:** 915/264-3707. **Contact:** Dr. Ron Brasel, Provost. **World Wide Web address:** http://www.hc.cc.tx.us. **Description:** A college for the deaf with an enrollment of approximately 105 students. The institute offers courses in liberal arts, technical, vocational/occupational, and developmental studies. The institute also offers numerous support services such as career advisement and job placement assistance. Founded in 1980. **NOTE:** An application must be submitted for any position. See website for job listings and applications. **Positions advertised include:** Men's Residence Hall Supervisor; Preparatory English Instructor; Fitness Center Director; Utility Maintenance Technician; Speech Instructor. **Parent company:** Howard County Junior College.

SOUTHWEST GENERAL HOSPITAL
7400 Barlite Boulevard, San Antonio TX 78224. 210/921-3439. **Fax:** 210/921-3450. **Recorded jobline:** 210/921-3439. **Contact:** Recruiter. **World Wide Web address:** http://www.swgeneralhospital.com. **Description:** A 319-bed, acute care hospital. Southwest General Hospital offers multiple diagnostic treatment and services in the following medical specialties: general and orthopedic surgery; physical therapy and rehabilitation, the treatment of strokes and complications resulting from diabetes; plastic and oral surgery; pediatrics; cardiac and pulmonary services; treatment of infectious diseases; and diabetes treatment. Southwest General Hospital offers a full range of psychiatric services including adult inpatient, adolescent inpatient, and partial hospitalization for adults. Founded in 1979. Southwest General has three sister facilities in Texas: Mid-Jefferson Hospital (Nederland TX); Odessa Regional Hospital (Odessa TX); and, Park Place Medical Center (Port Arthur TX). **NOTE:** Apply online at this hospital's website. **Positions advertised include:** RN; Biomedical Technician; Case Manager; LVN; Medical Technologist; Coder; Dietician. **Corporate headquarters location:** Franklin TN. **Other U.S. locations:** Nationwide. **Parent company:** IASIS Healthcare. **Operations at this facility include:** Administration; Service.

SOUTHWEST RESEARCH INSTITUTE
P.O. Drawer 28510, San Antonio TX 78228-0510. 210/522-2223. **Physical address:** 6220 Culebra Road, San Antonio TX 78238. **Fax:** 210/522-3990. **Contact:** Human Resources. **E-mail address:** humanresources@swri.org. **World Wide Web address:** http://www.swri.org. **Description:** An independent, nonprofit, applied engineering and physical science research and development organization. Research is conducted in areas such as automation, intelligent systems, and advanced computer technology; biosciences/bioengineering; nuclear waste regulatory analyses; electronic systems and instrumentation; encapsulation and polymer research; engines, fuels, and lubricants; environmental science; fire technology; fluid and machinery dynamics; engineering and materials sciences; nondestructive evaluation research and development; and space sciences. **Special programs:** Internships. **Corporate headquarters location:** This location. **Listed on:** Privately held. **Number of employees nationwide:** 2,800.

SOUTHWEST SECURITIES PRIVATE CLIENT GROUP, INC.
1201 Elm Street, Suite 3500, Dallas TX 75270-2180. 214/651-1800. **Contact:** Human Resources. **E-mail address:** careers@onlinepreferred.com. **World Wide Web address:** http://www.onlinepreferred.com. **Description:** Southwest Securities Group, Inc. is a holding company with subsidiaries engaged in providing securities brokerage, investment banking, and investment advisory services. The company also offers online banking and stock trading services. Founded in 1972. **Corporate headquarters location:** This location. **Other area locations:** Longview TX: Lufkin TX; Georgetown TX; San Antonio TX; Austin TX; Houston TX. **Other U.S. locations:** Chicago IL; Albuquerque NM; Santa Fe NM; Oklahoma City, OK. **Listed on:** New York Stock Exchange. **Stock exchange symbol:** SWS. **Number of employees worldwide:** 1,100.

SOUTHWEST TEXAS METHODIST HOSPITAL
METHODIST WOMEN'S & CHILDREN'S HOSPITAL
7700 Floyd Curl Drive, San Antonio TX 78229. 210/575-4000. **Recorded jobline:** 210/57-4562. **Contact:** Human Resources. **World Wide Web address:** http://www.sahealth.com. **Description:** A 626-bed hospital that offers both short- and long-term care. Methodist Women's & Children's Hospital is a 150-bed hospital that specializes in labor, delivery, and pediatrics. **NOTE:** Apply online at the hospital's website for open positions.

SOUTHWESTERN ADVENTIST UNIVERSITY
100 Hillcrest Drive, P.O. Box 567, Keene TX 76059. 817/645-3921. **Contact:** Human Resources. **World Wide Web address:** http://www.swau.edu. **Description:** A college affiliated with the Seventh Day Adventist Church and offering 40 undergraduate programs and two graduate-level programs. Over 1,100 students are enrolled.

SOUTHWESTERN BAPTIST THEOLOGICAL SEMINARY
P.O. Box 22000, Fort Worth TX 76122. 817/923-1921. **Physical address:** 2001 West Seminary Drive, Fort Worth TX 76115. **Contact:** Human Resources. **World Wide Web address:** http://www.swbts.edu. **Description:** A seminary college offering a variety of religious training programs. **NOTE:** Apply in person at the Human Resources Office. **Office hours:** Monday – Friday, 8:00 a.m. – 5:00 p.m.

SOUTHWESTERN PETROLEUM CORPORATION
P.O. Box 961005, Fort Worth TX 76161. 817/332-2336. **Toll-free phone:** 817/877-9372. **Fax:** 817/877-4047. **Contact:** Human Resources. **World Wide Web address:** http://www.swepcousa.com. **Description:** Manufactures protective coatings and specialty lubricants for the energy industry. **NOTE:** Apply online at this company's website. **Positions advertised include:** Sales Consultant. **Corporate headquarters location:** This location. **Other U.S. locations:** Nationwide. **International locations:** Worldwide. **Listed on:** Privately held.

SPAWGLASS CONSTRUCTION INC.
13800 West Road, Houston TX 77041. 281/970-5300. **Fax:** 281/970-5305. **Contact:** Human Resources. **E-mail address:** humanresources@spawglass.com. **World Wide Web address:** http://www.spawglass.com. **Description:** A general construction contractor. **NOTE:** Send resume via e-mail or visit the nearest location. See the company's website for locations' addresses. **Corporate headquarters location:** This location. **Other area locations:** San Antonio TX; Austin TX; Harlingen TX.

SPECIALTY HOSPITAL OF SAN ANTONIO
7310 Oak Manor Drive, San Antonio 78229. 210/308-0261. **Contact:** Jill Doire, Divisional Recruiter. **World Wide Web address:** http://www.tricare.com. **Description:** A long-Term, acute Care hospital. **Note:** Entry-level positions and part-time jobs are offered. **Positions advertised include:** Administrator. **Parent company:** Trans Healthcare.

SPECS LIQUOR WAREHOUSE
2410 Smith Street, Houston TX 77006. 713/526-8787. **Toll-free phone:** 888/526-8787. **Fax:** 713/526-6129. **Contact:** Human Resources. **World Wide Web address:** http://www.specsonline.com. **Description:** Operates a chain of 20 liquor stores throughout the Greater Houston area. **Positions advertised include:** Management; Retail Sales; Clerical; Stocker; Deli. **Corporate headquarters location:** This location.

SPINDLETOP MENTAL HEALTH & MENTAL RETARDATION
2750 South Eighth Street, Beaumont TX 77701. 409/839-1000. **Contact:** Human Resources. **Description:** A crisis resolution and counseling center providing addiction recovery programs throughout six counties in Texas.

SPORTS SUPPLY GROUP, INC.
P.O. Box 7726, 1901 Diplomat Drive, Dallas TX 75234. 972/484-9484. **Fax:** 972/884-7465. **Recorded jobline:** 972/884-7280. **Contact:** Human Resources. **E-mail address:** dallashr@sportsupplygroup.com. **World Wide Web address:** http://www.sportsupplygroup.com. **Description:** A catalog retailer of sporting goods and recreational products. **NOTE:** Fax or e-mail resumes with cover letters including a salary history. **Positions advertised include:** Outbound Sales Associate; Customer Care Associate; Government Sales Associate; Staff Accountant; Inside Sales Associate. **Corporate headquarters location:** This location. **Other U.S. locations:** Alabama. **Number of employees nationwide:** 250.

STAR FURNITURE COMPANY
P.O. Box 219169, Houston TX 77218-9169. **Physical address:** 16666 Barker Springs Road Houston TX 77084. 281/492-5445. **Fax:** 281/579-5909. **Contact:** Paige Olson, Human Resources Director. **World Wide Web address:** http://www.starfurniture.com. **Description:** Engaged in the retail sale of home furnishings. **NOTE:** Full-time and part-time shifts are offered. **Positions advertised include:** Sales Consultant; Office Associate; Service Assistant; Warehouse Worker; Driver's Helper. **Office hours:** Monday – Friday, 9:00 a.m. – 5:00 p.m. **Corporate headquarters location:** This location. **Other area locations:** Austin TX; Bryan TX; San Antonio TX. **Parent company:** Berkshire Hathaway Inc. **Operations at this facility include:** Administration; Sales; Service. **Listed on:** Privately held.

STAR-TELEGRAM
400 West Seventh Street, Fort Worth TX 76102. 817/390-7459. **Fax:** 817/336-3739. **Contact:** Diana Oliveros, Employment Coordinator. **World Wide Web address:** http://www.star-telegram.com. **Description:** Publishes a daily newspaper. **NOTE:** Entry-level positions are offered. See website for contact information. **Special programs:** Internships. **Parent company:** Knight Ridder. **Operations at this facility include:** Administration; Manufacturing; Sales.

STARLITE RECOVERY CENTER
Elm Pass Road, Center Point TX 78010-0317. 830/634-2212. **Contact:** Human Resources. **World Wide Web address:** http://www.starliterecovery.com. **Description:** A residential treatment center for adults and adolescents, offering specialized care for substance abusers. **Parent company:** CRC Health Corporation.

STATE FARM INSURANCE
17301 Preston Road, Dallas TX 75379. 972/732-5000. **Contact:** Human Resources. **World Wide Web address:** http://www.statefarm.com. **Description:** Offers automobile, health, homeowners, life, and renters insurance. **NOTE:** Apply at the nearest location. See website for addresses and job listings. **Corporate headquarters location:** Bloomington IL. **Other area locations:** Jollyville TX; Houston TX (Claims Service Center).**Operations at this facility include:** Regional Headquarters. **Number of employees nationwide:** 78,000.

STEELCASE INC.
3131 McKinney Avenue, Suite 300, Dallas TX 75204-2442. 214/871-3044. **Contact:** Human Resources. **World Wide Web address:** http://www.steelcase.com. **Description:** Manufactures metal and wood office furniture. **NOTE:** Full-time, hourly and temporary positions offered. See company's website for job listings and contact information. **Positions advertised include:** Workplace Consultant. **Corporate headquarters location:** Grand Rapids MI. **Operations at this facility:** This location is

a Regional Office. **Listed on:** New York Stock Exchange. **Stock exchange symbol:** SCS.

STEPHEN F. AUSTIN STATE UNIVERSITY
P.O. Box 13039, SFA Station, Nacogdoches TX 75962. 936/468-2304. **Recorded jobline:** 936/468-3003. **Contact:** Human Resources. **World Wide Web address:** http://www.sfasu.edu. **Description:** A four-year college offering bachelor's and master's degrees. **NOTE:** Job listings and requirements are available online. A complete application is required for any position. Some positions may require an assessment test or documentation of credentials. To apply in person, visit the Human Resources Office in Room 201 of the Austin Building. Applications can be downloaded also from the university's website and mailed. **Office hours:** Monday – Friday, 9:00 a.m. – 4:00 p.m.

STERLING CHEMICALS, INC.
P.O. Box 1311, Texas City TX 77592-1311. 409/945-4431. **Physical address:** 201 Bay Street, Texas City TX 77590. **Fax:** 409/942-3481. **Contact:** Human Resources. **E-mail address:** HumanResources@sterlingchemicals.com. **World Wide Web address:** http://www.sterlingchemicals.com. **Description:** Engaged in the production of sodium chlorate, lactic acid, acetic acid, plasticizers, and sodium cyanide. **Corporate headquarters location:** Houston TX. **Operations at this facility include:** Manufactures petrochemicals.

STERLING CHEMICALS, INC.
333 Clay Street, Suite 3600, Houston TX 77002. 713/650-3700. **Fax:** 713/654-9551. **Contact:** Human Resources. **E-mail address:** HumanResources@sterlingchemicals.com. **World Wide Web address:** http://www.sterlingchemicals.com. **Description:** A chemical manufacturer engaged in the production of sodium chlorate, lactic acid, acetic acid, plasticizers, and sodium cyanide. **Corporate headquarters location:** This location. **Operations at this facility include:** Administration.

STERLING FOODS INC.
1075 Arion Parkway, San Antonio TX 78216. 210/490-1669. **Contact:** Jim Keuhl, Human Resources Manager. **World Wide Web address:** http://www.sterlingfoodsusa.com. **Description:** Manufacturers of ready-to-eat bakery foods and snacks. **Number of employees at this location:** 250.

STERLING McCALL TOYOTA
9400 Southwest Freeway, Houston TX 77074. 713/270-3900. **Contact:** Human Resources. **World Wide Web address:** http://www.sterlingmccalltoyota.com. **Description:** Sells and services automobiles. **NOTE:** See website for job listings and contact information. **Positions advertised include:** Line Technician; Salesperson.

STEWART & STEVENSON INC.
2707 North Loop West, Houston TX 77008-7700. 713/868-7700. **Fax:** 713/868-7692. 4516 Harrisburg Boulevard, Houston TX 77011. 713/923-2161. **Contact:** Recruiter. **World Wide Web address:** http://www.ssss.com. **Description:** Manufactures a broad line of products, primarily diesel or gas turbine powered, serving a multitude of industries and markets. Stewart & Stevenson Inc. has four divisions: Engineered Products, Power Products, TUG Aircraft Ground Support; and Tactical Vehicle Systems. **NOTE:** See the company's website for open positions and specific contact names, e-mail addresses, and postal addresses. **Corporate headquarters location:** This location. **Other area locations:** Corpus Christi TX; Dallas TX: El Paso TX: Fort Worth TX: Longview TX; Lubbock TX; Odessa TX; Pharr-Valley TX; San Antonio TX; Waco TX; Wichita Falls TX. **Other U.S. locations:** Nationwide. **International locations:** Worldwide. **Listed on:** NASDAQ. **Stock exchange symbol:** SSSS. **Number of employees worldwide:** 3,600.

STITCHES INC.
1144 Vista De Oro Drive, El Paso TX 79935. 915/593-2990. **Contact:** Human Resources. **Description:** A textile sewing and cutting contractor. **Corporate headquarters location:** This location.

THE STRAND THEATRE
2317 Ships Mechanics Row, Galveston TX 77550. 409/763-4591. **Toll-free phone:** 877/STR-AND9. **Contact:** Human Resources. **World Wide Web address:** http://www.galveston-thestrand.org. **Description:** A 200-seat theatre that hosts films, comedy shows, concerts, and children's theatre productions. Founded in 1978. **NOTE:** The Strand Theatre welcomes applications for volunteer positions.

STRAUS-FRANK COMPANY/CAR QUEST
P.O. Box 600, San Antonio TX 78292-0600. 210/226-0101. **Contact:** Peggy Mamirez, Human Resources Manager. **Description:** A wholesaler of automobile parts. Straus-Frank Company is a partner with GPI who owns the retail chain automotive parts store Car Quest. **NOTE:** Car Quest has locations throughout Texas and the United States. Apply in person at the nearest location. See website for locations and addresses. **Corporate headquarters location:** This location.

STRIPLING & COX
6370 Camp Bowie Boulevard, Fort Worth TX 76116. 817/738-7361. **Contact:** Human Resources. **Description:** A department store offering men's and women's apparel and home furnishings. **Other area locations:** Arlington TX. **Parent company:** The Dunlop Company (Fort Worth TX).

S2 SYSTEMS, INC.
4965 Preston Park Boulevard, Suite 800, Plano TX 75093. 972/599-5600. **Toll-free phone:** 800/527-4131. **Fax:** 972/599-5611. **Contact:** Human Resources. **World Wide Web address:** http://www.s2systems.com. **Description:** A provider of data communications middleware and related professional services that bridge the gap between open distributed systems and legacy mainframe and midrange systems used for online applications. **NOTE:** Mail or fax resume and cover letter stating salary requirements. **Corporate headquarters location:** This location.

STYROCHEM INTERNATIONAL
3607 North Sylvania, Fort Worth TX 76111. 817/759-4400. **Contact:** Human Resources. **World Wide Web address:** http://www.styrochem.com. **Description:** StyroChem International manufactures raw plastic beads. **NOTE:** All hiring done through a staffing agency.

SUKATASH
4455 Lyndon B Johnson Freeway, Suite 810, Dallas TX 75244. 972/788-2160. **Toll-free phone:** 866/287-2848. **Fax:** 972/788-8151. **Contact:** Human Resources. **World Wide Web address:** http://www.sukatash.com. **Description:** Performs custom computer programming for multilevel marketing firms.

SULLINS & ASSOCIATES, INC.
McDONALD'S CORPORATION
122 South 12th Street, Suite 105, Corsicana TX 75110. 903/872-5611. **Fax:** 903/872-5613. **Contact:** Human Resources. **E-mail address:** personnel@sullinsandassociates.com. **Description:** A franchise owner of McDonald's restaurants in Texas. A leader in the fast-food industry, McDonald's offers quick-service meals, specializing in hamburgers. **NOTE:** Jobseekers may also apply in person in one of the franchises restaurants. **World Wide Web address:** http://www.sulliansandassociates.com. **Special programs:** Internships. **Other area locations:** Ennis TX; Greenville TX; Palestine TX; Terrell TX; Waxahachie TX.

SUMMIT ELECTRIC
P.O. Box 67, Houston TX 77001-0067. 713/236-0971. **Physical address:** 2929 McKinney Drive, Houston TX 77003. **Toll-free phone:** 800/232-0971. **Contact:** Human Resources. **World Wide Web address:** http://www.summit.com. **Description:** A wholesale supplier of electrical apparatus and equipment. This company has 20 service centers in Texas, New Mexico, Louisiana and Arizona. **NOTE:** See the company's website for job listings and contact information.

SUNOCO CHEMICALS CORPORATION
P.O. Box 1919, La Porte TX 77571. 281/291-2801. **Contact:** Human Resources. **World Wide Web address:** http://www.sunocochemicals.com. **Description:** Sunoco Chemicals Corporation is a diversified chemicals manufacturer, marketing a broad range of products that are converted into consumer items. Markets served include automotive, construction, marine, and recreational. The company's product lines include phenol, bisphenol-A, polypropylene, acrylic sheet, coal chemicals, dibasic acids, cumene, plasticizers, and unsaturated polyester resins. **NOTE:** Second and third shifts are offered. **Special programs:** Internships; Training; Co-ops; Summer Jobs. **Corporate headquarters location:** Philadelphia PA. **Other area locations:** Bayport TX. **U.S. locations:** OH; PA; WV. **Operations at this facility include:** This location manufactures polypropylene.

SUNTRON CORPORATION
1111 Gillingham Lane, Sugar Land TX 77478. 281/243-5000. **Toll-free phone:** 888/520-3382. **Fax:** 281/243-5107. **Contact:** Human Resources. **World Wide Web address:** http://www.suntroncorp.com. **Description:** A global provider of vertically integrated electronics manufacturing services supplying high mix solutions for aerospace, industrial controls and instrumentation, medical, semiconductor, networking and telecommunications industries. **NOTE:** Apply online at this company's website. **Positions advertised include:** Cables Manufacturing Supervisor; Manufacturing Engineer; Customer Business Manager; Product Engineer; Business Analyst. **Corporate headquarters location:** Phoenix AZ. **Listed on:** NASDAQ. **Stock exchange symbol:** SUNN.

SUPER S FOODS
401 Isom Road, Building 100, San Antonio TX 78216. 210/344-1960. **Fax:** 210/341-6326. **Contact:** Human Resources. **Description:** A corporate division of the retail grocery store chain Super S Foods. Super S Foods has stores throughout Texas. **NOTE:** A completed application must be mailed or faxed to the company. The application can be found on the company's website. **Positions advertised include:** Store Manager; Assistant Store Manager; Market Manager; Produce Manager. **Corporate headquarters location:** This location. **Parent company:** Mass Marketing, Inc.

SUSMAN GODFREY L.L.P.
1000 Louisiana Street, Suite 5100, Houston TX 77002-5096. 713/651-9366. **Contact:** Human Resources. **World Wide Web address:** http://www.susmangodfrey.com. **Description:** A law firm specializing in antitrust, energy and natural resources, libel, negligence, litigation, intellectual property, and product liability law. **Special programs:** Internships. **Other area locations:** Dallas TX. **Other U.S. locations:** CA; WA.

SUSQUEHANNA RADIO CORP.
3500 Maple Avenue, Suite 1600, Dallas TX 75219. 214/520-4305. **Fax:** 214/525-2525. **Contact:** Human Resources. **World Wide Web address:** http://www.dfwradio.com. **Description:** Operates four radio stations in the Dallas - Fort Worth area: 99.5 The Wolf, Big Talk 570, Merge 93.3 Net, and The Ticket Sports Radio. **NOTE:** Part-time positions offered. See the radio's website for job listings and contact information. **Positions advertised include:** Advertising Sales Account Manager; Researcher; Events Coordinator; Traffic Manager; Promotion Assistant. **Corporate headquarters location:** York PA.

SWIFT ENERGY COMPANY
16825 Northchase Drive, Suite 400, Houston TX 77060. 281/874-2700. **Fax:** 281/874-2164. **Contact:** Charles Lopez, Human Resources Manager. **World Wide Web address:** http://www.swiftenergy.com. **Description:** Sells oil and gas to industrial customers. **Listed on:** New York Stock Exchange. **Stock exchange symbol:** SFY.

SYLVAN LEARNING CENTER
4356 Dowlen Road, Beaumont TX 77706. 409/899-9798. **Recorded jobline:** 877/228-3224. **Contact:** Human Resources. **World Wide Web address:** http://www.educate.com. **Description:** Provides educational instruction and tutoring through reading and math programs, study skills courses, SAT/ACT prep classes, and homework support. **NOTE:** This company has locations throughout Texas and the U.S. See website for job listings and contact information. **Positions advertised include:** Teachers; Director of Education; Center Directors. **Other U.S. locations:** Nationwide. **Parent company:** Educate, Inc. provides educational services and programs to children. **Listed on:** NASDAQ. **Stock exchange symbol:** SLVN.

SYMONS CORPORATION
1989 Peachleaf Street, Houston TX 77039. 281/590-6670. **Fax:** 847/635-9287. **Contact:** Human Resources. **E-mail address:** jobs@symons.com. **World Wide Web address:** http://www.symons.com. **Description:** An international manufacturer of standard, custom, and fiberglass concrete-forming equipment. The company also manufactures chemical systems including acrylic sealers, bonding agents, construction grouts, and curing compounds. **NOTE:** This company has additional locations in Texas. See website for addresses, job listings and application information. **Corporate headquarters location:** Des Plaines IL.

SYSCO CORPORATION
1390 Enclave Parkway, Houston TX 77077-2099. 281/584-1390. **Contact:** Human Resources. **World Wide Web address:** http://www.sysco.com. **Description:** Engaged principally in the wholesale distribution of food and related products and services to the food service industry. Products include a full line of frozen foods. This company also products healthcare items. **NOTE:** For positions at the corporate location, apply online at the company's website. For all other positions, apply in person at the nearest location. **Positions advertised include:** Business Analyst; Business Development Manager; Cash Management Analyst; Claims Associate; Pension Benefits Coordinator;

Pricing Coordinator; Product Manger. **Corporate headquarters location:** This location. **Other area locations:** Austin TX; Dallas TX; San Antonio TX: Lubbock TX. **Listed on:** New York Stock Exchange. **Stock exchange symbol:** SYY.

TD INDUSTRIES, INC.
P.O. Box 819060, Dallas TX 75381-9060. 972/888-9505. **Physical address:** 13850 Diplomat Drive, Dallas TX 75234. **Fax:** 972/888-9507. **Contact:** Human Resources. **E-mail address:** tddallasjobs@tdindustries.com. **World Wide Web address:** http://www.tdindustries.com. **Description:** A national construction and service company that designs, installs, and repairs HVAC, plumbing, high-purity process piping, and energy management systems in commercial and industrial markets. Founded in 1946. **NOTE:** Entry-level positions are offered. See this company's website for job listings and contact information for all locations. **Positions advertised include:** Quickpen Software Operator; Mechanical Estimator; Building Technician; Administrative Assistant; Lead Change-out Technician; Scheduler; Project Manager; Job Cost Analyst. **Corporate headquarters location:** This location. **Other area locations:** Houston TX; Austin TX; San Antonio TX. **Other U.S. locations:** GA; AZ; Washington D.C. **Listed on:** Privately held.

TL MARKETING INC.
4407 Bee Caves Road, Building 6, 2nd Floor, Suite 622, Austin TX 78746. 512/371-7272. **Fax:** 512/371-0727. **Contact:** Human Resources. **Description:** A marketing firm representing manufacturers within the electrical industry. **Corporate headquarters location:** Dallas TX.

TMP WORLDWIDE ADVERTISING AND COMMUNICATIONS
1021 Main Street, Suite 1050, Houston TX 77002. 713/843-8600. **Fax:** 832/366-1185. **Contact:** Carolyn Gaither, Human Resources. **World Wide Web address:** http://www.tmp.com. **Description:** A human resources outsourcing firm. Operations include Monster.com, one of the largest and most successful recruiting Websites; recruitment advertising; executive search and selection; and yellow page advertising. **NOTE:** Apply online at this company's website. **Positions advertised include:** Outside Sales Account Executive. **Corporate headquarters location:** New York NY.

TXI, INC.
1341 West Mockingbird Lane, Dallas TX 75247-6913. 972/647-6700. **Fax:** 972/647-3312. **Contact:** Recruiter. **E-mail address:** recruiter@txi.com. **World Wide Web address:** http://www.txi.com. **Description:** A leading supplier of cement and structural steel primarily to the construction industry. **NOTE:** This company has several facilities throughout Texas. See website for job listings and contact information. **Special programs:** Internships. **Corporate headquarters location:** This location. **Other U.S. locations:** CA; OK; LA. **Subsidiaries include:** Riverside Cement Company. **Listed on:** New York Stock Exchange. **Stock exchange symbol:** TXI.

TABS DIRECT
1002 Texas Parkway, Stafford TX 77477. 281/499-0417. **Toll-free phone:** 800/231-0697. **Fax:** 281/499-7098. **Contact:** Recruiter. **E-mail address:** tabs.HR.resumes@tabsdirect.com. **World Wide Web address:** http://www.tabsdirect.com. **Description:** A direct mail firm with five subsidiaries engaged in data processing and offset printing. Tabs Direct also has lettershop capabilities. **Special programs:** Internships. **Corporate headquarters location:** Atlanta GA. **Other U.S. locations:** Los Angeles CA; Chicago IL. **Parent company:** Omnicom. **Operations at this facility include:** Service. **Listed on:** New York Stock Exchange. **Stock exchange symbol:** OMC.

TACO CABANA, INC.
8918 Tesoro Drive, Suite 200, San Antonio TX 78217. 210/804-0990. **Fax:** 210/804-2425. **Recorded jobline:** 800/357-9924x326. **Contact:** Human Resources. **E-mail address:** recruiting@tacocabana.com. **World Wide Web address:** http://www.tacocabana.com. **Description:** Taco Cabana operates a chain of Mexican restaurants. Founded in 1978. **NOTE:** Jobseekers may also apply at the nearest Taco Cabana restaurant. See the company's website for locations. **Corporate headquarters location:** This location. **Parent company:** Carrols Corporation.

TANDY BRANDS ACCESSORIES
690 East Lamar Boulevard, Suite 200, Arlington TX 76011. 817/548-0090. **Contact:** Human Resources. **World Wide Web address:** http://www.tandybrands.com. **Description:** Designs, manufactures, and markets belts, ties, suspenders, and other leather products sold in department stores. **Corporate headquarters location:** This location. **Other area locations:** Yoakum TX (Manufacturing; Distribution); Dallas TX (Distribution). **Operations at this facility include:** Administration; Marketing; Sales. **Listed on:** NASDAQ. **Stock exchange symbol:** TBAC.

TANDY WIRE AND CABLE COMPANY
1920 Eighth Avenue, Fort Worth TX 76110. 817/415-4000. **Contact:** Human Resources. **Description:** Engaged in the manufacture of wire and cable including computer cable. **Parent company:** Radio Shack. **Operations at this facility include:** Manufacturing.

TANKNOLOGY-NDE INTERNATIONAL, INC.
8900 Shoal Creek Boulevard, Building 200, Austin TX 78757. 512/451-6334. **Toll-free phone:** 800/964-0010x119. **Contact:** Human Resources Department. **E-mail address:** thebestjobsare@tankology.com. **World Wide Web address:** http://www.tanknde.com. **Description:** Through its subsidiaries, Tanknology-NDE provides environmental compliance, information, and management services to owners and operators of underground storage tanks. The company has three principal lines of business: domestic underground storage tank testing; domestic tank management; and international underground storage tank testing. The company's primary service is tank tightness testing, tank integrity testing, or precision testing. This service involves testing underground storage tanks and associated piping to determine if they are leaking. **NOTE:** See company's website for job listings and contact information.

TARLETON STATE UNIVERSITY
Mail Stop T-510, Tarleton Station, Stephenville TX 76402. 254/968-9905. **Fax:** 254/968-9590. **Recorded jobline:** 254/968-9750. **Contact:** Mary Chenault, Employment Specialist. **World Wide Web address:** http://www.tarleton.edu. **Description:** A four-year state university offering bachelor's and master's degrees to approximately 6,300 students. Tarleton State University operates as part of the Texas A&M University System. **NOTE:** This university has a branch in Killen TX. See the university's website for job listings, skill assessment test and application procedures. **Office hours:** Monday – Friday, 8:00 a.m. – 5:00 p.m. **Corporate headquarters location:** College Station TX. **Operations at this facility include:** Administration.

TARRANT COUNTY JUNIOR COLLEGE
1500 Houston Street, Fort Worth TX 76102. 817/515-5100. **Contact:** Human Resources. **E-mail address:** jobs@tccd.edu. **World Wide Web address:** http://www.tcjc.cc.tx.us. **Description:** A two-year college offering associate's degrees and certificates. **NOTE:** This college requires jobseekers to complete a test online at its website. See website for additional information. **Positions advertised include:** Adjunct Instructor. **Corporate headquarters location:** This location. **Operations at this facility include:** Administration.

TAYLOR PUBLISHING COMPANY
1550 West Mockingbird Lane, Dallas TX 75235. 214/678-0209. **Toll-free phone:** 800/677-2800.214/819-8463. **Fax:** 214/819-8141. **Contact:** Stacey Young, Human Resources. **E-mail address:** syoung@taylorpub.com. **World Wide Web address:** http://www.taylorpub.com. **Description:** A publisher of yearbooks and specialty books. **NOTE:** Second shifts offered. See website for addresses and contact information for other Texas facilities. **Positions advertised include:** Prepress Production Specialists (PageMaker); Press Helpers; Machine Operators; Sales Representative. **Other area locations:** El Paso TX; San Angelo TX. **Other U.S. locations:** PA. **Operations at this facility include:** Administration; Manufacturing; Research and Development; Service.

TEAM INDUSTRIAL SERVICES, INC.
P.O. Box 123, Alvin TX 77512. 281/331-6154. **Physical address:** 200 Hermann Drive, Alvin TX 77511. **Contact:** Human Resources. **World Wide Web address:** http://www.teamindustrialservices.com. **Description:** Provides a wide variety of environmental services for industrial corporations including consulting, engineering, monitoring, and leak repair. Founded in 1973. **NOTE:** This company has 10 locations throughout Texas. See website for job listings, addresses and application. **Positions advertised include:** Field Machining Manager. **Corporate headquarters location:** This location. **Other U.S. locations:** Nationwide. **International locations:** Worldwide. **Listed on:** American Stock Exchange. **Stock exchange symbol:** TMI. **Number of employees worldwide:** 800.

TEAMSTAFF
2 Northpoint Drive, Suite 760, Houston TX 77060. 281/405-4300. **Toll-free phone:** 800/600-0374. **Contact:** Human Resources. **World Wide Web address:** http://www.teamstaff.com. **Description:** Offers a full line of services, which include payroll processing, permanent and temporary placement of personnel, in-house hardware and software systems, outsourcing, facility management, employee leasing, and insurance services, including employee benefits. **Corporate headquarters location:** Somerset NJ. **Listed on:** NASDAQ. **Stock exchange symbol:** TSTF.

TECCOR ELECTRONICS INC.
1800 Hurd Drive, Irving TX 75038. 972/580-1515. **Contact:** Human Resources. **World Wide Web address:** http://www.littelfuse.com. **Description:** Manufactures electronic power controls and related equipment. A second plant (also at this location) manufactures semiconductor power devices, solid-state relays, and a variety of silicon chips and rectifiers. **Corporate headquarters location:** This location. **Parent company:** Littlefuse.

TECHWORKS, INC.
4030 West Braker Lane, Suite 120, Austin TX 78759. 512/794-8533. **Fax:** 512/794-8520. **Contact:** Human Resources. **World Wide Web address:** http://www.techworks.com. **Description:** Manufactures and sells computer memory.

TECNOMATIX TECHNOLOGIES
2435 North Central Expressway, Suite 100, Richardson TX 75080-2722. 972/680-9700. **Fax:** 972/669-0563. **Contact:** Human Resources. **E-mail address:** jobs@us.tecnomatix.com. **World Wide Web address:** http://www.technomatix.com. **Description:** Develops, markets, and supports application-enabler software products for real-time monitoring, analysis, information management, and control solutions in worldwide industrial automation markets. Technomatix also develops, markets, and supports integrated hardware, software, and systems solutions for automated identification and data collection applications that are sold to a broad base of customers throughout North America. The company also acts as a full-service distributor and value-added re-marketer for manufacturers of bar code equipment. **Other U.S. locations:** Nationwide. **International locations:** Worldwide. **Operations at this facility include:** Administration; Divisional Headquarters; Research and Development; Sales; Service. **Listed on:** NASDAQ. **Stock exchange symbol:** TCNO.

TELECHECK SOUTHWEST
5251 Westheimer, Suite 1000, Houston TX 77056-5404. 713/331-7700. **Contact:** Human Resources. **World Wide Web address:** http://www.telecheck.com. **Description:** A check verification company. **NOTE:** Apply online at this company's website. **Corporate headquarters location:** This location. **Other U.S. locations:** Nationwide.

TELLABS TEXAS INC.
6565 MacArthur, Suite 225, Irving TX 75039. 972/869-4114. **Contact:** Human Resources. **World Wide Web address:** http://www.tellabs.com. **Description:** Tellabs designs and builds voice and data communication equipment used primarily by telephone companies. **NOTE:** Apply online at this company's website. **Corporate headquarters location:** Naperville IL. **Other area locations:** Dallas TX. **Other U.S. locations:** Nationwide. **International locations:** Parent company: Tellabs, Inc. **Operations at this facility include:** This location is a sales office. **Listed on:** NASDAQ. **Stock exchange symbol:** TLAB. **Number of employees worldwide:** 3,000.

TEMPLE-INLAND, INC.
P.O. Box 40, Austin TX 78767. 512/434-5800. **Contact:** Human Resources. **World Wide Web address:** http://www.templeinland.com. **Description:** A holding company offering corrugated packaging, bleached paperboard, building products, and financial services. **Other area locations:** Diboll TX; Houston TX; Dallas TX; Bellville TX; McKinney TX; San Antonio TX. **Positions advertised include:** Account Executive; Advertising Manager; Banking Center Manager; Business Analyst. **Corporate headquarters location:** This location. **Listed on:** New York Stock Exchange. **Stock exchange symbol:** TIN.

TENET HEALTHCARE CORPORATION
TENET DALLAS
13737 Noel Road, Dallas TX 75240. 469/893-2200. **Fax:** 469/893-1321. **Contact:** Manager of Recruitment. **World Wide Web address:** http://www.tenethealth.com. **Description:** A multibillion-dollar, multi-hospital corporation that, with its subsidiaries, owns or operates approximately 100 acute care facilities nationwide. In Texas, it operates 13 hospitals. **NOTE:** Apply online at this company's website for corporate positions. This company also provides hyperlinks to its hospitals' job listings. **Positions advertised include:** RN; Employee Performance Analyst; Quality Control Representative; Corporate Recruiter; Financial Analyst; Managed Care Regional Director;; Clinical Manager. **Corporate headquarters location:** Santa Monica CA. **Other U.S. locations:** Nationwide. **Operations at this facility include:** Administration; Regional Headquarters. **Listed on:** New York Stock Exchange. **Stock exchange symbol:** THC. **Number of employees nationwide:** 106,900.

TESORO PETROLEUM CORPORATION
300 Concord Plaza Drive, San Antonio TX 78216. 210/828-8484. **Toll-free phone:** 800/837-6762. **Recorded jobline:** 210/283-2600. **Contact:** Melinda Schott, Human Resources. **World Wide Web address:** http://www.tesoropetroleum.com. **Description:** Engaged in the refining, transportation, and marketing of natural gas, crude oil, and related products. Other operations include exploration and oil field services such as supplying lubricants, fuels, and specialty products to the U.S. drilling industry. Tesoro Petroleum has refining facilities in Alaska, exploration and production facilities in Texas, and sells its products to customers primarily in Alaska, the Far East, and the Rocky Mountain region. **NOTE:** This company only accepts resumes and applications for open positions. See its website for job listings. **Positions advertised include:** Solutions Delivery Analyst Family; Commercial Analyst; Card and Loyalty Programs Coordinator; Internal Auditor; Lease Crude Accountant; Programs Specialist; Services Coordinator. **Corporate headquarters location:** This location. **Listed on:** New York Stock Exchange. **Stock exchange symbol:** TSO.

TEX TAN WESTERN LEATHER COMPANY
808 South U.S. Highway 77A, Yoakum TX 77995. 361/293-2314. **Fax:** 361/293-2369. **Contact:** Human Resources. **World Wide Web address:** http://www.textan.com. **Description:** Tex Tan Western Leather Company is a manufacturer of various leather products including saddles, riding equipment, belts, and other sundry products. Tex Tan Western Leather Company provides these products to dealers worldwide. **Listed on:** Privately held.

TEX-TUBE COMPANY
1503 North Post Oak, Houston TX 77055. 713/686-4351. **Fax:** 713/685-3222. **Contact:** Human Resources. **World Wide Web address:** http://www.tex-tube.com. **Description:** Manufactures steel pipe and tubular products. **Corporate headquarters location:** Greer SC. **Other U.S. locations:** MD; ME; OH. **Operations at this facility include:** Manufacturing; Sales. **Listed on:** Privately held.

TEXACE CORPORATION
402 West Nueva, San Antonio TX 78207-0429. 210/227-7551. **Toll-free phone:** 800/835-8973. **Fax:** 210/227-4237. **Contact:** Human Resources. **World Wide Web address:** http://www.texace.com. **Description:** Texace Corporation manufactures a variety of headwear including golf caps and visors.

TEXAS A&M UNIVERSITY
809 East University Drive, Suite 101A, College Station TX 77843-1475. 979/845-5154. **Fax:** 979/847-8877. **Contact:** Human Resources. **E-mail address:** employoffice@tamu.edu. **World Wide Web address:** http://www.tamujobs.tamu.edu. **Description:** A university that offers a wide range of bachelor's, master's, doctoral and professional programs. Texas A&M also provides continuing education programs that serve the needs of area businesses and professionals. **NOTE:** Texas A&M University has 17 locations throughout the state. Its website provides a job listings for all locations. Apply online at the university's website or visit the Human Resources Office in Suite 101A. **Office hours:** Monday – Friday, 8:00 a.m. – 5:00 p.m. **Corporate headquarters location:** This location.

TEXAS CENTER FOR INFECTIOUS DISEASE
2303 SE Military Drive, San Antonio TX 78223. 210/534-8857x2255. **Fax:** 210/531-4504. **Contact:** Human Resources Director. **World Wide Web address:** http://www.tdh.state.tx.us/tcid. **Description:** A hospital that provides acute and chronic care to all patients referred for evaluation. **NOTE:** Texas Center for Infectious Disease offers career opportunities in the following areas: Chronic Respiratory Disease Services, which allows individuals to work with inpatient respiratory disease patients with a concentration on physical rehabilitation, patient education, and lifestyle adaptations; Diabetic Services, in which care includes medical evaluation and patient teaching; Chest Disease Services, through which the hospital treats diseases such as lung cancer, fungal disease, and tuberculosis; and Ambulatory Services, which offers an opportunity to work in a variety of clinics to include chest, Hansen's Disease, diabetes, and infectious diseases. The Texas Center for Infectious Disease also has a Tuberculosis Education Center. **NOTE:** Apply online at this organization's website. **Special programs:** Internships. **Corporate headquarters location:** Austin TX. **Operations at this facility include:** Administration; Research and Development; Service.

TEXAS CHILDREN'S HOSPITAL
Wells Fargo Building, Second Floor, 6631 South Main Street, MC 404230, Houston TX 77030. 832/824-2020. **Recorded jobline:** 832/824-2022. **Contact:** Human Resources. **World Wide Web address:** http://www.texaschildrenshospital.org. **Description:** A pediatric hospital. **NOTE:** A completed application is required for any position. Apply online at the hospital's website or in person at the Human Resources Office. **Positions advertised include:** RN; Account Representative; Clinical Nurse; Case Manager; Business Analyst; Financial Counselor; Education Coordinator; Medical Auditor Patient Care Assistant; Receptionist; Radiographer; Transplant Coordinator. **Office hours:** Monday – Friday, 8:00 a.m. – 4:00 p.m. **Operations at this facility include:** Administration; Research and Development; Service.

TEXAS CHIROPRACTIC COLLEGE
5912 Spencer Highway, Pasadena TX 77505. 281/998-6003. **Toll-free phone:** 800/468-6839. **Fax:** 281/991-5237. **Contact:** Human Resources Director. **E-mail address:** HR@txchiro.edu. **World Wide Web address:** http://www.txchiro.edu. **Description:** Offers Doctor of Chiropractic and Bachelor of Science in Human Biology degrees. **Positions advertised include**: Moody Health Center Director.

TEXAS CHRISTIAN UNIVERSITY
P.O. Box 298200, Fort Worth TX 76129. 817/257-7790. **Fax:** 817/257-7979. **Recorded jobline:** 817/257-7791. **Contact:** John Weif, Director of Employee Relations. **World Wide Web address:** http://www.tcu.edu. **Description:** A university offering undergraduate and graduate programs to approximately 7,000 students. **NOTE:** Clerical, staff, and faculty positions offered. See website for application information and contact. Some positions require a typing test and credential documentation. **Positions advertised include:** Data Control Specialist; Administrative Assistant; Computer Support Specialist; Financial Assistant; Horticultural Assistant; Musical Accompanist; Minister to the University; Athletic Director; Dean; Fund Officer; Professor (Various). **Corporate headquarters location:** This location.

TEXAS DEPARTMENT OF CRIMINAL DEFENSE
P.O. Box 13084, Capitol Station, Austin TX 78711-3084. 936/437-4141. **Physical Address:** 209 West 14th Street, Austin TX 78701. **Contact:** Human Resources. **E-mail address:** human.res@tdcj.state.tx.us. **World Wide Web address:** http://www.tdcj.state.tx.us. **Description:** Manages the state's extensive prison system. **NOTE:** Part-time positions are available. A completed application is required for any position. Applications can be downloaded online at the website. The website provides job listings for all the Texas correctional facilities. See website for all locations and their job openings. Apply online. **Special programs:** Correctional Training; Internships. **Positions advertised include:** Correctional Officer; Parole Officer; Parole Caseworker; Clerk, Food Service Manager; Laundry Manager.

TEXAS DEPARTMENT OF HEALTH
1100 West 49th Street, Austin TX 78756-3199. 512/458-7111. **Toll-free phone:** 888/963-7111. **Contact:** Human Resources. **E-mail address:** HHSJobs@tdh.state.tx.us. **World Wide Web address:** http://www.tdh.state.tx.us. **Description:** Employing 6,300 people statewide, the Texas Department of Health is a government department offering health services across the state. **NOTE:** Apply online at this organization's website. **Positions advertised include:** Environmental Specialist; Program Specialist; Network Specialist; Medical Technologist; Administrative Assistant. **Special programs:** Internships. **Corporate headquarters location:** This location. **Operations at this facility include:** Administration.

TEXAS DEPARTMENT OF HUMAN SERVICES
P.O. Box 149030, 701 West 55th Street, Austin TX 78751. 512/438-3011. **Toll-free phone:** 888/834-7406. **Contact:** Human Resources. **World Wide Web address:** http://www.dhs.state.tx.us. **Description:** This location houses the welfare office, which provides food stamps and oversees Medicaid services. **NOTE:** See this organization's website for job listings, application requirements and contact information. **Positions advertised include:** Program Consultant; Attorney; Accountant; Nurse; Pharmacist

TEXAS DEPARTMENT OF MENTAL HEALTH AND MENTAL RETARDATION, CENTRAL OFFICE
909 West 45th Street, Austin TX 78751. 512/454-3761. **Contact:** Human Resources. **World Wide Web address:** http://www.mhmr.state.tx.us. **Description:** Administrative offices for mental health and retardation services and facilities statewide. **NOTE:** Part-time positions are available. This website provides job listings for all the Texas mental health and retardation facilities, including schools and hospitals. An application is required for any position. Apply online. **Positions advertised include:** Reimbursement Officer; Clerk; Interpreter; Aquatics Instructor; Services Aide; Therapist Technician; Food Service Worker; Cook; LVN; RN; Pharmacist; Physician; Psychiatrist; Psychologist; Social Worker; Therapist.

TEXAS DEPARTMENT OF PUBLIC SAFETY
P.O. Box 4087, Austin TX 78773-0001. 512/424-2000. **Physical address:** 5805 North Lamar Boulevard, Austin TX 78752-4422. **Contact:** Human Resources. **World Wide Web address:** http://www.txdps.state.tx.us. **Description:** Administrative offices for motor vehicles, including safety and drivers licenses. This location is also the state office for crime investigations and the central office for Texas state patrol officers. **NOTE:** See website for job listings and applications. Mail all resumes and completed applications to the P.O. Box address, Attention: Human Resources, unless a job posting states otherwise. **Positions advertised include:** Administrative Assistant; Inspector; Research Specialist; Crime Lab Evidence Technician; Program Specialist; Security Worker; Data Entry Operator; Trooper Trainee. Special Programs: State Trooper Training.

TEXAS DEPARTMENT OF TRANSPORTATION
P.O. Drawer 15426, Austin TX 78761.512/416-2994. **Toll-free phone:** 800/893-6817. **Recorded jobline:** 800/893-6848. **Contact:** Human Resources. **World Wide Web address:** http://www.dot.state.tx.us. **Description:** Designs, builds, and maintains roads and highways throughout the state of Texas. **NOTE:** This organization provides job listings for its locations throughout Texas. See website for job listings and apply online.

TEXAS EASTMAN
P.O. Box 7444, Longview TX 75607. 903/237-5000. **Contact:** Human Resources. **World Wide Web address:** http://www.eastman.com. **Description:** Manufactures more than 40 chemical and plastic products. The company primarily uses propane and ethane to create its products. **NOTE:** See this company's website for job listings and application requirements. **Corporate headquarters location:** Kingsport TN. **Other area locations:** Ennis TX. **Parent company:** Eastman Chemicals. **Listed on:** New York Stock Exchange. **Stock exchange symbol:** EMN. **Number of employees worldwide:** 30,000.

TEXAS FIRST BANK
6501 Stewart Road, Galveston TX 77552. 409/744-6353. **Contact:** Manager. **World Wide Web address:** http://www.texasfirstbanks.com. **Description:** A full-service bank. **Other area locations:** Crystal Beach TX; Dickinson TX; Friendswood TX; Hitchcock TX; Kemah TX; La Marque TX; League City TX; Santa Fe TX; Texas City TX. **NOTE:** This bank lists has additional branches in Galveston. Its website lists all locations. Apply in person at the nearest bank location.

TEXAS HEALTH RESOURCES
611 Ryan Plaza Drive, Suite 900, Arlington TX 76011. 817/462-7900. **Toll-free phone:** 800/749-6877. **Fax:** 866/889-8975. **Contact:** Human Resources. **E-mail address:** thrjobpostings@texashealth.org. **World Wide Web address:** http://www.texashealth.org. **Description:** One of the largest nonprofit health care systems in Texas including a nursing home, 13 acute care hospitals, clinics, and home health services. **NOTE:** Part-time jobs and second and third shifts are offered. This company's website provides job listings for all its facilities. Apply online. **Corporate headquarters location:** This location. **Other area locations:** Greenville TX; Kaufman TX; Plano TX; Winnsboro TX.

TEXAS HIGHER EDUCATION COORDINATING BOARD
P.O. Box 12788, Austin TX 78711-2788. 512/427-6101. **Recorded jobline:** 512/427-6574. **Contact:** Betty Sharp, Personnel Director. **World Wide Web address:** http://www.thecb.state.tx.us. **Description:** A governmental board that regulates educational issues in Texas. **NOTE:** A completed application is required for any position. See the organization's website for application information and job listings. **Office hours:** Monday – Friday, 8:00 a.m. – 5:00 p.m.

TEXAS INSTRUMENTS, INC. (TI)
12500 TI Boulevard, Dallas TX 75243-4136. **Toll-free phone:** 800/336-5236. **Contact:** Human Resources. **World Wide Web address:** http://www.ti.com. **Description:** One of the world's largest technology companies, with sales and manufacturing operations in more than 25 countries. Texas Instruments (TI) is one of the world's largest suppliers of semiconductor products. TI's defense electronics business is a leading supplier of avionics, infrared, and weapons guidance systems to the U.S. Department of Defense and U.S. allies. The company is also a technology leader in high-performance notebook computers and model-based software development tools. TI sensors monitor and regulate pressure and temperature in products ranging from automobiles to air conditioning systems. **NOTE:** This company has job listings on its website for all its Texas and U.S. locations. Apply online. **Other area locations:** Houston TX (Manufacturing). **Corporate headquarters location:** This location. **Operations at this facility include:** Administration: Manufacturing; Sales. **Listed on:** New York Stock Exchange. **Stock exchange symbol:** TXN. **Number of employees worldwide:** 35,000.

TEXAS MEDICAL AND SURGICAL ASSOCIATES
8440 Walnut Hill Lane, Dallas TX 75231. 214/345-1400. **Contact:** Human Resources. **World Wide Web address:** http://www.texasmedicalandsurgical.com. **Description:** A private clinic. **Office hours:** Monday - Friday, 8:30 a.m. - 5:00 p.m. **Other area locations:** Garland TX.

TEXAS MEDICAL CENTER
2151 West Holcombe Boulevard, Houston TX 77030-3303. 713/791-6400. **Contact:** Christy Clark, Associate Vice President of Human Resources. **Fax:** 713/791-6402. **World Wide Web address:** http://www.tmc.edu. **Description:** A private, non-profit medical center.

TEXAS MONTHLY
P.O. Box 1569, Austin TX 78767. 512/320-6900. **Fax:** 512/476-9007. **Contact:** Angela Hollinsworth, Human Resources. **E-mail address:** humanresources@texasmonthly.com. **World Wide Web address:** http://www.texasmonthly.com. **Description:** *Texas Monthly* is a regional, general interest magazine. Articles range from health and travel to true crime. The magazine has a circulation of approximately 300,000. Founded in 1972. **Positions advertised include:** National Account Manager; Advertising Sales Manager. **Special programs:** Internships. **Corporate headquarters location:** This location. **Parent company:** Emmis Communications (Indianapolis IN).

TEXAS-NEW MEXICO POWER COMPANY
P.O. Box 2943, Fort Worth TX 76133. 817/731-0099. **Physical address:** 4100 International Plaza, Tower II, Fort Worth TX 76109. **Contact:** Suzy McGovern, Human Resources. **E-mail address:** smcgovern@tnpe.com. **World Wide Web address:** http://www.tnpe.com. **Description:** A public utility engaged in the purchase, transmission, distribution, and sale of electrical power in Texas and New Mexico. It has approximately 240,000 customers in northern Texas and southern New Mexico. **Positions advertised include:** Supervisor of IT Market Operations; Credit/Collections Operations Analyst; Energy Technician; Customer Technician; Manager of Compensation and Benefits. **NOTE:** See this company's website for job listings and e-mail resumes. **Corporate headquarters location:** This location. **Parent company:** TNP Enterprises Inc. **Listed on:** Privately held.

TEXAS ORTHOPEDIC HOSPITAL
7401 South Main, Houston TX 77030. 713/799-8600. **Toll-free phone:** 800/678-4501. **Contact:** Human Resources. **World Wide Web address:** http://www.texasorthopedic.com. **Description:** An orthopedic hospital offering specialty surgery, sports medicine, and rehabilitation services. Texas Orthopedic Hospital is an affiliate of Columbia/HCA Healthcare Corporation. Founded in 1995. **NOTE:** Part-time and volunteer positions offered. Apply online at this hospital's website. **Positions advertised include:** House Supervisor; Medical Technologist; Occupational Therapist; Pharmacist; RN; Security Representative; Surgical Technician.

TEXAS PARKS & WILDLIFE
4200 Smith School Road, Austin TX 78744. 512/389-4800. **Toll-free phone:** 800/792-1112. **Recorded jobline:** 512/389-4954. **Contact:** Human Resources. **World Wide Web address:** http://www.tpwd.state.tx.us. **Description:** Dedicated to preserving the nature and wildlife of Austin and the surrounding Texas area. **NOTE:** This organization's website provides job listings for its locations throughout Texas. Apply online for open positions.

TEXAS PETROCHEMICALS CORPORATION (TPC)
Three Riverway, Suite 1500, Houston TX 77056-1935. 713/627-7474. **Contact:** Human Resources. **Description:** Manufactures, markets and trades natural gas through facilities in Texas, Louisiana, Mississippi, and other locations throughout the Gulf Coast. **NOTE:** Submit resume online at this company's website. **Corporate headquarters location:** This location. **Other area locations:** Galena Park TX; Pearland TX; Texas City TX. **Other U.S. locations:** NY. **Parent company:** PacifiCorp.

TEXAS RECREATION CORPORATION
P.O. Box 539, Wichita Falls TX 76307. 940/322-4463. **Contact:** Human Resources. **World Wide Web address:** http://www.texasrec.com. **Description:** Manufactures soft foam products including pool flotation devices.

TEXAS REFINERY CORPORATION
P.O. Box 711, Fort Worth TX 76101. 817/332-1161. **Physical address:** One Refinery Place, 840 North Main Street, Fort Worth TX 76101. **Toll-free phone:** 800/827-0711. **Contact:** Jim Peel, Human Resources. **E-mail address:** trcsales@texasrefinery.com. **World Wide Web address:** http://www.texasrefinery.com. **Description:** Manufactures specialty lubricant products and building maintenance products such as roof coatings. **NOTE:** A completed application must accompany a resume. Apply online at this company's website. **Positions advertised include:** Sales Representative.

TEXAS SOUTHERN UNIVERSITY
3100 Cleburne Avenue, Houston TX 77004. 713/313-7011. **Contact:** Human Resources. **World Wide Web address:** http://www.tsu.edu. **Description:** A four-year university offering both undergraduate and graduate degree programs. **NOTE:** See this university's website for job listings and application. **Positions advertised include:** Security Officer; Assistant Band Director; Program Director; Archivist; Professor (Various).

TEXAS SPECIALTY HOSPITAL
7955 Harry Heinz Boulevard, Dallas TX 75235. 214/637-0000. **Fax:** 214/905-0566. **Contact:** Jill Doire, Divisional Recruiter. **World Wide Web address:** http://www.tricare.com. **Description:** A long-term, acute care hospital. **NOTE:** Entry-level and part-time positions are available. **Parent company:** Trans Healthcare.

TEXAS STADIUM
2401 East Airport Freeway, Irving TX 75062. 972/438-7676. **Contact:** Human Resources. **Description:** A sporting arena. Texas Stadium is the home field of the Dallas Cowboys professional football team.

TEXAS STATE AUDITOR'S OFFICE
P.O. Box 12067, Austin TX 78711. 512/936-9500. **Fax:** 512/936-9400. **Contact:** Dennis Wilson, Human Resources Officer. **World Wide Web address:** http://www.sao.state.tx.us. **Description:** The independent auditor for the Texas state government. Texas State Auditor's Office provides legislators, agency management, and the citizens of Texas with information about the operations of state-run agencies and universities. Additional duties include the management of control audits, statewide financial and compliance audits, special investigations, classification compliance audits, briefing reports, legislative requests, and special issue areas. **NOTE:** An application is required. See the office's website for job listings and application. **Positions advertised include:** Senior Auditor; Senior Information Systems Audit Analyst; Staff Auditor; Texas State Auditor. **Special programs:** Internships; Training.

TEXAS STATE UNIVERSITY—SAN MARCOS
601 University Drive, J.C. Kellam Building, Suite 340, San Marcos TX 78666. 512/245-2557. **Fax:** 512/245-3911. **Contact:** Human Resources. **E-mail address:** hr@txstate.edu. **World Wide Web address:** http://www.humanresources.swt.edu. **Description:** A college offering undergraduate, graduate and doctoral degrees. **NOTE:** For more information about the university, visit http://www.txstate.edu. To apply for staff positions, a completed application must accompany a resume. Download application at the website. For faculty and other positions, see website for application procedures. Walk-in applications are accepted in the Human Resources office during regular business hours. **Positions advertised include:** Administrative Assistant; Grant Secretary; Data Entry Operator; Residence Hall Director; Business Manager, Microcomputer Lab Assistant; Professor (Various). **Office hours:** Monday – Friday, 8:00 a.m. – 5:00 p.m.

TEXAS TECH UNIVERSITY
P.O. Box 41093, Lubbock TX 79409-1093. 806/742-3851. **Contact:** James A. Brown, Managing Director. **E-mail address:** employment@ttu.edu. **World Wide Web address:** http://www.ttu.edu. **Description:** A state university. The university offers undergraduate and graduate degrees in liberal arts, law, applied health, and medicine. **NOTE:** Texas Tech University has campus locations throughout Texas. See website for locations, job listings and application requirements. **Positions advertised include:** Administrative Assistant; Analyst; Professor (Various); Chief Accountant; Chief of Police; Coordinator; Custodian; Development Officer; Lead Advisor; Medical Lab Technician; Patient Services Supervisor; Proposal Writer; Section Manager. **Corporate headquarters location:** This location.

TEXAS UTILITIES COMPANIES
1601 Bryan Street, Dallas TX 75201-3411. 214/812-4600. **Fax:** 214/812-8419. **Recorded jobline:** 214/812-8633. **Contact:** Human Resources. **World Wide Web address:** http://www.txu.com. **Description:** A large, investor-owned, electric utility providing electric service to 2 million customers in north, central, and west Texas. **NOTE:** This company only accepts online applications. See its website. **Positions advertised include:** Call Center Supervisor; Trainer; Senior Analyst; Welder; Meter Reader Trainee. **Special programs:** Internships. **Corporate headquarters location:** This location. **Subsidiaries include:** TXU Energy; TXU Gas; Oncor; TXU Australia. **Parent company:** TXU Corporation. **Listed on:** New York Stock Exchange. **Stock exchange symbol:** TXU. **Number of employees nationwide:** 18,000.

TEXAS VETERINARY MEDICAL DIAGNOSTIC LABORATORY
P.O. Box 3200, Amarillo TX 79116-3200. 806/353-7478. **Physical address:** 6610 Amarillo Boulevard West, Amarillo TX 79106. **Toll-free phone:** 888/646-5624. **Fax:** 806/359-0636. **Contact:** Human Resources. **World Wide Web address:** http://tvmdl.tamu.edu. **Description:** A diagnostic laboratory that performs medical testing on animals to assist veterinarians with diagnosis and prognosis. Test fields include chemistry, hematology, urology, toxicology, serology, histology, bacteriology, and necropsies. **Office hours:** Monday - Friday, 8:00 a.m. - 5:00 p.m.; Saturday, 8:00 a.m. - 12:00 p.m. **Other U.S. locations:** College Station TX; Gonzales TX; Center TX.

TEXAS WESLEYAN UNIVERSITY
1201 Wesleyan Street, Fort Worth TX 76105. 817/531-4403. **Fax:** 817/531-4402. **Contact:** Human Resources. **E-mail address:** hr@txwes.edu. **World Wide Web address:** http://www.txwesleyan.edu. **Description:** A small, private university affiliated with the United Methodist Church. Texas Wesleyan University offers a variety of undergraduate and graduate degrees to approximately 3,000 students. Founded in 1890. **NOTE:** To apply, submit cover letter, resume and references. **Positions advertised include:** Benefactor/Colleague Data Base Administrator; module Support Specialist; Associate Dean; Provost and Senior Vice President; Assistant Professor (Various); Dean. **Corporate headquarters location:** This location.

TEXOIL, INC.
110 Cypress Station Drive, Suite 220, Houston TX 77090. 281/537-9920. **Fax:** 281/537-8324. **Contact:** Human Resources. **World Wide Web address:** http://www.texoil.com. **Description:** Engaged in oil and gas exploration and development. **Corporate headquarters location:** This location. **Listed on:** NASDAQ. **Stock exchange symbol:** TXLI.

TEXOMA MEDICAL CENTER (TMC)
1000 Memorial Drive, Denison TX 75020. 903/416-4085. **Fax:** 903/416-4087. **Recorded jobline:** 800/566-1211. **Contact:** Joni Horn, Human Resources. **World Wide Web address:** http://www.thcs.org. **Description:** Texoma Medical Center (TMC) is an acute care hospital with 300 beds. TMC offers general medical and surgical services, intensive care, and pediatric care. Founded in 1965. **NOTE:** Second and third shifts are offered. This hospital provides job listings on its website. **Office hours:** Monday, 8:00 a.m. – 4:00 p.m.; Tuesday – Friday, 8:00 a.m. – 5:00 p.m. **Positions advertised include:** LVN; Preoperative Core Technician; Training Service Specialist; Medical Assistant; Cleaning Technician; Floor Technician; Dietitian; Building Maintenance Operator. **Special programs:** Co-ops; Summer Jobs. **Corporate headquarters location:** This location. **Other U.S. locations:** OK. **Subsidiaries include:** Times Medical Equipment. **Parent company:** Texoma Healthcare Systems, Inc. (also at this location). **Operations at this facility include:** Administration; Support Services.

THAI AIRWAYS INTERNATIONAL LTD.
8700 North Stemmons Freeway, Suite 133, Dallas TX 75247. 800/426-5204. **Contact:** Human Resources. **World Wide Web address:** http://www.thaiair.com. **Description:** One of Asia's leading airlines, offering flights to 72 cities in 37 countries. **Corporate headquarters location:** Bangkok.

TRANSWESTERN PUBLISHING
9211 Waterford Centre Boulevard Street, Austin TX 78758. 512/451-2121. **Fax:** 512/451-7595. **Contact:** Human Resources. **World Wide Web address:** http://www.twpsite.com. Founded in 1980. **Description:** creates and distributes directories in more than 20 states. **Positions advertised include:** Account Executive. **NOTE:** Apply online. **Corporate headquarters location:** San Diego CA. **Operations at this facility include:** This is primarily a sales location. **Listed on:** Privately held. **Number Of employees nationwide:** 2,000.

THERMON MANUFACTURING COMPANY
P.O. Box 609, San Marcos TX 78667-0609. 512/396-5801. **Physical address:** 100 Thermon Drive, San Marcos TX 78666. **Contact:** Human Resources. **E-mail address:** human.resources@thermon.com. **World Wide Web address:** http://www.thermon.com. **Description:** A manufacturer of heat tracings. **Corporate headquarters location:** This location. **Other U.S. locations:** CA; DE; LA; NC. **International locations:** Worldwide.

THINKSPARK
4835 LBJ Freeway, Suite 1100, Dallas TX 75244. 972/392-0955. **Toll-free phone:** 888/262-6043. **Contact:** Human Resources. **World Wide Web address:** http://www.thinkspark.com. **Description:** Offers services in four main areas: Database Services, which includes database administration and monitoring services; E-Business Solutions, which includes knowledge management, enterprise resource planning, and e-commerce; System Services, which includes systems integration and interface design; and Education Services. Founded in 1987. **Positions advertised include:** Territory Manager. **Other area locations:** Austin TX; Houston TX; San Antonio TX. **Other U.S. locations:** NV; OK.

THOMPSON & KNIGHT LLP
1700 Pacific Avenue, Suite 3300, Dallas TX 75201. 214/969-1700. **Contact:** Human Resources. **World Wide Web address:** http://www.tklaw.com. **Description:** A law firm specializing in a wide variety of law disciplines including bankruptcy, corporate, intellectual property, real estate, and environmental. **NOTE:** This law firm has recruiters for each of its location. See its website for contact names and information. **Special programs:** Internships. **Other area locations:** Austin TX; Houston TX; San Antonio TX. **Other U.S. locations:** Monterrey CA. **International locations:** Algiers; Paris; Rio de Janeiro.

J. WALTER THOMPSON
1845 Woodall Rodgers Freeway, Dallas TX 75201. 214/754-9316. **Contact:** Human Resources. **World Wide Web address:** http://www.jwtworld.com. **Description:** One of the largest advertising agencies in the nation. **NOTE:** Apply online at this company's website. **Special programs:** Marketing Fellowship. **Positions advertised include:** Traffic Coordinator. **Corporate headquarters location:** New York NY. **Other U.S. locations**: Nationwide. **Other area locations:** Worldwide. **Parent company:** WWP. **Number of employees worldwide:** 8,500.

THORNTON STEEL COMPANY INC.
2700 West Pafford, Fort Worth TX 76110. 817/926-3324. **Fax:** 817/926-0758. **Contact:** Human Resources. **World Wide Web address:** http://www.thornsteel.com. **Description:** A structural steel fabricator. **Corporate headquarters location:** This location. **Operations at this facility include:** Manufacturing; Sales. **Number of employees at this location:** 15.

THORPE CORPORATION
P.O. Box 33047, Houston TX 77233. 713/644-1247. **Fax:** 713/644-3011. **Contact:** Human Resources. **World Wide Web address:** http://www. thorpeproducts.com. **Description:** An engineering, construction, and refractory company. **NOTE:** Entry-level positions are offered. **Corporate headquarters location:** This location. **Other area locations:** Beaumont TX; Dallas TX. **Other U.S. locations:** Gonzales LA. **Subsidiaries include:** J.T. Thorpe (also at this location); Leacon-Sunbelt, Inc.; Thorpe Products. **Operations at this facility include:** Administration; Manufacturing; Sales; Service. **Listed on:** Privately held.

3D/INTERNATIONAL
1900 West Loop South, Suite 400, Houston TX 77027. 713/871-7000. **Contact:** Personnel. **World Wide Web address:** http://www.3di.com. **Description:** An architectural and interior design firm. The company also provides construction management, engineering, environmental consulting, and program management systems. **NOTE:** This company provides its job listings for all its Texas and U.S. locations online at its website. Apply online. **Positions advertised include:** Receptionist; Project Manager; General Superintendent. **Corporate headquarters location:** This location. **Other area locations:** Austin TX; San Antonio TX. **Other U.S. locations:** NM, CA; MI; MN; FL; AZ; UT; Washington D.C. **Operations at this facility include:** Administration; Sales; Service.

3M
6801 River Place Boulevard, Austin TX 787726-9000. 512/984-1800. Fax: 512/984-1800. **Recorded jobline:** 512/984-6908. **Contact:** Human Resources. **World Wide Web address:** http://www.3m.com. **Description:** 3M manufactures products in three sectors: Industrial and Consumer; Information, Imaging, and Electronic; and Life Sciences. The Industrial and Consumer Sector manufactures a variety of products under brand names including 3M, Scotch, Post-it, Scotch-Brite, and Scotchgard. The Information, Imaging, and Electronic Sector is a leader in several high-growth global industries including telecommunications, electronics, electrical, imaging, and memory media. The Life Science Sector serves two broad market categories: health care, and traffic and personal safety. In the health care market, 3M is a leading provider of medical and surgical supplies, drug-delivery systems, and dental products; in traffic and personal safety, 3M is a leader in products for worker protection, vehicle and sign graphics, and out-of-home advertising. **NOTE:** Apply online at this company's website. **Positions advertised include:** Sales Representative; Financial Analyst. **Corporate headquarters location:** St. Paul MN. **Other area locations:** Brownswood TX (Manufacturing). **Operations at this facility include:** Regional office. **Listed on:** New York Stock Exchange. **Stock exchange symbol:** MMM.

3M
4501 Hwy. 377 South, Brownwood TX 76801. 325/646-3551. **Fax:** 325/646-5863. **Recorded jobline:** 512/984-6908. **Contact:** Human Resources. **World Wide Web address:** http://www.3m.com. **Description:** 3M manufactures products in three sectors: Industrial and Consumer; Information, Imaging, and Electronic; and Life Sciences. The Industrial and Consumer Sector manufactures a variety of products under brand names including 3M, Scotch, Post-it, Scotch-Brite, and Scotchgard. The Information, Imaging, and Electronic Sector is a leader in several high-growth global industries including telecommunications, electronics, electrical, imaging, and memory media. The Life Science Sector serves two broad market categories: health care, and traffic and personal safety. In the health care market, 3M is a leading provider of medical and surgical supplies, drug-delivery systems, and dental products; in traffic and personal safety, 3M is a leader in products for worker protection, vehicle and sign graphics, and out-of-home advertising. **NOTE:** Apply online at this company's website. **Corporate headquarters location:** St. Paul MN. **Other area locations:** Austin TX; Houston TX. **Operations at this facility include:** Display and Graphics. **Listed on:** New York Stock Exchange. **Stock exchange symbol:** MMM.

3M
16727 Aldine Westfield, Houston TX 77032-1349. 281/821-4990. **Fax:** 281/821-2525. **Recorded jobline:** 512/984-6908. **Contact:** Human Resources. **World Wide Web address:** http://www.3m.com. **Description:** 3M manufactures products in three sectors: Industrial and Consumer; Information, Imaging, and Electronic; and Life Sciences. The Industrial and Consumer Sector manufactures a variety of products under brand names including 3M, Scotch, Post-it, Scotch-Brite, and Scotchgard. The Information, Imaging, and Electronic Sector is a leader in several high-growth global industries including telecommunications, electronics, electrical, imaging, and memory media. The Life Science Sector serves two broad market categories: health care, and traffic and personal safety. In the health care market, 3M is a leading provider of medical and surgical supplies, drug-delivery systems, and dental products; in traffic and personal safety, 3M is a leader in products for worker protection, vehicle and sign graphics, and out-of-home advertising. **NOTE:** Apply online at this company's website. **Corporate headquarters location:** St. Paul MN. **Other area locations:** Austin TX; Brownwood TX. **Operations at this facility include:** Industrial Business. **Listed on:** New York Stock Exchange. **Stock exchange symbol:** MMM.

TIDEWATER
7815 Harborside Drive, Galveston TX 77554. 409/744-9500. **Contact:** Human Resources. **World Wide Web address:** http://www.tidewater-construction.com. **Description:** Provides offshore marine transportation services. **NOTE:** See this company's website for additional Texas and U.S. locations and job listings. **Corporate headquarters location:** New Orleans, LA.

TIME WARNER CABLE
8400 West Tidwell Road, Houston TX 77040. 713/462-9000. **Contact:** Human Resources. **World Wide Web address:** http://www.twchouston.com. **Description:** Provides residential cable television services. **NOTE:** To see job listings, go to the parent' company's website at http://timewarner.com/careers. Apply online. **Positions advertised include:** PAC Representative; Customer Technical Support Specialist; General Manager. **Parent company:** Time Warner Inc.

TOM THUMB FOOD & PHARMACY
3663 Briar Park, Houston TX 77042. **Fax:** 713/435-2499. **Recorded jobline:** 214/355-7444. **Contact:** Recruitment Office. **E-mail address:** employment@tomthumb.com. **World Wide Web address:** http://www.tomthumb.com. **Description:** A chain of supermarkets, including Randall's stores. **NOTE:** This company also has recorded joblines for its Randall's stores. For positions at Randall's in Houston, call 713/268-3404. For positions at Randall's in Austin, call 512/427-2557. All resumes should be mailed to the Briar Park address. Interested jobseekers may also apply online at the company's website or at the nearest store location. **Special programs:** Internships. **Corporate headquarters location:** Houston TX. **Parent company:** Safeway. **Operations at this facility include:** Sales; Service. **Listed on:** New York Stock Exchange. **Stock exchange symbol:** SWY.

TOMBALL REGIONAL HOSPITAL
P.O. Box 889, Tomball TX 77375. 281/401-7780. **Physical address:** 605 Holderrietch Road, Tomball TX 77375. **Jobline:** 281/401-7739. **Contact:** Human Resources. **E-mail address:** jobs@tomballhospital.org. **World Wide Web address:** http://www.tomballhospital.org. **Description:** A full-service hospital employing over 300 physicians. Founded in 1976. **NOTE:** Full-time and part-time shifts are available. An application is required for any position. For job listings and application, see this hospital's website. This company offers RN internships. For information, contact Carol Adolph at 281/401-7990 or via e-mail at cadolph@tomballhospital.org. **Positions advertised include:** Echo/Vascular Technician; Physical Therapist; Psychology Technician; Respiratory Therapist; RN; Aerobic Instructor; Cafeteria Worker; Clinical Dietitian; Cook. **Office hours:** Monday – Friday, 8:00 a.m. – 4:30 p.m.

TORO IRRIGATION
9455 Railroad Drive, El Paso TX 79924-6702. 915/757-2586. **Contact:** Human Resources. **Description:** Manufactures and assembles plastic molding injections for the irrigation industry. **Corporate headquarters location:** Riverside CA.

TOWN NORTH YMCA
4332 Northaven Road, Dallas TX 75229. 214/357-8431. **Fax:** 214/357-2986. **Contact:** Human Resources. **World Wide Web address:** http://www.ymcadallas.org. **Description:** One of the nation's largest and most comprehensive nonprofit service organizations. The YMCA provides health and fitness, social and personal development, sports and recreation, education and career development, and camps and conferences to children, teens, adults, seniors, families, disabled individuals, refugees and foreign nationals, YMCA residents, and community residents through a broad range of specific programs. **NOTE:** An application is required for any position at any YMCA. Applications can be found on the website and can be faxed. There are 18 other YMCAs in the Greater Dallas area. See website for additional locations and job listings. **Other U.S. locations:** Nationwide.

TOYOTA OF DALLAS INC.
2610 Forest Lane, Dallas TX 75234. 972/241-6655. **Toll-free phone:** 800/442-4349. **Contact:** James Deaton, Human Resources. **E-mail address:** jdeaton@vtaig.com. **World Wide Web address:** http://www.toyotaofdallas.com. **Description:** Specializes in the retail sale of new and used Toyota cars. **Positions advertised include:** Master Technician; Line Technician; Cash Office; Clerical; Service Advisor; Quick Service Technician. **Corporate headquarters location:** This location.

TRADESTAR INVESTMENTS
8201 Preston Road, Suite 270, Dallas TX 75209. 214/373-0066. **Toll-free phone:** 800/622-5484. **Contact:** Human Resources. **World Wide Web address:** http://www.fiserv.com. **Description:** A regional brokerage firm. **NOTE:** Apply online at this company's website. **Corporate headquarters location:** Brookfield, WI. **Listed on:** NASDAQ. **Stock exchange symbol:** FISV.

TRAMMELL CROW COMPANY
2001 Ross Avenue, Suite 3400, Dallas TX 75201-2997. 214/863-3000. **Fax:** 214/863-3138. **Contact:** Human Resources. **World Wide Web address:** http://www.trammellcrow.com. **Description:** A national real estate development and brokerage agency. Founded in 1948. **NOTE:** This company has other Texas locations. See its website for addresses, job listings and contact information. **Positions advertised include:** Accounting Associate; CPU Coordinator; Executive Assistant; Lead Operating Engineer; Local Marketing Services Engineer; Security Staff. **Special programs:** Internships. **Other area locations:** Carrolton, TX; Fort Worth, TX; Houston TX; Irving TX; Plano, TX; Richardson TX; San Antonio TX. **Listed on:** New York Stock Exchange. **Stock exchange symbol:** TCC.

THE TRANE COMPANY
P.O. Box 814609, Dallas TX 75381. 972/406-6000. **Fax:** 972/243-1349. **Contact:** Human Resources. **E-mail address:** tranejobs@netscape.net. **World Wide Web address:** http://www.trane.com. **Description:** Engaged in the development, manufacture, and sale of air conditioning equipment designed for use in central air conditioning systems for commercial, institutional, industrial, and residential buildings. The Trane Company's products are designed to cool water, and to cool, heat, humidify, dehumidify, move, and filter air. Other products include similar systems for buses and rapid transit vehicles, refrigeration equipment for trucks, and pollution control equipment. **NOTE:** Entry-level positions are offered. **Positions advertised include:** HVAC Service Technician; Service Account Manager; Equipment Estimator; Water Treatment Project Manager/Technician; Inside Sales Support. **Corporate headquarters location:** La Crosse WI. **Other area locations:** Fort Worth TX

(Training Center.) **Parent company:** American Standard. **Operations at this facility include:** Sales.

TRANSCORE INC.
19111 Dallas Parkway, Suite 300, Dallas TX 75287. 972/733-6600. **Fax:** 972/733-6699. **Contact:** Human Resources Department. **World Wide Web address:** http://www.transcore.com. **Description:** Manufactures electronic identification equipment. **Corporate headquarters location:** This location. **Listed on:** New York Stock Exchange.

TRANS HEALTHCARE, INC.
7310 Oak Manor Drive, San Antonio TX 78229. 210/308-0261. **Contact:** Jill Doire, Divisional Recruiter. **E-mail address:** jill.doire@his-inc.com. **World Wide Web address:** http://www.thicare.com. **Description:** A 138-bed acute care hospital offering a wide range of long- and short-term care services. **NOTE:** This company operates several hospitals in Dallas, Corpus Christi and El Paso TX. See company's website for information and job listings for these locations. Jill Doire is the contact for all the hospitals.

TRAULSEN & COMPANY, INC.
4401 Blue Mound Road, Fort Worth TX 76106. 817/625-9671. **Toll-free phone:** 800/825-8220. **Fax:** 817/624-4302. **Contact:** Susan Pereira, Human Resources. **World Wide Web address:** http://www.traulsen.com. **Description:** Manufactures an extensive line of commercial refrigerators and freezers. **Corporate headquarters location:** This location.

TRAVELHOST
10701 North Stemmons Freeway, Dallas TX 75220-2419. 972/556-0541. **Fax:** 972/432-8729. **Contact:** Human Resources. **World Wide Web address:** http://www.travelhost.com. **Description:** A travel, business, and entertainment magazine published weekly. Founded in 1967.

TRIANGLE FOOD SERVICES
16970 Dallas Parkway, Suite 701, Dallas TX 75248. 972/248-4145. **Fax:** 972/248-8116. **Contact:** Human Resources. **Description:** A cafeteria chain with 68 locations in five states. **Corporate headquarters location:** This location. **Listed on:** Privately held.

TRICO TECHNOLOGIES
1995 Billy Mitchell Boulevard, Brownsville TX 78521. 956/544-2722. **Fax:** 956/827-3272. **Contact:** Human Resources. **World Wide Web address:** http://www.tricoproducts.com. **Description:** A manufacturer of windshield wipers. **Special programs:** Training. **Corporate headquarters location:** Rochester Hills MI.

TRILOGY DEVELOPMENT GROUP
5001 Plaza on the Lake, Austin TX 78746. 512/874-3100. **Fax:** 512/874-8900. **Contact:** Human Resources. **E-mail address:** recruit_US@trilogy.com. **World Wide Web address:** http://www.trilogy.com. **Description:** A developer of configuration software for a variety of industries including automotive, utilities, insurance, shipping, and computers.

TRINITY INDUSTRIES, INC.
P.O. Box 568887, Dallas TX 75356-8887. 214/631-4420. **Physical address:** 2525 Stemmons Freeway, Dallas TX 75207-2401. **Contact:** Human Resources Department. **World Wide Web address:** http://www.trin.net. **Description:** Manufactures an assortment of railroad and construction equipment and replacement parts. Trinity Industries also offers related services for the transportation, construction, aerospace, commercial, and industrial markets. Products include railcars, gas processing systems, petroleum transportation systems, guardrails, bridge girders and beams, airport boarding bridges, barges, tugboats, military marine vessels, and precision welding products. Trinity Industries also manufactures concrete and aggregates and produces metal components for the petrochemical, industrial, processing, and power markets. **Positions advertised include:** Business Services Coordinator; Contract Administrator; Corporate Safety Manager; Customer Service Coordinator; Field Marketing Representative; Stress Engineer; Internal Auditor; Welding Engineer; Fabrication Supervisor; Fixture Design Engineer. **Corporate headquarters location:** This location. **Other area locations:** San Antonio TX; Longview TX; Houston TX; Fort Worth TX. **Operations at this facility include:** Administration; Sales; Service. **Listed on:** New York Stock Exchange. **Stock exchange symbol:** TRN.

TRINITY MEDICAL CENTER
4343 North Josey Lane, Carrollton TX 75010. 972/492-1010. **Contact:** Human Resources. **World Wide Web address:** http://www.trinitymedicalcenter.com. **Description:** A 137-bed acute care hospital that includes a neonatal intensive care unit. **NOTE:** A completed application is required for any position. Apply online. **Positions advertised include:** Scheduling Lead Coordinator; RN (Various); Mammography Technician; Admitting Director; Admitting Representative; Surgery Technician; Hospital Compliance Officer; Medical Records Coordinator. **Parent company:** Tenet Healthcare.

TRINITY UNIVERSITY
One Trinity Place, Box 91, San Antonio TX 78212-7200. 210/999-7507. **Fax:** 210/999-7542. **Recorded jobline:** 210/999-7510. **Contact:** Human Resources. **E-mail address:** humanresources@trinity.edu. **World Wide Web address:** http://www.trinity.edu. **Description:** A four-year college with majors including education, biology, communications, business administration, and engineering. Current enrollment is approximately 2,400. Founded in 1869. **NOTE:** Full-time, part-time and temporary positions offered. A completed application is required for certain positions. See website for listings and information. **Positions advertised include:** Senior Data Entry Clerk; Senior Secretary; Degree Audit Coordinator; Associate Director of Development; Information Resources Communications Officer; Assistant Director of Financial Aid; Assistant Director of Admissions, Professor (Various); Molecular Biologist.

TUESDAY MORNING CORPORATION
6250 LBJ Freeway, Dallas TX 75240. 972/387-3562. **Fax:** 972/387-1974. **Contact:** Human Resources. **World Wide Web address:** http://www.tuesdaymorning.com. **Description:** Operates a chain of over 400 discount retail stores under the name Tuesday Morning Inc. The stores sell close-out gift and houseware merchandise at prices ranging from 50 percent to 80 percent below retail prices. **Positions advertised include:** Store Manager; Assistant Store Manager; Senior Store Associate; Store Associate. **NOTE:** The stores are open to the public 10 times a year only for four- to eight-week sales events. **Corporate headquarters location:** This location. **Other U.S. locations:** Nationwide. **Listed on:** NASDAQ. **Stock exchange symbol:** TUES.

TURNER, COLLIE & BRADEN, INC.
P.O. Box 130089, Houston TX 77219. 713/780-4100. **Physical address:** 5757 Woodway, Suite 101 West, Houston TX 77057-1599. **Fax:** 713/784-1546. **Contact:** Human Resources. **World Wide Web address:** http://www.tcandb.com. **Description:** A consulting firm providing technical services including engineering and design for the transportation, public works, environmental, and land development industries and does engineering economics and feasibility studies. Founded in 1946. **NOTE:** Entry-level positions and part-time jobs are offered. **Positions advertised include:** Administrative Clerk. **Special programs:** Internships; Co-ops; Summer Jobs. **Office hours:** Monday - Friday, 7:30 a.m. - 4:30 p.m. **Corporate headquarters location:** This location. **Other area locations:** Austin TX; Dallas TX; San Antonio TX; Fort Worth TX; Pharr TX. **Other U.S. locations:** CO; CA; NV; IL. **Parent company:** AECOM. **Operations at this facility include:** Administration; Divisional Headquarters; Sales. **Listed on:** Privately held.

TWELVE OAKS MEDICAL CENTER
4200 Portsmouth Street, Houston TX 77027. 713/623-2500. **Fax:** 713/964-8906. **Contact:** Human Resources. **E-mail address:** employment@twelveoaksmedicalcenter.com. **World Wide Web address:** http://www.twelveoaksmedicalcenter.com. **Description:** A general hospital. **NOTE:** E-mail or fax resumes. **Positions advertised include:** RN; Speech Therapist; Phlebotomist; Speech Therapist; Anesthesia Technician.

TXI CHAPARRAL STEEL COMPANY
1341 West Mockingbird Lane, Dallas TX 75247. 972/647-6700. **Fax:** 972/647-3312. **Contact:** Human Resources. **E-mail address:** recruiter@txi.com. **World Wide Web address:** http://www.txi.com. **Description:** A steel works company. Founded in 1975. **NOTE:** Please visit website to view job listings. **Positions advertised include:** Human Resources Analyst; Operational Accountant; Plant Helper; Rail Unloader; Senior Java Developer. **Corporate headquarters location:** This location. Parent company: TXI. **Listed on:** New York Stock Exchange. **Stock exchange symbol:** TXI. **CEO:** Mel G. Brekhus.

TYCO VALVES AND CONTROLS
3950 Greenbriar, Stafford TX 77477. 281/274-4400. **Fax:** 281/274-6916. **Contact:** Human Resources. **World Wide Web address:** http://www.tycovalves.com. **Description:** Engaged in the designing, engineering, manufacturing, and marketing of special purpose and conventional precision valves for use in the petroleum, chemical, natural gas transmission, and power generation industries. Product lines include safety relief valves used for overpressure protection; hand valves and instrument manifolds used in conjunction with pressure and flow measuring devices; and a variety of other valve and valve-related products. **NOTE:** This company provides job listings on its website for all of its locations. Apply online. **Other area locations:** Angleton TX; Pasadena TX; Baytown TX. **Other U.S. locations:** Baton Rouge, LA.

TYLER PIPE INDUSTRIES, INC.
P.O. Box 2027, Tyler TX 75710. 903/882-5511. **Toll-free phone:** 800/527-8478. **Fax:** 800/248-9537. **Contact:** Human Resources. **World Wide Web address:** http://www.tylerpipe.com. **Description:** Manufactures and distributes soil pipe and pipefittings. Tyler Pipe Industries, Inc. is also a national producer of both plastic and iron piping for large-volume users.

TYSON FOODS INC.
1484 North East Loop 436, Carthage TX 75633. 903/693-7101. **Contact:** Human Resources. **World Wide Web address:** http://www.tyson.com. **Description:** Tyson Foods Inc. is one of the world's largest fully integrated producers, processors, and marketers of poultry-based food products. The company also produces other entrees and convenience food items. Products include Tyson Holly Farms Fresh Chicken, Weaver, Louis Kemp Crab, Lobster Delights, Healthy Portion, Beef Stir Fry, Crab Delights Stir Fry, Chicken Fried Rice Kits, Pork Chops with Cinnamon Apples, Salmon Grill Kits, Fish'n Chips Kits, and Rotisserie Chicken. **NOTE:** Tyson Foods has 13 locations throughout Texas. See its website for locations; job listings and application information. **Special programs:** Internships. **Corporate headquarters location:** Springdale AR. **Other U.S. locations:** Nationwide. **Operations at this facility include:** This location is a poultry processing plant. **Listed on:** New York Stock Exchange. **Stock exchange symbol:** TSN. **Number of employees nationwide:** 124,000.

TYSON FRESH MEATS, INC.
P.O. Box 30500, Amarillo TX 79187. 806/335-1531. **Contact:** Human Resources Department. **World Wide Web address:** http://www.tysonfoodsinc.com **Description:** A beef and pork meat processor. **NOTE:** See company's website for job listings.

UBS FINANCIAL SERVICES INC.
100 Crescent Court, Suite 600, Dallas TX 75201. 214/220-0400. **Contact:** Branch Manager. **World Wide Web address:** http://www.ubs.com. **Description:** A full-service securities firm with over 300 offices nationwide. Services include investment banking, asset management, merger and acquisition consulting, municipal securities underwriting, estate planning, retirement programs, and transaction management. Clients include corporations, governments, institutions, and individuals. Founded in 1879. **NOTE:** This company has more than 30 locations throughout Texas. See website for job listings, locations and application information. **Positions advertised include:** Experienced Financial Advisor. **Special programs:** Internships; MBA Training. **Corporate headquarters location:** New York NY. **Other U.S. locations:** Nationwide.

UMR COMMUNICATIONS
2400 Lone Star Drive, Dallas TX 75212. 214/630-6495. **Contact:** Human Resources. **World Wide Web address:** http://www.umr.org. **Description:** Publishes religious articles including the *United Methodist Reporter* and the *National Christian Reporter*. Founded in 1847.

URS CORPORATION
P.O. Box 201088, Austin TX 78720-1088. 512/454-4797. **Contact:** Human Resources. **World Wide Web address:** http://www.urscorp.com. **Description:** An architectural, engineering, and environmental consulting firm that specializes in air transportation, environmental solutions, surface transportation, and industrial environmental and engineering concerns. Founded in 1969. **NOTE**: See this company's website for all job listings in Texas. Apply online. **Positions advertised include:** Accounting Clerk; Contract Administrator; Environmental Engineer; Geologist; Scientist; Senior Chemical Engineer; Technical Assistant. **Corporate headquarters location:** This location. **Other area locations:** Dallas TX; Freeport TX; Houston TX; San Antonio TX. **Listed on:** New York Stock Exchange. **Stock exchange symbol:** URS.

URS CORPORATION
9801 Westheimer, Suite 500, Houston TX 77042. 713/789-9801. Fax: 713/789-8404. **Contact:** Human Resources. **World Wide Web address:** http://www.urscorp.com. **Description:** An architectural, engineering, and environmental consulting firm that specializes in air transportation, environmental solutions, surface transportation, and industrial environmental and engineering concerns. Founded in 1969. **NOTE**: See this company's website for all job listings in Texas. Apply online. **Positions advertised**

include: Accounting Clerk; Contract Administrator; Environmental Engineer; Geologist; Scientist; Senior Chemical Engineer; Technical Assistant. **Corporate headquarters location:** This location. **Other area locations:** Austin TX; Freeport TX; Houston TX; San Antonio TX. **Listed on:** New York Stock Exchange. **Stock exchange symbol:** URS.

URS CORPORATION
3010 LBJ Freeway, Suite 1300, Dallas TX 75234. 972/406-6950. **Fax:** 972/406-6951. **Contact:** Human Resources. **World Wide Web address:** http://www.urscorp.com. **Description:** An architectural, engineering, and environmental consulting firm that specializes in air transportation, environmental solutions, surface transportation, and industrial environmental and engineering concerns. Founded in 1969. **NOTE:** See this company's website for all job listings in Texas. Apply online. **Positions advertised include:** Accounting Clerk; Contract Administrator; Environmental Engineer; Geologist; Scientist; Senior Chemical Engineer; Technical Assistant. **Corporate headquarters location:** This location. **Other area locations:** Austin TX; Freeport TX; Houston TX; San Antonio TX. **Listed on:** New York Stock Exchange. **Stock exchange symbol:** URS.

U.S. DEPARTMENT OF VETERANS AFFAIRS
AMARILLO VA HEALTH CARE SYSTEM
6010 West Amarillo Boulevard, Amarillo TX 79106. 806/355-9703. **Fax:** 806/354-7860. **Recorded jobline:** 806/354-7828. **Contact:** Human Resources. **World Wide Web address:** http://www.va.gov. **Description:** Part of the U.S. Veterans Administration, this organization is composed of healthcare facilities that include 200 beds for acute, geriatric and extended care. Serves the Childress, Lubbock, Stratford TX communities, Clovis NM, and Liberal KS. This location is also a teaching facility. **NOTE:** Apply in person at this facility's Human Resources office. Monday – Friday, 7:30 a.m. – 4:30 p.m.

U.S. DEPARTMENT OF VETERANS AFFAIRS
CENTRAL TEXAS VETERANS HEALTH CARE SYSTEM
1901 Veterans Memorial Drive, Temple TX 76504-7451. 254/778-4811ext.4048. **Toll-free phone:** 800/423-2111. **Contact:** Human Resources. **World Wide Web address:** http://www.central-texas.med.va.gov. **Description:** This system consists of two medical centers and several outpatient and community-based clinics. A full-service and teaching hospital with approximately 300 beds. It provides medical, nursing, and hospice care. **NOTE:** See website for additional locations in this system and for job listings. A complete application is required for any position. Apply online. **Positions advertised include:** Physicians; Medical Technicians; Pharmacists; RN; LVN; Nuclear Medicine Technician; Physical Therapist. **Other area locations:** Waco TX (Medical Center); Austin TX (Outpatient Clinic.)

U.S. DEPARTMENT OF VETERANS AFFAIRS
EL PASO VA HEALTH CARE SYSTEM
5001 North Pledras Street, El Paso TX 79930-4211. 915/564-6100. **Fax:** 915/564-7920. **Contact:** Human Resources. **World Wide Web address:** http://www.va.gov. **Description:** This system provides acute medical care for military personnel. It is also a teaching facility with residences in internal medicine and psychiatry. **NOTE:** Apply in person at the Human Resources Office.

U.S. DEPARTMENT OF VETERANS AFFAIRS
HOUSTON VETERANS BENEFITS ADMINISTRATION OFFICE
6900 Almeda Road Houston TX 77030. 713/794-3669. **Toll-free phone:** 800/827-1000. **Contact:** Human Resources. **World Wide Web address:** http://www.va.gov. **Description:** Provides federal benefits to veterans and their dependents. It is one of the largest cabinet departments and operates nationwide medical hospitals, national cemeteries and assistance programs. **NOTE:** For administrative and support positions, apply online at the office's website. For healthcare positions, apply online at http://www.vacareers.com. **Other area locations:** Waco TX (Regional Office).

U.S. DEPARTMENT OF VETERANS AFFAIRS
HOUSTON VA MEDICAL CENTER
2002 Holcombe Boulevard, Houston TX 77030-4298. 713/791-1414. **Toll-free phone:** 800/553-2278. **Contact:** Human Resources. **World Wide Web address:** http://www.houston.med.va.gov. **Description:** A medical facility to provide specialized medical care to veterans. Services include cancer treatments; heart surgery; digestive disorders, and spinal cord injury. One of the VA's centers for the study of Parkinson's Disease. A teaching hospital affiliated with Baylor College of Medicine. **NOTE:** Apply online at http://www.vacareers.com for job listings and contact information for this specific location. **Other area locations:** Beaumont TX (Outpatient Clinic); Lufkin TX (Outpatient Clinic).

U.S. DEPARTMENT OF VETERANS AFFAIRS
NORTH TEXAS HEALTH CARE SYSTEM
4500 South Lancaster Road, Dallas TX 75216. 214/742-8387. **Contact:** Human Resources. **World Wide Web address:** http://www.north-texas.med.va.gov. **Description:** This location is a flagship medical center specializing in spinal cord treatment. Also provides medical services to homeless veterans. **NOTE:** Interested jobseekers should apply online at http://ww.usajobs.opm.gov or call 912/757-3000. **Special programs:** Volunteer. **Other area locations:** Bonham TX (Medical Center); Fort Worth TX (Outpatient Clinic).

U.S. DEPARTMENT OF VETERANS AFFAIRS
SOUTH TEXAS VETERANS HEALTH CARE SYSTEM
740 Merton Minter Boulevard, San Antonio TX 78229. 210/617-5300. **Contact:** Human Resources. **World Wide Web address:** http://www.vasthcs.med.va.gov. **Description:** A medical center with nearly 1,500 beds for medical, psychiatric and rehabilitative services. Affiliated with the Veterans Administration and the Texas Health Science Center. It has a number of outpatient clients and community-based clinics, including homeless programs, throughout surrounding Texas locations. **NOTE:** apply online. **Other area locations:** Kerrville TX (Medical Center).

U.S. DEPARTMENT OF VETERANS AFFAIRS
WEST TEXAS VA HEALTH CARE SYSTEM
300 Veterans Boulevard, Big Spring, TX 79720. 325/263-7361. **Fax:** 325/264-4834. **Contact:** Human Resources. **World Wide Web address:** http://www.va.gov. **Description:** A medical center consisting of about 100 beds and serves nearly 50 West Texas and New Mexico communities. Ophthalmology is a specialty. A teaching facility.

U.S. ENVIRONMENTAL PROTECTION AGENCY (EPA)
1445 Ross Avenue, Dallas TX 75202-2733. 214/665-6444. **Toll-free phone:** 800/887-6063. **Fax:** 214/665-7113. **Contact:** Human Resources **World Wide Web address:** http://www.epa.gov/region06/. **Description:** The EPA is dedicated to improving and preserving the quality of the environment, both nationally and globally, and protecting human health and the productivity of natural resources. The agency is committed to ensuring that federal environmental laws are implemented and enforced effectively; U.S. policy, both foreign and domestic, encourages the integration of economic development and environmental protection so that economic growth can be sustained over the long term; and public and private decisions affecting energy, transportation, agriculture, industry, international trade, and natural resources fully integrate considerations of environmental quality. Founded in 1970. **Special programs:** Internships. **Corporate headquarters location:** Washington DC. **Other U.S. locations:** Nationwide.

U.S. FEDERAL RESERVE BANK OF DALLAS
P.O. Box 655906, Dallas TX 75265-5906. 214/922-6000. **Physical address:** 2200 North Pearl Street, Dallas TX 75201. **Recorded jobline:** 214/922-6166. **Contact:** Employment. **Toll-free phone:** 800/333-4460. **World Wide Web address:** http://www.dallasfed.org. **Description:** One of 12 regional Federal Reserve banks that, along with the Federal Reserve Board of Governors in Washington DC and the Federal Open Market Committee, comprise the Federal Reserve System. As the nation's central bank, the Federal Reserve is charged with three major responsibilities: monetary policy, banking supervision and regulation, and processing payments. **NOTE:** This organization's website provides job listings and contact information for all of its Texas locations. See website. **Special programs:** Internships. **Other area locations:** Houston TX; San Antonio TX: El Paso TX. **Other U.S. locations:** Nationwide.

U.S. FOODSERVICE
950 South Shiloh Road, Garland TX 95042. 972/487-6200. **Fax:** 214/349-0279. **Contact:** Human Resources. **World Wide Web address:** http://www.usfoodservice.com. **Description:** An institutional food production and distribution company with clients in the restaurant and health care industries. Also produces specialty food items. **NOTE:** On its website, this company lists its openings by for all of its Texas and U.S. locations. Apply online. **Positions advertised include:** Contract Coordinator; Delivery Driver; Hot Shot Driver; Human Resources Director; Senior Human Resources Leader. **Corporate headquarters location:** Columbia MD. **Other area locations:** Dallas TX (Specialty); Austin TX (Distribution); Houston TX (Distribution); Lubbock TX (Distribution); Conroe TX (Specialty). **Other U.S. locations:** Nationwide. **Parent company:** Royal Ahold. **Operations at this facility include:** Distribution. **Listed on:** New York Stock Exchange. **Stock exchange symbol:** AHO.

U.S. HOME CORPORATION
P.O. Box 2863, Houston TX 77252-2863. 713/877-2311. **Physical address:** 10707 Clay Road, Houston TX 77041. **Contact:** Human Resources. **World Wide Web address:** http://www.ushome.com. **Description:** Builds and sells single-family houses. **NOTE:** This company has several locations throughout Texas. For job listings at a specific location, apply online at the corporate website. **Positions advertised include:** Internal Auditor. **Other area locations:** Austin TX; Dallas TX; San Antonio TX; Fort Worth TX; Fredericksburg TX. **Other U.S. locations:** AZ; CA; CO; FL; MD; MI; NV; NJ: NC; OH; VA; Washington D.C. **Parent company:** Lennar. **Listed on:** New York Stock Exchange. **Stock exchange symbol:** LEN. **Number of employees nationwide:** 7,700

U.S. LEGAL SUPPORT, INC.
519 North Sam Houston Parkway East, Houston TX 77060. 713/653-7100. **Toll-free phone:** 800/622-1107. **Fax:** 713/653-7171. **Contact:** Human Resources. **World Wide Web address:** http://www.uslegalsupport.com. **Description:** Provides support services in the areas of certified depositions, trial reporters, specialized video services, records retrieval, and other legal services. **NOTE:** This agency offers temporary and permanent positions within the legal field. **Other area locations:** Dallas TX; Austin TX; San Antonio TX; Corpus Christi TX.

U.S. ZINC CORPORATION
P.O. Box 611, Houston TX 77001. 713/926-1705. **Physical address:** 6020 Navigation, Houston TX 77011. **Fax:** 713/924-4824. **Contact:** Human Resources. **World Wide Web address:** http://www.uszinc.com. **Description:** A multi-state manufacturer of secondary zinc. Products include zinc dust (powder), zinc oxide, and zinc metal. The company is also a primary recycler of industrial scrap. Customers include tire makers, galvanizers, and chemical process facilities. **Corporate headquarters location:** This location. **Other U.S. locations:** GA; IL; TN. **Parent company:** IMCO Recycling Inc. **Operations at this facility include:** This is the headquarters for the company's Zinc Dust division. Administration, manufacturing, and sales activities are conducted at this location. **Listed on:** Privately held.

USAA REAL ESTATE COMPANY
9800 Fredersicksburg Road, San Antonio TX 78288. 210/498-1289. **Toll-free phone:** 800/531-8022. **Fax:** 210/498-8986. **Contact:** Human Resources. **World Wide Web address:** http://www. usaa.com. **Description:** Engaged in commercial real estate services for corporate, institutional, and private investors. **NOTE:** On its website, this company provides job listings, addresses, and contact information for its other locations. **Positions advertised include:** Senior Financial Advisor; Financial Analyst; Commercial Strategy Advisor; Managing Editor; Marketing Director; Teller; Shipper; Consumer Loan Processing; Legal Secretary; Employee Communications Writer; Credit Card Specialist. **Other U.S. locations:** AZ; VA; CO; FL; CA. **International locations:** London; Frankfurt.

USFI
12100 Ford Road, Suite 100, Dallas TX 75234. 972/444-8381. **Fax:** 972/402-8139. **World Wide Web address:** http://www.usfi.com. **Description:** provides marketing communications solutions. **NOTE:** Please apply for positions online. **Positions advertised include:** Account Manager; Graphic Designer; Staff Accountant; Software Engineer.

USFILTER
4415 East Greenwood Street, Baytown TX 77520. 281/383-7033. **Fax:** 281/383-3273. **Contact:** Human Resources. **World Wide Web address:** http://www.usfilter.com. **Description:** Produces filters, filtration equipment, strainers, and related items. USFilter also operates related research facilities. **NOTE:** Apply online at this company's website. **Positions advertised include:** Sales Representative; Field Service Technician; Sales Engineer. **Corporate headquarters location:** Palm Desert CA. **Other area locations:** Dallas TX; Conroe TX; Pflugerville, TX. **Other U.S. locations:** Nationwide. **International locations:** Canada. **Number of employee worldwide:** 15,000.

UTI DRILLING, LP
1950 Avenue S, Levelland TX 79336. 806/894-5479. **Fax:** 806/785-8400. **Contact:** Human Resources. **Description:** Operates oil and gas drilling rigs and provides contract drilling services to the oil and gas industry. **Parent company:** Patterson Energy.

ULTRAK INC.
1301 Waters Ridge Drive, Lewisville TX 75057. 972/353-6500. **Contact:** Human Resources. **World Wide Web address:** http://www.ultrak.com. **Description:** Manufactures security surveillance equipment. **NOTE:** Visit the Honeywell website for job listings: http://www.honeywell.com/careers. Apply online. **Special programs:** Internships. **Parent company:** Honeywell. **Listed on:** NASDAQ. **Stock exchange symbol:** ULTK.

UNISHIPPERS ASSOCIATION
800 West Airport Freeway, Suite 611, Lock Box 6065, Irving TX 75062. 972/445-0808. **Contact:** Human Resources. **World Wide Web address:** http://www.unishippers.com. **Description:** An authorized reseller of airplanes for airfreight companies. **NOTE:** This company has several Texas and U.S. locations. See its website to apply online for openings at specific locations. **Positions advertised include:** Operations; Sales. **Corporate headquarters location:** Salt Lake City UT. **Number of employees nationwide:** 800.

UNISYS CORPORATION
13105 NW Freeway, Suite 825, Houston TX 77040. 713/744-2666. **Contact:** Human Resources. **World Wide Web address:** http://www.unisys.com. **Description:** Unisys Corporation provides information services, technology, and software. The company's Enabling Software Team creates a variety of software projects that facilitate the building of user applications and the management of distributed systems. The company's Platforms Group is responsible for UNIX Operating Systems running across multiple processor server platforms including all peripheral and communication drivers. The Unisys Commercial Parallel Processing Team develops microkernel-based operating systems, I/O device drivers, ATM hardware, diagnostics, and system architectures. The System Management Group is in charge of the overall management of development programs for UNIX desktop and entry-server products. **NOTE:** Apply online. **Positions advertised include:** Helpdesk Agent; Curriculum Developer; Healthcare Systems Consultant; Information Technology; Call Center Supervisor; Portfolio Sales Executive; Bid Proposal Manager. **Special programs:** Internships. **Office hours:** Monday - Friday, 8:00 a.m. - 5:00 p.m. **Corporate headquarters location:** Blue Bell PA. **Other U.S. locations:** Nationwide. **International locations:** Worldwide. **Operations at this facility include:** This location manufactures and sells computers. **Number of employees nationwide:** 37,000.

UNITED INSURANCE COMPANIES INC.
4001 McEwen, Suite 200, Dallas TX 75244. 972/392-6700. **Fax:** 972/392-6737. **Contact:** Human Resources. **World Wide Web address:** http://www.uici.net. **Description:** Offers health and life insurance. **NOTE:** Entry-level positions are offered. **NOTE:** For career opportunity information, see this company's website. **Corporate headquarters location:** North Richland Hills TX. **Other U.S. locations:** Glendale AZ; Lakewood CO; St. Petersburg FL; Norcross GA; Oklahoma City OK; Sioux Falls SD. **Operations at this facility include:** Administration; Service. **Listed on:** New York Stock Exchange. **Stock exchange symbol:** UCI. **Number of employees at this location:** 1,200. **Number of employees worldwide:** 2,500.

UNITED PARCEL SERVICE (UPS)
P.O. Box 2047, Grapevine TX 76099-2047. 972/456-4928. **Recorded jobline:** 888/877-0924. **Contact:** Human Resources. **World Wide Web address:** http://www.ups.com. **Description:** United Parcel Service is a parcel pickup and delivery service organization that provides service to all 50 states and to more than 185 countries and territories worldwide. The company delivers approximately 12 million packages daily. **NOTE:** The jobline lists mainly part-time positions, including those at other Texas locations. Apply online. **Positions advertised include:** Account Executive; Regional Account Manager. **Operations at this facility include:** This location houses regional administrative offices.

UNITED REGIONAL HEALTHCARE SYSTEMS
1700 Seventh Street, Wichita Falls TX 76301. 940/764-7806. **Toll-free phone:** 800/301-3879. **Fax:** 940/764-7820. **Recorded jobline:** 940/764-7802. **Contact:** Kim Horton, Recruitment Specialist. **World Wide Web address:** http://www.urhcs.org. **Description:** A licensed, 300-bed, acute care facility. **NOTE:** Full-time and part-time positions offered. This organization's website provides job listings and contact information on its website. Apply online. **Positions advertised include:** Floor Care Technician; Health Information Resource Nurse; Patient Care Associate; Certified Scrub Technician; Diagnostic Radiological Technician; Emergency Department Services Technician; Phlebotomist; LVN;; Occupational Therapist; Patient Care Associate; Pharmacist; RN.

UNITED SPACE ALLIANCE COMPANY
600 Gemini Avenue, Houston TX 77058. 281/282-2000. **Contact:** Human Resources. **World Wide Web address:** http://www.unitedspacealliance.com. **Description:** A government contracted management and operations firm for the space shuttle program. **NOTE:** Apply online at this company's website. **Other U.S. locations:** FL; AL; CA; Washington D.C. **Operations at this facility include:** Administration; Service. **Parent company:** Boeing Company and Lockheed Martin Corporation.

UNITED SUPERMARKETS
7830 Orlando Avenue, Lubbock TX 79423. 806/792-0220. **Contact:** Human Resources. **E-mail address:** info@unitedtexas.com. **World Wide Web address:** http://www.unitedtexas.com. **Description:** This chain of supermarkets has more than 40 stores in Texas. **NOTE:** This company provides a list of all its locations on its website. For retail positions, apply at the nearest location. **Special programs:** Manager Training. **Corporate headquarters location:** This location.

UNITED WAY OF METROPOLITAN DALLAS
901 Ross Avenue, Dallas TX 75202. 214/978-0000. **Contact:** Human Resources. **World Wide Web address:** http://www.unitedwaydallas.com. **Description:** A nonprofit organization that helps to meet the health and human-care needs of Dallas area residents. Overall, the United Way includes approximately 1,900 organizations. **Special programs:** Internships. **Office hours:** Monday - Friday, 8:15 a.m. - 5:00 p.m. **Corporate headquarters location:** Alexandria VA.

UNITED WAY OF THE TEXAS GULF COAST
P.O. Box 924507, Houston TX 77292-4507. 713/685-2300. **Fax:** 713/956-2868. **Contact:** Human Resources. **E-mail address:** employment@uwtgc.org. **World Wide Web address:** http://www.uwtgc.org. **Description:** The United Way provides necessary job and life skills training in order to help people become independent, responsible citizens, capable of making a contribution to society; empowers communities and individuals to care for themselves; provides opportunities to maintain physical and mental well-being; supports all children with a safe, nurturing environment through positive role models, developmental experiences, social stimulation, and interaction; ensures the opportunity for individuals to maintain an independent life; provides resources that give people a safe and secure living environment and provides for basic needs; and provides social and emotional support to family members so that they can function in society at their optimal potential. **NOTE:** Apply online. **Positions advertised include:** 2-1-1 Information and Referral Coordinator; Director of Major Gifts and Leadership Giving.

UNIVERSAL COMPUTER SYSTEMS, INC. (UCS)
DEALER COMPUTER SYSTEMS, INC. (DCS)
6700 Hollister, Houston TX 77040. 713/718-1800. **Toll-free phone:** 800/883-3031. **Contact:** Human Resources. **E-mail address:** Careers@UniversalComputerSys.com. **World Wide Web address:** http://www.universalcomputersys.com. **Description:** Supplies computer software and hardware systems specifically designed for the business of automobile dealerships. **NOTE:** Entry-level positions, part-time jobs, and second and third shifts are offered. **Positions advertised include:** General Administrative Clerk; Systems Software Development; Windows Development; COBOL Programmers; Dutch Marketing Representative. Service Pricing Guide Installer; Demo Specialist; Network Technician; Systems Network Engineer. **Special programs:** Internships; Co-ops. **Corporate headquarters location:** This location. **Other area locations:** College Station TX. **Other U.S. locations:** Nationwide. **International locations:** Worldwide. **Listed on:** Privately held. **Number of employees nationwide:** 2,600.

UMC HEALTH SYSTEM
602 Indiana Avenue, Lubbock TX 79415. 806/775-9222. **Recorded jobline:** 806/775-9215. **Contact:** Human Resources Manager. **World Wide Web address:** http://www.teamumc.org. **Description:** A 354-bed facility that includes The Children's Hospital, The Southwest Cancer and Research Center, Level I Trauma Center, a Pre-Hospital Emergency Service, a Burn Intensive Care Unit, and Community Outreach Programs. **NOTE:** For nursing opportunities, call 806/775-8912. A complete application is required for any position. Visit the website to print an application or apply online. **Positions advertised include:** Accountant; Cafeteria Aide; Cardiac Sonographer; Health Unit Coordinator; RN, LVN, Patient/Staff Educator; Renovation Technician. **Special programs:** Volunteer.

UNIVERSITY OF HOUSTON/DOWNTOWN
One Main Street, Suite 9105 South, Houston TX 77002. 713/221-8427. **Recorded jobline:** 713/221-8609. **Contact:** Human Resources. **World Wide Web address:** http://www.dt.uh.edu. **Description:** The main campus of the University of Houston. **NOTE:** A complete application must accompany a resume. Resumes and applications are only accepted for current openings. For more information, an application and job listings, see the university's website. **Positions advertised include:** Professors (Various); Vice President of Student Affairs; Reference Librarian; Scholarship Counselor; Student Loan Coordinator; Staff Nurses; Dean.

UNIVERSITY OF NORTH TEXAS
P.O. Box 311010, Denton TX 76203-1010. 940/565-2281. **Fax:** 940/565-4382. **Recorded jobline:** 940/565-4070. **Contact:** Human Resources. **World Wide Web address:** http://www.unt.edu. **Description:** A university offering undergraduate and graduate programs of study in numerous fields. Enrollment at the university is approximately 25,000. **NOTE:** This university also has a Dallas campus called the System Center. See website for both locations' job listings and application information. **Special programs:** Internship; Work-Study.

UNIVERSITY OF NORTH TEXAS HEALTH SCIENCE AT FORT WORTH
3500 Camp Bowie Boulevard, Suite 735, Fort Worth TX 76107-2699. 817/735-2000. **Fax:** 817/735-0107. **Recorded jobline:** 817/735-2675. **Contact:** Human Resources. **E-mail address:** hr_ase@hsc.unt.edu. **World Wide Web address:** http://www.hsc.unt.edu. **Description:** A health science education center. **NOTE:** See website for job listings and specific contact information. Apply online for open positions. **Positions advertised include:** Certified Coder; Clinical Services Representative; Senior Administrative Clerk; Associate Director of Development and Alumni Relations; Communications Coordinator; Compliance Analyst; Financial Aid Counselor; Manager of News and Information; Senior Human Resource Representative; Laboratory Assistant; Postdoctoral Research Associate; Research Assistant; Research Scientist; Senior Research Assistant. **Corporate headquarters location:** This location. **Office hours:** Monday – Friday, 8:00 – 5:00 p.m. **Operations at this facility include:** Administration; Education; Research and Development.

UNIVERSITY OF ST. THOMAS
3800 Montrose Boulevard, Houston TX 77006. 713/522-7911. **Fax:** 713/525-3896. **Contact:** Human Resources. **World Wide Web address:** http://www.stthom.edu. **E-mail address:** hr@stthom.edu. **Description:** A liberal arts university affiliated with the Catholic Church. The university has an enrollment of 2,700 students. **NOTE:** Entry-level positions and part-time jobs are offered. See website for job listings and contact information. **Positions advertised include:** Vice President for Student Affairs; Dean of Scholarships & Financial Aid; Registrar; Records Clerk; Professor (Various). **Corporate headquarters location:** This location.

UNIVERSITY OF TEXAS AT ARLINGTON
1225 West Mitchell Street, Suite 112, Box 19176, Arlington TX 76019. 817/272-3461. **Fax:** 817/272-5798. **Contact:** Human Resources. **E-mail address:** employment@uta.edu. **World Wide Web address:** http://www.uta.edu. **Description:** A state university offering 55 bachelor's, 60 master's, and 19 doctoral degrees to approximately 20,000 students. Founded in 1895. **NOTE:** This university posts its staff and support job listings on its website. Apply online. Resumes for general consideration are not accepted. Jobseekers interested in faculty positions should visit the departments' separate web pages for openings. **Positions advertised include:** Continuing Education Director; Associate Registrar; Associate Director; Public Service Librarian; Software Systems Specialist; **Special programs:** Internships. **Office hours:** Monday – Friday, 8:00 a.m. – 5:00 p.m. **Corporate headquarters location:** Austin TX. **Operations at this facility include:** Administration; Research and Development; Sales; Service.

UNIVERSITY OF TEXAS AT AUSTIN
P.O. Box Drawer V, Austin TX 78713-8922. 512/471-3656. **Physical address:** University of Texas at Austin, Austin TX 78712. **Toll-free phone:** 800/687-8086. **Contact:** Jim DeWitt, Human Resources. **World Wide Web address:** http://www.utexas.edu. **Description:** One location of the state university. **NOTE:** Interested jobseekers can mail their applications; apply online at the school's website, or visit the Human Resources. See the website for staff job listings, additional application procedures and requirements. **Office hours:** Monday, Tuesday, Thursday, and Friday, 8:00 a.m. – 5:00 p.m. Wednesday, 9:00 a.m. – 5:00 p.m. **Operations at this facility include:** Administration; Research and Development; Service.

UNIVERSITY OF TEXAS AT BROWNSVILLE
80 Fort Brown Street, Brownsville TX 78520. 956/544-8205. **Fax:** 956/982-0175. **Contact:** Human Resources. **World Wide Web address:** http://www.utb.edu. **Description:** University of Texas at Brownsville and Texas Southmost College are partner institutions offering the following programs of study: College of Liberal Arts, College of Science, Mathematics & Technology, School of Business, School of

Education, and School of Health Sciences. Founded in 1973. **NOTE:** A completed application is required for any position. See website for job listings and application procedures. Applications and resumes may be mailed, faxed or delivered to the Human Resources Office located in the Cortez Building, Suite 129. **Positions advertised include:** Accounting Clerk; Accounting Group Supervisor; Chemistry Lab Coordinator; Child Care Assistant; Maintenance Worker; Librarian; Staff Nurse; Lecturer (Various); Professor (Various).

UNIVERSITY OF TEXAS AT DALLAS
Mail Station AD 35, P.O. Box 830688, Richardson TX 75083-0688. 972/883-2221. **Contact:** Human Resources. **E-mail address:** jobs@utdalla.edu. **World Wide Web address:** http://www.utdallas.edu. **Description:** A state university offering programs at the undergraduate, graduate, and doctoral levels. Enrollment at the university is approximately 10,000. There is also a campus in the Dallas TX area. **NOTE:** Apply online at the university's website. Part-time jobs are offered. **Positions advertised include:** Academic Advisor; Child Development Specialist; Admissions Counselor; Research Associate; Program Coordinator; Professor (Various).

UNIVERSITY OF TEXAS AT EL PASO
Human Resources Services, Administration Building, Room 216, El Paso TX 79968-0507. 915/747-5202. **Recorded jobline:** 915/747-8837. **Contact:** Human Resources. **World Wide Web address:** http://www.utep.edu. **Description:** One location of the state university with more than two-thirds of the student population representing the area's strong Mexican-American community. Bachelors, masters, and doctoral degrees offered in liberal arts and science fields. **NOTE:** See website for job listings, contact information and application requirements and procedures. **Positions advertised include:** Horticulturist; Coach (Various); Special Projects Manager; Database Administrator; Professor (Various); Lecturer (Various); Literacy Coordinator; Research Associate.

UNIVERSITY OF TEXAS AT TYLER
3900 University Boulevard, Administration Building 108, Tyler TX 75799. 903/566-7234. **Fax:** 903/566-5690. **Contact:** Human Resources. **E-mail address:** humanresources@mail.uttyl.edu. **World Wide Web address:** http://www.uttyl.edu. **Description:** A state university offering undergraduate and graduate programs of study. **NOTE:** A completed application is required for any position. Apply online at the website. **Positions advertised include:** Police Cadet; Guard; Tennis Coach. **Office hours:** Monday – Friday, 8:00 a.m. – 5:00 p.m.

UNIVERSITY OF TEXAS HEALTH CENTER AT TYLER
11937 U.S. Highway 271, Tyler TX 75708-3154. 903/877-7740. **Fax:** 903/877-7729. **Recorded jobline:** 903/877-7071 (Staff and Support Services); 800/297-3799 (Physician). **Contact:** Human Resources. **E-mail address:** jobs@uthct.edu. **World Wide Web address:** http://www.uthct.edu. **Description:** A non-profit hospital engaged in patient care, education, and research. **NOTE:** A completed application is required for any position. To apply in person, visit the Human Resources Office in Room 179B. **Positions advertised include:** Nurse Clinician; Staff Nurse; Attorney; Exercise Technician; Staff Pharmacist; Research Associate; Respiratory Therapist; Laboratory Technician. **Office hours:** Monday – Friday, 7:00 a.m. – 5:00 p.m.

UNIVERSITY OF TEXAS MEDICAL BRANCH
301 University Boulevard, Galveston TX 77551. 409/772-2758. **Contact:** Employment Office. **World Wide Web address:** http://www.hr.utmb.edu. **Description:** Educates health professionals and offers extensive medical services through a network of hospitals and health clinics. Founded in 1891. **NOTE:** Part-time, hourly and temporary positions offered. Apply online at the university's website. This location does not accept walk-in applicants. **Positions advertised include:** Nurse Researcher; Simulator Technician; Librarian; Psychiatrist; Dentist; Professors (Various); Speech Pathologist; RN; Auditor. **Special programs:** Volunteer.

UNIVERSITY OF TEXAS SOUTHWESTERN MEDICAL CENTER AT DALLAS
5323 Harry Hines Boulevard, Dallas TX 75139-9023. 214/648-9827. **Fax:** 214/648-9875. **Recorded jobline:** 214/648-5627. **Contact:** Human Resources. **World Wide Web address:** http://www.swmed.edu. **Description:** An academic medical center affiliated with Southwestern Medical School, Southwestern Graduate School of Biomedical Sciences, and Southwestern Allied Health Sciences School. **NOTE:** Entry-level, part-time and temporary positions are offered. Apply online at the website for all positions. **Positions advertised include:** RN: LVN, Medical Technologist; Dentist; Dental Hygienist; Research Technician; Administrative Staff Assistant; Clinical Staff Assistant; Accountant; Financial Accountant; Budgeter; Billing; Animal Technician; Plumber, Groundskeeper, Electrician. **Special programs:** Internships. **Operations at this facility include:** Administration; Research and Development.

UNIVERSITY OF TEXAS-PAN AMERICAN
1201 West University Drive, Edinburg TX 78539. 956/381-2511. **Fax:** 956/381-2340. **Recorded jobline:** 956/381-2551. **Contact:** Human Resources. **World Wide Web address:** http://www.panam.edu. **Description:** One location of the state university. **NOTE:** A complete application is required for any position. To apply, visit the website or the Human Resources. Jobseekers may also call for an application. See website for job listings, contact information, and application procedures and requirements. **Positions advertised include:** Orientation Coordinator; Business/Economic Research Assistant; Coordinator of Student Development; Library Clerk; Duplicating Equipment Operator; Staff Nurse; Student Development Specialist. **Office hours:** Monday - Friday, 8:00 a.m. - 5:00 p.m. **Corporate headquarters location:** Austin TX. **Operations at this facility include:** Administration; Service.

UNIVERSITY OF THE INCARNATE WORD
4301 Broadway Street, Box 320, San Antonio TX 78209. 210/829-6019. **Fax:** 210/829-3847. **Contact:** Human Resources. **E-mail address:** uiwhr@university.uiwtx.edu. **World Wide Web address:** http://www.uiw.edu. **Description:** A Catholic, co-educational, four-year university offering liberal arts and professional studies. The university offers such majors as fine arts, nursing, pre-professional studies, business, and education. The enrollment for the college is approximately 3,000 undergraduate and graduate students. Founded in 1881. **NOTE:** An application is required for every position. See website for application. **Positions advertised include:** Dean (Various); Academic Counselor; Director of Student Services; Professor (Various); Librarian; Admissions Secretary; Office Assistant; Resident Director. **Office hours:** Monday – Friday, 8:00 a.m. – 5:00 p.m.

US ONCOLOGY
16825 Northchase, Suite 1300, Houston TX. 77060. 832/601-8766. **Contact:** Human Resources. **World Wide Web address:** http://www.usoncology.com. **Description:** One of the world's largest companies devoted to providing outpatient care to treating cancer patients. US Oncology has cancer research facilities. It has more than 70 cancer centers across 27 states. **Positions advertised include:** Financial Systems Implementation Specialist; Application Engineer; Radiation Therapist. Marketing Director; Project Manager; Regulatory Coordinator; Medical Oncologist; Radiation Oncologist. **Other area locations:** Statewide. **Other U.S. locations:** Nationwide. **Listed on:** NASDAQ. **Stock exchange symbol:** USON.

UTEX INDUSTRIES INC.
10810 Old Katy Road, Houston TX 77043. 713/467-1000. **Toll-free phone:** 800/359-9229. **Fax:** 800/359-9230. 979/725-8503. **Contact:** Human Resources. **World Wide Web address:** http://www.utexind.com. **Description:** Manufactures gaskets, o-rings, and related products for the oil industry. This company also has a manufacturing location in Houston. **NOTE:** Apply online. **Corporate headquarters:** This location. **Other area locations:** Weimar TX (Manufacturing); Conroe TX (Manufacturing). **Operations at this facility include:** Administration; Sales.

VF FACTORY OUTLET
805 Factory Outlet Drive, Hempstead TX 77445-5604. 979/826-8277. **Contact:** Human Resources. **World Wide Web address:** http://www.vffo.com. **Description:** One location of a discount retailer of jeanswear, sportswear, activewear, intimate apparel, and occupational apparel. **NOTE:** Jobseekers interested in management positions should mail their resumes to: Human Resources Manager, Dept. W., VF Outlet, 801 Hill Avenue, Reading PA 19610-3026. Jobseekers interested in other positions should apply online or at the nearest store location. **Positions advertised include:** Store Management Trainee; Sales Associates; Warehouse Security Associates; Custodial Maintenance. **Corporate headquarters location:** Reading PA. **Other area locations:** Corsicana TX; Le Marque TX; Livingston TX; Mineral Wells TX; San Marcos TX; Sulphur Springs TX. **Other U.S. locations:** Nationwide.

VNU BUSINESS MEDIA
ADWEEK
3102 Maple Avenue, Suite 210, Dallas TX 75201. 214/871-9550. **Contact:** Human Resources. **World Wide Web address:** http://www.vnubusinessmedia.com **Description:** Publishes trade magazines; produces online content, and organizes trade shows and conferences. **Other U.S. locations:** Nationwide. **International locations:** Switzerland; United Kingdom. **Parent company:** VNU Business Media (New York NY). **Operations at this facility include:** Publishing.

VTEL CORPORATION
9208 Waterford Centre Boulevard, Austin TX 78758. 512/821-7000. **Contact:** Human Resources. **World Wide Web address:** http://www.vtel.com. **Description:** A leading provider of interactive videoconferencing systems in the distance learning and health care markets. VTEL products are distributed primarily through resellers and co-marketers. **NOTE:** Fax resumes to Amanda in Human Resources at 512/821-7133. **Corporate headquarters location:** This location. **Listed on:** Privately held.

VALERO ENERGY CORPORATION
P.O. Box 500, San Antonio TX 78292. 210/370-2000. **Physical address:** One Valero Place, San Antonio TX 78212. **Toll-free phone:** 800/531-7911. **Fax:** 210/370-2646. **Contact:** Human Resources. **World Wide Web address:** http://www.valero.com. **Description:** Valero Energy Corporation has an extensive refining system with a throughput capacity of nearly 2 million barrels per day. The company's geographically diverse refining network stretches from Canada to the U.S. Gulf Coast, and West Coast. Valero has almost 5,000 retail sites in the United States and Canada, branded as Valero, Diamond Shamrock, Ultramar, Beacon, and Total. Valero is a leading producer of premium environmentally clean products, such as reformulated gasoline, (CARB) Phase II gasoline, low-sulfur diesel and oxygenates. The company also operates a credit card program with over 500,000 active accounts. **NOTE:** Part-time positions offered. Apply on this company's website for all positions. **Positions advertised include:** Pipeline Integrity Engineer; Human Resources Analyst; Optimization and Performance Analysis Manager; Systems Specialist; Control Systems Engineer; Chief Refining Inspector; Engineering Associate; Customer Account Representative; Store Manager; Assistant Store Manager. **Corporate headquarters location:** This location. **Other area locations:** Corpus Christi TX; Houston TX; Krotz Springs, TX; McKee TX; Three Rivers TX; Sunray TX. **Listed on:** New York Stock Exchange. **Stock exchange symbol:** VLO. **Number of employees worldwide:** 20,000.

VALERO ENERGY CORPORATION
CREDIT CARD CENTER
P.O. Box 300, Amarillo TX 79105. 806/324-4601. **Contact:** Human Resources. **World Wide Web address:** http://www.valero.com. **Description:** Valero Energy Corporation, an energy refining system, operates its own credit card program with more than 500,000 active accounts. NOTE: Apply online at the company's website for all positions. **Corporate headquarters location:** San Antonio TX. **Operations at this facility include:** Accounting; Sales.

VALLEN CORPORATION
521 North Sam Houston Parkway East, Suite 300, Houston TX 77060. 281/500-4500. **Fax:** 713/462-4510. **Contact:** Human Resources. **World Wide Web address:** http://www.vallen.com. **Description:** Manufactures and distributes safety products. Founded in 1947. **NOTE:** Apply online or fax resumes. **Corporate headquarters location:** This location. **Other U.S. locations:** Nationwide. **International locations:** Canada; Mexico. **Subsidiaries include:** Vallen Safety Supply Company. **Parent company:** Hagemeyer N.V. Company. **Number of employees nationwide:** 1,000.

VALLEY BAPTIST MEDICAL CENTER
P.O. Drawer 2588, Harlingen TX 78550. 956/389-4703. **Physical address:** 2101 Pease Street, Harlingen TX 78550. **Toll-free phone:** 800/828-8262. **Recorded jobline:** 956/389-2330. **Contact:** Human Resources. **E-mail address:** humanresources@valleybaptist.net. **World Wide Web address:** http://www.vbmc.org. **Description:** A 588-bed, nonprofit, acute care, medical center. **NOTE:** Part-time, second and third shifts are offered. A completed application is required for any position. Apply online or fax or mail application. Walk-in applicants are also accepted in Human Resources during regular office hours. **Positions advertised include:** Accounting; Speech Language Pathologist; Electro-Physiology Technologist; Corporate Communications Coordinator; Licensed Physical Therapist; Bereavement Coordinator; Nurse Recruiter; RN; LVN; Medication Aide; Buyer—Project Coordinator. **Special programs:** Internships; Co-ops; Summer Jobs. **Corporate headquarters location:** This location.

VALLEY REGIONAL MEDICAL CENTER
100A East Alton Gloor Boulevard, Brownsville TX 78526. 956/350-7000. **Contact:** Human Resources. **World Wide Web address:** http://www.valleyregionalmedicalcenter.com. **Description:** This 171-bed, acute care medical center offers services such as skilled nursing, rehabilitation, and various medical specialties. **NOTE:** Part-time, weekend, flex-time positions offered. Apply online at the center's website. **Positions advertised include:** Director of Imaging; Case Manager; RN; Director of Therapeutic Services; Speech Therapist. **Special programs:** Volunteers.

VARCO INTERNATIONAL, INC.
2000 West Sam Houston Parkway South, Houston TX 77042. 281/953-2200. **Contact:** Human Resources. **E-mail address:** careers@varco.com. **World Wide Web address:** http://www.tuboscope.com. **Description:** Manufactures and distributes coatings for pipes. This company also provides services to enhance pipeline operations and management. **NOTE:** In addition to its corporate headquarters, this company has more than 20 manufacturing and sales locations throughout Texas. See website for locations and addresses. **Listed on:** New York Stock Exchange. **Stock exchange symbol:** VRC.

VECTA
1800 South Great SW Parkway, Grand Prairie TX 75051. 972/641-2860. **Contact:** Human Resources. **World Wide Web address:** http://www.vecta.com. **Description:** Custom manufactures office furniture. **Other area locations:** GA; IL: CA: NY; MI. **Parent company:** Steelcase (Grand Rapids MI). **Operations at this facility include:** Manufacturing. **Number of employees nationwide:** 300.

VERITAS D.G.C.
10300 Town Park Drive, Houston TX 77072. 832/351-8300. **Fax:** 832/8701. **Contact:** Human Resources. **World Wide Web address:** http://www.veritasdgc.com. **Description:** Engaged in land and marine seismic surveying, as well as the processing of collected work. **NOTE:** This company provides job listings for all its Texas and U.S. locations. Apply online. **Corporate headquarters location:** This location. **International locations:** Canada. **Listed on:** New York Stock Exchange. **Stock exchange symbol:** VTS.

VERIZON COMMUNICATIONS
6210 Rothway Street, Houston TX 77040. 713/867-6600. **Contact:** Human Resources. **World Wide Web address:** http://www.verizon.com. **Description:** A full-service communications services provider. Verizon offers residential local and long distance telephone services and Internet access; wireless service plans, cellular phones, and data services; a full-line of business services including Internet access, data services, and telecommunications equipment and services; and government network solutions including Internet access, data services, telecommunications equipment and services, and enhanced communications services. This location provides telecommunications equipment and services. **NOTE:** Resumes must be submitted via the Website: http://www.verizon.com/careers. **Corporate headquarters location:** New York NY. **Operations at this facility include:** Manufacturing; Distribution; Sales. **Listed on:** New York Stock Exchange. **Stock exchange symbol:** VZ.

VERIZON COMMUNICATIONS CREDIT CARD SERVICES
1255 Corporate Drive, Irving TX 75038. 972/507-5000. **Contact:** Human Resources. **World Wide Web address:** http://www.verizon.com. **Description:** A full-service communications services provider. This location manages administrative services and customer accounts. **NOTE:** Resumes must be submitted via the Website: http://www.verizon.com/careers. **Corporate headquarters location:** New York NY. **Operations at this facility include:** Administration; Sales. **Listed on:** New York Stock Exchange. **Stock exchange symbol:** VZ.

VERIZON COMMUNICATIONS INTERNET SOLUTIONS TEXAS
P.O. Box 152212, Irving TX 75015-22212. 972/717-7700. **Physical address:** 500 East John Carpenter Freeway, Irving TX 75062. **Contact:** Human Resources. **World Wide Web address:** http://www.verizon.com. **Description:** A full-service communications services provider. This location provides business services including Internet access, data services, telecommunications equipment and services, and government network solutions, and enhanced communications services. **NOTE:** Resumes must be submitted via the Website: http://www.verizon.com/careers. **Corporate headquarters location:** New York NY. **Operations at this facility include:** Sales; Distribution. **Listed on:** New York Stock Exchange. **Stock exchange symbol:** VZ.

VERIZON COMMUNICATIONS LAW ENFORCEMENT ASSISTANCE
2701 South Johnson Street, San Angelo TX 76904. **Toll-free phone:** 888/483-2600. **Contact:** Human Resources. **World Wide Web address:** http://www.verizon.com. **Description:** A full-service communications services provider. **NOTE:** Resumes must be submitted via the Website: http://www.verizon.com/careers. **Corporate headquarters location:** New York NY. **Listed on:** New York Stock Exchange. **Stock exchange symbol:** VZ.

VERIZON NEW MEDIA SERVICES
P.O. Box 619810, DFW Airport TX 75261-9810. 972/453-7000. **Physical address:** One Verizon Place, West Airfield Drive, DFW Airport, TX 75261-9810. **Contact:** Human Resources. **World Wide Web address:** http://www.verizon.com. **Description:** This location is engaged in Yellow Pages publishing. Overall, Verizon Communications is a full-service communications services provider. **NOTE:** Resumes must be submitted via the Website: http://www.verizon.com/careers. **Corporate headquarters location:** New York NY. **Operations at this facility include:** Service; Distribution. **Listed on:** New York Stock Exchange. **Stock exchange symbol:** VZ.

VERTEXRSI ANTENNA PRODUCTS
2600 North Longview Street, Kilgore TX 75662. 903/984-0555. **Fax:** 903/984-1826. **Contact:** Personnel. **World Wide Web address:** http://www.tripointglobal.com. **Description:** Designs and manufactures satellite Earth station antennas that use domestic, international, and military radio frequencies. The company also offers a complete line of standard antenna products. **NOTE:** Entry-level positions are offered. This company also has another Kilgore location at 1104 Energy Drive, Kilgore TX 75662; 903/984-7811. It primarily is a sales and marketing location. See website for job listings for all Texas, U.S. and international locations. **Corporate headquarters location:** Richardson TX. **Other area locations:** Worthham TX (Manufacturing); Longview TX (Manufacturing). **Other U.S. locations:** NJ; PA; GA. **International locations:** Germany, India; Estonia. **Parent company:** General Dynamics. **Operations at this facility include:** Administration; Manufacturing; Research and Development; Sales; Service.

VIA METROPOLITAN TRANSIT
1021 San Pedro, San Antonio TX 78212. 210/362-2240. **Contact:** Human Resources. **E-mail address:** hr.emp@viainfo.net. **World Wide Web address:** http://www.viainfo.net. **Description:** A bus line for the city of San Antonio. **NOTE:** Apply at Human Resources office. **Positions advertised include:** Strategic Planning Coordinator; Shop Attendant; Bus Operator; Paratransit Operator; Substitute Teacher; Temporary Clerical Pool. **Office hours:** Monday – Friday, 7:30 a.m. – 5:00 p.m. **Corporate headquarters location:** This location.

VICTORIAN CONDO HOTEL & CONFERENCE CENTER
6300 Seawall Boulevard, Galveston TX 77550. 409/740-3555. **Toll-free phone:** 800/231-6363. **Contact:** Human Resources. **World Wide Web address:** http://www.galveston.com/victorian. **Description:** A full-service hotel and conference center.

VIGNETTE CORPORATION
1301 South Mopac Expressway, Building 3, Austin TX 78746-5776. 512/741-4300. **Toll-free phone:** 888/608-9900. **Fax:** 512/741-1403. **Contact:** Human Resources. **World Wide Web address:** http://www.vignette.com. **Description:** Supplies e-business applications to online business clients. **NOTE:** Apply online at this company's website. **Positions advertised include:** Customer Support Engineer; Technical Writer; Systems Administrator; Copywriter/Editor; Customer Reference Specialist; Marketing Programs Manager; Financial Analyst. **Corporate headquarters location:** This location. **Listed on:** NASDAQ. **Stock exchange symbol:** VIGN.

VIRGINIA KMP CORPORATION
4100 Platinum Way, Dallas TX 75237. 214/330-7731. **Toll-free number:** 800/285-8567. **Contact:** Human Resources. **World Wide Web address:** http://www.virginiakmp.com. **Description:** Manufactures and sells chemicals, filter dryers, refrigeration accumulators, and air conditioners.

VIRTUOSO
500 Main Street, Suite 400, Fort Worth TX 76102. 817/870-0300. **Fax:** 817/870-4645. **Contact:** Rick Doolittle, Recruitment Director. **World Wide Web address:** http://www.virtuoso.com. **Description:** A travel consortium specializing in leisure travel. **NOTE:** Apply online.

VISITING NURSE ASSOCIATION
1440 West Mockingbird Lane, Suite 500, Dallas TX 75247. 214/689-0055. **Fax:** 214/689-2977. **Contact:** Human Resources. **E-mail address:** hr@vnatexas.org. **World Wide Web address:** http://www.vnatexas.org. **Description:** A home health care agency that provides intermittent in-home visits. **NOTE:** This website has job listings for all the association's Texas locations. Apply online. **Positions advertised include:** Pediatric Physical Therapist; Home Care RN; Pediatric Occupational Therapist; Child Life Specialist. **Other area locations:** Collins TX; Kaufman TX; Tarrant TX; Denton TX. **Office hours:** Monday – Friday, 8:00 a.m. – 4:00 p.m. **Other U.S. locations:** Nationwide.

THE VISTAWALL GROUP
P.O. Box 629, 803 Airport Road, Terrell TX 75160. 972/551-6100. **Toll-free phone:** 800/869-4567. **Fax:** 972/551-6210. **Contact:** Human Resources. **E-mail address:** careers@vistawall.com. **World Wide Web address:** http://www.vistawall.com. **Description:** The Vistawall Group, through its subsidiaries, designs, manufactures, and distributes entrances, storefront and low-rise framing systems, skylight systems, and engineered curtain wall systems. **Positions advertised include:** Contracts Manager/Project Management. **Corporate headquarters location:** This location. **Other area locations:** Dallas TX; Houston TX. **Subsidiaries include:** Moduline Window Systems; Naturalite Skylight Systems; Skywall Translucent Systems; Vistawall Architectural Products. **Parent company:** Butler Manufacturing Company.

VOUGHT AIRCRAFT INDUSTRIES
PO Box 655907, Dallas TX 75265. 972/946-4238. **Fax:** 972/946-3438. **Contact:** Human Resources. **World Wide Web address:** http://www.voughtaircraft.com. **Description:** Develops and manufactures aerostructures for military and commercial use worldwide. **Positions advertised include:** Numerical Control Programmer; Quality Analyst; Logistics Engineer; Reliability Engineer; Quality Assurance Engineer; Assembly Supervisor; Structural Analyst; Structural Design Engineer.

VULCAN MATERIALS
4303 North FM 1604 East, San Antonio TX 78247. 210/494-9555. **Contact:** Human Resources. **World Wide Web address:** http://www.vulcanmaterials.com. **Description:** Fabricators of concrete, asphalt, and other stone products. **NOTE:** Vulcan has many manufacturing plants and sales locations throughout Texas. See its website for job listings and addresses. **Corporate headquarters location:** Birmingham AL. **Listed on:** New York Stock Exchange. **Stock exchange symbol:** VMC.

VULCAN MATERIALS
14047 Industrial Road, Houston TX 77015. 713/455-1465. **Fax:** 713/455-9666. **Contact:** Human Resources. **World Wide Web address:** http://www.vulcanmaterials.com. **Description:** Fabricators of concrete, asphalt, and other stone products. **NOTE:** Vulcan has many manufacturing plants and sales locations throughout Texas. See its website for job listings and addresses. **Corporate headquarters location:** Birmingham AL. **Listed on:** New York Stock Exchange. **Stock exchange symbol:** VMC.

VULCAN MATERIALS
1111 Gilbert Pit Road, Weatherford TX 76066. 817/594-4524. **Contact:** Human Resources. **World Wide Web address:** http://www.vulcanmaterials.com. **Description:** Fabricators of concrete, asphalt, and other stone products. **NOTE:** Vulcan has many manufacturing plants and sales locations throughout Texas. See its website for job listings and addresses. **Corporate headquarters location:** Birmingham AL. **Listed on:** New York Stock Exchange. **Stock exchange symbol:** VMC.

VULCRAFT
P.O. Box 186, Grapeland TX 75844-0186. 936/687-4665. **Fax:** 936/687-4290. **Contact:** Human Resources. **World Wide Web address:** http://www.vulcraft.com. **Description:** Manufactures steel joists and steel decking. **Parent company:** Nucor Corporation is a steel and steel products manufacturer with mills in North and South Carolina, Nebraska, Texas, Utah, and Arizona. Products include hot-rolled and cold-finished steel shapes, girders, and beams.

WACHOVIA SECURITIES
200 Crescent Court, Suite 1080, Dallas TX. 214/740-3200. **Toll-free phone:** 800/327-6861. **Fax:** 214/740-3250. **Contact:** Human Resources. **World Wide Web address:** http://www.wachoviasec.com. **Description:** Provides a broad range of financial services, including asset management, lending, trust services, and investment banking. **Corporate headquarters location:** Richmond VA. **Other area locations:** Major metropolitan cities in TX. **Other U.S. locations:** Nationwide.

WACO TRIBUNE-HERALD
900 Franklin Avenue, Waco TX 76701. 254/757-5757. **Toll-free phone:** 800/678-8742. **Contact:** Lura Hancock, Human Resources Director. **World Wide Web address:** http://www.wacotrib.com. **Description:** Publishes a daily newspaper. **Parent company:** Cox Communication.

WADLEY REGIONAL MEDICAL CENTER
1000 Pine Street, Texarkana TX 75501. 903/798-7160. **Fax:** 903/798-7177. **Recorded jobline:** 903/798-7161. **Contact:** Human Resources. **E-mail address:** resumes@wadleyrmc.com. **World Wide Web address:** http://www.wadleyrmc.com. **Description:** A nonprofit, acute care hospital with 448 beds. The services offered at Wadley Regional Medical Center include a skilled nursing facility, a Cancer Treatment & Diagnostic Imaging Center, a day surgery center, and a Community Oriented Medical Plan Clinic. Founded in 1959. **NOTE:** Second and third shifts are offered. A completed application is required for any position. Apply online. **Positions advertised include:** LVN; Respiratory Therapist; Nursing Technician; Radiology Clerk. **Special programs:** Summer Jobs; Volunteer.

WAID AND ASSOCIATES
14205 Burnet Road, Suite 600, Austin TX 78728. 512/255-9999. **Fax:** 512/255-8780. **Contact:** Human Resources. **E-mail address:** waid@waid.com. **World Wide Web address:** http://www.waid.com. **Description:** An engineering and environmental services firm. The company specializes in air quality services for industrial clients, particularly involving emissions control; permitting and compliance. Waid and Associates also provides services in waste and wastewater management, environmental management, and environmental information systems. Founded in 1978. **NOTE:** Entry-level positions are offered. **Office hours:** Monday - Friday, 8:00 a.m. - 5:00 p.m. **Corporate headquarters location:** This location. **Other area locations:** Houston TX; Midland TX. **Parent company:** Waid Corporation. **Listed on:** Privately held.

WAL-MART STORES, INC.
3159 South Garland Road, Garland TX 75041. 972/278-8077. **Contact:** Human Resources. **World Wide Web address:** http://www.walmart.com. **Description:** One of the largest retail merchandise chains in the country, operating full-service discount department stores, combination grocery and discount stores, and warehouse stores requiring membership. **NOTE:** Wal-mart has many locations throughout Texas. For management positions, apply online at its website. For hourly positions, visit the nearest store location. **Special programs:** Internships. **Corporate headquarters location:** Bentonville AR. **Other U.S. locations:** Nationwide.

WALGREEN COMPANY
8110 Kempwood, Houston TX 77055. 713/973-5800. **Contact:** Human Resources. **World Wide Web address:** http://www.walgreens.com. **Description:** Walgreen is a retail drug store chain with more than 3,600 stores nationwide. The company sells prescription and proprietary drugs and also carries cosmetics, toiletries, tobacco, and general merchandise. **NOTE:** Apply online for corporate, support, and retail positions. **Corporate headquarters location:** Deerfield IL. **Operations at this facility include:** This location is a district office and warehouse. **Listed on:** New York Stock Exchange. **Stock exchange symbol:** WAG.

WALLS INDUSTRIES, INC.
P.O. Box 98, Cleburne TX 76033. 817/645-4366. **Contact:** Human Resources. **World Wide Web address:** http://www.wallsoutdoors.com. **Description:** Manufactures outerwear for men, women, and children. **Corporate headquarters location:** This location.

WALLS INDUSTRIES, INC.
P.O. Box 196, Sweetwater TX 79556-0196. 325/235-5456. **Fax:** 915/235-8512. **Contact:** Human Resources. **World Wide Web address:** http://www.wallsoutdoors.com. **Description:** Manufactures outerwear for men, women, and children. This location is an outlet store. **Corporate headquarters location:** Cleburne TX.

WARRANTECH CORPORATION
2200 Highway 121 Suite 100, Bedford TX 76021. 817/785-6601. **Toll-free phone:** 800/833-8801. **Contact:** Human Resources. **World Wide Web address:** http://www.warrantech.com. **Description:** Provides extended service contracts and limited warranties to retailers, distributors, and manufacturers of automobiles, recreational vehicles, automotive components, home appliances, home entertainment products, computers and peripherals, and office and communications equipment. **NOTE:** Apply online. **Positions advertised include:** Application Developer. **Corporate headquarters location:** This location. **Other U.S. locations:** Stamford CT.

WASHINGTON GROUP INTERNATIONAL
5220 Spring Valley Road, Suite 204, Dallas TX 75254. 972/385-1635. **Contact:** Human Resources. **World Wide Web address:** http://www.wgint.com. **Description:** Provides a variety of technical construction services including design, engineering, and consulting with a customer base consisting mainly of petroleum refining, petrochemical, and chemical plants.

WASTE MANAGEMENT, INC.
1001 Fannin Street, Suite 4000, Houston TX 77002. 713/512-6200. **Contact:** Human Resources. **World Wide Web address:** http://www.wm.com. **Description:** An international provider of comprehensive waste management services as well as engineering, construction, industrial, and related service. **NOTE:** This company has several locations throughout Texas and the U.S. For corporate positions, apply online. For positions at specific locations, see website for addresses and contact information. **Positions advertised include:** ETL Programmer; Strategic Sourcing Manager; Toxic Tort Manager; Administrative Assistant; Training Manager; Senior Internal Auditor. **Corporate headquarters location:** This location. **Other U.S. locations:** Nationwide. **Operations at this facility include:** Administration. **Listed on:** New York Stock Exchange. **Stock exchange symbol:** WMI.

WAUSAU INSURANCE COMPANIES
P.O. Box 152800, Irving TX 75015-2800. 972/650-1955. **Physical address:** 105 Decker Court, Suite 600, Irving TX 75062-2272. **Contact:** Human Resources. **World Wide Web address:** http://www.wausau.com. **Description:** Offers casualty, property, and group insurance products to commercial customers through 100 service offices located throughout the United States. **NOTE:** Entry-level positions are offered. Apply online for all positions. **Positions advertised include:** Senior Account Executive; Claims Specialist; Insurance Assistant; Customer Claims Representative; Secretary; Law Clerk. **Corporate headquarters location:** Wausau WI. **Other area locations:** Houston TX; San Antonio TX; Carrollton TX; Spring TX. **Other U.S. locations:** Nationwide. **Operations at this facility include:** Administration; Divisional Headquarters; Sales.

WEATHERFORD INTERNATIONAL, INC.
P.O. Box 27608, Houston TX 77227. 713/693-4000. **Physical address:** 515 Post Oak Boulevard, Suite 200, Houston TX 77027. **Contact:** Human Resources. **World Wide Web address:** http://www.weatherford.com. **Description:** Manufactures and services oil field equipment. **NOTE:** See website for job listings and contact information. **Positions advertised include:** Rotating Fishing Project Coordinator; Rotating Fishing Tool Supervisor; Supervisor. **Corporate headquarters location:** This location. **Other area locations:** Statewide. **Other U.S. locations:** Nationwide. **International locations:** Worldwide. **Listed on:** New York Stock Exchange. **Stock exchange symbol:** WFT. **Number of employees nationwide:** 14,000.

WEBB, STOKES & SPARKS, L.L.P.
P.O. Box 1271, San Angelo TX 76902. 915/653-6866. **Physical address:** 314 West Harris Avenue, San Angelo TX 76903. **Toll-free phone:** 800/727-4529. **Fax:** 915/655-1250. **Contact:** Human Resources Department. **World Wide Web address:** http://www.webbstokessparks.com. **Description:** A law office specializing in personal injury cases.

DAVID WEEKLEY HOMES
1111 North Post Oak Road, Houston TX 77055. 713/963-0500. **Fax:** 713/963-0322. **Contact:** Human Resources. **World Wide Web address:** http://www.davidweekleyhomes.com. **Description:** Builds energy-efficient homes and offers multilevel warranties. **NOTE:** Apply online. **Positions advertised include:** Help Desk Associate; Residential Sales Consultant; Residential Construction Superintendent; Marketing Coordinator. **Other area locations:** Austin TX; Dallas TX; San Antonio TX. **Other U.S. locations:** GA; NC; FL; GA; SC; CO; TN.

WEINGARTEN REALTY INVESTORS
P.O. Box 924133, Houston TX 77292-4133. 713/866-6000. **Physical address:** 2600 Citadel Plaza Drive, Suite 300, Houston TX 77008. **Fax:** 713/866-6993. **Contact:** Human Resources. **E-mail address:** jobs@weingarten.com. **World Wide Web address:** http://www.weingarten.com. **Description:** Buys, sells, and manages shopping centers and industrial properties. **Positions advertised include:** Accounting Assistant; Regional Property Manager; Leasing Representative; Senior Leasing Executive; Regional Director of New Developer. **Stock exchange symbol:** WRI.

WELCOM SOFTWARE TECHNOLOGY
15990 North Barkers Landing, Suite 350, Houston TX 77079. 281/558-0514. **Fax:** 281/584-7828. **Contact:** Human Resources. **E-mail address:** personnel@welcom.com. **World Wide Web address:** http://www.welcom.com. **Description:** Designs, develops, and markets project- and cost-management software. Founded in 1983. **NOTE:** Entry-level positions are offered. **Positions advertised include:** Earned Value and Project Management Consultant. **Special programs:** Internships; Training; Summer Jobs. **Office hours:** Monday - Friday, 8:00 a.m. - 5:00 p.m. **Corporate headquarters location:** This location. **International locations:** United Kingdom; France. **Number of employees worldwide:** 80.

WELLS FARGO BANK
P.O. Box 1241, Lubbock TX 79408-1241. 806/765-8861. **Physical address:** 1500 Broadway Street, Lubbock TX 79401. **Contact:** Human Resources. **World Wide Web address:** http://www.wellsfargo.com. **Description:** A diversified financial institution with more than $200 billion in assets. Wells Fargo serves more than 17 million customers through 5,000 independent locations worldwide. The company also maintains several stand-alone ATMs and branches within other retail outlets. Services include community banking, credit and debit cards, home equity and mortgage loans, online banking, student loans, and insurance. Wells Fargo also offers a complete line of commercial and institutional financial services. Founded in 1852. This location provides notary service and Spanish-speaking tellers. **Positions advertised include:** Banker; Teller. **NOTE:** Jobseekers are encouraged to submit resumes via the Website: http://www.wfjobs.com. **Corporate headquarters location:** San Francisco CA. **Other U.S. locations:** Nationwide. **International locations:** Worldwide. **Listed on:** New York Stock Exchange. **Stock exchange symbol:** WFC. **Number of employees worldwide:** 123,000.

WELLS FARGO BANK
P.O. Box 1891, San Angelo TX 76902. 915/657-8600. **Physical address:** 36 West Beauregard Avenue, San Angelo TX 76903. **Contact:** Human Resources. **World Wide Web address:** http://www.wellsfargo.com. **Description:** A main branch location of Wells Fargo, a diversified financial institution billions of dollars in assets. In addition to commercial and institutional financing, this location offers its customers Spanish-speaking services and a notary public. **Positions advertised include:** Banker; Teller. **NOTE:** Jobseekers are encouraged to submit resumes via the Website: http://www.wfjobs.com. **Corporate headquarters location:** San Francisco CA. **Other U.S. locations:** Nationwide. **International locations:** Worldwide. **Listed on:** New York Stock Exchange. **Stock exchange symbol:** WFC. **Number of employees worldwide:** 123,000.

WELLS FARGO BANK
P.O. Box 1790, Alice TX 78333. 361/668-2400. **Physical address:** 601 East Main Street, Alice TX 78332. **Contact:** Human Resources. **World Wide Web address:** http://www.wellsfargo.com. **Description:** A worldwide diversified financial institution. Services at this location include: A talking ATM; Spanish-speaking tellers; a notary; and wheel-chair access. **Positions advertised include:** Banker; Teller. **NOTE:** Jobseekers are encouraged to submit resumes via the Website: http://www.wfjobs.com. **Corporate headquarters location:** San Francisco CA. **Other U.S. locations:** Nationwide. **International locations:** Worldwide. **Listed on:** New York Stock Exchange. **Stock exchange symbol:** WFC. **Number of employees worldwide:** 123,000.

WELLS FARGO BANK
P.O. Box 699, Laredo TX 78042. 956/726-8200. **Physical address:** 1100 Matamoros Street, Laredo TX 78040. **Contact:** Human Resources. **World Wide Web address:** http://www.wellsfargo.com. **Description:** A diversified financial institution with more than 17 million customers through 5,300 independent locations worldwide. The company also maintains several stand-alone ATMs and branches. Wells Fargo also offers a complete line of commercial and institutional financial services. Founded in 1852. Services at this location include cashier checks; notary services; traveler's checks and Spanish-speaking tellers. This location is also wheelchair accessible. **Positions advertised include:** Banker; Teller. **NOTE:** Jobseekers are encouraged to submit resumes via the Website: http://www.wfjobs.com. **Corporate headquarters location:** San Francisco CA. **Other U.S. locations:** Nationwide. **International locations:** Worldwide. **Listed on:** New York Stock Exchange. **Stock exchange symbol:** WFC. **Number of employees worldwide:** 123,000.

WEST OAKS HOSPITAL
6500 Hornwood Drive, Houston TX 77074. 713/995-0909. **Fax:** 713/995-5249. **Contact:** Human Resources. **World Wide Web address:** http://www.psysolutions.com **Description:** A freestanding psychiatric hospital that provides care on inpatient, day treatment, residential treatment, and outpatient bases to children, adolescents, and adults. **NOTE:** Apply online at the hospital's website. **Special programs:** Summer Jobs. **Corporate headquarters location:** Austin TX. **Parent company:** Psychiatric Solutions Inc. **Listed on:** NASDAQ. **Stock exchange symbol:** PSYS.

WESTIN PARK CENTRAL HOTEL
12720 Merit Drive, Dallas TX 75251. 972/385-3000. **Fax:** 324/889-7970. **World Wide Web address:** http://westin-dallas.felcor.com. **Description:** Provides centrally located accommodations in the city of Dallas. **Positions advertised include:** Accounts Payable Clerk; Accounts Receivable Clerk.

WEST TELESERVICES
10931 Laureate Drive, Building 3000, San Antonio TX 78249. 210/690-6900. **Toll-free phone:** 800/521-6000. **Contact:** Human Resources. **World Wide Web address:** http://www.west.com. **Description:** A telemarketing company that deals with both outbound (phone sales) and inbound (phone orders) calls. This location handles inbound and outbound calling for *Fortune* 500 companies. **NOTE:** This company requires that interested jobseekers apply in person. The website provides job listings for each location as well as location addresses and office hours. **Positions advertised include:** Customer Service Representative; Interactive Sales Representative; Marketing Representative; Teleservices Representative. **Special programs:** Internships. **Other area locations:** Beaumont TX; El Paso TX; Harlingen TX; Killeen TX; Lubbock TX; Universal City TX; Waco TX; Sherman TX. **Listed on:** NASDAQ. **Stock exchange symbol:** WSTC.

WEST UNIVERSITY PLACE, CITY OF
3800 University Boulevard, Houston TX 77005. 713/668-4441. **Contact:** Human Resources. **World Wide Web address:** http://www.ci.west-university-place.tx.us. **Description:** Houses administrative and government offices for city departments including public works, the city manager, parks/recreation, and senior services. **NOTE:** A complete application is required for any position. For job listings and an application, see the city's website. **Positions advertised include:** Administrative Assistant for Fire and Human Resources; Refuse Collector/Solid Waste Driver; Senior Services Activity Coordinator.

WESTERN GEOPHYSICAL COMPANY
P.O. Box 2469, Houston TX 77252. 713/789-9600. **Contact:** Human Resources. **World Wide Web address:** http://www.westerngeo.com. **Description:** Provides a full range of geophysical services for oil and gas exploration. Services include land and marine seismic surveys, geophysical programming, and data processing and interpretation. **NOTE:** Apply online at this company's website. **Special programs:** Internships. **Positions advertised include:** Earth Scientist; Quality Control Inspector; Slickline Operator; Research Engineer; Well Data Analyst; Senior Mechanical Engineer; Petroleum Engineer. **Corporate headquarters location:** This location. **Other U.S. locations:** AK; CA; CO. **International locations:** Australia; Bolivia; Brazil; Colombia; Egypt; England; Guatemala; Italy; Pakistan; Saudi Arabia; Singapore; Tunisia. **Parent company:** Schlumberger (New York City NY). **Operations at this facility include:** Administration; Manufacturing; Research and Development; Sales; Service. **Listed on:** New York Stock Exchange. **Stock exchange symbol:** SLB.

WESTERN PLAYLAND INC.
6900 Delta Drive, El Paso TX 79905. 915/772-3953. **Contact:** Human Resources. **World Wide Web address:** http://www.westernplayland.com. **Description:** An amusement park. **NOTE:** A completed application is required for any position. Download application online and mail it.

WEYERHAEUSER COMPANY
P.O. Box 1209, Sealy TX 77474. 979/885-4191. **Contact:** Human Resources. **World Wide Web address:** http://www.weyerhaeuser.com. **Description:** Weyerhaeuser Company's principal businesses are the growing and harvesting of timber; the manufacture, distribution, and sale of forest products including logs, wood chips, and building products; real estate development and construction; and financial services. Weyerhaeuser is one of the world's largest private owners of marketable softwood timber and one of the largest producers of softwood lumber and pulp. The company is also one of North America's largest producers of forest products and recyclers of office wastepaper, newspaper, and corrugated boxes. In addition to its limber and paper products, the company provides water shipping and real estate development services. This location manufactures corrugated packaging. Founded in 1900. **NOTE:** Apply online at its website. **Corporate headquarters location:** Federal Way WA. **Other U.S. locations:** Nationwide. **International locations:** Worldwide. **Listed on:** New York Stock Exchange. **Stock exchange symbol:** WY. **Number of employees worldwide:** 47,000.

WEYERHAEUSER COMPANY
8800 Sterling Street, Irving TX 75063. 972/929-8581. **Contact:** Human Resources. **World Wide Web address:** http://www.weyerhaeuser.com. **Description:** Weyerhaeuser Company's principal businesses are the growing and harvesting of timber for building and manufacturing use. This location is an enterprise technology site. **NOTE:** Mail resume to this location. **Corporate headquarters location:** Federal Way WA. **Other U.S. locations:** Nationwide. **International locations:** Worldwide. **Listed on:** New York Stock Exchange. **Stock exchange symbol:** WY. **Number of employees worldwide:** 47,000.

WHATABURGER, INC.
4600 Parkdale Drive, Corpus Christi TX 78411. 361/878-0650. **Contact:** Director of Human Resources. **World Wide Web address:** http://www.whataburger.com. **Description:** Operates 500 restaurants in the Sunbelt area. Founded in 1950. **NOTE:** This website has job listings for all of its locations. Apply online. **Positions advertised include:** General Manager; Manager; Help Desk Support; Purchasing Manager. **Corporate headquarters location:** This location. **Other U.S. locations:** AZ.

WHITING-TURNER COMPANY
2301 West Plano Parkway, Suite 104, Plano TX 75075. 469/429-0800. **Fax:** 469/429-0801. **Contact:** Human Resources. **World Wide Web address:** http://www.whiting-turner.com. **Description:** A construction company that builds state-of-the-art retail and office buildings. Founded in 1909. **NOTE:** Send resume directly to the office. **Positions advertised include:** Architectural Engineers; Civil Engineers; Electrical Engineers; Mechanical Engineers; Structural Engineers; Building Technicians; Construction Managers. **Corporate headquarters location:** Baltimore MD. **Other U.S. locations:** Nationwide.

WHOLE FOODS MARKET INC.
601 North Lamar Boulevard, Suite 300, Austin TX 78703. 512/477-4455. **Contact:** Human Resources. **World Wide Web address:** http://www.wholefoods.com. **Description:** Owns and operates a chain of natural foods supermarkets. **NOTE:** This company has other Texas locations. See its website for job listings for all its locations. Apply online. **Positions advertised include:** Business Systems Analyst; National Replenishment Coordinator; Purchasing Systems Team Lead; Senior Buyer/Product Developer. **Other U.S. locations:** CA; LA; MA; NC; RI. **Operations at this facility include:** Regional Headquarters. **Listed on:** NASDAQ. **Stock exchange symbol:** WFMI.

WHOLESALE ELECTRIC SUPPLY CO., INC.
4040 Gulf Freeway, Houston TX 77004. 713/748-6100. **Contact:** Human Resources. **World Wide Web address:** http://www.wholesaleelectric.com. **Description:** Distributes switches and electrical equipment for the commercial, OEM, chemical, petrochemical, refining, and utility industries.

WICHITA FALLS STATE HOSPITAL
P.O. Box 300, Wichita Falls TX 76307. 940/552-9901. **Fax:** 940/689-5735. **Contact:** Staffing. **Description:** A nonprofit, forensic and mental health hospital. **Special programs:** Internships. **Corporate headquarters location:** Austin TX. **Other area locations:** Vernon TX. **Parent company:** Texas Department of Mental Health. **Operations at this facility include:** Administration.

WILDWOOD MANAGEMENT GROUP
18585 Sigimi, Suite 101, San Antonio TX 78258. 210/403-9785. **Contact:** Human Resources. **Description:** Engaged in property management for apartments and condominiums.

WILLIAMS GAS PIPELINES-TRANSCO
P.O. Box 1396, Houston TX 77251. 713/215-2000. **Physical address:** 2800 Post Oak Boulevard, Houston TX 77056. **Contact:** Human Resources. **World Wide Web address:** http://www.williams.com. **Description:** Transports natural gas to the southeastern and northeastern United States. **NOTE:** Apply online. **Positions advertised include:** Environmental Specialist. **Corporate headquarters location:** This location. **Parent company:** Williams Energy. **Listed on:** New York Stock Exchange. **Stock exchange symbol:** WMB.

WILLIAMSON PRINTING CORPORATION
6700 Denton Drive, Dallas TX 75235. 214/904-2100. **Toll-free phone:** 800/843-5423. **Recorded jobline:** 214/904-2603. **Contact:** Human Resources. **E-mail address:** jobs@twpc.com. **World Wide Web address:** http://www.twpc.com. **Description:** A commercial printing company. **NOTE:** Entry-level positions and second and third shifts are offered. Apply online. **Positions advertised include:** Customer Service Representative; Jogger; Handworker. **Special programs:** Summer Jobs. **Corporate headquarters location:** This location. **Subsidiaries include:** Williamson Express, Printing Resource Management, The Fulfillment Center. **Listed on:** Privately held.

WILLIAMSON-DICKIE MANUFACTURING COMPANY
P.O. Box 1779, Fort Worth TX 76101. 817/336-7201. **Contact:** Melissa Petty, Human Resources. **World Wide Web address:** http://www.dickies.com. **Description:** Manufactures apparel for men and boys including casual slacks and work pants. **NOTE:** Job listings for all locations can be found on Dickie's website. Apply online. **Positions advertised include:** Assistant Manager; Corporate Industrial Engineer; Pattern Maker; Production Planner; Product Costing Analyst; Sales Associate. **Corporate headquarters location:** This location.

WILLIAMSON-DICKIE MANUFACTURING COMPANY
P.O. Box 295, Weslaco TX 78596. 956/968-1567. **Contact:** Human Resources. **World Wide Web address:** http://www.dickies.com. **Description:** Williamson-Dickie Manufacturing Company manufactures apparel for men and boys including casual slacks and work pants. **NOTE:** Apply online at this company's website. **Corporate headquarters location:** Fort Worth TX. **Operations at this facility include:** This location is primarily engaged in apparel sewing.

WILLIAMSON-DICKIE MANUFACTURING COMPANY
6110 South 42nd Street, McAllen TX 78503. 956/686-6541. **Contact:** Human Resources. **World Wide Web address:** http://www.dickies.com. **Description:** Williamson-Dickie Manufacturing Company manufactures apparel for men and boys including casual slacks and work pants. **NOTE:** Apply online at this company's website. **Corporate headquarters location:** Fort Worth TX. **Operations at this facility include:** This location manufactures men's work pants.

WINDHAM SCHOOL DISTRICT
P.O. Box 40, Huntsville TX 77342-0040. 936/291-5321. **Fax:** 936/291-4622. **Contact:** Minnie Madison, Human Resources. **E-mail address:** personnel@wsdtx.org. **World Wide Web address:** http://www.windhamschooldistrict.org. **Description:** Responsible for correctional education for the Texas Department of Criminal Justice. **NOTE:** Windham School District is governed by the Texas Education Agency and hires only certified teachers and administrators, some positions requiring a degree, and clerical positions. See the district's website for job listings for all locations. **Operations at this facility include:** Administration; Regional Headquarters.

WINSTEAD SECHREST & MINICK P.C.
5400 Renaissance Tower, 1201 Elm Street, Dallas TX 75270. 214/745-5211. **Contact:** Patty Stewart, Recruiting. **World Wide Web address:** http://www.winstead.com. **Description:** A law firm offering services in a variety of practice areas including environmental, insurance, real estate, and tax. **NOTE:** This company offers attorney, staff, and student positions. See website for job listings and contact and application information. **Other area locations:** Austin TX; Fort Worth TX; Houston TX; San Antonio TX; The Woodlands TX. **Other U.S. locations:** Washington D.C. **International locations:** Mexico City. **Number of employees worldwide:** 700.

WITHERSPOON ADVERTISING & PUBLIC RELATIONS
P.O. Box 2137, Fort Worth TX 76113. 817/335-1373. **Contact:** Mike Wilie, Chairman and Chief Executive Officer. **World Wide Web address:** http://www.witherspoon.com. **Description:** A national advertising and public relations agency. **Corporate headquarters location:** This location. **Operations at this facility include:** Service.

WOLF CAMERA
3264 Westheimer, Houston TX 77098. 713/528-3332. Recorded jobline: 888/994-4413. **Contact:** Human Resources. **E-mail address:** recruiter@ritzcamera.com. **World Wide Web address:** http://www.wolfcamera.com. **Description:** One location of a company that provides photography services, such as a one-hour photo development lab. The company also sells film, frames, and other photography products. **NOTE:** An application is required for any position. To obtain one, visit this company's website and apply online. An interested jobseeker may also download an application online and mail to Ritz Cameras Centers, Inc., 6711 Ritz Way, Beltsville MD 20706, Attention: Recruiter – Online, or fax it to 301/419-7047. The application may also be dropped off at the nearest Wolf Camera location. See website for additional Texas locations. **Parent company:** Ritz Camera.

WOOD GROUP PRESSURE CONTROL
17420 Katy Freeway, Suite 300, Houston TX 77094. 281/828-3500. **Fax:** 281/828-3525. **Contact:** Human Resources. **E-mail address:** careers@woodgroup.com. **World Wide Web address:** http://www.woodgroup.co.uk. **Description:** Manufactures and remanufactures wellheads and other oil field equipment. **NOTE:** E-mail resume.

Corporate headquarters location: United Kingdom. **Operations at this facility include:** This location is the corporate office for its U.S. business.

WORLD FINANCIAL GROUP
2600 Via Fortuna, Suite 220, Austin TX 78746. 512/328-4220. **Contact:** Human Resources. **World Wide Web address:** http://www.wfg-online.com. **Description:** Offers a wide variety of financial services including mutual funds, debt consolidation, securities, mortgages, health insurance, and life insurance. **Parent company:** AEGON.

WUKASCH COMPANY
1810 Guadalupe Street, Austin TX 78701. 512/472-4700. **Contact:** Don C. Wukasch, President. **Description:** A diversified real estate and securities investment company providing real estate property management and securities portfolio management. **Special programs:** Internships. **Corporate headquarters location:** This location. **Listed on:** Privately held.

WYNDHAM GREENSPOINT
12400 Greenspoint Drive, Houston TX 77060. 281/875-2222. **Contact:** Human Resources. **World Wide Web address:** http://www.wyndham.com. **Description:** A large upscale, luxury hotel chain with locations throughout the world. **NOTE:** Search and apply for positions online. **Listed on:** American Stock Exchange. **Stock exchange symbol:** WBR.

WYNDHAM INTERNATIONAL
P.O. Box 224108, Dallas TX 75222-4108. 214/863-1000. **Contact:** Human Resources. **World Wide Web address:** http://www.wyndham.com. **Description:** A large upscale, luxury hotel chain with locations throughout the world. **NOTE:** Apply online for corporate positions. **Positions advertised include**: Recruiting Manager; Property Accountant; Manager of Office Services; Accounting Operations Manager; Manager of Sales and Catering Systems; Project Manager; Administrative Assistant. **Listed on:** American Stock Exchange. **Stock exchange symbol:** WBR.

WYNDHAM ANATOLE HOTEL
2201 Stemmons Freeway, Dallas TX 75207. 214/748-1200. **Contact:** Human Resources. **World Wide Web address:** http://www.wyndham.com. **Description:** A luxury convention hotel with more than 1,600 rooms. **NOTE:** Apply online at this company's website. **Positions advertised include:** Assistant Telecommunications Manager. **Operations at this facility include:** Service.

WYNNE/JACKSON, INC.
600 North Pearl Street, Suite 650, Lock Box 149, Dallas TX 75201. 214/880-8600. **Fax:** 214/880-8709. **Contact:** Frank Murphy, Senior Vice President and Chief Financial Officer. **World Wide Web address:** http://www.wynnejackson.com. **Description:** A commercial real estate development and property management company. **Corporate headquarters location:** This location.

XCEL ENERGY
P.O. Box 1261, Amarillo TX 79170-0001. 806/378-2121. **Contact:** Human Resources. **World Wide Web address:** http://www.xcelenergy.com. **Description:** Provides electric service to the Amarillo area. **NOTE:** Entry-level positions offered. Apply online for all positions. **Special programs:** Internships. **Corporate headquarters location:** Minneapolis MN. **Listed on:** New York Stock Exchange. **Stock exchange symbol:** XEL.

XEROX CORPORATION
1301 Ridgeview Drive, Lewisville TX 75057. 972/830-4000. **Contact:** Human Resources. **World Wide Web address:** http://www.xerox.com. **Description:** Xerox Corporation is a leader in the global document market providing document solutions that enhance business productivity. Xerox develops, manufactures, markets, sells, and services a full range of document processing products. **Corporate headquarters location:** Stamford CT. **Operations at this facility include:** This location is a sales and service office. **Listed on:** New York Stock Exchange. **Stock exchange symbol:** XRX.

XEROX CORPORATION
6836 Austin Center Boulevard, Suite 300, Austin TX 78731. 512/343-5600. **Contact:** Human Resources Center. **World Wide Web address:** http://www.xerox.com. **Description:** Xerox is a leader in the global document market providing document solutions that enhance business productivity. Xerox develops, manufactures, markets, sells, and services a full range of document processing products and solutions. **NOTE:** Apply online. **Positions advertised include:** Sales Manager. **Corporate headquarters location:** Stamford CT. **Operations at this facility include:** This location is a regional sales and service office. **Listed on:** New York Stock Exchange. **Stock exchange symbol:** XRX.

XEROX OMNIFAX
9715 Burnet Road, Austin TX 78758. 512/719-5566 **Toll-free phone:** 800/221-5566. **Fax:** 512/719-5567 **Contact:** Human Resources. **World Wide Web address:** http://www.omnifax.com. **Description:** Manufactures communications systems, telewriters, and facsimile recording devices. **NOTE:** Apply online at the parent company's website: http://www.xerox.com. **Parent company:** Xerox Corporation. **Listed on:** New York Stock Exchange. **Stock exchange symbol:** XRX.

YMCA OF METROPOLITAN FORT WORTH
512 Lamar Street, Fort Worth TX 76102. 817/332-3281. **Contact:** Human Resources. **World Wide Web address:** http://www.ymcafw.org. **Description:** One of the nation's largest and most comprehensive service organizations. The YMCA provides health and fitness, social and personal development, sports and recreation, education and career development, and camps and conferences to children, youths, adults, the elderly, families, the disabled, refugees and foreign nationals, YMCA residents, and community residents, through a broad range of specific programs. **NOTE:** The YMCA has several locations in Fort Worth TX. See its website for other area locations, job listings and contact information. **Other U.S. locations:** Nationwide.

OFFICES OF NORMAN A. ZABLE, P.C.
5757 Alpha Road, Suite 504, Dallas TX 75240. 972/386-6900. **Contact:** Human Resources Department. **Description:** A civil law practice specializing in business and bankruptcy law.

H.B. ZACHRY COMPANY
537 Logwood, San Antonio TX 78221. 210/475-8000. **Fax:** 210/475-8775. **Recorded jobline:** 800/JOB-SUSA. **Contact:** Larry Cantwell, Professional Employment Manager. **World Wide Web address:** http://www.zachry.com. **Description:** A construction management company operating through the following seven divisions: Process, Power, Heavy, Maintenance & Service, Commercial, International, and Pipeline. The company primarily builds power plants, highways, and pipelines in the southern United States, as well as in foreign countries. H.B. Zachry Company does not handle residential construction contracts. Founded in 1923. **NOTE:** Entry-level positions are offered. This company's website has a complete job listings on its website. Apply online. **Positions advertised include:** Documents Controls; Legal Secretary; Construction Electrical Facilitator; Design Technician; Mechanical Equipment Reliability Improvement Coordinator; Maintenance Supervisor; Civil Field Superintendents; Secretary **Special programs:** Summer Jobs. **Corporate headquarters location:** This location. **Listed on:** Privately held.

H.B. ZACHRY COMPANY
10111 Richmond Avenue, Houston Texas 77042. 832/242-1019. **Contact:** Human Resources. **World Wide Web address:** http://www.zachry.com. **Description:** H.B. Zachry is an industrial construction management company operating through the following divisions: Process; Power; Heavy; Maintenance & Service; Commercial; International; and Pipeline. The company builds power plants, highways, and pipelines in the southern United States, as well as in foreign countries. H.B. Zachry Company does not handle residential construction contracts. Founded in 1923. **Corporate headquarters location:** San Antonio TX. **Operations at this facility include:** This location is a project management and consulting office. **Listed on:** Privately held.

ZALE CORPORATION
901 West Walnut Hill Lane, Mail Station 5B-12, Irving TX 75038. 972/580-4000. **Fax:** 972/580-5266. **Contact:** Manager of Corporate Staffing. **World Wide Web address:** http://www.zalecorp.com. **Description:** A specialty retail firm engaged in selling fine jewelry and related products. **NOTE:** Entry-level positions are offered. Apply online at the company's website or mail or fax resumes. **Positions advertised include:** Senior Insurance Accountant; Distribution Sale Lead; Advertising Project Manager; Training Specialist; Real Estate Attorney; Records Clerk; Curriculum Designer; Merchandise Planning Director. **Corporate headquarters location:** This location. **Other U.S. locations:** Nationwide. **Listed on:** New York Stock Exchange. **Stock exchange symbol:** ZLC. **Number of employees worldwide:** 20,000.

ZALE LIPSHY UNIVERSITY HOSPITAL
UNIVERSITY OF TEXAS SOUTHWESTERN MEDICAL CENTER CAMPUS
5151 Harry Hines Boulevard, Dallas TX 75235-7786. 214/879-2660 **Fax:** 214/879-2652 **Recorded jobline:** 214/590-3484. **Contact:** Human Resources. **World Wide Web address:** http://www.zluh.org. **Description:** Zale Lipshy University Hospital at Southwestern Medical Center was built to serve University of Texas Southwestern Medical Center at Dallas as its private, nonprofit, adult referral hospital for specialized tertiary care. The facilities consist of 152 hospital beds (20 intensive care unit beds, 89 medical/surgical beds, 22 rehabilitation beds, and 21 psychiatric beds) and 12 operating room suites for specialized surgical care in the areas of neurological surgery, orthopedics, urology, gynecology, otorhinolaryngology (ear, nose, and throat), ophthalmology, cardiothoracic surgery, oral and maxillofacial surgery, vascular surgery, and plastic and reconstructive surgery. Founded in 1989. **NOTE:** Second and third shifts are offered. A complete application is required for any position. Applications and resumes may be faxed, mailed or delivered in person. Interested jobseekers may also apply online at the website. **Positions advertised include:** Lead Medical Therapist; Phlebotomist; Business Systems Manager; Lab Manager; RN; Assistant Nursing Manager; Systems Analyst; Billing Supervisor; Buyer II; Performance Improvement Analyst. **Office hours:** Monday – Friday, 8:00 a.m. – 4:30 p.m. **Operations at this facility include:** Administration; Service.

ZILKER BOTANICAL GARDEN
2220 Barton Springs Road, Austin TX 78746. 512/477-8672. **Contact:** Human Resources. **World Wide Web address:** http://www.zilkergarden.org. **Description:** Covering 22 acres of land, Zilker Botanical Garden is comprised of a multitude of individual gardens including Xeriscape Garden, Herb and Fragrance Garden, and Rose Garden. **Special programs:** Volunteer.

ZIMMER, INC.
9900 Spectrum Drive, Austin TX 78717. 512/432-9900. **Fax:** 512/432-9200. **Recorded jobline:** 512/432-9283. **Contact:** Human Resources. **World Wide Web address:** http://www.centerpulsorthropedics.com. **Description:** A worldwide leader in the manufacture and distribution of orthopedic implants for knees, hips, and shoulders. **NOTE:** Apply online at this company's website or in person at the Human Resources Office. **Positions advertised include:** Associate Scientist; Internal System Auditor; Temporary Machinist; Sales Support Representative.

ZIMMERMAN SIGN COMPANY
3013 North Jackson, Jacksonville TX 75766. 903/589-2100. **Fax:** 903/589-2101. **Contact:** Human Resources . **World Wide Web address:** http://www.zimmermansign.com. **Description:** Manufactures electric signs. **Corporate headquarters location:** This location.

ZONAGEN INC.
2408 Timberloch Place, Suite B-4, The Woodlands TX 77380. 281/367-5892. **Contact:** Human Resources. **World Wide Web address:** http://www.zonagen.com. **Description:** Researches, develops, and markets biopharmaceutical products that deal with a variety of issues including sexual dysfunction, urology, fertility, and contraception. **Corporate headquarters location:** This location. **Listed on:** NASDAQ. **Stock exchange symbol:** ZONA.

A&K RAILROAD MATERIALS
P.O. Box 30076, Salt Lake City UT 84130. 801/974-5484. **Physical address:** 1505 South Redwood, Salt Lake City UT 84130. **Toll-free phone:** 800/453-8812. **Fax:** 801/972-2041. **Contact:** Human Resources. **E-mail address:** info@akrailroad.com. **World Wide Web address:** http://www.akrailroad. com. **Description:** A wholesaler of materials used to build railroads. **Corporate headquarters location:** This location. **Other U.S. locations:** Nationwide.

ALTIRIS
588 West 400 South, Lindon UT 84042. 801/226-8500. **Toll-free phone:** 888/252-5551. **Fax:** 801/226-8506. **Contact:** Human Resources. **E-mail address:** hr@altiris.com. **World Wide Web address:** http://www.altiris.com. **Description:** A software company. Founded 1998. **Positions advertised include:** Senior Consultant; Regional Sales Manager; Field Systems Engineer; Strategic Alliance Account Manager; SAS Account Manager. **Corporate headquarters location:** This location. **International locations:** Germany; Australia. **Listed on:** NASDAQ. **Stock exchange symbol:** ATRS. **President/CEO:** Greg Butterfield.

ATK THIOKOL PROPULSION
P.O. Box 707, Brigham City UT 84302-0707. 435/863-3511. **Fax:** 435/863-2234. **Contact:** Employee Relations Manager. **World Wide Web address:** http://www.atk.com. **Description:** Thiokol is a manufacturer of propulsion, gas generator, fastening, and ordnance systems and products for the aerospace, industrial, transportation, and military markets. Products are used in satellites, aircraft, missiles, space shuttles, and munitions. **NOTE:** Federal Express mailing address is 160 North Highway 83, Corinne UT 84307. **Positions advertised include:** Material Planning and Control Analyst; Quality Engineer; Scientist. **Special programs:** Internships. **Corporate headquarters location:** Edina MN. **Other area locations:** Magna UT. **Parent company:** ATK. **Operations at this facility include:** This location manufactures rocket motors for space shuttles.

ARUP LABORATORIES
500 Chipeta Way, Salt Lake City UT 84108. 801/583-2787. **Toll-free phone:** 800/242-2787. **Fax:** 801/584-2712. **Contact:** Recruitment. **World Wide Web address:** http://www.arup-lab.com. **Description:** Performs esoteric and general laboratory testing for hospitals, reference laboratories, and independent laboratory clients. ARUP Laboratories provides a broad range of tests including analytical determinations on biological fluids and tissues. **Positions advertised include:** Medical Technologist; Assistant Director; Community Relations Representative; Industrial Engineer; Mobile Equipment Technologist; Phlebotomist; Technical Writer. **Corporate headquarters location:** This location. **Number of employees nationwide:** 1,400.

ABBOTT LABORATORIES
4455 Atherton Drive, Salt Lake City UT 84124. 801/262-2688. **Contact:** Human Resources Department. **World Wide Web address:** http://www. abbott.com. **Description:** A *Fortune* 500 company engaged in the design and manufacture of disposable medical devices for hemodynamic monitoring and fluid collection. **NOTE:** Please visit website to search for jobs and apply online. **Positions advertised include:** District Manager. **Corporate headquarters location:** Lake County IL. **Other U.S. locations:** Nationwide. **International locations:** Worldwide. **Listed on:** New York Stock Exchange. **Stock exchange symbol:** ABT. **Number of employees worldwide:** 70,000.

ALBERTSON'S, INC.
140 North 900 West, Salt Lake City UT 84116. 801/532-7530. **Contact:** Human Resources. **World Wide Web address:** http://www.albertsons.com. **Description:** One of the largest retail food-drug chains in the U.S. The company operates approximately 2,500 stores in 37 states. **Corporate headquarters location:** Boise ID. **Listed on:** New York Stock Exchange. **Stock exchange symbol:** ABS. **Number of employees nationwide:** 200,000.

ALCOA ENGINEERED PRODUCTS
1550 Kirby Lane, Spanish Fork UT 84660. 801/798-8730. **Contact:** Human Resources. **World Wide Web address:** http://www.alcoa.com. **Description:** ALCOA is engaged in all aspects of the aluminum industry including mining, refining, smelting, fabricating, and recycling. The company also manufactures ceramic packaging for the semiconductor industry, alumina chemicals, plastic bottle closures, vinyl siding, packaging machinery, and electrical distribution systems for automobiles. **Special programs:** Internships; Co-ops. **Corporate headquarters location:** Pittsburgh PA. **Operations at this facility include:** This location is engaged in the extrusion of aluminum. **Listed on:** New York Stock Exchange. **Stock exchange symbol:** AA.

ALLEN COMMUNICATIONS
5 Triad Center, 5th Floor, Salt Lake City UT 84180. 801/537-7800. **Toll-free phone:** 866/310-7800. **Fax:** 801/537-7805. **Contact:** Shelley Duggar, Human Resources Manager. **E-mail address:** shellyd@allencomm.com. **World Wide Web address:** http://www.allencomm.com. **Description:** Provides computer-based training (CBT) and Web-based training solutions to businesses. **NOTE:** Entry-level positions and part-time jobs are offered. **Positions advertised include:** Instructional Designer. **Special programs:** Internships; Apprenticeships; Training; Summer Jobs. **Office hours:** Monday - Friday, 7:30 a.m. - 5:30 p.m. **Corporate headquarters location:** This location. **Other U.S. locations:** PA; TX. **International locations:** United Kingdom. **Parent company:** Mentergy. **CEO:** Ron Zamir.

ALLSTATE INSURANCE COMPANY
P.O. Box 57995, Salt Lake City UT 84157. 801/264-2000. **Physical address:** 6056 Fashionsquare Drive, Suite 100, Salt Lake City UT 84107. **Contact:** Human Resources. **World Wide Web address:** http://www.allstate.com. **Description:** Provides homeowner's and auto insurance. **NOTE:** Please visit website for online application form. **Positions advertised include:** Claim Trainee. **Special programs:** Internships. **Corporate headquarters location:** Northbrook IL. **Other U.S. locations:** Nationwide.

ALPHA PRO TECH
236 North 2200 West, Salt Lake City UT 84116. 801/363-2890. **Fax:** 801/355-2534. **Contact:** Personnel. **World Wide Web address:** http://www.alphaprotech.com. **Description:** Manufactures safety apparel and products used in cleanrooms and the food and pharmaceutical manufacturing industries. Products include disposable facemasks, eye goggles, and the "Aqua Track" shoe cover worn for traction on slippery surfaces. **Corporate headquarters location:** Ontario, Canada. **Other U.S. locations:** Janesville WI; Nogales AZ; Richboro PA; Valdosta GA. **International locations:** Benjamin Hill, Mexico. **Listed on:** American Stock Exchange. **Stock exchange symbol:** APT. **Number of employees worldwide:** 230.

ALPINE HEALTH INDUSTRIES
1525 West Business Park Drive, Orem UT 84058. 801/225-5525x123. **Toll-free phone:** 800/572-5076. **Fax:** 801/225-5899. **Contact:** Human Resources. **Description:** A contract manufacturer for the pharmaceutical industry. The company provides convenience packet filling, substantial mixing capacity, encapsulating and tableting, and multiple packaging services. **NOTE:** Part-time jobs and second and third shifts are offered. **Special programs:** Summer Jobs. **Office hours:** Monday - Friday, 8:00 a.m. - 5:00 p.m. **Corporate headquarters location:** Texarkana TX.

ALPINE SCHOOL DISTRICT
575 North 100 East, American Fork UT 84003. 801/756-8400. **Contact:** Human Resources. **World Wide Web address:** http://www.alpine.k12.ut.us. **Description:** Operates 33 elementary schools, 8 junior high schools, and 7 senior high schools. **Positions advertised include:** Administrator of Schools; Director of Human Resources; Elementary Library Media Specialist; Elementary Teacher; Head Elementary Custodian; Head Sweeper; Lead Secretary Elementary; Secondary Teacher; Special Education Para-Educator; Special Education Teacher; Sweeper; Teacher's Assistant.

ALTA INDUSTRIES
1887 South 700 West, Salt Lake City UT 84110. 801/972-8160. **Contact:** Human Resources. **World Wide Web address:** http://www.alta-steel.com. **Description:** A holding company. **Subsidiaries include:** Alta Computer manufactures computer-related equipment. MBCI manufactures roofing materials. Steelco manufactures steel.

ALTA SKI AREA
P.O. Box 8007, Alta UT 84092-8007. 801/359-1078. **Fax:** 801/799-2340. **Contact:** Human Resources. **E-mail address:** info@altaskiarea.com. **World Wide Web address:** http://www.altaskiarea.com. **Description:** Operates a variety of ski trails. Founded in 1938. **NOTE:** Employment is seasonal. Positions are available from November to April. Please visit website for online application form, and to see specific contact for position. **Positions advertised include:** Lift Operator; Snow Cat Operator; Kitchen Help; Snowmaker; Building Maintenance Worker; Ticket Seller; Watson's Shelter Worker; PSIA Certified Instructor; Ski School Sales Personnel; Snow Remover; Ski Patroller; Alf's Restaurant Worker; Ski Shop Employee; Ski Area Mechanic; Parking Attendant.

THE AMALGAMATED SUGAR COMPANY
P.O. Box 1520, Ogden UT 84402. 801/399-3431. **Physical address:** 2427 Lincoln Avenue, Ogden UT 84401. **Fax:** 801/393-8042. **Contact:** Human Resources. **World Wide Web address:** http://www.amalgamatedsugar.com. **Description:** One of the largest producers of sugar. The company's White Satin brand sugar is sold primarily to industrial users in pacific, intermountain, and midwestern states. **Corporate headquarters location:** This location. **Other U.S. locations:** Paul ID; American Falls ID; Nampa ID; Mount Home ID; Nyssa OR; Twin Falls ID. **Parent company:** Valhi, Inc.

AMERICA FIRST CREDIT UNION
P.O. Box 9199, Ogden UT 84409-0199. 801/965-3225. **Physical address:** 1344 West 4675 South, Riverdale UT 84405. **Contact:** Human Resources. **World Wide Web address:** http://www.americafirst.com. **Description:** A credit union. **NOTE:** Please visit website to download application form. **Positions advertised include:** Maintenance Service Representative. Monday – Friday, 9:30 a.m. – 5:30 p.m.; Saturday, 9:00 a.m. – 3:00 p.m. **Corporate headquarters location:** This location. **Other area locations:** Statewide.

AMERICAN CANCER SOCIETY
941 East 3300 South, Salt Lake City UT 84106. 801/483-1560. **Fax:** 801/483-1558. **Contact:** Human Resources. **World Wide Web address:** http://www.cancer.org. **Description:** A nationwide, community-based, nonprofit, voluntary health organization dedicated to eliminating cancer as a major health problem by funding cancer research and public education. The society helps patients directly by offering services including transportation to treatment and rehabilitation services. **NOTE:** Volunteer positions are also available. Please see website for details on how to apply for specific positions. **Positions advertised include:** Director of Government Relations. **Special programs:** Internships. **Corporate headquarters location:** Atlanta GA. **Other area locations:** Orem UT. **Other U.S. locations:** Nationwide.

AMERICAN RED CROSS
P.O. Box 3836, Salt Lake City UT 84110-3836. 801/323-7000. **Physical address:** 465 South 400 East, Salt Lake City UT. **Toll-free phone:** 800/328-9272. **Contact:** Human Resources. **E-mail address:** info@utahredcross.org. **World Wide Web address:** http://www.redcross.org; http://www.utahredcross.org. **Description:** A humanitarian organization that aids disaster victims, gathers blood for crisis distribution, trains individuals to respond to emergencies, educates individuals on various diseases, and raises funds for other charitable establishments. **NOTE:** Please visit website to search for jobs, register, and apply online. **Other U.S. locations:** Nationwide. **International locations:** Worldwide.

AMERICOLD LOGISTICS, LLC
P.O. Box 160441, Clearfield UT 84016. 801/773-6886. **Physical address:** 755 East 1700 South, Clearfield UT 84106. **Toll-free phone:** 888/484-4877. **Fax:** 801/773-0887. **Contact:** Human Resources. **World Wide Web address:** http://www.amclog.com. **Description:** A freezer/storage company that operates a refrigerated food warehouse facility that stores frozen beef for food processing. **Corporate headquarters location:** Atlanta GA. **Other U.S. locations:** Nationwide.

AMSCO WINDOWS
P.O. Box 25368, Salt Lake City UT 84125. 801/972-6441; 801/978-5000. **Physical address:** 1880 South 1045 West, Salt Lake City UT. **Toll-free phone:** 800/748-4661. **Fax:** 801/978-5058. **Contact:** Human Resources. **World Wide Web address:** http://www.amscowindows.com. **Description:** A window manufacturer. **Office hours:** Monday – Friday, 8:00 a.m. – 5:00 p.m. **Corporate headquarters location:** This location.

ANIXTER
1837 South 4130 West, Building E, Salt Lake City UT 84104. 801/973-2121. **Fax:** 801/973-4472. **Contact:** Human Resources. **World Wide Web address:** http://www.anixter.com. **Description:** Anixter is a value-added provider of industrial wire and cabling solutions that support voice and data applications. Solutions include customized pre- and postsale services and products from the world's leading manufacturers. **NOTE:** Please visit website to search for jobs and apply online. **Positions advertised include:** Inside Sales Representative. **Corporate headquarters location:** Glenview IL. **Other U.S. locations:** Nationwide. **International locations:** Worldwide. **Operations at this facility include:** This location is a distribution center that houses wire cable, construction cable, and networking departments.

ARCTIC CIRCLE RESTAURANTS
P.O. Box 339, Midvale UT 84047. 801/561-3620. **Physical address:** 411 West 7200 South, Suite 200, Midvale UT. **Contact:** Human Resources. **World Wide Web**

address: http://www.arcticcirclerest.com. **Description:** Owns and operates the Arctic Circle restaurant chain. **Corporate headquarters location:** This location. **Other U.S. locations:** ID; CA; WA; OR; WY; NE; MT.

ARNOLD MACHINERY
P.O. Box 30020, Salt Lake City UT 84130-0020. 801/972-4000. **Physical address:** 2975 West 2100 South, Salt Lake City UT 84119. **Fax:** 801/975-4080. **Contact:** Human Resources. **World Wide Web address:** http://www.arnoldmachinery.com. **Description:** A wholesaler of mining, construction, and material handling equipment. **Corporate headquarters location:** This location. **Other U.S. locations:** OR; NV; AZ; ID; MT. **CEO:** Russ Fleming.

ARROWHEAD DENTAL LABORATORIES
11170 South State Street, Sandy UT 84070. 801/572-7200. **Toll-free phone:** 800/800-7200. **Fax:** 801/572-7290. **Contact:** Brent Burge, Human Resources. **E-mail address:** resumes@arrowheaddental.com. **World Wide Web address:** http://www.arrowheaddental.com. **Description:** A laboratory that manufactures dental prosthetics such as dentures, crowns, and bridges.

ASSOCIATED FOOD STORES, INC.
1850 West 2100 South, Salt Lake City UT 84119. 801/973-4400. **Fax:** 801/978-8851. **Recorded jobline:** 800/574-9000 Ext. 8699. **Contact:** Fred Ferguson, Human Resources Manager. **World Wide Web address:** http://www.afstores.com. **Description:** A wholesale food company. **NOTE:** Contact Human Resources at 800/574-9000 Ext. 8368. For retail positions, call Dave Wirthlin at 801/978-8201, or e-mail at join@afstores.com. **Positions advertised include:** Retail Workers. **Corporate headquarters location:** This location. **Operations at this facility include:** Divisional Headquarters; Regional Headquarters; Research and Development; Sales. **Listed on:** Privately held.

AUTO METER PRODUCTS, INC.
350 West Center Street, Pleasant Grove UT 84062. 801/785-0051. **Fax:** 801/785-8699. **Contact:** Personnel. **World Wide Web address:** http://www.autometer.com. **Description:** Manufactures high-performance automobile gauges, industrial gauges, and tester units. **NOTE:** Entry-level positions are offered. **Corporate headquarters location:** Sycamore IL. **Other area locations:** Ephraim UT. **Operations at this location include:** OEM Instrumentation Headquarters. **Listed on:** Privately held.

AUTOLIV
3350 Airport Road, Ogden UT 84405. 801/625-9200. **Fax:** 801/625-4911. **Contact:** Human Resources. **World Wide Web address:** http://www. autoliv.com. **Description:** Manufactures a variety of safety products for automobiles including air bags, antiwhiplash seats, child restraints, and leg protection. This location also hires seasonally. **NOTE:** Please visit website to search for jobs and apply online. **Positions advertised include:** Design Engineer. **Corporate headquarters location:** This location. **Other area locations:** Brigham City UT; Tremonton UT; Promontory UT. **Other U.S. locations:** Auburn Hills MI; Aurora CO; Indianapolis IN; Columbia City IN; Madisonville KY. **International locations:** Worldwide. **Number of employees nationwide:** 8,000.

AUTOLIV
1360 North 1000 West, Tremonton UT 84337. 435/257-1000. **Fax:** 435/257-1010. **Contact:** Human Resources. **World Wide Web address:** http://www.autoliv.com. **Description:** Manufactures a variety of safety products for automobiles including air bags, antiwhiplash seats, child restraints, and leg protection. This location also hires seasonally. **NOTE:** Entry-level positions and second and third shifts are offered. Please visit website to search for jobs and apply online. **Special programs:** Training. **Corporate headquarters location:** Odgen UT. **Other area locations:** Brigham City UT; Promontory UT. **Other U.S. locations:** Auburn Hills MI; Aurora CO; Indianapolis IN; Columbia City IN; Madisonville KY. **International locations:** Worldwide. **Number of employees nationwide:** 8,000.

AXONIX CORPORATION
844 South 200 East, Salt Lake City UT 84111. 801/521-9797. **Toll-free phone:** 800/866-9797. **Contact:** Human Resources. **World Wide Web address:** http://www.axonix.com. **Description:** Manufactures peripherals for laptop computers.

BMC WEST
1350 West 200 South, Lindon UT 84042. 801/785-8787. **Fax:** 801/785-6728. **Contact:** Human Resources. **World Wide Web address:** http://www.bmcwest.com. **Description:** BMC West manufactures wood trusses used in roof construction. **NOTE:** Please visit website to post resume for interest in general employment. **Positions advertised include:** Manager; Sales Personnel; Designer; Production Personnel. **Corporate headquarters location:** Boise ID. **Other area locations:** Ogden UT; Orem UT; Salt Lake City UT. **Other U.S. locations:** West Coast and Midwest.

BANK OF UTAH
2605 Washington Boulevard, Ogden UT 84401. 801/409-5000. **Contact:** Human Resources. **World Wide Web address:** http://www.bankofutah.com. **Description:** Operates a full-service commercial bank with a wide range of traditional banking services including online and telephone banking. **Corporate headquarters location:** This location. **Other area locations:** Statewide.

BANK ONE
80 West Broadway, Suite 200, Salt Lake City UT 84101. 801/481-5350. **Contact:** Human Resources. **World Wide Web address:** http://www.bankone.com. **Description:** A full-service bank and financial institution. Founded in 1868. **NOTE:** Entry-level positions are offered. Please visit website for online application form. **Positions advertised include:** Administrative Assistant; Cash Services Vault Teller; Customer Service Associate. **Special programs:** Training. **Other area locations:** Nationwide. **Other U.S. locations:** Nationwide. **International locations:** Worldwide.

BANTA BOOK GROUP
2600 North Main Street, Spanish Fork UT 84660. 801/798-0800. **Contact:** Deborah Steadman, Personnel Director. **E-mail address:** apply@banta.com. **World Wide Web address:** http://www.banta.com. **Description:** Provides complete software project management including software documentation printing, magnetic disk and CD-ROM replication, electronic document indexing and retrieval software, CD-ROM mastering, software packaging services, complete turnkey literature management, electronic order fulfillment, toll-free phone order services, and customer product inventory management. **NOTE:** Please visit website for online application form. **Positions advertised include:** Saddle Stitcher Operator. **Corporate headquarters location:** Menasha WI. **Other U.S. locations:** Nationwide. **Parent company:** Banta Corporation is a technology and market leader in printing and digital imaging. The corporation serves publishers of educational and general books, special interest magazines, consumer and business catalogs, and direct marketing materials. In addition to printing and digital imaging, Banta Corporation offers multimedia and software packages, interactive media, point-of-purchase materials, and single-use products. Banta operates through the following groups: Banta Book Group; Banta Catalog Group; Banta Digital Group; Banta Direct Marketing Group; Banta Information Services Group; Banta Publications Group; Signs, Displays, Labels & Stamps; and Single-Use Products. **Listed on:** New York Stock Exchange. **Stock exchange symbol:** BN.

C.R. BARD ACCESS SYSTEMS
5425 West Amelia Earhart Drive, Salt Lake City UT 84116. 801/595-0700. **Toll-free phone:** 800/443-5505. **Fax:** 801/595-4947. **Contact:** Human Resources. **E-mail address:** Denver.smith@crbard.com. **World Wide Web address:** http://www.crbard.com. **Description:** Develops, manufactures, and markets medical devices that focus on oncology, urology, and vascular disease. C.R. Bard Access Systems also offers specialty products that focus on hemostasis, hernia repair, and performance irrigation. **NOTE:** Entry-level positions and second and third shifts are offered. **Positions advertised include:** Director of Marketing Developments; Marketing Manager; Manger/Director of International Marketing; Materials Manager; Compliance Specialist. **Special programs:** Internships; Training. **Office hours:** Monday - Friday, 8:00 a.m. - 5:00 p.m. **Corporate headquarters location:** Murray Hill NJ. **Other U.S. locations:** Pittsburgh PA; Lowell MA; Billerica MA; Covington GA; Tempe AZ; Cranston RI. **International locations:** Worldwide. **Operations at this facility include:** Divisional Headquarters. **Stock exchange symbol:** BCR. **Number of employees at this location:** 275.

BARNES & NOBLE
1104 East 2100 South, Salt Lake City UT 84106. 801/463-2610. **Contact:** Human Resources. **World Wide Web address:** http://www.bn.com. **Description:** A bookstore chain operating nationwide. This location has a cafe and music department in addition to its book departments. **Corporate headquarters location:** New York NY. **Listed on:** New York Stock Exchange. **Stock exchange symbol:** BKS.

BD MEDICAL
9450 South State Street, Sandy UT 84070. 801/565-2300. **Toll-free phone:** 888/237-2762. **Fax:** 800/847-2220. **Contact:** Human Resources. **World Wide Web address:** http://www.bd.com. **Description:** Becton Dickinson Vascular Access produces surgical and medical instruments and apparatus. **NOTE:** Please visit website to search for jobs and apply online. **Positions advertised include:** Material Development Manager; Manager of Capability Systems; Senior Process Engineer. **Special programs:** Internships; Co-ops. **Corporate headquarters location:** Franklin Lakes NJ. **Other U.S. locations:** Nationwide. **Parent company:** Becton Dickinson & Company manufactures and sells a broad range of medical supplies, devices, and diagnostic systems for use by health professionals, medical research institutions, and the general public. The infectious disease diagnostics sector focuses on providing accurate and timely diagnostic information. The cellular analysis diagnostics sector focuses on providing the products and systems that enable researchers and clinicians to control, regulate, and analyze cells and cell functions. The drug delivery sector provides products that create a safer health care workplace, enhance therapy, and lower the total cost of patient care. The technique products sector focuses on products that enhance surgical and critical care procedures, improving health care worker safety, and lowering the total cost of medical care. **Operations at this facility include:** This location manufactures a variety of products including peripheral venous access, central venous access, site maintenance, fluid maintenance, and EKG-related equipment.

BEEHIVE MACHINERY INC.
P.O. Box 5002, Sandy UT 84091-5002. 801/561-4211. **Physical address:** 9100 South 500 West, Sandy UT 84070-5002. **Toll-free phone:** 800/621-8438. **Fax:** 801/562-9123. **Contact:** Controller. **World Wide Web address:** http://www.weilerinc.com. **Description:** Engaged in the research, development, engineering, and manufacturing of food-processing machinery. Products are used to process meat, fish, poultry, fruits, and vegetables. **Corporate headquarters location:** Whitewater WI. **Parent company:** Weiler and Company, Inc.

BIG-D CONSTRUCTION CORPORATION
420 East South Temple, Suite 550, Salt Lake City UT 84111. 801/415-6000. **Fax:** 801/415-6900. **Contact:** Human Resources Representative. **E-mail address:** rprice@big-d.com. **World Wide Web address:** http://www.big-d.com. **Description:** A commercial construction firm. Founded in 1967. **Positions advertised include:** Senior Project Manager. **Corporate headquarters location:** This location. **Listed on:** Privately held. **CEO:** Jack Livingood.

BLACK DIAMOND EQUIPMENT LTD.
2084 East 3900 South, Salt Lake City UT 84124. 801/278-5552. **Fax:** 801/ 278-5544. **Contact:** Human Resources. **World Wide Web address:** http://www.bdel.com. **Description:** Manufactures a variety of outdoor recreational equipment including cross-country skiing, mountaineering, rock climbing, and ice climbing gear. **NOTE:** Human Resources phone is 801/278-5552 Ext. 800. **International locations:** Reinach Switzerland.

BLUE SQUIRREL
686 East 8400 South, Sandy UT 84070. 801/352-1551. **Toll-free phone:** 800/ 999-2734. **Fax:** 801/912-6032. **Contact:** Human Resources. **World Wide Web address:** http://www.bluesquirrel.com. **Description:** Develops Internet and content management software including WebWhacker, WebSeeker, ClickBook, Grab-a-Site, TechSeeker, and LegalSeeker. **Parent company:** ForeFront Group, Inc. **Listed on:** NASDAQ. **Stock exchange symbol:** FFGI.

BOART LONGYEAR COMPANY
2640 West 1700 South, Salt Lake City UT 84104. 801/972-6430. **Fax:** 801/977-3374. **Contact:** Director of Human Resources. **World Wide Web address:** http://www.boartlongyear.com. **Description:** Serves the minerals and environmental drilling industries worldwide. The company designs and manufactures a line of core drills, diamond bits, and down-hole tools. Products include the LM and LMP models of long feed hydraulic and multipurpose drills, the induction-hardened Q wireline drill rods, and the "Series" impregnated bits. The company also offers contract drilling services in the fields of mineral exploration, geotechnical investigation, environmental monitoring, and oil and gas exploration. **Positions advertised include:** Driller; Assistant Driller. **Corporate headquarters location:** South Africa. **Other U.S. locations:** Nationwide. **International locations:** Worldwide. **Number of employees worldwide:** 6,700.

THE BOEING COMPANY
1215 North 2200 West, Salt Lake City UT 84116. 801/537-6400. **Contact:** Human Resources. **E-mail address:** employmentoperations@boeing.com. **World Wide Web address:** http://www.boeing.com. **Description:** Boeing is a major manufacturer of high-technology aerospace products including military and commercial aircraft, space systems, and missiles. **NOTE:** Please visit website to apply online. **Corporate headquarters location:** Chicago IL. **Other U.S. locations:** Nationwide. **Operations at this facility include:** This location manufactures fuselages for a variety of aircraft.

BOISE CASCADE OFFICE PRODUCTS CORPORATION
2675 South 900 West, Salt Lake City UT 84119. 801/972-5142. **Toll-free phone:** 800/472-6473. **Fax:** 801/972-5142. **Contact:** Human Resources. **World Wide Web address:** http://www.officemaxsolutions.com. **Description:** Boise Cascade Office Products Corporation is a producer and distributor of pulp and paper, a direct distributor of office products, and a manufacturer and distributor of building products. The company has more than 90 manufacturing and distribution locations in 27 states. Boise Cascade Office Products Corporation's paper is used for commercial printing and publishing, forms, envelopes, reprographics, tablets, and packaging. Overnight delivery and direct-mail has made the company one of the largest distributors of its kind in the United States. Boise Cascade Office Products Corporation provides customers with direct delivery of virtually any office product including office and computer supplies and xerographic paper. Boise Cascade Corporation produces engineered wood products such as laminated veneer lumber and wood I-joists. Founded in 1957. **NOTE:** Please visit website for online application form. **Office hours:** Monday – Friday, 8:00 a.m. – 5:00 p.m. **Corporate headquarters location:** Boise ID. **Other U.S. locations:** Nationwide. **Operations at this facility include:** This location is an office products distribution center. **Listed on:** New York Stock Exchange. **Stock exchange symbol:** BCC.

BONNEVILLE COMMUNICATIONS
55 North 300 Westt, Salt Lake City UT 84180. 801/237-2600. **Toll-free phone:** 888/8-BONCOM. **Fax:** 801/237-2614. **Contact:** Human Resources. **E-mail address:** bonneville@bonneville.com. **World Wide Web address:** http://www.boneville.com. **Description:** An advertising agency specializing in public service announcements and direct response. **Corporate headquarters location:** This location.

BONNEVILLE INTERNATIONAL CORPORATION
55 North 300 West, Salt Lake City UT 84110-1160. 801/575-7663. **Contact:** Employee Relations. **World Wide Web address:** http://www.bonnint. com. **Description:** Operates a television station, 15 radio stations, a full-service advertising agency, a video production house, a nationwide special service radio network, a news bureau in Washington DC, a signatory and corporate sales company, and a satellite transmission company. Bonneville International operates broadcast stations in Los Angeles, San Francisco, Salt Lake City, Chicago, and Washington DC. Founded in 1964. **NOTE:** Entry-level positions and part-time jobs are offered. **Corporate headquarters location:** This location. **Subsidiaries include:** Bonneville Communications (Salt Lake City UT) is an advertising agency that specializes in public service announcements and direct response; The Bonneville Media Group; Bonneville Worldwide Entertainment provides 24-hour programming for members of The Church of Jesus Christ of Latter-Day Saints; The Bonneville Satellite Company provides uplinking and downlinking services, primarily for The Church of Jesus Christ of Latter-Day Saints.

BOURNS INC.
693 West 1700 South, Logan UT 84321-1900. 435/750-7394. **Fax:** 435/753-5709. **Contact:** Human Resources Department. **World Wide Web address:** http://www.bourns.com. **Description:** Manufactures network resistor products. **Corporate headquarters location:** Riverside CA. **Other U.S. locations:** Barrington IL. **International locations:** Worldwide. **Listed on:** Privately held. **CEO:** Gordon Bourns. **Number of employees at this location:** 55.

BRIGHAM YOUNG UNIVERSITY
Provo UT 84602. 801/422-3563. **Contact:** Assistant Vice President of Human Resources. **E-mail address:** staff_employment@byu.edu; hrs@byu.edu. **World Wide Web address:** http://www.byu.edu. **Description:** A private, coeducational university with approximately 32,000 students enrolled. **NOTE:** For faculty positions, please visit website to download BYU employment application online. For other positions, please visit website to register and apply online. Administrative and staff applications are kept on file for one year; those for full-time employees are kept on file for three years. **Positions advertised include:** Academic Advisor; University Photography Manager; Service Engineer; Donor Liaison; Bookstore Cashier; Faculty – Various Departments; Police Officer; Reserve Patrol Officer; On Call Dispatcher; Radiology Technician; Traffic Clerk; **Special programs:** Internships.

BROADCAST INTERNATIONAL
7050 Union Park Center, #600, Salt Lake City UT 84047. 801/562-2252. **Toll-free phone:** 800/722-0400. **Fax:** 801/562-1773. **Contact:** Human Resources. **World Wide Web address:** http://www.brin.com. **Description:** Provides satellite networking and teleconferencing services. **CEO:** Rod Tiede.

BROWNING COMPANY
One Browning Place, Morgan UT 84050. 801/876-2711. **Toll-free phone:** 800/333-3288. **Fax:** 801/876-3331. **Contact:** Human Resources. **E-mail address:** hr2002@browning.com. **World Wide Web address:** http://www.browning.com. **Description:** Manufactures sporting goods, rifles, shotguns, boots, safes, and archery products. **Office hours:** Monday – Friday, 8:00 a.m. – 4:30 p.m. **Corporate headquarters location:** This location. **Other area locations:** Springville UT. **Other U.S. locations:** Arnold MO; Springfield MO; Tucson AZ; Morgantown NC.

BRYCE CANYON LODGE
Bryce Canyon National Park, UT 84717. 435/834-5361. **Fax:** 435/834-5464. **Contact:** Human Resources. **E-mail address:** jobs-bryce@xanterra.com. **Description:** A resort affiliated with one of Utah's National Parks. **NOTE:** Please visit website for online application form. Hiring begins in December and continues throughout the season. **Positions advertised include:** Accounting Clerk; Night Auditor; Kitchen Utility; Cook; Food & Beverage Server; Busser; Hostess/Host; Bartender; Storekeeper; Guest Room Attendant; Laundry Attendant; Night Security Personnel; Dorm Procter; Retail Sales Associate; Camper Store Clerk; Retail Terminal Operator; Management Positions. **Corporate headquarters location:** Aurora CO. **Parent company:** Xanterra Parks and Resorts.

BRYCE CANYON NATIONAL PARK
P.O. Box 170001, Bryce Canyon UT 84717-0001. 435/834-5322. **Contact:** Human Resources. **World Wide Web address:** http://www.nps.gov/brca. **Description:** A National Park. **NOTE:** Please visit http://www.usajobs.opm.gov. to see job listings.

BURDETT APPAREL
3550 South West Temple, Salt Lake City UT 84115. 801/262-6163. **Contact:** Human Resources. **Description:** A contract manufacturer of children's and unisex sportswear.

BURLINGTON COAT FACTORY
340 East University Parkway, Orem UT 84058-7602. 801/224-1700. **Contact:** Human Resources. **E-mail address:** employment. Opportunities@coat.com. **World Wide Web address:** http://www.coat.com. **Description:** An apparel discount store. All-name-brand apparel lines include coats, sportswear, children's wear, men's wear, juvenile furniture, linens, shoes, and accessories. **NOTE:** Please contact your local store to learn about immediate employment opportunities. You may also contact corporate headquarters through mail or email to learn about positions nationwide. Corporate headquarters address is 1830 Route 130, Burlington NJ 08016. Contact Human Resources. **Positions advertised include:** Store Manager; Merchandising Assistant Store Manager; Operations Manager; Department Sales Manager; Customer Service Manager; Customer Service Supervisor; Receiving Supervisor; Sales Associate; Cashier; Computer Operator; Accounting Room Auditor; Loss Prevention Personnel; Fitting Room Sales Associate; Maintenance Personnel. **Corporate headquarters location:** Burlington NJ. **Other area locations:** Murray UT. **Other U.S. locations:** Nationwide.

BURRELLE'S INFORMATION SERVICES
1687 West 820 North, Provo UT 84601. 801/374-6920. **Contact:** Human Resources. **World Wide Web address:** http://www.burrellesluce.com. **Description:** Provides press clippings. **Corporate headquarters location:** Livingston NJ.

CH2M HILL
215 South State Street, Suite, 1000 Salt Lake City UT 84111. 801/350-5200. **Contact:** Human Resources. **E-mail address:** hr@ch2m.com. **World Wide Web address:** http://www.ch2m.com. **Description:** A group of employee-owned companies operating under the names CH2M Hill, Inc., Industrial Design Corporation, Operations Management International, CH2M Hill International, and CH2M Hill Engineering. The company provides planning, engineering design, and operation and construction management services to help clients apply technology, safeguard the environment, and develop infrastructure. The professional staff includes specialists in environmental engineering and waste management, water management, transportation, industrial facilities, and a broad spectrum of infrastructure systems. Founded in 1946. **Corporate headquarters location:** Englewood CO.

CABLES TO GO OEM
2351 South 2300 West, Salt Lake City UT 84119. 801/872-6242. **Fax:** 801/977-3888. **Contact:** Human Resources Department. **E-mail address:** oem@cablestogo-oem.com. **World Wide Web address:** http://www.cablestogo-oem.com. **Description:** Manufactures cable assemblies for the electronics industry. **Corporate headquarters location:** Dayton OH. **International locations:** Taiwan; China.

CALLISTER, NEBEKER & McCULLOUGH
10 East South Temple, Suite 900, Salt Lake City UT 84133. 801/530-7300. **Fax:** 801/364-9127. **Contact:** Human Resources Department. **World Wide Web address:** http://www.cnmlaw.com. **Description:** A law firm with a wide range of practice areas excluding criminal law. **NOTE:** Please visit website to fill out recruiting form.

CAMPBELL SCIENTIFIC
815 West 1800 North, Logan UT 84321-1784. 435/753-2342. **Fax:** 435/750-9540. **Contact:** Human Resources. **E-mail address:** info@campbellsci.com. **World Wide Web address:** http://www.campbellsci.com. **Description:** Manufactures data acquisition systems, which are used in weather stations. **NOTE:** Please visit website to download application form. **Positions advertised include:** Software Support Applications Engineer; Water Resources Applications Engineer. **Corporate headquarters location:** This location. **Other U.S. locations:** Nationwide. **International locations:** Worldwide.

CARR PRINTING COMPANY
P.O. Box 888, Bountiful UT 84011-0888. 801/295-2321. **Physical address:** 580 West 100 North, Bountiful UT. **Fax:** 801/295-5489. **Contact:** Human Resources. **World Wide Web address:** http://www.carrprinting.com. **Description:** Engaged in commercial printing including election-related materials, yearbooks, and phone directories for the North and South Davis counties.

CASELLE, INC.
P.O. Box 100, Spanish Fork UT 84660-0100. 801/798-9851. **Physical address:** 1570 North Main Street, Spanish Fork UT. **Toll-free phone:** 800/228-9851. **Contact:** Merril D. Frost, Human Resources Manager. **E-mail address:** jobs@caselle.com. **World Wide Web address:** http://www.caselle.com. **Description:** Develops specialized accounting software for use by local government offices.

CENTAUR PRINT PARTNERS
5600 North University Avenue, Provo UT 84604. 801/225-2299. **Toll-free phone:** 800/752-4083. **Contact:** Human Resources. **World Wide Web address:** http://www.centaurprint.com. **Description:** A book printer and bookbinding firm with complete prepress facilities including typesetting, paste-up, camera, color/black & white presses, and multicolor presses. Community Press also offers a complete hardcover bookbinding line with cover making, embossing, stamping, and other services. **Corporate headquarters location:** This location. **CEO:** Brent Penrod.

CENTRAL UTAH ENTERPRISES
1170 South 350 East, Provo UT 84606. 801/375-0414. **Fax:** 801/374-8086. **Contact:** Human Resources. **Description:** Provides job skill training for jobseekers with disabilities.

CEPHALON, INC.
4745 Wiley Post Way, Salt Lake City UT 84116. 801/595-1405. **Fax:** 801/595-1406. **Contact:** Recruitment Manager. **World Wide Web address:** http://www.cephalon.com. **Description:** Develops, manufactures, and markets pharmaceutical products for the treatment of neurological disorders, sleep disorders, and cancer. Founded in 1987. **NOTE:** Please you're your resume to the corporate office location, at 145 Brandywine Parkway, West Chester PA 19380. You may also fax to 610/738-6312. Make sure to list the position code on your resume or cover letter. Your resume will be kept on file for six months. **Positions advertised include:** Analytical Chemist; Biochemist; Biostatic Specialist; Clinical Operations Specialist; Commercial Operations Specialist; Development Manufacturer; Human Resources Personnel; Information Technology Specialist; Medical Personnel; Sales and Marketing Specialist. **Corporate headquarters location:** West Chester PA. **International locations:** Germany; France. **Listed on:** NASDAQ. **Stock exchange symbol:** CEPH.

CERAMATEC, INC.
2425 South 900 West, Salt Lake City UT 84119. 801/972-2455. **Fax:** 801/972-1925. **Contact:** Human Resources. **E-mail address:** hr@ ceramatec.com. **World Wide Web address:** http://www.ceramatec.com. **Description:** Manufactures ceramic parts for analyzer equipment in the medical field. **NOTE:** Please visit website to print application form.

CHICAGO, BRIDGE, & IRON (CB&I)
P.O. Box 1447, Provo UT 84603. 801/373-8150. **Physical address:** 550 East 700 South, Provo UT 84601. **Fax:** 801/373-1147. **Contact:** Human Resources. **World Wide Web address:** http://www.chicago-bridge.com. **Description:** A large Dutch engineering and construction company. Founded 1889. **Corporate headquarters**

location: The Netherlands. **Listed on:** New York Stock Exchange. **Stock exchange symbol:** CBI. **Number of employees worldwide:** 8,000.

CHROMALOX
2150 North Rulon White Boulevard, Ogden UT 84404. 801/782-3030. **Contact:** Human Resources. **World Wide Web address:** http://www.chromalox.com. **Description:** Manufactures industrial heating equipment including parts for water heaters. **Corporate headquarters location:** Pittsburg PA. **Other area locations:** Morgan UT. **Other U.S. locations:** Nationwide. **International locations:** Worldwide.

CIMETRIX, INC.
6979 South High Tech Drive, Midvale UT 84047. 801/256-6500. **Toll-free phone:** 800/344-7292. **Fax:** 801/256-6510. **Contact:** Director of Human Resources. **World Wide Web address:** http://www.cimetrix.com. **Description:** Builds open architecture software for SMT equipment, robots, and assembly cells. Founded in 1989. **Office hours:** Monday - Friday, 8:00 a.m. - 5:30 p.m. **Corporate headquarters location:** This location. **CEO:** Robert H. Reback.

CIRQUE CORPORATION
2463 South 3850 West, Suite A, Salt Lake City UT 84120. 801/467-1100. **Toll-free phone:** 800/454-3375. **Fax:** 801/467-0208. **Contact:** Human Resources. **World Wide Web address:** http://www.glidepoint.com. **Description:** Manufactures the "glide point" computer apparatus that can be used instead of a mouse. **NOTE:** Please visit website for online application form.

CIS CORPORATION
857 West South Jordan Parkway, Suite 200, South Jordan UT 84095. 801/302-8930. **Fax:** 801/302-8934. **Contact:** Human Resources. **E-mail address:** webcontact@cis.com. **World Wide Web address:** http://www.cis.com. **Description:** Provides technical business services to companies.

CITI COMMERCE SOLUTIONS
2195 University Park Boulevard, Layton UT 84041. 801/779-7002. **Contact:** Employment Manager. **World Wide Web address:** http://www.careers.citicards.com. **Description:** Provides private-label credit programs and operational outsourcing services. **NOTE:** Please visit website to register, search for jobs, and apply online. **Positions advertised include:** Human Resources Manager.

CLEAR ONE COMMUNICATIONS CORPORATION
1825 Research Way, Salt Lake City UT 84119. 801/975-7200. **Toll-free phone:** 800/945-7730. **Fax:** 801/977-0087. **Contact:** Human Resources. **E-mail address:** hr@clearone.com. **World Wide Web address:** http://www.clearone.com. **Description:** Develops, markets, and distributes audio conferencing products and services for use in the broadcast and teleconferencing markets. Clear One Communications also manufactures listening products that provide amplification at places such as sporting events, museums, and tour buses for those who are hearing impaired. **Positions advertised include:** Administrative Assistant; Direct Sales Channel Manager; Conferencing Sales Director; Wireless RF Engineer; Audio DSP Firmware Engineer; Drafter; Electrical Hardware Engineer; Call Center Agent – Part time; Project Manager; New Account Sales Representative; Technical Repairer. **Corporate headquarters location:** This location. **Other U.S. locations:** Golden Valley MN. **International locations:** Germany; United Kingdom; Canada. **Listed on:** Pink Sheets. **Stock exchange symbol:** CLRO.

COCA-COLA BOTTLING COMPANY OF OGDEN
2860 Pennsylvania Avenue, Ogden UT 84401. 801/627-1310. **Contact:** Human Resources. **World Wide Wed Address:** http://www.coca-cola.com. **Description:** A bottling plant for Coca-Cola, one of the world's largest soft drink producers. Brand names include Coca-Cola, Diet Coke, Coca-Cola Light (international), Sprite, Diet Sprite, Mr. PiBB, Mello Yello, Fanta, TAB, Fresca, Fruitopia, PowerAde, and Minute Maid. **Parent company:** The Coca-Cola Company owns 100 supporting brands around the world including PowerAde, Aquarius, Hi-C, Georgia (canned coffee, sold in Japan), Thums Up & Limca (India), Sparletta Brands (South Africa), Nestea (distributed by Coca-Cola Enterprises Inc.), and Seiryusabo (Japan).

COLDWELL BANKER PREMIER REALTY
2180 South 1300 East, Suite 140, Salt Lake City UT 84106. 801/486-3175. **Toll-free phone:** 800/720-3826. **Fax:** 801/485-4468. **Contact:** Human Resources. **E-mail address:** craig.lelis.utahhomes.com. **World Wide Web address:** http://www.coldwellbanker.com; http://www.utahhomes.com. **Description:** A real estate firm specializing in residential properties. **Other area locations:** Statewide. **Other U.S. locations:** Nationwide. **Number of employees worldwide:** 80,000.

COLDWELL BANKER RESIDENTIAL BROKERAGE
4699 Harrison Boulevard, Suite 200, Ogden UT 84403. 801/479-9300. **Fax:** 801/479-0127. **Contact:** Linda Pearson, Human Resources. **E-mail address:** linda.pearson@utahhomes.com. **World Wide Web address:** http://www.utahhomes.com. **Description:** One of the largest Utah-based real estate companies with over 400 full-time agents and 11 offices located along the Wasatch range. **Other area locations:** Statewide. **Parent company:** Coldwell Banker. **Listed on:** New York Stock Exchange. **Stock exchange symbol:** CD. **Number of employees worldwide:** 112,000.

COLDWELL BANKER
1346 South Legend Hills Drive, Layton UT 84040. 801/774-1500. **Contact:** Human Resources. **World Wide Web address:** http://www.utahhomes.com. **Description:** A real estate agency. **Parent company:** Coldwell Banker.

COLLISION SAFETY ENGINEERING
150 South Mountainway Drive, Orem UT 84058. 801/229-6200. **Fax:** 801/229-6203. **Contact:** Personnel. **E-mail address:** mail@cselc.com. **World Wide Web address:** http://www.collisionsafety.com. **Description:** Performs automobile accident reconstruction and automobile safety research.

COMPEQ INTERNATIONAL CORPORATION
620 North John Glenn Road, Salt Lake City UT 84116. 801/990-2000. **Fax:** 801/924-0319. **Contact:** Human Resources. **E-mail address:** michliu@compeq.com.tw. **World Wide Web address:** http://www.compeq.com. **Description:** Manufactures printed circuit boards. **NOTE:** Entry-level positions are offered. **Corporate headquarters location:** Taiwan. **Other U.S. locations:** Chandler AZ; Fremont CA. **International locations:** China. **CEO:** W.C. Chang. **Number of employees at this location:** 413. **Number of employees worldwide:** 5,249.

COMPUTER ASSOCIATES
11778 South Election Drive, Suite 100, Draper UT 84020. 801/619-7500. **Contact:** Human Resources. **World Wide Web address:** http://ca.com. **Description:** A leading international provider of computer services for businesses. **NOTE:** Please mail your resume to corporate headquarters at One Computer Associates Plaza, Islandia NY 11749; phone is 800/454-3788. Or visit website for online application form – online application is preferred. **Corporate headquarters location:** New York NY. **Other U.S. locations:** Nationwide. **International locations:** Worldwide. **Listed on:** New York Stock Exchange. **Stock exchange symbol:** CA.

CONDIE'S FOODS
4850 South 5300 West, Salt Lake City UT 84118. 801/969-1448. **Contact:** Personnel. **Description:** Sells salad ingredients and other food products to restaurants.

CONNECT PUBLIC RELATIONS
80 East 100 North, Provo UT 84606. 801/373-7888. **Fax:** 801/373-8680. **Contact:** Janeen Bullock, Human Resources. **E-mail address:** janeenb@connectpr.com. **World Wide Web address:** http://www.connectpr.com. **Description:** A public relations and marketing firm with clients in the computer networking field. Founded in 1990. **Special programs:** Internships. **Corporate headquarters location:** This location. **Other U.S. locations:** San Francisco CA. **Listed on:** Privately held.

CONNECTING EDGE, INC.
P.O. Box 95551, Salt Lake City UT 84095-0551. 801/446-4243. **Fax:** 801/446-4244. **Contact:** Personnel. **E-mail address:** info@connecting-edge.com. **World Wide Web address:** http://www.connecting-edge.com. **Description:** Designs and manufactures data communications equipment including multiprotocol switches and fiber-optic networking equipment.

CONVERGYS
1400 West 4400 South, Ogden UT 84405. 801/629-6423. **Toll-free phone:** 800/543-6423. **Contact:** Human Resources. **World Wide Web address:** http://www.convergys.com. **Description:** Provides integrated marketing services. Telephone marketing services include consumer inbound and outbound telephone sales, catalog order processing, dealer locator information, and fulfillment; customized consumer telephone sales, service, database maintenance, and fulfillment; business-to-business sales and marketing; and market research including focus groups, computerized telephone surveys, and quantitative and qualitative services. Convergys also assists international clients in executing marketing strategies in European marketplaces. The company handles 375,000 outbound calls and 480,000 inbound calls per day, and has over 3,600 workstations. Founded in 1976. **Other area locations:** Statewide. **Other U.S. locations:** Nationwide. **International locations:** Worldwide. **Parent company:** Cincinnati Bell.

CONVERGYS
2460 West Highway 56, Suite 1, Cedar City UT 84720. 435/867-3000. **Contact:** Human Resources. **World Wide Web address:** http://www.convergys.com. **Description:** Provides integrated marketing services. Telephone marketing services include consumer inbound and outbound telephone sales, catalog order processing, dealer locator information, and fulfillment; customized consumer telephone sales, service, database maintenance, and fulfillment; business-to-business sales and marketing; and market research, including focus groups, computerized telephone surveys, and quantitative and qualitative services. Convergys also assists international clients in executing marketing strategies in European marketplaces. The company handles 375,000 outbound calls and 480,000 inbound calls per day, and has over 3,600 workstations. Founded in 1976. **Other area locations:** Statewide. **Other U.S. locations:** Nationwide. **International locations:** Worldwide.

COTTONWOOD MILL
12757 South Minute Man Drive, Draper UT 84020. 801/572-6550. **Contact:** Human Resources. **E-mail address:** cottonwood@utah-inter.net. **World Wide Web address:** http://www.cottonwoodcabinets.com. **Description:** Manufactures kitchen and bathroom cabinets and drawers.

DHI COMPUTING SERVICE, INC.
P.O. Box 51427, Provo UT 84605-1427. 801/373-8518. **Physical address:** 1525 West 820 North, Provo UT 84601. **Toll-free phone:** 800/453-9400. **Fax:** 801/374-5316. **Contact:** Human Resources. **World Wide Web address:** http://www.dhiprovo.com. **Description:** Develops business software and installs hardware that is used mainly by dairies.

DMJM
220 East Morris Avenue, Suite 300, Salt Lake City UT 84115. 801/484-9884. **Contact:** Human Resources. **Description:** Provides a full range of architectural and engineering services. **World Wide Web address:** http://www.dmjm.com. **Description:** An architecture design firm. **NOTE:** Resumes for engineering positions should be addressed to Ed Patience. Resumes regarding architectural positions should be sent to Ralph Stanislaw. **Special programs:** Internships. **Corporate headquarters location:** Los Angeles CA. **Other U.S. locations:** Nationwide. **International locations:** Saudi Arabia. **Operations at this facility include:** Divisional Headquarters; Service.

THE DAILY HERALD
P.O. Box 717, Provo UT 84603-0717. 801/373-5050. **Physical address:** 1555 North Freedom Boulevard, Provo UT 84604. **Toll-free phone:** 800/880-8075. **Contact:** Office Manager. **World Wide Web address:** http://www.heraldextra.com. **Description:** A daily newspaper with 36,000 subscribers.

DAIRY FARMERS OF AMERICA
1140 South 3200 West, Salt Lake City UT 84104. 801/977-3000. **Contact:** Human Resources. **World Wide Web address:** http://www.dfamilk.com. **Description:** Produces milk and other dairy products. **Corporate headquarter location:** Kansas City MO. **Other U.S. locations:** Nationwide.

DAVIS, COUNTY OF
P.O. Box 618, Farmington UT 84025-0618. 801/451-3415. **Physical address:** 28 East State Street, Farmington UT 84025. **Recorded jobline:** 801/451-3484. **Contact:** Human Resources. **World Wide Web address:** http://www.daviscountyutah.gov/default.cfm. **Description:** Provides a diversified range of countywide services, as well as certain municipal services. Countywide services include tax assessing and collection, auditing, budgeting, surveying, recording, marriage licenses, passports, and elections; health services, such as health promotion, nursing clinics, well-child exams and immunizations, environmental health, and vehicle inspection programs; human service programs including Council on Aging, public safety services such as emergency dispatch, paramedic, ambulance, emergency services, and corrections; and functions such as Antelope Island Visitors Center, public works, flood control, animal control, libraries, golf courses, tourism, economic development, planning and zoning, agricultural extension services, county fair activities, and county support services. Davis County has 220,000 citizens. **NOTE:** Please visit website to download the Davis County Employment Application. You must submit this application in order to be considered for employment. **Positions advertised include:** Community Health Nurse; Golf Course Grounds Worker; Deputy Sheriff;

Paramedic; Dispatcher; Driver; FairPark Concession Aide; I/M Technician; Office Specialist; Correctional Officer; Custodian. **Office hours:** Monday – Friday, 8:00 a.m. – 5:00 p.m. **Corporate headquarters location:** This location. **Operations at this facility include:** Administration.

DAVIS BEHAVIORAL HEALTH
P.O. Box 689, Farmington UT 84025. 801/447-8887. **Physical address:** 117 West 200 South, Farmington UT. **Fax:** 801/451-6331. **Contact:** Personnel Director. **Description:** Provides mental health and alcohol and drug services for adults and children. Services include inpatient, outpatient, residential, prevention, day treatment, 24-hour emergency response, evaluation, and therapeutic foster care. **NOTE:** Entry-level positions are offered. **Positions advertised include:** Counselor; Licensed Practical Nurse; Physician; Psychologist; Registered Nurse; Secretary; Social Worker. **Other area locations:** Layton UT; Bountiful UT.

DAVIS COUNTY SCHOOL DISTRICT
45 East State Street, Farmington UT 84025. 801/402-5261. **Fax:** 801/444-5354. **Contact:** Human Resources. **World Wide Web address:** http://www.davis.k12.ut.us. **Description:** Operates the public schools in Davis County. **NOTE:** Entry-level positions are offered. **Positions advertised include:** Custodian – Part-time; Transition Assistant; Educational Interpreter; Certified Occupational Therapy Assistant. **Special programs:** Internships; Training. **Corporate headquarters location:** This location. **Other area locations:** Salt Lake City; Ogden.

DELOITTE & TOUCHE
50 South Main Street, Suite 1800, Salt Lake City UT 84144-0458. 801/328-4706. **Fax:** 801/355-7515. **Contact:** Personnel. **E-mail address:** dtcareers@deloitte.com. **World Wide Web address:** http://www. us.deloitte.com. **Description:** An international firm of certified public accountants providing professional accounting, auditing, tax, and management consulting services to widely diversified clients. **Positions advertised include:** Audit Senior. **Special programs:** Internships. **Corporate headquarters location:** New York NY. **Other U.S. locations:** Nationwide. **International locations:** Worldwide. **Number of employees worldwide:** 120,000.

DEER VALLEY LODGING
P.O. Box 3000 Park City UT 84060. 435/649-4040. **Physical address:** 1375 Deer Valley Drive South, Park City UT. **Toll-free phone:** 800/782-4813. **Fax:** 435/655-4816. **Contact:** Human Resources. **E-mail address:** hrdept@deervalleylodging.com. **World Wide Web address:** http://www.deervalleylodging.com. **Description:** Rents condominium-style accommodations to visitors to the Deer Valley area. **NOTE:** Please visit website for online application form. **Positions advertised include:** Accounting Clerk; Housekeeping Director.

DENTRIX DENTAL SYSTEMS
727 East Utah Valley Drive, Suite 500, American Fork UT 84003. 801/763-9300. **Toll-free phone:** 800/DENTRIX. **Fax:** 801/763-9336. **Contact:** Human Resources. **World Wide Web address:** http://www.dentrix.com. **Description:** Develops clinical and practice management software for dentists. Founded 1989. **NOTE:** No phone calls regarding employment. Please visit website for online application form. Online applications are preferred. **Positions advertised include:** Technical Support Personnel; Trade Show Coordinator; Software Engineer Medical Personnel; Software Architect Medical Personnel; Area Sales Manager – Chicago; Inside Sales Representative; Order Processor. **Corporate headquarters location:** This location.

DESERET BOOK COMPANY
P.O. Box 30178, Salt Lake City UT 84130. 801/534-1515. **Physical address:** 40 East South Temple, Salt Lake City UT 84130. **Contact:** Andrea Barker, Human Resources. **E-mail address:** hrdept@deseretbook.com. **World Wide Web address:** http://deseretbook.com. **Description:** Deseret Book Company is a wholesaler, retailer, and publisher of books. The company publishes primarily church-oriented books as well as some self-help and children's books. **NOTE:** Please visit website for online application form. **Positions advertised include:** Purchasing Agent; Inventory Manager. **Office hours:** Monday – Friday, 8:00 a.m. – 5:00 p.m. **Other area locations:** Statewide. **Other U.S. locations:** ID; NV; AZ; CA; OR; CO; NM; WA. **Operations at this facility include:** This location is both a retail location and a publishing facility.

DESERET LABORATORIES
1414 East 3850 South, St. George UT 84790. 435/628-8786. **Toll-free phone:** 800/632-2993. **Fax:** 435/673-1202. **Contact:** Human Resources. **E-mail address:** hrmgr@deseretlabs.com. **World Wide Web address:** http://www.deseretlabs.com. **Description:** Manufactures vitamins and botanicals and conducts research and development pertaining to its product line. **Positions advertised include:** Granulators; Mechanic; Warehouse Specialist.

DESERET MUTUAL BENEFIT ADMINISTRATORS
P.O. Box 45530, Salt Lake City UT 84145-0530. 801/578-5600. **Toll-free phone:** 800/777-3622. **Fax:** 801/578-5910. **Contact:** Human Resources. **World Wide Web address:** http://www.dmba.com. **Description:** Provides life, medical, dental, and disability insurance as well as retirement and savings plans. **NOTE:** Human Resources phone is 801/78-5640. **Positions advertised include:** Case Management Nurse. **Office hours:** Monday, Tuesday, Thursday, Friday, 8:00 a.m. – 5:00 p.m.; Wednesday, 9:00 a.m. – 5:00 p.m.

DESERET NEWS
P.O. Box 1257, Salt Lake City UT 84110. 801/237-2137. **Physical address:** 30 East 100 South, Salt Lake City UT 84111. **Fax:** 801/237-2121. **Contact:** Personnel Director. **World Wide Web address:** http://www.deseretnews.com. **Description:** Publishes a locally-owned, daily newspaper with a circulation of more than 70,000. Advertising, production, and circulation activities are carried out jointly with competitor *Salt Lake Tribune* through Newspaper Agency Corporation (Salt Lake City UT). **NOTE:** This location does not have an editorial division. **Office hours:** Monday – Friday, 8:00 a.m. – 5:00 p.m. **Corporate headquarters location:** This location. **Listed on:** Privately held.

DIGISPEC
115 South State Street, Linden UT 84042. 801/785-5000. **Toll-free phone:** 800/755-8218. **Fax:** 801/785-0339. **Contact:** Human Resources. **World Wide Web address:** http://www.datapad.com. **Description:** Manufactures custom mouse pads. Founded 1984.

DIRECT MORTGAGE CORPORATION
6995 South Union Park Center, Suite 380, Midvale UT 84047. 801/924-2300. **Fax:** 801/924-2394. **Contact:** Human Resources. **E-mail address:** Employment@DirectMortgageWholesale.com. **World Wide Web address:** http://www.directmortgagewholesale.com. **Description:** A wholesale mortgage company. **NOTE:** Search and apply for positions online. **Positions advertised include:** Account Executive; Broker Coordinator; Underwriting. **Other area locations:** Midvale UT. **Other U.S. locations:** Sacramento CA.

DISCOVER CARD SERVICES
8475 South Sandy Parkway, Sandy UT 84070. 801/542-5440. **Contact:** Human Resources. **World Wide Web address:** http://www.discover card.com. **Description:** Provides customer service for Discover credit card holders and also engages in payment collection. **NOTE:** Please visit website for online application form. **Corporate headquarters location:** Riverwoods IL. **Other area locations:** Salt Lake City UT. **Other U.S. locations:** Nationwide. **International locations:** United Kingdom. **Number of employees nationwide:** 18,000.

DORR-OLIVER EIMCO
P.O. Box 300, Salt Lake City UT 84110-0300. 801/526-2000. 2403. **Physical address:** 669 West 200 South, Salt Lake City UT 84101. **Fax:** 801/526-2005. **Contact:** Human Resources. **World Wide Web address:** http://www.glv.com. **Description:** Produces a broad line of machinery and equipment used for liquid/solid separation in various process industries and for municipal and industrial waste treatment. **Corporate headquarters location:** Orillia, Ontario Canada. **Other U.S. locations:** Nationwide. **International locations:** Worldwide. **Parent company:** GL&V Canada Inc. **Operations at this facility include:** Administration; Divisional Headquarters; Manufacturing; Research and Development; Sales; Service.

DUKE ENERGY
305 West North Temple, Salt Lake City UT 84180. 801/531-4400. **Contact:** General Manager. **World Wide Web address:** http://www.dukeenergy.com. **Description:** Principally involved in natural gas pipeline operations. The company owns and operates an interstate natural gas transmission system that consists of more than 4,300 miles of pipeline. **NOTE:** Please contact corporate headquarters regarding employment opportunities. Their phone is 713/627-5400. **Corporate headquarters location:** Houston TX. **Parent company:** Panhandle Eastern Corporation.

DYNIX
400 West Dynix Drive, Provo UT 84604. 801/223-5200. **Toll-free phone:** 800/288-8020. **Fax:** 801/223-5202. **Recorded jobline:** 801/223-5627; or 800/288-8020 Ext. 5627. **Contact:** Manager of Employment. **World Wide Web address:** http://www.dynix.com. **Description:** Installs automated computer networks at libraries. **NOTE:** Please visit website for online application form. **Positions advertised include:** Product Manager; Purchasing Agent; Senior Quality Assurance Engineer; Senior Software Engineer; Systems Analyst. **Other U.S. locations:** Evanston IL. **International locations:** Worldwide.

EFI ELECTRONICS CORPORATION
1751 South 4800 West, Salt Lake City UT 84104. 801/977-9009. **Toll-free phone:** 800/877-1174. **Fax:** 801/977-3474. **Contact:** Human Resources. **E-mail address:** kspencer@efinet.com. **World Wide Web address:** http://www.efinet.com. **Description:** Manufactures and markets TVSS (transient voltage surge suppression) products. The company's TVSS products protect electronic equipment from electrical disturbances such as lightning, grid switching, and electrical accidents, which can lead to hardware failure, data communication disruptions, equipment damage, and/or down time. **NOTE:** Please email resume, or stop by the offices to pick up an application. **Corporate headquarters location:** This location. **Other U.S. locations:** DE. **International locations:** Spain; Singapore;

EASTON TECHNICAL PRODUCTS
5040 Harold Gatty Drive, Salt Lake City UT 84116. 801/539-1400. **Contact:** Human Resources. **World Wide Web address:** http://www.eastonarchery.com. **Description:** Manufactures aluminum sports equipment. **Operations at this facility include:** This location manufactures archery arrows and tent tubing.

EDO CORPORATION
2645 South 300 West, Salt Lake City UT 84115. 801/486-7481. **Contact:** Human Resources. **E-mail address:** hr@edoceramic.com. **World Wide Web address:** http://www.edocorp.com. **Description:** EDO Corporation designs and manufactures advanced electronic and specialized equipment for military, general aviation, marine, and industrial markets. Principal products include sonar equipment, mine countermeasure systems, and aircraft stores suspension and ejection mechanisms; flight instruments and automatic flight control systems for general aviation aircraft; piezoelectric ceramic components for acoustic and video scanning systems; and fiber-reinforced composite components for the aviation industry. The company conducts extensive research and development and operates in three business segments: Military Systems; Aviation Products; and Marine Systems and Specialized Products. **Corporate headquarters location:** New York NY. **Other U.S. locations:** Nationwide. **Operations at this facility include:** This location is a manufacturing facility for the company's Marine Systems and Specialized Products segment. **Number of employees nationwide:** 2,800.

EDO FIBER SCIENCE
506 North Billy Mitchell Road, Salt Lake City UT 84116. 801/537-1800. **Contact:** Human Resources. **E-mail address:** kjaussi@edoceramic.com. **World Wide Web address:** http://www.edocorp. com. **Description:** Manufactures composite structural products in support of several industries including aviation/commercial aircraft, aerospace, and marine. **Corporate headquarters location:** New York NY. **Other U.S. locations:** Nationwide. **Operations at this facility include:** Administration; Divisional Headquarters; Manufacturing; Research and Development; Sales; Service. **Number of employees nationwide:** 2,800.

C.R. ENGLAND & SONS, INC.
P.O. Box 27728, Salt Lake City UT 84127-0728. 801/972-2712. **Physical address:** 4701 West 2100 South, Salt Lake City UT 84120. **Toll-free phone:** 800/356-5046. **Contact:** Human Resources. **E-mail address:** For Driver positions – debbier@crengland.com; For Staff positions – carriejo@crengland.com. **World Wide Web address:** http://www.crengland.com. **Description:** A long-haul trucking company. **NOTE:** For Driver positions, please visit website for application form. **Positions advertised include:** Driver. **Corporate headquarters location:** This location. **President:** Eugene England. **CEO:** Daniel England.

EQUITABLE LIFE & CASUALTY INSURANCE COMPANY
P.O. Box 2460, Salt Lake City UT 84110. 801/579-3400. **Physical address:** 5 Triad Center, Suite 200, Salt Lake City UT 84180-1200. **Toll-free phone:** 888/352-5120. **Contact:** Director of Human Resources. **World Wide Web address:** http://www.equilife.com. **Description:** Provides health, medical, and life insurance policies. **Corporate headquarters location:** This location.

ERNST & YOUNG LLP
60 East South Temple, Suite 800, Salt Lake City UT 84111-1036. 801/350-3300. **Fax:** 801/350-3456. **Contact:** Human Resources. **World Wide Web address:** http://www.ey.com. **Description:** A certified public accounting firm that also provides

management consulting services. Services include data processing, financial modeling, financial feasibility studies, production planning and inventory management, management sciences, health care planning, human resources, cost accounting, and budgeting systems. **NOTE:** Please visit website for online application form. **Positions advertised include:** Tax Compliance Manager; Tax Consulting Specialist; Tax Consulting Senior. **Special programs:** Internships. **Corporate headquarters location:** New York NY. **Other U.S. locations:** Nationwide. **International locations:** Worldwide.

ESIGNAL
3 Triad Center, Suite 100, Salt Lake City UT 84180. 801/532-3400. **Fax:** 801/532-3202. **Contact:** Human Resources. **World Wide Web address:** http://www.esignal.com. **Description:** Provides data-on-command to the financial information marketplace. **Corporate Headquarters location:** Hayward CA. **Parent company:** Interactive Data Corporation. **Listed on:** New York Stock Exchange. **Stock exchange symbol:** IDC.

EVANS & SUTHERLAND COMPUTER CORPORATION
600 Komas Drive, Salt Lake City UT 84108. 801/588-1000. **Fax:** 801/588-4500. **Contact:** Human Resources. **E-mail address:** staffing@es.com. **World Wide Web address:** http://www.es.com. **Description:** Designs, manufactures, sells, and services special purpose 3-D computer graphics hardware and software. The products are developed to help people solve complicated problems and to help train people to perform complex tasks. Uses of this equipment include visual simulation systems for pilot training and engineering workstations for molecular modeling or engineering design. The majority of Evans & Sutherland's customers are in the aerospace and defense-related markets. Founded in 1968. **NOTE:** Human Resources phone is 801/588-1603. **Corporate headquarters location:** This location. **Other U.S. locations:** Orlando FL. **International locations:** England; Germany; China; United Arab Emirates. **Operations at this facility include:** Administration; Manufacturing; Research and Development; Sales; Service. **President/CEO:** James R. Oyler. **Listed on:** NASDAQ. **Stock exchange symbol:** ESCC.

FMC JETWAY SYSTEMS
3100 Pennsylvania Avenue, Ogden UT 84401. 801/627-6600. **Fax:** 801/629-3474. **Contact:** Human Resources. **World Wide Web address:** http://www.jetway.com. **Description:** Manufactures passenger boarding bridges for airplanes. **Number of employees nationwide:** 8,500.

FAIRCHILD SEMICONDUCTOR CORPORATION
3333 West 9000 South, West Jordan UT 84088. 801/562-7000. **Contact:** Human Resources. **World Wide Web address:** http://www.fairchildsemi.com. **Description:** Manufactures semiconductors for use in telecommunications, personal computing, and digital video applications. **Corporate headquarters location:** South Portland ME. **Other U.S. locations:** Irving TX. **International locations:** China; England; Japan; Korea.

FEATURE FILMS FOR FAMILIES
5286 Commerce Drive, Suite A-116, Salt Lake City UT 84107. 801/263-9205. **Contact:** Recruiting. **World Wide Web address:** http://www.familytv.com. **Description:** A G-rated video production and distribution company. The company has produced more than 10 family movies. **NOTE:** Second and third shifts are available. **Special programs:** Training. **Other area locations:** Roy UT; Price UT; Logan UT; Orem UT; Murray UT. **Other U.S. locations:** Marshalltown IA; Evanston WY.

FETZER'S, INC.
1436 South West Temple, Salt Lake City UT 84115. 801/484-6103. **Fax:** 801/484-6122. **Contact:** Human Resources. **E-mail address:** fetzers@fetzersinc.com. **World Wide Web address:** http://www.fetzersinc.com. **Description:** Designs and manufactures custom store fixtures and commercial furniture. **NOTE:** No phone calls regarding employment. You may apply in person Tuesday through Friday, from 1:00 p.m. to 4:30 p.m. Please visit website for online application form.

FIELDCREST CABINETS INC.
Building D6, Freeport Center, Clearfield UT 84016. 801/773-9663. **Contact:** Human Resources. **World Wide Web address:** http://www.fieldcrest.net. **Description:** Fieldcrest Corporation manufactures wooden cabinets. **Other area locations:** Sandy UT.

FIFE ROCK PRODUCTS COMPANY INC.
P.O. Box 479, Brigham City UT 84302. 435/723-3478. **Physical address:** 620 East 500 South, Brigham City UT 84302. **Contact:** General Manager. **Description:** Produces ready-mix concrete and other construction products. **Corporate headquarters location:** This location.

FIRST HEALTH
2650 South Decker Lake Lane, P.O. Box 30089, Salt Lake City UT 84119. 801/974-6550. **Contact:** Human Resources. **World Wide Web address:** http://www.firsthealth.com. **Description:** One of the nation's largest independent health care cost management companies. From a nationwide network of sales, administration, and utilization review offices, FIRST HEALTH offers integrated health care cost management services to the private, self-funded, and government markets. **NOTE:** Please visit website for online application form. **Corporate headquarters location:** Downers Grove IL. **Subsidiaries include:** FIRST HEALTH Strategies offers a full range of integrated health care management services including outsourcing, claims administration, data analysis, provider networks, disability management, health care management, and prescription drug management. FIRST HEALTH Services serves as a Medicaid fiscal agent, a pharmacy program administrator, and as a managed care contractor. Viable Information Processing Systems offers a full range of software products and services in all arenas of the health care information industry. Genex Services is a medical cost containment services company whose system helps companies gain substantial savings in worker's compensation, health care, disability, and casualty claims. **Other U.S. locations:** Nationwide. **Listed on:** NASDAQ. **Stock exchange symbol:** FHCC. **President/CEO:** Edward L. Wristen. **Number of employees nationwide:** 5,500.

FLOWSERVE CORPORATION
1350 North Mountain Springs Parkway, Springville UT 84663. 801/489-8611. **Recorded jobline:** 801/489-2220. **Contact:** Ryan Murray, Human Resources. **World Wide Web address:** http://www.flowserve.com. **Description:** Manufactures and distributes a full range of automatic control valves. Founded in 1965. **NOTE:** Resumes and applications are only accepted when there are open positions. You may pick up an application in person at the reception area of the offices in Springville. Call Human Resources Contact directly at 801/489-2486. **Office hours:** Monday – Friday, 8:00 a.m. – 5:00 p.m. **Corporate headquarters location:** Irving TX. **Other area locations:** Salt Lake City UT; Murray UT. **Other U.S. locations:** Nationwide. **International locations:** Worldwide. **Parent company:** Duriron Company. **Number of employees worldwide:** 14,000.

FORSGREN ASSOCIATES
370 East 500 South, Suite 200, Salt Lake City UT 84111. 801/364-4785. **Toll-free phone:** 800/826-9304. **Fax:** 801/364-4802. **Contact:** Human Resources. **E-mail address:** ckemp@forsgren.com. **World Wide Web address:** http://www.forsgren.com. **Description:** A civil engineering firm. **Other area locations:** Farmington UT. **Other U.S. locations:** Wenatchee WA; Boise ID; Rexburg ID; Evanston WY; Ouray CO; Sacramento CA.

FORT KNOX SECURITY PRODUCTS
993 North Industrial Park Road, Orem UT 84057. 801/224-7233. **Toll-free phone:** 800/821-5216. **Fax:** 801/226-5493. **Contact:** Human Resources. **World Wide Web address:** http://www.ftknox.com. **Description:** Manufactures home security vaults.

FRAME RATE
10150 Centennial Parkway, Sandy UT 84070. 801/456-3711. **Fax:** 801/382-1110. **Contact:** Human Resources. **E-mail address:** jobs@framerate.com. **World Wide Web address:** http://www.framerate.com. **Description:** Provides businesses and individuals with digital and multimedia services. Founded 1993.

FRANKLIN COVEY
2200 West Parkway Boulevard, Salt Lake City UT 84119. 801/975-1776. **Toll-free phone:** 800/827-1776. **Contact:** Human Resources. **World Wide Web address:** http://www.franklincovey.com. **Description:** Provides training seminars and products designed to improve individual productivity through effective time management. The company also offers other training and consulting services. **International locations:** Worldwide. **Listed on:** New York Stock Exchange. **Stock exchange symbol:** FC. **Number of employees worldwide:** 2,500.

FRESENIUS MEDICAL CARE
475 West 13th Street, Ogden UT 84404. 801/626-4515. **Contact:** Human Resources Manager. **World Wide Web address:** http://www.fmcna.com. **Description:** A pharmaceutical drug manufacturer specializing plastic blood-banking disposables, intravenous devices, and specialty solutions. The company markets these products to both home care patients and medical institutions in the United States and abroad. **Corporate headquarters location:** Lexington MA. **Other U.S. locations:** Nationwide.

GE CAPITAL FINANCIAL
4246 South Riverboat Road, Salt Lake City UT 84123. 801/517-5000. **Contact:** Human Resources. **World Wide Web address:** http://www.ge.com. **Description:** Provides second mortgage and home equity loans as well as corporate credit cards. **NOTE:** Please visit website to search for jobs and apply online. **Positions advertised include:** General Counsel. **Listed on:** New York Stock Exchange. **Stock exchange symbol:** GE. **Number of employees worldwide:** 315,000.

KEN GARFF AUTOMOTIVE GROUP
531 South State Street, Salt Lake City UT 84111. 801/521-6111. **Contact:** Human Resources. **World Wide Web address:** http://www.kengarff.com. **Description:** An automotive dealer group with six locations and 14 automotive product lines. **NOTE:** Entry-level positions are offered. **Special programs:** Apprenticeships; Training. **Corporate headquarters location:** This location.

GART SPORTS
5550 South 900 East, Murray UT 84117. 801/263-3633. **Contact:** Human Resources. **World Wide Web address:** http://www.gartsports.com. **Description:** A retailer of outdoor goods such as athletic wear, hunting gear, fishing gear, and camping gear. **Positions advertised include:** Store Associate – Full-time, Part-time. **Office hours:** Monday – Saturday, 9:00 a.m. – 9:00 p.m.; Sunday 10:00 a.m. – 6:00 p.m. **Corporate headquarters location:** Englewood CO. **Other U.S. locations:** ID; MT; NM; WY.

GAS-N-GO
P.O. Box 1903, Provo UT 84603. 801/375-1412. **Physical address:** 47 East 300 North, Suite B, Provo UT. **Contact:** Human Resources. **Description:** Operates a chain of automotive service stations that includes gas stations, car washes, and oil change stations. **Corporate headquarters location:** This location. **Other area locations:** Magna UT; Orem UT; Wellington UT.

GENERAL DISTRIBUTING COMPANY INC.
5350 Amelia Earhart Drive, Salt Lake City UT 84116-2900. 801/531-7895. **Contact:** Office Manager. **Description:** Engaged in the wholesale distribution of Budweiser. **Corporate headquarters location:** This location.

GLOBAL ACCESSORIES
80 Golf Course Road, Logan UT 84321. 435/752-1000. **Fax:** 435/792-1298. **Contact:** Human Resources. **World Wide Web address:** http://www.global-accessories.com. **Description:** A manufacturer and distributor of automotive aftermarket products including car seat covers and front-end covers. **NOTE:** Entry-level positions are offered. **Corporate headquarters location:** This location.

BILL GOOD MARKETING
12393 Gateway Parkplace, Suite 600, Draper UT 84020. 801/572-1480. **Fax:** 801/572-1496. **Contact:** Human Resources Manager. **World Wide Web address:** http://www.billgood.com. **Description:** Develops and markets software used by stockbrokers. **Corporate headquarters location:** This location. **Listed on:** Privately held. **Number of employees at this location:** 100.

GOSSNER FOODS
1051 North 1000 West, Logan UT 84321-6852. 435/713-6100. **Fax:** 435/713-6200. **Contact:** Human Resources. **World Wide Web address:** http://www.gossner.com. **Description:** Processes and distributes a variety of cheese products. Founded 1966. **Corporate headquarters location:** This location.

GRANITE FURNITURE
1475 West 9000 South, West Jordan UT 84088. 801/566-4444. **Contact:** Human Resources. **World Wide Web address:** http://www.granitefurniture.com. **Description:** Manufactures residential furniture and sells it at retail locations. **NOTE:** Please visit website for online application form. **Other area locations:** Sugar House UT; Layton UT; Oren UT.

GRANITE SCHOOL DISTRICT
340 East 3545 South, Salt Lake City UT 84115-4697. 801/685-5000. **Physical address:** Administration Building, Room 37, 340 East 3545 South. **Contact:** Human Resources. **World Wide Web address:** http://www.granite.k12.ut.us. **Description:** Operates 89 public schools with an enrollment of 76,000 students. **NOTE:** Human Resources phone is 801/685-4511. Fax is 801/685-4204.

HK SYSTEMS
515 East 100 South, Salt Lake City UT 84102. 801/530-4000. **Toll-free phone:** 800/453-3550. **Fax:** 801/530-4476. **Contact:** Human Resources. **World Wide Web address:** http://www.hksystems.com. **Description:** HK Systems designs and manufactures computer-controlled machinery for manufacturing and for various warehousing processes. **Positions advertised include:** Account Executive; Pharmaceutical Industry Account Executive; Director of Sales; Proposal Manager; Maintenance Technician. **Corporate headquarters location:** New Berlin WI. **Operations at this facility include:** This location develops inventory control and management software.

JOHN H. HARLAND COMPANY
4867 Harold Gatty Drive, Salt Lake City UT 84116. 801/537-1040. **Contact:** Human Resources. **World Wide Web address:** http://www.harland.net. **Description:** A financial printing firm. Products include business and personal checks, as well as other forms and documents for the banking industry, and are marketed throughout the United States. Harland is also engaged in direct marketing campaign management and provides financial institutions with database marketing software and loan and deposit origination software. **Corporate headquarters location:** Atlanta GA. **Subsidiaries include:** Harland Printed Products; Harland Financial Solutions; Scantron; Scantron Service Group. **Listed on:** New York Stock Exchange. **Stock exchange symbol:** JH.

HART SCIENTIFIC
799 East Utah Valley Drive, American Fork UT 84003-9775. 801/763-1600. **Toll-free phone:** 800/438-4278. **Fax:** 801/763-1010. **Contact:** Human Resources Manager. **World Wide Web address:** http://www.hartscientific.com. **Description:** Manufactures temperature calibration equipment. **NOTE:** Please visit website to complete an e-mail form that will be sent directly to Human Resources contact. **Corporate headquarters location:** This location. **President:** Chris Juchau.

HEMISPHERE SOFTWARE
2815 East 3300 South, Salt Lake City UT 84109. 801/466-8899. **Toll-free phone:** 800/866-4364. **Fax:** 801/486-1938. **Contact:** Human Resources. **World Wide Web address:** http://www.hemicorp.com. **Description:** Develops accounting software used by contractors.

HERALD JOURNAL
P.O. Box 487, Logan UT 84323-1487. 435/752-2121. **Physical address:** 75 West 300 North, Logan UT. **Toll-free phone:** 888/259-7631. **Fax:** 435/753-6642. **Contact:** Human Resources. **World Wide Web address:** http://hjnews.townnews.com. **Description:** A local newspaper serving the Logan Utah area.

HEWLETT-PACKARD COMPANY
348 East Winchester, Suite 100, Salt Lake City UT 84107. 801/265-6200. **Contact:** Human Resources. **World Wide Web address:** http://www.hp.com. **Description:** Hewlett-Packard designs and manufactures measurement and computation products and systems used in business, engineering, science, health care, and education. Principal products are integrated instrument and computer systems including hardware and software, computer systems and peripheral products, and medical electronic equipment and systems. **NOTE:** Jobseekers are encouraged to apply via the Website: http://www.jobs.hp.com. **Corporate headquarters location:** Palo Alto CA. **Other U.S. locations:** Nationwide. **International locations:** Worldwide. **Operations at this facility include:** This location manufactures advanced computer-aided engineering tools. **Listed on:** New York Stock Exchange. **Stock exchange symbol:** HPQ. **Number of employees worldwide:** 140,000.

HOLME, ROBERTS & OWEN
299 South Main Street, Suite 1800 Salt Lake City UT 84111-2263. 801/521-5800. **Fax:** 801/521-9639. **Contact:** Human Resources. **World Wide Web address:** http://www.hro.com. **Description:** A law firm specializing in corporate and tax law. **NOTE:** Please visit website for online application form, and for details on applying for specific positions. **Positions advertised include:** IP Associate; Legal Opportunities; Staff Opportunities. **Corporate headquarters location:** Denver CO.

HONEYWELL CONSUMER PRODUCTS GROUP
P.O. Box 160437, Building C-13, Clearfield UT 84016-0437. 801/773-1484. **Physical address:** Freeport Center, Clearfield UT. **Contact:** Personnel. **World Wide Web address:** http://www.honeywell.com. **Description:** Honeywell is engaged in the research, development, manufacture, and sale of advanced technology products and services in the fields of chemicals, electronics, automation, and controls. The company's major businesses are home and building automation and control, performance polymers and chemicals, industrial automation and control, space and aviation systems, and defense and marine systems. **NOTE:** Please visit website to search for jobs and apply online. **Positions advertised include:** Customer Advocate. **Special programs:** Internships. **Corporate headquarters location:** Morristown NJ. **Other area locations:** Salt Lake City UT; Lehi UT; West Valley City UT. **Other U.S. locations:** Nationwide. **International locations:** Worldwide. **Operations at this facility include:** This location manufactures filters for automotive and related applications. **Listed on:** New York Stock Exchange. **Stock exchange symbol:** HON.

HOYT USA INC.
543 North Neil Armstrong Road, Salt Lake City UT 84116. 801/363-2990. **Toll-free phone:** 800/522-HOYT. **Fax:** 801/537-1470. **Contact:** Human Resources. **World Wide Web address:** http://www.hoytusa.com. **Description:** A manufacturer of archery equipment and accessories.

HUISH DETERGENT COMPANY
1987 South 3540 West, Salt Lake City UT 84104. 801/975-3100. **Fax:** 801/ 975-3249. **Contact:** Human Resources. **E-mail address:** employment@huish.com. **World Wide Web address:** http://www.huish.com. **Description:** Manufactures laundry detergent, fabric softener, and related products. **NOTE:** Mail resumes to the main office at P.O. Box 25057, Salt Lake City UT 84125. **Corporate headquarters location:** This location.

HUNTSMAN CORPORATION
500 Huntsman Way, Salt Lake City UT 84108. 801/584-5700. **Contact:** Human Resources. **World Wide Web address:** http://www.huntsman.com. **Description:** Manufactures chemicals and plastic products including ethylene, propylene, ethanlolamines, alkylalkanolamines, olefins, and a variety of others. **NOTE:** Please see website for details on Graduate Recruitment. **Corporate headquarters location:** This location. **Other U.S. locations:** TX; IL; LA; MO; FL; NJ; NH. **International locations:** Worldwide.

HURCO INDUSTRIES
P.O. Box 9119, Ogden UT 84409. 801/394-9471. **Physical address:** 200 West 33rd Street, Ogden UT 84401. **Fax:** 801/394-8218. **Contact:** Human Resources. **World Wide Web address:** http://www.hurcoind.com. **Description:** Produces wooden partitions and various fixtures. **Corporate headquarters location:** This location.

I-O CORPORATION
1490 North 2200 West, Suite 100, Salt Lake City UT 84116. 801/973-6767. **Fax:** 801/974-5683. **Contact:** Human Resources. **World Wide Web address:** http://www.iocorp.com. **Description:** Manufactures peripheral equipment for mainframes.

ICI PAINTS
2179 South 300 West, Suite 1, Salt Lake City UT 84115. 801/486-2211. **Contact:** Human Resources. **World Wide Web address:** http://www. icipaints.com. **Description:** Manufactures and distributes a complete range of paints, varnishes, lacquers, rust inhibitors, and similar products. **Corporate headquarters location:** Slough UK. **Other U.S. locations:** Nationwide. **International locations:** Worldwide. **Parent company:** ICI Group. **CEO:** David Hamill. **Number of employees worldwide:** 15,610.

ICON HEALTH & FITNESS, INC.
1500 South 1000 West, Logan UT 84321. 435/750-5000. **Contact:** Human Resources. **World Wide Web address:** http://www.iconfitness.com. **Description:** One of the largest manufacturers of home fitness equipment in the world. Brand names include Image, Jumpking, ProForm, Weilder, NordicTrack, and Weslo products. **Positions advertised include:** Receiving Lead; Fitness Consultant; Administrative Assistant; Electrical/Manufacturing Engineer; Drafter – Entry Level; Mechanical Engineer; Tooling Specialist; Seasonal Batch Picker; Punch Press Operator; PowderCoat Loader; MRB Coordinator; Translator; Coordinator; Saw Operator; Materials Lead; Quality Control Auditor. **Corporate headquarters location:** This location. **Other area locations:** Clearfield UT; Smithfield UT. **Other U.S. locations:** Charleston SC; Colorado Springs CO. **CEO:** Scott Watterson. **Number of employees worldwide:** 4,200.

IDAHO TECHNOLOGY, INC.
390 Wakara Way, Salt Lake City UT 84108. 801/736-6354. **Toll-free phone:** 800/735-6544. **Fax:** 801/588-0507. **Contact:** Human Resources. **E-mail address:** hr@idahotech.com. **World Wide Web address:** http://www.idahotech.com. **Description:** A research and development company for molecular biological equipment. Idaho Technology also manufactures and assembles thermocyclers. **NOTE:** Please visit website for online application form if desired. **Positions advertised include:** Scientist and Research Associate; Laboratory Technologist. **Corporate headquarters location:** This location.

INFINIA AT GRANITE HILLS
950 East 3300 South, Salt Lake City UT 84106. 801/486-5121. **Contact:** Human Resources. **Description:** A religious and non-medical long-term care facility for patients who have suffered traumatic brain injuries. **Other area locations:** Ogden UT; Alta UT.

INSURQUOTE SYSTEMS, INC.
1125 West Center Street, Orem UT 84057. 801/373-7345. **Toll-free phone:** 800/658-8778. **Fax:** 801/377-4152. **Contact:** Personnel. **World Wide Web address:** http://www.insurquote.com. **Description:** Designs software for the insurance industry. **Corporate headquarters location:** This location. **CEO:** Bill Woahn.

INTEL CORPORATION
3740 West 13400 South, Riverton UT 84065. 801/445-8080. **Contact:** Human Resources. **World Wide Web address:** http://www.intel.com. **Description:** Intel is one of the largest semiconductor manufacturers in the world. Other operations include supercomputers; embedded control chips and flash memories; video technology software; multimedia hardware; personal computer enhancement products; and designing, making, and marketing microcomputer components, modules, and systems. Intel sells its products to original equipment manufacturers and other companies that incorporate them into their products. **NOTE:** Please visit website to submit resume electronically. **Corporate headquarters location:** Santa Clara CA. **Other U.S. locations:** Nationwide. **International locations:** Worldwide. **Operations at this facility include:** This location manufactures network hardware for Macintosh and IBM computers. **Listed on:** NASDAQ. **Stock exchange symbol:** INTC. **Number of employees worldwide:** 78,000.

INTERCONTINENTAL HOTELS GROUP
1275 West 2240 South, Salt Lake City UT 84119. 801/975-3000. **Fax:** 801/975-3040. **Contact:** Human Resources. **World Wide Web address:** http://www.sixcontinentshotels.com. **Description:** A reservation center receiving calls from the United States and Canada for the Intercontinental Hotels Group, which includes the Holiday Inn, Staybridge Suites, Crowne Plaza, and Candlewood Suites hotel chains.

IOMEGA CORPORATION
1821 West Iomega Way, Roy UT 84067. 801/332-1000. **Contact:** Human Resources. **World Wide Web address:** http://www.iomega.com. **Description:** Creates information storage solutions that enhance the usefulness of personal computers and workstations in a variety of applications. Iomega's products help people manage their information storage needs. The company's products include Zip drives which are three drives in one, offering expansion for hard drives, mobile storage with portable convenience, and backup information. Founded in 1980. **Positions advertised include:** Magnetic Read/Write Channel Engineer; MR Head Test Engineer; Project Specialist; Firmware Design Engineer; Developer – Data Warehouse and Business Objects. **Corporate headquarters location:** San Diego CA. **Other U.S. locations:** Houston TX. **International locations:** Singapore; Switzerland; Canada. **Listed on:** New York Stock Exchange. **Stock exchange symbol:** IOM. **CEO:** Werner Heid. **Number of employees worldwide:** 590.

JACOBSEN CONSTRUCTION COMPANY, INC.
P.O. Box 27608, Salt Lake City UT 84127-0608. 801/973-0500. **Physical address:** 3131 West 2210 South, Salt Lake City UT 84119. **Fax:** 801/973-7496. **Contact:** Human Resources Department. **E-mail address:** hr-dept@jacobconstruction.com. **World Wide Web address:** http://www.jacobsen-const.com. **Description:** A general contractor involved in large commercial, industrial, manufacturing, public works, and institutional projects. Founded in 1922. **NOTE:** Entry-level positions are offered. Please visit website to download application form. **Special programs:** Apprenticeships; Training; Summer Jobs. **Corporate headquarters location:** This location. **Other U.S. locations:** Jackson WY. **Subsidiaries include:** Jacobsen Construction Services. **Listed on:** Privately held. **President/CEO:** Lonnie M. Bullard. **Number of employees nationwide:** 450.

JONES, WALDO, HOLBROOK & McDONOUGH
170 South Main Street, Suite 1500, Salt Lake City UT 84101-1644. 801/521-3200. **Fax:** 801/328-0537. **Contact:** Kyle V. Leishman, Recruitment Committee Coordinator. **E-mail address:** kleishman@joneswaldo.com. **World Wide Web address:** http://www.joneswaldo.com. **Description:** A law firm specializing in corporate law, litigation, and real estate law. **NOTE:** Please visit website for information on who to contact for more specific employment information. **Corporate headquarters location:** This location. **Other area locations:** St. George UT.

JORDAN SCHOOL DISTRICT
9361 South 300 East, Sandy UT 84070. 801/567-8100. **Fax:** 801/567-8030. **Contact:** Human Resources. **World Wide Web address:** http://www.jordan.k12.ut.us. **Description:** Operates the public schools in southern Salt Lake County, servicing more than 73,000 students. **NOTE:** When applying for a general position, please be sure to include a resume, cover letter, application form (available on the website, or in he Human Resource Department), and a typing test (which should be certified by Job Services). When applying for a Licensed Position, be sure to include an application, a transcript of credit showing the degree you have attained and where you received it from, a copy of your placement file, and a copy of your Utah Teaching license. **Positions advertised include:** Speech-Language Pathologist – Full-time and Part-time; Campus Monitor. **Office hours:** Monday – Friday, 8:00 a.m. – 5:00 p.m.

JOY MINING MACHINERY
P.O. Box 89, Wellington UT 84542. 435/637-6161. **Physical address:** 1275 West Ridge Road, Wellington UT. **Fax:** 435/637-8942. **Contact:** Human Resources. **E-mail address:** contactjoy@joy.com. **World Wide Web address:** http://www.joy.com. **Description:** One of the world's most prominent manufacturers of capital equipment for coal mining, oil and gas wells, air pollution control, air compression, ore processing, minerals and metals mining, and various other industries. Products are manufactured in more than 30 plants and are distributed worldwide. **Corporate headquarters location:** Warrendale PA. **Other area locations:** Price UT. **Other U.S. locations:** Nationwide. **International locations:** Worldwide. **Number of employees worldwide:** 4,500.

KPMG
15 West South Temple, Suite 1500, Salt Lake City UT 84101. 801/333-8000. **Contact:** Human Resources Director. **World Wide Web address:** http://www.us.kpmg.com. **Description:** KPMG delivers a wide range of value-added assurance, tax, and consulting services. **Corporate headquarters location:** Montvale NJ. **Other U.S. locations:** Nationwide. **International location:** Worldwide. **Parent company:** KPMG International has more than 100,000 employees worldwide including 6,500 partners and 60,000 professional staff, serving clients in 844 cities in 155 countries. KPMG International is a leader among professional services firms engaged in capturing, managing, assessing, and delivering information to create knowledge that will help its clients maximize shareholder value. **CEO:** Eugene D. O'Kelly.

KSL BROADCAST HOUSE
KSL Broadcast House, 55 North 300 West, Salt Lake City UT 84180. 801/ 575-5555. **Fax:** 801/575-5820. **Recorded jobline:** 801/575-5780. **Contact:** Human Resources. **E-mail address:** kslhr@ksl.com. **World Wide Web address:** http://www.ksl.com. **Description:** Operates an AM radio station and a NBC-affiliated television station (Channel 5). **NOTE:** Please visit website to download application form. **Positions advertised include:** *TV* – On-Call News Graphic Artist; On-Call Production Operator/Assistant (Temporary); Studio Technician – Part-time; On-going Account Executive; On-Call Video Editor; News Reporter; On-Call Associate Producer; On-Call Desk Assistant. *Radio* – News Anchor/ Reporter/ Producer/Editor; Control Room Operator – Part-time; On-Call Radio News Anchor/Reporter/Producer/Editor; Overnight Control/Feed Room Operator – Part-time. **Special programs:** Internships.

KTVX TELEVISION
ABC 4/KTVX, 2175 West 1700 South, Salt Lake City UT 84104. 801/975-4444. **Contact:** Human Resources. **World Wide Web address:** http://www. 4utah.com. **Description:** Operates Channel 4, an ABC-affiliated television station. **NOTE:** Please visit website for specific contacts for open positions. No phone calls regarding employment. **Positions advertised include:** Character Generator Operator – Part-time; PM Character Generator Operator – Full-time; Satellite Truck Operator/Photographer; Photographer; Producer.

KUTV
CHANNEL 2
299 South Main Street Suite 150, Salt Lake City UT 84111. 801/973-3000. **Fax:** 801/973-3349. **Contact:** Ronda K. Porter, Human Resources. **World Wide Web address:** http://www.kutv.com. **Description:** A television broadcasting station owned and operated by CBS. **NOTE:** Direct contact phone is 801/973-3462. **Positions advertised include:** General Assignment Reporter; Utah County Reporter; TV Studio Tech/Master Control Operator; Accountant; Investigative Producer; News Producer. **Special programs:** Internships. **Corporate headquarters location:** New York NY. **Parent company:** Westinghouse Electric.

KENCRAFT, INC.
119 East 200 North, Alpine UT. 801/756-6916. **Toll-free phone:** 800/377-4368. **Contact:** Human Resources. **World Wide Web address:** http://www.kencraftcandy.com. **Description:** A confectioner that manufactures hand-decorated lollipops and candy sticks under their own label.

KENNECOTT UTAH COPPER CORPORATION
P.O. Box 6001, Magna UT 84044-6001. 801/252-3000. **Physical address:** 8315 West 3595 South, Magna UT 84044. **Fax:** 801/569-6045. **Recorded jobline:** 801/252-3036. **Contact:** Human Resources. **E-mail address:** info@kennecott.com. **World Wide Web address:** http://www. kennecott.com. **Description:** A mining and processing company with primary products that include copper, precious metals, and molybdenum. **NOTE:** If you are unable to reach an office location, you may register over the phone, at 801/468-0053. **Positions advertised include:** Operations Supervisor; Maintenance Supervisor; Technical Superintendent. **Office hours:** Monday - Friday, 8:00 a.m. - 4:30 p.m. **Corporate headquarters location:** This location. **Parent company:** Rio Tinto (London, England). **Listed on:** Privately held. **CEO:** Bill Champion.

KIMBERLY-CLARK HEALTHCARE
12050 Lone Peak Parkway, Draper UT 84020. 801/572-6800. **Fax:** 801/572-6999. **Contact:** Human Resources. **World Wide Web address:** http://www.kchealthcare.com. **Description:** Manufactures a wide variety of medical products used in intensive care units, emergency rooms, gastrointestinal and radiology procedure rooms, main operating rooms, burn units, and outpatient/satellite surgical centers. **NOTE:** Please visit corporate website to submit resume. **Special programs:** Internships; Co-ops. **Corporate headquarters location:** Roswell GA. **Parent company:** Kimberly-Clark. **Listed on:** New York Stock Exchange. **Stock exchange symbol:** KMB.

KIMBERLY-CLARK CORPORATION
2010 North Rulon White Boulevard, Ogden UT 84404. 801/782-2500. **Contact:** Human Resources. **World Wide Web address:** http://www.kimberly-clark.com. **Description:** Kimberly-Clark Corporation manufactures and markets products for personal, business, and industrial uses throughout the world. The name brands of Kimberly-Clark Corporation also include Kleenex facial and bathroom tissue, Pull-Ups training pants, Kotex and New Freedom feminine care products, Depends and Poise incontinence care products, Hi-Dri household towels, Kimguard sterile wrap, Kimwipes industrial wipers, and Classic business and correspondence papers. Most of the company's products are made from natural and synthetic fibers using advanced technologies in absorbency, fibers, and nonwovens. Kimberly-Clark Corporation has extensive overseas operations in Europe and Asia. **NOTE:** Please visit website to submit resume electronically. Resumes and applications are kept on file for two years. Jobseekers should register with the Work Force Services, 480 27th Street, Ogden UT 84404. Applications sent to the plant location will not be accepted. **Office hours:** Monday – Friday 7:30 a.m. – 4:00 p.m. **Corporate headquarters location:** Neenah WI. **International locations:** Worldwide. **Operations at this facility include:** This location manufactures Huggies diapers. **Listed on:** New York Stock Exchange. **Stock exchange symbol:** KMB.

KIRTON McCONKIE
60 East South Temple, Suite 1800, Salt Lake City UT 84111. 801/328-3600. **Fax:** 801/321-4893. **Contact:** Hiring Partner. **World Wide Web address:** http://www.kmclaw.com. **Description:** A law firm that specializes in corporate law and litigation.

KITCO
1625 North 1100 West, Springville UT 84663. 801/489-2000. **Fax:** 801/489-2199. **Contact:** Human Resources. **E-mail address:** jobs@wencor.com. **World Wide Web address:** http://www.kitcoinc.com. **Description:** Manufactures and assembles aircraft systems repair kits and modification kits for military aircraft owned by the U.S. government and some foreign governments. **NOTE:** Please visit website to download application form. Mail application and resume to P.O. Box 514, Springville UT 84663. **Positions advertised include:** Accountant; Product Research Supervisor; Product Research Specialist; Wencor PMA Product Line Manager; Product Line Manager; Inside Sales Representative; Machining Operations Manager. **Corporate headquarters location:** This location. **Other U.S. locations:** Atlanta GA; Miami FL; Bensenville IL. **International locations:** Amsterdam, Netherlands.

KLUNE INDUSTRIES
1800 North 300 West, Spanish Fork UT 84660. 801/798-7401. **Fax:** 801/798-1006. **Contact:** Human Resources. **World Wide Web address:** http://www.klune.com. **Description:** A manufacturing and engineering company that specializes in laser cutting and welding, sheet metal forming, and assembly of products for aerospace companies. **NOTE:** Please visit website for online application form. **Other U.S. locations:** North Hollywood CA.

KOMATSU EQUIPMENT COMPANY
P.O. Box 26737, Salt Lake City UT 84026. 801/972-3660. **Physical address:** 2350 West 1500 South, Salt Lake City UT 84104. **Toll-free phone:** 888/325-5582. **Fax:** 801/975-1354. **Contact:** Christine Hale, Human Resources Manager. **World Wide Web address:** http://www.komatsueq.com. **Description:** Sells and services heavy equipment and parts. **Company slogan:** Quality and reliability. **Office hours:** Monday - Friday, 8:00 a.m. - 5:00 p.m. **Corporate headquarters location:** This location. **Other U.S. locations:** Elico NV; Las Vegas NV; Sparks NV; Gillette WY. **Parent company:** KomatsuAmerica. **Number of employees nationwide:** 180.

LDS HOSPITAL
8th Avenue and C Street, Salt Lake City UT 84143-0001. 801/480-1091. **Contact:** Human Resources. **World Wide Web address:** http://www.ihc.com/ldsh. **Description:** A hospital with 520 beds and various units including a women's health center, cardiac unit, and organ transplant unit. **NOTE:** Applications and resumes are only accepted online. **Positions advertised include:** Food Service Worker; LPN; Medical Technologist/MLT; Patient Service Representative; Imaging Clerk; RN – Various Departments; Medical Director – IHC Community and School Clinics; HR Consultant; Nurse Practitioner; Ultrasonographer; Lead Medical Student; Occupational Therapist Assistant; Echocardiographer; Nurse Educator. **Parent company:** Intermountain Health Care.

L-3 COMMUNICATION SYSTEMS WEST
640 North 2200 West, Salt Lake City UT 84116. 801/594-2000. **Fax:** 801/594-3572. **Contact:** Human Resources. **World Wide Web address:** http://www.l-3com.com/csw. **Description:** Provides communications systems for high-performance intelligence collection, imagery processing, and satellite communications for Department of Defense (DoD) and other government agencies. The company provides high-data rate, wideband, secure, real-time communications systems for surveillance, reconnaissance and other airborne intelligence collection systems. **Positions advertised include:** Antenna Assembler Specialist; Applications Developer; Assembler Specialist; Engineering Technician; Financial Analyst; Financial Analyst; HR Recruiter, Technical; Sr. IT Telecommunications Analyst.

LA-Z-BOY CHAIR COMPANY
P.O. Box 280, 350 West 1000 North, Tremonton UT 84337. 435/257-5282. **Fax:** 435/257-6004. **Contact:** Thom Smith, Human Resources Manager. **World Wide Web address:** http://www.la-z-boy.com. **Description:** Manufactures upholstered seating and one of the nation's largest overall manufacturers of residential furniture. La-Z-Boy is best known for its upholstered recliners. La-Z-Boy operates 24 plants in the United States and Canada, with its products being sold through over 10,000 retail locations. The company operates in five divisions. La-Z-Boy Residential manufactures stationary chairs, sofas and love seats, recliners, reclining sofas, sleeper sofas, and modular seating groups. La-Z-Boy Canada manufactures residential seating and markets La-Z-Boy residential products in Canada. Hammary manufactures tables, living room cabinets, wall entertainment units, and upholstered furniture, as well as CompaTables. Kincaid makes solid-wood bedroom and dining room furniture. La-Z-Boy Contract Furniture Group includes La-Z-Boy Business Furniture, La-Z-Boy Healthcare Furniture (hospital chairs, recliners, and special mobile recliners marketed through contract dealers and medical sales companies), and La-Z-Boy Hospitality Furniture (specially engineered La-Z-Boy recliners that are sold directly to major hotel and motel chains and through hospitality sales companies. **NOTE:** Contact Human Resources Manager directly at 435/257-9308. **Corporate headquarters location:** Monroe MI.

LABEL EXPRESS
1305 South 630 East, American Fork UT 84003. 801/642-3500. **Fax:** 801/642-3510. **Contact:** Human Resources. **E-mail address:** info@ labelexp.com. **World Wide Web address:** http://www.labelexp.com. **Description:** Prints flexographic labels used on a broad range of products.

LABORATORY CORPORATION OF AMERICA (LABCORP)
5199 South Green Street, Murray UT 84123. 801/288-9000. **Toll-free phone:** 800/444-4522. **Contact:** Human Resources. **World Wide Web address:** http://www.labcorp.com. **Description:** One of the nation's leading clinical laboratory companies, providing services primarily to physicians, hospitals, clinics, nursing homes, and other clinical labs nationwide. LabCorp performs tests on blood, urine, and other body fluids and tissue, aiding the diagnosis of disease. **Positions advertised include:** Laboratory Assistant; Laboratory Services Team Leader; Medical Technologist; Microbiology Department; Microbiology Senior Medical Technologist. **Corporate headquarters location:** Burlington NC. **Other U.S. locations:** Nationwide. **Listed on:** New York Stock Exchange. **Stock exchange symbol:** LH. **Number of employees nationwide:** 23,000.

LAKEVIEW HOSPITAL
630 East Medical Drive, Bountiful UT 84010. 801/299-2200. **Fax:** 801/299-2198. **Recorded jobline:** 801/299-2563. **Contact:** Human Resources. **World Wide Web address:** http://www.lakeviewhospital.com. **Description:** A hospital with services that include cardiac rehabilitation, trauma, Alzheimer's assessment, and oncology. **NOTE:** Human Resources phone is 801/299-2566. Please visit website for details on contacts for specific positions. Volunteer positions are also available. **Positions advertised include:** RN – Various Departments; Director – Surgical Services; Pharmacist; Occupational Therapist; Physical Therapist; Respiratory Therapist. **Office hours:** 8:30 a.m. – 4:30 p.m. **Corporate headquarters location:** Nashville TN. **Parent company:** Columbia/HCA.

LARSON DAVIS, INC.
1681 West 820 North, Provo UT 84601. 801/375-0177. **Toll-free phone:** 888/258-3222. **Fax:** 801/375-0182. **Contact:** Human Resources. **World Wide Web address:** http://www.larsondavis.com. **Description:** Develops, manufactures, and markets precision measuring instrumentation and accompanying computer hardware and software technology. The company sells its measurement instruments to private industry and governmental agencies for both industrial and military applications.

LAYTON CONSTRUCTION
8911 South Sandy Parkway, Sandy UT 84070. 801/568-9090. **Fax:** 801/563-3695. **Contact:** Human Resources. **E-mail address:** hr@laytoncompanies.com. **World Wide Web address:** http://www. layton-const.com. **Description:** Engaged in industrial and commercial construction. **NOTE:** Please visit website to download application form. Resumes are only accepted when accompanies by the application form. **Positions advertised include:** Senior Construction Manager; Project Administrator/Project Assistant; Superintendent.

LEGATO SYSTEMS, INC.
71 South 1380 West, Lindon UT 84042. 801/922-9101. **Fax:** 801/223-0199. **Contact:** Human Resources. **World Wide Web address:** http://www.legato.com. **Description:** Produces storage management software that allows data to be moved, managed, and protected. **NOTE:** Please visit website to register, search for jobs, and apply online. **Corporate headquarters location:** Mountain View CA. **Other U.S. locations:** Nationwide. **International locations:** Worldwide. **Parent company:** EMC Corporation. **Listed on:** New York Stock Exchange. **Stock exchange symbol:** EMC.

LEGGETT & PLATT
2695 West Highway 56, Cedar City UT 84720. 435/586-9948. **Fax:** 435/586-0242. **Contact:** Human Resources. **World Wide Web address:** http://www.goer.com. **Description:** Manufactures a wide variety of store fixtures including display cases. **Corporate headquarters location:** Carthage MO. **Other U.S. locations:** Nationwide. **Listed on:** New York Stock Exchange. **Stock exchange symbol:** LEG. **CEO:** Felix E. Wright.

THE LENDING COMPANY
7084 South 2300 East, Suite 200, Salt Lake City UT 84124. 801/944-4422. **Toll-free phone:** 888/472-9500. **Fax:** 801/942-9225. **Contact:** Personnel. **Description:** A mortgage lending institution.

LEVOLOR HOME FASHIONS
1330 West 3300 South, Ogden UT 84401. 801/627-2450. **Contact:** Human Resources. **World Wide Web address:** http://www.levolor.com. **Description:** Produces a line of nationally-advertised specialty draperies and drapery hardware. **Corporate headquarters location:** Hoboken NJ. **Parent company:** Newell Operating Company.

LEXISNEXIS
2222 South 950 East, Provo UT 84606. 801/354-8000. **Toll-free phone:** 800/500-3627. **Contact:** Human Resources Department. **World Wide Web address:** http://www.lexisnexis.com. **Description:** Develops document assembly software. **NOTE:** Jobseekers are encouraged to apply via the Website: http://www.lexisnexis.com/employment. **Positions advertised include:** Template Editor. **Corporate headquarters location:** Dayton OH. **Other U.S. locations:** Nationwide. **International locations:** Worldwide. **Parent company:** Reed Elsevier. **Number of employees worldwide:** 12,000.

LIBERTY SAFE
999 West Utah Avenue, Payson UT 84651. 801/925-1000. **Toll-free phone:** 800/247-5625. **Fax:** 801/465-2712. **Contact:** Human Resources. **World Wide Web address:** http://www.libertysafe.com. **Description:** Manufactures safes for use in residential homes. **Corporate headquarters location:** This location.

LIFETIME PRODUCTS
P.O. Box 160010, Freeport Center, Building D-11, Clearfield UT 84016-0010. 801/776-1532. **Fax:** 801/776-4397. **Contact:** Human Resources Department. **E-mail address:** employment@lifetime.com. **World Wide Web address:** http://www.lifetime.com. **Description:** Manufactures basketball stands and hoops, picnic tables, and ping-pong tables.

LOOMIS, FARGO & CO.
563 West 500 South, Suite 340, Bountiful UT 84010. 801/397-8507. **Fax:** 801/397-8155. **E-mail address:** loomisfargo@loomisfargo.com. **World Wide Web address:** http://www.loomisfargo.com. **Description:** Provides security escorts, armored transportation, and protection services. **Positions advertised include:** Driver/Guard; Branch Manager; Customer Service Representative; Transportation Supervisor. **Corporate headquarters location:** Houston TX. **Other area locations:** Salt Lake City UT; Saint George UT. **Other U.S. locations:** Nationwide. **Parent company:** Securitas AB.

MACLEAN QUALITY COMPOSITES
3392 West 8600 South, West Jordan UT 84088. 801/565-8003. **Fax:** 801/565-8225. **Contact:** Human Resources. **E-mail address:** info@ macqc.com. **World Wide Web address:** http://www.macqc.com. **Description:** Manufactures composite tubing used in a variety of products including bicycle components and windsurfing masts. **Corporate headquarters location:** This location. **Other U.S. locations:** Vista CA. **International locations:** Hangzhou China.

MALNOVE INC.
P.O. Box 160128, Clearfield UT 84016-0128. 801/773-7400. **Physical address:** Freeport Center, Building A-16F, Clearfield UT. **Fax:** 801/774-8441. **Contact:** Human Resources. **World Wide Web address:** http://www.malnove.com. **Description:** A packaging company that manufactures cardboard boxes. **Other U.S. locations:** Jacksonville FL; Omaha NE.

MANAGEMENT & TRAINING CORPORATION
500 North Marketplace Drive, P.O. Box 10, Centerville UT 84014. 801/693-2600. **Fax:** 801/693-2900. **Contact:** Human Resources. **World Wide Web address:** http://www.mtctrains.com. **Description:** As a government contractor, Management & Training Corporation manages the operation of Job Corps centers nationwide; manages the operations of low- to minimum-security correctional facilities; and provides building maintenance services. **Special programs:** Internships; Training. **Corporate headquarters location:** This location. **Other area locations:** Clearfield UT. **Other U.S. locations:** Nationwide. **International locations:** Ontario Canada; Queensland Australia. **Listed on:** Privately held.

MARCH OF DIMES BIRTH DEFECTS FOUNDATION
515 East 4500 South, Suite G-200, Salt Lake City UT 84107. 801/293-3300. **Toll-free phone:** 877/881-9255. **Fax:** 801/293-3387. **Contact:** Human Resources. **E-mail address:** UT469@marchofdimes.com. **World Wide Web address:** http://www.marchofdimesutah.org; http://www.modimes.org. **Description:** An organization dedicated to preventing birth defects and infant mortality through the Campaign for Healthier Babies, which includes programs of research, community services, education, and advocacy. March of Dimes chapters across the country work with their communities to determine and meet the needs of women, children, and families. Through specially designed programs, women are provided access to prenatal care. **Corporate headquarters location:** White Plain NY.

MARKER USA
P.O. Box 680520, Park City UT 84068. 435-940-0006. **Physical address:** 890 Main Street, Suite 5101, Park Cit UT 84060. **Fax:** 435/940-1116. **Contact:** Human Resources. **World Wide Web address:** http://www.markerusa.com. **Description:** Distributes German-made ski equipment and apparel. **NOTE:** Entry-level positions and part-time jobs are offered. **Corporate headquarters location:** This location. **Other U.S. locations:** West Lebanon NH.

MAS COMPUTERS
1005 North State Street, Orem UT 84057. 801/226-1892. **Fax:** 801/226-2129. **Contact:** Human Resources. **World Wide Web address:** http://www.mascomputersonline.com. **Description:** Resells new and used computers, computer components, and software. **President:** Tim Bird.

McKAY-DEE HOSPITAL CENTER
4401 Harrison Boulevard, Ogden UT 84403. 801/627-2800. **Contact:** Human Resources. **World Wide Web address:** http://www.ihc.com/xp/ihc/mckaydee. **Description:** A private, nonprofit, full-service, 415-bed, community hospital owned and administered by Intermountain Health Care, Inc. McKay-Dee's services include The Heart Institute, Women and Children's Services, Northern Utah's high-risk birthing center; prenatal testing and treatment facilities; an around-the-clock trauma team; the Community Health Information Center, offering information on health issues to men, women, children, and seniors; and a chemical dependency treatment program. **NOTE:** Please visit website to search for jobs and to apply online. Human Resources phone is 801/387-7700. **Positions advertised include:** Ultrasonographer; Central Processing Technician; RN – Various Departments; Food Service Worker/Dishwasher; Cook; Cashier; Dietary Technician; Licensed Counselor; Pharmacist. **Special programs:** Internships. **Parent company:** Intermountain Health Care – IHC.

McLEOD USA
1401 North Highway 89, Farmington UT 84025. 801/451-0248. **Contact:** Human Resources. **World Wide Web address:** http://www.mcleodusa.com. **Description:** Provides long-distance service for businesses and residences. **NOTE:** Please visit website to search for jobs and apply online. **Corporate headquarters location:** Cedar Rapids IA. **Other U.S. locations:** Nationwide. **Listed on:** NASDAQ. **Stock exchange symbol:** MCLD. **CEO:** Chris A. Davis. **Number of employees nationwide:** 3,119.

MERIT MEDICAL SYSTEMS, INC.
1600 West Merit Parkway, South Jordan UT 84095. 801/253-1600. **Fax:** 801/253-1687. **Contact:** Susan Kubiak, Vice President; Robin Nielsen, Employment Supervisor Organizational Development. **E-mail address:** skubiak@merit.com; robinn@merit.com. **World Wide Web address:** http://www.merit.com. **Description:** Develops, manufactures, and distributes disposable proprietary medical products used in interventional diagnostic procedures, primarily in cardiology and radiology. The company serves client hospitals worldwide. Founded in 1987. **NOTE:** For employment information, dial Extension 150 for Susan Kubiak, 107 for Robin Nielsen. **Corporate headquarters location:** This location. **Other U.S. locations:** Santa Clara CA; Angleton TX. **International locations:** Ireland; Netherlands; France. **Subsidiaries include:** Merit Sensor Systems. **Listed on:** NASDAQ. **Stock exchange symbol:** NMS. **President/CEO:** Fred P. Lampropoulos.

MERRILL LYNCH
P.O. Box 2610, Salt Lake City UT 84110-2610. 801/535-1300. **Physical address:** 60 East South Temple Street, Salt Lake City UT 84111. **Fax:** 801/355-3410. **Contact:** Human Resources. **World Wide Web address:** http://www.ml.com. **Description:** A diversified financial service organization. The company is a major broker in securities, option contracts, commodities and financial futures contracts, and insurance. Merrill Lynch also deals with corporate and municipal securities and investment banking. **NOTE:** Please visit website to search for jobs and apply online. **Positions advertised include:** Loan Accountant; Consulting Relationship Manager; Receptionist. **Corporate headquarters location:** New York NY. **Other area locations:** Statewide. **Other U.S. locations:** Nationwide. **International locations:** Worldwide.

MINING SERVICES INTERNATIONAL CORPORATION (MSI)
5505 South 900 East, Suite 300, Salt Lake City UT 84117. 801/233-6000. **Contact:** Human Resources. **World Wide Web address:** http://www.miningservices.com. **Description:** Develops explosive technologies and supplies chemicals to the mining industry. The company also produces aqueous sodium cyanide, a chemical used in gold mining operations, at its CYANCO plant located outside Winnemucca NV. **Office hours:** Monday – Friday, 8:00 a.m. – 5:00 p.m. **Corporate headquarters location:** This location. **Other U.S. locations:** MT; WY; WV. **International locations:** Australia; Canada; Chile; France; India; South Africa.

MITY-LITE, INC.
1301 West 400 North, Orem UT 84057-4442. 801/224-0589. **Toll-free phone:** 800/327-1692. **Fax:** 801/224-6191. **Contact:** Human Resources. **World Wide Web address:** http://www.mitylite.com. **Description:** Manufactures lightweight, durable, plastic folding-leg tables and upholstered stacking chairs. Founded in 1987. **NOTE:** Entry-level positions and part-time jobs are offered. **Office hours:** Monday - Friday, 7:30 a.m. - 5:30 p.m. **Corporate headquarters location:** This location. **International locations:** Australia. **Parent company:** Mity Enterprises. **Listed on:** NASDAQ. **Stock exchange symbol:** MITY. **CEO:** Brad Nielson.

MOOG AIRCRAFT GROUP
2268 South 3270 West, Salt Lake City UT 84119-1193. 801/973-4300. **Fax:** 801/974-7581. **Contact:** Human Resources. **E-mail address:** jobinquiry.slc@moog.com. **World Wide Web address:** http://www.moog.com. **Description:** Focuses on two major business areas: electronic systems and control systems. The electronic business area is a leading producer of both civil and military ground-based air navigation aids and air traffic control systems. The control systems business area is a major provider of mechanical, electromechanical, hydraulic, and pneumatic actuation systems and solenoids to the aerospace, defense, and industrial markets. The Salt Lake division also supplies the fin actuation systems for the TOW, Maverick, and Hellfire missiles. The company also performs aircraft maintenance, repair, overhaul, and modification services. **Positions advertised include:** Senior Logistics Analyst. **Corporate headquarters location:** East Aurora NY. **Other U.S. locations:** Chatsworth CA; Torrance CA. **International locations:** Worldwide. **Parent company:** Raytheon. **Listed on:** New York Stock Exchange. **Stock exchange symbol:** Mog.A; Mog.B.

MOORE WALLACE
630 West 1000 North, Logan UT 84321. 435/752-9175. . **Fax:** 435/755-4280. **Contact:** Human Resources Manager. **World Wide Web address:** http://www.rrdonnelley.com. **Description:** Produces images and words, and provides printing and mailing services to companies in publishing, healthcare, and retail industries, among others. **Other U.S. locations:** Nationwide. **International locations:** Worldwide. **Parent company:** RR Donnelley. **Number of employees worldwide:** 50,000.

MORONI FEED PROCESSING
P.O. Box 308, Moroni UT 84632. 435/436-8211. **Contact:** Kent Barton. **World Wide Web address:** http://www.norbest.com/a_moroni_feed.cfm. **Description:** A poultry processing plant. **Corporate headquarters location:** This location. **Parent company:** Norbest, Inc. **Number of employees nationwide:** 850.

MORRIS MURDOCK TRAVEL
240 East Morris Avenue, Salt Lake City UT 84115. 801/487-9731. **Toll-free phone:** 800/888-6699. **Fax:** 801/483-6338. **Contact:** Personnel Manager. **World Wide Web address:** http://www.morrismurdock.com. **Description:** A large travel agency. **Corporate headquarters location:** This location. **Other area locations:** Statewide. **Other U.S. locations:** ID; MT; HI. **CEO:** Mark Slack.

MORTON SALT
P.O. Box 506, Grantsville UT 84029. 801/250-6335. **Physical address:** Highway I-80, Exit 84, Flux Grantsville UT. **Contact:** Human Resources. **World Wide Web address:** http://www.mortonsalt.com. **Description:** This division of Morton International manufactures table salt. **NOTE:** This firm does not accept unsolicited resumes. Please only respond to advertised openings. **Other U.S. locations:** Nationwide. **International locations:** Canada. **Parent company:** Morton International.

MOUNTAIN STATES STEEL, INC.
325 South Geneva Road, Lindon UT 84042. 801/785-5085. **Fax:** 801/785-1100. **Contact:** Human Resources. **E-mail address:** mssteel@mssteel.com. **World Wide Web address:** http://www.mssteel.com. **Description:** Engaged in structural steel fabrication. Founded in 1987. **NOTE:** Entry-level positions and second and third shifts are offered. **Positions advertised include:** Welder; Fitter. **Special programs:** Apprenticeships; Training. **Corporate headquarters location:** This location. **Listed on:** Privately held.

MOXTEK, INC.
452 West 1260 North, Orem UT 84057. 801/225-0930. **Fax:** 801/221-1121. **Contact:** Human Resources. **World Wide Web address:** http://www.moxtek.com. **Description:** Manufactures components for analytical instruments and engineers new products for X-ray analysis of materials.

MRS. FIELD'S ORIGINAL COOKIES, INC.
2855 East Cottonwood Parkway, Suite 400, Salt Lake City UT 84121-7050. 801/736-5600. **Contact:** Personnel. **World Wide Web address:** http://www.mrsfields.com. **Description:** Produces cookies. Founded in 1978. **Special programs:** Internships; Apprenticeships; Summer Jobs. **Corporate headquarters location:** This location. **Other U.S. locations:** Nationwide. **International locations:** Worldwide. **Listed on:** Privately held.

MYRIAD GENETICS
320 Wakara Way, Salt Lake City UT 84108. 801/582-3600. **Fax:** 801/584-3640. **Contact:** Human Resources. **E-mail address:** jobs@myriad.com. **World Wide Web address:** http://www.myriad.com. **Description:** Researches genetic links to breast cancer and heart disease. **NOTE:** No phone calls regarding employment. **Positions advertised include:** Account Executive; Customer Service Specialist; Laboratory Technician; National Accounts Manager; Regional Medical Specialist; Research Associate; Vice President of Clinical Research. **Corporate headquarters location:** This location. **CEO:** Peter D. Meldrum.

NPS PHARMACEUTICALS
420 Chipeta Way, Salt Lake City UT 84108. 801/583-4939. **Fax:** 801/583-4961. **Contact:** Human Resources. **World Wide Web address:** http://www.npsp.com. **Description:** Engaged in treatment therapy research for diseases such as osteoporosis. **NOTE:** Human Resources phone is 801/583-4961. Please visit website to search for jobs and apply online. **Positions advertised include:** Administrative Assistant; Bioanalytical Chemist; Corporate Safety Manager; Pharmacokineticist; Senior Neuropharmacologist; Toxicologist. **Corporate headquarters location:** This location. **Other U.S. locations:** Parsippany NJ. **International locations:** Ontario Canada.

NACO INDUSTRIES, INC.
395 West 1400 North, Logan UT 84341. 435/753-8020. **Toll-free phone:** 800/445-4151. **Fax:** 435/752-7041. **Contact:** Human Resources Manager. **World Wide Web address:** http://www.naco-industries.com. **Description:** Manufactures polyvinyl chloride products, primarily pipe fittings and valves. These products are distributed by wholesalers to the irrigation, construction, industrial, and utility industries. **Corporate headquarters location:** This location. **Other U.S. locations:** Lodi CA; Garden City KS.

NACT TELECOMMUNICATIONS
191 West 5200 North, Provo UT 84604. 801/802-3000. **Fax:** 801/802-2000. **Contact:** Human Resources. **E-mail address:** resumes@nact.com. **World Wide Web address:** http://www.nact.com. **Description:** Provides switching systems to the telecommunications industry. **Parent company:** Verso Technologies.

NATURE'S SUNSHINE
P.O. Box 19005, Provo UT 84605-9005. 801/342-4300. **Physical address:** 75 East 1700 South, Provo UT. **Fax:** 801/798-4126. **Contact:** Human Resources. **E-mail address:** hr@natr.com. **World Wide Web address:** http://www.naturessunshine.com. **Description:** Produces herbs and vitamins in capsule form. Nature's Sunshine manufactures over 200 vitamin and health products. **Positions advertised include:** Manager – International Accounting; Packaging Operator. **Corporate headquarters location:** This location. **Other area locations:** Spanish Fork, UT. **International locations:** Worldwide.

NATURE'S WAY
10 Mountain Springs Parkway, Springville UT 84663. 801/489-1500. **Toll-free phone:** 800/962-8873. **Fax:** 801/489-1700. **Recorded jobline:** 801/489-1501. **Contact:** Andrea Clifford, Personnel. **E-mail address:** andreacl@naturesway.com. **World Wide Web address:** http://www. naturesway.com. **Description:** Manufactures health foods including herbs and vitamins. Founded in 1969. **NOTE:** Entry-level positions and second and third shifts are offered. This firm does not accept unsolicited resumes. An application must be submitted in order to be considered for employment. Applications are available to pick up at 1375 North Mountain Springs Parkway in Springville, Monday – Friday, 8:00 a.m. – 5:00 p.m. Please call the jobline for a list of available positions. **Company slogan:** To advance healthy living through natural choices. **Corporate headquarters location:** This location. **Parent company:** Murdock Madaus Schwabe. **Listed on:** Privately held.

NEPHI RUBBER PRODUCTS (NRP)
255 West 1100 North, Nephi UT 84648. 435/623-1740. **Fax:** 435/623-2638. **Contact:** Human Resources Department. **World Wide Web address:** http://www.nrpjones.com. **Description:** Manufactures a variety of rubber and plastic fabricated products, primarily hoses. **Corporate headquarters location:** LaPorte IN.

NESTLE'S FROZEN FOODS
815 West Raymond Klauck Way, Springville UT 84663. 801/489-8621. **Contact:** Human Resources. **World Wide Web address:** http://www.nestle.com. **Description:** Manufactures frozen foods for retail sale. **NOTE:** Please visit career site - http://www.nestleusa.com/careers – to search for jobs and apply online. **Positions advertised include:** Pediatric Nutrition Representative. **Other U.S. locations:** Nationwide. **International locations:** Worldwide. **Number of employees worldwide:** 230,000.

NEWAYS, INC.
2089 West Neways Drive, Springville UT 84663. 801/418-2000. **Fax:** 801/418-2195. **Contact:** Human Resources. **World Wide Web address:** http://www.neways.com. **Description:** Manufactures personal care products. The Neways product line includes hair care, skin care, nail care, and dental care products. **Positions advertised include:** Training Manager; Distributor Relations Manager. **Corporate headquarters locations:** This location. **Other area locations:** Salem UT. **Number of employees at this location:** 400. **Number of employees worldwide:** 850.

NEWSPAPER AGENCY CORPORATION (NAC)
P.O. Box 45838, Salt Lake City UT 84145. 801/237-2800. **Fax:** 801/237-2856. **Physical address:** 143 South Main Street, Salt Lake City 84111. **Contact:** Karen Ruff, Human Resources. **E-mail address:** kruff@nacorp.com. **World Wide Web address:** http://www.nacorp.com/NAC2. **Description:** Provides business management, advertising, circulation, and production services for two editorially independent Salt Lake City newspapers published under the names *Salt Lake Tribune* and *Deseret Morning News*. **NOTE:** Call Human Resources contact directly at 801/237-2793. **Corporate headquarters location:** This location.

NORDSTROM, INC.
50 South Main Street, Salt Lake City UT 84144-2012. 801/322-4200. **Contact:** Human Resources Department. **World Wide Web address:** http://www.nordstrom.com. **Description:** A specialty retailer that sells apparel, shoes, and accessories for the family. Nordstrom, Inc. also has a mail-order catalog division. **Office hours:** Monday – Saturday, 10:00 a.m. – 9:00 p.m.; Sunday, 12:00 p.m. – 6:00 p.m. **Corporate headquarters location:** Seattle WA. **Other area locations:** Murray UT; Orem UT. **Other U.S. locations:** Nationwide.

NOVELL, INC.
1800 South Novell Place, Provo UT 84606. 801/861-7000. **Toll-free phone:** 800/453-1267. **Contact:** Staffing Department. **World Wide Web address:** http://www.novell.com. **Description:** Novell, Inc. develops software tools and systems, works in partnership with other companies, and provides computer network management services. Products include NetWare 5.1, GroupWise 5.5, ManageWise 2.7, and Novell Net Publisher. **NOTE:** Contact Human Resources toll-free at 888/475-4631. **Positions advertised include:** Applications Engineer; Business Systems Analyst; Contract Manager; Documentation Specialist; Help Desk Support Engineer; Inside Sales Representative; International Tax Accountant; Managed Services Engineer; Marketing Communications Manager; Network Security Administrator; Public Relations Manager; Security Specialist; Senior Auditor; Senior Consultant; Software Engineer Senior; Tax Accountant; Technical Support Engineer; Web Developer. **Corporate headquarters location:** Waltham MA. **Other area locations:** Salt Lake City UT. **Other U.S. locations:** Nationwide. **International locations:** Worldwide. **Operations at this facility include:** This location provides networking services. **Number of employees at this location:** 3,000.

NU SKIN INTERNATIONAL, INC.
One Nu Skin Plaza, 75 West Center Street, Provo UT 84601-4483. 801/345-1000. **Fax:** 801/345-2799. **Contact:** Human Resources. **E-mail address:** jobs@nuskin.com. **World Wide Web address:** http://www.nuskin.com. **Description:** Manufactures and markets personal care and nutritional products. The personal care products division includes hair care, skin care, nail care, sun protection, and oral health care products. The Interior Design Nutritional division operates a weight management lifestyle program. The program consists of nutritional products, weight management supplements, instructional materials, and an interactive health and fitness assessment and counseling program. Founded in 1984. **Positions advertised include:** QA Engineer; ISS Phone Tech; ERP Business Analyst; Work Force Management Analyst. **Office hours:** 8:00 a.m. – 5: 00 p.m. **Corporate headquarters location:** This location. **International locations:** Worldwide. **Listed on:** New York Stock Exchange. **Stock exchange symbol:** NUS. **President:** Lori Bush.

NUCOR STEEL UTAH
P.O. Box 100, Plymouth UT 84330. 435/458-2353. **Physical address:** 7285 West 21200 North Plymouth UT. **Toll-free phone:** 800/453-2886. **Fax:** 435/458-2309. **Contact:** Human Resources. **World Wide Web address:** http://www.nsutah.com. **Description:** This location operates as part of the parent company's Nucor Steel Division, which produces bars, angles, light structural, sheet, and special steel products. In addition to selling steel on the open market, these mills assure an economical supply of steel for the parent company's other divisions. **Parent company:** Nucor Corporation manufactures steel products. Other divisions include Vulcraft, one of the nation's largest producers of steel joists and joist girders; Nucor Cold Finish, which produces cold-finished steel bars used extensively for shafting and machined precision parts; Nucor Grinding Balls, which produces steel grinding balls in Utah for the mining industry; Nucor Fastener, a steel bolt-making facility; Nucor Bearing Products, Inc., which produces steel bearings and machined steel parts; and Nucor Building Systems, which produces metal buildings and components.

NUTRACEUTICAL CORPORATION
1400 Kearns Boulevard, Park City UT 84060. 435/655-6000. **Toll-free phone:** 800/669-8877. **Fax:** 800/767-8514. **Recorded jobline:** 800/669-3009. **Contact:** Human Resources. **World Wide Web address:** http://www.nutraceutical.com. **Description:** Produces nutritional and herbal supplements. **NOTE:** Entry-level positions, part-time jobs, and second and third shifts are offered. **NOTE:** Please visit website to search for jobs and apply online. **Positions advertised include:** Marketing Analyst; Product Brand Manager. **Special programs:** Internships; Summer Jobs. **Corporate headquarters location:** This location. **Other area locations:** Lindon UT; Ogden UT. **Subsidiaries include:** Au Naturel; Monarch Labs. **Listed on:** Privately held. **Number of employees worldwide:** 600. **CEO:** Frank W. Gay II.

OEC MEDICAL SYSTEMS
384 Wright Brothers Drive, Salt Lake City UT 84116. 801/328-9300. **Contact:** Human Resources. **World Wide Web address:** http://www.gemedical systems.com. **Description:** Manufactures portable X-ray machines. **NOTE:** Please visit website to search for jobs and apply online. **Parent company:** GE Medical Systems.

OGDEN, CITY OF
2549 Washington Boulevard, Suite 220, Ogden UT 84401. 801/629-8730. **Fax:** 801/629-8735. **Contact:** Human Resources Office. **World Wide Web address:** http://www.ogdencity.com. **Description:** The largest city in Weber County with 64,000 residents, the city government of Ogden provides municipal services to the public. **NOTE:** Please visit website to see listings of various employment opportunities. You may apply online, or print an application. **Office hours:** Monday – Friday, 8:00 a.m. – 5:00 p.m.

OGDEN MARRIOTT
247 24th Street, Ogden UT 84401. 801/627-1190. **Fax:** 801/394-6312. **Contact:** Sales Manager. **World Wide Web address:** http://www.marriott.com. **Description:** One location of the Marriott chain. The hotel has a private club and a full-service restaurant. **Corporate headquarters location:** Washington D.C. **Other U.S. locations:** Nationwide. **International locations:** Worldwide. **Listed on:** New York Stock Exchange. **Stock exchange symbol:** MAR.

OGDEN REGIONAL MEDICAL CENTER
5475 South 500 East, Ogden UT 84405. 801/479-2111. **Contact:** Human Resources Department. **World Wide Web address:** http://www.ogden regional.com. **Description:** A 239-bed hospital. Columbia Ogden Regional Medical Center's services include women's and children's health services, cardiac care, cancer treatment, orthopedics, physical medicine and rehabilitation, behavioral health services, alcohol and chemical dependency treatment, and health education and wellness services. **NOTE:** Please visit website for online application form. Contact Human Resources directly at 801/479-2071. Volunteer positions are also available. **Positions advertised include:** Clinical Dietician; Food and Nutrition Culinary Coordinator; Donor Services Trainer; Donor Technician; Medical Lab Technician; Mobile Team Supervisor; RN – Various Departments; Pharmacist; COTA; Occupational Therapist; Physical Therapist; Physical Therapy Assistant; Radiology Technician; Sonographer; Special Procedures Technician.

OSBORN SPECIALTY SEWING
7095 West 3500 South, West Valley City UT 84128. 801/250-1865. **Fax:** 801/250-6099. **Toll-free phone:** 800/592-7195. **Toll-free fax:** 800/688-1865. **Contact:** Cade Osborn, Human Resources Manager. **E-mail address:** cade@cobblestones.com. **World Wide Web address:** http://www. cobblestones.com. **Description:** Manufactures a wide range of sportswear and activewear under the trade name Cobblestones Activewear. **Corporate headquarters location:** This location.

OTTO & SONS
4980 West 9470 South, West Jordan UT 84088. 801/280-0166. **Fax:** 801/280-3540. **Contact:** Human Resources. **E-mail address:** recruiter@osigroup.com. **World Wide Web address:** http://www.osigroup.com. **Description:** Otto & Sons processes hamburger meat for McDonald's Restaurants. Please contact the corporate headquarters for career information. **Corporate headquarters location:** Aurora IL. **Parent company:** OSI Group. **Other U.S. locations:** Nationwide. **International locations:** Worldwide.

PACIFICORP
UTAH POWER
One Utah Center, 201 South Main Street, Salt Lake City UT 84111. 801/220-2000. **Fax:** 801/220-2798. **Contact:** Employment. **E-mail address:** hrquestions@pacificorp.com. **World Wide Web address:** http://www. utahpower.net. **Description:** PacifiCorp, through Pacific Power (another subsidiary) and Utah Power, serves 1.3 million customers in seven western states, making it one of the largest electric companies west of the Rocky Mountains. PacifiCorp is one of the nation's lowest-cost producers of coal-fired energy, and also has low-cost hydro resources. PacifiCorp interconnects with more than 50 other utilities, most of which have higher system power costs. PacifiCorp also holds a telecommunications utility known as Pacific Telecom. **NOTE:** Please visit website to search for jobs and apply online. Do not send resumes to listed e-mail address. **Positions advertised include:** Distribution Operations Supervisor; Journeyman Substation Lineman. **Corporate headquarters location:** Portland ME. **Other area locations:** Statewide. **Other U.S. locations:** Nationwide. **International locations:** Canada. **Parent Company:** Pacificorp.

PACKAGING CORPORATION OF AMERICA
460 West 500 South, Salt Lake City UT 84101. 801/359-8681. **Fax:** 801/355-7721. **Contact:** Human Resources. **World Wide Web address:** http://www.packagingcorp.com. **Description:** Manufactures containerboard and corrugated packaging products. **NOTE:** To inquire about job opportunities, please call the corporate location Human Resources department at 847/482-2111, or fax 847/482-2238. **Corporate headquarters location:** Lake Forest IL. **Other U.S. locations:** Nationwide.

PARK CITY GROUP INC.
P.O. Box 5000, Park City UT 84060. 435/649-2221. **Physical address:** 333 Main Street, Park City UT 84060. **Toll-free phone:** 800/772-4556. **Fax:** 435/645-2010. **Contact:** Human Resources. **E-mail address:** jobs@parkcitygroup.com. **World Wide Web address:** http://www. parkcitygroup.com. **Description:** Manufactures inventory report software for the retail industry. **Positions advertised include:** Corporate Communications Manager; Product Specialist; Product Trainer; Product Implementer; Software Sales Specialist; Technical Writer; Software Developer – Java; Account Manager. **CEO:** Randall K. Fields.

PARKER HANNIFIN CORPORATION
CONTROL SYSTEMS DIVISION
1425 West 2675 North, Ogden UT 84404-2696. 801/786-3000. **Fax:** 801/786-3045. **Contact:** Personnel. **World Wide Web address:** http://www.parker.com. **Description:** Parker Hannifin makes motion control products including fluid power systems, electromechanical controls, and related components. Products are sold through direct sales employees and more than 4,900 distributors. The motion and control group makes hydraulic pumps, power units, control valves, accumulators, cylinders, actuators, and automation devices to remove contaminants from air, fuel, oil, water, and other fluids. Fluid Connectors Group makes connectors, tube and hose fittings, hoses, and couplers that transmit fluid. Seal Group makes sealing devices, gaskets, and packing that insure leak-proof connections. Automotive and refrigeration groups make components for use in industrial and automotive air conditioning and refrigeration systems. Principal products of aerospace segment are hydraulic, pneumatic, and fuel systems and components. **NOTE:** Please visit website t register, search for jobs, and apply online. **Positions advertised include:** New Business Development Manager – Hydromechanical Market. **Office hours:** Monday – Friday, 7:30 a.m. – 4:30 p.m. **Corporate headquarters location:** Cleveland OH. **Other U.S. locations:** Nationwide. **International location:** Worldwide. **Operations at this facility include:** This location manufactures aircraft equipment, primarily flight and other control mechanisms. **Listed on:** New York Stock Exchange. **Stock exchange symbol:** PH.

JACK B. PARSON COMPANIES
P.O. Box 3429, Ogden UT 84409. 801/731-1111. **Fax:** 801/731-8800. **Physical address:** 2350 South 1900 West, Ogden UT 84401. **Contact:** Human Resources. **World Wide Web address:** http://www.jbparson.com. **Description:** One of the intermountain region's largest producers of sand, gravel, and ready-mix concrete, and asphalt. The company also offers paving and construction services. Founded in 1952. **NOTE:** Entry-level positions are offered. **Internship information:** Summer internships are occasionally available for assistant construction/asphalt estimators. **Corporate headquarters location:** This location. **Other area locations:** Statewide. **Other U.S. locations:** Idaho. **Subsidiaries include:** Bannock Paving Company; Idaho Sand & Gravel Company. **Operations at this facility include:** Divisional Headquarters. **Listed on:** NASDAQ. **Stock exchange symbol:** CRHCY. **Number of employees nationwide:** 2,000.

PARSONS, BEHLE & LATIMER
P.O. Box 45898, Salt Lake City UT 84145-0898. 801/532-1234. **Physical address:** 201 South Main Street, Suite 1800, Salt Lake City UT 84111-2218. **Fax:** 801/536-6111. **Contact:** Darcie Koski, Recruitment Specialist. **E-mail address:** dkoski@pblutah.com. **World Wide Web address:** http://www. pblutah.com. **Description:** A law firm with a wide variety of specialties including corporate, environmental, litigation, and tax law. **Special programs:** Internships; Summer Associate Training. **Other area locations:** Lindon UT.

PAYCHEX, INC.
6955 South Union Park Center, Suite 260, Midvale UT 84047. 801/561-3473. **Fax:** 801/561-3644. **Contact:** Human Resources Manager. **E-mail address:** fieldrecruiting@paychex.com; jobopps@paychex.com. **World Wide Web address:** http://www.paychex.com. **Description:** A national payroll processing and payroll tax preparation company for small to medium-sized businesses. The company also provides human resource products and services including employee handbook services, Section 125 cafeteria plans, insurance services, and 401(k) record keeping. Paychex has 94 locations and serves nearly 225,000 clients nationwide. **NOTE:** Positions listed may not apply to this specific location. Check with desired location for specific available positions. **Positions advertised include:** Account Executive; Branch Manager; Branch Trainer; Client Service Advisor; Client Service Manager – New Markets and Paychex Online; Client Service Representative; Computer Operator; Delphi Developer; Distribution Specialist; District Sales Assistant; Human Resources Manager; Payroll Specialist; Receptionist; Sales Management; Sales Representative; Selling Sales Manager; Technical Support Specialist. **Special programs:** Internships; Co-ops. **Corporate headquarters location:** Rochester NY. **Other U.S. locations:** Nationwide.

PETERSEN INCORPORATED
1527 North 2000 West, Ogden UT 84404. 801/732-2000. **Fax:** 801/732-2098. **Toll-free phone:** 800/410-6789. **Contact:** Dave Dixon, Human Resources. **E-mail address:** daved@petersen-inc.com. **World Wide Web address:** http://www.petersen-inc.com. **Description:** Engaged in steel fabrication. Founded in 1961. **Corporate headquarters location:** This location.

PHONE DIRECTORIES COMPANY
P.O. Box 2277, Orem UT 84059-2277. 801/225-0801. **Physical address:** 135 South Mountain Way Drive, Orem UT 84058. **Fax:** 801/225-0991. **Contact:** Human Resources. **E-mail address:** hr@phonedir.com. **World Wide Web address:** http://www.phonedir.com. **Description:** An independent publisher of telephone directories. **Corporate headquarters location:** This location. **Other U.S. locations:** Nationwide. **International locations:** Canada. **Positions advertised include:** Collector; Sales Representative; Graphic Designer; Advertising Proofer; Receptionist – Part-time; Final Editor; Special Sections Book Editor; Accounts Payable Clerk; Outside Sales Representative; Inside Sales Advertising Consultants; Contract Coordination Team Member; Inside Sales Representative.

POWDER RIVER, INC.
P.O. Box 50758, Provo UT 84606. 801/538-0327. **Physical address:** 388 East 900 South, Provo UT 84606. **Toll-free phone:** 800/453-5318. **Contact:** General Manager. **World Wide Web address:** http://www.powderriver.com. **Description:** Manufactures livestock handling equipment such as a "squeeze shoot" used for containing cattle.

PREMIER COMPUTING TECHNOLOGIES
385 West 2880 South, Salt Lake City UT 84115. 801/487-8400. **Fax:** 801/487-8416. **Contact:** Human Resources. **E-mail address:** dpotter@premiercomputing.com. **World Wide Address:** http://www.premiercomputing.com. **Description:** Provides information technology products and services to institutions, governmental agencies,

and corporations worldwide. Founded in 1977. **Office hours:** Monday - Friday, 8:00 a.m. - 5:00 p.m.

PRESTIGE FINANCIAL
1420 South 500 West, Salt Lake City UT 84115. 866/PFS-CREDIT. **Contact:** Human Resources. **E-mail address:** careers@gopfs.com. **World Wide Web address:** http://www.prestige-financial.com. **Description:** A nationwide financial lending company. **Positions advertised include:** Software Developer. **Corporate headquarters location:** This location. **Other U.S. locations:** Nationwide.

PRICEWATERHOUSECOOPERS
36 South State Street, Suite 1700, Salt Lake City UT 84111. 801/531-9666. **Fax:** 801/933-8106. **Contact:** Personnel. **World Wide Web address:** http://www.pricewaterhousecoopers.com. **Description:** One of the largest certified public accounting firms in the world. PricewaterhouseCoopers provides public accounting, business advisory, management consulting, and taxation services. **NOTE:** Please visit website to search for jobs and apply online. **Corporate headquarters location:** New York NY. **Other area locations:** Ogden UT. **Other U.S. locations:** Nationwide. **International locations:** Worldwide.

PRIMARY CHILDREN'S MEDICAL CENTER
100 North Medical Drive, Salt Lake City UT 84113-1100. 801/588-2000. **Contact:** Recruiter. **World Wide Web address:** http://www.ihc.com/xp/ihc/primary/. **Description:** A 232-bed facility equipped and staffed to treat children with complex illnesses and injuries. The pediatric center serves five states in the Intermountain West. The hospital is affiliated with the Department of Pediatrics at the University of Utah. Specialized services for children include cancer treatment, a cardiology unit, child abuse/neglect counseling, infant special care, pediatric surgery, and trauma treatment. Founded in 1922. **NOTE:** Human Resources phone is 801/588-2203. **Positions advertised include:** Pediatric Technician; ED Health Unit Coordinator; Medical Secretary; PCA – Various Departments; ED Health Unit Coordinator; Patient Account Representative; Research Assistant; Echo Technician; Respiratory Care Therapist; Food and Nutrition Department Educator; Pharmacist; Occupational Therapist; Medical Technologist; EGG Technician; Director of Pediatric Education Services; Human Resources Consultant; Surgical Technologist. **Parent company:** Intermountain Health Care.

PROMODEL CORPORATION
556 East Technology Avenue, Orem UT 84097. 801/223-4600. **Fax:** 801/226-6046. **Contact:** Human Resources. **E-mail address:** hr@promodel.com. **World Wide Web address:** http://www.promodel.com. **Description:** Develops and sells simulation software that is used in a wide range of industries including health care and manufacturing. **Positions advertised include:** Regional Director; Pharmaceutical Sales Representative. **Corporate headquarters location:** Bethlehem PA.

PROVO CITY CORPORATION
P.O. Box 1849, Provo UT 84601. 801/852-6180. **Physical address:** 351 West Center Street, Provo UT. **Fax:** 801/852-6190. **Recorded jobline:** 801/852-6187. **Contact:** Human Resources. **World Wide Web address:** http://www.provo.org. **Description:** Provides city government services. **NOTE:** Please visit website for more details on available positions. **Positions advertised include:** Animal Control Officer; Assistant Library Services Manager; Property Room Cadet – Part-time; Water Safety Instructor/Lifeguard – Part-time; Youth Soccer Referee – Part-time/Seasonal; Track and Field Instructor – Part-time/Seasonal; 911 Dispatcher; Aquatics Specialist; Clerk; Customer Service Representative; Crossing Guard; Meter Reader; Gymnastics Instructor; Laborer; Office Specialist; Referee; Police Officer; Firefighter; Power Line Worker; Security Worker; Systems Analyst. **Office hours:** Monday – Thursday, 7:00 a.m. – 6:00 p.m. **Corporate headquarters location:** This location.

Q COMM INTERNATIONAL, INC.
510 East Technology Avenue, Building C, Orem UT 84097. 801/226-4222. **Fax:** 801/222-9555. **Toll-free phone:** 800/626-9941. **Contact:** Human Resources. **E-mail address:** info@qcomm.com. **World Wide Web address:** http://www.qcomm.com. **Description:** A telecommunications services provider that mainly sells prepaid calling cards.

QUESTAR CORPORATION
P.O. Box 45433, Salt Lake Cit UT 84145-0433. 801/324-5000. **Physical address:** 180 East 100 South, Sale Lake City 84139. **Recorded jobline:** 801/324-5795. **Contact:** Human Resources. **World Wide Web address:** http://www.questarcorp.com. **Description:** A utility holding company. **NOTE:** Hiring is conducted through the Department of Workforce Services. You can reach them at 801/468-0097. **Subsidiaries include:** Questar Gas; Questar Pipeline Company; Questar Exploration and Production; Questar Energy Trading Co.

QUESTAR GAS
P.O. Box 45360, Salt Lake City UT 84145-0360. 801/324-2550. **Physical address:** 180 East 100 South Salt Lake City UT 84145. **Toll-free phone:** 800/323-5517. **Recorded jobline:** 801/324-5795. **Contact:** Human Resources. **World Wide Web address:** http://www.questargas.com. **Description:** Questar Gas is a fuel wholesaler. **NOTE:** Hiring is conducted through the Department of Workforce Services. You can reach them at 801/468-0097.

RGL GALLAGHER
136 East South Temple, Suite 1770, Salt Lake City UT 84111. 801/355-0400. **Fax:** 801/355-5577. **Contact:** Personnel. **World Wide Web address:** http://www.rglslc.com. **Description:** A certified public accounting firm. **NOTE:** Please visit website to post your resume. **Corporate headquarters location:** Englewood CO. **Other U.S. locations:** Nationwide. **International locations:** London England; Dublin Ireland; Sydney Australia; Perth Australia; Tokyo Japan. **Parent company:** RGL International. **CEO:** Sherlyn W. Farrell.

RACORE COMPUTER PRODUCTS INC.
4125 South 6000 West, West Valley City UT 84128. 801/973-9779. **Toll-free phone:** 877/252-9779. **Fax:** 801/973-2005. **Contact:** Human Resources. **E-mail address:** hrjobs@racore.com. **World Wide Web address:** http://www.racore.com. **Description:** Manufactures network boards. **Corporate headquarters location:** This location.

RADIX INTERNATIONAL
4855 Wiley Post Way, Salt Lake City UT 84116. 801/537-1717. **Toll-free phone:** 800/367-9258. **Fax:** 801/328-3401. **Contact:** Human Resources. **E-mail address:** careers@radix-md.co.uk. **World Wide Web address:** http://www.radix-intl.com. **Description:** Manufactures hand-held computer systems used in meter readings and other applications. **Corporate headquarters location:** This location. **International locations:** United Kingdom.

RED MAN PIPE & SUPPLY COMPANY
P.O. Box 540448, North Salt Lake City UT 84054. 801/298-4605. **Physical address:** 485 North 400 West, North Salt Lake City UT 84054. **Fax:** 801/295-9191. **Contact:** Human Resources. **E-mail address:** jobs@red-man.com. **World Wide Web address:** http://www.red-man.com. **Description:** A wholesale distributor of pipes, valves, and fittings. **NOTE:** Please visit website to download employment application form. Send resumes to 8023 East 63rd Place, Suite 800, Tulsa OK 74133, or fax to 918/461-5380. Reach this office by phone at 918/461-5386. **Other area locations:** Price UT; Roosevelt UT; Vernal UT. **Other U.S. locations:** Nationwide. **President/CEO:** Craig Ketchum.

REGENCE BLUE CROSS & BLUE SHIELD OF UTAH, INC.
P.O. Box 30270, Salt Lake City UT 84130-0270. 801/333-2100. **Physical address:** 2890 East Cottonwood Parkway, Salt Lake City UT 84121. **Toll-free phone:** 800/624-6519. **Recorded jobline:** 801/333-2060. **Contact:** Employment Coordinator. **World Wide Web address:** http://www.ut.regence.com. **Description:** A health insurance provider. **NOTE:** This firm does not accept unsolicited resumes. Please call the jobline for a list of available positions. Please visit website to download application form. If you are interested in more than one job, you must submit a resume or application for each position. **Positions advertised include:** Vice President of Claims; Medical Management Coordinator; Administrative Support; TriCare Provider Relations Specialist. **Special programs:** Internships. **Office hours:** 8:00 a.m. – 5:00 p.m. **Corporate headquarters location:** This location. **Other area locations:** Ogden UT; Provo UT. **Number of employees nationwide:** 880.

RICHARDS LABORATORIES OF UTAH, INC.
55 East Center Street, Pleasant Grove UT 84062. 801/785-2500. **Contact:** Human Resources. **Description:** A microbiology laboratory, an environmental laboratory, and a bioremediation facility.

ROADWAY EXPRESS INC.
1234 South 3200 West, Salt Lake City UT 84104. 801/973-7399. **Fax:** 801/975-9916. **Contact:** Human Resources. **World Wide Web address:** http://www.roadway.com. **Description:** Operates a freight consolidation and distribution terminal for one of the largest common carriers in the United States, with terminals nationwide. The company operates in all 50 states. Founded in 1930. **Corporate headquarters location:** Akron OH. **Other area locations:** Orem UT. **Other U.S. locations:** Nationwide. **Subsidiaries include:** Roadway Services is a transportation holding company with subsidiaries involved in long-haul, air freight, small package, and custom logistics services. Other subsidiaries of the parent company include Roadway Global Air, with worldwide air freight service through 230 service centers; Roadway Package System, with 271 terminals in the United States and a dozen in Canada; Roadway Express, a motor freight transportation company that offers service in all 50 states, Canada, and Mexico; and four regional short-haul freight carriers. The company also offers indirect service to Latin America, Guam, Europe, the Middle East, and the Pacific Rim. **Parent company:** Yellow Roadway Corporation. **Number of employees nationwide:** 24,800.

ROBOTRONICS
1610 West 1600 South, Springville UT 84663. 801/489-4466. **Toll-free phone:** 800/762-6876. **Fax:** 801/489-8241. **Contact:** Human Resources. **World Wide Web address:** http://www.robotronics.com. **Description:** Builds robots that assist in children's safety education. Customers include various schools, police departments, and fire departments.

RONALD McDONALD HOUSE
935 East South Temple, Salt Lake City UT 84102-1411. 801/363-4663. **Fax:** 801/363-0092. **Contact:** Human Resources. **World Wide Web address:** http://www.rmhc.com. **Description:** Offers housing for families of children who are hospitalized due to acute or chronic illnesses. The facility allows families to remain close to the medical facilities that are caring for their children. **NOTE:** Volunteer positions also available. **Corporate headquarters location:** Oak Brook IL. **Other U.S. locations:** Nationwide. **International locations:** Worldwide.

SME STEEL CONTRACTORS
5955 West Wells Park Road, West Jordan UT 84088. 801/280-0711. **Fax:** 801/280-3460. **Contact:** Jeff Archibold, Human Resources Manager. **E-mail address:** jeffa@smesteel.com. **World Wide Web address:** http://www.smesteel.com. **Description:** Fabricates and erects structural steel for large buildings. The company serves clients throughout Utah, Nevada, and California. **NOTE:** Please visit website for online application form. **Corporate headquarters location:** This location. **Other U.S. locations:** Pocatello ID. **Listed on:** Privately held.

SOSYSTEMS
720 East Timpanogos Parkway, Orem UT 84097-6214. 801/222-0200. **Toll-free phone:** 800/385-5567. **Fax:** 801/222-0250. **Contact:** Human Resources Department. **E-mail address:** resume@so-sys.com. **World Wide Web address:** http://www.so-sys.com. **Description:** Develops and sells operations software used by credit unions. Founded in 1976. **Positions advertised include:** Technical Support Representative; Trainer. **Corporate headquarters location:** This location. **Listed on:** Privately held. **CEO:** Dave Smart. **Number of employees at this location:** 66.

SAFFIRE, INC.
734 East Utah Valley Drive, American Fork UT 84003. 801/847-1400. **Fax:** 801/847-1401. **Contact:** Human Resources. **E-mail address:** hr@saffire.com. **World Wide Web address:** http://www.saffire.com. **Description:** Develops computer and video game software. Numerous products are licensed for the Super Nintendo and Sega Genesis game systems. **CEO:** Mark Kendall.

ST. GEORGE STEEL FABRICATORS
1301 East 700 North, St. George UT 84770. 435/673-4856. **Fax:** 435/628-4139. **Contact:** Personnel. **E-mail address:** info@stgeorgesteel.com. **World Wide Web address:** http://www.stgeorgesteel.com. **Description:** Engaged in structural steel and plate steel fabrication and repair. **Corporate headquarters location:** This location. **Other area locations:** Murray UT. **Operations at this facility include:** Administration; Manufacturing; Sales. **President:** John Campos.

ST. MARK'S HOSPITAL
1200 East 3900 South, Salt Lake City UT 84124. 801/268-7111. **Toll-free phone:** 800/965-7778. **Fax:** 801/270-3393. **Recorded jobline:** 801/268-7127. **Contact:** Human Resources. **E-mail address:** employment@ mountainstarhealth.com. **World Wide Web address:** http://www.stmarkshospital.com. **Description:** A 300-bed, acute care hospital that specializes in cardiology, women's health services, orthopedics, and oncology services. **NOTE:** Human Resources phone is 801/268-7066. Please visit website to download application form. **Positions advertised include:** Cardiovascular Technician; EP Coordinator; Childbirth Educator; Clinical Resource Manager; Housekeeper; Medical Assistant; RN – Various Departments; Occupational Therapist; Pharmacist; Mammography Technician; Respiratory Therapist.

SALT LAKE COUNT
2001 South State Street, Suite N4600, Sale Lake City UT 84190-3150. 801/468-2351. **Fax:** 801/468-2172. **Contact:** Director of Personnel Division. **World Wide Web address:** http://www.slco.org. **Description:** Responsible for hiring town officials and workers for the county of Salt Lake. **NOTE:** Please visit website to search for jobs and download application form. You may also pick up an application form in person at the address listed. **Positions advertised include:** 4-H Outreach Program Assistant; Accountant; Accounts Receivable Specialist; Administrative & Fiscal Manager; Administrative Assistant; Adoption Program Coordinator; Air Pollution Control Specialist; Animal Control Officer; Architect; Archivist; Billing Specialist; Building Inspection Field Supervisor; Chief Deputy Sheriff. **Office hours:** Monday – Friday, 8:00 a.m. – 5:00 p.m. **Number of employees at this location:** 5,000.

SALT LAKE COMMUNITY COLLEGE
4600 South Redwood Road, Salt Lake City UT 84123. 801/957-4917. **Fax:** 801/957-4721. **Recorded jobline:** 801/957-4133. **Contact:** Jenny Archuleta, Employment Specialist. **E-mail address:** archulje@slcc.edu. **World Wide Web address:** http://www.slcc.edu. **Description:** A two-year community college with over 16,000 students. The college offers an associate of arts degree; an associate of science degree; an associate of applied science degree; one-year certificates; and a certificate of completion. The associate of science and associate of arts degrees are transferable to four-year colleges. The student to faculty ratio is 20 to one. The college is fully accredited by the Northwest Association of Schools and Colleges. The two main campuses are the Redwood Campus and the South City Campus. The college also has four satellite locations and three teaching centers. **NOTE:** Please visit website to download application form or to apply online. **Positions advertised include:** Nursing Faculty; Visual Art and Design Faculty; Administrative Assistant; Accounting Clerk; Secretary; Biology Lab Instructor; Site Facilitator; Lifeguard; Licensed Clinical Social Worker; Employment Technician.

SALT LAKE TRIBUNE
143 South Main Street, Salt Lake City UT 84111. 801/237-8504. **Fax:** 801/257-8525. **Contact:** Sharyn Weiser, Human Resource Manager. **E-mail address:** sweiser@sltrib.com. **World Wide Web address:** http://www.sltrib.com. **Description:** Publishes an independent newspaper with a daily circulation of more than 126,000 and 162,000 on Sunday. Advertising, production, and circulation activities are carried out jointly with competitor *Deseret News* through Newspaper Agency Corporation. **NOTE:** Human Resources phone is 801/257-8504. Part-time jobs are offered. **Special programs:** Internships; Summer Jobs. **Office hours:** Monday - Friday, 7:00 a.m. - 2:00 a.m. **Corporate headquarters location:** This location. **Operations at this facility include:** Administration. **Listed on:** Privately held.

SAN SEGAL SPORTSWEAR
611 West 9560 South, Sandy UT 84070. 801/566-3248. **Toll-free phone:** 800/338-6048. **Fax:** 801/566-3350. **Contact:** Human Resources. **World Wide Web address:** http://www.sansegal.com. **Description:** Engaged in screen printing and embroidering men's and women's sportswear for apparel companies. **Positions advertised include:** Sales Representative; Graphic Artist. **Office hours:** Monday – Friday, 8:00 a.m. – 5:00 p.m.

SANDLOT CORPORATION
250 West Center Street, 2nd Floor, Provo UT 84601. 801/373-2246. **Fax:** 801/373-5066. **Contact:** Personnel. **E-mail address:** jobs@sandlot.com. **World Wide Web address:** http://www.sandlot.com. **Description:** Develops database software for publishing companies. **Positions advertised include:** Quality Assurance Personnel. **Other U.S. locations:** Princeton NJ. **International locations:** United Kingdom.

THE SCO GROUP
355 South 520 West, Suite 100, Lindon UT 84042. 801/765-4999. **Fax:** 801/765-1313. **Contact:** Human Resources. **E-mail address:** jobs@sco.com. **World Wide Web address:** http://www.thescogroup.com. **Description:** Provides software, including UNIX, to small businesses. Founded 1994. **Positions advertised include:** Computer Instructor; Senior Software Engineer; Inside Sales Manager. **Corporate headquarters location:** This location. **International locations:** Worldwide. **Lusted on:** NASDAQ. **Stock exchange symbol:** SCOX. **President/CEO:** Darl C. McBride.

SECURITAS SECURITY SERVICES
5525 South 900 East, Salt Lake City UT 84117. 801/262-5678. **Toll-free phone:** 800/232-7465. **Fax:** 801/266-7935. **Contact:** Branch Manager. **World Wide Web address:** http://www.securitas.com. **Description:** One of the world's largest suppliers of global, total security solutions. The company provides a broad array of security-related services to address the protection needs of more than 20,000 customers through 220 offices in the United States, Canada, Mexico, Europe, and Asia. Pinkerton counts approximately half of the *Fortune* 500 companies as its clients. **NOTE:** Please visit website to search for jobs and apply online. **Corporate headquarters location:** Stockholm Sweden. **Other area locations:** South Jordan UT; Sandy UT; Magna UT. **Other U.S. locations:** Nationwide. **Number of employees worldwide:** 200,000.

SELECT PORTFOLIO SERVICING
P.O. Box 65250, Salt Lake City UT 84165-0250. 801/293-1883. **Contact:** Human Resources. **E-mail address:** Pam.Gurmankin@spservicing.com. **World Wide Web address:** http://www.spservicing.com. **Description:** A financial services company that engages in the servicing of single-family residential mortgage loans. It also services impaired credit loans and non-performing loans for a variety of clients. Founded in 1989. **Positions advertised include:** Accounts Payable Specialist; Bankruptcy Supervisor; Bankruptcy Specialist; Entry Level Office Position; Manager, Investor Reporting; Mortgage Collections Certified Real Estate Appraiser; Programmer Analyst. **Corporate headquarters location:** This location. **Other U.S. locations:** Hatboro PA; Jacksonville FL.

SENTINEL CONSUMER PRODUCTS
Freeport Center, #C12, Clearfield UT 84015. 801/825-5671. **Contact:** Human Resources Department. **World Wide Web address:** http://www.sentinelconsumer.com. **NOTE:** Please visit website for online application form, or send your resume to the corporate office – 7750 Tyler Boulevard, Mentor OH 44060-4887. **Description:** Manufactures cotton balls, cotton swabs, and cotton insoles. **Corporate headquarters location:** Mentor OH. **Other U.S. locations:** Anniston AL.

SHAW BENECO
7090 South Union Park Avenue, Midvale UT 84042. 801/565-1122. **Fax:** 801/565-1761. **Contact:** Human Resources. **World Wide Web address:** http://www.shawbeneco.com. **Description:** A construction management company. **Corporate headquarters location:** This location. **Other U.S. locations:** Nationwide. **Parent company:** The Shaw Group.

SKYWEST, INC.
444 South River Road, St. George UT 84790. 435/634-3000. **Fax:** 435/634-3105. **Contact:** Personnel Department. **World Wide Web address:** http://www.skywest.com. **Description:** A holding company. **NOTE:** Please visit website to search for jobs, access the application online, and sign up for the Career Mailing List – you will receive weekly updates about available jobs. **Positions advertised include:** Flight Attendant; Customer Service Agent; Ramp Agent; Cross Utilized Agent. **Special programs:** Internships. **Corporate headquarters location:** This location. **Subsidiaries include:** SkyWest Airlines is a large regional airline that operates as a Delta Connection carrier and offers scheduled passenger and cargo air services to 42 cities in 12 western states. Scenic Airlines provides air tours, general aviation, and scheduled airline services to Arizona, Nevada, and Utah. National Parks Transportation, Inc. rents Avis vehicles in five of the airport locations served by SkyWest and Scenic Airlines. **Operations at this facility include:** Administration. **Listed on:** NASDAQ. **Stock exchange symbol:** SKYW.

SII MEGADIAMOND
275 West 2230 North, Provo UT 84604. 801/377-3474. **Toll-free phone:** 800/453-1370. **Fax:** 801/818-4549. **Contact:** Human Resources. **World Wide Web address:** http://www.megadiamond.com. **Description:** Manufactures synthetic diamond inserts for drill heads and other drilling tools. **NOTE:** Human Resources phone is 801/818-4518. **International locations:** Scurelle Italy. **Parent company:** Smith International.

SMITH'S FOOD & DRUG CENTERS
1550 South Redwood Road, Salt Lake City UT 84104. 801/974-1400. **Contact:** Human Resources. **World Wide Web address:** http://www.smithsfoodanddrug.com. **Description:** Smith's Food & Drug Centers are designed for one-stop shopping and have specialty departments such as one-hour photo processing, hot prepared foods, delicatessen, seafood counter, frozen yogurt counter, bakery, florist, and pharmacy. **NOTE:** Please visit website to search for jobs and apply online. **Positions advertised include:** Retail Personnel; Pharmacy Workers; Manufacturers; Corporate Personnel. **Special programs:** Internships. **Corporate headquarters location:** This location. **Parent company:** The Kroger Company. **Listed on:** New York Stock Exchange. **Stock exchange symbol:** KR.

SMURFIT-STONE CONTAINER CORPORATION
2357 South 900 West, Salt Lake City UT 84119. 801/972-3005. **Toll-free phone:** 877/772-2999. **Contact:** Human Resources Manager. **World Wide Web address:** http://www.smurfit-stone.com. **Description:** One of the world's leading paper-based packaging companies. Smurfit-Stone Container Corporation's main products include corrugated containers, folding cartons, and multiwall industrial bags. The company is also one of the world's largest collectors and processors of recycled products that are then sold to a worldwide customer base. Smurfit-Stone Container Corporation also operates several paper tube, market pulp, and newsprint production facilities. **Corporate headquarters location:** Chicago IL. **Other U.S. locations:** Nationwide. **International locations:** China; Mexico; Canada. **Listed on:** NASDAQ. **Stock exchange symbol:** SSCC. **Number of employees nationwide:** 38,600.

SNOW, CHRISTENSEN & MARTINEAU
P.O. Box 45000, Salt Lake City UT 84145-5000. 800/748-4313. **Physical address:** 10 Exchange Place, 11th Floor, Salt Lake City UT. **Fax:** 801/363-0400. **Contact:** Recruiting. **E-mail address:** bmiller@scmlaw.com. **World Wide Web address:** http://www.scmlaw.com. **Description:** A law firm with a variety of specialties including employment, insurance, and real estate law. **NOTE:** Direct phone for contact is 801/322-9126. Please visit website for details on contact information, depending on your location and area of interest. **Corporate headquarters location:** This location.

SNOW COLLEGE
150 East College Avenue, Ephraim UT 84627. 435/283-7057. **Fax:** 435/ 283-6285. **Contact:** Claudia Jarrett, Director of Human Resources Department. **E-mail address:** bonnie.edwards@snow.edu. **World Wide Web address:** http://www.snow.edu. **Description:** A two-year community college. **NOTE:** Entry-level positions are offered. Human Resources phone is 435/283-7057. Please visit website to download application form, and for more details on he application procedure. **Positions advertised include:** Adjunct Biology Professor; Assistant Professor of Communications; Upward Bound Administrative Assistant.

SONIC INNOVATIONS, INC.
2795 East Cottonwood Parkway, Suite 660, Salt Lake City UT 84141. 801/365-2800. **Fax:** 801/365-3000. **Contact:** Human Resources. **E-mail address:** info@sonici.com. **World Wide Web address:** http://www.sonici.com. **Description:** Designs and manufactures advanced hearing aids, using a successful and tiny chip. **Corporate headquarters location:** This location. **International locations:** Canada; Denmark, Australia; New Zealand. **Listed on:** NASDAQ. **Stock exchange symbol:** SNCI. **President/CEO:** Andrew G. Raguskus.

SORENSON BIOSCIENCE
6507 South 400 West, Salt Lake City UT 84107. 801/266-9334. **Fax:** 801/262-0433; 801/892-0465. **Contact:** Human Resources. **E-mail address:** sbiinfo@sorbio.com. **World Wide Web address:** http://www.sorbio.com. **Description:** Manufactures plastic ends for pipettes that are used in genetic research. Founded 1981.

SORENSON MEDIA
4393 South Riverboat Road, Suite 300, Salt Lake City UT 84123. 801/287-9400. **Fax:** 801/287-9401. **Contact:** Human Resources. **World Wide Web address:** http://www.sorenson.com. **Description:** Provides video technology for internet purposes. Founded 2000. **Corporate headquarters location:** This location. **CEO:** James L. Sorenson, Jr.

SOUTH VALLEY HEALTH CENTER
3706 West 9000 South, West Jordan UT 84088-8866. 801/280-2273. **Contact:** Human Resources. **Description:** A nursing home with 120 beds. The center also provides rehabilitation services and physical and speech therapy.

SOUTHERN UTAH UNIVERSITY
351 West Center Street, Cedar City UT 84720. 435/586-7754. **Fax:** 435/ 865-8420. **Contact:** Human Resources Department. **World Wide Web address:** http://www.suu.edu. **Description:** A public, state-assisted university. The university offers programs in over 80 fields including arts, letters, and humanities; business, technology, and communication; and education. The college offers master's, bachelor's, and associate's degrees as well as certification programs. The university has approximately 6,000 students enrolled. The campus includes a land observatory and an archeology site. Founded in 1897. **NOTE:** Please visit website to download appropriate application form, or to register to receive future job announcements. **Positions advertised include:** Assistant Professor – Various Departments; Adjunct Instructor – Various Departments; Dean – College of Performing and Visual Arts; Director of

Bands; Director of Master of Fine Arts Program in Arts Administration; Director of Sponsored Research and Grants. **Special programs:** Internships. **Office hours:** Monday - Friday, 8:00 a.m. - 5:00 p.m. **Corporate headquarters location:** Salt Lake City UT.

SOUTHWIRE COMPANY
3295 West 8600 South, West Jordan UT 84088. 801/568-2300. **Contact:** Human Resources. **World Wide Web address:** http://www.mysouthwire.com. **Description:** Manufactures wire for all types of end uses. **Corporate headquarters location:** Carrollton GA. **CEO:** Stu Thorn.

STANDARD-EXAMINER
P.O. Box 12790, Ogden UT 84412. 801/625-4200. **Physical address:** 332 Standard Way, Ogden UT. **Toll-free phone:** 800/234-5505. **Fax:** 801/625-4508. **Contact:** Jayne Dunn, Human Resources Director. **World Wide Web address:** http://www.standard.net. **Description:** Publishes an independent daily newspaper with a circulation of more than 60,000. **NOTE:** Contact Human Resources directly at 801/625-4522. Fax: is 801/625-4535. **Corporate headquarters location:** This location. **Number of employees at this location:** 390.

STOCK BUILDING SUPPLY
ANDERSON LUMBER
P.O. Box 9459, Ogden UT 84409. 801/479-3400. **Physical address:** 1843 West 4000 South, Roy UT 84409. **Fax:** 801/476-1953. **Contact:** Human Resources. **E-mail address:** heather.mccullen@stocksupply.com. **World Wide Web address:** http://www.stockbuildingsupply.com. **Description:** A contracting company. Stock Building Supply is one of the United States' largest construction material providers. **NOTE:** Please send resumes to Carolina Holdings, P.O. Box 58515, Raleigh NC 27658. **Corporate headquarters location:** Raleigh NC. **Other area locations:** Statewide. **Other U.S. locations:** Nationwide. **Parent company:** Wolseley. **Listed on:** New York Stock Exchange. **Stock exchange symbol:** WOS.

STORAGETEK
376 East 400 South, Suite 308, Salt Lake City UT 84111. 801/322-3435. **Fax:** 801/533-9718. **Contact:** Human Resources. **E-mail address:** stkjobs@storagetek.com. **World Wide Web address:** http://www.stortek.com. **Description:** Storage Technology Corporation manufactures, markets, and services high-performance computer information storage and retrieval systems for mainframe and mid-frame computers and networks. Products include automated cartridge systems, random access subsystems, and fault-tolerant disk arrays. The company also distributes equipment; sells new peripherals, software, and hardware; and offers support services. **NOTE:** Please visit website to search for jobs and apply online. The online application method is preferred by the company, but you may also build a resume on the website, or email your resume. **Corporate headquarters location:** Louisville CO. **Other U.S. locations:** Nationwide. **International locations:** Worldwide. **Operations at this facility include:** This location is an administrative facility. **Listed on:** New York Stock Exchange. **Stock exchange symbol:** STK. **Number of employees worldwide:** 7,000.

SUNKIST GROWERS INC.
102 West 500 South, Suite 605, Salt Lake City UT 84101. 801/364-2733. **Contact:** Human Resources. **World Wide Web address:** http://www.sunkist.com. **Description:** Produces citrus fruits and products under the Sunkist brand name.

SWEET CANDY COMPANY
P.O. Box 22450, Salt Lake City UT 84122. 801/886-1444. **Physical address:** 3780 West Directors Row, Salt Lake City UT 84104. **Toll-free phone:** 800/669-8669. **Fax:** 801/866-1404. **Contact:** Human Resources. **E-mail address:** mail@sweetcandy.com. **World Wide Web address:** http://www.sweetcandy.com. **Description:** Manufactures a wide range of candy and confectionery goods.

SYMANTEC CORPORATION
796 East Utah Valley Drive, Suite 100, American Fork UT 84003. 801/224-5306. **Fax:** 801/227-3766. **Contact:** Human Resources Department. **World Wide Web address:** http://www.symantec.com. **Description:** Provides Internet security, including virus protection and firewall networks. Develops software for consumers that secures their computer passwords and personal computer files. **Positions advertised include:** Senior Software Engineer; Principal Software Engineer; Senior Human Factors Engineer. **Corporate headquarters location:** Cupertino CA. **Other U.S. locations:** Nationwide. **International locations:** Worldwide. **Listed on:** NASDAQ. **Stock exchange symbol:** SYMC. **Number of employees worldwide:** 5,000.

O.C. TANNER
1930 South State Street, Salt Lake City UT 84115. 801/486-2430. **Toll-free phone:** 800/453-7490. **Contact:** Human Resources. **E-mail address:** jobs@octanner.com. **World Wide Web address:** http://www.octanner.com. **Description:** A full-service provider and manufacturer of corporate recognition awards and programs. **Positions advertised include:** Proposal Specialist/Administrative Assistant; Client Representative; Sales Representative. **Corporate headquarters location:** This location. **Listed on:** Privately held. **President/CEO:** Kent Murdock. **Number of employees worldwide:** 2,000.

TARGET
7025 Park Center Drive, Salt Lake City UT 84121-6619. 801/255-2292. **Description:** A nationwide chain of retail stores. **NOTE:** Please visit website to register, search for jobs, and apply online. **Positions advertised include:** Pharmacist; Executive Team Leader; Store Team Leader. **Corporate headquarters location:** Minneapolis MN. **Other area locations:** Orem UT; West Valley City UT. **Other U.S. locations:** Nationwide. **Parent company:** Target Corporation. **Listed on:** New York Stock Exchange. **Stock exchange symbol:** TGT.

TESCO WILLIAMSEN
P.O. Box 26864, Salt Lake City UT 84126. 801/973-9400. **Physical address:** 1925 West Indiana Avenue, Salt Lake City UT 84104-3610. **Toll-free phone:** 800/828-9847. **Fax:** 801/973-2838. **Contact:** Human Resources. **World Wide Web address:** http://www.tescowilliamsen.com. **Description:** Manufactures and sells truck trailers, truck and bus bodies, and custom mobile equipment. **Corporate headquarters location:** This location.

3M HEALTH INFORMATION SYSTEMS
575 West Murray Boulevard, Murray UT 84123-4611. 801/265-4400. **Fax:** 801/263-3658. **Contact:** Personnel. **E-mail address:** resumes@3mjobs.com. **World Wide Web address:** http://www.3mhis.com. **Description:** A systems integrator to more than 3,000 hospitals, health networks and enterprises, managed care organizations, outpatient facilities, and medical group practices. The company provides the health care market with clinical information systems that have data integration, total quality management, and expert system technology capabilities. **NOTE:** Entry-level positions are offered. **Positions advertised include:** Data Innovation System Installer; Inpatient Clinical Consultant/Project Leader; Senior Manager of Outpatient Services; Software Quality Assurance Manager; Business Development Analyst; Product Marketing Manager for Coding/Reimbursement Modules; Products Marketing Manager; Product Marketing/Business Development Manager; Deputy Project Manager; Sales Representative Specialist for Home Health; Advanced Software Engineer; Advanced Product Analyst. **Special programs:** Internships; Training; Co-ops. **Corporate headquarters location:** This location. **Other U.S. locations:** Atlanta GA; Westchester IL; Wallingford CT; Burtonsville MD; Washington D.C. **Parent company:** 3M. **Listed on:** New York Stock Exchange. **Stock exchange symbol:** MMM.

TRANSCORE
488 East 6400 South, Suite 375, Murray UT 84107. 801/293-1920. **Fax:** 801/293-1921. **Contact:** Human Resources. **World Wide Web address:** http://www.transcore.com. **Description:** Transcore is a traffic engineering and transportation-planning firm. **NOTE:** Mail resumes to 8158 Adams Drive, Hummelstown PA 17036, or fax to 717/564-8439. **Other U.S. locations:** Nationwide. **Positions advertised include:** Advanced Traffic Management System Inspector. **Office hours:** Monday – Friday, 8:00 a.m. – 5:00 p.m. **Parent company:** Science Applications International Corporation (SAIC), also at this location is a technology firm that provides products and services relating to transportation, health care, energy, and national security. SAIC's primary business is government and military contracting.

U.S. BANK
15 West South Temple Street, Suite 200, Salt Lake City UT 84101. 801/534-6164. **Toll-free phone:** 800/USB-ANKS. **Contact:** Human Resources. **World Wide Web address:** http://www.usbank.com. **Description:** Provides full-service banking including investment and trust services. **NOTE:** Please visit website to search for jobs and apply online. **Positions advertised include:** Administrative Assistant; Branch Manager; Branch Operations Specialist; District Operations Manager; In Store Banker; In Store Branch Assistant; Personal Banker; Teller; Teller Coordinator. **Office hours:** Monday – Friday 9:00 a.m. – 5:00 p.m. **Parent company:** U.S. Bancorp. **Other U.S. locations:** Nationwide. **Listed on:** New York Stock Exchange. **Stock exchange symbol:** USB. **President/CEO:** Jerry A. Grundhofer.

U.S. DEPARTMENT OF VETERANS AFFAIRS
VETERANS ADMINISTRATION MEDICAL CENTER
500 Foothill Drive, Salt Lake City UT 84148. 801/582-1565. **Fax:** 801/584-1289. **Contact:** Human Resources. **World Wide Web address:** http://www.va.gov. **Description:** A medical center. From 54 hospitals in 1930, the VA health care system has grown to include more than 170 medical centers; more than 364 outpatient, community, and outreach clinics; 130 nursing home care units; and 37 domiciliary residences. VA operates at least one medical center in each of the 48 contiguous states, Puerto Rico, and the District of Columbia. With approximately 76,000 medical center beds, VA treats nearly 1 million patients in VA hospitals; 75,000 in nursing home care units; and 25,000 in domiciliary residences. VA's outpatient clinics register approximately 24 million visits per year. **NOTE:** Human Resources phone is 801/584-1284. Fax is 801/584-2588. Visit USAJOBS website to search for positions. **Positions advertised include:** Biological Science Laboratory Technician; Informational Technology Specialist; Pharmacist; Medical Instrument Technician; Medical Instrument Technician; Registered Respiratory Therapist; Diagnostic Radiology Technician. **Other area locations:** Fountain Green UT; Nephi UT; Orem UT; Roosevelt UT; South Ogden UT; St. George UT. **Other U.S. locations:** Nationwide. **Parent company:** U.S. Department of Veterans Affairs.

U.S. FEDERAL RESERVE BANK OF SAN FRANCISCO
P.O. Box 30780, Salt Lake City 84130-0780. 801/322-7900. **Physical address:** 120 South State Street, Salt Lake City UT 84111. **Contact:** Sherilyn Ranstrom, Personnel Manager. **World Wide Web address:** http://www.frbsf.org. **Description:** One of 12 regional Federal Reserve banks that along with the Federal Reserve Board of Governors in Washington DC, and the Federal Open Market Committee (FOMC), comprise the Federal Reserve System, the nation's central bank. As the nation's central bank, the Federal Reserve is charged with three major responsibilities: monetary policy, banking supervision and regulation, and processing payments. **Office hours:** Monday – Friday, 8:00 a.m. – 4:45 p.m. **Corporate headquarters location:** San Francisco. **Other U.S. locations:** AK; AZ; CA; HI; ID; NV; OR; WA. **International locations:** American Samoa; Guam; Mariana Islands.

U.S. XPRESS ENTERPRISES, INC.
1901 West 2100 South, Salt Lake City UT 84119. 801/975-2513. **Contact:** Human Resources. **World Wide Web address:** http://www.usxpress.com. **Description:** A nationwide truckload carrier. **Corporate headquarters location:** Chattanooga TN. **Operations at this facility include:** Administration; Sales; Service. **Listed on:** NASDAQ. **Stock exchange symbol:** XPRSA.

UINTA BUSINESS SYSTEMS INC.
332 West Bugatti Avenue, Salt Lake City UT 84115. 801/461-7600. **Toll-free phone:** 800/735-0234. **Fax:** 801/486-4720. **Contact:** Jeune Ellis. **E-mail address:** jeunee@uinta.com. **World Wide Web address:** http://www.uinta.com. **Description:** One of Utah's largest systems resellers. Uinta Business Systems sells, leases, and services office machinery including computers, fax machines, and photocopiers. **NOTE:** Unita's employment opportunities are filled through TechStaff, an in-house staffing group. Please e-mail your resume to Jeune Ellis, or call her at 801/461-7655. **Positions advertised include:** Microsoft Certified Systems Engineer; Certified Novell Engineer; LAN/WAN; Desktop Support Specialist; Help Desk Support Specialist; PC Technician; Unix Administrator. **Other U.S. locations:** Las Vegas NV. **Subsidiaries include:** Unita Information Solutions; Unita eSolutions; Unita Document Systems.

ULTRADENT PRODUCTS INC.
505 West 10200 South, South Jordan UT 84095. 801/572-4200. **Toll-free phone:** 800/496-8337. **Fax:** 801/553-4642. **Recorded jobline:** 801/553-4233. **Contact:** Human Resources. **E-mail address:** hr@ultradent.com. **World Wide Web address:** http://www.ultradent.com. **Description:** Manufactures products for use by dentists including syringes and opalescent whitening gel. **Positions advertised include:** Accounts Receivable Clerk; Dental Lab Technician/Ceramist; Thermoform Operator; Material Tester/Engineering Technician; Packaging Engineer; Territory Account Manger. **Corporate headquarters location:** This location. **Number of employees at this location:** 600.

UNICITY INTERNATIONAL
748 North 1340 West, Orem UT 84057. 801/764-1800. **Contact:** Human Resources. **World Wide Web address:** http://www.enrich.com. **Description:** Develops, manufactures, markets, and distributes herbs and health food products. **Office hours:** 7:00 a.m. – 9:00 p.m. **Corporate headquarters location:** This location.

UNISYS CORPORATION
P.O. Box 16800, Salt Lake City UT 84116-0800. 801/594-5000. **Physical address:** 480 North 2200 West, Salt Lake City UT 84116. **Fax:** 801/594-5660. **Contact:** Human

Resources. **World Wide Web address:** http://www.unisys.com. **Description:** Unisys Corporation provides information services, technology, and software. Unisys specializes in developing critical business solutions based on open information networks. The company's Enabling Software Team creates a variety of software projects that facilitate the building of user applications and the management of distributed systems. The company's Platforms Group is responsible for UNIX Operating Systems running across a wide range of multiple processor server platforms including all peripheral and communication drivers. The Unisys Commercial Parallel Processing Team develops microkernel-based operating systems, I/O device drivers, ATM hardware, diagnostics, and system architectures. The System Management Group is in charge of the overall management of development programs for UNIX desktop and entry-server products. **Corporate headquarters location:** Blue Bell PA. **Other U.S. locations:** Nationwide. **International locations:** Worldwide. **Operations at this facility include:** This location is involved in scaleable commercial transaction processing systems based on distributed computing technologies. **Listed on:** New York Stock Exchange. **Stock exchange symbol:** UIS. **Number of employees worldwide:** 37,000.

UNITED PARCEL SERVICE (UPS)
2040 Parkway Boulevard, Suite 100, West Valley City UT 84119. 801/973-3600. **Fax:** 801/973-3795. **Contact:** Human Resources Manager. **World Wide Web address:** http://www.ups.com. **Description:** A package pickup and delivery service organization providing service to all 50 states and to more than 185 countries and territories worldwide, delivering approximately 12 million packages daily. **NOTE:** Please visit http://www.upsjobs.com to search for jobs. **Corporate headquarters location:** Atlanta GA. **Other area locations:** Logan UT; Ogden UT; Provo UT; Salt Lake City UT. **Other U.S. locations:** Nationwide. **International locations:** Worldwide.

UNIVERSAL SYSTEMS, INC. (USI)
1356 East 3300 South, Salt Lake City UT 84106. 801/484-9151. **Contact:** Human Resources. **E-mail address:** employment@usicomputer.com. **World Wide Web address:** http://www.usicomputer.com. **Description:** Develops workflow and document management software and provides systems integration services. The company provides turnkey solutions to *Fortune* 500 and government clients utilizing the latest in client/server platforms and SQL compliant databases. **Office hours:** 8:00 a.m. – 6:00 p.m. **Corporate headquarters location:** This location.

UNIVERSITY HOSPITALS & CLINICS
420 Wakara Way, Suite 105, Salt Lake City UT 84108. 801/581-2169. **Fax:** 801/581-4579. **Contact:** Human Resources. **E-mail address:** employment@hr.utah.edu. **World Wide Web address:** http://www.med.utah.edu. **Description:** University Hospitals & Clinics is comprised of University of Utah Hospital, a 392-bed tertiary and acute care facility. University Hospitals serves as the clinical arm for the medical school and the college of health, nursing, and pharmacy. Hospital inpatient admissions, clinic visits, and emergency department visits total more than 250,000 annually. Special research centers include the Institute for Human Genetics, which houses the Howard Hughes Medical Institute, a world-class genetics research program. Other centers include the Center for Human Toxicology; the Cardiovascular Research and Training Institute; the Institute for Biomedical Engineering/Division of Artificial Organs; and the Center for Diagnostic Imaging Research in the radiology department. As a major referral facility, University Hospitals has numerous specialties including burns and trauma; heart, kidney, and bone marrow transplants; newborn intensive care; shock wave lithotripsy; and cancer care. University Hospitals has expanded to include the University Neuropsychiatric Institute. **NOTE:** Entry-level and volunteer positions are offered. Please visit website to search for jobs and apply online. **Positions advertised include:** Coordinator of Special Events; Executive Secretary; Production Manager; Survey Clerk; Senior Laboratory Specialist; Lab Technician; Outpatient Clinical Representative; Research Nurse; Medical Storekeeper; RN – Various Departments; Compensation Analyst; Medical Assistant; Education Specialist; Accounting Specialist; Computer Operator; Customer Service Representative; Nutrition Care Aide; Library Aide; EMT; Insurance Account Representative; Psychiatric Technician; Drug/Alcohol Counselor; Pharmacist; Clinical Nurse – Various Departments; LPN. **Corporate headquarters location:** This location. **Other area locations:** Park City UT; Sugarhouse UT; Wendover UT.

UNIVERSITY OF UTAH
420 Wakara Way, Suite 105, Salt Lake City UT 84108. 801/581-2169. **Fax:** 801/581-4579. **Contact:** Human Resources. **E-mail address:** employment@hr.utah.edu. **World Wide Web address:** http://www.utah.edu. **Description:** A state university offering more than 70 undergraduate degree programs and more than 90 graduate majors. **Positions advertised include:** Clerk; Dispatcher; Executive Secretary; Academic Coordinator; Accounting Clerk; Community Liaison; Education Specialist; Academic Advisor; Office Assistant; Computer Operator; Lab Technician; Vehicle Operator.

UTAH ADMINISTRATIVE OFFICE OF THE COURTS
450 South State, P.O. Box 140241, Salt Lake City UT 84114-0241. 801/578-3800. **Fax:** 801/238-7814. **Contact:** Human Resources. **World Wide Web address:** http://www.utcourts.gov. **Description:** The Utah Administrative Office of the Courts implements the standards, policies, and rules established by the judicial council; organizes and administers all of the nonjudicial activities of the court; prepares the state judicial budget; conducts studies; and develops procedures to further the administration of the courts. The administrative offices serve as staff to the judicial council, rules committee, board of judges, standing and ad hoc committees, and nominating commissions. The Utah Judicial Council is the policy-making body of the judiciary. It has the constitutional authority to adopt uniform rules for the administration of all courts in the state. The council also sets standards for judicial performance, court facilities, support services, and judicial and nonjudicial staff levels. The Utah district court system is comprised of two appellate courts: the supreme court and the court of appeals, and four trial courts: the district, juvenile, circuit, and justice courts. **NOTE:** Please visit website to search for jobs, and to download an application form. **Positions advertised include:** Juvenile Court Probation Officer; Deputy Court Clerk; Deputy Probation Officer; Juvenile Court Probation Officer; Deputy Court Clerk; Juvenile Court Judge.

UTAH COUNTY GOVERNMENT
100 East Center Street, Suite 2200, Provo UT 84606. 801/370-8158. **Recorded jobline:** 801/851-8585. **Fax:** 801/851-8166. **Contact:** Personnel. **E-mail address:** ucadm.utahcnty@state.ut.us. **World Wide Web address:** http://www.co.utah.ut.us. **Description:** Utah County Government provides public health and welfare services; offers fire protection; licenses businesses and trades; records property mortgages, deeds, and other legal documents; purchases and controls property; and erects and maintains buildings necessary for the use of the county. The county government also assists business growth in the community. County government is headed by a board consisting of three commissioners. **NOTE:** Please visit website to apply online, or to download the application form. Resumes are not accepted; you must submit an application. **Positions advertised include:** Corrections Registered Nurse; Deputy Sheriff; Substance Abuse Counselor; Office Specialist; District Manager – North Pointe Solid Waste.

UTAH DEPARTMENT OF CORRECTIONS
14717 South Minuteman Boulevard, Draper UT 84020. 801/545-5500. **Fax:** 801/545-5670. **Contact:** Human Resources Office. **E-mail address:** corrections@utah.gov. **World Wide Web address:** http://www.udc.state.ut.us. **Description:** Protects the community while providing offenders with the tools necessary to enhance their prospects for success in society. The Division of Institutional Operations provides a continuum of confinement to control committed offenders so that they may function in a manner that will not be harmful to themselves, staff, other offenders, or society. **Positions advertise include:** Correctional Officer; Registered Nurse; Corrections Support Services Officer. **Special programs:** Internships. **Operations at this facility include:** Divisional Headquarters.

UTAH DEPARTMENT OF HUMAN RESOURCE MANAGEMENT
2120 State Office Building, P.O. Box 141531, Salt Lake City UT 84114-1531. 801/538-3025. **Fax:** 801/538-3081. **Contact:** Human Resources Department. **E-mail address:** hrchat@utah.gov. **World Wide Web address:** http://www.dhrm.state.ut.us. **Description:** Hires for a range of state departments in the Executive Branch of the state of Utah including the attorney general's office, the chamber of commerce, and the governor's office. The department also oversees agencies that have their own human resources departments including the Department of Administrative Services and the Department of Transportation.

UTAH DEPARTMENT OF HUMAN SERVICES
120 North 200 West, Room 427, Salt Lake City UT 84145. 801/538-4222. **Fax:** 801/538-4446. **Contact:** Human Resources Department. **World Wide Web address:** http://www.dhs.state.ut.us. **Description:** Administers state programs for mental health, public assistance, child welfare, and programs supported under the Older Americans Act. Other programs include substance abuse, service for people with disabilities, family services, youth corrections, and child support enforcement. The Department of Human Services also oversees and administers the Utah State Department Center in American Fork and the Utah State Hospital in Provo.

UTAH DEPARTMENT OF NATURAL RESOURCES
P.O. Box 145610, 1594 West North Temple Street, Salt Lake City UT 84114-5610. 801/538-7200. **Contact:** Human Resources Department. **World Wide Web address:** http://www.nr.utah.gov. **Description:** Conserves, protects, and develops the state's natural resources. Department of Natural Resources is broken down into several divisions. The Division of Oil, Gas, and Mining regulates exploration for and development of oil, gas, coal, and other mineral resources. This division also ensures that when exploration and developmental activities are completed, oil and gas wells are properly abandoned and mining sites are satisfactorily reclaimed. The Division of Parks and Recreation protects, preserves, and manages many of Utah's natural and cultural resources. The Division of State Lands and Forestry is broken down into two organizations: the first manages nontrust and sovereign lands and handles the state forestry and fire control programs. The second half is responsible for administering trust lands granted by the state at time of statehood. The Division of Water Resources plans, develops, uses, and protects the state's water resources. The Division of Water Rights is responsible for the general supervision and management of the use of the state's waters. Activities regulated by the division include appropriation, distribution and adjudication of water, dam safety, stream channel alterations, geothermal, and water well drilling. The Division of Wildlife regulates hunting, fishing and trapping, and promotes recreational, educational, scientific, and aesthetic enjoyment of wildlife resources. **NOTE:** To learn about employment opportunities, contact the Department of Human Resource Management at 801/538-3062. **Office hours:** Monday – Friday, 8:00 a.m. – 5:00 p.m.

UTAH DEPARTMENT OF PUBLIC SAFETY
P.O. Box 141775, 4501 South 2700 West, Salt Lake City UT 84114-1775. 801/965-4461. **Toll-free phone:** 800/222-0038. **Contact:** Human Resources. **World Wide Web address:** http://publicsafety.utah.gov. **Description:** The Utah Department of Public Safety provides a safe environment for Utah state citizens by ensuring that citizens operating motor vehicles in the state possess the proper qualifications and obey traffic laws and regulations; monitoring highway safety and investigating the causes of injury, loss of life, and property damage due to motor vehicle accidents; planning for mitigation and prevention of natural or man-made disasters; preventing criminal activity and identifying and apprehending persons violating state criminal statutes; assisting other criminal justice agencies throughout the state in the investigation, detection, identification, and apprehension of those involved in criminal activity; providing training to recruits entering the law enforcement community by assessing and meeting their continuing educational needs; ensuring compliance with the Utah Liquor Control Act and Utah's controlled substance statutes; assisting in the determination of fires of unknown origin and to ensure compliance with Utah's fire prevention regulations; ensuring the integrity of those participating in the federal Medicaid program; maintaining a vital communications network throughout Utah; regulating individuals and organizations as determined by the Legislature; and responding to the call of the governor and providing assistance as requested. **NOTE:** Please submit our resume to the Department of Human Resource Management - 120 State Office Building, P.O. Box 141531, Salt Lake City UT 84114-1531. **Positions advertised include:** Accountant; Auditor; Bureau Chief Criminal Investigator; Data Terminal Technician; Division Director; Human Resource Technician; LAN Administrator; Accounting Technician; Program Specialist; Programmer Analyst; Planner; Safety Officer; Secretary; Secretary/Legal Office Clerk; Support Services Technician; DPS Officer; Radio Dispatcher; Archival Technician; Clerk; Fleet Manager; Mail Clerk; Micrographic Technician; Technical Support Specialist; Warehouse Worker.

UTAH FUN DOME
4998 South 360 West, Murray UT 84123. 801/293-0800. **Fax:** 801/265-3869. **Contact:** Human Resources. **E-mail address:** info@fundome.com. **World Wide Web address:** http://www.fundome.com. **Description:** Operates an indoor entertainment facility that includes arcade games, a bowling alley, and miniature golf.

UTAH MEDICAL PRODUCTS, INC.
7043 South 300 West, Midvale UT 84047-1048. 801/566-1200. **Toll-free phone:** 800/533-4984. **Fax:** 801/566-2062. **E-mail address:** careers@utahmed.com. **Contact:** Human Resources. **World Wide Web address:** http://www.utahmed.com. **Description:** Utah Medical Products, Inc. develops, manufactures, assembles, and markets a broad range of products serving the critical care and obstetrics/gynecology markets. Products include a line of transducers and catheters used in monitoring blood pressure and uterine contraction pressure, an electrosurgery generator and disposable electrodes used in a new treatment to remove precancerous cervical tissue, a line of disposable infant oxygen therapy products, and female incontinence therapy products. The company's markets include specialties where new treatment techniques are being performed in hospitals, outpatient surgery centers, and doctors' offices. Founded in 1978. **NOTE:** Entry-level positions and second and third shifts are offered. **Positions**

advertised include: Technician. **Corporate headquarters location:** This location. **Other U.S. locations:** Redmond OR. **International locations:** Athlone, Ireland. **Operations at this facility include:** Administration; Divisional Headquarters; Manufacturing; Regional Headquarters; Research and Development; Sales; Service. **Listed on:** NASDAQ. **Stock exchange symbol:** UTMD.

UTAH REFRACTORIES CORPORATION
2200 North 1100 West, Lehi UT 84043. 801/768-3591. **Contact:** Human Resources. **Description:** Manufactures high temperature bricks, cement, and mortar for use in glass furnaces at steel mills.

UTAH STATE HOSPITAL
P.O. Box 270, Provo UT 84603-0270. 801/344-4400. **Physical address:** 1300 East Center Street, Provo UT 84606. **Fax:** 801/344-4225. **Contact:** Human Resources. **World Wide Web address:** http://www.hsush.state.ut.us. **Description:** A hospital. Specialized programs include a children's unit, an adolescent unit, four adult units, a geriatric unit, and a forensic unit. The children's unit has a capacity of 22 patients, serving children between the ages of 6 and 13 who have psychiatric and/or behavioral disorders. The unit offers individual therapy, group therapy, family therapy, and recreational therapy. The adolescent unit has a capacity of 50 patients and serves as a residential treatment center for emotionally disturbed youth between the ages of 13 and 18. Various treatment programs are used with emphasis on peer and group processes, stressing responsibility and concern for self and others. The adult programs, treating chronically-ill patients, are broken down into four units with a total capacity for 149 patients. The geriatric unit, for patients age 55 and over, has a 60-bed patient capacity. The Forensic Unit, with a capacity for 54 people, is designed to meet the needs of patients of different legal status. **NOTE:** Please send your resume to the address listed above, as well as to the Utah Department of Human Resource Management - 2120 State Office Building, P.O. Box 141531, Salt Lake City UT 84114-1531. **Positions advertised include:** Registered Nurse; Psychiatrist; Licensed Practical Nurse.

UTAH STATE UNIVERSITY
9510 Old Main Hill, Logan UT 84328. 435/797-1000. **Contact:** Personnel Services. **World Wide Web address:** http://www.usu.edu. **Description:** A four-year state university with an enrollment of approximately 20,000 students. **NOTE:** please visit website to search for jobs, and to find details on application process for specific positions. **Positions advertised include:** Department Head – Various Departments; Assistant Professor – Various Departments; Senior Lecturer & Executive in Residence – Business Administration; Early Childhood Teacher; Research Assistant – Special Education and Rehabilitation; Faculty – Music; Research Associate; Extension Educator; Medical Laboratory Technologist; Cataloger; Clinical Instructor; System Administrator; Fire Marshall; SAAVI Coordinator; Safety Coordinator; Director – Institutional Developer; Programmer/Analyst; Accountant; Clothing/Gifts Buyer; Atmospheric Scientist. **Special programs:** Internships. **Corporate headquarters location:** This location.

UTAH SYMPHONY
Abravanel Hall, 123 West South Temple, Salt Lake City UT 84101-1496. 801/533-5626. **Fax;** 801/869-9026. **Contact:** Shelley Gifford, Orchestra Personnel Assistant. **E-mail address:** sgifford@utahsymphonyopera.org. **World Wide Web address:** http://www.utahsymphony.org. **Description:** A symphony that performs year round. **NOTE:** No phone calls regarding employment. **Positions advertised include:** Artistic Administrator; Principal Bassoon; Viola Player; Director of Foundations and Planned Giving.

UTAH TRANSIT AUTHORITY
P.O. Box 30810. Salt Lake City UT 84130-0810. 801/262-5626. **Physical address:** 3600 South 700 West, Salt Lake City UT. **Toll-free phone:** 888/743-3882. **Recorded jobline:** 801/287-4617. **Contact:** Human Resources. **E-mail address:** jobs@utabus.com. **World Wide Web address:** http://www.utabus.com. **Description:** Operates the mass transit bus system. **Positions advertised include:** Rail Service Employee. **Office hours:** Monday – Saturday, 6:00 a.m. – 7:00 p.m. **Corporate headquarters location:** This location. **Other area locations:** Orem UT; Ogden UT.

UTAH VALLEY REGIONAL MEDICAL CENTER
1034 North 500 West, Provo UT 84604-3337. 801/373-7850. **Contact:** Human Resources. **World Wide Web address:** http://www.ihc.com/xp/ihc/uvrmc. **Description:** With 350 beds, Utah Valley Regional is one of the largest hospitals in the nonprofit Intermountain Health Care system. The hospital is a tertiary referral center for Utah County and the south and central counties of the state. The center includes an open-heart program, dialysis center, two MRIs, trauma care, newborn intensive care, three heart catheter labs, and a radiation oncology center. **NOTE:** Human Resources phone is 801/357-7035. Please visit website to register, search for jobs, and apply online. **Positions advertised include:** RN – Various Departments; Ultrasonographer; Health Unit Coordinator; Media Manager; Medical Technologist; Cook; Housekeeper; Pharmacy Manager; Radiology Technician; Mammography Technologist; Licensed Psychologist; CT Technologist.

UTAH WOOL MARKETING ASSOCIATION
855 South 500 West, Salt Lake City UT 84101. 801/328-1507. **Fax:** 801/531-6838. **Contact:** Will Hart Griggs, Manager. **Description:** Provides a variety of marketing and related business and financial services to ranchers, processors, and retailers involved in the production and sale of wool and related products. **Office hours:** Monday – Friday, 8:00 a.m. – 4:30 p.m. **Corporate headquarters location:** This location.

UTAH ZOOLOGICAL SOCIETY
2600 East Sunnyside Avenue, Salt Lake City UT 84108. 801/582-1631. **Fax:** 801/584-1770. **Contact:** Human Resources. **World Wide Web address:** http://www.hoglezoo.org. **Description:** A nonprofit organization that operates the Hogle Zoo. This location also hires seasonally. **NOTE:** The society offers volunteer opportunities. Entry-level positions and part-time jobs are offered. Human Resources phone is 801/584-1728. **Positions advertised include:** Graphics Assistant. **Special programs:** Internships; Summer Jobs. **Corporate headquarters location:** This location.

VARIAN X-RAY TUBE PRODUCTS
1678 South Pioneer Road, Salt Lake City UT 84104-4298. 801/972-5000. **Fax:** 801/973-5050. **Contact:** Human Resources Representative. **E-mail address:** industrial@xtp.varian.com; jobs@us.varian.com. **World Wide Web address:** http://www.varian.com. **Description:** Varian is a diversified, international manufacturing company. Varian operates manufacturing facilities in seven nations and has sales and service offices worldwide. The company is organized around the following core businesses: Health Care Systems, Instruments, Electronic Devices, and Semiconductor Equipment. Varian medical linear accelerators, treatment stimulators, and information management systems are used in hospitals and clinics worldwide. The company is also a leading supplier of X-ray tubes for imaging systems and instruments used in research against diseases. Varian also makes instruments used to regulate the quality of diverse products ranging from petroleum and pharmaceuticals to ice cream and champagne, as well as vacuum pumps and leak detectors that are essential to many processes that require a vacuum environment. Varian is a worldwide leader in the manufacture of devices that generate, amplify, and define signals for radio and television broadcasting and satellite communications. Varian's products are also used in air traffic control, navigation, radar, fusion energy, and other scientific research applications. **NOTE:** Please send resume to corporate headquarters at 911 Hansen Way, Palo Alto CA 94304, or fax to 650/424-5920. **Positions advertised include:** Senior Accountant; Senior Accountant Analyst; Electrical Engineer; Manufacturing Engineer; Product Assurance Engineer; Software Engineer; Test Engineer; Manager – Facilities Engineering; Customer Support Representative; Field Service Representative; Product Support Engineer; Senior Compensation Analyst; Systems Analyst; Digital Media Designer; Product Manager; Inventory Control Specialist; Warehouse Supervisor; Mechanical Technician; Quality Assurance Specialist; Sales Representative; Regional Sales Manager; Applications Specialist; Product Training Specialist. **Corporate headquarters location:** Palo Alto CA. **Other U.S. locations:** CA; VA; NV; GA; IL; NJ. **International locations:** Worldwide. **Operations at this facility include:** This location produces electron tubes for use in medical equipment. **Listed on:** New York Stock Exchange. **Stock exchange symbol:** VAR. **CEO:** Richard M. Levy.

WAL-MART STORES, INC.
1330 South Providence Center Drive, Cedar City UT 84720. 435/674-0454. **Contact:** Human Resources. **World Wide Web address:** http://www.walmart.com. **Description:** Wal-Mart Stores is one of the largest retail merchandise chains in the country, operating full-service discount department stores, combination grocery and discount stores, and warehouse stores requiring membership. Founded in 1962. **Corporate headquarters location:** Bentonville AR. **Operations at this facility include:** One location of the nationwide department store chain.

WATSON LABS-UTAH
417 Wakara Way, Salt Lake City UT 84108. 801/588-6200. **Contact:** Human Resources. **World Wide Web address:** http://www.watsonutah.com. **Description:** A researcher, developer, and manufacturer of drug delivery systems. **NOTE:** Please visit website to register, search for jobs, and apply online. **Positions advertised include:** Biostatistician; Clinical Data Specialist; Manager – Analytical R&D; Chemist; Process Operator; Scientist; Clinical Programmer Analyst; Direct Quality Assurance; Process Operator; Maintenance Supervisor; Secretary; General Maintenance Mechanic; Process Operator; Validation Engineer; Packaging Operator; Data Entry Clerk; Quality Auditor Associate. **Corporate headquarters location:** Corona CA. **Parent company:** Watson Pharmaceuticals. **Listed on:** New York Stock Exchange. **Stock exchange symbol:** WPI. **Number of employees at this location:** 242.

WE R MEMORY KEEPERS
P.O. Box 16509, Salt Lake City UT 84116. 801/521-2411. **Toll-free phone:** 877/742-5937. **Contact:** Human Resources. **World Wide Web address:** http://www.weronthenet.com. **Description:** Offers bookbinding and other commercial printing services. We R Memory Keepers also manufactures custom loose-leaf binders, software packaging, and leather goods. **Corporate headquarters location:** This location.

WEBER STATE UNIVERSITY
Miller Administration Building, Room 111, 1016 University Circle, Ogden UT 84408-1016. 801/626-6032. **Fax:** 801/626-6925. **Contact:** Holly Hirst, Employment Specialist. **E-mail address:** hhirst@weber.edu, hr@weber.edu. **World Wide Web address:** http://www.weber.edu. **Description:** A state university with approximately 14,000 students enrolled. **Positions advertised include:** Dean of Student Affairs; Assistant Professor – Various Departments; Automotive Technology Faculty; Faculty – First Year Coordinator; Nursing Lab Coordinator; Employee Wellness Program Coordinator; Financial Aid Counselor; Web Administrator; Secretary. **Corporate headquarters location:** This location.

WEIDER NUTRITION GROUP, INC.
2002 South 5070 West, Salt Lake City UT 84104. 801/975-5000. **Contact:** Human Resources. **World Wide Web address:** http://www.weidernutrition.biz. **Description:** Weider Nutrition Group manufactures vitamins. **Listed on:** New York Stock Exchange. **Stock exchange symbol:** WNI. **CEO:** Bruce J. Wood.

WEIR SPECIALTY PUMPS
P.O. Box 209, Salt Lake City UT 84110-0209. 801/359-8731. **Physical address:** 440 West 800 South, Salt Lake City UT 84101. **Fax:** 801/355-9303. **World Wide Web address:** http://www.weirsp.com. **Contact:** Human Resources. **Description:** Manufactures industrial pumps and pump systems. The company also manufactures rubber products for industrial and mining applications and is engaged in bulk injection molding. **Special programs:** Internships. **Corporate headquarters location:** This location. **Parent company:** The Weir Group PLC.

WELLS FARGO BANK
299 South Main Street, Salt Lake City UT 84111. 801/246-1300. **Contact:** Human Resources. **World Wide Web address:** http://www.wellsfargo.com. **Description:** A diversified financial institution with over $234 billion in assets. Wells Fargo serves over 17 million customers through 5,300 independent locations worldwide. The company also maintains several stand-alone ATMs and branches within other retail outlets. Services include community banking, credit and debit cards, home equity and mortgage loans, online banking, student loans, and insurance. Wells Fargo also offers a complete line of commercial and institutional financial services. Founded in 1852. **NOTE:** Please visit website to register, search for jobs, and apply online. **Positions advertised include:** Teller; Loan Documentation Representative; Business Lending Underwriter; Personal Banker; Teller; Lead Teller; Loan Servicing Representative. **Office hours:** Monday – Friday, 9:00 a.m. – 5:00 p.m.; Saturday, 9:00 a.m. – 3:00 p.m. **Corporate headquarters location:** San Francisco CA. **Other U.S. locations:** Nationwide. **International locations:** Worldwide. **Listed on:** New York Stock Exchange. **Stock exchange symbol:** WFC.

WESTGATE SOFTWARE INC.
12345 South 300 East, Draper UT 84020. 801/495-1200. **Fax:** 801/495-1208. **Contact:** Human Resources Department. **E-mail address:** info@westgatesoftware.com. **World Wide Web address:** http://www.westgatesoftware.com. **Description:** Develops software for use in film processing and the dry cleaning industry. **Office hours:** Monday – Friday, 8:00 a.m. – 5:00 p.m. **Corporate headquarters location:** This location. **International locations:** United Kingdom.

WESTMINSTER COLLEGE
106 Bamberger Hall, 1840 South 1300 East, Salt Lake City UT 84105. 801/484-7651. **Fax:** 801/832-3107. **Contact:** Human Resources. **E-mail address:** jobs@westminstercollege.edu. **World Wide Web address:** http://www.wcslc.edu. **Description:** A small, private, four-year college offering bachelor's and master's degree

programs. **NOTE:** For Adjunct Professor positions, please contact the Adjunct Professor Office at 211 Bamberger Hall, Attention Betsy Price, or call at 801/832-2587, and fax at 801/484-6450. **Positions advertised include:** Administrative Assistant; Associate Director of Admissions; Campus Patrol Officer; Chief Flight Instructor; Executive Director of Communications; Graduate Program Marketing/Recruitment Specialist; Seasonal Groundskeeper; Dean of Nursing; Faculty – Various Departments. **Office hours:** Monday – Friday, 8:00 a.m. – 5:00 p.m.

WHITEWATER WHIRLPOOL BATHS & SYSTEMS
195 South Geneva Road, Lindon UT 84042. 801/785-3554. **Contact:** Human Resources. **World Wide Web address:** http://www.whitewaterinc.com. **Description:** Manufactures cultured marble and onyx for bathtubs, showers, and bathroom vanities. **Other area locations:** Salt Lake City UT; Layton UT; St. George UT.

WILLIAMS GAS PIPELINES
P.O. Box 58900, Salt Lake City UT 84158-0900. 801/583-8800. **Physical address:** 295 Chipeta Way, Salt Lake City UT 84108. **Fax:** 801/584-6483. **Contact:** Human Resources Department. **E-mail address:** e-resumes@williams.com. **World Wide Web address:** http://www.williams.com. **Description:** Owns and operates a natural gas pipeline system including gas storage facilities in the western United States. The company serves customers in California, Colorado, Idaho, Nevada, Oregon, Utah, Washington, and Wyoming. **Corporate headquarters location:** Tulsa OK.

WILSON AUDIO
2233 Mountain Vista Lane, Provo UT 84606. 801/377-2233. **Fax:** 801/377-2282. **Contact:** Personnel. **E-mail address:** was@wilsonaudio.com. **World Wide Web address:** http://www.wilsonaudio.com. **Description:** Manufactures high-end audio equipment including stereo speakers.

WINDER DAIRY
400 West 4100 South, West Valley City UT 84120. 801/969-3401. **Toll-free phone:** 800/WINDER. **Fax:** 801/969-2223. **Contact:** Robin Goodwin, Human Resources Manager. **E-mail address:** robingoodwin@winderdairy.com. **World Wide Web address:** http://www.winderdairy.com. **Description:** Produces a full range of dairy products for area distribution. **Positions advertised include:** Route Sales Personnel/Driver; Door-to-Door Representative. **Corporate headquarters location:** This location.

WINDSOR DOOR
2943 West Parkway Boulevard, West Valley City UT 84119. 801/974-0226. **Fax:** 801/974-0407. **Contact:** Human Resources. **E-mail address:** employment@windsordoor.com. **World Wide Web address:** http://www.windsordoor.com/default2.asp. **Description:** A wholesaler of wooden garage doors. **NOTE:** Please visit website for online application form. Send resumes to corporate office at P.O. Box 8915, Little Rock AR 72219. **Corporate headquarters location:** Little Rock AR.

THE WIRTHLIN WORLDWIDE
1998 South Columbia Lane, Orem UT 84097. 801/226-1524. **Fax:** 801/226-3483. **Contact:** Human Resources. **E-mail address:** resumes@wirthlin.com. **World Wide Web address:** http://www.wirthlin.com. **Description:** Conducts political phone research and data analysis including public opinion polls for political candidates. **NOTE:** Please send resumes to corporate office at 1920 Association Drive, Reston VA 20191, or fax to 703/832-8974. **Corporate headquarters location:** Reston VA. **Other area locations:** Salt Lake City UT. **Other U.S. locations:** New York, NY; Dallas TX; Chicago IL; Detroit MI; Grand Rapids MI; Cincinnati OH. **International locations:** England; Belgium; Australia; China; Hong Kong.

WON-DOOR CORPORATION
1865 South 3480 West, Salt Lake City UT 84104. 801/973-7500. **Toll-free phone:** 800/453-8494. **Fax:** 801/977-9749. **Contact:** Personnel. **E-mail address:** personnel@wondoor.com. **World Wide Web address:** http://www.wondoor.com. **Description:** Manufactures sliding partition doors and swinging fire doors. **Corporate headquarters location:** This location. **Other U.S. locations:** Nationwide. **International locations:** Canada; Taiwan; United Kingdom; New Zealand; Singapore; Germany.

WONDERBREAD/HOSTESS CAKES
P.O. Box 108, Ogden UT 84402. 801/394-5743. **Physical address:** 2557 Grant Avenue, Ogden UT 84401. **Contact:** Human Resources. **World Wide Web address:** http://www.wonderbread.com. **Description:** Wonderbread/Hostess Cakes is a baking company manufacturing products of the same name. **Corporate headquarters location:** Kansas City MO. **Other area locations:** Salt Lake City UT. **Parent company:** Interstate Bakeries Corporation. **Listed on:** New York Stock Exchange. **Stock exchange symbol:** IBC. **Number of employees nationwide:** 34,000.

XACTWARE INFORMATION SERVICES
1426 East 750 North, Orem UT 84097. 801/764-5900. **Fax:** 801/224-5218. **Contact:** K.J. Norton, Human Resources. **E-mail address:** xadmin@xactware.com. **World Wide Web address:** http://www.xactware.com. **Description:** Manufactures software for the insurance and construction industries. **Office hours:** Monday – Friday, 7:00 a.m. – 5:00 p.m. **Corporate headquarters location:** This location.

XEROX CORPORATION
675 East 500 South, Suite 100, Salt Lake City UT 84102. 801/535-8500. **Contact:** Manager. **World Wide Web address:** http://www.xerox.com. **Description:** Manufactures business machines, copiers, computer systems, and word processors. The company also publishes educational materials through various subsidiaries, and manufactures other products such as aerospace systems and components, electrostatic printers, microfiche printers, and many other related products and services. In addition, Xerox provides international communications services and systems. **NOTE:** Please visit website to search for jobs and apply online. **Positions advertised include:** Document Solutions Representative; Graphic Arts Sales Executive. **Corporate headquarters location:** Stamford CT. **Other U.S. locations:** Nationwide. **International locations:** Worldwide. **Operations at this facility include:** This location provides sales and service for a variety of Xerox products. **Listed on:** New York Stock Exchange. **Stock exchange symbol:** XRX. **Number of employees worldwide:** 61,100.

XPEDX
P.O. Box 30000, Salt Lake City UT 84130. 801/972-2661. **Physical address:** 3700 West 1987 South, Salt Lake City UT 84104. **Fax:** 801/972-9541. **E-mail address:** xpedx.recruiting@xpedx.com. **World Wide Web address:** http://www.xpedx.com. **Contact:** Human Resources. **Description:** A wholesale distribution center for graphics, printing, and industrial papers, and related products. **Other U.S. locations:** Nationwide.

YWCA
322 East 300 South, Salt Lake City UT 84111-2699. 801/537-8600. **Fax:** 801/355-2826. **Contact:** Human Resources. **World Wide Web address:** http://www.ywca.com. **Description:** Provides counseling, physical fitness activities, a shelter, and daycare programs for women. **NOTE:** You must complete an employment application in order to be considered for a position. Please visit website to download employment application. Volunteer positions are also available. **Positions advertised include:** Receptionist; Social Worker – Bilingual; Child Advocate. **Corporate headquarters location:** Washington D.C. **Other area locations:** Brigham City UT. **Other U.S. locations:** Nationwide.

YELLOW TRANSPORTATION
2410 South 2700 West, West Valley City UT 84119. 801/977-6200. **Fax:** 801/977-6220. **Contact:** Human Resources Manager. **World Wide Web address:** http://www.yellowfreight.com. **Description:** Yellow Freight Systems is a national long-haul truckload carrier, with over 585 terminal locations in all 50 states, Puerto Rico, and many Canadian provinces. **NOTE:** Please contact the company for specific hiring procedures. **Corporate headquarters location:** Overland Park KS.

YORK INTERNATIONAL CORPORATION
4402 South Century Drive, Salt Lake City UT 84123. 801/261-1200. **Fax:** 801/261-0999. **Contact:** Human Resources. **E-mail address:** cal.arnold@york.com. **World Wide Web address:** http://www.york.com. **Description:** York International Corporation manufactures a full line of residential commercial, industrial air conditioning and refrigeration equipment and systems, heating systems, and food systems. Founded 1874. **NOTE:** Resumes should be sent to Human Resources, P.O. Box 1592 – 36BH, York PA 17405. **Corporate headquarters location:** York PA. **Other U.S. locations:** Nationwide. **International locations:** Worldwide. **Operations at this facility include:** This location is a district sales office. **Listed on:** New York Stock Exchange. **Stock exchange symbol:** YRK. **Number of employees worldwide:** 23,000.

YOUNG ELECTRIC SIGN COMPANY
2401 Foothill Drive, Salt Lake City UT 84109. 801/464-4600. **Fax:** 801/483-0998. **Contact:** Human Resources Director. **E-mail address:** jobs@yesco.com. **World Wide Web address:** http://www.yesco.com. **Description:** Manufactures and sells outdoor signs and displays. **Positions advertised include:** Sign Service Technician; Account Executive; Electronics Design Engineer; Sign Service Apprentice; Junior Software Developer; Service Manager; Branch Manager; **Corporate headquarters location:** This location. **Other area locations:** Ogden UT; Orem UT; St. George UT. **Other U.S. locations:** MI; CA; AZ; NV; CO; ID; OR.

ZELLERBACH
2255 South 300 East, Salt Lake City UT 84115. 801/484-4461. **Fax:** 801/488-1997. **Contact:** Human Resources. **World Wide Web address:** http://www.zellerbachonline.com. **Description:** Distributes printing paper, packaging equipment, and commercial and industrial supplies throughout the country.

ZERO ENCLOSURES
P.O. Box 540310, North Salt Lake UT 84054. 801/397-8700. **Physical address:** 500 West 200 North, North Salt Lake UT 84054. **Fax:** 801/299-7389. **Contact:** Human Resources. **World Wide Web address:** http://www.zerocases.com. **Description:** A manufacturer of specialized metal enclosures and accessories for the electronics industry. **Corporate headquarters location:** Los Angeles CA. **International locations:** United Kingdom.

ZEVEX INTERNATIONAL INC.
4314 Zevex Park Lane, Salt Lake City UT 84123. 801/264-1001. **Toll-free phone:** 800/970-2337. **Fax:** 801/264-1051. **Contact:** Barbara Newbould, Human Resources. **E-mail address:** barbara.newbould@zevex.com; hr@zevex.com. **World Wide Web address:** http://www.zevex.com. **Description:** A research and development, design, and manufacturing facility for ultrasonic medical equipment. **NOTE:** Contact Human Resources directly at 800/970-2337 Ext. 107. No phone applications. **Positions advertised include:** Customer Service Representative; Senior Regulatory Affairs Specialist; Engineering Technician; Designer; Independent Clinical Coordinator. **Corporate headquarters location:** This location.

ZIONS FIRST NATIONAL BANK
One South Main Street, Suite 800, Salt Lake City UT 84111. 801/524-4916. **Contact:** Director of Human Resources. **E-mail address:** jobs@zionbank.com. **World Wide Web address:** http://www.zionsbank.com. **Description:** A national bank engaged in a wide range of commercial banking and trust activities including checking and savings accounts, loan services, credit services, trust services, and other traditional banking. **Positions advertised include:** Commercial Loan Officer; Private Banking Commercial Loan Officer; Real Estate Residential Loan Officer; Small Business Acquisitions Officer; Corporate Operating Risk Management Manager; Loan Specialist; Field Examiner; Test Infrastructure Manager; Programmer – Middleware Developer; Programmer Analyst; Project Manager; Chief Architect; Database Administrator; ETL Developer; Information Security Analyst; Auditor; Investment Financial Consultant; Personal Banking Representative; Direct Branch Sales Specialist; Administrative Assistant; Head of Client Advisory Services; Telephone Client Service Provider; Head of Marketing; Chief Financial Officer. **Corporate headquarters location:** This location. **Other area locations:** Nationwide. **Other U.S. locations:** AZ; CA; CO; ID; NV; NM; WA. **Parent company:** Zions Bancorporation. **Operations at this facility include:** Administration; Divisional Headquarters; Regional Headquarters; Service. **CEO:** A. Scott Anderson.

ADC
P.O. Box 759, Water Street, North Bennington VT 05257. 802/442-5411. **Fax:** 802/447-3845. **Contact:** Human Resources. **World Wide Web address:** http://www.adc.com. **Description:** Manufactures fiber-optic cable. Founded in 1928. **Corporate headquarters location:** Centennial CO. **Other locations:** Marlton NJ; Sidney NE. **Operations at this facility include:** Fiber Optic Research & Development; Manufacturing Center.

ARD, INC.
159 Bank Street, Suite 300, Burlington VT 05401. 802/658-3890. **Fax:** 802/658-4247. **Contact:** Jim Thorn. **World Wide Web address:** http://www.ardinc.com. **Description:** ARD is an international development and consulting firm that works mainly with the U.S. Agency for International Development (USAID) and other multilateral development agencies specializing in issues relating to agriculture, rural development, energy conservation, the environment, local governance, and organizational development. Founded in 1977. **NOTE:** The company offers overseas consulting and management opportunities. **Positions advertised include:** Rural Enterprise Development Specialist; Rural Productivity Development Specialist; Senior Water Associate. **Other locations:** Washington DC. **International locations:** Worldwide. **Listed on:** Privately held.

GEORGE F. ADAMS & COMPANY, INC.
Mill Road, P.O. Box 248, Moscow VT 05662. 802/253-7510. **Contact:** Human Resources. **Description:** A manufacturer of wood products including knobs, buttons, and beads.

J.K. ADAMS COMPANY, INC.
P.O. Box 248, Dorset VT 05251. 802/362-2303. **Physical address:** 1430 Route 30, Dorset VT 05251. **Toll-free phone:** 800/451-6118. **Fax:** 802/362-5472. **Contact:** Human Resources. **E-mail address:** info@jkadams.com. **World Wide Web address:** http://www.jkadams.com. **Description:** Manufactures wood products including tripods, leveling rods, and house wares. Founded in 1944. **Corporate headquarters location:** This location. **Other locations:** Chimacum WA. **Operations at this facility include:** Manufacturing; Sales and Administration; Retail Outlet. **President:** Malcolm Cooper.

ALCOA INTERNATIONAL HOLDINGS COMPANY
P.O. Box 1491, Burlington VT 05402-1491. 802/658-2726. **Physical address:** 5 Burlington Square, Burlington VT. **Contact:** Human Resources. **World Wide Web address:** http://www.alcoa.com. **Description:** Engaged in all aspects of the aluminum industry including mining, refining, smelting, fabricating, and recycling. ALCOA also manufactures ceramic packaging for the semiconductor industry, alumina chemicals, plastic bottle closures, vinyl siding, packaging machinery, and electrical distribution systems for automobiles. **NOTE:** Contact Human Resources at the parent company: 412/553-4545. **Corporate headquarters location:** Pittsburgh PA. **Other U.S. locations:** Nationwide. **International Locations:** Worldwide. **Parent company:** Alcoa Inc. **Operations at this facility include:** Legal and accounting offices. In Rutland VT the company operates a Reynolds Food Packaging facility. **Listed on:** New York Stock Exchange. **Stock exchange symbol:** AA. **Chairman/President/CEO:** Alain J. P. Belda. **Annual sales/revenues:** $20.3 billion. **Number of employees at this location:** 2. **Number of employees worldwide:** 129,000.

AMERICAN HEALTH CARE SOFTWARE
99 Swift Street, Suite 300, South Burlington VT 05403. 802/872-3484. **Toll-free phone:** 800/336-1776. **Fax:** 802/872-3476. **Contact:** Marcia DeRosia, Owner. **E-mail address:** derosiam@ahconline.com. **World Wide Web address:** http://www.ahconline.com. **Description:** Develops software for the nursing home industry and home health care agencies. Founded in 1977. **Positions advertised include:** Sales and Marketing Representative; Programmer/Analyst; Installer/Trainer; Customer Service Representative. **Office hours:** Monday – Thursday, 8:00 a.m. – 7:00 p.m., Friday, 8:00 a.m. – 5:00 p.m.

AMERICAN RED CROSS
32 North Prospect Street, Burlington VT 05401. 802/658-6400. **Fax:** 802/658-6120. **Contact:** Human Resources. **World Wide Web address:** http://www.newenglandblood.org. **Description:** A humanitarian organization that aids disaster victims, gathers blood for crisis distribution, trains individuals to respond to emergencies, educates individuals on various diseases, and raises funds for other charitable establishments. **NOTE:** Resumes accepted by e-mail or fax. No phone calls please. **Positions advertised include:** Laboratory Assistant.

BARRY CALLEBAUT U.S.A. INC.
400 Industrial Park Road, St. Albans VT 05478. 802/524-9711. **Fax:** 802/526-1608. **Contact:** Human Resources. **World Wide Web address:** http://www.barry-callebaut.com. **Description:** Manufactures cocoa butter, chocolate liqueur, chocolate chips, and retail and novelty chocolates operating 30 production facilities in 16 countries. **NOTE:** Human Resources extension: x234. **Number of employees at this location:** 160. **Number of employees worldwide:** 7,500.

BEN & JERRY'S HOMEMADE INC.
30 Community Drive, South Burlington VT 05403-6828. 802/846-1500. **Fax:** 802/846-1520. **Recorded jobline:** 802/846-1543 x7584. **Contact:** HR Staffing. **E-mail address:** jobs@benjerry.com. **World Wide Web address:** http://www.benjerry.com. **Description:** Ben & Jerry's manufactures and distributes traditional as well as original flavors of ice cream and low-fat frozen yogurt. Franchised stores are located in Vermont and surrounding states. **Positions advertised include:** Senior Integrated Marketing Specialist; UNIX/Windows Administrator; Retail Brand Manager. **Corporate headquarters location:** This location. **Other area locations:** Bellows Falls VT; Burlington VT; St. Albans VT; Waterbury VT. **Parent company:** Unilever. **President/CEO:** Yves Couette.

BEN & JERRY'S HOMEMADE INC.
89 Main Street, Montpelier VT 05602. 802/223-5530. **Contact:** HR Staffing. **E-mail address:** jobs@benjerry.com. **World Wide Web address:** http://www.benjerry.com. **Description:** Ben & Jerry's manufactures and distributes traditional as well as original flavors of ice cream and low-fat frozen yogurt. Franchised stores are located in Vermont and surrounding states. **Other area locations:** Bellows Falls VT; Burlington VT; St. Albans VT; Waterbury VT. **Parent company:** Unilever. **President/CEO:** Yves Couette.

BENNINGTON COLLEGE
One College Drive, Bennington VT 05201. 802/440-4423. **Fax:** 802/440-4424. **Contact:** Heather Faley, Director Human Resources. **E-mail address:** hroffice@bennington.edu. **World Wide Web address:** http://www.bennington.edu. **Description:** A four-year private college with 800 students in southern Vermont offering bachelor's and master's degrees. **Positions advertised include:** Drama Professor; Literature/Writing Professor; Director of Communications; Director of Major Gifts; Special Assistant, External Relations; Development Associate.

BIJUR LUBRICATING CORPORATION
50 Kocher Drive, Bennington VT 05201. 802/447-2174. **Fax:** 802/447-1365. **Contact:** Human Resources Manager. **E-mail address:** bijurhr@bijurlube.com. **World Wide Web address:** http://www.bijur.com. **Description:** Manufactures automatic lubricating pumps. Founded in 1923. **NOTE:** Resumes should be sent to the parent company's location: Human Resource Manager, Bijur Lubricating Corporation, 808 Aviation Parkway, Suite 1400, Morrisville NC 27560-6600; Phone: 919/465-4448; Fax: 919/465-0516. **Corporate headquarters location:** Morrisville NC. **Other locations:** Irving TX. **International locations:** China; France; Germany; Ireland; Switzerland. **Parent company:** Vesper Lubrication Group (Morrisville NC).

BIO-TEK INSTRUMENTS
P.O. Box 998, Winooski VT 05404-0998. 888/451-5171. **Physical address:** Highland Industrial Park, Winooski VT 05404. **Toll-free phone:** 888/451-5171. **Fax:** 802/655-7941. **Contact:** Human Resources. **E-mail address:** Hrresumes@biotek.com. **World Wide Web address:** http://www.biotek.com. **Description:** Bio-Tek is a worldwide leader in biomedical and laboratory instrumentation. Bio-Tek designs, develops, and markets biomedical and laboratory instruments, associated software programs, and integrated system solutions. **Positions advertised include:** Senior Embedded Software Engineer; Principal Optical Engineer; Mechanical Engineer; Electrical Engineer. **Corporate headquarters location:** This location.

G.S. BLODGETT CORPORATION
44 Lakeside Avenue, Burlington VT 05401. 802/860-3700. **Toll-free phone:** 800/331-5842. **Fax:** 802/864-0183. **Contact:** S.M. Branon, Human Resources. **E-mail address:** employment@blodgett.com. **World Wide Web address:** http://www.blodgett.com. **Description:** Manufactures commercial baking and roasting ovens, char broilers, and fryers. Founded in 1848. **NOTE:** Resumes accepted for open positions only. **Corporate headquarters location:** This location. **Other locations include:** Bow NH. **Operations at this facility include:** Corporate Administration; Sales; Service; Manufacturing, Research and Development of ovens and combination ovens/steamers. **Listed on:** Privately held. **Number of employees at this location:** 330. **Number of employees nationwide:** 700. **Number of employees worldwide:** 730.

BLUE CROSS AND BLUE SHIELD OF VERMONT
P.O. Box 186, Montpelier VT 05601. 800/255-4550. **Contact:** Human Resources. **E-mail address:** hrapps@bcbsvt.com. **World Wide Web address:** http://www.bcbsvt.com. **Description:** Offers customers high quality, financially sound health benefit products, supporting Vermont's unique, community-based health care system. **Positions advertised include:** Administrative Assistant; Application Configuration Specialist; Clinical Improvement Activity Coordinator; Wellness & Community Outreach Coordinator. **Number of employees:** 360.

BOGNER OF AMERICA, INC.
172 Bogner Drive, P.O. Box 644, Newport VT 05855. 802/334-6507. **Contact:** Human Resources. **World Wide Web address:** http://www.bogner.com. **Description:** Manufactures ski and golf clothing. **NOTE:** Human Resources phone extension: x137. **Corporate headquarters location:** This location.

BOOTH BROTHERS DAIRY/H.P. HOOD INC.
219 Allen Street Extension, P.O. Box 301, Barre VT 05641. 802/476-6605. **Fax:** 802/476-7497. **Contact:** Human Resources. **Description:** Produces and bottles dairy products such as milk and cream.

BRATTLEBORO RETREAT
Anna Marsh Lane, P.O. Box 803, Brattleboro VT 05302. 802/258-3703. **Fax:** 802/258-3797. **Contact:** Susan Dorais, Human Resources Department. **E-mail address:** sdorais@retreathealthcare.org. **World Wide Web address:** http://www.bratretreat.org. **Description:** A center offering a full continuum of both inpatient and outpatient treatment services for psychiatric patients. Founded in 1834. **Positions advertised include:** Unit Clerk; Senior Program Therapist; Mental Health Worker; Psychiatrist; Psychiatric Registered Nurse; Licensed Practical Nurse. **Number of employees at this location:** 650.

BRYANT GRINDER CORPORATION
65 Pearl Street, Springfield VT 05150. 802/885-5161. **Fax:** 802/885-9444. **Contact:** Human Resources. **World Wide Web address:** http://www.bryantgrinder.com. **Description:** Manufactures precision grinding machinery for a variety of industrial applications. Founded in 1909. **Parent company:** Vermont Machine Tool Corporation.

THE BURLINGTON FREE PRESS
191 College Street, Burlington VT 05401. 802/863-3441. **Fax:** 802/651-4804. **Contact:** Bobbi Hart, Human Resources Administrative Assistant. **E-mail address:** bhart@bfp.burlingtonfreepress.com. **World Wide Web address:** http://www.burlingtonfreepress.com. **Description:** Publisher of *The Burlington Free Press*, Vermont's largest daily newspaper. **Positions advertised include:** Driving-Route Carrier; Walking-Route Carrier; Advertising Account Executive. **Corporate headquarters location:** Arlington VA. **Parent company:** Gannett Company, Inc. **Number of employees at this location:** 270.

BURLINGTON HEALTH AND REHABILITATION CENTER
P.O. Box 1107, 300 Pearl Street, Burlington VT 05401. 802/658-4200. **Fax:** 802/863-8016. **Contact:** Human Resources. **Description:** A 168-bed, for-profit, nursing home that provides long-term and subacute care, including the providing IV and antibiotic therapy, pain management, wound care, rehabilitation and pulmonary/ventilator care, social services and respite care. **NOTE:** Part-time jobs and second and third shifts are offered. **Positions advertised include:** Certified Nurses Aide; Physical Therapist; Registered Nurse; Social Worker. **Special programs:** Training. **Parent company:** CPL Long Term Care Real Estate Investment Trust (Toronto, Canada).

C&S WHOLESALE GROCERS, INC.
P.O. Box 821, 47 Old Ferry Road, Brattleboro VT 05302. 802/257-4371. **Fax:** 802/257-6032. **Contact:** Recruiting Department. **E-mail address:** recruiting@cswg.com. **World Wide Web address:** http://www.cswg.com. **Description:** The largest grocery wholesalers in New England distributing more than 53,000 grocery, produce, and nonfood items to 4,000 supermarkets and chains from Maine to Maryland including Grand Union and Safeway. Founded in 1918. **Positions advertised include:** Central Support Advertising Analyst; Advertising and Marketing Coordinator; Merchandising Analyst; Budget Analyst; Financial Analyst; Cafeteria Manager; Router. **Office hours:** 8:00 a.m. – 4:30 p.m. **Corporate headquarters location:** This location. **Other locations:** MA; MD; NJ; NY; OH; PA. **Operations at this facility include:** Corporate Administration; Freezer and Dry Grocery Warehouse; Distribution. **Listed on:** Privately held. **Chairman/CEO:** Richard B. (Rick) Cohen. **Annual sales/revenues:** $9.7 billion. **Number of employees at this location:** 1,200. **Number of employees nationwide:** 7,500.

CPC OF VERMONT INC.
P.O. Box 706, Pond Lane, Middlebury VT 05753. 802/388-6381. **Fax:** 802/388-2545. **Contact:** Jill Nutting, Personnel Manager. **Description:** Designs and manufactures molds and custom injection molding. **NOTE:** Hires through temp agencies. **Annual sales/revenues:** $4.5 million. **President:** Mike Funk. **Number of employees at this location:** 175.

CABOT CREAMERY COOPERATIVE
One Home Farm Way, Montpelier VT 05602. 888/792-2268. **Contact:** Human Resources. **World Wide Web address:** http://www.cabotcheese.com. **Description:** A dairy cooperative producing Cabot-brand cheese, butter, and cultured dairy products. The company is owned by 1500 farm families in New England and upstate New York. Founded in 1919. **NOTE:** Second and third shifts are offered. Job hotline: 800/346-9449. **Positions advertised include:** Marketing Administrative Assistant; Cut and Wrap Technician; Maintenance Mechanic; Warehouse Crew Member; Cut and Wrap Sanitation Technician; Night Sanitation Technician; Laboratory Technician. **Office hours:** Monday – Friday, 8:00 a.m. – 8:00 p.m. **Corporate headquarters location:** This location. **Other U.S. locations:** Cabot VT; West Springfield MA; Suffolk VA; Waterbury VT. **Subsidiaries/Affiliates include:** McCadam Cheese. **Parent company:** Agri-Mark, Inc. (Methuen MA).

CAPITAL CITY PRESS, INC.
P.O. Box 546, Montpelier VT 05601. 802/223-5207. **Fax:** 802/229-1090. **Contact:** Elizabeth Madigan, Human Resources Generalist. **E-mail address:** emadigan@capcitypress.com. **World Wide Web address:** http://www.capcitypress.com. **Description:** A full-service printing company that providing editorial, composition, and typesetting services through mailing and fulfillment for publishers of scientific, medical, and educational journals. The company operates a manufacturing facility in Berlin VT, editorial and composition services in Barre VT, and warehouses in Williamstown VT. Founded in 1908. **NOTE:** Second and third shifts are offered. **Positions advertised include:** Issue Manager. **Corporate headquarters location:** This location. **Listed on:** Privately held. **Other locations:** Barre VT; Berlin VT; Williamstown VT. **Parent company:** Sheridan Group. **Operations at this facility include:** Manufacturing; Printing Press; Corporate Administration. **Number of employees:** 275.

J.P. CARRARA & SONS, INC.
P.O. Box 60, North Clarendon VT 05759. 802/775-2301. **Fax:** 802/775-1048. **Contact:** Philip Varney, Human Resources. **E-mail address:** jpcarrara@aol.com. **Description:** A building and foundation construction company. Products include ready-mix concrete, sand, stone, and precast concrete. Founded in 1962. **Other locations:** Middlebury VT; Rutland VT. **President/GM:** Paul J. Carrara. **Number of employees at this location:** 125.

CARRIS REELS, INC.
439 West Street, Rutland VT 05701-2639. 802/773-9111. **Fax:** 802/770-3581. **Contact:** Karen McGrath, Human Resources Executive. **World Wide Web address:** http://www.carris.com. **Description:** Manufactures reels of wood, metal, tin, and plastic for wire and cord. Carris Reels has manufacturing plants and assembly and distribution centers nationwide. Founded in 1951. **Other U.S. locations:** AZ; CA; CT; IN; MI; NC; VA; WA. **International locations:** Brazil; Mexico. **Subsidiaries/Affiliates include:** Vermont Tubs; Killington Wood Products. **Operations at this facility include:** Plywood Division; Plastics Division; Manufacturing; Corporate Administration. **Number of employees:** 1,200.

CASTLETON STATE COLLEGE
86 Seminary Street, Castleton VT 05735. 802/468-5611. **Contact:** Lyn Sawyer, Director of Human Resources. **E-mail address:** lyn.sawyer@castleton.edu. **World Wide Web address:** http://www.castleton.edu. **Description:** A four year state college serving 1700 students. Castleton offers more than 30 undergraduate programs of study, as well as graduate programs in Education and Forensic Psychology. Founded in 1787. **NOTE:** Contact the Human Resources Office at: 62 Alumni Drive, Castleton VT 05735. Phone: 802/468-1207 or 802/468-1208. **Positions advertised include:** Assistant Women's Lacrosse Coach; Security Officer; Custodian/Housekeeper; English Professor; Physics Professor; African/World History Professor; Biology Professor; Reference/Instruction Librarian. **President:** Dave Wolk.

CENTRAL VERMONT MEDICAL CENTER
P.O. Box 547, Barre VT 05641. 802/371-4100. **Fax:** 802/371-4700. **Contact:** Human Resources. **World Wide Web address:** http://www.cvmc.hitchcock.org. **Description:** Central Vermont Hospital is a not-for-profit 122-bed facility offering comprehensive in-patient and out-patient care services along with 24-hour emergency care. Other hospital services include cardiology, neurology, ophthalmology, orthopedics, urology, psychiatry inpatient services, physical and occupational therapy and renal dialysis. **President and CEO:** Daria Mason. **Number of employees nationwide:** 1,100.

CENTRAL VERMONT PUBLIC SERVICE CORPORATION
77 Grove Street, Rutland VT 05701. 800/238-2877. **Fax:** 802/747-2198. **Contact:** Joan F. Gamble, VP Strategic Change & Business Services. **E-mail address:** ngombos@cvps.com. **World Wide Web address:** http://www.cvps.com. **Description:** Central Vermont Public Service provides energy and energy-related services to customers in nearly three-quarters of Vermont. Founded in 1929. **NOTE:** Human Resources phone: 802/747-5730. **Positions advertised include:** Accounting Research Analyst; Director, Organizational Development; Resource Scheduler; Tax Accountant; Telecommunications Technician; Senior Energy Consultant; Electrician; Lineworker. **Special programs:** Internships. **Corporate headquarters location:** This location. **Subsidiaries include:** Catamount Energy Corporation; Connecticut Valley Electric Company, Inc.; SmartEnergy Services Inc.; The Home Service Store. **Operations at this facility include:** Administration; Sales; Service. **Listed on:** New York Stock Exchange. **Stock exchange symbol:** CV. **President/CEO:** Robert H. (Bob) Young. **Annual sales/revenues:** $303 million. **Number of employees:** 550.

CHAMPLAIN CABLE CORPORATION
175 Hercules Drive, Colchester VT 05446. 802/655-2121. **Toll-free phone:** 800/451-5162. **Fax:** 802/654-4234. **Contact:** Human Resources. **World Wide Web address:** http://www.champcable.com. **Description:** Manufactures cable and wire for the automotive industry, data communications companies, and other industrial corporations. **Parent company:** Huber & Suhner, Inc.

PARA RESEARCH, INC.
dba CHAMPLAIN SOFTWARE
30 Steeplebush Road, Essex Junction VT 05452. 802/872-9672. **Fax:** 802/872-1178. **Contact:** Human Resources. **World Wide Web address:** http://www.champlainsoftware.com. **Description:** Develops computer programs for higher education administration. **NOTE:** Contact parent company address: 85 Eastern Avenue, Gloucester MA 01930. 978/282-1100. **Parent company:** Para Research, Inc.

CHITTENDEN BANK
P.O. Box 820, Burlington VT 05402-0820. 802/658-4000. **Fax:** 802/660-2300. **Contact:** Human Resources. **E-mail address:** jobs@chittenden.com. **World Wide Web address:** http://www.chittenden.com. **Description:** A full-service bank offering a broad range of financial services throughout the state including deposit accounts and services; consumer, commercial, and public sector loans; and investment and trust services to individuals. Founded in 1974. **Positions advertised include:** Technology Services Manager; Payroll Specialist; Technical Specialist; Audit Manager; Technical Support Clerk; Bank Sales & Service Representative; Quality Assurance Analyst; Senior Credit Analyst; Senior Compliance Officer; Mortgage Loan Officer; Account Manager; Investment Assistant. **Corporate headquarters location:** This location. **Other area locations:** Statewide. **Subsidiaries/Affiliates include:** Flagship Bank and Trust; The Bank of Western Massachusetts; Maine Bank & Trust; CUMEX (Credit Union Mortgage Exchange); First Savings of New Hampshire; Pomerleau Insurance Agency; Ocean National Bank; Granite State Bankshares. **Parent company:** Chittenden Corporation (also at this location).

COLDWELL BANKER HICKOK & BOARDMAN REALTY
345 Shelburne Road, Burlington VT 05401. 802/863-1500. **Toll-free phone:** 800/639-5520. **Fax:** 802/658-7616. **Contact:** Leslee MacKenzie, President. **World Wide Web address:** http://www.hickokandboardman.com. **Description:** Provides residential and commercial real estate services. **Positions advertised include:** Real Estate Associates

THE COMMUNICATORS GROUP
P.O. Box 1980, Brattleboro VT 05302-1980. 802/257-4321. **Physical address:** 122 Oak Street, Brattleboro VT 05301. **Fax:** 802/257-2143. **Contact:** Human Resources. **World Wide Web address:** http://www.communicatorsgroup.com. **Description:** An advertising agency operating in print, radio, and television. **Number of employees:** 14.

COMMUNITY COLLEGE OF VERMONT
Wasson Hall, P.O. Box 120, Waterbury VT 05676-0120. 802/241-3535. **Fax:** 802/241-3526. **Contact:** Human Resources. **World Wide Web address:** http://www.ccv.vsc.edu. **Description:** A non-campus, community college offering courses and degree programs at twelve locations throughout the state and online. **NOTE:** For faculty positions contact the Site Coordinator at each location. **Positions advertised include:** Burlington Coordinator of Academic Services; Rutland Site Office Manager; Rutland Evening Receptionist; Part-time Accounting Instructor; Part-time Business Instructor. **Office hours:** Monday – Friday, 8:30 a.m. – 4:30 p.m. **Other locations:** Bennington VT; Brattleboro VT; Burlington VT; Middlebury VT; Montpelier VT; Morrisville VT; Newport VT; Rutland VT; St. Albans VT; St. Johnsbury VT; Springfield VT; Upper Valley VT. **Operations at this facility include:** Administrative Offices; Financial Aid; Registrar. **Number of employees:** 125 staff employees and 750 Part-time instructors.

COMMUNITY NATIONAL BANK
4811 U.S. Route 5, P.O. Box 259, Derby VT 05829. 802/334-7915. **Contact:** Kathy Austin, Human Resources. **E-mail address:** derby@communitynationalbank.com. **World Wide Web address:** http://www.communitynationalbank.com. **Description:** A full-service bank providing a complete line of retail banking services to the residents of northeastern and central Vermont. **Other locations:** Barton VT; Derby Line VT; Island Pond VT; Montpelier VT; Newport VT; St. Johnsbury VT; Troy VT.

WILLIAM E. DAILY, INC.
1424 Vermont Route 7A, Shaftsbury VT 05262. 802/442-9923. **Fax:** 802/442-9927. **Contact:** Human Resources. **Description:** Manufactures ready-mixed concrete, precast concrete culvert pipes, and washed sand and stone. **President:** William E. Daily III. **Number of employees at this location:** 70.

A.N. DERINGER, INC.
64-66 North Main Street, P.O. Box 1309, St. Albans VT 05478-1012. 802/524-8110. **Toll-free phone:** 800/523-4357. **Fax:** 802/524-8297. **Contact:** Human Resources. **World Wide Web address:** http://www.anderinger.com. **Description:** Offers a wide range of international trade services from customs house brokerage and freight forwarding to warehousing, cargo insurance, global transportation and confidential business consultation operating 33 offices coast to coast in the U.S. and agents worldwide. Founded in 1919. **NOTE:** Human Resources phone: 802/524-8116. **Positions advertised include:** Credit and Collections Manager. **Other area locations:** Burlington VT; Derby Line VT; Highgate Springs VT. Norton VT; St. Albans VT. **Other U.S. locations:** Nationwide. **International locations:** Worldwide. **Chairman:** Kenneth J. Holzscheiter. **Number of employees:** 550.

DOWLING'S
91 Catamount Drive, P.O. Box 1001, Milton VT 05468. 802/893-5100. **Fax:** 802/893-5110. **Contact:** Maria Burns, Human Resources. **Description:** Sells tobacco, candy, health and beauty aids, groceries, and beverages. **Parent company:** Burlington Drug, Inc. (also at this location).

DYNAPOWER CORPORATION
1020 Hinesburg road, P.O. Box 9210, South Burlington VT 05407. 802/860-7200. **Toll-free phone:** 800/292-6792. **Fax:** 802/864-3782. **Contact:** Stefanie Pollard, Human Resources. **E-mail address:** resumes@dynapower.com. **World Wide Web address:** http://www.dynapower.com. **Description:** A custom designer and manufacturer of DC power supplies, rectifiers, and coil transformers.

EHV-WEIDMANN INDUSTRIES, INC.
One Gordon Mills Way, P.O. Box 903, St. Johnsbury VT 05819-0903. 802/748-8106. **Fax:** 802/751-3377. **Contact:** Human Resources. **Description:** Manufactures electrical insulation products primarily for transformers. The company also produces electrical systems. **Operations at this facility include:** Administration; Manufacturing; Research and Development; Sales. **Listed on:** Privately held. **Number of employees at this location:** 350.

EDLUND COMPANY INC.
159 Industrial Parkway, P.O. Box 929, Burlington VT 05401. 802/862-9661. **Fax:** 802/862-4822. **Contact:** Human Resources. **World Wide Web address:** http://www.edlundco.com. **Description:** Develops and manufactures equipment and supplies for commercial and institutional food service. Products include can crushers; can openers; scales; and knife sharpeners.

ENGELBERTH CONSTRUCTION, INC.
463 Mountain View Drive, Colchester VT 05446. 802/655-0100. **Contact:** Gina Catanzarita, Director of Human Resources. **E-mail address:** ginac@Engelberth.com. **World Wide Web address:** http://www.engelberth.com. **Description:** An industrial construction company and general contractor with ongoing contracts at area churches and schools while maintaining a core business in hospital construction. At regional ski resorts, including Killington, Stratton Mountain, and Stowe, the company has construction contracts for building housing and expanding base lodges. **Other**

locations: Bedford NH; Keene NH. **Corporate headquarters location:** This location. **Annual sales/revenues:** $95 million. **Number of employees:** 280.

ENTERGY NUCLEAR OPERATIONS, INC.
dba VERMONT YANKEE NUCLEAR POWER CORPORATION
185 Old Ferry Road, P.O. Box 7002, Brattleboro VT 05302-7002. 802/257-5271. **Fax:** 802/258-2123. **Contact:** Human Resources Department. **World Wide Web address:** http://www.entergy.com. **Description:** Operator of boiling-water reactor of nuclear power plant. **Positions advertised include:** Senior Nuclear Engineer; Secretary; Control Instrument Specialist. **Special programs:** Internships; Training. **Corporate headquarters location:** This location. **Other area locations:** Vernon VT (Yankee Plant). **Other U.S. locations:** AR; CT; District of Columbia; IL; LA; MA; NY; TX. **International locations:** Bulgaria. **Parent company:** Entergy Corporation (New Orleans LA). **Operations at this facility include:** Corporate Administration. **Listed on:** New York Stock Exchange. **Stock exchange symbol:** ETR. **Chairman:** Robert Luft. **Annual sales/revenues:** $8.3 billion. **Number of employees at this location:** 345. **Number of employees worldwide:** 15,000.

ETHAN ALLEN INC.
1280 Route 253, P.O. Box 217, Beecher Falls VT 05902. 802/266-3355. **Fax:** 802/266-7765. **Contact:** Human Resources. **World Wide Web address:** http://www.ethanallen.com. **Description:** Manufactures and distributes household furniture under the Ethan Allen brand name operating 17 manufacturing plants, 3 saw mills, and 300 retail outlets. Founded in 1932. **NOTE:** Human Resources phone extension at this plant: x236. For administrative positions at the company headquarters, other manufacturing positions, or positions at wholly-owned retail stores contact: Manager of Employment, Ethan Allen Inc., Ethan Allen Drive, P.O. Box 1966, Danbury CT 06813-1966. Phone: 203/743-8000. Fax: 203/743-8609. **Company slogan:** Everyone's At Home With Ethan Allen. **Corporate headquarters location:** Danbury CT. **Other area locations:** Orleans VT (Manufacturing plant). **Parent company:** Ethan Allen Interiors Inc. **Operations at this location include:** Manufacturing plant. **Listed on:** New York Stock Exchange. **Stock exchange symbol:** ETH. **Chairman/President/CEO:** M. Farooq Kathwari. **Annual sales/revenues:** $892 million. **Number of employees:** 7,600.

ETHAN ALLEN INTERIORS INC.
dba ETHAN ALLEN HOME INTERIORS
2735 Shelburne Road, Shelburne, VT 05482. 802/985-8028. **Fax:** 802/985-8795. **Contact:** Michael Lash. **E-mail address:** info@shelburne.ethanallen.com. **World Wide Web address:** http://www.ethanallen.com. **Description:** Household furniture retail chain of 102 company-owned retail outlets and 200 independently owned and authorized stores distributing manufactured goods under the trade name Ethan Allen. Founded in 1932. **NOTE:** For administrative positions at the company headquarters, manufacturing positions, or positions at wholly-owned retail stores contact: Manager of Employment, Ethan Allen Inc., Ethan Allen Drive, P.O. Box 1966, Danbury CT 06813-1966. Phone: 203/743-8000. Fax: 203/743-8609. **Company slogan:** Everyone's At Home With Ethan Allen. **Positions advertised include:** Manager; Retail Salesperson; Home Fashion Designer; Receptionist; Delivery Person. **Corporate headquarters location:** Danbury CT. **Subsidiaries include:** Ethan Allen Inc.; *Interiors Magazine.* **Operations at this location include:** Independently owned retail outlet. **Listed on:** New York Stock Exchange. **Stock exchange symbol:** ETH. **Chairman/President/CEO:** M. Farooq Kathwari. **Annual sales/revenues:** $892 million. **Number of employees:** 7,600.

FACTORY POINT NATIONAL BANK OF MANCHESTER CENTER
P.O. Box 1567, Manchester Center VT 05255-1567. 802/362-2424. **Fax:** 802/362-4101. **Contact:** Jill Smith, Human Resources. **World Wide Web address:** http://www.factorypoint.com. **Description:** A full-service regional bank serving southern Vermont with primary activities in residential real estate lending, small business loan and deposit services, consumer banking services, and trust and investment services. Founded in 1883. **NOTE:** Human Resources phone extension: x252. **Positions advertised include:** Customer Service Representative; Financial Services Representative. **Other locations:** Arlington VT; Dorset VT; Ludlow VT; Rutland VT; Springfield VT. **Parent company:** Factory Point Bancorp Inc. (also at this location). **Listed on:** Over the Counter. **Stock exchange symbol:** FAPB. **Chairman:** Thomas P. Whalen. **Annual sales/revenues:** $3.5 million. **Number of employees:** 100.

FAIRBANKS SCALES INC.
2176 Portland Street, Suite 1, St. Johnsbury VT 05819-8802. 802/748-5111. **Fax:** 802/748-5216. **Contact:** Human Resources. **World Wide Web address:** http://www.fairbanks.com. **Description:** A manufacturer of industrial and personal scales with two manufacturing facilities and 40 customer support centers nationwide. Fairbanks Scales also repairs scales and manufactures the individual component parts for sale to consumers and businesses. Founded in 1830. **Positions advertised include:** Quality Assurance Manager; Manufacturing Engineer; Design Engineer; Service Technician; Area Service Manager; Area Sales Manager; Programmer. **Corporate headquarters location:** Kansas City MO. **Operations at this facility include:** Manufacturing. **Number of employees at this facility:** 110. **Number of employees nationwide:** 800.

FIBERMARK, INC.
161 Wellington Road, P.O. Box 498, Brattleboro VT 05302-0498. 802/257-0365. **Fax:** 802/258-2743. **Contact:** Human Resources. **E-mail address:** hr@fibermark.com. **World Wide Web address:** http://www.fibermark.com. **Description:** Operates 12 manufacturing facilities nationwide specializing in fiber-based materials in four product lines: Filer media segment for liquid and air filters, and vacuum cleaner bags; the technical specialties unit produces sandpaper and printed circuit boards; the office products division manufactures binders and report covers; and the durable specialties unit produces tape substrates for masking and surgical tape. **NOTE:** Entry-level positions and second and third shifts are offered. **Special programs:** Internships; Summer Jobs. **Corporate headquarters location:** This location. **Other U.S. locations:** MA; NJ; NY; PA; RI. **International locations:** France; Germany; Hong Kong; United Kingdom. **Subsidiaries include:** Decorative Specialties International. **Operations at this facility include:** Corporate Administration; Office Products Division manufacturing. **Listed on:** New York Stock Exchange. **Stock exchange symbol:** FMK. **Chairman/CEO:** Alex Kwader. **Annual sales/revenues:** $365 million. **Number of employees at this location:** 250. **Number of employees worldwide:** 2,000.

FLETCHER ALLEN HEALTHCARE
111 Colchester Avenue, Burlington VT 05401. 802/847-0000. **Physical address:** 150 Colchester Avenue, Burlington VT 05401. **Recorded jobline:** 802/847-2722. **Contact:** Employment Office. **E-mail address:** fahcjobs@vtmednet.org. **World Wide Web address:** http://www.fahc.org. **Description:** Operates a full-service, acute care hospital with 500 beds and operates offices in northeastern Vermont. Fletcher Allen Healthcare offers general medical and surgical care, cancer and heart programs, a birthing center, and other services. **NOTE:** Applicants are requested to submit information through the company's Website using the Online Resume. **Positions advertised include:** Nurse Manager; Assistant Nurse Manager; Directory of Therapy; Director of Professional Revenue; Quality Improvement Consultant.

FOODSCIENCE CORPORATION
20 New England Drive, Essex Junction VT 05453. 802/878-5508. **Toll-free phone:** 800/874-9444. **Fax:** 802/878-0549. **Contact:** Gina Walter, Personnel Director. **E-mail address:** hr@foodsciencecorp.com. **World Wide Web address:** http://www.foodsciencecorp.com. **Description:** Manufactures vitamins, minerals, and health food supplements. **Subsidiaries include:** FoodScience of Vermont; Vetri-Science Laboratories of Vermont; DaVinci Laboratories of Vermont; U.S. Animal Nutritionals of Vermont; Mountain Naturals of Vermont; Pet Naturals of Vermont.

G.S. PRECISION, INC.
101 John Seitz Drive, Brattleboro VT 05301-3642. 802/257-5200. **Fax:** 802/257-7937. **Contact:** Richard Kaufmann, Employee Relations Manager. **Description:** Manufactures high-precision machine parts and subassemblies for the aerospace, jet engine, automotive, and computer industries. Founded in 1958.

GE AIRCRAFT ENGINES
210 Columbian Avenue, Rutland VT 05701. 802/773-9121. **Fax:** 802/773-2402. **Contact:** Human Resources. **World Wide Web address:** http://www.geae.com. **Description:** Manufactures jet, turboprop, and turboshaft engines for cargo, executive, and passenger jets, bombers, and helicopters as well as aircraft engine derivatives for marine propulsion and industrial power sources. The Engine Services unit contracts to maintain, service, and provide spare parts for transportation companies. **NOTE:** Apply for positions via the company Website. **Positions advertised include:** Account Representative. **Special programs:** Internships; Co-ops; **Corporate headquarters location:** Evandale OH. **Other locations:** KY; MA; MD; NC; HH; NM. **International locations:** Canada. **Subsidiaries include:** GE Engine Services. **Parent company:** General Electric. **Operations at this location include:** Fan and Compressor Airfoil production; Spare Parts manufacturing. **President/CEO:** David L. Calhoun. **Annual sales/revenues:** $11.4 billion.

GW PLASTICS, INC.
P.O. Box 56, Bethel VT 05032. 802/234-9941. **Physical address:** 239 Pleasant Street, Bethel VT 05032. **Fax:** 802/234-5814. **Contact:** Cathy Tempesta, Human Resources Coordinator. **World Wide Web address:** http://www.gwplastics.com. **Description:** Manufactures close tolerance, custom precision molded components, thermoplastics, injection molding, and dies. **Positions advertised include:** Administrative Assistant; Machine Maintenance Technician; Manufacturing Quality Engineer; Production and Inventory Control Manager; Team Leader. **Corporate headquarters location:** This location. **Other area locations:** Royalton VT (manufacturing facility). **Other U.S. locations:** San Antonio TX; Tucson AZ. **Operations at this facility include:** Corporate Administration; Manufacturing. **Number of employees at this location:** 240.

GENERAL DYNAMICS
ARMAMENT AND TECHNICAL PRODUCTS
128 Lakeside Avenue, Burlington VT 05401. 802/657-7400. **Fax:** 802/657-6292. **Contact:** Human Resources Department, Burlington Operations. **E-mail address:** staffing@gdarm.com. **World Wide Web address:** http://www.gdarm.com. **Description:** Designs, develops, and produces defense products for defense departments of the U.S. government and 33 allied countries specializing in composites technology and production, chemical/biological detection, protection systems, and integrated armament products for air, land, and sea platforms. **NOTE:** Entry-level positions are offered. **Positions advertised include:** Business Area Finance Manager; Principal Mechanical Engineer; Advanced Programs Manager; Quality Engineer; Mechanical Design Specialist; Senior Principal Systems Engineer; Principal Mechanical Systems Engineer; Principal Systems Engineer; Principal Electrical Systems Engineer; Contract Administrator/Senior Contract Administrator; Senior Quality Assurance Specialist; Program Manager; Strategic Planning Manager; Senior/Principal Business Process Specialist; CInternet Content Specialist; Proposal Development Specialist; Senior Hardware Design Engineer; Senior Mechanical Systems Engineer; Deputy Program Manager; Rockets & Tactical Systems Engineering Manager; Principal Program Planner; Senior Test Engineer; Principal Staffing Specialist. **Corporate headquarters location:** Charlotte NC. **Other area locations:** Jericho VT. **Other U.S. locations:** AR; FL; ME; NE; NY; VA. **Parent company:** General Dynamics Corporation (Falls Church VA). **Operations at this facility include:** Corporate Administration; Engineering and Manufacturing; Research and Development; Supply Chain Management. **Number of employees at this location:** 720.

GOODRICH CORPORATION
100 Panton Road, Vergennes VT 05491. 802/877-4799. **Fax:** 802/877-4111. **Contact:** Diana McCormick, Human Resources Representative. **E-mail address:** Diana.mccormick@Goodrich.com. **World Wide Web address:** http://www.goodrich.com. **Description:** The Goodrich Corporation, formerly the BF Goodrich tire maker, is now focused on its aerospace business: Airframe Systems, Electronic Systems, and Engine Systems. The company also services Boeing and Airbus with aircraft maintenance and repair, and operates 133 facilities in 20 countries. **NOTE:** The company receives resumes via their Online Resume Tool. **Positions advertised include:** Program Manager; Sales Representative. **Corporate headquarters location:** Charlotte NC. **Other U.S. locations:** Nationwide. **International locations:** Worldwide. **Operations at this facility include:** Goodrich Aerospace Aircraft Wheel & Brake Overhaul facility; JcAIR Avionics Equipment Testing Systems (New Century KS). **Listed on:** New York Stock Exchange. **Stock exchange symbol:** GR. **Chairman/CEO:** Marshall O. Larsen. **Annual sales/revenues:** $4 billion. **Number of employees at this location:** 700. **Number of employees worldwide:** 19,200.

GRANITE IMPORTERS, INC.
16 South Vine Street, P.O. Box 712, Barre VT 05641. 802/476-5812. **Fax:** 802/476-7349. **Contact:** Human Resources. **World Wide Web address:** http://www.graniteimporters.com. **Description:** A fully developed architectural stone fabricating company specializing in cubic work, special moldings, columns, steps, coping, paving, and veneer for residential and commercial projects. The company operates a block saw plant and a production plant offering complete fabrication services from budgeting for design development through engineering, anchorage design, drafting, fabrication and delivery of finished stone. Founded in 1971.

GREEN MOUNTAIN ANTIBODIES, INC.
One Mill Street, Suite 1-7, Burlington VT 05402. 802/865-6230. **Fax:** 802/865-0115. **Contact:** Human Resources. **E-mail address:** info@greenmoab.com. **World Wide Web address:** http://www.greenmoab.com. **Description:** Manufactures murine monoclonal antibodies for use in research. **President:** Bill Church.

GREEN MOUNTAIN COFFEE ROASTERS, INC.
33 Coffee Lane, Waterbury VT 05676. 802/244-5621. **Toll-free phone:** 800/545-2326. **Fax:** 802/244-6570. **Contact:** Human Resources. **World Wide Web address:** http://www.greenmountaincoffee.com. **Description:** Roasts over 25 types of arabica beans to produce over 70 varieties of coffee, which are sold to over 7,000 wholesale customers including supermarkets, convenience stores, resorts, and office delivery services under the Newman's Own Organics and Green Mountain Coffee brands as well as through catalogs and the Internet. Founded in 1981. **Positions advertised include:** Corporate Controller; Graphic Designer; Merchandiser; Production Manager. **Corporate headquarters location:** This location. **Other locations:** AZ; CA; CT; FL; MA; NH; NY; PA. **Parent company:** Green Mountain Coffee, Inc. **Listed on:** NASDAQ. **Stock exchange symbol:** GMCR. **Chairman/President/CEO:** Robert (Bob) P. Stiller. **Annual sales/revenues:** $100 million. **Number of employees at this location:** 200. **Number of employees nationwide:** 529.

GREEN MOUNTAIN POWER CORPORATION
163 Acorn Lane, Colchester VT 05446-6611. 802/864-5731. **Fax:** 802/655-8445. **Contact:** Human Resources Department. **World Wide Web address:** http://www.gmpvt.com. **Description:** An electric utility company supplying some 87,000 residential and commercial customers. The company purchases most of its power from other utilities and markets wholesale electricity. **NOTE:** Application form available from the company Website. **Corporate headquarters location:** This location. **Listed on:** New York Stock Exchange. **Stock exchange symbol:** GMP. **Chairman:** Nordahl L. Brue. **Annual sales/revenues:** $275 million. **Number of employees:** 193.

HEB MANUFACTURING COMPANY, INC.
P.O. Box 188, Chelsea VT 05038. 802/685-4821. **Toll-free phone:** 800/639-4187. **Fax:** 802/685-7755. **Contact:** Human Resources. **E-mail address:** mail@hebmfg.com. **World Wide Web address:** http://www.hebmfg.com. **Description:** Manufactures wireforming, stamping, roll-threading weldments, and strip and wire fourslides. Operates tool and die facilities, automatic presses and offers full design and engineering services.

HARBOUR INDUSTRIES, INC.
4744 Shelburne Road, P.O. Box 188, Shelburne VT 05482. 802/985-3311. **Fax:** 802/985-4170. **Contact:** Human Resources. **World Wide Web address:** http://www.harbourind.com. **Description:** Manufactures high-performance wire and cable. **NOTE:** Entry-level positions and second and third shifts are offered. **Corporate headquarters location:** This location. **Other U.S. locations:** Nationwide. **International locations:** Canada. **Parent company:** The Marmon Group. **Operations at this facility include:** Wire and cable manufacturing; Coaxial cable production; Corporate Administration. **Listed on:** Privately held. **Number of employees at this location:** 125. **Number of employees nationwide:** 155.

HAYWARD TYLER PUMP COMPANY, INC.
480 Roosevelt Highway, P.O. Box 680, Colchester VT 05446. 802/655-4444. **Fax:** 802/655-4682. **Contact:** Human Resources. **E-mail address:** steph@htyler.com. **World Wide Web address:** http://www.haywardtyler.com. **Description:** Manufactures engineered pumps and sealed or sealless motor products serving the electric utility, nuclear power, chemical, desalination and other industries worldwide. Founded in 1971. **Corporate headquarters location:** This location. **Parent company:** Hayward Tyler Group Limited (Luton, England). **Operations at this facility include:** Administrative offices; Warehouse; Manufacturing facility.

HAZELETT STRIP-CASTING CORPORATION
135 West Lake Shore Drive, P.O. Box 600, Colchester VT 05446. 802/863-6376. **Fax:** 802/863-1523. **Contact:** Human Resources. **E-mail address:** hazelett@hazelett.com. **World Wide Web address:** http://www.hazelett.com. **Description:** Manufactures continuous casting machinery for nonferrous and ferrous metals. **Positions advertised include:** Mechanical Design Engineer; Mechanical Engineering Design Supervisor; Machinist.

HEMMINGS MOTOR NEWS
222 Main Street, P.O. Box 256, Bennington VT 05201. 802/442-3101. **Toll-free phone:** 800/227-4373. **Fax:** 802/447-9600. **Contact:** Human Resources. **E-mail address:** jobs@hemmings.com. **World Wide Web address:** http://www.hemmings.com. **Description:** Publishes 800-page monthly *Hemmings Motor News* car magazine with 260,000 circulation as well as *Hemmings Rods & Performance, Special Interest Autos* magazines, and *Hemmings' Collector-Car Almanac*. The company posts classified listings, auto shows, and events on its interactive Website; produces a line of collectible die-cast model trucks; publishes an antique-car calendar; and operates a full-service Sunoco Filling Station at 216 Main Street in Bennington. Founded in 1954. **Parent company:** American City Business Journals (Charlotte NC). **Listed on:** Privately held. **Chairman:** Ray Shaw. **Number of employees at this location:** 115.

HIGH MEADOW BUSINESS SOLUTIONS, INC.
P.O. Box 1546, Manchester Center VT 05255. 802/362-2296. **Physical address:** 343 High Meadow Way, Manchester VT 05254. **Toll-free phone:** 800/755-9692. **Fax:** 802/362-2298. **Contact:** Human Resources. **E-mail address:** info@retailedge.com. **World Wide Web address:** http://www.highmeadow.com. **Description:** Manufactures a line of cash register, retail management, and point-of-sale software under the brand name RetailEdge. Founded in 1989.

HOLIDAY INN EXPRESS
818 Charlestown Road, Springfield VT 05156. 802/885-4516. **Contact:** Human Resources. **World Wide Web address:** http://www.holiday-inn.com. **Description:** An 88-room hotel, which is part of the worldwide hotel chain.

HOLIDAY INN RUTLAND/KILLINGTON
476 US Route 7 South, Rutland VT 05701. 802/775-1911. **Toll-free phone:** 800/462-4810. **Fax:** 802/775-0113. **Contact:** Raminder Chatha, General Manager. **World Wide Web address:** www.holidayinn-vermont.com. **Description:** A full-service, independently-owned franchise of the international hotel chain, with 150 rooms offering complete amenities and close to several area ski resorts. **Positions advertised include:** Assistant General Manager.

IDX SYSTEMS CORPORATION
40 IDX Drive, South Burlington VT 05402-1070. 802/862-1022. **Fax:** 802/863-9288. **Contact:** Administrative Manager. **World Wide Web address:** http://www.idx.com. **Description:** Develops medical software for hospitals. IDX Systems Corporation provides access to health care information for physician groups and academic medical centers across the country. Founded in 1969. **NOTE:** The company does not accept hardcopy resumes. Apply online via the company Website. **Positions advertised include:** Account Manager; Accounts Payable Associate; Connectivity Architect; Data Analyst; Electronic Production Specialist; Carecast Consultant. **Special programs:** Internships available. **Corporate headquarters location:** This location. **Other U.S. locations:** Nationwide. **Listed on:** NASDAQ. **Subsidiaries include:** EDiX. **Stock exchange symbol:** IDXC. **Chairman:** Richard E. Tarrant. **Annual sales/revenues:** $460 million. **Number of employees:** 4,750.

JANOS TECHNOLOGY INC.
1068 Grafton Road, Townshend VT 05353-9605. 802/365-7714. **Fax:** 802/365-4596. **Contact:** Lisa Egan, Director of Human Resources. **E-mail address:** personnel@janostech.com. **World Wide Web address:** http://www.janostech.com. **Description:** Manufactures and designs high tech precision optics assemblies, custom infrared optics, sophisticated optical analysis systems, infrared zoom systems, diamond machined mirrors, optical assemblies, photonics testing instruments, and measurement equipment used in astronomy, lasers, space applications, and the defense industry. **Parent company:** The Monroe Group, Inc. (Northbrook IL).

THE A. JOHNSON CO.
995 South 116 Road, Bristol VT 05443. 802/453-4884. **Fax:** 802/453-3844. **Contact:** Ann Johnson, Partner. **E-mail address:** ajohnson@gmavt.net. **Description:** Produces kiln-dried hardwood lumber. **Positions advertised include:** Bookkeeper. **Number of employees:** 50.

KAMTECH PLASTICS CO.
3 Graves Street, P.O. Box 572, Montpelier VT 05601. 802/223-5012. **Fax:** 802/223-6145. **Contact:** Human Resources. **Description:** Manufactures custom injection molds and thermoplastic engineering resins. **NOTE:** Second and third shifts are offered. **Corporate headquarters location:** This location. **Annual sales/revenues:** Less than $5 million. **Number of employees at this location:** 50.

KEYBANK N.A.
149 Bank Street, Burlington VT 05401. 802/660-4160. **Toll-free phone:** 888/539-7247. **Contact:** Human Resources Manager. **World Wide Web address:** http://www.keybank.com. **Description:** A stock savings bank offering a full line of installment, mortgage, and commercial loans. **Positions advertised include:** Client Relations Representative; Senior Relationship Manager; Cash Vault Specialist. **Parent company:** KeyCorp (Cleveland OH).

KILLINGTON LTD.
4763 Killington Road, Killington VT 05751. 802/422-3333. **Contact:** Human Resources. **World Wide Web address:** http://www.killington.com. **Description:** A resort located in central Vermont, with an 18-hole golf course, a tennis school (USPTA), and winter skiing. **NOTE:** Part-Time, Temporary, and Seasonal positions are available. Applications for winter employment are accepted beginning in August. **Positions advertised include:** Conference Sales Manager; Front Desk Agent; Administrative Assistant; Snow Removal Equipment Operator; Lift Mechanic; Guest Service Representative; Shuttle Driver; Ticket Checker; Nurse; Food Service Worker; Cashier; Dishwasher. **Special programs:** Internships. **Corporate headquarters location:** This location.

LANDMARK COLLEGE
River Road South, P.O. Box 820, Putney VT 05346. 802/387-6871. **Fax:** 802/387-7111. **Contact:** Director of Human Resources. **E-mail address:** tbrown@landmark.edu. **World Wide Web address:** http://www.landmark.edu. **Description:** A two-year liberal arts college designed specifically for students with Dyslexia, Attention Deficit Hyperactivity Disorder, and other learning disabilities and differences. **Positions advertised include:** Director of Major Gifts; Manager, Foundations and Corporate Relations; Associate Director, National Institute; Associate Dean, Short-Term and Special Programs; Administrative Assistant; Library Assistant; Housekeeper; Web Designer; Associate Director of Admissions, Summer and Special Programs; Enrollment Services Associate. **President:** Lynda J. Katz, Ph.D.

LEAHY PRESS, INC.
P.O. Box 428, Montpelier VT 05601. 802/223-2100. **Physical address:** 79 River Street, Montpelier VT 05602. **Fax:** 802/229-4149. **Contact:** Human Resources. **E-mail address:** leahy@leahypress.com. **World Wide Web address:** http://www.leahypress.com. **Description:** Commercial printer offering full-service commercial offset printing, design, and typesetting with in-house capacity for one to five+ color printing production. The company produces catalogs, magazines, calendars, and folders as well as providing desktop publishing and graphic design services. **Company slogan:** Professional Touch in Printing. **Positions advertised include:** Bindery Worker; Cost Estimator; Customer Service Representative; Graphic Artist; Management Analyst/Consultant; Printing Press Operator; Quality Control Supervisor; Secretary. **Number of employees at this location:** 25.

LOVEJOY TOOL CO., INC.
133 Main Street, P.O. Box 949, Springfield VT 05156. 802/885-2194. **Toll-free phone:** 800/843-8376. **Fax:** 802/885-9511. **Contact:** Human Resources. **E-mail address:** lovejoy@lovejoytool.com. **World Wide Web address:** http:/www.lovejoytool.com. **Description:** Manufactures metal cutting tools including inserted blade type, counterbores, flywheels, end mills, arbors, and boring heads. Founded in 1917. **Number of employees:** 85.

MACE SECURITY INTERNATIONAL, INC. (MSI)
160 Benmont Avenue, Suite 1, Bennington VT 05201. 802/447-1503. **Fax:** 802/442-3823. **Contact:** Human Resources. **World Wide Web address:** http://www.mace.com. **Description:** A leading producer of Mace brand personal defense chemical sprays and protection devices, alarms, and door braces for the consumer market as well as operating 55 Super Bright car washes nationwide. **NOTE:** Send resumes and cover letters to the attention of: Ronald Pirollo, Mace Security International, 1000 Crawford Place, Suite 400, Mt. Laurel NJ 08054; or e-mail: pirollor@mace-security.com. **Corporate headquarters location:** Mt. Laurel NJ. **Other locations:** Fort Lauderdale FL. **Operations at this facility include:** Personal Security Products Division. **Listed on:** NASDAQ. **Stock exchange symbol:** MACE. **Chairman/President/CEO:** Louis D. Paolino Jr. **Annual sales/revenues:** $48 million. **Number of employees nationwide:** 1,825.

MACK GROUP
dba MACK MOLDING COMPANY NORTHERN DIV.
608 Warm Brook Road, Arlington VT 05250. 802/375-2511. **Fax:** 802/375-0792. **Contact:** Nancy Cefalo, Human Resources. **World Wide Web address:** http://www.mack.com. **Description:** Mack Molding Company is a custom molder and manufacturer of injection-molding plastic products with 12 locations worldwide supplying contract manufacturing services and injection molded plastic parts to high technology companies and serving the server/mass storage, business equipment, medical, telecommunications, industrial and consumer products markets, and specializes in producing components, housing for computers, and packaging. Founded in 1920. **Positions advertised include:** Manufacturing Supervisor; Procurement Specialist; Accounts Receivable/Credit Manager. **Corporate headquarters location:**

This location. **Other locations:** Chelmsford MA; Statesville NC; Inman SC; Cavendish VT; Pownal VT. **Operations at this facility include:** Manufacturing; Corporate Administration. **Listed on:** Privately held. **Annual sales/revenues:** $400 million. **Number of employees at this location:** 200. **Number of employees nationwide:** 800. **Number of employees worldwide:** 1,900.

MAPLE GROVE FARMS OF VERMONT
1052 Portland Street, St. Johnsbury VT 05819. 802/748-5141. **Contact:** Michelle Magoon, Director of Human Resources. **World Wide Web address:** http://www.maplegrove.com. **Description:** Largest packer of Pure Maple Syrup producing maple products distributed worldwide. The company operates the Maple Museum and gives tours of the maple factory which manufactures maple syrup, sugar, maple candy and confections, salad dressing, mint candies, gift packs, jams and jellies, and steak sauce.

McCORMACK, GUYETTE & ASSOCIATES, PC
66 Grove Street, Rutland VT 05701. 802/775-3221. **Fax:** 802/775-1850. **Contact:** Human Resources. **E-mail address:** mga@cpa-vermont.com. **World Wide Web address:** http://www.cpa-vermont.com. **Description:** A certified public accounting agency providing a variety of accounting services including payroll, tax preparation, and audits. **Number of employees:** 10.

McKENZIE OF VERMONT
P.O. Box 4059, South Burlington VT 05406. 802/864-4585. **Physical address:** 160 Flynn Avenue, Burlington VT 05401. **Contact:** Controller. **Description:** A meat packing company. Products include sausage, sausage products, smoked hams, bacon, and processed meats.

MERCHANTS BANCSHARES, INC.
dba MERCHANTS BANK
P.O. Box 1009, South Burlington VT 05402-9969. 802/658-3400. **Physical address:** 275 Kennedy Drive, South Burlington VT 05403 **Fax:** 802/865-1698. **Recorded jobline:** 802/865-1881. **Contact:** Personnel Systems Administrator. **E-mail address:** jobs@mbvt.com. **World Wide Web address:** http://www.mbvt.com. **Description:** A full-service bank specializing in residential and commercial mortgages as well as offering commercial, construction, agricultural, and consumer loans. It operates 38 branches throughout the state offering checking, money market, and savings accounts and CDs. **NOTE:** Human Resources phone: 802/865-1807. **Positions advertised include:** Teller/Customer Service Representative. **Subsidiaries include:** Merchants Trust Company; Merchants Properties. **Operations at this location include:** Corporate Administration. **Listed on:** NASDAQ. **Stock exchange symbol:** MBVT. **Chairman:** Raymond C. Pecor Jr. **Annual sales/revenues:** $62.5 million. **Number of employees:** 289.

MIDDLEBURY COLLEGE
84 Self Service Road, Middlebury VT 05753. 802/443-5000. **Fax:** 802/443-2058. **Contact:** Human Resources. **E-mail address:** hr@middlebury.edu. **World Wide Web address:** http://www.middlebury.edu. **Description:** A small, independent, liberal arts college with approximately 2,200 undergraduates enrolled. The college offers programs of study in the Arts, Foreign Languages, History and Humanities, Interdisciplinary Programs, Natural Sciences, Social Sciences, and Independent Studies. Founded in 1800. **NOTE:** Send resumes and applications materials to: Human Resources, Middlebury College, Service Building, Second Floor, Middlebury VT 05753. Human Resources phone: 802/443-5465. Candidates for faculty positions: see website for application deadlines and specific contact information. **Positions advertised include:** Associate Director, Health Center; Senior Development Officer; Reference and Instruction Librarian, Sciences; Assistant Director of Annual Giving; Events Scheduler; Prep Cook; Counter Worker; Lodge Caretaker; Special Events Staffer; Visiting Assistant Professor, Behavioral Neuroscience; Visiting Assistant Professor, Social Philosophy; Lecturer, Modern Standard Arabic; Associate Instructor, Organic Chemistry.

MILTOPE CORPORATION
76 Pearl Street, Springfield VT 05156. 802/885-4100. **Contact:** John Keefe, Office Manager. **World Wide Web address:** http://www.miltope.com. **Description:** Designs, develops, and manufactures rugged computers, workstations, printers, mass storage devices, and related computer equipment for ground-based or airborne military applications that must operate in demanding and severe battlefield conditions. Founded in 1975. **NOTE:** Resumes should be sent to the company's headquarters: Edward F. Crowell, Vice President Human Resources, Miltope Corporation, Human Resources Department, 3800 Richardson Road, South Hope Hull, AL 36043. Fax: 334/613-6591. E-mail: ed.crowell@miltope.com. **Positions advertised include:** Electronics Technician; Electrical Engineer. **Corporate headquarters location:** Hope Hull AL. **Other locations:** Boulder CO; New Orleans LA. **Parent company:** Miltope Group, Inc (Hope Hull AL). **Operations at this facility include:** Mass Storage Systems design and production facility. **Listed on:** NASDAQ. **Stock exchange symbol:** MILT. **President and CEO:** Thomas R. Dickinson. **Annual sales/revenues:** $45.2 million. **Number of employees nationwide:** 156.

MOUNT SNOW RESORT
P.O. Box 2810, West Dover VT 05356. 802/464-4233. **Physical address:** Route 100, West Dover VT 05356. **Fax:** 802/464-4135. **Contact:** Human Resources. **E-mail address:** jobs@mountsnow.com. **World Wide Web address:** http://www.mountsnow.com. **Description:** One of the largest ski resorts in the east. **NOTE:** Seasonal positions available. **Positions advertised include:** Cashier; Café Worker; Snowmaker; Parking Attendant; Lift Attendant; Housekeeper; Laundry Attendant; Nail Technician; Switchboard Operator; Massage Therapist; Childcare Staff Worker; Development Ski Coach; Snowboard Shop Sales Associate.

MYLAN LABORATORIES INC.
dba MYLAN TECHNOLOGIES INC.
110 Lake Street, St. Albans VT 05478. 802/527-7792. **Toll-free phone:** 800/532-5226. **Fax:** 802/527-0486. **Contact:** Human Resources Manager. **E-mail address:** mtihr@mylanlabs.com. **World Wide Web address:** http://www.mylan.com. **Description:** A pharmaceutical company manufacturing generic antibiotics, antidepressants, anti-inflammatories, beta-blockers, and laxatives. The company also manufactures transdermal drug delivery systems, coating and laminates for the transdermal administration of drugs, patches for wound care therapy, and surgical drapes. Founded in 1961. **NOTE:** Many positions are second or third shift. **Positions advertised include:** Manager, Pharmaceutical Quality Assurance. **Corporate headquarters location:** Pittsburgh PA. **Other locations:** IL; NC; PA; WV. **Subsidiaries/Affiliates include:** Bertek Pharmaceuticals Inc.; Mylan Pharmaceuticals Inc.; UDL Laboratories Inc. **Parent company:** Mylan Laboratories Inc. (Pittsburgh PA). **Listed on:** New York Stock Exchange. **Stock exchange symbol:** MYL. **Chairman:** Milan Puskar. **Annual sales/revenues:** $1.1 billion. **Number of employees nationwide:** 2,200.

NATIONAL LIFE INSURANCE COMPANY
SENTINEL FUNDS
P.O. Box 1499. Montpelier VT 05601. 802/229-3333. **Physical address:** One National Life Drive, Montpelier VT 05604. **Fax:** 802/229-3313. **Contact:** Joan Witham, Human Resources. **E-mail address:** jwitham@nationallife.com. **World Wide Web address:** http://www.nlv.com. **Description:** An insurance firm providing customers with life and disability policies. Sentinel Funds (also at this location, 802/229-3900) is an affiliate of National Life Insurance Company and a regulated investment company. Founded in 1934. **Positions advertised include:** Producer Compensation Specialist; Director, Sales Strategy; Agency Specialist; Security Operations Representative; Shareholder Accounting Specialist; Financial Control Supervisor; Marketing Specialist; Equity Analyst; Portfolio Manager.

NEW ENGLAND CENTRAL RAILROAD, INC.
2 Federal Street, Suite 201, St. Albans VT 05478. 802/527-3500. **Fax:** 802/527-3482. **Contact:** Louise Corbiere, Office Manager. **Description:** A railroad company operating 366 miles of tracks between East Albugh VT and New London CT serving Vermont, New Hampshire, Massachusetts, and Connecticut. **General Manager:** Mike Olmstead.

NEW ENGLAND CULINARY INSTITUTE
250 Main Street, Montpelier VT 05602. 877/223-6324. **Contact:** Human Resources. **E-mail address:** greatjobs@neci.edu. **World Wide Web address:** http://www.neci.edu. **Description:** A culinary school offering certificate programs, associate's degrees, and bachelor's degrees in various culinary related programs. New England Culinary Institute has campus locations in Montpelier VT, Essex VT, and the British Virgin Islands. **Positions advertised include:** Adjunct Chef Instructor; Baker; Executive Sous Chef; Host; Student Accounts Coordinator; Student Services Coordinator. **International locations:** Tortola, British Virgin Islands. **Number of employees worldwide:** 509.

NEWPORT PLASTICS CORPORATION
P.O. Box 988, Lyndonville VT 05851. 802/626-4000. **Physical address:** Rural Route 122, Lyndonville VT 05851. **Contact:** Human Resources. **Description:** A composite plastics manufacturer producing specialty fiberglass products and a variety of plastic components including fiberglass aircraft parts, computer housings, aircraft seat covers, and industrial equipment housings.

NEXUS CUSTOM ELECTRONICS, INC.
402 Prospect Street, P.O. Box 250, Brandon VT 05733-0250. 802/247-6811. **Fax:** 802/247-3946. **Contact:** Mr. Del Cook, Human Resources. **E-mail address:** delcS@nexuscei.com. **World Wide Web address:** http://www.nexuscei.com. **Description:** Manufactures custom-designed electronic components including magnetic, temperature control, and other related products. Nexus Custom Electronics offers surface-mount, thru-hole, and mixed PCB technologies; global test resources; and total systems integration. **Corporate headquarters location:** This location. **Other locations:** Woburn MA. **Parent company:** Jaco Electronics, Inc. distributes computer systems, computer subsystems, electronic components, and electromechanical devices.

NORTH HARTLAND TOOL CORPORATION
14 Evarts Road, P.O. Box 38, North Hartland VT 05052. 802/295-3196. **Fax:** 802/295-1692. **Contact:** Human Resources. **World Wide Web address:** http://www.nhtool.com. **Description:** Manufactures gages, fixtures, special tools, and precision parts. **NOTE:** Entry-level positions and part-time jobs are offered. **Positions advertised include:** Controller; Draftsperson; MIS Specialist; Production Manager; Purchasing Agent/Manager; Sales Representative; Secretary; Mechanical Engineer. **Special programs:** Apprenticeships; Co-ops; Summer Jobs. **Parent company:** Netam Industries Inc. (Jupiter FL). **Listed on:** Privately held. **President:** John M. Mullen. **Annual sales/revenues:** $5 million. **Number of employees at this location:** 55.

NORTHEASTERN HEATING, VENTILATING & AIR CONDITIONING
32 Boyer Circle, Williston VT 05495. 802/865-8008. **Fax:** 802/862-9227. **Contact:** Human Resources. **Description:** Manufactures sheet metal products and performs air conditioning and heating installation and service for commercial customers. **Number of employees at this location:** 50.

NORTHEASTERN LOG HOMES
P.O. Box 126, Groton VT 05046-0126. 802/584-3336. **Physical address:** 492 Scott Highway, Groton VT 05046. **Contact:** Human Resources. **World Wide Web address:** http://www.northeasternlog.com. **Description:** Manufactures precut log, post, and beam homes. Founded in 1972. **Corporate headquarters location:** This location. **Other locations:** Kenduskeag ME; Louisville KY; Westfield MA; York ME. **Listed on:** Privately held. **President:** Jon French. **Number of employees at this location:** 90.

NORTHEASTERN VERMONT REGIONAL HOSPITAL
1315 Hospital Drive, St. Johnsbury VT 05819. 802/748-8141. **Fax:** 802/748-7398. **Contact:** Trish Noyes, Human Resources Coordinator. **E-mail address:** t.noyes@nvrh.org. **World Wide Web address:** http://www.nvrh.org. **Description:** A community-based, non-profit, 75-bed acute care facility providing primary care, internal medicine, surgical and specialty services, inpatient and outpatient care, and 24-hour services, as well as operating an emergency room; a walk-in clinic; a birth unit; a speech therapy department; a respiratory therapy department; a nuclear medicine department; an ultrasound department; and outpatient clinics for dermatology, cardiology, oncology, and neurology. **NOTE:** Human Resources phone: 802/748-7415. **Company slogan:** We Treat You Like Family. **Positions advertised include:** Director, Surgical and Ambulatory Services; Imaging Technologist; Clinical Applications Specialist; Medical Technologist; Licensed Practical Nurse; Occupational Health Nurse. **Chairman:** Patricia Burnham.

NORWICH UNIVERSITY
158 Harmon Drive, Northfield VT 05663. 800/468-6679. **Contact:** Human Resources. **World Wide Web address:** http://www.norwich.edu. **Description:** A private military college founded in 1819. Norwich University is a diversified academic institution that educates traditional age students in a Corps of Cadets or as civilians, and adult students. **Positions advertised include:** Athletic Trainer; Assistant Football Coach; Campus Security Officer; Custodian/Floor Crew; Director of Engineering Admissions; Groundskeeper; Assistant Director/Associate Director. **Number of employees:** 492.

THE OFFSET HOUSE, INC.
89 Sand Hill Road, P.O. Box 8329, Essex VT 05451-8329. 802/878-4440. **Fax:** 802/879-4865. **Contact:** Human Resources. **E-mail address:** jobs@offsethouse.com. **World Wide Web address:** http://www.offsethouse.com. **Description:** Engaged in the printing of manuals, booklets, and brochures, as well as handling direct mail printing and mailing services. Founded in 1972. **Positions advertised include:** Sales Professional. **Number of employees at this location:** 130.

OMYA INC.
61 Main Street, Proctor VT 05765. 802/459-3311. **Contact:** Human Resources. **E-mail address:** jobs.us@omya.com. **World Wide Web address:** http://www.omya-na.com. **Description:** Formerly Pluess-Staufer Industries, Omya operates 140 facilities in 30 countries manufacturing ground calcium carbonate, a material used in the paper, paint, plastics, food and pharmaceutical industries as well as other industrial applications. Founded in 1891. **Positions advertised include:** Administrative Specialist. **Other U.S. locations:** Nationwide. **International locations:** Worldwide. **Parent company:** Omya AG (Oftringen, Switzerland).

THE ORVIS COMPANY INC.
dba ORVIS RETAIL STORE
Historic Route 7A, Manchester VT 05254. 802/362-1300. **Fax:** 802/362-0141. **Contact:** Mary Cheddie, Human Resources. **E-mail address:** careers@orvis.com. **World Wide Web address:** http://www.orvis.com. **Description:** The company sells hunting and fishing clothing, home furnishings, and country life gifts as well as arranging guided fishing, hunting trips, and travel; selling through mail-order catalogs; operating a Website; and distributing to 500 independently-run stores worldwide. The company also operates over 40 company stores in the U.S. and Britain and runs fly-fishing and shooting seminars. Founded in 1856. **Corporate headquarters location:** This location. **Other U.S. locations:** Roanoke VA; Sunderland VT. **Listed on:** Privately held. **Chairman:** Leigh Perkins Sr.

PIZZAGALLI CONSTRUCTION COMPANY
50 Joy Drive, P.O. Box 2009, South Burlington VT 05403. 802/658-4100. **Fax:** 802/651-1208. **Contact:** Jim Carabell, Human Resources. **E-mail address:** resumes@pizzagalli.com. **World Wide Web address:** http://www.pizzagalli.com. **Description:** A general contractor that handles projects including water and wastewater treatment plants; government work including army barracks and prisons; and high school renovations and additions. **NOTE:** Human Resources phone: 802/651-1255. **Positions advertised include:** Director, Health and Safety; Estimator; Project Engineer; Project Manager; Superintendent; Treasurer. **Special programs:** Training; Internships; Coops. **Corporate headquarters location:** This location. **Other U.S. locations:** Garner NC; South Portland ME. **Subsidiaries/Affiliates include:** Pizzagalli Properties, LLC. **Number of employees at this location:** 95. **Number of employees nationwide:** 1,200.

POLHEMUS, INC.
40 Hercules Drive, P.O. Box 560, Colchester VT 05446. 802/655-3159. **Fax:** 802/655-1439. **Contact:** Human Resources. **World Wide Web address:** http://www.polhemus.com. **Description:** Develops, designs, manufactures, and sells electromagnetic measuring systems, 3D motion tracking systems, 3D scanners, and real-time eye tracking systems that measure the position and orientation of objects in three-dimensional space, which are used in image-guided surgery, biomechanics, simulation and training, television/motion picture animation, video games, virtual reality applications, and head tracking systems. Founded in 1969. **President:** Al Rodgers.

PRECI MANUFACTURING INC.
400 Weaver Street, Winooski VT 05404. 802/655-2414. **Fax:** 802/655-0796. **Contact:** Paul Daigle, Plant Manager. **E-mail address:** pdaigle@preci.com. **World Wide Web address:** http://www.preci.com. **Description:** Manufactures precision mechanical components for the aerospace, medical, and computer industries. **Positions advertised include:** Mechanical Engineer. **Number of employees at this location:** 55.

ROCK OF AGES CORPORATION
P.O. Box 482, Barre VT 05641. 802/476-3121. **Physical address:** 772 Graniteville Road, Graniteville VT 05654. **Fax:** 802/476-2245. **Contact:** Human Resources. **World Wide Web address:** http://www.rockofages.com. **Description:** A granite quarrier, manufacturer, and retailer of granite memorials for cemeteries, operating 10 quarries and 5 manufacturing and sawing facilities, and distributing through over 100 company-owned retail outlets nationwide and 75 authorized dealers. Founded in 1885. **Positions advertised include:** Administrative Assistant; CAD Designer. **Corporate headquarters location:** This location. **Other U.S. locations:** Nationwide. **Operations at this facility include:** Quarry Division; Corporate Administration; Visitor Center; Memorial Division; Manufacturing/Sawing Division. **Listed on:** NASDAQ. **Stock exchange symbol:** ROAC. **Chairman/President/CEO:** Kurt M. Swenson. **Annual sales/revenues:** $92.5 million. **Number of employees:** 900.

ROCK-TENN COMPANY
P.O. Box 98, Sheldon Springs VT 05485. 802/933-7733. **Fax:** 802/933-5326. **Contact:** Manager of Human Resources. **World Wide Web address:** http://www.rocktenn.com. **Description:** A manufacturer of 100 percent recycled paperboard and paperboard products. Both clay-coated and uncoated recycled paperboard is manufactured at eight mills from Vermont to Texas. Over two-thirds of paperboard production is used by the company's own converting plants to produce folding cartons, book and notebook covers, components for the furniture industry, and solid-fiber partitions used in shipping glass and plastic containers. **Corporate headquarters location:** Norcross GA. **Other locations:** Nationwide. **Listed on:** New York Stock Exchange. **Stock exchange symbol:** RKT.

ROSSIGNOL SKI COMPANY INC.
P.O. Box 298, Industrial Avenue, Williston VT 05495. 802/863-2511. **Contact:** Human Resources Administrator. **World Wide Web address:** http://www.rossignol.com. **Description:** Distributes alpine skis and tennis racquets, which are manufactured in Europe. **Corporate headquarters location:** Voiron, France.

JOHN A. RUSSELL CORPORATION
170 South Main Street, Suite 6, Rutland VT 05701-4599. 802/775-3325. **Fax:** 802/775-8292. **Contact:** Chris Lackney, Human Resources. **E-mail address:** clackney@russellconstructionservices.com. **World Wide Web address:** http://www.jarc.com. **Description:** A construction company and general contractor that builds schools, warehouses, and grocery stores. **NOTE:** Human Resources phone extension: x212. **Positions advertised include:** Project Manager; Superintendent; Project Engineer; Field Engineer.

RUTLAND REGIONAL MEDICAL CENTER
160 Allen Street, Rutland VT 05701. 802/775-7111. **Fax:** 802/747-6248. **Contact:** Anna White, Employee Specialist/Recruiter. **E-mail address:** awhite@rrmc.org or jobs@rrmc.org. **World Wide Web address:** http://www.rrmc.org. **Description:** A 188-bed hospital providing educational, preventive, ambulatory, emergency, secondary, and selected tertiary and long-term care services to Rutland County, central and southern Vermont, and bordering communities in New York. Founded in 1896. **NOTE:** For nursing positions contact: Cathy Dudley, RN Recruiter. E-mail address: cdudley@rrmc.org. Phone: 802/747-3666. A. White's phone: 802/747-1604. **Positions advertised include:** Chief Nursing Officer; Phlebotomist; Medical Technologist; MRI Technologist; Pharmacist; Respiratory Therapist; Food Service Assistant; Licensed Practical Nurse; Occupational Therapist; Pathology Secretary; Registered Nurse; ; Radiologic Technologist; Speech Language Pathologist; Security Officer. **Affiliates include:** Okemo Regional Medical Center; Vermont Orthopedic Clinic. **Parent company:** Rutland Regional Health Services. **Chairman:** Michael McCormack. **Number of employees:** 1,500.

SB ELECTRONICS, INC.
131 South Main Street, Suite 1, Barre VT 05641-4854. 802/476-4146. **Fax:** 802/476-4149. **Contact:** Human Resources. **World Wide Web address:** http://www.sbelectronics.com. **Description:** The company, formerly the Sprague Electric company, designs and manufactures film capacitor products as well as axial leaded film capacitors specializing in high voltage, tight tolerance, demanding peak currents, and high frequency capacitors. Founded in 1959.

SCA TISSUE NORTH AMERICA LLC
210 Riverside Drive, Brattleboro VT 05301. 802/257-0511. **Contact:** Human Resources. **World Wide Web address:** http://www.scatissue.com. **Description:** Paper company with 12 manufacturing sites nationwide producing hygiene products, packaging, and graphic papers. Brand names include Tork, Park Avenue Ultra, Coronet, Main Street, and Second Nature. **Corporate headquarters location:** Neenah WI. **Other U.S. locations:** Nationwide. **Number of employees nationwide:** 2,600.

ST. ALBANS COOPERATIVE CREAMERY, INC
140 Federal Street, St. Albans VT 05478. 802/524-6581. **Fax:** 802/527-1769. **Contact:** Bart Tatro. **World Wide Web address:** http://www.stalbanscooperative.com. **Description:** A milk and cream processing facility producing over 300,000 gallons of milk per day marketed and manufactured for milk products including powdered milk, ice cream, and skim milk. Founded in 1919. **President:** Harold Howrigan. **Annual sales/revenues:** $200 million. **Number of employees:** 60.

SAPUTO CHEESE USA, INC.
10516 Route 116, Hinesburg VT 05461. 802/482-2121. **Fax:** 802/482-2115. **Contact:** Lisa Osgood, Human Resources. **World Wide Web address:** http://www.saputo.com. **Description:** Manufactures feta cheese. The company sells its products to food service organizations in bulk and in small packages of shredded varieties. **NOTE:** Send resumes and applications to the company's U.S. headquarters address: Human Resources Department, 25 Tri-State International Office Center, Suite 250, Lincolnshire IL 60069. Fax: 847/267-1134. E-mail address: cv2@saputo.com. **Positions advertised include:** Regional Quality Assurance Manager; Independent Zone Manager, Northeast. **Corporate headquarters location:** Saint-Léonard, Québec, Canada. **Listed on:** Toronto Stock Exchange. **Stock exchange symbol:** SAP.TO. **Annual sales/revenues:** $160 million. **Number of employees at this location:** 100.

SEVERN TRENT LABORATORIES, INC.
208 South Park Drive, Suite 1, Colchester VT 05446. 802/655-1203. **Fax:** 802/655-1248. **Contact:** Human Resources. **World Wide Web address:** http://www.stl-inc.com. **Description:** Provides a complete range of environmental testing services to private industry, engineering consultants, and government agencies in support of federal and state environmental regulations. The company also possesses analytical capabilities in the fields of air toxins, field analytical services, radiochemistry/mixed waste, and advanced technology.

SHELBURNE CORPORATION
P.O. Box 158, Shelburne VT 05482. 802/985-3321. **Contact:** Human Resources. **World Wide Web address:** http://www.barrecrafters.com. **Description:** Manufactures household and builders hardware; wire forms and stampings; mechanical and electromechanical assemblies; and ski and bicycle products. **Number of employees at this location:** 100.

SHERATON BURLINGTON HOTEL AND CONFERENCE CENTER
870 Williston Road, South Burlington VT 05403. 802/865-6600. **Fax:** 802/865-6671. **Contact:** Abby Welman, Human Resources. **E-mail address:** burlingtonvt.hr@Sheraton.com. **World Wide Web address:** http://www/sheratonburlington.com. **Description:** Vermont's largest hotel and conference center. **NOTE:** Human Resources Phone: 802/865-6691.

SMITH, INC.
Winhall Station Road, P.O. Box 87, South Londonderry VT 05155. 802/824-5515. **Fax:** 802/824-6664. **Contact:** Human Resources. **Description:** Manufacturer of kiln-dried hardwood, pine-glued dimension stock, and wood chips. **Owner:** Dick Smith.

SOLO CUP COMPANY
15 Lower Newton Street, St. Albans VT 05478. 802/524-5966. **Contact:** Human Resources. **World Wide Web address:** http://www.solocup.com. **Description:** Manufactures paper products, disposable tableware, and plastic packaging operating 17 manufacturing facilities and eight distribution centers nationwide.

SPECIALTY FILAMENTS INC.
P.O. Box 1029, Burlington VT 05402. 802/863-6333. **Physical address:** One Howard Street, Burlington VT 05401. **Contact:** Barb Dusablon Human Resources Coordinator. **E-mail address:** bdusablon@specialtyfilaments.com. **World Wide Web address:** http://www.specialtyfilaments.com. **Description:** Manufactures thermoplastic monofilaments used in the production of brushes. **Corporate headquarters location:** Andover MA.

SPRINGFIELD HOSPITAL
25 Ridgewood Road, P.O. Box 2003, Springfield VT 05156. 802/885-2151. **Contact:** Janet Laraway, Human Resources Director. **E-mail address:** jlaraway@springfieldhospital.org. **World Wide Web address:** http://www.springfieldhospital.org. **Description:** A nonprofit, general hospital. **NOTE:** Entry-level positions and second and third shifts are offered. This location also offers volunteer opportunities. Human Resources phone: 802/885-7640. **Positions advertised include:** Radiographer; Speech Therapist; Nutritional Services Aide; Adult Day Care Aide; Registered Nurse; Pharmacist. **Special programs:** Apprenticeships; Summer Jobs.

STINEHOUR PRESS
853 Lancaster Road, Lunenburg VT 05906. 802/328-2507. **Fax:** 802/328-3960. **Contact:** Human Resources. **World Wide Web address:** http://www.stinehourpress.com. **Description:** A printing company with products that include art reproductions, museum catalogs, and posters. **Number of employees at this location:** 55. **CEO:** Warren D. Bingham.

STRATTON CORPORATION
RR1 Box 145, Stratton Mountain VT 05155. 802/297-4107. **Fax:** 802/297-4238. **Contact:** Recruiting Manager. **World Wide Web address:** http://www.stratton.com. **Description:** Operates a large ski resort, Stratton Mountain, with 92 trails serviced by

12 lifts. The resort covers 178 acres and also features cross-country skiing in two areas, as well as a golf course. **NOTE:** Part-time and seasonal positions offered. **Positions advertised include:** Property Supervisor; Maintenance Engineer; Community Manager; Childcare Administrator; Childcare Aide; Information Technology Support Specialist; Grooming Mechanic; Groomer; Resort Electrician; Housekeeper; Night Laundry Staffer; Dishwasher/Prep Cook; Front Desk Clerk. **Number of employees at this location:** 280.

SUPERIOR TECHNICAL CERAMICS CORPORATION
600 Industrial Park Road, P.O. Box 1028, St. Albans Industrial Park, St. Albans VT 05478. 802/527-7726. **Fax:** 802/527-1181. **Contact:** Charles Mayhood, Human Resources Manager. **E-mail address:** cmayhood@superiortechceramics.com. **World Wide Web address:** http://www.superiortechceramics.com. **Description:** Manufactures technical ceramic parts for electronics and heliarc welding. **Positions advertised include:** Machinist; Communications Network Control Programmer.

SUSS MICROTECH AMERICA, INC.
228 Suss Drive, Waterbury Center VT 05677. 802/244-5181. **Fax:** 802/244-5329. **Contact:** Human Resources. **E-mail address:** hr@suss.com. **World Wide Web address:** http://www.suss.com. **Description:** Manufactures electronics equipment including mask aligners, spinners, and coating equipment for use in the semiconductor industry. **Number of employees at this location:** 110. **CEO:** Dr. Frank Richter.

TIVOLY INC.
434 Baxter Avenue, Derby Line VT 05830. 802/873-3106. **Fax:** 802/873-3535. **Contact:** Janice Lamoureux, Human Resources Director. **World Wide Web address:** http://www.tivolyinc.com. **Description:** Manufactures cutting tools, dies, and counterbores specializing in hand taps, production taps, performance taps, Application taps, Carbide taps, reamers, and drills for consumers and businesses. **President/CEO:** Philippe Bourg. **Number of employees:** 150.

TRAPP FAMILY LODGE
700 Trapp Hill Road, P.O. Box 1428, Stowe VT 05672. 802/253-8511. **Fax:** 802/253-5757. **Contact:** Human Resources. **E-mail address:** hr@trappfamily.com. **World Wide Web address:** http://www.trappfamilylodge.com. **Description:** A 2,700 acre cross country ski lodge and resort owned and operated by the von Trapp family. **Positions advertised include:** Guest House Crew Leader; Guest House Cleaner; Villa Housekeeper; Outdoor Maintenance/Groundskeeper; Conference Set-Up Staff Worker. **Special Programs:** Internships available. **President:** Johannes von Trapp.

TRIDYNE INTERNATIONAL, INC.
dba TRIDYNE PROCESS SYSTEMS
80 Allen Road, South Burlington VT 05403. 802/863-6873. **Fax:** 802/860-1591. **Contact:** Emmy Madigan, Office Manager. **World Wide Web address:** http://www.tridyneinc.com. **Description:** Designs and manufactures state-of-the-art automatic weighing and weight counting systems that weigh, measure, or count materials into precise portions before packaging them. The company specializes in frictionless bearing scales and load cell base systems from smaller table top to multiple lane units and provides complete solutions by working with packaging machinery manufacturers. Founded in 1963. **President:** Susith Wijetunga. **Number of employees:** 12.

TUTTLE LAW PRINT, INC.
dba TUTTLE PRINTING & ENGRAVING
P.O. Drawer 110, Rutland VT 05702. 802/773-9171. **Physical address:** Quality Lane, Rutland VT 05701. **Toll-free phone:** 800/776-7682. **Contact:** Human Resources. **E-mail address:** info@tuttleprinting.com. **World Wide Web address:** http://www.tuttleprinting.com. **Description:** Provides printed stationery and related products for law and other professional offices. Founded in 1912. **Number of employees at this location:** 60.

ULTRAMAR ENERGY, INC.
dba ULTRAMAR HOMENERGY
282 South Main Street, P.O. Box 711, St. Albans VT 05478. 802/527-7755. **Contact:** Human Resources. **Description:** Distributor of home heating oil servicing 250,000 customers in Eastern Canada and the Northeastern U.S. offering technical advice and a range of energy products and services. Ultramar Energy operates 12 refineries in Canada and the U.S., and over 5,000 retail outlets as well as operations in petrochemicals and home heating oil. **Corporate headquarters location:** Montreal, Quebec, Canada. **Other area locations:** Bennington VT; Manchester VT; Middlebury VT; Montpelier VT; Morrisville VT; Woodstock VT. **Other U.S. locations:** Nationwide. **Parent company:** Valero Energy Corporation (San Antonio TX). **Annual sales/revenues:** $30 billion.

UNION MUTUAL GROUP
UNION MUTUAL OF VERMONT COMPANIES
P.O. Box 158, Montpelier VT 05601-0158. 802/223-5261. **Physical address:** 139 State Street, Montpelier VT 05602. **Contact:** Human Resources. **Description:** Provides various lines of property and casualty insurance to residential and commercial clients throughout Vermont, New Hampshire, Maine, Massachusetts, and New York. Founded in 1874. **Positions advertised include:** Property and Casualty Claims Representative. **Corporate headquarters location:** This location. **Other locations:** Greenville NY; South Paris ME. **Subsidiaries include:** Union Mutual Fire Insurance Company; New England Guaranty Insurance Company, Inc.; Eastern Mutual Insurance Company. **Chairman:** John F. McLaughlin. **Number of employees at this location:** 65.

UNITED WAY OF WINDHAM COUNTY
28 Vernon Street, Suite 410, Brattleboro VT 05301. 802/257-4011. **Fax:** 802/257-4715. **Contact:** Andrea Livermore, Executive Director. **World Wide Web address:** http://www.unitedwaywindham.org. **Description:** Through a network of volunteers and service programs, United Way of Windham County helps to meet the health and human care needs of its community through 40 annual programs as well as conducting needs assessments, reviewing agency programs, raising money for service programs, and offering comprehensive information and referrals through a help line.

UNIVERSITY OF VERMONT
228 Waterman Building, 85 South Prospect Street, Burlington VT 05405. 802/656-3494. **Fax:** 802/656-3476. **Recorded jobline:** 802/656-2248. **Contact:** Employment Office. **E-mail address:** employment@uvm.edu. **World Wide Web address:** http://www.uvm.edu. **Description:** A state university offering a liberal arts curriculum with over 90 undergraduate majors, 72 master's and 20 PhD programs. Colleges at the University of Vermont include Agriculture and Life Sciences, Allied Health Sciences, Business Administration, Education, Engineering, and Nursing. Founded in 1791. **NOTE:** Employment Office phone: 802/656-4490. **Positions advertised include:** Assistant Business Manager; Assistant Professor, Nutrition and Food Sciences; Assistant Professor, Orthopedic Rehabilitation; Assistant to Director, Career Services; Chairperson, Plant and Soil Sciences; Dairy Farm Management Educator; Director, Conferences and Events; Help Desk Specialist. **Number of employees:** 3,000.

VELAN VALVE CORPORATION
94 Avenue C, Williston VT 05495-9732. 802/863-2562. **Fax:** 802/862-4014. **Contact:** Labor Relations Manager. **E-mail address:** hr.us@velanvalve.com. **World Wide Web address:** http://www.velan.com. **Description:** Manufactures cast and forged steel control valves. Founded in 1950. **Special programs:** Summer Jobs. **Corporate headquarters location:** Montreal, Canada. **International locations:** Worldwide. **Parent company:** Velan Inc. **Operations at this facility include:** Manufacturing; Regional Headquarters; Sales. **Listed on:** Privately held. **President/Chairman:** A.K. Velan. **Number of employees at this location:** 205.

VERMONT AEROSPACE MANUFACTURING, INC.
966 Industrial Parkway, P.O. Box 1148, Lyndonville VT 05851. 802/748-8705. **Fax:** 802/748-8437. **Contact:** Human Resources. **E-mail address:** roxann@vtaerospace.com. **World Wide Web address:** http://www.vtaerospace.com. **Description:** A contract manufacturer of precision CNC machining and fabrication for the aircraft and defense industries including Northrop Grumman, Lockheed Martin, Fairchild, and General Dynamics, which use components in rapid-fire 20mm and 30mm gun systems, the M1A1 tank, the Bradley Fighting Vehicle, and commercial aircraft including Airbus, Bell, Boeing, Canadair, and Sikorsky. **Positions advertised include:** Computer Network Controlled Milling Set Up; Computer Network Control Operator; Computer Network Controlled Lathe Set Up; Tool Maker; Armament Quality Supervisor; Aircraft Quality Supervisor; Customer Service Representative; Manufacturing Engineer; Mechanical Engineer; Materials Purchaser. **Annual sales/revenues:** $12 million. **Number of employees:** 140.

VERMONT AGENCY OF TRANSPORTATION
National Life Building, P.O. Drawer 33, Montpelier VT 05633. 802/828-2625. **Fax:** 802/828-2894. **Contact:** Richard C. Carey, Chief of Human Resources. **E-mail address:** rick.carey@state.vt.us. **World Wide Web address:** http://www.aot.state.vt.us. **Description:** Handles transportation issues in the state of Vermont. **Positions advertised include:** Equipment Technician; Maintenance Supervisor; Manager; Civil Engineer; Motor Vehicle Records Chief; Audit Chief.

VERMONT DEPARTMENT OF TOURISM & MARKETING
6 Baldwin Street, P.O. Drawer 33, Montpelier VT 05633. 802/828-3676. **Contact:** Personnel. **World Wide Web address:** http://www.travel-vermont.com. **Description:** Promotes Vermont as a vacation destination through advertising and public relations. **NOTE:** All staffing is done through the Vermont Department of Personnel; contact for more information. Phone: 802/828-3483. World Wide Web address: http://www.state.vt.us/pers.

VERMONT ELECTRIC POWER COMPANY (VELCO)
366 Pinnacle Ridge Road, Rutland VT 05701. 802/773-9161. **Contact:** Carol Byrne, Personnel Director. **E-mail address:** cbyrne@velco.com. **World Wide Web address:** http://www.velco.com. **Description:** Provides power transmission services to customers. The company supplies and transmits electrical power across the state of Vermont, selling it to utilities for use by residential and commercial customers. Founded in 1956. Personnel phone: 802/770-6271. **Positions advertised include:** Electrical Designer and Projects Commissioning Engineer. **President and CEO:** Martin Miller. **Number of employees at this location:** 90.

VERMONT MEDICAL, INC.
Industrial Park, P.O. Box 556, Bellows Falls VT 05101. 802/463-9976. **Fax:** 802/463-9318. **Contact:** Kristina Utton, Sales Manager. **E-mail address:** kutton@vermed.com. **World Wide Web address:** http://www.vermed.com. **Description:** Manufactures disposable medical monitoring electrodes and other special purpose medical electrodes. Vermont Medical also distributes medical monitoring accessories. Angiolaz (also at this location) manufactures scopes for various medical uses including exploratory surgical procedures. Founded in 1978. **NOTE:** Entry-level positions are offered. **Subsidiaries include:** Angiolaz (also at this location). **Listed on:** Privately held. **Number of employees at this location:** 90.

VERMONT MUTUAL INSURANCE COMPANY
P.O. Box 188, Montpelier VT 05601-0188. 802/229-7634. **Physical address:** 89 State Street, Montpelier VT 05602. **Toll-free phone:** 800/451-5000. **Fax:** 802/229-7670. **Contact:** Heather Schmidt, Human Resources Manager. **E-mail address:** hschmidt@vermontmutual.com. **World Wide Web address:** http://www.vermontmutual.com. **Description:** A property and casualty insurance company. **NOTE:** Human Resources phone: 802/229-7634. **Positions advertised include:** Senior Casualty Claim Adjuster; Claims Program Manager, Property; Security Analyst. **Corporate headquarters location:** This location. **Subsidiaries include:** Granite Mutual Insurance Company; Northern Security Insurance Company. **Number of employees at this location:** 185.

VERMONT NETWORK AGAINST DOMESTIC VIOLENCE & SEXUAL ASSAULT
P.O. Box 405, Montpelier VT 05601. 802/223-1302. **Fax:** 802/223-6943. **Contact:** Coordinator. **World Wide Web address:** http://www.vtnetwork.org. **Description:** A nonprofit, public education and advocacy organization composed of 16 member organizations offering services to battered women and their children. Activities of the coalition include public education and advocacy; technical assistance to member groups; information and technical assistance to public agencies and legislative committees; and professional training for law enforcement and human service workers.

VERMONT PUBLIC TELEVISION (VPT)
88 Ethan Allen Avenue, Colchester VT 05446. 802/655-4800. **Fax:** 802/655-6593. **Contact:** Rob Cunningham, Human Resources Department. **E-mail address:** hresources@vpt.org. **World Wide Web address:** http://www.vpt.org. **Description:** Vermont Public Television (VPT) is a member of Public Broadcasting Service (PBS) and carries a complete schedule of PBS programming, as well as programs purchased from other national sources. VPT produces programming of local interest and has several weekly series. Founded in 1967. **NOTE:** Entry-level positions are offered. **Office hours:** Monday - Friday, 8:30 a.m. - 5:00 p.m. **President:** John King. **Number of employees:** 45.

VERMONT PURE HOLDINGS, LTD.
117 Route 66, Catamount Commercial Park, P.O. Box C, Randolph VT 05060. 802/728-3600. **Fax:** 802/728-7294. **Contact:** Sandee Flood, Human Resources Administrator. **E-mail address:** sflood@vermontpure.com. **World Wide Web address:** http://www.vermontpure.com. **Description:** Bottles, markets, and distributes a full line of natural spring water and office refreshment products and services including coffee service, snacks, beverages, and complete mini-kitchen services marketing and distributing under the Vermont Pure, Crystal Rock, and Vermont Hidden Spring brands. **NOTE:** Human Resources phone: 802/728-7207. **Corporate**

headquarters location: This location. **Listed on:** American Stock Exchange. **Stock exchange symbol:** VPS. **Chairman/CEO:** Timothy G. Fallon. **Annual sales/revenues:** $71.7 million. **Number of employees:** 369.

VERMONT STATE HOSPITAL
103 South Main Street, Weeks Building, Waterbury VT 05671-1601. 802/241-1000. **Fax:** 802/241-3001. **Contact:** Human Resources. **World Wide Web address:** http://www.state.vt.us/dmh. **Description:** A 70-bed psychiatric hospital offering inpatient services run by the state's Department of Developmental and Mental Health Services.

THE VERMONT TEDDY BEAR COMPANY, INC.
6655 Shelburne Road, Shelburne VT 05482. 802/985-3001. **Fax:** 802/985-1330. **Recorded jobline:** 802/985-1397 ext.1718. **Contact:** Human Resources. **E-mail address:** ddukette@vtbear.com. **World Wide Web address:** http://www.vermontteddybear.com. **Description:** Designs and manufactures hand-crafted teddy bears and markets them primarily as gifts called Bear-Grams, which are personalized teddy bears delivered directly to the recipient with a card and candy for special occasions. Founded in 1983. **Positions advertised include:** Facilities Supervisor; Pajama Development Coordinator; Product Sales Analyst; Operations Trainer. **Corporate headquarters location:** This location. **Other area locations:** Newport VT. **Subsidiaries/Affiliates include:** The PajamaGram Company; The TastyGram Company. **Listed on:** NASDAQ. **Stock exchange symbol:** BEAR. **President/CEO:** Elisabeth B. Robert. **Annual sales/revenues:** $39 million. **Number of employees at this location:** 311.

VERMONT TRANSIT COMPANY INC.
345 Pine Street, Burlington VT 05401. 802/864-6811. **Fax:** 802/862-7812. **Contact:** Human Resources. **World Wide Web address:** http://www.vermonttransit.com. **Description:** A bussing company that serves Vermont, New Hampshire, Maine, New York, and Massachusetts. **NOTE:** Apply online or at the terminal. **Positions advertised include:** Terminal Employee; Maintenance Technician; Service Worker; Motorcoach Operator. **Corporate headquarters location:** This location. **Other locations:** Boston MA; Portland ME; Rutland VT; White River Junction VT.

VISHAY TANSITOR
P.O. Box 230, West Road, Bennington VT 05201. 802/442-5473. **Contact:** Gail Wysocki, Personnel Director. **World Wide Web address:** http://www.vishay.com. **Description:** Manufactures tantalum capacitors used in light bulb filaments.

WNNE-TV
P.O. Box 1310, White River Junction VT 05001. 802/295-3100. **Contact:** News Director. **World Wide Web address:** http://www.wnne.com. **Description:** An NBC-affiliated television broadcasting station serving Vermont and New Hampshire.

WASHINGTON COUNTY MENTAL HEALTH SERVICES, INC.
P.O. Box 647, Montpelier VT 05601-0647. 802/229-0591. **Fax:** 802/223-8623. **Contact:** Susan Loynd, Human Resources. **E-mail address:** personnel@wcmhs.org. **World Wide Web address:** http://www.wcmhs.org. **Description:** Provides comprehensive, community-based services to adults with serious and persistent mental illness; developmental disabilities, mental retardation and autism; children with severe emotional disturbances and their families; children and adults with acute behavioral problems; and a wide range of other challenging behaviors. Their services include individualized residential and day treatment. **NOTE:** Search for open positions at http://www.jobsinvt.com.

WHITNEY BLAKE COMPANY
20 Industrial Drive, P.O. Box 579, Bellows Falls VT 05101. 802/463-9558. **Fax:** 802/463-3926. **Contact:** Alice Relihan, Human Resources Administrator. **E-mail address:** relihan_alice@wblake.com. **World Wide Web address:** http://www.wblake.com. **Description:** Manufactures plastic and rubber retractable cord.

WICOR AMERICAS MANAGEMENT INC.
P.O. Box 407, St. Johnsbury VT 05819. 802/748-8727. **Physical address:** 79 Gordon Mills Way, St. Johnsbury VT. **Contact:** Linda Gilman, Manager of Benefits. **Description:** Manufactures and wholesales printing paper, insulators, and electrical and insulation materials through its subsidiaries.

YORK CAPACITOR CORPORATION
450 Weaver Street, P.O. Box 278, Winooski VT 05404. 802/655-2550. **Fax:** 802/655-4307. **Contact:** Human Resources. **E-mail address:** info@yorkcapacitor.com. **World Wide Web address:** http://www.yorkcapacitor.com. **NOTE:** Hires through a temp agency**.** **Description:** Manufactures electrical motors and capacitors. Founded in 1924.

ABB POWER T&D COMPANY, INC.
State Route 42, P.O. Box 38, Bland VA 24315. 276/688-3325. **Contact:** Human Resources. **World Wide Web address:** http://www.abb.com. **Description:** Manufactures commercial, industrial, and seismic transformers. **NOTE:** Search and apply for positions online. **Parent company:** ABB Ltd. **Listed on:** New York Stock Exchange. **Stock exchange symbol:** ABB. **Number of employees at this location:** 300. **Number of employees nationwide:** 10,000. **Number of employees worldwide:** 115,000.

ABB POWER T&D COMPANY, INC.
P.O. Box 920, South Boston VA 24592. 434/575-7971. **Physical address:** 2135 Philpott Road, South Boston VA 24592. **Contact:** Wanda Blythe, Human Resources. **World Wide Web address:** http://www.abb.com. **Description:** Manufactures commercial, industrial, and seismic transformers. **NOTE:** Search and apply for positions online. **Parent company:** ABB Ltd. **Listed on:** New York Stock Exchange. **Stock exchange symbol:** ABB. **Number of employees at this location:** 300. **Number of employees nationwide:** 10,000. **Number of employees worldwide:** 115,000.

AC TECHNOLOGIES, INC.
2751 Prosperity Avenue, Suite 500, Fairfax VA 22031. 703/698-4300. Fax: 703/698-4381. **E-mail:** jobs@ac-tech.com. **World Wide Web address:** http://www.ac-tech.com. **Description:** AC Technologies, Inc. provides a range of management and IT services and solutions to government agencies and companies nationwide. Founded in 1993. **NOTE:** Search and apply for positions online. **Positions advertised include:** J2EE Developer; Testing/IV&V configuration Analyst; Principal IV&V Test Engineer; IV&V software Test Technician. **Corporate headquarters location:** This location. **Other area locations:** Alexandria VA; Washington DC; Suitland MD. **Other U.S. locations:** Albany NY; Chicago IL; Montgomery AL; Oakland CA; Tuscaloosa AL.

THE AES CORPORATION
4300 Wilson Avenue, Arlington VA 22203. 703/522-1315. **Fax:** 703/528-4510. **Contact:** Human Resources. **World Wide Web address:** http://www.aesc.com. **Description:** The AES Corporation develops, owns, and operates independent electric power generating facilities. The company operates in 27 countries on five continents through 17 distribution businesses serving over 11 million customers. **Corporate headquarters location:** This location. **Listed on:** New York Stock Exchange. **Stock exchange symbol:** AES. **Number of employees worldwide:** 30,000.

AMF BOWLING PRODUCTS, INC.
8100 AMF Drive, Richmond VA 23111. 804/559-8600. **Fax:** 804/559-8650. **Contact:** Human Resources. **World Wide Web address:** http://www.amf.com **Description:** AMF Bowling Worldwide Inc. is the world's largest owner and operator of bowling centers, with about 385 U.S. bowling centers and over 100 international bowling centers, and is also a leader in the manufacturing and marketing of bowling and billiards products. **NOTE:** Search and apply for positions online. **Other area locations:** Mechanicsville VA. **Number of employees worldwide:** 16,000.

ASG SOFTWARE SOLUTIONS
12700 Sunrise Valley Drive, Reston VA 20191-5804. 703/464-1300. **Toll-free phone:** 800/333.8666. **Fax:** 703/464-4918. **Contact:** Human Resources. **World Wide Web address:** http://www.asg.com. **Description:** ASG provides businesses with services and software solutions for security, applications, operations, information, performance, and infrastructure management. ASG helps mainframe clients mobilize their resources to boost productivity and enhance performance through intelligent use of technology. ASG has more than 40 offices worldwide with 900 employees. Founded in 1986. **NOTE:** Search and apply for positions online. **Positions advertised include:** Distribution/Facilities Coordinator; Account Executive; Senior Solution Architect; Systems Engineer; Professional Services Consultant; Senior Software Engineer; **Corporate headquarters location:** Naples FL.

AT&T GOVERNMENT SOLUTIONS, INC.
1900 Gallows Road, Vienna VA 22182. 703/506-5000. **Contact:** Human Resources. **World Wide Web address:** http://www.att.com. **Description:** Creates large-scale decision support systems and software engineering environments, applies operations research and mathematical modeling to business and management systems, and implements advanced database technology. AT&T Government Solutions, Inc. also provides studies and analysis capabilities for policy development and planning; modeling and simulation of hardware and software used in real-time testing of sensor, weapon, and battlefield management command, control, and communication systems; and testing and evaluation. The company's services are offered primarily to government and commercial customers. **NOTE:** Search and apply for positions or submit resume online. **Positions advertised include:** Remedy Engineer; Programmer/Analyst; Information Assurance Engineer; Test Engineer; Senior Computer Systems Engineer. **Corporate headquarters location:** This location. **Other U.S. locations:** Nationwide. **Parent company:** AT&T Corporation. **Listed on:** New York Stock Exchange. **Stock exchange symbol:** T. **Number of employees worldwide:** 3,000.

AT&T GOVERNMENT SOLUTIONS, INC.
2901 South Lynnhaven Road, Suite 400, Virginia Beach VA 23452. 757/631-4460. **Contact:** Human Resources. **World Wide Web address:** http://www.att.com. **Description:** AT&T Government Solutions, Inc. is a provider of knowledge-based professional services and technology-based product solutions to government and commercial customers. The company's activities encompass sophisticated telecommunications products, network systems analysis, and network software development operations for the commercial market. The company creates large-scale decision-support systems and software engineering environments, applies operations research and mathematical modeling to business and management systems, and implements advanced database technology. AT&T Government Solutions, Inc. also provides studies and analysis for policy development and planning; modeling and simulation of hardware and software used in real-time testing of sensor, weapon, and battlefield management command, control, and communication systems; and testing and evaluation. **NOTE:** Search and apply for positions or submit resume online. **Corporate headquarters location:** Vienna VA. **Other U.S. locations:** Nationwide. **Operations at this facility include:** This location provides computer training for a broad customer base. **Parent company:** AT&T Corporation. **Listed on:** New York Stock Exchange. **Stock exchange symbol:** T. **Number of employees worldwide:** 3,000.

ABBOTT LABORATORIES
Business Route 29 North, P.O. Box 479, Altavista VA 24517. 434/369-3100. **Contact:** Human Resources. **World Wide Web address:** http://www.abbott.com. **Description:** Manufactures pharmaceuticals and liquid nutrition products including Similac, Pedialyte, and Ensure. The company also manufactures anesthetics, blood pressure monitors, and I.V. systems. **NOTE:** Offers internships. Search and apply for positions online. **Corporate headquarters location:** Abbott Park IL. **Other U.S. locations:** Nationwide. **International locations:** Worldwide. **Listed on:** New York Stock Exchange. **Stock exchange symbol:** ABT. Number of employees worldwide: 70,000.

ABOUTWEB
2106D Gallows Road, Vienna VA 22182. 703/448-5048. **Fax:** 703/448-5048. **Contact:** Human Resources. **E-mail address:** info@aboutweb.com. **World Wide Web address:** http://www.aboutweb.com. **Description:** Aboutweb offers Staff Augmentation and IT Project solution services. **NOTE:** Search and apply for positions at website. **Positions advertised include:** Internet Advertising Sales; Lead Microsoft Network Engineer; Web Developer; Financial Systems Analysts; System Engineers. **Corporate Headquarters:** Rockville MD

ACCENTURE
11951 Freedom Drive, Reston VA 20190. 703/947-2000. **Fax:** 703/947-2200 **Contact:** Human Resources. **World Wide Web address:** http://www.accenture.com. **Description:** Accenture is a management consulting, technology services, and outsourcing company. **NOTE:** Search and apply for positions online. **Positions advertised include:** Entry-Level Programmers; Java/J2EE Sr. Programmer; Cobol Sr. Programmer; CICS Support Analyst; Federal Government Security Lead; Marketing Manager; Transaction Attorney; Technology Integration Consultant. **Number of employees worldwide:** 90,000.

ADVANCE AUTO PARTS, INC.
5673 Airport Road NW, Roanoke VA 24012. 540/362-4911. **Fax:** 540/561-6930. **Contact:** Director of Human Resources. **World Wide Web address:** http://www.advanceautoparts.com. **Description:** Operates a chain of 2,500 auto part stores in 39 states, Puerto Rico, and the Virgin Islands. **NOTE:** Submit application online. **Corporate headquarters location:** This location. **Listed on:** New York Stock Exchange. **Stock exchange symbol:** AAP. **Number of employees nationwide:** 33,000.

ADVANCED ENGINEERING & RESEARCH ASSOCIATES, INC. (AERA)
2800 Shirlington Road, Arlington VA 22206. 703/824-5000. **Fax:** 703/824-5003. **Contact:** Human Resources. **E-mail address:** opportunities@aera.com. **World Wide Web address:** http://www.aera.com. **Description**: AERA provides services in information technology, acquisition logistics, systems engineering, interactive multimedia, and facilities engineering with areas of expertise including marine and aviation propulsion engineering, computer-based training, digital storage systems, and electronic performance support systems. Services include consulting, systems design, systems integration, and testing. **NOTE:** Search and apply for positions online. **Positions advertised include:** Management Analyst; Senior Engineer; Analyst. **Corporate headquarters location:** This location. **Other U.S. locations:** FL; GA; MD; NC; PA; VT. **Parent company:** EDO Corporation.

ADVANCED LOGIC INDUSTRIES (ALI)
922 University City Boulevard, Blacksburg VA 24060. 540/552-6108. **Fax:** 540/552-6126. **Contact:** Human Resources. **E-mail address:** employment@ali-inc.com. **World Wide Web address:** http://www.ali-inc.com. **Description:** Provides consulting, software development, Internet services, product procurement. Support services, and training services. **Other area locations:** Forest VA; Roanoke VA.

ADVANCED MANAGEMENT TECHNOLOGY, INC.
1515 Wilson Boulevard, Suite 1100, Arlington VA 22209. 703/841-2684. **Fax:** 703/841-1486. **Contact:** Recruiter/Staffing Specialist. **E-Mail Address:** recruiter@amti.com. **World Wide Web address:** http://www.amti.com. **Description:** Provides information systems management, Internet/intranet development; multimedia product design and distribution, system engineering, and aviation services. Founded in 1987. **NOTE:** Entry-level positions are offered. Search and apply for positions online. **Company slogan:** Our employees are integral to our continued success. **Special programs:** Training. **Office hours:** Monday - Friday, 8:30 a.m. - 5:30 p.m. **Corporate headquarters location:** This location. **Other U.S. locations:** Los Angeles CA; Atlanta GA; Jamaica NY; Fort Worth TX. **International locations:** New Delhi, India. **Parent company:** Tetra Tech, Inc. **President/CEO:** Anita Talwar. **Number of employees at this location:** 50. **Number of employees nationwide:** 415.

ADVANCED RESOURCE TECHNOLOGIES, INC. (ARTI)
1555 King Street, Suite 400, Alexandria VA 22314. 703/682-4740. **Fax:** 703/682-4823. **Contact:** Human Resources. **E-mail address:** recruiter@team-arti.com. **World Wide Web address:** http://www.team-arti.com. **Description:** A diversified, employee-owned information services provider and systems integrator with expertise in providing information systems engineering, IT security services, network engineering services, security services and management, and program management. **NOTE:** Search and apply for positions or submit resume online. **Positions advertised include:** Senior Account Manager. **Special programs:** Internships. **Other U.S. locations:** Huntsville AL; St. Louis MO; Tridelphia WV. **Listed on:** Privately held. **Number of employees nationwide:** 280.

AERUS
300 East Valley Drive, Bristol VA 24201. 276/466-2942. **Contact:** Human Resources. **World Wide Web address:** http://www.aerusonline.com. **Description:** A manufacturer and retailer of vacuums with more than 500 locations in the U.S. and Canada. **Corporate headquarters location:** Dallas TX. **Parent company:** Electrolux AB. **Listed on:** NASDAQ. **Stock exchange symbol:** ELUX.

AETHER
13625 Dulles Technology Drive, Suite B, Herndon, Virginia 20171. 703/793-2523. **Fax:** 703/793-8725. **Contact:** Human Resources. **World Wide Web address:** http://www.aethersystems.com. **Description:** Aether Systems provides wireless and mobile data solutions that increase efficiency and productivity for the transportation, fleet management, and public safety markets. Founded in 1966. **NOTE:** Search and apply for positions or submit resume online. **Positions advertised include:** Sr. Software Engineer. **Corporate headquarters location:** Owings Mills MD. **Other U.S. locations:** Marlborough MA; Richardson TX; Joplin MO.

ALION SCIENCE AND TECHNOLOGY
1750 Tysons Boulevard, Suite 1300, McLean, VA 22102. 703/918-4480. **Contact:** Human Resources. **World Wide Web address:** http://www.alionscience.com. **Description:** A privately held, employee-owned global research and development company primarily serving the U.S. government. Founded in 1936. **NOTE:** Search and apply for positions online. **Number of employees worldwide:** 1,700.

ALCOA HOME EXTERIORS, INC.
185 Johnson Drive, Stuarts Draft VA 24477-0538. 540/337-3663. **Contact:** Human Resources. **World Wide Web address:** http://www.alcoa.com. **Description:** Manufactures vinyl siding for sale to distributors. **NOTE:** Search and apply for positions online. **Corporate headquarters location:** Pittsburgh PA. **Other U.S. locations:** Denison TX; Gaffney SC; Sidney OH; Atlanta GA. **Parent company:** Alcoa, Inc. **Listed on:** New York Stock Exchange. **Stock exchange symbol:** AA. **Number of employees nationwide:** 1,600.

ALEXANDRIA ANIMAL HOSPITAL
2660 Duke Street, Alexandria VA 22314. 703/751-2022. **Fax:** 703/751-6426. **Contact:** Manager. **World Wide Web address:** http://www.alexandriaanimalhospital.com. **Description:** An animal hospital for pets providing medical, dental, and surgical services. **Positions advertised include:** Receptionist; Veterinarian. **Number of employees at this location:** 100.

ALLIED PLYWOOD CORPORATION
6100 Farrington Avenue, Alexandria VA 22304. 703/256-5800. **Toll-free phone:** 800/733-8480. **Fax:** 727/545-4685. **Contact:** Human Resources. **E-mail address:** employment@alliedplywood.com. **World Wide Web address:** http://www.alliedplywood.com. **Description:** A wholesale lumber company that includes industrial products, Flex Wood, molding, laminates, and other wood products. **NOTE:** Only e-mailed or faxed resumes accepted. No phone calls. **Other area locations:** Marshall VA; Norfolk VA; Richmond VA. **Other U.S. locations:** Jacksonville FL; Orlando FL; Pinellas Park FL; Marietta GA; Rockville MD; Waldorf MD; Charlotte NC; Knoxville TN.

ALLIED DEFENSE GROUP, INC.
8000 Towers Crescent Drive, Suite 260, Vienna VA 22182. 703/847-5268. **Toll-free phone:** 800/847-5322. **Fax:** 703/847-5334. **Contact:** Human Resources Department. **E-mail address:** headquarters@allieddefensegroup.com. **World Wide Web address:** http://www.allieddefensegroup.com. **Description:** A holding company that provides defense and commercial electronic security services through its subsidiaries, which include: MECAR (medium caliber ammunition and mortars), Titan Dynamics Systems (pyrotechnics used in warfare training and simulation), NS Microwave (microwave surveillance equipment), VSK Group (electronic security and fire detection systems), and SeaSpace Corporation (remote sensing equipment used with satellites). **Corporate headquarters location:** This location. **Listed on:** American Stock Exchange. **Stock exchange symbol:** ADG. **Number of employees worldwide:** 500.

ALLSTATE INSURANCE COMPANY
12011 Lee Jackson Highway, Suite 306, Fairfax VA 22033. 703/591-0440. **Fax:** 703/591-0443. **Contact:** Human Resources Department. **E-mail address:** careers@allstate.com. **World Wide Web address:** http://www.allstate.com. **Description:** As one of the nation's largest insurance companies, Allstate Insurance provides a complete line of property, liability, life, reinsurance, and commercial lines of insurance. Founded in 1931. **NOTE:** Internships offered. Search and apply for positions online. **Company slogan:** You're in good hands with Allstate. **Positions advertised include:** Claim Representative; Education Administrator; Insurance Agent/Broker; Underwriter/Assistant Underwriter. **Corporate headquarters location:** Northbrook IL. **Other U.S. locations:** Nationwide. **Listed on:** New York Stock Exchange. **Stock exchange symbol:** ALL.

ALPHA INDUSTRIES INC.
14155 Sullyfield Circle, Suite G, Chantilly VA 20151. 703/378-1420. **Fax:** 703/378-4910. **Contact:** Human Resources Department. **World Wide Web address:** http://www.alphaindustries.com. **Description:** A manufacturer of military clothing. Founded in 1959. **Positions advertised include:** Sales Representative. **Other U.S. locations:** Knoxville TN.

ALPHAINSIGHT CORPORATION
3130 Fairview Park Drive, Suite 600, Falls Church VA 22042. 703/243-8700. **Fax:** 703/243-8226. **Contact:** Technical Recruiter. **E-mail address:** recruiting@alphainsight.com. **World Wide Web address:** http://www.alphainsight.com. **Description:** Provides e-strategies/web applications development, network engineering support and administration, and information security and assurance. Founded in 1989. **NOTE:** Search and apply for positions or submit resume online. Entry-level positions are offered. **Positions advertised include:** System Administrator; Accounting Manager; Database Administrator; COMSEC Analyst-Vault; Information Security Trainer; System Certifier; Site Certifier; Network Engineer; Sr. Technical Writer; Security Analyst; Software Support Specialist. **Corporate headquarters location:** This location. **Listed on:** Privately held. **President:** Mr. Kwang Kim.

ALPHATECH, INC.
3811 North Fairfax Drive, Suite 500, Arlington, VA 22203. 703/524-6263. **Fax:** 703/524-6280. **Contact:** Human Resources. **World Wide Web address:** http://www.alphatech.com. **Description:** Provides information processing, software development, and systems engineering services. Founded in 1979. **NOTE:** Search and apply for positions online. **Positions advertised include:** Lead Engineer; Sr. Software Engineer; Sr. Human Resources Generalist. **Corporate headquarters location:** Burlington MA. **Other U.S. locations:** San Diego CA. **Number of employees nationwide:** 250.

AMERICAN BUILDING MAINTENANCE (ABM)
113 Clermont Avenue, Alexandria VA 22304. 703/461-7501. **Contact:** Human Resources. **World Wide Web address:** http://www.abm.com. **Description:** Provides maintenance services for area offices. ABM operates 76 branch offices in 40 states. **Corporate headquarters location:** San Francisco CA. **Other U.S. locations:** Nationwide. **Operations at this facility include:** Service. **Listed on:** New York Stock Exchange. **Stock exchange symbol:** ABM. Number of employees nationwide: 43,000.

AMERICAN CHEMISTRY COUNCIL, INC.
1300 Wilson Boulevard, Arlington VA 22209. 703/741-5000. **Fax:** 703/741-6083. **Contact:** Human Resources. **E-mail address:** hr@americanchemistry.com. **World Wide Web address:** http://www.americanchemistry.com. **Description:** A trade association representing the chemical industry. The organization coordinates public policy issues, online training seminars, research and testing programs, and workshops and administers environmental, health, and safety regulations. NOTE: Submit resume and cover letter with salary requirements via e-mail or fax. **Positions advertised include:** Communications Group Associate; Staff Accountant; Director, Public Health/Technical; Paralegal; Managing Director; Communications Group Editor; Associate A/P; Director. **Subsidiaries include:** American Chemistry Council Multimedia (also at this location) provides multimedia, computer training, and telecommunications services to its members and the public.

AMERICAN FLAT GLASS DISTRIBUTORS, INC. (AFGD)
6200 Gorman Road, Richmond VA 23231. 804/222-0120. **Fax:** 804/226-1859. **Contact:** Human Resources Generalist. **World Wide Web address:** http://www.afgd.com. **Description:** American Flat Glass Distributors specializes in architectural insulated units and custom tempering. The firm manufactures a complete line of insulated units for commercial and residential applications. The product line includes clear, tint, and reflective float glass; laminated, low-emissivity, tempered, acrylic, mirror, obscure, insulated, and polished wire glass; as well as a complete line of glass handling, storage, and transportation equipment. **NOTE:** Search and apply for positions online. **Positions advertised include:** Inside Sales Representative. **Corporate headquarters location:** Atlanta GA. **Other U.S. locations:** Nationwide. **Parent company:** AFG Industries. **Operations at this facility include:** Manufacturing; Sales. **Listed on:** Privately held. **Number of employees at this location:** 75. **Number of employees nationwide:** 1,000.

AMERICAN NATIONAL BANK AND TRUST COMPANY
P.O. Box 191, Danville VA 24543. 434/792-5111. **Physical address:** 628 Main Street, Danville VA 24541. **Toll-free phone:** 800/240-8190/ **Contact:** Human Resources. **World Wide Web address:** http://www.amnb.com. **Description:** A full-service bank with 14 branch locations. Founded in 1909. **Corporate headquarters location:** This location. **Subsidiaries include:** ANB Mortgage Corp.; AND Investor Services. **Listed on:** NASDAQ. **Stock exchange symbol:** AMNB.

AMERICAN PRESS, LLC
One American Place, Gordonsville VA 22942. 540/832-2253. **Fax:** 540/832-7253. **Contact:** Human Resources. **Description:** A web offset printer of magazines and catalogs. **NOTE:** Entry-level positions are offered. **Other U.S. locations:** Nationwide. **Operations at this facility include:** Administration; Divisional Headquarters; Manufacturing. **Listed on:** Privately held. **Annual sales/revenues:** $21 - $50 million. **Number of employees at this location:** 300.

AMERICAN RED CROSS
8111 Gatehouse Road, Falls Church VA 22042. 703/206-7330. **Contact:** Human Resources. **World Wide Web address:** www.redcross.org/jobs. **Description:** A humanitarian organization that aids disaster victims, gathers blood for crisis distribution, trains individuals to respond to emergencies, educates individuals on various diseases, and raises funds for other charitable establishments. **NOTE:** Search and apply for positions online. **Positions advertised include:** Manager, Configuration Management; Senior Analyst, Software Development; Senior Analyst, IT Field Regulatory Compliance.

AMERICAN SAFETY RAZOR COMPANY
One Razor Blade Lane, Verona VA 24482. 540/248-8000. **Fax:** 540/248-9773. **Contact:** Reginald Ryals, Human Resources Administrator. **E-mail address:** jobs2@asrco.com. **World Wide Web address:** http://www.asrco.com. **Description:** American Safety Razor Company designs, manufactures, and markets razors and blades, bladed hand tools, specialty industrial blades, and medical blades. **NOTE:** Search and apply for positions online. **Positions advertised include:** Production Supervisor; Marketing Administrator; Product Manager. **Corporate headquarters location:** Cedar Knolls NJ. **Other U.S. locations:** TN; AZ. **International locations:** Canada; England; Mexico; Puerto Rico; Israel. **Number of employees nationwide:** 1,630.

AMERICAN SYSTEMS CORPORATION (ASC)
13990 Park East Circle, Chantilly VA 20151-2272. 703/968-6300. **Toll-free phone:** 800/733-2721. **Fax:** 703/968-5151. **Contact:** Human Resources. **E-mail address:** recruiting@2asc.com. **World Wide Web address:** http://www.2asc.com. **Description:** Provides information technology services to the Department of Defense and other government agencies, the intelligence community, and commercial clients. Core businesses include systems engineering and network integration services; enterprise-wide structured cable plant installations; training services; and outsourcing of technical and administrative services. **NOTE:** Search and apply for positions online. **Positions advertised include:** Account Executive; Accountant; Cable Installer; Software Engineer; Systems Engineer; Facilities Assistant; Project Manager. **Corporate headquarters location:** This location. **Other area locations:** Arlington VA; Norfolk VA; /Dumfries VA; Springfield VA. **Other U.S. locations:** GA; LA; MD; CT; CA; DC; RI; FL; PA; WA; SC. **Subsidiaries include:** American Communications Corporation. **Listed on:** Privately held. **Annual sales/revenues:** $175 million. **Number of employees at this location:** 250. **Number of employees nationwide:** 1,350.

AMERICAN TRUCKING ASSOCIATIONS, INC.
2200 Mill Road, Alexandria VA 22314-4677. 703/838-1726. **Fax:** 703/836-5880. **Contact:** Kay Perkins, Vice President of Personnel. **World Wide Web address:** http://www.trucking.org. **Description:** This national federation of the trucking industry represents all types of trucking companies. **Corporate headquarters location:** This location.

AMERICAN WOODMARK CORPORATION
P.O. Box 1980, Winchester VA 22604. 540/665-9100. **Physical address:** 3102 Shawnee Drive, Winchester VA 22601-4208. **Contact:** Human Resources. **World Wide Web address:** http://www.americanwoodmark.com. **Description:** Manufactures and distributes kitchen cabinets and vanities. The company's products are sold nationally through a network of independent distributors, home centers, major builders, and home manufacturers. Founded in 1980. **NOTE:** Entry-level positions and part-time jobs are offered. **Company slogan:** Creating value through people. **Corporate headquarters location:** This location. **Other U.S. locations:** AZ; GA; IN; KY; MN; OK; TN; WV. **Listed on:** NASDAQ. **Stock exchange symbol:** AMWD. **Annual sales/revenues:** $564 million. **Number of employees at this location:** 220. **Number of employees nationwide:** 2,600.

AMERIGROUP CORPORATION,
4425 Corporation Lane, Virginia Beach, VA 23462. 757/490-6900. **Fax:** 757/518-3600. **Contact:** Human Resources. **E-mail address:** hrvacorp@amerigroupcorp.com. **World Wide Web address:** http://www.amerigroupcorp.com. **Description:** A multi-state managed health care company serving people who receive health care benefits through publicly sponsored programs. **Positions advertised include:** Recovery Analyst; HRIS Analyst; Manager, M&A Underwriting; Manager, Operational Audit; RN, Telephonic Triage. **Corporate headquarters location:** This location. **Other U.S. locations:** TX; NJ; MD; IL; FL; Washington DC.

AMERIND, INC.
1310 Braddock Place, Suite 400, Alexandria VA 22314-1651. 703/836-5900. **Fax:** 703/836-8691. **Contact:** Manager of Personnel Department. **E-mail address:** jobs@amerind.com. **World Wide Web address:** http://www.amerind.com. **Description:** Provides business process re-engineering, data management, document processing systems solutions, performance measurement and evaluation, program support, and instructional systems analysis. Founded in 1983. **NOTE:** Search and apply for positions online. **Positions advertised include:** Contracts and Accounting Manager; Program Manager. **Corporate headquarters location:** This location. **Other area locations:** Reston VA; Virginia Beach VA. **Other U.S. locations:** DC; MD; CA; CO; FL; GA; PA; WA. **Parent company:** FCBS. **Listed on:** Privately held. **Number of employees nationwide:** 200.

ANALEX CORPORATION
5904 Richmond Highway, Suite 300, Alexandria VA 22303. 703/329-9400. **Fax:** 703/329-8187. **Contact:** Human Resources. **E-mail address:** jobs@analex.com. **World Wide Web address:** http://www.analex.com. **Description:** A technical services

company operating through its subsidiaries. **Subsidiaries include:** Advanced Biosystems conducts R&D of medical defenses against biological weapons and products to treat or prevent infectious diseases; SyCom Services, Inc. is a computer engineering firm. **NOTE:** Search and apply for positions online. **Positions advertised include:** S/W Developer; Service Development Engineer; UNIX/WINTEL Systems Administrator. **Listed on:** American Stock Exchange. **Stock exchange symbol:** NLX.

ANALYSTS INTERNATIONAL
4136 Innslake Drive, Suite A, Glen Allen, VA 23060. 804/217-8490. **Toll-free phone:** 877/840-7860. **Fax:** 804/217-8493. **Contact:** Human Resources. **E-mail address:** jobs@analysts.com. **World Wide Web address:** http://www.analysts.com. **Description:** A diversified IT services company offering staffing, network infrastructure, and outsourcing services. Founded in 1966. NOTE: Search and apply for positions online. **Positions advertised include:** Sr. Business Systems Analyst; Systems Administrator; Business Analyst. **Corporate headquarters location:** Minneapolis MN. **Other U.S. locations:** Nationwide.

ANALYTICAL MECHANICS ASSOCIATES, INC. (AMA)
303 Butler Farm Road, Suite 104A, Hampton VA 23666. 757/865-0944. **Fax:** 575/865-1881. **Contact:** Human Resources. **E-mail address:** resumes@ama-inc.com. **World Wide Web address:** http://www.ama-inc.com. **Description:** Provides aerospace consulting to NASA. **Positions advertised include:** Multimedia Specialist; Software Engineer; Software Developer; Programmer; Project Engineer; Software Manager; Senior Analyst; Systems Analyst. **Other U.S. locations:** CA; AL.

ANDREW CORPORATION
19700 Janelia Farm Boulevard, Ashburn VA 20147. 703/726-5500. **Fax:** 703/726-5600. **Contact:** Human Resources. **World Wide Web address:** http://www.andrew.com. **Description:** Designs, manufactures, and supplies communications equipment, services, and systems. **NOTE:** Search and apply for positions or submit resume online. **Corporate headquarters location:** Orland Park IL. **Listed on:** NASDAQ. **Stock exchange symbol:** DNDW. **Number of employees worldwide:** 7,000.

ANHEUSER-BUSCH, INC.
7801 Pocahontas Trail, Williamsburg VA 23185. 757/253-3600. **Contact:** Human Resources. **Recorded jobline:** 800/545-4342. **World Wide Web address:** http://www.anheuser-busch.com. **Description:** This location is a beer brewing facility. **Corporate headquarters location:** St. Louis MO. **Parent company:** Anheuser-Busch's operations and resources are focused on beer, adventure park entertainment and packaging. Anheuser-Busch also has interests in aluminum beverage container recycling, malt production, rice milling, real estate development, turf farming, metalized paper label printing and transportation services. The company is one of the largest domestic brewers, operating 14 breweries in the U.S. and overseas and distributing through over 900 independent wholesalers. Anheuser-Busch is also one of the largest operators of amusement parks in the United States, with locations in Florida, Virginia, Texas, Ohio, and California. Through subsidiary Campbell Taggart Inc., Anheuser-Busch is also one of the largest commercial baking companies in the United States, producing foods under the Colonial brand name, among others. Founded in 1852. **NOTE:** Search and apply for positions online. **Corporate headquarters location:** St Louis MO. **Listed on:** New York Stock Exchange. **Stock exchange symbol:** BUD.

ANIXTER INC.
45075 Old Ox Road, Suite 100, Dulles VA 20166. 703/318-2300. **Fax:** 703/318-2324. **Contact:** Human Resources. **World Wide Web address:** http://www.anixter.com. **Description:** A distributor of communication products, electrical and electronic wire and cable and a leading distributor of fasteners and other small parts to original equipment manufacturers. Operates locations in 180 cities in 42 countries. Founded in 1957. **NOTE:** Search and apply for positions online. **Corporate headquarters location:** Glenview IL. **Listed on:** New York Stock Exchange. **Stock exchange symbol:** AXE. **Number of employees worldwide:** 5,000.

ANSER (ANALYTIC SERVICES INC.)
2900 South Quincy Street, Suite 800, Arlington VA 22206. 703/416-2000. Toll-free phone: 866/226-5697. **Fax:** 703/416-3019. **Contact:** Human Resources Department. **E-mail address:** jobs@anser.org. **World Wide Web address:** http://www.anser.org. **Description:** An independent, nonprofit, public research institute that provides analytic and technical support to federal agencies in the areas of homeland security, aerospace systems development, acquisition, operations, requirements definition, technology evaluation, testing, and planning; aerospace science and technology program planning and management; modernization planning; information systems planning and acquisition; C3I program planning; and foreign technology analyses. **NOTE:** Search and apply for jobs online. **Positions advertised include:** Accountant; Analyst; Contracts Administrator; Facilities Administrator; Information Technology Technician; Senior Analyst; Senior Systems Engineer; Systems Analyst. **Special programs:** Internships. **Corporate headquarters location:** This location. **Other area locations:** Hampton VA. **Other U.S. locations:** Colorado Springs CO. **Operations at this facility include:** Research and Development. **Number of employees at this location:** 480.

ANTEON CORPORATION
3211 Jermantown Road, Fairfax VA 22030. 703/246-0200. **Contact:** Human Resources. **E-mail address:** careers@anteon.com. **World Wide Web address:** http://www.anteon.com. **Description:** Provides information technology solutions and advanced engineering services to government clients. The company designs, integrates, maintains, and upgrades state-of-the-art systems for national defense, intelligence, emergency response, and other high-priority missions. **Positions advertised include:** Accounting Associate; Collections Specialist; Corporate Real Estate Planner; Director of Proposals; Financial Analyst; Functional Analyst; Marketing Analyst; Security Officer; Software Architect; Sr. Network Engineer; Sr. Proposal Specialist; Tax Analyst. **Corporate headquarters location:** This location. **Listed on:** New York Stock Exchange. **Stock exchange symbol:** ANT. **Number of employees worldwide:** 7,600 in more than 100 offices.

ANTHEM BLUE CROSS BLUE SHIELD
2015 Staples Mill Road, Richmond VA 23230. 804/354-7000. **Contact:** Recruitment & Staffing. **World Wide Web address:** http://www.anthem.com. **Description:** A health insurance provider. **NOTE:** Search and apply for positions, or submit resume online. **Positions advertised include:** Account Executive; Account Manager; Data Analyst; Data Mining Analyst; Director, Medical; Manager, Business Project and Support; Nurse Consultant; Nutritional Consultant; Sr. Product Manager; Sr. Enterprise Systems Management Analyst/Advisor. **Corporate headquarters location:** Indianapolis IN. **Other area locations:** Roanoke VA; Virginia Beach VA. **Other U.S. locations:** OH; IN; KY; CO; NF; CT; ME; NH. **Operations at this facility include:** Administration; Divisional Headquarters; Regional Headquarters; Sales; Service. **Listed on:** Privately held. **Number of employees at this location:** 3,200. **Number of employees nationwide:** 4,000.

ANVICOM, INC.
1934 Old Gallows Road, Suite 200, Vienna VA 22182. 703/970-7300. **Fax:** 703/876-6338. **Contact:** Human Resources. **E-mail address:** jobs@anvi.com. **Description:** Provides IT engineering and support services to the U.S. Government and Department of Defense. **NOTE:** Search and apply for positions online. **Positions advertised include:** Contract Specialist; Network Engineer; Principal System Engineer; Sr. Network Administrator; Technical Recruiter; Sales Engineer; Research and Marketing Assistant. **Number of employees at this location:** 200.

APPLIED ORDNANCE TECHNOLOGY, INC.
100 Greenspring Drive, Stafford VA 22554. 540/288-2680. **Fax:** 540/288-9905. **Contact:** Human Resources. **World Wide Web address:** http://www.aot.com. **Description:** Provides engineering and management services to support weapons engineering, environmental engineering, ordnance design, information technology, system safety, and gun and ammunition systems. **NOTE:** Search and apply for positions online. **Positions advertised include:** Program Analyst; Systems Engineer.

ASH LAWN OPERA SUMMER FESTIVAL
2000 Holiday Drive, Suite 100, Charlottesville VA 22901. 434/293-4500. **Fax:** 434/293-0736 **Contact:** Ms. Judith Walker, General Director. **Description:** A summer festival that produces two operas and one musical theatrical production each season. Ash Lawn-Highland Summer Festival offers preperformance lectures; presents Music at Twilight (including classical and contemporary programs); and offers Summer Saturdays, a theater and music production for children. **Special programs:** Internships; Apprenticeships. **Internship information:** There are two summer internships available in Production and Arts Management/Production. There are four summer and academic year internships available in Press, Development, Marketing, and Administration. For more information or to apply, please contact Saskia Santen-Arts, Intern Coordinator. **Corporate headquarters location:** This location. **Number of employees at this location:** 60.

ATLANTIC COAST AIRLINES HOLDINGS, INC.
45200 Business Court, Suite 100, Dulles VA 20166. 703/650-6000. **Recorded jobline:** 866/975-4222. **Contact:** Director of Human Resources. **World Wide Web address:** http://www.atlanticcoast.com. **Description:** One of the largest regional airlines operating in the United States, flying to 84 destinations in the U.S. and Canada with approximately 850 scheduled departures each weekday. Atlantic Coast Airlines operates as United Express, Delta Connection, and Independence Air. Positions advertised include: Manager, Aircraft Records; Training Coordinator; Senior Analyst; Lead Receiving Inspector; Aircraft Inspector; Corporate Security Specialist; Operations Manager; Irregular Operations Manager; System Control Instructor; Document Editor; Avionics Technician. **NOTE:** Application information for specific openings available online. **Corporate headquarters location:** This location. **Listed on:** NASDAQ. **Stock exchange symbol:** ACAI. **Number of employees nationwide:** 5,000.

ATLANTIC COAST COTTON
14251 John Marshall Highway, Gainesville VA 20155. 703/753-7000. **Contact:** Human Resources. **E-mail address:** accfirst@aol.com. **World Wide Web address:** http://www.atlanticcoastcotton.com. **Description:** A wholesale distributor of a variety of sportswear and clothing products including T-shirts, sweatshirts, sweatpants, hats, fleecewear, and sleepwear. **Positions advertised include:** Part-time Warehouse Worker.

ATLANTIC COAST FORESTRY INC.
PO Box 1233, Madison VA 22727. 540/948-5330. **Contact:** Human Resources. **Description:** Develops and cultivates forests to provide services for the paper industry.

ATLANTIC RESEARCH CORPORATION
5945 Wellington Road, Gainesville VA 20155. 703/754-5000. **Contact:** Susan Imperatore, Human Resources. **E-mail address:** hr@atlanticresearchcorp.com. **World Wide Web address:** http://www.atlanticresearchcorp.com. **Description:** ARC is a leading developer and manufacturer of advanced solid rocket propulsion systems, gas generators and auxiliary rocket motors for both space and defense applications. **Corporate headquarters location:** This location. Other U.S. locations: AR; CA; UT. **Parent company:** GenCorp.

ATLAS ALEXANDRIA PACKAGING & SUPPLY
7398 Ward Park Lane, Springfield VA 22153. 703/644-5550. **Contact:** Human Resources. **E-mail address:** info@alexpkg.com. **World Wide Web address:** http://www.alexpkg.com. **Description:** Operates a packaging and crating company, for both local and international customers through five divisions: wood crating and packing, foam manufacturing, corrugated box manufacturing, mil-spec. packing and packaging, and packaging supplies. Founded in 1972.

ATLAS COPCO DRILLING SOLUTIONS
7500 Shadwell Drive, Roanoke VA 24019. 540/362-3321. **Contact:** Human Resources. **World Wide Web address:** http://www.irco.com. **Description:** Manufactures drilling equipment and accessories for the worldwide construction, mining, quarrying, and waterwell drilling industries. **Headquarters location:** Stockholm Sweden.

AVALONBAY COMMUNITIES, INC.
2900 Eisenhower Avenue, 3rd Floor, Alexandria VA 22314. 703/329-6300. **Fax:** 703/329-9130. **Contact:** Rita Grazda, Director of Human Resources. **World Wide Web address:** http://www.avalonbay.com. **Description:** A self-administered and self-managed equity real estate investment trust that specializes in the development, construction, acquisition, and management of apartment communities in the mid-Atlantic and northeastern United States. AvalonBay owns or operates 143 apartment communities in ten states and D.C. **NOTE:** Search and apply for positions online. **Positions advertised include:** Accounts Payable Analyst; Circuit Program Participant; Comp Support Specialist; Financial Analyst; Staff Accountant. **Corporate headquarters location:** This location. **Listed on:** New York Stock Exchange. **Stock exchange symbol:** AVB.

AVERETT UNIVERSITY
420 West Main Street, Danville VA 24541. 434/791-5600. **Contact:** Faye Dix, Human Resources. **World Wide Web address:** http://www.averett.edu. **Description:** A private, co-ed, four-year, liberal arts college. Averett offers bachelor of arts and bachelor of science degrees in 30 undergraduate programs, as well as a master of business administration, a master of arts and teaching, and a master of education. Total enrollment is 2,800.

BAE SYSTEMS NORTH AMERICA
1215 Jefferson Davis Highway, Arlington VA 22202. 703/416-7800. **Fax:** 703/415-1459. **Contact:** Director of Human Resources. **World Wide Web address:** http://www.baesystems.com. **Description:** Designs, develops, integrates, manufactures, and supports a wide range of advanced aerospace products and intelligent electronic systems for government and commercial customers. Maintains operations in 30 states.

NOTE: Search and apply for positions online. **Corporate headquarters location:** Rockville MD. **Parent company:** BAE Systems plc. **Number of employees nationwide:** 25,000.

BAE SYSTEMS
2525 Network Place, Herndon VA 20171. 703/563-7500. **Contact:** Human Resources. **World Wide Web address:** http://www.digitalnet.com. **Description:** DigitalNet specializes in end-to-end networking computer solutions for the government. **Positions advertised include:** Business Services director; Management Consultant; Assoc Systems Administrator; Accounting Specialist; Principal Systems Analyst; Supervisor Computer Systems; Technical Writer/Editor. **NOTE:** Search and apply for positions online. **Operations at this facility include:** This location is a sales office for government contracts. **Listed on:** NASDAQ. **Stock exchange symbol:** DNET.

BHA GROUP, INC.
11864 Canon Boulevard, Suite 105, Newport News VA 23606-4223. 757/595-7982. **Contact:** Human Resources. **E-mail address:** hr@bha.com. **World Wide Web address:** http://www.bhagroup.com. **Description:** BHA Group, Inc. designs, manufactures, and sells replacement parts and accessories for electrostatic precipitators and for fabric filter dust collection equipment. The company also provides rehabilitation and conversion services for the industrial air pollution control equipment it produces. BHA operates nine manufacturing facilities. **NOTE:** Search and apply for positions online. **Positions advertised include:** Application Engineer; Digital Engineer. **Corporate headquarters location:** Kansas City MO. **Operations at this facility include:** This location provides the U.S. electrostatic precipitator markets with replacement parts, control systems, and services. Electrostatic precipitators are a type of air pollution control equipment. **Listed on:** NASDAQ. **Stock exchange symbol:** BHAG.

B.I.A. CAPITAL CORPORATION
15120 Enterprise Court, Suite 100, Chantilly VA 20151. 703/818-8115. **Fax:** 703/803-3299. **Contact:** Human Resources. **E-mail address:** hr@bia.com. **World Wide Web address:** http://www.biacompanies.com. **Description:** A consulting firm for television and radio broadcasting.

MICHAEL BAKER CORPORATION
3601 Eisenhower Avenue, Suite 600, Alexandria VA 22304. 703/960-8800. **Fax:** 703/960-9125. **Contact:** Human Resources Department. **World Wide Web address:** http://www.mbakercorp.com. **Description:** Provides engineering consulting and design services, construction services, and operations and maintenance services. As the company's core business, the engineering group encompasses a broad range of disciplines required to plan, design, and inspect the construction of architectural and engineering projects. Michael Baker's construction group consists of construction management and design, heavy and highway construction, and general construction. Maintains offices in 21 states and six other countries. **NOTE:** Search and apply for positions online. **Positions advertised include:** Technical Manager; Business Systems Analyst; Civil Associate; Civil Engineer; GIS Specialist; Software Systems Developer; Public Relations Specialist; Marketing Coordinator; Planning Associate; Project Manager; Operations Manager; Technical Writer. **Corporate headquarters location:** Moon Township PA. **Other U.S. locations:** Nationwide. **International locations:** Worldwide. **Listed on:** AMEX. **Stock exchange symbol:** BKR. Number of employees nationwide: 4,400.

BALMAR PRINTING AND GRAPHICS, INC.
2818 Fallfax Drive, Falls Church VA 22042-2804. 703/289-9000. **Fax:** 703/876-9657. **Contact:** Human Resources. **World Wide Web address:** http://www.balmar.com. **Description:** A commercial lithographic printer. **Positions advertised include:** Press Operator. **Corporate headquarters location:** This location. **Number of employees at this location:** 100.

BANK OF AMERICA
1111 East Main Street, P.O. Box 27025, Richmond VA 23219. 804/788-2121. **Contact:** Staffing. **E-mail address:** careers@bankofamerica.com. **World Wide Web address:** http://www.bankofamerica.com. **Description:** Bank of America is one of the world's largest financial institutions, serving individual consumers, small businesses and large corporations with a range of banking, investing, asset management and other financial and risk-management products and services. **NOTE:** Search and apply for positions online. **Positions advertised include:** Sr. Telephone Sales Associate; Teller; Customer Service Rep; Systems Engineer; Full Service Financial Advisor; Sr. Process Design Engineer. **Corporate headquarters location:** Charlotte NC. **Listed on:** New York Stock Exchange. **Stock exchange symbol:** BAC. **Number of employees worldwide:** 180,000.

BANK OF AMERICA
One Commercial Place, Norfolk VA 23510. 757/441-4770. **Contact:** Human Resources Department. **E-mail address:** careers@bankofamerica.com. **World Wide Web address:** http://www.bankofamerica.com. **Description:** Bank of America is one of the world's largest financial institutions, serving individual consumers, small businesses and large corporations with a range of banking, investing, asset management and other financial and risk-management products and services. **NOTE:** Search and apply for positions online. **Positions advertised include:** Customer Service Rep; Operations Analyst; Trust Assistant; Collector; Master Black Belt I. **Corporate headquarters location:** Charlotte NC. **Listed on:** New York Stock Exchange. **Stock exchange symbol:** BAC. **Number of employees worldwide:** 180,000.

BANK OF CLARKE COUNTY
EAGLE FINANCIAL SERVICES, INC.
P.O. Box 391, Berryville VA 22611. 540/955-2510. **Physical address:** 2 East Main Street, Berryville VA 22611. **Toll-free phone:** 800/650-8723. **Contact:** Kaley Crosen, Vice President of Human Resources. **World Wide Web address:** http://www.bankofclarke.com. **Description:** Bank of Clarke County grants commercial, financial, agricultural, residential, and consumer loans to customers in Virginia and eastern West Virginia. Bank of Clarke County also provides general banking services at nine locations. Founded in 1881. **Corporate headquarters location:** This location. **Parent company:** Eagle Financial Services. **Number of employees nationwide:** 65.

BANNER AEROSPACE
45025 Aviation Drive, Suite 400, Dulles VA 20166-7516. 703/478-5800. **Fax:** 703/478-5795. **Contact:** Human Resources Department. **World Wide Web address:** http://www.fairchild.com. **Description:** An aerospace distribution business that stocks and distributes a wide variety of parts to aircraft operators and aerospace customers providing aircraft parts and services to customers worldwide. **Corporate headquarters location:** This location. **Parent company:** Fairchild Corporation.

BARBER & ROSS COMPANY
255 Fort Collier Road, Winchester VA 22603. 540/722-9199. **Contact:** Human Resources. **Description:** Manufactures window units, interior and exterior door units, door entrance products, and other door products and accessories. **Corporate headquarters location:** This location. **Other area locations:** Richmond VA. **Other U.S. locations:** Mebane NC; Knox IN. **Number of employees nationwide:** 1,200.

BASSETT FURNITURE INDUSTRIES, INC.
P.O. Box 626, Bassett VA 24055. 276/629-6000. **Physical address:** 3525 Fairystone Park Highway, Bassett VA 24055. **Contact:** Manager of Human Resources Department. **E-mail address:** bassett@bassettfurniture.com. **World Wide Web address:** http://www.bassettfurniture.com. **Description:** Manufactures and sells a full-line of furniture for the home such as bedroom and dining suites, accent pieces, tables, wall and entertainment units, upholstered sofas, chairs and love seats, recliners, and mattresses and box springs. Also operates more than 100 Bassett Furniture Direct stores. **Corporate headquarters location:** This location. **Other U.S. locations:** Nationwide. **Listed on:** NASDAQ. **Stock exchange symbol:** BSET. **Number of employees nationwide:** 7,800.

BENCHMARK BANKSHARES, INC.
BENCHMARK COMMUNITY BANK
100 South Broad Street P.O. Box 569, Kenbridge VA 23944. 434/676-9054. **Fax:** 434/676-1875. **Contact:** Jennifer Clarke, Human Resources Officer. **E-mail address:** Jenny.Clark@bcbonline.com. **World Wide Web address:** http://www.bcbonline.com. **Description:** A holding company for Benchmark Community Bank, a savings and loan institution with nine branch offices located in southern Virginia. **NOTE:** Search for positions and download application forms online. **Corporate headquarters location:** This location.

BETATECH
344 Maple Avenue West, Suite 182, Vienna VA 22180. 703/276-0039. **Fax:** 703/276-1666. **Contact:** Human Resources. **E-Mail:** jobs@betatech.com. **World Wide Web address:** http://www.betatech.com. **Description:** Provides search and placement services for Technical, Accounting, Financial, and Sales Candidates. **Positions advertised include:** Civil Engineer; Architect/Financial Systems; Accounts Payable Specialist; Sr. Sales Rep. **Corporate Headquarters:** Kensington MD.

BOAR'S HEAD PROVISION COMPANY, INC.
P.O. Box 277, Jarratt VA 23867. 434/535-8581. **Contact:** Vanessa Butts, Human Resources Manager. **World Wide Web address:** http://www.boarshead.com. **Description:** Boar's Head Provision Company, Inc. produces a variety of deli products including ham, beef, bologna, hot dogs, and salami. **Positions advertised include:** Safety and Health Manager; Employee Services Technician. **Other area locations:** Petersburg VA. **Other U.S. locations:** Brooklyn NJ; Edison NJ; Forrest City AR; Holland MI; Sarasota FL. **Operations at this facility include:** This location is primarily a production plant.

BOATU.S.
880 South Pickett Street, Alexandria VA 22304. 703/823-9550. **Fax:** 703/461-4395. **Recorded jobline:** 703/461-4691. **Contact:** Evelyn Matey, Director of Human Resources. **E-mail address:** humanresources@boatus.com. **World Wide Web address:** http://www.boatus.com. **Description:** One of the largest national associations of recreational boat owners. BoatU.S. provides marine insurance to its members, representation in Congress, water towing services, and discount boating equipment. Founded in 1966. **NOTE:** Search for positions online. **Positions advertised include:** Service Rep; File Clerk; Towing Service Rep; Image Coordinator; Membership marketing Coordinator; Print Buyer; Web Specialist. **Corporate headquarters location:** This location. **Operations at this facility include:** Administration; Sales; Service. **Number of employees at this location:** 500. **Number of employees nationwide:** 1,000.

BOOZ-ALLEN & HAMILTON, INC.
8283 Greensboro Drive, McLean VA 22102. 703/902-5000. **Fax:** 703/902-3333. **Contact:** Recruiting Manager. **E-mail address:** recruiting_feedback@bah.com. **World Wide Web address:** http://www.bah.com. **Description:** A diversified, international, management consulting organization offering services in both the commercial and public sectors. The company's areas of expertise include strategy operations and technology. Specific services include corporate strategy and long-range planning; organization design; management changes; human resources management; financial management and control; acquisitions and divestiture; information systems and automation; manufacturing, inventory, and distribution control; marketing strategy and positioning; venture management; transportation and environmental systems; technology research; new products and process development; government programs; and regulatory compliance. **Positions advertised include:** .NET Developer; .NET Developer, Junior; Accountant, Mid; Data Analyst; Strategic Energy Associate. **Corporate headquarters location:** This location. **International locations:** Worldwide. **Operations at this facility include:** Service. **Number of employees at this location:** 3,600. **Number of employees worldwide:** 14,000.

BOWL AMERICA INC.
6446 Edsall Road, Alexandria VA 22312. 703/941-6300. **Contact:** Human Resources. **Description:** Engaged in the operation of 18 bowling centers. **Corporate headquarters location:** This location. **Other area locations:** Richmond VA. **Other U.S. locations:** Washington DC; Jacksonville FL; Orlando FL; Baltimore MD. **Listed on:** American Stock Exchange. **Stock exchange symbol:** BWL. **Number of employees nationwide:** 700.

BRANCH BANKING & TRUST COMPANY
6400 Arlington Boulevard, Falls Church VA 22042. 703/241-4866. **Contact:** Human Resources. **World Wide Web address:** http://www.bbandt.com. **Description:** BB&T is a financial holding company operating more than 1,400 branch offices. **NOTE:** Search and apply for positions online. Positions advertised include: Institutional Trust Services Sales Associate; Private Banker; Private Banking Manager; Senior Interior Designer. **Corporate headquarters location:** Winston-Salem NC. **Other U.S. locations:** AL; DC; FL; GA; IN; KY; MD; NC; SC; TN; WV.

BRENCO, INC.
2580 Frontage Road, P.O. Box 389, Petersburg VA 23804. 804/732-0202. **Fax:** 804/732-4722. **Contact:** Human Resources. **E-mail address:** resumes@brencoqbs.com. **World Wide Web address:** http://www.brencoqbs.com. **Description:** Manufactures tapered roller bearings and component parts for railroad cars. The company sells tapered roller bearings to most major railroads and railroad car builders worldwide. Automotive forgings are sold principally to automobile manufacturers. **Positions advertised include:** Production Worker; Programmer; Electrician; Machinist; Security Guard. **Corporate headquarters location:** This location. **Subsidiaries include:** Quality Bearing Service specializes in bearing reconditioning and the sale of replacement bearings; Rail Link, Inc. provides third-

party contract switching services to large industrial rail users. **Parent company:** AMSTED Industries Inc.

BRIEFINGS PUBLISHING GROUP
1101 King Street, Suite 110, Alexandria VA 22334. 703/548-3800. **Toll-free phone:** 800/722-9221. **Fax:** 703/684-2136. **Contact:** Human Resources. **World Wide Web address:** http://www.briefings.com. **Description:** Publishes business advice in various formats including newsletters, tip books, reports, and videos.

THE BRINK'S COMPANY
1801 Bayberry Court, P.O. Box 18100, Richmond VA 23226. 804/289-9600. **Fax:** 804/289-9768. **Contact:** Human Resources. **E-mail address:** info@BrinksCompany.com. **World Wide Web address:** http://www.pittston.com. **Description:** The Brink's Company is a global leader in business and security services with three operating units: Brink's, Incorporated, a provider of secure transportation and cash management services; Brink's Home Security, a residential alarm company; and BAX Global, providing supply chain management and transportation solutions. **NOTE:** Search and apply for positions online. **Positions advertised include:** Internal Auditor; Controls Assessment Analyst. **Corporate headquarters location:** This location. **Other U.S. locations:** Darien CT. **Listed on:** New York Stock Exchange. **Stock exchange symbol:** PZB. **Annual sales/revenues:** $4 billion. **Number of employees worldwide:** 50,000.

BRISTOL COMPRESSORS
15185 Industrial Park Road, Bristol VA 24202. 276/466-4121. **Fax:** 276/645-2423. **Contact:** Joe Pendergast, Manager, Human Resources. E-mail address: joe.pendergast@bristolcompressors.com. **World Wide Web address:** http://www.bristolcompressors.com. **Description:** Manufactures compressors used in air conditioning and heat pump applications. **Corporate headquarters location:** This location. **Other U.S. locations:** Arkadelphia AR.

BURLINGTON KLOPMAN FABRICS
797 Main Street, P.O. Box 2000, Hurt VA 24563. 434/324-4211. **Contact:** Human Resources. **World Wide Web address:** http://www.burlington.com. **Description:** An apparel dyeing and finishing plant. **Parent company:** Burlington Industries, Inc. is a manufacturer of men's and women's clothing. **NOTE:** Offers summer internships.

BUSCH GARDENS/WATER COUNTRY USA
One Busch Gardens Boulevard, Williamsburg VA 23187-8785. **Fax:** 757/253-3013. **Recorded jobline:** 757/253-3020. **Contact:** Human Resources. **World Wide Web address:** http://www.buschgardens.com. **Description:** A theme park. **Office hours:** Monday - Saturday, 9:00 a.m. - 4:00 p.m. **Parent company:** Anheuser-Busch. **Listed on:** New York Stock Exchange. **Stock exchange symbol:** BUD.

CACI INTERNATIONAL, INC.
1100 North Glebe Road, Arlington VA 22201. 703/841-7800. **Fax:** 703/679-4510. **Contact:** Human Resources. **E-mail address:** jobs@caci.com. **World Wide Web address:** http://www.caci.com. **Description:** Provides IT and network solutions including system integration, knowledge management, engineering, simulation, and information assurance for the government and international commercial customers. CACI maintains 100 offices in the U.S. and overseas. **NOTE:** Search and apply for positions online. **Positions advertised include:** Applications Support Analyst; Web Applications Developer; Strategic Planning Specialist; Portal Services Team Leader; functional Analyst Expert/Mathematician; Database Developer; Senior Portfolio Analyst; System Analyst; Software Engineer. **Corporate headquarters location:** This location. **Other area locations:** Alexandria VA; Chantilly VA; Chesapeake VA; Fairfax VA; Herndon VA; Manassas VA. **Other U.S. locations:** Nationwide. **International locations:** Worldwide. **Operations at this facility include:** Administration. **Listed on:** NASDAQ. **Stock exchange symbol:** CACI. **Number of employees worldwide:** 7,500.

CB RICHARD ELLIS
7501 Boulders View Drive, Suite 600, Richmond VA 23225. 804/320-5500. **Fax:** 804/320-4839. **Contact:** Human Resources. **E-mail address:** opps@crbe.com. **World Wide Web address:** http://www.cbrichardellis.com. **Description:** A real estate services company offering property sales and leasing, property and facility management, mortgage banking, and investment management services. More than 250 locations worldwide. **NOTE:** Search and apply for positions online. **Positions advertised include:** Financial Analyst; Marketing Assistant; Research Assistant; Finance Manager. **Corporate headquarters location:** Los Angeles CA. **Other U.S. locations:** Nationwide. **International locations:** Worldwide. **Number of employees at this location:** 60. **Number of employees worldwide:** 13,500.

CI TRAVEL
CRUISE INTERNATIONAL
101 West Main Street, Suite 800, Norfolk VA 23510. 757/627-8000. **Toll-free phone:** 888/734-0775. **Contact:** Human Resources. **World Wide Web address:** http://www.citravel.com. **Description:** An ocean cruise line.

CPFILMS INC.
P.O. Box 5068, Martinsville VA 24115. 276/627-3000. **Fax:** 276/627-3032. **Contact:** Human Resources. **E-mail address:** CPFilms@cpfilms.com. **World Wide Web address:** http://www.cpfilms.com. **Description:** Processes dyed, coated, laminated, and metalized films for solar control. **Other area locations:** Axton VA; Fieldale VA. **Other U.S. locations:** Canoga Park CA. **Parent company:** Solutia. **Listed on:** New York Stock Exchange. **Stock exchange symbol:** SOI. **Number of employees nationwide:** 700.

CSX CORPORATION
P.O. Box 85629, Richmond VA 23285-5629. 804/782-1400. **Fax:** 904/359-3932. **Physical address:** 901 East Cary Street, Richmond VA 23219. **Contact:** Human Resources. **World Wide Web address:** http://www.csx.com. **Description:** An operator of container ship lines, railcars, and barges. CSX also provides intermodal and logistics services, operates a resort, and conducts real estate activities. The company's rail system consists of 23,000 miles of track in 23 states and Canada. **NOTE:** Search for jobs online. Application procedures vary according to position. **Corporate headquarters location:** This location. **Listed on:** New York Stock Exchange. **Stock exchange symbol:** CSX. **Annual sales/revenues:** $7.8 billion. **Number of employees worldwide:** 40,000.

CTI INC.
3951 Pender Drive, Suite 120, Fairfax VA 22030-6035. 703/383-7200. **Toll-free phone:** 800/765-7208. **Fax:** 703/352-6765. **Contact:** Carol Ismer, Human Resources Manager. **World Wide Web address:** http://www.cti.com. **Description:** Provides systems integration services and products and language translation services for the federal government and commercial healthcare markets. Founded in 1980.

CADMUS COMMUNICATIONS CORPORATION
1801 Bayberry Court, Suite 200, Richmond VA 23226. 804/287-5680. **Fax:** 804/583-6780. **Contact:** Barbara Strickland, Human Resources. **E-mail address:** strickland@cadmus.com. **World Wide Web address:** http://www.cadmus.com. **Description:** Cadmus provides integrated graphic communications services to professional publishers, not-for-profit societies and corporations. Cadmus is the world's largest provider of content management and production services to scientific, technical and medical journal publishers, the fourth largest periodicals printer in North America, and a provider of specialty packaging and promotional printing services. **NOTE:** Search and apply for positions online. **Positions advertised include:** Bindery Operator; Bindery Assistant; Material Handler; Production Manager; Web Press Assistant. **Corporate headquarters location:** This location. **Other U.S. locations:** GA; DE; NY; TX; MD; NC; PA; VA. **Listed on:** NASDAQ. **Stock exchange symbol:** CDMS. **Number of employees nationwide:** 3,000.

CADMUS SPECIALTY PUBLICATIONS
2901 Byrdhill Road, Richmond VA 23228-5867. 804/261-3000. **Contact:** Human Resources. **World Wide Web address:** http://www.cadmus.com. **Description:** Provides production services for business-to-business and special interest publishers. **Special programs:** Internships. **Other U.S. locations:** Easton MD; Linthicum MD. **Parent company:** Cadmus Communications Corporation. **Listed on:** New York Stock Exchange. **Stock exchange symbol:** CDMS.

CALIBER ASSOCIATES
10530 Rosehaven Street, Suite 400, Fairfax VA 22030. 703/385-3200. **Fax:** 703/385-3206. **Contact:** Human Resources. **E-mail:** careers@caliber.com. **World Wide Web Address:** http://www.caliber.com. **Description:** Caliber Associates is an employee-owned consulting firm, providing research and consulting services that help clients develop and manage effective human services programs and policies for the public good. **Positions advertised include:** Administrative Associate; Coldfusion Developer; Research Assistant; Education Programs Manager; Technical Assistance Coordinator.

CAMELLIA FOODS
P.O. Box 2320, Norfolk VA 23501. 757/855-3371. **Contact:** Human Resources. **Description:** Operates three chains of grocery stores: Meatland, Food City, and Fresh Pride. **Corporate headquarters location:** This location.

CANON VIRGINIA, INC.
12000 Canon Boulevard, Newport News VA 23606. 757/881-6300. **Fax:** 757/881-6024. **Recorded jobline:** 757/881-6020. **Contact:** Human Resources Department. **E-mail address:** cvi_hr@cvi.canon.com. **World Wide Web address:** http://www.usa.canon.com. **Description:** Manufactures office products including copiers, facsimiles, printers, and computers. **NOTE:** Search and apply for positions online. Summer internships are offered. **Corporate headquarters location:** Lake Success NY. **Parent company:** Canon USA. **Operations at this facility include:** Manufacturing. **Listed on:** New York Stock Exchange. **Stock exchange symbol:** CAJ. **Annual sales/revenues:** More than $100 million. **Number of employees at this location:** 1,200. **Number of employees nationwide:** 10,000.

CAPITAL ONE FINANCIAL CORPORATION
1680 Capital One Drive, McLean VA 22102. 703/875-1000. **Contact:** Management Recruiter. **E-mail address:** jobs@capitalone.com. **World Wide Web address:** http://www.capitalone.com. **Description:** A holding company. Its principal subsidiaries, Capital One Bank and Capital One, F.S.B., offer consumer lending products and are among the largest providers of MasterCard and Visa credit cards in the world. Positions advertised include: Group Manager, Portfolio Trading; Business Analyst; Securitization Attorney; Tax Controversy Associate; Securities Attorney; Engagement Manager. **Corporate headquarters location:** This location. **Other U.S. locations:** CA; FL; ID; MA; TX; WA. **Listed on:** New York Stock Exchange. **Stock exchange symbol:** COF. **Number of employees at this location:** 1,000. **Number of employees nationwide:** 2,600.

CARBONE OF AMERICA
540 Branch Drive, Salem VA 24153. 504/389-7535. **Fax:** 540/389-7538. **Contact:** Human Resources. **World Wide Web address:** http://www.carboneced.com. **Description:** Manufactures carbon brushes for automobile parts such as starters, alternators, and fan belts. **Parent company:** Le Carbone-Lorraine France.

CARGILL TURKEY PRODUCTS
P.O. Box 549, Harrisonburg VA 22803. 540/568-1542. **Contact:** Human Resources. **World Wide Web address:** http://www.cargill.com. **Description:** A producer and marketer of poultry food products. **Special programs:** Internships.

CARILION BEDFORD MEMORIAL HOSPITAL
1613 Oakwood Street, Bedford VA 24523-0688. 540/586-2441. **Recorded jobline:** 800/816-1090. **Contact:** Human Resources. **World Wide Web address:** http://www.bmhva.com. **Description:** A nonprofit, JCAHO-accredited medical facility. Carilion Bedford Memorial Hospital serves as a 110-bed nursing home and a 55-bed hospital. **NOTE:** Search and apply for positions online. **Positions advertised include:** Certified Nursing Assistant; Licensed Practical Nurse; Registered Nurse; Respiratory Care Therapist; Radiologic Technologist. **Parent company:** Carilion Health Systems. **Number of employees at this location:** 400.

CARILION NEW RIVER VALLEY MEDICAL CENTER
P.O. Box 5, Radford VA 24141. 540/731-2000. **Physical address:** 2900 Tyler Road, Christianburg VA 24073. **Recorded jobline:** 800/816-1090. **Contact:** Human Resources. **World Wide Web address:** http://www.carilion.com. **Description:** An acute care facility with 175 licensed beds. The hospital offers the following community services: Lifeline, a personal emergency response system; Meals on Wheels; Viva Club, a health club for people 55 and older; and Home Health Plus, a home health agency that provides nursing and other in-home services. The hospital also offers critical care, dietary services, emergency care, emergency medical services, extended care, endoscopic services, intravenous therapy, neurology, obstetrics, pediatric care, patient education, patient financial services, physical therapy, progressive care, radiology, respiratory care services, same-day surgery, and a sleep disorder center. **Positions advertised include:** Certified Registered Nurse Anesthetist; Licensed Practical Nurse; Multi-Skilled Technologist; Nuclear Medicine Technologist; Nurse Manager; Pharmacist; Radiologic Technologist; Registered Nurse; Sonographer. **Parent company:** Carilion Health Systems.

CARPENTER COMPANY
5016 Monument Avenue, Richmond VA 23230. 804/359-0800. **Toll-free phone:** 800/288-3834. **Fax:** 804/804/278-9689. **Contact:** Andrea Hale. **E-mail address:** andrea.hale@carpenter.com. **World Wide Web address:** http://www.carpenter.com. **Description:** Manufactures urethane-related products for use in carpet padding, insulation, packaging, furniture, and bedding. **NOTE:** Entry-level positions are offered. NOTE: Search and apply for positions online. **Positions advertised include:** Sr.

Assistant Credit Administrator; Product Development Assistant; Associate Research Engineer. **Corporate headquarters location:** This location. **Listed on:** Privately held. **Number of employees at this location:** 300. **Number of employees nationwide:** 4,600. **Number of employees worldwide:** 6,800.

CATAWBA HOSPITAL
P.O. Box 200, Catawba VA 24070-0200. 540/375-4200. **Fax:** 540/375-4359. **Physical address:** 5525 Catawba Hospital Drive, Catawba VA 24070. **Fax:** 540/375-4359. **Contact:** Human Resources. **World Wide Web address:** http://www.catawba.state.va.us. **Description:** A 270-bed, state operated, mental health hospital for adults and geriatrics. Affiliated with the University of Virginia School of Medicine. NOTE: Search for positions online. All applications require a State Employment Application available online. **Positions advertised include:** Registered Nurse; Nursing Assistant; Adult Psychiatrist; Therapist; Licensed Practical Nurse.

CEL-SCI CORPORATION
8229 Boone Boulevard, Suite 802, Vienna VA 22182. 703/506-9460. **Fax:** 703/506-9471. **Contact:** Human Resources. **World Wide Web address:** http://www.cel-sci.com. **Description:** Develops immune system-based treatments for cancer and infectious diseases. CEL-SCI Corporation is involved in the research and development of natural human interleukin-2 and cytokine-related products and processes using proprietary cell culture technologies. Founded in 1983. **Corporate headquarters location:** This location. **Subsidiaries include:** Viral Technologies, Inc. is a privately held company engaged in the development of a vaccine for AIDS. **Listed on:** American Stock Exchange. **Stock exchange symbol:** CVM. **Number of employees at this location:** 10. **Number of employees nationwide:** 30.

THE CENTECH GROUP, INC.
4600 North Fairfax Drive, Suite 400, Arlington VA 22203. 703/525-4444. **Fax:** 703/525-2349. **Contact:** Personnel. **E-mail address:** recruiting@centechgroup.com. **World Wide Web address:** http://www.centechgroup.com. **Description:** Specializes in providing information technology integration services to the federal government. **NOTE:** Entry-level positions are offered. **Positions advertised include:** Business Development Manager; Jr. Network Administrator; Sr. Technical Editor; Training Specialist; Sr. Systems Analyst; Creative Media Specialist; QA Documentation Specialist; Database Administrator. **Office hours:** Monday - Friday, 8:00 a.m. - 5:30 p.m. **Corporate headquarters location:** This location. **Other U.S. locations:** Hugo OK; Montgomery AL. **President:** Fernando V. Galaviz.

CENTRA HEALTH INC.
1920 Atherholt Road, Lynchburg VA 24501. 434/947-4738. **Contact:** Employment Coordinator. **World Wide Web address:** http://www.centrahealth.com. **Description:** A regional, nonprofit health care system that operates through two hospitals in central Virginia. **NOTE:** Search for positions online. **Positions advertised include:** Analysts, Coding; Clinical Documentation Specialist; Counselor, Financial LTC; Reimbursement Specialist; Financial Analyst; Health Information Analyst; Database Administrator; Patient Accounting Specialist. **Corporate headquarters location:** This location. **Number of employees at this location:** 3,300.

CENTRAL VIRGINIA BANKSHARES, INC.
CENTRAL VIRGINIA BANK
P.O. Box 39, Powhatan VA 23139. 804/598-4217. **Physical address:** 2501 Anderson Highway, Powhatan VA 23139. **Contact:** Shirley G. Boelt, Assistant Vice President of Human Resources. **E-mail address:** sboelt@centralvabank.com. **World Wide Web address:** http://www.centralvabank.com. **Description:** Central Virginia Bankshares, Inc. is the holding company for Central Virginia Bank (also at this location.) Central Virginia Bank offers a wide range of services including checking and savings accounts; certificates of deposit; installment, construction, and permanent residential mortgage loans; and other consumer lending services. The bank also offers related services such as traveler's checks, safe deposit, deposit transfer, customer note payment, collections, notary public, and escrow. **NOTE:** Entry-level positions and part-time jobs are offered. **Company slogan:** More than just a bank, we're a member of the community. **Special programs:** Summer Jobs. **Corporate headquarters location:** This location. **Other area locations:** Brandermill VA; Cartersville VA; Midlothian VA; Cumberland VA. **Listed on:** NASDAQ. **Stock exchange symbol:** CVBK. **Annual sales/revenues:** $11 - $20 million. **Number of employees nationwide:** 90.

CENTRAL VIRGINIA TRAINING CENTER
P.O. Box 1098, Lynchburg VA 24505. 434/947-6000. **Fax:** 434/947-2140. **Toll-free phone:** 866/897-6095. **Contact:** Human Resources. **World Wide Web address:** http://www.cvtc.state.va.us. **Description:** A state residential facility for individuals with mental retardation. **NOTE:** Search for positions online. A state application, which may be downloaded online, must accompany any resumes. **Positions advertised include:** RN; Psychiatrist; LPN; Facility Director; Respiratory Therapy Tech; Psychology Asst; Pharmacist. **Number of employees at this location:** 1,400.

CENTURY 21 NEW MILLENNIUM
5990 Kingstowne Towne Center, Alexandria VA 22315. 703/922-4010. **Toll-free phone:** 800/708-7085. **Fax:** 703/922-7888. **Contact:** Steve Kon, Director of Career Development. **E-mail address:** careers@c21nm.com. **World Wide Web address:** http://www.c21nm.com. **Description:** A full-service real estate agency servicing the Washington DC metropolitan area's commercial and residential markets.

CHESAPEAKE CORPORATION
1021 East Cary Street, Richmond VA 23219. 804/697-1000. **Contact:** Human Resources. **E-mail address:** careers@cskcorp.com. **World Wide Web address:** http://www.cskcorp.com. **Description:** Provides specialty paperboard and plastic packaging for pharmaceutical, healthcare, international and branded products, food and household, agrochemical, specialty chemical, and beverage markets. Founded in 1918. **Corporate headquarters location:** This location. **Other U.S. locations:** Lexington NC. **International locations:** Worldwide. **Listed on:** New York Stock Exchange. **Stock exchange symbol:** CSK. **Number of employees nationwide:** 5,200.

CHESAPEAKE RESTAURANT GROUP
1960 Gallows Road, Suite 200, Vienna VA 22182. 703/827-0320. **Fax:** 703/893-1536. **Contact:** Connie Ohm, Director of Human Resources. **E-mail address:** info@chesapeakerestaurants.com. **World Wide Web address:** http://www.chesapeakerestaurants.com. **Description:** Operates 8 Chesapeake Bay Seafood Houses, 23 Chili's, and 3 On the Border, restaurants. **Positions advertised include:** Restaurant Manager. **Special programs:** Internships. **Corporate headquarters location:** This location. **Operations at this facility include:** Administration; Research and Development. **Listed on:** Privately held. **Annual sales/revenues:** Less than $5 million. **Number of employees nationwide:** 3,000.

CHILDREN'S HOSPITAL OF THE KING'S DAUGHTERS
601 Children's Lane, Norfolk VA 23507-1910. 757/668-7000. **Fax:** 757/668-7745. **Recorded jobline:** 757/668-9123. **Contact:** Human Resources. **E-mail address:** jobs@chkd.org. **World Wide Web address:** http://www.chkd.org. **Description:** A 186-bed, nonprofit medical center, treating children from birth to age 21. This location also serves as a regional pediatric referral center. **NOTE:** Search and apply for positions online. **Positions advertised include:** Clinical Practice and Education Specialist; Neonatal Nurse Practitioner; Sleep Lab Tech; Surgical Tech; Radiology Tech; Occupational Health Nurse; Respiratory Care Practitioner; Respiratory Operations Coordinator; ER Technician; Occupational Therapist; Medical Transcriptionist; Data Quality Manager; Lead Teacher; Patient Interviewer; Licensed Clinical Psychologist; RN; Nurse Manager; Director of Operating Room.

CHILDREN'S REGIONAL OUTPATIENT CENTER
8501 Arlington Boulevard, Suite 200, Fairfax VA 22031. 571/226-8380. **Fax:** 571/226-8362. **Toll-free phone:** 800/787-0467. **Contact:** Human Resources. **Description:** Offers comprehensive home care programs and is a regional pediatric trauma center. Over the years, the center has pioneered studies on antibiotic resistance and on the causes of severe respiratory tract infection; developed a special form of Vitamin D to treat kidney failure; performed one of the first bone marrow and heart transplants; and identified three viruses that cause infant pneumonia, infant diarrhea, and croup.

THE CHRISTOPHER COMPANIES
10306 Eaton Place, Suite 450, Fairfax VA 22030. 703/352-5950. **Fax:** 703/352-0960. **Contact:** Human Resources Department. **World Wide Web address:** http://www.christophercompanies.com. **Description:** Engaged in the building of customized homes, condominiums, and townhouse developments in the northern Virginia area. Founded in 1974.

CHRISTOPHER NEWPORT UNIVERSITY
One University Place, Newport News VA 23606. 757/594-7000. **Contact:** Human Resources. **World Wide Web address:** http://www.cnu.edu. **Description:** A four-year comprehensive, coeducational, state-supported institution within Virginia's public university system. The university has an enrollment of approximately 5,000 students and offers 115 academic majors and programs. **NOTE:** Search for positions online. **Positions advertised include:** Manager of Records and Research; Human Resources Coordinator; Business Manager; Coordinator for Corporate Recruitment; vice President for University Advancement; Assistant Professor (various subjects). **Number of employees at this location:** 932.

CIBA SPECIALTY CHEMICALS
2301 Wilroy Road, Suffolk VA 23434. 757/538-3700. **Fax:** 757/538-3989. **Contact:** Human Resources. **E-mail address:** career@cibasc.com. **World Wide Web address:** http://www.cibasc.com. **Description:** Manufactures specialty chemicals through five segments: plastic additives, coating effects, textile effects; home and personal care, and water and paper treatments. **Other U.S. locations:** Nationwide. **International locations:** Worldwide. **Listed on:** New York Stock Exchange. **Stock exchange symbol:** CSB.

CINTAS CORPORATION
P.O. Box 1207, Culpeper VA 22701. 540/825-2300. **Contact:** Human Resources. **World Wide Web address:** http://www.cintas.com. **Description:** Provides uniform rental, industrial laundering, and restroom cleaning services. Operates 365 facilities in the U.S. and Canada, including 14 manufacturing plants and seven distribution centers. **Corporate headquarters location:** Cincinnati OH. **Other U.S. locations:** Nationwide. **Operations at this facility include:** Administration; Divisional Headquarters; Manufacturing; Regional Headquarters; Sales; Service. **Listed on:** NASDAQ. **Stock exchange symbol:** CTAS. **Number of employees at this location:** 140. **Number of employees worldwide:** 27,000.

CIRCUIT CITY STORES, INC.
9954 Mayland Drive, Richmond VA 23233-1464. 804/527-4000. **Toll-free phone:** 888/773-2489. **Fax:** 804/527-4086. **Contact:** Staffing & Planning. **E-mail address:** cc-jobs@circuitcity.com. **World Wide Web address:** http://www.circuitcity.com. **Description:** One of the largest U.S. retailers of brand-name consumer electronics and major appliances, as well as personal computers, music, and software. The company also sells used cars at CarMax Auto Superstores. Circuit City has over 600 Circuit City and Circuit City Express stores in operation nationwide. Founded in 1949. **NOTE:** Search and apply for positions online. **Positions advertised include:** Inside Sales Representative; Media Planner/Buyer; Segment Marketing Manager; Statistician, Marketing; District Human Resources Manager. **Special programs:** Internships. **Office hours:** Monday - Friday, 8:30 a.m. - 5:00 p.m. **Corporate headquarters location:** This location. **Other U.S. locations:** Nationwide. **Listed on:** New York Stock Exchange. **Stock exchange symbol:** CC. **Annual sales/revenues:** Nearly $10 billion. **Number of employees at this location:** 3,000. **Number of employees nationwide:** 40,000.

CITIZENS AND FARMERS BANK
C&F FINANCIAL CORPORATION
P.O. Box 391, West Point VA 23181. 804/843-2360. **Physical address:** 802 Main Street, West Point VA 23181. **Fax:** 804/843-3017. **Contact:** Human Resources. **World Wide Web address:** http://www.cffc.com. **Description:** C&F Financial Corporation is the holding company for Citizens and Farmers Bank (also at this location.) The bank is a savings and loan institution with 10 branch locations in Virginia, and two Citizens & Commerce Bank branch locations. Other subsidiaries of C&F Financial Corporation include C&F Mortgage Corporation, which originates and sells mortgages; and C&F Investment Services, Inc., which offers brokerage services. **Positions advertised include:** Data Processing Technician; General Bookkeeper. **Corporate headquarters location:** This location. **Other area locations:** Norge VA; Providence Forge VA; Quinton VA; Richmond VA; Saluda VA; Tappahannock VA; Williamsburg VA. **Listed on:** NASDAQ. **Stock exchange symbol:** CFFI. **President/CEO:** Larry Dillon. **Number of employees nationwide:** 95.

CLEAN HARBORS ENVIRONMENTAL SERVICES, INC.
7515 Harvest Road, Prince George VA 23875. 804/452-1800. **Contact:** Human Resources. **World Wide Web address:** http://www.cleanharbors.com. **Description:** This location is a regional environmental service center. Clean Harbors, Inc., through its subsidiaries, provides environmental and waste management services in 36 states, Canada, Mexico, and Puerto Rico. The company's hazardous waste management services include treatment, storage, recycling, transportation, risk analysis, site assessment, laboratory analysis, site closure, and disposal of hazardous materials through environmentally sound methods including incineration. Environmental remediation services include emergency response, surface remediation, groundwater restoration, industrial maintenance, and facility decontamination. **NOTE:** Search and apply for positions online. **Positions advertised include:** Field Service Foreman; field Technician; Field Service Supervisor; Field Operations Manager. **Corporate headquarters location:** Braintree MA. **Other U.S. locations:** Nationwide. **Listed on:** NASDAQ. **Stock exchange symbol:** CLHB. **Number of employees nationwide:** 1,400.

COLLEGE OF WILLIAM AND MARY
P.O. Box 8795, Thiemes House, Williamsburg VA 23187-8795. 757/221-3169. **Fax:** 757/221-3156. **Recorded jobline:** 757/221-3167. **Contact:** Office of Personnel Services. **World Wide Web address:** http://www.wm.edu. **Description:** A four-year college offering bachelor's, master's (including MBAs), first professional, and doctoral degrees. Approximately 5,250 undergraduate and 2,400 graduate students attend the College of William and Mary. **NOTE:** Search for positions online. Applications must be submitted online; paper applications will not be accepted. **Positions advertised include:** Administrative Officer; EIS Project Coordinator; Office Manager; Journal Center Administrative Assistant. **Number of employees nationwide:** 2,000.

COLONIAL NATIONAL HISTORICAL PARK
P.O. Box 210, Yorktown VA 23690. 757/898-3400. **Contact:** Annette Spragan, Personnel Management Specialist. **World Wide Web address:** http://www.nps.gov/colo. **Description:** A national historical park that preserves, protects, and interprets the site of the first permanent English settlement in the New World (Jamestown) and the site of the last major battle of the American Revolutionary War.

THE COLONIAL WILLIAMSBURG FOUNDATION
P.O. Box 1776, Williamsburg VA 23187. 757/229-1000. **Toll-free phone:** 800/HISTORY. **Fax:** 757/220-7259. **Recorded jobline:** 757/220-7129. **Contact:** Sherri Ashby, Human Resources Representative. **E-mail address:** sashby@cwf.org. **World Wide Web address:** http://www.history.org. **Description:** A nonprofit educational organization that acts to preserve and restore 18th-century Williamsburg through historical interpretation. Founded in 1926. **NOTE:** Entry-level positions, part-time jobs, and second and third shifts are offered. Search and apply for positions online. **Special programs:** Internships; Apprenticeships; Summer Jobs. **Corporate headquarters location:** This location. **Number of employees at this location:** 3,500.

COLUMBIA SERVICES GROUP, INC.
11350 Random Hills Road, Suite 650, Fairfax VA 22030. 703/207-1000. **Fax:** 703/207-1000. **Contact:** Human Resources Specialist. **E-mail address:** info@columbiaservices.com. **World Wide Web address:** http://www.columbiaservices.com. **Description:** Provides IT services in the areas of systems integration, LAN infrastructure support, Help Desk support, and technical support services. Founded in 1984. **NOTE:** Search and apply for positions online. **Positions advertised include:** Trainer; Hardware Installation Technician; Systems Engineer; Systems Analyst; Senior Systems Architect; Communications Specialist. **Corporate headquarters location:** This location. **Other U.S. locations:** Nationwide. **Listed on:** Privately held. **President/CEO:** Emmett R. Anderson.

COMDIAL CORPORATION
1180 Seminole Trail, Charlottesville VA 22901. 434/978-2200. **Contact:** Human Resources. **E-mail address:** employment@comdial.com. **World Wide Web address:** http://www.comdial.com. **Description:** Designs, manufactures, and markets small to medium-sized business telephone systems. The company also offers a broad range of advanced telecommunications products and systems solutions based on computer telephone integration, primarily for the hospitality industry. Founded in 1977. **Corporate headquarters location:** Sarasota FL. **Subsidiaries include:** American Phone Centers, Inc.; American Telecommunications Corporation; Comdial Business Communications Corporation; Comdial Consumer Communications Corporation; Comdial Enterprise Systems, Inc.; Comdial Telecommunications International, Inc.; Comdial Telecommunications, Inc.; Scott Technologies Corporation. **Listed on:** NASDAQ. **Stock exchange symbol:** CMDL. **Number of employees nationwide:** 790.

COMMAND TECHNOLOGIES, INC.
405 Belle Air Lane, Warrenton VA 20186. 540/349-8623. **Fax:** 540/347-7105. **Contact:** Human Resources. **E-mail address:** hrdept@commtechinc.com. **World Wide Web address:** http://www.commtechinc.com. **Description:** A computer systems engineering firm offering technical services, logistic support services, training services, technology applications, information systems engineering, network systems support, and research and development. Founded in 1988. **Positions advertised include:** Junior Multimedia Developer. **Corporate headquarters location:** This location. **Other U.S. locations:** TX; FL. **Number of employees nationwide:** 500.

COMMONWEALTH BANKSHARES, INC.
BANK OF THE COMMONWEALTH
403 Boush Street, Norfolk VA 23510. 757/446-6900. **Contact:** Human Resources. **World Wide Web address:** http://www.bankofthecommonwealth.com. **Description:** A bank holding company with a subsidiary, Bank of the Commonwealth (also at this location), that provides a complete line of banking, investment, and trust services to businesses and individuals. The bank operates nine branch offices. Founded in 1971. **Corporate headquarters location:** This location. **Other area locations:** Virginia Beach VA. **Listed on:** NASDAQ. **Stock exchange symbol:** CWBS. **Chairman of the Board:** E.J. Woodard.

COMMUNITY MEMORIAL HEALTHCENTER
125 Buena Vista Circle, South Hill VA 23970. 434/447-3151. **Fax:** 434/774-2519. **Contact:** Human Resources. **World Wide Web address:** http://www.cmh-sh.org. **Description:** A not-for-profit 144-bed hospital and 140-bed nursing home, offering both emergency and skilled care. Founded in 1954. **NOTE:** Search for positions online. **Positions advertised include:** RN's; CNA's; LPN's; Speech Therapist; Physical Therapist; Radiologic Technologist; Respiratory Therapist; Assistant Volunteer Coordinator; Area Technician. **Number of employees at this location:** 700.

COMPUTER ASSOCIATES INTERNATIONAL, INC.
2291 Wood Oak Drive, Herndon VA 20171. 703/708-3000. **Fax:** 703/709-4580. **Contact:** Janet Nguyen, Director of Human Resources. **World Wide Web address:** http://www.ca.com. **Description:** Computer Associates International is a provider of solutions and services for the management of IT infrastructure, business information and application development. The company provides solutions for enterprise management, storage management, security management, application life cycle management, data management and application development, and portal and business intelligence. Computer Associates International serves major business, government, research, and educational organizations. Founded in 1976. **NOTE:** Search and apply for positions or submit resume online. **Positions advertised include:** Public Relations Manager; Associate Project Manager; Consultant; Principal Consultant; Project Coordinator; Senior Consultant; Senior Project Manager. **Corporate headquarters location:** Islandia NY. **Other U.S. locations:** Nationwide. **International locations:** Worldwide. **Operations at this facility include:** Divisional Headquarters. **Listed on:** New York Stock Exchange. **Stock exchange symbol:** CA. **CEO:** Sanjay Kumar. **Annual sales/revenues:** More than $3 billion. **Number of employees at this location:** 700. **Number of employees nationwide:** 5,000. Number of employees worldwide: 16,000.

COMPUTER SCIENCES CORPORATION (CSC)
3170 Fairview Park Drive, Falls Church VA 22042. 703/876-1000. **Fax:** 703/876-1376. **Contact:** Human Resources. **World Wide Web address:** http://www.csc.com. **Description:** CSC is a leading IT Consulting and outsourcing firm providing: application outsourcing; business process outsourcing, credit services, customer relationship management, enterprise application integration, enterprise solutions, hosting services, IT infrastructure outsourcing, knowledge management, legal solutions, management consulting, research services, risk management and claims, security, and supply chain management. **NOTE:** Search and apply for positions online. **Positions advertised include:** Technician. **Corporate headquarters location:** El Segundo CA. **International locations:** Worldwide. **Listed on:** New York Stock Exchange. **Stock exchange symbol:** CSC. **Number of employees nationwide:** 20,000. Number of employees worldwide: 90,000.

CONSUMER PORTFOLIO SERVICES
860 Greenbrier Circle, Suite 600, Chesapeake VA 23320. **Fax:** 757/413-5374. **Contact:** Human Resources. **World Wide Web address:** http://www.consumerportfolio.com. **Description:** Consumer Portfolio Services, Inc. is a specialty finance company that provides indirect automobile financing to vehicle purchasers with past credit problems, low incomes, or limited credit histories by purchasing retail installment sales contracts from factory franchised automobile dealers, securing them, accumulating the contracts into pools, and selling the pooled contracts to investors in the form of "AAA" rated asset-backed securities. Founded in 1991. Purchases contracts in 41 states from approximately 3,800 dealers. **Corporate headquarters location:** Irvine CA. **Listed on:** NASDAQ. **Stock exchange symbol:** CPSS.

COORS BREWING COMPANY
5135 South Eastside Highway, Elkton VA 22827. 540/289-8000. **Contact:** Human Resources. **World Wide Web address:** http://www.coors.com. **Description:** Coors Brewing Company is one of the largest brewers in the United States. Key brands include Coors Light, Coors Original, Zima, and Killian's Irish Red. **NOTE:** Internships offered. **Positions advertised include:** Temporary Operations; Team Leader. **Corporate headquarters location:** Golden CO. **Parent company:** Adolph Coors Company. **Operations at this facility include:** This location is a packaging facility. **Listed on:** New York Stock Exchange. **Stock exchange symbol:** RKY.

CORNING INC.
265 Corning Drive, Danville VA 24541-6262. 434/793-9511. **Fax:** 434/797-6323. **Contact:** Human Resources. **World Wide Web address:** http://www.corning.com. **Description:** Corning Inc. is a diverse manufacturer of specialty glass and glass ceramic products. Products include fiber optic and copper cables, frequency control devices, coaxial interconnects and microwave connectors, glass for LCD displays, emissions controls, laboratory products, eyeglass lenses, optical fiber products, photonic materials, semiconductor optics, and technical materials. Brand names include Corning and Pyrex. The company produces over 60,000 products through 70 manufacturing locations. **NOTE:** Search and apply for positions or submit resume online. **Positions advertised include:** Shift Coordinator. **Corporate headquarters location:** Corning NY. **Operations at this facility include:** This location is a manufacturing plant that primarily produces eyeglass lenses. **Listed on:** New York Stock Exchange. **Stock exchange symbol:** GLW. Number of employees worldwide: 20,000.

CORT BUSINESS SERVICES
11250 Waples Mill Road, Suite 500, Fairfax VA 22030. 703/968-8500. **Toll-free phone:** 888/669-2678. **Fax:** 703/968-8550. **Contact:** Director of Human Resources. **World Wide Web address:** http://www.cort1.com. **Description:** A leading national provider of rental furniture, accessories, and related services in the rent-to-rent segment of the furniture rental industry. The segment serves both corporate and individual customers. CORT focuses on corporate customers by offering office and residential furniture and related accessories through a direct sales force of approximately 450 salespeople and a network of 94 showrooms in 26 states and the District of Columbia. Corporate customers include *Fortune* 500 companies, small businesses and professionals, and owners and operators of apartment communities. The company operates under two names: CORT Furniture Rental, which attracts mostly corporate customers and upper-income individuals; and General Furniture Leasing, which focuses on middle-income individuals and residential customers. **Corporate headquarters location:** This location.

COVANCE LABORATORIES INC.
9200 Leesburg Pike, Vienna VA 22182. 703/893-5400. **Contact:** Human Resources. **World Wide Web address:** http://www.covance.com. **Description:** A life sciences firm providing drug development services. Clients include global pharmaceutical and biotech companies. **NOTE:** Search and apply for positions online. **Positions advertised include:** Administrative Assistant; Associate, Scientific Director, Clinical Pathology; Logistics Supervisor; Study Coordinator, Bioanalytical Services; Archive Technician. **International locations:** 18 countries. **Operations at this facility include:** Administration; Research and Development. **Listed on:** New York Stock Exchange. **Stock exchange symbol:** CVD. Number of employees worldwide: 6,500.

COX COMMUNICATIONS
3080 Centerville Road, Herndon VA 20171. 703/378-8400. **Contact:** Human Resources. **World Wide Web address:** http://www.cox.com. **Description:** The fourth largest cable provider in the U.S., with operations in 23 states. **Corporate headquarters location:** Atlanta GA. **Listed on:** New York Stock Exchange. **Stock exchange symbol:** COX. **Number of employees nationwide:** 20,000.

CROWN CORK & SEAL COMPANY, INC.
P.O. Box 2820, Winchester VA 22604. 540/662-2591. **Fax:** 540/662-5644. **Contact:** Human Resources. **World Wide Web address:** http://www.crowncork.com. **Description:** Crown Cork & Seal Company is a worldwide manufacturer and distributor of a wide range of crowns, seals, and aluminum/steel cans including aerosol and beverage cans. Crown Cork & Seal Company also manufactures bottling equipment. **Corporate headquarters location:** Philadelphia PA. **International locations:** France; Singapore. **Operations at this facility include:** This location manufactures metal parts for beverage cans. **Listed on:** New York Stock Exchange. **Stock exchange symbol:** CCK.

CRYPTEK SECURE COMMUNICATIONS, LLC
1501 Morgan Road, Sterling VA 20166. 571/434-2000. **Toll-free phone:** 800/753-0706. **Fax:** 571/434-2001. **Contact:** Human Resources Department. **E-mail address:** careers@cryptek.com. **World Wide Web address:** http://www.cryptek.com. **Description:** Designs, produces, and markets secure communications products for the government and private sectors. Founded in 1986. **Positions advertised include:** Firmware Engineer; Gigabit Architect; Operating Systems Engineer; Security

applications Engineer; Senior Operating Systems Engineer; Senior Security Engineer; Senior Software Engineer. **Corporate headquarters location:** This location.

CUISINE SOLUTIONS INC.
85 South Bragg Street, Suite 600, Alexandria 22312. 703/270-2900. **Toll-free phone:** 888/285-4679. **Fax:** 703/750-9519. **Contact:** Human Resources. **World Wide Web address:** http://www.cuisinesolutions.com. **Description:** Develops, produces, and markets fully cooked entrees and sauces for the banquet, airline, passenger rail service, retail, military, and restaurant industries. **NOTE:** Submit resume online. **Corporate headquarters location:** This location. **International locations:** France; Norway. **Operations at this facility include:** Administration; Divisional Headquarters; Manufacturing; Sales. **Number of employees at this location:** 100.

CUMBERLAND HOSPITAL FOR CHILDREN & ADOLESCENTS
9407 Cumberland Road, New Kent VA 23124. 804/966-2242. **Toll-free phone:** 800/368-3472. **Fax:** 804/966-5639. **Contact:** Lee Byrd, Human Resources Manager. **World Wide Web address:** http://www.cumberlandhospital.com. **Description:** An 84-bed pediatric hospital. **NOTE:** Second and third shifts are offered. **Positions advertised include:** CEO; **Office hours:** Monday - Friday, 9:00 a.m. - 5:00 p.m. **Parent company:** Ardent Health Services. **Number of employees at this location:** 250.

CYBERNETICS
111 Cybernetics Way, Yorktown VA 23693. 757/833-9000. **Contact:** Human Resources. **E-mail address:** careers@cybernetics.com. **World Wide Web address:** http://www.cybernetics.com. **Description:** Designs, manufactures, markets, and services disk and tape storage solutions. Founded in 1978.

DCS CORPORATION
1330 Braddock Place, Alexandria VA 22314. 571/227-6000. **Fax:** 571/227-6001. **Contact:** Human Resources. **E-mail address:** info@dcscorp.com. **World Wide Web address:** http://www.dcscorp.com. **Description:** A research and development firm providing services and products for the government and private industry in areas such as navigation and avionics systems and integration; integrated information systems technology; electro-optics development and engineering; and acquisition, logistics, test, and evaluation management. Founded in 1977. **NOTE:** Internships offered. Search and apply for positions online. **Positions advertised include:** A/P Accountant; Information Systems Analyst; Project/Task Leader; Analyst III; Computer Engineer; Electro-Optics Design and Engineering manager; Electrical Engineer; Network Architect; Senior Modeling and Simulation Engineer. **Office hours:** Monday - Friday, 8:00 a.m. - 5:00 p.m. **Corporate headquarters location:** This location. **Other U.S. locations:** AL; CA; FL; MD. **Listed on:** Privately held. **Number of employees at this location:** 195. **Number of employees nationwide:** 400.

DSD LABORATORIES, INC.
INFORMATION TECHNOLOGY SOLUTIONS GROUP
3959 Pender Drive, Suite 109, Fairfax VA 22030. 703/385-5298. **Fax:** 703/385-5299. **Contact:** Human Resources. **World Wide Web address:** http://www.dsditsg.com. **Description:** Provides leading-edge technical services including web-based applications development, and a full-range of network services, to a wide range of customers, both locally and nationally. **Corporate headquarters location:** Sudbury MA. **Other area locations:** Hampton VA; Reston VA.

DAN RIVER, INC.
2291 Memorial Drive, Danville VA 24541. 434/799-7000. **Contact:** Manager of Recruiting. **World Wide Web address:** http://www.danriver.com. **Description:** A manufacturer and marketer of textile products for the home fashions and apparel fabrics markets. Dan River manufactures a coordinated line of home fashions products consisting of packaged bedroom furnishings such as comforters, sheets, pillowcases, shams, bedskirts, decorative pillows, and draperies. The company also manufactures a broad range of woven and knit cotton and cotton-blend apparel fabrics, and is a leading domestic supplier of men's dress shirt fabrics, primarily oxford and pinpoint oxford cloth. **NOTE:** Search and apply for positions online. May also mail resume to PO Box 261, Danville VA 24543. **Positions advertised include:** Senior Programmer; Graphic Artist. **Corporate headquarters location:** This location. **Other U.S. locations:** TN; GA; NC. **Subsidiaries include:** Dan River Factory Stores, Inc. operates six factory outlet stores. **Listed on:** New York Stock Exchange. **Stock exchange symbol:** DRF. Number of employees nationwide: 6,600.

DAN RIVER, INC.
P.O. Box 280, Brookneal VA 24528. 434/376-2311. **Contact:** Human Resources. **World Wide Web address:** http://www.danriver.com. **Description:** A manufacturer and marketer of textile products for the home fashions and apparel fabrics markets. Dan River manufactures a coordinated line of home fashions products consisting of packaged bedroom furnishings such as comforters, sheets, pillowcases, shams, bedskirts, decorative pillows, and draperies. The company also manufactures a broad range of woven and knit cotton and cotton-blend apparel fabrics and is a leading domestic supplier of men's dress shirting fabrics, primarily oxford and pinpoint oxford cloth. Dan River distributes home fashions products through a full range of domestic distribution channels, including department stores, specialty home fashions stores, direct marketers, national chains, mass merchants, and regional discounters. **Corporate headquarters location:** Danville VA. **Other U.S. locations:** GA; TN; NC. **Subsidiaries include:** Dan River Factory Stores, Inc. operates six factory outlet stores. **Listed on:** New York Stock Exchange. **Stock exchange symbol:** DRF.

DANAHER MOTION
201 West Rock Road, Radford VA 24141. 540/639-2495. **Fax:** 540/731-5675. **Contact:** Human Resources. **E-mail address:** thodge@kollmorgen.com. **World Wide Web address:** http://www.kollmorgen.com. **Description:** Manufactures DC torque motors, amplifiers, electromechanical actuators and controllers, and other advanced motion control products. The company also designs and supplies submarine periscopes, weapons directors, and military optics for the U.S. government and other allied nations. **Corporate headquarters location:** Northampton MA.

DATALUX CORPORATION
155 Aviation Drive, Winchester VA 22602. 540/662-1500. **Toll-free phone:** 800/328-2589. **Contact:** Human Resources. **E-mail address:** info@datalux.com. **World Wide Web address:** http://www.datalux.com. **Description:** A manufacturer of computer products for use in environments that require durable and compact designs. **Corporate headquarters location:** This location. Other U.S. locations: GA; IL; CA.

DATATEL INC.
4375 Fair Lakes Court, Fairfax VA 22033. 703/968-9000. **Contact:** Human Resources. **E-mail address:** datatel@rpc.webhire.com. **World Wide Web address:** http://www.datatel.com. **Description:** Develops and markets software applications for higher education. Founded in 1968. **NOTE:** Internships available. Search and apply for positions online. **Positions advertised include:** Accountant; Business Practices Managers; Developer; Senior Developer; Developer/Designer; Documentation Manager; Financial Solutions Consultant; Instructional Designer/Developer; Lead Consultant; Marketing Product Manager; Quality Assurance Analysts. **Corporate headquarters location:** This location. **Other U.S. locations:** San Francisco CA; Dallas TX. **Number of employees nationwide:** 470.

DELEX SYSTEMS INC.
1953 Gallows Road, Suite 700, Vienna VA 22182. 703/734-8300. **Fax:** 703/893-5338. **Contact:** Human Resources. **E-mail address:** hr@delex.com. **World Wide Web address:** http://www.delex.com. **Description:** Provides information technology, program management, modeling and simulation, research and analysis, and training solutions for domestic and international customers. Founded in 1968. **Positions advertised include:** A/P Accountant; EP-3E/Naval Flight Officer. **Corporate headquarters location:** This location. Other area locations: Arlington VA; Virginia Beach VA. **Other U.S. locations:** CA; MD; WA. **Listed on:** Privately held. **Number of employees at this location:** 140. **Number of employees nationwide:** 250.

DELOITTE & TOUCHE
1750 Tysons Boulevard, Suite 800, McLean VA 22102-4219. 703/251-1000. **Fax:** 703/251-3400. **Contact:** Human Resources. **World Wide Web address:** http://www.us.deloitte.com. **Description:** An international firm of certified public accountants providing professional accounting, auditing, tax, and management consulting services to widely diversified clients. The company has a specialized program consisting of national industry groups and functional groups that cross industry lines. Groups are involved in various disciplines including accounting, auditing, taxation management advisory services, small and growing businesses, mergers and acquisitions, and computer applications. Positions advertised include: Administrative Energy-Knowledge Manager; Business Development Manager; Senior Audit Manager; Senior Consultant Business Process and IT Controls; Property Tax Senior. **Parent company:** Deloitte Touche Tohmatsu. **Other U.S. locations:** Nationwide.

DELTEK SYSTEMS INC.
13880 Dulles Corner Lane, Herndon VA 20171. 703/734-8606. **Toll-free phone:** 800/456-2009. **Fax:** 703/734-1146. **Contact:** Human Resources. **E-mail address:** jobs@deltek.com. **World Wide Web address:** http://www.deltek.com. **Description:** Designs, develops, and supports advanced enterprise-level software for project-oriented companies. Deltek focuses on the architecture/engineering/construction, IT/systems integration, professional services and government contracting markets. Services include implementation consulting, training, software maintenance, and support. Founded in 1983. **NOTE:** Search and apply for positions online. **Positions advertised include:** Cognos System Consultant; Managing Director; Materials Management Consultant; New Business Development Associate; Quality Assurance Analyst; Sr. Data Conversion Consultant; Sr. Technical Consultant; System Consultant; Tax Analyst. **Corporate headquarters location:** This location. **Other U.S. locations:** Portland OR; St. Petersburg FL; Cambridge MA. **International locations:** Philippines; United Kingdom. **Listed on:** Privately owned. **Number of employees at this worldwide:** 650.

DEPAUL MEDICAL CENTER
150 Kingsley Lane, Norfolk VA 23505. 757/489-5000. **Contact:** Human Resources. **World Wide Web address:** http://www.bonsecourshamptonroads.com. **Description:** A 366-bed, nonprofit medical center. DePaul Medical Center is both an inpatient and outpatient acute care teaching hospital, offering residencies in medicine, obstetrics/gynecology, pediatrics, urology, radiology, surgery, and ENT. Specialized treatment centers include The Cancer Center, The Center for Birth, The Laser Center, The Diabetes Center, and the Elise and Henry Clay Hofheimer II Gerontology Center. **NOTE:** Search and apply for positions online. **Positions advertised include:** Cardiovascular Tech; Certified Registered Nurse Anesthetist; Clinical Coordinator; Clinical Instructor; CNA's; Direct Main Coordinator/Database Manager; Financial Services Rep; LPN's; Phlebotomist; Plant Operations Manager; Radiation Therapist; Respiratory Therapist; RN's; Vascular Technician. **Parent company:** Bon Secours Hampton Roads Health System.

DEWBERRY & DAVIS
8401 Arlington Boulevard, Fairfax VA 22031-4666. 703/849-0100. **Fax:** 703/849-0185. **Contact:** Richard A. Penner, Director of Personnel. **E-mail address:** hr@dewberry.com. **World Wide Web address:** http://www.dewberryanddavis.com. **Description:** A full-service architectural and engineering firm. Operations include planning, engineering, architecture, program management, surveying and mapping. Founded in 1956. **NOTE:** Entry-level positions are offered. Search and apply for positions online. **Positions advertised include:** Civil Engineer, Transportation; Project Architect; Training and Development Specialist (IT). **Special programs:** Internships. **Office hours:** Monday - Friday, 8:00 a.m. - 5:00 p.m. **Corporate headquarters location:** This location. **Other U.S. locations:** 27 offices in 12 states. **Listed on:** Privately held. **Annual sales/revenues:** More than $100 million. **Number of employees at this location:** 800. **Number of employees nationwide:** 1,500.

DIMON INC.
P.O. Box 681, Danville VA 24543-0681. 434/792-7511. **Fax:** 434/791-0377. **Physical address:** 512 Bridge Street, Danville VA 24541. **Contact:** Human Resources. **World Wide Web address:** http://www.dimon.com. **Description:** An independent leaf tobacco merchant, purchasing and processing tobacco in more than 40 countries, and supplying customers in 90 countries. Founded in 1995. **Corporate headquarters location:** This location. **Listed on:** New York Stock Exchange. **Stock exchange symbol:** DMN. **Number of employees worldwide:** 20,000.

DOLLAR TREE STORES, INC.
500 Volvo Parkway, Chesapeake VA 23320. 757/321-5000. **Fax:** 757/321-5555. **Contact:** David McDearman, Director of Human Resources. **E-mail address:** corprecruiter@dollartree.com. **World Wide Web address:** http://www.dollartree.com. **Description:** A leading operator of discount variety stores offering merchandise for $1. The company's stores offer a wide assortment of everyday general merchandise. The company operates more than 2,500 stores in 47 states. **NOTE:** Search and apply for positions online. **Positions advertised include:** Inventory Accounting Manager; Tax Analyst; IT Audit Manager; Payroll Supervisor; Operations Analyst; Internal Controls Manager; Systems Analyst; Associate Buyer; Corporate Trainer; Production Assistant. **Corporate headquarters location:** This location. **Subsidiaries include:** Dollar Tree Distribution, Inc.; Dollar Tree Management, Inc. **Operations at this facility include:** Administration; Warehouse/Distribution. **Listed on:** NASDAQ. **Stock exchange symbol:** DLTR. **Number of employees nationwide:** 4,500.

DOMINION HOSPITAL
2960 Sleepy Hollow Road, Falls Church VA 22044. 703/536-2000. **Fax:** 703/533-9650. **Contact:** Human Resources. **E-mail address:** dominionhr@hcahealthcare.com. **World Wide Web address:** http://www.dominionhospital.com. **Description:** A short-term psychiatric hospital offering inpatient services covering a wide range of problems including substance abuse, eating disorders, sleep disorders, sexual abuse, emotional

trauma, and depression. **NOTE:** Search and apply for positions online. **Parent company:** Columbia/HCA Healthcare Corporation.

DOMINION
P.O. Box 26666, Richmond VA 23261. 804/819-2000. **Physical address:** 120 Tredegar Street, Richmond VA 23219. **Contact:** Human Resources Manager. **E-mail address:** human_resources@dom.com. **World Wide Web address:** http://www.dom.com. **Description:** Produces and distributes electric power and natural gas to 5 million customers in nine states. **NOTE:** Offers co-op, intern, and minority scholarship programs. Search and apply for positions online. **Positions advertised include:** Accountant; Credit Analyst; Energy Market Analyst; Energy Trading Specialist; Oil Analyst; Project Designer; Risk Management Analyst; Senior Computational/Quantitative Programming Manager. **Corporate headquarters location:** This location. **Listed on:** New York Stock Exchange. **Stock exchange symbol:** D. **Annual sales/revenues:** More than $100 million. **Number of employees nationwide:** 11,030.

R.R. DONNELLEY & SONS COMPANY
4201 Murray Place, P.O. Box 11829, Lynchburg VA 24501. 434/522-7400. **Contact:** Human Resources. **World Wide Web address:** http://www.rrdonnelley.com. **Description:** R.R. Donnelley & Sons is a world leader in managing, reproducing, and distributing print and digital information for publishing, merchandising, and information technology customers. The company is one of the largest commercial printers in the world, producing catalogs, inserts, magazines, books, directories, computer documentation, and financial printing. R.R. Donnelley has more than 180 sales offices and production facilities. Principal services offered by the company include conventional and digital prepress operations, computerized printing and binding, and sophisticated pool shipping and distribution services for printed products; information repackaging into multiple formats (print, magnetic, and optical media); database management, list rental, list enhancement, and direct mail production services; turnkey computer documentation services (outsourcing, translation, printing, binding, diskette replication, kitting, licensing, republishing, and fulfillment); reprographics and facilities management; creative design and communication services; and digital and conventional map creation and related services. **Positions advertised include:** Electronic Technician; Building Services Apprentice. **Corporate headquarters location:** Chicago IL. **Other U.S. locations:** Nationwide. **International locations:** Worldwide. **Operations at this facility include:** This location is a commercial printer. **Listed on:** New York Stock Exchange. **Stock exchange symbol:** RRD. **Annual sales/revenues:** $4.8 billion. **Number of employees nationwide:** 30,000. **Number of employees worldwide:** 50,000.

R.R. DONNELLEY & SONS COMPANY
2347 Kratzer Road, Harrisonburg VA 22802-8303. 540/434-8833. **Contact:** Barbara Miller, Human Resources Manager. **World Wide Web address:** http://www.rrdonnelley.com. **Description:** R.R. Donnelley & Sons is a world leader in managing, reproducing, and distributing print and digital information for publishing, merchandising, and information technology customers. The company is one of the largest commercial printers in the world, producing catalogs, inserts, magazines, books, directories, computer documentation, and financial printing. R.R. Donnelley has more than 180 sales offices and production facilities. Principal services offered by the company include conventional and digital prepress operations, computerized printing and binding, and sophisticated pool shipping and distribution services for printed products; information repackaging into multiple formats (print, magnetic, and optical media); database management, list rental, list enhancement, and direct mail production services; turnkey computer documentation services (outsourcing, translation, printing, binding, diskette replication, kitting, licensing, republishing, and fulfillment); reprographics and facilities management; creative design and communication services; and digital and conventional map creation and related services. **Corporate headquarters location:** Chicago IL. **Other U.S. locations:** Nationwide. **International locations:** Worldwide. **Operations at this facility include:** This location is a book printing and binding plant. **Listed on:** New York Stock Exchange. **Stock exchange symbol:** RRD.

DOUBLE ENVELOPE COMPANY
7702 Plantation Road, Roanoke VA 24019. 540/362-3311. **Contact:** Human Resources. **Description:** Manufactures a variety of paper products including labels, order forms, and envelopes.

DUNHAM-BUSH INC.
P.O. Box 20000, Harrisonburg VA 22801. 540/434-0711. **Fax:** 540/434-2448. **Contact:** Human Resources. **E-mail address:** jswope@dunham-bush.com. **World Wide Web address:** http://www.dunham-bush.com. **Description:** A manufacturer of heating, ventilation, and air conditioning components for commercial, institutional, and industrial use. **Other U.S. locations:** Hartford CT.

E.I. DUPONT DE NEMOURS & COMPANY
400 DuPont Boulevard, Waynesboro VA 22980. 540/949-2000. **Contact:** Human Resources. **E-mail address:** info@dupont.com. **World Wide Web address:** http://www.dupont.com. **Description:** Operating in more than 70 countries, the company offers a wide range of products and services to markets including agriculture, nutrition, electronics, communications, safety and protection, home and construction, transportation and apparel. Operates in more than 70 countries worldwide with 135 manufacturing and processing facilities. **NOTE:** Search and apply for positions online. **Corporate headquarters location:** Wilmington DE. **Operations at this facility include:** This location manufactures Lycra and nylon. **Listed on:** New York Stock Exchange. **Stock exchange symbol:** DD. **Annual sales/revenues:** More than $100 million. **Number of employees worldwide:** 77,000.

E.I. DUPONT DE NEMOURS & COMPANY
5401 Jefferson Davis Highway, Richmond VA 23234. 804/383-2000. **Recorded jobline:** 804/383-3037. **Contact:** Human Resources. **E-mail address:** info@dupont.com. **World Wide Web address:** http://www.dupont.com. **Description:** Operating in more than 70 countries, the company offers a wide range of products and services to markets including agriculture, nutrition, electronics, communications, safety and protection, home and construction, transportation and apparel. Operates in more than 70 countries worldwide with 135 manufacturing and processing facilities. **NOTE:** Search and apply for positions online. **Positions advertised include:** Application Research Engineer. **Corporate headquarters location:** Wilmington DE. **Operations at this facility include:** This location manufactures Teflon, Kevlar, Tyvek, and Nomex. **Listed on:** New York Stock Exchange. **Stock exchange symbol:** DD. **Chairman/CEO:** Charles O. Holliday, Jr. **Annual sales/revenues:** $27 billion. **Number of employees worldwide:** 77,000.

DYNAMIC DETAILS, INC.
1200 Severn Way, Sterling VA 20166. 703/652-2200. **Fax:** 703/652-2295. **Contact:** Human Resources. **World Wide Web address:** http://www.ddiglobal.com. **Description:** Designs and manufactures printed circuit boards. Founded in 1975. **Positions advertised include:** Engineer; Quality Manager; Methods Engineer; Staff Accountant. **Special programs:** Training. Other U.S. locations: CA; CO; TX. **International locations:** Canada; United Kingdom. **Operations at this facility include:** Administration; Manufacturing; Research and Development; Sales. **Listed on:** Privately held.

DYNEX CAPITAL
4551 Cox Road, Suite 300, 3rd Floor, Glen Allen VA 23060. 804/217-5800. **Fax:** 804/217-5825. **Contact:** Human Resources. **E-mail address:** askdx@dynexcapital.com. **World Wide Web address:** http://www.dynexcapital.com. **Description:** a financial services company, which invests in loans and securities consisting of or secured by, single-family mortgage loans, commercial mortgage loans, manufactured housing installment loans and delinquent property tax receivables. **Corporate headquarters location:** This location. **Listed on:** New York Stock Exchange. **Stock exchange symbol:** DX.

EDS (ELECTRONIC DATA SYSTEMS CORPORATION)
13600 EDS Drive, Herndon VA 20171. 703/742-2000. **Fax:** 703/742-4032. **Contact:** Staffing Department. **E-mail address:** careers@eds.com. **World Wide Web address:** http://www.eds.com. **Description:** EDS provides a portfolio of business and technology solutions to help its clients improve their business performance. EDS' core portfolio comprises information-technology, applications and business process services, as well as information-technology transformation services. Founded in 1962. NOTE: Search and apply for positions online. Positions advertised include: Consultant Architect; Contract Specialist; Telecommunications Analyst; Financial Analyst; Technical Delivery Team Manager; Senior Systems Engineer. **Corporate headquarters location:** Plano TX. **Other U.S. locations:** Nationwide. **International locations:** Worldwide. **Listed on:** New York Stock Exchange. **Stock exchange symbol:** EDS. **Number of employees nationwide:** 64,000. **Number of employees worldwide:** 130,000.

EMC CORPORATION
8444 Westpark Drive, Suite 700, McLean VA 22102. 703/970-5800. **Fax:** 703/893-2562. **Contact:** Human Resources. **E-mail address:** resumes@emc.com. **World Wide Web address:** http://www.emc.com. **Description:** EMC designs, manufactures, markets, and supports high-performance data storage and management products to industry and government customers. **NOTE:** Search and apply for positions online. **Positions advertised include:** Client Solutions Lead; Account Manager; Senior Account Manager; Technical Business Consultant. **Corporate headquarters location:** Hopkinton MA. **Listed on:** New York Stock Exchange. **Stock exchange symbol:** EMC.

EPLUS, INC.
13595 Dulles Technology Drive, Herndon VA 20171-3413. 703/984-8400. **Toll-free phone:** 888/482-5718. **Fax:** 703/984-8600. **Contact:** Human Resources. **E-mail address:** info@eplus.com. **World Wide Web address:** http://www.eplus.com. **Description:** Provides enterprise cost management solutions. EPlus offer expertise in financial services, e-procurement, content management, supplier enablement, document imaging and collaboration and asset management. Founded in 1990. **Corporate headquarters location:** This location. **Other U.S. locations:** CA; CT; FL; GA; IL; MD; MA; MI; NJ; NY; NC; PA; TX; UT. **Listed on:** NASDAQ. **Stock exchange symbol:** PLUS.

ETS INTERNATIONAL, INC.
1401 Municipal Road NW, Roanoke VA 24012-1309. 540/265-0004. **Fax:** 540/265-0131. **Contact:** Personnel. **E-mail address:** etsi@infionline.net. **World Wide Web address:** http://www.etsi-inc.com. **Description:** ETS is an environmental service firm specializing in air emissions control, testing, training, troubleshooting, and testimony. **Corporate headquarters location:** This location. **Other U.S. locations:** Sanford FL.

EAGLE-PICHER AUTOMOTIVE GROUP
WOLVERINE GASKET DIVISION
201 Industrial Park Road, Blacksburg VA 24060. 540/552-7674. **Fax:** 540/552-6082. **Contact:** Human Resources. **E-mail address:** career.automotive@eaglepicher.com. **World Wide Web address:** http://www.epcorp.com. **Description:** Eagle-Picher Automotive Group develops, markets, and manufactures automotive components worldwide. **NOTE:** Submit resume online. **Other U.S. locations:** MI; FL. **Operations at this facility include:** This location manufactures gaskets. **Parent company:** Eagle-Picher Industries.

EASTERN SHORE NEWS
P.O. Box 288, Tasley VA 23418. 757/787-1200. **Contact:** Human Resources. **Description:** Publishes weekly and bi-weekly newspapers and resort publications in Delaware, Maryland, and Virginia. **Operations at this facility include:** Administration.

DAVIS H. ELLIOT COMPANY INC.
P.O. Box 12707, Roanoke VA 24027-2707. 540/992-2865. **Fax:** 540/344-9888. **Contact:** Karen Cobble, Human Resources Director. **World Wide Web address:** http://www.davishelliot.com. **Description:** A construction service provider that specializes in commercial and industrial electrical construction, the design and manufacturing of electric control panels, and transmission and distribution line construction and repair. Founded in 1946. **NOTE:** Entry-level positions are offered. **Special programs:** Apprenticeships. **Office hours:** Monday - Friday, 8:00 a.m. - 5:00 p.m. **Corporate headquarters location:** This location. **Other U.S. locations:** Lexington KY; Broken Arrow OK.

EMCOR CONSTRUCTION SERVICES
1420 Spring Hill Road, Suite 500, McLean VA 22102. 703/556-8000. **Fax:** 703/556-0890. **Contact:** Lynn Mauer, Human Resources. **World Wide Web address:** http://www.emcorgroup.com. **Description:** A national electrical construction contractor. **NOTE:** Search and apply for positions online. **Parent company:** EMCOR Group Inc. **Listed on:** New York Stock Exchange. **Stock exchange symbol:** EME.

EMCOR FACILITIES SERVICES INC.
320 23rd Street S, Arlington VA 22202. 866/200-9796. **Fax:** 703/769-1063. **Contact:** Human Resources. **World Wide Web address:** http://www.emcorgroup.com. **Description:** Provides operation, maintenance, and support services to building management systems. **NOTE:** Search and apply for positions online. **Positions advertised include**: Production Specialist/Coordinator; Proposal Manager/Writer; Program Development Manager; Proposal Production Manager. **Parent company:** EMCOR Group Inc. **Listed on:** New York Stock Exchange. **Stock exchange symbol:** EME.

ENCORE NETWORKS
45472 Holiday Drive, Dulles VA 20166. 703/318-4350. **Fax:** 703/318-4371. **Contact:** Human Resources. **E-mail address:** jobs@encorenetworks.com. **World Wide Web**

address: http://www.fastcomm.com. **Description:** Develops secure, converged, broadband networks for carriers and enterprise customers. **NOTE:** Search and apply for positions online. **Positions advertised include:** Manager of Marketing Communications; Technical Support Engineer; VPN Software Development Engineer; Product Manager.

ENSCO, INC.
3110 Fairview Park Drive, Fall Church VA 22042-4501. 703/321-9000. **Toll-free phone:** 800/367-2682. **Contact:** Professional Staffing. **E-mail address:** hr@ensco.com. **World Wide Web address:** http://www.ensco.com. **Description:** Provides engineering, science and advanced technology solutions for the defense, security, transportation, environment, aerospace, and intelligent automation industries. Founded in 1969. **NOTE:** Internships and co-op programs offered. Search and apply for positions online. Resumes not accepted at e-mail address. **Positions advertised include:** HR Assistant; Director of Facilities Management. **Corporate headquarters location:** This location. **Other U.S. locations:** AL; CA; FL; IN; MI; NY. **Operations at this facility include:** Administration; Research and Development. **Listed on:** Privately held. **Number of employees at this location:** 140. **Number of employees nationwide:** 700.

EQUANT
2355 Dulles Corner Boulevard, Building 3, Herndon VA 20171. 703/689-6000. **Contact:** Human Resources. **E-mail address:** careers@equant.com. **World Wide Web address:** http://www.equant.com. **Description:** Equant provides global telecommunications services for multinational businesses. Its network operates in 220 countries and territories. **NOTE:** Submit resumes to e-mail address: **Other U.S. locations:** GA; MA; IL; CA; NY. **Parent company:** France Telecom Group. **Listed on:** New York Stock Exchange. **Stock exchange symbol:** ENT.

ETHYL CORPORATION
330 South 4th Street, Richmond VA 23219. 804/788-5600. **Fax:** 804/788-5688. **Contact:** Human Resources. **E-mail address:** employment@ethyl.com. **World Wide Web address:** http://www.ethyl.com. **Description:** Manufactures fuel and lubricant additives including products for gas and diesel fuels, engine oils, automatic transmission fluids, gear oils, hydraulic fluids, and industrial oils. Founded in 1921. **Corporate headquarters location:** This location. Other U.S. locations: Houston TX; Orangeburg SC; Sauget IL. International locations: Belgium; Brazil; Canada. **Listed on:** New York Stock Exchange. **Stock exchange symbol:** EY. **Number of employees at this location:** 690. **Number of employees nationwide:** 2,000.

EXPONENT, INC.
1800 Diagonal Road, Suite 300, Alexandria VA 22314. 571/227-7200. **Fax:** 571/227-7299. **Contact:** Human Resources. **E-mail address:** hr@exponent.com. **World Wide Web address:** http://www.exponent.com. **Description:** An engineering and scientific consulting firm that performs in-depth scientific research and analysis and rapid-response evaluations for clients' technical problems. Founded in 1967. **NOTE:** Search and apply for positions online. **Positions advertised include:** Managing Scientist; Engineer/Scientist; Cost Engineer/Senior Cost Engineer; Senior Systems Engineer. **Corporate headquarters location:** Menlo Park CA. **International locations:** Germany; United Kingdom. **Listed on:** NASDAQ. **Stock exchange symbol:** EXPO.

EXXONMOBIL CORPORATION
3225 Gallows Road, Fairfax VA 22037. 703/846-3000. **Fax:** 703/849-2020. **Contact:** Staffing and Training. **World Wide Web address:** http://www.exxon.mobil.com. **Description:** An integrated oil company engaged in petroleum and chemical products marketing, refining, manufacturing, exploration, production, transportation, and research and development worldwide. Other products include fabricated plastics, films, food bags, housewares, garbage bags, and building materials. The company also has subsidiaries involved in real estate development and mining operations. **NOTE:** Search and apply for positions online. **Corporate headquarters location:** Irving TX. **Other U.S. locations:** Nationwide. **International locations:** Worldwide. **Operations at this facility include:** A regional office of ExxonMobil Aviation. **Listed on:** New York Stock Exchange. **Stock exchange symbol:** XOM. **Annual sales/revenues:** More than $100 million.

FAIRFAX IDENTITY LABORATORY
3025 Hamaker Court, Suite 103, Fairfax VA 22031. 703/698-3919. **Fax:** 703/698-7971. **Contact:** Human Resources. **E-mail address:** jobs@givf.com. **World Wide Web address:** http://www.fairfaxidlab.com. **Description:** Provides diagnostic, treatment, genetic and reproductive testing, and cryobank services. **Parent company:** Genetics & IVF Institute.

FAIRFAX MEDICAL LABORATORIES
4200 Pleasant Valley Road, Chantilly VA 20151. 703/222-2313. **Fax:** 703/263-7961. **Contact:** Human Resources Manager. **World Wide Web address:** http://www.fairfaxmedicallab.com. **Description:** A full-service medical laboratory that provides comprehensive clinical laboratory services. Founded in 1984. **Positions advertised include:** Medical Technologist; Phlebotomist.

FAUQUIER HOSPITAL
500 Hospital Drive, Warrenton VA 20186-3099. 540/347-2550. **Fax:** 540/341-0823. **Recorded jobline:** 540/349-0535. **Contact:** Human Resources Department. **E-mail address:** humanresources@fauquierhospital.org. **World Wide Web address:** http://www.fauquierhospital.org. **Description:** An 84-bed, acute care, nonprofit hospital providing inpatient, outpatient, and emergency care. The hospital is also affiliated with Warrenton Overlook Health and Rehabilitation Center, a 115-bed long-term and rehabilitative care facility. **Number of employees at this location:** 600.

FAXPLUS, INC.
1011 Arlington Boulevard, Suite 375, Arlington VA 22209. 703/807-1000. **Toll-free phone:** 800/755-1508. **Fax:** 703/527-4308. **Contact:** Human Resources. **World Wide Web address:** http://www.faxplusinc.com. **Description:** Sells and services digital copiers, fax machines, and other office products primarily to the government. Founded in 1986. **Corporate headquarters location:** This location.

FEDERAL-MOGUL CORPORATION
300 Industrial Park Road SE, Blacksburg VA 24060. 540/557-3300. **Fax:** 540/953-4690. **Contact:** Human Resources. **World Wide Web address:** http://www.federal-mogul.com. **Description:** An international manufacturer of bearings for automobile, tractor, truck, and heavy-equipment engines. **NOTE:** Submit resumes to: Corporate Human Resources Staffing, Federal-Mogul corporation, 26555 Northwestern Highway, Southfield MI 48034. **Corporate headquarters location:** Southfield MI. **Annual sales/revenues:** $5.5 billion. **Number of employees at this location:** 430. **Number of employees worldwide:** 45,000.

FEDERAL-MOGUL FRICTION PRODUCTS
P.O. Box 3250, Winchester VA 22604. 540/662-3871. **Fax:** 540/662-5875. **Physical address:** 2410 Papermill Road, Winchester VA 22601. **Contact:** Human Resources. **World Wide Web address:** http://www.federal-mogul.com. **Description:** Manufactures disc pads, brake blocks, and drum linings. **NOTE:** Submit resumes to: Corporate Human Resources Staffing, Federal-Mogul corporation, 26555 Northwestern Highway, Southfield MI 48034. **Corporate headquarters location:** Southfield MI. **Annual sales/revenues:** $5.5 billion. **Number of employees at this location:** 400. **Number of employees worldwide:** 45,000.

FELD ENTERTAINMENT, INC.
8607 Westwood Center Drive, Vienna VA 22182. 703/448-4000. **Fax:** 703/448-4100. **Contact:** Human Resources. **E-mail address:** feld@alexus.com. **World Wide Web address:** http://www.feldentertainment.com. **Description:** Operates circuses including Ringling Bros. and Barnum & Bailey Circus, television productions, and ice shows including Walt Disney's World on Ice. Founded in 1967. **Positions advertised include:** Accountant; Administrative Assistant; Brand Manager; Database Analyst; Director of Business Operations; Financial Analyst; Operations Coordinator; Print Buying Manager; Senior Contracts Manager; Systems Engineer. **Corporate headquarters location:** This location. Other U.S. locations: MD; FL.

FERGUSON ENTERPRISES, INC.
P.O. Box 2777, Newport News VA 23602. 757/874-7400. **Contact:** Recruiting Department. **E-mail address:** resumes@ferguson.com. **World Wide Web address:** http://www.ferguson.com. **Description:** A coast-to-coast wholesale distributor, supplying8plumbing and builder products, industrial pipe, valves and fittings, heating and cooling equipment, waterworks products, and tool and safety products. Ferguson Enterprises operates over 500 locations in 49 states, D.C. Puerto Rico, and Mexico. Founded in 1953. **NOTE:** Offers entry-level positions. **Positions advertised include:** Instructional Designer/Technical Writer; computer Programmer; Software Tester; Network Support Analyst. **Other U.S. locations:** Nationwide. **International locations:** Mexico; Puerto Rico.

FINE'S MEN'S SHOPS INC.
1164 Azalea Garden Road, Norfolk VA 23513. 757/857-6013. **Contact:** Mitchell Fine, President. **Description:** Operates a chain of men's clothing stores. **Corporate headquarters location:** This location.

FIRST INFORMATION TECHNOLOGY SERVICES, INC.
2011 Crystal Drive, Suite 308, Arlington VA 22202. 703/271-2014. **Contact:** Keith Paige. **E-mail address:** ktpaige@1stinfotech.com. **World Wide Web address:** http://www.1stinfotech.com. **Description:** An information system services provider specializing in security engineering and systems integration for computer systems with enhanced security requirements. **Positions advertised include:** Web Developer; Network Engineer; Security Analyst.

THE FLIGHT INTERNATIONAL GROUP, INC.
Newport News/Williamsburg International Airport, One Lear Drive, Newport News VA 23602. 757/886-5500. **Fax:** 757/874-7481. **Contact:** Human Resources. **World Wide Web address:** http://www.fltintl.com. **Description:** Provides electronic warfare simulation training and equipment calibration to the U.S. Navy and other government customers. **Parent company:** L-3 Communications Vertex Aerospace LLC. **Number of employees nationwide:** 135.

FORD NORFOLK ASSEMBLY PLANT
2424 Ford Drive, Norfolk VA 23523-2495. 757/494-2000. **Contact:** Human Resources Department. **World Wide Web address:** http://www.ford.com. **Description:** Ford is engaged in the design, development, manufacture, and sale of cars, trucks, tractors, and related components and accessories. Ford is also one of the largest providers of financial services in the United States. The company has manufacturing, assembly, and sales affiliates in 29 countries outside the United States. The company's three core businesses are the Automotive Group, the Financial Services Group, and Hertz, the world's largest car rental organization. **NOTE:** Search and apply for positions online. **Corporate headquarters location:** Dearborn MI. **Operations at this facility include:** This location is a truck manufacturing facility.

FOUNDERS FURNITURE
P.O. Box 848, Appomattox VA 24522. 804/352-7181. **Physical address:** Highway 460, Appomattox VA 24522. **Contact:** Human Resources. **World Wide Web address:** http://www.foundersfurniture.com. **Description:** A manufacturer and marketer of bedroom furniture. **Parent company:** Thomasville Furniture Industries.

FREDDIE MAC
8200 Jones Branch Drive, McLean VA 22102. 703/903-2000. **Contact:** Director of Employment. **World Wide Web address:** http://www.freddiemac.com. **Description:** Provides mortgage credit services and secondary mortgages. Founded in 1970. **NOTE:** Second and third shifts are offered. Search and apply for positions online. **Positions advertised include:** Collections Specialist; Control Manager; Business Planning and Development Manager; Marketing Communication Specialist; Business Applications Analyst; Financial Analyst; Senior Economist; Examiner; Operational Management Director; Website Production Manager; Research Analyst. **Special programs:** Internships; Co-ops. **Corporate headquarters location:** This location. **Other U.S. locations:** Woodland Hills CA; Washington DC; Atlanta GA; Chicago IL; New York NY; Carrollton TX. **Listed on:** New York Stock Exchange. **Stock exchange symbol:** FRE. **Number of employees nationwide:** 3,500.

GE FINANCIAL ASSURANCE
6604 West Broad Street, Richmond VA 23230. 804/281-6000. **Contact:** Director of Human Resources. **World Wide Web address:** http://www.gefinancialassurance.com. **Description:** A life insurance company that also offers financial management products. **Corporate headquarters location:** Fairfield CT. **Other U.S. locations:** CA; CO; CT; NY; PA; WA. **Parent company:** General Electric Company. **Listed on:** New York Stock Exchange. **Stock exchange symbol:** GE.

GANNETT COMPANY, INC.
7950 Jones Branch Drive, McLean VA 22107. 703/854-6000. **Fax:** 703/854-2009. **Contact:** Human Resources. **E-mail address:** corpjobs@gannett.com. **World Wide Web address:** http://www.gannett.com. **Description:** A nationwide news and information company with operations in 43 states that publishes 101 newspapers including *USA Today*, and is one of the largest outdoor advertising companies in North America. Gannett also owns and operates 22 television stations, 130 websites, advertising operations, direct marketing services, commercial printing, and database marketing operations. Positions advertised include: Analyst; Senior Analyst; Project Leader; IT Specialist; Senior Telecommunications Analyst; Director, Financial Analysis; **Special programs:** Internships. **Corporate headquarters location:** This location. **Other U.S. locations:** Nationwide. **International locations:** Great Britain;

Guam; Hong Kong; Columbia; Belgium; Germany; Italy. **Listed on:** New York Stock Exchange. **Stock exchange symbol:** GCI. **Annual sales/revenues:** $6.7 billion. **Number of employees worldwide:** 53,000.

GEICO CORPORATION
One GEICO Boulevard, Fredericksburg VA 22412. 540/286-4441. **Fax:** 540/372-3899. **Recorded jobline:** 800/841-7445. **Contact:** Human Resources. **E-mail address:** jobs@geico.com. **World Wide Web address:** http://www.geico.com. **Description:** GEICO and its affiliates: GEICO General Insurance Company; GEICO Indemnity Company; and GEICO Casualty Company, insure private passenger automobiles and provide homeowner and other types of insurance for qualified applicants. The companies market collectively under the trademarks GEICO and GEICO Direct. Founded in 1936. **NOTE:** Resumes not accepted by e-mail. Search and apply for positions online. Positions advertised include: Auto Damage Adjusters; claims Service Representative; Customer Service Insurance Counselor; Sales Insurance Coordinator. **Corporate headquarters location:** Chevy Chase MD. **Parent company:** Berkshire Hathaway.

GENERAL DYNAMICS ADVANCED INFORMATION SYSTEMS
1421 Jefferson Davis Highway, Suite 600, Arlington VA 22202. 703/271-7300. **Fax:** 703/271-7301. **Contact:** Human Resources. **E-mail address:** careers.info@veridian.com. **World Wide Web address:** http://www.veridian.com. **Description:** A provider of information-based systems, integrated solutions and services with core capabilities in network security and enterprise protection; intelligence, surveillance and reconnaissance; knowledge discovery and decision support; chemical, biological and nuclear detection; network and enterprise management; and systems engineering services. **Number of employees worldwide:** 7,000.

GENERAL DYNAMICS CORPORATION
2941 Fairview Park Drive, Suite 100, Falls Church VA 22042-4523. 703/876-3000. **Fax:** 703/876-3125. **Contact:** Human Resources. **World Wide Web address:** http://www.generaldynamics.com. **Description:** General Dynamics is involved in business aviation and aircraft services, land and amphibious combat systems, mission-critical information systems and technologies, and shipbuilding and marine systems. The company is a leading supplier of sophisticated defense systems to the United States and its allies. Founded in 1952. **NOTE:** Search and apply for positions online. **Corporate headquarters location:** This location. **Other U.S. locations:** CT; MI; NJ; OH; RI. **Listed on:** New York Stock Exchange. **Stock exchange symbol:** GD. **Annual sales/revenues:** $16.6 billion. **Number of employees at this location:** 60. **Number of employees nationwide:** 31,000. **Number of employees worldwide:** 67,000.

GENERAL ELECTRIC COMPANY
125 Apple Valley Road, Winchester VA 22602. 540/667-5990. **Contact:** Human Resources. **World Wide Web address:** http://www.ge.com. **Description:** General Electric operates in the following areas: aircraft engines (jet engines, replacement parts, and repair services for commercial, military, executive, and commuter aircraft); appliances; broadcasting (NBC); industrial (lighting products, electrical distribution and control equipment, transportation systems products, electric motors and related products, a broad range of electrical and electronic industrial automation products, and a network of electrical supply houses); materials (plastics, ABS resins, silicones, superabrasives, and laminates); power systems (products for the generation, transmission, and distribution of electricity); technical products and systems (medical systems and equipment, as well as a full range of computer-based information and data interchange services for both internal use and external commercial and industrial customers); and capital services (consumer services, financing, and specialty insurance.) **NOTE:** Search and apply for positions online. **Corporate headquarters location:** Fairfield CT. **Operations at this facility include:** This location manufactures light bulbs. **Listed on:** New York Stock Exchange. **Stock exchange symbol:** GE. **Number of employees worldwide:** 315,000.

GENERAL ELECTRIC COMPANY
1501 Roanoke Boulevard, Room 118, Salem VA 24153. 540/387-7000. **Contact:** Personnel. **World Wide Web address:** http://www.ge.com. **Description:** General Electric operates in the following areas: aircraft engines (jet engines, replacement parts, and repair services for commercial, military, executive, and commuter aircraft); appliances; broadcasting (NBC); industrial (lighting products, electrical distribution and control equipment, transportation systems products, electric motors and related products, a broad range of electrical and electronic industrial automation products, and a network of electrical supply houses); materials (plastics, ABS resins, silicones, superabrasives, and laminates); power systems (products for the generation, transmission, and distribution of electricity); technical products and systems (medical systems and equipment, as well as a full range of computer-based information and data interchange services for both internal use and external commercial and industrial customers); and capital services (consumer services, financing, and specialty insurance.) **NOTE:** Search and apply for positions online. **Corporate headquarters location:** Fairfield CT. **Operations at this facility include:** This location manufactures AC-DC drivers and panels. **Listed on:** New York Stock Exchange. **Stock exchange symbol:** GE. **Number of employees worldwide:** 315,000.

GENERAL FOAM PLASTICS CORPORATION
3321 East Princess Anne Road, Norfolk VA 23502. 757/857-0153. **Contact:** Laura Williams, Personnel Director. **Description:** Manufactures a variety of plastic products including holiday decorations and swimming pools.

GENERAL KINETICS INC.
10688-D Crestwood Drive, Manassas VA 20109-3464. 703/331-8033. **Fax:** 703/331-5592. **Contact:** Human Resources. **E-mail address:** info@gki.com. **World Wide Web address:** http://www.gki.com. **Description:** Custom designs and manufactures electronic enclosures and systems for severe environments. General Kinetics' customers include computer, government, military, telecommunications, and industrial clients. Founded in 1954. **Corporate headquarters location:** This location. **Other U.S. locations:** Johnstown PA. **Number of employees nationwide:** 120.

GEORGE MASON UNIVERSITY
4400 University Drive, Fairfax VA 22030-4444. 703/993-1000. **Fax:** 703/993-2601. **Recorded jobline:** 703/993-4000. **Contact:** Human Resources. **World Wide Web address:** http://www.gmu.edu. **Description:** A four-year university offering bachelor's, master's (including MBAs), first professional, and doctoral degrees. Approximately 28,000 students attend George Mason University. **NOTE:** Search for positions online. **Other area locations:** Arlington VA; Manassas VA.

GEORGIA-PACIFIC CORPORATION
P.O. Drawer D, Emporia VA 23847. 434/634-5123. **Fax:** 434/634-9385. **Physical address:** 634 Davis Street, Emporia VA 23847. **Contact:** Human Resources. **World Wide Web address:** http://www.gp.com. **Description:** Georgia-Pacific Corporation is a manufacturer, wholesaler, and distributor of building products, industrial wood products, pulp, paper, packaging, and related chemicals. The company is one of the world's largest manufacturers of forest products, with 400 facilities in the U.S., Canada, and 11 other countries. Georgia-Pacific Corporation owns 6 million acres of forestland in North America. Founded in 1927. **NOTE:** Search and apply for positions online. **Positions advertised include:** Safety Supervisor. **Corporate headquarters location:** Atlanta GA. **Operations at this facility include:** This location manufactures plywood. **Listed on:** New York Stock Exchange. **Stock exchange symbol:** GP. **Number of employees worldwide:** 61,000.

GLOBAL VILLAGE PUBLISHING, INC. (GVPI)
1101 King Street, Suite 190, Alexandria VA 22314-2944. 703/548-9595. **Toll-free phone:** 800/394-4874. **Fax:** 703/548-9598. **Contact:** Human Resources. **World Wide Web address:** http://www.gvpi.com. **Description:** Provides software and services for organizations involved in electronic publishing of information for internal or external distribution. Founded in 1987.

GOLD'S GYM
2955 South Glebe Road, Arlington VA 22206. 703/683-4653. **Contact:** Human Resources. **World Wide Web address:** http://www.goldsgym.com. **Description:** A full-service health and fitness club. Each club is complete with weights and cardiovascular equipment, fitness and aerobic instruction, tanning, personal training, and childcare facilities. Overall, Gold's Gym is one of the world's largest health club chains, with over 550 locations. **Corporate headquarters location:** Palm Springs CA.

GOLD'S GYM
14290 Sullyfield Circle, Suite 400, Chantilly VA 20151. 703/378-4653. **Contact:** Human Resources. **World Wide Web address:** http://www.goldsgym.com. **Description:** A full-service health and fitness club. Each club is complete with weights and cardiovascular equipment, fitness and aerobic instruction, tanning, personal training, and childcare facilities. Overall, Gold's Gym is one of the world's largest health club chains, with over 550 locations. **Corporate headquarters location:** Palm Springs CA.

GOODYEAR TIRE & RUBBER COMPANY
1901 Goodyear Boulevard, Danville VA 24541. 434/791-9200. **Contact:** Human Resources. **World Wide Web address:** http://www.goodyear.com. **Description:** Goodyear Tire & Rubber Company's principal business is the development, manufacture, distribution, and sale of tires for most applications worldwide. Goodyear also manufactures and sells a broad spectrum of rubber products and rubber-related chemicals for various industrial and consumer markets and provides auto repair services. The company operates 32 plants in the United States, 42 plants in 28 other countries, and more than 1,800 retail tire and service centers and other distribution facilities around the globe. **NOTE:** Offers co-op and internship programs. **Corporate headquarters location:** Akron OH. **Other U.S. locations:** Nationwide. **International locations:** Worldwide. **Operations at this facility include:** This location manufactures truck and airplane tires. **Subsidiaries include:** Celeron; Goodyear Asia; Goodyear Europe; Goodyear Latin America; Goodyear Racing; Kelly-Springfield; North American Tire. **Listed on:** New York Stock Exchange. **Stock exchange symbol:** GT. **Number of employees worldwide:** 88,000.

GOVERNMENT TECHNOLOGY SERVICES, INC. (GTSI)
3901 Stonecroft Boulevard, Chantilly VA 20151-1010. 703/502-2000. **Fax:** 703/222-5240. **Toll-free phone:** 800/999-4874. **Contact:** Human Resources. **E-mail address:** careers@gtsi.com. **World Wide Web address:** http://www.gtsi.com. **Description:** Provides IT solutions to government customers in such areas as high performance computing, advanced networking, mobile and wireless, web portals, high availability storage, and information assurance. Founded in 1983. **NOTE:** Search and apply for positions online. **Positions advertised include:** Director Information Security; Sales Support specialist; Buyer I; EGT Technologist; Sun Systems Engineer; Network Engineer; PAR I; Account Executive; Business Development Executive; Director of Quality. **Special programs:** Internships. **Corporate headquarters location:** This location. **Operations at this facility include:** Administration; Sales; Service. **Listed on:** NASDAQ. **Stock exchange symbol:** GTSI. **Annual sales/revenues:** More than $100 million. **Number of employees at this location:** 400.

W.W. GRAINGER
1401 Sewells Point Road, Norfolk VA 23502. 757/855-3153. **Fax:** 757/855-9542. **Contact:** Human Resources. **World Wide Web address:** http://www.grainger.com. **Description:** Distributes a variety of equipment and components to the industrial, commercial, contracting, and institutional markets nationwide. The company operates 337 branches in all 50 states and Puerto Rico. Products include equipment and components for motors, air tools, hydraulic products, refrigeration items, power and hand tools, office equipment, computer supplies, storage equipment, replacement parts, industrial products, safety items, cold weather clothing, and sanitary supplies. **NOTE:** Search and apply for positions online. **Corporate headquarters location:** Lake Forest IL. **Listed on:** New York Stock Exchange. **Stock exchange symbol:** GWW.

GUEST SERVICES
3055 Prosperity Avenue, Fairfax VA 22031. 703/849-9300. **Toll-free phone:** 800/345-7534. **Contact:** Human Resources Department. **E-mail address:** biondif@guestservices.com. **World Wide Web address:** http://www.guestservices.com. **Description:** Manages a variety of contract food and hospitality services. Founded in 1917. **NOTE:** Apply for positions online. **Corporate headquarters location:** This location. **Operations at this facility include:** Regional Headquarters. **Number of employees at this location:** 80. **Number of employees nationwide:** 3,500.

GUNSTON HALL PLANTATION
10709 Gunston Rd, Mason Neck VA 22079. 703/550-9220. **Fax:** 703/550-9480. **Contact:** Human Resources. **World Wide Web address:** http://www.gunstonhall.org. **Description:** A 550-acre plantation house operating as a museum. In the 1700s the plantation was home to George Mason, the author of the Virginia declaration of rights. **NOTE:** Volunteer positions available.

HALIFAX CORPORATION
5250 Cherokee Avenue, Alexandria VA 22312. 703/750-2202. **Fax:** 703/658-2444. **Contact:** Human Resources. **E-mail address:** info@hxcorp.com. **World Wide Web address:** http://www.hxcorp.com. **Description:** Performs a variety of computer-related services such as systems integration, consulting, computer maintenance and repair, facilities management, and outsourcing. Founded in 1967. **NOTE:** Submit resumes to: drandles@hxcorp.com. **Corporate headquarters location:** This location. **Other U.S. locations:** Nationwide. **Operations at this facility include:** Administration; Sales; Service. **Listed on:** American Stock Exchange. **Stock exchange symbol:** HX. **Annual sales/revenues:** $51 - $100 million. **Number of employees at this location:** 70. **Number of employees nationwide:** 680.

HAMILTON BEACH/PROCTOR-SILEX, INC.
4421 Waterfront Drive, Glen Allen VA 23060. 804/273-9777. **Contact:** Human Resources. **World Wide Web address:** http://www.hamiltonbeach.com. **Description:** Manufactures small appliances including blenders, can openers, coffee makers, food processors, irons, mixers, steamers, and toasters. **NOTE:** Positions posted on Monster.com. **Positions advertised include:** Senior Sourced Buyer; Project Engineer. **Corporate headquarters location:** This location.

HAMPTON UNIVERSITY
Office of Human Resources, Armstrong-Slater Hall, Room 110, Hampton VA 23668. 757/727-5250. **Contact:** Director of Human Resources. **World Wide Web address:** http://www.hamptonu.edu. **Description:** A four-year university offering bachelor's and master's degrees, including MBAs. Approximately 5,700 students attend Hampton University.

HECHT'S
685 North Glebe Road, Arlington VA 22203-2199. 703/558-1200. **Contact:** Human Resources. **World Wide Web address:** http://www.hechts.com. **Description:** A general merchandise and apparel retailer, operating 61 stores. NOTE: Apply for positions online. **Office hours:** Monday - Friday, 9:00 a.m. - 5:00 p.m. **Corporate headquarters location:** This location.

HERSHEY CHOCOLATE USA
P.O. Box 1028, Stuarts Draft VA 24477. 540/337-4700. **Physical address:** 120 Harold Cook Drive, Stuarts Draft VA 24477. **Contact:** Employee Relations. **World Wide Web address:** http://www.hersheys.com. **Description:** Manufactures Hershey chocolates. **NOTE:** Please call for application procedures. **Corporate headquarters location:** Hershey PA. **Parent company:** Hershey Foods Corporation makes and sells a wide selection of confectionery, chocolate, and pasta products with over 50 brands marketed throughout the world. The company operates through the following primary segments: Hershey Chocolate USA, Hershey International, Hershey Pasta Group, and Hershey Canada Inc. Brands of confections include Kit Kat, Reese's, Almond Joy, and Kisses. Pasta brands include Ronzoni, Skinner, P&R, Light 'n Fluffy, and American Beauty. **Listed on:** New York Stock Exchange. **NOTE:** Search and apply for positions online. **Stock exchange symbol:** HSY.

HILB, ROGAL AND HAMILTON COMPANY
4951 Lake Brook Drive, Suite 500, Glen Allen VA 23060. 804/747-6500. **Fax:** 804/747-3146. **Contact:** Human Resources. **E-mail address:** opportunities@hrh.com. **World Wide Web address:** http://www.hrh.com. **Description:** Provides customized insurance and risk management solutions as well as employee benefits consulting for businesses, associations, and individuals. Operates 120 offices nationwide. **NOTE:** Search and apply for positions online. **Positions available include:** Assistant Controller; Accounting Assistant. **Corporate headquarters location:** This location. **Other U.S. locations:** Nationwide. **Listed on:** New York Stock Exchange. **Stock exchange symbol:** HRH. **Number of employees nationwide:** 1,630.

HITACHI DATA SYSTEMS
951 East Byrd Street, Suite 950, Riverfront Plaza, Richmond VA 23219-4075. 804/644-7200. **Fax:** 804/643-1254. **Contact:** Human Resources. **World Wide Web address:** http://www.hds.com. **Description:** Provides data storage solutions in government and private sectors. **NOTE:** Search and apply for positions or submit resume online. **Corporate headquarters location:** Santa Clara CA. **Other U.S. locations:** Nationwide. **International locations:** Worldwide. **Parent company:** Hitachi, Ltd. **Operations at this facility include:** This location serves as a sales and marketing office. **Number of employees worldwide:** 2,700.

HONEYWELL
4101 Bermuda Hundred Road, Chesterfield VA 23836. 804/530-6000. **Contact:** Human Resources. **World Wide Web address:** http://www.honeywell.com. **Description:** Honeywell is engaged in the research, development, manufacture, and sale of advanced technology products and services in the fields of chemicals, electronics, automation, and controls. The company's major businesses are home and building automation and control, performance polymers and chemicals, industrial automation and control, space and aviation systems, and defense and marine systems. **NOTE:** Search and apply for positions or submit resume online. **Corporate headquarters location:** Morristown NJ. **Operations at this facility include:** This location produces a variety of chemicals. **Listed on:** New York Stock Exchange. **Stock exchange symbol:** HON.

HONEYWELL
15801 Woods Edge Road, Colonial Heights VA 23834. 804/520-3000. **Contact:** Human Resources. **World Wide Web address:** http://www.honeywell.com. **Description:** Honeywell is engaged in the research, development, manufacture, and sale of advanced technology products and services in the fields of chemicals, electronics, automation, and controls. The company's major businesses are home and building automation and control, performance polymers and chemicals, industrial automation and control, space and aviation systems, and defense and marine systems. **NOTE:** Search and apply for positions or submit resume online. **Positions advertised include:** Human Resources Leader. **Corporate headquarters location:** Morristown NJ. **Operations at this facility include:** This location is a technical research center. **Listed on:** New York Stock Exchange. **Stock exchange symbol:** HON.

HOPPMANN CORPORATION
13129 Airpark Drive, Suite 120, Elkwood VA. 540/829-2564. **Toll-free phone:** 800/368-3582. **Fax:** 540/829-1724. **Contact:** Human Resources. **E-mail address:** bambrose@hoppmann.com. **World Wide Web address:** http://www.hoppmann.com. **Description:** Produces automated parts handling systems. Founded in 1955. **Positions advertised include:** Electrical Technician. **Corporate headquarters location:** This location. **Other area locations:** Lynchburg VA. Madison Heights VA. **International locations:** Verden Germany. **Number of employees at this location:** 150.

HUNTON & WILLIAMS
1751 Pinnacle Drive, Suite 1700, McLean VA 22102. 703/714-7400. **Fax:** 703/714-7410. **Contact:** Trish McClendon, Human Resources. **E-mail address:** pmcclendon@hunton.com. **World Wide Web address:** http://www.hunton.com. **Description:** A law firm specializing in a wide variety of areas including constitutional, corporate, patent, and real estate law. Founded in 1901. Maintains 17 offices with 850 attorneys. **Corporate headquarters location:** Richmond VA.

ICF CONSULTING
9300 Lee Highway, Fairfax VA 22031. 703/934-3000. **Fax:** 703/934-3740. **Contact:** Employment Manager. **E-mail address:** info@icfconsulting.com. **World Wide Web address:** http://www.icfconsulting.com. **Description**: ICF Consulting is a management, technology, and policy consulting firm that develops solutions in five markets: energy, environment, homeland security, community development, and transportation. Since 1969, ICF Consulting has served major corporations, government at all levels, and multinational institutions. **NOTE:** Entry-level positions available. Search and apply for positions online. **Positions advertised include:** Associate; Associate for Emergency Management; Configuration Management Specialist; Contracts Specialist; Data Administrator; Director/VP, Business Development, Homeland Security; Energy Management and Efficiency Expert; Housing and Community Development Associate. **Corporate headquarters location:** This location. **International locations:** Lisbon, Portugal; London, England; Moscow, Russia; Rio de Janeiro, Brazil; Toronto, Canada.

IPC TECHNOLOGIES, INC.
7200 Glen Forest Drive, Richmond VA 23226. 804/285-9300. **Fax:** 804/285-4492. **Contact:** Human Resources. **World Wide Web address:** http://www.ipctech.com. **Description:** Provides computer-consulting services. The company specializes in GUI application and database design. **NOTE:** Search and apply for positions online. **Positions advertised include:** Technical Recruiter; Software Engineer; Web Developer; Network Administrator; Network Engineer; Programmer/Analyst; GUI Developer. **Corporate headquarters location:** This location.

ITC LEARNING CORPORATION
1616 Anderson Road, Suite 109, McLean VA 22102. 703/442-0670. **Toll-free phone:** 800/638-3757. **Fax:** 703/852-7174. **Contact:** Personnel. **E-mail address:** learning@itclearning.com. **World Wide Web address:** http://www.itclearning.com. **Description:** A full-service training company specializing in the development, production, marketing, and sale of both off-the-shelf and custom-designed multimedia training courseware for commercial, educational, and government organizations. The company also markets, sells, and distributes linear training products (primarily videotape and text-based) through its Training Department. Founded in 1977. **Corporate headquarters location:** This location. **Other U.S. locations:** Atlanta GA. **International locations:** Australia; United Kingdom. **Subsidiaries include:** CI Acquisition Corporation. **Annual sales/revenues:** $21 - $50 million. **Number of employees at this location:** 45. **Number of employees nationwide:** 100.

ITT DEFENSE PRODUCTS & SERVICES
1650 Tysons Boulevard, Suite 1700, McLean VA 22102. 703/790-6300. **Fax:** 703/790-6360. **Contact:** Human Resources. **World Wide Web address:** http://www.defense.itt.com. **Description:** Manufactures electronic defense products primarily for the U.S. military and allied nations. The company operates through the following divisions: tactical communications, radar, night vision, electronic warfare, operations and maintenance, and space systems. **NOTE:** Search for positions online. **International locations:** Hong Kong; Kuwait; Saudi Arabia; Switzerland; United Kingdom. **Parent company:** ITT Industries. **Listed on:** New York Stock Exchange. **Stock exchange symbol:** ITT.

ITW PAKTRON
1205 McConville Road, Lynchburg VA 24502. 434/239-6941. **Fax:** 434/239-4730. **Contact:** Ms. Terri J. Brown, Human Resources Manager. **E-mail address:** itwpaktron@paktron.com. **World Wide Web address:** http://www.paktron.com. **Description:** Manufactures film capacitors. **Corporate headquarters location:** Chicago IL. **Operations at this facility include:** Divisional Headquarters; Manufacturing.

INFODATA SYSTEMS INC.
13454 Sunrise Valley Drive, Suite 500, Herndon VA 20171-3282. 703/934-5205. **Toll-free phone:** 800/336-4939. **Fax:** 703/934-7154. **Contact:** Human Resources. **E-mail address:** hr@infodata.com. **World Wide Web address:** http://www.infodata.com. **Description:** Provides complete electronic document management systems solutions to address developing client/server technologies, through the sale of products and software integration services. The company also offers product support services including training, a telephone hotline service, product enhancements, and maintenance releases. Founded in 1968. **NOTE:** Search and apply for positions online. **Positions advertised include:** Software Engineer; Senior Systems Integrator; Senior Developer, Documentum; C++ Developer; Web Developer; XML Analyst; Database Engineer; Configuration Management Specialist; Senior INFOSEC Engineer. **Corporate headquarters location:** This location. **Listed on:** NASDAQ. **Number of employees at this location:** 80.

INFORMATION ANALYSIS INC.
11240 Waples Mill Road, Suite 400, Fairfax VA 22030. 703/383-3000. **Fax:** 703/293-7979. **Contact:** Kathy Hommas, Personnel Director. **World Wide Web address:** http://www.infoa.com. **Description:** IAI provides a full range of IT services specializing in e-business solutions, enterprise portals, system migration and modernization, and enterprise application integration. Founded in 1979. **NOTE:** Search and apply for jobs or submit resume online. **Positions advertised include:** Forms Technician. **Corporate headquarters location:** This location.

INFORMATION 1ST, INC.
11710 Plaza America Drive, Suite 1200, Reston VA 20190. 703/691-2480. **Fax:** 703/691-4649. **Contact:** Human Resources. **E-mail address:** recruiting@information1st.com. **World Wide Web address:** http://www.information1st.com. **Description:** Develops scalable web-based solutions that enable organizations to effectively capture, track, and manage issues throughout their lifecycle. Their solutions for information management initiatives include knowledge management, document management, workflow processing, and records management. **Parent company:** STG, Inc.

INFORMATION MANAGEMENT CONSULTANTS, INC. (IMC)
11480 Commerce Park Drive, Reston VA 20191. 703/871-8700. **Fax:** 703/871-8900. **Contact:** Human Resources. **World Wide Web address:** http://www.imc.com. **Description:** Provides a wide range of information systems planning, development, and implementation services to public and private sector clients in the United States and abroad. Services include image and document management, knowledge management, workflow automation, data warehousing, information navigation and retrieval, web-based applications, and Internet-enabled distribution of public information. Founded in 1981. **NOTE:** Entry-level positions are offered. **Positions advertised include:** Senior Financial Analyst; Proposals Manager; EDM Delivery Manager; Network Administrator; Programmer Analyst; Senior Enterprise Document Management Analyst. **Special programs:** Training. **Subsidiaries:** KEVRIC; Intrinsic Management Consultants. **Operations at this facility include:** Administration; Regional Headquarters; Sales. **Listed on:** Privately held. **Annual sales/revenues:** $21 - $50 million. **Number of employees at this location:** 300.

INOVA ALEXANDRIA HOSPITAL
4320 Seminary Road, Alexandria VA 22304. 703/504-3000. **Contact:** Director of Human Resources. **E-mail address:** jobs@inova.com. **World Wide Web address:** http://www.inova.com. **Description:** A 339-bed general medical and surgical hospital. Special departments of Alexandria Hospital include a Level II trauma center, a cancer center, a cardiac surgery unit, radiology, pediatrics, a women's specialty unit, and a

mental health and behavioral center. **Positions advertised include:** Management Coordinator; Respiratory Therapist; Director, Radiology, Oncology, and Infusion; Radiologic Technologist; Medical Technologist; Sonographer; Education Coordinator; Physical Therapist; Computed Tomography Tech; Nuclear Medicine Tech; Registered Nurse. **Parent company:** Inova Health System.

INOVA EMERGENCY CARE CENTER
4315 Chain Bridge Road, Fairfax VA 22030. 703/591-9322. **Contact:** Human Resources. **E-mail address:** jobs@inova.com. **World Wide Web address:** http://www.inova.com. **Description:** A 24-hour emergency care center with laboratory and X-ray services. **Positions advertised include:** Emergency Medical Technician; Registered Nurse; Security Officer. **Other area locations:** Reston VA. **Parent company:** Inova Health System.

INOVA EMERGENCY CARE CENTER
11901-A Baron Cameron Avenue, Reston VA 20191. 703/471-0175. **Contact:** Human Resources. **E-mail address:** jobs@inova.com. **World Wide Web address:** http://www.inova.com. **Description:** A 24-hour emergency care center with laboratory and X-ray services. **Positions advertised include:** Medical Technologist; Registered Nurse; Patient Registration Rep. **Other area locations:** Fairfax VA. **Parent company:** Inova Health System.

INOVA FAIR OAKS HOSPITAL
3600 Joseph Siewick Drive, Fairfax VA 22033. 703/391-3600. **Contact:** Human Resources. **E-mail address:** jobs@inova.com. **World Wide Web address:** http://www.inova.com. **Description:** A 160-bed full-service hospital that provides maternal and infant health care. **Positions advertised include:** Emergency Medical Technician; Care Team Assistant; Pharmacy Technician; Business Manager; Radiologic Technologist; Medical Technologist; Pharmacist; Registered Nurse. **Parent company:** Inova Health System.

INOVA FAIRFAX HOSPITAL
3300 Gallows Road, Falls Church VA 22042-3300. 703/698-1110. **Contact:** Human Resources. **E-mail address:** jobs@inova.com. **World Wide Web address:** http://www.inova.com. **Description:** A full-service, 656-bed, inpatient and outpatient care hospital. Inova Fairfax Hospital provides cancer treatment services, 24-hour emergency services, newborn intensive care, and general medical and surgical care. **Positions advertised include:** Management Coordinator; Registered Nurse; Medical Technologist; Physician; Radiologic Technologist; Sonographer; Phlebotomist; Physical Therapist; Surgical Physician Assistant. **Parent company:** Inova Health System.

INOVA MOUNT VERNON HOSPITAL
2501 Parker's Lane, Alexandria VA 22306. 703/664-7000. **Contact:** Human Resources. **E-mail address:** jobs@inova.com. **World Wide Web address:** http://www.inova.com. **Description:** A full-service hospital. The hospital has emergency, cardiac, rehabilitation, and psychiatry units; the Mount Vernon Cancer Institute; and outpatient surgery. **Positions advertised include:** Speech Pathologist; Medical Records Supervisor; Occupational Therapist; Physical Therapist; Pharmacist; Registered Nurse; Medical Technologist. **Parent company:** Inova Health System.

INSTITUTE OF DEFENSE ANALYSES
4850 Mark Center Drive, Alexandria VA 22311-1882. 703/845-2000. **Fax:** 240/282-8314. **Contact:** Employment Office. **E-mail address:** resumes@ida.org. **World Wide Web address:** http://www.ida.org. **Description:** Provides defense system evaluation, testing, and simulation for the government. The non-profit, federally funded Institute of Defense Analyses also offers technical support services. **Positions advertised include:** Administrative Officer; Network System Analyst; Micro-Computer Technician; Research Assistant; Analyst, Intelligent Systems; Defense Resource Analyst; Satellite Test and Evaluation Analyst; Undersea Warfare Analyst; Cost Research and Analysis. **Special programs:** Internships. **Internship information:** The institute offers several paid internships every summer. Applications are accepted January through March. Candidates are asked to send a cover letter and resume by fax or e-mail. **Corporate headquarters location:** This location. **Number of employees at this location:** 750.

INTEGIC CORPORATION
14585 Avion Parkway, Chantilly VA 20151. 703/222-2840. **Contact:** Human Resources. **World Wide Web address:** http://www.integic.com. **E-mail address:** careers@integic.com. **Description:** Targeting the health care and life sciences industries as well as government agencies, Integic develops enterprise application integration software and provides e-business systems integration services for connecting legacy computer systems and applications to the Internet and other networks. **Positions advertised include:** Business Analyst; Business Development Manager; Developer; Govt Financial/Systems Analyst; Installation Engineer; JAVA Developer; Network Engineer; Programmer Analyst; Web Developer. **Corporate headquarters location:** This location. Other U.S. locations: CA; MD; MA; NJ; NY; NC; OH; PA.

INTEGRATED SYSTEMS ANALYSTS, INC.
2800 Shirlington Road, Suite 1100, Arlington VA 22206-3601. 703/824-0700. **Contact:** Human Resources. **World Wide Web address:** http://www.isa.com. **Description:** Provides systems engineering and computer systems support to government agencies and commercial clients. Founded in 1980. **NOTE:** Search and apply for positions online. **Other U.S. locations:** Detroit MI; Dallas TX; San Diego CA. **Number of employees nationwide:** 600.

INTERMET CORPORATION
P.O. Box 11589, Lynchburg VA 24506. 434/528-8702. **Contact:** Human Resources Manager. **World Wide Web address:** http://www.intermet.com. **Description:** A cast metals manufacturing operation supplying ductile iron castings to the automobile industry. **Corporate headquarters location:** Troy MI. **Other area locations:** Radford VA. **Other U.S. locations:** Columbus GA; Decatur IL; Havana IL; Hibbing MN. **International locations:** Germany. **Operations at this facility include:** Manufacturing. **Listed on:** NASDAQ. **Stock exchange symbol:** INMT. **Number of employees at this location:** 700.

INTERNATIONAL ASSOCIATION OF CHIEFS OF POLICE
515 North Washington Street, Alexandria VA 22314. 703/836-6767. **Contact:** Human Resources Manager. **World Wide Web address:** http://www.theiacp.org. **Description:** National headquarters for the trade association representing police chiefs and other law enforcement officials. **Positions advertised include:** Research Fellow; Research Intern.

INTERNATIONAL PAPER COMPANY
34040 Union Camp Drive, P.O. Box 178, Franklin VA 23851. 757/569-4705. **Contact:** Human Resources. **World Wide Web address:** http://www.internationalpaper.com. **Description:** International Paper Company manufactures pulp and paper, packaging, wood products, and a range of specialty products. The company is organized into five business segments: Printing Papers, with principal products that include uncoated papers, coated papers, bristles, and pulp; Packaging, which includes industrial packaging, consumer packaging, and Kraft and specialty papers; Distribution, including the sale of printing papers, graphic arts equipment and supplies, packaging materials, industrial supplies, and office products; Specialty Products, which includes imaging products, specialty panels, nonwovens, chemicals, and minerals; and Forest Products which includes logging and wood products. Founded in 1898, the company has operations in nearly 40 countries. **NOTE:** Search and apply for positions online. **Corporate headquarters location:** Stamford CT. **Operations at this facility include:** This facility manufactures pulp, particleboard, fine paper, and related products. **Listed on:** New York Stock Exchange. **Stock exchange symbol:** IP. **Number of employees worldwide:** 83,000.

ISOMET CORPORATION
5263 Port Royal Road, Springfield VA 22151. 703/321-8301. **Fax:** 703/321-8546. **Contact:** Vivian Hudson, HR Manager. **E-mail address:** isomet@isomet.com. **World Wide Web address:** http://www.isomet.com. **Description:** Designs and manufactures acousto-optic devices that are used in graphic arts, semiconductor wafer inspection, military systems, and biophotonics. **NOTE:** Submit resumes to e-mail address above. **Corporate headquarters location:** This location.

JC COMPUTER SERVICES, INC.
4705 Eisenhower Avenue, Alexandria VA 22304. 703/461-0860. **Fax:** 703/370-4017. **Contact:** Dianne Lamb, Vice President of Administration. **E-mail address:** info@jccs.com. **World Wide Web address:** http://www.jccs.com. **Description:** Provides network support, software development, management consulting, training, and other IT related services. Founded in 1985. **NOTE:** Entry-level positions are offered. **Corporate headquarters location:** This location. **Listed on:** Privately held. **Number of employees at this location:** 50.

JAMES MADISON UNIVERSITY
800 South Main Street, Harrisonburg VA 22807. 540/568-6211. **Fax:** 540/568-1796. **Contact:** Human Resources Department. **E-mail address:** jobs@jmu.edu. **World Wide Web address:** http://www.jmu.edu/humanresources. **Description:** A four-year university offering bachelor's and master's degrees. Approximately 15,000 students attend James Madison University. **NOTE:** Search and apply for positions online. A state application, which can be downloaded from website, must be submitted for each opening. **Positions advertised include:** HelpDesk Consultant; Security Engineer; Instructor; Lecturer; Visiting Assistant Professor; Clinical Instructor; Assistant Professor; Management Lecturer; Coordinator of Information Technology; Capital Gifts Officer; Grant Writer; Director of Development. **Corporate headquarters location:** This location. **Number of employees at this location:** 1,400.

JAMES RIVER COAL COMPANY
901 East Byrd Street, Suite 1600, Richmond VA 23219-4528. 804/780-3000. Fax: 804/780-0643. **Contact:** Human Resources. **World Wide Web address:** http://www.jamesrivercoal.com. **Description:** James River Coal Company mines coal.

JAMESTOWN-YORKTOWN FOUNDATION
P.O. Box 1607, Williamsburg VA 23187-1607. 757/253-4838. **Toll-free phone:** 888/593-4682. **Fax:** 757/253-5299. **Contact:** Debbie Jarvis, Human Resources. **World Wide Web address:** http://www.historyisfun.org. **Description:** An institution of the commonwealth of Virginia that operates Jamestown Settlement and Yorktown Victory Center, museums that preserve and interpret the first English settlement in the New World and the story of the American Revolution. **Number of employees at this location:** 466 full- and part-time staff and 1,100 volunteers.

KAISER PERMANENTE
14139 Potomac Mills Road, Woodbridge VA 22192. 703/490-8400. **Contact:** Human Resources. **World Wide Web address:** http://www.kaiserpermanente.org. **Description:** A nonprofit, public benefit and charitable health care corporation that enrolls members and arranges for their medical, hospital, and related services nationwide. **NOTE:** Search and apply for positions online. Resumes may be sent to Human Resources, 2101 East Jefferson Street, Rockville MD 20849, or faxed to 301/962-4100. **Positions advertised include:** Ambulatory Care Pharmacist; Clinical RN; Phlebotomist.

KAISER PERMANENTE
6501 Loisdale Court, Springfield VA 22150. 703/922-1000. **Contact:** Human Resources. **World Wide Web address:** http://www.kaiserpermanente.org. **Description:** A nonprofit, public benefit and charitable health care corporation that enrolls members and arranges for their medical, hospital, and related services nationwide. **NOTE:** Search and apply for positions online. Resumes may be sent to Human Resources, 2101 East Jefferson Street, Rockville MD 20849, or faxed to 301/962-4100. **Positions advertised include:** Clinical Assistant; Medical Diagnostic Sonographer; Orthopedic Technician.

KEARNEY AND COMPANY
4501 Ford Avenue, Suite 1400, Alexandria VA 22302. 703/931-5600. **Fax:** 703-931-3655. **Contact:** Human Resources. **World Wide Web address:** http://www.kearneyco.com. **Description:** Kearney & Company is a CPA firm founded in 1985 that specializes in providing accounting, audit, and information technology services to the federal government. **Positions advertised Include:** Staff Accountant/Auditor; Audit Manager; Systems Programmer; Information Security Analyst.

LANDAMERICA FINANCIAL GROUP, INC.
LAWYERS TITLE INSURANCE CORPORATION
101 Gateway Centre Parkway, Gateway One, Richmond VA 23235. 804/267-8000. **Contact:** Human Resources. **E-mail address:** corprecruiter@landam.com. **World Wide Web address:** http://www.landam.com. **Description:** Provides title insurance and real estate-related services on commercial and residential transactions in the United States, Canada, the Bahamas, Puerto Rico, and the U.S. Virgin Islands. Lawyers Title Insurance Corporation also provides search and examination services and closing services for a broad-based customer group that includes lenders, developers, real estate brokers, attorneys, and homebuyers. Founded in 1925. **NOTE:** Search and apply for positions online. **Positions advertised include:** State Manager/Area Direct Closing Manager; Operations Analyst; Corporate Legal Secretary. **Corporate headquarters location:** This location. **Other U.S. locations:** Nationwide. **Listed on:** New York Stock Exchange. **Stock exchange symbol:** LFG.

LANDMARK COMMUNICATIONS, INC.
150 West Brambleton Avenue, Norfolk VA 23510. 757/446-2010. **Contact:** Charlie Hill, Vice President of Human Resources. **World Wide Web address:** http://www.landmarkcom.com. **Description:** A privately held media company with interests in newspapers, television broadcasting, cable programming and electronic

publishing. The company operates KLAS-TV Channel 8 (Las Vegas NV) and the NewsChannel 5 Network (Nashville TN). Publishing operations are conducted through Falcon Publishing (Helena MT), which publishes regional recreational guides; and Landmark Specialty Publications (also at this location), which has businesses including Antique Trader Publications, Tuff Stuff Publications, Landmark Specialty Books, and Collector's Super Mall. **Number of employees nationwide:** 5,000.

LANDSTAR GOVERNMENT TRANSPORTATION
6225 Brandon Avenue, Suite 320, Springfield VA 22150. 703/912-6808. **Contact:** Human Resources. **World Wide Web address:** http://www.landstar.com. **Description:** The government transportation services office of one of the largest multimodal transportation service companies in North America. **NOTE:** Resumes should be sent to Landstar System, Inc., P.O. Box 19135, Jacksonville FL 32245. **Corporate headquarters location:** Jacksonville FL. **Other U.S. locations:** Madisonville KY; Romulus MI. **Parent company:** Landstar System, Inc. is divided into specialized freight transportation segments. Its business is a mix of regular accounts and spot hauls. Subsidiaries of the parent company include: Landstar Expedited, Inc.; Landstar Express America, Inc.; Landstar Gemini, Inc.; Landstar Inway, Inc.; Landstar ITCO, Inc.; Landstar Ligon, Inc.; Landstar Poole, Inc.; Landstar Ranger, Inc.; Landstar T.L.C., Inc.; and Landstar Transportation Service, Inc. **Listed on:** NASDAQ. **Stock exchange symbol:** LSTR. **Number of employees nationwide:** 2,500.

LEAR CORPORATION
P.O. Box 181, Strasburg VA 22657. 540/465-3741. **Physical address:** 806 East Queen Street, Strasburg VA 22657. **Contact:** Human Resources. **World Wide Web address:** http://www.lear.com. **Description:** Manufactures and distributes automotive trim and accessories. Nationally, Lear's Automotive Industries division designs and manufactures interior trim systems and blow-molded plastic parts including gas tank shields, radiator coolant overflow reservoirs, and complete door panel assemblies. **NOTE:** Search and apply for positions online. Lear only accepts resumes for current job openings. **Corporate headquarters location:** Southfield MI. **Listed on:** New York Stock Exchange. **Stock exchange symbol:** LEA.

LEGG MASON, INC.
8444 Westpark Drive, Suite 100, McLean VA 22102. 703/821-9100. **Fax:** 703/821-7597. **Contact:** Human Resources. **World Wide Web address:** http://www.leggmason.com. **Description:** Legg Mason is a holding company with subsidiaries engaged in securities brokerage and trading; investment management of mutual funds and individual and institutional accounts; underwriting of corporate and municipal securities and other investment banking activities; sales of annuities and banking services; and the provision of other financial services. The company serves its brokerage clients through 128 offices. **NOTE:** Search and apply for positions online. **Positions advertised include:** Client Services Representative. **Corporate headquarters location:** Baltimore MD. **Subsidiaries include:** Legg Mason Wood Walker, Inc. (Baltimore MD) and Howard, Weil, Labouisse, Friedrichs, Inc. (New Orleans LA). Founded in 1899. **Listed on:** New York Stock Exchange. **Stock exchange symbol:** LM. **Number of employees nationwide:** 4,200.

LEGUM & NORMAN
4401 Ford Avenue, 12th Floor, Alexandria VA 22302. 703/600-6000. **Toll-free phone:** 800/255-3486. **Fax:** 703/848-0982. **Contact:** Personnel. **E-mail address:** careers@legumnorman.com. **World Wide Web address:** http://www.legumnorman.com. **Description:** A privately owned real estate services company offering property and facility management services. **NOTE:** Submit resume online. **Corporate headquarters location:** This location. **Other U.S. locations:** Chicago IL; Ocean City MD.

LEXISNEXIS
701 East Water Street, Charlottesville VA 22902. 434/972-7600. **Toll-free phone:** 800/446-3410. **Contact:** Human Resources. **World Wide Web address:** http://www.lexisnexis.com. **Description:** A publisher of legal, tax, and regulatory information for legal, corporate, government, and academic markets. **NOTE:** Search and apply for positions online. Part-time jobs and second and third shifts are offered. **Special programs:** Internships. **Office hours:** Monday - Friday, 8:00 a.m. - 4:30 p.m. **Other U.S. locations:** Nationwide. **Parent company:** Reed Elsevier Inc.

LIBERTY UNIVERSITY
1971 University Boulevard, Lynchburg VA 24502. 434/582-2000. **Contact:** Laura Wallace, Director of Personnel. **World Wide Web address:** http://www.liberty.edu. **Description:** A four-year liberal arts university offering bachelor's and master's degree programs.

LIFECARE MEDICAL TRANSPORTS, INC.
1170 International Parkway, Fredericksburg VA 22406. 540/752-7721. **Fax:** 540/752-5194. **Contact:** Human Resources. **World Wide Web address:** http://www.lifecare94.com. **Description:** An ambulance service. **NOTE:** Application form available online. **Positions advertised include:** ALS/BLS Field Technician; Administrative Assistant; Billing Coordinator; Service Technician; Wheelchair Van Driver.

LILLIAN VERNON CORPORATION
2600 International Parkway, Virginia Beach VA 23452. 757/427-7700. **Fax:** 757/427-7819. **Recorded job hotline:** 757/427-7901. **Contact:** Staffing Specialist. **E-mail address:** hrvb@lillianvernon.com. **World Wide Web address:** http://www.lillianvernon.com. **Description:** Lillian Vernon is a specialty catalog company that markets gift, household, gardening, decorative, Christmas, and children's products. **Corporate headquarters location:** Rye NY. **Operations at this facility include:** This location is the company's national distribution center. **Listed on:** American Stock Exchange. **Stock exchange symbol:** LVC.

LOCKHEED MARTIN MISSION SYSTEMS
P.O. Box 1339, Manassas VA 20108. 703/367-2371. **Physical address:** 9255 Wellington Road, Manassas VA 20110. **Contact:** Human Resources Director. **World Wide Web address:** http://www.lmco.com. **Description:** Lockheed Martin is an aerospace and technology company engaged in the design, manufacture, and management of systems and products for the fields of space, defense, electronics, communications, information management, energy, and materials. **NOTE:** Search and apply for positions or submit resume online. **Positions advertised include:** Sys Integration Analyst; Electrical Engineer; Sr. Field Technician; Sr. Facilities Engineer; Operations Engineering Manager; Market Research Planner. **Corporate headquarters location:** Bethesda MD. **Operations at this facility include:** This location performs research and development for electronics and aerospace applications. **Listed on:** New York Stock Exchange. **Stock exchange symbol:** LMT.

LORD & TAYLOR
7950 Tysons Corner Center, McLean VA 22102. 703/506-1156. **Contact:** Human Resources. **World Wide Web address:** http://www.lordandtaylor.com. **Description:** A full-line department store carrying clothing, accessories, and home furnishings. **NOTE:** Part-time jobs are offered. Request interview online. **Corporate headquarters location:** New York NY. **Parent company:** The May Department Stores Company. **Listed on:** New York Stock Exchange. **Stock exchange symbol:** MAY. **Number of employees at this location:** 300.

LOUDOUN HOSPITAL CENTER
44045 Riverside Parkway, Leesburg VA 20176. 703/858-6000. **Toll-free phone:** 888/542-8477. **Contact:** Human Resources. **World Wide Web address:** http://www.loudounhospital.org. **Description:** A full-service, general care hospital. **NOTE:** Search and apply for positions online. **Positions advertised include:** Biomedical Technician; Clinical Nurse Specialist; Clinical Systems Analyst; Communication Associate; Lab Assistant; LPN's; Medical Records Specialist; Medical Technologist; Patient Care Tech; Pharmacist; RN's; Radiology Technologist; Security Officer.

LOUDOUN MUTUAL INSURANCE COMPANY
15609 High Street, Waterford VA 20197. 540/882-3232. **Contact:** Human Resources. **Description:** A property and casualty insurance company operating exclusively in Virginia. **Number of employees at this location:** 15.

LUMENOS
1801 North Beauregard Street, Suite 10, Alexandria VA 22311. 888/339-7950. **Contact:** Human Resources. **E-mail address:** jobss@lumenos.com. **World Wide Web address:** http://www.lumenos.com. **Description:** A consumer health care benefits company.

LYNCHBURG GENERAL HOSPITAL
1901 Tate Springs Road, Lynchburg VA 24501. 434/947-3000. **Contact:** Human Resources. **Description:** A 270-bed emergency and critical care center specializing in cardiology, emergency medicine, orthopedics, neurology, and neurosurgery. **NOTE:** Search and apply for positions online. **Positions advertised include:** Radiologic Technologist; Cardiac Sonographer; Phlebotomist II; EEG Tech; Environmental Services Tech; RN; Pharmacist; Pharmacy Tech; Speech Pathologist. **Parent company:** Centra Health.

MCI, INC.
22001 Loudoun County Parkway, Ashburn VA 20147. 703/416-0760. **Contact:** Human Resources. **Description:** A global communications provider with more than 20 million customers, delivering communications connectivity to businesses, governments, and consumers in 150 countries. Founded in 1963. **NOTE:** Search and apply for positions online. **Positions advertised include:** Sr. Accountant; Technical Consultant; Sr. Staff Specialist; Sr. Systems Analyst. **Number of employees worldwide:** 50,000.

M&G ELECTRONICS
889 Sea Hawk Circle, Virginia Beach VA 23452. 757/468-6000. **Fax:** 757/468-5442. **Contact:** Audra Riddle, Human Resources Manager. **World Wide Web address:** http://www.mgelectronic.com. **Description:** Assembles wiring harnesses and installs gauges for boat dashboards. Founded in 1975. **NOTE:** Entry-level positions and second and third shifts are offered. **Corporate headquarters location:** This location. **Other U.S. locations:** NC; SC. **Operations at this facility include:** Administration; Customer Service; Manufacturing; Sales. **Listed on:** Privately held. **Annual sales/revenues:** $21 - $50 million. **Number of employees at this location:** 500. **Number of employees nationwide:** 530.

MHM SERVICES
1593 Spring Hill Road, Suite 610, Vienna VA 22182. 703/749-4600. **Toll-free phone:** 800/416-3649. **Fax:** 703/749-4604. **Contact:** Human Resources. **E-mail address:** jobs@mhm-services.com. **World Wide Web address:** http://www.mhm-services.com. **Description:** Provides behavioral health services. MHM Corrections provides on-site mental health services to private and government agencies including correctional facilities. MHM Solutions specializes in long-term contract staffing for healthcare facilities. MHM Community Care manages behavioral health programs. **NOTE:** Search and apply for positions online. **Positions advertised include:** Accounts Payable Clerk; Executive Assistant; Payroll Specialist. **Corporate headquarters location:** This location. **Other U.S. locations:** Montgomery AL; Atlanta GA; Nashville TN; Monticello FL. **Number of employees nationwide:** 510.

MKS INC.
12450 Fair Lakes Circle, Suite 400, Fairfax VA 22033. 703/803-3343. **Fax:** 703/803-3344. **Contact:** Human Resources. **World Wide Web address:** http://www.mks.com. **Description:** Provides enterprise software configuration management products to enable companies to better manage and control the process of software development. Founded in 1984. **Corporate headquarters location:** Waterloo, Canada. Other U.S. locations: Lombard IL; Burlington MA.

MARKEL CORPORATION
4521 Highwoods Parkway, Glen Allen VA 23060. 804/747-0136. **Fax:** 804/527-3845. **Contact:** Wendy Killeen, Employment Coordinator. **E-mail address:** hr@markelcorp.com. **World Wide Web address:** http://www.markelcorp.com. **Description:** Markets and underwrites specialty insurance products and programs for a variety of niche markets. Markel Corporation provides underwriting for professional and product liability, excess and surplus lines, specialty programs, and specialty personal lines. Professional liability coverage is offered to physicians and health care professionals, insurance companies, directors and officers, attorneys, architects, and engineers. Product liability is provided to manufacturers and distributors. Property/casualty insurance for nonstandard and hard-to-place risks is underwritten on an excess and surplus line basis. Specialty program insurance includes coverages for camps, youth and recreation, health and fitness, and agribusiness organizations, as well as accident and health insurance for colleges. The company also underwrites personal lines insurance for watercraft and motorcycles, and maintains wholesale and retail brokerage operations that produce business primarily for its insurance subsidiaries. **Positions advertised include:** Underwriter; Sr. Claims Examiner; Staff Internal Auditor; Assistant Catastrophe Analyst; Staff Investment Accountant; Pricing Analyst. **Special programs:** Internships. **Corporate headquarters location:** This location. **Listed on:** New York Stock Exchange. **Stock exchange symbol:** MKL. **Number of employees at this location:** 470.

THE MARTIN AGENCY
One Shockoe Plaza, Richmond VA 23219-4132. 804/698-8000. **Contact:** Ana Reilly, Recruiter. **E-mail address:** info_hr@martinagency.com. **World Wide Web address:** http://www.martinagency.com. **Description:** An advertising agency. **Other U.S. locations:** New York NY.

MARTIN FOCUS GROUP
1199 North Fairfax Street, Suite 150, Alexandria VA 22314. 703/519-5800. **Fax:** 703/519-0704. **Contact:** Human Resources. **World Wide Web address:**

http://www.martinfocus.com. **Description:** Designs and conduct focus groups throughout the state. **Other area locations:** Richmond VA; Roanoke VA.

MARY IMMACULATE HOSPITAL
2 Bernadine Drive, Newport News VA 23602. 757/886-6600. **Contact:** Human Resources. **World Wide Web address:** http://www.bonsecours.org. **Description:** A 110-bed, acute care, general hospital. Mary Immaculate Hospital offers a Discovery Care Center (child care facility) and two MedCare centers providing walk-in general care. This hospital has three centers to aid its community: St. Francis Nursing Center, which provides 10 beds for skilled care and 105 beds for intermediate care; Kiosk, which provides free weekly blood pressure screenings; and Family Focus, which provides support for parents and families. Founded in 1952. **NOTE:** Search and apply for positions online. **Positions advertised include:** Admissions Nurse; Clinical Coordinator; CNA's; Critical Care Educator; Histotechnologist; LPN's; Nurse Manager; Radiology Therapist; Respiratory Therapist. **Parent company:** Bon Secours Health System.

MARYMOUNT UNIVERSITY
2807 North Glebe Road, Arlington VA 22207-4299. 703/284-1680. **Contact:** Human Resource Services. **World Wide Web address:** http://www.marymount.edu. **Description:** A coeducational university affiliated with the Catholic Church, enrolling approximately 2,200 students in undergraduate studies and 1,600 students in graduate studies. Marymount University offers associate's, bachelor's, and master's degrees. The university's various degrees are offered in the schools of Arts and Sciences, Business Administration, Education and Human Services, and Nursing. **NOTE:** Search and apply for positions online. **Positions advertised include:** Library Specialist; Director of Residence Life; Assistant/Associate Professor of Nursing; Physical Plant Director; Assistant Professor of Graphic Design; Nursing Lab and Technology Coordinator.

MARYVIEW MEDICAL CENTER
3636 High Street, Portsmouth VA 23707. 757/398-2200. **Contact:** Human Resources Manager. **World Wide Web address:** http://www.bonsecours.org. **Description:** A 346-bed acute care hospital, which includes a 54-bed Behavioral Medicine Center. **NOTE:** Search and apply for positions online. **Positions advertised include:** Admission Nurse; CNA's; Education Coordinator; Executive Director, Foundation; HR Assistant; Insurance Verifier; Manager of Staffing and Administrative Services; Radiation Therapist; Radiology Technologist; RN's; Respiratory Therapist. **Parent company:** Bon Secours Health System.

McKESSON MEDICAL GROUP
8741 Landmark Road, Richmond VA 23228. 804/264-7500. **Fax:** 804/264-7679. **Contact:** Human Resources. **E-mail address:** webmail@mckgenmed.com. **World Wide Web address:** http://www.mckgenmed.com. **Description:** A medical equipment wholesaler with distribution and service centers in 24 states. **NOTE:** Search and apply for positions online. **Positions advertised include:** Accountant; Pharmacy Technician; Vice President, Acute Care Sales; Inventory Analyst; Product manager, Laboratory Marketing; contract Associate. **Corporate headquarters location:** This location. **Parent company:** McKesson Corporation. **Listed on:** New York Stock Exchange. **Stock exchange symbol:** MCK. **Number of employees nationwide:** 4,000.

MEDECO SECURITY LOCKS, INC.
P.O. Box 3075, Salem VA 24153-0330. 540/380-5000. **Physical address:** 3625 Allegheny Drive, Salem VA 24153. **Fax:** 540/380-1791. **Contact:** Human Resources. **E-mail address:** employment@medeco.com. **World Wide Web address:** http://www.medeco.com. **Description:** A manufacturer of high-security locks. **NOTE:** Search and apply for positions online. **Positions advertised include:** Marketing Assistant; Electrical Engineer, Product Development. **Parent company:** ASSA ABLOY Group.

MERCER HUMAN RESOURCE CONSULTING
4600 Cox Road, Suite 400, Glen Allen VA 23060. 804/747-0275. **Fax:** 804/527-2428. **Contact:** Human Resources. **World Wide Web address:** http://www.mercerhr.com. **Description:** One of the world's largest actuarial and human resources management consulting firms, providing advice to organizations on all aspects of employee/management relationships. Services include retirement, health and welfare, performance and rewards, communication, investment, human resources administration, risk, finance and insurance, and health care provider consulting. **NOTE:** Search and apply for positions online. **Positions advertised include:** Actuarial Analyst; Actuarial Intern. **Corporate headquarters location:** New York NY. **Parent company:** Marsh & McLennan Companies, Inc. **Number of employees worldwide:** 15,000.

MERCK & COMPANY, INC.
P.O. Box 7, Elkton VA 22827. 540/298-1211. **Contact:** Human Resources. **World Wide Web address:** http://www.merck.com. **Description:** Merck is a worldwide organization engaged in discovering, developing, producing, and marketing products for the maintenance of health and the environment. Products include human and animal pharmaceuticals and chemicals sold to the health care, oil exploration, food processing, textile, paper, and other industries. Merck also runs an ethical drug mail-order marketing business. **Positions advertised include:** Manufacturing Engineer/Chemist/Biologist. **Corporate headquarters location:** Whitehouse Station NJ. **Operations at this facility include:** This location manufactures pharmaceuticals. **Listed on:** New York Stock Exchange. **Stock exchange symbol:** MRK.

METRO MACHINE CORPORATION
P.O. Box 1860, Norfolk VA 23501. 757/543-6801. **Contact:** Don Fisher, Personnel Director. **World Wide Web address:** http://www.memach.com. **Description:** Engaged in shipbuilding and repair. **Other U.S. locations:** Philadelphia PA; Erie PA.

METROCALL WIRELESS, INC.
6910 Richmond Highway, Alexandria VA 22306. 703/660-6677. **Contact:** Human Resources. **World Wide Web address:** http://www.metrocall.com. **Description:** A leading provider of local and regional paging services in the Northeast, mid-Atlantic, and southeast regions of the United States, as well as California, Nevada, and Arizona. Metrocall also provides nationwide wireless communications for pagers, data terminals, personal computers, and personal digital assistants. **NOTE:** Search and apply for positions online. **Positions advertised include:** Senior Manager, Government Sales; Creative Design Manager; PBX Administrator; State and Local Tax Manager; Senior Network Engineer; Systems Sales Specialist. **Corporate headquarters location:** This location. **Number of employees nationwide:** 2,500.

MITEL, INC.
MITEL TELECOMMUNICATIONS SYSTEMS
205 Van Buren Street, Suite 400, Herndon VA 20170-5336. 703/318-7020. **Fax:** 703/736-3168. **Contact:** Human Resources. **World Wide Web address:** http://www.mitel.com. **Description:** A leading global provider of enterprise and small business communications solutions and services, including advanced voice, video and data communications platforms, desktop phones and Internet appliances, intuitive applications for customer relationship management and mobility, messaging and multimedia collaboration. The company now focuses its efforts on Internet Protocol (IP) and the benefits it enables through the convergence of voice, video and data over a single broadband network. Through strategic relationships, Mitel Networks can offer businesses the choice and flexibility of an end-to-end converged Local Area Network or seamless interoperability with any existing infrastructure. **NOTE:** Search and apply for positions online. **Corporate headquarters location:** Canada. **Other U.S. locations:** Nationwide. **International locations:** Worldwide. **Number of employees worldwide:** 2,000.

MODIS
2809 Emerywood Parkway, Suite 380, Richmond VA 23294. 804/672-7558. **Fax:** 804/672-1386. **Contact:** Human Resources. **E-mail address:** resume@modisit.com. **World Wide Web address:** http://www.modisit.com. **Description:** Provides information technology resource management in the areas of staff augmentation, direct placement, and project management. **NOTE:** Search and apply for positions online. **Positions advertised include:** Java Developer; Data Warehouse Supervisor; ETL Specialist; Cognos Reporting Specialist; Business Systems Analyst; Configuration/Change Management Analyst; Unisys Testing Analyst; Middleware Quality Analyst; Client Server Developer; Technical Writer/Editor. **Corporate headquarters location:** Jacksonville FL. **Other U.S. locations:** Nationwide. **Parent company:** MPS Group, Inc.

MOLINS RICHMOND, INC.
3900 Carolina Avenue, Richmond VA 23222. 804/329-9081. **Fax:** 804/321-5862. **Contact:** Human Resources. **E-mail address:** molins.richmond@molins.com. **World Wide Web address:** http://www.molins.com. **Description:** A specialist engineering company that manufactures equipment for the tobacco, food processing, and consumer goods industries. Founded in 1931. **Number of employees at this location:** 130.

MOOG COMPONENTS GROUP
1213 North Main Street, Blacksburg VA 24060. 540/552-3011. **Fax:** 540/557-6400. **Contact:** Human Resources. **E-mail address:** mvaden@moog.com. **World Wide Web address:** http://www.moog.com. **Description:** Manufactures motion control and data-transmission devices; principal products are electrical and fiber-optic slip rings, brushless DC motors, and electromechanical actuators. Parent company: MOOG Inc.

MOTIENT CORPORATION
10802 Parkridge Boulevard, Reston VA 20191. 703/758-6000. **Contact:** Human Resources. **E-mail address:** resume@motient.com. **World Wide Web address:** http://www.motient.com. **Description:** Provides wireless communications services and solutions nationwide including satellite mobile messaging systems, wireless e-mail services, and two-way wireless data services. **NOTE:** Send resumes to Motient Corporation, Attn: Human Resources, 300 Knightsbridge Parkway, Lincolnshire IL 60069 or via e-mail address above. **Corporate headquarters location:** Lincolnshire IL. **Number of employees nationwide:** 470.

MOUNT REGIS CENTER
405 Kimball Avenue, Salem VA 24153. 540/389-4761. **Toll-free phone:** 800/477-3447. **Contact:** Human Resources. **World Wide Web address:** http://www.mtregis.com. **Description:** A drug and alcohol treatment facility. Mount Regis Center has a 25-bed residential treatment center; day and outpatient services are available. Founded in 1947.

NCI INFORMATION SYSTEMS, INC.
11730 Plaza America Drive, Reston VA 20190. 703/707-6900. **Toll-free phone:** 888/409-5457. **Fax:** 703/707-6901. **Contact:** Human Resources. **E-mail address:** contactus@nciinc.com. **World Wide Web address:** http://www.nciinc.com. **Description:** Provides both government agencies and commercial clients with IT solutions and services. NCI Information Systems is comprised of six business units: Enterprise Management and Support; Systems Development and Integration; Systems Engineering; Risk Management; Electronic Data Management; and Facilities Management. Founded in 1986. **NOTE:** Search and apply for positions online. **Positions advertised include:** Capture Manager; Technical Specialist, Principal; Technical Writer. **Corporate headquarters location:** This location. Other U.S. locations: AL; AZ; CO; MI; NJ; GA; IL; MD; OH; TN.

NEC AMERICA INC.
14040 Park Center Road, Herndon VA 22071. 703/834-4000. **Fax:** 703/437-7178. **Contact:** Human Resources. **E-mail address:** resumes@hn.va.nec.com. **World Wide Web address:** http://www.nec.com. **Description:** Provides solutions for broadband networking and mobile Internet with focus on IT-network integrated solutions and semiconductors. **NOTE:** Search and apply for positions online. **Positions advertised include:** Program Manager. **Operations at this facility include:** Headquarters for the Optical Network Systems Division, which oversees the development, sales, installation, and service of optical telecommunications products.

NVR, INC.
7601 Lewinsville Road, Suite 300, McLean VA 22102. 703/761-2000. **Fax:** 703/761-2030. **Contact:** Human Resources. **E-mail address:** info@nvrinc.com. **World Wide Web address:** http://www.nvrinc.com. **Description:** A national homebuilder and mortgage company. Founded in 1948. **NOTE:** Entry-level positions and part-time jobs are offered. Search and apply for positions online. **Positions advertised include:** Audit Supervisor; Accounting Operational Auditor; Human Resources Manager; Sr. Human Resources Representative. **Special programs:** Internships; Training; Co-ops; Summer Jobs. **Office hours:** Monday - Friday, 8:00 a.m. - 5:00 p.m. **Corporate headquarters location:** This location. **Other U.S. locations:** DE; MD; NC; NJ; NY; OH; PA; SC; TN. **Listed on:** American Stock Exchange. **Stock exchange symbol:** NVR. **Annual sales/revenues:** More than $100 million. **Number of employees at this location:** 75. **Number of employees nationwide:** 3,500.

NSGDATACOM, INC.
3863 Centerview Drive, Chantilly VA 20151-3232. 703/793-2001. **Fax:** 703/793-2001. **Contact:** Human Resources. **E-mail address:** hr@nsgdata.com. **World Wide Web address:** http://www.nsgdata.com. **Description:** Designs, manufactures, sells, and supports a range of voice and data communication products for wire-line and wireless networks. **NOTE:** Search and apply for positions online. **Positions advertised include:** Senior Sales Executive. **Corporate headquarters location:** This location. **Other U.S. locations:** Fredrick MD. **International locations:** United Kingdom; Hong Kong. **Number of employees worldwide:** 295.

NATIONAL ALLIANCE FOR THE MENTALLY ILL (NAMI)
2107 Wilson Boulevard, Suite 300, Arlington VA 22201. 703/524-7600. **Contact:** Human Resources. **World Wide Web address:** http://www.nami.org. **Description:** Provides a wide range of services to families living with mental illness including support groups and special interest networks; up-to-date, scientific information through

publications; a toll-free helpline; annual Mental Illness Awareness Week campaigns; advocacy for services; and support for research. Founded in 1979.

NATIONAL AUTOMOBILE DEALERS ASSOCIATION
8400 Westpark Drive, McLean VA 22102. 703/821-7000. **Contact:** Human Resources. **E-mail address:** recruiter@nada.org. **World Wide Web address:** http://www.nada.org. **Description:** A trade organization representing nearly 20,000 new car and truck dealerships. The association publishes a used car guide for dealers that offers insurance information and retirement plans for dealerships. **Corporate headquarters location:** This location. **Operations at this facility include:** Administration; Research and Development; Sales; Service. **Number of employees at this location:** 400.

NATIONAL FRUIT PRODUCT COMPANY, INC.
550 Fairmont Avenue, Winchester VA 22601. 540/662-3401. **Contact:** Herb Glass, Corporate Human Resources Manager. **E-mail address:** hglass@nfpc.com. **World Wide Web address:** http://www.whitehousefoods.com. **Description:** A food processor. National Fruit primarily produces apple juice, applesauce, vinegar, apple butter, apple slices, and pie fillings. Positions advertised include: Quality Assurance Manager. **Corporate headquarters location:** This location. **Operations at this facility include:** Administration; Manufacturing; Research and Development; Sales. **Listed on:** Privately held. **Number of employees at this location:** 500. **Number of employees nationwide:** 1,000.

NATIONAL RURAL ELECTRIC COOPERATIVE ASSOCIATION
4301 Wilson Boulevard, Arlington VA 22203-1860. 703/907-5500. **Contact:** Jennifer Anderson, Human Resources. **World Wide Web address:** http://www.nreca.org. **Description:** The national organization representing the interests of cooperative electric utilities and the consumers they serve. NRECA has nearly 1,000 member cooperatives that serve 36 million people in 47 states. Most of the 875 distribution systems are consumer-owned cooperatives; some are public power districts. NRECA is an advocate for consumer-owned cooperatives on energy and operational issues as well as rural community and economic development. Founded in 1942. **NOTE:** Search and apply for positions online. **Positions advertised include:** Executive Assistant, Business Development; Manager, Employee Relations and Service, HR; Senior Marketing Associate; Senior Writer, Communications; Marketing Communications Senior Specialist; Senior Advisor, Business Integrator and Production Support; Systems Integrator, IT; Operations Manager, Education and Training. **Corporate headquarters location:** This location.

NATIONAL RURAL UTILITIES COOPERATIVE FINANCE CORPORATION
2201 Cooperative Way, Herndon VA 20171. 703/709-6700. **Contact:** Human Resources. **World Wide Web address:** http://www.nrucfc.org. **Description:** A nonprofit financial institution owned by more than 1,000 rural electric systems and related organizations. National Rural Utilities Cooperative Finance Corporation offers its members/owners a variety of loan, investment, service, and specialized financing options to supplement the loan programs of the Rural Utilities Service of the United States Department of Agriculture. **NOTE:** Search and apply for positions or submit resume online. **Positions advertised include:** Commercial Lender; External Reporting Assistant; Information Technologies Analyst; Senior Communications/Writer. **Corporate headquarters location:** This location. **Number of employees nationwide:** 1,040.

NATIONAL SCIENCE FOUNDATION
4201 Wilson Boulevard, Arlington VA 22230. 703/292-5111. **Contact:** Human Resources. **World Wide Web address:** http://www.nsf.gov. **Description:** An independent agency of the U.S. government, established in 1950, that provides funding for scientific and engineering research and education. **NOTE:** Search and apply for positions online. **Positions advertised include:** Equal Employment Manager; Program Director, Biological Sciences; Management Analyst; Director, Division of Chemical and Transport Systems; Director, Division of Ocean Sciences; Program Director for the Developmental and Learning Sciences Program; Program Director for Electronics, Photonics, and Device Technologies; Physical Scientist; Science Education Administrator.

NATIONAL WILDLIFE FEDERATION
11100 Wildlife Center Drive, Reston VA 20190-5362. **Toll-free phone:** 800/822-9919. **Contact:** Human Resources. **World Wide Web address:** http://www.nwf.org. **Description:** A nonprofit, conservation society dedicated to preserving the nation's wildlife. Founded in 1936. **NOTE:** Search and apply for positions online. **Special programs:** Internships. **Internship information:** Cover letters and resumes should be directed to 1400 16th Street NW, Washington DC 20036. **Corporate headquarters location:** This location. **Other U.S. locations:** Washington DC; Atlanta GA; Winchester VA. **Number of employees at this location:** 300. **Number of employees nationwide:** 500.

NATIONWIDE HOMES, INC.
1100 Rives Road, P.O. Box 5511, Martinsville VA 24115. 276/632-7100. **Toll-free phone:** 800/216-7001. **Fax:** 276/666-2537. **Contact:** John Adams, Human Resources Director. **World Wide Web address:** http://www.nationwide-homes.com. **Description:** Builder of modular single-family homes, commercial structures, multi-family residences, and remodeling additions. **NOTE:** Entry-level positions are offered. **Special programs:** Apprenticeships; Summer Jobs. **Office hours:** Monday - Friday, 8:00 a.m. - 5:00 p.m. **Listed on:** Privately held. **President/CEO:** Ronald Evans. **Annual sales/revenues:** $21 - $50 million. **Number of employees at this location:** 450.

NAUTILUS INTERNATIONAL INC.
709 Powerhouse Road, Independence VA 24348. 276/773-2881. **Contact:** Human Resources Manager. **World Wide Web address:** http://www.nautilus.com. **Description:** Manufactures a variety of exercise equipment including the Nautilus Time Machine and Personal Circuit lines. Founded in 1974.

NESTLE USA, INC.
201 Airside Drive, Danville VA 24540. 434/822-4000. **Contact:** Human Resources Manager. **World Wide Web address:** http://www.nestleusa.com. **Description:** Produces food and beverage products under various brand names including Nestle, Stouffer's, Ortega, and Taster's Choice. **NOTE:** Search and apply for positions online. **Parent company:** Nestle S.A. **Number of employees nationwide:** 21,000.

NEWSPAPER ASSOCIATION OF AMERICA
1921 Gallows Road, Suite 600, Vienna VA 22182. 703/902-1600. **Fax:** 703/917-0636. **Contact:** Human Resources. **E-mail address:** jobs@naa.org. **World Wide Web address:** http://www.naa.org. **Description:** A nonprofit, professional association dedicated to the marketing, public policy, diversity, industry development, and other operations of the newspaper publishing industry. **NOTE:** search and apply for positions online. **Positions advertised include:** Vice President, Media Relations.

NEXTEL COMMUNICATIONS
2001 Edmund Halley Drive, Reston VA 20191. 703/433-4000. **Contact:** Human Resources. **World Wide Web address:** http://www.nextel.com. **Description**: A leading provider of fully integrated wireless communications services with the largest all-digital wireless network in the country covering thousands of communities across the United States. **NOTE:** Search and apply for positions online. **Positions advertised include:** Senior Recruiter; Counsel, Public Sector; Systems Manager Operations; Sr. Analyst Ops; Staff Attorney; Senior Project Manager; Senior Analyst, Revenue Assurance; Engineer IV, Network; Network Planner; Manager, Engineering Services; Director, Channel Marketing; Sr. Business Systems Analyst; Pricing Analyst. **Corporate headquarters location:** This location. **Listed on:** NASDAQ. **Stock exchange symbol:** NXTL. **Number of employees nationwide:** 17,000.

NISSAN MOTOR COMPANY
196 Van Buren Street, Suite 400, Herndon VA 20170. 703/318-4400. **Contact:** Human Resources. **World Wide Web address:** http://www.nissandriven.com. **Description:** A manufacturer of automobiles. **NOTE:** Search and apply for positions online. **Listed on:** NASDAQ. **Stock exchange symbol:** NSANY.

NOLAND COMPANY
2700 Warwick Boulevard, Newport News VA 23607. 757/928-9000. **Fax:** 757/928-9170. **Contact:** Human Resources. **World Wide Web address:** http://www.noland.com. **Description**: Noland is an independent wholesale distributor of mechanical equipment and supplies to the construction industry and manufacturing, with nearly 100 locations across the eastern and southern United States. **Positions advertised include:** Outside Sales Professional. **Listed on:** NASDAQ. **Stock exchange symbol:** NOLD. **Number of employees nationwide:** 1,400.

NORFOLK SOUTHERN CORPORATION
3 Commercial Place, Norfolk VA 23510-9227. 757/629-2600. **Recorded jobline:** 800/214-3609. **Contact:** Manager of Recruiting. **E-mail address:** careers@nscorp.com. **World Wide Web address:** http://www.nscorp.com. **Description:** A railroad freight transportation and holding company controlling Norfolk Southern Railway, and subsidiaries. The company's rail lines extend 21,800 miles through 22 eastern states, the District of Columbia and the province of Ontario. **NOTE:** Entry-level positions are offered. **Special programs:** Internships. **Corporate headquarters location:** This location. **Other U.S. locations:** Nationwide. **Listed on:** New York Stock Exchange. **Stock exchange symbol:** NSC. **Annual sales/revenues:** More than $100 million. **Number of employees nationwide:** 28,000.

NORFOLK STATE UNIVERSITY
700 Park Avenue, Norfolk VA 23504. 757/823-8600. **Fax:** 757/823-2078. **Contact:** Human Resources. **World Wide Web address:** http://www.nsu.edu. **Description:** A university offering undergraduate and graduate programs. The university has an enrollment of approximately 8,000. Founded in 1979.

NORSHIPCO
750 West Berkley Avenue, Norfolk VA 23523. 757/494-4000. **Fax:** 757/494-4030. **Recorded jobline:** 757/494-2964. **Contact:** Human Resources Manager. **E-mail address:** human_resources@norshipco.com. **World Wide Web address:** http://www.norshipco.com. **Description:** Performs non-nuclear ship repair, modernization, conversion, and overhaul. **Positions advertised include:** Outside Machinist. **Parent company:** United States Marine Repair.

NORTHERN VIRGINIA COMMUNITY COLLEGE
4001 Wakefield Chapel Road, Annandale VA 22003-3796. 703/323-3124. **Contact:** Diane Kownacki, Director of Human Resources. **E-mail address:** resumes@nvcc.edu. **World Wide Web address:** http://www.nv.cc.va.us/hr. **Description:** A two-year, nonprofit college offering transfer and occupational/technical programs. Northern Virginia Community College has five campuses and an Extended Learning Institute. **NOTE:** Second and third shifts are offered. A Virginia State Employment Application is required to apply for all positions. Search for positions online. **Special programs:** Training. **Office hours:** Monday - Friday, 8:30 a.m. - 5:00 p.m. **Corporate headquarters location:** This location. **Number of employees nationwide:** 600.

NORTHERN VIRGINIA COMMUNITY HOSPITAL
601 South Carlin Springs Road, Arlington VA 22204-1096. 703/671-1200. **Fax:** 703/578-2281. **Contact:** Human Resources. **World Wide Web address:** http://www.nvchospital.com. **Description:** A 164-bed hospital with emergency, intensive care, and long-term acute care facilities. The hospital's services include an outpatient surgery center offering eye laser treatment, a gastroenterology and GI endoscopic lab, a pain management center, and a urodynamics lab; a wide range of urological services; MRI and CAT scans; a cardiac catheterization lab; a sleep disorders lab; and inpatient and partial-day psychiatric programs. Founded in 1961. **NOTE:** Search and apply for positions online. **Number of employees at this location:** 550. **Parent company:** Columbia/HCA Healthcare.

NORTHROP GRUMMAN INFORMATION TECHNOLOGY
2411 Dulles Corner Park, Suite 500, Herndon VA 20171. 703/713-4000. **Contact:** Human Resources. **World Wide Web address:** http://www.northgrum.com. **Description**: A provider of IT, systems engineering, and systems integration for the Department of Defense, national intelligence, federal civilian and state/local agencies and commercial customers, with solutions that support simulation and training, information assurance, combat systems, software engineering, weather systems, military intelligence, enterprise systems, secure communications, and space systems. **NOTE:** Search and apply for positions online. **Positions advertised include:** Director, Data Center Consolidation; Business Process Writer; Manager, Business Systems; Proposal Analyst; Technical Product Support Rep; IS Technologist; Manager, Proposal Analysis. **Corporate headquarters location:** Los Angeles CA. **Parent company:** Northrop Grumman Corporation manufactures military aircraft, commercial aircraft parts, radar equipment, and electronic systems. Northrop Grumman has developed the B-2 Stealth Bomber, as well as parts for the F/A-18 and the Boeing 747. Other operations include computer systems development for management and scientific applications. **Listed on:** New York Stock Exchange. **Stock exchange symbol:** NOC. **Number of employees worldwide:** 22,500.

NORTHROP GRUMMAN NEWPORT NEWS
4101 Washington Avenue, Newport News VA 23607. 757/380-4878. **Fax:** 757/380-3114. **Recorded jobline:** 757/380-2142. **Contact:** Human Resources. **World Wide Web address:** http://www.nn.northropgrumman.com/index.asp. **Description:** Engaged in the design, construction, repair, overhaul, and refueling of conventional and nuclear-powered merchant and naval surface ships and submarines. **Positions advertised include:** Designer; Medical Records Supervisor: Engineer; Rigger; VCS Product Planner; Operations Coordinator; Construction Manager; Sr. Engineer; Project Engineer; Financial Analyst. **Corporate headquarters location:** This location. **Parent company:** Northrop Grumman. **Operations at this facility include:** Administration;

Manufacturing; Research and Development. **Listed on:** New York Stock Exchange. **Stock exchange symbol:** NOC. **Number of employees at this location:** 17,000.

NOVA CHEMICALS
5100 Bainbridge Boulevard, Chesapeake VA 23320. 757/494-2500. **Recorded jobline:** 888/371-0161. **Contact:** Dina Beimler, Personnel Manager. **World Wide Web address:** http://www.novachem.com. **Description:** Manufactures crystal, impact, and specialty polystyrene. **NOTE:** Search and apply for positions online. Unsolicited resumes not accepted. **Corporate headquarters location:** Calgary Canada. **Listed on:** New York Stock Exchange. **Stock exchange symbol:** NCX. **Number of employees at this location:** 240.

NTELOS INC.
401 Spring Lane, Suite 300, P.O. Box 1990, Waynesboro VA 22980. 540/946-3500. **Contact:** Human Resources. **World Wide Web address:** http://www.ntelos.com. **Description**: An integrated communications provider. NTELOS provides products and services to customers in Virginia, West Virginia, Kentucky, Tennessee and North Carolina, including wireless digital PCS, dial-up Internet access, high-speed DSL, and local and long distance telephone services. **NOTE:** Unsolicited resumes not accepted. Search and apply for positions online. **Positions advertised include:** Corporate Tax Analyst. **Corporate headquarters location:** This location.

OLD DOMINION ANIMAL HEALTH CENTER
6719 Lowell Avenue, McLean VA 22101. 703/356-5582. **Contact:** Human Resources. **World Wide Web address:** http://www.odahcenter.com. **Description:** An animal hospital offering both routine and emergency care.

OLD DOMINION ELECTRIC COOPERATIVE
4201 Dominion Boulevard, Suite 300, Glen Allen VA 23060. 804/747-0592. **Contact:** Human Resources. **World Wide Web address:** http://www.odec.com. **Description:** A nonprofit wholesale power supply cooperative. Old Dominion Electric Cooperative provides wholesale electric service to 12 member distribution cooperatives engaged in the retail sale of power to member-consumers located in Virginia, Maryland, Delaware, and West Virginia. **NOTE:** Search and apply for positions online. Unsolicited resumes not accepted. **Corporate headquarters location:** This location. **Number of employees nationwide:** 70.

OLD DOMINION UNIVERSITY
Hampton Boulevard, Norfolk VA 23529. 757/683-3000. **Contact:** Human Resources. **World Wide Web address:** http://www.odu.edu. **Description:** A four-year university offering bachelor's, master's, and doctoral degree programs. Approximately 21,000 students are enrolled. Founded in 1930. **NOTE:** Search and apply for positions online. Only online applications accepted.

OLIFF & BERRIDGE, PLC
277 South Washington Street, Suite 500, Alexandria VA 22314. 703/836-6400. **Fax:** 703/836-2787. **Contact:** Human Resources. **E-mail address:** hr@oliff.com. **World Wide Web address:** http://www.oliff.com. **Description:** An intellectual property law firm. Founded in 1983. **Positions advertised include:** Floater Patent Secretary; Paralegal. **Corporate headquarters location:** This location.

OLYMPUS IMPORTED AUTO PARTS CORPORATION
5168 Eisenhower Avenue, Alexandria VA 22304. 703/370-0850. **Fax:** 703/370-8399. **Contact:** Human Resources. **World Wide Web address:** http://www.olyonline.com. **Description:** Supplies automobile replacement parts.

OPTICAL CABLE CORPORATION
5290 Concourse Drive, Roanoke VA 24019. 540/265-0690. **Fax:** 540/265-0724. **Contact:** Human Resources. **World Wide Web address:** http://www.occfiber.com. **Description:** Manufactures tight-buffered fiber-optic cables for high bandwidth transmission of data, video, and audio communications. **Corporate headquarters location:** This location. **Listed on:** NASDAQ. **Stock exchange symbol:** OCCF.

ORACLE CORPORATION
1900 Oracle Way, Reston VA 20190-4735. 703/478-9000. **Fax:** 703/318-6340. **Contact:** Clancy Bucy, Human Resources. **World Wide Web address:** http://www.oracle.com. **Description:** Designs and manufactures database and information management software for businesses and provides consulting services. **Special programs:** Training. **NOTE:** Search and apply for positions online. **Corporate headquarters location:** Redwood Shores CA. **Other area locations:** Chesapeake VA; Richmond VA. **Other U.S. locations:** Nationwide. **Listed on:** NASDAQ. **Stock exchange symbol:** ORCL.

ORBIMAGE
21700 Atlantic Boulevard, Dulles VA 20166. 703/931-5600. **Fax:** 703/931-3655. **Contact:** Human Resources. **E-Mail address:** recruiter@orbimage.com. **World Wide Web address:** http://www.orbimage.com. **Description:** Orbimage is a leading global provider of geospatial imagery products and services, with a constellation of digital remote sensing satellites complemented by data from other optical, aerial and radar sources. **NOTE:** Search and apply for positions on Website.

ORBITAL SCIENCES CORPORATION
21839 Atlantic Boulevard, Dulles VA 20166. 703/406-5000. **Fax:** 703/406-5511. **Contact:** Emily Bender, Employment Manager. **E-mail address:** staffing@orbital.com. **World Wide Web address:** http://www.orbital.com. **Description:** Orbital Sciences Corporation develops and manufactures small space and missile systems for commercial, civil government and military customers. The company's primary products are satellites and launch vehicles. Orbital also offers space-related technical services to government agencies and develops and builds satellite-based transportation management systems for public transit agencies and private vehicle fleet operators. Founded in 1982. **Positions advertised include:** Test Engineer, I&T; Senior Scientist, RF; Principal Finance Analyst; Manager, Mechanical Analysis Group; Senior Manufacturing Development Specialist; Senior Manufacturing Technician. **Special programs:** Internships. **Corporate headquarters location:** This location. Other U.S. locations: AZ; MD; CA. **Listed on:** New York Stock Exchange. **Stock exchange symbol:** ORB. **Number of employees worldwide:** 2,200.

THE ORKAND CORPORATION
7799 Leesburg Pike, Suite 700 North, Falls Church VA 22043-2499. 703/610-4200. **Contact:** Recruitment Manager. **E-mail address:** resumes@orkand.com. **World Wide Web address:** http://www.orkand.com. **Description:** Develops information systems under government contracts and for private industry. Founded in 1970. **NOTE:** Search and apply for positions online. **Positions advertised include:** Director of Business Development; Graphic Designer/Production Coordinator; Manager of Corporate Communications; Proposal Manager; Project Accountant; **Corporate headquarters location:** This location. **Other U.S. locations:** Memphis TN; Norman OK.

OVERNITE TRANSPORTATION, INC.
P.O. Box 1216, Richmond VA 23218-1216. 804/231-8000. **Physical address:** 1000 Semmes Avenue, Richmond VA 23224. **Fax:** 804/291-5104. **Recorded jobline:** 804/291-5627. **Contact:** Staffing Services. **World Wide Web address:** http://www.overnite.com. **Description:** A trucking company that transports goods nationwide. NOTE: Search for positions online. Mail for fax resume. **Positions advertised include:** Customer Service Associate. **Other U.S. locations:** Nationwide. **Parent company:** Overnite Corporation. **Listed on:** NASDAQ. **Stock exchange symbol:** OVNT. **Annual sales/revenues:** More than $100 million.

OWENS & MINOR
P.O. Box 27626, Richmond VA 23060. 804/747-9794. **Fax:** 804/270-7281. **Contact:** Erika Davis, Vice President of Human Resources. **World Wide Web address:** http://www.owens-minor.com. **Description:** One of the nation's largest wholesale distributors of national branded medical, surgical, and nontraditional supplies. The distribution centers of Owens & Minor serve hospitals, integrated health care systems, primary care facilities, and group purchasing organizations throughout the United States. The company also helps customers control health care costs and improve inventory management through services in supply chain management, logistics, and technology. **NOTE:** Search and apply for positions online. **Positions advertised include:** Manager, Clinical Technology Implementation; OMSolutions Analyst; Compensation Analyst; Data Coordinator; Director, Internal Audit; Consulting Director, Supply Chain Integration. **Special programs:** Internships. **Corporate headquarters location:** This location. **Other U.S. locations:** Nationwide. **Listed on:** New York Stock Exchange. **Stock exchange symbol:** OMI. **Annual sales/revenues:** More than $100 million. **Number of employees at this location:** 3,000.

PEC SOLUTIONS, INC.
12730 Fair Lakes Circle, Fairfax VA 22033. 703/679-4900. **Fax:** 703/679-4901. **Contact:** Human Resources. **Description:** A professional services firm that helps Government clients use information technology to improve mission performance. The company provides customized solutions for Homeland Security, criminal justice and intelligence, defense, and civilian agencies within the Federal Government and first responders and other components at state and local levels. **NOTE:** Search and apply for positions online. **Positions advertised include:** CMR Operations Engineer; Computer Technician; Contracts Administrator; Database Administrator; J2EE Software Engineer; Lotus Notes Developer.

PSI INTERNATIONAL, INC.
10306 Eaton Place, Suite 400, Fairfax VA 22030. 703/352-8700. **Fax:** 703/352-8236. **Contact:** Human Resources Representative. **E-mail address:** jobs@psiint.com. **World Wide Web address:** http://www.psiint.com. **Description:** Provides information technology solutions to government and private sectors, focusing on scientific, pharmaceutical, biotech and regulatory industries worldwide. The company specializes in integrating information technology services with subject matter expertise in health and social sciences. Founded in 1977. **Positions advertised include:** Business Development Manager. **Corporate headquarters location:** This location. **Listed on:** Privately held. **Number of employees at this location:** 25. **Number of employees nationwide:** 175.

PEEBLES DEPARTMENT STORES
One Peebles Street, South Hill VA 23970. 434/447-5297. **Contact:** Tim Moyer, Training and Recruitment Director. **World Wide Web address:** http://www.peebles-stores.com. **Description:** Operates a department store chain of 140 stores in 17 states. NOTE: Apply for positions online. **Corporate headquarters location:** This location. **Number of employees at this location:** 2,200. **Number of employees nationwide:** 2,340.

PENDER VETERINARY CLINIC
4001 Legato Road, Fairfax VA 22033. 703/591-3304. **Fax:** 703/591-6936. **Contact:** Human Resources. **World Wide Web address:** http://www.pendervet.com. **Description:** An animal clinic providing both routine and emergency care. Founded in 1971.

PERRY JUDD'S INCORPORATED
One Shenandoah Valley Drive, Strasburg VA 22657. 540/465-6606. **Fax:** 540/465-6610. **Contact:** Carl Dysart, Human Resources Manager. **E-mail address:** cdysart@perryjudds.com. **World Wide Web address:** http://www.perryjudds.com. **Description:** Provides commercial printing services of publications and catalogs. **Positions advertised include:** Entry-level. **Corporate headquarters location:** Waterloo WI. **Other U.S. locations:** IA. **Number of employees at this location:** 800.

PHILIP MORRIS USA
615 Maury Street, Richmond VA 23224. 804/274-2000. **Contact:** Manager of Placement and EEO. **World Wide Web address:** http://www.philipmorrisusa.com. **Description:** In the tobacco industry, Philip Morris USA and Philip Morris International together form one of the largest international cigarette operations in the world. U.S. brand names include Marlboro, Parliament, Virginia Slims, Benson & Hedges, and Merit. **Parent company:** Altria Group, Inc. **NOTE:** Search and apply for positions online. **Positions advertised include:** Financial Analyst; Real Estate Purchasing Agent; Toxicologist; Research Analyst; Engineer; Key Account Analyst; Training Design Senior Specialist; Counsel; Information Systems Controls Analysts. **Corporate headquarters location:** This location. **Listed on:** New York Stock Exchange. **Stock exchange symbol:** MO.

PIEDMONT BEHAVIORAL HEALTH CENTER
P.O. Box 2547, Leesburg VA 20177. **Physical address:** 42009 Victory lane, Leesburg VA 20176. **Toll-free phone:** 800/777-8855. **Contact:** Human Resources. **Description:** A psychiatric medical center offering both inpatient and outpatient treatment in the areas of alcohol and drug dependency, depression, and marital problems.

PIEDMONT GERIATRIC HOSPITAL
5001 East Patrick Henry Highway, P.O. Box 427, Burkeville VA 23922. 434/767-4401. **Contact:** Human Resources. **World Wide Web address:** http://www.pgh.state.va.us. **Description:** A Virginia state facility that provides inpatient treatment to elderly patients with mental illnesses. **Special programs:** Internships. **Corporate headquarters location:** Richmond VA. **Parent company:** Department of Mental Health. **Number of employees at this location:** 450.

PIERCE ASSOCIATES
4216 Wheeler Avenue, Alexandria VA 22304. 703/751-2400. **Fax:** 703/751-2479. **Contact:** John Dunleavy, Senior Vice President. **World Wide Web address:** http://www.pierceassociates.com. **Description:** A contractor specializing in mechanical construction (HVAC, plumbing, and fire protection.) **Corporate headquarters location:** This location. **Listed on:** Privately held. **Number of employees at this location:** 40.

PILGRIM'S PRIDE CORPORATION
P.O. Box 7275, Broadway VA 22815-7000. 540/896-7000. **Fax:** 540/896-0850. **Contact:** Personnel. **World Wide Web address:** http://www.pilgrimspride.com. **Description:** A fully integrated poultry and turkey processor, marketer, and distributor. Pilgrim's Pride offers over 250 poultry and related products and operates processing plants and packaging facilities. **NOTE:** Search for positions online. **Positions advertised include:** Safety Manager. **Corporate headquarters location:** Pittsburg TX. **Listed on:** New York Stock Exchange. **Stock exchange symbol:** CHX. **Number of employees worldwide:** 40,000.

POLYONE CORPORATION
1944 Valley Avenue, Winchester VA 22601. 540/667-6666. **Physical address:** 1944 Valley Avenue, Winchester VA. **Contact:** Human Resources. **World Wide Web address:** http://www.polyone.com. **Description:** Provides polymer products, services, and solutions including plastic compounds, colorants, thermoplastic elastomers, specialty vinyl resins, polyurethanes and engineered films, plus specialty additives. **NOTE:** Unsolicited resumes not accepted. **Corporate headquarters location:** Cleveland OH. **Other U.S. locations:** Nationwide. **International locations:** Worldwide. **Listed on:** New York Stock Exchange. **Stock exchange symbol:** POL.

POTOMAC HOSPITAL
2300 Opitz Boulevard, Woodbridge VA 22191. 703/670-1313. **Recorded jobline:** 703/670-1836. **Contact:** Human Resources. **World Wide Web address:** http://www.potomachospital.com. **Description:** A 153-bed nonprofit general hospital. Potomac Hospital offers clinical services including a 24-hour emergency room, critical care, progressive care, maternal and infant care, neonatology, LDRs, pediatrics, Lamaze/expectant parent classes, an operating room, ambulatory care surgery, post anesthesia care, surgery, medicine/oncology, hospice care, mental health-adult/adolescent care, cardiology services, physical medicine and rehabilitation services, radiation oncology, respiratory services, radiology/angiography, ultrasound, nuclear medicine, a CT scanner, MRI, laboratory, occupational therapy, and an inpatient/retail pharmacy service. **Parent company:** Inova Health System. **Number of employees at this location:** 1,000.

PRAGMATICS, INC.
7926 Jones Branch Drive, Suite 711, McLean VA 22102. 703/761-4033. **Fax:** 703/761-4089. **Contact:** Corporate Recruiter. **E-mail address:** Recruiter@pragmatics.com. **World Wide Web address:** http://www.pragmatics.com. **Description:** Offers services in software and system engineering, information assurance, and program management acquisition and consulting. Founded in 1985. **NOTE:** Search and apply for positions online. Most positions require an active security clearance. **Positions advertised include:** GEMS Schedule Analyst; Technical Writer; Intermediate Systems Engineer; Java Developer; DoD Program Manager; Senior Testing Engineer; Meeting Coordinator; Mid Systems Coordinator.

PRESTO PRODUCTS COMPANY
Plant Highway 58 West, P.O. Box 527, South Boston VA 24592. 434/572-6961. **Contact:** Wayne Connor, Plant Manager. **World Wide Web address:** http://www.prestoproducts.com. **Description:** Supplies products including private label food and disposer bags, packaging closures, soil stabilization materials, and specialty stretch films. **Parent company:** Alcoa Consumer Products. **Number of employees at this location:** 300.

PRICEWATERHOUSECOOPERS
1751 Pinnacle Drive, Suite 800, McLean VA 22102-3811. 703/918-3000. **Contact:** Personnel. **World Wide Web address:** http://www.pwc.com. **Description:** One of the largest certified public accounting firms in the world. PricewaterhouseCoopers provides public accounting, business advisory, management consulting, and taxation services. **NOTE:** Search and apply for positions online. **Positions advertised include:** Change & Learning Sr. Associate. **Corporate headquarters location:** New York NY. **Other U.S. locations:** Nationwide. **Number of employees worldwide:** 120,000.

PRINCE WILLIAM/MANASSAS CVB
8609 Sudley Road, Suite 105, Manassas VA 20110. 703/396-7130. **Fax:** 703/396-7160. **Contact:** Human Resources Department. **World Wide Web address:** http://www.visitpwc.com. **Description:** The offices of the convention and visitors bureau serving Prince William County. **Positions advertised include:** Tourism Marketing Manager.

PRINCE WILLIAM HOSPITAL
8700 Sudley Road, Manassas VA 20110. 703/369-8000. **Contact:** Susan Barrett, Employment Coordinator. **World Wide Web address:** http://www.pwhs.org. **Description:** A nonprofit, 170-bed, community hospital. Founded in 1964. **NOTE:** Search and apply for positions online. **Positions advertised include:** Coding Manager; Director, Emergency Services Department; Director, Radiology; Manager, Engineering; Manager, Customer Service and Billing; Registered Nurses; Oncology Technician; Surgical Technician; Licensed Practical Nurse; Cardiopulmonary Technician; Clinical Dietitian; Medical Librarian/CME Coordinator. **Number of employees at this location:** 1,000.

PROGRESS PRINTING COMPANY
2677 Waterlick Road, Lynchburg VA 24502. 434/239-9213. **Contact:** Human Resources Manager. **World Wide Web address:** http://www.progprint.com. **Description:** Prints annual reports, direct mailings, college brochures, and pocket folders in four, six, and eight color presses. Founded in 1962. **Number of employees at this location:** 300.

PUBLIC BROADCASTING SYSTEM (PBS)
1320 Braddock Place, Alexandria VA 22314. 703/739-5000. **Contact:** Human Resources. **E-mail address:** jobs@pbs.org. **World Wide Web address:** http://www.pbs.org. **Description:** A private, non-profit media organization owned and operated by the nation's 349 public television stations. Founded in 1969. **NOTE:** Internships available. Search and apply for positions online. **Positions advertised include:** Assistant Director, Marketing; Associate Director, Station Relations; Associate Director, National Outreach; Associate Producer; Director, Professional Development; Executive Coordinator. **Corporate headquarters location:** This location. **President:** Ervin Duggan, President.

PULASKI COMMUNITY HOSPITAL
P.O. Box 759, Pulaski VA 24301. 540/980-6822. **Fax:** 540/994-8423. **Recorded jobline:** 540/994-8522. **Contact:** Katie Kirk, Human Resources Director. **World Wide Web address:** http://www.pch-va.com. **Description:** A 147-bed acute care hospital. The hospital has various services and units including home health, cardiac rehabilitation, family birthing center, intensive care unit, cardiac care unit, progressive care unit, oncology, emergency center, physical therapy, and orthopedic care. Founded in 1973. **Positions advertised include:** CRNA; Director, Health Information Management; LPN; Registered Nurse; Occupational Therapist; Physical Therapist; Nuclear Medicine Tech; Radiology Tech. **Number of employees at this location:** 400.

PULASKI FURNITURE CORPORATION
One Pulaski Square, Pulaski VA 24301. 540/980-7330. **Contact:** Diane Hall, Human Resources Director. **World Wide Web address:** http://www.pulaskifurniture.com. **Description:** Manufactures bedroom and dining room furniture. **Corporate headquarters location:** This location. **Number of employees nationwide:** 1,000.

PULSECOM
2900 Towerview Road, Herndon VA 20171. 703/471-2900. **Fax:** 703/471-2903. **Contact:** Human Resources Director. **E-mail address:** hr@pulse.com. **World Wide Web address:** http://www.pulse.com. **Description:** Produces telecommunications products including channel books, frame relay systems, test access systems, digital loop carriers, and network management systems; and remote control supervisory systems for industrial processes. **Corporate headquarters location:** This location. **Parent company:** Hubbell, Inc. **Operations at this facility include:** Administration; Divisional Headquarters; Manufacturing; Research and Development; Sales; Service. **Listed on:** New York Stock Exchange. **Stock exchange symbol:** HUB.

QED SYSTEMS, INC.
4646 North Witchduck Road, Virginia Beach VA 23455. 757/490-5046. **Contact:** James Lyons, Human Resources Manager. **World Wide Web address:** http://www.qedsysinc.com. **Description:** A government contracting facility. QED Systems, Inc. handles marine engineering, manufactures technical manuals, and performs shipboard inspections. Founded in 1970. **Corporate headquarters location:** This location.

QUADRAMED
12110 Sunset Hills Road, Suite 600, Reston VA 20190-3224. 703/709-2300. **Toll-free phone:** 800/576-4562. **Fax:** 703/709-2490. **Contact:** Personnel. **E-mail address:** resume@quadramed.com. **World Wide Web address:** http://www.quadramed.com. **Description:** Develops and markets specialized decision support software designed to improve the organizational and clinical effectiveness of hospitals, academic medical centers, managed care providers, large physician groups, and other health care providers. **NOTE:** Search and apply for positions online. **Positions advertised include:** Contract Administrator; Business Systems Analyst; Software Architect, Database; Sr. Software Engineer; Management Analyst; Installation Specialist; Procurement Manager; Quality Assurance Analyst; Senior Financial Analyst. **Corporate headquarters location:** This location. **Listed on:** NASDAQ. **Stock exchange symbol:** QMDC.

QWEST COMMUNICATIONS
4250 North Fairfax Drive, Arlington VA 22203. **Toll-free phone:** 800/296-0220. **Recorded jobline:** 888/793-7811. **Contact:** Human Resources. **World Wide Web address:** http://www.qwest.com. **Description:** A long-distance telecommunications carrier that provides a broad array of domestic and international voice, data, and Internet services to commercial and residential customers. Qwest Communications provides service to customers through its network of digital fiber-optic facilities. **Positions advertised include:** Lead Financial Analyst; Information Systems Engineer; Sr. Logistics Coordinator; Sr. Property Manager; Sr. Sales Engineer; Sr. Account Executive. **Corporate headquarters location:** Denver CO. **Operations at this facility include:** Location of the Qwest Government Services Division. **Listed on:** New York Stock Exchange. **Stock exchange symbol:** Q.

RWS ENTERPRISES
dba COUNTRY COOKING
4335 Brambleton Avenue, Roanoke VA 24018. 540/774-0613. **Contact:** Human Resources. **Description:** Operates the Country Cooking restaurant chain with locations throughout Virginia. **Corporate headquarters location:** This location.

RADVA CORPORATION
P.O. Box 2900, Radford VA 24143. 540/639-2458. **Contact:** Human Resources Director. **World Wide Web address:** http://www.radva.com. **Description:** Designs and manufactures protective packaging and shape-molded foam products. **Corporate headquarters location:** This location. **Other U.S. locations:** Portsmouth VA. **Subsidiaries include:** Radva RU, Inc.; Thermastructure, Ltd.

RAPPAHANNOCK GENERAL HOSPITAL
101 Harris Drive, Kilmarnock VA 22482. 804/435-8000. **Contact:** Human Resources Manager. **World Wide Web address:** http://www.rgh-hospital.com. **Description:** An acute care, community-owned, nonprofit hospital with 76 beds. Rappahannock General Hospital offers an array of services including a 24-hour emergency room, a stationary MRI, Rappahannock Home Health Agency, physical therapy, a maternity center, diagnostic X-ray, mammography, and ultrasonography. **Positions advertised include:** Registered Nurse; Physical Therapist; CNA; Exercise Physiologist; Licensed Practical Nurse; Occupational Therapist; Respiratory Therapist. **Number of employees at this location:** 425.

RAYTHEON SYSTEMS COMPANY
7700 Arlington Boulevard, Falls Church VA 22042. 703/560-5000. **Fax:** 703/849-1510. **Contact:** Human Resources. **World Wide Web address:** http://www.raytheon.com. **Description:** A systems contractor in the areas of remote-controlled reconnaissance, information processing and display, electronic combat operations, digitally controlled communications, and intrusion detection. **NOTE:** Search and apply for positions online. **Positions advertised include:** Systems Engineer, Information Systems Security Officer; Program Security Representative; TCS Program Manager; Chief Communications System Engineer; Deputy Program Manager; Technical Support Engineer; Program Manager; EW Engineer; UAV Systems Design. **Corporate headquarters location:** Waltham MA. **Parent company:** Raytheon Company. **Operations at this facility include:** Divisional Headquarters; Manufacturing; Research and Development. **Listed on:** New York Stock Exchange. **Stock exchange symbol:** RTN.

REHAU INC.
P.O. Box 1706, Leesburg VA 20177. 703/777-5255. **Physical address:** 1501 Edwards Ferry Road, Leesburg VA 20176. **Fax:** 703/777-6508. **Contact:** Human Resources. **E-mail address:** hr.leesburg@rehau-na.com. **World Wide Web address:** http://www.rehau-na.com. **Description:** Processes polymers and compounds used in the manufacture of more than 40,000 products. Founded in 1948. **Corporate headquarters location:** North American headquarters at this location.

REHRIG INTERNATIONAL
1301 Battery Brooke Parkway, Richmond VA 23237. 804/743-9600. **Toll-free phone:** 800/446-2729. **Fax:** 804/743-9420. **Contact:** Human Resources Manager. **World Wide Web address:** http://www.rehrig.com. **Description:** Manufactures plastic shopping carts and hand baskets.

RESEARCH TRIANGLE INSTITUTE (RTI)
One Enterprise Parkway, Suite 310, Hampton VA 23666. 757/827-1160. **Fax:** 757/827-3273. **Contact:** Human Resources Department. **E-mail address:** jobs@rti.org. **World Wide Web address:** http://www.rti.org. **Description:** A nonprofit, independent research organization involved in many scientific fields, under contract to business; industry; federal, state, and local governments; industrial associations; and public service agencies. RTI works in the areas of health, environmental protection, advanced technology, education and training, and economic and social development. **NOTE:** Search and apply for positions online. **Corporate headquarters location:** Research Triangle Park NC. **Other U.S. locations:** Washington DC; Cocoa Beach FL; Atlanta GA; Rockville MD; Chicago IL; Waltham MA; Anniston AL. **Number of employees nationwide:** 2,300.

RESTON HOSPITAL CENTER
1850 Town Center Parkway, Reston VA 20190. 703/689-9000. **Fax:** 703/689-0840. **Contact:** Human Resources. **World Wide Web address:** http://www.restonhospital.net. **Description:** A 127-bed general hospital offering 24-hour emergency, critical, and progressive care services. **Positions advertised include:** PBX Operator; Case Manager; HR Assistant; Medical Transcriptionist; DRG Coder; RN; LPN; Sterile Processing Technician; Pharmacist; Scheduling Representative.

J. SERGEANT REYNOLDS COMMUNITY COLLEGE
P.O. Box 85622, Richmond VA 23285-5622. 804/371-3249. **Contact:** Human Resources. Department **World Wide Web address:** http://www.jsr.cc.va.us. **Description:** A community college offering one- and two-year programs of study in business, liberal arts, community service, education, and science. **NOTE:** Search for positions online. **Positions advertised include:** Coordinator of Medical Laboratory distance Education; Dean, School of Information Systems, Business, and Public Safety; Librarian; Vice President of Finance and Administration; Nursing Instructor. **Corporate headquarters location:** This location. **Operations at this facility include:** Administration. **Number of employees at this location:** 1,000.

RICHMOND TIMES-DISPATCH
300 East Franklin Street, Richmond VA 23293. 804/649-6000. **Fax:** 804/649-6761. **Contact:** Human Resources. **World Wide Web address:** http://www.timesdispatch.com. **Description:** A newspaper publisher. **Corporate headquarters location:** This location. **Parent company:** Media General. **Listed on:** New York Stock Exchange. **Stock exchange symbol:** MEG. **Number of employees nationwide:** 7,300.

RIVERSIDE HEALTH SYSTEM
606 Denbigh Boulevard, Suite 601, Newport News VA 23608. 757/875-7500. **Contact:** Larry Boyles, Vice President of Human Resources. **World Wide Web address:** http://www.riverside-online.com. **Description:** An integrated health care provider operating three acute-care hospitals, a physical rehabilitation hospital, ambulatory centers, seven long-term care facilities, two continuing care retirement communities, home health care services, and five wellness and fitness centers. **Number of employees at this location:** 20.

ROANOKE COLLEGE
221 College Lane, Salem VA 24153. 540/375-2500. **Contact:** Kathy Page, Human Resources Manager. **World Wide Web address:** http://www.roanoke.edu. **Description:** One of the oldest Lutheran colleges in the nation. This four-year liberal arts undergraduate college offers 29 majors, 28 minors, and 13 concentrations. Roanoke College has an enrollment of 1,750 students. Founded in 1842. **Positions advertised include:** Visiting Assistant Professor;.

ROANOKE ELECTRIC STEEL CORPORATION
P.O. Box 13948, Roanoke VA 24038. 540/342-1831. **Physical address:** 102 Westside Boulevard, NW, Roanoke VA 24017. **Toll-free phone:** 800/765-6567. **Fax:** 540/342-9437. **Contact:** Sam Miller, Director of Human Resources. **E-mail address:** info@roanokesteel.com. **World Wide Web address:** http://www.roanokesteel.com. **Description:** Manufactures, fabricates, processes, and markets merchant steel products, billets, industrial truck sections, truck trailer crossmembers, manufactured housing beams, open-web steel joists, and reinforcing bars. **Listed on:** NASDAQ. **Stock exchange symbol:** RESC. **Number of employees at this location:** 750.

ROANOKE GAS COMPANY
519 Kimball Avenue, Roanoke VA 24016. 540/983-3800. **Contact:** Jane O'Keefe, Human Resources Director. **World Wide Web address:** http://www.roanokegas.com. **Description:** A public utility engaged in the distribution of natural gas to approximately 48,500 residential, commercial, and industrial customers in the cities of Roanoke, Salem, and Bluefield VA, and Bluefield WV. Roanoke Gas also serves approximately 5,700 propane customers in southwestern Virginia and southern West Virginia, as well as several natural gas industrial transportation customers by brokerage of natural gas supplies through a subsidiary. Founded in 1883. **NOTE:** Unsolicited resumes not accepted. **Corporate headquarters location:** This location. **Subsidiaries include:** Bluefield Gas Company; Highland Propane Company. **Parent company:** RGC Resources, Inc. **Listed on:** NASDAQ. **Stock exchange symbol:** RGCO.

ROBBINS-GIOIA, INC.
11 Canal Center Plaza, Suite 200, Alexandria VA 22314. 703/548-7006. **Fax:** 703/548-3724. **Contact:** Human Resources. E-mail address: resume@robbinsgioia.com. **World Wide Web address:** http://www.rgalex.com. **Description:** A management consulting firm. The company's services include cost management, risk management, communication management, configuration management, document management, portfolio management, material management, quality management, issues tracking, requirements/scope management, vendor selection, and planning and scheduling. Founded in 1980. **NOTE:** Entry-level positions are offered. Search and apply for positions online. **Positions advertised include:** MS Project Business Consultant; Content Editor; Accountant; Human Resources Assistant. **Corporate headquarters location:** This location. **Other U.S. locations:** Nationwide. **Operations at this facility include:** Administration; Sales; Service. **Listed on:** Privately held. **Number of employees nationwide:** 450.

THE ROCHESTER CORPORATION
751 Old Brandy Road, Culpeper VA 22701. 540/825-2111. **Fax:** 540/825-2238. **Contact:** Human Resources. **World Wide Web address:** http://www.rochestercables.com. **Description:** Manufactures wire rope and electromechanical cable used in television antennas, underwater cables, and oil fields. Founded in 1794. **Parent company:** Tyco International Ltd. **Listed on:** New York Stock Exchange. **Stock exchange symbol:** TYC.

ROCKINGHAM MEMORIAL HOSPITAL
235 Cantrell Avenue, Harrisonburg VA 22801. 540/433-4100. **Fax:** 540/564-5446. **Contact:** Diane Ray, Recruitment/Employment Manager. **World Wide Web address:** http://www.rmhonline.com. **Description:** A 330-bed, nonprofit, community hospital. NOTE: Download application and mail to: Human Resources Department at above address. Electronic applications not accepted. Search for positions online. **Positions advertised include:** LPN; RN; Compliance Review Coordinator; Clinical Resource Specialist; Staff Physical Therapist; Clinical Pharmacist; Polysomnographic Technologist; Nuclear Med Staff Technologist. **Operations at this facility include:** Service. **Number of employees at this location:** 1,500.

ROWE FURNITURE
2121 Gardner Street, Elliston VA 24087. 540/389-8671. **Fax:** 540/444-5072. **Contact:** Human Resources. **E-mail address:** employment@rowefurniture.com. **World Wide Web address:** http://www.rowefurniture.com. **Description:** A leading designer and manufacturer of upholstered furniture. Products include sofas, sleeper sofas, loveseats, chairs, and motion furniture. Rowe sells its furniture nationwide through its commissioned sales force to over 1,200 national, regional, and local retailers. **NOTE:** Search and apply for positions online. **Positions advertised include:** JIT Inventory Analyst; Customer Service Representative. **Other U.S. locations:** MO.

RUBBERMAID COMMERCIAL PRODUCTS, INC.
3124 Valley Avenue, Winchester VA 22601. 540/667-8700. **Fax:** 540/542-8770. **Contact:** Human Resources Manager. **E-mail address:** careers@rubbermaidcommercial.com. **World Wide Web address:** http://www.rcpworksmarter.com. **Description:** Manufactures plastic products for the maintenance, refuse, food service, and agriculture markets. **NOTE:** Search and apply for positions online. **Positions advertised include:** CAD Engineer; Product Engineer. **Corporate headquarters location:** Freeport IL. **Parent company:** Newell Rubbermaid, Inc. **Operations at this facility include:** Administration; Divisional Headquarters; Manufacturing; Research and Development; Sales. **Listed on:** New York Stock Exchange. **Stock exchange symbol:** NWL. **Number of employees at this location:** 900.

S&K FAMOUS BRANDS, INC.
11100 West Broad Street, Richmond VA 23060. 804/346-2500. **Contact:** Human Resources. **World Wide Web address:** http://www.skmenswear.com. **Description:** Engaged in the retail sale of men's clothing, furnishings, sportswear, and accessories. S&K Famous Brands operates over 240 stores. **NOTE:** Search and apply for positions online. **Positions advertised include:** Visual Communications Manager; Direct Marketing Database Manager. **Corporate headquarters location:** This location. **Operations at this facility include:** Administration; Distribution. **Listed on:** NASDAQ. **Stock exchange symbol:** SKFB. **Number of employees nationwide:** 1,575.

SER SOLUTIONS, INC.
Loudoun Tech Center, 21680 Ridgetop Circle, Dulles VA 20166. 703/948-5500. **Toll-free phone:** 800/274-5676. **Fax:** 703/430-7738. **Contact:** Human Resources. **E-mail address:** jobs.usa@ser.com. **World Wide Web address:** http://www.sersolutions.com. **Description:** Provides software solutions in the areas of accounts payable, shared service centers, banking and financial service operations, contact centers, and customer service operations. **NOTE:** Search and apply for positions online. **Positions advertised include:** Systems Engineer. **Other U.S. locations:** Rochester Hills MI; Norwalk CT. **International locations:** UK.

STG, INC.
11710 Plaza America Drive, Suite 1200, Reston VA 20190. 703/691-2480. **Fax:** 703/691-3467. **Contact:** Recruiting. **E-mail address:** recruiting@stginc.com. **World Wide Web address:** http://www.stginc.com. **Description:** A full-service information technology, engineering, and scientific services firm. STG provides high-tech consulting services to the federal government and commercial sector. Founded in 1986. **NOTE:** Search and apply for positions online. **Positions advertised include:** Linguists; Principal Security Administrator; Project Controller. **Special programs:** Training. **Corporate headquarters location:** This location. **Other U.S. locations:** MD; PA; CO. **Subsidiaries include:** Information 1st; DSTI. **Listed on:** Privately held. **Annual sales/revenues:** $11 - $20 million. **Number of employees worldwide:** 1,700.

SCIENCE & TECHNOLOGY CORPORATION
10 Basil Sawyer Drive, Hampton VA 23666-1393. 757/766-5800. **Fax:** 757/865-4009. **Contact:** Human Resources. **E-mail address:** jobs@stcnet.com. **World Wide Web address:** http://www.stcnet.com. **Description:** A research and development government contractor engaged in atmospheric sciences and meteorology, remote sensing, scientific data processing and modeling, chemical/biological defense, test and evaluation, programming support, and biology, astrobiology and microgravity research. Founded in 1979. **NOTE:** Search and apply for positions online. **Corporate headquarters location:** This location. **Other U.S. locations:** AL; CA; CO; FL; MD; NH; TX; UT. **Listed on:** Privately held. **President/CEO:** Dr. Adarsh Deepak. **Annual sales/revenues:** $21 - $50 million. **Number of employees at this location:** 65. **Number of employees nationwide:** 300.

SCIENCE APPLICATIONS INTERNATIONAL CORPORATION (SAIC)
1710 SAIC Drive, P.O. Box 1303, McLean VA 22102. 703/821-4300. **Contact:** Human Resources. **World Wide Web address:** http://www.saic.com. **Description:** A research and engineering firm offering information technology, systems integration and eSolutions to commercial and government customers in the areas of national and homeland security, energy, the environment, space, telecommunications, health care, and logistics. Founded in 1969. **NOTE:** Internships offered. Search and apply for positions online. **Positions advertised include:** Business Development Manager; Senior contract Representative; Pricing Analyst; Policy Analyst; Business and Information Analyst; Military Historian; Intelligence Analyst; Senior Engineer/Scientist; Senior Systems Engineer; Project Control Analyst; Project Administrator; Enterprise Architect; Application Developer; Systems Engineer; NCI Biophotographer; Subcontracts Administrator. **Corporate headquarters location:** San Diego CA. **Other U.S. locations:** Nationwide. **Number of employees worldwide:** 43,000.

SCOTT & STRINGFELLOW INC.
909 East Main Street, Richmond VA 23219. 804/643-1811. **Toll-free phone:** 800/552-7757. **Fax:** 804/643-3786. **Contact:** Jordan Ball, Manager. **World Wide Web address:** http://www.scottstringfellow.com. **Description:** A full-service regional brokerage and investment banking firm serving individual, institutional, corporate, and municipal clients in Virginia, North Carolina, and South Carolina. **NOTE:** Search and apply for positions online. **Positions advertised include:** Public Finance Assistant; Marketing Assistant; Administrative Assistant. **Corporate headquarters location:** This location. **Parent company:** BB&T Corporation. **Listed on:** New York Stock Exchange. **Stock exchange symbol:** BBT. **Number of employees nationwide:** 600.

SENET INTERNATIONAL CORPORATION
3040 Williams Drive, Suite 510 Fairfax VA 22031. 703/206-9383. **Fax:** 703/206-9666. **Contact:** Human Resources. **E-mail address:** careers@senet-int.com. **World Wide Web address:** http://www.senet-int.com. **Description:** An Information and network e-

security consulting firm. **Positions advertised include:** Security Engineer; Information Security Analyst; Network Engineer; Server Engineer; Network Security Specialist.

SENTARA CAREPLEX HOSPITAL
3000 Coliseum Drive, Hampton VA 23666. 757/736-1000. **Contact:** Human Resources. **World Wide Web address:** http://www.sentara.com. **Description:** Opened in December 2002, Sentara CarePlex Hospital is an acute care facility with 194 private patient rooms and advanced operating, diagnostic, and monitoring systems. **NOTE:** Search and apply for positions online. **Positions advertised include:** Cardiovascular Invasive Specialist; Clinical Nurse; Laboratory Manager; Physical Therapist; RN's; Respiratory Therapist; Staff Development Educator; Team Leader, SPD.

SENTARA HEALTHCARE
6015 Poplar Hall Drive, Norfolk VA 23502. 757/455-7200. **Contact:** Human Resources. **E-mail address:** jobs@sentara.com. **World Wide Web address:** http://www.sentara.com. **Description:** A nonprofit, regional health management organization. Sentara Health System operates six acute care hospitals, one extended care hospital, more than 70 sites of care, 25 primary care practices, a full range of health coverage plans, home health and hospice services, physical therapy and rehabilitation services, urgent care facilities, ground medical transport services, mobile diagnostic vans and two health and fitness facilities. **NOTE:** Search and apply for positions online. **Positions advertised include:** Benefits Consultant. **Number of employees nationwide:** 15,000.

SENTARA NORFOLK GENERAL HOSPITAL
600 Gresham Drive, Norfolk VA 23507. 757/668-3000. **Contact:** Human Resources. **World Wide Web address:** http://www.sentara.com. **Description:** A 644-bed, tertiary care hospital with the area's only Level I Trauma Center and burn trauma unit. **NOTE:** Search and apply for positions online. **Positions advertised include:** Cardiac Tech II; Cardiovascular Invasive Specialist; Clinical Manager, Nursing Unit; Laboratory Technician; MRI Technologist; Marketing/Public Relation Specialist; RN's; Physical Therapist; Occupational Therapist; Transplant Coordinator; Vascular Lab Tech. **Number of employees at this location:** 3,300.

SERCO
2650 Park Tower Drive, Suite 800, Vienna VA 22180. 571/226-5000. **Contact:** Human Resources. **E-mail address:** resumes@serco.com. **World Wide Web address:** http://www.serco-na.com. **Description:** Serco provides a broad range of services to the U.S. Military, the U.S. Postal Service, US Federal Aviation Administration, Canadian Department of National Defence, Ontario Ministry of Transportation, as well as other federal civilian agencies, state and local governments, and commercial customers. **NOTE:** Search and apply for positions online. **Positions advertised include:** Software Engineer and Systems Analyst; Director Of Communications. **Special programs:** Training. **Corporate headquarters location:** This location. **Other U.S. locations:** Nationwide. **International locations:** Worldwide. **Number of employees nationwide:** 6,000. **Number of employees worldwide:** 40,000.

SETA CORPORATION
6862 Elm Street, Suite 600, McLean VA 22101-3833. 703/821-8178. **Fax:** 703/821-8274. **Contact:** Human Resources Director. **E-mail address:** resume@seta.com. **World Wide Web address:** http://www.seta.com. **Description:** A government contractor providing information technology services primarily in the area of systems engineering support of telecommunication networks essential to national defense, homeland security, and benefits programs. **NOTE:** Search and apply for positions online. **Positions advertised include:** Sr. Java Software Developer; QoS MPLS Network Engineer; Systems Administrator, UNIX/Win2000. **Other area locations:** Norfolk VA; Baltimore MD. **Other U.S. locations:** CA; WA; MO; IL; OH; AL; NY; PA; HI.

7-ELEVEN, INC.
7-ELEVEN CONVENIENCE STORES
5300 Shawnee Road, Alexandria VA 22312. 703/642-0711. **Toll-free phone:** 800/547-5711. **Fax:** 703/941-4687. **Recorded jobline:** 800/711-JOBS. **Contact:** Division Recruiter. **World Wide Web address:** http://www.7-eleven.com. **Description:** This location houses administrative offices. 7-Eleven operates 24,000 stores worldwide. Founded in 1927. **NOTE:** Search and apply for positions online. **Positions advertised include:** Field Consultant. **Special programs:** Internships. **Corporate headquarters location:** Dallas TX. **Operations at this facility include:** Divisional Headquarters; Sales; Service. **Listed on:** New York Stock Exchange. **Stock exchange symbol:** SE. **Number of employees nationwide:** 40,000.

SHELTERING ARMS REHABILITATION HOSPITAL
8266 Atlee Road, Mechanicsville VA 23116. 804/342-4370. **Fax:** 804/342-4316. **Contact:** Human Resources. **E-mail address:** jobs@shelteringarms.com. **World Wide Web address:** http://www.shelteringarms.com. **Description:** A nonprofit hospital providing comprehensive services to individuals with physical and cognitive disabilities. **Positions advertised include:** Occupational Therapist; Physical Therapist; Rehabilitation Technician; Aquatic Specialist; Fitness Specialist; Patient Access Representative; LPN; RN. **Office hours:** Monday - Friday, 8:00 a.m. - 4:30 p.m. **Corporate headquarters location:** This location. **Operations at this facility include:** Administration. **Number of employees at this location:** 350.

SHENANDOAH UNIVERSITY
1460 University Drive, Winchester VA 22601. 540/665-4500. **Contact:** Human Resources. **World Wide Web address:** http://www.su.edu. **Description:** A private, coeducational university offering over 60 programs of study at the undergraduate, graduate, doctorate and professional levels at the main campus, Health Professions Building on the campus of the Winchester Medical Center, and Northern Virginia Campus in Leesburg. Shenandoah University is affiliated with the United Methodist Church. There are about 2,500 students enrolled at the university. Founded in 1875. **NOTE:** Search for positions online. Positions advertised include: Associate/Assistant Professor of OT; Director of the Leadership Circle; Director of Residence Life; Pharmacy Faculty; Director of Clinical Education; Education Faculty.

SICPA
8000 Research Way, Springfield VA 22153. 703/455-8050. **Fax:** 703/455-4518. **Contact:** Human Resources. **World Wide Web address:** http://www.sicpa.com. **Description:** SICPA manufactures inks for the purpose of securing value documents and for a variety of packaging, printing, and industrial applications. **Corporate headquarters location:** Switzerland. **Other U.S. locations:** Kingsport TN; Fort Worth TX. **International locations:** Switzerland. **Operations at this facility include:** This location houses the company's U.S. headquarters and manufactures ink.

SIEMENS AUTOMOTIVE
615 Bland Boulevard, Newport News VA 23602. 757/875-7000. **Contact:** Human Resources. **World Wide Web address:** http://www.us.siemens.com. **Description:** Manufactures automotive electronics including engine and powertrain management systems, electrical distribution systems, navigation systems, sensors, exhaust emission controls, and safety systems. **NOTE:** Search and apply for positions online. **Positions advertised include:** Mfg. Engineer; Quality Planner; Manufacturing Technician; Engineer, Sensors. **Parent company:** Siemens AG. **Listed on:** New York Stock Exchange. **Stock exchange symbol:** SI.

SIGNAL CORPORATION
3040 Williams Drive, Suite 200, Fairfax VA 22031. 703/205-0500. **Fax:** 703/560-0463. **Contact:** Human Resources. **World Wide Web address:** http://www.signalcorp.com. **Description**: Provides information technology and engineering & management products and services to industry and Government. Signal Solutions' information technology services include design, installation, and administration of LAN/WANs; help desk services; software development; system design and engineering; facility operations; and system and database administration. Engineering & management services consist of system, hardware and software engineering; in-service engineering; acquisition management; logistics planning and engineering; training; technical and financial planning; and administrative support. **NOTE:** Search and apply for positions online. **Positions advertised include:** Accounts Payable Supervisor; Transit Safety and Security Analyst; Sr. Director of Business Development; Project Manager; Sr. Systems Analyst. **Parent company:** General Dynamics.

SMITHFIELD FOODS INC.
200 Commerce Street, Smithfield VA 23430. 757/365-3000. **Contact:** Human Resources. **World Wide Web address:** http://www.smithfieldfoods.com. **Description:** Produces and sells food products, primarily pork, under 50 brand names. **NOTE:** Search and apply for positions or submit resume online. **Positions advertised include:** Distribution Manager; Director of Financial Reporting; QA Inspector; Employee Relations Manager; Corporate Recruiter; Staff Accountant. **Corporate headquarters location:** This location. **Listed on:** New York Stock Exchange. **Stock exchange symbol:** SFD. **Annual sales/revenues:** More than $100 million.

SNACK ALLIANCE
P.O. Box 1909, Bristol VA 24203. 276/669-6194. **Physical address:** 225 Commonwealth Avenue, Bristol VA 24201. **Toll Free Number:** 800/665-3880. **Contact:** Human Resources. **World Wide Web Address:** http://www.snackalliance.com. **Description:** Manufactures and distributes snack foods including potato chips, tortilla chips, and popcorn. The company also buys and sells its own brand of crackers. Founded in 1924. **Number of employees at this location:** 500.

SOUTHSIDE COMMUNITY HOSPITAL
800 Oak Street, Farmville VA 23901. 434/392-8811. **Fax:** 434/315-2439. **Contact:** Judy Black, Director of Human Resources. **World Wide Web address:** http://www.sch-farmville.org. **Description:** A nonprofit hospital. Joining the Medical College of Virginia's Massey Cancer Center, the hospital offers an Oncology Clinic to area cancer patients. Southside Community Hospital also offers the following services: dialysis, pharmacy, respiratory therapy, Home Health, Lifeline (personal emergency response system), social services, Anatomical & Clinical Laboratory, radiology, nuclear medicine, Cardiac Diagnostic Unit, surgery, outpatient surgery, anesthesiology, Mobile Lithostar System (state-of-the-art technology to remove kidney stones), physical therapy, patient teaching, speech therapy, pain management, obstetrics, nursery, pediatrics, Residency Program, organ donation, Mobile Health Fair Program (free medical screening to area businesses and their employees), and a speakers bureau. Founded in 1927. **NOTE:** Search and apply for jobs online. **Positions advertised include:** RN's; Patient Registration Supervisor; Staff Pharmacist.

SOUTHTRUST BANK
300 East Main Street, Norfolk VA 23510. 757/446-6600. **Contact:** Human Resources. **World Wide Web address:** http://www.southtrust.com. **Description:** One location of the bank holding company that operates 717 financial centers and offers banking and other related financial services to commercial and retail customers. **NOTE:** Search and apply for jobs online. **Positions advertised include:** Investment Sales Rep; Financial Center Manager. **Corporate headquarters location:** Birmingham AL. **Other U.S. locations:** FL; GA; MS; NC; SC; TN; TX. **Listed on:** NASDAQ. **Stock exchange symbol:** SOTR. **Number of employees nationwide:** 170.

SPARKS PERSONNEL SERVICES
11490 Commerce Park Drive, Suite 100, Reston VA 20191. 703/620-6444. **Fax:** 703/620-2968. **Contact:** Human Resources. **World Wide Web address:** http://www.sparkspers.com. **Description:** Staffing firm that places personnel In a variety of businesses and positions. **NOTE:** Search and apply for positions through website. **Positions advertised include:** Administrative Assistant; Customer Service Rep; Executive Assistant; Receptionist; Marketing Specialist.

SPARTA
1911 North Fort Myer Drive, Suite 1100, Arlington VA 22209. 703/558-0036. **Fax:** 703/558-0045. **Contact:** Human Resources. **World Wide Web address:** http://www.sparta.com. **Description:** Sparta is a systems engineering and advanced technology company. Sparta is dedicated to serving America's needs within core business areas such as strategic defense and offense systems, tactical weapon systems, space systems, and information systems. **NOTE:** Search and apply for positions on Website. **Positions advertised include:** Division Manager; Staff Action Officer; Senior T&E Engineer; Chem-Bio Defense Program Engineer/Analyst.

STANDARD TECHNOLOGY INC.
5109 Leesburg Pike, Suite 208, Falls Church VA 22041. 703/379-2500. **Contact:** Human Resources. **World Wide Web address:** http://www.stic2.com. **Description:** Provides information technology solutions, engineering, and technical support to various businesses. Founded in 1985.

STANLEY FURNITURE COMPANY, INC.
1641 Fairystone Park Highway, P.O. Box 30, Stanleytown VA 24168. 276/627-2000. **Contact:** Nola Turner, Human Resources. **E-mail address:** hroffice@stanleyfurniture.com. **World Wide Web address:** http://www.stanleyfurniture.com. **Description:** Manufactures dining room and bedroom furniture. **Other U.S. locations:** NC. **Listed on:** NASDAQ. **Stock exchange symbol:** STLY. **Number of employees nationwide:** 3,000.

STEEL CLOUD
1306 Squire Court, Dulles VA 20166-8908. 703/450-0400. **Fax:** 703/450-0406. **Contact:** Human Resources. **E-mail address:** jobs@steelcloud.com. **World Wide Web address:** http://www.steelcloud.com. **Description:** Steel Cloud provides custom-configured computer systems and professional services to government and commercial customers. **Positions advertised include:** Account Manager; Federal Software Sales Rep; Sales Engineer; Software Engineer; Network Administrator. **Listed on:** NASDAQ. **Exchange symbol:** SCLD.

STIHL INC.
536 Viking Drive, Virginia Beach VA 23452. 757/486-9100. **Fax:** 757/486-9125. **Contact:** Human Resources. **E-mail address:** employment@stihlhr.com. **World Wide Web address:** http://www.stihlusa.com. **Description:** Manufactures portable outdoor power equipment. **NOTE:** Entry-level positions are offered. Search and apply for positions online. **Positions advertised include:** Process Engineer; Machine Operator; Assembler; Sales Planning Assistant. **Corporate headquarters location:** Stutgart, Germany. **Other U.S. locations:** CT; WA. **Parent company:** Andreas Stihl. **Operations at this facility include:** Administration; Divisional Headquarters; Manufacturing; Sales. **Listed on:** Privately held. **Annual sales/revenues:** More than $100 million. **Number of employees at this location:** 730.

STRONGWELL
P.O. Box 580, Bristol VA 24203. 276/645-8000. **Physical address:** 400 Commonwealth Avenue, Bristol VA 24201. **Fax:** 276/645-8132. **Contact:** Mitch Williams, Human Resources Manager. **World Wide Web address:** http://www.strongwell.com. **Description:** Manufactures reinforced plastics and fiberglass dealing with pultrusions, extrusions, molds, and composites. Founded in 1970. **Corporate headquarters location:** This location. **Other area locations:** Abingdon VA. **Other U.S. locations:** MN; TN; CA. **Number of employees at this location:** 400.

STUDENT LOAN MARKETING ASSOCIATION (SALLIE MAE)
11600 Sallie Mae Drive, Reston VA 20193. 703/810-3000. **Contact:** Employment. **World Wide Web address:** http://www.salliemae.com. **Description:** A major financial intermediary to the educational financing market in the U.S. The company provides student loan services, as well as other financial and management services to loan originators. The association also provides financing for academic equipment. Founded in 1972. **NOTE:** Search and apply for positions online. **Positions advertised include:** Director Systems Development; Business Solutions Analyst; Account Executive; Director Credit; Corporate communications Rep; Manager of Corporate Finance; Sr. Loan Accountant. **Corporate headquarters location:** This location. **Parent company:** SLM Corporation (also at this location.) **Number of employees nationwide:** 3,275.

SUNRISE ASSISTED LIVING, INC.
7902 Westpark Drive, McLean VA 22102. 703/273-7500. **Fax:** 703/744-1601. **Recorded jobline:** 888/686-8830. **Contact:** Human Resources. **E-mail address:** careers@mail.sunrise-al.com. **World Wide Web address:** http://www.sunrise-al.com. **Description:** Operates assisted living communities for seniors. Founded in 1981. **Corporate headquarters location:** This location. **Other U.S. locations:** Nationwide. **Listed on:** New York Stock Exchange. **Stock exchange symbol:** SRZ. **Annual sales/revenues:** More than $100 million.

SUNTRUST BANKS, INC.
1001 Semmes Avenue, Richmond VA 23224. 804/675-9600. **Fax:** 804/319-1811. **Contact:** Human Resources. **World Wide Web address:** http://www.suntrust.com. **Description:** SunTrust Banks is a bank holding company with 1,200 subsidiary banking offices located primarily in Florida, Georgia, Maryland, Tennessee, Virginia, and the District of Columbia. **NOTE:** Search and apply for positions online. **Corporate headquarters location:** Atlanta GA. **Subsidiaries include:** SunTrust Bank. **Listed on:** New York Stock Exchange. **Stock exchange symbol:** STI.

SUPERVALU INC.
8258 Richfood Road, Mechanicsville VA 23116. 804/746-6000. **Contact:** Human Resources Department. **E-mail address:** super.careers@supervalu.com. **World Wide Web address:** http://www.supervalu.com. **Description:** Operates as a food retailer and wholesaler. **Corporate headquarters location:** Eden Prairie MN. **Listed on:** New York Stock Exchange. **Stock exchange symbol:** SVU. **Number of employees nationwide:** 57,400.

SWEDISH MATCH
7300 Beaufont Springs Drive, Suite 400, P.O. Box 13297, Richmond VA 23225. 804/287-1700. **Fax:** 804/302-1760. **Contact:** Human Resources Director. **World Wide Web address:** http://www.swedishmatch.com. **Description:** Manufactures snuff and chewing tobacco, cigars and pipe tobacco, matches and lighters. Smokeless tobacco brand names include Redman, Golden Blend, and Renegades. **Corporate headquarters location:** Stockholm, Sweden. **Listed on:** NASDAQ. **Stock exchange symbol:** SWMAY. **Number of employees at this location:** 60.

SWISSPORT USA
Washington Dulles International Airport, 45025 Aviation Drive, Suite 350, Dulles VA 20166. 703/742-4300. **Fax:** 703/742-4321. **Contact:** Human Resources. **E-mail address:** william.rodriguez@swissport-usa.com. **World Wide Web address:** http://www.swissport.com. **Description:** Provides a wide range of ground-handling services for airlines and airports. Services include maintenance, inspections, spare parts inventory, into-plane fueling, cargo handling, cabin cleaning, and ramp services. Swissport USA also operates reservation centers for airlines. Founded in 1964. **Parent company:** Alpha Airports Group. **Annual sales/revenues:** More than $100 million. **Number of employees at this location:** 50. **Number of employees nationwide:** 6,000.

SYSTEM PLANNING CORPORATION
1000 Wilson Boulevard, Suite 3000, Arlington VA 20009. 703/351-8200. **Fax:** 703/351-8261. **Contact:** Director of Staff Development. **E-mail address:** recruiting@sysplan.com. **World Wide Web address:** http://www.sysplan.com. **Description:** Provides high-technology systems and support for national security initiatives and policy. Customers include state and local governments, major aerospace companies, and architectural and engineering firms. **NOTE:** Search and apply for positions online. **Positions advertised include:** Fire Service/Emergency Medical Service Researchers; Electronic Systems Engineer; Combat Technology Analyst; F-18 Avionics Systems Engineer. **Corporate headquarters location:** This location.

SYSTEMS RESEARCH & APPLICATION (SRA)
4300 Fair Lakes Court, Fairfax VA 22033. 703/803-1500. **Fax:** 703/803-1509. **Contact:** Human Resources. **World Wide Web address:** http://www.sra.com. **Description:** SRA provides information technology services and solutions, including strategic consulting, systems design, development and integration, and outsourcing and operations management, to clients in national security, civil government, and health care and public health. **NOTE:** Search and apply for positions online. **Positions advertised include:** Sr. KM Project Manager; Plumtree Developer/Administrator; Mid Level Pricing Analyst; Pre-Sales Engineer; Business Development Manager; Sr. Systems Engineer; Sr. Database Engineer. **Listed on:** New York Stock Exchange. **Stock exchange symbol:** SRX.

TMP WORLDWIDE INC.
8280 Greensboro Drive, Suite 900, McLean VA 22102. 703/269-0100. **Fax:** 703/269-0115. **Contact:** Human Resources. **World Wide Web address:** http://www.tmp.com. **Description:** An advertising and public relations firm specializing in corporate and marketing communications. **Positions advertised include:** Marketing and Communications Account Executive; Contract Administrator; Senior Account Executive. **Parent company:** Monster Worldwide. **Listed on:** NASDAQ. **Stock exchange symbol:** TMPW.

TRW AUTOMOTIVE
1100 Wilson Boulevard, Arlington VA 22209. 703/224-0932. **Fax:** 703/224-0937. **Contact:** Human Resources. **World Wide Web address:** http://www.trwauto.com. **Description:** Manufactures components including chassis systems and safety systems, for automakers such as DaimlerChrysler, Ford, and GM. **Corporate headquarters location:** Livonia MI. **Listed on:** New York Stock Exchange. **Stock exchange symbol:** TRW.

TALLYGENICOM CORPORATION
4500 Daly Drive, Suite 100, Chantilly VA 20151. 703/633-8700. **Fax:** 703/222-7629. **Contact:** Dick Gooch, Manager of Human Resources. **World Wide Web address:** http://www.genicom.com. **Description:** TallyGenicom offers a wide selection of ultra-reliable business and industrial printers, printing solutions, printer supplies, printer parts, and service. They provide a full range of impact and laser printers, including line matrix, serial matrix, industrial ink jet, monochrome laser and color laser. **NOTE:** Search and apply for positions online. **Positions advertised include:** HR Representative. **Corporate headquarters location:** This location. **Other area locations:** Waynesboro VA. **Other U.S. locations:** Kent WA. **Operations at this facility include:** This location manufactures printers and relays. **Number of employees nationwide:** 2,150.

TELLABS
45085 University Drive, Ashburn VA 20147. 703/729-6400. **Toll-free phone:** 800/443-0726. **Fax:** 703/729-6152. **Contact:** Human Resources Department. **World Wide Web address:** http://www.tellabs.com. **Description:** Develops, manufactures, and markets voice enhancement products for wireless (including digital cellular), satellite-based, and wireline telecommunications systems throughout the world. **NOTE:** Entry-level positions are offered. Search and apply for positions online. **Special programs:** Internships. **Corporate headquarters location:** Naperville IL. **Operations at this facility include:** Divisional Headquarters. **Listed on:** NASDAQ. **Stock exchange symbol:** TLAB. **Annual sales/revenues:** More than $100 million. **Number of employees at this location:** 300. **Number of employees nationwide:** 7,000.

TELOS CORPORATION
19886 Ashburn Road, Ashburn VA 20147. 703/724-3800. **Toll-free phone: 800/444-9628. Fax:** 703/724-3860. **Contact:** Human Resources. **World Wide Web address:** http://www.telos.com. **Description**: Provides solutions in the areas of information assurance, secure wireless networking, secure message handling, secure local area networks ("LAN") data integration, and enterprise risk management. Founded in 1968. **NOTE:** Search and apply for positions online. **Positions advertised include:** AMHS Engineer; Assistant Program Manager; Contract Recruiter; Deputy director Security Programs; Logistics Manager; Network Administrator; Security Analyst; Technical Program Manager; Wireless LAN Sustainment Engineer. **Corporate headquarters location:** This location. **Subsidiaries include:** Xacta. **Operations at this facility include:** Administration; Manufacturing; Research and Development; Sales; Service. **Number of employees at this location:** 280. **Number of employees nationwide:** 345.

TETRA TECH, INC.
10306 Eaton Place, Suite 340, Fairfax VA 22030. 703/385-6000. **Contact:** Human Resources. **World Wide Web address:** http://www.tetratech.com. **Description:** Provides consulting, engineering, and technical services to commercial and government clients. **Corporate headquarters location:** Pasadena CA. **Listed on:** NASDAQ. **Stock exchange symbol:** TTEK. Number of employees worldwide: 9,000.

TETRA TECH, INC.
5205 Leesburg Pike, Suite 1400, Falls Church VA 22041. 703/931-9301. **Contact:** Human Resources. **World Wide Web address:** http://www.tetratech.com. **Description:** An environmental consulting firm. **Corporate headquarters location:** Pasadena CA. **Listed on:** NASDAQ. **Stock exchange symbol:** TTEK. Number of employees worldwide: 9,000.

TEXTRON/AMSCO PRODUCTS
345 East Marshall Street, Wytheville VA 24382. 276/228-8141. **Contact:** Human Resources. **Description:** Manufactures screws used primarily in automobiles and appliances.

TIDEWATER SKANSKA, INC.
809 South Military Highway, Virginia Beach VA 23464. 757/578-4100. Fax: 757/420-3551. **Contact:** Human Resources. **E-mail address:** mail@tidewaterskanska.com. **World Wide Web address:** http://www.usacivil.skanska.com. **Description:** A heavy industrial, highway, and bridge contractor with primary operations in the Southeast. **Positions advertised include:** Marine/Bridge Superintendent; Estimator; Project Engineer; Senior Structural/Civil Engineer; Joint Venture Project Manager. **Corporate headquarters location:** This location. **Parent company:** Skanska USA Civil, Inc. **Listed on:** Privately held. **Annual sales/revenues:** More than $100 million. **Number of employees at this location:** 90. **Number of employees nationwide:** 600.

TIME-LIFE INC.
2000 Duke Street, Alexandria VA 22314. 703/838-7000. **Contact:** Human Resources. **World Wide Web address:** http://www.timelife.com. **Description:** Publishes a wide range of trade books including children's, educational, health issues, and cookbooks.

THE TITAN CORPORATION
13135 Lee Jackson Highway, Suite 300, Fairfax VA 22033. 703/449-7600. **Contact:** Human Resources. **World Wide Web address:** http://www.titan.com. **Description:** An information technology company providing networking services, systems integration, and systems engineering to the government and other customers. **NOTE:** Search and apply for positions online. **Positions advertised include:** Accounts Payable Specialist; Analyst; Contract Administrator; Director, Business Development; Enterprise Architect; Software Applications Engineer; Security Specialist. **Corporate headquarters location:** San Diego CA. **Other U.S. locations:** Nationwide. **Listed on:** New York Stock Exchange. **Stock exchange symbol:** TTN. **Number of employees worldwide:** 12,000.

THE TITAN CORPORATION
CIVIL GOVERNMENT SERVICES GROUP (CGSG)
1593 Spring Hill Road, Suite 700, Vienna VA 22182-2249. 703/827-2606. **Contact:** Human Resources. **World Wide Web address:** http://www.titan.com. **Description:** Offers networking and systems integration services to the government. **Corporate**

headquarters location: San Diego CA. **Other U.S. locations:** Nationwide. **Listed on:** New York Stock Exchange. **Stock exchange symbol:** TTN.

TRANSACTION NETWORK SERVICES, INC. (TNS)
1939 Roland Clarke Place, Reston VA 20191. 703/453-8300. **Contact:** Human Resources. **World Wide Web address:** http://www.tnsi.com. **Description:** Provides data communications services for transaction-oriented applications. TNS has four divisions: point-of services, telecom services, financial services, and international systems.

TREEV
13454 Sunrise Valley Dr., Fourth Floor, Herndon VA 20171. 703/478-2260. **Toll-free phone:** 800/254-0994. **Fax:** 703/481-6920. **Contact:** Human Resources. **E-mail address:** jobs@treev.com. **World Wide Web address:** http://www.treev.com. **Description:** TREEV provides software solutions and consulting services that enable financial institutions to transform paper-intensive operations into more efficient digital and automated processes. Founded in 1986. **NOTE:** Search and apply for positions online. **Positions advertised include:** Mid-Level Technical Writer. **Corporate headquarters location:** This location. **Number of employees nationwide:** 115.

US AIRWAYS, INC.
2345 Crystal Drive, Arlington VA 22227. 703/872-7000. **Contact:** Senior Vice President of Human Resources. **World Wide Web address:** http://www.usairways.com. **Description:** Provides air transportation of passengers, property, and mail; reservations and ground support services to commuter carriers; aircraft remarketing; aircraft appraisal services; general aviation and spare parts sales; fixed-based operations; fuel services; and other aviation-related activities. **NOTE:** Search and apply for positions online. **Positions advertised include:** Manager, Domestic Pricing; Loyalty Project Lead; Sr. Financial Analyst; Financial Analyst; Tax Manager; Project Manager. **Corporate headquarters location:** This location. **Listed on:** New York Stock Exchange. **Stock exchange symbol:** U. **Annual sales/revenues:** More than $100 million.

U.S. CENTRAL INTELLIGENCE AGENCY (CIA)
P.O. Box 4090, Reston VA 20195. 703/613-7126. **Contact:** Recruitment Center. **World Wide Web address:** http://www.cia.gov. **Description:** Provides foreign intelligence and conducts counterintelligence operations on issues related to national security as directed by the president. Founded in 1947. **NOTE:** Search and apply for positions online.

U.S. DEPARTMENT OF VETERANS AFFAIRS MEDICAL CENTER
1201 Broad Rock Road, Building 507, Richmond VA 23249. 804/675-5000x4784. **Toll-free phone:** 800/368-6008. **Fax:** 804/675-5585. **Contact:** Personnel Office. **World Wide Web address:** http://www.va.gov. **Description:** The Hunter Holmes McGuire VA Medical Center is a 427-bed facility offering primary, secondary, and tertiary health care in medicine, surgery, neurology, rehabilitation medicine, intermediate care, acute and sustaining spinal cord injury, skilled nursing home care, and palliative care. Primary and secondary levels of care are provided in psychiatry beds, along with a substance abuse rehabilitation program. Affiliated with the Medical College of Virginia.

U.S. DRUG ENFORCEMENT AGENCY (DEA)
2401 Jefferson Davis Highway, Alexandria VA 22301. 202/307-8869. **Contact:** Office of Personnel. **World Wide Web address:** http://www.usdoj.gov/dea. **Description:** A federal law enforcement agency responsible for combating drug abuse. The DEA was established to control narcotic and dangerous drug abuse through enforcement and prevention. The DEA is responsible for the laws and statutes relating to narcotic drugs, marijuana, depressants, stimulants, anabolic steroids, and hallucinogenic drugs. The administration has 19 domestic field divisions and 49 foreign country offices. Additionally, it has numerous resident offices throughout the United States and overseas. The DEA also regulates the legal trade in narcotics and dangerous drugs, which includes establishing import, export, and manufacturing quotas for some controlled drugs. It provides federal, state, local, and foreign law enforcement officers with specialized training in narcotic and dangerous drug control. The Office of Forensic Sciences is the laboratory testing division of the DEA, where chemists scientifically identify new compounds, analyze evidence, provide expert testimony in courts, and develop intelligence data used to determine trends. **Corporate headquarters location:** This location.

U.S. FARM CREDIT ADMINISTRATION
1501 Farm Credit Drive, McLean VA 22102-5090. 703/883-4000. **Contact:** *OCAO. **E-mail address:** info-line@fca.gov. **World Wide Web address:** http://www.fca.gov. **Description:** A government agency that regulates and examines the Farm Credit System. The agency has four field locations. **Corporate headquarters location:** This location. **Operations at this facility include:** Administration.

U.S. FEDERAL RESERVE BANK OF RICHMOND
P.O. Box 27622, Richmond VA 23261. 804/697-8000. **Physical address:** 701 East Byrd Street, Richmond VA 23219. **Fax:** 804/697-8490. **Contact:** Human Resources. **World Wide Web address:** http://www.rich.frb.org. **Description:** A branch bank of the Federal Reserve System, which consists of 12 regional Federal Reserve banks that, along with the Federal Reserve Board of Governors in Washington DC, comprise the Federal Reserve System, the nation's central bank. As the nation's central bank, the Federal Reserve is charged with three major responsibilities: monetary policy, banking supervision and regulation, and processing payments. **Other U.S. locations:** Denver CO; Miami FL; Atlanta GA; Chicago IL; Boston MA; Minneapolis MN; St. Louis MO; Charlotte NC; New York NY; Philadelphia PA; Dallas TX; Houston TX; Salt Lake City UT.

U.S. PATENT AND TRADEMARK OFFICE
2011 Crystal Park One, Suite 707, Arlington VA 22202. 703/305-8231. **Toll-free phone:** 800/786-9199. **Contact:** Office of Human Resources. **World Wide Web address:** http://www.uspto.gov. **Description:** Reviews applications for patents and makes legal determinations concerning the granting of patents. **NOTE:** Resumes should be sent to Human Resources, P.O. Box 171, Washington DC 20231. **Corporate headquarters location:** This location. **Other U.S. locations:** Washington DC. **Parent company:** U.S. Department of Commerce. **Number of employees nationwide:** 1,000.

U.S. SECURITIES AND EXCHANGE COMMISSION
MS 0-1, 6432 General Green Way Drive, Alexandria VA 22312. **Fax:** 703/914-0556. **Recorded jobline:** 202/942-4150. **Contact:** Office of Human Resources. **World Wide Web address:** http://www.sec.gov. **Description:** A regulatory commission ensuring that securities markets and investors are engaged in fair operations.

UTD INC.
8350 Alban Road, Suite 700, Springfield VA 22150. 703/440-8834. **Fax:** 703/455-4676. **Contact:** Human Resources. **World Wide Web address:** http://www.utdinc.com. **Description:** A facilities engineering, design, development and protection consultancy. Primarily serves the DoD. **NOTE:** Search for positions online. **Positions advertised include:** Civil Engineer; Proposal Manager; Senior Electrical Engineer.

UXB INTERNATIONAL, INC.
21641 Beaumeade Circle, Suite 301, Ashburn VA 20147-6002. 703/724-9600. **Fax:** 703/724-3528. **Contact:** Human Resources. **E-mail address:** HR@uxb.com. **World Wide Web address:** http://www.uxb.com. **Description:** Provides ordnance and explosive waste services for the United States Army. The company specializes in chemical warfare identification, recovery, and disposal; extraction and transportation of reactive materials; geophysical studies; metal detection; seismic refraction; and humanitarian remining. **Positions advertised include:** UXO Supervisor; Technician; UXO Safety Officer; Quality Control Specialist. **Corporate headquarters location:** This location.

UNISYS CORPORATION
12010 Sunrise Valley Drive, Reston VA 20191-3499. 703/620-7000. **Fax:** 703/620-7022. **Contact:** Mary Moore, Recruiting and Staffing. **World Wide Web address:** http://www.unisys.com. **Description:** Unisys Corporation provides information services, technology, and software. Unisys specializes in developing critical business solutions based on open information networks. Primary vertical markets are financial services, the public sector, transportation, communications and media as well as other commercial industries. Unisys operates in more than 100 countries around the world. **NOTE:** Search and apply for positions online. **Positions advertised include:** Sr. Proposal Manager; Program Controller; Project Controller Consultant; Engagement Manager; Director, Marketing Communications; Architect; Financial Analyst; Enterprise Architect. **Corporate headquarters location:** Blue Bell PA. **Other U.S. locations:** Nationwide. **Operations at this facility include:** This location offers various computer services to the federal government. **Listed on:** New York Stock Exchange. **Stock exchange symbol:** UIS. **Number of employees worldwide:** 37,000.

UNITED DOMINION REALTY TRUST, INC.
400 East Cary Street, Richmond VA 23219. 804/780-2691. **Fax:** 804/343-1912. **Contact:** Human Resources. **World Wide Web address:** http://www.udrt.com. **Description:** One of the largest real estate investment trusts specializing in residential apartment communities in the Southeast. United Dominion is a fully integrated real estate company handling acquisition, construction, and property management. The trust owns 138 properties including over 75,000 apartments in 120 communities, 14 neighborhood shopping centers, and four other commercial properties. Founded in 1972. **NOTE:** Search and apply for positions online. **Positions advertised include:** Construction Manager. **Corporate headquarters location:** This location. **Listed on:** New York Stock Exchange. **Stock exchange symbol:** UDR.

UNITED WAY OF AMERICA
701 North Fairfax Street, Alexandria VA 22314-2045. 703/836-7112. **Fax:** 703/683-7811. **Contact:** Human Resources. **World Wide Web address:** http://www.unitedway.org. **Description:** This location is the national service and training center, supporting its members with services that include advertising, training, corporate relations, research, networks, and government relations. Overall, through a vast network of volunteers and local charities, local United Way organizations throughout America help meet the health needs of millions. United Way's history is built on local organizations helping people in their communities. The United Way system includes approximately 1,400 community-based organizations. **Positions advertised include:** Senior Associate, Administrative. **Corporate headquarters location:** This location.

UNIVERSAL CORPORATION
P.O. Box 25099, Richmond VA 23260. 804/359-9311. **Physical address:** 1501 North Hamilton Street, Richmond VA 23230. **Contact:** Mike Oberschmidt Jr., Vice President of Human Resources. **World Wide Web address:** http://www.universalcorp.com. **Description:** An agricultural products holding company with interests in tobacco; agri-products including tea, rubber, nuts, dried fruit, and canned and frozen foods; and lumber and building products in Europe. Founded in 1918. **NOTE:** Job openings in Virginia are posted through the Virginia Employment Commission at www.vaworkforce.com. **Corporate headquarters location:** This location. **Listed on:** New York Stock Exchange. **Stock exchange symbol:** UVV. **Annual sales/revenues:** More than $100 million. **Number of employees worldwide:** 28,000.

UNIVERSAL SYSTEMS & TECHNOLOGY, INC. (UNITECH)
5870 Trinity Parkway, 4th Floor, Centreville VA 20120. 703/502-9600. **Fax:** 703/502-9300. **Contact:** Staffing. **E-mail address:** careers@unitech1.com. **World Wide Web address:** http://www.unitech1.com. **Description:** A professional services and solutions company concentrating in the areas of training and simulation, government and aviation solutions, sustaining operations, and homeland security for federal, state and local, and commercial customers. **NOTE:** Search and apply for positions online. **Positions advertised include:** Business Development Account Manager; Instructional Systems Designer. **Special programs:** Internships; Training. **Corporate headquarters location:** This location. **Other U.S. locations:** FL; NM; IA; SC; OK; DC. **Operations at this facility include:** Regional Headquarters. **Annual sales/revenues:** $21 - $50 million.

UNIVERSITY OF VIRGINIA
914 Emmett Street, Charlottesville VA 22904. 434/924-4598. **Fax:** 434/924-6911. **Recorded jobline:** 434/924-4400. **Contact:** Human Resources. **E-mail address:** hrdept@virginia.edu. **World Wide Web address:** http://www.hrs.virginia.edu. **Description:** A state university with 19,000 undergraduate and graduate students enrolled. **NOTE:** Search for positions online. **Special programs:** Internships. **Corporate headquarters location:** This location. **Operations at this facility include:** Administration; Research and Development; Service. **Number of employees at this location:** 11,000.

URGENT MEDICAL CARE LAKERIDGE
12449 Hedges Run Drive, Lake Ridge VA 22192. 703/494-6160. **Contact:** Human Resources. **Description:** A walk-in medical facility specializing in the treatment of minor illnesses and injuries. The center also has on-site X-ray and laboratory facilities.

USER TECHNOLOGY ASSOCIATES (UTA)
950 North Glebe Road, Suite 100, Arlington VA 22203. 703/522-5132. **Contact:** Human Resources. **E-mail address:** info@utanet.com. **World Wide Web address:** http://www.utanet.com. **Description:** Builds, integrates and manages enterprise network computing solutions for government organizations. **NOTE:** Search and apply for positions online. **Positions advertised include:** Help Desk Technician. **Corporate headquarters location:** This location.

VSE CORPORATION
2550 Huntington Avenue, Alexandria VA 22303-1499. 703/960-4600. **Fax:** 703/960-2688. **Recorded jobline:** 703/329-4784. **Contact:** Human Resources. **E-mail address:** hr@vsecorp.com. **World Wide Web address:** http://www.vsecorp.com. **Description:** Offers engineering services, logistical support services, and data processing services. **NOTE:** Search and apply for positions online. **Positions advertised include:** Engineering Technician. **Other U.S. locations:** NJ; MD; FL; CA; MI; GA. **Listed on:** NASDAQ. **Stock exchange symbol:** VSEC. **Number of employees at this location:** 200. **Number of employees nationwide:** 1,200.

VALUEMARK WEST END BEHAVIORAL HEALTH CARE SYSTEM
12800 West Creek Parkway, Richmond VA 23238. 804/784-2200. **Contact:** Human Resources. **Description:** An acute care psychiatric facility that houses 84 beds that serve children, adolescents, adults, and geriatrics. Founded in 1964.

VERISIGN, INC.
21355 Ridgetop Circle, Dulles VA 20166. 703/948-3200. **Contact:** Human Resources. **E-mail address:** jobs@verisign.com. **World Wide Web address:** http://www.verisign.com. **Description:** Provides infrastructure services to improve Internet and telecommunications networks. **NOTE:** Search and apply for positions online. **Positions advertised include:** Senior Financial Analyst; Network Program manager; Sr. Engineer; Technical Writer; Infrastructure Director; Marketing Manager. **Corporate headquarters location:** Mountain View CA. **Listed on:** NASDAQ. **Stock exchange symbol:** VRSN.

VERIZON COMMUNICATIONS
1310 North Courthouse Road, Arlington VA 22201. 703/974-3000. **Contact:** Human Resources. **World Wide Web address:** http://www.verizon.com. **Description:** A full-service communications services provider. Verizon offers residential local and long-distance telephone services and Internet access; wireless service plans, cellular phones, and data services; a full-line of business services including Internet access, data services, and telecommunications equipment and services; and government network solutions including Internet access, data services, telecommunications equipment and services, and enhanced communications services. **NOTE:** Search and apply for positions online. **Positions advertised include:** Federal Business Development Manager; DoD Staff Consultant; Regulatory Director; Project Manager; Coordinator, Business Sales Support. **Corporate headquarters location:** New York NY. **Listed on:** New York Stock Exchange. **Stock exchange symbol:** VZ.

VERSAR, INC.
6850 Versar Center, Springfield VA 22151. 703/750-3000. **Fax:** 703/642-6807. **Contact:** Human Resources. **World Wide Web address:** http://www.versar.com. **Description:** Versar is a professional services firm working in the areas of environment, energy, architecture/engineering/construction, defense, information technology, and management and policy consulting. Founded in 1969. **Positions advertised include:** Director of Procurement; Environmental Scientist. **Other U.S. locations:** Tempe AZ; Sacramento CA; Northglenn CO; Lombard IL; Columbia MD; Eden Beaver Creek OH; Oklahoma City OK; Horsham PA; San Antonio TX. **Subsidiaries include:** GEOMET Technologies, Inc., 8577 Atlas Drive, Gaithersburg MD. **Listed on:** American Stock Exchange. **Stock exchange symbol:** VSR. **Number of employees nationwide:** 495.

VIRGINIA BAPTIST HOSPITAL
3300 Rivermont Avenue, Lynchburg VA 24503. 434/947-4000. **Contact:** Human Resources. **Description:** A 317-bed hospital serving Central Virginia as the regional hospital for cancer care, women's and children's care, mental health and chemical dependency treatment, outpatient surgery, physical rehabilitation, and home health. **NOTE:** Search and apply for positions online. **Positions advertised include:** C-Section Technician; Educator; Radiologic Technologist; LPN; RN; Shift Manager, Nursing; Certified Nursing Assistant; Health Information Analyst; Counselor II; Health Unit Coordinator. **Parent company:** Centra Health.

VIRGINIA HOSPITAL CENTER-ARLINGTON
1701 North George Mason Drive, Arlington VA 22205-3698. 703/558-5000. **Contact:** Human Resources. **World Wide Web address:** http://www.virginiahospitalcenter.net. **Description:** A full-service, nonprofit tertiary care facility. Arlington Hospital operates outpatient clinics, a cancer center, and a cardiac unit. **Positions advertised include:** Assistant Director of Radiography; Assistant Patient Care Director; Case Manager; Clinical Specialist; Manager of Systems Administration; Public Relations Director; RN; LPN; Physical Therapist.

VIRGINIA POLYTECHNICAL INSTITUTE (VIRGINIA TECH)
Southgate Center, 1st Floor, Blacksburg VA 24061-0318. 540/231-5301. **Fax:** 540/231-3830. **Contact:** Personnel Services. **E-mail address:** perserv@vt.edu. **World Wide Web address:** http://www.vt.edu. **Description:** A land grant university that provides advanced instruction, research, and outreach programs. Continuing education is also offered at Roanoke Graduate Center, Northern Virginia Graduate Center, and Tidewater Graduate Center. NOTE: Search for positions online. **Corporate headquarters location:** This location. **Operations at this facility include:** Administration; Education; Research and Development. **Number of employees at this location:** 6,000.

VIRGINIA POWER
P.O. Box 26666, Richmond VA 23261. 804/771-3000. **Physical address:** One James River Plaza, 701 East Cary Street, Richmond VA 23219. **Fax:** 804/771-4792. **Contact:** Human Resources. **World Wide Web address:** http://www.dom.com. **Description:** A regulated public utility that generates, transmits, distributes, and sells electricity to more than 2 million homes and businesses in Virginia and North Carolina. The company sells electricity to retail customers including government agencies, as well as to wholesale customers such as rural electric cooperatives and municipalities. Founded in 1909. **Positions advertised include:** Electrical Engineer; Electric Scheduler; Operational Accounting Analyst; Natural Gas Trading Analyst; Training Specialist. **Corporate headquarters location:** This location. **Parent company:** Dominion Resources Inc. **Operations at this facility include:** Administration. **Listed on:** New York Stock Exchange. **Stock exchange symbol:** D. **Number of employees at this location:** 2,000. **Number of employees nationwide:** 10,500.

WACHOVIA BANK N.A.
1311 Dolley Madison Boulevard, McLean VA 22101. 703/556-7785. **Contact:** Human Resources. **World Wide Web address:** http://www.wachovia.com. **Description:** A full-service savings bank. **Parent company:** Wachovia Corporation. **Listed on:** New York Stock Exchange. **Stock exchange symbol:** WB.

WALTER GRINDERS, INC.
5160 Lad Land Drive, Fredericksburg VA 22407. 540/898-3700. **Fax:** 540/898-2811. **Contact:** Human Resources. **E-mail address:** info.wg@walter-ag.com. **World Wide Web address:** http://www.walter-ag.com. **Description:** Manufactures grinding machinery and related parts. **NOTE:** Search and apply for positions online. **Positions advertised include:** Applications Engineer. **Corporate headquarters location:** This location. **Parent company:** Walter AG (Germany).

WASHINGTON BUSINESS JOURNAL
1555 Wilson Boulevard, Suite 400, Arlington VA 22209-2405. 703/875-2200. **Fax:** 703/875-2231. **Contact:** Human Resources. **E-mail address:** Washington@bizjournals.com. **World Wide Web address:** http://www.bizjournals.com/washington. **Description:** Publishers of a weekly business newspaper. **Special programs:** Internships. **Parent company:** American City Business Journals (Charlotte NC). **Operations at this facility include:** Administration; Publishing; Sales; Service. **Number of employees at this location:** 45.

MARY WASHINGTON COLLEGE
George Washington Hall, Room 24, 1301 College Avenue, Fredericksburg VA 22401. 540/654-1000. **Contact:** Personnel Office. **World Wide Web address:** http://www.mwc.edu. **Description:** A four-year, coeducational, state-supported, residential college of the liberal arts and sciences. Mary Washington College has a full-time enrollment of approximately 3,500 students. **NOTE:** Search for positions online. Positions advertised include: Director of User Services.

MARY WASHINGTON HOSPITAL
2217 Princess Ann, Suite 105-1, Fredericksburg VA 22401. 540/741-1561. **Fax:** 540/899-2571. **Recorded jobline:** 540/741-1001. **Contact:** Human Resources. **World Wide Web address:** http://www.medicorp.org. **Description:** An acute care hospital with 318 beds. Services also include a nursing home, an assisted living center, a retirement center, a free-standing psychiatric hospital, a same-day surgery center, and an urgent care center. **NOTE:** Search and apply for positions online. **Positions advertised include:** Physical therapist; Diagnostic Technologist; Orthopedic Specialty Coordinator; RN's; LPN; Respiratory Therapist; Radiation Therapist; Ultrasonographer; Network/System Analyst. **Parent company:** MediCorp Health System.

WESTERN STATE HOSPITAL
1301 Richmond Avenue, P.O. Box 2500, Staunton VA 24402. 540/332-8300. **Fax:** 540/332-8305. **Recorded jobline:** 540/332-8315. **Contact:** Ms. Jeanne Brown, Human Resources Analyst. **World Wide Web address:** http://www.wsh.state.va.us. **Description:** A 465-bed hospital operated by the Commonwealth of Virginia, Department of Mental Health, Mental Retardation, and Substance Abuse **NOTE:** Search for positions online. **Number of employees at this location:** 870.

WILLIAMS INDUSTRIES INC.
P.O. Box 1770, Manassas VA 20109. 703/335-7800. **Physical address:** 8624 J.D. Reading Drive, Manassas VA 20109. **Fax:** 703/335-7802. **Contact:** Human Resources. **World Wide Web address:** http://www.wmsi.com. **Description:** A general construction company for the industrial, commercial, and institutional construction markets. Founded in 1970. **NOTE:** Entry-level positions and second and third shifts are offered. **Special programs:** Apprenticeships. **Office hours:** Monday - Friday, 8:30 a.m. - 4:30 p.m. **Corporate headquarters location:** This location. **Listed on:** NASDAQ. **Stock exchange symbol:** WMSI. **Number of employees nationwide:** 600.

WILLIAMS WHITTLE ASSOCIATES, INC.
711 Princess Street, Alexandria VA 22314. 703/836-9222. **Contact:** Human Resources. **World Wide Web address:** http://www.williamswhittle.com. **Description:** An advertising and public relations firm in categories such as restaurants, health care, telecommunications, real estate, automotive, and women's personal products.

XEROX CORPORATION
8180 Greensboro Drive, McLean VA 22102. 703/902-2520. **Contact:** Human Resources. **E-mail address:** xerox@isearch.com. **World Wide Web address:** http://www.xerox.com. **Description:** Develops, manufactures, markets, services, and finances information-processing products, including copiers, scanners, electronic printing systems, word processing systems, personal computers, and computer peripherals. **NOTE:** Search and apply for positions online. **Corporate headquarters location:** Stamford CT. **Listed on:** New York Stock Exchange. **Stock exchange symbol:** XRX.

XEROX CORPORATION
1700 Bayberry Court, Suite 200, Richmond VA 23226. 804/289-5400. **Contact:** Human Resources. **E-mail address:** xerox@isearch.com. **World Wide Web address:** http://www.xerox.com. **Description:** Develops, manufactures, markets, services, and finances information-processing products, including copiers, scanners, electronic printing systems, word processing systems, personal computers, and computer peripherals. **NOTE:** Search and apply for positions online. **Corporate headquarters location:** Stamford CT. **Listed on:** New York Stock Exchange. **Stock exchange symbol:** XRX.

XO COMMUNICATIONS
11111 Sunset Hills Road, Reston VA 20190. 703/547-2000. **Fax:** 703/547-2881. **Contact:** Human Resources. **E-mail address:** professional.services@xo.com. **World Wide Web address:** http://www.xo.com. **Description:** Provides communication services to businesses, large enterprises, and carriers. **NOTE** Search and apply for positions online. **Positions advertised include:** Accountant; Commodity Manager; Business Analyst; Financial Analyst; Internal Audit Manager; Corporate Development, Sr. Analyst.

AAA SEATTLE
330 Sixth Avenue North, Seattle WA 98109. 206/448-5353. **Contact:** Human Resources. **E-mail address:** hr@aaawa.com. **World Wide Web address:** http://www.aaawa.com. **Description:** Provides insurance, travel, and a wide variety of services to motorists through a network of over 50 branch offices. **Corporate headquarters location:** Heathrow FL.

ACI COMMUNICATIONS, INC.
23413 66th Avenue South, Kent WA 98032. 253/854-9802. **Fax:** 253/813-1001. **Contact:** Lan Mosher, Director of Human Resources. **E-mail address:** lmosher@acicomms.com. **World Wide Web address:** http://www.acicomms.com. **Description:** Designs and produces a broad range of electromechanical products used for the interconnection of circuits in electronic applications. The company manufactures interconnection hardware accessories including high-performance sockets, switches, connectors, and test and packaging systems for the computer, mobile communication, test, and consumer electronics market. The wiring systems division manufactures products for automotive and related industries including automotive connectors, terminal blocks, power distribution centers, cables and specialty wiring harnesses, safety devices, audio systems, and built-in cellular phones. **Corporate headquarters location:** This location.

ADM MILLING COMPANY
601 1st Street, Cheney WA 99004. 509/235-6216. **Contact:** Personnel. **World Wide Web address:** http://www.admworld.com. **Description:** Processes wheat, barley, corn, oats, and rice. The company specializes in milling wheat for flour, cakes, cookies, and pasta. **Corporate headquarters location:** Decatur IL. **Listed on:** New York Stock Exchange. **Stock exchange symbol:** ADM.

ADT SECURITY SERVICES
841 Powell Avenue SW, Suite 101, Renton WA 98055. 206/624-3103. **Contact:** Human Resources. **World Wide Web address:** http://www.adtsecurityservices.com. **Description:** Designs, installs, sells, and monitors fire and burglar alarm systems for commercial and industrial retail customers. The company also offers armed and unarmed security guards. **Corporate headquarters location:** Boca Raton FL. **Other U.S. locations:** Nationwide.

ADT SECURITY SERVICES
528 South Cannon Street, Spokane WA 99204-1717. 509/838-8283. **Contact:** Human Resources. **World Wide Web address:** http://www.adtsecurityservices.com. **Description:** Designs, installs, sells, and monitors fire and burglar alarm systems for commercial and industrial retail customers. The company also offers armed and unarmed security guards. **Corporate headquarters location:** Boca Raton FL. **Other U.S. locations:** Nationwide.

A.P.A. - THE ENGINEERED WOOD ASSOCIATION
7011 South 19th Street, Tacoma WA 98466. 253/565-6600. **Fax:** 253/565-7265. **Contact:** Human Resources. **E-mail address:** hr@apawood.org. **World Wide Web address:** http://www.apawood.org. **Description:** A nonprofit trade association providing research, quality testing, and marketing services for its member mills. Members of the A.P.A. produce plywood, OSB, and I-joists. Founded in 1936. **Special programs:** Training. **Corporate headquarters location:** This location. **Other U.S. locations:** Nationwide. **Number of employees at this location:** 170.

ABATIX ENVIRONMENTAL CORPORATION
1808 B Street NW, Suite 190, Auburn WA 98001. 253/735-1960. **Fax:** 214/381-9513. **Contact:** Human Resources. **E-mail address:** hr@abatix.com. **World Wide Web address:** http://www.abatix.com. **Description:** A full-line supplier of durable and nondurable supplies to the asbestos and lead abatement, hazardous material remediation, and construction industries. Products include industrial safety supplies, construction tools, general safety products such as protective clothing and eyewear, and clean-up equipment. **Corporate headquarters location:** Dallas TX. **Listed on:** NASDAQ. **Stock exchange symbol:** ABIX.

ACKERLEY PARTNERS
1301 Fifth Avenue, Suite 3525, Seattle WA 98101. 206/624-2888. **Contact:** Personnel Department. **World Wide Web address:** http://www.ackerleypartners.com. **Description:** Operates a group of media and entertainment companies. The Ackerley Group's national operations include an outdoor advertising agency, 14 television stations, three radio stations, and a sports/entertainment division that operates the NBA's Seattle SuperSonics and the WNBA's Seattle Storm. **Corporate headquarters location:** This location. **Listed on:** New York Stock Exchange. **Stock exchange symbol:** AK.

ACRO-WOOD CORPORATION
4425 South 3rd Avenue, P.O. Box 1028, Everett WA 98206. 425/258-3555. **Fax:** 425/252-7622. **Contact:** Controller. **World Wide Web address:** http://www.acrowood.com. **Description:** Operates a pulp and paper mill offering such products as plywood, particleboard, and machinery for the lumber industry. **Corporate headquarters location:** New York NY.

ACTIVE VOICE CORPORATION
2033 Sixth Avenue, Suite 500, Seattle WA 98121. 206/441-4700. **Fax:** 206/441-4784. **Contact:** Human Resources. **E-mail address:** personnel@activevoice.com. **World Wide Web address:** http://www.activevoice.com. **Description:** A leading provider of PC-based voice processing systems and CTI solutions. The company's software products enable small to medium-sized businesses and offices to communicate more effectively by integrating their traditional office telephone systems with voicemail, automated attendant, and interactive voice response functions. The company's products are utilized by a broad variety of enterprises in manufacturing, retail, service, health care, governmental, and institutional settings. Founded in 1983. **Positions advertised include:** Senior Software Engineer. **Corporate headquarters location:** This location. **International locations:** Australia; Canada; China; France; India; South Africa; Sweden; the Netherlands; United Kingdom. **Subsidiaries include:** Pronexus, Inc., Ontario, Canada. **Listed on:** NASDAQ. **Stock exchange symbol:** ACVC. **Number of employees at this location:** 175.

ADDUS HEALTHCARE, INC.
1010 North Normandie Street, Suite 303, Spokane WA 99202. 509/326-1090. **Fax:** 847/303-5376. **Contact:** Human Resources. **E-mail address:** personnel@addus.com. **World Wide Web address:** http://www.addus.com. **Description:** Provides home health care services for the elderly and disabled. Services include skilled nursing, respiratory therapy, rehabilitation, and home medical equipment. **Corporate headquarters location:** Palatine IL.

ADOBE SYSTEMS, INC.
801 North 34th Street, Seattle WA 98103. 206/470-7000. **Contact:** Personnel Department. **World Wide Web address:** http://www.adobe.com. **Description:** Adobe Systems develops, markets, and supports computer software products and technologies for Macintosh, Windows, and OS/2 platforms that enable users to create, display, print, and communicate electronic documents. The company distributes its products through a network of original equipment manufacturer customers, distributors and dealers, and value-added resellers and system integrators. The company has operations in the Americas, Europe, and the Pacific Rim. **Corporate headquarters location:** San Jose CA. **Operations at this facility include:** This location develops several of the company's software products and provides sales and support services. **Listed on:** NASDAQ. **Stock exchange symbol:** ADBE.

ADVANCED BUSINESSLINK CORPORATION
5808 Lake Washington Boulevard NE, Suite 100, Kirkland WA 98033. 425/602-4777. **Contact:** Human Resources. **E-mail address:** jobs@businesslink.com. **World Wide Web address:** http://www.businesslink.com. **Description:** Develops web-to-host and remote access software for IBM AS/400 servers. **Positions advertised include:** Account Executive; Outside Sales Representative; Marketing Director; Media Relations Manager. **Corporate headquarters location:** San Jose CA.

ADVANCED DIGITAL INFORMATION CORPORATION
11431 Willows Road NE, Redmond WA 98052. 425/881-8004. **Toll-free phone:** 800/336-1233. **Fax:** 425/881-2296. **Contact:** Human Resources. **E-mail address:** jobs@adic.com. **World Wide Web address:** http://www.adic.com. **Description:** Designs, manufactures, and markets hardware and software products for data storage and protection. Founded in 1983. **Positions advertised include:** Mechanical Engineer; Product Test Engineer. **Corporate headquarters location:** This location. **Parent company:** Lockheed Martin Corporation. **Listed on:** NASDAQ. **Stock exchange symbol:** ADIC. **Annual sales/revenues:** $51 - $100 million.

ADVO, INC.
4103 C Street NE, Auburn WA 98002. 253/395-8075. **Contact:** Human Resources. **World Wide Web address:** http://www.advo.com. **Description:** One of the nation's largest full-service direct mail marketing companies. **Company slogan:** The targeter of choice. **Corporate headquarters location:** Windsor CT. **Listed on:** New York Stock Exchange. **Stock exchange symbol:** AD.

AEROJET
P.O. Box 97009, Redmond WA 98073-9709. 425/885-5000. **Physical address:** 11411 139th PL N.E., Redmond WA 98052. **Contact:** Human Resources. **E-mail address:** careers@aerojet.com. **World Wide Web address:** http://www.rocket.com. **Description:** Aerojet is a world-recognized aerospace and defense leader principally serving the missile and space propulsion, and defense and armaments markets. **NOTE:** Website applications are preferred; visit http://www.aerojet.com for more information. **Positions advertised include:** Assembly Technician; Electron Beam Welder; Engineer; Engineering Intern; Passivation Technician; Program Planner; Quality Engineering Manager. **Corporate headquarters location:** Sacramento, CA. **Other U.S. locations:** Nationwide. **Parent Company:** GenCorp, Inc. **Listed on:** New York Stock Exchange. **Stock exchange symbol:** GY.

AGILENT TECHNOLOGIES
8600 Soper Hill Road, Everett WA 98205-1209. 425/335-2000. **Contact:** Staffing Department. **World Wide Web address:** http://www.agilent.com. **Description:** Operates through four business segments: chemical analysis, healthcare solutions, semiconductor products, and test and measurement. **Positions advertised include:** Senior Solution Architect. **Corporate headquarters location:** Palo Alto CA. **Listed on:** New York Stock Exchange. **Stock exchange symbol:** A.

AGILENT TECHNOLOGIES
24001 East Mission Avenue, Liberty Lake WA 99019. 509/921-4001. **Fax:** 509/921-4300. **Contact:** Personnel Department. **World Wide Web address:** http://www.agilent.com. **Description:** Engaged in the design and manufacture of measurement and computation products and systems used in business, industry, engineering, science health care, and education. **Corporate headquarters location:** Palo Alto CA. **Other U.S. locations:** Nationwide. **Listed on:** New York Stock Exchange. **Stock exchange symbol:** A.

AGRINORTHWEST
P.O. Box 2308, Tri-Cities WA 99302. 509/547-8879. **Physical address:** 2810 West Clearwater Street, Kennewick WA 99336. **Fax:** 509/734-5075. **Contact:** Mark Knight, Human Resources Manager. **Description:** One of the largest diversified agricultural operations in the western United States. Agrinorthwest is engaged in the production of a variety of food crops including potatoes, grain, corn, and apples. **Number of employees nationwide:** 700.

AIKEN, ST. LOUIS & SILJEG, P.S.
801 Second Avenue, Suite 1200, Seattle WA 98104. 206/624-2650. **Contact:** Personnel. **World Wide Web address:** http://www.aiken.com. **Description:** A law firm specializing in corporate, tax, insurance, and environmental law. **Corporate headquarters location:** This location.

AIM AVIATION INC.
P.O. Box 9011, Renton WA 98057. 425/235-2750. **Physical address:** 705 SW Seventh Street, Renton WA 98055. **Contact:** Human Resources Department. **E-mail address:** recruiting@aimseattle.com. **World Wide Web address:** http://www.aimaviation.com. **Description:** Manufactures a wide variety of products for aircraft interiors. **Corporate headquarters location:** England.

AIM AVIATION INC.
1530 22nd Street NW, Auburn WA 98001-3300. 253/804-3355. **Contact:** Human Resources. **World Wide Web address:** http://www.aimaviation.com. **Description:** Manufactures a wide variety of products for aircraft interiors. **Corporate headquarters location:** England.

AIR LIQUIDE CORPORATION
4230 East Trent Avenue, Spokane WA 99202. 509/536-7484. **Contact:** Human Resources. **World Wide Web address:** http://www.airliquide.com. **Description:** Air Liquide Corporation is a diversified manufacturer engaged in the recovery and sale of atmospheric industrial gases, the manufacture and sale of oil field equipment and supplies, and the distribution of welding and industrial equipment and supplies. **Corporate headquarters location:** Houston TX. **International locations:** Worldwide. **Operations at this facility include:** This location processes and distributes industrial and medical gases.

AIR LIQUIDE CORPORATION
41304 South Piert Road, Kennewick WA 99337. 509/582-5168. **Contact:** Human Resources. **World Wide Web address:** http://www.airliquide.com. **Description:** Air Liquide Corporation is a diversified manufacturer engaged in the recovery and sale of atmospheric industrial gases, the manufacture and sale of oil field equipment and

supplies, and the distribution of welding and industrial equipment and supplies. **Corporate headquarters location:** Houston TX. **International locations:** Worldwide. **Operations at this facility include:** This location processes and distributes carbon dioxide for the manufacture of dry ice.

AIR VAN MOVING GROUP
10510 NE Northup Way, Suite 110, Kirkland WA 98033. **Toll-free phone:** 800/326-3683. **Contact:** Personnel Director. **World Wide Web address:** http://www.navlagent.com/airvan. **Description:** A freight forwarding company with operations in domestic moving services. **Corporate headquarters location:** This location.

AJILON CONSULTING
11711 SE 8th, Suite 303, Bellevue WA 98005. 425/455-1004. **Fax:** 425/455-5098. **Contact:** Human Resources. **E-mail address:** recruit.seattle@ajilon.com. **World Wide Web address:** http://www.ajilonconsulting.com. **Description:** Offers computer consulting services, project support, and end user services. **Positions advertised include:** Seibel/Genesys Architect; Senior Reports Analyst. **Other U.S. locations:** Nationwide.

ALASKAN COPPER WORKS
P.O. Box 3546, Seattle WA 98124-3546. 206/623-5800. **Physical address:** 3223 Sixth Avenue South, Seattle WA 98134. **Recorded jobline:** 206/382-8221. **Contact:** Human Resources. **World Wide Web address:** http://www.alascop.com. **Description:** Produces fabricated pipe and other metal products including heat exchangers and process equipment. **Parent company:** Alaskan Copper Companies.

ALBERTSON'S, INC.
14500 15th Avenue NE, Shoreline WA 98155. 206/365-2422. **Contact:** Human Resources. **E-mail address:** employment@albertsons.com. **World Wide Web address:** http://www.albertsons.com. **Description:** A full-service supermarket. **Corporate headquarters location:** Boise ID. **Listed on:** New York Stock Exchange. **Stock exchange symbol:** ABS.

ALCIDE CORPORATION
P.O. Box 89, Redmond WA 98073-0089. 425/882-2555. **Physical address:** 8561 154th Avenue NE, Redmond WA 98052. **Fax:** 425/861-0173. **Contact:** Human Resources. **World Wide Web address:** http://www.alcide.com. **Description:** Researches, develops, and markets antimicrobial products for industrial, human, and animal health uses and for direct application to food in order to control food-borne pathogens. Alcide has developed several disinfectants and a sterilant to kill microorganisms on surface areas and to reduce the threat of disease transmission in health care facilities. In the animal health field, the company has marketed technology to prevent mastitis in dairy cattle. **Positions advertised include:** Lab Chemist; Clerk/Receptionist. **Corporate headquarters location:** This location. **Listed on:** NASDAQ. **Stock exchange symbol:** ALCO.

ALL-STAR TOYOTA INC.
13355 Lake City Way NE, Seattle WA 98125. 206/367-0080. **Contact:** Personnel Department. **Description:** A retailer and wholesaler of automobile parts and services.

ALLPAK CONTAINER, INC.
1100 SW 27th Street, Renton WA 98055. 425/227-0400. **Fax:** 425/227-0197. **Contact:** Human Resources Manager. **E-mail address:** humanresources@allpak.com. **World Wide Web address:** http://www.allpak.com. **Description:** Produces recycled paperboard and paper packaging products including corrugated containers, specialty corrugated products, and folding cartons. **Corporate headquarters location:** This location.

ALLSTATE INSURANCE COMPANY
18911 North Creek Parkway, Suite 301, Bothell WA 98011. 425/489-2200. **Contact:** Human Resources. **World Wide Web address:** http://www.allstate.com. **Description:** Provides a full line of property, liability, life, reinsurance, and commercial lines of insurance. **Positions advertised include:** Claims Associate; Claims Service Adjuster. **Corporate headquarters location:** Northbrook IL. **Parent company:** Sears, Roebuck & Company. **Operations at this facility include:** Administration; Regional Headquarters; Sales; Service. **Listed on:** New York Stock Exchange. **Stock exchange symbol:** S. **Number of employees at this location:** 1,500. **Number of employees nationwide:** 53,000.

AMAZON.COM, INC.
2646 Rainier Avenue South, Seattle WA 98144. 206/622-2335. **Contact:** Strategic Growth. **E-mail address:** jobs@amazon.com. **World Wide Web address:** http://www.amazon.com. **Description:** An online store engaged in the sale of books, videos, music, toys, and electronics. Amazon.com also offers online auctions. Founded in 1995. **NOTE:** If sending a resume via e-mail, please be sure the information is in an ASCII-text format. **Positions advertised include:** Technical Program/Product Manager; Senior Buyer; Software Development Engineer. **Corporate headquarters location:** This location. **Other U.S. locations:** New Castle DE; McDonough GA; Coffeyville KS; Cambellsville KY; Lexington KY; Fernley NV. **International locations:** Europe. **Listed on:** NASDAQ. **Stock exchange symbol:** AMZN. **President/CEO:** Jeffrey Bezos.

AMERICAN AIRLINES, INC.
Seattle-Tacoma International Airport, Seattle WA 98158-1277. 206/433-3951. **Contact:** Human Resources. **World Wide Web address:** http://www.americanair.com. **Description:** Provides scheduled jet service to more than 170 destinations throughout North America, the Caribbean, Latin America, Europe, and the Pacific. **NOTE:** All resumes should be sent to: American Airlines, Inc., Human Resources, P.O. Box 619616, Mail Drop 5105, DFW Airport TX 75261-9040. **Corporate headquarters location:** Fort Worth TX. **Parent company:** AMR Corporation's operations fall within three major lines of business: the Air Transportation Group, the SABRE Group, and the AMR Management Services Group.

AMERICAN BUILDING MAINTENANCE
16 East Columbia Drive, Kennewick WA 99336. 509/582-9776. **Toll-free phone:** 800/678-4270. **Fax:** 509/582.5224. **Contact:** Human Resources. **World Wide Web address:** http://www.cbvcp.com. **Description:** American Building Maintenance (ABM) provides nationwide maintenance services to commercial and residential facilities. ABM was founded over 75 years ago. ABM offers a variety of services including janitorial, lighting maintenance, floor care, janitorial supplies, window cleaning, and carpet cleaning. **Positions advertised include:** Janitorial; Maintenance. **Corporate headquarters location:** This location. **Other U.S. locations:** Nationwide.

AMERICAN GENERAL FINANCE
10740 Meridian Avenue North, Suite 105, Seattle WA 98133. 206/362-4566. **Contact:** Human Resources. **World Wide Web address:** http://www.agfinance.com. **Description:** One of the country's largest public insurance companies. American General Finance also provides financial services including mortgage loans, real estate investment and development, investment counseling, and management and distribution of mutual funds. **Corporate headquarters location:** New York NY. **Parent company:** American General Corporation. **Listed on:** New York Stock Exchange. **Stock exchange symbol:** AGC.

AMERICAN RED CROSS
1900 25th Avenue South, Seattle WA 98144-4708. 206/323-2345. **Contact:** Human Resources. **World Wide Web address:** http://www.redcross.org. **Description:** A humanitarian organization that aids disaster victims, gathers blood for crisis distribution, trains individuals to respond to emergencies, educates individuals on various diseases, and raises funds for other charitable establishments. **Corporate headquarters location:** Washington DC.

AMERICANWEST BANCORPORATION
9506 North Newport Highway, Spokane WA 99218. 509/467-6949. **Contact:** Human Resources. **World Wide Web address:** http://www.awbank.net. **Description:** A bank holding company. **Corporate headquarters location:** This location.

AMGEN
1201 Amgen Court West, Seattle WA 98119-3105. 206/265-7000. **Fax:** 206/621-1399. **Contact:** Human Resources. **World Wide Web address:** http://www.amgen.com. **Description:** A leading biopharmaceutical company focused on the discovery, manufacture, and marketing of products to treat immune system disorders. **NOTE:** Apply online. **Positions advertised include:** Business Analyst; Engineer; Facilities Maintenance Technician; Global Project Manager. **Corporate headquarters location:** Thousand Oaks CA. **Other area locations:** Bothell WA. **Operations at this facility include:** Administration; Manufacturing; Research and Development.

AMGEN
21507 23rd Drive SE, Bothell WA 98021. 206/265-7000. **Contact:** Human Resources. **World Wide Web address:** http://www.amgen.com. **Description:** Amgen is a leading biopharmaceutical company focused on the discovery, manufacture, and marketing of products to treat immune system disorders. **NOTE:** Apply online. **Corporate headquarters location:** Thousand Oaks CA. **Operations at this facility include:** This location is a manufacturing plant.

ANALYSTS INTERNATIONAL CORPORATION (AIC)
10655 NE Fourth Street, Suite 400, Bellevue WA 98004-5022. 425/454-2500. **Toll-free phone:** 800/698-9411. **Contact:** Human Resources Department. **E-mail address:** jobs@analysts.com. **World Wide Web address:** http://www.analysts.com. **Description:** An international computer consulting firm. The company assists clients in developing systems in a variety of industries using different programming languages and software. Founded in 1966. **Office hours:** Monday - Friday, 8:00 a.m. - 5:00 p.m. **Corporate headquarters location:** Minneapolis MN. **Other U.S. locations:** Nationwide. **International locations:** Cambridge, England; Toronto, Canada. **Listed on:** NASDAQ. **Stock exchange symbol:** ANLY. **Annual sales/revenues:** More than $100 million. **Number of employees at this location:** 250.

ANIXTER-SEATTLE
21419 64th Avenue South, Kent WA 98032. 253/872-6200. **Contact:** Human Resources. **E-mail address:** jobs@anixter.com. **World Wide Web address:** http://www.anixter.com. **Description:** A value-added provider of industrial wire and cabling solutions that support voice and data applications. Solutions include customized pre- and postsale services, a wide range of technology products from the world's leading manufacturers, and logistics management through a global distribution network. Founded in 1957. **Corporate headquarters location:** Skokie IL. **Parent company:** Anixter International. **Operations at this facility include:** Administration; Sales; Service. **Listed on:** New York Stock Exchange. **Stock exchange symbol:** AXE. **Annual sales/revenues:** More than $100 million. **Number of employees at this location:** 50. **Number of employees nationwide:** 3,500. **Number of employees worldwide:** 5,000.

ANVIL CORPORATION
1675 West Bakerview Road, Bellingham WA 98226. 360/671-1450. **Contact:** Johanna Snyder, Human Resources. **E-mail address:** jsnyder@anvilcorp.com. **World Wide Web address:** http://www.anvilcorp.com. **Description:** An engineering and technical services company that provides a variety of services to the mining, environmental, utilities, transportation, and chemical industries. **Positions advertised include:** NDE Technician. **Corporate headquarters location:** This location.

APPLIED INDUSTRIAL TECHNOLOGIES
2747A R.W. Johnson Boulevard SW, Olympia WA 98512. 360/754-4363. **Contact:** Human Resources. **E-mail address:** career@applied.com. **World Wide Web address:** http://www.applied.com. **Description:** A distributor of bearings, power transmitters, hydraulic power units, and rubber products for use in various industries. **Corporate headquarters location:** Cleveland OH. **Listed on:** New York Stock Exchange. **Stock exchange symbol:** AIT.

APPLIED INDUSTRIAL TECHNOLOGIES
1701 Portland Avenue, Tacoma WA 98421. 253/383-5363. **Contact:** Human Resources. **E-mail address:** career@applied.com. **World Wide Web address:** http://www.applied.com. **Description:** A distributor of bearings, power transmitters, hydraulic power units, and rubber products for use in various industries. **Corporate headquarters location:** Cleveland OH. **Listed on:** New York Stock Exchange. **Stock exchange symbol:** AIT.

APPLIED INDUSTRIAL TECHNOLOGIES
4021 6th Avenue, P.O. Box 24345, Seattle WA 98124-0345. 206/223-5255. **Fax:** 206/682-6919. **Contact:** Human Resources Department. **E-mail address:** career@apz-applied.com. **World Wide Web address:** http://www.appliedindustrial.com. **Description:** A distributor of bearings, power transmitters, hydraulic power units, and rubber products for use in various industries. **Corporate headquarters location:** Cleveland OH. **Listed on:** New York Stock Exchange. **Stock exchange symbol:** AIT.

APPLIED INDUSTRIAL TECHNOLOGIES
2910 Kauffman Avenue, Vancouver WA 98660. 360/695-3326. **Contact:** Human Resources. **E-mail address:** career@apz-applied.com. **World Wide Web address:** http://www.appliedindustrial.com. **Description:** A distributor of bearings, power transmitters, hydraulic power units, and rubber products for use in various industries. **Corporate headquarters location:** Cleveland OH. **Listed on:** New York Stock Exchange. **Stock exchange symbol:** AIT.

APRIA HEALTHCARE GROUP INC.
P.O. Box 3039, Redmond WA 98073-3039. 425/881-8500. **Physical address:** 14945 NE 87th Street, Redmond WA 98052. **Contact:** Human Resources. **World Wide Web**

address: http://www.apria.com. **Description:** One of the largest national providers of home health care products and services including a broad range of respiratory therapy services, home medical equipment, and infusion therapy services. Apria's home health care services are provided to patients who have been discharged from hospitals, skilled nursing facilities, or convalescent homes and are being treated at home. In conjunction with medical professionals, Apria personnel deliver, install, and service medical equipment, as well as provide appropriate therapies and coordinate plans of care for their patients. Apria personnel also instruct patients and caregivers in the correct use of equipment and monitor the equipment's effectiveness. **Positions advertised include:** Staff Pharmacist; Branch Pharmacy Manager; Regional Respiratory Therapy Manager. **Corporate headquarters location:** Costa Mesa CA. **Listed on:** New York Stock Exchange. **Stock exchange symbol:** AHG.

ARKEMA GROUP
2901 Taylor Way, Tacoma WA 98421. 253/627-9101. **Contact:** Human Resources. **World Wide Web address:** http://www.atofina.com. **Description:** Atofina Chemicals is a diversified chemicals manufacturer. **Headquarters location:** Philadelphia PA. **Operations at this facility include:** This location manufactures chlorate.

ASH GROVE CEMENT COMPANY
3801 East Marginal Way South, Seattle WA 98134. 206/623-5596. **Contact:** Human Resources. **World Wide Web address:** http://www.ashgrove.com. **Description:** Operates cement and lime plants in nine states across the country. With an annual production capacity of more than 4.6 million tons of cement, Ash Grove is one of the largest cement manufacturers in the United States. The Portland and masonry cements produced at the company's plants are used in the construction of highways, bridges, commercial and industrial complexes, residential homes, and a myriad of other structures. In addition to cement operations, the company operates two lime plants with total production capacity of 270,000 tons per year. Ash Grove lime products are used in steel and paper manufacturing, municipal water treatment, agriculture, and construction. **Positions advertised include:** Plant Manager; Product Manager; Maintenance Manager; Process Engineer; Chief Chemist; Human Resources Manager. **Office hours:** Monday - Friday, 7:00 a.m. - 4:00 p.m. **Corporate headquarters location:** Overland Park KS.

ASIX
10900 NE Eighth Avenue, Suite 700, Bellevue WA 98004. 425/635-0709. **Toll-free phone:** 800/335-2525. **Contact:** Personnel. **E-mail address:** resumes@asix.com. **World Wide Web address:** http://www.asix.com. **Description:** Provides computer consulting services.

ASSOCIATED GROCERS, INC.
P.O. Box 3763, Seattle WA 98124-2263. 206/762-2100. **Fax:** 206/767-8785. **Recorded jobline:** 206/767-8788. **Contact:** Human Resources Department. **E-mail address:** jobs@agsea.com. **World Wide Web address:** http://www.agsea.com. **Description:** Provides general merchandise and grocery products to over 400 independently owned retail markets in several western states. The company also offers a variety of related services including retail promotion, human resources, accounting, procurement, warehousing, and transportation. Founded in 1934. **Positions advertised include:** Meat Specialist; Order Selector. **NOTE:** Jobseekers interested in driver or warehouse positions must call the Human Resources Department to set up an application appointment. All driver and warehouse positions are part-time, on-call positions, and applicants must be at least 18 years old. **Company slogan:** The food people. **Office hours:** Monday - Friday, 8:00 a.m. - 5:00 p.m. **Corporate headquarters location:** This location. **Other area locations:** Kent WA. **Annual sales/revenues:** More than $100 million. **Number of employees nationwide:** 1,400.

ATLAS FOUNDRY & MACHINERY COMPANY
3021 South Wilkeson Street, Tacoma WA 98409. 253/475-4600. **Fax:** 253/471-7037. **Contact:** Personnel. **World Wide Web address:** http://www.atlasfoundry.com. **Description:** Produces a diversified range of steel and stainless steel castings for the construction, transportation, maritime, oil, and nuclear industries. The firm also has fabrication and machining capabilities in large, complex weldings and castings. **Corporate headquarters location:** This location.

ATTACHMATE CORPORATION
P.O. Box 90026, Bellevue WA 98009-9026. 425/644-4010. **Toll-free phone:** 800/426-6283. **Contact:** Recruiter. **E-mail address:** cooljobs@attachmate.com. **World Wide Web address:** http://www.attachmate.com. **Description:** Designs, manufactures, and markets personal computer to mainframe data communications products worldwide. Products are marketed under the IRMA, Crosstalk, and Quickappbrand names. Founded in 1982. **Positions advertised include:** Software Test Engineer; Senior Database Engineer; Technical Architect; Senior Administrative Assistant; User Interface Developer. **Special programs:** Internships. **Office hours:** Monday - Friday, 9:00 a.m. - 5:00 p.m. **Corporate headquarters location:** This location. **Other U.S. locations:** Nationwide. **International locations:** Worldwide. **Listed on:** Privately held. **Number of employees nationwide:** 1,000.

AUTO-CHLOR SYSTEM OF WASHINGTON
P.O. Box 94263, Seattle WA 98124-6563. 206/622-0900. **Physical address:** 4315 Seventh Avenue South, Seattle WA 98108. **Contact:** Personnel Department. **World Wide Web address:** http://www.autochlor.net. **Description:** Manufactures and distributes commercial dishwashers and related supplies. **Positions advertised include:** Route Sales Trainee. **Corporate headquarters location:** Los Altos CA.

AVISTA CORPORATION
1411 East Mission Avenue, Spokane WA 99220-3727. 509/489-0500. **Contact:** Employment. **World Wide Web address:** http://www.avistacorp.com. **Description:** Provides natural gas and electricity to customers in eastern Washington, northern Idaho, Oregon, and Northern California. **NOTE:** This firm does not accept unsolicited resumes. Please only respond to advertised openings. **Positions advertised include:** Large Format Copy Technician. **Special programs:** Internships. **Corporate headquarters location:** This location. **Other U.S. locations:** South Lake Tahoe CA; Medford CT; Klammath OR. **Operations at this facility include:** Administration. **Listed on:** New York Stock Exchange. **Stock exchange symbol:** AVA. **Number of employees at this location:** 900. **Number of employees nationwide:** 1,400.

AVOCENT CORPORATION
9911 Willows Road NE, Redmond WA 98052. 425/861-5858. **Contact:** Human Resources Department. **E-mail address:** hr@avocent.com. **World Wide Web address:** http://www.avocent.com. **Description:** Manufactures a variety of computer components such as concentrated switches. **Positions advertised include:** Auditor; Quality Engineer; Business Analyst; Help Desk Technician; Product Manager; Web Developer. **Listed on:** NASDAQ. **Stock exchange symbol:** AVCT.

AVTECH CORPORATION
3400 Wallingford Avenue North, Seattle WA 98103. 206/634-2540. **Contact:** Personnel Director. **E-mail address:** hr@avtcorp.com. **World Wide Web address:** http://www.avtcorp.com. **Description:** Manufactures a variety of electronic equipment products including interior lighting and flight deck audio control panels. **Positions advertised include:** QA Supervisor. **Corporate headquarters location:** This location.

AZTECA RESTAURANTS
133 SW 158th Street, Burien WA 98166. 206/243-7021. **Contact:** Human Resources. **World Wide Web address:** http://www.aztecamex.com. **Description:** Owns and operates a chain of Mexican restaurants. **Corporate headquarters location:** This location.

BJ'S PAINT'N PLACE INC.
6528 Capitol Boulevard South, Tumwater WA 98501. 360/943-3232. **Contact:** Human Resources. **World Wide Web address:** http://www.bjspaint.com. **Description:** A retail store offering paints, stains, wallpaper, fabric, finishes, brushes, and similar products.

BOC GASES
4715 NE 78th Street, Vancouver WA 98665. 360/695-1255. **Contact:** Human Resources. **E-mail address:** jobs@us.gases.boc.com. **World Wide Web address:** http://www.boc.com. **Description:** Manufactures and markets industrial gases and related products. BOC Gases also provides full engineering and technical services. **Listed on:** New York Stock Exchange. **Stock exchange symbol:** BOX.

BAINBRIDGE ISLAND SCHOOL DISTRICT
8489 Madison Avenue NE, Bainbridge Island WA 98110. 206/842-4714. **Contact:** Dixie Brown, Personnel Specialist. **E-mail address:** dbrown@bainbridge.wednet.edu. **World Wide Web address:** http://www.bainbridge.wednet.edu. **Description:** A public school district that is comprised of one high school, one middle school, three elementary schools, and an alternative learning program. **Operations at this facility include:** Administration. **Number of employees at this location:** 400.

BANK OF AMERICA
800 Fifth Avenue, 33rd Floor, Seattle WA 98104. 206/461-0800. **Contact:** Human Resources Department. **World Wide Web address:** http://www.bankofamerica.com/careers. **Description:** Bank of America is a full-service banking and financial institution. The company operates through four business segments: Global Corporate and Investment Banking, Principal Investing and Asset Management, Commercial Banking, and Consumer Banking. **Corporate headquarters location:** Charlotte NC. **Other U.S. locations:** Nationwide. **Operations at this facility include:** This location is a bank. **Listed on:** New York Stock Exchange. **Stock exchange symbol:** BAC.

BARNES & NOBLE BOOKSTORES
626 106th Avenue NE, Bellevue WA 98004. 425/451-8463. **Contact:** Human Resources. **World Wide Web address:** http://www.bn.com. **Description:** A bookstore chain operating nationwide. This location has a cafe and music department in addition to its book departments. **Corporate headquarters location:** New York NY. **Listed on:** New York Stock Exchange. **Stock exchange symbol:** BKS.

BARTELL DRUGS
4727 Denver Avenue South, Seattle WA 98134. 206/763-2626. **Contact:** Personnel Department. **E-mail address:** hr@bartelldrugs.com. **World Wide Web address:** http://www.bartelldrugs.com. **Description:** Operates a chain of drug stores in the Seattle area. **Positions advertised include:** Pharmacy Assistant; Pharmacist; Management Trainee. **Corporate headquarters location:** This location. **Number of employees nationwide:** 600.

E.J. BARTELLS COMPANY
P.O. Box 4160, Renton WA 98057-4160. 425/228-4111. **Physical address:** 700 Powell Avenue SW, Renton WA 98055. **Fax:** 425/228-8807. **Contact:** Human Resources Department. **World Wide Web address:** http://www.ejbartells.com. **Description:** A wholesale distributor, fabricator, and manufacturer of insulation and refractory products. **Corporate headquarters location:** This location. **Other area locations:** Kennewick WA; Spokane WA. **Other U.S. locations:** Anchorage AK; Denver CO; Billings MT; Eugene OR; Medford OR; Portland OR; Salt Lake City UT. **Subsidiaries include:** Bartells Materials Management, Inc. **Operations at this facility include:** Administration. **Number of employees nationwide:** 700.

ROBERT E. BAYLEY CONSTRUCTION
8005 SE 28th Street, Suite 100, Mercer Island WA 98040-9004. 206/621-8884. **Fax:** 206/343-7728. **Contact:** Personnel Department. **World Wide Web address:** http://www.bayley.net. **Description:** A general building contractor specializing in commercial construction. **Corporate headquarters location:** This location.

R.W. BECK, INC.
1001 Fourth Avenue, Suite 2500, Seattle WA 98154. 206/695-4700. **Contact:** Mr. Van Finger, Director of Personnel. **World Wide Web address:** http://www.rwbeck.com. **Description:** A diversified professional, technical, and management consulting firm. The company provides construction, environmental, technical, energy, solid waste, and water/wastewater services nationwide. **NOTE:** Apply online. **Positions advertised include:** Senior Project Manager. **Corporate headquarters location:** This location. **Number of employees at this location:** 175. **Number of employees nationwide:** 500.

BEKINS NORTHWEST
6501 216th Street SW, Mount Lake Terrace WA 98043. 425/775-8950. **Fax:** 206/527-1429. **Contact:** Personnel Director. **E-mail address:** hr@nekins.net. **World Wide Web address:** http://www.bekinsnorthwest.com. **Description:** Engaged in the transporting and warehousing of household goods, office and industrial equipment, electronics, and business records. Founded in 1903. **Corporate headquarters location:** Seattle WA.

BELLEVUE COMMUNITY COLLEGE
3000 Landerholm Circle SE, Bellevue WA 98007-6484. 425/564-2247. **Recorded jobline:** 425/564-2082. **Contact:** Human Resources. **World Wide Web address:** http://www.bcc.ctc.edu. **Description:** A community college operating as part of the Washington State Community College System. Over 18,000 students are enrolled each quarter.

THE BELLINGHAM HERALD
P.O. Box 1277, Bellingham WA 98227-1277. 360/676-2600. **Contact:** Personnel. **World Wide Web address:** http://www.bellinghamherald.com. **Description:** Publishes a local evening newspaper.

BELSHAW BROTHERS, INC.
1750 22nd Avenue South, Seattle WA 98144-4590. 206/322-5474. **Contact:** Personnel Department. **E-mail address:** jobs@belshaw.com. **World Wide Web address:** http://www.belshaw.com. **Description:** Manufactures bakery equipment. The company's products include donut fryers, glazers, finishing tables, and automatic conveyors. **Corporate headquarters location:** This location.

BERGER/ABAM ENGINEERS INC.
33301 Ninth Avenue South, Suite 300, Federal Way WA 98003-2600. 206/431-2300. **Fax:** 206/431-2250. **Contact:** Personnel. **E-mail address:** employment@abam.com. **World Wide Web address:** http://www.abam.com. **Description:** A civil engineering and consulting firm specializing in the design of piers and waterfront structures, tanks and reservoirs, bridges, transit guideways, buildings, floating structures, and offshore drilling platforms. Berger/Abam Engineers Inc. also performs concrete material research, advanced computer design analysis, and construction management services. **Positions advertised include:** Document Production Specialist; Civil Engineer. **Corporate headquarters location:** This location.

BEST WESTERN BELLEVUE INN
11211 Main Street, Bellevue WA 98004. 425/455-5240. **Fax:** 425/455-0654. **Contact:** Human Resources. **World Wide Web address:** http://www.bestwestern.com. **Description:** A 180-room hotel franchise offering rental car services, restaurants, and meeting facilities. **Corporate headquarters location:** Phoenix AZ.

BESTFOODS BAKING COMPANY
155 NE 100th Street, Suite 100, Seattle WA 98125. 206/522-9983. **Contact:** Human Resources. **World Wide Web address:** http://www.bestfoods.com. **Description:** Bestfoods Baking Company produces and distributes a line of cakes, cookies, doughnuts, and various baked products. **Corporate headquarters location:** Englewood Cliffs NJ. **Operations at this facility include:** This location houses administrative offices.

BIO-RAD LABORATORIES
6565 185th Avenue NE, Redmond WA 98052. 425/881-8300. **Contact:** Human Resources. **World Wide Web address:** http://www.bio-rad.com. **Description:** Engaged in the research and development of diagnostic test equipment used to detect blood viral disease.

BIRDSEYE FOODS
P.O. Box 11046, Tacoma WA 98411-0046. 253/383-1621. **Physical address:** 3303 South 35th Street, Tacoma WA 98409. **Contact:** Personnel. **World Wide Web address:** http://www.birdseyefoods.com. **Description:** A food manufacturing company with products that include a variety of vegetables and other foods.

THE BOEING COMPANY
P.O. Box 3707, Mail Stop 6H-PH, Seattle WA 98124-2207. 206/655-1131. **Contact:** Employment Office. **World Wide Web address:** http://www.boeing.com. **Description:** One of the world's largest aerospace firms. Boeing applies advanced aerospace technology to a wide range of space, defense, electronic, and computing programs. The Boeing Company is divided into four business segments: Commercial Airplanes, Missile Aircraft and Missile Systems, Space and Communications, and Phantom Works, the company's advanced research and development segment. The Commercial Airplane Group is the company's largest operating unit. **Positions advertised include:** Strategy Analyst; Maintenance Analyst; Human Resources Specialist; Internal Auditor. **Corporate headquarters location:** Chicago IL. **Listed on:** New York Stock Exchange. **Stock exchange symbol:** BA. **Annual sales/revenues:** More than $100 million.

BOISE CASCADE CORPORATION
P.O. Box 1729, Yakima WA 98907-0051. 509/453-3131. **Contact:** Human Resources. **World Wide Web address:** http://www.bc.com. **Description:** An integrated paper and forest products company with operations located throughout the United States. The company manufactures and distributes paper and paper products, office products, and building products and owns and manages timberland to support these operations. Boise Cascade is one of the largest pulp and paper producers in the United States. Founded in 1957. **Corporate headquarters location:** Boise ID. **Other U.S. locations:** Emmett ID. **Listed on:** New York Stock Exchange. **Stock exchange symbol:** BCC.

THE BON MARCHE
Third Avenue & Pine, Seattle WA 98181. 206/344-2121. **Contact:** Personnel. **World Wide Web address:** http://www.federated-fds.com. **Description:** Operates a retail department store. **Parent company:** Federated Department Stores. **Number of employees nationwide:** 3,750.

BOSTON SCIENTIFIC CORPORATION
15340 NE 92nd Street, Building B, Redmond WA 98052. 425/556-1540. **Contact:** Human Resources. **World Wide Web address:** http://www.bsci.com. **Description:** Develops noninvasive surgical products and procedures. **Corporate headquarters location:** Natick MA. **Listed on:** New York Stock Exchange. **Stock exchange symbol:** BSX.

BRANDRUD FURNITURE, INC.
1502 20th Street NW, Auburn WA 98001-3428. 253/922-6167. **Contact:** Personnel. **World Wide Web address:** http://www.brandrud.com. **Description:** Manufactures furniture for office, health care, and institutional settings. **Corporate headquarters location:** This location.

BRANOM INSTRUMENT COMPANY
P.O. Box 80307, Seattle WA 98108-0307. 206/762-6050. **Toll-free phone:** 800/767-6051. **Fax:** 206/762-9351. **Contact:** Personnel Department. **World Wide Web address:** http://www.branom.com. **Description:** A wholesaler of electronic parts and equipment including timing and counting, temperature, pressure, flow, level, and AC/DC instruments. Founded in 1947. **NOTE:** Resumes may be sent to the above e-mail address. **Office hours:** Monday - Friday, 8:00 a.m. - 5:00 p.m. **Corporate headquarters location:** This location. **CEO:** William W. Branom. **Sales Manager:** Joanne Nunn. **Annual sales/revenues:** $5 - $10 million. **Number of employees at this location:** 40. **Number of employees nationwide:** 80.

BEN BRIDGE CORPORATION
P.O. Box 1908, Seattle WA 98111-1908. 206/448-8800. **Contact:** Human Resources. **World Wide Web address:** http://www.benbridge.com. **Description:** A retailer of fine jewelry and related accessories. **Positions advertised include:** Quality Assurance Specialist; Watchmaker; Clerical and Administrative Associate. **Corporate headquarters location:** This location. **Other U.S. locations:** AL; CA; HI; NV; OR. **Operations at this facility include:** Administration; Sales. **Number of employees at this location:** 80. **Number of employees nationwide:** 475.

BROWN & CALDWELL
701 Pike Place, Suite 1200, Seattle WA 98101. 206/624-0100. **Contact:** Personnel. **E-mail address:** resumes@brwncald.com. **World Wide Web address:** http://www.brownandcaldwell.com. **Description:** An employee-owned environmental engineering and consulting firm specializing in the planning, engineering, and design of waste management systems. The company is also engaged in construction management and analytical environmental testing. **Positions advertised include:** Engineer; Office Support Associate. **Corporate headquarters location:** Walnut Creek CA.

BUFFELEN WOODWORKING COMPANY
1901 Taylor Way, P.O. Box 1383, Tacoma WA 98401-1383. 253/627-1191. **Contact:** Human Resources Department. **Description:** A large millwork manufacturing company. **Corporate headquarters location:** This location. **Operations at this facility include:** Administration; Manufacturing; Sales; Service.

BUNZL EXTRUSION
3110 70th Avenue East, Tacoma WA 98424-3608. 253/284-8000. **Contact:** Human Resources. **World Wide Web address:** http://www.bunzlextrusion.com. **Description:** Manufactures plastic extrusions specializing in core, fence, and highway products. **Corporate headquarters location:** Richmond VA.

BURKE GIBSON INC.
702 Third Street SW, Auburn WA 98001-5278. 253/735-4444. **Fax:** 253/833-2916. **Contact:** Human Resources. **World Wide Web address:** http://www.burkegibsoninc.com. **Description:** Designs and manufactures point-of-purchase advertising displays for retail and warehouse sales. **Corporate headquarters location:** This location.

THE BURKE MUSEUM OF NATURAL HISTORY & CULTURE
University of Washington, P.O. Box 353010, Seattle WA 98195-3010. 206/543-5590. **Contact:** Department of Human Resources. **World Wide Web address:** http://www.washington.edu/burkemuseum. **Description:** A museum that explores the natural and cultural history of the Pacific Northwest region. The museum houses more than 3 million geological, anthropological, and zoological specimens.

CB RICHARD ELLIS
1420 Fifth Avenue, Suite 1700, Seattle WA 98101-2314. 206/292-1600. **Contact:** Human Resources. **E-mail address:** opps@cbre.com. **World Wide Web address:** http://www.cbrichardellis.com. **Description:** A fully-integrated real estate and real estate-related service company. **Corporate headquarters location:** Los Angeles CA.

CH2M HILL
P.O. Box 91500, Bellevue WA 98009-2050. 425/453-5000. **Physical address:** 777 108th Avenue NE, Suite 800, Bellevue WA 98004. **Contact:** Human Resources. **World Wide Web address:** http://www.ch2m.com. **Description:** CH2M Hill is group of employee-owned companies operating under the names CH2M Hill, Inc., Industrial Design Corporation, Operations Management International, CH2M Hill International, and CH2M Hill Engineering. The company provides planning, engineering design, and operation and construction management services to help clients apply technology, safeguard the environment, and develop infrastructure. The professional staff includes specialists in environmental engineering and waste management, water management, transportation, industrial facilities, and a broad spectrum of infrastructure systems. Founded in 1946. **Corporate headquarters location:** Denver CO. **Other U.S. locations:** Nationwide. **Number of employees at this location:** 350. **Number of employees nationwide:** 4,000.

CADET MANUFACTURING COMPANY
2500 West 4th Plain Boulevard, P.O. Box 1675, Vancouver WA 98660-1675. 360/693-2505. **Contact:** Personnel. **World Wide Web address:** http://www.cadetco.com. **Description:** Manufactures electric heaters, thermostats, and air cleaning systems. Founded in 1957. **Corporate headquarters location:** This location.

CALLISON ARCHITECTURE
1420 Fifth Avenue, Suite 2400, Seattle WA 98101. 206/623-4646. **Fax:** 206/623-4625. **Contact:** Human Resources. **E-mail address:** employment@callison.com. **World Wide Web address:** http://www.callison.com. **Description:** Provides architectural and design services to the healthcare, hospitality, residential, and retail markets. **Positions advertised include:** Administrative Assistant; Designer; Specification Writer. **Corporate headquarters location:** This location.

CAMP DRESSER & McKEE INC. (CDM)
P.O. Box 3885, Bellevue WA 98009. 425/453-8383. **Physical address:** 11811 NE First Street, Suite 201, Bellevue WA 98005. **Fax:** 425/646-9523. **Contact:** Human Resources Department. **E-mail address:** hr@cdm.com. **World Wide Web address:** http://www.cdm.com. **Description:** A worldwide provider of environmental engineering, scientific, planning, and management services. The company focuses on professional activities for the management of water resources, hazardous and solid wastes, wastewater, infrastructure, and environmental systems for industry and government. **Positions advertised include:** Senior Wastewater Engineer; Senior O&M Technician; Assistant Project Manager. **Other U.S. locations:** Nationwide. **International locations:** Worldwide.

CAPGEMINI
105000 NE Eight Street. Suite 1400, Bellevue WA 98004. 425/818-3300. **Fax:** 425/818-3301. **Contact:** Human Resources. **World Wide Web address:** http://www.us.capgemini.com. **Description:** A leading provider of information technology consulting services with over 40 branch offices worldwide. The company provides its clients with the solutions needed to achieve business and operational goals. CapGemini focuses on three major activities: consultancy, implementation, and systems integration. **Corporate headquarters location:** New York NY.

CAPITAL DEVELOPMENT COMPANY
649 Woodland Square Loop SE, Lacey WA 98503. 360/493-8124. **Contact:** Human Resources. **Description:** Engaged in a variety of construction activities including contracting, leasing, and property development and management.

CAPTARIS
10885 NE 14th Street, Suite 400, Bellevue WA. 425/455-6000. **Contact:** Human Resources. **World Wide Web address:** http://www.captaris.com. **Description:** Develops, manufactures, markets, and supports a broad line of open systems-based, computer technology software products and systems that automate call answering. **Positions advertised include:** Financial Analyst; Configuration Management Engineer. **Corporate headquarters location:** This location. **Listed on:** NASDAQ. **Stock exchange symbol:** CAPA.

CARDINAL DISTRIBUTION
P.O. Box 1589, Auburn WA 98001-1589. 253/939-5550. **Physical address:** 801 C Street NW, Auburn WA. **Fax:** 253/833-9402. **Contact:** Human Resources. **World Wide Web address:** http://www.cardinal.com. **Description:** A nationwide wholesale distributor of pharmaceuticals, medical and surgical products, and related health supplies. The company also distributes merchandise typically sold in retail drug stores, hospitals, and health care provider facilities. Cardinal Distribution also provides its clients with such specialized support services as order entry and confirmation, inventory control, monitoring pricing strategies, and financial reporting. The company has developed an in-pharmacy computer system that provides prices, patient profiles, financial data, and management services. **Corporate headquarters location:** Dublin OH. **Other U.S. locations:** Nationwide. **Operations at this facility include:** Regional Headquarters; Warehouse/Distribution; Wholesaling. **Number of employees at this location:** 175. **Number of employees nationwide:** 3,000.

CARE CENTER AT KELSEY CREEK
2700 152nd Avenue NE, Redmond WA 98052. 425/957-2400. **Contact:** Human Resources. **E-mail address:** recruiters.i@ghc.org. **World Wide Web address:** http://www.ghc.org. **Description:** A skilled nursing home that offers hospice care and general long-term care. **Positions advertised include:** Visiting Nurse Hospice Case Manager; Pharmacy Technician; Physical Therapy Assistant; Occupational Therapist; Physical Therapist. **Parent company:** Group Health Cooperative.

CASCADE NATURAL GAS CORPORATION
P.O. Box 24464, Seattle WA 98124-0464. 206/624-3900. **Physical address:** 222 Fairview Avenue North, Seattle WA 98109. **Contact:** Personnel Director. **World Wide Web address:** http://www.cngc.com. **Description:** Engaged in the distribution and transportation of natural gas to customers. **Corporate headquarters location:** This location. **Operations at this facility include:** Administration. **Listed on:** New York Stock Exchange. **Stock exchange symbol:** CGC.

CATERPILLAR INC.
6811 East Mission Avenue, Spokane WA 99212. 509/924-5700. **Contact:** Human Resources. **E-mail address:** employment@cat.com. **World Wide Web address:** http://www.cat.com. **Description:** Caterpillar is one of the world's largest manufacturers of construction and mining equipment, natural gas engines, and industrial gas turbines; and a leading global supplier of diesel engines. Products range from track-type tractors to hydraulic excavators, backhoe loaders, motor graders, and off-highway trucks. They are used in the construction, road building, mining, forestry, energy, transportation, and materials industries. **Other U.S. locations:** Nationwide. **International locations:** Worldwide. **Operations at this facility include:** This location stores and wholesales machine parts for the company. **Listed on:** New York Stock Exchange. **Stock exchange symbol:** CAT.

CELL THERAPEUTICS, INC.
201 Elliott Avenue West, Seattle WA 98119. 206/282-7100. **Fax:** 206/272-4010. **Recorded jobline:** 800/656-2355. **Contact:** Human Resources. **E-mail address:** resume@ctiseattle.com. **World Wide Web address:** http://www.cticseattle.com. **Description:** Researches and develops oncology products designed to manage cancer and cancer treatment side effects. Founded in 1992. **Corporate headquarters location:** This location. **Listed on:** NASDAQ. **Annual sales/revenues:** $5 - $10 million. **Number of employees at this location:** 190.

CELLULAR TECHNICAL SERVICES COMPANY (CTS)
2815 Second Avenue, Suite 100, Seattle WA 98121. 206/443-6400. **Fax:** 206/269-1404. **Contact:** Bruce York, Manager. **E-mail address:** hr@celtech.com. **World Wide Web address:** http://www.cellulartech.com. **Description:** Develops and markets real-time information management software systems used for fraud detection, billing, and customer service. Cellular Technical Services Company serves clients in the wireless communications industry. **Corporate headquarters location:** This location. **Listed on:** New York Stock Exchange. **Stock exchange symbol:** CTSC.

CENTRAL KITSAP SCHOOL DISTRICT
P.O. Box 8, Silverdale WA 98383. 360/662-1680. **Physical address:** 9210 Silverdale Way NW, Silverdale WA 98383. **Fax:** 360/662-1611. **Recorded jobline:** 360/662-1699. **Contact:** Personnel Department. **E-mail address:** tiffanyw@cksd.wednet.edu. **World Wide Web address:** http://www.cksd.wednet.edu. **Description:** Administrative offices for the school district. **Positions advertised include:** Executive Director of Secondary Teaching & Learning; Assistant Superintendent of Human Resources; Director of Special Services. **Corporate headquarters location:** This location. **Number of employees at this location:** 1,500.

CENTRAL WASHINGTON UNIVERSITY
400 East Eighth Avenue, Ellensburg WA 98926. 509/963-1202. **Recorded jobline:** 509/963-1562. **Contact:** Human Resources. **E-mail address:** humanres@cwu.edu. **World Wide Web address:** http://www.cwu.edu. **Description:** A regional university offering baccalaureate and graduate degrees in more than 90 academic programs serving nearly 8,000 students. **Number of employees at this location:** 1,000.

CENTURYTEL
P.O. Box 9901, Vancouver WA 98668-8701. 360/905-5800. **Physical address:** 805 Broadway, Vancouver WA 98660. **Contact:** Manager of Employment and Administration. **E-mail address:** staffing@centurytel.com. **World Wide Web address:** http://www.centurytel.com. **Description:** A holding company providing administrative and other services to its subsidiaries, whose operations include providing telephone services. **Positions advertised include:** Customer Service Representative. **Other area locations:** Cheney WA; Gig Harbor WA. **Other U.S. locations:** Anchorage AK; Kalispell MT; Lebanon OR; Tomah WI. **Listed on:** New York Stock Exchange. **Stock exchange symbol:** CTL. **Number of employees at this location:** 500. **Number of employees nationwide:** 3,000.

CENVEO
6520 South 190th Street, Suite 100, Kent WA 98032-2169. 206/576-4300. **Toll-free phone:** 800/347-6989. **Fax:** 206/574-8013. **Contact:** Human Resources Department. **World Wide Web address:** http://www.mwseattle.com. **Description:** Manufactures envelopes and related paper products. Founded in 1921. **Corporate headquarters location:** Englewood CO.

CHILDCARE INTERNATIONAL
715 West Orchard Drive, Suite 7, Bellingham WA 98225. 360/647-2283. **Contact:** Human Resources. **World Wide Web address:** http://www.childcare-intl.org. **Description:** Dedicated to the global relief of children in need. The organization's programs include feeding and sponsorship of these children. Founded in 1981.

CHILDREN'S HOSPITAL AND MEDICAL CENTER
4800 Sand Point Way NE, Seattle WA 98105-0371. 206/987-2000. **Toll-free phone:** 866/987-2000. **Recorded jobline:** 206/987-2230. **Contact:** Human Resources. **E-mail address:** jobs@chmc.org. **World Wide Web address:** http://www.chmc.org. **Description:** A tertiary pediatric hospital and medical center that serves Washington, Alaska, Idaho, and Montana. Children's Hospital also provides research and educational facilities. **Positions advertised include:** Lab Aide; Equipment and Logistics Technician; Food Service Worker; Nurse Technician. **Operations at this facility include:** Service. **Number of employees at this location:** 2,400.

CHIQUITA PROCESSED FOODS
P.O. Box 458, Walla Walla WA 99362. 541/938-4461. **Contact:** Personnel Department. **E-mail address:** jobs@chiquita.com. **World Wide Web address:** http://www.chiquita.com. **Description:** Manufactures and processes canned peas, carrots, corn, asparagus, green beans, and spinach. **Positions advertised include:** Business Account Manager; Director of New Business Development; Distribution Center Supervisor; Operations Manager. **Corporate headquarters location:** New Richmond WI. **Listed on:** New York Stock Exchange. **Stock exchange symbol:** CQB. **Number of employees nationwide:** 1,500.

THE CHRONICLE
321 North Pearl Street, P.O. Box 580, Centralia WA 98531. 360/736-3311. **Contact:** Human Resources. **World Wide Web address:** http://www.chronline.com. **Description:** Publishes a daily newspaper with a circulation of approximately 15,500. **Corporate headquarters location:** This location. **Number of employees at this location:** 100.

CHUBB GROUP INSURANCE
601 Union Street, Suite 3800, Seattle WA 98101. 206/624-2100. **Contact:** Human Resources. **World Wide Web address:** http://www.chubb.com. **Description:** One of the largest property and casualty insurers in the United States, with more than 110 offices in 30 countries worldwide. The company offers a broad range of specialty insurance products and services designed for individuals and businesses, including high-technology, financial institutions, and general manufacturers. **Corporate headquarters location:** Warren NJ. **Other U.S. locations:** Nationwide. **Listed on:** New York Stock Exchange. **Stock exchange symbol:** CB.

CINGULAR
P.O. Box 97061, Redmond WA 98073. 206/624-5700. **Contact:** Human Resources. **World Wide Web address:** http://www.cingular.com. **Description:** One of the nation's largest digital wireless networks providing wireless voice and data communication. **Other U.S. locations:** Nationwide.

CLOVER PARK SCHOOL DISTRICT
10903 Gravelly Lake Drive SW, Lakewood WA 98499. 253/583-5095. **Recorded jobline:** 253/583-5003. **Fax:** 253/589-7440. **Contact:** Lori Liedes, Recruitment Coordinator. **E-mail address:** Lliedes@cloverpark.k12.wa.us. **World Wide Web address:** http://cpsd.cloverpark.k12.wa.us. **Description:** Administrative offices of the Clover Park school district. **Positions advertised include:** Counselor; Math Teacher; Science Teacher; English Teacher; Social Studies Teacher. **Number of employees at this location:** 1,800.

COCA-COLA BOTTLING COMPANY
3333 South 38th Street, Tacoma WA 98409. 253/474-9567. **Contact:** Human Resources. **World Wide Web address:** http://www.coca-cola.com. **Description:** A bottling company packaging Coca-Cola, Barq's and Dr. Pepper brand beverages. **Corporate headquarters location:** Bellevue WA. **Parent company:** Coca-Cola Company is one of the world's largest marketers, distributors, and producers of bottled and canned products. Coca-Cola Enterprises, part of the Coca-Cola Company, is in the liquid, nonalcoholic refreshment business, which includes traditional carbonated soft drinks, still and sparkling waters, juices, isotonics, and teas. The company operates in 38 states, the District of Columbia, the U.S. Virgin Islands, the Islands of Tortola and Grand Cayman, and the Netherlands. Coca-Cola Enterprises operates 268 facilities, approximately 24,000 vehicles, and over 860,000 vending machines, beverage dispensers, and coolers used to market, distribute, and produce the company's products. **Listed on:** New York Stock Exchange. **Stock exchange symbol:** COKE.

COCHRAN ELECTRIC COMPANY INC.
P.O. Box 33524, Seattle WA 98133-0524. 206/367-1900. **Physical address:** 12500 Aurora Avenue North, Seattle WA 98133. **Fax:** 206/368-3218. **Contact:** Personnel Department. **E-mail address:** jobs@cochraninc.com. **World Wide Web address:** http://www.cochran-inc.com. **Description:** Engaged in commercial and industrial electrical work and powerline engineering. **Corporate headquarters location:** This location.

COEUR D'ALENE COMPANY
P.O. Box 2610, Spokane WA 99220-2610. 509/924-6363. **Toll-free phone:** 800/824-0505. **Fax:** 509/924-6924. **Contact:** Human Resources. **World Wide Web address:** http://www.coeurdal.com. **Description:** Engaged in the distribution, processing, and fabrication of steel and related products. Operations consist of the custom production of finished metal structures or products in accordance with a customer's specifications. The fabrication and processing operations include activities such as cutting, bending, drilling, riveting, welding, assembling, and painting metals. Items produced have included liners for aluminum, magnesium, or other metal producers; structural metal components for the construction of buildings; and structural metal supports for highway signs. **Corporate headquarters location:** This location. **Listed on:** New York Stock Exchange. **Stock exchange symbol:** CDE. **Number of employees at this location:** 70.

COLUMBIA BANK
P.O. Box 2156, Mail Stop 2500, Tacoma WA 98401. 253/305-1900. **Recorded jobline:** 253/305-0717. **Contact:** Human Resources. **World Wide Web address:** http://www.columbiabank.com. **Description:** A full-service bank. **Corporate headquarters location:** This location. **Listed on:** NASDAQ. **Stock exchange symbol:** COLB.

COLUMBIA LIGHTING INC.
3808 North Sullivan Road, P.O. Box 2787, Spokane WA 99220-2787. 509/924-7000. **Fax:** 509/921-7539. **Contact:** Human Resources. **E-mail address:** hresources@columbia-ltg.com. **World Wide Web address:** http://www.columbialighting.com. **Description:** Manufactures lighting equipment for commercial and industrial use. The company is also a wholesaler of lighting fixtures. **Parent company:** USI. **Operations at this facility include:** Administration; Manufacturing; Sales; Service. **Listed on:** New York Stock Exchange. **Stock exchange symbol:** USI. **Number of employees at this location:** 620.

THE COLUMBIAN PUBLISHING COMPANY
P.O. Box 180, Vancouver WA 98666-0180. 360/694-3391. **Physical address:** 701 West Eighth Street, Vancouver WA 98660. **Contact:** Personnel. **E-mail address:** jobs@columbian.com. **World Wide Web address:** http://www.columbian.com. **Description:** Publishes the *Columbian*, a daily newspaper. **Corporate headquarters**

location: This location. **Operations at this facility include:** Manufacturing; Sales; Service. **Number of employees at this location:** 350.

COMCAST
900 132nd Street SW, Everett WA 98204. **Toll-free phone:** 877/824-2288. **Contact:** Human Resources. **World Wide Web address:** http://www.comcast.com. **Description:** One of the nation's largest cable television and broadband services companies.

COMMUNITY COLLEGE OF SPOKANE
P.O. Box 6000, Spokane WA 99217-6000. 509/434-5040. **Physical address:** 501 North Riverpoint Boulevard, Spokane WA 99202. **Fax:** 509/434-5055. **Recorded jobline:** 509/533-2013. **Contact:** Manager of Human Resources Department. **E-mail address:** hr@ccs.spokane.edu. **World Wide Web address:** http://www.ccs.spokane.edu. **Description:** Provides academic and vocational education and training to more than 22,000 full- and part-time students in six northeastern Washington counties. Community College of Spokane operates two colleges, Spokane Community College and Spokane Falls Community College, as well as the Institute for Extended Learning, which is responsible for a variety of off-campus programs and services. **Number of employees at this location:** 1,900.

COMPUTER ASSOCIATES INTERNATIONAL, INC.
12131 113th Avenue NE, Suite 300, Kirkland WA 98034. 425/825-2600. **Contact:** Human Resources. **World Wide Web address:** http://www.cai.com. **Description:** Computer Associates International is one of the world's leading developers of client/server and distributed computing software. The company develops, markets, and supports enterprise management, database and applications development, business applications, and consumer software products for a broad range of mainframe, midrange, and desktop computers. Computer Associates serves major business, government, research, and educational organizations. Founded in 1976. **Office hours:** Monday - Friday, 8:00 a.m. - 5:00 p.m. **Corporate headquarters location:** Islandia NY. **Other U.S. locations:** Nationwide. **Operations at this facility include:** This location develops software. **Listed on:** New York Stock Exchange. **Stock exchange symbol:** CA. **Annual sales/revenues:** More than $100 million. **Number of employees nationwide:** 4,000. **Number of employees worldwide:** 9,000.

COMTECH AHA CORPORATION
2345 Northeast Hopkins Court, Pullman WA 99163-5601. 509/334-1000. **Fax:** 509/334-9000. **Contact:** Human Resources. **E-mail address:** hr@aha.com. **World Wide Web address:** http://www.aha.com. **Description:** Manufactures products for data storage, digital communications, and digital hard copy. **Corporate headquarters location:** This location.

CONCRETE TECHNOLOGY CORPORATION
P.O. Box 2259, Tacoma WA 98401-2259. 253/383-3545. **Physical address:** 1123 Port of Tacoma Road, Tacoma WA 98421. **Contact:** Personnel Director. **World Wide Web address:** http://www.concretetech.com. **Description:** Manufactures concrete for a variety of end-use applications. **Corporate headquarters location:** This location.

CONNELLY SKIS INC.
P.O. Box 716, Lynnwood WA 98046. 425/775-5416. **Physical address:** 20621 52nd Avenue West, Lynnwood WA 98036. **Contact:** Human Resources. **World Wide Web address:** http://www.connellyskis.com. **Description:** Manufactures water skis, tubes, wet suits, and related accessories. **Corporate headquarters location:** This location.

CONOCOPHILLIPS
3901 Unick Road, Ferndale WA 98248. 360/384-1011. **Fax:** 360/384-8246. **Contact:** Human Resources. **World Wide Web address:** http://www.conocophillips.com. **Description:** Refines petroleum and related products. **Special programs:** Internships. **Corporate headquarters location:** Houston TX. **Other U.S. locations:** Nationwide. **Listed on:** New York Stock Exchange. **Stock exchange symbol:** COP. **Number of employees at this location:** 300. **Number of employees nationwide:** 2,000.

CONSOLIDATED FREIGHTWAYS
805 Broadway, Suite 205, Vancouver WA 98660. 208/232-8727. **Contact:** Personnel. **E-mail address:** cinfo@cfwy.com. **World Wide Web address:** http://www.cfwy.com. **Description:** A motor freight carrier and air freight forwarder operating in all 50 states. Operations include export/import brokerage, overseas forwarding, and warehousing and distribution services. **Corporate headquarters location:** Vancouver WA. **Listed on:** NASDAQ. **Stock exchange symbol:** CFWY.

CONTINENTAL VAN LINES INC.
4501 West Marginal Way, P.O. Box 3963, Seattle WA 98124-3963. 206/937-2261. **Contact:** Personnel. **E-mail address:** jobs@continentalvan.com. **World Wide Web address:** http://www.continentalvan.com. **Description:** Engaged in interstate moving and storage. **Positions advertised include:** Class A Drivers; Packers; Loaders/Drivers; Customer Service Staff. **Corporate headquarters location:** Fort Wayne IN.

CORBIS CORPORATION
710 Second Avenue, Suite 200 Seattle WA 98007. 206/373-6000. **Contact:** Human Resources. **World Wide Web address:** http://www.corbis.com. **Description:** Develops and sells digital images to businesses. **Positions advertised include:** Assistant to General Counsel; Staff Accountant; Client Services Technician; Account Executive. **Corporate headquarters location:** This location.

CORUM GROUP LTD.
10500 NE Eighth Street, Suite 1500, Bellevue WA 98004. 425/455-8281. **Fax:** 425/455-1415. **Contact:** Gina Stanhope, Human Resources. **World Wide Web address:** http://www.corumgroup.com. **Description:** Assists software companies to successfully execute company mergers and alliances. **Corporate headquarters location:** This location.

COSTCO WHOLESALE
999 Lake Drive, Issaquah WA 98027. 425/313-8100. **Fax:** 425/313-8103. **Contact:** Human Resources. **World Wide Web address:** http://www.costco.com. **Description:** A nationwide retailer of food, clothing, and numerous other products at wholesale prices. **Corporate headquarters location:** This location. **Listed on:** NASDAQ. **Stock exchange symbol:** COST. **Annual sales/revenues:** More than $100 million.

CRAY INC.
Merrill Place, 411 First Avenue South, Suite 600, Seattle WA 98104-2860. 206/701-2000. **Fax:** 206/701-2500. **Contact:** Corporate Recruiter. **E-mail address:** resumes@cray.com. **World Wide Web address:** http://www.cray.com. **Description:** Develops high-end supercomputers. **Positions advertised include:** Floor Plan Engineer; Release Engineer; Platform Manager; Program Manager. **Corporate headquarters location:** This location. **Listed on:** NASDAQ. **Stock exchange symbol:** CRAY.

CROWN CORK & SEAL COMPANY, INC.
1202 Fones Road SE, Olympia WA 98501. 360/491-4900. **Contact:** Human Resources. **World Wide Web address:** http://www.crowncork.com. **Description:** Crown Cork & Steel is a worldwide manufacturer and distributor of a wide range of crowns, seals, and aluminum and steel cans including aerosol and beverage cans. The company also manufactures bottling equipment. **Corporate headquarters location:** Philadelphia PA. **Operations at this facility include:** This location manufactures aluminum and steel beverage cans. **Listed on:** New York Stock Exchange. **Stock exchange symbol:** CCK.

CRYSTAL MOUNTAIN RESORT
33914 Crystal Mountain Boulevard, Crystal Mountain WA 98022. 360/663-2265. **Contact:** Human Resources. **World Wide Web address:** http://www.crystalmt.com. **Description:** A ski resort and lodge.

CUMMINS NORTHWEST
811 South West Grady Way, P.O. Box 9811, Renton WA 98057. 425/235-3440. **Contact:** Human Resources. **World Wide Web address:** http://www.cummins.com. **Description:** One of the world's leading producers of diesel engines, engine parts, and power train systems for the mining, military, construction, transportation, agriculture, and industrial markets. **Positions advertised include:** Product Manager. **Corporate headquarters location:** Portland OR. **Listed on:** New York Stock Exchange. **Stock exchange symbol:** CUM.

CUMMINS NORTHWEST
926 NW Maryland Avenue, Chehalis WA 98532. 360/748-8841. **Contact:** Human Resources. **World Wide Web address:** http://www.cummins.com. **Description:** One of the world's leading producers of diesel engines, engine parts, and power train systems for the mining, military, construction, transportation, agriculture, and industrial markets. **Corporate headquarters location:** Portland OR. **Listed on:** New York Stock Exchange. **Stock exchange symbol:** CUM.

CUMMINS-ALLISON CORPORATION
6118 Sixth Avenue South, Seattle WA 98108. 206/763-3900. **Fax:** 847/299-4940. **Contact:** Human Resources. **E-mail address:** jobs@cumminsallison.com. **World Wide Web address:** http://www.cumminsallison.com. **Description:** Manufactures paper shredders and coin-counting machines. **Positions advertised include:** Sales Representative. **Corporate headquarters location:** Mount Prospect IL. **Operations at this facility include:** This location is a sales office.

CUSHMAN & WAKEFIELD OF WASHINGTON INC.
1420 Fifth Avenue, Seattle WA 98101. 206/682-0666. **Contact:** Human Resources. **World Wide Web address:** http://www.cushwake.com/us. **Description:** A real estate services firm offering sales, property management, and appraisal services. **Corporate headquarters location:** New York NY.

CUTLER-HAMMER SENSORS
720 80th Street SW, Everett WA 98203. 425/513-5300. **Contact:** Human Resources. **World Wide Web address:** http://www.cutler-hammer.com. **Description:** A manufacturer of electrical control products and equipment. **Parent company:** Eaton Corporation. **Listed on:** New York Stock Exchange. **Stock exchange symbol:** ETN.

DDB SEATTLE
1008 Western Avenue, Suite 601, Seattle WA 98104. 206/442-9900. **Contact:** Human Resources. **World Wide Web address:** http://www.ddbseattle.com. **Description:** An advertising agency. **Positions advertised include:** Online Coordinator. **Parent company:** DDB Needham Worldwide, Inc.

DLR GROUP
900 Fourth Avenue, Suite 700, Seattle WA 98164. 206/461-6000. **Contact:** Jill Star, Recruiter. **E-mail address:** jstar@dlrgroup.com. **World Wide Web address:** http://www.dlrgroup.com. **Description:** An architectural design firm that specializes in educational, judicial, medical, and recreational projects.

THE DAILY HERALD COMPANY
P.O. Box 930, Everett WA 98206. 425/339-3000. **Physical address:** 1213 California Street, Everett WA 98201. **Recorded jobline:** 425/339-3009. **Contact:** Human Resources. **E-mail address:** jobs@heraldnet.com. **World Wide Web address:** http://www.heraldnet.com. **Description:** Publishes one daily newspaper and five weekly newspapers. The daily circulation of the *Herald* is approximately 55,000. This firm does not accept unsolicited resumes. Please call the jobline for a list of openings. **Positions advertised include:** Inside Sales Representative. **Special programs:** Internships. **Internship information:** Summer internships in news, photography, and advertising are sometimes offered. **Corporate headquarters location:** This location. **Number of employees at this location:** 375.

DAILY RECORD
PIONEER PUBLISHING
401 North Main Street, Ellensburg WA 98926. 509/925-1414. **Toll-free phone:** 800/676-4850. **Fax:** 509/925-5696. **Contact:** Managing Editor. **E-mail address:** dailyrecord@kvnews.com. **World Wide Web address:** http://www.kvnews.com. **Description:** Publishes a daily regional/community newspaper with a circulation of 6,000. Founded in 1899. **Special programs:** Internships. **Corporate headquarters location:** Seattle WA. **Publisher:** Bill Kunerth. **Information Systems Manager:** Joe Johnson. **Number of employees at this location:** 40.

DAILY SUN NEWS
600 South 6th Street, P.O. Box 878, Sunnyside WA 98944. 509/837-4500. **Contact:** Human Resources. **World Wide Web address:** http://www.sunnyside.net. **Description:** Publishes a daily newspaper. **Parent company:** Eagle Newspapers, Inc.

THE DAILY WORLD
315 South Michigan Street, P.O. Box 269, Aberdeen WA 98520. 360/532-4000. **Contact:** Human Resources. **World Wide Web address:** http://www.thedailyworld.com. **Description:** Publishes a newspaper with a circulation of approximately 15,000.

DAIRY FARMERS OF WASHINGTON
4201 198th Street SW, Suite 101, Lynnwood WA 98036-6751. 425/672-0687. **Contact:** Personnel Department. **World Wide Web address:** http://www.eatsmart.org. **Description:** A commission engaged in the promotion of Washington's milk and dairy products.

DAISHOWA AMERICA COMPANY, LTD.
P.O. Box 271, Port Angeles WA 98362. 360/457-4474. **Fax:** 360/452-9004. **Contact:** David Flodstrom, Human Resources Manager. **Description:** Manufactures telephone directory paper. The company also operates pulp and de-ink facilities. **Corporate**

headquarters location: This location. **Annual sales/revenues:** More than $100 million. **Number of employees at this location:** 300.

WAYNE DALTON CORPORATION
2001 Industrial Drive, Centralia WA 98531. 360/736-7651. **Toll-free phone:** 877/827-3667. **Contact:** John Peterson, Human Resources. **World Wide Web address:** http://www.wayne-dalton.com. **Description:** Manufactures garage doors and related items. **Corporate headquarters location:** Mt. Hope OH. **Parent company:** Hardsco Corporation.

DANZAS AEI
600 Oakesdale Avenue SW, Suite 101, Renton WA 98055. 425/917-2600. **Contact:** Personnel. **World Wide Web address:** http://www.danzas.com. **Description:** A leading provider of logistics solutions. Services include air, road, rail, and sea transportation, as well as distribution and warehousing. **Corporate headquarters location:** Darien CT. **International locations:** Worldwide.

DANZAS AEI
18850 Eighth Avenue South, Suite 800, Sea Tac WA 98148. 206/835-7193. **Contact:** Human Resources. **World Wide Web address:** http://www.danzas.com. **Description:** A leading provider of logistics solutions. Services include air, road, rail, and sea transportation, as well as distribution and warehousing. **Corporate headquarters location:** Darien CT. **International locations:** Worldwide.

DATA I/O CORPORATION
P.O. Box 97046, Redmond WA 98073-9746. 425/881-6444. **Physical address:** 10525 Willows Road NE, Redmond WA 98052. **Recorded jobline:** 425/867-6963. **Contact:** Employment Department. **World Wide Web address:** http://www.data-io.com. **Description:** Manufactures programmable integrated circuit chips. **Special programs:** Internships. **Corporate headquarters location:** This location. **Other U.S. locations:** Nationwide. **Listed on:** NASDAQ. **Stock exchange symbol:** DAIO. **Annual sales/revenues:** $51 - $100 million. **Number of employees at this location:** 285. **Number of employees nationwide:** 320.

DAVIS WIRE CORPORATION
19411 80th Avenue South, Kent WA 98032. 253/872-8910. **Fax:** 253/395-3729. **Contact:** Dan Kay, Manager of Human Resources. **World Wide Web address:** http://www.daviswire.com. **Description:** Manufactures steel wire and related products. **Corporate headquarters location:** San Ramon CA. **Other U.S. locations:** Irwindale CA; Pueblo CO. **Operations at this facility include:** Divisional Headquarters. **Number of employees at this location:** 200. **Number of employees nationwide:** 600.

DEALER INFORMATION SYSTEMS CORPORATION (DIS)
1315 Cornwall Avenue, Bellingham WA 98225. 360/733-7610. **Contact:** Human Resources. **World Wide Web address:** http://www.discorp.com. **Description:** Develops management software for agricultural, construction, and automobile dealerships throughout the United State and Canada. DIS Corporation also offers its customers communications equipment and technical support. **Corporate headquarters location:** This location.

DEL MONTE FOODS
P.O. Box 1528, Yakima WA 98907. 509/575-6584. **Physical address:** 108 West Walnut Street, Yakima WA 98902. **Contact:** Personnel. **World Wide Web address:** http://www.delmonte.com. **Description:** Del Monte Foods is a producer of canned fruits and vegetables, tomato sauces, condiments, and dessert products for the consumer, institutional, and military markets. The company operates over 60 plants worldwide where it processes food and makes, labels, and packs its own cans. Brand names include Del Monte, Morton Munchwich, Snack Cups, Bonanza, Ortega, Sunkist Plus, and Summer Crisp. **Corporate headquarters location:** San Francisco CA. **Operations at this facility include:** This location processes canned fruits. **Listed on:** New York Stock Exchange. **Stock exchange symbol:** DLM.

DELOITTE & TOUCHE
925 Fourth Avenue, Suite 3300, Seattle WA 98104-1126. 206/447-8345. **Contact:** Human Resources Manager. **World Wide Web address:** http://www.us.deloitte.com. **Description:** An international firm of certified public accountants providing professional accounting, auditing, tax, and management consulting services to widely diversified clients. The company has a specialized program consisting of national industry groups and functional groups that cross industry lines. Groups are involved in various disciplines including accounting, auditing, taxation management advisory services, small and growing businesses, mergers and acquisitions, and computer applications. **Corporate headquarters location:** Wilton CT.

DHL
3101 Western Avenue, Seattle WA 98121. 206/830-4600. **Contact:** Recruiting. **World Wide Web address:** http://www.dhl.com. **Description:** A domestic and international air express, air, and ocean freight services company. Operations include both domestic and international door-to-door, next-day delivery, and door-to-airport freight services. Airborne Express operates a fleet of more than 14,000 delivery vehicles. **Positions advertised include:** Claims Examiner; Corporate Accountant; Customer Service Representative; International Accounting Specialist; Payroll Coordinator.

DIADORA AMERICA, INC.
6419 South 228th Street, Kent WA 98032-1874. 253/520-8868. **Contact:** Human Resources. **World Wide Web address:** http://www.diadoraamerica.com. **Description:** One of the world's largest manufacturers of soccer shoes and apparel, athletic clothing, and shoes for a variety of sports. Internationally, the company also produces a line of outdoor footwear, ski apparel, and cycling gear. **Parent company:** Diadora SpA.

DIAMOND PARKING SERVICES, INC.
3161 Elliott Avenue, Suite 200, Seattle WA 98121. 206/284-3100. **Contact:** Personnel. **E-mail address:** hr@diamondparking.com. **World Wide Web address:** http://www.diamondparking.com. **Description:** Owns parking facilities and is involved in real estate. **Corporate headquarters location:** This location. **Number of employees at this location:** 200.

DOWL ENGINEERS
8320 154th Avenue NE, Redmond WA 98052. 425/869-2670. **Fax:** 425/869-2679. **Contact:** Linda Finch, Human Resources. **E-mail address:** lfinch@dowl.com. **World Wide Web address:** http://www.dowl.com. **Description:** Offers specialized environmental engineering services to a variety of clients in government and industry. The company also provides civil engineering and surveying services to municipal and private development clients. **Positions advertised include:** Civil Engineer; Transportation/Traffic Engineer; Auto CAD Technician; Construction Inspector; Licensed Surveyor; Geologist.

DYNACARE LABORATORY
1229 Madison Street, Suite 500, Seattle WA 98104. 206/386-2672. **Fax:** 206/386-2991. **Contact:** Human Resources. **E-mail address:** jobsdnw@dynacare.com. **World Wide Web address:** http://www.dynacare.com. **Description:** A medical laboratory. **Positions advertised include:** Lab Assistant; Phlebotomist; Medical Technologist; Assistant Supervisor of Specimen Processing; Route Representative. **Listed on:** NASDAQ. **Stock exchange symbol:** DNCR.

EDS (ELECTRONIC DATA SYSTEMS CORPORATION)
19351 Eighth Avenue NE, Suite B, Poulsbo WA 98370. 360/697-3330. **Contact:** Human Resources. **E-mail address:** careers@eds.com. **World Wide Web address:** http://www.eds.com. **Description:** Provides consulting, systems development, systems integration, and systems management services for large-scale and industry-specific applications. Founded in 1962. **Corporate headquarters location:** Plano TX. **Other U.S. locations:** Nationwide. **International locations:** Worldwide. **Listed on:** New York Stock Exchange. **Stock exchange symbol:** EDS. **Number of employees worldwide:** 115,000.

EZ LOADER BOAT TRAILERS INC.
P.O. Box 3263, Spokane WA 99220-3263. 509/489-0181. **Physical address:** 717 North Hamilton Street, Spokane WA 99202. **Contact:** Human Resources. **World Wide Web address:** http://www.ezloader.com. **Description:** Manufactures boat trailers. **Corporate headquarters location:** This location. **Operations at this facility include:** Administration; Manufacturing; Research and Development.

EASTERN WASHINGTON UNIVERSITY
314 Showalter Hall, Cheney WA 99004-2431. 509/359-2381. **Fax:** 509/359-2874. **Recorded jobline:** 509/359-4390. **Contact:** Human Resources Department. **E-mail address:** hr@mail.ewu.edu. **World Wide Web address:** http://www.ewu.edu. **Description:** A four-year university offering undergraduate and graduate degrees to approximately 8,500 students. **Corporate headquarters location:** This location. **Operations at this facility include:** Administration. **Number of employees at this location:** 1,100.

EDAW INC.
1505 Western Avenue, Suite 601, Seattle WA 98101. 206/622-1176. **Fax:** 206/343-9809. **Contact:** Human Resources. **E-mail address:** humanresources@edaw.com. **World Wide Web address:** http://www.edaw.com. **Description:** Engaged in landscape architecture, environmental planning, and urban design services worldwide. **Corporate headquarters location:** San Francisco CA. **Other U.S. locations:** Irvine CA; Denver CO; Atlanta GA; Alexandria VA. **Operations at this facility include:** Administration; Service. **Number of employees at this location:** 15. **Number of employees nationwide:** 200. **Number of employees worldwide:** 250.

EDDIE BAUER, INC.
P.O. Box 97000, Redmond WA 98073-9700. 425/755-6100. **Physical address:** 15010 NE 36th Street, Redmond WA 98052. **Toll-free phone:** 800/625-7935. **Fax:** 425/755-7696. **Contact:** Human Resources. **World Wide Web address:** http://www.eddiebauer.com. **Description:** A multi-unit, private-label retailer and catalog company for apparel and home accessories. **Corporate headquarters location:** This location. **Other U.S. locations:** Nationwide. **Parent company:** Spiegel, Inc. **Listed on:** NASDAQ. **Stock exchange symbol:** SPGLE. **Number of employees at this location:** 1,000. **Number of employees nationwide:** 10,000.

EDMONDS COMMUNITY COLLEGE
20000 68th Avenue West, Lynnwood WA 98036. 425/640-1400. **Recorded jobline:** 425/640-1510. **Contact:** Human Resources. **E-mail address:** jobs@edcc.edu. **World Wide Web address:** http://www.edcc.edu. **Description:** A community college that operates as part of the Washington State Public Higher Education System. **NOTE:** Please call the jobline for a listing of available positions. **Positions advertised include:** Media Maintenance Technician; ESL Instructor; Mathematics Instructor; Chemistry Instructor. **Number of employees at this location:** 1,000.

EKONO INC.
11061 NE Second Street, Suite 107, Bellevue WA 98004. 425/455-5969. **Fax:** 425/455-3091. **Contact:** Heikki Mannisto, President. **E-mail address:** mannisto.heikki@ekono.com. **World Wide Web address:** http://www.ekono.com. **Description:** An engineering consulting firm serving the pulp and paper industry. **Corporate headquarters location:** This location. **Parent company:** Duoplan Oy.

ELDEC CORPORATION
16700 13th Avenue West, P.O. Box 97027, Lynnwood WA 98046-9727. 425/743-1313. **Fax:** 425/743-8234. **Contact:** Employment Department. **E-mail address:** staffing@eldec.com. **World Wide Web address:** http://www.eldec.com. **Description:** Custom designs precision electronic and electromechanical equipment. Eldec markets its products to commercial and military aircraft companies. **Corporate headquarters location:** This location.

ELTON-WOLF PUBLISHING
2505 Second Avenue, Suite 515, Seattle WA 98121. 206/748-0345. **Fax:** 206/748-0343. **Contact:** Human Resources. **E-mail address:** info@elton-wolf.com. **World Wide Web address:** http://www.elton-wolf.com. **Description:** Publishes author-subsidized cookbooks, autobiographies, fiction, poetry, computer manuals and business manuals. **Other U.S. locations:** Denver CO; Portland OR. **International locations:** Vancouver, British Columbia.

EMERALD CITY GRAPHICS
23328 66th Avenue South, Kent WA 98032. 253/520-2600. **Toll-free phone:** 877/631-5178. **Fax:** 253/520-2607. **Contact:** Human Resources Department. **E-mail address:** marks@emeraldcg.com. **World Wide Web address:** http://www.emeraldcg.com. **Description:** Prints manuals, manufactures custom binders, and offers electronic publishing services. **Parent company:** Consolidated Graphics. **Listed on:** New York Stock Exchange. **Stock exchange symbol:** CGX.

EPOCH PHARMACEUTICALS, INC.
21720 23rd Drive SE 150, Bothell WA 98021. 425/482-5555. **Fax:** 425/482-5550. **Contact:** Human Resources. **World Wide Web address:** http://www.epochpharm.com. **Description:** A biomedical company focused on the development of oligonucleotides as new therapeutic compounds and for use in diagnostic testing. Utilizing proprietary and unique technology in the design, synthesis, and chemical modification of oligonucleotides, the company is developing gene blockers that act by specifically binding to and inactivating the DNA of disease-associated genes; protein blockers that act by selective inhibition of certain proteins that are central to the growth and reproduction of cells and viruses; and DNA probe-based diagnostic systems for the rapid identification of certain disease pathogens. **Listed on:** NASDAQ. **Stock exchange symbol:** EBIO.

ERNST & YOUNG LLP
999 Third Avenue, Suite 3500, Seattle WA 98104. 206/621-1800. **Contact:** Human Resources. **World Wide Web address:** http://www.ey.com. **Description:** A certified public accounting firm that also provides management consulting services. Services include data processing, financial modeling, financial feasibility studies, production planning and inventory management, management sciences, health care planning, human resources, cost accounting, and budgeting systems. **Positions advertised include:** Technology & Security Risk Services Manager; Tax Consulting Manager. **Corporate headquarters location:** New York NY. **Number of employees nationwide:** 25,000. **Number of employees worldwide:** 73,000.

ESTERLINE TECHNOLOGIES
500 108th Avenue NE, Bellevue WA 98004. 425/453-9400. **Fax:** 425/453-2916. **Contact:** Personnel Department. **E-mail address:** hr@esterline.com. **World Wide Web address:** http://www.esterline.com. **Description:** A manufacturing company serving several market areas including commercial aerospace, the defense industry, and the electronics industries. The company is divided into three business groups: Advanced Materials, Aerospace, and Automation. **Corporate headquarters location:** This location. **Subsidiaries include:** Armtec Defense Products Company, Coachella CA; Auxitrol S.A., France; Excellon Automation Company, Torrance CA; Kirkhill Rubber Company, Brea CA; Korry Electronics Company, Seattle WA; W.A. Whitney Company, Rockford IL. **Listed on:** New York Stock Exchange. **Stock exchange symbol:** ESL. **CEO:** Wendell P. Hurlbut.

EVERETT, CITY OF
2930 Wetmore Avenue, Suite 6A, Everett WA 98201. 425/257-8767. **Recorded jobline:** 425/257-8768. **Fax:** 425/257-8754. **Contact:** Personnel. **E-mail address:** employment-HR@ci.everett.wa.us. **World Wide Web address:** http://www.ci.everett.wa.us. **Description:** Houses the city of Everett's administrative offices and city hall. The city's population is approximately 84,000. **Office hours:** Monday - Friday, 8:00 a.m. - 5:00 p.m. **Corporate headquarters location:** This location.

EVERETT CLINIC
3901 Hoyt Avenue, Everett WA 98201. 425/259-0966. **Contact:** Human Resources Department. **E-mail address:** hr@everettclinic.com. **World Wide Web address:** http://www.everettclinic.com. **Description:** A multispecialty group medical clinic operating through eight sites in Snohomish County. **Positions advertised include:** Behavioral Health Technician; Staff Registered Nurse; Nursing Supervisor.

EVERETT COMMUNITY COLLEGE
2000 Tower Street, Everett WA 98201. 425/388-9229. **Contact:** Human Resources Department. **World Wide Web address:** http://www.evcc.ctc.edu. **Description:** A two-year, community college. **Positions advertised include:** Dean of Communication and Social Sciences; Nursing Instructor.

EVERGREEN COMMUNITY HOME HEALTH CARE
12910 Totem Lake Boulevard, Suite 3204, Kirkland WA 98034. 425/899-3300. **Contact:** Human Resources Department. **World Wide Web address:** http://www.evergreenhealthcare.com. **Description:** Offers health services including nursing care, physical therapy, speech therapy, occupational therapy, home health aides, and social work, with specializations in oncology, pediatrics, and diabetic management. Evergreen Community Home Health Care staff help with the transition from the hospital or nursing home back to the primary residence. **Positions advertised include:** Registered Nurse; Licensed Practical Nurse; Certified Nursing Assistant; Housekeeper.

EVERGREEN HOSPITAL MEDICAL CENTER
12040 NE 128th Street, Kirkland WA 98034. 425/899-1000. **Fax:** 425/899-2510. **Contact:** Human Resources. **E-mail address:** jobs@evergreenhealthcare.org. **World Wide Web address:** http://www.evergreenhealthcare.org. **Description:** A medical center housing an acute care hospital, a surgery center, a hospice center, a head injury rehabilitation center, a telemarketing center, and a home health department. **Positions advertised include:** Clinical Nurse Specialist. **Operations at this facility include:** Administration. **Number of employees at this location:** 1,500.

EXCELL DATA
1756 114th Avenue SE, Suite 220, Bellevue WA 98004. 425/974-2000. **Toll-free phone:** 800/5-EXCELL. **Fax:** 425/974-2001. **E-mail address:** info@excell.com. **World Wide Web address:** http://www.excell.com. **Description:** Excell Data delivers value-add services: Systems Integration; IT Outsourcing; Technology Procurement Services; Contract Consulting; Custom Application Development; Infrastructure Services; Event Technical Support. **Positions advertised include:** Access/Excel Project Manager; Access/Excel VBA Developer; API Tester with C# Skills; Software Designer; NET Developer for User Interfaces; NET Developer with Server Technologies; NET Developers; NET Web Applications Developer. **Corporate headquarters location:** This location. **Other U.S. locations:** Nationwide. **President and COO:** Rick Jorgensen. **Number of employees nationwide:** 3,500 employees.

EXOTIC METALS FORMING COMPANY
5411 South 226th Street, Kent WA 98032. 253/395-3710. **Fax:** 253/458-3538. **Contact:** Human Resources. **E-mail address:** jobs@exoticmetals.com. **World Wide Web address:** http://www.emfcowa.com. **Description:** Manufactures aircraft engine parts. **Positions advertised include:** Material Manager; Programmer/Analyst; NDT Technician. **Corporate headquarters location:** This location.

EXPEDITORS INTERNATIONAL OF WASHINGTON, INC.
1015 Third Avenue, 12th Floor, Seattle WA 98104. 206/674-3400. **Contact:** Personnel. **World Wide Web address:** http://www.expd.com. **Description:** Engaged in the business of international air and ocean freight forwarding. The company also acts as a customs broker in its domestic overseas offices. **Positions advertised include:** Staff Accountant; Administrative Assistant; EDI Coordinator; Database Administrator; Senior JAVA Developer; IS Project Manager; UI Designer. **Corporate headquarters location:** This location. **Listed on:** NASDAQ. **Stock exchange symbol:** EXPD.

EXPORTS INC.
435 Martin Street, Suite 4000, Blaine WA 98230. 360/332-5239. **Contact:** Human Resources. **Description:** A property management firm involved in the financial management of corporate properties.

FCB SEATTLE
1011 Western Avenue, Suite 1000, Seattle WA 98104. 206/467-6585. **Fax:** 206/223-2765. **Contact:** Human Resources. **E-mail address:** jobs@seattle.fcb.com. **World Wide Web address:** http://www.seattle.fcb.com. **Description:** A full-service advertising agency. FCB Seattle also offers public relations services including corporate relations, marketing support, employee relations, financial relations, government affairs, and community relations. The staff includes specialists in marketing, media, account service, creative work, research, public relations, finance, agriculture, and broadcast affairs. **Corporate headquarters location:** New York NY.

FIC INSURANCE GROUP
2101 Fourth Avenue, Suite 700, Seattle WA 98121. 206/441-1942. **Contact:** Personnel Department. **E-mail address:** hr@ficgroup.com. **World Wide Web address:** http://www.ficgroup.com. **Description:** Sells life and disability insurance. **Corporate headquarters location:** Austin TX. **Parent company:** Merrill Lynch & Co., Inc. **Number of employees at this location:** 420.

FARM CREDIT SERVICES
P.O. Box 2515, Spokane WA 99224. 509/340-5300. **Toll-free phone:** 800/743-2125. **Fax:** 800/255-1789. **Contact:** Human Resources. **E-mail address:** hrdept@farm-credit.com. **World Wide Web address:** http://www.farm-credit.com. **Description:** Provides long-, intermediate-, and short-term financing to agricultural producers, farm-related businesses, fisherman, part-time farmers, and country homeowners. The banks and related associations provide credit and credit-related services to eligible borrowers for qualified agricultural purposes. **Positions advertised include:** Mortgage Loan Officer. **Corporate headquarters location:** This location. **Other U.S. locations:** AK; ID; MT.

FILENET CORPORATION
720 Fourth Avenue, Suite 100, Kirkland WA 98033. 425/893-7000. **Contact:** Human Resources. **E-mail address:** cooljobs@filenet.com. **World Wide Web address:** http://www.filenet.com. **Description:** FileNET develops and markets electronic content management software and e-business solutions. Products and services are used to help corporations and organizations build intranets, create electronic portals to streamline information management, and to create, process, edit, organize, and store all forms of digital content for Internet applications. Founded in 1983. **Company slogan:** Putting documents to work. **Special programs:** Internships. **Corporate headquarters location:** Costa Mesa CA. **Other U.S. locations:** Nationwide. **International locations:** Worldwide. **Listed on:** NASDAQ. **Stock exchange symbol:** FILE. **Number of employees nationwide:** 1,700.

FIREMAN'S FUND INSURANCE COMPANY
2101 Fourth Avenue, Suite 1100, Seattle WA 98121. 206/728-5100. **Contact:** Human Resources. **World Wide Web address:** http://www.the-fund.com. **Description:** Offers a variety of commercial insurance products and services. **Corporate headquarters location:** Novato CA. **Parent company:** Allianz AG. **Operations at this facility include:** Administration; Service.

FIRST MUTUAL BANK
400 108th Avenue NE, P.O. Box 1647, Bellevue WA 98009. 425/453-5301. **Fax:** 425/455-7300. **Contact:** Human Resources. **World Wide Web address:** http://www.firstmutual.com. **Description:** A savings bank primarily offering real estate loan services. The company also offers a variety of depository and banking services. Founded in 1953. **Positions advertised include:** Assistant Branch Manager; Consumer Loan Servicing Representative; Sales Finance Assistant; Wholesale Loan Representative; Workflow Analyst. **Corporate headquarters location:** This location. **Other area locations:** Issaquah WA; Ballard WA; Bellingham WA; Monroe WA; Redmond WA; Seattle WA.

FISHERIES SUPPLY COMPANY
1900 North Northlake Way, Suite 10, Seattle WA 98103. 206/632-4462. **Contact:** Personnel Department. **World Wide Web address:** http://www.fisheries-supply.com. **Description:** A wholesaler of marine hardware and supplies. **Corporate headquarters location:** This location.

FLOW INTERNATIONAL CORPORATION
23500 64th Avenue South, Kent WA 98032. 253/850-3500. **Toll-free phone:** 800/446-3569. **Fax:** 253/813-2710. **Contact:** Human Resources. **E-mail address:** hr@flowcorp.com. **World Wide Web address:** http://www.flowcorp.com. **Description:** One of the world's leading manufacturers of ultrahigh-pressure (UHP) waterjet cutting and cleaning systems, and factory-automated equipment. Flow International has three main product categories: UHP cutting and cleaning, HydroMilling and HydroCleaning services, and powered access systems equipment. The company provides environmentally sound solutions for the manufacturing, industrial cleaning, and factory automation markets. Flow International offers a wide range of robotics articulation capabilities, automated assembly systems, and other specialized manufacturing components. The company sells original equipment and spare parts. **Corporate headquarters location:** This location. **International locations:** Worldwide. **Listed on:** NASDAQ. **Stock exchange symbol:** FLOW. **CEO:** Ronald Tarrant. **Facilities Manager:** Doug Sweeney. **Purchasing Manager:** Jim Arndt.

FLUKE CORPORATION
P.O. Box 9090, Everett WA 98206-9090. 425/347-6100. **Physical address:** 6920 Seaway Boulevard, Everett WA 98203. **Contact:** Personnel Department. **E-mail address:** jobs@fluke.com. **World Wide Web address:** http://www.fluke.com. **Description:** A manufacturer of electronic instrumentation for test measurement and calibration. **Positions advertised include:** Engineering Manager; Accounts Payable/Payroll Manager; Test Engineer. **Corporate headquarters location:** This location. **Parent company:** Danaher Corporation. **Listed on:** New York Stock Exchange. **Stock exchange symbol:** DHR.

FLUOR FEDERAL SERVICES
P.O. Box 1050, Richland WA 99352. 509/372-2000. **Contact:** Human Resources. **World Wide Web address:** http://www.fluor.com. **E-mail address:** ffshr@flour.com. **Description:** A full-service engineering and construction company serving the power, industrial, hydrocarbon, and process industries, as well as the federal government. **Parent company:** Fluor Corporation (Irvine CA) is engaged in engineering and construction, as well as the production of various natural resources. Fluor Corporation provides its services to energy, natural resource, industrial, commercial, utility, and government clients. Natural resources mined include gold, silver, lead, zinc, iron ore, coal, oil, and gas. The corporation also provides contract drilling services. **Listed on:** New York Stock Exchange. **Stock exchange symbol:** FLR. **Number of employees worldwide:** 20,000.

FOAMEX INTERNATIONAL, INC.
19635 78th Avenue South, Kent WA 98032. 253/872-0170. **Contact:** Personnel Manager. **E-mail address:** careers@foamex.com. **World Wide Web address:** http://www.foamex.com. **Description:** One of the nation's largest manufacturers of flexible polyurethane foam products. Foamex products are classified into four groups: cushion foams, carpet cushion foams, automotive foams, and technical foams. Cushion foams are used for mattresses, quilting and borders, home and office furniture, computer and electronics packaging, and padding foams for health care. Foamex carpet cushion foams include prime, bonded, sponge rubber, felt carpet cushion, synthetic grass turf, and a variety of textured carpeting and wall coverings. Automotive foams

include foams for cushioning and seating, acoustical foams, headliner foams, trim foams, and foams for door panel parts. Technical foams include those for filtration, reservoiring, sound absorption and transmission, carburetors, high-speed inkjet printers, speaker grilles, oxygenators, and EKG pads, as well as cosmetic applicators, mop heads, paint brushes, and diapers. **Corporate headquarters location:** Linwood PA. **Listed on:** NASDAQ. **Stock exchange symbol:** FMXI. **Annual sales/revenues:** More than $100 million. **Number of employees worldwide:** 3,600.

FOOD SERVICES OF AMERICA
18430 East Valley Highway, Kent WA 98032. 425/251-9100. **Contact:** Human Resources. **World Wide Web address:** http://www.fsafood.com. **Description:** A food service company specializing in the distribution of fruit, fresh seafood, canned and frozen goods, and fresh meat. **Positions advertised include:** Associate Services Specialist; Day Delivery Driver. **Corporate headquarters location:** Seattle WA.

FOSS HOME & VILLAGE
13023 Greenwood Avenue North, Seattle WA 98133. 206/364-1300. **Contact:** Human Resources. **World Wide Web address:** http://www.fosscare.org. **Description:** A long-term care facility that offers skilled nursing and assisted living services.

FOSS MARITIME
660 West Ewing Street, Seattle WA 98119. 206/281-3800. **Contact:** Personnel Department. **E-mail address:** fossjobs@foss.com. **World Wide Web address:** http://www.fossmaritime.com. **Description:** Provides maritime carrier services; deep-sea forum services; domestic, coastwide, and intercoastal transportation; and ship repair and services. **Corporate headquarters location:** This location.

FOSTER PEPPER & SHEFELMAN PLLC
1111 Third Avenue, Suite 3400, Seattle WA 98101. 206/447-7296. **Contact:** Meg Clara, Director of Human Resources. **E-mail address:** claram@foster.com. **World Wide Web address:** http://www.foster.com. **Description:** A law firm specializing in corporate and environmental law. Founded in 1904. **Other area locations:** Bellevue WA; Spokane WA. **Other U.S. locations:** Anchorage AK; Portland OR. **Number of employees at this location:** 350.

TETRA TECH FW, INC.
12100 NE 195th Street, Suite 200, Bothell WA 98011. 425/482-7600. **Fax:** 425/482-7652. **Contact:** Human Resources Manager. **World Wide Web address:** http://www.tetratech.com. **Description:** A worldwide environmental consulting and engineering firm. **Positions advertised include:** Design/Task Construction Order Manager; Field Construction Engineer; Quality Control Inspector; Senior Associate Cost Engineer. **Corporate headquarters location:** Pasadena CA. **Other U.S. locations:** Nationwide. **Listed on:** NASDAQ. **Stock exchange symbol:** TTEK. **Number of employees nationwide:** 9000.

FOUR SEASONS OLYMPIC HOTEL
411 University Street, Seattle WA 98101. 206/621-1700. **Recorded jobline:** 206/287-4047. **Contact:** Personnel. **World Wide Web address:** http://www.fourseasons.com. **Description:** A 450-room hotel with 20,000 square feet of meeting and function space, three restaurants, a health club, and a retail arcade with 14 international shops. Four Seasons Hotels & Resorts operates approximately 50 luxury hotels and resorts in 22 countries. **Corporate headquarters location:** Ontario, Canada. **Other U.S. locations:** Nationwide. **International locations:** Worldwide. **Listed on:** New York Stock Exchange. **Stock exchange symbol:** FS. **Number of employees at this location:** 585.

FRANKLIN PIERCE SCHOOL DISTRICT
315 129th Street South, Tacoma WA 98444. 253/537-0211. **Fax:** 253/536-0797. **Contact:** Mrs. Jamie Siegel, Executive Director of Personnel. **E-mail address:** jamies@fp.k12.wa.us. **World Wide Web address:** http://www.midland.fp.k12.wa.us. **Description:** Public school district for the Tacoma area. **Positions advertised include:** Special Education Teacher; Physical Therapist; Elementary School Counselor; Music/Movement Teacher. **Operations at this facility include:** Administration.

FRED MEYER, INC.
14300 First Avenue South, Seattle WA 98168. 206/433-6404. **Contact:** Personnel Department. **E-mail address:** fredmeyer@webhire.com. **World Wide Web address:** http://www.fredmeyer.com. **Description:** A major retailer of food and general merchandise on the West Coast operating through more than 400 stores in 26 states. Products include food, apparel, appliances, jewelry, health and beauty aids, and pharmaceuticals. **Corporate headquarters location:** Portland OR. **Other U.S. locations:** AK; CA; ID; MT; OR; UT. **Parent company:** The Kroger Company. **Listed on:** New York Stock Exchange. **Stock exchange symbol:** KR. **Number of employees nationwide:** 2,440.

FRITO-LAY, INC.
4808 NW Fruit Valley Road, Vancouver WA 98660. 360/694-8478. **Contact:** Human Resources. **World Wide Web address:** http://www.fritolay.com. **Description:** A worldwide manufacturer and wholesaler of snack products including Fritos Corn Chips, Lays Potato Chips, and Doritos Tortilla Chips. **NOTE:** All job openings are posted with the Washington State Job Service. Call 360/735-5000 for more information. **Corporate headquarters location:** Plano TX. **Parent company:** PepsiCo, Inc. (Purchase NY). **Listed on:** New York Stock Exchange. **Stock exchange symbol:** PEP.

FUNTASIA FAMILY FUN PARK
7212 220th Street SW, Edmonds WA 98026. 425/775-2174. **Contact:** Human Resources. **World Wide Web address:** http://www.familyfunpark.com. **Description:** An amusement park offering a variety of recreational facilities including a go-cart track, a mini-golf course, bumper cars and boats, a video arcade, and batting cages.

GM NAMEPLATE INC.
INTAQ KEY PANELS
2040 15th Avenue West, Seattle WA 98119. 206/284-2200. **Fax:** 206/284-3705. **Contact:** Human Resources. **E-mail address:** humanresources@gnnameplate.com. **World Wide Web address:** http://www.gmnameplate.com. **Description:** Involved in coating, engraving, allied services, paper coatings, and glazing. GM Nameplate is also a manufacturer of a variety of metal products. **Positions advertised include:** Business Programmer/Analyst. **Corporate headquarters location:** This location.

GACO WESTERN INC.
P.O. Box 88698, Seattle WA 98138-2698. 206/575-0450. **Contact:** Yolanda Sewell, Human Resources Manager. **E-mail address:** ysewell@gaco.com. **World Wide Web address:** http://www.gaco.com. **Description:** Manufactures elastomeric coatings. **Corporate headquarters location:** This location.

GAI'S NORTHWEST BAKERIES
P.O. Box 24327, Seattle WA 98124. 206/322-0931. **Contact:** Human Resources. **World Wide Web address:** http://www.gaisbakery.com. **Description:** A regional wholesale baking company. **NOTE:** This Bakery is partnered with Franz Family Bakeries, also in Seattle. **Annual sales/revenues:** $51 - $100 million. **Parent company:** Untied States Bakery.

GENERAL CHEMICAL CORPORATION
8579 North Texas Road, Anacortes WA 98221. 360/293-2171. **Contact:** Human Resources. **E-mail address:** hrinfo@genchem.com. **World Wide Web address:** http://www.genchem.com. **Description:** Manufactures sulfuric acid and other inorganic chemicals. **Corporate headquarters location:** Parsippany NJ. **Parent company:** The General Chemical Group, Inc.

GENERAL DYNAMICS
P.O. Box 97009, Redmond WA 98073-9709. 425/885-5000. **Fax:** 425/882-5746. **Contact:** Employment. **World Wide Web address:** http://www.generaldynamics.com. **Description:** The Aerospace & Electronics Division develops space propulsion, solid propellant, and electronics systems for the aerospace, defense, and electronics industries. Overall, General Dynamics is a defense and aerospace company that, in addition to this division, also operates through its Ordinance and Tactical Systems Division. **Corporate headquarters location:** Falls Church VA.

GENIE INDUSTRIES
P.O. Box 97030, Redmond WA 98073. 425/881-1800. **Physical address:** 18340 NE 76th Street, Redmond WA 98052. **Contact:** Human Resources. **World Wide Web address:** http://www.genieind.com. **Description:** Designs, manufactures, and services lifts, aerial platforms, and booms. Products are used primarily in warehouses and at distribution facilities, as well as in construction projects. **Parent company:** Terex.

GEORGIA-PACIFIC CORPORATION
300 West Laurel Street, Bellingham WA 98225. 360/733-4410. **Contact:** Human Resources Manager. **World Wide Web address:** http://www.gp.com. **Description:** Manufactures, wholesales, and distributes building products, industrial wood products, pulp, paper, packaging, and related chemicals. **Other U.S. locations:** Nationwide. **Listed on:** New York Stock Exchange. **Stock exchange symbol:** GP.

GEORGIA-PACIFIC CORPORATION
401 NE Adams Street, Camas WA 98607. 360/834-4444. **Contact:** Personnel Director. **World Wide Web address:** http://www.gp.com. **Description:** Manufactures, wholesales, and distributes building products, industrial wood products, pulp, paper, packaging, and related chemicals. **Other U.S. locations:** Nationwide. **Listed on:** New York Stock Exchange. **Stock exchange symbol:** GP.

GETRONICS
22425 East Appleway Road, Liberty Lake WA 99019. 509/927-5600. **Contact:** Human Resources. **World Wide Web address:** http://www.getronics.com. **Description:** Provides information and communication technology solutions and support services worldwide. Getronics conducts its business through two major sectors: Systems Integration and Networked Technology Services includes enterprise system integration, managed services and infrastructure outsourcing, and network integration; and Business Solutions and Consulting includes software services, consulting, industry business solutions, and financial business solutions. **Corporate headquarters location:** Billerica MA. **International locations:** Worldwide.

GOLD RESERVE INC.
926 West Sprague Avenue, Suite 200, Spokane WA 99201. 509/623-1500. **Toll-free phone:** 800/625-9550. **Fax:** 509/623-1634. **Contact:** Human Resources. **World Wide Web address:** http://www.goldreserveinc.com. **Description:** A mining company engaged, through foreign subsidiaries, in the acquisition and exploration of gold and other mineral properties. Gold Reserve has focused its attention on mining opportunities in Venezuela due to the enormous mineral resources believed to be contained within the country. **Corporate headquarters location:** This location. **Listed on:** AMEX. **Stock exchange symbol:** GRZ.

GONZAGA UNIVERSITY
502 East Boone, Spokane WA 99258-0080. 509/328-5996. **Physical address:** 414 East Sharp, Spokane WA 99258-0080. **Fax:** 509/323-5813. **Recorded jobline:** 509/323-5916. **Contact:** Tracy Kelly, Employment and HR Specialist. **E-mail address:** kelly@gonzaga.edu. **World Wide Web address:** http://www.gonzaga.edu. **Description:** A university offering coursework in a number of fields including arts and sciences, business administration, education, engineering, law, nursing, and military science. Gonzaga University enrolls approximately 3,000 undergraduate and 2,000 graduate students.

GOODRICH AVIATION
3100 112th Street, Everett WA 98204. 425/347-3030. **Contact:** Human Resources. **World Wide Web address:** http://www.goodrich.com. **Description:** Provides aircraft systems, components, and services, and manufactures a wide range of specialty chemicals. Goodrich Aviation operates an international network of sales offices and aircraft service centers and has manufacturing facilities in seven countries. **Listed on:** New York Stock Exchange. **Positions advertised include:** Senior Tooling Engineer. **Stock exchange symbol:** GR.

GOODWILL INDUSTRIES
307 West Columbia Street, Pasco WA 99301. 509/547-7717. **Contact:** Employment. **World Wide Web address:** http://www.goodwill.org. **Description:** Goodwill Industries is a nonprofit provider of employment training for the disabled and the poor, and operates 1,400 thrift stores nationwide. **Corporate headquarters location:** Bethesda MD. **Operations at this facility include:** This location houses the area administrative offices and a thrift store.

GRAINGER
5706 East Broadway Avenue, Spokane WA 99212. 509/535-9882. **Contact:** Human Resources. **World Wide Web address:** http://www.grainger.com. **Description:** Distributes a variety of equipment and components to the industrial, commercial, contracting, and institutional markets nationwide. Products include equipment and components for motors, air tools, hydraulic products, refrigeration items, power and hand tools, office equipment, computer supplies, storage equipment, replacement parts, industrial products, safety items, cold weather clothing, and sanitary supplies. **Positions advertised include:** Outside Sales Account Manager; Market Development Specialist. **Corporate headquarters location:** Chicago IL. **Listed on:** New York Stock Exchange. **Stock exchange symbol:** GWW.

GRAINGER
6725 Todd Boulevard, Tukwila WA 98188. 425/251-5030. **Contact:** Human Resources. **World Wide Web address:** http://www.grainger.com. **Description:** Distributes a variety of equipment and components to the industrial, commercial, contracting, and institutional markets nationwide. Products include equipment and components for motors, air tools, hydraulic products, refrigeration items, power and

hand tools, office equipment, computer supplies, replacement parts, industrial products, safety items, cold weather clothing, and storage equipment. **Positions advertised include:** Outside Sales Account Manager; Market Development Specialist. **Corporate headquarters location:** Chicago IL. **Listed on:** New York Stock Exchange. **Stock exchange symbol:** GWW.

GRANGE INSURANCE GROUP
ROCKY MOUNTAIN FIRE & CASUALTY
200 Cedar Street, Seattle WA 98121. 206/448-4911. **Fax:** 206/448-0942. **Contact:** Human Resources Department. **E-mail address:** hr@grange.com. **World Wide Web address:** http://www.grange.com. **Description:** A property and casualty insurance firm. Founded in 1894. **Corporate headquarters location:** This location.

GRAYBAR ELECTRIC COMPANY
P.O. Box 3727, Seattle WA 98124. 206/292-4848. **Contact:** Personnel Manager. **E-mail address:** opportunities@graybaronline.com **World Wide Web address:** http://www.gbe.com. **Description:** Distributes electrical and telecommunications equipment including wire, transformers, lighting fixtures, power transmission equipment, telephone station apparatus, and other hardware, primarily to independent telephone companies and public power utilities. Founded in 1869. **Corporate headquarters location:** St. Louis MO. **Number of employees nationwide:** 7,660.

GREAT REPUBLIC LIFE INSURANCE
1900 West Nickerson Street, Suite 200, Seattle WA 98119. 206/285-1422. **Fax:** 206/282-5865. **Contact:** Personnel Department. **World Wide Web address:** http://www.grlins.com. **Description:** A health insurance underwriting company.

GROUP HEALTH COOPERATIVE
P.O. Box 34586Y, Seattle WA 98124. 206/448-2748. **Physical address:** 12501 East Marginal Way, Tukwila WA 98168. **Contact:** Human Resources. **World Wide Web address:** http://www.ghc.org. **Description:** A health maintenance organization and hospital operator. **Corporate headquarters location:** This location. **Number of employees at this location:** 9,000.

GROUP HEALTH EASTSIDE HOSPITAL
2700 152nd Avenue NE, Redmond WA 98052. 425/883-5151. **Contact:** Human Resources. **E-mail address:** recruiters.i@ghc.org. **World Wide Web address:** http://www.ghc.org. **Description:** An acute care hospital that also offers physical therapy and pediatric care.

GUIDANT CORPORATION
6645 185th Avenue NE, Suite 100, Redmond WA 98052. 425/376-1300. **Fax:** 425/376-1426. **Contact:** Human Resources. **World Wide Web address:** http://www.guidant.com. **Description:** Guidant Corporation designs, develops, manufactures, and markets a wide range of products for use in cardiac rhythm management, coronary artery disease intervention, and other forms of minimally invasive surgery. **Corporate headquarters location:** Indianapolis IN. **Operations at this facility include:** This location is engaged in research and development. **Listed on:** New York Stock Exchange. **Stock exchange symbol:** GDT. **Annual sales/revenues:** More than $100 million.

H.O. SPORTS
17622 NE 67th Court, Redmond WA 98052. 425/885-3505. **Toll-free phone:** 800/938-4040. **Fax:** 425/867-5327. **Contact:** Human Resources. **E-mail address:** info@hosports.com. **World Wide Web address:** http://www.hosports.com. **Description:** Manufactures a variety of outdoor recreation equipment including water skis and snowboards. **Corporate headquarters location:** This location.

HAGGEN, INC.
TOP FOOD & DRUG
P.O. Box 9704, Bellingham WA 98227. 360/733-8720. **Recorded jobline:** 888/HAG-GENS. **Fax:** 360/752-6424. **Contact:** Human Resources Manager. **E-mail address:** careers@haggen.com. **World Wide Web address:** http://www.haggen.com. **Description:** Operates over 25 grocery stores throughout the Pacific Northwest. **Special programs:** Internships. **Corporate headquarters location:** This location.

HARBORVIEW MEDICAL CENTER
325 Ninth Avenue, Seattle WA 98104. 206/223-3000. **Contact:** Human Resources. **World Wide Web address:** http://www.uwmedicine.org. **Description:** A unit of the University of Washington Academic Medical Center. The Harborview Medical Center contains an adult and pediatric trauma center and a regional burn center.

HARRISON MEMORIAL HOSPITAL
2520 Cherry Avenue, Bremerton WA 98310. 360/792-6720. **Fax:** 360/792-6724. **Recorded jobline:** 360/792-6729. **Contact:** Sue Wallace, Recruiter. **E-mail address:** suewallace@hmh.westsound.net. **World Wide Web address:** http://www.harrisonhospital.org. **Description:** A 297-bed, full-service hospital specializing in cardiology care, diagnostic imaging, emergency and urgent care, oncology, radiation therapy, and retinal and laparoscopic surgery. Founded in 1918. **Positions advertised include:** Radiologic Technologist; Medical Imaging Aide; Surgical Technician; Supply Support Technician; Speech Language Pathologist; Physical Therapist; Occupational Therapist. **Number of employees at this location:** 1,400.

HART CROWSER
1910 Fairview Avenue East, Seattle WA 98102. 206/324-9530. **Contact:** Human Resources. **E-mail address:** staffing@hartcrowser.com. **World Wide Web address:** http://www.hartcrowser.com. **Description:** An environmental consulting firm offering site development, remediation, and waste management services. Founded in 1974. **Corporate headquarters location:** This location. **Other U.S. locations:** AK; CA; CO; IL; NJ; OR.

HAWORTH INC.
5701 6th Avenue South, Seattle WA 98108. 206/623-8035. **Contact:** Human Resources. **World Wide Web address:** http://www.haworth.com. **Description:** A leading manufacturer of office furniture including desks, storage and filing cabinets, and seating products. **Corporate headquarters location:** Holland MI.

HELLY HANSEN INC.
3326 160th Avenue SE, Suite 200, Bellevue WA 98008. 425/883-8823. **Fax:** 425/882-4932. **Contact:** Human Resources. **World Wide Web address:** http://www.hellyhansen.com. **Description:** Manufactures outdoor apparel. Product types include waterproof, winter, and work apparel. Founded in 1877. **International locations:** Moss, Norway.

HEMPHILL BROTHERS INC.
P.O. Box 80786, Seattle WA 98108. 206/762-7622. **Contact:** Personnel Department. **Description:** A manufacturer of crushed limestone and silica sand. **Corporate headquarters location:** This location.

HERAEUS SHIN-ETSU AMERICA INC.
4600 NW Pacific Rim Boulevard, Camas WA 98607. 360/834-4004. **Contact:** Office Administrator. **Description:** Manufactures quartz products for the semiconductor industry. **Office hours:** Monday - Friday, 8:00 a.m. - 5:00 p.m. **Corporate headquarters location:** Duluth GA. **Number of employees at this location:** 50.

HEWLETT-PACKARD COMPANY
3380 146th Place SE, Suite 200, Bellevue WA 98007. 425/643-4000. **Contact:** Human Resources. **World Wide Web address:** http://www.hp.com. **Description:** Hewlett-Packard is engaged in the design and manufacture of measurement and computation products and systems used in business, industry, engineering, science, health care, and education. Principal products are integrated instrument and computer systems including hardware and software, peripheral products, and medical electronic equipment and systems. **NOTE:** Jobseekers should send resumes to Employment Response Center, Hewlett-Packard Company, Mail Stop 20-APP, 3000 Hanover Street, Palo Alto CA 94304-1181. **Corporate headquarters location:** Palo Alto CA. **Other U.S. locations:** Nationwide. **Operations at this facility include:** This location is engaged in the sale of electronic measurement and computing products. **Listed on:** New York Stock Exchange. **Stock exchange symbol:** HPQ. **Number of employees at this location:** 225.

HEWLETT-PACKARD COMPANY
18110 SE 34th Street, Vancouver WA 98683. 360/212-2493. **Contact:** Personnel Manager. **World Wide Web address:** http://www.hp.com. **Description:** Hewlett-Packard is engaged in the design and manufacture of measurement and computation products and systems used in business, industry, engineering, science, health care, and education. Principal products are integrated instrument and computer systems including hardware and software, peripheral products, and medical electronic equipment and systems. **NOTE:** Jobseekers should send resumes to Employment Response Center, Hewlett-Packard Company, Mail Stop 20-APP, 3000 Hanover Street, Palo Alto CA 94304-1181. **Corporate headquarters location:** Palo Alto CA. **Other U.S. locations:** Nationwide. **Operations at this facility include:** This location produces workstation printers including serial impact and serial ink-jet printers. **Listed on:** New York Stock Exchange. **Stock exchange symbol:** HPQ.

HEXCEL CORPORATION
P.O. Box 97004, Kent WA 98064. 253/872-7500. **Contact:** Human Resources. **World Wide Web address:** http://www.hexcel.com. **Description:** Manufactures structural materials including aerospace products, nonaerospace honeycomb, resin-impregnated industrial fabrics, and nonimpregnated fabrics; and specialty chemicals including bulk pharmaceuticals, custom and special-purpose chemicals, specialty resins, and industrial maintenance chemicals. **Corporate headquarters location:** Stamford CT.

HIGHLINE COMMUNITY COLLEGE
P.O. Box 98000, Des Moines WA 98198-9800. 206/878-3710. **Physical address:** 2400 South 240th Street, Des Moines WA. **Fax:** 206/870-4853. **Contact:** Human Resources. **World Wide Web address:** http://www.highline.ctc.edu. **Description:** A community college with an enrollment of approximately 10,000 students. Founded in 1961.

HOLLAND AMERICA LINE WESTOURS
300 Elliott Avenue West, Seattle WA 98119. 206/281-3535. **Fax:** 206/281-7110. **Contact:** Personnel. **World Wide Web address:** http://www.hollandamerica.com. **Description:** Owns hotels, cruise ships, and sail ships, and operates a motor coach transportation division.

HOLLISTER-STIER LABORATORIES, LLC
3525 North Regal Street, Spokane WA 99207. 509/489-5656. **Fax:** 509/482-1792. **Contact:** Human Resources. **E-mail address:** human_resources@Hollister-stier.com. **World Wide Web address:** http://www.hollister-stier.com. **Description:** Engaged in the development and manufacture of allergy medication. **Positions advertised include:** Senior Validation Specialist; Accountant; Environmental Monitoring Technician; Warehouse Clerk; Pollen Collector.

HOLY FAMILY HOSPITAL
5633 North Lidgerwood Street, Spokane WA 99207. 509/482-2111. **Fax:** 509/482-2178. **Contact:** Human Resources. **World Wide Web address:** http://www.holy-family.org. **Description:** A 272-bed acute care hospital that offers a full range of medical, outpatient, and surgical care. **Positions advertised include:** Registered Nurse; Speech Pathologist; Pharmacist; Social Worker; Lab Assistant.

HONEYWELL
15001 NE 36th Street, Redmond WA 98073. 425/885-3711. **Fax:** 425/885-8781. **Contact:** Human Resources. **World Wide Web address:** http://www.honeywell.com. **Description:** Honeywell is engaged in the research, development, manufacture, and sale of advanced technology products and services in the fields of chemicals, electronics, automation, and controls. The company's major businesses are home and building automation and control, performance polymers and chemicals, industrial automation and control, space and aviation systems, and defense and marine systems. **Other U.S. locations:** Nationwide. **Operations at this facility include:** This location designs and manufactures avionics systems for commercial and military aircraft.

HONEYWELL
15128 East Euclid Avenue, Spokane WA 99216. 509/252-2200. **Contact:** Human Resources. **World Wide Web address:** http://www.honeywell.com. **Description:** Honeywell is engaged in the research, development, manufacture, and sale of advanced technology products and services in the fields of chemicals, electronics, automation, and controls. The company's major businesses are home and building automation and control, performance polymers and chemicals, industrial automation and control, space and aviation systems, and defense and marine systems. **Operations at this facility include:** This location is a manufacturer of components for the electronics industry.

HORIZON AIR
P.O. Box 48309, Seattle WA 98148. 206/241-6757. **Toll-free phone:** 800/356-5993. **Contact:** Human Resources. **World Wide Web address:** http://www.horizonair.com. **Description:** A passenger and freight air transportation company.

HOTEL LUSSO
One North Post Street, Spokane WA 99201. 509/747-9750. **Fax:** 509/363-2389. **Contact:** Personnel. **World Wide Web address:** http://www.westcoasthotels.com. **Description:** A boutique-style, luxury hotel offering reception and conference rooms. **Parent company:** Westcoast Hotels.

HUGHES SUPPLY INC
10013 Martin Luther King Jr. Way South, Seattle WA 98178. 206/722-4800. **Contact:** Personnel. **Description:** A company engaged in the wholesale of industrial waterworks supplies. **Corporate headquarters location:** This location. **Operations at this facility include:** Administration; Sales; Service.

HUNTER DOUGLAS NORTHWEST
1905 Raymond Avenue SW, Renton WA 98055. 425/430-6110. **Contact:** Human Resources. **World Wide Web address:** http://www.hunterdouglas.com. **Description:** Manufactures Venetian blinds. **Office hours:** Monday - Friday, 8:00 a.m. - 4:30 p.m.

HUTTIG BUILDING PRODUCTS
P.O. Box 1049, Auburn WA 98071-1049. 253/941-2600. **Fax:** 253/735-9370. **Contact:** Director of Employee Relations. **World Wide Web address:** http://www.huttig.com. **Description:** A wholesale distributor of building materials. **Positions advertised include:** Branch Manager; Outside Sales Representative. **Corporate headquarters location:** Chesterfield MO.

IAM CARES
4700 42nd Avenue, Southwest Suite 570, Seattle WA 98116. 206/938-1253. **Toll-free phone:** 800/763-1301. **Fax:** 206/764-0452. **Contact:** Area Project Director. **World Wide Web address:** http://www.iamcareswa.org. **Description:** A nonprofit agency sponsored by the Machinist Union (IAM & AW). IAM Cares provides employment and training services to individuals with disabilities. Founded in 1980. **Special programs:** Internships. **Corporate headquarters location:** Upper Marlboro MD. **Other U.S. locations:** Nationwide. **International locations:** Canada. **Number of employees at this location:** 15. **Number of employees nationwide:** 150.

IBM CORPORATION
3600 Carillon Point, Kirkland WA 98033. 425/803-0600. **Toll-free phone:** 800/796-9876. **Contact:** Human Resources. **World Wide Web address:** http://www.ibm.com. **Description:** IBM is a developer, manufacturer, and marketer of advanced information processing products including computers and microelectronic technology, software, networking systems, and information technology-related services. **NOTE:** Jobseekers should send a resume to IBM Staffing Services, 1DPA/051, 3808 Six Forks Road, Raleigh NC 27609. **Corporate headquarters location:** Armonk NY. **Other U.S. locations:** Nationwide. **Operations at this facility include:** This location is a programming center. **Subsidiaries include:** IBM Credit Corporation; IBM Instruments, Inc.; IBM World Trade Corporation.

ICICLE SEAFOODS INC.
4019 21st Avenue W, Seattle WA 98119. 206/282-0988. **Fax:** 206/282-7222. **Contact:** Personnel. **World Wide Web address:** http://www.icicleseafoods.com. **Description:** Manufactures canned and frozen fish, shellfish, and shrimp products. **Positions advertised include:** Accounts Payable Representative; Inventory Control Specialist; Human Resources Manager.

ICOS CORPORATION
22021 20th Avenue SE, Bothell WA 98021. 425/485-1900. **Fax:** 425/489-0356. **Contact:** Human Resources. **E-mail address:** hr@icos.com. **World Wide Web address:** http://www.icos.com. **Description:** Discovers and develops new pharmaceuticals by targeting early stages of the chronic inflammatory process and by seeking points of intervention that may lead to more specific and efficacious drugs. ICOS's signal transduction programs in PDE inhibitors and cell cycle checkpoint modulators have yielded additional approaches to treating inflammatory conditions, as well as male erectile dysfunction, cardiovascular diseases, and cancer. **Positions advertised include:** Building Facilities Coordinator; Clinical Pharmacist; Purchasing Assistant; Payroll Specialist; Senior Staff Scientist. **Corporate headquarters location:** This location. **Number of employees at this location:** 200.

IDD AEROSPACE CORPORATION
P.O. Box 97056, Redmond WA 98073. 425/885-4353. **Contact:** Human Resources. **World Wide Web address:** http://www.iddaerospace.com. **Description:** Manufactures illuminated displays and other lighting products and electrical components for the aerospace industry. **Positions advertised include:** Quality Engineer; Six Sigma/Lean Engineer; Mechanical Engineer.

THE IMAGE BANK, INC.
601 North 34th Street, Seattle WA 98103. 206/925-5000. **Toll-free phone:** 888/888-5889. **Contact:** Personnel. **World Wide Web address:** http://www.imagebank.com. **Description:** Stocks and sells photographs, illustrations, and film obtained from photographers and artists. **Corporate headquarters location:** This location. **International locations:** Worldwide. **Parent company:** Getty Images.

INFORMATION BUILDERS INC.
520 Pike Street, Seattle WA 98101. 206/624-9055. **Contact:** Human Resources. **E-mail address:** employment_opportunities@ibi.com. **World Wide Web address:** http://www.informationbuilders.com. **Description:** Develops software for client/server technology and application development. **Corporate headquarters location:** New York NY. **Other U.S. locations:** Nationwide. **Number of employees nationwide:** 1,500.

INTEL CORPORATION
2800 Center Drive, DuPont WA 98327-5050. 253/371-8080. **Toll-free phone:** 800/628-8686. **Contact:** Human Resources. **E-mail address:** resumes@intel.com. **World Wide Web address:** http://www.intel.com. **Description:** Intel Corporation is a manufacturer of computer microprocessors and computer related parts. **NOTE:** Resumes should be sent to Intel Corporation, Staffing Department, P.O. Box 549263, Suite 281, Waltham MA 02454. **Corporate headquarters location:** Santa Clara CA. **Operations at this facility include:** This location manufactures PCs for original equipment manufacturers who market the computers under their own brand names. **Subsidiaries include:** Shiva Corporation produces a line of direct-dial products and remote access servers. **Listed on:** NASDAQ. **Stock exchange symbol:** INTC. **Number of employees worldwide:** 78,000.

INTERLINQ SOFTWARE CORPORATION
11980 NE 24th Street, Bellevue WA 98005. 425/827-1112. **Fax:** 425/827-0927. **Contact:** Human Resources. **E-mail address:** talent@interlinq.com. **World Wide Web address:** http://www.interlinq.com. **Description:** A leading provider of PC-based software solutions for the residential mortgage lending industry. The company's MortgageWare Enterprise product line is sold to banks, savings institutions, mortgage banks, mortgage brokers, and credit unions. The MortgageWare Enterprise product line is a complete PC-based software system that automates all aspects of the loan origination and secondary marketing processes, from qualifying a borrower to processing, settling, closing, and selling loans. MortgageWare Enterprise also includes tools to help lenders track and manage loans in their system, as well as a proprietary electronic communications system that enables data to be transferred via modem between headquarters, branch offices, and laptop origination systems. **Corporate headquarters location:** This location. **Listed on:** NASDAQ. **Stock exchange symbol:** INLQ. **Number of employees at this location:** 180.

INTERMEC CORPORATION
6001 36th Avenue West, Everett WA 98203. 425/348-2600. **Contact:** Human Resources. **World Wide Web address:** http://www.intermec.com. **Description:** Develops and manufactures automated data collection systems and mobile computing systems. Founded in 1966. **Parent company:** Unova Company. **Listed on:** New York Stock Exchange. **Stock exchange symbol:** UNA.

INTERNATIONAL ABSORBENTS INC.
P.O. Box 1587, Bellingham WA 98227-1587. 360/734-7415. **Physical address:** 1051 Hilton Avenue, Bellingham WA 98225. **Fax:** 360/671-1588. **Contact:** Human Resources. **World Wide Web address:** http://www.absorbent.com. **Description:** Develops, produces, and markets absorbent products for use in the marine spill clean-up, general industrial, oil/water filtration, animal litter/bedding, and commercial markets. **Corporate headquarters location:** This location. **Subsidiaries include:** Absorption Corp. **Operations at this facility include:** Manufacturing; Sales.

INTERPACIFIC INVESTORS SERVICES, INC.
2623 Second Avenue, Seattle WA 98121-1294. 206/269-5050. **Fax:** 206/269-5055. **Contact:** Human Resources. **World Wide Web address:** http://www.iisbonds.com. **Description:** A regional securities broker/dealer specializing in conservative investments such as corporate and municipal bonds, mutual funds, stocks, and life insurance. **Sales Manager:** Bill Shultheis.

INTERPOINT CORPORATION
10301 Willow Road NE, Redmond WA 98052. 425/882-3100. **Toll-free phone:** 800/822-8782. **Fax:** 425/882-3100. **Recorded jobline:** 425/895-5005. **Contact:** Human Resources Department. **E-mail address:** careers@intp.com. **World Wide Web address:** http://www.interpoint.com. **Description:** Manufactures microelectronic power-conversion products for the aerospace, space, military, medical, industrial, and commercial markets. Products include DC-DC converters, EMI Filters, and custom-designed microcircuits. **Corporate headquarters location:** This location.

INTERSTATE BRANDS CORPORATION
P.O. Box 98949, Lakewood WA 98498. 253/444-1000. **Contact:** Personnel Department. **Description:** Manufactures and distributes a line of bread and cake products under the Wonderbread and Hostess brand names. **Operations at this facility include:** Manufacturing. **Corporate headquarters location:** Kansas City MO.

INTERWORLD ELECTRONICS & COMPUTER INDUSTRIES, INC.
P.O. Box 1280, Point Roberts WA 98281. **Toll-free phone:** 877/902-2979. **Contact:** Human Resources Department. **World Wide Web address:** http://www.interwld.com. **Description:** Distributes industrial computer solutions including software, hardware, and electronics. Interworld Electronics & Computer Industries also provides tech-support and custom design services. **International locations:** Australia.

INVENSYS BUILDING SYSTEMS
7222 East Nora Avenue, Spokane WA 99212. 509/892-1121. **Contact:** Human Resources. **World Wide Web address:** http://www.invensysibs.com. **Description:** Provides heating, ventilation, and air conditioning services.

IOLINE CORPORATION
14140 200th Street NE, Woodinville WA 98072. 425/398-8282. **Fax:** 425/398-8383. **Contact:** Human Resources. **E-mail address:** resume@ioline.com. **World Wide Web address:** http://www.ioline.com. **Description:** Manufactures plotters for computers. **Positions advertised include:** Apparel Systems Specialist; Sales/Marketing Director. **Corporate headquarters location:** This location.

ITRON, INC.
P.O. Box 15288, Spokane WA 99215. 509/924-9900. **Physical address:** 2818 North Sullivan Road, Spokane WA 99216. **Toll-free phone:** 800/635-5461. **Fax:** 800/462-6119. **Contact:** Human Resources. **E-mail address:** itron@webhire.com. **World Wide Web address:** http://www.itron.com. **Description:** A leading supplier of data acquisition and wireless communications products for the remote data management needs of electric, gas, and water utilities worldwide. The company also designs, manufactures, markets, installs, and services hardware, software, and integrated systems for automatic meter reading and other related applications. **NOTE:** Resumes should be sent to Human Resources, P.O. Box 430, Burlington MA 01803. **Company slogan:** Collect data, deliver information, enable innovation. **Positions advertised include:** Sales Order Planner; Marketing Manager; Quality Service Analyst; Principal Service Analyst. **Corporate headquarters location:** This location. **Other U.S. locations:** Waseca MN; Raleigh NC; Pittsburgh PA; Philadelphia PA. **Listed on:** NASDAQ. **Stock exchange symbol:** ITRI. **Annual sales/revenues:** More than $100 million. **Number of employees nationwide:** 1,000.

JCV CONSTRUCTORS
325 South Kenyon Street, P.O. Box 80346, Seattle WA 98108-0346. 206/762-4219. **Contact:** Personnel Department. **Description:** Engaged in general contract construction. Founded in 1991. **Annual sales/revenues:** $11 - $20 million. **Number of employees at this location:** 10.

JWT SPECIALIZED COMMUNICATIONS
316 Occidental Avenue South, Seattle WA 98104. 206/623-2620. **Contact:** Human Resources. **World Wide Web address:** http://www.jwtworks.com. **Description:** A national advertising agency specializing in personnel recruitment advertising, human resources management systems, and employee communications. **Corporate headquarters location:** Los Angeles CA. **Parent company:** WPP Group.

JENSEN DISTRIBUTION SERVICES
314 West Riverside Avenue, P.O. Box 3708, Spokane WA 99220. 509/624-1321. **Toll-free phone:** 800/234-1321. **Fax:** 509/838-2432. **Contact:** Personnel. **E-mail address:** darrelanc@jensenonline.com. **World Wide Web address:** http://www.jensenonline.com. **Description:** A wholesale distributor of hardware goods. **Corporate headquarters location:** This location.

JORGENSEN FORGE CORPORATION
8531 East Marginal Way South, Seattle WA 98108-4018. 206/762-1100. **Fax:** 206/763-0848. **Contact:** Human Resources. **E-mail address:** jobs@jorgensenforge.com. **World Wide Web address:** http://www.jorgensenforge.com. **Description:** Provides services including melting, forging, heat treating, and machining of steel and aluminum forgings. **Corporate headquarters location:** This location. **Operations at this facility include:** Administration; Manufacturing. **Number of employees at this location:** 200.

K-PLY INC.
439 Marine Drive, Port Angeles WA 98363. 360/457-4421. **Contact:** Pam Anderson, Human Resources Director. **World Wide Web address:** http://www.kplyinc.com. **Description:** A manufacturer of lumber products for use in home applications including exterior siding. **Corporate headquarters location:** This location. **Parent company:** Klukwan Inc. **Number of employees nationwide:** 300.

KCTS-TV CHANNEL 9
401 Mercer Street, Seattle WA 98109. 206/728-6463. **Recorded jobline:** 206/443-4800. **Fax:** 206/443-6691. **Contact:** Human Resources Office. **E-mail address:** jobs@kcts.org. **World Wide Web address:** http://www.kcts.org. **Description:** A public television station. **Positions advertised include:** Network Administrator; Public Television Sponsorship Sales Representative. **Corporate headquarters location:** This location. **Other U.S. locations:** Washington DC. **Subsidiaries include:** Pacific Coast Public TV (Vancouver, Canada). **Number of employees at this location:** 300.

KIRO-TV
2807 Third Avenue, Seattle WA 98121. 206/728-8285. **Recorded jobline:** 206/728-5205. **Contact:** Human Resources. **World Wide Web address:** http://www.kirotv.com. **Description:** A television broadcasting company. **Positions advertised include:** Audio Operator; Production Assistant; Promotion Writer; Producer; Reporter. **Special programs:** Internships. **Internship information:** Applicants for internships must be in their junior or senior years of college or be in their final year of community college or vocational school. Resumes and letters of interest are required. **Corporate headquarters location:** Atlanta GA. **Parent company:** Cox Broadcasting, Inc. **Facilities Manager:** LeRoy Gates. **Sales Manager:** Sandy Zogg. **Number of employees at this location:** 240.

KL MANUFACTURING COMPANY
2726 North Monroe Street, Spokane WA 99205-3355. 509/326-2350. **Fax:** 509/326-2350. **Contact:** Christine M. Green, Personnel Manager. **Description:** A garment mill engaged in the manufacture of clothing and backpacks. **Office hours:** Monday - Friday, 7:30 a.m. - 5:00 p.m. **Corporate headquarters location:** This location. **Other area locations:** Chewelah WA. **Facilities Manager:** Michael E. Doohan. **Number of employees at this location:** 135. **Number of employees nationwide:** 225.

KOMO-TV CHANNEL 4
FISHER BROADCASTING INC.
100 Fourth Avenue North, Seattle WA 98109. 206/404-4000. **Contact:** Human Resources. **World Wide Web address:** http://www.komotv.com. **Description:** An ABC-affiliated television station. Fisher Broadcasting (also at this location) is engaged in television and radio broadcasting. **Parent company:** Fisher Companies, Inc. **Listed on:** NASDAQ. **Stock exchange symbol:** FSCI.

K.P. CORPORATION
2001 22nd Avenue South, Seattle WA 98144. 206/328-4919. **Toll-free phone:** 800/328-3284. **Contact:** Human Resources. **E-mail address:** jobs@kpcorp.com. **World Wide Web address:** http://www.kpcorp.com. **Description:** A commercial lithographic printer. **Corporate headquarters location:** San Ramon CA.

KPMG
801 2nd Avenue, Suite 904, Seattle WA 98104. 206/292-1500. **Contact:** Paige Haapala, Human Resources. **World Wide Web address:** http://www.kpmg.com. **Description:** Delivers a wide range of value-added assurance, tax, and consulting services. **Corporate headquarters location:** Montvale NJ. **Parent company:** KPMG International is a leader among professional services firms engaged in capturing, managing, assessing, and delivering information to create knowledge that will help its clients maximize shareholder value. **Listed on:** NASDAQ. **Stock exchange symbol:** KCIN.

K2 CORPORATION
19215 Vashon Highway SW, Vashon WA 98070. 206/463-3631. **Contact:** Personnel Director. **E-mail address:** employment@k2snowboarding.com. **World Wide Web address:** http://www.k2sports.com. **Description:** Manufactures outdoor recreation equipment. **Positions advertised include:** Web Content/Brand Images Specialist. **Corporate headquarters location:** This location. **Listed on:** New York Stock Exchange. **Stock exchange symbol:** KTO. **Number of employees nationwide:** 800.

KWJZ FM RADIO
KSRB AM RADIO
3650 131st Avenue SE, Suite 550, Bellevue WA 98006. 425/373-5536. **Contact:** Promotions Director. **World Wide Web address:** http://www.kwjz.com. **Description:** An FM radio station. KSRB (also at this location) is an AM radio station. **Parent company:** Sandusky Radio.

KAYE-SMITH BUSINESS GRAPHICS INC.
P.O. Box 956, Renton WA 98057. 425/228-8600. **Contact:** Human Resources Department. **World Wide Web address:** http://www.kayesmith.com. **Description:** A commercial lithographic printer.

KEANE, INC.
636 120th Avenue NE, Bellevue WA 98005. 425/451-8272. **Contact:** Human Resources. **E-mail address:** careers@keane.com. **World Wide Web address:** http://www.keane.com. **Description:** Keane offers businesses a variety of computer consulting services. Keane also develops, markets, and manages software for its clients and assists in project management. Founded in 1965. **NOTE:** Mail resume to Ms. Chris Miller, 383 Collins Road NE, Suite 200, Cedar Rapids IA 52402. **Corporate headquarters location:** Boston MA. **Other U.S. locations:** Nationwide. **Operations at this facility include:** This location is an office of the healthcare solutions division. **Listed on:** American Stock Exchange. **Stock exchange symbol:** KEA. **Number of employees nationwide:** 4,500.

KELLY-MOORE PRESERVATIVE PAINTS
5400 Airport Way South, Seattle WA 98108. 206/763-0300. **Contact:** Personnel Department. **World Wide Web address:** http://www.kellymoore.com. **Description:** The Kelly-Moore Paint Company manufactures and sells paint through four manufacturing facilities and more than 150 retail locations in 10 states. **Corporate headquarters location:** San Carlos CA. **Other U.S. locations:** AZ; AR; CA; CO; ID; NV; OK; OR; TX; UT. **International locations:** Guam. **Operations at this facility include:** This location manufactures industrial paint coatings.

KENT SCHOOL DISTRICT
12033 SE 256th Street, Kent WA 98030. 253/373-7209. **Contact:** Human Resources. **World Wide Web address:** http://www.kent.wednet.edu. **Description:** Provides administrative support to the 36 schools in the Kent school system. **Operations at this facility include:** Administration. **Number of employees at this location:** 2,500.

KENWORTH TRUCK COMPANY
P.O. Box 1000, Kirkland WA 98038. 425/828-5000. **Physical address:** 10630 NE 38th Place, Kirkland WA 98033. **Fax:** 425/828-5054. **Contact:** Human Resources Department. **E-mail address:** kw.jobs@paccar.com. **World Wide Web address:** http://www.kenworth.com. **Description:** Manufactures Class 8 trucks. **Positions advertised include:** Senior Programmer/Analyst. **Special programs:** Internships. **Corporate headquarters location:** Bellevue WA. **Parent company:** PACCAR, Inc. **Operations at this facility include:** Administration; Divisional Headquarters; Sales; Service. **Listed on:** NASDAQ. **Stock exchange symbol:** PCAR. **Number of employees nationwide:** 2,500.

FERGUSON
4100 West Marginal Way SW, Seattle WA 98106. 206/682-8700. **Contact:** Administrative Manager. **World Wide Web address:** http://www.ferguson.com. **Description:** A wholesale distributor of industrial pipe, valves, and fittings for commercial, industrial, marine, and nuclear applications. The company is also engaged in the distribution of valve automation products. **Corporate headquarters location:** Newport News VA. **Parent company:** Wolseley Company. **Operations at this facility include:** Administration; Sales.

KEY TECHNOLOGY, INC.
150 Avery Street, Walla Walla WA 99362. 509/529-2161. **Fax:** 509/527-1331. **Contact:** Sherrie Mason, Human Resources Manager. **E-mail address:** jobs@keyww.com. **World Wide Web address:** http://www.keyww.com. **Description:** A leading designer and manufacturer of process automation systems for the food processing industry. The company's automated systems convey, clean, grade, inspect, and process a wide variety of food products including vegetables, snacks, cereals, nuts, and poultry. Key Technology is also a leader in the design and manufacture of high-speed machine vision systems. These systems inspect moving products for flaws in color, size, or other customer-established criteria, and remove those items that do not meet the quality specifications. **Positions advertised include:** Product Marketing Manager; Production Welder; Upgrade & Parts Sales Coordinator. **Corporate headquarters location:** This location. **Listed on:** NASDAQ. **Stock exchange symbol:** KTEC. **Number of employees at this location:** 440. **Number of employees worldwide:** 480.

KEY TRONIC CORPORATION
4424 North Sullivan Road, Spokane WA 99216. 509/928-8000. **Fax:** 509/927-5383. **Contact:** Personnel. **E-mail address:** jobs@keytronic.com. **World Wide Web address:** http://www.keytronic.com. **Description:** One of the world's largest independent manufacturers of computer keyboards and input devices. Key Tronic designs, develops, and manufactures standard and custom keyboards for integration with personal computers, terminals, and word processors made by original equipment manufacturers. Founded in 1969. **Positions advertised include:** Buyer/Planner. **Special programs:** Internships. **Internship information:** Internships are offered on an as needed basis. The company has year-round internships, but primarily has openings in the summer and recruits through local colleges. Please call this location for more information. **Corporate headquarters location:** This location. **Other U.S. locations:** Las Cruces NM; El Paso TX. **International locations:** Dundalk, Ireland; Juarez, Mexico. **Listed on:** NASDAQ. **Stock exchange symbol:** KTCC. **Annual sales/revenues:** More than $100 million. **Number of employees at this location:** 550. **Number of employees nationwide:** 650. **Number of employees worldwide:** 3,000.

KEYBANK N.A.
1119 Pacific Avenue, Mail Stop WA 31-03-0850, Tacoma WA 98402-5500. 253/305-7750. **Fax:** 253/305-7908. **Contact:** Personnel Director. **World Wide Web address:** http://www.keybank.com. **Description:** A bank. **NOTE:** Please send resumes to KeyBank N.A., Human Resources, P.O. Box 92933, Cleveland OH 44101. **Positions advertised include:** Underwriting Officer; Portfolio Manager; Client Relations Representative; Sales and Service Associate. **Special programs:** Internships. **Corporate headquarters location:** Cleveland OH. **Other U.S. locations:** Nationwide. **Parent company:** KeyCorp. **Operations at this facility include:** Administration; Sales; Service. **Listed on:** New York Stock Exchange. **Stock exchange symbol:** KEY. **Number of employees at this location:** 4,000. **Number of employees nationwide:** 33,000.

KIEWIT COMPANIES
719 V Street, Vancouver WA 98661. 360/693-1478. **Fax:** 360/693-5582. **Contact:** Human Resources Manager. **E-mail address:** human.resources@kiewit.com. **World Wide Web address:** http://www.kiewit.com. **Description:** One of the largest construction companies in the country. Kiewit's primary markets are building, power, transportation, water resources, and mining. Types of projects include highways, bridges, high-rise buildings, office complexes, railroads, tunnels, subways, dams, airports, power plants, canals, water treatment facilities, offshore petroleum platforms, and other heavy civil projects. The company has district offices throughout North America. **Positions advertised include:** Engineer; Project Manager. **Corporate headquarters location:** Omaha NE.

KIMBERLY-CLARK
2600 Federal Avenue, Everett WA 98201. 425/259-7333. **Contact:** Staffing and Compensation Manager. **World Wide Web address:** http://www.kimberly-clark.com. **Description:** Processes pulp and paper used in making tissues. **Corporate headquarters location:** Neenah WI. **Listed on:** New York Stock Exchange. **Stock exchange symbol:** KMB.

KING COUNTY JOURNAL, EASTSIDE
1705 132nd Avenue NE, Bellevue WA 98005-2251. 425/455-2222. **Fax:** 425/635-0602. **Contact:** Human Resources. **E-mail address:** hr@eastsidejournal.com. **World Wide Web address:** http://www.kingcountyjournal.com. **Description:** Publishes a daily newspaper with a circulation of approximately 30,000. **Parent company:** Horvitz Newspapers Group.

KING COUNTY JOURNAL, SOUTH COUNTY
600 Washington Avenue, Kent WA 98032. 253/872-6600. **Fax:** 253/854-1006. **Contact:** Human Resources. **E-mail address:** hr-kent@kingcountyjournal. **World Wide Web address:** http://www.kingcountyjournal.com. **Description:** A daily newspaper. **Positions advertised include:** Delivery Assistant; Customer Calling Representative; Inside Sales Representative. **Special programs:** Internships. **Number of employees at this location:** 200.

KING ELECTRICAL MANUFACTURING COMPANY
9131 10th Avenue South, Seattle WA 98108. 206/762-0400. **Fax:** 206/763-7738. **Contact:** Human Resources. **World Wide Web address:** http://www.king-electric.com. **Description:** Manufactures a wide range of electric heating equipment for the home. **Corporate headquarters location:** This location.

KING 5 TELEVISION
333 Dexter Avenue North, Seattle WA 98109. 206/448-5555. **Contact:** Human Resources Department. **E-mail address:** hr@king5.com. **World Wide Web address:** http://www.king5.com. **Description:** An NBC-affiliated television station. Programming includes daily newscasts, *Evening Magazine*, *Almost Live*, and *Watch This!* **Positions advertised include:** Account Executive; Desktop Support Analyst; Sales Assistant; News Anchor; Photographer/Editor. **Number of employees nationwide:** 225.

KORRY ELECTRONICS
901 Dexter Avenue North, Seattle WA 98109. 206/281-1300. **Fax:** 206/286-5545. **Contact:** Human Resources. **World Wide Web address:** http://www.korry.com. **Description:** A manufacturer of lighted push-button switches, annunciators, panels, keyboards, and accessories. **Positions advertised include:** Accounts Receivable Associate; Quality Engineer; Test/Environmental Technician; Business Development Manager. **Corporate headquarters location:** Bellevue WA. **Parent company:** Esterline Technologies. **Listed on:** New York Stock Exchange. **Stock exchange symbol:** ESL. **Number of employees at this location:** 400.

LABOR READY, INC.
P.O. Box 2910, Tacoma WA 98402-2910. 253/383-9101. **Toll-free phone:** 800/610-8920. **Fax:** 800/850-9559. **Contact:** Human Resources. **World Wide Web address:** http://www.laborready.com. **Description:** Provides temporary employees, primarily to construction, warehousing, landscaping, and manufacturing businesses. Founded in 1989. **Corporate headquarters location:** This location. **Other U.S. locations:** Nationwide. **International locations:** Canada; Puerto Rico; United Kingdom. **Listed on:** New York Stock Exchange. **Stock exchange symbol:** LRW. **Annual sales/revenues:** More than $100 million.

LABORATORY CORPORATION OF AMERICA (LABCORP)
21903 68th Avenue South, Kent WA 98032-2427. 253/395-4000. **Contact:** Human Resources. **World Wide Web address:** http://www.labcorp.com. **Description:** One of the nation's leading clinical laboratory companies, providing services primarily to physicians, hospitals, clinics, nursing homes, and other clinical labs nationwide. LabCorp performs tests on blood, urine, and other body fluids and tissue, aiding the diagnosis of disease. **Positions advertised include:** Account Representative; Medical Laboratory Sales Representative. **Corporate headquarters location:** Burlington NC. **Listed on:** New York Stock Exchange. **Stock exchange symbol:** LH.

LAFARGE CORPORATION
5400 West Marginal Way SW, Seattle WA 98106. 206/937-8025. **Contact:** Human Resources. **World Wide Web address:** http://www.lafarge-na.com. **Description:** Produces cement, concrete, aggregates, and related products. The company operates 15 full-production cement plants and 420 construction materials facilities. **Corporate headquarters location:** Reston VA. **Subsidiaries include:** Systech Environmental Corporation is a processor and recycler of industrial waste products into fuel for cement kilns. **Listed on:** New York Stock Exchange. **Stock exchange symbol:** LAF.

LAIDLAW TRANSIT INC.
6405 218th Street SW, Mouthlake Terrace WA 98043. 206/764-9700. **Contact:** Human Resources. **World Wide Web address:** http://www.laidlawtransit.com. **Description:** Provides bus service for Seattle and charter bus service to private customers. The company is also a school bus contractor. **Parent company:** Laidlaw, Inc. provides solid waste collection, compaction, transportation, treatment, transfer, and disposal services; provides hazardous waste services; operates hazardous waste facilities and wastewater treatment plants; and operates passenger and school buses, transit system buses, and tour and charter buses. **Corporate headquarters location:** Mt. Lake Terrace WA. **Listed on:** American Stock Exchange. **Stock exchange symbol:** GLL.

LAIRD PLASTICS
650 South Industrial Way, Seattle WA 98108. 206/623-4900. **Contact:** Human Resources. **World Wide Web address:** http://www.laird-plastics.com. **Description:** A distributor of a wide range of plastics and plastics materials including films, rods, sheets, tubes, and related products. **Corporate headquarters location:** West Palm Beach FL.

LAKELAND VILLAGE
P.O. Box 200, Medical Lake WA 99022. 509/299-1800. **Contact:** Human Resources. **Description:** A state residential habilitation facility for individuals with developmental disabilities.

LAMB WESTON, INC.
P.O. Box 1900, Tri-Cities WA 99302. 509/735-4651. **Fax:** 509/736-0386. **Contact:** Personnel Administrator. **E-mail address:** resume@lambweston.com. **World Wide Web address:** http://www.lamb-weston.com. **Description:** Processes a broad line of nationally distributed frozen potato products including french fries and potato wedges. **Corporate headquarters location:** This location. **Parent company:** ConAgra, Inc. is a diversified, international food company. Products range from prepared foods to supplies farmers need to grow their crops. ConAgra has major businesses in branded grocery products including shelf-stable and frozen foods, processed meats, chicken and turkey products, and cheeses, as well as major businesses in potato products, private-label grocery products, beef, pork, seafood, grain and pulse merchandising, grain processing, specialty trailing, crop protection chemicals, fertilizers, and animal feed. ConAgra is a family of independent operating companies. **Listed on:** New York Stock Exchange. **Stock exchange symbol:** CAG.

LAPLINK.COM, INC.
10210 NE Points Drive, Suite 400, Kirkland WA 98033. 425/952-6000. **Fax:** 425/952-6002. **Contact:** Human Resources. **E-mail address:** hotjobs@laplink.com. **World Wide Web address:** http://www.laplink.com. **Description:** Develops software for businesses and individuals enabling access to private and public computer networks, the Internet, and individual PCs. Founded in 1982. **Company slogan:** The remote access champion. **Office hours:** Monday - Friday, 8:00 a.m. - 5:00 p.m. **Corporate headquarters location:** This location. **Annual sales/revenues:** $21 - $50 million. **Number of employees at this location:** 80. **Number of employees worldwide:** 90.

LEMASTER & DANIELS
601 West Riverside Avenue, Suite 700, Spokane WA 99201. 509/624-4315. **Contact:** Human Resources. **World Wide Web address:** http://www.lemasterdaniels.com. **Description:** An accounting firm providing accounting, auditing, and tax services to clients. Founded in 1908. **Positions advertised include:** Accountant; Director of Reimbursement. **Corporate headquarters location:** This location.

LEVITON VOICE & DATA
2222 222nd Street SE, Suite 100, Bothell WA 98021. 425/486-2222. **Contact:** Human Resources. **E-mail address:** hr@levitonvoicedata.com. **World Wide Web address:** http://www.levitonvoicedata.com. **Description:** Produces system solutions for network infrastructure. The company offers frame-to-station solutions; fiber and copper systems; horizontal and backbone infrastructure; and voice, data, and video connections. **Corporate headquarters location:** Littleneck NY.

LIFELONG AIDS ALLIANCE
1002 East Seneca, Seattle WA 98122. 206/328-8979. **Fax:** 206/325-2689. **Contact:** Human Resources. **E-mail address:** jobs@lifelongaidsalliance.org. **World Wide Web address:** http://www.lifelongaidsalliance.org. **Description:** Provides case management, financial advocacy, and housing assistance to individuals infected with the AIDS virus.

LINDAL CEDAR HOMES INC.
4300 South 104th Place, Seattle WA 98178. 206/725-0900. **Fax:** 206/725-1615. **Contact:** Personnel Department. **E-mail address:** employment@lindal.com. **World Wide Web address:** http://www.lindal.com. **Description:** Manufactures cedar homes and sunrooms. Lindal also provides wholesale lumber, building materials, and related services. **Positions advertised include:** Area Manager. **Corporate headquarters location:** This location.

LOCKDOWN NETWORKS, INC.
100 West Harrison, North Tower, Suite 300, Seattle WA 98119. 206/285-8080. **Fax:** 206/285-8081. **Contact:** Human Resources. **E-mail address:** careers@lockdownnetworks.com. **World Wide Web address:** http://www.lockdownnetworks.com. **Description:** A provider of appliance-based vulnerability management for securing wired and wireless enterprise networks. Their appliances audit, prioritize, remediate, report, and eliminate network security vulnerabilities. **Positions advertised include:** Senior Software Engineer. **Corporate headquarters location:** This location.

LOOMIS FARGO & COMPANY
3716 South G Street, Tacoma WA 98418. 253/475-4225. **Fax:** 253-475-2356. **Contact:** Personnel. **World Wide Web address:** http://www.loomisfargo.com. **Description:** An armored security service specializing in transporting currency. **NOTE:** Applications will not be mailed to jobseekers. They must be picked up in person. **Other U.S. locations:** Nationwide.

LONGVIEW FIBRE COMPANY
300 Fibre Way, P.O. Box 639, Longview WA 98632. 360/425-1550. **Fax:** 360/575-5934. **Contact:** Human Resources. **E-mail address:** info@longfibre.com. **World Wide Web address:** http://www.longviewfibre.com. **Description:** Owns and operates tree farms in Oregon and Washington and is a major pulp, wood, and paper products manufacturer. The company also produces shipping containers, merchandise, and grocery bags. **Listed on:** New York Stock Exchange. **Stock exchange symbol:** LFB.

LUTHERAN COMMUNITY SERVICES
433 Minor Avenue North, Seattle WA 98109. 206/694-5700. **Contact:** Human Resources. **World Wide Web address:** http://www.lcsnw.org. **Description:** Provides a variety of social services including counseling, family support, grassroots, and foster care services. Annually, the organization serves more than 20,000 individuals.

LYNDEN INC.
P.O. Box 3757, Seattle WA 98124-3757. 206/241-8778. **Physical address:** 1800 International Boulevard, Suite 800, Seattle WA 98188. **Fax:** 206/243-8415. **Contact:** Personnel Department. **World Wide Web address:** http://www.lynden.com. **Description:** Provides transportation and construction services for barge, air freight, and trucking companies. **Corporate headquarters location:** This location.

LYNX MEDICAL SYSTEMS
15325 SE 30th Place, Suite 200, Bellevue WA 98007. 425/641-4451. **Contact:** Human Resources. **E-mail address:** humanresources@lynxmed.com. **World Wide Web address:** http://www.lynxmed.com. **Description:** Offers coding, billing, transcription, and consulting services to professional medical groups, health care facilities and systems, and third-party payers. **Positions advertised include:** CDM Coordinator; Inpatient/Outpatient Coding Specialist; Sales Manager; Executive Assistant. **Corporate headquarters location:** This location. **Other U.S. locations:** Waterloo IA.

MDS PHARMA SERVICES
2204 30th Drive SE, Bothell WA 98021-4444. 425/487-8200. **Contact:** Human Resources. **World Wide Web address:** http://www.mdsps.com. **Description:** Engaged in pharmaceutical research and development.

MTS
12600 SE 38th Street, Suite 250, Bellevue WA 98006. 425/401-1000. **Toll-free phone:** 800/900-8725. **Fax:** 425/401-1700. **Contact:** Human Resource Department. **E-mail address:** employment@mtsint.com. **World Wide Web address:** http://www.mtsint.com. **Description:** Develops software for the telecommunications industry. **Corporate headquarters location:** This location. **Other U.S. locations:** Piscataway NJ. **Listed on:** NASDAQ. **Stock exchange symbol:** MTSL.

MALLORY AND CHURCH CORPORATION
676 South Industrial Way, Seattle WA 98108. 206/587-2100. **Toll-free phone:** 800/255-TIES. **Fax:** 206/587-2971. **Contact:** Human Resources. **World Wide Web address:** http://www.malloryandchurch.com. **Description:** One of the world's largest manufacturers of neckties. Founded in 1908. **Corporate headquarters location:** This location. **Other U.S. locations:** Corona CA; Roswell GA; New York NY; Pittsburgh PA.

MAR LAC PARTS PLUS
P.O. Box 1896, Auburn WA 98071-1896. 206/322-2626. **Contact:** Human Resources. **Description:** A distributor of automotive parts. **Corporate headquarters location:** This location. **Parent company:** Mar Lac Distributing Company.

MARCO SEATTLE
2300 West Commodore Way, Seattle WA 98199. 206/285-3200. **Contact:** Hank Schlapp, Personnel Director. **E-mail address:** personnel@marcocorp.com. **World Wide Web address:** http://www.marcoseattle.com. **Description:** Manufactures commercial marine machinery, fishing gear, equipment, and vessels. Other operations include oil spill management systems and related pollution control items. **Number of employees nationwide:** 600.

MARSH ADVANTAGE OF AMERICA
1215 Fourth Avenue, Suite 600, Seattle WA 98161. 206/613-7700. **Contact:** Human Resources. **E-mail address:** hr.maa@seabury.com. **World Wide Web address:** http://www.marshadvantage.com. **Description:** An insurance brokerage. Marsh Advantage of America is an international insurance broker engaged in insurance booking, risk management, and benefits consulting.

MARTHA & MARY NURSING HOME
P.O. Box 127, Poulsbo WA 98370. 360/779-7500. **Physical address:** 19160 Front Street NE, Poulsbo WA 98370. **Fax:** 360/779-8400. **Contact:** Human Resources. **E-mail address:** healthsvc@mmhc.org. **World Wide Web address:** http://www.marthaandmary.org. **Description:** A 180-bed nursing home that provides activities, horticulture therapy, intergenerational programs, pet therapy, and rehabilitation. **Positions advertised include:** Licensed Practical Nurse; Registered Nurse; Certified Nursing Assistant.

MARTINGALE & CO.
20205 144th Avenue NE, Woodinville WA 98072. 425/483-3313. **Contact:** Human Resources. **World Wide Web address:** http://www.patchwork.com. **Description:** Publishes instructional quilt-making books and home decoration gift books.

VIRGINIA MASON MEDICAL CENTER
1100 Ninth Avenue, Seattle WA 98101. 206/223-6600. **Contact:** Human Resources. **World Wide Web address:** http://www.vmmc.org. **Description:** A complete health care system that operates a 336-bed, acute care hospital, 16 regional clinics, an AIDS facility, and research laboratories. Founded in 1920. **Positions advertised include:** Administrative Assistant; Biomedical Equipment Technician; Clinic Service Representative; Orthopedics Coordinator; File Clerk; Customer Service Representative. **Special programs:** Internships.

MATSUSHITA KOTOBUKI ELECTRONICS INDUSTRIES OF AMERICA, INC.
2001 Kotobuki Way, Vancouver WA 98660. 360/695-1338. **Fax:** 360/695-3155. **Contact:** Human Resources. **Description:** Manufactures combination TV/VCR units. **Listed on:** New York Stock Exchange. **Stock exchange symbol:** MC. **President:** Kenzo Hayashi.

MAVERICK INTERNATIONAL
8214 44th Avenue West, Mukilteo WA 98275. 425/355-7474. **Physical address:** 8217 44th Avenue West, Mukilteo WA 98275. **Contact:** Human Resources. **E-mail address:** hr@mav.com. **World Wide Web address:** http://www.mav.com. **Description:** Manufactures desktop check encoders for use in the financial industry. **Positions advertised include:** Accountant; Manufacturing Engineer; Material Control Manager.

McNAUL, EBEL, NAWROT, HELGREN & VANCE
600 University Street, One Union Square, Suite 2700, Seattle WA 98101. 206/467-1816. **Fax:** 206/624-5128. **Contact:** Mike Cason, Office Administrator. **E-mail address:** mcason@mcnaul.com. **World Wide Web address:** http://www.mcnaul.com. **Description:** A law firm specializing in the areas of real estate, litigation, and business.

MEDICAL CENTER OF TACOMA
P.O. Box 34586, Seattle WA 98124. 253/596-3300. **Physical address:** 209 Martin Luther King Jr. Way, Tacoma WA 98405. **Contact:** Human Resources. **World Wide Web address:** http://www.ghc.org. **Description:** A full-service medical center that also offers optometry and women's health care services. **Positions advertised include:** Administrative Assistant III; Medical Center Manager; Registered Nurse; Patient Care Representative; Office Assistant III; Vehicle Operator; Analyst/Programmer; Manager Accounting.

MEDTRONIC PHYSIO-CONTROL INC.
P.O. Box 97006, Redmond WA 98073-9706. 425/867-4000. **Physical address:** 11811 Willows Road NE, Redmond WA 98052. **Contact:** Human Resources. **World Wide Web address:** http://www.physiocontrol.com. **Description:** Manufactures, sells, and services defibrillators, monitors, and pacemakers. **Positions advertised include:** Administrative Assistant; Business Director; Commercial Sales Consultant; Commercial Segment Manager; Data Communications Systems Manager. **Parent company:** Medtronic, Inc. **Operations at this facility include:** Administration; Manufacturing; Research and Development; Sales; Service. **Listed on:** New York Stock Exchange. **Stock exchange symbol:** MDT.

MERCER ISLAND, CITY OF
9611 SE 36th Street, Mercer Island WA 98040. 206/236-5326. **Fax:** 206/236-3651. **Contact:** Human Resources Manager. **E-mail address:** hr@ci.mercer-island.wa.us. **World Wide Web address:** http://www.ci.mercer-island.wa.us. **Description:** City government offices for Mercer Island, a suburb of Seattle with over 21,000 residents. **Positions advertised include:** Development Engineer; Parks Maintenance Manager; Recreation Leader. **Special programs:** Internships. **Corporate headquarters location:** This location. **Operations at this facility include:** Administration. **Annual sales/revenues:** $11 - $20 million. **Number of employees at this location:** 170.

MERIDIAN VALLEY CLINICAL LAB, INC.
515 West Harrison Street, Suite 9, Kent WA 98032. 253/859-8700. **Contact:** Human Resources Department. **World Wide Web address:** http://www.meridianvalleylab.com. **Description:** Engaged in testing related to adrenal steroids and allergies. The lab also performs stool analyses. **Corporate headquarters location:** This location.

MERRILL LYNCH
601 108th Avenue NE, Suite 2100, Bellevue WA 98004. 425/462-8158. **Contact:** Human Resources. **World Wide Web address:** http://www.ml.com. **Description:** One of the largest securities brokerage firms in the United States, Merrill Lynch provides financial services in the following areas: securities, extensive insurance, and real estate and related services. The company also brokers commodity futures, commodity options, and corporate and municipal securities. In addition, Merrill Lynch is engaged in investment banking activities. **Positions advertised include:** Senior Underwriter; Investment Officer; Cash Flow Associate. **Corporate headquarters location:** New York NY. **Listed on:** NASDAQ. **Stock exchange symbol:** MITT.

MERRILL LYNCH HOWARD JOHNSON
1700 Seventh Avenue, Suite 2200, Seattle WA 98101. 206/625-1040. **Contact:** Human Resources. **World Wide Web address:** http://www.ml.com. **Description:** An international benefits consulting company. The company works mainly with 401(k) plans and group benefits for corporations.

MICROSOFT CORPORATION
One Microsoft Way, Redmond WA 98052-6399. 425/882-8080. **Contact:** Recruiting Department. **World Wide Web address:** http://www.microsoft.com/careers. **Description:** Designs, sells, and supports a product line of systems and applications software for business, home, and professional use. Microsoft also produces related books and hardware products. Software products include spreadsheet, desktop publishing, project management, graphics, word processing, and database applications, as well as operating systems and programming languages. **Corporate headquarters location:** This location. **Listed on:** NASDAQ. **Stock exchange symbol:** MSFT. **Annual sales/revenues:** More than $100 million.

MIKRON INDUSTRIES
1034 Sixth Avenue North, Kent WA 98032. 253/854-8020. **Contact:** Amy Rhodes, Human Resources. **E-mail address:** amy_rhodes@mikronvinyl.com. **World Wide Web address:** http://www.mikronvinyl.com. **Description:** Engaged in the extrusion of custom vinyl profiles, primarily for windows and doors. **Corporate headquarters location:** This location.

MILLER BREWING COMPANY
100 Custer Way, Tumwater WA 98501. 360/754-5000. **Fax:** 360/754-5107. **Contact:** Human Resources. **E-mail address:** miller@webhire.com (Please do not include any attachments). **World Wide Web address:** http://www.millerbrewing.com. **Description:** Produces and distributes beer and other malt beverages. Principal beer brands include Miller Lite, Lite Ice, Miller Genuine Draft, Miller Genuine Draft Light, Miller High Life, Miller Reserve, Lowenbrau, Milwaukee's Best, Meister Brau, as well as Red Dog and Icehouse brewed at the Plank Road Brewery. Miller also produces Sharp's, a nonalcoholic brew. **Corporate headquarters location:** Milwaukee WI.

MILLIMAN USA
1301 Fifth Avenue, Suite 3800, Seattle WA 98101-2605. 206/624-7940. **Fax:** 206/340-1380. **Contact:** Personnel Department. **E-mail address:** seattle.office@milliman.com. **World Wide Web address:** http://www.milliman.com. **Description:** A nationwide actuarial and consulting firm. **Positions advertised include:** Actuary; Pension Analyst. **Corporate headquarters location:** This location. **Operations at this facility include:** Administration; Service.

MODERN MACHINERY
22431 83rd Avenue South, Kent WA 98032. 253/872-3500. **Fax:** 253/872-3519. **Contact:** Human Resources. **World Wide Web address:** http://www.pneco.com. **Description:** Engaged in the sale and service of construction and logging equipment.

MODIS, INC.
2101 4th Avenue, Suite 220, Seattle WA 98121. 206/441-0707. **Contact:** Human Resources. **E-mail address:** resume@modisit.com. **World Wide Web address:** http://www.modisit.com. **Description:** An IT consulting firm. Founded in 1986. **Corporate headquarters location:** Jacksonville FL. **Parent company:** MPS.

MOSS ADAMS LLP
1001 Fourth Avenue, Suite 2830, Seattle WA 98154. 206/223-1820. **Contact:** Human Resources. **World Wide Web address:** http://www.mossadams.com. **Description:** One of the nation's largest accounting and consulting firms. Founded in 1913. **Positions advertised include:** Assurance Services Manager; Tax Analyst; Research and Development Manager; Senior IT Consultant. **Corporate headquarters location:** This location. **Other U.S. locations:** CA; OR.

MOSS ADAMS LLP
1301 A Street, Suite 600, Tacoma WA 98402. 253/572-4100. **Contact:** Human Resources. **World Wide Web address:** http://www.mossadams.com. **Description:** One of the nation's largest accounting and consulting firms. Founded in 1913. **Corporate headquarters location:** Seattle WA. **Other U.S. locations:** CA; OR.

MOTOROLA, INC.
24000 35th Avenue SE, Bothell WA 98021. 425/487-1234. **Contact:** Human Resources. **World Wide Web address:** http://www.motorola.com. **Description:** Provides applied research, development, manufacturing, and marketing of high-technology electronic systems and components for industry and government in the fields of communications, automotive, controls, semiconductor, information systems, and office information. Motorola manufactures communications equipment and electronic products including car radios, cellular phones, semiconductors, computer systems, cellular infrastructure equipment, pagers, cordless phones, and LAN systems. **Corporate headquarters location:** Schaumburg IL. **Listed on:** New York Stock Exchange. **Stock exchange symbol:** MOT. **Number of employees worldwide:** 107,000.

MOUNTAIN SAFETY RESEARCH
3800 First Avenue South, Seattle WA 98134. 206/624-8573. **Toll-free phone:** 800/531-9531. **Fax:** 800/583-7583. **Contact:** Human Resources. **E-mail address:** info@msrgear.com. **World Wide Web address:** http://www.msrcorp.com. **Description:** A manufacturer of high quality outdoor sporting goods including stoves, snow equipment, poles, cookware, water treatment, and tents. **Corporate headquarters location:** This location. **Positions advertised include:** International Sales Manager.

LANCE MUELLER & ASSOCIATES
130 Lakeside Avenue, Suite 250, Seattle WA 98122. 206/325-2553. **Fax:** 206/328-0554. **Contact:** Lance Mueller, Principal. **E-mail address:** lmueller@lmueller.com. **World Wide Web address:** http://www.lma-architects.com. **Description:** An architectural firm that specializes in commercial projects.

MUZAK LLC
P.O. Box 80416, Seattle WA 98108. 206/763-2517. **Physical address:** 200 South Orcas Street, Seattle WA 98108. **Contact:** Personnel Department. **E-mail address:** corporate@nbbi.com. **World Wide Web address:** http://www.muzak.com. **Description:** Provides satellite delivered and on-site music services to commercial and retail establishments delivered both directly and through franchised dealers worldwide. Muzak serves approximately 300,000 locations worldwide through over 200 sales and service locations. **Corporate headquarters location:** Fort Mill SC.

NBBJ ARCHITECTURE DESIGN PLANNING
111 South Jackson Street, Seattle WA 98104. 206/223-5555. **Fax:** 206/621-2300. **Contact:** Personnel. **World Wide Web address:** http://www.nbbj.com. **Description:** An architectural design firm. NBBJ specializes in commercial buildings, health facilities, sports and entertainment complexes, airports, retail centers, government buildings, and senior living facilities. The company is also heavily engaged in urban planning and design, campus planning, and graphic design services. **Positions advertised include:** Architect; Planner; Interior Designer; Graphic Designer. **Other U.S. locations:** Los Angeles CA; San Francisco CA; Research Triangle Park NC; New York NY; Columbus OH. **International locations:** Japan; Norway; Taiwan. **Operations at this facility include:** Service.

NC MACHINERY COMPANY
P.O. Box 3562, Seattle WA 98124. 425/251-9800. **Contact:** Human Resources. **World Wide Web address:** http://www.ncmachinery.com. **Description:** Sells heavy equipment including generators, backhoes, and asphalt cutters as part of Caterpillar's worldwide dealer network. **Number of employees nationwide:** 600.

NATIONAL ASIAN PACIFIC CENTER ON AGING
Melborne Tower, 1511 Third Avenue, Suite 914, Seattle WA 98101. 206/624-1221. **Toll-free phone:** 800/336-2722. **Fax:** 206/624-1023. **Contact:** Director. **World Wide Web address:** http://www.napca.org. **Description:** A nonprofit, private organization that operates in conjunction with the Older Americans Act. National Asian Pacific Center on Aging maintains a national network of service agencies, compiles statistics on the Asian Pacific population, provides technical assistance to local Asian Pacific community groups so they may be better able to meet the needs of older people, conducts workshops and training programs to educate health care and social service professionals, disseminates information on support groups, and finds employment for older people through its Seniors' Community Service Employment Program. **Corporate headquarters location:** This location. **Other U.S. locations:** Los Angeles CA. **Parent company:** Administration on Aging.

NATIONAL FROZEN FOODS CORPORATION
P.O. Box 9366, Seattle WA 98109. 206/322-8900. **Fax:** 206/322-4458. **Contact:** Human Resources. **World Wide Web address:** http://www.nationalfrozenfoods.com. **Description:** Processes, packages, and distributes frozen fruits and vegetables. Founded in 1912. **Company slogan:** The Best of the Great Northwest. **Special programs:** Co-ops.

NATIONAL MUSIC SERVICE
P.O. Box 5378, Spokane WA 99205. 509/327-7784. **Toll-free phone:** 800/541-2671. **Fax:** 509/328-4208. **Contact:** Human Resources. **World Wide Web address:** http://www.natlmusic.com. **Description:** Manufactures and distributes music and video systems for funeral homes, mausoleums, churches, and hospitals.

NATIONAL SECURITIES CORPORATION
1001 Fourth Avenue, Suite 2200, Seattle WA 98154. 206/622-7200. **Contact:** Human Resources Manager. **World Wide Web address:** http://www.nationalsecurities.com. **Description:** A securities brokerage providing services such as asset management, investment banking, and institutional sales and research. **Corporate headquarters location:** This location.

NEORX CORPORATION
300 Elliot Avenue West, Suite 500, Seattle WA 98119. 206/281-7001. **Fax:** 206/284-7112. **Contact:** Human Resources. **E-mail address:** hr@neorx.com. **World Wide Web address:** http://www.neorx.com. **Description:** Develops treatments for cancer and cardiovascular disease. The company's focus is on targeting therapeutic agents on diseased or injured cells, while sparing normal tissues the full impact of these treatments. The company's cardiovascular program is focused primarily on reducing reclosure of coronary arteries following balloon angioplasty. **Corporate headquarters location:** This location. **Listed on:** NASDAQ. **Number of employees at this location:** 80.

NETMANAGE, INC.
11332 NE 122nd Way, Kirkland WA 98034. 425/814-9255. **Contact:** Human Resources. **World Wide Web address:** http://www.netmanage.com. **Description:** Develops, markets, and supports Windows-based connectivity software and associated applications tools. The company's software products provide PC users easy access to computer applications and data residing on multiple host mainframes and minicomputers in enterprisewide information systems networks. **NOTE:** Job seekers may search for and apply for positions online. **Corporate headquarters location:** Cupertino CA. **Listed on:** NASDAQ. **Stock exchange symbol:** NETM.

NEUVANT AEROSPACE
11002 29th Avenue West, Paine Field Everett WA 98204. 425/353-8080. **Fax:** 425/355-7933. **Contact:** Elizabeth Hollar, Human Resources. **E-mail address:** elizabeth.hollar@neuvant.com. **World Wide Web address:** http://www.neuvant.com. **Description:** Manufactures aerostructure details. Allfab Aerospace builds parts for airplanes and missiles for commercial clients.

NINTENDO OF AMERICA
P.O. Box 957, Redmond WA 98073. 425/882-2040. **Contact:** Human Resources. **World Wide Web address:** http://www.nintendo.com. **Description:** An importer, wholesaler, and manufacturer of electronic games, home video systems, home video games, and watches. **Corporate headquarters location:** This location.

NORD COMPANY
300 West Marine View Drive, P.O. Box 1187, Everett WA 98201. 425/259-9292. **Contact:** Personnel Department. **Description:** Produces wood-style and rail-panel doors, louver products, columns and posts, and arch spindles. **Corporate headquarters location:** Clamout Falls OR.

NORDSTROM, INC.
1617 Sixth, Seattle WA 98101. 206/628-2111. **Contact:** Personnel. **World Wide Web address:** http://www.nordstrom.com. **Description:** This location is the flagship store of one of the largest independently owned fashion retailers in the United States. The company operates more than 100 full-line stores across the nation. Founded in 1901. **Positions advertised include:** Corporate Expense Keyer; Data Warehouse Analyst; Administrative Assistant; Sales Audit Representative; Senior Accountant; Project Manager; Quality Assurance Analyst. **Corporate headquarters location:** This location. **Listed on:** New York Stock Exchange. **Stock exchange symbol:** JWN. **Annual sales/revenues:** More than $100 million.

NORDSTROM RACK
1601 Second Avenue, Seattle WA 98101. 206/448-8522. **Contact:** Human Resources. **World Wide Web address:** http://www.nordstrom.com. **Description:** Nordstom is one of the largest independently owned fashion retailers in the United States. The company operates more than 60 full-line stores across the nation along with over 20 clearance, boutique, and leased shoe departments in 12 department stores in Hawaii and Guam. Founded in 1901. **Operations at this facility include:** This location is a discounted outlet store. **Listed on:** New York Stock Exchange. **Stock exchange symbol:** JWN. **Annual sales/revenues:** More than $100 million. **Number of employees at this location:** 500.

NORTHLAND COMMUNICATIONS CORPORATION
101 Stewart Street, Suite 700, Seattle WA 98101. 206/621-1351. **Toll-free phone:** 800/448-0273. **Fax:** 315/671-6268. **Contact:** Rheta Angeoes, Human Resources Manager. **E-mail address:** rangeoes@dreamscape.com. **World Wide Web address:** http://www.northlandtel.com. **Description:** Provides cable television services, local news production, and local advertising for small-market radio and cable systems. **Positions advertised include:** Account Executive; Accountant; Customer Service Representative; Network Operations Technician; PBX Technician; Systems Administrator. **Corporate headquarters location:** This location. **Other U.S. locations:** Nationwide. **Operations at this facility include:** Administration. **Listed on:** Privately held. **Number of employees at this location:** 50. **Number of employees nationwide:** 470.

NORTHSHORE UTILITY DISTRICT
6830 NE 185th Street, Kenmore WA 98028. 425/398-4400. **Fax:** 425/398-4430. **Contact:** Alcien Cockbain, Human Resources. **E-mail address:** alliec@nud.net. **World Wide Web address:** http://www.nud.net. **Description:** A special purpose water and sewer utility company. **Positions advertised include:** Meter Technician.

NORTHWEST AIRLINES
Seattle-Tacoma International Airport, Seattle WA 98158. **Recorded jobline:** 612/726-3600. **Contact:** Human Resources. **World Wide Web address:** http://www.nwa.com. **Description:** One of the world's largest airlines and one of America's oldest carriers. Northwest Airlines serves more than 250 cities in Asia, Europe, North America, and Australia. The U.S. system spans 49 states and the District of Columbia. Hub cities are located in Detroit, Minneapolis/St. Paul, Memphis, and Tokyo. Maintenance bases are in Atlanta and Minneapolis/St. Paul. Crew bases are in Anchorage, Chicago, Detroit, Memphis, San Francisco, Minneapolis/St. Paul, New York, Seattle/Tacoma, Boston, Los Angeles, Honolulu, and several international cities. The company maintains a fleet of over 400 aircraft that fly approximately 2,600 flights each day. Founded in 1926. **NOTE:** The company recommends calling the jobline or viewing postings on the Website first. Resumes should be sent to Northwest Airlines, 5101 Northwest Drive, Mail Stop A1410, St. Paul MN 55111-3034. **Corporate headquarters location:** Eagan MN. **Listed on:** NASDAQ. **Stock exchange symbol:** NWAC. **Number of employees worldwide:** 53,000.

NORTHWEST COMPOSITES, INC.
12810 State Avenue, Marysville WA 98271. 360/653-2211. **Fax:** 360/653-2112. **Contact:** Human Resources. **E-mail address:** hr@nwcomposites.com. **World Wide Web address:** http://www.nwcomposites.com. **Description:** Manufactures composite products for airplane interiors including luggage bins and door latches.

NORTHWEST HARDWOODS
20015 67th Avenue NE, P.O. Box 7, Arlington WA 98223. 360/435-8502. **Contact:** Personnel. **Description:** Produces maple and alder woods used in furniture construction.

NORTHWEST HOSPITAL
1550 North 115th Street, Suite 1, Seattle WA 98133. 206/368-1785. **Recorded jobline:** 206/368-1791. **Contact:** Human Resources Department. **World Wide Web address:** http://www.nwhospital.org. **Description:** A full-service nonprofit hospital that specializes in brain, breast, and prostate cancer; treatment and rehabilitation for diabetes and vascular disease; radioactive seed implantation; neurological disorders; and rehabilitation therapy. Founded in 1960. **Positions advertised include:** Authorization Referral Representative; Nursing Assistant; Exercise Specialist; Inventory Coordinator; Lab Assistant; EKG Technician.

NORTHWEST PROTECTIVE SERVICES, INC.
2700 Elliott Avenue, Seattle WA 98121. 206/448-4040. **Fax:** 206/448-2461. **Contact:** Human Resources. **World Wide Web address:** http://www.nwprotective.com. **Description:** Provides contract security services. **Positions advertised include:** Security Officer. **Corporate headquarters location:** This location. **Other area locations:** Spokane WA; Tacoma WA. **Other U.S. locations:** Portland OR. **Operations at this facility include:** Service. **Number of employees nationwide:** 700.

NORTHWESTERN INDUSTRIES INC.
2500 West Jameson Street, Seattle WA 98199-1294. 206/285-3140. **Fax:** 206/285-3603. **Toll-free phone:** 800/426-2771. **Contact:** Human Resources. **World Wide Web address:** http://www.nwiglass.com. **Description:** One of the largest glass fabricators in the United States. The company offers tempered, laminated, and insulated glass products. Founded in 1975. **Corporate headquarters location:** This location.

NUCOR STEEL
2424 SW Andover Street, Seattle WA 98106. 206/933-2222. **Toll-free phone:** 800/677-1012. **Contact:** Human Resources Department. **World Wide Web address:** http://www.nucorbar.com. **Description:** Birmingham Steel operates minimills in the United States that produce steel and steel products on a low-cost basis. Primary products are steel reinforced bar (rebar) used in the construction industry, and rounds, squares, flats, angles, channels, and strips (merchant products), which are sold to fabricators and other merchants. **Subsidiaries include:** B&M American Steel and Wire manufactures steel rod and wire from semi-finished billets. These products are marketed to the automotive, agricultural, industrial fastener, welding, appliance, and aerospace industries. **Corporate headquarters location:** Charlotte NC. **Operations at this facility include:** This location manufactures rebar. **Number of employees at this location:** 300.

OCEAN SPRAY CRANBERRIES
1480 State Route 105, Aberdeen WA 98520. 360/648-2201. **Contact:** Human Resources. **World Wide Web address:** http://www.oceanspray.com. **Description:** Ocean Spray Cranberries is a nationally recognized food processor engaged in the packaging, processing, and marketing of fresh cranberries, cranberry sauces, and cranberry and grapefruit juices. **Corporate headquarters:** Lakeville-Middleboro MA. **Other U.S. locations:** Vero Beach FL; Bordenton NJ; Sulphur Springs TX; Kenosha WI. **Operations at this facility include:** This location processes cranberry juices and sauces.

THE OLYMPIAN
P.O. Box 407, Olympia WA 98507. 360/754-5490. **Physical address:** 111 Bethel Street NE, Olympia WA 98506. **Contact:** Carol Achatz, Director of Human Resources Department. **E-mail address:** cachatz@theolympian.com. **World Wide Web address:** http://www.theolympian.com. **Description:** Publishes a daily newspaper with a circulation of approximately 40,000 weekdays, and a Sunday circulation of approximately 50,000. **Positions advertised include:** Retail Sales Kiosk Representative; Health Care Account Executive; Strategic Marketing and Development Coordinator; Health/Social Services Reporter; Customer Services Representative. **Parent company:** Gannett Newspapers. **Listed on:** New York Stock Exchange. **Stock exchange symbol:** GCI.

OLYMPIC COLLEGE
1600 Chester Avenue, 5th Floor, College Service Center, Bremerton WA 98337-1699. 360/475-7300. **Fax:** 360/475-7302. **Contact:** Linda Yerger, Personnel Director. **E-mail:** jobs@oc.ctc.edu. **World Wide Web address:** http://www.oc.ctc.edu. **Description:** A two-year community college that offers associate degrees in arts and science, transfer programs, and various technical degrees. **Corporate headquarters location:** This location.

OLYMPIC NATIONAL PARK
NATIONAL PARK SERVICE
600 East Park Avenue, Port Angeles WA 98362-6798. 360/452-4501. **Contact:** Human Resources Department. **World Wide Web address:** http://www.olympic.national-park.com. **Description:** A national park that includes glacier-capped mountains, over 60 miles of Pacific coastline, and parts of old growth and temperate rain forests. **Special programs:** Internships. **Corporate headquarters location:** Washington DC. **Parent company:** Department of the Interior. **Operations at this facility include:** Administration; Research and Development; Service. **Number of employees at this location:** 300.

OLYMPIC RESOURCE MANAGEMENT
P.O. Box 1780, Poulsbo WA 98370. 360/697-5932. **Physical address:** 19245 10th Avenue NE, Poulsbo WA 98370. **Contact:** Human Resources. **World Wide Web address:** http://www.orm.com. **Description:** Plants and harvests trees sold as timber to the domestic market. This company is also engaged in real estate development. **Parent company:** Pope Resources.

ONYX SOFTWARE CORPORATION
1100 112th Avenue NE, Suite 100, Bellevue WA 98004. 425/451-8060. **Fax:** 425/990-3343. **Contact:** Recruiting Department. **E-mail address:** recruiting@onyxcorp.com. **World Wide Web address:** http://www.onyx.com. **Description:** Develops customer management software.

ORACLE CORPORATION
500 108th Avenue NE, Suite 1300, Bellevue WA 98004. 425/646-0200. **Contact:** Human Resources. **World Wide Web address:** http://www.oracle.com. **Description:** Oracle Corporation designs and manufactures database and information management software for business and provides consulting services. **NOTE:** For commercial consultant positions, address resumes to Tammy Yeager. For sales positions, address resumes to Virginia Wagner. **Corporate headquarters location:** Redwood Shores CA. **Other U.S. locations:** Nationwide. **International locations:** Worldwide. **Operations at this facility include:** Administration; Regional Headquarters; Sales. **Listed on:** NASDAQ. **Stock exchange symbol:** ORCL. **Annual sales/revenues:** More than $100 million. **Number of employees at this location:** 230. **Number of employees nationwide:** 41,000.

ORIENT OVERSEAS CONTAINER LINE LTD. (OOCL)
18912 North Creek Parkway, Suite 208, Bothell WA 98011. 425/488-5080. **Contact:** Human Resources. **World Wide Web address:** http://www.oocl.com. **Description:** An international containerized transportation company. OOCL owns and operates several container vessels, terminals, and chassis throughout the world. The company also maintains a support group consisting of several depots, warehouses, and trucking companies to support its ocean-based transport operations. **Corporate headquarters location:** Hong Kong. **International locations:** Worldwide.

OUTDOOR EMPIRE PUBLISHING
P.O. Box 19000, Seattle WA 98109. 206/624-3845. **Fax:** 206/695-8512. **Contact:** Patricia Waterhouse, Human Resources Department. **E-mail address:** staff@fishingandhuntingnews.com. **World Wide Web address:** http://www.fhnews.com. **Description:** Publishes *Fishing and Hunting News*, a semimonthly magazine.

OUTPUT TECHNOLOGY CORPORATION
3808 North Sullivan Road, Building 3, Spokane WA 99216. 509/536-0468. **Contact:** Personnel Administration. **Email address:** hr@output.com. **World Wide Web address:** http://www.output.com. **Description:** Manufactures and distributes printers and related products. **Corporate headquarters location:** This location. **Number of employees at this location:** 130.

OVERLAKE HOSPITAL MEDICAL CENTER
1035 116th Avenue NE, Bellevue WA 98004. 425/688-5201. **Fax:** 425/688-5758. **Contact:** Human Resources Department. **World Wide Web address:** http://www.overlakehospital.org. **Description:** A 227-bed, nonprofit, acute care medical center. Overlake Hospital specializes in open-heart surgery and offers a comprehensive cardiac program. **Special programs:** Internships. **Annual sales/revenues:** $5 - $10 million. **Number of employees at this location:** 1,900.

OVERLAKE SERVICE LEAGUE
P.O. Box 53203, Bellevue WA 98015-3203. 425/451-1175. **Fax:** 425/451-1088. **Contact:** Special Services. **World Wide Web address:** http://www.overlakeserviceleague.com. **Description:** A social services organization that provides emergency financial assistance, develops and offers several youth programs, and operates a thrift store. Founded in 1911.

PACCAR INC.
777 106th Avenue NE, Bellevue WA 98004. 425/468-7400. **Fax:** 425/468-8216. **Contact:** Human Resources. **World Wide Web address:** http://www.paccar.com. **Description:** Manufactures, leases, and finances heavy-duty on- and off-road trucks and industrial winches for industrial and commercial use. Brand names include Peterbilt, Foden, DAF, and Kenworth. **Special programs:** Internships. **Corporate headquarters location:** This location. **Other U.S. locations:** Nationwide. **International locations:** Australia; Canada; Mexico; the Netherlands; United Kingdom. **Annual sales/revenues:** More than $100 million. **Number of employees at this location:** 425. **Number of employees nationwide:** 10,000.

PACIFIC COAST FEATHER COMPANY, INC.
1964 4th Avenue South, Seattle WA 98134. 206/624-1057. **Toll-free phone:** 888/297-1778 **Contact:** Personnel Department. **World Wide Web address:** http://www.pacificcoast.com. **Description:** Manufactures pillows, comforters, and featherbeds.

PACIFIC LUMBER & SHIPPING COMPANY
1301 Fifth Avenue, Suite 3131, Seattle WA 98111. 206/682-7262. **Fax:** 206/622-1072. **Contact:** Personnel. **E-mail address:** info@pls-lumber.com. **World Wide Web address:** http://www.pls-lumber.com. **Description:** A worldwide lumber wholesaler providing both hardwoods and softwoods. **Corporate headquarters location:** This location. **Other area locations:** Everett WA; Longview WA. **Number of employees at this location:** 30.

PACIFIC NORTHWEST NATIONAL LABORATORY
P.O. Box 999, 902 Battelle Boulevard, Richland WA 99352. 509/375-2121. **Toll-free phone:** 888/375-PNNL. **Contact:** Human Resources. **World Wide Web address:** http://www.pnl.gov. **Description:** A national laboratory engaged in basic and applied research in energy, material and chemical sciences, earth and environmental engineering, waste technology, environmental restoration, and nuclear-related areas. **Positions advertised include:** Duty Forecaster; Senior Atmospheric Scientist; HR Generalist; Program Director. **Special programs:** Internships. **Corporate headquarters location:** Columbus OH. **Operations at this facility include:** Research and Development. **Number of employees at this location:** 4,800.

PACIFIC SEASONINGS
21612 88th Avenue South, Kent WA 98031. 253/395-9400. **Fax:** 253/395-3330. **Contact:** Personnel Department. **Description:** Produces foods such as raw and salted nuts, spices, extracts, and seasoning mixes.

PACIFIC TRAIL INC.
1700 Westlake Avenue North, Suite 200, Seattle WA 98109. 206/270-5300. **Fax:** 206/270-5301. **Contact:** Human Resources. **World Wide Web address:** http://www.pacifictrail.com. **Description:** Designs, manufactures, and markets outerwear for active, casual, and performance use. Founded in 1945. **Parent company:** London Fog.

PACMED CLINIC
1200 12th Avenue South, Seattle WA 98144. 206/621-4111. **Fax:** 206/621-4031. **Contact:** Human Resources. **World Wide Web address:** http://www.pacmed.org. **Description:** A nonprofit medical center operating clinics throughout the Seattle area. **Positions advertised include:** Coding Manager; Senior Supervisor of Health Data Services; Clinical RN; Medical Assistant; Physical Therapist; Healthcare Application Analyst. **Office hours:** Monday - Friday, 8:00 a.m. - 4:00 p.m. **Number of employees at this location:** 1,200.

PAINE ELECTRONICS
2401 South Bayview Street, Seattle WA 98144. 206/329-8600. **Fax:** 206/329-1615. **Contact:** Human Resources. **World Wide Web address:** http://www.painecorp.com. **Description:** Engaged in the manufacture of pressure-measuring instruments and thick-film microcircuits.

PARAMETRIX, INC.
P.O. Box 460, Sumner WA 98390. 253/863-5128. **Contact:** Human Resources. **World Wide Web address:** http://www.parametrix.com. **Description:** An environmental and engineering consulting firm. The company is also engaged in environmental surveying. Founded in 1969. **Positions advertised include:** Structural Design Engineer; Bridge Design Engineer; Senior Word Processor; Marketing Database Coordinator. **Corporate headquarters location:** This location.

THE PARAMOUNT HOTEL
724 Pine Street, Seattle WA 98101. 206/292-9500. **Fax:** 206/292-8610. **Contact:** Human Resources. **World Wide Web address:** http://www.westcoasthotels.com. **Description:** A 146-room, chateau-style hotel featuring the Blowfish Asian Cafe and two meeting rooms. **Parent company:** Westcoast Hotels.

PARKER, SMITH & FEEK, INC.
2233 112th Avenue NE, Bellevue WA 98004. 425/709-3600. **Toll-free phone:** 800/457-0220. **Fax:** 425/709-7472. **Contact:** Employee Relations. **World Wide Web address:** http://www.psfinc.com. **Description:** Provides a variety of insurance services including commercial property/casualty, health, life, and personal lines. Founded in 1937. **Corporate headquarters location:** This location. **Other U.S. locations:** Anchorage AK. **sales/revenues:** $11 - $20 million.

PARSONS BRINCKERHOFF INC.
999 Third Avenue, Suite 2200, Seattle WA 98104-4020. 206/382-5200. **Fax:** 206/382-5222. **Contact:** Personnel. **World Wide Web address:** http://www.pbworld.com. **Description:** An engineering and design firm engaged in the design of bridges, tunnels, rapid transit systems, hydroelectric facilities, water supply systems, and marine facilities worldwide. **Corporate headquarters location:** New York NY.

PATHOLOGY ASSOCIATES MEDICAL LABORATORIES
110 West Cliff Avenue, Spokane WA 99204. 509/755-8600. **Contact:** Human Resources. **E-mail address:** hr@paml.com. **World Wide Web address:** http://www.paml.com. **Description:** A laboratory that performs blood, tissue, and drug tests. **Corporate headquarters location:** This location.

PEMCO FINANCIAL SERVICES
P.O. Box 778, Seattle WA 98111. 206/628-4090. **Toll-free phone:** 800/552-7430. **Fax:** 206/628-6072. **Recorded jobline:** 206/628-8740. **Contact:** Human Resources. **E-mail address:** jobs@pfcenter.com. **World Wide Web address:** http://www.pemco.com. **Description:** Provides insurance, banking, and credit union services through its subsidiaries. Founded in 1936. **Positions advertised include:** Sales Supervisor; Individual Life Underwriter; Document Services Specialist; Training Consultant; Risk Management Representative. **Special programs:** Training. **Corporate headquarters location:** This location. **Subsidiaries include:** PEMCO Insurance Companies; PEMCO Life Insurance Company; Washington School Employees Credit Union; PEMCO Corporation; EvergreenBank. **Number of employees at this location:** 800. **Number of employees nationwide:** 1,030.

PENDLETON WOOLEN MILLS
2 17th Street, P.O. Box 145, Washougal WA 98671. 360/835-2131. **Fax:** 360/835-5451. **Contact:** Human Resources. **World Wide Web address:** http://www.pendleton-usa.com. **Description:** Processes and manufactures wool to create fabric and clothing.

PENINSULA DAILY NEWS
P.O. Box 1330, Port Angeles WA 98362. 360/452-2345. **Fax:** 360/417-3521. **Contact:** Publisher. **World Wide Web address:** http://www.peninsuladailynews.com. **Description:** A daily newspaper with a weekday circulation of 5,800 and a Sunday circulation of 17,600. **Corporate headquarters location:** Bellevue WA. **Parent company:** Northwest Media. **Operations at this facility include:** Divisional Headquarters. **Number of employees at this location:** 70. **Number of employees nationwide:** 350.

PEPSI-COLA COMPANY
2300 26th Avenue South, Seattle WA 98144. 206/323-2932. **Fax:** 206/326-7484. **Contact:** Human Resources. **World Wide Web address:** http://www.pepsico.com. **Description:** Bottles and distributes Pepsi-Cola. **Parent company:** PepsiCo, Inc. (Purchase NY) consists of Frito-Lay Company, Pepsi-Cola Company, Quaker Oats Company, and Tropicana Products, Inc. **Number of employees at this location:** 1,300.

PHILIP SERVICES CORPORATION
20245 77th Avenue South, Kent WA 98032. 253/872-8030. **Contact:** Human Resources. **World Wide Web address:** http://www.contactpsc.com. **Description:** Philip Services Corporation is divided into three groups: Northwest By-Products Management; Metals Recovery; and Industrial Services. Founded in 1970. **Operations at this facility include:** This location is a hazardous-waste treatment facility. **Annual sales/revenues:** More than $100 million.

PHILIPS MEDICAL SYSTEMS
P.O. Box 3003, Bothell WA 98041-3003. 425/487-7000. **Physical address:** 22100 Bothell Everett Highway, Bothell WA 98021-3003. **Toll-free phone:** 800/722-7900. **Fax:** 425/485-6080. **Contact:** Personnel. **World Wide Web address:** http://www.medical.philips.com. **Description:** Engaged in the development and manufacture of medical diagnostic ultrasound systems. These systems serve a variety of uses in radiology, cardiology, obstetrics/gynecology, vascular, musculoskeletal, and intraoperative applications. Founded in 1969. **Company slogan:** We are ultrasound. **Special programs:** Internships; Training. **Corporate headquarters location:** This location.

PIONEER INDUSTRIES
7440 West Marginal Way South, Seattle WA 98106. 206/768-1990. **Fax:** 206/768-8910. **Contact:** Human Resources Department. **World Wide Web address:** http://www.pioneerhumanserv.com. **Description:** A contract manufacturer of aircraft components and sheet metal products for a variety of industrial uses. Founded in 1966. **Positions advertised include:** Chemical Dependency Counselor; Residential Supervisor; Case Manager; Sheet Metal Instructor. **Special programs:** Training. **Corporate headquarters location:** This location. **Parent company:** Pioneer Human Services operates rehabilitation and job training programs for work-release prisoners and people recovering from addictions. **Annual sales/revenues:** Approximately $55 million. **Number of employees at this location:** 700.

PLUM CREEK TIMBER COMPANY, INC.
999 Third Avenue, Suite 4300, Seattle WA 98104-4096. 206/467-3600. **Toll-free phone:** 800/858-5347. **Fax:** 206/467-3786. **Contact:** Personnel Department. **E-mail address:** info@plumcreek.com. **World Wide Web address:** http://www.plumcreek.com. **Description:** Manufactures softwood, hardwood, lumber, plywood, fiber bands, and laminates.

POTLATCH CORPORATION
601 West Riverside Avenue, Suite 1100, Spokane WA 99201. 509/835-1516. **Fax:** 509/835-1559. **Contact:** Employee Relations Administrator. **E-mail address:** info@potlatchcorp.com. **World Wide Web address:** http://www.potlatchcorp.com. **Description:** A fully-integrated manufacturer of forest products including lumber, plywood, paper, bleached paperboard, and consumer products. Wood products are produced at plants in Arkansas, Idaho, and Minnesota and are marketed through company sales representatives to wholesalers for distribution nationwide. Coated papers for magazines, catalogs, and direct-mail advertising are produced in Minnesota and sold mostly to merchants. **Corporate headquarters location:** Lewiston ID. **Listed on:** New York Stock Exchange. **Stock exchange symbol:** PCH. **Number of employees worldwide:** 7,000.

PRECISION DIGITAL IMAGES CORPORATION
8520 15th Avenue NE, Redmond WA 98011. 425/882-0218. **Fax:** 425/867-9177. **Contact:** Human Resources. **World Wide Web address:** http://www.precisionimages.com. **Description:** Designs image processing and image collection subsystems for computers. Products are sold to original equipment manufacturers primarily for such applications as machine vision, desktop video conferencing and medical imaging. Founded in 1992.

PRECOR, INC.
20031 142nd Avenue, P.O. Box 7202, Woodinville WA 98072. 425/486-9292. **Fax:** 425/398-3005. **Contact:** Human Resources. **E-mail address:** hr@precor.com. **World Wide Web address:** http://www.precor.com. **Description:** One of the world's leading designers, manufacturers, and marketers of fitness equipment for home and commercial use. Products include treadmills, stairclimbers, cyclers, and elliptical crosstrainers. **Corporate headquarters location:** This location. **International locations:** England; Germany; Singapore. **Subsidiaries include:** Pacific Fitness. **Parent company:** Premark International (Deerfield IL) is a *Fortune* 500 company. **President:** Bill Potts.

PREMERA BLUE CROSS
3900 East Sprague, Spokane WA 99202. 509/536-4700. **Recorded jobline:** 888/647-3628. **Contact:** Human Resources. **World Wide Web address:** http://www.premera.com. **Description:** A nonprofit health care insurance provider.

PREMIER INDUSTRIES INC.
1019 Pacific Avenue, Suite 1501, Tacoma WA 98402. 253/572-5111. **Fax:** 253/383-7100. **Contact:** Human Resources. **World Wide Web address:** http://www.premier-industries.com. **Description:** Manufactures integrated plastic products.

PRICEWATERHOUSECOOPERS
1001 Fourth Avenue, Suite 4200, Seattle WA 98154-1101. 206/622-1505. **Fax:** 206/398-3100. **Contact:** Human Resources Department. **World Wide Web address:** http://www.pricewaterhousecoopers.com. **Description:** One of the largest certified public accounting firms in the world. PricewaterhouseCoopers provides public accounting, business advisory, management consulting, and taxation services. **Corporate headquarters location:** New York NY. **Other U.S. locations:** Nationwide.

PRICEWATERHOUSECOOPERS
999 Third Avenue, Suite 4400, Seattle WA 98104-4045. 206/622-8700. **Contact:** Personnel. **World Wide Web address:** http://www.pricewaterhousecoopers.com. **Description:** One of the largest certified public accounting firms in the world. PricewaterhouseCoopers provides public accounting, business advisory, management consulting, and taxation services. **Corporate headquarters location:** New York NY. **Other U.S. locations:** Nationwide.

PRINCESS TOURS
2815 Second Avenue, Suite 400, Seattle WA 98121. 206/336-6000. **Fax:** 206/336-6100. **Contact:** Personnel. **World Wide Web address:** http://www.princess.com. **Description:** Operates rail and motorcoach tours in Alaska and the Canadian Rockies for land-only touring, or in conjunction with cruise ships. The company also owns and operates seasonal and year-round hotels in Alaska. **Corporate headquarters location:** This location. **Other U.S. locations:** AK. **Operations at this facility include:** Administration; Sales. **Number of employees at this location:** 150. **Number of employees nationwide:** 300.

PROCYTE CORPORATION
8511 154th Avenue NE, Building A, Redmond WA 98052. 425/869-1239. **Contact:** Human Resources. **World Wide Web address:** http://www.procyte.com. **Description:** Develops copper peptide complex-based products designed for hair care, skin care, and tissue repair. The company also offers contract manufacturing services to biotech and pharmaceutical companies. **Corporate headquarters location:** This location.

PROVIDENCE EVERETT MEDICAL CENTER
1321 Colby Avenue, Everett WA 98206. 425/261-4460. **Fax:** 425/261-4470. **Contact:** Human Resources. **World Wide Web address:** http://www.providence.org. **Description:** A full-service, acute care hospital. The Center also specializes in advanced cancer treatment and heart surgery.

PROVIDENCE HOSPICE OF SEATTLE
425 Pontius Avenue North, Suite 300, Seattle WA 98109-5452. 206/320-4000. **Fax:** 206/320-2280. **Contact:** Human Resources. **Description:** Provides skilled nursing and other home and hospice services.

PROVIDENCE MOTHER JOSEPH CARE CENTER
3333 Ensign Road NE, Olympia WA 98506. 360/493-4900. **Fax:** 360/493-4000. **Contact:** Human Resources. **World Wide Web address:** http://www.providence.org. **Description:** A 152-bed skilled nursing home that also operates a special care facility for Alzheimer's residents.

PROVIDENCE MOUNT ST. VINCENT
4831 35th Avenue SW, Seattle WA 98126. 206/937-3700. **Fax:** 206/938-8999. **Contact:** Human Resources. **World Wide Web address:** http://www.providence.org. **Description:** A long-term care facility that offers assisted living and skilled nursing services, an intergenerational learning center, and rehabilitation programs.

PRUDENTIAL MACPHERSON
18551 Aurora Avenue North, Suite 100, Shoreline WA 98133. 206/546-4124. **Contact:** Personnel Department. **World Wide Web address:** http://www.macphersons.com. **Description:** A real estate company that also operates apartment buildings and provides related services.

PUBLICIS
424 Second Avenue West, Seattle WA 98119. 206/285-2222. **Contact:** Personnel Department. **E-mail address:** resume@publicis-usa.com. **World Wide Web address:** http://www.publicisinthewest.com. **Description:** An advertising and public relations agency specializing in the areas of technology, health care, retail, and consumer goods. **Corporate headquarters location:** New York NY.

PUGET SOUND FREIGHT LINES INC.
P.O. Box 24526, Seattle WA 98124. 206/623-1600. **Physical address:** 3720 Airport Way South, Seattle Washington 98134. **Contact:** Personnel Department. **E-mail address:** hr@psfl.com. **World Wide Web address:** http://www.psfl.com. **Description:** A regional common carrier using both company drivers and owner/operators in truckload operations. **Corporate headquarters location:** This location. **Other U.S. locations:** OR.

PURE NETWORKS, INC.
2815 Eastlake Avenue E, Suite 201, Seattle WA 98102. 206/322-0002. **Fax:** 206/322-9283. **Contact:** Human Resources. **E-mail address:** PureRecruiting@purenetworks.com. **World Wide Web address:** http://www.purenetworks.com. **Description:** Provider of home networking software and services. **Positions advertised include:** Director of Operations; Web Services Development Manager. **Corporate headquarters location:** This location.

QUALITY FOOD CENTERS
10116 NE Eighth Street, Bellevue WA 98004. 425/455-3761. **Contact:** Human Resources. **World Wide Web address:** http://www.qfconline.com. **Description:** Operates a chain of retail supermarkets. **Corporate headquarters location:** Cincinnati OH. **Parent company:** The Kroger Company. **Number of employees nationwide:** 2,600.

QUEST DIAGNOSTICS INCORPORATED
1737 Airport Way South, Suite 200, Seattle WA 98134. 206/623-8100. **Fax:** 206/624-5488. **Contact:** Human Resources Department. **World Wide Web address:** http://www.questdiagnostics.com. **Description:** One of the largest clinical laboratories in North America, providing a broad range of clinical laboratory services to health care clients, which include physicians, hospitals, clinics, dialysis centers, pharmaceutical companies, and corporations. The company offers and performs tests on blood, urine, and other bodily fluids and tissues to provide information for health and well-being. **Positions advertised include:** Specimen Processor; Phlebotomy Services Representative; Pricing Manager.

QUINTON
3303 Monte Villa Parkway, Bothell WA 98021-8906. 425/402-2000. **Fax:** 425/402-2015. **Contact:** Human Resources. **E-mail address:** employment@quinton.com. **World Wide Web address:** http://www.quinton.com. **Description:** Manufactures, markets, and distributes cardiopulmonary instrumentation and devices such as cardiac stress test systems, electrocardiographs, and treadmills. **Positions advertised include:** Accounts Payable Clerk; Contract Administrator. **Corporate headquarters location:** This location. **Listed on:** NASDAQ. **Stock exchange symbol:** QUIN.

RAF TECHNOLOGY, INC.
15400 NE 90th Street, Suite 300, Redmond WA 98052. 425/867-0700. **Contact:** Human Resources. **World Wide Web address:** http://www.raf.com. **Description:** A provider of advanced recognition, verification and identity authentication solutions for government and commercial clients. **Positions advertised include:** QA Engineer; System Quality Assurance and Program Management; Technical Services Consultant. **Corporate headquarters location:** This location.

RSG FOREST PRODUCTS, INC.
985 NW Second Street, Kalama WA 98625. 360/673-2825. **Fax:** 360/673-5558. **Contact:** Human Resources. **World Wide Web address:** http://www.rsgfp.com. **Description:** A lumber company producing primarily cedar fencing. **Corporate headquarters location:** This location. **Other U.S. locations:** OR.

RAGEN MACKENZIE INCORPORATED
999 Third Avenue, Suite 4300, Seattle WA 98104. 206/343-5000. **Fax:** 206/389-8245. **Contact:** Personnel Department. **World Wide Web address:** http://www.ragen-mackenzie.com. **Description:** Engaged in investment banking. Founded in 1982.

RAYONIER INC.
3033 Ingram Street, Hoquiam, WA 98158. 360/533-7000. **Contact:** Human Resources. **World Wide Web address:** http://www.rayonier.com. **Description:** Rayonier is a leading international forest products company engaged in the trading, merchandising, and manufacturing of logs, timber, and wood products, and in the production and sale of high-value specialty pulps. Rayonier owns, buys, and harvests timber stumpage and purchases delivered logs, primarily in North America and New Zealand, for subsequent sale into export markets (primarily Japan, Korea, and China), as well as to domestic lumber and pulp mills. Rayonier also produces dimension and specialty products for residential construction and industrial uses. **Positions advertised include:** Timber Resource Manager; International Wood Products Controller. **Corporate headquarters location:** Jacksonville FL. **Operations at this facility include:** This location markets

logs, lumber products, and pulp. **Listed on:** New York Stock Exchange. **Stock exchange symbol:** RYN.

RAYTHEON SYSTEMS COMPANY
1050 NE Hostmark, Poulsbo WA 98370. 360/697-6600. **Contact:** Personnel. **World Wide Web address:** http://www.raytheon.com. **Description:** Manufactures defense and commercial electronics systems and business aviation and special mission aircraft. **Corporate headquarters location:** Lexington MA.

RAYTHEON AIRCRAFT COMPANY
7001 Perimeter Road South, Suite 104, Seattle WA 98108. 206-763-8421. **Contact:** Personnel. **World Wide Web address:** http://www.raytheon.com. **Description:** Manufactures defense and commercial electronics systems and business aviation and special mission aircraft. **Corporate headquarters location:** Lexington MA.

RAYTHEON ENGINEERS & CONSTRUCTION, INC.
10900 Northeast 8th Street, Suite 500, Bellevue WA 98004. 425-451-4500. **Contact:** Personnel. **World Wide Web address:** http://www.raytheon.com. **Description:** Manufactures defense and commercial electronics systems and business aviation and special mission aircraft. **Corporate headquarters location:** Lexington MA.

RAYTHEON TECHNICAL SERVICES COMPANY
16300 Christensen Road, Tukwila, WA 98188. 206-244-4616. **Contact:** Personnel. **World Wide Web address:** http://www.raytheon.com. **Description:** Manufactures defense and commercial electronics systems and business aviation and special mission aircraft. **Corporate headquarters location:** Lexington MA.

REALNETWORKS
P.O. Box 91123, Seattle WA 98111-9223. 206/674-2700. **Fax:** 206/674-2699. **Contact:** Human Resources. **World Wide Web address:** http://www.realnetworks.com. **Description:** Develops software that allows users to listen to audio applications over the Internet. **NOTE:** Jobseekers may submit applications online. **Listed on:** NASDAQ. **Stock exchange symbol:** RNWK.

RECREATIONAL EQUIPMENT INC. (REI)
P.O. Box 1938, Sumner WA 98390. 253/395-5500. **Physical address:** 6750 South 228th Street, Kent WA 98032. **Recorded jobline:** 253/395-4694. **Contact:** Human Resources Department. **World Wide Web address:** http://www.rei.com/jobs. **Description:** A retailer of outdoor clothing and a wide variety of recreational equipment. **NOTE:** Jobseekers may apply and submit resumes online. **Corporate headquarters location:** Kent WA. **Operations at this facility include:** Administration. **Number of employees nationwide:** 3,000.

RED DOT CORPORATION
P.O. Box 58270, Seattle WA 98138-1270. 206/575-3840. **Fax:** 206/575-8267. **Contact:** Human Resources. **World Wide Web address:** http://www. reddotcorp.com. **Description:** A manufacturer and wholesaler of heating and air conditioning equipment for heavy vehicles such as semi-trucks and off-road vehicles. **Office hours:** Monday - Friday, 7:45 a.m. - 4:30 p.m. **Corporate headquarters location:** This location.

REGENCE BLUESHIELD
1800 Ninth Avenue, Seattle WA 98101. 206/464-3600. **Contact:** Human Resources. **World Wide Web address:** http://www.wa.regence.com. **Description:** A health care service contractor that has been providing health care coverage to Washington residents for more than 86 years. Regence BlueShield has a roster of more than 19,000 physicians, dentists, and other providers serving more than 1 million members. **Positions advertised include:** Actuary Assistant, Business System Analyst; Director of Sales and Service. **Number of employees:** 2,300 employees.

RENTON, CITY OF
1055 South Grady Way, Renton WA 98055. 425/430-7650. **Fax:** 425/430-7665. **Recorded jobline:** 425/430-7652. **Contact:** Mike Webby, Human Resources. **World Wide Web address:** http://www.ci.renton.wa.us. **Description:** The administrative offices for the city of Renton. **Number of employees at this location:** 560.

RENTON SCHOOL DISTRICT
300 SW Seventh Street, Renton WA 98055. 425/204-2354. **Fax:** 425/204-2383. **Recorded jobline:** 425/204-2305. **Contact:** Marcia Rochabrand, Recruiting Coordinator. **E-mail address:** mrochabrand@renton.wednet.edu. **World Wide Web address:** http://www.renton.wednet.edu. **Description:** Administrative offices for the Renton public school district. **Office hours:** Monday - Friday, 7:30 a.m. - 4:30 p.m. **Number of employees at this location:** 1,400.

RENTON TECHNICAL COLLEGE
3000 NE Fourth Street, Renton WA 98056. 425/235-2352. **Fax:** 425/235-7832. **Recorded jobline:** 425/235-2354. **Contact:** Human Resources. **World Wide Web address:** http://www.renton-tc.ctc.edu. **Description:** A technical college operated by the State Board for Community and Technical Colleges.

RESTAURANTS UNLIMITED INC.
1818 North Northlake Way, Seattle WA 98103-9097. 206/634-3082. **Fax:** 206/547-4829. **Contact:** Director of Staffing. **World Wide Web address:** http://www.restaurants-unlimited.com. **Description:** Owns and operates a chain of full-service dinner houses. Founded in 1969. **Corporate headquarters location:** This location. **Operations at this facility include:** Administration.

REXAM BEVERAGE CAN COMPANY
1220 Second Avenue North, Kent WA 98032. 253/854-9950. **Contact:** Human Resources. **Wide Web address:** http://www.rexam.com. **Description:** Manufactures a variety of container products. **Corporate headquarters location:** London, England. **Listed on:** London Stock Exchange. **Stock exchange symbol:** REX.L. **CEO:** Rolf Borjesson.

RIDE SNOWBOARD COMPANY
19215 Vashon Highway SW, Vashon WA 98070. 206/463-3631. **Toll-free phone:** 800/757-5806. **Fax:** 206/463-2861. **Contact:** Human Resources. **World Wide Web address:** http://www.ridesnowboards.com. **Description:** A leading designer, manufacturer, and marketer of snowboards, clothing, and related products under the Ride, Liquid, Preston, Cappel, and SMP brand names. Founded in 1992. **Special programs:** Internships. **Corporate headquarters location:** This location. **Subsidiaries include:** Ride - Canada, Toronto, Canada; Ride Manufacturing, Corona CA; SMP, Chula Vista CA. **Parent company:** Ride Inc. **Listed on:** NASDAQ. **Stock exchange symbol:** RIDE. **Annual sales/revenues:** $51 - $100 million. **Number of employees at this location:** 90. **Number of employees nationwide:** 250.

RITE AID CORPORATION
110 SW 148th Street, Burien WA 98166. 206/835-0166. **Fax:** 206/835-0991. **Contact:** Employee Relations Manager. **World Wide Web address:** http://www.riteaid.com. **Description:** Rite Aid Corporation operates 3800 retail drug stores in 30 states and the District of Columbia. Founded in 1939. **Special programs:** Internships. **Corporate headquarters location:** Harrisburg PA. **Other U.S. locations:** Nationwide. **Operations at this facility include:** This location houses administrative offices. **Listed on:** New York Stock Exchange. **Stock exchange symbol:** RAD. **Number of employees nationwide:** 40,000.

RIVERDEEP/THE LEARNING COMPANY
6727 185th Avenue NE, Building A, Redmond WA 98052. 425/556-8400. **Contact:** Human Resources. **E-mail address:** resumes@riverdeep.net. **World Wide Web address:** http://www.riverdeep.net. **Description:** Develops, publishes, and markets educational software and other products for the early childhood and special education markets. **Corporate headquarters location:** Novato CA; Boston MA. **Listed on:** NASDAQ. **Stock exchange symbol:** RVDP. **Number of employees at this location:** 150.

THE ROBBINS COMPANY
22445 76th Avenue South, Kent WA 98032. 253/872-0500. **Fax:** 253/872-0199. **Contact:** Human Resources Department. **World Wide Web address:** http://www.robbinstbm.com. **Description:** Designs and manufactures mining machinery and equipment. **Corporate headquarters location:** Solon OH. **Other U.S. locations:** Oak Hill WV.

ROCKWELL AUTOMATION
15375 SE 30th Place, Suite 150, Bellevue WA 98007. 425/746-2840. **Contact:** Human Resources. **World Wide Web address:** http://www.automation.rockwell.com. **Description:** Engaged in the production of industrial control equipment, software-based control equipment, magnetic materials, and electronic components. Founded in 1904. **Corporate headquarters location:** Milwaukee WI.

ROPAK NORTHWEST
2108 B Street Northwest, Suite 110, Building A, Auburn WA 98001. 253/804-0343. **Toll-free phone:** 866/607-6748. **Fax:** 253/804/6982. **Contact:** Human Resources. **E-mail address:** tammie_gaull@ropakcorp.com. **World Wide Web address:** http://www.ropakcorp.com. **Description:** Manufactures plastic packaging and materials handling products. **International locations:** Worldwide.

FRANK RUSSELL COMPANY
909 A Street, Tacoma WA 98402. 253/596-3056. **Fax:** 253/594-1727. **Recorded jobline:** 253/596-5454. **Contact:** Personnel. **E-mail address:** empsvc@russell.com. **World Wide Web address:** http://www.russell.com. **Description:** Provides a variety of financial services such as investment management, mutual funds, and investment consulting. Founded in 1936. **NOTE:** Jobseekers may submit applications and resumes online. **Corporate headquarters location:** This location. **Other U.S. locations:** Boston MA; New York NY. **International locations:** Australia; Canada; France; Italy; New Zealand; Singapore; South Africa; United Kingdom. **Number of employees at this location:** 1,000. **Number of employees nationwide:** 1,200.

S&W/CENTERFOODS MANAGEMENT COMPANY
20062 19th Avenue NE, Seattle WA 98155. 206/362-2255. **Fax:** 206/362-8850. **Contact:** Human Resources. **World Wide Web address:** http://www.centerfoods.com. **Description:** Owns and operates several fast-food restaurants located in malls, which are part of the national chains Orange Julius, A&W, Dairy Queen, and Auntie Anne's. Founded in 1971. **Special programs:** Internships; Training. **Internship information:** The company has a paid internship program for hotel/restaurant or business management students. To apply, submit a letter of application and include goals, schedule, and time frame. Call for more information. **Corporate headquarters location:** This location. **Number of employees at this location:** 300.

SAS CARGO
2427 South 161st Street, Seattle WA 98158. 206/433-5151. **Fax:** 201/896-3724. **Contact:** Human Resources. **World Wide Web address:** http://www.sascargo.com. **Description:** A cargo shipping company.

SEA, INC.
7030 220th Street SW, Mountlake Terrace WA 98043. 425/771-2182. **Fax:** 425/771-2650. **Contact:** Human Resources. **World Wide Web address:** http://www.sea-dmi.com. **Description:** Manufactures and markets electronics including radio and telephone systems for land and ocean applications, and ocean depth sounders and related instrumentation. **Office hours:** Monday - Friday, 8:00 a.m. - 5:00 p.m. **Parent company:** Datamarine International, Inc.

SEH AMERICA INC.
4111 Northeast 112th Avenue, Vancouver WA 98682. 360/883-7000. **Fax:** 360/883-7074. **Contact:** Human Resources. **E-mail address:** resume@sehamerica.com. **World Wide Web address:** http://sehamerica.com. **Description:** Manufactures silicon wafers used primarily for the semiconductor industry.

SI TECHNOLOGIES, INC.
6925 216th Street Southwest, Mountlake Terrace WA 98043. 425/672-2620. **Contact:** Human Resources. **World Wide Web address:** http://www.sitechnologies.com. **Description:** Manufactures mobile and stationary weighing systems, fleet information systems, and force measurement devices. **NOTE:** Jobseekers should send resumes to: Human Resources, P.O. Box 1744, Cumberland MD 21502, or fax it to 301/722-7346. **Corporate headquarters location:** Tustin CA. **Other U.S. locations:** IN; OR; PA; TX. **International locations:** Canada. **Subsidiaries include:** Advanced Recording Instruments; Evergreen Weigh, Inc.; Load Measurement Corporation. **Listed on:** NASDAQ. **Stock exchange symbol:** SISI. **President/CEO:** Rick Beets.

SAFECO INSURANCE CORPORATION
Safeco Plaza, Seattle WA 98185. 206/545-5000. **Recorded jobline:** 800/753-5330. **Contact:** Personnel Director. **World Wide Web address:** http://www.safeco.com. **Description:** A diversified financial services company with operations including property and liability, life and health insurance, pension plans, mutual funds, commercial credit, and real estate development. **Positions advertised include:** Actuarial Assistant; Agency Incentive Compensation Manager; Analyst; Application Developer; Business Recovery Developer. **Special programs:** Internships. **Corporate headquarters location:** This location. **Other area locations:** Redmond WA. **Other U.S. locations:** Nationwide. **Annual sales/revenues:** More than $100 million.

SAFECO LIFE INSURANCE COMPANY
P.O. Box 34690, Seattle WA 98124. 425/376-8000. **Contact:** Human Resources. **World Wide Web address:** http://www.safeco.com. **Description:** Provides life and health insurance. **Parent company:** Safeco Insurance Corporation. **Positions**

advertised include: Actuarial Assistant; Agency Incentive Compensation Manager; Analyst; Application Developer; Business Recovery Developer.

SAFEWAY, INC.
3020 NE 45th Street, Seattle WA 98105. 206/522-8350. **Contact:** Human Resources. **World Wide Web address:** http://www.safeway.com. **Description:** Safeway Inc. is one of the world's largest food retailers. The company operates approximately 1,660 stores in the western, Rocky Mountain, southwestern, and mid-Atlantic regions of the United States and in western Canada. In support of its stores, the company has an extensive network of distribution, manufacturing, and food processing facilities. Safeway, Inc. also holds a 49 percent interest in Casa Ley, S.A. de C.V., which operates food/variety, clothing, and wholesale outlet stores in western Mexico. **Subsidiaries include:** Dominick's Supermarkets is a Chicago-area chain with 112 stores. **Listed on:** New York Stock Exchange. **Stock exchange symbol:** SWY.

SAFEWAY, INC.
3820 Rainier Avenue South, Seattle WA 98118. 206/725-9575. **Contact:** Human Resources. **World Wide Web address:** http://www.safeway.com. **Description:** Safeway Inc. is one of the world's largest food retailers. The company operates approximately 1,660 stores in the western, Rocky Mountain, southwestern, and mid-Atlantic regions of the United States and in western Canada. In support of its stores, the company has an extensive network of distribution, manufacturing, and food processing facilities. Safeway, Inc. also holds a 49 percent interest in Casa Ley, S.A. de C.V., which operates food/variety, clothing, and wholesale outlet stores in western Mexico. **Subsidiaries include:** Dominick's Supermarkets is a Chicago-area chain with 112 stores. **Listed on:** New York Stock Exchange. **Stock exchange symbol:** SWY.

SAGEM MORPHO, INC.
1145 Broadway Plaza, Suite 200, Tacoma WA 98402-3253. 253/383-3617. **Fax:** 253/272-2934. **Contact:** Manager of Human Resources. **World Wide Web address:** http://www.morpho.com. **Description:** Manufactures and sells automated fingerprinting technologies to law enforcement and other civil service agencies. **Positions advertised include:** Customer Support Engineer. **Special programs:** Internships. **Corporate headquarters location:** This location. **Parent company:** Sagem SA. **Annual sales/revenues:** $21 - $50 million. **Number of employees at this location:** 150. **Number of employees nationwide:** 350.

ST. JOSEPH HOSPITAL
2901 Squalicum Parkway, Bellingham WA 98225. 360/734-5400. **Contact:** Personnel Office. **World Wide Web address:** http://www.peacehealth.org. **Description:** A 253-bed medical center and trauma center that provides a full range of inpatient and outpatient care including cancer care, emergency and trauma care, heart surgery, and neurosurgery. **Positions advertised include:** Registered Nurse; Certified Nurse Manger; Clinical Manager; Coder; Database System Administrator; Internal Auditor; Medical Technologist; Pharmacist; Speech Pathologist; Surgical Technologist.

SAINT-GOBAIN GLASS CONTAINER CORPORATION
5801 East Marginal Way South, Seattle WA 98134-2413. 206/762-0660. **Fax:** 206/768-6266. **Contact:** Jason Noble, Human Resources Manager. **Description:** Manufactures glass bottles and jars. **Parent company:** The Ball Corporation.

SALOMON SMITH BARNEY
999 Third Avenue, Suite 4500, Seattle WA 98104. 206/344-3500. **Contact:** Personnel Department. **World Wide Web address:** http://www.salomonsmithbarney.com. **Description:** An international investment banking, market making, and research firm serving corporations, state and local governments, sovereign and provincial governments and their agencies, central banks, and other financial institutions. **Corporate headquarters location:** New York NY.

SALOMON SMITH BARNEY
411 108th Avenue NE, Suite 1600, Bellevue WA 98004. 425/453-3450. **Contact:** Human Resources. **World Wide Web address:** http://www.salomonsmithbarney.com. **Description:** An international investment banking, market making, and research firm serving corporations, state and local governments, sovereign and provincial governments and their agencies, central banks, and other financial institutions. **Corporate headquarters location:** New York NY.

SANDVIK SPECIAL METALS
P.O. Box 6027, Kennewick WA 99336. 509/586-4131. **Fax:** 509/582-3552. **Contact:** Human Resources. **World Wide Web address:** http://www.sandvik.com. **Description:** Manufactures nuclear and aerospace tubing and bicycle frames and tubing. **Number of employees at this location:** 300.

SCANDINAVIAN AIRLINES
1301 Fifth Avenue, Suite 3101, Seattle WA 98101. 206/682-5250. **Fax:** 206/625-9057. **Contact:** Human Resources. **World Wide Web address:** http://www.scandinavian.net. **Description:** Scandinavian Airlines is an air transport company. **Operations at this facility include:** This location is the western regional sales office.

SCHWABE, WILLIAMSON & WYATT, P.C.
1420 Fifth Avenue, Suite 3010, Seattle WA 98101-2339. 206/622-1711. **Contact:** Recruitment. **World Wide Web address:** http://www.schwabe.com. **Description:** A law firm operating through two departments: Transactions and Litigation. The Transactions Department provides a wide range of legal services to area businesses, specializing in general business, corporate tax, energy, environment, natural resources, and real estate. The Litigation Department specializes in admiralty, commercial litigation, intellectual property, product liability, workers' compensation, and insurance. Founded in 1892. **Corporate headquarters location:** Portland OR. **Other area locations:** Vancouver WA.

SCHWABE, WILLIAMSON & WYATT, P.C.
1111 Main Street, Suite 410, Vancouver WA 98660. 360/694-7551. **Contact:** Recruitment. **World Wide Web address:** http://www.schwabe.com. **Description:** A law firm operating through two departments: Transactions and Litigation. The Transactions Department provides a wide range of legal services to area businesses, specializing in general business, corporate tax, energy, environment, natural resources, and real estate. The Litigation Department specializes in admiralty, commercial litigation, intellectual property, product liability, workers' compensation, and insurance. Founded in 1892. **Corporate headquarters location:** Portland OR. **Other area locations:** Seattle WA.

SEA-TAC MARRIOTT
3201 South 176th Street, Seattle WA 98188. 206/241-2000. **Fax:** 206/241-2235. **Contact:** Personnel Office. **World Wide Web address:** http://www.marriott.com. **Description:** A 465-room, full-service hotel featuring convention and banquet facilities and a restaurant. **Other U.S. locations:** Nationwide.

SEARS, ROEBUCK & CO.
15711 Aurora Avenue North, Seattle WA 98133. 206/364-9000. **Contact:** Human Resources. **World Wide Web address:** http://www.sears.com. **Description:** The company's structure is divided into three groups: Sears Merchandise Group, Allstate Insurance Group, and Corporate Business. With its network of mall-based stores, Sears is a leading retailer of apparel, home, and automotive products and related services for families throughout North America. **Positions advertised include:** District Technical Manager. **Corporate headquarters location:** Chicago IL. **Subsidiaries include:** Allstate Insurance Group; PMI Mortgage Insurance Company; Homart; Prodigy; Advantis**Listed on:** New York Stock Exchange. **Stock exchange symbol:** S.

SEATTLE ATHLETIC CLUB/DOWNTOWN
2020 Western Avenue, Seattle WA 98121. 206/443-1111. **Fax:** 206/443-2632. **Contact:** Human Resources. **World Wide Web address:** http://www.sacdt.com. **Description:** A full-service athletic club offering a variety of classes, personal training services, and extensive free weights and cardiovascular equipment. Other club amenities include a swimming pool, a whirlpool, saunas and steam rooms, and basketball and squash courts.

SEATTLE CENTER
305 Harrison Street, Seattle WA 98109-4645. 206/684-7202. **Fax:** 206/233-3932. **Contact:** Personnel. **World Wide Web address:** http://www.seattlecenter.com. **Description:** An entertainment complex. The Seattle Center is home to many cultural and athletic organizations including the Seattle Symphony, Seattle Opera, the NBA's Seattle SuperSonics, and the WNBA's Seattle Storm.

SEATTLE CENTRAL COMMUNITY COLLEGE
1500 Harvard Avenue, Seattle WA 98122. 206/587-4155. **Fax:** 206/587-4158. **Contact:** Human Resources. **E-mail address:** jobs@sccd.ctc.edu. **World Wide Web address:** http://www.sccd.ctc.edu. **Description:** A community college. **Number of employees at this location:** 800.

SEATTLE CHORAL COMPANY
1518 NE 143rd Street, Seattle WA 98125. 206/365-8765. **Fax:** 206/365-8714. **Contact:** Mr. Fred Coleman, Artistic Director. **World Wide Web address:** http://www.seattlechoralcompany.org. **Description:** An oratorio society performing symphonic and a cappella masterworks. Founded in 1980. **Corporate headquarters location:** This location.

SEATTLE DAILY JOURNAL OF COMMERCE
83 Columbia Street, Seattle WA 98104. 206/622-8272. **Fax:** 206/622-8416. **Contact:** Hiring Manager. **World Wide Web address:** http://www.djc.com. **Description:** Publishes a daily newspaper with a circulation of approximately 5,000.

SEATTLE DAYS INN TOWN CENTER
2205 Seventh Avenue, Seattle WA 98121. 206/448-3434. **Contact:** Personnel. **World Wide Web address:** http://www.daysinn.com. **Description:** A 91-room hotel. This location also houses a restaurant and lounge.

SEATTLE FILMWORKS
1260 16th Avenue West, Seattle WA 98119. 206/281-1390. **Fax:** 206/273-8373. **Contact:** Personnel. **E-mail address:** jobs@photoworks.com. **World Wide Web address:** http://www.filmworks.com. **Description:** Processes and sells 35mm film via mail order. Seattle Filmworks has the capabilities to deliver customers' pictures over the Internet. **Positions advertised include:** Vice President of Sales and Marketing. **Corporate headquarters location:** This location. **Operations at this facility include:** Administration; Manufacturing; Research and Development; Sales. **Number of employees at this location:** 400.

SEATTLE MARINE FISHING SUPPLY COMPANY
P.O. Box 99098, Seattle WA 98199-0098. 206/285-5010. **Physical address:** 2121 West Commodore Way, Seattle WA 98199. **Fax:** 206/285-7925. **Contact:** Personnel Department. **World Wide Web address:** http://www.seamar.com. **Description:** A wholesaler of marine supplies and hardware.

THE SEATTLE MARINERS
P.O. Box 4100, Seattle WA 98104. 206/346-4000. **Fax:** 206/346-4050. **Contact:** Personnel Department. **World Wide Web address:** http://www.mariners.org. **Description:** A professional baseball team playing in Major League Baseball's American League West division. Founded in 1977.

SEATTLE PACIFIC UNIVERSITY
330 West Nickerson, Seattle WA 98119. 206/281-2809. **Fax:** 206/281-2846. **Recorded jobline:** 206/281-2065. **Contact:** Kathleen Abbott, Employment Manager. **World Wide Web address:** http://www.spu.edu. **Description:** A Christian university of arts and sciences with an enrollment of approximately 3,400. **NOTE:** Jobseekers are encouraged to submit both the SPU Employment Application and the specific application for the position. **Positions advertised include:** Assistant Professor of Accounting; Physical Education Instructor; Residence Life Coordinator; Senior Administrative Assistant.

SEATTLE POLICE DEPARTMENT
610 Third Avenue, 15th Floor, Seattle WA 98104-1886. 206/684-5464. **Fax:** 206/386-9022. **Contact:** Personnel. **World Wide Web address:** http://www.ci.seattle.wa.us. **Description:** Seattle's police department. **NOTE:** To obtain an application for an entry-level police officer position, call the City of Seattle Civil Service Commission at 206/386-1303. **Corporate headquarters location:** This location. **Number of employees at this location:** 1,200.

SEATTLE POST-INTELLIGENCER
P.O. Box 1909, Seattle WA 98111. 206/448-8000. **Physical address:** 101 Elliott Avenue West, Seattle WA 98119. **Fax:** 206/448-8299. **Contact:** Personnel Manager. **World Wide Web address:** http://www.seattlep-i.com. **Description:** A daily morning newspaper with a weekday circulation in excess of 200,000. *Seattle Post-Intelligencer* is part of the Hearst Newspaper Group. Under terms of a joint operating agreement, circulation, advertising, and production operations for the newspaper are handled by the Seattle Times Company.

THE SEATTLE TIMES COMPANY
P.O. Box 70, Seattle WA 98111. 206/464-2121. **Recorded jobline:** 206/464-2118. **Contact:** Personnel. **World Wide Web address:** http://www.seattletimes.com. **Description:** Publishers of the *Seattle Times* newspaper. The company also conducts circulation, advertising, and production operations for *Seattle Post-Intelligencer*.

SECURITAS USA
2510 North Pines Road, Suite 1, Spokane WA 99206. 509/927-2552. **Contact:** Human Resources. **World Wide Web address:** http://www.securitas.com. **Description:** One

of the world's largest suppliers of global, total security solutions. The company provides a broad array of security-related services including business intelligence, investigations, security systems integration, and consulting.

SEDRO-WOOLLEY SCHOOL DISTRICT
801 Trail Road, Sedro-Woolley WA 98284. 360/855-3500. **Fax:** 360/855-3501. **Contact:** Personnel. **World Wide Web address:** http://www.swsd.k12.wa.us. **Description:** Offices of the Sedro-Woolley school system.

7-ELEVEN, INC.
2089 72nd Avenue South, Kent WA 98032. 253/796-7100. **Fax:** 253/796-7120. **Contact:** Human Resources. **World Wide Web address:** http://www.7-eleven.com. **Description:** Owns and operates 7-Eleven convenience stores. **Positions advertised include:** Field Consultant. **Corporate headquarters location:** Dallas TX.

SEVERN TRENT LABORATORIES, INC.
2800 George Washington Way, Richland WA 99352. 509/375-3131. **Fax:** 509/375-5590. **Contact:** Human Resources. **World Wide Web address:** http://www.stlinc.com. **Description:** Provides a complete range of environmental testing services to private industry, engineering consultants, and government agencies in support of federal and state environmental regulations. **Corporate headquarters location:** St. Louis MO.

SHAKERTOWN CORPORATION
1200 Kerron Street, P.O. Box 400, Winlock WA 98596. 360/785-3501. **Toll-free phone:** 800/426-8970. **Fax:** 360/785-3076. **Contact:** Personnel Department. **World Wide Web address:** http://www.shakertown.com. **Description:** Manufactures cedar shingle siding and roofing panels.

SHANNON & WILSON, INC.
P.O. Box 300303, Seattle WA 98103. 206/632-8020. **Physical address:** 400 North 34th Street, Suite 100, Seattle WA 98103. **Fax:** 206/633-6777. **Contact:** Human Resources. **E-mail address:** jobs@shanwil.com. **World Wide Web address:** http://www.shannonwilson.com. **Description:** Provides geotechnical consulting services to a variety of industrial and government clients. Services include foundation engineering studies, waste management, and construction monitoring. **Positions advertised include:** Office Support Clerk. **Corporate headquarters location:** This location.

SHARP MICROELECTRONICS USA
5700 NW Pacific Rim Boulevard, Camas WA 98607. 360/834-8700. **Fax:** 360/817-7544. **Contact:** Human Resources. **World Wide Web address:** http://www.sharp-usa.com. **Description:** Sharp Corporation develops business products, consumer electronics, and electronic components. **Corporate headquarters location:** Mahwah NJ. **Operations at this facility include:** This location is a sales and marketing facility. **Parent company:** Sharp Corporation.

SHORELINE COMMUNITY COLLEGE
16101 Greenwood Avenue North, Shoreline WA 98133-5696. 206/546-4101. **Fax:** 206/546-5850. **Recorded jobline:** 206/546-5894x3306. **Contact:** Human Resources. **E-mail address:** scchr@ctc.edu. **World Wide Web address:** http://www.shore.ctc.edu. **Description:** A community college with an enrollment of approximately 8,000. Founded in 1965. **Positions advertised include:** Geography Instructor. **Number of employees at this location:** 850.

SHURGARD STORAGE CENTERS INC.
1155 Valley Street, Suite 400, Seattle WA 98109. 206/624-8100. **Fax:** 206/624-1645. **Contact:** Human Resources. **World Wide Web address:** http://www.shurgard.com. **Description:** Specializes in the self-storage industry. Shurgard Storage Centers Inc. is a self-administered, real estate investment trust. As one of the largest self-storage center operators in the United States, the company operates over 280 storage centers nationally and abroad. Shurgard owns approximately 60 percent of these centers. **Corporate headquarters location:** This location. **Listed on:** New York Stock Exchange. **Stock exchange symbol:** SHU.

SIEMENS BUSINESS SERVICES, INC.
4500 150th Avenue NE, Overlake North, Building A, Redmond WA 98052. 425/556-3800. **Contact:** Personnel. **World Wide Web address:** http://www.siemens.com. **Description:** Provides systems integration, help desk, and PC repair services to *Fortune* 1000 companies and federal clients. **Corporate headquarters location:** Norwalk CT. **Other U.S. locations:** Nationwide. **Listed on:** New York Stock Exchange. **Stock exchange symbol:** SI.

SIEMENS ULTRASOUND
P.O. Box 7002, Issaquah WA 98027-7002. 425/392-9180. **Physical address:** 22010 SE 51st Street, Issaquah WA 98029. **Contact:** Human Resources. **World Wide Web address:** http://www.siemensultrasound.com. **Description:** Develops and manufactures ultrasound systems. **Positions advertised include:** Technical Instructor. **Corporate headquarters location:** This location.

SIERRA, INC.
3060 139th Avenue SE, Suite 500, Bellevue WA 98005. 425/649-9800. **Fax:** 425/641-7617. **Contact:** Human Resources. **E-mail address:** recruit@sierra.com. **World Wide Web address:** http://www.sierra.com. **Description:** Develops and distributes entertainment and educational software. The company's products are designed for IBM compatible and Macintosh systems. Founded in 1979. **NOTE:** Jobseekers may apply for positions online. **Positions advertised include:** Game Designer; Associate Producer; Production Assistant. **Corporate headquarters location:** Oakhurst CA. **Other U.S. locations:** Nationwide. **International locations:** France; Germany. **Annual sales/revenues:** More than $100 million. **Number of employees at this location:** 450.

THE SIMPSON DOOR COMPANY
400 Simpson Avenue, McCleary WA 98557. 360/495-3291. **Fax:** 360/495-3295. **Contact:** Human Resources. **World Wide Web address:** http://www.simpsondoor.com. **Description:** Manufactures doors. Founded in 1912. **NOTE:** Unsolicited resumes/applications are not accepted. Employment opportunities are usually listed in the corresponding community's newspaper. **Corporate headquarters location:** This location.

SIMPSON INVESTMENT COMPANY
1301 fifth Avenue, Suite 2800, Seattle WA 98101-2613. 206/224-5000. **Contact:** Human Resources. **World Wide Web address:** http://www.simpson.com. **Description:** Produces and markets lumber, plywood, and wood chips for the lumber and paper industries. **NOTE:** Unsolicited resumes/applications are not accepted. Employment opportunities are usually listed in the corresponding community's newspaper. **Corporate headquarters location:** This location. **Subsidiaries include:** Simpson Timber Company; Simpson Paper Company; Simpson Tacoma Kraft Company. **Operations at this facility include:** Administration; Sales.

SIMPSON TACOMA KRAFT COMPANY
P.O. Box 2133, Tacoma WA 98401-2133. 253/572-2150. **Contact:** Human Resources. **Description:** Manufactures bleached and unbleached kraft pulp and liverboard. **NOTE:** Unsolicited resumes/applications are not accepted. Employment opportunities are usually listed in the corresponding community's newspaper.

SIMPSON RESOURCE COMPANY
P.O. Box 460, Shelton WA 98584. 360/426-3381. **Contact:** Human Resources. **World Wide Web address:** http://www.simpson.com. **Description:** Produces and markets lumber, plywood, and wood chips for the lumber and paper industries. **NOTE:** Unsolicited resumes/applications are not accepted. Employment opportunities are usually listed in the corresponding community's newspaper. **Corporate headquarters location:** Seattle WA. **Number of employees at this location:** 1,200.

SIRACH CAPITAL MANAGEMENT INC.
520 Pike Street, Suite 2800, Seattle WA 98101-1389. 206/624-3800. **Fax:** 206/626-5410. **Contact:** Personnel. **World Wide Web address:** http://www.sirachcap.com. **Description:** An investment advisory firm specializing in managing the assets of institutions and high-worth individuals. Services include mutual funds, 401(k) plan, investment, and trust fund management. **Number of employees at this location:** 45.

SIX STATES DISTRIBUTORS
3711 East Trent Avenue, Spokane WA 99202-4420. 509/535-7671. **Fax:** 509/535-9105. **Contact:** Rick Baird, Manager. **World Wide Web address:** http://www.sixstates.com. **Description:** Primarily engaged in the wholesaling of truck parts. The company also manufactures systems for trucks including transmissions and drive lines.

SKAGIT VALLEY COLLEGE
2405 East College Way, Mount Vernon WA 98273. 360/416-7748. **Fax:** 360/416-7878. **Recorded jobline:** 360/416-7800. **Contact:** Human Resources. **E-mail address:** employ@skagit.edu. **World Wide Web address:** http://www.skagit.edu. **Description:** A community college offering degrees in more than 20 disciplines.

SKAGIT VALLEY HOSPITAL
1415 East Kincaid, P.O. Box 1376, Mount Vernon WA 98273-1376. 360/428-8228. **Fax:** 360/428-2416. **Recorded jobline:** 360/416-8345. **Contact:** Human Resources. **World Wide Web address:** http://www.skagitvalleyhospital.org. **Description:** A nonprofit, regional health system offering a full line of medical services. **Positions advertised include:** Patient Services Secretary; Monitor Telemetry Technician; Unit Assistant; Imaging Manager; Certified Nursing Assistant; Registered Nurse. **Corporate headquarters location:** This location. **Operations at this facility include:** Administration. **Number of employees at this location:** 1,200.

SMITHS AEROSPACE
2720 West Washington Avenue, Yakima WA 98903. 509/248-5000. Fax: 509/452-7022. **Contact:** Cheryl Dale, Human Resources Director. **World Wide Web address:** http://www.smiths-aerospace.com. **Description:** Manufactures hydraulic and pneumatic valves used in military and commercial fixed-wing aircraft and helicopters, tanks, and the national aerospace program. **Positions advertised include:** Systems Engineer; Video/Graphics Engineer; Avionics Systems Engineer; Test Equipment Builder; Business Development Manager. **Operations at this facility include:** Administration; Manufacturing; Sales. **Number of employees worldwide:** 33,000.

SMURFIT-STONE CONTAINER CORPORATION
P.O. Box 479, Renton WA 98057. 877/772-2999. **Contact:** Human Resources Department. **World Wide Web address:** http://www.smurfit-stone.com. **Description:** Smurfit-Stone Container Corporation is one of the world's leading paper-based packaging companies. The company's main products include corrugated containers, folding cartons, and multiwall industrial bags. The company is also one of the world's largest collectors and processors of recycled products that are then sold to a worldwide customer base. Smurfit-Stone Container Corporation also operates several paper tube, market pulp, and newsprint production facilities. **Corporate headquarters location:** Chicago IL. **Other U.S. locations:** Nationwide. **Operations at this facility include:** This location manufactures folding cartons. **Listed on:** NASDAQ. **Stock exchange symbol:** SSCC.

SMURFIT-STONE CONTAINER CORPORATION
8030 South 194th Street, Kent WA 98032. 253/437-1038. **Contact:** Human Resources. **World Wide Web address:** http://www.smurfit-stone.com. **Description:** Smurfit-Stone Container Corporation is one of the world's leading paper-based packaging companies. The company's main products include corrugated containers, folding cartons, and multiwall industrial bags. The company is also one of the world's largest collectors and processors of recycled products that are then sold to a worldwide customer base. Smurfit-Stone Container Corporation also operates several paper tube, market pulp, and newsprint production facilities. **Corporate headquarters location:** Chicago IL. **Other U.S. locations:** Nationwide. **Operations at this facility include:** This location is a paper mill that produces containerboard. **Listed on:** NASDAQ. **Stock exchange symbol:** SSCC.

SNOKIST GROWERS
P.O. Box 1587, Yakima WA 98907-1587. 509/453-5631. **Physical address:** 18 West Mead Avenue, Yakima WA 98902. **Contact:** Personnel. **World Wide Web address:** http://www.snokist.com. **Description:** A processor of fruit including plums, apples, and cherries. **Number of employees at this location:** 400.

SOCIETY EXPEDITIONS, INC.
2001 Western Avenue, Suite 300, Seattle WA 98121. 206/728-9400. **Fax:** 206/728-2301. **Contact:** Human Resources Manager. **E-mail address:** employment@societyexpeditions.com. **World Wide Web address:** http://www.societyexpeditions.com. **Description:** An expedition cruise line offering service to Alaska, Antarctica, and the South Pacific. **Positions advertised include:** Expedition Leader; Staff Assistant; Lecturer. **International locations:** Bremen, Germany.

SOLUCIENT
411 108th Avenue NE, Suite 800, Bellevue WA 98004. 425/455-2652. **Toll-free phone:** 800/290-8982. **Fax:** 425/451-9736. **Contact:** Human Resources. **E-mail address:** becareers@solucient.com. **World Wide Web address:** http://www.solucient.com. **Description:** Provides data processing services and develops software for the health care industry. **Positions advertised include:** Quality Assurance Manager; Receptionist; Senior Program Manager; Senior Technical Writer. **Corporate headquarters location:** Evanston IL.

SOUND FORD INC.
750 Rainier Avenue South, Renton WA 98055. 425/235-1000. **Contact:** Human Resources. **World Wide Web address:** http://www.soundford.com. **Description:** An automotive dealership. **Positions advertised:** Sales; Management.

SOUTH KITSAP SCHOOL DISTRICT
1962 Hoover Avenue SE, Port Orchard WA 98366. 360/874-7075. **Fax:** 360/876-7076. **Contact:** Manager of Human Resources Department. **E-mail address:** skjobs@skitsap.wednet.edu. **World Wide Web address:** http://www.skitsap.wednet.edu. **Description:** Administrative offices of the South Kitsap area school district. **NOTE:** Employment applications can be downloaded from the website. **Positions advertised include:** Principal; Special Education Teacher; Nurse; Speech/Language Pathologist. **Number of employees at this location:** 1,100.

SOUTH PUGET SOUND COMMUNITY COLLEGE
2011 Mottman Road SW, Olympia WA 98512-6218. 360/754-7711. **Recorded jobline:** 360/754-7711 ext. 7. **Contact:** Human Resources. **World Wide Web address:** http://www.spscc.ctc.edu. **Description:** A two-year, community college with over 5,000 full- and part-time students enrolled.

SPACELABS MEDICAL, INC.
P.O. Box 7018, Issaquah WA 98027-7018. 425/657-7200. **Fax:** 425/657-7211. **Contact:** Human Resources Department. **E-mail address:** resumes@slmd.com. **World Wide Web address:** http://www.spacelabs.com. **Description:** Manufactures patient monitoring equipment, clinical information systems, ambulatory monitoring products, and monitoring supplies. **Positions advertised include:** Product Evaluation Specialist; CV Technologist. **Corporate headquarters location:** This location. **Other U.S. locations:** AZ; CA; CO; FL; NY; NC; OR. **Operations at this facility include:** Administration; Manufacturing; Research and Development. **Number of employees at this location:** 1,200. **Number of employees nationwide:** 1,700.

SPECTRUM CONTROLS, INC.
P.O. Box 5533, Bellevue WA 98006. 425/746-9481. **Physical address:** 2700 Richards Road, Suite 200, Bellevue WA 98005. **Fax:** 425/641-9473. **Contact:** Lynn Robbins, Personnel Manager. **World Wide Web address:** http://www.spectrumcontrols.com. **Description:** Designs and manufactures electronic industrial control products for the industrial automation market. Founded in 1983. **Company slogan:** We are a product leadership company. **Other U.S. locations:** GA; MI; TX. **President:** Bruce Wanta. **Annual sales/revenues:** $5 - $10 million. **Number of employees at this location:** 40.

THE SPOKESMAN REVIEW
COWLES PUBLISHING COMPANY
P.O. Box 2160, Spokane WA 99210. 509/459-5000. **Contact:** Human Resources. **World Wide Web address:** http://www.spokesmanreview.com. **Description:** Publishes the *Spokesman Review*, a daily newspaper with a circulation of approximately 98,000.

SQUARE D COMPANY
7525 SE 24th Street, Suite 320, Mercer Island WA 98040. 206/232-9702. **Contact:** Human Resources. **World Wide Web address:** http://www.squared.com. **Description:** A manufacturer of electrical distribution products for the construction industry. Products are used in commercial and residential construction, industrial facilities, and machinery and original equipment manufacturers' products. **Corporate headquarters location:** Palatine IL. **Other U.S. locations:** AZ; CA; KY; MO; NE; OH; SC; TN. **Parent company:** Groupe Schneider possesses global expertise in electrical contracting, industrial engineering, and construction. Groupe Schneider has five major operating companies: Jeumont-Schneider Industrie, Merlin Gerin, Spie Batignolles, Square D, and Telemecanique.

STANISLAW ASHBAUGH, LLP
4400 Bank of America Tower, 701 Fifth Avenue, Seattle WA 98104-7012. 206/386-5900. **Fax:** 206/344-7400. **Contact:** Francine Wright, Administrator. **World Wide Web address:** http://www.stanislaw.com. **Description:** A law firm specializing in business, construction, employment, and insurance law. **Number of employees at this location:** 40.

STARBUCKS COFFEE CORPORATION
P.O. Box 34067, Seattle WA 98124. 206/447-1575. **Physical address:** 2401 Utah Avenue South, Seattle WA 98134. **Fax:** 206/447-0828. **Recorded jobline:** 206/447-4123. **Contact:** Human Resources. **World Wide Web address:** http://www.starbucks.com. **Description:** Sells whole-bean coffees, along with hot coffees and Italian-style espresso beverages through more than 2,500 retail stores worldwide. The company purchases green coffee beans for its coffee varieties from coffee-producing regions throughout the world and custom roasts them. In addition to coffee beans and beverages, the company's stores offer a selection of coffee-making equipment, accessories, pastries, and confections. Also, the company sells whole-bean coffees through specialty sales groups, a national mail-order operation, and supermarkets. **Corporate headquarters location:** This location. **Other U.S. locations:** Nationwide. **International locations:** Worldwide. **Number of employees worldwide:** 37,000.

STERLING SAVINGS ASSOCIATION
111 North Wall Street, Spokane WA 99201. 509/458-2711. **Fax:** 509/358-6161. **Contact:** Human Resources. **World Wide Web address:** http://www.sterlingsavingsbank.com. **Description:** Provides full-service banking services including deposits and originating consumer, business banking, commercial real estate, and residential construction loans. The company operates 77 branches. **Subsidiaries include:** Action Mortgage Company operates residential loan production offices; Harbor Financial Services provides nonbank investments including mutual funds, variable annuities, and tax-deferred annuities to clients through regional representatives; INTERVEST-Mortgage Investment Company provides commercial real estate lending. **Number of employees nationwide:** 860.

STEVENS MEMORIAL HOSPITAL
21727 76th Avenue West, #102, Edmonds WA 98026. 425/640-4190. **Fax:** 425/640-4449. **Contact:** Human Resources Department. **World Wide Web address:** http://www.stevenshealthcare.org. **Description:** A 217-bed, acute care medical center offering a full range of health care services including emergency care, critical care, surgery, a birthing center, orthopedic care, comprehensive cancer care, mental health services, diagnostic imaging, and outpatient services. Founded in 1964.

STRAND HUNT CONSTRUCTION INC.
12015 115th Avenue NE, Kirkland WA 98034. 425/823-1954. **Fax:** 425/823-8635. **Contact:** Human Resources. **E-mail address:** hr@strandhunt.com. **World Wide Web address:** http://www.strandhunt.com. **Description:** Engaged in general contract construction.

THE SUMMIT AT SNOQUALMIE
P.O. Box 1068, 101 State Route 906, Snoqualmie Pass WA 98068. 425/434-7669. **Contact:** Manager of Human Resources Department. **World Wide Web address:** http://www.summitatsnoqualmie.com. **Description:** Operates four ski areas in the metropolitan Seattle area. This location also hires seasonally. **Corporate headquarters location:** This location. **Number of employees at this location:** 1,200.

SUN NEWSPAPER
P.O. Box 259, 545 Fifth Street, Bremerton WA 98337. 206/842-5696. **Contact:** Personnel. **World Wide Web address:** http://www.thesunlink.com. **Description:** Publishes an evening newspaper with a circulation of approximately 40,000. **Number of employees at this location:** 240.

SUNGARD
13513 NE 126th Place, Suite B, Kirkland WA 98034. 425/814-4000. **Fax:** 425/814-4001. **Contact:** Human Resources. **World Wide Web address:** http://www.sungard.com. **Description:** Develops schedule management software for electric utility companies. **Corporate headquarters location:** Wayne PA.

SUNSET MAGAZINE
500 Union Street, Suite 600, Seattle WA 98101. 206/682-3993. **Fax:** 650/324-5727. **Recorded jobline:** 650/324-5706. **Contact:** Personnel Department. **E-mail address:** jobs@sunset.com. **World Wide Web address:** http://www.sunsetmagazine.com. **Description:** Publishes the Pacific Northwest edition of *Sunset Magazine*, focusing on Western cooking, gardening, and travel. **NOTE:** Mail resumes to: 80 Willow Road, Menlo Park CA 94025. For current openings, call the job-line listed above. **Positions advertised include:** Style Editor; Photo Editor; Home Program Manager; Consumer Marketing Manager.

SUPERVALU INC.
1525 East D Street, Tacoma WA 98421. 253/404-4200. **Fax:** 253/404-4288. **Contact:** Human Resources Manager. **E-mail address:** super.careers@supervalu.com. **World Wide Web address:** http://www.supervalu.com. **Description:** SUPERVALU Inc. is one of the nation's largest food retailers and distribution companies, supplying grocery, health and beauty, and general merchandise products to over 6,100 customers. In the corporate retail sector, SUPERVALU operates over 1,100 stores under the Bigg's, Cub Foods, Shop'n Save, Save-A-Lot, Scott's Foods, Laneco, and Hornbachers names. **Special programs:** Internships. **Corporate headquarters location:** Eden Prairie MN. **Subsidiaries include:** Hazelwood Farms Bakeries manufactures frozen bakery products. **Operations at this facility include:** This location houses administrative offices. **Listed on:** New York Stock Exchange. **Stock exchange symbol:** SVU. **Number of employees at this location:** 935.

SWEDISH MEDICAL CENTER
747 Broadway, Seattle WA 98122. 206/386-2141. **Recorded jobline:** 206/386-2888. **Fax:** 206/386-2145. **Contact:** Human Resources. **World Wide Web address:** http://www.swedish.org. **Description:** An 860-bed, full-service, acute care medical center that also provides a wide range of specialty services. **Positions advertised include:** Administrative Assistant; Medical Records Clerk; Nurse Manager; Registered Nurse; Accountant; Revenue Analyst. **Number of employees at this location:** 4,000.

SYSCO FOOD SERVICES OF SEATTLE, INC.
P.O. Box 97054, Kent WA 98064. 206/622-2261. **Physical address:** 22820 54th Avenue South, Kent WA 98032. **Fax:** 206/721-1559. **Recorded jobline:** 206/721-5484. **Contact:** Human Resources. **E-mail address:** jobs@syscoseattle.com. **World Wide Web address:** http://www.syscoseattle.com. **Description:** Engaged in the wholesale distribution of food and related products and services to other businesses such as hotels and schools. **Positions advertised include:** Outside Sales Representative. **Corporate headquarters location:** Houston TX.

TTM TECHNOLOGIES
17550 Northeast 67th Court, Redmond WA 98052. 425/883-7575. **Fax:** 425/882-1268**Contact:** Human Resources. **World Wide Web address:** http://www.ttmtech.com. **Description:** Manufactures circuit boards and related electrical components. **Positions advertised include:** Mechanical Engineer. **Corporate headquarters location:** This location.

TACOMA, CITY OF
747 Market Street, Room 1336, Tacoma WA 98402-3764. 253/591-5400. **Recorded jobline:** 253/591-5795. **Contact:** Human Resources. **World Wide Web address:** http://www.cityoftacoma.org. **Description:** Government offices for the city of Tacoma. **Positions advertised include:** Convention Center Manager; Senior Financial Analyst; Water Control Plant Supervisor; Civil Engineer. **Special programs:** Internships. **Corporate headquarters location:** This location. **Number of employees nationwide:** 3,000.

TACOMA GOODWILL INDUSTRIES
REHABILITATION CENTER INC.
714 South 27th Street, Tacoma WA 98409. 253/272-5166. **Fax:** 253/428-4162. **Contact:** Human Resources. **E-mail address:** resumes@tacomagoodwill.org. **World Wide Web address:** http://www.tacomagoodwill.org. **Description:** Provides vocational rehabilitation programs. **Positions advertised include:** Loss Prevention Analyst; Custodian; Maintenance Worker. **Corporate headquarters location:** Bethesda MD. **Number of employees at this location:** 600.

TACOMA GUITARS
4615 East 192 2nd Street, Tacoma WA 98446. 253/847-6508. **Contact:** Human Resources. **World Wide Web address:** http://www.tacomaguitars.com. **Description:** Manufactures a line of guitars and related accessories.

TACOMA LUTHERAN HOME
1301 North Highlands Parkway, Tacoma WA 98406. 253/752-7112. **Contact:** Human Resources. **World Wide Web address:** http://www.tacomalutheran.com. **Description:** A retirement community providing skilled nursing, assisted living, and independent living services.

TACOMA NEWS, INC.
P.O. Box 11000, Tacoma WA 98411. 253/597-8575. **Contact:** Human Resources. **World Wide Web address:** http://www.tribnet.com. **Description:** Publishes a morning newspaper with a daily circulation of approximately 122,000 and a circulation of approximately 140,000 on Sunday.

TACOMA PUBLIC UTILITIES
747 Market Street, Room 1336, Tacoma WA 98402-3764. 253/591-5400. **Recorded jobline:** 253/591-5795. **Contact:** Human Resources. **World Wide Web address:** http://www.cityoftacoma.org. **Description:** Provides water and electricity services.

P.J. TAGGARES COMPANY
850 North Broadway, Othello WA 99344. 509/488-3356. **Contact:** Personnel. **Description:** A farmer-owned agribusiness firm. The farmers raise vegetables that are then sold to processing plants and grain distributors for local consumption.

TALLYGENICOM
8301 South 180th Street, Kent WA 98032. 425/251-5500. **Fax:** 425/251-5520. **Toll-free phone:** 800/843-1347. **Contact:** Personnel. **E-mail address:** hrd@tally.com. **World Wide Web address:** http://www.tallygenicom.com. **Description:** Manufactures laser, serial, and line matrix printers. **Office hours:** Monday - Friday, 7:45 a.m. - 4:15 p.m.

TARGETED GENETICS CORPORATION
1100 Olive Way, Suite 100, Seattle WA 98101. 206/623-7612. **Fax:** 206/521-4782. **Recorded jobline:** 206/521-7300. **Contact:** Human Resources. **E-mail address:** careers@targen.com. **World Wide Web address:** http://www.targen.com. **Description:** Develops gene therapy products for the treatment of certain acquired and inherited diseases. The principal focus is on three product development programs that address high-risk diseases for which there are no known cures: cytoxic T lymphocyte, (CTL)-based, immunotherapy for infectious diseases and cancer; in vivo adeno-associated virus, (AAV)-based, therapy for cystic fibrosis and other diseases; and stem cell therapy. The company approaches gene therapy through multiple delivery systems including retroviral vector delivery, AAV vector delivery, and nonviral vector delivery. **Positions advertised include:** Quality Assurance Associate. **Special programs:** Internships. **Corporate headquarters location:** This location. **Operations at this facility include:** Research and Development. **Annual sales/revenues:** Less than $5 million. **Listed on:** NASDAQ. **Stock exchange symbol:** TGEN. **Number of employees at this location:** 80.

TELDON CALENDARS
P.O. Box 653, Blaine WA 98230. 360/945-1211. **Toll-free phone:** 800/755 1211. **Contact:** Human Resources Department. **E-mail address:** jobs@teldon.com. **World Wide Web address:** http://www.teldon.com. **Description:** Publishes promotional calendars. **Parent company:** Teldon International Inc. manufactures promotional products, and prints logos on a variety of items including mugs, pens, and towels.

TELECT, INC.
2111 North Molter Road, Liberty Lake WA 99019. 509/926-6000. **Fax:** 509/927-0852. **Contact:** Human Resources. **World Wide Web address:** http://www.telect.com. **Description:** An international designer and manufacturer of fiber-optic, digital, analog, professional audio/video, power, and electronic monitoring and control equipment. Founded in 1982. **Positions advertised include:** Mechanical Engineer. **Special programs:** Internships; Training. **Corporate headquarters location:** This location. **International locations:** Guadalajara, Mexico. **Annual sales/revenues:** More than $100 million. **Number of employees at this location:** 900. **Number of employees nationwide:** 950. **Number of employees worldwide:** 1,150.

TELTONE CORPORATION
P.O. Box 945, Bothell WA 98041. 425/487-1515. **Physical Address:** 22522 29th Drive SE, Suite 201, Canyon Business Park, Bothell WA 98021. **Fax:** 425/402-7222. **Contact:** Human Resources. **E-mail address:** hr@teltone.com. **World Wide Web address:** http://www.teltone.com. **Description:** Manufactures telecommunications equipment including testing equipment for the communications industry and telecommuting products. **Special programs:** Internships. **NOTE:** Applications can be directed by mail to Human Resources at P.O. Box 945 Bothell WA 98041-0945. Unsolicited applications are not accepted. **Corporate headquarters location:** This location. **Operations at this facility include:** Administration; Manufacturing; Research and Development; Sales; Service. **Number of employees at this location:** 75.

TEMPO TEXTRON
11001 31st Place West, Everett WA 98204. 425/355-0590. **Contact:** Personnel Department. **World Wide Web address:** http://www.tempo.textron.com. **Description:** Manufactures high-technology support equipment, digital test equipment, and related products. **Parent company:** Greenlee Textron. **Operations at this facility include:** Administration; Manufacturing; Research and Development; Sales; Service.

TESORO PETROLEUM
P.O. Box 700, Anacortes WA 98221. 360/293-9119. **Contact:** Personnel Director. **World Wide Web address:** http://www.tesoropetroleum.com. **Description:** A refinery engaged in the production of automobile and airplane fuels, kerosene, and diesel products. **Corporate headquarters location:** San Antonio TX.

THRIFTWAY STORES INC.
400 NW 56th Street, Seattle WA 98107. 206/783-7922. **Fax:** 206/315-4410. **Contact:** Personnel. **World Wide Web address:** http://www.thriftway.com. **Description:** Operates a retail grocery chain with over 100 outlets. **Corporate headquarters location:** This location.

TIME OIL COMPANY
P.O. 24447, Seattle WA 98124-0447. 206/285-2400. **Physical address:** 2737 West Commodore Way, Seattle WA 98199. **Fax:** 206/286-6453. **Contact:** Elynor Lemon. Human Resources. **E-mail address:** hr@timeoil.com. **World Wide Web address:** http://www.timeoil.com. **Description:** Operates retail gasoline service stations, wholesales petroleum products, and retails fuel oil heaters.

TIME-LIFE LIBRARIES
1100 Olive Way, Suite 320, Seattle WA 98010. 206/748-0626. **Contact:** Human Resources. **Description:** Time-Life Libraries is a book publisher. **Operations at this facility include:** This location is a telemarketing office. **Parent company:** Time-Life.

TODD PACIFIC SHIPYARDS CORPORATION
P.O. Box 3806, Seattle WA 98124. 206/623-1635. **Physical address:** 1806 16th Avenue SW, Seattle WA 98134. **Fax:** 206/442-8505. **Contact:** Personnel. **E-mail address:** jobs@toddpacific.com. **World Wide Web address:** http://www.toddpacific.com. **Description:** Engaged in the construction, maintenance, and repair of commercial ships, both domestic and foreign, and of ships for the U.S. Navy and other government agencies. **Positions advertised include:** Project Manager; Senior Financial Analyst; CVN Zone Manager.

TONE COMMANDER SYSTEMS INC.
11609 49th Place West, Mukilteo WA 982754255. 425/349-1000. **Fax:** 425/349-1010. **Contact:** Personnel. **World Wide Web address:** http://www.tonecommander.com. **Description:** Manufactures telecommunications equipment including Centrex attendant consoles and ISDN equipment. **Corporate headquarters location:** This location. **Annual sales/revenues:** $5 - $10 million. **Number of employees at this location:** 40.

TRANSNATION TITLE INSURANCE COMPANY
1206 Sixth Avenue, Suite 100, Seattle WA 98101. 206/628-3540. **Contact:** Louise Condon, Personnel Administrator. **World Wide Web address:** http://www.ttic-nw.com. **Description:** One of the nation's leading providers of title insurance. **Office hours:** Monday - Friday, 8:00 a.m. - 5:00 p.m.

TREE TOP, INC.
P.O. Box 248, Selah WA 98942. 509/697-7251. **Contact:** Personnel Department. **E-mail address:** jobs@treetop.com. **World Wide Web address:** http://www.treetop.com. **Description:** An agricultural cooperative owned by 2,500 apple and pear growers in Washington, Oregon, and Idaho. The cooperative was formed to process and market its members' processor-grade fruit. Tree Top also produces and sells an array of dried, frozen, and concentrated fruit products in bulk as ingredients used in the food industry. Founded in 1960. **Number of employees nationwide:** 1,000.

TRI NORTH DEPARTMENT STORES
5700 Sixth Avenue South, Suite 214, Seattle WA 98108-2511. 206/767-7600. **Contact:** Human Resources. **Description:** Owns and operates a chain of retail clothing department stores located primarily throughout the Pacific Northwest. **Corporate headquarters location:** This location.

TRIPATH IMAGING, INC.
8271 154th Avenue NE, Redmond WA 98052. 425/869-7284. **Toll-free phone:** 800/636-7284. **Fax:** 425/869-5325. **Contact:** Human Resources. **World Wide Web address:** http://www.tripathimaging.com. **Description:** Engaged in the research and development of technologies to automate the interpretation of medical images. The company's initial products are automated screening systems that are used to analyze and classify Pap smears. These screening systems use high-speed video microscopes, image interpretation software, and field-of-view computers to recognize, analyze, and classify individual cells within the complex images on a Pap smear. These products include the AutoPap QC and the AutoPap Screener. **Corporate headquarters location:** Burlington NC. **Number of employees at this location:** 100.

TRI-CITY HERALD
P.O. Box 2608, Tri-Cities WA 99302. 509/582-1476. **Contact:** Kelly Janicek, Human Resources Manager. **World Wide Web address:** http://www.tri-cityherald.com. **Description:** Publishes a daily newspaper with a circulation of over 40,000. **Special programs:** Internships. **Corporate headquarters location:** Sacramento CA. **Parent company:** McClatchey Newspapers Group.

URM STORES, INC.
P.O. Box 3365, Spokane WA 99220. 509/467-2620. **Contact:** Personnel Department. **World Wide Web address:** http://www.urmstores.com. **Description:** A grocery and general merchandise business. **Number of employees nationwide:** 2,000.

URS CORPORATION
Century Square, 1501 Fourth Avenue, Suite 1440, Seattle WA 98101-1616. 206/438-2700. **Contact:** Human Resources. **World Wide Web address:** http://www.urscorp.com. **Description:** An architectural, engineering, and environmental consulting firm that specializes in air transportation, environmental solutions, surface transportation, and industrial environmental and engineering concerns. **Positions advertised include:** Civil Geotechnical Engineer; Electrical Senior Designer; Environmental Technician; Graduate Civil Engineer; Graduate Geologist; Marketing Services Manager; Mechanical Engineer; Principal Environmental Scientist; Project Toxicologist; CADD Designer; Senior Estimator.

US AIRWAYS, INC.
Seattle-Tacoma International Airport, Seattle WA 98158. 206/433-7858. **Contact:** Manager. **World Wide Web address:** http://www.usairways.com. **Description:** US Airways offers service to 155 cities in the United States, Canada, the Bahamas, Bermuda, Puerto Rico, the Virgin Islands, France, and Germany. The company's primary hubs are located in Charlotte, Pittsburgh, Baltimore/Washington, and Philadelphia. **Corporate headquarters location:** Arlington VA. **Parent company:** United Airlines, Inc.

U.S. ARMY CIVILIAN RECRUITING OFFICE
P.O. Box 3957, Seattle WA 98124-3957. 206/764-3592. **Physical address:** 4735 East Marginal Way South, Seattle 98134-2329. **Contact:** Human Resources. **Description:** Recruits civilians as support staff for the Eighth U.S. Army. **Number of employees worldwide:** 3,200.

U.S. ARMY CORPS OF ENGINEERS
201 North Third Street, Walla Walla WA 99362-9265. 509/527-7027. **Contact:** Recruitment/Placement. **World Wide Web address:** http://www.nww.usace.army.mil. **Description:** A federal government agency engaged in water resource engineering.

U.S. BANK OF WASHINGTON
1420 Fifth Avenue, Seattle WA 98101. 206/344-3619. **Contact:** Human Resources. **World Wide Web address:** http://www.usbank.com. **Description:** A commercial and consumer banking institution. U.S. Bank provides a full range of commercial real estate products and services, cash management services and consultation, and merchant services and sales. The Homepartners family of mortgage loan products provides down payment assistance, flexible underwriting and repayment terms, and homebuyer education for first-time and low- to moderate-income buyers. **Corporate headquarters location:** Portland OR. **Parent company:** U.S. Bancorp. **Number of employees nationwide:** 3,500.

U.S. DEPARTMENT OF VETERANS AFFAIRS
VA PUGET SOUND HEALTHCARE SYSTEM
1660 South Columbian Way, Seattle WA 98108. 206/764-2135. **Contact:** Human Resources. **World Wide Web address:** http://www.puget-sound.med.va.gov. **Description:** A 488-bed, critical care hospital affiliated with the University of Washington Medical School. The VA health care system includes 171 medical centers; more than 364 outpatient, community, and outreach clinics; 130 nursing home care units; and 37 domiciliary residences nationwide. **NOTE:** Employment forms may be downloaded from website. **Office hours:** Monday - Friday, 8:00 a.m. - 4:30 p.m. **Parent company:** U.S. Department of Veterans Affairs. **Number of employees at this location:** 1,800.

U.S. DEPARTMENT OF VETERANS AFFAIRS
JONATHAN M. WAINWRIGHT MEMORIAL VA MEDICAL CENTER
77 Wainwright Drive, Walla Walla WA 99362. 509/525-5200. Fax: 509/527-3452. **Contact:** Human Resources. **Description:** A 66-bed facility providing traditional primary and secondary care plus psychiatry and substance abuse residential rehabilitation and CWT programs.

U.S. ENVIRONMENTAL PROTECTION AGENCY (EPA)
1200 Sixth Avenue, OMP-077, Seattle WA 98101. 206/553-4973. **Contact:** Human Resources. **World Wide Web address:** http://www.epa.gov. **Description:** The EPA is dedicated to improving and preserving the quality of the environment, both nationally and globally, and protecting human health and the productivity of natural resources. The agency is committed to ensuring that federal environmental laws are implemented and enforced effectively; U.S. policy, both foreign and domestic, encourages the integration of economic development and environmental protection so that economic growth can be sustained over the long term; and public and private decisions affecting energy, transportation, agriculture, industry, international trade, and natural resources fully integrate considerations of environmental quality. Founded in 1970. **Special programs:** Internships. **Corporate headquarters location:** Washington DC. **Other U.S. locations:** San Francisco CA; Denver CO; Atlanta GA; Chicago IL; Kansas City KS; Boston MA; New York NY; Philadelphia PA; Dallas TX. **Number of employees nationwide:** 19,000.

U.S. MARINE
BAYLINER MARINE CORPORATION
P.O. Box 9029, Everett WA 98206. 360/435-5571. **Fax:** 360/403-4249. **Contact:** Human Resources. **World Wide Web address:** http://www.baylinerboats.com. **Description:** Builds pleasure boats. **Corporate headquarters location:** Arlington WA. **Other U.S. locations:** Nationwide. **Parent company:** Brunswick Corporation. **Operations at this facility include:** Divisional Headquarters. **Number of employees at this location:** 900. **Number of employees nationwide:** 3,600.

U.S. NATURAL RESOURCES
P.O. Box 310, Woodland WA 98674. 360/225-8267. **Fax:** 360/383-7659. **Contact:** Human Resources. **Description:** Manufactures sawmill machinery. **Corporate headquarters location:** This location.

U.S. OIL & REFINING COMPANY
P.O. Box 2255, Tacoma WA 98401. 253/383-1651. **Physical address:** 3001 Marshall Avenue, Tacoma WA 98421. **Fax:** 253/383-9970. **Contact:** Marcia E. Nielsen, Administration Services Manager. **E-mail address:** men@usor.com. **World Wide Web address:** http://www.usor.com. **Description:** A petroleum refinery. **Special programs:** Summer Jobs. **Number of employees at this location:** 155.

UNIGARD INSURANCE COMPANY
15805 NE 24th Street, Bellevue WA 98008-2409. 425/644-5236. **Fax:** 425/671-0109. **Contact:** Personnel. **World Wide Web address:** http://www.unigard.com. **Description:** An insurance company specializing in property and casualty insurance. **Positions advertised include:** Administrative Services Representative; Agency Relations Manager. **Other U.S. locations:** AZ; CA; ID; NY; NC; UT. **Parent company:** Winterthur Group. **Number of employees at this location:** 500. **Number of employees nationwide:** 630.

UNIONBAY SPORTSWEAR
P.O. Box 58710, Seattle WA 98138. 206/282-8889. **Fax:** 206/298-2146. **Contact:** Human Resources. **World Wide Web address:** http://www.unionbay.com. **Description:** Manufactures a line of sportswear geared toward young men and women. **Positions advertised include:** Designer; Financial Analyst; National Sales Manager; Sales Planner; Sales Representative Girls. **Office hours:** Monday - Friday, 7:30 a.m. - 5:30 p.m. **Corporate headquarters location:** Kent WA.

UNISEA
P.O. Box 97019, Redmond WA 98073. 425/881-8181. **Physical address:** 15400 NE 90th Street, Redmond WA 98053. **Fax:** 425/861-5276. **Contact:** Human Resources. **World Wide Web address:** http://www.unisea.com. **Description:** Processes seafood and related products. **Subsidiaries include:** Dutch Harbor Seafoods, Ltd. (also at this location) manufactures seafood products for sale at retail grocery stores.

UNITED DATA
15305 NE 95th Street, Redmond WA 98052. 425/881-7000. **Fax:** 425/8853282. **Contact:** Personnel Administrator. **World Wide Web address:** http://www.proctorinc.com. **Description:** Manufactures electronic equipment for the telephone industry including range extenders, test equipment, and security equipment. The company is also a leading developer of 9-1-1 backup systems. Founded in 1957. **Parent company:** Proctor.

UNITED SAVINGS AND LOAN BANK
601 South Jackson Street, Seattle WA 98104. 206/624-7581. **Fax:** 206/624-2326. **Contact:** Personnel Department. **Description:** A full-service bank. **Corporate headquarters location:** This location. **Operations at this facility include:** Administration; Service. **Number of employees at this location:** 50.

UNIVAR USA
8201 South 212th Street, Kent WA 98032. 425/656-8380. **Fax:** 425/889-3671. **Contact:** Human Resources. **World Wide Web address:** http://www.univarusa.com. **Description:** Manufactures and wholesales chemical pesticides and industrial chemicals. **Positions advertised include:** Administrative Assistant; Sales Engineer.

UNIVERSAL SODEXHO
1113 A Street, Tacoma WA 98402. 253/383-9200. **Contact:** Personnel Department. **World Wide Web address:** http://www.universalsodexho.com. **Description:** A catering service specializing in providing services to remote locations.

UNIVERSITY OF PUGET SOUND
1500 North Warner Street, Tacoma WA 98416. 253/879-3100. **Recorded jobline:** 253/879-3368. **Contact:** Human Resources Department. **World Wide Web address:** http://www.ups.edu. **Description:** A four-year, liberal arts college.

UNIVERSITY SWAGING CORPORATION
840 NW 45th Street, Seattle WA 98107. 206/784-8000. **Fax:** 206/784-8004. **Contact:** Human Resources Department. **World Wide Web address:** http://www.universityswaging.com. **Description:** Manufactures aerospace and marine parts by performing a highly specialized cold metal forming process for fitting various types of metal fittings to multistrand cable. University Swaging Corporation is one of the few companies worldwide to utilize the swaging process to make a variety of aerospace parts from aluminum tubing for applications where minimal weight and maximum strength are a necessity, such as for braces and for moving parts. **Annual sales/revenues:** $11 - $20 million. **Number of employees at this location:** 60.

UNIVERSITY OF WASHINGTON
4945 Brooklyn Avenue NE, Seattle WA 98195. 206/543-2354. **Fax:** 206/685-0636. **Contact:** Lisa Anderson, HR Employment Specialist. **E-mail address:** lindaa@u.washington.edu. **World Wide Web address:** http://www.washington.edu. **Description:** The oldest public university on the west coast, offering 140 majors, 90 minors, and numerous graduate programs.

UTILX CORPORATION
P.O. Box 97009, Kent WA 98064-9709. 253/395-0200. **Fax:** 253/395-1040. **Contact:** Personnel. **E-mail address:** jobs@utilx.com. **World Wide Web address:** http://www.utilx.com. **Description:** Provides installation and maintenance services for underground utilities including electricity, water, gas, and telephone. UTILX's technologies include the FlowMole guided drilling system and the CableCure service for injecting silicon fluids into utility cables to repair damage from water. The company's services are marketed domestically while their products are sold primarily in international markets. **Corporate headquarters location:** This location. **Subsidiaries include:** Flow Mole Limited (UK). **Number of employees at this location:** 100. **Number of employees nationwide:** 500.

VAAGEN BROTHERS LUMBER INC.
565 West Fifth Street, Colville WA 99114. 509/684-5071. **Fax:** 509/684-2168. **Contact:** Personnel. **World Wide Web address:** http://www.vaagenbros.com. **Description:** A lumber producer. **Number of employees at this location:** 480.

VALIN NORTHWEST
1850 130th Avenue NE, Suite 1, Bellevue WA 98005-2244. 425/885-0372. **Fax:** 425/885-5579. **Contact:** Human Resources. **E-mail address:** resumes@valin.com. **World Wide Web address:** http://www.valinonline.com. **Description:** A supplier of fluid handling, measurement and control products for a wide range of industrial process applications. **Corporate headquarters location:** Sunnyvale CA.

VANTEON CORPORATION
8700 148th Avenue NE, Redmond WA 98052. 425/250-0000. **Contact:** Ruth Lobe, Recruiter. **E-mail address:** resume@vanteon.com. **World Wide Web address:** http://www.vanteon.com. **Description:** Custom designs software solutions for clients engaged in e-commerce services. **NOTE:** E-mail resume. **Corporate headquarters location:** Pittsford NY.

VENTURI TECHNOLOGY PARTNERS
11255 Kirkland Way, Kirkland WA 98033. 425/202-8135. **Contact:** Human Resources Department. **World Wide Web address:** http://www.venturipartners.com. **Description:** Offers software consulting services. Venturi Technology Partners provides businesses with support for mainframes, personal computers, systems configurations, information systems, and software testing.

VERISIGN
P.O. Box 2909, Olympia WA 98501. 360/493-6000. **Physical address:** 4501 Intelco Loop SE, Olympia WA 98507. **Contact:** Human Resources. **E-mail address:** jobs@verisign.com. **World Wide Web address:** http://www.verisign.com. **Description:** Provides web presence services, security services, payment services, and telecommunications services. **Corporate headquarters location:** Mountain View CA. **Listed on:** NASDAQ. **Stock exchange symbol:** VRSN.

VERIZON COMMUNICATIONS
1800 41st Street, Everett WA 98201. 425/261-5321. **Fax:** 425/258-5901. **Contact:** Human Resources. **World Wide Web address:** http://www.verizon.com. **Description:** Provides a wide variety of communications services ranging from local telephone services for the home and office to highly complex voice and data services for governments and commercial industries. **Other U.S. locations:** Nationwide.

THE VICTORY STUDIOS
2247 15th Avenue West, Seattle WA 98119. 206/282-1776. **Toll-free phone:** 888/282-1776. **Fax:** 206/282-3535. **Contact:** Human Resources. **World Wide Web address:** http://www.victorystudios.com. **Description:** Provides video duplication, audio and editing services, and computer graphics services. **Corporate headquarters location:** This location. **Other U.S. locations:** North Hollywood CA. **Operations at this facility include:** Administration. **Annual sales/revenues:** $5 - $10 million. **Number of employees at this location:** 50. **Number of employees nationwide:** 75.

VISITING NURSE PERSONAL SERVICES
600 Birchwood Avenue, Suite 100, Bellingham WA 98225. 360/734-9662. **Contact:** Human Resources. **World Wide Web address:** http://www.vnaa.org. **Description:** Provides home health care and hospice services.

VYKOR, INC.
200 Mill Avenue South, Suite 100, Renton WA 98055. 425/264-2601. **Fax:** 425/264-2600. **Contact:** Human Resources. **E-mail address:** jobs@vykor.com. **World Wide Web address:** http://www.vykor.com. **Description:** Provides engineered parts management sourcing solutions to industrial manufacturing companies. **Positions advertised include:** Senior Test Engineer. **Corporate headquarters location:** This location. **CEO:** Rob Eleveld.

THE WACKENHUT CORPORATION
1035 Andover Park West, Suite 210, Tukwila WA 98188. 253/872-1555. **Fax:** 253/395-8099. **Contact:** Human Resources. **World Wide Web address:** http://www.wackenhut.com. **Description:** Provides physical security services, correction services, and related products to businesses, governments, and individuals from more than 150 offices worldwide. Specific services include security guard services; corrections staffing; private investigative services; the assembly and sale of electronic security equipment and systems; the training of security guards and fire and crash rescue personnel; providing fire protection and emergency ambulance service to municipalities; security consulting; planning, designing, and implementing integrated security systems; and providing specialized services to the nuclear power industry. **Corporate headquarters location:** Palm Beach Gardens FL. **Other U.S. locations:** Nationwide. **Number of employees nationwide:** 40,000.

WACOM TECHNOLOGY COMPANY
1311 SE Cardinal Court, Vancouver WA 98683. 360/896-9833. **Fax:** 360/896-9724. **Contact:** Human Resources. **World Wide Web address:** http://www.wacom.com. **Description:** Manufactures image-enhancing software, animation software, and graphic digitizing equipment.

WAGSTAFF INC.
3910 North Flora Road, Spokane WA 99216. 509/922-1404. **Contact:** Human Resources. **World Wide Web address:** http://www.wagstaff.com. **Description:** Manufactures casting equipment for the aluminum industry. **Positions advertised include:** Research Engineer; Automation Specialist; Customer Service Representative. **Corporate headquarters location:** This location.

WARDS COVE PACKING COMPANY INC.
88 East Hamlin Street, Seattle WA 98102. 206/323-3200. **Fax:** 206/323-9165. **Recorded jobline:** 206/325-4621. **Contact:** Personnel Department. **Description:** Operates seasonal salmon canneries in Alaska. Founded in 1912. **Corporate headquarters location:** This location. **Other U.S. locations:** AK. **Parent company:** Wards Cove Packing. **Number of employees at this location:** 150. **Number of employees nationwide:** 7,000.

WASHINGTON FEDERAL SAVINGS & LOAN ASSOCIATION
425 Pike Street, Seattle WA 98101. 206/624-7930. **Fax:** 206/624-2334. **Contact:** Human Resources. **World Wide Web address:** http://www.washingtonfederal.com. **Description:** Offers a full range of banking services through 85 branch offices. Subsidiaries of the company are also involved in real estate development and insurance brokerage operations. **NOTE:** A Human Resources Coordinator can be reached at 206/777-8247. **Positions advertised include:** Customer Service Representative; Loan Coordinator. **Corporate headquarters location:** This location. **Other U.S. locations:** AZ; ID; OR; UT. **Listed on:** NASDAQ. **Stock exchange symbol:** WFSL.

WASHINGTON MUTUAL SAVINGS BANK
P.O. Box 834, SAS0108, Seattle WA 98101. 206/461-6400. **Contact:** Human Resources. **World Wide Web address:** http://www.wamu.com. **Description:** One of the largest independently owned and locally managed banks in Washington state. Washington Mutual offers a wide array of financial products and services through the bank and its affiliates including deposit accounts, loans, annuities, mutual funds, full-service securities brokerage, and travel services. **Positions advertised include:** Technology Analyst; Integration Engineer; Technical Project Manager. **Special programs:** Internships. **Corporate headquarters location:** This location. **Other U.S. locations:** CA; FL; ID; MT; OR; TX; UT. **Subsidiaries include:** Composite Research & Management Company; Murphey Favre; Mutual Travel; WM Insurance Services; WM Life Insurance. **Listed on:** American Stock Exchange; NASDAQ; New York Stock Exchange. **Annual sales/revenues:** More than $100 million.

WASHINGTON STATE APPLE COMMISSION
P.O. Box 18, Wenatchee WA 98807. 509/663-9600. **Fax:** 509/662-5824. **Contact:** Personnel. **World Wide Web address:** http://www.bestapples.com. **Description:** A commission engaged in the promotion of Washington's apple industry.

WASHINGTON STATE DEPARTMENT OF REVENUE
2409 Pacific Avenue NE, P.O. Box 47463, Olympia WA 98504-7463. 360/570-6183. **Contact:** Human Resources Manager. **World Wide Web address:** http://dor.wa.gov. **Description:** Administers state tax laws; acts as revenue advisor to the Governor, the Legislature, and other state and local agencies; and oversees the administration of property tax laws. **Positions advertised include:** Tax Policy Specialist; Excise Tax Examiner; IT Recruiter. **Number of employees at this location:** 500.

WASHINGTON, STATE OF
DEPARTMENT OF PERSONNEL
521 Capital Way South, P.O. Box 47500, Olympia WA 98504-7500. 360/664-1960. **Recorded jobline:** 360/664-6226. **Contact:** Personnel. **World Wide Web address:** http://hr.dop.wa.gov. **Description:** Engaged in the recruitment and examination of candidates for the purpose of establishing a register of qualified personnel for all state agencies and all job classifications. TDD: 360/664-0389. **NOTE:** This department does not accept unsolicited resumes. Please only respond to advertised openings. **Special programs:** Internships; Summer Jobs. **Internship information:** Both resident and nonresident students are eligible to apply for state internships. Undergraduate internships are offered to students who have completed one full term or semester of undergraduate work and are currently enrolled in an undergraduate program. Application materials should be submitted to the recruiting agency and contact person noted on the job bulletin. Executive fellowships, lasting either one or two years, are offered to students who have completed one academic year of graduate school, and who are pursuing a graduate degree. Students must be currently enrolled to be eligible. Permanent Washington State employees are eligible for fellowships regardless of academic status, though a recommendation letter from the appropriate agency director is required. Please contact the Department of Personnel for more information. **Office hours:** Monday - Friday, 8:00 a.m. - 5:00 p.m. **Corporate headquarters location:** This location.

WASHINGTON STATE UNIVERSITY
P.O. Box 641014, Pullman WA 99164-1014. 509/335-4521. **Fax:** 509/335-1259. **Recorded jobline:** 509/335-7637. **Contact:** Human Resources. **E-mail address:** hrs@wsu.edu. **World Wide Web address:** http://www.wsu.edu. **Description:** A state university. Approximately 15,000 undergraduate and 2,000 graduate students are enrolled in almost 100 programs of study. **Special programs:** Summer Jobs. **Office hours:** Monday - Friday, 8:00 a.m. - 5:00 p.m. **President:** V. Lane Rawlins, President.

WEATHERVANE WINDOW COMPANY
P.O. Box 2424, Kirkland WA 98083. 425/827-9669. **Toll-free phone:** 800/634-3433. **Fax:** 425/822-9797. **Contact:** Human Resources. **World Wide Web address:** http://www.weathervanewindows.com. **Description:** Manufactures wood, aluminum-clad wood, and vinyl windows.

WEB PRESS CORPORATION
22023 68th Avenue South, Kent WA 98032. 253/395-3343. **Fax:** 253/395-4492. **Contact:** Human Resources. **World Wide Web address:** http://www.webpresscorp.com. **Description:** Manufactures and sells rotary offset, web-fed printing presses. These products are designed for use in printing newspapers, advertising inserts, paperback books, and similar products. **Corporate headquarters location:** This location. **Number of employees at this location:** 50.

WELLS, ST. JOHN, ROBERTS, GREGORY & MATKIN P.S.
601 West First Avenue, Suite 1300, Spokane WA 99201. 509/624-4276. **Contact:** Recruitment. **World Wide Web address:** http://www.wellsstjohn.com. **Description:** A law firm specializing in copyrights, patents, and trademarks.

THE WEST SEATTLE HELPLINE
4517 California Avenue SW, Suite A, P.O. Box 16738, Seattle WA 98116. 206/932-4357. **Fax:** 206/933-8174. **Contact:** Human Resources. **World Wide Web address:** http://www.seattlewesthelpline.org. **Description:** Provides financial assistance to families facing homelessness. The West Seattle Helpline also works closely with other community organizations to provide clothing and food for these families.

WESTCOAST VANCE HOTEL
620 Stewart Street, Seattle WA 98101. 206/441-4200. **Fax:** 206/441-8612. **Contact:** Human Resources. **World Wide Web address:** http://www.westcoasthotels.com. **Description:** A 165-room, boutique style, luxury hotel featuring the Yakima Grill Restaurant. **Parent company:** Westcoast Hotels.

WESTERN NATIONAL INSURANCE GROUP
9706 4th Avenue NE, Suite 200, Seattle WA 98115. 206/526-5900. **Toll-free phone:** 800492-9020. **Contact:** Personnel. **World Wide Web address:** http://www.wnins.com. **Description:** An insurance brokerage company.

WESTERN RECREATIONAL VEHICLE, INC.
P.O. Box 9547, Yakima WA 98909-0547. 509/457-4133. **Fax:** 509/457-8184. **Contact:** Human Resources. **World Wide Web address:** http://www.wrv.com. **Description:** Manufactures a variety of recreational vehicles including travel trailers and campers.

WESTERN WASHINGTON UNIVERSITY
Mail Stop 5221, Bellingham WA 98225. 360/650-3774. **Fax:** 360/650-2810. **Contact:** Human Resources. **World Wide Web address:** http://www.wwu.edu. **Description:** A four-year university.

WESTFARM FOODS
P.O. Box 79007, Seattle WA 98119. 206/284-7220. **Toll-free phone:** 800/333-MILK. **Fax:** 206/216-2871. **Contact:** Human Resources. **E-mail address:** jobs@westfarm.com. **World Wide Web address:** http://www.westfarm.com. **Description:** Manufactures, sells, and distributes dairy products. WestFarm Foods is divided into two groups: Consumer Products and Manufactured Products. The Consumer Products division produces and markets dairy-based products for the wholesale, retail market, and foodservice markets. The Manufactured Products division produces butter, whey powder, cheeses, and dry milk powder in bulk quantities and then markets its products to institutions, food brokers, and food processing companies. **Positions advertised include:** Administrative Assistant; Director of Bulk Milk Sales; Director of Communications; Creative Services Manager. **Corporate headquarters location:** This location. **Other area locations:** Chehalis WA; Issaquah WA; Lynden WA; Spokane WA; Sunnyside WA; Yakima WA. **Other U.S. locations:** Los Angeles CA; San Jose CA; Boise ID; Caldwell ID; Eugene OR; Medford OR; Portland OR. **Number of employees at this location:** 660. **Number of employees nationwide:** 1,800.

WHITE RUNKLE ASSOCIATES
518 West Riverside, Spokane WA 99201. 509/747-6767. **Fax:** 509/747-9211. **Contact:** Human Resources. **World Wide Web address:** http://www.whiterunkle.com. **Description:** A full-service advertising, marketing, and public relations firm serving clients throughout the Northwest. Founded in 1980. **Special programs:** Internships. **Corporate headquarters location:** This location. **Number of employees at this location:** 20.

WHITMAN COLLEGE
345 Boyer Avenue, Walla Walla WA 99362. 509/527-5172. **Fax:** 509/527-5859. **Contact:** Personnel Director. **E-mail address:** luckstd@whitman.edu. **World Wide Web address:** http://www.whitman.edu. **Description:** A four-year, liberal arts college with an enrollment of approximately 1,300. Founded in 1859. **Positions advertised include:** Director of Admission; Director of Foundation & Corporate Relations; Executive Director of Development; Physics Technician and Laboratory Coordinator.

WHITWORTH COLLEGE
300 West Hawthorne Road, Spokane WA 99251. 509/777-1000. **Fax:** 509/777-3773. **Recorded jobline:** 509/777-3202. **Contact:** Human Resources. **World Wide Web address:** http://www.whitworth.edu. **Description:** A private, liberal arts college affiliated with the Presbyterian Church. Academic programs include majors in 17 departments, interdisciplinary areas of concentration, off-campus internships and foreign studies, graduate learning opportunities, and career preparation programs. **President:** Bill Robinson.

WILLIAMS & HELDE
711 Sixth Avenue North, Suite 200, Seattle WA 98109. 206/285-1940. **Fax:** 206/283-8897. **Contact:** Human Resources Department. **World Wide Web address:** http://www.williams-helde.com. **Description:** An advertising agency. Founded in 1970. **Number of employees at this location:** 10.

WILLIS
505 Fifth Avenue, Suite 200, Seattle WA 98104. 206/386-7400. **Fax:** 206/386-7960. **Contact:** Human Resources. **World Wide Web address:** http://www.willis.com. **Description:** An international insurance broker engaged in commercial property, liability, fidelity, security, and life insurance, as well as group benefits. **Positions advertised include:** Client Services Manager. **Special programs:** Internships. **Listed on:** New York Stock Exchange. **Stock exchange symbol:** WSH.

WOODLAND PARK ZOO
601 North 59th Street, Seattle WA 98103-5858. 206/684-4800. **Contact:** Personnel. **World Wide Web address:** http://www.zoo.org. **Description:** A zoo located on 92 acres of botanical gardens. Exhibits include over 300 different animal species, as well as the African Savannah, Elephant Forest, Northern Trail, and the Tropical Rain Forest. **Positions advertised include:** Classes/Camp Assistant; Cashier; Drafting and Design Specialist; Outreach and Education Coordinator; Security Officer.

HOWARD S. WRIGHT CONSTRUCTION COMPANY
425 Pontius Avenue North, Seattle WA 98109. 206/447-7654. **Fax:** 206/447-7727. **Contact:** Personnel. **World Wide Web address:** http://www.hswright.com. **Description:** A general contracting company for nonresidential buildings.

YAKIMA HERALD-REPUBLIC
114 North 4th Street, Yakima WA 98901. 509/577-7741. **Toll-free phone:** 800/343-2799. **Fax:** 509/577-7765**Contact:** Human Resources. **E-mail address:** hr@yakima-herald.com. **World Wide Web address:** http://www.yakima-herald.com. **Description:** Publishes a daily newspaper with a circulation of approximately 44,000.

ZONES, INC.
1102 15th Street SW, Suite 102, Auburn WA 98001-6509. 253/205-3000. **Fax:** 253/205-3450. **Contact:** Human Resources. **E-mail address:** resumes@zones.com. **World Wide Web address:** http://www.zones.com. **Description:** Zones, Inc. and its subsidiaries are single-source, multi-vendor direct marketing resellers of name-brand information technology products. Zones serve the small- to medium-sized business market, as well as enterprise and public sector accounts. **Positions advertised include:** Account Executive; Manager In Training. **Corporate headquarters location:** This location. **Listed on:** NASDAQ. **Stock exchange symbol:** ZONS.

ABB INC.
843 North Jefferson Street, Lewisburg WV 24901. 304/647-4358. **Contact:** Human Resources. **World Wide Web address:** http://www.abb.com/us. **Description:** Manufactures analytical equipment for commercial and industrial use. **Special Programs:** Global Trainee Program for Finance and Business Control. **Corporate headquarters location:** Norwalk CT. **Other U.S. locations:** Nationwide. **International locations:** Worldwide. **Parent company:** ABB Ltd. **President:** Donald Aiken.

AFG INDUSTRIES, INC.
Rural Route 3, Box 151N, Bridgeport WV 26330. 304/842-8193. **Contact:** Human Resources. **World Wide Web address:** http://www.afgglass.com. **Description:** A leading manufacturer and distributor of flat glass for commercial and residential applications. Products include clear float, tint, solar, patterned, and tempered glass. **Corporate headquarters location:** Kingsport, TN. **CEO:** D. Roger Kennedy. **Parent company:** Asahi Glass America, Inc.

ALLEGHENY POWER
1310 Fairmont Avenue, Fairmont WV 26555-1392. 304/366-3000. **Fax:** 724/830-5801. **Recorded jobline:** 877/276-7364. **Contact:** Organizational Development Team. **E-mail address:** resumes@alleghenyenergy.com. **World Wide Web address:** http://www.alleghenyenergy.com. **Description:** An electric utility company that supplies power to northern and eastern West Virginia, southwestern and central Pennsylvania, and western Maryland. **NOTE:** With the exception of power station openings, send resumes to: 800 Cabin Hill Drive, Greensburg PA 15601. **Positions advertised include:** Administrative Assistant; Business Account Specialist; Customer Service Representative; Meter Reader; Power Station Worker; Lineworker Apprentice; Substation Electrician Apprentice; System Security Technician. **Corporate headquarters location:** Hagerstown MD. **Parent company:** Allegheny Energy, Inc. **Listed on:** New York Stock Exchange. **Stock exchange symbol:** AYE.

ALLIANCE CONSULTING
124 Philpott Lane, Beaver WV 25813. 304/255-0491. **Fax:** 307/275-4232. **Contact:** Jody Lilly. **Email:** Jlilly@aci.wbv.com. **World Wide Web address:** http://www.aci-ecs.com. **Description:** Provides environmental consulting and engineering services.

ALLIED WASTE INDUSTRIES, INC.
D.B.A. BROWNING-FERRIS INDUSTRIES, INC.
P.O. Box 2828, Fairmont WV 26555. 304/366-8900. **Physical address:** 2 Twelfth Street, Fairmont WV 26555. **Toll free phone:** 800/696-3173. **Contact:** Human Resources Department. **World Wide Web address:** http://www.alliedwaste.com. **Description:** Engaged primarily in the collection and disposal of solid waste for commercial, industrial, and residential customers. Services provided include landfill services, waste-to-energy programs, hazardous waste removal, and liquid waste removal. The company has worldwide operations at more than 500 facilities. **Corporate headquarters location:** Scottsdale AZ. **Listed on:** New York Stock Exchange. **Stock exchange symbol:** AW.

AMES-TRUE TEMPER
465 Rail Road, Camp Hill WV 17011. 304/424-3000. **Toll-free phone:** 800/393-1846. **Fax:** 304/480-4005. **Contact:** Donna Sweeney, Human Resources. **World Wide Web address:** http://www.ames.com. **Description:** Manufactures hand tools. **Corporate headquarters location:** This location. **Other U.S. locations:** Nationwide. **International locations:** Canada. **Operations at this facility include:** Administration; Manufacturing; Research and Development; Sales; Service. **Annual sales/revenues:** More than $100 million. **Number of employees at this location:** 1,000.

ARCH COAL, INC.
Catenary Coal Campbell's Creek Complex, 42 Rensford Star Route, Charleston WV 25306. 304/925-9361. **Contact:** Human Resources. **E-mail address:** careers@archcoal.com. **World Wide Web address:** http://www.archcoal.com. **Description:** Mines, processes, markets, and distributes low-sulfur bituminous coal marketed primarily in the eastern United States and in Europe. Arch Coal accounts for approximately one-tenth of the United States' coal supply and has a reserve base of approximately 3.5 billion tons. **NOTE:** Send resumes to: One CityPlace Drive Suite 300, St. Louis MO 63141. **Positions advertised include:** Senior Planning Engineer. **Corporate headquarters location:** St. Louis MO. **Other U.S. locations:** CO; KS; UT; VA; WY. **Listed on:** New York Stock Exchange. **Stock exchange symbol:** ACI.

ARCH COAL, INC.
Arch of West Virginia, HC61, Box 156, Yolyn WV 25654. 304/792-8200. **Physical address:** Rum Creek Road, Yolyn WV 25654. **Contact:** Human Resources Manager. **World Wide Web address:** http://www.archcoal.com. **Description:** Mines, processes, markets, and distributes low-sulfur bituminous coal marketed primarily in the eastern United States and in Europe. Arch Coal has about 688 million tons of proven and probable low-sulfur coal reserves located in southern West Virginia and eastern Kentucky. **NOTE:** Send resumes to: One CityPlace Drive Suite 300, St. Louis MO 63141. **Corporate headquarters location:** St. Louis MO. **Other U.S. locations:** CO; KS; UT; VA; WY. **Listed on:** New York Stock Exchange. **Stock exchange symbol:** ACI.

BAYER CORPORATION
State Route 2, P.O. Box 500, New Martinsville WV 26155. 304/455-4400. **Fax:** 304/457/2962 **Contact:** Human Resources. **World Wide Web address:** http://www.bayerjobs.com. **Description:** Produces pigments and synthetic resins. **Special programs:** Co-Ops; Internships; Entry Level Positions. **Corporate headquarters location:** Pittsburgh PA. **Parent company:** Bayer USA. **Operations at this facility include:** Manufacturing. **Listed on:** New York Stock Exchange. **Stock exchange symbol:** BAY.

BLUEFIELD STATE COLLEGE
219 Rock Street, Bluefield WV 24701-2198. 304/327-4277. **Fax:** 304/325-7747. **Contact:** Elizabeth Belcher, Human Resource Director. **E-mail address:** ebelcher@bscvax.wvnet.edu. **World Wide Web address:** http://www.bluefield.wvnet.edu. **Description:** A state-supported commuter college with a primary focus on career and technical two- and four-year programs. The college offers associate's and bachelor's degrees and certificate programs. **Positions advertised include:** Adjunct Instructors; Part-Time Head Women's Volleyball Coach; Campus Service Worker-Grounds. **Corporate headquarters location:** This location. **Operations at this facility include:** Administration. **Number of employees at this location:** 200.

BOWLES RICE McDAVID GRAFF & LOVE
600 Quarrier Street, P.O. Box 1386, Charleston WV 25301-1386. 304/347-1100. **Contact:** Elizabeth D. Harter, Human Resources Department Chair. **Email address:** bharter@bowlesrice.com. **World Wide Web address:** http://www.bowlesrice.com. **Description:** A corporate law firm. **Special Programs:** Summer Clerkship Programs. **Other area locations:** Fairmont WV; Martinsburg WV; Morgantown WV; Parkersburg WV. **Other U.S. locations:** Lexington KY; Winchester VA.

BRALEY & THOMPSON
906 A-3 Grand Central Avenue, Vienna WV 26105. 304/295-5175. **Toll-free phone:** 800/969-5170. **Fax:** 304/295-5176. **Contact:** Patty Clark, Unit Administrator. **World Wide Web address:** http://www.btkids.com. **Description:** Provides foster care services and family preservation support. **NOTE:** send resumes to 1600 7th Street, Parkersburg WV 26101. **Office hours:** Monday – Friday, 8:30 a.m. – 4:30 p.m. **Other area locations:** St. Albans WV; Huntington WV.

BURGESS & NIPLE, LTD.
1124 Smith Street, Suite 105, Charleston WV 25301. 304/343-9370. **Contact:** Human Resources. **E-mail address:** hr@burnip.com. **World Wide Web address:** http://www.burgessniple.com. **Description:** An engineering and architecture firm engaged in study, analysis, and design services. The company specializes in waterworks, wastewater, industrial services, hydropower, energy conservation, transportation, systems analysis, HVAC, and geotechnical. Founded in 1912. **NOTE:** Send Resumes to: Human Resources, Burgess & Niple, 5085 Reed Road, Columbus OH 43220. **Positions advertised include:** Travel Demand Forecaster. **Corporate headquarters location:** Columbus OH. **Other U.S. locations:** AZ; KY; IN; OH; PA; VA.

CHARLESTON AREA MEDICAL CENTER
P.O. Box 1574, Charleston WV 25326. 304/388-7458. **Physical address:** 511 Brooks Street Charleston WV 25301. **Toll-free phone:** 800/323-5157. **Contact:** Employment Services. **World Wide Web address:** http://www.camcare.com. **Description:** Charleston Area Medical Center has 914 beds divided among three divisions: General (general medical and surgical, trauma, renal, neurology, and orthopedics); Women and Children; and Memorial (cardiac and oncology.) **NOTE:** You can also apply online. Candidates for Physician positions may contact the Physician Recruitment Office at 304/ 388-7546 or 866/551-8927 for more information. **Positions advertised include:** Medical Technologist; MRI Technologist; Nuclear Technologist; Occupational Therapist; Pharmacist; Pharmacy Technician; Physical Therapist; Physical Therapist Assistant; Radiologic Technologist; Respiratory Therapist; Technical Assistant; Phlebotomist; Senior Biostatistician; LPN, Open Heart Surgery; LPN, Renal; Registered Nurse; Clinical Nurse; Anesthesiologist; Cardiologist; Endocrinologist; Endovascular Specialist; Gastroenterologist; General Surgeon; Hematologist; Hospitalist; Neurologist; OB Program Director; Gynecologist; Orthopedic Surgeon; Pathologist; Pediatrician; Reproductive Endocrinologist; Rheumatologist; Urologist. **Parent company:** CAMC Health System. **Office hours:** Monday-Friday, 7:30 a.m.- 4:30 p.m.

CHARLES TOWN RACES AND SLOTS
U.S. Route 340 Charles Town WV 25414. 304/724-4639. **Toll-free phone:** 800/795-7001. **Fax:** 304/724-4368. **Recorded jobline:** 304/724-4308. **E-mail address:** ctrhr@pngaming.com. **World Wide Web Address:** http://www.ctownraces.com. **Description:** Live horse racing, as well as gaming facilities and various dining and drinking selections. Founded in 1933. **Note:** Contact appropriate department supervisors with questions regarding specific positions. All other inquiries related to benefits or employment should be addressed to Human Resources at 304/ 724-4237. **Positions advertised include:** Audit Clerk; Bartender; Busperson; Cage Cashier; Cage Cashier Lead; Cocktail Server; Coin Impressment Team Member; Concession Cashier; Cook-all levels; Dishwasher; Count Team Member; Count Team Leader; HVAC Technician; HVAC Supervisor; Mutuel Teller (Terminal Operator); Player's Choice Representative; Receptionist/Swithcboard; Recruiting Assistant; Warehouse Assistant; Cage Manager; Human Resources Trainer; Parking Supervisor; Food and Beverage Supervisor.

CITIZENS NATIONAL BANK
211-213 Third Street, P.O. Box 1519, Elkins WV 26241. 304/636-4095. **Toll-free phone:** 800/797-5790. **Fax:** 304/636-6924. **Contact:** Carla R. Fisher, Human Resources. **World Wide Web address:** http://www.cnbelkins.com. **Description:** A bank holding company with a subsidiary that performs commercial banking operations and other related financial activities. **Special programs:** Internships available. **Number of employees at this location:** 65.

CITY HOLDING COMPANY
25 Gatewater Road, Charleston WV 25313. 304/769-1100. **Toll-free phone:** 800/922-9236. **Fax:** 304/769-1313. **Contact:** Human Resources. **World Wide Web address:** http://www.cityholding.com. **Description:** A holding company that, through a number of banking-related subsidiaries, performs commercial banking operations, mortgage banking, brokerage services, and related activities. **NOTE:** Send resumes to: City Holding Company, Attention: Human Resources, 25 Gatewater Road, Cross Lanes WV 25313. **Positions advertised include:** Branch Manager. **Other area locations:** Statewide. **Other U.S. locations:** OH. **Listed on:** NASDAQ. **Stock exchange symbol:** CHCO. **President and CEO:** Gerald R. Francis.

COLUMBIA GAS TRANSMISSION CORPORATION
P.O. Box 1273, Charleston WV 25325. 304/357-2000. **Physical address:** 1700 MacCorkle Avenue SE, Charleston WV 25314. **Contact:** Human Resources. **E-mail address:** hrquestions@nisource.com. **World Wide Web address:** http://www.columbiagastrans.com. **Description:** Engaged in natural gas transmission. **NOTE:** Send Resumes to: Columbia Gas Transmission, Human Resources Service Center, 1700 MacCorkle Avenue Southeast, Charleston WV 25314. See parent company's website for current job listings. **Special programs:** Internships available. **Corporate headquarters location:** Fairfax VA. **Parent company:** NiSource Inc. **Operations at this facility include:** Administration. **Listed on:** New York Stock Exchange. **Stock exchange symbol:** NI.

CONCORD COLLEGE
P.O. Box 1000, Athens WV 24712-1000. 304/384-5121. **Toll-free phone:** 800/344-6679. **Contact:** Human Resources. **E-mail address:** info@concord.edu. **World Wide Web address:** http://www.concord.wvnet.edu. **Description:** A four-year public college with a student enrollment of over 3,000. Founded in 1872. **Number of employees at this location:** 300.

CYTEC INDUSTRIES
Cytec Industries Inc, One Heilman Avenue, Willow Island WV 26134. 304/665-2422. **Contact:** Human Resources. **World Wide Web address:** http://www.cytec.com. **Description:** Processes raw materials for the production of biochemicals. **NOTE:** Does not accept unsolicited resumes. Check Website for details on where to send resume for desired positions. **Corporate headquarters location:** West Paterson NJ. **Other U.S. locations:** Nationwide. **International locations:** Worldwide. **Listed on:** New York Stock Exchange. **Stock exchange symbol:** CYT. **President and CEO:** David Lilley.

DELOITTE & TOUCHE
1215 Laidley Tower, Charleston WV 25301. 304/342-5300. **Toll-free phone:** 888/277-5938. **Contact:** Managing Partner. **E-mail address:** dtcareers@deloitte.com. **World**

Wide Web address: http://www.us.deloitte.com. **Description:** An international firm of certified public accountants providing professional accounting, auditing, tax, and management consulting services to widely diversified clients. The company has a specialized program consisting of national industry groups and functional groups that cross industry lines. Groups are involved in various disciplines including accounting, auditing, taxation management advisory services, small and growing businesses, mergers and acquisitions, and computer applications. **Special Programs:** Internships; Vacation Work Programs; Continuing Education. **Other U.S. locations:** Nationwide. **International locations:** Worldwide. **Parent company:** Deloitte Touche Tohmatsu.

DOMINION TRANSMISSION
445 West Main Street, Clarksburg WV 26301. 304/627-3000. **Recorded jobline:** 304/627-3177. **Contact:** Human Resources. **E-mail address:** human_resources@dom.com. **World Wide Web address:** http://www.dom.com. **Description:** An interstate gas pipeline that provides transportation and storage services to the Midwest, Northeast, and Mid-Atlantic markets. Dominion Transmission also operates one of the world's largest underground natural gas storage systems. **NOTE:** Submitting resumes online is strongly recommended. **Positions advertised include:** Sales and Operations Coordinator. **Special Programs:** Cooperative Education Program; Internship Program; Scholarship Programs. **Operations at this facility include:** Administration; Divisional Headquarters; Sales. **Other U.S. Locations:** Nationwide.

THE DOW CHEMICAL COMPANY
437 MacCorkle Avenue SW, P.O. Box 8004, South Charleston WV 25303. 304/747-7000. **Fax:** 304/747-3084. **Contact:** Human Resources. **World Wide Web address:** http://www.dow.com. **Description:** One of the largest chemical companies in the United States, Dow manufactures industrial and consumer products. Consumer products include Saran Wrap, Spray 'N Wash, Dow bathroom cleaners, prescription drugs, and over-the-counter health care products. Industrial chemicals are used in the food processing, pharmaceuticals, and utilities markets. Plastics are manufactured for the automotive, electronics, packaging, and recreation markets. Other operations include cogeneration and steam power for the utility market and petrochemical production. **NOTE:** Dow prefers applications through their website. **Special Programs:** Internships; Co-ops. **Corporate headquarters location:** Midland MI. **Other U.S. locations:** Nationwide. **International locations:** Worldwide. **Listed on:** New York Stock Exchange. **Stock exchange symbol:** DOW.

DUPONT BELLE
901 West DuPont Avenue, Belle WV 25015. 304/357-1000. **Contact:** Human Resources. **E-mail address:** info@Dupont.com. **World Wide Web address:** http://www.dupont.com. **Description:** E.I. DuPont de Nemours & Company's activities include the manufacturing of biomedical, industrial, and consumer products (such as photographic, data-recording, and video devices); the production of man-made fiber products (with applications in a variety of consumer and commercial industries); polymer products (such as plastic resins, elastomers, and films); agricultural and industrial chemicals (such as herbicides and insecticides, pigments, fluorochemicals, petroleum additives, and mineral acids); the exploration and production of crude oil and natural gas; the refining, marketing, and downstream transportation of petroleum; and the mining and distribution of steam and metallurgical coals. The company supplies the aerospace, agriculture, apparel, transportation, health care, and printing and publishing industries. **NOTE:** Candidates for Ph.D. and Science positions should contact Dr. Lin Wang. Candidates for student employment should contact Mickey Candia. Resumes are only accepted through the company's online system. The above email address is for questions only. **Special programs:** Internships; Co-ops; Early Career Development Programs; Marketing Leadership Development Programs. **Corporate headquarters location:** Wilmington DE. **Operations at this location include:** manufactures synthetics, inorganic industrial chemicals, and agricultural chemicals. **Listed on:** New York Stock Exchange. **Stock exchange symbol:** DD. **CEO:** Charles Holliday, Jr. **Annual sales/revenues:** More than $100 million. **Number of employees worldwide:** 94,000.

EASTERN AMERICAN ENERGY CORPORATION
501 56th Street SE, Floor 3, Charleston WV 25304-2393. 304/925-6100. **Contact:** Human Resources. **Description:** Purchases, distributes, and supplies natural gas; conducts developmental natural gas drilling and production operations; markets natural gas; and conducts exploratory and developmental oil drilling and production operations.

EASTERN ASSOCIATED COAL CORPORATION
P.O. Box 1233, Charleston WV 25324. 304/344-0300. **Contact:** Elizabeth Wills, Personnel Manager. **World Wide Web address:** http://www.peabodyenergy.com. **Description:** A coal mining company. **Corporate headquarters location:** St. Louis MO. **Parent company:** Peabody Energy Corporation. **Listed on:** New York Stock Exchange. **Stock exchange symbol:** BTU. **CEO:** Irl F. Engelhardt.

FIRST COMMUNITY BANCSHARES, INC.
FIRST COMMUNITY BANK
1001 Marshall Street, P.O. Box 5939, Princeton WV 24740. 304/487-9000. **Contact:** Human Resources. **World Wide Web address:** http://www.fcbinc.com. **Description:** A holding company with subsidiaries that operate 48 banks. **NOTE:** Entry-level positions are offered. **Special programs:** Internships; Summer Jobs. **Corporate headquarters location:** Bluefield VA. **Subsidiaries include:** Blue Ridge Bank; FCBank of Mercer County, Inc.; FCBank of Southwest Virginia, Inc.; FCBank, Inc.; First Community Bank (also at this location.) **Listed on:** NASDAQ. **Stock exchange symbol:** FCBC. **President and CEO:** John M. Mendez. **Annual sales/revenues:** $11 - $20 million. **Number of employees at this location:** 85. **Number of employees nationwide:** 530.

FMW COMPOSITE SYSTEMS INC
1200 West Benedum Industrial Drive, Bridgeport WV 26330. 304/624-8028. **Fax:** 304/624-0170. **Contact:** Human Resources. **World Wide Web address:** http://www.fmwcomposite.com. **Description:** Originally formed to provide subcontract-manufacturing services to Telenyde Vehicle Systems, FMW is now a full scale composite and filament company, providing engineering, development and manufacturing, and expertise in production to commercial companies and the United States military. **Positions advertised include:** Program Manager.

GENERAL MOTORS CORPORATION
P.O. Box 1248, Martinsburg WV 25402. 304/267-5600. **Physical address:** 1000 Warm Springs Avenue, Martinsburg WV 25401. **Contact:** Personnel Director. **World Wide Web address:** http://www.gm.com. **Description:** This facility serves as a warehousing location and distribution center for motor vehicle parts. General Motors Corporation is one of the world's largest full-line vehicle manufacturers, and also has substantial interests in information technology, electronics, and finance. GM conducts business through the following sectors: North American Automotive Operations, International Operations, General Motors Acceptance Corporation (GMAC), Electronic Data Systems Corporation (EDS), and GM Hughes Electronics Corporation. North American Automotive Operations includes Sales/Service Groups (Buick, Cadillac, Chevrolet, GMC Truck, Oldsmobile, Pontiac, and Saturn) and Vehicle Development Groups (Powertrain, Truck Group, Small Car Group, and Midsize/Luxury Car Group.) International Operations include GM Europe; Asia Pacific Operations; and Latin America, Africa, Middle East Operations. GMAC, which provides financing and insurance to GM customers and dealers, consists of North American Operations, International Operations, Motors Insurance Corporation, and GMAC Mortgage Group. EDS applies information technologies to more than 8,000 customers globally in the communications, energy/chemical, insurance, public sector, travel and transportation, financial services, manufacturing, and retail industries. GM Hughes Electronics Corporation is involved in automotive, telecommunications, space, and defense electronics. Founded in 1908. **Corporate headquarters location:** Detroit MI. **Listed on:** New York Stock Exchange. **Stock exchange symbol:** GM.

GOODRICH AEROSPACE
ICE PROTECTION SYSTEMS DIVISION
HC 75, Box 1, Stringtown Road, Union WV 24983. 304/772-3062. **Contact:** Human Resources. **World Wide Web address:** http://www.goodrich.com. **Description:** The aerospace segment of the company manufactures aircraft systems and components and provides aircraft services worldwide. **NOTE:** Please submit resume via their Website. **Positions advertised include:** Elastomeric Technical Section Engineer; Elastomeric Mechanical Engineer. **Corporate headquarters location:** Charlotte NC. **Parent company:** The Goodrich Company. **Listed on:** New York Stock Exchange. **Operations at this facility include:** This location manufactures aircraft deicers. **Stock exchange symbol:** GR.

GRANT COUNTY BANK
P.O. Box 929, Petersburg WV 26847-0929. 304/257-4111. **Physical address:** 3 North Main Street, Petersburg WV 26847. **Contact:** Human Resources. **Description:** A multibank holding company engaged in commercial banking, insurance services, and other related financial activities. **Other area locations:** Riverton WV; Keyser WV; Moorefield WV. **President:** C.E. Porter.

HEALTHSOUTH MOUNTAINVIEW HOSPITAL
1160 Van Voorhis Road, Morgantown WV 26505. 304/598-1100. **Fax:** 304/592-1103. **Contact:** Trisha Plevich, Director of Human Resources. **World Wide Web address:** http://www.healthsouth.com. **Description:** An acute care, rehabilitation hospital with 80 beds that also offers outpatient services. **NOTE:** Call 304/285-1034 to reach the Office of Human Resources directly. **Corporate headquarters location:** Birmingham AL. **Other area locations:** Beckley WV; Bluefield WV; Parkersburg WV; Princeton WV; Vienna WV. **Other U.S. Locations:** Nationwide. **Parent company:** HealthSouth Corporation. **Listed on:** New York Stock Exchange. **Stock exchange symbol:** HRC.

HOMER LAUGHLIN CHINA COMPANY
Sixth and Harrison Street, Newell WV 26050. 304/387-1300. **Toll-free phone:** 800/452-4462. **Fax:** 304/387-0593. **Contact:** Eric E. Furbee, Human Resources Manager. **E-mail address:** hlc@hlchina.com. **World Wide Web address:** http://www.hlchina.com. **Description:** Manufactures ceramic dinnerware sold to restaurants and retailers for consumer use. Founded in 1871. **NOTE:** Do not send resumes via email. **Office Hours:** Monday – Friday, 8:00 a.m. – 5:00 p.m. **Corporate headquarters location:** This location. **President:** Marcus Aaron II. **Annual sales/revenues:** $51 - $100 million. **Number of employees at this location:** 1,150.

HUNTINGTON BANK
230 West Pike Street, Clarksburg WV 26301. 304/623-7100. **Contact:** Human Resources. **World Wide Web address:** http://www.huntington.com. **Description:** A full-service bank. **NOTE:** Apply online or mail to: Huntington National Banks of West Virginia, Human Resources, 103 Adams Street, Fairmont WV 26555. **Positions advertised include:** Customer Service Representative; Security Investigator. **Parent company:** Huntington Bancshares Inc. (Columbus OH.) **Listed on:** NASDAQ. **Stock exchange symbol:** HBAN.

HUNTINGTON INTERNAL MEDICINE GROUP
1115 20th Street, Huntington WV 25703. 304/528-4600. **Contact:** Human Resources. **E-mail address:** hr@uhswv.com. **World Wide Web address:** http://www.uhswv. com. **Description:** A group of approximately 40 physicians who treat clients on an outpatient basis. Specializations include internal medicine and cardiology. Founded in 1969. **NOTE:** For physician positions contact Sandra Franklin the Director of Physician Recruitment. Phone: 304/528-4657. E-mail: sfranklin@uhswv.com. **Positions advertised include:** Cardiologist; Family Practitioner; Pulmonary Specialist; Gastroenterologist; Oncologist; Hospitalist; Internal Medicine Practitioner. **Other area locations:** Barboursville WV; Putnam County WV; Westmoreland WV. **Parent company:** Ultimate Health Services, Inc.

JOHNS MANVILLE CORPORATION
2905 Third Avenue, Vienna WV 26105. 304/295-9361. **Contact:** Human Resources. **E-mail address:** humanresources@jm.com. **World Wide Web address:** http://www.jm.com. **NOTE:** Send resumes to: P.O. Box 5108, Denver CO 80217. Unsolicited resumes are not considered. **Description:** Manufactures insulation and building materials. The company consists of three major divisions: Insulation, Roofing Systems, and Engineered Products. **Corporate headquarters location:** Denver CO. **Operations at this facility include:** Manufacturing. **Number of employees worldwide:** 9,000.

KANAWHA STONE COMPANY
P.O. Box 503, Nitro WV 25143. 304/755-8271. **Physical address:** 401 Jacobson Drive, Poca WV 25159. **Fax:** 304/755-8274. **Contact:** Dave Lawman. **E-mail address:** dave.lawman@kanawhastone.com. **World Wide Web address:** http://www.kanawhastone.com. **Description:** Specializing in unusual excavation and construction jobs, with an emphasis on time and budget constraints. Founded in 1973. **NOTE:** Does not accept job inquiries or applications online. **Number of employees at this location:** 220.

LABYRINTH SOLUTIONS, INC.
P.O. Box 573, Morgantown WV 26507-0434. 304/292-7700. **Physical address:** 235 High Street, Suite 416, Morgantown WV 26505. **Contact:** Human Resources. **World Wide Web address:** http://www.labyrinth.net. **Description:** A local provider of Internet access. **NOTE:** Please only respond to openings posted on the company's Website. No phone calls please.

LIBRARY CORPORATION
Research Park, Inwood WV 25428. 304/229-0100. **Toll-free phone:** 800/325-7759. **Fax:** 304/229-0295. **Contact:** Human Resources. **E-mail address:** hr@tlcdelivers.com. **World Wide Web address:** http://www.tlcdelivers.com. **Description:** Develops, manufactures, and markets software that allows libraries to automate their cataloguing systems. Founded in 1974. **Note:** Prefers applications through their website. **Positions advertised include:** Senior Client/Server Developer; Graphic Designer. **Other U.S.**

locations: Denver CO; Brandon FL. **International locations:** Singapore. **CEO:** Annette Harwood Murphy.

LIFEBRIDGE
One United Way Square, Charleston WV 25301. 304/340-3500. **Contact:** Human Resources. **E-mail address:** internal@uwaychwv.org. **World Wide Web address:** http://www.uwaychaswv.org. **Description:** United Way of Kanawha Valley and Community Council of Kanawha Valley merged to form LifeBridge. Through a vast network of volunteers and local charities, local United Way organizations throughout America help meet the health needs of millions of people. United Way's over 100-year history is built on local organizations helping people in their own communities. The United Way system includes approximately 1,900 community-based organizations. **President:** Marilyn Donnellan.

LOGAN CORPORATION
555 Seventh Avenue, P.O. Box 58, Huntington WV 25706. 304/526-4700. **Toll-free phone:** 888/853-4751. **Fax:** 304/526-4747. **World Wide Web address:** http://www.logancorp.com. **Description:** Specializes in product lines for mining, industrial and construction companies. Logan Corporation also provides rental, sales and service of construction and industrial equipment. Founded in 1904. **Corporate Headquarters location:** This location. **Other area locations:** Charleston WV; Clarksburg WV. **Other U.S. locations:** Prestonburg KY; Middlesboro KY. **Operations at this facility include:** The locomotive parts renewal warehouse is located adjacent to the corporate headquarters at this location.

MARSH BELLOFRAM
State Route 2, P.O. Box 305, Newell WV 26050. 304/387-1200. **Toll-free phone:** 800/727-5646. **Fax:** 304/387-1212. **Contact:** Human Resources. **E-mail address:** humanresources@marshbellofram.com. **World Wide Web address:** http://www.marshbellofram.com. **Description:** Manufactures precision instruments including pressure gauges, thermometers, and needle valves. **Operations at this facility include:** Administration; Manufacturing; Research and Development; Sales. **International location:** Nottingham England.

MARSHALL UNIVERSITY
207 Old Main, One John Marshall Drive, Huntington WV 25755. 304/696-6455. **Fax:** 304/696-6844. **Contact:** Jim Stephens, Director of Human Resources. **E-mail address:** human-resources@marshall.edu. **World Wide Web address:** http://www.marshall.edu. **Description:** A university. **Positions advertised include:** Adjunct Instructor; Assistant Professor, Biochemistry; Assistant Professor, Molecular Biology; Assistant Professor, Family and Community Health; Assistant Professor, General English; Assistant Professor, Forensic Science; Assistant Professor of Pediatric Infectious Disease; Assistant Professor of Statistics; Assistant Professor, Music; Assistant Professor, Physical Education; Assistant Professor, Spanish; Director/Faculty, Statewide Deaf Education; General Surgeon; Information Services Librarian; Minority Fellow; Vascular Surgeon; Assistant Dean of Enrollment Management; Campus Service Worker; Campus Trade Worker; Certified Psychologist, Autism Training Center; Director of Alumni Relations; Epidemiologist; Executive Dean, College of Education and Human Services; Information Technology Consultant; Network Specialist; Project Coordinator; Public Affairs Specialist; Research Associate; Research Genetic Counselor; Resident Director/Graduate Assistant; Senior Accountant; Site Manager. **Operations at this facility include:** Administration.

McJUNKIN CORPORATION
P.O. Box 513, Charleston WV 25322. 304/348-5211. **Physical address:** 835 Hillcrest Drive, Charleston WV 25311. **Fax:** 304/348-4922. **Contact:** Human Resources. **E-mail address:** info@mcjunkin.com. **World Wide Web address:** http://www.mcjunkin. com. **Description:** A distributor of industrial supplies including pipes, valves, and fittings. **NOTE:** Accepts unsolicited resumes. **Corporate headquarters location:** This location. **Operations at this facility include:** Administration; Manufacturing; Research and Development; Sales; Service.

MOUNTAIN CAD
P.O. Box 8517, 339 Sixth Avenue SW, South Charleston WV 25303. 304/744-7911. **Fax:** 304/744-8049. **Contact:** Human Resources. **E-mail address:** info@mtncad.com. **World Wide Web address:** http://www.mtncad.com. **Description:** An AutoCAD dealer specializing in mapping and GIS solutions.

MTR GAMING GROUP, INC.
MOUNTAINEER RACE TRACK & GAMING RESORT
P.O. Box 358, Route 2 South, Chester WV 26034. 304/387-2400. **Fax:** 304/387-8417. **Contact:** Human Resources. **E-mail address:** mchevront@mtrgaming.com. **World Wide Web address:** http://www.mtrgaming.com. **Description:** Owns and operates gaming resorts offering slot machines, racetracks, and table gambling. **Positions advertised include:** Corporate Accountant; Dining Room Assistant Manager; Buffet Sous Chef; Buffet Attendant; Massage Therapist; Cosmetologist; Receptionist. **Corporate headquarters location:** This location. **Other U.S. locations:** Las Vegas NV; Reno NV. **Listed on:** NASDAQ. **Stock exchange symbol:** MNTG.

MOUNTAIN V OIL AND GAS, INC.
P.O. Box 470, Bridgeport WV 26330. 304/842-6320. **Physical address:** 712 Masonic Drive, Bridgeport WV 26330. **Fax:** 304/842-0016. **Contact:** Mike Shaver. **E-mail address:** smshaver@earthlink.net. **World Wide Web address:** http://www.mountainvoilandgas.com. **Description:** An independent oil and gas exploration and production company. **Other U.S. Locations:** PA.

MYLAN PHARMACEUTICALS, INC.
781 Chestnut Ridge Road, P.O. Box 4310, Morgantown WV 26504. 304/599-2595. **Toll-free phone:** 800/826-9526. **Fax:** 304/598-5406. **Contact:** Human Resources. **E-mail address:** resume@mylanlabs.com. **World Wide Web address:** http://www.mylan.com. **Description:** Manufactures a broad range of pharmaceuticals including analgesics, antibiotics, antidepressants, anti-inflammatory drugs, diuretics, and muscle relaxants. Founded in 1961. **NOTE:** Second and third shifts are offered. **Positions advertised include:** Quality Control Chemist; Development/Validation Chemist; Bioanalytical Chemist; Business Specialist; Electronic Technician; Statistician. **Special programs:** Internships; Summer Jobs. **Corporate headquarters location:** Pittsburgh PA. **Parent company:** Mylan Laboratories Inc. (Pittsburgh PA.) **Listed on:** New York Stock Exchange. **Stock exchange symbol:** MYL. **CEO:** Milan Puskar. **Annual sales/revenues:** More than $100 million. **Number of employees at this location:** 900. **Number of employees nationwide:** 1,750.

OGLEBAY RESORT & CONFERENCE CENTER
Route 88 North-Oglebay Park, Wheeling WV 26003. 304/243-4000. **Toll-free phone:** 800/624-6988. **Contact:** Human Resources. **World Wide Web address:** http://www.oglebay-resort.com. **Description:** A 212-room resort and conference center that also offers a golf course and zoo. **NOTE:** Entry level applications are accepted on a continual basis and kept on file for three months. **Positions advertised include:** Electrician; Animal Keeper; Cottage Attendant; Bingo Attendant; Laundry Attendant; Steward; Security Officer. **Internship information:** Horticulture Intern; Zoo Education Intern; Public Relations/Communications Intern; Marketing Intern; Animal Care Intern; Graphic Arts Intern.

OHIO VALLEY MEDICAL CENTER
OHIO VALLEY HEALTH SERVICES AND EDUCATION CORPORATION
2000 Eoff Street, Wheeling WV 26003. 304/234-8615. **Contact:** Human Resources. **World Wide Web address:** http://www.ohiovalleymedicalcenter.com. **Description:** An acute care facility with 450 beds that offers a wide range of services including general medical and surgical procedures, a heart program, a cancer program, and a birthing center. **NOTE:** All resumes should be directed to the parent company. **Positions advertised include:** Recreational Therapist; Staff Nurse; Medical Technician; Phlebotomist; Senior Staff Pharmacist; Therapist. **Parent company:** Ohio Valley Health Services and Education Corporation (also at this location.)

PPG INDUSTRIES, INC.
P.O. Box 191, New Martinsville WV 26155. 304/845-5300. **Physical address:** State Route 2, New Martinsville 26155. **Fax:** 304/455-2385. **Contact:** Human Resources. **World Wide Web address:** http://www.ppg.com. **Description:** PPG Industries is a supplier of products for manufacturing, building, automotive, processing, and numerous other world industries. The company makes decorative and protective coatings, flat glass and fabricated glass products, continuous-strand fiberglass, and industrial and specialty chemicals. PPG operates manufacturing facilities throughout the United States and abroad. Founded in 1883. **Corporate headquarters location:** Pittsburgh PA. **Other U.S. locations:** Nationwide. **International locations:** Canada; China; France; Germany; Ireland; Italy; Mexico; The Netherlands; Portugal; Spain; Taiwan; United Kingdom. **Operations at this facility include:** Manufacturing. **Listed on:** New York Stock Exchange. **Stock exchange symbol:** PPG.

PARSONS BRINCKERHOFF INC.
1000 Marion Center, Suite 101, Fairmont WV 26554. 304/534-4405. **Fax:** 304/534-4406. **Contact:** Human Resources. **E-mail address:** careers@pbworld.com. **World Wide Web address:** http://www.pbworld.com. **Description:** Provides total engineering and construction management services including the development of major bridges, tunnels, highways, marine facilities, buildings, industrial complexes, and railroads. Founded in 1885. **Special Programs:** Internships; College Campus Visits. **Corporate headquarters location:** New York NY.

PETERSON REHABILITATION HOSPITAL AND GERIATRIC CENTER
Homestead Avenue, Wheeling WV 26003. 304/234-0500. **Contact:** Human Resources. **World Wide Web address:** http://www.ohiovalleymedicalcenter.com. **Description:** Peterson Rehabilitation Hospital and Geriatric Center has 172 beds and is divided into three divisions: skilled care (step-down from ICU); long-term care; and rehabilitation. Both inpatient and outpatient services are offered. **NOTE:** All resumes should be sent to the parent company at 2000 Eoff Street, Wheeling WV 26003. **Parent company:** Ohio Valley Health Services and Education Corp.

PETROLEUM DEVELOPMENT CORPORATION
P.O. Box 26, Bridgeport WV 26330. 304/842-3597. **Physical address:** 103 East Main Street, Bridgeport WV 26330. **Toll-free phone:** 800/624-3821. **Contact:** Human Resources. **E-mail address:** petd@petd.com. **World Wide Web address:** http://www.petd.com. **Description:** Involved in oil and gas exploration, production, and development, as well as related property management. The company grants credit to purchasers of oil and gas and the owners of managed properties, almost all of who are located in the Appalachian Basin area of West Virginia, Tennessee, Pennsylvania, and Ohio. **Corporate headquarters location:** This location. **Listed on:** NASDAQ. **Stock exchange symbol:** PETD. **CEO:** James Ryan.

PHILIPS LIGHTING COMPANY
Rural Route 3, Box 505, Fairmont WV 26554. 304/367-3500. **Fax:** 304/367-3578. **Contact:** Paul Zepp, Human Relations Manager. **World Wide Web address:** http://www.lighting.philips.com. **Description:** Manufactures and markets lighting products and systems for industry and home including incandescent, fluorescent, automotive, high-intensity discharge, compact fluorescent, specialty, and projection lamps. **Parent company:** Philips Electronics North America Corporation is one of the largest industrial companies in the United States. Philips concentrates its efforts primarily in the fields of consumer electronics, consumer products, electrical and electronics components, and professional equipment. **Listed on:** New York Stock Exchange. **Stock exchange symbol:** PHG.

POCAHONTAS BANKSHARES CORPORATION
FIRST CENTURY BANK
500 Federal Street, P.O. Box 1559, Bluefield WV 24701. 304/325-8181. **Contact:** Human Resources. **World Wide Web address:** http://www.firstcentury.com. **Description:** A bank holding company that, through its subsidiaries, provides commercial banking operations, credit card services, and related activities. **Other area locations:** Hilton WV; Oceana WV; Pineville WV; Princeton WV. **Listed on:** OTC BB. **Stock exchange symbol:** FCBS. **Other U.S. locations:** VA. **CEO:** R.W. Wilkinson.

PRESTERA CENTER
3375 U.S. Route 60 East, Huntington WV 25705. 304/525-7851. **Fax:** 304/525-1504. **Contact:** Linda Persun, Director of Human Resources. **E-mail address:** lpersun@prestera.com. **World Wide Web address:** http://www.prestera.org. **Description:** A nonprofit, community, mental health center that offers outpatient and residential treatment for children, adolescents, and adults with behavioral problems, mental illness, or substance addictions. Founded in 1967. **NOTE:** Entry-level positions are offered. **Positions advertised include:** Therapist; Therapist/Team Leader; Case Manager; Staff Psychiatrist; Physicians Assistant; Registered Nurse; LPN. **Special programs:** Internships; Summer Jobs. **Corporate headquarters location:** This location. **Executive Director:** Robert Hansen. **Number of employees at this location:** 400.

QUEBECOR WORLD
871 Baker Road, Martinsburg WV 25401. 304/267-3600. **Contact:** Human Resources. **E-mail address:** usa.careers@quebecorworld.com. **World Wide Web address:** http://www.quebecorworld.com. The world's largest commercial printer, with over 160 facilities worldwide. **Special programs:** Internships. **Corporate headquarters location:** Montreal, Canada. **Listed on:** New York Stock Exchange. **Stock exchange symbol:** IQW. **Number of employees at this location:** 400. **Number of employees worldwide:** 39,000.

CHARLES RYAN ASSOCIATES
300 Summers Street, Suite 1100, Charleston WV 25301. 304/342-0161. **Toll-free Phone:** 877/342-0161. **Fax:** 304/342-1941. **Contact:** Human Resources. **E-mail address:** resume@charlesryan.com. **World Wide Web address:** http://www.cryanassoc.com. **Description:** A public relations agency. Founded in 1974.

NOTE: Resume forms may be completed online. **Positions advertised include:** Art Director. **Other U.S. locations:** Richmond, VA; Lexington, KY. **CEO:** Charles Ryan.

SMC ELECTRICAL PRODUCTS
P.O. Box 880, Barboursville WV 25504. 304/736-4541. **Physical address:** 6072 Ohio River Road, Huntington WV 25702. **Fax:** 304/736-4541. **Contact:** Jerry Porter, Manager of Personnel. **E-mail address:** humanres@smcelectrical.com. **World Wide Web address:** http://www.smcelectrical.com. **Description:** Manufactures electrical components for mining equipment.

SMURFIT-STONE CONTAINER CORPORATION
2333 Commerce Street, Wellsburg WV 26070. 304/737-3311. **Contact:** Human Resources. **World Wide Web address:** http://www.smurfit-stone.com. **Description:** Smurfit-Stone Container Corporation is one of the world's leading paper-based packaging companies. The company's main products include corrugated containers, folding cartons, and multiwall industrial bags. The company is also one of the world's largest collectors and processors of recycled products that are then sold to a worldwide customer base. Smurfit-Stone Container Corporation also operates several paper tube, market pulp, and newsprint production facilities. **NOTE:** Does not accept resumes. Company uses local employment service. **Corporate headquarters location:** Chicago IL. **Other U.S. locations:** Nationwide. **Operations at this facility include:** This location manufactures paper bags. **Listed on:** NASDAQ. **Stock exchange symbol:** SSCC. **Annual sales/revenues:** More than $100 million.

SPECIAL METALS
3200 Riverside Drive, Huntington WV 25705. 304/526-5100. **Toll-free phone:** 800/334-4626. **Fax:** 304/526-5309. **Contact:** Human Resources. **E-mail address:** smc_hr@smcwv.com. **World Wide Web address:** http://www.smcwv.com. **Description:** Develops, manufactures, and markets high-nickel alloy products in a variety of mill forms. Primary customers are in the aerospace, marine, petro-chemical, and environmental industries. **NOTE:** Entry-level positions are offered. **Positions advertised include:** Process Engineer; Electronics Technician. **Special programs:** Internships; Co-ops. **Corporate headquarters location:** This location. **Other U.S. locations:** IL; IN; KY; NC. **International locations:** Worldwide. **Annual sales/revenues:** More than $100 million. **Number of employees nationwide:** 1,720.

STEEL OF WEST VIRGINIA
P.O. Box 2547, Huntington WV 25726. 304/696-8200. **Physical address:** Seventeenth Street and Second Avenue, Huntington WV 25703. **Toll-free phone:** 800/624-3492. **Fax:** 304/529-1479. **Contact:** Personnel. **E-mail address:** steel@swvainc.com. **World Wide Web address:** http://www.swvainc.com. **Description:** Fabricates mine beams, rail, steel mine ties, and other locomotive-related products. **Other U.S. locations:** Memphis, TN.

SUMMIT COMMUNITY BANK
P.O. Box 179, Moorefield WV 26836. 304/538-2353. **Physical address:** 310 North Main Street, Moorefield WV 26836. **Fax:** 304/538-7053. **Contact:** Human Resources. **World Wide Web address:** http://www.sbvnb.com. **Description:** A commercial banking company. **President:** Pat Frye. **Number of employees at this location:** 55.

UNIVERSITY OF CHARLESTON
2300 MacCorkle Avenue SE, Charleston WV 25304. 304/357-4736. **Toll-free phone:** 800/995-4682. **Fax:** 304/357-4832. **Contact:** Roy Howell, Department of Human Resources. **Email address:** hr@ucwv.edu. **World Wide Web address:** http://www.uchaswv.edu. **Description:** A private, undergraduate university with an enrollment of 1,500 students. **Positions advertised include:** Assistant Professor, Business; Biology Professor; History Professor; Chair, Department of Radiological Science; Assistant Professor, English; Associate Librarian. **Corporate headquarters location:** This location. **Operations at this facility include:** Administration; Service. **President:** Dr. Edwin Welch.

VECELLIO & GROGAN, INC.
P.O. Box 2438, Beckley WV 25802-2438. 304/252-6575. **Physical address:** 2251 Robert C. Byrd Drive, Beckley WV 25801. **Toll-free phone:** 800/255-6575. **Fax:** 304/252-4131. **Contact:** Penny Jones, Personnel Manager. **E-mail address:** HR@VecellioGrogan.com. **World Wide Web address:** http://www.vecelliogrogan.com. **Description:** A construction company specializing in highways and bridges. **NOTE:** Interested candidates can complete an online form and/or fax a resume to the number listed above. **Positions advertised include:** Foreman; Equipment Operator; Truck Driver; Field Mechanics; Survey Crew; Laborer.

VERIZON COMMUNICATIONS
1500 MacCorkle Avenue SE, Charleston WV 25314. **Toll-free phone:** 800/925-3775. **Contact:** Human Resources. **World Wide Web address:** http://www.verizon.com. **Description:** A full-service communications services provider. Verizon offers residential local and long distance telephone services and Internet access; wireless service plans, cellular phones, and data services; a full-line of business services including Internet access, data services, and telecommunications equipment and services; and government network solutions including Internet access, data services, telecommunications equipment and services, and enhanced communications services. **NOTE:** Apply online for open positions. **Positions advertised include:** Corporate Account Manager. **Special Programs:** Internships; Co-ops. **Corporate headquarters location:** New York NY. **Listed on:** New York Stock Exchange. **Stock exchange symbol:** VZ.

CECIL I. WALKER MACHINERY COMPANY
1400 East Dupont Avenue, Belle WV 25015. 304/949-6400. **Toll-free phone:** 800/642-8203. **Fax:** 304/949-7380. **Contact:** Human Resources. **E-mail address:** jobs@walker-cat.com. **World Wide Web address:** http://www.walker-cat.com. **Description:** Engaged in the sale and service of industrial machinery and equipment. **NOTE:** Email resumes, or send to: P.O. Box 2427, Charleston WV 25329. **Positions advertised include:** Mechanic; Warehouse Person; Parts Counterperson; Sales Associate; Manager. **Other area locations:** Parkersburg WV; Huntington WV; Crab Orchard WV; Summersville WV; Lyburg WV; Sophia WV; Nitro WV; Parkersburg WV. **Other U.S. locations:** Jackson OH. **Listed on:** Privately held. **Number of employees nationwide:** 480.

WEIRTON STEEL
400 Three Springs Drive, Weirton WV 26062. 304/797-4678. **Fax:** 304/797-2792. **Contact:** Robert Rubicky, Human Resources. **E-mail address:** Robert.rubicky@weirton.com. **World Wide Web address:** http://www.weirton.com. **Description:** An integrated manufacturer of flat-rolled carbon steel and tin for the construction, automotive, food and beverage, electrical, container, appliance, service center, and commercial equipment markets. The company also sells its products to other steel milling companies. **NOTE:** Offers online applications and only accepts resumes for current job openings. **Subsidiaries include:** Crown Cork & Seal Company, a major U.S. can producer. **CEO and Director:** D. Leonard Wise.

WESBANCO WHEELING
141 Zane Street, Wheeling WV 26003. 304/232-2760. **Contact:** Human Resources. **E-mail address:** humanresources@wesbanco.com. **World Wide Web address:** http://www.wesbanco.com. **Description:** A commercial bank. **NOTE:** Entry level positions available. To contact Human Resources directly call: 304/234-9268. Applications are accepted for available positions only. **Positions advertised include:** Part-Time Teller; Part-Time Clerk; Senior Accounting Officer; Investment Officer. **Other area locations:** Statewide. **Other U.S. locations:** OH, PA. **Parent company:** Wesbanco, Inc. **Listed on:** NASDAQ. **Stock exchange symbol:** WSBC. **Number of employees at this location:** 400.

WEST VIRGINIA UNIVERSITY
P.O. Box 6640, One Waterfront Place, Second Floor, Morgantown WV 26506. 304/293-3405. **Recorded jobline:** 304/293-7234. **Contact:** James A. Morris, Director of Employment. **World Wide Web address:** http://www.wvu.edu. **Description:** A state university. **NOTE:** Go to http://www.hr.wvu.edu for an employment application, or contact Human Resources directly at 304/293-5700. **Positions advertised include:** Assistant Professor, English; Assistant Professor, Psychology; Assistant Professor, Mathematics; Assistant Professor, Political Science; Assistant Professor, Scenic and Costume Design; Professor and Chair, Engineering and Mineral Sources; Program Coordinator, Freshman Engineering; Director of Career Development; Education Coordinator, Health Services; Nurse Educator; University Grants Manager; Data Network Specialist; Campus Services Supervisor; Research Assistant, Department of Forestry; Administrative Assistant; Accounting Assistant; Traffic Enforcement Assistant.

WEST VIRGINIA UNIVERSITY HOSPITALS
Medical Center Drive, P.O. Box 8121, Morgantown WV 26506-8121. 304/598-4075. **Toll-free phone:** 800/453-5708. **Fax:** 304/598-4264. **Contact:** Human Resources. **E-mail address:** wvuhjobs@rcbhsc.wvu.edu. **World Wide Web address:** http://www.health.wvu.edu. **Description:** A 375-bed hospital and Level I-trauma center. The hospital houses the Children's Hospital and the Jon Michael Moore Trauma Center. Founded in 1986. **NOTE:** Second and third shifts are offered. Temporary, Per Diem, and Weekend positions also available. **Positions advertised include:** Radiology Technician; Cardiac Monitor Technician; Respiratory Therapist; Pharmacist; Clinical care Coordinator; Nursing Manager; Social Worker; Speech Pathologist; Registered Nurse; Part-Time Assistant Teacher; Part-Time Traffic and Transportation Officer.

WHEELING-PITTSBURGH STEEL CORPORATION
1134 Market Street, Wheeling WV 26003. 304/234-2400. **Fax:** 304/234-2442. **Contact:** Director of Personnel. **World Wide Web address:** http://www.wpsc.com. **Description:** An integrated producer of flat-rolled, tin coated, galvanized, and corrugated steel products. **NOTE:** Jobs are regularly posted on http://www.monster.com. **Special programs:** Internships; Co-ops. **Corporate headquarters location:** New York NY. **Other U.S. locations:** AL; KS; OH; PA; TX. **Parent company:** WHX Corporation. **Operations at this facility include:** Administration; Manufacturing; Sales; Service. **Listed on:** New York Stock Exchange. **Stock exchange symbol:** WHX. **Annual sales/revenues:** More than $100 million. **Number of employees at this location:** 5,000.

A-C COMPRESSOR CORPORATION
401 East South Island Street, Appleton WI 54914. 920/830-0499. **Fax:** 920/225-1560. **Contact:** Personnel. **World Wide Web address:** http://www.accompressor.com. **Description:** Manufactures compressors that are customized to customers' requirements. **Corporate headquarters location:** This location. **Parent company:** GE Power Systems.

AAA WISCONSIN
664 West Washington Avenue, Madison WI 53703. 608/257-6222. **Fax:** 608/836-7240. **Contact:** Human Resources. **E-mail address:** applyonline@aaawisc.com. **World Wide Web address:** http://www.aaawisc.com. **Description:** Provides insurance, travel, and a wide variety of motorist services to its members through a network of 14 branch offices. **NOTE:** Entry-level positions are offered. Resumes are accepted only for current open positions. **Positions advertised include:** Member Representative. **Special programs:** Training. **Corporate headquarters location:** This location. **Other U.S. locations:** Nationwide

AB DATA
8050 North Port Washington Road, Milwaukee WI 53217. 414/352-4404. **Fax:** 414/352-3994. **Contact:** Human Resources. **World Wide Web address:** http://www.abdata.com. **Description:** A full-service, direct mail marketing company that primarily serves nonprofit and democratic political clients. **NOTE:** Entry-level positions are offered. **Corporate headquarters location:** This location. **Other U.S. locations:** Washington DC. **Listed on:** Privately held. **Annual sales/revenues:** $5 - $10 million. **Number of employees at this location:** 85. **Number of employees nationwide:** 100.

ABS GLOBAL, INC.
1525 River Road, P.O. Box 459, De Forest WI 53532. 608/846-3721. **Toll-free phone:** 800/356-5331. **Fax:** 608/846-6442. **Contact:** Human Resources. **E-mail address:** hr_abs@absglobal.com. **World Wide Web address:** http://www.absglobal.com. **Description:** Manufactures artificial insemination products for cattle. The company is a world leader in bovine DNA, in vitro fertilization, and cell cloning research. **Positions advertised include:** ABS Representative; Accountant; Customer Service Representative.

A.N.S. HOME HEALTH SERVICES
2711 South 84th Street, Milwaukee WI 53227. 414/481-9800. **Fax:** 414/481-9808. **Contact:** Human Resources Department. **World Wide Web address:** http://www.anshomecare.com. **Description:** An agency that provides home health care services.

AQS, INC.
1325 Walnut Ridge Drive, Hartland WI 53029-8894. 262/367-5495. **Fax:** 262/369-7501. **Contact:** Human Resources. **World Wide Web address:** http://www.aqssys.com. **Description:** Develops software for the insurance industry. **Positions advertised include:** Sales Support Specialist; Database Administration Technician; Program Manager; Business Analyst; Director of Marketing.

ASI
741 North Grand Avenue, Waukesha WI 53186. 262/574-9000. **Fax:** 262/574-9090. **Contact:** Human Resources. **World Wide Web address:** http://www.anlt.com. **Description:** A firm specializing in computerized utility mapping and software. **NOTE:** Search and apply for positions or submit resume online.

ACE WORLD WIDE MOVING & STORAGE
1900 East College Avenue, Cudahy WI 53110. 414/764-1000. **Fax:** 414/764-1650 **Contact:** Human Resources. **World Wide Web address:** http://www.aceworldwide.com. **Description:** An international moving and storage company. **NOTE:** Fill out application.

ACTION FLOOR SYSTEMS LLC
4781 North U.S. Highway 51, Mercer WI 54547-9708. 715/476-3512. **Fax:** 715/476-3585. **Toll-free phone:** 800/746-3512. **Contact:** Vicki Meyer, Human Resources Department. **World Wide Web address:** http://www.actionfloors.com. **Description:** A manufacturer of hardwood flooring.

ADECCO EMPLOYMENT SERVICES
2300 North Mayfair Road, Suite 680, Milwaukee WI 53226-1508. 414/771-6005. **Contact:** Human Resources. **World Wide Web address:** http://www.adeccousa.com. **Description:** Adecco's services encompass staffing, career services, executive search and e-recruitment. **Other U.S. locations:** Nationwide. **Listed on:** New York Stock Exchange. **Stock exchange symbol:** ADO.

ADVANCED LASER MACHINING INC.
600 Cashman Drive, Chippewa Falls WI 54729. 715/720-8093. **Fax:** 715/720-8094. **Contact:** Human Resources. **World Wide Web address:** http://www.laser27.com. **Description:** Fabricates steel, stainless steel, and aluminum.

AERIAL COMPANY, INC.
2300 Aerial Drive, P.O. Box 197, Marinette WI 54143. 715/735-9323. **Fax:** 715/735-6991. **Contact:** Human Resources Department. **World Wide Web address:** http://www.aerialcompany.com. **Description:** A wholesale distributor of professional beauty salon products. **Number of employees nationwide:** 650.

AIR WISCONSIN AIRLINES CORPORATION
W6390 Challenger Drive, Suite 203, Appleton WI 54914-9120. 920/739-5123. **Recorded jobline:** 888/354-4505. **Contact:** Human Resources. **World Wide Web address:** http://www.airwis.com. **Description:** Provides air transportation services. **Positions advertised include:** Director of Information Systems and Services; Flight Following Auditor; Shift Supervisor; Technical Acceptance Specialist. **Corporate headquarters location:** This location.

ALLIANCE FOR CHILDREN & FAMILIES
11700 West Lake Park Drive, Milwaukee WI 53224. 414/359-1040. **Toll-free phone:** 800/221-2681. **Fax:** 414/359-1074. **Contact:** Human Resources Department. **World Wide Web address:** http://www.alliance1.org. **Description:** A national membership organization that provides resources and leadership to over 300 private, nonprofit child- and family-serving organizations in the U.S. and Canada. Founded in 1911. **Parent company:** Families International, Inc.

ALLIANT ENERGY
1 Parker Place, Madison WI 53707-1007. 608/458-3311. **Toll-free phone:** 800/255-4268. **Fax:** 608/458-0120. **Recorded jobline:** 800/851-0658. **Contact:** Staffing Coordinator. **World Wide Web address:** http://www.alliantenergy.com. **Description:** A utility company. **NOTE:** Search and apply for positions online. **Positions advertised include:** Administrative Assistant; Senior Data Center Administrator; Regulatory Planning Associate; Team Leader, Customer and Operations System Support. **CEO:** Erroll Davis Jr.

AMERICAN AG-TEC INTERNATIONAL, LTD.
1711 Woolsey Street, P.O. Box 569, Delavan WI 53115-0569. 262/728-8815. **Fax:** 262/728-8131. **E-mail address:** info@ag-tec.com. **Contact:** Human Resources. **E-mail address:** info@ag-tec.com. **World Wide Web address:** http://www.ag-tec.com. **Description:** dedicated to international markets within the agriculture industry, focusing primarily on genetic development and biotechnology, technology transfers and licensing, seeds and seed production, and agricultural production.

AMERICAN APPRAISAL ASSOCIATES
411 East Wisconsin Avenue, Suite 1900, Milwaukee WI 53202. 414/271-7240. **Contact:** Colleen Stoltmann, Human Resources Manager. **E-mail address:** careers@american-appraisal.com. **World Wide Web address:** http://www.american-appraisal.com. **Description:** An independent international valuation consulting organization specializing in tangible and intangible assets; closely held securities; insurance services; and merger, acquisition, and investment services. Founded in 1896. **NOTE:** Search and apply for positions online. **Positions advertised include:** Associate Appraiser/Valuation Consultant. **Corporate headquarters location:** This location. **Operations at this facility include:** Administration; Regional Headquarters; Sales. **Listed on:** Privately held. **Number of employees worldwide:** 900.

AMERICAN EXPRESS FINANCIAL ADVISORS
1400 Lombardi Avenue, Suite 201 South, IDS Center, Green Bay WI 54304. 920/499-2141. **Fax:** 920/498/9588. **Contact:** Human Resources Department. **World Wide Web address:** http://www.amercianexpress.com. **Description:** Provides a variety of financial products and services to help individuals, businesses, and institutions establish and achieve their financial goals. American Express Financial Advisors has a field of more than 10,000 financial advisors in the United States and offers financial planning, annuities, mutual funds, insurance, investment certificates, and institutional investment advisory trust, tax preparation, and retail securities brokerage services.

AMERICAN EXPRESS FINANCIAL ADVISORS
3241A Business Park Drive, Stevens Point WI 54481. 715/341-2500. **Fax:** 715/341-7182. **Contact:** Human Resources Department. **World Wide Web address:** http://www.amercianexpress.com. **Description:** Provides a variety of financial products and services to help individuals, businesses, and institutions establish and achieve their financial goals. American Express Financial Advisors has a field of more than 8,000 financial advisors in the United States and offers financial planning, annuities, mutual funds, insurance, investment certificates, and institutional investment advisory trust, tax preparation, and retail securities brokerage services.

AMERICAN FAMILY INSURANCE GROUP
6000 American Parkway, Madison WI 53783-0001. 608/249-2111. **Fax:** 608/243-6529. **Contact:** Monica Smith, Human Resources. **World Wide Web address:** http://www.amfam.com. **Description:** A multiline mutual insurance company operating in 17 states. **NOTE:** Search and apply for positions online. **Positions advertised include:** Actuarial Loss Reserves Analyst; Audio Visual Technician; Managing Actuary; Network Transport Specialist; Physical Damage Claim Analyst. **Special programs:** Internships. **Corporate headquarters location:** This location. **Annual sales/revenues:** More than $100 million. **Number of employees at this location:** 2,400.

AMERICAN FLOOR COVERING
2914 Latham Drive, Suite B, Madison WI 53713. 608/276-3440. **Fax:** 608/276-3441. **Contact:** Human Resources. **Description:** A wholesale distributor of floor covering materials including ceramic tile and industrial flooring supplies.

AMERICAN FOODS GROUP
544 Acme Street, P.O. Box 8547, Green Bay WI 54308. 920/437-6330. **Fax:** 920/436-6510. **Contact:** Human Resources. **World Wide Web address:** http://www.american-foods.com. **Description:** American Foods Group processes and markets beef and pork products. **Corporate headquarters location:** This location. **Number of employees at this location:** 1,200.

AMERICAN GIRL, INC.
8400 Fairway Place, Middleton WI 53562. 608/836-4848. **Fax:** 608/836-1999. **Contact:** Recruiting. **World Wide Web address:** http://www.americangirl.com. **Description:** Operates in four divisions: consumer catalogue and direct mail sales; book publishing, which markets The American Girls Collection and American Girl Library; the magazine division which publishes *American Girl* magazine; and customer programs, which provides programs and special events centered on an American Girl theme. Founded in 1986. **NOTE:** Search and apply for positions online. **Positions advertised include:** Business Systems Analyst; Sales Representative; Director, Licensing and New Business Development. **Office hours:** Monday - Thursday, 8:00 a.m. - 5:00 p.m.; Friday 8:00 a.m. - 1:00 p.m. **Corporate headquarters location:** This location. **Other area locations:** DeForest WI; Eau Claire WI; Wilmot WI. **Other U.S. locations:** Chicago IL. **Parent company:** Mattel, Inc. is one of the world's leading toy manufacturers. **Listed on:** Privately held. **President/Owner:** Pleasant Rowland. **Number of employees at this location:** 750. **Number of employees nationwide:** 1,000.

AMERICAN HEART ASSOCIATION (AHA)
660 East Mason Street, Milwaukee WI 53202. 414/271-9999. **Fax:** 414/271-3299. **Contact:** Personnel. **World Wide Web address:** http://www.americanheart.org. **Description:** One of the oldest and largest national, nonprofit, voluntary health associations dedicated to reducing disability and death from cardiovascular diseases and stroke. The AHA, also called the Heart Fund, is a community-based organization with approximately 2,100 state and metropolitan affiliates, divisions, and branches throughout the United States and Puerto Rico. The American Heart Association runs interactive public education programs and trains 5 million Americans per year in emergency care procedures. Founded in 1924. **Corporate headquarters location:** Dallas TX.

AMERICAN MEDICAL SECURITY
3100 AMS Boulevard, P.O. Box 19032, Green Bay WI 54313. 920/661-1111. **Toll-free phone:** 800/232-5432. **Fax:** 920/661-2059. **Recorded jobline:** 800/232-5432, ext14625. **Contact:** Human Resources. **E-mail address:** resume@eams.com. **World Wide Web address:** http://www.eams.com. **Description:** AMS markets, administers, and designs insurance coverages such as medical, dental, term life, and short-term disability through professional independent agents. Founded in 1988. **NOTE:** Entry-level positions and second and third shifts are offered. **Positions advertised include:** Tax Accountant; Sr. Database Administrator; Marketing Implementation Coordinator; Subrogation Assistant; Training and Design Specialist. **Corporate headquarters location:** This location. **Other U.S. locations:** Indianapolis IN. **Parent company:**

United Wisconsin Services. **Annual sales/revenues:** More than $100 million. **Number of employees at this location:** 2,500.

AMERICAN RED CROSS
4860 Sheboygan Avenue, Madison WI 53705. 608/233-9300. **Fax:** 608/227-1439. **Contact:** Joanne Krantz, Personnel Director. **E-mail address:** jkrantz@arcbadger.org. **World Wide Web address:** http://www.redcross.org/wi/badger. **Description:** A humanitarian organization that aids disaster victims, gathers blood for crisis distribution, trains individuals to respond to emergencies, educates individuals on various diseases, and raises funds for other charitable establishments. **Positions advertised include:** Chief Executive Officer; emergency Services Director. **Other U.S. locations:** Nationwide.

AMERICOLD LOGISTICS, LLC
110th Street and Highway 54, P.O. Box 675, Plover WI 54467. 715/421-3200. **Fax:** 715/424-3921. **Toll-free phone:** 888/484-4877. **Contact:** Human Resources Department. **World Wide Web address:** http://www.americold.net. **Description:** Provider of temperature-controlled food distribution services. **Corporate headquarters location:** Atlanta GA. **Other area locations:** Babcock WI: Tomah WI. **Other U.S. locations:** Nationwide. **Number of employees nationwide:** 6,000.

AMSCO
311 West Coleman Street, Rice Lake WI 54868. 715/234-9061. **Fax:** 715/234-1816. **Contact:** Human Resources. **World Wide Web address:** http://www.amsco1.com. **Description:** A manufacturer of aluminum window screens for the Andersen Corporation. **Positions advertised include:** Product Development Engineer. **Parent company:** Quanex. **Operations at this facility include:** Manufacturing; Research and Development. **Listed on:** New York Stock Exchange. **Number of employees at this location:** 260. **Number of employees nationwide:** 2,500.

AMTELCO
4800 Curtin Drive, McFarland WI 53558. 608/838-4194. **Toll-free phone:** 800/356-9148. **Fax:** 608/838-8367. **Contact:** Human Resources. **E-mail address:** info@amtelco.com. **World Wide Web address:** http://www.amtelco.com. **Description:** Manufactures telemessaging systems for call answering. Products and services include voice mail, speed call handling, and multiple call handling.

ANCHOR FOOD PRODUCTS
555 Hickory Farm Lane, Appleton WI 54914. 920/997-2828. **Fax:** 920/997-7605. **Contact:** Personnel. **World Wide Web address:** http://www.1800poppers.com. **Description:** Engaged in the production of a variety of appetizers for retail sale. **Parent company:** McCain Foods.

APACHE STAINLESS EQUIPMENT CORPORATION
2910 Apache Drive, P.O. Box 370, Plover WI 54467. 715/344-4636. **Fax:** 715/344-3811. **Contact:** Jean Thompson, Human Resources. **World Wide Web address:** http://www.apachestainless.com. **Description:** Fabricates stainless steel tanks for a variety of industrial uses. **Positions advertised include:** Quality Assurance manager; Fabrication Sales; Heli-Arc Welder; Stainless Metal Finisher. **Other area locations:** Beaver Dam WI.

APPLIED INDUSTRIAL TECHNOLOGIES
2400 North Sandra Street, Appleton WI 54911-8666. 920/739-5351. **Fax:** 920/739-8453. **Contact:** Personnel. **E-mail address:** career@applied.com. **World Wide Web address:** http://www.appliedindustrial.com. **Description:** A distributor of industrial, fluid power and engineered products and systems with 440 locations in 47 states, Canada, Puerto Rico, and Mexico. **Corporate headquarters location:** Cleveland OH. **Number of employees worldwide:** 4,300.

ARTESYN TECHNOLOGIES
ARTESYN COMMUNICATIONS PRODUCTS, INC.
8310 Excelsior Drive, Madison WI 53717. 608/831-5500. **Toll-free phone:** 800/356-9602. **Fax:** 608/826-8004. **Contact:** Human Resources. **E-mail address:** jobs@artesyncp.com. **World Wide Web address:** http://www.artesyn.com. **Description:** Designs, manufactures, and services power conversion products and communications subsystems for the computing and communications industries. **Positions advertised include:** ESS Software Design Engineering Intern; Product Marketing Manager; Senior Financial Analyst; Buyer. **Listed on:** NASDAQ. **Stock exchange symbol:** ATSN.

ASHLEY FURNITURE INDUSTRIES INC.
One Ashley Way, Arcadia WI 54612. 608/323-3377. **Toll-free phone:** 800/477-2222. **Fax:** 608/323-6008. **Contact:** Human Resources. **World Wide Web address:** http://www.ashleyfurniture.com. **Description:** Manufactures furniture and operates stores. **NOTE:** Search and apply for positions online. **Positions advertised include:** Application Developer; Cost Accountant; Internal Auditor; Replenishment Planner; Demand Planner; Business Planner; Project Coordinator; Human Resource Director; Database Administrator; MRO Purchasing Specialist.

ASSOCIATED BANC-CORP
1200 Hansen Road, Green Bay WI 54304. 920/491-7000. **Toll-free phone:** 800/682-4989. **Fax:** 920/491-7110. **Contact:** Lola LaCount, Human Resources. **World Wide Web address:** http://www.assocbank.com. **Description:** A diversified, multibank holding company providing a complete range of business, retail, trust/asset management, correspondent, leasing, insurance, mortgage banking, real estate, and investment services. Operates 200 banking locations in Wisconsin, Illinois, and Minnesota. Founded in 1970. **NOTE:** Search and apply for positions online. **Positions advertised include:** Business Banker; Building Engineer; Corporate Controller; Corporate Investment Portfolio Manager; Distribution Specialist; Network Engineer; Treasurer. **Corporate headquarters location:** This location. **Other U.S. locations:** IL; MN. **Listed on:** NASDAQ. **Stock exchange symbol:** ASBC.

AURORA HEALTH CARE
3000 West Mountain Street, Milwaukee WI 53215. 414/647-3000. **Fax:** 414/671-8111. **Contact:** Human Resources Department. **World Wide Web address:** http://www.aurorahealthcare.org. **Description:** Owns and operates several hospitals, medical groups, and walk-in clinics. Aurora Health Care is one of the largest not-for-profit health care corporations in Wisconsin. **Corporate headquarters location:** This location.

AURORA LAKELAND MEDICAL CENTER
W3985 County Road NN, P.O. Box 1002, Elkhorn WI 53121. 262/741-2000. **Fax:** 262/741-2482. **Recorded jobline:** 262/741-2833. **Contact:** Kathy Tews, Human Resources Supervisor. **World Wide Web address:** http://www.aurorahealthcare.org. **Description:** A 99-bed hospital. **NOTE:** Search and apply for positions or submit resume online. **Positions advertised include:** CNA; Occupational Therapist; Registered Nurses; Medical Transcriptionist; Radiology Technologist; Certified Nursing Assistant; Respiratory Therapist; Anesthesia Technician. **Corporate headquarters location:** Milwaukee WI. **CEO:** Loren Anderson. **Annual sales/revenues:** $21 - $50 million. **Number of employees at this location:** 500.

AUTOMATIC DATA PROCESSING (ADP)
330 East Kilborn, Suite 875, Milwaukee WI 53202. 414/273-4444. **Contact:** Human Resources Department. **World Wide Web address:** http://www.adp.com. **Description:** Offers technology-based solutions through four business units: employer services offers HR, payroll and benefits administration; brokerage services provides securities processing and investor communication services; dealer services provides computing solutions for auto and truck dealers; and claims services provides auto repair estimating and claims processing. **NOTE:** Search and apply for positions online. **Positions advertised include:** Major Accounts Sales Representatives; SBS Sales Outside Sales Associates. **Corporate headquarters location:** Roseland NJ. **Listed on:** New York Stock Exchange. **Stock exchange symbol:** ADP.

AUTOMATIC FIRE PROTECTION
3265 North 126th Street, Suite B, Brookfield WI 53005. 262/781-9665. **Toll-free phone:** 800/686-9665. **Fax:** 262/781-1152. **Contact:** Sue Packel, Human Resources. **E-mail address:** spackel@autofire.com. **World Wide Web address:** http://www.autofire.com. **Description:** Sells and services equipment for industrial, institutional, and commercial applications.

AZCO, INC.
806 Valley Road, Menasha WI 54952. 920/734-5791. **Fax:** 920/734-7432. **Contact:** Recruiter. **E-mail address:** smitchell@azco-inc.com. **World Wide Web address:** http://www.azco-inc.com. **Description:** An employee-owned full-service integrated construction firm specializing in machinery installation, structural steel construction, construction management, pipe and sheet metal installations, and boiler repair and installation. **Positions advertised include:** Project Manager; Superintendent; Quality control Inspector; Safety Representative; Project Coordinators. **Other area locations:** Appleton WI.

BCI, INC.
N7 W2205 Johnson Road, Waukesha WI 53186-1856. 262/542-3100. **Toll-free phone:** 800/558-2345. **Fax:** 262/542-2301. **Contact:** Human Resources. **E-mail address:** hr@smiths-bci.com. **World Wide Web address:** http://www.smiths-bci.com. **Description:** Manufactures noninvasive patient equipment that monitors respiration, exhaled gases, anesthetic agents, blood pressure, and temperature. **Corporate headquarters locations:** This location. **Parent company:** Smiths Medical. **Numbers of employees at this location:** 100.

BDO SEIDMAN, LLP
330 East Kilbourn Avenue, Suite 950, Milwaukee WI 53202-3143. 414/272-5900. **Fax:** 414/272-1090. **Contact:** Human Resources Department. **World Wide Web address:** http://www.bdo.com. **Description:** A public accounting and consulting firm. **NOTE:** Search and apply for positions online. **Positions advertised include:** Business Development Manager; Assurance Senior. **Other U.S. locations:** Nationwide. **CEO:** Denis Field.

BADGER METER, INC.
4545 West Brown Deer Road, P.O. Box 245036, Milwaukee WI 53224-9536. 414/355-0400. **Fax:** 414/371-5949. **Contact:** Human Resources. **World Wide Web address:** http://www.badgermeter.com. **Description:** Manufactures and markets flow measurement and control products. The company serves industrial and utility markets worldwide. Its products are used to measure and control the flow of liquids and gases in a variety of applications. The company's Industrial Division provides flow meter and control products for markets including energy and petroleum, food and beverage, pharmaceutical, chemical, water and wastewater, process waters, and concrete. The Utilities Division manufactures and markets a complete line of flow measurement products and associated systems for public and private water utilities and selected meter reading products for public and private natural gas utilities. **Corporate headquarters location:** This location. **Other U.S. locations:** Tulsa OK. **Listed on:** American Stock Exchange. **Stock exchange symbol:** BMI.

ROBERT W. BAIRD & COMPANY
777 East Wisconsin Avenue, P.O. Box 672, Milwaukee WI 53201-0672. 414/765-3500. **Toll-free phone:** 800/792-2473. **Fax:** 414/765-7303. **Contact:** Human Resources. **World Wide Web address:** http://www.rwbaird.com. **Description:** A full-service investment firm. Founded in 1919. **NOTE:** Entry-level positions and part-time jobs are offered. **Positions advertised include:** Trading Support Specialist; Equity Research Associate; Branch Registered Sales Associate; Computer Operations Analyst; Retirement Plans Field Consultant; Experience Financial Advisor. **Office hours:** Monday - Friday, 9:00 a.m. - 6:30 p.m. **Corporate headquarters location:** This location. **Number of employees at this location:** 1,200. **Number of employees nationwide:** 2,300.

BANK MUTUAL
201 North Monroe Avenue, Green Bay WI 54301. 920/437-7101. **Contact:** Human Resources. **World Wide Web address:** http://www.bankmutual.com. **Description:** Provides full personal and commercial banking services. **Other area locations:** Statewide.

BANC ONE WISCONSIN CORPORATION
111 East Wisconsin Avenue, Suite 100, Milwaukee WI 53202. 414/765-2121. **Fax:** 414/765-2054. **Contact:** Employee Relations. **World Wide Web address:** http://www.bancone.com. **Description:** A banking services organization engaged in commercial, retail, and trust services. **NOTE:** Search and apply for positions online. **Positions advertised include:** Customer Service Associate; Insurance Specialist; Relationship Banker. **Corporate headquarters location:** Chicago IL. **Parent company:** Banc One Corporation (Chicago IL) is one of the nation's largest bank holding companies. Banc One operates an affiliate network of over 75 banks with more than 1,500 banking locations. In addition, Banc One operates corporations involved in data processing, venture capital, investment and merchant banking, trust, brokerage, investment management, leasing, mortgage banking, consumer finance, and insurance.

BANK ONE
22 East Mifflin Street, Madison WI 53703. 608/282-6020. **Contact:** Human Resources. **World Wide Web address:** http://www.bankone.com. **Description:** A full-service bank. Banc One Corporation (Chicago IL) operates an affiliate network of over 75 banks with more than 1,500 banking locations. In addition, Banc One operates corporations involved in data processing, venture capital, investment and merchant banking, trust, brokerage, investment management, leasing, mortgage banking, consumer finance, and insurance. **Positions advertised include:** Relationship Banker; Customer Service Associate. **Other area locations:** Statewide. **Other U.S. locations:** Nationwide.

BANK ONE RACINE
4930 Douglas Avenue, Racine WI 53402. 262/681-4265. **Contact:** Human Resources. **World Wide Web address:** http://www.bankone.com. **Description:** A full-service bank. **Positions advertised include:** Relationship Banker; Customer Service Associate; **Parent company:** Banc One Corporation (Chicago IL) is one of the nation's largest bank holding companies. Banc One operates an affiliate network of over 75 banks with more than 1,500 banking locations. In addition, Banc One operates corporations involved in data processing, venture capital, investment and merchant banking, trust, brokerage, investment management, leasing, mortgage banking, consumer finance, and insurance.

BANTA CORPORATION
225 Main Street, P.O. Box 8003, Menasha WI 54952-8003. 920/751-7777. **Fax:** 920/751-7787. **Contact:** Human Resources. **E-mail address:** apply@banta.com. **World Wide Web address:** http://www.banta.com. **Description:** Offers a variety of printing services to publishers of educational and general books, special-interest magazines, custom consumer and business catalogs, and direct marketing materials. Banta Corporation also offers supply-chain management, serving as a global outsourcing partner for companies in technology, pharmaceutical and medical device sectors, and is a leading manufacturer and distributor of disposable healthcare and dental products. **NOTE:** Search and apply for positions online. **Positions advertised include:** Corporate Business Analyst; Corporate Financial Analyst; Data Security Analyst; Support Analyst. **Corporate headquarters location:** This location. **Other U.S. locations:** CA; CT; GA; IL; MA; MN; MO; NJ; NY; OH; PA; TN; TX; UT; VA; WA. **International locations:** Ireland; Mexico; Singapore. **Subsidiaries include:** Banta Book Group; Banta Catalog Group; Banta Digital Group; Banta Direct Marketing Group; Banta Global Turnkey Group; Banta Healthcare Products; Banta Publications Group. **Listed on:** New York Stock Exchange. **Stock exchange symbol:** BN. **Annual sales:** $1.5 billion. **Number of employees worldwide:** 8,000.

BANTA DIGITAL GROUP
1457 Earl Street, Menasha WI 54952. 920/751-7800. **Fax:** 920/751-7899. **Contact:** Jim Fulcer, Human Resources. **World Wide Web address:** http://www.banta.com. **Description:** Activities include data management for the creation of film and printing plates such as electronic and conventional prepress services; preparation and storage of customers' digital electronic files containing text and images; high-speed transmission of digitized text and graphics; digital photography; electronic layout and design; one- and four-color digital printing; television identity campaigns; corporate image videos; and interactive and alternative media programming. **Parent company:** Banta Corporation.

BANTA HEALTHCARE GROUP
570 Enterprise Drive, Neenah WI 54956. 920/751-4300. **Fax:** 920/751-4456. **Contact:** Sharon Haines, Human Resources Representative. **World Wide Web address:** http://www.bantahealthcare.com. **Description:** Manufactures single-use paper, gauze, and cotton products for the health care industry. Brand names include TIDI and Encore. **Positions advertised include:** National Accounts Manager; Sr. Programmer Analyst.

BAYLAKE BANK CORPORATION
P.O. Box 9, Sturgeon Bay WI 54235. 920/743-5551. **Fax:** 920/746-6989. **Toll-free phone:** 800/267-3610. **Contact:** Human Resources. **World Wide Web address:** http://www.baylake.com. **Description:** A full-service banking corporation with 26 locations in northeastern and central Wisconsin. **NOTE:** Search for positions online.

BAYMONT INN & SUITES
100 East Wisconsin Avenue, Suite 1800, Milwaukee WI 53202-4119. 414/905-1000. **Fax:** 414/905-2415. **Contact:** Corporate Recruiter. **E-mail address:** recruiter@baymontinns.com. **World Wide Web address:** http://www.baymontinns.com. **Description:** A hospitality company operating a wide variety of hotels, theaters, entertainment centers, and restaurants. Lodging operations are partly comprised of 190 limited-service hotels located in 31 states. Founded in 1973. **Positions advertised include:** General Manager; Assistant General Manager; Front Desk Clerk. **Special programs:** Internships. **Office hours:** Monday - Friday, 8:30 a.m. - 5:00 p.m. **Corporate headquarters location:** This location. **Parent company:** The Marcus Corporation. **Listed on:** New York Stock Exchange. **Stock exchange symbol:** MCS. **President:** Greg Marcus. **Number of employees at this location:** 170. **Number of employees nationwide:** 4,000.

BEACON RESOURCE GROUP, INC.
12308 North Corporate Parkway, Suite 100, Mequon WI 53092-3380. 262/243-6100. **Fax:** 262/243-1207. **Contact:** Richard Omdahl, Human Resources Department. **Description:** Provides services and distributes instructional literature, pamphlets, and videos to a variety of home care providers.

BEAVER DAM COMMUNITY HOSPITAL
707 South University Avenue, Beaver Dam WI 53916. 920/887-7181. **Fax:** 920/887-4101. **Recorded jobline:** 920/887-4102. **Contact:** Employee Services Department. **World Wide Web address:** http://www.bdch.com. **Description:** A nonprofit hospital offering a 125-bed acute care facility, a 123-bed skilled nursing facility, as well as home health services. **NOTE:** Entry-level positions as well as second and third shifts are offered. Search and apply for positions online. **Positions advertised include:** Registered Nurses; Licensed Practical Nurses. **Special programs:** Internships; Training. **Annual sales/revenues:** $21 - $50 million. **Number of employees at this location:** 750.

BELLIN MEMORIAL HOSPITAL
P.O. Box 23400, Green Bay WI 54305-3400. 920/433-3422. **Physical address:** 744 South Webster Street, Green Bay WI. **Fax:** 920/431-5507. **Recorded jobline:** 920/433-3559. **Contact:** Human Resources Specialist. **World Wide Web address:** http://www.bellin.org. **Description:** A 167-bed acute care hospital. **NOTE:** Search and apply for positions online. **Positions advertised include:** AODA Therapist; Certified Registered Nurse Anesthetist; Counselor; Nuclear Medicine Technologist; Registered Nurse; Surgical Technologist; Ultrasonographer. **Number of employees at this location:** 2,300.

BELMARK
600 Hertitage Road, P.O. Box 5310, De Pere WI 54115-5310. 920/336-2848. **Contact:** Human Resources Department. **World Wide Web address:** http://www.belmark.com. **Description:** A printer of labels, packaging. and folding cartons. **President:** Bruce A. Bell. **Number of employees at this location:** 290.

BELOIT COLLEGE
762 Church Street, Beloit WI 53511. 608/363-2630. **Fax:** 608/363-2221. **Contact:** Lori Rhead, Director of Personnel. **World Wide Web address:** http://www.beloit.edu. **Description:** A four-year college offering a liberal arts curriculum. Founded in 1847. **Positions advertised include:** Area Hall Director; Assistant Director of Admissions; Assistant Director for Computing Infrastructure; Assistant Professor, Spanish. **NOTE:** Search for positions online.

BELOIT SCHOOL DISTRICT
Kolak Education Center, 1633 Keeler Avenue, Beloit WI 53511. 608/361-4018. **Fax:** 608/361-4123. **Contact:** Ronald Nortier, Assistant Superintendent Business Services. **World Wide Web address:** http://www.sdb.k12.wi.us. **Description:** A public school district with 12 elementary, two middle, one high, and one charter school. **NOTE:** Only online applications are accepted. Apply for positions with the School District through the Wisconsin Education Career Access Network at: http://careers.education.wisc.edu/wecan.

BEMIS MANUFACTURING COMPANY
300 Mill Street, P.O. Box 901, Sheboygan Falls WI 53085-0901. 920/467-4621. **Toll-free phone:** 800/558-7651. **Fax:** 920/467-5230. **Contact:** Human Resources. **E-mail address:** humanresources@bemismfg.com. **World Wide Web address:** http://www.bemismfg.com. **Description:** Manufactures toilet seats, cutting boards, deck furniture, air purifiers, planters, gutters, and disposable medical products. **NOTE:** Search and apply for positions online. **Positions advertised include:** Market Research Analyst. **Corporate headquarters location:** This location. **Other area locations:** Menomonee Falls.

BIRDSEYE FOODS
520 North Broadway, P.O. Box 19027, Green Bay WI 54307-9027. 920/435-5300. **Contact:** Human Resources Department. **World Wide Web address:** http://www.birdseyefoods.com. **Description:** A food processing and marketing company. **NOTE:** Search and apply for positions online. **Positions advertised include:** Production Planner; Senior Programmer Analyst.

BLUE CROSS AND BLUE SHIELD UNITED OF WISCONSIN
401 West Michigan Street, Milwaukee WI 53203. 414/226-5000. **Contact:** Human Resources. **World Wide Web address:** http://www.bluecrosswisconsin.com. **Description:** A nonprofit health care insurance organization providing managed health care plans to both individuals and groups. Blue Cross and Blue Shield offers Point-of-Service, individual health, and HMO plans, as well as dental insurance. **NOTE:** Search and apply for positions online.

THE BOELTER COMPANIES
11100 West Silver Spring Road, Milwaukee WI 53225. 414/461-3400. **Toll-free phone:** 800/392-3278. **Fax:** 414/461-5058. **Contact:** Human Resources. **World Wide Web address:** http://www.boelter.com. **Description:** A wholesale distributor of restaurant supplies and equipment. **Positions advertised include:** Retail Sales Representative. **Corporate headquarters location:** This location. **Other area locations:** IL; MI; MN.

BOLDT COMPANY
2525 North Roemer Road, Appleton WI 54911. 920/739-6321. **Fax:** 920/739-4409. **Contact:** Gary Tornes, Vice President of Human Resources. **E-mail address:** resume@boldt.com. **World Wide Web address:** http://www.theboldtcompany.com. **Description:** A construction services firm specializing in the pulp and paper, engineering, and construction industries. **Corporate headquarters location:** This location. **Other area locations:** Madison WI, Milwaukee WI. **Other U.S. locations:** GA, IL, MN, OK.

BORG INDAK, INC.
701 Enterprise Drive, Delavan WI 53115. 262/728-5531. **Fax:** 262/728-3788. **Contact:** Human Resources Director. **E-mail address:** info@borgindak.com. **World Wide Web address:** http://www.borgindak.com. **Description:** A manufacturer and designer of electrical/electronic devices for the automotive and appliance industry. Founded in 1936. **NOTE:** Search for positions online. **Positions advertised include:** Chief Engineer. **Special programs:** Internships; Co-ops. **Corporate headquarters location:** This location. **Listed on:** Privately held. **Number of employees at this location:** 250.

BRADY CORPORATION
BRADY FINANCIAL COMPANY
P.O. Box 571, Milwaukee WI 53201-0571. 414/358-6600. **Toll-free phone:** 800/541-1686. **Fax:** 800/292-2289. **Contact:** Human Resources. **World Wide Web address:** http://www.bradycorp.com. **Description:** Develops, manufactures, and markets industrial identification products and coated materials. Brady Financial Company (also at this location) provides treasury, insurance, credit, collection, and other services to Brady Corporation operations. **NOTE:** Internships offered. Search and apply for positions online. **Positions advertised include:** Flow Process Engineer; Benefits Supervisor; collection Coordinator; Internal Auditor; Sr. Tax Analyst; Sr. Organizational Effectiveness Consultant. **Number of employees worldwide:** 3,100.

BRIGGS & STRATTON
12301 North Wirth Street, Wauwatosa WI 53222. 414/259-5333. **Fax:** 920/674-4370. **Contact:** Human Resources. **E-mail address:** jobs@bsppgroup.com. **World Wide Web address:** http://www.briggsandstratton.com. **Description:** Manufactures air-cooled gasoline engines used in outdoor power equipment. The company also produces car and truck locking mechanisms. **Corporate headquarters location:** Wauwatosa WI. Other area locations: Menomonee Falls WI. Other U.S. locations: AL; KY; MO; GA; FL. **Listed on:** New York Stock Exchange. **Stock exchange symbol:** BGG.

BROWN, COUNTY OF
Northern Building, 305 East Walnut Street, Room 620, Green Bay WI 54301. **Recorded jobline:** 920/448-6276. **Contact:** Human Resources Department. **E-mail address:** BC_Human_Resources@co.brown.wi.us. **World Wide Web address:** http://www.co.brown.wi.us. **Description:** Provides government services in the areas of human services, health care, and recreation. This location also houses the offices of the Clerk of Courts, the county treasurer, the Register of Deeds, and the sheriff's department. **NOTE:** Search for positions online. **Positions advertised include:** Court Reporter; Account Clerk; Certified Nursing Assistant; Licensed practical Nurse; Library Director. **Number of employees at this location:** 1,400.

BROWN COUNTY PUBLISHING COMPANY
138 Main Street, Denmark WI 54208. 920/863-2154. **Fax:** 920/863-6102. **Contact:** Roger Wanek, Human Resources Director. **World Wide Web address:** http://www.doorcountyadvocate.com. **Description:** A publisher of a variety of newspapers, as well as newsletters and brochures for businesses. **NOTE:** Entry-level positions are offered. **Special programs:** Internships. **Corporate headquarters location:** This location. **Listed on:** Privately held. **Number of employees at this location:** 150. **Number of employees nationwide:** 250.

BUILDING SERVICE INC. (BSI)
11925 West Carmen Avenue, Milwaukee WI 53225-2134. 414/353-3600. **Fax:** 414/358-5092. **Contact:** Human Resources Department. **World Wide Web address:**

http://www.buildingservice.com. **Description:** Offers interior design and space planning to construction management services for renovations and new construction.

BUSINESS MARKETING ASSOCIATES, INC.
3520 County Road, Wausau WI 54401. 715/675-3900. **Contact:** Human Resources Department. **Description:** Engaged in advertising, marketing, and public relations for individual consumers, as well as business-to-business. Business Marketing Associates specializes in the health care and manufacturing industries. **Positions advertised include:** Account Executives.

CNI NEWSPAPERS
P.O. Box 510210, New Berlin WI 53151. 262/938-5000. **Contact:** Human Resources. **World Wide Web address:** http://www.cninewsonline.com. **Description:** Publishes 23 weekly newspapers covering a wide range of subjects.

CAMERA CORNER/CONNECTING POINT
529 North Monroe Street, Green Bay WI 54301. 920/435-5353. **Fax:** 920/435-3619. **Contact:** Human Resources Department. **World Wide Web address:** http://www.cccp.com. **Description:** Sells cameras and computer systems. Camera Corner/Connecting Point also provides service and technical support. **Corporate headquarters location:** This location.

CAMTRONICS MEDICAL SYSTEMS
900 Walnut Ridge Drive, P.O. Box 950, Hartland WI 53029. 262/367-0700. **Fax:** 262/369-3192. **Contact:** Human Resources. **E-mail address:** employment@camtronics.com. **World Wide Web address:** http://www.camtronics.com. **Description:** Camtronics Medical Systems manufactures diagnostic imaging equipment for cardiology and radiology procedures. Founded in 1986. **NOTE:** Search and apply for positions online. **Positions advertised include:** Customer Service Operations Analyst; Technical Instructor. **Corporate headquarters location:** This location. **Operations at this facility include:** This location is the main office and manufacturing facility.

CAPESIDE COVE GOOD SAMARITAN CENTER
23926 Fourth Avenue South, Siren WI 54872. 715/349-2292. **Fax:** 715/349-7218. **Contact:** Administrator. **World Wide Web address:** http://www.good-sam.com. **Description:** A nonprofit company providing long-term, short-term, and respite care services to adults. The center also has an outpatient therapy clinic that provides services for physical and occupational therapy, pain management, wound care, ostomy care, incontinence, podiatry, and behavioral management. **NOTE:** Entry-level positions and second and third shifts are offered. **Special programs:** Apprenticeships; Training. **Corporate headquarters location:** Sioux Falls SD. **Other U.S. locations:** Nationwide. **Parent company:** Evangelical Lutheran Good Samaritan Society.

CARSON PIRIE SCOTT & COMPANY
331 West Wisconsin Avenue, Milwaukee WI 53203. 414/347-1152. **Fax:** 414/347-5337. **Contact:** Human Resources Department. **World Wide Web address:** http://www.saksincorporated.com. **Description:** A department store chain, with more than 50 stores located in the Midwest. The company operates 27 Carson Pirie Scott stores in greater Chicago, Indiana, and Minnesota; 12 Boston stores in Wisconsin; and 12 Bergner's stores in central Illinois. **NOTE:** Search and apply for positions online. **Positions advertised include:** Manager, Planning and Allocation; Division Merchandise Manager; Labor Management Staff Planner; VP, Divisional Merchandise Manager. **Corporate headquarters location:** This location. **Parent company:** Saks Incorporated **Listed on:** New York Stock Exchange. **Stock exchange symbol:** SKS. **Number of employees at this location:** 700. **Number of employees nationwide:** 14,000.

CARVER BOAT CORPORATION
7090 Markham Drive, P.O. Box 1010, Pulaski WI 54162-1010. 920/822-1600. **Fax:** 920/822-8820. **Contact:** Human Resources. **World Wide Web address:** http://www.carveryachts.com. **Description:** A manufacturer of cabin cruisers and yachts. **NOTE:** Search and apply for positions online. **Positions advertised include:** Bilingual Supervisor; CAD Drafter; Manufacturing Supervisor.

CASE IH
700 State Street, Racine WI 53404. 262/636-6011. **Contact:** Human Resources Department. **E-mail address:** employment@casecorp.com. **World Wide Web address:** http://www.caseih.com. **Description:** Engaged in the manufacture and distribution of agricultural and construction equipment and accessories. **NOTE:** Search and apply for positions online. **Positions advertised include:** Technical Support Specialist; Sales and Use Tax Analyst; Credit Analyst; Marketing Director; Human Resources Representative. **Corporate headquarters location:** This location. **Parent company:** CNH. **Annual sales/revenues:** More than $100 million.

CATALYST INTERNATIONAL
8989 North Deerwood Drive, Milwaukee WI 53223. 414/362-6800. **Fax:** 414/362-6794. **Contact:** Human Resources. **E-mail address:** careers@catalystinternational.com. **World Wide Web address:** http://www.catalystwms.com. **Description:** Manufactures software for supply chain systems. **NOTE:** Search and apply for positions online. **Positions advertised include:** Project Consultant; system Analyst; Sales Administrator; Manager, Internal Support. **Corporate headquarters location:** This location. **Other U.S. locations:** Newtown PA. **International locations:** England; France; Italy; Mexico; South America.

CHILDREN'S HOSPITAL OF WISCONSIN
9000 West Wisconsin Avenue, Wauwatosa WI 53226. 414/266-2000. **Fax:** 414/266-6138. **Contact:** Human Resources. **World Wide Web address:** http://www.chw.org. **Description:** A hospital specializing in pediatric care. **NOTE:** Search and apply for positions online. **Positions advertised include:** Registered Nurses; Sr. Benefits Analyst; Clinical Dietitian; Pharmacy Technician; Utilization Management Specialist; Outcomes Statistical Analyst; Human Resources Recruiter; Health Unit Coordinator.

CHILDREN'S SERVICE SOCIETY OF WISCONSIN
611 56th Street, Suite 300, Kenosha WI 53140. 262/652-5522. **Contact:** Human Resources. **World Wide Web address:** http://www.cssw.org. **Description:** A state agency offering counseling, adoption, and foster parent services. **NOTE:** Search and apply for positions online. **Positions advertised include:** Child and Family Therapist.

CHIMERX
6143 North 60th Street, Milwaukee WI 53218. 414/535-9506. **Toll-free phone:** 800/626-7833. **Fax:** 414/535-9508. **Contact:** Human Resources. **World Wide Web address:** http://www.chimerx.com. **Description:** Produces research quality DNA/RNA modifying enzymes. **NOTE:** Internships offered. **Other area locations:** Madison WI. **Parent company:** Molecular Biology Resources, Inc.

CHRISTIAN HOME, INC.
331 Bly Street, Waupun WI 53963. 920/324-9051. **Fax:** 920/324-4724. **Contact:** Human Resources. **Description:** An 84-bed, skilled nursing facility that provides rehabilitative, physical, occupational, speech, and respiratory therapy. Christian Home, Inc. offers both subacute and long-term care. **Annual sales/revenues:** Less than $5 million.

CHURNY COMPANY
705 West Fulton Street, Waupaca WI 54981. 715/258-4040. **Fax:** 715/285-4046. **Contact:** Human Resources. **Description:** A manufacturer of cheese. **Parent company:** Kraft Foods, Inc.

CITATION CASTINGS
P.O. Box 98, County Highway M, Browntown WI 53522. 608/966-3261. **Contact:** Human Resources. **World Wide Web address:** http://www.citationcorp.com. **Description:** Manufactures steel castings for a broad range of industrial uses.

CITATION CORPORATION
W 139 N 5470 Oak Lane, P.O. Box 300, Menomonee Falls WI 53052-0300. 262/781-8210. **Fax:** 262/781-9165. **Contact:** Patty Pokwinski, Director of Human Resources. **World Wide Web address:** http://www.citation.net. **Description:** A high-volume, long-run, contract machining organization serving the automotive, construction equipment, and computer industries. **NOTE:** Entry-level positions and second and third shifts are offered. **Special programs:** Training. **Corporate headquarters location:** Birmingham AL. **Listed on:** Privately held. **Annual sales/revenues:** $51 - $100 million.

THEDA CLARK MEDICAL CENTER
130 Second Street, P.O. Box 2021, Neenah WI 54956. 920/729-3100. **Fax:** 920/720-7290. **Recorded jobline:** 920/729-2024. **Contact:** Employment Coordinator. **E-mail address:** humanresources@thedacare.org. **World Wide Web address:** http://www.thedacare.org. **Description:** A 250-bed hospital located on Neenah's Doty Island. Specialized services include emergency department and trauma services including a Chest Pain Center; ThedaStar, a medical helicopter service; and Theda Clark Regional Birth Center, which offers single-room maternity care, high-risk obstetrical services, and neonatal intensive care. With a Level III nursery, Theda Clark is a designated perinatal center for the area. The Center for Rehabilitation Services treats trauma, stroke, orthopedic, and neuromuscular conditions. Theda Heart Center provides imaging and diagnostic services, medical and surgical treatment, and a complete cardiac rehabilitation program. The Center for Recovery provides a continuum of mental health and addiction services offered in inpatient, residential, and outpatient settings. Theda Clark Regional Medical Center also operates a comprehensive Neurosciences Center, providing surgical intervention and diagnostic rehabilitation services, and intensive care and surgical units including laser and outpatient services. **NOTE:** Search and apply for positions online. Mail resume to P.O. Box 8025, 122 East College Avenue, Appleton WI 54912. **Positions advertised include:** Physical Therapist; Licensed Practical Nurse; Registered Nurse; CNA. **Corporate headquarters location:** Appleton WI. **Parent company:** ThedaCare. **Number of employees at this location:** 1,400.

CLIFTON GUNDERSON L.L.C.
123 North Court Street, Suite One, P.O. Box 329, Sparta WI 54656. 608/269-2424. **Fax:** 608/269-2549. **Contact:** Human Resources. **World Wide Web address:** http://www.cliftoncpa.com. **Description:** A certified public accounting and consulting firm with offices in 14 states and the District of Columbia. **NOTE:** Search and apply for positions online. **Other U.S. locations:** Nationwide. **CEO:** Carl George. **Number of employees nationwide:** 1,500.

COLDWELL BANKER
928 Grand Avenue, Schofield WI 54476. 715/359-0521. **Fax:** 715/359-4826. **Contact:** Human Resources. **World Wide Web address:** http://www.coldwellbanker.com. **Description:** One of the three largest residential real estate companies in the United States and Canada in total home sales transactions. Coldwell Banker has 3,500 independently owned and operated offices. **Corporate headquarters location:** Parsippany NJ. **Parent company:** Cendant Corporation.

COLOR ARTS, INC.
1840 Oakdale Avenue, P.O. Box 081158, Racine WI 53408-1158. 262/634-0040. **Toll-free phone:** 800/236-7751. **Fax:** 262/633-3008. **Contact:** Human Resources Department. **World Wide Web address:** http://www.colorarts.com. **Description:** A screen printer and digital image producer.

COLUMBIA ST. MARY'S HOSPITAL OZAUKEE
13111 North Port Washington Road, Mequon WI 53097. 262/243-7300. **Fax:** 262/243-7532. **Contact:** Human Resources. **World Wide Web address:** http://www.columbia-stmarys.org. **Description:** A nonprofit, acute care hospital with affiliated clinics. **NOTE:** Entry-level positions, part-time jobs, and second and third shifts are offered. **Advertised positions include:** Cardiovascular Tech; Clinical Nurse Specialist; Emergency Care Technician; Registered Nurse; Speech Language Pathologist. **Parent company:** Columbia St. Mary's. **Listed on:** Privately held. **Number of employees at this location:** 850.

COLUMBIA ST. MARY'S COLUMBIA
2025 East Newport Avenue, Milwaukee WI 53211. 414/961-3750. **Contact:** Human Resources. **World Wide Web address:** http://www.columbia-stmarys.org. **Description:** A hospital affiliated with Columbia St. Mary's. **NOTE:** Search and apply for positions online. **Positions advertised include:** Case Manager; Director of Performance Improvement and Accreditation; RN Clinical Instructor.

COOPER ENVIRONMENTAL & ENGINEERING RESOURCES, INC.
5569 Peters Drive, West Bend WI 53095. 262/338-9697. **Fax:** 262/338-9645. **Contact:** Human Resources. **Description:** An environmental services firm with risk assessment and cleanup-level determination, site development and remedial strategies, site investigations, remediation design, and construction monitoring.

COOPER POWER SYSTEMS
2300 Badger Drive, Waukesha, WI 53188. 262/524-3300. **Fax:** 262/524-3313. **Contact:** Human Resources. **World Wide Web address:** www.cooperpower.com. **E-mail address:** cooper@cooperpower.com. **Description:** Cooper Power Systems manufactures equipment, components, and systems for distributing and managing electrical energy. Products are used by electric utility companies in bringing electric power to homes, industries, businesses, and institutions worldwide. **NOTE:** Entry-level positions are offered. **Positions advertised include:** Senior Financial Analyst; Systems Administrator; Product Specialist; International Customer Services Representative. **Special programs:** Training. **Corporate headquarters location:** Houston TX. **International locations:** Brazil; China. **Parent company:** Cooper Industries, Inc. **Listed on:** New York Stock Exchange. **Stock exchange symbol:** CBE. **Annual**

sales/revenues: More than $100 million. **Number of employees at this location:** 575. **Number of employees worldwide:** 50,000.

CORE PRODUCTS
1505 Parker Avenue, Chetek WI 54728-0627. 715/924-4525. **Physical address:** 625 Fourth Street, Chetek WI 54728. **Fax:** 715/924-2662. **Contact:** Human Resources. **Description:** Manufactures orthopedic softgoods including medical braces.

COVANCE, INC.
3301 Kinsman Boulevard, Madison WI 53704. 608/241-4471. **Fax:** 608/242-2624. **Contact:** Human Resources Manager. **World Wide Web address:** http://www.covance.com. **Description:** A life sciences firm providing biological and chemical research services. Covance is also a supplier of laboratory animals and biological products. Clients include research institutes, industrial companies, government agencies, and manufacturers of pharmaceuticals, chemicals, food, and cosmetics. **Positions advertised include:** Research Associate; Study Coordinator; Analyst; Client Service Coordinator; Operations Manager. **Corporate headquarters location:** Princeton NJ. **Other U.S. locations:** Nationwide. **International locations:** Worldwide. **Listed on:** New York Stock Exchange. **Stock exchange symbol:** CVD.

CRESTLINE
1000 Southview Drive, Mosinee WI 54455. 715/693-7000. **Fax:** 715/693-8505. **Contact:** Personnel. **World Wide Web address:** http://www.crestlinewindows.com. **Description:** A manufacturer of windows, patio doors, and skylights under the Vetter and Crestline labels. Founded in 1892. **NOTE:** Entry-level positions are offered. **Parent company:** The Peachtree Companies, Inc.

CRISPELL-SNYDER, INC.
700 Geneva Parkway, P.O. Box 550, Lake Geneva WI 53147. 262/348-5600. **Toll-free phone:** 800/203-7700. **Fax:** 262/348-9979. **Contact:** Maggie Mentel, Human Resources Director. **E-mail address:** mentelm@crispell-snyder.com. **World Wide Web address:** http://www.crispell-snyder.com. **Description:** Consulting engineers specializing in civil engineering for small municipalities in southeastern and eastern Wisconsin. Crispell-Snyder provides services in the areas of transportation, water resources, wastewater treatment, general public works engineering, studies, grant writing, and structural engineering. **NOTE:** Entry-level positions and part-time jobs are offered. **Positions advertised include:** Senior Public Works Engineer. **Special programs:** Internships; Co-ops; Summer Jobs. **Corporate headquarters location:** This location. **Other area locations:** Racine WI; Germantown WI. **Listed on:** Privately held. **President:** Douglas Mushel. **Annual sales/revenues:** Less than $5 million. **Number of employees at this location:** 45. **Number of employees nationwide:** 75.

CRITICARE SYSTEMS, INC.
20925 Crossroads Circle, Suite 100, Waukesha WI 53186-4054. 262/798-8282. **Fax:** 262/-798-8290. **Contact:** Human Resources. **World Wide Web address:** http://www.csiusa.com. **Description:** Designs, manufactures, and markets patient monitoring systems and noninvasive sensors. Founded in 1984. **Corporate headquarters location:** This location. **International locations:** Australia; Denmark; Japan; Singapore; Spain. **Listed on:** NASDAQ. **Stock exchange symbol:** CXIM.

CUNA MUTUAL GROUP
5910 Mineral Point Road, Madison WI 53701-0391. 608/238-5851. **Fax:** 608/231-8527. **Contact:** Human Resources. **World Wide Web address:** http://www.cunamutual.com. **Description:** Provides insurance and financial services to credit unions and credit union members. **NOTE:** Search and apply for positions online. **Positions advertised include:** VP, Solution Development Leader; Product Administration Specialist; Project Services Consultant; Sr. Investment Officer; CU Financial Solutions Consultant; Tax Manager; Corporate Recruiter; Sr. Human Resources Consultant. **Corporate headquarters location:** This location. **Other U.S. locations:** Nationwide.

CURTIS INDUSTRIES, INC.
2400 South 43rd Street, Milwaukee WI 53219. 414/649-4200. **Fax:** 414/649-4279. **Contact:** Jay Livingston, Human Resources Manager. **World Wide Web address:** http://www.curtisind.com. **Description:** An electronic components company that builds, designs, and manufactures a variety of electronic equipment including terminal blocks, EMI/RFI filters, liquid level controls, and relay sockets. **Parent company:** Powers Holdings, Inc. **Operations at this facility include:** Administration; Manufacturing; Research and Development; Sales; Service.

DAIRYLAND POWER COOPERATIVE
P.O. Box 817, La Crosse WI 54602-0817. 608/788-4000. **Physical address:** 3200 East Avenue South, La Crosse WI 54601. **Fax:** 608/787-1465. **Recorded jobline:** 608/787-1293. **Contact:** Human Resources. **E-mail address:** jobs@dairynet.com. **World Wide Web address:** http://www.dairynet.com. **Description:** Provides wholesale electrical requirements and other services for 25 electric distribution cooperatives and 20 municipal utilities. **NOTE:** Search and apply for positions online. **Positions advertised include:** Instrument Technician; Lineworker; Telecommunications Technician; Plant Engineer; Power Plant Operator Trainee; Relay and Control Engineer.

DANE COUNTY PARENT COUNCIL
HEAD START
2096 Red Arrow Trail, Madison WI 53711. 608/275-6740. **Fax:** 608/275-6756. **Contact:** Human Resources. **Description:** A family service center that offers a wide range of basic support services for parents including a GED program and free clothing. Head Start (also at this location) is an educational program for children.

DEAN HEALTH PLAN, INC.
1277 Deming Way, Madison WI 53717. 608/836-1400. **Fax:** 608/827-4002. **Recorded jobline:** 800/356-7344. **Contact:** Human Resources Manager. **World Wide Web address:** http://www.deancare.com. **Description:** A managed health care company. Founded in 1983. **Positions advertised include:** Manager of Claims Integrity; Corporate Training Specialist; Provider Database Analyst; Accountant; Data Warehouse Developer; Project Manager/Business Analyst; Software Engineer. **Office hours:** Monday - Friday, 8:00 a.m. - 4:30 p.m. **Corporate headquarters location:** This location. **Listed on:** Privately held. **Number of employees at this location:** 250.

DEAN MEDICAL CENTER
1808 West Beltline Highway, Madison WI 53713. 608/250-1500. **Fax:** 608/250-1441. **Recorded jobline:** 608/250-3326. **Contact:** Human Resources. **E-mail address:** deancareers@deancare.com. **World Wide Web address:** http://www.deancare.com. **Description:** A multispecialty group practice with over 30 locations in southwestern Wisconsin. **Positions advertised include:** Certified Nursing Assistant; Certified Medical Assistant; Database Administrator; Licensed Practical Nurses; Registered Nurses; Supervisor of Clinic Services; Drug Information Pharmacist. **Corporate headquarters location:** This location. **President/CAO:** Kevin R. Hayden.

ED DEBEVIC'S RESTAURANT
780 North Jefferson Street, Milwaukee WI 53202. 414/226-2200. **Fax:** 414/226-2456. **Contact:** Human Resources. **World Wide Web address:** http://www.eddebevics.com. **Description:** One location of the casual dining restaurant chain. Ed Debevic's serves American cuisine and operates a gift shop. **Corporate headquarters location:** Chicago, IL. **Other U.S. locations:** Beverly Hills CA; Chicago IL; Phoenix AZ.

DECRANE AIRCRAFT SEATING COMPANY, INC.
701 Maple Street, Peshtigo WI 54157. 715/582-4517. **Fax:** 715/582-2899. **Contact:** Human Resources Department. **E-mail address:** employment@dasc-inc.com. **World Wide Web address:** http://www.decraneseats.com. **Description:** Manufactures custom aircraft seating, upholstery, tables, and cabinetry hinges.

DEDICATED COMPUTING
N26 W23880 Commerce Circle, Waukesha WI, 53188. 262/951-7200. **Toll-free phone:** 877/523-3301. **Fax:** 262/523-2266. **Contact:** Human Resources. **E-mail address:** hr@dedicatedcomputing.com. **World Wide Web address:** http://www.dedicatedcomputing.com. **Description:** Dedicated Computing is a manufacturer and integrator of OEM computer engines. **NOTE:** Search and apply for positions online. **Positions advertised include:** Cell Member; Project Engineer; Server Cell Member; Account Manager. **Parent company:** Omni Tech Corporation.

DEL MONTE CORPORATION
1400 Plover Road, Plover WI 54467. 715/344-8285. **Fax:** 715/344-5862. **Contact:** Human Resources Department. **World Wide Web address:** http://www.delmonte.com. **Description:** An international processor and distributor of foods operating in the following business segments: Processed Foods, Fresh Fruit, Transportation, and Institutional Services. The Processed Foods Division processes canned, frozen, dried, and chilled foods in more than 40 domestic and 20 foreign plants. Del Monte Corporation's support operations include can manufacturing, label printing, seed production, and agricultural and scientific research. The company's products are distributed in more than 60 countries under the brand names Del Monte, Granny Goose, and Award.

DELPHI ENERGY & ENGINE MANAGEMENT SYSTEMS
7929 South Howell Avenue, Oak Creek WI 53154. 414/768-2000. **Contact:** Human Resources. **World Wide Web address:** http://www.delphi.com. **Description:** Manufactures catalytic converters for automobiles. **Parent company:** General Motors Corporation.

DERCO AEROSPACE INC.
8000 West Tower Avenue, P.O. Box 25549, Milwaukee WI 53223. 414/355-3066. **Fax:** 414/355-6129. **Contact:** Human Resources. **E-mail address:** resumes@dercoaerospace.com. **World Wide Web address:** http://www.dercoaerospace.com. **Description:** Distributes OEM spare parts, components, and ground support equipment for aircraft. **Positions advertised include:** Capture Manager; Logistician; Avionics Engineer; Contracts Administration Specialist. **Corporate headquarters location:** This location. **Parent company:** United Technologies Corporation. **Annual sales/revenues:** $51 - $100 million. **Number of employees at this location:** 300.

DEXM ENGINEERED PRODUCTS
N22 W23977 Ridge View Parkway, Suite 100, Waukesha WI 53188. 262/523-4670. **Fax:** 262/523-4675. **Contact:** Human Resources. **Description:** Specializes in producing high quality, precision metal fabricated components.

DICKTEN & MASCH MANUFACTURING COMPANY
N44 W33341 Watertown Plank Road, Nashotah WI 53058-9700. 262/369-5555. **Fax:** 262/367-5630. **Contact:** Dawn Korth, Human Resources Manager. **World Wide Web address:** http://www.dicktenplastics.com. **Description:** A custom plastic injection thermoset and thermoplastic molder. **Number of employees at this location:** 400.

DOMTAR
100 Wisconsin River Drive, Port Edwards WI 54469. 715/887-5111. **Fax:** 715/887-5214. **Contact:** Personnel. **World Wide Web address:** http://www.domtar.com. **Description:** A paper mill. **NOTE:** Internships offered. Submit resume online. **Number of employees at this location:** 825.

DOVER DIVERSIFIED
2607 North Grandview Boulevard, Suite 105, Waukesha WI 53188. 262/548-6060. **Fax:** 262/548-6069. **Contact:** Human Resources Department. **Description:** A company that provides a broad range of financial services.

DUNSIRN INDUSTRIES
AVERY DENNISON
P.O. Box 785, Neenah WI 54957. 920/725-3814. **Fax:** 920/725-9102. **Contact:** Human Resources Department. **World Wide Web address:** http://www.averydennison.com. **Description:** A paper conversion facility. **Number of employees at this location:** 120.

DYNAMATICS
3122 14th Avenue, Kenosha WI 53140. 262/656-4011. **Fax:** 262/656-4430. **Contact:** Human Resources. **World Wide Web address:** http://www.dynamatics.com. **Description:** Manufactures a wide range of products serving the automotive, industrial, commercial, and defense markets. Principal products include truck transmission and axles, engine components, and electrical equipment and controls. The electrical and electronic controls production is divided into three groups: industrial and commercial controls, automotive and applicative controls, and specialty controls.

ECM MOTOR COMPANY
1099 Proctor Drive, Elkhorn WI 53121. 414/723-6400. **Fax:** 414/723-7373. **Contact:** Human Resources. **World Wide Web address:** http://www.ecmmotor.com. **Description:** A manufacturer of subfractional horsepower motors and gearmotors. **NOTE:** Entry-level positions are offered. **Corporate headquarters location:** This location. **Parent company:** BTR/FASCO. **Operations at this facility include:** Administration; Manufacturing. **Number of employees at this location:** 600. **Number of employees nationwide:** 670.

ESE, INC.
3600 Downwind drive, Marshfield WI 54449-7107. 715/387-4778. **Fax:** 715/387-0125. **Contact:** Rosemarie Webber, Human Resources. **E-mail address:** hr@ese1.com. **World Wide Web address:** http://www.ese1.com. **Description:** Designs and engineers process control systems for the food, dairy, brewery, and pharmaceutical industries. Founded in 1981. **Positions advertised include:** Controls Engineering Manager. **Office hours:** Monday - Friday, 8:00 a.m. - 5:00 p.m. **Corporate headquarters location:** This location. **Number of employees at this location:** 30.

EASTBAY
111 South First Avenue, Wausau WI 54401. 715/845-5538. **Fax:** 715/261-9549. **Contact:** Human Resources. **E-mail address:** jobs@eastbay.com. **World Wide Web address:** http://www.eastbay.com. **Description:** A direct marketer of sporting goods and apparel such as sneakers and sweatshirts. **NOTE:** Search for positions online. **Positions advertised include:** Marketing Specialist; Quantitative Analyst. Other area locations: Green Bay WI; Oshkosh WI. **Parent company:** Foot Locker, Inc.

ECK INDUSTRIES, INC.
1602 North 8th Street, Manitowoc WI 54221-0967. 920/682-4618. **Fax:** 920/682-9298. **Contact:** Personnel. **World Wide Web address:** http://www.eckindustries.com. **Description:** Manufactures aluminum castings for automobiles and motorcycles.

EDWARD JONES
212 East Main Street, Sun Prairie WI 53590. 608/837-2700. **Fax:** 888/672-2353. **Contact:** Personnel. **World Wide Web address:** http://www.edwardjones.com. **Description:** A securities brokerage firm. **NOTE:** Apply online. **Corporate headquarters location:** Maryland Heights MD. **Listed on:** Privately held. **Number of employees at this location:** 5. **Number of employees nationwide:** 7,000.

EDWARD JONES
500 West Franklin Street, Appleton WI 54911. 920/739-7719. **Contact:** Personnel. **World Wide Web address:** http://www.edwardjones.com. **Description:** A securities brokerage firm. **Corporate headquarters location:** Maryland Heights MD. **Other U.S. locations:** Sun Prairie WI. **Listed on:** Privately held. **Number of employees nationwide:** 7,000.

ELECTRONICS TELE-COMMUNICATIONS, INC.
1915 MacArthur Road, Waukesha WI 53188. 262/542-5600. **Fax:** 262/542-1524. **Contact:** Human Resources. **E-mail address:** hrmgr@etcia.com **World Wide Web address:** http://www.etcia.com. **Description:** Develops, manufactures, markets, services, and leases interactive voice systems for the telephone industry. Services include software design, equipment installation, recording services, and technical support. **Corporate headquarters location:** This location. **Other U.S. locations:** Pleasanton CA; Atlanta GA.

ELECTROTEK CORPORATION
7745 South 10th Street, Oak Creek WI 53154. 414/762-1390. **Fax:** 414/762-1510. **Contact:** Human Resources. **World Wide Web address:** http://www.boards4u.com. **Description:** Manufactures printed circuit boards. Founded in 1968. **NOTE:** Entry-level positions and second and third shifts are offered. **Special programs:** Training. **Corporate headquarters location:** This location. **Listed on:** Privately held. **Annual sales/revenues:** $11 - $20 million. **Number of employees at this location:** 160.

EMMPAK FOODS INC.
200 South Emmber Lane, Milwaukee WI 53233. 414/645-6500. **Contact:** Paul H. Sobczak, Human Resources Director. **Description:** A manufacturer of processed meats and boneless beef.

ENCORE SENIOR VILLAGE
5555 Burke Road, Madison WI 53704. 608/829-0909. **Fax:** 608/829-3040. **Contact:** Human Resources Department. **World Wide Web address:** http://www.encoresl.com. **Description:** A facility that specializes in caring for individuals with Alzheimer's disease. **NOTE:** Apply for positions online. **Corporate headquarters location:** Portland OR.

ENERQUIP INC.
611 North Road, P.O. Box 467, Medford WI 54451-0467. 715/748-5888. **Fax:** 715/748-6484. **Contact:** Personnel. **World Wide Web address:** http://www.enerquip.com. **Description:** Manufactures heat exchangers, pressure vessels, and tanks for the food, dairy, pharmaceutical industries. Enerquip custom designs to ASME and other codes. **Corporate headquarters location:** This location.

EPIC SYSTEMS CORPORATION
5301 Tokay Boulevard, Madison WI 53711. 608/271-9000. **Fax:** 608/271-7237. **Contact:** Human Resources. **E-mail address:** jobs@epicsystems.com. **World Wide Web address:** http://www.epicsystems.com. **Description:** A healthcare software company. **Positions advertised include:** Clinical Informatics; Consultants; Pharmacy Software Advocate; Problem Solver; Software Developer; UNIX or VMS Systems Engineer. **Corporate headquarters location:** This location.

MARSHALL ERDMAN AND ASSOCIATES
5117 University Avenue, Madison WI 53705. 608/238-0211. **Toll-free phone:** 800/322-5117. **Fax:** 608/218-4336. **Contact:** Sarah Carpenter. **E-mail address:** scarpenter@erdman.com. **World Wide Web address:** http://www.erdman.com. **Description:** Designs and constructs healthcare facilities nationwide. **NOTE:** Entry-level positions and second and third shifts are offered. **Positions advertised include:** Development Analyst; Project Engineer, Electrical; Project Engineer, Plumbing. **Special programs:** Internships. **Corporate headquarters location:** This location. **Other U.S. locations:** Denver CO; Hartford CT; Washington DC; Atlanta GA; Dallas TX. **Listed on:** Privately held. **Annual sales/revenues:** More than $100 million. **Number of employees at this location:** 270. **Number of employees nationwide:** 410.

ESKER SOFTWARE
465 Science Drive, Madison WI 53711. 608/273-6000. **Toll-free phone:** 800/368-5283. **Fax:** 608/273-8227. **Contact:** Personnel. **E-mail address:** recruiting@esker.com. **World Wide Web address:** http://www.esker.com. **Description:** Develops communications software to help users automate document creation and delivery. Founded in 1982. **NOTE:** Search for and apply for positions online. **Positions advertised include:** Software Product Manager; Technical Support manager; Technical Support Specialist. **Office hours:** Monday - Friday, 8:30 a.m. - 5:00 p.m. **Corporate headquarters location:** France. **Other U.S. locations:** Stillwater OK. Lake Forest CA. **International locations:** Worldwide. **Listed on:** Euronext.

EXEL INNS OF AMERICA, INC.
4706 East Washington Avenue, Madison WI 53704. 608/241-5271. **Fax:** 608/241-3224. **Contact:** Director of Personnel. **E-mail address:** hrdir@excelinns.com. **World Wide Web address:** http://www.exelinns.com. **Description:** A limited-service motel chain with 35 locations, primarily in the Midwest. Founded in 1973. **NOTE:** Search and apply for positions online. **Corporate headquarters location:** This location. **Other U.S. locations:** MN; IA; IL; MI; TX; ND. **Listed on:** Privately held. **Annual sales/revenues:** $21 - $50 million. **Number of employees nationwide:** 750.

EXPRESS TECHNOLOGIES CORPORATION
400 Reid Street, Suite 0, De Pere WI 54115. 920/337-1640. **Toll-free phone:** 800/654-9548. **Fax:** 920-337-1643. **Contact:** Human Resources. **World Wide Web address:** http://www.exptech.com. **Description:** A developer of software called World Watch, displaying real time geographical locations throughout the world, as well as illuminated patterns that delineate regions currently experiencing daylight. Express products are also available as World Watch screen savers.

EXTENDICARE HEALTH SERVICES
111 West Michigan Street, Milwaukee WI 53203-2903. 414/908-8000. **Fax:** 414/908-8143. **Contact:** Angela Komarek. **E-mail address:** akomarek@extendicare.com. **World Wide Web address:** http://www.extendicare.com. **Description:** Operates 275 long-term care facilities in North America. Services include medical rehabilitation, respiratory services, cardiac rehabilitation, infusion therapy, and wound care. **Positions advertised include:** Nursing Home Administrator; Community Care Branch Manager; Director of Nursing/Care; Nurse Consultant; Registered Nurse; Registered Dietician. **Other U.S. locations:** Nationwide. **Operations at this facility include:** Administration.

FWD/SEAGRAVE
105 East 12th Street, Clintonville WI 54929. 715/823-2141. **Fax:** 715/823-5768. **Contact:** Human Resources. **E-mail address:** jobs@seagrave.com. **World Wide Web address:** http://www.seagrave.com. **Description:** FWD/Seagrave is engaged principally in the design and manufacture of heavy-duty, on/off-highway, all-wheel drive trucks, as well as Seagrave firefighting apparatus including components and service parts for all units. Founded in 1881. **Positions advertised include:** Product Design Engineer; Quality Engineer; Manufacturing Engineer. **Corporate headquarters location:** This location. **Operations at this facility include:** This location manufactures fire trucks. **Listed on:** Privately held. **Number of employees at this location:** 400.

FAIRBANKS MORSE ENGINE
701 White Avenue, Beloit WI 53511. 608/364-4411. **Toll-free phone:** 800/356-6955. **Fax:** 608/364-8039. **Contact:** Human Resources Department. **E-mail address:** fmhr@fairbanksmorse.com. **World Wide Web address:** http://www.fairbanksmorse.com. **Description:** Manufactures large diesel and dual fuel engines used for power generation, marine propulsion, and locomotives. **NOTE:** Second and third shifts are offered. **Positions advertised include:** Field Service Engineer. **Special programs:** Internships. **Corporate headquarters location:** This location. **Parent company:** EnPro Industries. **Operations at this facility include:** Administration; Manufacturing; Research and Development; Sales; Service. **Annual sales/revenues:** More than $100 million. **Number of employees at this location:** 500.

THE FALK CORPORATION
P.O. Box 492, Milwaukee WI 53201-0492. 414/342-3131. **Fax:** 414/937-4359. **Contact:** Human Resources. **World Wide Web address:** http://www.falkcorp.com. **Description:** Manufactures gears, power transmission parts, and various other parts used in industrial machinery. **Corporate headquarters location:** This location. **Parent company:** Hamilton Sundstrand.

FAMILY SERVICE
128 East Olin Avenue, Suite 100, Madison WI 53713. 608/252-1325x1127. **Fax:** 608/252-1333. **Contact:** Nancy Caray, Human Resources Coordinator. **Description:** A private, nonprofit mental health agency with programs that include ATA (Alternatives to Aggression), SAH (Safe at Home), FIT (Families in Transition), and CCCS (Consumer Credit Counseling Services). Founded in 1910. **Special programs:** Internships. **President/CEO:** David Johnson. **Annual sales/revenues:** Less than $5 million. **Number of employees at this location:** 55.

FAMOUS FOOTWEAR
7010 Mineral Point Road, Madison WI 53717-1701. 608/829-3668. **Contact:** Recruitment Manager. **World Wide Web address:** http://www.famousfootwear.com. **Description:** A shoe retailer operating over 920 stores in 50 states plus Guam and Puerto Rico. **NOTE:** Search and apply for positions or submit resume online. **Positions advertised include:** Buyer; Controller, Retail Finance; Copywriter; Customer Insight Specialist; Location Planning Manager; Real Estate Associate. **Special programs:** Internships. **Corporate headquarters location:** This location. **Other U.S. locations:** Nationwide. **Parent company:** Brown Shoe Company, Inc. **Number of employees nationwide:** 10,000.

FEDERAL-MOGUL POWERTRAIN SYSTEMS
2318 Waldo Boulevard, P.O. Box 910, Manitowoc WI 54221-0910. 920/684-7881. **Fax:** 920/684-1641. **Contact:** Human Resources. **World Wide Web address:** http://www.federal-mogul.com. **Description:** Supplies automotive components, subsystems, modules and systems to original equipment manufacturers and the aftermarket. Operates 130 manufacturing facilities in 24 countries. **NOTE:** Internship and co-op programs offered. Submit resume to: Federal-Mogul Corporation, Attn: Corporate Human Resources Staffing, 26555 Northwestern Highway, Southfield MI 48034. **Corporate headquarters location:** Southfield MI. **Number of employees at this location:** 585. **Number of employees worldwide:** 45,000.

FIGI'S GIFTS INC.
3200 South Maple Avenue, Marshfield WI 54449. 715/387-6311. **Fax:** 715/384-1420. **Contact:** Human Resources. **World Wide Web address:** http://www.figis.com. **Description:** A leader in mail-order/catalog food gifts, with a full line of products including cheese, sausage, smokehouse specialties, candy, cookies, nuts, cakes, fruits, plants, and a variety of nonfood gifts. Founded in 1944. **Parent company:** Fingerhut. **Annual sales/revenues:** More than $100 million. **Number of employees nationwide:** 2,500.

FIGI'S GIFTS INC.
2525 South Roddis Avenue, Marshfield WI 54449. 715/384-1425. **Toll-free phone:** 800/360-6542. **Fax:** 715/384-1177. **Contact:** Mike Oemig, Human Resources Recruiter. **World Wide Web address:** http://www.figis.com. **Description:** A leader in mail-order/catalog food gifts, with a full line of products including cheese, sausage, smokehouse specialties, candy, cookies, nuts, cakes, fruits, plants, and a variety of nonfood gifts. This location also hires seasonally. Founded in 1944. **NOTE:** Part-time jobs are offered. **Special programs:** Internships. **Corporate headquarters location:** This location. **Other area locations:** Neillsville WI; Stevens Point WI. **Parent company:** Fingerhut. **Annual sales/revenues:** More than $100 million. **Number of employees at this location:** 2,250. **Number of employees nationwide:** 2,500.

FIRST STATE BANK - NEW LONDON
113 West North Water Street, P.O. Box 268, New London WI 54961-0268. 920/982-3300. **Fax:** 920/982-4498. **Contact:** Human Resources. **World Wide Web address:** http://www.bankfirststate.com. **Description:** This location is the main branch of the local commercial bank. Founded in 1933. **NOTE:** Search and apply for positions online. **Positions advertised include:** Deposit Operations Manager; Human Resources Manager; Retail Loan Officer; VP of Marketing.

FIRSTLOGIC, INC.
100 Harborview Plaza, La Crosse WI 54601-4071. 608/782-5000. **Toll-free phone:** 888/215-6442. **Fax:** 608/788-1188. **Contact:** Employment Specialist. **E-mail address:** hr@firstlogic.com. **World Wide Web address:** http://www.firstlogic.com. **Description:** Develops and manufactures software for postal automation, document processing, and database management. Founded in 1984. **NOTE:** Entry-level positions are offered. Search and apply for positions online. **Positions advertised include:** Product Test Engineer; Instructor/Consultant; Senior Consultant; Software Engineer. **Corporate headquarters location:** This location. **Other U.S. locations:** Nationwide. **President/CEO:** Doug Schmidt. **Number of employees at this location:** 200. **Number of employees nationwide:** 400.

FISERV, INC.
255 Fiserv Drive, P.O. Box 979, Brookfield WI 53045. 262/879-5000. **Fax:** 262/879-5013. **Contact:** Human Resources Department. **World Wide Web address:** http://www.fiserv.com. **Description:** Provides information management systems and services to the financial industry, including transaction processing, outsourcing, business process outsourcing and software and systems solutions. **NOTE:** Search and apply for positions online. **Positions advertised include:** Business Analyst; Client Services Supervisor; Conversion Programmer Analyst; Corporate Attorney; Specialist, Project Management; Director of Marketing Services; HRIS Administrator; MicroProducts Systems Analyst; Network Engineer. **Corporate headquarters location:** This location. **Listed on:** NASDAQ. **Stock exchange symbol:** FISV. **Annual sales/revenues:** More than $100 million. **Number of employees at this location:** 8,500.

FISKARS, INC.
2537 Daniels Street, Madison WI 53718. 608/259-1649. **Contact:** Human Resources. **World Wide Web address:** http://www.fiskars.com. **Description:** Manufactures scissors and shears of all types. **Positions advertised include:** Sr. LAN/WAN Engineer; Sr. Product Design Engineer; IT Server Engineer. **Corporate headquarters location:** This location. **Parent company:** Fiskars Brands, Inc.

FLAD & ASSOCIATES, INC.
644 Science Drive, Madison WI 53711. 608/238-2661. **Fax:** 608/238-6727. **Contact:** Human Resources. **E-mail address:** humanresources@flad.com. **World Wide Web address:** http://www.flad.com. **Description:** An architectural and engineering firm specializing in the planning and design of facilities for academic, healthcare, and research, development and production clients. Founded in 1927. **NOTE:** Search and apply for positions online. **Positions advertised include:** Human Resources/Training; Lab Planner; Project Manager; Project Manager, Healthcare; Senior Interior Designer, Healthcare. **Number of employees nationwide:** 300.

FOREMOST FARMS USA COOPERATIVE
E10889A Penny Lane, P.O. Box 111, Baraboo WI 53913. **Toll-free phone:** 800/362-9196. **Contact:** Human Resources. **E-mail address:** humanresources@foremostfarms.com. **World Wide Web address:** http://www.foremostfarms.com. **Description:** Foremost Farms USA Cooperative is a cooperative that provides dairy producers a financially strong business that efficiently assembles, processes and markets milk and related dairy products. **Positions advertised include:** Database Systems Manager; Materials Planner; Operations Intern; Production Associates; Production Supervisor. **Cooperative Headquarters:** This location.

FOX RIVER PAPER
100 West Lawrence Street, Appleton WI 54911. 920/733-7341. **Fax:** 920/733-2975. **Contact:** Human Resources. **E-mail address:** webmail@frpaper.com. **World Wide Web address:** http://www.foxriverpaper.com. **Description:** Manufacturer of premium uncoated writing, text, cover, and specialty papers. **Subsidiaries:** Gilbert Paper. **Parent company:** Fox Valley Corporation. **Number of employees at this location:** 340.

FRANCISCAN SKEMP MEDICAL CENTER
700 West Avenue South, La Crosse WI 54601. 608/791-9756. **Toll-free phone:** 800/246-6499. **Fax:** 608/791-9504. **Contact:** Human Resources Department. **World Wide Web address:** http://www.franciscanskemp.org. **Description:** A Mayo Health System affiliate providing health services to the tri-state communities of Iowa, Minnesota, and Wisconsin. The system includes hospitals, clinics, elderly care services, behavioral health, and services for women. **NOTE:** Entry-level positions are offered. Search and apply for positions online. **Positions advertised include:** Anesthesiologist; Dermatologist; Diabetes Nurse Educator; Hematologist/Oncologist; Invasive Cardiovascular Technologist; Mammography Technologist; Occupational Therapist; Neurosurgeon; Registered Nurses. **Corporate headquarters location:** This location. **Operations at this facility include:** Administration. **Number of employees at this location:** 2,900.

FRESH BRANDS, INC.
2215 Union Avenue, Sheboygan WI 53081. 920/457-4433. **Fax:** 920/457-6295. **Contact:** Human Resources Manager. **World Wide Web address:** http://www.fresh-brands.com. **Description:** A supermarket retailer and grocery wholesaler through corporate-owned retail, franchised and independent supermarkets. The corporate-owned and franchised retail supermarkets currently operate under the Piggly Wiggly and Dick's Supermarkets brands. Fresh Brands currently has 77 franchised supermarkets, 29 corporate-owned supermarkets and two corporate-owned convenience stores, all of which are served by two distribution centers and a centralized bakery/deli production facility. Supermarkets are located in Wisconsin, northern Illinois and northeastern Iowa. **Corporate headquarters location:** This location. **Listed on:** NASDAQ. **Stock exchange symbol:** FRSH. **Number of employees nationwide:** 1,700.

FRISKIES PETCARE COMPANY
150 West Riverview Drive, Jefferson WI 53549. 920/674-4100. **Fax:** 920/674-5022. **Contact:** Human Resources. **World Wide Web address:** http://www.friskies.com. **Description:** Manufactures and sells the Alpo brand of premium canned dog foods and Friskies brand of premium canned cat foods. Friskies PetCare Company is one of the largest dog and cat food manufacturers and distributors in the United States. **Positions advertised include:** Training and Safety Manager. **Other U.S. locations:** PA. **Parent company:** Nestle.

FRONTIER TECHNOLOGIES
10201 North Port Washington Road, Mequon WI 53092. 414/241-4555. **Contact:** Human Resources. **World Wide Web address:** http://www.frontiertech.com. **Description:** Develops network software solutions and digital signature software.

GE HEALTHCARE
3000 North Grandview Boulevard, Waukesha WI 53188. 414/355-5000. **Toll-free phone:** 800/558-5120. **Fax:** 414/355-3790. **Contact:** Human Resources. **World Wide Web address:** http://www.gehealthcare.com. **Description:** A global leader in the medical monitoring and diagnostic equipment market. The company designs and manufactures medical electronic equipment, software, and systems for the diagnosis, monitoring, and computerized charting of patients. Major product lines include electrocardiographic equipment, patient monitors, clinical information systems, defibrillators, and instruments for respiratory and anesthetic gas analysis. An international field service organization and a complete line of supplies support all product lines. Principal markets include health care systems, major medical institutions, and teaching hospitals, as well as smaller hospitals, medical clinics, physician offices, government hospitals, research institutions, and emergency care providers. **NOTE:** Search and apply for positions online. **Positions advertised include:** GEHC Technology Security Director; Development Engineer; XRay Downstream Marketing Manager; Financial Analyst. **Parent company:** General Electric.

G&L MOTION CONTROL, LLC
672 South Military Road, Fond du Lac WI 54935. 920/921-7100. **Contact:** Human Resources. **World Wide Web address:** http://www.glcontrols.com. **Description:** Manufactures and sells industrial control products including programmable industrial controls, servo motors and drives, operator interfaces, and software. **NOTE:** Entry-level positions are offered. **Special programs:** Internships. **International locations:** England; Germany. **Parent company:** ThyssenKrupp Technologies. **Listed on:** NASDAQ. **Stock exchange symbol:** GIDL. **Number of employees at this location:** 200. **Number of employees nationwide:** 2,500.

GKN SINTER METALS
N112 W18700 Mequon Road, P.O. Box 1009, Germantown WI 53051. 262/255-9050. **Contact:** Human Resources. **World Wide Web address:** http://www.gknsintermetals.com. **Description:** Manufactures powdered metal parts that are used in a wide range of products. Operates 40 facilities in 13 countries. **NOTE:** Search and apply for positions online. **Positions advertised include:** Manufacturing Engineering Manager. **Corporate headquarters location:** Auburn Hills MI. **Number of employees worldwide:** 7,500.

GARDNER BENDER
6100 North Baker Road, Milwaukee WI 53209. 414/352-4160. **Fax:** 414/352-2377. **Contact:** Human Resources. **World Wide Web address:** http://www.gardnerbender.com. **Description:** Manufactures and distributes electrical products. **NOTE:** Entry-level positions are offered. Search and apply for positions online. **Positions advertised include:** Applications Developer, Java; Electronic Commerce Administrator. **Special programs:** Internships; Training. **Corporate headquarters location:** This location. **International locations:** Canada.

GEHL COMPANY
143 Water Street, West Bend WI 53095. 262/334-9461. **Fax:** 262/338-7517. **Contact:** Human Resources. **World Wide Web address:** http://www.gehl.com. **Description:** A manufacturer of agricultural and construction equipment. The company is a leading manufacturer of agricultural implements in North America offering a comprehensive product line of equipment for haymaking, forage harvesting, feed-making, manure-handling, and materials-handling. Gehl Company's mobile construction equipment line includes a diversified offering of skid steer loaders; rough-terrain, telescoping-boom forklifts; and paving equipment. **Corporate headquarters location:** This location. **Other U.S. locations:** Belvidere IL; Madison SD; Yankton SD. **Listed on:** NASDAQ. **Stock exchange symbol:** GEHL. **Number of employees at this location:** 850.

GENERAC
900 North Parkway, P.O. Box 299, Jefferson WI 53549. 920/674-3750. **Fax:** 920/674-4370. **Contact:** Human Resources Department. **E-mail address:** jobs@bsppgroup.com. **World Wide Web address:** http://www.generac-portables.com. **Description:** A manufacturer of pressure washers and generators for a wide variety of industries. **Positions advertised include:** Program Manager. **Parent company:** Briggs & Stratton Corporation.

GENTIVA HEALTH SERVICES
10909 West Greenfield, Suite 201, West Allis WI 53214. 414/257-1156. **Fax:** 414/257-1733. **Contact:** Human Resources. **World Wide Web address:** http://www.gentiva.com. **Description:** Gentiva Health Services provides home health care services, pharmaceutical support, and supplemental staffing services. **NOTE:** Search and apply for positions online. **Positions advertised include:** Registered Nurse; Nurse Manager/Pediatrics; Branch Director; Physical Therapists. **Corporate headquarters location:** Melville NY. **Other area locations:** Racine WI. **Operations at this facility include:** This location is a home health care agency.

GEORGIA-PACIFIC CORPORATION
P.O. Box 19130, Green Bay WI 54307-9130. 920/435-8821. **Physical address:** 1919 South Broadway, Green Bay WI 54304. **Contact:** Senior Recruiter. **World Wide Web address:** http://www.gp.com. **Description:** Manufactures, wholesales, and distributes building products, industrial wood products, pulp, paper, packaging materials, and related chemicals. The company is one of the world's largest manufacturers of forest products. **NOTE:** Entry-level positions, second and third shifts, and part-time jobs are offered. Search and apply for positions online. **Positions advertised include:** Engineer; Process Engineer; Project Engineer; Maintenance Supervisor. **Office hours:** Monday - Friday, 7:30 a.m. - 4:00 p.m. **Corporate headquarters location:** Atlanta GA. **Other U.S. locations:** Nationwide. **International locations:** Worldwide. **Listed on:** New York Stock Exchange. **Stock exchange symbol:** GP. **CEO:** Miles Marsh. **Annual sales/revenues:** More than $100 million. **Number of employees at this location:** 3,000.

THE GESSERT GROUP
5369 North 118th Court, Milwaukee WI 53225. 414/466-3400. **Fax:** 414/466-9369. **Contact:** Human Resources Department. **World Wide Web address:** http://www.gessert.com. **Description:** A marketing and multimedia communications company specializing in the health care industry. The company's services also include print work and video production. **Corporate headquarters location:** This location.

GILBERT PAPER
100 West Lawrence Street, P.O. Box 2215, Appleton WI 54912-2215. 920/733-7341. **Contact:** Human Resources. **World Wide Web address:** http://www.gilbertpaper.com. **Description:** A paper manufacturer.

GOLDEN GUERNSEY COMPANY
2101 Delafield Street, Waukesha WI 53188. 262/547-1700. **Fax:** 262/312-5026. **Contact:** Human Resources. **Description:** A manufacturer of dairy products.

GOOD HUMOR-BREYERS ICE CREAM
909 Packerland Drive, Green Bay WI 54303. 920/499-5151. **Fax:** 920/497-6523. **Contact:** Personnel. **E-mail address:** jobs.ghbhr@unilever.com. **World Wide Web address:** http://www.icecreamusa.com. **Description:** A major producer of frozen packaged ice cream and novelties distributed nationally.

GOODYEAR TIRE & RUBBER COMPANY
143 Goodyear Street, Sun Prairie WI 53590. 608/825-1800. **Fax:** 608/825-1802. **Contact:** Human Resources. **World Wide Web address:** http://www.goodyear.com. **Description:** Goodyear Tire & Rubber Company's principal business is the development, manufacture, distribution, and sale of tires. Goodyear also manufactures and sells a broad spectrum of rubber products and rubber-related chemicals for various industrial and consumer markets, and provides auto repair services. **Other U.S. locations:** Nationwide. **International locations:** Worldwide. **Subsidiaries include:** North American Tire; Kelly-Springfield, Goodyear Europe; Goodyear Latin America; Goodyear Asia; Celeron; and Goodyear Racing. **Operations at this facility include:** Manufacture of hose products. **Number of employees worldwide:** 92,000.

GRAEF, ANHALT, SCHLOEMER & ASSOCIATES, INC.
125 South 84th Street, Suite 401, Milwaukee WI 53214-1470. 414/259-1500. **Fax:** 414/259-0037. **Contact:** Carrie Kopischkie, Human Resources Assistant. **World Wide Web address:** http://www.gasai.com. **Description:** A full-service civil engineering and consulting firm. Founded in 1961. **NOTE:** Entry-level positions are offered. Search and apply for positions online. **Positions advertised include:** Accounting Manager; Architects and Architectural Technicians; Electrical Engineer; Environmental Scientists; Human Resources Assistant; Hydrologist; Municipal Project Manager. **Special programs:** Co-ops. **Corporate headquarters location:** This location. **Other area locations:** Green Bay WI; Madison WI. **Other U.S. locations:** Chicago IL; Davenport IA. **Number of employees at this location:** 175. **Number of employees nationwide:** 230.

GRANITE MICROSYSTEMS
10202 North Enterprise Drive, Mequon WI 53092. 262/242-8800. **Toll-free phone:** 800/822-2983. **Fax:** 22/242-8825. **Contact:** Human Resources. **E-mail address:** info2@granitemicrosystems.com. **World Wide Web address:** http://www.granitem.com. **Description:** Develops, customizes, and manufactures hardware. In addition, the company develops software and offers research and development, consulting, and technical support services. **NOTE:** Search and apply for positions online.

GRANT THORNTON LLP
10 College Avenue, Suite 300 Appleton WI 54911. 920/968-6700. **Fax:** 920/968-6719. **Contact:** Personnel. **World Wide Web address:** http://www.grantthornton.com. **Description:** An international, certified, public accounting firm offering a comprehensive scope of consulting and accounting services, as well as strategic and tactical planning assistance to a diverse clientele. **Other U.S. locations:** Nationwide.

GRANT THORNTON LLP
2 East Gilman Street, Madison WI 53703. 608/257-6761. **Toll-free phone:** 800/356-4049. **Fax:** 608/257-6760. **Contact:** Linda Peterson, Human Resources Department. **World Wide Web address:** http://www.grantthornton.com. **Description:** An international, certified, public accounting firm offering a comprehensive scope of management consulting and accounting services, as well as strategic and tactical planning assistance to a diverse clientele. **Other U.S. locations:** Nationwide.

GREAT LAKES HIGHER EDUCATION CORPORATION
2401 International Lane, Madison WI 53704. 608/246-1800. **Toll-free phone:** 800/274-4611. **Fax:** 608/246-1600. **Recorded jobline:** 608/240-1150. **Contact:** Human Resources Department. **E-mail address:** hresource@glhec.org. **World Wide Web address:** http://www.mygreatlakes.com. **Description:** A leading guarantor and servicer of student loans. **NOTE:** Entry-level positions are offered. Search and apply for positions online. **Positions advertised include:** Loan Counselor; Sr. Data Administrator; IT Project Manager; Project Engineering Deployment Specialist. **Special programs:** Internships. **Corporate headquarters location:** This location. **Other U.S. locations:** Oak Brook IL; St. Paul MN; Columbus OH; Eau Claire WI. **Number of employees at this location:** 550. **Number of employees nationwide:** 700.

GREAT NORTHERN CORPORATION
P.O. Box 939, Appleton WI 54912-0939. 920/739-3671. **Physical address:** 395 Stoebe Road, Appleton WI 54914. **Toll-free phone:** 800/236-3671. **Fax:** 920/739-7096. **Contact:** Human Resources Department. **World Wide Web address:** http://www.gnc-net.com. **Description:** A designer and manufacturer of corrugated containers and related products. **NOTE:** Search for positions online. **Other area locations:** Racine WI; Dale WI. **Other U.S. locations:** PA; FL; CA; OR;

GREATLAND CORPORATION
3130 South Ridge Road, Green Bay WI 54304. 920/339-4480. **Contact:** Jenny Nowak. **E-mail address:** menglebert@greatland.com. **World Wide Web address:** http://www.greatland.com. **Description:** A national provider of products and services for the financial, tax and accounting services markets. Founded in 1974. **Positions advertised include:** Accounts Receivable/Collections Clerk; Assistant Marketing Manager; Business Development Manager; Market Specialist; Project Manager; Senior Systems Analyst; Software Support Associate; Requirements and Technical Writing Analyst. **Corporate headquarters location:** This location.

GREDE FOUNDRIES, INC.
P.O. Box 26499, Milwaukee WI 53226. 414/257-3600. **Physical address:** 9898 West Bluemound Road, Milwaukee WI 53226. **Fax:** 414/256-9399. **Contact:** Human Resources. **World Wide Web address:** http://www.grede.com. **Description:** Produces gray and ductile iron castings for a variety of different industries. **NOTE:** Search and apply for positions online. **Positions advertised include:** Sr. Programmer Analyst. **Special programs:** Internships; Co-ops. **Corporate headquarters location:** This location. **Other U.S. locations:** SC; MI; IN; MN; KS. **International locations:** Worldwide. **Listed on:** Privately held. **Annual sales/revenues:** More than $100 million. **Number of employees at this location:** 130. **Number of employees nationwide:** 5,000.

GREEN BAY, CITY OF
100 North Jefferson Street, Green Bay WI 54301. 920/448-3010. **Fax:** 920/448-6277. **Recorded jobline:** 920/448-3149. **Contact:** Human Resources. **E-mail address:** gbcity@ci.green-bay.wi.us. **World Wide Web address:** http://www.ci.green-bay.wi.us. **Description:** This location houses all of the government services offices for the city of Green Bay. **NOTE:** Search for positions online and download job application form. **Positions advertised include:** Sr. Landscape Architect; Neighborhood Education Specialist; Humane Officer. **Number of employees at this location:** 1,000.

GREEN BAY PACKERS
1265 Lombardi Avenue, Green Bay WI 54304. 920/496-5700. **Contact:** Human Resources Department. **World Wide Web address:** http://www.packer.com. **Description:** The administrative offices for the National Football League team. **Corporate headquarters location:** This location.

GREENHECK FAN CORPORATION
P.O. Box 410, Schofield WI 54476-0410. 715/355-2236. **Fax:** 715/355-2444. **Contact:** Human Resources. **E-mail address:** hr@greenheck.com. **World Wide Web address:** http://www.greenheck.com. **Description:** Manufactures rooftop ventilators, sidewall fans, centrifugal fans, and kitchen ventilation systems. **NOTE:** Search and apply for positions online. **Positions advertised include:** Application Engineer; International Application Engineer; Product Development Engineer; Materials Specialist. **Special programs:** Internships. **Corporate headquarters location:** This location. **Other U.S. locations:** Sacramento CA; Frankfort KY. **Operations at this facility include:** Administration; Manufacturing; Research and Development; Sales. **Annual sales/revenues:** More than $100 million. **Number of employees nationwide:** 1,400.

GUNDERSEN LUTHERAN MEDICAL CENTER
1900 South Avenue, La Crosse WI 54601-5467. 608/782-7300. **Toll-free phone:** 800/362-9567. **Contact:** Human Resource Services. **E-mail address:** careers@gundluth.org. **Recorded jobline:** 866/651-1942. **Description:** Not-for-profit healthcare system that includes a 325-bed teaching hospital with a Level II Trauma and Emergency Center, 26 medical clinics, seven behavioral health clinics, four reproductive care clinics, 11 vision centers, two affiliated hospitals, and four affiliated nursing homes. **NOTE:** Search and apply for positions online. **Positions advertised include:** Administrative Director, Orthopaedics; Advanced Practice Nurse; Allergist; Budget Analyst; Cardiologist; Data Specialist; Dermatologist; Echocardiographer; Financial Analyst; Gastroenterologist; Coding Specialist; Medical Assistant; Pediatrician; Pharmacist; Radiologist; RN's. **Number of employees at this location:** 5,500.

HK SYSTEMS
2855 South James Drive, New Berlin WI 53151-3662. 262/860-7000. **Fax:** 262/860-7010. **Contact:** Human Resources. **E-mail address:** hr.mke@hksystems.com. **World Wide Web address:** http://www.hksystems.com. **Description:** HK Systems designs and manufactures computer-controlled machinery for manufacturing and various warehousing processes. **NOTE:** Search and apply for positions online. **Positions advertised include:** Account Executives; Proposal Manager; Pharmaceutical Industry Account Executive. **Corporate headquarters location:** This location. **Other U.S. locations:** UT; KY; AL. **International locations:** Canada. **Operations at this facility include:** This location houses the corporate offices only.

HADER SEITZ MANUFACTURING, INC.
15600 West Lincoln Avenue, P.O. Box 510260, New Berlin WI 53151. 262/641-6000. **Toll-free number:** 877/388-2101. **Fax:** 877/385-8114. **Contact:** Personnel. **World Wide Web address:** http://www.hader-seitz.com. **Description:** Engaged in the manufacture of hydraulic cylinders, accumulators, and rotary swivel valves. **Corporate headquarters location:** This location. **Parent company:** Hader Industries. **Operations at this facility include:** Administration; Manufacturing; Sales.

HARLEY-DAVIDSON, INC.
3700 West Juneau Avenue, Milwaukee WI 53208. 414/342-4680. **Fax:** 414/343-8230. **Contact:** Personnel. **World Wide Web address:** http://www.harley-davidson.com. **Description:** Harley-Davidson Motor company the only major U.S.-based motorcycle manufacturer, produces heavyweight motorcycles and offers a line of motorcycle parts, accessories, apparel, and general merchandise. **NOTE:** Search and apply for positions online. **Positions advertised include:** Manufacturing Process Engineer; Manufacturing Engineer; Sr. Project Engineer; Case Management Coordinator. **Corporate headquarters location:** This location. **Other U.S. locations:** Talladega AL; York PA; Tomahawk WI. **Subsidiaries include:** Buell Motorcycle Company; Harley-Davidson Financial Services. **Listed on:** New York Stock Exchange. **Stock exchange symbol:** HDI. **Number of employees nationwide:** 8,200.

HARMAN BECKER AUTOMOTIVE SYSTEMS
38023 Airport Lane, Prairie du Chien WI 53821. 608/326-8989. **Fax:** 608/326-5525. **Contact:** Human Resources. **World Wide Web address:** http://www.harman.com. **Description:** This location assembles loudspeakers. **Listed on:** New York Stock Exchange. **Stock exchange symbol:** HAR.

HARRISDATA
13555 Bishop's Court, Suite 300, Brookfield WI 53005-6277. 262/784-9099. **Toll-free phone:** 800/225-0585. **Fax:** 262/784-5994. **Contact:** Human Resources. **E-mail address:** hr@harrisdata.com. **World Wide Web address:** http://www.harrisdata.com. **Description:** Manufactures software that facilitates a variety of operations including human resources, financial services, and distribution. **Corporate headquarters location:** This location.

HEARTLAND BUSINESS SYSTEMS
1700 Stephen Street, PO Box 347, Little Chute WI 54140. 920/788-7720. **Toll-free phone:** 800/236-7914. **Fax:** 920/788-7739. **Contact:** Human Resources. **World Wide Web address:** http://www.hbs.net. **Description:** Heartland Business Systems is a provider of value added integration services and networking technologies. Heartland has developed services and support programs for commercial, industrial, government, and education clients throughout Wisconsin. **Positions advertised include:** Computer Engineer and Trainer; Receiving and Purchasing Associate; Senior System Engineer. **Corporate headquarters location:** This location. **Other area locations:** Milwaukee WI.

HEIN-WERNER
2110 Pewaukee Road, #A Waukesha WI 53188. 262/542-6611. **Fax:** 262/542-7890. **Contact:** Personnel. **World Wide Web address:** http://www.heinwerner.com. **Description:** A manufacturer and marketer of collision repair equipment. **Parent company:** Snap-on Inc.

HERALD TIMES REPORTER
P.O. Box 790, Manitowoc WI 54220. 920/684-4433. **Contact:** Human Resources. **World Wide Web address:** http://www.htrnews.com. **Description:** A daily newspaper with a circulation of approximately 19,000 serving the Manitowoc County area. **Parent company:** The Gannett Company.

HILLSHIRE FARM AND KAHN'S
N3620 County Road D, New London WI 54961. 920/982-2611. **Toll-free phone:** 800/558-8440. **Fax:** 920/982-1272. **Contact:** Robin Ludwikowski, Human Resources Manager. **World Wide Web address:** http://www.hillshirefarm.com. **Description:** Manufacturers of packaged meats including sausages, luncheon meats, hot dogs, and breakfast sandwiches. **NOTE:** Entry-level positions and second and third shifts are offered. **Special programs:** Internships; Training; Summer Jobs. **Corporate headquarters location:** Cincinnati OH. **Other U.S. locations:** Claryville KY. **Parent company:** Sara Lee. **Number of employees at this location:** 1,300. **Number of employees nationwide:** 2,600.

HOFFER'S COATINGS INC.
310 South Bellis Street, Wausau WI 54403. 715/845-7221. **Contact:** Human Resources. **World Wide Web address:** http://www.hciinfo.com. **Description:** Manufactures a wide variety of paints and coatings. Hoffer's also manufactures the Enviro-Prep system, which aids in lead paint disposal. **Corporate headquarters location:** This location. **Number of employees at this location:** 300.

HOME ENTRY SERVICES
2605 Kennedy Road, Janesville WI 53545. 608/757-2445. **Fax:** 608/757-0012. **Contact:** Human Resources. **Description:** Employs data entry workers who work out of their homes. The company handles data from a wide range of industries.

HOMES FOR INDEPENDENT LIVING (HIL)
P.O. Box 278, Douseman WI 53118. 262/569-5520. **Fax:** 262/569-9962. **Contact:** HIL Employment. **World Wide Web address:** http://www.hil-wi.com. **Description:** A for-profit agency providing residential support services to people with developmental disabilities through over 70 regionally organized programs in 10 Wisconsin counties. Founded in 1977. **NOTE:** Entry-level positions and second and third shifts are offered. Apply for employment online. **Corporate headquarters location:** Oconomowoc WI. **Parent company:** Oconomowoc Residential Programs, Inc. provides a variety of human services.

HUF-NORTH AMERICA
9020 West Dean Road, Milwaukee WI 53224. 414/365-4950. **Fax:** 424/365-8211. **Contact:** Human Resources. **Description:** A manufacturer of key locksets used in the automotive industry. **Corporate headquarters location:** Germany. **Other U.S. locations:** Greenville TN. **International locations:** Korea. **Listed on:** Privately held. **Annual sales/revenues:** $21 - $50 million. **Number of employees at this location:** 140.

HUFCOR INC.
P.O. Box 591, Janesville WI 53547-0591. 608/756-1242. **Physical address:** 2101 Kennedy road, Janesville WI 53545. **Toll-free phone:** 800/542-2371. **Fax:** 608/758-8253. **Contact:** Vice President of Human Resources. **E-mail address:** hiring@hufcor.com. **World Wide Web address:** http://www.hufcor.com. **Description:** Manufactures partitions of various sizes. **Positions advertised include:** Production Facilitator; Electronic Tool Maker; Cost Accountant.

HUFFY SPORTS
N53 W24700 South Corporate Circle, Sussex WI 53089. 262/820-3440. **Toll-free phone:** 800/558-5234. **Fax:** 262/558-6757. **Contact:** Human Resources. **World Wide Web address:** http://www.huffysports.com. **Description:** A sporting goods manufacturer.

HUMANA
1100 Employers Boulevard, Green Bay WI 54344. 920/336-1100. **Toll-free phone:** 800/558-4444. **Fax:** 920/337-5285. **Recorded jobline:** 920/337-5395. **Contact:** Human Resources. **World Wide Web address:** http://www.humana.com. **Description:** A service center for Humana, a leading provider of a broad range of employee benefits products to small businesses. The company provides managed care group insurance, group life, dental, disability income, and flexible benefits services. The company also provides administrative and managed care services for medium-sized and large employers and health insurance purchasing pool marketing and administration. **NOTE:** Search and apply for positions online. **Positions advertised include:** Technology Applications Engineer; Product Development/Project Analyst; Actuarial Analyst; Consultant; Grievance and Appeal Process Manager; Agency Management Specialist. **Corporate headquarters location:** Louisville KY. **Other area locations:** De Pere WI; Hartland WI; Madison WI; Milwaukee WI.

HUSCO INTERNATIONAL
P.O. Box 257, Waukesha WI 53187-0257. 262/513-4200. **Physical address:** W239 N218 Pewaukee Road, Waukesha WI 53188. **Fax:** 262/513-4514. **Contact:** Jim Tarkowski, Vice President of Human Resources. **World Wide Web address:** http://www.huscointl.com. **Description:** Designs and manufactures electrohydraulic and hydraulic controls for mobile equipment in construction, material handling, agricultural, and automotive markets worldwide. **NOTE:** Need to fill out an application. Entry-level positions are offered. Search for positions online. **Special programs:** Internships. **Corporate headquarters location:** This location. **Other area locations:** Whitewater WI. **Parent company:** HUSCO International Limited (England). **Operations at this facility include:** Administration; Manufacturing; Research and Development; Sales; Service. **Listed on:** Privately held. **Annual sales/revenues:** More than $100 million. **Number of employees at this location:** 475. **Number of employees worldwide:** 600.

IFS
12000 West Park Place, Milwaukee WI 53224. 414/359-9800. **Fax:** 414/359-9011. **Contact:** Sharon Ryczek, Human Resources. **E-mail address:** info@ifsna.com. **World Wide Web address:** http://www.ifsworld.com. **Description:** Develops enterprise application components used in manufacturing, supply chain management, customer relationship management, service provision, financials, product development, maintenance, and human resource administration. Founded in 1983. **Parent company:** Industrial & Financial Systems. **Number of employees worldwide:** 3,200.

ITW BEE LEITZKE
2000 Industrial Road, Iron Ridge, WI 53035. 920/625-2342. **Fax:** 920/625-2643. **Contact:** Human Resources. E-mail address: info@itwbeeleitzke.com. **Description:** Manufactures a variety of fasteners for industrial applications.

IDEXX LABORATORIES
2536 Alpine Road, Eau Claire WI 54703. 715/834-0355. **Fax:** 715/834-0165. **Contact:** Human Resources. **World Wide Web address:** http://www.idexx.com. **Description:** Develops and sells software for veterinarians. **NOTE:** Search and apply for positions online. **Positions advertised include:** Sr. Call Center Specialist; Trainer; National Sales Manager, Computer Systems; Programmer/Analyst. **Corporate headquarters location:** Portland ME. **Number of employees worldwide:** 2,400.

INACOM INFORMATION SYSTEMS
3001 West Beltline Highway, Madison WI 53713. 608-661-7700. **Toll-free phone:** 877-462-2664. **Fax:** 608-661-7701. **Contact:** Corporate Recruiter. **E-mail address:** jobs@inacom-msn.com. **World Wide Web address:** http://www.inacom.com. **Description:** A locally owned and operated information technology consulting and training firm, offering business solutions in the areas of application development, education, networking, product procurement, project management, security, storage, and voice, video, and data convergence. **NOTE:** Search and apply for positions online. **Positions advertised include:** Outbound Sales Position; Microsoft Certified Instructor; Microsoft Networking Specialist. **Other area locations:** Brookfield WI; Appleton WI; Holmen WI.

INDIANHEAD COMMUNITY ACTION AGENCY
209 East third Street South, P.O. Box 40, Ladysmith WI 54848-0040. 715/532-5594. **Fax:** 715/532-7808. **Contact:** Georgette Bembenek, Human Resources Director. **World Wide Web address:** http://www.indianheadcaa.org. **Description:** A nonprofit agency providing a variety of social services including home health care, Head Start programs, a home weatherizing program, and a clothing center. Founded in 1964. **NOTE:** Entry-level positions and part-time jobs are offered. **Office hours:** Monday - Friday, 8:00 a.m. - 4:30 p.m. **Corporate headquarters location:** This location. **Executive Director:** Jerome Drahos. **Number of employees at this location:** 35. **Number of employees nationwide:** 950.

INNOTEK E-P
300 Sussex Street, Pewaukee WI 53072. 262/691-2200. **Fax:** 262/691-4430. **Contact:** Human Resources. **World Wide Web address:** http://www.innotek-ep.com. **Description:** Distributes wholesale hydraulic and pneumatic equipment. **Special programs:** Internships.

INTEGRATED COMMUNICATION SERVICES, INC.
44 East Mifflin Street, Suite 500, Madison WI 53703. 608/251-8008. **Fax:** 608/251-7679. **Contact:** Human Resources. **Description:** A telecommunications answering service. **Corporate headquarters location:** This location. **Parent company:** Telephone & Data Systems, Inc. (TDS) **Number of employees at this location:** 25.

INTERMET RACINE
8213 Durand Avenue, Sturtevant WI 53177. 262/504-3366. **Contact:** Human Resources Department. **World Wide Web address:** http://www.intermet.com. **Description:** A high-tech manufacturer of nonferrous castings, machining, assemblies, and other tools. Ganton Technologies supplies products to major automotive and blue chip companies. **Corporate headquarters location:** Troy MI.

INTERNATIONAL PAPER COMPANY
600 Thilmany Road, P.O. Box 600, Kaukauna,WI 54130. 920/766-4611. **Contact:** Human Resources. **World Wide Web address:** http://www.ipaper.com. **Description:** Manufacturer of specialty packaging, pressure sensitive papers, converted products. **NOTE:** Search and apply for positions online. **Positions advertised include:** Sr. Product Development Engineer. **Corporate headquarters location:** Stamford CT. **Number of employees at this location:** 1,100.

INTERNETWORX SYSTEMS, INC.
325 North Corporate Drive, Suite 280, Brookfield WI 53045. 262/792-0050. **Fax:** 262/792-0620. **Contact:** Human Resources Department. **E-mail address:** careers@internetworxsystems.com. **World Wide Web address:** http://www.internetworxsystems.com. **Description:** Designs enterprise resource planning software for manufacturing facilities. **Other U.S. locations:** Chicago IL.

INVITROGEN CORPORATION
501 Charmany Drive, Madison WI 53719. 608/204-5000. **Toll-free phone:** 800/791-1400. **Fax:** 608/204-5200. **Contact:** Human Resources. **World Wide Web address:** http://www.panvera.com. **Description:** Manufactures drug discovery screening products and services. **NOTE:** Search and apply for positions online. **Positions advertised include:** Drug Discovery Business Area Manager; Research Associate; Scientist; Sr. Scientist. **Parent company:** Invitrogen.

JOCKEY INTERNATIONAL, INC.
2300 60th Street, P.O. Box 1417, Kenosha WI 53141-1417. 262/658-8111. **Fax:** 262/653-3014. **Contact:** Human Resources. **E-mail address:** human_resource@jockey.com. **World Wide Web address:** http://www.jockey.com. **Description:** One of the world's largest privately-owned underwear, sportswear, and hosiery companies. Founded in 1876. **NOTE:** Entry-level positions are offered. Search and apply for positions online. **Positions advertised include:** Fabric and Fiber Technologist; Visual Merchandiser; Retail Database Marketing Analyst; Associate Buyer; Resource Planner; Internal Auditor. **Special programs:** Internships. **Corporate headquarters location:** This location. **Other U.S. locations:** Nationwide. **International locations:** Canada; Hong Kong; United Kingdom. **Annual sales/revenues:** More than $100 million. **Number of employees at this location:** 380. **Number of employees nationwide:** 5,000. **Number of employees worldwide:** 5,600.

JOHNSON CONTROLS, INC.
5757 North Green Bay Avenue, P.O. Box 591, Milwaukee WI 53201-0591. 414/228-1200. **Fax:** 414/524-2299. **Contact:** Human Resources. **E-mail address:** erecruit@jci.com. **World Wide Web address:** http://www.jci.com. **Description:** A leader in automotive systems and facility management and control. In the automotive market, it is a supplier of integrated seating and interior systems, and batteries. For nonresidential facilities, Johnson Controls provides control systems and services including comfort, energy and security management. **NOTE:** Search and apply for positions online. **Corporate headquarters location:** This location. **Other U.S. locations:** Nationwide. **International locations:** Worldwide. **Operations at this facility include:** Administration; Automotive Group activities. **Listed on:** New York Stock Exchange. **Stock exchange symbol:** JCI. **Annual sales/revenues:** More than $100 million. **Number of employees at this location:** 300. **Number of employees nationwide:** 89,000.

JOHNSON CONTROLS, INC.
507 East Michigan Street, P.O. Box 423, Milwaukee WI 53202-9780. 414/524-4000. **Toll-free phone:** 800/333-2222. **Contact:** Human Resources. **E-mail address:** erecruit@jci.com. **World Wide Web address:** http://www.jci.com. **Description:** A leader in automotive systems and facility management and control. In the automotive market, it is a supplier of integrated seating and interior systems, and batteries. For nonresidential facilities, Johnson Controls provides control systems and services including comfort, energy and security management. **NOTE:** Search and apply for positions online. **Other U.S. locations:** Nationwide. **International locations:** Worldwide. **Operations at this facility include:** Controls Group activities. **Listed on:** New York Stock Exchange. **Stock exchange symbol:** JCI. **Annual sales/revenues:** More than $100 million. **Number of employees nationwide:** 89,000.

JORGENSEN CONVEYORS INC.
10303 North Baehr Road, Mequon WI 53092-4611. 262/242-3089. **Fax:** 262/242-4382. **Contact:** Personnel. **E-mail address:** info@jorgensenconveyors.com. **World Wide Web address:** http://www.jorgensenconveyors.com. **Description:** Manufactures metal conveyor belts for use in various industries. Founded in 1950. Privately owned and operated. **Positions advertised include:** Project Engineer; Designer/Drafter; Inspector; Receptionist; Accounting Supervisor; Purchasing Assistant. **Corporate headquarters location:** This location. **Annual sales/revenues:** $5 - $10 million. **Number of employees at this location:** 110.

JOY GLOBAL, INC.
100 E. Wisconsin Ave., Ste. 2780, Milwaukee, WI 53202 . 414/319-8500. **Fax:**

414/319-8510. **Contact:** Human Resources. **World Wide Web address:** http://www.joyglobal.com. **Description:** Produces machinery for the surface mining and quarrying industries. **Subsidiaries include:** Joy Mining Equipment; P&H Mining Equipment. **Listed on:** NASDAQ. **Stock exchange symbol:** JOYG.

KI
P.O. Box 8100, Green Bay WI 54308-8100. 920/468-8100. **Physical address:** 1330 Bellevue Street, Green Bay WI 54302. **Fax:** 920/468-2232. **Contact:** Human Resources Department. **E-mail address:** info@ki.com. **World Wide Web address:** http://www.ki.com. **Description:** A manufacturer of a broad range of office, commercial, institutional, and educational furniture. Founded in 1941. **NOTE:** Search and apply for positions online. **Positions advertised include:** Sales Force Automation Analyst; Market Development Analyst; Project Coordinator. **Number of employees worldwide:** 3,500.

KEANE, INC.
11270 West Park Place, Suite 400, Milwaukee WI 53224. 414/410-2000. **Toll-free phone:** 800/442-9902. **Fax:** 414/359-1610. **Contact:** Nancy Basile, Recruiter. **E-mail address:** info.milw@keane.com. **World Wide Web address:** http://www.keane.com. **Description:** Designs, develops, and manages software for corporations and health care facilities. Keane, Inc.'s services enable clients to leverage existing information systems and develop and manage new software applications more rapidly and proficiently. Founded in 1965. **NOTE:** Search and apply for positions online. **Positions advertised include:** Programmer/Analyst; Web Application Developer; Application Specialist. **Corporate headquarters location:** Boston MA. **Other U.S. locations:** Nationwide. **Listed on:** American Stock Exchange. **Stock exchange symbol:** KEA. **Annual sales/revenues:** More than $100 million. **Number of employees at this location:** 200.

J.J. KELLER & ASSOCIATES, INC.
3003 West Breezewood Lane, P.O. Box 368, Neenah WI 54957-0368. 920/722-2848. **Fax:** 920/727-7522. **Recorded jobline:** 920/720-7800. **Contact:** Human Resources. **World Wide Web address:** http://www.jjkeller.com. **Description:** A provider of safety- and regulatory-based publications, training materials, printed forms, and services to various industries. Founded in 1953. **NOTE:** Entry-level positions are offered. Search and apply for positions online. **Positions advertised include:** Business Systems Specialist: Software Developer; Web Developer; Editor/Writer; Sr. Catalog Copywriter; National Account Executive; Inside Sales Representative; Account Management Sales. **Corporate headquarters location:** This location. **Listed on:** Privately held. **Number of employees at this location:** 800.

KENOSHA BEEF
BIRCHWOOD FOODS
P.O. Box 639, Kenosha WI 53141. 262/859-2272. **Physical address:** 3111 152nd Avenue, Kenosha WI 53144. **Toll-free phone:** 800/541-1685. **Fax:** 262/859-2078. **Contact:** Phyllis Murray, Director of Personnel. **E-mail address:** bwinfo@bwfoods.com. **World Wide Web address:** http://www.bwfoods.com. **Description:** A beef packer with a product line that includes boxed beef for large quantity sales both nationwide and internationally. Kenosha Beef also produces hamburger patties for Burger King, Dairy Queen, A&W, Hardee's, and under the company's own label. The company also supplies mixed and cooked ground beef to Taco Bell. Founded in 1936. **NOTE:** Entry-level positions and second and third shifts are offered. **Corporate headquarters location:** This location. **Other U.S. locations:** Atlanta GA; Columbus OH; Frankfort IN. **Subsidiaries include:** Birchwood Transport. **Listed on:** Privately held. **Annual sales/revenues:** More than $100 million. **Number of employees at this location:** 400. **Number of employees nationwide:** 750.

KENOSHA NEWS
715 58th Street, Kenosha WI 53140. 262/657-1000. **Fax:** 262/657-6226. **Contact:** Human Resources. **World Wide Web address:** http://www.kenoshacounty.com. **Description:** A daily newspaper. **NOTE:** Entry-level positions are offered. **Special programs:** Internships; Apprenticeships. **Subsidiaries include:** Bulletin; Zion/Benton News. **Parent company:** United Communications Corporation. **Listed on:** Privately held. **Number of employees at this location:** 300.

KENOSHA YOUTH FOUNDATION
720 59th Place, Kenosha WI 53140. 262/654-7292. **Contact:** Human Resources Department. **World Wide Web address:** http://www.kyf.org. **Description:** Provides a wide range of social and educational services for the area's youth.

KIMBERLY-CLARK CORPORATION
2100 Winchester Road, Neenah WI 54956. 920/721-2631. **Fax:** 920/721-4219. **Contact:** Nancy Bowers, Recruiting Specialist. **E-mail address:** opportunities@kc-careers.com. **World Wide Web address:** http://www.kimberly-clark.com. **Description:** A leading manufacturer of personal care, tissue, and health care products. The company's name brands include Huggies, Pull-Ups, Kotex, Depend, Kleenex, Scott, Kimberly-Clark, Tecnol, Kimwipes, and Wypall. Other brands sold outside of the United States include Andrex, Scottex, Page, Popee, and Kimbies. Kimberly-Clark is also a major producer of premium business, correspondence, and technical papers. Worldwide, the company has operations in 38 countries and its products are sold in more than 150 countries. Founded in 1872. **NOTE:** Entry-level positions are offered. **Positions advertised include:** Sr. Internal Communication Manager; Casualty Risk Manager; Safety Coordinator; Learning and Development Coordinator; Packaging Engineer; Research Microbiologist; **Company slogan:** Where people who think differently think together. **Special programs:** Internships; Co-ops. **Corporate headquarters location:** Dallas TX. **Other U.S. locations:** Nationwide. **International locations:** Worldwide. **Listed on:** New York Stock Exchange. **Stock exchange symbol:** KMB. **Number of employees nationwide:** 22,300. **Number of employees worldwide:** 64,000.

KOHL'S DEPARTMENT STORE
N56 W17000 Ridgewood Drive, Menomonee Falls WI 53051. 262/703-7000. **Fax:** 262/703-6363. **Contact:** Manager of College Relations. **World Wide Web address:** http://www.kohls.com. **Description:** A value-oriented, family-focused, specialty department store. The company operates nearly 600 stores nationwide. **NOTE:** Search and apply for positions online. **Positions advertised include:** Broadcast/Production Coordinator; Concept Writer; Content Production Coordinator; Financial Analyst; Senior Compensation Analyst; LAN Technician; Oracle DBA; Sr. Systems Analyst; Coordinator Import Compliance; Manager of Store Finance. **Corporate headquarters location:** This location. **Other U.S. locations:** Nationwide. **Listed on:** New York Stock Exchange. **Stock exchange symbol:** KSS. **Annual sales/revenues:** More than $100 million. **Number of employees at this location:** 1,500. **Number of employees nationwide:** 50,000.

KOHL'S DEPARTMENT STORE DISTRIBUTION CENTER
13901 Woodale Drive, Menomonee Falls WI 53051. 262/783-4907. **Contact:** Human Resources. **World Wide Web address:** http://www.kohls.com. **Description:** A value-oriented, family-focused, specialty department store. The company operates nearly 600 stores nationwide. **NOTE:** Search and apply for positions online. **Corporate headquarters location:** Menomonee Falls WI. **Other U.S. locations:** Nationwide. **Operations at this facility include:** One of eight distribution centers nationwide. **Listed on:** New York Stock Exchange. **Stock exchange symbol:** KSS. **Annual sales/revenues:** More than $100 million. **Number of employees nationwide:** 22,250.

KOHLER COMPANY
444 Highland Drive, Kohler WI 53044. 920/457-4441. **Fax:** 920/459-1818. **Contact:** Human Resources Department. **World Wide Web address:** http://www.kohlerco.com. **Description:** Kohler, one of the largest privately-owned companies in the United States, is a manufacturer of plumbing products, furniture, engines, and generators. Kohler's three plants in the United States specialize in the manufacture of plumbing products for homes, businesses, and institutions. Kohler's Power Systems Group manufactures generators, transfer switches, and accessories for power and recreational vehicles. The Engine Division manufactures air-cooled, 4-cycle engines. The Interiors Group specializes in home furnishings and interior design. The Hospitality and Real Estate Group provides hospitality and land development to businesses nationwide. Kohler also has a design center that promotes new innovations for kitchens and baths. **NOTE:** Search and apply for positions online. **Positions advertised include:** Operations Analyst; Corporate Communications Specialist; CAD Design Drafter; Design Analyst; Human Factors Analyst; Industrial Designer; Process Engineer; Project Engineer; Sr. Mechanical Project Engineer; Production Supervisor; Sr. Systems Project Leader. **Corporate headquarters location:** This location. **Other U.S. locations:** AR; SC; NC; AL; TN; MS; MI; OR; CA; TX. **International locations:** Worldwide. **Number of employees nationwide:** 15,000.

KOLBE & KOLBE MILLWORK
1323 South 11th Avenue, Wausau WI 54401-5998. 715/842-5666. **Fax:** 715/845-8270. **Contact:** Christina Williams, Human Resources. **E-mail address:** cwilliams@kolbe-kolbe.com. **World Wide Web address:** http://www.kolbe-kolbe.com. **Description:** Manufactures wooden doors and wood-framed windows. **NOTE:** Search for positions online. **Positions advertised include:** Pro-E Technician. **Corporate headquarters location:** This location. **Subsidiaries include:** K-K Sales distributes products throughout the Midwest; K-K Way transports products throughout the Midwest; KVW manufactures vinyl windows and doors. **Number of employees at this location:** 1,300.

KONICA MINOLTA BUSINESS SOLUTIONS U.S.A., INC.
5133 W. Terrace Drive, Suite 101, Madison WI 53718. 608/257-6315. **Contact:** Human Resources. **E-mail address:** dnichols@kmbs.konicaminolta.us. **World Wide Web address:** http://www.kmbs.konicaminolta.us. **Description:** MBS is a leader in document imaging, providing its customers with solutions for document creation, production and management. The company provides the essentials of imaging to companies and organizations ranging from small office/home office to workgroups and departments and to large production operations with its technologically advanced line products and services. **Positions advertised include:** Account Executive; Copier/Printer Technician; Digital Product Specialist; Major Account Print Production Specialist; Sales Representative. **Corporate headquarters location:** Ramsey NJ.

KOSS CORPORATION
4129 North Port Washington Avenue, Milwaukee WI 53212-1052. 414/964-5000. **Toll-free phone:** 800/872-5677. **Fax:** 414/964-8615. **Contact:** Cheryl Mike, Director of Human Resources. **World Wide Web address:** http://www.koss.com. **Description:** Designs, manufactures, and sells stereo headphones, audio/video loudspeakers, and related accessory products. The company's products are sold through audio specialty stores, catalog showrooms, regional department store chains, military exchanges, and national retailers under the Koss name and dual label. The company has more than 1,600 domestic dealers, and its products are carried in more than 11,000 domestic retail outlets. **Corporate headquarters location:** This location. **International locations:** Canada; Switzerland.

LSI NEW GLARUS
200 Industrial Drive, New Glarus WI 53574. 608/527-2131. **Fax:** 608/527-2931. **Contact:** Human Resources. **Description:** A specialty foods manufacturer of meat snacks, sausages, and processed meats. **NOTE:** Entry-level positions are offered. **Special programs:** Apprenticeships; Training. **Corporate headquarters location:** This location. **Listed on:** Privately held. **Annual sales/revenues:** $21 - $50 million. **Number of employees at this location:** 150.

LACROSSE FOOTWEAR, INC.
1629 Caledonia Street, La Crosse WI 54602-1328. 608/782-3020. **Contact:** Human Resources. **E-mail address:** hr@lacrossefootwear.com. **World Wide Web address:** http://www.lacrosse-outdoors.com. **Description:** A leading producer of protective footwear for the sporting, occupational, and recreational markets. The company markets its products primarily under the LaCrosse, Danner, Lake of the Woods, and Red Ball brand names. Founded in 1897. **Corporate headquarters location:** Portland OR. **Other area locations:** Clintonville WI; Hillsboro WI. **Other U.S. locations:** Claremont NH. **Operations at this facility include:** Administration; Manufacturing; Sales; Service. **Listed on:** NASDAQ. **Stock exchange symbol:** BOOT. **Annual sales/revenues:** $51 - $100 million. **Number of employees at this location:** 800. **Number of employees nationwide:** 1,300.

LADISH COMPANY, INC.
5481 South Packard Avenue, P.O. Box 8902, Cudahy WI 53110-8902. 414/747-2611. **Fax:** 414/747-3540. **Contact:** Human Resources. **E-mail address:** hrdept@ladishco.com. **World Wide Web address:** http://www.ladishco.com. **Description:** A manufacturer of fabricated metals and services for aerospace and industrial manufacturers. **Listed on:** NASDAQ. **Stock exchange symbol:** LDSH.

LAIDLAW TRANSIT, INC.
6015 52nd Street, Kenosha WI 53144. 262/657-7155. **Fax:** 262/657-6044. **Contact:** Human Resources Department. **E-mail address:** careers@laidlawjobs.com. **World Wide Web address:** http://www.laidlaw.com. **Description:** Provides bus service for Kenosha and provides charter bus service to private customers. The company is also a school bus contractor. **Parent company:** Laidlaw International, Inc.

LAKESIDE FOODS, INC.
P.O. Box 1327, Manitowac WI 54221-1327. 920/684-3356. **Physical address:** 508 Jay Street, Manitowac WI 54220. **Fax:** 920/686-4033. **Contact:** Thomas Reilly, Human Resources. **E-mail address:** treilly@lakesidefoods.com. **World Wide Web address:** http://www.lakesidefoods.com. **Description:** Processes vegetables and other foods. **NOTE:** Search for positions online. **Positions advertised include:** Maintenance Supervisor.

LANDS' END, INC.
One Lands' End Lane, Dodgeville WI 53595. 608/935-9341. **Fax:** 608/935-4260. **Contact:** Human Resources. **World Wide Web address:** http://www.landsend.com.

Description: An international direct merchant of a wide variety of casual clothing for men, women, and children; accessories; shoes; and soft luggage. The company's products are offered through its monthly catalogs, the Internet, and stores. **NOTE:** Search and apply for positions online. **Positions advertised include:** Middleware Administrator; Quality Assurance Analyst; Planner; HR Generalist; Compensation Analyst; Graphic Designer; Merchandise Manager; Sr. Learning Manager. **Corporate headquarters location:** This location. **International locations:** England; Japan. **Parent company:** Sears, Roebuck and Company. **Number of employees worldwide:** 4,700.

GUSTAVE A. LARSON COMPANY
W233 N2869 Roundy Circle West, P.O. Box 910, Pewaukee WI 53072-0910. 262/542-0200. **Fax:** 262/542-1400. **Contact:** Human Resources. **E-mail address:** info@egalco.com. **World Wide Web address:** http://www.galarson.com. **Description:** A wholesale distributor of a broad range of HVACR equipment, parts, and supplies. **NOTE:** Search for positions online.

LEGGETTE, BRASHEARS & GRAHAM, INC.
6525 Grand Teton Plaza, Madison WI 53719. 608/833-5555. **Fax:** 608/833-5551. **Contact:** Human Resources. **E-mail address:** Wisconsin@lbgweb.com. **World Wide Web address:** http://www.lbgweb.com. **Description:** A professional groundwater and environmental engineering services company. **NOTE:** Search and apply for positions online. **Other U.S. locations:** Nationwide.

LEVEL VALLEY CREAMERY
807 Pleasant Valley Road, West Bend WI 53095-9761. 262/675-6533. **Fax:** 262/675-2827. **Contact:** Human Resources. **E-mail address:** contact@levelvalley.com. **World Wide Web address:** http://www.levelvalley.com. **Description:** A producer of butter, cream cheese, and a variety of evaporated and dried milk products. **Corporate headquarters location:** This location. **Other U.S. locations:** Antioch TN. **Annual sales/revenues:** More than $100 million. **Number of employees at this location:** 160. **Number of employees nationwide:** 250.

LIBERTY MUTUAL INSURANCE COMPANY
15700 West Bluemound Road, Brookfield WI 53005. 262/782-9500. **Toll-free phone:** 800/341-0599. **Fax:** 262/782-5682. **Contact:** Human Resources Department. **World Wide Web address:** http://www.libertymutual.com. **Description:** A full-line insurance firm offering life, medical, and business insurance, as well as investment and retirement plans. **NOTE:** Search and apply for jobs online. **Positions advertised include:** Sr. Underwriter, CM; Sales Associate; Account Representative.

LOOMIS FARGO & COMPANY
603 South Oneida Street, Green Bay WI 54303. 920/494-0124. **Fax:** 920/494-0749. **Contact:** Personnel. **World Wide Web address:** http://www.loomisfargo.com. **Description:** An armored security service specializing in transporting currency. **NOTE:** Applications will not be mailed to jobseekers. They must be picked up in person. **Other U.S. locations:** Nationwide.

M&I BANK
221 West College Avenue, P.O. Box 239, Appleton WI 54911. 920/738-3800. **Contact:** Human Resources. **World Wide Web address:** http://www.mibank.com. **Description:** One M&I retail banking location. **Parent company:** Marshall & Ilsley Corporation.

MPI - WISCONSIN MACHINING
528 E Tyranena Park Road, P.O. Box 4, Lake Mills WI 53551. 920/648-3438. **Fax:** 920/648-8773. **Contact:** Human Resources. **E-mail address:** humanresources@mpi-int.com. **Description:** Manufactures automotive parts. **NOTE:** Job seekers may apply to MPI International, Inc. Attn: Human Resources, 2129 Austin Avenue, Rochester Hills Michigan 48309. **Parent company:** MPI International, Inc.

MADISON, CITY OF
210 Martin Luther King Jr. Boulevard, Room 403, Madison WI 53710. 608/266-4611. **Fax:** 608/267-8671. **Recorded jobline:** 608/266-6500. **Contact:** Human Resources. **E-mail address:** hr@ci.madison.wi.us. **World Wide Web address:** http://www.ci.madison.wi.us. **Description:** Provides services to the city of Madison. **NOTE:** Search for positions online. Applications for employment will not be accepted via e-mail.

MADISON CHILDREN'S MUSEUM
100 State Street, Madison WI 53703. 608/256-6445. **Contact:** Executive Director. **World Wide Web address:** http://www.madisonchildrensmuseum.com. **Description:** A children's museum offering a wide variety of activities and programs weekly and monthly.

MADISON CIVIC CENTER
MADISON REPERTORY THEATRE
211 State Street, Madison WI 53703-2287. 608/258-4177. **Fax:** 608/258-4971. **Contact:** Human Resources Department. **E-mail address:** civiccenter@ci.madison.wi.us. **World Wide Web address:** http://www.madcivic.org. **Description:** Offers performances by the Madison Symphony Orchestra, the Madison Opera, the Madison Repertory Theatre (also at this location), and the Children's Theatre of Madison. **NOTE:** The Civic Center is an agency of the City of Madison. Job seekers may visit: http://www.ci.madison.wi.us/hr/jobopen.html for open positions.

MADISON OPERA & GUILD
333 Glenway Street, Madison WI 53705. 608/238-8085. **Fax:** 608/233-3431. **World Wide Web address:** http://www.madisonopera.org. **Contact:** Human Resources. **E-mail address:** info@madisonopera.org. **Description:** Holds performances throughout the year at the Madison Civic Center. **Corporate headquarters location:** This location.

MADISON SYMPHONY ORCHESTRA
6314 Odana Road, Madison WI 53719. 608/257-3734. **Fax:** 608/280-6192. **Contact:** Human Resources Department. **World Wide Web address:** http://www.madisonsymphony.org. **Description:** This location houses the administrative offices, as well as the box office for the Madison Symphony Orchestra.

MANITOWOC COMPANY INC.
2400 South 44th Street, P.O. Box 66, Manitowac WI 54220. 920/684-4410. **Fax:** 920/652-9778. **Contact:** Jan Nesper, Human Resources. **World Wide Web address:** http://www.manitowoc.com. **Description:** Manufactures lifting equipment for the global construction industry, foodservice equipment, and provides shipbuilding, repair and conversion services. **NOTE:** Search and apply for positions online. **Positions advertised include:** Sr. Engineer; Engineer. **Listed on:** New York Stock Exchange. **Stock exchange symbol:** MTW. **Number of employees nationwide:** 7,700.

MARKESAN RESIDENT HOME, INC.
1130 North Margaret Street, P.O. Box 130, Markesan WI 53946. 920/398-2751. **Fax:** 920/398-3937. **Contact:** Business Office Manager. **Description:** A nonprofit nursing home with residential assisted living and Alzheimer's units. **NOTE:** Second and third shifts are offered. **Special programs:** Internships; Training. **Corporate headquarters location:** This location. **Listed on:** Privately held. **Number of employees at this location:** 90.

MARQUETTE UNIVERSITY
915 West Wisconsin Avenue, East Hall, Room 185, P.O. Box 1881, Milwaukee WI 53201-1881. 414/288-7305. **Fax:** 414/288-7425. **Recorded jobline:** 414/288-7000. **Contact:** Human Resources. **E-mail address:** resume@marquette.edu. **World Wide Web address:** http://www.marquette.edu. **Description:** A four-year, Jesuit-affiliated university with approximately 7,600 undergraduate and 3,400 graduate students. Founded in 1881. **NOTE:** Resumes accepted for open positions. Search for positions online. E-mail applications for non-exempt or entry level positions to: jobs@margette.edu.

MARSHALL & ILSLEY CORPORATION
770 North Water Street, 8th Floor, Milwaukee WI 53202. 414/765-7801. **Recorded jobline:** 414/765-8300. **Contact:** Human Resources. **World Wide Web address:** http://www.mibank.com. **Description:** Operates nearly 250 retail banking offices in Wisconsin, Arizona, Minnesota, Missouri, Nevada, Florida, and Illinois. M&I also provides trust and investment management, equipment leasing, mortgage banking, financial planning, investments, insurance services and data processing. Founded in 1847. **NOTE:** Search and apply for positions online. **Subsidiaries include:** Metavante Corporation. **Listed on:** New York Stock Exchange. **Stock exchange symbol:** MI.

MARSHFIELD CLINIC
1000 North Oak Avenue, Marshfield WI 54449. 715/387-5511. **Toll-free phone:** 800/782-8581. **Contact:** Human Resources. **World Wide Web address:** http://www.marshfieldclinic.org. **Description:** Marshfield Clinic is the largest private group medical practice in Wisconsin and one of the largest in the United States, with 724 physicians representing 86 different medical specialties, 5,696 additional employees, and 41 regional centers/sites in 34 Wisconsin communities. **NOTE:** Search and apply for positions online. **Number of employees at this location:** 450.

MATTHEWS PAINT COMPANY
8201 100th Street, Pleasant Prairie WI 53158. 262/947-0700. **Toll-free phone:** 800/323-6593. **Fax:** 262/947-0444. **Contact:** Human Resources. **E-mail address:** mpcmail@ppg.com. **World Wide Web address:** http://www.signpaint.com. **Description:** A manufacturer of paints. This location manufactures base colors with suppliers making up custom colors. **Corporate headquarters location:** This location. **Number of employees at this location:** 40.

MAXAIR INC.
West 6381 Columbia Drive, Appleton WI 54914. 920/738-3020. **Toll-free phone:** 800/833-1544. **Fax:** 920/738-3026. **Contact:** Human Resources. **World Wide Web address:** http://www.maxair-inc.com. **Description:** Provides air chartering services and airplane rentals, and operates a flight school.

MAYNARD STEEL CASTING COMPANY
2856 South 27th Street, Milwaukee WI 53215-3603. 414/645-0440. **Fax:** 414/645-7378. **Contact:** Personnel. **World Wide Web address:** http://www.maynardsteel.com. **Description:** A steel foundry producing castings for construction, mining and railroad, and other industries. **Corporate headquarters location:** This location. **Other area locations:** Beaver Dam WI. **Operations at this facility include:** Administration; Manufacturing; Sales. **Listed on:** Privately held. **Number of employees at this location:** 425.

MAYSTEEL LLC
PO Box 1240, Menomonee Falls WI 53052-1240. 262/251-1632. **Physical address:** N89 W14700 Patrita Drive, Menomonee Falls WI 53051. **Fax:** 262/251-8307. **Contact:** Human Resources. **World Wide Web address:** http://www.maysteel.com. **Description:** Specializes in the custom fabrication of metal enclosures, assemblies, and components on both a contract basis and via proprietary products used in the distribution of electric power. Founded in 1936. **NOTE:** Search and apply for positions online. **Positions advertised include:** CAM/CNC Programmer; Continuous Improvement Technician; Engineering Project Manager; Production Supervisor; Project Engineer. **Other area locations:** Allenton WI; Columbus WI.

MAYVILLE ENGINEERING COMPANY INC.
715 South Street, Mayville WI 53050. 920/387-4500. **Fax:** 920/387-2682. **Contact:** Human Resources. **E-mail address:** jobs@mayvl.com. **World Wide Web address:** http://www.mayvl.com. **Description:** A contract metalworking manufacturer serving OEM's nationwide.

MEAD & HUNT, INC.
6501 Watts Road, Madison WI 53719. 608/273-6380. **Fax:** 608/273-6391. **Contact:** Human Resources. **E-mail address:** hr@meadhunt.com. **World Wide Web address:** http://www.meadhunt.com. **Description:** Provides a wide range of services in all areas of engineering. **NOTE:** Search and apply for positions online. **Positions advertised include:** Electrical Engineer; Sr. Electrical Engineer; Water Resources Sr. Project Manager. **Other area locations:** Green Bay WI; La Crosse WI; Milwaukee WI. **Other U.S. locations:** CA: OR; DC; MI; MN. **Number of employees nationwide:** 270.

MEDA-CARE AMBULANCE SERVICE
2515 West Vliet Street, Milwaukee WI 53205. 414/342-1148. **Fax:** 414/342-0888. **Contact:** Linda Wiedmann, Director of Operations. **World Wide Web address:** http://www.meda-care.com. **Description:** Provides both emergency and nonemergency transportation via ambulance. **NOTE:** Second and third shifts are offered. **Positions advertised include:** Emergency Medical Technicians; Paramedics; Registered Nurses; Respiratory Therapists. **Special programs:** Training. **Corporate headquarters location:** This location. **Listed on:** Privately held. **Annual sales/revenues:** $5 - $10 million. **Number of employees at this location:** 140.

MEDICAL COLLEGE OF WISCONSIN
8701 Watertown Plank Road, Milwaukee WI 53226. 414/456-8296. **Recorded jobline:** 414/456-8193. **Contact:** Human Resources. **E-mail address:** mcw_emp@mcw.edu. **World Wide Web address:** http://www.mcw.edu. **Description:** A medical school offering a four-year M.D. program prior to residency. Medical College of Wisconsin enrolls approximately 1,200 students. Founded in 1893. Number of employees at this location: 4,370. **NOTE:** Search for positions and download application online. **Positions advertised include:** Research Scientist; Medical Education Coordinator; Accountant; Biostatistician; Case Manager; Nurse Practitioner; Systems Analyst; Assistant/Associate Professors.

MEG TEC SYSTEMS
830 Prosper Road, De Pere WI 54115-0030. 920/336-5715. **Fax:** 920/337-1429. **Contact:** Human Resources. **World Wide Web address:** http://www.megtec.com. **Description:** Manufactures pollution control systems and graphic art dryers for the printing industry. **NOTE:** Search and apply for positions online. **Positions advertised include:** Worldwide Supply Chain Director; Manufacturing Engineer; Manager, Human Resources; Field Service Representative; Mechanical Project Engineer. **Parent company:** Sequa Corporation. **Number of employees worldwide:** 800.

MENARD, INC.
4777 Menard Drive, Eau Claire, WI 54703-9604. 715/876-5911. **Fax:** 715/876-2868. **Contact:** Employment Office. **World Wide Web address:** http://www.menards.com. **Description:** Operates a chain of home improvement stores. **NOTE:** Business or human resources graduates may obtain information about the Manager Trainee Program by contacting Personnel Recruiters, 5136 Old Mill Plaza, Eau Claire WI 54703. **Other U.S. locations:** MN; IA; IL; NB; ND; SD; ID; MI.

MENASHA CORPORATION
1645 Bergstrom Road, Neenah WI 54956. 920/751-1000. **Toll-free phone:** 800/558-5073. **Contact:** Melanie Collins. **E-mail address:** hr@menasha.com. **World Wide Web address:** http://www.menasha.com. **Description:** A manufacturer of packaging, engineered plastics, and labeling, and provides consumer promotions. Founded in 1849. **Positions advertised include:** Design Manager; Manufacturing Area Manager; Treasury Analyst. **Corporate headquarters location:** This location. **Other U.S. locations:** Nationwide. **Operations at this facility include:** Administration; Manufacturing. **Listed on:** Privately held. **Number of employees at this location:** 200. **Number of employees nationwide:** 5,000.

MENASHA, TOWN OF
2000 Municipal Drive, Neenah WI 54956-5665. 920/720-7100. **Fax:** 920/720-7112. **Contact:** Human Resources. **World Wide Web address:** http://www.town-menasha.com. **Description:** The municipal offices for the town of Menasha.

MERCURY MARINE
W6250 West Pioneer Road, P.O. Box 1939, Fond du Lac WI 4936-1939. 920/929-5040. **Fax:** 920/929-5893. **Contact:** Human Resources. **Description:** Mercury Marine is the leading producer of marine engines in the world. Primary products include Mercury and Mariner outboard engines, Mercury MerCruiser sterndrive and inboard engines, Mercury Precision Parts and accessories, MotorGuide trolling motors and Teignbridge propellers. **NOTE:** Search and apply for positions online. **Positions advertised include:** Accounts Payable Manager; Benchmark Engineer; Buyer; Calibration Engineer; Commodity Manager; Cost Engineer; Director of Engineering Information Systems; Production Supervisor; Quality Engineer. **Other U.S. locations:** Stillwater OK; St. Cloud FL. **Parent company:** Brunswick Corporation

MERCY HEALTH SYSTEM
1000 Mineral Point Avenue, P.O. Box 5003, Janesville WI 53547. 608/756-6721. **Fax:** 608/756-5627. **Recorded jobline:** 608/741-6979. **Contact:** Human Resources. **E-mail address:** hr@mhsjvl.org. **World Wide Web address:** http://www.mercyhealthsystem.org. **Description:** A health care system with 50 facilities in 21 communities that includes acute-care hospitals, skilled nursing centers, an independent living facility, and several ambulatory care centers. Mercy Health System also offers full residency training for diagnostic radiology, general surgery, and internal medicine. **NOTE:** Entry-level positions and second and third shifts are offered. **Positions advertised include:** Physical Therapist; Speech Therapist; Staff Pharmacist; CT Tech; Histo Tech; MRI Tech; Radiology Tech; Respiratory Therapist; Ultrasound Tech; Radiation Therapist; RN's; LPN's. **Special programs:** Internships; Training; Summer Jobs. **Office hours:** Monday - Friday, 8:00 a.m. - 5:00 p.m. **Corporate headquarters location:** This location. **Other U.S. locations:** CA; IL; PA. **CEO:** Javon Bea. **Number of employees at this location:** 2,300.

MERITER HEALTH SERVICES INC.
202 South Park Street, Madison WI 53715. 608/267-6134. **Fax:** 608/267-6568. **Recorded jobline:** 608/267-6055. **Contact:** Michelle Burmester, Employment Coordinator. **E-mail address:** employment@meriter.com. **World Wide Web address:** http://www.meriter.com. **Description:** A full-service health care provider that includes Meriter Hospital, a 448-bed, nonprofit, acute care hospital; Meriter Retirement Services; Meriter Home Health; General Medical Laboratories; and The Meriter Foundation. **Positions advertised include:** Director, Medical Records; Patient Safety Administrator; Epic Support Analyst; Programmer Analyst; Registered Nurse; Nurse Manager; Pharmacy Technician; Phlebotomist; Clinical Nurse Educator. **Special programs:** Internships. **Corporate headquarters location:** This location.

MERRICK'S, INC.
2415 Parview Road, P.O. Box 620307, Middleton WI 53562-0307. 608/831-3440. **Toll-free phone:** 800/637-7425. **Fax:** 608/836-8943. **Contact:** Human Resources. **World Wide Web address:** http://www.merricks.com. **Description:** Manufactures animal feed ingredients for the agricultural industry such as milk replacers for baby animals. The milk replacers are derived from a variety of sources including milk protein, animal plasma, and plant protein. **International locations:** Worldwide. **Parent company:** Merrick Management Group LLC. **Listed on:** Privately held. **Annual sales/revenues:** $51 - $100 million.

METAVANTE CORPORATION
4900 West Brown Deer Road, Milwaukee WI 53223. 414/357-2290. **Contact:** Human Resources. **World Wide Web address:** http://www.metavante.com. **Description:** Provides technology for financial institutions including customer relationship management, electronic banking, electronic funds transfer, financial account processing, and wealth management. **NOTE:** Entry-level positions and second and third shifts are offered. **Special programs:** Internships; Training; Summer Jobs. **Corporate headquarters location:** This location. Other U.S. locations: GA; CA; MI; FL; MA; IL; NJ. **Parent company:** Marshall & Ilsley Corporation's **Operations at this facility include:** Administration; Research and Development; Sales; Service. **Listed on:** New York Stock Exchange. **Stock exchange symbol:** MI.

METSO PAPER, INC.
2111 North Sandra Street, Appleton WI 54911-8667. 920/733-7361. **Fax:** 920/733-1048. **Contact:** Human Resources Department. **World Wide Web address:** http://www.metso.com. **Description:** A supplier of process industry machinery and systems, The company's core businesses are fiber and paper technology (Metso Paper), rock and mineral processing (Metso Minerals) and automation and control technology (Metso Automation). **Corporate headquarters location:** Finland. **Other U.S. locations:** Atlanta GA; Biddeford ME; Charlotte NC; Hudson Falls NY; Houston TX.

METSO PAPER, INC.
1280 Willowbrook Road, Beloit WI 53511. 608/365-3319. **Fax:** 608/364-7013. **Contact:** Human Resources Department. **World Wide Web address:** http://www.metso.com. **Description:** Designs, manufactures, and markets paper-making machinery and related equipment. Primary customers are producers of pulp and paper products including tissue, newsprint, fine paper, and multiply board. **Corporate headquarters location:** This location. **Other U.S. locations:** Atlanta GA; Biddeford ME; Charlotte NC; Hudson Falls NY; Houston TX. **Operations at this facility include:** Administration; Manufacturing; Research and Development; Sales.

METSO PAPER, INC.
618 South Oneid Street, Appleton WI 54915. 920/749-4393. **Fax:** 920/733-5548. **Contact:** Denise Vanderloop, Manager of Human Resources. **World Wide Web address:** http://www.metso.com. **Description:** A manufacturer of paper and finishing systems with production facilities worldwide. **Other area locations:** Beloit WI. **Other U.S. locations:** Atlanta GA; Biddeford ME; Charlotte NC; Hudson Falls NY; Houston TX.

C.R. MEYER AND SONS COMPANY
895 West 20th Street, P.O. Box 2157, Oshkosh WI 54903-2157. 920/235-3350. **Fax:** 920/235-3419. **Contact:** Human Resources Manager. **E-mail address:** info@crmeyer.com. **World Wide Web address:** http://www.crmeyer.com. **Description:** A privately owned, full-service construction company. Founded in 1888. **Corporate headquarters location:** This location. **Other area locations:** Rhinelander WI. **Other U.S. locations:** Kalamazoo MI; Coleraine MN; Tulsa OK.

MICHAEL, BEST & FRIEDRICH
100 East Wisconsin Avenue, Suite 3300, Milwaukee WI 53202-4108. 414/271-6560. **Fax:** 414/277-0656. **Contact:** Tammy A. McCormack, Human Resources Director. **E-mail address:** tamccormack@mbf-law.com. **World Wide Web address:** http://www.mbf-law.com. **Description:** A legal services firm specializing in all types of corporate law. **Positions advertised include:** Business/Corporate Partner; Land and Resources Partner; Tax Partner. **Other area locations:** Manitowoc WI; Waukesha WI; Madison WI. **Other U.S. locations:** Chicago IL; Center Valley PA.

MIDWEST AIR GROUP, INC.
6744 South Howell Avenue, HQ-22, Oak Creek WI 53154-1402. 414/570-4000. **Toll-free phone:** 800/452-2022. **Fax:** 414/570-9666. **Contact:** Personnel. **E-mail address:** meacareers@Midwest-express.com. **World Wide Web address:** http://www.midwestexpress.com. **Description:** An airline specializing in passenger air transportation throughout the Midwest. **NOTE:** Resumes accepted only for open positions. **Positions advertised include:** Accounting and Reporting Specialist; Facility Maintenance Technician; Powerplant Engineer. **Listed on: New York Stock Exchange.** Stock exchange symbol: MEH.

MIDWEST DENTAL MANAGEMENT
680 Hehli Way, P.O. Box 69, Mondovi WI 54755. 715/926-5050. **Toll-free phone:** 800/782-7186. **Fax:** 715/926-5405. **Contact:** Human Resources. **E-mail address:** hr@midwest-dental.com. **World Wide Web address:** http://www.midwest-dental.com. **Description:** Midwest Dental Management is a statewide dental practice management company providing dental services through 28 offices in Wisconsin and one office in Minnesota. Founded in 1968. **NOTE:** Entry-level positions are offered. **Special programs:** Internships. **Corporate headquarters location:** This location. **Operations at this facility include:** This location houses administrative offices. **CEO:** Yvonne Mayberry. **Annual sales/revenues:** $11 - $20 million. **Number of employees at this location:** 250.

MILLER BREWING COMPANY
P.O. Box 482, Milwaukee WI 53201-0482. 414/931-2000. **Physical address:** 3939 West Highland Boulevard, Milwaukee WI 53208-2866. **Contact:** Corporate Recruiter. **World Wide Web address:** http://www.millerbrewing.com. **Description:** Produces and distributes beer and other malt beverages. Principal beer brands include Miller Lite, Lite Ice, Miller Genuine Draft, Miller Genuine Draft Light, Miller High Life, Miller Reserve, Lowenbrau, Milwaukee's Best, Meister Brau, Red Dog, and Icehouse. Miller also produces Sharp's, a non-alcoholic brew. **NOTE:** Search and apply for positions online. **Positions advertised include:** Business Analyst; Compensation Analyst; Corporate Sr. Buyer; Corporate Human Resources Manager; Corporate Pricing Manager; Distributor Development and Strategy Manager; Industrial Engineer; Financial Project Specialist, Operations. **Corporate headquarters location:** This location. **Other U.S. locations:** Irwindale CA; Albany GA; Eden NC; Trenton OH; Fort Worth TX. **Subsidiaries include:** The Jacob Leinenkugel Brewing Company (Chippewa Falls WI) brews Leinenkugel's Original Premium, Leinenkugel's Light, Leinie's Ice, Leinenkugel's Limited, Leinenkugel's Red Lager, and four seasonal beers: Leinenkugel's Genuine Bock, Leinenkugel's Honey Weiss, Leinenkugel's Autumn Gold, and Leinenkugel's Winter Lager. Miller owns and operates one of the largest beer importers in the United States, Molson Breweries U.S.A., Inc., based in Reston VA, which imports Molson beers from Canada, as well as Foster's Lager and many other brands. **Number of employees nationwide:** 155,000.

MILLER ELECTRIC
1635 West Spencer Street, P.O. Box 1079, Appleton WI 54912-1079. 920/734-9821. **Fax:** 920/735-4038. **Contact:** Amy Blasewitz. **E-mail address:** ablase@millerwelds.com. **World Wide Web address:** http://www.millerwelds.com. **Description:** Manufactures arc welding and cutting equipment. **Positions advertised include:** Electrical Engineer; Mechanical Engineer; Welding Engineer.

MILLER ENGINEERS & SCIENTISTS
5308 South 12th Street, Sheboygan WI 53081-8099. 920/458-6164. **Toll-free phone:** 800/969-7013. **Fax:** 920/458-0369. **Contact:** Human Resources. **World Wide Web address:** http://www.startwithmiller.com. **Description:** An environmental consulting firm that also performs land surveying and materials testing.

MILWAUKEE BALLET COMPANY, INC.
504 West National Avenue, Milwaukee WI 53204. 414/643-7677. **Fax:** 414/649-4066. **Contact:** Controller. **World Wide Web address:** http://www.milwaukeeballet.org. **Description:** A nonprofit professional dance company. Milwaukee Ballet Company also operates a ballet school with over 800 students. The ballet has five series of performances each year and over 25 performances of *The Nutcracker* each December. **Special programs:** Apprenticeships. **Corporate headquarters location:** This location. **Subsidiaries include:** Milwaukee Ballet Orchestra. **Annual sales/revenues:** Less than $5 million. **Number of employees at this location:** 250.

MILWAUKEE ELECTRIC TOOL CORPORATION
13135 West Lisbon Road, Brookfield WI 53005. 262/781-3600. **Toll-free phone:** 800/729-3878. **Fax:** 262/783-8228. **Contact:** Human Resources. **World Wide Web address:** http://www.milawaukeetool.com. **Description:** Engaged in the design, manufacture, sale, and service of portable power tools. **NOTE:** Entry-level positions are offered. Search and apply for positions online. **Positions advertised include:** Sr. Engineering Lab Technician; Design Drafter. **Corporate headquarters location:** This

location. **Other U.S. locations:** AR; MS. **Parent company:** Atlas-Copco. **Number of employees at this location:** 900. **Number of employees nationwide:** 2,000.

MILWAUKEE JOURNAL SENTINEL, INC.
333 West State Street, Milwaukee WI 53203. 414/224-2000. **Fax:** 414/224-2897. **Contact:** Employment Manager. **E-mail address:** hr@journalsentinel.com. **World Wide Web address:** http://www.jsonline.com. **Description:** A newspaper with a daily circulation of 290,000 and 500,000 on Sundays. Founded in 1882. **NOTE:** Entry-level positions are offered. **Special programs:** Internships; Apprenticeships; Summer Jobs. **Office hours:** Monday - Friday, 8:00 a.m. - 5:00 p.m. **Corporate headquarters location:** This location. **Parent company:** Journal Communications (also at this location). **Operations at this facility include:** Administration; Manufacturing; Sales; Service. **President:** Keith Spore. **Number of employees at this location:** 3,000.

MILWAUKEE PUBLIC MUSEUM
800 West Wells Street, Milwaukee WI 53233. 414/278-6186. **Fax:** 414/278-6100. **Recorded jobline:** 414/278-6151. **Contact:** Human Resources. **World Wide Web address:** http://www.mpm.edu. **Description:** A museum open to the public year-round. Exhibits include The Streets of Old Milwaukee, Third Planet Dinosaur Hall, and Costa Rican Rainforest. The museum also operates the Humphrey IMAX Dome Theater and a turn-of-the-century exhibit called A Sense of Wonder. The museum also offers weekend family programs called Afternoon Adventures. **NOTE:** Search for positions online. **Positions advertised include:** Graphic Designer; Gift Officer; Director of Corporate Relations.

MILWAUKEE PUBLIC SCHOOLS
P.O. Box 2181, Milwaukee WI 53201-2182. 414/475-8220. **Fax:** 414/475-8722. **Contact:** Human Resources. **World Wide Web address:** http://www.milwaukee.k12.wi.us. **Description:** Manages the public school system for the city of Milwaukee, which includes 21 high schools, 24 middle schools, 119 elementary schools, 36 community schools, and 10 early childhood contract sites with 105,000 students. The Milwaukee Public Schools also offers alternative certification programs for teachers. Founded in 1836. **NOTE:** Download application form. **Company slogan:** High standards start here. **Positions advertised include:** Certified Teacher; Substitute; Secretary. **Special programs:** Internships; Training; Co-ops; Summer Jobs. **Office hours:** Monday - Friday, 8:00 a.m. - 5:00 p.m. **Corporate headquarters location:** This location. **Annual sales/revenues:** Less than $5 million. **Number of employees at this location:** 12,000.

MILWAUKEE REPERTORY THEATRE
108 East Wells Street, Milwaukee WI 53202. 414/224-1761. **Fax:** 414/224-9097. **Contact:** Personnel. **World Wide Web address:** http://www.milwaukeerep.com. **Description:** A theater producing a broad range of classical and contemporary theater pieces. **NOTE:** Search for positions online.

MILWAUKEE SCHOOL OF ENGINEERING
1025 North Broadway Street, Milwaukee WI 53202-3109. 414/277-7132. **Fax:** 414/277-2233. **Recorded jobline:** 414/277-4546. **Contact:** Kevin Morin, Director of Human Resources. **E-mail address:** hr@msoe.edu. **World Wide Web address:** http://www.msoe.edu. **Description:** A technical university that offers bachelor's and master's degrees and certificate programs in the areas of engineering, engineering technology, technical communication, and business. **Corporate headquarters location:** This location. **Operations at this facility include:** Administration; Service.

MODINE MANUFACTURING COMPANY
1500 DeKoven Avenue, Racine WI 53403-2552. 262/636-1200. **Fax:** 262/636-1424. **Contact:** Kelly Horon, Employment/Recruiting Manager. **World Wide Web address:** http://www.modine.com. **Description:** An independent, worldwide leader in heat transfer technology, serving vehicular (passenger car, van, truck, off-highway equipment, earth moving equipment, construction equipment, and agricultural equipment); industrial (a mixed category of OEM customers including the makers of engines, air compressors, refrigeration equipment, and hydraulic-pneumatic devices); commercial; and building/HVAC markets. The company's major products include radiators, oil coolers, vehicular air conditioning condensers and evaporators, building/HVAC products, charge-air coolers, and radiator cores. **Positions advertised include:** Web Architect/Developer; ABAP Programmer Analyst; Sr. Financial Operations Analyst; Applications Engineer. **Corporate headquarters location:** This location. **Other U.S. locations:** Nationwide. **Subsidiaries include:** Langerer & Reich (L&R); Austria Warmetauscher GmbH (AWG).

THE MONROE CLINIC
515 22nd Avenue, Monroe WI 53566. 608/324-1152. **Fax:** 608/324-1114. **Contact:** Sharon Mitchell, Human Resources Department. **E-mail address:** Sharon_Mitchell@themonroeclinic.com. **World Wide Web address:** http://www.themonroeclinic.org. **Description:** A nonprofit, multispecialty, 100-bed general hospital with outpatient facilities. Founded in 1939. **NOTE:** Second and third shifts are offered. **Company slogan:** A proud tradition of caring. **Positions advertised include:** Registered Nurse; Licensed Practical Nurse; Respiratory Therapist; Medical Laboratory Technician; Phlebotomist; Interface Programmer; . **Special programs:** Internships. **Office hours:** Monday - Friday, 8:00 a.m. - 5:00 p.m. **Corporate headquarters location:** This location. **Annual sales/revenues:** $21 - $50 million. **Number of employees at this location:** 920.

MOORE WALLACE RESPONSE MARKETING
1333 Scheuring Road, Depere WI 54115. 920/499-0811. **Fax:** 920/339-1676. **Contact:** Human Resources. **World Wide Web address:** http://www.moore.com. **Description:** Provides a wide range of direct mailing services. **Parent company:** RR Donnelley.

MORROW MEMORIAL HOME FOR THE AGED, INC.
331 South Water Street, Sparta WI 54656. 608/269-3168. **Fax:** 608/269-7642. **Contact:** Human Resources Director. **World Wide Web address:** http://www.morrowhome.org. **Description:** A nonprofit nursing home offering long-term care. Founded in 1917. **NOTE:** Entry-level positions, part-time jobs, and second and third shifts are offered. **Company slogan:** Four Cs - Christian, Compassionate Care with Competence. **Special programs:** Internships; Apprenticeships; Training; Co-ops; Summer Jobs. **Corporate headquarters location:** This location. **Executive Director:** Anita Genrich. **Number of employees at this location:** 130.

MORTGAGE GUARANTY INSURANCE CORP.
250 East Kilbourn Avenue, Milwaukee WI 53202. 414/347-6575. **Toll-free phone:** 800/424-6442. **Fax:** 414/347-4866. **Contact:** Human Resources. **World Wide Web address:** http://www.mgic.com. **Description:** Provides private mortgage insurance. **Positions advertised include:** Operating Systems Analyst/Administrator; Underwriting Analysis Coordinator; Information Security Analyst; Technology Assistance Specialist.

MOUNT MARY COLLEGE
2900 North Menomonee River Parkway, Milwaukee WI 53222-4597. 414/258-4810. **Fax:** 414/443-3600. **Contact:** Madeline Smith, Director of Human Resources. **E-mail address:** hrads@mtmary.edu. **World Wide Web address:** http://www.mtmary.edu. **Description:** A four-year Catholic, women's, liberal arts institution with approximately 1,500 students. **Positions advertised include:** Financial Aid counselor; Admission Counselor. **Number of employees at this location:** 300.

NCL GRAPHIC SPECIALTIES, INC.
North 29 West 22960 Marjean Lane, Waukesha WI 53186. 262/832-6100. **Fax:** 262/832-6272. **Contact:** Human Resources. **E-mail address:** recruiter@nclgs.com. **World Wide Web address:** http://www.nclgraphicspecialties.com. **Description:** An offset web press printer, specializing in large-volume production of labels, on-pak, in-pak, and around-pak commercial printing. **NOTE:** Search and apply for positions online. **Positions advertised include:** Operators. **Corporate headquarters location:** This location. **Other area locations:** Brookfield WI. **Listed on:** Privately held. **Annual sales/revenues:** $21 - $50 million. **Number of employees at this location:** 200.

NANIK SPRINGS WINDOW FASHIONS
7200 Stewart Avenue, Wausau WI 54401. 715/843-4653. **Fax:** 715/843-8182. **Contact:** Human Resources. **Description:** Manufactures wooden interior blinds of all styles. **Corporate headquarters location:** This location. **Number of employees at this location:** 450.

NESTLE FOOD COMPANY
1200 Nestle Avenue, Eau Claire WI 54703. 715/839-9440. **Contact:** Human Resources. **World Wide Web address:** http://www.nestle.com. **Description:** Nestle Food Company is an international food and beverage company. **Corporate headquarters location:** Switzerland. **Operations at this facility include:** This location manufactures baby formula.

NEW GLARUS HOME INC.
600 Second Avenue, New Glarus WI 53574. 608/527-2126. **Fax:** 608/527-5365. **Contact:** Jaqui Haldiman, Human Resources Manager. **Description:** A nursing and retirement home. **Annual sales/revenues:** Less than $5 million. **Number of employees at this location:** 100.

NORTH AMERICAN MECHANICAL, INC.
6135 North American Lane, Deforest WI 53532. 608/241-4328. **Fax:** 608/241-2710. **Contact:** Personnel Department. **E-mail address:** personnel@naminc.com. **World Wide Web address:** http://www.naminc.com. **Description:** A commercial HVAC contractor. **NOTE:** Entry-level positions and part-time jobs are offered. **Special programs:** Internships; Apprenticeships; Summer Jobs. **Corporate headquarters location:** This location. **Parent company:** Comfort Systems USA, Inc. **Listed on:** New York Stock Exchange. **Stock exchange symbol:** FIX. **Number of employees at this location:** 165.

NORTH CENTRAL HEALTH CARE FACILITIES
1100 Lake View Drive, Wausau WI 54403. 715/848-4600. **Fax:** 715/845-5398. **Contact:** Human Resources. **Description:** A psychiatric hospital that provides diagnostic treatment of mental health disorders, alcohol and drug abuse, and developmental disabilities. The hospital also provides a variety of geriatric services. **Corporate headquarters location:** This location. **Number of employees at this location:** 850.

NORTHERN LAKE SERVICE, INC.
400 North Lake Avenue, Crandon WI 54520-1298. 715/478-2777. **Toll-free phone:** 800/278-1254. **Fax:** 715/478-3060. **Contact:** Personnel. **E-mail address:** norlake@northernlakeservice.com. **World Wide Web address:** http://www.northernlakeservice.com. **Description:** An environmental analytical laboratory that conducts a wide range of tests on soil and water samples to determine whether contaminants are present.

THE NORTHWESTERN MUTUAL LIFE INSURANCE COMPANY
720 East Wisconsin Avenue, Milwaukee WI 53202. 414/271-1444. **Fax:** 414/665-2690. **Recorded jobline:** 414/665-7070. **Contact:** Human Resources. **World Wide Web address:** http://www.nmfn.com. **Description:** Specializes in individual life insurance coverage. The company's product portfolio includes permanent and term insurance, CompLife, disability income insurance, and annuity plans for the personal, business, estate, and pension planning markets. Founded in 1857. **NOTE:** Search and apply for positions online. **Positions advertised include:** Audit Specialist; BACC Operations Manager; Commodity Specialist; Data Warehouse Technical Lead; Diversity Consultant; Financial Services Attorney; Mutual Fund Accounting Specialist. **Special programs:** Internships. **Corporate headquarters location:** This location. **Other U.S. locations:** Nationwide. **Operations at this facility include:** Administration; Service. **Annual sales/revenues:** More than $100 million. **Number of employees at this location:** 4,400.

NORTHWOODS MEDICAL CENTER
2383 State Highway 17, Phelps WI 54554. 715/545-2313. **Contact:** Human Resources. **Description:** A hospital with numerous facilities that offer a full range of medical services.

OAK CREEK WOOD PRODUCTS
P.O. Box 110, Oak Creek WI 53154. 414/762-7170. **Fax:** 414/762-3070. **Contact:** Human Resources. **Description:** Manufactures wooden boxes, crates, pallets, and skids.

OCEAN SPRAY CRANBERRIES, INC.
7800 60th Avenue, Kenosha WI 53142. 262/694-5200. **Fax:** 262/694-5533. **Contact:** Human Resources. **World Wide Web address:** http://www.oceanspray.com. **Description:** Ocean Spray is a nationally recognized food processor engaged in the packaging, processing, and marketing of fresh cranberries, cranberry sauces, and cranberry and grapefruit juices. **NOTE:** Search and apply for positions online. **Positions advertised include:** Operations Supervisor. **Corporate headquarters location:** Lakeville MA. **Other U.S. locations:** MA; NJ; NV; WA. **Operations at this facility include:** This location processes juice products.

OLYMPIA RESORT & CONFERENCE CENTER
1350 Royale Mile Road, Oconomowoc WI 53066. 262/369-4976. **Toll-free phone:** 800/558-9573. **Fax:** 262/369-4998. **Contact:** Mark Mayfield, Human Resources Director. **E-mail address:** mmayfield@charterinternet.net. **World Wide Web address:** http://www.olympiaresort.com. **Description:** A hotel with a health spa, indoor and outdoor pools, child care facility, restaurant, and golf course. **Positions advertised include:** Engineer; Fitness Supervisor.

OMNI RESOURCES INC.
450 North Sunnyslope Road, Suite 180, Brookfield WI 53005. 262/797-0600. **Fax:** 262/797-8866. **Contact:** Human Resources. **E-mail address:** resumes@omniresources.com. **World Wide Web address:** http://www.omniresource.com. **Description:** An information systems consulting firm. Founded in 1984. **NOTE:** Search and apply for positions online. **Positions advertised include:** BW Analyst; SMS Engineer; SAP SD Functional Consultant; Software Testing Technician; Consultant, CCAT; Sr. AIX UNIX System Administrator; Java Developer; Oracle Financials Developer/Analyst. **Corporate headquarters location:** Milwaukee WI. **Other area locations:** Madison WI; Appleton WI. **Other U.S. locations:** Tampa FL; Minneapolis MN. **Listed on:** Privately held. **Number of employees at this location:** 100. **Number of employees nationwide:** 500.

OMNI RESOURCES INC.
131 West Wilson Street, Suite 505, Madison WI 53703. 608/284-2040. **Fax:** 608/284-2050. **Contact:** Human Resources. **E-mail address:** resumes@omniresources.com. **World Wide Web address:** http://www.omniresource.com. **Description:** An information systems consulting firm. Founded in 1984. **NOTE:** Search and apply for positions online. **Positions advertised include:** Mainframe/Network Security Administrator; Oracle DBA; Technical Writer; Novell Engineer; SQL Server DBA. **Corporate headquarters location:** Milwaukee WI. **Other area locations:** Appleton WI. **Other U.S. locations:** Tampa FL; Minneapolis MN. **Listed on:** Privately held. **Number of employees nationwide:** 500.

OMNI TECH CORPORATION
N27 W23676 Paul Road, Pewaukee WI 53072. 262/523-3300. **Contact:** Human Resources. **World Wide Web address:** http://www.otcwi.com. **Description:** Manufactures personal computers and offers custom networking services. **Subsidiaries:** Dedicated Computing.

ONEIDA BINGO & CASINO
P.O. Box 365, Oneida WI 54155. 920/494-7900. Toll-free phone: 800/238-4263. **Contact:** Human Resources. **World Wide Web address:** http://www.oneidabingoandcasino.net. **Description:** A casino. **Corporate headquarters location:** This location. **Number of employees at this location:** 3,500.

OPPORTUNITIES INC.
200 East Cramer Street, Fort Atkinson WI 53538-0278. 920/563-2437. **Toll-free phone:** 800/314-4567. **Fax:** 920/563-4651. **Contact:** Bonnie Kraush, Human Resources. **World Wide Web address:** http://www.oppinc.com. **Description:** A vocational rehabilitation facility serving adults with all ranges of disabilities. Includes vocational skill training, job placement, employment counseling, assessment, and a full range of therapy services. The company is engaged in subcontract work for other companies in the areas of printing, bindery, mailings, assembly, packaging, and metal fabrication. **Special programs:** Internships. **Number of employees nationwide:** 500.

OSCAR MAYER FOODS CORPORATION
910 Mayer Avenue, P.O. Box 7188, Madison WI 53707. 608/241-3311. **Fax:** 608/242-6107. **Contact:** Human Resources. **World Wide Web address:** http://www.oscar-mayer.com. **Description:** A nationwide meat and poultry processor. **Corporate headquarters location:** This location. **Other U.S. locations:** Englewood CO; Chicago IL. **Parent company:** Kraft Foods.

OSHKOSH B'GOSH INC.
P.O. Box 300, Oshkosh WI 54902. 920/231-8800. **Fax:** 920/231-8621. **Contact:** Human Resources. **E-mail address:** careers@bgosh.com. **World Wide Web address:** http://www.oshkoshbgosh.com. **Description:** A manufacturer of rugged adult workwear for farmers and railroad workers. The company also manufactures children's wear, bib overalls, shorts, shirts, dresses, activewear, swimwear, and accessories sold under the OshKosh B'Gosh and Baby B'Gosh labels; and youthwear under the Genuine Girl and Genuine Blues labels. The company also manufactures footwear, bedding, outerwear, and eyewear. Founded in 1895. **Positions advertised include:** Art Operations Technician; Assistant Buyer, Sourcing; Director of Accounting. **Corporate headquarters location:** This location. **International locations:** Worldwide. **Listed on:** NASDAQ. **Stock exchange symbol:** GOSHA.

OSHKOSH CORRECTIONAL INSTITUTION
1730 West Snell Road, Oshkosh WI 54901. 920/231-4010. **Contact:** Human Resources. **Description:** Part of the Wisconsin Correctional System.

OSHKOSH NORTHWESTERN
P.O. Box 2926, Oshkosh WI 54901. 920/235-7700. 920/235-7700. **Toll-free phone:** 800/924-6168. **Contact:** Human Resources Department. **World Wide Web address:** http://www.thenorthwestern.com. **Description:** Publishes a daily newspaper. **Corporate headquarters location:** This location.

OSHKOSH TRUCK CORPORATION
P.O. Box 2566, Oshkosh WI 54903-2566. 920/235-9151. **Physical address:** 2307 Oregon Street, Oshkosh WI 54902. **Fax:** 920/233-9268. **Contact:** Human Resources. **E-mail address:** jobline@oshtruck.com. **World Wide Web address:** http://www.oshkoshtruck.com. **Description:** Manufactures specialty trucks and truck bodies for the defense, fire and emergency, concrete placement and refuse hauling markets. **NOTE:** Search and apply for positions online. **Positions advertised include:** Accounting Supervisor; Materials Analyst/Planner; Quality Specialist; Project Engineer; Industrial Engineer; Model and Simulation Engineer; Lead Business Analyst. **Corporate headquarters location:** This location. **Listed on:** New York Stock Exchange. **Stock exchange symbol:** OSK. **Annual sales/revenues:** $1.9 billion.

OSMONICS AUTOTROL CORPORATION
5730 North Glen Park Road, Milwaukee WI 53209. 262/238-4400. **Fax:** 262/238-4418. **Contact:** Laura Bruder, Human Resources Manager. **Description:** A manufacturer of controls and systems for the water conditioning industry.

P&H MINING EQUIPMENT
4400 West National Avenue, Milwaukee WI 53214. 414/671-4400. **Fax:** 414/671-7618. **Recorded Jobline:** 800/244-9777. **Contact:** Employment Manager, Human Resources. **E-mail address:** milwrecruitment@phmining.com. **World Wide Web address:** http://www.phmining.com. **Description:** Manufactures and services large excavating and drilling machines used in mining operations. **NOTE:** Search and apply for positions online. **Positions advertised include:** Audit Consultant; Supervisor Production Control; Telecom Analyst; Service Engineer; Technical Illustrator; Project Engineer. **International locations:** Australia; Brazil; South Africa; Japan. **Parent company:** Joy Global, Inc.

PIC WISCONSIN
1002 Deming Way, P. O. Box 45650, Madison WI 53717. 608/831-8331. **Fax:** 608/831-0084. **Contact:** Human Resources. **E-mail address:** Human_Resources@picwisconsin.com. **World Wide Web address:** http://www.picwisconsin.com. **Description:** A carrier of medical liability insurance. The company serves the insurance needs of physicians, hospitals, and clinics. **NOTE:** Search and apply for positions online. **Positions advertised include:** Risk Management Consultant; Distribution Manager; Sr. Underwriter. **Corporate headquarters location:** This location. **Annual sales/revenues:** $21 - $50 million. **Number of employees at this location:** 60.

PKWARE, INC.
9025 North Deerwood Drive, Brown Deer WI 53223-2480. 414/354-8699. **Fax:** 414/354-8559. **Contact:** Human Resources. **E-mail address:** hr@pkware.com. **World Wide Web address:** http://www.pkware.com. **Description:** Develops data compression software including PKZIP. **NOTE:** Search and apply for positions online. **Positions advertised include:** Sr. Software Sales; Webmaster; Financial Analyst. **Other U.S. locations:** Miamisburg OH; Redwood Shores CA.

PTC (PARAMETRIC TECHNOLOGY CORPORATION)
Crossroads Corporate Center II, 20800 Swenson Drive, Suite 250, Waukesha WI 53186. 262/798-9494. **Fax:** 262/798-9467. **Contact:** Office Manager. **World Wide Web address:** http://www.ptc.com. **Description:** Parametric Technology Corporation designs and develops fully-integrated software products for mechanical engineering and automated manufacturing. The company has offices in 23 countries. **NOTE:** Search and apply for positions online. **Corporate headquarters location:** Needham MA. **Other U.S. locations:** WA. **Operations at this facility include:** This location serves as a regional sales office. **Listed on:** NASDAQ. **Stock exchange symbol:** PMTC.

PACON CORPORATION
2325 North Casaloma Drive, P.O. Box 7170, Appleton WI 54912-7068. 920/830-5050. **Toll-free phone:** 800/333-2545. **Fax:** 800/332-5099. **Contact:** Human Resources. **World Wide Web address:** http://www.pacon.com. **Description:** Producer of paper products for the art and school industries.

PALMER JOHNSON YACHTS
P.O. Box 109, Sturgeon Bay WI 54235. 920/743-4412. **Contact:** Human Resources. **World Wide Web address:** http://www.palmerjohnson.com. **Description:** Builds, refits, brokers, and charters luxury high-performance yachts. Founded in 1918. **Positions advertised include:** Design Engineer; Joiner; Mechanic; Rigger; Upholsterer; Electrician; Painter; Welder; Sales Executive.

PAPER CONVERTING MACHINE COMPANY
P.O. Box 19005, Green Bay WI 54307-9005. 920/494-5601. **Fax:** 920/494-8865. **Contact:** Human Resources. **World Wide Web address:** http://www.pcmc.com. **Description:** Designs and builds converting machinery for the paper, film, and foil industries. **Corporate headquarters location:** This location. **Listed on:** Privately held. **Number of employees at this location:** 860.

PARAGON DEVELOPMENT SYSTEMS, INC.
1823 Executive Drive, P.O. Box 128, Oconomowoc WI 53066. 262/569-5300. **Toll-free phone:** 800/966-6090. **Fax:** 262/569-5390. **E-mail address:** info@pdspc.com. **Contact:** Human Resources. **World Wide Web address:** http://www.pdspc.com. **Description:** Assists medium- to large-sized organizations plan for, procure, deploy, manage, support, and retire IT assets. **NOTE:** Search for positions online. **Other area locations:** Milwaukee WI; Madison WI.

PARKER HANNIFIN CORPORATION
533 North Oak Street, Grantsburg WI 54840. 715/463-2561. **Fax:** 715/463-6313. **Contact:** Human Resources. **World Wide Web address:** http://www.parker.com. **Description:** A manufacturing facility of the Parker Hannifin Corporation Quick Coupling Division. **Other area locations:** Chetek WI. **Corporate headquarters location:** Cleveland OH. **Operations at this facility include:** This location manufactures fluid and hydraulic couplers.

PERRY JUDD'S INC.
575 West Madison Street, Waterloo WI 53594. 920/478-3551. **Toll-free phone:** 800/737-7948. **Fax:** 920/478-1536. **Contact:** Human Resources. **E-mail address:** information@perryjudds.com. **World Wide Web address:** http://www.perryjudds.com. **Description:** A printer of catalogs and magazines. **Corporate headquarters location:** This location. **Other U.S. locations:** Nationwide. **Operations at this facility include:** Administration; Manufacturing; Sales. **Number of employees at this location:** 1,400.

PHILLIPS PLASTICS CORPORATION
7 Longlake Drive, Phillips WI 54555. 715/339-3005. **Fax:** 715/339-3092. **Contact:** Human Resources. **World Wide Web address:** http://www.phillipsplastics.com. **Description:** Engaged in the custom injection molding of plastics and metal. The company's services include high engineering and tooling. **NOTE:** Search and apply for positions online. **Corporate headquarters location:** This location. **Other U.S. locations:** Minneapolis MN. **Operations at this facility include:** Manufacturing; Sales. **Number of employees at this location:** 325. **Number of employees nationwide:** 1,600.

PLEXUS CORP.
55 Jewelers Park Drive, Neenah WI 54957-0677. 920/722-3451. **Fax:** 920/751-5395. **Contact:** Amy Sabac, Human Resources. **World Wide Web address:** http://www.plexus.com. **Description:** Services include mechanical, electronic and software design, printed circuit board development, prototyping services, new product introduction, material procurement and management, printed circuit board and higher level assembly, test development, in-circuit and functional testing, final system box build, fulfillment and sustaining services. Founded in 1980. **NOTE:** Search and apply for positions online. **Positions advertised include:** Financial Analyst; Focus Factory Manager; VP of Medical Market Sector; Engineering Manager; Staff Test Engineer. **Special programs:** Internships. **Corporate headquarters location:** This location. **Other area locations:** Appleton WI. **Other U.S. locations:** Ayer MA; Raleigh NC; Louisville CO; Fremont CA; Nampa ID; Hillsboro OR; Bothell WA. **Subsidiaries include:** Plexus Technology Group. **Operations at this facility include:** Administration; Manufacturing. **Listed on:** NASDAQ. **Stock exchange symbol:** PLXS. **Annual sales/revenues:** More than $100 million. **Number of employees at this location:** 2,100. **Number of employees nationwide:** 2,600.

POLARIS INDUSTRIES
805 Seminole Avenue, Osceola WI 54020. 715/294-3370. **Fax:** 715/294-4175. **Contact:** Personnel. **World Wide Web address:** http://www.polarisindustries.com. **Description:** Polaris Industries manufactures recreational vehicles including snowmobiles and all-terrain vehicles. Other products include personal watercraft and garments and accessories, such as snowmobile suits and leathers, wet suits, helmets, goggles, activewear, and tennis shoes, all bearing the Polaris logo. Polaris products are

sold around the world through a network of nearly 2,000 dealers in North America and 55 distributors covering 82 countries worldwide. **NOTE:** Search and apply for positions online. **Positions advertised include:** Advanced Manufacturing Engineer; Design Engineer; Manufacturing Supervisor; Powertrain Product Manager; Project Engineer; Sr. Test Engineer. **Operations at this facility include:** This location manufactures engines and components. **Listed on:** New York Stock Exchange. **Stock exchange symbol:** PII.

POWERWARE
N9246 Highway 80 South, Necedah WI 54646. 608/565-7200. **Fax:** 608/565-2221. **Contact:** Human Resources. **World Wide Web address:** http://www.powerware.com. **Description:** A designer, manufacturer, and marketer of power protection products for PCs, LANs, WANs, and global networks. Best Power also provides support services. **Corporate headquarters location:** Raleigh NC.

PRECISION DRIVE & CONTROL
504 11th Street, P.O. Box 537, Monroe WI 53566. 608/328-5600. **Contact:** Human Resources Department. **Description:** An electronic contractor that is also involved in the repair and service of electric motors and related components.

PRENT CORPORATION
2225 Kennedy Road, P.O. Box 471, Janesville WI 53547-0471. 608/754-0276. **Fax:** 608/754-2410. **Contact:** Human Resources Director. **E-mail address:** apply@prent.com. **World Wide Web address:** http://www.prent.com. **Description:** Manufacturer of custom thermoformed plastic packaging parts, 60 percent of which are used by the medical products industry. **Positions advertised include:** Sales Representative. **Corporate headquarters:** This location. **Other U.S. locations:** Flagstaff AZ. **International locations:** Malaysia; Singapore. **Operations at this facility include:** Administration; Manufacturing. **Listed on:** Privately held.

PRESCOTT'S SUPERMARKETS, INC.
1719 South Main Street, West Bend WI 53095. 262/338-5620. **Fax:** 262/338-5630. **Contact:** Human Resources. **World Wide Web address:** http://www.prescotts.com. **Description:** A retail grocer with six store locations throughout Wisconsin. **NOTE:** Entry-level positions are offered. **Corporate headquarters location:** This location. **Listed on:** Privately held. **Annual sales/revenues:** More than $100 million.

PROCTER & GAMBLE
700 Eastman Avenue, Green Bay WI 54302. 920/430-2101. **Contact:** Human Resources Department. **World Wide Web address:** http://www.pg.com. **Description:** Procter & Gamble manufactures over 300 laundry, cleaning, paper, beauty, health care, food, and beverage products in more than 140 countries. Brand name products include Cover Girl, Max Factor, Vidal Sassoon, Clearasil, and Noxzema health and beauty products; Pepto-Bismol, Vicks, and NyQuil health care products; Bounce, Downy, Tide, Comet, and Mr. Clean cleaning products; Luvs, Pampers, Always, Tampax, Bounty, Charmin, and Puffs paper products; and Crisco, Folgers, Millstone, Sunny Delight, and Pringles food and beverage products. **Corporate headquarters location:** Cincinnati OH. **Other U.S. locations:** Nationwide. **Listed on:** New York Stock Exchange. **Stock exchange symbol:** PG.

PROMEGA CORPORATION
2800 Woods Hollow Road, Madison WI 53711. 608/274-4330. **Toll-free phone:** 800/356-9526. **Fax:** 800/277-2516. **Contact:** Human Resources Department. **E-mail address:** hr@promega.com. **World Wide Web address:** http://www.promega.com. **Description:** Designs and manufactures biological reagents and systems for the life sciences industry. Founded in 1978. **NOTE:** Search and apply for positions online. **Positions advertised include:** R& D Scientist; Production Scientist; Sr. Software Developer; VP Marketing; Marketing Coordinator; Director of Human Resources; Associate General Counsel; **Corporate headquarters location:** This location.

PROTOPROBE, INC.
10437 Innovation Drive, Suite 303, Milwaukee WI 53226-4815. 414/774-2670. **Toll-free phone:** 800/432-3711. **Fax:** 414/774-0767. **Contact:** Human Resources. **World Wide Web address:** http://www.protoprobe.com. **Description:** Researches protein chemistry, immunology, molecular and cellular biology, and focuses on antibody technology and tools to research and treat cancer in humans. Research is performed for the federal government and research companies.

QMR PLASTICS
434 Highland Drive, River Falls WI 54022. 715/426-4700. **Fax:** 715/426-5115. **Contact:** Human Resources. **World Wide Web address:** http://www.qmrplastics.com. **Description:** Engaged in plastic injection molding. **NOTE:** Entry-level positions, part-time jobs, and second and third shifts are offered. **Special programs:** Internships; Training. **Office hours:** Monday - Friday, 8:00 a.m. - 5:00 p.m. **Corporate headquarters location:** Minneapolis MN. **International locations:** France; Singapore. **Listed on:** Privately held. **Annual sales/revenues:** $11 - $20 million. **Number of employees at this location:** 65. **Number of employees nationwide:** 1,500. **Number of employees worldwide:** 2,000.

QUAD/GRAPHICS, INC.
W224 N3322 Duplainville Road, Pewaukee WI 53072. 414/566-6000. **Contact:** Human Resources. **E-mail address:** quadjobs@qg.com. **World Wide Web address:** http://www.qg.com. **Description:** A printing company. **NOTE:** Search and apply for positions online. **Positions advertised include:** Corporate Trainee; Material Handler; Driver; Trip Planner/Dispatcher. **Corporate headquarters location:** This location. **Other area locations:** Sussex WI; Hartford WI, Lomira WI, West Allis WI. **Other U.S. locations:** CA; GA; MA; NJ; NY; OH; WV. **International locations:** Argentina; Brazil; Poland. **Number of employees worldwide:** 12,000.

QUALITY LOGISTICS
2121 American Boulevard, Suite A, De Pere WI 54115. 920/388-1154. **Fax:** 920/338-1164. **Contact:** Human Resources. **E-mail address:** info@qualitylogistics.com. **World Wide Web address:** http://www.qualitylogistics.com. **Description:** Manufactures packaging, and provides warehousing, support, distribution, and logistics services.

RBC DAIN RAUSCHER INC.
4010 West Spencer Street, Appleton WI 54914-4064. 920/739-6311. **Toll-free phone:** 800/365-0050. **Fax:** 920/739-9447. **Contact:** Ed Heyes, Human Resources Representative. **World Wide Web address:** http://www.rbcdain.com. **Description:** A financial consulting and securities firm. **NOTE:** Search and apply for positions online. **Other U.S. locations:** Nationwide. **Parent company:** Royal Bank of Canada. **Number of employees worldwide:** 6,000.

RBP CHEMICAL TECHNOLOGY
150 South 118th Street, P.O. Box 14069, Milwaukee WI 53214-0069. 414/258-0911. **Toll-free phone:** 800/558-0747. **Fax:** 414/258-7908. **Contact:** Human Resources. **World Wide Web address:** http://www.rbpchemical.com. **Description:** Manufactures chemicals for the graphic arts and for the production of printed circuit boards. **Special programs:** Internships. **Corporate headquarters location:** This location. **Operations at this facility include:** Manufacturing; Research and Development. **Number of employees at this location:** 50.

RANCH COMMUNITY SERVICES
West 187 North 8661 Maple Road, Menomonee Falls WI 53051-1800. 262/251-8670. **Fax:** 262/251-8878. **Contact:** Human Resources Coordinator. **E-mail address:** careers@ranchwi.org. **World Wide Web address:** http://www.ranchwi.org. **Description:** A nonprofit human services organization devoted to assisting adults with developmental disabilities by helping them to find jobs and providing them with community activities. There are additional locations in Waukesha and Milwaukee Counties. Founded in 1960. **NOTE:** Entry-level positions and second and third shifts are offered. **Positions advertised include:** Certified Nursing Assistant; Community Integration Specialist. **Special programs:** Internships; Training. **Corporate headquarters location:** This location. **Annual sales/revenues:** Less than $5 million. **Number of employees at this location:** 150.

RAYOVAC CORPORATION
601 Rayovac Drive, Madison WI 53711. 608/275-3340. **Contact:** Human Resources. **World Wide Web address:** http://www.rayovac.com. **Description:** Manufactures batteries and battery-operated lighting devices. **NOTE:** Search and apply for positions online. **Positions advertised include:** Operations Finance Analyst; Mechanical Designer; Sales Information Analyst; Project Engineer; Sr. Programmer Analyst; Test Engineer; Manager of Internal Audit; Graphic Artist; Inventory Manager. **Other area locations:** Fennimore WI; Portage WI. **Operations at this facility include:** Administration; Research and Development; Sales. **Number of employees at this location:** 600. **Number of employees worldwide:** 3,300. **Listed on:** New York Stock Exchange. **Stock exchange symbol:** ROV.

REGAL BELOIT CORPORATION
200 State Street, Beloit WI 53511-6254. 608/364-8800. **Fax:** 608/364-8818. **Contact:** Human Resources Department. **E-mail address:** regal@regal-beloit.com. **World Wide Web address:** http://www.regal-beloit.com. **Description:** Manufactures mechanical and electrical motion control products for a variety of markets. **NOTE:** Search and apply for positions online. **Positions advertised include:** Corporate Accountant; Director of Human Resources; **Corporate headquarters:** This location. **Listed on:** American Stock Exchange. **Stock exchange symbol:** RBC. **Annual sales/revenue:** $600 million.

REGAL WARE, INC.
1675 Reigle Drive, Kewaskum WI 53040. 262/626-2121. **Contact:** Human Resources. **World Wide Web address:** http://www.regalware.com. **Description:** Manufactures stainless steel cookware, giftware, bakeware, specialty items, portable electrical appliances, coffee makers, food processors, electric knives, and microwave cookware.

REIMAN PUBLICATIONS
5400 South 60th Street, Greendale WI 53129. 414/423-0100. **Fax:** 414/423-3840. **Contact:** Human Resources. **E-mail address:** hr@reimanpub.com. **World Wide Web address:** http://www.reimanpub.com. **Description:** Publishes ten magazines focusing on country life, food, gardening, and nostalgia. Each magazine is supported solely by subscriptions. Also offers calendars and books. **NOTE:** Search and apply for positions online. **Positions advertised include:** Business Analyst; Assistant Circulation Manager; marketing Analyst; Inventory Planner; Associate Editor; Editor-in-Chief.

REINHART, BOERNER, VAN DEUREN
1000 North Water Street, Suite 2100, Milwaukee WI 53202. 414/298-1000. **Fax:** 414/298-8097. **Contact:** Human Resources. **World Wide Web address:** http://www.reinhartlaw.com. **Description:** A law firm that specializes in cases in real estate, corporate, banking, and tax law. **Other area locations:** Madison WI; Waukesha WI.

THE REPORTER
P.O. Box 630, Fond du Lac WI 54936-0630. 920/922-4600. **Physical address:** 33 West Second Street, Fond du Lac WI 54935. **Fax:** 920/922-5388. **Contact:** Human Resources Department. **World Wide Web address:** http://www.fdlreporter.com. **Description:** A daily newspaper. Founded in 1870. **Parent company:** The Gannett Co.

REXNORD PLASTICS DIVISION
1272 Dakota Drive, P.O. Box 480, Grafton WI 53024. 262/376-4600. **Fax:** 262/376-4740. **Contact:** Human Resources Department. **World Wide Web address:** http://www.rexnordplastics.com. **Description:** Involved in plastic injection molding. **Other U.S. locations:** Clinton TN; Milwaukee WI.

THE RICHLAND CENTER FOUNDRY COMPANY
1000 Foundry Drive, P.O. Box 609, Richland Center WI 53581. 608/647-6121. **Fax:** 608/647-6126. **Contact:** Karen Knoble, Human Resources Manager. **E-mail address:** hr@rcfoundry.com. **World Wide Web address:** http://www.rcfoundry.com. **Description:** A short- to medium-run gray and ductile iron foundry. **Positions advertised include:** General Production Associate. **Corporate headquarters location:** This location. **Operations at this facility include:** Administration; Manufacturing; Sales. **Listed on:** Privately held. **Number of employees at this location:** 300.

ROCKWELL AUTOMATION
1201 South Second Street, P.O. Box 2086, Milwaukee WI 53201-2496. 414/382-2000. **Fax:** 414/382-4499. **Contact:** Vicki Schmidt, Human Resources Department. **World Wide Web address:** http://www.rockwell.com. **Description:** Engaged in the production of industrial control equipment, software-based control equipment, magnetic materials, and electronic components. **NOTE:** Search and apply for positions online. **Positions advertised include:** Commodity Director; Manager, Global Employee Communications; Marketing Manager; Sr. Development Engineer; Analyst, UNIX Systems; Materials Engineer. **Listed on:** New York Stock Exchange. **Stock exchange symbol:** ROK. **Number of employees worldwide:** 23,000.

ROCKWELL AUTOMATION
777 East Wisconsin Avenue, Suite 1400, Milwaukee WI 53202. 414/212-5200. **Fax:** 414/212-5346. **Contact:** Human Resources Department. **World Wide Web address:** http://www.rockwell.com. **Description:** Manufactures products for the printing, military, automotive, and aerospace industries through its electronics, automotive, and graphics divisions. Products include military and commercial communication equipment, guidance systems, electronics, components for automobiles, and printing presses. Rockwell International provides the U.S. government with parts and services for bombers, as well as power systems for the space station. The company is also a contractor for the Space Shuttle Orbiter program. **NOTE:** Search and apply for positions online. **Positions advertised include:** Human Resources Manager. **Corporate headquarters location:** This location. **Listed on:** New York Stock Exchange. **Stock exchange symbol:** ROK.

ROCKWELL SOFTWARE
2424 South 102nd Street, West Allis WI 53227. 414/328-2000. **Fax:** 414/328-2211. **Contact:** Human Resources. **World Wide Web address:** http://www.software.rockwell.com. **Description:** A manufacturer of software for various industrial applications. **NOTE:** Search and apply for positions online. **Other U.S. locations:** Mayfield Village, OH.

ROUNDY'S INC.
875 East Wisconsin Avenue, Suite 100, Milwaukee WI 53202. 414/231-5000. **Fax:** 262/953-6580. **Recorded jobline:** 262/524-5700. **Contact:** Human Resources. **World Wide Web address:** http://www.roundys.com. **Description:** Manufactures and distributes food products to warehouses and supermarkets throughout the Midwest. Founded in 1875. **NOTE:** Entry-level positions and second and third shifts are offered. Search and apply for positions online. **Positions advertised include:** Installation Specialist; Business Analyst; Technical Architect; Programmer Analyst; Security Analyst. **Corporate headquarters location:** This location. **Annual sales/revenues:** More than $100 million. **Number of employees at this location:** 200. **Number of employees nationwide:** 5,000.

RUDER, WARE & MICHLER
500 Third Street, Suite 700, P.O. Box 8050, Wausau WI 54402-8050. 715/845-4336. **Fax:** 715/845-2718. **Contact:** Human Resources Department. **E-mail address:** ruder@ruder.com. **World Wide Web address:** http://www.ruder.com. **Description:** A law firm. Primary clients are government and industrial businesses. Founded in 1921.

RYERSON TULL
500 South 88th Street, Milwaukee WI 53214. 414/453-8000. **Fax:** 414/453-8013. **Contact:** Human Resources Department. **World Wide Web address:** http://www.ryersontull.com. **Description:** One of the nation's largest distributors and processors of steel, aluminum, nickel alloys, copper, brass, and industrial plastics. Plant operations are located in 28 cities, carry 350,000 tons of metal in stock, and serve 100,000 customers. Founded in 1842. **NOTE:** Entry-level positions are offered. **Positions advertised include:** Quality Assurance Representative. **Special programs:** Training. **Corporate headquarters location:** Chicago IL. **Listed on:** New York Stock Exchange. **Stock exchange symbol:** RT. **Annual sales/revenues:** More than $100 million. **Number of employees worldwide:** 5,000.

SBC COMMUNICATIONS INC.
7419 West Bradley Road, Milwaukee WI 53223. 414/357-7015. **Toll-free phone:** 800/924-3675. **Fax:** 414/678-6941. **Recorded jobline:** 866/695-6271. **Contact:** Human Resources. **World Wide Web address:** http://www.sbc.com. **Description:** One of the largest telephone holding companies in the United States, providing local telephone service to over 17 million customers in 13 states. **Positions advertised include:** Sr. Sales Support Manager. **Corporate headquarters location:** Chicago IL. **Other U.S. locations:** AR; CA; CO; KA; MO; NV; OK; TX; IN; MI; OH. **Subsidiaries include:** Ameritech Mobile is a wireless communications company that provides services to 1 million clients and over 500,000 pagers. Subsidiaries of Ameritech provide advertising, publishing, research and development, messaging, financing, and leasing services. **Listed on:** New York Stock Exchange. **Stock exchange symbol:** SBC **Number of employees worldwide:** 168,000.

S.C. JOHNSON
1525 Howe Street, Racine WI 53403-5011. 262/260-2000. **Toll-free phone:** 800/494-4855. **Contact:** Human Resources. **World Wide Web address:** http://www.scjohnson.com. **Description:** Manufactures consumer products such as furniture polish, cleaning products, and air fresheners. **NOTE:** Submit resume online. **Positions advertised include:** Sr. Unix Administrator; Process IT Administrator; Research Scientist. **Number of employees worldwide:** 9,500.

SSI TECHNOLOGIES, INC.
3200 Palmer Drive, P.O. Box 5011, Janesville WI 53547-5011. 608/757-2000. **Toll-free phone:** 888/477-4320. **Fax:** 608/373-2392. **Contact:** Human Resources. **World Wide Web address:** http://www.ssitechnologies.com. **Description:** Produces components such as sensors and sensor-based monitoring systems, coil assemblies, and solenoids for the automotive industry, and powdered-metal components for automotive and industrial applications. **Positions advertised include:** Product Engineer; Sr. Product Engineer; Sr. Manufacturing Engineer; Manufacturing Engineer; EHS Facilitator. **Other U.S. locations:** Farmington Hills MI. **Number of employees worldwide:** 1,100.

SPX PROCESS EQUIPMENT
611 Sugar Creek Road, Delavan WI 53115. 262/728-1900. **Fax:** 262/728-4904. **Contact:** Human Resources. **World Wide Web address:** http://www.spxprocessequipment.com. **Description:** Manufactures stainless steel valves, pumps, and fittings for the food and dairy industry. **Corporate headquarters location:** This location. **Operations at this facility include:** Accounting/Auditing; Manufacturing; Research and Development; Sales; Service. **Parent company:** SPX Corporation.

ST. CAMILLUS CAMPUS
10200 West Bluemound Road, Wauwatosa WI 53226. 414/259-6333. **Fax:** 414/259-7739. **Contact:** Pam Loveless, Human Resources Director. **E-mail address:** hrd@stcam.com. **World Wide Web address:** http://www.stcam.com. **Description:** A nonprofit health care center offering home health care services, supportive living, adult day services, and a subacute unit. **NOTE:** Entry-level positions and second and third shifts are offered. **Positions advertised include:** Registered Nurse; Licensed Practical Nurse; Registered Nurse Case Manager; Home Health Aide. **Special programs:** Training. **Office hours:** Monday - Friday, 8:00 a.m. - 5:00 p.m. **Corporate headquarters location:** This location. **Number of employees at this location:** 625.

ST. COLETTA'S OF WISCONSIN
West 4955 Highway 18, Jefferson WI 53549-9799. 920/674-4330. **Fax:** 920/674-4603. **Contact:** Human Resources. **E-mail address:** recruiter@stcolettawi.org. **World Wide Web address:** http://www.stcolettawi.org. **Description:** A facility for individuals with developmental disabilities that houses a school and other programs. **Number of employees at this location:** 300.

ST. FRANCIS BANK, F.S.B.
3545 South Kinnickinnic Avenue, St. Francis WI 53235-3700. 414/744-8600. **Fax:** 262/787-8776. **Recorded jobline:** 414/747-7699. **Contact:** Human Resources. **World Wide Web address:** http://www.stfrancisbank.com. **Description:** A bank with 23 full-service locations in Wisconsin. **NOTE:** Resumes only accepted for open positions. Resumes may be submitted online or mailed to 13400 Bishops Lane, Suite 350, Brookfield WI 53005. **Parent company:** MidAmerica Bank.

ST. JOSEPH'S HOSPITAL
611 Saint Joseph's Avenue, Marshfield WI 54449-1898. 715/387-1713. **Toll-free phone:** 800/221-3733 **Fax:** 715/387-7001. **Contact:** Human Resource Services. **E-mail address:** sjhjobs@stjosephs-marshfield.org. **World Wide Web address:** http://www.stjosephs-marshfield.org. **Description:** A 504-bed, tertiary referral center and teaching hospital. **Positions advertised include:** Certified Nursing Assistant; Communication Specialist; EMS Coordinator; General Practice Pharmacy Resident; Physical Therapist; Respiratory Therapist; Radiology Technologist; Registered Nurse. **Corporate headquarters location:** Milwaukee WI. **Parent company:** Sisters of the Sorrowful Mother Ministry Corporation. **Operations at this facility include:** Administration. **Number of employees at this location:** 2,100.

ST. LUKE'S MEDICAL CENTER
2900 West Oklahoma Avenue, Milwaukee WI 53215. 414/649-6000. **Fax:** 414/649-7982. **Contact:** Human Resources. **World Wide Web address:** http://www.aurorahealthcare.org. **Description:** A medical center providing a full range of health services. **Positions advertised include:** Phlebotomist; Supervisor, Endocrine Center; Radiologic Technologist; Coordinator, Research RN; Reimbursement Analyst; Pharmacist; Instructional Designer; Sr. Medical Imaging Technician; Registered Nurse.

ST. VINCENT HOSPITAL
835 South Van Buren Avenue, P.O. Box 13508, Green Bay WI 54307-3508. 920/433-0111. **Recorded jobline:** 920/431-3279. **Fax:** 920/431-3151. **Contact:** Human Resources Department. **World Wide Web address:** http://www.stvincenthospital.org. **Description:** A 547-bed, acute care hospital offering a wide variety of medical and diagnostic services. **Positions advertised include:** CT Tech, Radiology; Cancer Registrar; Cath Lab Registered Nurse; Certified Nursing Assistant; Director, Pediatrics; Director, Radiology; Echocardiographer; Medical Technologist; Medical Transcriptionist; Pharmacist. **Number of employees at this location:** 1,700.

SANNES SKOGDALEN
P.O. Box 177, 101 Sunshine Boulevard, Soldiers Grove WI 54655. 608/624-5244. **Fax:** 608/624-3478. **Contact:** Donald A. Sannes, Administrator. **Description:** A nursing home. **Corporate headquarters location:** This location. **Parent company:** Milam Inc. **Listed on:** Privately held. **Annual sales/revenues:** Less than $5 million. **Number of employees at this location:** 90.

SCHNEIDER NATIONAL, INC.
3101 South Packerland Drive, P.O. Box 2545, Green Bay WI 54306-2545. 920/592-2000. **Toll-free phone:** 800/558-6767. **Fax:** 920/592-3252. **Contact:** Human Resources. **E-mail address:** recruiting@schneider.com. **World Wide Web address:** http://www.schneider.com. **Description:** Offers a wide range of transportation and logistics services. Schneider National's transportation sector offers van, intermodal, flatbed, and bulk tank services. The company also offers solutions to supply chain management problems. Founded in 1935. **NOTE:** Entry-level positions, part-time jobs, and second and third shifts are offered. **Positions advertised include:** Application Development Technical Architecture; Business Analyst; Data communication Analyst; Desktop Integration Specialist; Infrastructure Architect; Project Manager; Facility Manager; Logistics Manager. **Special programs:** Internships; Training; Co-ops; Summer Jobs. **Corporate headquarters location:** This location. **Other U.S. locations:** Nationwide. **International locations:** Canada; Mexico. **Listed on:** Privately held. **Annual sales/revenues:** More than $100 million. **Number of employees nationwide:** 16,000.

SCHREIBER FOODS INC.
P.O. Box 19010, Green Bay WI 54307-9010. 920/437-7601. **Toll-free phone:** 800/344-0333. **Fax:** 920/437-1617. **Contact:** Human Resources. **World Wide Web address:** http://www.sficorp.com. **Description:** A dairy products food processing company. **Positions advertised include:** Recruiter; Export Business Sales Manager; Marketing Manager; Collections/Deductions Analyst; Telecommunications Analyst. **Corporate headquarters location:** This location. **Number of employees worldwide:** 4,200.

SCHUMANN PRINTERS, INC.
701 South Main Street, Fall River WI 53932. 920/484-3348. **Fax:** 920/484-3661. **Contact:** Personnel. **World Wide Web address:** http://www.spiweb.com. **Description:** Prints, binds, and mails publications and magazines. Founded in 1963. **NOTE:** Entry-level positions and second and third shifts are offered. **Corporate headquarters location:** This location. **Annual sales/revenues:** $21 - $50 million. **Number of employees at this location:** 170.

SECURITAS USA
2501 South Oneida Street, Appleton WI 54915. 920/739-9271. **Fax:** 920/739-6252. **Contact:** Human Resources. **World Wide Web address:** http://www.securitas.com. **Description:** Securitas offers a full range of specialized protective services including Premier Property/High-Rise Services, Healthcare/Hospital Services, Special Event Services, ATM Services, and Patrol Services. The company serves thousands of companies worldwide with investigation services, threat assessment services, executive protection, and more. **NOTE:** Applicants may be required to take a drug screening test. **Operations at this facility include:** This location is a district office of the international investigation and security company. **Parent company:** Securitas.

SENSIENT TECHNOLOGIES CORPORATION
777 East Wisconsin Avenue, Milwaukee WI 53202-5304. 414/271-6755. **Toll-free phone:** 800/558-9892. **Fax:** 414/347-4783. **Contact:** Employment Manager. **E-mail address:** employment@sensient-tech.com. **World Wide Web address:** http://www.sensient-tech.com. **Description:** A producer of food, dairy, and beverage flavors; food, drug, and cosmetic colors; fragrances, and specialty chemicals for inkjet inks. **Corporate headquarters location:** This location. **Other U.S. locations:** CA; IN; MO; NJ. **International locations:** Worldwide. **Operations at this facility include:** Administration; Sales; Service. **Listed on:** New York Stock Exchange. **Stock exchange symbol:** SXT.

SEVEN OAKS
6263 North Green Bay Road, Glendale WI 53209. 414/351-0543. **Fax:** 414/351-0239. **Contact:** Minnie Harris, Human Resources Director. **Description:** A 94-bed nursing home. **NOTE:** Entry-level positions are offered. **Corporate headquarters location:** Waukesha WI. **Parent company:** Laureate Group. **Number of employees at this location:** 150.

SHOPKO STORES, INC.
P.O. Box 19060, Green Bay WI 54307-9060. 920/497-2211. **Physical address:** 700 Pilgrim Way, Green Bay WI 54304. **Fax:** 920/429-4799. **Contact:** Human Resources. **E-mail address:** careers@shopko.com. **World Wide Web address:** http://www.shopko.com. **Description:** A leading regional retailer operating 141 ShopKo Stores and 218 Pamida stores in 23 states. The company's stores carry a wide selection of branded and private-label goods such as women's, men's, and children's apparel; shoes; jewelry; accessories; and home textiles; and hardline goods such as housewares; small appliances; furniture; music/videos; toys; sporting goods; cosmetics;

and seasonal items. Most of ShopKo's stores also include pharmacy centers and optical centers. **Positions advertised include:** Business Analyst; Corporate Traffic Manager; Fleet Equipment Manager; Accountant; Networking Engineering Architect. **Corporate headquarters location:** This location. **Listed on:** New York Stock Exchange. **Stock exchange symbol:** SKO.

SIERRA INC.
566 State Street, Racine WI 53402. 262/638-1851. **Toll-free phone:** 800/644-7267. **Fax:** 262/638-1852. **Contact:** Human Resources Department. **World Wide Web address:** http://www.sierrainc.com. **Description:** Sells and services computers for large retailers.

SILICON GRAPHICS, INC.
890 Industrial Boulevard, Chippewa Falls WI 54729. 715/726-8000. **Fax:** 715/726-7110. **Contact:** Staffing. **World Wide Web address:** http://www.sgi.com. **Description:** SGI manufactures a family of workstation and server systems that are used by engineers, scientists, and other creative professionals to develop, analyze, and simulate complex, three-dimensional objects. **NOTE:** Search and apply for positions online. **Positions advertised include:** Director Strategic Tech Initiatives. **Corporate headquarters location:** Mountain View CA. **Operations at this facility include:** This location manufactures supercomputers.

SKAALEN RETIREMENT SERVICES
400 North Morris Street, Stoughton WI 53589. 608/873-5651. **Fax:** 608/873-5748. **Contact:** Barb Kroda, R.N., Director of Nursing. **World Wide Web address:** http://www.skaalen.com. **Description:** A 266-bed nursing home. **NOTE:** Entry-level positions are offered. **Positions advertised include:** Registered Nurse; Licensed Practical Nurse; Certified Nursing Assistant. **Annual sales/revenues:** $5 - $10 million. **Number of employees at this location:** 300.

SKYWARD, INC.
5233 Coye Drive, Stevens Point WI 54481. **Toll-free phone:** 800/236-7274. **Fax:** 715/341-1370. **Contact:** Human Resources Department. **World Wide Web address:** http://www.skyward.com. **Description:** Develops school administration data processing software. Founded in 1980. **NOTE:** Entry-level positions are offered. **Positions advertised include:** Programmer. **Corporate headquarters location:** This location. **Other U.S. locations:** Bloomington IL; Waite Park MN; Okemos MI; Austin TX. **Listed on:** Privately held. **Annual sales/revenues:** $5 - $10 million. **Number of employees at this location:** 110.

A.O. SMITH CORPORATION
11270 West Park Place, Suite 170, Milwaukee WI 53224. 414/359-4000. **Fax:** 414/359-4064. **Contact:** Personnel. **World Wide Web address:** http://www.aosmith.com. **Description:** A.O. Smith Corporation consists of two operating units: the Electrical Products Company manufactures a variety of electrical motors used in commercial and consumer applications; and A.O. Smith Water Products Company manufactures water heaters. **Corporate headquarters location:** This location. **Other U.S. locations:** Nationwide. **International locations:** Canada; China; England; Hungary; Ireland; Mexico; Netherlands. **Listed on:** New York Stock Exchange. **Stock exchange symbol:** AOS.

SNAP-ON INC.
2801 80th Street, Kenosha WI 53141. 262/656-5200. **Fax:** 262/656-4961. **Contact:** Recruiter. **E-mail address:** corporatestaffing@snapon.com. **World Wide Web address:** http://www.snapon.com. **Description:** Manufactures and distributes tools, storage units, and diagnostic equipment for professional repair, maintenance, and industrial use. Snap-On's line includes over 14,000 tools, tool chests, custom tools, and diagnostic instruments. Products are supplied through over 5,000 independent dealers and franchises and more than 500 sales representatives. **NOTE:** Search and apply for positions online. **Positions advertised include:** Sr. NT Administrator; Financial Analyst; Associate Product Manager; Sr. Internal Auditor; Manager, IT Business Integration; Director, Operational Excellence; Corporate Operations Improvement Facilitator. **Corporate headquarters location:** This location. **Operations at this facility include:** Administration; Manufacturing; Research and Development. **Listed on:** New York Stock Exchange. **Stock exchange symbol:** SNA. **Number of employees at this location:** 1,000. **Number of employees worldwide:** 12,200.

SONIC FOUNDRY, INC.
222 West Washington Avenue, Suite 775, Madison WI 53703. 608/443-1600. **Fax:** 608/443-1601. **Contact:** Personnel. **World Wide Web address:** http://www.sfoundry.com. **Description:** Develops enterprise media communications technology. Founded in 1991. **Positions advertised include:** Inside Sales Representative. **Other U.S. locations:** Pittsburgh PA. **Listed on:** NASDAQ. **Stock exchange symbol:** SOFO.

SPHERION
4811 South 76th Street, Suite 110, Milwaukee WI 53220. 414/282-2112. **Contact:** Staffing. **World Wide Web address:** http://www.spherion.com. **Description:** Provides staffing, recruiting, and workforce solutions nationwide from 750 locations. Spherion places individuals in flexible and full-time jobs ranging from administrative and light industrial positions to professions that include accounting, finance, sales, marketing, manufacturing, engineering, law, human resources, and technology. **NOTE:** Apply online. **Positions advertised include:** Account Manager; Forklift Driver; Customer Service Supervisor; Benefits Coordinator; Director of Sales. **Corporate headquarters location:** Fort Lauderdale FL. **Other U.S. locations:** Nationwide. **Parent company:** Interim. **Listed on:** New York Stock Exchange. **Stock exchange symbol:** SFN.

STOP-N-GO
2934 Fish Hatchery Road, Madison WI 53713-3175. 608/271-4433. **Fax:** 608/271-1222. **Contact:** Mark Kiley, Director of Human Resources. **E-mail address:** contact@stop-n-go.com. **World Wide Web address:** http://www.stop-n-go.com. **Description:** Operates a chain of 42 convenience stores in southern Wisconsin and northern Illinois and has developed partnerships with several food service entities. Founded in 1963. **NOTE:** Entry-level positions, part-time jobs, and second and third shifts are offered. **Company slogan:** 100% customer satisfaction, every store, every time. **Positions advertised include:** Customer Service Representative; Sales Manager. **Special programs:** Training; Summer Jobs. **Corporate headquarters location:** This location. **Annual sales/revenues:** $51 - $100 million. **Number of employees nationwide:** 320.

STORA ENSO NORTH AMERICA
231 1st Avenue North, Wisconsin Rapids WI 54495-2774. 715/422-3111. **Contact:** External Recruiter. **World Wide Web address:** http://www.storaenso.com. **Description:** Manufactures enamel papers, specialty papers, paperboard, and corrugated products for the print communication, food, and consumer product packaging industries. The company controls seven manufacturing facilities in Wisconsin. **Listed on:** New York Stock Exchange. **Stock exchange symbol:** SEO. **Number of employees worldwide:** 43,000.

STRATAGEM, INC.
200 Woodland Prime, Suite 300, Menomonee Falls WI 53051. 262/532-2700. **Toll-free phone:** 800/228-4422. **Fax:** 262/532-2701. **Contact:** Human Resources. **E-mail address:** careers@stratagemnet.com. **World Wide Web address:** http://www.stratagemconsulting.com. **Description:** Offers comprehensive information technology consulting services. Founded in 1986. **Positions advertised include:** Project Manager; Systems Analyst; Design Architect; Developer. **Office hours:** Monday - Friday, 8:00 a.m. - 5:00 p.m. **Corporate headquarters location:** This location. **Other area locations:** Appleton WI; Madison WI. **Listed on:** Privately held. **President:** Gary Krieger. **Facilities Manager:** Cornel Rosario. **Information Systems Manager:** Keith Campbell. **Purchasing Manager:** Cornel Rosario. **Sales Manager:** Jerry Tobin. **Annual sales/revenues:** $21 - $50 million. **Number of employees at this location:** 250. **Number of employees nationwide:** 450.

STRONG CAPITAL MANAGEMENT
100 Heritage Reserve, Menomonee Falls WI 53051. 414/359-1400. **Contact:** Human Resources Department. **World Wide Web address:** http://www.strong-funds.com. **Description:** A mutual fund retailer and investment firm with offices in Wisconsin, Minnesota, Illinois, and Indiana. **Positions advertised include:** Senior Marketing and Database Analyst; Compliance Manager. **Corporate headquarters location:** This location. **Number of employees at this location:** 800.

SUNRISE MEDICAL
5001 Joerns, Stevens Point WI 54481-5040. 715/341-3600. **Fax:** 303/928-5759. **Contact:** Human Resources. **World Wide Web address:** http://www.sunrisemedical.com. **Description:** Manufactures homecare and extended care products Founded in 1983. **NOTE:** Entry-level positions are offered. Search for positions online. **Special programs:** Training. **Corporate headquarters location:** Carlsbad CA. **Parent company:** Sunrise Medical. **Listed on:** New York Stock Exchange. **Stock exchange symbol:** SMD. **Annual sales/revenues:** $11 - $20 million. **Number of employees at this location:** 70. **Number of employees nationwide:** 2,000. **Number of employees worldwide:** 3,200.

SUTTLE-STRAUS
1000 Uniek Drive, P.O.Box 370, Waunakee WI 53597. 608/849-1000. **Fax:** 608/849-8264. **Contact:** Donna Shriver, Human Resources Manager. **E-mail address:** donna.shriver@suttle-straus.com. **World Wide Web address:** http://www.suttle-straus.com. **Description:** A commercial printing company providing flat-color and full-color printed products to a growing base of commercial customers. Founded in 1969. **NOTE:** Entry-level positions and second and third shifts are offered. **Corporate headquarters location:** This location. **Parent company:** TDS (Telephone and Data Systems, Inc.). **Annual sales/revenues:** $5 - $10 million. **Number of employees at this location:** 75. **Number of employees nationwide:** 8,000.

SWING-N-SLIDE CORPORATION
1317 Barberry Drive, Janesville WI 53545. 608/755-4760. **Contact:** Human Resources. **World Wide Web address:** http://www.swing-n-slide.com. **Description:** A leading designer, manufacturer, and marketer of do-it-yourself, wooden home playground equipment. Swing-N-Slide's kits are designed to be assembled by the consumer, and most kits can be combined with each other and the company's Cool Wave Slides. Swing-N-Slide also manufactures and markets the Tuff Kids line of commercial playground equipment and the Clubhouse, a wooden and plastic outdoor playhouse. **Corporate headquarters location:** This location. **Parent company:** PlayCore, Inc. **Number of employees at this location:** 230.

SYSTEMS & PROGRAMMING SOLUTIONS
530 North 108th Place, Suite 100, Wauwatosa WI 53226. 414/302-2929. **Toll-free phone:** 800/353-7774. **Fax:** 414/302-2930. **Contact:** Human Resources. **E-mail address:** hr@spsinet.com. **World Wide Web address:** http://www.spsinet.com. **Description:** Provides software and hardware consulting services for AS/400, Internet PC, and network systems including systems planning, design and development, project management, capacity planning, hardware configuration and procurement, hardware/software installations and conversions. Founded in 1987. **Other area locations:** Madison WI. **Number of employees at this location:** 40.

TDS INFORMATION SERVICES
8401 Greenway Boulevard, Suite 230, Middleton WI 53562-0980. 608/664-8600. **Contact:** Human Resources. **E-mail address:** careers@teldta.com. **World Wide Web address:** http://www.tdscs.com. **Description:** Provides information technology and services to assist customers in reaching their business objectives. TDS Computing Services offers system integration, development, support, and processing. The company also provides bill printing and mailing services for customers. **Positions advertised include:** Accountant; Financial Analyst; Applications Systems Analyst; SAP Business Systems Analyst. **Corporate headquarters location:** Chicago IL. **Parent company:** Telephone & Data Systems, Inc.'s (TDS) business units include United States Cellular Corporation, which manages and invests in cellular systems throughout the nation, and American Paging, Inc., which operates paging and voicemail systems, offering a wide variety of service packages including basic local paging service; statewide, regional, and nationwide paging; and voicemail with fax options. TDS's associated service companies include American Communications Consultants, Inc., an engineering and management consulting company, and Suttle Press, Inc., a commercial printing subsidiary. **Number of employees at this location:** 320.

TDS TELECOM
301 South Westfield Road, Madison WI 53705. 608/664-4000. **Toll-free phone:** 877/741-5627. **Fax:** 608/664-4485. **Contact:** National Recruitment and Selection Team. **E-mail address:** resume@tdstelecom.com. **World Wide Web address:** http://www.tdstelecom.com. **Description:** Provides local telephone and access service to rural and suburban areas across the nation and pursues an active program of acquiring operating telephone companies. **Positions advertised include:** Accounts Payable Assistant; Customer Center Operations Manager; Residential Sales Advisor; Human Resources and Staffing Administrator; Sr. Database Analyst; Infrastructure Specialist. **Corporate headquarters location:** This location. **Other U.S. locations:** Nationwide. **Parent company:** Telephone & Data Systems, Inc.'s (TDS) business units include United States Cellular Corporation, which manages and invests in cellular systems throughout the nation, and American Paging, Inc., which operates paging and voicemail systems, offering a wide variety of service packages including basic local paging service; statewide, regional, and nationwide paging; and voicemail with fax options. TDS's associated service companies include American Communications Consultants, Inc., an engineering and management consulting company; Suttle Press, Inc., a commercial printing subsidiary; and TDS Computing Services, Inc., an information systems subsidiary. **Annual sales/revenues:** More than $100 million. **Number of employees at this location:** 115. **Number of employees nationwide:** 2,600.

TRW AUTOMOTIVE ELECTRONICS
20175 West Mill Road, P.O. Box 717, Galesville WI 54630. 608/582-2251. **Fax:** 608/582-2963. **Contact:** Human Resources. **World Wide Web address:** http://www.trw.com. **Description:** A full-service contract manufacturer of switches and controls, primarily for the automotive industry. **NOTE:** Search and apply for positions online. **Corporate headquarters location:** Livonia MI. **Number of employees worldwide:** 61,000.

TAPEDISK CORPORATION
500 Main Street, Suite 318, Menomonie WI 54751. 715/235-3388. **Fax:** 715/235-3818. **Contact:** Roy Ostenso, CEO. **E-mail address:** tapedisk@tapedisk.com. **World Wide Web address:** http://www.tapedisk.com. **Description:** A software developer for tape-based secondary storage systems and disaster recovery. Founded in 1992.

TARGET STORES
4777 South 27th Street, Greenfield WI 53221. 414/282-1000. **Contact:** Personnel. **World Wide Web address:** http://www.target.com. **Description:** A discount department store. **NOTE:** Entry-level positions are offered. **Parent company:** Dayton Hudson Corporation. **Number of employees at this location:** 215.

TAX AIRFREIGHT
5975 South Howell Avenue, Milwaukee WI 53207. 414/769-6565. **Fax:** 414/769-0529. **Contact:** Recruiting Manager. **E-mail address:** careers@taxair.com. **World Wide Web address:** http://www.taxair.com. **Description:** An air courier service.

TEKLYNX
1529 Continental Drive, Eau Claire WI 5470. 715/833-2331. **Fax:** 715/833-1995. **Contact:** Human Resources. **E-mail address:** info@teklynx.com. **World Wide Web address:** http://www.teklynx.com. **Description:** A developer and marketer of bar code labeling software. **NOTE:** Apply online.

3M
P.O. Box 1207, Wausau WI 54402-1207. 715/845-7241. **Fax:** 715/845-0271. **Contact:** Human Resources Department. **World Wide Web address:** http://www.3m.com. **Description:** 3M manufactures products in three sectors: Industrial and Consumer; Information, Imaging, and Electronic; and Life Sciences. The Industrial and Consumer Sector includes a variety of products under brand names including 3M, Scotch, Post-it, Scotch-Brite, and Scotchgard. The Information, Imaging, and Electronic Sector is a leader in several high-growth global industries including telecommunications, electronics, electrical, imaging, and memory media. The Life Sciences Sector serves two broad market categories: health care, and traffic and personal safety. In the health care market, 3M is a leading provider of medical and surgical supplies, drug delivery systems, and dental products; in traffic and personal safety, 3M is a leader in products for transportation safety, worker protection, vehicle and sign graphics, and out-of-home advertising. **NOTE:** Search and apply for positions online. **Positions advertised include:** Manufacturing Engineer; Mechanical Engineer; Process Graphics Engineer. **Corporate headquarters location:** St. Paul MN. **Operations at this facility include:** This location manufactures roofing granules.

3M TOUCH SYSTEMS
7025 West Marcia Road, Milwaukee WI 53223. 414/365-3555. **Fax:** 414/365-1133. **Contact:** Human Resources. **World Wide Web address:** http://www.3m.com. **Description:** Manufactures touch screens. Founded in 1993. **Positions advertised include:** Spec Technician; Drafter. **NOTE:** Entry-level positions are offered. **Other U.S. locations:** Methuen MA.

THRIVENT FINANCIAL FOR LUTHERANS
4321 North Ballard Road, Appleton WI 54919-0001. 920/734-5721. **Contact:** Human Resources Department. **World Wide Web address:** http://www.thrivent.com. **Description:** A provider of life and health insurance, as well as investment capital management and annuities. **NOTE:** Search and apply for positions online. **Positions advertised include:** Senior Litigation Attorney; Retirement Plan consultant; Program Manager; Technical System Designer; Lead IT Methodologist; Senior Research Analyst; Technical Systems Analyst. **Corporate headquarters location:** This location. **Annual sales/revenues:** More than $100 million.

TOMAH HEALTH CARE CENTER
1505 Butts Avenue, Tomah WI 54660. 608/372-3241. **Contact:** Human Resources. **Description:** A geriatric rehabilitation and health center.

TOMAH MEMORIAL HOSPITAL
321 Butts Avenue, Tomah WI 54660. 608/372-2181. **Fax:** 608/374-6615. **Contact:** Human Resources. **E-mail address:** breinert@tomahhospital.org. **World Wide Web address:** http://www.tomahhospital.org. **Description:** A nonprofit, 49-bed general hospital. **NOTE:** Part-time jobs and second and third shifts are offered. Search and apply for positions online. **Positions advertised include:** Certified Occupational Therapy Assistant. **Number of employees at this location:** 200.

TOUCHPOINT HEALTH PLAN
5 Innovation Court, Appleton WI 54914. 920/735-6300. **Fax:** 920/831-6886. **Contact:** Human Resources. **World Wide Web address:** http://www.touchpointhealth.com. **Description:** A health plan with 145,000 members

TOWN & COUNTRY ELECTRIC
2662 American Drive, Appleton WI 54915. 920/738-1500. **Toll-free phone:** 800/677-1506. **Fax:** 920/738-8984. **Contact:** Human Resources. **World Wide Web address:** http://www.encompass.com. **Description:** A commercial and industrial electrical contractor. **NOTE:** Need to fill out an application. **Corporate headquarters location:** This location. **Listed on:** New York Stock Exchange. **Stock exchange symbol:** ESR.

TRANE
3600 Pammel Creek Road, La Crosse WI, 54601. **Contact:** Staff Employment Dept. 349. **E-mail address:** hqstaffemp@trane.com. **World Wide Web address:** http://www.trane.com. **Description:** A leading global provider of heating, cooling, dehumidifying and air cleaning systems for residential, commercial, institutional and industrial applications. **Positions advertised include:** Accountant; Business Systems Analyst; Compressor Designer; Embedded Software Engineer; Heat Transfer Engineer; Laboratory HVAC Technician; LAN Systems Administrator; Modeling Engineer. **Parent company:** American Standard.

TRI-PHASE AUTOMATION, INC.
604 North Shore Drive, Hartland WI 53029. 262/367-6900. **Fax:** 262/367-6910. **Contact:** Human Resources. **World Wide Web address:** http://www.tri-phase.com. **Description:** A distributor of mechanical engineering products. **Corporate headquarters location:** This location.

TUFCO TECHNOLOGIES
3161 South Ridge Road, P.O. Box 23500, Green Bay WI 54305-3500. 920/336-0054. **Toll-free phone:** 800/558-8145. **Fax:** 920/336-9041. **Contact:** Human Resources. **World Wide Web address:** http://www.tufco.com. **Description:** A leading specialty printer and converter of custom paper and nonwoven materials. Tufco's contract manufacturing division custom-converts paper, tissue, and polyethylene film into such products as cleaning wipes and medical drapes. The company's business imaging products include specialty paper rolls and precision-sheeted products. The company provides custom converting services for industrial uses and converting of specialty and fine printing papers and paperboard, polyethylene film, and coated products. **Corporate headquarters location:** This location. **Other U.S. locations:** Newton NC. **Listed on:** NASDAQ. **Stock exchange symbol:** TFCO.

U.S. BANK
777 East Wisconsin Avenue, Milwaukee WI 53202. 414/765-4035. **Contact:** Human Resources Manager. **World Wide Web address:** http://www.usbank.com. **Description:** A commercial bank. **NOTE:** Search and apply for positions online. **Positions advertised include:** Mutual Funds Specialist; Operations Manager; Paralegal; Private Client Group Trust Business Development Officer. **Parent company:** U.S. Bancorp operates 2,275 banking offices in 24 states.

U.S. COUNSELING SERVICES, INC.
120 Bishop's Way, Suite 100, Brookfield WI 53008-0951. **Toll-free phone:** 800/558-6377. **Fax:** 262/784-5779. **Contact:** Human Resources Assistant. **E-mail address:** resume@usconnect.com. **World Wide Web address:** http://www.uscounselingservices.com. **Description:** Provides equipment asset management services, such as instrument and equipment maintenance management, physical inventory tracking, and cost-of-ownership analysis, to the pharmaceutical and healthcare industries. Founded in 1969. **Corporate headquarters location:** This location. **Other U.S. locations:** Nationwide. **Parent company:** Thermo Electron Corporation (Waltham MA). **Number of employees nationwide:** 175.

U.S. OIL COMPANY, INC.
425 South Washington Street, Combined Locks WI 54113. 920/739-6101. **Fax:** 920/788-0531. **Contact:** Personnel. **World Wide Web address:** http://www.usoil.com. **E-mail address:** generalinfo@usoil.com. **Description:** A wholesale distributor of petroleum products and automotive parts. Services include petroleum equipment consulting and environmental laboratory services. Retail divisions include convenience stores and plumbing and heating outlets. **Corporate headquarters location:** This location. **Other U.S. locations:** St. Louis MO; Chicago IL; Minneapolis MN; Milwaukee WI. **Operations at this facility include:** Administration; Sales. **Listed on:** Privately held. **Number of employees at this location:** 900.

UNICO INC.
3725 Nicholson Road, Franksville WI 53126-0505. 262/886-5678. **Fax:** 262/504-7734. **Contact:** Jim Kudulis, Personnel Manager. **E-mail address:** kudulisj@unicous.com. **World Wide Web address:** http://www.unicous.com. **Description:** Develops, manufactures, and services drive products and systems for the motion-control market. **Corporate headquarters location:** This location. **Other U.S. locations:** Nationwide. **Operations at this facility include:** Administration; Manufacturing; Research and Development; Sales; Service. **International locations:** Canada; Venezuela; England; Germany; China; Japan. **Listed on:** Privately held. **Number of employees at this location:** 185.

UNITED MIGRANT OPPORTUNITY SERVICES, INC. (UMOS, INC.)
2607 South 5th Street, Milwaukee WI 53207. 414/389-6000. **Toll-free phone:** 800/279-8667. **Fax:** 414/671-4833. **Contact:** Claudia Lovo, Human Resources Specialist. **World Wide Web address:** http://www.umos.org. **Description:** A nonprofit company offering a wide range of employment, training, and educational programs and services statewide to enable migrant, seasonal farm workers and other disadvantaged clients to obtain full employment **Corporate headquarters location:** This location. **Number of employees at this location:** 30.

UNIVERSITY OF WISCONSIN/EAU CLAIRE
105 Garfield Avenue, Room 220, Eau Claire WI 54702-4004. 715/836-2637. **Fax:** 715/836-3051. **Contact:** Personnel Services. **World Wide Web address:** http://www.uwec.edu. **Description:** A campus of the state university with approximately 10,500 students. **NOTE:** Search and apply for positions online. **Positions advertised include:** Associate Dean of Student Development; Dean of the College of Arts and Sciences; Director of Intercollegiate Athletics; Director of Office of Multicultural Affairs. **Number of employees at this location:** 1,150.

UNIVERSITY OF WISCONSIN/GREEN BAY
2420 Nicolet Drive, Green Bay WI 54311-7001. 920/465-2390. **Fax:** 920/465-5104. **Contact:** Personnel Services. **World Wide Web address:** http://www.uwgb.edu. **Description:** A campus of the state university with approximately 5,400 students. **NOTE:** Search and apply for positions online. **Positions advertised include:** Assistant Professor of Communication and the Arts; Lecturer and Social Work Field Education Coordinator; Assistant/Associate Professor of Social Work; Nursing Program Lecturer; Assistant Professor of Natural and Applied Sciences, Chemistry. **Number of employees at this location:** 675.

UNIVERSITY OF WISCONSIN/LA CROSSE
1725 State Street, La Crosse WI 54601. 608/785-8013. **Fax:** 608/785-8525. **Contact:** Human Resources. **World Wide Web address:** http://www.uwlax.edu. **Description:** A campus of the state university with approximately 8,700 students. **NOTE:** Search and apply for positions online. **Positions advertised include:** Assistant Professor, Chemistry; Chair, Geography/Earth Science; Associate Counselor.

UNIVERSITY OF WISCONSIN/MADISON
500 Lincoln Drive, 166 Bascom Hall, Madison WI 53706. 608/263-6561. **Fax:** 608/262-5203. **Contact:** Academic Personnel Office. **World Wide Web address:** http://www.wisc.edu/ohr. **Description:** A campus of the state university with an enrollment of 42,000. UW Madison is a research university. **NOTE:** Search and apply for positions online. **Positions advertised include:** Microbiologist; IS Systems Development Services Professional; Licensed Practical Nurse; Assistant Professors; Director of Research and Sponsored Programs; Associate Dean. **Operations at this facility include:** Administration; Research and Development; Sales; Service. **Number of employees nationwide:** 16,000.

UNIVERSITY OF WISCONSIN/MILWAUKEE
2033 East Hartford Avenue, P.O. Box 413, Milwaukee WI 53201. 414/229-4463. **Fax:** 414/229-4102. **Contact:** Personnel Department. **World Wide Web address:** http://www.uwm.edu. **Description:** A campus of the state university with approximately 26,000 students. **NOTE:** Search and apply for positions online. **Positions advertised include:** Chair of Global Studies and International Business;

Professors; Assistant/Associate Professors; Senior Development Specialist; Administrative Program Manager; Research Specialist; Outreach Program Manager.

UNIVERSITY OF WISCONSIN/OSHKOSH
800 Algoma Boulevard, Oshkosh WI 54901. 920/424-1234. **Fax:** 920/424-2021. **Contact:** Personnel Department. **World Wide Web address:** http://www.uwosh.edu. **Description:** A campus of the state university. **NOTE:** Search and apply for positions online. **Positions advertised include:** Assistant/Associate Professors; Associate Student Services Specialist; Lecturers; Professional Coordinator.

UNIVERSITY OF WISCONSIN/PARKSIDE
900 Wood Road, Box 2000, Kenosha WI 53141-2000. 262/595-2204. **Fax:** 262/595-2206. **Contact:** Human Resources Department. **World Wide Web address:** http://www.uwp.edu. **Description:** A campus of the state university with approximately 4,700 students.

UNIVERSITY OF WISCONSIN/STEVENS POINT
2100 Main Street, Stevens Point WI 54481. 715/346-01123. **Contact:** Personnel Department. **World Wide Web address:** http://www.uwsp.edu. **Description:** A campus of the state university with an enrollment of 8,700 students. **NOTE:** Search and apply for positions online. **Positions advertised include:** Dean of the college of Letters and Science; Executive Director of Campus Life; Assistant Professors; Media Specialist; Admissions Counselor. **Number of employees at this location:** 950.

UNIVERSITY OF WISCONSIN/STOUT
P.O. Box 790, Menomonie WI 54751. 715/232-2415. **Fax:** 715/232-1527. **Contact:** Personnel Department. **World Wide Web address:** http://www.uwstout.edu. **Description:** A campus of the state university with approximately 8,000 students.

UNIVERSITY OF WISCONSIN/WHITEWATER
800 West Main Street, Whitewater WI 53190. 262/472-1234. **Fax:** 262/472-5668. **Contact:** Personnel. **World Wide Web address:** http://www.uww.edu. **Description:** A campus of the state university with approximately 10,000 students. **NOTE:** Search and apply for positions online. **Positions advertised include:** Art History Faculty; Accounting Faculty; Laboratory Manager; Dean of Graduate Studies; Director of Admissions; Director of Advancement; Facilities Planning and Management Director.

VALLEY PACKAGING INDUSTRIES, INC.
1325 South Perkins Street, Appleton WI 54914. 920/749-5840. **Fax:** 920/749-5850. **Contact:** Human Resources. **E-mail address:** hr@vpind.com. **World Wide Web address:** http://www.vpind.com. **Description:** A nonprofit corporation that provides a broad range of vocational rehabilitation services for disabled persons. The majority of participants are engaged in production line packaging and product assembly. The corporation also offers an Early Intervention Program for children with developmental delays, vocational evaluations, work adjustment training, extended employment, transitional employment, vocational support programs, and a School-to-Work Program. The company also has two other locations in Appleton. Founded in 1956. **Positions advertised include:** Truck Driver; Program Assistant. **Special programs:** Internships. **Office hours:** Monday - Friday, 7:45 a.m. - 4:15 p.m. **Corporate headquarters location:** This location. **Subsidiaries include:** Madison Packaging & Assembly (Madison WI). **Executive Director:** Robert Russo. **Number of employees at this location:** 250. **Number of employees nationwide:** 900.

VERNON MANOR
E7404A, County Road BB, Viroqua WI 54665. 608/637-5400. **Fax:** 608/637-5441. **Contact:** Administrator. **Description:** A nursing home. Founded in 1981. **NOTE:** Entry-level positions are offered. **Special programs:** Internships. **Office hours:** Monday - Friday, 8:30 a.m. - 4:30 p.m. **Corporate headquarters location:** This location. **Parent company:** Vernon County. **Annual sales/revenues:** Less than $5 million. **Number of employees at this location:** 120.

VISITING NURSE ASSOCIATION
520 North 32nd Avenue, Wausau WI 54401. 715/847-2600. **Fax:** 715/847-2607. **Contact:** Human Resources. **Description:** Provides health services to patients in their home or place of residence. Services include nursing, physical therapy, occupational therapy, speech pathology, nutritional therapy, mental health and enterostomal therapy, medical social services, and hospice care.

VON BRIESEN & ROPER
P.O. Box 3262, Milwaukee WI 53201-3262. 414/276-1122. **Physical address:** 411 East Wisconsin Avenue, 7th Floor, Milwaukee WI 53202. **Toll-free phone:** 800/622-0607. **Contact:** Human Resources. **World Wide Web address:** http://www.vonbriesen.com. **Description:** A law firm specializing in corporate, divorce, and environmental law. **NOTE:** Search and apply for positions online. **Positions advertised include:** Experienced Health Care Associate; Law Clerk; Experienced Estate Planning Attorney; Accounting Manager.

WE ENERGIES
333 West Everett Street, Milwaukee WI 53290-0001. 414/221-3333. **Recorded jobline:** 414/221-3091. **Fax:** 414/221-3340. **Contact:** Human Resources Department. **World Wide Web address:** http://www.we-energies.com. **Description:** We Energies is the trade name of Wisconsin Electric Power Co. and Wisconsin Gas Co., which supply one million customers with wholesale electric services and natural gas. **NOTE:** Search and apply for positions online. **Positions advertised include:** Auditor; Nuclear Drafting Engineer; Gas System Operations Analyst. **Corporate headquarters location:** This location. **Parent company:** Wisconsin Energy Corporation. **Listed on:** New York Stock Exchange. **Stock exchange symbol:** WEC.

WPC BRANDS
1 Repel Road, Jackson WI 53037-0198. 262/677-4121. **Toll-free phone:** 800/558-6614. **Fax:** 262/677-9006. **Contact:** Human Resources. **World Wide Web address:** http://www.wpcbrands.com. **Description:** WPC Brands manufactures and distributes specialty chemical and branded consumer products in the leisure market (insect repellents; sunscreens; lip balms; chemical fish attractants; biodegradable fishing lures; scent cleansing, masking, and luring products for hunters; water purification tablets; a lotion used to relieve the itching effects of insect bites; citronella candles; scented candles; and a hand cleaner and odor eliminator); the household market (Disposer Care, a product to clean and deodorize garbage disposals); and the institutional care market (Chlorazene antiseptic powder, which is used in hydrotherapy tanks in hospitals, nursing homes, and rehabilitation centers to treat open wounds). **Corporate headquarters location:** This location.

WYOU COMMUNITY TV
609 East Washington Street, Madison WI 53703-2913. 608/258-9644. **Fax:** 608/258-8803. **Contact:** Human Resources. **E-mail address:** wyou@danenet.org. **Description:** A public access cable television station. **Corporate headquarters location:** This location.

WALGREEN HEALTH INITIATIVES
1435 North 113th Street, Milwaukee WI 53226. 414/256-7234. **Fax:** 414/908-2530. **Contact:** Human Resources. **E-mail address:** corporate.opportunities@walgreens.com. **World Wide Web address:** http://www.walgreenshealth.com. **Description:** Sells medical supplies and equipment to nursing homes, operates institutional pharmacies for long-term care facilities, and provides home health care services. Founded in 1986. **Corporate headquarters location:** Deerfield IL.

WALTHERS TRAINS
5601 West Florist Avenue, Milwaukee WI 53218-1622. 414/527-0770. **Fax:** 414/527-4423. **Contact:** Lisa Buth, Human Resources Manager. **World Wide Web address:** http://www.walthers.com. **Description:** Develops, markets, and manufactures model railroad products and provides information on model railroading. **NOTE:** Entry-level positions are offered. **Corporate headquarters location:** This location. **Listed on:** Privately held. **Annual sales/revenues:** $21 - $50 million. **Number of employees at this location:** 150.

WARD ADHESIVES
North 27 West 23539 Paul Road, Pewaukee WI 53072. 262/523-6300. **Fax:** 262/523-6301. **Contact:** Human Resources. **Description:** A wholesale distributor of industrial adhesives to major local manufacturers.

WASHINGTON MUTUAL HOME LOANS
11200 West Parkland Avenue, Milwaukee WI 53224. 414/359-9300. **Contact:** Human Resources. **World Wide Web address:** http://www.wamuhomeloans.com. **Description:** Provides single-family residential mortgages.

WATERTOWN DAILY TIMES
113-115 West Main Street, P.O. Box 140, Watertown WI 53094-0140. 920/261-5161. **Contact:** Human Resources Department. **World Wide Web address:** http://www.wdtimes.com. **Description:** A daily newspaper with a circulation of 10,000.

WAUKESHA MEMORIAL HOSPITAL, INC.
725 American Avenue, Waukesha WI 53188. 262/928-7969. **Toll-free phone:** 800/326-2011. **Fax:** 262/544-6437. **Contact:** Barb Dyer, Human Resources Coordinator. **E-mail address:** careers@phci.org. **World Wide Web address:** http://www.waukeshamemorial.org. **Description:** A 300-bed acute care hospital that offers state-of-the-art technology and care in the areas of open heart surgery, cancer care, neonatal intensive care, physical rehabilitation, and behavioral health services. The hospital operates as part of Waukesha Hospital System, Inc., a private, nonprofit, integrated health care delivery system that provides a wide range of services. Founded in 1914. **NOTE:** Entry-level positions and second and third shifts are offered. **Positions advertised include:** Accountant; CT Technologist; Registered Nurse; Clinical Dietician; Echo Lab Coordinator; Licensed Practical Nurse; Info System Clinical Specialist. **Parent company:** ProHealth Care, Inc. **Listed on:** Privately held. **Annual sales/revenues:** More than $100 million. **Number of employees at this location:** 2,600.

WAUSAU, CITY OF
407 Grant Street, Wausau WI 54403. 715/261-6500. **Contact:** Human Resources Manager. **World Wide Web address:** http://www.ci.wausau.wi.us. **Description:** The administrative offices for the city of Wausau. **Number of employees at this location:** 300.

WAUSAU FINANCIAL SYSTEMS INC.
875 Indianhead Drive, P.O. Box 37, Mosinee WI 54455-0037. 715/359-0427. **Contact:** Human Resources. **World Wide Web address:** http://www.wausaufs.com. **Description:** Sells banking equipment such as automated teller machines, check processing machines, and programming systems for banks. **NOTE:** Search and apply for positions online. **Positions advertised include:** Associate System Analyst; Marketing Analyst; Configuration Programmer; Technical Trainer; Documentation Analyst; Implementation Specialist. **Corporate headquarters location:** This location. **Other U.S. locations:** Fridley MN; Oklahoma City OK; Kirkland WA.

WAUSAU HOMES, INC.
P.O. Box 8005, Wausau WI 54402-8005. 715/359-7272. **Contact:** Human Resources. **World Wide Web address:** http://www.wausauhomes.com. **Description:** A home-builder. **NOTE:** Search and apply for positions online. **Positions advertised include:** Cost Accountant; Associate Buyer. **Corporate headquarters location:** This location. **Number of employees at this location:** 500.

WAUSAU INSURANCE COMPANIES
P.O. Box 8017, Wausau WI 54402-8017. 715/842-0747. **Physical address:** 2000 Westwood Drive, Wausau WI 54401-7881. **Toll-free phone:** 800/435-4401. **Contact:** Human Resources. **World Wide Web address:** http://www.wausau.com. **Description:** A business insurance company selling casualty, property, and other commercial insurance products to medium- and large-sized companies through roughly 100 service offices located throughout the United States. **Corporate headquarters location:** This location. **Number of employees at this location:** 2,500.

WAUSAU MOSINEE PAPER CORPORATION
100 Paper Place, Mosinee WI 54455-9099. 715/693-4470. **Contact:** Human Resources. **World Wide Web address:** http://www.wausaumosinee.com. **Description:** Manufactures specialty papers; towel and tissue papers; and laminated, saturated, and coated products. **Corporate headquarters location:** This location. **Other area locations:** Brokaw WI; Rhinelander WI; Appleton WI; Columbus WI. Other U.S. locations: ME; NH; OH; KY; MS. **Listed on:** New York Stock Exchange. **Stock exchange symbol:** WMO.

WESTSIDE SENIOR DAY CENTER
5920 West Center Street, Milwaukee WI 53210. 414/442-2117. **Fax:** 414/442-2184. **Contact:** Human Resources. **E-mail address:** hr@mcfi.net. **World Wide Web address:** http://www.mcfi.net. **Description:** A state-certified elderly daycare center. **NOTE:** Entry-level positions are offered. **Special programs:** Internships. **Parent company:** Milwaukee Center for Independence. **Number of employees at this location:** 15.

WEYERHAEUSER COMPANY
200 North Grand Avenue, Rothschild WI 54474. 715/359-3101. **Contact:** Human Resources. **E-mail address:** careers@weyerhaeuser.com. **World Wide Web address:** http://www.weyerhaeuser.com. **Description:** Weyerhaeuser Company is a producer of forest products. Its principal businesses are the growing and harvesting of timber; the manufacture, distribution, and sale of forest products including logs, wood chips, building products, pulp, paper, and packaging products; real estate development and construction; and financial services. The company is one of the world's largest private

owners of marketable softwood timber and a large producer of softwood lumber and market pulp. It is also one of the largest North American producers of forest products and recyclers of office wastepaper, newspaper, and corrugated boxes. **NOTE:** Search and apply for positions online. **Corporate headquarters location:** Tacoma WA. **Other U.S. locations:** Nationwide. **Operations at this facility include:** This location manufactures fine paper. **Listed on:** New York Stock Exchange. **Stock exchange symbol:** WY. **Number of employees at this location:** 500. **Number of employees worldwide:** 60,000.

WIDEN ENTERPRISES
6911 Mangrove Lane, Madison WI 53713. 608/222-1296. **Toll-free phone:** 800/444-2828. **Fax:** 608/222-4005. **Contact:** Human Resources Director. **E-mail address:** hr@widen.com. **World Wide Web address:** http://www.widen.com. **Description:** A graphic communications firm that provides prepress, digital printing, and information management services for the packaging, retail, catalog, and specialty markets. Founded in 1948. **NOTE:** Search and apply for positions online. **Positions advertised include:** Data Assistant; Java Developer; Sr. Java Developer; Technical Project Coordinator. **Corporate headquarters location:** This location. **Annual sales/revenues:** $11 - $20 million. **Number of employees at this location:** 140.

WINGRA TECHNOLOGIES, INC.
525 Junction Road, Suite 2500, Madison WI 53717. 608/662-4400. **Fax:** 608/662-0545. **Contact:** Personnel. **E-mail address:** personnel@wingra.com. **World Wide Web address:** http://www.wingra.com. **Description:** Provides enterprise messaging integration and migration solutions. **Corporate headquarters location:** This location.

WIPFLI ULLRICH BERTELSON
11 Scott Street, Wausau WI 54403. 715/845-3111. **Fax:** 715/842-7272. **Contact:** Sue Kozifek, Human Resources. **World Wide Web address:** http://www.wipfli.com. **Description:** Offers management consulting services in: accounting, auditing, and tax; strategic business planning; human resource consulting; business valuation services; family business services; and marketing consulting. **NOTE:** Search and apply for positions online. **Positions advertised include:** Proofreader; Staff Accountant, Benefit Plan Services. **Corporate headquarters location:** This location. **Other area locations:** Statewide. **Other U.S. locations:** St Paul MN.

WISCONSIN ENERGY CORPORATION
P.O. Box 1331, Milwaukee WI 53201. 414/221-2345. **Physical address:** 231 W. Michigan St, Milwaukee WI 53203. **Contact:** Human Resources. **World Wide Web address:** http://www.wisconsinenergy.com. **Description:** An energy holding company formed in 1987 with utility and non-utility subsidiaries. The company, through We Energies and its utility subsidiary Edison Sault Electric Company, serves more than one million electric customers in Wisconsin and Michigan's Upper Peninsula and 980,000 natural gas customers in Wisconsin. We Energies is the trade name of Wisconsin Electric Power Company and Wisconsin Gas Company, the company's principal utility subsidiaries. Its non-utility businesses include energy development, pump manufacturing, recycling and renewable energy and real estate development. **Listed on:** New York Stock Exchange. **Stock exchange symbol:** WEC. **Number of employees nationwide:** 9,000.

WISCONSIN HUMANE SOCIETY
4500 West Wisconsin Avenue, Milwaukee WI 53208. 414/264-6257. **Contact:** Human Resources. **World Wide Web address:** http://www.wihumane.org. **Description:** A nonprofit, community-based organization that provides shelter and veterinary care for stray, unwanted, feral, and wild animals and prevents the mistreatment of animals through education and law enforcement. Founded in 1879. **NOTE:** Entry-level positions, part-time jobs, and second and third shifts are offered. **Positions advertised include:** Development Director; Veterinary Technician; Animal Care Technician. **Special programs:** Internships; Summer Jobs. **Office hours:** Monday - Friday, 10:00 a.m. - 8:30 p.m.; Saturday, 10:00 a.m. - 6:00 p.m. **Listed on:** Privately held. **Annual sales/revenues:** Less than $5 million.

WISCONSIN MANAGEMENT COMPANY
2040 South Park Street, Madison WI 53713. 608/258-2080. **Contact:** Human Resources. **Description:** A real estate management company that handles apartment complexes, condominiums, and dormitories.

WISCONSIN PUBLIC SERVICE CORPORATION
700 North Adams Street, P.O. Box 19002, Green Bay WI 54307-9002. 920/433-1598. **Toll-free phone:** 800/450-7260. **Contact:** Human Resources. **World Wide Web address:** http://www.wisconsinpublicservice.com. **Description:** A gas and electric utility company. **Positions advertised include:** Staff Accountant; financial Reporting and Research Accountant. **Number of employees at this location:** 1,100.

YASKAWA DRIVES & SYSTEMS
16555 West Ryerson Road, New Berlin WI 53151. 262/782-0200. **Contact:** Human Resources. **World Wide Web address:** http://www.drives.com. **Description:** Yaskawa Drives & Systems is a designer, manufacturer, and marketer of electrical, electronic, and industrial components and products. The company also offers services and repair support for its components. **Operations at this facility include:** This location manufactures small electronic parts for the drive systems of electric motors.

ZENS MANUFACTURING
2435 North Martin Luther King Drive, P.O. Box 12504, Milwaukee WI 53212-0504. 414/372-7060. **Contact:** Human Resources. **Description:** A knitting manufacturer that operates two divisions, both of which are housed at this location. One division knits medical hosiery and the other division makes industrial tubing, such as the tubes that are found in environmental cleanup equipment. **Corporate headquarters location:** This location.

AMERICAN NATIONAL BANK
1912 Capitol Avenue, P.O. Box 1528, Cheyenne WY 82003. 307/634-2121. **Contact:** Human Resources. **E-mail address:** sbordson@andbwy.com. **World Wide Web address:** http://www.anbwy.com. **Description:** A full service community banking institution. **Parent Company:** The Sturm Financial Group. **Other area locations include:** Casper; Pine Bluffs.

AVIAT AIRCRAFT, INC.
P.O. Box 1240, Afton WY 83110. 307/885-3151. **Contact:** Human Resources Department. **E-mail address:** stu@aviataircraft.com. **World Wide Web address:** http://www.aviataircraft.com. **Description:** Manufactures small aircraft for recreational, government, agricultural, and commercial applications. Aviat Aircraft also offers repair services. **Positions advertised include:** Designated Engineering Representative; Designated Airworthiness Representative. **Corporate headquarters location:** This location.

AXIOHM TRANSACTION SOLUTIONS, INC.
860 College View Drive, Riverton WY 82501. 307/856-4821. **Contact:** Paul Gardner, Director of Human Resources. **E-mail address:** paul.gardner@axiohm.com. **World Wide Web address:** http://www.axiohm.com. **Description:** Designs, manufactures, and markets transaction printers including the production of thermal and impact printheads. Axiohm Transaction Solutions also designs and manufactures bar code printers, magnetic card and strip readers and writers, card printers, dot matrix impact printheads, magnetic heads, and labeling systems. Products are used in the retail, manufacturing, health care, banking, hospitality, unattended kiosk, government, and gaming industries. **Positions advertised include:** Software Applications Lead Developer; Software Application Engineer; Senior Web Developer. **Other U.S. locations:** Garden Grove CA; San Diego CA; Golden CO; Ithaca NY. **International locations:** Worldwide. **Annual sales/revenues:** More than $100 million. **Number of employees worldwide:** 1,325.

CAMPBELL COUNTY MEMORIAL HOSPITAL
P.O. Box 3011, Gillette WY 82717. 307/682-8811. **Physical address:** 501 South Burma Avenue, Gillette WY 82716. **Toll-free phone:** 800/208-2043. **Contact:** Human Resources. **E-mail address:** humanresources@ccmh.net. **World Wide Web address:** http://www.ccmh.net. **Description:** A 119-bed, acute care hospital. The hospital is designated as a Level II Trauma Center and a Level II Intensive Care Nursery. The hospital also has a Special Care Nursery for older infants who require hospital care. The hospital also offers outpatient care services, intensive and critical care services, home health services, radiology and imaging services, emergency services, rehabilitation services, laboratory services, cardiopulmonary services, and mental and behavioral health services. Campbell County Memorial Hospital is accredited by the Joint Commission on Accreditation of Healthcare Organizations. **Positions advertised include:** Wright Physical Therapist; Occupational Therapist; Speech Therapist; Clinical Informatics Analyst; Child Care Technician; Admitting Clerk; Human Resources Manager; Assistant Administrator; Patient Care Observer; RN; LPN; Paramedic.

COASTAL CHEM, INC.
P.O. Box 1287, Cheyenne WY 82003. 307/637-2700. **Contact:** Human Resources. **Description:** Processes and provides ammonia products. Coastal's product line includes anhydrous ammonia, nitric acid, ammonium nitrate, urea, UAN solution, and ATS solution. Anhydrous ammonia is used as an agricultural fertilizer, industrial chemical, and as the basic ingredient for all of the other nitrogen products. Nitrogen-based products are sold to agricultural, mining, and industrial customers. Founded in 1964.

DORNAN
P.O. Box 39, Moose WY 83012. 307/733-2415. **Contact:** Dawn Gersten. **E-mail address:** dawn@dornans.com. **World Wide Web address:** http://www.dornans. com. **Description:** A family owned resort operating cabins, a trading post, bar, restaurant, and gift shop. **Positions advertised include:** Dishwasher; Cook; Baker; Server; Cashier; Janitor; Retail Associate; Housekeeper; Bartender; Night Auditor.

ELKHORN CONSTRUCTION
71 Allegiance Circle, P.O. Box 809, Evanston WY 82931-0809. 307/789-1595. **Contact:** Staffing. **World Wide Web address:** http://www.elkhornconstruction.com. **Description:** Provides industrial and plant construction and maintenance catering to the oil, gas, power, and mining industries. Founded in 1984. **Positions advertised include:** Welder; Pipefitter; Laborer; Concrete Helper; Equipment Operator; Insulator; Tubing Fitter; Carpenter; Painter; Craft Foreman; Project Foreman. **Corporate headquarters location:** This location. **Other U.S. locations include:** CO; NM; UT; KS. **Subsidiaries include:** Dynamic Services; HOAD, Inc.

FMC CORPORATION
P.O. Box 872, Green River WY 82935. 307/875-2580. **Contact:** Human Resources. **World Wide Web address:** http://www.fmc.com. **Description:** FMC is one of the world's leading producers of chemicals and machinery for industry, government, and agriculture. FMC divides its business into five major segments: Agricultural Products, Energy Systems, Food and Transportation Systems, Industrial Chemicals, and Specialty Chemicals. **Corporate headquarters location:** Philadelphia PA. **Other U.S. locations:** Nationwide. **International locations:** Worldwide. **Operations at this facility include:** This location is a soda ash manufacturer. **Listed on:** New York Stock Exchange. **Stock exchange symbol:** FMC.

FRONTIER REFINING
P.O. Box 1588, Cheyenne WY 82003. 307/634-3551. **Fax:** 307/771-8794. **Contact:** Human Resources Manager. **World Wide Web address:** http://www.frontier-refinery.com. **Description:** Manufactures a full line of high-grade fuels from locally produced Wyoming crude oils. More than one-half of the refinery's products are distributed locally and throughout southern Wyoming. The company is also one of the major suppliers of petroleum products to western Nebraska and the Colorado Front Range. The remaining product is shipped from the refinery through Continental Pipeline, which travels east to Nebraska; and WYCO Pipeline, which travels south to Colorado. The refinery's products are sold to major oil companies as well as smaller independents that have retail operations in the region. **NOTE:** Second and third shifts are offered. **Positions advertised include:** Turnaround Supervisor. **Office hours:** Monday - Friday, 8:00 a.m. - 5:00 p.m. **Corporate headquarters location:** Houston TX. **Other U.S. locations:** Denver CO; El Dorado KS. **Parent company:** Frontier Refining & Marketing Inc. **Listed on:** New York Stock Exchange. **Stock exchange symbol:** FTO. **Number of employees at this location:** 260.

GENERAL CHEMICAL CORPORATION
P.O. Box 551, Green River WY 82935. 307/875-3350. **Contact:** Human Resources. **World Wide Web address:** http://www.genchem.com. **Description:** A supplier of soda ash to the glass, chemical, paper, and detergent industries. General Chemical is one of the only North American producers of both natural soda ash and synthetic ash. The Green River site is part of General Chemical's 50-plant network and contains an underground trona mine and a surface plant to process the ore into soda ash. With an operating capacity of approximately 2.2 million tons of trona per year, the facility has trona reserves containing over 500 million tons of high-grade ore. Founded in 1968. **Positions advertised include:** General Manager; Financial Manager. **Corporate headquarters location:** Parsippany NJ.

HOLLAND & HART LLP
P.O. Box 1347, Cheyenne WY 82003. 307/778-4200. **Fax:** 307/778-8175. **Contact:** Brad Cabe, Hiring Partner. **World Wide Web address:** http://www.hollandhart.com. **Description:** A full-service law firm. Founded in 1978. **Positions advertised include:** Partner, Intern; Associate. **Office hours:** Monday - Friday, 8:00 a.m. - 5:00 p.m. **Other U.S. locations:** CO; ID; MT; NM; UT. **Annual sales/revenues:** $51 - $100 million. **Number of employees at this location:** 35. **Number of employees nationwide:** 250.

JACKSON HOLE MOUNTAIN RESORT
P.O. Box 290, Teton Village WY 83025. 307/733-2292. **Fax:** 307/739-6255. **Recorded jobline:** 307/739-2604. **Contact:** Human Resources. **World Wide Web address:** http://www.jacksonhole.com. **Description:** A ski resort offering a full range of activities throughout the year. Facilities include numerous ski slopes, snow mobile trails, a golf course, hiking trails, and bike trails. Jackson Hole Mountain Resort also offers ski instruction. **Positions advertised include:** Grounds Keeper; Maintenance; Child Care Worker; Food & Beverage Manager; Snowmaker; Front Office Worker; Trail Groomer; Ticket Sales.

KMART CORPORATION
4000 East Second Street, Casper WY 82609. 307/265-0808. **Contact:** Personnel. **World Wide Web address:** http://www.bluelight.com. **Description:** Kmart Corporation is one of the largest retailers in the United States. The company operates approximately 2,200 discount general merchandise department stores throughout the United States, Puerto Rico, the U.S. Virgin Islands, and Guam. **Corporate headquarters location:** Troy MI. **International locations:** Czech Republic; Mexico; Puerto Rico; Singapore; Slovakia. **Listed on:** New York Stock Exchange. **Stock exchange symbol:** KM. **Annual sales/revenues:** More than $100 million. **Number of employees nationwide:** 275,000.

LIFE-LINK INTERNATIONAL, INC.
P.O. Box 2913, Jackson Hole WY 83001. 307/733-2266. **Contact:** Human Resources. **World Wide Web address:** http://www.life-link.com. **Description:** A manufacturer of backcountry skiing and avalanche prevention products and tools. **Other U.S. locations:** Bozeman MT.

MAVERIK COUNTRY STORES, INC.
391 Washington Street, Afton WY 83110. 307/885-9412 **Contact:** Mr. Val Dee Swenson, Payroll Supervisor. **World Wide Web address:** http://www.maverik.com. **Description:** Operates a chain of convenience stores that include bakeries. Maverik Country Stores operates over 130 locations in the western United States. **Corporate headquarters location:** This location. **Other U.S. locations:** AZ; CO; ID; MT; NV; UT.

MEMORIAL HOSPITAL OF CONVERSE COUNTY
P.O. Box 1450, Douglas WY 82633. 307/358-2122. **Physical address:** 111 South Fifth Street, Douglas WY 82633. **Fax:** 307/358-9216. **Contact:** Linda York, Human Resources Officer. **World Wide Web address:** http://www.conversehospital.com. **Description:** A nonprofit, 44-bed county hospital. **NOTE:** Entry-level positions and part-time jobs are offered. **Positions advertised include:** RN; LPN; Critical Care Manager; Assistant Buyer; Family Practice Pediatrician; Orthopedic Surgeon. **Office hours:** Monday - Friday, 8:30 a.m. - 5:00 p.m. **Corporate headquarters location:** This location. **Facilities Manager:** Chuck Kern. **Purchasing Manager:** Steve Sibrel. **Number of employees at this location:** 150.

MEMORIAL HOSPITAL OF SWEETWATER COUNTY
P.O. Box 1359, Rock Springs WY 82902. 307/362-3711. **Fax:** 307/362-8391. **Contact:** Bob Walters, Director of Human Resources. **E-mail address:** mhschr@mineralhospital.com. **World Wide Web address:** http://www.minershospital.com. **Description:** A 99-bed, acute care hospital. Services include anesthesiology, emergency care, general surgery, internal medicine, obstetrics, ophthalmology, plastic surgery, radiology, and urology. **Positions advertised include:** RN; CNA; Radiological Technologist; Respiratory Therapist; Physical Therapist. **Number of employees at this location:** 365.

PITTSBURG & MIDWAY COAL MINING COMPANY
P.O. Box 950, Kemmerer WY 83101. 307/828-2200. **Contact:** Human Resources. **Description:** Produces approximately 3.8 million tons of coal a year. **Parent company:** Chevron Company. **Number of employees at this location:** 300.

STROUT ARCHITECTS
85 West Snow King, Jackson Hole WY 83025. 307/733-5778. **Contact:** Human Resources Department. **E-mail address:** szabriskie@stroutarchitects.com. **World Wide Web address:** http://www.stroutarchitects.com. **Description:** A commercial and residential architecture firm.

TETON DATA SYSTEMS
dba STAT!REF
P.O. Box 4798, Jackson WY 83001. 307/733-5494. **Toll-free phone:** 800/755-7828. **Fax:** 307/739-1229. **Contact:** Human Resources Department. **E-mail address:** info@tetondata.com. **World Wide Web address:** http://www.tetondata.com. **Description:** Manufactures and distributes medical reference software. The company's primary product is STAT!Ref. **Positions advertised include:** Data Translator. **Office hours:** Monday - Friday, 8:30 a.m. - 5:00 p.m. **Number of employees at this location:** 25.

TETON HOMES
P.O. Box 2349, Mills WY 82644. 307/235-1525. **Contact:** Human Resources. **World Wide Web address:** http://www.tetonhomes.com. **Description:** Teton Homes is a manufacturer of RVs. The company's RV line includes the Grand, the Prestige, and the Tradition. Founded in 1967.

TETON PINES RESORT & COUNTRY CLUB
P.O. Box 14090, Jackson WY 83002. 307/733-1005. **Physical address:** 3450 North Country Club Drive, Jackson WY 83002. **Toll-free phone:** 800/238-2223. **Contact:** Human Resources Department. **World Wide Web address:** http://www.tetonpines. com. **Description:** A vacation resort offering lodging, dinning, golf, hiking, hunting/fishing, skiing, and swimming. **Positions advertised include:** Server; Busser; Cashier/Host; Bartender; Cook; Greenskeeper; Front Desk Assistant; Housekeeper; Pool Attendant; Tennis Instructor.

TRILEGIANT
3001 East Pershing Boulevard, Cheyenne WY 82001. 307/771-2700. **Contact:** Human Resources. **World Wide Web address:** http://www.trilegiant.com. **Description:** Provides services to protect against lost credit cards. **Corporate headquarters location:** Norwalk CT. **Operations at this facility include:** Administration; Sales; Service. **Number of employees nationwide:** 3,000.

U.S. DEPARTMENT OF VETERANS AFFAIRS
VETERANS ADMINISTRATION MEDICAL CENTER
2360 East Pershing Boulevard, Mail Stop 05, Cheyenne WY 82001. 307/778-7331. **Contact:** Human Resources. **World Wide Web address:** http://www.va.gov. **Description:** Provides primary and secondary inpatient and outpatient services to veterans. Comprehensive programs at the facility include counseling and treatment for post-combat trauma, substance abuse, and chronic mental illness.

UNILINK INC.
P.O. Box 1630, Jackson WY 83001. 307/733-1666. **Fax:** 888/456-8015. **Contact:** Human Resources. **World Wide Web address:** http://www.unilink-inc.com. **Description:** Develops software for the accounting industry. **Corporate headquarters location:** This location. **Office hours:** Monday - Friday, 8:00 a.m. - 5:00 p.m.

UNITED MEDICAL CENTER
UMC West, 214 East 23rd Street, Cheyenne WY 82001. 307/634-2273. **Fax:** 307/633-7714. **Recorded jobline:** 307/633-7764. **Contact:** Human Resources. **E-mail address:** rdagenhart@umcwy.org. **World Wide Web address:** http://www.umcwy.org. **Description:** A 219-bed medical center providing a wide range of medical services including cardiac services that covers acute cardiac care; emergency care for trauma, coronary, adult, and pediatric cases; a 17-bed oncology unit with a low patient to nurse ratio; a short-term, 16-bed, behavioral health unit; maternal/child services with six labor and delivery rooms, a general nursery, and post-partum care; a 15-bed rehabilitation unit operated by Spalding Rehabilitation Hospital; and a series of surgical procedures. **Positions advertised include:** LPN; RN; Radiology Transporter; CNA; Radiologic Technologist; Executive Secretary; Echosonographer; Personal Wellness Trainer; RIS/PACS Coordinator; Housekeeper; Biomedical Technician; Admissions Clerk; Physical Therapist Assistant.

UNIVERSITY OF WYOMING
139 Wyo Hall, P.O. Box 3422, Laramie WY 82071. 307/766-2215. **Fax:** 307/766-5607. **Contact:** Human Resources. **E-mail address:** jobapps@uwyo.edu. **World Wide Web address:** http://www.uwyo.edu/hr. **Description:** A state university offering bachelor's, master's, and doctoral degree programs. **NOTE:** Part-time jobs are offered. **Positions advertised include:** Academic Professional Lecturer; Assistant Professor; Associate Professor; Director, Teacher Education; Neurobiologist;. **Special programs:** Internships; Summer Jobs. **Corporate headquarters location:** This location. **Operations at this facility include:** Administration; Education; Regional Headquarters. **Number of employees at this location:** 2,600.

WELLS FARGO BANK
P.O. Box 2799, Casper WY 82602. 307/235-7797. **Contact:** Personnel. **World Wide Web address:** http://www.wellsfargo.com. **Description:** A diversified financial institution with over $234 billion in assets. Wells Fargo serves over 17 million customers through 5,300 independent locations worldwide. The company also maintains several stand-alone ATMs and branches within other retail outlets. Services include community banking, credit and debit cards, home equity and mortgage loans, online banking, student loans, and insurance. Wells Fargo also offers a complete line of commercial and institutional financial services. Founded in 1852. **Corporate headquarters location:** San Francisco CA. **Other U.S. locations:** Nationwide. **International locations:** Worldwide. **Listed on:** New York Stock Exchange. **Stock exchange symbol:** WFC. **Annual sales/revenues:** More than $100 million. **Number of employees worldwide:** 104,000.

WEST PARK HOSPITAL
707 Sheridan Avenue, Cody WY 82414. 307/527-7501. **Toll-free phone:** 800/654-9447. **Contact:** Human Resources Department. **World Wide Web address:** http://www.westparkhospital.org. **Description:** West Park Hospital is a 46-bed, nonprofit hospital. Physicians in 13 specialties treat approximately 8,500 patients a year. The hospital also offers a 14-bed chemical dependency center, providing medically supervised alcoholism and drug abuse recovery. The program includes detoxification, evaluation, and education and group, individual, and family therapy as well as aftercare. The hospital holds the contract with Yellowstone Park Medical Services and also operates a 105-bed long-term care center, providing skilled and intermediate nursing home care. West Park Hospital is accredited by the Joint Commission on Accreditation of Healthcare Organizations. **Positions advertised include:** RN; Certified Nursing Assistant; Unit Coordinator; Ultrasonographer; Physical Therapist; Speech Therapist; Personal Care Coordinator; Visual Observation Staff. **Number of employees at this location:** 300.

WYOMING MEDICAL CENTER
1233 East Second Street, Casper WY 82601. 307/577-7201. **Toll-free phone:** 800/822-7201. **Contact:** Personnel. **World Wide Web address:** http://www.wmcnet.org. **Description:** A 282-bed, nonprofit hospital. Approximately 90 physicians specialize in numerous areas including cardiac and reconstructive surgery, neurology, internal medicine, oncology, orthopedics, rheumatology, and rehabilitation. The hospital provides diagnostic resources including catheterization, vascular and stress testing, echocardiogram, and nuclear medicine facilities. At the oncology facility, known as the Central Wyoming Oncology Center, patient care is provided by a team of radiation oncologists. **Positions advertised include:** SSP II; Transcriptionist; Certified Surgical Technologist; EEG Technician; Lab Resources Technician; Radiology Technician; Respiratory Therapist; RN; LPN; Application Specialist; Cancer Registrar; Pharmacist; Assistant Teacher; Food Service Manager. **Number of employees at this location:** 1,000.

WYOMING STATE HOSPITAL
P.O. Box 177, Evanston WY 82931-0177. 307/789-3464. **Fax:** 307/789-7373. **Contact:** Bob Stahl, Human Resources Specialist. **Description:** A psychiatric hospital. **Special programs:** Internships. **Corporate headquarters location:** Cheyenne WY. **Operations at this facility include:** Administration. **Number of employees at this location:** 450.

WYOMING TRIBUNE-EAGLE
702 West Lincolnway, Cheyenne WY 82001. 307/634-3361. **Contact:** Human Resources. **World Wide Web address:** http://www.wyomingnews.com. **Description:** A daily newspaper. **Parent company:** Cheyenne Newspapers, Inc.

THE BASICS OF JOB WINNING: A CONDENSED REVIEW

This chapter is divided into four sections. The first section explains the fundamentals that every jobseeker should know, especially first-time jobseekers. The next three sections deal with special situations faced by specific types of jobseekers: those who are currently employed, those who have lost a job, and college students.

THE BASICS: Things Everyone Needs to Know

Career Planning

The first step to finding your ideal job is to clearly define your objectives. This is better known as career planning (or life planning if you wish to emphasize the importance of combining the two). Career planning has become a field of study in and of itself.

If you are thinking of choosing or switching careers, we particularly emphasize two things. First, choose a career where you will enjoy most of the day-to-day tasks. This sounds obvious, but most of us have at some point found the idea of a glamour industry or prestigious job title attractive without thinking of the key consideration: Would we enjoy performing the *everyday* tasks the position entails?

The second key consideration is that you are not merely choosing a career, but also a lifestyle. Career counselors indicate that one of the most common problems people encounter in jobseeking is that they fail to consider how well-suited they are for a particular position or career. For example, some people, attracted to management consulting by good salaries, early responsibility, and high-level corporate exposure, do not adapt well to the long hours, heavy travel demands, and constant pressure to produce. Be sure to ask yourself how you might adapt to the day-to-day duties and working environment that a specific position entails. Then ask yourself how you might adapt to the demands of that career or industry as a whole.

Choosing Your Strategy

Assuming that you've established your career objectives, the next step of the job search is to develop a strategy. If you don't take the time to develop a plan, you may find yourself going in circles after several weeks of randomly searching for opportunities that always seem just beyond your reach.

The most common jobseeking techniques are:

- following up on help-wanted advertisements (in the newspaper or online)
- using employment services
- relying on personal contacts
- contacting employers directly (the Direct Contact method)

Each of these approaches can lead to better jobs. However, the Direct Contact method boasts twice the success rate of the others. So unless you have specific reasons to employ other strategies, Direct Contact should form the foundation of your job search.

If you choose to use other methods as well, try to expend at least half your energy on Direct Contact. Millions of other jobseekers have already proven that Direct Contact has been twice as effective in obtaining employment, so why not follow in their footsteps?

Setting Your Schedule

Okay, so now that you've targeted a strategy it's time to work out the details of your job search. The most important detail is setting up a schedule. Of course, since job searches aren't something most people do regularly, it may be hard to estimate how long each step will take. Nonetheless, it is important to have a plan so that you can monitor your progress.

When outlining your job search schedule, have a realistic time frame in mind. If you will be job-searching full-time, your search could take at least two months or more. If you can only devote part-time effort, it will probably take at least four months.

You probably know a few people who seem to spend their whole lives searching for a better job in their spare time. Don't be one of them. If you are presently working and don't feel like devoting a lot of energy to jobseeking right now, then wait. Focus on enjoying your present position, performing your best on the job, and storing up energy for when you are really ready to begin your job search.

The first step in beginning your job search is to clearly define your objectives.

Those of you who are currently unemployed should remember that *job-hunting is tough work, both physically and emotionally*. It is also intellectually demanding work that requires you to be at your best. So don't tire yourself out by working on your job campaign around the clock. At the same time, be sure to discipline yourself. The most logical way to manage your time while looking for a job is to keep your regular working hours.

If you are searching full-time and have decided to choose several different strategies, we recommend that you divide up each week, designating some time for each method. By trying several approaches at once, you can evaluate how promising each seems and alter your schedule accordingly. Keep in mind that the *majority of openings are filled without being advertised.* Remember also that positions advertised on the Internet are just as likely to already be filled as those found in the newspaper!

If you are searching part-time and decide to try several different contact methods, we recommend that you try them sequentially. You simply won't have enough time to put a meaningful amount of effort into more than one method at once. Estimate the length of your job search, and then allocate so many weeks or months for each contact method, beginning with Direct Contact. The purpose of setting this schedule is not to rush you to your goal but to help you periodically evaluate your progress.

The Direct Contact Method

Once you have scheduled your time, you are ready to begin your search in earnest. Beginning with the Direct Contact method, the first step is to develop a checklist for categorizing the types of firms for which you'd like to work. You might categorize firms by product line, size, customer type (such as industrial or consumer), growth prospects, or geographical location. Keep in mind, the shorter the list the easier it will be to locate a company that is right for you.

Next you will want to use *The National JobBank* to assemble your list of potential employers. Choose firms where *you* are most likely to be able to find a job. Try matching your skills with those that a specific job demands. Consider where your skills might be in demand, the degree of competition for employment, and the employment outlook at each company.

Separate your prospect list into three groups. The first 25 percent will be your primary target group, the next 25 percent will be your secondary group, and the remaining names will be your reserve group.

After you form your prospect list, begin working on your resume. Refer to the Resumes and Cover Letters section following this chapter for more information.

Once your resume is complete, begin researching your first batch of prospective employers. You will want to determine whether you would be happy working at the firms you are researching and to get a better idea of what their employment needs might be. You also need to obtain enough information to sound highly informed about the company during phone conversations and in mail correspondence. But don't go all out on your research yet! You probably won't be able to arrange interviews with some of these firms, so save your big research effort until you start to arrange interviews. Nevertheless, you should plan to spend several hours researching each firm. Do your research in batches to save time and energy. Start with this book, and find out what you can about each of the firms in your primary target group. For answers to specific questions, contact any pertinent professional associations that may be able to help you learn more about an employer. Read industry publications looking for articles on the firm. Then look up the company on the Internet or try additional resources at your local library. Keep organized, and maintain a folder on each firm.

The more you know about a company, the more likely you are to catch an interviewer's eye. (You'll also face fewer surprises once you get the job!)

Information to look for includes: company size; president, CEO, or owner's name; when the company was established; what each division does; and benefits that are important to you. An abundance of company information can now be found electronically, through the World Wide Web or commercial online services. Researching companies online is a convenient means of obtaining information quickly and easily. If you have access to the Internet, you can search from your home at any time of day.

You may search a particular company's Website for current information that may be otherwise unavailable in print. In fact, many companies that maintain a site update their information daily. In addition, you may also search articles written about the company online. Today, most of the nation's largest newspapers, magazines, trade publications, and regional business periodicals have online versions of their publications. To find additional resources, use a search engine like Yahoo! or Alta Vista and type in the keyword "companies" or "employers."

If you discover something that really disturbs you about the firm (they are about to close their only local office), or if you discover that your chances of getting a job there are practically nil (they have just instituted a hiring freeze), then cross them off your prospect list. If possible, supplement your research efforts by contacting individuals who know the firm well. Ideally you should make an informal contact with someone at that particular firm, but often a direct competitor or a major customer will be able to supply you with just as much information. At the very least, try to obtain whatever printed information the company has available -- not just annual reports, but product brochures, company profiles, or catalogs. This information is often available on the Internet.

Getting the Interview

Now it is time to make Direct Contact with the goal of arranging interviews. If you have read any books on job-searching, you may have noticed that most of these books tell you to avoid the human resources office like the plague. It is said that the human resources office never hires people; they screen candidates. Unfortunately, this is often the case. If you can identify the appropriate manager with the authority to hire you, you should try to contact that person directly.

The obvious means of initiating Direct Contact are:

- Mail (postal or electronic)
- Phone calls

DEVELOPING YOUR CONTACTS: NETWORKING

Some career counselors feel that the best route to a better job is through somebody you already know or through somebody to whom you can be introduced. These counselors recommend that you build your contact base beyond your current acquaintances by asking each one to introduce you, or refer you, to additional people in your field of interest.

The theory goes like this: You might start with 15 personal contacts, each of whom introduces you to three additional people, for a total of 45 additional contacts. Then each of these people introduces you to three additional people, which adds 135 additional contacts. Theoretically, you will soon know every person in the industry.

Of course, developing your personal contacts does not work quite as smoothly as the theory suggests because some people will not be able to introduce you to anyone. The further you stray from your initial contact base, the weaker your references may be. So, if you do try developing your own contacts, try to begin with as many people that you know personally as you can. Dig into your personal phone book and your holiday greeting card list and locate old classmates from school. Be particularly sure to approach people who perform your personal business such as your lawyer, accountant, banker, doctor, stockbroker, and insurance agent. These people develop a very broad contact base due to the nature of their professions.

Mail contact is a good choice if you have not been in the job market for a while. You can take your time to prepare a letter, say exactly what you want, and of course include your resume. Remember that employers receive many resumes every day. Don't be surprised if you do not get a response to your inquiry, *and don't spend weeks waiting for responses that may never come.* If you do send a letter, follow it up (or precede it) with a phone call.

DON'T BOTHER WITH MASS MAILINGS OR BARRAGES OF PHONE CALLS

Direct Contact does not mean burying every firm within a hundred miles with mail and phone calls. Mass mailings rarely work in the job hunt. This also applies to those letters that are personalized -- but dehumanized -- on an automatic typewriter or computer. Don't waste your time or money on such a project; you will fool no one but yourself.

The worst part of sending out mass mailings, or making unplanned phone calls to companies you have not researched, is that you are likely to be remembered as someone with little genuine interest in the firm, who lacks sincerity -- somebody who nobody wants to hire.

HELP WANTED ADVERTISEMENTS

Only a small fraction of professional job openings are advertised. Yet the majority of jobseekers -- and quite a few people not in the job market -- spend a lot of time studying the help wanted ads. As a result, the competition for advertised openings is often very severe.

A moderate-sized employer told us about their experience advertising in the help wanted section of a major Sunday newspaper:

It was a disaster. We had over 500 responses from this relatively small ad in just one week. We have only two phone lines in this office and one was totally knocked out. We'll never advertise for professional help again.

If you insist on following up on help wanted ads, then research a firm before you reply to an ad. Preliminary research might help to separate you from all of the other professionals responding to that ad, many of whom will have only a passing interest in the opportunity. It will also give you insight about a particular firm, to help you determine if it is potentially a good match. That said, your chances of obtaining a job through the want ads are still much smaller than they are with the Direct Contact method.

This will increase your impact, and because of the initial research you did, will underscore both your familiarity with and your interest in the firm. Bear in mind that your goal is to make your name a familiar one with prospective employers, so that when a position becomes available, your resume will be one of the first the hiring manager seeks out.

If you send a fax, always follow with a hard copy of your resume and cover letter in the mail. Often, through no fault of your own, a fax will come through illegibly and employers do not often have time to let candidates know.

Another alternative is to make a "cover call." Your cover call should be just like your cover letter: concise. Your first statement should interest the employer in you. Then try to subtly mention your familiarity with the firm. Don't be overbearing; keep your introduction to three sentences or less. Be pleasant, self-confident, and relaxed. This will greatly increase the chances of the person at the other end of the line developing the conversation. But don't press. If you are asked to follow up with "something in the mail," this signals the conversation's natural end. Don't try to prolong the conversation once it has ended, and don't ask what they want to receive in the mail. Always send your resume and a highly personalized follow-up letter, reminding the addressee of the phone conversation. *Always* include a cover letter if you are asked to send a resume, and treat your resume and cover letter as a total package. Gear your letter toward the specific position you are applying for and prove why you would be a "good match" for the position.

Unless you are in telephone sales, making smooth and relaxed cover calls will probably not come easily. Practice them on your own, and then with your friends or relatives.

If you obtain an interview as a result of a telephone conversation, be sure to send a thank-you note reiterating the points you made during the conversation. You will appear more professional and increase your impact. However, unless specifically requested, don't mail your resume once an interview has been arranged. Take it with you to the interview instead.

You should never show up to seek a professional position without an appointment. Even if you are somehow lucky enough to obtain an interview, you will appear so unprofessional that you will not be seriously considered.

Preparing for the Interview

As each interview is arranged, begin your in-depth research. You should arrive at an interview knowing the company upside-down and inside-out. You need to know the company's products, types of customers, subsidiaries, parent company, principal locations, rank in the industry, sales and profit trends, type of ownership, size, current plans, and much more. By this time you have probably narrowed your job search to one industry. Even if you haven't, you should still be familiar with common industry terms, the trends in the firm's industry, the firm's principal competitors and their relative performance, and the direction in which the industry leaders are headed.

Dig into every resource you can! Surf the Internet. Read the company literature, the trade press, the business press, and if the company is public, call your stockbroker (if you have one) and ask for additional information. If possible, speak to someone at the firm before the interview, or if not, speak to someone at a competing firm. The more time you spend, the better. Even if you feel extremely pressed for time, you should set aside several hours for pre-interview research.

If you have been out of the job market for some time, don't be surprised if you find yourself tense during your first few interviews. It will probably happen every time you re-enter the market, not just when you seek your first job after getting out of school.

You should arrive at an interview knowing the company upside-down and inside-out.

Tension is natural during an interview, but knowing you have done a thorough research job should put you more at ease. Make a list of questions that you think might be asked in each interview. Think out your answers carefully and practice them with a friend. Tape record your responses to the problem questions. (*See also in this chapter: Informational Interviews.*) If you feel particularly unsure of your interviewing skills, arrange your first interviews at firms you are not as interested in. (But remember it is common courtesy to seem enthusiastic about the possibility of working for any firm at which you interview.) Practice again on your own after these first few interviews. Go over the difficult questions that you were asked.

Take some time to really think about how you will convey your work history. Present "bad experiences" as "learning experiences." Instead of saying "I hated my position as a salesperson because I had to bother people on the phone," say "I realized that cold-calling was not my strong suit. Though I love working with people, I decided my talents would be best used in a more face-to-face atmosphere." Always find some sort of lesson from previous jobs, as they all have one.

Interview Attire

How important is the proper dress for a job interview? Buying a complete wardrobe, donning new shoes, and having your hair styled every morning are not enough to guarantee you a career position as an investment banker. But on the other hand, if you can't find a clean, conservative suit or won't take the time to wash your hair, then you are just wasting your time by interviewing at all.

Personal grooming is as important as finding appropriate clothes for a job interview. Careful grooming indicates both a sense of thoroughness and self-confidence. This is not the time to make a statement -- take out the extra earrings and avoid any garish hair colors not found in nature. Women should not wear excessive makeup, and both men and women should refrain from wearing any perfume or cologne (it only takes a small spritz to leave an allergic interviewer with a fit of sneezing and a bad impression of your meeting). Men should be freshly shaven, even if the interview is late in the day, and men with long hair should have it pulled back and neat.

Men applying for any professional position should wear a suit, preferably in a conservative color such as navy or charcoal gray. It is easy to get away with wearing the same dark suit to consecutive interviews at the same company; just be sure to wear a different shirt or tie for each interview.

Women should also wear a business suit. Professionalism still dictates a suit with a skirt, rather than slacks, as proper interview garb for women. This is usually true even at companies where pants are acceptable attire for female employees. As much as you may disagree with this guideline, the more prudent time to fight this standard is after you land the job.

SKIRT VS. PANTS: An Interview Dilemma

For those women who are still convinced that pants are acceptable interview attire, listen to the words of one career counselor from a prestigious New England college:

I had a student who told me that since she knew women in her industry often wore pants to work, she was going to wear pants to her interviews. Almost every recruiter commented that her pants were "too casual," and even referred to her as "the one with the pants." The funny thing was that one of the recruiters who commented on her pants had been wearing jeans!

The final selection of candidates for a job opening won't be determined by dress, of course. However, inappropriate dress can quickly eliminate a first-round candidate. So while you shouldn't spend a fortune on a new wardrobe, you should be sure that your clothes are adequate. The key is to dress at least as formally or slightly more formally and more conservatively than the position would suggest.

What to Bring

Be complete. Everyone needs a watch, a pen, and a notepad. Finally, a briefcase or a leather-bound folder (containing extra, *unfolded*, copies of your resume) will help complete the look of professionalism.

Sometimes the interviewer will be running behind schedule. Don't be upset, be sympathetic. There is often pressure to interview a lot of candidates and to quickly fill a demanding position. So be sure to come to your interview with good reading material to keep yourself occupied and relaxed.

The Interview

The very beginning of the interview is the most important part because it determines the tone for the rest of it. Those first few moments are especially crucial. Do you smile when you meet? Do you establish enough eye contact, but not too much?

Do you walk into the office with a self-assured and confident stride? Do you shake hands firmly? Do you make small talk easily without being garrulous? It is human nature to judge people by that first impression, so make sure it is a good one. But most of all, try to be yourself.

The interviewer's job is to find a reason to turn you down; your job is to not provide that reason.

-John L. LaFevre, author,
How You Really Get Hired

Often the interviewer will begin, after the small talk, by telling you about the company, the division, the department, or perhaps, the position. Because of your detailed research, the information about the company should be repetitive for you, and the interviewer would probably like nothing better than to avoid this regurgitation of the company biography. So if you can do so tactfully, indicate to the interviewer that you are very familiar with the firm. If he or she seems intent on providing you with background information, despite your hints, then acquiesce.

BE PREPARED:
Some Common Interview Questions

Tell me about yourself.

Why did you leave your last job?

What excites you in your current job?

Where would you like to be in five years?

How much overtime are you willing to work?

Tell me about a difficult situation that you faced at your previous/present job.

What are your greatest strengths/weaknesses?

Describe a work situation where you took initiative.

Why should we hire you?

But be sure to remain attentive. If you can manage to generate a brief discussion of the company or the industry at this point, without being forceful, great. It will help to further build rapport, underscore your interest, and increase your impact.

Soon (if it didn't begin that way) the interviewer will begin the questions, many of which you will have already practiced. This period of the interview usually falls into one of two categories (or somewhere in between): either a structured interview, where the interviewer has a prescribed set of questions to ask; or an unstructured interview, where the interviewer will ask only leading questions to get you to talk about yourself, your experiences, and your goals. Try to sense as quickly as possible in which direction the interviewer wishes to proceed. This will make the interviewer feel more relaxed and in control of the situation.

Remember to keep attuned to the interviewer and make the length of your answers appropriate to the situation. If you are really unsure as to how detailed a response the interviewer is seeking, then ask.

As the interview progresses, the interviewer will probably mention some of the most important responsibilities of the position. If applicable, draw parallels between your experience and the demands of the position as detailed by the interviewer. Describe your past experience in the same manner that you do on your resume: emphasizing results and achievements and not merely describing activities. But don't exaggerate. Be on the level about your abilities.

The first interview is often the toughest, where many candidates are screened out. If you are interviewing for a very competitive position, you will have to make an impression that will last. Focus on a few of your greatest strengths that are relevant to the position. Develop these points carefully, state them again in different words, and then try to summarize them briefly at the end of the interview.

Often the interviewer will pause toward the end and ask if you have any questions. Particularly in a structured interview, this might be the one chance to really show your knowledge of and interest in the firm. Have a list prepared of specific questions that are of real interest to you. Let your questions subtly show your research and your knowledge of the firm's activities. It is wise to have an extensive list of questions, as several of them may be answered during the interview.

Do not turn your opportunity to ask questions into an interrogation. Avoid reading directly from your list of questions, and ask questions that you are fairly certain the interviewer can answer (remember how you feel when you cannot answer a question during an interview).

Even if you are unable to determine the salary range beforehand, do not ask about it during the first interview. You can always ask later. Above all, don't ask about fringe benefits until you have been offered a position. (Then be sure to get all the details.)

Try not to be negative about anything during the interview, particularly any past employer or any previous job. Be cheerful. Everyone likes to work with someone who seems to be happy. Even if you detest your current/former job or manager, do not make disparaging comments. The interviewer may construe this as a sign of a potential attitude problem and not consider you a strong candidate.

Don't let a tough question throw you off base. If you don't know the answer to a question, simply say so -- do not apologize. Just smile. Nobody can answer every question -- particularly some of the questions that are asked in job interviews.

Before your first interview, you may be able to determine how many rounds of interviews there usually are for positions at your level. (Of course it may differ quite a bit even within the different levels of one firm.) Usually you can count on attending at least two or three interviews, although some firms are known to give a minimum of six interviews for all professional positions. While you should be more relaxed as you return for subsequent interviews, the pressure will be on. The more prepared you are, the better.

Depending on what information you are able to obtain, you might want to vary your strategy quite a bit from interview to interview. For instance, if the first interview is a screening interview, then be sure a few of your strengths really stand out. On the other hand, if later interviews are primarily with people who are in a position to veto your hiring, but not to push it forward, then you should primarily focus on building rapport as opposed to reiterating and developing your key strengths.

If it looks as though your skills and background do not match the position the interviewer was hoping to fill, ask him or her if there is another division or subsidiary that perhaps could profit from your talents.

After the Interview

Write a follow-up letter immediately after the interview, while it is still fresh in the interviewer's mind. Not only is this a thank-you, but it also gives you the chance to provide the interviewer with any details you may have forgotten (as long as they can be tactfully added in). If you haven't heard back from the interviewer within a week of sending your thank-you letter, call to stress your continued interest in the firm and the position. If you lost any points during the interview for any reason, this letter can help you regain footing. Be polite and make sure to stress your continued interest and competency to fill the position. Just don't forget to proofread it thoroughly. If you are unsure of the spelling of the interviewer's name, call the receptionist and ask.

THE BALANCING ACT:
Looking for a New Job While Currently Employed

For those of you who are still employed, job-searching will be particularly tiring because it must be done in addition to your normal work responsibilities. So don't overwork yourself to the point where you show up to interviews looking exhausted or start to slip behind at your current job. On the other hand, don't be tempted to quit your present job! The long hours are worth it. Searching for a job while you have one puts you in a position of strength.

Making Contact

If you must be at your office during the business day, then you have additional problems to deal with. How can you work interviews into the business day? And if you work in an open office, how can you even call to set up interviews? Obviously, you should keep up the effort and the appearances on your present job. So maximize your use of the lunch hour, early mornings, and late afternoons for calling. If you keep trying, you'll be surprised how often you will be able to reach the executive you are trying to contact during your out-of-office hours. You can catch people as early as 8 a.m. and as late as 6 p.m. on frequent occasions.

Scheduling Interviews

Your inability to interview at any time other than lunch just might work to your advantage. If you can, try to set up as many interviews as possible for your lunch hour. This will go a long way to creating a relaxed atmosphere. But be sure the interviews don't stray too far from the agenda on hand.

Lunchtime interviews are much easier to obtain if you have substantial career experience. People with less experience will often find no alternative to taking time off for interviews. If you have to take time off, you have to take time off. But try to do this as little as possible. Try to take the day off in order to avoid being blatantly obvious about your job search, and try to schedule two to three interviews for the same day. Explain to the interviewer why you might have to juggle your interview schedule; he/she should honor the respect you're showing your current employer by minimizing your days off and will probably appreciate the fact that another prospective employer is interested in you.

Try calling as early as 8 a.m. and as late as 6 p.m. You'll be surprised how often you will be able to reach the executive you want during these times of the day.

References

What do you tell an interviewer who asks for references from your current employer? Just say that while you are happy to have your former employers contacted, you are trying to keep your job search confidential and would rather that your current employer not be contacted until you have been given a firm offer.

IF YOU'RE FIRED OR LAID OFF:
Picking Yourself Up and Dusting Yourself Off

If you've been fired or laid off, you are not the first and will not be the last to go through this traumatic experience. In today's changing economy, thousands of professionals lose their jobs every year. Even if you were terminated with just cause, do not lose heart. Remember, being fired is not a reflection on you as a person. It is usually a reflection of your company's staffing needs and its perception of your recent job performance and attitude. And if you were not performing up to par or enjoying your work, then you will probably be better off at another company anyway.

Be prepared for the question "Why were you fired?" during job interviews.

A thorough job search could take months, so be sure to negotiate a reasonable severance package, if possible, and determine to what benefits, such as health insurance, you are still legally entitled. Also, register for unemployment compensation immediately. Don't be surprised to find other professionals collecting unemployment compensation -- it is for everyone who has lost their job.

Don't start your job search with a flurry of unplanned activity. Start by choosing a strategy and working out a plan. Now is not the time for major changes in your life. If possible, remain in the same career and in the same geographical location, at least until you have been working again for a while. On the other hand, if the only industry for which you are trained is leaving, or is severely depressed in your area, then you should give prompt consideration to moving or switching careers.

Avoid mentioning you were fired when arranging interviews, but be prepared for the question "Why were you fired?" during an interview. If you were laid off as a result of downsizing, briefly explain, being sure to reinforce that your job loss was not due to performance. If you were in fact fired, be honest, but try to detail the reason as favorably as possible and portray what you have learned from your mistakes. If you are confident one of your past managers will give you a good reference, tell the interviewer to contact that person. Do not to speak negatively of your past employer and try not to sound particularly worried about your status of being temporarily unemployed.

Finally, don't spend too much time reflecting on why you were let go or how you might have avoided it. Think positively, look to the future, and be sure to follow a careful plan during your job search.

THE COLLEGE STUDENT:
Conducting Your First Job Search

While you will be able to apply many of the basics covered earlier in this chapter to your job search, there are some situations unique to the college student's job search.

Perhaps the biggest problem college students face is lack of experience. Many schools have internship programs designed to give students exposure to the field of their choice, as well as the opportunity to make valuable contacts. Check out your school's career services department to see what internships are available. If your school does not have a formal internship program, or if there are no available internships that appeal to you, try contacting local businesses and offering your services. Often, businesses will be more than willing to have an extra pair of hands (especially if those hands are unpaid!) for a day or two each week. Or try contacting school alumni to see if you can "shadow" them for a few days, and see what their daily duties are like.

THE GPA QUESTION

You are interviewing for the job of your dreams. Everything is going well: You've established a good rapport, the interviewer seems impressed with your qualifications, and you're almost positive the job is yours. Then you're asked about your GPA, which is pitifully low. Do you tell the truth and watch your dream job fly out the window?

Never lie about your GPA (they may request your transcript, and no company will hire a liar). You can, however, explain if there is a reason you don't feel your grades reflect your abilities, and mention any other impressive statistics. For example, if you have a high GPA in your major, or in the last few semesters (as opposed to your cumulative college career), you can use that fact to your advantage.

Informational Interviews

Although many jobseekers do not do this, it can be extremely helpful to arrange an informational interview with a college alumnus or someone else who works in your desired industry. You interview them about their job, their company, and their industry with questions you have prepared in advance. This can be done over the phone but is usually done in person. This will provide you with a contact in the industry who may give you more valuable information -- or perhaps even a job opportunity -- in the future. Always follow up with a thank you letter that includes your contact information.

The goal is to try to begin building experience and establishing contacts as early as possible in your college career.

What do you do if, for whatever reason, you weren't able to get experience directly related to your desired career? First, look at your previous jobs and see if there's anything you can highlight. Did you supervise or train other employees? Did you reorganize the accounting system, or boost productivity? Accomplishments like these demonstrate leadership, responsibility, and innovation -- qualities that most companies look for in employees. And don't forget volunteer activities and school clubs, which can also showcase these traits.

On-Campus Recruiting

Companies will often send recruiters to interview on-site at colleges. This gives students a chance to interview with companies that may not have interviewed them otherwise. This is particularly true if a company schedules "open" interviews, in which the only screening process is who is first in line at the sign-ups. Of course, since many more applicants gain interviews in this format, this also means that many more people are rejected. The on-campus interview is generally a screening interview, to see if it is worth the company's time to invite you in for a second interview. Do everything possible to make yourself stand out from the crowd.

The first step is to check out any and all information your school's career center has on the company. If the information seems out of date, check out the company on the Internet or call the company's headquarters and ask for any printed information.

Many companies will host an informational meeting for interviewees, often the evening before interviews are scheduled to take place. DO NOT MISS THIS MEETING. The recruiter will almost certainly ask if you attended. Make an effort to stay after the meeting and talk with the company's representatives. Not only does this give you an opportunity to find out more information about the company and the position, it also makes you stand out in the recruiter's mind. If there's a particular company that you had your heart set on, but you weren't able to get an interview with them, attend the information session anyway. You may be able to persuade the recruiter to squeeze you into the schedule. (Or you may discover that the company really isn't the right fit for you.)

Try to check out the interview site beforehand. Some colleges may conduct "mock" interviews that take place in one of the standard interview rooms. Or you may be able to convince a career counselor to let you sneak a peek during off-hours. Either way, having an idea of the room's setup will help you to prepare.

Arrive at least 15 minutes early to the interview. The recruiter may be ahead of schedule, and might meet you early. But don't be surprised if previous interviews have run over, resulting in your 30-minute slot being reduced to 20 minutes (or less). Don't complain or appear anxious; just use the time you do have as efficiently as possible to showcase the reasons *you* are the ideal candidate. Staying calm and composed in these situations will work to your advantage.

LAST WORDS

A parting word of advice. Again and again during your job search you will face rejection. You will be rejected when you apply for interviews. You will be rejected after interviews. Don't let rejections slow you down. Keep reminding yourself that the sooner you go out, start your job search, and get those rejections flowing in, the closer you will be to obtaining the job you want.

GET YOUR ACT TOGETHER!

When filling a position, an employer will often have 100-plus applicants, but time to interview only a handful of the most promising ones. As a result, he or she will reject most applicants after only briefly skimming their resumes.

Unless you have phoned and talked to the employer -- which you should do whenever you can -- you will be chosen or rejected for an interview entirely on the basis of your resume and cover letter. *Your cover letter must catch the employer's attention, and your resume must hold it.* (But remember -- a resume is no substitute for a job search campaign. *You* must seek a job. Your resume is only one tool, albeit a critical one.)

RESUME FORMAT:
Mechanics of a First Impression

The Basics

Employers dislike long resumes, so unless you have an unusually strong background with many years of experience and a diversity of outstanding achievements, keep your resume length to one page. If you must squeeze in more information than would otherwise fit, try using a smaller typeface or changing the margins. Watch also for "widows" at the end of paragraphs. You can often free up some space if you can shorten the information enough to get rid of those single words taking up an entire line. Another tactic that works with some word processing programs is to decrease the font size of your paragraph returns and changing the spacing between lines.

Always print your resume on standard 8 1/2" x 11" paper. Since recruiters often get resumes in batches of hundreds, a smaller-sized resume may be lost in the pile. Oversized resumes are likely to get crumpled at the edges, and won't fit easily in their files.

First impressions matter, so make sure the recruiter's first impression of your resume is a good one. Never hand-write your resume (or cover letter)! Print your resume on quality paper that has weight and texture, in a conservative color such as white, ivory, or pale gray. Good resume paper is easy to find at many stores that sell stationery or office products. It is even available at some drug stores. Use *matching* paper and envelopes for both your resume and cover letter. One hiring manager at a major magazine throws out all resumes that arrive on paper that differs in color from the envelope!

Whatever you do, don't buy fancy paper covered with images of fluffy clouds and rainbows in the background or anything that looks like casual stationery that you would send to your favorite aunt or best friend. Do not spray perfume or cologne on your resume. Do not include your picture with your resume unless you have a specific and appropriate reason to do so.

Another helpful tip: Do a test print of your resume (and cover letter), to make sure the watermark is on the same side as the text so that you can read it. Also make sure it is right-side up. As trivial as this may sound, some recruiters check for this! One recruiter at a law firm in New Hampshire sheepishly admitted this is the first thing he checks. *"I open each envelope and check the watermarks on the resume and cover letter. Those candidates that have it wrong go into a different pile."*

Getting it on Paper

Modern photocomposition typesetting gives you the clearest, sharpest image, a wide variety of type styles, and effects such as italics, bold-facing, and book-like justified margins. It is also too expensive for many jobseekers. The quality of today's laser printers means that a computer-generated resume can look just as impressive as one that has been professionally typeset.

A computer with a word processing or desktop publishing program is the most common way to generate your resume. This allows you the flexibility to make changes almost instantly and to store different drafts on disk. Word processing and desktop publishing programs also offer many different fonts to choose from, each taking up different amounts of space. (It is generally best to stay between 9-point and 12-point font size.) Many other options are also available, such as bold-facing or italicizing for emphasis and the ability to change and manipulate spacing. It is generally recommended to leave the right-hand margin unjustified as this keeps the spacing between the text even and therefore easier to read. It is not wrong to justify both margins of text, but if possible try it both ways before you decide.

For a resume on paper, the end result will be largely determined by the quality of the printer you use. Laser printers will generally provide the best quality. Do not use a dot matrix printer.

Many companies now use scanning equipment to screen the resumes they receive, and certain paper, fonts, and other features are more compatible with this technology. White paper is preferable, as well as a standard font such as Courier or Helvetica. You should use at least a 10-point font, and avoid bolding, italics, underlining, borders, boxes, or graphics.

Household typewriters and office typewriters with nylon or other cloth ribbons are *not* good enough for typing your resume. If you don't have access to a quality word processing program, hire a professional with the resources to prepare your resume for you. Keep in mind that businesses such as Kinko's (open 24 hours) provide access to computers with quality printers.

Don't make your copies on an office photocopier. Only the human resources office may see the resume you mail. Everyone else may see only a copy of it, and copies of copies quickly become unreadable. Furthermore, sending photocopies of your resume or cover letter is completely unprofessional. Either print out each copy individually, or take your resume to a professional copy shop, which will generally offer professionally-maintained, extra-high-quality photocopiers and charge fairly reasonable prices. You want your resume to represent you with the look of polished quality.

Proof with Care

Whether you typed it or paid to have it produced professionally, mistakes on resumes are not only embarrassing, but will usually remove you from consideration (particularly if something obvious such as your name is misspelled). No matter how much you paid someone else to type, write, or typeset your resume, *you* lose if there is a mistake. So proofread it as carefully as possible. Get a friend to help you. Read your draft aloud as your friend checks the proof copy. Then have your friend read aloud while you check. Next, read it letter by letter to check spelling and punctuation.

If you are having it typed by a resume service or a printer, and you don't have time to proof it, pay for it and take it home. Proof it there and bring it back later to get it corrected and printed.

> **The one piece of advice I give to everyone about their resume is: Show it to people, show it to people, show it to people. Before you ever send out a resume, show it to at least a dozen people.**
>
> -Cate Talbot Ashton, Associate Director, Career Services, Colby College

If you wrote your resume with a word processing program, use the built-in spell checker to double-check for spelling errors. Keep in mind that a spell checker will not find errors such as "to" for "two" or "wok" for "work." Many spell check programs do not recognize missing or misused punctuation, nor are they set to check the spelling of capitalized words. It's important that you still proofread your resume to check for grammatical mistakes and other problems, even after it has been spellchecked.

If you find mistakes, do not make edits in pen or pencil or use white-out to fix them on the final copy!

Electronic Resumes

As companies rely increasingly on emerging technologies to find qualified candidates for job openings, you may opt to create an electronic resume in order to remain competitive in today's job market. Why is this important? Companies today sometimes request that resumes be submitted by e-mail, and many hiring managers regularly check online resume databases for candidates to fill unadvertised job openings. Other companies enlist the services of electronic employment database services, which charge jobseekers a nominal fee to have their resumes posted to the database to be viewed by potential employers. Still other companies use their own automated applicant tracking systems, in which case your resume is fed through a scanner that sends the image to a computer that "reads" your resume, looking for keywords, and files it accordingly in its database.

Whether you're posting your resume online, e-mailing it directly to an employer, sending it to an electronic employment database, or sending it to a company you suspect uses an automated applicant tracking system, you must create some form of electronic resume to take advantage of the technology. Don't panic! An electronic resume is simply a modified version of your conventional resume. An electronic resume is one that is sparsely formatted, but filled with keywords and important facts.

In order to post your resume to the Internet -- either to an online resume database or through direct e-mail to an employer -- you will need to change the way your resume is formatted. Instead of a Word, WordPerfect, or other word processing document, save your resume as a plain text, DOS, or ASCII file. These three terms are basically interchangeable, and describe text at its simplest, most basic level, without the formatting such as boldface or italics that most jobseekers use to make their resumes look more interesting. If you use e-mail, you'll notice that all of your messages are written and received in this format. First, you should remove all formatting from your resume including boldface, italics, underlining, bullets, differing font sizes, and graphics. Then, convert and save your resume as a plain text file. Most word processing programs have a "save as" feature that allows you to save files in different formats. Here, you should choose "text only" or "plain text."

Another option is to create a resume in HTML (hypertext markup language), the text formatting language used to publish information on the World Wide Web. However, the real usefulness of HTML resumes is still being explored. Most of the major online databases do not accept HTML resumes, and the vast majority of companies only accept plain text resumes through their e-mail.

Finally, if you simply wish to send your resume to an electronic employment database or a company that uses an automated applicant tracking system, there is no need to convert your resume to a plain text file. The only change you need to make is to organize the information in your resume by keywords. Employers are likely to do keyword searches for information, such as degree held or knowledge of particular types of software. Therefore, using the right keywords or key phrases in your resume is critical to its ultimate success. Keywords are usually nouns or short phrases that the computer searches for which refer to experience, training, skills, and abilities. For example, let's say an employer searches an employment database for a sales representative with the following criteria:

BS/BA
exceeded quota
cold calls
high energy
willing to travel

Even if you have the right qualifications, neglecting to use these keywords would result in the computer passing over your resume. Although there is no way to know for sure which keywords employers are most likely to search for, you can make educated guesses by checking the help-wanted ads or online job postings for your type of job. You should also arrange keywords in a keyword summary, a paragraph listing your qualifications that immediately follows your name and address (see sample letter in this chapter). In addition, choose a nondecorative font with clear, distinct characters, such as Helvetica or Times. It is more difficult for a scanner to accurately pick up the more unusual fonts. Boldface and all capital letters are best used only for major section headings, such as "Experience" and "Education." It is also best to avoid using italics or underlining, since this can cause the letters to bleed into one another.

Types of Resumes

The most common resume formats are the functional resume, the chronological resume, and the combination resume. (Examples can be found at the end of this chapter.) A functional resume focuses on skills and de-emphasizes job titles, employers, etc. A functional resume is best if you have been out of the work force for a long time or are changing careers. It is also good if you want to highlight specific skills and strengths, especially if all of your work experience has been at one company. This format can also be a good choice if you are just out of school or have no experience in your desired field.

Choose a chronological format if you are currently working or were working recently, and if your most recent experiences relate to your desired field. Use reverse chronological order and include dates. To a recruiter your last job and your latest schooling are the most important, so put the last first and list the rest going back in time.

A combination resume is perhaps the most common. This resume simply combines elements of the functional and chronological resume formats. This is used by many jobseekers with a solid track record who find elements of both types useful.

Organization

Your name, phone number, e-mail address (if you have one), and a complete mailing address should be at the top of your resume. Try to make your name stand out by using a slightly larger font size or all capital letters. Be sure to spell out everything. Never abbreviate St. for Street or Rd. for Road. If you are a college student, you should also put your home address and phone number at the top. Change your message on your answering machine if necessary -- RUSH blaring in the background or your sorority sisters screaming may not come across well to all recruiters. If you think you may be moving within six months then include a second address and phone number of a trusted friend or relative who can reach you no matter where you are.

Remember that employers will keep your resume on file and may contact you months later if a position opens that fits your qualifications. All too often, candidates are unreachable because they have moved and had not previously provided enough contact options on their resume.

Next, list your experience, then your education. If you are a recent graduate, list your education first, unless your experience is more important than your education. (For example, if you have just graduated from a teaching school, have some business experience, and are applying for a job in business, you would list your business experience first.)

Keep everything easy to find. Put the dates of your employment and education on the left of the page. Put the names of the companies you worked for and the schools you attended a few spaces to the right of the dates. Put the city and state, or the city and country, where you studied or worked to the right of the page.

The important thing is simply to break up the text in some logical way that makes your resume visually attractive and easy to scan, so experiment to see which layout works best for your resume. However you set it up, stay consistent. Inconsistencies in fonts, spacing, or tenses will make your resume look sloppy. Also, be sure to use tabs to keep your information vertically lined up, rather than the less precise space bar.

RESUME CONTENT:
Say it with Style

Sell Yourself

You are selling your skills and accomplishments in your resume, so it is important to inventory yourself and know yourself. If you have achieved something, say so. Put it in the best possible light, but avoid subjective statements, such as "I am a hard worker" or "I get along well with my coworkers." Just stick to the facts.

While you shouldn't hold back or be modest, don't exaggerate your achievements to the point of misrepresentation. Be honest. Many companies will immediately drop an applicant from consideration (or fire a current employee) upon discovering inaccurate or untrue information on a resume or other application material.

USE ACTION VERBS

How you write your resume is just as important as *what* you write. In describing previous work experiences, the strongest resumes use short phrases beginning with action verbs. Below are a few you may want to use. (This list is not all-inclusive.)

achieved	developed	integrated	purchased
administered	devised	interpreted	recreated
advised	directed	interviewed	reduced
analyzed	discovered	invented	regulated
arranged	distributed	launched	reported
assembled	eliminated	maintained	researched
assisted	established	managed	resolved
attained	evaluated	marketed	restored
budgeted	examined	mediated	revamped
built	executed	monitored	revised
calculated	expanded	negotiated	scheduled
collaborated	expedited	obtained	selected
collected	facilitated	operated	served
compiled	formulated	ordered	sold
completed	founded	organized	solved
computed	generated	participated	stocked
conducted	headed	performed	studied
consolidated	identified	planned	supervised
constructed	implemented	prepared	supplied
consulted	improved	presented	supported
controlled	increased	processed	tested
coordinated	initiated	produced	trained
created	installed	proposed	updated
designed	instituted	provided	upgraded
determined	instructed	published	wrote

Write down the important (and pertinent) things you have done, but do it in as few words as possible. Your resume will be scanned, not read, and short, concise phrases are much more effective than long-winded sentences. Avoid the use of "I" when emphasizing your accomplishments. Instead, use brief phrases beginning with action verbs.

While some technical terms will be unavoidable, you should try to avoid excessive "technicalese." Keep in mind that the first person to see your resume may be a human resources person who won't necessarily know all the jargon -- and how can they be impressed by something they don't understand?

Keep it Brief

Also, try to hold your paragraphs to six lines or less. If you have more than six lines of information about one job or school, put it in two or more paragraphs. A short resume will be examined more carefully. Remember: Your resume usually has between eight and 45 seconds to catch an employer's eye. So make every second count.

Job Objective

A functional resume may require a job objective to give it focus. One or two sentences describing the job you are seeking can clarify in what capacity your skills will be best put to use. Be sure that your stated objective is in line with the position you're applying for.

Examples:

- An entry-level editorial assistant position in the publishing industry.
- A senior management position in a telecommunications firm.

Don't include a job objective on a chronological resume unless your previous work experiences are completely unrelated to the position for which you're applying. The presence of an overly specific job objective might eliminate you from consideration for other positions that a recruiter feels are a better match for your qualifications. But even if you don't put an objective on paper, having a career goal in mind as you write can help give your resume a solid sense of direction.

Education

Keep it brief if you have more than two years of career experience. Elaborate more if you have less experience. If you are a recent college graduate, you may choose to include any high school activities that are directly relevant to your career. If you've been out of school for a while you don't need to list your education prior to college.

Mention degrees received and any honors or special awards. Note individual courses or projects you participated in that might be relevant for employers. For example, if you are an English major applying for a position as a business writer, be sure to mention any business or economics courses. Previous experience such as Editor-in-Chief of the school newspaper would be relevant as well.

If you are uploading your resume to an online job hunting site, action verbs are still important, but the key words or key nouns that a computer would search for become more important. For example, if you're seeking an accounting position, key nouns that a computer would search for such as "GAAP" or "CPA" or "payroll" become very important.

Highlight Impressive Skills

Be sure to mention any computer skills you may have. You may wish to include a section entitled "Additional Skills" or "Computer Skills," in which you list any software programs you know. An additional skills section is also an ideal place to mention fluency in a foreign language.

Personal Data

This section is optional, but if you choose to include it, keep it brief. A one-word mention of hobbies such as fishing, chess, baseball, cooking, etc., can give the person who will interview you a good way to open up the conversation. Team sports experience is looked at favorably. It doesn't hurt to include activities that are somewhat unusual (fencing, Akido, '70s music) or that somehow relate to the position or the company to which you're applying. For instance, it would be worth noting if you are a member of a professional organization in your industry of interest. Never include information about your age, alias, date of birth, health, physical characteristics, marital status, religious affiliation, or political/moral beliefs.

Those things (marital status, church affiliations, etc.) have no place on a resume. Those are illegal questions, so why even put that information on your resume?

-Becky Hayes, Career Counselor, Rice University

References

The most that is needed is the sentence "References available upon request" at the bottom of your resume. If you choose to leave it out, that's fine. This line is not really necessary. It is understood that references will most likely be asked for and provided by you later on in the interviewing process. Do not actually send references with your resume and cover letter unless specifically requested.

HIRING A RESUME WRITER:
Is it the Right Choice for You?

If you write reasonably well, it is to your advantage to write your own resume. Writing your resume forces you to review your experiences and figure out how to explain your accomplishments in clear, brief phrases. This will help you when you explain your work to interviewers. It is also easier to tailor your resume to each position you're applying for when you have put it together yourself.

If you write your resume, everything will be in your own words; it will sound like you. It will say what you want it to say. If you are a good writer, know yourself well, and have a good idea of which parts of your background employers are looking for, you should be able to write your own resume better than someone else. If you decide to write your resume yourself, have as many people as possible review and proofread it. Welcome objective opinions and other perspectives.

When to Get Help

If you have difficulty writing in "resume style" (which is quite unlike normal written language), if you are unsure which parts of your background to emphasize, or if you think your resume would make your case better if it did not follow one of the standard forms outlined either here or in a book on resumes, then you should consider having it professionally written.

Even some professional resume writers we know have had their resumes written with the help of fellow professionals. They sought the help of someone who can be objective about their background, as well as provide an experienced sounding board to help focus their thoughts.

If You Hire a Pro

The best way to choose a writer is by reputation: the recommendation of a friend, a personnel director, your school placement officer, or someone else knowledgeable in the field.

Important questions:

- "How long have you been writing resumes?"
- "If I'm not satisfied with what you write, will you go over it with me and change it?"
- "Do you charge by the hour or a flat rate?"

There is no sure relation between price and quality, except that you are unlikely to get a good writer for less than $50 for an uncomplicated resume and you shouldn't have to pay more than $300 unless your experience is very extensive or complicated. There will be additional charges for printing. Assume nothing no matter how much you pay. It is your career at stake if there are mistakes on your resume!

Few resume services will give you a firm price over the phone, simply because some resumes are too complicated and take too long to do for a predetermined price. Some services will quote you a price that applies to almost all of their customers. Once you decide to use a specific writer, you should insist on a firm price quote *before* engaging their services. Also, find out how expensive minor changes will be.

COVER LETTERS:
Quick, Clear, and Concise

Always mail a cover letter with your resume. In a cover letter you can show an interest in the company that you can't show in a resume. You can also point out one or two of your skills or accomplishments the company can put to good use.

Make it Personal

The more personal you can get, the better, so long as you keep it professional. If someone known to the person you are writing has recommended that you contact the company, get permission to include his/her name in the letter. If you can get the name of a person to send the letter to, address it directly to that person (after first calling the company to verify the spelling of the person's name, correct title, and mailing address). Be sure to put the person's name and title on both the letter and the envelope. This will ensure that your letter will get through to the proper person, even if a new person now occupies this position. It will not always be possible to get the name of a person. Always strive to get at least a title.

Be sure to mention something about why you have an interest in the company -- *so many candidates apply for jobs with no apparent knowledge of what the company does!* This conveys the message that they just want any job.

Type cover letters in full. Don't try the cheap and easy ways, like using a computer mail merge program or photocopying the body of your letter and typing in the inside address and salutation. You will give the impression that you are mailing to a host of companies and have no particular interest in any one.

Print your cover letter on the same color and same high-quality paper as your resume.

Cover letter basic format

Paragraph 1: State the specific position you are seeking. It is not always necessary to state how you found out about the position -- often you will apply without knowing that a position is open.

Paragraph 2: Include what you know about the company and why you are interested in working there. Mention any prior contact with the company or someone known to the hiring person if relevant. Briefly state your qualifications and what you can offer. (Do not talk about what you cannot do).

Paragraph 3: Close with your phone number and where/when you can be reached. Make a request for an interview. State when you will follow-up by phone (or mail or e-mail if the ad requests no phone calls). Do not wait long -- generally five working days. If you say you're going to follow-up, then actually do it! This phone call can get your resume noticed when it might otherwise sit in a stack of 225 other resumes.

Cover letter do's and don'ts

- *Do* keep your cover letter brief and to the point.
- *Do* be sure it is error-free.
- *Do* accentuate what you can offer the company, not what you hope to gain.
- *Do* be sure your phone number and address is on your cover letter just in case it gets separated from your resume (this happens!).
- *Do* check the watermark by holding the paper up to a light -- be sure it is facing forward so it is readable -- on the same side as the text, and right-side up.
- *Do* sign your cover letter (or type your name if you are sending it electronically). Blue or black ink are both fine. Do not use red ink.
- *Don't* just repeat information verbatim from your resume.
- *Don't* overuse the personal pronoun "I."
- *Don't* send a generic cover letter -- show your personal knowledge of and interest in that particular company.

THANK YOU LETTERS:
Another Way to Stand Out

As mentioned earlier, *always* send a thank you letter after an interview (see the sample later in this section). So few candidates do this and it is yet another way for you to stand out. Be sure to mention something specific from the interview and restate your interest in the company and the position.

It is generally acceptable to handwrite your thank you letter on a generic thank you card (but *never* a postcard). Make sure handwritten notes are neat and legible. However, if you are in doubt, typing your letter is always the safe bet. If you met with several people it is fine to send them each an individual thank you letter. Call the company if you need to check on the correct spelling of their names.

Remember to:

- Keep it short.
- Proofread it carefully.
- Send it *promptly*.

FUNCTIONAL RESUME

Jennifer T. Moore
33 Park Street
Boston, MA 02215
617.555.1876

OBJECTIVE:
To contribute over two years experience in promotion, communications, and administration to an entry-level position in advertising.

SUMMARY OF QUALIFICATIONS:

- Experienced business writer and communicator.
- Performed advertising duties for small business.
- General knowledge of office management.
- Demonstrated ability to work well in both supervisory and support staff roles.
- Type 75 words per minute.

SELECTED ACHIEVEMENTS AND RESULTS:
Promotion:
Compose, edit, and proofread correspondence and PR materials for own catering service. Manage large-scale mailings.

Communication:
Instruct and evaluate students; curriculum and lesson planning; conduct parent-teacher conferences; develop educational materials. Train and supervise clerks.

Computer Skills:
Proficient in MS Word, Lotus 1-2-3, Excel, and Filemaker Pro. Familiar with both Macintosh and IBM-compatible formats.

Administration:
Record-keeping and file organization. Data processing and computer operations, accounts receivable, accounts payable, inventory control, and customer relations. Scheduling, office management, and telephone reception.

WORK HISTORY:
Teacher; Floor Manager; Administrative Assistant; Accounting Clerk.

EDUCATION:
Simmons College, Boston, MA, BA in Communications, 2003.

CHRONOLOGICAL RESUME

Frank Flores
38 Winchester Street
Newton, MA 02459
617.555.1924

EDUCATION

Boston College, Chestnut Hill MA
Bachelor of Arts in Elementary Education, 2003
- Graduated *magna cum laude*
- Physical education minor
- Kappa Delta Pi member, inducted 2001

EXPERIENCE

September 2003-Present

Remy Elementary School, Norwell MA
Part-time Kindergarten Teacher
- Instruct kindergartners in reading, spelling, language arts, and music.
- Participate in the selection of textbooks and learning aids.
- Organize and supervise class field trips and coordinate in-class presentations.

Summers 2001-2003

Friendly Fenway Youth Center, Boston MA
Child-care Counselor
- Oversaw summer program for low-income youth.
- Budgeted and coordinated special events and field trips, working with program director to initiate variations in the program.
- Served as Youth Advocate in cooperation with social worker to address the social needs and problems of participants.

Spring 2001

Heritage Day School, Brookline MA
Student Teacher
- Taught third-grade class in all elementary subjects.
- Designed and implemented a two-week unit on Native Americans.
- Assisted in revision of third-grade curriculum.

Fall 2000

Family First Daycare Center, Dorchester MA
Daycare Worker
- Supervised preschool children on the playground and during art activities.
- Created a "Wishbone Corner," where children could quietly look at books or take a voluntary "time-out."

ADDITIONAL INTERESTS

Adult literacy volunteer, little league coach, reading, running, theater.

GENERAL MODEL FOR A COVER LETTER

Your mailing address
Date

Contact's name
Contact's title
Company
Company's mailing address

Dear Mr./Ms. _________:

Immediately explain why your background makes you the best candidate for the position that you are applying for. Describe what prompted you to write (want ad, article you read about the company, networking contact, etc.). Keep the first paragraph short and hard-hitting.

Detail what you could contribute to this company. Show how your qualifications will benefit this firm. Describe your interest in the corporation. Subtly emphasizing your knowledge about this firm and your familiarity with the industry will set you apart from other candidates. Remember to keep this letter short; few recruiters will read a cover letter longer than half a page.

If possible, your closing paragraph should request specific action on the part of the reader. Include your phone number and the hours when you can be reached. Mention that if you do not hear from the reader by a specific date, you will follow up with a phone call. Lastly, thank the reader for their time, consideration, etc.

Sincerely,

(signature)

Your full name (typed)

Enclosure (use this if there are other materials, such as your resume, that are included in the same envelope)

COVER LETTER SAMPLE

38 Winchester Street
Newton MA 02459
July 9, 200-

Mr. William James
Principal
Lansdowne Elementary School
17 Lansdowne Street
Boston MA 02215

Dear Mr. James:

Ramon Garcia recently informed me of a possible opening for a third grade teacher at Lansdowne Elementary School. With my experience instructing third-graders, both in schools and in summer programs, I feel I would be an ideal candidate for the position. Please accept this letter and the enclosed resume as my application.

Lansdowne Elementary School's educational philosophy that every child can learn and succeed interests me, since it mirrors my own. My current position at Remy Elementary School has reinforced this philosophy, heightening my awareness of the different styles and paces of learning and increasing my sensitivity toward special needs children. Furthermore, as a direct result of my student teaching experience at Heritage Day School, I am comfortable, confident, and knowledgeable working with third-graders.

I look forward to discussing the position and my qualifications for it in more detail. I can be reached at 617.555.1924 evenings or 617.555.1317 weekdays. If I do not hear from you before Tuesday of next week, I will call to see if we can schedule a time to meet. Thank you for your time and consideration.

Sincerely,

Frank Flores

Frank Flores

GENERAL MODEL FOR A FOLLOW-UP LETTER

Your mailing address
Date

Contact's name
Contact's title
Company
Company's mailing address

Dear Mr./Ms.__________:

Remind the interviewer of the reason (i.e., a specific opening, an informational interview, etc.) you were interviewed, as well as the date. Thank him/her for the interview, and try to personalize your thanks by mentioning some specific aspect of the interview.

Confirm your interest in the organization (and in the opening, if you were interviewing for a particular position). Use specifics to re-emphasize that you have researched the firm in detail and have considered how you would fit into the company and the position. This is a good time to say anything you wish you had said in the initial meeting. Be sure to keep this letter brief; a half-page is plenty.

If appropriate, close with a suggestion for further action, such as a desire to have an additional interview, if possible. Include your phone number and the hours that you can be reached. Alternatively, you may prefer to mention that you will follow up with a phone call in several days. Once again, thank the person for meeting with you, and state that you would be happy to provide any additional information about your qualifications.

Sincerely,

(signature)

Your full name (typed)

INDEX OF COMPANIES BY INDUSTRY

ACCOUNTING & MANAGEMENT CONSULTING

ALABAMA
Frazier & Deeter LLC

ARIZONA
Comprehensive Business Services
Deloitte & Touche
Ernst & Young LLP
KPMG
PricewaterhouseCoopers

CALIFORNIA
AON Consulting
Bain & Company
BearingPoint, Inc.
Benson & Neff
Crawford Pimentel & Company
Deloitte & Touche
Ernst & Young LLP
H&R Block
Mercer Human Resource Consulting
PricewaterhouseCoopers

COLORADO
Arthur Andersen
BBC Research & Consulting
Clifton Gunderson LLP
Deloitte & Touche LLP
Grant Thornton LLP
MMS
PricewaterhouseCoopers

CONNECTICUT
Charles P. Myrick, CPA
Deloitte & Touche
Ernst & Young LLP
The Futures Group International
KPMG
McGladrey & Pullen, LLP
Mercer Human Resource Consulting
PricewaterhouseCoopers

DELAWARE
Belfint, Lyons & Schuman
Gunnip & Co.
Phillips & Cohen Associates, Ltd.
TransUnion

DISTRICT OF COLUMBIA
American Institute of Certified Public Accountants (AICPA)
Charles P. Myrick CPA
Deloitte & Touche
Ernst & Young LLP/The E&Y Kenneth Leventhal Real Estate Group Division
Gardiner, Kamya & Associates
KPMG
Native American Consultants, Inc.
PricewaterhouseCoopers

FLORIDA
Deloitte & Touche
Ernst & Young LLP
KPMG
O'Sullivan Creel, LLP
PricewaterhouseCoopers

GEORGIA
AON Consulting
Booz Allen Hamilton
Deloitte & Touche
Draffin & Tucker
Ernst & Young LLP
Georgia Management Services
H&R Block
Hay Group
Hewitt Associates
KPMG
PricewaterhouseCoopers

HAWAII
Deloitte & Touche

ILLINOIS
BDO Seidman, LLP
Bansley & Kiener
The Chicago Group, Inc.
Clifton Gunderson L.L.C.
Hewitt Associates
KPMG
A.T. Kearney Procurement Solutions
George S. May International
McGladrey & Pullen, LLP
PricewaterhouseCoopers
RSM McGladrey

INDIANA
BKD LLP
Blue & Co., LLC
Deloitte & Touche
Ernst & Young LLP
Geminus Corporation
KPMG

IOWA
RSM McGladrey

MAINE
Baker Newman & Noyes
MacDonald Page Schatz Fletcher

MARYLAND
Aronson & Company
Beatty Satchell Business Services, Inc.
Clifton Gunderson LLP
Ernst & Young LLP
GE Global Exchange Services
Grant Thornton LLP
Hariton, Mancuso & Jones, P.C.
KPMG
National Association of Black Accountants
PricewaterhouseCoopers

MASSACHUSETTS
ABT Associates Inc.
BDO Seidman, LLP
Bain & Company, Inc.
Ceridian Employer Services
Ernst & Young LLP
The Forum Corporation
Grant Thornton LLP
H&R Block
KPMG
A.T. Kearney, Inc.
Arthur D. Little, Inc.
MicroCal LLC.
PricewaterhouseCoopers LLP
GT Reilly & Co.

MICHIGAN
Plante & Moran, LLP
United American Healthcare

MINNESOTA
EMA Services, Inc.
Ernst & Young LLP
Grant Thornton LLP
Hewitt Associates
KPMG
McGladrey & Pullen, LLP
Personnel Decisions International (PDI)
RSM McGladrey, Inc.
Schechter Dokken Kanter
Towers Perrin

MISSISSIPPI
Horne CPA Group
Huffman & Company, CPA

MISSOURI
Deloitte & Touche
Ernst & Young LLP
H&R Block
KPMG
PricewaterhouseCoopers
Rubin, Brown, Gornstein & Co. LLP

NEVADA
Deloitte & Touche
Grant Thornton LLP
Kafoury Armstrong & Co.
PricewaterhouseCoopers

NEW JERSEY
AON Consulting
Bowman & Company LLP
Deloitte & Touche
Ernst & Young LLP
Jackson Hewitt Inc.
KPMG
Kepner-Tregoe, Inc.
Mercer Human Resources Consulting
Kurt Salmon Associates, Inc.
Sibson Consulting

NEW MEXICO
Gilmore, Gannaway, Andrews, Smith & Company
KPMG

NEW YORK
CT Corporation System
Delloitte Touche Tohmatsu/dba Deloitte & Touche LLP

AEROSPACE

APPAREL, FASHION, AND TEXTILES

Darlington Fabrics Corporation
Donnkenny, Inc.
Fab Industries, Inc.
Victor Forstmann, Inc./The Forstmann Company
G-III Apparel Group, Ltd.
Galey & Lord, Inc.
Garan Inc.
Hickey Freeman Company Inc.
JLM Couture, Inc.
Jordache Enterprises
Kenneth Cole Productions
The Leslie Fay Companies, Inc.
Liz Claiborne
J.B. Martin Company
Milliken & Company
Movie Star, Inc.
National Spinning Company Inc.
New Era Cap Company, Inc.
Paxar
Phillips-Van Heusen Corporation
Polo Ralph Lauren
Salant Corporation
F. Schumacher & Company
Springs Industries, Inc.
Standard Manufacturing Company Inc.
Tote Isotoner Inc.
The Warnaco Group, Inc.
West Point Stevens, Inc.

NORTH CAROLINA

Acme-McCrary Corporation
Alba-Waldensian, Inc.
American & Efird, Inc.
Burke Mills, Inc.
Clayton Marcus
Coats North America
Collins & Aikman Holdings Corporation
Cone Mills Corporation
Cross Creek Apparel Inc.
Galey & Lord, Inc.
Granite Knitwear, Inc.
Guilford Mills, Inc.
Hanes Industries
Holt Hosiery
Holt Sublimation
Honeywell
International Textile Group
Invista
Kayser-Roth Corporation
Kimberly-Clark Corporation
Lee Industries
National Spinning Company Inc.
Performance Fibers
Regal Manufacturing Company
Rocky Mount Cord Company
Royal Home Fashions Inc.
Sara Lee Hosiery
Sara Lee Intimate Apparel
Shadowline Inc.
M.J. Soffe Company, Inc.
Thomasville Furniture
Unifi, Inc.
VF Corporation
Waverly Mills Incorporated

NORTH DAKOTA

Sioux Manufacturing Corporation

OHIO

Betlin, Inc.
Fechheimer Brothers Company
Holloway Sportswear
Mitchellace Inc.
Rocky Shoes & Boots Inc.

OREGON

Adidas America
Columbia Sportswear Company
Danner Shoe Manufacturing Company
Dennis Uniform Manufacturing Company
Hickory Springs Manufacturing Company
Jantzen, Inc.
Nike, Inc.
Nike, Inc./Western Regional Customer Service
Pendleton Woolen Mills Inc.

PENNSYLVANIA

Alfred Angelo, Inc.
Bayer Clothing Group, Inc.
Bollman Hat Company
City Shirt Company
Congoleum Corporation
Cove Shoe Company
Craftex Mills, Inc.
Dallco Industries Inc.
Delta Wundies
Double-H Boot Company
Good Lad Apparel
Hutspah Shirts
Jones Apparel Group, Inc.
Kleinert's Inc.
Kraemer Textiles, Inc.
Pincus Brothers, Inc.
Seton Company
Sure Fit Inc.
Tama Manufacturing Company Inc.
Valley Forge Flag Company, Inc.
Warnaco
Woolrich, Inc.

RHODE ISLAND

A & H Manufacturing
Cranston Print Works Company
Donnelly's School Apparel
Eastern Color and Chemical Company

SOUTH CAROLINA

American Fiber & Finishing
BASF Corporation
Delta Woodside Industries, Inc.
Greenwood Mills, Inc.
Hampshire Designers, Inc.
Honeywell
JPS Industries
KoSa
Propex
Tietex International

TENNESSEE

AlbaHealth
Altama Delta Corporation
BBA Fiberweb Reemay, Inc.
Carhartt Inc.
Charleston Hosiery Inc.
Crescent Hosiery Mills
Mohawk Yarn, Inc.
Genesco, Inc.
Georgia Boot Inc.
Invista
Leggett & Platt, Inc.
Levi Strauss & Company
OshKosh B'Gosh Inc.
Red Kap Industries
Rockford Manufacturing Company
Shaw Industries Inc.
Texas Boot, Inc.
United Knitting
Wilson Sporting Goods

TEXAS

Border Apparel Laundry Ltd.
C C Creations
Conti Window Fashions
Custom Drapery, Blinds, & Carpet
Dilly Uniform Company
Haggar Clothing Company
HATCO
Houston Wiper & Mill Supply Company
Justin Boot Company
Kast Fabrics
Tony Lama Company
Lucchese Boot Company
Pindler & Pindler Inc.
Savane International Corporation
Scope Imports Inc.
Stitches Inc.
Tex Tan Western Leather Company
Texace Corporation
Walls Industries, Inc.
Williamson-Dickie Manufacturing Company

UTAH

Burdett Apparel
Levolor Home Fashions
Osborn Specialty Sewing
San Segal Sportswear

VERMONT

Bogner of America, Inc.

VIRGINIA

Alpha Industries Inc.
Atlantic Coast Cotton
Burlington Klopman Fabrics
Dan River, Inc.
E.I. DuPont de Nemours & Company

WASHINGTON

Diadora America, Inc.
Helly Hansen Inc.
KL Manufacturing Company
Mallory and Church Corporation
Pacific Trail Inc.

Pendleton Woolen Mills
Unionbay Sportswear

WISCONSIN
Eastbay
Jockey International, Inc.
LaCrosse Footwear, Inc.
OshKosh B'Gosh Inc.

ARCHITECTURE/ CONSTRUCTION/ ENGINEÉRING (MISC.)

ALABAMA
BE&K Engineering Company
Cavalier Homes, Inc./ Cavalier Homes of Alabama
Tec-Masters, Inc.
Wyle Laboratories

ALASKA
Arctic Slope Regional Corporation
Chugach Alaska Corporation (CAC)

ARIZONA
Arizona Engineering Company
R.W. Beck & Associates
Burgess & Niple, Inc.
CH2M Hill, Inc.
Exponent, Inc.
Goettl Air Conditioning Inc.
JMC Mechanical
Jacobs Sverdrup
Johnson Controls, Inc.
Kinetics Systems
Kitchell Corporation
Larsen Supply Company
Andrew Lauren Interiors
McCarthy Building Companies, Inc.
Palm Harbor Homes Inc.
Perini Building Company
Pulte Homes, Inc.
Chas Roberts Air Conditioning
Stantec Consulting
The Sundt Companies, Inc.
Sundt Construction, Inc.
Sunvek
Swengel-Robbins, Inc.
Western Technologies, Inc.

CALIFORNIA
ABS Consulting
ACCO Engineered Systems
AECOM Technology Corporation
Advanced Foam
Amelco Corporation
Anthony and Sylvan Pools
Barker Mechanical Services Inc.
Bechtel Corporation
Bechtel Nevada
Boyle Engineering Corporation
Burke Mercer
CH2M Hill California Inc.
Cal-Air Conditioning
Calprop Corporation
Capital Pacific Holdings
The Clark Construction Group, Inc.
Coast Foundry & Manufacturing Company
DMJM
Elixir Industries
Exponent, Inc.
FM Global
Ferguson Enterprises, Inc.
Fluor Corporation
Gardco Lighting
Gensler
Granite Construction Inc.
Hathaway Dinwiddie Construction Company
Holmes and Narver Inc.
Hunter Douglas
Jacobs Engineering Group Inc.
Jensen Industries, Inc.
Kawneer Company Inc.
Lathrop Construction Associates, Inc.
Locus Technologies
Matich Corporation
McElroy Metal Inc.
Parex Inc.
Parsons Brinckerhoff Inc.
Rimkus Consulting Group
Roel Construction Company
The Ryland Group, Inc.
Southdown California Cement
Standard Pacific Homes
Swinerton Incorporated
Trans-Pacific Consultants
URS Corporation
Wentz Group
George H. Wilson, Inc./ Mechanical Contractors

COLORADO
Air Purification Company
Arinc Research Corporation
Black & Veatch
Boyle Engineering Corporation
CH2M Hill
Centex Homes
Creative Touch Interiors
Hensel Phelps Construction
ISEC, Inc.
Jacobs Engineering Group, Inc./Jacobs Facilities, Inc.
Kellogg LLC
Kiewit Western Company
Merrick & Company
Natkin Contracting
Nexus Corporation
Gerald H. Phipps, Inc.
George T. Sanders Company
Trane Company
U.S. Engineering Company
United Pipeline Systems, Inc.
Vanguard Research, Inc.
Washington Group International
Wright Water Engineers Inc.

CONNECTICUT
ABB Inc.
BVH Integrated Services, Inc.
J. Brown/LMC Group
Carrier Corporation
Fluidyne Ansonia
O&G Industries Inc.

DELAWARE
Baltimore Aircoil Company
Chicago Bridge and Iron Co.
M. Davis & Sons Inc.
Deacon Industrial Supply Company Incorporated
Edward J. DeSeta Co., Inc.
Homsey Architecture Inc.
Snyder, Crompton & Associates, Inc.
J.F. Sobieski Mechanical Contractors, Inc.
Speakman Company
Tilcon Delaware Inc.

DISTRICT OF COLUMBIA
AEPA Architects Engineers PC
Horning Brothers
J.A. Jones/Tompkins Builders
Parsons Brinckerhoff Inc.
Thomas Somerville Company

FLORIDA
AJT & Associates, Inc.
ATC Associates
Aluma Systems
APAC Inc.
Ashley Aluminum, LLC/dba Cameron Ashley Building Products
Atlantic Marine, Inc./ Atlantic Dry Dock Corporation
Bertram Yacht, Inc.
Catalina Yachts
Centex Rooney
J.W. Conner & Sons, Inc.
Devcon International Corporation
Exponent, Inc.
Florida Crushed Stone Company
Florida Engineered Construction Products
The Haskell Company
Hubbard Construction Company
Jenkins and Charland, Inc.
Misener Marine Construction
Nobility Homes, Inc.
Oriole Homes Corporation
Palm Harbor Homes
Palmer Electric Company/ Showcase Lighting
Post, Buckley, Schuh, and Jernigan, Inc.
RWA, Inc.
Reynolds, Smith, and Hills, Inc.
Scotty's, Inc.
Treadway Industries, LLC
Tri-City Electrical Contractors
Walt Disney Imagineering
Walter Industries
Wilson Miller

GEORGIA
Abco Builders Inc.

ARTS, ENTERTAINMENT, SPORTS, AND RECREATION

AUTOMOTIVE

Arvin Meritor
Autoalliance International, Inc.
Borg-Warner Automotive
Robert Bosch Corporation
The Budd Company
Chivas Industries
Cooper-Standard Automotive/ The Standard Products Company
Crotty Corporation
The Crown Group, Inc.
DaimlerChrysler Corporation
Dana Corporation
Davis Tool and Engineering Inc.
Delphi Automotive Systems Corporation
Denso International America, Inc.
Denso Manufacturing Michigan, Inc.
Dodge City/Warren Truck Division
Draw-Tite Inc.
Dura Convertible Systems
Durakon Industries Inc.
Eagle-Picher Automotive Group
Eaton Corporation
Emhart Automotive
Engineering Service, Inc.
Enterprise Automotive Systems
Federal-Mogul Corporation
Flex-N-Gate
Ford Motor Company
GKN Automotive Inc.
GM Powertrain
General Motors Corporation
General Motors Technical Center
Georgie Boy Manufacturing Inc.
Hahn Elastomer
Hastings Manufacturing Company
Hayes Lemmerz International, Inc.
Johnson Controls, Inc.
Key Safety Systems, Inc.
Lear Corporation
Magna Donnelly Corporation
Martinrea Industries Inc.
Mesco (Manufacturers Equpment and Supply Company)
Michigan Rubber Products
Modern Engineering Inc.
Morgan Olson
Nabco Inc.
Norgren Automotive
PPG Industries, Inc./Automotive Technical Center
Plastech
Prestige Stamping, Inc.
Pullman Industries Inc.
Raytech Automotive
Rieter Automotive North America
Rolls-Royce & Bentley Motor Cars Inc.
Roush Industries
Saturn Corporation
Saturn Electronics and Engineering, Inc.
Spartan Motors
Stellar Engineering Inc.
TRMI, Inc.
TRW Automotive Electronics Group
TRW Steering & Suspension Systems
TRW Vehicle Safety Systems Inc.
Tower Automotive
U.S. Manufacturing Corporation
Unique Fabricating Inc.
Valiant International Inc.
Visteon Corporation
Volkswagen of America
Wagon Engineering
Ziebart International Corporation

MINNESOTA

Clore Automotived
Crysteel Manufacturing
Ford Motor Company
NOVUS Auto Glass Repair & Replacement
PAM Companies
Sheldahl Inc.
TRW Automotive Electronics
Universal Co-Op Inc.

MISSISSIPPI

Borg-Warner Automotive
CalsonicKansei North America, Inc
Delphi Packard Electric Systems
Nissan North America

MISSOURI

DaimlerChrysler Corporation
Ford Motor Company
General Motors Corporation

NEBRASKA

Eaton Corporation

NEVADA

Auto Diesel Electric
General Motors Corporation
Mr. Gasket
United Engine & Machine Company

NEW HAMPSHIRE

Collins & Aikman Corporation

NEW JERSEY

BMW of North America, Inc.
Ford Motor Company
KEM Manufacturing Company Inc.
Mercedes-Benz USA, LLC
Subaru of America
Volvo Cars of North America, Inc.

NEW MEXICO

Firestone Tire & Service Center
GCR Truck Tire Centers, Inc.
Nova BUS Inc.

NEW YORK

Arlen Corporation
Audiovox Corporation
Bombardier Transportation
Ford Motor Company
Hahn Automotive Warehouse, Inc.
Honeywell Transportation & Power Systems/Friction Materials Division
Mark IV Industries, Inc.
Meridian Automotive Systems
Purolator Products Company
Standard Motor Products Inc.
Trayer Products Inc.
Truck-Lite Company Inc.

NORTH CAROLINA

AW North Carolina
Goerlich's Exhaust Systems
Hackney & Sons Inc.
Stanadyne Automotive Corporation
Thomas Built Buses, Inc.

NORTH DAKOTA

IR Bobcat Company

OHIO

AAP St. Marys Corporation
ArvinMeritor Automotive
Behr Dayton Thermal Products
The Budd Company/Plastics Division
DaimlerChrysler Corporation
Findlay Industries Inc.
Ford Motor Company
GM Powertrain
General Motors Corporation
Honeywell Consumer Products Group
Janesville Products
Kenworth Truck Company
Lear Corporation
Myers Industries Inc.
Navistar International Transportation Corporation
Pilkington Libbey-Owens-Ford Company
TS Trim Industries Inc.
TTC
Tenneco Automotive
Thor Industries
Toledo Molding & Die Inc.
Venture Corporation
ZF Batavia

OKLAHOMA

Mark IV Automotive
Unit Parts Company

OREGON

America's Tire Company
Beaver Motor Coaches
Consolidated Metco Inc.
Warn Industries Inc.

PENNSYLVANIA

Altec Industries, Inc.
Carbone of America
Cardone Industries
Dana Corporation
Dana Corporation/Parish Division
EMI Company
East Penn Manufacturing Company Inc.
Federal-Mogul Corporation
General Motors Corporation
Harley-Davidson Motor Company, Inc.
Johnson Matthey Inc.
Lear Corporation
Mack Trucks Inc.
Motion Control Industries Inc.

BANKING/SAVINGS & LOANS/ OTHER DEPOSITORY INSTITUTIONS (MISC.)

BIOTECHNOLOGY/ PHARMACEUTICALS/ SCIENTIFIC R&D (MISC.)

BD Biosciences
Bayer Corporation
Beckman Coulter, Inc.
Biocatalytics Inc.
Biogen Idec
Bio-Rad Laboratories
BioSource International, Inc.
BioTime, Inc.
B. Braun/McGaw Inc.
Calgene, Inc.
Cancervax Corporation
Celera
Cell Genesys, Inc.
Chiron Corporation
Cholestech Corporation
Cortex Pharmaceuticals Inc.
Cosmodyne Inc.
Cygnus, Inc.
Dade Behring, Inc.
Diagnostic Products Corporation
Elan Pharmaceuticals, Inc.
Exelixis, Inc.
Fisher Scientific Company
Genelabs Technologies, Inc.
Genentech, Inc.
Gilead Sciences
HemaCare Corporation
Hycor Biomedical Inc.
I-Flow Corporation
Immune Response Corporation
Inamed Corporation
InSite Vision Incorporated
International Remote Imaging Systems, Inc. (IRIS)
Irwin Naturals For Health/ Nature's Secret
Isis Pharmaceuticals, Inc.
La Jolla Pharmaceutical Company (LJP)
Lawrence Berkeley National Laboratory
Laboratory Corporation of America (LabCorp)
Lawrence Livermore National Laboratory
Ligand Pharmaceuticals Inc.
Merck Research Laboratories
Metallurgical Labs Inc.
Nektar Therapeutics
Nuclear Pharmacy Services
Oncology Therapeutics Network
Onyx Pharmaceuticals, Inc.
Protein Design Labs, Inc.
Psychemedics Corporation
Quest Diagnostics
Quest Diagnostics at Nichols Institute
Questcor Pharmaceuticals Corporation
QUIDEL Corporation
Rockwell Scientific Company LLC
SRI International
Scios Inc.
Shaklee Corporation
SkyePharma
Tanabe Research Laboratories USA, Inc.
Thermo Electron
Vical Inc.
Watson Pharmaceuticals, Inc.
Xencor
Xenogen Corporation

COLORADO

Amgen Inc.
AspenBio, Inc.
Baxter Hemoglobin Therapeutics
Bolder BioTechnology, Inc.
Colorado Serum Company
The Hach Company
NatureSmart/NBTY
OSI Pharmaceuticals, Inc.
Quest Diagnostics Incorporated
Replidyne, Inc.
Roche Colorado
Sandoz Inc.
Sirna Therapeutics, Inc.
Sciona, Inc.
University Corporation for Atmospheric Research

CONNECTICUT

Applera Corporation
Bayer Corporation
Boehringer Ingelheim Pharmaceuticals, Inc.
Bristol-Myers Squibb Company
Clinical Laboratory Partners
DIANON Systems, Inc.
Foley Laboratory Services, Inc.
Moore Medical Corporation
Neurogen Corporation
Pfizer Inc.
Purdue Pharma L.P.
Quest Diagnostics/Patient Service Center
Vion Pharmaceuticals
Watson Pharmaceuticals, Inc.

DELAWARE

AstraZeneca Pharmaceuticals
Dade Behring Inc.
Quest Pharmaceutical Services
Laboratory Corporation of America (LabCorp)

DISTRICT OF COLUMBIA

Genentech, Inc.
GlaxoSmithKline
Hoffmann-La Roche Inc.
National Academy of Sciences/ National Research Council
Research Triangle Institute (RTI)

FLORIDA

ABC Research Corporation
Beckman Coulter, Inc.
IVAX Corporation
IVAX Pharmaceuticals
The Monticello Company
Nabi Biopharmaceuticals
Noven Pharmaceuticals, Inc.
PharMerica/Pharmacy Management Services (PMS)
Quest Diagnostics Incorporated
Research Triangle Institute (RTI)
Rexall Showcase International
Schering-Plough
Scientific Instruments, Inc.

GEORGIA

Bard Medical Division
Cryolife
Huber Engineered Materials
Immucor
Laboratory Corporation of America (LABCORP)
Merck & Company, Inc.
Merial Ltd.
Micromeritics Instrument Corporation
Mikart
Pfizer
Quest Diagnostics Incorporated
Solvay Pharmaceuticals
Universal Solutions Inc.

HAWAII

Cyanotech Corporation

ILLINOIS

Abbott Laboratories
ALRA Laboratories, Inc.
American Pharmaceutical Services
Argonne National Laboratory
Cole-Parmer Instrument Company
DSM Desotech Inc.
Dade Behring, Inc.
The Female Health Company
Fermi National Accelerator Laboratory
Ferro Pfanstiehl Laboratories, Inc.
Fujisawa Healthcare, Inc.
GE Health
Leica North America
NeighborCare
Northfield Laboratories, Inc.
Quest Diagnostics Incorporated
Sargent-Welch Scientific Co.
Silliker Laboratories Group, Inc.

INDIANA

Bayer Corporation
Bindley Western Industries, Inc.
Central Indiana Regional Blood Center
Covance Laboratories Inc.
Eli Lilly and Company
Mead Johnson Nutritionals
Mid-America Clinical Labs
Pathologists Associated
Schwarz Pharma Manufacturing
Seradyn Inc.

IOWA

Ain Company, LLC
Ames Laboratory
BioForce Nanosciences
Fort Dodge Animal Health, Inc.
Integrated DNA Technologies
NewLink Genetics Corporation
Novartis Animal Health US Inc.
Pharmacom Corporation
Phytodyne Inc.
Pioneer Hi-Bred International

BUSINESS SERVICES/ NON-SCIENTIFIC RESEARCH

CHEMICALS/RUBBER AND PLASTICS

ICI Paints
NACO Industries, Inc.
Nephi Rubber Products
Sorenson Bioscience

VERMONT
CPC of Vermont Inc.
GW Plastics, Inc.
Kamtech Plastics Co.
Mack Group/dba Mack Molding Company Northern Division
Specialty Filaments Inc.
Whitney Blake Company

VIRGINIA
American Chemistry Council, Inc.
Carpenter Company
Ciba Specialty Chemicals
E.I. DuPont de Nemours & Co.
Goodyear Tire & Rubber Company
Honeywell
Nova Chemicals
Polyone Corporation
Presto Products Company
Radva Corporation
REHAU Inc.
Rubbermaid Commercial Products, Inc.
SICPA
Strongwell

WASHINGTON
Air Liquide Corporation
Alcide Corporation
Arkema Group
BOC Gases
Bunzl Extrusion
Foamex International, Inc.
Gaco Western Inc.
General Chemical Corporation
Hexcel Corporation
Kelly-Moore Preservative Paints
Laird Plastics
Mikron Industries
Premier Industries Inc.
Univar USA

WEST VIRGINIA
Bayer Corporation
Cytec Industries
Dow Chemical Company
DuPont Belle
PPG Industries, Inc.

WISCONSIN
Dickten & Masch Manufacturing Company
Goodyear Tire & Rubber Company
Hoffer's Coatings Inc.
Matthews Paint Company
Phillips Plastics Corporation
Prent Corporation
QMR Plastics
RBP Chemical Technology
Rexnord Plastics Division

WYOMING
Coastal Chem, Inc.
FMC Corporation

COMMUNICATIONS: TELECOMMUNICATIONS/ BROADCASTING

ALABAMA
ADTRAN, Inc.
Interconnect Systems Corporation

ALASKA
General Communication, Inc. (GCI)
Matanuska Telephone Association, Inc. (MTA)

ARIZONA
Anixter
Corning Gilbert, Inc.
Cox Communications
Inter-Tel Inc.
KISS-FM
KKLT-FM
KNIX-FM
KPHO-TV5
KPNX-TV 12
KTAR-AM 620
KTVK-TV/Channel 3
microHelix, Inc.
Vodavi Communications, Inc.

ARKANSAS
AETN
ALLTEL Corporation

CALIFORNIA
ABC Family
ABC, Inc.
ABC7/KGO-TV
ADC Telecommunications, Inc./ Wireline Systems Division
Accom, Inc.
Allied Telesyn, Inc.
Applied Signal Technology
Aspect Communications Corporation
Axxcelera Broadband Wireless
CBS Corporation
CXR Telcom
CNet Networks, Inc.
Comcast Spotlight
Cox Communications, Inc.
DMX Music LLC
Dantel, Inc.
Discovery Communications Inc.
Earthlink
Fox Television/KTTV-Fox 11
Freedom Communications Inc.
Grass Valley Group
Harris Corporation
JDS Uniphase Corporation
KCRA-TV
L3 Communications
Lucent Technologies Internetworking Systems
NextiraOne
QUALCOMM Incorporated
SS8 Networks
Siemens Business Communications
Stratex Networks
TCI (Technology for Communications International)
TelASIC Communications
Unisys Pulsepoint Communications
Verizon Communications
Verizon Wireless
Westwood One Inc.

COLORADO
Anixter
Avaya Inc.
Ball Corporation
Cingular Wireless
Global Crossing Conferencing
ICG Communications, Inc.
Infinity Broadcasting Corporation
Liberty Media Corporation
MCI, Inc.
Qwest Communications
Starz Encore Group LLC
Time Warner Telecom
UnitedGlobalCom, Inc.
Verizon Wireless

CONNECTICUT
Cognitronics Corporation
Connecticut Public Broadcasting
Cox Radio, Inc.
Dictaphone Corporation
Farmstead Telephone Group, Inc.
Woodbury Telephone Company
World Wrestling Federation Entertainment, Inc.

DELAWARE
Advanced Networking, Inc.
WILM News Radio
AT&T Wireless

DISTRICT OF COLUMBIA
ABC News
BET Services/ Black Entertainment Television Network
CBS News/Washington Bureau
CNN (Cable News Network)
INTELSAT
National Public Radio (NPR)
Radio Free Europe/ Radio Liberty, Inc.
WJLA-TV
WRC NBC Channel 4
XM Satellite Radio

FLORIDA
Aerotron-Repco Systems, Inc.
America II Corp., Inc.
appliedlogx
Dictaphone Corporation
Dycom Industries, Inc.

Broadbeam Corporation
Intel Corporation
Lucent Technologies Inc.
Mikros Systems Corporation
Nextel Communications
RCN Corporation
RFL Electronics Inc.
Telcordia Technologies
Verizon Communications
WFPG-FM 96.9
Western Union Corporation

NEW MEXICO
Citadel Communications Corporation
Community Cable Channel 27
Frontier Corporation
KCHF-TV 11
KNME-TV
KOB-TV 4
KRQE-TV 13
Qwest Communications International, Inc.

NEW YORK
ABC, Inc.
ACC Business, Inc.
ACTV Inc.
CBS Broadcasting Inc.
CNN News Group (Cable News Network)
Cablevision Systems Corporation
C-Cor.net Corporation
Choice One Communications
Comtech Telecommunications Corporation
Comverse Technology Inc.
Contec Corporation
CopyTele, Inc.
Crescent Telephone Company
DHB Industries, Inc.
Dynalec Corporation
Fox News Network LLC/dba Fox News Channel
Frontier Corporation
Granite Broadcasting Corporation
Hearst-Argyle Television, Inc.
King World Productions
L-3 Communications Holdings, Inc.
Loral Space & Communications LTD
Lucent Technologies Inc.
Lynch Interactive Corporation
NBC (National Broadcast Company, Inc.)
Nice Systems Inc.
Petry Media Corporation/dba Blair Television, Inc.
Porta Systems Corporation
Roanwell Corporation
Time Warner Cable
Veramark Technologies Inc.
Viacom Inc.
WSKG Public TV and Radio

NORTH CAROLINA
Acterna
CSA Wireless
Draka Comteq
Ericsson Inc.
Jefferson-Pilot Communications
Lucent Technologies Inc.
Nortel Networks
Scotty Technologies of the Americas
Sumitomo Electric Lightwave Corporation
University of North Carolina Center for Public Television
Verizon Communications

NORTH DAKOTA
MidContinent Communications
WDAY-TV-AM

OHIO
ALLTEL Communications/ ALLTEL Information Services
Amerilink Corporation/ RadioShack Installation Services
Applied Innovation Inc.
Cincinnati Bell, Inc.
R.L. Drake Company
Lucent Technologies Inc.
Preformed Line Products Company
SBC Corporation
The E.W. Scripps Company
Time Warner Cable Communications
Time Warner Telecom
WBNS-TV/Dispatch Broadcast Group
WLWT-Channel 5
Xetron Corporation

OKLAHOMA
AMCAT (American Computer & Telephone, Inc.)
Cable One
Gemstar-TV Guide International
Xeta Technologies

OREGON
AT&T Broadband
Integra Telecom
KPTV 12
Metro One Telecommunications
nCube
Oregon Public Broadcasting (OPB)
Qwest Communications

PENNSYLVANIA
AM Communications
AT&T Broadband
AT&T Wireless Services
Adelphia Communications Corporation
Agere Systems
CTI Data Solutions Inc.
Capsule Communications
Charter Communications
Comcast Corporation.
Denver & Ephrata Telephone and Telegraph Company (D&E)
Greater Philadelphia Radio Group
KDKA Channel 2
Motorola, Inc./Broadband Communications Sector
NBC 10-WCAU
North Pittsburgh Telephone Company
QVC Network, Inc.
Verizon Communications
WBEB-FM
WPXI Channel 11
WQED Channel 13
WTAE Channel 4

RHODE ISLAND
ABC Channel 6/WLNE – TV
KVH, Inc.
LIN Television Corporation

SOUTH CAROLINA
Comcast Cablevision
The Liberty Corporation
Pirelli Cable Corporation
Rock Hill Telephone Company

SOUTH DAKOTA
DISH Network
Midcom, Inc.
Nextel Partners

TENNESSEE
AFL Communications
Asurion
MTV Networks Nashville/ Country Music Television (CMT)
TDS Telecom
Time Warner Telecom
U.S.A. Mobility

TEXAS
Alcatel USA Inc.
Andrew Corporation
Belo Corporation/ The Dallas Morning News
Channel 2 KPRC-TV
Clear Channel Communications
Corning Cable Systems
Decibel Products Inc.
Ericsson Inc.
Fujitsu Network Communications (FNC)
General Cable Company
KFDA-TV/News Channel 10
KLBK-TV
KRLD/Texas State Networks
KVII-TV
KVIL-AM/FM 103.7
KXXV-TV
Lucent Technologies Inc.
Motorola, Inc.
NEC America Inc.
Nokia USA
QVC
RF Monolithics, Inc.
SBC Communications Inc./ Southwestern Bell
Susquehanna Radio Corp.
Tellabs Texas Inc.
Time Warner Cable
VTEL Corporation
Verizon Communications

COMPUTER HARDWARE, SOFTWARE, AND SERVICES

Select, Inc.
Siebel Systems, Inc.
Siemens Business Services
Sky Computers Inc.
Smart Modular Technologies, Inc.
SoftTech, Inc.
SpyGlass Integration
StorageTek
Stratus Technologies
Stream International
Sun Microsystems, Inc.
Sybase, Inc.
Systems Engineering, Inc.
SystemSoft Corporation
Taxware International, Inc.
Technical Communications Corporation (TCC)
Telco Systems Inc.
3Com Corporation
3M Touch Systems
Titan Corporation
Turbine Inc.
Unisys Corporation
Viryanet
Webhire, Inc.
Xyvision Enterprise Solutions, Inc.
Zoom Telephonics Inc.

MICHIGAN

ABL Electronic Service, Inc.
Advantage Computing Systems, Inc.
Air Gage Corporation
Analysts International Corporation (AIC)
Ann Arbor Computer
CTG (Computer Task Group)
Ciber, Inc.
Computer Decisions International Inc.
Computer Methods Corporation
Compuware Corporation
Core Technology Corporation
Covansys
Creative Solutions
Data Systems Network Corporation
EDS PLM Solutions
Federal APD, Inc.
Fisher/Unitech Inc.
Forest Computer Inc.
Future Three Software Inc.
GEAC Comshare
Gedas, Inc.
MTS Systems Corporation
Manatron Inc.
The Medstat Group, Inc.
Miracle Software
National Tech Team, Inc.
Nematron Corporation
Parametric Technology Corporation
Printek, Inc.
QAD Inc.
SER Solutions, Inc.
Softech
Systems Integration Specialists, Inc. (SISCO)
TechSmith Corporation
Unisys Corporation
Virtual Services
Xycom Automation
Zenacomp

MINNESOTA

APA Cables and Networks
ASI DataMyte
Affiliated Computer Services
Analysts International Corporation (AiC)
BLM Technologies Inc.
Bankers Systems, Inc.
Ceridian
Ciber, Inc.
CIM Software Corporation
Comdisco, Inc.
Computer Associates International, Inc.
Computer Network Technology Corporation
Compuware Corporation
Cray Inc.
Digi International Inc.
EFI
Electronics for Imaging
Epicor Software Corporation
Fourth Shift Corporation
Health Outcome Management Inc.
Hutchinson Technology Inc.
IBM Corporation
Image Systems Corporation
Imation Corporation
International Assessment Network
Jasc Software
Kroll Ontrack Inc.
Laser Design Inc.
Lawson Software
Lockheed Martin Tactical Defense Systems
McKesson Provider Technologies
Metafile Information Systems Inc.
Multi-Tech Systems Inc.
Pearson NCS
netASPx
PC Solutions
PC Wholesale
Plasmon IDE
Retek
Rimage Corporation
SPSS, Inc.
Sagebrush Corporation
Seagate Technology
Software AG Americas
StorageTek
Syntegra, Inc.
Transition Networks
TREEV, Inc.
Trimin Systems Inc.
Velos, Inc.
Xata Corporation
Zomax Incorporated

MISSISSIPPI

Creative Controllers Inc.
Diversified Technology, Inc.

MISSOURI

ACS
AOS Global Solutions
Accenture
Ajilon Services Inc.
Analysts International Corporation (AIC)
Brick Network
Cerner Citation, Inc.
Cerner Corporation
Ciber Information Services
DST Systems, Inc.
Daugherty Systems
Diagraph Corporation
FairCom
Financial Information Technology Inc.
Heartland Technology Solutions
Hewlett-Packard Company
Jack Henry and Associates, Inc.
IBM Corporation
Impact Technologies, Inc.
JBM Electronics Company
Missouri Information Solutions
Multidata Systems International Corporation
The Newberry Group
Quality Software Engineering
Reynolds & Reynolds
SAVVIS Communications Inc.
SIRSI Corporation
Skywalker Communications
Sockett Internet
TALX Corporation
Tripos Inc.
Wave Thomson Learning
World Wide Technology Inc.
Xyquad Inc.

MONTANA

5 Star Business Technology Group
Logistics Systems Inc.
MSE Technology Applications, Inc.
Northrop Grumman Mission Systems
RightNow Technologies

NEBRASKA

ACI Worldwide
Achala Creative Solutions
Analysts International Corporation (AIC)
Automated Systems, Inc.
Booz Allen Hamilton
Centurion Wireless Technologies Inc.
Computer Cable Connection
Damacreg Corporation
Ex-Cel Solutions, Inc.
Imagine Technology
Information Technology, Inc.
Modis
Northrop Grumman

NEVADA

Acuity Solutions
Arcata Associates, Inc.
ComGlobal Systems Inc.
Cubix Corporation

ELECTRONIC/INDUSTRIAL ELECTRICAL EQUIPMENT AND COMPONENTS

COLORADO

CONNECTICUT

DELAWARE

DISTRICT OF COLUMBIA

FLORIDA

GEORGIA

ENVIRONMENTAL & WASTE MANAGEMENT SERVICES

FABRICATED METAL PRODUCTS AND PRIMARY METALS

RHODE ISLAND
Amtrol, Inc.
Deutsche Nickel America, Inc.
Wolverine Joining Technologies

SOUTH CAROLINA
ALCOA (Aluminum Company of America)
CeramTec North America
Hydro Aluminum
Nucor Steel
Owen Steel Company
The Shaw Group, Inc./dba B.F. Shaw, Inc.
Spartanburg Steel Products Inc.

SOUTH DAKOTA
ALCOA (Aluminum Company of America)

TENNESSEE
ALCOA (Aluminum Company of America)
Alltrista Zinc Products, L.P.
BetterBilt Smyrna
Gerdau Ameristeel Corporation
Conley Frog Switch & Forge
Gerdau AmeriSteel
Mueller Gas Products
Ormet Aluminum Mill Products
Philips Services Corporation
Plant Maintenance Service Corporation
U.S. Pipe and Foundry Company
Vestal Manufacturing

TEXAS
Alamo Iron Works, Inc.
ALCOA (Aluminum Company of America)
Amerimax Building Products, Inc.
Amfels, Inc.
Asarco Inc.
Cargill Steel & Wire
Friedman Industries, Inc.
G.H. Hensley Industries, Inc.
Houston Wire and Cable Company
Lewis & Lambert Metal
The Lofland Company
Lone Star Steel Company
Martin Sprocket & Gear Inc.
Merchants Metals
Metals USA, Inc.
NCI Building Systems
Parkview Metal Products Inc.
Quanex Corporation
Safety Steel Service Inc.
SEMCO Dot Metal Products
TXI Chaparral Steel Company
Tex-Tube Company
Thornton Steel Company Inc.
Trinity Industries, Inc.
U.S. Zinc Corporation
Vulcraft

UTAH
ALCOA Engineered Products
Chicago Bridge & Iron (CB&I)
Mountain States Steel, Inc.
Nucor Steel Utah
Petersen Incorporated
SME Steel Contractors
St. George Steel Fabricators
Southwire Company
Zero Enclosures

VERMONT
ALCOA International Holdings Company
HEB Manufacturing Company, Inc.
Velan Valve Corporation

VIRGINIA
Crown Cork & Seal Company, Inc.
Roanoke Electric Steel Corporation

WASHINGTON
Alaskan Copper Works
Atlas Foundry & Machinery Co.
Coeur d'Alene Company
Crown Cork & Seal Company, Inc.
Davis Wire Corporation
GM Nameplate Inc.
Jorgensen Forge Corporation
Nucor Steel
Pioneer Industries
Sandvik Special Metals

WEST VIRGINIA
Special Metals
Steel of West Virginia
Weirton Steel
Wheeling-Pittsburgh Steel Corporation

WISCONSIN
Advanced Laser Machining
Apache Stainless Equipment Corporation
Citation Corporation
DexM Engineered Products
GKN Sinter Metals
Grede Foundries, Inc.
Ladish Company, Inc.
Maynard Steel Casting Company
Maysteel LLC
Mayville Engineering Company Inc.
The Richland Center Foundry Company
Ryerson Tull

FINANCIAL SERVICES (MISCELLANEOUS)

ALABAMA
Alabama Central Credit Union
Alabama Credit Union
Harbert Management Corporation

ALASKA
Alaska USA Trust Company

ARIZONA
AXA Advisors
Conseco Finance
First Investors Corporation
KHIMETRICS
Merrill Lynch
Morgan Stanley Dean Witter & Company
Prudential Securities
RBC Dain Rauscher
Smith Barney
SunAmerica Securities
UBS Financial Services Inc.

ARKANSAS
Stephens, Inc.

CALIFORNIA
Aames Financial Corporation
ACS (Affiliated Computer Services)
American Express Company
American General Finance
Barclays Global Investors
Bear, Stearns & Company, Inc.
California First Leasing Corporation
California Fringe Benefit
The Capital Group Companies/ American Funds Distributors
Charles Schwab & Co., Inc.
Citicorp/Citibank
Commonwealth Financial Corporation
Consumer Portfolio Services, Inc.
Countrywide Credit Industries
George Elkins Mortgage Banking Company
E*Trade
First American Title Company
First Mortgage Corporation
Franklin Resources, Inc.
GATX Capital Corporation
GE Commercial Finance
Household Finance Corporation
Impac Companies
Itex Corporation
Jefferies & Company, Inc.
Merrill Lynch
Morgan Stanley
Pacific Life Insurance
Prominent USA
Providian Financial
Prudential Financial
RBC Dain Raucher
SEI Investments Company
SunAmerica Inc.
Transamerica Corporation
UBS Financial Services, Inc.
Visa International
WFS Financial
Washington Mutual
Wausau Mortgage Corporation
Wedbush Morgan Securities
Wells Fargo Foothill

COLORADO
American Century Investments
Countrywide Funding Corporation
Founders Asset Management
Janus Capital

HEALTH CARE SERVICES, EQUIPMENT, AND PRODUCTS (MISC.)

RHODE ISLAND

SOUTH CAROLINA

SOUTH DAKOTA

TENNESSEE

INSURANCE

Metlife, Inc.
The MONY Group
Mutual of America
National Benefit Life Insurance
New York Life Insurance Company
OneBeacon Insurance Group
Radian Reinsurance Inc.
Security Mutual Life Insurance of New York
TIAA-CREF
Transatlantic Holdings, Inc.
Utica National Insurance Group
Universal American Financial Corp.
Willis of New York, Inc.

NORTH CAROLINA
Blue Cross and Blue Shield of North Carolina
GMAC Insurance
Investors Title Insurance Company
North Carolina Mutual Life Insurance Company
Sterling Healthcare
Royal & SunAlliance USA

NORTH DAKOTA
Blue Cross and Blue Shield of North Dakota
Clarica Life Insurance Company

OHIO
American Commerce Insurance Company
American Financial Group (AFG)
Cincinnati Financial Corporation
Grange Insurance Companies
Great American Insurance Company
Hilb Rogal & Hobbs (HRH)
Lawyers Title Insurance Corporation
McGowan & Company, Inc.
Motorists Insurance Companies
Nationwide Insurance Enterprise
Norman-Spencer McKernan Agency, Inc.
The Ohio Casualty Group
Ohio Mutual Insurance Group/ United Ohio Insurance Company
Progressive Corporation
State Auto Insurance Companies
Western and Southern Life Insurance Company
Westfield Group
Willis of Ohio, Inc.

OKLAHOMA
Blue Cross Blue Shield of Oklahoma

OREGON
Nationwide Direct
ODS Health Plans
Orion Auto
The Standard

PENNSYLVANIA
Aetna U.S. Healthcare
Allstate Insurance Company
AON Risk Services
Chubb Group of Insurance Companies
Colonial Penn
Fidelity Mutual Life Insurance Company
Harleysville Insurance Companies
The Hartford/ITT Hartford
Independence Blue Cross of Greater Philadelphia
Liberty Mutual Insurance Group
Lincoln National Corporation (LNC)/dba Lincoln Financial Group
Marsh USA, Inc.
OneBeacon Insurance
The PMA Insurance Group
Penn Mutual Life Insurance Company
Penn Treaty American Corporation
Prudential Insurance Company of America
Radian Guaranty Inc.
Union Fidelity Life Insurance Company

RHODE ISLAND
AAA Southern New England
Amica Mutual Insurance Company

SOUTH CAROLINA
Canal Insurance Company
Colonial Life & Accident Insurance Company
Kanawha Insurance Company, Inc.
Liberty Insurance Services Corporation
The Seibels Bruce Group, Inc.

TENNESSEE
America Service Group/ Prison Health Services Inc.
American General Life and Accident Insurance Company
Blue Cross and Blue Shield of Tennessee
Harleysville Insurance
Haulers Insurance Company, Inc.
Lawyers Title Insurance Corporation
Marsh, Inc.
Permanent General and Tennessee Insurance
State Farm Insurance Agency
UnumProvident Corporation
Willis Corporation

TEXAS
ACAP Corporation
American General Corporation
American National Insurance Company
Blue Cross Blue Shield of Texas
CNA Commercial Insurance
Chicago Title Insurance Company
Chubb Group of Insurance Companies
Citizens, Inc.
Crum & Forster Insurance
FIC Insurance Group
Farmers Insurance Group
General Reinsurance Corporation
Lawyers Title Insurance Corporation
National Foundation Life Insurance Company
Principal Financial Group
Progressive County Mutual Insurance Company
Ranger Insurance Company
State Farm Insurance
St. Paul Travelers Company
United Insurance Companies Inc.
Wausau Insurance Companies

UTAH
Allstate Insurance Company
Deseret Mutual Benefit Administrators
First Relliance Mortgage
Equitable Life & Casualty Insurance Company
FIRST HEALTH
Regions Blue Cross & Blue Shield of Utah, Inc.

VERMONT
Blue Cross and Blue Shield of Vermont
National Life Insurance Co./ Sentinal Funds
Union Mutual Group/Union Mutual of Vermont Companies
Vermont Mutual Insurance Company

VIRGINIA
Allstate Insurance Company
Anthem Blue Cross Blue Shield
GE Financial Assurance
GEICO Corporation
Hilb, Rogal and Hamilton Company
Kaiser Permanente
LandAmerica Financial Group, Inc. Lawyers Title Insurance Corp.
Loudoun Mutual Insurance Company
Markel Corporation

WASHINGTON
Allstate Insurance Company
American General Finance
Chubb Group Insurance
FIC Insurance Group
Fireman's Fund Insurance Company
Grange Insurance Group/Rocky Mountain Fire & Casualty
Great Republic Life Insurance
Group Health Cooperative
Marsh Advantage of America
Parker, Smith & Feek, Inc.
PEMCO Financial Services
Premera Blue Cross
Safeco Insurance Corporation
Safeco Life Insurance Company
Transnation Title Insurance Co.
Unigard Insurance Company
Western National Insurance Group
Willis

WEST VIRGINIA
Grant County Bank

MANUFACTURING: MISCELLANEOUS CONSUMER

MANUFACTURING: MISCELLANEOUS INDUSTRIAL

PAPER AND WOOD PRODUCTS

PRINTING AND PUBLISHING

REAL ESTATE

TRANSPORTATION/TRAVEL

UTILITIES: ELECTRIC/GAS/WATER

MISCELLANEOUS WHOLESALING